wwnorton.com/naal

The StudySpace site that accompanies *The Norton Anthology of American Literature* is FREE, but you will need the code below to register for a password that will allow you to access the copyrighted materials on the site.

AMER-ICAN

THE NORTON ANTHOLOGY OF

AMERICAN
LITERATURE

SHORTER EIGHTH EDITION

Beginnings to 1700   •   FRANKLIN

American Literature 1700–1820   •   GURA

Native American Literatures   •   KRUPAT

American Literature 1820–1865   •   LEVINE   •   KRUPAT

American Literature 1865–1914   •   BAYM   •   LEVINE   •   KRUPAT   •   REESMAN

American Literature 1914–1945   •   LOEFFELHOLZ

American Literature since 1945   •   KLINKOWITZ   •   WALLACE

THE NORTON ANTHOLOGY OF

AMERICAN
LITERATURE

SHORTER EIGHTH EDITION

Nina Baym, *General Editor*

SWANLUND CHAIR AND CENTER FOR
ADVANCED STUDY PROFESSOR EMERITA OF ENGLISH
JUBILEE PROFESSOR OF LIBERAL ARTS AND SCIENCES
University of Illinois at Urbana-Champaign

Robert S. Levine, *Associate General Editor*

DISTINGUISHED UNIVERSITY PROFESSOR OF ENGLISH
AND DISTINGUISHED SCHOLAR–TEACHER
University of Maryland, College Park

W · W · NORTON & COMPANY
NEW YORK · LONDON

W. W. Norton & Company has been independent since its founding in 1923, when William Warder Norton and Mary D. Herter Norton first published lectures delivered at the People's Institute, the adult education division of New York City's Cooper Union. The firm soon expanded its program beyond the Institute, publishing books by celebrated academics from America and abroad. By midcentury, the two major pillars of Norton's publishing program—trade books and college texts—were firmly established. In the 1950s, the Norton family transferred control of the company to its employees, and today—with a staff of four hundred and a comparable number of trade, college, and professional titles published each year—W. W. Norton & Company stands as the largest and oldest publishing house owned wholly by its employees.

Editor: Julia Reidhead
Associate Editor: Carly Fraser Doria
Managing Editor, College: Marian Johnson
Manuscript Editors: Michael Fleming, Katharine Ings, Candace Levy,
Susan Joseph, Pam Lawson
Electronic Media Editor: Eileen Connell
Project Editor: Rachel Mayer
Marketing Manager, Literature: Kimberly Bowers
Production Manager: Sean Mintus
Photo Editor: Stephanie Romeo
Photo Research: Jane Sanders Miller
Permissions Manager: Megan Jackson
Permissions Clearing: Nancy Rodwan
Text Design: Jo Anne Metsch
Art Director: Rubina Yeh
Composition: The Westchester Book Group
Manufacturing: LSC Communications, Crawfordsville

The text of this book is composed in Fairfield Medium with the display set in Aperto.

Library of Congress Cataloging-in-Publication Data

The Norton anthology of American literature / Nina Baym, general editor;
Robert S. Levine, associate general editor. — 8th ed.
      p. cm.
   Includes bibliographical references and index.
    ISBN 978-0-393-93476-2 (pbk., v. A) — ISBN 978-0-393-93477-9 (pbk., v. B) —
ISBN 978-0-393-93478-6 (pbk., v. C) — ISBN 978-0-393-93479-3 (pbk., v. D) —
ISBN 978-0-393-93480-9 (pbk., v. E)   1. American literature.   2. United States—
Literary collections.   I. Baym, Nina.   II. Levine, Robert S. (Robert Steven), 1953–
   PS507.N65 2012
   810.8—dc23

                                                                    2011038279

ISBN 978-0-393-91885-4

W. W. Norton & Company, Inc., 500 Fifth Avenue, New York, NY 10110-0017
wwnorton.com

W. W. Norton & Company Ltd., 15 Carlisle Street, London W1D 3BS

7 8 9 0

Contents

American Literature 1700–1820

American Literature 1820–1865

American Literature 1865–1914

American Literature 1914–1945

American Literature since 1945

Preface to the Shorter Eighth Edition

This edition of *The Norton Anthology of American Literature* is the last for me as General Editor, and I am delighted to announce that Robert S. Levine, the editor of "American Literature 1820–1865," will take over as General Editor for the next and subsequent editions. Here he joins me as Associate Editor; together we have continued the work for which Norton has achieved its leading position among American literature anthologies. It has been a great pleasure to work on this anthology, to make contact with teachers and students around the country—indeed around the world. I know I leave *The Norton Anthology of American Literature* in immensely capable hands.

From the anthology's inception in 1979, the editors have had three main aims: first, to present a rich and substantial enough variety of works to enable teachers to build courses according to their own ideals (thus, teachers are offered more authors and more selections than they will probably use in any one course); second, to make the anthology self-sufficient by featuring many works in their entirety along with extensive selections for individual authors; third, to balance traditional interests with developing critical concerns in a way that points to a coherent American literary history. As early as 1979, we anthologized work by Anne Bradstreet, Mary Rowlandson, Sarah Kemble Knight, Phillis Wheatley, Margaret Fuller, Harriet Beecher Stowe, Frederick Douglass, Sarah Orne Jewett, Kate Chopin, Mary E. Wilkins Freeman, Booker T. Washington, Charles Chesnutt, Edith Wharton, W. E. B. Du Bois, and other writers who were not yet part of a standard canon. Yet we never shortchanged writers like Franklin, Emerson, Whitman, Hawthorne, Melville, Dickinson, Hemingway, Fitzgerald, and Faulkner, whose work students expected to read in their American literature courses, and whom teachers then and now would not think of doing without.

Although the so-called canon wars of the 1980s and 1990s have subsided, they initiated a review of our understanding of American literature that has enlarged the number and diversity of authors now recognized as contributors to the totality of American literature. The traditional writers, who look different in this expanded context, also appear different according to which of their works are selected. Teachers and students remain committed to the idea of the literary—that writers strive to produce artifacts that are both intellectually serious and formally skillful—but believe more than ever that writers should also be understood in relation to their cultural and historical situations. In endeavoring to do justice to these complex realities, we have worked, as in previous editions, with detailed suggestions from many teachers and, through those teachers, the students who use the anthology. Thanks to questionnaires, comment cards, face-to-face and phone discussions, letters, and email, we have been able to listen to those for whom this book is intended. For this Shorter Eighth Edition, we have drawn on the careful commentary of over 170 reviewers.

Our new materials continue the work of broadening the canon by representing five new writers in depth, without sacrificing widely assigned writers, many of whose selections have been reconsidered, reselected, and expanded. Our aim is always to provide extensive enough selections to do the writers justice, including complete works wherever possible. Of the 16 complete longer texts in the anthology, 2—Eugene O'Neill's *Long Day's Journey into Night* and Tennessee Williams's *A Streetcar Named Desire*—are exclusive to *The Norton Anthology of American Literature*. Charles Brockden Brown, Louisa May Alcott, Martin Luther King Jr., and Junot Díaz are all new to the Shorter Eighth Edition, which has expanded and in some cases reconfigured such central figures as Emerson, Hawthorne, Melville, Dickinson, and Twain, offering new approaches in the headnotes and section introductions. In fact, over the last two editions, the headnotes and, in many cases, selections for such frequently assigned authors as Benjamin Franklin, Washington Irving, James Fenimore Cooper, William Cullen Bryant, Henry Wadsworth Longfellow, Ralph Waldo Emerson, Harriet Beecher Stowe, Mark Twain, William Dean Howells, Henry James, Kate Chopin, W. E. B. Du Bois, Edith Wharton, Willa Cather, and William Faulkner have been revised, updated, and in some cases entirely rewritten in light of recent scholarship. The Shorter Eighth Edition further expands its selections of women writers and writers from diverse ethnic, racial, and regional backgrounds—always with attention to the critical acclaim that recognizes their contributions to the American literary record. Recently added clusters on "Native Americans: Contact and Conflict" and "Native Americans: Removal and Resistance," introduced and annotated by Native American specialist Arnold Krupat, enable teachers to bring early Native American writing and oratory into their syllabuses, or should they prefer, to focus on these selections as a free-standing unit leading toward the moment after 1945 when Native writers fully entered the mainstream of literary activity.

We are pleased to continue our popular innovation of topical gatherings of short texts that illuminate the cultural, historical, intellectual, and literary concerns of their respective periods. Designed to be taught in a class period or two, or used as background, each of the 8 clusters consists of brief, carefully excerpted primary and (in one case) secondary texts, about 6–10 per cluster, and an introduction. Diverse voices—many new to the anthology—highlight a range of views current when writers of a particular time period were active, and thus allow students better to understand some of the large issues that were being debated at particular historical moments. For example, in "Slavery, Race, and the Making of American Literature," texts by David Walker, William Lloyd Garrison, Angelina Grimké, Sojourner Truth, and Martin R. Delany speak to the great paradox of pre–Civil War America, addressed by numerous authors of the period: the contradictory rupture between the realities of slavery and the nation's ideals of freedom.

The Shorter Eighth Edition strengthens this feature with four new clusters attuned to the requests of teachers. To help students address the controversy over race and aesthetics in *Adventures of Huckleberry Finn*, we introduce a cluster in "American Literature 1865–1914" that shows what some of the leading critics of the past few decades have thought was at stake in reading and interpreting Twain's canonical novel. Entitled "Critical Controversy: Race and the Ending of *Adventures of Huckleberry Finn*," the cluster brings together selections by Toni Morrison, Jane Smiley, Leo Marx, Justin Kaplan, Julius Lester, Shelley Fisher Fishkin, and David L. Smith. For the contemporary period in "Literature Since 1945," we print for the first time "Creative Nonfiction," a much-requested topic showcasing a newly important (and highly popular) literary genre, with selections by Edward Abbey, Barry Lopez, Jamaica Kincaid, Joan Didion, and Edwidge Danticat, among others. New to "Beginnings to 1700" is a cluster on "First Encounters: Early European Accounts of Native Americans," while "American Literature 1820–1865" has a revised cluster, "Section, Region, Nation, Hemisphere," which puts new emphasis on the expanding U.S. nation in the larger context of the Americas, and "American Literature 1865–1914" offers "Realism and Naturalism," with selections by Theodore Dreiser, Frank Norris, William Dean Howells, and others.

The Shorter Eighth Edition of *The Norton Anthology of American Literature* features a dramatic expansion of our illustrations, including not only the color plates so popular in the last edition, but also over 80 black-and-white illustrations added throughout the volumes. In selecting color plates—from Juan de la Cosa's world map at the start of the sixteenth century to *The Gates* by Christo and Jeanne-Claude at the beginning of the twenty-first—the editors aimed to provide images relevant to literary works in the anthology while depicting arts and artifacts representative of each era. Throughout the Shorter Eighth Edition, we have similarly added visually striking black-and-white images that will provoke discussion. In addition, graphic works—segments from Art Spiegelman's canonical graphic novel *Maus*, and a facsimile page of an Emily Dickinson manuscript, along with a number of the new illustrations—open possibilities for teaching visual texts.

Period-by-Period Revisions

Beginnings to 1820. "Beginnings to 1700," edited by Wayne Franklin, continues to feature narratives by early European explorers of the North American continent as they encountered and attempted to make sense of the diverse cultures they met, and as they attempted to justify their aim of claiming the territory for Europeans. These are precisely the issues foregrounded by the new cluster on "First Encounters," which gathers writings by Hernán Cortés, Samuel de Champlain, Robert Juet, and others. In addition to the recently added material from Roger Williams and Edward Taylor, we continue to offer selections from Rowlandson's enormously influential *A Narrative of the Captivity and Restoration of Mrs. Mary Rowlandson*. The heightened attention in this section to the combined religious and territorial aspirations of the Anglo settlers, which fail to take account of the perspectives of the Native American writers, gives students a fuller sense of the inevitable conflicts ensuing from the European perception that North America was a "New World" rather than a long-settled world with its own history and traditions. We note, too, the important role of the experiences of, and narratives by, women in the early European settlement of the future United States.

In "American Literature 1700–1820," edited by Philip Gura, we approach the eighteenth century as a period of consolidation and development in an emergent American literature. The inclusion of a long excerpt from one of Charles Brockden Brown's major novels, *Edgar Huntly*, new to the Shorter Eighth Edition, calls attention to the Americanization of such important literary developments as the gothic. We have also added new selections by Benjamin Franklin and Thomas Jefferson. The cluster "Native Americans: Contact and Conflict," collects speeches and accounts by Pontiac, Samson Occom, Chief Logan (as cited by Thomas Jefferson), Red Jacket, and Tecumseh, which, as a group, underscore a centuries-long pattern of initial friendly contact mutating into bitter and violent conflict between Native Americans and whites. This cluster, which focuses on Native Americans' points of view, wonderfully complements the new cluster on "First Encounters," which focuses on European colonizers' points of view.

American Literature 1820–1865. Under the editorship of Robert S. Levine, this section is now much more diverse. Emerson's *Nature*, Douglass's *Narrative*, and Whitman's *Song of Myself* are still complete in this volume, as well as novellas by Melville, Davis's *Life in the Iron Mills*, and other frequently assigned works. Aware of the important role of African American writers in the period, the omnipresence of race and slavery as literary and political themes, and the recognition of literary value in a previously ignored population, we have recently added the major African American writer Frances E. W. Harper, as well as more chapters from Stowe's *Uncle Tom's Cabin* (including a new chapter for the Shorter Eighth Edition) and the cluster "Slavery, Race, and the Making of American Literature," which help to remind students of how central slavery was to the literary and political life of the nation during this period. "Native Americans: Resistance and Removal," gathers oratory and writings—by Native Americans such as Black Hawk, Petelasharo, Elias Boudinot, and the collective authors of the Cherokee Memorials as well as by whites such as Ralph Waldo Emerson—protesting Andrew Jackson's ruthless national policy of Indian removal. Political themes, far from diluting the literary imagination of American authors, served to inspire some of the most memorable writing of the day.

Recently added prose fiction includes chapters from Cooper's *Last of the Mohicans* and Poe's "The Black Cat." Poetry by Emily Dickinson is now presented in the texts recently established by R. W. Franklin (we retain the traditional Thomas Johnson numbers in brackets for reference) and includes a facsimile page from Fascicle 10. For the Shorter Eighth Edition there are a number of substantial additions, including new poems and letters by Dickinson and a new section on Louisa May Alcott featuring her Civil War story "My Contraband." Other selections added to this edition include Washington Irving's "The Author's Account of Himself," a key chapter from Harriet Beecher Stowe's *Uncle Tom's Cabin* (on the death of Little Eva), and Frances Harper's "Learning to Read."

American Literature 1865–1914. Edited by Nina Baym, Robert S. Levine, and Jeanne Campbell Reesman, this section over the last two editions has taken on a striking new look. To our well-received complete longer works— Twain's *Adventures of Huckleberry Finn*, Chopin's *The Awakening*, and

James's *Daisy Miller*—we have added complete texts of Stephen Crane's *Maggie: A Girl of the Streets* and Abraham Cahan's *The Imported Bridegroom*, as well as chapters from Theodore Dreiser's *Sister Carrie* and Twain's *Roughing It*. Also recently added are Edith Wharton's "The Other Two" and "Roman Fever," and works by Sui Sin Far, Zitkala Ša, and Ambrose Bierce. Additional writings by Walt Whitman and Emily Dickinson help students bridge the years between the Civil War and the industrializing 1890s. As mentioned above, a new critical cluster on *Huckleberry Finn* will help instructors to engage their students in debates about some of the most controversial aspects of Twain's novel. Another cluster takes up key political and literary disputes from the era: In "Realism and Naturalism," critical writings by William Dean Howells, Henry James, Frank Norris, Theodore Dreiser, and Jack London illuminate the turn to realism and naturalism, styles developed to represent and deal with the rapidly changing character of the American nation as it entered the industrial era with a markedly more diverse and larger population. By request of instructors and students, we have added a new poet, Paul Laurence Dunbar, a new story by Kate Chopin, "The Story of an Hour," and a new selection by Sui Sin Far, authors who underscore the emergence of a literary culture in which voices from diverse ethnic, racial, and regional backgrounds became part of American literary culture.

American Literature 1914–1945. Edited by Mary Loeffelholz, "American Literature 1914–1945" offers a number of complete longer works—Eugene O'Neill's *Long Day's Journey into Night* (exclusive to the Norton Anthology), Willa Cather's *Neighbour Rosicky*, Susan Glaspell's *Trifles*, T.S. Eliot's *The Waste Land*, and Ernest Hemingway's *The Snows of Kilimanjaro*. Reconsidered selections by Ezra Pound, T. S. Eliot, Marianne Moore, Hart Crane, and Langston Hughes encourage students and teachers to contemplate the interrelation of modernist aesthetics with ethnic, regional, and popular writing. An illuminating cluster, newly added to the Shorter Eighth Edition, addresses central events of the modern period: In "Modernist Manifestos," F. T. Marinetti, Mina Loy, Ezra Pound, Willa Cather, William Carlos Williams, and Langston Hughes show how the manifesto as a form exerted a powerful influence on international modernism in all the arts.

American Literature since 1945. "American Literature since 1945," jointly edited by Jerome Klinkowitz and Patricia B. Wallace, features a period introduction in which prose and poetry intermingle and for which "Postwar" no longer explains a period that grows longer with every edition. The result is a rich representation of the period's literary activity, and a more accurate presentation of the writers themselves, many of whom write in multiple genres. The volume continues to offer the complete texts of Tennessee Williams's *A Streetcar Named Desire* (exclusive to this anthology), Arthur Miller's *Death of a Salesman*, and Allen Ginsberg's *Howl*. Introduced in the Seventh Edition, Art Spiegelman's prize-winning *Maus* opens possibilities for teaching the graphic novel. Another innovation from the Seventh Edition was the inclusion of teachable stand-alone segments from important novels by Saul Bellow (*The Adventures of Augie March*) and Jack Kerouac (*Big Sur*), and we continue to print those chapters. Newly anthologized writers include Martin Luther King Jr., and the Dominican-American fiction writer Junot Díaz, whose 2008 novel, *The Brief Wondrous Life of Oscar Wao*, won the Pulitzer Prize and was an international sensation. New to the Shorter Eighth Edition is a cluster on "Creative Nonfiction." Here students are introduced to writers such as Joan Didion and Edward Abbey who self-consciously blend fiction and nonfiction, creating works that over the past few decades have become enormously popular and influential.

In all, we are delighted to offer this revised Shorter Eighth Edition to teachers and students, and we welcome your comments.

Additional Resources from the Publisher

The Shorter Eighth Edition retains the flexible formats—a one-volume paperback version and two-volume paperback splits—that have been welcomed by instructors and students. These formats accommodate instructors who use the anthology in either a one- or two-semester survey. To give instructors even more flexibility, the publisher is making available the full list of 220 Norton Critical Editions, including such frequently assigned novels as Harriet Beecher Stowe's *Uncle Tom's Cabin*, Herman Melville's *Moby-Dick*, Edith Wharton's *The House of Mirth*, and William Faulkner's *The Sound and the Fury*, among many others. A Norton Critical Edition can be included with any volume for free. Each Norton Critical Edition gives students an authoritative, carefully annotated text accompanied by rich contextual and critical materials prepared by an expert in the subject.

For students using *The Norton Anthology of American Literature*, the publisher provides a wealth of resources on the free StudySpace website (wwnorton.com/naal). Students who activate the password included in each new copy of the anthology gain access to more than 70 reading-comprehension quizzes with extensive feedback; bulleted period summaries and period review quizzes with feedback; timelines; maps; audio readings of public domain texts; Literary Workshops that show students step-by-step how to read, analyze, and respond in writing to a work of literature; and a new "Literary Places" feature that uses Google Tours tools to let students (virtually) visit Thoreau's Walden Pond, Faulkner's Oxford, Mississippi, home, Cather's Nebraska plains, and other literary places. The rich gathering of content on StudySpace is designed to help students understand individual works and appreciate the places, sounds, and sights of literature.

The publisher also provides extensive instructor-support materials. Designed to enhance large or small lecture environments, the Instructor Resource Disc, expanded for the Eighth Edition, features more than 300 images with explanatory captions; lecture PowerPoint slides for each period introduction and for most topic clusters; and audio recordings (MP3). Much praised by both new and experienced instructors, *Teaching with The Norton Anthology of American Literature: A Guide for Instructors* by Edward Whitley, Lehigh University, and Bruce Michelson, University of Illinois at Urbana-Champaign, provides detailed reading lists for a variety of approaches—the historical approach, the "major authors" approach, the literary traditions approach, and the approach by genre or theme. Each author/work entry offers teaching suggestions, discussion questions, and suggestions for incorporating multimedia from the Instructor Resource Disc, the *American Passages* website, as well as other outside resources. The Guide is available both in print and in a searchable online format. Finally, Norton Coursepacks bring high-quality digital media into a new or existing online course. The Coursepacks include all content from the StudySpace website, short-answer questions with suggested answers, and a bank of discussion questions adapted from the Guide. Norton's Coursepacks are available in a variety of formats, including Blackboard/WebCT, Desire2Learn, Angel, and Moodle, at no cost to instructors or students.

Instructors who adopt *The Norton Anthology of American Literature* have access to an extensive array of films and videos. In addition to videos of the plays by O'Neill, Williams, and Miller in the anthology, segments of the award-winning video series *American Passages: A Literary Survey* are available without charge on orders of specified quantities of the Norton Anthology. Funded by Annenberg/CPB, produced by Oregon Public Broadcasting, and developed with the Norton Anthology as its exclusive companion anthology, *American Passages* contains sixteen segments, each covering a literary movement or period by exploring two or three authors in depth. The videos are supported by the *American Passages* Archive, a searchable online archive of over 3,000 items, including visual art, audio files, primary-source materials, and additional texts, which may be accessed through the link on the StudySpace student website. A print instructor's guide and student guide are also available. For information about the videos, contact your Norton representative.

Editorial Procedures

As in past editions, editorial features—period introductions, headnotes, annotations, and bibliographies—are designed to be concise yet full and to give students necessary information without imposing an interpretation. The editors have updated all apparatus in response to new scholarship: period introductions have been entirely or substantially rewritten, as have many headnotes. All Selected Bibliographies and each period's general-resources bibliographies categorized by Reference Works, Histories, and Literary Criticism have been thoroughly updated. The Shorter Eighth Edition retains three editorial features that help students place their reading in historical and cultural context—a Texts/Contexts timeline following each period introduction and maps on the endpaper of each volume.

Our policy has been to reprint each text in the form that accords, as far as it is possible to determine, to the intention of its author. There is one exception: we have modernized most spellings and (very sparingly) the punctuation in "Beginnings to 1700" and "American Literature 1700–1820" on the principle that archaic spellings and typography pose unnecessary problems for beginning students. We have used square brackets to indicate titles supplied by the editors for the convenience of students. Whenever a portion of a text has been omitted, we have indicated that omission with three asterisks. If the omitted portion is important for following the plot or argument, we give a brief summary within the text or in a footnote. After each work, we cite (when known) the date of composition on the left and the date of first publication on the right; in some instances, the latter is followed by the date of a revised edition for which the author was responsible.

The editors have benefited from commentary offered by hundreds of teachers throughout the country. Those teachers who prepared detailed critiques, or who offered special help in preparing texts, are listed under Acknowledgments, on a separate page. We also thank the many people at Norton who contributed to the Shorter Eighth Edition: Julia Reidhead, who supervised the Shorter Eighth Edition; Marian Johnson, managing editor, college; Carly Fraser Doria, associate editor; Eileen Connell, electronic media editor; Michael Fleming, Candace Levy, Katharine Ings, and Susan Joseph, manuscript editors; Rachel Mayer, Pam Lawson, Jack Borrebach, Sophie Hagen, Diane Cipollone, project editors; Hannah Blaisdell, editorial assistant; Benjamin Reynolds and Sean Mintus, production managers; Jo Anne Metsch, designer; Trish Marx, manager, photo department; Stephanie Romeo, photo editor; Jane Sanders Miller, photo researcher; Debra Morton Hoyt, art director; Megan Jackson, permissions manager; and Margaret Gorenstein, who cleared permissions. We also wish to acknowledge our debt to the late George P. Brockway, former president and chairman at Norton, who invented this anthology, and to M. H. Abrams, Norton's advisor on English texts. All have helped us to create an anthology that, more than ever, is testimony to the continuing richness of American literary traditions.

NINA BAYM, General Editor
ROBERT S. LEVINE, Associate General Editor

Acknowledgments

Among our many critics, advisors, and friends, the following were of especial help toward the preparation of the Shorter Eighth Edition, either with advice or by providing critiques of particular periods of the anthology: Stephen Adams (University of Western Ontario); Jacob Agatucci (Central Oregon Community College/Cochise College); M. Lee Alexander (College of William and Mary); Booker T. Anthony (Fayetteville State University); Carolyn Bergonzo; Susanne George Bloomfield (University of Nebraska–Kearney); Amy Branam (Frostburg State University); Dr. David Brottman; Alan Brown (University of West Alabama); P. Michael Campbell (Coastal Carolina University); Randall Cluff (Southern Virginia University); Edward S. Cutler (Brigham Young University); Michael Drexler (Bucknell University); Matt Dube (William Woods University); Annamaria Formichella Elsden (Buena Vista University); Daniel Fineman (Occidental College); Lorie Watkins Fulton (William Carey University); James Gill (Northwest Christian University); Rachel Golland (St. Thomas Aquinas College); Charlotte Gordon (Endicott College); Carey Goyette (Clinton Community College); Dr. Lisa Grunberger (Temple University); Jeff Gundy (Bluffton University); Laura Hammons (Hinds Community College); John R. Hart (Motlow State Community College); Trenton Hickman (Brigham Young University); Wenching Ho (Feng Chia University); Greg Horn (Southwest Virgina Community College); Robert Jakubovic (Cincinnati State Technical and Community College); Paul Jones (Ohio University); Virginia Kennedy (Cornell University); Mabel Khawaja (Hampton University); Dr. Matt Klauza (Erskine College); Peter J. Kvidera (John Carroll University); Gretchen Lieb (Vassar College); Shuchin Lin (Tunghai University); Trish Loughran (University of Illinois); Kristina Lucas (NHTI); Scott Richard Lyons (University of Michigan–Ann Arbor); Adam McKible (John Jay College); Irvin Morris (Navajo Community College); Paul Ohler (Kwantlen Polytechnic University); Laura Osborne (New River Community College); H. Daniel Peck (Vassar College); Jay Peterson (Atlantic Cape Community College); Lily Phillips (North Carolina State University); Roxanna Pisiak (Morrisville State College); Paula Reif (Carl Albert State College); Debby Rosenthal (John Carroll University); Peter Sattler (Lakeland College); Brandon R. Schrand (University of Idaho); Gabriela Serrano (Angelo State University); Larry Severeid (Utah State University–College of Eastern Utah); Scott R. Stankey (Anoka Ramsey Community College); Jeffrey Steele (University of Wisconsin); Terri L. Stricker (Washington Bible College); Hsiu-chih Tsai (National Taiwan University); Rebecca A. Wall (Winston-Salem State University); Edward

Whitelock (Gordon College); Russell Winn (J. F. Drake State Technical College); David A. Wright (Furman University); Scott D. Yarbrough (Charleston Southern University); Elizabeth Young (Mount Holyoke College). Finally, congratulations to Cecilia Gigliotti (New Britain High School, CT) and Shanell Sharpe (University of Connecticut), winners of the 2011 Norton Anthology Student Recitation Contest.

THE NORTON ANTHOLOGY OF

AMERICAN LITERATURE

SHORTER EIGHTH EDITION

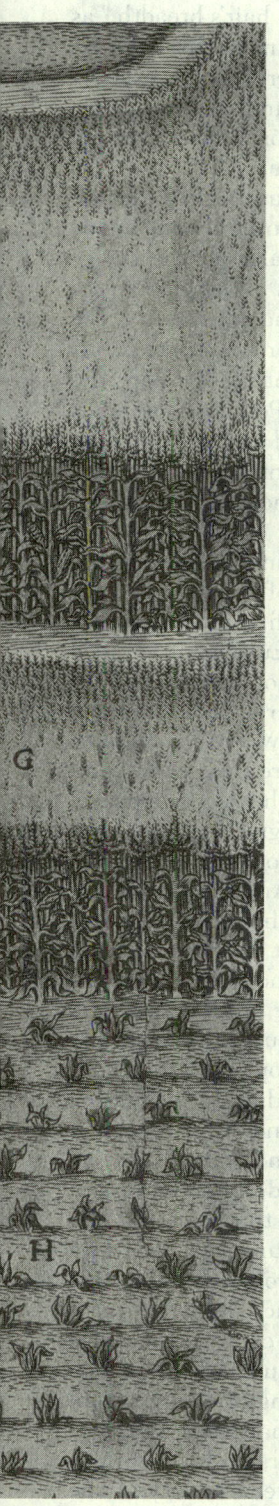

G

H

Beginnings to 1700

THE MARVELS OF SPAIN— AND AMERICA

In 1494 a man who had crossed the Atlantic in a large ship returned home to amaze those whom he had left behind with tales of a new world full of "marvels." None of those who listened to him had accomplished anything remotely like this. None had heard of this other world, let alone seen it, and none could begin to comprehend what its discovery might mean for their own familiar universe. As they listened with rapt attention, the voyager told of things undreamed of, plants and animals and most of all strange peoples whose uncanny customs, costumes, and beliefs astonished all who heard him.

The man in question might have been Christopher Columbus or any of the dozens of Europeans who accompanied him on his first voyage, but he was not. In fact, this teller of tales did join in that voyage, but he had not sailed from Palos, Spain, with the other men on August 6, 1492, and had not been with them when, at two in the morning of October 12, they sighted the Bahamian island they named San Salvador. Twice he crossed the Atlantic with Columbus, but in reverse: first to Spain from the Indies and then back again. We do not know his original name, but we know that he was a Taino Indian from the Bahamas, one of seven Natives whom Columbus seized and took to Spain. There he was baptized and renamed Diego Colón, after the son of Columbus himself. (Colón was the Spanish version of the family's name.) Of the other natives, all of whom were similarly rechristened, one remained in Spain, where he died within a few years. Four others

John White, **Indian Village of Secoton** (detail), 1585. For more information about this image, see the color insert in this volume.

died of sickness on the passage back to America with Columbus and Colón. Colón and the sixth man escaped the same fate only "by a hair's breadth," as the fleet's physician, Diego Alvarez Chanca, wrote in his important letter on the second voyage. Returned to the Caribbean, the two served as translators for the much larger party of Spaniards, perhaps fifteen hundred strong, who arrived in seventeen ships early in November 1493. Colón himself already had seen service as an intermediary during the first voyage.

Of the two men, only Colón is reported by the historian Andrés Bernáldez, who knew Columbus and used the mariner's own lost account of the second voyage, to have regaled the other Natives with tales of "the things which he had seen in Castile and the marvels of Spain, . . . the great cities and fortresses and churches, . . . the people and horses and animals, . . . the great nobility and wealth of the sovereigns and great lords, . . . the kinds of food, . . . the festivals and tournaments [and] bull-fighting." Perhaps the other man had died by this point in the second voyage. Perhaps Columbus singled out Colón for special mention because Colón had learned Castilian well enough to speak it and had shown himself to be an intelligent man and a good guide. He was to accompany Columbus on the whole of this voyage, which lasted three years.

The story of Colón catches in miniature the extraordinary changes that were to occur as natives of Europe encountered natives of the Americas for the first time in recorded history. His story reminds us first that discovery was mutual rather than one-sided. To be sure, far more Europeans voyaged to America than Americans to Europe, and they sent home thousands of reports and letters detailing what they saw and did there. Because many of these European travelers came to America to stay, however, the Indians soon had a colonial imitation of Europe developing before their eyes, complete with fortresses, churches, horses, new foods (on the second voyage, Columbus brought wheat, melons, onions, radishes, salad greens, grapevines, sugar cane, and various fruit trees), and much else that Colón in 1493 could have found only in Europe. Over time the Natives of America could discover Europe encroaching on their villages and fields as the imported European landscape vied with their own. Europe was present in the textiles on the colonists' bodies, in the tools in their hands (for both of which the American Indians traded), and in the institutions of the church and state (slavery being the most obvious example) that had begun to reshape the identities and reorganize the lives of Native American peoples. In such concrete terms a new world was being created in the West Indies. It was not the new world Columbus himself was speaking of near the end of his life when he wrote in 1500 to the Spanish sovereigns Ferdinand and Isabella that he had "brought under [their] dominion . . . another world, whereby Spain, which was called poor, is now most rich." The new world that mattered was not just an expanse of space previously unknown to Europeans; it was a genuinely new set of social relationships that would evolve over the next centuries as Europe and the Americas continued to interact. With the European introduction of African slaves early in the sixteenth century, the terms of this new world became much more complex. The cultural and social relations of Americans took their origin in a great mixing of peoples from the whole Atlantic basin during the first century and a half after 1492.

Discovery began with wonder—that of Colón's listeners on his return in 1494 and that of Columbus as he descanted on the green beauty of the

Columbus Landing in the Indies, from *La Lettera dell'isole che ha trovata nouovamenta il re di'spagna,* 1493. This woodcut was created to accompany a metrical version, by the Florentine poet Giuliano Dati, of the letter Columbus wrote describing his first voyage. It is of interest for its symbolic presentation of European authority (in the person of Ferdinand of Spain) and its early conceptualization of what the Taino Indians looked like.

islands—evoking a mood that has remained strong in American writing ever since: he saw "trees of a thousand kinds" on San Salvador in November 1492, trees that seemed to "touch the sky . . . as green and as lovely as they are in Spain in May." But beyond that transcendent moment, discovery entailed a many-sided process of influence and exchange that ultimately produced the hybrid cultural universe of the Atlantic world, of which the English colonies were one small part. Much of this universe came through struggle rather than cooperation. Each people used its own traditions or elements recently borrowed from others to endure or conquer or outwit its opposite numbers, and violence often swallowed up the primal wonder glimpsed in the earliest documents. With gunpowder and steel, Europeans had the technological edge in warfare, and it would seem that—despite centuries of propaganda to the contrary—they were more violent than the American Indians. The Natives at first found the scale of European warfare appalling. In New England, soldier John Underhill thus noted in his *Newes from America* (1638) the complaint of the colonists' Native allies against the Pequot tribe in 1637. "The manner of *English* men's fight is too furious, and slays too many men." The Natives were quick to adopt European weapons and tactics, however, applying them to their own disputes and to their disputes with the Europeans. The ferocity of what Europeans have called the

"Indian wars" was the violent recoil in the face of violence from interlopers who threatened the very life of the Native peoples.

Almost literally from 1492, Native peoples began to die in large numbers, if not from war then from enslavement, brutal mistreatment, despair, or disease. One of the more insidious forms of "exchange" involved the transfer to the American Indians of the microbes to which Europeans had become inured but to which the Indians had virtually no resistance. Nothing better displays the isolation of the continents and the drama of encounter that began in 1492 than the epidemic disasters that smallpox, measles, typhus, and other European maladies unleashed on the Native Americans. Whole populations plummeted as such diseases, combined with the other severe stresses placed on the Natives, spread throughout the Caribbean and then on the mainland of Central and South America. The institutional disease of slavery further decimated the Native peoples. It is widely agreed that the original population of the island of Hispaniola (estimated at anywhere from one hundred thousand to eight million in 1492) plunged once the Spanish took over the island, partly through disease and partly through the abuses of the *encomienda* system of virtual enslavement. In the face of this sudden decline in available Native labor, Spain introduced African slavery into Hispaniola as early as 1501. By the middle of the sixteenth century the Native population had been so completely displaced by African slaves that the Spanish historian Antonio de Herrera called the island "an effigy or an image of Ethiopia itself." Thus the destruction of one people was accompanied by the displacement and enslavement of another. By that point, the naive "wonder" of discovery was all but unrecoverable.

It would be inaccurate to picture the Indians, however, as merely victims, suffering decline. The Natives made shrewd use of the European presence in America to forward their own aims, as Colón reminds us. In 1519 the disaffected Natives in the Aztec Empire clearly threw their lot in with Cortés because they saw in him a chance to settle the score with their overlord Montezuma, which they assuredly did. In New England, the Pequot War of 1637 saw a similar alignment on the English side of such tribes as the Narragansetts and the Mohegans, who had grievances with the fierce Pequots in the region. Under ordinary circumstances, as with the Iroquois in the Northeast, European technology and the European market were seized on as a means of consolidating advantages gained before the arrival of the colonists. The Iroquois had begun to organize their famous League of the Five Nations before European settlement, but they solidified their earlier victories over other Native peoples by forging canny alliances with the Dutch and then the English in New York. In the Southeast, remnant peoples banded together in the early eighteenth century to create the Catawba, a new political group that constructed what one historian has called a "new world" for itself. No longer known by a bewildering diversity of names, the former Nassaw and Suttirie and Charra and Succa peoples banded together with several others in an attempt to deal more effectively with the encroaching Euro-Americans of Charleston and the Low Country. This hardly was a case of diminishment or reduction. Even as fewer and fewer of the original millions remained, they showed themselves resourceful in resisting, transforming, and exploiting the exotic cultures the Europeans were imposing on their original landscape.

NATIVE AMERICAN ORAL LITERATURE

When Columbus sailed from Europe in 1492, he left behind him a number of relatively centralized nation-states with largely agricultural economies. Europeans spoke some two or three dozen languages, most of them closely related; and they were generally Christian in religious belief and worldview, although many groups had had contact—and conflict—with adherents of Judaism and Islam. A written alphabet had been used by Europeans to preserve and communicate information for many centuries, and Gutenberg's invention of moveable type in the mid-1400s had shown the way to a mechanical means of "writing"; by 1492, Europe was on its way to becoming a print culture.

By contrast, in 1492 in North America, Native people spoke hundreds of languages belonging to entirely different linguistic families (e.g., Athapascan, Uto-Aztecan, Chinookan, Siouan, and Algonquian) and structured their societies in widely diverse forms. In the Great Basin of the West, small, loosely organized bands of Utes eked out a bare subsistence by hunting and gathering, while the sedentary Pueblo peoples of the Southwest and the Iroquoians of the Northeast had both highly developed agricultural economies and complex modes of political organization. In spite of some common features, religious and mythological beliefs were also diverse. Among North American peoples alone, eight different types of creation stories have been cataloged, most of these quite different from those found in Judaism, Christianity, and Islam.

Also unlike European cultures, Native Americans north of what is now Mexico did not use a written alphabet. Theirs were oral cultures, relying on spoken words—whether chanted, sung, or presented in lengthy narratives— and the memory of those words to preserve important cultural information. The term *literature* comes from the Latin *littera,* "letter." Native American literatures were not, until long after the arrival of the Europeans, written "littera-tures." Indeed, as the phrase *oral literature* might appear to be a contradiction in terms, some have chosen to call the expressions of the oral tradition *orature.*

These expressions were, like the languages, political economies, and religious beliefs of Native American peoples, extremely various. Europeans in 1492 could name the tragedy, the comedy, the epic, the ode, and a variety of lyric forms as types of literature. In Native America there were almost surely (*almost,* because we have no actual records that predate 1492) such things as Winnebago trickster tale cycles, Apache jokes, Hopi personal naming and grievance chants, Yaqui deer songs, Yuman dream songs, Piman shamanic chants, Iroquois condolence rituals, Navajo curing and blessing chants, and Chippewa songs of the Great Medicine Society, to name only some of the types of Native American verbal expression.

That there are many such types is unquestionable, but are these "literary" types? This question would not make sense to traditional Native peoples, who do not have a category of language use corresponding to our category of literature. From a Western perspective, however, the types of Native American verbal expression could be considered as literature only after that late-eighteenth- and early-nineteenth-century revolution in European consciousness known as Romanticism. In that period the concept of literature shifted away from being defined by the *medium* of expression (all language preserved in *letters*) to the *kind* of expression (those texts that emphasized the imaginative and emotional possibilities of language). With this shift in the meaning of *literature,* many Native American verbal types could quite comfortably be considered literary.

But bringing them to the page in English involves two issues of translation, not just one. In addition, that is, to the usual question of how to translate foreign languages (and, in this case, non-European languages) into English, there is also the question of how to translate from oral to written. Oral performances are dramatic events in time, language presented to the ears of listeners who are physically present. Written literature, however, presents a silent array of marks: letters, objects, as it were, in space for the eyes of an audience that is for the most part not known to the author. In oral performance, a pause, a quickening of pace, a lowering or raising of the voice can affect the audience's understanding. And, typically, the performance is in turn affected by audience response. Can anything be done to convey such things on the page? Indeed, should translators even try to convey such things on the page? Not surprisingly, there are many different answers to these questions. Some translations have experimented with a special typography and layout where type size and page design attempt to present analogs for the eye of what the ear would have heard—what Dennis Tedlock has called a "performable text." Others, convinced that no arrangement of black marks on a page can actually reproduce the effect of a living voice, have simply chosen to translate in formats that look like either poetry or prose.

It needs to be emphasized, however, that in oral performance poetry can be distinguished from prose only when it can be shown to have what Dan Ben-Amos has called a regular "metric sub-structure." But a great many performances with no such metric regularity at all—oral narratives, for example—have been printed to *look like* what *we* call poetry on the page. This is strictly a decision made by the translator or transcriber, usually one who wishes to emphasize the literary quality of the story in question.

VOYAGES OF DISCOVERY

Columbus was still making voyages to America (1492–93, 1493–96, 1498, and 1502–04) as other Europeans, following his example, found their way to the West Indies. Giovanni Caboto (known as John Cabot to the English for whom he sailed) and his fellow Italian Amerigo Vespucci both crossed the ocean before 1500, as did the Portuguese Pedro Cabral. After that date the voyagers became too many to track. Unlike the Viking expeditions of five hundred years before, which had established modest coastal settlements in North America that Native Americans soon wiped out, this second European wave quickly gathered momentum and extended itself far to the north and south of the Caribbean basin that Columbus explored. Cabot was near the mouth of the Saint Lawrence in Canada the year before Vespucci found that of the Amazon, nearly five thousand miles away in South America. Soon the Europeans were establishing colonies everywhere. The first Spanish colonists lingered on the Caribbean island of Hispaniola after the departure of Columbus in 1493, and although that small settlement of La Navidad was soon destroyed in a clash with Taino natives under the cacique Caonabo of Maguana, the massive second voyage in 1493 came equipped to stay. From that point on Spain and Europe generally maintained an aggressive presence in the West Indies. The constant battles along vague frontiers with Native peoples added fuel to the dissension and political in-fighting among the settlers themselves, whose riots and mutinies nearly ruined settlement after settlement. John Smith's experience during the first Jamestown voyage of 1607 provides probably the most famous example from Anglo-America. Arrested and nearly executed (probably for offending his "betters," something he had the habit of doing) en route to America in 1607, Smith was released in Virginia when the colony's sealed instructions were opened, revealing that this apparently low-ranking soldier had been named to the prestigious governing council even before the ships had left England. Columbus himself became the focus of fierce competition among greedy settlers and officials in Hispaniola by the time of his third voyage and, stripped of his property and powers by a royal official enraged by the uproar, was taken back to Spain in chains in 1500.

Europe continued to expand in the Americas amid the disorder within settlement walls and the great violence outside. Columbus found the mainland of South America in 1498 and Central America in 1502, by which time Cabot and the Portuguese Corte-Real brothers, Gaspar and Miguel, had been down the coast of North America from Labrador to the Chesapeake, and Cabral and Vespucci had covered the east coast of South America from the Orinoco River in present-day Venezuela to well south of the Río de la Plata on the border of present-day Uruguay and Argentina. Between 1515 and the 1520s, Spain, under the reign of Charles V, aggressively reached out over the Gulf of Mexico, toward the Yucatán Peninsula and Mexico and

New World Natives, from an anonymous German woodcut, c. 1505. The text accompanying this detailed early illustration comments on Native Americans and their customs, praising their physical appearance and healthfulness as well as their distaste for both private property and public government. Only in passing does it assert that they kill and eat their enemies, smoking the dead bodies above their fires, as on closer inspection the woodcut indicates.

Florida and the Isthmus of Panama, then sent expeditions into the heart of North America from the 1520s to the 1540s, covering a vast region stretching from Florida west to the Gulf of California and north as far as Kansas and the Tennessee River. At the same time, other Spanish explorers and conquistadors spread out over South America, especially its west coast, where in imitation of Cortés's conquest of Mexico a decade earlier Francisco Pizarro overcame the Incan Empire, recently weakened by civil war. In that same period, the Portuguese established their first permanent settlements in Brazil, and the French explorer Jacques Cartier sailed into the Gulf of Saint Lawrence, then up its chief river as far as the site of the future Montreal. Within fifty years of 1492, then, the east coasts of much of both continents had been explored and many of their interior regions had been traversed; the most powerful and sophisticated of their peoples, the Aztecs and the Incas, had been conquered; and Europe had settled in for a long stay.

Under Ferdinand and Isabella and their grandson Charles V, Spain took the most aggressively expansive role in America. Other European nations, most conspicuously France and England, were more self-absorbed, awakening slowly to what was happening across the sea. Their first explorers enjoyed bad luck and inconsistent support. John and Sebastian Cabot had sailed for English merchants and the monarchs Henry VII and Henry VIII, but the first Cabot was lost on his voyage in 1498, and the second kept his interest in America alive only by entering the service of the Spanish Crown after 1512. A return to his adopted homeland of England and a royal pension from Edward VI came to him only in the 1540s, by which time he had committed himself to the search for an eastward route to China via the seas north of Russia. In France, Cartier enjoyed early support from Francis I, but his failure to find gold and other riches in the Saint Lawrence valley and his dispute with the nobleman Roberval, whom the king appointed to command Cartier's third voyage in 1541, led to profound disenchantment in France. Fishermen from both nations continued to harvest the fabulous riches of the shoals off North America and summered on the shore, drying their catch. But not until the 1570s for England and the beginning of the next century for France, as a new generation of adventurers arose and a period of commercial expansion set in, did broad public support and governmental sanction combine to stir lasting curiosity and investment. A series of luckless North American voyages by the English under Martin Frobisher, Humphrey Gilbert, and then Walter Ralegh ended in the tragedy of the "Lost Colony" of Roanoke Island in the 1580s. For another twenty years few English explorers made serious new efforts, although the press bubbled with publications regarding the New World, particularly the works of Richard Hakluyt the younger, whose great collections gathered the fugitive records of English, and indeed European, expansion overseas. Hakluyt's masterwork, *The Principall Navigations* (1598–1600), brought the literary productions of countless European mariners to the attention of a public newly stirred by what Shakespeare would soon call this "brave new world" of Euro-America. Hakluyt notwithstanding, only in 1606 did a second Virginia colony set forth, and this one faltered grievously at the start with a shipwreck on Bermuda (which was to inspire Shakespeare's *The Tempest*), riots at Jamestown, near starvation, and violent encounters with the Natives. By 1603 French interest had revived under the direction of a group of explorers and expansionists, Samuel de Champlain most significantly, who hoped to profit from America and, even more, to find a route through it to the fabled riches of Asia. Seasoned from his voyages to Spanish America, Champlain picked up where Cartier had left off sixty years earlier, founded permanent settlements in the Saint Lawrence valley, and through his agents and followers pushed French exploration as far west as Lake Superior at a time when the English were still struggling in Virginia and the settlement of New England had just begun at Plymouth.

LITERARY CONSEQUENCES OF 1492

The period of European exploration in the Americas produced a surprisingly large and intriguing body of literature. While many manuscripts were archived and out of reach until the nineteenth century, a number of texts found their way into print and were widely dispersed, thanks to the establishment of printing in the half century before 1492. Shortly after Columbus's return to Spain in early 1493, there appeared in print his letter to the court official Luis de Santangel, narrating the voyage and lushly describing the perpetual spring Columbus had found in the West Indies the previous autumn. From the appearance of that letter on, the printing press and the European expansion into America were reciprocal parts of a single engine. Without the ready dispersal of texts rich with imagery that stirred individual imagination and national ambition in regard to the West Indies, Europe's movement westward would have been blunted and perhaps thwarted. The sword of conquest found in the pen, and in the printing press, an indispensable ally.

The great mass of early American writings came from the hands of Europeans rather than the Native peoples of the Western Hemisphere; fortunately, there are important exceptions. The Native Americans had a lively oral culture that valued memory over mechanical means of preserving texts, although among some groups, such as the Aztecs, written traditions existed (in North America these records included shellwork belts and painted animal hides, tepees, and shields), and many more groups used visual records in subtle and sophisticated ways. Such cataclysms as the Conquest of Mexico produced not only the Spanish narratives of Cortés, Bernal Díaz del Castillo, and others but also native responses, many of which perished with those who knew them. Those that survived in original native characters or in transliterated form have inestimable ethnographic and literary value. For instance, anonymous Native writers working in the Nahuatl language of the Aztecs in 1528—significantly, they used the Roman alphabet introduced by the Spanish—lamented the fall of their capital to Cortés in the following lines:

> Broken spears lie in the roads;
> we have torn our hair in our grief.
> The houses are roofless now, and their walls
> are red with blood.

No one reading these four lines will easily glorify the Conquest of Mexico or of the Americas more generally. The story of the transoceanic encounter, however, ceases to be a matter of easy contrasts once one reads widely in the texts on either side. Although Europeans committed atrocities in the American, often they did so as a result of blundering and miscommunication rather than cool, deliberate policy. In fact, the split between policy and action goes to the heart of the infant Atlantic world of the sixteenth century and is mirrored in and influenced by the character of the writing that survives from the period. The great distance separating the hemispheres made the coordination of intention and performance extremely difficult. The authorities at home lacked the knowledge to form prudent or practical policy; as a result many texts written by explorers or colonists were intended as "briefs" meant to inform or influence policy decisions made at a distance. To cite a simple example, Columbus himself wrote a point-by-point description of his second voyage in 1495, addressed to Ferdinand and Isabella in a series of "items" to which the specific responses of the sovereigns were added by a court scribe. More complexly, Cortés sought to justify his patently illegal invasion of Mexico in 1519 by sending several long letters to Charles V defending his actions and promising lavish returns if his conquest could proceed.

Most documents sent from America to the European powers reveal such generally political intentions. Europe responded by issuing directives aimed at controlling events across the sea. Even when good policies were articulated in Europe, however, applying them in America entailed further problems. By the time instructions arrived in Hispaniola, Mexico, Jamestown, or Quebec, new events in the colony might have rendered them pointless. Distance made control both crucial and difficult. Whereas formal authority typically resided in Europe, power as an informal fact of life and experience and circumstance belonged to those in America who could seize and use it or who acquired it by virtue of what they did rather than the official investitures they bore. Mutiny became so pervasive a fact or fear in America precisely because individuals and groups had, morally and geographically, great latitude in the thinly populated colonial enclaves. If writing served in this fluid, ambiguous universe as a means to influence official policy at home, it also emerged as a means of justifying actions (as with Cortés) that violated or ignored European directives.

Early American writing had, though, a third and more compelling purpose as a literature of witness. That we know so much about the European devastation of the West Indies comes from the fact that some Europeans responded powerfully to that devastation in writing. Although no one typifies this mood better than Bartolomé de las Casas (1474–1566) who assailed Spain's ruthless destruction of whole peoples in America, it is the rare European document that does not reveal the bloody truths of Europe's colonial dreams. Starting with the Columbian voyages themselves and flowering in the Spanish West Indies, especially in the 1540s and 1550s when debates about the mistreatment of the Natives earnestly moved the clerics and government officials at home, America inspired an outpouring of written expression. Not all the literature of witness speaks to specific issues of policy or particular public debates, but in many of the texts one senses a critical eye, a point of view not likely to be swayed by the slogans of empire or faith or even wealth. Writers such as Diaz del Castillo, the chronicler of Cortés, and England's John Smith came from the underclass of their native countries, where but for the opportunities represented by America they might well have spent their days in silence. As a result, their writing could be subversive, even mutinous, achieving its greatest depth when it captured a vision of America as not just a dependent province of Europe, but a place where much that was genuinely new might be learned.

PILGRIM AND PURITAN

The establishment of Plymouth Plantation on the South Shore of Massachusetts in 1620 brought to North America a new kind of English settler. The founders of the colony (later called Pilgrims by their leader and historian William Bradford) shared with their allies, the Puritans, a wish to purify Christian belief and practice. Whereas the Puritans were initially willing to work within the confines of the established Church of England, the Pilgrims thought it so corrupt that they wished to separate themselves from it completely. While still in England, they set up their own secret congregation in the village of Scrooby in Nottinghamshire. Often subject to persecution and imprisonment, the Scrooby Separatists (as they were also called) saw little chance for remaining true to their faith as long as they remained in England. In 1608, five years after Queen Elizabeth was succeeded by James Stuart, an enemy of all such reformers, the Scrooby congregation left England and settled in the Netherlands, where, William Bradford tells us, they saw "fair and beautiful cities"—but, as foreigners, they were confronted by the "grisly face of poverty." Isolated by their language and unable to farm, they took up trades like weaving, Bradford's choice, that promised a living. Eventually, fearing that they might lose their religious identity as their children were swallowed up in Dutch culture, they petitioned for the right to settle in the vast American territories of England's Virginia Company. Backed by English investors, the venture was commercial as well as religious in nature. Among the hundred people on the *Mayflower* there were almost three times as many secular settlers as Separatists. This initial group, set down on the raw Massachusetts shore in November 1620, made hasty arrangements to face the winter. The colonists survived this "starving time" by virtue of their own fortitude and the essential aid of the nearby Wampanoag Indians and their leader, Massasoit. From these "small beginnings," as Bradford was eager to declare, grew a community of mythical import to the later nation.

Much larger at its start was the well-financed effort that brought a contingent of Puritans under John Winthrop to Massachusetts Bay, not far north of Plymouth, in 1630. Although these settlers initially expressed no overt intention to sever their ties with the Church of England, and are generally regarded as nonseparating dissenters, the distance they put between themselves and church hierarchy was eloquent testimony of a different purpose. On other issues, they shared with the Pilgrims the same basic beliefs: both agreed with Martin Luther that no pope or bishop had a right to impose any law on a Christian without consent and both accepted John Calvin's view that God freely chose (or "elected") those he would save and those he would damn eternally. By 1691, when a new charter subsumed Plymouth as an independent colony under Massachusetts Bay, the Pilgrims and Puritans had merged in all but memory.

Too much can be made of the Calvinist doctrine of election; those who have not read the actual Puritan sermons often come away from secondary sources with the mistaken notion that Puritans talked about nothing but damnation. Puritans did indeed hold that God had chosen, before their birth, those whom he wished to save; but it does not follow that Puritans considered most of us to be born damned. Puritans argued that Adam broke the "Covenant of Works" (the promise God made to Adam that he was immortal and could live in Paradise forever as long as he obeyed God's commandments) when he disobeyed and ate of the tree of knowledge of good and evil, thereby bringing sin and death into the world. Their central doctrine, however, was the new "Covenant of Grace," a binding agreement that Christ made with all people who believed in him and that he sealed with his Crucifixion, promising them eternal life. Puritans thus addressed themselves not to the hopelessly unregenerate but to the indifferent, and they addressed the heart more often than the mind, always distinguishing between "historical" or rational understanding and heartfelt "saving faith." There is more joy in Puritan life and thought than we often credit, and this joy is the direct result of meditation on the doctrine of Christ's redeeming power. Edward Taylor is not alone in making his rapturous litany of Christ's attributes: "He is altogether lovely in everything, lovely in His person, lovely in His natures, lovely in His properties, lovely in His offices, lovely in His titles, lovely in His practice, lovely in His purchases and lovely in His relations." All of Taylor's art is a meditation on the miraculous gift of the Incarnation, and in this respect his sensibility is typically Puritan. Anne Bradstreet, who is remarkably frank about confessing her religious doubts, told her children that it was "upon this rock Christ Jesus" that she built her faith.

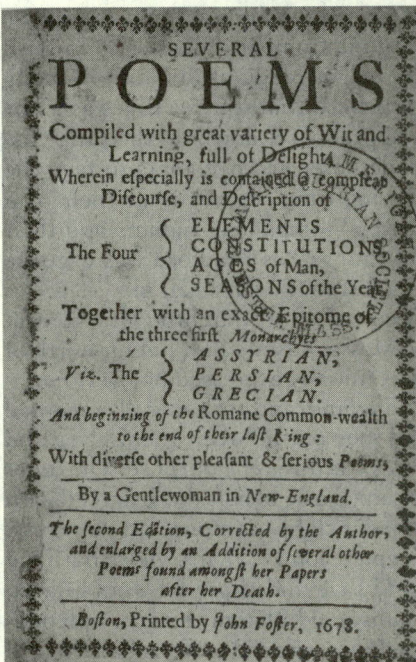

The Tenth Muse. Anne Bradstreet's first book appeared in London in 1650, with the title *The Tenth Muse, Lately Sprung up in America*. There were nine muses in the classical world, so including "a Gentlewoman in those parts" among that select company was a notable honor. In 1678, a second edition appeared in Boston.

Not surprisingly, the Puritans held to the strictest requirements regarding communion, or, as they preferred to call it, the Lord's Supper. It was the more important of the two sacraments they recognized (baptism being the other), and they guarded it with a zeal that set them apart from all other dissenters. In the beginning communion was regarded as a sign of election, to be taken only by those who had become church members by standing before their minister and elders and giving an account of their conversion. This insistence on challenging their members made these New England churches more rigorous than any others and confirmed the feeling that they were a special few. Thus when John Winthrop addressed the immigrants to the Bay Colony aboard the flagship *Arbella* in 1630, he told them that the eyes of the world were on them and that they would be an example for all, a "city upon a hill." Like William Bradford for the Pilgrims, Winthrop in his history of the Puritans wished to record the actualization of that dream.

WRITING IN TONGUES

While the New England colonies have conventionally been regarded as the centerpiece of early American literature, the first North American settlements had been founded elsewhere many years earlier. Saint Augustine, Jamestown, Santa Fe, Albany, and New York, for instance, are all older than Boston. More important, English was not the only language in which early North American texts were written. Indeed, it was a tardy arrival in America, and its eventual emergence as the dominant language of classic American literature was hardly inevitable. To some extent, the large initial immigration to Boston in the 1630s, the high articulation of Puritan cultural ideals, and the early establishment of a college and a printing press in Cambridge all gave New England a substantial edge. In time, political events would make English a useful lingua franca for the colonies at large and, in time, the literary medium of choice.

Before 1700, however, and often long after it, other languages remained actively in use not only for mundane purposes but also as expressive vehicles. Particularly beyond the vague borders of the English colonial world (the shifting lines between French Canada and New England as well as the southern colonies and Spanish Florida, for example), those other languages were completely dominant. Even within the limits of the eventual thirteen colonies, there existed large enclaves of speakers of languages other than English, especially in the middle colonies. Among the noteworthy settlers of New Netherland, for instance, were Belgian Walloons, near neighbors of the Dutch in Europe but speakers of a radically different language. The mix of "foreigners" in Albany, begun as a fur trade post by Netherlander merchants on the upper Hudson, made it a minority Dutch town, its population made up mainly of settlers of Scandinavian, French, Portuguese, English, Irish, Scots, German, African, and West Indian derivation—even people from Spain, then the enemy of the Netherlanders, and from faraway Croatia. For two centuries after New Netherland and its capital, New Amsterdam, were conquered by the English in 1664 and both renamed New York, Dutch and other languages were widely used there in public and private life before eventually dying out. Similar linguistic transformations, with the social and personal losses they bring, occurred in other English-controlled regions that would eventually form the United States. In Pennsylvania, where large groups of Protestants from continental Europe were welcomed by the colony's founder, William Penn, German in particular remains a vital language to this day, although the friction between these German communities and "the English" reminds us that language is a ground of contest between ethnic groups, not just of self-expression within each. In fact, the first item printed in Pennsylvania, although it issued from the press established by an immigrant Englishman, was in German, as was the largest book printed in any of the colonies before the Revolution. When we read American history backward, looking for early precedents of national institutions, practices, and values, we are likely to miss the radical linguistic and cultural diversity of the colonial world. Readers of the colonial record need to attend to the many tongues with which the colonists articulated their experiences, visions, and values.

AMERICAN LITERATURE IN 1700

Along the eastern seaboard by 1700, most of the colonies that were to unite in seeking independence from Britain toward the end of the eighteenth century had been founded—Georgia was to follow in the 1730s. As Britain sought to consolidate and unify its overseas possessions, the map began to resemble that of 1776, and English had already emerged as a powerful inter-colonial tool. But up and down the coast, a surprising variety of peoples was becoming accustomed to the transatlantic or local publication of their writings. At the end of the first full century of European colonization, the printing press was active in many areas, from Cambridge and Boston to New York, Philadelphia, and Annapolis. From 1696 to 1700, to be sure, only about 250 separate items were issued in all these places combined. Although this is a small number compared to the output of the printers in London at the time, it must be remembered that printing was established in the American colonies *before* it was allowed in most of England, where restrictive laws, the last of them repealed as late as 1693, had long confined printing to four locations: London, York, Oxford, and Cambridge. In this regard, if only because of the transatlantic isolation of America, the colonies ventured into the modern world earlier than their provincial English counterparts.

The literary situation in America three centuries ago is suggested by a brief examination of the products of the presses then in operation. Among those 250 items published at the seventeenth century's end was a whole library of texts by the most prolific colonial author, Cotton Mather. In this period, he published more than three dozen titles, including his account of the "tearful decade" (1688–98) of warfare between New England and New France and the latter's Indian allies, which contains his famous narrative of the bloody escape of Hannah Dustan from her captors. Mather also published several biographies of New England's founding ministers and penned treatises on the proper behavior of servants toward their masters, on the "well-ordered family," and on the spiritual risks faced by seamen. He also issued a warning against "impostors pretending to be ministers."

Despite their tendency to mirror the self-regarding aspect of Puritan thought, even Mather's works remind us that America in 1700 was opening outward. In the *Magnalia Christi Americana*, published just after the start of the new century, Mather himself told an anecdote that conveys the change at hand. A newly trained minister who had journeyed north from Massachusetts Bay to Maine was preaching to a group of hardened fishermen. He was urging his listeners not to "contradict the main end of Planting this Wilderness," the service of God and God's purposes, when a member of the makeshift gathering had the effrontery to contradict *him*: "Sir, you are mistaken, you think you are Preaching to the People at the Bay; our main end was to catch Fish." Even in New England, Mather suggests, "main ends" differed profoundly from place to place and from community to community. Elsewhere, the rich array of purposes was reflected in the diverse items issued by American printers at the time when Mather's *Magnalia* was just appearing (this large book was first published in London, not in Boston, it might be noted). There was a pair of texts, for instance, dealing with the Native Americans of New York that suggest how colonialism was altered by the drive toward cross-cultural interaction. One reported on a conference held in 1696 between the governor of that "province," as all the colonies were then being called, and the "Five . . . Nations of Indians," the Iroquois, a dynamic confederacy of peoples who had long controlled much of New York's territory and exacted tribute from far distant Native peoples as well. This was a kind of text that proliferated throughout New York's colonial era, when the governor and his agents made regular visits to the important Iroquois capital at Onondaga to listen to the concerns of these allies of the English. The second text concerning Native peoples in New York also reflected this unique cross-cultural pattern. In the 1690s, when the French and English empires were coming into serious conflict in America, Native peoples were frequently swept up in the fray. The "Propositions Made by the Five Nations of Indians" to New York's governor in 1698 accordingly entreated him to protect the Iroquois from harassment by New France's Indian allies, who were moving eastward into Iroquoia and fiercely raiding the villages there.

Such texts, reaching across the boundaries between the Indian nations and colonial powers, catch the diplomatic tone of cross-cultural relations in the Midatlantic region. The complexity of the political culture in early America is borne out in other texts of the era as well, such as *God's Protecting Providence* (1699), Philadelphian Jonathan Dickinson's much-reprinted account of his shipwreck and Indian captivity in Spanish Florida, which combined piety, adventure, and exoticism. Similarly exotic was *Barbarian Cruelties* (1700), in which British author Francis Brooks told of European captives in North Africa, an area of the globe that was long to be the focus of Westerners' anxieties and, in the post-Revolutionary era, an American war or two. But such adventurous narratives were not all sited in exotic and distant locales. Some, like the seemingly mundane textbook on the English language written by Francis Daniel Pastorius and aimed not only at young Americans but also (as the author's own Germanic-sounding English suggested) at "those who from foreign countries and nations come to settle amongst us," suggest less dramatic but still important cross-cultural concerns. Religion, a dominant theme in the American press in 1700, was itself linked to strong social issues, as demonstrated by Daniel Gould's account of the 1660 execution of Quaker dissenters in Boston, a work published in New York in 1700. The printer of Gould's book, in fact, also issued a pair of dissenting tracts by the Quaker and Salem merchant Thomas Maule, including one called *New England's Persecutors Mauled with Their Own Weapons*. (Maule's name would become famous to later generations of readers through Nathaniel Hawthorne's none too accurate association of it with the curse dooming the Pyncheon family in his Salem novel *The House of the Seven Gables*.) Finally, rounding out the century, came *The Selling of Joseph* by Samuel Sewall, among the earliest antislavery tracts written and published in America and thus a work of great importance to the future. The published items from this half decade of the seventeenth century also included almanacs and governmental publications. Such more mundane items contributed as well to the establishment of print culture and, ultimately, of literary traditions in British America. It was the almanac, one recalls, that helped make Benjamin Franklin's fortune as a printer, and it was Franklin who converted that everyday form into a vehicle of rare wit and sturdy English.

Beginnings to 1700

TEXTS	CONTEXTS
Peoples indigenous to the Americas orally perform and transmit a variety of "literary" genres that include, among others, speeches, songs, and stories	
	1000–1300 Anasazi communities inhabit southwestern regions
	1492 Christopher Columbus arrives in the Bahamas • between 4 and 7 million Native Americans estimated in what is now the United States, including Alaska
1493 Columbus, **"Letter to Luis de Santangel Regarding the First Voyage"**	
	1500 Native American populations begin to be ravaged by European diseases
	1514 Bartolomé de las Casas petitions Spanish Crown to treat Native American peoples as humanely as other subject populations
	1519–21 Cortés conquers Aztecs in Mexico
	1526 Spanish explorers bring first African slaves to South Carolina
	1539 First printing press in the Americas set up in Mexico City • Hernando de Soto invades Florida
1542 Álvar Núñez Cabeza de Vaca, *The Relation of Álvar Núñez Cabeza de Vaca*	
1552 Bartolomé de las Casas, *The Very Brief Relation of the Devastation of the Indies*	
	1558–1603 Reign of Elizabeth I
	1584 Walter Ralegh lands on "island" of Roanoke; names it "Virginia" for Queen Elizabeth
	1603–13 Samuel de Champlain explores the Saint Lawrence River; founds Québec
	1607 Jamestown is established in Virginia • Powhatan confederacy saves colonists from starving; teaches them to plant tobacco
	1619 Twenty Africans arrive in Jamestown on a Dutch vessel as indentured servants
	1620 *Mayflower* drops anchor in Plymouth Harbor
	1621 First Thanksgiving, at Plymouth
1624 John Smith, *The General History of Virginia, New England, and the Summer Isles*	

Boldface titles indicate works in the anthology.

TEXTS	CONTEXTS
1630 John Winthrop delivers his sermon "**A Model of Christian Charity**" (pub. 1838)	**1630–43** Immigration of English Puritans to Massachusetts Bay
1630–50 William Bradford writes *Of Plymouth Plantation* (pub. 1856)	
1637 Thomas Morton, *New English Canaan*	**1637** Pequot War
	1638 Anne Hutchinson banished from Bay Colony for challenging Puritan beliefs
1643 Roger Williams, *A Key into the Language of America*	
1650 Anne Bradstreet, *The Tenth Muse*	
1662 Michael Wigglesworth, *The Day of Doom*	
1673–1729 Samuel Sewall keeps his *Diary* (pub. 1878–82)	
	1675–76 King Philip's War destroys power of Native American tribes in New England
	1681 William Penn founds Pennsylvania
1682 Mary Rowlandson's *Narrative of the Captivity and Restoration*	
1682–1725 Edward Taylor writing his *Preparatory Meditations* (pub. 1939, 1960)	
1690 *The New-England Primer*	
	1692 Salem witchcraft trials
1702 Cotton Mather, *Magnalia Christi Americana*	

THE IROQUOIS CREATION STORY

The people known collectively as the Iroquois were made up of the Mohawk, Seneca, Oneida, Onondaga, and Cayuga nations. Joined in the early eighteenth century by the Tuscarora of North Carolina, the Five Nations became the Six Nations. The original Five Nations occupied lands that ranged from the area northeast of Lakes Ontario and Erie around the Saint Lawrence and Ottawa Rivers, then south of the lakes, and eastward almost to the Hudson River. Named Iroquois by the French (the Dutch and English called all these peoples Mohawk, Maqua, or Seneca), the Six Nations called themselves People of the Longhouse (*Haudenosaunee* in Seneca, *Kanosoni* in Mohawk), in reference to their primary type of dwelling. Iroquois longhouses were some twenty feet wide and from forty to two hundred feet long, accommodating several families who shared cooking fires. The largest towns of the Iroquois contained as many as two thousand people.

The Iroquois creation myth exists in some twenty-five versions, the earliest of which was taken down by the Frenchman Gabriel Sagard in 1623. There is, however, no actual transcription and translation of an Iroquois cosmogonic myth by a Native person until that of David Cusick, a Tuscarora, in the nineteenth century.

David Cusick was born around 1780 on the Oneida Reservation in New York, in Madison County. His father, Nicholas, an important leader among his people, was a Christian who had served on the American side during the Revolution. Educated by the missionary Samuel Kirkland, Cusick became a physician as well as an artist. The woodcuts at the front of the second edition (1828) of his *Sketches of the Ancient History of the Six Nations* are his work. Largely forgotten until recently, Cusick's *Sketches*

Atotarho. This is one of four engravings that David Cusick included in the second edition (1828) of *Sketches of the Ancient History of the Six Nations*. It shows the war chief of the Onondagas, Atotarho, said to be a sorcerer, with a twisted body and snakes in his hair. Several times Atotarho rejected Deganawidah and Hiawatha's pleas that he join them in forming the Great League of Peace of the Iroquois. Finally, after they healed him and combed the tangles from his hair, he agreed and became the traditional "firekeeper" of the Iroquois League.

was well known in its time and an important source for Henry Rowe Schoolcraft's *Notes on the Iroquois* (1847).

Although the story Cusick tells, with its monsters and supernatural events, cannot help but strike us as myth, Cusick calls the work a *history*, a history of the establishment of the Iroquois Confederacy. This serves, as the scholar Maureen Konkle has written, to link historical knowledge to political authority. Indeed, the urgency that Cusick reveals in the preface to his work—he states that he was "so small educated that it was impossible for [him] to compose the work without much difficulty" but that no one else would undertake it—may well derive from a strong sense of the current threat to his peoples' continued political existence. Cusick published on the eve of Andrew Jackson's election to the presidency and was well aware of Jackson's stated intention of "removing" eastern Indians to lands west of the Mississippi. Although we print material only from Part I of Cusick's *Sketches*, dealing with the foundation and establishment of the Iroquois world, Parts II and III present the ancient Iroquois as defending themselves long ago against monsters or other tribes by means that may well continue to serve the Iroquois in their defense against expansionist Americans.

We have selected Cusick's version of the Iroquois creation story because it is early, because it is by a Native person (Cusick was the first Native American to record on his own the founding myths of his people), and because it is fairly accessible to the contemporary reader.

The Iroquois Creation Story[1]

A Tale of the Foundation of the Great Island, Now North America;— the Two Infants Born, and the Creation of the Universe

Among the ancients there were two worlds in existence. The lower world was in great darkness;—the possession of the great monster; but the upper world was inhabited by mankind; and there was a woman conceived[2] and would have the twin born. When her travail drew near, and her situation seemed to produce a great distress on her mind, and she was induced by some of her relations to lay herself on a mattress which was prepared, so as to gain refreshments to her wearied body; but while she was asleep the very place sunk down towards the dark world.[3] The monsters[4] of the great water were alarmed at her appearance of descending to the lower world; in consequence all the species of the creatures were immediately collected into where it was expected she would fall. When the monsters were assembled, and they made consultation, one of them was appointed in haste to search the great deep, in order to procure some earth, if it could be obtained; accordingly the monster descends, which succeeds, and returns to the place. Another requisition was presented, who would be capable to secure the woman from the terrors of the great water, but none was able to comply except a large turtle came forward and made proposal to them to endure her lasting weight, which was accepted. The woman was yet descending from a great distance. The turtle executes

1. The text is from the first edition of *Sketches of the Ancient History of the Six Nations* (1827).
2. The woman who conceives is, in most Iroquois accounts of the creation, the second generation of sky women to become pregnant without sexual activity. "Mankind": i.e., humans rather than "monsters"—undefined creatures of a time before the world as we know it was established—although these humans have powers quite different from those that humans usually possess.
3. Other versions have Sky Woman either being pushed out of the upper world or accidentally falling.
4. In other versions the monsters are a variety of familiar animal. Cusick conveys the mysterious and dangerous state of affairs in the as-yet-unformed universe.

upon the spot, and a small quantity of earth was varnished on the back part of the turtle. The woman alights on the seat prepared, and she receives a satisfaction.[5] While holding her, the turtle increased every moment and became a considerable island of earth, and apparently covered with small bushes. The woman remained in a state of unlimited darkness, and she was overtaken by her travail to which she was subject. While she was in the limits of distress one of the infants in her womb was moved by an evil opinion and he was determined to pass out under the side of the parent's arm, and the other infant in vain endeavoured to prevent his design.[6] The woman was in a painful condition during the time of their disputes, and the infants entered the dark world by compulsion, and their parent expired in a few moments. They had the power of sustenance without a nurse, and remained in the dark regions. After a time the turtle increased to a great Island and the infants were grown up, and one of them possessed with a gentle disposition, and named ENIGORIO, i.e. the good mind. The other youth possessed an insolence of character, and was named ENIGONHAHETGEA, i.e. the bad mind.[7] The good mind was not contented to remain in a dark situation, and he was anxious to create a great light in the dark world; but the bad mind was desirous that the world should remain in a natural state. The good mind determines to prosecute his designs, and therefore commences the work of creation. At first he took the parent's head, (the deceased) of which he created an orb, and established it in the centre of the firmament, and it became of a very superior nature to bestow light to the new world, (now the sun) and again he took the remnant of the body and formed another orb, which was inferior to the light (now moon). In the orb a cloud of legs appeared to prove it was the body of the good mind, (parent). The former was to give light to the day and the latter to the night; and he also created numerous spots of light, (now stars): these were to regulate the days, nights, seasons, years, etc. Whenever the light extended to the dark world the monsters were displeased and immediately concealed themselves in the deep places, lest they should be discovered by some human beings. The good mind continued the works of creation, and he formed numerous creeks and rivers on the Great Island, and then created numerous species of animals of the smallest and the greatest, to inhabit the forests, and fishes of all kinds to inhabit the waters. When he had made the universe he was in doubt respecting some being to possess the Great Island; and he formed two images of the dust of the ground in his own likeness, male and female, and by his breathing into their nostrils he gave them the living souls, and named them EA-GWE-HOWE, i.e., a real people;[8] and he gave the Great Island all the animals of game for their maintenance and he appointed

---

5. I.e., she lands safely, without harm.

6. Other versions of the story have Sky Woman give birth to a daughter, who again becomes supernaturally pregnant (perhaps by the spirit of the turtle), and it is *she* who conceives the twins. The twins argue even in the womb, the Evil Twin deciding not to be born in the normal way but to burst through his mother's side, which leads to her death. The theme of rival twins is widespread in the Americas.

7. More commonly, the Good Twin is called Tharonhiawagon (Sky-Grasper, Creator, or Upholder of the Heavens), and the Evil Twin is named Tawiscaron (Evil-Minded, Flint, Ice, Patron of Winter, and other disasters). Cusick's Enigorio is

a rough translation of the Tuscarora word for "good-minded" into Mohawk, and his Enigonhahetgea is an equally rough translation into Seneca, Onondaga, or Cayuga of the Tuscarora word for "bad-minded." Cusick has probably changed the Tuscarora words best known to him into these other Iroquois languages because they were considered to be more prestigious than Tuscarora, the Tuscaroras having only recently joined the Iroquois Confederacy.

8. Humans. "EA-GWE-HOWE": Tuscarora term used by speakers of all the languages of the Six Nations; today, it simply means Indian, or Indians.

thunder to water the earth by frequent rains, agreeable of the nature of the system; after this the Island became fruitful and vegetation afforded the animals subsistence. The bad mind, while his brother was making the universe, went throughout the Island and made numerous high mountains and falls of water, and great steeps, and also creates various reptiles which would be injurious to mankind; but the good mind restored the Island to its former condition. The bad mind proceeded further in his motives and he made two images of clay in the form of mankind; but while he was giving them existence they became apes;[9] and when he had not the power to create mankind he was envious against his brother; and again he made two of clay. The good mind discovered his brothers contrivances, and aided in giving them living souls, (it is said these had the most knowledge of good and evil). The good mind now accomplishes the works of creation, notwithstanding the imaginations of the bad mind were continually evil; and he attempted to enclose all the animals of game in the earth, so as to deprive them from mankind; but the good mind released them from confinement, (the animals were dispersed, and traces of them were made on the rocks near the cave where it was closed). The good mind experiences that his brother was at variance with the works of creation, and feels not disposed to favor any of his proceedings, but gives admonitions of his future state. Afterwards the good mind requested his brother to accompany him, as he was proposed to inspect the game, etc., but when a short distance from their moninal[1] [sic] residence, the bad mind became so unmanly that he could not conduct his brother any more.[2] The bad mind offered a challenge to his brother and resolved that who gains the victory should govern the universe; and appointed a day to meet the contest. The good mind was willing to submit to the offer, and he enters the reconciliation with his brother; which he falsely mentions that by whipping with flags would destroy his temporal life;[3] and he earnestly solicits his brother also to notice the instrument of death, which he manifestly relates by the use of deer horns, beating his body he would expire. On the day appointed the engagement commenced, which lasted for two days: after pulling up the trees and mountains as the track of a terrible whirlwind, at last the good mind gained the victory by using the horns, as mentioned the instrument of death, which he succeeded in deceiving his brother and he crushed him in the earth; and the last words uttered from the bad mind were, that he would have equal power over the souls of mankind after death; and he sinks down to eternal doom, and became the Evil Spirit.[4] After this tumult the good mind repaired to the battle ground, and then visited the people and retires from the earth.[5]

9. Cusick may have seen an ape or a depiction of apes (there are no apes native to the New World) and decided to name them as the creatures made by the Evil Twin in contrast to the humans made by the Good Twin. John Buck and Chief John Gibson, in their later renditions of the Iroquois creation narrative, also refer to apes at this point in the narrative.

1. Cusick perhaps means *nominal*, their named or designated residence.

2. I.e., the Evil Twin became so rude and obnoxious that the Good Twin could not lead ("conduct") his brother to the appointed place any longer.

3. The Good Twin tells his brother that he can be killed by being beaten with corn stalks, rushes, reeds, or cattails. Cusick calls this a deception; other accounts treat it as a confession of weakness. Next, the Evil Twin admits that he would die if beaten with the antlers of deer.

4. This may reflect an awareness of the Christian belief in the devil as the evil spirit, ruler over the lower depths.

5. Other versions go on to say that the Good Twin teaches the people how to grow corn and how to avoid harm by means of prayer and ritual.

CHRISTOPHER COLUMBUS
1451–1506

B orn into a family of wool workers near the once supreme Mediterranean port of Genoa, Christopher Columbus turned to the sea as a young man, developed a plan to find a commercially viable Atlantic route to Asia, and in 1492 won the support of the Spanish monarchs, Ferdinand and Isabella, for this "enterprise of the Indies." His series of four voyages between 1492 and 1504 produced a brief moment of wonder followed by a long series of disasters and disappointments. Apparently friendly relations with the Taino Indians on the island of Hispaniola in 1492 turned sour as the settlers Columbus left behind demanded gold and sexual partners from their hosts; on his return there in 1494, none of the Europeans were alive. A new settlement established on the island after this discovery fell into such disorder during the absence of Columbus in Cuba and Jamaica that in 1496 he was forced to return to Spain to clear his name of politically motivated charges made against him by other Europeans in the West Indies. A third voyage, begun in 1498, took him for the first time to the South American mainland; the lushness of nature there made him believe himself near paradise, but that illusion vanished when, on his return to Hispaniola, he encountered Spanish settlers there in open rebellion against his authority. Able to reach a truce only at the expense of the Taino Indians, who were to be virtually enslaved by the rebels, Columbus soon found himself under arrest, sent in chains to Spain in 1500 to answer yet more charges. His last voyage, intended to recoup his tarnished reputation, resulted in a long period of suffering in Panama and shipwreck in Jamaica, and these outer woes were accompanied by nearly delusional periods as Columbus underwent a virtual breakdown. Rescued at last from this extremity, he returned to Europe, where soon afterward he died. The West Indies, as his discoveries were called, remained disordered and bloody.

Several documents regarding the four voyages survive from Columbus's hand. The supposed *Journal* of his first voyage is actually a summary prepared by the cleric and reformer Bartolomé de las Casas. A letter sent by Columbus to Luis de Santangel, a royal official and an early supporter of his venture, provides a more authentic account and served as the basis for the first printed description of America, issued in 1493 in Spain and widely translated and reprinted across Europe. A memorandum regarding the second voyage, intended by Columbus for the Spanish monarchs (whose responses to each point also survive), offers useful insights into the emerging ambiguities and problems of the colony on Hispaniola. For the third and fourth voyages, three letters from Columbus, two sent to the Crown and one to a woman of the Spanish court, detail his deepening worldly and spiritual troubles.

The texts are from *Select Documents Illustrating the Four Voyages of Columbus*, translated and edited by Cecil Jane (1930–33).

From Letter to Luis de Santangel[1] Regarding the First Voyage

[At sea, February 15, 1493]

Sir,

As I know that you will be pleased at the great victory with which Our Lord has crowned my voyage, I write this to you, from which you will learn how in thirty-three days, I passed from the Canary Islands to the Indies with the fleet which the most illustrious king and queen our sovereigns gave to me. And there I found very many islands filled with people innumerable, and of them all I have taken possession for their highnesses, by proclamation made and with the royal standard unfurled, and no opposition was offered to me. To the first island which I found I gave the name *San Salvador*,[2] in remembrance of the Divine Majesty, Who has marvelously bestowed all this; the Indians call it "Guanahani." To the second I gave the name *Isla de Santa María de Concepción*; to the third, *Fernandina*; to the fourth, *Isabella*; to the fifth, *Isla Juana*,[3] and so to each one I gave a new name.

When I reached Juana I followed its coast to the westward, and I found it to be so extensive that I thought that it must be the mainland, the province of Catayo.[4] And since there were neither towns nor villages on the seashore, but only small hamlets, with the people of which I could not have speech because they all fled immediately, I went forward on the same course, thinking that I should not fail to find great cities and towns. And at the end of many leagues,[5] seeing that there was no change and that the coast was bearing me northwards, which I wished to avoid since winter was already beginning and I proposed to make from it to the south, and as moreover the wind was carrying me forward, I determined not to wait for a change in the weather and retraced my path as far as a certain harbor known to me. And from that point I sent two men inland to learn if there were a king or great cities. They traveled three days' journey and found an infinity of small hamlets and people without number, but nothing of importance. For this reason they returned.

I understood sufficiently from other Indians, whom I had already taken, that this land was nothing but an island. And therefore I followed its coast eastwards for one hundred and seven leagues to the point where it ended. And from that cape I saw another island distant eighteen leagues from the former, to the east, to which I at once gave the name "Española."[6] And I went there and followed its northern coast, as I had in the case of Juana, to the eastward for one hundred and eighty-eight great leagues in a straight line. This island and all the others are very fertile to a limitless degree, and this island is extremely so. In it there are many harbors on the coast of the sea, beyond comparison with others which I know in Christendom, and many rivers, good and large, which is marvelous. Its lands are high, and there are in

---

1. A former merchant and a court official since 1478 who had supported Columbus's proposal to the Spanish Crown and had helped secure financing for the first voyage.
2. The precise identity of the Bahamian island Columbus named San Salvador is not known today, although many theories have been put forward, most positing that Watling Island is the likeliest site.
3. Of these four islands, only the identity of Juana (Cuba) is today certain.
4. I.e., China (or "Cathay").
5. Renaissance units of measurement were inexact. Columbus's "league" was probably about four miles.
6. I.e., Hispaniola, where the countries of Haiti and the Dominican Republic are located.

it very many sierras and very lofty mountains, beyond comparison with the island of Tenerife.[7] All are most beautiful, of a thousand shapes, and all are accessible and filled with trees of a thousand kinds and tall, and they seem to touch the sky. And I am told that they never lose their foliage, as I can understand, for I saw them as green and as lovely as they are in Spain in May, and some of them were flowering, some bearing fruit, and some in another stage, according to their nature. And the nightingale was singing and other birds of a thousand kinds in the month of November there where I went. There are six or eight kinds of palm, which are a wonder to behold on account of their beautiful variety, but so are the other trees and fruits and plants. In it are marvelous pine groves, and there are very large tracts of cultivatable lands, and there is honey,[8] and there are birds of many kinds and fruits in great diversity. In the interior are mines of metals, and the population is without number. Española is a marvel.

1493

From Letter to Ferdinand and Isabella Regarding the Fourth Voyage[1]

[Jamaica, July 7, 1503]

* * *

Of Española, Paria,[2] and the other lands, I never think without weeping. I believed that their example would have been to the profit of others; on the contrary, they are in an exhausted state; although they are not dead, the infirmity is incurable or very extensive; let him who brought them to this state come now with the remedy if he can or if he knows it; in destruction, everyone is an adept. It was always the custom to give thanks and promotion to him who imperiled his person. It is not just that he who has been so hostile to this undertaking should enjoy its fruits or that his children should. Those who left the Indies, flying from toils and speaking evil of the matter and of me, have returned with official employment.[3] So it has now been ordained in the case of Veragua.[4] It is an ill example and without profit for the business and for justice in the world.

The fear of this, with other sufficient reasons, which I saw clearly, led me to pray your highnesses before I went to discover these islands and Terra Firma, that you would leave them to me to govern in your royal name. It pleased you; it was a privilege and agreement, and under seal and oath, and you granted me the title of viceroy and admiral and governor general of all. And you fixed the boundary, a hundred leagues beyond the Azores and the Cape Verde Islands, by a line passing from pole to pole, and you gave me

7. The largest of the Canary Islands.
8. The honeybee, presumably the source of the honey found on the island, is not native to the Western Hemisphere. Nor is the nightingale, mentioned above.
1. Written on Jamaica in 1503, this letter was hand carried from there to Hispaniola by Diego Mendez.
2. Paria was the mainland region of what is now

Venezuela, near the island of Trinidad. Columbus, who had first landed in South America ("Terra Firma," as he terms it later) in 1498, argued that the terrestrial paradise lay nearby.
3. Although it appears that Columbus has specific personal enemies in mind, it is not clear whom he means.
4. I.e., Panama, where Columbus was shipwrecked earlier in this voyage.

wide power over this and over all that I might further discover. The document states this very fully.

The other most important matter, which calls aloud for redress, remains inexplicable to this moment. Seven years I was at your royal court, where all to whom this undertaking was mentioned, unanimously declared it to be a delusion. Now all, down to the very tailors, seek permission to make discoveries. It can be believed that they go forth to plunder, and it is granted to them to do so, so that they greatly prejudice my honor and do very great damage to the enterprise. It is well to give to God that which is His due and to Caesar that which belongs to him.[5] This is a just sentiment and based on justice.

The lands which here obey Your Highnesses are more extensive and richer than all other Christian lands. After I, by the divine will, had placed them under your royal and exalted lordship, and was on the point of securing a very great revenue, suddenly, while I was waiting for ships to come to your high presence with victory and with great news of gold, being very secure and joyful, I was made a prisoner and with my two brothers was thrown into a ship, laden with fetters, stripped to the skin, very ill-treated, and without being tried or condemned. Who will believe that a poor foreigner could in such a place rise against Your Highnesses, without cause, and without the support of some other prince, and being alone among your vassals and natural subjects, and having all my children at your royal court?

I came to serve at the age of twenty-eight years, and now I have not a hair on my body that is not gray, and my body is infirm, and whatever remained to me from those years of service has been spent and taken away from me and sold, and from my brothers, down to my very coat, without my being heard or seen, to my great dishonor. It must be believed that this was not done by your royal command. The restitution of my honor, the reparation of my losses, and the punishment of him who did this, will spread abroad the fame of your royal nobility. The same punishment is due to him who robbed me of the pearls, and to him who infringed my rights as admiral.[6] Very great will be your merit, fame without parallel will be yours, if you do this, and there will remain in Spain a glorious memory of Your Highnesses, as grateful and just princes.

The pure devotion which I have ever borne to the service of Your Highnesses, and the unmerited wrong that I have suffered, will not permit me to remain silent, although I would fain do so; I pray Your Highnesses to pardon me. I am so ruined as I have said; hitherto I have wept for others; now, Heaven have mercy upon me, and may the earth weep for me. Of worldly goods, I have not even a blanca[7] for an offering in spiritual things. Here in the Indies I have become careless of the prescribed forms of religion. Alone in my trouble, sick, in daily expectation of death, and encompassed about by a million savages, full of cruelty and our foes, and so separated from the holy Sacraments of Holy Church, my soul will be forgotten if it here leaves my body. Weep for me, whoever has charity, truth, and justice.

I did not sail upon this voyage to gain honor or wealth; this is certain, for already all hope of that was dead. I came to Your Highnesses with true

5. cf. "Render therefore unto Caesar the things which are Caesar's, and unto God the things that are God's" (Matthew 22.21).
6. The reference is to Alonso de Ojeda (1468–

c. 1516), who had taken pearls (part of what was reserved to Columbus under his agreement with the Spanish Crown) from Paria to Española.
7. A small Spanish coin.

devotion and with ready zeal, and I do not lie. I humbly pray Your Highnesses that if it please God to bring me forth from this place, that you will be pleased to permit me to go to Rome and to other places of pilgrimage. May the Holy Trinity preserve your life and high estate, and grant you increase of prosperity.

Done in the Indies in the island of Jamaica, on the seventh of July, in the year one thousand five hundred and three.

1505

ÁLVAR NÚÑEZ CABEZA DE VACA
c. 1490–1558

Among those who may have witnessed the disgrace of Columbus as he passed in chains through Cadiz in 1498 was a boy from the nearby village of Jerez de la Frontera. Álvar Núñez Cabeza de Vaca was the son of the village alderman, grandson of the conqueror of the Guanache people of Grand Canary Island, and a descendant on his mother's side from a hero of the wars against the Moors who was given the family name "Cabeza de Vaca" (or "cow's head") when he used a cow's skull to mark a strategic route through an unguarded mountain pass. Mindful of this family heritage, as a young man Cabeza de Vaca went off to the wars in Italy (he later was to say that the American Indians of Texas were as shrewd in battle "as if they had been reared in Italy in continual feuds"), then fought in Spain itself before, in 1527, he sailed on Panfilo de Narváez's Florida expedition as *aquacil mayor* (provost marshal) and treasurer.

The expedition endured many disasters. Narváez, an impetuous, self-centered man and a poor leader, first took his six hundred men to Hispaniola, where a quarter of them deserted, and then to Cuba, where two of the six ships were lost in a hurricane. Ten months after leaving Spain the expedition landed in the vicinity of what is now known as Sarasota Bay, on Florida's west coast. Against Cabeza de Vaca's advice, Narváez sent the ships farther along the shore in search of a rumored port where his army might rejoin them, but the ships were never seen again. Effectually stranded, Narváez took possession of Florida while the inhabitants of Sarasota Bay (probably Calusa Indians) made "many signs and threats [that] left little doubt that they were bidding us to go." Soon the expedition, reduced to eating its horses, sought to escape other groups of Florida Indians, from the Timucuan of the Suwannee River area to the Apalachees of the Panhandle, by building clumsy "barges" and retreating to the sea. Narváez took the best oarsmen in his own craft and left the other barges behind him as they neared Mobile Bay; when he pulled away from the others he told them, with false magnanimity, that "it was no longer a time when one should command another"—that is, every man for himself! With that, Narváez and his crew disappeared, apparently lost at sea.

The other rafts passed the mouth of what must have been the Mississippi, and finally wrecked on Galveston Island, now Texas, in November 1528. Here began a further whittling away of the survivors and a time of extraordinary struggle for Cabeza de Vaca and the three men who survived with him: the Spaniards Andrés Dorantes and Alonso del Castillo Maldonado and Dorantes's black slave, Estevánico, a native of the Moroccan town of Azemmor. The itinerary of Cabeza de Vaca's North

American odyssey was long and involved. Alone or with drifting groups of other survivors, he spent his first two years on the Texas coast as a prisoner and slave of the Han and Capoque clans of the Karankawa Indians and then gradually progressed north and west, gaining status and power among the Caddos, Atakapas, Coahuiltecans, and other natives from his activities as a merchant and especially his skill as a healer. By 1535, he reached present-day New Mexico, where he encountered the Jumanos and Conchos, then headed southwest into Mexico as the leader of a vast crowd of Pimas and Opatas who, revering him, followed him from village to village.

The heady mood of the journey dissipated the following March, however, when the wanderers encountered a party of Spanish slave hunters under Diego de Alcaraz in western Mexico. Seeing the terror of his American Indian escorts at these "Christian slavers," as he acerbically called them, Cabeza de Vaca became openly critical of Alcaraz, who arrested him, sent him south, and seized as slaves the six hundred natives in his company. From Mexico City, where he agitated against the cruel (and strictly illegal) activities of the likes of Alcaraz, Cabeza de Vaca went to Spain in 1537, intent on making similar protestations to Emperor Charles V. Allowed to lead an expedition himself to South America, Cabeza de Vaca hoped to enact an enlightened American Indian policy, but his Río de la Plata colonists, profiting from the old injustices, removed him forcibly from office and sent him in chains back to Spain in 1545. After long delays in settling the dispute, in 1551 he was exiled to what is now Algeria and forbidden to return to America.

During the three years he spent in Spain before his departure for Río de la Plata in 1540, Cabeza de Vaca completed his first narrative of the Narváez expedition. It was published in Spain in 1542; a corrected and expanded version that includes the story of his later American experience appeared in 1555. Addressed to Charles V, the 1542 account sought to justify his conclusions regarding Spanish policy and behavior in America as well as to argue for renewed explorations and settlement in the regions he had traversed (several later Spanish expeditions, including those of Coronado and de Soto, clearly drew on Cabeza de Vaca's arguments and knowledge). More important, however, *The Relation of Álvar Núñez Cabeza de Vaca* sought to recount (with remarkable understatement) his sufferings and many brushes with death and to explore his complex feelings regarding the Native Americans and his countrymen's dealings with them.

From The Relation of Álvar Núñez Cabeza de Vaca[1]

[DEDICATION]

Sacred Caesarian Catholic Majesty:

Among all the princes who have reigned, I know of none who has enjoyed the universal esteem of Your Majesty[2] at this day, when strangers vie in approbation with those motivated by religion and loyalty.

Although everyone wants what advantage may be gained from ambition and action, we see everywhere great inequalities of fortune, brought about not by conduct but by accident, and not through anybody's fault but as the will of God. Thus the deeds of one far exceed his expectation, while another can show no higher proof of purpose than his fruitless effort, and even the effort may go unnoticed.

---

1. The text is based on *Adventures in the Unknown Interior of America,* edited and translated by Cyclone Covey (1961).

2. Emperor Charles V (1500–1558), grandson and successor of Ferdinand and Isabella.

I can say for myself that I undertook the march abroad, on royal authorization, with a firm trust that my service would be as evident and distinguished as my ancestors', and that I would not need to speak to be counted among those Your Majesty honors for diligence and fidelity in affairs of state. But my counsel and constancy availed nothing toward those objectives we set out to gain, in your interests, for our sins. In fact, no other of the many armed expeditions into those parts has found itself in such dire straits as ours, or come to so futile and fatal a conclusion.

My only remaining duty is to transmit what I saw and heard in the nine years I wandered lost and miserable over many remote lands. I hope in some measure to convey to Your Majesty not merely a report of positions and distances, flora and fauna, but of the customs of the numerous, barbarous people I talked with and dwelt among, as well as any other matters I could hear of or observe. My hope of going out from among those nations was always small; nevertheless, I made a point of remembering all the particulars, so that should God our Lord eventually please to bring me where I am now, I might testify to my exertion in the royal behalf.

Since this narrative, in my opinion, is of no trivial value for those who go in your name to subdue those countries and bring them to a knowledge of the true faith and true Lord and bring them under the imperial dominion, I have written very exactly. Novel or, for some persons, difficult to believe though the things narrated may be, I assure you they can be accepted without hesitation as strictly factual. Better than to exaggerate, I have minimized all things; it is enough to say that the relation is offered Your Majesty for truth.

I beg that it may be received as homage, since it is the most one could bring who returned thence naked.

* * *

[THE MALHADO WAY OF LIFE]

The people[3] we came to know there are tall and well built. Their only weapons are bows and arrows, which they use with great dexterity. The men bore through one of their nipples, some both, and insert a joint of cane two and a half palms long by two fingers thick. They also bore their lower lip and wear a piece of cane in it half a finger in diameter.

Their women toil incessantly.

From October to the end of February every year, which is the season these Indians live on the island, they subsist on the roots I have mentioned,[4] which the women get from under water in November and December. Only in these two months, too, do they take fish in their cane weirs. When the fish is consumed, the roots furnish the one staple. At the end of February the islanders go into other parts to seek sustenance, for then the root is beginning to grow and is not edible.

These people love their offspring more than any in the world and treat them very mildly.

If a son dies, the whole village joins the parents and kindred in weeping. The parents set off the wails each day before dawn, again at noon, and at sunset, for one year. The funeral rites occur when the year of mourning is up.

3. The Capoques and Hans of coastal Texas, near today's Galveston Island, which Cabeza de Vaca calls *Malhado*, or the Island of Doom.

4. I.e., "certain roots which taste like nuts, mostly grubbed from [under] the water with great labor."

Following these rites, the survivors wash off the smoke stain of the ceremony in a symbolic purgation. All the dead are lamented this way except the aged, who merit no regrets. The dead are buried, except medicine-men, who are cremated. Everybody in the village dances and makes merry while the pyre of a medicine-man kindles, and until his bones become powder. A year later, when his rites are celebrated, the entire village again participating, this powder is presented in water for the relatives to drink.

Each man has an acknowledged wife, except the medicine-men, who may have two or three wives apiece. The several wives live together in perfect amity.

When a daughter marries, she must take everything her husband kills in hunting or catches in fishing to the house of her father, without daring to eat or to withhold any part of it, and the husband gets provided by female carrier from his father-in-law's house. Neither the bride's father nor mother may enter the son-in-law's house after the marriage, nor he theirs; and this holds for the children of the respective couples. If a man and his in-laws should chance to be walking so they would meet, they turn silently aside from each other and go a crossbow-shot out of their way, averting their glance to the ground. The woman, however, is free to fraternize with the parents and relatives of her husband. These marriage customs prevail for more than fifty leagues inland from the island.

At a house where a son or brother may die, no one goes out for food for three months, the neighbors and other relatives providing what is eaten. Because of this custom, which the Indians literally would not break to save their lives, great hunger reigned in most houses while we resided there, it being a time of repeated deaths. Those who sought food worked hard, but they could get little in that severe season. That is why Indians who kept me left the island by canoe for oyster bays on the main.

Three months out of every year they eat nothing but oysters and drink very bad water. Wood is scarce; mosquitoes, plentiful. The houses are made of mats; their floors consist of masses of oyster shells. The natives sleep on these shells—in animal skins, those who happen to own such.

Many a time I would have to go three days without eating, as would the natives. I thought it impossible that life could be so prolonged in such protracted hunger; though afterwards I found myself in yet greater want, as shall be seen.

The Indians who had Alonso del Castillo, Andrés Dorantes, and the others of their barge who remained alive, spoke a different dialect and claimed a different descent from these I lived among. They frequented the opposite shore of the main to eat oysters, staying till the first of April, then returning.

The distance to the main is two leagues at the widest part of the channel. The island itself, which supports the two tribes commodiously, is half a league wide by five long.

The inhabitants of all these parts go naked, except that the women cover some part of their persons with a wool that grows on trees,[5] and damsels dress in deerskin.

The people are generous to each other with what little they have. There is no chief. All belonging to the same lineage keep together. They speak two languages: Capoque and Han.

---

5. I.e., Spanish moss.

They have a strange custom when acquaintances meet or occasionally visit, of weeping for half an hour before they speak. This over, the one who is visited rises and gives his visitor all he has. The latter accepts it and, after a while, carries it away, often without a word. They have other strange customs, but I have told the principal and most remarkable of them.

In April [1529] we went to the seashore and ate blackberries all month, a time of [dance ceremonies] and *fiestas* among the Indians.

* * *

[OUR LIFE AMONG THE AVAVARES AND ARBADAOS]

All the Indians of this region[6] are ignorant of time, either by the sun or moon; nor do they reckon by the month or year. They understand the seasons in terms of the ripening of fruits, the dying of fish, and the position of stars, in which dating they are adept.

The Avavares always treated us well. We lived as free agents, dug our own food, and lugged our loads of wood and water. The houses and our diet were like those of the nation we had just come from, but the Avavares suffer yet greater want, having no corn, acorns, or pecans. We always went naked like them and covered ourselves at night with deerskins.

Six of the eight months we dwelled with these people we endured acute hunger; for fish are not found where they are either. At the end of the eight months, when the prickly pears were just beginning to ripen again [mid-June 1535], I traveled with the Negro—unknown to our hosts—to others a day's journey farther on: the Maliacones.[7] When three days had passed, I sent Estevánico to fetch Castillo and Dorantes.

When they got there, the four of us set out with the Maliacones, who were going to find the small fruit of certain trees which they subsist on for ten or twelve days while the prickly pears are maturing. They joined another tribe, the Arbadaos, who astonished us by their weak, emaciated, swollen condition.

We told the Maliacones with whom we had come that we wanted to stop with these Arbadaos. The Maliacones despondently returned the way they came, leaving us alone in the brushland near the Arbadao houses. The observing Arbadaos talked among themselves and came up to us in a body. Four of them took each of us by the hand and led us to their dwellings.

Among them we underwent fiercer hunger than among the Avavares. We ate not more than two handfuls of prickly pears a day, and they were still so green and milky they burned our mouths. In our lack of water, eating brought great thirst. At nearly the end of our endurance we bought two dogs for some nets, with other things, and a skin I used for cover.

I have already said that we went naked through all this country; not being accustomed to going so, we shed our skins twice a year like snakes. The sun and air raised great, painful sores on our chests and shoulders, and our heavy loads caused the cords to cut our arms. The region is so broken and so overgrown that often, when we gathered wood, blood flowed from us in many

6. At this point in his story, having escaped from his captivity among the Capoques and Hans, Cabeza de Vaca is among the Avavares and Arbadaos in inland Texas.

7. Neighbors of the Avavares and Arbadaos. "The Negro": Estevánico, a Moorish slave from the west coast of Morocco.

places where the thorns and shrubs tore our flesh. At times, when my turn came to get wood and I had collected it at heavy cost in blood, I could neither drag nor bear it out. My only solace in these labors was to think of the sufferings of our Redeemer, Jesus Christ, and the blood He shed for me. How much worse must have been his torment from the thorns than mine here!

I bartered with these Indians in combs I made for them and in bows, arrows, and nets. We made mats, which are what their houses consist of and for which they feel a keen necessity. Although they know how to make them, they prefer to devote their full time to finding food; when they do not, they get too pinched with hunger.

Some days the Indians would set me to scraping and softening skins. These were my days of greatest prosperity in that place. I would scrape thoroughly enough to sustain myself two or three days on the scraps. When it happened that these or any people we had left behind gave us a piece of meat, we ate it raw. Had we put it to roast, the first native who came along would have filched it. Not only did we think it better not to risk this, we were in such a condition that roasted meat would have given us pain. We could digest it more easily raw.

Such was our life there, where we earned our meager subsistence by trade in items which were the work of our own hands.

[CUSTOMS OF THAT REGION]

From the Island of Doom to this land, all the Indians we saw have the custom of not sleeping with their wives from the time they are discovered pregnant to two years after giving birth. Children are suckled until they are twelve, when they are old enough to find their own support. We asked why they thus prolonged the nursing period, and they said that the poverty of the land frequently meant—as we witnessed—going two or three days without eating, sometimes four; if children were not allowed to suckle in seasons of scarcity, those who did not famish would be weaklings.

Anyone who chances to fall sick on a foraging trip and cannot keep up with the rest is left to die, unless he be a son or brother; him they will help, even to carrying on their back.

It is common among them all to leave their wives when there is disagreement, and directly reconnect with whomever they please. This is the course of men who are childless. Those who have children never abandon their wives.

When Indian men get into an argument in their villages, they fist-fight until exhausted, then separate. Sometimes the women will go between and part them, but men never interfere. No matter what the disaffection, they do not resort to bows and arrows. After a fight, the disputants take their houses (and families) and go live apart from each other in the scrub wood until they have cooled off; then they return and from that moment are friends as if nothing had happened. No intermediary is needed to mend their friendship.

In case the quarrelers are single men, they repair to some neighboring people (instead of the scrub wood), who, even if enemies, welcome them warmly and give so largely of what they have that when the quarrelers' animosity subsides, they return to their home village rich.

* * *

[THE FIRST CONFRONTATION]

When we saw for certain that we were drawing near the Christians, we gave thanks to God our Lord for choosing to bring us out of such a melancholy and wretched captivity. The joy we felt can only be conjectured in terms of the time, the suffering, and the peril we had endured in that land.

The evening of the day we reached the recent campsite, I tried hard to get Castillo or Dorantes to hurry on three days, unencumbered, after the Christians who were now circling back into the area we had assured protection. They both reacted negatively, excusing themselves for weariness, though younger and more athletic than I; but they being unwilling, I took the Negro and eleven Indians next morning to track the Christians. We went ten leagues, past three villages where they had slept.

The day after that, I overtook four of them on their horses. They were dumbfounded at the sight of me, strangely undressed and in company with Indians. They just stood staring for a long time, not thinking to hail me or come closer to ask questions.

"Take me to your captain," I at last requested; and we went together half a league to a place where we found their captain, Diego de Alcaraz.

When we had talked awhile, he confessed to me that he was completely undone, having been unable to catch any Indians in a long time; he did not know which way to turn; his men were getting too hungry and exhausted. I told him of Castillo and Dorantes ten leagues away with an escorting multitude. He immediately dispatched three of his horsemen to them, along with fifty of his Indian allies. The Negro went, too, as a guide; I stayed behind.

I asked the Christians to furnish me a certificate of the year, month, and day I arrived here, and the manner of my coming; which they did.[8] From this river to the Christian town, Sant Miguel[9] within the government of the recently created province of New Galicia, is a distance of thirty leagues.

[THE FALLING-OUT WITH OUR COUNTRYMEN]

After five days, Andrés Dorantes and Alonso del Castillo arrived with those who had gone for them; and they brought more than 600 natives of the vicinity whom the Indians who had been escorting us drew out of the woods and took to the mounted Christians, who thereupon dismissed their own escort.

When they arrived, Alcaraz begged us to order the villagers of this river out of the woods in the same way to get us food. It would be unnecessary to command them to bring food, if they came at all; for the Indians were always diligent to bring us all they could.

We sent our heralds to call them, and presently there came 600 Indians with all the corn they possessed. They brought it in clay-sealed earthen pots which had been buried. They also brought whatever else they had; but we wished only a meal, so gave the rest to the Christians to divide among themselves.

After this we had a hot argument with them, for they meant to make slaves of the Indians in our train. We got so angry that we went off forgetting the many Turkish-shaped bows, the many pouches, and the five emerald arrow-

---

8. It was probably March 1536.
9. I.e., Culiacán, the northernmost Spanish set-

tlement in Mexico at that time, located in Sinaloa near the mouth of the Gulf of California.

heads, etc., which we thus lost. And to think we had given these Christians a supply of cowhides and other things that our retainers had carried a long distance!

It proved difficult to persuade our escorting Indians to go back to their homes, to feel apprehensive no longer, and to plant their corn. But they did not want to do anything until they had first delivered us into the hands of other Indians, as custom bound them. They feared they would die if they returned without fulfiling this obligation whereas, with us, they said they feared neither Christians nor lances.

This sentiment roused our countrymen's jealousy. Alcaraz bade his interpreter tell the Indians that we were members of his race who had been long lost; that his group were the lords of the land who must be obeyed and served, while we were inconsequential. The Indians paid no attention to this. Conferring among themselves, they replied that the Christians lied: We had come from the sunrise, they from the sunset; we healed the sick, they killed the sound; we came naked and barefoot, they clothed, horsed, and lanced; we coveted nothing but gave whatever we were given, while they robbed whomever they found and bestowed nothing on anyone.

* * *

To the last I could not convince the Indians that we were of the same people as the Christian slavers. Only with the greatest effort were we able to induce them to go back home. We ordered them to fear no more, reestablish their towns, and farm.

Already the countryside had grown rank from neglect. This is, no doubt, the most prolific land in all these Indies. It produces three crops a year; the trees bear a great variety of fruit; and beautiful rivers and brimming springs abound throughout. There are gold- and silver-bearing ores. The people are well disposed, serving such Christians as are their friends with great good will. They are comely, much more so than the Mexicans. This land, in short, lacks nothing to be regarded as blest.

When the Indians took their leave of us they said they would do as we commanded and rebuild their towns, if the Christians let them. And I solemnly swear that if they have not done so it is the fault of the Christians.

After we had dismissed the Indians in peace and thanked them for their toil in our behalf, the Christians subtly sent us on our way in the charge of an *alcalde* named Cebreros, attended by two horsemen.[1] They took us through forests and wastes so we would not communicate with the natives and would neither see nor learn of their crafty scheme afoot. Thus we often misjudge the motives of men; we thought we had effected the Indians' liberty, when the Christians were but poising to pounce.

* * *

c. 1536–40   1542

---

1. I.e., they were, in effect, under arrest.

First Encounters: Early European Accounts of Native America

From the first voyage of Columbus, European voyagers and colonists put much time into writing reports on their ventures. Probably the most important subject of such colonial discourses was the land itself, since its nature and potential mattered immediately to European powers and commercial companies. But the Native peoples occupying the land quickly emerged as a subject of immense curiosity and interest as well. In describing the greatly varied inhabitants of the Western Hemisphere for European eyes and minds, these writers crafted something like a notion of culture. Anthropology, as various scholars have argued, was created in the expansion of Europe to the West after 1492.

Pilgrim leaders William Bradford and Edward Winslow, among others, called the initial contact between Europeans and Native Americans the "First Encounter." It is of course not possible to isolate the very first moment, either historically or textually, from the flow of events and words. Yet it is instructive to imagine the First Encounter as a moment of special importance in human history. Although Europeans with their primitive firearms and disease-wracked bodies were not all that different from the inhabitants of the Western Hemisphere, the contrasts for both sides were evident. European ideology allowed no place either for this other hemisphere or the peoples that dwelled in it. For centuries after 1492, scholars in Europe struggled to account for the biblical failure to mention the "Indians." Even if we leave aside that thorny religious issue, European description of the habits and attitudes of Native Americans caused widespread reflection on the question of what key traits defined human nature globally.

Bafflement over such questions existed uneasily alongside more worldly feelings—greed for land and its potential wealth, fear for the vulnerability of exposed European colonies that before long dotted the shores of the Americas, and jealousy over the efforts of other colonizing powers. Nor were the Native Americans without their own range of emotions. Europeans brought technologies and practices that bemused, aided, and (often at the same time) outraged Native peoples. Moreover, European incursions, although small in scale at first, soon became major factors in the economic, political, medical, and cultural life of tribal groups. They disrupted the life of individual tribes and upset rough balances of power and interest that had existed before 1492. European expressions of astonishment at the new landscape and its inhabitants were soon overwhelmed by invasions of American space that forever altered, and in many cases destroyed, Native territories and peoples.

The set of selections included here, representing reports of some of these early encounters, exemplifies several aspects of the complex process. It illustrates, for one thing, the sheer geographical range of the phenomenon: in reading of Cortés in Mexico in 1519–21 and Champlain and Hudson some ninety years later in the hinterlands of what would become New York State, one senses exactly how much territory was at stake in the early period, and the scope of the resulting transformations. Moreover, some of the themes in the narratives of these figures are broadly consistent despite the range of space and context. Cortés took advantage of preexisting jealousies between the Aztecs and some of the surrounding subject peoples. Champlain, surrounding himself with Indian allies from the Saint Lawrence valley, did the same—thereby winning a victory over the powerful and much-feared Iroquois. In the two narratives touching on Hudson's 1609 voyage, one from a crewman and the other collected some two hundred years later from Native sources far from New York, one may detect the same sense of guarded strategy that allowed both Cortés and Champlain to succeed. That Hudson's crew exploited not only weaponry but also liquor as tools for dealing with the Natives reveals the unscrupulous methods often employed by their successors.

These selections also possess other interests. Cortés laid waste to Mexico City in an effort to improvise (in defiance of Spanish authority) a better colonial policy. In his wondering descriptions of the complex beauty of Montezuma's capital, one catches the innocent opening of his soon-bloody career as a conquistador. Empire is always implicit, often explicit, in these texts. Champlain and Hudson in fact came into upstate New York at precisely the same moment, in 1609. Neither man was on his first voyage or his last. But their forays south and north into what we now call the Hudson–Champlain corridor mapped out the future setting of many battles among European powers and their Native allies. Here in this very terrain the English successors of the Dutch (who had employed Hudson) would grapple with the French in a series of wars, including that which produced the legends used by James Fenimore Cooper in *The Last of the Mohicans* (1826). Here too the American rebels in 1775 would capture Ticonderoga, originally a French fort, but more recently a British one, on their way to a failed invasion of Canada. And in 1777, when the British under General John Burgoyne moved south out of Canada intent on destroying the rebellious colonies and ending the Revolution, they were defeated by a suddenly effective American army at Saratoga. Reading about Champlain and Hudson helps one imagine the long imperial process set in motion by their apparently simple incursions in 1609.

One similarity between these two explorers is the amount of violence that accompanied their penetration into Native lands, described in especially graphic detail by Champlain. This issue is worth pausing over. It is crucial to put early American violence into a proper historical context. It occurred, of course, on both sides, although European apologists often sought to blame it on Native resistance or what they soon were describing as the inherent "savagery" of the Native peoples. Even a quick reading of the Champlain and Hudson narratives dispels such arguments. Although the Indian allies accompanying Champlain indeed carried out shocking tortures on one of their Iroquois prisoners, their behavior had complex historical sources—it was hardly the expression of some supposedly innate evil. For one thing, as their taunting of that prisoner indicates, they viewed his torture as payback for "the cruelties which he and his friends" had "practiced upon them." The Iroquois, a powerful league of Algonquian tribes occupying much of the present state of New York, had been carrying out aggressive warfare against other Native peoples, including those of eastern Canada, when the European powers first ventured into that part of the continent. They therefore were much feared and much resisted by the ancestors of Champlain's allies.

Even without European involvement, intertribal wars in this region could be bloody and widely destructive. However, it is also clear that the coming of Europeans into Native regions exacerbated preexisting tensions. The Iroquois surely viewed Champlain's alliance with the Huron and Montagnais and other northern peoples as an ominous development. And the traditional enemies of the Iroquois, cheered by that same alliance, surely saw it as a guarantee that they could behave toward the aggressive Iroquois with more vigor than they otherwise might have. In short, the presence of Europeans deepened and sharpened Native-on-Native violence.

Furthermore, the Europeans not only caused an escalation of Native violence but also brought their own traditions of bloody warfare with them. Aside from such special cases as those of the Iroquois in the Northeast or the Navajo in the Southwest, Native Americans of the conquest period typically waged war in a restrained, even ritualized, manner as compared with Europeans. In another of the selections in this grouping, there is further insight into this issue. In 1636–37, the English colonists of New England joined forces to mount a campaign against one of the more feared Native peoples in their region, the Pequots of coastal Connecticut. Previous aggressions by the Pequots against other tribes helped the English persuade some Pequot enemies, including the Mohegans and the Narragansetts, to join in what became a war of virtual extermination. Although these Native allies had little love for the Pequot, they nonetheless found the methods of the English army shockingly bloody. We know this because one of the English soldiers, John Underhill of Massachusetts, reported that sort of reaction on the part of the Narragansett. Underhill's small book *Newes from America*, issued in London in 1638, sought to defend the justness of the English cause. But in conveying the Native perception that English warfare was evil because it killed too many people, Underhill provided evidence of the savagery of which European settlers were capable. He thus provides a fitting end to this group of readings.

HERNÁN CORTÉS

Typical in some ways of the class of colonial agents that quickly developed in Spain and its American possessions after 1492, Hernán Cortés (1485–1543) had much experience in Hispaniola and Cuba before he was given command of an expedition that was sent out, in 1519, to round up stranded Spaniards on the mainland of Yucatan. When, owing to conflicts between Cortés and the governor of Cuba, Diego Velázquez, the expedition was cancelled at the last minute, Cortés disobeyed his recall and forged ahead. Once on the Mexican coast, he destroyed his ships so his men could not go back. He then plunged inland, gathered Native allies for what proved, against heavy odds, a remarkable conquest of Montezuma's Aztec Empire. The five letters he wrote to Charles V of Spain were intended to create a rationale for the technically illegal actions that had led to this outcome. The present selection derives from the second letter, written after the Spaniards had arrived in Tenochtitlan (Mexico City) but before they began their bloody conquest of Montezuma and his Aztec forces.

From Second Letter to the Spanish Crown[1]

[DESCRIPTION OF TENOCHTITLAN]

This great city of Temixtitan * * * is as big as Seville or Córdoba.[2] The main streets are very wide and very straight; some of these are on the land, but the rest and all the smaller ones are half on land, half canals where they paddle their canoes. All the streets have openings in places so that the water may pass from one canal to another. Over all these openings, and some of them are very wide, there are bridges made of long and wide beams joined together very firmly and so well made that on some of them ten horsemen may ride abreast.

Seeing that if the inhabitants of this city wished to betray us they were very well equipped for it by the design of the city, for once the bridges had

---

1. The text is from *Hernán Cortés: Letters from Mexico*, edited and translated by A. R. Pagden (1971).
2. Prominent cities in Spain. Temixitan, also known as Tenochtitlan, is modern Mexico City, where Mutezuma (Montezuma) ruled over the Aztec Empire and its subordinate states.

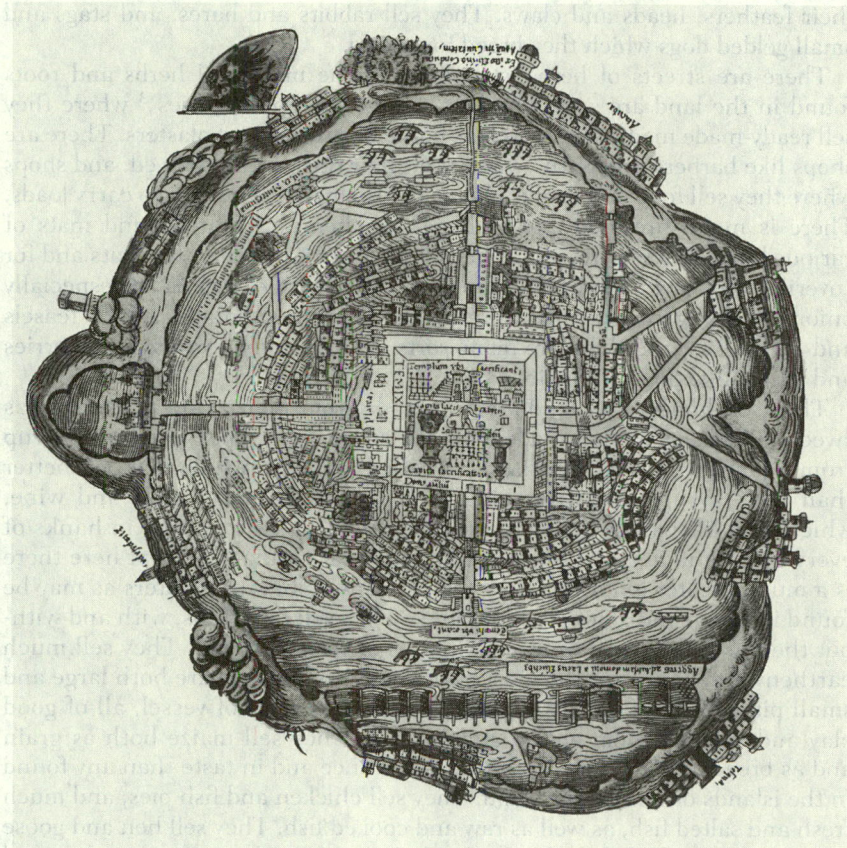

Tenochtitlan, or Mexico City, from *Praeclara Ferdinādi Cortesii de Nova maris Oceani Hyspania Narratio,* 1524. This German map of the Aztec capital of Tenochtitlan, based on a sketch reportedly made for Cortés, accompanied a translation of his second and third letters to Charles V. It displays the material complexity documented in his prose.

been removed they could starve us to death without our being able to reach the mainland, as soon as I entered the city I made great haste to build four brigantines, and completed them in a very short time. They were such as could carry three hundred men to the land and transport the horses whenever we might need them.

This city has many squares where trading is done and markets are held continuously. There is also one square twice as big as that of Salamanca, with arcades all around, where more than sixty thousand people come each day to buy and sell, and where every kind of merchandise produced in these lands is found; provisions as well as ornaments of gold and silver, lead, brass, copper, tin, stones, shells, bones, and feathers. They also sell lime, hewn and unhewn stone, adobe bricks, tiles, and cut and uncut woods of various kinds. There is a street where they sell game and birds of every species found in this land: chickens, partridges and quails, wild ducks, flycatchers, widgeons, turtledoves, pigeons, cane birds, parrots, eagles and eagle owls, falcons, sparrow hawks and kestrels, and they sell the skins of some of these birds of prey with their feathers, heads and claws. They sell rabbits and hares, and stags and small gelded dogs which they breed for eating.

There are streets of herbalists where all the medicinal herbs and roots found in the land are sold. There are shops like apothecaries',[3] where they sell ready-made medicines as well as liquid ointments and plasters. There are shops like barbers' where they have their hair washed and shaved, and shops where they sell food and drink. There are also men like porters to carry loads. There is much firewood and charcoal, earthenware braziers and mats of various kinds like mattresses for beds, and other, finer ones, for seats and for covering rooms and hallways. There is every sort of vegetable, especially onions, leeks, garlic, common cress and watercress, borage, sorrel, teasels and artichokes; and there are many sorts of fruit, among which are cherries and plums like those in Spain.

They sell honey, wax, and a syrup made from maize canes, which is as sweet and syrupy as that made from the sugar cane. They also make syrup from a plant which in the islands is called *maguey*,[4] which is much better than most syrups, and from this plant they also make sugar and wine, which they likewise sell. There are many sorts of spun cotton, in hanks of every color, and it seems like the silk market at Granada, except here there is a much greater quantity. They sell as many colors for painters as may be found in Spain and all of excellent hues. They sell deerskins, with and without the hair, and some are dyed white or in various colors. They sell much earthenware, which for the most part is very good; there are both large and small pitchers, jugs, pots, tiles, and many other sorts of vessel, all of good clay and most of them glazed and painted. They sell maize both as grain and as bread and it is better both in appearance and in taste than any found in the islands or on the mainland. They sell chicken and fish pies, and much fresh and salted fish, as well as raw and cooked fish. They sell hen and goose eggs, and eggs of all the other birds I have mentioned, in great number, and they sell *tortillas* made from eggs.

Finally, besides those things which I have already mentioned, they sell in the market everything else to be found in this land, but they are so many and so varied that because of their great number and because I cannot remember many of them nor do I know what they are called I shall not mention them. Each kind of merchandise is sold in its own street without any mixture whatever; they are very particular in this. Everything is sold by number and size, and until now I have seen nothing sold by weight. There is in this great square a very large building like a courthouse, where ten or twelve persons sit as judges. They preside over all that happens in the markets, and sentence criminals. There are in this square other persons who walk among the people to see what they are selling and the measures they are using; and they have been seen to break some that were false.

There are, in all districts of this great city, many temples or houses for their idols. They are all very beautiful buildings, and in the important ones there are priests of their sect who live there permanently; and, in addition to the houses for the idols, they also have very good lodgings. All these priests dress in black and never comb their hair from the time they enter the priesthood until they leave; and all the sons of the persons of high rank, both the lords and honored citizens also, enter the priesthood and wear the habit

3. Drugstores.
4. A large spiked plant (also called aloe) from which both a sweet syrup and a strong liquor (pulque) are still produced today.

from the age of seven or eight years until they are taken away to be married; this occurs more among the first-born sons, who are to inherit, than among the others. They abstain from eating things, and more at some times of the year than at others; and no woman is granted entry nor permitted inside these places of worship.

Amongst these temples there is one, the principal one, whose great size and magnificence no human tongue could describe, for it is so large that within the precincts, which are surrounded by a very high wall, a town of some five hundred inhabitants could easily be built. All round inside this wall there are very elegant quarters with very large rooms and corridors where their priests live. There are as many as forty towers, all of which are so high that in the case of the largest there are fifty steps leading up to the main part of it; and the most important of these towers is higher than that of the cathedral of Seville. They are so well constructed in both their stone and woodwork that there can be none better in any place, for all the stonework inside the chapels where they keep their idols is in high relief, with figures and little houses, and the woodwork is likewise of relief and painted with monsters and other figures and designs. All these towers are burial places of chiefs, and the chapels therein are each dedicated to the idol which he venerated.

There are three rooms within this great temple for the principal idols, which are of remarkable size and stature and decorated with many designs and sculptures, both in stone and in wood. Within these rooms are other chapels, and the doors to them are very small. Inside there is no light whatsoever; there only some of the priests may enter, for inside are the sculptured figures of the idols, although, as I have said, there are also many outside.

The most important of these idols, and the ones in whom they have most faith, I had taken from their places and thrown down the steps; and I had those chapels where they were cleaned, for they were full of the blood of sacrifices; and I had images of Our Lady and of other saints put there, which caused Mutezuma and the other natives some sorrow. First they asked me not to do it, for when the communities learnt of it they would rise against me, for they believed that those idols gave them all their worldly goods, and that if they were allowed to be ill treated, they would become angry and give them nothing and take the fruit from the earth leaving the people to die of hunger. I made them understand through the interpreters how deceived they were in placing their trust in those idols which they had made with their hands from unclean things. They must know that there was only one God, Lord of all things, who had created heaven and earth and all else and who made all of us; and He was without beginning or end, and they must adore and worship only Him, not any other creature or thing. And I told them all I knew about this to dissuade them from their idolatry and bring them to the knowledge of God our Saviour. All of them, especially Mutezuma, replied that they had already told me how they were not natives of this land, and that as it was many years since their forefathers had come here, they well knew that they might have erred somewhat in what they believed, for they had left their native land so long ago; and as I had only recently arrived from there, I would better know the things they should believe, and should explain to them and make them understand, for they would do as I said was best. Mutezuma and many of the chieftains of the city were with me until the idols were removed, the chapel cleaned and the images set up, and I urged them not to sacrifice living creatures to the idols, as they were accustomed, for, as well as being most abhorrent to God, Your Sacred Majesty's laws forbade it and ordered that he who kills shall be killed. And from then on they ceased to do it, and in all the time I stayed in that city I did not see a living creature killed or sacrificed.

The figures of the idols in which these people believe are very much larger than the body of a big man. They are made of dough from all the seeds and vegetables which they eat, ground and mixed together, and bound with the blood of human hearts which those priests tear out while still beating. And also after they are made they offer them more hearts and anoint their faces with the blood. Everything has an idol dedicated to it, in the same manner as the pagans who in antiquity honored their gods. So they have an idol whose favor they ask in war and another for agriculture; and likewise for each thing they wish to be done well they have an idol which they honor and serve.

There are in the city many large and beautiful houses, and the reason for this is that all the chiefs of the land, who are Mutezuma's vassals, have houses in the city and live there for part of the year; and in addition there are many rich citizens who likewise have very good houses. All these houses have very large and very good rooms and also very pleasant gardens of various sorts of flowers both on the upper and lower floors.

Along one of the causeways to this great city run two aqueducts made of mortar. Each one is two paces wide and some six feet deep, and along one of them a stream of very good fresh water, as wide as a man's body, flows into the heart of the city and from this they all drink. The other, which is empty, is used when they wish to clean the first channel. Where the aqueducts cross the bridges, the water passes along some channels which are as wide as an ox; and so they serve the whole city.

Canoes paddle through all the streets selling the water; they take it from the aqueduct by placing the canoes beneath the bridges where those channels are, and on top there are men who fill the canoes and are paid for their work. At all the gateways to the city and at the places where these canoes are unloaded, which is where the greater part of the provisions enter the city, there are guards in huts who receive a *certum quid*[5] of all that enters. I have not yet discovered whether this goes to the chief or to the city, but I think to the chief, because in other markets in other parts I have seen this tax paid to the ruler of the place. Every day, in all the markets and public places there are many workmen and craftsmen of every sort, waiting to be employed by the day. The people of this city are dressed with more elegance and are more courtly in their bearing than those of the other cities and provinces, and because Mutezuma and all those chieftains, his vassals, are always coming to the city, the people have more manners and politeness in all matters. Yet so as not to tire Your Highness with the description of the things of this city (although I would not complete it so briefly), I will say only that these people live almost like those in Spain, and in as much harmony and order as there, and considering that they are barbarous and so far from the knowledge of God and cut off from all civilized nations, it is truly remarkable to see what they have achieved in all things.

* * *

1522

5. A certain part (Latin).

SAMUEL DE CHAMPLAIN

Born into a seafaring family near La Rochelle on France's Atlantic coast, Champlain (c. 1570–1635), more than any other Frenchman of his time, deepened his country's interest in North America and planted that interest solidly in American soil. He had already crossed the ocean six times by 1603, when (as "geographer royal" under the command of François Pont-Gravé) he sailed up the Saint Lawrence River as far as the future site of Montreal, where the expedition took on valuable furs before returning to France. Early in 1604, Champlain published his official report, *Des Sauvages* (Of the Indians), illustrated with his own maps, and in April returned to America under the command of the Sieur de Monts, a Protestant merchant who was a native of Champlain's own region. Champlain came back again in 1608 and founded Quebec City. From that base the following year, gathering Indian allies from several tribes in the Saint Lawrence valley and the mountains to the north, he went up the Richelieu River into the long, narrow lake to the south that bears his name today. While on this expedition, which he wrote about in his next book, *Les Voyages* (1613), he and his allies met and defeated a party of Mohawk Indians from what is now central New York. The violent encounter helped turn most Mohawk and their kin in the Iroquois Confederation against the French for the next 150 years.

From The Voyages of the Sieur de Champlain[1]

[THE IROQUOIS]

We departed on the following day, pursuing our way up the river as far as the entrance to the lake.[2] * * *

On the following day we entered the lake * * * in which I saw four beautiful islands[3] * * * which, like the Iroquois river, were formerly inhabited by Indians: but have been abandoned, since they have been at war with one another. There are also several rivers flowing into the lake, on whose banks are many fine trees of the same varieties we have in France, with many of the finest vines I had seen anywhere. * * *

Continuing our way along this lake in a westerly direction and viewing the country, I saw towards the east very high mountains on the tops of which there was snow. I enquired of the natives whether these parts were inhabited. They said they were, and by the Iroquois, and that in those parts there were beautiful valleys and fields rich in corn such as I have eaten in that country, along with other products in abundance. And they said that the lake went close to the mountains, which, as I judged, might be some twenty-five leagues away from us. Towards the south I saw others which were not less lofty than the first-mentioned, but there was no snow on these. The Indians told me that it was there that we were to meet their enemies, that the mountains

---

1. The text is from *The Works of Samuel de Champlain in Six Volumes*, vol. 2, edited by H. P. Biggar and translated by John Squair (1925).
2. Called by Champlain "the river of the Iroquois," this is today known as the Richelieu.
3. The lake, ever since known as Lake Champlain, contains a number of large islands near where the Richelieu flows out of its north end.

were thickly populated, and that we had to pass a rapid which I saw afterwards. Thence they said we had to enter another lake.[4] * * *

Now as we began to get within two or three days' journey of the home of their enemy, we proceeded only by night, and during the day we rested. Nevertheless, they kept up their usual superstitious ceremonies in order to know what was to happen to them in their undertakings, and often would come and ask me whether I had had dreams and had seen their enemies. I would tell them that I had not, but nevertheless continued to inspire them with courage and good hope. When night came on, we set off on our way until the next morning. Then we retired into the thick woods where we spent the rest of the day. Towards ten or eleven o'clock, after walking around our camp, I went to take a rest, and while asleep I dreamed that I saw in the lake near a mountain our enemies, the Iroquois, drowning before our eyes. I wanted to succour them, but our Indian allies said to me that we should let them all perish; for they were bad men. When I awoke they did not fail to ask me as usual whether I had dreamed anything. I told them what I had seen in my dream. This gave them such confidence that they no longer had any doubt as to the good fortune awaiting them.

Evening having come, we embarked in our canoes in order to proceed on our way, and as we were paddling along very quietly, and without making any noise, about ten o'clock at night on the twenty-ninth of [July], at the extremity of a cape[5] which projects into the lake on the west side, we met the Iroquois on the war-path. Both they and we began to utter loud shouts and each got his arms ready. We drew out into the lake and the Iroquois landed and arranged all their canoes near one another. Then they began to fell trees with the poor axes which they sometimes win in war, or with stone axes; and they barricaded themselves well.

Our Indians all night long also kept their canoes close to one another and tied to poles in order not to get separated, but to fight all together in case of need. We were on the water within bowshot of their barricades. And when they were armed, and everything in order, they sent two canoes which they had separated from the rest, to learn from their enemies whether they wished to fight, and these replied that they had no other desire, but that for the moment nothing could be seen and that it was necessary to wait for daylight in order to distinguish one another. They said that as soon as the sun should rise, they would attack us, and to this our Indians agreed. Meanwhile the whole night was spent in dances and songs on both sides, with many insults and other remarks, such as the lack of courage of our side, how little we could resist or do against them, and that when daylight came our people would learn all this to their ruin. Our side too was not lacking in retort, telling the enemy that they would see such deeds of arms as they had never seen, and a great deal of other talk, such as is usual at the siege of a city. Having sung, danced, and flung words at one another for some time, when daylight came, my companions and I were still hidden, lest the enemy should see us, getting our fire-arms ready as best we could, being however still separated, each in a canoe of the Montagnais Indians.[6] After we were armed

4. Now known as Lake George, this body of water is connected to Lake Champlain through the short La Chute River, site of the rapids mentioned in the previous sentence.
5. Now known as Crown Point, in the southern part of Lake Champlain.

6. Members of this group of peoples, from the mountainous region north of the Saint Lawrence River, accompanied Champlain in his expedition into the territory of their ancient enemies, the Iroquois.

with light weapons, we took, each of us, an arquebus[7] and went ashore. I saw the enemy come out of their barricade to the number of two hundred, in appearance strong, robust men. They came slowly to meet us with a gravity and calm which I admired; and at their head were three chiefs. Our Indians likewise advanced in similar order, and told me that those who had the three big plumes were the chiefs, and that there were only these three, whom you could recognize by these plumes, which were larger than those of their companions; and I was to do what I could to kill them. I promised them to do all in my power, and told them that I was very sorry they could not understand me, so that I might direct their method of attacking the enemy, all of whom undoubtedly we should thus defeat; but that there was no help for it, and that I was very glad to show them, as soon as the engagement began, the courage and readiness which were in me.

As soon as we landed, our Indians began to run some two hundred yards towards their enemies, who stood firm and had not yet noticed my companions who went off into the woods with some Indians. Our Indians began to call to me with loud cries; and to make way for me they divided into two groups, and put me ahead some twenty yards, and I marched on until I was within some thirty yards of the enemy, who as soon as they caught sight of me halted and gazed at me and I at them. When I saw them make a move to draw their bows upon us, I took aim with my arquebus and shot straight at one of the three chiefs, and with this shot two fell to the ground and one of their companions was wounded who died thereof a little later. I had put four bullets into my arquebus. As soon as our people saw this shot so favorable for them, they began to shout so loudly that one could not have heard it thunder, and meanwhile the arrows flew thick on both sides. The Iroquois were much astonished that two men should have been killed so quickly, although they were provided with shields made of cotton thread woven together and wood, which were proof against their arrows. This frightened them greatly. As I was reloading my arquebus, one of my companions fired a shot from within the woods, which astonished them again so much that, seeing their chiefs dead, they lost courage and took to flight, abandoning the field and their fort, and fleeing into the depth of the forest, whither I pursued them and laid low still more of them. Our Indians also killed several and took ten or twelve prisoners. The remainder fled with the wounded. Of our Indians fifteen or sixteen were wounded with arrows, but these were quickly healed.

After we had gained the victory, our Indians wasted time in taking a large quantity of Indian corn and meal belonging to the enemy, as well as their shields, which they had left behind, the better to run. Having feasted, danced, and sung, we three hours later set off for home with the prisoners. The place where this attack took place is in 43° and some minutes of latitude, and was named Lake Champlain.

* * *

Having gone about eight leagues, the Indians, towards evening, took one of the prisoners to whom they made a harangue on the cruelties which he and his friends without any restraint had practiced upon them, and that similarly he should resign himself to receive as much, and they ordered him to sing, if he had the heart. He did so, but it was a very sad song to hear.

---

7. An early, relatively heavy kind of gun.

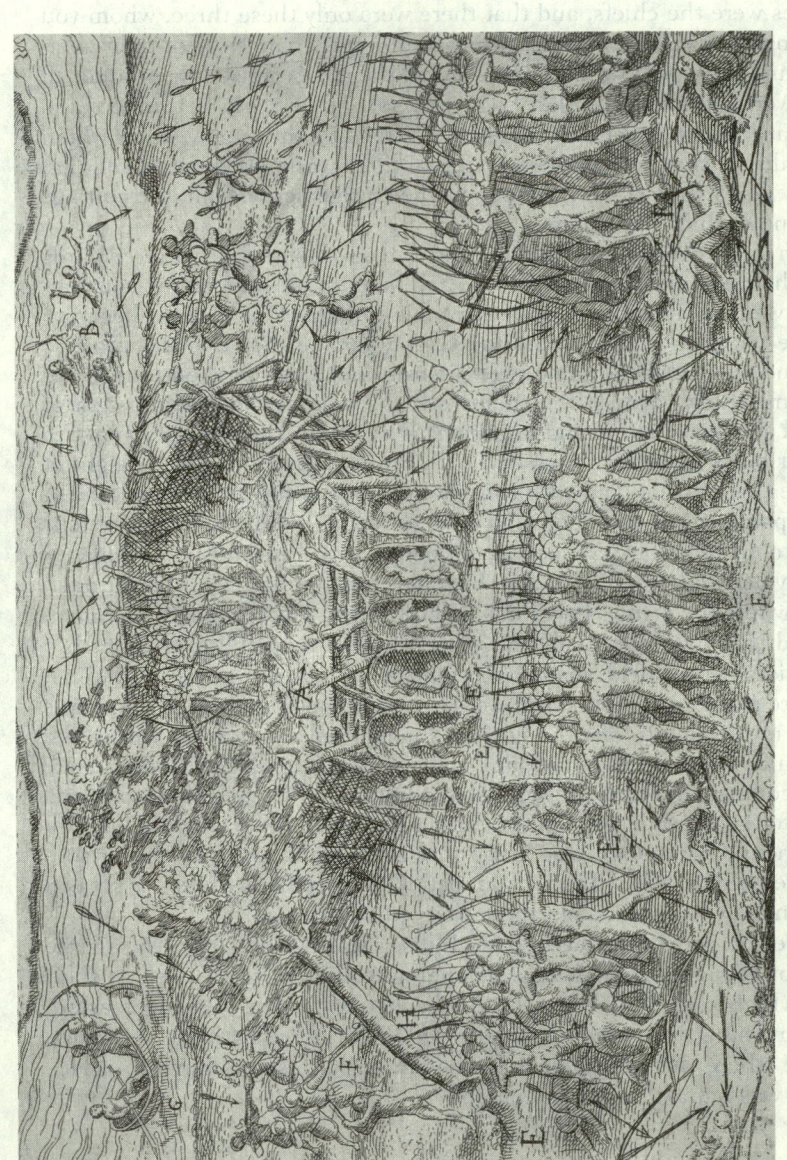

Fort des Yroquois, from *Les Voyages du Sieur de Champlain*, 1613. This woodcut depicts a French attack on an Iroquois fort during a second expedition undertaken in 1610. The fort (A) was a typical palisade constructed of horizontal and vertical logs but could not adequately protect the Iroquois, who (B) threw themselves into the river to escape the French (F) and what Champlain called "all our Indian allies" (E). The attackers also cut down high trees (H) "in order to demolish the Iroquois Fort."

Meanwhile our Indians kindled a fire, and when it was well lighted, each took a brand and burned this poor wretch a little at a time in order to make him suffer the greater torment. Sometimes they would leave off, throwing water on his back. Then they tore out his nails and applied fire to the ends of his fingers and to his [penis]. Afterwards they scalped him and caused a certain kind of gum to drip very hot upon the crown of his head. Then they pierced his arms near the wrists and with sticks pulled and tore out his sinews by main force, and when they saw they could not get them out, they cut them off. This poor wretch uttered strange cries, and I felt pity at seeing him treated in this way. Still he bore it so firmly that sometimes one would have said he felt scarcely any pain. They begged me repeatedly to take fire and do like them. I pointed out to them that we did not commit such cruelties, but that we killed people outright, and that if they wished me to shoot him with the arquebus, I should be glad to do so. They said no; for he would not feel any pain. I went away from them as if angry at seeing them practice so much cruelty on his body. When they saw that I was not pleased, they called me back and told me to give him a shot with the arquebus. I did so, without his perceiving anything, and with one shot caused him to escape all the tortures he would have suffered rather than see him brutally treated. When he was dead, they were not satisfied; they opened his body and threw his bowels into the lake. Afterwards they cut off his head, arms and legs, which they scattered about; but they kept the scalp, which they had flayed, as they did with those of all the others whom they had killed in their attack. They did another awful thing, which was to cut his heart into several pieces and to give it to a brother of the dead man to eat and to others of his companions who were prisoners. These took it and put it into their mouths, but would not swallow it. Some of the Algonquin Indians who were guarding the prisoners made them spit it out and threw it into the water. That is how these people act with regard to those whom they capture in war. And it would be better for them to die fighting, and be killed at once, as many do, rather than to fall into the hands of their enemies. When this execution was over, we set out upon our return with the rest of the prisoners, who went along continually singing, without other expectation than to be tortured like him of whom we have spoken. When we arrived at the rapids of the river of the Iroquois, the Algonquins returned into their own country and the [Hurons] also with some of the prisoners, all much pleased at what had taken place in the war, and because I had gone with them willingly. So we all separated with great protestations of mutual friendship, and they asked me if I would not go to their country, and aid them continually like a brother. I promised them I would.

* * *

1613

WILLIAM BRADFORD   EDWARD WINSLOW

Although readers may be familiar with William Bradford's grand narrative of the legendary landing of the Pilgrims on Plymouth Rock in his retrospective history, *Of Plymouth Plantation*, a contemporary account of that event that he co-authored with his good friend Edward Winslow and published in 1622 as *Mourt's Relation* portrays it as a tentative move made up of small events. That earlier account is a narrative of confused movements and puzzling discoveries—a "black thing" seen on the beach along with buried caches of corn and deserted clusters of Indian wigwams. Even the confusion between wolves and men, of which Bradford and Winslow make a good deal, is redolent of the larger ambiguity of the colonizing efforts in which all these writers took part. For Bradford and Winslow, happily, one can examine how colonial actors later sought to dispel at least some of the fuzziness. For in the ninth chapter of the first book of *Of Plymouth Plantation*, included later in this anthology, Bradford retells the Cape Cod story in an instructively varied form.

Bradford (1590–1657) grew up among radical nonconforming Protestants of rural northern England who early earned his allegiance and whom he accompanied on their exile in the Lowlands early in the seventeenth century. By contrast, Winslow (1595–1655) had been brought up in relative ease in Worcestershire, closer to London, largely untouched by spiritual concerns. He encountered Bradford and the other exiles while traveling in Leyden and, finding new purpose in their spiritual life, joined them in their voyage to America in 1620. Once the colonists had established themselves at Plymouth, both men became important public figures: each, for instance, served several terms as governor. The book they wrote together during the first months ashore in America is a mark of their common purpose and shared viewpoint. In later decades, however, the two were separated when Winslow, sent back to England on public business in 1646, became involved in the Puritan government of Oliver Cromwell. Winslow died in the West Indies in the aftermath of an unsuccessful military campaign against the Spanish colony of Santo Domingo.

From Mourt's Relation[1]

[CAPE COD FORAYS]

Wednesday the sixth of December [1620] we set out, being very cold and hard weather, we were a long while after we launched from the ship, before we could get clear of a sandy point, which lay within less than a furlong of the same. In which time, two were very sick, and *Edward Tilley* had like to have sounded with cold; the Gunner was also sick unto Death, (but hope of trucking[2] made him to go) and so remained all that day, and the next night; at length we got clear of the sandy point, and got up our sails, and within an hour or two we got under the weather shore,[3] and then had smoother water and better sailing, but it was very cold, for the water froze on our clothes,

---

1. The text is from *Mourt's Relation, or Journal of the Plantation at Plymouth*, edited by Henry Martyn Dexter (1865).

2. Trading. "Sounded": fainted.
3. The shore from which the wind was blowing.

and made them many times like coats of Iron: we sailed six or seven leagues by the shore, but saw neither river nor creek, at length we met with a tongue of Land, being flat off from the shore, with a sandy point, we bore up to gain the point, and found there a fair income or road,[4] of a Bay, being a league over at the narrowest, and some two or three in length, but we made right over to the land before us, and left the discovery of this *Income* till the next day: as we drew near to the shore, we espied some ten or twelve *Indians*, very busy about a black thing, what it was we could not tell, til afterwards they saw us, and ran to and fro, as if they had been carrying some thing away, we landed a league or two from them, and had much ado to put ashore anywhere, it lay so full of flat sands, when we came to shore, we made us a Baricado, and got firewood, and set out our Sentinels, and betook us to our lodging, such as it was; we saw the smoke of the fire which the Savages made that night, about four or five miles from us, in the morning we divided our company, some eight in the Shallop,[5] and the rest on the shore went to discover this place, but we found it only to be a Bay, without either river or creek coming into it, yet we deemed it to be as good an harbor as Cape Cod, for they that sounded it, found a ship might ride in five fathom water, we on the land found it to be a level soil, but none of the fruitfulest; we saw two becks[6] of fresh water, which were the first running streams that we saw in the Country, but one might stride over them: we found also a great fish, called a *Grampus* dead on the sands, they in the Shallop found two of them also in the bottom of the bay, dead in like sort, they were cast up at high water, and could not get off for the frost and ice; they were some five or six paces long, and about two inches thick of fat, and fleshed like a Swine, they would have yielded a great deal of oil, if there had been time and means to have taken it, so we finding nothing for our turn, both we and our Shallop returned. We then directed our course along the Sea sands, to the place where we first saw the *Indians*, when we were there, we saw it was also a *Grampus* which they were cutting up, they cut it into long rands or pieces, about an ell long, and two handfuls broad, we found here and there a piece scattered by the way, as it seemed, for haste: this place the most were minded[7] we should call, the *Grampus Bay*, because we found so many of them there: we followed the track of the *Indians'* bare feet a good way on the sands, at length we saw where they struck into the Woods by the side of a Pond, as we went to view the place, one said, he thought he saw an *Indian* house among the trees, so went up to see: and here we and the Shallop lost sight one of another till night, it being now about nine or ten o'clock, so we light on a path, but saw no house, and followed a great way into the woods, at length we found where Corn had been set, but not that year, anon we found a great burying place, one part whereof was encompassed with a large Palazado, like a Churchyard, with young spires[8] four or five yards long, set as close one by another as they could two or three foot in the ground within it was full of Graves, some bigger, and some less, some were also paled about, and others had like an *Indian* house made over them, but not matted: those Graves were more sumptuous than those at *Corne-hill,* yet we digged none of them up, but only viewed them,

4. Protected inlet or roadstead.
5. Small sailing vessel often used in coastal exploration. "Baricado": barricade.
6. Brooks.

7. Thought. "Rands": strips.
8. Saplings. "Been set": planted. "Palazado": fence of thin posts or pales (hence palisade).

and went our way; without[9] the Palazado were graves also, but not so costly: from this place we went and found more Corn ground, but not of this year. As we ranged we light on four or five *Indian* houses, which had been lately dwelt in, but they were uncovered and had no mats about them, else they were like those we found at *Corne-hill*, but had not been so lately dwelt in, there was nothing left but two or three pieces of old matts, a little sedge,[1] also a little further we found two Baskets full of parched Acorns hid in the ground, which we supposed had been Corn when we began to dig the same, we cast earth thereon again and went our way. All this while we saw no people, we went ranging up and down till the Sun began to draw low, and then we hasted out of the woods, that we might come to our Shallop, which when we were out of the woods, we espied a great way off, and called them to come unto us, the which they did as soon as they could, for it was not yet high water, they were exceeding glad to see us, (for they feared because they had not seen us in so long a time) thinking we would have kept by the shoreside, so being both weary and faint, for we had eaten nothing all that day, we fell to make our Rendezvous[2] and get firewood, which always cost us a great deal of labor, by [the] time we had done, and our Shallop come to us, it was within night, and we fed upon such victuals as we had, and betook us to our rest, after we had set out our watch. About midnight we heard a great and hideous cry, and our Sentinel called, *Arm, Arm.* So we bestirred ourselves and shot off a couple of Muskets, and noise ceased; we concluded, that it was a company of Wolves or Foxes, for one told us, he had heard such a noise in *New-found-land.* About five o'clock in the morning we began to be stirring, and two or three which doubted whether their Pieces would go off or no made trial of them, and shot them off, but thought nothing at all, after Prayer we prepared ourselves for breakfast, and for a journey, and it being now the twilight in the morning, it was thought meet to carry the things down to the Shallop: some said, it was not best to carry the Armor down, others said, they would be readier, two or three said, they would not carry theirs, till they went themselves, but mistrusting nothing at all: as it fell out, the water not being high enough, they laid the things down upon the shore, and came up to breakfast. Anon, all upon a sudden, we heard a great and strange cry, which we knew to be the same voices, though they varied their notes, one of our company being abroad came running in, and cried, *They are men, Indians, Indians,*[3] and withal, their arrows came flying amongst us, our men ran out with all speed to recover their arms, as by the good Providence of God they did. In the meantime, Captain *Miles Standish*, having a snaphance[4] ready, made a shot, and after him another, after they two had shot, other two of us were ready, but he wished us not to shoot, till we could take aim, for we knew not what need we should have, and there were four only of us, which had their arms there ready, and stood before the open side of our Baricado, which was first assaulted, they thought it best to defend it, lest the enemy should take it and our stuff, and so have the more vantage against us, our care was no less for the Shallop, but we hoped all the rest would defend it; we called

9. Outside. "*Indian* house": Native American wigwams were constructed of timber frames and covered with woven mats. "*Corne-hill*": a spot on Cape Cod where they had unearthed buried stores of grain. Corn Hill was also an ancient ward in London.

1. Reed used for roofing.
2. Camp.
3. As opposed to the wolves or foxes that the Englishmen had earlier thought the men to be.
4. An early version of a flintlock gun.

unto them to know how it was with them, and they answered, Well, Well, every one, and be of good courage: we heard three of their Pieces go off, and the rest called for a fire-brand to light their matches,[5] one took a log out of the fire on his shoulder and went and carried it unto them, which was thought did not a little discourage our enemies. The cry of our enemies was dreadful, especially, when our men ran out to recover their Arms, their note was after this manner, *Woath woach ha ha hach woach*: our men were no sooner come to their Arms, but the enemy was ready to assault them.

There was a lusty man and no wit less valiant,[6] who was thought to be their Captain, stood behind a tree within half a musket shot of us, and there let his arrows fly at us; he was seen to shoot three arrows, which were all avoided, for he at whom the first arrow was aimed, saw it, and stooped down and it flew over him, the rest were avoided also: he stood three shots of a Musket, at length one took full aim at him, after which he gave an extraordinary cry and away they went all, we followed them about a quarter of a mile, but we left six to keep our Shallop, for we were careful of our business: then we shouted all together two several[7] times, and shot off a couple of muskets and so returned: this we did that they might see we were not afraid of them nor discouraged. Thus it pleased God to vanquish our Enemies and give us deliverance, by their noise we could not guess that they were less than thirty or forty, though some thought that they were many more yet in the dark of the morning, we could not so well discern them among the trees, as they could see us by our fireside, we took up eighteen of their arrows which we have sent to *England* by Master *Jones*, some whereof were headed with brass, others with Harts horn,[8] and others with Eagles' claws many more no doubt were shot, for these we found, were almost covered with leaves: yet by the especial providence of God, none of them either hit or hurt us, though many came close by us, and on every side of us, and some coats which hung up in our Baricado, were shot through and through. So after we had given God thanks for our deliverance, we took our Shallop and went on our Journey, and called this place, *The first Encounter.* * * *

1622

5. Wax-coated fuses used with guns lacking snaphance devices.
6. Strong and courageous.

7. Separate.
8. I.e., points made from deer antlers.

JOHN UNDERHILL

A native of Warwickshire, where his family served the earls of Leicester, John Underhill (c. 1597–1672) sought a military career early in life. Like many another Englishman of the time, he gained experience by joining the Protestant cause in the Lowlands, where the northern provinces under William of Orange were at war with the Spanish Crown. Underhill immigrated to Massachusetts Bay with the English Puritans in 1630 and was employed as a soldier in New England once more, especially during the war of 1636–37 against the Pequot people. Orthodox enough at that time, he soon became affiliated with the Antinomians, one of several more radical splinter groups that arose against the Puritan way. His spiritual insurgency caused his dismissal as a soldier, the confiscation of his arms, and the loss of his right to vote in Boston. He thereupon left for England, where he wrote *Newes from America* (1638), in which, while narrating the bloody Pequot War and mentioning his own troubles with the powers that be, he nonetheless held out the promise of fresh opportunity for his English readers. On his return to America shortly afterward, he sought a second chance in New Hampshire. Before long, however, fresh troubles forced him to relocate first to Massachusetts, then to Connecticut, and finally to New Netherland. Having helped in the English conquest of that Dutch colony in 1664 and then having served in the provincial government of New York, he ended his days on Long Island.

From News from America[1]

[THE ATTACK ON PEQUOT FORT]

Having embarked our soldiers, we weighed anchor at *Saybrook* Fort, and set sail for the *Narraganset Bay*,[2] deluding the *Pequots* thereby, for they expected us to fall into *Pequot* River; but crossing their expectation, bred in them a security: we landed our men in the *Narraganset Bay*, and marched over land above two day's journey before we came to *Pequot*;[3] quartering the last night's march within two miles of the place, we set forth about one of the clock in the morning, having sufficient intelligence that they knew nothing of our coming: Drawing near to the Fort yielded up ourselves to God, and entreated his assistance in so weighty an enterprise. We set on our march to surround the Fort,[4] Captain *John Mason*, approaching to the West end, where it had an entrance to pass into it, myself marching to the South side, surrounding the Fort, placing the *Indians*, for we had about three hundred of them, without side of our soldiers in a ring battalia, giving a volley of shot upon the Fort, so remarkable it appeared to us, as we could not but admire[5] at the providence of God in it, that soldiers so inexpert in the use of their arms, should give so complete a volley, as though the finger of God had touched both match and flint[6] which volley being given at break of day, and themselves fast asleep for the most part, bred in them such a terror, that they broke forth into a most doleful cry, so as if God had not fitted the hearts of men for the service, it would have bred in them a commiseration toward them:[7] but every man being bereaved of pity fell upon the work without compassion, considering the blood they had shed of our native Countrymen, and how barbarously they had dealt with them, and slaine first and last about thirty persons. Having given fire, we approached near to the entrance which they had stopped full, with arms of trees, or brakes:[8] myself approaching to the entrance found the work too heavy for me, to draw out all those

1. The text is from the first edition of *Newes from America; or, A New and Experimentall Discoverie of New England, Containing a True Relation of Their War-like Proceedings These Two Yeares Last Past, with a Figure of the Indian Fort or Palizado* (1638).
2. The body of water on which Rhode Island is centered. Saybrook Fort was an English fortification on the west shore at the mouth of the Connecticut River.
3. The main settlement of the Pequot Indians, west of Narragansett Bay near New London in southeastern Connecticut.
4. "This Fort or palisado, was [nearly] an acre of ground which was surrounded with trees, and

half trees set into the ground three feet deep, and fastened close one to another, as you may see more clearly [depicted] in the figure of it before the book" [Underhill's note. See the following page for the figure].
5. Be amazed by. "Battalia": circular arrangement of troops.
6. Reference to the two ways of firing a contemporary gun: by lighting a match, a kind of wick that conveys fire to the gunpowder in a matchlock gun, or by striking a piece of flint stone against a metal part on a flintlock gun, producing sparks that ignite the powder.
7. I.e., the Pequots.
8. Bushes or briars.

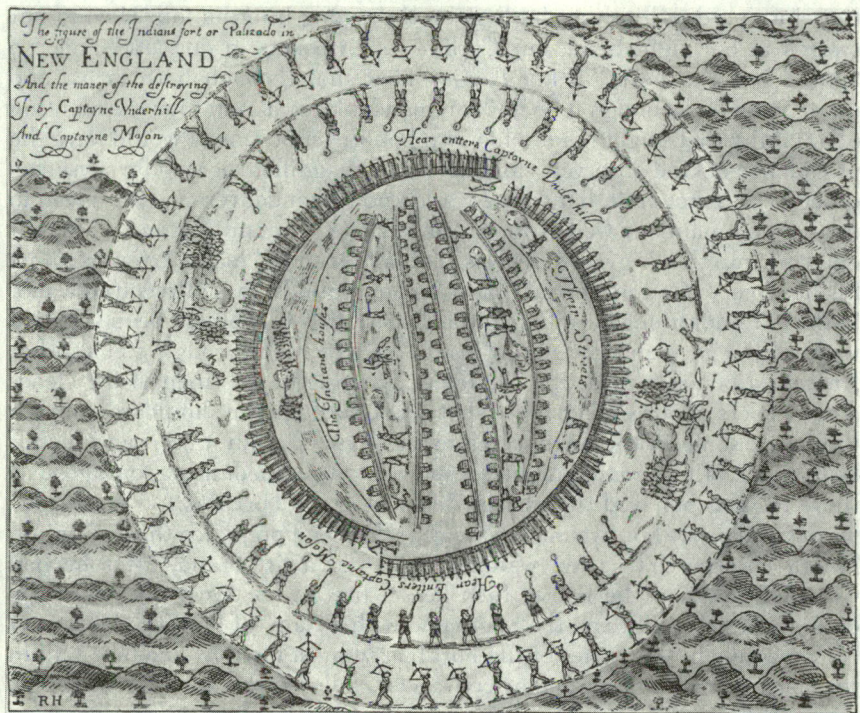

The figure of the Indians' fort *or Palisado in* NEW ENGLAND *and the maner of the destroying It by Captayne Underhill and Capatyne Mason,* from John Underhill, *News from America,* 1638. Although this representation of the battle at Pequot Fort in 1637 is clearly schematic, it does convey much information about the Pequot manner of living in the settlement and many details about the strategy of encirclement used by the English in destroying it.

which were strongly forced in. We gave order to one Master *Hedge,* and some other soldiers to pull out those brakes, having this done, and laid them between me and the entrance, and without order themselves, proceeded first on the South end of the Fort: but remarkable it was to many of us; men that run before they are sent, most commonly have an ill reward. Worthy Reader, let me entreat you to have a more charitable opinion of me (though unworthy to be better thought of) than is reported in the other Book:[9] you may remember there is a passage unjustly laid upon me, that when we should come to the entrance, I should put forth this question: "shall we enter?" others should answer again: "What came we hither for else?" It is well known to many, it was never my practise in time of my command, when we are in garrison, much to consult with a private soldier, or to ask his advice in point of War, much less in a matter of so great a moment as that was, which experience had often taught me, was not a time to put forth such a question, and

9. Reference to Philip Vincent, *A True Relation of the Late Battle Fought in New-England between the English and the Savages* (1638), an account written by an English minister who appears to have traveled in America and witnessed the war. Vincent, who shows an attitude more tolerant of the Pequots, claimed that one Pequot prisoner dared Underhill's men to kill him, at which point, tying one of his legs to a post and grabbing the other, twenty soldiers literally tore him limb from limb. Underhill then reportedly shot him.

therefore pardon him that hath given the wrong information. Having our swords in our right hand, our Carbines or Muskets in our left hand, we approached the Fort. Master *Hedge* being shot through both arms, and more[1] wounded; though it be not commendable for a man to make mention of anything that might tend to his own honor; yet because I would have the providence of God observed,[2] and his Name magnified, as well for myself as others, I dare not omit, but let the world know, that deliverance was given to us that command, as well as to private soldiers. Captain *Mason* and myself entering into the Wigwams, he was shot, and received many Arrows against his headpiece, God preserved him from any wounds; myself received a shot in the left hip, through a sufficient Buff coat,[3] that if I had not been supplied with such a garment, the Arrow would have pierced through me; another I received between neck and shoulders, hanging in the linen of my Headpiece, others of our soldiers were shot, some through the shoulders, some in the faces, some in the head, some in the legs: Captain *Mason* and myself losing each of us a man, and had near twenty wounded: most courageously these *Pequots* behaved themselves: but seeing the Fort was too hot for us, we devised a way how we might save ourselves and prejudice them, Captain *Mason* entering into a Wigwam, brought out a fire-brand, after he had wounded many in the house, then he set fire on the West side where he entered, myself set fire on the South end with a train[4] of Powder, the fires of both meeting in the center of the Fort blazed most terribly, and burnt all in the space of half an hour; many courageous fellows were unwilling to come out, and fought most desperately through the Palisadoes, so as they were scorched and burnt with the very flame, and were deprived of their arms, in regard[5] the fire burnt their very bowstrings, and so perished valiantly: mercy they did deserve for their valor, could we have had opportunity to have bestowed it; many were burnt in the Fort, both men, women, and children, others forced out, and came in troops to the *Indians*, twenty, and thirty at a time, which our soldiers received and entertained with the point of the sword; down fell men, women, and children, those that escaped us, fell into the hands of the *Indians*, that were in the rear of us; it is reported by themselves, that there were about four hundred souls in this Fort, and not above five of them escaped out of our hands. Great and doleful was the bloody sight to the view of young soldiers that never had been in War, to see so many souls lie gasping on the ground so thick in some places, that you could hardly pass along. It may be demanded, "Why should you be so furious (as some have said) should not Christians have more mercy and compassion?" But I would refer you to *David's* war, when a people is grown to such a height of blood, and sin against God and man, and all confederates in the action,[6] there he hath no respect to persons, but harrows[7] them, and

1. Others. According to Vincent's narrative, Hedge was a young gentleman from Northamptonshire in central England who had in fact countered Underhill's question "Shall we enter?" by boldly replying, "What came we hither for else?" (i.e., "Why else did we come here?").
2. Noticed. Puritan theology stressed the power of God to intervene in human experience through his providential powers.
3. A heavy-duty military coat made of oxhide. John Mason (c. 1600–1672) was commander of the Connecticut troops in the Pequot War and

author of *A Brief History of the Pequot War* (first published in 1676). "Headpiece": helmet.
4. A makeshift fuse. "Prejudice": hurt.
5. So that. "Palisadoes": fences made of thin posts or pales.
6. I.e., when everyone is implicated in the evil. "David's War": See 1 Samuel 17. King David of the Israelites famously defeated the giant Goliath, champion of the Philistines, to whom Underhill compares the Pequots.
7. I.e., punishes. A harrow is an agricultural tool with teeth that pulverize the soil.

saws them, and puts them to the sword, and the most terriblest death that may be: sometimes the Scripture declareth women and children must perish with their parents; sometimes the case alters: but we will not dispute it now. We had sufficient light from the word of God for our proceedings.

Having ended this service, we drew our forces together to battallia, being ordered, the *Pequots* came upon us with their prime men, and let fly at us, myself fell on scarce with twelve or fourteen men to encounter with them;[8] but they finding our bullets to outreach their arrows, forced themselves often to retreat: when we saw we could have no advantage against them in the open field, we requested our *Indians* for to entertain fight with them,[9] our end was that we might see the nature of the *Indian* war: which they granted us and fell out; the *Pequots*, *Narragansets*, and *Mohigeners* changing a few arrows together after such a manner, as I dare boldly affirm, they might fight seven years and not kill seven men: they came not near one another, but shot remote, and not point-blank, as we often do with our bullets, but at rovers,[1] and then they gaze up in the sky to see where the Arrow falls, and not until it is fallen do they shoot again. This fight is more for pastime, than to conquer and subdue enemies. But spending a little time this way, we were forced to cast our eyes upon our poor maimed soldiers, many of them lying upon the ground, wanting[2] food and such nourishable things as might refresh them in this faint state: but we were not supplied with any such things whereby we might relieve them, but only were constrained to look up to God, and to entreat him for mercy toward them: most were thirsty but could find no water; the provision we had for food was very little; many distractions seized upon us at the present, a Chirurgion we wanted, our Chirurgion not accustomed to war, durst not hazard himself where we ventured our lives, but like a fresh-water soldier[3] kept aboard, and by this means our poor maimed soldiers were brought to a great strait and faintness, some of them swounding away[4] for want of speedy help, but yet God was pleased to preserve the lives of them, though not without great misery, and pain to themselves for the present. Distractions multiplying, strength and courage began to fail with many. Our *Indians* that had stood close to us hitherto, were fallen into consultation, and were resolved for to leave us in a land we knew not which way to get out: suddenly after their resolution, fifty of the *Narraganset Indians* fell off from the rest returning home. The *Pequots* spying them pursued after them; then came the *Narragansets* to Captain *Mason*, and myself, crying, "oh help us now, or our men will be all slain." We answered, "how dare you crave aid of us, when you are leaving of us in this distressed condition, not knowing which way to march out of the Country? But yet you shall see it is not the nature of *Englishmen* to deal like Heathens, to requite evil for evil, but we will succour you." Myself falling on with thirty men, in the space of an hour rescued their men, and in our recreat to the body,[5] slew and wounded above a hundred *Pequots*, all fighting men that charged us both in rear and flanks. Having overtaken the body, we were resolved to march to a certain neck of land that lay by the seaside,

8. I.e., although they were outnumbered.
9. I.e., to engage with the Pequots. "Outreach": carry farther than.
1. At random. The Mohegans (*Mohigeners*), a Connecticut tribe closely related to the Pequots, sided with the English against the Pequots in this war.
2. Lacking.
3. An inexperienced, therefore squeamish person.
4. Swooning or fainting. "Chirurgion": surgeon. "Durst": dared.
5. The main part of the English army.

where we intended to quarter[6] that night, because we knew not how to get our maimed men to *Pequot* River. As yet we saw not our Pinnaces sail along, but feared the Lord had crossed them, which also the master of the Bark[7] much feared. We gave them order to set sail on the *Narraganset Bay*, about midnight, as we were to fall upon the Fort in the morning, so that they might meet us in *Pequot* River in the afternoon; but the wind being cross bred in them a great perplexity what would become of us, knowing that we were but slenderly provided, both with munition and provision: but they being in a distracted condition lifted up their hearts to God for help: about twelve of the clock the wind turned about and became fair, it brought them along in sight of us, and about ten o'clock in the morning carried them into *Pequot* River, coming to an anchor at the place appointed, the wind turned as full against them as ever it could blow. How remarkable this providence of God was I leave to a Christian eye to judge; Our *Indians* came to us, and much rejoiced at our victories, and greatly admired the manner of *English* men's fight: but cried *mach it, mach it;*[8] that is, it is naught, it is naught, because it is too furious, and slays too many men. Having received their desires, they freely promised, and gave up themselves to march along with us, wherever we would go. God having eased us from that oppression that lay upon us, thinking we should have been left in great misery for want of our vessels, we diverted our thoughts from going to that neck of land; and faced about, marching to the river where our vessels lay at anchor. One remarkable passage.[9] The *Pequots* playing upon our flanks, one Sergeant *Davis*, a pretty courageous soldier, spying something black upon the top of a rock, stepped forth from the body with a Carbine of three foot long, and at a venture[1] gave fire, supposing it to be an *Indian's* head, turning him over with his heels upward; the *Indians* observed this, and greatly admired that a man should shoot so directly. The *Pequots* were much daunted at the shot, and forbore approaching so near upon us. Being come to the *Pequot* river we met with Captain *Patrick*, who under his command had forty able soldiers, who were ready to begin a second attempt: but many of our men being maimed and much wearied, we forbore that night and embarked ourselves, myself setting sail for *Saybrook* Fort. Captain *Mason*, and Captain *Patrick* marching overland, burned and spoiled the Country between the *Pequot* and Connecticut River, where we received them. The *Pequots* having received so terrible a blow, and being much affrighted with the destruction of so many, the next day fell into consultation, assembling their most ablest men together [and] propounded these three things, first whether they would set upon a sudden revenge upon the *Narragansets*, or attempt an enterprise upon the *English*, or fly; they were in great dispute one amongst another, *Sasachus*[2] their chief commander was all for blood, the rest for flight, alleging these arguments: we are a people bereaved of courage, our hearts are sadded with the death of so many of our dear friends; we see upon what advantage the *English* lie, what sudden and deadly blows they strike [and] what advantage they have of their pieces to us who are not able to reach them with our arrows at distance. They are supplied with everything neces-

---

6. Camp.
7. Small ship. "Pinnaces": small sailing vessels. "Crossed": doomed.
8. Also spelled *machit* (Algonquian), defined by Roger Williams in *A Key into the Language of*
America (1643) as "evil."
9. Event.
1. At random.
2. Sassacus (c. 1560–1637) had become the chief of the Pequots in 1632.

sary, they are flote[3] and heartened in their victory; to what end shall we stand it out with them? We are not able, therefore let us rather save some than lose all. This prevailed. Suddenly after they spoiled all those goods they could not carry with them, broke up their tents and Wigwams, and betook themselves to flight. *Sasachus* flying toward Connecticut plantation, quartered by the river side, there he met with a Shallop[4] sent down to *Saybrook* Fort, which had in it three men, they let fly upon them, shot many arrows into them. Courageous were the *English*, and died in their hands, but with a great deal of valor. The forces which were prepared in the *Bay*[5] were ready for to set forth: myself being taken on but for three months, and the soldiers willing to return to the *Bay*, we embarked ourselves, and set to sail; in our journey we met with certain Pinnaces, in them a hundred able and well-appointed soldiers under the conduct of one Captain *Stoughton*, and other inferior officers; and in company with them one Mr. *John Wilson*, who was sent to instruct the Company; these falling into *Pequot* River, met with many of the distressed *Indians*, some they slew, others they took prisoners.

3. I.e., floated or buoyed up. "Pieces": guns.
4. A heavy boat propelled by either oars or a sail.

5. Massachusetts Bay.

JOHN SMITH
1580–1631

Under the patent granted to Sir Walter Ralegh by Queen Elizabeth I in 1584, the English undertook their first serious effort at colonization in Virginia. By 1590 this attempt, in the vicinity of Roanoke, had ended in disaster. When the English renewed their involvement in America in the 1600s, they replaced the older heroic model of exploration and colonization with a more corporate one. Under this new model, the single controlling figure of Ralegh's era was replaced by larger companies of investors (often merchants), which had more capital to support costly expansion overseas. In fact, King James I split the vaguely defined region of Virginia, which ran from Florida to Canada, into two more manageable parts, giving the direction of each to separate but related groups of investors who together composed the Virginia Company. The southern part (including the area now known as the state of Virginia) came under the care of the company's members from London, while the northern part (from which New England was to be developed) fell to members in the West Country towns of Bristol, Plymouth, and Exeter. Although the so-called First Charter was succeeded by new ones in 1609 and 1612, its broad base of formalized support set the pattern for English colonial practice over the next hundred years. As a compromise between large-scale governmental action and isolated individual effort, the format of the colonial "company" proved both useful and enduring.

The push toward corporate structures did not mean that interesting individuals disappeared. Indeed, one of the most colorful of all the Englishmen ever involved in America, the legendary Captain John Smith, proved by his crucial role in the establishment and continuance of the new colony at Jamestown that success in such ventures still required individual initiative and commitment. Few people had more pertinent preparation to reteach the English this old lesson. When named by the London partners to the ruling council (that is, the local governing committee) for the Virginia colony sent out in late December 1606, John Smith brought rich experience to his charge. His early life was deceptively mundane: born into a farmer's family in Lincolnshire, he was apprenticed at fifteen to a shopkeeper near his home. But tales of exploration, piracy, and military adventure had already stirred his imagination. In 1593 he may have tried to join a punitive expedition Sir Francis Drake was thought to be readying against England's enemy Spain, although his father apparently intervened. Shortly after his father's death in 1596, the fiery sixteen-year-old managed to have his indenture to the shopkeeper canceled and went to the Netherlands as a soldier to fight for the Dutch in their long war of independence from Philip II.

Following his tour of duty in the Netherlands, he saw action in the Mediterranean aboard a privateer, winning a good share of the prize money when a Venetian galley was captured. Smith next joined the Austrian army in its continuing war (1593–1606) against the Turks, and while in the Austrian service, he fought valiantly in Hungary and was promoted to a captaincy. Eventually, after defeating and beheading a succession of three Turkish officers in single combat in Rumania (his coat of arms, awarded later, showed the three severed heads), Smith was wounded in battle, taken prisoner, and sold into slavery to a Turk. Smith was passed from place to place until, held prisoner on the Black Sea, he murdered his master and fled back to Rumania via Russia and Poland, returning to England in the winter of 1604–05.

Many of these details come to us only through Smith's own at times garbled narratives, most of them penned long after the events. But when the Jamestown backers encountered him as they readied their expedition, he must have had the air of someone deeply experienced in the skills that the quasi-military venture would require. Smith's military background (and temperament), however, also carried liabilities in that age when warfare was brutal and soldiers were far from professional: he sometimes used force unnecessarily, and his hard-to-control temper and stubborn self-reliance made him an often troublesome companion. Already on the voyage over, Smith ran afoul of those in charge, was placed under arrest while the fleet was near the Canary Islands in February 1607, and was threatened with execution in the West Indies the following month. By June 10, some weeks after the arrival in Virginia and the opening of the heretofore secret list of the council members (not revealed sooner so as to prevent difficulties on shipboard), Smith had been given a reprieve and was sworn in to his seat on the council. From then until his final departure for England in October 1609, he was in the middle of the tumultuous colony's affairs. Smith survived the grim period of sickness in 1607 and missed the bleaker "starving time" that came shortly after his departure, but during his years there, he was always at the epicenter of the various political earthquakes that rocked early Virginia.

Placed in charge of its supplies in the fall of 1607, he was elected president of the council—in effect, the colony's governor—the following year, after a series of wide-ranging explorations that made him the most knowledgeable of the settlers regarding the new land. The explorations also led to his imprisonment at the hands of Powhatan, overlord of the Chesapeake Bay Indians, from whom he claimed (much later) that the king's young daughter Pocahontas had rescued him. Whatever role Pocahontas played, what Smith took to be his impending execution may have been nothing more than a harmless adoption ceremony inducting him into Powhatan's tribe. In this episode as in others, Smith's volatile and unpredictable relations with the Native Americans were characteristic. Also characteristic was the fact that as a writer Smith milked the story of his rescue by Pocahontas. Although he failed to have the lasting influence on Virginia's affairs that he sought, in recasting that story fifteen years after the fact he finally found the immortality that had thus far eluded him. How easily we forget that on his return to Jamestown from Powhatan's village he was charged with the loss of two soldiers and would have been hanged had a fleet with much-needed supplies not arrived from England. Or that when he left Virginia in 1609 (never to return), it was because he had been severely injured when his gunpowder bag mysteriously exploded in his lap while he napped on the deck of an exploring vessel.

Smith and his works form an important bridge between Virginia and New England, the first two permanent English colonies in North America. The first of his publications, *A True Relation of Such Occurrences and Accidents of Note as Hath Happened in Virginia* (1608), was a badly edited version of a letter he had sent back from the colony without intending that it be published. It was followed by a work to which many colonists, including Smith, contributed, *A Map of Virginia, with a Description of the Country . . . [and] The Proceedings of those Colonies* (sic) (1612). Some years later, Smith enlarged this book by adding more texts by other hands, expanding his own prose, and extending its geographical range and chronological coverage. More its editor than its author, Smith published the resulting *General History of Virginia, New England, and the Summer Isles* (that is, Bermuda) in 1624. This book demonstrated the later reach of Smith's American ambitions beyond Virginia proper, for his knowledge of New England was based on a voyage he made there in 1614 and on his continuing involvement with the region—which in fact he, not the Puritans, named. During his life, Smith published more works on New England than on Virginia (*A Description of New England*, 1616; *New England's Trials*, 1620 and 1622; and *Advertisements for the Inexperienced Planters of New England, or Anywhere*, 1631). But for some unfortunate setbacks (bad weather several times forced him to abandon other voyages for New England), he might well have become more famous for this second aspect of his American career than for the first. An energetic promoter of the potential of this new region for English settlers, Smith offered the Pilgrims his services as guide for their voyage in 1620, but they chose instead to put Smith's helpful books in the hands of the more temperate Myles Standish. From that point on Smith's America was not the geographical region about which he had entertained such bright hopes at the century's start but rather the verbal realm he continued to explore in his later writings. When he closed the Virginia part of his *General History* by writing "Thus far have I travelled in this Wilderness of Virginia," he was revealing how much Virginia had become a country of his mind. Long gone from that still-struggling colony by then, he had internalized it so well that he helped to make it a permanent part of the English—and the Anglo-American—imagination.

The texts are from *Travels and Works of Captain John Smith*, edited by Edward Arber and A. G. Bradley (1910).

From The General History of Virginia, New England, and the Summer Isles[1]

From *The Third Book*

FROM CHAPTER 2. WHAT HAPPENED TILL THE FIRST SUPPLY

Being thus left to our fortunes, it fortuned that within ten days[2] scarce ten amongst us could either go, or well stand, such extreme weakness and sickness oppressed us. And threat none need marvel, if they consider the cause and reason, which was this:

---

1. The Bermuda Islands. The Third Book is titled "The Proceedings and Accidents of the English Colony in Virginia" and is derived from Smith's Virginia book of 1612. The bulk of this chapter, which opens with an account of dire sickness, may have been written by John Smith himself, although at its publication in 1612 it was credited solely to Thomas Studley, chief storekeeper of the colony. In 1624, Smith added to Studley's signature at the end of this section of the text not only his own initials but also the names of Robert Fenton and Edward Harrington as part authors. Studley died early in the first year, on August 28, 1607, four days after Harrington, so neither could have written much of what is in part attributed to them. Of Robert Fenton nothing is known.

2. By the end of June 1607, after Captain Christopher Newport (d. 1617) left to fetch new supplies from England. "Fortuned": happened.

Whilst the ships stayed, our allowance was somewhat bettered, by a daily proportion of biscuit, which the sailors would pilfer to sell, give, or exchange with us, for money, Sassafras,[3] furs, or love. But when they departed, there remained neither tavern, beer house, nor place of relief, but the common kettle.[4] Had we been as free from all sins as [from] gluttony, and drunkenness, we might have been canonized for Saints; but our President would never have been admitted, for engrossing to his private, oatmeal, sack, oil, aqua vitae, beef, eggs, or what not, but the kettle;[5] that indeed he allowed equally to be distributed, and that was half a pint of wheat, and as much barley boiled with water for a man a day, and this having fried some twenty-six weeks in the ship's hold, contained as many worms as grains, so that we might truly call it rather so much bran then corn; our drink[6] was water, our lodgings castles in the air.

With this lodging and diet, our extreme toil in bearing and planting palisades, so strained and bruised us, and our continual labor in the extremity of the heat had so weakened us, as were cause sufficient to have made us as miserable in our native country, or any other place in the world.

From May, to September [1607], those that escaped, lived upon sturgeon, and sea crabs. Fifty in this time we buried, the rest seeing the President's[7] projects to escape these miseries in our pinnace by flight (who all this time had neither felt want nor sickness) so moved our dead spirits, as we deposed him and established Ratcliffe in his place, (Gosnold being dead, Kendall deposed). Smith newly recovered, Martin[8] and Ratcliffe were by his care preserved and relieved, and the most of the soldiers recovered with the skillful diligence of Master Thomas Wotton our general surgeon.

But now was all our provision spent, the sturgeon gone, all helps abandoned, each hour expecting the fury of the savages, when God the patron of all good endeavors, in that desperate extremity so changed the hearts of the savages, that they brought such plenty of their fruits, and provision, as no man wanted.[9]

And now where some affirmed it was ill done of the Council to send forth men so badly provided, this incontradictable reason will show them plainly they are too ill advised to nourish such ill conceits: first, the fault of our going was our own; what could be thought fitting or necessary we had; but what we should find, or want, or where we should be, we were all ignorant, and supposing to make our passage in two months, with victual to live, and the advantage of the spring to work; we were at sea five months, where we both spent our victual and lost the opportunity of the time and season to plant, by the unskilfull presumption of our ignorant transporters, that understood not at all, what they undertook.

3. The bark of the sassafras tree, sold for its supposed medicinal qualities, was a valuable commodity in London.
4. I.e., the communal resources.
5. I.e., President Edward Maria Wingfield (c. 1560–1613), a man of high connections in England, would not have been canonized because he diverted many supplies (everything except the contents of the common kettle) for his own use, including sack (wine) and aqua vitae (brandy).
6. "Drink," here used ironically, customarily referred to wine or beer. "Corn": grain.
7. I.e., Wingfield.
8. Captain John Martin (c. 1567–1632?) was a colonist best known for his contentiousness. "Captain John Ratcliffe" was an alias of John Sickle-more, master of one of the vessels on the voyage over and a member of the local council. The most enigmatic figure in Jamestown, he was elected president of the council in September 1607, but later fell out with Smith. Captain Bartholomew Gosnold (ca. 1572–1607), who had explored New England before the first Jamestown voyage, probably had been responsible for Smith's recruitment to the venture. Captain George Kendall was executed for mutiny later in the year.
9. I.e., was in want.

Such actions have ever since the world's beginning been subject to such accidents, and everything of worth is found full of difficulties: but nothing so difficult as to establish a commonwealth so far remote from men and means, and where men's minds are so untoward[1] as neither do well themselves, nor suffer others. But to proceed.

The new President and Martin, being little beloved, of weak judgment in dangers, and less industry in peace, committed the managing of all things abroad[2] to Captain Smith: who by his own example, good words, and fair promises, set some to mow, others to bind thatch, some to build houses, others to thatch them, himself always bearing the greatest task for his own share, so that in short time, he provided most of them lodgings, neglecting any for himself.

This done, seeing the savages' superfluity begin to decrease [Smith] (with some of his workmen) shipped himself in the shallop[3] to search the country for trade. The want[4] of the language, knowledge to manage his boat without sails, the want of a sufficient power (knowing the multitude of the savages), apparel for his men, and other necessaries, were infinite impediments yet no discouragement.

Being but six or seven in company he went down the river to Kecoughtan[5] where at first they scorned him as a famished man, and would in derision offer him a handful of corn, a piece of bread, for their swords and muskets, and such like proportions also for their apparel. But seeing by trade and courtesy there was nothing to be had, he made bold to try such conclusions as necessity enforced; though contrary to his commission, [he] let fly[6] his muskets, ran his boat on shore, whereat they all fled into the woods.

So marching towards their houses, they might see great heaps of corn: much ado he had to restrain his hungry soldiers from present taking of it, expecting as it happened that the savages would assault them, as not long after they did with a most hideous noise. Sixty or seventy of them, some black, some red, some white, some particoloured, came in a square order, singing and dancing out of the woods, with their Okee (which was an Idol made of skins, stuffed with moss, all painted and hung with chains and copper) borne before them, and in this manner, being well armed with clubs, targets, bows and arrow, they charged the English that so kindly received them with their muskets loaded with pistol shot, that down fell their God, and divers lay sprawling on the ground; the rest fled again to the woods, and ere long sent one of their Quiyoughkasoucks[7] to offer peace, and redeem their Okee.

Smith told them, if only six of them would come unarmed and load his boat, he would not only be their friend, but restore them their Okee, and give them beads, copper, and hatchets besides, which on both sides was to their contents[8] performed, and then they brought him venison, turkeys, wild fowl, bread, and what they had, singing and dancing in sign of friendship till they departed.

In his return he discovered the town and country of Warraskoyack.[9]

1. Intractable.
2. I.e., outside the palisade.
3. An open boat.
4. Inability to speak.
5. A village near the mouth of the James River whose inhabitants, the Kecoughtans, were members of the Powhatan Confederacy.
6. Fired.
7. Smith elsewhere defines this term as referring to the "petty gods" of the Algonquian-speaking peoples, but here it may be used to mean priests. "Particolored": i.e. painted for battle. "Square order": formation. "Targets": small shields. "So kindly" in such a way. "Divers." several.
8. I.e., in mutual contentment.
9. A village on the south side of the James River near the mouth of the modern Pagan River, approximately opposite Smithfield.

Thus God unboundless by His power,
Made them thus kind, would us devour.

Smith perceiving (notwithstanding their late misery) not any regarded but from hand to mouth[1] (the company being well recovered) caused the pinnace to be provided with things fitting to get provision for the year following, but in the interim he made three or four journeys and discovered the people of Chickahominy.[2] Yet what he carefully provided the rest carelessly spent.

Wingfield and Kendall living in disgrace * * * strengthened themselves with the sailors and other confederates, to regain their former credit and authority, or at least such means aboard the pinnace, (being fitted to sail as Smith had appointed for trade) to alter her course and to go for England.

Smith, unexpectedly returning, had the plot discovered to him, much trouble he had to prevent it, till with store of saker[3] and musket shot he forced them stay or sink in the river: which action cost the life of Captain Kendall.

These brawls are so disgustful, as some will say they were better forgotten, yet all men of good judgment will conclude, it were better their baseness should be manifest to the world, than the business bear the scorn and shame of their excused disorders.[4]

The President and Captain Archer[5] not long after intended also to have abandoned the country, which project also was curbed, and suppressed by Smith.

The Spaniard never more greedily desired gold then he victual, nor his soldiers more to abandon the country, than he to keep it. But [he found] plenty of corn in the river of Chickahominy, where hundreds of savages in divers places stood with baskets expecting his coming.

And now the winter approaching, the rivers became so covered with swans, geese, ducks, and cranes that we daily feasted with good bread, Virginia peas, pumpkins, and putchamins, fish, fowl, and divers sorts of wild beasts as fat as we could eat them, so that none of our Tuftaffety humorists[6] desired to go for England.

But our comedies never endured long without a tragedy, some idle exceptions[7] being muttered against Captain Smith, for not discovering the head of Chickahominy river, and [he being] taxed by the council to be too slow in so worthy an attempt. The next voyage he proceeded so far that with much labor by cutting of trees asunder he made his passage, but when his barge could pass no farther, he left her in a broad bay out of danger of shot, commanding none should go ashore till his return; himself with two English and two savages went up higher in a canoe, but he was not long absent but his men went ashore, whose want of government gave both occasion and oppor-

---

1. I.e., none of the settlers, despite their recent sufferings, gave any thought to gathering a store of provision for the future.
2. The region along the Chickahominy River, which empties into the James River a short distance west of Jamestown.
3. Shot for a small cannon used in sieges and on shipboard. "Discovered": revealed.
4. I.e., it is necessary to recount these troubles and lay the blame on the responsible individuals (Wingfield and Kendall), rather than let the whole "business" of the colony suffer ill repute.

5. Gabriel Archer (c. 1575–1609?) had been an associate of Bartholomew Gosnold before the Jamestown voyage. Having gone back to England in 1608 as a confirmed opponent of Smith, he showed up in Virginia again the following year to head an anti-Smith faction but died during the starving time the next winter. Ratcliffe (Sicklemore) was still president.
6. Self-indulgent persons who might be given to wearing lace. "Putchamins": persimmons.
7. Objections.

tunity to the savages to surprise one George Cassen, whom they slew and much failed not to have cut off the boat and all the rest.[8]

Smith little dreaming of that accident, being got to the marshes at the river's head twenty miles in the desert, had his two men slain (as is supposed) sleeping by the canoe, whilst himself by fowling sought them victual, who finding he was beset with 200 savages, two of them he slew, still defending himself with the aid of a savage his guide, whom he bound to his arm with his garters, and used him as a buckler,[9] yet he was shot in his thigh a little, and had many arrows that stuck in his clothes but no great hurt, till at last they took him prisoner.

When this news came to Jamestown, much was their sorrow for his loss, few expecting what ensued.

Six or seven weeks those barbarians kept him prisoner, many strange triumphs and conjurations they made of him, yet he so demeaned[1] himself amongst them, as he not only diverted them from surprising the fort, but procured his own liberty, and got himself and his company such estimation amongst them, that those savages admired him more than their owne Quiyoughkasoucks.

The manner how they used and delivered him, is as followeth:

The savages having drawn from George Cassen whither Captain Smith was gone, prosecuting that opportunity they followed him with 300 bowmen, conducted by the King of Pamunkey, who in divisions searching the turnings of the river, found Robinson and Emry[2] by the fireside; those they shot full of arrows and slew. Then finding the Captain, as is said, that used the savage that was his guide as his shield (three of them being slain and divers other so galled[3]) all the rest would not come near him. Thinking thus to have returned to his boat, regarding them, as he marched, more than his way, [he] slipped up to the middle in an oozy creek and his savage with him, yet dared they not come to him till being near dead with cold, he threw away his arms. Then according to their composition[4] they drew him forth and led him to the fire, where his men were slain. Diligently they chafed his benumbed limbs.

He demanding for their captain, they showed him Opechancanough,[5] King of Pamunkey, to whom he gave a round ivory double compass dial. Much they marveled at the playing of the fly[6] and needle, which they could see so plainly and yet not touch it because of the glass that covered them. But when he demonstrated by that globe-like jewell, the roundness of the earth, and skies, the sphere of the sun, moon, and stars, and how the sun did chase the night round about the world continually, the greatness of the land and sea, the diversity of nations, variety of complexions, and how we were to them antipodes,[7] and many other such like matters, they all stood as amazed with admiration.

---

8. I.e., only through fault of their own did they fall to wipe out Cassen's whole party. "Government": discipline.
9. Shield. "Desert": wilderness. "Garters": laces used for tying clothing.
1. Behaved.
2. The two men mentioned above as having been killed while they slept. Thomas Emry was a carpenter. John Robinson was a "gentleman."

3. Wounded.
4. Agreement for surrender.
5. Powhatan's younger half-brother (d. 1644) and Smith's captor, who led the Indian Confederacy's attack on the colonists in 1622 and as late as 1644 attempted one last time to expel them from the country.
6. Compass card.
7. On the opposite side of the globe.

Notwithstanding, within an hour after, they tied him to a tree, and as many as could stand about him prepared to shoot him, but the King holding up the compass in his hand, they all laid down their bows and arrows, and in a triumphant manner led him to Orapaks,[8] where he was after their manner kindly feasted, and well used.

Their order in conducting him was thus: Drawing themselves all in file, the King in the midst had all their pieces and swords borne before him. Captain Smith was led after him by three great savages holding him fast by each arm, and on each side six went in file with their arrows nocked.[9] But arriving at the town (which was but only thirty or forty hunting houses made of mats, which they remove as they please, as we our tents), all the women and children staring to behold him, the soldiers first all in file performed the form of a Bissom[1] so well as could be, and on each flank, officers as sergeants to see them keep their orders. A good time they continued this exercise and then cast themselves in a ring, dancing in such several postures and singing and yelling out such hellish notes and screeches; being strangely painted, every one [had] his quiver of arrows and at his back a club, on his arm a fox or an otter's skin or some such matter for his vambrace, their heads and shoulders painted red, with oil and pocones mingled together, which scarlet-like color made an exceeding handsome show, his bow in his hand, and the skin of a bird with her wings abroad[2] dryed, tied on his head, a piece of copper, a white shell, a long feather with a small rattle growing at the tails of their snakes tied to it, or some such like toy. All this while, Smith and the King stood in the midst, guarded as before is said, and after three dances they all departed. Smith they conducted to a long house where thirty or forty tall fellows did guard him, and ere long more bread and venison was brought him than would have served twenty men. I think his stomach at that time was not very good; what he left they put in baskets and tied over his head. About midnight they set the meat again before him; all this time not one of them would eat a bit with him, till the next morning they brought him as much more, and then did they eat all the old, and reserved the new as they had done the other, which made him think they would fat him to eat him. Yet in this desperate estate, to defend him from the cold, one Maocassater brought him his gown, in requital[3] of some beads and toys Smith had given him at his first arrival in Virginia.

Two days after, a man would have slain him (but that the guard prevented it) for the death of his son, to whom they conducted him to recover the poor man then breathing his last. Smith told them that at Jamestown he had a water would do it, if they would let him fetch it, but they would not permit that, but made all the preparations they could to assault Jamestown, craving his advice, and for recompence he should have life, liberty, land, and women. In part of a table book[4] he wrote his mind to them at the fort, what was intended, how they should follow that direction to affright the messengers, and without fail send him such things as he wrote for. And an inventory with them. The difficulty and danger, he told the savages, of the mines, great

---

8. A village located farther inland, later the residence of Powhatan.

9. Notched; i.e., with their arrows fitted on the bowstring ready for use.

1. From an Italian term denoting a snakelike formation.

2. Outspread. "Vambrace": forearm protection. "Pocones": a dye of vegetative origin.

3. Payment.

4. A notebook.

guns, and other engines[5] exceedingly affrighted them, yet according to his request they went to Jamestown in as bitter weather as could be of frost and snow, and within three days returned with an answer.

But when they came to Jamestown, seeing men sally out as he had told them they would, they fled, yet in the night they came again to the same place where he had told them they should receive an answer and such things as he had promised them, which they found accordingly, and with which they returned with no small expedition to the wonder of them all that heard it, that he could either divine[6] or the paper could speak.

Then they led him to the Youghtanunds, the Mattapanients, the Piankatanks, the Nantaughtacunds, and Onawmanients upon the rivers of Rappahannock and Potomac, over all those rivers, and back again by divers other several nations,[7] to the King's habitation at Pamunkey where they entertained him with most strange and fearful conjurations:[8]

> As if near led to hell,
> Amongst the devils to dwell.

Not long after, early in a morning, a great fire was made in a long house, and a mat spread on the one side as on the other; on the one they caused him to sit, and all the guard went out of the house, and presently came skipping in a great grim fellow all painted over with coal[9] mingled with oil, and many snakes' and weasels' skins stuffed with moss, and all their tails tied together so as they met on the crown of his head in a tassel, and round about the tassel was as a coronet of feathers, the skins hanging round about his head, back, and shoulders and in a manner covered his face, with a hellish voice, and a rattle in his hand. With most strange gestures and passions he began his invocation and environed[1] the fire with a circle of meal; which done, three more such like devils came rushing in with the like antic tricks, painted half black, half red, but all their eyes were painted white and some red strokes like mustaches along their cheeks. Round about him those fiends danced a pretty while, and then came in three more as ugly as the rest, with red eyes and white strokes over their black faces. At last they all sat down right against him, three of them on the one hand of the chief priest, and three on the other. Then all with their rattles began a song; which ended, the chief priest laid down five wheat corns; then straining his arms and hands with such violence that he sweat and his veins swelled, he began a short oration;[2] at the conclusion they all gave a short groan and then laid down three grains more. After that, began their song again, and then another oration, ever laying down so many corns as before till they had twice encircled the fire; that done, they took a bunch of little sticks prepared for that purpose, continuing still their devotion, and at the end of every song and oration they laid down a stick betwixt the divisions of corn. Till night, neither he nor they did either eat or drink, and then they feasted merrily with the best provisions they could make. Three days they used this ceremony; the

5. Weaponry.
6. Perform magic. "Expedition": speed.
7. Other Algonquian-speaking groups. The named groups were part of the confederacy that was under the rule of Powhatan.
8. Incantations. However, Smith derived the following couplet from a translation of Seneca pub-

lished by Martin Fotherby in his *Atheomastix* (1622).
9. I.e., charcoal.
1. Encircled.
2. Prayer. "Wheat corns": i.e., five kernels of Indian corn.

meaning whereof, they told him, was to know if he intended them well or no. The circle of meal signified their country, the circles of corn the bounds of the sea, and the sticks his country. They imagined the world to be flat and round, like a trencher,[3] and they in the midst.

After this they brought him a bag of gunpowder, which they carefully preserved till the next spring, to plant as they did their corn, because they would be acquainted with the nature of that seed.

Opitchapam, the King's brother,[4] invited him to his house, where, with as many platters of bread, fowl, and wild beasts as did environ him, he bid him welcome, but not any of them would eat a bit with him but put up all the remainder in baskets.

At his return to Opechancanough's, all the King's women and their children, flocked about him for their parts,[5] as a due by custom, to be merry with such fragments:

> But his waking mind in hideous dreams did oft see wondrous shapes,
> Of bodies strange, and huge in growth, and of stupendous makes.[6]

At last they brought him to Werowocomoco,[7] where was Powhatan, their Emperor. Here more than two hundred of those grim courtiers stood wondering at him, as [if] he had been a monster, till Powhatan and his train had put themselves in their greatest braveries.[8] Before a fire upon a seat like a bedstead, he sat covered with a great robe made of raccoon skins and all the tails hanging by. On either hand did sit a young wench of sixteen or eighteen years and along on each side [of] the house, two rows of men and behind them as many women, with all their heads and shoulders painted red, many of their heads bedecked with the white down of birds, but every one with something, and a great chain of white beads about their necks.

At his entrance before the King, all the people gave a great shout. The Queen of Appomattoc[9] was appointed to bring him water to wash his hands, and another brought him a bunch of feathers, instead of a towel to dry them; having feasted him after their best barbarous manner they could, a long consultation was held, but the conclusion was, two great stones were brought before Powhatan; then as many as could, laid hands on him, dragged him to them, and thereon laid his head and being ready with their clubs to beat out his brains, Pocahontas,[1] the King's dearest daughter, when no entreaty could prevail, got his head in her arms and laid her own upon his to save him from death, whereat the Emperor was contented he should live to make him hatchets, and her bells, beads, and copper, for they thought him as well of all occupations as themselves.[2] For the King himself will make his own robes, shoes, bows, arrows, pots; plant, hunt, or do any thing so well as the rest.

---

3. A flat wood dish.
4. Actually the chief's half-brother; he succeeded Powhatan in 1618.
5. Gifts.
6. From a translation of Lucretius by Fotherby.
7. Powhatan's village on the north shore of the York River, almost due north of Jamestown.
8. Finery; i.e., costumes.
9. Opossunoquonuske was the weroansqua, or leader, of a small village (Appamatuck) near the

future site of Petersburg, Virginia. In 1610, she was killed by the English in retaliation for the deaths of fourteen settlers.
1. Daughter of Powhatan (c. 1591–1617), she was mentioned in Smith's earlier versions of his captivity narrative, but first emerged as its heroine only in the *History*, which was published seven years after her death in England.
2. I.e., they thought him as variously skilled as themselves.

"Map of the old Virginia," by Robert Vaughan, from John Smith, *The Generall History of Virginia, the Somer Isles, and New Englánd*, 1624. This map of Old Virginia, the part of coastal North Carolina where the first English explorations and settlements took place in the 1580s, is surrounded by images portraying John Smith's warlike encounters around Jamestown some twenty years later. The panel in the lower right corner shows the supposed intervention of Pocahontas in the planned execution of Smith.

> They say he bore a pleasant show,
> But sure his heart was sad.
> For who can pleasant be, and rest,
> That lives in fear and dread:
> And having life suspected, doth
> It still suspected lead.[3]

Two days after, Powhatan having disguised himself in the most fearfulest manner he could, caused Captain Smith to be brought forth to a great house in the woods and there upon a mat by the fire to be left alone. Not long after, from behind a mat that divided the house, was made the most dolefulest noise he ever heard; then Powhatan more like a devil than a man, with some two hundred more as black as himself, came unto him and told him now they were friends, and presently he should go to Jamestown, to send him two great guns and a grindstone for which he would give him the Country of Capahowasic and for ever esteem him as his son Nantaquoud.[4]

3. Derived from a translation of Euripides by Fotherby.

4. I.e., Powhatan would esteem him as highly as his own son Nantaquoud. Capahowasic was along the York River near where Smith was held prisoner.

So to Jamestown with twelve guides Powhatan sent him. That night they quartered in the woods, he still expecting (as he had done all this long time of his imprisonment) every hour to be put to one death or other, for all their feasting. But almighty God (by His divine providence) had mollified the hearts of those stern barbarians with compassion. The next morning betimes they came to the fort, where Smith having used the savages with what kindness he could, he showed Rawhunt, Powhatan's trusty servant, two demi-culverins[5] and a millstone to carry [to] Powhatan; they found them somewhat too heavy, but when they did see him discharge them, being loaded with stones, among the boughs of a great tree loaded with icickles, the ice and branches came so tumbling down that the poor savages ran away half dead with fear. But at last we regained some conference with them and gave them such toys and sent to Powhatan, his women, and children such presents as gave them in general full content.

Now in Jamestown they were all in combustion, the strongest preparing once more to run away with the pinnace; which with the hazard of his life, with saker falcon[6] and musket shot, Smith forced now the third time to stay or sink.

Some no better than they should be, had plotted with the President the next day to have put him to death by the Levitical[7] law, for the lives of Robinson and Emry; pretending the fault was his that had led them to their ends: but he quickly took such order with such lawyers that he laid them by the heels till he sent some of them prisoners for England.

Now ever once in four or five days, Pocahontas with her attendants brought him so much provision that saved many of their lives, that else for all this had starved with hunger.

> Thus from numb death our good God sent relief,
> The sweet assuager of all other grief.[8]

His relation of the plenty he had seen, especially at Werowocomoco, and of the state and bounty of Powhatan (which till that time was unknown), so revived their dead spirits (especially the love of Pocahontas)[9] as all men's fear was abandoned.

Thus you may see what difficulties still crossed any good endeavor; and the good success of the business being thus oft brought to the very period of destruction; yet you see by what strange means God hath still delivered it.

* * *

From *The Fourth Book*

[SMITH'S FAREWELL TO VIRGINIA]

Thus far I have traveled in this Wilderness of Virginia, not being ignorant for all my pains this discourse will be wrested, tossed and turned as many

---

5. Large cannons.
6. Small artillery piece.
7. "And he that killeth any man shall surely be put to death" (Leviticus 24.17).
8. Apparently the first line is Smith's own, based on Fotherby, but the second is borrowed directly

from Fotherby's translation from a quotation of Euripides found in Plutarch.
9. I.e., the evident affection of Pocahontas for Smith and the English was instrumental in reviving the colonists' spirits.

ways as there is leaves;[1] that I have written too much of some, too little of others, and many such like objections. To such I must answer, in the Company's name I was requested to do it,[2] if any have concealed their approved experiences from my knowledge, they must excuse me: as for every fatherless or stolen relation,[3] or whole volumes of sophisticated rehearsals, I leave them to the charge of them that desire them. I thank God I never undertook anything yet [for which] any could tax me of carelessness or dishonesty, and what[4] is he to whom I am indebted or troublesome? Ah! were these my accusers but to change cases and places with me [for] but two years, or till they had done but so much as I, it may be they would judge more charitably of my imperfections. But here I must leave all to the trial of time, both myself, Virginia's preparations, proceedings and good events, praying to that great God the protector of all goodness to send them as good success as the goodness of the action[5] and country deserveth, and my heart desireth.

1624

From A Description of New England

Who can desire more content, that hath small means; or but only his merit to advance his fortune, than to tread, and plant that ground he hath purchased by the hazard of his life? If he have but the taste of virtue and magnanimity, what to such a mind can be more pleasant, than planting and building a foundation for his posterity, got from the rude earth, by God's blessing and his own industry, without prejudice[1] to any? If he have any grain of faith or zeal in religion, what can he do less hurtful to any; or more agreeable to God, than to seek to convert those poor savages to know Christ, and humanity, whose labors with discretion will triple requite thy charge and pains? What so truly suits with honor and honesty, as the discovering things unknown? erecting towns, peopling countries, informing the ignorant, reforming things unjust, teaching virtue; and gaining to our native mother country a kingdom to attend her, finding employment for those that are idle, because they know not what to do: so far from wronging any, as to cause posterity to remember thee; and remembering thee, ever honor that remembrance with praise?

* * *

Then, who would live at home idly (or think in himself any worth to live) only to eat, drink, and sleep, and so die? Or by consuming that carelessly, [which] his friends got worthily? Or by using that miserably, that maintained virtue honestly? Or for being descended nobly, pine with the vain vaunt of great kindred, in penury?[2] Or (to maintain a silly show of bravery) toil out thy heart, soul, and time, basely, by shifts,[3] tricks, cards, and dice? Or by

---

1. Pages.
2. Smith was not requested to write the whole *General History* by the Virginia Company, so it is not clear what his reference is here. Possibly the discourse to which he refers is the brief summary of recommendations for the "reformation" of Virginia that ends The Fourth Book and that he drew up at the request of the royal commissioners charged with effecting that reformation.

3. I.e., anonymous or "fugitive" narratives. "Approved": proven.
4. Who; i.e., he has been a burden to nobody.
5. Venture. "Events": results.
1. Harm. "Magnanimity": greatness of spirit.
2. I.e., live in poverty while claiming great ancestors.
3. Expedients. "Bravery": fine appearances.

relating news of others' actions, shark[4] here or there for a dinner, or supper; deceive thy friends, by fair promises, and dissimulation, in borrowing where thou never intendest to pay; offend the laws, surfeit with excess, burden thy country, abuse thyself, despair in want, and then cozen[5] thy kindred, yea even thine own brother, and wish thy parents' death (I will not say damnation) to have their estates? though thou seest what honors, and rewards, the world yet hath for them will seek them and worthily deserve them.

* * *

Let this move you to embrace employment, for those whose educations, spirits, and judgments want but your purses; not only to prevent such accustomed dangers, but also to gain more thereby than you have. And you fathers that are either so foolishly fond, or so miserably covetous, or so wilfully ignorant, or so negligently careless, as that you will rather maintain your children in idle wantonness, till they grow your masters; or become so basely unkind, as they wish nothing but your deaths; so that both sorts grow dissolute: and although you would wish them anywhere to escape the gallows, and ease your cares; though they spend you here one, two, or three hundred pound a year; you would grudge to give half so much in adventure with them, to obtain an estate, which in a small time but with a little assistance of your providence,[6] might be better than your own. But if an angel should tell you, that any place yet unknown can afford such fortunes; you would not believe him, no more than Columbus was believed there was any such land as is now the well-known abounding America; much less such large regions as are yet unknown, as well in America, as in Africa, and Asia, and Terra Incognita; where were courses for gentlemen (and them that would be so reputed) more suiting their qualities, than begging from their Prince's generous disposition, the labors of his subjects, and the very marrow of his maintenance.

I have not been so ill bred, but I have tasted of plenty and pleasure, as well as want and misery: nor doth necessity yet, or occasion of discontent, force me to these endeavors: nor am I ignorant what small thank I shall have for my pains; or that many would have the World imagine them to be of great judgment, that can but blemish these my designs, by their witty objections and detractions: yet (I hope) my reasons with my deeds, will so prevail with some, that I shall not want[7] employment in these affairs, to make the most blind see his own senselessness, and incredulity; hoping that gain will make them affect that, which religion, charity, and the common good cannot. It were but a poor device in me, to deceive myself; much more the king, state, my friends and country, with these inducements: which, seeing his Majesty hath given permission, I wish all sorts of worthy, honest, industrious spirits, would understand: and if they desire any further satisfaction, I will do my best to give it: Not to persuade them to go only;[8] but go with them: Not leave them there; but live with them there.

I will not say, but by ill providing and undue managing, such courses may be taken, [that] may make us miserable enough:[9] But if I may have the

---

4. Sponge.
5. Deceive. "Excess": overindulgence.
6. Provision.
7. Lack.

8. Alone.
9. I.e., he won't promise that even with bad management they'll succeed.

execution of what I have projected; if they want to eat, let them eat or never digest me.[1] If I perform what I say, I desire but that reward out of the gains [which] may suit my pains, quality, and condition. And if I abuse you with my tongue, take my head for satisfaction. If any dislike at the year's end, defraying their charge,[2] by my consent they should freely return. I fear not want of company sufficient, were it but known what I know of those countries; and by the proof of that wealth I hope yearly to return, if God please to bless me from such accidents, as are beyond my power in reason to prevent: For, I am not so simple to think, that ever any other motive than wealth, will ever erect there a commonwealth; or draw company from their ease and humors at home, to stay in New England to effect my purposes.

And lest any should think the toil might be insupportable, though these things may be had by labor, and diligence: I assure myself there are who delight extremely in vain pleasure, that take much more pains in England, to enjoy it, than I should do here to gain wealth sufficient: and yet I think they should not have half such sweet content: for, our pleasure here is still gains; in England charges and loss. Here nature and liberty affords us that freely, which in England we want, or it costeth us dearly. What pleasure can be more, than (being tired with any occasion[3] a-shore, in planting vines, fruits, or herbs, in contriving their own grounds, to the pleasure of their own minds, their fields, gardens, orchards, buildings, ships, and other works, &c.) to recreate themselves before their own doors, in their own boats upon the sea; where man, woman and child, with a small hook and line, by angling, may take diverse sorts of excellent fish, at their pleasures? And is it not pretty sport, to pull up two pence, six pence, and twelve pence, as fast as you can haul and veer a line?[4] He is a very bad fisher [that] cannot kill in one day with his hook and line, one, two, or three hundred cods: which dressed and dried, if they be sold there for ten shillings the hundred (though in England they will give more than twenty) may not both the servant, the master, and merchant, be well content with this gain? If a man work but three days in seven, he may get more than he can spend, unless he will be excessive. Now that carpenter, mason, gardener, tailor, smith, sailor, forgers,[5] or what other, may they not make this a pretty recreation though they fish but an hour in a day, to take more than they eat in a week? or if they will not eat it, because there is so much better choice; yet sell it, or change it, with the fishermen, or merchants, for anything they want. And what sport doth yield a more pleasing content, and less hurt or charge than angling with a hook; and crossing the sweet air from isle to isle, over the silent streams of a calm sea? Wherein the most curious may find pleasure, profit, and content.

Thus, though all men be not fishers: yet all men, whatsoever, may in other matters do as well. For necessity doth in these cases so rule a commonwealth, and each in their several functions, as their labors in their qualities may be as profitable, because there is a necessary mutual use of all.

For Gentlemen, what exercise should more delight them, than ranging daily those unknown parts, using fowling and fishing, for hunting and hawking? and yet you shall see the wild hawks give you some pleasure, in seeing them stoop (six or seven after one another) an hour or two together, at the

---

1. I.e., or never read Smith's works.
2. I.e., once they have paid the cost of their support for the year.
3. Task.
4. I.e., fish.
5. I.e., ironworkers.

schools of fish in the fair harbors, as those ashore at a fowl; and never trouble nor torment yourselves, with watching, mewing,[6] feeding, and attending them: nor kill horse and man with running and crying, See you not a hawk?[7] For hunting also: the woods, lakes, and rivers afford not only chase sufficient, for any that delights in that kind of toil, or pleasure; but such beasts to hunt, that besides the delicacy of their bodies for food, their skins are so rich, as may well recompence thy daily labor, with a captains pay.

For laborers, if those that sow hemp, rape,[8] turnips, parsnips, carrots, cabbage, and such like; give twenty, thirty, forty, fifty shillings yearly for an acre of ground, and meat, drink, and wages to use it, and yet grow rich; when better, or at least as good ground, may be had, and cost nothing but labor; it seems strange to me, any such should there grow poor.

My purpose is not to persuade children [to go] from their parents; men from their wives; nor servants from their masters: only, such as with free consent may be spared: But that each parish, or village, in city, or country, that will but apparell their fatherless children, of thirteen or fourteen years of age, or young married people, that have small wealth to live on; here by their labor may live exceedingly well: provided always that first there be a sufficient power to command them, houses to receive them, means to defend them, and meet provisions for them; for, any place may be overlain:[9] and it is most necessary to have a fortress (ere this grow to practice) and sufficient masters (as, carpenters, masons, fishers, fowlers, gardeners, husbandman, sawyers, smiths, spinsters, tailors, weavers , and such like) to take ten, twelve, or twenty, or as there is occasion, for apprentices. The masters by this may quickly grow rich; these may learn their trades themselves, to do the like; to a general and an incredible benefit, for king, and country, master, and servant.

1616

6. Keeping in a cage. "Stoop": swoop down.
7. Smith contrasts the delight of watching wild hawks hunt their prey in America with the tedious care that keepers of trained hawks in England must give their birds—as when such birds fly away and must be hunted for all over the countryside.
8. I.e., the rape plant.
9. Overcome.

WILLIAM BRADFORD
1590–1657

William Bradford epitomizes the spirit of determination and self-sacrifice that seems to us characteristic of our first "Pilgrims," a word Bradford himself was the first to use to describe the community of believers who sailed from Southampton, England, on the *Mayflower* and settled in Plymouth, Massachusetts, in 1620. For Bradford, as well as for the other members of this community, the decision to settle at Plymouth was the last step in a long march of exile from England, and the hardships they suffered in the new land were tempered with the knowledge that they were in a place they had chosen for themselves, safe at last from persecution. Shortly after their arrival Bradford was elected governor. His duties involved more than that title might imply today: he was chief judge and jury, oversaw agriculture and trade, and made allotments of land. It would be hard to imagine a historian better prepared to write the history of this colony.

Bradford's own life provides a model of the life of the community as a whole. He was born in Yorkshire, in the town of Austerfield, of parents who were modestly well off. Bradford's father died when he was an infant. His mother remarried in 1593, and he was brought up by his paternal grandparents and uncles. He did not receive a university education; instead, he was taught the arts of farming. When he was only twelve or thirteen, he heard the sermons of the Nonconformist minister Richard Clyfton, who preached in a neighboring parish; these sermons changed Bradford's life. For Clyfton was the religious guide of a small community of believers who met at the house of William Brewster in Scrooby, Nottinghamshire, and it was this group that Bradford joined in 1606. Much against the opposition of uncles and grandparents, he left home and joined them. They were known as "Separatists," because unlike the majority of Puritans, they saw no hope of reforming the Church of England from within. They wished to follow Calvin's model and to set up "particular" churches, each one founded on a formal covenant, entered into by those who professed their faith and swore to the covenant. Their model was the Old Testament covenant God made with Adam and renewed through Christ. In their covenanted churches God offered himself as a contractual partner to each believer; it was a contract freely initiated but perpetually binding. They were not sympathetic to the idea of a national church. Separating was, however, by English law an act of treason, and many believers paid a high price for their dreams of purity. Sick of the hidden life that the Church of England forced on them, the Scrooby community took up residence in the Netherlands. Bradford joined them in 1609 and there learned to be a weaver. When he came into his inheritance he went into business for himself.

Living in a foreign land was not easy, and eventually the Scrooby community petitioned for a grant of land in North America. Their original grant was for land in the Virginia territory, but high seas prevented them from reaching those shores and they settled instead at Plymouth, Massachusetts. In the second book of Bradford's history he describes the signing of the Mayflower Compact, a civil covenant designed to allow the temporal state to serve the godly citizen. It was the first of a number of plantation covenants designed to protect the rights of citizens beyond the reach of established governments.

Bradford was a self-educated man, deeply committed to the Puritan cause. Cotton Mather, in his ecclesiastical history of New England, describes him as "a person for study as well as action; and hence notwithstanding the difficulties which he passed in his youth, he attained unto a notable skill in languages. . . . But the Hebrew he most of all studied, because, he said, he would see with his own eyes the ancient oracles of God in their native beauty. . . . The crown of all his life was his holy, prayerful, watchful and fruitful walk with God, wherein he was exemplary." Bradford served as governor for all but five of the remaining years of his life.

The manuscript of Bradford's *History,* although known to early historians, disappeared from Boston after the Revolution. The first book (through chapter IX) had been copied into the Plymouth church records and was thus preserved, but the second book was presumed lost. The manuscript was eventually found in the residence of the bishop of London and published for the first time in 1856. In 1897 it was returned to this country by ecclesiastical decree and was deposited in the State House in Boston.

Of Plymouth Plantation[1]

From *Book I*

CHAPTER IX. OF THEIR VOYAGE, AND HOW THEY PASSED THE SEA;
AND OF THEIR SAFE ARRIVAL AT CAPE COD

September 6. These troubles being blown over,[2] and now all being compact together in one ship, they put to sea again with a prosperous wind, which continued divers days together, which was some encouragement unto them; yet, according to the usual manner, many were afflicted with seasickness. And I may not omit here a special work of God's providence. There was a proud and very profane young man, one of the seamen, of a lusty,[3] able body, which made him the more haughty; he would always be contemning the poor people in their sickness, and cursing them daily with grievous execrations, and did not let[4] to tell them, that he hoped to help to cast half of them overboard before they came to their journey's end, and to make merry with what they had; and if he were by any gently reproved, he would curse and swear most bitterly. But it pleased God before they came half seas over, to smite this young man with a grievous disease, of which he died in a desperate manner, and so was himself the first that was thrown overboard. Thus his curses lighted on his own head; and it was an astonishment to all his fellows, for they noted it to be the just hand of God upon him.

After they had enjoyed fair winds and weather for a season, they were encountered many times with cross winds, and met with many fierce storms, with which the ship was shroudly[5] shaken, and her upper works made very leaky; and one of the main beams in the midships was bowed and cracked, which put them in some fear that the ship could not be able to perform the voyage. So some of the chief of the company, perceiving the mariners to fear the sufficiency of the ship, as appeared by their mutterings, they entered into serious consultation with the master and other officers of the ship, to consider in time of the danger; and rather to return than to cast themselves into a desperate and inevitable peril. And truly there was great distraction and difference of opinion amongst the mariners themselves; fain would they do what could be done for their wages' sake (being now half the seas over) and on the other hand they were loath to hazard their lives too desperately. But in examining of all opinions, the master and others affirmed they knew the ship to be strong and firm underwater; and [as] for the buckling of the main beam, there was a great iron screw the passengers brought out of Holland, which would raise the beam into his place; the which being done, the carpenter and master affirmed that with a post put under it, set firm in the lower deck, and otherways bound, he would make it sufficient. And as for the decks and upper works they would caulk them as well as they could, and though with the working of the ship they would not long keep staunch,[6] yet there would otherwise be no great danger, if they did not overpress her with sails. So they committed themselves to the will of God, and resolved

---

1. The text is adapted from *Bradford's History "Of Plimoth Plantation." From the Original Manuscript* (1897).
2. Some of Bradford's community sailed on the *Speedwell* from Delftshaven early in August 1620, but the ship's unseaworthiness forced their

transfer to the *Mayflower*.
3. Strong, energetic.
4. Hesitate.
5. Shrewdly, in its original sense of badly or dangerously.
6. Watertight.

to proceed. In sundry of these storms the winds were so fierce, and the seas so high, as they could not bear a knot of sail, but were forced to hull,[7] for divers days together. And in one of them, as they thus lay at hull, in a mighty storm, a lusty young man (called John Howland) coming upon some occasion above the gratings, was, with a seele[8] of the ship thrown into [the] sea; but it pleased God that he caught hold of the topsail halyards, which hung overboard, and ran out at length; yet he held his hold (though he was sundry fathoms under water) till he was hauled up by the same rope to the brim of the water, and then with a boat hook and other means got into the ship again, and his life saved; and though he was something ill with it, yet he lived many years after, and became a profitable member both in church and commonwealth. In all this voyage there died but one of the passengers, which was William Butten, a youth, servant to Samuel Fuller, when they drew near the coast. But to omit other things (that I may be brief) after long beating at sea they fell with that land which is called Cape Cod; the which being made and certainly known to be it, they were not a little joyful. After some deliberation had amongst themselves and with the master of the ship, they tacked about and resolved to stand for the southward (the wind and weather being fair) to find some place about Hudson's River for their habitation. But after they had sailed that course about half the day, they fell amongst dangerous shoals and roaring breakers, and they were so far entangled therewith as they conceived themselves in great danger; and the wind shrinking upon them withal, they resolved to bear up again for the Cape, and thought themselves happy to get out of those dangers before night overtook them, as by God's providence they did. And the next day they got into the Cape Harbor,[9] where they rid in safety. A word or two by the way of this cape; it was thus first named by Captain Gosnold and his company, Anno[1] 1602, and after by Captain Smith was called Cape James, but it retains the former name amongst seamen. Also that point which first showed those dangerous shoals unto them, they called Point Care, and Tucker's Terror, but the French and Dutch to this day call it Malabarr,[2] by reason of those perilous shoals, and the losses they have suffered there.

Being thus arrived in a good harbor and brought safe to land, they fell upon their knees and blessed the God of heaven, who had brought them over the vast and furious ocean, and delivered them from all the perils and miseries thereof, again to set their feet on the firm and stable earth, their proper element. And no marvel if they were thus joyful, seeing wise Seneca was so affected with sailing a few miles on the coast of his own Italy; as he affirmed, that he had rather remain twenty years on his way by land, than pass by sea to any place in a short time, so tedious and dreadful was the same unto him.[3]

But here I cannot but stay and make a pause, and stand half amazed at this poor people's present condition, and so I think will the reader, too, when he well considers the same. Being thus passed the vast ocean, and a sea of troubles before in their preparation (as may be remembered by that which went before), they had now no friends to welcome them, nor inns to entertain

---

7. Drift before the weather under very little sail.
8. Roll.
9. They arrived at present-day Provincetown Harbor on November 11, 1620, after sixty-five days at sea.
1. In the year (Latin).

2. The prefix *mal* means "bad," a reference to the dangerous sandbars.
3. Bradford cites the *Moral Epistles to Lucilius* of the Roman Stoic philosopher Seneca (4? B.C.E.–65 C.E.).

or refresh their weatherbeaten bodies, no houses or much less towns to repair to, to seek for succor. It is recorded in scripture as a mercy to the apostle and his shipwrecked company, that the barbarians showed them no small kindness in refreshing them,[4] but these savage barbarians, when they met with them (as after will appear) were readier to fill their sides full of arrows than otherwise. And for the season it was winter, and they that know the winters of that country know them to be sharp and violent, and subject to cruel and fierce storms, dangerous to travel to known places, much more to search an unknown coast. Besides, what could they see but a hideous and desolate wilderness, full of wild beasts and wild men? And what multitudes there might be of them they knew not. Neither could they, as it were, go up to the top of Pisgah,[5] to view from this wilderness a more goodly country to feed their hopes; for which way soever they turned their eyes (save upward to the heavens) they could have little solace or content in respect of any outward objects. For summer being done, all things stand upon them with a weatherbeaten face, and the whole country, full of woods and thickets, represented a wild and savage hue. If they looked behind them, there was the mighty ocean which they had passed, and was now as a main bar and gulf to separate them from all the civil parts of the world. If it be said they had a ship to succor them, it is true; but what heard they daily from the master and company? but that with speed they should look out a place with their shallop,[6] where they would be at some near distance; for the season was such as he would not stir from thence till a safe harbor was discovered by them where they would be, and he might go without danger; and that victuals consumed apace, but he must and would keep sufficient for themselves and their return. Yea, it was muttered by some, that if they got not a place in time, they would turn them and their goods ashore and leave them. Let it also be considered what weak hopes of supply and succor they left behind them, that might bear up their minds in this sad condition and trials they were under; and they could not but be very small. It is true, indeed, the affections and love of their brethren at Leyden was cordial and entire towards them, but they had little power to help them, or themselves; and how the case stood between them and the merchants at their coming away, hath already been declared. What could now sustain them but the spirit of God and His grace? May not and ought not the children of these fathers rightly say: "Our fathers were Englishmen which came over this great ocean, and were ready to perish in this wilderness; but they cried unto the Lord, and He heard their voice, and looked on their adversity,"[7] "Let them therefore praise the Lord, because He is good, and His mercies endure forever." "Yea, let them which have been redeemed of the Lord, show how He hath delivered them from the hand of the oppressor. When they wandered in the desert wilderness out of the way, and found no city to dwell in, both hungry, and thirsty, their soul was overwhelmed in them. Let them confess before the Lord His loving kindness, and His wonderful works before the sons of men."[8]

4. See Acts 28.1–2.
5. Mountain from which Moses saw the Promised Land (Deuteronomy 34.1–4).
6. Small vessel fitted with one or more masts.
7. Deuteronomy 26.6–8 [Bradford's note].
8. Psalm 107.1, 2, 4, 5, 8 [Bradford's note].

CHAPTER X. SHOWING HOW THEY SOUGHT OUT A PLACE OF HABITATION;
AND WHAT BEFELL THEM THEREABOUT

Being thus arrived at Cape Cod the 11th of November, and necessity calling them to look out a place for habitation (as well as the master's and mariners' importunity), they having brought a large shallop with them out of England, stowed in quarters in the ship, they now got her out and set their carpenters to work to trim her up; but being much bruised and shattered in the ship with foul weather, they saw she would be long in mending. Whereupon a few of them tendered themselves to go by land and discover those nearest places, whilst the shallop was in mending, and the rather because as they went into that harbor there seemed to be an opening some two or three leagues off, which the master judged to be a river. It was conceived there might be some danger in the attempt, yet seeing them resolute, they were permitted to go, being sixteen of them, well armed, under the conduct of Captain Standish,[9] having such instructions given them as was thought meet. They set forth the 15th of November, and when they had marched about the space of a mile by the seaside, they espied five or six persons with a dog coming towards them, who were savages, but they fled from them, and ran up into the woods, and the English followed them, partly to see if they could speak with them, and partly to discover if there might not be more of them lying in ambush. But the Indians seeing themselves thus followed, they again forsook the woods, and ran away on the sands as hard[1] as they could, so as they could not come near them, but followed them by the track of their feet sundry miles, and saw that they had come the same way. So, night coming on, they made their rendezvous and set out their sentinels, and rested in quiet that night, and the next morning followed their track till they had headed a great creek, and so left the sands, and turned another way into the woods. But they still followed them by guess, hoping to find their dwellings, but they soon lost both them and themselves, falling into such thickets as were ready to tear their clothes and armor in pieces, but were most distressed for want of drink. But at length they found water and refreshed themselves, being the first New England water they drunk of, and was now in their great thirst as pleasant unto them as wine or beer had been in foretimes. Afterwards they directed their course to come to the other shore, for they knew it was a neck of land they were to cross over, and so at length got to the seaside, and marched to this supposed river, and by the way found a pond of clear fresh water, and shortly after a good quantity of clear ground where the Indians had formerly set corn, and some of their graves. And proceeding further they saw new stubble where corn had been set the same year, also they found where lately a house had been, where some planks and a great kettle was remaining, and heaps of sand newly paddled with their hands, which they, digging up, found in them divers fair Indian baskets filled with corn, and some in ears, fair and good, of divers colors, which seemed to them a very goodly sight (having never seen any such before). This was near the place of that supposed river they came to seek, unto which they went and found it to open itself into two arms with a high cliff of sand in the entrance, but more like to be creeks of salt water than any fresh, for aught they saw, and that there was good harborage for their shallop,

9. Myles Standish (1584?–1656), a professional soldier who had fought in the Netherlands, was in the employ of the Pilgrims.
1. Fast.

leaving it further to be discovered by their shallop when she was ready. So their time limited them being expired, they returned to the ship, lest they should be in fear of their safety, and took with them part of the corn, and buried up the rest, and so like the men from Eshcol[2] carried with them of the fruits of the land, and showed their brethren, of which, and their return, they were marvelously glad, and their hearts encouraged.

After this, the shallop being got ready, they set out again for the better discovery of this place, and the master of the ship desired to go himself, so there went some thirty men, but found it to be no harbor for ships but only for boats. There was also found two of their houses covered with mats, and sundry of their implements in them, but the people were run away and could not be seen.[3] Also there was found more of their corn, and of their beans of various colors. The corn and beans they brought away, purposing to give them full satisfaction when they should meet with any of them (as about some six months afterward they did, to their good content). And here is to be noted a special providence of God, and a great mercy to this poor people, that here they got seed to plant them corn the next year, or else they might have starved, for they had none, nor any likelihood to get any till the season had been past (as the sequel did manifest). Neither is it likely they had had this, if the first voyage had not been made, for the ground was now all covered with snow, and hard frozen. But the Lord is never wanting unto his in their greatest needs; let his holy name have all the praise.

The month of November being spent in these affairs, and much foul weather falling in, the 6th of December they sent out their shallop again with ten of their principal men, and some seamen, upon further discovery, intending to circulate that deep bay of Cape Cod. The weather was very cold, and it froze so hard as the spray of the sea lighting on their coats, they were as if they had been glazed; yet that night betimes they got down into the bottom of the bay, and as they drew near the shore they saw some ten or twelve Indians very busy about something.[4] They landed about a league or two from them, and had much ado to put ashore anywhere, it lay so full of flats. Being landed, it grew late, and they made themselves a barricade with logs and boughs as well as they could in the time, and set out their sentinel and betook them to rest, and saw the smoke of the fire the savages made that night. When morning was come they divided their company, some to coast along the shore in the boat, and the rest marched through the woods to see the land, if any fit place might be for their dwelling. They came also to the place where they saw the Indians the night before, and found they had been cutting up a great fish like a grampus,[5] being some two inches thick of fat like a hog, some pieces whereof they had left by the way; and the shallop found two more of these fishes dead on the sands, a thing usual after storms in that place, by reason of the great flats of sand that lie off. So they ranged up and down all that day, but found no people, nor any place they liked. When the sun grew low, they hasted out of the woods to meet with their shallop, to whom they made signs to come to them into a creek hard by, the which they did at high water, of which they were very glad, for they had not seen each other all that day, since the morning. So they made them a barri-

2. In Numbers 13.23–26, scouts sent out by Moses to search the wilderness return after forty days with clusters of grapes picked near a brook they called "Eschol."

3. Descendants of these Nauset Indians reside today at Mashpee on Cape Cod.
4. Near present-day Eastham.
5. Probably a pilot whale.

cado (as usually they did every night) with logs, stakes, and thick pine boughs, the height of a man, leaving it open to leeward, partly to shelter them from the cold and wind (making their fire in the middle, and lying round about it), and partly to defend them from any sudden assaults of the savages, if they should surround them.

So being very weary, they betook them to rest. But about midnight, they heard a hideous and great cry, and their sentinel called, "Arm! arm," so they bestirred them and stood to their arms, and shot off a couple of muskets, and then the noise ceased. They concluded it was a company of wolves, or such like wild beasts, for one of the seamen told them he had often heard such a noise in Newfoundland. So they rested till about five of the clock in the morning, for the tide, and their purpose to go from thence, made them be stirring betimes. So after prayer they prepared for breakfast, and it being day dawning, it was thought best to be carrying things down to the boat. But some said it was not best to carry the arms down, others said they would be the readier, for they had lapped them up in their coats from the dew. But some three or four would not carry theirs till they went themselves, yet as it fell out, the water being not high enough, they laid them down on the bank-side, and came up to breakfast. But presently, all on the sudden, they heard a great and strange cry, which they knew to be the same voices they heard in the night, though they varied their notes, and one of their company being abroad came running in, and cried, "Men, Indians, Indians," and withal, their arrows came flying amongst them. Their men ran with all speed to recover their arms, as by the good providence of God they did. In the meantime, of those that were there ready, two muskets were discharged at them, and two more stood ready in the entrance of their rendezvous, but were commanded not to shoot till they could take full aim at them, and the other two charged again with all speed, for there were only four had arms there, and defended the barricado, which was first assaulted. The cry of the Indians was dreadful, especially when they saw their men run out of the rendezvous toward the shallop, to recover their arms, the Indians wheeling about upon them. But some running out with coats of mail on, and cutlasses in their hands, they soon got their arms, and let fly amongst them, and quickly stopped their violence. Yet there was a lusty man, and no less valiant, stood behind a tree within half a musket shot, and let his arrows fly at them. He was seen [to] shoot three arrows, which were all avoided. He stood three shots of a musket, till one taking full aim at him, made the bark or splinters of the tree fly about his ears, after which he gave an extraordinary shriek, and away they went all of them. They[6] left some to keep the shallop, and followed them about a quarter of a mile, and shouted once or twice, and shot off two or three pieces, and so returned. This they did, that they might conceive that they were not afraid of them or any way discouraged. Thus it pleased God to vanquish their enemies, and give them deliverance; and by His special providence so to dispose that not any one of them were either hurt, or hit, though their arrows came close by them, and on every side them, and sundry of their coats, which hung up in the barricado, were shot through and through. Afterwards they gave God solemn thanks and praise for their deliverance, and gathered up a bundle of their arrows, and sent them into

6. The English.

England afterward by the master of the ship, and called that place the "First Encounter." From hence they departed, and coasted all along, but discerned no place likely for harbor, and therefore hasted to a place that their pilot (one Mr. Coppin, who had been in the country before) did assure them was a good harbor, which he had been in, and they might fetch it before night, of which they were glad, for it began to be foul weather. After some hours' sailing, it began to snow and rain, and about the middle of the afternoon, the wind increased, and the sea became very rough, and they broke their rudder, and it was as much as two men could do to steer her with a couple of oars. But their pilot bade them be of good cheer, for he saw the harbor; but the storm increasing, and night drawing on, they bore what sail they could to get in, while they could see. But herewith they broke their mast in three pieces, and their sail fell overboard, in a very grown sea, so as they had like to have been cast away; yet by God's mercy they recovered themselves, and having the flood[7] with them, struck into the harbor. But when it came to, the pilot was deceived in the place, and said, the Lord be merciful unto them, for his eyes never saw that place before, and he and the master's mate would have run her ashore, in a cove full of breakers, before the wind. But a lusty seaman which steered, bade those which rowed, if they were men, about with her, or else they were all cast away, the which they did with speed. So he bid them be of good cheer and row lustily, for there was a fair sound before them, and he doubted not but they should find one place or other where they might ride in safety. And though it was very dark, and rained sore, yet in the end they got under the lee of a small island, and remained there all that night in safety. But they knew not this to be an island till morning, but were divided in their minds: some would keep the boat for fear they might be amongst the Indians; others were so weak and cold, they could not endure, but got ashore, and with much ado got fire (all things being so wet) and the rest were glad to come to them, for after midnight the wind shifted to the northwest, and it froze hard. But though this had been a day and night of much trouble and danger unto them, yet God gave them a morning of comfort and refreshing (as usually He doth to His children), for the next day was a fair sunshining day, and they found themselves to be on an island secure from the Indians, where they might dry their stuff, fix their pieces,[8] and rest themselves, and gave God thanks for His mercies, in their manifold deliverances. And this being the last day of the week, they prepared there to keep the Sabbath. On Monday they sounded the harbor, and found it fit for shipping, and marched into the land, and found divers cornfields, and little running brooks, a place (as they supposed) fit for situation.[9] At least it was the best they could find, and the season, and their present necessity, made them glad to accept of it. So they returned to their ship again with this news to the rest of their people, which did much comfort their hearts.

On the 15th of December they weighed anchor to go to the place they had discovered, and came within two leagues of it, but were fain to bear up again, but the 16th day the wind came fair, and they arrived safe in this harbor, and afterwards took better view of the place, and resolved where to

---

7. Flood tide.
8. Weapons.
9. The landing (at modern Plymouth) occurred

on December 21, 1620. "Sounded": measured the depth of.

pitch their dwelling, and the 25th day began to erect the first house for common use to receive them and their goods.

From *Book II*

* * *

FROM CHAPTER XI.[1] THE REMAINDER OF ANNO 1620

I shall a little return back and begin with a combination[2] made by them before they came ashore, being the first foundation of their government in this place, occasioned partly by the discontented and mutinous speeches that some of the strangers[3] amongst them had let fall from them in the ship (that when they came ashore they would use their own liberty; for none had power to command them, the patent[4] they had being for Virginia, and not for New England, which belonged to another Government, with which the Virginia Company had nothing to do), and partly that such an act by them done (this their condition considered) might be as firm as any patent, and in some respects more sure.

The form was as followeth.

In the name of God, Amen. We whose names are underwritten, the loyal subjects of our dread sovereign Lord, King James, by the grace of God, of Great Britain, France, and Ireland king, defender of the faith, etc., having undertaken, for the glory of God, and advancement of the Christian faith, and honor of our king and country, a voyage to plant the first colony in the northern parts of Virginia, do by these presents solemnly and mutually in the presence of God, and one of another, covenant and combine ourselves together into a civil body politic, for our better ordering and preservation and furtherance of the ends aforesaid; and by virtue hereof to enact, constitute, and frame such just and equal laws, ordinances, acts, constitutions, and offices, from time to time, as shall be thought most meet and convenient for the general good of the Colony, unto which we promise all due submission and obedience. In witness whereof we have hereunder subscribed our names at Cape Cod the 11th of November, in the year of the reign of our sovereign lord, King James, of England, France, and Ireland the eighteenth, and of Scotland the fifty-fourth. Anno Domini[5] 1620.

After this they chose, or rather confirmed, Mr. John Carver[6] (a man godly and well approved amongst them) their governor for that year. And after they had provided a place for their goods, or common store, (which were long in unlading[7] for want of boats, foulness of the winter weather, and sickness of divers) and begun some small cottages for their habitation, as time would admit, they met and consulted of laws and orders, both for their civil and military government, as the necessity of their condition did require, still adding thereunto as urgent occasion in several times, and as cases did require.

---

1. Bradford did not number the chapters in Book II.
2. A form of union.
3. Not all the voyagers were "saints" (that is, members of Bradford's church); those who came along for economic gain he generally called "strangers."

4. A document signed by a sovereign granting privileges to those named in it.
5. "In the year of the Lord" (Latin).
6. A tradesman, like Bradford, and an original member of the group that went to Holland. After his death, Bradford was elected governor.
7. Unloading.

[DIFFICULT BEGINNINGS]

In these hard and difficult beginnings they found some discontents and mur-murings arise amongst some, and mutinous speeches and carriages in other; but they were soon quelled and overcome by the wisdom, patience, and just and equal carriage of things by the governor and better part, which clave[8] faithfully together in the main. But that which was most sad and lamentable was, that in two or three months' time half of their company died, especially in January and February, being the depth of winter, and wanting houses and other comforts; being infected with the scurvy and other diseases, which this long voyage and their inaccommodate condition had brought upon them; so as there died sometimes two or three of a day, in the foresaid time; that of one hundred and odd persons, scarce fifty remained. And of these in the time of most distress, there was but six or seven sound persons, who, to their great commendations be it spoken, spared no pains, night nor day, but with abundance of toil and hazard of their own health, fetched them wood, made them fires, dressed them meat, made their beds, washed their loathsome clothes, clothed and unclothed them; in a word, did all the homely[9] and necessary offices for them which dainty and queasy stomachs cannot endure to hear named; and all this willingly and cheerfully, without any grudging in the least, showing herein their true love unto their friends and brethren, a rare example and worthy to be remembered. Two of these seven were Mr. William Brewster, their reverend elder, and Myles Standish, their captain and military commander, unto whom myself and many others were much beholden in our low and sick condition. And yet the Lord so upheld these persons, as in this general calamity they were not at all infected either with sickness or lameness. And what I have said of these, I may say of many others who died in this general visitation, and others yet living, that whilst they had health, yea, or any strength continuing, they were not want-ing[1] to any that had need of them. And I doubt not but their recompense is with the Lord.

But I may not here pass by another remarkable passage not to be forgotten. As this calamity fell among the passengers that were to be left here to plant, and were hasted ashore and made to drink water, that the seamen might have the more beer, and one[2] in his sickness, desiring but a small can of beer, it was answered, that if he were their own father he should have none. The dis-ease began to fall amongst them also, so as almost half of their company died before they went away, and many of their officers and lustiest men, as the boatswain, gunner, three quartermasters, the cook, and others. At which the master was something stricken and sent to the sick ashore and told the gover-nor he should send for beer for them that had need of it, though he drunk water homeward bound. But now amongst his company there was far another kind of carriage in this misery than amongst the passengers: for they that before had been boon companions in drinking and jollity in the time of their health and welfare, began now to desert one another in this calamity, saying they would not hazard their lives for them, they should be infected by coming to help them in their cabins, and so, after they came to die by it, would do

---

8. Past tense of *cleave*. "Carriages": attitudes.
9. Intimate, domestic.
1. Lacking in attention.

2. Which was this author himself [Bradford's note].

little or nothing for them, but if they died let them die. But such of the passengers as were yet aboard showed them what mercy they could, which made some of their hearts relent, as the boatswain (and some others), who was a proud young man, and would often curse and scoff at the passengers. But when he grew weak, they had compassion on him and helped him; then he confessed he did not deserve it at their hands, he had abused them in word and deed. "O!" saith he, "you, I now see, show your love like Christians indeed one to another, but we let one another lie and die like dogs." Another lay cursing his wife, saying if it had not been for her he had never come this unlucky voyage, and anon cursing his fellows, saying he had done this and that, for some of them, he had spent so much, and so much, amongst them, and they were now weary of him, and did not help him, having need. Another gave his companion all he had, if he died, to help him in his weakness; he went and got a little spice and made him a mess of meat once or twice, and because he died not so soon as he expected, he went amongst his fellows, and swore the rogue would cozen[3] him, he would see him choked before he made him any more meat; and yet the poor fellow died before morning.

[DEALINGS WITH THE NATIVES]

All this while the Indians came skulking about them, and would sometimes show themselves aloof off, but when any approached near them, they would run away. And once they stole away their tools where they had been at work, and were gone to dinner. But about the 16th of March a certain Indian came boldly amongst them, and spoke to them in broken English, which they could well understand, but marveled at it.[4] At length they understood by discourse with him, that he was not of these parts, but belonged to the eastern parts, where some English ships came to fish, with whom he was acquainted, and could name sundry of them by their names, amongst whom he had got his language. He became profitable to them in acquainting them with many things concerning the state of the country in the east parts where he lived, which was afterwards profitable unto them; as also of the people here, of their names, number, and strength; of their situation and distance from this place, and who was chief amongst them. His name was *Samoset;* he told them also of another Indian whose name was *Squanto,* a native of this place, who had been in England and could speak better English than himself. Being, after some time of entertainment and gifts, dismissed, a while after he came again, and five more with him, and they brought again all the tools that were stolen away before, and made way for the coming of their great Sachem, called *Massasoit,* who, about four or five days after, came with the chief of his friends and other attendance, with the aforesaid *Squanto.* With whom, after friendly entertainment, and some gifts given him, they made a peace with him (which hath now continued this twenty-four years)[5] in these terms:

1. That neither he nor any of his, should injure or do hurt to any of their people.

---

3. Cheat. "Mess": meal.
4. The Abnaki chief Samoset had encountered English fishing vessels in southern Maine; he picked up his English there and may have come south with Captain Thomas Dermer.
5. Bradford's aside indicates that, having begun his history in 1630, he was writing this part in 1644.

2. That if any of his did any hurt to any of theirs, he should send the offender, that they might punish him.

3. That if anything were taken away from any of theirs, he should cause it to be restored, and they should do the like to his.

4. If any did unjustly war against him, they would aid him; if any did war against them, he should aid them.

5. He should send to his neighbors confederates, to certify them of this, that they might not wrong them, but might be likewise comprised in the conditions of peace.

6. That when their men came to them, they should leave their bows and arrows behind them.

After these things he returned to his place called *Sowams,* some forty mile from this place, but *Squanto* continued with them, and was their interpreter, and was a special instrument sent of God for their good beyond their expectation. He directed them how to set their corn, where to take fish, and to procure other commodities, and was also their pilot to bring them to unknown places for their profit, and never left them till he died. He was a native of this place, and scarce any left alive besides himself. He was carried away with divers others by one Hunt, a master of a ship, who thought to sell them for slaves in Spain; but he got away for England, and was entertained by a merchant in London, and employed to Newfoundland and other parts, and lastly brought hither into these parts by one Mr. Dermer, a gentleman employed by Sir Ferdinando Gorges and others, for discovery, and other designs in these parts. Of whom I shall say something, because it is mentioned in a book set forth Anno 1622 by the President and Council for New England, that he made the peace between the savages of these parts and the English, of which this plantation, as it is intimated, had the benefit.[6] But what a peace it was, may appear by what befell him and his men.

This Mr. Dermer was here the same year that these people came, as appears by a relation written by him, and given me by a friend, bearing date June 30, Anno 1620. And they came in November following, so there was but four months difference. In which relation to his honored friend, he hath these passages of this very place:

> I will first begin (saith he) with that place from whence *Squanto,* or *Tisquantum,* was taken away, which in Capt. Smith's map[7] is called Plymouth (and I would that Plymouth had the like commodities). I would that the first plantation might here be seated, if there come to the number of fifty persons, or upward. Otherwise at Charlton,[8] because there the savages are less to be feared. The *Pokanokets,* which live to the west of Plymouth, bear an inveterate malice to the English, and are of more strength than all the savages from thence to Penobscot.[9] Their desire of revenge was occasioned by an Englishman, who having many of them on board, made a great slaughter with their murderers[1] and small shot, when as (they say) they offered no injury on their parts. Whether they were English or no, it may be doubted; yet they believe they were, for

6. Gorges (c. 1566–1647), who had a patent for settling in northern New England, had published *A Briefe Relation of the Discovery and Plantation of New England* in 1622.

7. John Smith (1580–1631) published his *Description of New England* in 1616, after his 1614 voyage. Tisquantum was Squanto's Indian name.

8. Near the mouth of the Charles River, in present-day Boston and Charlestown.

9. A large bay on Maine's central coast. "*Pokanokets*": the Wampanoags, the tribe of Massasoit.

1. Small cannons.

the French have so possessed them; for which cause *Squanto* cannot deny but they would have killed me when I was at *Namasket,* had he not entreated hard for me. The soil of the borders of this great bay, may be compared to most of the plantations which I have seen in Virginia. The land is of diverse sorts, for *Patuxet* is a hardy but strong soil, *Nauset* and *Satucket* are for the most part a blackish and deep mould, much like that where groweth the best tobacco in Virginia.[2] In the bottom of that great bay is store of cod and bass, or mullet, etc.

But above all he commends *Pokanoket* for the richest soil, and much open ground fit for English grain, etc.

Massachusetts is about nine leagues from Plymouth, and situate in the midst between both, is full of islands and peninsulas, very fertile for the most part.

(With sundry such relations which I forbear to transcribe, being now better known than they were to him.)

He was taken prisoner by the Indians at *Monomoit*[3] (a place not far from hence, now well known). He gave them what they demanded for his liberty, but when they had got what they desired, they kept him still and endeavored to kill his men, but he was freed by seizing on some of them, and kept them bound till they gave him a canoe's load of corn. Of which, see Purchas, lib. 9, fol. 1778.[4] But this was Anno 1619.

After the writing of the former relation he came to the Isle of *Capawack*[5] (which lies south of this place in the way to Virginia), and the foresaid *Squanto* with him, where he going ashore amongst the Indians to trade, as he used to do, was betrayed and assaulted by them, and all his men slain, but one that kept the boat; but himself got aboard very sore wounded, and they had cut off his head upon the cuddy of the boat, had not the man rescued him with a sword. And so they got away, and made shift to get into Virginia, where he died, whether of his wounds or the diseases of the country, or both together, is uncertain. By all which it may appear how far these people were from peace, and with what danger this plantation was begun, save as the powerful hand of the Lord did protect them. These things were partly the reason why they[6] kept aloof and were so long before they came to the English. Another reason (as after themselves made known) was how about three years before, a French ship was cast away at Cape Cod, but the men got ashore, and saved their lives, and much of their victuals, and other goods. But after the Indians heard of it, they gathered together from these parts, and never left watching and dogging them till they got advantage, and killed them all but three or four which they kept, and sent from one Sachem to another, to make sport with, and used them worse than slaves (of which the foresaid Mr. Dermer redeemed two of them) and they conceived this ship[7] was now come to revenge it.

2. If Dermer was not lying about the soil, it obviously has been much degraded since his visit. Patuxet ("at the little falls") was the Indian name for Plymouth. Nauset, named for the local Indian tribe, was near present-day Eastham. Satucket ("near the mouth of the stream") was a Nauset village close to the town of Brewster.

3. Once a harbor near Orleans and Harwich.

4. Samuel Purchas (1577–1626) was an English clergyman and collector of travel writings, famous for compiling the four-volume work to which Bradford refers: *Purchas His Pilgrimes* (1625). "Lib.": abbreviation for *liber,* or "book" (Latin). "Fol.": abbreviation for *folio,* or "sheet" or page (Latin). (Bradford refers to p. 1778 in Purchas's ninth book, found in volume 4.)

5. Martha's Vineyard.

6. The Indians.

7. The *Mayflower.*

Also, as after was made known, before they came to the English to make friendship, they got all the *Powachs*[8] of the country, for three days together, in a horrid and devilish manner to curse and execrate them with their conjurations, which assembly and service they held in a dark and dismal swamp.

But to return. The spring now approaching, it pleased God the mortality began to cease amongst them, and the sick and lame recovered apace, which put as it were new life into them, though they had borne their sad affliction with much patience and contentedness, as I think any people could do. But it was the Lord which upheld them, and had beforehand prepared them; many having long borne the yoke, yea from their youth. Many other smaller matters I omit, sundry of them having been already published in a journal made by one of the company,[9] and some other passages of journeys and relations already published, to which I refer those that are willing to know them more particularly. And being now come to the 25th of March, I shall begin the year 1621.

FROM CHAPTER XIX. ANNO 1628

* * *

[MR. MORTON OF MERRYMOUNT]

About some three or four years before this time, there came over one Captain Wollaston, a man of pretty parts,[1] and with him three or four more of some eminency, who brought with them a great many servants, with provisions and other implements for to begin a plantation, and pitched themselves in a place within the Massachusetts which they called, after their Captain's name, Mount Wollaston. Amongst whom was one Mr. Morton,[2] who, it should seem, had some small adventure of his own or other men's amongst them, but had little respect amongst them, and was slighted by the meanest servants. Having continued there some time, and not finding things to answer their expectations, nor profit to arise as they looked for, Captain Wollaston takes a great part of the servants, and transports them to Virginia, where he puts them off at good rates, selling their time to other men;[3] and writes back to one Mr. Rasdall, one of his chief partners, and accounted their merchant, to bring another part of them to Virginia likewise, intending to put them off there as he had done the rest. And he, with the consent of the said Rasdall, appointed one Fitcher to be his lieutenant, and govern the remains of the plantation, till he or Rasdall returned to take further order thereabout. But this Morton abovesaid, having more craft then honesty (who had been a kind of pettifogger, of Furnivals Inn) in the other's absence, watches an opportunity (commons being but hard amongst them) and got some strong drink and other junkets, and made them a feast;[4] and after they were merry, he began to tell them, he would give them good counsel. "You see," saith he, "that many of

8. Medicine men.
9. *Mourt's Relation*; see p. 48.
1. I.e., of a clever nature.
2. Very little is known of Captain Wollason or Thomas Morton other than what Bradford tells. Morton (c. 1579–1647) trained as a lawyer in London, came to New England in the 1620s. He tangled with Bradford, in part because of his enthusiastic response to the New England scene, evident in his *New English Canaan* (1637).
3. A servant was someone employed in agricul-

tural or domestic labor; the servants in this case were indentured, meaning that their time had been purchased by their original employers (or masters), in exchange for their transportation, and hence the remainder of their time could be sold to others.
4. The shifty lawyer (or "pettifogger") Morton, knowing that the settlers' ordinary food ("commons") was in short supply, threw a feast of delicacies ("junkets") to win over the hearts and minds of the remaining servants.

your fellows are carried to Virginia; and if you stay till this Rasdall return, you will also be carried away and sold for slaves with the rest. Therefore I would advise you to thrust out this Lieutenant Fitcher; and I, having a part in the Plantation, will receive you as my partners and consociates; so may you be free from service, and we will converse, trade, plant, and live together as equals, and support and protect one another," or to like effect. This counsel was easily received; so they took opportunity, and thrust Lieutenant Fitcher out [of] doors, and would suffer him to come no more amongst them, but forced him to seek bread to eat, and other relief from his neighbors, till he could get passage for England. After this they fell to great licentiousness, and led a dissolute life, pouring out themselves into all profaneness. And Morton became lord of misrule,[5] and maintained (as it were) a school of Atheism. And after they had got some good into their hands, and got much by trading with the Indians, they spent it as vainly, in quaffing and drinking both wine and strong waters in great excess, and, as some reported, £10 worth in a morning. They also set up a maypole, drinking and dancing about it many days together, inviting the Indian women, for their consorts, dancing and frisking together, like so many fairies, or furies rather, and worse practices. As if they had anew revived and celebrated the feasts of the Roman Goddess Flora, or the beastly practices of the mad Bacchinalians.[6] Morton likewise (to show his poetry) composed sundry rhymes and verses, some tending to lasciviousness, and others to the detraction and scandal of some persons, which he affixed to this idle or idol maypole. They changed also the name of their place, and instead of calling it Mount Wollaston, they call it Merrymount, as if this jollity would have lasted ever. But this continued not long, for after Morton was sent for England (as follows to be declared) shortly after came over that worthy gentleman, Mr. John Endicott, who brought over a patent under the broad seal, for the government of the Massachusetts, who visiting those parts caused that maypole to be cut down, and rebuked them for their profaneness, and admonished them to look there should be better walking; so they now, or others, changed the name of their place again, and called it Mount Dagon.[7]

Now to maintain this riotous prodigality and profuse excess, Morton, thinking himself lawless, and hearing what gain the French and fishermen made by trading of pieces,[8] powder, and shot to the Indians, he, as the head of this consortship, began the practise of the same in these parts; and first he taught them how to use them, to charge and discharge, and what proportion of powder to give the piece, according to the size or bigness of the same; and what shot to use for fowl, and what for deer. And having thus instructed them, he employed some of them to hunt and fowl for him, so as they became far more active in that employment than any of the English, by reason of their swiftness of foot, and nimbleness of body, being also quick-sighted, and by continual exercise well knowing the haunts of all sorts of game. So as when they saw the execution that a piece would do, and the benefit that might come by the same, they became mad, as it were, after

5. The master of the carnival-like atmosphere of old English holidays, especially at Christmas.
6. At the revels in honor of Bacchus, the Roman god of wine, frenzied worshipers drank, danced, and even tore apart wild animals and devoured them. Flora, the Roman goddess of flowers and vegetation, was the center of a cult that put on highly indecent farces.
7. Reference to the Philistines, who captured and tortured Samson, who, however, at last brought down Dagon's temple (Judges 16.23–31).
8. Guns.

them, and would not stick to give any price they could attain to for them, accounting their bows and arrows but baubles in comparison of them.

* * *

This Morton having thus taught them the use of pieces, he sold them all he could spare, and he and his consorts determined to send for many out of England, and had by some of the ships sent for above a score. The which being known, and his neighbors meeting the Indians in the woods armed with guns in this sort, it was a terror unto them, who lived stragglingly,[9] and were of no strength in any place. And other places (though more remote) saw this mischief would quickly spread over all, if not prevented. Besides, they saw they should keep no servants, for Morton would entertain any, how vile soever, and all the scum of the country, or any discontents, would flock to him from all places, if this nest was not broken; and they should stand in more fear of their lives and goods (in short time) from this wicked and debauched crew, than from the savages themselves.

So sundry of the chief of the straggling plantations, meeting together, agreed by mutual consent to solicit those of Plymouth (who were then of more strength than them all) to join with them, to prevent the further growth of this mischief, and suppress Morton and his consorts before they grew to further head and strength. Those that joined in this action (and after contributed to the charge of sending him for England) were from Piscataqua, Naumkeag, Winnisimmett, Wessaguset, Nantasket, and other places where any English were seated. Those of Plymouth being thus sought to by their messengers and letters, and weighing both their reasons, and the common danger, were willing to afford them their help, though themselves had least cause of fear or hurt. So, to be short, they first resolved jointly to write to him, and in a friendly and neighborly way to admonish him to forbear these courses, and sent a messenger with their letters to bring his answer. But he was so high as he scorned all advice, and asked who had to do with him; he had and would trade pieces with the Indians in despite of all, with many other scurillous terms full of disdain. They sent to him a second time, and bade him be better advised, and more temperate in his terms, for the country could not bear the injury he did; it was against their common safety, and against the King's proclamation. He answered in high terms as before, and that the King's proclamation was no law, demanding what penalty was upon it. It was answered, more than he could bear, His Majesty's displeasure. But insolently he persisted, and said the King was dead and his displeasure with him, and many the like things; and threatened withal that if any came to molest him, let them look to themselves, for he would prepare for them. Upon which they saw there was no way but to take him by force, and having so far proceeded, now to give over would make him far more haughty and insolent. So they mutually resolved to proceed, and obtained of the governor of Plymouth to send Captain Standish, and some other aid with him, to take Morton by force. The which accordingly was done. But they found him to stand stiffly in his defense, having made fast his doors, armed his consorts, set divers dishes of powder and bullets ready on the table; and if they had not been over-armed with drink, more hurt might have been done. They summoned

9. In a scattered fashion.

him to yield, but he kept his house, and they could get nothing but scoffs and scorns from him; but at length, fearing they would do some violence to the house, he and some of his crew came out, but not to yield, but to shoot; but they were so steeled[1] with drink as their pieces were too heavy for them; himself with a carbine (over-charged and almost half filled with powder and shot, as was after found) had thought to have shot Captain Standish, but he stepped to him, and put by his piece, and took him. Neither was there any hurt done to any of either side, save that one was so drunk that he ran his own nose upon the point of a sword that one held before him as he entered the house, but he lost but a little of his hot blood.[2] Morton they brought away to Plymouth, where he was kept, till a ship went from the Isle of Shoals for England, with which he was sent to the Council of New England; and letters written to give them information of his course and carriage; and also one was sent at their common charge to inform their Honors more particularly, and to prosecute against him. But he fooled of the messenger, after he was gone from hence, and though he went for England, yet nothing was done to him, not so much as rebuked, for aught was heard; but returned the next year. Some of the worst of the company were dispersed, and some of the more modest kept the house till he should be heard from. But I have been too long about so unworthy a person, and bad a cause.

*　*　*

FROM CHAPTER XXIII. ANNO 1632

*　*　*

[PROSPERITY WEAKENS COMMUNITY]

Also the people of the plantation began to grow in their outward estates, by reason of the flowing of many people into the country, especially into the Bay of the Massachusetts, by which means corn and cattle rose to a great price, by which many were much enriched, and commodities grew plentiful; and yet in other regards this benefit turned to their hurt, and this accession of strength to their weakness. For now as their stocks increased, and the increase vendible,[3] there was no longer any holding them together, but now they must of necessity go to their great lots; they could not otherwise keep their cattle; and having oxen grown, they must have land for plowing and tillage. And no man now thought he could live, except he had cattle and a great deal of ground to keep them, all striving to increase their stocks. By which means they were scattered all over the bay, quickly, and the town, in which they lived compactly till now, was left very thin, and in a short time almost desolate. And if this had been all, it had been less, though too much; but the church must also be divided, and those that had lived so long together in Christian and comfortable fellowship must now part and suffer many divisions. First, those that lived on their lots on the other side of the bay (called Duxbury) they could not long bring their wives and children to the public worship and church meetings here, but with such burthen, as, growing to some competent number, they sued to be dismissed and become a body of themselves; and so they were dismissed (about this time), though

1. Insensible.
2. In his own book, Morton refers to Standish as "Captain Shrimp" and says it would have been easy for him to destroy these "nine worthies" like "a flock of wild geese," but that he loathed violence and asked for his freedom to leave. He suggests that he was treated brutally because the Pilgrims wished to shame him before the Indian revelers.
3. Salable.

very unwillingly. But to touch this sad matter, and handle things together that fell out afterward: to prevent any further scattering from this place, and weakening of the same, it was thought best to give out some good farms to special persons, that would promise to live at Plymouth, and likely to be helpful to the church or commonwealth, and so tie the lands to Plymouth as farms for the same; and there they might keep their cattle and tillage by some servants, and retain their dwellings here. And so some special lands were granted at a place general, called Green's Harbor, where no allotments had been in the former division, a place very well meadowed, and fit to keep and rear cattle, good store. But alas! this remedy proved worse than the disease; for within a few years those that had thus got footing there rent themselves away, partly by force, and partly wearing the rest with importunity and pleas of necessity, so as they must either suffer them to go, or live in continual opposition and contention. And others still, as they conceived themselves straitened,[4] or to want accommodation, break away under one pretense or other, thinking their own conceived necessity, and the example of others, a warrant sufficient for them. And this, I fear, will be the ruin of New England, at least of the churches of God there, and will provoke the Lord's displeasure against them.

* * *

4. Financially hampered.

JOHN WINTHROP
1588–1649

John Winthrop, the son of Adam Winthrop, a lawyer, and Anne Browne, the daughter of a tradesman, was born in Groton, England, on an estate that his father had purchased from Henry VIII. It was a prosperous farm, and Winthrop had all the advantages that his father's social and economic position would allow. He went to Cambridge University for two years and married at the age of seventeen. It was probably at Cambridge that Winthrop was exposed to Puritan ideas. Unlike Bradford and the Pilgrims, however, Winthrop was not a Separatist; that is, he wished to reform the national church from within, purging it of everything that harked back to Rome, especially the hierarchy of the clergy and all the traditional Catholic rituals. For a time Winthrop thought of becoming a clergyman himself, but instead he turned to the practice of law.

In the 1620s severe economic depression in England made Winthrop realize that he could not depend on the support of his father's estate. The ascension to the throne of Charles I—who was known to be sympathetic to Roman Catholicism and impatient with Puritan reformers—was also taken as an ominous sign for Puritans, and Winthrop was not alone in predicting that "God will bring some heavy affliction upon the land, and that speedily." Winthrop came to realize that he could not antagonize the king by expressing openly the Puritan cause without losing all that he possessed. The only recourse seemed to be to obtain the king's permission to emigrate. In March 1629 a group of enterprising merchants, all ardent Puritans, was able to get a charter from the Council for New England for land in America. They called themselves "The Company of Massachusetts Bay in New England."

From four candidates, Winthrop was chosen governor in October 1629; for the next twenty years most of the responsibility for the colony rested in his hands. On April 8, 1630, an initial group of some seven hundred emigrants sailed from England. The ship carrying Winthrop was called the *Arbella*. Either just before departing from England or on the high seas, Winthrop delivered his sermon *A Model of Christian Charity*. It set out clearly and eloquently the ideals of a harmonious Christian community and reminded all those on board that they would stand as an example to the world either of the triumph or the failure of this Christian enterprise. When Cotton Mather wrote his history of New England some fifty years after Winthrop's death, he chose Winthrop as his model of the perfect earthly ruler. Although the actual history of the colony showed that Winthrop's ideal of a perfectly selfless community was impossible to realize in fact, Winthrop emerges from the story as a man of unquestioned integrity and deep humanity.

A Model of Christian Charity[1]

I

A MODEL HEREOF

God Almighty in His most holy and wise providence, hath so disposed of the condition of mankind, as in all times some must be rich, some poor, some high and eminent in power and dignity; others mean and in subjection.

THE REASON HEREOF

First, to hold conformity with the rest of His works, being delighted to show forth the glory of His wisdom in the variety and difference of the creatures; and the glory of His power, in ordering all these differences for the preservation and good of the whole; and the glory of His greatness, that as it is the glory of princes to have many officers, so this great King will have many stewards, counting Himself more honored in dispensing His gifts to man by man, than if He did it by His own immediate hands.

Secondly, that He might have the more occasion to manifest the work of His Spirit: first upon the wicked in moderating and restraining them, so that the rich and mighty should not eat up the poor, nor the poor and despised rise up against their superiors and shake off their yoke; secondly in the regenerate, in exercising His graces, in them, as in the great ones, their love, mercy, gentleness, temperance, etc., in the poor and inferior sort, their faith, patience, obedience, etc.

Thirdly, that every man might have need of other, and from hence they might be all knit more nearly together in the bonds of brotherly affection. From hence it appears plainly that no man is made more honorable than another or more wealthy, etc., out of any particular and singular respect to himself, but for the glory of his Creator and the common good of the creature, man. Therefore God still reserves the property of these gifts to Himself

1. The text is from Old South Leaflets, Old South Association, Old South Meetinghouse, Boston, Massachusetts, No. 207, edited by Samuel Eliot Morison. The original manuscript for Winthrop's sermon is lost, but a copy made during Winthrop's lifetime was published by the Massachusetts Historical Society in 1838.

as [in] Ezekiel: 16.17. He there calls wealth His gold and His silver.[2] [In] Proverbs: 3.9, he claims their service as His due: honor the Lord with thy riches, etc.[3] All men being thus (by divine providence) ranked into two sorts, rich and poor; under the first are comprehended all such as are able to live comfortably by their own means duly improved; and all others are poor according to the former distribution.

There are two rules whereby we are to walk one towards another: justice and mercy. These are always distinguished in their act and in their object, yet may they both concur in the same subject in each respect; as sometimes there may be an occasion of showing mercy to a rich man in some sudden danger of distress, and also doing of mere justice to a poor man in regard of some particular contract, etc.

There is likewise a double law by which we are regulated in our conversation one towards another in both the former respects: the law of nature and the law of grace, or the moral law or the law of the Gospel, to omit the rule of justice as not properly belonging to this purpose otherwise than it may fall into consideration in some particular cases. By the first of these laws man as he was enabled so withal [is] commanded to love his neighbor as himself.[4] Upon this ground stands all the precepts of the moral law, which concerns our dealings with men. To apply this to the works of mercy, this law requires two things: first, that every man afford his help to another in every want or distress; secondly, that he performed this out of the same affection which makes him careful of his own goods, according to that of our Savior. Matthew: "Whatsoever ye would that men should do to you."[5] This was practiced by Abraham and Lot in entertaining the Angels and the old man of Gibeah.[6]

The law of grace or the Gospel hath some difference from the former, as in these respects: First, the law of nature was given to man in the estate of innocency; this of the Gospel in the estate of regeneracy.[7] Secondly, the former propounds one man to another, as the same flesh and image of God; this as a brother in Christ also, and in the communion of the same spirit and so teacheth us to put a difference between Christians and others. *Do good to all, especially to the household of faith*: Upon this ground the Israelites were to put a difference between the brethren of such as were strangers though not of Canaanites.[8] Thirdly, the law of nature could give no rules for dealing with enemies, for all are to be considered as friends in the state of innocency, but the Gospel commands love to an enemy. Proof. If thine Enemy hunger, feed him; Love your Enemies, do good to them that hate you. Matthew: 5.44.

2. "Thou hast also taken thy fair jewels of my gold and of my silver, which I had given thee, and madest to thyself images of men, and didst commit whoredom with them."
3. "Honour the Lord with thy substance, and with the firstfruits of all thine increase: So shall thy barns be filled with plenty, and thy presses shall burst out with new wine" (Proverbs 3.9–10).
4. Matthew 5.43, 19.19.
5. "Therefore all things whatsoever ye would that men should do to you, do ye even so to them: for this is the law of the prophets" (Matthew 7.12).
6. In Judges 19.16–21, an old citizen of Gibeah offered shelter to a traveling priest or Levite and defended him from enemies from a neighboring city. Abraham entertains the angels in Genesis 18: "And the Lord appeared unto him in the plains of Mamre: and he sat in the tent door in the heat of the day; And he lift up his eyes and looked, and, lo, three men stood by him: and when he saw them, he ran to meet them" (Genesis 18.1–2). Lot was Abraham's nephew, and he escaped the destruction of the city of Sodom because he defended two angels who were his guests from a mob (Genesis 19.1–14).
7. Humanity lost its natural innocence when Adam and Eve fell; that state is called unregenerate. When Christ came to ransom humankind for Adam and Eve's sin, he offered salvation for those who believed in him and who thus became regenerate, or saved.
8. People who lived in Canaan, the Land of Promise for the Israelites.

This law of the Gospel propounds likewise a difference of seasons and occasions. There is a time when a Christian must sell all and give to the poor, as they did in the Apostles' times.[9] There is a time also when a Christian (though they give not all yet) must give beyond their ability, as they of Macedonia, Corinthians: 2.8.[1] Likewise community of perils calls for extraordinary liberality, and so doth community in some special service for the Church. Lastly, when there is no other means whereby our Christian brother may be relieved in his distress, we must help him beyond our ability, rather than tempt God in putting him upon help by miraculous or extraordinary means.

This duty of mercy is exercised in the kinds, *giving, lending* and *forgiving.*—

Quest. What rule shall a man observe in giving in respect of the measure?

Ans. If the time and occasion be ordinary, he is to give out of his abundance. Let him lay aside as God hath blessed him. If the time and occasion be extraordinary, he must be ruled by them; taking this withal, that then a man cannot likely do too much, especially if he may leave himself and his family under probable means of comfortable subsistence.

Objection. A man must lay up for posterity, the fathers lay up for posterity and children and he "is worse than an infidel" that "provideth not for his own."

Ans. For the first, it is plain that it being spoken by way of comparison, it must be meant of the ordinary and usual course of fathers and cannot extend to times and occasions extraordinary. For the other place, the Apostle speaks against such as walked inordinately, and it is without question, that he is worse than an infidel who through his own sloth and voluptuousness shall neglect to provide for his family.

Objection. "The wise man's eyes are in his head" saith Solomon, "and foreseeth the plague,"[2] therefore we must forecast and lay up against evil times when he or his may stand in need of all he can gather.

Ans. This very argument Solomon useth to persuade to liberality, Ecclesiastes: "Cast thy bread upon the waters," and "for thou knowest not what evil may come upon the land."[3] Luke: 16.9. "Make you friends of the riches of iniquity."[4] You will ask how this shall be? very well. For first he that gives to the poor, lends to the Lord and He will repay him even in this life an hundred fold to him or his—The righteous is ever merciful and lendeth and his seed enjoyeth the blessing; and besides we know what advantage it will be to us in the day of account when many such witnesses shall stand forth for us to witness the improvement of our talent.[5] And I would know of those who plead so much for laying up for time to come, whether they hold that

9. In Luke, Jesus tells a ruler who asks him what he must do to gain eternal life: "sell all that thou hast, and distribute unto the poor, and thou shalt have treasure in heaven: and come, follow me" (Luke 18.22).

1. "Moreover, brethren, we do you to wit of the grace of God bestowed on the churches of Macedonia; How that in a great trial of affliction, the abundance of their joy and their deep poverty abounded unto the riches of their liberality. For to their power, I bear record, yea, and beyond their power they were willing of themselves; Praying us with much intreaty that we would receive the gift, and take upon us the fellowship of the ministering to the saints" (2 Corinthians 8.1–4).

2. Ecclesiastes 2.14. Solomon was the son of David and successor to David as king of all Israel.

3. "Cast thy bread upon the waters: for thou shalt find it after many days. Give a portion to seven, and also to eight; for thou knowest not what evil shall be upon the earth" (Ecclesiastes 11.1–2). Winthrop either makes his own translations from the Bible or uses the King James or Geneva versions; his quotations, therefore, differ occasionally from the King James version used in these notes.

4. The passage in Luke refers to the servant who, removed from his stewardship, resolves to be received in the houses of his master's debtors and cuts their bills in half. "And I say unto you, Make to yourselves friends of the mammon of unrighteousness; that, when ye fail, they may receive you into everlasting habitations" (Luke 16.9).

5. Originally a measure of money.

to be Gospel, Matthew: 6.19: "Lay not up for yourselves treasures upon earth,"[6] etc. If they acknowledge it, what extent will they allow it? if only to those primitive times, let them consider the reason whereupon our Savior grounds it. The first is that they are subject to the moth, the rust, the thief. Secondly, they will steal away the heart; where the treasure is there will the heart be also. The reasons are of like force at all times. Therefore the exhortation must be general and perpetual, with always in respect of the love and affection to riches and in regard of the things themselves when any special service for the church or particular distress of our brother do call for the use of them; otherwise it is not only lawful but necessary to lay up as Joseph[7] did to have ready upon such occasions, as the Lord (whose stewards we are of them) shall call for them from us. Christ gives us an instance of the first, when He sent his disciples for the ass, and bids them answer the owner thus, the Lord hath need of him.[8] So when the tabernacle was to be built He sends to His people to call for their silver and gold, etc.; and yields them no other reason but that it was for His work. When Elisha comes to the widow of Sareptah and finds her preparing to make ready her pittance for herself and family, He bids her first provide for Him; he challengeth first God's part which she must first give before she must serve her own family.[9] All these teach us that the Lord looks that when He is pleased to call for His right in anything we have, our own interest we have must stand aside till His turn be served. For the other, we need look no further than to that of John: 1: "He who hath this world's goods and seeth his brother to need and shuts up his compassion from him, how dwelleth the love of God in him," which comes punctually to this conclusion: if thy brother be in want and thou canst help him, thou needst not make doubt, what thou shouldst do, if thou lovest God thou must help him.

Quest. What rule must we observe in lending?

Ans. Thou must observe whether thy brother hath present or probable, or possible means of repaying thee, if there be none of these, thou must give him according to his necessity, rather than lend him as he requires. If he hath present means of repaying thee, thou art to look at him not as an act of mercy, but by way of commerce, wherein thou art to walk by the rule of justice; but if his means of repaying thee be only probable or possible, then is he an object of thy mercy, thou must lend him, though there be danger of losing it, Deuteronomy: 15.7: "If any of thy brethren be poor," etc., "thou shalt lend him sufficient."[1] That men might not shift off this duty by the apparent hazard, He tells them that though the year of Jubilee[2] were at hand (when he must remit it, if he were not able to repay it before) yet he must lend him and that cheerfully: "It may not grieve thee to give him" saith He; and because some might object; "why so I should soon impoverish

---

6. "Lay not up for yourselves treasures upon earth, where moth and rust doth corrupt, and where thieves break through and steal: But lay up for yourselves treasures in heaven, where neither moth nor rust doth corrupt, and where thieves do not break through nor steal" (Matthew 6.19–20).

7. The son of Jacob and Rachel, who stored up the harvest in the seven good years before the famine (Genesis 41).

8. Matthew 21.5–7.

9. 1 Kings 17.8–24.

1. "If there be among you a poor man of one of thy brethren within any of thy gates in thy land which the Lord thy God giveth thee, thou shalt not harden thine heart, nor shut thine hand from thy poor brother: But thou shalt open thine hand wide unto him, and shalt surely lend him sufficient for his need, in that which he wanteth" (Deuteronomy 15.7–8).

2. According to Mosaic law, every seventh year the lands would lie fallow, all work would cease, and all debts would be canceled. The Jubilee year concluded a cycle of seven sabbatical years.

myself and my family," He adds "with all thy work,"[3] etc.; for our Savior, Matthew: 5.42: "From him that would borrow of thee turn not away."

Quest. What rule must we observe in forgiving?

Ans. Whether thou didst lend by way of commerce or in mercy, if he have nothing to pay thee, [you] must forgive, (except in cause where thou hast a surety or a lawful pledge) Deuteronomy: 15.2. Every seventh year the creditor was to quit that which he lent to his brother if he were poor as appears—verse 8: "Save when there shall be no poor with thee." In all these and like cases, Christ was a general rule, Matthew: 7.12: "Whatsoever ye would that men should do to you, do ye the same to them also."

Quest. What rule must we observe and walk by in cause of community of peril?

Ans. The same as before, but with more enlargement towards others and less respect towards ourselves and our own right. Hence it was that in the primitive church they sold all, had all things in common, neither did any man say that which he possessed was his own. Likewise in their return out of the captivity, because the work was great for the restoring of the church and the danger of enemies was common to all, Nehemiah exhorts the Jews to liberality and readiness in remitting their debts to their brethren, and disposing liberally of his own to such as wanted, and stand not upon his own due, which he might have demanded of them.[4] Thus did some of our forefathers in times of persecution in England, and so did many of the faithful of other churches, whereof we keep an honorable remembrance of them; and it is to be observed that both in Scriptures and later stories of the churches that such as have been most bountiful to the poor saints, especially in these extraordinary times and occasions, God hath left them highly commended to posterity, as Zacheus, Cornelius, Dorcas, Bishop Hooper, the Cuttler of Brussells[5] and divers others. Observe again that the Scripture gives no caution to restrain any from being over liberal this way; but all men to the liberal and cheerful practice hereof by the sweetest promises; as to instance one for many, Isaiah: 58.6: "Is not this the fast I have chosen to loose the bonds of wickedness, to take off the heavy burdens, to let the oppressed go free and to break every yoke, to deal thy bread to the hungry and to bring the poor that wander into thy house, when thou seest the naked to cover them. And then shall thy light break forth as the morning, and thy health shall grow speedily, thy righteousness shall go before God, and the glory of the Lord shall embrace thee; then thou shalt call and the Lord shall answer thee" etc. [Verse] 10: "If thou pour out thy soul to the hungry, then shall thy light spring out in darkness, and the Lord shall guide thee continually, and satisfy thy soul in drought, and make fat thy bones; thou shalt be like a watered garden, and they shalt be of thee that shall build the old waste places" etc. On the contrary, most heavy curses are laid upon such as are straightened towards the Lord and His people, Judges: 5.[23]: "Curse ye

---

3. "The seventh year, the year of release, is at hand; and thine eye be evil against thy poor brother, and thou givest him nought; and he cry unto the Lord against thee, and it be sin unto thee. Thou shalt surely give him, and thine heart shall not be grieved when thou givest unto him: because that for this thing the Lord thy God shall bless thee in all thy works, and in all that thou puttest thine hand unto" (Deuteronomy 15.9–10).

4. Nehemiah was sent by King Artaxerxes to repair the walls of the city of Jerusalem; he saved the city as governor when he persuaded those lending money to charge no interest, and to think first of the common good (see Nehemiah 3).

5. Christian martyrs.

Meroshe because ye came not to help the Lord," etc. Proverbs: [21.13]: "He who shutteth his ears from hearing the cry of the poor, he shall cry and shall not be heard." Matthew: 25: "Go ye cursed into everlasting fire" etc. "I was hungry and ye fed me not." 2 Corinthians: 9.6: "He that soweth sparingly shall reap sparingly."

Having already set forth the practice of mercy according to the rule of God's law, it will be useful to lay open the grounds of it also, being the other part of the commandment, and that is the affection from which this exercise of mercy must arise. The apostle[6] tells us that this love is the fulfilling of the law, not that it is enough to love our brother and so no further; but in regard of the excellency of his parts giving any motion to the other as the soul to the body and the power it hath to set all the faculties on work in the outward exercise of this duty. As when we bid one make the clock strike, he doth not lay hand on the hammer, which is the immediate instrument of the sound, but sets on work the first mover or main wheel, knowing that will certainly produce the sound which he intends. So the way to draw men to works of mercy, is not by force of argument from the goodness or necessity of the work; for though this course may enforce a rational mind to some present act of mercy, as is frequent in experience, yet it cannot work such a habit in a soul, as shall make it prompt upon all occasions to produce the same effect, but by framing these affections of love in the heart which will as natively bring forth the other, as any cause doth produce effect.

The definition which the Scripture gives us of love is this: "Love is the bond of perfection." First, it is a bond or ligament. Secondly it makes the work perfect. There is no body but consists of parts and that which knits these parts together gives the body its perfection, because it makes each part so contiguous to others as thereby they do mutually participate with each other, both in strength and infirmity, in pleasure and pain. To instance in the most perfect of all bodies: Christ and His church make one body. The several parts of this body, considered apart before they were united, were as disproportionate and as much disordering as so many contrary qualities or elements, but when Christ comes and by His spirit and love knits all these parts to Himself and each to other, it is become the most perfect and best proportioned body in the world. Ephesians: 4.16: "Christ, by whom all the body being knit together by every joint for the furniture thereof, according to the effectual power which is the measure of every perfection of parts," "a glorious body without spot or wrinkle," the ligaments hereof being Christ, or His love, for Christ is love (1 John: 4.8). So this definition is right: "Love is the bond of perfection."

From hence we may frame these conclusions. 1. First of all, true Christians are of one body in Christ, 1 Corinthians: 12.12, 27: "Ye are the body of Christ and members of their part." Secondly: The ligaments of this body which knit together are love. Thirdly: No body can be perfect which wants its proper ligament. Fourthly: All the parts of this body being thus united are made so contiguous in a special relation as they must needs partake of each other's strength and infirmity; joy and sorrow, weal and woe. 1 Corinthians: 12.26: "If one member suffers, all suffer with it, if one be in honor, all rejoice with it." Fifthly: This sensibleness and sympathy of each other's

6. Saint Paul in his Epistle to the Romans 9.31.

conditions will necessarily infuse into each part a native desire and endeavor to strengthen, defend, preserve and comfort the other.

To insist a little on this conclusion being the product of all the former, the truth hereof will appear both by precept and pattern. 1 John: 3.10: "Ye ought to lay down your lives for the brethren." Galatians: 6.2: "bear ye one another's burthens and so fulfill the law of Christ." For patterns we have that first of our Savior who out of His good will in obedience to His father, becoming a part of this body, and being knit with it in the bond of love, found such a native sensibleness of our infirmities and sorrows as He willingly yielded Himself to death to ease the infirmities of the rest of His body, and so healed their sorrows. From the like sympathy of parts did the apostles and many thousands of the saints lay down their lives for Christ. Again, the like we may see in the members of this body among themselves. Romans: 9. Paul could have been contented to have been separated from Christ, that the Jews might not be cut off from the body. It is very observable what he professeth of his affectionate partaking with every member: "who is weak" saith he "and I am not weak? who is offended and I burn not;"[7] and again, 2 Corinthians: 7.13. "therefore we are comforted because ye were comforted." Of Epaphroditus[8] he speaketh, Philippians: 2.30. that he regarded not his own life to do him service. So Phoebe[9] and others are called the servants of the church. Now it is apparent that they served not for wages, or by constraint, but out of love. The like we shall find in the histories of the church in all ages, the sweet sympathy of affections which was in the members of this body one towards another, their cheerfulness in serving and suffering together, how liberal they were without repining, harborers without grudging and helpful without reproaching; and all from hence, because they had fervent love amongst them, which only make the practice of mercy constant and easy.

The next consideration is how this love comes to be wrought. Adam in his first estate[1] was a perfect model of mankind in all their generations, and in him this love was perfected in regard of the habit. But Adam rent himself from his creator, rent all his posterity also one from another; whence it comes that every man is born with this principle in him, to love and seek himself only, and thus a man continueth till Christ comes and takes possession of the soul and infuseth another principle, love to God and our brother. And this latter having continual supply from Christ, as the head and root by which he is united, gets the predomining[2] in the soul, so by little and little expels the former. 1 John: 4.7. "love cometh of God and every one that loveth is born of God," so that this love is the fruit of the new birth, and none can have it but the new creature. Now when this quality is thus formed in the souls of men, it works like the spirit upon the dry bones. Ezekiel: 37: "bone came to bone." It gathers together the scattered bones, of perfect old man Adam,[3] and knits them into one body again in Christ, whereby a man is become again a living soul.

7. 2 Corinthians 11.29.
8. Saint Paul tells the Philippians that he will send to them as a spiritual guide "Epaphroditus, my brother, and companion in labour, and fellow soldier, but your messenger, and he that ministered to my wants" (Philippians 2.25).
9. A Christian woman praised by Saint Paul in

Romans 16.1.
1. I.e., in his innocence.
2. Predominance.
3. Jesus Christ has traditionally been called the "New Adam" to signify the redemption of humankind from the original sin of "Old Adam."

The third consideration is concerning the exercise of this love which is twofold, inward or outward. The outward hath been handled in the former preface of this discourse. For unfolding the other we must take in our way that maxim of philosophy *simile simili gaudet*, or like will to like; for as it is things which are turned with disaffection to each other, the ground of it is from a dissimilitude arising from the contrary or different nature of the things themselves; for the ground of love is an apprehension of some resemblance in things loved to that which affects it. This is the cause why the Lord loves the creature, so far as it hath any of His image in it; He loves His elect because they are like Himself, He beholds them in His beloved son. So a mother loves her child, because she thoroughly conceives a resemblance of herself in it. Thus it is between the members of Christ. Each discerns, by the work of the spirit, his own image and resemblance in another, and therefore cannot but love him as he loves himself. Now when the soul, which is of a sociable nature, finds anything like to itself, it is like Adam when Eve was brought to him. She must have it one with herself. This is flesh of my flesh (saith the soul) and bone of my bone. She conceives a great delight in it, therefore she desires nearness and familiarity with it. She hath a great propensity to do it good and receives such content in it, as fearing the miscarriage of her beloved she bestows it in the inmost closet of her heart. She will not endure that it shall want any good which she can give it. If by occasion she be withdrawn from the company of it, she is still looking towards the place where she left her beloved. If she heard it groan, she is with it presently. If she find it sad and disconsolate, she sighs and moans with it. She hath no such joy as to see her beloved merry and thriving. If she see it wronged, she cannot hear it without passion. She sets no bounds to her affections, nor hath any thought of reward. She finds recompense enough in the exercise of her love towards it. We may see this acted to life in Jonathan and David.[4] Jonathan, a valiant man endowed with the spirit of Christ, so soon as he discovers the same spirit in David, had presently his heart knit to him by this lineament of love, so that it is said he loved him as his own soul. He takes so great pleasure in him, that he strips himself to adorn his beloved. His father's kingdom was not so precious to him as his beloved David. David shall have it with all his heart, himself desires no more but that he may be near to him to rejoice in his good. He chooseth to converse with him in the wilderness even to the hazard of his own life, rather than with the great courtiers in his father's palace. When he sees danger towards him, he spares neither rare pains nor peril to direct it. When injury was offered his beloved David, he would not bear it, though from his own father; and when they must part for a season only, they thought their hearts would have broke for sorrow, had not their affections found vent by abundance of tears. Other instances might be brought to show the nature of this affection, as of Ruth and Naomi,[5] and many others; but this truth is cleared enough.

If any shall object that it is not possible that love should be bred or upheld without hope of requital, it is granted; but that is not our cause; for this love is always under reward. It never gives, but it always receives with advantage; first, in regard that among the members of the same body, love and affection

---

4. The story of David and Jonathan is told in 1 Samuel 19 ff.
5. Naomi was the mother-in-law of Ruth, whom Ruth refused to leave when her husband died, telling her, "For whither thou goest, I will go; and where thou lodgest, I will lodge" (Ruth 1.16).

are reciprocal in a most equal and sweet kind of commerce. Secondly, in regard of the pleasure and content that the exercise of love carries with it, as we may see in the natural body. The mouth is at all the pains to receive and mince the food which serves for the nourishment of all the other parts of the body, yet it hath no cause to complain; for first the other parts send back by several passages a due proportion of the same nourishment, in a better form for the strengthening and comforting the mouth. Secondly, the labor of the mouth is accompanied with such pleasure and content as far exceeds the pains it takes. So is it in all the labor of love among Christians. The party loving, reaps love again, as was showed before, which the soul covets more than all the wealth in the world. Thirdly: Nothing yields more pleasure and content to the soul than when it finds that which it may love fervently, for to love and live beloved is the soul's paradise, both here and in heaven. In the state of wedlock there be many comforts to bear out the troubles of that condition; but let such as have tried the most, say if there be any sweetness in that condition comparable to the exercise of mutual love.

From former considerations arise these conclusions.

First: This love among Christians is a real thing, not imaginary.

Secondly: This love is as absolutely necessary to the being of the body of Christ, as the sinews and other ligaments of a natural body are to the being of that body.

Thirdly: This love is a divine, spiritual nature free, active, strong, courageous, permanent; undervaluing all things beneath its proper object; and of all the graces, this makes us nearer to resemble the virtues of our Heavenly Father.

Fourthly: It rests in the love and welfare of its beloved. For the full and certain knowledge of these truths concerning the nature, use, and excellency of this grace, that which the Holy Ghost hath left recorded, 1 Corinthians: 13, may give full satisfaction, which is needful for every true member of this lovely body of the Lord Jesus, to work upon their hearts by prayer, meditation, continual exercise at least of the special [influence] of His grace, till Christ be formed in them and they in Him, all in each other, knit together by this bond of love.

II

It rests now to make some application of this discourse by the present design, which gave the occasion of writing of it. Herein are four things to be propounded: first the persons, secondly the work, thirdly the end, fourthly the means.

First, For the persons. We are a company professing ourselves fellow members of Christ, in which respect only though we were absent from each other many miles, and had our employments as far distant, yet we ought to account ourselves knit together by this bond of love, and live in the exercise of it, if we would have comfort of our being in Christ. This was notorious in the practice of the Christians in former times; as is testified of the Waldenses,[6] from the mouth of one of the adversaries *Æneas Sylvius*[7] "mutuo [ament] penè

6. The Waldenses took their name from Pater Valdes, an early French reformer of the church. They still survive as a religious community.
7. *Solent amare* is a closer approximation of the

Latin than Morison's suggestion of *ameni*. Aeneas Sylvius Piccolomini (1405–1464), Pope Pius II, was a historian and scholar.

antequam norunt," they used to love any of their own religion even before they were acquainted with them.

Secondly, for the work we have in hand. It is by a mutual consent, through a special overvaluing providence and a more than an ordinary approbation of the Churches of Christ, to seek out a place of cohabitation and consortship under a due form of government both civil and ecclesiastical. In such cases as this, the care of the public must oversway all private respects, by which, not only conscience, but mere civil policy, doth bind us. For it is a true rule that particular estates cannot subsist in the ruin of the public.

Thirdly. The end is to improve our lives to do more service to the Lord; the comfort and increase of the body of Christ whereof we are members; that ourselves and posterity may be the better preserved from the common corruptions of this evil world, to serve the Lord and work out our salvation under the power and purity of His holy ordinances.

Fourthly, for the means whereby this must be effected. They are twofold, a conformity with the work and end we aim at. These we see are extraordinary, therefore we must not content ourselves with usual ordinary means. Whatsoever we did or ought to have done when we lived in England, the same must we do, and more also, where we go. That which the most in their churches maintain as a truth in profession only, we must bring into familiar and constant practice, as in this duty of love. We must love brotherly without dissimulation; we must love one another with a pure heart fervently. We must bear one another's burthens. We must not look only on our own things, but also on the things of our brethren, neither must we think that the Lord will bear with such failings at our hands as he doth from those among whom we have lived; and that for three reasons.

First, In regard of the more near bond of marriage between Him and us, where-in He hath taken us to be His after a most strict and peculiar manner, which will make Him the more jealous of our love and obedience. So He tells the people of Israel, you only have I known of all the families of the earth, therefore will I punish you for your transgressions. Secondly, because the Lord will be sanctified in them that come near Him. We know that there were many that corrupted the service of the Lord, some setting up altars before His own, others offering both strange fire and strange sacrifices also; yet there came no fire from heaven or other sudden judgment upon them, as did upon Nadab and Abihu,[8] who yet we may think did not sin presumptuously. Thirdly. When God gives a special commission He looks to have it strictly observed in every article. When He gave Saul a commission to destroy Amaleck, He indented with him upon certain articles,[9] and because he failed in one of the least, and that upon a fair pretense, it lost him the kingdom which should have been his reward if he had observed his commission.

Thus stands the cause between God and us. We are entered into covenant[1] with Him for this work. We have taken out a commission, the Lord

8. "And Nadab and Abihu, the sons of Aaron, took either of them his censer, and put fire therein, and put incense thereon, and offered strange fire before the Lord, which he commanded them not. And there went out fire from the Lord, and devoured them, and they died before the Lord" (Leviticus 10.1–2). Winthrop's point is that the chosen people are often punished more severely than unbelievers.
9. I.e., made an agreement with him on parts of a contract or agreement. Saul was instructed to destroy the Amalekites and all that they possessed, but he spared their sheep and oxen, and in doing so disobeyed the Lord's commandment and was rejected as king (1 Samuel 15.1–34).
1. A legal contract. The Israelites entered into a covenant with God in which he promised to protect them if they kept his word and were faithful to him.

hath given us leave to draw our own articles. We have professed to enterprise these actions, upon these and those ends, we have hereupon besought Him of favor and blessing. Now if the Lord shall please to hear us, and bring us in peace to the place we desire, then hath He ratified this covenant and sealed our commission, [and] will expect a strict performance of the articles contained in it; but if we shall neglect the observation of these articles which are the ends we have propounded, and, dissembling with our God, shall fall to embrace this present world and prosecute our carnal intentions, seeking great things for ourselves and our posterity, the Lord will surely break out in wrath against us; be revenged of such a perjured people and make us know the price of the breach of such a covenant.

Now the only way to avoid this shipwreck, and to provide for our posterity, is to follow the counsel of Micah,[2] to do justly, to love mercy, to walk humbly with our God. For this end, we must be knit together in this work as one man. We must entertain each other in brotherly affection, we must be willing to abridge ourselves of our superfluities, for the supply of other's necessities. We must uphold a familiar commerce together in all meekness, gentleness, patience and liberality. We must delight in each other, make other's conditions our own, rejoice together, mourn together, labor and suffer together, always having before our eyes our commission and community in the work, our community as members of the same body. So shall we keep the unity of the spirit in the bond of peace. The Lord will be our God, and delight to dwell among us as His own people, and will command a blessing upon us in all our ways, so that we shall see much more of His wisdom, power, goodness and truth, than formerly we have been acquainted with. We shall find that the God of Israel is among us, when ten of us shall be able to resist a thousand of our enemies; when He shall make us a praise and glory that men shall say of succeeding plantations, "the Lord make it like that of NEW ENGLAND." For we must consider that we shall be as a city upon a hill.[3] The eyes of all people are upon us, so that if we shall deal falsely with our God in this work we have undertaken, and so cause Him to withdraw His present help from us, we shall be made a story and a by-word through the world. We shall open the mouths of enemies to speak evil of the ways of God, and all professors for God's sake. We shall shame the faces of many of God's worthy servants, and cause their prayers to be turned into curses upon us till we be consumed out of the good land whither we are agoing.

And to shut up this discourse with that exhortation of Moses, that faithful servant of the Lord, in his last farewell to Israel, Deuteronomy 30.[4] Beloved, there is now set before us life and good, death and evil, in that we are commanded this day to love the Lord our God, and to love one another, to walk

---

2. An 8th-century-B.C.E. prophet whose words are presented in the Book of Micah. Micah speaks continually of the judgment of God on his people and the necessity to hope for salvation: "I will bear the indignation of the Lord, because I have sinned against him, until he plead my cause, and execute judgment for me: he will bring me forth to the light, and I shall behold his righteousness" (Micah 7.9).

3. "Ye are the light of the world. A city that is set on a hill cannot be hid. Neither do men light a candle, and put it under a bushel, but on a candlestick; and it giveth light unto all that are in the house" (Matthew 5.14–15).

4. "And it shall come to pass, when all these things are come upon thee, the blessing and the curse, which I have set before thee, and thou shalt call them to mind among all the nations, whither the Lord thy God hath driven thee, and shalt return unto the Lord thy God, and shalt obey his voice according to all that I command thee this day, thou and thy children, with all thine heart, and with all thy soul; That then the Lord thy God will turn thy captivity, and have compassion upon thee, and will return and gather thee from all the nations, whither the Lord thy God hath scattered thee" (Deuteronomy 30.1–3).

in His ways and to keep His commandments and His ordinance and His laws, and the articles of our covenant with Him, that we may live and be multiplied, and that our Lord our God may bless us in the land whither we go to possess it. But if our hearts shall turn away, so that we will not obey, but shall be seduced, and worship other gods, our pleasures and profits, and serve them; it is propounded unto us this day, we shall surely perish out of the good land whither we pass over this vast sea to possess it.

Therefore let us choose life,
that we and our seed
may live by obeying His
voice and cleaving to Him,
for He is our life and
our prosperity.

1630   1838

ROGER WILLIAMS
c. 1603–1683

In his journal for January 1636, John Winthrop notes that when the governor of Massachusetts and his assistants met to reconsider the charge of divisiveness against Roger Williams, they agreed that they could not wait until spring to banish him from the commonwealth. They had to move immediately and ship him back to England. His opinions were dangerous and spreading. When they went to Salem to seize him and "carry him aboard the ship," however, they found he "had been gone 3 days before, but whither they could not learn." Williams had, of course, fled Massachusetts for Rhode Island. He found shelter there with the Narragansett Indians and, from that time until his death almost fifty years later, Williams and Providence Plantation were synonymous with the spirit of religious liberty. Rhode Island became a sanctuary for those who found the strictures of the Massachusetts Bay insufferable: Separatists, Baptists, Seekers, Antinomians, Jews, and Quakers all found a home there. In 1663 Rhode Island received a royal charter from Charles II in which freedom of conscience was guaranteed. It was something of which not even Englishmen were assured, and it became so indelibly "American" an idea that provision was made for it in our 1791 Bill of Rights.

Williams had infuriated and threatened the leaders of Massachusetts by taking four rather extreme positions, any one of which seriously undermined the theocracy that was at the heart of the Bay Colony government. He denied, first, that Massachusetts had a proper title to its land, arguing that King Charles I could not bestow a title to something that belonged to the Natives. Second, he argued that no unregenerate person could be required either to pray in churches or to swear on oath in a court of law; third, that Massachusetts Bay Colony ministers, who had persuaded the king of England when they left their native country that they wished to remain a part of the national church, should not only separate from the Church of England but repent that they had ever served it; last, that civil authority was limited to civil matters and that magistrates had no jurisdiction over the soul. Williams, as the historian Perry Miller has put it, wanted to "build a wall of separation between state and church not to prevent the state from becoming an instrument of 'priestcraft,' but in order to keep the holy and pure religion of Jesus Christ from contamination by the slightest taint of earthly support." It was a disturbing position to Separatist and non-Separatist alike, and Williams has the distinction of having made himself unwelcome in both Plymouth and Boston.

Williams and his wife, Mary, arrived in Boston aboard the ship *Lyon* in 1631. He had graduated from Cambridge University in 1627 and sometime before 1629 took holy orders and served as a chaplain to Sir William Masham at Otis in the county of Essex. It was there that Williams's interest in church reform developed. Years later he said that it was Archbishop Laud (who required an oath of loyalty to the Church of England from all clerics) who "pursued" him "out of this land." When, shortly after his arrival in America, he refused a call to the prestigious First Church of Boston because he "durst not officiate to an unseparated people," Massachusetts authorities must have had their first inkling of just how assured Williams was in matters of belief. It was in October 1635 that he was first accused of holding "new and dangerous opinions against the authority of magistrates."

The Massachusetts authorities did not cite Williams's attitude toward the American Indians in their charges against him, but in this regard as well, his position was antithetical to their own. From the beginning, he wrote, his "soul's desire was to do the natives good, and to that end to have their language." Although he was not interested in assimilating their culture, Williams nevertheless saw that the American Indians were no better or worse than the "rogues" who dealt with them, and that in fact they possessed a marked degree of civility. Williams must have known that when he prepared his *Key into the Language of America* (1634) his book would prove useful to those who wished to convert Native Americans to Christianity, but Williams was not primarily interested in the conversion of others. *Anyone* not regenerate (that is, "born again"), Williams argued, was outside the people of God, and to refer to the American Indians as "heathen" was "improperly sinful" and "unchristianly." Williams himself remained a Seeker and detached from the community of any church for most of his life. His great disappointment was that despite his efforts to befriend the Narragansetts, they joined their brothers in King Philip's War and burned the settlements at both Warwick and Providence. By the time Williams died, sometime between January and March of 1683, the question of the future role of the Narragansetts became moot. The great tribe would never recover from the losses incurred during that war.

From A Key into the Language of America[1]

To My Dear and Well-Beloved Friends and Countrymen, in Old and New England

I present you with a key; I have not heard of the like, yet framed, since it pleased God to bring that mighty continent of America to light. Others of my countrymen have often, and excellently, and lately written of the country (and none that I know beyond the goodness and worth of it).

This key, respects the native language of it, and happily may unlock some rarities concerning the natives themselves, not yet discovered.

I drew the materials in a rude lump at sea, as a private help to my own memory, that I might not, by my present absence, lightly lose what I had so dearly bought in some few years hardship, and charges among the barbarians. Yet being reminded by some, what pity it were to bury those materials

---

1. The text is from a reprint of the first edition (1643), published by the Rhode Island and Providence Tercentenary Committee (1936).

in my grave at land or sea; and withal, remembering how oft I have been importuned by worthy friends of all sorts, to afford them some helps this way. I resolved (by the assistance of The Most High) to cast those materials into this key, pleasant and profitable for all, but especially for my friends residing in those parts.

A little key may open a box, where lies a bunch of keys.

With this I have entered into the secrets of those countries, wherever English dwell about two hundred miles, between the French and Dutch plantations; for want of this, I know what gross mistakes myself and others have run into.

There is a mixture of this language north and south, from the place of my abode, about six hundred miles; yet within the two hundred miles (afore-mentioned) their dialects do exceedingly differ; yet not so, but (within that compass) a man may, by this help, converse with thousands of natives all over the country: and by such converse it may please the Father of Mercies to spread civility, (and in His own most holy season) Christianity. For one candle will light ten thousand, and it may please God to bless a little leaven to season the mighty lump of those peoples and territories.

It is expected, that having had so much converse with these natives, I should write some little of them.

Concerning them (a little to gratify expectation) I shall touch upon four heads:

First, by what names they are distinguished.

Secondly, their original[2] and descent.

Thirdly, their religion, manners, customs, etc.

Fourthly, that great point of their conversion.

To the first, their names are of two sorts:

First, those of the English giving: as natives, savages, Indians, wildmen (so the Dutch call them *wilden*), Abergeny[3] men, pagans, barbarians, heathen.

Secondly, their names which they give themselves.

I cannot observe that they ever had (before the coming of the English, French or Dutch amongst them) any names to difference themselves from strangers, for they knew none; but two sorts of names they had, and have amongst themselves:

First, general, belonging to all natives, as Nínnuock, Ninnimissinnûwock, Eniskeetompaûwog, which signifies Men, Folk, or People.

Secondly, particular names, peculiar to several nations, of them amongst themselves, as Nanhigganġuck, Massachusêuck, Cawasumsêuck, Cowwesġuck, Quintikóock, Qunnipiġuck, Pequttóog, etc.

They have often asked me, why we call them Indians, natives, etc. And understanding the reason, they will call themselves Indians, in opposition to English, etc.

For the second head proposed, their original and descent:

From Adam and Noah[4] that they spring, it is granted on all hands.

But for their later descent, and whence they came into those parts, it seems as hard to find, as to find the wellhead of some fresh stream, which running many miles out of the country to the salt ocean, hath met with many mixing streams by the way. They say themselves, that they have sprung and grown up in that very place, like the very trees of the wilderness.

2. Place of origin.
3. Aboriginal.

4. After the great flood described in the Bible only Noah and his family remain.

They say that their great god Kautántowwìt created those parts, as I observed in the chapter of their religion. They have no clothes, books, nor letters, and conceive their fathers never had; and therefore they are easily persuaded that the God that made Englishmen is a greater God, because He hath so richly endowed the English above themselves. But when they hear that about sixteen hundred years ago, England and the inhabitants thereof were like unto themselves, and since have received from God, clothes, books, etc. they are greatly affected with a secret hope concerning themselves.

Wise and judicious men, with whom I have discoursed, maintain their original to be northward from Tartaria:[5] and at my now taking ship, at the Dutch plantation, it pleased the Dutch Governor, (in some discourse with me about the natives), to draw their line from Iceland, because the name Sackmakan (the name for an Indian prince, about the Dutch) is the name for a prince in Iceland.

Other opinions I could number up: under favor I shall present (not mine opinion, but) my observations to the judgment of the wise.

First, others (and myself) have conceived some of their words to hold affinity with the Hebrew.

Secondly, they constantly anoint their heads as the Jews did.

Thirdly, they give dowries for their wives, as the Jews did.

Fourthly (and which I have not so observed amongst other nations as amongst the Jews, and these:) they constantly separate their women (during the time of their monthly sickness) in a little house alone by themselves four or five days, and hold it an irreligious thing for either father or husband or any male to come near them.

They have often asked me if it be so with women of other nations, and whether they are so separated: and for their practice they plead nature and tradition. Yet again I have found a greater affinity of their language with the Greek tongue.

2. As the Greeks and other nations, and ourselves call the seven stars (or Charles' Wain, the Bear,)[6] so do they Mosk or Paukunnawaw, the Bear.

3. They have many strange relations of one Wétucks, a man that wrought great miracles amongst them, and walking upon the waters, etc., with some kind of broken resemblance to the Son of God.

Lastly, it is famous that the Sowwest (Sowaniu) is the great subject of their discourse. From thence their traditions. There they say (at the southwest) is the court of their great god Kautántowwìt: at the southwest are their forefathers' souls: to the southwest they go themselves when they die; from the southwest came their corn, and beans out of their great god Kautántowwìt's field: and indeed the further northward and westward from us their corn will not grow, but to the southward better and better. I dare not conjecture in these uncertainties. I believe they are lost, and yet hope (in the Lord's holy season) some of the wildest of them shall be found to share in the blood of the Son of God. To the third head, concerning their religion, customs, manners etc. I shall here say nothing, because in those 32 chapters of the whole book,[7] I have briefly touched those of all sorts, from their birth to their burials, and have endeavored (as the nature of the work would give way) to bring some short observations and applications home to Europe from America.

---

5. Mongolia.
6. I.e., the constellation known as Ursa Major (Great Bear), the Big Dipper, or Charlemagne's wagon ("wain").
7. I.e., the thirty-two chapters of William's *Key*.

Therefore fourthly, to that great point of their conversion, so much to be longed for, and by all New-English so much pretended,[8] and I hope in truth.

For myself I have uprightly labored to suit my endeavors to my pretenses: and of later times (out of desire to attain their language) I have run through varieties of intercourses[9] with them day and night, summer and winter, by land and sea, particular passages tending to this, I have related divers, in the chapter of their religion.

Many solemn discourses I have had with all sorts of nations of them, from one end of the country to another (so far as opportunity, and the little language I have could reach).

I know there is no small preparation in the hearts of multitudes of them. I know their many solemn confessions to myself, and one to another of their lost wandering conditions.

I know strong convictions upon the consciences of many of them, and their desires uttered that way.

I know not with how little knowledge and grace of Christ the Lord may save, and therefore, neither will despair, nor report much.

But since it hath pleased some of my worthy countrymen to mention (of late in print) Wequash, the Péquot captain, I shall be bold so far to second their relations, as to relate mine own hopes of him (though I dare not be so confident as others).

Two days before his death, as I passed up to Qunníhticut[1] River, it pleased my worthy friend Mr. Fenwick, (whom I visited at his house in Saybrook Fort at the mouth of that river,) to tell me that my old friend Wequash lay very sick. I desired to see him, and himself was pleased to be my guide two miles where Wequash lay.

Amongst other discourse concerning his sickness and death (in which he freely bequeathed his son to Mr. Fenwick) I closed[2] with him concerning his soul: he told me that some two or three years before he had lodged at my house, where I acquainted him with the condition of all mankind, & his own in particular; how God created man and all things; how man fell from God, and of his present enmity against God, and the wrath of God against him until repentance. Said he, "your words were never out of my heart to this present;" and said he "me much pray to Jesus Christ." I told him so did many English, French, and Dutch, who had never turned to God, nor loved Him. He replied in broken English: "Me so big naughty heart, me heart all one stone!" Savory expressions using to breathe from compunct and broken hearts, and a sense of inward hardness and unbrokenness. I had many discourses with him in his life, but this was the sum of our last parting until our General Meeting.[3]

Now, because this is the great inquiry of all men: what Indians have been converted? what have the English done in those parts? what hopes of the Indians receiving the knowledge of Christ?

And because to this question, some put an edge from the boast of the Jesuits in Canada and Maryland, and especially from the wonderful conversions made by the Spaniards and Portugals in the West-Indies, besides what I have here written, as also, beside what I have observed in the chapter of their reli-

8. Asserted, proffered (with none of the modern connotations of deceit).
9. Conversations.

1. Connecticut.
2. Came to the end of his talk.
3. I.e., Judgment Day.

gion, I shall further present you with a brief additional discourse concerning this great point, being comfortably persuaded that that Father of Spirits, who was graciously pleased to persuade Japhet (the Gentiles) to dwell in the tents of Shem[4] (the Jews), will, in His holy season (I hope approaching), persuade these Gentiles of America to partake of the mercies of Europe, and then shall be fulfilled what is written by the prophet Malachi,[5] from the rising of the sun (in Europe) to the going down of the same (in America), My name shall be great among the Gentiles. So I desire to shope and pray,

Your unworthy countryman,
ROGER WILLIAMS

From The Bloody Tenet of Persecution, for Cause of Conscience, in a Conference between Truth and Peace[1]

To every Courteous Reader.

While I plead the cause of *truth* and *innocency* against the bloody *doctrine* of *persecution* for cause of *conscience,* I judge it not unfit to give *alarm* to myself, and all men to prepare to be *persecuted* or hunted for cause of *conscience.*

Whether thou standest charged with ten or but two talents,[2] if thou huntest any for cause of *conscience,* how canst thou say thou followest the *Lamb of God* who so abhorred that practice?

If Paul, if Jesus Christ, were present here at London, and the question were proposed what religion would they approve of: the Papists, Prelatists,[3] Presbyterians, Independents, etc. would each say, "Of mine, of mine."

But put the second question, if one of the several sorts should by major vote attain the sword of steel: what weapons doth Christ Jesus authorize them to fight with in His cause? Do not all men hate the persecutor, and every conscience true or false complain of cruelty, tyranny? etc.

Two mountains of crying guilt lie heavy upon the backs of all that name the name of Christ in the eyes of Jews, Turks, and Pagans.

First, the blasphemies of their idolatrous inventions, superstitions, and most unchristian conversations.

Secondly, the bloody, irreligious and inhumane oppressions and destructions under the mask or veil of the name of Christ, etc.

O how like is the jealous Jehovah, the consuming fire to end these present slaughters in a greater slaughter of the holy witnesses? Revelation 11.

Six years preaching of so much truth of Christ (as that time afforded in King Edward's days) kindles the flames of Queen Mary's bloody persecutions.[4]

---

4. Japhet was the third son of Noah and, in some traditions, the progenitor of the Indo-European race (see Genesis 9.18).
5. "For from the rising of the sun even unto the going down of the same my name shall be great among the Gentiles" (Malachi 1.11).
1. The text is from *The Writings of Roger Williams,* vol. 3 (1866–74). Williams wrote this tract while in London attempting to get a patent for Providence Plantation. It is one of a series of

tracts in which Williams debated John Cotton on the question of freedom of conscience. Neither the author's name nor the publisher appeared on the title page, and copies were burned by order of Parliament because of its democratic implications.
2. Individuals.
3. Episcopalians.
4. Many Protestants were burned at the stake during the reign of Queen Mary, 1553–58. Edward VI was King from 1547 to 1553.

Who can now but expect that after so many scores of years preaching and professing of more truth, and amongst so many great contentions amongst the very best of Protestants, a fiery furnace should be heat, and who sees not now the fires kindling?

I confess I have little hopes till those flames are over, that this discourse against the doctrine of persecution for cause of conscience should pass current (I say not amongst the wolves and lions, but even amongst the sheep of Christ themselves) yet *liberavi animam meam*,[5] I have not hid within my breast my soul's belief; and although sleeping on the bed either of the pleasures or profits of sin thou thinkest thy conscience bound to smite at him that dares to waken thee? Yet in the midst of all these civil and spiritual wars[6] I hope we shall agree in these particulars.

First, however, the proud (upon the advantage of an higher earth or ground) overlook the poor and cry out schismatics, heretics, etc. shall blasphemers and seducers escape unpunished, etc. Yet there is a sorer punishment in the Gospel for despising of Christ than Moses, even when the despiser of Moses was put to death without mercy, Hebrews 10.28–29. "He that believeth not shall be damned," Mark 16.16.

Secondly, whatever worship, ministry, ministration, the best and purest are practiced without faith and true persuasion that they are the true institutions of God, they are sin, sinful worships, ministries, etc. And however in civil things we may be servants unto men, yet in divine and spiritual things the poorest peasant must disdain the service of the highest prince: "Be ye not the servants of men," I Corinthians 14.

Thirdly, without search and trial no man attains this faith and right persuasion, I Thessalonians 5. "Try all things."

In vain have English Parliaments permitted English Bibles in the poorest English houses, and the simplest man or woman to search the Scriptures, if yet against their soul's persuasion from the Scripture, they should be forced (as if they lived in Spain or Rome itself without the sight of a Bible) to believe as the Church believes.

Fourthly, having tried, we must hold fast, I Thessalonians 5, upon the loss of a crown, Revelation 13, we must not let go for all the flea bitings of the present afflictions, etc. having bought truth dear, we must not sell it cheap, not the least grain of it for the whole world, no not for the saving of souls, though our own most precious; least of all for the bitter sweetening of a little vanishing pleasure.

For a little puff of credit and reputation from the changeable breath of uncertain sons of men.

For the broken bags of riches on eagles' wings: For a dream of these, any or all of these which on our deathbed vanish and leave tormenting stings behind them: Oh, how much better is it from the love of truth, from the love of the Father of Lights, from whence it comes, from the love of the Son of God, who is the way and the truth, to say as He, John 18.37: "For this end was I born, and for this end came I into the world that I might bear witness to the truth."

1643–44   1644

A Letter to the Town of Providence[1]

That ever I should speak or write a tittle,[2] that tends to such an infinite liberty of conscience, is a mistake, and which I have ever disclaimed and abhorred. To prevent such mistakes, I shall at present only propose this case: There goes many a ship to sea, with many hundred souls in one ship, whose weal and woe is common, and is a true picture of a commonwealth, or a human combination or society. It hath fallen out sometimes, that both Papists and Protestants, Jews and Turks, may be embarked in one ship; upon which supposal I affirm, that all the liberty of conscience, that ever I pleaded for, turns upon these two hinges—that none of the Papists, Protestants, Jews, or Turks be forced to come to the ship's prayers or worship, nor compelled from their own particular prayers or worship, if they practice any. I further add, that I never denied, that notwithstanding this liberty, the commander of this ship ought to command the ship's course, yea, and also command that justice, peace, and sobriety be kept and practiced, both among the seamen and all the passengers. If any of the seamen refuse to perform their services, or passengers to pay their freight; if any refuse to help, in person or purse, towards the common charges or defense; if any refuse to obey the common laws and orders of the ship, concerning their common peace or preservation; if any shall mutiny and rise up against their commanders and officers; if any should preach or write that there ought to be no commanders or officers, because all are equal in Christ, therefore no masters nor officers, no laws nor orders, nor corrections nor punishments; I say, I never denied, but in such cases, whatever is pretended, the commander or commanders may judge, resist, compel, and punish such transgressors, according to their deserts and merits. This if seriously and honestly minded, may, if it so please the Father of Lights, let in some light to such as willingly shut not their eyes.

I remain studious of your common peace and liberty.

Roger Williams

1655   1874

---

1. The text is from *The Writings of Roger Williams,* vol. 6 (1866–74). Williams wrote this letter after his return to Providence from England in 1654 in hopes of settling a controversy that divided the town over the question of religious autonomy and civil restraint.
2. I.e., write even as much as a dot, the smallest part.

ANNE BRADSTREET
c. 1612–1672

Anne Bradstreet's father, Thomas Dudley, was the manager of the country estate of the Puritan Earl of Lincoln, and his daughter was very much the apple of his eye. He took great care to see that she received an education superior to that of most young women of the time. When she was only sixteen she married the young Simon Bradstreet, a recent graduate of Cambridge University, who was associated with her father in conducting the affairs of the earl of Lincoln's estate. He also shared her father's Puritan beliefs. A year after the marriage her husband was appointed to assist in the preparations of the Massachusetts Bay Company, and the following year the Bradstreets and the Dudleys sailed with Winthrop's fleet. Bradstreet tells us that when she first "came into this country" she "found a new world and new manners," at which her "heart rose" in resistance. "But after I was convinced it was the way of God, I submitted to it and joined the church at Boston."

We know very little of Bradstreet's daily life, except that it was a hard existence. The wilderness, Samuel Eliot Morison once observed, "made men stern and silent, children unruly, servants insolent." William Bradford's wife, Dorothy, staring at the barren dunes of Cape Cod, is said to have chosen the certainty of drowning over the unknown life ashore. Added to the hardship of daily living was the fact that Bradstreet was never very strong. She had rheumatic fever as a child and as a result suffered recurrent periods of severe fatigue; nevertheless, she risked death by childbirth eight times. Her husband was secretary to the company and later governor of the Bay Colony, was always involved in the colony's diplomatic missions, and in 1661 went to England to renegotiate the Bay Company charter with Charles II. Simon's tasks must have added to her responsibilities at home. And like any good Puritan she added to the care of daily life the examination of her conscience. She tells us in one of the "Meditations" written for her children that she was troubled many times about the truth of the Scriptures, that she never saw any convincing miracles, and that she always wondered if those of which she read "were feigned." What proved to her finally that God exists was not her reading but the evidence of her own eyes. She is the first in a long line of American poets who took their consolation not from theology but from the "wondrous works," as she wrote, "that I see, the vast frame of the heaven and the earth, the order of all things, night and day, summer and winter, spring and autumn, the daily providing for this great household upon the earth, the preserving and directing of all to its proper end."

When Bradstreet was a young girl she had written poems to please her father, and he made much of their reading them together. After her marriage she continued writing. Quite unknown to her, her brother-in-law, John Woodbridge, pastor of the Andover church, brought with him to London a manuscript collection of her poetry and had it printed there in 1650. *The Tenth Muse* was the first published volume of poems written by a resident of America and was widely read. The Reverend Edward Taylor, also a poet and living in the frontier community of Westfield, Massachusetts, had a copy of the second edition of Bradstreet's poems (1678) in his library. Although she herself probably took greatest pride in her long meditative poems on the ages of humankind and on the seasons, the poems that have attracted present-day readers are the more intimate ones, which reflect her concern for her family and home and the pleasures she took in everyday life rather than in anticipation of the life to come.

The text is the *Works of Anne Bradstreet*, edited by Jeannine Hensley (1967).

The Prologue

1

To sing of wars, of captains, and of kings,
Of cities founded, commonwealths begun,
For my mean[1] pen are too superior things:
Or how they all, or each their dates have run
Let poets and historians set these forth,   5
My obscure lines shall not so dim their worth.

2

But when my wond'ring eyes and envious heart
Great Bartas'[2] sugared lines do but read o'er,
Fool I do grudge the Muses[3] did not part
'Twixt him and me that overfluent store;   10
A Bartas can do what a Bartas will
But simple I according to my skill.

3

From schoolboy's tongue no rhet'ric we expect,
Nor yet a sweet consort[4] from broken strings,
Nor perfect beauty where's a main defect: 15
My foolish, broken, blemished Muse so sings,
And this to mend, alas, no art is able,
'Cause nature made it so irreparable.

4

Nor can I, like that fluent sweet tongued Greek,
Who lisped at first, in future times speak plain.[5]   20
By art he gladly found what he did seek,
A full requital of his striving pain.
Art can do much, but this maxim's most sure:
A weak or wounded brain admits no cure.

5

I am obnoxious to each carping tongue   25
Who says my hand a needle better fits,
A poet's pen all scorn I should thus wrong,
For such despite they cast on female wits:
If what I do prove well, it won't advance,
They'll say it's stol'n, or else it was by chance.   30

1. Humble.
2. Guillaume du Bartas (1544–1590), a French writer much admired by the Puritans. He was most famous as the author of *The Divine Weeks,* an epic poem translated by Joshua Sylvester and intended to recount the great moments in Christian history.
3. In Greek mythology, the nine goddesses of the arts and sciences. "Fool": i.e., like a fool.
4. Accord, harmony of sound.
5. The Greek orator Demosthenes (c. 383–322 B.C.E.) conquered a speech defect.

6

But sure the antique Greeks were far more mild
Else of our sex, why feigned they those nine
And poesy made Calliope's[6] own child;
So 'mongst the rest they placed the arts divine:
But this weak knot they will full soon untie.   35
The Greeks did nought, but play the fools and lie.

7

Let Greeks be Greeks, and women what they are;
Men have precedency and still excel,
It is but vain unjustly to wage war;
Men can do best, and women know it well   40
Preeminence in all and each is yours;
Yet grant some small acknowledgment of ours.

8

And oh ye high flown quills[7] that soar the skies,
And ever with your prey still catch your praise,
If e'er you deign these lowly lines your eyes   45
Give thyme or parsley wreath, I ask no bays;[8]
This mean and unrefined ore of mine
Will make your glist'ring gold but more to shine.

                                                               1650

Contemplations

1

Some time now past in the autumnal tide,
When Phoebus[1] wanted but one hour to bed,
The trees all richly clad, yet void of pride,
Were gilded o'er by his rich golden head.
Their leaves and fruits seemed painted, but was true,   5
Of green, of red, of yellow, mixed hue;
Rapt were my senses at this delectable view.

2

I wist[2] not what to wish, yet sure thought I,
If so much excellence abide below,
How excellent is He that dwells on high,   10
Whose power and beauty by His works we know?
Sure He is goodness, wisdom, glory, light,

---

6. The muse of epic poetry.
7. Pens.
8. Garlands of laurel, used to crown a poet.

1. Apollo, the sun god.
2. Know.

That hath this under world so richly dight;[3]
More heaven than earth was here, no winter and no night.

3

Then on a stately oak I cast mine eye,   15
Whose ruffling top the clouds seemed to aspire;
How long since thou wast in thine infancy?
Thy strength, and stature, more thy years admire,
Hath hundred winters past since thou wast born?
Or thousand since thou brakest thy shell of horn?   20
If so, all these as nought, eternity doth scorn.

4

Then higher on the glistering Sun I gazed,
Whose beams was shaded by the leafy tree;
The more I looked, the more I grew amazed,
And softly said, "What glory's like to thee?"   25
Soul of this world, this universe's eye,
No wonder some made thee a deity;
Had I not better known, alas, the same had I.

5

Thou as a bridegroom from thy chamber rushes,
And as a strong man, joys to run a race;[4]   30
The morn doth usher thee with smiles and blushes;
The Earth reflects her glances in thy face.
Birds, insects, animals with vegative,
Thy heat from death and dullness doth revive,
And in the darksome womb of fruitful nature dive.   35

6

Thy swift annual and diurnal course,
Thy daily straight and yearly oblique path,
Thy pleasing fervor and thy scorching force,
All mortals here the feeling knowledge hath.
Thy presence makes it day, thy absence night,   40
Quaternal seasons caratuséd by thy might:
Hail creature, full of sweetness, beauty, and delight.

7

Art thou so full of glory that no eye
Hath strength thy shining rays once to behold?
And is thy splendid throne erect so high,   45
As to approach it, can no earthly mold?
How full of glory then must thy Creator be,

---

3. Furnished, adorned.
4. The sun "is as a bridegroom coming out of his   chamber, and rejoiceth as a strong man to run a
race" (Psalm 19.5).

Who gave this bright light luster unto thee?
Admired, adored for ever, be that Majesty.

8

Silent alone, where none or[5] saw, or heard,   50
In pathless paths I lead my wand'ring feet,
My humble eyes to lofty skies I reared
To sing some song, my mazéd[6] Muse thought meet.
My great Creator I would magnify,
That nature had thus decked liberally;   55
But Ah, and Ah, again, my imbecility!

9

I heard the merry grasshopper then sing.
The black-clad cricket bear a second part;
They kept one tune and played on the same string,
Seeming to glory in their little art.   60
Shall creatures abject thus their voices raise
And in their kind resound their Maker's praise
Whilst I, as mute, can warble forth no higher lays?

10

When present times look back to ages past,
And men in being fancy those[7] are dead,   65
It makes things gone perpetually to last,
And calls back months and years that long since fled.
It makes a man more aged in conceit[8]
Than was Methuselah,[9] or's grandsire great,
While of their persons and their acts his mind doth treat.   70

11

Sometimes in Eden fair he seems to be,
Sees glorious Adam there made lord of all,
Fancies the apple, dangle on the tree,
That turned his sovereign to a naked thrall.[1]
Who like a miscreant's driven from that place,   75
To get his bread with pain and sweat of face,
A penalty imposed on his backsliding race.

12

Here sits our grandame in retired place,
And in her lap her bloody Cain new-born;
The weeping imp oft looks her in the face,   80
Bewails his unknown hap[2] and fate forlorn;
His mother sighs to think of Paradise,

---

5. Either.
6. Amazed.
7. I.e., those who.
8. Apprehension, the processes of thought.

9. Thought to have lived 969 years (Genesis 5.27).
1. Slave.
2. Fortune, circumstances.

And how she lost her bliss to be more wise,
Believing him that was, and is, father of lies.[3]

13

Here Cain and Abel come to sacrifice,   85
Fruits of the earth and fatlings[4] each do bring.
On Abel's gift the fire descends from skies,
But no such sign on false Cain's offering;
With sullen hateful looks he goes his ways,
Hath thousand thoughts to end his brother's days,   90
Upon whose blood his future good he hopes to raise.

14

There Abel keeps his sheep, no ill he thinks;
His brother comes, then acts his fratricide:
The virgin Earth of blood her first draught drinks,
But since that time she often hath been cloyed.   95
The wretch with ghastly face and dreadful mind
Thinks each he sees will serve him in his kind,
Though none on earth but kindred near then could he find.

15

Who fancies not his looks now at the bar,
His face like death, his heart with horror fraught,   100
Nor malefactor ever felt like war,
When deep despair with wish of life hath fought,
Branded with guilt and crushed with treble woes,
A vagabond to Land of Nod[5] he goes.
A city builds, that walls might him secure from foes.   105

16

Who thinks not oft upon the father's ages,
Their long descent, how nephew's sons they saw,
The starry observations of those sages,
And how their precepts to their sons were law,
How Adam sighed to see his progeny,   110
Clothed all in his black sinful livery,
Who neither guilt nor yet the punishment could fly.

17

Our life compare we with their length of days
Who to the tenth of theirs doth now arrive?
And though thus short, we shorten many ways,   115
Living so little while we are alive;

---

3. By believing in the "father of lies," Eve lost
Paradise in her desire to gain wisdom (Genesis
3). Her elder son, Cain, slew his brother, Abel
(Genesis 4.8).

4. Animals fattened for slaughter.
5. An unidentified region east of Eden where
Cain dwelled after slaying Abel (Genesis 4.16).

In eating, drinking, sleeping, vain delight
So unawares comes on perpetual night,
And puts all pleasures vain unto eternal flight.

18

When I behold the heavens as in their prime,   120
And then the earth (though old) still clad in green,
The stones and trees, insensible of time,
Nor[6] age nor wrinkle on their front are seen;
If winter come and greenness then do fade,
A spring returns, and they more youthful made;   125
But man grows old, lies down, remains where once he's laid.

19

By birth more noble than those creatures all,
Yet seems by nature and by custom cursed,
No sooner born, but grief and care makes fall
That state obliterate he had at first;   130
Nor youth, nor strength, nor wisdom spring again,
Nor habitations long their names retain,
But in oblivion to the final day remain.

20

Shall I then praise the heavens, the trees, the earth
Because their beauty and their strength last longer?   135
Shall I wish there, or never to had birth,
Because they're bigger, and their bodies stronger?
Nay, they shall darken, perish, fade, and die,
And when unmade, so ever shall they lie,
But man was made for endless immortality.   140

21

Under the cooling shadow of a stately elm
Close sat I by a goodly river's side,
Where gliding streams the rocks did overwhelm,
A lonely place, with pleasures dignified.
I once that loved the shady woods so well,   145
Now thought the rivers did the trees excel,
And if the sun would ever shine, there would I dwell.

22

While on the stealing stream I fixt mine eye,
Which to the longed-for ocean held its course,
I marked, nor crooks, nor rubs,[7] that there did lie   150
Could hinder aught,[8] but still augment its force.
"O happy flood," quoth I, "that holds thy race

6. Neither   8. Anything.
7. Difficulties.

Till thou arrive at thy beloved place,
Nor is it rocks or shoals that can obstruct thy pace,

23

Nor is't enough, that thou alone mayst slide   155
But hundred brooks in thy clear waves do meet,
So hand in hand along with thee they glide
To Thetis' house,[9] where all embrace and greet.
Thou emblem true of what I count the best,
O could I lead my rivulets to rest,   160
So may we press to that vast mansion, ever blest."

24

Ye fish, which in this liquid region 'bide,
That for each season have your habitation,
Now salt, now fresh where you think best to glide
To unknown coasts to give a visitation,   165
In lakes and ponds you leave your numerous fry;
So nature taught, and yet you know not why,
You wat'ry folk that know not your felicity.

25

Look how the wantons frisk to taste the air,
Then to the colder bottom straight they dive;   170
Eftsoon to Neptune's[1] glassy hall repair
To see what trade they great ones there do drive,
Who forage o'er the spacious sea-green field,
And take the trembling prey before it yield,
Whose armor is their scales, their spreading fins their shield. 175

26

While musing thus with contemplation fed,
And thousand fancies buzzing in my brain,
The sweet-tongued Philomel[2] perched o'er my head
And chanted forth a most melodious strain
Which rapt me so with wonder and delight,   180
I judged my hearing better than my sight,
And wished me wings with her a while to take my flight.

27

"O merry Bird," said I, "that fears no snares,
That neither toils nor hoards up in thy barn,
Feels no sad thoughts nor cruciating[3] cares   185
To gain more good or shun what might thee harm.

---

9. I.e., the sea. Thetis, a sea nymph, was Achilles' mother.
1. Roman god of the ocean. "Eftsoon": soon afterward.
2. I.e., the nightingale. Philomela, the daughter

of King Attica, was transformed into a nightingale after her brother-in-law raped her and tore out her tongue.
3. I.e., excruciating, painful.

Thy clothes ne'er wear, thy meat is everywhere,
Thy bed a bough, thy drink the water clear,
Reminds not what is past, nor what's to come dost fear."

28

"The dawning morn with songs thou dost prevent,[4]   190
Sets hundred notes unto thy feathered crew,
So each one tunes his pretty instrument,
And warbling out the old, begin anew,
And thus they pass their youth in summer season,
Then follow thee into a better region,   195
Where winter's never felt by that sweet airy legion."

29

Man at the best a creature frail and vain,
In knowledge ignorant, in strength but weak,
Subject to sorrows, losses, sickness, pain,
Each storm his state, his mind, his body break,   200
From some of these he never finds cessation,
But day or night, within, without, vexation,
Troubles from foes, from friends, from dearest, near'st relation.

30

And yet this sinful creature, frail and vain,
This lump of wretchedness, of sin and sorrow,   205
This weatherbeaten vessel wracked with pain,
Joys not in hope of an eternal morrow;
Nor all his losses, crosses, and vexation,
In weight, in frequency and long duration
Can make him deeply groan for that divine translation.[5]   210

31

The mariner that on smooth waves doth glide
Sings merrily and steers his bark with ease,
As if he had command of wind and tide,
And now become great master of the seas:
But suddenly a storm spoils all the sport,   215
And makes him long for a more quiet port,
Which 'gainst all adverse winds may serve for fort.

32

So he that saileth in this world of pleasure,
Feeding on sweets, that never bit of th' sour,
That's full of friends, of honor, and of treasure,   220
Fond fool, he takes this earth ev'n for heav'n's bower.
But sad affliction comes and makes him see

4. Anticipate.   5. Transformation.

Here's neither honor, wealth, nor safety;
Only above is found all with security.

33

O Time the fatal wrack[6] of mortal things,   225
That draws oblivion's curtains over kings;
Their sumptuous monuments, men know them not,
Their names without a record are forgot,
Their parts, their ports, their pomp's[7] all laid in th' dust
Nor wit nor gold, nor buildings scape time's rust; 230
But he whose name is graved in the white stone[8]
Shall last and shine when all of these are gone.

               1678

The Author to Her Book[1]

Thou ill-formed offspring of my feeble brain,
Who after birth didst by my side remain,
Till snatched from thence by friends, less wise than true,
Who thee abroad, exposed to public view,
Made thee in rags, halting to th' press to trudge, 5
Where errors were not lessened (all may judge).
At thy return my blushing was not small,
My rambling brat (in print) should mother call,
I cast thee by as one unfit for light,
Thy visage was so irksome in my sight;   10
Yet being mine own, at length affection would
Thy blemishes amend, if so I could:
I washed thy face, but more defects I saw,
And rubbing off a spot still made a flaw.
I stretched thy joints to make thee even feet,[2] 15
Yet still thou run'st more hobbling than is meet;
In better dress to trim thee was my mind,
But nought save homespun cloth i' th' house I find.
In this array 'mongst vulgars[3] may'st thou roam.
In critic's hands beware thou dost not come,   20
And take thy way where yet thou art not known;
If for thy father asked, say thou hadst none;
And for thy mother, she alas is poor,
Which caused her thus to send thee out of door.

               1678

---

6. Destroyer.
7. Vanity. "Parts": features. "Ports": places of refuge.
8. "To him that overcometh will I give to eat of the hidden manna and will give him a white stone, and in the stone a new name written, which no man knoweth saving he that receiveth it" (Reve-lation 2.17). "Scape": Escape.
1. *The Tenth Muse* was published in 1650 with-out Bradstreet's knowledge. She is thought to have written this poem in 1666 when a 2nd edi-tion was contemplated.
2. I.e., metrical feet; thus to smooth out the lines.
3. The common people.

Before the Birth of One of Her Children

All things within this fading world hath end,
Adversity doth still our joys attend;
No ties so strong, no friends so dear and sweet,
But with death's parting blow is sure to meet.
The sentence past is most irrevocable, 5
A common thing, yet oh, inevitable.
How soon, my Dear, death may my steps attend,
How soon't may be thy lot to lose thy friend,
We both are ignorant, yet love bids me
These farewell lines to recommend to thee, 10
That when that knot's untied that made us one,
I may seem thine, who in effect am none.
And if I see not half my days that's due,
What nature would, God grant to yours and you;
The many faults that well you know I have 15
Let be interred in my oblivious grave;
If any worth or virtue were in me,
Let that live freshly in thy memory
And when thou feel'st no grief, as I no harms,
Yet love thy dead, who long lay in thine arms, 20
And when thy loss shall be repaid with gains
Look to my little babes, my dear remains.
And if thou love thyself, or loved'st me,
These O protect from stepdame's[1] injury.
And if chance to thine eyes shall bring this verse, 25
With some sad sighs honor my absent hearse;
And kiss this paper for thy love's dear sake,
Who with salt tears this last farewell did take.

1678

To My Dear and Loving Husband

If ever two were one, then surely we.
If ever man were loved by wife, then thee;
If ever wife was happy in a man,
Compare with me, ye women, if you can.
I prize thy love more than whole mines of gold 5
Or all the riches that the East doth hold.
My love is such that rivers cannot quench,
Nor ought but love from thee, give recompense.
Thy love is such I can no way repay,
The heavens reward thee manifold, I pray. 10
Then while we live, in love let's so persevere
That when we live no more, we may live ever.

1678

1. I.e., stepmother's.

A Letter to Her Husband, Absent upon Public Employment

My head, my heart, mine eyes, my life, nay, more,
My joy, my magazine[1] of earthly store,
If two be one, as surely thou and I,
How stayest thou there, whilst I at Ipswich[2] lie?
So many steps, head from the heart to sever,   5
If but a neck, soon should we be together.
I, like the Earth this season, mourn in black,
My Sun is gone so far in's zodiac,
Whom whilst I 'joyed, nor storms, nor frost I felt,
His warmth such frigid colds did cause to melt.   10
My chilled limbs now numbed lie forlorn;
Return, return, sweet Sol, from Capricorn;[3]
In this dead time, alas, what can I more
Than view those fruits which through thy heat I bore?
Which sweet contentment yield me for a space,   15
True living pictures of their father's face.
O strange effect! now thou art southward gone,
I weary grow the tedious day so long;
But when thou northward to me shalt return,
I wish my Sun may never set, but burn   20
Within the Cancer[4] of my glowing breast,
The welcome house of him my dearest guest.
Where ever, ever stay, and go not thence,
Till nature's sad decree shall call thee hence;
Flesh of thy flesh, bone of thy bone,   25
I here, thou there, yet both but one.

1678

In Memory of My Dear Grandchild Elizabeth Bradstreet, Who Deceased August, 1665, Being a Year and a Half Old

1

Farewell dear babe, my heart's too much content,
Farewell sweet babe, the pleasure of mine eye,
Farewell fair flower that for a space was lent,
Then ta'en away unto eternity.
Blest babe, why should I once bewail thy fate,   5
Or sigh thy days so soon were terminate,
Sith[1] thou art settled in an everlasting state.

---

1. Warehouse, storehouse.
2. Ipswich, Massachusetts, is north of Boston.
3. Capricorn, the tenth sign of the zodiac, represents winter. "Sol": sun.

4. Cancer, the fourth sign of the zodiac, represents summer.
1. Since.

2

By nature trees do rot when they are grown,
And plums and apples thoroughly ripe do fall,
And corn and grass are in their season mown, 10
And time brings down what is both strong and tall.
But plants new set to be eradicate,
And buds new blown to have so short a date,
Is by His hand alone that guides nature and fate.

1678

Here Follows Some Verses upon the Burning of Our House, July 10th, 1666

Copied Out of a Loose Paper

In silent night when rest I took
For sorrow near I did not look
I wakened was with thund'ring noise
And piteous shrieks of dreadful voice.
That fearful sound of "Fire!" and "Fire!" 5
Let no man know is my desire.
I, starting up, the light did spy,
And to my God my heart did cry
To strengthen me in my distress
And not to leave me succorless. 10
Then, coming out, beheld a space
The flame consume my dwelling place.
And when I could no longer look,
I blest His name that gave and took,[1]
That laid my goods now in the dust. 15
Yea, so it was, and so 'twas just.
It was His own, it was not mine,
Far be it that I should repine;
He might of all justly bereft
But yet sufficient for us left. 20
When by the ruins oft I past
My sorrowing eyes aside did cast,
And here and there the places spy
Where oft I sat and long did lie:
Here stood that trunk, and there that chest, 25
There lay that store I counted best.
My pleasant things in ashes lie,
And them behold no more shall I.
Under thy roof no guest shall sit,
Nor at thy table eat a bit. 30
No pleasant tale shall e'er be told,
Nor things recounted done of old.
No candle e'er shall shine in thee,

---

1. "The Lord gave, and the Lord hath taken away; blessed be the name of the Lord" (Job 1.21).

Nor bridegroom's voice e'er heard shall be.
In silence ever shall thou lie,   35
Adieu, Adieu, all's vanity.[2]
Then straight I 'gin my heart to chide,
And did thy wealth on earth abide?
Didst fix thy hope on mold'ring dust?
The arm of flesh didst make thy trust?   40
Raise up thy thoughts above the sky
That dunghill mists away may fly.
Thou hast an house on high erect,
Framed by that mighty Architect,
With glory richly furnished,   45
Stands permanent though this be fled.
It's purchaséd and paid for too
By Him who hath enough to do.
A price so vast as is unknown
Yet by His gift is made thine own;   50
There's wealth enough, I need no more,
Farewell, my pelf,[3] farewell my store.
The world no longer let me love,
My hope and treasure lies above.

1867

To My Dear Children

This book by any yet unread,
I leave for you when I am dead,
That being gone, here you may find
What was your living mother's mind.
Make use of what I leave in love,
And God shall bless you from above.
                                                    A. B.

My dear children,

   I, knowing by experience that the exhortations of parents take most
effect when the speakers leave to speak,[1] and those especially sink deepest
which are spoke latest, and being ignorant whether on my death bed I shall
have opportunity to speak to any of you, much less to all, thought it the
best, whilst I was able, to compose some short matters (for what else to call
them I know not) and bequeath to you, that when I am no more with you,
yet I may be daily in your remembrance (although that is the least in my
aim in what I now do), but that you may gain some spiritual advantage by
my experience. I have not studied in this you read to show my skill, but to
declare the truth, not to set forth myself, but the glory of God. If I had
minded the former, it had been perhaps better pleasing to you, but seeing
the last is the best, let it be best pleasing to you.

   The method I will observe shall be this: I will begin with God's dealing
with me from my childhood to this day.

2. Empty, worthless.   falsely gained.
3. Possessions, usually in the sense of being   1. I.e., stop speaking.

In my young years, about 6 or 7 as I take it, I began to make conscience of my ways, and what I knew was sinful, as lying, disobedience to parents, etc., I avoided it. If at any time I was overtaken with the like evils, it was as a great trouble, and I could not be at rest till by prayer I had confessed it unto God. I was also troubled at the neglect of private duties though too often tardy that way. I also found much comfort in reading the Scriptures, especially those places I thought most concerned my condition, and as I grew to have more understanding, so the more solace I took in them.

In a long fit of sickness which I had on my bed I often communed with my heart and made my supplication to the most High who set me free from that affliction.

But as I grew up to be about 14 or 15, I found my heart more carnal,[2] and sitting loose from God, vanity and the follies of youth take hold of me.

About 16, the Lord laid His hand sore upon me and smote me with the smallpox. When I was in my affliction, I besought the Lord and confessed my pride and vanity, and He was entreated of me and again restored me. But I rendered not to Him according to the benefit received.

After a short time I changed my condition and was married, and came into this country, where I found a new world and new manners, at which my heart rose. But after I was convinced it was the way of God, I submitted to it and joined to the church at Boston.

After some time I fell into a lingering sickness like a consumption together with a lameness, which correction I saw the Lord sent to humble and try me and do me good, and it was not altogether ineffectual.

It pleased God to keep me a long time without a child, which was a great grief to me and cost me many prayers and tears before I obtained one, and after him gave me many more of whom I now take the care, that as I have brought you into the world, and with great pains, weakness, cares, and fears brought you to this, I now travail[3] in birth again of you till Christ be formed in you.

Among all my experiences of God's gracious dealings with me, I have constantly observed this, that He hath never suffered me long to sit loose from Him, but by one affliction or other hath made me look home, and search what was amiss; so usually thus it hath been with me that I have no sooner felt my heart out of order, but I have expected correction for it, which most commonly hath been upon my own person in sickness, weakness, pains, sometimes on my soul, in doubts and fears of God's displeasure and my sincerity towards Him; sometimes He hath smote a child with a sickness, sometimes chastened by losses in estate,[4] and these times (through His great mercy) have been the times of my greatest getting and advantage; yea, I have found them the times when the Lord hath manifested the most love to me. Then have I gone to searching and have said with David, "Lord, search me and try me, see what ways of wickedness are in me, and lead me in the way everlasting,"[5] and seldom or never but I have found either some sin I lay under which God would have reformed, or some duty neglected which He would have performed, and by His help I have laid vows and bonds upon my soul to perform His righteous commands.

If at any time you are chastened of God, take it as thankfully and joyfully as in greatest mercies, for if ye be His, ye shall reap the greatest benefit by it.

---

2. I.e., worldly.
3. Toil, labor.
4. Financial losses.
5. Psalm 139.23–24.

It hath been no small support to me in times of darkness when the Almighty hath hid His face from me that yet I have had abundance of sweetness and refreshment after affliction and more circumspection[6] in my walking after I have been afflicted. I have been with God like an untoward child, that no longer than the rod has been on my back (or at least in sight) but I have been apt to forget Him and myself, too. Before I was afflicted, I went astray, but now I keep Thy statutes.[7]

I have had great experience of God's hearing my prayers and returning comfortable answers to me, either in granting the thing I prayed for, or else in satisfying my mind without it, and I have been confident it hath been from Him, because I have found my heart through His goodness enlarged in thankfulness to Him.

I have often been perplexed that I have not found that constant joy in my pilgrimage and refreshing which I supposed most of the servants of God have, although He hath not left me altogether without the witness of His holy spirit, who hath oft given me His word and set to His seal that it shall be well with me. I have sometimes tasted of that hidden manna that the world knows not, and have set up my Ebenezer,[8] and have resolved with myself that against such a promise, such tastes of sweetness, the gates of hell shall never prevail; yet have I many times sinkings and droopings, and not enjoyed that felicity that sometimes I have done. But when I have been in darkness and seen no light, yet have I desired to stay myself upon the Lord, and when I have been in sickness and pain, I have thought if the Lord would but lift up the light of His countenance upon me, although He ground me to powder, it would be but light to me; yea, oft have I thought were I in hell itself and could there find the love of God toward me, it would be a heaven. And could I have been in heaven without the love of God, it would have been a hell to me, for in truth it is the absence and presence of God that makes heaven or hell.

Many times hath Satan troubled me concerning the verity of the Scriptures, many times by atheism how I could know whether there was a God; I never saw any miracles to confirm me, and those which I read of, how did I know but they were feigned? That there is a God my reason would soon tell me by the wondrous works that I see, the vast frame of the heaven and the earth, the order of all things, night and day, summer and winter, spring and autumn, the daily providing for this great household upon the earth, the preserving and directing of all to its proper end. The consideration of these things would with amazement certainly resolve me that there is an Eternal Being. But how should I know He is such a God as I worship in Trinity, and such a Savior as I rely upon? Though this hath thousands of times been suggested to me, yet God hath helped me over. I have argued thus with myself. That there is a God, I see. If ever this God hath revealed himself, it must be in His word, and this must be it or none. Have I not found that operation by it that no human invention can work upon the soul, hath not judgments befallen divers who have scorned and contemned it, hath it not been preserved through all ages maugre[9] all the heathen tyrants and all of the enemies who have opposed it? Is there any story but that which shows the beginnings of times, and how the world came to be as we see? Do we not know the prophecies in

---

6. Prudence.
7. Psalm 119.8.
8. In 1 Samuel 7.12, a stone monument to commemorate a victory over the Philistines. "Manna":

the "bread from heaven" (Exodus 16.4) that fed the Israelites in the wilderness.
9. In spite of. "Divers": various (people). "Contemned": despised.

it fulfilled which could not have been so long foretold by any but God Himself?

When I have got over this block, then have I another put in my way, that admit this be the true God whom we worship, and that be his word, yet why may not the Popish religion be the right? They have the same God, the same Christ, the same word. They only interpret it one way, we another.

This hath sometimes stuck with me, and more it would, but the vain fooleries that are in their religion together with their lying miracles and cruel persecutions of the saints, which admit were they as they term them, yet not so to be dealt withal.

The consideration of these things and many the like would soon turn me to my own religion again.

But some new troubles I have had since the world has been filled with blasphemy and sectaries,[1] and some who have been accounted sincere Christians have been carried away with them, that sometimes I have said, "Is there faith upon the earth?" and I have not known what to think; but then I have remembered the works of Christ that so it must be, and if it were possible, the very elect should be deceived. "Behold," saith our Savior, "I have told you before." That hath stayed my heart, and I can now say, "Return, O my Soul, to thy rest, upon this rock Christ Jesus will I build my faith, and if I perish, I perish"; but I know all the Powers of Hell shall never prevail against it. I know whom I have trusted, and whom I have believed, and that He is able to keep that I have committed to His charge.

Now to the King, immortal, eternal and invisible, the only wise God, be honor, and glory for ever and ever, Amen.

This was written in much sickness and weakness, and is very weakly and imperfectly done, but if you can pick any benefit out of it, it is the mark which I aimed at.

1867

1. Unbelievers, heretics.

MARY ROWLANDSON
c. 1637–1711

On June 20, 1675, Metacomet, who was called Philip by the colonists, led the first of a series of attacks on colonial settlements that lasted for more than a year. Before they were over, more than twelve hundred houses had been burned, about six hundred English colonials were dead, and three thousand American Indians killed. These attacks have become known as "King Philip's War." It was the direct result of the execution in Plymouth, Massachusetts, of three of Philip's Wampanoag tribesmen, but the indirect causes were many; not least was the fact that the Native Americans were starving and desperate to retain their lands. In a sense, the war may be seen as a last-ditch effort by the Wampanoags and their allies against further expansion by the colonists. By the time the war was over, in August

1676, with Philip slain and his wife and children sold into slavery in the West Indies, the independent power of American Indians in New England had ended.

Probably the most famous victim of these attacks is the author of *A Narrative of the Captivity and Restoration of Mrs. Mary Rowlandson,* the wife of the minister of the town of Lancaster. With the exception of the eleven weeks she spent as a captive among the Wampanoags, almost everything about Mrs. Rowlandson's life remains conjectural. She was born in Somersetshire, in the south of England around 1637, and brought to this country in 1639. Her father, John White, became a wealthy landholder in the Massachusetts Bay Colony who settled in Lancaster in 1653. About 1656 she married Joseph Rowlandson and for the next twenty years led a busy life as mother and minister's wife. The attack on Lancaster occurred on February 20, 1676, and she was not released until the second of May, having been ransomed for twenty pounds. The following year she went with her husband to Wethersfield, Connecticut; Mr. Rowlandson died there in 1678. The town voted to pay her an annuity "so long as she remains a widow among us." Literary scholar David Greene has verified that Mary Rowlandson married Captain Samuel Talcott in Wethersfield on August 6, 1679, and that she died in that Connecticut Valley town on January 5, 1711, thirty-five years after her famous ordeal.

Shortly after her return to Lancaster, Mrs. Rowlandson began to make a record of her life in captivity. Her *Narrative* (published in 1682 as *The Sovereignty and Goodness of God . . . Being a Narrative of the Captivity and Restoration of Mrs. Mary Rowlandson*) is the only evidence we have of her skill as a writer. The account of her captivity became one of the most popular prose works of the seventeenth century, both in this country and in England. It combined high adventure, heroism, and exemplary piety and is the first and, in its narrative skill and delineation of character, the best of what have become popularly known as "Indian captivities." As transformed into fictional form by writers like James Fenimore Cooper (in *The Last of the Mohicans*) and William Faulkner (in *Sanctuary*), it is a genre that has proven to be an integral part of our American literary consciousness.

From A Narrative of the Captivity and Restoration of Mrs. Mary Rowlandson[1]

On the tenth of February 1675,[2] came the Indians with great numbers upon Lancaster:[3] their first coming was about sunrising; hearing the noise of some guns, we looked out; several houses were burning, and the smoke ascending to heaven. There were five persons taken in one house; the father, and the mother and a sucking child, they knocked on the head; the other two they took and carried away alive. There were two others, who being out of their garrison[4] upon some occasion were set upon; one was knocked on the head,

1. The text used is *Original Narratives of Early American History, Narratives of Indian Wars 1675–1699*, vol. 14, edited by C. H. Lincoln (1952). All copies of Rowlandson's original edition have been lost. Like most modern editors, Lincoln has chosen to reprint the second "addition," printed in Cambridge, Massachusetts, by Samuel Green in 1682. The full title is *The sovereignty and goodness of GOD, together with the faithfulness of his promises displayed; being a narrative of the captivity and restoration of Mrs. Mary Rowlandson, commended by her, to all that desires to know the Lord's doings to, and dealings with her. Especially to her dear children and relations. The* second *Addition Corrected and amended. Written by her own hand for her private use, and now made public at the earnest desire of some friends, and for the benefit of the afflicted. Deut. 32.39. See now that I, even I am he, and there is no god with me; I kill and I make alive, I wound and I heal, neither is there any can deliver out of my hand.*
2. A Thursday. Using the present Gregorian calendar, adopted in 1752, February 20, 1676.
3. Lancaster, Massachusetts, was a frontier town of approximately fifty families, about thirty miles west of Boston.
4. I.e., houses in the town where people gathered for defense.

A Narrative. Rowlandson, whose narrative first appeared in 1682, had not fought against her Native Americans captors. But by 1773, when one of several editions issued at the time of the American Revolution was published, she had been given a gun and thus elevated into a defender of her realm—like the male patriots who at that time were opposing British policy.

the other escaped; another there was who running along was shot and wounded, and fell down; he begged of them his life, promising them money (as they told me) but they would not hearken to him but knocked him in head, and stripped him naked, and split open his bowels.[5] Another, seeing many of the Indians about his barn, ventured and went out, but was quickly shot down. There were three others belonging to the same garrison who were killed; the Indians getting up upon the roof of the barn, had advantage to shoot down upon them over their fortification. Thus these murderous wretches went on, burning, and destroying before them.

At length they came and beset our own house, and quickly it was the dolefulest day that ever mine eyes saw. The house stood upon the edge of a hill; some of the Indians got behind the hill, others into the barn, and others behind anything that could shelter them; from all which places they shot against the house, so that the bullets seemed to fly like hail; and quickly they wounded one man among us, then another, and then a third. About two hours (according to my observation, in that amazing time) they had been about the house before they prevailed to fire it (which they did with flax and hemp, which they brought out of the barn, and there being no defense about the house, only two flankers[6] at two opposite corners and one of them not finished); they fired it once and one ventured out and quenched it, but they quickly fired it again, and that took. Now is the dreadful hour come, that I have often heard of (in time of war, as it was the case of others), but now mine eyes see it. Some in our house were fighting for their lives, others wallowing in their blood, the house on fire over our heads, and the bloody heathen ready to knock us on the head, if we stirred out. Now might we hear mothers and children crying out for themselves, and one another, "Lord, what shall we do?" Then I took my children (and one of my sisters', hers) to go forth and leave the house: but as soon as we came to the door and appeared, the Indians shot so thick that the bullets rattled against the house, as if one had taken an handful of stones and threw them, so that we were fain to give back.[7] We

5. Belly.
6. Projecting fortifications.

7. I.e., eager to return the gunfire.

had six stout dogs belonging to our garrison, but none of them would stir, though another time, if any Indian had come to the door, they were ready to fly upon him and tear him down. The Lord hereby would make us the more acknowledge His hand, and to see that our help is always in Him. But out we must go, the fire increasing, and coming along behind us, roaring, and the Indians gaping before us with their guns, spears, and hatchets to devour us. No sooner were we out of the house, but my brother-in-law (being before wounded, in defending the house, in or near the throat) fell down dead, whereat the Indians scornfully shouted, and hallowed, and were presently upon him, stripping off his clothes, the bullets flying thick, one went through my side, and the same (as would seem) through the bowels and hand of my dear child in my arms. One of my elder sisters' children, named William, had then his leg broken, which the Indians perceiving, they knocked him on [his] head. Thus were we butchered by those merciless heathen, standing amazed, with the blood running down to our heels. My eldest sister being yet in the house, and seeing those woeful sights, the infidels hauling mothers one way, and children another, and some wallowing in their blood: and her elder son telling her that her son William was dead, and myself was wounded, she said, "And Lord, let me die with them," which was no sooner said, but she was struck with a bullet, and fell down dead over the threshold. I hope she is reaping the fruit of her good labors, being faithful to the service of God in her place. In her younger years she lay under much trouble upon spiritual accounts, till it pleased God to make that precious scripture take hold of her heart, "And he said unto me, my Grace is sufficient for thee" (2 Corinthians 12.9). More than twenty years after, I have heard her tell how sweet and comfortable that place was to her. But to return: the Indians laid hold of us, pulling me one way, and the children another, and said, "Come go along with us"; I told them they would kill me: they answered, if I were willing to go along with them, they would not hurt me.

Oh the doleful sight that now was to behold at this house! "Come, behold the works of the Lord, what desolations he has made in the earth."[8] Of thirty-seven persons who were in this one house, none escaped either present death, or a bitter captivity, save only one, who might say as he, "And I only am escaped alone to tell the News" (Job 1.15). There were twelve killed, some shot, some stabbed with their spears, some knocked down with their hatchets. When we are in prosperity, Oh the little that we think of such dreadful sights, and to see our dear friends, and relations lie bleeding out their heart-blood upon the ground. There was one who was chopped into the head with a hatchet, and stripped naked, and yet was crawling up and down. It is a solemn sight to see so many Christians lying in their blood, some here, and some there, like a company of sheep torn by wolves, all of them stripped naked by a company of hell-hounds, roaring, singing, ranting, and insulting, as if they would have torn our very hearts out; yet the Lord by His almighty power preserved a number of us from death, for there were twenty-four of us taken alive and carried captive.

I had often before this said that if the Indians should come, I should choose rather to be killed by them than taken alive, but when it came to the trial my mind changed; their glittering weapons so daunted my spirit, that I chose rather to go along with those (as I may say) ravenous beasts, than that

8. Psalm 46.8.

moment to end my days; and that I may the better declare what happened to me during that grievous captivity, I shall particularly speak of the several removes[9] we had up and down the wilderness.

The First Remove

Now away we must go with those barbarous creatures, with our bodies wounded and bleeding, and our hearts no less than our bodies. About a mile we went that night, up upon a hill within sight of the town, where they intended to lodge. There was hard by[1] a vacant house (deserted by the English before, for fear of the Indians). I asked them whether I might not lodge in the house that night, to which they answered, "What, will you love English men still?" This was the dolefulest night that ever my eyes saw. Oh the roaring, and singing and dancing, and yelling of those black creatures in the night, which made the place a lively resemblance of hell. And as miserable was the waste that was there made of horses, cattle, sheep, swine, calves, lambs, roasting pigs, and fowl (which they had plundered in the town), some roasting, some lying and burning, and some boiling to feed our merciless enemies; who were joyful enough, though we were disconsolate. To add to the dolefulness of the former day, and the dismalness of the present night, my thoughts ran upon my losses and sad bereaved condition. All was gone, my husband gone (at least separated from me, he being in the Bay;[2] and to add to my grief, the Indians told me they would kill him as he came homeward), my children gone, my relations and friends gone, our house and home and all our comforts—within door and without—all was gone (except my life), and I knew not but the next moment that might go too. There remained nothing to me but one poor wounded babe, and it seemed at present worse than death that it was in such a pitiful condition, bespeaking compassion, and I had no refreshing for it, nor suitable things to revive it. Little do many think what is the savageness and brutishness of this barbarous enemy, Ay, even those that seem to profess more than others among them, when the English have fallen into their hands.

Those seven that were killed at Lancaster the summer before upon a Sabbath day, and the one that was afterward killed upon a weekday, were slain and mangled in a barbarous manner, by one-eyed John, and Marlborough's Praying Indians, which Capt. Mosely brought to Boston, as the Indians told me.[3]

The Second Remove[4]

But now, the next morning, I must turn my back upon the town, and travel with them into the vast and desolate wilderness, I knew not whither. It is not my tongue, or pen, can express the sorrows of my heart, and bitterness of my spirit that I had at this departure: but God was with me in a wonderful manner, carrying me along, and bearing up my spirit, that it did not quite fail. One of the Indians carried my poor wounded babe upon a horse; it went moaning all along, "I shall die, I shall die." I went on foot after it,

9. I.e., departures; movings from place to place.
1. Close by.
2. I.e., Boston, or Massachusetts Bay.
3. On August 30, 1675, Captain Samuel Mosely, encouraged by a number of people who were skeptical of converted American Indians, brought to Boston by force fifteen Christianized American Indians who lived on their own lands in Marlborough, Massachusetts, and accused them of an attack on the town of Lancaster on August 22.
4. To Princeton, Massachusetts, near Mount Wachusett.

with sorrow that cannot be expressed. At length I took it off the horse, and carried it in my arms till my strength failed, and I fell down with it. Then they set me upon a horse with my wounded child in my lap, and there being no furniture upon the horse's back, as we were going down a steep hill we both fell over the horse's head, at which they, like inhumane creatures, laughed, and rejoiced to see it, though I thought we should there have ended our days, as overcome with so many difficulties. But the Lord renewed my strength still, and carried me along, that I might see more of His power; yea, so much that I could never have thought of, had I not experienced it.

After this it quickly began to snow, and when night came on, they stopped, and now down I must sit in the snow, by a little fire, and a few boughs behind me, with my sick child in my lap; and calling much for water, being now (through the wound) fallen into a violent fever. My own wound also growing so stiff that I could scarce sit down or rise up; yet so it must be, that I must sit all this cold winter night upon the cold snowy ground, with my sick child in my arms, looking that every hour would be the last of its life; and having no Christian friend near me, either to comfort or help me. Oh, I may see the wonderful power of God, that my Spirit did not utterly sink under my affliction: still the Lord upheld me with His gracious and merciful spirit, and we were both alive to see the light of the next morning.

The Third Remove[5]

The morning being come, they prepared to go on their way. One of the Indians got up upon a horse, and they set me up behind him, with my poor sick babe in my lap. A very wearisome and tedious day I had of it; what with my own wound, and my child's being so exceeding sick, and in a lamentable condition with her wound. It may be easily judged what a poor feeble condition we were in, there being not the least crumb of refreshing that came within either of our mouths from Wednesday night to Saturday night, except only a little cold water. This day in the afternoon, about an hour by sun, we came to the place where they intended, *viz.*[6] an Indian town, called Wenimesset, northward of Quabaug. When we were come, Oh the number of pagans (now merciless enemies) that there came about me, that I may say as David, "I had fainted, unless I had believed, etc." (Psalm 27.13). The next day was the Sabbath. I then remembered how careless I had been of God's holy time; how many Sabbaths I had lost and misspent, and how evilly I had walked in God's sight; which lay so close unto my spirit, that it was easy for me to see how righteous it was with God to cut off the thread of my life and cast me out of His presence forever. Yet the Lord still showed mercy to me, and upheld me; and as He wounded me with one hand, so he healed me with the other. This day there came to me one Robert Pepper (a man belonging to Roxbury) who was taken in Captain Beers's fight, and had been now a considerable time with the Indians; and up with them almost as far as Albany, to see King Philip, as he told me, and was now very lately come into these parts.[7] Hearing, I say, that I was in this Indian town, he obtained leave to come and see me. He told me he himself was wounded in the leg at Captain Beers's fight; and was not able some time to go, but as they carried him, and as he took

5. February 12–27; they stopped at a Native American village on the Ware River near New Braintree.
6. Abbreviation for *videlicet* (Latin), "namely" or "that is to say."
7. Captain Beers had attempted to save the garrison of Northfield, Massachusetts, on September 4, 1675.

oaken leaves and laid to his wound, and through the blessing of God he was able to travel again. Then I took oaken leaves and laid to my side, and with the blessing of God it cured me also; yet before the cure was wrought, I may say, as it is in Psalm 38.5–6, "My wounds stink and are corrupt, I am troubled, I am bowed down greatly, I go mourning all the day long." I sat much alone with a poor wounded child in my lap, which moaned night and day, having nothing to revive the body, or cheer the spirits of her, but instead of that, sometimes one Indian would come and tell me one hour that "your master will knock your child in the head," and then a second, and then a third, "your master will quickly knock your child in the head."

This was the comfort I had from them, miserable comforters are ye all, as he[8] said. Thus nine days I sat upon my knees, with my babe in my lap, till my flesh was raw again; my child being even ready to depart this sorrowful world, they bade me carry it out to another wigwam (I suppose because they would not be troubled with such spectacles) whither I went with a very heavy heart, and down I sat with the picture of death in my lap. About two hours in the night, my sweet babe like a lamb departed this life on Feb. 18, 1675. It being about six years, and five months old. It was nine days from the first wounding, in this miserable condition, without any refreshing of one nature or other, except a little cold water. I cannot but take notice how at another time I could not bear to be in the room where any dead person was, but now the case is changed; I must and could lie down by my dead babe, side by side all the night after. I have thought since of the wonderful goodness of God to me in preserving me in the use of my reason and senses in that distressed time, that I did not use wicked and violent means to end my own miserable life. In the morning, when they understood that my child was dead they sent for me home to my master's wigwam (by my master in this writing, must be understood Quinnapin, who was a Sagamore,[9] and married King Philip's wife's sister; not that he first took me, but I was sold to him by another Narragansett Indian, who took me when first I came out of the garrison). I went to take up my dead child in my arms to carry it with me, but they bid me let it alone; there was no resisting, but go I must and leave it. When I had been at my master's wigwam, I took the first opportunity I could get to go look after my dead child. When I came I asked them what they had done with it; then they told me it was upon the hill. Then they went and showed me where it was, where I saw the ground was newly digged, and there they told me they had buried it. There I left that child in the wilderness, and must commit it, and myself also in this wilderness condition, to Him who is above all. God having taken away this dear child, I went to see my daughter Mary, who was at this same Indian town, at a wigwam not very far off, though we had little liberty or opportunity to see one another. She was about ten years old, and taken from the door at first by a Praying Ind. and afterward sold for a gun. When I came in sight, she would fall aweeping; at which they were provoked, and would not let me come near her, but bade me be gone; which was a heart-cutting word to me. I had one child dead, another in the wilderness, I knew not where, the third they would not let me come near to: "Me (as he said) have ye bereaved of my Children, Joseph is not, and Simeon is not, and ye will take Benjamin also, all these things are against me."[1] I could not sit

---

8. I.e., as Job said. "I have heard many such things: miserable comforters are ye all" (Job 16.2).
9. A subordinate chief among the Algonquin Indians. Quinnapin was the husband of Weetamoo, and Rowlandson became her servant.
1. Jacob's lamentation in Genesis 42.36.

still in this condition, but kept walking from one place to another. And as I was going along, my heart was even overwhelmed with the thoughts of my condition, and that I should have children, and a nation which I knew not, ruled over them. Whereupon I earnestly entreated the Lord, that He would consider my low estate, and show me a token for good, and if it were His blessed will, some sign and hope of some relief. And indeed quickly the Lord answered, in some measure, my poor prayers; for as I was going up and down mourning and lamenting my condition, my son came to me, and asked me how I did. I had not seen him before, since the destruction of the town, and I knew not where he was, till I was informed by himself, that he was amongst a smaller parcel of Indians, whose place was about six miles off. With tears in his eyes, he asked me whether his sister Sarah was dead; and told me he had seen his sister Mary; and prayed me, that I would not be troubled in reference to himself. The occasion of his coming to see me at this time, was this: there was, as I said, about six miles from us, a small plantation of Indians, where it seems he had been during his captivity; and at this time, there were some forces of the Ind. gathered out of our company, and some also from them (among whom was my son's master) to go to assault and burn Medfield.[2] In this time of the absence of his master, his dame brought him to see me. I took this to be some gracious answer to my earnest and unfeigned desire. The next day, *viz.* to this, the Indians returned from Medfield, all the company, for those that belonged to the other small company, came through the town that now we were at. But before they came to us, Oh! the outrageous roaring and hooping that there was. They began their din about a mile before they came to us. By their noise and hooping they signified how many they had destroyed (which was at that time twenty-three). Those that were with us at home were gathered together as soon as they heard the hooping, and every time that the other went over their number, these at home gave a shout, that the very earth rung again. And thus they continued till those that had been upon the expedition were come up to the Sagamore's wigwam; and then, Oh, the hideous insulting and triumphing that there was over some Englishmen's scalps that they had taken (as their manner is) and brought with them. I cannot but take notice of the wonderful mercy of God to me in those afflictions, in sending me a Bible. One of the Indians that came from Medfield fight, had brought some plunder, came to me, and asked me, if I would have a Bible, he had got one in his basket. I was glad of it, and asked him, whether he thought the Indians would let me read? He answered, yes. So I took the Bible, and in that melancholy time, it came into my mind to read first the 28th chapter of Deuteronomy,[3] which I did, and when I had read it, my dark heart wrought on this manner: that there was no mercy for me, that the blessings were gone, and the curses come in their room, and that I had lost my opportunity. But the Lord helped me still to go on reading till I came to Chap. 30, the seven first verses, where I found, there was mercy promised again, if we would return to Him by repentance;[4] and though we were scattered from one end of the earth to the other, yet the Lord would gather us together, and turn all those curses upon our enemies. I do not desire to live to forget this Scripture, and what comfort it was to me.

---

2. The attack on Medfield, Massachusetts, occurred on February 21.
3. This chapter of Deuteronomy is concerned with blessings for obedience to God and curses for disobedience.

4. "That then the Lord thy God will turn thy captivity, and have compassion upon thee, and will return and gather thee from all the nations" (Deuteronomy 30.3).

Now the Ind. began to talk of removing from this place, some one way, and some another. There were now besides myself nine English captives in this place (all of them children, except one woman). I got an opportunity to go and take my leave of them. They being to go one way, and I another, I asked them whether they were earnest with God for deliverance. They told me they did as they were able, and it was some comfort to me, that the Lord stirred up children to look to Him. The woman, *viz.* goodwife[5] Joslin, told me she should never see me again, and that she could find in her heart to run away. I wished her not to run away by any means, for we were near thirty miles from any English town, and she very big with child, and had but one week to reckon, and another child in her arms, two years old, and bad rivers there were to go over, and we were feeble, with our poor and coarse entertainment. I had my Bible with me, I pulled it out, and asked her whether she would read. We opened the Bible and lighted on Psalm 27, in which Psalm we especially took notice of that, *ver. ult.,* "Wait on the Lord, Be of good courage, and he shall strengthen thine Heart, wait I say on the Lord."[6]

The Twelfth Remove[7]

It was upon a Sabbath-day morning, that they prepared for their travel. This morning I asked my master whether he would sell me to my husband. He answered me "Nux,"[8] which did much rejoice my spirit. My mistress, before we went, was gone to the burial of a papoose, and returning, she found me sitting and reading in my Bible; she snatched it hastily out of my hand, and threw it out of doors. I ran out and catched it up, and put it into my pocket, and never let her see it afterward. Then they packed up their things to be gone, and gave me my load. I complained it was too heavy, whereupon she gave me a slap in the face, and bade me go; I lifted up my heart to God, hoping the redemption was not far off; and the rather because their insolency grew worse and worse.

But the thoughts of my going homeward (for so we bent our course) much cheered my spirit, and made my burden seem light, and almost nothing at all. But (to my amazement and great perplexity) the scale was soon turned; for when we had gone a little way, on a sudden my mistress gives out; she would go no further, but turn back again, and said I must go back again with her, and she called her *sannup,* and would have had him gone back also, but he would not, but said he would go on, and come to us again in three days. My spirit was, upon this, I confess, very impatient, and almost outrageous.[9] I thought I could as well have died as went back; I cannot declare the trouble that I was in about it; but yet back again I must go. As soon as I had the opportunity, I took my Bible to read, and that quieting Scripture came to my hand, "Be still, and know that I am God" (Psalm 46.10). Which stilled my spirit for the present. But a sore time of trial, I concluded, I had to go through, my master being gone, who seemed to me the best friend that I had of an Indian, both in cold and hunger, and quickly so it proved. Down I sat, with my heart as full as it could hold, and yet so hungry that I could not sit neither; but going out to see what I could find, and walking among the trees, I found six acorns, and two chestnuts, which were some refreshment to me. Towards night I gathered some sticks for my own comfort, that I might

---

5. I.e., the mistress of a house.
6. Verse 14. *"Ver. ult.":* last verse (Latin abbrev.)
7. Sunday, April 9.
8. Yes.
9. Outraged.

not lie a-cold; but when we came to lie down they bade me to go out, and lie somewhere else, for they had company (they said) come in more than their own. I told them, I could not tell where to go, they bade me go look; I told them, if I went to another wigwam they would be angry, and send me home again. Then one of the company drew his sword, and told me he would run me through if I did not go presently. Then was I fain to stoop to this rude fellow, and to go out in the night, I knew not whither. Mine eyes have seen that fellow afterwards walking up and down Boston, under the appearance of a Friend Indian, and several others of the like cut. I went to one wigwam, and they told me they had no room. Then I went to another, and they said the same; at last an old Indian bade me to come to him, and his squaw gave me some ground nuts; she gave me also something to lay under my head, and a good fire we had; and through the good providence of God, I had a comfortable lodging that night. In the morning, another Indian bade me come at night, and he would give me six ground nuts, which I did. We were at this place and time about two miles from [the] Connecticut River. We went in the morning to gather ground nuts, to the river, and went back again that night. I went with a good load at my back (for they when they went, though but a little way, would carry all their trumpery[1] with them). I told them the skin was off my back, but I had no other comforting answer from them than this: that it would be no matter if my head were off too.

The Twentieth Remove[2]

It was their usual manner to remove, when they had done any mischief, lest they should be found out; and so they did at this time. We went about three or four miles, and there they built a great wigwam, big enough to hold an hundred Indians, which they did in preparation to a great day of dancing. They would say now amongst themselves, that the governor would be so angry for his loss at Sudbury, that he would send no more about the captives, which made me grieve and tremble. My sister being not far from the place where we now were, and hearing that I was here, desired her master to let her come and see me, and he was willing to it, and would go with her; but she being ready before him, told him she would go before, and was come within a mile or two of the place. Then he overtook her, and began to rant as if he had been mad, and made her go back again in the rain; so that I never saw her till I saw her in Charlestown. But the Lord requited many of their ill doings, for this Indian her master, was hanged afterward at Boston. The Indians now began to come from all quarters, against their merry dancing day. Among some of them came one goodwife Kettle. I told her my heart was so heavy that it was ready to break. "So is mine too," said she, but yet said, "I hope we shall hear some good news shortly." I could hear how earnestly my sister desired to see me, and I as earnestly desired to see her; and yet neither of us could get an opportunity. My daughter was also now about a mile off, and I had not seen her in nine or ten weeks, as I had not seen my sister since our first taking. I earnestly desired them to let me go and see them: yea, I entreated, begged, and persuaded them, but to let me see my daughter; and yet so hard-hearted were they, that they would not suffer it. They made use of their tyrannical power whilst they had it; but through the Lord's wonderful mercy, their time was now but short.

1. Worthless things.
2. April 28 to May 2, to an encampment at the southern end of Wachusett Lake, Princeton, Massachusetts.

On a Sabbath day, the sun being about an hour high in the afternoon, came Mr. John Hoar[3] (the council permitting him, and his own foreward spirit inclining him), together with the two forementioned Indians, Tom and Peter, with their third letter from the council. When they came near, I was abroad. Though I saw them not, they presently called me in, and bade me sit down and not stir. Then they catched up their guns, and away they ran, as if an enemy had been at hand, and the guns went off apace. I manifested some great trouble, and they asked me what was the matter? I told them I thought they had killed the Englishman (for they had in the meantime informed me that an Englishman was come). They said, no. They shot over his horse and under and before his horse, and they pushed him this way and that way, at their pleasure, showing what they could do. Then they let them come to their wigwams. I begged of them to let me see the Englishman, but they would not. But there was I fain to sit their pleasure. When they had talked their fill with him, they suffered me to go to him. We asked each other of our welfare, and how my husband did, and all my friends? He told me they were all well, and would be glad to see me. Amongst other things which my husband sent me, there came a pound of tobacco, which I sold for nine shillings in money; for many of the Indians for want of tobacco, smoked hemlock, and ground ivy. It was a great mistake in any, who thought I sent for tobacco; for through the favor of God, that desire was overcome. I now asked them whether I should go home with Mr. Hoar? They answered no, one and another of them, and it being night, we lay down with that answer. In the morning Mr. Hoar invited the Sagamores to dinner; but when we went to get it ready we found that they had stolen the greatest part of the provision Mr. Hoar had brought, out of his bags, in the night. And we may see the wonderful power of God, in that one passage, in that when there was such a great number of the Indians together, and so greedy of a little good food, and no English there but Mr. Hoar and myself, that there they did not knock us in the head, and take what we had, there being not only some provision, but also trading-cloth,[4] a part of the twenty pounds agreed upon. But instead of doing us any mischief, they seemed to be ashamed of the fact, and said, it were some matchit[5] Indian that did it. Oh, that we could believe that there is nothing too hard for God! God showed His power over the heathen in this, as He did over the hungry lions when Daniel was cast into the den.[6] Mr. Hoar called them betime to dinner, but they ate very little, they being so busy in dressing themselves, and getting ready for their dance, which was carried on by eight of them, four men and four squaws. My master and mistress being two. He was dressed in his holland[7] shirt, with great laces sewed at the tail of it; he had his silver buttons, his white stockings, his garters were hung round with shillings, and he had girdles of wampum upon his head and shoulders. She had a kersey[8] coat, and covered with girdles of wampum from the loins upward. Her arms from her elbows to her hands were covered with bracelets; there were handfuls of necklaces about her neck, and several sorts of jewels in her ears. She had fine red stockings, and white shoes, her hair powdered and face painted red, that

---

3. John Hoar was from Concord, Massachusetts. He had been delegated by Rowlandson's husband to represent him at the council for the Sagamore Indians and to bargain for Rowlandson's redemption.
4. Cloth used for barter.
5. Bad.
6. The prophet Daniel was cast into a den of lions, but they did not harm him (see Daniel 6.1–29).
7. Linen.
8. Coarse cloth woven from long wool and usually ribbed.

was always before black. And all the dancers were after the same manner. There were two others singing and knocking on a kettle for their music. They kept hopping up and down one after another, with a kettle of water in the midst, standing warm upon some embers, to drink of when they were dry. They held on till it was almost night, throwing out wampum to the standers by. At night I asked them again, if I should go home? They all as one said no, except[9] my husband would come for me. When we were lain down, my master went out of the wigwam, and by and by sent in an Indian called James the Printer,[1] who told Mr. Hoar, that my master would let me go home tomorrow, if he would let him have one pint of liquors. Then Mr. Hoar called his own Indians, Tom and Peter, and bid them go and see whether he would promise it before them three; and if he would, he should have it; which he did, and he had it. Then Philip[2] smelling the business called me to him, and asked me what I would give him, to tell me some good news, and speak a good word for me. I told him I could not tell what to give him. I would [give him] anything I had, and asked him what he would have? He said two coats and twenty shillings in money, and half a bushel of seed corn, and some tobacco. I thanked him for his love; but I knew the good news as well as the crafty fox. My master after he had had his drink, quickly came ranting into the wigwam again, and called for Mr. Hoar, drinking to him, and saying, he was a good man, and then again he would say, "hang him rogue." Being almost drunk, he would drink to him, and yet presently say he should be hanged. Then he called for me. I trembled to hear him, yet I was fain to go to him, and he drank to me, showing no incivility. He was the first Indian I saw drunk all the while that I was amongst them. At last his squaw ran out, and he after her, round the wigwam, with his money jingling at his knees. But she escaped him. But having an old squaw he ran to her; and so through the Lord's mercy, we were no more troubled that night. Yet I had not a comfortable night's rest; for I think I can say, I did not sleep for three nights together. The night before the letter came from the council, I could not rest, I was so full of fears and troubles, God many times leaving us most in the dark, when deliverance is nearest. Yea, at this time I could not rest night nor day. The next night I was overjoyed, Mr. Hoar being come, and that with such good tidings. The third night I was even swallowed up with the thoughts of things, *viz.* that ever I should go home again; and that I must go, leaving my children behind me in the wilderness; so that sleep was now almost departed from mine eyes.

On Tuesday morning they called their General Court (as they call it) to consult and determine, whether I should go home or no. And they all as one man did seemingly consent to it, that I should go home; except Philip, who would not come among them.

But before I go any further, I would take leave to mention a few remarkable passages of providence, which I took special notice of in my afflicted time.

1. Of the fair opportunity lost in the long march, a little after the fort fight, when our English army was so numerous, and in pursuit of the enemy, and so near as to take several and destroy them, and the enemy in such distress for food that our men might track them by their rooting in the earth for ground nuts, whilst they were flying for their lives. I say, that then our army

---

9. Unless.
1. Wowaus, an American Indian who assisted the Reverend John Eliot in his printing of the

Bible.
2. I.e. King Philip.

should want provision, and be forced to leave their pursuit and return homeward; and the very next week the enemy came upon our town, like bears bereft of their whelps, or so many ravenous wolves, rending us and our lambs to death. But what shall I say? God seemed to leave his People to themselves, and order all things for His own holy ends. Shall there be evil in the City and the Lord hath not done it?[3] They are not grieved for the affliction of Joseph, therefore shall they go captive, with the first that go captive.[4] It is the Lord's doing, and it should be marvelous in our eyes.

2. I cannot but remember how the Indians derided the slowness, and dullness of the English army, in its setting out. For after the desolations at Lancaster and Medfield, as I went along with them, they asked me when I thought the English army would come after them? I told them I could not tell. "It may be they will come in May," said they. Thus did they scoff at us, as if the English would be a quarter of a year getting ready.

3. Which also I have hinted before, when the English army with new supplies were sent forth to pursue after the enemy, and they understanding it, fled before them till they came to Banquaug river, where they forthwith went over safely; that that river should be impassable to the English. I can but admire to see the wonderful providence of God in preserving the heathen for further affliction to our poor country. They could go in great numbers over, but the English must stop. God had an over-ruling hand in all those things.

4. It was thought, if their corn were cut down, they would starve and die with hunger, and all their corn that could be found, was destroyed, and they driven from that little they had in store, into the woods in the midst of winter; and yet how to admiration did the Lord preserve them for His holy ends, and the destruction of many still amongst the English! strangely did the Lord provide for them; that I did not see (all the time I was among them) one man, woman, or child, die with hunger.

Though many times they would eat that, that[5] a hog or a dog would hardly touch; yet by that God strengthened them to be a scourge to His people.

The chief and commonest food was ground nuts. They eat also nuts and acorns, artichokes, lily roots, ground beans, and several other weeds and roots, that I know not.

They would pick up old bones, and cut them to pieces at the joints, and if they were full of worms and maggots, they would scald them over the fire to make the vermin come out, and then boil them, and drink up the liquor, and then beat the great ends of them in a mortar, and so eat them. They would eat horse's guts, and ears, and all sorts of wild birds which they could catch; also bear, venison, beaver, tortoise, frogs, squirrels, dogs, skunks, rattlesnakes; yea, the very bark of trees; besides all sorts of creatures, and provision which they plundered from the English. I can but stand in admiration to see the wonderful power of God in providing for such a vast number of our enemies in the wilderness, where there was nothing to be seen, but from hand to mouth. Many times in a morning, the generality of them would eat up all they had, and yet have some further supply against they wanted. It is said, "Oh, that my People had hearkened to me, and Israel had walked in my ways, I should soon have subdued their Enemies, and turned my hand against their Adversaries" (Psalm 81.13–n14). But now our perverse and evil carriages in the sight of the Lord, have so offended Him, that

3. Amos 3.6.
4. Amos 6.6–7.

5. I.e., that which.

instead of turning His hand against them, the Lord feeds and nourishes them up to be a scourge to the whole land.

5. Another thing that I would observe is the strange providence of God, in turning things about when the Indians was at the highest, and the English at the lowest. I was with the enemy eleven weeks and five days, and not one week passed without the fury of the enemy, and some desolation by fire and sword upon one place or other. They mourned (with their black faces) for their own losses, yet triumphed and rejoiced in their inhumane, and many times devilish cruelty to the English. They would boast much of their victories; saying that in two hours time they had destroyed such a captain and his company at such a place; and boast how many towns they had destroyed, and then scoff, and say they had done them a good turn to send them to Heaven so soon. Again, they would say this summer that they would knock all the rogues in the head, or drive them into the sea, or make them fly the country; thinking surely, Agag-like, "The bitterness of Death is past."[6] Now the heathen begins to think all is their own, and the poor Christians' hopes to fail (as to man) and now their eyes are more to God, and their hearts sigh heavenward; and to say in good earnest, "Help Lord, or we perish." When the Lord had brought His people to this, that they saw no help in anything but Himself; then He takes the quarrel into His own hand; and though they had made a pit, in their own imaginations, as deep as hell for the Christians that summer, yet the Lord hurled themselves into it. And the Lord had not so many ways before to preserve them, but now He hath as many to destroy them.

But to return again to my going home, where we may see a remarkable change of providence. At first they were all against it, except my husband would come for me, but afterwards they assented to it, and seemed much to rejoice in it; some asked me to send them some bread, others some tobacco, others shaking me by the hand, offering me a hood and scarf to ride in; not one moving hand or tongue against it. Thus hath the Lord answered my poor desire, and the many earnest requests of others put up unto God for me. In my travels an Indian came to me and told me, if I were willing, he and his squaw would run away, and go home along with me. I told him no: I was not willing to run away, but desired to wait God's time, that I might go home quietly, and without fear. And now God hath granted me my desire. O the wonderful power of God that I have seen, and the experience that I have had. I have been in the midst of those roaring lions, and savage bears, that feared neither God, nor man, nor the devil, by night and day, alone and in company, sleeping all sorts together, and yet not one of them ever offered me the least abuse of unchastity to me, in word or action. Though some are ready to say I speak it for my own credit; but I speak it in the presence of God, and to His Glory. God's power is as great now, and as sufficient to save, as when He preserved Daniel in the lion's den; or the three children in the fiery furnace.[7] I may well say as his Psalm 107.12, "Oh give thanks unto the Lord for he is good, for his mercy endureth for ever." Let the redeemed of the Lord say so, whom He hath redeemed from the hand of the enemy, especially that I should come away in the midst of so many hundreds of enemies quietly and peaceably, and not a dog moving his tongue. So I took my leave of them, and in coming along my heart melted into tears, more than all the while I was

6. 1 Samuel 15.32. Agag was the king of Amalek; he was defeated by Saul and thought himself spared, but was then slain by Samuel (see 1 Samuel 15).

7. Shadrach, Meshach, and Abednego refused to worship false gods and were cast into a fiery furnace but saved from death by an angel (see Daniel 3.13–30).

with them, and I was almost swallowed up with the thoughts that ever I should go home again. About the sun going down, Mr. Hoar, and myself, and the two Indians came to Lancaster, and a solemn sight it was to me. There had I lived many comfortable years amongst my relations and neighbors, and now not one Christian to be seen, nor one house left standing. We went on to a farmhouse that was yet standing, where we lay all night, and a comfortable lodging we had, though nothing but straw to lie on. The Lord preserved us in safety that night, and raised us up again in the morning, and carried us along, that before noon, we came to Concord. Now was I full of joy, and yet not without sorrow; joy to see such a lovely sight, so many Christians together, and some of them my neighbors. There I met with my brother, and my brother-in-law, who asked me, if I knew where his wife was? Poor heart! he had helped to bury her, and knew it not. She being shot down by the house was partly burnt, so that those who were at Boston at the desolation of the town, and came back afterward, and buried the dead, did not know her. Yet I was not without sorrow, to think how many were looking and longing, and my own children amongst the rest, to enjoy that deliverance that I had now received, and I did not know whether ever I should see them again. Being recruited[8] with food and raiment we went to Boston that day, where I met with my dear husband, but the thoughts of our dear children, one being dead, and the other we could not tell where, abated our comfort each to other. I was not before so much hemmed in with the merciless and cruel heathen, but now as much with pitiful, tender-hearted and compassionate Christians. In that poor, and distressed, and beggarly condition I was received in; I was kindly entertained in several houses. So much love I received from several (some of whom I knew, and others I knew not) that I am not capable to declare it. But the Lord knows them all by name. The Lord reward them sevenfold into their bosoms of His spirituals, for their temporals.[9] The twenty pounds, the price of my redemption, was raised by some Boston gentlemen, and Mrs. Usher, whose bounty and religious charity, I would not forget to make mention of. Then Mr. Thomas Shepard of Charlestown received us into his house, where we continued eleven weeks; and a father and mother they were to us. And many more tender-hearted friends we met with in that place. We were now in the midst of love, yet not without much and frequent heaviness of heart for our poor children, and other relations, who were still in affliction. The week following, after my coming in, the governor and council sent forth to the Indians again; and that not without success; for they brought in my sister, and goodwife Kettle. Their not knowing where our children were was a sore trial to us still, and yet we were not without secret hopes that we should see them again. That which was dead lay heavier upon my spirit, than those which were alive and amongst the heathen: thinking how it suffered with its wounds, and I was no way able to relieve it; and how it was buried by the heathen in the wilderness from among all Christians. We were hurried up and down in our thoughts, sometime we should hear a report that they were gone this way, and sometimes that; and that they were come in, in this place or that. We kept inquiring and listening to hear concerning them, but no certain news as yet. About this time the council had ordered a day of public thanksgiving. Though I thought I had still cause of mourning, and being unsettled in our minds, we thought we would ride toward the eastward, to see if we could hear anything concerning our children. And as we were riding

8. Refreshed.   9. Worldly goods and gifts.

along (God is the wise disposer of all things) between Ipswich and Rowley we met with Mr. William Hubbard, who told us that our son Joseph was come in to Major Waldron's, and another with him, which was my sister's son. I asked him how he knew it? He said the major himself told him so. So along we went till we came to Newbury; and their minister being absent, they desired my husband to preach the thanksgiving for them; but he was not willing to stay there that night, but would go over to Salisbury, to hear further, and come again in the morning, which he did, and preached there that day. At night, when he had done, one came and told him that his daughter was come in at Providence. Here was mercy on both hands. Now hath God fulfilled that precious Scripture which was such a comfort to me in my distressed condition. When my heart was ready to sink into the earth (my children being gone, I could not tell whither) and my knees trembling under me, and I was walking through the valley of the shadow of death; then the Lord brought, and now has fulfilled that reviving word unto me: "Thus saith the Lord, Refrain thy voice from weeping, and thine eyes from tears, for thy Work shall be rewarded, saith the Lord, and they shall come again from the Land of the Enemy."[1] Now we were between them, the one on the east, and the other on the west. Our son being nearest, we went to him first, to Portsmouth, where we met with him, and with the Major also, who told us he had done what he could, but could not redeem him under seven pounds, which the good people thereabouts were pleased to pay. The Lord reward the major, and all the rest, though unknown to me, for their labor of love. My sister's son was redeemed for four pounds, which the council gave order for the payment of. Having now received one of our children, we hastened toward the other. Going back through Newbury my husband preached there on the Sabbath day; for which they rewarded him many fold.

On Monday we came to Charlestown, where we heard that the governor of Rhode Island had sent over for our daughter, to take care of her, being now within his jurisdiction; which should not pass without our acknowledgments. But she being nearer Rehoboth than Rhode Island, Mr. Newman went over, and took care of her and brought her to his own house. And the goodness of God was admirable to us in our low estate, in that He raised up passionate[2] friends on every side to us, when we had nothing to recompense any for their love. The Indians were now gone that way, that it was apprehended dangerous to go to her. But the carts which carried provision to the English army, being guarded, brought her with them to Dorchester, where we received her safe. Blessed be the Lord for it, for great is His power, and He can do whatsoever seemeth Him good. Her coming in was after this manner: she was traveling one day with the Indians, with her basket at her back; the company of Indians were got before her, and gone out of sight, all except one squaw; she followed the squaw till night, and then both of them lay down, having nothing over them but the heavens and under them but the earth. Thus she traveled three days together, not knowing whither she was going; having nothing to eat or drink but water, and green hirtle-berries. At last they came into Providence, where she was kindly entertained by several of that town. The Indians often said that I should never have her under twenty pounds. But now the Lord hath brought her in upon free-cost, and given her to me the second time. The Lord make us a blessing indeed, each to others. Now have I seen that Scripture also fulfilled, "If any of thine be

1. Jeremiah 31.16.
2. Compassionate.

driven out to the outmost parts of heaven, from thence will the Lord thy God gather thee, and from thence will he fetch thee. And the Lord thy God will put all these curses upon thine enemies, and on them which hate thee, which persecuted thee" (Deuteronomy 30.4–7). Thus hath the Lord brought me and mine out of that horrible pit, and hath set us in the midst of tender-hearted and compassionate Christians. It is the desire of my soul that we may walk worthy of the mercies received, and which we are receiving.

Our family being now gathered together (those of us that were living), the South Church in Boston hired an house for us. Then we removed from Mr. Shephard's, those cordial friends, and went to Boston, where we continued about three-quarters of a year. Still the Lord went along with us, and provided graciously for us. I thought it somewhat strange to set up house-keeping with bare walls; but as Solomon says, "Money answers all things"[3] and that we had through the benevolence of Christian friends, some in this town, and some in that, and others; and some from England; that in a little time we might look, and see the house furnished with love. The Lord hath been exceeding good to us in our low estate, in that when we had neither house nor home, nor other necessaries, the Lord so moved the hearts of these and those towards us, that we wanted neither food, nor raiment for ourselves or ours: "There is a Friend which sticketh closer than a Brother" (Proverbs 18.24). And how many such friends have we found, and now living amongst? And truly such a friend have we found him to be unto us, in whose house we lived, *viz.* Mr. James Whitcomb, a friend unto us near hand, and afar off.

I can remember the time when I used to sleep quietly without workings in my thoughts, whole nights together, but now it is other ways with me. When all are fast about me, and no eye open, but His who ever waketh, my thoughts are upon things past, upon the awful dispensation of the Lord towards us, upon His wonderful power and might, in carrying of us through so many difficulties, in returning us in safety, and suffering none to hurt us. I remember in the night season, how the other day I was in the midst of thousands of enemies, and nothing but death before me. It is then hard work to persuade myself, that ever I should be satisfied with bread again. But now we are fed with the finest of the wheat, and, as I may say, with honey out of the rock.[4] Instead of the husk, we have the fatted calf.[5] The thoughts of these things in the particulars of them, and of the love and goodness of God towards us, make it true of me, what David said of himself, "I watered my Couch with my tears" (Psalm 6.6). Oh! the wonderful power of God that mine eyes have seen, affording matter enough for my thoughts to run in, that when others are sleeping mine eyes are weeping.

I have seen the extreme vanity of this world: One hour I have been in health, and wealthy, wanting nothing. But the next hour in sickness and wounds, and death, having nothing but sorrow and affliction.

Before I knew what affliction meant, I was ready sometimes to wish for it. When I lived in prosperity, having the comforts of the world about me, my relations by me, my heart cheerful, and taking little care for anything, and yet seeing many, whom I preferred before myself, under many trials and afflictions, in sickness, weakness, poverty, losses, crosses, and cares of the world,

---

3. Ecclesiastes 10.19.
4. He should have fed them also with the finest of the wheat: and with honey out of the rock

should I have satisfied thee" (Psalm 81.16).
5. And bring hither the fatted calf, and kill it; and let us eat, and be merry" (Luke 15.23).

I should be sometimes jealous least I should have my portion in this life, and that Scripture would come to my mind, "For whom the Lord loveth he chasteneth, and scourgeth every Son whom he receiveth" (Hebrews 12.6). But now I see the Lord had His time to scourge and chasten me. The portion of some is to have their afflictions by drops, now one drop and then another; but the dregs of the cup, the wine of astonishment, like a sweeping rain that leaveth no food, did the Lord prepare to be my portion. Affliction I wanted, and affliction I had, full measure (I thought), pressed down and running over. Yet I see, when God calls a person to anything, and through never so many difficulties, yet He is fully able to carry them through and make them see, and say they have been gainers thereby. And I hope I can say in some measure, as David did, "It is good for me that I have been afflicted."[6] The Lord hath showed me the vanity of these outward things. That they are the vanity of vanities, and vexation of spirit, that they are but a shadow, a blast, a bubble, and things of no continuance. That we must rely on God Himself, and our whole dependance must be upon Him. If trouble from smaller matters begin to arise in me, I have something at hand to check myself with, and say, why am I troubled? It was but the other day that if I had had the world, I would have given it for my freedom, or to have been a servant to a Christian. I have learned to look beyond present and smaller troubles, and to be quieted under them. As Moses said, "Stand still and see the salvation of the Lord" (Exodus 14.13).

Finis.

1682

6. Psalm 119.71.

EDWARD TAYLOR
c. 1642–1729

Given the importance of Edward Taylor's role in the town in which he lived for fifty-eight years, it is curious that we should know so little about his life. Taylor was probably born in Sketchly, Leicestershire County, England; his father was a "yeoman farmer"; that is, he was not a "gentleman" with large estates, but an independent landholder with title to his farm. Although Taylor's poetry contains no images that directly reflect his boyhood in Leicestershire, the dialect of that farming country is ever-present and gives his verse an air of provincial charm but also, it must be admitted, makes it difficult and complex for the modern reader. Taylor did not enter Harvard until he was twenty-nine years old and stayed only three years. It is assumed, therefore, that he had some university education in England, but it is not known where. We do know that he taught school and that he left his family and sailed to New England in 1668 because he would not sign an oath of loyalty to the Church of England. Rather than compromise his religious principles as a Puritan, he preferred exile in what he once called a "howling wilderness." It was at Harvard that he must have decided to leave teaching and prepare himself for the ministry.

In 1671 a delegation from the frontier town of Westfield, Massachusetts, asked Taylor to join them as their minister, and after a good deal of soul-searching he journeyed with them the hundred miles west to Westfield, where he remained the rest of his life. As by far the most educated member of that community, he served as minister, physician, and public servant. Taylor married twice and had fourteen children, many of whom died in infancy. A rigorous observer of all churchly functions, Taylor did not shy away from the religious controversies of the period. He was a strict observer of the "old" New England way, demanding a public account of conversion before admission to church membership and the right to partake of the sacrament of communion.

Taylor was a learned man as well as a pious one. Like most Harvard ministers, he knew Latin, Hebrew, and Greek. He had a passion for books and copied out in his own hand volumes that he borrowed from his college roommate, Samuel Sewall. He was known to Sewall and others as a good preacher, and on occasion he sent poems and letters to Boston friends, some parts of which were published during his lifetime. But Taylor's work as a poet was generally unknown until, in the 1930s, Thomas H. Johnson discovered that most of Taylor's poems had been deposited in the Yale University Library by Taylor's grandson, Ezra Stiles, a former president of Yale. It was one of the major literary discoveries of the twentieth century and revealed a body of work by a Puritan divine that was remarkable both in its quantity and quality.

Taylor's interest in poetry was lifelong, and he tried his hand at a variety of poetic genres: elegies on the death of public figures; lyrics in the manner of Elizabethan songs; a long poem, *God's Determinations,* in the tradition of the medieval debate; and an almost unreadable five-hundred-page *Metrical History of Christianity,* primarily a book of martyrs. But Taylor's best verse is to be found in a series called *Preparatory Meditations.* These poems, written for his own pleasure and never a part of any religious service, followed chiefly on his preparation for a sermon to be delivered at monthly communion. They gave the poet an occasion to summarize the emotional and intellectual content of his sermon and to speak directly and fervently to God. Sometimes these poems are gnarled and difficult to follow, but they also reveal a unique voice, unmistakably Taylor's. They are written in an idiom that harks back to the verse Taylor must have known as a child in England—the Metaphysical lyrics of John Donne and George Herbert—and so delight in puns and paradoxes and a rich profusion of metaphors and images. Nothing previously known about Puritan literature had suggested that there was a writer in New England who had sustained such a long-term love affair with poetry.

FROM PREPARATORY MEDITATIONS[1]

Prologue

> *Lord, Can a Crumb of Dust the Earth outweigh,*
> *Outmatch all mountains, nay, the Crystal sky?*
> *Embosom in't designs that shall Display*
> *And trace into the Boundless Deity?*

---

1. The full title is *Preparatory Meditations before my Approach to the Lord's Supper. Chiefly upon the Doctrine preached upon the Day of Administration [of Communion].* Taylor administered communion once a month to those members of his congregation who had made a declaration of their faith. He wrote these meditations in private; they are primarily the result of his contemplation of the biblical texts that served as the basis for the communion sermon. A total of 217 meditations survive, dating from 1682 to 1725. The text used here is from *Poems of Edward Taylor,* edited by Donald E. Stanford (1960).

Yea, hand a Pen whose moisture doth guide o'er   5
Eternal Glory with a glorious glore.[2]

If it its Pen had of an Angel's Quill,
    And sharpened on a Precious Stone ground tight,
And dipped in liquid Gold, and moved by Skill
    In Crystal leaves should golden Letters write,   10
    It would but blot and blur, yea, jag, and jar
    Unless Thou mak'st the Pen, and Scrivener.

I am this Crumb of Dust which is designed
    To make my Pen unto Thy Praise alone,
And my dull Fancy[3] I would gladly grind   15
    Unto an Edge on Zion's[4] Precious Stone.
    And Write in Liquid Gold upon Thy Name
    My Letters till Thy glory forth doth flame.

Let not th' attempts break down my Dust, I pray,
    Nor laugh Thou them to scorn but pardon give.   20
Inspire this crumb of Dust till it display
    Thy Glory through't: and then Thy dust shall live.
    Its failings then Thou'lt overlook, I trust,
    They being Slips slipped from Thy Crumb of Dust.

Thy Crumb of Dust breathes two words from its breast,   25
    That Thou wilt guide its pen to write aright
To Prove Thou art, and that Thou art the best
    And show Thy Properties to shine most bright.
    And then Thy Works will shine as flowers on Stems
    Or as in Jewelry Shops, do gems.   30

c. 1682   1939

Meditation 8 (First Series)

John 6.51. I am the Living Bread.[1]

I kenning through Astronomy Divine
    The World's bright Battlement,[2] wherein I spy
A Golden Path my Pencil cannot line,
    From that bright Throne unto my Threshold lie.
    And while my puzzled thoughts about it pour,   5
    I find the Bread of Life in't at my door.

2. Glory (Scottish).
3. I.e., imagination.
4. The hill in Jerusalem on which Solomon built his temple; the City of God on earth.
1. "The Jews then murmured at him, because he said, I am the bread which came down from heaven. And they said, Is not this Jesus, the son of Joseph, whose father and mother we know? how is it then that he saith, I came down from heaven? Jesus therefore answered[,] . . . Verily, verily, I say unto you, He that believeth on me hath everlasting life. I am that bread of life" (John 6.41–48). Jesus offers a "New Covenant of Faith" in place of the "Old Covenant of Works," which Adam broke when he disobeyed God's commandment.
2. I.e., discerning, by means of "divine astronomy," the towers of heaven. Taylor goes on to suggest that there is an invisible golden path from this world to the Gates of Heaven.

When that this Bird of Paradise[3] put in
    This Wicker Cage (my Corpse) to tweedle praise
Had pecked the Fruit forbade: and so did fling
    Away its Food; and lost its golden days;   10
    It fell into Celestial Famine sore:
    And never could attain a morsel more.

Alas! alas! Poor Bird, what wilt thou do?
    The Creatures' field no food for Souls e'er gave.
And if thou knock at Angels' doors they show   15
    An Empty Barrel: they no soul bread have.
    Alas! Poor Bird, the World's White Loaf is done.
    And cannot yield thee here the smallest Crumb.

In this sad state, God's Tender Bowels[4] run
    Out streams of Grace: and He to end all strife   20
The Purest Wheat in Heaven His dear-dear son
    Grinds, and kneads up into this Bread of Life.
    Which Bread of Life from Heaven down came and stands
    Dished on Thy Table up by Angels' Hands.

Did God mold up this Bread in Heaven, and bake,   25
    Which from His Table came, and to thine goeth?
Doth He bespeak thee thus, This Soul Bread take?
    Come Eat thy fill of this thy God's White Loaf?
    It's Food too fine for Angels, yet come, take
    And Eat thy fill. It's Heaven's Sugar Cake.   30

What Grace is this knead in this Loaf? This thing
    Souls are but petty things it to admire.
Ye Angels, help: This fill would to the brim
    Heav'ns whelmed-down[5] Crystal meal Bowl, yea and higher.
    This Bread of Life dropped in thy mouth, doth Cry: 35
    Eat, Eat me, Soul, and thou shalt never die.

June 8, 1684   1939

Upon Wedlock, and Death of Children[1]

A Curious Knot[2] God made in Paradise,
    And drew it out enameled[3] neatly Fresh.
It was the True-Love Knot, more sweet than spice,
    And set with all the flowers of Grace's dress.
    It's Wedden's[4] Knot, that ne're can be untied: 5
    No Alexander's Sword[5] can it divide.

---

3. I.e., the soul, which is like a bird kept in the body's cage.
4. Here used in the sense of the interior of the body, the "seat of the tender and sympathetic emotions," the heart.
5. Turned over. The *Oxford English Dictionary* quotes a passage from Dryden that is relevant: "That the earth is like a trencher and the Heavens a dish whelmed over it."

1. The text here is from *Poems of Edward Taylor*, edited by Donald E. Stanford (1960).
2. Flower bed.
3. Polished, shining.
4. I.e., wedding's.
5. Alexander the Great cut the Gordian knot devised by the king of Phyrgia when he learned that anyone who could undo it would rule Asia.

The slips[6] here planted, gay and glorious grow:
    Unless an Hellish breath do singe their Plumes.
Here Primrose, Cowslips, Roses, Lilies blow[7]
    With Violets and Pinks that void[8] perfumes: 10
    Whose beauteous leaves o'erlaid with Honey Dew,
    And Chanting birds Chirp out sweet Music true.

When in this Knot I planted was, my Stock[9]
    Soon knotted, and a manly flower out brake.[1]
And after it, my branch again did knot,   15
    Brought out another Flower, its sweet-breathed mate.
    One knot gave one tother[2] the tother's place.
    Whence Chuckling smiles fought in each other's face.

But Oh! a glorious hand from glory came
    Guarded with Angels, soon did crop this flower[3]   20
Which almost tore the root up of the same,
    At that unlooked for, Dolesome, darksome hour.
    In Prayer to Christ perfumed it did ascend,
    And Angels bright did it to heaven 'tend.

But pausing on't, this sweet perfumed my thought: 25
    Christ would in Glory have a Flower, Choice, Prime,
And having Choice, chose this my branch forth brought.
    Lord take't. I thank Thee, Thou tak'st ought of mine:
    It is my pledge in glory, part of me
    Is now in it, Lord, glorified with Thee.   30

But praying o're my branch, my branch did sprout,
    And bore another manly flower, and gay,[4]
And after that another, sweet brake[5] out,
    The which the former hand soon got away.
    But Oh! the tortures, Vomit, screechings, groans,   35
    and six week's Fever would pierce hearts like stones.[6]

Grief o'er doth flow: and nature fault would find
    Were not Thy Will, my Spell, Charm, Joy, and Gem:
That as I said, I say, take, Lord, they're Thine.
    I piecemeal pass to Glory bright in them.   40
    In joy, may I sweet flowers for glory breed,
    Whether thou get'st them green, or lets them seed.

c. 1682   1939

6. Cuttings.
7. Bloom.
8. Emit.
9. Stem, stalk.
1. Samuel Taylor was born on August 27, 1675, and lived to maturity.
2. To the other.

3. Elizabeth Taylor was born on December 27, 1676, and died on December 25, 1677.
4. James Taylor was born on October 12, 1678, and lived to maturity.
5. I.e., broke out.
6. Abigail Taylor was born on August 6, 1681, and died on August 22, 1682.

Upon a Wasp Chilled with Cold[1]

The Bear that breathes the Northern blast[2]
Did numb, Torpedo-like,[3] a Wasp
Whose stiffened limbs encramped, lay bathing
In Sol's[4] warm breath and shine as saving,
Which with her hands she chafes and stands   5
Rubbing her Legs, Shanks, Thighs, and hands.
Her petty toes, and fingers' ends
Nipped with this breath, she out extends
Unto the Sun, in great desire
To warm her digits at that fire.   10
Doth hold her Temples in this state
Where pulse doth beat, and head doth ache.
Doth turn, and stretch her body small,
Doth Comb her velvet Capital.[5]
As if her little brain pan were   15
A Volume of Choice precepts clear.
As if her satin jacket hot
Contained Apothecary's Shop
Of Nature's receipts,[6] that prevails
To remedy all her sad ails,   20
As if her velvet helmet high
Did turret[7] rationality.
She fans her wing up to the Wind
As if her Pettycoat were lined,
With reason's fleece, and hoists sails   25
And humming flies in thankful gales
Unto her dun Curled[8] palace Hall
Her warm thanks offering for all.

Lord, clear my misted sight that I
May hence view Thy Divinity,   30
Some sparks whereof Thou up dost hasp[9]
Within this little downy Wasp
In whose small Corporation[1] we
A school and a schoolmaster see,
Where we may learn, and easily find   35
A nimble Spirit bravely mind
Her work in every limb: and lace
It up neat with a vital grace,
Acting each part though ne'er so small
Here of this Fustian[2] animal,   40
Till I enravished Climb into
The Godhead on this Ladder do,

---

1. The text used here is from *Poems of Edward Taylor*, edited by Donald E. Stanford (1960).
2. The northern constellation the Big Dipper, also called Ursa Major, or the Great Bear.
3. The torpedo is a fish, like a stingray, that discharges a shock to one who touches it, causing numbness. Sir Thomas Browne writes: "Torpedoes deliver their opium at a distance and stupify beyond themselves" (1646).
4. The sun personified.
5. Head.
6. Remedies, prescriptions. "Apothecary's Shop": a drugstore or pharmacy.
7. Contain, encompass.
8. Dark curved.
9. Enclose, fasten.
1. Body.
2. Coarse-clothed.

Where all my pipes inspired upraise
An Heavenly music furred[3] with praise.

1960

Huswifery[1]

Make me, O Lord, Thy Spinning Wheel complete.
    Thy Holy Word my Distaff make for me.
Make mine Affections Thy Swift Flyers neat
    And make my Soul Thy holy Spool to be.
    My conversation make to be Thy Reel   5
    And reel the yarn thereon spun of Thy Wheel.[2]

Make me Thy Loom then, knit therein this Twine:
    And make Thy Holy Spirit, Lord, wind quills:[3]
Then weave the Web Thyself. The yarn is fine.
    Thine Ordinances make my Fulling Mills.[4]   10
    Then dye the same in Heavenly Colors Choice,
    All pinked with Varnished[5] Flowers of Paradise.

Then clothe therewith mine Understanding, Will,
    Affections, Judgment, Conscience, Memory,
My Words, and Actions, that their shine may fill   15
    My ways with glory and Thee glorify.
    Then mine apparel shall display before Ye
    That I am Clothed in Holy robes for glory.

1939

3. Trimmed or embellished, as with fur.
1. Housekeeping: used here to mean weaving. In Taylor's *Treatise Concerning the Lord's Supper*, he considers the significance of the sacrament of communion and takes as his text a passage from the New Testament: "And he saith unto him, Friend, how camest thou in hither not having a wedding garment? And he was speechless" (Matthew 22.12). Taylor argues that the wedding garment is the proper sign of the regenerate Christian. The text used here is from *Poems of Edward Taylor*, edited by Donald E. Stanford (1960).

2. In lines 1–6 Taylor refers to the working parts of a spinning wheel. "Distaff": holds the raw wool or flax. "Flyers": regulate the spinning. "Spool": twists the yarn. "Reel": Takes up the finished thread.
3. I.e., be like a spool or bobbin.
4. Where cloth is beaten and cleansed with fuller's earth, or soap.
5. Glossy, sparkling. "Pinked": adorned.

COTTON MATHER
1663–1728

Cotton Mather, as the eldest son of Increase Mather and the grandson of Richard Mather and John Cotton, was the heir apparent to the Congregational hierarchy that had dominated the churches of New England for almost fifty years. Like his father before him, Cotton Mather attended Harvard College. He was admitted at the age of twelve, and when he graduated in 1678, President Urian Oakes told the commencement audience that his hope was great that "in this youth, Cotton and Mather shall, in fact as well as name, joint together and once more appear in life." He was expected by his family to excel and did not disappoint them, but there is no doubt he had to pay a price for his ambition: he stammered badly when young, so much so that it was assumed he could never be a preacher, and he was subject all his life to nervous disorders that drove him alternately to ecstasy and despair. His enemies often complained that he was vain and aggressive. But he was also a genius of sorts, competent in the natural sciences and gifted in the study of ancient languages. He possessed a strong mind, and by the time he had stopped writing he could boast that he had published more than four hundred separate works. A worthy successor to his father's position as pastor of the Second Church of Boston, he remained connected with that church from 1685, when he was ordained, until his death forty-three years later.

Like Benjamin Franklin, Mather found great satisfaction in doing good works and organized societies for building churches, supported schools for the children of slaves, and worked to establish funds for indigent clergy. But for all his worldly success, Mather's life was darkened by disappointment and tragedy. He lost two wives and saw his third wife go insane, and of his fifteen children, only two lived until his death. More than one of his contemporaries observed that he never overcame his bitterness at being rejected for the presidency of Harvard. It was the one thing his father had achieved that eluded him.

Although he was a skillful preacher and an eminent theologian, it is his work as a historian that has earned Mather a significant place in American literature. No one has described more movingly the hopes of the first generation of Puritans, and what gives Mather's best writing its urgency is the sense that the Puritan community as he knew it was fading away. By the time that Mather was writing his history of New England, the issues that seemed most pressing to his parishioners were political and social rather than theological. In his diary of 1700 he noted that "there was hardly any but my father and myself to appear in defense of our invaded churches." Everything that Mather wrote can be seen as a call to defend the old order of church authority against the encroachment of an increasingly secular world. As an apologist for the "old New England way" Mather certainly left himself open to attack, and by the end of the seventeenth century he had become a scapegoat for the worst in Puritan culture. He is often blamed for the Salem witchcraft trials, for example, but he never actually attended one of them; his greatest crime was in not speaking out against those who he knew had exceeded the limits of authority. Mather saw the devil's presence in Salem as a final campaign to undermine and destroy religious community.

In spite of its rambling and sometimes self-indulgent nature, the *Magnalia Christi Americana* (the title may be translated as "A history of the wonderful works of Christ in America") remains Mather's most impressive work. It is described on the title page as an "ecclesiastical history of New England," and in the course of its seven books, Mather attempts to record for future readers not only a history of the New England churches and the college (Harvard) where its ministers were trained but representative biographies of "saint's" lives. Although it is true that Mather was so caught up in his vision of a glorious past that he was sometimes quite blind to the suffocating realities of the world in which he lived, no one has set forth more clearly the history of a people who saw themselves transforming a wilderness into a garden and the ideal of a harmonious community that has been characterized time and again as the American dream. It is, however, in Mather's biographical sketches—his lives of Bradford, Winthrop, Eliot, and Phips—that the *Magnalia* is most arresting, for it is in his account of a particular saint's reconciliation with God on earth that New England's story is most eloquently realized.

In addition to defending Puritan beliefs and attempting to record New England's history in the epic *Magnalia,* Mather experimented in a variety of forms that served the tastes of an emergent popular literary culture. Certainly that was the case in his handling of such tales as Hannah Dustan's, since the Indian captivity narrative was to be a prolific source for later American writers eager to reach a wide public. Dustan, who never published her own account of her harrowing and violent experience, told it to Mather herself. He included his version in his *Decennium Luctuosum* (Tearful Decade), a general chronicle of warfare between the New England colonists and Native Americans published in 1699, and reprinted it in his *Magnalia* two years later. But Mather's reach went further. His many forays into what in essence were "conduct books" (such as *Ornaments for the Daughters of Zion*, 1692, and *Bonifacius*, 1710, later reprinted as *Essays to Do Good*), even as they showed him seeking to replace the old political power of the clergy with moral chastisement and persuasion, pioneered a kind of writing that proliferated in England and America across the following century, helping ordinary people to imitate the manners and values of the elite and thus to rise in the world. Here, too, Mather shared an interest with Benjamin Franklin, whose *Poor Richards Almanack* would provide similar guidance for commoners.

From The Wonders of the Invisible World[1]

[A PEOPLE OF GOD IN THE DEVIL'S TERRITORIES]

The New Englanders are a people of God settled in those, which were once the devil's territories; and it may easily be supposed that the devil was exceedingly disturbed, when he perceived such a people here accomplishing the promise of old made unto our blessed Jesus, that He should have the utmost parts of the earth for His possession.[2] There was not a greater uproar among the Ephesians,[3] when the Gospel was first brought among them, than there was among the powers of the air (after whom those Ephesians walked) when first the silver trumpets of the Gospel here made the joyful sound. The devil thus irritated, immediately tried all sorts of methods to overturn this poor plantation: and so much of the church, as was fled into this wilderness, immediately found the serpent cast out of his mouth a flood for the carrying of it away. I believe that never were more satanical devices used for the unsettling of any people under the sun, than what have been employed for the extirpation of the vine which God has here planted, casting out the heathen, and preparing a room before it, and causing it to take deep root, and fill the land, so that it sent its boughs unto the Atlantic Sea eastward, and its branches unto the Connecticut River westward, and the hills were covered with a shadow thereof. But all those attempts of hell have hitherto been abortive, many an Ebenezer[4] has been erected unto the praise of God, by his poor people here; and having obtained help from God, we continue to this day. Wherefore the devil is now making one attempt more upon

1. In May 1692, Governor William Phips of Massachusetts appointed a court to "hear and determine" the cases against some nineteen persons in Salem accused of witchcraft. Mather had long been interested in the subject of witchcraft, and in this work, written at the request of the judges, he describes the case against the accused. Mather, like many others, saw the evidence of witchcraft as the devil's work, a last-ditch effort to undermine the Puritan ideal. Mather was himself skeptical of much of the evidence used against the accused, especially as the trials proceeded in the summer of 1692, but like a number of prominent individuals in the community, he made no public protest. First published in 1693,

the text used here is taken from the reprint by John Russell Smith (1862).

2. After Jesus was baptized he fasted in the desert for forty days; it was there that the devil tempted him and offered him the world (see Luke 4).

3. Ephesus was an ancient city in Asia Minor, famous for its temples to the goddess Diana. When Saint Paul preached there he received hostile treatment, and riots followed the sermons of missionaries who attempted to convert the Ephesians.

4. Stone of help (Hebrew, literal trans.); a commemorative monument like the one Samuel erected to note victory over the Philistines (1 Samuel 7.12).

us; an attempt more difficult, more surprising, more snarled with unintelligible circumstances than any that we have hitherto encountered; an attempt so critical, that if we get well through, we shall soon enjoy halcyon days with all the vultures of hell trodden under our feet. He has wanted his incarnate legions to persecute us, as the people of God have in the other hemisphere been persecuted: he has therefore drawn forth his more spiritual ones to make an attack upon us. We have been advised by some credible Christians yet alive, that a malefactor, accused of witchcraft as well as murder, and executed in this place more than forty years ago, did then give notice of an horrible plot against the country by witchcraft, and a foundation of witchcraft then laid, which if it were not seasonably discovered, would probably blow up, and pull down all the churches in the country. And we have now with horror seen the discovery of such a witchcraft! An army of devils is horribly broke in upon the place which is the center, and after a sort, the first-born of our English settlements: and the houses of the good people there are filled with the doleful shrieks of their children and servants, tormented by invisible hands, with tortures altogether preternatural. After the mischiefs there endeavored, and since in part conquered,[5] the terrible plague of evil angels hath made its progress into some other places, where other persons have been in like manner diabolically handled. These our poor afflicted neighbors, quickly after they become infected and infested with these demons, arrive to a capacity of discerning those which they conceive the shapes of their troublers; and notwithstanding the great and just suspicion that the demons might impose the shapes of innocent persons in their spectral exhibitions upon the sufferers (which may perhaps prove no small part of the witch-plot in the issue), yet many of the persons thus represented, being examined, several of them have been convicted of a very damnable witchcraft: yea, more than one [and] twenty have confessed, that they have signed unto a book, which the devil showed them, and engaged in his hellish design of bewitching and ruining our land. We know not, at least I know not, how far the delusions of Satan may be interwoven into some circumstances of the confessions; but one would think all the rules of understanding human affairs are at an end, if after so many most voluntary harmonious confessions, made by intelligent persons of all ages, in sundry towns, at several times, we must not believe the main strokes wherein those confessions all agree: especially when we have a thousand preternatural things every day before our eyes, wherein the confessors do acknowledge their concernment, and give demonstration of their being so concerned. If the devils now can strike the minds of men with any poisons of so fine a composition and operation, that scores of innocent people shall unite, in confessions of a crime, which we see actually committed, it is a thing prodigious, beyond the wonders of the former ages, and it threatens no less than a sort of a dissolution upon the world. Now, by these confessions 'tis agreed that the devil has made a dreadful knot of witches in the country, and by the help of witches has dreadfully increased that knot: that these witches have driven a trade of commissioning their confederate spirits to do all sorts of mischiefs to the neighbors, whereupon there have ensued such mischievous consequences upon the bodies and estates of the neighborhood, as could not otherwise be accounted for: yea, that at prodigious witch-meetings, the wretches

5. I.e., after the mischiefs were attempted there, and later partly overcome.

have proceeded so far as to concert and consult the methods of rooting out the Christian religion from this country, and setting up instead of it perhaps a more gross diabolism than ever the world saw before. And yet it will be a thing little short of miracle, if in so spread a business as this, the devil should not get in some of his juggles,[6] to confound the discovery of all the rest.

* * *

But I shall no longer detain my reader from his expected entertainment, in a brief account of the trials which have passed upon some of the male-factors lately executed at Salem, for the witchcrafts whereof they stood convicted. For my own part, I was not present at any of them; nor ever had I any personal prejudice at the persons thus brought upon the stage; much less at the surviving relations of those persons, with and for whom I would be as hearty a mourner as any man living in the world: The Lord comfort them! But having received a command[7] so to do, I can do no other than shortly relate the chief matters of fact, which occurred in the trials of some that were executed, in an abridgment collected out of the court papers on this occasion put into my hands. You are to take the truth, just as it was; and the truth will hurt no good man. There might have been more of these, if my book would not thereby have swollen too big; and if some other wor-thy hands did not perhaps intend something further in these collections; for which cause I have only singled out four or five, which may serve to illus-trate the way of dealing, wherein witchcrafts use to be concerned; and I report matters not as an advocate, but as an historian.

* * *

[THE TRIAL OF MARTHA CARRIER]

AT THE COURT OF OYER AND TERMINER,[8] HELD BY ADJOURNMENT AT SALEM, AUGUST 2, 1692

I. Martha Carrier was indicted for the bewitching certain persons, accord-ing to the form usual in such cases, pleading not guilty to her indictment; there were first brought in a considerable number of the bewitched persons who not only made the court sensible[9] of an horrid witchcraft committed upon them, but also deposed that it was Martha Carrier, or her shape, that grievously tormented them, by biting, pricking, pinching and choking of them. It was further deposed that while this Carrier was on her examination before the magistrates, the poor people were so tortured that every one expected their death upon the very spot, but that upon the binding of Carrier they were eased. Moreover the look of Carrier then laid the afflicted people for dead; and her touch, if her eye at the same time were off them, raised them again: which things were also now seen upon her trial. And it was testi-fied that upon the mention of some having their necks twisted almost round, by the shape of this Carrier, she replied, "It's no matter though their necks had been twisted quite off."

II. Before the trial of this prisoner, several of her own children had frankly and fully confessed not only that they were witches themselves, but

---

6. Tricks.
7. I.e., the request by the judges to explain the sentencing of people accused of witchcraft.
8. To hear and determine.
9. Aware.

that this their mother had made them so. This confession they made with great shows of repentance, and with much demonstration of truth. They related place, time, occasion; they gave an account of journeys, meetings and mischiefs by them performed, and were very credible in what they said. Nevertheless, this evidence was not produced against the prisoner at the bar,[1] inasmuch as there was other evidence enough to proceed upon.

III. Benjamin Abbot gave his testimony that last March was a twelvemonth,[2] this Carrier was very angry with him, upon laying out some land near her husband's: her expressions in this anger were that she would stick as close to Abbot as the bark stuck to the tree; and that he should repent of it afore seven years came to an end, so as Doctor Prescot should never cure him. These words were heard by others besides Abbot himself; who also heard her say, she would hold his nose as close to the grindstone as ever it was held since his name was Abbot. Presently after this, he was taken with a swelling in his foot, and then with a pain in his side, and exceedingly tormented. It bred into a sore, which was lanced by Doctor Prescot, and several gallons of corruption[3] ran out of it. For six weeks it continued very bad, and then another sore bred in the groin, which was also lanced by Doctor Prescot. Another sore then bred in his groin, which was likewise cut, and put him to very great misery: he was brought unto death's door, and so remained until Carrier was taken, and carried away by the constable, from which very day he began to mend, and so grew better every day, and is well ever since.

Sarah Abbot also, his wife, testified that her husband was not only all this while afflicted in his body, but also that strange, extraordinary and unaccountable calamities befell his cattle; their death being such as they could guess at no natural reason for.

IV. Allin Toothaker testified that Richard, the son of Martha Carrier, having some difference with him, pulled him down by the hair of the head. When he rose again he was going to strike at Richard Carrier but fell down flat on his back to the ground, and had not power to stir hand or foot, until he told Carrier he yielded; and then he saw the shape of Martha Carrier go off his breast.

This Toothaker had received a wound in the wars; and he now testified that Martha Carrier told him he should never be cured. Just afore the apprehending of Carrier, he could thrust a knitting needle into his wound four inches deep; but presently after her being seized, he was thoroughly healed.

He further testified that when Carrier and he some times were at variance, she would clap her hands at him, and say he should get nothing by it; whereupon he several times lost his cattle, by strange deaths, whereof no natural causes could be given.

V. John Rogger also testified that upon the threatening words of this malicious Carrier, his cattle would be strangely bewitched; as was more particularly then described.

VI. Samuel Preston testified that about two years ago, having some difference with Martha Carrier, he lost a cow in a strange, preternatural, unusual manner; and about a month after this, the said Carrier, having again some difference with him, she told him he had lately lost a cow, and

---

1. I.e., the defendant in court.
2. I.e., a year ago last March.

3. Pus; infected matter. "Lanced": cut open.

it should not be long before he lost another; which accordingly came to pass; for he had a thriving and well-kept cow, which without any known cause quickly fell down and died.

VII. Phebe Chandler testified that about a fortnight before the apprehension of Martha Carrier, on a Lordsday,[4] while the Psalm was singing in the Church, this Carrier then took her by the shoulder and shaking her, asked her, where she lived: she made her no answer, although as Carrier, who lived next door to her father's house, could not in reason but know who she was. Quickly after this, as she was at several times crossing the fields, she heard a voice, that she took to be Martha Carrier's, and it seemed as if it was over her head. The voice told her she should within two or three days be poisoned. Accordingly, within such a little time, one half of her right hand became greatly swollen and very painful; as also part of her face: whereof she can give no account how it came. It continued very bad for some days; and several times since she has had a great pain in her breast; and been so seized on her legs that she has hardly been able to go. She added that lately, going well to the house of God, Richard, the son of Martha Carrier, looked very earnestly upon her, and immediately her hand, which had formerly been poisoned, as is abovesaid, began to pain her greatly, and she had a strange burning at her stomach; but was then struck deaf, so that she could not hear any of the prayer, or singing, till the two or three last words of the Psalm.

VIII. One Foster, who confessed her own share in the witchcraft for which the prisoner stood indicted, affirmed that she had seen the prisoner at some of their witch-meetings, and that it was this Carrier, who persuaded her to be a witch. She confessed that the devil carried them on a pole to a witch-meeting; but the pole broke, and she hanging about Carrier's neck, they both fell down, and she then received an hurt by the fall, whereof she was not at this very time recovered.

IX. One Lacy, who likewise confessed her share in this witchcraft, now testified, that she and the prisoner were once bodily present at a witch-meeting in Salem Village; and that she knew the prisoner to be a witch, and to have been at a diabolical sacrament, and that the prisoner was the undoing of her and her children by enticing them into the snare of the devil.

X. Another Lacy, who also confessed her share in this witchcraft, now testified, that the prisoner was at the witch-meeting, in Salem Village, where they had bread and wine administered unto them.

XI. In the time of this prisoner's trial, one Susanna Sheldon in open court had her hands unaccountably tied together with a wheel-band[5] so fast that without cutting, it could not be loosed: it was done by a specter; and the sufferer affirmed it was the prisoner's.

Memorandum. This rampant hag, Martha Carrier, was the person of whom the confessions of the witches, and of her own children among the rest, agreed that the devil had promised her she should be Queen of Hebrews.

1692, 1693

---

4. Sunday.   5. A strap that goes around a wheel.

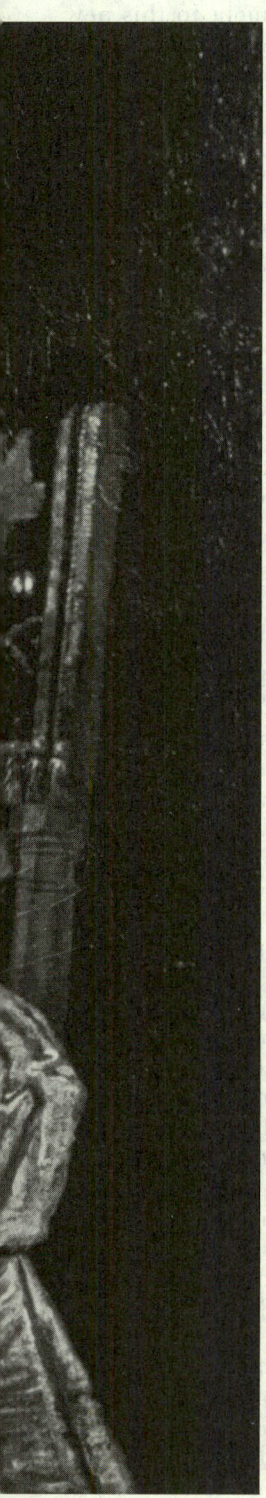

American Literature
1700–1820

AN EXPANDING WORLD
AND UNIVERSE

By the time of Cotton Mather's death in 1728, which symbolically marks the passing of Puritanism as the colonists had experienced it, the imaginative world he and other clerical writers strove to maintain was challenged in a variety of ways. The eighteenth century saw enormous changes—economic, social, philosophical, and scientific—that inevitably affected the influence and authority of clergymen like Mather and transformed the ways in which they understood the world. Most important, many intellectuals now believed in the power of the human mind to comprehend the universe as never before, particularly through the laws of physics as they recently had been described by the great Isaac Newton (1642–1727). Inevitably, then, scripture became more a handmaiden than a guide to metaphysics. Second, and of equal importance, through the influence of the English metaphysician John Locke (1632–1704) there arose new psychological paradigms that postulated human sympathy, rather than supernatural grace, as the basis for the moral life. As elaborated by Adam Smith and other thinkers, this reliance on human sympathy or "sentiment" as the catalyst for moral choice and action concomitantly encouraged the belief that each individual had the power to control his or her spiritual destiny. Such challenges to the theocentric world of the colonial clergy came with the immense changes in Western thought described by historians as the Enlightenment.

The Enlightenment had political as well as scientific and religious implications. By the end of the century,

Elizabeth Clarke Freake and Baby Mary, unknown artist, 1671–74. For more information about this image, see the color insert in this volume.

colonists were in the process of establishing a polity the likes of which the world had not yet seen. There would be a religious element to this new nation, but it would be only one component of a state whose destiny, while still thought of as divinely guaranteed, was understood to be achievable on earth through the spread of democratic principles. The literature of this century reflected and extended these and other new currents in Western thought and culture.

The eighteenth century brought a new world into being in the most basic and striking ways. The increase in population alone helps account for the greater diversity of opinion in religious as well as in political life that marked it and its literature. In 1670, for example, the population of the colonies numbered approximately 111,000. Thirty years later it was more than 250,000; by 1760, if one includes Georgia, it reached 1,600,000—and the settled area had tripled. The demand for and price of colonial goods increased in England, and vast fortunes were to be made in New England with any business connected with shipbuilding: especially timber, tar, and pitch. Virginia planters became rich through tobacco; and rice and indigo from the Carolinas were in constant demand. Further, compared with the crowded cities of Europe, the colonies were healthier and cheaper, and promotional literature as well as personal testimony painted British North America as a region in which one could take charge of and transform one's life. Thus those who could arrange their passage, either by paying for it outright or mortgaging it through indentured service, arrived in great numbers: Boston, for example, almost doubled in size from 1700 to 1720. The colonies were ethnically diverse; the great migration during the first half of the eighteenth century was not primarily English. Dutch and Germans came in large numbers and so did French Protestants. By this time, too, Jewish merchants and craftsmen had established themselves in New York and Philadelphia.

The rapid expansion of transatlantic trade—hallmark of what we now recognize as the beginning of modern consumerism—linked the colonies to other areas in what historians call the Atlantic Rim, a region encompassing Europe, Africa, and the Caribbean basin as well as North and South America. The rim had a complex, multiethnic, multiracial population united by little more than their status as laborers. Thus even as the new and seemingly insatiable desire for goods brought great wealth to planters and merchants, it created at the other end of the social spectrum the world's first multiethnic working class, one whose members often had to endure great cruelty. The numbers of enslaved Africans increased in this period, for example, even as some of them, typified here by Olaudah Equiano, began to speak out about their experiences and condition. Other groups like the New England Indians suffered in different ways. Estimated to number twenty-five thousand in 1600, they already had been reduced by one third during the plague of 1616–18 and declined steadily thereafter; many Native American communities disappeared entirely during this period of expansion in the Northeast. Their fate in the southern colonies and the Caribbean islands, often linked to plantation slavery, was no better.

The economic ferment affected the very warp and woof of social organization. New England towns, for example, long viewed as pillars of stability, were often full of acrimonious debate between first settlers and newcomers as they bickered over the disposition of land or the proper form and substance of worship. When the colonies' first towns were formed, for example, acreage was apportioned to settlers and allotted free; but by 1713 speculators in land were hard at work, buying as much as possible for as little as possible and selling at often-substantial profit. Many a town history records the wrangling of splinter groups and the establishment of a "second" church and the inevitable migration of families and groups who sought richer farm lands. Under new economic and religious pressures, the idea of a "community" of mutually helpful souls was fast disappearing, and the colonists' gradual awakening to the incongruity of the slavery that they tolerated or even encouraged only further stretched the capacity of their rhetoric of Christian charity.

While life in many parts of the colonies remained difficult, the hardships and dangers the first settlers faced were mostly overcome, and more and more colonists, particularly those along the coast, emulated the culture of metropolitan London. At the same time, once colonists began to expect the refinements made available by their extensive trading networks, they better understood what was special or unique about the society they were creating in the New World. United by the common experience of ocean passage and the desire to make new lives for themselves, these thousands of emigrants slowly but inexorably began to realize that they had more in common as inhabitants of America than they did as emigrants from a Europe that rapidly receded into memory. In 1702 no one would have dreamed of an independent union of colonies, but by the 1750s it was a distinct possibility.

ENLIGHTENMENT IDEALS

By the early eighteenth century, scientists and philosophers had posed great challenges to seventeenth-century beliefs, and the "modern" period as we understand it emerged from their efforts to envisage humans and their universe in new terms, even as they struggled to yoke this brave new world to what they learned from scripture. Indeed, scientists like Newton and philosophers like Locke sought to resolve implicit conflicts between their discoveries and traditionally held Christian truths. Because they believed that God worked in reasonable, comprehensible ways with humankind uppermost, they saw nothing heretical in arguing that the universe was an orderly system such that by the application of reason humanity would comprehend its laws, or that one's supreme moral obligation was to relate to one's fellows through an innate and thus natural power of sympathy. But the inevitable result of such inquiries made the universe seem much more rational and benevolent than it had been represented in Puritan doctrine. Similarly, people increasingly defined their highest duties in social rather than in spiritual terms.

Because science made the world seem more comprehensible, many put less stock in revealed religion. Often these new scientists and philosophers were avowedly, or were called, Deists; they deduced the existence of a supreme being from the construction of the universe itself rather than from the Bible. "A creation," as one distinguished historian has put it, "presupposes a creator." A harmonious universe proclaimed the beneficence of God. Characteristically seventeenth-century modes of thought—Bradford's and Winthrop's penchant for the allegorical and emblematic, seeing every natural and human event as a message from God, for instance—seemed anachronistic and quaint. People were less interested in the metaphysical verities of introspective divines than in the progress of ordinary individuals, relating now to their fellow beings through emotions and experiences they shared as colonists. This no doubt accounts for the widespread popularity of Benjamin Franklin's *Autobiography*. Many now assumed that humankind was naturally good and thus dwelt on neither the Fall nor the Incarnation, but rather on how thinking, feeling people shared the bonds of their common humanity. They were less interested in theology than in humankind's own nature, and frequently cited Alexander Pope's famous couplet:

> Know then thyself, presume not God to scan,
> The proper study of mankind is man.

Locke said that "our business" here on earth "is not to know all things, but those which concern our conduct." In suggesting that we are not born with a set of innate ideas of good or evil and that the mind is rather like a blank wax tablet (a *tabula rasa*) on which experiences are inscribed, Locke qualified traditional belief and suggested that the more that we understood and sympathized with our fellow men and women, the richer our social and spiritual lives would be.

REASON AND RELIGION: THE GREAT AWAKENING

But the old beliefs did not die easily, and as early as the 1730s a conservative reaction against the worldview of the new science and psychology followed as some intellectuals, aware of the new thought but intent on maintaining the final truth of revealed religion, resisted the religious implications of Enlightenment principles. But the genie had escaped from the bottle, and this reaction was itself indelibly marked by the new thought it opposed.

One unexpected result, for example, was that the first half of the eighteenth century witnessed a number of religious revivals in both England and America that in part were fueled by the new emphasis on emotion as a defining component of human experience. Although some historians view the revivals as desperate efforts to reassert outmoded Puritan values in the face of the new, but in fact the religious fires that burned so intensely between 1735 and 1750 were themselves the direct product of the new cult of feeling whose foundation Locke had laid. Now ministers as well as philosophers argued that our greatest pleasure was derived from the good we did for others, and that our sympathetic emotions (our joys as

George Whitefield, c. 1741, by John Wollaston. Transatlantic revivalist George Whitefield preaching to a crowded meeting during the Great Awakening.

well as our tears) were not signs of humankind's fallen state but rather a guarantee of our future glory. The African American poet Phillis Wheatley, for example, whose poem on the death of the itinerant Methodist George Whitefield (1714–1770) made her famous, said that Whitefield prayed that "grace in every heart might dwell" and longed to see "America excell." After his many successful religious revivals in England, Whitefield embarked on a preaching tour along the Atlantic seaboard colonies in 1739–40, a visit that was punctuated by great emotionalism. But in this he only followed the similarly "extraordinary circumstances" that had occurred in Northampton, Massachusetts, under the leadership of Jonathan Edwards in the 1730s and that have come to be synonymous with the "Great Awakening."

Edwards also had read his Locke and agreed that if his parishioners were to be awakened from their spiritual slumbers they had to experience religion in a more visceral way, not just strive to comprehend it intellectually. Thus, from his time as a young minister under the tutelage of his eminent grandfather, the Reverend Solomon Stoddard, Edwards began to rejuvenate the basic tenets of Calvinism, including that of unconditional election, the sixteenth-century doctrine most difficult for eighteenth-century minds to accept. Edwards insisted that such doctrines made sense in terms of Enlightenment science. Hammering at his congregation with what one historian has called a "rhetoric of sensation," he persuaded his listeners that God's sovereignty was not only the most reasonable doctrine but also the most "delightful" and that it revealed itself to him in an almost sensuous way as "exceeding pleasant, bright, and sweet." In carefully reasoned, calmly argued prose, as harmonious and as ordered as anything the age produced, Edwards brought many in his audience to accept that "if the great things of religion are rightly understood, they will affect the heart." Thus, while most people remember Edwards for his frightening sermon *Sinners in the Hands of an Angry God,* he was much more moved by the experience of joy that his faith brought him. More typical is his "Personal Narrative" or his apostrophe to Sarah Pierpont (whom he would marry), for both testify to how experientially moving he found true religious feeling. These are foundational texts for understanding the rise of the sentimental in American literature and Western culture generally.

The Awakening in turn engendered as many critics as supporters, for many believed that revivalists were too given over to "enthusiasm" at the expense of their reason. Thus Edwards and others who believed in the new light that God had shed over them had to expend much of their time and energy in pamphlet wars with prominent clergy such as Boston's Charles Chauncy who, from his pulpit in that city's First Church, compared the fervor of the revivalists to the hysteria that Anne Hutchinson had engendered a century earlier. Heirs to a rapid expansion of print culture that fueled the controversies over revival, rivals like Edwards and Chauncy, and others on both sides of the religious question, used the presses as never before to win over public opinion. Inevitably, the fires of revival burned lower; when Edwards himself tried to consolidate his success in Northampton and in 1749 demanded from applicants personal accounts of conversion before admitting them to church membership, he was accused of being a reactionary, removed from his pulpit, and effectively silenced. He spent the next few years as a missionary to the American Indians in Stockbridge, Massachusetts, a town forty miles west of Northampton, carrying on the work of the

Reverend David Brainard, a young man who, had he lived, would have married Edwards's daughter Jerusha. There Edwards remained until invited to become president of the College of New Jersey. His death in Princeton was the direct result of the smallpox inoculation he had received to set an example for his frightened and superstitious students; it serves as a vivid reminder of how complicated the response to the "new science" could become in any one individual.

IMPERIAL POLITICS

If religion occupied many colonists in the first half of the eighteenth century, after 1763, when Great Britain had consolidated its empire in the New World with victory over the French in Canada, politics dominated its second half. On June 7, 1776, at the second Continental Congress, Richard Henry Lee of Virginia moved that "these united colonies are, and of a right ought to be, free and independent states." A committee was duly appointed to prepare a declaration of independence, and it was issued on July 4. Although these motions and their swiftness took some delegates by surprise—the purpose of the congress had, after all, not been to declare independence but to protest the usurpation of rights by king and Parliament and to effect a compromise with the homeland—others saw them as the inevitable consequence of the events of the preceding decade. The Stamp Act of 1764, taxing all newspapers, legal documents, and licenses, had infuriated Bostonians and resulted in the burning of the governor's palace; the Virginian Patrick Henry had taken the occasion to speak passionately against taxation without representation. In 1770 a Boston mob had been fired on by British soldiers. Three years later came the famous Tea Party, when colonists disguised themselves

The Destruction of Tea at Boston Harbor, lithograph by Nathaniel Currier. The famed Boston Tea Party of 1763, when colonists, disguised as Native Americans, protested a new British tax on tea and other commodities.

as Native Americans and dumped English tea into Boston harbor to protest paying taxes on it and to test the limits of British rule. In adopting Native American dress, these protesters declared themselves antithetical to everything British. The news of the armed confrontation with the British in Concord and Lexington, Massachusetts, in April 1775 was still on everyone's tongue in Philadelphia when the Second Continental Congress convened a month later.

Although the drama of these events and the personal suffering they caused cannot be underestimated, colonists also were transformed into revolutionaries through the power of the word. Thomas Paine's pamphlet *Common Sense*, published in January 1776, has been credited with tipping the scales toward revolution, but it was preceded by a vast literature that took to heart the arguments of the Whig opposition in England. The Whigs, the so-called country as opposed to court party, inveighed against luxury and tyranny in terms that resonated across the Atlantic. In arguing that separation from England was the only reasonable course and that "the Almighty" had planted these feelings in us "for good and wise purposes," Paine appealed to basic tenets of the Enlightenment. His clarion call—"stand forth!"—to those who "love mankind," those "that dare oppose not only the tyranny but the tyrant," did not go unheeded. Americans needed a champion for the Revolution, and in December 1776, when Washington's troops were at their most demoralized, it was again Paine's first *Crisis* paper—popularly called *The American Crisis*—that was read to all the regiments and was said to have inspired their coming success.

Paine first came to America in 1774 with a note from Benjamin Franklin recommending him to publishers and editors. He was only one of a number of young writers who took advantage of the revolution in print culture that was to make authorship as we know it possible. This period was, in fact, the great age of the newspaper and the moral essay; Franklin tells us that he modeled his own style on the clarity, good sense, and simplicity of the English essayists Joseph Addison and Richard Steele. The first newspaper in the colonies appeared in 1704, and by the time of the Revolution there were almost fifty papers and forty magazines. The great cry was for a "national literature" (meaning anti-British), and the political events of the 1770s presented a dramatic opportunity for a career in letters. It is not surprising, then, that the most significant writings of the period are political, such as the essays Alexander Hamilton, John Jay, and James Madison wrote for New York newspapers in 1787 and 1788 in support of the new federal constitution, collectively known as *The Federalist Papers*. They provided an eloquent defense of the framework of the republic and remind us that in good measure the uniqueness of the nascent United States of America resided in the language of the documents, the very words, on which the nation was based. Together with such self-consciously American works as Benjamin Franklin's *Autobiography* and Hector St. John de Crèvecoeur's *Letters from an American Farmer,* they mark the beginning of a new sense of national identity as colonists from greatly different backgrounds and of varied nationalities now found reasons to call themselves "Americans." This gradual transformation was not easy. Washington Irving's fictional character Rip Van Winkle found the world radically different when, finally awakened from his slumbers, he tried to make sense of what he had missed, the American Revolution: "God knows, I'm not myself—I'm somebody else—that's me yonder—no—that's somebody else got into my shoes—I was myself last night, but I fell asleep on the mountain and everything's changed, and I'm changed, and I can't tell what's my name, or who I am!"

But Irving's characterization is fictional, and it is important to recall that during this same period other writers published utilitarian political and polite—aesthetically enjoyable—literature simultaneously. Philip Freneau, for example, succeeded first as a writer of anti-British satires; after publishing his *Poems Written Chiefly during the Late War* (1786) he turned to newspaper work, editing the *New York Daily Advertiser* and writing anti–Federalist Party essays, making himself an enemy of Alexander Hamilton in the process. Even Franklin got into the act. As early as 1747 he voiced his support for women—in this instance, for blame to be shared equally by man and woman in the case of an illegitimate birth—in his pseudonymous "Speech of Polly Baker," which appeared first in a London magazine. Other authors cut a different profile, publishing in local periodicals and newspapers but also contributing significantly to an extensive manuscript culture in which literary efforts were shared with a coterie of like-minded people. Most important, even women such as Judith Sargent Murray, Sarah Wentworth Morton, and others got into the act, and all found eager audiences for their work in such periodicals as Isaiah Thomas's *Massachusetts Magazine*. Although the conventions of the day required at least a show of anonymity, the women used feminine pen names and their identities were generally known, thus proclaiming the right of women to opine in print on public events and, as in the case of Murray, to try their hands at belles lettres as well.

In addition, by the late eighteenth century some writers began to publish the nation's first novels—fiction too lengthy to lend itself to either manuscript circulation or public reading. Primacy is usually given to William Hill Brown's epistolary novel, *The Power of Sympathy* (1789), but the next decade also saw the publication of important novels by women, particularly Susan-

Early American print shop. Authors in the young republic had their work published by printers working in such shops.

nah Rowson's *Charlotte Temple* (1794) and Hannah Webster Foster's *The Coquette* (1797), works that often treated, even as they exemplified, the right of women to be considered equals in the new nation's democratic experiment. In the last decade of the century, Charles Brockden Brown also published several novels, *Edgar Huntly* among them, that adapted the Gothic mode to the American landscape as well as to topics like Indian captivity and imperialism. Such later writers as Nathaniel Hawthorne and Edgar Allan Poe viewed his work as an important precursor to their own psychological fiction. These early novels were issued by enterprising printers who took a chance on publishing them in the hope that a title might emerge as a "steady seller,"—that is, remain in sufficient demand to warrant constant reprinting. In turn, such popularity was all the more likely because of a new and growing readership as literacy rates rose significantly in this period among both men and women.

But because neither the technological nor the economic infrastructure was yet in place to support a national audience and because people lived in widely separated and poorly connected villages or on remote farms, none of these early American writers, not even such popular novelists as Rowson and Foster, could live by the pen alone. The crisis in American life caused by the Revolution had made artists more aware of American subjects, but it was Washington Irving who best learned how to exploit this nascent self-consciousness, who had the distinction of being the first American writer to live on the income produced by his publications. His generation discovered ways of being American without compromising their integrity, and they successfully harnessed the world of print to their ambition to speak as professional authors.

PURSUING HAPPINESS

When John Winthrop described his "model" for a Christian community, he envisioned a group of men and women working together for the common good, each knowing his or her place in the stable social structure decreed by God. At all times, he said, "some must be rich, some poor, some high and eminent in power and dignity," others low and "in subjection." Ideally, it was to be a community of love, all made equal by their fallen nature and their shared concern for salvation, and it was to be a stable community. But by 1800, President John Adams witnessed social mobility of a kind and to an extent that Winthrop would not have dreamed possible. As historians have observed, European critics of America in the eighteenth and nineteenth centuries never understood that great social change was possible without social upheaval primarily because there was no feudal hierarchy to overthrow. When Crèvecoeur wanted to distinguish America from Europe, it was the lingering medievalism of the latter that he wished to stress. The visitor to America, he said, "views not the hostile castle, and the haughty mansion, contrasted with the clay-built hut and miserable cabin, where cattle and men help to keep each other warm, and dwell in meanness, smoke and indigence."

Of course, in 1820, many Americans were still not free. Some of the Founding Fathers, including George Washington and Thomas Jefferson, were themselves slave owners, even though they remained conflicted about

A New England Kitchen. A Hundred Years Ago, c. 1876. In the late eighteenth century, most women were still relegated to the domestic roles here illustrated, although some had begun to chafe against what they saw as restricted opportunities for intellectual advancement.

the institution's moral validity, as Jefferson's section on slavery in his *Notes on the State of Virginia* indicates. Men could not vote unless they owned property; women could not vote at all. Women were wards of their fathers until marriage, upon which their legal identity was merged with their husbands, so that they could not own property or keep for themselves any wages they might earn. Educated at home for domestic duties, young women were supposed to be excluded from public intellectual life. But, by the end of the eighteenth century, a movement to educate women like men—so that they could properly imbue their young children with patriotic ideals—had gained considerable strength. Every literary woman testified in her own way to the usefulness of all women in the public sphere. Fired by Enlightenment ideals of reason and equality, such women as Judith Sargent Murray and Hannah Foster began to speak and write on public subjects and to agitate for their rights as citizens.

The condition of Native Americans continued to deteriorate throughout the nineteenth century. Clearly understanding their vulnerability to colonial expansionist drives, many eastern tribes sided with the British during the Revolution. After the British defeat, they were exposed both to white vengeance and white greed. Entire tribes were systematically displaced from their traditional territories, pushed ever farther and farther west. Nevertheless, the same forces that earlier had undermined church authority in New England gradually affected the Americans' conception of what constituted the good society. If, as cultural historian Russel Nye once put it, the two assumptions held to be true by most eighteenth-century Americans were "the perfectibility of man, and the prospect of his future progress," American citizens had to ground those assumptions in the reality of their day-to-day relations with others whose plight had not yet been touched by the contagion of liberty. Thus much imaginative energy in the late eighteenth and early nineteenth centuries was expended in beginning to correct institutional and social injustices: the tyranny of monarchy, the tolerance for slavery, the misuse of prisons, the subjugation of women. Even as they agitated for an extension of the principles of liberty codified by the Revolutionary generation, few doubted that with the application of intelligence the human lot could be improved. Writers including Freneau, Franklin, and Crèvecoeur argued that, if it was not too late, the transplanted European might learn more about fellowship and manners from "the noble savages" than from rude white settlers, slave owners, and backwoods pioneers.

For many, it is Franklin who best represents the promise of the Enlightenment in America, even as his long and fruitful life also testified to the pitfalls accompanying an uncritical adoption of principles that enshrined the individual's concerns above those of the community. Franklin was self-educated, social, assured, a man of the world, ambitious and public-spirited, speculative about the nature of the universe, and in matters of religion content "to observe the actual conduct of humanity rather than to debate supernatural matters that are unprovable." When his friend Ezra Stiles asked him about his religion, Franklin said he believed in the "creator of the universe" but he doubted the "divinity of Jesus." He would never be dogmatic about it, however, because—as he wryly put it—he expected soon "an opportunity of knowing the truth with less trouble." Franklin always presents himself as a man depending on firsthand experience, too worldly wise to be caught off guard, and always minding "the main chance," as one character in Tyler's *The Contrast* counsels. This aspect of Franklin's persona, however, belies another side of him and of the eighteenth century: those idealistic assumptions on which the great public documents of the American Revolution, especially the Declaration of Independence, are grounded. Given the emblematic nature of Franklin's character, it seems right that of the documents most closely associated with the formation of the American republic—the Declaration of Independence, the treaty of alliance with France, the Treaty of Paris, and the Constitution—only he signed all four.

The fact that Americans in the last quarter of the eighteenth century held that "certain truths are self-evident, that all men are created equal, that they are endowed by their Creator with certain unalienable Rights, that among these are Life, Liberty and the pursuit of Happiness" was the result of their reading the Scottish philosophers, particularly Francis Hutcheson and Lord Kames (Henry Home), who argued that all people in all places possess a sense common to all—a moral sense—that contradicted the notion of the mind as an empty vessel awaiting experience. This idealism paved the way for such writers as Bryant, Emerson, Thoreau, and Whitman, but in the 1770s its presence is found chiefly in politics and ethics. The assurance of a universal sense of right and wrong made possible both the overthrow of tyrants and the restoration of order, and it allowed humankind to make new earthly covenants, not, as was the case with Bradford and Winthrop, for the glory of God, but, as Thomas Jefferson argued, for the individual's right to happiness on earth. How Americans used and abused that right in the service of self-interest would become the theme of countless writers after 1820, as a market revolution permanently elevated liberal principles over those of the civic republicanism that had inspirited the previous generation.

TEXTS	CONTEXTS
1704–05 Sarah Kemble Knight keeps *The Private Journal of a Journey from Boston to New York* (pub. 1825)	
	1718 French found New Orleans
	1726–56 The "Great Awakening"
1741 Jonathan Edwards, *Sinners in the Hands of an Angry God*	**1741** Vitus Bering discovers Alaska
	1755–63 French and Indian Wars
1768 Samson Occom, *A Short Narrative of My Life* (pub. 1982)	
1771–90 Benjamin Franklin continues his *Autobiography* (Part I pub. 1818)	
1773 Phillis Wheatley, *Poems on Various Subjects*	**1773** Boston Tea Party
1774 John Woolman, *The Journal of John Woolman*	
1774–83 John and Abigail Adams exchange letters (pub. 1840, 1875)	
	1775–83 War for American Independence
1776 Thomas Paine, *Common Sense*	**1776** Declaration of Independence
1780s Annis Boudinot Stockton publishes poems in magazines and newspapers	
1782 J. Hector St. John de Crèvecoeur, *Letters from an American Farmer*	
	1783 Britain opens "Old Northwest" (region south of Great Lakes) to United States after Treaty of Paris ends American Revolution
1786 Philip Freneau, *Poems*	
1787 Thomas Jefferson, *Notes on the State of Virginia* • Royall Tyler, *The Contrast*	**1787** U.S. Constitution adopted
1787–88 *The Federalist* papers	
1789 Olaudah Equiano, *The Interesting Narrative of the Life of Olaudah Equiano*	**1789** George Washington elected first president
1790 Judith Sargent Murray, *On the Equality of the Sexes*	

Boldface titles indicate works in the anthology.

TEXTS	CONTEXTS
1791 Susanna Rowson, *Charlotte: A Tale of Truth*	1791 Washington D.C. established as U.S. capital
1797 Hannah Foster, *The Coquette*	
1799 Charles Brockden Brown, *Edgar Huntly*	
	1803 United States buys Louisiana Territory from France
	1812–14 Second war against England
	1819 Spain exchanges Florida for U.S. assumption of $5 million in claims

SARAH KEMBLE KNIGHT
1666–1727

Like a number of the classics of early American literature, *The Private Journal* of Mrs. Sarah Kemble Knight was not published until the nineteenth century; it at once found an enthusiastic audience eager to read documents of social history from the American past. Knight's shorthand journal, as transcribed and edited by Theodore Dwight, provides a healthy contrast to the soul-searching journals of Knight's contemporaries and reminds us of the manifold ways in which provincial Americans absorbed transatlantic models for the expression of the most common and intimate details of their lives. As such, the journal links her frank narrative to the similarly revealing private writings of William Byrd and others who saw around them subjects for meditation on what made a provincial culture viable and mature. Knight was a keen observer of provincial America and a woman who did not suffer fools gladly. Something of Knight's tough-mindedness was undoubtedly the result of the fact that she had to make her way in the world with considerable ingenuity and that early on in life she displayed a gift for managing other people's affairs—a gift that, unfortunately, sometimes led her to arrogance.

Knight was the daughter of the Boston merchant Thomas Kemble and Elizabeth Trerice of Charlestown, Massachusetts. She married a man much older who was a sometime sea captain and London agent for an American company. After her father died in 1689, Knight assumed full responsibility for managing the household. While her husband was abroad, she kept a boardinghouse and taught school (hence the title "Madam Knight") and supposedly could number Benjamin Franklin and the Mather children among her pupils. Knight taught penmanship, made copies of court records, and wrote letters for people having business with the courts. Historians recently have demonstrated that such engagement in public affairs was not as exceptional as it once seemed, for in the early eighteenth century many women played significant economic roles. Thus she trained herself in the ways of the law and had a reputation for settling estates with skill. In 1704, while her husband was abroad, Knight took on herself the task of settling her cousin Caleb Trowbridge's estate on behalf of his young widow. Knight set out for New Haven, Connecticut, on Monday, October 2, 1704. From there she went to New York and returned home to Boston in March 1705. It was a hazardous journey, one not undertaken lightly in those years and almost unprecedented for a woman traveling alone.

In 1706 Knight apparently became a widow; her husband is not mentioned again after that date. In 1714 she followed her married daughter to Connecticut. Her last years were spent in New London, where she ran an inn and, true to her genius, made shrewd investments in property.

The text used here is from *The Journal of Madame Knight*, edited by George P. Winship (1920; reprinted 1935).

From The Private Journal of a Journey from Boston to New York

Saturday, October the Seventh

We set out early in the morning and being something unacquainted with the way, having asked it of some we met, they told us we must ride a mile or two and turn down a lane on the right hand, and by their direction we rode on but not yet coming to the turning, we met a young fellow and asked him how far it was to the lane which turned down towards Guilford [Connecticut]. He said we must ride a little further and turn down by the corner of Uncle Sam's lot. My guide vented his spleen at the lubber,[1] and we soon after came into the road, and keeping still on, without anything further remarkable, about two o'clock afternoon we arrived at New Haven, where I was received with all possible respects and civility. Here I discharged Mr. Wheeler with a reward to his satisfaction, and took some time to rest after so long and toilsome a journey, and informed myself of the manners and customs of the place and at the same time employed myself in the affair I went there upon.

They are governed by the same laws as we in Boston (or little differing) throughout this whole colony of Connecticut, and much the same way of church government, and many of them good, sociable people, and I hope religious too. But a little too much independent in their principles, and, as I have been told, were formerly in their zeal very rigid in their administrations towards such as their laws made offenders, even to a harmless kiss or innocent merriment among young people, whipping being a frequent and counted an easy punishment, about which as other crimes, the judges were absolute in their sentences. They told me a pleasant story about a pair of justices in those parts, which I may not omit the relation of.

A negro slave belonging to a man in the town stole a hogshead[2] from his master and gave or sold it to an Indian, native of the place. The Indian sold it in the neighborhood, and so the theft was found out. Thereupon the heathen[3] was seized and carried to the justice's house to be examined. But his Worship (it seems) was gone into the field, with a brother in office to gather in his pompions.[4] Whither the malefactor is hurried, and complaint made and satisfaction in the name of justice demanded. Their Worships can't proceed in form without a bench: whereupon they order one to be immediately erected, which, for want of fitter materials, they made with pompions—which being finished, down sets their Worships, and the malefactor called and by the senior Justice interrogated after the following manner: You, Indian, why did you steal from this man? You shouldn't do so—it's a grandy wicked thing to steal. "Hol't, hol't," cries Justice junior. "Brother, you speak negro to him. I'll ask him." "You, sirrah, why did you steal this man's hogshead?" "Hogshead?" (replies the Indian), "Me no stomany."[5] "No?" says his Worship, and pulling off his hat, patted his own head with his hand, says, "Tatapa—you, Tatapa—you; all one this. Hogshead all one this." "Hah!" says Netop, "Now me stomany that." Whereupon the company fell into a great fit

---

1. Clumsy fellow.
2. A large barrel or cask.
3. I.e., the Indian.
4. Pumpkins.
5. Understand.

of laughter, even to roaring. Silence is commanded, but to no effect: for they continued perfectly shouting. "Nay," says his Worship in an angry tone, "If it be so, *take me off the bench.*"

Their diversions in this part of the country are on lecture days and training days[6] mostly: on the former there is riding from town to town.

And on training days the youth divert themselves by shooting at the target, as they call it (but it very much resembles a pillory[7]), where he that hits nearest the white has some yards of red ribbon presented him which being tied to his hatband, the two ends streaming down his back, he is led away in triumph with great applause as the winners of the Olympiack games. They generally marry very young: the males oftener, as I am told, under twenty than above. They generally make public weddings and have a way something singular (as they say) in some of them, *viz.* just before joining hands the bridegroom quits the place, who is soon followed by the bridesmen and, as it were, dragged back to duty—being the reverse to the former practice among us, to steel[8] man's pride.

There are great plenty of oysters all along by the seaside as far as I rode in the colony and those very good. And they generally lived very well and comfortably in their families. But too indulgent (especially the farmers) to their slaves, suffering too great familiarity from them, permitting them to sit at table and eat with them (as they say, to save time), and into the dish goes the black hoof as freely as the white hand. They told me that there was a farmer lived near the town where I lodged who had some difference with his slave concerning something the master had promised him and did not punctually perform, which caused some hard words between them. But at length they put the matter to arbitration and bound themselves to stand to the award of such as they named—which done, the arbitrators having heard the allegations of both parties, order the master to pay 40[s9] to black face and acknowledge his fault. And so the matter ended, the poor master very honestly standing to[1] the award.

There are everywhere in the towns as I passed a number of Indians the natives of the country, and are the most savage[2] of all the savages of that kind that I had ever seen: little or no care taken (as I heard upon inquiry) to make them otherwise. They have in some places lands of their own, and governed by laws of their own making;—they marry many wives and at pleasure put them away, and on the least dislike or fickle humor, on either side. Saying *"stand away"* to one another is a sufficient divorce. And, indeed, those uncomely *"stand aways"* are too much in vogue among the English in this (indulgent colony) as their records plentifully prove, and that on very trivial matters, of which some have been told me, but are not proper to be related by a female pen, though some of that foolish sex have had too large a share in the story.

If the natives commit any crime on their own precincts among themselves the English takes no cognezens[3] of. But if on the English ground they are punishable by our laws. They mourn for their dead by blacking their faces

---

6. Days set aside for military exercises. "Lecture days": days when a less formal sermon was offered than the one prepared for Sundays.
7. A wooden frame on a post with holes for the head and arms, used as public punishment for offenders.

8. Fortify against.
9. Shillings, or two English pounds.
1. I.e., paying.
2. Unchristian.
3. Recognition; more properly, "cognizance."

and cutting their hair after an awkerd and frightful manner, but can't bear you should mention the names of their dead relations to them. They trade most for rum, for which they would hazard their very lives, and the English fit[4] them generally as well by seasoning it plentifully with water.

They give the title of merchant to every trader who rate their goods according to the time and spetia[5] they pay in: *viz.* pay, money, pay as money, and trusting. *Pay* is grain, pork, beef, &c. at the prices set by the General Court that year; *money* is pieces of eight, rials, or Boston or Bay shillings[6] (as they call them,) or good hard money, as sometimes silver coin is termed by them; also wampum, *viz.* Indian beads which serves for change. *Pay as money* is provisions, as aforesaid, one third cheaper than as the Assembly or General Court sets it, and *trust* as they and the merchant agree for time.

Now, when the buyer comes to ask for a commodity, sometimes before the merchant answers that he has it, he says, *"Is your pay ready?"* Perhaps the chap replies "Yes." "What do you pay in?" says the merchant. The buyer having answered, then the price is set; as suppose he wants a sixpenny knife, in pay it is 12d[7]—in pay as money eight pence, and hard money its own price, *viz. 6d.* It seems a very intricate way of trade and what *Lex Mercatoria*[8] had not thought of.

Being at a merchant's house, in comes a tall country fellow, with his alfogeos[9] full of tobacco; for they seldom lose their cud, but keep chewing and spitting as long as their eyes are open. He advanced to the middle of the room, makes an awkward nod, and spitting a large deal of aromatic tincture, he gave a scrape with his shovel-like shoe, leaving a small shovel full of dirt on the floor, made a full stop, hugging his own pretty body with his hands under his arms, stood staring round him like a cat let out of a basket. At last, like the creature Balaam rode on,[1] he opened his mouth and said: "Have you any ribinen for hatbands to sell, I pray?" The questions and answers about the pay being passed, the ribin is brought and opened. Bumpkin simpers, cries "It's confounded gay I vow"; and beckning to the door, in comes Joan Tawdry, dropping about 50 curtsies, and stands by him. He shows her the ribin. *"Law, you,"* says she, *"it's right gent,* do you take it, *tis dreadful[2] pretty."* Then she inquires *"Have you any hood silk[3] I pray?"* which being brought and bought, "Have you any *thread silk to sew it with?"* says she, which being accommodated with they departed. They generally stand after they come in a great while speechless, and sometimes don't say a word till they are asked what they want, which I impute to the awe they stand in of the merchants, who they are constantly almost indebted to, and must take what they bring without liberty to choose for themselves. But they serve them as well,[4] making the merchants stay long enough for their pay.

We may observe here the great necessity and benefit both of education and conversation; for these people have as large a portion of mother wit,[5] and sometimes a larger, than those who have been brought up in cities, but

---

4. Fix; cheat.
5. Actual coin or money; more properly, "specie." "Rate": calculate the price of.
6. Coin minted in the Massachusetts Bay Colony. "Pieces of eight": Spanish silver coins. "Rials": former English gold coins worth ten shillings.
7. Pence; from the Latin *denarius.*
8. The law of merchants (Latin).

9. Saddlebag-like cheeks; from the Spanish *alforges,* "pouch."
1. The ass of the Old Testament prophet Balaam spoke to him (Numbers 22).
2. Extremely. "Gent": genteel, stylish.
3. Silk cloth suitable for a hood.
4. I.e., treat them equally badly.
5. Native intelligence.

for want of improvements render themselves almost ridiculous, as above. I should be glad if they would leave such follies and am sure all that love clean houses (at least) would be glad on't too.

They are generally very plain in their dress, throughout all the colony, as I saw, and follow one another in their modes, that you may know where they belong, especially the women, meet them where you will.

Their chief red-letter day is St. Election,[6] which is annually observed according to charter, to choose their government, a blessing they can never be thankful enough for, as they will find if ever it be their hard fortune to lose it. The present governor in Connecticut is the Honorable John Winthrop, Esq. A gentleman of an ancient and honorable family whose father was governor here sometime before, and his grandfather had been governor of the Massachusetts.[7] This gentleman is a very courteous and affable person, much given to hospitality, and has by his good services gained the affection of the people as much as any who had been before him in that post.

From *December the Sixth*

* * *

The city of New York is a pleasant, well-compacted place, situated on a commodious river which is a fine harbor for shipping. The buildings brick generally, very stately and high, though not altogether like ours in Boston. The bricks in some of the houses are of divers colors and laid in checkers, being glazed look very agreeable. The inside of them are neat to admiration, the wooden work, for only the walls are plastered, and the sumers and gist[8] are planed and kept very white scowered as so is all the partitions if made of boards. The fireplaces have no jambs (as ours have) but the backs run flush with the walls, and the hearth is of tiles and is as far out into the room at the ends as before the fire, which is generally five foot in the lower rooms, and the piece over where the mantle tree should be is made as ours with joiners'[9] work, and as I suppose is fastened to iron rods inside. The house where the vendue[1] was, had chimney corners like ours, and they and the hearths were laid with the finest tile that I ever see, and the staircases laid all with white tile which is ever clean, and so are the walls of the kitchen which had a brick floor. They were making great preparations to receive their governor, Lord Cornbury[2] from the Jerseys, and for that end raised the militia to guard him on shore to the fort.

They are generally of the Church of England and have a New England gentleman for their minister, and a very fine church set out with all customary requisites. There are also a Dutch and divers conventicles as they call them, *viz.* Baptist, Quakers, etc. They are not strict in keeping the Sabbath as in Boston and other places where I had been, but seem to deal with great exactness as far as I see or deal with. They are sociable to one another and courte-

6. With the name "St. Election" day, Knight mockingly suggesting that the day is kept as sacred as a religious holiday.
7. In 1704 Fitz-John Winthrop (1638–1707) was the governor of Connecticut. His father, John Winthrop (1606–1676), founded New London and was governor from 1659 to 1676. Fitz-John Winthrop's grandfather, John Winthrop (1588–1649), was the first governor of the Massachusetts Bay

Colony.
8. Main beams and joists.
9. Craftsmen who constructed things by joining pieces of wood together. Their work was more finished than a carpenter's.
1. Auction.
2. Edward Hyde (1661–1723), royal governor of New York and New Jersey from 1702 to 1708.

A View of Fort George with the City of New York from the S.W. An engraving of New York showing its skyline (primarily church steeples) as it might have appeared to Sarah Kemble Knight in the early eighteenth century.

ous and civil to strangers and fare well in their houses. The English go very fashionable in their dress. But the Dutch, especially the middling sort, differ from our women, in their habit go loose, wear French muchets which are like a cap and a headband in one, leaving their ears bare, which are set out with jewels of a large size and many in number. And their fingers hooped with rings, some with large stones in them of many colors as were their pendants in their ears, which you should see very old women wear as well as young.

They have vendues very frequently and make their earnings very well by them, for they treat with good liquor liberally, and the customers drink as liberally and generally pay for't as well, by paying for that which they bid up briskly for, after the sack[3] has gone plentifully about, though sometimes good penny worths' are got there. Their diversions in the winter is riding sleighs about three or four miles out of town, where they have houses of entertainment at a place called the Bowery, and some go to friends' houses who handsomely treat them. Mr. Burroughs carried his spouse and daughter and myself out to one Madame Dowes, a gentlewoman that lived at a farm house, who gave us a handsome entertainment of five or six dishes and choice beer and metheglin,[4] cider, etc. all which she said was the produce of her farm. I believe we met 50 or 60 sleighs that day—they fly with great swiftness and some are so furious that they'll turn out of the path for none except a loaden cart. Nor do they spare for any diversion the place affords, and sociable to a degree, their tables being as free to their neighbors as to themselves.

Having here transacted the affair I went upon and some other that fell in the way, after about a fortnight's stay there I left New York with no little regret[.]* * *

---

3. Wine; specifically, white wine imported from Spain or the Canaries.

4. A spiced variety of mead. The cider offered was probably also alcoholic.

January the Sixth

Being now well recruited and fit for business I discoursed the person I was concerned with, that we might finish in order to my return to Boston. They delayed as they had hitherto done hoping to tire my patience. But I was resolute to stay and see an end of the matter let it be never so much to my disadvantage—So January 9th they come again and promise the Wednesday following to go through with the distribution of the estate which they delayed till Thursday and then come with new amusements.[5] But at length by the mediation of that holy good gentleman, the Rev. Mr. James Pierpont, the minister of New Haven, and with the advice and assistance of other our good friends we come to an accommodation and distribution, which having finished though not till February, the man that waited on me to York taking the charge of me I set out for Boston. We went from New Haven upon the ice (the ferry being not passable thereby) and the Rev. Mr. Pierpont with Madam Prout, cousin Trowbridge and divers others were taking leave, we went onward without anything remarkable till we come to New London and lodged again at Mr. Saltonstall's—and here I dismissed my guide, and my generous entertainer provided me Mr. Samuel Rogers of that place to go home with me—I stayed a day here longer than intended by the commands of the honorable Governor Winthrop to stay and take a supper with him whose wonderful civility I may not omit. The next morning I crossed the ferry to Groton, having had the honor of the company, of Madam Livingston (who is the governor's daughter) and Mary Christophers and divers others to the boat—and that night lodged at Stonington and had roast beef and pumpkin sauce for supper. The next night at Haven's and had roast fowl, and the next day we come to a river which by reason of the freshets coming down was swelled so high we feared it impassable and the rapid stream was very terrifying—However we must over and that in a small canoe. Mr. Rogers assuring me of his good conduct,[6] I after a stay of near an hour on the shore for consultation, went into the canoe, and Mr. Rogers paddled about 100 yards up the creek by the shore side, turned into the swift stream and dexterously steering her in a moment we come to the other side as swiftly passing as an arrow shot out of the bow by a strong arm. I stayed on the shore till he returned to fetch our horses, which he caused to swim over, himself bringing the furniture in the canoe. But it is past my skill to express the exceeding fright all their transactions formed in me. We were now in the colony of Massachusetts and taking lodgings at the first inn we come to, had a pretty difficult passage the next day which was the second of March by reason of the sloughy[7] ways then thawed by the sun. Here I met Capt. John Richards of Boston who was going home, so being very glad of his company we rode something harder than hitherto, and missing my way in going up a very steep hill, my horse dropped down under me as dead; this new surprise no little hurt me, meeting it just at the entrance into Dedham from whence we intended to reach home that night. But was now obliged to get another horse there and leave my own, resolving for Boston that night if possible. But in going over the causeway at Dedham the Bridge being overflowed by the high waters coming down, I very narrowly escaped falling over into the river

---

5. I.e., trifles that caused further delays.
6. Company for safekeeping.

7. Muddy.

horse and all which 'twas almost a miracle I did not—now it grew late in the afternoon and the people having very much discouraged us about the sloughy way which they said we should find very difficult and hazardous, it so wrought on me being tired and dispirited and disappointed of my desires of going home, that I agreed to lodge there that night which we did at the house of one Draper, and the next day being March 3d we got safe home to Boston, where I found my aged and tender mother and my dear and only child in good health with open arms ready to receive me, and my kind relations and friends flocking in to welcome me and hear the story of my transactions and travails, I having this day been five months from home and now I cannot fully express my joy and satisfaction. But desire sincerely to adore my great Benefactor for thus graciously carrying forth and returning in safety his unworthy handmaid.

1704–05   1825

JONATHAN EDWARDS
1703–1758

Although it is certainly true that, as the critic Perry Miller once put it, the real life of Jonathan Edwards is the life of a mind, the circumstances surrounding Edwards's career are not without their drama, and the story of his rise to eminence and fall from power remains one of the most moving in American literature.

Edwards was born in East Windsor, Connecticut, a town not far from Hartford, the son of the Reverend Timothy Edwards and Esther Stoddard Edwards. There was little doubt from the beginning as to his career. Edwards's mother was the daughter of the Reverend Solomon Stoddard of Northampton, Massachusetts, one of the most influential and independent figures in the religious life of New England. Western Massachusetts clergymen were so anxious for his approval that he was sometimes called the "Pope of the Connecticut Valley," and his gifted grandson, the only male child in a family of eleven children, was groomed to be his heir.

Edwards was a studious and dutiful child and from an early age showed remarkable gifts of observation and exposition. When he was eleven he wrote an essay, still very readable, on the flying spider. Most of Edwards's early education was at home. In 1716, when he was thirteen, Edwards was admitted to Yale College; he stayed on to read theology in New Haven for two years after his graduation in 1720. Like Benjamin Franklin, Edwards determined to perfect himself, and in one of his early notebooks he resolved "never to lose one moment of time, but to improve it in the most profitable way" he could. As a student he always rose at four in the morning, studied thirteen hours a day, and reserved part of each day for walking. It was a routine that Edwards varied little, even when, after spending two years in New York, he came to Northampton to assist his grandfather in his church. He married in 1727. In 1729 Solomon Stoddard died, and Edwards was named to succeed him. In the twenty-four years that Edwards lived in Northampton he managed to tend his duties as pastor of a growing congregation and deliver brilliant sermons, to write some of his most important books—concerned primarily with defining the nature of true religious experience—and watch his eleven children grow up. Until the mid-1740s his relations with the town were harmonious.

In spite of the awesome—even imposing—quality of Edwards's mind, all of his work is of a piece and, in essence, readily graspable. Edwards was trying to restore to his congregation and to his readers that original sense of religious commitment that he felt had been lost since the first days of the Puritan exodus to America, and he wanted to do this by transforming his congregation from mere believers who understood the logic of Christian doctrine to converted Christians who were genuinely moved by the principles of their belief. Edwards says that he read the work of the English philosopher John Locke (1632–1704) with more pleasure "than the greedy miser finds when gathering up handfuls of silver and gold, from some newly discovered treasure." For Locke confirmed Edwards's conviction that we must do more than comprehend religious ideas; we must be *moved* by them, we must know them experientially: the difference, as he says, is like that between reading the word *fire* and actually being burned. Basic to this newly felt belief is the recognition that nothing that an individual can do warrants his or her salvation, that people are motivated entirely by self-love, and that it is only supernatural grace that alters their natural depravity. In his progress as a Christian, Edwards says that he experienced several steps toward real Christian commitment but that his true conversion came only when he had achieved a "full and constant sense of the absolute sovereignty of God, and a delight in that sovereignty." The word *delight* reminds us that Edwards is trying to inculcate and describe a religious feeling that approximates a physical sensation, recognizing always that supernatural feelings and natural ones are actually very different. The word links him to the transatlantic community of those who recognized sentiment as the basic emotion that connects individuals to each other in manifold ways. In his patient and lucid prose Edwards became a master at the art of persuading his congregation that it could—and *must*—possess this intense awareness of humanity's precarious condition. The exaltation that his parishioners felt when they experienced delight in God's sovereignty was the characteristic fervid emotion of religious revivalism.

For fifteen years, beginning in 1734, this spirit of revivalism transformed complacent believers all along the eastern seaboard. This period of new religious fervor has been called the Great Awakening, and in its early years Edwards could do no wrong. His meetinghouse was filled with newly converted believers, and the details of the spiritual life of Edwards and his congregation were the subject of inquiry by Christian believers everywhere as his works describing his own experience in the revivals were widely published and distributed in a period of expanding print culture. But in his attempt to restore the church to the position of authority it held in the years of his grandfather's reign, Edwards went too far. When he named backsliders from his pulpit—including members of the best families in town—and tried to return to the old order of communion, permitting the sacrament to be taken only by those who had publicly declared themselves to be saved, the people of the town turned against him. Residents of the Connecticut Valley everywhere were tired of religious controversy, and the hysterical behavior of a few fanatics turned many against the spirit of revivalism. On June 22, 1750, by a vote of two hundred to twenty, Edwards was dismissed from his church and effectively silenced. Although the congregation had difficulty naming a successor to Edwards, they preferred to have no sermons rather than let Edwards preach. For the next seven years he served as missionary to the Housatonnuck Indians in Stockbridge, Massachusetts, a town thirty-five miles to the west of Northampton. There he wrote his monumental treatises debating the doctrine of the freedom of the will and defining the nature of true virtue: "that consent, propensity, and union of heart to Being in general, that is immediately exercised in a general good will." It was in Stockbridge that Edwards received, very reluctantly, a call to become president of the College of New Jersey (later called Princeton). Three months after his arrival in Princeton, Edwards died of smallpox, the result of the inoculation taken to prevent infection.

Personal Narrative[1]

I had a variety of concerns and exercises about my soul from my childhood; but had two more remarkable seasons of awakening[2] before I met with that change, by which I was brought to those new dispositions, and that new sense of things, that I have since had. The first time was when I was a boy, some years before I went to college, at a time of remarkable awakening in my father's congregation. I was then very much affected[3] for many months, and concerned about the things of religion, and my soul's salvation; and was abundant in duties. I used to pray five times a day in secret, and to spend much time in religious talk with other boys; and used to meet with them to pray together. I experienced I know not what kind of delight in religion. My mind was much engaged in it, and had much self-righteous pleasure; and it was my delight to abound in religious duties. I, with some of my schoolmates joined together, and built a booth in a swamp, in a very secret and retired place, for a place of prayer. And besides, I had particular secret places of my own in the woods, where I used to retire by myself; and used to be from time to time much affected. My affections seemed to be lively and easily moved, and I seemed to be in my element, when engaged in religious duties. And I am ready to think, many are deceived with such affections, and such a kind of delight, as I then had in religion, and mistake it for grace.

But in process of time, my convictions and affections wore off; and I entirely lost all those affections and delights, and left off secret prayer, at least as to any constant performance of it; and returned like a dog to his vomit, and went on in ways of sin.[4]

Indeed, I was at some times very uneasy, especially towards the latter part of the time of my being at college.[5] Till it pleased God, in my last year at college, at a time when I was in the midst of many uneasy thoughts about the state of my soul, to seize me with a pleurisy;[6] in which he brought me nigh to the grave, and shook me over the pit of hell.

But yet, it was not long after my recovery, before I fell again into my old ways of sin. But God would not suffer me to go on with any quietness; but I had great and violent inward struggles: till after many conflicts with wicked inclinations, and repeated resolutions, and bonds that I laid myself under by a kind of vows to God, I was brought wholly to break off all former wicked ways, and all ways of known outward sin; and to apply myself to seek my salvation, and practice the duties of religion: but without that kind of affection and delight, that I had formerly experienced. My concern now wrought more by inward struggles and conflicts, and self-reflections. I made seeking my salvation the main business of my life. But yet it seems to me, I sought

1. Because of Edwards's reference to an evening in January 1739, this essay must have been written after that date. Edwards's reasons for writing it are not known, and it was not published in his lifetime. After his death his friend Samuel Hopkins had access to his manuscripts and prepared *The Life and Character of the Late Rev. Mr. Jonathan Edwards*, which was published in 1765. In that volume the "Personal Narrative" appeared in section IV as a chapter titled "An Account of His Conversion, Experiences, and Religious Exercises, Given by Himself." The text here is from the Yale University Press *Works of Jonathan Edwards*, vol. 16, edited by George Claghorn.

2. I.e., spiritual awakenings, renewals. "Exercises": agitations.

3. Emotionally aroused, as opposed to merely understanding rationally the arguments for Christian faith.

4. "As a dog returneth to his vomit, so a fool returneth to his folly" (Proverbs 26.11).

5. Edwards was an undergraduate at Yale from 1716 to 1720 and a divinity student from 1720 to 1722.

6. A respiratory disorder.

after a miserable manner: which has made me sometimes since to question, whether ever it issued in that which was saving;[7] being ready to doubt, whether such miserable seeking was ever succeeded. But yet I was brought to seek salvation, in a manner that I never was before. I felt a spirit to part with all things in the world, for an interest in Christ. My concern continued and prevailed, with many exercising things and inward struggles; but yet it never seemed to be proper to express my concern that I had, by the name of terror.

From my childhood up, my mind had been wont to be full of objections against the doctrine of God's sovereignty, in choosing whom He would to eternal life and rejecting whom he pleased; leaving them eternally to perish, and be everlastingly tormented in hell. It used to appear like a horrible doctrine to me. But I remember the time very well, when I seemed to be convinced, and fully satisfied, as to this sovereignty of God, and his justice in thus eternally disposing of men, according to his sovereign pleasure. But never could give an account, how, or by what means, I was thus convinced; not in the least imagining, in the time of it, nor a long time after, that there was any extraordinary influence of God's Spirit in it: but only that now I saw further, and my reason apprehended the justice and reasonableness of it. However, my mind rested in it; and it put an end to all those cavils and objections, that had till then abode with me, all the preceeding part of my life. And there has been a wonderful alteration in my mind, with respect to the doctrine of God's sovereignty, from that day to this; so that I scarce ever have found so much as the rising of an objection against God's sovereignty, in the most absolute sense, in showing mercy on whom he will show mercy, and hardening and eternally damning whom he will.[8] God's absolute sovereignty, and justice, with respect to salvation and damnation, is what my mind seems to rest assured of, as much as of anything that I see with my eyes; at least it is so at times. But I have oftentimes since that first conviction, had quite another kind of sense of God's sovereignty, than I had then. I have often since, not only had a conviction, but a *delightful* conviction. The doctrine of God's sovereignty has very often appeared, an exceeding pleasant, bright and sweet doctrine to me: and absolute sovereignty is what I love to ascribe to God. But my first conviction was not with this.

The first that I remember that ever I found anything of that sort of inward, sweet delight in God and divine things, that I have lived much in since, was on reading those words, 1 Tim. 1.17, "Now unto the King eternal, immortal, invisible, the only wise God, be honor and glory for ever and ever, Amen." As I read the words, there came into my soul, and was as it were diffused through it, a sense of the glory of the divine being, a new sense, quite different from anything I ever experienced before. Never any words of Scripture seemed to me as these words did. I thought with myself, how excellent a Being that was; and how happy I should be, if I might enjoy that God, and be wrapt[9] up to God in heaven, and be as it were swallowed up in him. I kept saying, and as it were singing over these words of Scripture to myself; and went to prayer, to pray to God that I might enjoy him; and prayed in a manner quite different from what I used to do, with a new sort of affection. But it

7. I.e., truly redeeming, capable of making the penitent a "saint."
8. "Therefore hath he mercy on whom he will have mercy, and whom he will he hardeneth" (Romans 9.18).
9. Lifted.

never came into my thought, that there was anything spiritual, or of a saving nature in this.

From about that time, I began to have a new kind of apprehensions and ideas of Christ, and the work of redemption, and the glorious way of salvation by him. I had an inward, sweet sense of these things, that at times came into my heart; and my soul was led away in pleasant views and contemplations of them. And my mind was greatly engaged, to spend my time in reading and meditating on Christ; and the beauty and excellency of his person, and the lovely way of salvation, by free grace in him. I found no books so delightful to me, as those that treated of these subjects. Those words (Cant. 2:1) used to be abundantly with me: "I am the rose of Sharon, the lily of the valleys." The words seemed to me, sweetly to represent, the loveliness and beauty of Jesus Christ. And the whole book of Canticles[1] used to be pleasant to me; and I used to be much in reading it, about that time. And found, from time to time, an inward sweetness, that used, as it were, to carry me away in my contemplations; in what I know not how to express otherwise, than by a calm, sweet abstraction of soul from all the concerns o[f] this world; and a kind of vision, or fixed ideas and imaginations, of being alone in the mountains, or some solitary wilderness, far from all mankind, sweetly conversing with Christ, and wrapt and swallowed up in God. The sense I had of divine things, would often of a sudden as it were, kindle up a sweet burning in my heart; an ardor of my soul, that I know not how to express.

Not long after I first began to experience these things, I gave an account to my father, of some things that had passed in my mind. I was pretty much affected by the discourse we had together. And when the discourse was ended, I walked abroad alone, in a solitary place in my father's pasture, for contemplation. And as I was walking there, and looked up on the sky and clouds; there came into my mind, a sweet sense of the glorious majesty and grace of God, that I know not how to express. I seemed to see them both in a sweet conjunction: majesty and meekness joined together: it was a sweet and gentle, and holy majesty; and also a majestic meekness; an awful sweetness; a high, and great, and holy gentleness.

After this my sense of divine things gradually increased, and became more and more lively, and had more of that inward sweetness. The appearance of everything was altered: there seemed to be, as it were, a calm, sweet cast, or appearance of divine glory, in almost everything. God's excellency, his wisdom, his purity and love, seemed to appear in everything; in the sun, moon and stars; in the clouds, and blue sky; in the grass, flowers, trees; in the water, and all nature; which used greatly to fix my mind. I often used to sit and view the moon, for a long time; and so in the daytime, spent much time in viewing the clouds and sky, to behold the sweet glory of God in these things: in the meantime, singing forth with a low voice, my contemplations of the Creator and Redeemer. And scarce anything, among all the works of nature, was so sweet to me as thunder and lightning. Formerly, nothing had been so terrible to me. I used to be a person uncommonly terrified with thunder: and it used to strike me with terror, when I saw a thunderstorm rising. But now, on the contrary, it rejoiced me. I felt God at the

1. I.e., Song of Solomon.

first appearance of a thunderstorm. And used to take the opportunity at such times, to fix myself to view the clouds, and see the lightnings play, and hear the majestic and awful voice of God's thunder: which often times was exceeding entertaining, leading me to sweet contemplations of my great and glorious God. And while I viewed, used to spend my time, as it always seemed natural to me, to sing or chant forth my meditations; to speak my thoughts in soliloquies, and speak with a singing voice.

I felt then a great satisfaction as to my good estate.[2] But that did not content me. I had vehement longings of soul after God and Christ, and after more holiness; wherewith my heart seemed to be full, and ready to break: which often brought to my mind, the words of the Psalmist, Ps. 119:28, "My soul breaketh for the longing it hath." I often felt a mourning and lamenting in my heart, that I had not turned to God sooner, that I might have had more time to grow in grace. My mind was greatly fixed on divine things; I was almost perpetually in the contemplation of them. Spent most of my time in thinking of divine things, year after year. And used to spend abundance of my time, in walking alone in the woods, and solitary places, for meditation, soliloquy and prayer, and converse with God. And it was always my manner, at such times, to sing forth my contemplations. And was almost constantly in ejaculatory prayer, wherever I was. Prayer seemed to be natural to me; as the breath, by which the inward burnings of my heart had vent.

The delights which I now felt in things of religion, were of an exceeding different kind, from those forementioned, that I had when I was a boy. They were totally of another kind; and what I then had no more notion or idea of, than one born blind has of pleasant and beautiful colors. They were of a more inward, pure, soul-animating and refreshing nature. Those former delights, never reached the heart; and did not arise from any sight of the divine excellency of the things of God; or any taste of the soul-satisfying, and life-giving good, there is in them.

My sense of divine things seemed gradually to increase, till I went to preach at New York; which was about a year and a half after they began. While I was there, I felt them, very sensibly,[3] in a much higher degree, than I had done before. My longings after God and holiness, were much increased. Pure and humble, holy and heavenly Christianity, appeared exceeding amiable to me. I felt in me a burning desire to be in everything a complete Christian; and conformed to the blessed image of Christ: and that I might live in all things, according to the pure, sweet and blessed rules of the gospel. I had an eager thirsting after progress in these things. My longings after it, put me upon pursuing and pressing after them. It was my continual strife day and night, and constant inquiry, how I should be more holy, and live more holily, and more becoming a child of God, and disciple of Christ. I sought an increase of grace and holiness, and that I might live an holy life, with vastly more earnestness, than ever I sought grace, before I had it. I used to be continually examining myself, and studying and contriving for likely ways and means, how I should live holily, with far greater diligence and earnestness, than ever I pursued anything in my life: but with too great a dependence on my own strength, which afterwards proved a great damage to me. My experience had not then taught me, as it has done since, my extreme fee-

2. Condition of being.
3. Feelingly. Edwards was in New York from August 1722 to April 1723, assisting at a Presbyterian church.

bleness and impotence, every manner of way; and the innumerable and bottomless depths of secret corruption and deceit, that there was in my heart. However, I went on with my eager pursuit after more holiness; and sweet conformity to Christ.

The Heaven I desired was a heaven of holiness; to be with God, and to spend my eternity in divine love, and holy communion with Christ. My mind was very much taken up with contemplations on heaven, and the enjoyments of those there; and living there in perfect holiness, humility and love. And it used at that time to appear a great part of the happiness of heaven, that there the saints could express their love to Christ. It appeared to me a great clog and hindrance and burden to me, that what I felt within, I could not express to God, and give vent to, as I desired. The inward ardor of my soul, seemed to be hindered and pent up, and could not freely flame out as it would. I used often to think, how in heaven, this sweet principle should freely and fully vent and express itself. Heaven appeared to me exceeding delightful as a world of love. It appeared to me, that all happiness consisted in living in pure, humble, heavenly, divine love.

I remember the thoughts I used then to have of holiness. I remember I then said sometimes to myself, I do certainly know that I love holiness, such as the gospel prescribes. It appeared to me, there was nothing in it but what was ravishingly lovely. It appeared to me, to be the highest beauty and amiableness, above all other beauties: that it was a divine beauty; far purer than anything here upon earth; and that everything else, was like mire, filth and defilement, in comparison of it.

Holiness, as I then wrote down some of my contemplations on it, appeared to me to be of a sweet, pleasant, charming, serene, calm nature. It seemed to me, it brought an inexpressible purity, brightness, peacefulness and ravishment to the soul: and that it made the soul like a field or garden of God, with all manner of pleasant flowers; that is all pleasant, delightful and undisturbed; enjoying a sweet calm, and the gently vivifying beams of the sun. The soul of a true Christian, as I then wrote my meditations, appeared like such a little white flower, as we see in the spring of the year; low and humble on the ground, opening its bosom, to receive the pleasant beams of the sun's glory; rejoicing as it were, in a calm rapture; diffusing around a sweet fragrancy; standing peacefully and lovingly, in the midst of other flowers round about; all in like manner opening their bosoms, to drink in the light of the sun.

There was no part of creature-holiness, that I then, and at other times, had so great a sense of the loveliness of, as humility, brokenness of heart and poverty of spirit: and there was nothing that I had such a spirit to long for. My heart, as it were, panted after this to lie low before GOD, and in the dust; that I might be nothing, and that God might be all; that I might become as a little child.[4]

While I was there at New York, I sometimes was much affected with reflections on my past life, considering how late it was, before I began to be truly religious; and how wickedly I had lived till then: and once so as to weep abundantly, and for a considerable time together.

---

4. "Verily I say unto you, Whosoever shall not receive the kingdom of God as a little child, he shall not enter therein" (Mark 10.15).

On January 12, 1722–3, I made a solemn dedication of myself to God, and wrote it down; giving up myself, and all that I had to God; to be for the future in no respect my own; to act as one that had no right to himself, in any respect. And solemnly vowed to take God for my whole portion and felicity; looking on nothing else as any part of my happiness, nor acting as if it were: and his law for the constant rule of my obedience; engaging to fight with all my might, against the world, the flesh and the devil, to the end of my life. But have reason to be infinitely humbled, when I consider, how much I have failed of answering my obligation.

I had then abundance of sweet religious conversation in the family where I lived, with Mr. John Smith, and his pious mother. My heart was knit in affection to those, in whom were appearances of true piety; and I could bear the thoughts of no other companions, but such as were holy, and the disciples of the blessed Jesus.

I had great longings for the advancement of Christ's kingdom in the world. My secret prayer used to be in great part taken up in praying for it. If I heard the least hint of anything that happened in any part of the world, that appeared to me, in some respect or other, to have a favorable aspect on the interest of Christ's kingdom, my soul eagerly catched at it; and it would much animate and refresh me. I used to be earnest to read public news-letters, mainly for that end; to see if I could not find some news favorable to the interest of religion in the world.

I very frequently used to retire into a solitary place, on the banks of Hudson's River, at some distance from the city, for contemplation on divine things, and secret converse with God; and had many sweet hours there. Sometimes Mr. Smith and I walked there together, to converse of the things of God; and our conversation used much to turn on the advancement of Christ's kingdom in the world, and the glorious things that God would accomplish for his church in the latter days.

I had then, and at other times, the greatest delight in the holy Scriptures, of any book whatsoever. Oftentimes in reading it, every word seemed to touch my heart. I felt an harmony between something in my heart, and those sweet and powerful words. I seemed often to see so much light, exhibited by every sentence, and such a refreshing ravishing food communicated, that I could not get along in reading. Used oftentimes to dwell long on one sentence, to see the wonders contained in it; and yet almost every sentence seemed to be full of wonders.

I came away from New York in the month of April 1723, and had a most bitter parting with Madam Smith and her son. My heart seemed to sink within me, at leaving the family and city, where I had enjoyed so many sweet and pleasant days. I went from New York to Weathersfield[5] by water. As I sailed away, I kept sight of the city as long as I could; and when I was out of sight of it, it would affect me much to look that way, with a kind of melancholy mixed with sweetness. However, that night after this sorrowful parting, I was greatly comforted in God at Westchester, where we went ashore to lodge: and had a pleasant time of it all the voyage to Saybrook.[6] It was sweet to me to think of meeting dear Christians in heaven, where we should never part

---

5. Wethersfield, Connecticut, is very near his father's home in Windsor.

6. Westchester and Saybrook are in New York and Connecticut, respectively.

more. At Saybrook we went ashore to lodge on Saturday, and there kept sabbath; where I had a sweet and refreshing season, walking alone in the fields.

After I came home to Windsor, remained much in a like frame of my mind, as I had been in at New York; but only sometimes felt my heart ready to sink, with the thoughts of my friends at New York. And my refuge and support was in contemplations on the heavenly state; as I find in my diary of May 1, 1723. It was my comfort to think of that state, where there is fulness of joy; where reigns heavenly, sweet, calm and delightful love, without alloy; where there are continually the dearest expressions of this love; where is the enjoyment of the persons loved, without ever parting; where these persons that appear so lovely in this world, will really be inexpressibly more lovely, and full of love to us. And how sweetly will the mutual lovers join together to sing the praises of God and the Lamb![7] How full will it fill us with joy, to think, that this enjoyment, these sweet exercises will never cease or come to an end; but will last to all eternity!

Continued much in the same frame in the general, that I had been in at New York, till I went to New Haven, to live there as Tutor of the College; having some special season of uncommon sweetness: particularly once at Bolton, in a journey from Boston, walking out alone in the fields. After I went to New Haven, I sunk in religion; my mind being diverted from my eager and violent pursuits after holiness, by some affairs that greatly perplexed and distracted my mind.

In September 1725, was taken ill at New Haven; and endeavoring to go home to Windsor, was so ill at the North Village, that I could go no further: where I lay sick for about a quarter of a year. And in this sickness, God was pleased to visit me again with the sweet influences of his spirit. My mind was greatly engaged there on divine, pleasant contemplations, and longings of soul. I observed that those who watched with me, would often be looking out for the morning, and seemed to wish for it. Which brought to my mind those words of the Psalmist, which my soul with sweetness made its own language, "My soul waiteth for the Lord more than they that watch for the morning: I say, more than they that watch for the morning" [Ps. 130:6]. And when the light of the morning came, and the beams of the sun came in at the windows, it refreshed my soul from one morning to another. It seemed to me to be some image of the sweet light of God's glory.

I remember, about that time, I used greatly to long for the conversion of some that I was concerned with. It seemed to me, I could gladly honor them, and with delight be a servant to them, and lie at their feet, if they were but truly holy.

But sometime after this, I was again greatly diverted in my mind, with some temporal concerns, that exceedingly took up my thoughts, greatly to the wounding of my soul: and went on through various exercises, that it would be tedious to relate, that gave me much more experience of my own heart, than ever I had before.

Since I came to this town, I have often had sweet complacency[8] in God in views of his glorious perfections, and the excellency of Jesus Christ. God has appeared to me, a glorious and lovely being, chiefly on the account of

7. In Revelation the symbol of Christ.
8. Contentment. "This town": Northampton, Massachusetts, where, in 1726, Edwards came to help his grandfather in conducting the affairs of his parish.

his holiness. The holiness of God has always appeared to me the most lovely of all his attributes. The doctrines of God's absolute sovereignty, and free grace, in showing mercy to whom he would show mercy; and man's absolute dependence on the operations of God's Holy Spirit, have very often appeared to me as sweet and glorious doctrines. These doctrines have been much my delight. God's sovereignty has ever appeared to me, as great part of his glory. It has often been sweet to me to go to God, and adore him as a sovereign God, and ask sovereign mercy of him.

I have loved the doctrines of the gospel: they have been to my soul like green pastures. The gospel has seemed to me to be the richest treasure; the treasure that I have most desired, and longed that it might dwell richly in me. The way of salvation by Christ, has appeared in a general way, glorious and excellent, and most pleasant and beautiful. It has often seemed to me, that it would in a great measure spoil heaven, to receive it in any other way. That text has often been affecting and delightful to me, Is. 32:2, "A man shall be an hiding place from the wind, and a covert from the tempest," etc.

It has often appeared sweet to me, to be united to Christ; to have him for my head, and to be a member of his body: and also to have Christ for my teacher and prophet. I very often think with sweetness and longings and pantings of soul, of being a little child, taking hold of Christ, to be led by him through the wilderness of this world. That text, Matt. 18 at the beginning, has often been sweet to me, "Except ye be converted, and become as little children," etc. I love to think of coming to Christ, to receive salvation of him, poor in spirit, and quite empty of self; humbly exalting him alone; cut entirely off from my own root, and to grow into, and out of Christ: to have God in Christ to be all in all; and to live by faith in the Son of God, a life of humble, unfeigned confidence in him. That Scripture has often been sweet to me, Ps. 115:1, "Not unto us, O Lord, not unto us, but unto thy name give glory, for thy mercy, and for thy truth's sake." And those words of Christ, Luke 10:21, "In that hour Jesus rejoiced in spirit, and said, I thank thee, O Father, Lord of heaven and earth, that thou hast hid these things from the wise and prudent, and hast revealed them unto babes: even so Father, for so it seemed good in thy sight." That sovereignty of God that Christ rejoiced in, seemed to me to be worthy to be rejoiced in; and that rejoicing of Christ, seemed to me to show the excellency of Christ, and the spirit that he was of.

Sometimes only mentioning a single word, causes my heart to burn within me: or only seeing the name of Christ, or the name of some attribute of God. And God has appeared glorious to me, on account of the Trinity. It has made me have exalting thoughts of God, that he subsists in three persons; Father, Son, and Holy Ghost.

The sweetest joys and delights I have experienced, have not been those that have arisen from a hope of my own good estate; but in a direct view of the glorious things of the gospel. When I enjoy this sweetness, it seems to carry me above the thoughts of my own safe estate. It seems at such times a loss that I cannot bear, to take off my eye from the glorious, pleasant object I behold without me, to turn my eye in upon myself, and my own good estate.

My heart has been much on the advancement of Christ's kingdom in the world. The histories of the past advancement of Christ's kingdom, have been sweet to me. When I have read histories of past ages, the pleasantest thing in all my reading has been, to read of the kingdom of Christ being promoted. And when I have expected in my reading, to come to any such thing, I have lotted[9] upon it all the way as I read. And my mind has been much entertained and delighted, with the Scripture promises and prophecies, of the future glorious advancement of Christ's kingdom on earth.

I have sometimes had a sense of the excellent fullness of Christ, and his meetness and suitableness as a Savior; whereby he has appeared to me, far above all, the chief of ten thousands.[1] And his blood and atonement has appeared sweet, and his righteousness sweet; which is always accompanied with an ardency of spirit, and inward strugglings and breathings and groanings, that cannot be uttered, to be emptied of myself, and swallowed up in Christ.

Once, as I rid out into the woods for my health, *anno*[2] 1737; and having lit from my horse in a retired place, as my manner commonly has been, to walk for divine contemplation and prayer; I had a view, that for me was extraordinary, of the glory of the Son of God; as mediator between God and man; and his wonderful, great, full, pure and sweet grace and love, and meek and gentle condescension. This grace, that appeared to me so calm and sweet, appeared great above the heavens. The person of Christ appeared ineffably excellent, with an excellency great enough to swallow up all thought and conception. Which continued, as near as I can judge, about an hour; which kept me, the bigger part of the time, in a flood of tears, and weeping aloud. I felt withal, an ardency of soul to be, what I know not otherwise how to express, than to be emptied and annihilated; to lie in the dust, and to be full of Christ alone; to love him with a holy and pure love; to trust in him; to live upon him; to serve and follow him, and to be totally wrapt up in the fullness of Christ; and to be perfectly sanctified and made pure, with a divine and heavenly purity. I have several other times, had views very much of the same nature, and that have had the same effects.

I have many times had a sense of the glory of the third person in the Trinity, in his office of Sanctifier; in his holy operations communicating divine light and life to the soul. God in the communications of his Holy Spirit, has appeared as an infinite fountain of divine glory and sweetness; being full and sufficient to fill and satisfy the soul: pouring forth itself in sweet communications, like the sun in its glory, sweetly and pleasantly diffusing light and life.

I have sometimes had an affecting sense of the excellency of the word of God, as a word of life; as the light of life; a sweet, excellent, life-giving word: accompanied with a thirsting after that word, that it might dwell richly in my heart.

I have often since I lived in this town, had very affecting views of my own sinfulness and vileness; very frequently so as to hold me in a kind of loud weeping, sometimes for a considerable time together: so that I have often been forced to shut myself up.[3] I have had a vastly greater sense of my wickedness, and the badness of my heart, since my conversion, than ever I had before. It has often appeared to me, that if God should mark iniquity against me, I should appear the very worst of all mankind; of all that have been since the beginning of the world of this time: and that I should have by far the lowest place in hell. When others that have come to talk with me about their soul

---

9. Rejoiced.
1. "My beloved is white and ruddy, the chiefest among ten thousand" (Song of Solomon 5.10).

2. In the year (Latin).
3. I.e., retire to his study.

concerns, have expressed the sense they have had of their own wickedness, by saying that it seemed to them, that they were as bad as the devil himself; I thought their expressions seemed exceeding faint and feeble, to represent my wickedness. I thought I should wonder, that they should content themselves with such expressions as these, if I had any reason to imagine, that their sin bore any proportion to mine. It seemed to me, I should wonder at myself, if I should express my wickedness in such feeble terms as they did.

My wickedness, as I am in myself, has long appeared to me perfectly ineffable, and infinitely swallowing up all thought and imagination; like an infinite deluge, or infinite mountains over my head. I know not how to express better, what my sins appear to me to be, than by heaping infinite upon infinite, and multiplying infinite by infinite. I go about very often, for this many years, with these expressions in my mind, and in my mouth, "Infinite upon infinite. Infinite upon infinite!" When I look into my heart, and take a view of my wickedness, it looks like an abyss infinitely deeper than hell. And it appears to me, that were it not for free grace, exalted and raised up to the infinite height of all the fullness and glory of the great Jehovah,[4] and the arm of his power and grace stretched forth, in all the majesty of his power, and in all the glory of his sovereignty; I should appear sunk down in my sins infinitely below hell itself, far beyond sight of everything, but the piercing eye of God's grace, that can pierce even down to such a depth, and to the bottom of such an abyss.

And yet, I ben't in the least inclined to think, that I have a greater conviction of sin than ordinary. It seems to me, my conviction of sin is exceeding small, and faint. It appears to me enough to amaze me, that I have no more sense of my sin. I know certainly, that I have very little sense of my sinfulness. That my sins appear to me so great, don't seem to me to be, because I have so much more conviction of sin than other Christians, but because I am so much worse, and have so much more wickedness to be convinced of. When I have had these turns of weeping and crying for my sins, I thought I knew in the time of it, that my repentance was nothing to my sin.

I have greatly longed of late, for a broken heart, and to lie low before God. And when I ask for humility of God, I can't bear the thoughts of being no more humble, than other Christians. It seems to me, that though their degrees of humility may be suitable for them; yet it would be a vile self-exaltation in me, not to be the lowest in humility of all mankind. Others speak of their longing to be humbled to the dust. Though that may be a proper expression for them, I always think for myself, that I ought to be humbled down below hell. 'Tis an expression that it has long been natural for me to use in prayer to God. I ought to lie infinitely low before God.

It is affecting to me to think, how ignorant I was, when I was a young Christian, of the bottomless, infinite depths of wickedness, pride, hypocrisy and deceit left in my heart.

I have vastly a greater sense, of my universal, exceeding dependence on God's grace and strength, and mere good pleasure, of late, than I used formerly to have; and have experienced more of an abhorrence of my own righteousness. The thought of any comfort or joy, arising in me, on any consideration, or reflection on my own amiableness, or any of my performances or experiences, or any goodness of heart or life, is nauseous and detestable

---

4. The name used for God in the Old Testament.

to me. And yet I am greatly afflicted with a proud and self-righteous spirit; much more sensibly, than I used to be formerly. I see that serpent rising and putting forth its head, continually, everywhere, all around me.

Though it seems to me, that in some respects I was a far better Christian, for two or three years after my first conversion, than I am now; and lived in a more constant delight and pleasure: yet of late years, I have had a more full and constant sense of the absolute sovereignty of God, and a delight in that sovereignty; and have had more of a sense of the glory of Christ, as a mediator, as revealed in the Gospel. On one Saturday night in particular, had a particular discovery of the excellency of the gospel of Christ, above all other doctrines; so that I could not but say to myself; "This is my chosen light, my chosen doctrine": and of Christ, "This is my chosen prophet." It appeared to me to be sweet beyond all expression, to follow Christ, and to be taught and enlightened and instructed by him; to learn of him, and live to him.

Another Saturday night, January 1738–9, had such a sense, how sweet and blessed a thing it was, to walk in the way of duty, to do that which was right and meet to be done, and agreeable to the holy mind of God; that it caused me to break forth into a kind of a loud weeping, which held me some time; so that I was forced to shut myself up, and fasten the doors. I could not but as it were cry out, "How happy are they which do that which is right in the sight of God! They are blessed indeed, they are the happy ones!" I had at the same time, a very affecting sense, how meet and suitable it was that God should govern the world, and order all things according to his own pleasure; and I rejoiced in it, that God reigned, and that his will was done.

c. 1740   1765

Sarah Edwards's Narrative[1]

I have been particularly acquainted with many persons that have been the subjects of the high and extraordinary transports of the present day; and in the highest transports of any of the instances that I have been acquainted with, and where the affections of admiration, love and joy, so far as another could judge, have been raised to a higher pitch than in any other instances I have observed or been informed of, the following things have been united: viz. a very frequent dwelling, for some considerable time together, in such views of the glory of the divine perfections, and Christ's excellencies, that the soul in the meantime has been as it were perfectly overwhelmed, and swallowed up with light and love and a sweet solace, rest and joy of soul, that was altogether unspeakable; and more than once continuing for five or six hours together, without any interruption, in that clear and lively view or sense of the infinite beauty and amiableness of Christ's person, and the heavenly sweetness of his excellent and transcendent love; so that (to use the person's own expressions) the soul remained in a kind of heavenly Elysium, and did as it were swim in the rays of Christ's love, like a little mote swimming in the beams of the sun, or streams of his light that come in at a

---

1. Edwards includes his wife's narrative in *Some Thoughts Concerning the Present Revival of Religion* (1742).

window; and the heart was swallowed up in a kind of glow of Christ's love, coming down from Christ's heart in heaven, as a constant stream of sweet light, at the same time the soul all flowing out in love to him; so that there seemed to be a constant flowing and reflowing from heart to heart. The soul dwelt on high, and was lost in God, and seemed almost to leave the body; dwelling in a pure delight that fed and satisfied the soul; enjoying pleasure without the least sting, or any interruption, a sweetness that the soul was lost in; so that (so far as the judgment and word of a person of discretion may be taken, speaking upon the most deliberate consideration) what was enjoyed in each single minute of the whole space, which was many hours, was undoubtedly worth more than all the outward comfort and pleasure of the whole life put together; and this without being in any trance, or being at all deprived of the exercise of the bodily senses: and the like heavenly delight and unspeakable joy of soul, enjoyed from time to time, for years together; though not frequently so long together, to such an height: extraordinary views of divine things, and religious affections, being frequently attended with very great effects on the body, nature often sinking under the weight of divine discoveries, the strength of the body taken away, so as to deprive of all ability to stand or speak; sometimes the hands clinched, and the flesh cold, but senses still remaining; animal nature often in a great emotion and agitation, and the soul very often, of late, so overcome with great admiration, and a kind of omnipotent joy, as to cause the person (wholly unavoidably) to leap with all the might, with joy and mighty exultation of soul; the soul at the same time being so strongly drawn towards God and Christ in heaven, that it seemed to the person as though soul and body would, as it were of themselves, of necessity mount up, leave the earth and ascend thither.

These effects on the body did not begin now in this wonderful season, that they should be owing to the influence of the example of the times, but about seven years ago; and began in a much higher degree, and greater frequency, near three years ago, when there was no such enthusiastical season, as many account this, but it was a very dead time through the land. They arose from no distemper catched from Mr. Whitefield or Mr. Tennent, because they began before either of them came into the country; they began, as I said, near three years ago, in a great increase, upon an extraordinary self-dedication, and renunciation of the world, and resignation of all to God, made in a great view of God's excellency, and high exercise of love to him, and rest and joy in him; since which time they have been very frequent; and began in a yet higher degree, and greater frequency, about a year and [a] half ago, upon another new resignation of all to God, with a yet greater fervency and delight of soul; since which time the body has been very often fainting with the love of Christ; and began in a much higher degree still, the last winter, upon another resignation and acceptance of God, as the only portion and happiness of the soul, wherein the whole world, with the dearest enjoyments in it, were renounced as dirt and dung, and all that is pleasant and glorious, and all that is terrible in this world, seemed perfectly to vanish into nothing, and nothing to be left but God, in whom the soul was perfectly swallowed up, as in an infinite ocean of blessedness: since which time there have often been great agitations of body, and an unavoidable leaping for joy; and the soul as it were dwelling almost without interruption, in a kind of paradise; and very often, in high transports, disposed to speak of those great and glorious things of God and Christ, and the eternal world, that are in view, to others that are present, in a most earnest manner, and with a loud voice, so that it is next to impossible to avoid it: these effects on the body not arising from any bodily distemper or weakness, because the greatest of all have been in a good state of health. This great rejoicing has been a rejoicing with trembling, i.e. attended with a deep and lively sense of the greatness and majesty of God, and the person's own exceeding littleness and vileness: spiritual joys in this person never were attended, either formerly or lately, with the least appearance of any laughter or lightness of countenance, or manner of speaking; but with a peculiar abhorrence of such appearances in spiritual rejoicings, especially since joys have been greatest of all. These high transports when they have been past, have had abiding effects in the increase of the sweetness, rest and humility that they have left upon the soul; and a new engagedness of heart to live to God's honor, and watch and fight against sin. And these things not in one that is in the giddy age of youth, nor in a new convert, and unexperienced Christian, but in one that was converted above twenty-seven years ago; and neither converted nor educated in that enthusiastical town of Northampton (as some may be ready to call it), but in a town and family that none that I know of suspected of enthusiasm; and in a Christian that has been long, in an uncommon manner, growing in grace, and rising, by very sensible degrees, to higher love to God, and weanedness from the world, and mastery over sin and temptation, through great trials and conflicts, and long continued struggling and fighting with sin, and earnest and constant prayer and labor in religion, and engagedness of mind in the use of all means, attended with a great exactness of life: which growth has been attended, not only with a great increase of religious affections, but with a wonderful alteration of outward behavior, in many things, visible to those who are most intimately acquainted, so as lately to have become as it were a new person; and particularly in living so much more above the world, and in a greater degree of steadfastness and strength in the way of duty and self-denial, maintaining the Christian conflict against temptations, and conquering from time to time under great trials; persisting in an unmoved, untouched calm and rest; under the changes and accidents of time.

The person had formerly in lower degrees of grace, been subject to unsteadiness, and many ups and downs, in the frame of mind; the mind being under great disadvantages, through a vapory habit of body, and often subject to melancholy, and at times almost overborne with it, it having been so even from early youth: but strength of grace, and divine light has of a long time, wholly conquered these disadvantages, and carried the mind in a constant manner, quite above all such effects of vapors. Since that resignation spoken of before, made near three years ago, everything of that nature seems to be overcome and crushed by the power of faith and trust in God, and resignation to him; the person has remained in a constant uninterrupted rest, and humble joy in God, and assurance of his favor, without one hour's melancholy or darkness, from that day to this; vapors have had great effects on the body, such as they used to have before, but the soul has been always out of their reach. And this steadfastness and constancy has remained through great outward changes and trials; such as times of the most extreme pain, and apparent hazard of immediate death. What has been felt in late great transports is known to be nothing new in kind, but to be of the same nature with what was felt formerly, when a little child of about five or six years of age; but only in a vastly higher degree. These transporting views and rapturous affections are not attended with any enthusiastic disposition to follow impulses, or any supposed prophetical revelations; nor have they been observed to be attended with any appearance of spiritual pride, but very much of a contrary disposition, an increase of a spirit of humility and meekness, and a disposition in honor to prefer others [cf. Rom. 12:10]. And 'tis worthy to be remarked, that at a time remarkably distinguished from all others, wherein discoveries and holy affections were evidently at the greatest height that ever happened, the greatness and clearness of divine light being overwhelming, and the strength and sweetness of divine love altogether overpowering, which began early in the morning of the Holy Sabbath, and lasted for days together, melting all down in the deepest humility and poverty of spirit, reverence and resignation, and the sweetest meekness, and universal benevolence; I say, 'tis worthy to be observed, that there were these two things in a remarkable manner felt at that time, viz. a peculiar sensible aversion to a judging others that were professing Christians of good standing in the visible church, that they were not converted, or with respect to their degrees of grace; or at all intermeddling with that matter, so much as to determine against and condemn others in the thought of the heart; it appearing hateful, as not agreeing with that lamb-like humility, meekness, gentleness and charity, which the soul then, above other times, saw the beauty of, and felt a disposition to. The disposition that was then felt was, on the contrary, to prefer others to self, and to hope that they saw more of God and loved him better; though before, under smaller discoveries and feebler exercises of divine affection, there had been felt a disposition to censure and condemn others. And another thing that was felt at that time, was a very great sense of the importance of moral social duties, and how great a part of religion lay in them: there was such a new sense and conviction of this, beyond what had been before, that it seemed to be as it were a clear discovery then made to the soul. But in general, there has been a very great increase of a sense of these two things, as divine views and divine love have increased.

The things already mentioned have been attended also with the following things, viz. an extraordinary sense of the awful majesty and greatness of God, so as oftentimes to take away the bodily strength; a sense of the holiness of God, as of a flame infinitely pure and bright, so as sometimes to overwhelm soul and body; a sense of the piercing all-seeing eye of God, so as sometimes to take away the bodily strength; and an extraordinary view of the infinite terribleness of the wrath of God, which has very frequently been strongly impressed on the mind, together with a sense of the ineffable misery of sinners that are exposed to this wrath, that has been overbearing: sometimes the exceeding pollution of the person's own heart, as a sink of all manner of abomination, and a nest of vipers, and the dreadfulness of an eternal hell of God's wrath, opened to view both together; with a clear view of a desert of that misery, without the least degree of divine pity, and that by the pollution of the best duties; yea, only by the pollution and irreverence, and want of humility that attended once speaking of the holy name of God, when done in the best manner that ever it was done; the strength of the body very often taken away with a deep mourning for sin, as committed against so holy and good a God, sometimes with an affecting sense of actual sin, sometimes especially indwelling sin, sometimes the consideration of the sin of the heart as appearing in a particular thing, as for instance, in that there was no greater forwardness and readiness to self-denial for God and Christ, that had so denied himself for us; yea, sometimes the consideration of sin that was in only speaking one word concerning the infinitely great and holy God, has been so affecting as to overcome the strength of nature: very great sense of the certain truth of the great things revealed in the Gospel; an overwhelming sense of the glory of the work of redemption, and the way of salvation by Jesus Christ; the glorious harmony of the divine attributes appearing therein, as that wherein "mercy and truth are met together, and righteousness and peace have kissed each other" [Ps. 85:10]; a sight of the fulness and glorious sufficiency of Christ, that has been so affecting as to overcome the body: a constant immovable trust in God through Christ, with a great sense of his strength and faithfulness, the sureness of his covenant, and the immutability of his promises, so that the everlasting mountains and perpetual hills have appeared as mere shadows to these things: sometimes the sufficiency and faithfulness of God as the covenant God of his people, appearing in these words, "I AM THAT I AM" [Exod. 3:14], in so affecting a manner as to overcome the body: a sense of the glorious, unsearchable, unerring wisdom of God in his works, both of creation and providence, so as to swallow up the soul, and overcome the strength of the body: a sweet rejoicing of soul at the thoughts of God's being infinitely and unchangeably happy, and an exulting gladness of heart that God is self-sufficient, and infinitely above all dependence, and reigns over all, and does his will with absolute and uncontrollable power and sovereignty; a sense of the glory of the Holy Spirit, as the great Comforter, so as to overwhelm both soul and body; only mentioning the word, "the Comforter," has immediately taken away all strength; that word, as the person expressed it, seemed great enough to fill heaven and earth: a most vehement and passionate desire of the honor and glory of God's name; a sensible, clear and constant preference of it not only to the person's own temporal interest, but spiritual comfort in this world; and a willingness to suffer the hidings of God's face, and to live and die in darkness and horror if God's honor should require it, and to have no other reward for it but that God's name should be glorified, although so much of the sweetness of the light of God's countenance had been experienced: a great lamenting of ingratitude, and the lowness of the degree of love to God, so as to deprive of bodily strength; and very often vehement longings and faintings after more love to Christ, and greater conformity to him; especially longing after these two things, viz. to be more perfect in humility and adoration; the flesh and heart seems often to cry out for a lying low before God, and adoring him with greater love and humility: the thoughts of the perfect humility with which the saints in heaven worship God, and fall down before his throne, have often overcome the body, and set it into a great agitation.

A great delight in singing praises to God and Jesus Christ, and longing that this present life may be, as it were, one continued song of praise to God; longing, as the person expressed it, to sit and sing this life away; and an overcoming pleasure in the thoughts of spending an eternity in that exercise: a living by faith to a great degree; a constant and extraordinary distrust of own strength and wisdom; a great dependence on God for his help, in order to the performance of anything to God's acceptance, and being restrained from the most horrid sins, and running upon God, even on his neck, and "on the thick bosses of his bucklers" [Job 15:26]: such a sense of the black ingratitude of true saints' coldness and deadness in religion, and their setting their hearts on the things of this world, as to overcome the bodily frame:

a great longing that all the children of God might be lively in religion, fervent in their love, and active in the service of God; and when there have been appearances of it in others, rejoicing so in beholding the pleasing sight, that the joy of soul has been too great for the body: taking pleasure in the thoughts of watching and striving against sin, and fighting through the way to heaven, and filling up this life with hard labor, and bearing the cross for Christ, as an opportunity to give God honor; not desiring to rest from labors till arrived in heaven, but abhorring the thoughts of it, and seeming astonished that God's own children should be backward to strive and deny themselves for God: earnest longings that all God's people might be clothed with humility and meekness, like the Lamb of God, and feel nothing in their hearts but love and compassion to all mankind; and great grief when anything to the contrary seems to appear in any of the children of God, as any bitterness, or fierceness of zeal, or censoriousness, or reflecting uncharitably on others, or disputing with any appearance of heat of spirit; a deep concern for the good of others' souls; a melting compassion to those that looked on themselves as in a state of nature, and to saints under darkness, so as to cause the body to faint: an universal benevolence to mankind, with a longing as it were to embrace the whole world in the arms of pity and love; ideas of suffering from enemies the utmost conceivable rage and cruelty, with a disposition felt to fervent love and pity in such a case, so far as it could be realized in thought; fainting with pity to the world that lies in ignorance and wickedness; sometimes a disposition felt to a life given up to mourning alone in a wilderness over a lost and miserable world; compassion towards them being often to that degree, that would allow of no support or rest, but in going to God, and pouring out the soul in prayer for them; earnest desires that the work of God; that is now in the land, may be carried on, and that with greater purity, and freedom from all bitter zeal, censoriousness, spiritual pride, hot disputes, etc.

A vehement and constant desire for the setting up of Christ's kingdom through the earth, as a kingdom of holiness, purity, love, peace and happiness to mankind: the soul often entertained with unspeakable delight, and bodily strength overborne at the thoughts of heaven as a world of love, where love shall be the saints' eternal food, and they shall dwell in the light of love, and swim in an ocean of love, and where the very air and breath will be nothing but love; love to the people of God, or God's true saints, as such that have the image of Christ, and as those that will in a very little time shine in his perfect image, that has been attended with that endearment and oneness of heart, and that sweetness and ravishment of soul, that has been altogether inexpressible; the strength very often taken away with longings that others might love God more, and serve God better, and have more of his comfortable presence, than the person that was the subject of these longings, desiring to follow the whole world to heaven, or that everyone should go before, and be higher in grace and happiness, not by this person's diminution, but by others' increase: a delight in conversing of things of religion, and in seeing Christians together, talking of the most spiritual and heavenly things in religion, in a lively and feeling manner, and very frequently overcome with the pleasure of such conversation: a great sense often expressed, of the importance of the duty of charity to the poor, and how much the generality of Christians come short in the practice of it: a great sense of the need God's ministers have of much of the Spirit of God, at this day especially; and most earnest longings and wrestlings with God for them, so as to take away the bodily strength: the greatest, fullest, longest continued, and most constant assurance of the favor of God, and of a title to future glory, that ever I saw any appearance of in any person, enjoying, especially of late (to use the person's own expression) the riches of full assurance: formerly longing to die with something of impatience, but lately, since that resignation forementioned about three years ago, an uninterrupted entire resignation to God with respect to life or death, sickness or health, ease or pain, which has remained unchanged and unshaken, when actually under extreme and violent pains, and in times of threatenings of immediate death; but though there be this patience and submission, yet the thoughts of death and the day of judgment are always exceeding sweet to the soul. This resignation is also attended with a constant resignation of the lives of dearest earthly friends; and sometimes when some of their lives have been imminently threatened, often expressing the sweetness of the liberty of having wholly left the world, and renounced all for God, and having nothing but God, in whom is an infinite fulness.

These things have been attended with a constant sweet peace and calm and serenity of soul, without any cloud to interrupt it; a continual rejoicing in all the works of God's hands, the works of nature, and God's daily works of providence, all appearing with a sweet smile upon them; a wonderful access to God by prayer, as it were seeing him, and sensibly immediately conversing with him, as much oftentimes (to use the person's own expressions) as if Christ were here on earth, sitting on a visible throne, to be approached to and conversed with; frequent, plain, sensible and immediate answers of prayer; all tears wiped away; all former troubles and sorrows of life forgotten, and all sorrow and sighing fled away, excepting grief for past sins and for remaining corruption, and that Christ is loved no more, and that God is no more honored in the world, and a compassionate grief towards fellow creatures; a daily sensible doing and suffering everything for God for a long time past, eating for God, and working for God, and sleeping for God, and bearing pain and trouble for God, and doing all as the service of love, and so doing it with a continual, uninterrupted cheerfulness, peace and joy. "Oh how good," said the person once, "is it to work for God in the daytime, and at night to lie down under his smiles!" High experiences and religious affections in this person have not been attended with any disposition at all to neglect the necessary business of a secular calling, to spend the time in reading and prayer, and other exercises of devotion; but worldly business has been attended with great alacrity, as part of the service of God: the person declaring that it being done thus, 'tis found to be as good as prayer. These things have been accompanied with an exceeding concern and zeal for moral duties, and that all professors may with them adorn the doctrine of God their Saviour; and an uncommon care to perform relative and social duties, and a noted eminence in them; a great inoffensiveness of life and conversation in the sight of others; a great meekness, gentleness and benevolence of spirit and behavior; and a great alteration in those things that formerly used to be the person's failings; seeming to be much overcome and swallowed up by the late great increase of grace, to the observation of those that are most conversant and most intimately acquainted: in times of the brightest light and highest flights of love and joy, finding no disposition to any opinion of being now perfectly free from sin (agreeable to the notion of the Wesleys[2] and their followers, and some

2. John and Charles Wesley were 18th-century British clergy instrumental in the foundation of Methodism. They were awakened to religion through the efforts of George Whitefield, whom they knew at Oxford.

other high pretenders to spirituality in these days); but exceedingly the contrary: at such times especially, seeing how loathsome and polluted the soul is, soul and body and every act and word appearing like rottenness and corruption in that pure and holy light of God's glory: not slighting instruction or means of grace any more for having had great discoveries; on the contrary, never more sensible of the need of instruction than now. And one thing more may be added, viz. that these things have been attended with a particular dislike of placing religion much in dress, and spending much zeal about those things that in themselves are matters of indifference, or an affecting to shew humility and devotion by a mean habit, or a demure and melancholy countenance, or anything singular and superstitious.

Now if such things are enthusiasm, and the fruits of a distempered brain, let my brain be evermore possessed of that happy distemper! If this be distraction, I pray God that the world of mankind may be all seized with this benign, meek, beneficent, beatifical, glorious distraction!

1742

A Divine and Supernatural Light[1]

IMMEDIATELY IMPARTED TO THE SOUL BY THE SPIRIT OF GOD, SHOWN TO BE BOTH A SCRIPTURAL AND RATIONAL DOCTRINE

Matthew 16.17

> And Jesus answered and said unto him, Blessed art thou, Simon Barjona;[2] for flesh and blood hath not revealed it unto thee, but my Father which is in heaven.

Christ addresses these words to Peter upon occasion of his professing his faith in Him as the Son of God. Our Lord was inquiring of His disciples, whom men said that He was; not that He needed to be informed, but only to introduce and give occasion to what follows. They answer that some said He was John the Baptist, and some Elias, and others Jeremias, or one of the prophets.[3] When they had thus given an account whom others said that He was, Christ asks them, whom they said that He was? Simon Peter, whom we find always zealous and forward, was the first to answer: he readily replied to the question, Thou art Christ, the Son of the living God.

Upon this occasion, Christ says as He does to him and of him in the text: in which we may observe.

1. That Peter is pronounced blessed on this account.—Blessed art thou— "Thou art an happy man, that thou art not ignorant of this, that I am Christ, the Son of the living God. Thou art distinguishingly happy. Others are blinded, and have dark and deluded apprehensions, as you have now given an account, some thinking that I am Elias, and some that I am Jeremias, and some one thing, and some another: but none of them thinking right, all

1. Edwards delivered this sermon in Northampton, Massachusetts, in 1733; it was published the following year at the request of his congregation. The text here is from *The Works of Jonathan Edwards* (1829–30), vol. 6, edited by Sereno E. Dwight.

2. The apostle Peter (Simon, son of Jona).

3. Matthew 16.14. Elias is the name used in the New Testament for the prophet Elijah.

of them are misled. Happy art thou, that art so distinguished as to know the truth in this matter."

2. The evidence of this his happiness declared, viz., That God, and He only, had revealed it to him. This is an evidence of his being blessed.

First. As it shows how peculiarly favored he was of God above others; q.d.,[4] "How highly favored art thou, that others, wise and great men, the scribes, Pharisees,[5] and rulers, and the nation in general, are left in darkness, to follow their own misguided apprehensions; and that thou shouldst be singled out, as it were, by name, that My heavenly Father should thus set His love on thee, Simon Bar-jona.—This argues thee blessed, that thou shouldst thus be the object of God's distinguishing love."

Secondly. It evidences his blessedness also, as it intimates that this knowledge is above any that flesh and blood can reveal. "This is such knowledge as only my Father which is in heaven can give. It is too high and excellent to be communicated by such means as other knowledge is. Thou art blessed, that thou knowest what God alone can teach thee."

The original of this knowledge is here declared, both negatively and positively. Positively, as God is here declared the author of it. Negatively, as it is declared, that flesh and blood had not revealed it. God is the author of all knowledge and understanding whatsoever. He is the author of all moral prudence, and of the skill that men have in their secular business. Thus it is said of all in Israel that were wise-hearted and skilled in embroidering, that God had filled them with the spirit of wisdom. Exodus 28.3.[6]

God is the author of such knowledge; yet so that flesh and blood reveals it. Mortal men are capable of imparting the knowledge of human arts and sciences, and skill in temporal affairs. God is the author of such knowledge by those means: flesh and blood is employed as the mediate or second cause of it; He conveys it by the power and influence of natural means. But this spiritual knowledge, spoken of in the text, is what God is the author of, and none else: He reveals it, and flesh and blood reveals it not. He imparts this knowledge immediately, not making use of any intermediate natural causes, as He does in other knowledge.

What had passed in the preceding discourse naturally occasioned Christ to observe this; because the disciples had been telling how others did not know Him, but were generally mistaken about him, divided and confounded in their opinions of Him: but Peter had declared his assured faith, that He was the Son of God. Now it was natural to observe how it was not flesh and blood that had revealed it to him, but God; for if this knowledge were dependent on natural causes or means, how came it to pass that they, a company of poor fishermen, illiterate men, and persons of low education, attained to the knowledge of the truth, while the Scribes and Pharisees, men of vastly higher advantages, and greater knowledge and sagacity, in other matters, remained in ignorance? This could be owing only to the gracious distinguishing influence and revelation of the Spirit of God. Hence, what I would make the subject of my present discourse from these words, is this:

---

4. I.e., *quasi dicat*; as if he should say (Latin).
5. A sect hostile to Jesus and known for their arrogance and pride (Matthew 9.9–13). "Scribes": interpreters of the Jewish law.

6. This passage from Exodus refers to God's command to the people of Israel to make proper garments for Aaron's priesthood.

Doctrine

That there is such a thing as a spiritual and divine light, immediately imparted to the soul by God, of a different nature from any that is obtained by natural means. And on this subject I would,

    I. Show what this divine light is.
    II. How it is given immediately by God, and not obtained by natural means.
    III. Show the truth of the doctrine.
And then conclude with a brief improvement.[7]

    I. I would show what this spiritual and divine light is. And in order to it would show,

First, In a few things, what it is not. And here,

1. Those convictions that natural men may have of their sin and misery, is not this spiritual and divine light. Men, in a natural condition, may have convictions of the guilt that lies upon them, and of the anger of God, and their danger of divine vengeance. Such convictions are from the light of truth. That some sinners have a greater conviction of their guilt and misery than others is because some have more light, or more of an apprehension of truth than others. And this light and conviction may be from the Spirit of God; the Spirit convinces men of sin; but yet nature is much more concerned in it than in the communication of that spiritual and divine light that is spoken of in the doctrine; it is from the Spirit of God only as assisting natural principles, and not as infusing any new principles. Common grace differs from special in that it influences only by assisting of nature, and not by imparting grace, or bestowing anything above nature. The light that is obtained is wholly natural, or of no superior kind to what mere nature attains to, though more of that kind be obtained than would be obtained if men were left wholly to themselves; or, in other words, common grace only assists the faculties of the soul to do that more fully which they do by nature, as natural conscience or reason will by mere nature make a man sensible of guilt, and will accuse and condemn him when he has done amiss. Conscience is a principle natural to men; and the work that it doth naturally, or of itself, is to give an apprehension of right and wrong, and to suggest to the mind the relation that there is between right and wrong and a retribution. The Spirit of God, in those convictions which unregenerate men[8] sometimes have, assists conscience to do this work in a further degree than it would do if they were left to themselves. He helps it against those things that tend to stupify it, and obstruct its exercise. But in the renewing and sanctifying work of the Holy Ghost, those things are wrought in the soul that are above nature, and of which there is nothing of the like kind in the soul by nature; and they are caused to exist in the soul habitually, and according to such a stated constitution or law, that lays such a foundation for exercises in a continued course, as is called a principle of nature. Not only are remaining principles assisted to do their work more freely and fully, but those principles are restored that were utterly destroyed by the fall; and the mind thenceforward habitually exerts those acts that the dominion of sin had made it as wholly destitute of as a dead body is of vital acts.

---

7. Literally, turning something to profit; here used in the sense of the lesson to be learned.

8. Those who are not yet saved.

The Spirit of God acts in a very different manner in the one case, from what He doth in the other. He may, indeed, act upon the mind of a natural man, but He acts in the mind of a saint[9] as an indwelling vital principle. He acts upon the mind of an unregenerate person as an extrinsic occasional agent; for, in acting upon them, He doth not unite himself to them: for, notwithstanding all His influences that they may possess, they are still sensual, having not the Spirit. Jude 19.[1] But He unites himself with the mind of a saint, takes him for His temple, actuates and influences him as a new supernatural principle of life and action. There is this difference, that the Spirit of God, in acting in the soul of a godly man, exerts and communicates Himself there in His own proper nature. Holiness is the proper nature of the Spirit of God. The Holy Spirit operates in the minds of the godly, by uniting Himself to them, and living in them, and exerting His own nature in the exercise of their faculties. The Spirit of God may act upon a creature, and yet not in acting communicate Himself. The Spirit of God may act upon inanimate creatures, as, the Spirit moved upon the face of the waters,[2] in the beginning of the creation; so the Spirit of God may act upon the minds of men many ways, and communicate Himself no more than when He acts upon an inanimate creature. For instance, He may excite thoughts in them, may assist their natural reason and understanding, or may assist other natural principles, and this without any union with the soul, but may act, as it were, upon an external object. But as He acts in His holy influences and spiritual operations, He acts in a way of peculiar communication of Himself; so that the subject is thence denominated spiritual.

2. This spiritual and divine light does not consist in any impression made upon the imagination. It is no impression upon the mind, as though one saw anything with the bodily eyes. It is no imagination or idea of an outward light or glory, or any beauty of form or countenance, or a visible luster or brightness of any object. The imagination may be strongly impressed with such things; but this is not spiritual light. Indeed when the mind has a lively discovery of spiritual things, and is greatly affected with the power of divine light, it may, and probably very commonly doth, much affect the imagination; so that impressions of an outward beauty or brightness may accompany those spiritual discoveries. But spiritual light is not that impression upon the imagination, but an exceedingly different thing. Natural men may have lively impressions on their imaginations; and we cannot determine but that the devil, who transforms himself into an angel of light, may cause imaginations of an outward beauty, or visible glory, and of sounds and speeches, and other such things; but these are things of a vastly inferior nature to spiritual light.

3. This spiritual light is not the suggesting of any new truths or propositions not contained in the word of God. This suggesting of new truths or doctrines to the mind, independent of any antecedent revelations of those propositions, either in word or writing, is inspiration; such as the prophets and apostles had, and such as some enthusiasts[3] pretend to. But this spiritual light that I am speaking of, is quite a different thing from inspiration. It reveals no new doctrine, it suggests no new proposition to the mind, it

---

9. Here, a living Christian who has passed from mere understanding of Christ's doctrine to heartfelt commitment; such people were often called "visible saints."

1. "These be they who separate themselves, sensual, having not the Spirit."

2. Genesis 1.2.

3. People who erroneously claim to be inspired by the spirit of God.

teaches no new thing of God, or Christ, or another world, not taught in the Bible, but only gives a due apprehension of those things that are taught in the word of God.

4. It is not every affecting view that men have of religious things that is this spiritual and divine light. Men by mere principles of nature are capable of being affected with things that have a special relation to religion as well as other things. A person by mere nature, for instance, may be liable to be affected with the story of Jesus Christ, and the sufferings he underwent, as well as by any other tragical story. He may be the more affected with it from the interest he conceives mankind to have in it. Yea, he may be affected with it without believing it; as well as a man may be affected with what he reads in a romance, or sees acted in a stage play. He may be affected with a lively and eloquent description of many pleasant things that attend the state of the blessed in heaven, as well as his imagination be entertained by a romantic[4] description of the pleasantness of fairyland, or the like. And a common belief of the truth of such things, from education or otherwise, may help forward their affection. We read in Scripture of many that were greatly affected with things of a religious nature, who yet are there represented as wholly graceless, and many of them very ill[5] men. A person therefore may have affecting views of the things of religion, and yet be very destitute of spiritual light. Flesh and blood may be the author of this; one man may give another an affecting view of divine things with but common assistance; but God alone can give a spiritual discovery of them.—But I proceed to show.

Secondly, Positively what this spiritual and divine light is.

And it may be thus described: A true sense of the divine excellency of the things revealed in the word of God, and a conviction of the truth and reality of them thence arising. This spiritual light primarily consists in the former of these, viz., a real sense and apprehension of the divine excellency of things revealed in the word of God. A spiritual and saving conviction of the truth and reality of these things, arises from such a sight of their divine excellency and glory; so that this conviction of their truth is an effect and natural consequence of this sight of their divine glory. There is therefore in this spiritual light,

1. A true sense of the divine and superlative excellency of the things of religion; a real sense of the excellency of God and Jesus Christ, and of the work of redemption, and the ways and works of God revealed in the gospel. There is a divine and superlative glory in these things; an excellency that is of a vastly higher kind, and more sublime nature than in other things; a glory greatly distinguishing them from all that is earthly and temporal. He that is spiritually enlightened truly apprehends and sees it, or has a sense of it. He does not merely rationally believe that God is glorious, but he has a sense of the gloriousness of God in his heart. There is not only a rational belief that God is holy, and that holiness is a good thing, but there is a sense of the loveliness of God's holiness. There is not only a speculatively judging that God is gracious, but a sense how amiable God is on account of the beauty of this divine attribute.

There is a twofold knowledge of good of which God has made the mind of man capable. The first, that which is merely notional; as when a person only

---

4. Fanciful, imaginary.   5. I.e., evil.

speculatively judges that anything is, which by the agreement of mankind, is called good or excellent, viz., that which is most to general advantage, and between which and a reward there is a suitableness,—and the like. And the other is, that which consists in the sense of the heart; as when the heart is sensible[6] of pleasure and delight in the presence of the idea of it. In the former is exercised merely the speculative faculty, or the understanding, in distinction from the will or disposition of the soul. In the latter, the will, or inclination, or heart, are mainly concerned.

Thus there is a difference between having an opinion, that God is holy and gracious, and having a sense of the loveliness and beauty of that holiness and grace. There is a difference between having a rational judgment that honey is sweet, and having a sense of its sweetness. A man may have the former, that knows not how honey tastes; but a man cannot have the latter unless he has an idea of the taste of honey in his mind. So there is a difference between believing that a person is beautiful, and having a sense of his beauty. The former may be obtained by hearsay, but the latter only by seeing the countenance. When the heart is sensible of the beauty and amiableness of a thing, it necessarily feels pleasure in the apprehension. It is implied in a person's being heartily sensible of the loveliness of a thing, that the idea of it is pleasant to his soul; which is a far different thing from having a rational opinion that it is excellent.

2. There arises from this sense of the divine excellency of things contained in the word of God, a conviction of the truth and reality of them; and that, either indirectly or directly.

First, Indirectly, and that two ways:

1. As the prejudices of the heart, against the truth of divine things, are hereby removed; so that the mind becomes susceptive of the due force of rational arguments for their truth. The mind of man is naturally full of prejudices against divine truth. It is full of enmity against the doctrines of the gospel; which is a disadvantage to those arguments that prove their truth, and causes them to lose their force upon the mind. But when a person has discovered to him the divine excellency of Christian doctrines, this destroys the enmity, removes those prejudices, sanctifies the reason, and causes it to lie open to the force of arguments for their truth.

Hence was the different effect that Christ's miracles had to convince the disciples, from what they had to convince the Scribes and Pharisees. Not that they had a stronger reason, or had their reason more improved; but their reason was sanctified, and those blinding prejudices, that the Scribes and Pharisees were under, were removed by the sense they had of the excellency of Christ, and his doctrine.

It not only removes the hindrances of reason, but positively helps reason. It makes even the speculative notions more lively. It engages the attention of the mind, with more fixedness and intenseness to that kind of objects; which causes it to have a clearer view of them, and enables it more clearly to see their mutual relations, and occasions it to take more notice of them. The ideas themselves that otherwise are dim and obscure are by this means impressed with the greater strength, and have a light cast upon them, so that the mind can better judge of them. As he that beholds objects on the face

6. Aware.

of the earth, when the light of the sun is cast upon them, is under greater advantage to discern them in their true forms and natural relations, than he that sees them in a dim twilight.

The mind, being sensible of the excellency of divine objects, dwells upon them with delight; and the powers of the soul are more awakened and enlivened to employ themselves in the contemplation of them, and exert themselves more fully and much more to the purpose. The beauty of the objects draws on the faculties, and draws forth their exercises; so that reason itself is under far greater advantages for its proper and free exercises, and to attain its proper end, free of darkness and delusion.—But,

Secondly, A true sense of the divine excellency of the things of God's word doth more directly and immediately convince us of their truth; and that because the excellency of these things is so superlative. There is a beauty in them so divine and godlike, that it greatly and evidently distinguishes them from things merely human, or that of which men are the inventors and authors; a glory so high and great, that when clearly seen, commands assent to their divine reality. When there is an actual and lively discovery of this beauty and excellency, it will not allow of any such thought as that it is the fruit of men's invention. This is a kind of intuitive and immediate evidence. They believe the doctrines of God's word to be divine, because they see a divine, and transcendent, and most evidently distinguishing glory in them; such a glory as, if clearly seen, does not leave room to doubt of their being of God, and not of men.

Such a conviction of the truths of religion as this, arising from a sense of their divine excellency, is included in saving faith. And this original of it is that by which it is most essentially distinguished from that common assent, of which unregenerate men are capable.

II. I proceed now to the second thing proposed, viz., to show how this light is immediately given by God, and not obtained by natural means. And here,

1. It is not intended that the natural faculties are not used in it. They are the subject of this light: and in such a manner, that they are not merely passive, but active in it. God, in letting in this light into the soul, deals with man according to his nature, and makes use of his rational faculties. But yet this light is not the less immediately from God for that; the faculties are made use of as the subject, and not as the cause. As the use we make of our eyes in beholding various objects, when the sun arises, is not the cause of the light that discovers those objects to us.

2. It is not intended that outward means have no concern in this affair. It is not in this affair, as in inspiration, where new truths are suggested; for, by this light is given only a due apprehension of the same truths that are revealed in the word of God, and therefore it is not given without the word. The gospel is employed in this affair. This light is the "light of the glorious gospel of Christ" (2 Corinthians 4.3–4).[7] The gospel is as a glass, by which this light is conveyed to us (1 Corinthians 13.12): "Now we see through a glass."[8]—But,

---

7. "But if our gospel be hid, it is hid to them that are lost: In whom the god of this world hath blinded the minds of them which believe not, lest the light of the glorious gospel of Christ, who is the image of God, should shine unto them."
8. "For now we see through a glass, darkly; but then face to face."

3. When it is said that this light is given immediately by God, and not obtained by natural means, hereby is intended that it is given by God without making use of any means that operate by their own power or natural force. God makes use of means; but it is not as mediate causes to produce this effect. There are not truly any second causes of it; but it is produced by God immediately. The word of God is no proper cause of this effect, but is made use of only to convey to the mind the subject matter of this saving instruction: And this indeed it doth convey to us by natural force or influence. It conveys to our minds these doctrines; it is the cause of a notion of them in our heads, but not of the sense of their divine excellency in our hearts. Indeed a person cannot have spiritual light without the word. But that does not argue, that the word properly causes that light. The mind cannot see the excellency of any doctrine, unless that doctrine be first in the mind; but seeing the excellency of the doctrine may be immediately from the Spirit of God; though the conveying of the doctrine, or proposition, itself, may be by the word. So that the notions which are the subject matter of this light are conveyed to the mind by the word of God; but that due sense of the heart, wherein this light formally consists, is immediately by the Spirit of God. As, for instance, the notion that there is a Christ, and that Christ is holy and gracious, is conveyed to the mind by the word of God: But the sense of the excellency of Christ, by reason of that holiness and grace, is nevertheless, immediately the work of the Holy Spirit.—I come now,

III. To show the truth of the doctrine; that is, to show that there is such a thing as that spiritural light that has been described, thus immediately let into the mind by God. And here I would show, briefly, that this doctrine is both scriptural and rational.

First, It is scriptural. My text is not only full to the purpose, but it is a doctrine with which the Scripture abounds. We are there abundantly taught, that the saints differ from the ungodly in this; that they have the knowledge of God, and a sight of God, and of Jesus Christ. I shall mention but few texts out of many: 1 John 3.6: "Whosoever sinneth, hath not seen him, nor known him." 3 John 11: "He that doeth good, is of God: but he that doeth evil, hath not seen God." John 14.19: "The world seeth me no more; but ye see me." John 17.3: "And this is eternal life, that they might know thee, the only true God, and Jesus Christ whom thou hast sent." This knowledge, or sight of God and Christ, cannot be a mere speculative knowledge, because it is spoken of as that wherein they differ from the ungodly. And by these scriptures, it must not only be a different knowledge in degree and circumstances, and different in its effects, but it must be entirely different in nature and kind.

And this light and knowledge is always spoken of as immediately given of God; Matthew 11.25–27: "At that time, Jesus answered and said, I thank thee, O Father, Lord of heaven and earth, because thou hast hid these things from the wise and prudent, and hast revealed them unto babes. Even so, Father, for so it seemed good in thy sight. All things are delivered unto me of my Father: and no man knoweth the Father, save the Son, and he to whomsoever the Son will reveal him." Here this effect is ascribed exclusively to the arbitrary operation and gift of God bestowing this knowledge on whom He will, and distinguishing those with it who have the least natural advantage or means for knowledge, even babes, when it is denied to the wise and prudent. And imparting this knowledge is here appropriated to the Son of God, as His sole prerogative. And again, 2 Corinthians 4.6: "For God, who commanded the light to shine out of darkness, hath shined in our hearts, to give the light of the knowledge of the glory of God, in the face of Jesus Christ." This plainly shows, that there is a discovery of the divine superlative glory and excellency of God and Christ, peculiar to the saints: and, also, that it is as immediately from God, as light from the sun, and that it is the immediate effect of His power and will. For it is compared to God's creating the light by his powerful word in the beginning of the creation; and is said to be by the Spirit of the Lord, in the 18th verse of the preceding chapter. God is spoken of as giving the knowledge of Christ in conversion, as of what before was hidden and unseen; Galatians 1.15–16: "But when it pleased God, who separated me from my mother's womb, and called me by his grace, to reveal his son in me." The scripture also speaks plainly of such a knowledge of the word of God, as has been described as the immediate gift of God; Psalm 119.18: "Open thou mine eyes, that I may behold wondrous things out of thy law." What could the Psalmist mean, when he begged of God to open his eyes? Was he ever blind? Might he not have resort to the law, and see every word and sentence in it when he pleased? And what could he mean by those wondrous things? Were they the wonderful stories of the creation, and deluge, and Israel's passing through the Red Sea,[9] and the like? Were not his eyes open to read these strange things when he would? Doubtless, by wondrous things in God's law, he had respect to those distinguishing and wonderful excellencies, and marvelous manifestations of the divine perfections and glory contained in the commands and doctrines of the word, and those works and counsels of God that were there revealed. So the scripture speaks of a knowledge of God's dispensation, and covenant of mercy,[1] and way of grace towards His people, as peculiar to the saints, and given only by God; Psalm 25.14: "The secret of the Lord is with them that fear him; and he will show them his covenant."

And that a true and saving belief of the truth of religion is that which arises from such a discovery is, also, what the scripture teaches. As John 6.40: "And this is the will of him that sent me, that every one who seeth the Son, and believeth on him, may have everlasting life"; where it is plain that a true faith is what arises from a spiritual sight of Christ. And John 17.6–8: "I have manifested thy name unto the men which thou gavest me out of the world. Now, they have known, that all things whatsoever thou hast given me, are of thee. For I have given unto them the words which thou gavest me, and they have received them, and have known surely, that I came out from thee, and they have believed that thou didst send me"; where Christ's manifesting God's name to the disciples, or giving them the knowledge of God, was that whereby they knew that Christ's doctrine was of God, and that Christ Himself proceeded from Him, and was sent by Him. Again, John 12.44–46: "Jesus cried, and said, He that believeth on me, believeth not on me but on him that sent me. And he that seeth me, seeth him that sent me. I am come a light into the world, that whosoever believeth on me, should not abide in darkness." Their believing in Christ, and spiritually seeing Him, are parallel.

9. The waters of the Red Sea divided for the Israelites in their exodus from Egypt (Exodus 14.21).
1. The agreement between Christ and those who believe in him that they would be saved; also known as the Covenant of Faith, as distinct from the Covenant of Works, which Adam broke.

Christ condemns the Jews, that they did not know that He was the Messiah, and that His doctrine was true, from an inward distinguishing taste and relish of what was divine, in Luke 12.56–57. He having there blamed the Jews, that, though they could discern the face of the sky and of the earth, and signs of the weather, that yet they could not discern those times—or, as it is expressed in Matthew, the signs of those times—adds, "yea, and why even of your ownselves, judge ye not what is right?" i.e., without extrinsic signs. Why have ye not that sense of true excellency, whereby ye may distinguish that which is holy and divine? Why have ye not that savor of the things of God, by which you may see the distinguishing glory, and evident divinity of me and my doctrine?

The apostle Peter mentions it as what gave him and his companions good and well-grounded assurance of the truth of the gospel, that they had seen the divine glory of Christ. 2 Peter 1.16: "For we have not followed cunningly devised fables, when we made known unto you the power and coming of our Lord Jesus Christ, but were eye-witnesses of his majesty." The apostle has respect to that visible glory of Christ which they saw in His transfiguration. That glory was so divine, having such an ineffable appearance and semblance of divine holiness, majesty, and grace, that it evidently denoted Him to be a divine person. But if a sight of Christ's outward glory might give a rational assurance of His divinity, why may not an apprehension of His spiritual glory do so too? Doubtless Christ's spiritual glory is in itself as distinguishing, and as plainly shows His divinity, as His outward glory—nay, a great deal more, for His spiritual glory is that wherein His divinity consists; and the outward glory of His transfiguration showed Him to be divine, only as it was a remarkable image or representation of that spiritual glory. Doubtless, therefore, he that has had a clear sight of the spiritual glory of Christ, may say, "I have not followed cunningly devised fables, but have been an eyewitness of His majesty, upon as good grounds as the apostle, when he had respect to the outward glory of Christ that he had seen." But this brings me to what was proposed next, viz., to show that,

Secondly, This doctrine is rational.[2]

1. It is rational to suppose, that there is really such an excellency in divine things—so transcendent and exceedingly different from what is in other things—that if it were seen, would most evidently distinguish them. We cannot rationally doubt but that things divine, which appertain to the supreme Being, are vastly different from things that are human; that there is a high, glorious, and godlike excellency in them that does most remarkably difference them from the things that are of men, insomuch that if the difference were but seen, it would have a convincing, satisfying influence upon anyone that they are divine. What reason can be offered against it unless we would argue that God is not remarkably distinguished in glory from men.

If Christ should now appear to any one as he did on the mount at His transfiguration,[3] or if He should appear to the world in His heavenly glory, as He will do at the Day of Judgment,[4] without doubt, His glory and majesty would be such as would satisfy everyone that He was a divine person, and that His religion was true; and it would be a most reasonable, and well

---

2. Capable of being grasped by the mind, understandable.
3. In Matthew 17.1–8, Christ appeared to Peter, James, and John shining "as the sun" and his garments "white as the light."
4. See Revelation 4.

grounded conviction too. And why may there not be that stamp of divinity or divine glory on the word of God, on the scheme and doctrine of the gospel, that may be in like manner distinguishing and as rationally convincing, provided it be but seen? It is rational to suppose, that when God speaks to the world, there should be something in His word vastly different from men's word. Supposing that God never had spoken to the world, but we had notice that He was about to reveal Himself from heaven and speak to us immediately Himself, or that He should give us a book of His own inditing;[5] after what manner should we expect that He would speak? Would it not be rational to suppose, that His speech would be exceeding different from men's speech, that there should be such an excellency and sublimity in His word, such a stamp of wisdom, holiness, majesty, and other divine perfections, that the word of men, yea of the wisest of men, should appear mean and base in comparison of it? Doubtless it would be thought rational to expect this, and unreasonable to think otherwise. When a wise man speaks in the exercise of His wisdom, there is something in everything He says, that is very distinguishable from the talk of a little child. So, without doubt, and much more is the speech of God, to be distinguished from that of the wisest of men; agreeable to Jeremiah 23.28–29. God, having there been reproving the false prophets that prophesied in his name, and pretended that what they spake was His word, when indeed it was their own word, says, "The prophet that hath a dream, let him tell a dream; and he that hath my word let him speak my word faithfully: what is the chaff to the wheat? saith the Lord. Is not my word like as a fire? saith the Lord: and like a hammer that breaketh the rock in pieces?"

2. If there be such a distinguishing excellency in divine things, it is rational to suppose that there may be such a thing as seeing it. What should hinder but that it may be seen? It is no argument that there is no such distinguishing excellency, or that it cannot be seen, because some do not see it, though they may be discerning men in temporal matters. It is not rational to suppose, if there be any such excellency in divine things, that wicked men should see it. Is it rational to suppose that those whose minds are full of spiritual pollution, and under the power of filthy lusts, should have any relish or sense of divine beauty or excellency; or that their minds should be susceptive of that light that is in its own nature so pure and heavenly? It need not seem at all strange that sin should so blind the mind, seeing that men's particular natural tempers and dispositions will so much blind them in secular matters; as when men's natural temper is melancholy, jealous, fearful, proud, or the like.

3. It is rational to suppose that this knowledge should be given immediately by God, and not be obtained by natural means. Upon what account should it seem unreasonable that there should be any immediate communication between God and the creature? It is strange, that men should make any matter of difficulty of it. Why should not He that made all things still have something immediately to do with the things that He has made? Where lies the great difficulty, if we own the being of a God, and that He created all things out of nothing, of allowing some immediate influence of God on the creation still? And if it be reasonable to suppose it with respect to any part of the creation, it is especially so with respect to reasonable, intelligent creatures; who are next to God in the gradation of the different orders of beings, and whose business is most immediately with God; and reason teaches that

5. Composition.

man was made to serve and glorify his Creator. And if it be rational to suppose that God immediately communicates Himself to man in any affair, it is in this. It is rational to suppose that God would reserve that knowledge and wisdom, which is of such a divine and excellent nature, to be bestowed immediately by Himself, and that it should not be left in the power of second causes. Spiritual wisdom and grace is the highest and most excellent gift that ever God bestows on any creature; in this, the highest excellency and perfection of a rational creature consists. It is also immensely the most important of all divine gifts: it is that wherein man's happiness consists, and on which his everlasting welfare depends. How rational is it to suppose that God, however He has left lower gifts to second causes, and in some sort in their power, yet should reserve this most excellent, divine, and important of all divine communications in His own hands to be bestowed immediately by Himself, as a thing too great for second causes to be concerned in. It is rational to suppose that this blessing should be immediately from God, for there is no gift or benefit that is in itself so nearly related to the divine nature. Nothing which the creature receives is so much a participation of the Deity; it is a kind of emanation of God's beauty, and is related to God as the light is to the sun. It is, therefore, congruous and fit, that when it is given of God, it should be immediately from Himself, and by Himself, according to His own sovereign will.

It is rational to suppose, that it should be beyond man's power to obtain this light by the mere strength of natural reason; for it is not a thing that belongs to reason to see the beauty and loveliness of spiritual things; it is not a speculative thing, but depends on the sense of the heart. Reason, indeed, is necessary, in order to it, as it is by reason only that we are become the subjects of the means of it; which means, I have already shown to be necessary in order to it, though they have no proper causal influence in the affair. It is by reason that we become possessed of a notion of those doctrines that are the subject matter of this divine light or knowledge; and reason may many ways be indirectly and remotely an advantage to it. Reason has also to do in the acts that are immediately consequent on this discovery: for, seeing the truth of religion from hence, is by reason, though it be but by one step, and the inference be immediate. So reason has to do in that accepting of and trusting in Christ that is consequent on it. But if we take reason strictly—not for the faculty of mental perception in general, but for ratiocination, or a power of inferring by arguments—the perceiving of spiritual beauty and excellency no more belongs to reason than it belongs to the sense of feeling to perceive colors, or to the power of seeing to perceive the sweetness of food. It is out of reason's province to perceive the beauty or loveliness of anything; such a perception does not belong to that faculty. Reason's work is to perceive truth and not excellency. It is not ratiocination that gives men the perception of the beauty and amiableness of a countenance, though it may be many ways indirectly an advantage to it; yet it is no more reason that immediately perceives it than it is reason that perceives the sweetness of honey; it depends on the sense of the heart. Reason may determine that a countenance is beautiful to others, it may determine that honey is sweet to others, but it will never give me a perception of its sweetness.

I will conclude with a very brief improvement of what has been said.

First, this doctrine may lead us to reflect on the goodness of God, that has so ordered it, that a saving evidence of the truth of the Gospel is such as is attainable by persons of mean capacities and advantages, as well as those that are of the greatest parts and learning. If the evidence of the Gospel depended only on history and such reasonings as learned men only are capable of, it would be above the reach of far the greatest part of mankind. But persons with an ordinary degree of knowledge are capable, without a long and subtle train of reasoning, to see the divine excellency of the things of religion; they are capable of being taught by the Spirit of God, as well as learned men. The evidence that is this way obtained is vastly better and more satisfying than all that can be obtained by the arguings of those that are most learned and greatest masters of reason. And babes are as capable of knowing these things as the wise and prudent; and they are often hid from these when they are revealed to those. 1 Corinthians 1.26–27: "For ye see your calling, brethren, how that not many wise men, after the flesh, not many mighty, not many noble, are called. But God hath chosen the foolish things of the world."

Secondly, This doctrine may well put us upon examining ourselves, whether we have ever had this divine light let into our souls. If there be such a thing, doubtless it is of great importance whether we have thus been taught by the Spirit of God; whether the light of the glorious gospel of Christ, who is the image of God, hath shined unto us, giving us the light of the knowledge of the glory of God in the face of Jesus Christ; whether we have seen the Son, and believed on Him, or have that faith of gospel doctrines which arises from a spiritual sight of Christ.

Thirdly, All may hence be exhorted earnestly to seek this spiritual light. To influence and move to it, the following things may be considered.

1. This is the most excellent and divine wisdom that any creature is capable of. It is more excellent than any human learning; it is far more excellent than all the knowledge of the greatest philosophers or statesmen. Yea, the least glimpse of the glory of God in the face of Christ doth more exalt and ennoble the soul than all the knowledge of those that have the greatest speculative understanding in divinity without grace. This knowledge has the most noble object that can be, viz., the divine glory and excellency of God and Christ. The knowledge of these objects is that wherein consists the most excellent knowledge of the angels, yea, of God Himself.

2. This knowledge is that which is above all others sweet and joyful. Men have a great deal of pleasure in human knowledge, in studies of natural things; but this is nothing to that joy which arises from this divine light shining into the soul. This light gives a view of those things that are immensely the most exquisitely beautiful and capable of delighting the eye of the understanding. The spiritual light is the dawning of the light of glory in the heart. There is nothing so powerful as this to support persons in affliction, and to give the mind peace and brightness in this stormy and dark world.

3. This light is such as effectually influences the inclination and changes the nature of the soul. It assimilates our nature to the divine nature, and changes the soul into an image of the same glory that is beheld. 2 Corinthians 3.18: "But we all with open face, beholding as in a glass the glory of the Lord, are changed into the same image, from glory to glory, even as by the Spirit of the Lord." This knowledge will wean from[6] the world, and raise the

6. Draw us away from.

inclination to heavenly things. It will turn the heart to God as the fountain of good, and to choose Him for the only portion. This light, and this only, will bring the soul to a saving close with Christ. It conforms the heart to the gospel, mortifies its enmity and opposition against the scheme of salvation therein revealed; it causes the heart to embrace the joyful tidings, and entirely to adhere to, and acquiesce in, the revelation of Christ as our Savior; it causes the whole soul to accord and symphonize with it, admitting it with entire credit and respect, cleaving to it with full inclination and affection; and it effectually disposes the soul to give up itself entirely to Christ.

4. This light, and this only, has its fruit in an universal holiness of life. No merely notional or speculative understanding of the doctrines of religion will ever bring to this. But this light, as it reaches the bottom of the heart, and changes the nature, so it will effectually dispose to an universal obedience. It shows God as worthy to be obeyed and served. It draws forth the heart in a sincere love to God, which is the only principle of a true, gracious, and universal obedience, and it convinces of the reality of those glorious rewards that God has promised to them that obey Him.

1733   1734

Sinners in the Hands of an Angry God[1]

Deuteronomy 32.35

Their foot shall slide in due time.[2]

In this verse is threatened the vengeance of God on the wicked unbelieving Israelites, who were God's visible people, and who lived under the means of grace,[3] but who, notwithstanding all God's wonderful works towards them, remained (as in verse 28)[4] void of counsel, having no understanding in them. Under all the cultivations of heaven, they brought forth bitter and poisonous fruit, as in the two verses next preceding the text.[5] The expression I have chosen for my text, "Their foot shall slide in due time," seems to imply the following things, relating to the punishment and destruction to which these wicked Israelites were exposed.

1. That they were always exposed to destruction; as one that stands or walks in slippery places is always exposed to fall. This is implied in the manner of their destruction coming upon them, being represented by their foot

1. Edwards delivered this sermon in Enfield, Connecticut, a town about thirty miles south of Northampton, on Sunday, July 8, 1741. In Benjamin Trumbull's *A Complete History of Connecticut* (1797, 1818) we are told that Edwards read his sermon in a level voice with his sermon book in his left hand, and in spite of his calm, "there was such a breathing of distress, and weeping, that the preacher was obliged to speak to the people and desire silence, that he might be heard." The text here is from *The Works of Jonathan Edwards* (1829–30), vol. 7, edited by Sereno E. Dwight.
2. "To me belongeth vengeance, and recompense; their foot shall slide in due time: for the day of their calamity is at hand, and the things that shall come upon them make haste."

3. I.e., the Ten Commandments. For Protestants following the Westminster Confession (1646), the "means of grace" consist of "preaching of the word and the administration of the sacraments of baptism and the Lord's Supper."
4. "For they are a nation void of counsel, neither is there any understanding in them" (Deuteronomy 32.28).
5. "For their vine is of the vine of Sodom, and the fields of Gomorrah: their grapes are grapes of gall, their clusters are bitter: Their wine is the poison of dragons, and the cruel venom of asps" (Deuteronomy 32.32–33). Sodom and Gomorrah were wicked cities destroyed by a rain of fire and sulfur from heaven (Genesis 19.24).

sliding. The same is expressed, Psalm 73.18: "Surely thou didst set them in slippery places; thou castedst them down into destruction."

2. It implies that they were always exposed to sudden unexpected destruction. As he that walks in slippery places is every moment liable to fall, he cannot foresee one moment whether he shall stand or fall the next; and when he does fall, he falls at once without warning: which is also expressed in Psalm 73.18–19: "Surely thou didst set them in slippery places; thou castedst them down into destruction: How are they brought into desolation as in a moment!"

3. Another thing implied is, that they are liable to fall of themselves, without being thrown down by the hand of another; as he that stands or walks on slippery ground needs nothing but his own weight to throw him down.

4. That the reason why they are not fallen already, and do not fall now, is only that God's appointed time is not come. For it is said that when that due time, or appointed times comes, their foot shall slide. Then they shall be left to fall, as they are inclined by their own weight. God will not hold them up in these slippery places any longer, but will let them go; and then, at that very instant, they shall fall into destruction; as he that stands on such slippery declining ground, on the edge of a pit, he cannot stand alone, when he is let go he immediately falls and is lost.

The observation from the words that I would now insist upon is this. "There is nothing that keeps wicked men at any one moment out of hell, but the mere pleasure of God." By the mere pleasure of God, I mean His sovereign pleasure, His arbitrary will, restrained by no obligation, hindered by no manner of difficulty, any more than if nothing else but God's mere will had in the least degree, or in any respect whatsoever, any hand in the preservation of wicked men one moment. The truth of this observation may appear by the following considerations.

1. There is no want of power in God to cast wicked men into hell at any moment. Men's hands cannot be strong when God rises up. The strongest have no power to resist Him, not can any deliver[6] out of His hands. He is not only able to cast wicked men into hell, but He can most easily do it. Sometimes an earthly prince meets with a great deal of difficulty to subdue a rebel, who has found means to fortify himself, and has made himself strong by the numbers of his followers. But it is not so with God. There is no fortress that is any defense from the power of God. Though hand join in hand, and vast multitudes of God's enemies combine and associate themselves, they are easily broken in pieces. They are as great heaps of light chaff before the whirlwind; or large quantities of dry stubble before devouring flames. We find it easy to tread on and crush a worm that we see crawling on the earth; so it is easy for us to cut or singe a slender thread that any thing hangs by: thus easy is it for God, when he pleases, to cast His enemies down to hell. What are we, that we should think to stand before Him, at whose rebuke the earth trembles, and before whom the rocks are thrown down?

2. They deserve to be cast into hell; so that divine justice never stands in the way, it makes no objection against God's using His power at any moment to destroy them. Yea, on the contrary, justice calls aloud for an infinite punishment of their sins. Divine justice says of the tree that brings forth such

---

6. I.e., rescue others.

grapes of Sodom, "Cut it down, why cumbereth it the ground?" Luke 13.7. The sword of divine justice is every moment brandished over their heads, and it is nothing but the hand of arbitrary mercy, and God's will, that holds it back.

3. They are already under a sentence of condemnation to hell. They do not only justly deserve to be cast down thither, but the sentence of the law of God, that eternal and immutable rule of righteousness that God has fixed between Him and mankind, is gone out against them, and stands against them; so that they are bound over already to hell. John 3.18: "He that believeth not is condemned already." So that every unconverted man properly belongs to hell; that is his place; from thence he is, John 8.23: "Ye are from beneath." And thither he is bound; it is the place that justice, and God's word, and the sentence of his unchangeable law assign to him.

4. They are now the objects of that very same anger and wrath of God that is expressed in the torments of hell. And the reason why they do not go down to hell at each moment is not because God, in whose power they are, is not then very angry with them as He is with many miserable creatures now tormented in hell, who there feel and bear the fierceness of His wrath. Yea, God is a great deal more angry with great numbers that are now on earth: yea, doubtless, with many that are now in this congregation, who it may be are at ease, than He is with many of those who are now in the flames of hell.

So that it is not because God is unmindful of their wickedness, and does not resent it, that He does not let loose His hand and cut them off. God is not altogether such an one as themselves, though they may imagine Him to be so. The wrath of God burns against them, their damnation does not slumber; the pit is prepared, the fire is made ready, the furnace is now hot, ready to receive them; the flames do now rage and glow. The glittering sword is whet,[7] and held over them, and the pit hath opened its mouth under them.

5. The devil stands ready to fall upon them, and seize them as his own, at what moment God shall permit him. They belong to him; he has their souls in his possession, and under his dominion. The Scripture represents them as his goods, Luke 11.12.[8] The devils watch them; they are ever by them at their right hand; they stand waiting for them, like greedy hungry lions that see their prey, and expect to have it, but are for the present kept back. If God should withdraw His hand, by which they are restrained, they would in one moment fly upon their poor souls. The old serpent is gaping for them; hell opens its mouth wide to receive them; and if God should permit it, they would be hastily swallowed up and lost.

6. There are in the souls of wicked men those hellish principles reigning that would presently kindle and flame out into hell fire, if it were not for God's restraints. There is laid in the very nature of carnal men a foundation for the torments of hell. There are those corrupt principles, in reigning power in them, and in full possession of them, that are seeds of hell fire. These principles are active and powerful, exceeding violent in their nature, and if it were not for the restraining hand of God upon them, they would soon break out, they would flame out after the same manner as the same corruptions, the same enmity does in the hearts of damned souls, and would beget the same torments as they do in them. The souls of the wicked are in Scripture

7. Sharpened.
8. "Or if he shall ask an egg, will he offer him a scorpion?"

compared to the troubled sea, Isaiah 57.20.[9] For the present, God restrains their wickedness by His mighty power, as He does the raging waves of the troubled sea, saying, "Hitherto shalt thou come, but no further;"[1] but if God should withdraw that restraining power, it would soon carry all before it. Sin is the ruin and misery of the soul; it is destructive in its nature; and if God should leave it without restraint, there would need nothing else to make the soul perfectly miserable. The corruption of the heart of man is immoderate and boundless in its fury; and while wicked men live here, it is like fire pent up by God's restraints, whereas if it were let loose, it would set on fire the course of nature; and as the heart is now a sink of sin, so if sin was not restrained, it would immediately turn the soul into a fiery oven, or a furnace of fire and brimstone.

7. It is no security to wicked men for one moment that there are no visible means of death at hand. It is no security to a natural[2] man that he is now in health and that he does not see which way he should now immediately go out of the world by any accident, and that there is no visible danger in any respect in his circumstances. The manifold and continual experience of the world in all ages, shows this is no evidence that a man is not on the very brink of eternity, and that the next step will not be into another world. The unseen, unthought-of ways and means of persons going suddenly out of the world are innumerable and inconceivable. Unconverted men walk over the pit of hell on a rotten covering, and there are innumerable places in this covering so weak that they will not bear their weight, and these places are not seen. The arrows of death fly unseen at noonday;[3] the sharpest sight cannot discern them. God has so many different unsearchable ways of taking wicked men out of the world and sending them to hell, that there is nothing to make it appear that God had need to be at the expense of a miracle, or go out of the ordinary course of His providence, to destroy any wicked man at any moment. All the means that there are of sinners going out of the world are so in God's hands, and so universally and absolutely subject to His power and determination, that it does not depend at all the less on the mere will of God whether sinners shall at any moment go to hell than if means were never made use of or at all concerned in the case.

8. Natural men's prudence and care to preserve their own lives, or the care of others to preserve them, do not secure them a moment. To this, divine providence and universal experience do also bear testimony. There is this clear evidence that men's own wisdom is no security to them from death; that if it were otherwise we should see some difference between the wise and politic men of the world, and others, with regard to their liableness to early and unexpected death: but how is it in fact? Ecclesiastes 2.16: "How dieth the wise man? even as the fool."

9. All wicked men's pains and contrivance which they use to escape hell, while they continue to reject Christ, and so remain wicked men, do not secure them from hell one moment. Almost every natural man that hears of hell, flatters himself that he shall escape it; he depends upon himself for his own security; he flatters himself in what he has done, in what he is now

---

9. "But the wicked are like the troubled sea, when it cannot rest, whose waters cast up mire and dirt."
1. Job 38.11.

2. I.e., unregenerate, unsaved.
3. "Thou shalt not be afraid for the terror by night; nor for the arrow that flieth by day" (Psalm 91.5).

doing, or what he intends to do. Every one lays out matters in his own mind how he shall avoid damnation, and flatters himself that he contrives well for himself, and that his schemes will not fail. They hear indeed that there are but few saved, and that the greater part of men that have died heretofore are gone to hell; but each one imagines that he lays out matters better for his own escape than others have done. He does not intend to come to that place of torment; he says within himself that he intends to take effectual care, and to order matters so for himself as not to fail.

But the foolish children of men miserably delude themselves in their own schemes, and in confidence in their own strength and wisdom; they trust to nothing but a shadow. The greater part of those who heretofore have lived under the same means of grace, and are now dead, are undoubtedly gone to hell; and it was not because they were not as wise as those who are now alive: it was not because they did not lay out matters as well for themselves to secure their own escape. If we could speak with them, and inquire of them, one by one, whether they expected when alive, and when they used to hear about hell, ever to be the subjects of that misery, we doubtless, should hear one and another reply, "No, I never intended to come here: I had laid out matters otherwise in my mind; I thought I should contrive well for myself: I thought my scheme good. I intended to take effectual care; but it came upon me unexpected; I did not look for it at that time, and in that manner; it came as a thief: Death outwitted me: God's wrath was too quick for me. Oh, my cursed foolishness! I was flattering myself, and pleasing myself with vain dreams of what I would do hereafter; and when I was saying, peace and safety, then suddenly destruction came upon me."

10. God has laid Himself under no obligation by any promise to keep any natural man out of hell one moment. God certainly has made no promises either of eternal life or of any deliverance or preservation from eternal death but what are contained in the covenant of grace,[4] the promises that are given in Christ, in whom all the promises are yea and amen. But surely they have no interest in the promises of the covenant of grace who are not the children of the covenant, who do not believe in any of the promises, and have no interest in the Mediator of the covenant.[5]

So that, whatever some have imagined and pretended[6] about promises made to natural men's earnest seeking and knocking, it is plain and manifest that whatever pains a natural man takes in religion, whatever prayers he makes, till he believes in Christ, God is under no manner of obligation to keep him a moment from eternal destruction.

So that, thus it is that natural men are held in the hand of God, over the pit of hell; they have deserved the fiery pit, and are already sentenced to it; and God is dreadfully provoked. His anger is as great towards them as to those that are actually suffering the executions of the fierceness of His wrath in hell, and they have done nothing in the least to appease or abate that anger, neither is God in the least bound by any promise to hold them up one moment; the devil is waiting for them, hell is gaping for them, the flames gather and flash about them, and would fain lay hold on them, and swallow them up; the fire pent up in their own hearts is struggling to break out: and

---

4. The original covenant God made with Adam is called the Covenant of Works; the second covenant Christ made with fallen humanity—declaring that if they believed in him they would be saved—is called the Covenant of Grace.
5. I.e., Christ, who took upon himself the sins of the world and suffered for them.
6. Claimed.

they have no interest in any Mediator, there are no means within reach that can be any security to them. In short, they have no refuge, nothing to take hold of; all that preserves them every moment is the mere arbitrary will, and uncovenanted, unobliged forbearance of an incensed God.

Application

The use of this awful[7] subject may be for awakening unconverted persons in this congregation. This that you have heard is the case of every one of you that are out of Christ. That world of misery, that lake of burning brimstone, is extended abroad under you. There is the dreadful pit of the glowing flames of the wrath of God; there is hell's wide gaping mouth open; and you have nothing to stand upon, nor any thing to take hold of; there is nothing between you and hell but the air; it is only the power and mere pleasure of God that holds you up.

You probably are not sensible[8] of this; you find you are kept out of hell, but do not see the hand of God in it; but look at other things, as the good state of your bodily constitution, your care of your own life, and the means you use for your own preservation. But indeed these things are nothing; if God should withdraw His hand, they would avail no more to keep you from falling, than the thin air to hold up a person that is suspended in it.

Your wickedness makes you as it were heavy as lead, and to tend downwards with great weight and pressure towards hell; and if God should let you go, you would immediately sink and swiftly descend and plunge into the bottomless gulf, and your healthy constitution, and your own care and prudence, and best contrivance, and all your righteousness, would have no more influence to uphold you and keep you out of hell, than a spider's web would have to stop a fallen rock. Were it not for the sovereign pleasure of God, the earth would not bear you one moment; for you are a burden to it; the creation groans with you; the creature is made subject to the bondage of your corruption, not willingly; the sun does not willingly shine upon you to give you light to serve sin and Satan; the earth does not willingly yield her increase to satisfy your lusts; nor is it willingly a stage for your wickedness to be acted upon; the air does not willingly serve you for breath to maintain the flame of life in your vitals, while you spend your life in the service of God's enemies. God's creatures are good, and were made for men to serve God with, and do not willingly subserve to any other purpose, and groan when they are abused to purposes so directly contrary to their nature and end. And the world would spew you out, were it not for the sovereign hand of Him who hath subjected it in hope. There are black clouds of God's wrath now hanging directly over your heads, full of the dreadful storm, and big with thunder; and were it not for the restraining hand of God, it would immediately burst forth upon you. The sovereign pleasure of God, for the present, stays His rough wind; otherwise it would come with fury, and your destruction would come like a whirlwind, and you would be like the chaff of the summer threshing floor.

The wrath of God is like great waters that are dammed for the present; they increase more and more, and rise higher and higher, till an outlet is given; and the longer the stream is stopped, the more rapid and mighty is its course when once it is let loose. It is true that judgment against your evil

---

works has not been executed hitherto; the floods of God's vengeance have been withheld; but your guilt in the meantime is constantly increasing, and you are every day treasuring up more wrath; the waters are constantly rising, and waxing more and more mighty; and there is nothing but the mere pleasure of God that holds the waters back, that are unwilling to be stopped, and press hard to go forward. If God should only withdraw His hand from the floodgate, it would immediately fly open, and the fiery floods of the fierceness and wrath of God, would rush forth with inconceivable fury, and would come upon you with omnipotent power; and if your strength were ten thousand times greater than it is, yea, ten thousand times greater than the strength of the stoutest, sturdiest devil in hell, it would be nothing to withstand or endure it.

The bow of God's wrath is bent, and the arrow made ready on the string, and justice bends the arrow at your heart, and strains the bow, and it is nothing but the mere pleasure of God, and that of an angry God, without any promise or obligation at all, that keeps the arrow one moment from being made drunk with your blood. Thus all you that never passed under a great change of heart, by the mighty power of the Spirit of God upon your souls, all you that were never born again, and made new creatures, and raised from being dead in sin, to a state of new, and before altogether unexperienced light and life, are in the hands of an angry God. However you may have reformed your life in many things, and may have had religious affections, and may keep up a form of religion in your families and closets,[9] and in the house of God, it is nothing but His mere pleasure that keeps you from being this moment swallowed up in everlasting destruction. However unconvinced you may now be of the truth of what you hear, by and by you will be fully convinced of it. Those that are gone from being in the like circumstances with you see that it was so with them; for destruction came suddenly upon most of them; when they expected nothing of it and while they were saying, peace and safety: now they see that those things on which they depended for peace and safety, were nothing but thin air and empty shadows.

The God that holds you over the pit of hell, much as one holds a spider or some loathsome insect over the fire, abhors you, and is dreadfully provoked: His wrath towards you burns like fire; He looks upon you as worthy of nothing else but to be cast into the fire; He is of purer eyes than to bear to have you in His sight; you are ten thousand times more abominable in His eyes than the most hateful venomous serpent is in ours. You have offended Him infinitely more than ever a stubborn rebel did his prince; and yet it is nothing but His hand that holds you from falling into the fire every moment. It is to be ascribed to nothing else, that you did not go to hell the last night; that you was suffered to awake again in this world, after you closed your eyes to sleep. And there is no other reason to be given, why you have not dropped into hell since you arose in the morning, but that God's hand has held you up. There is no other reason to be given why you have not gone to hell, since you have sat here in the house of God, provoking His pure eyes by your sinful wicked manner of attending His solemn worship. Yea, there is nothing else that is to be given as a reason why you do not this very moment drop down into hell.

O sinner! Consider the fearful danger you are in: it is a great furnace of wrath, a wide and bottomless pit, full of the fire of wrath, that you are held

9. Studies; rooms for meditation. "Affections": feelings.

over in the hand of that God, whose wrath is provoked and incensed as much against you, as against many of the damned in hell. You hang by a slender thread, with the flames of divine wrath flashing about it, and ready every moment to singe it, and burn it asunder; and you have no interest in any Mediator, and nothing to lay hold of to save yourself, nothing to keep off the flames of wrath, nothing of your own, nothing that you ever have done, nothing that you can do, to induce God to spare you one moment. And consider here more particularly.

1. Whose wrath it is: it is the wrath of the infinite God. If it were only the wrath of man, though it were of the most potent prince, it would be comparatively little to be regarded. The wrath of kings is very much dreaded, especially of absolute monarchs, who have the possessions and lives of their subjects wholly in their power, to be disposed of at their mere will. Proverbs 20.2: "The fear of a king is as the roaring of a lion: Whoso provoketh him to anger, sinneth against his own soul." The subject that very much enrages an arbitrary prince is liable to suffer the most extreme torments that human art can invent, or human power can inflict. But the greatest earthly potentates in their greatest majesty, and strength, and when clothed in their greatest terrors, are but feeble, despicable worms of the dust, in comparison of the great and almighty Creator and King of heaven and earth. It is but little that they can do, when most enraged, and when they have exerted the utmost of their fury. All the kings of the earth, before God, are as grasshoppers; they are nothing, and less than nothing: both their love and their hatred is to be despised. The wrath of the great King of kings, is as much more terrible than theirs, as His majesty is greater. Luke 12.4–5: "And I say unto you, my friends, Be not afraid of them that kill the body, and after that, have no more that they can do. But I will forewarn you whom you shall fear: fear him, which after he hath killed, hath power to cast into hell: yea, I say unto you, Fear him."

2. It is the fierceness of His wrath that you are exposed to. We often read of the fury of God; as in Isaiah 59.18: "According to their deeds, accordingly he will repay fury to his adversaries." So Isaiah 66.15: "For behold, the Lord will come with fire, and with his chariots like a whirlwind, to render his anger with fury, and his rebuke with flames of fire." And in many other places. So, Revelation 19.15: we read of "the wine press of the fierceness and wrath of Almighty God."[1] The words are exceeding terrible. If it had only been said, "the wrath of God," the words would have implied that which is infinitely dreadful: but it is "the fierceness and wrath of God." The fury of God! the fierceness of Jehovah![2] Oh, how dreadful must that be! Who can utter or conceive what such expressions carry in them! But it is also "the fierceness and wrath of Almighty God." As though there would be a very great manifestation of His almighty power in what the fierceness of His wrath should inflict, as though omnipotence should be as it were enraged, and exerted, as men are wont to exert their strength in the fierceness of their wrath. Oh! then, what will be the consequence! What will become of the poor worms that shall suffer it! Whose hands can be strong? And whose heart can endure? To what a dreadful, inexpressible, inconceivable depth of misery must the poor creature be sunk who shall be the subject of this!

1. "He treadeth the winepress of the fierceness and wrath of Almighty God."

2. The name used for God in the Old Testament.

Consider this, you that are here present that yet remain in an unregenerate state. That God will execute the fierceness of His anger implies that He will inflict wrath without any pity. When God beholds the ineffable extremity of your case, and sees your torment to be so vastly disproportioned to your strength, and sees how your poor soul is crushed, and sinks down, as it were, into an infinite gloom; He will have no compassion upon you, He will not forbear the executions of His wrath, or in the least lighten His hand; there shall be no moderation or mercy, nor will God then at all stay His rough wind; He will have no regard to your welfare, nor be at all careful lest you should suffer too much in any other sense, than only that you shall not suffer beyond what strict justice requires. Nothing shall be withheld because it is so hard for you to bear. Ezekiel 8.18: "Therefore will I also deal in fury: mine eye shall not spare, neither will I have pity; and though they cry in mine ears with a loud voice, yet I will not hear them." Now God stands ready to pity you; this is a day of mercy; you may cry now with some encouragement of obtaining mercy. But when once the day of mercy is past, your most lamentable and dolorous cries and shrieks will be in vain; you will be wholly lost and thrown away of God as to any regard to your welfare. God will have no other use to put you to, but to suffer misery; you shall be continued in being to no other end; for you will be a vessel of wrath fitted to destruction; and there will be no other use of this vessel, but to be filled full of wrath. God will be so far from pitying you when you cry to Him, that it is said He will only "laugh and mock." Proverbs 1.25–26, etc.[3]

How awful are those words, Isaiah 63.3, which are the words of the great God: "I will tread them in mine anger, and will trample them in my fury, and their blood shall be sprinkled upon my garments, and I will stain all my raiment." It is perhaps impossible to conceive of words that carry in them greater manifestations of these three things, viz., contempt, and hatred, and fierceness of indignation. If you cry to God to pity you, He will be so far from pitying you in your doleful case, or showing you the least regard or favor, that instead of that, He will only tread you under foot. And though He will know that you cannot bear the weight of omnipotence treading upon you, yet He will not regard that, but He will crush you under His feet without mercy; He will crush out your blood, and make it fly and it shall be sprinkled on His garments, so as to stain all His raiment. He will not only hate you, but He will have you in the utmost contempt: no place shall be thought fit for you, but under His feet to be trodden down as the mire of the streets.

3. The misery you are exposed to is that which God will inflict to that end, that He might show what that wrath of Jehovah is. God hath had it on His heart to show to angels and men both how excellent His love is, and also how terrible His wrath is. Sometimes earthly kings have a mind to show how terrible their wrath is, by the extreme punishments they would execute on those that would provoke them. Nebuchadnezzar, that mighty and haughty monarch of the Chaldean empire, was willing to show his wrath when enraged with Shadrach, Meshech, and Abednego; and accordingly gave orders that the burning fiery furnace should be heated seven times hotter than it was before; doubtless, it was raised to the utmost degree of fierceness

3. "But ye have set at nought all my counsel, and would none of my reproof: I also will laugh at your calamity; I will mock you when your fear cometh."

that human art could raise it.[4] But the great God is also willing to show His wrath, and magnify His awful majesty and mighty power in the extreme sufferings of His enemies. Romans 9.22: "What if God, willing to show his wrath, and to make his power known, endure with much long-suffering the vessels of wrath fitted to destruction?" And seeing this is His design, and what He has determined, even to show how terrible the restrained wrath, the fury and fierceness of Jehovah is, He will do it to effect. There will be something accomplished and brought to pass that will be dreadful with a witness. When the great and angry God hath risen up and executed His awful vengeance on the poor sinner, and the wretch is actually suffering the infinite weight and power of His indignation, then will God call upon the whole universe to behold that awful majesty and mighty power that is to be seen in it. Isaiah 33.12–14: "And the people shall be as the burnings of lime, as thorns cut up shall they be burnt in the fire. Hear ye that are far off, what I have done; and ye that are near, acknowledge my might. The sinners in Zion are afraid; fearfulness hath surprised the hypocrites," etc.

Thus it will be with you that are in an unconverted state, if you continue in it; the infinite might, and majesty, and terribleness of the omnipotent God shall be magnified upon you, in the ineffable strength of your torments. You shall be tormented in the presence of the holy angels, and in the presence of the Lamb; and when you shall be in this state of suffering, the glorious inhabitants of heaven shall go forth and look on the awful spectacle, that they may see what the wrath and fierceness of the Almighty is; and when they have seen it, they will fall down and adore that great power and majesty. Isaiah 66.23–24: "And it shall come to pass, that from one new moon to another, and from one sabbath to another, shall all flesh come to worship before me, saith the Lord. And they shall go forth and look upon the carcasses of the men that have transgressed against me; for their worm shall not die, neither shall their fire be quenched, and they shall be an abhorring unto all flesh."

4. It is everlasting wrath. It would be dreadful to suffer this fierceness and wrath of Almighty God one moment; but you must suffer it to all eternity. There will be no end to this exquisite horrible misery. When you look forward, you shall see a long forever, a boundless duration before you, which will swallow up your thoughts, and amaze your soul; and you will absolutely despair of ever having any deliverance, any end, any mitigation, any rest at all. You will know certainly that you must wear out long ages, millions of millions of ages, in wrestling and conflicting with this almighty merciless vengeance; and then when you have so done, when so many ages have actually been spent by you in this manner, you will know that all is but a point to what remains. So that your punishment will indeed be infinite. Oh, who can express what the state of a soul in such circumstances is! All that we can possibly say about it gives but a very feeble, faint representation of it; it is inexpressible and inconceivable: For "who knows the power of God's anger?"[5]

How dreadful is the state of those that are daily and hourly in the danger of this great wrath and infinite misery! But this is the dismal case of every soul in this congregation that has not been born again, however moral and strict, sober and religious, they may otherwise be. Oh that you would consider it,

---

4. See Daniel 3.1–30.
5. "Who knoweth the power of thine anger? even

according to thy fear, so is thy wrath" (Psalm 90.11).

whether you be young or old! There is reason to think that there are many in this congregation now hearing this discourse that will actually be the subjects of this very misery to all eternity. We know not who they are, or in what seats they sit, or what thoughts they now have. It may be they are now at ease, and hear all these things without much disturbance, and are now flattering themselves that they are not the persons, promising themselves that they shall escape. If they knew that there was one person, and but one, in the whole congregation, that was to be the subject of this misery, what an awful thing would it be to think of! If we knew who it was, what an awful sight would it be to see such a person! How might all the rest of the congregation lift up a lamentable and bitter cry over him! But, alas! instead of one, how many is it likely will remember this discourse in hell? And it would be a wonder, if some that are now present should not be in hell in a very short time, even before this year is out. And it would be no wonder if some persons, that now sit here, in some seats of this meetinghouse, in health, quiet and secure, should be there before tomorrow morning. Those of you that finally continue in a natural condition, that shall keep out of hell longest will be there in a little time! your damnation does not slumber; it will come swiftly, and, in all probability, very suddenly upon many of you. You have reason to wonder that you are not already in hell. It is doubtless the case of some whom you have seen and known, that never deserved hell more than you, and that heretofore appeared as likely to have been now alive as you. Their case is past all hope; they are crying in extreme misery and perfect despair; but here you are in the land of the living and in the house of God, and have an opportunity to obtain salvation. What would not those poor damned hopeless souls give for one day's opportunity such as you now enjoy!

And now you have an extraordinary opportunity, a day wherein Christ has thrown the door of mercy wide open, and stands in calling and crying with a loud voice to poor sinners; a day wherein many are flocking to Him, and pressing into the kingdom of God. Many are daily coming from the east, west, north and south; many that were very lately in the same miserable condition that you are in are now in a happy state, with their hearts filled with love to Him who has loved them, and washed them from their sins in His own blood, and rejoicing in hope of the glory of God. How awful is it to be left behind at such a day! To see so many others feasting, while you are pining and perishing! To see so many rejoicing and singing for joy of heart, while you have cause to mourn for sorrow of heart, and howl for vexation of spirit! How can you rest one moment in such a condition? Are not your souls as precious as the souls of the people at Suffield,[6] where they are flocking from day to day to Christ?

Are there not many here who have lived long in the world, and are not to this day born again? and so are aliens from the commonwealth of Israel,[7] and have done nothing ever since they have lived, but treasure up wrath against the day of wrath? Oh, sirs, your case, in an especial manner, is extremely dangerous. Your guilt and hardness of heart is extremely great. Do you not see how generally persons of your years are passed over and left, in the present remarkable and wonderful dispensation of God's mercy? You had need to consider yourselves, and awake thoroughly out of sleep. You cannot bear the

6. A town in the neighborhood [Edwards's note].   7. I.e., not among the chosen people, the saved.

fierceness and wrath of the infinite God. And you, young men, and young women, will you neglect this precious season which you now enjoy, when so many others of your age are renouncing all youthful vanities, and flocking to Christ? You especially have now an extraordinary opportunity; but if you neglect it, it will soon be with you as with those persons who spent all the precious days of youth in sin, and are now come to such a dreadful pass in blindness and hardness. And you, children, who are unconverted, do not you know that you are going down to hell, to bear the dreadful wrath of that God, who is now angry with you every day and every night? Will you be content to be the children of the devil, when so many other children in the land are converted, and are become the holy and happy children of the King of kings?

And let every one that is yet of Christ, and hanging over the pit of hell, whether they be old men and women, or middle-aged, or young people, or little children, now hearken to the loud calls of God's word and providence. This acceptable year of the Lord, a day of such great favors to some, will doubtless be a day of as remarkable vengeance to others. Men's hearts harden, and their guilt increases apace at such a day as this, if they neglect their souls; and never was there so great danger of such person being given up to hardness of heart and blindness of mind. God seems now to be hastily gathering in His elect in all parts of the land; and probably the greater part of adult persons that ever shall be saved, will be brought in now in a little time, and that it will be as it was on the great outpouring of the Spirit upon the Jews in the apostles' days;[8] the election will obtain, and the rest will be blinded. If this should be the case with you, you will eternally curse this day, and will curse the day that ever you was born, to see such a season of the pouring out of God's Spirit, and will wish that you had died and gone to hell before you had seen it. Now undoubtedly it is, as it was in the days of John the Baptist, the ax is in an extraordinary manner laid at the root of the trees,[9] that every tree which brings not forth good fruit, may be hewn down and cast into the fire.

Therefore, let everyone that is out of Christ, now awake and fly from the wrath to come. The wrath of Almighty God is now undoubtedly hanging over a great part of this congregation: Let everyone fly out of Sodom: "Haste and escape for your lives, look not behind you, escape to the mountain, lest you be consumed."[1]

1741

---

8. In Acts 2 the apostle Peter admonishes a crowd to repent and be converted, saying, "Save yourselves from this untoward generation. Then they that gladly received his word were baptized: and the same day there were added unto them about three thousand souls" (Acts 2.40–41).

9. "And now also the ax is laid unto the root of the trees: therefore every tree which bringeth not forth good fruit is hewn down, and cast into the fire" (Matthew 3.10).
1. Genesis 19.17.

Native Americans:
Contact and Conflict

Well before the *Mayflower* Pilgrims sailed into Cape Cod Bay in 1620, Captain John Smith had published the story of a Pamunkey Indian woman from the Virginia tidewater called Pocahontas who, in 1607, had intervened to save him from death at the hands of her people. Pocahontas was not actually the young woman's name, for that word meant something like "playful girl" (it remains a matter of debate whether "playful" did or did not imply "wanton"), so there may have been many "pocahontases." This particular pocahontas was named Mataoka, and she was the eleven- or twelve-year-old daughter of Powhatan (also known as Wahunsunacock), an important Native American leader. Smith's salvation, in fact, was purely ceremonial, an act intended to bring him and his powerful English companions into reciprocal relations with the Chesapeake Bay Natives. The English did not understand this, however, and soon their relentless demand for Indian land and Indian submission to English law led to Indian resistance. In 1622, Pocahontas's people rose up against the English settlement in Jamestown, killing some five hundred of the colonists before the attack was put down.

This pattern of friendly contact between Europeans and Indians followed by bloody conflict would recur again and again until almost the turn of the twentieth century. Thus it was that in New England, later in the seventeenth century, initial cordial encounters between the Native population and the English invader-settlers turned hostile, leading to the Pequot War, which, at its conclusion in 1637, saw the near-extermination of the Pequots—a fate that also befell the Wampanoags under "King Philip" (his actual name was Metacom), in 1676, at the end of the so-called King Philip's War.

From the earliest period of contact the newcomers were impressed by Indian oratory. Yet, although we know many deeds of the seventeenth-century Indians, we know almost nothing of what they said. It was only in the eighteenth century that the first transcriptions and translations of Indian oratory began to appear; all but one of the selections reprinted here are records of this later period of Native American oratorical eloquence. Despite their differences, the oratorical documents all reflect the familiar pattern of friendly contact followed by bitter conflict. The selection from the autobiography of the Reverend Samson Occom, a Mohegan, is one of the first surviving texts written by a North American Indian, one who had sincerely accepted Christianity for all that he, too, records mistreatment by the whites.

The orators, as we have noted, speak on behalf of resistance, whether religious or military. Pontiac, citing a charismatic Delaware prophet, attempts to persuade Huron and Pottawatomi leaders to join his Ottawa people in armed resistance to the British, as Tecumseh would later seek to forge an Indian alliance against the expansionist Americans. Logan, as cited by Thomas Jefferson, explains the reasons for his violent resistance to the colonists his people had earlier welcomed. Although Red Jacket also worked to protect the lands of his Seneca people, his response to the Reverend Jacob Cram documents his people's insistence that their religion is as good for them as Christianity is for the Americans. Samson Occom's brief autobiography, while testifying to an enthusiastic acceptance of Christianity, also conveys a sense of the prejudice to which even Christian and "civilized" Indians might yet be subjected.

We have Occom's text as he wrote it. But the texts we have of Native American oratory were produced by hands other than those of the orators themselves, and vary widely in terms of their authenticity and accuracy. Some "famous" speeches are now known to be largely or entirely invented, while others almost surely represent the words actually spoken by an Indian person. Somewhere between these extremes are speeches that might be called "bicultural composites," speeches probably based in large measure on what an Indian person actually said, but whose final English text owes much to translators, transcribers, editors, and publishers. We do not print here (or anywhere in these volumes) any speech known to be a fabrication, and we attempt to indicate the status of the speeches we do include.

PONTIAC

Pontiac (1720?–1769) was an Ottawa Indian, born around 1720, between Lake Erie and Lake Huron, near present-day Detroit. *Ottawa* derives from the Algonquian *atawewin*, meaning "commerce" or "to trade," and in the eighteenth century the Ottawas had strong trading and diplomatic alliances with the French. But in 1760 the British defeated the French at Fort Detroit, and in 1762, Sir Jeffrey Amherst, commander-in-chief of British forces in North America, turned command of Detroit over to Henry Gladwin, a man who shared Amherst's contempt for Indians. Gladwin continued his predecessor's policies of refusing to supply food, arms, and, critically, gunpowder to the Indians as the French had done, and he also discarded the French policy of treating Indians as allies in favor of a policy of treating them as subjects of the British Crown.

The Delaware Indians (the name *Delaware* does not derive from a Native language; rather, it refers to Lord De La Warr, a British governor of Virginia) had long suffered at the hands of the British, who had defrauded them of most of their lands. By the 1760s, this Algonquian-speaking people had had extensive contact with tribes farther west. In 1760 or 1761, a young Delaware named Neolin (meaning "four" and referring to the sacred four directions) had a vision that—much as Wovoka's vision would do more than a hundred years later—led him to preach the necessity of largely abandoning the things and manners of the Europeans. Pontiac does not seem actually to have encountered the Delaware prophet, but he knew Neolin's message, which led him to organize what non-Indians called a "conspiracy" against the British. To persuade other tribes to join the Ottawas in resistance to the British, Pontiac is said to have given the speech printed here to an assembly of Ottawa, Huron, and Pottawatomi leaders on April 27, 1763. But neither the accuracy of the date nor the authenticity of the speech can be documented with any certainty.

All reprintings of Pontiac's speech derive from Francis Parkman's *The Conspiracy of Pontiac* (1851). Parkman gives as his source for the speech the "*Pontiac,* MS." taken from the "*M'Dougal,* MSS." This would seem to point to Lieutenant John McDougall, who was intimately involved with the history of this period—indeed, he was taken prisoner by the Indians and managed to escape. But no manuscript by him has been found. Did McDougall hear Pontiac speak? If so, who would have translated and transcribed Pontiac's words? The historical record is silent. We publish Pontiac's speech on the assumption—a guess, to be sure—that there is a strong likelihood that he spoke words to this effect on the basis of his knowledge of the Delaware prophet.

Speech at Detroit

* * *

"A Delaware Indian," said Pontiac, "conceived an eager desire to learn wisdom from the Master of Life; but, being ignorant where to find him, he had recourse to fasting, dreaming, and magical incantations. By these means it was revealed to him, that, by moving forward in a straight, undeviating course, he would reach the abode of the Great Spirit. He told his purpose to no one; and having provided the equipments of a hunter,—gun, powder-horn, ammunition, and a kettle for preparing his food,—he set out on his errand. For some time he journeyed on in high hope and confidence. On the evening of the eighth day, he stopped by the side of a brook at the edge of a meadow, where he began to make ready his evening meal, when, looking up, he saw three large openings in the woods before him, and three well-beaten paths which entered them. He was much surprised; but his wonder increased, when, after it had grown dark, the three paths were more clearly visible than ever. Remembering the important object of his journey, he could neither rest nor sleep; and, leaving his fire, he crossed the meadow, and entered the largest of the three openings. He had advanced but a short distance into the forest, when a bright flame sprang out of the ground before him, and arrested his steps. In great amazement, he turned back, and entered the second path, where the same wonderful phenomenon again encountered him; and now, in terror and bewilderment, yet still resolved to persevere, he took the last of the three paths. On this he journeyed a whole day without interruption, when at length, emerging from the forest, he saw before him a vast mountain, of dazzling whiteness. So precipitous was the ascent, that the Indian thought it hopeless to go farther, and looked around him in despair: at that moment, he saw, seated at some distance above, the figure of a beautiful woman arrayed in white who arose as he looked upon her, and thus accosted him: 'How can you hope, encumbered as you are, to succeed in your design? Go down to the foot of the mountain, throw away your gun, your ammunition, your provisions, and your clothing; wash yourself in the stream which flows there, and you will then be prepared to stand before the Master of Life.' The Indian obeyed, and again began to ascend among the rocks, while the woman, seeing him still discouraged, laughed at his faintness of heart, and told him that, if he wished for success, he must climb by the aid of one hand and one foot only. After great toil and suffering, he at length found himself at the summit. The woman had disappeared, and he was left alone. A rich and beautiful plain lay before him, and at a little distance he saw three great villages, far superior to the squalid wigwams of the Delawares. As he approached the largest, and stood hesitating whether he should enter, a man gorgeously attired stepped forth, and, taking him by the hand, welcomed him to the celestial abode. He then conducted him into the presence of the Great Spirit, where the Indian stood confounded at the unspeakable splendor which surrounded him. The Great Spirit bade him be seated, and thus addressed him:—

"'I am the Maker of heaven and earth, the trees, lakes, rivers, and all things else. I am the Maker of mankind; and because I love you, you must do my will. The land on which you live I have made for you, and not for others. Why do you suffer the white men to dwell among you? My children, you have forgotten the customs and traditions of your forefathers. Why do you not clothe yourselves in skins, as they did, and use the bows and arrows, and the stone-pointed lances, which they used? You have bought guns, knives, kettles, and blankets, from the white men, until you can no longer do without them; and, what is worse, you have drunk the poison fire-water, which turns you into fools. Fling all these things away; live as your wise forefathers lived before you. And as for these English,—these dogs dressed in red, who have come to rob you of your hunting-grounds, and drive away the game,—you must lift the hatchet against them. Wipe them from the face of the earth, and then you will win my favor back again, and once more be happy and prosperous. The children of your great father, the King of France, are not like the English. Never forget that they are your brethren. They are very dear to me, for they love the red men, and understand the true mode of worshiping me.'"

The Great Spirit next gave his hearer various precepts of morality and religion, such as the prohibition to marry more than one wife; and a warning against the practice of magic, which is worshipping the devil. A prayer, embodying the substance of all that he had heard, was then presented to the Delaware. It was cut in hieroglyphics upon a wooden stick, after the custom of his people; and he was directed to send copies of it to all the Indian villages.

* * *

SAMSON OCCOM

B orn in New London, Connecticut, Samson Occom (1723–1792) was a Mohegan, a member of the northernmost branch of the Pequot tribe. When he was sixteen, Occom tells us, he heard some of the Christian evangelical preachers who had come among the Indians and was so moved by their words that he converted to Christianity. Some few years later, Occom was accepted as a pupil by the Reverend Eleazar Wheelock, known to be particularly interested in training young Indian men to become missionaries to their people. After his studies with Wheelock, Occom ministered to the Indians in New London, and then to the Natives of Montauk, Long Island. In his eleven years with the Montauks, Occom married, raised a family, and was finally ordained by the Presbytery of Suffolk in 1759.

In 1765, Occom went to England along with the Reverend Nathaniel Whitaker to raise funds for his former mentor's Indian Charity-School. He delivered some three hundred sermons and collected nearly twelve thousand pounds. Wheelock had promised to care for Occom's family while he was away, but when Occom returned, he found his family sickly and in extreme poverty. Then he learned that Wheelock intended to use the money he had raised to move the Indian School to Hanover, New Hampshire (where it would later become Dartmouth College). Occom angrily predicted to Wheelock that his "College has too much worked by Grandeur for the Poor Indians, they'll never have much benefit of it." He was right. Dartmouth soon ceased to minister to Native American students, and Occom and Wheelock broke off their long relationship.

In dire financial straits, alienated from Wheelock, and feeling the vulnerability of his position as an "Indian preacher" in the church, Occom wrote a ten-page autobiography by way of self-justification. Dated September 17, 1768, the manuscript reposed in the Dartmouth archives and was not published until 1982. In it, Occom provides fascinating details of the day-to-day life of a rural minister in the eighteenth century. We learn that he tends his garden, his animals, and his congregation. He preaches to the Indians and teaches their children, shrewdly innovating to help those "who were Some what Dull" to learn their letters. All the time Occom is well aware that he is an *Indian* preacher and teacher, and he speculates that some of the criticisms leveled against him may arise, as he writes, simply because "I am a poor Indian."

Occom urged neutrality for the Indians at the outbreak of the Revolutionary War, and in the years after independence, he served as minister to the Native Americans at New Stockbridge. At the time of his death he was a teacher of the Tuscarora Indians in New York State, where the Tuscarora had moved in 1720 from their original homeland in North Carolina.

Our text, an unedited transcription of Occom's autobiography that preserves the original spelling and punctuation, is from *The Elders Wrote: An Anthology of Early Prose by North America Indians, 1768–1931*, edited by Bernd Peyer (1982).

From A Short Narrative of My Life

When I was 16 years of age, we heard a Strange Rumor among the English, that there were Extraordinary Ministers Preaching from Place to Place and a Strange Concern among the White People. This was in the Spring of the Year. But we Saw nothing of these things, till Some Time in the Summer, when Some Ministers began to visit us and Preach the Word of God; and the Common People all Came frequently and exhorted us to the things of God, which it pleased the Lord, as I humbly hope, to Bless and accompany with Divine Influence to the Conviction and Saving Conversion of a Number of us; amongst whom I was one that was Imprest with the things we had heard. These Preachers did not only come to us, but we frequently went to their meetings and Churches. After I was awakened[1] & converted, I went to all the meetings, I could come at; & Continued under Trouble of Mind about 6 months; at which time I began to Learn the English Letters; got me a Primer, and used to go to my English Neighbours frequently for Assistance in Reading, but went to no School. And when I was 17 years of age, I had, as I trust, a Discovery of the way of Salvation through Jesus Christ, and was enabl'd to put my trust in him alone for Life & Salvation. From this Time the Distress and Burden of my mind was removed, and I found Serenity and Pleasure of Soul, in Serving God. By this time I just began to Read in the New Testament without Spelling,—and I had a Stronger Desire Still to Learn to read the Word of God, and at the Same Time had an uncommon Pity and Compassion to my Poor Brethren According to the Flesh. I used to wish I was capable of Instructing my poor Kindred. I used to think, if I Could once Learn to Read I would Instruct the poor Children in Reading,—and used frequently to talk with our Indians Concerning Religion. This continued till I was in my 19th year: by this Time I could Read a little in the Bible. At this Time my Poor Mother was going to Lebanon, [Connecticut,] and having had Some Knowledge of Mr. Wheelock and hearing he had a Number of English youth under his Tuition,[2] I had a great Inclination to go to him and be with him a week or a Fortnight, and Desired my Mother to Ask Mr. Wheelock whether he would take me a little while to Instruct me in Reading. Mother

---

1. I.e., spiritually awakened to a sense of sin.   2. Tutelage, instruction.

did so; and when She Came Back, She Said Mr. Wheelock wanted to See me as Soon as possible. So I went up, thinking I Should be back again in a few Days; when I got up there, he received me With kindness and Compassion and in Stead of Staying a Fortnight or 3 Weeks, I Spent 4 Years with him.— After I had been with him Some Time, he began to acquaint his Friends of my being with him, and of his Intentions of Educating me, and my Circumstances. And the good People began to give Some Assistance to Mr. Wheelock, and gave me Some old and Some New Clothes. Then he represented the Case to the Honorable Commissioners at Boston, who were Commission'd by the Honorable Society in London for Propagating the gospel among the Indians in New England and parts adjacent, and they allowed him 60 £ in old Tender, which was about 6 £ Sterling,[3] and they Continued it 2 or 3 years, I can't tell exactly.—While I was at Mr. Wheelock's, I was very weakly and my Health much impaired, and at the End of 4 Years, I over Strained my Eyes to such a Degree, I Could not persue my Studies any Longer; and out of these 4 years I Lost Just about one year;—And was obliged to quit my Studies.

As soon as I left Mr. Wheelock, I endeavored to find Some Employ among the Indians; went to Nahantuck, thinking they may want a School Master but they had one; then went to Narraganset, and they were Indifferent about a School, and went back to Mohegan, and heard a number of our Indians were going to Montauk, on Long Island, and I went with them, and the Indians there were very desirous to have me keep a School amongst them and I Consented, and went back a while to Mohegan and Some time in November I went on the Island, I think it is 17 years ago last November I agreed to keep School with them Half a Year, and left it with them to give me what they Pleased. * * *

My Method in the School was, as Soon as the Children got together, and took their proper Seats, I Prayed with them, then began to hear them. I generally began (after some of them Could Spell and Read,) With those that were yet in their Alphabets, So around, as they were properly Seated till I got through and I obliged them to Study their Books, and to help one another. When they could not make out a hard word they Brought it to me—and I usually heard them, in the Summer Season 8 Times a Day 4 in the morning, and in ye after Noon.—In the Winter Season 6 Times a Day, As soon as they could Spell, they were obliged to Spell when ever they wanted to go out. I concluded with Prayer; I generally heard my Evening Scholars 3 Times Round, And as they go out the School, every one, that Can Spell, is obliged to Spell a Word, and to go out Leisurely one after another. I Catechised 3 or 4 Times a Week according to the Assembly's Shout or Catechism, and many Times Proposed Questions of my own, and in my own Tongue. I found Difficulty with Some Children, who were Some what Dull, most of these can soon learn to Say over their Letters, they Distinguish the Sound by the Ear, but their Eyes can't Distinguish the Letters, and the way I took to cure them was by making an Alphabet on Small bits of paper, and glued them on Small Chips of Cedar after this manner A B & C. I put these on Letters in order on a Bench then point to one Letter and bid a Child to take notice of it, and then I order the Child to fetch me the Letter from the Bench if he Brings the

3. Probably worth about $1,400 in present-day American currency.

Letter, it is well, if not he must go again and again till he brings ye right Letter. When they can bring any Letters this way, then I just Jumble them together, and bid them to set them in Alphabetical order, and it is a Pleasure to them; and they soon Learn their Letters this way. * * *

LOGAN   THOMAS JEFFERSON

Although he was a person of considerable renown, the exact origins and identity of the man known as Chief Logan (1725?–1780) are not entirely clear. He was a Mingo—the term generally used for Iroquoian Natives living outside their nations' homelands—of either Oneida or Cayuga background, whose Indian name was probably Tachnedorus, but was known in English as John Logan. In 1774 agents of Virginia governor Lord Dunmore provoked a brief "war" in the interest of appropriating Native lands. A particularly brutal event of this war was the Yellow Creek massacre led by Daniel Greathouse, whose party killed and scalped nine Indians, among them, Logan's pregnant sister, who was mutilated along with her unborn child. At the end of the war, Logan was asked to attend a treaty meeting with Dunmore. He refused but apparently sent a message through General John Gibson that eventually was transformed into a speech in English. Gibson, although married to Logan's sister, had fought against the Indians in this war (and lost his wife and unborn child). He would have understood whichever Iroquoian language Logan spoke.

Thomas Jefferson (1743–1826) said he heard Logan's speech directly from Gibson and that he wrote it down in his memo book. The speech first appeared in print in the *Pennsylvania Journal* on January 20, 1775, based on a copy sent by James Madison. (How Madison got the speech has not been determined.) Jefferson's text is almost identical to the Madison version. Known as "Logan's Lament," the speech became famous, appearing, for example, in the fourth and fifth editions of the *McGuffey Readers,* textbooks widely used in the nineteenth-century classroom; it was also noted approvingly by President Theodore Roosevelt. Nonetheless, in regard to, for example, Logan's statement to the colonists that "I had even thought to have lived with you," there is evidence that he was, to the contrary, intending to settle on the west bank of the Ohio River, far away from white settlers. Logan is also mistaken about the perpetrator of the Yellow Creek massacre; the guilty party, as we have noted was not Michael Cresap, as he says, but Daniel Greathouse. As to his claim to be utterly without kin, we do know that in addition to clan relatives, Logan had at least one blood relative, a nephew, for it was that nephew who killed him on his return from a visit to Detroit in 1780. He did this, the nephew later said, because Logan "was too great a man to live . . . he talked so strong that nothing could be carried contrary to his opinions." If that were the case, then, as Anthony Wallace remarked, "By a twist of fate, the eloquence that earned Logan immortality led also to his death."

Foremost among the drafters of the Declaration of Independence and serving as the third president of the United States, Jefferson was a man whose fame still shines brightly. His only book, *Notes on the State of Virginia*, was privately printed in France in 1784–85 and then issued in London in 1787. In his "Query VI. Productions Mineral, Vegetable, and Animal," Jefferson employed inductive reasoning to counter the deductive conclusions of the French Count de Buffon that the "productions" of the New World were in every way inferior to those of Europe. Jefferson also argued that the American Indians were not inherently inferior to the "civilized" whites and offered a strong defense of their "genius," pointing especially to their capacity for noble oratory. To illustrate this point, but also to confirm the useful notion for land speculators that Indians were a "vanishing race," he quoted Chief Logan's speech. When some claimed that the speech was a fraud, Jefferson responded by printing twenty-three pages of affidavits testifying to its authenticity in the 1801 edition of *Notes on the State of Virginia*. Nonetheless, it remains unclear just how much of this speech represents the words that Logan actually spoke. As we have them, they may indeed provide an illustration of Native genius, while also calling for Native justice.

The text used here is from the Norton edition of *Notes on the State of Virginia*, by Thomas Jefferson, edited by William Peden (1954).

From Chief Logan's Speech
Notes on the State of Virginia, Query VI

* * *

I may challenge the whole orations of Demosthenes and Cicero,[1] and of any more eminent orator, if Europe has furnished more eminent, to produce a single passage, superior to the speech of Logan, a Mingo chief, to Lord Dunmore,[2] when governor of this state. And, as a testimony of their talents in this line, I beg leave to introduce it, first stating the incidents necessary for understanding it. In the spring of the year 1774, a robbery was committed by some Indians on certain land-adventurers on the river Ohio. The whites in that quarter, according to their custom, undertook to punish this outrage in a summary way. Captain Michael Cresap,[3] and a certain Daniel Great-house, leading on these parties, surprised, at different times, traveling and hunting parties of the Indians, having their women and children with them, and murdered many. Among these were unfortunately the family of Logan, a chief celebrated in peace and war, and long distinguished as the friend of the whites. This unworthy return provoked his vengeance. He accordingly signalized himself in the war which ensued. In the autumn of the same year a decisive battle was fought at the mouth of the Great Kanhaway, between the collected forces of the Shawanese, Mingoes, and Delawares, and a detachment of the Virginia militia. The Indians were defeated, and sued for peace. Logan however disdained to be seen among the suppliants. But, lest the sincerity of a treaty should be distrusted, from which so distinguished a chief absented himself, he sent by a messenger the following speech to be delivered to Lord Dunmore.

"I appeal to any white man to say, if ever he entered Logan's cabin hungry, and he gave him not meat; if ever he came cold and naked, and he clothed him not. During the course of the last long and bloody war, Logan remained idle in his cabin, an advocate for peace. Such was my love for the whites, that my countrymen pointed as they passed, and said, 'Logan is the friend of white men.' I had even thought to have lived with you, but for the injuries of one man. Col. Cresap, the last spring, in cold blood, and unprovoked, murdered all the relations of Logan, not sparing even my women and children. There

---

1. The two most renowned classical orators. Demosthenes (c. 385–322 B.C.E.) was an Athenian. Marcus Tullius Cicero (106–43 B.C.E.) was a Roman.
2. John Murray, Earl of Dunmore (1732–1809),

was the colonial governor of Virginia from 1771 to 1775. "Mingo": Iroquoian Natives living outside their nations' homelands.
3. A Maryland soldier and frontiersman (1742–1775).

runs not a drop of my blood in the veins of any living creature. This called on me for revenge. I have sought it: I have killed many: I have fully glutted my vengeance. For my country, I rejoice at the beams of peace. But do not harbor a thought that mine is the joy of fear. Logan never felt fear. He will not turn on his heel to save his life. Who is there to mourn for Logan?— Not one."

RED JACKET

The Seneca orator known as Red Jacket (1758?–1830), for the red jacket the British awarded him for his services as a message runner during the Revolutionary War, may have had many Indian names, although the only one we know is Sagoyewatha, which means roughly "he keeps them awake," and apparently alludes to his abilities as an orator. After the War of 1812, he was involved in successful negotiations with the Americans to protect Seneca lands in western New York. Among many noteworthy orations, his most famous speech was the reply he gave to the missionary Jacob Cram in 1805.

Cram had been sent from Massachusetts to establish a mission station among the Senecas. To this end, he invited them to assemble at Buffalo Creek, New York. His address, delivered through an interpreter, essentially developed the assertion that, in Cram's words, "There is but one religion, and but one way to serve God, and if you do not embrace the right way, you cannot be happy hereafter."

After appropriate consultation with others of the Seneca delegation, Red Jacket delivered the speech reprinted here, outlining what has been called a "separatist" position—quite simply, the notion that while the ways of white Christians may be fine for them, they are not necessarily equally fine for non-white indigenous peoples who have their own religious beliefs.

Present at Red Jacket's speech was Erastus Granger, postmaster and Indian agent at Buffalo Creek and cousin to Gideon Granger, Thomas Jefferson's postmaster. His immediate subordinate was Joseph Parrish, who probably served as translator, as he had done on other occasions. Whoever transcribed the translation of Red Jacket's speech—perhaps Parrish himself—it appeared in print, in the April 1809 issue of the *Monthly Anthology*, and was reprinted many times throughout the nineteenth century.

The text used here is from William Leete Stone, *The Life and Times of Red-Jacket, or Sa-go-ye-wat-ha: Being the Sequel to the History of the Six Nations* (1841).

Portrait of Red Jacket. Red Jacket dealt with American presidents from Washington to Jackson, delivering major addresses to Washington, Adams, and Monroe in an effort to protect his people's lands.

Reply to the Missionary Jacob Cram

FRIEND AND BROTHER: It was the will of the Great Spirit that we should meet together this day. HE orders all things, and has given us a fine day for our Council. HE has taken his garment from before the sun, and caused it to shine with brightness upon us. Our eyes are opened, that we see clearly; our ears are unstopped, that we have been able to hear distinctly the words you have spoken. For all these favors we thank the Great Spirit; and HIM *only*.

BROTHER: This council fire was kindled by you. It was at your request that we came together at this time. We have listened with attention to what you have said. You requested us to speak our minds freely. This gives us great joy; for we now consider that we stand upright before you, and can speak what we think. All have heard your voice, and all speak to you now as one man. Our minds are agreed.

BROTHER: You say you want an answer to your talk before you leave this place. It is right you should have one, as you are a great distance from home, and we do not wish to detain you. But we will first look back a little, and tell you what our fathers have told us, and what we have heard from the white people.

BROTHER: Listen to what we say. There was a time when our forefathers owned this great island. Their seats extended from the rising to the setting sun. The Great Spirit had made it for the use of Indians. HE had created the buffalo, the deer, and other animals for food. HE had made the bear and the beaver. Their skins served us for clothing. HE had scattered them over the country, and taught us how to take them. HE had caused the earth to produce corn for bread. All this HE had done for his red children, because HE loved them. If we had some disputes about our hunting ground, they were generally settled without the shedding of much blood. But an evil day came upon us. Your forefathers crossed the great water and landed on this island. Their numbers were small. They found friends and not enemies. They told us they had fled from their own country for fear of wicked men, and had come here to enjoy their religion. They asked for a small seat. We took pity on them, granted their request; and they sat down amongst us. We gave them corn and meat; they gave us poison[1] in return.

The white people, BROTHER, had now found our country. Tidings were carried back, and more came amongst us. Yet we did not fear them. We took them to be friends. They called us brothers. We believed them and gave them a larger seat. At length their numbers had greatly increased. They wanted more land; they wanted our country. Our eyes were opened, and our minds became uneasy. Wars took place. Indians were hired to fight against Indians, and many of our people were destroyed. They also brought strong liquor amongst us. It was strong and powerful, and has slain thousands.

BROTHER: Our seats were once large and yours were small. You have now become a great people, and we have scarcely a place left to spread our blankets. You have got our country, but are not satisfied; you want to force your religion upon us.

BROTHER: Continue to listen. You say that you are sent to instruct us how to worship the Great Spirit agreeably to his mind, and, if we do not take hold

---

1. Rum [William Stone's note].

of the religion which you white people teach, we shall be unhappy hereafter. You say that you are right and we are lost. How do we know this to be true? We understand that your religion is written in a book. If it was intended for us as well as you, why has not the Great Spirit given to us, and not only to us, but why did he not give to our forefathers, the knowledge of that book, with the means of understanding it rightly? We only know what you tell us about it. How shall we know when to believe, being so often deceived by the white people?

BROTHER: You say there is but one way to worship and serve the Great Spirit. If there is but one religion, why do you white people differ so much about it? Why not all agreed, as you can all read the book?

BROTHER: We do not understand these things. We are told that your religion was given to your forefathers, and has been handed down from father to son. We also have a religion, which was given to our forefathers, and has been handed down to us their children. We worship in that way. It teaches us to be thankful for all the favors we receive; to love each other, and to be united. We never quarrel about religion.

BROTHER: The Great Spirit has made us all, but HE has made a great difference between his white and red children. HE has given us different complexions and different customs. To you HE has given the arts. To these HE has not opened our eyes. We know these things to be true. Since HE has made so great a difference between us in other things, why may we not conclude that he has given us a different religion according to our understanding? The Great Spirit does right. HE knows what is best for his children; we are satisfied.

BROTHER: We do not wish to destroy your religion, or take it from you. We only want to enjoy our own.

* * *

BROTHER: We are told that you have been preaching to the white people in this place. These people are our neighbors. We are acquainted with them. We will wait a little while, and see what effect your preaching has upon them. If we find it does them good, makes them honest and less disposed to cheat Indians, we will then consider again of what you have said.

BROTHER: You have now heard our answer to your talk, and this is all we have to say at present. As we are going to part, we will come and take you by the hand, and hope the Great Spirit will protect you on your journey, and return you safe to your friends.

TECUMSEH

In 1846 the historian Henry Trumbull called Tecumseh (1775?–1813) "the most extraordinary Indian that has appeared in history," and in 1961 Alvin Josephy echoed Trumbull in denominating Tecumseh "the Greatest Indian." This high estimate of Tecumseh is curious in that he was unwaveringly hostile to the Americans who relentlessly encroached on the lands of his Shawnee people in parts of the Old Northwest Territory, present-day Ohio and Indiana. In the Treaty of Fort Wayne in

1809, the Shawnees—despite the opposition of Tecumseh and his charismatic brother, Tenkswatawa, known as the Prophet—ceded huge tracts of land to the United States, prompting Tecumseh to attempt to organize a multitribal resistance to the Americans. Thus he was away in the south when William Henry Harrison decisively defeated the Prophet's forces at Tippecanoe in 1811. (In 1840, Harrison would be elected president of the United States with James Tyler as his vice president, running on the slogan, "Tippecanoe and Tyler too!") The Prophet's followers became disillusioned, and Tecumseh himself had no further success in bringing the tribes together in resistance. He fought on the side of the British in the War of 1812 and was killed at the Battle of the Thames, in southern Ontario, in 1813.

The brief speech printed here derives from the captivity narrative of John Dunn Hunter, published in 1823. Hunter, born about 1802, was taken captive by Osage Indians when he was no more than two or three years old and lived among them until about 1816. It was while he was with the Osages that he claims to have heard Tecumseh speak to them in either 1811 or 1812, a time when he himself would have been no more than ten years old. This should, of course, make us wary. And yet, although Tecumseh's visit to the Osages has not been substantiated, it is quite possible that he did speak to them and that the young and impressionable John Dunn Hunter was indeed present. Although we cannot authenticate this speech the way we could Red Jacket's speech, we nonetheless have here what Tecumseh may well have said in 1811, as reconstructed for us by John Dunn Hunter, who wrote that he was deeply moved by the words of "this untutored native of the forest . . . as no audience . . . either in ancient or modern times ever before witnessed."

The text is from John Dunn Hunter, *Memoirs of a Captivity among the Indians of North America* (1823), in Richard Drinnon's edition (1973).

Speech to the Osages

When the Osages and distinguished strangers had assembled, Tecumseh arose; and after a pause of some minutes, in which he surveyed his audience in a very dignified, though respectfully complaisant and sympathizing manner, he commenced as follows:

Brothers—We all belong to one family; we are all children of the Great Spirit; we walk in the same path; slake our thirst at the same spring; and now affairs of the greatest concern lead us to smoke the pipe around the same council fire!

Brothers—We are friends; we must assist each other to bear our burdens. The blood of many of our fathers and brothers has run like water on the ground, to satisfy the avarice of the white men. We, ourselves, are threatened with a great evil; nothing will pacify them but the destruction of all the red men.

Brothers—When the white men first set foot on our grounds, they were hungry; they had no place on which to spread their blankets, or to kindle their fires. They were feeble; they could do nothing for themselves. Our fathers commiserated their distress, and shared freely with them whatever the Great Spirit had given his red children. They gave them food when hungry, medicine when sick, spread skins for them to sleep on, and gave them grounds, that they might hunt and raise corn. Brothers, the white people are like poisonous serpents: when chilled, they are feeble and harmless; but invigorate them with warmth, and they sting their benefactors to death.

The white people came among us feeble; and now we have made them strong, they wish to kill us, or drive us back, as they would wolves and panthers.

Brothers—The white men are not friends to the Indians: at first, they only asked for land sufficient for a wigwam; now, nothing will satisfy them but the whole of our hunting grounds, from the rising to the setting sun.

Brothers—The white men want more than our hunting grounds; they wish to kill our warriors; they would even kill our old men, women, and little ones.

Brothers—Many winters ago, there was no land; the sun did not rise and set: all was darkness. The Great Spirit made all things. He gave the white people a home beyond the great waters. He supplied these grounds with game, and gave them to his red children; and he gave them strength and courage to defend them.

Brothers—My people wish for peace; the red men all wish for peace: but where the white people are, there is no peace for them, except it be on the bosom of our mother.

Brothers—The white men despise and cheat the Indians; they abuse and insult them; they do not think the red men sufficiently good to live.

The red men have borne many and great injuries; they ought to suffer them no longer. My people will not; they are determined on vengeance; they have taken up the tomahawk; they will make it fat with blood; they will drink the blood of the white people.

Brothers—My people are brave and numerous; but the white people are too strong for them alone. I wish you to take up the tomahawk with them. If we all unite, we will cause the rivers to stain the great waters with their blood.

Brothers—If you do not unite with us, they will first destroy us, and then you will fall an easy prey to them. They have destroyed many nations of red men because they were not united, because they were not friends to each other.

Brothers—The white people send runners amongst us; they wish to make us enemies, that they may sweep over and desolate our hunting grounds, like devastating winds, or rushing waters.

Brothers—Our Great Father, over the great waters, is angry with the white people, our enemies. He will send his brave warriors against them; he will send us rifles, and whatever else we want—he is our friend, and we are his children.

Brothers—Who are the white people that we should fear them? They cannot run fast, and are good marks to shoot at: they are only men; our fathers have killed many of them: we are not squaws, and we will stain the earth red with their blood.

Brothers—The Great Spirit is angry with our enemies; he speaks in thunder, and the earth swallows up villages, and drinks up the Mississippi. The great waters will cover their lowlands; their corn cannot grow; and the Great Spirit will sweep those who escape to the hills from the earth with his terrible breath.

Brothers—We must be united; we must smoke the same pipe; we must fight each other's battles; and more than all, we must love the Great Spirit: he is for us; he will destroy our enemies, and make all his red children happy.

BENJAMIN FRANKLIN
1706–1790

Benjamin Franklin was born on Milk Street in Boston, the tenth son in a family of fifteen children. His father, Josiah, was a tallow chandler and soap boiler who came to Boston in 1682 from Ecton in Northamptonshire, England, and was proud of his Protestant ancestors. He married Abiah Folger, whose father was a teacher to Native Americans. Josiah talked of offering his son Benjamin as his "tithe" to the church and enrolled him in Boston Grammar School as a preparation for the study of the ministry; but his plans were too ambitious, and Benjamin was forced to leave school and work for his father. He hated his father's occupation and threatened to run away to sea. A compromise was made, and when Benjamin was twelve he was apprenticed to his brother, a printer. He must have been a natural student of the printing trade; he loved books and reading, he learned quickly, and he liked to write. His brother unwittingly published Benjamin's first essay when he printed an editorial left on his desk signed "Silence Dogood." When his brother was imprisoned in 1722 for offending Massachusetts officials, Franklin carried on publication of the paper by himself.

In 1723 Franklin broke with his brother and ran away to Philadelphia. It was a defiant act for an apprentice, and his brother was justly indignant and angry. But the break was inevitable, for Franklin was proud and independent by nature and too clever by far for his brother. At seventeen, with little money in his pocket but already an expert printer, he proceeded to make his way in the world, subject to the usual "errata," as he liked to call his mistakes, but confident that he could profit from lessons learned and not repeat them. His most serious error was in trusting a foolish man, Pennsylvania governor Sir William Keith, who wanted to be important to everyone. As a result of Governor Keith's "favors," Benjamin found himself alone and without employment in London in 1724. He returned to the colonies two years later, at the very time when the colonies' print culture experienced a remarkable upsurgence that marked a period of increasing dependence on the printer as a disseminator of information. Franklin, ever an astute businessman, turned this to his advantage.

Franklin had an uncanny instinct for success and knew that the new commercialism demanded that anyone in business assume a public persona that best served his and his clients' interests, even if it masked one's true self. He taught himself French, Spanish, Italian, and Latin and yet was shrewd enough to know that people did not like to do business with merchants who were smarter than themselves. He dressed plainly and sometimes carried his own paper in a wheelbarrow through Philadelphia streets to assure prospective customers that he was hardworking and not above doing things for himself. By the time he was twenty-four he was the sole owner of a successful printing shop and was editor and publisher of the *Pennsylvania Gazette*. He offered his *Poor Richard's Almanac* for sale in 1733 and made it an American institution, filling it with maxims, most of which he coined himself, for achieving wealth and preaching hard work and thrift. Another of his popular writings was his pseudonymously published "Speech of Miss Polly Baker," which enjoyed wide transatlantic circulation and indicated his unusually progressive views of women for his time.

In that speech he had argued that in cases of illegitimate birth men should share equal blame with women, and he knew of what he spoke. In 1730 he married Deborah Read, the daughter of his first landlady, and they had two children. But Franklin also had one illegitimate child, and Deborah accepted Franklin's son William into the household. William was later to become governor of New Jersey and a Loyalist during the Revolution; Franklin addressed the first part of his *Autobiography* to him. Before he retired from business at the age of forty-two, Franklin had founded a library, invented a stove, established a fire company, subscribed to an academy that would become the University of Pennsylvania, and served as secretary to the American Philosophical Society. It was his intention when he retired to devote himself to public affairs and his lifelong passion for the natural sciences, especially the phenomena of sound, vapors, earthquakes, and electricity.

Franklin's observations on electricity were published in London in 1751 and, despite his disclaimers in the *Autobiography*, won him the applause of British scientists. Science was Franklin's great passion, the only thing, the American historian Charles Beard once said, about which Franklin was not ironic. His inquiring mind was challenged most by the mechanics of the world's seemingly ordinary phenomena, and he was convinced that his mind's rational powers could solve riddles that had puzzled humankind for centuries. Franklin believed that people were naturally innocent, that all the mysteries that charmed the religious mind could be explained to our advantage, and that education, properly undertaken, would transform our lives and set us free from the tyrannies of church and monarchy. Franklin had no illusions about the "errata" of humankind, but his editorial metaphor suggests that we can change and alter our past in a way that the word *sins* does not.

Franklin's remaining years, however, were spent not in a laboratory, but at diplomatic tables in London, Paris, and Philadelphia, where his gift for irony served him well. He was a born diplomat—detached, adaptable, witty, urbane, charming, and clever—and of the slightly more than forty years left to him after his retirement, more than half were spent abroad. In 1757 he went to England to represent the colonies and stayed for five years, returning in 1763. It was in England in 1768 that Franklin first noted his growing sense of alienation and the impossibility of compromise with the mother country. Parliament can make *all* laws for the colonies or *none,* he said, and "I think the arguments for the latter more numerous and weighty, than those for the former." When he returned to Philadelphia in May 1775, he was chosen as a representative to the Second Continental Congress, and he served on the committee to draft the Declaration of Independence. In October 1776, he was appointed minister to France, where he successfully negotiated a treaty of allegiance and became something of a cult hero. In 1781 he was a member of the American delegation to the Paris peace conference, and he signed the Treaty of Paris, which

Almanac for 1739. Writing under the pseudonym Richard Saunders, Franklin became famous for the aphorisms included in his immensely popular *Poor Richard's Almanac.*

brought the Revolutionary War to an official end. Franklin protested his too-long stay in Europe and returned to Philadelphia in 1785, serving as a delegate to the Constitutional Convention. By the time he died in 1790, he was one of the most beloved Americans. Twenty thousand people attended his funeral.

This hero of the eighteenth century, however, has not universally charmed readers of our own time; some find Franklin a garrulous but insensitive man of the world, too adaptable for a man of integrity and too willing to please. D. H. Lawrence is only one of a number of Franklin's critics who have charged him with indifference to the darker recesses of the soul. Beyond question, Franklin's reputation, like Emerson's, has suffered even from the admiration of reductionists who see him as a hero to those bent on seeking the way to wealth. But such single-mindedness does not do justice to Franklin's complexity. A reading of his finest prose will serve as a proper antidote; for the voice we find there is fully alert to the best and worst in all of humankind.

All the Franklin texts used here—with the exception of *The Autobiography*—are from *The Writings of Benjamin Franklin,* edited by Albert Henry Smyth (1905).

The Way to Wealth[1]

Preface to Poor Richard Improved

Courteous Reader,

I have heard that nothing gives an author so great pleasure, as to find his works respectfully quoted by other learned authors. This pleasure I have seldom enjoyed; for though I have been, if I may say it without vanity, an eminent author of almanacs annually now a full quarter of a century, my brother authors in the same way, for what reason I know not, have ever been very sparing in their applauses, and no other author has taken the least notice of me, so that did not my writings produce me some solid pudding, the great deficiency of praise would have quite discouraged me.

I concluded at length, that the people were the best judges of my merit; for they buy my works; and besides, in my rambles, where I am not personally known, I have frequently heard one or other of my adages repeated with "as Poor Richard says" at the end on 't; this gave me some satisfaction, as it showed not only that my instructions were regarded, but discovered likewise some respect for my authority; and I own, that to encourage the practice of remembering and repeating those wise sentences, I have sometimes quoted myself with great gravity.

Judge, then, how much I must have been gratified by an incident I am going to relate to you. I stopped my horse lately where a great number of people were collected at a vendue[2] of merchant goods. The hour of sale not being come, they were conversing on the badness of the times and one of the company called to a plain clean old man, with white locks, "Pray, Father Abraham, what think you of the times? Won't these heavy taxes quite ruin the country? How shall we be ever able to pay them? What would you advise us to?" Father Abraham stood up, and replied, "If you'd have my advice, I'll give it you in short, for a *word to the wise is enough, and many words won't*

---

1. Franklin wrote this essay for the twenty-fifth anniversary issue of his *Almanac*, the first issue of which, under the fictitious editorship of "Richard Saunders," appeared in 1733. For this essay Franklin brought together the best of his maxims in the guise of a speech by Father Abraham. It is frequently reprinted as "The Way to Wealth" but is also known by earlier titles: "Poor Richard Improved" and "Father Abraham's Speech."
2. Auction or sale.

fill a bushel, as Poor Richard says." They joined in desiring him to speak his mind, and gathering round him, he proceeded as follows:

"Friends," says he, "and neighbors, the taxes are indeed very heavy, and if those laid on by the government were the only ones we had to pay, we might more easily discharge them; but we have many others, and much more griev- ous to some of us. We are taxed twice as much by our idleness, three times as much by our pride, and four times as much by our folly; and from these taxes the commissioners cannot ease or deliver us by allowing an abatement. How- ever, let us hearken to good advice, and something may be done for us; *God helps them that help themselves,* as Poor Richard says, in his Almanac of 1733.

"It would be thought a hard government that should tax its people one- tenth part of their time, to be employed in its service. But idleness taxes many of us much more, if we reckon all that is spent in absolute sloth, or doing of nothing, with that which is spent in idle employments, or amusements, that amount to nothing. Sloth, by bringing on diseases, absolutely shortens life. *Sloth, like rust, consumes faster than labor wears; while the used key is always bright,* as Poor Richard says. *But dost thou love life, then do not squander time, for that's the stuff life is made of,* as Poor Richard says. How much more than is necessary do we spend in sleep, forgetting that *the sleeping fox catches no poul- try* and that *there will be sleeping enough in the grave,* as Poor Richard says.

"*If time be of all things the most precious, wasting time must be,* as Poor Rich- ard says, *the greatest prodigality;* since, as he elsewhere tells us, *lost time is never found again; and what we call time enough, always proves little enough:* let us then up and be doing, and doing to the purpose; so by diligence shall we do more with less perplexity. *Sloth makes all things difficult, but industry[3] all easy,* as Poor Richard says; *and he that riseth late must trot all day, and shall scarce overtake his business at night;* while *laziness travels so slowly, that poverty soon overtakes him,* as we read in Poor Richard, who adds, *drive thy business, let not that drive thee,* and *early to bed, and early to rise, makes a man healthy, wealthy, and wise.*

"So what signifies wishing and hoping for better times. We may make these times better, if we bestir ourselves. *Industry need not wish,* as Poor Richard says, *and he that lives upon hope will die fasting. There are no gains without pains; then help hands, for I have no lands,* or if I have, they are smartly taxed. And, as Poor Richard likewise observes, *he that hath a trade hath an estate; and he that hath a calling, hath an office of profit and honor;* but then the trade must be worked at, and the calling well followed, or neither the estate nor the office will enable us to pay our taxes. If we are industrious, we shall never starve; for, as Poor Richard says, *at the workingman's house hunger looks in, but dares not enter.* Nor will the bailiff or the constable enter, for *industry pays debts, while despair increaseth them,* says Poor Richard. What though you have found no treasure, nor has any rich relation left you a legacy, *diligence is the mother of good luck,* as Poor Richard says, and *God gives all things to industry. Then plow deep, while sluggards sleep, and you shall have corn to sell and to keep,* says Poor Dick. Work while it is called today, for you know not how much you may be hindered tomorrow, which makes Poor Richard says, *one today is worth two tomorrows,* and farther, *have you somewhat to do tomorrow, do it today.* If you were a servant, would you not be ashamed that a good mas- ter should catch you idle? Are you then your own master, *be ashamed to catch*

3. I.e., industriousness.

yourself idle, as Poor Dick says. When there is so much to be done for your-self, your family, your country, and your gracious king, be up by peep of day; *let not the sun look down and say, inglorious here he lies.* Handle your tools without mittens; remember that *the cat in gloves catches no mice,* as Poor Richard says. 'Tis true there is much to be done, and perhaps you are weak-handed, but stick to it steadily; and you will see great effects, for *constant dropping wears away stones,* and *by diligence and patience the mouse ate in two the cable;* and *little strokes fell great oaks,* as Poor Richard says in his Alma-nac, the year I cannot just now remember.

"Methinks I hear some of you say, 'must a man afford himself no leisure?' I will tell thee, my friend, what Poor Richard says, *employ thy time well, if thou meanest to gain leisure; and, since thou art not sure of a minute, throw not away an hour.* Leisure is time for doing something useful; this leisure the diligent man will obtain, but the lazy man never; so that, as Poor Richard says *a life of leisure and a life of laziness are two things.*[4] Do you imagine that sloth will afford you more comfort than labor? No, for as Poor Richard says, *trouble springs from idleness, and grievous toil from needless ease. Many without labor, would live by their wits only, but they break for want of stock.* Whereas industry gives comfort, and plenty, and respect: *fly[5] pleasures, and they'll follow you. The diligent spinner has a large shift;[6]* and now I have a sheep and a cow, every-body bids me good morrow; all of which is well said by Poor Richard.

"But with our industry, we must likewise be steady, settled, and careful, and oversee our own affairs with our own eyes, and not trust too much to others; for, as Poor Richard says

> *I never saw an oft-removed tree,*
> *Nor yet an oft-removed family,*
> *That throve so well as those that settled be.*

And again, *three removes[7] is as bad as a fire;* and again, *keep thy shop, and thy shop will keep thee;* and again, *if you would have your business done, go; if not, send.* And again,

> *He that by the plow would thrive,*
> *Himself must either hold or drive.*

And again, *the eye of a master will do more work than both his hands;* and again, *want[8] of care does us more damage than want of knowledge;* and again, *not to oversee workmen is to leave them your purse open.* Trusting too much to others' care is the ruin of many; for, as the Almanac says, *in the affairs of this world, men are saved, not by faith, but by the want of it;* but a man's own care is profitable; for, saith Poor Dick, *learning is to the studious,* and *riches to the careful,* as well as *power to the bold,* and *heaven to the virtuous,* and farther, *if you would have a faithful servant, and one that you like, serve your-self.* And again, he adviseth to circumspection and care, even in the smallest matters, because sometimes *a little neglect may breed great mischief;* add-ing, *for want of a nail the shoe was lost; for want of a shoe the horse was lost; and for want of a horse the rider was lost, being overtaken and slain by the enemy; all for want of care about a horseshoe nail.*

---

4. I.e., two different things.
5. Flee.
6. Wardrobe.

7. Moves.
8. Lack.

"So much for industry, my friends, and attention to one's own business; but to these we must add frugality, if we would make our industry more certainly successful. A man may, if he knows not how to save as he gets, keep his nose all his life to the grindstone, and die not worth a groat[9] at last. *A fat kitchen makes a lean will,* as Poor Richard says; and

> *Many estates are spent in the getting,*
> *Since women for tea forsook spinning and knitting,*
> *And men for punch forsook hewing and splitting.*

If you would be wealthy, says he, in another Almanac, *think of saving as well as of getting: the Indies have not made Spain rich, because her outgoes are greater than her incomes.*

"Away then with your expensive follies, and you will not then have so much cause to complain of hard times, heavy taxes, and chargeable families; for, as Poor Dick says,

> *Women and wine, game[1] and deceit,*
> *Make the wealth small and the wants great.*

And farther, *what maintains one vice would bring up two children.* You may think perhaps, that a little tea, or a little punch now and then, diet a little more costly, clothes a little finer, and a little entertainment now and then, can be no great matter; but remember what Poor Richard says, *many a little makes a mickle*; and farther, *Beware of little expenses; a small leak will sink a great ship*; and again, *who dainties[2] love shall beggars prove*; and moreover, *fools make feasts, and wise men eat them.*

"Here you are all got together at this vendue of fineries and knicknacks. You call them goods; but if you do not take care, they will prove evils to some of you. You expect they will be sold cheap, and perhaps they may for less than they cost; but if you have no occasion for them, they must be dear to you. Remember what Poor Richard says; *buy what thou hast no need of, and ere long thou shalt sell thy necessaries.* And again, *at a great penny-worth pause a while*: he means, that perhaps the cheapness is apparent only, and not real; or the bargain, by straightening[3] thee in thy business, may do thee more harm than good. For in another place he says, *many have been ruined by buying good pennyworths.* Again, Poor Richard says, *'tis foolish to lay out money in a purchase of repentance*; and yet this folly is practiced every day at vendues, for want of minding the Almanac. *Wise men,* as Poor Dick says, *learn by others' harms, fools scarcely by their own*; but *felix quem faciunt aliena pericula cautum.*[4] Many a one, for the sake of finery on the back, have gone with a hungry belly, and half-starved their families. *Silks and satins, scarlet and velvets,* as Poor Richard says, *put out the kitchen fire.*

"These are not the necessaries of life; they can scarcely be called the conveniences; and yet only because they look pretty, how many want to have them! The artificial wants of mankind thus become more numerous than the natural; and, as Poor Dick says, *for one poor person, there are an hundred indigent.* By these, and other extravagancies, the genteel are reduced to poverty, and forced to borrow of those whom they formerly despised, but who through industry and frugality have maintained their standing; in which case it appears

---

9. A silver coin worth about four pence.
1. Gambling.
2. Delicacies, luxuries. "Mickle": lot.

3. Restricting.
4. A Latin version of the proverb just quoted.

plainly, that *a plowman on his legs is higher than a gentleman on his knees*, as Poor Richard says. Perhaps they have had a small estate left them, which they knew not the getting of; they think, "'Tis day, and will never be night"; that a little to be spent out of so much is not worth minding; *a child and a fool*, as Poor Richard says, *imagine twenty shillings and twenty years can never be spent* but, *always taking out of the meal-tub, and never putting in, soon comes to the bottom*; as Poor Dick says, *when the well's dry, they know the worth of water*. But this they might have known before, if they had taken his advice; *if you would know the value of money, go and try to borrow some; for, he that goes a-borrowing goes a-sorrowing*; and indeed so does he that lends to such people, when he goes to get it in again. Poor Dick farther advises, and says,

> Fond[5] *pride of dress is sure a very curse;*
> E'er[6] *fancy you consult, consult your purse.*

And again, *pride is as loud a beggar as want, and a great deal more saucy.* When you have bought one fine thing, you must buy ten more, that your appearance may be all of a piece; but Poor Dick says, *'tis easier to suppress the first desire, than to satisfy all that follow it.* And 'tis as truly folly for the poor to ape the rich, as for the frog to swell, in order to equal the ox.

> Great estates may venture more,
> But little boats should keep near shore.

'Tis, however, a folly soon punished; for *pride that dines on vanity sups on contempt*, as Poor Richard says. And in another place, *pride breakfasted with plenty, dined with poverty, and supped with infamy.* And after all, of what use is this pride of appearance, for which so much is risked so much is suffered? It cannot promote health, or ease pain; it makes no increase of merit in the person, it creates envy, it hastens misfortune.

> What is a butterfly? At best
> He's but a caterpillar dressed.
> The gaudy fop's his picture just,

as Poor Richard says.

"But what madness must it be to run in debt for these superfluities! We are offered, by the terms of this vendue, *six months' credit*; and that perhaps has induced some of us to attend it, because we cannot spare the ready money, and hope now to be fine without it. But, ah, think what you do when you run in debt; you give to another power over your liberty. If you cannot pay at the time, you will be ashamed to see your creditor; you will be in fear when you speak to him; you will make poor pitiful sneaking excuses, and by degrees come to lose your veracity, and sink into base downright lying; for, as Poor Richard says, *the second vice is lying, the first is running in debt.* And again, to the same purpose, *lying rides upon debt's back.* Whereas a free-born Englishman ought not to be ashamed or afraid to see or speak to any man living. But poverty often deprives a man of all spirit and virtue: *'tis hard for an empty bag to stand upright*, as Poor Richard truly says.

"What would you think of that prince, or that government, who should issue an edict forbidding you to dress like a gentleman or a gentlewoman, on pain of imprisonment or servitude? Would you not say, that you were free, have a right to dress as you please, and that such an edict would be a breach of your privileges, and such a government tyrannical? And yet you are about to put yourself under that tyranny, when you run in debt for such dress! Your creditor has authority, at his pleasure to deprive you of your liberty, by confining you in gaol[7] for life, or to sell you for a servant, if you should not be able to pay him! When you have got your bargain, you may, perhaps, think little of payment; but *creditors*, Poor Richard tells us, *have better memories than debtors*; and in another place says, *creditors are a superstitious sect, great observers of set days and times.* The day comes round before you are aware, and the demand is made before you are prepared to satisfy it, or if you bear your debt in mind, the term which at first seemed so long will, as it lessens, appear extremely short. Time will seem to have added wings to his heels as well as shoulders. *Those have a short Lent,* saith Poor Richard, *who owe money to be paid at Easter.* Then since, as he says, *The borrower is a slave to the lender, and the debtor to the creditor,* disdain the chain, preserve your freedom; and maintain your independency: be industrious and free; be frugal and free. At present, perhaps, you may think yourself in thriving circumstances, and that you can bear a little extravagance without injury; but,

> *For age and want, save while you may;*
> *No morning sun lasts a whole day,*

as Poor Richard says. Gain may be temporary and uncertain, but ever while you live, expense is constant and certain; and *'tis easier to build two chimneys than to keep one in fuel*, as Poor Richard says. So, *rather go to bed supperless than rise in debt.*

> *Get[8] what you can, and what you get hold;*
> *'Tis the stone that will turn all your lead into gold,*

as Poor Richard says. And when you have got the philosopher's stone,[9] sure you will no longer complain of bad times, or the difficulty of paying taxes.

"This doctrine, my friends, is reason and wisdom; but after all, do not depend too much upon your own industry, and frugality, and prudence, though excellent things, for they may all be blasted without the blessing of heaven; and therefore, ask that blessing humbly, and be not uncharitable to those that at present seem to want it, but comfort and help them. Remember, Job[1] suffered, and was afterwards prosperous.

"And now to conclude, *experience keeps a dear[2] school, but fools will learn in no other, and scarce in that;* for it is true, *we may give advice, but we cannot give conduct,* as Poor Richard says: however, remember this, *they that won't be counseled, can't be helped,* as Poor Richard says: and farther, that, *if you will not hear reason, she'll surely rap your knuckles.*"

Thus the old gentleman ended his harangue. The people heard it, and approved the doctrine, and immediately practiced the contrary, just as if it had been a common sermon; for the vendue opened, and they began to buy extravagantly, notwithstanding his cautions and their own fear of taxes. I found the good man had thoroughly studied my almanacs, and digested all I had dropped on these topics during the course of five and twenty years.

---

7. Jail.
8. Earn.
9. A substance much sought by alchemists, thought to transform base metals into gold.

1. The Old Testament patriarch whose faith was tested by suffering.
2. Expensive.

The frequent mention he made of me must have tired any one else, but my vanity was wonderfully delighted with it, though I was conscious that not a tenth part of the wisdom was my own, which he ascribed to me, but rather the gleanings I had made of the sense of all ages and nations. However, I resolved to be the better for the echo of it; and though I had at first determined to buy stuff for a new coat, I went away resolved to wear my old one a little longer. Reader, if thou wilt do the same, thy profit will be as great as mine. I am, as ever, thine to serve thee,

Richard Saunders
July 7, 1757

1757   1758

The Speech of Miss Polly Baker[1]

*The SPEECH of Miss Polly Baker, before a Court of Judicature,
at Connecticut in New England, where she was prosecuted
the fifth Time for having a Bastard Child; which influenced the
Court to dispense with her Punishment, and induced one of her
Judges to marry her the next Day.*

May it please the Honourable Bench to indulge me a few Words: I am a poor unhappy Woman; who have no Money to Fee Lawyers to plead for me, being hard put to it to get a tolerable Living. I shall not trouble your Honours with long Speeches; for I have not the presumption to expect, that you may, by any Means, be prevailed on to deviate in your Sentence from the Law, in my Favour. All I humbly hope is, that your Honours would charitably move the Governor's Goodness on my Behalf, that my Fine may be remitted. This is the Fifth Time, Gentlemen, that I have been dragg'd before your Courts on the same Account; twice I have paid heavy Fines, and twice have been brought to public Punishment, for want of Money to pay those Fines. This may have been agreeable to the Laws; I do not dispute it: But since Laws are sometimes unreasonable in themselves, and therefore repealed; and others bear too hard on the Subject in particular Circumstances; and therefore there is left a Power somewhere to dispense with the Execution of them; I take the Liberty to say, that I think this Law, by which I am punished, is both unreasonable in itself, and particularly severe with regard to me, who have always lived an inoffensive Life in the Neighbourhood where I was born, and defy my Enemies (if I have any) to say I ever wrong'd Man, Woman, or Child. Abstracted from the Law, I cannot conceive (may it please your Honours) what the Nature of my Offence is. I have brought Five fine Children into the World, at the Risque of my Life: I have maintained them well by my own Industry, without burthening the Township, and could have done it better, if it had not been for the heavy Charges and Fines I have paid. Can it be a Crime (in the Nature of Things I mean) to add to the Number of the King's Subjects, in a new Country that really wants People? I own I should think it rather a Praise worthy, than a Punishable Action. I have debauch'd no other Woman's Husband, nor inticed any innocent Youth: These Things I never was charged with; nor has any one the least cause of Complaint against me,

---

1. The text is from *Gentleman's Magazine* (London), April 1747.

unless, perhaps the Minister, or the Justice, because I have had Children without being Married, by which they have miss'd a Wedding Fee. But, can even this be a Fault of mine? I appeal to your Honours. You are pleased to allow I don't want Sense; but I must be stupid to the last Degree, not to prefer the honourable State of Wedlock, to the Condition I have lived in. I always was, and still am, willing to enter into it; I doubt not my Behaving well in it, having all the Industry, Frugality, Fertility, and Skill in Oeconomy, appertaining to a good Wife's Character. I defy any Person to say I ever Refused an Offer of that Sort: On the contrary, I readily Consented to the only Proposal of Marriage that ever was made me, which was when I was a Virgin; but too easily confiding in the Person's Sincerity that made it, I unhappily lost my own Honour, by trusting to his; for he got me with Child, and then forsook me: That very Person you all know; he is now become a Magistrate of this County; and I had hopes he would have appeared this Day on the Bench, and have endeavoured to moderate the Court in my Favour; then I should have scorn'd to have mention'd it; but I must Complain of it as unjust and unequal, that my Betrayer and Undoer, the first Cause of all my Faults and Miscarriages (if they must be deemed such) should be advanced to Honour and Power, in the same Government that punishes my Misfortunes with Stripes and Infamy. I shall be told, 'tis like, that were there no Act of Assembly in the Case, the Precepts of Religion are violated by my Transgressions. If mine, then, is a religious Offence, leave it, Gentlemen, to religious Punishments. You have already excluded me from all the Comforts of your Church Communion: Is not that sufficient? You believe I have offended Heaven, and must suffer eternal Fire: Will not that be sufficient? What need is there, then, of your additional Fines and Whippings? I own, I do not think as you do; for, if I thought, what you call a Sin, was really such, I would not presumptuously commit it. But how can it be believed, that Heaven is angry at my having Children, when, to the little done by me towards it, God has been pleased to add his divine Skill and admirable Workmanship in the Formation of their Bodies, and crown'd it by furnishing them with rational and immortal Souls? Forgive me Gentlemen, if I talk a little extravagantly on these Matters; I am no Divine: But if you, great Men, (*)[2] must be making Laws, do not turn natural and useful Actions into Crimes, by your Prohibitions. Reflect a little on the horrid Consequences of this Law in particular: What Numbers of procur'd Abortions! and how many distress'd Mothers have been driven, by the Terror of Punishment and public Shame, to imbrue, contrary to Nature, their own trembling Hands in the Blood of their helpless Offspring! Nature would have induc'd them to nurse it up with a Parent's Fondness. 'Tis the Law therefore, 'tis the Law itself that is guilty of all these Barbarities and Murders. Repeal it then, Gentlemen; let it be expung'd for ever from your Books: And on the other hand, take into your wise Consideration, the great and growing Number of Batchelors in the Country, many of whom, from the mean Fear of the Expence of a Family, have never sincerely and honourably Courted a Woman in their Lives; and by their Manner of Living, leave unproduced (which I think is little better than Murder) Hundreds of their Posterity to the Thousandth Generation. Is not theirs a greater Offence against the Public Good, than mine? Compel them then, by a Law, either to Marry, or pay double the Fine of Fornication every Year. What must poor young Women do, whom Custom has forbid to solicit the Men, and who cannot force themselves upon Husbands, when the Laws take no Care to provide them any, and yet severely punish if they do their Duty without them? Yes, Gentlemen, I venture to call it a Duty; 'tis the Duty of the first and great Command of Nature, and of Nature's God, *Increase and multiply*: A Duty, from the steady Performance of which nothing has ever been able to deter me; but for it's Sake, I have hazarded the Loss of the public Esteem, and frequently incurr'd public Disgrace and Punishment; and therefore ought, in my humble Opinion, instead of a Whipping, to have a Statue erected to my Memory.

1747

Remarks Concerning the Savages of North America

Savages we call them, because their manners differ from ours, which we think the perfection of civility; they think the same of theirs.

Perhaps, if we could examine the manners of different nations with impartiality, we should find no people so rude, as to be without any rules of politeness; nor any so polite, as not to have some remains of rudeness.[1]

The Indian men, when young, are hunters and warriors; when old, counselors; for all their government is by counsel of the sages; there is no force, there are no prisons, no officers to compel obedience, or inflict punishment. Hence they generally study oratory, the best speaker having the most influence. The Indian women till the ground, dress the food, nurse and bring up the children, and preserve and hand down to posterity the memory of public transactions. These employments of men and women are accounted natural and honorable. Having few artificial wants, they have abundance of leisure for improvement by conversation. Our laborious manner of life, compared with theirs, they esteem slavish and base; and the learning, on which we value ourselves, they regard as frivolous and useless. An instance of this occurred at the Treaty of Lancaster, in Pennsylvania, *anno* 1744, between the government of Virginia and the Six Nations.[2] After the principal business was settled, the commissioners from Virginia acquainted the Indians by a speech, that there was at Williamsburg a college, with a fund for educating Indian youth; and that, if the Six Nations would send down half a dozen of their young lads to that college, the government would take care that they should be well provided for, and instructed in all the learning of the white people. It is one of the Indian rules of politeness not to answer a public proposition the same day that it is made; they think it would be treating it as a light matter, and that they show it respect by taking time to consider it, as of a matter important. They therefore deferred their answer till the day following; when their speaker began, by expressing their deep sense of the kindness of the Virginia government, in making them that offer; "for we know," says he, "that you highly esteem the kind of learning taught in those Colleges, and that the maintenance of our young men, while with you, would be very expensive to you. We are convinced, therefore, that you mean to do us good by your proposal; and we thank you heartily. But you, who are wise, must know that different nations have different conceptions of things; and you will therefore not take it amiss, if our ideas of this kind of education happen not to be the same with yours. We have had some experience of it; several

1. In Franklin's time not only unmannerly behavior but also, more broadly, unsophisticated and uncivilized behavior. "Politeness": not just mannerly behavior but also sophisticated and civilized behavior.
2. A confederation of Iroquois tribes: Seneca, Cayuga, Oneida, Onondaga, Mohawk, and Tuscarora. "*Anno*": in the year (Latin).

of our young people were formerly brought up at the colleges of the northern provinces; they were instructed in all your sciences; but, when they came back to us, they were bad runners, ignorant of every means of living in the woods, unable to bear either cold or hunger, knew neither how to build a cabin, take a deer, or kill an enemy, spoke our language imperfectly, were therefore neither fit for hunters, warriors, nor counselors; they were totally good for nothing. We are however not the less obliged by your kind offer, though we decline accepting it; and, to show our grateful sense of it, if the gentlemen of Virginia will send us a dozen of their sons, we will take great care of their education, instruct them in all we know, and make *men* of them."

Having frequent occasions to hold public councils, they have acquired great order and decency in conducting them. The old men sit in the foremost ranks, that warriors in the next, and the women and children in the hind-most. The business of the women is to take exact notice of what passes, imprint it in their memories (for they have no writing), and communicate it to their children. They are the records of the council, and they preserve traditions of the stipulations in treaties 100 years back; which, when we compare with our writings, we always find exact. He that would speak, rises. The rest observe a profound silence. When he has finished and sits down, they leave him 5 or 6 minutes to recollect, that, if he has omitted anything he intended to say, or has anything to add, he may rise again and deliver it. To interrupt another, even in common conversation, is reckoned highly indecent. How different this from the conduct of a polite British House of Commons, where scarce a day passes without some confusion, that makes the speaker hoarse in calling to *order;* and how different from the mode of conversation in many polite companies of Europe, where, if you do not deliver your sentence with great rapidity, you are cut off in the middle of it by the impatient loquacity of those you converse with, and never suffered to finish it!

The politeness of these savages in conversation is indeed carried to excess, since it does not permit them to contradict or deny the truth of what is asserted in their presence. By this means they indeed avoid disputes; but then it becomes difficult to know their minds, or what impression you make upon them. The missionaries who have attempted to convert them to Christianity all complain of this as one of the great difficulties of their mission. The Indians hear with patience the truths of the Gospel explained to them, and give their usual tokens of assent and approbation; you would think they were convinced. No such matter. It is mere civility.

A Swedish minister, having assembled the chiefs of the Susquehanah Indians, made a sermon to them, acquainting them with the principal historical facts on which our religion is founded; such as the fall of our first parents by eating an apple, the coming of Christ to repair the mischief, His miracles and suffering, etc. When he had finished, an Indian orator stood up to thank him. "What you have told us," he says, "is all very good. It is indeed bad to eat apples. It is better to make them all into cider. We are much obliged by your kindness in coming so far, to tell us these things which you have heard from your mothers. In return, I will tell you some of those we have heard from ours. In the beginning, our fathers had only the flesh of animals to subsist on; and if their hunting was unsuccessful, they were starving. Two of our young hunters, having killed a deer, made a fire in the woods to broil some part of it. When they were about to satisfy their hunger, they beheld a beautiful young woman descend from the clouds, and seat herself on that hill, which you see yonder among the blue mountains.

They said to each other, it is a spirit that has smelled our broiling venison, and wishes to eat of it; let us offer some to her. They presented her with the tongue; she was pleased with the taste of it, and said, 'Your kindness shall be rewarded; come to this place after thirteen moons, and you shall find something that will be of great benefit in nourishing you and your children to the latest generations.' They did so, and, to their surprise, found plants they had never seen before; but which, from that ancient time, have been constantly cultivated among us, to our great advantage. Where her right hand had touched the ground, they found maize; where her left hand had touched it, they found kidney-beans; and where her backside had sat on it, they found tobacco." The good missionary, disgusted with this idle tale, said, "What I delivered to you were sacred truths; but what you tell me is mere fable, fiction, and falsehood." The Indian, offended, replied, "My brother, it seems your friends have not done you justice in your education; they have not well instructed you in the rules of common civility. You saw that we, who understand and practice those rules, believed all your stories; why do you refuse to believe ours?"

When any of them come into our towns, our people are apt to crowd round them, gaze upon them, and incommode them, where they desire to be private; this they esteem great rudeness, and the effect of the want of instruction in the rules of civility and good manners. "We have," say they, "as much curiosity as you, and when you come into our towns, we wish for opportunities of looking at you, but for this purpose we hide ourselves behind bushes, where you are to pass, and never intrude ourselves into your company."

Their manner of entering one another's village has likewise its rules. It is reckoned uncivil in traveling strangers to enter a village abruptly, without giving notice of their approach. Therefore, as soon as they arrive within hearing, they stop and hollow,[3] remaining there till invited to enter. Two old men usually come out to them, and lead them in. There is in every village a vacant dwelling, called *the stranger's house.* Here they are placed, while the old men go round from hut to hut, acquainting the inhabitants, that strangers are arrived, who are probably hungry and weary; and every one sends them what he can spare of victuals, and skins to repose on. When the strangers are refreshed, pipes and tobacco are brought; and then, but not before, conversation begins, with inquiries who they are, whither bound, what news, etc.; and it usually ends with offers of service, if the strangers have occasion of guides, or any necessaries for continuing their journey; and nothing is exacted for the entertainment.[4]

The same hospitality, esteemed among them as a principal virtue, is practiced by private persons; of which Conrad Weiser, our interpreter, gave me the following instances. He had been naturalized among the Six Nations, and spoke well the Mohawk language. In going through the Indian country, to carry a message from our Governor to the Council at Onondaga, he called at the habitation of Canassatego, an old acquaintance, who embraced him, spread furs for him to sit on, placed before him some boiled beans and venison, and mixed some rum and water for his drink. When he was well refreshed, and had lit his pipe, Canassatego began to converse with him; asked how he had fared the many years since they had seen each other; whence he then came; what occasioned the journey, etc. Conrad answered

---

3. Cry out; announce themselves.   4. I.e., hospitality.

all his questions; and when the discourse began to flag, the Indian, to continue it, said, "Conrad, you have lived long among the white people, and know something of their customs; I have been sometimes at Albany, and have observed, that once in seven days they shut up their shops, and assemble all in the great house; tell me what it is for? What do they do there?" "They meet there," says Conrad, "to hear and learn *good things.*" "I do not doubt," says the Indian, "that they tell you so; they have told me the same; but I doubt the truth of what they say, and I will tell you my reasons. I went lately to Albany to sell my skins and buy blankets, knives, powder, rum, etc. You know I used generally to deal with Hans Hanson; but I was a little inclined this time to try some other merchant. However, I called first upon Hans, and asked him what he would give for beaver. He said he could not give any more than four shillings a pound; 'but,' says he, 'I cannot talk on business now; this is the day when we meet together to learn *good things,* and I am going to the meeting.' So I thought to myself, 'Since we cannot do any business today, I may as well go to the meeting too,' and I went with him. There stood up a man in black, and began to talk to the people very angrily. I did not understand what he said; but, perceiving that he looked much at me and at Hanson, I imagined he was angry at seeing me there; so I went out, sat down near the house, struck fire, and lit my pipe, waiting till the meeting should break up. I thought too, that the man had mentioned something of beaver, and I suspected it might be the subject of their meeting. So, when they came out, I accosted my merchant. 'Well, Hans,' says I, 'I hope you have agreed to give more than four shillings a pound.' 'No,' says he, 'I cannot give so much; I cannot give more than three shillings and sixpence.' I then spoke to several other dealers, but they all sung the same song,—three and sixpence,—three and sixpence. This made it clear to me, that my suspicion was right; and, that whatever they pretended of meeting to learn *good things,* the real purpose was to consult how to cheat Indians in the price of beaver. Consider but a little, Conrad, and you must be of my opinion. If they met so often to learn *good things,* they would certainly have learned some before this time. But they are still ignorant. You know our practice. If a white man, in traveling through our country, enters one of our cabins, we all treat him as I treat you; we dry him if he is wet, we warm him if he is cold, we give him meat and drink, that he may allay his thirst and hunger; and we spread soft furs for him to rest and sleep on; we demand nothing in return. But, if I go into a white man's house at Albany, and ask for victuals and drink, they say, 'Where is your money?' and if I have none, they say, 'Get out, you Indian dog.' You see they have not yet learned those little *good things,* that we need no meetings to be instructed in, because our mothers taught them to us when we were children; and therefore it is impossible their meetings should be, as they say, for any such purpose, or have any such effect; they are only to contrive *the cheating of Indians in the price of beaver.*"[5]

1784

5. "It is remarkable that in all ages and countries hospitality has been allowed as the virtue of those whom the civilized were pleased to call barbarians. The Greeks celebrated the Scythians for it. The Saracens possessed it eminently, and it is to this day the reigning virtue of the wild Arabs. St. Paul, too, in the relation of his voyage and shipwreck on the island of Melité says the barbarous people showed us no little kindness; for they kindled a fire, and received us every one, because of the present rain, and because of the cold" [Franklin's note]. St. Paul's account of his visit to Melita may be found in Acts 28. The Scythians were nomadic tribes of southeastern Europe known for their plundering.

The Autobiography   Franklin turned to the manuscript of *The Autobiography* on four different occasions over a period of nineteen years. The first part, addressed to his son William Franklin (1731–1813), governor of New Jersey when Franklin was writing this section, was composed while Franklin was visiting the country home of Bishop Jonathan Shipley at Twyford, a village about fifty miles from London. It was begun on July 30 and concluded on or about August 13, 1771. Franklin did not work on the manuscript again until he was living in France and was minister of the newly formed United States, about thirteen years later. The last two sections were written in August 1788 and the winter of 1789–90, when Franklin stopped because of illness. Before he died he carried his life up to the year 1758. The account ends, therefore, before Franklin's great triumphs as a diplomat and public servant.

The first part of *The Autobiography* was published in 1791 by Jacques Buisson in a French translation; William Temple Franklin, Franklin's grandson, published an edition of *The Autobiography* in 1818, but he did not possess the last section that his grandfather wrote because he unwittingly exchanged it for the French translator's Part One. It was not until 1868 that John Bigelow published *The Autobiography* as we know it, with all four sections complete.

The text for *The Autobiography* here reprinted is the first to have been taken directly from the manuscript itself (all other editors have merely corrected earlier printed texts). It was established by J. A. Leo Lemay and Paul Zall for their Norton Critical Edition of *The Autobiography* and is here reprinted with permission. The text has been only slightly modernized. All manuscript abbreviations and symbols have been expanded. The editors note that they omitted short dashes, which Franklin often wrote after sentences, and punctuation marks that "have been clearly superseded by revisions or additions." Careless slips have been corrected silently but may be found in the section on emendations in their text. Lemay and Zall were generous in letting us consult their footnotes and biographical sketches. Every student of *The Autobiography* must also acknowledge the helpful edition of Leonard W. Labaree et al. (1964).

From The Autobiography

[PART ONE]

Twyford, at the Bishop of St. Asaph's 1771.

Dear Son,

I have ever had a Pleasure in obtaining any little Anecdotes of my Ancestors. You may remember the Enquiries I made among the Remains[1] of my Relations when you were with me in England; and the Journey I took for that purpose. Now imagining it may be equally agreeable to you to know the Circumstances of *my* Life, many of which you are yet unacquainted with; and expecting a Week's uninterrupted Leisure in my present Country Retirement, I sit down to write them for you. To which I have besides some other Inducements. Having emerg'd from the Poverty and Obscurity in which I was born and bred, to a State of Affluence and some Degree of Reputation in the World, and having gone so far thro' Life with a considerable Share of Felicity, the conducting Means I made use of, which, with the Blessing of

---

1. I.e., the remaining representatives of a family. Franklin and his son toured England in 1758 and visited ancestral homes at Ecton and Banbury.

God, so well succeeded, my Posterity may like to know, as they may find some of them suitable to their own Situations, and therefore fit to be imitated. That Felicity, when I reflected on it, has induc'd me sometimes to say, that were it offer'd to my Choice, I should have no Objection to a Repetition of the same Life from its Beginning, only asking the Advantage Authors have in a second Edition to correct some Faults of the first. So would I if I might, besides correcting the Faults, change some sinister Accidents and Events of it for others more favorable, but tho' this were denied, I should still accept the Offer. However, since such a Repetition is not to be expected, the Thing most like living one's Life over again, seems to be a *Recollection* of that Life; and to make that Recollection as durable as possible, the putting it down in Writing. Hereby, too, I shall indulge the Inclination so natural in old Men, to be talking of themselves and their own past Actions, and I shall indulge it, without being troublesome to others who thro' respect to Age might think themselves oblig'd to give me a Hearing, since this may be read or not as any one pleases. And lastly, (I may as well confess it, since my Denial of it will be believ'd by no body) perhaps I shall a good deal gratify my own *Vanity*. Indeed I scarce ever heard or saw the introductory Words, *Without Vanity I may say,* etc. but some vain thing immediately follow'd. Most People dislike Vanity in others whatever Share they have of it themselves, but I give it fair Quarter wherever I meet with it, being persuaded that it is often productive of Good to the Possessor and to others that are within his Sphere of Action: And therefore in many Cases it would not be quite absurd if a Man were to thank God for his Vanity among the other Comforts of Life.

And now I speak of thanking God, I desire with all Humility to acknowledge, that I owe the mention'd Happiness of my past Life to his kind Providence, which led me to the Means I us'd and gave them Success. My Belief of This, induces me to *hope,* tho' I must not *presume,* that the same Goodness will still be exercis'd towards me in continuing that Happiness, or in enabling me to bear a fatal Reverso,[2] which I may experience as others have done, the Complexion of my future Fortune being known to him only: and in whose Power it is to bless to us even our Afflictions.

The Notes one of my Uncles (who had the same kind of Curiosity in collecting Family Anecdotes) once put into my Hands, furnish'd me with several Particulars, relating to our Ancestors. From those Notes I learned that the Family had liv'd in the same Village, Ecton in Northamptonshire, for 300 Years, and how much longer he knew not, (perhaps from the Time when the Name *Franklin* that before was the Name of an Order of People,[3] was assum'd by them for a Surname, when others took Surnames all over the Kingdom)[4] on a Freehold of about 30 Acres, aided by the Smith's Business which had continued in the Family till his Time, the eldest Son being always bred to that Business. A Custom which he and my Father both followed as to their eldest Sons. When I search'd the Register at Ecton, I found an Account of their Births, Marriages and Burials, from the Year 1555 only, there being no Register kept in that Parish at any time preceding. By that Register I perceiv'd that I was the youngest Son of the youngest Son for 5 Generations back. My Grandfather Thomas, who was born in 1598, lived at Ecton till he

---

2. I.e., a backhanded stroke, a word used in dueling with rapiers.
3. A "franklin" was a freeholder—an individual who owned land but was not of noble birth.
4. Here a note [Franklin intended to insert a note here, but did not].

grew too old to follow Business longer, when he went to live with his Son John, a Dyer at Banbury in Oxfordshire, with whom my Father serv'd an Apprenticeship. There my Grandfather died and lies buried. We saw his Gravestone in 1758. His eldest Son Thomas liv'd in the House at Ecton, and left it with the Land to his only Child, a Daughter, who with her Husband, one Fisher of Wellingborough, sold it to Mr. Isted, now Lord of the Manor there.

My Grandfather had 4 Sons that grew up, viz., Thomas, John, Benjamin and Josiah. I will give you what Account I can of them at this distance from my Papers, and if those are not lost in my Absence, you will among them find many more Particulars. Thomas was bred a Smith under his Father, but being ingenious, and encourag'd in Learning (as all his Brothers likewise were,) by an Esquire[5] Palmer then the principal Gentleman in that Parish, he qualified himself for the Business of Scrivener,[6] became a considerable Man in the County Affairs, was a chief Mover of all public Spirited Undertakings for the County or Town of Northampton and his own Village, of which many Instances were told us at Ecton, and he was much taken Notice of and patroniz'd by the then Lord Halifax. He died in 1702, Jan. 6, old Stile,[7] just 4 Years to a Day before I was born. The Account we receiv'd of his Life and Character from some old People at Ecton, I remember struck you as something extraordinary from its Similarity to what you knew of mine. Had he died on the same Day, you said one might have suppos'd a Transmigration.[8]

John was bred a Dyer, I believe of Woollens. Benjamin was bred a Silk Dyer, serving an Apprenticeship at London. He was an ingenious Man. I remember him well, for when I was a Boy he came over to my Father in Boston, and lived in the House with us some Years. He lived to a great Age. His Grandson Samuel Franklin now lives in Boston. He left behind him two Quarto[9] Volumes, Manuscript of his own Poetry, consisting of little occasional Pieces address'd to his Friends and Relations, of which the following sent to me, is a Specimen.[1] He had form'd a Shorthand of his own, which he taught me, but never practicing it I have now forgot it. I was nam'd after this Uncle, there being a particular Affection between him and my Father. He was very pious, a great Attender of Sermons of the best Preachers, which he took down in his Shorthand and had with him many Volumes of them. He was also much of a Politician, too much perhaps for his Station. There fell lately into my Hands in London a Collection he had made of all the principal Pamphlets relating to Public Affairs from 1641 to 1717. Many of the Volumes are wanting, as appears by the Numbering, but there still remains 8 Volumes Folio, and 24 in Quarto and Octavo. A Dealer in old Books met with them, and knowing me by my sometimes buying of him, he brought them to me. It seems my Uncle must have left them here when he went to America, which was above 50 Years since. There are many of his Notes in the Margins.

5. An honorific originally extended to a young man of gentle birth, but extended as a courtesy to any gentleman.
6. A professional copier of documents.
7. Until 1752 England used the Julian calendar, in which the new year began on March 25. Because the Julian calendar did not have leap years, it had fallen behind the astronomical year; the English skipped eleven days when adopting the Gregorian calendar. Franklin's birthday is either January 6, 1705–06, "old Stile," or January 17, 1706, New Style.

8. The passage of the soul, upon death, to another's body.
9. The terms *folio, quarto,* and *octavo* designate book sizes from large to small. A single sheet of paper folded once makes a folio, or four sides for printing; a quarto is obtained if the sheet is folded again; an octavo is the sheet folded once more.
1. Here insert it [Franklin's note, but the example was not included].

This obscure Family of ours was early in the Reformation, and continu'd Protestants thro' the Reign of Queen Mary,[2] when they were sometimes in Danger of Trouble on Account of their Zeal against Popery. They had got an English Bible,[3] and to conceal and secure it, it was fastened open with Tapes under and within the Frame of a Joint Stool.[4] When my Great Great Grandfather read in it to his Family, he turn'd up the Joint Stool upon his Knees, turning over the Leaves then under the Tapes. One of the Children stood at the Door to give Notice if he saw the Apparitor[5] coming, who was an Officer of the Spiritual Court. In that Case the Stool was turn'd down again upon its feet, when the Bible remain'd conceal'd under it as before. This Anecdote I had from my Uncle Benjamin. The Family continu'd all of the Church of England till about the End of Charles the Second's Reign,[6] when some of the Ministers that had been outed for Nonconformity, holding Conventicles[7] in Northamptonshire, Benjamin and Josiah adher'd to them, and so continu'd all their Lives. The rest of the Family remain'd with the Episcopal Church.

Josiah, my Father, married young, and carried his Wife with three Children unto New England, about 1682.[8] The Conventicles having been forbidden by Law, and frequently disturbed, induced some considerable Men of his Acquaintance to remove to that Country, and he was prevail'd with to accompany them thither, where they expected to enjoy their Mode of Religion with Freedom. By the same Wife he had 4 Children more born there, and by a second Wife ten more, in all 17, of which I remember 13 sitting at one time at his Table, who all grew up to be Men and Women, and married. I was the youngest Son and the youngest Child but two, and was born in Boston, New England.

My Mother the second Wife was Abiah Folger, a Daughter of Peter Folger, one of the first Settlers of New England, of whom honorable mention is made by Cotton Mather, in his Church History of that Country, (entitled Magnalia Christi Americana) as a *godly learned Englishman,* if I remember the Words rightly.[9] I have heard that he wrote sundry small occasional Pieces, but only one of them was printed which I saw now many Years since. It was written in 1675, in the homespun Verse of that Time and People, and address'd to those then concern'd in the Government there. It was in favor of Liberty of Conscience, and in behalf of the Baptists, Quakers, and other Sectaries,[1] that had been under Persecution; ascribing the Indian Wars and other Distresses that had befallen the Country to that Persecution, as so many Judgments of God, to punish so heinous an Offence; and exhorting a Repeal of those uncharitable Laws. The whole appear'd to me as written with a good deal of Decent Plainness and manly Freedom. The six last concluding Lines I remember, tho' I have forgotten the two first of the Stanza, but the Purport of them was that his Censures proceeded from *Goodwill,* and therefore he would be known as the Author,

---

2. From 1553 to 1558, Mary, the older sister of Elizabeth I, tried to restore Roman Catholicism as the national church.

3. The English Bible was also known as the "Geneva" version, translated by Reformed English Protestants living in Switzerland; this version, used by the Puritans, was outlawed by the Church of England.

4. A small four-legged stool.

5. An officer of an ecclesiastical court, in this case a court established to eliminate heresy.

6. Charles II (1630–1685) reigned from 1660 to 1685.

7. Secret and illegal meetings of Nonconformists, outlawed in 1664. Nonconformists refused to adopt the rituals and acknowledge the hierarchy of the Church of England.

8. More correctly, October 1683.

9. Cotton Mather's ecclesiastical history *The Wonderful Work of Christ in America,* which was published in London in 1702; the quotation is properly "an Able Godly Englishman."

1. Sectarians; believers or followers of a particular religious teaching.

> because to be a Libeler, (says he)
>   I hate it with my Heart.
> From Sherburne Town[2] where now I dwell,
>   My Name I do put here,
> Without Offence, your real Friend,
>   It is Peter Folgier.

My elder Brothers were all put Apprentices to different Trades. I was put to the Grammar School at Eight Years of Age, my Father intending to devote me as the Tithe[3] of his Sons to the Service of the Church. My early Readiness in learning to read (which must have been very early, as I do not remember when I could not read) and the Opinion of all his Friends that I should certainly make a good Scholar, encourag'd him in this Purpose of his. My Uncle Benjamin too approv'd of it, and propos'd to give me all his Shorthand Volumes of Sermons, I suppose as a Stock to set up with, if I would learn his Character.[4] I continu'd however at the Grammar School not quite one Year, tho' in that time I had risen gradually from the Middle of the Class of that Year to be the Head of it, and farther was remov'd into the next Class above it, in order to go with that into the third at the End of the Year. But my Father in the meantime, from a View of the Expense of a College Education which, having so large a Family, he could not well afford, and the mean Living many so educated were afterwards able to obtain, Reasons that he gave to his Friends in my Hearing, altered his first Intention, took me from the Grammar School, and sent me to a School for Writing and Arithmetic kept by a then famous Man, Mr. George Brownell, very successful in his Profession generally, and that by mild encouraging Methods. Under him I acquired fair Writing pretty soon, but I fail'd in the Arithmetic, and made no Progress in it.

At Ten Years old, I was taken home to assist my Father in his Business, which was that of a Tallow Chandler and Soap-Boiler.[5] A Business he was not bred to, but had assumed on his Arrival in New England and on finding his Dying Trade would not maintain his Family, being in little Request. Accordingly I was employed in cutting Wick for the Candles, filling the Dipping Mold, and the Molds for cast Candles, attending the Shop, going of Errands, etc. I dislik'd the Trade and had a strong Inclination for the Sea; but my Father declar'd against it; however, living near the Water, I was much in and about it, learned early to swim well, and to manage Boats, and when in a Boat or Canoe with other Boys I was commonly allow'd to govern, especially in any case of Difficulty; and upon other Occasions I was generally a Leader among the Boys, and sometimes led them into Scrapes, of which I will mention one Instance, as it shows an early projecting[6] public Spirit, tho' not then justly conducted. There was a Salt Marsh that bounded part of the Mill Pond, on the Edge of which at Highwater, we us'd to stand to fish for Minnows. By much Trampling, we had made it a mere Quagmire. My Proposal was to build a Wharf there fit for us to stand upon, and I show'd my Comrades a large Heap of Stones which were intended for a new House near the Marsh, and which would very well suit our Purpose. Accordingly in the Evening when the Workmen were gone, I assembled a Number of my Playfellows, and working with them diligently like so many Emmets,[7] sometimes two or

2. In the Island of Nantucket [Franklin's note].
3. I.e., as if his son were the tenth part of his income, traditionally given to the church.
4. Here, his system of shorthand.

5. Maker of candles and soap.
6. Enterprising. "Govern": steer.
7. Ants.

three to a Stone, we brought them all away and built our little Wharf. The next Morning the Workmen were surpris'd at Missing the Stones; which were found in our Wharf; Enquiry was made after the Removers; we were discovered and complain'd of; several of us were corrected by our Fathers; and tho' I pleaded the Usefulness of the Work, mine convinc'd me that nothing was useful which was not honest.

I think you may like to know something of his Person and Character. He had an excellent Constitution of Body, was of middle Stature, but well set and very strong. He was ingenious, could draw prettily, was skill'd a little in Music and had a clear pleasing Voice, so that when he play'd Psalm Tunes on his Violin and sung withal as he some times did in an Evening after the Business of the Day was over, it was extremely agreeable to hear. He had a mechanical Genius too, and on occasion was very handy in the Use of other Tradesmen's Tools. But his great Excellence lay in a sound Understanding, and solid Judgment in prudential Matters, both in private and public Affairs. In the latter indeed he was never employed, the numerous Family he had to educate and the Straitness of his Circumstances, keeping him close to his Trade, but I remember well his being frequently visited by leading People, who consulted him for his Opinion on Affairs of the Town or of the Church he belong'd to and show'd a good deal of Respect for his Judgment and Advice. He was also much consulted by private Persons about their Affairs when any Difficulty occur'd, and frequently chosen an Arbitrator between contending Parties. At his Table he lik'd to have as often as he could, some sensible Friend or Neighbor, to converse with, and always took care to start some ingenious or useful Topic for Discourse, which might tend to improve the Minds of his Children. By this means he turn'd our Attention to what was good, just, and prudent in the Conduct of Life; and little or no Notice was ever taken of what related to the Victuals on the Table, whether it was well or ill drest, in or out of season, of good or bad flavor, preferable or inferior to this or that other thing of the kind; so that I was brought up in such a perfect Inattention to those Matters as to be quite Indifferent what kind of Food was set before me; and so unobservant of it, that to this Day, if I am ask'd I can scarce tell, a few Hours after Dinner, what I din'd upon. This has been a Convenience to me in traveling, where my Companions have been sometimes very unhappy for want of a suitable Gratification of their more delicate because better instructed Tastes and Appetites.

My Mother had likewise an excellent Constitution. She suckled all her 10 Children. I never knew either my Father or Mother to have any Sickness but that of which they died, he at 89 and she at 85 Years of age. They lie buried together at Boston, where I some Years since plac'd a Marble stone over their Grave with this Inscription:

> Josiah Franklin
> And Abiah his Wife
> Lie here interred.
> They lived lovingly together in Wedlock
> Fifty-five Years.
> Without an Estate or any gainful Employment,[8]
> By constant Labor and Industry,

8. Privileged employment.

With God's Blessing,
They maintained a large Family
Comfortably;
And brought up thirteen Children,
And seven Grandchildren
Reputably.
From this Instance, Reader,
Be encouraged to Diligence in thy Calling,
And distrust not Providence.
He was a pious and prudent Man,
She a discreet and virtuous Woman.
Their youngest Son,
In filial Regard to their Memory,
Places this Stone.
J.F. born 1655—Died 1744. Ætat[9] 89
A.F. born 1667—died 1752——85.

By my rambling Digressions I perceive myself to be grown old. I us'd to write more methodically. But one does not dress for private Company as for a public Ball. 'Tis perhaps only Negligence.

To return. I continu'd thus employ'd in my Father's Business for two Years, that is till I was 12 Years old; and my Brother John[1] who was bred to that Business having left my Father, married and set up for himself at Rhode Island, there was all Appearance that I was destin'd to supply his Place and be a Tallow Chandler. But my Dislike to the Trade continuing, my Father was under Apprehensions that if he did not find one for me more agreeable, I should break away and get to Sea, as his Son Josiah had done to his great Vexation. He therefore sometimes took me to walk with him, and see Joiners, Bricklayers, Turners, Braziers,[2] etc. at their Work, that he might observe my Inclination, and endeavor to fix it on some Trade or other on Land. It has ever since been a Pleasure to me to see good Workmen handle their Tools; and it has been useful to me, having learned so much by it, as to be able to do little Jobs myself in my House, when a Workman could not readily be got; and to construct little Machines for my Experiments while the Intention of making the Experiment was fresh and warm in my Mind. My Father at last fix'd upon the Cutler's Trade, and my Uncle Benjamin's Son Samuel who was bred to that Business in London being about that time establish'd in Boston, I was sent to be with him some time on liking. But his Expectations of a Fee with me displeasing my Father, I was taken home again.

From a Child I was fond of Reading, and all the little Money that came into my Hands was ever laid out in Books. Pleas'd with the Pilgrim's Progress, my first Collection was of John Bunyan's[3] Works, in separate little Volumes. I afterwards sold them to enable me to buy R. Burton's[4] Historical Collections; they were small Chapmen's Books[5] and cheap, 40 or 50 in all. My Father's little Library consisted chiefly of Books in polemic Divinity,

9. Abbreviation of *ætatis,* "aged" (Latin).
1. John Franklin (1690–1756), Franklin's favorite brother; he was to become postmaster of Boston.
2. Woodworkers, bricklayers, latheworkers, brassworkers.
3. John Bunyan (1628–1688) published *Pilgrim's Progress* in 1678; his works were enormously popular and available in cheap one-shilling editions.

The book is an allegory in which the hero, Christian, flees the City of Destruction and makes his way to the Celestial City with the help of characters named Mr. Worldly-Wiseman, Faithful, Hopeful, etc.
4. "Burton": a pseudonym for Nathaniel Crouch (c. 1632–1725), a popularizer of British history.
5. Peddlers' books, hence inexpensive.

most of which I read, and have since often regretted, that at a time when I had such a Thirst for Knowledge, more proper Books had not fallen in my Way, since it was now resolv'd I should not be a Clergyman. Plutarch's Lives[6] there was, in which I read abundantly, and I still think that time spent to great Advantage. There was also a Book of Defoe's called an Essay on Projects[7] and another of Dr. Mather's call'd Essays to do Good,[8] which perhaps gave me a Turn of Thinking that had an Influence on some of the principal future Events of my Life.

This Bookish Inclination at length determin'd my Father to make me a Printer, tho' he had already one Son, (James) of that Profession. In 1717 my Brother James return'd from England with a Press and Letters[9] to set up his Business in Boston. I lik'd it much better than that of my Father, but still had a Hankering for the Sea. To prevent the apprehended Effect of such an Inclination, my Father was impatient to have me bound[1] to my Brother. I stood out some time, but at last was persuaded and signed the Indentures,[2] when I was yet but 12 Years old. I was to serve as an Apprentice till I was 21 Years of Age, only I was to be allow'd Journeyman's Wages[3] during the last Year. In a little time I made great Proficiency in the Business, and became a useful Hand to my Brother. I now had Access to better Books. An Acquaintance with the Apprentices of Booksellers enabled me sometimes to borrow a small one, which I was careful to return soon and clean. Often I sat up in my Room reading the greatest Part of the Night, when the Book was borrow'd in the Evening and to be return'd early in the Morning lest it should be miss'd or wanted. And after some time an ingenious Tradesman[4] who had a pretty[5] Collection of Books, and who frequented our Printing-House, took Notice of me, invited me to his Library, and very kindly lent me such Books as I chose to read. I now took a Fancy to Poetry, and made some little Pieces. My Brother, thinking it might turn to account encourag'd me, and put me on composing two occasional Ballads. One was called the *Light House Tragedy,* and contain'd an Account of the drowning of Capt. Worthilake with his Two Daughters; the other was a Sailor Song on the Taking of *Teach* or Blackbeard the Pirate.[6] They were wretched Stuff, in the Grubstreet Ballad Style,[7] and when they were printed he sent me about the Town to sell them. The first sold wonderfully, the Event being recent, having made a great Noise. This flatter'd my Vanity. But my Father discourag'd me, by ridiculing my Performances, and telling me Verse-makers were generally Beggars; so I escap'd being a Poet, most probably a very bad one. But as Prose Writing has been of great Use to me in the Course of my Life, and was a principal Means of my Advancement, I shall tell you how in such a Situation I acquir'd what little Ability I have in that Way.

6. Plutarch (c. 46–120 C.E.), Greek biographer who wrote *Parallel Lives* of noted Greek and Roman figures.
7. Daniel Defoe's (1659?–1731) *Essay on Projects* (1697) offered suggestions for economic improvement.
8. Cotton Mather published *Bonifacius: An Essay upon the Good* in 1710.
9. Type.
1. Apprenticed.
2. A contract binding him to work for his brother for nine years. James Franklin (1697–1735) had learned the printer's trade in England.

3. I.e., be paid for each day's work, having served his apprenticeship.
4. Mr. Matthew Adams [Franklin's note].
5. Exceptionally fine.
6. The full texts of these ballads cannot be found; George Worthylake, lighthouse keeper on Beacon Island, Boston Harbor, and his wife and daughter were drowned on November 3, 1718. The pirate Blackbeard, Edward Teach, was killed off the Carolina coast on November 22, 1718.
7. Grub Street in London was inhabited by poor literary hacks who churned out poems of topical interest.

There was another Bookish Lad in the Town, John Collins by Name, with whom I was intimately acquainted. We sometimes disputed, and very fond we were of Argument, and very desirous of confuting one another. Which disputatious Turn, by the way, is apt to become a very bad Habit, making People often extremely disagreeable in Company, by the Contradiction that is necessary to bring it into Practice, and thence, besides souring and spoiling the Conversation, is productive of Disgusts and perhaps Enmities where you may have occasion for Friendship. I had caught it by reading my Father's Books of Dispute about Religion. Persons of good Sense, I have since observ'd, seldom fall into it, except Lawyers, University Men, and Men of all Sorts that have been bred at Edinburgh.[8] A Question was once some how or other started between Collins and me, of the Propriety of educating the Female Sex in Learning, and their Abilities for Study. He was of Opinion that it was improper; and that they were naturally unequal to it. I took the contrary Side, perhaps a little for Dispute sake. He was naturally more eloquent, had a ready Plenty of Words, and sometimes as I thought bore me down more by his Fluency than by the Strength of his Reasons. As we parted without settling the Point, and were not to see one another again for some time, I sat down to put my Arguments in Writing, which I copied fair and sent to him. He answer'd and I replied. Three or four Letters of a Side had pass'd, when my Father happen'd to find my Papers, and read them. Without entering into the Discussion, he took occasion to talk to me about the Manner of my Writing, observ'd that tho' I had the Advantage of my Antagonist in correct Spelling and pointing[9] (which I ow'd to the Printing-House) I fell far short in elegance of Expression, in Method and in Perspicuity, of which he convinc'd me by several Instances. I saw the Justice of his Remarks, and thence grew more attentive to the *Manner* in Writing, and determin'd to endeavor at Improvement.

About this time I met with an odd Volume of the Spectator.[1] I had never before seen any of them. I bought it, read it over and over, and was much delighted with it. I thought the Writing excellent, and wish'd if possible to imitate it. With that View, I took some of the Papers, and making short Hints of the Sentiment in each Sentence, laid them by a few Days, and then without looking at the Book, tried to complete the Papers again, by expressing each hinted Sentiment at length and as fully as it had been express'd before, in any suitable Words that should come to hand.

Then I compar'd my Spectator with the Original, discover'd some of my Faults and corrected them. But I found I wanted a Stock of Words or a Readiness in recollecting and using them, which I thought I should have acquir'd before that time, if I had gone on making Verses, since the continual Occasion for Words of the same Import but of different Length, to suit the Measure,[2] or of different Sound for the Rhyme, would have laid me under a constant Necessity of searching for Variety, and also have tended to fix that Variety in my Mind, and make me Master of it. Therefore I took some of the Tales and turn'd them into Verse: And after a time, when I had

8. Scottish Presbyterians were noted for their argumentative nature.
9. Punctuation. Spelling and punctuation were not standardized at this time.
1. An English periodical published daily from March 1, 1711, to December 6, 1712, and revived in 1714. It contained essays by Joseph Addison (1672–1719) and Richard Steele (1672–1729) and addressed itself primarily to matters of literature and morality. Its aim was to "enliven morality with wit" and "temper wit with morality."
2. Meter.

pretty well forgotten the Prose, turn'd them back again. I also sometimes jumbled my Collections of Hints into Confusion, and after some Weeks, endeavor'd to reduce them into the best Order, before I began to form the full Sentences, and complete the Paper. This was to teach me Method in the Arrangement of Thoughts. By comparing my Work afterwards with the original, I discover'd many faults and amended them; but I sometimes had the Pleasure of Fancying that in certain Particulars of small Import, I had been lucky enough to improve the Method or the Language and this encourag'd me to think I might possibly in time come to be a tolerable English Writer, of which I was extremely ambitious.

My Time for these Exercises and for Reading, was at Night after Work, or before Work began in the Morning; or on Sundays, when I contrived to be in the Printing-House alone, evading as much as I could the common Attendance on public Worship, which my Father used to exact of me when I was under his Care: And which indeed I still thought a Duty; tho' I could not, as it seemed to me, afford the Time to practice it.

When about 16 Years of Age, I happen'd to meet with a Book written by one Tryon,[3] recommending a Vegetable Diet. I determined to go into it. My Brother being yet unmarried, did not keep House, but boarded himself and his Apprentices in another Family. My refusing to eat Flesh occasioned an Inconveniency, and I was frequently chid for my singularity. I made myself acquainted with Tryon's Manner of preparing some of his Dishes, such as Boiling Potatoes or Rice, making Hasty Pudding,[4] and a few others, and then propos'd to my Brother, that if he would give me Weekly half the Money he paid for my Board, I would board myself. He instantly agreed to it, and I presently found that I could save half what he paid me. This was an additional Fund for buying Books: But I had another Advantage in it. My Brother and the rest going from the Printing-House to their Meals, I remain'd there alone, and dispatching presently my light Repast, (which often was no more than a Biscuit or a Slice of Bread, a Handful of Raisins or a Tart from the Pastry Cook's, and a Glass of Water) had the rest of the Time till their Return, for Study, in which I made the greater Progress from that greater Clearness of Head and quicker Apprehension which usually attend Temperance in Eating and Drinking. And now it was that being on some Occasion made asham'd of my Ignorance in Figures, which I had twice fail'd in learning when at School, I took Cocker's Book of Arithmetic,[5] and went thro' the whole by myself with great Ease. I also read Seller's and Sturmy's Books of Navigation,[6] and became acquainted with the little Geometry they contain, but never proceeded far in that Science. And I read about this Time Locke on Human Understanding and the Art of Thinking by Messrs. du Port Royal.[7]

While I was intent on improving my Language, I met with an English Grammar (I think it was Greenwood's[8]) at the End of which there were two little Sketches of the Arts of Rhetoric and Logic, the latter finishing

---

3. Thomas Tryon, whose *Way to Health, Wealth, and Happiness* appeared in 1682; a digest titled *Wisdom's Dictates* appeared in 1691.
4. I.e., cornmeal or oatmeal mush.
5. Edward Cocker's *Arithmetic,* published in 1677, was reprinted twenty times by 1700.
6. John Seller published *An Epitome of the Art of Navigation* in 1681. Samuel Sturmy published *The Mariner's Magazine: Or Sturmy's Mathematical and Practical Arts* in 1699.
7. John Locke (1632–1704) published *An Essay Concerning Human Understanding* in 1690. Antoine Arnauld (1612–1694) and Pierre Nicole (1625?–1695), of Port Royal, published the English edition of *Logic: Or the Art of Thinking* in 1687. It was originally published in Latin in 1662.
8. James Greenwood wrote *An Essay towards a Practical English Grammar* (1711).

with a Specimen of a Dispute in the Socratic Method.[9] And soon after I procur'd Xenophon's Memorable Things of Socrates,[1] wherein there are many Instances of the same Method. I was charm'd with it, adopted it, dropped my abrupt Contradiction and positive Argumentation, and put on the humble Enquirer and Doubter. And being then, from reading Shaftesbury and Collins,[2] became a real Doubter in many Points of our Religious Doctrine, I found this Method safest for myself and very embarrassing to those against whom I used it, therefore I took a Delight in it, practic'd it continually and grew very artful and expert in drawing People even of superior Knowledge into Concessions the Consequences of which they did not foresee, entangling them in Difficulties out of which they could not extricate themselves, and so obtaining Victories that neither myself nor my Cause always deserved. I continu'd this Method some few Years, but gradually left it, retaining only the Habit of expressing myself in Terms of modest Diffidence, never using when I advance any thing that may possibly be disputed, the Words, *Certainly, undoubtedly,* or any others that give the Air of Positiveness to an Opinion; but rather say, *I conceive,* or *I apprehend* a Thing to be so or so, *It appears to me,* or *I should think it so or so for such and such Reasons,* or *I imagine* it to be so, or *it is so if I am not mistaken.* This Habit I believe has been of great Advantage to me, when I have had occasion to inculcate my Opinions and persuade Men into Measures that I have been from time to time engag'd in promoting. And as the chief Ends of Conversation are to *inform,* or to be *informed,* to *please* or to *persuade,* I wish well-meaning sensible Men would not lessen their Power of doing Good by a Positive assuming Manner that seldom fails to disgust, tends to create Opposition, and to defeat every one of those Purposes for which Speech was given us, to wit, giving or receiving Information, or Pleasure: For If you would *inform,* a positive dogmatical Manner in advancing your Sentiments, may provoke Contradiction and prevent a candid Attention. If you wish Information and Improvement from the Knowledge of others and yet at the same time express yourself as firmly fix'd in your present Opinions, modest sensible Men, who do not love Disputation, will probably leave you undisturb'd in the Possession of your Error; and by such a Manner you can seldom hope to recommend yourself in *pleasing* your Hearers, or to persuade those whose Concurrence you desire. Pope says, judiciously.

> *Men should be taught as if you taught them not,*
> *And things unknown propos'd as things forgot,*

farther recommending it to us,

> To *speak tho' sure, with seeming Diffidence.*[3]

And he might have coupled with this Line that which he has coupled with another, I think less properly,

---

9. I.e., in the form of a debate or dialectic.

1. Xenophon's (434?–355 B.C.E.) *The Memorable Things of Socrates* was translated by Edward Bysshe in 1712.

2. Anthony Ashley Cooper, third Earl of Shaftesbury (1671–1713), was a religious skeptic. Anthony Collins (1676–1729) argued that the world could satisfactorily be explained in terms of itself. Perhaps Franklin read Shaftesbury's *Characteristics of Men, Manners, Opinions, Times* (1711) and Collins's *A Discourse of Free Thinking* (1713).

3. From Alexander Pope's *An Essay on Criticism* (1711), lines 574–75 and 567, respectively. Franklin is quoting from memory. The first line should read, "Men must be taught as if you taught them not," and the third, "And speak, tho' sure, with seeming Diffidence."

For want of Modesty is want of Sense.

If you ask why *less properly*, I must repeat the Lines;

"Immodest Words admit of *no* Defence;
For Want of Modesty is Want of Sense."[4]

Now is not *Want of Sense*, (where a Man is so unfortunate as to want it) some Apology for his *Want of Modesty?* and would not the Lines stand more justly thus?

Immodest Words admit *but this* Defence,
That Want of Modesty is Want of Sense.

This however I should submit to better Judgments.

My Brother had in 1720 or 21, begun to print a Newspaper. It was the second[5] that appear'd in America, and was called *The New England Courant.* The only one before it, was *The Boston News Letter.* I remember his being dissuaded by some of his Friends from the Undertaking, as not likely to succeed, one Newspaper being in their Judgment enough for America. At this time 1771 there are not less than five and twenty. He went on however with the Undertaking, and after having work'd in composing the Types and printing off the Sheets I was employ'd to carry the Papers thro' the Streets to the Customers. He had some ingenious Men among his Friends who amus'd themselves by writing little Pieces for this Paper, which gain'd it Credit, and made it more in Demand; and these Gentlemen often visited us. Hearing their Conversations, and their Accounts of the Approbation their Papers were receiv'd with, I was excited to try my Hand among them. But being still a Boy, and suspecting that my Brother would object to printing any Thing of mine in his Paper if he knew it to be mine, I contriv'd to disguise my Hand, and writing an anonymous Paper I put it in at Night under the Door of the Printing-House.

It was found in the Morning and communicated to his Writing Friends when they call'd in as Usual. They read it, commented on it in my Hearing, and I had the exquisite Pleasure, of finding it met with their Approbation, and that in their different Guesses at the Author none were named but Men of some Character among us for Learning and Ingenuity. I suppose now that I was rather lucky in my Judges: And that perhaps they were not really so very good ones as I then esteem'd them. Encourag'd however by this, I wrote and convey'd in the same Way to the Press several more Papers,[6] which were equally approv'd, and I kept my Secret till my small Fund of Sense for such Performances was pretty well exhausted, and then I discovered[7] it; when I began to be considered a little more by my Brother's Acquaintance, and in a manner that did not quite please him, as he thought, probably with reason, that it tended to make me too vain. And perhaps this might be one Occasion of the Differences that we began to have about this Time. Tho' a Brother, he considered himself as my Master, and me as his Apprentice; and accordingly expected the same Services from me as he would from another; while I

4. Franklin is mistaken here: the lines are from Wentworth Dillon, fourth Earl of Roscommon (1633?–1685), from his *Essay on Translated Verse* (1684), lines 113–14. The second line should read, "For want of decency is want of sense." "Want": lack.

5. Actually the fifth; James Franklin's paper appeared on August 7, 1721.
6. The Silence Dogood letters (April 12–October 8, 1722), constituted the earliest essay series in America.
7. Revealed.

thought he demean'd me too much in some he requir'd of me, who from a Brother expected more Indulgence, Our Disputes were often brought before our Father, and I fancy I was either generally in the right, or else a better Pleader, because the Judgment was generally in my favor. But my Brother was passionate and had often beaten me, which I took extremely amiss; and thinking my Apprenticeship very tedious, I was continually wishing for some Opportunity of shortening it, which at length offered in a manner unexpected.[8]

One of the Pieces in our Newspaper, on some political Point which I have now forgotten, gave Offence to the Assembly. He was taken up, censur'd and imprison'd[9] for a Month by the Speaker's Warrant, I suppose because he would not discover his Author. I too was taken up and examin'd before the Council; but tho' I did not give them any Satisfaction, they contented themselves with admonishing me, and dismiss'd me; considering me perhaps as an Apprentice who was bound to keep his Master's Secrets. During my Brother's Confinement, which I resented a good deal, notwithstanding our private Differences, I had the Management of the Paper, and I made bold to give our Rulers some Rubs[1] in it, which my Brother took very kindly, while others began to consider me in an unfavorable Light, as a young Genius that had a Turn for Libeling and Satire.[2] My Brother's Discharge was accompanied with an Order of the House, (a very odd one) *that James Franklin should no longer print the Paper called the New England Courant.* There was a Consultation held in our Printing-House among his Friends what he should do in this Case. Some propos'd to evade the Order by changing the Name of the Paper; but my Brother seeing Inconveniences in that, it was finally concluded on as a better Way, to let it be printed for the future under the Name of *Benjamin Franklin.* And to avoid the Censure of the Assembly that might fall on him, as still printing it by his Apprentice, the Contrivance was, that my old Indenture should be return'd to me with a full Discharge on the Back of it, to be shown on Occasion; but to secure to him the Benefit of my Service I was to sign new Indentures for the Remainder of the Term, which were to be kept private. A very flimsy Scheme it was, but however it was immediately executed, and the Paper went on accordingly under my Name for several Months.[3] At length a fresh Difference arising between my Brother and me, I took upon me to assert my Freedom, presuming that he would not venture to produce the new Indentures. It was not fair in me to take this Advantage, and this I therefore reckon one of the first Errata[4] of my Life: But the Unfairness of it weigh'd little with me, when under the Impressions of Resentment, for the Blows his Passion too often urg'd him to bestow upon me. Tho' he was otherwise not an ill-natur'd Man: Perhaps I was too saucy and provoking.

When he found I would leave him, he took care to prevent my getting Employment in any other Printing-House of the Town, by going round and speaking to every Master, who accordingly refus'd to give me Work. I then

---

8. I fancy his harsh and tyrannical Treatment of me, might be a means of impressing me with that Aversion to arbitrary Power that has stuck to me thro' my whole Life [Franklin's note].

9. On June 11, 1722, the *Courant* hinted that there was collusion between local authorities and pirates raiding off Boston Harbor. James Franklin was jailed from June 12 to July 7. "Assembly":

Massachusetts legislative body; the lower house, with representatives elected by towns of the Massachusetts General Court.

1. Insults, annoyances.

2. Satirizing.

3. The paper continued under Franklin's name until 1726, nearly three years after he left Boston.

4. Printer's term for errors (Latin).

thought of going to New York as the nearest Place where there was a Printer: and I was the rather inclin'd to leave Boston, when I reflected that I had already made myself a little obnoxious to the governing Party; and from the arbitrary Proceedings of the Assembly in my Brother's Case it was likely I might if I stay'd soon bring myself into Scrapes; and farther that my indiscreet Disputations about Religion began to make me pointed at with Horror by good People, as an Infidel or Atheist; I determin'd on the Point: but my Father now siding with my Brother, I was sensible that if I attempted to go openly, Means would be used to prevent me. My Friend Collins therefore undertook to manage a little for me. He agreed with the Captain of a New York Sloop for my Passage, under the Notion of my being a young Acquaintance of his that had got a naughty Girl with Child, whose Friends would compel me to marry her, and therefore I could not appear or come away publicly. So I sold some of my Books to raise a little Money, was taken on board privately, and as we had a fair Wind, in three Days I found myself in New York near 300 Miles from home, a Boy of but 17, without the least Recommendation to or Knowledge of any Person in the Place, and with very little Money in my Pocket.

My Inclinations for the Sea, were by this time worn out, or I might now have gratified them. But having a Trade, and supposing myself a pretty good Workman, I offer'd my Service to the Printer of the Place, old Mr. William Bradford.[5] He could give me no Employment, having little to do, and Help enough already: But, says he, my Son at Philadelphia has lately lost his principal Hand, Aquila Rose, by Death. If you go thither I believe he may employ you. Philadelphia was 100 Miles farther. I set out, however, in a Boat for Amboy;[6] leaving my Chest and Things to follow me round by Sea. In crossing the Bay we met with a Squall that tore our rotten Sails to pieces, prevented our getting into the Kill,[7] and drove us upon Long Island. In our Way a drunken Dutchman, who was a Passenger too, fell overboard; when he was sinking I reach'd thro' the Water to his shock Pate[8] and drew him up so that we got him in again. His Ducking sober'd him a little, and he went to sleep, taking first out of his Pocket a Book which he desir'd I would dry for him. It prov'd to be my old favorite Author Bunyan's Pilgrim's Progress[9] in Dutch, finely printed on good Paper with copper Cuts,[1] a Dress better than I had ever seen it wear in its own Language. I have since found that it has been translated into most of the Languages of Europe, and suppose it has been more generally read than any other Book except perhaps the Bible. Honest John was the first that I know of who mix'd Narration and Dialogue, a Method of Writing very engaging to the Reader, who in the most interesting Parts finds himself as it were brought into the Company, and present at the Discourse. Defoe in his Crusoe, his Moll Flanders, Religious Courtship, Family Instructor, and other Pieces, has imitated it with Success.[2] And Richardson has done the same in his Pamela,[3] etc.

5. William Bradford (1663–1752), one of the first American printers and father of Andrew Bradford (1686–1742), Franklin's future competitor in Philadelphia.
6. Perth Amboy, New Jersey.
7. The narrow channel that separates Staten Island, New York, from New Jersey.
8. Shaggy head of hair.
9. See n. 3, p. 254.

1. Engravings.
2. Daniel Defoe (1659?–1731) published *Robinson Crusoe* in 1719, *Moll Flanders* in 1722, *Religious Courtship* in 1772, and *The Family Instructor* in 1715–18.
3. Samuel Richardson (1689–1761) published his novel *Pamela: Or Virtue Rewarded* in 1740. Franklin reprinted it in 1744 and in doing so published the first novel in America.

When we drew near the Island we found it was at a Place where there could be no Landing, there being a great Surf on the stony Beach. So we dropped Anchor and swung round towards the Shore. Some People came down to the Water Edge and hallow'd to us, as we did to them. But the Wind was so high and the Surf so loud, that we could not hear so as to understand each other. There were Canoes on the Shore, and we made Signs and hallow'd that they should fetch us, but they either did not understand us, or thought it impracticable. So they went away, and Night coming on, we had no Remedy but to wait till the Wind should abate, and in the mean time the Boatman and I concluded to sleep if we could, and so crowded into the Scuttle[4] with the Dutchman who was still wet, and the Spray beating over the Head of our Boat, leak'd thro' to us, so that we were soon almost as wet as he. In this Manner we lay all Night with very little Rest. But the Wind abating the next Day, we made a Shift to reach Amboy before Night, having been 30 hours on the Water without Victuals, or any Drink but a Bottle of filthy Rum: The Water we sail'd on being salt.

In the Evening I found myself very feverish, and went ill to Bed. But having read somewhere that cold Water drank plentifully was good for a Fever, I follow'd the Prescription, sweat plentifully most of the Night, my Fever left me, and in the Morning crossing the Ferry, proceeded on my Journey, on foot, having 50 Miles to Burlington,[5] where I was told I should find Boats that would carry me the rest of the Way to Philadelphia.

It rain'd very hard all the Day, I was thoroughly soak'd, and by Noon a good deal tir'd, so I stopped at a poor Inn, where I stayed all Night, beginning now to wish I had never left home. I cut so miserable a Figure too, that I found by the Questions ask'd me I was suspected to be some runaway Servant, and in danger of being taken up on that Suspicion. However I proceeded the next Day, and got in the Evening to an Inn within 8 or 10 Miles of Burlington, kept by one Dr. Browne.[6]

He entered into Conversation with me while I took some Refreshment, and finding I had read a little, became very sociable and friendly. Our Acquaintance continu'd as long as he liv'd. He had been, I imagine, an itinerant Doctor, for there was no Town in England, or Country in Europe, of which he could not give a very particular Account. He had some Letters,[7] and was ingenious, but much of an Unbeliever, and wickedly undertook some Years after to travesty the Bible in doggerel Verse as Cotton had done Virgil.[8] By this means he set many of the Facts in a very ridiculous Light, and might have hurt weak minds if his Work had been publish'd: but it never was. At his House I lay that Night, and the next Morning reach'd Burlington. But had the Mortification to find that the regular Boats were gone a little before my coming, and no other expected to go till Tuesday, this being Saturday. Wherefore I return'd to an old Woman in the Town of whom I had bought Gingerbread to eat on the Water, and ask'd her Advice; she invited me to lodge at her House till a Passage by Water should offer; and being tired with my foot Traveling, I accepted the Invitation. She understanding I was a Printer, would have

---

4. A hole or opening in a ship's deck provided with a movable cover or lid.

5. Then the capital of West Jersey, about eighteen miles north of Philadelphia.

6. Dr. John Browne (c. 1667–1737), innkeeper in Burlington and a noted religious skeptic as

well as physician.

7. I.e., formal education.

8. Charles Cotton (1630–1687) parodied the first and fourth books of the *Aeneid* in his *Scarronides* (1664). The opening lines are: "I sing the Man (read it who list), / A Trojan true as ever pissed."

had me stay at that Town and follow my Business, being ignorant of the Stock necessary to begin with. She was very hospitable, gave me a Dinner of Ox Cheek with great Goodwill, accepting only of a Pot of Ale in return. And I thought myself fix'd till Tuesday should come. However walking in the Evening by the Side of the River a Boat came by, which I found was going towards Philadelphia with several People in her. They took me in, and as there was no Wind, we row'd all the Way; and about Midnight not having yet seen the City, some of the Company were confident we must have pass'd it, and would row no farther, the others knew not where we were, so we put towards the Shore, got into a Creek, landed near an old Fence with the Rails of which we made a Fire, the Night being cold, in October, and there we remain'd till Daylight. Then one of the Company knew the Place to be Cooper's Creek a little above Philadelphia, which we saw as soon as we got out of the Creek, and arriv'd there about 8 or 9 aClock, on the Sunday morning, and landed at the Market Street Wharf.[9]

I have been the more particular in this Description of my Journey, and shall be so of my first Entry into that City, that you may in your Mind compare such unlikely Beginning with the Figure I have since made there. I was in my working Dress, my best Clothes being to come round by Sea. I was dirty from my Journey; my Pockets were stuff'd out with Shirts and Stockings; I knew no Soul, nor where to look for Lodging. I was fatigu'd with Traveling, Rowing and Want of Rest. I was very hungry, and my whole Stock of Cash consisted of a Dutch Dollar and about a Shilling in Copper. The latter I gave the People of the Boat for my Passage, who at first refus'd it on Account of my Rowing; but I insisted on their taking it, a Man being sometimes more generous when he has but a little Money than when he has plenty, perhaps thro' Fear of being thought to have but little. Then I walk'd up the Street, gazing about, till near the Market House I met a Boy with Bread. I had made many a Meal on Bread, and inquiring where he got it, I went immediately to the Baker's he directed me to in Second Street; and ask'd for Biscuit, intending such as we had in Boston, but they it seems were not made in Philadelphia, then I ask'd for a three-penny Loaf, and was told they had none such: so not considering or knowing the Difference of Money and the greater Cheapness nor the Names of his Bread, I bad him give me three pennyworth of any sort. He gave me accordingly three great Puffy Rolls. I was surpris'd at the Quantity, but took it, and having no Room in my Pockets, walk'd off, with a Roll under each Arm, and eating the other. Thus I went up Market Street as far as Fourth Street, passing by the Door of Mr. Read, my future Wife's Father, when she standing at the Door saw me, and thought I made as I certainly did a most awkward ridiculous Appearance. Then I turn'd and went down Chestnut Street and part of Walnut Street, eating my Roll all the Way, and coming round found myself again at Market Street Wharf, near the Boat I came in, to which I went for a Drought of the River Water, and being fill'd with one of my Rolls, gave the other two to a Woman and her Child that came down the River in the Boat with us and were waiting to go farther. Thus refresh'd I walk'd again up the Street, which by this time had many clean dress'd People in it who were all walking the same Way; I join'd them, and thereby was led into the great Meeting

9. October 6, 1723.

House of the Quakers near the Market. I sat down among them, and after looking round a while and hearing nothing said, being very drowsy thro' Labor and want of Rest the preceding Night, I fell fast asleep, and continu'd so till the Meeting broke up, when one was kind enough to rouse me. This was therefore the first House I was in or slept in, in Philadelphia.

Walking again down towards the River, and looking in the Faces of People, I met a young Quaker Man whose Countenance I lik'd, and accosting him requested he would tell me where a Stranger could get Lodging. We were then near the Sign of the Three Mariners. Here, says he, is one Place that entertains Strangers, but it is not a reputable House; if thee wilt walk with me, I'll show thee a better. He brought me to the Crooked Billet in Water Street. Here I got a Dinner. And while I was eating it, several sly Questions were ask'd me, as it seem'd to be suspected from my youth and Appearance, that I might be some Runaway. After Dinner my Sleepiness return'd: and being shown to a Bed, I lay down without undressing, and slept till Six in the Evening; was call'd to Supper; went to Bed again very early and slept soundly till the next Morning. Then I made myself as tidy as I could, and went to Andrew Bradford the Printer's. I found in the Shop the old Man his Father, whom I had seen at New York, and who traveling on horse back had got to Philadelphia before me. He introduc'd me to his Son, who receiv'd me civilly, gave me a Breakfast, but told me he did not at present want a Hand, being lately supplied with one. But there was another Printer in town lately set up, one Keimer,[1] who perhaps might employ me; if not, I should be welcome to lodge at his House, and he would give me a little Work to do now and then till fuller Business should offer.

The old Gentleman said, he would go with me to the new Printer: And when we found him, Neighbor, says Bradford, I have brought to see you a young Man of your Business, perhaps you may want such a One. He ask'd me a few Questions, put a Composing Stick[2] in my Hand to see how I work'd, and then said he would employ me soon, tho' he had just then nothing for me to do. And taking old Bradford whom he had never seen before, to be one of the Townspeople that had a Goodwill for him, enter'd into a Conversation on his present Undertaking and Prospects; while Bradford not discovering that he was the other Printer's Father; on Keimer's Saying he expected soon to get the greatest Part of the Business into his own Hands, drew him on by artful Questions and starting little Doubts, to explain all his Views, what Interest he relied on, and in what manner he intended to proceed. I who stood by and heard all, saw immediately that one of them was a crafty old Sophister,[3] and the other a mere Novice. Bradford left me with Keimer, who was greatly surpris'd when I told him who the old Man was.

Keimer's Printing-House I found, consisted of an old shatter'd Press and one small worn-out Font of English,[4] which he was then using himself, composing in it an Elegy on Aquila Rose[5] before-mentioned, an ingenious young Man of excellent Character much respected in the Town, Clerk of the Assembly,[6] and a pretty Poet. Keimer made Verses, too, but very indifferently.

1. Samuel Keimer (c. 1688–1742), a printer in London before coming to Philadelphia.
2. An instrument of adjustable width in which type is set before being put on a galley.
3. Trickster, rationalizer. "Discovering": revealing.
4. An oversized type, not practicable for books and newspapers.

5. Journeyman printer (c. 1695–1723) for Andrew Bradford; his son Joseph apprenticed with Franklin.
6. One who has charge of the records, documents, and correspondence of any organized body; here, the Pennsylvania legislative council.

He could not be said to write them, for his Manner was to compose them in the Types directly out of his Head; so there being no Copy, but one Pair of Cases,[7] and the Elegy likely to require all the Letter, no one could help him. I endeavor'd to put his Press (which he had not yet us'd, and of which he understood nothing) into Order fit to be work'd with; and promising to come and print off his Elegy as soon as he should have got it ready, I return'd to Bradford's who gave me a little Job to do for the present, and there I lodged and dieted.[8] A few Days after Keimer sent for me to print off the Elegy. And now he had got another Pair of Cases, and a Pamphlet to reprint, on which he set me to work.

These two Printers I found poorly qualified for their Business. Bradford had not been bred to it, and was very illiterate; and Keimer tho' something of a Scholar, was a mere Compositor, knowing nothing of Presswork. He had been one of the French Prophets[9] and could act their enthusiastic Agitations. At this time he did not profess any particular Religion, but something of all on occasion; was very ignorant of the World, and had, as I afterwards found, a good deal of the Knave in his Composition. He did not like my Lodging at Bradford's while I work'd with him. He had a House indeed, but without Furniture, so he could not lodge me: But he got me a Lodging at Mr. Read's before-mentioned, who was the Owner of his House. And my Chest and Clothes being come by this time, I made rather a more respectable Appearance in the Eyes of Miss Read, than I had done when she first happen'd to see me eating my Roll in the Street.

I began now to have some Acquaintance among the young People of the Town, that were Lovers of Reading with whom I spent my Evenings very pleasantly and gaining Money by my Industry and Frugality, I lived very agreeably, forgetting Boston as much as I could, and not desiring that any there should know where I resided except my Friend Collins who was in my Secret, and kept it when I wrote to him. At length an Incident happened that sent me back again much sooner than I had intended.

I had a Brother-in-law, Robert Homes,[1] Master of a Sloop that traded between Boston and Delaware. He being at New Castle[2] 40 Miles below Philadelphia, heard there of me, and wrote me a Letter, mentioning the Concern of my Friends in Boston at my abrupt Departure, assuring me of their Goodwill to me, and that everything would be accommodated to my Mind if I would return, to which he exhorted me very earnestly. I wrote an Answer to his Letter, thank'd him for his Advice, but stated my Reasons for quitting Boston fully, and in such a Light as to convince him I was not so wrong as he had apprehended. Sir William Keith[3] Governor of the Province, was then at New Castle, and Captain Homes happening to be in Company with him when my Letter came to hand, spoke to him of me, and show'd him the Letter. The Governor read it, and seem'd surpris'd when he was told my Age. He said I appear'd a young Man of promising Parts, and therefore should be encouraged: The Printers at Philadelphia were wretched ones, and if I would set up there, he made no doubt I should succeed; for his Part, he would procure me the public Business, and do me every other Service in

---

7. Two shallow trays that contain uppercase and lowercase type.
8. Boarded.
9. An English sect that preached doomsday and cultivated emotional fits.
1. Husband of Franklin's sister Mary, and a ship's

captain (d. before 1743).
2. Delaware.
3. Keith (1680–1749) was governor of Pennsylvania from 1717 to 1726; he fled to England in 1728 to escape debtor's prison.

his Power. This my Brother-in-Law afterwards told me in Boston. But I knew as yet nothing of it; when one Day Keimer and I being at Work together near the Window, we saw the Governor and another Gentleman (which prov'd to be Colonel French, of New Castle) finely dress'd, come directly across the Street to our House, and heard them at the Door.

Keimer ran down immediately, thinking it a Visit to him. But the Governor enquir'd for me, came up, and with a Condescension[4] and Politeness I had been quite unus'd to, made me many Compliments, desired to be acquainted with me, blam'd me kindly for not having made myself known to him when I first came to the Place, and would have me away with him to the Tavern where he was going with Colonel French to taste as he said some excellent Madeira. I was not a little surpris'd, and Keimer star'd like a Pig poison'd. I went however with the Governor and Colonel French, to a Tavern the Corner of Third Street, and over the Madeira he propos'd my Setting up my Business, laid before me the Probabilities of Success, and both he and Colonel French assur'd me I should have their Interest and Influence in procuring the Public-Business of both Governments. On my doubting whether my Father would assist me in it, Sir William said he would give me a Letter to him, in which he would state the Advantages, and he did not doubt of prevailing with him. So it was concluded I should return to Boston in the first Vessel with the Governor's Letter recommending me to my Father.

In the meantime the Intention was to be kept secret, and I went on working with Keimer as usual, the Governor sending for me now and then to dine with him, a very great Honor I thought it, and conversing with me in the most affable, familiar, and friendly manner imaginable. About the End of April 1724, a little Vessel offer'd for Boston. I took Leave of Keimer as going to see my Friends. The Governor gave me an ample Letter, saying many flattering things of me to my Father, and strongly recommending the Project of my setting up at Philadelphia, as a Thing that must make my Fortune. We struck on a Shoal in going down the Bay and sprung a Leak, we had a blustring time at Sea, and were oblig'd to pump almost continually, at which I took my Turn. We arriv'd safe however at Boston in about a Fortnight. I had been absent Seven Months and my Friends had heard nothing of me, for my Brother Homes was not yet return'd; and had not written about me. My unexpected Appearance surpris'd the Family; all were however very glad to see me and made me Welcome, except my Brother.

I went to see him at his Printing-House: I was better dress'd than ever while in his Service, having a genteel new Suit from Head to foot, a Watch, and my Pockets lin'd with near Five Pounds Sterling in Silver. He receiv'd me not very frankly, look'd me all over, and turn'd to his Work again. The Journeymen were inquisitive where I had been, what sort of a Country it was, and how I lik'd it? I prais'd it much, and the happy Life I led in it; expressing strongly my Intention of returning to it; and one of them asking what kind of Money we had there, I produc'd a handful of Silver and spread it before them, which was a kind of Raree-Show[5] they had not been us'd to, Paper being the Money of Boston. Then I took an Opportunity of letting them see my Watch: and lastly, (my Brother still grum and sullen) I gave them a Piece of Eight to drink[6] and

4. A disregard for difference in rank or station.
5. A sidewalk peep show. Silver coins were rare in the colonies.

6. A Spanish dollar with which they could buy drinks.

took my Leave. This Visit of mine offended him extremely. For when my Mother some time after spoke to him of a Reconciliation, and of her Wishes to see us on good Terms together, and that we might live for the future as Brothers, he said, I had insulted him in such a Manner before his People that he could never forget or forgive it. In this however he was mistaken.

My Father receiv'd the Governor's Letter with some apparent Surprise; but said little of it to me for some Days; when Captain Homes returning, he show'd it to him, ask'd if he knew Keith, and what kind of a Man he was: Adding his Opinion that he must be of small Discretion, to think of setting a Boy up in Business who wanted yet 3 Years of being at Man's Estate. Homes said what he could in favor of the Project; but my Father was clear in the Impropriety of it; and at last gave a flat Denial to it. Then he wrote a civil Letter to Sir William thanking him for the Patronage he had so kindly offered me, but declining to assist me as yet in Setting up, I being in his Opinion too young to be trusted with the Management of a Business so important; and for which the Preparation must be so expensive.

My Friend and Companion Collins, who was a Clerk at the Post-Office, pleas'd with the Account I gave him of my new Country, determin'd to go thither also: And while I waited for my Father's Determination,[7] he set out before me by Land to Rhode Island, leaving his Books which were a pretty Collection of Mathematics and Natural Philosophy,[8] to come with mine and me to New York where he propos'd to wait for me. My Father, tho' he did not approve Sir William's Proposition, was yet pleas'd that I had been able to obtain so advantageous a Character from a Person of such Note where I had resided, and that I had been so industrious and careful as to equip myself so handsomely in so short a time: therefore seeing no Prospect of an Accommodation between my Brother and me, he gave his Consent to my Returning again to Philadelphia, advis'd me to behave respectfully to the People there, endeavor to obtain the general Esteem, and avoid lampooning and libeling to which he thought I had too much Inclination; telling me, that by steady Industry and a prudent Parsimony, I might save enough by the time I was One and Twenty to set me up, and that if I came near the Matter he would help me out with the Rest. This was all I could obtain, except some small Gifts as Tokens of his and my Mother's Love, when I embark'd again for New York, now with their Approbation and their Blessing.

The Sloop putting in at Newport, Rhode Island, I visited my Brother John, who had been married and settled there some Years. He received me very affectionately, for he always lov'd me. A Friend of his, one Vernon, having some Money due to him in Pennsylvania, about 35 Pounds Currency, desired I would receive it for him, and keep it till I had his Directions what to remit it in. Accordingly he gave me an Order. This afterwards occasion'd me a good deal of Uneasiness. At Newport we took in a Number of Passengers for New York: Among which were two young Women, Companions, and a grave, sensible Matron-like Quaker-Woman with her Attendants. I had shown an obliging Readiness to do her some little Services which impress'd her I suppose with a degree of Goodwill towards me. Therefore when she saw a daily growing Familiarity between me and the two Young Women, which they appear'd to encourage, she took me aside and said, Young Man, I am

7. Decision.   8. I.e., natural science.

concern'd for thee, as thou has no Friend with thee, and seems not to know much of the World, or of the Snares Youth is expos'd to; depend upon it those are very bad Women, I can see it in all their Actions, and if thee art not upon thy Guard, they will draw thee into some Danger: they are Strangers to thee, and I advise thee in a friendly Concern for thy Welfare, to have no Acquaintance with them. As I seem'd at first not to think so ill of them as she did, she mention'd some Things she had observ'd and heard that had escap'd my Notice; but now convinc'd me she was right. I thank'd her for her kind Advice, and promis'd to follow it. When we arriv'd at New York, they told me where they liv'd, and invited me to come and see them: but I avoided it. And it was well I did: For the next Day, the Captain miss'd a Silver Spoon and some other Things that had been taken out of his Cabin, and knowing that these were a Couple of Strumpets, he got a Warrant to search their Lodgings, found the stolen Goods, and had the Thieves punish'd. So tho' we had escap'd a sunken Rock which we scrap'd upon in the Passage, I thought this Escape of rather more Importance to me.

At New York I found my Friend Collins, who had arriv'd there some Time before me. We had been intimate from[9] Children, and had read the same Books together. But he had the Advantage of more time for Reading, and Studying and a wonderful Genius for Mathematical Learning in which he far outstripped me. While I liv'd in Boston most of my Hours of Leisure for Conversation were spent with him, and he continu'd a sober as well as an industrious Lad; was much respected for his Learning by several of the Clergy and other Gentlemen, and seem'd to promise making a good Figure in Life: but during my Absence he had acquir'd a Habit of Sotting with[1] Brandy; and I found by his own Account and what I heard from others, that he had been drunk every day since his Arrival at New York, and behav'd very oddly. He had gam'd too and lost his Money, so that I was oblig'd to discharge[2] his Lodgings, and defray his Expences to and at Philadelphia: Which prov'd extremely inconvenient to me. The then Governor of New York, Burnet,[3] Son of Bishop Burnet, hearing from the Captain that a young Man, one of his Passengers, had a great many Books, desired he would bring me to see him. I waited upon him accordingly, and should have taken Collins with me but that he was not sober. The Governor treated me with great Civility, show'd me his Library, which was a very large one, and we had a good deal of Conversation about Books and Authors. This was the second Governor who had done me the Honor to take Notice of me, which to a poor Boy like me was very pleasing.

We proceeded to Philadelphia. I received on the Way Vernon's Money, without which we could hardly have finish'd our Journey. Collins wish'd to be employ'd in some Counting House; but whether they discover'd his Dramming by his Breath, or by his Behavior, tho' he had some Recommendations, he met with no Success in any Application, and continu'd Lodging and Boarding at the same House with me and at my Expense. Knowing I had that Money of Vernon's he was continually borrowing of me, still promising Repayment as soon as he should be in Business. At length he had got so much of it, that I was distress'd to think what I should do, in case of being call'd on to remit it. His Drinking continu'd, about which we sometimes

---

9. I.e., since we were.
1. Getting stupefied on.
2. To release him from debt by paying his bills.

3. William Burnet (1688–1729), governor of New York and New Jersey from 1720 to 1728, and governor of Massachusetts from 1728 to 1729.

quarrel'd, for when a little intoxicated he was very fractious. Once in a Boat on the Delaware with some other young Men, he refused to row in his Turn: I will be row'd home, says he. We will not row you, says I. You must, says he, or stay all Night on the Water, just as you please. The others said, Let us row; What signifies it? But my Mind being soured with his other Conduct, I continu'd to refuse. So he swore he would make me row, or throw me overboard; and coming along stepping on the Thwarts[4] towards me, when he came up and struck at me, I clapped my Hand under his Crotch, and rising, pitch'd him headforemost into the River. I knew he was a good Swimmer, and so was under little Concern about him; but before he could get round to lay hold of the Boat, we had with a few Strokes pull'd her out of his Reach. And ever when he drew near the Boat, we ask'd if he would row, striking a few Strokes to slide her away from him. He was ready to die with Vexation, and obstinately would not promise to row; however seeing him at last beginning to tire, we lifted him in; and brought him home dripping wet in the Evening. We hardly exchang'd a civil Word afterwards; and a West India Captain who had a Commission to procure a Tutor for the Sons of a Gentleman at Barbados,[5] happening to meet with him, agreed to carry him thither. He left me then, promising to remit me the first Money he should receive in order to discharge the Debt. But I never heard of him after.

The Breaking into this Money of Vernon's was one of the first great Errata of my Life. And this Affair show'd that my Father was not much out in his Judgment when he suppos'd me too Young to manage Business of Importance. But Sir William, on reading his Letter, said he was too prudent. There was great Difference in Persons, and Discretion did not always accompany Years, nor was Youth always without it. And since he will not set you up, says he, I will do it myself. Give me an Inventory of the Things necessary to be had from England, and I will send for them. You shall repay me when you are able; I am resolv'd to have a good Printer here, and I am sure you must succeed. This was spoken with such an Appearance of Cordiality, that I had not the least doubt of his meaning what he said. I had hitherto kept the Proposition of my Setting up a Secret in Philadelphia, and I still kept it. Had it been known that I depended on the Governor, probably some Friend that knew him better would have advis'd me not to rely on him, as I afterwards heard it as his known Character to be liberal of Promises which he never meant to keep. Yet unsolicited as he was by me, how could I think his generous Offers insincere? I believ'd him one of the best Men in the World.

I presented him an Inventory of a little Printing-House, amounting by my Computation to about 100 Pounds Sterling. He lik'd it, but ask'd me if my being on the Spot in England to choose the Types and see that everything was good of the kind, might not be of some Advantage. Then, says he, when there, you may make Acquaintances and establish Correspondences in the Bookselling, and Stationery Way. I agreed that this might be advantageous. Then says he, get yourself ready to go with Annis;[6] which was the annual Ship, and the only one at that Time usually passing between London and Philadelphia. But it would be some Months before Annis sail'd, so I continu'd working with Keimer, fretting about the Money Collins had got from me,

4. The seat on which an oarsman sits.
5. Island in the British West Indies.
6. Thomas Annis, captain of the *London Hope,*

the packet boat on which Franklin sailed to London in 1724.

and in daily Apprehensions of being call'd upon by Vernon, which however did not happen for some Years after.

I believe I have omitted mentioning that in my first Voyage from Boston, being becalm'd off Block Island,[7] our People set about catching Cod and haul'd up a great many. Hitherto I had stuck to my Resolution of not eating animal Food; and on this Occasion, I consider'd with my Master Tryon, the taking every Fish as a kind of unprovok'd Murder, since none of them had or ever could do us any Injury that might justify the Slaughter. All this seem'd very reasonable. But I had formerly been a great Lover of Fish, and when this came hot out of the Frying Pan, it smelt admirably well. I balanc'd some time between Principle and Inclination: till I recollected, that when the Fish were opened, I saw smaller Fish taken out of their Stomachs: Then, thought I, if you eat one another, I don't see why we mayn't eat you. So I din'd upon Cod very heartily and continu'd to eat with other People, returning only now and then occasionally to a vegetable Diet. So convenient a thing it is to be a *reasonable Creature,* since it enables one to find or make a Reason for everything one has a mind to do.

Keimer and I liv'd on a pretty good familiar Footing and agreed tolerably well: for he suspected nothing of my Setting up. He retain'd a great deal of his old Enthusiasms, and lov'd an Argumentation. We therefore had many Disputations. I us'd to work him so with my Socratic Method, and had trapann'd[8] him so often by Questions apparently so distant from any Point we had in hand, and yet by degrees led to the Point, and brought him into Difficulties and Contradictions, that at last he grew ridiculously cautious, and would hardly answer me the most common Question, without asking first, *What do you intend to infer from that?* However it gave him so high an Opinion of my Abilities in the Confuting Way, that he seriously propos'd my being his Colleague in a Project he had of setting up a new Sect. He was to preach the Doctrines, and I was to confound all Opponents. When he came to explain with me upon the Doctrines, I found several Conundrums[9] which I objected to, unless I might have my Way a little too, and introduce some of mine. Keimer wore his Beard at full Length, because somewhere in the Mosaic Law it is said, *thou shalt not mar the Corners of thy Beard.*[1] He likewise kept the seventh-day Sabbath; and these two Points were Essentials with him. I dislik'd both, but agreed to admit them upon Condition of his adopting the Doctrine of using no animal Food. I doubt, says he, my Constitution will not bear that. I assur'd him it would, and that he would be the better for it. He was usually a great Glutton, and I promis'd myself some Diversion in half-starving him. He agreed to try the Practice if I would keep him Company. I did so and we held it for three Months. We had our Victuals dress'd and brought to us regularly by a Woman in the Neighborhood, who had from me a List of 40 Dishes to be prepar'd for us at different Times, in all which there was neither Fish Flesh nor Fowl, and the Whim suited me the better at this time from the Cheapness of it, not costing us about 18 Pence Sterling each, per Week. I have since kept several Lents most strictly, leaving the common Diet for that, and that for the common, abruptly, without the least Inconvenience: So that I think there is little in the Advice of

7. Off the coast of Rhode Island.
8. Trapped.
9. Puzzles, difficult questions.
1. "Ye shall not round the corners of your heads, neither shalt thou mar the corners of thy beard" (Leviticus 19.27). Keimer probably also wore his hair long.

making those Changes by easy Gradations. I went on pleasantly, but Poor Keimer suffer'd grievously, tir'd of the Project, long'd for the Flesh Pots of Egypt,[2] and order'd a roast Pig. He invited me and two Women Friends to dine with him, but it being brought too soon upon table, he could not resist the Temptation, and ate it all up before we came.

I had made some Courtship during this time to Miss Read. I had a great Respect and Affection for her, and had some Reason to believe she had the same for me: but as I was about to take a long Voyage, and we were both very young, only a little above 18, it was thought most prudent by her Mother to prevent our going too far at present, as a Marriage if it was to take place would be more convenient after my Return, when I should be as I expected set up in my Business. Perhaps too she thought my Expectations not so well founded as I imagined them to be.

My chief Acquaintances at this time were, Charles Osborne, Joseph Watson, and James Ralph;[3] All Lovers of Reading. The two first were Clerks to an eminent Scrivener or Conveyancer in the Town, Charles Brockden;[4] the other was Clerk to a Merchant. Watson was a pious sensible young Man, of great integrity. The others rather more lax in their Principles of Religion, particularly Ralph, who as well as Collins had been unsettled by me, for which they both made me suffer. Osborne was sensible, candid, frank, sincere, and affectionate to his Friends; but in literary Matters too fond of Criticizing. Ralph, was ingenious, genteel in his Manners, and extremely eloquent; I think I never knew a prettier Talker. Both of them great Admirers of Poetry, and began to try their Hands in little Pieces. Many pleasant Walks we four had together, on Sundays into the Woods near Skuylkill,[5] where we read to one another and conferr'd on what we read. Ralph was inclin'd to pursue the Study of Poetry, not doubting but he might become eminent in it and make his Fortune by it, alledging that the best Poets must when they first began to write, make as many Faults as he did. Osborne dissuaded him, assur'd him he had no Genius for Poetry, and advis'd him to think of nothing beyond the Business he was bred to; that in the mercantile way tho' he had no Stock, he might by his Diligence and Punctuality recommend himself to Employment as a Factor,[6] and in time acquire wherewith to trade on his own Account. I approv'd the amusing oneself with Poetry now and then, so far as to improve one's Language, but no farther. On this it was propos'd that we should each of us at our next Meeting produce a Piece of our own Composing, in order to improve by our mutual Observations, Criticisms and Corrections. As Language and Expression was what we had in View, we excluded all Considerations of Invention,[7] by agreeing that the Task should be a Version of the 18th Psalm, which describes the Descent of a Deity.[8] When the Time of our Meeting drew nigh, Ralph call'd on me first, and let me know his Piece was ready. I told him I had been busy, and having little Inclination had done nothing. He then show'd me his Piece for my Opinion; and I much approv'd it, as

2. "And the whole congregation of the children of Israel murmured against Moses and Aaron in the wilderness: And the children of Israel said unto them, Would to God we had died by the hand of the Lord in the land of Egypt, when we sat by the flesh pots, and when we did eat bread to the full" (Exodus 16.2–3).
3. Ralph (c. 1695–1762) became well known as a political journalist. Charles Osborne's dates are unknown. Joseph Watson died about 1728.
4. Brockden (1683–1769) came to Philadelphia in 1706. "Conveyancer": one who draws up leases and deeds.
5. A river at Philadelphia.
6. Business agent.
7. I.e., originality.
8. "He bowed the heavens also, and came down: and darkness was under his feet" (Psalm 18.9).

it appear'd to me to have great Merit. Now, says he, Osborne never will allow the least Merit in any thing of mine, but makes 1000 Criticisms out of mere Envy. He is not so jealous of you. I wish therefore you would take this Piece, and produce it as yours. I will pretend not to have had time, and so produce nothing. We shall then see what he will say to it. It was agreed, and I immediately transcrib'd it that it might appear in my own hand. We met.

Watson's Performance was read: there were some Beauties in it: but many Defects. Osborne's was read: It was much better. Ralph did it Justice, remark'd some Faults, but applauded the Beauties. He himself had nothing to produce. I was backward, seem'd desirous of being excus'd, had not had sufficient Time to correct; etc., but no Excuse could be admitted, produce I must. It was read and repeated; Watson and Osborne gave up the Contest; and join'd in applauding it immoderately. Ralph only made some Criticisms and propos'd some Amendments, but I defended my Text. Osborne was against Ralph, and told him he was no better a Critic than Poet; so he dropped the Argument. As they two went home together, Osborne express'd himself still more strongly in favor of what he thought my Production, having restrain'd himself before as he said, lest I should think it Flattery. But who would have imagin'd, says he, that Franklin had been capable of such a Performance; such Painting, such Force! such Fire! He has even improv'd the Original! In his common Conversation, he seems to have no Choice of Words; he hesitates and blunders; and yet, good God, how he writes!

When we next met, Ralph discover'd the Trick we had played him, and Osborne was a little laughed at. This Transaction fix'd Ralph in his Resolution of becoming a Poet. I did all I could to dissuade him from it, but he continu'd scribbling Verses, till *Pope*[9] cur'd him. He became however a pretty good Prose Writer. More of him hereafter. But as I may not have occasion again to mention the other two, I shall just remark here, that Watson died in my Arms a few Years after, much lamented, being the best of our Set. Osborne went to the West Indies, where he became an eminent Lawyer and made Money, but died young. He and I had made a serious Agreement, that the one who happen'd first to die, should if possible make a friendly Visit to the other, and acquaint him how he found things in that separate State. But he never fulfill'd his Promise.

The Governor, seeming to like my Company, had me frequently to his House; and his Setting me up was always mention'd as a fix'd thing. I was to take with me Letters recommendatory to a Number of his Friends, besides the Letter of Credit to furnish me with the necessary Money for purchasing the Press and Types, Paper, etc. For these Letters I was appointed to call at different times, when they were to be ready, but a future time was still[1] named. Thus we went on till the ship whose Departure too had been several times postponed was on the Point of sailing. Then when I call'd to take my Leave and receive the Letters, his Secretary, Dr. Bard,[2] came out to me and said the Governor was extremely busy, in writing, but would be down at New Castle before the Ship, and there the Letters would be delivered to me.

9. In the 2nd edition of the *Dunciad* (1728), a poem that attacks ignorance of all kinds, Alexander Pope responded to Ralph's slur against him in *Sawney*: "Silence, ye Wolves: while Ralph to Cynthia howls. / And makes Night hideous—Answer him ye Owls" (book 3, lines 159–60). In the 1742 edition Pope included another dig at Ralph: "And see: The very Gazeteers give o'er, / Ev'n Ralph repents" (book 1, lines 215–16).
1. Always.
2. Patrick Bard, or Baird, resided in Philadelphia as port physician after 1720.

Ralph, tho' married and having one Child, had determined to accompany me in this Voyage. It was thought he intended to establish a Correspondence, and obtain Goods to sell on Commission. But I found afterwards, that thro' some Discontent with his Wife's Relations, he purposed to leave her on their Hands, and never return again. Having taken leave of my Friends, and interchang'd some Promises with Miss Read, I left Philadelphia in the Ship, which anchor'd at New Castle. The Governor was there. But when I went to his Lodging, the Secretary came to me from him with the civilest Message in the World, that he could not then see me being engag'd in Business of the utmost Importance, but should send the Letters to me on board, wish'd me heartily a good Voyage and a speedy Return, etc. I return'd on board, a little puzzled, but still not doubting.

Mr. Andrew Hamilton,[3] a famous Lawyer of Philadelphia, had taken Passage in the same Ship for himself and Son: and with Mr. Denham[4] a Quaker Merchant, and Messrs. Onion and Russel Masters of an Iron Work in Maryland, had engag'd the Great Cabin; so that Ralph and I were forc'd to take up with a Berth in the Steerage: And none on board knowing us, were considered as ordinary Persons. But Mr. Hamilton and his Son (it was James, since Governor) return'd from New Castle to Philadelphia the Father being recall'd by a great Fee to plead for a seized Ship. And just before we sail'd Colonel French coming on board, and showing me great Respect, I was more taken Notice of, and with my Friend Ralph invited by the other Gentlemen to come into the Cabin, there being now Room. Accordingly we remov'd thither.

Understanding that Colonel French had brought on board the Governor's Dispatches, I ask'd the Captain for those Letters that were to be under my Care. He said all were put into the Bag together; and he could not then come at them; but before we landed in England, I should have an Opportunity of picking them out. So I was satisfied for the present, and we proceeded on our Voyage. We had a sociable Company in the Cabin, and lived uncommonly well, having the Addition of all Mr. Hamilton's Stores, who had laid in plentifully. In this Passage Mr. Denham contracted a Friendship for me that continued during his Life. The Voyage was otherwise not a pleasant one, as we had a great deal of bad Weather.

When we came into the Channel, the Captain kept his Word with me, and gave me an Opportunity of examining the Bag for the Governor's Letters. I found none upon which my Name was put, as under my Care; I pick'd out 6 or 7 that by the Handwriting I thought might be the promis'd Letters, especially as one of them was directed to Basket[5] the King's Printer, and another to some Stationer. We arriv'd in London the 24th of December, 1724. I waited upon the Stationer who came first in my Way, delivering the Letter as from Governor Keith. I don't know such a Person, says he: but opening the Letter, O, this is from Riddlesden,[6] I have lately found him to be a complete Rascal, and I will have nothing to do with him, nor receive any Letters from him. So putting the Letter into my Hand, he turn'd on his Heel

---

3. Andrew Hamilton (c. 1678–1741), American-born lawyer. His successful defense of John Peter Zenger against a charge of libel established freedom of the press in the colonies and earned him the sobriquet "the Philadelphia Lawyer." His son James Hamilton (c. 1710–1783) was governor of Pennsylvania four times between 1748 and 1773.

4. Thomas Denham (d. 1728), merchant and benefactor, left Bristol, England, in 1715.

5. John Baskett (d. 1742).

6. William Riddlesden (d. before 1733), well known in Maryland as a man of "infamy."

and left me to serve some Customer. I was surprised to find these were not the Governor's Letters. And after recollecting and comparing Circumstances, I began to doubt his Sincerity. I found my Friend Denham, and opened the whole Affair to him. He let me into Keith's Character, told me there was not the least Probability that he had written any Letters for me, that no one who knew him had the smallest Dependence on him, and he laughed at the Notion of the Governor's giving me a Letter of Credit, having as he said no Credit to give. On my expressing some Concern about what I should do: He advis'd me to endeavor getting some Employment in the Way of my Business. Among the Printers here, says he, you will improve yourself; and when you return to America, you will set up to greater Advantage.

We both of us happen'd to know, as well as the Stationer, that Riddlesden the Attorney, was a very Knave. He had half ruin'd Miss Read's Father by drawing him in to be bound[7] for him. By his Letter it appear'd, there was a secret Scheme on foot to the Prejudice of Hamilton, (Suppos'd to be then coming over with us,) and that Keith was concern'd in it with Riddlesden. Denham, who was a Friend of Hamilton's, thought he ought to be acquainted with it. So when he arriv'd in England, which was soon after, partly from Resentment and Ill-Will to Keith and Riddlesden, and partly from Goodwill to him: I waited on him, and gave him the Letter. He thank'd me cordially, the Information being of Importance to him. And from that time he became my Friend, greatly to my Advantage afterwards on many Occasions.

But what shall we think of a Governor's playing such pitiful Tricks, and imposing so grossly on a poor ignorant Boy! It was a Habit he had acquired. He wish'd to please everybody; and having little to give, he gave Expectations. He was otherwise an ingenious sensible Man, a pretty good Writer, and a good Governor for the People, tho' not for his Constituents the Proprietaries,[8] whose Instructions he sometimes disregarded. Several of our best Laws were of his Planning, and pass'd during his Administration.

Ralph and I were inseparable Companions. We took Lodgings together in Little Britain[9] at 3 shillings 6 pence per Week, as much as we could then afford. He found some Relations, but they were poor and unable to assist him. He now let me know his Intentions of remaining in London, and that he never meant to return to Philadelphia. He had brought no Money with him, the whole he could muster having been expended in paying his Passage. I had 15 Pistoles.[1] So he borrowed occasionally of me, to subsist while he was looking out for Business. He first endeavor'd to get into the Playhouse, believing himself qualified for an Actor; but Wilkes,[2] to whom he applied, advis'd him candidly not to think of that Employment, as it was impossible he should succeed in it. Then he propos'd to Roberts, a Publisher in Paternoster Row,[3] to write for him a Weekly Paper like the Spectator, on certain Conditions, which Roberts did not approve. Then he endeavor'd to get Employment as a Hackney Writer[4] to copy for the Stationers and Lawyers about the Temple[5] but could find no Vacancy.

7. I.e., as a cosigner of a document and legally bound to be responsible for his debts.
8. Members of the Penn family were the Proprietors of Pennsylvania and its legal owners. "Constituents": those who appointed him their representative; in this case, the Penn family, which retained control of Pennsylvania until the Revolution.
9. A street in London near St. Paul's Cathedral.

1. Spanish gold coin worth approximately eighteen shillings.
2. Robert Wilks (1665?–1732), an Irish actor, dominated London theater life from 1709 to 1730.
3. The center of the London printing business.
4. A copyist.
5. The Inner and Middle Temples were two of four buildings in London that were centers for the legal profession.

I immediately got into Work at Palmer's, then a famous Printing-House in Bartholomew Close;[6] and here I continu'd near a Year. I was pretty diligent; but spent with Ralph a good deal of my Earnings in going to Plays and other Places of Amusement. We had together consum'd all my Pistoles, and now just rubb'd[7] on from hand to mouth. He seem'd quite to forget his Wife and Child, and I by degrees my Engagements with Miss Read, to whom I never wrote more than one Letter, and that was to let her know I was not likely soon to return. This was another of the great Errata of my Life, which I should wish to correct if I were to live it over again. In fact, by our Expenses, I was constantly kept unable to pay my Passage.

At Palmer's I was employ'd in Composing for the second Edition of Wollaston's Religion of Nature.[8] Some of his Reasonings not appearing to me well-founded, I wrote a little metaphysical Piece, in which I made Remarks on them. It was entitled, *A Dissertation on Liberty and Necessity, Pleasure and Pain*.[9] I inscrib'd it to my Friend Ralph. I printed a small Number. I occasion'd my being more consider'd by Mr. Palmer, as a young Man of some Ingenuity, tho' he seriously expostulated with me upon the Principles of my Pamplet which to him appear'd abominable. My printing this Pamphlet was another Erratum.

While I lodg'd in Little Britain I made an Acquaintance with one Wilcox a Bookseller, whose Shop was at the next Door. He had an immense Collection of second-hand Books. Circulating Libraries were not then in Use; but we agreed that on certain reasonable Terms which I have now forgotten, I might take, read and return any of his Books. This I esteem'd a great Advantage, and I made as much Use of it as I could.

My Pamphlet by some means falling into the Hands of one Lyons,[1] a Surgeon, Author of a Book entitled *The Infallibility of Human Judgment*, it occasioned an Acquaintance between us; he took great Notice of me, call'd on me often, to converse on these Subjects, carried me to the Horns a pale Ale-House in [blank] Lane, Cheapside, and introduc'd me to Dr. Mandeville,[2] Author of the Fable of the Bees who had a Club there, of which he was the Soul, being a most facetious entertaining Companion. Lyons too introduc'd me to Dr. Pemberton, at Batson's Coffee House,[3] who promis'd to give me an Opportunity some time or other of seeing Sir Isaac Newton,[4] of which I was extremely desirous; but this never happened.

I had brought over a few Curiosities among which the principal was a Purse made of the Asbestos, which purifies by Fire. Sir Hans Sloane[5] heard of it, came to see me, and invited me to his House in Bloomsbury Square; where he show'd me all his Curiosities, and persuaded me to let him add that to the Number, for which he paid me handsomely.

6. Just off Little Britain, and a square known for its printers and typesetters.
7. Proceeded with difficulty.
8. William Wollaston's *Religion of Nature* was first published in 1725. Franklin set the type for the 4th edition, which appeared in April 1726.
9. Franklin's pamphlet, of which only four copies are known to survive. By denying the existence of virtue and vice Franklin laid himself open to accusations of atheism.
1. William Lyons, a surgeon and author of *The Infallibility, Dignity, and Excellence of Human Judgment* (1719).
2. Bernard Mandeville (c. 1670–1733), a Dutch physician and man of letters residing in London. His *Fable of the Bees* was published in 1723.
3. Batson's in Cornhill was a favorite meeting place of physicians. Henry Pemberton (1694–1771) was a friend of Isaac Newton's and a member of the Royal Society.
4. Newton (1642–1727), best known for explaining the theories of gravity, light, and color, was president of the Royal Society from 1703 to 1727.
5. Physician and naturalist (1660–1753), who was the successor to Newton as president of the Royal Society. His library and museum served as the basis for the present collection at the British Museum.

In our House there lodg'd a young Woman, a Millener, who I think had a shop in the Cloisters.[6] She had been genteelly bred, was sensible and lively, and of most pleasing Conversation. Ralph read Plays to her in the Evenings, they grew intimate, she took another Lodging, and he follow'd her. They liv'd together some time, but he being still out of Business, and her Income not sufficient to maintain them with her Child, he took a Resolution of going from London, to try for a Country School, which he thought himself well qualified to undertake, as he wrote an excellent Hand, and was a Master of Arithmetic and Accounts. This however he deem'd a Business below him, and confident of future better Fortune when he should be unwilling to have it known that he once was so meanly employ'd, he chang'd his Name, and did me the Honor to assume mine. For I soon after had a Letter from him, acquainting me, that he was settled in a small Village in Berkshire, I think it was, where he taught reading and writing to 10 or a dozen Boys at 6 pence each per Week, recommending Mrs. T. to my Care, and desiring me to write to him directing for Mr. Franklin Schoolmaster at such a Place. He continu'd to write frequently, sending me large Specimens of an Epic Poem, which he was then composing, and desiring my Remarks and Corrections. These I gave him from time to time, but endeavor'd rather to discourage his Proceeding. One of Young's Satires was then just publish'd.[7] I copied and sent him a great Part of it, which set in a strong Light the Folly of pursuing the Muses with any Hope of Advancement by them. All was in vain. Sheets of the Poem continu'd to come by every Post. In the mean time Mrs. T. having on his Account lost her Friends and Business, was often in Distresses, and us'd to send for me, and borrow what I could spare to help her out of them. I grew fond of her Company, and being at this time under no Religious Restraints, and presuming on my Importance to her, I attempted Familiarities, (another Erratum) which she repuls'd with a proper Resentment, and acquainted him with my Behavior. This made a Breach between us, and when he return'd again to London, he let me know he thought I had cancel'd all the Obligations he had been under to me. So I found I was never to expect his Repaying me what I lent to him or advanc'd for him. This was however not then of much Consequence, as he was totally unable. And in the Loss of his Friendship I found myself reliev'd from a Burden. I now began to think of getting a little Money beforehand; and expecting better Work, I left Palmer's to work at Watts's[8] near Lincoln's Inn Fields, a still greater Printing-House. Here I continu'd all the rest of my Stay in London.

At my first Admission into this Printing-House, I took to working at Press, imagining I felt a Want of the Bodily Exercise I had been us'd to in America, where Presswork is mix'd with Composing. I drank only Water; the other Workmen, near 50 in Number, were great Guzzlers of Beer. On occasion I carried up and down Stairs a large Form of Types[9] in each hand, when others carried but one in both Hands. They wonder'd to see from this and several Instances that the Water-American as they call'd me was *stronger* than themselves who drunk *strong*[1] Beer. We had an Alehouse Boy who attended always in the House to supply the Workmen. My Companion at the Press drank every day a Pint before Breakfast, a Pint at Breakfast with his Bread

---

6. Probably near St. Bartholomew's Church, London.
7. Edward Young (1683–1765) published the first four parts of *Love of Fame, the Universal Passion* in 1725.
8. John Watts (c. 1678–1763).
9. Type set and locked in metal frames.
1. With high alcohol content.

and Cheese; a Pint between Breakfast and Dinner; a Pint at Dinner; a Pint in the Afternoon about Six o'clock, and another when he had done his Day's Work. I thought it a detestable Custom. But it was necessary, he suppos'd, to drink *strong* Beer that he might be *strong* to labor. I endeavor'd to convince him that the Bodily Strength afforded by Beer could only be in proportion to the Grain or Flour of the Barley dissolved in the Water of which it was made; that there was more Flour in a Penny-worth of Bread, and therefore if he would eat that with a Pint of Water, it would give him more Strength than a Quart of Beer. He drank on however, and had 4 or 5 Shillings to pay out of his Wages every Saturday Night for that muddling Liquor; an Expense I was free from. And thus these poor Devils keep themselves always under.[2]

Watts after some Weeks desiring to have me in the Composing-Room, I left the Pressmen. A new *Bienvenu*[3] or Sum for Drink, being 5 Shillings, was demanded of me by the Compositors.[4] I thought it an Imposition, as I had paid below. The Master thought so too, and forbad my Paying it. I stood out two or three Weeks, was accordingly considered as an Excommunicate, and had so many little Pieces of private Mischief done me, by mixing my Sorts,[5] transposing my Pages, breaking my Matter,[6] etc., etc. if I were ever so little out of the Room, and all ascrib'd to the Chapel[7] Ghost, which they said ever haunted those not regularly admitted, that notwithstanding the Master's Protection, I found myself oblig'd to comply and pay the Money; convinc'd of the Folly of being on ill Terms with those one is to live with continually. I was now on a fair Footing with them, and soon acquir'd considerable Influence. I propos'd some reasonable Alterations in their Chapel Laws, and carried them against all Opposition. From my Example a great Part of them, left their muddling Breakfast of Beer and Bread and Cheese, finding they could with me be supplied from a neighboring House with a large Porringer of hot Water-gruel, sprinkled with Pepper, crumb'd with Bread, and a Bit of Butter in it, for the Price of a Pint of Beer, viz., three halfpence. This was a more comfortable as well as cheaper Breakfast, and kept their Heads clearer. Those who continu'd sotting with Beer all day, were often, by not paying, out of Credit at the Alehouse, and us'd to make Interest with me to get Beer, *their Light,* as they phras'd it, *being out.* I watch'd the Pay table on Saturday Night, and collected what I stood engag'd for them, having to pay some times near Thirty Shillings a Week on their Accounts. This and my being esteem'd a pretty good Riggite,[8] that is a jocular verbal Satirist, supported my Consequence in the Society. My constant Attendance, (I never making a St. Monday),[9] recommended me to the Master; and my uncommon Quickness at Composing, occasion'd my being put upon all Work of Dispatch, which was generally better paid. So I went on now very agreeably.

My Lodging in Little Britain being too remote, I found another in Duke Street opposite to the Romish Chapel.[1] It was two pair of Stairs backwards at an Italian Warehouse. A Widow Lady kept the House; she had a Daughter and a Maid Servant, and a Journeyman who attended the Warehouse, but lodg'd abroad. After sending to enquire my Character at the House where

---

2. I.e., in poverty.
3. Welcome (French, literal trans.).
4. Typesetters.
5. Type, letters.
6. Type set up for printing.
7. "A Printing House is always called a Chapel by the Workmen" [Franklin's note]. The workers

set their own customs, practices, and fines.
8. One who makes fun of others.
9. Taking Monday off as if it were a religious holiday.
1. The Roman Catholic Chapel of St. Anselm and St. Cecilia.

I last lodg'd, she agreed to take me in at the same Rate, 3 Shillings 6 Pence per Week, cheaper as she said from the Protection she expected in having a Man lodge in the House. She was a Widow, an elderly Woman, had been bred a Protestant, being a Clergyman's Daughter, but was converted to the Catholic Religion by her Husband, whose Memory she much revered, had lived much among People of Distinction, and knew a 1000 Anecdotes of them as far back as the Times of Charles the second. She was lame in her Knees with the Gout, and therefore seldom stirr'd out of her Room, so sometimes wanted Company; and hers was so highly amusing to me that I was sure to spend an Evening with her whenever she desired it. Our Supper was only half an Anchovy each, on a very little Strip of Bread and Butter, and half a Pint of Ale between us. But the Entertainment was in her Conversation. My always keeping good Hours, and giving little Trouble in the Family, made her unwilling to part with me; so that when I talk'd of a Lodging I had heard of, nearer my Business, for 2 Shillings a Week, which, intent as I now was on saving Money, made some Difference; she bid me not think of it, for she would abate me two Shillings a Week for the future, so I remain'd with her at 1 Shilling 6 Pence as long as I stayed in London.

In a Garret of her House there lived a Maiden Lady of 70 in the most retired Manner, of whom my Landlady gave me this Account, that she was a Roman Catholic, had been sent abroad when young and lodg'd in a Nunnery with an Intent of becoming a Nun: but the Country not agreeing with her, she return'd to England, where there being no Nunnery, she had vow'd to lead the Life of a Nun as near as might be done in those Circumstances: Accordingly She had given all her Estate to charitable Uses, reserving only Twelve Pounds a year to live on, and out of this Sum she still gave a great deal in Charity, living herself on Watergruel only, and using no Fire but to boil it. She had lived many Years in that Garret, being permitted to remain there gratis by successive catholic Tenants of the House below, as they deem'd it a Blessing to have her there. A Priest visited her, to confess her every Day. I have ask'd her, says my Landlady, how she, as she liv'd, could possibly find so much Employment for a Confessor? O, says she, it is impossible to avoid *vain Thoughts*. I was permitted once to visit her: She was cheerful and polite, and convers'd pleasantly. The Room was clean, but had no other Furniture than a Mattress, a Table with a Crucifix and Book, a Stool, which she gave me to sit on, and a Picture over the Chimney of St. *Veronica*,[2] displaying her Handkerchief with the miraculous Figure of Christ's bleeding Face on it, which she explain'd to me with great Seriousness. She look'd pale, but was never sick, and I give it as another Instance on how small an Income Life and Health may be supported.

At Watts's Printing-House I contracted an Acquaintance with an ingenious young Man, one Wygate, who having wealthy Relations, had been better educated than most Printers, was a tolerable Latinist, spoke French, and lov'd Reading. I taught him, and a Friend of his, to swim at twice going into the River, and they soon became good Swimmers. They introduc'd me to some Gentlemen from the Country who went to Chelsea by Water to see the College and Don Saltero's Curiosities.[3] In our Return, at the Request

2. According to tradition, as Christ bore the Cross, St. Veronica wiped his face with a cloth that miraculously retained the image of his face.
3. James Salter was a former barber for Sir Hans Sloane; he kept supposed relics, like Job's tears and pieces of the true Cross, on view. He was dubbed Don Saltero by the *Tatler*. "College": i.e., Chelsea Hospital, erected on the site of the former Chelsea College.

of the Company, whose Curiosity Wygate had excited, I stripped and leaped into the River, and swam from near Chelsea to Blackfriars,[4] performing on the Way many Feats of Activity both upon and under Water, that surpris'd and pleas'd those to whom they were Novelties. I had from a Child been ever delighted with this Exercise, had studied and practic'd all Thevenot's[5] Motions and Positions, added some of my own, aiming at the graceful and easy, as well as the Useful. All these I took this Occasion of exhibiting to the Company, and was much flatter'd by their Admiration. And Wygate, who was desirous of becoming a Master, grew more and more attach'd to me on that account, as well as from the Similarity of our Studies. He at length propos'd to me traveling all over Europe together, supporting ourselves every where by working at our Business. I was once inclin'd to it. But mentioning it to my good Friend Mr. Denham, with whom I often spent an Hour when I had Leisure, he dissuaded me from it; advising me to think only of returning to Pennsylvania, which he was now about to do.

I must record one Trait of this good Man's Character. He had formerly been in Business at Bristol, but fail'd in Debt to a Number of People, compounded[6] and went to America. There, by a close Application to Business as a Merchant, he acquir'd a plentiful Fortune in a few Years. Returning to England in the Ship with me, He invited his old Creditors to an Entertainment, at which he thank'd them for the easy Composition[7] they had favor'd him with, and when they expected nothing but the Treat, every Man at the first Remove[8] found under his Plate an Order on a Banker for the full Amount of the unpaid Remainder with Interest.

He now told me he was about to return to Philadelphia, and should carry over a great Quantity of Goods in order to open a Store there: He propos'd to take me over as his Clerk, to keep his Books (in which he would instruct me), copy his Letters, and attend the Store. He added, that as soon as I should be acquainted with mercantile Business he would promote me by sending me with a Cargo of Flour and Bread, etc., to the West Indies, and procure me Commissions from others; which would be profitable, and if I manag'd well, would establish me handsomely. The Thing pleas'd me, for I was grown tired of London, remember'd with Pleasure the happy Months I had spent in Pennsylvania, and wish'd again to see it. Therefore I immediately agreed, on the Terms of Fifty Pounds a Year, Pennsylvania Money; less indeed than my then Gettings as a Compositor, but affording a better Prospect.

I now took Leave of Printing, as I thought for ever, and was daily employ'd in my new Business; going about with Mr. Denham among the Tradesmen, to purchase various Articles, and see them pack'd up, doing Errands, calling upon Workmen to dispatch, etc., and when all was on board, I had a few Days' Leisure. On one of these Days I was to my Surprise sent for by a great Man I knew only by Name, a Sir William Wyndham and I waited upon him. He had heard by some means or other of my Swimming from Chelsey to Blackfriars, and of my teaching Wygate and another young Man to swim in a few Hours. He had two Sons about to set out on their Travels; he wish'd to have them first taught Swimming; and propos'd to gratify me handsomely if I would teach them. They were not yet come to Town and my Stay was uncertain, so I could not undertake it. But from this Incident I thought

---

4. I.e., more than three miles.
5. Melchisédeck de Thevenot, *The Art of Swimming* (1699).
6. Settled part payment on his debts.

7. Conditions for accepting a declaration of bankruptcy.
8. I.e., the first time the plates were cleared.

it likely, that if I were to remain in England and open a Swimming School, I might get a good deal of Money. And it struck me so strongly, that had the Overture been sooner made me, probably I should not so soon have returned to America. After Many Years, you and I had something of more Importance to do with one of these Sons of Sir William Wyndham,[9] become Earl of Egremont, which I shall mention in its Place.[1]

Thus I spent about 18 Months in London. Most Part of the Time, I work'd hard at my Business, and spent but little upon myself except in seeing Plays, and in Books. My Friend Ralph had kept me poor. He owed me about 27 Pounds; which I was now never likely to receive; a great Sum out of my small Earnings. I lov'd him notwithstanding, for he had many amiable Qualities. Tho' I had by no means improv'd my Fortune, I had pick'd up some very ingenious Acquaintance whose Conversation was of great Advantage to me, and I had read considerably.

We sail'd from Gravesend on the 23d of July 1726. For The Incidents of the Voyage, I refer you to my Journal, where you will find them all minutely related. Perhaps the most important Part of that Journal is the *Plan*[2] to be found in it which I formed at Sea for regulating my future Conduct in Life. It is the more remarkable, as being form'd when I was so young, and yet being pretty faithfully adhered to quite thro' to old Age. We landed in Philadelphia the 11th of October, where I found sundry Alterations. Keith was no longer Governor, being superseded by Major Gordon:[3] I met him walking the Streets as a common Citizen. He seem'd a little asham'd at seeing me, but pass'd without saying anything. I should have been as much asham'd at seeing Miss Read, had not her Friends despairing with Reason of my Return, after the Receipt of my Letter, persuaded her to marry another, one Rogers, a Potter, which was done in my Absence. With him however she was never happy, and soon parted from him, refusing to cohabit with him, or bear his Name. It being now said that he had another Wife. He was a worthless Fellow tho' an excellent Workman which was the Temptation to her Friends. He got into Debt, and ran away in 1727 or 28, went to the West Indies, and died there. Keimer had got a better House, a Shop well supplied with Stationery, plenty of new Types, a number of Hands tho' none good, and seem'd to have a great deal of Business.

Mr. Denham took a Store in Water Street, where we open'd our Goods. I attended the Business diligently, studied Accounts, and grew in a little Time expert at selling. We lodg'd and boarded together, he counsel'd me as a Father, having a sincere Regard for me: I respected and lov'd him: and we might have gone on together very happily: But in the Beginning of February 1726/7 when I had just pass'd my 21st Year, we both were taken ill. My Distemper was a Pleurisy,[4] which very nearly carried me off: I suffered a good deal, gave up the Point[5] in my own Mind, and was rather disappointed when I found myself recovering; regretting in some degree that I must now sometime or other have all that disagreeable Work to do over again. I forget what his Distemper was. It held him a long time, and at length carried him off. He left me a small Legacy in a nuncupative Will,[6] as a Token of his Kind-

9. Chancellor of the exchequer and Tory leader in Parliament (1687–1740).
1. Franklin does not mention Charles Wyndham (1710–1763) again.
2. Only the "Outline" and "Preamble" of Franklin's *Plan* survive.

3. Patrick Gordon (1644–1736), governor of Pennsylvania from 1726 to 1736.
4. A disease of the lungs.
5. End; i.e., resigned himself to death.
6. An oral will.

ness for me, and he left me once more to the wide World. For the Store was taken into the Care of his Executors, and my Employment under him ended: My Brother-in-law Homes, being now at Philadelphia, advis'd my Return to my Business. And Keimer tempted me with an Offer of large Wages by the Year to come and take the Management of his Printing-House that he might better attend his Stationer's Shop. I had heard a bad Character of him in London, from his Wife and her Friends, and was not fond of having any more to do with him. I tried for farther Employment as a Merchant's Clerk; but not readily meeting with any, I clos'd again with Keimer.

I found in *his* House these Hands; Hugh Meredith[7] a Welsh-Pennsylvanian, 30 Years of Age, bred to Country Work: honest, sensible, had a great deal of solid Observation, was something of a Reader, but given to drink: Stephen Potts,[8] a young Country Man of full Age, bred to the Same, of uncommon natural Parts[9] and great Wit and Humor, but a little idle. These he had agreed with at extreme low Wages, per Week, to be rais'd a Shilling every 3 Months, as they would deserve by improving in their Business, and the Expectation of these high Wages to come on hereafter was what he had drawn them in with. Meredith was to work at Press, Potts at Bookbinding, which he by Agreement, was to teach them, tho' he knew neither one nor t'other. John ——— a wild Irishman brought up to no Business, whose Service for 4 Years Keimer had purchas'd[1] from the Captain of a Ship. He too was to be made a Pressman. George Webb,[2] an Oxford Scholar, whose Time for 4 Years he had likewise bought, intending him for a Compositor: of whom more presently. And David Harry,[3] a Country Boy, whom he had taken Apprentice. I soon perceiv'd that the Intention of engaging me at Wages so much higher than he had been us'd to give, was to have these raw cheap Hands form'd thro' me, and as soon as I had instructed them, then, they being all articled to him, he should be able to do without me. I went on however, very cheerfully; put his Printing-House in Order, which had been in great Confusion, and brought his Hands by degrees to mind their Business and to do it better.

It was an odd Thing to find an Oxford Scholar in the Situation of a bought Servant. He was not more than 18 Years of Age, and gave me this Account of himself; that he was born in Gloucester, educated at a Grammar School there, had been distinguish'd among the Scholars for some apparent Superiority in performing his Part when they exhibited Plays; belong'd to the Witty Club there, and had written some Pieces in Prose and Verse which were printed in the Gloucester Newspapers. Thence he was sent to Oxford; there he continu'd about a Year, but not well-satisfied, wishing of all things to see London and become a Player. At length receiving his Quarterly Allowance of 15 Guineas, instead of discharging his Debts, he walk'd out of Town, hid his Gown in a Furz Bush,[4] and footed it to London, where having no Friend to advise him, he fell into bad Company, soon spent his Guineas, found no means of being introduc'd among the Players, grew necessitous, pawn'd his Clothes and wanted Bread. Walking the Street very hungry, and not knowing

7. Hugh Meredith (c. 1696–1749), later a business partner of Franklin's.

8. Later a bookseller and innkeeper (d. 1758).

9. I.e., handsome.

1. I.e., Keimer had paid for his passage in exchange for his service.

2. Later a member of Franklin's Junto Club and printer (1708–1736?).

3. A Welsh Quaker (1708–1760) and later first printer in Barbados.

4. An evergreen shrub; gorse. "Gown": academic robe worn regularly by Oxford students. "Player": actor.

what to do with himself, a Crimp's Bill[5] was put into his Hand, offering immediate Entertainment and Encouragement to such as would bind themselves to serve in America. He went directly, sign'd the Indentures, was put into the Ship and came over; never writing a Line to acquaint his Friends what was become of him. He was lively, witty, good-natur'd and a pleasant Companion, but idle, thoughtless and imprudent to the last Degree.

John the Irishman soon ran away. With the rest I began to live very agreeably; for they all respected me, the more as they found Keimer incapable of instructing them, and that from me they learned something daily. We never work'd on a Saturday, that being Keimer's Sabbath. So I had two Days for Reading. My Acquaintance with ingenious People in the Town increased. Keimer himself treated me with great Civility and apparent Regard; and nothing now made me uneasy but my Debt to Vernon, which I was yet unable to pay, being hitherto but a poor Economist. He however kindly made no Demand of it.

Our Printing-House often wanted Sorts,[6] and there was no Letter Founder in America. I had seen Types cast at James's[7] in London, but without much Attention to the Manner: However I now contriv'd a Mold, made use of the Letters we had as Puncheons, struck the Matrices[8] in Lead, and thus supplied in a pretty tolerable way all Deficiencies. I also engrav'd several Things on occasion. I made the Ink, I was Warehouse-man and everything, in short quite a Factotum.[9]

But however serviceable I might be, I found that my Services became every Day of less Importance, as the other Hands improv'd in the Business. And when Keimer paid my second Quarter's Wages, he let me know that he felt them too heavy, and thought I should make an Abatement. He grew by degrees less civil, put on more of the Master, frequently found Fault, was captious and seem'd ready for an Out-breaking. I went on nevertheless with a good deal of Patience, thinking that his encumber'd Circumstances were partly the Cause. At length a Trifle snapped our Connection. For a great Noise happening near the Courthouse, I put my Head out of the Window to see what was the Matter. Keimer being in the Street look'd up and saw me, call'd out to me in a loud Voice and angry Tone to mind my Business, adding some reproachful Words, that nettled me the more for their Publicity, all the Neighbors who were looking out on the same Occasion being Witnesses how I was treated. He came up immediately into the Printing-House, continu'd the Quarrel, high Words pass'd on both Sides, he gave me the Quarter's Warning we had stipulated, expressing a Wish that he had not been oblig'd to so long a Warning: I told him his Wish was unnecessary for I would leave him that Instant; and so taking my Hat walk'd out of Doors; desiring Meredith whom I saw below to take care of some Things I left, and bring them to my Lodging.

Meredith came accordingly in the Evening, when we talk'd my Affair over. He had conceiv'd a great Regard for me, and was very unwilling that I should leave the House while he remain'd in it. He dissuaded me from returning to my native Country[1] which I began to think of. He reminded me that Keimer

5. An advertisement for free passage to the colonies for those who would work as indentured servants.
6. See n. 5, p. 277.
7. Thomas James's foundry in London.

8. Molds for casting type. "Puncheons": stamping tools.
9. Jack-of-all-trades.
1. I.e., Boston.

was in debt for all he possess'd, that his Creditors began to be uneasy, that he kept his Shop miserably, sold often without Profit for ready Money, and often trusted without keeping Account. That he must therefore fail; which would make a Vacancy I might profit of. I objected my Want of Money. He then let me know, that his Father had a high Opinion of me, and from some Discourse that had pass'd between them, he was sure would advance Money to set us up, if I would enter into Partnership with him. My Time, says he, will be out with Keimer in the Spring. By that time we may have our Press and Types in from London: I am sensible I am no Workman. If you like it, Your Skill in the Business shall be set against the Stock I furnish; and we will share the Profits equally. The Proposal was agreeable, and I consented. His Father was in Town, and approv'd of it, the more as he saw I had great Influence with his Son, had prevail'd on him to abstain long from Dram-drinking,[2] and he hop'd might break him of that wretched Habit entirely, when we came to be so closely connected. I gave an Inventory to the Father, who carried it to a Merchant; the Things were sent for; the Secret was to be kept till they should arrive, and in the mean time I was to get Work if I could at the other Printing-House. But I found no Vacancy there, and so remain'd idle a few Days, when Keimer, on a Prospect of being employ'd to print some Paper-money, in New Jersey, which would require Cuts and various Types that I only could supply, and apprehending Bradford might engage me and get the Job from him, sent me a very civil Message, that old Friends should not part for a few Words, the Effect of sudden Passion, and wishing me to return. Meredith persuaded me to comply, as it would give more Opportunity for his Improvement under my daily Instructions. So I return'd, and we went on more smoothly than for some time before. The New Jersey Job was obtain'd. I contriv'd a Copper-Plate Press for it, the first that had been seen in the Country. I cut several Ornaments and Checks for the Bills. We went together to Burlington,[3] where I executed the Whole to Satisfaction, and he received so large a Sum for the Work, as to be enabled thereby to keep his Head much longer above Water.

    At Burlington I made an Acquaintance with many principal People of the Province. Several of them had been appointed by the Assembly a Committee to attend the Press, and take Care that no more Bills were printed than the Law directed. They were therefore by Turns constantly with us, and generally he who attended brought with him a Friend or two for Company. My Mind having been much more improv'd by Reading than Keimer's, I suppose it was for that Reason my Conversation seem'd to be more valu'd. They had me to their Houses, introduc'd me to their Friends and show'd me much Civility, while he, tho' the Master, was a little neglected. In truth he was an odd Fish, ignorant of common Life, fond of rudely opposing receiv'd Opinions, slovenly to extreme dirtiness, enthusiastic[4] in some Points of Religion, and a little Knavish withal. We continu'd there near 3 Months, and by that time I could reckon among my acquired Friends, Judge Allen, Samuel Bustill, the Secretary of the Province, Isaac Pearson, Joseph Cooper and several of the Smiths, Members of Assembly, and Isaac Decow the Surveyor General. The latter was a shrewd sagacious old Man, who told me that he began for himself when young by wheeling Clay for the Brickmakers, learned to write

2. Frequently drinking small measures of alcohol.   4. Highly emotional.
3. New Jersey.

after he was of Age, carried the Chain for Surveyors, who taught him Surveying, and he had now by his Industry acquir'd a good Estate; and says he, I foresee, that you will soon work this Man out of his Business and make a Fortune in it at Philadelphia. He had not then the least Intimation of my Intention to set up there or anywhere. These Friends were afterwards of great Use to me, as I occasionally was to some of them. They all continued their Regard for me as long as they lived.

Before I enter upon my public Appearance in Business, it may be well to let you know the then State of my Mind, with regard to my Principles and Morals, that you may see how far those influenc'd the future Events of my Life. My Parents had early given me religious Impressions, and brought me through my Childhood piously in the Dissenting Way.[5] But I was scarce 15 when, after doubting by turns of several Points as I found them disputed in the different Books I read, I began to doubt of Revelation itself. Some Books against Deism fell into my Hands; they were said to be the Substance of Sermons preached at Boyle's Lectures.[6] It happened that they wrought an Effect on me quite contrary to what was intended by them: For the Arguments of the Deists which were quoted to be refuted, appeared to me much Stronger than the Refutations. In short I soon became a thorough Deist. My Arguments perverted some others, particularly Collins and Ralph: but each of them having afterwards wrong'd me greatly without the least Compunction, and recollecting Keith's Conduct towards me, (who was another Freethinker) and my own towards Vernon and Miss Read which at Times gave me great Trouble, I began to suspect that this Doctrine tho' it might be true, was not very useful. My London pamphlet, which had for its Motto those Lines of Dryden

> ——Whatever is, is right
> Tho' purblind Man Sees but a Part of
> The Chain, the nearest Link,
> His Eyes not carrying to the equal Beam,
> That poizes all, above.[7]

[And from the Attributes of God, his infinite Wisdom, Goodness and Power concluded that nothing could possibly be wrong in the World, and that Vice and Virtue were empty Distinctions, no such Things existing:] appear'd now not so clever a Performance as I once thought it; and I doubted whether some Error had not insinuated itself unperceiv'd into my Argument, so as to infect all that follow'd, as is common in metaphysical Reasonings. I grew convinc'd that *Truth, Sincerity* and *Integrity* in Dealings between Man and Man, were of the utmost Importance to the Felicity of Life, and I form'd written Resolutions, (which still remain in my Journal Book) to practice them ever while I lived. Revelation had indeed no weight with me as such; but I entertain'd an Opinion, that tho' certain Actions might not be bad *because* they were forbidden by it, or good *because* it commanded them; yet probably those Actions might be forbidden *because* they were bad for us, or commanded *because* they were beneficial to us, in their own Natures, all

5. I.e., in the Congregational or Presbyterian way, as opposed to the Church of England.
6. Robert Boyle (1627–1691), English physicist and chemist, endowed a series of lectures for discussing the existence of God and preaching against "infidels." Deism accepts a supreme being as the author of finite existence, but denies Christian doctrines of revelation and supernaturalism.
7. The first line is not from John Dryden (1631–1700) but from Alexander Pope's *Essay on Man* (1733), Epistle I, line 294; however, Dryden's line is close: "Whatever is, is in its Causes just." The rest of the poem is recalled accurately from Dryden's *Oedipus* (3.1.244–48).

the Circumstances of things considered. And this Persuasion, with the kind hand of Providence, or some guardian Angel, or accidental favorable Circumstances and Situations, or all together, preserved me (thro' this dangerous Time of Youth and the hazardous Situations I was sometimes in among Strangers, remote from the Eye and Advice of my Father) without any *willful* gross Immorality or Injustice that might have been expected from my Want of Religion. I say *willful,* because the Instances I have mentioned, had something of *Necessity* in them, from my Youth, Inexperience, and the Knavery of others. I had therefore a tolerable Character to begin the World with, I valued it properly, and determin'd to preserve it. STOP

We had not been long return'd to Philadelphia, before the New Types arriv'd from London. We settled with Keimer, and left him by his Consent before he heard of it. We found a House to hire near the Market, and took it. To lessen the Rent, (which was then but 24 Pounds a Year tho' I have since known it let for 70) we took in Thomas Godfrey a Glazier,[8] and his Family, who were to pay a considerable Part of it to us, and we to board with them. We had scarce opened our Letters and put our Press in Order, before George House, an Acquaintance of mine, brought a Countryman to us; whom he had met in the Street enquiring for a Printer. All our Cash was now expended in the Variety of Particulars we had been obliged to procure, and this Countryman's Five Shillings, being our First Fruits and coming so seasonably, gave me more Pleasure than any Crown[9] I have since earn'd; and from the Gratitude I felt towards House, has made me often more ready than perhaps I should otherwise have been to assist young Beginners.

There are Croakers in every Country always boding its Ruin. Such a one then lived in Philadelphia, a Person of Note, an elderly Man, with a wise Look and very grave Manner of Speaking. His Name was Samuel Mickle. This Gentleman, a Stranger to me, stopped one Day at my Door, and ask'd me if I was the young Man who had lately opened a new Printing-House: Being answer'd in the Affirmative; He said he was sorry for me; because it was an expensive Undertaking, and the Expense would be lost, for Philadelphia was a sinking[1] Place, the People already half Bankrupts or near being so; all Appearances of the contrary such as new Buildings and the Rise of Rents, being to his certain Knowledge fallacious, for they were in fact among the Things that would soon ruin us. And he gave me such a Detail of Misfortunes now existing or that were soon to exist, that he left me half-melancholy. Had I known him before I engag'd in this Business, probably I never should have done it. This Man continu'd to live in this decaying Place, and to declaim in the same Strain, refusing for many Years to buy a House there, because all was going to Destruction, and at last I had the Pleasure of seeing him give five times as much for one as he might have bought it for when he first began his Croaking.

I should have mention'd before, that in the Autumn of the preceding Year, I had form'd most of my ingenious Acquaintance into a Club, for mutual Improvement, which we call'd the Junto.[2] We met on Friday Evenings. The Rules I drew up, requir'd that every Member in his Turn should produce one or more Queries on any Point of Morals, Politics or Natural Philosophy, to

8. A man who sets glass for windowpanes.
9. A coin worth five shillings.
1. Economically declining.

2. I.e., a small, select group (the name is taken from the Spanish word *junta,* "council").

be discuss'd by the Company, and once in three Months produce and read an Essay of his own Writing on any Subject he pleased. Our Debates were to be under the Direction of a President, and to be conducted in the sincere Spirit of Enquiry after Truth, without fondness for Dispute, or Desire of Victory; and to prevent Warmth, all expressions of Positiveness in Opinion, or of direct Contradiction, were after some time made contraband and prohibited under small pecuniary Penalties. The first Members were, Joseph Breintnall,[3] a Copier of Deeds for the Scriveners; a good-natur'd friendly middle-ag'd Man, a great Lover of Poetry, reading all he could meet with, and writing some that was tolerable; very ingenious in many little Nicknackeries, and of sensible Conversation. Thomas Godfrey,[4] a self-taught Mathematician, great in his Way, and afterwards Inventor of what is now call'd Hadley's Quadrant.[5] But he knew little out of his way, and was not a pleasing Companion, as like most Great Mathematicians I have met with, he expected unusual Precision in everything said, or was forever denying or distinguishing upon Trifles, to the Disturbance of all Conversation. He soon left us. Nicholas Scull,[6] a Surveyor, afterwards Surveyor-General, Who lov'd Books, and sometimes made a few Verses. William Parsons,[7] bred a Shoemaker, but loving Reading, had acquir'd a considerable Share of Mathematics, which he first studied with a View to Astrology that he afterwards laughed at. He also became Surveyor General. William Maugridge, a Joiner,[8] and a most exquisite Mechanic, and a solid sensible Man. Hugh Meredith, Stephen Potts, and George Webb, I have Characteris'd before. Robert Grace,[9] a young Gentleman of some Fortune, generous, lively and witty, a Lover of Punning and of his Friends. And William Coleman,[1] then a Merchant's Clerk, about my Age, who had the coolest clearest Head, the best Heart, and the exactest Morals, of almost any Man I ever met with. He became afterwards a Merchant of great Note, and one of our Provincial Judges: Our Friendship continued without Interruption to his Death, upwards of 40 Years. And the Club continu'd almost as long and was the best School of Philosophy, Morals and Politics that then existed in the Province; for our Queries which were read the Week preceding their Discussion, put us on reading with Attention upon the several Subjects, that we might speak more to the purpose: and here too we acquired better Habits of Conversation, everything being studied in our Rules which might prevent our disgusting each other. From hence the long Continuance of the Club, which I shall have frequent Occasion to speak farther of hereafter; But my giving this Account of it here, is to show something of the Interest I had, everyone of these exerting themselves in recommending Business to us.

Breintnall particularly procur'd us from the Quakers, the Printing 40 Sheets of their History, the rest being to be done by Keimer: and upon this we work'd exceeding hard, for the Price was low. It was a Folio, Pro Patria Size, in Pica with Long Primer Notes.[2] I compos'd of it a Sheet a Day, and Meredith work'd it off at Press. It was often 11 at Night and sometimes later, before I had finish'd my Distribution[3] for the next day's Work: For the little

3. Breintnall (d. 1746) shared Franklin's interest in science. "Warmth": anger. "Positiveness": certainty.
4. Godfrey (1704–1749).
5. An instrument for measuring altitudes in navigation and astronomy.
6. Nicholas Scull II (1687–1761).
7. Parsons (1701–1757) became surveyor general

in 1741 and librarian of the Library Company.
8. A ship's carpenter (d. 1766).
9. Franklin's landlord for thirty-seven years.
1. Coleman (1704–1769).
2. A book of large size, with the main text in twelve-point type and the notes in ten-point type.
3. I.e., of type, returning letters to their cases so that they may be used again.

Jobs sent in by our other Friends now and then put us back. But so determin'd I was to continue doing a Sheet a Day of the Folio, that one Night when having impos'd my Forms,[4] I thought my Day's Work over, one of them by accident was broken and two Pages reduc'd to Pie,[5] I immediately distributed and compos'd it over again before I went to bed. And this Industry visible to our Neighbors began to give us Character and Credit; particularly I was told, that mention being made of the new Printing Office at the Merchants' Every-night-Club, the general Opinion was that it must fail, there being already two Printers in the Place, Keimer and Bradford; but Doctor Baird (whom you and I saw many Years after at his native Place, St. Andrews in Scotland) gave a contrary Opinion; for the Industry of that Franklin, says he, is superior to anything I ever saw of the kind: I see him still at work when I go home from Club; and he is at Work again before his Neighbors are out of bed. This struck the rest, and we soon after had Offers from one of them to supply us with Stationery. But as yet we did not choose to engage in Shop Business.

I mention this Industry the more particularly and the more freely, tho' it seems to be talking in my own Praise, that those of my Posterity who shall read it, may know the Use of that Virtue, when they see its Effects in my Favor throughout this Relation.

George Webb, who had found a Friend that lent him wherewith to pur-chase his Time of Keimer, now came to offer himself as a Journeyman to us. We could not then employ him, but I foolishly let him know, as a Secret, that I soon intended to begin a Newspaper, and might then have Work for him. My Hopes of Success as I told him were founded on this, that the then only Newspaper,[6] printed by Bradford was a paltry thing, wretchedly manag'd, no way entertaining; and yet was profitable to him. I therefore thought a good Paper could scarcely fail of good Encouragement. I requested Webb not to mention it, but he told it to Keimer, who immediately, to be beforehand with me, published Proposals for Printing one himself, on which Webb was to be employ'd. I resented this, and to counteract them, as I could not yet begin our Paper, I wrote several Pieces of Entertainment for Bradford's Paper, under the Title of the Busy Body which Breintnall continu'd some Months.[7] By this means the Attention of the Public was fix'd on that Paper, and Keimer's Proposals which we burlesqu'd and ridicul'd, were disregarded. He began his Paper however, and after carrying it on three Quarters of a Year, with at most only 90 Subscribers, he offer'd it to me for a Trifle, and I having been ready some time to go on with it, took it in hand directly, and it prov'd in a few Years extremely profitable to me.[8]

I perceive that I am apt to speak in the singular Number, though our Partnership still continu'd. The Reason may be, that in fact the whole Man-agement of the Business lay upon me. Meredith was no Compositor, a poor Pressman, and seldom sober. My Friends lamented my Connection with him, but I was to make the best of it.

Our first Papers made a quite different Appearance from any before in the Province, a better Type and better printed: but some spirited Remarks of my Writing on the Dispute then going on between Governor Burnet[9] and the

---

4. Locked the type into its form and readied it for printing.
5. A confused pile.
6. The *American Weekly Mercury*.
7. From February 4, 1728, to September 25, 1729.

8. Franklin took over Keimer's *The Universal Instructor in All Arts and Sciences: and Pennsyl-vania Gazette* in October 1729 and shortened the name to the *Pennsylvania Gazette*.
9. See n. 3, p. 268.

Massachusetts Assembly, struck the principal People, occasion'd the Paper and the Manager of it to be much talk'd of, and in a few Weeks brought them all to be our Subscribers. Their Example was follow'd by many, and our Number went on growing continually. This was one of the first good Effects of my having learned a little to scribble. Another was, that the leading Men, seeing a Newspaper now in the hands of one who could also handle a Pen, thought it convenient to oblige and encourage me. Bradford still printed the Votes and Laws and other Public Business. He had printed an Address of the House[1] to the Governor in a coarse blundering manner; We reprinted it elegantly and correctly, and sent one to every Member. They were sensible of the Difference, it strengthen'd the Hands of our Friends in the House, and they voted us their Printers for the Year ensuing.

Among my Friends in the House I must not forget Mr. Hamilton[2] before-mentioned, who was then returned from England and had a Seat in it. He interested himself[3] for me strongly in that Instance, as he did in many others afterwards, continuing his Patronage till his Death. Mr. Vernon about this time put me in mind of the Debt I ow'd him: but did not press me. I wrote him an ingenuous Letter of Acknowledgments, crav'd his Forbearance a little longer which he allow'd me, and as soon as I was able I paid the Principal with Interest and many Thanks. So that Erratum was in some degree corrected.

But now another Difficulty came upon me, which I had never the least Reason to expect. Mr. Meredith's Father, who was to have paid for our Printing-House according to the Expectations given me, was able to advance only one Hundred Pounds, Currency, which had been paid, and a Hundred more was due to the Merchant; who grew impatient and su'd us all. We gave Bail, but saw that if the Money could not be rais'd in time, the Suit must come to a Judgment and Execution, and our hopeful Prospects must with us be ruined, as the Press and Letters must be sold for Payment, perhaps at half-Price. In this Distress two true Friends whose Kindness I have never forgotten nor ever shall forget while I can remember anything, came to me separately unknown to each other, and without any Application from me, offering each of them to advance me all the Money that should be necessary to enable me to take the whole Business upon myself if that should be practicable, but they did not like my continuing the Partnership with Meredith, who as they said was often seen drunk in the Streets, and playing at low Games in Alehouses, much to our Discredit. These two Friends were *William Coleman* and *Robert Grace*.

I told them I could not propose a Separation while any Prospect remain'd of the Merediths fulfilling their Part of our Agreement. Because I thought myself under great Obligations to them for what they had done and would do if they could. But if they finally fail'd in their Performance, and our Partnership must be dissolv'd, I should then think myself at Liberty to accept the Assistance of my Friends. Thus the matter rested for some time. When I said to my Partner, perhaps your Father is dissatisfied at the Part you have undertaken in this Affair of ours, and is unwilling to advance for you and me what he would for you alone: If that is the Case, tell me, and I will resign the whole to you and go about my Business. No—says he, my Father has really been

---

1. I.e., the Pennsylvania Assembly.
2. Andrew Hamilton.
3. "I got his Son once £500" [Franklin's note].

Franklin was able to get the legislature to pay Governor James Hamilton his salary when they were at odds with him.

disappointed and is really unable; and I am unwilling to distress him farther. I see this is a Business I am not fit for. I was bred a Farmer, and it was a Folly in me to come to Town and put myself at 30 Years of Age an Apprentice to learn a new Trade. Many of our Welsh People are going to settle in North Carolina where Land is cheap: I am inclin'd to go with them, and follow my old Employment. You may find Friends to assist you. If you will take the Debts of the Company upon you, return to my Father the hundred Pound he has advanc'd, pay my little personal Debts, and give me Thirty Pounds and a new Saddle, I will relinquish the Partnership and leave the whole in your Hands. I agreed to this Proposal. It was drawn up in Writing, sign'd and seal'd immediately. I gave him what he demanded and he went soon after to Carolina; from whence he sent me next Year two long Letters, containing the best Account that had been given of that Country, the Climate, Soil, Husbandry, etc., for in those Matters he was very judicious. I printed them in the Papers,[4] and they gave great Satisfaction to the Public.

As soon as he was gone, I recurr'd to my two Friends; and because I would not give an unkind Preference to either, I took half what each had offered and I wanted, of one, and half of the other; paid off the Company Debts, and went on with the Business in my own Name, advertising that the Partnership was dissolved. I think this was in or about the Year 1729.[5]

About this Time there was a Cry among the People for more Paper-Money, only 15,000 Pounds being extant in the Province and that soon to be sunk.[6] The wealthy Inhabitants oppos'd any Addition, being against all Paper Currency, from an Apprehension that it would depreciate as it had done in New England to the Prejudice of all Creditors. We had discuss'd this Point in our Junto, where I was on the Side of an Addition, being persuaded that the first small Sum struck in 1723 had done much good, by increasing the Trade, Employment, and Number of Inhabitants in the Province, since I now saw all the old Houses inhabited, and many new ones building, where as I remember'd well, that when I first walk'd about the Streets of Philadelphia, eating my Roll, I saw most of the Houses in Walnut Street between Second and Front Streets with Bills[7] on their Doors, to be let; and many likewise in Chestnut Street, and other Streets; which made me then think the Inhabitants of the City were one after another deserting it. Our Debates possess'd me so fully of the Subject, that I wrote and printed an anonymous Pamphlet on it, entitled, *The Nature and Necessity of a Paper Currency*.[8] It was well receiv'd by the common People in general; but the Rich Men dislik'd it; for it increas'd and strengthen'd the Clamor for more Money; and they happening to have no Writers among them that were able to answer it, their Opposition slacken'd, and the Point was carried by a Majority in the House. My Friends there, who conceiv'd I had been of some Service, thought fit to reward me, by employing me in printing the Money,[9] a very profitable Job, and a great Help to me. This was another Advantage gain'd by my being able to write. The Utility of this Currency became by Time and Experience so evident, as never afterwards

4. In the *Pennsylvania Gazette*, May 6 and 13, 1732.
5. More accurately, July 14, 1730.
6. Destroyed. In 1723 paper money had become so scarce that the Assembly issued new money secured by real estate mortgages; when the mortgages were paid off, the bills were "sunk." But by 1729 the value of the currency was so low that the money was recalled before the mortgages were paid.
7. Signs.
8. *A Modest Inquiry into the Nature and Necessity of a Paper Currency* (April 3, 1729).
9. Franklin received the contract to print money in 1731.

to be much disputed, so that it grew soon to 55,000 Pounds, and in 1739 to 80,000 Pounds, since which it arose during War to upwards of 350,000 Pounds—Trade, Building and Inhabitants all the while increasing. Tho' I now think there are Limits beyond which the Quantity may be hurtful.

I soon after obtain'd, thro' my Friend Hamilton, the Printing of the New Castle[1] Paper Money, another profitable Job, as I then thought it; small Things appearing great to those in small Circumstances. And these to me were really great Advantages, as they were great Encouragements. He procured me also the Printing of the Laws and Votes of that Government which continu'd in my Hands as long as I follow'd the Business.

START I now open'd a little Stationer's Shop.[2] I had in it Blanks of all Sorts the correctest that ever appear'd among us, being assisted in that by my Friend Breintnall; I had also Paper, Parchment, Chapmen's Books,[3] etc. One Whitmarsh[4] a Compositor I had known in London, an excellent Workman now came to me and work'd with me constantly and diligently, and I took an Apprentice the Son of Aquila Rose. I began now gradually to pay off the Debt I was under for the Printing-House. In order to secure my Credit and Character as a Tradesman, I took care not only to be in *Reality* Industrious and frugal, but to avoid all *Appearances* of the contrary. I dressed plainly; I was seen at no Places of idle Diversion; I never went out a-fishing or shooting; a Book, indeed, sometimes debauch'd me from my Work; but that was seldom, snug, and gave no Scandal: and to show that I was not above my Business, I sometimes brought home the Paper I purchas'd at the Stores, thro' the Streets on a Wheelbarrow. Thus being esteem'd an industrious thriving young Man, and paying duly for what I bought, the Merchants who imported Stationery solicited my Custom, others propos'd supplying me with Books, and I went on swimmingly. In the mean time Keimer's Credit and Business declining daily, he was at last forc'd to sell his Printing-House to satisfy his Creditors. He went to Barbados, and there lived some Years, in very poor Circumstances. STOP

His Apprentice David Harry, whom I had instructed while I work'd with him, set up in his Place at Philadelphia, having bought his Materials. I was at first apprehensive of a powerful Rival in Harry, as his Friends were very able, and had a good deal of Interest. I therefore propos'd a Partnership to him; which he, fortunately for me, rejected with Scorn. He was very proud, dress'd like a Gentleman, liv'd expensively, took much Diversion and Pleasure abroad, ran in debt, and neglected his Business, upon which all Business left him; and finding nothing to do, he follow'd Keimer to Barbados; taking the Printing-House with him. There this Apprentice employ'd his former Master as a Journeyman. They quarrel'd often. Harry went continually behind-hand, and at length was forc'd to sell his Types, and return to his Country Work in Pennsylvania. The Person that bought them employ'd Keimer to use them, but in a few years he died. There remain'd now no Competitor with me at Philadelphia, but the old one, Bradford, who was rich and easy, did a little Printing now and then by straggling Hands, but was not very anxious about the Business. However, as he kept the Post Office, it was imagined he had better Opportunities of obtaining News, his Paper was thought a

1. In Delaware. Delaware had a separate legislature but the same proprietary governor as Pennsylvania.
2. In July 1730.

3. Inexpensive paper pamphlets.
4. Thomas Whitmarsh (d. 1733); the following year Whitmarsh went to South Carolina.

better Distributer of Advertisements than mine, and therefore had many more, which was a profitable thing to him and a Disadvantage to me. For tho' I did indeed receive and send Papers by the Post, yet the public Opinion was otherwise; for what I did send was by Bribing the Riders[5] who took them privately: Bradford being unkind enough to forbid it: which occasion'd some Resentment on my Part; and I thought so meanly of him for it, that when I afterwards came into his Situation,[6] I took care never to imitate it.

I had hitherto continu'd to board with Godfrey who lived in Part of my House with his Wife and Children, and had one Side of the Shop for his Glazier's Business, tho' he work'd little, being always absorb'd in his Mathematics. Mrs. Godfrey projected a Match for me with a Relation's Daughter, took Opportunities of bringing us often together, till a serious Courtship on my Part ensu'd, the Girl being in herself very deserving. The old Folks encourag'd me by continual Invitations to Supper, and by leaving us together, till at length it was time to explain. Mrs. Godfrey manag'd our little Treaty. I let her know that I expected as much Money with their Daughter as would pay off my Remaining Debt for the Printing-House, which I believe was not then above a Hundred Pounds.[7] She brought me Word they had no such Sum to spare. I said they might mortgage their House in the Loan Office. The Answer to this after some Days was, that they did not approve the Match; that on Enquiry of Bradford they had been inform'd the Printing Business was not a profitable one, the Types would soon be worn out and more wanted, that S. Keimer and D. Harry had fail'd one after the other, and I should probably soon follow them; and therefore I was forbidden the House, and the Daughter shut up.

Whether this was a real Change of Sentiment, or only Artifice, on a Supposition of our being too far engag'd in Affection to retract, and therefore that we should steal a Marriage, which would leave them at Liberty to give or withhold what they pleas'd, I know not: But I suspected the latter, resented it, and went no more. Mrs. Godfrey brought me afterwards some more favorable Accounts of their Disposition, and would have drawn me on again: But I declared absolutely my Resolution to have nothing more to do with that Family. This was resented by the Godfreys, we differ'd, and they removed, leaving me the whole House, and I resolved to take no more Inmates. But this Affair having turn'd my Thoughts to Marriage, I look'd round me, and made Overtures of Acquaintance in other Places; but soon found that the Business of a Printer being generally thought a poor one, I was not to expect Money with a Wife unless with such a one, as I should not otherwise think agreeable. In the mean time, that hard-to-be-govern'd Passion of Youth, had hurried me frequently into Intrigues with low Women that fell in my Way, which were attended with some Expense and great Inconvenience, besides a continual Risk to my Health by a Distemper[8] which of all Things I dreaded, tho' by great good Luck I escaped it.

A friendly Correspondence as Neighbors and old Acquaintances, had continued between me and Mrs. Read's Family who all had a Regard for me from the time of my first Lodging in their House. I was often invited there

5. I.e., the postal riders or carriers. Franklin bribed them to have his papers delivered on the same day as Bradford's.
6. Franklin assumed Bradford's office as postmaster of Philadelphia in October 1737.

7. Franklin's expectations were not unusual: marriage arrangements often hinged on agreeable financial considerations.
8. I.e., syphilis.

and consulted in their Affairs, wherein I sometimes was of Service. I pitied poor Miss Read's unfortunate Situation, who was generally dejected, seldom cheerful, and avoided Company. I consider'd my Giddiness and Inconstancy when in London as in a great degree the Cause of her Unhappiness; tho' the Mother was good enough to think the Fault more her own than mine, as she had prevented our Marrying before I went thither, and persuaded the other Match in my Absence. Our mutual Affection was revived, but there were now great Objections to our Union. That Match was indeed look'd upon as invalid, a preceding Wife being said to be living in England; but this could not easily be prov'd, because of the Distance, etc. And tho' there was a Report of his Death, it was not certain. Then, tho' it should be true, he had left many Debts which his Successor might be call'd upon to pay. We ventured however, over all these Difficulties, and I took her to Wife Sept. 1, 1730.[9] None of the Inconveniencies happened that we had apprehended, she prov'd a good and faithful Helpmate, assisted me much by attending the Shop, we throve together, and have ever mutually endeavor'd to make each other happy. Thus I corrected that great Erratum as well as I could.

About this Time our Club meeting, not at a Tavern, but in a little Room of Mr. Grace's set apart for that Purpose; a Proposition was made by me, that since our Books were often referr'd to in our Disquisitions upon the Queries, it might be convenient to us to have them all together where we met, that upon Occasion they might be consulted; and by thus clubbing our Books to a common Library, we should, while we lik'd to keep them together, have each of us the Advantage of using the Books of all the other Members, which would be nearly as beneficial as if each owned the whole. It was lik'd and agreed to, and we fill'd one End of the Room with such Books as we could best spare. The Number was not so great as we expected; and tho' they had been of great Use, yet some Inconveniencies occurring for want of due Care of them, the Collection after about a Year was separated, and each took his Books home again.

And now I set on foot my first Project of a public Nature, that for a Subscription Library. I drew up the Proposals, got them put into Form by our great Scrivener Brockden, and by the help of my Friends in the Junto, procur'd Fifty Subscribers of 40 Shillings each to begin with and 10 Shillings a Year for 50 Years, the Term our Company was to continue. We afterwards obtain'd a Charter, the Company being increas'd to 100. This was the Mother of all the North American Subscription Libraries now so numerous. It is become a great thing itself, and continually increasing. These Libraries have improv'd the general Conversation of the Americans, made the common Tradesmen and Farmers as intelligent as most Gentlemen from other Countries, and perhaps have contributed in some degree to the Stand so generally made throughout the Colonies in Defense of their Privileges.

Memo.

Thus far was written with the Intention express'd in the Beginning and therefore contains several little family Anecdotes of no Importance to others. What follows was written many Years after in compliance with the Advice contain'd in these Letters, and accordingly intended for the Public. The Affairs of the Revolution occasion'd the Interruption.

9. Because there was no proof that John Rogers, Deborah Read's first husband, was dead, she and Franklin entered into a common-law marriage without civil ceremony.

[PART TWO]¹

LETTER FROM MR. ABEL JAMES,² WITH NOTES ON MY LIFE,
(RECEIVED IN PARIS)

My dear and honored Friend.

I have often been desirous of writing to thee, but could not be reconciled to the Thought that the Letter might fall into the Hands of the British,³ lest some Printer or busy Body should publish some Part of the Contents and give our Friends Pain and myself Censure.

Some Time since there fell into my Hands to my great Joy about 23 Sheets in thy own handwriting containing an Account of the Parentage and Life of thyself, directed to thy Son ending in the Year 1730 with which there were Notes⁴ likewise in thy writing, a Copy of which I enclose in Hopes it may be a means if thou continuedst it up to a later period, that the first and latter part may be put together; and if it is not yet continued, I hope thou wilt not delay it. Life is uncertain as the Preacher tells us, and what will the World say if kind, humane and benevolent Ben Franklin should leave his Friends and the World deprived of so pleasing and profitable a Work, a Work which would be useful and entertaining not only to a few, but to millions.

The Influence Writings under that Class have on the Minds of Youth is very great, and has no where appeared so plain as in our public Friends' Journals. It almost insensibly leads the Youth into the Resolution of endeavoring to become as good and as eminent as the Journalist. Should thine for Instance when published, and I think it could not fail of it, lead the Youth to equal the Industry and Temperance of thy early Youth, what a Blessing with that Class would such a Work be. I know of no Character living nor many of them put together, who has so much in his Power as Thyself to promote a greater Spirit of Industry and early Attention to Business, Frugality and Temperance with the American Youth. Not that I think the Work would have no other Merit and Use in the World, far from it, but the first is of such vast Importance, that I know nothing that can equal it.

The foregoing letter and the minutes accompanying it being shown to a friend, I received from him the following:

LETTER FROM MR. BENJAMIN VAUGHAN⁵

My Dearest Sir,   *Paris, January* 31, 1783.

When I had read over your sheets of minutes of the principal incidents of your life, recovered for you by your Quaker acquaintance; I told you I would send you a letter expressing my reasons why I thought it

1. Franklin wrote the second part of his autobiography at the Hôtel de Valentenois in Passy, a Paris suburb. He had been sent to Paris as American representative to the peace treaty, officially ending the war with Britain on September 3, 1783. Franklin remained in Paris until July 1785, when Thomas Jefferson replaced him as minister.
2. A Quaker merchant in Philadelphia (c. 1726–1790).

3. James's letter was written in 1782, when Britain was still at war with the colonies.
4. Franklin's outline for his *Autobiography,* written in 1771. Reprinted in the Yale University edition (1964).
5. The wealthy son (1751–1835) of a Jamaican merchant and Maine mother; private secretary to Lord Shelburne, and personal emissary to Franklin during the Paris peace talks (1782–85).

would be useful to complete and publish it as he desired. Various concerns have for some time past prevented this letter being written, and I do not know whether it was worth any expectation: happening to be at leisure however at present, I shall by writing at least interest and instruct myself; but as the terms I am inclined to use may tend to offend a person of your manners, I shall only tell you how I would address any other person, who was as good and as great as yourself, but less diffident. I would say to him, Sir, I *solicit* the history of your life from the following motives.

Your history is so remarkable, that if you do not give it, somebody else will certainly give it; and perhaps so as nearly to do as much harm, as your own management of the thing might do good.

It will moreover present a table of the internal circumstances of your country, which will very much tend to invite to it settlers of virtuous and manly minds. And considering the eagerness with which such information is sought by them, and the extent of your reputation, I do not know of a more efficacious advertisement than your Biography would give.

All that has happened to you is also connected with the detail of the manners and situation of *a rising* people; and in this respect I do not think that the writings of Caesar and Tacitus[6] can be more interesting to a true judge of human nature and society.

But these, Sir, are small reasons in my opinion, compared with the chance which your life will give for the forming of future great men; and in conjunction with your *Art of Virtue,*[7] (which you design to publish) of improving the features of private character, and consequently of aiding all happiness both public and domestic.

The two works I allude to, Sir, will in particular give a noble rule and example of *self-education.* School and other education constantly proceed upon false principles, and show a clumsy apparatus pointed at a false mark; but your apparatus is simple, and the mark a true one; and while parents and young persons are left destitute of other just means of estimating and becoming prepared for a reasonable course in life, your discovery that the thing is in many a man's private power, will be invaluable!

Influence upon the private character late in life, is not only an influence late in life, but a weak influence. It is in *youth* that we plant our chief habits and prejudices; it is in youth that we take our party[8] as to profession, pursuits, and matrimony. In youth therefore the turn is given; in youth the education even of the next generation is given; in youth the private and public character is determined: and the term of life extending from youth to age, life ought to begin well from youth; and more especially *before* we take our party as to our principal objects.

But your Biography will not merely teach self-education, but the education of *a wise man;* and the wisest man will receive lights and improve his progress, by seeing detailed the conduct of another wise man. And why are weaker men to be deprived of such helps, when we see our race

---

6. Gaius Julius Caesar (100–44 B.C.E.) and Publius Cornelius Tacitus (late 1st and early 2nd centuries C.E.).
7. Vaughan is referring to Franklin's intention to write "a little work for the benefit of youth" to be called *The Art of Virtue.* Part Two of the *Autobiography* is, in part, a response to Vaughan's reminder.
8. Make our decision.

has been blundering on in the dark, almost without a guide in this particular, from the farthest trace of time. Show then, Sir, how much is to
be done, *both to sons and fathers;* and invite all wise men to become like
yourself; and other men to become wise.

When we see how cruel statesmen and warriors can be to the humble
race, and how absurd distinguished men can be to their acquaintance, it
will be instructive to observe the instances multiply of pacific acquiescing manners; and to find how compatible it is to be great and *domestic;*
enviable and yet *good-humored.*

The little private incidents which you will also have to relate, will have
considerable use, as we want above all things, *rules of prudence in ordinary affairs;* and it will be curious to see how you have acted in these. It
will be so far a sort of key to life, and explain many things that all men
ought to have once explained to them, to give them a chance of becoming wise by foresight.

The nearest thing to having experience of one's own, is to have other
people's affairs brought before us in a shape that is interesting; this is
sure to happen from your pen. Your affairs and management will have an
air of simplicity or importance that will not fail to strike; and I am convinced you have conducted them with as much originality as if you had
been conducting discussions in politics or philosophy; and what more
worthy of experiments and system, (its importance and its errors considered) than human life!

Some men have been virtuous blindly, others have speculated fantastically, and others have been shrewd to bad purposes; but you, Sir, I am
sure, will give under your hand, nothing but what is at the same moment,
wise, practical, and good.

Your account of yourself (for I suppose the parallel I am drawing for
Dr. Franklin, will hold not only in point of character but of private history), will show that you are ashamed of no origin; a thing the more
important, as you prove how little necessary all origin is to happiness,
virtue, or greatness.

As no end likewise happens without a means, so we shall find, Sir,
that even you yourself framed a plan by which you became considerable;
but at the same time we may see that though the event is flattering, the
means are as simple as wisdom could make them; that is, depending
upon nature, virtue, thought, and habit.

Another thing demonstrated will be the propriety of every man's waiting for his time for appearing upon the stage of the world. Our sensations being very much fixed to the moment, we are apt to forget that
more moments are to follow the first, and consequently that man should
arrange his conduct so as to suit the *whole* of a life. Your attribution
appears to have been applied to your *life,* and the passing moments of it
have been enlivened with content and enjoyment, instead of being tormented with foolish impatience or regrets. Such a conduct is easy for
those who make virtue and themselves their standard, and who try to
keep themselves in countenance by examples of other truly great men,
of whom patience is so often the characteristic.

Your Quaker correspondent, Sir (for here again I will suppose the subject of my letter resembling Dr. Franklin,) praised your frugality, diligence, and temperance, which he considered as a pattern for all youth:

but it is singular that he should have forgotten your modesty, and your disinterestedness, without which you never could have waited for your advancement, or found your situation in the mean time comfortable; which is a strong lesson to show the poverty of glory, and the importance of regulating our minds.

If this correspondent had known the nature of your reputation as well as I do, he would have said; your former writings and measures would secure attention to your Biography, and Art of Virtue; and your Biography and Art of Virtue, in return, would secure attention to them. This is an advantage attendant upon a various character, and which brings all that belongs to it into greater play; and it is the more useful, as perhaps more persons are at a loss for the *means* of improving their minds and characters, than they are for the time or the inclination to do it.

But there is one concluding reflection, Sir, that will show the use of your life as a mere piece of biography. This style of writing seems a little gone out of vogue, and yet it is a very useful one; and your specimen of it may be particularly serviceable, as it will make a subject of comparison with the lives of various public cut-throats and intriguers, and with absurd monastic self-tormentors, or vain literary triflers. If it encourages more writings of the same kind with your own, and induces more men to spend lives fit to be written; it will be worth all Plutarch's Lives put together.

But being tired of figuring to myself a character of which every feature suits only one man in the world, without giving him the praise of it; I shall end my letter, my dear Dr. Franklin, with a personal application to your proper self.

I am earnestly desirous then, my dear Sir, that you should let the world into the traits of your genuine character, as civil broils may otherwise tend to disguise or traduce it. Considering your great age, the caution of your character, and your peculiar style of thinking, it is not likely that any one besides yourself can be sufficiently master of the facts of your life, or the intentions of your mind.

Besides all this, the immense revolution of the present period, will necessarily turn our attention towards the author of it; and when virtuous principles have been pretended in it, it will be highly important to show that such have really influenced; and, as your own character will be the principal one to receive a scrutiny, it is proper (even for its effects upon your vast and rising country, as well as upon England and upon Europe), that it should stand respectable and eternal. For the furtherance of human happiness, I have always maintained that it is necessary to prove that man is not even at present a vicious and detestable animal; and still more to prove that good management may greatly amend him; and it is for much the same reason, that I am anxious to see the opinion established, that there are fair characters existing among the individuals of the race; for the moment that all men, without exception, shall be conceived abandoned, good people will cease efforts deemed to be hopeless, and perhaps think of taking their share in the scramble of life, or at least of making it comfortable principally for themselves.

Take then, my dear Sir, this work most speedily into hand: show yourself good as you are good, temperate as you are temperate; and above all things, prove yourself as one who from your infancy have loved justice, liberty, and concord, in a way that has made it natural and consistent for you to have acted, as we have seen you act in the last seventeen years of your life. Let Englishmen be made not only to respect, but even to love you. When they think well of individuals in your native country, they will go nearer to thinking well of your country; and when your countrymen see themselves well thought of by Englishmen, they will go nearer to thinking well of England. Extend your views even further; do not stop at those who speak the English tongue, but after having settled so many points in nature and politics, think of bettering the whole race of men.

As I have not read any part of the life in question, but know only the character that lived it, I write somewhat at hazard. I am sure however, that the life, and the treatise I allude to (on the *Art of Virtue*), will necessarily fullfil the chief of my expectations; and still more so if you take up the measure of suiting these performances to the several views above stated. Should they even prove unsuccessful in all that a sanguine admirer of yours hopes from them, you will at least have framed pieces to interest the human mind; and whoever gives a feeling of pleasure that is innocent to man, has added so much to the fair side of a life otherwise too much darkened by anxiety, and too much injured by pain.

In the hope therefore that you will listen to the prayer addressed to you in this letter, I beg to subscribe myself, my dearest Sir, etc., etc.

Signed   BENJ. VAUGHAN.

CONTINUATION OF THE ACCOUNT OF MY LIFE.
BEGUN AT PASSY, 1784.

It is some time since I receiv'd the above Letters, but I have been too busy till now to think of complying with the Request they contain. It might too be much better done if I were at home among my Papers, which would aid my Memory, and help to ascertain Dates. But my Return being uncertain, and having just now a little Leisure, I will endeavor to recollect and write what I can; if I live to get home, it may there be corrected and improv'd.

Not having any Copy here of what is already written, I know not whether an Account is given of the means I used to establish the Philadelphia public Library, which from a small Beginning is now become so considerable, though I remember to have come down to near the Time of that Transaction, 1730. I will therefore begin here, with an Account of it, which may be struck out if found to have been already given.

At the time I establish'd myself in Pennsylvania, there was not a good Bookseller's Shop in any of the Colonies to the Southward of Boston. In New York and Philadelphia the Printers were indeed Stationers, they sold only Paper, etc., Almanacs, Ballads, and a few common School Books. Those who lov'd Reading were oblig'd to send for their Books from England. The Members of the Junto had each a few. We had left the Alehouse where we first met, and hired a Room to hold our Club in. I propos'd that we should all of us bring our Books to that Room, where they would not only be ready to consult in our Conferences, but become a common Benefit, each of us being at Liberty to borrow such as he wish'd to read at home. This was accordingly done, and for some time contented us. Finding the Advantage of this little Collection, I propos'd to render the Benefit from Books more common by commencing a Public Subscription Library. I drew a Sketch of the Plan and Rules that would be necessary, and got a skillful Conveyancer Mr. Charles Brockden[9] to put the whole in Form of Articles of Agreement to be subscribed, by which each Subscriber engag'd to pay a certain Sum down for the first Purchase of Books and an annual Contribution for increasing them. So few were the Readers at that time in Philadelphia, and the Majority of us so poor, that I was not able with great Industry to find more than Fifty Persons, mostly young Tradesmen, willing to pay down for this purpose Forty shillings each, and Ten Shillings per Annum. On this little Fund we began. The Books were imported. The Library was open one Day in the Week for lending them to the Subscribers, on their Promissory Notes to pay Double the Value if not duly returned. The Institution soon manifested its Utility, was imitated by other Towns and in other Provinces, the Libraries were augmented by Donations, Reading became fashionable, and our People having no public Amusements to divert their Attention from Study became better acquainted with Books, and in a few Years were observ'd by Strangers to be better instructed and more intelligent than People of the same Rank generally are in other Countries.

When we were about to sign the above-mentioned Articles, which were to be binding on us, our Heirs, etc., for fifty Years, Mr. Brockden, the Scrivener, said to us, "You are young Men, but it is scarce probable that any of you will live to see the Expiration of the Term fix'd in this Instrument." A Number of us, however, are yet living: But the Instrument was after a few Years rendered null by a Charter that incorporated and gave Perpetuity to the Company.

The Objections, and Reluctances I met with in Soliciting the Subscriptions, made me soon feel the Impropriety of presenting oneself as the Proposer of any useful Project that might be suppos'd to raise one's Reputation in the smallest degree above that of one's Neighbors, when one has need of their Assistance to accomplish that Project. I therefore put myself as much as I could out of sight, and stated it as a Scheme of *a Number of Friends,* who had requested me to go about and propose it to such as they thought Lovers of Reading. In this way my Affair went on more smoothly, and I ever after practic'd it on such Occasions; and from my frequent Successes, can heartily recommend it. The present little Sacrifice of your Vanity will afterwards be amply repaid. If it remains a while uncertain to whom the Merit belongs, someone more vain than yourself will be encourag'd to claim it, and then even Envy will be dispos'd to do you Justice, by plucking those assum'd Feathers, and restoring them to their right Owner.

This Library afforded me the Means of Improvement by constant Study, for which I set apart an Hour or two each Day; and thus repair'd in some Degree the Loss of the Learned Education my Father once intended for me. Reading was the only Amusement I allow'd myself. I spent no time in Taverns, Games, or Frolics of any kind. And my Industry in my Business continu'd as indefatigable as it was necessary. I was in debt for my Printing-House, I had a young Family[1] coming on to be educated, and I had to contend with for Business two Printers who were establish'd in the Place before me. My Circumstances however grew daily easier: my original Habits of Frugality continuing. And My Father having among his Instructions to me when a Boy, frequently repeated a Proverb of Solomon, *"Seest thou a Man*

---

9. Philadelphia's leading drafter of legal documents (1683–1769). "Conveyancer": an attorney who specializes in the transfer of real estate and property.
1. Franklin had three children: William, born c. 1731; Francis, born in 1732; Sarah, born in 1743.

diligent in his Calling, he shall stand before Kings, he shall not stand before mean Men."[2] I from thence consider'd Industry as a Means of obtaining Wealth and Distinction, which encourag'd me: tho' I did not think that I should ever literally stand before Kings, which however has since happened; for I have stood before five,[3] and even had the honor of sitting down with one, the King of Denmark, to Dinner.

START We have an English Proverb that says,

> He that would thrive
> Must ask his Wife,[4]

it was lucky for me that I had one as much dispos'd to Industry and Frugality as myself. She assisted me cheerfully in my Business, folding and stitching Pamphlets, tending Shop, purchasing old Linen Rags for the Paper-makers, etc., etc. We kept no idle Servants, our Table was plain and simple, our Furniture of the cheapest. For instance my Breakfast was a long time Bread and Milk, (no Tea,) and I ate it out of a two penny earthen Porringer[5] with a Pewter Spoon. But mark how Luxury will enter Families, and make a Progress, in Spite of Principle. Being Call'd one Morning to Breakfast, I found it in a China[6] Bowl with a Spoon of Silver. They had been bought for me without my Knowledge by my Wife, and had cost her the enormous Sum of three and twenty Shillings, for which she had no other Excuse or Apology to make, but that she thought *her* Husband deserv'd a Silver Spoon and China Bowl as well as any of his Neighbors. This was the first Appearance of Plate[7] and China in our House, which afterwards in a Course of Years as our Wealth increas'd, augmented gradually to several Hundred Pounds in Value.

I had been religiously educated as a Presbyterian, and tho' some of the Dogmas of that Persuasion, such as the Eternal Decrees of God, Election, Reprobation,[8] etc., appear'd to me unintelligible, others doubtful, and I early absented myself from the Public Assemblies of the Sect, Sunday being my Studying-Day, I never was without some religious Principles; I never doubted, for instance, the Existence of the Deity, that he made the World, and govern'd it by his Providence; that the most acceptable Service of God was the doing Good to Man; that our Souls are immortal; and that all Crime will be punished and Virtue rewarded either here or hereafter; these I esteem'd the Essentials of every Religion, and being to be found in all the Religions we had in our Country I respected them all, tho' with different degrees of Respect as I found them more or less mix'd with other Articles which without any Tendency to inspire, promote or confirm Morality, serv'd principally to divide us and make us unfriendly to one another. This Respect to all, with an Opinion that the worst had some good Effects, induc'd me to avoid all Discourse that might tend to lessen the good Opinion another might have of his own Religion; and as our Province increas'd in People and new Places of worship were continually wanted, and generally erected by voluntary Contribution, my Mite[9] for such purpose, whatever might be the Sect, was never refused.

---

2. Proverbs 22.29.
3. Louis XV and Louis XVI of France, George II and George III of England, and Christian VI of Denmark.
4. More commonly: "He that will thrive must ask leave of his wife."

5. Small bowl.
6. I.e., porcelain.
7. Silver.
8. Punishment. "Election": God's determining who is to be saved and who is to be damned.
9. Small contribution.

Tho I seldom attended any Public Worship, I had still an Opinion of its Propriety, and of its Utility when rightly conducted, and I regularly paid my annual Subscription for the Support of the only Presbyterian Minister or Meeting we had in Philadelphia. He us'd to visit me sometimes as a Friend, and admonish me to attend his Administrations, and I was now and then prevail'd on to do so, once for five Sundays successively. Had he been, *in my Opinion,* a good Preacher perhaps I might have continued, notwithstanding the occasion I had for the Sunday's Leisure in my Course of Study: But his Discourses were chiefly either polemic Arguments, or Explications of the peculiar Doctrines of our Sect, and were all to me very dry, uninteresting and unedifying, since not a single moral Principle was inculcated or enforc'd, their Aim seeming to be rather to make us Presbyterians than good Citizens. At length he took for his Text that Verse of the 4th Chapter of Philippians, *Finally, Brethren, Whatsoever Things are true, honest, just, pure, lovely, or of good report, if there be any virtue, or any praise, think on these Things;*[1] and I imagin'd in a Sermon on such a Text, we could not miss of having some Morality: But he confin'd himself to five Points only as meant by the Apostle, viz., 1. Keeping holy the Sabbath Day. 2. Being diligent in Reading the Holy Scriptures. 3. Attending duly the Public Worship. 4. Partaking of the Sacrament. 5. Paying a due Respect to God's Ministers. These might be all good Things, but as they were not the kind of good Things that I expected from that Text, I despaired of ever meeting with them from any other, was disgusted, and attended his Preaching no more. I had some Years before compos'd a little Liturgy or Form of Prayer for my own private Use, viz., in 1728, entitled, *Articles of Belief and Acts of Religion.*[2] I return'd to the Use of this, and went no more to the public Assemblies. My Conduct might be blameable, but I leave it without attempting farther to excuse it, my present purpose being to relate Facts, and not to make Apologies for them.

It was about this time that I conceiv'd the bold and arduous Project of arriving at moral Perfection. I wish'd to live without committing any Fault at anytime; I would conquer all that either Natural Inclination, Custom, or Company might lead me into. As I knew, or thought I knew, what was right and wrong, I did not see why I might not *always* do the one and avoid the other. But I soon found I had undertaken a Task of more Difficulty than I had imagined: While my Care was employ'd in guarding against one Fault, I was often surpris'd by another. Habit took the Advantage of Inattention. Inclination was sometimes too strong for Reason. I concluded at length, that the mere speculative Conviction that it was our Interest to be completely virtuous, was not sufficient to prevent our Slipping, and that the contrary Habits must be broken and good Ones acquired and established, before we can have any Dependence on a steady uniform Rectitude of Conduct. For this purpose I therefore contriv'd the following Method.

In the various Enumerations of the moral Virtues I had met with in my Reading, I found the Catalog more or less numerous, as different Writers included more or fewer Ideas under the same Name. Temperance, for Example, was by some confin'd to Eating and Drinking, while by others it was extended to mean the moderating every other Pleasure, Appetite, Inclination

---

1. A paraphrase of Philippians 4.8.
2. Only the first part of Franklin's *Articles of Belief and Acts of Religion* survives. It can be found in *The Papers of Benjamin Franklin,* vol. 1, edited by Leonard W. Labaree et al. (1964).

or Passion, bodily or mental, even to our Avarice and Ambition. I propos'd to myself, for the sake of Clearness, to use rather more Names with fewer Ideas annex'd to each, than a few Names with more Ideas; and I included after Thirteen Names of Virtues all that at that time occurr'd to me as necessary or desirable, and annex'd to each a short Precept, which fully express'd the Extent I gave to its Meaning.

These Names of Virtues with their Precepts were

1. TEMPERANCE.

Eat not to Dullness. Drink not to Elevation.

2. SILENCE.

Speak not but what may benefit others or yourself. Avoiding trifling Conversation.

3. ORDER.

Let all your Things have their Places. Let each Part of your Business have its Time.

4. RESOLUTION.

Resolve to perform what you ought. Perform without fail what you resolve.

5. FRUGALITY.

Make no Expense but to do good to others or yourself: i.e., Waste nothing.

6. INDUSTRY.

Lose no Time. Be always employ'd in something useful. Cut off all unnecessary Actions.

7. SINCERITY.

Use no hurtful Deceit. Think innocently and justly; and, if you speak; speak accordingly.

8. JUSTICE.

Wrong none, by doing Injuries or omitting the Benefits that are your Duty.

9. MODERATION.

Avoid Extremes. Forbear resenting Injuries so much as you think they deserve.

10. CLEANLINESS.

Tolerate no Uncleanness in Body, Clothes or Habitation.

11. TRANQUILITY.

Be not disturbed at Trifles, or Accidents common or unavoidable.

12. CHASTITY.

Rarely use Venery but for Health or Offspring; Never to Dullness, Weakness, or the Injury of your own or another's Peace or Reputation.

13. HUMILITY.

Imitate Jesus and Socrates.

My intention being to acquire the *Habitude*[3] of all these Virtues, I judg'd it would be well not to distract my Attention by attempting the whole at once,

---

3. I.e., making these virtues an integral part of his nature.

TEMPERANCE.

Eat not to Dulness.
Drink not to Elevation.

	S	M	T	W	T	F	S
T							
S	• •	•		•		•	
O	•	•	•		•	•	•
R			•			•	
F		•			•		
I			•				
S							
J							
M							
Cl.							
T							
Ch							
H							

but to fix it on one of them at a time, and when I should be Master of that, then to proceed to another, and so on till I should have gone thro' the thirteen. And as the previous Acquisition of some might facilitate the Acquisition of certain others, I arrang'd them with that View as they stand above. *Temperance* first, as it tends to procure that Coolness and Clearness of Head, which is so necessary where constant Vigilance was to be kept up, and Guard maintained, against the unremitting Attraction of ancient Habits, and the Force of perpetual Temptations. This being acquir'd and establish'd, *Silence* would be more easy, and my Desire being to gain Knowledge at the same time that I improv'd in Virtue, and considering that in Conversation it was obtain'd rather by the Use of the Ears than of the Tongue, and therefore wishing to break a Habit I was getting into of Prattling, Punning and Joking, which only made me acceptable to trifling Company, I gave *Silence* the second Place. This, and the next, *Order,* I expected would allow me more Time for attending to my Project and my studies; RESOLUTION once become habitual, would keep me firm in my Endeavors to obtain all the subsequent Virtues; *Frugality* and *Industry,* by freeing me from my remaining Debt, and producing Affluence and Independence would make more easy the Practice of *Sincerity* and *Justice,* etc., etc. Conceiving then that agreeable to the Advice of Pythagoras[4] in his Golden Verses, daily Examination would be necessary, I contriv'd the following Method for conducting that Examination.

I made a little Book in which I allotted a Page for each of the Virtues. I rul'd each Page with red Ink so as to have seven Columns, one for each Day of the Week, marking each Column with a Letter for the Day. I cross'd these Columns with thirteen red Lines, marking the Beginning of each Line with the first Letter of one of the Virtues, on which Line and in its proper Column I might mark by a little black Spot every Fault I found upon Examination, to have been committed respecting that Virtue upon that Day.

I determined to give a Week's strict Attention to each of the Virtues successively. Thus in the first Week my great Guard was to avoid every the least Offence against Temperance, leaving the other Virtues to their ordinary Chance, only marking every Evening the Faults of the Day. Thus if in the first Week I could keep my first Line marked T clear of Spots, I suppos'd the Habit of that Virtue so much strengthen'd and its opposite weaken'd, that I might venture extending my Attention to include the next, and for the following Week keep both Lines clear of Spots. Proceeding thus to the last, I could go thro' a Course complete in Thirteen Weeks, and four Courses in a Year. And like him who having a Garden to weed, does not attempt to eradicate all the bad Herbs at once, which would exceed his Reach and his Strength, but works on one of the Beds at a time, and having accomplish'd the first proceeds to a second; so I should have, (I hoped) the encouraging Pleasure of seeing on my Pages the Progress I made in Virtue, by clearing successively my Lines of their Spots, till in the End by a Number of Courses, I should be happy in viewing a clean Book after a thirteen Weeks' daily Examination.

This my little Book had for its Motto these Lines from *Addison's Cato,*[5]

---

4. Pythagoras (6th century B.C.E.), a Greek philosopher and mathematician. Franklin added a note here: "Insert those Lines that direct it in a Note," and wished to include verses translated: "Let sleep not close your eyes till you have thrice examined the transactions of the day: where have I strayed, what have I done, what good have I omitted?"

5. Joseph Addison, *Cato, a Tragedy* (1713; 5.1.15–18). Franklin also used these lines as an epigraph for his *Articles of Belief and Acts of Religion.*

> *Here will I hold: If there is a Pow'r above us,*
> *(And that there is, all Nature cries aloud*
> *Thro' all her Works) he must delight in Virtue,*
> *And that which he delights in must be happy.*

Another from *Cicero.*[6]

> *O Vitæ Philosophia Dux! O Virtutum indagatrix, expultrixque vitiorum!*
> *Unus dies bene, et ex præceptis tuis actus, peccanti immortalitati est*
> *anteponendus.*

Another from the Proverbs of Solomon speaking of Wisdom or Virtue;

> Length of Days is in her right hand, and in her Left Hand Riches and
> Honors; Her Ways are Ways of Pleasantness, and all her Paths are
> Peace.
>
> III, 16, 17

And conceiving God to be the Fountain of Wisdom, I thought it right and necessary to solicit his Assistance for obtaining it; to this End I form'd the following little Prayer, which was prefix'd to my Tables of Examination, for daily Use.

> *O Powerful Goodness! bountiful Father! merciful Guide! Increase in me*
> *that Wisdom which discovers my truest Interests; Strengthen my Resolu-*
> *tions to perform what that Wisdom dictates. Accept my kind Offices to thy*
> *other Children, as the only Return in my Power for thy continual Favors*
> *to me.*

I us'd also sometimes a little Prayer which I took from *Thomson's*[7] Poems, viz.,

> *Father of Light and Life, thou Good supreme,*
> *O teach me what is good, teach me thy self!*
> *Save me from Folly, Vanity and Vice,*
> *From every low Pursuit, and fill my Soul*
> *With Knowledge, conscious Peace, and Virtue pure,*
> *Sacred, substantial, neverfading Bliss!*

The Precept of *Order* requiring that *every Part of my Business should have its allotted Time*, one Page in my little Book contain'd the following Scheme of Employment for the Twenty-four Hours of a natural Day.

I enter'd upon the Execution of this Plan for Self-examination, and continu'd it with occasional Intermissions for some time. I was surpris'd to find myself so much fuller of Faults than I had imagined, but I had the Satisfaction of seeing them diminish. To avoid the Trouble of renewing now and then my little Book, which by scraping out the Marks on the Paper of old Faults to make room for new Ones in a new Course, became full of Holes: I transferr'd my Tables and Precepts to the Ivory Leaves of a Memorandum Book, on which the Lines were drawn with red Ink that made a durable Stain, and on those Lines I mark'd my Faults with a black Lead Pencil, which Marks I could easily wipe out with a wet Sponge. After a while I went thro'

6. Marcus Tullius Cicero (106–43 B.C.E.), Roman philosopher and orator. The quotation is from *Tusculan Disputations* (5.2.5), but several lines are omitted after *vitiorum*: Oh, philosophy, guide of life: Oh, searcher out of virtues and expeller of vices! . . . One day lived well and according to thy precepts is to be preferred to an eternity of sin (Latin).

7. James Thomson (1700–1748), *The Seasons*, "Winter" (1726), lines 218–23.

The Morning Question, What Good shall I do this Day?	5	}	Rise, wash, and address *Powerful Goodness;* contrive Day's Business and take the Resolution of the Day; prosecute the present Study: and breakfast.—
	6		
	7		
	8	}	Work.
	9		
	10		
	11		
	12	}	Read, or overlook my Accounts, and dine.
	1		
	2	}	Work.
	3		
	4		
	5		
	6	}	Put Things in their Places, Supper, Musick, or Diversion, or Conversation, Examination of the Day.
	7		
	8		
	9		
Evening Question, What Good have I done to day?	10	}	Sleep.—
	11		
	12		
	1		
	2		
	3		
	4		

one Course only in a Year, and afterwards only one in several Years; till at length I omitted them entirely, being employ'd in Voyages and Business abroad with a Multiplicity of Affairs, that interfered. But I always carried my little Book with me.

My Scheme of ORDER, gave me the most Trouble, and I found, that tho' it might be practicable where a Man's Business was such as to leave him the Disposition of his Time, that of a Journeyman Printer for instance, it was not possible to be exactly observ'd by a Master, who must mix with the World, and often receive People of Business at their own Hours. *Order* too, with regard to Places for Things, Papers, etc., I found extremely difficult to acquire. I had not been early accustomed to it, and having an exceeding good Memory, I was not so sensible of the Inconvenience attending Want of Method. This Article therefore cost me so much painful Attention and my Faults in it vex'd me so much, and I made so little Progress in Amendment, and had such frequent Relapses, that I was almost ready to give up the Attempt, and content myself with a faulty Character in that respect. Like the Man who in buying an Ax of a Smith my Neighbor, desired to have the whole of its Surface as bright as the Edge; the Smith consented to grind it bright for him if he would turn the Wheel. He turn'd while the Smith press'd the broad Face of the Ax hard and heavily on the Stone, which made the Turning of it very fatiguing. The Man came every now and then from the Wheel to see how the Work went on; and at length would take his Ax as it was without farther Grinding. No, says the Smith, Turn on, turn on; we shall have it bright by and by; as yet 'tis only speckled. Yes, says the Man; but—I *think I like a speckled Ax best.*—And I believe this may have been the Case with many who having for want of some such Means as I employ'd found the Difficulty of obtaining good, and breaking bad Habits, in other Points of Vice and Virtue, have given up the Struggle, and concluded that *a speckled Ax was best.* For something that pretended to be Reason was every now and then suggesting to me, that such extreme Nicety as I exacted of myself might be a kind of Foppery in Morals, which if it were known would make me ridiculous; that a perfect Character might be attended with the Inconvenience of being envied and hated; and that a benevolent Man should allow a few Faults in himself, to keep his Friends in Countenance. *STOP*

In Truth I found myself incorrigible with respect to *Order;* and now I am grown old, and my Memory bad, I feel very sensibly the want of it. But on the whole, tho' I never arrived at the Perfection I had been so ambitious of obtaining, but fell far short of it, yet I was by the Endeavor made a better and a happier Man than I otherwise should have been, if I had not attempted it; As those who aim at perfect Writing by imitating the engraved Copies,[8] tho' they never reach the wish'd for Excellence of those Copies, their Hand is mended by the Endeavor, and is tolerable while it continues fair and legible.

And it may be well my Posterity should be informed, that to this little Artifice, with the Blessing of God, their Ancestor ow'd the constant Felicity of his Life down to his 79th Year in which this is written. What Reverses may attend the Remainder is in the Hand of Providence: But if they arrive, the Reflection on past Happiness enjoy'd ought to help his Bearing them with more Resignation. To *Temperance* he ascribes his long-continu'd Health, and what is still left to him of a good Constitution. To *Industry* and *Frugality* the early Easiness of his Circumstances, and Acquisition of his Fortune, with

---

8. I.e., the models in the printed book.

all that Knowledge which enabled him to be an useful Citizen, and obtain'd for him some Degree of Reputation among the Learned. To *Sincerity* and *Justice* the Confidence of his Country, and the honorable Employs it conferr'd upon him. And to the joint Influence of the whole Mass of the Virtues, even in their imperfect State he was able to acquire them, all that Evenness of Temper, and that Cheerfulness in Conversation which makes his Company still sought for, and agreeable even to his younger Acquaintance. I hope therefore that some of my Descendants may follow the Example and reap the Benefit.

It will be remark'd[9] that, tho' my Scheme was not wholly without Religion there was in it no Mark of any of the distinguishing Tenets of any particular Sect. I had purposely avoided them; for being fully persuaded of the Utility and Excellency of my Method, and that it might be serviceable to People in all Religions, and intending some time or other to publish it, I would not have anything in it that should prejudice anyone of any Sect against it. I purposed writing a little Comment on each Virtue, in which I would have shown the Advantages of possessing it, and the Mischiefs attending its opposite Vice; and I should have called my Book the ART *of Virtue,* because it would have shown the *Means and Manner* of obtaining Virtue; which would have distinguish'd it from the mere Exhortation to be good, that does not instruct and indicate the Means; but is like the Apostle's Man of verbal Charity, who only, without showing to the Naked and the Hungry *how* or where they might get Clothes or Victuals, exhorted them to be fed and clothed. *James II,* 15, 16.[1]

But it so happened that my Intention of writing and publishing this Comment was never fulfilled. I did indeed, from time to time put down short Hints of the Sentiments, Reasonings, etc., to be made use of in it; some of which I have still by me: But the necessary close Attention to private Business in the earlier part of Life, and public Business since, have occasioned my postponing it. For it being connected in my Mind with a *great and extensive Project* that required the whole Man to execute, and which an unforeseen Succession of Employs prevented my attending to, it has hitherto remain'd unfinish'd.

In this Piece it was my Design to explain and enforce this Doctrine, that vicious Actions are not hurtful because they are forbidden, but forbidden because they are hurtful, the Nature of Man alone consider'd: That it was therefore every one's Interest to be virtuous, who wish'd to be happy even in this World. And I should from this Circumstance (there being always in the World a Number of rich Merchants, Nobility, States and Princes, who have need of honest Instruments for the Management of their Affairs, and such being so rare) have endeavored to convince young Persons, that no Qualities were so likely to make a poor Man's Fortune as those of Probity and Integrity.

My List of Virtues contain'd at first but twelve: But a Quaker Friend having kindly inform'd me that I was generally thought proud; that my Pride show'd itself frequently in Conversation; that I was not content with being in the right when discussing any Point, but was overbearing and rather insolent; of which he convinc'd me by mentioning several Instances; I determined endeavoring to cure myself if I could of this Vice or Folly among the

9. Observed.
1. "If a brother or sister be naked, and destitute of daily food, And one of you say unto them, Depart in peace, be ye warmed and filled: notwithstanding ye give them not those things which are needful to the body; what doth it profit?"

rest, and I added *Humility* to my List, giving an extensive Meaning to the Word. I cannot boast of much Success in acquiring the *Reality* of this Virtue; but I had a good deal with regard to the *Appearance* of it. I made it a Rule to forbear all direct Contradiction to the Sentiments of others, and all positive Assertion of my own. I even forbid myself, agreeable to the old Laws of our Junto, the Use of every Word or Expression in the Language that imported[2] a fix'd Opinion; such as *certainly, undoubtedly,* etc., and I adopted instead of them, I *conceive,* I *apprehend,* or I *imagine* a thing to be so or so, or it so appears to me at present. When another asserted something that I thought an Error, I denied myself the Pleasure of contradicting him abruptly, and of showing immediately some Absurdity in his Proposition; and in answering I began by observing that in certain Cases or Circumstances his Opinion would be right, but that in the present case there *appear'd* or *seem'd* to me some Difference, etc., I soon found the Advantage of this Change in my Manners. The Conversations I engag'd in went on more pleasantly. The modest way in which I propos'd my Opinions, procur'd them a readier Reception and less Contradiction; I had less Mortification when I was found to be in the wrong, and I more easily prevail'd with others to give up their Mistakes and join with me when I happen'd to be in the right. And this Mode, which I at first put on, with some violence to natural Inclination, became at length so easy and so habitual to me, that perhaps for these Fifty Years past no one has ever heard a dogmatical Expression escape me. And to this Habit (after my Character of Integrity) I think it principally owing, that I had early so much Weight with my Fellow Citizens, when I proposed new Institutions, or Alterations in the old; and so much Influence in public Councils when I became a Member. For I was but a bad Speaker, never eloquent, subject to much Hesitation in my choice of Words, hardly correct in Language, and yet I generally carried my Points.

In reality there is perhaps no one of our natural Passions so hard to subdue as *Pride.* Disguise it, struggle with it, beat it down, stifle it, mortify it as much as one pleases, it is still alive, and will every now and then peep out and show itself. You will see it perhaps often in this History. For even if I could conceive that I had completely overcome it, I should probably be proud of my Humility.

Thus far written at Passy, 1784.

2. Suggested.

J. HECTOR ST. JOHN DE CRÈVECOEUR
1735–1813

Crèvecoeur was a man with a mysterious past, and a number of details of his life have puzzled his biographers. He was born Michel-Guillaume Jean de Crèvecoeur in Caen, Normandy, in 1735. When he was nineteen, he sailed to England, where he lived with distant relatives. He planned to marry, but his fiancée died before the ceremony could take place, and in 1755 he went to Canada; he enlisted in the Canadian militia, served the government as a surveyor and cartographer, and was wounded in the defense of Quebec. His military career came to an end in 1759, at which time he traveled to New York and changed his name to Hector St. John, later expanding his surname to St. John de Crèvecoeur and adding an initial. For the next ten years Crèvecoeur traveled extensively in the colonies as a surveyor and trader with American Indians. In 1769 he bought land in Orange County, New York, and, newly married, settled into the life of an American farmer.

Given Crèvecoeur's restlessness, it is hard to know whether he would have been happy forever on his farm at Pine Hill, but the advent of the American Revolution and his Tory sympathies were enough to prompt his return to France. He claimed that he wished to reestablish ownership of family lands, and it is ironic, given his political sympathies, that he was arrested and imprisoned as a rebel spy when he tried to sail from the British-held port of New York. Not until 1780 did Crèvecoeur succeed in reaching London. He remained in France until 1783, when he returned as French consul to New York, Connecticut, and New Jersey, only to learn that his farm had been burned in an Indian attack, his wife was dead, and his children were housed with strangers.

Crèvecoeur was a great success as a diplomat—he was made an honorary citizen of a number of American cities, and the town of St. Johnsbury, Vermont, was named in his honor—but he did not remain long in America. He returned to France in 1785 and after 1790 remained there permanently, first living in Paris and retiring, after 1793, to Normandy. He died at his daughter's home outside Paris.

The first year that Crèvecoeur spent at Pine Hill he began to write a series of essays about America based on his travels and experience as a farmer. In some he assumed the persona of "Farmer James," which lends an air of fiction to what otherwise appear straightforward letters. He brought them to London in 1780 and, suppressing those essays most unsympathetic to the American cause, sold them to the bookseller Thomas Davies. *Letters from an American Farmer* appeared in 1782 and was an immediate success. Crèvecoeur found himself a popular hero when the expanded French edition appeared two years later. Its publication followed closely enough on the American Revolution to satisfy an almost insatiable demand for all things American and confirmed, for most readers, a vision of a new land, rich and promising, where enterprise prevailed over class and fashion. George Washington said the book was "too flattering" to be true, but careful readers of the twelve letters will note an ambiguous attitude throughout: Crèvecoeur's hymn to the land does not make him blind to the ignorant frontier settlers or the calculating slaveholder.

The text used is from *Letters from an American Farmer,* edited by Albert Boni and Charles Boni (1925).

From Letters from an American Farmer

From *Letter III. What Is an American*

I wish I could be acquainted with the feelings and thoughts which must agitate the heart and present themselves to the mind of an enlightened Englishman, when he first lands on this continent. He must greatly rejoice that he lived at a time to see this fair country discovered and settled; he must necessarily feel a share of national pride, when he views the chain of settlements which embellishes these extended shores. When he says to himself, this is the work of my countrymen, who, when convulsed by factions,[1]

1. Disputes.

afflicted by a variety of miseries and wants, restless and impatient, took refuge here. They brought along with them their national genius,[2] to which they principally owe what liberty they enjoy, and what substance they possess. Here he sees the industry of his native country displayed in a new manner, and traces in their works the embryos of all the arts, sciences, and ingenuity which flourish in Europe. Here he beholds fair cities, substantial villages, extensive fields, an immense country filled with decent houses, good roads, orchards, meadows, and bridges, where an hundred years ago all was wild, woody, and uncultivated! What a train of pleasing ideas this fair spectacle must suggest; it is a prospect which must inspire a good citizen with the most heartfelt pleasure. The difficulty consists in the manner of viewing so extensive a scene. He is arrived on a new continent; a modern society offers itself to his contemplation, different from what he had hitherto seen. It is not composed, as in Europe, of great lords who possess everything, and of a herd of people who have nothing. Here are no aristocratical families, no courts, no kings, no bishops, no ecclesiastical dominion, no invisible power giving to a few a very visible one; no great manufacturers employing thousands, no great refinements of luxury. The rich and the poor are not so far removed from each other as they are in Europe. Some few towns excepted, we are all tillers of the earth, from Nova Scotia to West Florida. We are a people of cultivators, scattered over an immense territory, communicating with each other by means of good roads and navigable rivers, united by the silken bands of mild government, all respecting the laws, without dreading their power, because they are equitable. We are all animated with the spirit of an industry which is unfettered and unrestrained, because each person works for himself. If he travels through our rural districts he views not the hostile castle, and the haughty mansion, contrasted with the clay-built hut and miserable cabin, where cattle and men help to keep each other warm, and dwell in meanness, smoke, and indigence. A pleasing uniformity of decent competence appears throughout our habitations. The meanest of our log-houses is a dry and comfortable habitation. Lawyer or merchant are the fairest titles our towns afford; that of a farmer is the only appellation of the rural inhabitants of our country. It must take some time ere he can reconcile himself to our dictionary, which is but short in words of dignity, and names of honor. There, on a Sunday, he sees a congregation of respectable farmers and their wives, all clad in neat homespun, well mounted, or riding in their own humble wagons. There is not among them an esquire, saving the unlettered magistrate. There he sees a parson as simple as his flock, a farmer who does not riot[3] on the labor of others. We have no princes, for whom we toil, starve, and bleed; we are the most perfect society now existing in the world. Here man is free as he ought to be; nor is this pleasing equality so transitory as many others are. Many ages will not see the shores of our great lakes replenished with inland nations, nor the unknown bounds of North America entirely peopled. Who can tell how far it extends? Who can tell the millions of men whom it will feed and contain? for no European foot has as yet traveled half the extent of this mighty continent!

The next wish of this traveler will be to know whence came all these people? They are a mixture of English, Scotch, Irish, French, Dutch, Germans and Swedes. From this promiscuous breed, that race now called Ameri-

---

2. Spirit; distinctive national character.   3. I.e., indulge himself.

cans have arisen. The eastern provinces[4] must indeed be excepted, as being the unmixed descendants of Englishmen. I have heard many wish that they had been more intermixed also: for my part, I am no wisher, and think it much better as it has happened. They exhibit a most conspicuous figure in this great and variegated picture; they too enter for a great share in the pleasing perspective displayed in these thirteen provinces. I know it is fashionable to reflect on them, but respect them for what they have done; for the accuracy and wisdom with which they have settled their territory; for the decency of their manners; for their early love of letters; their ancient college,[5] the first in this hemisphere; for their industry, which to me who am but a farmer is the criterion of everything. There never was a people, situated as they are, who with so ungrateful a soil have done more in so short a time. Do you think that the monarchical ingredients which are more prevalent in other governments have purged them from all foul stains? Their histories assert the contrary.

In this great American asylum, the poor of Europe have by some means met together, and in consequence of various causes; to what purpose should they ask one another what countrymen they are? Alas, two thirds of them had no country. Can a wretch who wanders about, who works and starves, whose life is a continual scene of sore affliction or pinching penury, can that man call England or any other kingdom his country? A country that had no bread for him, whose fields procured him no harvest, who met with nothing but the frowns of the rich, the severity of the laws, with jails and punishments; who owned not a single foot of the extensive surface of this planet? No! Urged by a variety of motives, here they came. Everything has tended to regenerate them; new laws, a new mode of living, a new social system; here they are become men: in Europe they were as so many useless plants, wanting vegetative mold and refreshing showers; they withered, and were mowed down by want, hunger, and war; but now by the power of transplantation, like all other plants they have taken root and flourished! Formerly they were not numbered in any civil lists[6] of their country, except in those of the poor; here they rank as citizens. By what invisible power has this surprising metamorphosis been performed? By that of the laws and that of their industry. The laws, the indulgent laws, protect them as they arrive, stamping on them the symbol of adoption; they receive ample rewards for their labors; these accumulated rewards procure them lands; those lands confer on them the title of freemen, and to that title every benefit is affixed which men can possibly require. This is the great operation daily performed by our laws. From whence proceed these laws? From our government. Whence the government? It is derived from the original genius and strong desire of the people ratified and confirmed by the crown. This is the great chain which links us all, this is the picture which every province exhibits, Nova Scotia excepted. There the crown has done all;[7] either there were no people who had genius, or it was not much attended to: the consequence is that the province is very thinly inhabited indeed; the power of the crown in conjunction with the mosquitoes has prevented men from settling there. Yet some parts of it flourished once, and it contained a mild, harmless set of people. But for the fault of a few leaders, the whole were banished. The greatest political error

---

4. New England.
5. Harvard College was founded in 1636. "Reflect": censure or blame.
6. Recognized employees of the civil government: ambassadors, judges, secretaries, etc.
7. In 1755 the French Acadians were banished from Nova Scotia by the British, who had taken it in 1710.

the crown ever committed in America was to cut off men from a country which wanted nothing but men!

What attachment can a poor European emigrant have for a country where he had nothing? The knowledge of the language, the love of a few kindred as poor as himself, were the only cords that tied him: his country is now that which gives him land, bread, protection, and consequence: *Ubi panis ibi patria*[8] is the motto of all emigrants. What then is the American, this new man? He is either a European, or the descendant of a European, hence that strange mixture of blood, which you will find in no other country. I could point out to you a family whose grandfather was an Englishman, whose wife was Dutch, whose son married a French woman, and whose present four sons have now four wives of different nations. *He* is an American, who, leaving behind him all his ancient prejudices and manners, receives new ones from the new mode of life he has embraced, the new government he obeys, and the new rank he holds. He becomes an American by being received in the broad lap of our great *Alma Mater*.[9] Here individuals of all nations are melted into a new race of men, whose labors and posterity will one day cause great changes in the world. Americans are the western pilgrims, who are carrying along with them that great mass of arts, sciences, vigor, and industry which began long since in the east; they will finish the great circle. The Americans were once scattered all over Europe; here they are incorporated into one of the finest systems of population which has ever appeared, and which will hereafter become distinct by the power of the different climates they inhabit. The American ought therefore to love this country much better than that wherein either he or his forefathers were born. Here the rewards of his industry follow with equal steps the progress of his labor; his labor is founded on the basis of nature, *self-interest*; can it want a stronger allurement? Wives and children, who before in vain demanded of him a morsel of bread, now, fat and frolicsome, gladly help their father to clear those fields whence exuberant crops are to arise to feed and to clothe them all; without any part being claimed, either by a despotic prince, a rich abbot, or a mighty lord. Here religion demands but little of him; a small voluntary salary to the minister, and gratitude to God; can he refuse these? The American is a new man, who acts upon new principles; he must therefore entertain new ideas, and form new opinions. From involuntary idleness, servile dependence, penury, and useless labor, he has passed to toils of a very different nature, rewarded by ample subsistence.—This is an American.

British America is divided into many provinces, forming a large association, scattered along a coast 1,500 miles extent and about 200 wide. This society I would fain examine, at least such as it appears in the middle provinces; if it does not afford that variety of tinges and gradations which may be observed in Europe, we have colors peculiar to ourselves. For instance, it is natural to conceive that those who live near the sea must be very different from those who live in the woods; the intermediate space will afford a separate and distinct class.

Men are like plants; the goodness and flavor of the fruit proceeds from the peculiar soil and exposition in which they grow. We are nothing but what we derive from the air we breathe, the climate we inhabit, the government we

---

8. Where there is bread, there is one's fatherland (Latin).

9. Dear mother (Latin, literal trans.).

obey, the system of religion we profess, and the nature of our employment. Here you will find but few crimes; these have acquired as yet no root among us. I wish I was able to trace all my ideas; if my ignorance prevents me from describing them properly, I hope I shall be able to delineate a few of the outlines, which are all I propose.

Those who live near the sea feed more on fish than on flesh, and often encounter that boisterous element. This renders them more bold and enterprising; this leads them to neglect the confined occupations of the land. They see and converse with a variety of people, their intercourse with mankind becomes extensive. The sea inspires them with a love of traffic, a desire of transporting produce from one place to another; and leads them to a variety of resources which supply the place of labor. Those who inhabit the middle settlements, by far the most numerous, must be very different; the simple cultivation of the earth purifies them, but the indulgences of the government, the soft remonstrances of religion, the rank of independent freeholders, must necessarily inspire them with sentiments, very little known in Europe among people of the same class. What do I say? Europe has no such class of men; the early knowledge they acquire, the early bargains they make, give them a great degree of sagacity. As freemen they will be litigious; pride and obstinacy are often the cause of lawsuits; the nature of our laws and governments may be another. As citizens it is easy to imagine that they will carefully read the newspapers, enter into every political disquisition, freely blame or censure governors and others. As farmers they will be careful and anxious to get as much as they can, because what they get is their own. As northern men they will love the cheerful cup. As Christians, religion curbs them not in their opinions; the general indulgence leaves everyone to think for themselves in spiritual matters; the laws inspect our actions, our thoughts are left to God. Industry, good living, selfishness, litigiousness, country politics, the pride of freemen, religious indifference are their characteristics. If you recede still farther from the sea, you will come into more modern settlements; they exhibit the same strong lineaments, in a ruder appearance. Religion seems to have still less influence, and their manners are less improved.

Now we arrive near the great woods, near the last inhabited districts;[1] there men seem to be placed still farther beyond the reach of government, which in some measure leaves them to themselves. How can it pervade every corner; as they were driven there by misfortunes, necessity of beginnings, desire of acquiring large tracts of land, idleness, frequent want of economy,[2] ancient debts; the reunion of such people does not afford a very pleasing spectacle. When discord, want of unity and friendship; when either drunkenness or idleness prevail in such remote districts; contention, inactivity, and wretchedness must ensue. There are not the same remedies to these evils as in a long-established community. The few magistrates they have are in general little better than the rest; they are often in a perfect state of war; that of man against man, sometimes decided by blows, sometimes by means of the law; that of man against every wild inhabitant of these venerable woods, of which they are come to dispossess them. There men appear to be no better than carnivorous animals of a superior rank, living on the flesh of wild animals when they can catch them, and when they are not able, they subsist

1. I.e., the frontier; the land west of the original colonies and east of the Mississippi.

2. I.e., they were improvident and spent beyond their means.

on grain. He who would wish to see America in its proper light, and have a true idea of its feeble beginnings and barbarous rudiments, must visit our extended line of frontiers where the last settlers dwell, and where he may see the first labors of settlement, the mode of clearing the earth, in all their different appearances; where men are wholly left dependent on their native tempers and on the spur of uncertain industry, which often fails when not sanctified by the efficacy of a few moral rules. There, remote from the power of example and check of shame, many families exhibit the most hideous parts of our society. They are a kind of forlorn hope, preceding by ten or twelve years the most respectable army of veterans which come after them. In that space, prosperity will polish some, vice and the law will drive off the rest, who uniting again with others like themselves will recede still farther; making room for more industrious people, who will finish their improvements, convert the loghouse into a convenient habitation, and rejoicing that the first heavy labors are finished, will change in a few years that hitherto barbarous country into a fine fertile, well-regulated district. Such is our progress, such is the march of the Europeans toward the interior parts of this continent. In all societies these are offcasts; this impure part serves as our precursors or pioneers; my father himself was one of that class,[3] but he came upon honest principles, and was therefore one of the few who held fast; by good conduct and temperance, he transmitted to me his fair inheritance, when not above one in fourteen of his contemporaries had the same good fortune.

Forty years ago his smiling country was thus inhabited; it is now purged, a general decency of manners prevails throughout, and such has been the fate of our best countries.

Exclusive of those general characteristics, each province has its own, founded on the government, climate, mode of husbandry, customs, and peculiarity of circumstances. Europeans submit insensibly to these great powers, and become, in the course of a few generations, not only Americans in general, but either Pennsylvanians, Virginians, or provincials under some other name. Whoever traverses the continent must easily observe those strong differences, which will grow more evident in time. The inhabitants of Canada, Massachusetts, the middle provinces, the southern ones will be as different as their climates; their only points of unit will be those of religion and language.

As I have endeavored to show you how Europeans become Americans, it may not be disagreeable to show you likewise how the various Christian sects introduced wear out, and how religious indifference becomes prevalent. When any considerable number of a particular sect happen to dwell contiguous to each other, they immediately erect a temple, and there worship the Divinity agreeably to their own peculiar ideas. Nobody disturbs them. If any new sect springs up in Europe it may happen that many of its professors[4] will come and settle in America. As they bring their zeal with them, they are at liberty to make proselytes if they can, and to build a meeting and to follow the dictates of their consciences; for neither the government nor any other power interferes. If they are peaceable subjects, and are industrious, what is it to their neighbors how and in what manner they think fit to address their prayers to the Supreme Being? But if the sectaries are not settled close together, if they are mixed with other denominations,

---

3. His father never came to America.   4. Believers.

their zeal will cool for want of fuel, and will be extinguished in a little time. Then the Americans become as to religion what they are as to country, allied to all. In them the name of Englishman, Frenchman, and European is lost, and in like manner, the strict modes of Christianity as practiced in Europe are lost also. This effect will extend itself still farther hereafter, and though this may appear to you as a strange idea, yet it is a very true one. I shall be able perhaps hereafter to explain myself better; in the meanwhile, let the following example serve as my first justification.

Let us suppose you and I to be traveling; we observe that in this house, to the right, lives a Catholic, who prays to God as he has been taught, and believes in transubstantiation;[5] he works and raises wheat, he has a large family of children, all hale and robust; his belief, his prayers offend nobody. About one mile farther on the same road, his next neighbor may be a good honest plodding German Lutheran, who addresses himself to the same God, the God of all, agreeably to the modes he has been educated in, and believes in consubstantiation;[6] by so doing he scandalizes nobody; he also works in his fields, embellishes the earth, clears swamps, etc. What has the world to do with his Lutheran principles? He persecutes nobody, and nobody persecutes him, he visits his neighbors, and his neighbors visit him. Next to him lives a seceder, the most enthusiastic of all sectaries;[7] his zeal is hot and fiery, but separated as he is from others of the same complexion, he has no congregation of his own to resort to, where he might cabal and mingle religious pride with worldly obstinacy. He likewise raises good crops, his house is handsomely painted, his orchard is one of the fairest in the neighborhood. How does it concern the welfare of the country, or of the province at large, what this man's religious sentiments are, or really whether he has any at all? He is a good farmer, he is a sober, peaceable, good citizen: William Penn[8] himself would not wish for more. This is the visible character, the invisible one is only guessed at, and is nobody's business. Next again lives a Low Dutchman, who implicitly believes the rules laid down by the synod of Dort.[9] He conceives no other idea of a clergyman than that of a hired man; if he does his work well he will pay him the stipulated sum; if not he will dismiss him, and do without his sermons, and let his church be shut up for years. But notwithstanding this coarse idea, you will find his house and farm to be the neatest in all the country; and you will judge by his wagon and fat horses that he thinks more of the affairs of this world than of those of the next. He is sober and laborious, therefore he is all he ought to be as to the affairs of this life; as for those of the next, he must trust to the great Creator. Each of these people instruct their children as well as they can, but these instructions are feeble compared to those which are given to the youth of the poorest class in Europe. Their children will therefore grow up less zealous and more indifferent in matters of religion than their parents. The foolish vanity, or rather the fury of making proselytes, is unknown here; they have no time,

---

5. The doctrine followed by Roman Catholics that the substance of the bread and wine used in the sacrament of communion is changed at the consecration to the substance of the body and blood of Christ.

6. As distinguished from transubstantiation; the doctrine that affirms that Christ's body is not present in or under the elements of bread and wine, but that the bread and wine are signs of Christ's presence through faith.

7. One who dissents or withdraws from an established church. "Seceder": a Presbyterian who has separated from the established Church of Scotland.

8. English Quaker and founder of Pennsylvania (1644–1718).

9. The Synod of Dort met in Holland in 1618 and attempted to settle disputes between Protestant reformed churches. "Low Dutchman": someone from Holland, not Belgium.

the seasons call for all their attention, and thus in a few years, this mixed neighborhood will exhibit a strange religious medley, that will be neither pure Catholicism nor pure Calvinism. A very perceptible indifference, even in the first generation, will become apparent; and it may happen that the daughter of the Catholic will marry the son of the seceder, and settle by themselves at a distance from their parents. What religious education will they give their children? A very imperfect one. If there happens to be in the neighborhood any place of worship, we will suppose a Quaker's meeting; rather than not show their fine clothes, they will go to it, and some of them may perhaps attach themselves to that society. Others will remain in a perfect state of indifference; the children of these zealous parents will not be able to tell what their religious principles are, and their grandchildren still less. The neighborhood of a place of worship generally leads them to it, and the action of going thither is the strongest evidence they can give of their attachment to any sect. The Quakers are the only people who retain a fondness for their own mode of worship; for be they ever so far separated from each other, they hold a sort of communion with the society, and seldom depart from its rules, at least in this country. Thus all sects are mixed as well as all nations; thus religious indifference is imperceptibly disseminated from one end of the continent to the other; which is at present one of the strongest characteristics of the Americans. Where this will reach no one can tell, perhaps it may leave a vacuum fit to receive other systems. Persecution, religious pride, the love of contradiction are the food of what the world commonly calls religion. These motives have ceased here; zeal in Europe is confined; here it evaporates in the great distance it has to travel; there it is a grain of powder inclosed, here it burns away in the open air, and consumes without effect.

But to return to our back settlers. I must tell you that there is something in the proximity of the woods which is very singular. It is with men as it is with the plants and animals that grow and live in the forests; they are entirely different from those that live in the plains. I will candidly tell you all my thoughts but you are not to expect that I shall advance any reasons. By living in or near the woods, their actions are regulated by the wildness of the neighborhood. The deer often come to eat their grain, the wolves to destroy their sheep, the bears to kill their hogs, the foxes to catch their poultry. This surrounding hostility immediately puts the gun into their hands; they watch these animals, they kill some; and thus by defending their property, they soon become professed hunters; this is the progress; once hunters, farewell to the plow. The chase renders them ferocious, gloomy, and unsociable; a hunter wants no neighbor, he rather hates them, because he dreads the competition. In a little time their success in the woods makes them neglect their tillage. They trust to the natural fecundity of the earth, and therefore do little; carelessness in fencing often exposes what little they sow to destruction; they are not at home to watch; in order therefore to make up the deficiency, they go oftener to the woods. That new mode of life brings along with it a new set of manners, which I cannot easily describe. These new manners, being grafted on the old stock, produce a strange sort of lawless profligacy, the impressions of which are indelible. The manners of the Indian natives are respectable, compared with this European medley. Their wives and children live in sloth and inactivity; and having no proper pursuits, you may judge what education the latter receive. Their tender minds have nothing else to contemplate but the example of their parents; like them they grow up a mongrel breed, half civilized, half savage, except nature stamps on them some constitutional propensities. That rich, that voluptuous sentiment is gone that struck them so forcibly; the possession of their freeholds[1] no longer conveys to their minds the same pleasure and pride. To all these reasons you must add their lonely situation, and you cannot imagine what an effect on manners the great distances they live from each other has! Consider one of the last settlements in its first view: of what is it composed? Europeans who have not that sufficient share of knowledge they ought to have, in order to prosper; people who have suddenly passed from oppression, dread of government, and fear of laws into the unlimited freedom of the woods. This sudden change must have a very great effect on most men, and on that class particularly. Eating of wild meat, whatever you may think, tends to alter their temper: though all the proof I can adduce is that I have seen it: and having no place of worship to resort to, what little society this might afford is denied them. The Sunday meetings, exclusive of religious benefits, were the only social bonds that might have inspired them with some degree of emulation in neatness. Is it then surprising to see men thus situated, immersed in great and heavy labors, degenerate a little? It is rather a wonder the effect is not more diffusive. The Moravians[2] and the Quakers are the only instances in exception to what I have advanced. The first never settle singly, it is a colony of the society which emigrates; they carry with them their forms, worship, rules, and decency: the others never begin so hard, they are always able to buy improvements, in which there is a great advantage, for by that time the country is recovered from its first barbarity. Thus our bad people are those who are half cultivators and half hunters; and the worst of them are those who have degenerated altogether into the hunting state. As old plowmen and new men of the woods, as Europeans and new-made Indians, they contract the vices of both; they adopt the moroseness and ferocity of a native, without his mildness, or even his industry at home. If manners are not refined, at least they are rendered simple and inoffensive by tilling the earth; all our wants are supplied by it, our time is divided between labor and rest, and leaves none of the commission of great misdeeds. As hunters it is divided between the toil of the chase, the idleness of repose, or the indulgence of inebriation. Hunting is but a licentious idle life, and if it does not always pervert good dispositions; yet, when it is united with bad luck, it leads to want: want stimulates that propensity to rapacity and injustice, too natural to needy men, which is the fatal gradation. After this explanation of the effects which follow by living in the woods, shall we yet vainly flatter ourselves with the hope of converting the Indians? We should rather begin with converting our back-settlers; and now if I dare mention the name of religion, its sweet accents would be lost in the immensity of these woods. Men thus placed are not fit either to receive or remember its mild instructions; they want[3] temples and ministers, but as soon as men cease to remain at home, and begin to lead an erratic life, let them be either tawny or white, they cease to be its disciples.

* * *

1. Land held outright for a specified period of time.
2. Followers of Jacob Hutter, who was executed in 1536. They were Christian family communities who gave up private property and were noted for their industry and thrift. They suffered a number of persecutions in the 17th century and emigrated to other lands.
3. Lack.

Europe contains hardly any other distinctions but lords and tenants; this fair country alone is settled by freeholders, the possessors of the soil they cultivate, members of the government they obey, and the framers of their own laws, by means of their representatives. This is a thought which you have taught me to cherish; our difference from Europe, far from diminishing, rather adds to our usefulness and consequence as men and subjects. Had our forefathers remained there, they would only have crowded it, and perhaps prolonged those convulsions which had shook it so long. Every industrious European who transports himself here may be compared to a sprout growing at the foot of a great tree; it enjoys and draws but a little portion of sap; wrench it from the parent roots, transplant it, and it will become a tree bearing fruit also. Colonists are therefore entitled to the consideration due to the most useful subjects; a hundred families barely existing in some parts of Scotland will here in six years cause an annual exportation of 10,000 bushels of wheat; 100 bushels being but a common quantity for an industrious family to sell, if they cultivated good land. It is here then that the idle may be employed, the useless become useful, and the poor become rich; but by riches I do not mean gold and silver, we have but little of those metals; I mean a better sort of wealth, cleared lands, cattle, good houses, good clothes, and an increase of people to enjoy them.

There is no wonder that this country has so many charms, and presents to Europeans so many temptations to remain in it. A traveler in Europe becomes a stranger as soon as he quits his own kingdom; but it is otherwise here. We know, properly speaking, no strangers; this is every person's country; the variety of our soils, situations, climates, governments, and produce hath something which must please everybody. No sooner does a European arrive, no matter of what condition, than his eyes are opened upon the fair prospect; he hears his language spoken, he retraces many of his own country manners, he perpetually hears the names of families and towns with which he is acquainted; he sees happiness and prosperity in all places disseminated; he meets with hospitality, kindness, and plenty everywhere; he beholds hardly any poor; he seldom hears of punishments and executions; and he wonders at the elegance of our towns, those miracles of industry and freedom. He cannot admire enough our rural districts, our convenient roads, good taverns, and our many accommodations; he involuntarily loves a country where everything is so lovely.

* * *

After a foreigner from any part of Europe is arrived, and become a citizen, let him devoutly listen to the voice of our great parent, which says to him, "Welcome to my shores, distressed European; bless the hour in which thou didst see my verdant fields, my fair navigable rivers, and my green mountains!—If thou wilt work, I have bread for thee; if thou wilt be honest, sober, and industrious, I have greater rewards to confer on thee—ease and independence. I will give thee fields to feed and clothe thee; a comfortable fireside to sit by, and tell thy children by what means thou hast prospered; and a decent bed to repose on. I shall endow thee beside with the immunities of a freeman. If thou wilt carefully educate thy children, teach them gratitude to God, and reverence to that government, the philanthropic government, which has collected here so many men and made them happy. I will also provide for thy progeny; and to every good man this ought to be the most holy, the most powerful, the most earnest wish he can possibly form, as well as the most consolatory prospect when he dies. Go thou and work and till; thou shalt prosper, provided thou be just, grateful, and industrious."

From *Letter IX. Description of Charles-Town; Thoughts on Slavery; on Physical Evil; A Melancholy Scene*

Charles-Town is, in the north, what Lima is in the south; both are capitals of the richest provinces of their respective hemispheres: you may therefore conjecture, that both cities must exhibit the appearances necessarily result-ing from riches. Peru abounding in gold, Lima is filled with inhabitants who enjoy all those gradations of pleasure, refinement, and luxury, which proceed from wealth. Carolina produces commodities, more valuable perhaps than gold, because they are gained by greater industry; it exhibits also on our northern stage, a display of riches and luxury, inferior indeed to the former, but far superior to what are to be seen in our northern towns. Its situation is admirable, being built at the confluence of two large rivers, which receive in their course a great number of inferior streams; all navigable in the spring, for flat-boats. Here the produce of this extensive territory concenters; here therefore is the seat of the most valuable exportation; their wharfs, their docks, their magazines,[4] are extremely convenient to facilitate this great commercial business. The inhabitants are the gayest in America; it is called the center of our beau monde, and it [is] always filled with the richest planters of the province, who resort hither in a quest of health and pleasure. Here are always to be seen a great number of valetudinarians from the West Indies, seeking for the renovation of health, exhausted by the debilitating nature of their sun, air, and modes of living. Many of these West Indians have I seen, at thirty, loaded with the infirmities of old age; for nothing is more common in those countries of wealth, than for persons to lose the abilities of enjoying the comforts of life, at a time when we northern men just begin to taste the fruits of our labor and prudence. The round of pleasure, and the expenses of those citizens' tables, are much superior to what you would imagine: indeed the growth of this town and province has been astonishingly rapid. It is [a] pity that the narrowness of the neck on which it stands prevents it from increasing; and which is the reason why houses are so dear. The heat of the climate, which is sometimes very great in the interior parts of the country, is always temperate in Charles-Town; though sometimes when they have no sea breezes the sun is too powerful. The climate renders excesses of all kinds very dangerous, particularly those of the table; and yet, insensible or fearless of danger, they live on, and enjoy a short and a merry life: the rays of their sun seem to urge them irresistably to dissipation and pleasure: on the contrary, the women, from being abstemious, reach to a longer period of life, and seldom die without having had several husbands. An European at his first arrival must be greatly surprised when he sees the elegance of their houses, their sumptuous furniture, as well as the magnificence of their tables. Can he imagine himself in a country, the establishment of which is so recent?

The three principal classes of inhabitants are, lawyers, planters, and mer-chants; this is the province which has afforded to the first the richest spoils,

4. Warehouses.

for nothing can exceed their wealth, their power, and their influence. They have reached the *ne plus ultra*[5] of worldly felicity; no plantation is secured, no title is good, no will is valid, but what they dictate, regulate, and approve. The whole mass of provincial property is become tributary to this society; which, far above priests and bishops, disdain to be satisfied with the poor Mosaical portion of the tenth.[6] I appeal to the many inhabitants, who, while contending perhaps for their right to a few hundred acres, have lost by the mazes of the law their whole patrimony. These men are more properly law givers than interpreters of the law; and have united here, as well as in most other provinces, the skill and dexterity of the scribe with the power and ambition of the prince: who can tell where this may lead in a future day? The nature of our laws, and the spirit of freedom, which often tends to make us litigious, must necessarily throw the greatest part of the property of the colonies into the hands of these gentlemen. In another century, the law will possess in the north, what now the church possesses in Peru and Mexico.

While all is joy, festivity, and happiness in Charles-Town, would you imagine that scenes of misery overspread in the country? Their ears by habit are become deaf, their hearts are hardened; they neither see, hear, nor feel for the woes of their poor slaves, from whose painful labors all their wealth proceeds. Here the horrors of slavery, the hardship of incessant toils, are unseen; and no one thinks with compassion of those showers of sweat and of tears which from the bodies of Africans, daily drop, and moisten the ground they till. The cracks of the whip urging these miserable beings to excessive labor, are far too distant from the gay capital to be heard. The chosen race eat, drink, and live happy, while the unfortunate one grubs up the ground, raises indigo, or husks the rice; exposed to a sun full as scorching as their native one; without the support of good food, without the cordials of any cheering liquor. This great contrast has often afforded me subjects of the most afflicting meditation. On the one side, behold a people enjoying all that life affords most bewitching and pleasurable, without labor, without fatigue, hardly subjected to the trouble of wishing. With gold, dug from Peruvian mountains, they order vessels to the coasts of Guinea; by virtue of that gold, wars, murders, and devastations are committed in some harmless, peaceable African neighborhood, where dwelt innocent people, who even knew not but that all men were black. The daughter torn from her weeping mother, the child from the wretched parents, the wife from the loving husband; whose families swept away and brought through storms and tempests to this rich metropolis! There, arranged like horses at a fair, they are branded like cattle, and then driven to toil, to starve, and to languish for a few years on the different plantations of these citizens. And for whom must they work? For persons they know not, and who have no other power over them than that of violence; no other right than what this accursed metal has given them! Strange order of things! Oh, Nature, where are thou?—Are not these blacks thy children as well as we? On the other side, nothing is to be seen but the most diffusive misery and wretchedness, unrelieved even in thought or wish! Day after day they drudge on without any prospect of ever reaping for themselves; they are obliged to devote their lives, their limbs, their will, and every vital

5. No more beyond (Latin, literal trans.); the point of highest achievement.
6. The practice of tithing (offering one tenth of one's worldly goods to God) was begun by Abra-ham (Genesis 14.20). It is "Mosaical" because the first five books of the Old Testament are traditionally ascribed to Moses.

exertion to swell the wealth of masters; who look not upon them with half the kindness and affection with which they consider their dogs and horses. Kindness and affection are not the portion of those who till the earth, who carry the burdens, who convert the logs into useful boards. This reward, simple and natural as one would conceive it, would border on humanity; and planters must have none of it!

* * *

A clergyman settled a few years ago at George-Town, and feeling as I do now, warmly recommended to the planters, from the pulpit, a relaxation of severity; he introduced the benignity of Christianity, and pathetically made use of the admirable precepts of that system to melt the hearts of his congregation into a greater degree of compassion toward their slaves than had been hitherto customary; "Sir (said one of his hearers) we pay you a genteel salary to read to us the prayers of the liturgy, and to explain to us such parts of the Gospel as the rule of the church directs; but we do not want you to teach us what we are to do with our blacks." The clergyman found it prudent to withhold any farther admonition. Whence this astonishing right, or rather this barbarous custom, for most certainly we have no kind of right beyond that of force? We are told, it is true, that slavery cannot be so repugnant to human nature as we at first imagine, because it has been practiced in all ages, and in all nations: the Lacedemonians[7] themselves, those great assertors of liberty, conquered the Helotes with the design of making them their slaves; the Romans, whom we consider as our masters in civil and military policy, lived in the exercise of the most horrid oppression; they conquered to plunder and to enslave. What a hideous aspect the face of the earth must then have exhibited! Provinces, towns, districts, often depopulated; their inhabitants driven to Rome, the greatest market in the world, and there sold by thousands! The Roman dominions were tilled by the hands of unfortunate people, who had once been, like their victors free, rich, and possessed of every benefit society can confer; until they became subject to the cruel right of war, and to lawless force. Is there then no superintending power who conducts the moral operations of the world, as well as the physical? The same sublime hand which guides the planets round the sun with so much exactness, which preserves the arrangement of the whole with such exalted wisdom and paternal care, and prevents the vast system from falling into confusion; doth it abandon mankind to all the errors, the follies, and the miseries, which their most frantic rage, and their most dangerous vices and passions can produce?

* * *

Everywhere one part of the human species are taught the art of shedding the blood of the other; of setting fire to their dwellings; of leveling the works of their industry: half of the existence of nations regularly employed in destroying other nations. What little political felicity is to be met with here and there, has cost oceans of blood to purchase; as if good was never to be the portion of unhappy man. Republics, kingdoms, monarchies, founded either on fraud or successful violence, increase by pursuing the steps of the same policy, until they are destroyed in their turn, either by the influence of their own crimes, or by more successful but equally criminal enemies.

7. Another name for the Spartans, who enslaved the people of Helos, a town in Laconia.

If from this general review of human nature, we descend to the examination of what is called civilized society; there the combination of every natural and artificial want, makes us pay very dear for what little share of political felicity we enjoy. It is a strange heterogeneous assemblage of vices and virtues, and of a variety of other principles, forever at war, forever jarring, forever producing some dangerous, some distressing extreme. Where do you conceive then that nature intended we should be happy? Would you prefer the state of men in the woods, to that of men in a more improved situation? Evil preponderates in both; in the first they often eat each other for want of food, and in the other they often starve each other for want of room. For my part, I think the vices and miseries to be found in the latter, exceed those of the former; in which real evil is more scarce, more supportable, and less enormous. Yet we wish to see the earth peopled; to accomplish the happiness of kingdoms, which is said to consist in numbers. Gracious God! to what end is the introduction of so many beings into a mode of existence in which they must grope amidst as many errors, commit as many crimes, and meet with as many diseases, wants, and sufferings!

The following scene will I hope account for these melancholy reflections, and apologize for the gloomy thoughts with which I have filled this letter: my mind is, and always has been, oppressed since I became a witness to it. I was not long since invited to dine with a planter who lived three miles from——, where he then resided. In order to avoid the heat of the sun, I resolved to go on foot, sheltered in a small path, leading through a pleasant wood. I was leisurely traveling along, attentively examining some peculiar plants which I had collected, when all at once I felt the air strongly agitated; though the day was perfectly calm and sultry. I immediately cast my eyes toward the cleared ground, from which I was but at a small distance, in order to see whether it was not occasioned by a sudden shower; when at that instant a sound resembling a deep rough voice, uttered, as I thought, a few inarticulate monosyllables. Alarmed and surprised, I precipitately looked all round, when I perceived at about six rods distance something resembling a cage, suspended to the limbs of a tree; all the branches of which appeared covered with large birds of prey, fluttering about, and anxiously endeavoring to perch on the cage. Actuated by an involuntary motion of my hands, more than by any design of my mind, I fired at them; they all flew to a short distance, with a most hideous noise: when, horrid to think and painful to repeat, I perceived a Negro, suspended in the cage, and left there to expire! I shudder when I recollect that the birds had already picked out his eyes, his cheek bones were bare; his arms had been attacked in several places, and his body seemed covered with a multitude of wounds. From the edges of the hollow sockets and from the lacerations with which he was disfigured, the blood slowly dropped, and tinged the ground beneath. No sooner were the birds flown, than swarms of insects covered the whole body of this unfortunate wretch, eager to feed on his mangled flesh and to drink his blood. I found myself suddenly arrested by the power of affright and terror; my nerves were convulsed; I trembled, I stood motionless, involuntarily contemplating the fate of this Negro, in all its dismal latitude. The living specter, though deprived of his eyes, could still distinctly hear, and in his uncouth dialect begged me to give him some water to allay his thirst. Humanity herself would have recoiled back with horror; she would have balanced whether to lessen such reliefless distress, or mercifully with one blow to end this dreadful scene of agonizing torture! Had I had a ball in my gun, I certainly should have dispatched him; but finding myself unable to perform so kind an office, I sought, though trembling, to relieve him as well as I could. A shell ready fixed to a pole, which had been used by some Negroes, presented itself to me; filled it with water, and with trembling hands I guided it to the quivering lips of the wretched sufferer. Urged by the irresistible power of thirst, he endeavored to meet it, as he instinctively guessed its approach by the noise it made in passing through the bars of the cage. "Tankè, you whitè man, tankè you, putè somè poison and givè me." "How long have you been hanging there?" I asked him. "Two days, and me no die; the birds, the birds; aaah me!" Oppressed with the reflections which this shocking spectacle afforded me, I mustered strength enough to walk away, and soon reached the house at which I intended to dine. There I heard that the reason for this slave being thus punished was on account of his having killed the overseer of the plantation. They told me that the laws of self-preservation rendered such executions necessary; and supported the doctrine of slavery with the arguments generally made use of to justify the practice; with the repetition of which I shall not trouble you at present.

Adieu.

THOMAS PAINE
1737–1809

The author of two of the most popular books in eighteenth-century America, and the most persuasive rhetorician of the cause for independence, Thomas Paine was born in England in 1737 and did not come to America until he was thirty-seven years old and the rebellion was looming. Paine's early years prepared him to be a supporter of the Revolution. The discrepancy between his high intelligence and the limitations imposed on him by poverty and caste made him long for a new social order. The son of a Quaker father and an Anglican mother, he once said that a sermon he heard at the age of eight impressed him with the cruelty inherent in Christianity and made him a rebel forever. By the time he arrived in Philadelphia with letters of introduction from Benjamin Franklin, recommending him as an "ingenious, worthy young man," he had already had a remarkably full life. He went to grammar school until he was thirteen and was then apprenticed in his father's corset shop; at nineteen he ran away from home to go to sea. From 1757 to 1774 he was, by turns, a corset maker, a tobacconist and grocer, a schoolteacher, and an exciseman (a government employee who taxed goods). His efforts to organize the excisemen and make Parliament raise their salary was unprecedented. He lost his job when he admitted he had stamped as inspected goods that had not been examined at all. His first wife died less than a year after his marriage, and he was separated from his second wife after three years. Scandals about his private life and questions about his integrity while he was employed as an exciseman provided his critics with ammunition for the rest of his life. Franklin was right, however, in recognizing Paine's genius; for, like Franklin himself, Paine was a remarkable man, self-taught and curious about everything, from the philosophy of law to natural science.

In Philadelphia he found himself as a journalist, and he quickly made his way in that city, first as a spokesman against slavery and then as the anonymous author of *Common Sense*, the first pamphlet published in the colonies to urge immediate independence from Britain. Paine was obviously the right man in the right place at the right time. Relations with England were at their lowest ebb: Boston was under siege, and the Second Continental Congress had convened in Philadelphia. *Common Sense* sold phenomenally well, and its authorship could not be kept a secret for long. (This revelation was followed inevitably by the charge of treason.) Paine enlisted in the Revolutionary Army and served as an aide-de-camp in battles in New York, New Jersey, and Pennsylvania. He followed the triumph of *Common Sense* with the first of sixteen pamphlets titled *Crisis*. The first *Crisis* paper ("These are the times that try men's souls") was read to Washington's troops at Trenton and did much to shore up the spirits of the Revolutionary soldiers.

Paine received a number of political appointments as rewards for his services as a writer for the American cause, but too indiscreet and hot-tempered for public employment, he misused his privileges and lost the most lucrative offices. In 1787 he returned to England, determined to get financial assistance to construct an iron bridge. His plans came to nothing. But in England he wrote his second-most successful work, his *Rights of Man* (1791–92), an impassioned plea against hereditary monarchy, the traditional institution Paine never tired of arguing against. Paine was charged with treason and fled to France, where he was made a citizen and lionized as a spokesman for revolution. The horrors of the French Revolution, however, brought home to Paine the fact that the overthrow of monarchy did not necessarily usher in light and order. When he protested the execution of Louis XVI, he was accused of sympathy with the Crown and imprisoned. He was saved from trial by the American ambassador, James Monroe, who offered him renewed American citizenship and safe passage back to New York.

Paine spent the last years of his life in New York City and in New Rochelle, New York. They were unhappy, impoverished years, and his reputation suffered enormously as a result of *The Age of Reason* (1794). Paine's attempt to define his beliefs was viewed as an attack on Christianity and, by extension, on conventional society. He was ridiculed and despised. Even George Washington, who had supported Paine's early writing, thought English criticism of him was "not a bad thing." Paine had clearly outlived his time—or was living ahead of it, for soon enough his deistic ideas assumed new life and form in American Romanticism. He was buried on his farm at New Rochelle after his request for a Quaker gravesite was refused. Ten years later an enthusiastic admirer exhumed his bones with the intention of having him reburied in England, but this plan came to nothing; the whereabouts of Paine's remains is, at present, unknown.

Paine's great gift as a stylist was "plainness." He said he needed no "ceremonious expressions." "It is my design," he wrote, "to make those who can scarcely read understand," to put arguments in a language "as plain as the alphabet," and to shape everything "to fit the powers of thinking and the turn of language to the subject, so as to bring out a clear conclusion that shall hit the point in question and nothing else."

From Common Sense[1]

Introduction

Perhaps the sentiments contained in the following pages are not yet sufficiently fashionable to procure them general favor; a long habit of not thinking

---

1. The full title is *Common Sense: Addressed to the Inhabitants of America, on the following Interesting Subjects: viz.: I. Of the Origin and Design of Government in General; with Concise Remarks on the English Constitution. II. Of Monarchy and* *Hereditary Succession. III. Thoughts on the Present State of American Affairs. IV. Of the Present Ability of America; with some Miscellaneous Reflections.* The text used here is from *The Writings of Thomas Paine* (1894–96), vol. 1, edited by M. D. Conway.

a thing wrong gives it a superficial appearance of being right, and raises at first a formidable outcry in defence of custom. But the tumult soon subsides. Time makes more converts than reason.

As a long and violent abuse of power is generally the means of calling the right of it in question (and in matters too which might never have been thought of, had not the sufferers been aggravated into the inquiry), and as the King of England hath undertaken in his own right, to support the Parliament in what he calls theirs, and as the good people of this country are grievously oppressed by the combination, they have an undoubted privilege to inquire into the pretensions of both, and equally to reject the usurpation of either.

In the following sheets, the author hath studiously avoided everything which is personal among ourselves. Compliments as well as censure to individuals make no part thereof. The wise and the worthy need not the triumph of a pamphlet; and those whose sentiments are injudicious or unfriendly will cease of themselves, unless too much pains is bestowed upon their conversions.

The cause of America is in a great measure the cause of all mankind. Many circumstances have, and will, arise which are not local, but universal, and through which the principles of all lovers of mankind are affected, and in the event of which their affections are interested. The laying a country desolate with fire and sword, declaring war against the natural rights of all mankind, and extirpating the defenders thereof from the face of the earth, is the concern of every man to whom nature hath given the power of feeling; of which class, regardless of party censure, is

The Author

From III. Thoughts on the Present State of American Affairs

In the following pages I offer nothing more than simple facts, plain arguments, and common sense: and have no other preliminaries to settle with the reader, than that he will divest himself of prejudice and prepossession, and suffer his reason and his feelings to determine for themselves: that he will put on, or rather that he will not put off, the true character of a man, and generously enlarge his views beyond the present day.

Volumes have been written on the subject of the struggle between England and America. Men of all ranks have embarked in the controversy, from different motives, and with various designs; but all have been ineffectual, and the period of debate is closed. Arms as the last resource decide the contest; the appeal was the choice of the King, and the continent has accepted the challenge.

It hath been reported of the late Mr. Pelham[2] (who though an able minister was not without his faults) that on his being attacked in the House of Commons on the score that his measures were only of a temporary kind, replied, "they will last my time." Should a thought so fatal and unmanly possess the colonies in the present contest, the name of ancestors will be remembered by future generations with detestation.

The sun never shined on a cause of greater worth. 'Tis not the affair of a city, a county, a province, or a kingdom; but of a continent—of at least one eighth part of the habitable globe. 'Tis not the concern of a day, a year, or

---

2. Henry Pelham (1696–1754), prime minister of Britain (1743–54).

an age; posterity are virtually involved in the contest, and will be more or less affected even to the end of time, by the proceedings now. Now is the seed time of continental union, faith and honor. The least fracture now will be like a name engraved with the point of a pin on the tender rind of a young oak; the wound would enlarge with the tree, and posterity read it in full grown characters.

By referring the matter from argument to arms, a new era for politics is struck—a new method of thinking hath arisen. All plans, proposals, etc., prior to the nineteenth of April, i.e., to the commencement of hostilities,[3] are like the almanacs of the last year; which though proper then, are superseded and useless now. Whatever was advanced by the advocates on either side of the question then, terminated in one and the same point, viz., a union with Great Britain; the only difference between the parties was the method of effecting it; the one proposing force, the other friendship; but it hath so far happened that the first hath failed, and the second hath withdrawn her influence.

As much hath been said of the advantages of reconciliation, which, like an agreeable dream, hath passed away and left us as we were, it is but right that we should examine the contrary side of the argument, and inquire into some of the many material injuries which these colonies sustain, and always will sustain, by being connected with and dependent on Great Britain. To examine that connection and dependence, on the principles of nature and common sense, to see what we have to trust to, if separated, and what we are to expect, if dependent.

I have heard it asserted by some, that as America has flourished under her former connection with Great Britain, the same connection is necessary towards her future happiness, and will always have the same effect. Nothing can be more fallacious than this kind of argument. We may as well assert that because a child has thrived upon milk, that it is never to have meat, or that the first twenty years of our lives is to become a precedent for the next twenty. But even this is admitting more than is true; for I answer roundly, that America would have flourished as much, and probably much more, had no European power taken any notice of her. The commerce by which she hath enriched herself are the necessaries of life, and will always have a market while eating is the custom of Europe.

But she has protected us, say some. That she hath engrossed[4] us is true, and defended the continent at our expense as well as her own, is admitted; and she would have defended Turkey from the same motive, viz., for the sake of trade and dominion.

Alas! we have been long led away by ancient prejudices and made large sacrifices to superstition. We have boasted the protection of Great Britain without considering that her motive was interest not attachment; and that she did not protect us from our enemies on our account; but from her enemies on her own account, from those who had no quarrel with us on any other account, and who will always be our enemies on the same account. Let Britain waive her pretensions to the continent, or the continent throw off the dependence, and we should be at peace with France and Spain, were they

3. The Minutemen of Lexington, Massachusetts, defended their ammunition stores against the British on April 19, 1775, and engaged in the first

armed conflict of the American Revolution.
4. Dominated.

at war with Britain. The miseries of Hanover's last war[5] ought to warn us against connections.

It hath lately been asserted in Parliament, that the colonies have no relation to each other but through the parent country, i.e., that Pennsylvania and the Jerseys,[6] and so on for the rest, are sister colonies by the way of England; this is certainly a very roundabout way of proving relationship, but it is the nearest and only true way of proving enmity (or enemyship, if I may so call it). France and Spain never were, nor perhaps ever will be, our enemies as Americans, but as our being the subjects of Great Britain.

But Britain is the parent country, say some. Then the more shame upon her conduct. Even brutes do not devour their young, nor savages make war upon their families; wherefore, the assertion, if true, turns to her reproach; but it happens not to be true, or only partly so, and the phrase parent or mother country hath been jesuitically[7] adopted by the King and his parasites, with a low papistical design of gaining an unfair bias on the credulous weakness of our minds. Europe, and not England, is the parent country of America. This new world hath been the asylum for the persecuted lovers of civil and religious liberty from every part of Europe. Hither have they fled, not from the tender embraces of the mother, but from the cruelty of the monster; and it is so far true of England, that the same tyranny which drove the first emigrants from home, pursues their descendants still.

In this extensive quarter of the globe, we forget the narrow limits of three hundred and sixty miles (the extent of England) and carry our friendship on a larger scale; we claim brotherhood with every European Christian, and triumph in the generosity of the sentiment.

It is pleasant to observe by what regular gradations we surmount the force of local prejudices, as we enlarge our acquaintance with the world. A man born in any town in England divided into parishes, will naturally associate most with his fellow parishioners (because their interests in many cases will be common) and distinguish him by the name of neighbor; if he meet him but a few miles from home, he drops the narrow idea of a street, and salutes him by the name of townsman; if he travel out of the county and meet him in any other, he forgets the minor divisions of street and town, and calls him countryman, i.e., countyman: but if in their foreign excursions they should associate in France, or any other part of Europe, their local remembrance would be enlarged into that of Englishmen. And by a just parity of reasoning, all Europeans meeting in America, or any other quarter of the globe, are countrymen; for England, Holland, Germany, or Sweden, when compared with the whole, stand in the same places on the larger scale, which the divisions of street, town, and county do on the smaller ones; distinctions too limited for continental minds. Not one third of the inhabitants, even of this province,[8] are of English descent. Wherefore, I reprobate the phrase of parent or mother country applied to England only, as being false, selfish, narrow and ungenerous.

But, admitting that we were all of English descent, what does it amount to? Nothing. Britain, being now an open enemy, extinguishes every other name

5. King George III of Great Britain was a descendant of the German House of Hanover. Paine is referring to the Seven Years' War (1756–63), which originally involved Prussia and Austria and grew to involve all the major European powers. American losses in what is also called the French and Indian Wars were heavy, even though the war was settled in Britain's favor.

6. The colony was divided into East and West Jersey.

7. I.e., cunningly.

8. I.e., Pennsylvania.

and title: and to say that reconciliation is our duty is truly farcical. The first King of England of the present line (William the Conqueror) was a Frenchman, and half the peers of England are descendants from the same country; wherefore, by the same method of reasoning, England ought to be governed by France.

Much hath been said of the united strength of Britain and the colonies, that in conjunction they might bid defiance to the world: but this is mere presumption; the fate of war is uncertain, neither do the expressions mean anything; for this continent would never suffer itself to be drained of inhabitants to support the British arms in either Asia, Africa, or Europe.

Besides, what have we to do with setting the world at defiance? Our plan is commerce, and that, well attended to, will secure us the peace and friendship of all Europe; because it is the interest of all Europe to have America a free port. Her trade will always be a protection, and her barrenness of gold and silver secure her from invaders.

I challenge the warmest advocate for reconciliation to show a single advantage that this continent can reap by being connected with Great Britain. I repeat the challenge; not a single advantage is derived. Our corn[9] will fetch its price in any market in Europe, and our imported goods must be paid for buy them where we will.

But the injuries and disadvantages which we sustain by that connection, are without number; and our duty to mankind at large, as well as to ourselves, instruct us to renounce the alliance: because, any submission to, or dependence on, Great Britain tends directly to involve this continent in European wars and quarrels, and set us at variance with nations who would otherwise seek our friendship, and against whom we have neither anger nor complaint. As Europe is our market for trade, we ought to form no partial connection with any part of it. It is the true interest of America to steer clear of European contentions, which she never can do, while, by her dependence on Britain, she is made the makeweight in the scale of British politics.

Europe is too thickly planted with kingdoms to be long at peace, and whenever a war breaks out between England and any foreign power, the trade of America goes to ruin, because of her connection with Britain. The next war may not turn out like the last,[1] and should it not, the advocates for reconciliation now will be wishing for separation then, because neutrality in that case would be a safer convoy than a man of war. Everything that is right or reasonable pleads for separation. The blood of the slain, the weeping voice of nature cries, "'Tis time to part." Even the distance at which the Almighty hath placed England and America is a strong and natural proof that the authority of the one over the other was never the design of Heaven. The time likewise at which the continent was discovered adds weight to the argument, and the manner in which it was peopled increases the force of it. The Reformation was preceded by the discovery of America: as if the Almighty graciously meant to open a sanctuary to the persecuted in future years, when home should afford neither friendship nor safety.

The authority of Great Britain over this continent is a form of government which sooner or later must have an end: and a serious mind can draw no true pleasure by looking forward, under the painful and positive conviction that

---

9. I.e., wheat, not what Americans now call corn.
1. The Seven Years' War concluded with the Treaty of Paris (1763), by which Britain gained Canada from France.

what he calls "the present constitution" is merely temporary. As parents, we can have no joy, knowing that this government is not sufficiently lasting to insure anything which we may bequeath to posterity: and by a plain method of argument, as we are running the next generation into debt, we ought to do the work of it, otherwise we use them meanly and pitifully. In order to discover the line of our duty rightly, we should take our children in our hand, and fix our station a few years farther into life; that eminence will present a prospect which a few present fears and prejudices conceal from our sight.

Though I would carefully avoid giving unnecessary offense, yet I am inclined to believe that all those who espouse the doctrine of reconciliation may be included within the following descriptions.

Interested men who are not to be trusted, weak men who cannot see, prejudiced men who will not see, and a certain set of moderate men who think better of the European world than it deserves; and this last class, by an ill-judged deliberation, will be the cause of more calamities to this continent than all the other three.

It is the good fortune of many to live distant from the scene of present sorrow; the evil is not sufficiently brought to their doors to make them feel the precariousness with which all American property is possessed. But let our imaginations transport us a few moments to Boston;[2] that seat of wretchedness will teach us wisdom, and instruct us forever to renounce a power in whom we can have no trust. The inhabitants of that unfortunate city, who but a few months ago were in ease and affluence, have now no other alternative than to stay and starve, or turn out to beg. Endangered by the fire of their friends if they continue within the city, and plundered by the soldiery if they leave it, in their present situation they are prisoners without the hope of redemption, and in a general attack for their relief they would be exposed to the fury of both armies.

Men of passive tempers look somewhat lightly over the offenses of Great Britain, and, still hoping for the best, are apt to call out, "Come, come, we shall be friends again for all this." But examine the passions and feelings of mankind: bring the doctrine of reconciliation to the touchstone of nature, and then tell me whether you can hereafter love, honor, and faithfully serve the power that hath carried fire and sword into your land? If you cannot do all these, then are you only deceiving yourselves, and by your delay bringing ruin upon posterity. Your future connection with Britain, whom you can neither love nor honor, will be forced and unnatural, and, being formed only on the plan of present convenience, will in a little time fall into a relapse more wretched than the first. But if you say, you can still pass the violations over, then I ask, hath your house been burnt? Hath your property been destroyed before your face? Are your wife and children destitute of a bed to lie on, or bread to live on? Have you lost a parent or a child by their hands, and yourself the ruined and wretched survivor? If you have not, then are you not a judge of those who have. But if you have, and can still shake hands with the murderers, then are you unworthy the name of husband, father, friend, or lover, and whatever may be your rank or title in life, you have the heart of a coward, and the spirit of a sycophant.

This is not inflaming or exaggerating matters, but trying them by those feelings and affections which nature justifies, and without which we should

2. Boston was under British military occupation and was blockaded for six months.

be incapable of discharging the social duties of life, or enjoying the felicities of it. I mean not to exhibit horror for the purpose of provoking revenge, but to awaken us from fatal and unmanly slumbers, that we may pursue determinately some fixed object. 'Tis not in the power of Britain or of Europe to conquer America, if she doth not conquer herself by delay and timidity. The present winter is worth an age if rightly employed, but if lost or neglected the whole continent will partake of the misfortune; and there is no punishment which that man doth not deserve, be he who, or what, or where he will, that may be the means of sacrificing a season so precious and useful.

'Tis repugnant to reason, to the universal order of things, to all examples from former ages, to suppose that this continent can long remain subject to any external power. The most sanguine in Britain doth not think so. The utmost stretch of human wisdom cannot, at this time, compass a plan, short of separation, which can promise the continent even a year's security. Reconciliation is now a fallacious dream. Nature hath deserted the connection, and art cannot supply her place. For, as Milton wisely expresses, "never can true reconcilement grow where wounds of deadly hate have pierced so deep."[3]

* * *

A government of our own is our natural right: and when a man seriously reflects on the precariousness of human affairs, he will become convinced that it is infinitely wiser and safer to form a constitution of our own in a cool deliberate manner, while we have it in our power, than to trust such an interesting event to time and chance. If we omit it now, some Massanello[4] may hereafter arise, who, laying hold of popular disquietudes, may collect together the desperate and the discontented, and by assuming to themselves the powers of government, finally sweep away the liberties of the continent like a deluge. Should the government of America return again into the hands of Britain, the tottering situation of things will be a temptation for some desperate adventurer to try his fortune; and in such a case, what relief can Britain give? Ere she could hear the news, the fatal business might be done; and ourselves suffering like the wretched Britons under the oppression of the conqueror. Ye that oppose independence now, ye know not what ye do: ye are opening a door to eternal tyranny by keeping vacant the seat of government. There are thousands and tens of thousands, who would think it glorious to expel from the continent that barbarous and hellish power, which hath stirred up the Indians and the Negroes to destroy us; the cruelty hath a double guilt: it is dealing brutally by us, and treacherously by them.

To talk of friendship with those in whom our reason forbids us to have faith, and our affections wounded through a thousand pores instruct us to detest, is madness and folly. Every day wears out the little remains of kindred between us and them; and can there be any reason to hope, that as the relationship expires, the affection will increase, or that we shall agree better when we have ten times more and greater concerns to quarrel over than ever?

Ye that tell us of harmony and reconciliation, can ye restore to us the time that is past? Can ye give to prostitution its former innocence? Neither can ye reconcile Britain and America. The last cord now is broken, the people of

---

3. *Paradise Lost* (1667), 4.98–99.
4. Thomas Anello, otherwise Massanello, a fisherman of Naples, who after spiriting up his countrymen in the public market place, against the oppression of the Spaniards, to whom the place was then subject, prompted them to revolt, and in the space of a day became King [Paine's note].

England are presenting addresses against us. There are injuries which nature cannot forgive; she would cease to be nature if she did. As well can the lover forgive the ravisher of his mistress, as the continent forgive the murders of Britain. The Almighty hath implanted in us these unextinguishable feelings for good and wise purposes. They are the guardians of His image in our hearts. They distinguish us from the herd of common animals. The social compact would dissolve, and justice be extirpated from the earth, or have only a casual existence were we callous to the touches of affection. The robber and the murderer would often escape unpunished, did not the injuries which our tempers sustain provoke us into justice.

O! ye that love mankind! Ye that dare oppose not only the tyranny but the tyrant, stand forth! Every spot of the old world is overrun with oppression. Freedom hath been hunted round the globe. Asia and Africa have long expelled her. Europe regards her like a stranger, and England hath given her warning to depart. O! receive the fugitive, and prepare in time an asylum for mankind.

1776

The Crisis,[1] No. 1

These are the times that try men's souls. The summer soldier and the sun-shine patriot will, in this crisis, shrink from the service of their country; but he that stands it now, deserves the love and thanks of man and woman. Tyranny, like hell, is not easily conquered; yet we have this consolation with us, that the harder the conflict, the more glorious the triumph. What we obtain too cheap, we esteem too lightly: it is dearness only that gives everything its value. Heaven knows how to put a proper price upon its goods; and it would be strange indeed if so celestial an article as freedom should not be highly rated. Britain, with an army to enforce her tyranny, has declared that she has a right (not only to tax) but "to bind us in all cases whatsoever," and if being bound in that manner is not slavery, then is there not such a thing as slavery upon earth. Even the expression is impious; for so unlimited a power can belong only to God.

Whether the independence of the continent was declared too soon, or delayed too long, I will not now enter into as an argument; my own simple opinion is, that had it been eight months earlier, it would have been much better. We did not make a proper use of last winter, neither could we, while we were in a dependent state. However, the fault, if it were one, was all our own;[2] we have none to blame but ourselves. But no great deal is lost yet. All that Howe has been doing for this month past is rather a ravage than a

1. The first of sixteen pamphlets that appeared under this title. Paine sometimes referred to this particular essay as *The American Crisis*. There were three pamphlet editions in one week: one undated, one dated December 19, and the one reprinted here, dated December 23. The text used here is from *The Writings of Thomas Paine 1894–96*, vol. 1, edited by M. D. Conway.
2. "The present winter is worth an age, if rightly employed; but, if lost or neglected, the whole continent will partake of the evil; and there is no punishment that man does not deserve, be he who, or what, or where he will, that may be the means of sacrificing a season so precious and useful" [Paine's note, taken from *Common Sense*]. Paine wanted an immediate declaration of independence, uniting the colonies and enlisting the aid of France and Spain.

conquest, which the spirit of the Jerseys,[3] a year ago, would have quickly repulsed, and which time and a little resolution will soon recover.

I have as little superstition in me as any man living, but my secret opinion has ever been, and still is, that God Almighty will not give up a people to military destruction, or leave them unsupportedly to perish, who have so earnestly and so repeatedly sought to avoid the calamities of war, by every decent method which wisdom could invent. Neither have I so much of the infidel in me as to suppose that He has relinquished the government of the world, and given us up to the care of devils; and as I do not, I cannot see on what grounds the King of Britain can look up to heaven for help against us: a common murderer, a highwayman, or a housebreaker has as good a pretense as he.

'Tis surprising to see how rapidly a panic will sometimes run through a country. All nations and ages have been subject to them: Britain has trembled like an ague[4] at the report of a French fleet of flat-bottomed boats; and in the fourteenth century the whole English army, after ravaging the kingdom of France, was driven back like men petrified with fear; and this brave exploit was performed by a few broken forces collected and headed by a woman, Joan of Arc.[5] Would that heaven might inspire some Jersey maid to spirit up her countrymen, and save her fair fellow sufferers from ravage and ravishment! Yet panics, in some cases, have their uses; they produce as much good as hurt. Their duration is always short; the mind soon grows through them, and acquires a firmer habit than before. But their peculiar advantage is that they are the touchstones of sincerity and hypocrisy, and bring things and men to light, which might otherwise have lain forever undiscovered. In fact, they have the same effect on secret traitors, which an imaginary apparition would have upon a private murderer. They sift out the hidden thoughts of man, and hold them up in public to the world. Many a disguised tory[6] has lately shown his head, that shall penitentially solemnize with curses the day on which Howe arrived upon the Delaware.

As I was with the troops at Fort Lee, and marched with them to the edge of Pennsylvania, I am well acquainted with many circumstances, which those who live at a distance know but little or nothing of. Our situation there was exceedingly cramped, the place being a narrow neck of land between the North River[7] and the Hackensack. Our force was inconsiderable, being not one fourth so great as Howe could bring against us. We had no army at hand to have relieved the garrison, had we shut ourselves up and stood on our defense. Our ammunition, light artillery, and the best part of our stores had been removed on the apprehension that Howe would endeavor to penetrate the Jerseys, in which case Fort Lee could be of no use to us; for it must occur to every thinking man, whether in the army or not, that these kind of field forts are only for temporary purposes, and last in use no longer than the enemy directs his force against the particular object, which such forts are raised to defend. Such was our situation and condition at Fort Lee on the morning of the 20th of November, when an officer arrived with information that the enemy with 200 boats had landed about seven miles above: Major General Green,[8] who commanded the garrison, immediately ordered them

---

3. The colony was divided into East and West Jersey. Lord William Howe (1729–1814), commander of the British Army in America from 1775 to 1778.
4. I.e., like one who is chilled.
5. Joan led the French to victory over the

English in 1429 (not the "fourteenth century").
6. Supporter of the king.
7. The Hudson River.
8. Major General Nathanael Greene (1742–1786). Paine was his aide-de-camp.

under arms, and sent express to General Washington at the town of Hacken-sack, distant, by the way of the ferry, six miles. Our first object was to secure the bridge over the Hackensack, which laid up the river between the enemy and us, about six miles from us, and three from them. General Washington arrived in about three quarters of an hour, and marched at the head of the troops towards the bridge, which place I expected we should have a brush for; however, they did not choose to dispute it with us, and the greatest part of our troops went over the bridge, the rest over the ferry, except some which passed at a mill on a small creek, between the bridge and the ferry, and made their way through some marshy grounds up to the town of Hackensack, and there passed the river. We brought off as much baggage as the wagons could contain, the rest was lost. The simple object was to bring off the garrison, and march them on till they could be strengthened by the Jersey or Pennsylvania militia, so as to be enabled to make a stand. We staid four days at Newark, collected our outposts with some of the Jersey militia, and marched out twice to meet the enemy, on being informed that they were advancing, though our numbers were greatly inferior to theirs. Howe, in my little opinion, commit-ted a great error in generalship in not throwing a body of forces off from Staten Island through Amboy, by which means he might have seized all our stores at Brunswick, and intercepted our march into Pennsylvania; but if we believe the power of hell to be limited, we must likewise believe that their agents are under some providential control.[9]

I shall not now attempt to give all the particulars of our retreat to the Delaware; suffice it for the present to say, that both officers and men, though greatly harassed and fatigued, frequently without rest, covering, or provision, the inevitable consequences of a long retreat, bore it with a manly and mar-tial spirit. All their wishes centered in one, which was that the country would turn out and help them to drive the enemy back. Voltaire has remarked that King William never appeared to full advantage but in difficulties and in action;[1] the same remark may be made on General Washington, for the character fits him. There is a natural firmness in some minds which cannot be unlocked by trifles, but which, when unlocked, discovers a cabinet[2] of fortitude; and I reckon it among those kind of public blessings, which we do not immediately see, that God hath blessed him with uninterrupted health, and given him a mind that can even flourish upon care.

I shall conclude this paper with some miscellaneous remarks on the state of our affairs; and shall begin with asking the following question: Why is it that the enemy have left the New England provinces, and made these middle ones the seat of war? The answer is easy: New England is not infested with tories, and we are. I have been tender in raising the cry against these men, and used numberless arguments to show them their danger, but it will not do to sacrifice a world either to their folly or their baseness. The period is now arrived, in which either they or we must change our sentiments, or one or both must fall. And what is a tory? Good God! what is he? I should not be afraid to go with a hundred whigs[3] against a thousand tories, were they to

9. The American losses were larger than Paine implies. General Howe took three thousand pris-oners and a large store of military supplies when he captured Fort Lee. Paine wrote The Crisis, No. 1 while serving with Washington's army as it retreated through New Jersey.

1. Voltaire (1694–1778) made this remark about King William III of England (1650–1702) in his History of Louis the Fourteenth (1751).
2. Storehouse.
3. Supporters of the Revolution.

attempt to get into arms. Every tory is a coward; for servile, slavish, self-interested fear is the foundation of toryism; and a man under such influence, though he may be cruel, never can be brave.

But, before the line of irrecoverable separation be drawn between us, let us reason the matter together: Your conduct is an invitation to the enemy, yet not one in a thousand of you has heart enough to join him. Howe is as much deceived by you as the American cause is injured by you. He expects you will all take up arms, and flock to his standard, with muskets on your shoulders. Your opinions are of no use to him, unless you support him personally, for 'tis soldiers, and not tories, that he wants.

I once felt all that kind of anger, which a man ought to feel, against the mean principles that are held by the tories: a noted one, who kept a tavern at Amboy,[4] was standing at his door, with as pretty a child in his hand, about eight or nine years old, as I ever saw, and after speaking his mind as freely as he thought was prudent, finished with this unfatherly expression, "Well! give me peace in my day." Not a man lives on the continent but fully believes that a separation must some time or other finally take place, and a generous parent should have said, "If there must be trouble, let it be in my day, that my child may have peace"; and this single reflection, well applied, is sufficient to awaken every man to duty. Not a place upon earth might be so happy as America. Her situation is remote from all the wrangling world, and she has nothing to do but to trade with them. A man can distinguish himself between temper and principle, and I am as confident, as I am that God governs the world, that America will never be happy till she gets clear of foreign dominion. Wars, without ceasing, will break out till that period arrives, and the continent must in the end be conqueror; for though the flame of liberty may sometimes cease to shine, the coal can never expire.

America did not, nor does not, want force; but she wanted a proper application of that force. Wisdom is not the purchase of a day, and it is no wonder that we should err at the first setting off. From an excess of tenderness, we were unwilling to raise an army, and trusted our cause to the temporary defense of a well-meaning militia. A summer's experience has now taught us better; yet with those troops, while they were collected, we were able to set bounds to the progress of the enemy, and thank God! they are again assembling. I always considered militia as the best troops in the world for a sudden exertion, but they will not do for a long campaign. Howe, it is probable, will make an attempt on this city;[5] should he fail on this side of the Delaware, he is ruined: if he succeeds, our cause is not ruined. He stakes all on his side against a part on ours; admitting he succeeds, the consequence will be that armies from both ends of the continent will march to assist their suffering friends in the middle states; for he cannot go everywhere, it is impossible. I consider Howe as the greatest enemy the tories have; he is bringing a war into their country, which, had it not been for him and partly for themselves, they had been clear of. Should he now be expelled, I wish with all the devotion of a Christian, that the names of whig and tory may never more be mentioned; but should the tories give him encouragement to come, or assistance if he come, I as sincerely wish that our next year's arms may expel them from the continent, and the congress appropriate their possessions to the relief of those who have suffered in well-doing. A single successful battle next year

---

4. Paine was stationed at Perth Amboy, New Jersey, while in the Continental Army.   5. I.e., Philadelphia.

will settle the whole. America could carry on a two years' war by the confiscation of the property of disaffected persons, and be made happy by their expulsion. Say not that this is revenge; call it rather the soft resentment of a suffering people, who, having no object in view but the good of all, have staked their own all upon a seemingly doubtful event. Yet it is folly to argue against determined hardness; eloquence may strike the ear, and the language of sorrow draw forth the tear of compassion, but nothing can reach the heart that is steeled with prejudice.

Quitting this class of men, I turn with the warm ardor of a friend to those who have nobly stood, and are yet determined to stand the matter out: I call not upon a few, but upon all; not on this state or that state, but on every state: up and help us; lay your shoulders to the wheel; better have too much force than too little, when so great an object is at stake. Let it be told to the future world that in the depth of winter, when nothing but hope and virtue could survive, that the city and the country, alarmed at one common danger, came forth to meet and to repulse it. Say not that thousands are gone, turn out your tens of thousands;[6] throw not the burden of the day upon Providence, but "show your faith by your works"[7] that God may bless you. It matters not where you live, or what rank of life you hold, the evil or the blessing will reach you all. The far and the near, the home counties and the back,[8] the rich and poor will suffer or rejoice alike. The heart that feels not now is dead: the blood of his children will curse his cowardice who shrinks back at a time when a little might have saved the whole, and made them happy. I love the man that can smile in trouble, that can gather strength from distress, and grow brave by reflection. 'Tis the business of little minds to shrink; but he whose heart is firm, and whose conscience approves his conduct, will pursue his principles unto death. My own line of reasoning is to myself as straight and clear as a ray of light. Not all the treasures of the world, so far as I believe, could have induced me to support an offensive war, for I think it murder; but if a thief breaks into my house, burns and destroys my property, and kills or threatens to kill me, or those that are in it, and to "bind me in all cases whatsoever"[9] to his absolute will, am I to suffer it? What signifies it to me, whether he who does it is a king or a common man; my countryman or not my countryman; whether it be done by an individual villain, or an army of them? If we reason to the root of things we shall find no difference; neither can any just cause be assigned why we should punish in the one case and pardon in the other. Let them call me rebel, and welcome, I feel no concern from it; but I should suffer the misery of devils were I to make a whore of my soul by swearing allegiance to one whose character is that of a sottish, stupid, stubborn, worthless, brutish man. I conceive likewise a horrid idea in receiving mercy from a being, who at the last day shall be shrieking to the rocks and mountains to cover him, and fleeing with terror from the orphan, the widow, and the slain of America.

There are cases which cannot be overdone by language, and this is one. There are persons, too, who see not the full extent of the evil which threatens them; they solace themselves with hopes that the enemy, if he succeed, will be merciful. It is the madness of folly to expect mercy from those who have refused to do justice; and even mercy, where conquest is the object, is only

6. "Saul hath slain his thousands, and David his ten thousands" (1 Samuel 18.7).
7. "Shew me thy faith without thy works, and I will shew thee my faith by my works" (James 2.18).

8. I.e., the backwoods.
9. From the Declaratory Act of Parliament, February 24, 1766, establishing British authority over the American colonies.

a trick of war; the cunning of the fox is as murderous as the violence of the wolf, and we ought to guard equally against both. Howe's first object is, partly by threats and partly by promises, to terrify or seduce the people to deliver up their arms and receive mercy. The ministry recommended the same plan to Gage, and this is what the tories call making their peace, "a peace which passeth all understanding"[1] indeed! A peace which would be the immediate forerunner of a worse ruin than any we have yet thought of. Ye men of Pennsylvania, do reason upon these things! Were the back counties to give up their arms, they would fall an easy prey to the Indians, who are all armed: this perhaps is what some tories would not be sorry for. Were the home counties to deliver up their arms, they would be exposed to the resentment of the back counties, who would then have it in their power to chastise their defection at pleasure. And were any one state to give up its arms, that state must be garrisoned by all Howe's army of Britons and Hessians[2] to preserve it from the anger of the rest. Mutual fear is the principal link in the chain of mutual love, and woe be to that state that breaks the compact. Howe is mercifully inviting you to barbarous destruction, and men must be either rogues or fools that will not see it. I dwell not upon the vapors of imagination: I bring reason to your ears, and, in language as plain as A, B, C, hold up truth to your eyes.

I thank God that I fear not. I see no real cause for fear. I know our situation well, and can see the way out of it. While our army was collected, Howe dared not risk a battle; and it is no credit to him that he decamped from the White Plains,[3] and waited a mean opportunity to ravage the defenseless Jerseys; but it is great credit to us, that, with a handful of men, we sustained an orderly retreat for near an hundred miles, brought off our ammunition, all our field pieces, the greatest part of our stores, and had four rivers to pass. None can say that our retreat was precipitate, for we were near three weeks in performing it, that the country[4] might have time to come in. Twice we marched back to meet the enemy, and remained out till dark. The sign of fear was not seen in our camp, and had not some of the cowardly and disaffected inhabitants spread false alarms through the country, the Jerseys had never been ravaged. Once more we are again collected and collecting; our new army at both ends of the continent is recruiting fast, and we shall be able to open the next campaign with sixty thousand men, well armed and clothed. This is our situation, and who will may know it. By perseverance and fortitude we have the prospect of a glorious issue; by cowardice and submission, the sad choice of a variety of evils—a ravaged country—a depopulated city— habitations without safety, and slavery without hope—our homes turned into barracks and bawdyhouses for Hessians, and a future race to provide for, whose fathers we shall doubt of. Look on this picture and weep over it! and if there yet remains one thoughtless wretch who believes it not, let him suffer it unlamented.

Common Sense

1776

1. "And the peace of God, which passeth all understanding, shall keep your hearts and minds through Christ Jesus" (1787) (Philippians 4.7). General Thomas Gage (1721–1787), who commanded the British armies in America from 1763 to 1775, before Howe.

2. German mercenaries.
3. In New York, where, on October 28, 1776, General Howe successfully overcame Washington's troops but failed to take full advantage of his victory.
4. I.e., the local volunteers.

THOMAS JEFFERSON
1743–1826

President of the United States, first secretary of state, minister to France, governor of Virginia, and congressman, Thomas Jefferson once said that he wished to be remembered for only three things: drafting the Declaration of Independence, writing and supporting the Virginia Statute for Religious Freedom (1786), and founding the University of Virginia. Jefferson might well have included a number of other accomplishments in this list: he was a remarkable architect and designed the Virginia state capitol, his residence Monticello, and the original buildings for the University of Virginia; he farmed thousands of acres and built one of the most beautiful plantations in America; he had a library of some ten thousand volumes, which served as the basis for the Library of Congress, and a collection of paintings and sculpture that made him America's greatest patron of the arts; and he was known the world over for his spirit of scientific inquiry and as the creator of a number of remarkable inventions. The three acts for which he wished to be remembered, however, have this in common: they all testify to Jefferson's lifelong passion to liberate the human mind from tyranny, whether imposed by the state, the church, or our own ignorance.

Jefferson was born at Shadwell, in what is now Albermarle County, Virginia. His mother, Jane Randolph, came from one of the most distinguished families in Virginia. Peter Jefferson, his father, was a county official and surveyor. He made the first accurate map of Virginia, something of which his son Thomas was always proud. Jefferson tells us in his *Autobiography* that his father's education had been "quite neglected" but that he was always "eager after information" and determined to improve himself. When Peter Jefferson died Thomas was only fourteen, the inheritor of 2,750 acres of land, and he added to this acreage until he died; at one time he owned almost 10,000 acres. In 1760, when Jefferson entered the College of William and Mary in Williamsburg, Virginia, he had mastered Latin and Greek, played the violin respectably, and was a skilled horseman. Williamsburg was the capital of Virginia as well as a college town, and Jefferson was fortunate enough to make the acquaintance of three men who strongly influenced his life: Governor Francis Fauquier, a fellow of the Royal Society; George Wythe, one of the best teachers of law in the country; and Dr. William Small, an emigrant from Scotland who taught mathematics and philosophy and who introduced Jefferson, as Garry Wills has put it, "to the invigorating realms of the Scottish Enlightenment," especially the work of Francis Hutcheson, author of *An Inquiry into the Original of Our Ideas of Beauty and Virtue* (1725), and Henry Home, Lord Kames, author of *Essays on the Principles of Morality and Natural Religion* (1751).

Jefferson stayed on in Williamsburg to study law after graduation and was admitted to the bar. In 1769 he was elected to the Virginia House of Burgesses and began a distinguished career in the legislature. In 1774 he wrote an influential and daring pamphlet called *A Summary View of the Rights of British America*, denying all parliamentary authority over America and arguing that ties to the British monarchy were voluntary and not irrevocable. Jefferson's reputation as a writer preceded him to Philadelphia, where he was a delegate to the Second Continental Congress, and on June 11, 1776, he was appointed to join Benjamin Franklin, John Adams, Roger Sherman, and Robert Livingston in drafting a declaration of independence. Although committee members made suggestions, the draft was very much Jefferson's own. As Wills has recently shown, Jefferson was unhappy with the changes made by Congress to his draft, and rightly so; for congressional changes went contrary to some of his basic arguments. Jefferson wished to place the British *people* on record as the ultimate cause of the Revolution, because they tolerated a corrupt Parliament and king; and he wished to include a strong statement against slavery. Congress tolerated neither passage. Jefferson was justified, however, in asking that he be remembered as the author of the Declaration. It was, as Dumas Malone, Jefferson's biographer, once put it, a "dangerous but glorious opportunity." Whether as the result of these frustrations or merely Jefferson's wish to be nearer his family, he left the Congress in September 1776 and entered the Virginia House of Delegates. In 1779 he was elected governor, and although reelected the following year, Jefferson's term of office soon came to an ignominious end. After the British captured Richmond in 1781, Jefferson and the legislature moved to Charlottesville, and he and the legislators barely escaped imprisonment when the pursuing British Army descended on them at Monticello. Jefferson's ensuing resignation and the lack of preparations for the defense of the city were held against him, and it was some time before he regained the confidence of Virginians.

From 1781 to 1784 Jefferson withdrew from public life and remained at Monticello, completing his only book, *Notes on the State of Virginia*. In 1784 he was appointed minister to France and served with Benjamin Franklin on the commission that signed the Treaty of Paris, which ended the Revolutionary War. He returned to Monticello in 1789, and in 1790 Washington appointed him the first secretary of state under the newly adopted Constitution. After three years he announced his retirement once again and withdrew to Monticello, where he rotated his crops and built a grist mill. But Jefferson's political blood was too thick for retirement, and in 1796 he ran for the office of president, losing to John Adams and taking the office of vice president instead. In 1800 he was elected president, the first to be inaugurated in Washington, D.C. He named Benjamin Latrobe surveyor of public buildings and worked with Latrobe in planning a great city.

When Jefferson returned to Monticello in 1809, he knew that his public life was over. For the final seventeen years of his life he kept a watchful eye on everything that grew in Monticello. But Jefferson was never far from the world. He rose every morning to attack his voluminous correspondence. The Library of Congress holds more than fifty-five thousand Jefferson manuscripts and letters, and the most recent edition of his writings will run to sixty volumes. Jefferson left no treatise on political philosophy and, in a sense, was no political thinker. He was always more interested in the practical consequences of ideas. Although in drafting the Declaration and elsewhere he had argued for the freedom of slaves, he evinced the same prejudices as most of his contemporaries in the colonies and then the United States. Unable to imagine blacks integrated into American society, he counseled their colonization elsewhere. On the other hand, in all likelihood he fathered one or more children with one of his younger slaves, Sally Hemings. He remained an agrarian aristocrat all his life, and it is to the liberty of mind and the values of the land that he always returned. As Dumas Malone puts it, he was a "homely aristocrat in manner of life and personal tastes; he distrusted all rulers and feared the rise of an industrial proletariat, but more than any of his eminent contemporaries, he trusted the common man, if measurably enlightened and kept in rural virtue." Jefferson died a few hours before John Adams on the Fourth of July, 1826.

From The Autobiography of Thomas Jefferson[1]

From *The Declaration of Independence*

* * *

It appearing in the course of these debates, that the colonies of New York, New Jersey, Pennsylvania, Delaware, Maryland, and South Carolina were not yet matured for falling from the parent stem, but that they were fast advancing to that state, it was thought most prudent to wait a while for them, and to postpone the final decision to July 1st; but, that this might occasion as little delay as possible, a committee was appointed to prepare a Declaration of Independence. The committee were John Adams, Dr. Franklin, Roger Sherman, Robert R. Livingston, and myself. Committees were also appointed, at the same time, to prepare a plan of confederation for the colonies, and to state the terms proper to be proposed for foreign alliance. The committee for drawing the Declaration of Independence, desired me to do it. It was accordingly done, and being approved by them, I reported it to the House on Friday, the 28th of June, when it was read, and ordered to lie on the table. On Monday, the 1st of July, the House resolved itself into a committee of the whole, and resumed the consideration of the original motion made by the delegates of Virginia, which, being again debated through the day, was carried in the affirmative by the votes of New Hampshire, Connecticut, Massachusetts, Rhode Island, New Jersey, Maryland, Virginia, North Carolina and Georgia. South Carolina and Pennsylvania voted against it. Delaware had but two members present, and they were divided. The delegates from New York declared they were for it themselves, and were assured their constituents were for it; but that their instructions having been drawn near a twelve-month before, when reconciliation was still the general object, they were enjoined by them to do nothing which should impede that object. They, therefore, thought themselves not justifiable in voting on either side, and asked leave to withdraw from the question: which was given them. The committee rose and reported their resolution to the House. Mr. Edward Rutledge, of South Carolina, then requested the determination might be put off to the next day, as he believed his colleagues, though they disapproved of the resolution, would then join in it for the sake of unanimity. The ultimate question, whether the House would agree to the resolution of the committee, was accordingly postponed to the next day, when it was again moved, and South Carolina concurred in voting for it. In the meantime, a third member had come post[2] from the Delaware counties, and turned the vote of that colony in favor of the resolution. Members of a different sentiment attending that morning from Pennsylvania also, her vote was changed, so that the whole twelve colonies who were authorized to vote at all, gave their voices for it; and, within a few days, the convention of New York approved of it, and thus supplied the void occasioned by the withdrawing of her delegates from the vote.

1. On June 7, 1776, Richard Henry Lee of Virginia proposed to the Second Continental Congress, meeting in Philadelphia, that "these united Colonies are, and of a right ought to be, free and independent states." On June 11, a committee of five—John Adams of Massachusetts, Benjamin Franklin of Pennsylvania, Roger Sherman of Connecticut, Robert Livingston of New York, and Thomas Jefferson of Virginia—was instructed to draft a declaration of independence. The draft presented to Congress on June 28 was primarily the work of Jefferson. Lee's resolution was passed on July 2, and the Declaration was adopted on July 4 with the changes noted by Jefferson in this text, taken from his *Autobiography*. On August 2 a copy in parchment was signed by all the delegates but three; they signed later. The text used here is from *The Writings of Thomas Jefferson*, edited by A. A. Lipscomb and A. E. Bergh (1903).
2. Speedily, posthaste.

Congress proceeded the same day to consider the Declaration of Independence, which had been reported and lain on the table the Friday preceding, and on Monday referred to a committee of the whole. The pusillanimous idea that we had friends in England worth keeping terms with, still haunted the minds of many. For this reason, those passages which conveyed censures on the people of England were struck out, lest they should give them offense. The clause too, reprobating the enslaving the inhabitants of Africa, was struck out in complaisance to South Carolina and Georgia, who had never attempted to restrain the importation of slaves, and who, on the contrary, still wished to continue it. Our northern brethren also, I believe, felt a little tender under those censures; for though their people had very few slaves themselves, yet they had been pretty considerable carriers of them to others. The debates, having taken up the greater parts of the 2d, 3d, and 4th days of July, were, on the evening of the last, closed; the Declaration was reported by the committee, agreed to by the House, and signed by every member present, except Mr. Dickinson.[3] As the sentiments of men are known not only by what they receive, but what they reject also, I will state the form of the Declaration as originally reported. The parts struck out by Congress shall be distinguished by a black line drawn under them, and those inserted by them shall be placed in the margin, or in a concurrent column.

A DECLARATION BY THE REPRESENTATIVES OF THE UNITED STATES OF AMERICA, IN GENERAL CONGRESS ASSEMBLED.

When, in the course of human events, it becomes necessary for one people to dissolve the political bands which have connected them with another, and to assume among the powers of the earth the separate and equal station to which the laws of nature and of nature's God entitle them, a decent respect to the opinions of mankind requires that they should declare the causes which impel them to the separation.

We hold these truths to be self evident: that all men are created equal;[4] that they are endowed by their Creator with inherent and inalienable rights; that among these are life, liberty, and the pursuit of happiness;[5] that to secure these rights, governments are instituted among men, deriving their just powers from the consent of the governed; that whenever any form of government becomes destructive of these ends, it is the right of the people to alter or to abolish it, and to institute new government, laying its foundation on such principles, and organizing its powers in such form, as to them shall seem most likely to effect their safety and happiness. Prudence, indeed, will dic-

certain

3. John Dickinson of Pennsylvania, who opposed it.
4. Garry Wills, in his study of the Declaration (*Inventing America*, 1978), tells us that Jefferson means *equal* in possessing a moral sense: "The moral sense is not only man's *highest* faculty, but the one that is *equal* to all men."
5. In his *Second Treatise on Government* (1689) John Locke defined man's natural rights to "life, liberty, and property." Jefferson's substitution of "pursuit of happiness" has puzzled a number of critics. Wills suggests that Jefferson was less influenced by Locke than by the Scottish philosophers, particularly Francis Hutcheson and his *Inquiry into the Original of Our Ideas of Beauty and Virtue* (1725). Wills tells us that "the pursuit of happiness is a phenomenon both obvious and paradoxical. It supplies us with the ground of human right and the goal of human virtue. It is the basic drive of the self, and the only means given for transcending the self. . . . Men in the eighteenth century felt they could become conscious of their freedom only by discovering how they were bound: When they found what they *must* pursue, they knew they had a *right* to pursue it."

tate that governments long established should not be changed for light and transient causes; and accordingly all experience hath shown that mankind are more disposed to suffer while evils are sufferable, than to right themselves by abolishing the forms to which they are accustomed. But when a long train of abuses and usurpations, begun at a distinguished[6] period and pursuing invariably the same object, evinces a design to reduce them under absolute despotism, it is their right, it is their duty to throw off such government, and to provide new guards for their future security. Such has been the patient sufferance of these colonies; and such is now the necessity which constrains them to expunge their former systems of government. [alter] The history of the present king of Great Britain[7] is a history of unremitting injuries and usurpations, among which appears [repeated] no solitary fact to contradict the uniform tenor of the rest, [all having] but all have in direct object the establishment of an absolute tyranny over these states. To prove this, let facts be submitted to a candid world for the truth of which we pledge a faith yet unsullied by falsehood.

He has refused his assent to laws the most wholesome and necessary for the public good.

He has forbidden his governors to pass laws of immediate and pressing importance, unless suspended in their operation till his assent should be obtained; and, when so suspended, he has utterly neglected to attend to them.

He has refused to pass other laws for the accommodation of large districts of people, unless those people would relinquish the right of representation in the legislature, a right inestimable to them, and formidable to tyrants only.

He has called together legislative bodies at places unusual, uncomfortable, and distant from the depository of their public records, for the sole purpose of fatiguing them into compliance with his measures.

He has dissolved representative houses repeatedly and continually for opposing with manly firmness his invasions on the rights of the people.

He has refused for a long time after such dissolutions to cause others to be elected, whereby the legislative powers, incapable of annihilation, have returned to the people at large for their exercise, the state remaining, in the meantime, exposed to all the dangers of invasion from without and convulsions within.

He has endeavored to prevent the population of these states; for that purpose obstructing the laws for naturalization of foreigners, refusing to pass others to encourage their migrations hither, and raising the conditions of new appropriations of lands.

He has suffered the administration of justice totally to cease [obstructed] in some of these states refusing his assent to laws for establish- [by] ing judiciary powers.

6. I.e., discernible.   7. King George III (1738–1820).

He has made <u>our</u> judges dependent on his will alone for the tenure of their offices, and the amount and payment of their salaries.

He has erected a multitude of new offices, <u>by a self-assumed power</u> and sent hither swarms of new officers to harass our people and eat out their substance.

He has kept among us in times of peace standing armies <u>and ships of war</u> without the consent of our legislatures.

He has affected to render the military independent of, and superior to, the civil power.

He has combined with others[8] to subject us to a jurisdiction foreign to our constitutions and unacknowledged by our laws, giving his assent to their acts of pretended legislation for quartering large bodies of armed troops among us; for protecting them by a mock trial from punishment for any murders which they should commit on the inhabitants of these states; for cutting off our trade with all parts of the world; for imposing taxes on us without our consent; for depriving us [ ] of the benefits of trial by jury; for transporting us beyond seas to be tried for pretended offenses; for abolishing the free system of English laws in a neighboring province,[9] establishing therein an arbitrary government, and enlarging its boundaries, so as to render it at once an example and fit instrument for introducing the same absolute rule into these <u>states</u>; for taking away our charters, abolishing our most valuable laws, and altering fundamentally the forms of our governments; for suspending our own legislatures, and declaring themselves invested with power to legislate for us in all cases whatsoever. *in many cases* *colonies;*

He has abdicated government here <u>withdrawing his governors, and declaring us out of his allegiance and protection.</u> *by declaring us out of his protection, and waging war against us.*

He has plundered our seas, ravaged our coasts, burnt our towns, and destroyed the lives of our people.

He is at this time transporting large armies of foreign mercenaries[1] to complete the works of death, desolation and tyranny already begun with circumstances of cruelty and perfidy [ ] unworthy the head of a civilized nation. *scarcely paralleled in the most barbarous ages, and totally*

He has constrained our fellow citizens taken captive on the high seas, to bear arms against their country, to become the executioners of their friends and brethren, or to fall themselves by their hands.

He has [ ] endeavored to bring on the inhabitants of our frontiers, the merciless Indian savages, whose known rule of warfare is an undistinguished destruction of all ages, sexes and conditions <u>of existence.</u> *excited domestic insurrection among us, and has*

He has <u>incited treasonable insurrections of our fellow citizens, with the allurements of forfeiture and confiscation of our property.</u>

---

8. I.e., the British Parliament.
9. The Quebec Act of 1774 recognized the Roman Catholic religion in Quebec and extended the borders of the province to the Ohio River; it restored French civil law and thus angered the New England colonies. It was often referred to as one of the "intolerable acts."
1. German soldiers hired by the king for colonial service.

He has waged cruel war against human nature itself, violating its most sacred rights of life and liberty in the persons of a distant people who never offended him, captivating and carrying them into slavery in another hemisphere, or to incur miserable death in their transportation thither. This piratical warfare, the opprobrium of infidel powers, is the warfare of the christian king of Great Britain. Determined to keep open a market where men should be bought and sold, he has prostituted his negative for suppressing every legislative attempt to prohibit or to restrain this execrable commerce. And that this assemblage of horrors might want no fact of distinguished die, he is now exciting those very people to rise in arms among us, and to purchase that liberty of which he has deprived them, by murdering the people on whom he also obtruded them: thus paying off former crimes committed against the LIBERTIES of one people, with crimes which he urges them to commit against the lives of another.

In every stage of these oppressions we have petitioned for redress in the most humble terms: our repeated petitions have been answered only by repeated injuries.

A prince whose character is thus marked by every act which may define a tyrant is unfit to be the ruler of a [ ] people who mean to be free. Future ages will scarcely believe that the hardiness of one man adventured, within the short compass of twelve years only, to lay a foundation so broad and so undisguised for tyranny over a people fostered and fixed in principles of freedom.

free

Nor have we been wanting in attentions to our British brethren. We have warned them from time to time of attempts by their legislature to extend a jurisdiction over these our states. We have reminded them of the circumstances of our emigration and settlement here, no one of which could warrant so strange a pretension: that these were effected at the expense of our own blood and treasure, unassisted by the wealth or the strength of Great Britain: that in constituting indeed our several forms of government, we had adopted one common king, thereby laying a foundation for perpetual league and amity with them: but that submission to their parliament was no part of our constitution, nor ever in idea, if history may be credited: and, we [ ] appealed to their native justice and magnanimity as well as to the ties of our common kindred to disavow these usurpations which were likely to interrupt our connection and correspondence. They too have been deaf to the voice of justice and of consanguinity, and when occasions have been given them, by the regular course of their laws, of removing from their councils the disturbers of our harmony, they have, by their free election, reestablished them in power. At this very time too, they are permitting their chief magistrate to send over not only soldiers of our common blood, but Scotch and foreign mercenaries to invade and destroy us. These facts have given the last stab to agonizing affection, and manly spirit bids us to renounce forever these unfeeling

an unwarrantable / us

have
and we have
conjured
them by
would
inevitably

brethren. <u>We must endeavor to forget our former love for them, and hold them as we hold the rest of mankind, enemies in war, in peace friends. We might have been a free and a great people together; but a communication of grandeur and of freedom, it seems, is below their dignity. Be it so, since they will have it. The road to happiness and to glory is open to us, too. We will tread it apart from them, and</u> acquiesce in the necessity which denounces[2] our eternal separation [ ]!

We must therefore and hold them as we hold the rest of mankind, enemies in war, in peace friends.

We therefore the representatives of the United States of America in General Congress assembled, do in the name, and by the authority of the good people of these <u>states reject and renounce all allegiance and subjection to the kings of Great Britain and all others who may hereafter claim by, through or under them; we utterly dissolve all political connection which may heretofore have subsisted between us and the people or parliament of Great Britain: and finally we do assert and declare these colonies to be free and independent states,</u> and that as free and independent states, they have full power to levy war, conclude peace, contract alliances, establish commerce, and to do all other acts and things which independent states may of right do.

And for the support of this declaration, we mutually pledge to each other our lives, our fortunes, and our sacred honor.

We, therefore, the representatives of the United States of America in General Congress assembled, appealing to the supreme judge of the world for the rectitude of our intentions, do in the name, and by the authority of the good people of these colonies, solemnly publish and declare, that these united colonies are, and of right ought to be free and independent states; that they are absolved from all allegiance to the British crown, and that all political connection between them and the state of Great Britain is, and ought to be, totally dissolved; and that as free and independent states, they have full power to levy war, conclude peace, contract alliances, establish commerce, and to do all other acts and things which independent states may of right do.

And for the support of this declaration, with a firm reliance on the protection of divine providence, we mutually pledge to each other our lives, our fortunes, and our sacred honor.

The Declaration thus signed on the 4th, on paper, was engrossed[3] on parchment, and signed again on the 2d of August.

1821   1829

THE FEDERALIST

When Richard Henry Lee, a Virginia delegate to the Continental Congress, proposed on June 7, 1776, his resolution for independence from Britain, he also suggested that a "plan of confederation be prepared and transmitted to the respective colonies for their consideration and approbation." On July 12, 1776, the Articles of Confederation were presented to Congress; they were debated for a year; they were ratified and adopted as the bylaws of the nation on March 1, 1781. The central question before the Constitutional Convention meeting in Philadelphia six years later was whether to try to salvage these articles by a number of complicated amendments or to draw up the framework of a new national government. Delegates to the convention decided on the latter and, in September 1787, received copies of the proposed Constitution which they, in turn, were to submit to their state legislatures for ratification. Advocates of the new Constitution, dubbed Federalists, and their Antifederalist opponents quickly rose to the occasion, and a great debate followed. Many were fearful at what they saw as the loss of states' rights and the power of a large, impersonal government to dominate the lives of individual citizens, and they cited the absence of a bill of rights; others thought that the Constitution favored urban over rural populations; still others bemoaned the end of the slave trade.

The debate took ten months, nowhere more seriously than in the state of New York, where adoption was not inevitable and a number of states' rights supporters objected to strengthening the power of the federal government. The discussion there produced a number of significant documents, none more enduring than the eighty-five essays that appeared in New York newspapers from October 1787 to April 1788, signed with the pen name Publius and later collected in two volumes called *The Federalist*. These essays were written by Alexander Hamilton (1757–1804), a brilliant and quick-tempered man who was a secretary and aide to General Washington and, later, secretary of the treasury; John Jay (1745–1829), who would be first chief justice of the United States Supreme Court and governor of the state of New York; and a Virginian, James Madison (1751–1836), a lawyer of distinction who would

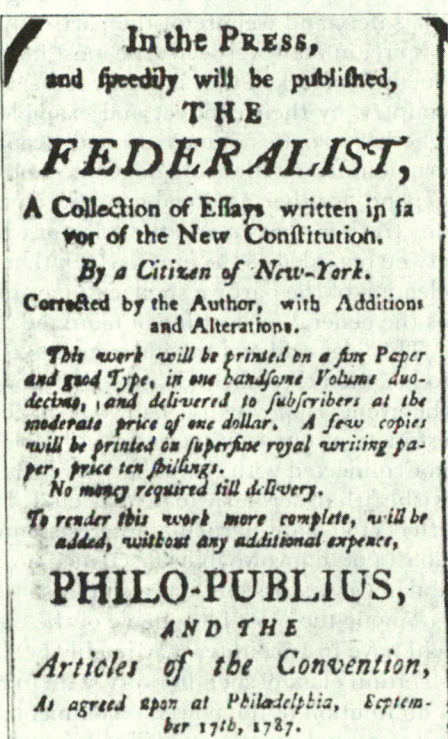

In the PRESS, and speedily will be published, THE FEDERALIST, A Collection of Essays written in favor of the New Constitution. By a Citizen of New-York. Corrected by the Author, with Additions and Alterations.

This work will be printed on a fine Paper and good Type, in one handsome Volume duodecimo, and delivered to subscribers at the moderate price of one dollar. A few copies will be printed on superfine royal writing paper, price ten shillings.

No money required till delivery.

To render this work more complete, will be added, without any additional expence,

PHILO-PUBLIUS, AND THE Articles of the Convention, As agreed upon at Philadelphia, September 17th, 1787.

The Federalist. Beginning in 1787, Alexander Hamilton, James Madison, and John Jay wrote eighty-five essays in support of the new Constitution that eventually were published in book form as *The Federalist*.

be fourth president of the United States. The pseudonym Publius was used for the sake of anonymity, but the authorship was generally known.

As originally conceived, *The Federalist* had only one purpose: to persuade reluctant New Yorkers to adopt the proposed new Constitution. It did not set out to define the nature of government; yet it has turned out to be far more lasting than most political treatises. Its essential argument is that individuals have a natural right to "liberty, dignity, and happiness" and that to ensure these rights government must "secure the public good, and private rights, against the dangers of a majority," at the same time preserving the "spirit and form of a popular government." This difficult balancing that *The Federalist* argues for goes to the very heart of American democracy.

The text used here is from *The Federalist* (1961), edited by Jacob E. Cooke.

From The Federalist

No. 1 [*Alexander Hamilton*]

To the People of the State of New York.   October 27, 1787

After an unequivocal experience of the inefficacy of the subsisting[1] federal government, you are called upon to deliberate on a new Constitution for the United States of America. The subject speaks its own importance; comprehending in its consequences nothing less than the existence of the Union, the safety and welfare of the parts of which it is composed, the fate of an empire, in many respects, the most interesting in the world. It has been frequently remarked that it seems to have been reserved to the people of this country, by their conduct and example, to decide the important question whether societies of men are really capable or not of establishing good government from reflection and choice, or whether they are forever destined to depend, for their political constitutions, on accident and force. If there be any truth in the remark, the crisis at which we are arrived may with propriety be regarded as the era in which that decision is to be made; and a wrong election of the part we shall act, may, in this view, deserve to be considered as the general misfortune of mankind.

This idea will add the inducements of philanthropy to those of patriotism to heighten the solicitude, which all considerate and good men must feel for the event. Happy will it be if our choice should be directed by a judicious estimate of our true interests, unperplexed and unbiased by considerations not connected with the public good. But this is a thing more ardently to be wished than seriously to be expected. The plan offered to our deliberations affects too many particular interests, innovates[2] upon too many local institutions, not to involve in its discussion a variety of objects foreign to its merits, and of views, passions and prejudices little favorable to the discovery of truth.

Among the most formidable of the obstacles which the new Constitution will have to encounter may readily be distinguished the obvious interest of a certain class of men in every state to resist all changes which may hazard a diminution of the power, emolument and consequence of the offices they hold under the state establishments—and the perverted ambition of another class of men, who will either hope to aggrandize themselves by the confusions of their country, or will flatter themselves with fairer prospects of elevation from the subdivision of the empire into several partial confederacies, than from its union under one government.

1. Existing; present.   2. Makes changes.

It is not, however, my design to dwell upon observations of this nature. I am well aware that it would be disingenuous to resolve indiscriminately the opposition of any set of men (merely because their situations might subject them to suspicion) into interested or ambitious views: candor will oblige us to admit, that even such men may be actuated by upright intentions; and it cannot be doubted that much of the opposition which has made its appearance, or may hereafter make its appearance, will spring from sources, blameless at least, if not respectable, the honest errors of minds led astray by preconceived jealousies and fears. So numerous indeed and so powerful are the causes, which serve to give a false bias to the judgment, that we upon many occasions see wise and good men on the wrong as well as on the right side of questions of the first magnitude to society. This circumstance, if duly attended to, would furnish a lesson of moderation to those, who are ever so much persuaded of their being in the right in any controversy. And a further reason for caution, in this respect, might be drawn from the reflection that we are not always sure that those who advocate the truth are influenced by purer principles than their antagonists. Ambition, avarice, personal animosity, party opposition, and many other motives, not more laudable than these, are apt to operate as well upon those who support as upon those who oppose the right side of a question. Were there not even these inducements to moderation, nothing could be more ill judged than that intolerant spirit, which has, at all times, characterized political parties. For, in politics as in religion, it is equally absurd to aim at making proselytes by fire and sword. Heresies in either can rarely be cured by persecution.

And yet however just these sentiments will be allowed to be, we have already sufficient indications that it will happen in this as in all former cases of great national discussion. A torrent of angry and malignant passions will be let loose. To judge from the conduct of the opposite parties, we shall be led to conclude that they will mutually hope to evince the justness of their opinions, and to increase the number of their converts by the loudness of their declamations, and by the bitterness of their invectives. An enlightened zeal for the energy and efficiency of government will be stigmatized, as the offspring of a temper fond of despotic power and hostile to the principles of liberty. An overscrupulous jealousy of danger to the rights of the people, which is more commonly the fault of the head than of the heart, will be represented as mere pretense and artifice; the bait for popularity at the expense of public good. It will be forgotten, on the one hand, that jealousy is the usual concomitant of violent love, and that the noble enthusiasm of liberty is too apt to be infected with a spirit of narrow and illiberal distrust. On the other hand, it will be equally forgotten that the vigor of government is essential to the security of liberty; that in the contemplation of a sound and well-informed judgment, their interest can never be separated; and that a dangerous ambition more often lurks behind the specious mask of zeal for the rights of the people than under the forbidding appearance of zeal for the firmness and efficiency of government. History will teach us that the former has been found a much more certain road to the introduction of despotism than the latter, and that of those men who have overturned the liberties of republics the greatest number have begun their career by paying an obsequious court to the people, commencing demagogues and ending tyrants.

In the course of the preceding observations I have had an eye, my fellow citizens, to putting you upon your guard against all attempts, from whatever quarter, to influence your decision in a matter of the utmost moment to your welfare by any impressions other than those which may result from the evidence of truth. You will, no doubt, at the same time, have collected from the general scope of them that they proceed from a source not unfriendly to the new Constitution. Yes, my countrymen, I own to you, that, after having given it an attentive consideration, I am clearly of opinion it is your interest to adopt it. I am convinced that this is the safest course for your liberty, your dignity, and your happiness. I effect not reserves, which I do not feel. I will not amuse you with an appearance of deliberation, when I have decided. I frankly acknowledge to you my convictions, and I will freely lay before you the reasons on which they are founded. The consciousness of good intentions disdains ambiguity. I shall not however multiply professions on this head. My motives must remain in the depository of my own breast: my arguments will be open to all, and may be judged of by all. They shall at least be offered in a spirit which will not disgrace the cause of truth.

I propose in a series of papers to discuss the following interesting particulars—the utility of the Union to your political prosperity—the insufficiency of the present confederation to preserve that Union—the necessity of a government at least equally energetic with the one proposed to the attainment of this object—the conformity of the proposed constitution to the true principles of republican government—its analogy to your own state constitution—and lastly, the additional security which its adoption will afford to the preservation of that species of government, to liberty and to property.

In the progress of this discussion I shall endeavor to give a satisfactory answer to all the objections which shall have made their appearance that may seem to have any claim to your attention.

It may perhaps be thought superfluous to offer arguments to prove the utility of the Union, a point, no doubt, deeply engraved on the hearts of the great body of the people in every state, and one, which it may be imagined, has no adversaries. But the fact is that we already hear it whispered in the private circles of those who oppose the new constitution that the thirteen states are of too great extent for any general system, and that we must of necessity resort to separate confederacies of distinct portions of the whole.[3] This doctrine will, in all probability, be gradually propagated, till it has votaries enough to countenance an open avowal of it. For nothing can be more evident, to those who are able to take an enlarged view of the subject, than the alternative of an adoption of the new Constitution, or a dismemberment of the Union. It will therefore be of use to begin by examining the advantages of that Union, the certain evils and the probable dangers to which every state will be exposed from its dissolution. This shall accordingly constitute the subject of my next address.

Publius[4]

No. 10 [*James Madison*]

To the People of the State of New York.   November 22, 1787
Among the numerous advantages promised by a well-constructed Union, none deserves to be more accurately developed than its tendency to break

3. The same idea, tracing the arguments to their consequences, is held out in several of the late publications against the new Constitution [Publius's note].

4. A Latin proper name and the collective pseudonym adopted by Hamilton, Madison, and Jay as the authors of *The Federalist*; their authorship was well known.

and control the violence of faction. The friend of popular governments never finds himself so much alarmed for their character and fate as when he contemplates their propensity to this dangerous vice. He will not fail therefore to set a due value on any plan which, without violating the principles to which he is attached, provides a proper cure for it. The instability, injustice and confusion introduced into the public councils have in truth been the mortal diseases under which popular governments have everywhere perished; as they continue to be the favorite and fruitful topics from which the adversaries to liberty derive their most specious declamations. The valuable improvements made by the American constitutions on the popular models, both ancient and modern, cannot certainly be too much admired; but it would be an unwarrantable partiality to contend that they have as effectually obviated the danger on this side as was wished and expected. Complaints are everywhere heard from our most considerate and virtuous citizens, equally the friends of public and private faith and of public and personal liberty; that our governments are too unstable; that the public good is disregarded in the conflicts of rival parties; and that measures are too often decided not according to the rules of justice and the rights of the minor party, but by the superior force of an interested and overbearing majority. However anxiously we may wish that these complaints had no foundation, the evidence of known facts will not permit us to deny that they are in some degree true. It will be found indeed, on a candid review of our situation, that some of the distresses under which we labor have been erroneously charged on the operation of our governments; but it will be found, at the same time, that other causes will not alone account for many of our heaviest misfortunes; and particularly, for that prevailing and increasing distrust of public engagements, and alarm for private rights, which are echoed from one end of the continent to the other. These must be chiefly, if not wholly, effects of the unsteadiness and injustice with which a factious spirit has tainted our public administrations.

By a faction I understand a number of citizens, whether amounting to a majority or minority of the whole, who are united and actuated by some common impulse of passion or of interest, adverse to the rights of other citizens, or to the permanent and aggregate interests of the community.

There are two methods of curing the mischiefs of faction: the one, by removing its causes; the other, by controlling its effects.

There are again two methods of removing the causes of faction: the one by destroying the liberty which is essential to its existence; the other, by giving to every citizen the same opinions, the same passions, and the same interests.

It could never be more truly said than of the first remedy, that it is worse than the disease. Liberty is to faction, what air is to fire, an aliment[5] without which it instantly expires. But it could not be a less folly to abolish liberty, which is essential to political life, because it nourishes faction, than it would be to wish the annihilation of air, which is essential to animal life, because it imparts to fire its destructive agency.

The second expedient is as impracticable as the first would be unwise. As long as the reason of man continues fallible, and he is at liberty to exercise it, different opinions will be formed. As long as the connection subsists between his reason and his self-love, his opinions and his passions will have a reciprocal influence on each other; and the former will be objects to which

5. Nutriment; sustenance.

the latter will attach themselves. The diversity in the faculties of men from which the rights of property originate is not less an insuperable obstacle to a uniformity of interests. The protection of these faculties is the first object of government. From the protection of different and unequal faculties of acquiring property, the possession of different degrees and kinds of property immediately results: and from the influence of these on the sentiments and views of the respective proprietors ensues a division of the society into different interests and parties.

The latent causes of faction are thus sown in the nature of man; and we see them everywhere brought into different degrees of activity, according to the different circumstances of civil society. A zeal for different opinions concerning religion, concerning government and many other points, as well of speculation as of practice; an attachment to different leaders ambitiously contending for pre-eminence and power; or to persons of other descriptions whose fortunes have been interesting to the human passions have in turn divided mankind into parties, inflamed them with mutual animosity, and rendered them much more disposed to vex and oppress each other than to cooperate for their common good. So strong is this propensity of mankind to fall into mutual animosities that where no substantial occasion presents itself, the most frivolous and fanciful distinctions have been sufficient to kindle their unfriendly passions and excite their most violent conflicts. But the most common and durable source of factions has been the various and unequal distribution of property. Those who hold and those who are without property have ever formed distinct interests in society. Those who are creditors and those who are debtors fall under a like discrimination. A landed interest, a manufacturing interest, a mercantile interest, a monied interest, with many lesser interests, grow up of necessity in civilized nations, and divide them into different classes, actuated by different sentiments and views. The regulation of these various and interfering interests forms the principal task of modern legislation, and involves the spirit of party and faction in the necessary and ordinary operations of government.

No man is allowed to be a judge in his own cause, because his interest would certainly bias his judgment and, not improbably, corrupt his integrity. With equal, nay with greater, reason a body of men are unfit to be both judges and parties at the same time; yet what are many of the most important acts of legislation but so many judicial determinations, not indeed concerning the rights of single persons, but concerning the rights of large bodies of citizens; and what are the different classes of legislators but advocates and parties to the causes which they determine? Is a law proposed concerning private debts? It is a question to which the creditors are parties on one side and the debtors on the other. Justice ought to hold the balance between them. Yet the parties are and must be themselves the judges; and the most numerous party, or, in other words, the most powerful faction, must be expected to prevail. Shall domestic manufactures be encouraged, and in what degree, by restrictions on foreign manufactures? are questions which would be differently decided by the landed and the manufacturing classes; and probably by neither, with a sole regard to justice and the public good. The apportionment of taxes on the various descriptions of property is an act which seems to require the most exact impartiality; yet, there is perhaps no legislative act in which greater opportunity and temptation are given to a predominant party to trample on the rules of justice. Every shilling with which they overburden the inferior number is a shilling saved to their own pockets.

It is in vain to say that enlightened statesmen will be able to adjust these clashing interests and render them all subservient to the public good. Enlightened statesmen will not always be at the helm; nor, in many cases, can such an adjustment be made at all, without taking into view indirect and remote considerations, which will rarely prevail over the immediate interest which one party may find in disregarding the rights of another, or the good of the whole.

The inference to which we are brought is that the *causes* of faction cannot be removed, and that relief is only to be sought in the means of controlling its *effects*.

If a faction consists of less than a majority, relief is supplied by the republican principle, which enables the majority to defeat its sinister views by regular vote. It may clog the administration, it may convulse the society, but it will be unable to execute and mask its violence under the forms of the Constitution. When a majority is included in a faction, the form of popular government on the other hand enables it to sacrifice to its ruling passion or interest both the public good and the rights of other citizens. To secure the public good and private rights against the danger of such a faction, and at the same time to preserve the spirit and the form of popular government, is then the great object to which our inquiries are directed. Let me add that it is the great desideratum[6] by which alone this form of government can be rescued from the opprobrium under which it has so long labored and be recommended to the esteem and adoption of mankind.

By what means is this object attainable? Evidently by one of two only. Either the existence of the same passion or interest in a majority at the same time must be prevented; or the majority, having such co-existent passion or interest, must be rendered, by their number and local situation, unable to concert and carry into effect schemes of oppression. If the impulse and the opportunity be suffered to coincide, we well know that neither moral nor religious motives can be relied on as an adequate control. They are not found to be such on the injustice and violence of individuals, and lose their efficacy in proportion to the number combined together; that is, in proportion as their efficacy becomes needful.

From this view of the subject, it may be concluded, that a pure democracy, by which I mean a society consisting of a small number of citizens who assemble and administer the government in person, can admit of no cure for the mischiefs of faction. A common passion or interest will, in almost every case, be felt by a majority of the whole; a communication and concert results from the form of government itself; and there is nothing to check the inducements to sacrifice the weaker party, or an obnoxious individual. Hence it is that such democracies have ever been spectacles of turbulence and contention; have ever been found incompatible with personal security, or the rights of property; and have in general been as short in their lives, as they have been violent in their deaths. Theoretic politicians, who have patronized this species of government, have erroneously supposed that by reducing mankind to a perfect equality in their political rights, they would, at the same time, be perfectly equalized and assimilated in their possessions, their opinions, and their passions.

A republic, by which I mean a government in which the scheme of representation takes place, opens a different prospect, and promises the cure for which we are seeking. Let us examine the points in which it varies from pure

6. Thing which is desired; that which is felt to be missing and needed (Latin).

democracy, and we shall comprehend both the nature of the cure, and the efficacy which it must derive from the Union.

The two great points of difference between a democracy and a republic are, first, the delegation of the government, in the latter, to a small number of citizens elected by the rest: secondly, the greater number of citizens, and greater sphere of country, over which the latter may be extended.

The effect of the first difference is, on the one hand, to refine and enlarge the public views by passing them through the medium of a chosen body of citizens, whose wisdom may best discern the true interest of their country, and whose patriotism and love of justice will be least likely to sacrifice it to temporary or partial considerations. Under such a regulation, it may well happen that the public voice pronounced by the representatives of the people will be more consonant to the public good than if pronounced by the people themselves convened for the purpose. On the other hand, the effect may be inverted. Men of factious tempers, of local prejudices, or of sinister designs may, by intrigue, by corruption or by other means, first obtain the suffrages,[7] and then betray the interests of the people. The question resulting is whether small or extensive republics are most favorable to the election of proper guardians of the public weal: and it is clearly decided in favor of the latter by two obvious considerations.

In the first place it is to be remarked that however small the republic may be, the representatives must be raised to a certain number in order to guard against the cabals[8] of a few; and that however large it may be, they must be limited to a certain number in order to guard against the confusion of a multitude. Hence the number of representatives in the two cases, not being in proportion to that of the constituents, and being proportionally greatest in the small republic, it follows, that if the proportion of fit characters be not less in the large than in the small republic, the former will present a greater option, and consequently a greater probability of a fit choice.

In the next place, as each representative will be chosen by a greater number of citizens in the large than in the small republic, it will be more difficult for unworthy candidates to practice with success the vicious arts, by which elections are too often carried; and the suffrages of the people being more free will be more likely to center on men who possess the most attractive merit, and the most diffusive and established characters.

It must be confessed that in this, as in most other cases, there is a mean, on both sides of which inconveniencies will be found to lie. By enlarging too much the number of electors, you render the representative too little acquainted with all their local circumstances and lesser interests; as by reducing it too much, you render him unduly attached to these, and too little fit to comprehend and pursue great and national objects. The federal Constitution forms a happy combination in this respect; the great and aggregate interests being referred to the national, the local, and, particular, to the state legislatures.

The other point of difference is the greater number of citizens and extent of territory which may be brought within the compass of republican, than of democratic[9] government; and it is this circumstance principally which ren-

7. Votes.
8. Plots.
9. Republicans are Federalists and are willing to have an elected few represent the whole; Democrats are anti-Federalists and are carefully guarding the individual's right to vote.

ders factious combinations less to be dreaded in the former than in the latter. The smaller the society, the fewer probably will be the distinct parties and interests composing it; the fewer the distinct parties and interests, the more frequently will a majority be found of the same party; and the smaller the number of individuals composing a majority, and smaller the compass within which they are placed, the more easily will they concert and execute their plans of oppression. Extend the sphere, and you take in a greater variety of parties and interests; you make it less probable that a majority of the whole will have a common motive to invade the rights of other citizens; or if such a common motive exists, it will be more difficult for all who feel it to discover their own strength, and to act in unison with each other. Besides other impediments, it may be remarked, that where there is a consciousness of unjust or dishonorable purposes, communication is always checked by distrust, in proportion to the number whose concurrence is necessary.

Hence it clearly appears that the same advantage which a republic has over a democracy, in controlling the effects of faction, is enjoyed by a large over a small republic—is enjoyed by the Union over the states composing it. Does this advantage consist in the substitution of representatives, whose enlightened views and virtuous sentiments render them superior to local prejudices, and to schemes of injustice? It will not be denied, that the representation of the Union will be most likely to possess these requisite endowments. Does it consist in the greater security afforded by a greater variety of parties, against the event of any one party being able to outnumber and oppress the rest? In an equal degree does the increased variety of parties, comprised within the Union, increase this security? Does it, in fine,[1] consist in the greater obstacles opposed to the concert and accomplishment of the secret wishes of an unjust and interested majority? Here, again, the extent of the Union gives it the most palpable advantage.

The influence of factious leaders may kindle a flame within their particular states, but will be unable to spread a general conflagration through the other states: a religious sect may degenerate into a political faction in a part of the confederacy, but the variety of sects dispersed over the entire face of it must secure the national councils against any danger from that source: a rage for paper money, for an abolition of debts, for an equal division of property, or for any other improper or wicked project, will be less apt to pervade the whole body of the Union than a particular member of it; in the same proportion as such a malady is more likely to taint a particular county or district than an entire state.

In the extent and proper structure of the Union, therefore, we behold a republican remedy for the diseases most incident to republican government. And according to the degree of pleasure and pride we feel in being republicans, ought to be our zeal in cherishing the spirit, and supporting the character of Federalists.

Publius

1787   1788

---

1. In conclusion.

OLAUDAH EQUIANO
1745?–1797

*T*he *Interesting Narrative of the Life of Olaudah Equiano, or Gustavus Vassa, the African* was published in London in 1789 and found an enthusiastic American audience when it was reprinted in New York in 1791. In the next five years it went through eight more editions, and it was reprinted again in the 1800s. This publication history suggests the book's centrality to the antislavery cause. No black voice before Frederick Douglass spoke so movingly to American readers about inhumanity, and no work before Douglass's own *Narrative* had such an impact. Incorporating the vocabulary and ideals of the Enlightenment—particularly the belief that sentiment linked all human beings and thus argued for the universality of human rights—Equiano spoke for the countless disenfranchised and exploited workers whose labor fueled the new mercantilism. In a literature replete with self-made figures who voyage from innocence to experience—some fictive, some not—Equiano's story, in view of the actual horrors he suffered, stands in a class quite by itself. He defined himself as neither African American (his first owner in the New World was a Virginian) nor Anglo African (after he settled in London), and he came to exemplify the Atlantic Rim, someone who at various times called Africa, North America, South America, and Europe his home.

Equiano writes that he was born in about 1745 in what is now Nigeria, in an otherwise unknown Ibo village called Essaka; he was sold to British slavers in 1756 and transported first to the Barbadoes in the West Indies and then to a plantation in Virginia. Recent scholarship has questioned these claims, suggesting that Equiano may have been born in the Carolinas. If this is true, it would mean that the narrative constitutes his decision to assume an African heritage, the testimony of someone from a marginalized group who speaks in the first person for the entire group's history. To make his own life appear more representative, Equiano thus merges his personal story with that of the voiceless African who has had to endure the horrors of the Middle Passage. His account of his later years, however, is corroborated by existing documents. He was with his second owner, Lieutenant Michael Henry Pascal, throughout the Seven Years' War between England and France and was present at the siege of Fort Louisburg on Cape Breton Island in Nova Scotia. Eventually, he was sold to a Quaker merchant from Philadelphia, Robert King, who conducted much of his business in the West Indies. King often traded in "live cargo," or slaves, and Equiano saw much that made him grateful for his Quaker master's treatment of him, though he had no illusions about what the loss of his freedom entailed. He saw the ugliest side of American life in both the North and the South. Even in Philadelphia, a city built on the premise of brotherly love, Equiano observed that the freed black was treated with profound contempt, "plundered" and "universally insulted," with no possibility of redress. King, however, did make it possible for Equiano to purchase his freedom in 1766. Having gained his liberty by paying forty pounds—money earned by carrying on his own business while managing King's—he never set foot on American soil again.

It was Equiano's intention to settle in London for the rest of his life. He made his living there as a free servant, a musician (he played the French horn), and a barber. But Equiano's skill as a seaman, and his always remarkable curiosity, made him restless for new adventures, and before he died he had traveled as far as Turkey; had attended the opera in Rome; and had seen Jamaica, Honduras, and Nicaragua. In 1783 Equiano brought the case of the infamous ship *Zong* to the British public: the owners had thrown 132 shackled slaves overboard and later made insurance claims against their loss. He lectured widely on the abolition of slavery and urged a project to resettle poor blacks in Sierra Leone, Africa. He was, in fact, given an official post in this undertaking, but lost it after he made accusations of corruption against government officials. Although he always spoke about his desire to return to the place of his birth, Africa always lay beyond his reach. In a letter written to his hosts in Birmingham, England, after lecturing there, he wrote:

> These acts of kindness and hospitality have filled me with a longing desire to see these worthy friends on my own estate in Africa, where the richest produce of it should be devoted to their entertainment. There they should partake of the luxuriant pineapples, and the well-flavored virgin palm-wine, and to heighten the bliss I would burn a certain tree, that would afford us light as clear and brilliant as the virtue of my guests.

In 1792 Equiano married Susanna Cullen, and their marriage was duly reported in the London *Gentleman's Magazine*. He died on March 31, 1797, and one of his daughters died shortly after.

The text used here is taken from the 1st edition, published in two volumes for the author in London in 1789. The original paragraphing has been altered to facilitate reading.

From The Interesting Narrative of the Life of Olaudah Equiano, or Gustavas Vassa, the African, Written by Himself

From *Chapter I*

I believe it is difficult for those who publish their own memoirs to escape the imputation of vanity; nor is this the only disadvantage under which they labor: it is also their misfortune, that what is uncommon is rarely, if ever, believed, and what is obvious we are apt to turn from with disgust, and to charge the writer with impertinence. People generally think those memoirs only worthy to be read or remembered which abound in great or striking events; those, in short, which in a high degree excite either admiration or pity: all others they consign to contempt and oblivion. It is therefore, I confess, not a little hazardous in a private and obscure individual, and a stranger too, thus to solicit the indulgent attention of the public; especially when I own[1] I offer here the history of neither a saint, a hero, nor a tyrant. I believe there are few events in my life, which have not happened to many: it is true the incidents of it are numerous; and, did I consider myself an European, I might say my sufferings were great: but when I compare my lot with that of most of my countrymen, I regard myself as a *particular favorite of Heaven,* and acknowledge the mercies of Providence in every occurrence of my life. If, then, the following narrative does not appear sufficiently interesting to engage general attention, let my motive be some excuse for its publication. I am not so foolishly vain as to expect from it either immortality or literary reputation. If it affords any satisfaction to my numerous friends, at whose request it has been written, or in the smallest degree promotes the interests of humanity, the ends for which it was undertaken will be fully attained, and every wish of my heart gratified. Let it therefore be remembered, that, in wishing to avoid censure, I do not aspire to praise.

1. Acknowledge.

That part of Africa, known by the name of Guinea, to which the trade for slaves is carried on, extends along the coast above 3400 miles, from Senegal to Angola, and includes a variety of kingdoms. Of these the most considerable is the kingdom of Benin, both as to extent and wealth, the richness and cultivation of the soil, the power of its king, and the number and warlike disposition of the inhabitants. It is situated nearly under the line,[2] and extends along the coast about 170 miles, but runs back into the interior part of Africa to a distance hitherto, I believe, unexplored by any traveler; and seems only terminated at length by the empire of Abyssinnia, near 1500 miles from its beginning. This kingdom is divided into many provinces or districts: in one of the most remote and fertile of which, I was born, in the year 1745, situated in a charming fruitful vale, named Essaka. The distance of this province from the capital of Benin and the sea coast must be very considerable: for I had never heard of white men or Europeans, nor of the sea; and our subjection to the king of Benin was little more than nominal; for every transaction of the government, as far as my slender observation extended, was conducted by the chief or elders of the place. The manners and government of a people who have little commerce with other countries, are generally very simple; and the history of what passes in one family or village, may serve as a specimen of the whole nation. My father was one of those elders or chiefs I have spoken of, and was styled Embrenche; a term, as I remember, importing the highest distinction, and signifying in our language a *mark* of grandeur. This mark is conferred on the person entitled to it, by cutting the skin across at the top of the forehead, and drawing it down to the eyebrows: and while it is in this situation applying a warm hand, and rubbing it until it shrinks up into a thick *weal* across the lower part of the forehead. Most of the judges and senators were thus marked; my father had long borne it: I had seen it conferred on one of my brothers, and I also was *destined* to receive it by my parents. Those Embrenche or chief men, decided disputes and punished crimes; for which purpose they always assembled together. The proceedings were generally short: and in most cases the law of retaliation prevailed.* * *

We are almost a nation of dancers, musicians and poets. Thus every great event, such as a triumphant return from battle, or other cause of public rejoicing, is celebrated in public dances, which are accompanied with songs and music suited to the occasion. The assembly is separated into four divisions, which dance either apart or in succession, and each with a character peculiar to itself. The first division contains the married men, who in their dances frequently exhibit feats of arms, and the representation of a battle. To these succeed the married women, who dance in the second division. The young men occupy the third: and the maidens the fourth. Each represents some interesting scene of real life, such as a great achievement, domestic employment, a pathetic story, or some rural sport; and as the subject is generally founded on some recent event, it is therefore ever new. This gives our dances a spirit and variety which I have scarcely seen elsewhere.[3]

* * *

2. I.e., the equator.
3. When I was in Smyrna I have frequently seen the Greeks dance after this manner [Equiano's note].

Chapter II

I hope the reader will not think I have trespassed on his patience in introducing myself to him, with some account of the manners and customs of my country. They had been implanted in me with great care, and made an impression on my mind, which time could not erase, and which all the adversity and variety of fortune I have since experienced, served only to rivet and record; for, whether the love of one's country be real or imaginary, or a lesson of reason, or an instinct of nature, I still look back with pleasure on the first scenes of my life, though that pleasure has been for the most part mingled with sorrow.

I have already acquainted the reader with the time and place of my birth. My father, besides many slaves, had a numerous family, of which seven lived to grow up, including myself and a sister, who was the only daughter. As I was the youngest of the sons, I became, of course, the greatest favorite with my mother, and was always with her; and she used to take particular pains to form my mind. I was trained up from my earliest years in the art of war: my daily exercise was shooting and throwing javelins; and my mother adorned me with emblems, after the manner of our greatest warriors. In this way I grew up till I was turned the age of eleven, when an end was put to my happiness in the following manner:—generally when the grown people in the neighborhood were gone far in the fields to labor, the children assembled together in some of the neighboring premises to play; and commonly some of us used to get up a tree to look out for any assailant, or kidnapper, that might come upon us—for they sometimes took those opportunities of our parents' absence, to attack and carry off as many as they could seize. One day as I was watching at the top of a tree in our yard, I saw one of those people come into the yard of our next neighbor but one to kidnap, there being many stout[4] young people in it. Immediately on this I gave the alarm of the rogue, and he was surrounded by the stoutest of them, who entangled him with cords, so that he could not escape till some of the grown people came and secured him. But, alas! ere long it was my fate to be thus attacked, and to be carried off, when none of the grown people were nigh. One day, when all our people were gone out to their works as usual, and only I and my dear sister were left to mind the house, two men and a woman got over our walls, and in a moment seized us both, and, without giving us time to cry out, or make resistance, they stopped our mouths, and ran off with us into the nearest wood. Here they tied our hands, and continued to carry us as far as they could, till night came on, when we reached a small house, where the robbers halted for refreshment, and spent the night. We were then unbound, but were unable to take any food; and, being quite overpowered by fatigue and grief, our only relief was some sleep, which allayed our misfortune for a short time. The next morning we left the house, and continued traveling all the day. For a long time we had kept the woods, but at last we came into a road which I believed I knew. I had now some hopes of being delivered; for we had advanced but a little way before I discovered some people at a distance, on which I began to cry out for their assistance; but my cries had no other effect than to make them tie me faster and stop my mouth, and then they put me into a large sack. They also stopped my sister's mouth, and tied her hands;

4. Strong.

and in this manner we proceeded till we were out of sight of these people. When we went to rest the following night, they offered us some victuals, but we refused it; and the only comfort we had was in being in one another's arms all that night, and bathing each other with our tears. But alas! we were soon deprived of even the small comfort of weeping together. The next day proved a day of greater sorrow than I had yet experienced; for my sister and I were then separated, while we lay clasped in each other's arms. It was in vain that we besought them not to part us; she was torn from me, and immediately carried away, while I was left in a state of distraction not to be described. I cried and grieved continually; and for several days did not eat any thing but what they forced into my mouth. At length, after many days traveling, during which I had often changed masters, I got into the hands of a chieftain, in a very pleasant country. This man had two wives and some children, and they all used me extremely well, and did all they could to comfort me; particularly the first wife, who was something like my mother. Although I was a great many days' journey from my father's house, yet these people spoke exactly the same language with us. This first master of mine, as I may call him, was a smith,[5] and my principal employment was working his bellows, which were the same kind as I had seen in my vicinity. They were in some respects not unlike the stoves here in gentlemen's kitchens, and were covered over with leather; and in the middle of that leather a stick was fixed, and a person stood up, and worked it in the same manner as is done to pump water out of a cask with a hand pump. I believe it was gold he worked, for it was of a lovely bright yellow color, and was worn by the women on their wrists and ankles. I was there I suppose about a month, and they at last used to trust me some little distance from the house. This liberty I used in embracing every opportunity to inquire the way to my own home; and I also sometimes, for the same purpose, went with the maidens, in the cool of the evenings, to bring pitchers of water from the springs for the use of the house. I had also remarked where the sun rose in the morning, and set in the evening, as I had traveled along; and I had observed that my father's house was towards the rising of the sun. I therefore determined to seize the first opportunity of making my escape, and to shape my course for that quarter; for I was quite oppressed and weighed down by grief after my mother and friends; and my love of liberty, ever great, was strengthened by the mortifying circumstance of not daring to eat with the free-born children, although I was mostly their companion. While I was projecting my escape one day, an unlucky event happened, which quite disconcerted my plan, and put an end to my hopes. I used to be sometimes employed in assisting an elderly slave to cook and take care of the poultry; and one morning, while I was feeding some chickens, I happened to toss a small pebble at one of them, which hit it on the middle, and directly killed it. The old slave, having soon after missed the chicken, inquired after it; and on my relating the accident (for I told her the truth, for my mother would never suffer me to tell a lie), she flew into a violent passion, and threatened that I should suffer for it; and, my master being out, she immediately went and told her mistress what I had done. This alarmed me very much, and I expected an instant flogging, which to me was uncommonly dreadful, for I had seldom been beaten at home. I therefore resolved to fly; and accordingly I ran into a thicket that was hard by, and hid myself in the bushes. Soon afterwards my mistress and the slave returned, and, not seeing me, they searched all the

5. A metalworker; here, a goldsmith.

house, but not finding me, and I not making answer when they called to me, they thought I had run away, and the whole neighborhood was raised in the pursuit of me. In that part of the country, as in ours, the houses and villages were skirted with woods, or shrubberies, and the bushes were so thick that a man could readily conceal himself in them, so as to elude the strictest search. The neighbors continued the whole day looking for me, and several times many of them came within a few yards of the place where I lay hid. I expected every moment, when I heard a rustling among the trees, to be found out, and punished by my master; but they never discovered me, though they were often so near that I even heard their conjectures as they were looking about for me; and I now learned from them that any attempts to return home would be hopeless. Most of them supposed I had fled towards home; but the distance was so great, and the way so intricate, that they thought I could never reach it, and that I should be lost in the woods. When I heard this I was seized with a violent panic, and abandoned myself to despair. Night, too, began to approach, and aggravated all my fears. I had before entertained hopes of getting home, and had determined when it should be dark to make the attempt; but I was now convinced it was fruitless, and began to consider that, if possibly I could escape all other animals, I could not those of the human kind; and that, not knowing the way, I must perish in the woods. Thus was I like the hunted deer—

> —"Every leaf and every whisp'ring breath,
> Convey'd a foe, and every foe a death."[6]

I heard frequent rustlings among the leaves, and being pretty sure they were snakes, I expected every instant to be stung by them. This increased my anguish, and the horror of my situation became now quite insupportable. I at length quitted the thicket, very faint and hungry, for I had not eaten or drank any thing all the day, and crept to my master's kitchen, from whence I set out at first, which was an open shed, and laid myself down in the ashes with an anxious wish for death, to relieve me from all my pains. I was scarcely awake in the morning, when the old woman slave, who was the first up, came to light the fire, and saw me in the fire place. She was very much surprised to see me, and could scarcely believe her own eyes. She now promised to intercede for me, and went for her master, who soon after came, and, having slightly reprimanded me, ordered me to be taken care of, and not ill treated.

Soon after this, my master's only daughter, and child by his first wife, sickened and died, which affected him so much that for some time he was almost frantic, and really would have killed himself, had he not been watched and prevented. However, in short time afterwards he recovered, and I was again sold. I was now carried to the left of the sun's rising, through many dreary wastes and dismal woods, amidst the hideous roarings of wild beasts. The people I was sold to used to carry me very often, when I was tired, either on their shoulders or on their backs. I saw many convenient well built sheds along the road, at proper distances, to accommodate the merchants and travelers, who lay in those buildings along with their wives, who often accompany them; and they always go well armed.

From the time I left my own nation, I always found somebody that understood me till I came to the sea coast. The languages of different nations did not totally differ, nor were they so copious as those of the Europeans,

6. From Sir John Denham's *Cooper's Hill* (1642), a topographical poem with moral reflections.

particularly the English. They were therefore, easily learned; and, while I was journeying thus through Africa, I acquired two or three different tongues. In this manner I had been traveling for a considerable time, when, one evening, to my great surprise, whom should I see brought to the house where I was but my dear sister! As soon as she saw me, she gave a loud shriek, and ran into my arms—I was quite overpowered: neither of us could speak; but, for a considerable time, clung to each other in mutual embraces, unable to do any thing but weep. Our meeting affected all who saw us; and, indeed, I must acknowledge, in honor of those sable destroyers of human rights, that I never met with any ill treatment, or saw any offered to their slaves, except tying them, when necessary, to keep them from running away. When these people knew we were brother and sister, they indulged us to be together; and the man, to whom I supposed we belonged, lay with us, he in the middle, while she and I held one another by the hands across his breast all night; and thus for a while we forgot our misfortunes, in the joy of being together; but even this small comfort was soon to have an end; for scarcely had the fatal morning appeared when she was again torn from me forever! I was now more miserable, if possible, than before. The small relief which her presence gave me from pain was gone, and the wretchedness of my situation was redoubled by my anxiety after her fate, and my apprehensions lest her sufferings should be greater than mine, when I could not be with her to alleviate them. Yes, thou dear partner of all my childish sports! thou sharer of my joys and sorrows! happy should I have ever esteemed myself to encounter every misery for you and to procure your freedom by the sacrifice of my own.—Though you were early forced from my arms, your image has been always riveted in my heart, from which neither time nor fortune have been able to remove it; so that, while the thoughts of your sufferings have damped my prosperity, they have mingled with adversity and increased its bitterness. To that Heaven which protects the weak from the strong, I commit the care of your innocence and virtues, if they have not already received their full reward, and if your youth and delicacy have not long since fallen victims to the violence of the African trader, the pestilential stench of a Guinea ship, the seasoning in the European colonies, or the lash and lust of a brutal and unrelenting overseer.

I did not long remain after my sister. I was again sold, and carried through a number of places, till after traveling a considerable time, I came to a town called Tinmah, in the most beautiful country I had yet seen in Africa. It was extremely rich, and there were many rivulets which flowed through it, and supplied a large pond in the center of the town, where the people washed. Here I first saw and tasted cocoa nuts, which I thought superior to any nuts I had ever tasted before; and the trees which were loaded, were also interspersed among the houses, which had commodious shades adjoining, and were in the same manner as ours, the insides being neatly plastered and whitewashed. Here I also saw and tasted for the first time, sugar cane. Their money consisted of little white shells, the size of the finger nail. I was sold here for one hundred and seventy-two of them, by a merchant who lived and brought me there. I had been about two or three days at his house, when a wealthy widow, a neighbor of his, came there one evening, and brought with her an only son, a young gentleman about my own age and size. Here they saw me; and, having taken a fancy to me, I was bought of the merchant, and went home with them. Her house and premises were situated close to one of those rivulets I have mentioned, and were the finest I ever saw in Africa: they were very extensive, and she had a number of slaves to attend her. The next day I was washed and perfumed, and when mealtime came, I was led into the presence of my mistress, and ate and drank before her with her son. This filled me with astonishment; and I could scarce help expressing my surprise that the young gentleman should suffer[7] me, who was bound, to eat with him who was free; and not only so, but that he would not at any time either eat or drink till I had taken first, because I was the eldest, which was agreeable to our custom. Indeed, every thing here, and all their treatment of me, made me forget that I was a slave. The language of these people resembled ours so nearly, that we understood each other perfectly. They had also the very same customs as we. There were likewise slaves daily to attend us, while my young master and I, with other boys, sported with our darts and bows and arrows, as I had been used to do at home. In this resemblance to my former happy state, I passed about two months; and I now began to think I was to be adopted into the family, and was beginning to be reconciled to my situation, and to forget by degrees my misfortunes, when all at once the delusion vanished; for, without the least previous knowledge, one morning early, while my dear master and companion was still asleep, I was awakened out of my reverie to fresh sorrow, and hurried away even amongst the uncircumcised.

Thus, at the very moment I dreamed of the greatest happiness, I found myself most miserable; and it seemed as if fortune wished to give me this taste of joy only to render the reverse more poignant.—The change I now experienced, was as painful as it was sudden and unexpected. It was a change indeed, from a state of bliss to a scene which is inexpressible by me, as it discovered to me an element I had never before beheld, and till then had no idea of, and wherein such instances of hardship and cruelty continually occurred, as I can never reflect on but with horror.

All the nations and people I had hitherto passed through, resembled our own in their manners, customs, and language: but I came at length to a country, the inhabitants of which differed from us in all those particulars. I was very much struck with this difference, especially when I came among a people who did not circumcise, and ate without washing their hands. They cooked also in iron pots, and had European cutlasses and cross bows, which were unknown to us, and fought with their fists among themselves. Their women were not so modest as ours, for they ate, and drank, and slept with their men. But above all, I was amazed to see no sacrifices or offerings among them. In some of those places the people ornamented themselves with scars, and likewise filed their teeth very sharp. They wanted sometimes to ornament me in the same manner, but I would not suffer them; hoping that I might some time be among a people who did not thus disfigure themselves, as I thought they did. At last I came to the banks of a large river which was covered with canoes, in which the people appeared to live with their household utensils, and provisions of all kinds. I was beyond measure astonished at this, as I had never before seen any water larger than a pond or a rivulet: and my surprise was mingled with no small fear when I was put into one of these canoes, and we began to paddle and move along the river. We continued going on thus till night, and when we came to land, and made fires on the banks, each family by themselves; some dragged their canoes on shore, others stayed and cooked in theirs, and laid in them all night. Those on the land had mats, of which they made tents, some in the shape of little houses; in these we slept; and after the morning meal, we embarked again and proceeded as before. I

7. Allow.

was often very much astonished to see some of the women, as well as the men, jump into the water, dive to the bottom, come up again, and swim about.—Thus I continued to travel, sometimes by land, sometimes by water, through different countries and various nations, till, at the end of six or seven months after I had been kidnapped, I arrived at the sea coast. It would be tedious and uninteresting to relate all the incidents which befell me during this journey, and which I have not yet forgotten; of the various hands I passed through, and the manners and customs of all the different people among whom I lived—I shall therefore only observe, that in all the places where I was, the soil was exceedingly rich; the pumpkins, eadas,[8] plaintains, yams, etc., etc., were in great abundance, and of incredible size. There were also vast quantities of different gums, though not used for any purpose, and every where a great deal of tobacco. The cotton even grew quite wild, and there was plenty of red-wood. I saw no mechanics[9] whatever in all the way, except such as I have mentioned. The chief employment in all these countries was agriculture, and both the males and females, as with us, were brought up to it, and trained in the arts of war.

The first object which saluted my eyes when I arrived on the coast, was the sea, and a slave ship, which was then riding at anchor, and waiting for its cargo. These filled me with astonishment, which was soon converted into terror, when I was carried on board. I was immediately handled, and tossed up to see if I were sound, by some of the crew; and I was now persuaded that I had gotten into a world of bad spirits, and that they were going to kill me. Their complexions, too, differing so much from ours, their long hair, and the language they spoke (which was very different from any I had ever heard), united to confirm me in this belief. Indeed, such were the horrors of my views and fears at the moment, that, if ten thousand worlds had been my own, I would have freely parted with them all to have exchanged my condition with that of the meanest slave in my own country. When I looked round the ship too, and saw a large furnace of copper boiling, and a multitude of black people of every description chained together, every one of their countenances expressing dejection and sorrow, I no longer doubted of my fate; and, quite overpowered with horror and anguish, I fell motionless on the deck and fainted. When I recovered a little, I found some black people about me, who I believed were some of those who had brought me on board, and had been receiving their pay; they talked to me in order to cheer me, but all in vain. I asked them if we were not to be eaten by those white men with horrible looks, red faces, and long hair. They told me I was not: and one of the crew brought me a small portion of spirituous liquor in a wine glass, but, being afraid of him, I would not take it out of his hand. One of the blacks, therefore, took it from him and gave it to me, and I took a little down my palate, which, instead of reviving me, as they thought it would, threw me into the greatest consternation at the strange feeling it produced, having never tasted any such liquor before. Soon after this, the blacks who brought me on board went off, and left me abandoned to despair.

I now saw myself deprived of all chance of returning to my native country, or even the least glimpse of hope of gaining the shore, which I now considered as friendly; and I even wished for my former slavery in preference to my present situation, which was filled with horrors of every kind, still heightened by my ignorance of what I was to undergo. I was not long suffered to

---

8. Or eddoes, edible roots found in the tropics. 9. Artisans, manual workers.

indulge my grief; I was soon put down under the decks, and there I received such a salutation in my nostrils as I had never experienced in my life: so that, with the loathsomeness of the stench, and crying together, I became so sick and low that I was not able to eat, nor had I the least desire to taste any thing. I now wished for the last friend, death, to relieve me; but soon, to my grief, two of the white men offered me eatables; and, on my refusing to eat, one of them held me fast by the hands, and laid me across, I think the windlass, and tied my feet, while the other flogged me severely. I had never experienced any thing of this kind before, and although not being used to the water, I naturally feared that element the first time I saw it, yet, nevertheless, could I have got over the nettings, I would have jumped over the side, but I could not; and besides, the crew used to watch us very closely who were not chained down to the decks, lest we should leap into the water; and I have seen some of these poor African prisoners most severely cut, for attempting to do so, and hourly whipped for not eating. This indeed was often the case with myself. In a little time after, amongst the poor chained men, I found some of my own nation, which in a small degree gave ease to my mind. I inquired of these what was to be done with us? They gave me to understand we were to be carried to these white people's country to work for them. I then was a little revived, and thought, if it were no worse than working, my situation was not so desperate; but still I feared I should be put to death, the white people looked and acted, as I thought, in so savage a manner; for I had never seen among any people such instances of brutal cruelty; and this not only shown towards us blacks, but also to some of the whites themselves. One white man in particular I saw, when we were permitted to be on deck, flogged so unmercifully with a large rope near the foremast, that he died in consequence of it; and they tossed him over the side as they would have done a brute. This made me fear these people the more; and I expected nothing less than to be treated in the same manner. I could not help expressing my fears and apprehensions to some of my countrymen; I asked them if these people had no country, but lived in this hollow place (the ship)? They told me they did not, but came from a distant one. "Then," said I, "how comes it in all our country we never heard of them?" They told me because they lived so very far off. I then asked where were their women? had they any like themselves? I was told they had. "And why," said I, "do we not see them?" They answered, because they were left behind. I asked how the vessel could go? they told me they could not tell; but that there was cloth put upon the masts by the help of the ropes I saw, and then the vessel went on; and the white men had some spell or magic they put in the water when they liked, in order to stop the vessel. I was exceedingly amazed at this account, and really thought they were spirits. I therefore wished much to be from amongst them, for I expected they would sacrifice me; but my wishes were vain—for we were so quartered that it was impossible for any of us to make our escape.

While we stayed on the coast I was mostly on deck; and one day, to my great astonishment, I saw one of these vessels coming in with the sails up. As soon as the whites saw it, they gave a great shout, at which we were amazed; and the more so, as the vessel appeared larger by approaching nearer. At last, she came to an anchor in my sight, and when the anchor was let go, I and my countrymen who saw it, were lost in astonishment to observe the vessel stop—and were now convinced it was done by magic. Soon after this the other ship got her boats out, and they came on board of us, and the people of both ships seemed very glad to see each other.—Several of the strangers also shook hands with us black people, and made motions with their hands, signifying I suppose, we were to go to their country, but we did not understand them.

At last, when the ship we were in had got in all her cargo, they made ready with many fearful noises, and we were all put under deck, so that we could not see how they managed the vessel. But this disappointment was the least of my sorrow. The stench of the hold while we were on the coast was so intolerably loathsome, that it was dangerous to remain there for any time, and some of us had been permitted to stay on the deck for the fresh air; but now that the whole ship's cargo were confined together, it became absolutely pestilential. The closeness of the place, and the heat of the climate, added to the number in the ship, which was so crowded that each had scarcely room to turn himself, almost suffocated us. This produced copious perspirations, so that the air soon became unfit for respiration, from a variety of loathsome smells, and brought on a sickness among the slaves, of which many died— thus falling victims to the improvident avarice, as I may call it, of their purchasers. This wretched situation was again aggravated by the galling of the chains, now become insupportable, and the filth of the necessary tubs, into which the children often fell, and were almost suffocated. The shrieks of the women, and the groans of the dying, rendered the whole a scene of horror almost inconceivable. Happily perhaps, for myself, I was soon reduced so low here that it was thought necessary to keep me almost always on deck; and from my extreme youth I was not put in fetters. In this situation I expected every hour to share the fate of my companions, some of whom were almost daily brought upon deck at the point of death, which I began to hope would soon put an end to my miseries. Often did I think many of the inhabitants of the deep much more happy than myself. I envied them the freedom they enjoyed, and as often wished I could change my condition for theirs. Every circumstance I met with, served only to render my state more painful, and heightened my apprehensions, and my opinion of the cruelty of the whites.

One day they had taken a number of fishes; and when they had killed and satisfied themselves with as many as they thought fit, to our astonishment who were on deck, rather than give any of them to us to eat, as we expected, they tossed the remaining fish into the sea again, although we begged and prayed for some as well as we could, but in vain; and some of my countrymen, being pressed by hunger, took an opportunity, when they thought no one saw them, of trying to get a little privately; but they were discovered, and the attempt procured them some very severe floggings. One day, when we had a smooth sea and moderate wind, two of my wearied countrymen who were chained together (I was near them at the time), preferring death to such a life of misery, somehow made through the nettings and jumped into the sea: immediately, another quite dejected fellow, who, on account of his illness, was suffered to be out of irons, also followed their example; and I believe many more would very soon have done the same, if they had not been prevented by the ship's crew, who were instantly alarmed. Those of us that were the most active, were in a moment put down under the deck, and there was such a noise and confusion amongst the people of the ship as I never heard before, to stop her, and get the boat out to go after the slaves. However, two of the wretches were drowned, but they got the other, and afterwards flogged him unmercifully, for thus attempting to prefer death to slavery. In this manner we continued to undergo more hardships than I can now relate, hardships which are inseparable from this accursed trade. Many a time we were near suffocation from the want of fresh air, which we were often without for whole days together. This, and the stench of the necessary tubs, carried off many.

During our passage, I first saw flying fishes, which surprised me very much; they used frequently to fly across the ship, and many of them fell on the deck. I also now first saw the use of the quadrant; I had often with astonishment seen the mariners make observations with it, and I could not think what it meant. They at last took notice of my surprise; and one of them, willing to increase it, as well as to gratify my curiosity, made me one day look through it. The clouds appeared to me to be land, which disappeared as they passed along. This heightened my wonder; and I was now more persuaded than ever, that I was in another world, and that every thing about me was magic. At last, we came in sight of the island of Barbadoes,[1] at which the whites on board gave a great shout, and made many signs of joy to us. We did not know what to think of this; but as the vessel drew nearer, we plainly saw the harbor, and other ships of different kinds and sizes, and we soon anchored amongst them, off Bridgetown. Many merchants and planters now came on board, though it was in the evening. They put us in separate parcels,[2] and examined us attentively. They also made us jump, and pointed to the land, signifying we were to go there. We thought by this, we should be eaten by these ugly men, as they appeared to us; and, when soon after we were all put down under the deck again, there was much dread and trembling among us, and nothing but bitter cries to be heard all the night from these apprehensions, insomuch, that at last the white people got some old slaves from the land to pacify us. They told us we were not to be eaten, but to work, and were soon to go on land, where we should see many of our country people. This report eased us much. And sure enough, soon after we were landed, there came to us Africans of all languages.

We were conducted immediately to the merchant's yard, where we were all pent up together, like so many sheep in a fold, without regard to sex or age. As every object was new to me, every thing I saw filled me with surprise. What struck me first, was, that the houses were built with bricks and stories,[3] and in every other respect different from those I had seen in Africa; but I was still more astonished on seeing people on horseback. I did not know what this could mean; and, indeed, I thought these people were full of nothing but magical arts. While I was in this astonishment, one of my fellow prisoners spoke to a countryman of his, about the horses, who said they were the same kind they had in their country. I understood them, though they were from a distant part of Africa; and I thought it odd I had not seen any horses there; but afterwards, when I came to converse with different Africans, I found they had many horses amongst them, and much larger than those I then saw.

We were not many days in the merchant's custody, before we were sold after their usual manner, which is this:—On a signal given (as the beat of a drum), the buyers rush at once into the yard where the slaves are confined, and make choice of that parcel they like best. The noise and clamor with which this is attended, and the eagerness visible in the countenances of the buyers, serve not a little to increase the apprehension of terrified Africans, who may well be supposed to consider them as the ministers of that

1. In the West Indies.
2. Groups.

3. I.e., the buildings were two-storied.

destruction to which they think themselves devoted. In this manner, without scruple, are relations and friends separated, most of them never to see each other again. I remember, in the vessel in which I was brought over, in the men's apartment, there were several brothers, who, in the sale, were sold in different lots; and it was very moving on this occasion, to see and hear their cries at parting. O, ye nominal Christians![4] might not an African ask you— Learned you this from your God, who says unto you, Do unto all men as you would men should do unto you? Is it not enough that we are torn from our country and friends, to toil for your luxury and lust of gain? Must every tender feeling be likewise sacrificed to your avarice? Are the dearest friends and relations, now rendered more dear by their separation from their kindred, still to be parted from each other, and thus prevented from cheering the gloom of slavery, with the small comfort of being together, and mingling their sufferings and sorrows? Why are parents to lose their children, brothers their sisters, or husbands their wives? Surely, this is a new refinement in cruelty, which, while it has no advantage to atone for it, thus aggravates distress, and adds fresh horrors even to the wretchedness of slavery.

From *Chapter III*

I now totally lost the small remains of comfort I had enjoyed in conversing with my countrymen; the women too, who used to wash and take care of me were all gone different ways, and I never saw one of them afterwards.

I stayed in this island for a few days; I believe it could not be above a fortnight; when I, and some few more slaves, that were not salable amongst the rest, from very much fretting, were shipped off in a sloop for North America. On the passage we were better treated than when we were coming from Africa, and we had plenty of rice and fat pork. We were landed up a river a good way from the sea, about Virginia county, where we saw few or none of our native Africans, and not one soul who could talk to me. I was a few weeks weeding grass, and gathering stones in a plantation; and at last all my companions were distributed different ways, and only myself was left. I was now exceedingly miserable, and thought myself worse off than any of the rest of my companions; for they could talk to each other, but I had no person to speak to that I could understand. In this state, I was constantly grieving and pining,[5] and wishing for death rather than any thing else. While I was in this plantation, the gentleman, to whom I suppose the estate belonged, being unwell, I was one day sent for to his dwelling house to fan him; when I came into the room where he was I was very much affrighted at some things I saw, and the more so as I had seen a black woman slave as I came through the house, who was cooking the dinner, and the poor creature was cruelly loaded with various kinds of iron machines; she had one particularly on her head, which locked her mouth so fast that she could scarcely speak; and could not eat nor drink. I was much astonished and shocked at this contrivance, which I afterwards learned was called the iron muzzle. Soon after I had a fan put in my hand, to fan the gentleman while he slept; and so I did indeed with great fear. While he was fast asleep I indulged myself a great deal in looking about the room, which to me appeared very fine and curious. The first object that engaged my attention was a watch which hung on the chimney, and was going. I was quite surprised at the noise it made, and was

4. Christians in name only.   5. Suffering.

afraid it would tell the gentleman any thing I might do amiss; and when I immediately after observed a picture hanging in the room, which appeared constantly to look at me, I was still more affrighted, having never seen such things as these before. At one time I thought it was something relative to magic; and not seeing it move, I thought it might be some way the whites had to keep their great men when they died, and offer them libations as we used to do our friendly spirits. In this state of anxiety I remained till my master awoke, when I was dismissed out of the room, to my no small satisfaction and relief; for I thought that these people were all made up of wonders. In this place I was called Jacob; but on board the African Snow, I was called Michael. I had been some time in this miserable forlorn, and much dejected state, without having any one to talk to, which made my life a burden, when the kind and unknown hand of the Creator (who in very deed leads the blind in a way they know not) now began to appear, to my comfort; for one day the captain of a merchant ship, called the Industrious Bee, came on some business to my master's house. This gentleman, whose name was Michael Henry Pascal, was a lieutenant in the royal navy, but now commanded this trading ship, which was somewhere in the confines of the county many miles off. While he was at my master's house, it happened that he saw me, and liked me so well that he made a purchase of me. I think I have often heard him say he gave thirty or forty pounds sterling for me; but I do not remember which. However, he meant me for a present to some of his friends in England: and as I was sent accordingly from the house of my then master (one Mr. Campbell), to the place where the ship lay; I was conducted on horseback by an elderly black man (a mode of traveling which appeared very odd to me). When I arrived I was carried on board a fine large ship, loaded with tobacco, etc., and just ready to sail for England. I now thought my condition much mended; I had sails to lie on, and plenty of good victuals to eat; and everybody on board used me very kindly, quite contrary to what I had seen of any white people before; I therefore began to think that they were not all of the same disposition. A few days after I was on board we sailed for England. I was still at a loss to conjecture my destiny. By this time, however, I could smatter a little imperfect English; and I wanted to know as well as I could where we were going. Some of the people of the ship used to tell me they were going to carry me back to my own country, and this made me very happy. I was quite rejoiced at the idea of going back; and thought if I could get home what wonders I should have to tell. But I was reserved for another fate, and was soon undeceived when we came within sight of the English coast. While I was on board this ship, my captain and master named me *Gustavus Vassa*. I at that time began to understand him a little, and refused to be called so, and told him as well as I could that I would be called Jacob; but he said I should not, and still called me Gustavus: and when I refused to answer to my new name, which I at first did, it gained me many a cuff; so at length I submitted, and by which I have been known ever since. The ship had a very long passage; and on that account we had very short allowance of provisions. Towards the last, we had only one pound and a half of bread per week, and about the same quantity of meat, and one quart of water a day. We spoke with only one vessel the whole time we were at sea, and but once we caught a few fishes. In our extremities the captain and people told me in jest they would kill and eat me; but I thought them in earnest, and was depressed beyond measure, expecting every moment to be my last. While I was in this situation, one evening they caught, with a good deal of trouble, a large shark, and got it on board. This gladdened my poor heart exceedingly, as I thought it would serve the people to eat instead of their eating me; but very soon, to my astonishment, they cut off a small part of the tail, and tossed the rest over the side. This renewed my consternation; and I did not know what to think of these white people, though I very much feared they would kill and eat me. There was on board the ship a young lad who had never been at sea before, about four or five years older than myself: his name was Richard Baker. He was a native of America, had received an excellent education, and was of a most amiable temper. Soon after I went on board, he showed me a great deal of partiality and attention, and in return I grew extremely fond of him. We at length became inseparable; and, for the space of two years, he was of very great use to me, and was my constant companion and instructor. Although this dear youth had many slaves of his own, yet he and I have gone through many sufferings together on shipboard; and we have many nights lain in each other's bosoms when we were in great distress. Thus such a friendship was cemented between us as we cherished till his death, which, to my very great sorrow, happened in the year 1759, when he was up the Archipelago, and on board his Majesty's ship the Preston: an event which I have never ceased to regret, as I lost at once a kind interpreter, an agreeable companion, and a faithful friend; who, at the age of fifteen, discovered a mind superior to prejudice; and who was not ashamed to notice, to associate with, and to be the friend and instructor of one who was ignorant, a stranger, of a different complexion, and a slave!

* * *

From *Chapter IV*

It was now between two and three years since I first came to England, a great part of which I had spent at sea; so that I became inured[6] to that service, and began to consider myself as happily situated, for my master treated me always extremely well; and my attachment and gratitude to him were very great. From the various scenes I had beheld on shipboard, I soon grew a stranger to terror of every kind, and was, in that respect at least, almost an Englishman. I have often reflected with surprise that I never felt half the alarm at any of the numerous dangers I have been in, that I was filled with at the first sight of the Europeans, and at every act of theirs, even the most trifling, when I first came among them, and for some time afterwards. That fear, however, which was the effect of my ignorance, wore away as I began to know them. I could now speak English tolerably well, and I perfectly understood every thing that was said. I not only felt myself quite easy with these new countrymen, but relished their society and manners. I no longer looked upon them as spirits, but as men superior to us; and therefore I had the stronger desire to resemble them, to imbibe their spirit, and imitate their manners. I therefore embraced every occasion of improvement, and every new thing that I observed I treasured up in my memory. I had long wished to be able to read and write; and for this purpose I took every opportunity to gain instruction, but had made as yet very little progress. However, when I went to London with my master, I had soon an opportunity of improving myself, which I gladly embraced. Shortly after my arrival, he sent me to wait upon

6. Accustomed.

the Miss Guerins, who had treated me with much kindness when I was there before; and they sent me to school.

While I was attending these ladies, their servants told me I could not go to Heaven unless I was baptized. This made me very uneasy, for I had now some faint idea of a future state. Accordingly I communicated my anxiety to the eldest Miss Guerin, with whom I was become a favorite, and pressed her to have me baptized; when to my great joy, she told me I should. She had formerly asked my master to let me be baptized, but he had refused. However she now insisted on it; and he being under some obligation to her brother, complied with her request. So I was baptized in St. Margaret's church, Westminster, in February, 1759, by my present name. The clergyman at the same time, gave me a book, called a Guide to the Indians, written by the Bishop of Sodor and Man.[7] On this occasion, Miss Guerin did me the honor to stand as god-mother, and afterwards gave me a treat. I used to attend these ladies about the town, in which service I was extremely happy; as I had thus many opportunities of seeing London, which I desired of all things. I was sometimes, however, with my master at his rendezvous house,[8] which was at the foot of Westminster bridge. Here I used to enjoy myself in playing about the bridge stairs, and often in the waterman's wherries,[9] with other boys. On one of these occasions there was another boy with me in a wherry, and we went out into the current of the river; while we were there, two more stout boys came to us in another wherry, and abusing us for taking the boat, desired me to get into the other wherry boat. Accordingly, I went to get out of the wherry I was in, but just as I had got one of my feet into the other boat, the boys shoved it off, so that I fell into the Thames; and, not being able to swim, I should unavoidably have been drowned, but for the assistance of some watermen who providentially came to my relief.

The Namur being again got ready for sea, my master, with his gang,[1] was ordered on board; and, to my no small grief, I was obliged to leave my schoolmaster, whom I liked very much, and always attended while I stayed in London, to repair on board with my master. Nor did I leave my kind patronesses, the Miss Guerins, without uneasiness and regret. They often used to teach me to read, and took great pains to instruct me in the principles of religion and the knowledge of God. I therefore parted from those amiable ladies with reluctance, after receiving from them many friendly cautions how to conduct myself, and some valuable presents.

When I came to Spithead,[2] I found we were destined for the Mediterranean, with a large fleet, which was now ready to put to sea. We only waited for the arrival of the Admiral, who soon came on board. And about the beginning of the spring of 1759, having weighed anchor, and got under way, sailed for the Mediterranean; and in eleven days, from the Land's End, we got to Gibralter. While we were here I used to be often on shore, and got various fruits in great plenty, and very cheap.

I had frequently told several people, in my excursions on shore, the story of my being kidnapped with my sister, and of our being separated, as I have related before; and I had as often expressed my anxiety for her fate, and my sorrow at having never met her again. One day, when I was on shore, and

7. Present-day Hebrides and the Isle of Man.
8. Private residence.
9. Small rowboats.

1. I.e., crew.
2. On the southern coast of England; a common rendezvous for the British fleet.

mentioning these circumstances to some persons, one of them told me he knew where my sister was, and if I would accompany him, he would bring me to her. Improbable as this story was, I believed it immediately, and agreed to go with him, while my heart leaped for joy; and, indeed, he conducted me to a black young woman, who was so like my sister, that at first sight, I really thought it was her; but I was quickly undeceived. And, on talking to her, I found her to be of another nation.

While we lay here, the Preston came in from the Levant.[3] As soon as she arrived, my master told me I should now see my old companion, Dick, who was gone in her when she sailed for Turkey. I was much rejoiced at this news, and expected every minute to embrace him; and when the captain came on board of our ship, which he did immediately after, I ran to inquire after my friend; but, with inexpressible sorrow, I learned from the boat's crew that the dear youth was dead! and that they had brought his chest, and all his other things, to my master. These he afterwards gave to me, and I regarded them as a memorial of my friend, whom I loved, and grieved for, as a brother.

* * *

After our ship was fitted out again for service, in September she went to Guernsey,[4] where I was very glad to see my old hostess, who was now a widow, and my former little charming companion, her daughter. I spent some time here very happily with them, till October, when we had orders to repair to Portsmouth. We parted from each other with a great deal of affection; and I promised to return soon, and see them again, not knowing what all powerful fate had determined for me. Our ship having arrived at Portsmouth, we went into the harbor, and remained there till the latter end of November, when we heard great talk about a peace,[5] and, to our very great joy, in the beginning of December we had orders to go up to London with our ship, to be paid off. We received this news with loud huzzas, and every other demonstration of gladness; and nothing but mirth was to be seen throughout every part of the ship. I, too, was not without my share of the general joy on this occasion. I thought now of nothing but being freed, and working for myself, and thereby getting money to enable me to get a good education; for I always had a great desire to be able at least to read and write; and while I was on ship-board, I had endeavored to improve myself in both. While I was in the Etna, particularly, the captain's clerk taught me to write, and gave me a smattering of arithmetic, as far as the Rule of Three.[6] There was also one Daniel Queen, about forty years of age, a man very well educated, who messed[7] with me on board this ship, and he likewise dressed and attended the captain. Fortunately this man soon became very much attached to me, and took very great pains to instruct me in many things. He taught me to shave and dress hair a little, and also to read in the Bible, explaining many passages to me, which I did not comprehend. I was wonderfully surprised to see the laws and rules of my own country written almost exactly here; a circumstance which I believe tended to impress our manners and customs more deeply on my memory. I used to tell him of this resemblance, and many a time we have sat up the whole night together at this employment. In short, he was like a father

---

3. The eastern shore of the Mediterranean.
4. One of the Channel Islands in the English Channel.
5. The Seven Years' War between England and France began in 1756.

6. A method of finding a fourth (unknown) number from three given numbers. Etna was the name of the ship.
7. Took meals.

to me, and some even used to call me after his name; they also styled me the black Christian. Indeed, I almost loved him with the affection of a son. Many things I have denied myself that he might have them; and when I used to play at marbles, or any other game, and won a few half-pence, or got any little money, which I sometimes did, for shaving any one, I used to buy him a little sugar or tobacco, as far as my stock of money would go. He used to say, that he and I never should part; and that when our ship was paid off, as I was as free as himself, or any other man on board, he would instruct me in his business, by which I might gain a good livelihood. This gave me new life and spirits; and my heart burned within me, while I thought the time long till I obtained my freedom. For though my master had not promised it to me, yet, besides the assurances I had received, that he had no right to detain me, he always treated me with the greatest kindness, and reposed in me an unbounded confidence; he even paid attention to my morals, and would never suffer me to deceive him, or tell lies, of which he used to tell me the consequences; and that if I did so, God would not love me. So that, from all this tenderness, I had never once supposed, in all my dreams of freedom, that he would think of detaining me any longer than I wished.

In pursuance of our orders, we sailed from Portsmouth for the Thames, and arrived at Deptford the 10th of December, where we cast anchor just as it was high water. The ship was up about half an hour, when my master ordered the barge to be manned; and all in an instant, without having before given me the least reason to suspect any thing of the matter, he forced me into the barge, saying, I was going to leave him, but he would take care I should not. I was so struck with the unexpectedness of this proceeding, that for some time I did not make a reply, only I made an offer to go for my books and chest of clothes, but he swore I should not move out of his sight, and if I did, he would cut my throat, at the same time taking his hanger.[8] I began, however, to collect myself, and plucking up courage, I told him I was free, and he could not by law serve me so. But this only enraged him the more: and he continued to swear, and said he would soon let me know whether he would or not, and at that instant sprung himself into the barge from the ship, to the astonishment and sorrow of all on board. The tide, rather unluckily for me, had just turned downward, so that we quickly fell down the river along with it, till we came among some outward-bound West Indiamen; for he was resolved to put me on board the first vessel he could get to receive me. The boat's crew, who pulled against their will, became quite faint, different times, and would have gone ashore, but he would not let them. Some of them strove then to cheer me, and told me he could not sell me, and that they would stand by me, which revived me a little, and I still entertained hopes; for, as they pulled along, he asked some vessels to receive me, but they would not. But, just as we had got a little below Gravesend, we came along side of a ship which was going away the next tide for the West Indies. Her name was the Charming Sally. Captain James Doran, and my master went on board, and agreed with him for me; and in a little time I was sent for into the cabin. When I came there, Captain Doran asked me if I knew him. I answered that I did not. "Then," said he, "you are now my slave." I told him my master could not sell me to him, nor to any one else. "Why," said he, "did not your master buy you?" I confessed he did. "But I have served him," said I, "many years, and he has taken all my wages and prize money, for I had only got one

8. Small sword.

sixpence during the war; besides this I have been baptized, and by the laws of the land no man has a right to sell me." And I added that I had heard a law-yer and others at different times tell my master so. They both then said that those people who told me so were not my friends; but I replied, "It was very extraordinary that other people did not know the law as well as they." Upon this, Captain Doran said I talked too much English; and if I did not behave myself well, and be quiet, he had a method on board to make me. I was too well convinced of his power over me to doubt what he said; and my former sufferings in the slave ship presenting themselves to my mind, the recollec-tion of them made me shudder. However, before I retired I told them that, as I could not get any right among men here, I hoped I should hereafter in Heaven; and I immediately left the cabin, filled with resentment and sorrow. The only coat I had with me my master took away with him, and said, "If your prize money had been £ 10,000, I had a right to it all, and would have taken it." I had about nine guineas, which, during my long seafaring life, I had scraped together from trifling perquisites and little ventures; and I hid it at that instant, lest my master should take that from me likewise, still hop-ing that by some means or other I should make my escape to the shore; and indeed some of my old shipmates told me not to despair, for they would get me back again; and that, as soon as they could get their pay, they would imme-diately come to Portsmouth to me, where the ship was going. But, alas! all my hopes were baffled, and the hour of my deliverance as was yet far off. My master, having soon concluded his bargain with the captain, came out of the cabin, and he and his people got into the boat and put off. I followed them with aching eyes as long as I could, and when they were out of sight I threw myself on the deck, with a heart ready to burst with sorrow and anguish.

From *Chapter V*

* * *

About the middle of May, when the ship was got ready to sail for England, I all the time believing that fate's blackest clouds were gathering over my head, and expecting their bursting would mix me with the dead, Captain Doran sent for me ashore one morning, and I was told by the messenger that my fate was then determined. With trembling steps and fluttering heart, I came to the captain, and found with him one Mr. Robert King, a Quaker, and the first merchant in the place. The captain then told me my former master had sent me there to be sold; but that he had desired him to get me the best master he could, as he told him I was a very deserving boy, which Captain Doran said he found to be true; and if he were to stay in the West Indies, he would be glad to keep me himself; but he could not venture to take me to London, for he was very sure that when I came there I would leave him. I at that instant burst out a crying, and begged much of him to take me to England with him, but all to no purpose. He told me he had got me the very best master in the whole island, with whom I should be as happy as if I were in England, and for that reason he chose to let him have me, though he could sell me to his own brother-in-law for a great deal more money than what he got from this gentle-man. Mr. King, my new master, then made a reply, and said the reason he had bought me was on account of my good character; and as he had not the least doubt of my good behavior, I should be very well off with him. He also told me he did not live in the West Indies, but at Philadelphia, where he was going soon; and, as I understood something of the rules of arithmetic, when we got there he would put me to school, and fit me for a clerk. This conversation relieved my mind a little, and I left those gentlemen considerably more at ease in myself than when I came to them; and I was very thankful to Captain Doran, and even to my old master, for the character they had given me. A character which I afterwards found of infinite service to me. I went on board again, and took leave of all my shipmates, and the next day the ship sailed. When she weighed anchor, I went to the waterside and looked at her with a very wishful and aching heart, and followed her with my eyes until she was totally out of sight. I was so bowed down with grief, that I could not hold up my head for many months; and if my new master had not been kind to me, I believe I should have died under it at last. And, indeed, I soon found that he fully deserved the good character which Captain Doran gave me of him; for he possessed a most amiable disposition and temper, and was very charitable and humane. If any of his slaves behaved amiss he did not beat or use them ill, but parted with them. This made them afraid of disobliging him; and as he treated his slaves better than any other man on the island, so he was better and more faithfully served by them in return. By this kind treatment I did at last endeavor to compose myself; and with fortitude, though moneyless, determined to face whatever fate had decreed for me. Mr. King soon asked me what I could do; and at the same time said he did not mean to treat me as a common slave. I told him I knew something of seamanship, and could shave and dress hair pretty well; and I could refine wines, which I had learned on shipboard, where I had often done it; and that I could write, and understood arithmetic tolerably well, as far as the Rule of Three. He then asked me if I knew any thing of guaging; and, on my answering that I did not, he said one of his clerks should teach me to guage.[9]

Mr. King dealt in all manner of merchandize, and kept from one to six clerks. He loaded many vessels in a year; particularly to Philadelphia, where he was born; and was connected with a great mercantile house in that city. He had, besides, many vessels and droggers,[1] of different sizes, which used to go about the island; and others, to collect rum, sugar, and other goods. I understood pulling and managing those boats very well. And this hard work, which was the first that he set me to, in the sugar seasons used to be my constant employment. I have rowed the boat, and slaved at the oars, from one hour to sixteen in the twenty-four; during which I had fifteen pence sterling per day to live on, though sometimes only ten pence. However, this was considerably more than was allowed to other slaves that used to work often with me, and belonged to other gentlemen on the island. Those poor souls had never more than nine-pence per day, and seldom more than six-pence, from their masters or owners, though they earned them three or four pistareens.[2] For it is a common practice in the West Indies for men to purchase slaves, though they have not plantations themselves, in order to let them out to planters and merchants at so much a piece by the day, and they give what allowance they choose out of this product of their daily work to their slaves, for subsistence; this allowance is often very scanty. My master often gave the owners of the slaves two and a half of these pieces per day, and found the poor fellows in victuals himself, because he thought their owners did not feed them well enough according to the work they did.

9. To measure the depth of a vessel when fully loaded.
1. Slow West Indian vessels that sail along the coast.
2. These pistareens are of a value of a shilling [Equiano's note].

* * *

Once, for a few days, I was let out to fit a vessel, and I had no victuals allowed me by either party; at last I told my master of this treatment, and he took me away from it. In many of the estates, on the different islands where I used to be sent for rum or sugar, they would not deliver it to me, or any other negro; he was therefore obliged to send a white man along with me to those places; and then he used to pay him from six to ten pistareens a day. From being thus employed, during the time I served Mr. King, in going about the different estates on the island,[3] I had all the opportunity I could wish for, to see the dreadful usage of the poor men; usage that reconciled me to my situation, and made me bless God for the hands into which I had fallen.

I had the good fortune to please my master in every department in which he employed me; and there was scarcely any part of his business, or household affairs, in which I was not occasionally engaged. I often supplied the place of a clerk, in receiving and delivering cargoes to the ships, in tending stores, and delivering goods. And besides this, I used to shave and dress my master when convenient, and take care of his horse; and when it was necessary, which was very often, I worked likewise on board of different vessels of his. By these means I became very useful to my master, and saved him, as he used to acknowledge, above a hundred pounds a year. Nor did he scruple to say I was of more advantage to him than any of his clerks; though their usual wages in the West Indies are from sixty to a hundred pounds current a year.

I have sometimes heard it asserted that a Negro cannot earn his master the first cost; but nothing can be further from the truth. I suppose nine tenths of the mechanics throughout the West Indies are Negro slaves; and I well know the coopers[4] among them earn two dollars a day, the carpenters the same, and often times more; as also the masons, smiths, and fisherman, etc. And I have known many slaves whose masters would not take a thousand pounds current for them. But surely this assertion refutes itself; for, if it be true, why do the planters and merchants pay such a price for slaves? And, above all, why do those who make this assertion exclaim the most loudly against the abolition of the slave trade? So much are men blinded, and to such inconsistent arguments are they driven by mistaken interest! I grant, indeed, that slaves are sometimes, by half-feeding, half-clothing, over-working and stripes,[5] reduced so low, that they are turned out as unfit for service, and left to perish in the woods, or expire on the dunghill.

My master was several times offered, by different gentlemen, one hundred guineas for me, but he always told them he would not sell me, to my great joy. And I used to double my diligence and care, for fear of getting into the hands of those men who did not allow a valuable slave the common support of life. Many of them even used to find fault with my master for feeding his slaves so well as he did; although I often went hungry, and an Englishman might think my fare very indifferent;[6] but he used to tell them he always would do it, because the slaves thereby looked better and did more work.

While I was thus employed by my master, I was often a witness to cruelties of every kind, which were exercised on my unhappy fellow slaves. I used frequently to have different cargoes of new Negroes in my care for sale; and it was almost a constant practice with our clerks, and other whites, to com-

3. Equiano remained in the West Indies from 1763 to 1766.
4. Barrel makers.
5. Lashes.
6. Poor, unsatisfactory.

mit violent depredations on the chastity of the female slaves; and these I was, though with reluctance, obliged to submit to at all times, being unable to help them. When we have had some of these slaves on board my master's vessels, to carry them to other islands, or to America, I have known our mates to commit these acts most shamefully, to the disgrace, not of Christians only, but of men. I have even known them to gratify their brutal passion with females not ten years old; and these abominations, some of them practiced to such scandalous excess, that one of our captains discharged the mate and others on that account. And yet in Montserrat[7] I have seen a Negro man staked to the ground, and cut most shockingly, and then his ears cut off bit by bit, because he had been connected with a white woman, who was a common prostitute. As if it were no crime in the whites to rob an innocent African girl of her virtue; but most heinous in a black man only to gratify a passion of nature, where the temptation was offered by one of a different color, though the most abandoned woman of her species.

Another Negro man was half hanged, and then burnt, for attempting to poison a cruel overseer. Thus, by repeated cruelties, are the wretched first urged to despair, and then murdered, because they still retain so much of human nature about them as to wish to put an end to their misery, and retaliate on their tyrants! These overseers are indeed for the most part persons of the worst character of any denomination of men in the West Indies. Unfortunately, many humane gentlemen, but not residing on their estates, are obliged to leave the management of them in the hands of these human butchers, who cut and mangle the slaves in a shocking manner on the most trifling occasions, and altogether treat them in every respect like brutes. They pay no regard to the situation of pregnant women, nor the least attention to the lodging of the field Negroes. Their huts, which ought to be well covered, and the place dry where they take their little repose, are often open sheds, built in damp places; so that when the poor creatures return tired from the toils of the field, they contract many disorders, from being exposed to the damp air in this uncomfortable state, while they are heated, and their pores are open. This neglect certainly conspires with many others to cause a decrease in the births as well as in the lives of the grown Negroes. I can quote many instances of gentlemen who reside on their estates in the West Indies, and then the scene is quite changed; the Negroes are treated with lenity and proper care, by which their lives are prolonged, and their masters profited. To the honor of humanity, I knew several gentlemen who managed their estates in this manner, and they found that benevolence was their true interest. And, among many I could mention in several of the islands, I knew one in Montserrat whose slaves looked remarkably well, and never needed any fresh supplies of Negroes; and there are many other estates, especially in Barbadoes, which, from such judicious treatment, need no fresh stock of Negroes at any time. I have the honor of knowing a most worthy and humane gentleman, who is a native of Barbadoes, and his estates there.[8] This gentleman has written a treatise on the usage of his own slaves. He allows them two hours of refreshment at midday, and many other indulgencies and comforts, particularly in their lodging; and, besides this, he raises more provisions on his estate than they can destroy; so that by these attentions he saves the lives of his Negroes, and keeps them healthy, and as happy as the

7. An island in the West Indies seven miles from Antigua.

8. Two of Equiano's notes identifying these men are omitted.

condition of slavery can admit. I myself, as shall appear in the sequel,[9] managed an estate, where, by those attentions, the Negroes were uncommonly cheerful and healthy, and did more work by half than by the common mode of treatment they usually do. For want,[1] therefore, of such care and attention to the poor Negroes, and otherwise oppressed as they are, it is no wonder that the decrease should require 20,000 new Negroes annually, to fill up the vacant places of the dead.

* * *

From *Chapter VI*

In the preceding chapter I have set before the reader a few of those many instances of oppression, extortion, and cruelty, which I have been a witness to in the West Indies; but were I to enumerate them all, the catalog would be tedious and disgusting. The punishments of the slaves on every trifling occasion are so frequent, and so well known, together with the different instruments with which they are tortured, that it cannot any longer afford novelty to recite them; and they are too shocking to yield delight either to the writer or the reader. I shall therefore hereafter only mention such as incidentally befell myself in the course of my adventures.

* * *

Some time in the year 1763, kind Providence seemed to appear rather more favorable to me. One of my master's vessels, a Bermudas sloop, about sixty tons burthen, was commanded by one captain Thomas Farmer, an Englishman, a very alert and active man, who gained my master a great deal of money by his good management in carrying passengers from one island to another; but very often his sailors used to get drunk and run away from the vessel, which hindered him in his business very much. This man had taken a liking to me, and many times begged of my master to let me go a trip with him as a sailor; but he would tell him he could not spare me, though the vessel sometimes could not go for want of hands, for sailors were generally very scarce in the island. However, at last, from necessity or force, my master was prevailed on, though very reluctantly, to let me go with this captain; but he gave him great charge to take care that I did not run away, for if I did he would make him pay for me. This being the case, the captain had for some time a sharp eye upon me whenever the vessel anchored; and as soon as she returned I was sent for on shore again. Thus was I slaving, as it were, for life, sometimes at one thing, and sometimes at another. So that the captain and I were nearly the most useful men in my master's employment. I also became so useful to the captain on ship-board, that many times, when he used to ask for me to go with him, though it should be but for twenty-four hours, to some of the islands near us, my master would answer he could not spare me, at which the captain would swear, and would not go the trip, and tell my master I was better to him on board than any three white men he had; for they used to behave ill in many respects, particularly in getting drunk; and then they frequently got the boat stove,[2] so as to hinder the vessel from coming back as soon as she might have done. This my master knew

9. I.e., later.
1. Lack.

2. Put a hole in the boat.

very well; and at last, by the captain's constant entreaties, after I had been several times with him, one day to my great joy, told me the captain would not let him rest, and asked whether I would go aboard as a sailor, or stay on shore and mind the stores, for he could not bear any longer to be plagued in this manner. I was very happy at this proposal, for I immediately thought I might in time stand some chance by being on board to get a little money, or possibly make my escape if I should be used ill. I also expected to get better food, and in greater abundance; for I had oftentimes felt much hunger, though my master treated his slaves, as I have observed, uncommonly well. I therefore, without hesitation, answered him, that I would go and be a sailor if he pleased. Accordingly I was ordered on board directly. Nevertheless, between the vessel and the shore, when she was in port, I had little or no rest, as my master always wished to have me along with him. Indeed he was a very pleasant gentleman, and but for my expectations on ship-board, I should not have thought of leaving him. But the captain liked me also very much, and I was entirely his right hand man. I did all I could to deserve his favor, and in return I received better treatment from him than any other, I believe, ever met with in the West Indies, in my situation.

After I had been sailing for some time with this captain, at length I endeavored to try my luck, and commence merchant. I had but a very small capital to begin with; for one single half bit,[3] which is equal to three pence in England, made up my whole stock. However, I trusted to the Lord to be with me; and at one of our trips to St. Eustatia,[4] a Dutch island, I bought a glass tumbler with my half bit, and when I came to Montserrat, I sold it for a bit, or six pence. Luckily we made several successive trips to St. Eustatia (which was a general mart for the West Indies, about twenty leagues from Montserrat), and in our next, finding my tumbler so profitable, with this one bit I bought two tumblers more; and when I came back, I sold them for two bits, equal to a shilling sterling. When we went again, I bought with these two bits four more of these glasses, which I sold for four bits on our return to Montserrat. And in our next voyage to St. Eustatia, I bought two glasses with one bit, and with the other three I bought a jug of Geneva,[5] nearly about three pints in measure. When we came to Montserrat, I sold the gin for eight bits, and the tumblers for two, so that my capital now amounted in all to a dollar, well husbanded[6] and acquired in the space of a month or six weeks, when I blessed the Lord that I was so rich. As we sailed to different islands, I laid this money out in various things occasionally, and it used to turn out to very good account, especially when we went to Guadaloupe, Grenada, and the rest of the French islands. Thus was I going all about the islands upwards of four years, and ever trading as I went, during which I experienced many instances of ill usage, and have seen many injuries done to other Negroes in our dealings with whites. And, amidst our recreations, when we have been dancing and merry-making, they, without cause, have molested and insulted us. Indeed, I was more than once obliged to look up to God on high, as I had advised the poor fisherman some time before. And I had not been long trading for myself in the manner I have related above, when I experienced the like trial in company with him as follows:—This man, being used to the water,

---

3. In the West Indies, a small silver coin a fraction of the Spanish dollar.
4. I.e., St. Eustatius, one of the Leeward Islands

in the West Indies.
5. The original name of gin.
6. Managed.

was upon an emergency put on board of us by his master, to work as another hand, on a voyage to Santa Cruz; and at our sailing he had brought his little all for a venture, which consisted of six bits' worth of limes and oranges in a bag; I had also my whole stock, which was about twelve bits' worth of the same kind of goods, separate in two bags, for we had heard these fruits sold well in that island. When we came there, in some little convenient time, he and I went ashore to sell them; but we had scarcely landed, when we were met by two white men, who presently took our three bags from us. We could not at first guess what they meant to do, and for some time we thought they were jesting with us; but they too soon let us know otherwise, for they took our ventures immediately to a house hard by, and adjoining the fort, while we followed all the way begging of them to give us our fruits, but in vain. They not only refused to return them, but swore at us, and threatened if we did not immediately depart they would flog us well. We told them these three bags were all we were worth in the world, and that we brought them with us to sell when we came from Montserrat, and showed them the vessel. But this was rather against us, as they now saw we were strangers, as well as slaves. They still therefore swore, and desired us to be gone, and even took sticks to beat us; while we, seeing they meant what they said, went off in the greatest confusion and despair. Thus, in the very minute of gaining more by three times than I ever did by any venture in my life before, was I deprived of every farthing I was worth. An unsupportable misfortune! but how to help ourselves we knew not. In our consternation we went to the commanding officer of the fort, and told him how we had been served by his people, but we obtained not the least redress. He answered our complaints only by a volley of imprecations against us, and immediately took a horse-whip, in order to chastise us, so that we were obliged to turn out much faster than we came in. I now, in the agony of distress and indignation, wished that the ire of God in his forked lightning might transfix these cruel oppressors among the dead. Still, however, we persevered; went back again to the house, and begged and besought them again and again for our fruits, till at last some other people that were in the house asked if we would be contented if they kept one bag and gave us the other two. We, seeing no remedy whatever, consented to this; and they, observing one bag to have both kinds of fruit in it, which belonged to my companion, kept that; and the other two, which were mine, they gave us back. As soon as I got them, I ran as fast as I could, and got the first Negro man I could to help me off. My companion, however, stayed a little longer to plead; he told them the bag they had was his, and likewise all that he was worth in the world; but this was of no avail, and he was obliged to return without it. The poor old man wringing his hands, cried bitterly for his loss; and, indeed, he then did look up to God on high, which so moved me in pity for him, that I gave him nearly one-third of my fruits. We then proceeded to the markets to sell them; and Providence was more favorable to us than we could have expected, for we sold our fruits uncommonly well; I got for mine about thirty-seven bits. Such a surprising reverse of fortune in so short a space of time seemed like a dream, and proved no small encouragement for me to trust the Lord in any situation. My captain afterwards frequently used to take my part, and get me my right, when I have been plundered or used ill by these tender Christian depredators; among whom I have shuddered to observe the unceasing blasphemous execrations which are wantonly thrown out by persons of all ages and conditions, not only without occasion, but even as if they were indulgencies and pleasure.

* * *

The reader cannot but judge of the irksomeness of this situation to a mind like mine, in being daily exposed to new hardships and impositions, after having seen many better days, and been, as it were, in a state of freedom and plenty; added to which, every part of the world I had hitherto been in, seemed to me a paradise in comparison to the West Indies. My mind was therefore hourly replete with inventions and thoughts of being freed, and, if possible, by honest and honorable means; for I always remembered the old adage, and I trust it has ever been my ruling principle, that "honesty is the best policy;" and likewise that other golden precept—"To do unto all men as I would they should do unto me." However, as I was from early years a pre-destinarian, I thought whatever fate had determined must ever come to pass; and, therefore, if ever it were my lot to be freed, nothing could prevent me, although I should at present see no means or hope to obtain my freedom; on the other hand, if it were my fate not to be freed, I never should be so, and all my endeavors for that purpose would be fruitless. In the midst of these thoughts, I therefore looked up with prayers anxiously to God for my liberty; and at the same time used every honest means, and did all that was possible on my part to obtain it. In process of time, I became master of a few pounds, and in a fair way of making more, which my friendly captain knew very well; this occasioned him sometimes to take liberties with me; but whenever he treated me waspishly, I used plainly to tell him my mind, and that I would die before I would be imposed upon as other Negroes were, and that to my life had lost its relish when liberty was gone. This I said, although I foresaw my then well-being or future hopes of freedom (humanly speaking) depended on this man. However, as he could not bear the thoughts of my not sailing with him, he always became mild on my threats. I therefore continued with him; and, from my great attention to his orders and his business, I gained him credit, and through his kindness to me, I at last procured my liberty. While I thus went on, filled with the thoughts of freedom, and resisting oppression as well as I was able, my life hung daily in suspense, particularly in the surfs I have formerly mentioned, as I could not swim. These are extremely violent throughout the West Indies, and I was ever exposed to their howling rage and devouring fury in all the islands. I have seen them strike and toss a boat right up on end, and maim several on board. Once in the Grenada islands, when I and about eight others were pulling a large boat with two puncheons[7] of water in it, a surf struck us, and drove the boat, and all in it, about half a stone's throw, among some trees, and above the high water mark. We were obliged to get all the assistance we could from the nearest estate to mend the boat, and launch it into the water again. At Montserrat, one night, in pressing hard to get off the shore on board, the punt was overset with us four times, the first time I was very near being drowned; however, the jacket I had on kept me up above water a little space of time, when I called on a man near me, who was a good swimmer, and told him I could not swim; he then made haste to me, and, just as I was sinking, he caught hold of me, and brought me to sounding,[8] and then he went and brought the punt also. As soon as we had turned the water out of her, lest we should be used ill for being absent, we attempted again three times more, and as often the horrid

7. Large casks.
8. I.e., where one could stand. "Punt": narrow, flat-bottomed boat.

surfs served us as at first; but at last, the fifth time we attempted, we gained our point, at the imminent hazard of our lives. One day also, at Old Road, in Montserrat, our captain, and three men besides myself, were going in a large canoe in quest of rum and sugar, when a single surf tossed the canoe an amazing distance from the water, and some of us, near a stone's throw from each other. Most of us were very much bruised; so that I and many more often said, and really thought, that there was not such another place under the heavens as this. I longed, therefore, much to leave it, and daily wished to see my master's promise performed, of going to Philadelphia.

While we lay in this place, a very cruel thing happened on board our sloop, which filled me with horror; though I found afterwards such practices were frequent. There was a very clever and decent free young mulatto man, who sailed a long time with us; he had a free woman for his wife, by whom he had a child, and she was then living on shore, and all very happy. Our captain and mate, and other people on board, and several elsewhere, even the natives of Bermudas, all knew this young man from a child that he was always free, and no one had ever claimed him as their property. However, as might too often overcomes right in these parts, it happened that a Bermudas captain, whose vessel lay there for a few days in the road, came on board of us, and seeing the mulatto man, whose name was Joseph Clipson, he told him he was not free, and that he had orders from his master to bring him to Bermudas. The poor man could not believe the captain to be in earnest, but he was very soon undeceived, his men laying violent hands on him; and although he showed a certificate of his being born free in St. Kitts, and most people on board knew that he served his time to[9] boat building, and always passed for a free man, yet he was forcibly taken out of our vessel. He then asked to be carried ashore before the Secretary or Magistrates, and these infernal invaders of human rights promised him he should; but instead of that, they carried him on board of the other vessel. And the next day, without giving the poor man any hearing on shore, or suffering him even to see his wife or child, he was carried away, and probably doomed never more in this world to see them again. Nor was this the only instance of this kind of barbarity I was a witness to. I have since often seen in Jamaica and other islands, free men, whom I have known in America, thus villainously trepanned[1] and held in bondage. I have heard of two similar practices even in Philadelphia. And were it not for the benevolence of the Quakers in that city, many of the sable[2] race, who now breathe the air of liberty, would, I believe, be groaning indeed under some planter's chains. These things opened my mind to a new scene of horror, to which I had been before a stranger. Hitherto I had thought slavery only dreadful, but the state of a free negro appeared to me now equally so at least, and in some respects even worse, for they live in constant alarm for their liberty; which is but nominal, for they are universally insulted and plundered, without the possibility of redress; for such is the equity of the West Indian laws, that no free Negro's evidence will be admitted in their courts of justice. In this situation, is it surprising that slaves, when mildly treated, should prefer even the misery of slavery to such a mockery of freedom? I was now completely disgusted with the West Indies, and thought I never should be entirely free until I had left them.

---

9. Was apprenticed at.   2. Black.
1. Trapped.

* * *

About the latter end of the year 1764, my master bought a larger sloop, called the Prudence, about seventy or eighty tons, of which my captain had the command. I went with him in this vessel, and we took a load of new slaves for Georgia and Charlestown. My master now left me entirely to the captain, though he still wished me to be with him; but I, who always much wished to lose sight of the West Indies, was not a little rejoiced at the thoughts of seeing any other country. Therefore, relying on the goodness of my captain, I got ready all the little venture I could; and, when the vessel was ready, we sailed, to my great joy. When we got to our destined places, Georgia and Charlestown, I expected I should have an opportunity of selling my little property to advantage. But here, particularly in Charlestown, I met with buyers, white men, who imposed on me as in other places. Notwithstanding, I was resolved to have fortitude, thinking no lot or trial too hard when kind Heaven is the rewarder.

We soon got loaded again, and returned to Montserrat; and there, amongst the rest of the islands, I sold my goods well; and in this manner I continued trading during the year 1764—meeting with various scenes of imposition, as usual. After this, my master fitted out his vessel for Philadelphia, in the year 1765; and during the time we were loading her, and getting ready for the voyage, I worked with redoubled alacrity, from the hope of getting money enough by these voyages to buy my freedom, in time, if it should please God; and also to see the town of Philadelphia, which I had heard a great deal about for some years past. Besides which, I had always longed to prove my master's promise the first day I came to him. In the midst of these elevated ideas, and while I was about getting my little stock of merchandize in readiness, one Sunday my master sent for me to his house. When I came there, I found him and the captain together; and, on my going in, I was struck with astonishment at his telling me he heard that I meant to run away from him when I got to Philadelphia. "And therefore," said he, "I must tell you again, you cost me a great deal of money, no less than forty pounds sterling; and it will not do to lose so much. You are a valuable fellow," continued he, "and I can get any day for you one hundred guineas, from many gentlemen in this island." And then he told me of Captain Doran's brother-in-law, a severe master, who ever wanted to buy me to make me his overseer. My captain also said he could get much more than a hundred guineas for me in Carolina. This I knew to be a fact; for the gentleman that wanted to buy me came off several times on board of us, and spoke to me to live with him, and said he would use me well. When I asked him what work he would put me to, he said, as I was a sailor, he would make me a captain of one of his rice vessels. But I refused; and fearing at the same time, by a sudden turn I saw in the captain's temper, he might mean to sell me, I told the gentleman I would not live with him on any condition, and that I certainly would run away with his vessel: but he said he did not fear that, as he would catch me again, and then he told me how cruelly he would serve me if I should do so. My captain, however, gave him to understand that I knew something of navigation, so he thought better of it; and, to my great joy, he went away. I now told my master, I did not say I would run away in Philadelphia; neither did I mean it, as he did not use me ill, nor yet the captain; for if they did, I certainly would have made some attempts before now; but as I thought that if it were God's will

I ever should be freed, it would be so, and, on the contrary, if it was not His will, it would not happen. So I hoped if ever I were freed, whilst I was used well, it should be by honest means; but as I could not help myself, he must do as he pleased; I could only hope and trust to the God of Heaven; and at that instant my mind was big with inventions, and full of schemes to escape. I then appealed to the captain, whether he ever saw any sign of my making the least attempt to run away, and asked him if I did not always come on board according to the time for which he gave me liberty; and, more particularly, when all our men left us at Guadeloupe, and went on board of the French fleet, and advised me to go with them, whether I might not, and that he could not have got me again. To my no small surprise, and very great joy, the captain confirmed every syllable that I had said, and even more; for he said he had tried different times to see if I would make any attempt of this kind, both at St. Eustatia and in America, and he never found that I made the smallest; but, on the contrary, I always came on board according to his orders; and he did really believe, if I ever meant to run away, that, as I could never have had a better opportunity, I would have done it the night the mate and all the people left our vessel at Guadeloupe. The captain then informed my master, who had been thus imposed on by our mate (though I did not know who was my enemy), the reason the mate had for imposing this lie upon him; which was, because I had acquainted the captain of the provisions the mate had given away or taken out of the vessel. This speech of the captain was like life to the dead to me, and instantly my soul glorified God; and still more so, on hearing my master immediately say that I was a sensible fellow, and he never did intend to use me as a common slave; and that but for the entreaties of the captain, and his character of me, he would not have let me go from the shores about as I had done. That also, in so doing, he thought by carrying one little thing or other to different places to sell, I might make money. That he also intended to encourage me in this, by crediting me with half a puncheon of rum and half a hogshead[3] of sugar at a time; so that, from being careful, I might have money enough, in some time, to purchase my freedom; and, when that was the case, I might depend upon it he would let me have it for forty pounds sterling money, which was only the same price he gave for me. This sound gladdened my poor heart beyond measure; though indeed it was no more than the very idea I had formed in my mind of my master long before, and I immediately made him this reply: "Sir, I always had that very thought of you, indeed I had, and that made me so diligent in serving you." He then gave me a large piece of silver coin, such as I never had seen or had before, and told me to get ready for the voyage, and he would credit me with a tierce[4] of sugar, and another of rum; he also said that he had two amiable sisters in Philadelphia, from whom I might get some necessary things. Upon this my noble captain desired me to go aboard; and, knowing the African metal,[5] he charged me not to say any thing of this matter to any body; and he promised that the lying mate should not go with him any more. This was a change indeed: in the same hour to feel the most exquisite pain, and in the turn of a moment the fullest joy. It caused in me such sensations as I was only able to express in my looks; my heart was so overpowered with gratitude, that I could have kissed both of their feet. When I left the room, I immediately went, or rather flew, to the vessel; which being loaded,

3. Large barrel.
4. A third of a barrel.

5. I.e., character.

my master, as good as his word, trusted me with a tierce of rum, and another of sugar, when we sailed, and arrived safe at the elegant town of Philadelphia. I sold my goods here pretty well; and in this charming place I found every thing plentiful and cheap.

While I was in this place, a very extraordinary occurrence befell me. I had been told one evening of a wise woman, a Mrs. Davis, who revealed secrets, foretold events, etc., etc. I put little faith in this story at first, as I could not conceive that any mortal could foresee the future disposals of Providence, nor did I believe in any other revelation than that of the Holy Scriptures; however, I was greatly astonished at seeing this woman in a dream that night, though a person I never before beheld in my life. This made such an impression on me, that I could not get the idea the next day out of my mind, and I then became as anxious to see her as I was before indifferent. Accordingly in the evening, after we left off working, I inquired where she lived, and being directed to her, to my inexpressible surprise, beheld the very woman in the very same dress she appeared to me to wear in the vision. She immediately told me I had dreamed of her the preceding night; related to me many things that had happened with a correctness that astonished me, and finally told me I should not be long a slave. This was the more agreeable news; as I believed it the more readily from her having so faithfully related the past incidents of my life. She said I should be twice in very great danger of my life within eighteen months, which, if I escaped, I should afterwards go on well. So, giving me her blessing, we parted. After staying here sometime till our vessel was loaded, and I had bought in my little traffic, we sailed from this agreeable spot for Montserrat, once more to encounter the raging surfs.

* * *

We soon came to Georgia, where we were to complete our landing, and here worse fate than ever attended me; for one Sunday night, as I was with some negroes in their master's yard, in the town of Savannah, it happened that their master, one Doctor Perkins, who was a very severe and cruel man, came in drunk; and not liking to see any strange negroes in his yard, he and a ruffian of a white man, he had in his service, beset me in an instant, and both of them struck me with the first weapons they could get hold of. I cried out as long as I could for help and mercy; but, though I gave a good account of myself, and he knew my captain, who lodged hard by him,[6] it was to no purpose. They beat and mangled me in a shameful manner, leaving me near dead. I lost so much blood from the wounds I received, that I lay quite motionless, and was so benumbed that I could not feel any thing for many hours. Early in the morning, they took me away to the jail. As I did not return to the ship all night, my captain, not knowing where I was, and being uneasy that I did not then make my appearance, made inquiry after me; and having found where I was, immediately came to me. As soon as the good man saw me so cut and mangled, he could not forbear weeping; he soon got me out of jail to his lodgings, and immediately sent for the best doctors in the place, who at first declared it as their opinion that I could not recover. My captain on this went to all the lawyers in the town for their advice, but they told him they could do nothing for me as I was a negro. He then went to Doctor Perkins, the hero who had vanquished me, and menaced him, swearing he would be revenged on him, and challenged him to fight.—But cowardice is ever the

6. I.e., close by him.

companion of cruelty—and the Doctor refused. However, by the skillfullness of one Dr. Brady of that place, I began at last to amend; but, although I was so sore and bad with the wounds I had all over me, that I could not rest in any posture, yet I was in more pain on account of the captain's uneasiness about me, than I otherwise should have been. The worthy man nursed and watched me all the hours of the night; and I was, through his attention and that of the doctor, able to get out of bed in about sixteen or eighteen days. All this time I was very much wanted on board, as I used frequently to go up and down the river for rafts, and other parts of our cargo, and stow them, when the mate was sick or absent. In about four weeks, I was able to go on duty, and in a fortnight after, having got in all our lading, our vessel set sail for Montserrat; and in less than three weeks we arrived there safe towards the end of the year. This ended my adventures in 1764, for I did not leave Montserrat again till the beginning of the following year.

From *Chapter VII*

Every day now brought me nearer my freedom, and I was impatient till we proceeded again to sea, that I might have an opportunity of getting a sum large enough to purchase it. I was not long ungratified; for, in the beginning of the year 1766, my master bought another sloop, named the Nancy, the largest I had ever seen. She was partly laden, and was to proceed to Philadelphia; our captain had his choice of three, and I was well pleased he chose this, which was the largest; for, from his having a large vessel, I had more room, and could carry a larger quantity of goods with me. Accordingly, when we had delivered our old vessel, the Prudence, and completed the lading of the Nancy, having made near three hundred per cent. by four barrels of pork I brought from Charlestown, I laid in as large a cargo as I could, trusting to God's providence to prosper my undertaking. With these views I sailed for Philadelphia. On our passage, when we drew near the land, I was for the first time surprised at the sight of some whales, having never seen any such large sea monsters before; and as we sailed by the land, one morning, I saw a puppy whale close by the vessel; it was about the length of a wherry boat, and it followed us all the day till we got within the Capes.[7] We arrived safe, and in good time at Philadelphia, and I sold my goods there chiefly to the Quakers. They always appeared to be a very honest, discreet sort of people, and never attempted to impose on[8] me; I therefore liked them, and ever after chose to deal with them in preference to any others.

One Sunday morning, while I was here, as I was going to church, I chanced to pass a meetinghouse. The doors being open, and the house full of people, it excited my curiosity to go in. When I entered the house, to my great surprise, I saw a very tall woman standing in the midst of them, speaking in an audible voice something which I could not understand. Having never seen any thing of this kind before, I stood and stared about me for some time, wondering at this odd scene. As soon as it was over, I took an opportunity to make inquiry about the place and people, when I was informed they were called Quakers. I particularly asked what that woman I saw in the midst of them had said, but none of them were pleased to satisfy me; so I quitted them, and soon after, as I was returning, I came to a church crowded with people; the churchyard was full likewise, and a number of people were even mounted

7. Equiano may be referring to Cape May in
southern New Jersey.   8. Cheat.

on ladders looking in at the windows. I thought this a strange sight, as I had never seen churches, either in England or the West Indies, crowded in this manner before. I therefore made bold to ask some people the meaning of all this, and they told me the Rev. Mr. George Whitefield was preaching. I had often heard of this gentleman, and had wished to see and hear him; but I never before had an opportunity. I now therefore resolved to gratify myself with the sight, and pressed in amidst the multitude. When I got into the church, I saw this pious man exhorting the people with the greatest fervor and earnestness, and sweating as much as I ever did while in slavery on Montserrat beach. I was very much struck and impressed with this; I thought it strange I had never seen divines exert themselves in this manner before, and was no longer at a loss to account for the thin congregations they preached to.

When we had discharged our cargo here, and were loaded again, we left this fruitful land once more, and set sail for Montserrat. My traffic had hitherto succeeded so well with me, that I thought, by selling my goods when we arrived at Montserrat, I should have enough to purchase my freedom. But as soon as our vessel arrived there, my master came on board, and gave orders for us to go to St. Eustatia, and discharge our cargo there, and from thence proceed for Georgia. I was much disappointed at this; but thinking, as usual, it was of no use to encounter with the decrees of fate, I submitted without repining, and we went to St. Eustatia. After we had discharged our cargo there, we took in a live cargo (as we call a cargo of slaves). Here I sold my goods tolerably well; but, not being able to lay out all my money in this small island to as much advantage as in many other places, I laid out only part, and the remainder I brought away with me net. We sailed from hence for Georgia, and I was glad when we got there, though I had not much reason to like the place from my last adventure in Savannah; but I longed to get back to Montserrat and procure my freedom, which I expected to be able to purchase when I returned. As soon as we arrived here, I waited on my careful doctor, Mr. Brady, to whom I made the most grateful acknowledgments in my power, for his former kindness and attention during my illness.

* * *

When we had unladen the vessel, and I had sold my venture, finding myself master of about forty-seven pounds—I consulted my true friend, the captain, how I should proceed in offering my master the money for my freedom. He told me to come on a certain morning, when he and my master would be at breakfast together. Accordingly, on that morning I went, and met the captain there, as he had appointed. When I went in I made my obeisance to my master, and with my money in my hand, and many fears in my heart, I prayed him to be as good as his offer to me, when he was pleased to promise me my freedom as soon as I could purchase it. This speech seemed to confound him, he began to recoil, and my heart that instant sunk within me. "What," said he, "give you your freedom? Why, where did you get the money? Have you got forty pounds sterling?" "Yes, sir," I answered. "How did you get it?" replied he. I told him, very honestly. The captain then said he knew I got the money honestly, and with much industry, and that I was particularly careful. On which my master replied, I got money much faster than he did; and said he would not have made me the promise he did if he had thought I should have got the money so soon. "Come, come," said my worthy captain, clapping my master on the back, "Come, Robert (which was his name), I think you must let him have his freedom;—you have laid your money out very well; you have received a very good interest for it all this time, and here is now the principal at last. I know Gustavus has earned you more than a hundred a year, and he will save you money, as he will not leave you.—Come, Robert, take the money." My master then said he would not be worse than his promise; and, taking the money, told me to go to the Secretary at the Register Office, and get my manumission[9] drawn up. These words of my master were like a voice from Heaven to me. In an instant all my trepidation was turned into unutterable bliss; and I most reverently bowed myself with gratitude, unable to express my feelings, but by the overflowing of my eyes, and a heart replete with thanks to God, while my true and worthy friend, the captain, congratulated us both with a peculiar degree of heartfelt pleasure. As soon as the first transports of my joy were over, and that I had expressed my thanks to these my worthy friends, in the best manner I was able, I rose with a heart full of affection and reverence, and left the room, in order to obey my master's joyful mandate of going to the Register Office. As I was leaving the house I called to mind the words of the Psalmist, in the 126th Psalm, and like him, "I glorified God in my heart, in whom I trusted." These words had been impressed on my mind from the very day I was forced from Deptford to the present hour, and I now saw them, as I thought, fulfilled and verified. My imagination was all rapture as I flew to the Register Office; and, in this respect, like the apostle Peter[1] (whose deliverance from prison was so sudden and extraordinary, that he thought he was in a vision), I could scarcely believe I was awake. Heavens! who could do justice to my feelings at this moment! Not conquering heroes themselves, in the midst of a triumph—Not the tender mother who has just regained her long lost infant, and presses it to her heart—Not the weary hungry, mariner, at the sight of the desired friendly port—Not the lover, when he once more embraces his beloved mistress, after she has been ravished from his arms! All within my breast was tumult, wildness, and delirium! My feet scarcely touched the ground, for they were winged with joy; and, like Elijah, as he rose to Heaven,[2] they "were with lightning sped as I went on." Every one I met I told of my happiness, and blazed about the virtue of my amiable master and captain.

When I got to the office and acquainted the Register with my errand, he congratulated me on the occasion, and told me he would draw up my manumission for half price, which was a guinea. I thanked him for his kindness; and, having received it, and paid him, I hastened to my master to get him to sign it, that I might be fully released. Accordingly he signed the manumission that day; so that, before night, I, who had been a slave in the morning, trembling at the will of another, was become my own master, and completely free. I thought this was the happiest day I had ever experienced; and my joy was still heightened by the blessings and prayers of many of the sable race, particularly the aged, to whom my heart had ever been attached with reverence.

* * *

As the form of my manumission has something peculiar in it, and expresses the absolute power and dominion one man claims over his fellow, I shall beg leave to present it before my readers at full length:

---

9. Document declaring his freedom.
1. "Acts xii.9" [Equiano's note]. "And he went out and followed him; and wist not that it was true which was done by the angel; but thought he saw a vision."
2. The Lord takes Elijah into heaven in 2 Kings 2.11.

Montserrat.—To all men unto whom these presents[3] shall come: I, Robert King, of the parish of St. Anthony, in the said island, merchant, send greeting. Know ye, that I, the aforesaid Robert King, for and in consideration of the sum of seventy pounds current money of the said island,[4] to me in hand paid, and to the intent that a negro man slave, named Gustavus Vassa, shall and may become free, having manumitted, emancipated, enfranchised, and set free, and by these presents do manumit, emancipate, enfranchise, and set free, the aforesaid negro man slave, named Gustavus Vassa, for ever; hereby giving, granting, and releasing unto him, the said Gustavus Vassa, all right, title, dominion, sovereignty, and property, which, as lord and master over the aforesaid Gustavus Vassa, I had, or now have, or by any means whatsoever I may or can hereafter possibly have over him, the aforesaid negro, for ever. In witness whereof, I, the above said Robert King, have unto these presents set my hand and seal, this tenth day of July, in the year of our Lord one thousand seven hundred and sixty-six.

ROBERT KING.

Signed, sealed, and delivered in the presence of Terry Legay, Montserrat.

Registered the within manumission at full length, this eleventh day of July, 1766, in liber[5] D.

TERRY LEGAY, REGISTER.

* * *

1789

3. The present words; this document.
4. The exchange rate favored the West Indians in this period: forty pounds sterling equaling seventy pounds in "local" currency.
5. Book (Latin).

JUDITH SARGENT MURRAY
1751–1820

Judith Sargent Murray found her most important subject—the independent female mind—in her first published essay, "The Utility of Encouraging a Degree of Self-Complacency, Especially in Female Bosoms." Writing under the pen name "Constantia," she advises young women that though a "pleasing form is undoubtedly advantageous," a developed mind is much more important. An intellectual woman in a culture that regarded women as men's mental inferiors, a professional writer in an era when almost no one—male or female—made a living by writing, Murray powerfully demonstrated the validity of her own precepts.

She was born and spent much of her life in Gloucester, Massachusetts, a coastal town about forty miles north of Boston. Both her mother, Judith Saunders, and her father, Winthrop Sargent, came from hardworking, seafaring families. The Sargents showed their independence in many ways. One was in allowing Judith to be tutored by the local clergyman along with her younger brother Winslow in college preparatory subjects like Latin, Greek, and mathematics. Another was in their liberal theology, which questioned the strict Calvinist doctrine of election and damnation. Murray, her parents, and her first husband, John Stevens, whom she married in 1769, knew

How blest the Maid whose bosom no headstrong passion knows,
Her days in Joy she Passes, her nights in soft repose.

BE SURE TO AVOID MANY TROUBLES WHICH OTHERS INDURE: KEEP WITHIN COMPASS AND YOU SHALL BE SURE

KEEP WITHIN COMPASS

A Virtuous Woman is a Crown to her Husband.

ENTER NOT INTO THE WAY OF THE WICKED, AND GO NOT IN THE PATH OF EVIL MEN.

"Keep within Compass," c. 1795. In this contemporary engraving, women are encouraged to remain outside the public sphere occupied by men. Judith Sargent Murray, among others, challenged this view.

the teachings of the English Universalist James Relly, which proclaimed that salvation was available to anyone who accepted Jesus Christ. Relly was sure that a rational God would never condemn members of his human flock to hell. The Sargents and Stevens were thus ready to welcome Relly's greatest disciple, John Murray, who had left England and was preaching his way up the eastern seaboard; he came to Gloucester in 1774. The first Universalist church in America was dedicated there in 1780. It was no coincidence that the Universalist church in America was the first to ordain women as ministers. Judith Sargent Murray's later advocacy of cultivating independent, intellectually alert women was totally compatible with her religious position. In 1788, about a year after the death of John Stevens in the West Indies, she married John Murray, and her career as a writer began in earnest.

In an increasingly secular world, essays and novels with moral subtexts would make readers into new congregations, and the growing number of magazines like Boston's *Massachusetts Magazine* or *The Gentleman's and Lady's Town and Country Magazine: or, Repository of Instruction and Entertainment,* where Murray's first essay appeared in 1784, would supplant many pulpits in the years to come. Eighteenth-century readers liked a moral commentary firmly rooted in the Ten Commandments without the additional trappings of the old theology. But while Murray found her true subject and an audience early on, it was not easy for her to make a living by the pen. In the volatile world of print culture, magazines changed hands frequently and many disappeared without trace, while publishers assumed that contributors would be so eager to see their name in print that no payment was necessary. Washington Irving was the first American writer to live on income derived solely from his writing.

Murray's most important work and her greatest financial success was a three-volume compilation of her work, published in 1798 as *The Gleaner*. Like many publications of the period, it was financed by subscribers, whose names were listed inside. Murray gathered 759 names, among which were Sarah Wentworth Morton and Mercy Otis Warren. She dedicated *The Gleaner* to John and Abigail Adams, who also subscribed. The book, a true miscellany, included two plays, eulogies, and a series of historical essays. Most of it consisted of essays Murray had written for the *Massachusetts Magazine* under the pen name of Mr. Vigilius, who styled himself a "gleaner"—that is, one who picked up bits of ungathered grain after a harvest. Some of these essays told a connected narrative about Mr. Vigilius's adopted daughter, Margaretta; there were also religious essays with Universalist themes; political essays on American foreign and domestic policy (a religious liberal, Murray was a political conservative); and didactic essays in the narrative style of early-eighteenth-century English periodical writing. At the end of the work, Murray "unmasked" Mr. Vigilius and came forward as a woman, explaining that she had hidden her sex because she feared that if she were known to be a woman, her writing would not be taken seriously.

Murray never repeated the financial success of *The Gleaner;* the work itself was not reissued until 1992. She seems to have published nothing new from 1796 to 1802, when she offered some poems in a new Boston publication that hoped to take up where the defunct *Massachusetts Magazine* left off. Her major efforts went to the care of her ailing and improvident husband. She edited his *Letters and Sketches of Sermons* (1812–13) and his posthumously published autobiography (1816). With her work on Murray's behalf completed, she left New England and made a final home with her daughter in Natchez, Mississippi, where she died in 1820.

From The Gleaner

Chapter XI[1]

[HISTORY OF MISS WELLWOOD]

> When crimes despotic in the bosom reign,
> The tears of weeping beauty flow in vain.

Scarce an hour had elapsed, after Margaretta had forwarded her letter to Miss Worthington, when the following interesting account from that young lady, which had been written some days before, was put into her hand.

---

1. This chapter is one of several that treat the story of Margaretta Melworth, the young ward of the Worthington family who became infatuated with the rake Courtland. Here, Amelia Worthington relates a cautionary tale of a woman who had a similar experience.

Miss Worthington *to* Miss Melworth.

New-Haven, July 25th, 1789.

Gracious Heaven, what are my sensations! Never did I expect to address my dear Miss Melworth under a consciousness of having contributed (as the event may prove) to her ruin: But in deed, and in truth, we have not intentionally erred; and surely the tale which I have to unfold, will banish from a mind, where integrity and every other virtue have taken up their abode, a wretch, who ought never to have profaned a temple so sacred.

My poor mother weeps incessantly; she says she shall never know peace again, if you are not enabled to assure her, that tranquillity is restored to a bosom, where she hath been accessary in planting so sharp a thorn. Listen, my beloved Margaretta, to the recital I have to make; and let the virtues of Hamilton obtain their due estimation.

About six years since, a gentleman by the name of Wellwood, was one of the most respectable dwellers in this city; his family consisted only of his lady and daughter, with their domestics; his daughter had been educated with the exactest care, and she was, at eighteen, a beautiful and accomplished young woman. Just at this important period, Mr. Wellwood paid the great debt of nature; and so deep an impression did this melancholy and calamitous event make upon the mind of Mrs. Wellwood, who was one of the first of women, that after languishing a few weeks, under all the pressure of a rapid decline she also obtained her passport, resigning her life, a confessed and lamented martyr to grief.

Thus, in a very short interval, the unfortunate Frances Wellwood saw herself precipitated from a situation the most eligible, with which the dispositions of paternal Providence can possibly endow a young creature, to that of an unprotected orphan; no guardian father, no indulgent mother remained, to direct her steps, or to approbate her movements! She had been accustomed to regard her parents as the source of wisdom; no design had she ever executed, unsanctioned by the parental voice, unpropitiated by the maternal smile; and the authors of her existence had, in every sense, continued the prop and the confidence of the being they had reared. Neither Mr. nor Mrs. Wellwood were natives of this city; none of their kindred resided among us: So that the beauteous orphan viewed herself as alone in the universe; and when she cast her distracted gaze upon the clay cold tenements of a father and a mother; upon those eyes, now for ever closed, which, while the least vestige of life remained, had still darted upon her the most benign and unequivocal testimonies of affectionate tenderness; upon those lips never again to be unsealed, which had opened but to enrich her with advice, admonitions, directions, or benedictions; when, with folded arms, she contemplated those trophies of relentless death, the unutterable anguish of her spirit, depriving her for a time of reason, suspended the operation of the silent sorrow, which afterward reduced her to the very verge of the grave! Not a benevolent heart in this city, but deeply felt for the lovely mourner; never did I see a more pathetically interesting object. But time, that sovereign physician, and the soothing of those friends, to whom her virtues and her misfortunes had inexpressibly endeared her, at length effectuated in her bosom precisely that state of tender melancholy, which, in a delicate and sentimental mind, is described as finding a luxury in tears; and her youth ᵃnd an excellent constitution, surmounting the ravages which had been made ʰᵉalth, she was gradually restored to a pensive kind of serenity.

The effects, of which Mr. Wellwood had died possessed, exclusive of his household moveables, which were very genteel, consisting altogether of navigation and articles of merchandize, he had directed in his will that they should be immediately converted into ready money; and the gentleman whom he had appointed his executor, with that integrity and dispatch, which are such conspicuous traits in his character, speedily disbursing every arrearage, and adjusting every affair relative to his trust, delivered into the hands of Miss Wellwood the sum of two thousand pounds in casts; this being the whole amount, after such settlement, of what remained of her deceased father's estate; and of this her patrimony, she was, agreeably to his direction, the sole and uncontrolled possessor. Behold her then, before she had completed her nineteenth year, absolute mistress of herself and fortune: Her apartments were elegantly furnished; she was in possession of a handsome library, and two thousand pounds in ready specie; but her discretion was unquestionable, and no one presumed to dictate to Miss Wellwood.

Just at this crisis, Courtland made his first appearance at New-Haven. His exterior and deportment, we have mutually agreed, are pleasingly fascinating, and our unguarded sex are but too easily captivated. His arts of seduction must be prodigious. When I see you, I will recount the gradual advances, by which he undermined a virtue, that would have been proof against a common assailant. Hoodwinking her reason, and misleading her judgment by arguments the most sophistical, *he induced her to view, as the result of human regulations, the marriage vow*; it was not to be found in the law of God, and it (or rather, the calling a priest to witness it) was calculated only for the meridian of common souls: True, the institution answered political purposes, and it might be necessary to preserve a character; but for him—his nuptial hour—should it take place previous to the death of a capriciously obstinate old uncle, who was a bachelor, and who had made his succeeding to his estate to depend upon his continuing single, would mark him the most imprudent of men. Mean time, his love for Miss Wellwood was unbounded; he could not possibly exist without her; he could not bear the idea of seeing her hourly exposed to the solicitations of those numerous pretenders, who thronged about her, while he was conscious that he possessed no superior claim to her attention; and surely, as they had the sole disposal of themselves, they might, in the sight of Heaven, exchange their vows; while that Heaven, which would record the deed, would also sanction and crown with success, a union so pure, so disinterested, and formed so wholly under its own sacred auspices; this transaction would in fact constitute their real nuptials, and upon the demise of the old gentleman, they would immediately submit to authorise their union by modern rites.

Miss Wellwood loved the villain—Horrid wretch!—he succeeded but too well, and she was involved in the deepest ruin! My tears blot the paper—would to God that they could cancel her faults, and serve as a *lethe* for her sufferings. Not a soul was apprized of their intercourse; and so well were their measures taken, that when, six months after, the young lady disappeared, amid the various conjectures which were formed, not even the shadow of suspicion glanced upon Courtland; every one expressed, in their own way, his or her wonder, grief, and apprehension; the whole town took an interest in her unexpected removal, and Courtland was with the foremost to express his astonishment; but as Miss Wellwood was entirely independent, no one was authorised to commence an active inquiry or pursuit.

The attention excited by any extraordinary event, after having its run, at length subsides; and Miss Wellwood ceased by degrees to be the subject of conversation; nor hath her strange flight been in any sort accounted for, until two days since, when Bridget introduced into our breakfasting parlour this forlorn female, who, immediately upon fixing her eyes on my mother, sunk down almost breathless at her feet! It is hardly necessary to add, that we instantly raised the hapless orphan, and that after recognizing, with some difficulty, the well-known features of Miss Wellwood, we received from her lips the foregoing particulars.

Upon her quitting New-Haven, she repaired directly to apartments, which had been taken for her by Courtland, in a distant village; her patrimony, you will not doubt, was relinquished to her betrayer. After sacrificing her honour, every thing else became a trifle. At first, he vouchsafed to support her; but for these two last years, either wanting ability or inclination, she has not been able to obtain from him the smallest sum! Of her furniture, of her valuable library, of every thing she is stripped; and for some months past she hath been reduced to the necessity of parting with her clothes, and of availing herself of her skill in needle work, for the subsistence of herself and three sons whom she hath borne to Courtland; and the little wretches, with their injured mother, have long been in want of the common necessaries of life! Yet, through all this, she hath been supported, being buoyed up by the hope of an ultimate residence with the father of her children: By the laws of Heaven, she regards herself as already his wife, while she hath repeatedly, with floods of tears, besought the abandoned man to confer upon her, by the rites of the church, a title so honourable; and, though still repulsed, and often with severity, she hath never despaired, until the tidings that Courtland was on the point of marriage with a young lady, who had abode for some time with us, reached her ears; this heart-rending intelligence produced her, upon the before mentioned morning, in our parlour; this hath also procured you the sorrow, which so melancholy a recital will doubtless occasion.

The once beautiful form of Miss Wellwood is now surprisingly emaciated; the few past weeks hath made dreadful havoc in her constitution; we assay to pour into her lacerated bosom what consolation is in our power; we have made her acquainted with your character, with its marked integrity and uniform consistency; and we have encouraged her to hope every thing from a goodness so perfect. The desolated sufferer will herself address you. Alas, alas! what further can I say! it is with difficulty that I have written thus far; but this information we have judged absolutely necessary. May God preserve my dear Miss Melworth from so black a villain—every thing is to be feared. For myself, I stand, in my own apprehension, as a culprit before you. Forgive, I entreat you, my sorrowing mother; and with your wonted kindness, for-give—O forgive—your truly affectionate, and greatly afflicted

AMELIA WORTHINGTON.

MISS WELLWOOD *to* MISS MELWORTH.

[*Inclosed in the preceding.*]

NEW-HAVEN, July 25th, 1789.

Will the most faultless of her sex deign to receive a line from one, who, but for the infatuation of a fatal and illusive passion, meeting her upon equal ground, might have drawn from so bright an example, a model by which she might have shaped her course, through an *event-judging* and *unfeeling* world. I am told that your virtues partake the mildest qualities, and that pity, bland and healing, is empress in your breast; if so, sweet mercy must administer there; and you will then not only tolerate the address of an unhappy stranger, but you will be impelled to lend to the prayer of my petition, a propitious ear. Miss Worthington hath condescended to become my introducer, and she informs me that she hath unfolded to you the story of my woes!

For myself, I write not, most respected young lady, either to exonerate myself, or to criminate an unfortunate man, who hath had the presumption to aspire to such daring heights! Registered in the uncontrovertible records of heaven, the wife of Courtland, in walks so reprehensible, it would ill become me to be found. No, Madam, I write to supplicate, and on my bended knees I am prostrated before you—I write to supplicate you to use your interest in the heart of Courtland, in my favour. Help me, O thou unblemished votary of virtue! help me to reclaim a husband, who, not naturally bad, hath too long wandered in the dangerous paths of dissipation; who hath drank too deeply of the empoisoned cup of error; and who, if he is not soon roused from his visionary career, may suddenly be precipitated into the gulph of perdition!

I said that Mr. Courtland was not naturally bad; and believe me, good young lady, I have, in a thousand instances, observed the rectitude of his heart. Early indulgence, and a mistaken mode of education, hath been his ruin; but the amiable qualities which are natal in his bosom, have, nevertheless, through the weeds by which they have been well nigh choaked, occasionally discovered themselves. Yet, whatever are his faults, they can never obliterate my errors; *doubtless he observed in me some blameable weakness*, or he would never have taken those unwarrantable steps, which were the consequence of our acquaintance; and now, circumstanced as we are, a failure of duty in him, can never apologize for the want of every proper exertion on my side. He is the father of my children; I have a presentiment that he may be recovered to the bosom of equity; and, if he will permit me, I will watch over him as my dearest treasure. Let him but acknowledge the honourable and endearing ties, father and husband; let him but sanction them in the face of the world, and I will soothe his aching head; I will smooth his thorny pillow; and, in every circumstance, in sickness and in health, I will continue that faithful Fanny, whom he hath so often sworn never to forsake, and whom, in the fulness of his heart, he hath called Heaven to witness, he would ever prefer to all created beings.

Perhaps he can no more command the sums which I have yielded into his hands—be it so, they were mine, I made them his, and he had a right to dispose of them—Nay, I think I had rather find him destitute; for such a situation will acquit him of that cruelty, with which he is otherwise chargeable on account of his late neglects. What are pecuniary emoluments, compared to that real felicity, which is to be derived from a mutual, a faithful, and an unbroken attachment? I have made the experiment, and I can confidently pronounce it in truth a fact—*that we want but little here below*. Let him know, Madam, that I will draw the impenetrable veil of silence over the past; that we will commence anew the voyage of life; and that if he will at length be just, his returning kindness, by invigorating once more this poor, this enervated frame, will restore alacrity to my efforts; and that I am, in that case, positive, our combined exertions will procure for ourselves, and our little ones, the *necessaries of life*.

What can I say? It is for my children I am thus importunate; were it not for their dear sakes, the story of my sufferings should never interrupt the felicity of Miss Melworth. No, believe me, no—but I would seek some turfed pillow, whereon to rest my weary head; and, closing forever these humid lids, I would haste to repose me in that vault, which entombs the remains of my revered parents, and where only I can rationally expect to meet the tranquillity for which I sigh. Innocent little sufferers!—observe them, dearest lady; to you their hands are uplifted—Courtland's features are imaged in their faces, and they plead the cause of equity.

Nor will we, my children, despair—we cannot sue in vain: Miss Melworth being our auxiliary, doubtless we shall again be reinstated in the bosom of your father.

Forgive, inestimable young lady, forgive this incoherent rambling—distraction not seldom pervades my mind. But grant, I beseech you, the prayer of my petition, and entitle yourself to the eternal gratitude of the now wretched

FRANCES WELLWOOD.

It was well that my girl had discarded Courtland from her heart, and that she had almost entirely recovered her tranquillity, previous to the receipt of these letters; otherwise, the sudden revolution they would have occasioned, must, in a young and impassioned mind, have uprooted her reason.

Old Mr. Wellwood had been one of the first of my friends; and from his countenance and advice, on my setting out in life, I had derived material advantages. The disappearance of his daughter had much perplexed me. I was fearful she was ill advised, but from the idea I had entertained of her discretion, I had not the least suspicion of the truth. Yet she never rushed upon my memory, without giving birth in my bosom to sensations truly painful; and I had been constantly solicitous to discover the place of her retreat.

Thus, under the influence of equity and gratitude, I hope my readers will do me the justice to believe, that in Miss Wellwood's affairs, I found myself naturally impelled to take a very active part. Margaretta speedily responded to both the ladies; but as her letter to Miss Worthington is not absolutely essential to my narration, I shall omit it: The following is a copy of her reply to Miss Wellwood.

MISS MELWORTH to MISS WELLWOOD.

Village of ———, August 1st, 1789.

I have, my dear Madam, received your pathetically plaintive epistle; and, over the melancholy recital of your woes, I have shed many tears. I lament your sorrows, and I honour the propriety of your present feelings and wishes; but a letter which I yesterday wrote to Miss Worthington, and which she will soon receive, will, I persuade myself, convince you of the indelicacy and inutility of my interference relative to Mr. Courtland. Before the name of Miss Wellwood had been announced to me, I had been convinced of my error, in entertaining the most distant views of a serious connexion with that gentleman; and the preference my inexperienced heart had avowed for him, was eradicated from my bosom.

Doubtless, if the ever honoured guardians of my unwary steps, had not still been continued to me, *ensnared as I too certainly was*, Miss Wellwood's *wrongs would not have exhibited a solitary trait in the history of the unfeeling* despoiler! You must excuse me, Madam, if I do not adopt *your mildness of expression*, when speaking of a *betrayer*, whose atrocious conduct hath blasted in their early blow, the opening prospects of a young lady, whose fair mind seems eminently formed for all those social and tender intercourses, which constitute and brighten the pleasing round of domestic life. Surely, Miss Wellwood—yet, sensible that painful retrospection will avail us nothing, I stop short.

But, my amiable panegyrist, though I, myself, am ineligible as a mediatress, between parties whose interests *ought indeed to be considered as one*, I am authorized to offer you the extricating hands, and protecting arms of those matchless benefactors, who, with unexampled condescension, have dignified the *orphan* Margaretta, by investing her with the title of *their daughter*; nor is this an empty title; their parental wisdom, their parental indulgence—*but come and see*. I am commanded to solicit you immediately to repair to an asylum, and to hearts, which will ever be open for your reception. My father, Madam, confesses essential and various obligations to your deceased parent; and he hath long been anxiously desirous to render the arrears, which were due to Mr. Wellwood, into the hands of his ever lovely representative. The bearer of this letter is commissioned to pay you the sum of fifty pounds, which you are requested to receive, as a *part of the interest*, which hath been, for such a length of time, your due; it may answer your present exigencies, and the *principal* is still in reserve. It is with much pleasure, I avail myself of the orders which are given me, to repeat my solicitations, that you would, without hesitation, hasten to this mansion. An elderly man and woman, who are to return to our village in the next stage, and who have long been our very respectable neighbours, will call upon you at Colonel Worthington's, to take your commands; and if you will be so obliging as to put yourself under their care, they will see you conveyed in safety to one, who, in addition to the general and unquestionable humanity of his character, feels his heart operated upon, in regard to Miss Wellwood, by the ancient and inviolable claims of gratitude.

Mr. Courtland, though not at present our visitor, is still a resident in this neighbourhood; and my father bids me assure you, that every rational step shall be taken, which can be supposed to have the remotest tendency toward the restoration of your peace. He himself will undertake your cause; and as his plans are always the result of wisdom and penetration, he is not seldom gratified by the accomplishment of his wishes. He will seek Mr. Courtland; he will assail him by those invincible arguments, with which equity, reason and nature will furnish him; and should he still remain obdurate, my dear and commiserating father will, nevertheless, aid you by his counsel, and continue unto you his protection; he will assist you in educating your young people, and in disposing of them in a manner, which will render them *useful members of society*: In short, no efforts which benevolence can command, will be wanting, to alleviate your misfortunes. Cheer up then, lovely mourner; the orphan's friend again is ours: I predict that the smile of tranquillity will again illumine your grief-worn countenance; and should I yet have to raise to you the voice of felicitation, *good, in that event, will be educed from evil*, and I shall then cease to regret a circumstance, which at present, as often as it is remembered, tinges my cheek with the blush of confusion. Were it necessary, I would add, that no means shall be left unassayed, which may be within the reach of, dear Madam, your truly commiserating, and sincere well-wisher,

MARGARETTA MELWORTH.

Taking it for granted, that the candid reader will allow for the partiality of a young creature, *whose high sense of common benefits*, and whose gratitude had rendered her almost an enthusiast,—I intrude no comment thereon. Margaretta's letter soon produced Miss Wellwood in our family; and upon the morning after her arrival, I sat off in pursuit of Mr. Courtland. My most direct course brought me to rap at the door of his lodgings, and as I was rather early, I made myself sure of finding him within. My astonishment, however, was not equal to my regret, when I was informed by his landlady, that a writ of attachment, being the evening before served upon him, at the suit of Mr. ———, and he not being able to procure sureties, he was taken lodged in the county jail. I hesitated not in regard to the measures which were best to be taken; a few moments produced me in that abode of the miserable; and I found little difficulty in obtaining an interview with the prisoner.

Courtland—never shall I forget his appearance—all those airs of importance, which had marked his innate consciousness of superiority, were whelmed in the storm of adversity, that had at length burst upon him. His haggard looks proclaimed, that sleep, in her accustomed manner, had forsaken his dreary abode; his dress was neglected; his hair in disordered ringlets hung upon his shoulders: In short, scarce a vestige of the finished gentleman remained; and his folded arms and vacant countenance, as I beheld him unobserved, were almost descriptive of insanity: But the jailer announcing my name, his agonized and unaffected discomposure commanded my utmost commiseration; an expression indicative of mingling confusion, surprise and apprehension, instantly suffused his cheek; and, with extreme perturbation, he exclaimed, "Good God! Mr. Vigillius—this is too much—but, forgive me, Sir, *the uniformity of your character* will not permit a continuance of the idea, that you are come hither either to reproach or insult me."

"To insult you, Mr. Courtland! God forbid. I come hither rather the petitioner of your favour; and it is a truth, that I at this moment feel, in regard to you, all the father predominating in my bosom; but, having matter for your private ear, I must beg the indulgence of this gentleman for a few moments."

The humane keeper withdrew with much civility; and the consternation of our delinquent was unutterable, while I proceeded to inform him of the early knowledge I had obtained of the commencement and progress of his career; of my information in regard to the ruined state of his affairs; and of my actual correspondence with his principal creditors. "I have opened my business, Sir," I added, "by this exordium, on purpose to let you know how well qualified I am to serve you; and however you may have smarted, while I have thus taken it upon me to probe your wounds, I flatter myself you may be induced to bless the hand, which is furnished also with a specific. In short, Sir, I am this morning authorized to act in your affairs—*a fair plaintiff hath constituted me her attorney, and I come to offer you terms of accommodation*—Miss Wellwood, Sir—" At the sound of this name he changed colour, bit his lips, groaned deeply, and vehemently articulated—*"Jesus God, have mercy on me!"* and, as if that injured female herself had been present, he thus continued: "Miss Wellwood—*lovely, but too credulous fair one—wretched woman!—I have undone thee; but, Madam, my death shall soon present you the only compensation in my power."*

"I came not, Sir," interrupted I, *"to point to the defenceless bosom the shaft of despair*: If you please, I will read a letter, which was written by Miss Wellwood to my daughter." I read; and, as I folded the paper, I beheld with astonishment, the tear of contrition bedewing his pallid cheek! *"Welcome stranger!"* he exclaimed—*"lovely woman—injured saint—forgiving martyr!— Yes, Heaven is my witness, that the tenderest affection of which this obdurate heart hath ever been capable, hath still been the undivided, unalienated posses- sion of* Fanny Wellwood—but, Sir, she knows not the depth of my misery— God of heaven! my crimes have *already precipitated me into the gulph of perdition,* and there remains no remedy."

But not to fatigue my readers by further circumlocution, I found that our gentleman had become as wax in my hand; and I proposed to him, that if I could procure his enlargement, he should retire immediately to my dwell- ing, where he would meet Miss Wellwood; and that the nuptial ceremony being *legally* performed, my house should become his castle; that I myself would undertake his affairs, thoroughly investigate every point, and endeav- our to adjust matters with his creditors.

My proposal was accepted, *with the most extravagant and rapturous demon- strations of joy*; and my interest, combined with that of a substantial neigh- bour's, soon liberating the captive, produced him a *happy and a grateful bridegroom.* The rites of the church were performed; not a single ceremony was omitted—while Margaretta and Serafina, blooming as Hebe, and cheer- ful as the morning, officiated as bride-maids.

Agreeably to my promise, I very soon opened my negociation with the dif- ferent claimants upon Mr. Courtland. New-Haven furnished me with many auxiliaries; it was sufficient to produce the daughter of Mr. Wellwood, to command, in her favour, the most energetic efforts: We speedily obtained a very advantageous compromise; our debtor was, by the joint assistance of many respectable characters, set up in business; and the deficiencies of nature and education, which we have noted in him, were abundantly sup- plied, *by the abilities, application, and economical arrangements* of Mrs. Courtland. Every year, a regular dividend of the profits of their business is remitted to their creditors; a large part of the old arrears is discharged; and they bid fair, in the run of a few revolving seasons, to possess themselves of a very handsome competency.

1798

PHILIP FRENEAU
1752–1832

Philip Freneau had all the advantages of wealth and social position, and the Fre- neau household in Manhattan was frequently visited by well-known writers and painters. Philip received a good education at the hands of tutors and at fifteen entered the sophomore class at the College of New Jersey (now Princeton Univer- sity). There he became fast friends with his roommate, James Madison, who would one day be president, and a classmate, Hugh Henry Brackenridge, who became a successful novelist. In their senior year Freneau and Brackenridge composed an ode on *The Rising Glory of America,* and Brackenridge read the poem at commencement.

It establishes early in Freneau's career his recurrent vision of a glorious future in which America would fulfill the collective hope of humankind:

> Paradise anew
> Shall flourish, by no second Adam lost,
> No dangerous tree with deadly fruit shall grow,
> No tempting serpent to allure the soul
> From native innocence. . . . The lion and the lamb
> In mutual friendship linked, shall browse the shrub,
> And timorous deer with softened tigers stray
> O'er mead, or lofty hill, or grassy plain.

For a short time Freneau taught school. He hoped to make a career as a writer, but it was an impractical wish. When he was offered a position as secretary on a plantation in the West Indies in 1776, he sailed to St. Croix and remained there almost three years. It was on that island, where "Sweet orange groves in lonely valleys rise," that Freneau wrote some of his most sensuous lyrics, but as he tells us in "To Sir Toby," he could not talk of "blossoms" and an "endless spring" forever in a land that abounded in poverty and misery and where the owners grew wealthy on a slave economy. In 1778 he returned home and enlisted as a seaman on a blockade runner; two years later he was captured at sea and imprisoned on the British ship *Scorpion,* anchored in New York harbor. He was treated brutally, an experience he described in his most popular poem, "The British Prison Ship" (1781), after his release from the hospital ship *Hunter.*

Freneau was to spend ten more years at sea, first as master of a merchant ship in 1784, and again in 1803, but immediately after he regained his health, he moved to Philadelphia to work in the post office, and it was in that city that he won his reputation as a journalist, satirist, and poet. As editor of the *Freeman's Journal,* Freneau wrote impassioned verse in support of the American Revolution and turned all his rhetorical gifts against anyone thought to be in sympathy with the British monarchy. It was during this period in his life that he became identified as the "Poet of the American Revolution." In 1791, after Freneau returned from duties at sea, Thomas Jefferson, as secretary of state, offered him a position as translator in his department, with the understanding that Freneau would have plenty of free time to devote to his newspaper, the *National Gazette.* Like Thomas Paine, Freneau was a strong supporter of the French Revolution, and he had a sharp eye for anyone not sympathetic to the democratic cause. He had a special grudge against Alexander Hamilton, secretary of the treasury, as chief spokesman for the Federalists. President Washington thought it was ironic that "that rascal Freneau" should be employed by his administration when he attacked it so outspokenly.

The *National Gazette* ceased publication in 1793, and after Jefferson resigned his office, Freneau left Philadelphia for good, alternating between ship's captain and newspaper editor in New York and New Jersey. He spent his last years on his New Jersey farm, unable to make it self-supporting and with no hope of further employment. Year after year he sold off the land he had inherited from his father and was finally reduced to applying for a pension as a veteran of the American Revolution. He died impoverished and unknown, lost in a blizzard.

Freneau's biographer, Lewis Leary, subtitled his book *A Study in Literary Failure* and began that work by observing that "Philip Freneau failed in almost everything he attempted." Freneau's most sympathetic readers believe that he was born in a time not ripe for poetry and that his genuine lyric gifts were always in conflict with his political pamphleteering. Had he been born fifty years later, perhaps he could have joined Cooper and Irving in a life devoted exclusively to letters. There is no doubt that he did much to pave the way for these later writers. Freneau is not "the father of American poetry" (as his readers, eager for an advocate for a national literary consciousness, liked to call him), but his obsession with the beautiful, transient things of nature and the conflict in his art between the sensuous and the didactic are among the central concerns of American poetry.

Texts used are *The Poems of Philip Freneau* (1902), edited by F. L. Pattee; *The Poems of Freneau* (1929), edited by H. H. Clark; and *The Last Poems of Philip Freneau* (1945), edited by Lewis Leary.

The Wild Honey Suckle

Fair flower, that dost so comely grow,
Hid in this silent, dull retreat,
Untouched thy honeyed blossoms blow,[1]
Unseen thy little branches greet:
   No roving foot shall crush thee here,   5
   No busy hand provoke a tear.

By Nature's self in white arrayed,
She bade thee shun the vulgar[2] eye,
And planted here the guardian shade,
And sent soft waters murmuring by;   10
   Thus quietly thy summer goes,
   Thy days declining to repose.

Smit with those charms, that must decay,
I grieve to see your future doom;
They died—nor were those flowers more gay,   15
The flowers that did in Eden bloom;
   Unpitying frosts, and Autumn's power
   Shall leave no vestige of this flower.

From morning suns and evening dews
At first thy little being came: 20
If nothing once, you nothing lose,
For when you die you are the same;
   The space between, is but an hour,
   The frail duration of a flower.

1786

The Indian Burying Ground

In spite of all the learned have said,
I still my old opinion keep;
The *posture*, that *we* give the dead,
Points out the soul's eternal sleep.

Not so the ancients of these lands—   5
The Indian, when from life released,
Again is seated[1] with his friends,
And shares again the joyous feast.

1. Bloom.
2. Common; unfeeling.
1. The North American Indians bury their dead in a sitting posture; decorating the corpse with wampum, the images of birds, quadrupeds, etc.: And (if that of a warrior) with bows, arrows, toma-hawks and other military weapons [Freneau's note].

His imaged birds, and painted bowl,
And venison, for a journey dressed,   10
Bespeak the nature of the soul,
Activity, that knows no rest.

His bow, for action ready bent,
And arrows, with a head of stone,
Can only mean that life is spent,   15
And not the old ideas gone.

Thou, stranger, that shalt come this way,
No fraud upon the dead commit—
Observe the swelling turf, and say
They do not *lie*, but here they *sit*.   20

Here still a lofty rock remains,
On which the curious eye may trace
(Now wasted, half, by wearing rains)
The fancies of a ruder race.

Here still an agéd elm aspires,   25
Beneath whose far-projecting shade
(And which the shepherd still admires)
The children of the forest played!

There oft a restless Indian queen
(Pale Sheba,[2] with her braided hair)   30
And many a barbarous form is seen
To chide the man that lingers there.

By midnight moons, o'er moistening dews,
In habit for the chase arrayed,
The hunter still the deer pursues,   35
The hunter and the deer, a shade!

And long shall timorous fancy see
The painted chief, and pointed spear,
And Reason's self shall bow the knee
To shadows and delusions here.   40

                                              1788

On the Religion of Nature

The power, that gives with liberal hand
    The blessings man enjoys, while here,
And scatters through a smiling land
    Abundant products of the year;
        That power of nature, ever blessed,   5
        Bestowed religion with the rest.

---

2. Sheba is the queen who visited Solomon to test his wisdom (1 Kings 10.1–13).

Born with ourselves, her early sway
  Inclines the tender mind to take
The path of right, fair virtue's way
  Its own felicity to make.   10
    This universally extends
    And leads to no mysterious ends.

Religion, such as nature taught,
  With all divine perfection suits;
Had all mankind this system sought   15
  Sophists[1] would cease their vain disputes,
    And from this source would nations know
    All that can make their heaven below.

This deals not curses on mankind,
  Or dooms them to perpetual grief,   20
If from its aid no joys they find,
  It damns them not for unbelief;
    Upon a more exalted plan
    Creatress nature dealt with man—

Joy to the day, when all agree   25
  On such grand systems to proceed,
From fraud, design, and error free,
  And which to truth and goodness lead:
    Then persecution will retreat
    And man's religion be complete.   30

                                                             1815

1. Teachers of philosophy.

PHILLIS WHEATLEY
c. 1753–1784

Phillis Wheatley was either nineteen or twenty years old when her *Poems on Various Subjects, Religious and Moral* was published in London in 1773. At the time of its publication she was the object of considerable public attention because, in addition to being a child prodigy, Wheatley was a black slave, born in Africa (probably in present-day Senegal or Gambia) and brought to Boston in 1761. She had been purchased by a wealthy tailor, John Wheatley, for his wife, Susannah, as a companion, and named for the vessel that carried her to America. Wheatley was fortunate in her surroundings, for Susannah Wheatley was sympathetic toward this very frail and remarkably intelligent child. In an age in which even few white women were given an education, Wheatley was taught to read and write and, in a short time, began to read Latin writers. She came to know the Bible well, and three English poets—Milton, Pope, and Gray—touched her deeply and exerted a strong influence on her verse. The Wheatleys moved in a circle of enlightened Boston Christians, and Phillis was introduced early on to a community that challenged the keeping of slaves as incompatible with Christian life. Wheatley's poem on the death of the Reverend George

Phillis Wheatley. This engraving accompanied an early edition of Wheatley's poetry; it emphasizes her race and social position.

Whitefield, the great egalitarian English evangelist who frequently toured New England, made her famous. In June 1773, she arrived in London with her manuscript in the company of the Wheatleys' son Nathaniel. She had come to England partly for reasons of health and partly to seek support for her first book. Benjamin Franklin and the lord mayor of London were among those who paid their respects. Her literary gifts, intelligence, and piety were a striking example to her English and American admirers of the triumph of the human spirit over the circumstances of birth. Her poems appeared early in September, and the governor of Massachusetts and John Wheatley and John Hancock were among the eighteen prominent citizens testifying that "under the Disadvantage of serving as a Slave in a Family in this Town," Wheatley "had been examined and thought qualified to write them."

Wheatley did not remain long enough in London to witness their publication; she was called back to Boston with the news that Susannah Wheatley was dying. Early in the fall of 1773 she was granted manumission. Susannah Wheatley died in 1774 and John Wheatley four years later. In that same year, 1778, she married John Peters, a freedman, about whom almost nothing is known other than that the Wheatleys did not like him, that he petitioned for a license to sell liquor in 1784, and that he may have been in debtor's prison when Phillis Wheatley died, having endured poverty and the loss of two children in her last years. On her deathbed her third child lay ill beside her and succumbed shortly after Wheatley herself. They were buried together in an unmarked grave. Five years earlier, and only one year after her marriage, a proposal appeared for a second volume of poetry to include thirteen letters and thirty-three poems. The volume was never published, and most of the poems and letters have yet to be found.

Wheatley's poetry was rediscovered in the 1830s by the New England abolitionists, but it is no exaggeration to say that she has never been better understood than at the present. Her recent critics have not only corrected a number of biographical errors but, more important, have provided a context in which her work can best be read and her life understood. This reconsideration shows Wheatley to be a bold and canny spokesperson for her faith and her politics; she early joined the cause of American independence and the abolition of slavery, anticipating her friend the Reverend Samuel Hopkins's complaint that when African Americans first heard the "sons of liberty" cry out for freedom they were shocked by the indifference to their own "abject slavery and utter wretchedness." It doesn't take a philosopher, Wheatley told Samson Occom, a Presbyterian minister and Mohegan tribesman, to see that the exercise of slavery cannot be reconciled with a "principle" that God has implanted in every human breast, "Love of Freedom." She was mistaken in thinking that the conservative earl of Dartmouth (William Legge) might be sympathetic to the American cause but correct in reminding him that there could be no justice anywhere if people in authority were deaf to the cries of human sorrow:

Should you, my lord, while you peruse my song,
Wonder from whence my love of Freedom sprung,
Whence flow these wishes for the common good,
By feeling hearts best understood,
I, young in life, by seeming cruel fate
Was snatched from Afric's fancied happy seat:
What pangs excruciating must molest,
What sorrows labor in my parent's breast?
Steeled was that soul and by no misery moved
That from a father seized his babe beloved:
Such, such my case. And can I then but pray
Others may never feel tyrannic sway?

With the publication of Wheatley's *Poems,* Henry Louis Gates Jr. has argued, "Wheatley launched two traditions at once—the black American literary tradition *and* the black woman's literary tradition. It is extraordinary that not just one but both of these traditions were founded simultaneously by a black woman—certainly an event unique in the history of literature—it is also ironic that this important fact of common, coterminous literary origin seems to have escaped most scholars."

On Being Brought from Africa to America

'Twas mercy brought me from my pagan land,
Taught my benighted soul to understand
That there's a God, that there's a Savior too:
Once I redemption neither sought nor knew.
Some view our sable[1] race with scornful eye,   5
"Their color is a diabolic dye."
Remember, Christians, Negroes, black as Cain,[2]
May be refined, and join the angelic train.

1773

To the Right Honourable William, Earl of Dartmouth,[1] His Majesty's Principal Secretary of State for North America, &c.

Hail, happy day, when, smiling like the morn,
Fair Freedom rose New England to adorn:
The northern clime beneath her genial ray,
Dartmouth, congratulates thy blissful sway:
Elate with hope her race no longer mourns,   5
Each soul expands, each grateful bosom burns,
While in thine hand with pleasure we behold
The silken reins, and Freedom's charms unfold.

1. Black.
2. Cain slew his brother Abel and was "marked" by God for doing so. This mark has sometimes been taken to be the origin of dark-skinned peoples (Genesis 4.1–15).
1. William Legge (1731–1801), second Earl of Dartmouth, was appointed secretary in charge of the American colonies in August 1772. Though sympathetic to the Methodist movement in England, he was not sympathetic to the cause of the American Revolution.

Long lost to realms beneath the northern skies
She shines supreme, while hated faction dies: 10
Soon as appeared the Goddess[2] long desired,
Sick at the view, she[3] languished and expired;
Thus from the splendors of the morning light
The owl in sadness seeks the caves of night.

No more, America, in mournful strain   15
Of wrongs, and grievance unredressed complain,
No longer shalt thou dread the iron chain,
Which wanton Tyranny with lawless hand
Had made, and with it meant t' enslave the land.

Should you, my lord, while you peruse my song,   20
Wonder from whence my love of Freedom sprung,
Whence flow these wishes for the common good,
By feeling hearts alone best understood,
I, young in life, by seeming cruel fate
Was snatch'd from Afric's fancied happy seat: 25
What pangs excruciating must molest,
What sorrows labor in my parent's breast?
Steeled was that soul and by no misery moved
That from a father seized his babe beloved:
Such, such my case. And can I then but pray   30
Others may never feel tyrannic sway?

For favors past, great Sir, our thanks are due,
And thee we ask thy favors to renew,
Since in thy power,[4] as in thy will before,
To sooth the griefs, which thou did'st once deplore.   35
May heavenly grace the sacred sanction give
To all thy works, and thou forever live
Not only on the wings of fleeting Fame,
Though praise immortal crowns the patriot's name,
But to conduct to heavens refulgent fane,[5]   40
May fiery coursers sweep th' ethereal plain,[6]
And bear thee upwards to that blest abode,
Where, like the prophet, thou shalt find thy God.

1773

To the University of Cambridge,[1] in New England

While an intrinsic ardor prompts to write,
The muses promise to assist my pen;
'Twas not long since I left my native shore
The land of errors, and Egyptian gloom:[2]

---

2. Freedom.
3. Faction.
4. I.e., since it is in thy power.
5. Shining temple.
6. The heavens. "Coursers": steeds; horses.
1. Harvard.

2. "And Moses stretched forth his hand toward heaven; and there was a thick darkness in all the land of Egypt three days" (Exodus 10.22). "Errors": i.e., theological errors, because Africa was unconverted.

Father of mercy, 'twas Thy gracious hand   5
Brought me in safety from those dark abodes.

Students, to you 'tis given to scan the heights
Above, to traverse the ethereal space,
And mark the systems of revolving worlds.
Still more, ye sons of science[3] ye receive   10
The blissful news by messengers from Heaven,
How Jesus' blood for your redemption flows.
See Him with hands out-stretched upon the cross;
Immense compassion in his bosom glows;
He hears revilers, nor resents their scorn: 15
What matchless mercy in the Son of God!
When the whole human race by sin had fallen,
He deigned to die that they might rise again,
And share with Him in the sublimest skies,
Life without death, and glory without end.   20

Improve[4] your privileges while they stay,
Ye pupils, and each hour redeem, that bears
Or good or bad report of you to Heaven.
Let sin, that baneful evil to the soul,
By you be shunned, nor once remit your guard;   25
Suppress the deadly serpent in its egg.
Ye blooming plants of human race divine,
An Ethiop[5] tells you 'tis your greatest foe;
Its transient sweetness turns to endless pain,
And in immense perdition sinks the soul.   30

1767   1773

On the Death of the Rev. Mr. George Whitefield,[1] 1770

Hail, happy saint, on thine immortal throne,
Possessed of glory, life, and bliss unknown;
We hear no more the music of thy tongue,
Thy wonted auditories[2] cease to throng.
Thy sermons in unequalled accents flow'd,   5
And every bosom with devotion glowed;
Thou didst in strains of eloquence refined
Inflame the heart, and captivate the mind.
Unhappy we the setting sun deplore,
So glorious once, but ah! it shines no more.   10

Behold the prophet in his towering flight!
He leaves the earth for heav'n's unmeasured height,
And worlds unknown receive him from our sight.

3. Knowledge.
4. Take advantage of.
5. Ethiopian. In Wheatley's time "Ethiopian" was
a conventional name for the black peoples of
Africa.
1. British clergyman (1714–1770). Whitefield was

the best-known revivalist in the 18th century. He
made several visits to America and died in Newburyport, Massachusetts. This was Wheatley's
first published poem, and it made her famous.
2. Listeners. "Wonted": accustomed.

There Whitefield wings with rapid course his way,
And sails to Zion[3] through vast seas of day.   15
Thy prayers, great saint, and thine incessant cries
Have pierced the bosom of thy native skies.
Thou moon hast seen, and all the stars of light,
How he has wrestled with his God by night.
He prayed that grace in every heart might dwell,   20
He longed to see America excel;
He charged[4] its youth that every grace divine
Should with full luster in their conduct shine;
That Savior, which his soul did first receive,
The greatest gift that even a God can give,   25
He freely offered to the numerous throng,
That on his lips with listening pleasure hung.

      "Take Him, ye wretched, for your only good,
"Take Him ye starving sinners, for your food;
"Ye thirsty, come to this life-giving stream,   30
"Ye preachers, take Him for your joyful theme;
"Take Him my dear Americans, he said,
"Be your complaints on His kind bosom laid:
"Take Him, ye Africans, He longs for you,
"Impartial Savior is His title due: 35
"Washed in the fountain of redeeming blood,
"You shall be sons, and kings, and priests to God."

      Great *Countess*,[5] we Americans revere
Thy name, and mingle in thy grief sincere;
New England deeply feels, the orphans mourn,   40
Their more than father will no more return.

      But, though arrested by the hand of death,
Whitefield no more exerts his laboring breath,
Yet let us view him in the eternal skies,
Let every heart to this bright vision rise;   45
While the tomb safe retains its sacred trust,
Till life divine re-animates his dust.

1770   1770, 1773

Thoughts on the Works of Providence

Arise, my soul, on wings enraptured, rise
To praise the monarch of the earth and skies,
Whose goodness and beneficence appear
As round its center moves the rolling year,
Or when the morning glows with rosy charms,   5
Or the sun slumbers in the ocean's arms:
Of light divine be a rich portion lent

---

3. Here, the heavenly city of God.
4. Exhorted.
5. Selina Shirley Hastings (1707–1791), Countess
of Huntingdon, was a strong supporter of George
Whitefield and active in Methodist church affairs.

To guide my soul, and favor my intend.
Celestial muse, my arduous flight sustain
And raise my mind to a seraphic[1] strain!   10

    Adored for ever be the God unseen,
Which round the sun revolves this vast machine,
Though to His eye its mass a point appears:
Adored the God that whirls surrounding spheres,
Which first ordained that mighty Sol[2] should reign   15
The peerless monarch of the ethereal train:
Of miles twice forty millions is His height,
And yet His radiance dazzles mortal sight
So far beneath—from Him the extended earth
Vigor derives, and every flowery birth: 20
Vast through her orb she moves with easy grace
Around her Phoebus[3] in unbounded space;
True to her course the impetuous storm derides,
Triumphant o'er the winds, and surging tides.

    Almighty, in these wond'rous works of Thine,   25
What Power, what Wisdom, and what Goodness shine!
And are Thy wonders, Lord, by men explored,
And yet creating glory unadored!

    Creation smiles in various beauty gay,
While day to night, and night succeeds to day: 30
That Wisdom, which attends Jehovah's ways,
Shines most conspicuous in the solar rays:
Without them, destitute of heat and light,
This world would be the reign of endless night:
In their excess how would our race complain,   35
Abhorring life! how hate its lengthened chain!
From air adust[4] what numerous ills would rise?
What dire contagion taint the burning skies?
What pestilential vapors, fraught with death,
Would rise, and overspread the lands beneath?   40

    Hail, smiling morn, that from the orient main[5]
Ascending dost adorn the heav'nly plain!
So rich, so various are thy beauteous dyes,
That spread through all the circuit of the skies,
That, full of thee, my soul in rapture soars,   45
And thy great God, the cause of all adores.

    O'er beings infinite His love extends,
His Wisdom rules them, and His Pow'r defends.
When tasks diurnal[6] tire the human frame,
The spirits faint, and dim the vital flame,   50
Then too that ever active bounty shines,
Which not infinity of space confines.

---

1. Angelic.   4. Dried up.
2. The sun.   5. Ocean. "Orient": eastern.
3. Apollo, the Greek sun god.   6. Daily.

The sable veil, that Night in silence draws,
Conceals effects, but shows the Almighty Cause,
Night seals in sleep the wide creation fair,   55
And all is peaceful but the brow of care.
Again, gay Phoebus, as the day before,
Wakes every eye, but what shall wake no more;
Again the face of nature is renewed,
Which still appears harmonious, fair, and good.   60
May grateful strains salute the smiling morn,
Before its beams the eastern hills adorn!

     Shall day to day, and night to night conspire
To show the goodness of the Almighty Sire?
This mental voice shall man regardless hear,   65
And never, never raise the filial prayer?
Today, O hearken, nor your folly mourn
For time mispent, that never will return.

     But see the sons of vegetation rise,
And spread their leafy banners to the skies.   70
All-wise Almighty providence we trace
In trees, and plants, and all the flowery race;
As clear as in the nobler frame of man,
All lovely copies of the Maker's plan.
The power the same that forms a ray of light,   75
That called creation from eternal night.
"Let there be light," He said. From his profound[7]
Old Chaos heard, and trembled at the sound:
Swift as the word, inspired by power divine,
Behold the light around its Maker shine,   80
The first fair product of the omnific God,
And now through all his works diffused abroad.

     As reason's powers by day our God disclose,
So we may trace Him in the night's repose:
Say what is sleep? and dreams how passing strange!   85
When action ceases, and ideas range
Licentious and unbounded o'er the plains,
Where Fancy's[8] queen in giddy triumph reigns.
Hear in soft strains the dreaming lover sigh
To a kind fair,[9] or rave in jealousy;   90
On pleasure now, and now on vengeance bent,
The lab ring passions struggle for a vent.
What power, O man! thy reason then restores,
So long suspended in nocturnal hours?
What secret hand returns the mental train,   95
And gives improv'd thine active powers again?
From thee, O man, what gratitude should rise!
And, when from balmy sleep thou op'st thine eyes,
Let thy first thoughts be praises to the skies.
How merciful our God who thus imparts   100

---

7. Depths. "And God said, Let there be light: and there was light" (Genesis 1.3).

8. The imagination in its image-making aspect.

9. Woman.

O'erflowing tides of joy to human hearts,
When wants and woes might be our righteous lot,
Our God forgetting, by our God forgot!

Among the mental powers a question rose,
"What most the image of the Eternal shows?"   105
When thus to Reason (so let Fancy rove)
Her great companion spoke, immortal Love.

"Say, mighty power, how long shall strife prevail,
"And with its murmurs load the whispering gale?
"Refer the cause to Recollection's shrine,   110
"Who loud proclaims my origin divine,
"The cause whence heaven and earth began to be,
"And is not man immortalized by me?
"Reason let this most causeless strife subside."
Thus Love pronounced, and Reason thus replied.   115

    "Thy birth, celestial queen! 'tis mine to own,
"In thee resplendent is the Godhead shown;
"Thy words persuade, my soul enraptured feels
"Resistless beauty which thy smile reveals."
Ardent she spoke, and, kindling at her charms,   120
She clasped the blooming goddess in her arms.

    Infinite Love where'er we turn our eyes
Appears: this every creature's wants supplies;
This most is heard in Nature's constant voice,
This makes the morn, and this the eve rejoice;   125
This bids the fostering rains and dews descend
To nourish all, to serve one gen'ral end,
The good of man: yet man ungrateful pays
But little homage, and but little praise.
To him, whose works arrayed with mercy shine,   130
What songs should rise, how constant, how divine!

1773

To S. M.,[1] a Young African Painter, on Seeing His Works

To show the laboring bosom's deep intent,
And thought in living characters to paint,
When first thy pencil did those beauties give,
And breathing figures learnt from thee to live,
How did those prospects give my soul delight,   5
A new creation rushing on my sight?
Still, wondrous youth! each noble path pursue,
On deathless glories fix thine ardent view:
Still may the painter's and the poet's fire
To aid thy pencil, and thy verse conspire!   10

---

1. Scipio Moorhead, a servant to the Reverend John Moorhead of Boston.

And may the charms of each seraphic[2] theme
Conduct thy footsteps to immortal fame!
High to the blissful wonders of the skies
Elate thy soul, and raise thy wishful eyes.
Thrice happy, when exalted to survey   15
That splendid city, crown'd with endless day,
Whose twice six gates[3] on radiant hinges ring:
Celestial Salem[4] blooms in endless spring.

   Calm and serene thy moments glide along,
And may the muse inspire each future song!   20
Still, with the sweets of contemplation blest,
May peace with balmy wings your soul invest!
But when these shades of time are chased away,
And darkness ends in everlasting day,
On what seraphic pinions shall we move,   25
And view the landscapes in the realms above?
There shall thy tongue in heavenly murmurs flow,
And there my muse with heavenly transport glow:
No more to tell of Damon's[5] tender sighs,
Or rising radiance of Aurora's[6] eyes,   30
For nobler themes demand a nobler strain,
And purer language on the ethereal plain.
Cease, gentle muse! the solemn gloom of night
Now seals the fair creation from my sight.

1773

To His Excellency General Washington[1]

Sir. I have taken the freedom to address your Excellency in the enclosed
poem, and entreat your acceptance, though I am not insensible of its
inaccuracies. Your being appointed by the Grand Continental Congress to
be Generalissimo of the armies of North America, together with the fame
of your virtues, excite sensations not easy to suppress. Your generosity,
therefore, I presume, will pardon the attempt. Wishing your Excellency all
possible success in the great cause you are so generously engaged in. I am,
      Your Excellency's most obedient humble servant,
              Phillis Wheatley

Providence, Oct. 26, 1775.
His Excellency Gen. Washington.

   Celestial choir! enthroned in realms of light,
Columbia's[2] scenes of glorious toils I write.

---

2. Angelic.
3. Heaven, like the city of Jerusalem, is thought
to have had twelve gates (as many gates as tribes
of Israel).
4. Heavenly Jerusalem.
5. In classical mythology Damon pledged his life
for his friend Pythias.
6. The Roman goddess of the dawn.

1. This poem was first published in the *Pennsylvania Magazine* when Thomas Paine was editor.
After reading it, Washington invited Wheatley to
meet him in Cambridge, Massachusetts, in February 1776.
2. This reference to America as "the land Columbus found" is believed to be the first in print.

While freedom's cause her anxious breast alarms,
She flashes dreadful in refulgent arms.
See mother earth her offspring's fate bemoan,   5
And nations gaze at scenes before unknown!
See the bright beams of heaven's revolving light
Involved in sorrows and the veil of night!
    The goddess comes, she moves divinely fair,
Olive and laurel[3] binds her golden hair: 10
Wherever shines this native of the skies,
Unnumbered charms and recent graces rise.
    Muse! bow propitious while my pen relates
How pour her armies through a thousand gates,
As when Eolus[4] heaven's fair face deforms,   15
Enwrapped in tempest and a night of storms;
Astonished ocean feels the wild uproar,
The refluent surges beat the sounding shore;
Or thick as leaves in Autumn's golden reign,
Such, and so many, moves the warrior's train.   20
In bright array they seek the work of war,
Where high unfurled the ensign[5] waves in air.
Shall I to Washington their praise recite?
Enough thou know'st them in the fields of fight.
Thee, first in place and honors—we demand   25
The grace and glory of thy martial band.
Famed for thy valor, for thy virtues more,
Hear every tongue thy guardian aid implore!
    One century scarce performed its destined round,
When Gallic[6] powers Columbia's fury found;   30
And so may you, whoever dares disgrace
The land of freedom's heaven-defended race!
Fixed are the eyes of nations on the scales,
For in their hopes Columbia's arm prevails.
Anon Britannia droops the pensive head,   35
While round increase the rising hills of dead.
Ah! cruel blindness to Columbia's state!
Lament thy thirst of boundless power too late.
    Proceed, great chief, with virtue on thy side,
Thy every action let the goddess guide.   40
A crown, a mansion, and a throne that shine,
With gold unfading, WASHINGTON! be thine.

1775–76   1776, 1834

---

3. Emblems of victory.
4. Ruler of the winds.
5. Flag or banner.

6. The French and Indian Wars (1754–63), between France and England, ended the French colonial empire in North America.

CHARLES BROCKDEN BROWN
1771–1810

The emergence of early American fiction in the 1790s owed much to the reading public's interest in the culture of sentiment. Of equal concern, however, was the vexed and ambiguous situation of women in the new republic. Widely viewed as repositories of virtue whose attention to the domestic sphere guaranteed the success of the nation's new political experiment, women quickly began to chafe at the intellectual and emotional restrictions such views of them entailed. Moreover, with its emphasis on the individual's capacity for self-improvement, republican ideology itself implied an enlarged role for women, one that such protofeminists as Judith Sargent Murray, among others, began to explore. Influenced in part by British author Mary Wollstonecraft's *Vindication of the Rights of Woman* (1792), these writers argued that truly republican marriages required women to be treated as men's equals. The emergent province of fiction provided an imaginative space that was useful for testing, celebrating, and sometimes rejecting this and other radical implications of revolutionary ideology.

No one better understood the usefulness of fiction for gauging the emotional depths of men and women than Charles Brockden Brown. Influenced by the gothic tradition in fiction as exemplified by the work of such English writers as William Godwin (Wollstonecraft's husband), Brown used its conventions to probe his generation's often uncritical embrace of Enlightenment principles. For him, the sentimental plot was just a starting point for very different kinds of explorations. His fiction overturned readers' Enlightenment faith in the rationality of human behavior and indicated that the emotional and obsessive, as much as the logical, were touchstones to character. Brown thus began to explore a rich vein in American fiction that Poe, Melville, and Hawthorne subsequently mined with great success.

Raised by Quaker parents in Philadelphia, one of the new nation's largest and most significant cultural centers, Brown prepared for a career in law. But as the time approached for him to strike out on his own, he gravitated instead to the world of belles-lettres. He might well have succeeded in Philadelphia, which by the 1790s—it was home to important publishers, including Mathew Carey—had become a place where a writer could aspire to the emergent profession of authorship. But Brown opted instead for New York City, where in the 1790s he met and befriended, among others, the Hartford wit and future president of Yale, Timothy Dwight; lexicographer Noah Webster; and Elihu Hubbard Smith, who in 1793 published the first anthology of American poetry. A bona fide member of the nascent American republic of letters, Brown read widely in English literature and, beginning in 1798, published seven important novels in the gothic mode, produced in a mere four years.

The first of these, *Wieland,* is the best known. It was followed by *Ormond* (1799), in which the main character, a freethinker recently returned from the Continent, tries the virtue of Constantia, an epitome of republican womanhood. In *Edgar Huntly* (1799), which is excerpted here, the novelist capitalized on the public's continuing interest in tales of Indian captivity and the wilderness generally, even as he teased readers, as in *Wieland,* with a rational explanation—in this case, sleepwalking—of the strange behavior of one of his central characters. Brown turned to his home city for the setting of *Arthur Mervyn* (1799–1800), whose melodramatic plot, centered on a Godwinian character, has as its background Philadelphia's yellow fever outbreak of 1793. With *Clara Howard* and *Jane Talbot*, both published in 1801, Brown concluded his remarkably fecund career as a novelist.

Although his novels were reissued in a uniform edition after his death in 1827, the first American novelist to have this honor, in his own lifetime Brown had a difficult time making a living through writing fiction alone. To augment his income he involved himself in other publishing ventures. Over the course of a decade, for example, he founded and edited *The Monthly Magazine and American Review* (1799–1800), *The Literary Magazine and American Register* (1803–07), and the *American Register, or General Repository of History, Politics, and Science* (1807–10), all of which provided outlets for his varied talents and ambitions. He contributed many essays to these and other journals, his most important effort being "Alcuin," a lengthy dialogue on women's rights that shows Wollstonecraft's influence, which appeared in the *Philadelphia Weekly Magazine* in 1798. His pamphlet *An Address to the Government of the United States on the Cession of Louisiana to the French* (1803) helped sway public opinion toward the purchase of the Louisiana Territory, and his translation of C. F. Volney's *A View of the Soil and Climate of the United States of America* (1804), with his own commentary, introduced this important thinker to many Americans.

Although he is sometimes termed America's first professional author, Brown did not enjoy the kind of success available to his immediate successors, Washington Irving and James Fenimore Cooper, primarily because the technological infrastructure for the rapid printing and widespread distribution of such work was not yet fully developed. His significance thus resides in his ability to identify those topics—like the limits of rationality and the role of the senses in epistemology—that were of growing interest to the American readership and in his willingness to explore the implications of republican ideology on gender relations.

Edgar Huntly offers an instructive mixture of gothic and sentimental elements that illustrates Brown's wish to transfer European modes to an American setting. The former are introduced at the beginning of the novel, with Edgar, who lives with his uncle and cousins in the countryside near Philadelphia, distraught at the recent murder of his friend Waldegrave. Revisiting the site of the death, Edgar finds Clithero Edny, a servant from an adjacent farm, digging in the earth and crying loudly, actions that Edgar believes link him to the crime. On further observation, he also concludes that Clithero has been sleepwalking. Edgar later confronts him concerning Waldegrave, but Clithero denies any complicity, instead relating a long story about his earlier life in Ireland (the substance of the chapters printed here) in which Brown uses a variety of devices from the culture of sentiment. In Ireland Clithero had been under the patronage of a Mrs. Lorimer, to whose ward, Clarice, he was engaged. In self-defense, Clithero asserts, he kills Mrs. Lorimer's dissolute brother, Wiatte, whom, despite his reprehensible behavior, she still loves dearly. Believing that the knowledge of her brother's death will destroy her, Edgar returns to Mrs. Lorimer's home and tries to stab her to death to spare her the agony, convinced that his action would be benevolent. His attempt fails, but she then learns what he has tried to keep from her and apparently dies of shock. Clithero abruptly leaves the family, flees to the New World, and finds his way to Philadelphia.

Brown later forwards his plot through the trope of captivity among the Native Americans, a device subsequently used by other early American novelists, most notably James Fenimore Cooper and Catharine Maria Sedgwick. One night Edgar awakens in a cave, hungry, thirsty, bruised, and beaten. He encounters a panther, kills the beast, and feasts on it, only to descend further into savagery when he finds in the same cave a group of Native Americans holding a white woman hostage. He kills her captors and flees with her through the wilderness. After the two return to safety and come upon Clithero, who also had been held captive and is wounded, the novel takes a more philosophical turn, with Edgar's counsel of the still-despairing Clithero, obsessed with what he continues to believe is his role in Mrs. Lorimer's death, and with Edgar's own struggle to come to terms with the virtues of civilization versus those of the savagery to which he had been reduced in his recent experiences in the wilderness. He subsequently encounters his former mentor Sarsefield, who condemns his recent violent actions and newfound resistance to social authority. The novel ends with Edgar's futile attempts to comfort Clithero and with Clitherto's suicide, caused in part by his continued anguish over the effects of his past actions. Edgar also learns that when he was in the wilderness he, too, had been sleepwalking, that Native Americans (perhaps the very ones whom he fought) were responsible for Waldegrave's death, and that Mrs. Lorimer is alive and has arrived in America.

The text is from the first edition, *Edgar Huntly; or, Memoirs of a Sleepwalker* (1799).

From Edgar Huntly

Chapter IV

You call upon me for a confession of my offences. What a strange fortune is mine! That an human being, in the present circumstances, should make this demand, and that I should be driven, by an irresistible necessity to comply with it! That here should terminate my calamitous series! That my destiny should call upon me to lie down and die, in a region so remote from the scene of my crimes; at a distance, so great, from all that witnessed and endured their consequences!

You believe me to be an assassin. You require me to explain the motives that induced me to murder the innocent. While this is your belief, and this the scope of your expectations, you may be sure of my compliance. I could resist every demand but this.

For what purpose have I come hither? Is it to relate my story? Shall I calmly sit here, and rehearse the incidents of my life? Will my strength be adequate to this rehearsal? Let me recollect the motives that governed me, when I formed this design. Perhaps, a strenuousness may be imparted by them, which, otherwise, I cannot hope to obtain. For the sake of those, I consent to conjure up the ghost of the past, and to begin a tale that, with a fortitude like mine, I am not sure that I shall live to finish.

You are unacquainted with the man before you. The inferences which you have drawn, with regard to my designs, and my conduct, are a tissue of destructive errors. You, like others, are blind to the most momentous consequences of your own actions. You talk of imparting consolation. You boast the benificence of your intentions. You set yourself to do me a benefit. What are the effects of your misguided zeal, and random efforts? They have brought my life to a miserable close. They have shrouded the last scene of it in blood. They have put the seal to my perdition.

My misery has been greater than has fallen to the lot of mortals. Yet it is but beginning. My present path, full as it is of asperities,[1] is better than that into which I must enter, when this is abandoned. Perhaps, if my pilgrimage had been longer, I might, at some future day, have lighted upon hope. In consequence of your interference, I am forever debarred from it. My existence is henceforward to be invariable. The woes that are reserved for me, are incapable alike of alleviation or intermission.

But I came not hither to recriminate. I came not hither to accuse others but myself. I know the retribution that is appointed for guilt like mine. It is just. I may shudder at the foresight of my punishment and shrink in the endurance of it; but I shall be indebted for part of my torment to the vigour

1. Difficulties.

of my understanding, which teaches me that my punishment is just. Why should I procrastinate my doom and strive to render my burthen more light. It is but just that is should crush me. Its procrastination is impossible. The stroke is already felt. Even now I drink of the cup of retribution. A change of being cannot agravate my woe. Till consciousness itself be extinct, the worm that gnaws me will never perish.

Fain would I be relieved from this task. Gladly would I bury in oblivion the transactions of my life: but no. My fate is uniform. The dæmon that controuled me at first is still in the fruition of power. I am entangled in his fold, and every effort that I make to escape only involves me in deeper ruin. I need not conceal, for all the consequences of disclosure are already experienced. I cannot endure a groundless imputation, though to free me from it, I must create and justify imputations still more atrocious. My story may at least be brief. If the agonies of remembrance must be awakened afresh, let me do all that in me lies to shorten them.

I was born in the county of Armagh.[2] My parents were of the better sort of peasants, and were able to provide me with the rudiments of knowledge. I should doubtless have trodden in their footsteps, and have spent my life in the cultivation of their scanty fields, if an event had not happened, which, for a long time, I regarded as the most fortunate of my life; but which I now regard as the scheme of some infernal agent and as the primary source of all my calamities.

My father's farm was a portion of the demesne[3] of one who resided wholly in the metropolis, and consigned the management of his estates to his stewards and retainers. This person married a lady, who brought him great accession of fortune. Her wealth was her only recommendation in the eyes of her husband, whose understanding was depraved by the prejudices of luxury and rank, but was the least of her attractions in the estimate of reasonable beings.

They passed some years together. If their union were not a source of misery to the lady, she was indebted for her tranquility to the force of her mind. She was, indeed, governed, in every action of her life by the precepts of duty, while her husband listened to no calls but those of pernicious dissipation. He was immersed in all the vices that grow out of opulence and a mistaken education.

Happily for his wife his career was short. He was enraged at the infidelity of his mistress, to purchase whose attachment, he had lavished two thirds of his fortune. He called the paramour, by whom he had been supplanted, to the field. The contest was obstinate, and terminated in the death of the challenger.

This event freed the lady from many distressful and humiliating obligations. She determined to profit by her newly acquired independence, to live thence-forward conformable to her notions of right, to preserve and improve, by schemes of economy, the remains of her fortune, and to employ it in the diffusion of good. Her plans made it necessary to visit her estates in the distant provinces.

During her abode in the manor of which my father was a vassal, she visited his cottage. I was at that time a child. She was pleased with my vivacity and promptitude, and determined to take me under her own protection. My parents joyfully acceded to her proposal, and I returned with her to the capital.

2. Region in northern Ireland. 3. Property, possession.

She had an only son of my own age. Her design, in relation to me, was, that I should be educated with her child, and that an affection, in this way, might be excited in me towards my young master, which might render me, when we should attain to manhood, one of his most faithful and intelligent dependents. I enjoyed, equally with him, all the essential benefits of education. There were certain accomplishments, from which I was excluded, from the belief that they were unsuitable to my rank and station. I was permitted to acquire others, which, had she been actuated by true discernment, she would, perhaps, have discovered to be far more incompatible with a servile station. In proportion as my views were refined and enlarged by history and science, I was likely to contract a thirst of independence, and an impatience of subjection and poverty.

When the period of childhood and youth was past, it was thought proper to send her son, to improve his knowledge and manners, by a residence on the continent. This young man was endowed with splendid abilities. His errors were the growth of his condition. All the expedients that maternal solicitude and wisdom could suggest, were employed to render him an useful citizen. Perhaps this wisdom was attested by the large share of excellence which he really possessed; and, that his character was not unblemished, proved only, that no exertions could preserve him from the vices that are inherent in wealth and rank, and which flow from the spectacle of universal depravity.

As to me, it would be folly to deny, that I had benefited by my opportunities of improvement. I fulfilled the expectation of my mistress, in one respect. I was deeply imbued with affection for her son, and reverence for herself. Perhaps the force of education was evinced in those particulars, without reflecting any credit on the directors of it. Those might merit the name of defects, which were regarded by them as accomplishments. My unfavorable qualities, like those of my master, were imputed to my condition, though, perhaps, the difference was advantageous to me, since the vices of servitude are less hateful than those of tyranny.

It was resolved that I should accompany my master in his travels in quality of favourite domestic. My principles, whatever might be their rectitude, were harmonious and flexible. I had devoted my life to the service of my patron. I had formed conceptions of what was really conducive to his interest, and was not to be misled by specious appearances. If my affection had not stimulated my diligence, I should have found sufficient motives in the behaviour of his mother. She condescended to express her reliance on my integrity and judgment. She was not ashamed to manifest, at parting, the tenderness of a mother, and to acknowledge that, all her tears were not shed on her son's account. I had my part in the regrets that called them forth.

During our absence, I was my master's constant attendant. I corresponded with his mother, and made the conduct of her son the principal theme of my letters. I deemed it my privilege, as well as duty, to sit in judgment on his actions, to form my opinions without regard to selfish considerations, and to avow them whenever the avowal tended to benefit. Every letter which I wrote, particularly those in which his behaviour was freely criticised, I allowed him to peruse. I would, on no account, connive at, or participate in the slightest irregularity. I knew the duty of my station, and assumed no other controul than that which resulted from the avoiding of deceit, and the open expression of my sentiments. The youth was of a noble spirit, but his firmness was wavering. He yielded to temptations which a censor less rigorous than I would have regarded as venial, or, perhaps laudable. My duty required me to set before him the consequences of his actions, and to give impartial and timely information to his mother.

He could not brook a monitor. The more he needed reproof, the less supportable it became. My company became every day less agreeable, till at length, there appeared a necessity of parting. A seperation took place, but not as enemies. I never lost his respect. In his representations to his mother, he was just to my character and services. My dismission was not allowed to injure my fortune, and his mother considered this event merely as a new proof of the inflexible consistency of my principles.

On this change in my situation, she proposed to me to become a member of her own family. No proposal could be more acceptable. I was fully acquainted with the character of this lady, and had nothing to fear from injustice and caprice. I did not regard her with filial familiarity, but my attachment and reverence would have done honour to that relation. I performed for her the functions of a steward. Her estates in the city were put under my direction. She placed boundless confidence in my discretion and integrity, and consigned to me the payment, and in some degree, the selection and government of her servants. My station was a servile one, yet most of the evils of servitude were unknown to me. My personal ease and independence were less infringed than that of those who are accounted the freeest members of society. I derived a sort of authority and dignity from the receipt and disbursement of money. The tenants and debtors of the lady were, in some respects, mine. It was, for the most part, on my justice and lenity that they depended for their treatment. My lady's household establishment was large and opulent. Her servants were my inferiors and menials. My leisure was considerable, and my emoluments large enough to supply me with every valuable instrument of improvement or pleasure.

These were reasons why I should be contented with my lot. These circumstances alone would have rendered it more eligible than any other, but it had additional, and far more powerful recommendations, arising from the character of Mrs. Lorimer, and from the relation in which she allowed me to stand to her.

How shall I enter upon this theme? How shall I expatiate upon excellencies, which it was my fate to view in their genuine colours, to adore with an immeasurable and inextinguishable ardour, and which, nevertheless, it was my hateful task to blast and destroy? Yet I will not be spared. I shall find in the rehearsal, new incitements to sorrow. I deserve to be supreme in misery, and will not be denied the full measure of a bitter retribution.

No one was better qualified to judge of her excellencies. A casual spectator might admire her beauty, and the dignity of her demeanour. From the contemplation of those, he might gather motives for loving or revering her. Age was far from having withered her complexion, or destroyed the evenness of her skin; but no time could rob her of the sweetness and intelligence which animated her features. Her habitual beneficence was bespoken in every look. Always in search of occasions for doing good, always meditating scenes of happiness, of which she was the author, or of distress, for which she was preparing relief, the most torpid insensibility was, for a time, subdued, and the most depraved smitten by charms, of which, in another person, they would not perhaps have been sensible.

A casual visitant might enjoy her conversation, might applaud the rectitude of her sentiments, the richness of her elocution, and her skill in all the offices of politeness. But it was only for him, who dwelt constantly under the same roof, to mark the inviolable consistency of her actions and opinions, the ceaseless flow of her candour, her cheerfulness, and her benevolence. It was only for one who witnessed her behaviour at all hours, in sickness and in health, her management of that great instrument of evil and good, money, her treatment of her son, her menials, and her kindred, rightly to estimate her merits.

The intercourse between us was frequent, but of a peculiar kind. My office in her family required me often to see her, to submit schemes to her consideration, and receive her directions. At these times she treated me in a manner, in some degree, adapted to the difference of rank, and the inferiority of my station, and yet widely dissimilar from that, which a different person would have adopted, in the same circumstances. The treatment was not that of an equal and a friend, but still more remote was it from that of a mistress. It was merely characterised by affability and condescention, but as such it had no limits.

She made no scruple to ask my council in every pecuniary affair, to listen to my arguments, and decide conformably to what, after sufficient canvassings and discussions, should appear to be right. When the direct occasions of our interview were dismissed, I did not of course withdraw. To detain or dismiss me was indeed at her option, but, if no engagement interfered, she would enter into general conversation. There was none who could with more safety to herself have made the world her confessor; but the state of society in which she lived, imposed certain limitations on her candour. In her intercourse with me there were fewer restraints than on any other occasion. My situation had made me more intimately acquainted with domestic transactions, with her views respecting her son, and with the terms on which she thought proper to stand with those whom old acquaintance or kindred gave some title to her good offices. In addition to all those motives to a candid treatment of me, there were others which owed their efficacy to her maternal regard for me, and to the artless and unsuspecting generosity of her character.

Her hours were distributed with the utmost regularity, and appropriated to the best purposes. She selected her society without regard to any qualities but probity and talents. Her associates were numerous, and her evening conversations embellished with all that could charm the senses or instruct the understanding. This was a chosen field for the display of her magnificence, but her grandeur was unostentatious, and her gravity unmingled with hautiness. From these my station excluded me, but I was compensated by the freedom of her compensated by the freedom of her communications in the intervals. She found pleasure in detailing to me the incidents that passed on those occasions, in rehearsing conversations and depicting characters. There was an uncommon portion of dramatic merit in her recitals, besides valuable and curious information. One uniform effect was produced in me by this behaviour. Each day, I thought it impossible for my attachment to receive any new accessions, yet the morrow was sure to produce some new emotion of respect or of gratitude, and to set the unrivalled accomplishments of this lady in a new and more favourable point of view. I contemplated no change in my condition. The necessity of change, whatever were the alternative, would have been a subject of piercing regret. I deemed my life a cheap sacrifice in her cause. No time would suffice to discharge the debt of gratitude that was due to her. Yet it was continually accumulating. If an anxious thought ever invaded my bosom it arose from this source.

It was no difficult task faithfully to execute the functions assigned to me. No merit could accrue to me from this source. I was exposed to no temptation. I had passed the feverish period of youth. No contagious example had contaminated my principles. I had resisted the allurements of sensuality and dissipation incident to my age. My dwelling was in pomp and splendor. I had amassed sufficient to secure me, in case of unforeseen accidents, in the enjoyment of competence. My mental resources were not despicable, and the external means of intellectual gratification were boundless. I enjoyed an unsullied reputation. My character was well known in that sphere which my lady occupied, not only by means of her favourable report, but in numberless ways in which it was my fortune to perform personal services to others.

Chapter V

Mrs. Lorimer had a twin brother. Nature had impressed the same image upon them, and had modelled them after the same pattern. The resemblance between them was exact to a degree almost incredible. In infancy and childhood they were perpetually liable to be mistaken for each other. As they grew up nothing to a superficial examination appeared to distinguish them but the sexual characteristics. A sagacious[4] observer would, doubtless, have noted the most essential differences. In all those modifications of the features which are produced by habits and sentiments, no two persons were less alike. Nature seemed to have intended them as examples of the futility of those theories, which ascribe every thing to conformation and instinct, and nothing to external circumstances; in what different modes the same materials may be fashioned, and to what different purposes the same materials may be applied. Perhaps the rudiments of their intellectual character as well as of their form, were the same; but the powers, that in one case, were exerted in the cause of virtue, were, in the other, misapplied to sordid and flagitious[5] purposes.

Arthur Wiatte, that was his name, had ever been the object of his sister's affection. As long as he existed she never ceased to labour in the promotion of his happiness. All her kindness was repaid by a stern and inexorable hatred. This man was an exception to all the rules which govern us in our judgments of human nature. He exceeded in depravity all that has been imputed to the arch-foe of mankind. His wickedness was without any of those remorseful intermissions from which it has been supposed that the deepest guilt is not entirely exempt. He seemed to relish no food but pure unadulterated evil. He rejoiced in proportion to the depth of that distress of which he was the author.

His sister, by being placed most within the reach of his enmity, experienced its worst effects. She was the subject on which, by being acquainted with the means of influencing her happiness, he could try his malignant experiments with most hope of success. Her parents being high in rank and wealth, the marriage of their daughter was, of course, an object of anxious attention. There is no event on which our felicity and usefulness more materially depends, and with regard to which, therefore, the freedom of choice and the exercise of our own understanding ought to be less infringed,

---

4. Wise.   5. Wicked, criminal.

but this maxim is commonly disregarded in proportion to the elevation of our rank and extent of our property.

The lady made her own election, but she was one of those who acted on a comprehensive plan, and would not admit her private inclination to dictate her decision. Her happiness of others, though founded on mistaken views, she did not consider as unworthy of her regard. The choice was such as was not likely to obtain the parental sanction, to whom the moral qualities of their son-in-law, though not absolutely weightless in the balance, were greatly inferior to the considerations of wealth and dignity.

The brother set no value on any thing but the means of luxury and power. He was astonished at that perverseness which entertained a different conception of happiness from himself. Love and friendship he considered as groundless and chimerical, and believed that those delusions, would, in people of sense, be rectified by experience; but he knew the obstinacy of his sister's attachment to these phantoms, and that to bereave her of the good they promised was the most effectual means of rendering her miserable. For this end he set himself to thwart her wishes. In the imbecility and false indulgence of his parents he found his most powerful auxiliaries. He prevailed upon them to forbid that union which wanted nothing but their concurrence, and their consent to endow her with a small portion of their patrimony to render completely eligible. The cause was that of her happiness and the happiness of him on whom she had bestowed her heart. It behoved her, therefore, to call forth all her energies in defence of it, to weaken her brother's influence on the minds of her parents, or to win him to be her advocate. When I reflect upon her mental powers, and the advantages which should seem to flow from the circumstance of pleading in the character of daughter and sister, I can scarcely believe that her attempts miscarried. I should have imagined that all obstacles would yield before her, and particularly in a case like this, in which she must have summoned all her forces, and never have believed that she had struggled sufficiently.

Certain it is that her lot was fixed. She was not only denied the husband of her choice, but another was imposed upon her, whose recommendations were irresistible in every one's apprehension but her own. The discarded lover was treated with every sort of contumely.[6] Deceit and violence were employed by her brother to bring his honour, his liberty, and even his life into hazard. All these iniquities produced no considerable effect on the mind of the lady. The machinations to which her love was exposed, would have exasperated him into madness, had not her most strenuous exertions been directed to appease him.

She prevailed on him at length to abandon his country, though she thereby merely turned her brother's depravity into a new channel. Her parents died without conciousness of the evils they inflicted, but they experienced a bitter retribution in the conduct of their son. He was the darling and stay of an ancient and illustrious house, but his actions reflected nothing but disgrace upon his ancestry, and threatened to bring the honours of their line to a period in his person. At their death the bulk of their patrimony devolved upon him. This he speedily consumed in gaming and riot. From splendid, he descended to meaner vices. The efforts of his sister to recall him to virtue were unintermitted and fruitless. Her affection for him he converted into a means of prolonging his selfish gratifications. She decided for the best. It

6. Reproach, abuse.

was no argument of weakness that she was so frequently deceived. If she had judged truly of her brother, she would have judged not only without example, but in opposition to the general experience of mankind. But she was not to be forever deceived. Her tenderness was subservient to justice. And when his vices had led him from the gaming table to the highway, when seized at length by the ministers of law, when convicted and sentenced to transportation, her intercession was solicited, when all the world knew that pardon would readily be granted to a supplicant of her rank, fortune, and character, when the criminal himself, his kindred, his friends, and even indifferent persons implored her interference, her justice was inflexible: She knew full well the incurableness of his depravity; that banishment was the mildest destiny that would befall him; that estrangement from ancient haunts and associates was the condition from which his true friends had least to fear.

Finding intreaties unavailing, the wretch delivered himself to the suggestions of his malice, and he vowed to be bloodily revenged on her inflexibility. The sentence was executed. That character must indeed be monstrous from which the execution of such threats was to be dreaded. The event sufficiently shewed that our fears on this head were well grounded. This event, however, was at a great distance. It was reported that the felons, of whom he was one, mutinied on board the ship in which they had been embarked. In the affray[7] that succeeded it was said that he was killed.

Among the nefarious deeds which he perpetrated was to be numbered the seduction of a young lady, whose heart was broken by the detection of his perfidy.[8] The fruit of this unhappy union was a daughter. Her mother died shortly after her birth. Her father was careless of her destiny. She was consigned to the care of an hireling,[9] who, happily for the innocent victim, performed the maternal offices for her own sake, and did not allow the want of a stipulated recompence to render her cruel or neglectful.

This orphan was sought out by the benevolence of Mrs. Lorimer and placed under her own protection. She received from her the treatment of a mother. The ties of kindred, corroborated by habit, was not the only thing that united them. That resemblance to herself, which had been so deplorably defective in her brother, was completely realized in his offspring. Nature seemed to have precluded every difference between them but that of age. This darling object excited in her bosom more than maternal sympathies. Her soul clung to the happiness of her *Clarice*, with more ardour than to that of her own son. The latter was not only less worthy of affection, but their separation necessarily diminished their mutual confidence.

It was natural for her to look forward to the future destiny of *Clarice*. On these occasions she could not help contemplating the possibility of a union between her son and niece. Considerable advantages belonged to this scheme, yet it was the subject of hope rather than the scope of a project. The contingencies were numerous and delicate on which the ultimate desirableness of this union depended. She was far from certain that her son would be worthy of this benefit, or that, if he were worthy, his propensities would not select for themselves a different object. It was equally dubious whether the young lady would not think proper otherwise to dispose of her affections. These uncertainties could be dissipated only by time. Meanwhile she was chiefly solicitous to render them virtuous and wise.

---

7. Battle.
8. Deceit, treachery.

9. Servant.

As they advanced in years, the hopes that she had formed were annihilated. The youth was not exempt from egregious errors. In addition to this, it was manifest that the young people were disposed to regard each other in no other light than that of brother and sister. I was not unapprised of her views. I saw that their union was impossible. I was near enough to judge of the character of Clarice. My youth and intellectual constitution made me peculiarly susceptible to female charms. I was her playfellow in childhood, and her associate in studies and amusements at a mature age. This situation might have been suspected of a dangerous tendency. This tendency, however, was obviated by motives of which I was, for a long time, scarcely conscious.

I was habituated to consider the distinctions of rank as indelible. The obstructions that existed, to any wish that I might form, were like those of time and space, and as, in their own nature, insuperable.

Such was the state of things previous to our setting out upon our travels. Clarice was indirectly included in our correspondence. My letters were open to her inspection, and I was sometimes honoured with a few complimentary lines under her own hand. On returning to my ancient abode, I was once more exposed to those sinister influences which absence had, at least, suspended. Various suitors had, meanwhile, been rejected. Their character, for the most part, had been such as to account for her refusal, without resorting to the supposition of a lurking or unavowed attachment.

On our meeting she greeted me in a respectful but dignified manner. Observers could discover in it nothing not corresponding to that difference of fortune which subsisted between us. If her joy, on that occasion, had in it some portion of tenderness, the softness of her temper, and the peculiar circumstances in which we had been placed, being considered, the most rigid censor could find no occasion for blame or suspicion.

A year passed away, but not without my attention being solicited by something new and inexplicable in my own sensations. At first I was not aware of their true cause; but the gradual progress of my feelings left me not long in doubt as to their origin. I was alarmed at the discovery, but my courage did not suddenly desert me. My hopes seemed to be extinguished the moment that I distinctly perceived the point to which they led. My mind had undergone a change. The ideas with which it was fraught were varied. The sight, or recollection of Clarice, was sure to occasion my mind to advert to the recent discovery, and to revolve the considerations naturally connected with it. Some latent glows and secret trepidations were likewise experienced, when, by some accident, our meetings were abrupt or our interviews unwitnessed; yet my usual tranquility was not as yet sensibly diminished. I could bear to think of her marriage with another without painful emotions, and was anxious only that her choice should be judicious and fortunate.

My thoughts could not long continue in this state. They gradually became more ardent and museful. The image of Clarice occurred with unseasonable[1] frequency. Its charms were enhanced by some nameless and indefinable additions. When it met me in the way I was irresistibly disposed to stop and survey it with particular attention. The pathetic cast of her features, the deep glow of her cheek, and some catch of melting music, she had lately breathed, stole incessantly upon my fancy. On recovering from my thoughtful moods, I sometimes found my cheeks wet with tears, that had fallen unperceived, and my bosom heaved with involuntary sighs.

---

1. Not in accordance with the occasion.

These images did not content themselves with invading my wakeful hours; but, likewise, incroached upon my sleep. I could no longer resign myself to slumber with the same ease as before. When I slept, my visions were of the same impassioned tenor.

There was no difficulty in judging rightly of my situation. I knew what it was that duty exacted from me. To remain in my present situation was a chimerical[2] project. That time and reflection would suffice to restore me to myself was a notion equally fallacious. Yet I felt an insupportable reluctance to change it. This reluctance was owing, not wholly or chiefly to my growing passion, but to the attachment which bound me to the service of my lady. All my contemplations had hither to been modelled on the belief of my remaining in my present situation during my life. My mildest anticipations had never fashioned an event like this. Any misfortune was light in comparison with that which tore me from her presence and service. But should I ultimately resolve to separate, how should I communicate my purpose. The pain of parting would scarcely be less on her side than on mine. Could I consent to be the author of disquietude to her? I had consecrated all my faculties to her service. This was the recompence which it was in my power to make for the benefits that I had received. Would not this procedure bear the appearance of the basest ingratitude? The shadow of an imputation like this was more excruciating than the rack.

What motive could I assign for my conduct? The truth must not be told. This would be equivalent to supplicating for a new benefit. It would more become me to lessen than increase my obligations. Among all my imaginations on this subject, the possibility of a mutual passion never occurred to me. I could not be blind to the essential distinctions that subsist among men. I could expatiate,[3] like others, on the futility of ribbonds[4] and titles, and on the dignity that was annexed to skill and virtue; but these, for the most part, were the incoherences of speculation, and in no degree influenced the stream of my actions, and practical sentiments. The barrier that existed in the present case, I deemed insurmountable. This was not even the subject of doubt. In disclosing the truth, I should be conceived to be soliciting my lady's mercy and intercession; but this would be the madness of presumption. Let me impress her with any other opinion than that I go in search of the happiness that I have lost under her roof. Let me save her generous heart from the pangs which this persuasion would infallibly produce.

I could form no stable resolutions. I seemed unalterably convinced of the necessity of separation, and yet could not execute my design. When I had wrought up my mind to the intention of explaining myself on the next interview,[5] when the next interview took place my tongue was powerless. I admitted any excuse for postponing my design, and gladly admitted any topic, however foreign to my purpose.

It must not be imagined that my health sustained no injury from this conflict of my passions. My patroness perceived this alteration. She inquired with the most affectionate solicitude, into the cause. It could not be explained. I could safely make light of it, and represented it as something which would probably disappear of itself, as it originated without any adequate cause. She was obliged to acquiesce in my imperfect account.

---

2. Fanciful, imaginery.
3. Talk at length.

4. Ribbons, as in decorations of honor.
5. Meeting.

Day after day passed in this state of fluctuation. I was conscious of the dangers of delay, and that procrastination, without rendering the task less necessary, augmented its difficulties. At length, summoning my resolution, I demanded an audience. She received me with her usual affability. Common topics were started; but she saw the confusion and trepidation of my thoughts, and quickly relinquished them. She then noticed to me what she had observed, and mentioned the anxiety which these appearances had given her. She reminded me of the maternal regard which she had always manifested towards me, and appealed to my own heart whether any thing could be said in vindication of that reserve with which I had lately treated her, and urged me as I valued her good opinion, to explain the cause of a dejection *that was too visible.*

To all this I could make but one answer: Think me not, Madam, perverse or ungrateful. I came just now to apprise you of a resolution that I had formed. I cannot explain the motives that induce me. In this case, to lie to you would be unpardonable, and since I cannot assign my true motives, I will not mislead you by false representations. I came to inform you of my intention to leave your service, and to retire with the fruits of your bounty, to my native village, where I shall spend my life, I hope, in peace.

Her surprise at this declaration was beyond measure. She could not believe her ears. She had not heard me rightly. She compelled me to repeat it. Still I was jesting. I could not possibly mean what my words imported.

I assured her, in terms still more explicit, that my resolution was taken and was unalterable, and again intreated her to spare me the task of assigning my motives.

This was a strange determination. What could be the grounds of this new scheme? What could be the necessity of hiding them from her? This mystery was not to be endured. She could by no means away with it. She thought it hard that I should abandon her at this time, when she stood in particular need of my assistance and advice. She would refuse nothing to make my situation eligible. I had only to point out where she was deficient in her treatment of me and she would endeavour to supply it. She was willing to augment my emoluments in any degree that I desired. She could not think of parting with me; but, at any rate, she must be informed of my motives.

It is an hard task, answered I, that I have imposed upon myself. I foresaw its difficulties, and this foresight has hitherto prevented me from undertaking it; but the necessity by which I am impelled, will no longer be withstood. I am determined to go; but to say why, is impossible. I hope I shall not bring upon myself the imputation of ingratitude; but this imputation, more intolerable than any other, must be borne, if it cannot be avoided but by this disclosure.

Keep your motives to yourself, said she. I have too good an opinion of you to suppose that you would practice concealment without good reason. I merely desire you to remain where you are. Since you will not tell me why you take up this new scheme, I can only say that it is impossible there should be any advantage in this scheme. I will not hear of it I tell you. Therefore, submit to my decree with a good grace.

Notwithstanding this prohibition I persisted in declaring that my determination was fixed, and that the motives that governed me would allow of no alternative.

So, you will go, will you, whether I will or no? I have no power to detain you? You will regard nothing that I can say?

Believe me, madam, no resolution ever was formed after a more vehement struggle. If my motives were known, you would not only cease to oppose, but would hasten my departure. Honour me so far with your good opinion, as to believe that, in saying this, I say nothing but the truth, and render my duty less burthensome by cheerfully acquiescing in its dictates.

I would, replied my lady, I could find somebody that has more power over you than I have. Whom shall I call in to aid me in this arduous task?

Nay, dear madam, if I can resist your intreaties, surely no other can hope to succeed.

I am not sure of that, said my friend, archly: there is one person in the world whose supplications, I greatly suspect, you would not withstand.

Whom do you mean? said I, in some trepidation.

You will know presently. Unless I can prevail upon you, I shall be obliged to call for assistance.

Spare me the pain of repeating that no power on earth can change my resolution.

That's a fib, she rejoined, with increased archness. You know it is. If a certain person intreat you to stay, you will easily comply. I see I cannot hope to prevail by my own strength. That is a mortifying consideration, but we must not part, that is a point settled. If nothing else will do, I must go and fetch my advocate. Stay here a moment.

I had scarcely time to breathe, before she returned, leading in Clarice. I did not yet comprehend the meaning of this ceremony. The lady was overwhelmed with sweet confusion. Averted eyes and reluctant steps, might have explained to me the purpose of this meeting, if I had believed that purpose to be possible. I felt the necessity of new fortitude, and struggled to recollect the motives that had hitherto sustained me.

There, said my patroness, I have been endeavouring to persuade this young man to live with us a little longer. He is determined, it seems, to change his abode. He will not tell why, and I do not care to know, unless I could shew his reasons to be groundless. I have merely remonstrated with him on the folly of his scheme, but he has proved refractory to all I can say. Perhaps your efforts may meet with better success.

Clarice said not a word. My own embarrassment equally disabled me from speaking. Regarding us both, for some time, with a benign aspect, Mrs. Lorimer resumed, taking an hand of each and joining them together.

I very well know what it was that suggested this scheme. It is strange that you should suppose me so careless an observer as not to note, or not to understand your situation. I am as well acquainted with what is passing in your heart as you yourself are, but why are you so anxious to conceal it. You know less of the adventurousness of love than I should have suspected. But I will not trifle with your feelings.

You, Clithero, know the wishes that I once cherished. I had hoped that my son would have found, in this darling child, an object worthy of his choice, and that my girl would have preferred him to all others. But I have long since discovered that this could not be. They are nowise suited to each other. There is one thing in the next place desirable, and now my wishes are accomplished. I see that you love each other, and never, in my opinion, was a passion more rational and just. I should think myself the worst of beings if I did not contribute all in my power to your happiness. There is not the shadow of objection to your union. I know your scruples, Clithero, and am sorry to see that you harbour them for a moment. Nothing is more unworthy of your good sense.

I found out this girl long ago. Take my word for it, young man, she does not fall short of you in the purity and tenderness of her attachment. What need is there of tedious preliminaries. I will leave you together, and hope you will not be long in coming to a mutual understanding. Your union cannot be completed too soon for my wishes. Clarice is my only and darling daughter. As to you Clithero, expect henceforth that treatment from me, not only to which your own merit intitles you, but which is due to the husband of my daughter.—With these words she retired and left us together.

Great God! deliver me from the torments of this remembrance. That a being by whom I was snatched from penury[6] and brutal ignorance, exalted to some rank in the intelligent creation, reared to affluence and honour, and thus, at last, spontaneously endowed with all that remained to complete the sum of my felicity, that a being like this—but such thoughts must not yet be—I must shut them out, or I shall never arrive at the end of my tale. My efforts have been thus far successful. I have hitherto been able to deliver a coherent narrative. Let the last words that I shall speak afford some glimmering of my better days. Let me execute without faltering the only task that remains for me.

Chapter VI

How propitious, how incredible was this event! I could scarcely confide in the testimony of my senses. Was it true that Clarice was before me, that she was prepared to countenance my presumption, that she had slighted obstacles which I had deemed insurmountable, that I was fondly beloved by her, and should shortly be admitted to the possession of so inestimable a good? I will not repeat the terms in which I poured forth, at her feet, the raptures of my gratitude. My impetuosity soon extorted from Clarice, a confirmation of her mother's declaration. An unrestrained intercourse was thenceforth established between us. Dejection and languor gave place, in my bosom, to the irradiations of joy and hope. My flowing fortunes seemed to have attained their utmost and immutable height.

Alas! They were destined to ebb with unspeakably greater rapidity, and to leave me, in a moment, stranded and wrecked.

Our nuptials would have been solemnised without delay, had not a melancholy duty interfered. Clarice had a friend in a distant part of the kingdom. Her health had long been the prey of a consumption.[7] She was now evidently tending to dissolution. In this extremity she intreated her friend to afford her the consolation of her presence. The only wish that remained was to die in her arms.

This request could not but be willingly complied with. It became me patiently to endure the delay that would thence arise to the completion of my wishes. Considering the urgency and mournfulness of the occasion, it was impossible for me to murmur, and the affectionate Clarice would suffer nothing to interfere with the duty which she owed to her dying friend. I accompanied her on this journey, remained with her a few days, and then parted from her to return to the metropolis. It was not imagined that it would be necessary to prolong her absence beyond a month. When I bade

6. Poverty.   7. Tuberculosis.

her farewell, and informed her on what day I proposed to return for her, I felt no decay of my satisfaction. My thoughts were bright and full of exultation. Why was not some intimation afforded me of the snares that lay in my path? In the train laid for my destruction, the agent had so skillfully contrived that my security was not molested by the faintest omen.

I hasten to the crisis of my tale. I am almost dubious of my strength. The nearer I approach to it, the stronger is my aversion. My courage, instead of gathering force as I proceed, decays. I am willing to dwell still longer on preliminary circumstances. There are other incidents without which my story would be lame. I detail them because they afford me a kind of respite from horrors, at the thought of which every joint in my frame trembles. They must be endured, but that infirmity may be forgiven, which makes me inclined to procrastinate my suffering.

I mentioned the lover whom my patroness was compelled, by the machinations of her brother, to discard. More than twenty years had passed since their separation. His birth was mean and he was without fortune. His profession was that of a surgeon. My lady not only prevailed upon him to abandon his country, but enabled him to do this by supplying his necessities from her own purse. His excellent understanding was, for a time, obscured by passion; but it was not difficult for my lady ultimately to obtain his concurrence to all her schemes. He saw and adored the rectitude of her motives, did not disdain to accept her gifts, and projected means for maintaining an epistolary intercourse[8] during their separation.

Her interest procured him a post in the service of the East-India company.[9] She was, from time to time, informed of his motions. A war broke out between the Company and some of the native powers. He was present at a great battle in which the English were defeated.[1] She could trace him by his letters and by other circumstances thus far, but here the thread was discontinued, and no means which she employed could procure any tidings of him. Whether he was captive, or dead, continued, for several years, to be merely matter of conjecture.

On my return to Dublin, I found my patroness engaged in conversation with a stranger. She introduced us to each other in a manner that indicated the respect which she entertained for us both. I surveyed and listened to him with considerable attention. His aspect was noble and ingenious, but his sun-burnt and rugged features bespoke a various and boisterous pilgrimage. The furrows of his brow were the products of vicissitude and hardship, rather than of age. His accents were fiery and energetic, and the impassioned boldness of his address, as well as the tenor of his discourse, full of allusions to the past, and regrets that the course of events had not been different, made me suspect something extraordinary in his character.

As soon as he left us, my lady explained who he was. He was no other than the object of her youthful attachment, who had, a few days before, dropped among us as from the skies. He had a long and various story to tell. He had accounted for his silence by enumerating the incidents of his life. (He had escaped from the prisons of Hyder, had wandered on foot, and under various

---

8. Communication through letters.
9. A British joint-stock company chartered in 1600 to carry on trade with the East Indies.
1. A reference to the Second Anglo-Mysore War (1780–84), fought between England and the

Indian region of Mysore, allied to France. Thus the battle, in which Indian leader Haidar Ali defeated the British colonel William Baillie, concerned the imperial plans of two chief European powers.

disguises, through the northern district of Hindoostaun.[2] He was sometimes a scholar of Benares, and sometimes a disciple of the Mosque.[3] According to the exigencies of the times, he was a pilgrim to Mecca or to Jagunaut.[4] By a long, circuitous, and perilous route, he at length arrived at the Turkish capital. Here he resided for several years, deriving a precarious subsistence from the profession of a surgeon. He was obliged to desert this post, in consequence of a duel between two Scotsmen. One of them had embraced the Greek religion,[5] and was betrothed to the daughter of a wealthy trader of that nation. He perished in the conflict, and the family of the lady not only procured the execution of his antagonist, but threatened to involve all those who were known to be connected with him in the same ruin.

His life being thus endangered, it became necessary for him to seek a new residence. He fled from Constantinople with such precipitation as reduced him to the lowest poverty. He had traversed the Indian conquests of Alexander,[6] as a mendicant.[7] In the same character, he now wandered over the native country of Philip and Philœpamen.[8] He passed safely through multiplied perils, and finally, embarking at Salonichi,[9] he reached Venice. He descended through the passes of the Apennine[1] into Tuscany. In this journey he suffered a long detention from banditti,[2] by whom he was waylaid. In consequence of his harmless deportment, and a seasonable display of his chirurgical[3] skill, they granted him his life, though they, for a time restrained him of his liberty, and compelled him to endure their society. The time was not misemployed which he spent immured in caverns and carousing with robbers. His details were eminently singular and curious, and evinced the accuteness of his penetration, as well the steadfastness of his courage.

After emerging from these wilds, he found his way along the banks of the Arno to Leghorn.[4] Thence he procured a passage to America, whence he had just returned, with many additions to his experience, but none to his fortune.

This was a remarkable event. It did not at first appear how far its consequences would extend. The lady was, at present, disengaged and independent. Though the passion which clouded her early prosperity was extinct, time had not diminished the worth of her friend, and they were far from having reached that age when love becomes chimerical and marriage folly. A confidential intercourse was immediately established between them. The bounty of Mrs. Lorimer soon divested her friend of all fear of poverty. At any rate, said she, he shall wander no further, but shall be comfortably situated for the rest of his life. All his scruples were vanquished by the reasonableness of her remonstrances and the vehemence of her solicitations.

A cordial intimacy grew between me and the newly arrived. Our interviews were frequent, and our communications without reserve. He detailed to me the result of his experience, and expatiated without end on the history of his actions and opinions. He related the adventures of his youth, and dwelt upon all the circumstances of his attachment to my patroness. On this subject I had heard only general details. I continually found cause, in the

---

2. Popular name for India. Hyder Ali was The Mysore leader (see n. 1, p. 427).
3. I.e., of the Muslim faith. Benares is a city on the Ganges River in India, considered a holy place.
4. I.e., Jagannath, India. Mecca is in modern-day Saudi Arabia. Both are holy cities.
5. Eastern Orthodox faith.
6. Alexander the Great (356–323 B.C.E.); also known as Alexander III or Macehon. King of Macedonia who conquered an immense area of Asia.

7. Beggar.
8. Macedonian rulers; Philip was the father of Alexander the Great.
9. Thessalonika, capital of the region of Macedonia, in Greece.
1. Chain of mountains in northwest Italy.
2. Bandits, thieves.
3. Surgical, medical.
4. A port city in western Tuscany. The Arno River flows through Florence.

course of his narrative, to revere the illustrious qualities of my lady, and to weep at the calamities to which the infernal malice of her brother had subjected her.

The tale of that man's misdeeds, amplified and dramatised, by the indignant eloquence of this historian, oppressed me with astonishment. If a poet had drawn such a portrait I should have been prone to suspect the soundness of his judgment. Till now I had imagined that no character was uniform and unmixed, and my theory of the passions did not enable me to account for a propensity gratified merely by evil, and delighting in shrieks and agony for their own sake.

It was natural to suggest to my friend, when expatiating on this theme, an inquiry as to how far subsequent events had obliterated the impressions that were then made, and as to the plausibility of reviving, at this more auspicious period, his claims on the heart of his friend. When he thought proper to notice these hints, he gave me to understand that time had made no essential alteration in his sentiments in this respect, that he still fostered an hope, to which every day added new vigour, that whatever was the ultimate event, he trusted in his fortitude to sustain it, if adverse, and in his wisdom to extract from it the most valuable consequences, if it should prove prosperous.

The progress of things was not unfavourable to his hopes. She treated his insinuations and professions with levity; but her arguments seemed to be urged, with no other view than to afford an opportunity of confutation; and, since there was no abatement of familiarity and kindness, there was room to hope that the affair would terminate agreeably to his wishes.

Chapter VII

Clarice, meanwhile, was absent. Her friend seemed, at the end of a month, to be little less distant from the grave than at first. My impatience would not allow me to wait till her death. I visited her, but was once more obliged to return alone. I arrived late in the city, and being greatly fatigued, I retired almost immediately to my chamber.

On hearing of my arrival, Sarsefield hastened to see me. He came to my bedside, and such, in his opinion, was the importance of the tidings which he had to communicate, that he did not scruple to rouse me from a deep sleep. . . . .

At this period of his narrative, Clithero stopped. His complexion varied from one degree of paleness to another. His brain appeared to suffer some severe constriction. He desired to be excused, for a few minutes, from proceeding. In a short time he was relieved from this paroxysm,[5] and resumed his tale with an accent tremulous at first, but acquiring stability and force as he went on.

On waking, as I have said, I found my friend seated at my bed-side. His countenance exibited various tokens of alarm. As soon as I perceived who it was, I started, exclaiming What is the matter?

He sighed. Pardon, said he, this unseasonable intrusion. A light matter would not have occasioned it. I have waited, for two days past, in an agony of impatience, for your return. Happily, you are, at last, come. I stand in the utmost need of your council and aid.

_____

5. Violent attack, as by disease.

Heaven defend! cried I. This is a terrible prelude. You may, of course, rely upon my assistance and advice. What is it that you have to propose?

Tuesday evening, he answered, I spent here. It was late before I returned to my lodgings. I was in the act of lifting my hand to the bell, when my eye was caught by a person standing close to the wall, at the distance of ten paces. His attitude was that of one employed in watching my motions. His face was turned towards me, and happened, at that moment, to be fully illuminated by the rays of a globe-lamp[6] that hung over the door. I instantly recognized his features. I was petrified. I had no power to execute my design, or even to move, but stood, for some seconds gazing upon him. He was, in no degree, disconcerted by the eagerness of my scrutiny. He seemed perfectly indifferent to the consequences of being known. At length he slowly turned his eyes to another quarter, but without changing his posture, or the sternness of his looks. I cannot describe to you the shock which this encounter produced in me. At last I went into the house, and have ever since been excessively uneasy.

I do not see any ground for uneasiness

You do not then suspect who this person is?

No. . . .

It is Arthur Wiatte. . . .

Good heaven! It is impossible. What, my lady's brother?

The same. . . .

It cannot be. Were we not assured of his death? That he perished in a mutiny on board the vessel in which he was embarked for transportation?

Such was rumour, which is easily mistaken. My eyes cannot be deceived in this case. I should as easily fail to recognize his sister, when I first met her, as him. This is the man, whether once dead or not, he is, at present, alive, and in this city.

But has any thing since happened to confirm you in this opinion.

Yes, there has. As soon as I had recovered from my first surprise, I began to reflect upon the measures proper to be taken. This was the identical Arthur Wiatte. You know his character. No time was likely to change the principles of such a man, but his appearance sufficiently betrayed the incurableness of his habits. The same sullen and atrocious passions were written in his visage. You recollect the vengeance which Wiatte denounced against his sister. There is every thing to dread from his malignity. How to obviate the danger, I know not. I thought, however, of one expedient. It might serve a present purpose, and something better might suggest itself on your return.

I came hither early the next day. Old Gowan the porter is well acquainted with Wiatte's story. I mentioned to him that I had reason to think that he had returned. I charged him to have a watchful eye upon every one that knocked at the gate, and that if this person should come, by no means to admit him. The old man promised faithfully to abide by my directions. His terrors, indeed, were greater than mine, and he knew the importance of excluding Wiatte from these walls.

Did you not inform my lady of this?

No. In what way could I tell it to her? What end could it answer? Why should I make her miserable? But I have not done. Yesterday morning Gowan took me aside, and informed me that Wiatte had made his appearance, the day before, at the gate. He knew him, he said, in a moment. He demanded to see the lady, but the old man told him she was engaged, and could not be seen.

6. Round glass cover for a candle.

He assumed peremtory and haughty airs, and asserted that his business was of such importance as not to endure a moment's delay. Gowan persisted in his first refusal. He retired with great reluctance, but said he should return tomorrow, when he should insist upon admission to the presence of the lady. I have inquired, and find that he has not repeated his visit. What is to be done?

I was equally at a loss with my friend. This incident was so unlooked for. What might not be dreaded from the monstrous depravity of Wiatte? His menaces of vengeance against his sister still rung in my ears. Some means of eluding them were indispensable. Could law be resorted to? Against an evil like this, no legal provision had been made. Nine years had elapsed since his transportation. Seven years was the period of his exile. In returning, therefore, he had committed no crime. His person could not be lawfully molested. We were justified, merely, in repelling an attack. But suppose we should appeal to law, could this be done without the knowledge and concurrence of the lady? She would never permit it. Her heart was incapable of fear from this quarter. She would spurn at the mention of precautions against the hatred of her brother. Her inquietude would merely be awakened on his own account.

I was overwhelmed with perplexity. Perhaps if he were sought out, and some judgment formed of the kind of danger to be dreaded from him, by a knowledge of his situation and views, some expedient might be thence suggested.

But how should his haunts be discovered? This was easy. He had intimated the design of applying again for admission to his sister. Let a person be stationed near at hand, who, being furnished with an adequate description of his person and dress, shall mark him when he comes, and follow him, when he retires, and shall forthwith impart to us the information on that head which he shall be able to collect.

My friend concurred in this scheme. No better could, for the present, be suggested. Here ended our conference.

I was thus supplied with a new subject of reflection. It was calculated to fill my mind with dreary forbodings. The future was no longer a scene of security and pleasure. It would be hard for those to partake of our fears, who did not partake of our experience. The existence of Wiatte, was the canker[7] that had blasted the felicity of my patroness. In his reappearance on the stage, there was something portentous. It seemed to include in it, consequences of the utmost moment, without my being able to discover what these consequences were.

That Sarsefield should be so quickly followed by his Arch-foe; that they started anew into existence, without any previous intimation, in a manner wholly unexpected, and at the same period. It seemed as if there lurked, under those appearances, a tremendous significance, which human sagacity could not uncover. My heart sunk within me when I reflected that this was the father of my Clarice. He by whose cruelty her mother was torn from the injoyment of untarnished honour, and consigned to infamy and an untimely grave: He by whom herself was abandoned in the helplessness of infancy, and left to be the prey of obdurate avarice, and the victim of wretches who traffic in virgin innocence: Who had done all that in him lay to devote her youth to guilt and misery. What were the limits of his power? How may he exert the parental prerogatives?

To sleep, while these images were haunting me, was impossible. I passed the night in continual motion. I strode, without ceasing, across the floor of my

7. Worm, sore.

apartment. My mind was wrought to an higher pitch than I had ever before experienced. The occasion, accurately considered, was far from justifying the ominous inquietudes which I then felt. How then should I account for them?

Sarsefield probably enjoyed his usual slumber. His repose might not be perfectly serene, but when he ruminated on impending or possible calamities, his tongue did not cleave to his mouth, his throat was not parched with unquenchable thirst, he was not incessantly stimulated to employ his superfluous fertility of thought in motion. If I trembled for the safety of her whom I loved, and whose safety was endangered by being the daughter of this miscreant, had he not equal reason to fear for her whom he also loved, and who, as the sister of this ruffian, was encompassed by the most alarming perils. Yet he probably was calm while I was harassed by anxieties.

Alas! The difference was easily explained. Such was the beginning of a series ordained to hurry me to swift destruction. Such were the primary tokens of the presence of that power by whose accursed machinations I was destined to fall. You are startled at this declaration. It is one to which you have been little accustomed. Perhaps you regard it merely as an effusion of phrenzy. I know what I am saying. I do not build upon conjectures and surmises. I care not indeed for your doubts. Your conclusion may be fashioned at your pleasure. Would to heaven that my belief were groundless, and that I had no reason to believe my intellects to have been perverted by diabolical instigations.

I could procure no sleep that night. After Sarsefield's departure I did not even lie down. It seemed to me that I could not obtain the benefits of repose otherwise than by placing my lady beyond the possibility of danger.

I met Sarsefield the next day. In pursuance of the scheme which had been adopted by us on the preceding evening, a person was selected and commissioned to watch the appearance of Wiatte. The day passed as usual with respect to the lady. In the evening she was surrounded by a few friends. Into this number I was now admitted. Sarsefield and myself made a part of this company. Various topics were discussed with ease and sprightliness. Her societies were composed of both sexes, and seemed to have monopolized all the ingenuity and wit that existed in the metropolis.

After a slight repast the company dispersed. This separation took place earlier than usual on account of a slight indisposition in *Mrs. Lorimer.* Sarsefield and I went out together. We took that opportunity of examining our agent, and receiving no satisfaction from him, we dismissed him, for that night, enjoining him to hold himself in readiness for repeating the experiment to-morrow. My friend directed his steps homeward, and I proceeded to execute a commission, with which I had charged myself.

A few days before, a large sum had been deposited in the hands of a banker, for the use of my lady. It was the amount of a debt which had lately been recovered. It was lodged here for the purpose of being paid on demand of her or her agents. It was my present business to receive this money. I had deferred the performance of this engagement to this late hour, on account of certain preliminaries which were necessary to be adjusted.

Having received this money, I prepared to return home. The inquietude which had been occasioned by Sarsefield's intelligence, had not incapacitated me from performing my usual daily occupations. It was a theme, to which, at every interval of leisure from business or discourse, I did not fail to return. At those times I employed myself in examining the subject on all sides; in supposing particular emergencies, and delineating the conduct that was proper to be observed on each. My daily thoughts were, by no means, so fear-inspiring as the meditations of the night had been.

As soon as I left the banker's door, my meditations fell into this channel. I again reviewed the recent occurrences, and imagined the consequences likely to flow from them. My deductions were not, on this occasion, peculiarly distressful. The return of darkness had added nothing to my apprehensions. I regarded Wiatte merely as one against whose malice it was wise to employ the most vigilant precautions. In revolving these precautions nothing occurred that was new. The danger appeared without unusual aggravations, and the expedients that offered themselves to my choice, were viewed with a temper not more sanguine or despondent than before.

In this state of mind I began and continued my walk. The distance was considerable between my own habitation and that which I had left. My way lay chiefly through populous and well frequented streets. In one part of the way, however, it was at the option of the passenger either to keep along the large streets, or considerably to shorten the journey, by turning into a dark, crooked, and narrow lane. Being familiar with every part of this metropolis, and deeming it advisable to take the shortest and obscurest road, I turned into the alley. I proceeded without interruption to the next turning. One night officer, distinguished by his usual ensigns,[8] was the only person who passed me. I had gone three steps beyond when I perceived a man by my side. I had scarcely time to notice this circumstance, when an hoarse voice exclaimed. "Damn ye villain, ye're a dead man!"

At the same moment a pistol flashed at my ear, and a report followed. This, however, produced no other effect, than, for a short space, to overpower my senses. I staggered back, but did not fall.

The ball, as I afterwards discovered, had grazed my forehead, but without making any dangerous impression. The assassin, perceiving that his pistol had been ineffectual, muttered, in an enraged tone,—This shall do your business—At the same time, he drew a knife forth from his bosom.

I was able to distinguish this action by the rays of a distant lamp, which glistened on the blade. All this passed in an instant. The attack was so abrupt that my thoughts could not be suddenly recalled from the confusion into which they were thrown. My exertions were mechanical. My will might be said to be passive, and it was only by retrospect and a contemplation of consequences, that I became fully informed of the nature of the scene.

If my assailant had disappeared as soon as he had discharged the pistol, my state of extreme surprise might have slowly given place to resolution and activity. As it was, my sense was no sooner struck by the reflection from the blade, than my hand, as if by spontaneous energy, was thrust into my pocket. I drew forth a pistol—

He lifted up his weapon to strike, but it dropped from his powerless fingers. He fell and his groans informed me that I had managed my arms with more skill than my adversary. The noise of this encounter soon attracted spectators. Lights were brought and my antagonist discovered bleeding at my feet. I explained, as briefly as I was able, the scene which they witnessed. The prostrate person was raised by two men, and carried into a public house,[9] nigh at hand.

8. Military insignia.   9. Tavern, inn.

I had not lost my presence of mind. I, at once, perceived the propriety of administering assistance to the wounded man. I dispatched, therefore, one of the by-standers for a surgeon of considerable eminence, who lived at a small distance, and to whom I was well known. The man was carried into an inner apartment and laid upon the floor. It was not till now that I had a suitable opportunity of ascertaining who it was with whom I had been engaged. I now looked upon his face. The paleness of death could not conceal his well known features. It was Wiatte himself who was breathing his last groans at my feet! . . . .

The surgeon, whom I had summoned, attended; but immediately perceived the condition of his patient to be hopeless. In a quarter of an hour he expired. During this interval, he was insensible to all around him. I was known to the surgeon, the landlord and some of the witnesses. The case needed little explanation. The accident reflected no guilt upon me. The landlord was charged with the care of the corse till the morning, and I was allowed to return home, without further impediment.

Chapter VIII

Till now my mind had been swayed by the urgencies of this occasion. These reflections were excluded, which rushed tumultuously upon me, the moment I was at leisure to receive them. Without foresight of a previous moment, an entire change had been wrought in my condition.

I had been oppressed with a sense of the danger that flowed from the existence of this man. By what means the peril could be annihilated, and we be placed in security from his attempts, no efforts of mind could suggest. To devise these means, and employ them with success, demanded, as I conceived, the most powerful sagacity and the firmest courage. Now the danger was no more. The intelligence in which plans of mischief might be generated, was extinguished or flown. Lifeless were the hands ready to execute the dictates of that intelligence. The contriver of enormous evil, was, in one moment, bereft of the power and the will to injure. Our past tranquility had been owing to the belief of his death. Fear and dismay had resumed their dominion when the mistake was discovered. But now we might regain possession of our wonted[1] confidence. I had beheld with my own eyes the lifeless corpse of our implacable adversary. Thus, in a moment, had terminated his long and flagitious[2] career. His restless indignation, his malignant projects, that had so long occupied the stage, and been so fertile of calamity, were now at an end!

In the course of my meditations, the idea of the death of this man had occurred, and it bore the appearance of a desirable event. Yet it was little qualified to tranquilise my fears. In the long catalogue of contingencies, this, indeed, was to be found; but it was as little likely to happen as any other. It could not happen without a series of anterior events paving the way for it. If his death came from us, it must be the theme of design. It must spring from laborious circumvention and deep laid stratagems.

No. He was dead. I had killed him. What had I done? I had meditated nothing. I was impelled by an unconscious necessity. Had the assailant been my father the consequence would have been the same. My understanding had been neutral. Could it be? In a space so short, was it possible that so tremendous a deed had been executed? Was I not deceived by some

---

1. Usual.   2. Wicked, atrocious.

portentous vision? I had witnessed the convulsions and last agonies of Wyatte. He was no more, and I was his destroyer!

Such was the state of my mind for some time after this dreadful event. Previously to it I was calm, considerate, and self-collected. I marked the way that I was going. Passing objects were observed. If I adverted to the series of my own reflections, my attention was not seized and fastened by them. I could disengage myself at pleasure, and could pass, without difficulty, from attention to the world within, to the contemplation of that without.

Now my liberty, in this respect, was at an end. I was fettered, confounded, smitten with excess of thought, and laid prostrate with wonder! I no longer attended to my steps. When I emerged from my stupor, I found that I had trodden back the way which I had lately come, and had arrived within sight of the banker's door. I checked myself, and once more turned my steps homeward.

This seemed to be an hint for entering into new reflections. The deed, said I, is irretrievable. I have killed the brother of my patroness, the father of my love.

This suggestion was new. It instantly involved me in terror and perplexity. How shall I communicate the tidings? What effect will they produce? My lady's sagacity is obscured by the benevolence of her temper. Her brother was sordidly wicked. An hoary[3] ruffian, to whom the language of pity was as unintelligible as the gabble[4] of monkeys. His heart was fortified against compunction, by the atrocious habits of forty years: he lived only to interrupt her peace, to confute the promises of virtue, and convert to rancour and reproach the fair fame of fidelity.

He was her brother still. As an human being, his depravity was never beyond the health-restoring power of repentance. His heart, so long as it beat, was accessible to remorse. The singularity of his birth had made her regard this being as more intimately her brother, than would have happened in different circumstances. It was her obstinate persuasion that their fates were blended. The rumour of his death she had never credited. It was a topic of congratulation to her friends, but of mourning and distress to her. That he would one day reappear upon the stage, and assume the dignity of virtue, was a source of consolation with which she would never consent to part.

Her character was now known. When the doom of exile was pronounced upon him, she deemed it incumbent on her to vindicate herself from aspersions founded on misconceptions of her motives in refusing her interference. The manuscript, though unpublished, was widely circulated. None could resist her simple and touching eloquence, nor rise from the perusal without resigning his heart to the most impetuous impulses of admiration, and enlisting himself among the eulogists of her justice and her fortitude. This was the only monument, in a written form, of her genius. As such it was engraven on my memory. The picture that it described was the perpetual companion of my thoughts.

Alas! It had, perhaps, been well for me if it had been buried in eternal oblivion. I read in it the condemnation of my deed, the agonies she was preparing to suffer, and the indignation that would overflow upon the author of so signal a calamity.

I had rescued my life by the sacrifice of his. Whereas I should have died. Wretched and precipitate coward! What had become of my boasted gratitude?

---

3. White-haired, aged.   4. Chattering.

Such was the zeal that I had vowed to her. Such the services which it was the business of my life to perform. I had snatched her brother from existence. I had torn from her the hope which she so ardently and indefatigably cherished. From a contemptible and dastardly regard to my own safety I had failed in the moment of trial, and when called upon by heaven to evince the sincerity of my professions.

She had treated my professions lightly. My vows of eternal devotion she had rejected with lofty disinterestedness. She had arraigned my impatience of obligation as criminal; and condemned every scheme I had projected for freeing myself from the burthen which her beneficence had laid upon me. The impassioned and vehement anxiety with which, in former days, she had deprecated the vengeance of her lover against Wiatte, rung in my ears. My senses were shocked anew by the dreadful sounds "Touch not my brother. Wherever you meet with him, of whatever outrage he be guilty, suffer him to pass in safety. Despise me: abandon me: kill me. All this I can bear even from you, but spare, I implore you, my unhappy brother. The stroke that deprives him of life will not only have the same effect upon me, but will set my portion in everlasting misery."

To these supplications I had been deaf. It is true I had not rushed upon him unarmed, intending no injury nor expecting any. Of that degree of wickedness I was, perhaps; incapable. Alas! I have immersed myself sufficiently deep in crimes. I have trampled under foot every motive dear to the heart of honour. I have shewn myself unworthy the society of men.

Such were the turbulent suggestions of that moment. My pace slackened. I stopped and was obliged to support myself against a wall. The sickness that had seized my heart penetrated every part of my frame. There was but one thing wanting to complete my distraction. . . . My lady, said I, believed her fate to be blended with that of Wiatte. Who shall affirm that the persuasion is a groundless one. She had lived and prospered, notwithstanding the general belief that her brother was dead. She would not hearken to the rumour. Why? Because nothing less than indubitable evidence would suffice to convince her? Because the counter-intimation flowed from an infalible source? How can the latter supposition be confuted? Has she not predicted the event?

The period of terrible fulfillment has arrived. The same blow that bereaved *him* of life, has likewise ratified her doom.

She has been deceived. It is nothing more, perhaps, than a fond imagination. . . . It matters not. Who knows not the cogency of faith? That the pulses of life are at the command of the will? The bearer of these tidings will be the messenger of death. A fatal sympathy will seize her. She will shrink, and swoon, and perish at the news!

Fond and short-sighted wretch! This is the price thou hast given for security. In the rashness of thy thought thou said'st, Nothing is wanting but his death to restore us to confidence and safety. Lo! the purchase is made. Havock[5] and despair, that were restrained during his life, were let loose by his last sigh. Now only is destruction made sure. Thy lady, thy Clarice, thy friend, and thyself, are, by this act, involved in irretrievable and common ruin!

I started from my attitude. I was scarcely conscious of any transition. The interval was fraught with stupor and amazement. It seemed as if my senses had been hushed in sleep, while the powers of locomotion were uncon-

---

5. I.e., havoc.

sciously exerted to bear me to my chamber. By whatever means the change was effected, there I was. . . .

I have been able to proceed thus far. I can scarcely believe the testimony of my memory that assures me of this. My task is almost executed, but whence shall I obtain strength enough to finish it? What I have told is light as gossamer,[6] compared with the insupportable and crushing horrors of that which is to come. Heaven, in token of its vengeance, will enable me to proceed. It is fitting that my scene should thus close.

My fancy began to be infected with the errors of my understanding. The mood into which my mind was plunged was incapable of any propitious intermission. All within me was tempestuous and dark. My ears were accessible to no sounds but those of shrieks and lamentations. It was deepest midnight, and all the noises of a great metropolis were hushed. Yet I listened as if to catch some strain of the dirge that was begun. Sable[7] robes, sobs and a dreary solemnity encompassed me on all sides. I was haunted to despair by images of death, imaginary clamours, and the train of funeral pageantry. I seemed to have passed forward to a distant era of my life. The effects which were to come were already realized. The foresight of misery created it, and set me in the midst of that hell which I feared.

From a paroxysm like this the worst might reasonably be dreaded, yet the next step to destruction was not suddenly taken. I paused on the brink of the precipice, as if to survey the depth of that phrensy that invaded me; was able to ponder on the scene, and deliberate, in a state that partook of calm, on the circumstances of my situation. My mind was harrassed by the repetition of one idea. Conjecture deepened into certainty. I could place the object in no light which did not corroborate the persuasion that, in the act committed, I had ensured the destruction of my lady. At length my mind, somewhat relieved from the tempest of my fears, began to trace and analize the consequences which I dreaded.

The fate of Wiatte would inevitably draw along with it that of his sister. In what way would this effect be produced? Were they linked together by a sympathy whose influence was independent of sensible communication? Could she arrive at a knowledge of his miserable end by other than verbal means? I had heard of such extraordinary co-partnerships in being and modes of instantaneous intercourse among beings locally distant. Was this a new instance of the subtlety of mind? Had she already endured his agonies, and like him already ceased to breathe.

Every hair bristled at this horrible suggestion. But the force of sympathy might be chimerical. Buried in sleep, or engaged in careless meditation, the instrument by which her destiny might be accomplished, was the steel of an assassin. A series of events, equally beyond the reach of foresight, with those which had just happened, might introduce, with equal abruptness, a similar disaster. What, at that moment, was her condition? Reposing in safety in her chamber, as her family imagined. But were they not deceived? Was she not a mangled corpse? Whatever were her situation, it could not be ascertained, except by extraordinary means, till the morning. Was it wise to defer the scrutiny till then? Why not instantly investigate the truth?

These ideas passed rapidly through my mind. A considerable portion of time and amplification of phrase are necessary to exhibit, verbally, ideas

---

6. Light, thin fabric.   7. Black.

contemplated in a space of incalculable brevity. With the same rapidity I conceived the resolution of determining the truth of my suspicions. All the family, but myself, were at rest. Winding passages would conduct me, without danger of disturbing them, to the hall from which double staircases ascended. One of these led to a saloon[8] above, on the east side of which was a door that communicated with a suit of rooms, occupied by the lady of the mansion. The first was an antechamber,[9] in which a female servant usually lay. The second was the lady's own bed-chamber. This was a sacred recess, with whose situation, relative to the other apartments of the building, I was well acquainted, but of which I knew nothing from my own examination, having never been admitted into it.

Thither I was now resolved to repair. I was not deterred by the sanctity of the place and hour. I was insensible to all consequences but the removal of my doubts. Not that my hopes were balanced by my fears. That the same tragedy had been performed in her chamber and in the street, nothing hindered me from believing with as much cogency as if my own eyes had witnessed it, but the reluctance with which we admit a detestable truth.

To terminate a state of intolerable suspense, I resolved to proceed forthwith to her chamber. I took the light and paced, with no interruption, along the galleries.[1] I used no precaution. If I had met a servant or robber, I am not sure that I should have noticed him. My attention was too perfectly engrossed to allow me to spare any to a casual object. I cannot affirm that no one observed me. This, however, was probable from the distribution of the dwelling. It consisted of a central edifice and two wings, one of which was appropriated to domestics, and the other, at the extremity of which my apartment was placed, comprehended a library, and rooms for formal, and social, and literary conferences. These, therefore, were deserted at night, and my way lay along these. Hence it was not likely that my steps would be observed.

I proceeded to the hall. The principal parlour was beneath her chamber. In the confusion of my thoughts I mistook one for the other. I rectified, as soon as I detected my mistake. I ascended, with a beating heart, the staircase. The door of the antichamber was unfastened. I entered, totally regardless of disturbing the girl who slept within. The bed which she occupied was concealed by curtains. Whether she were there, I did not stop to examine. I cannot recollect that any tokens were given of wakefulness or alarm. It was not till I reached the door of her own apartment that my heart began to falter.

It was now that the momentousness of the question I was about to decide, rushed with its genuine force, upon my apprehension. Appaled and aghast, I had scarcely power to move the bolt. If the imagination of her death was not to be supported, how should I bear the spectacle of wounds and blood? Yet this was reserved for me. A few paces would set me in the midst of a scene, of which I was the abhorred contriver. Was it right to proceed? There were still the remnants of doubt. My forebodings might possibly be groundless. All within might be safety and serenity. A respite might be gained from the execution of an irrevocable sentence. What could I do? Was not any thing easy to endure in comparison with the agonies of suspense? If I could not obviate the evil I must bear it, but the torments of suspense were susceptible of remedy.

I drew back the bolt, and entered with the reluctance of fear, rather than the cautiousness of guilt. I could not lift my eyes from the ground. I advanced

8. Large room.
9. Entryway.

1. Balcony.

to the middle of the room. Not a sound like that of the dying saluted my ear. At length, shaking off the fetters of hopelessness, I looked up. . . .

I saw nothing calculated to confirm my fears. Every where there reigned quiet and order. My heart leaped with exultation. Can it be, said I, that I have been betrayed with shadows? . . . . But this is not sufficient. . . .

Within an alcove was the bed that belonged to her. If her safety were inviolate, it was here that she reposed. What remained to convert torment-ing doubt into ravishing certainty? I was insensible to the perils of my pres-ent situation. If she, indeed, were there, would not my intrusion awaken her? She would start and perceive me, at this hour, standing at her bed-side. How should I account for an intrusion so unexampled[2] and audacious? I could not communicate my fears. I could not tell her that the blood with which my hands were stained had flowed from the wounds of her brother.

My mind was inaccessible to such considerations. They did not even modify my predominant idea. Obstacles like these, had they existed, would have been trampled under foot.

Leaving the lamp, that I bore, on the table, I approached the bed. I slowly drew aside the curtain and beheld her tranquilly slumbering. I listened, but so profound was her sleep that not even her breathings could be overheard. I dropped the curtain and retired.

How blissful and mild were the illuminations of my bosom at this discov-ery. A joy that surpassed all utterance succeeded the fierceness of despera-tion. I stood, for some moments, wrapt in delightful contemplation. Alas! It was a luminous but transient interval. The madness, to whose black sugges-tions it bore so strong a contrast, began now to make sensible approaches on my understanding.

True, said I, she lives. Her slumber is serene and happy. She is blind to her approaching destiny. Some hours will at least be rescued from anguish and death. When she wakes the phantom that soothed her will vanish. The tidings cannot be withheld from her. The murderer of thy brother cannot hope to enjoy thy smiles. Those ravishing accents, with which thou hast used to greet me, will be changed. Scouling[3] and reproaches, the invectives of thy anger and the maledictions of thy justice will rest upon my head.

What is the blessing which I made the theme of my boastful arrogance? This interval of being and repose is momentary. She will awake but only to perish at the spectacle of my ingratitude. She will awake only to the con-sciousness of instantly impending death. When she again sleeps she will wake no more. I her son, I, whom the law of my birth doomed to poverty and hardship, but whom her unsolicited beneficence snatched from those evils, and endowed with the highest good known to intelligent beings, the consola-tions of science and the blandishments of affluence; to whom the darling of her life, the offspring in whom are faithfully preserved the linaments of its angelic mother, she has not denied!. . . . What is the recompense that I have made? How have I discharged the measureless debt of gratitude to which she is entitled? Thus!. . . .

Cannot my guilt be extenuated? Is there not a good that I can do thee? Must I perpetrate unmingled evil? Is the province assigned me that of an infernal emissary, whose efforts are concentred in a single purpose and that purpose a malignant one? I am the author of thy calamities. What-ever misery is reserved for thee, I am the source whence it flows. Can I

2. Unusual.   3. Scowling.

not set bounds to the stream? Cannot I prevent thee from returning to a consciousness which, till it ceases to exist, will not cease to be rent[4] and mangled?

Yes. It is in my power to screen thee from the coming storm: to accelerate thy journey to rest. I will do it. . . .

The impulse was not to be resisted. I moved with the suddenness of lightning. Armed with a pointed implement that lay . . . it was a dagger. As I set down the lamp, I struck the edge. Yet I saw it not, or noticed it not till I needed its assistance. By what accident it came hither, to what deed of darkness it had already been subservient, I had no power to inquire. I stepped to the table and seized it.

The time which this action required was insufficient to save me. My doom was ratified by powers which no human energies can counterwork. . . . Need I go farther? Did you entertain any imagination of so frightful a catastrophe? I am overwhelmed by turns with dismay and with wonder. I am prompted by turns to tear my heart from my breast, and deny faith to the verdict of my senses.

Was it I that hurried to the deed? No. It was the dæmon that possessed me. My limbs were guided to the bloody office by a power foreign and superior to mine. I had been defrauded, for a moment, of the empire of my muscles. A little moment for that sufficed.

If my destruction had not been decreed why was the image of Clarice so long excluded? Yet why do I say long? The fatal resolution was conceived, and I hastened to the execution, in a period too brief for more than itself to be viewed by the intellect.

What then? Were my hands embrued in this precious blood? Was it to this extremity of horror that my evil genius was determined to urge me? Too surely this was his purpose; too surely I was qualified to be its minister.

I lifted the weapon. Its point was aimed at the bosom of the sleeper. The impulse was given. . . .

At the instant a piercing shriek was uttered behind me, and a stretched-out hand, grasping the blade, made it swerve widely from its aim. It descended, but without inflicting a wound. Its force was spent upon the bed.

O! for words to paint that stormy transition! I loosed my hold of the dagger. I started back, and fixed eyes of frantic curiosity on the author of my rescue. He that interposed to arrest my deed, that started into being and activity at a moment so pregnant with fate, without tokens of his purpose or his coming being previously imparted, could not, me-thought, be less than divinity.

The first glance that I darted on this being corroborated my conjecture. It was the figure and the linaments of Mrs. Lorimer. Neglegently habited in flowing and brilliant white, with features bursting with terror and wonder, the likeness of that being who was stretched upon the bed, now stood before me.

All that I am able to conceive of angel was comprised in the moral constitution of this woman. That her genius had overleaped all bounds, and interposed to save her, was no audacious imagination. In the state in which my mind then was no other belief than this could occupy the first place.

My tongue was tied. I gazed by turns upon her who stood before me, and her who lay upon the bed, and who, awakened by the shriek that had been uttered, now opened her eyes. She started from her pillow, and, by assuming a new and more distinct attitude, permitted me to recognize *Clarice herself!*

---

4. Torn, cut.

Three days before, I had left her, beside the bed of a dying friend, at a solitary mansion in the mountains of Donnegal. Here it had been her resolution to remain till her friend should breathe her last. Fraught with this persuasion; knowing this to be the place and hour of repose of my lady, hurried forward by the impetuosity of my own conceptions, deceived by the faint gleam which penetrated through the curtain and imperfectly irradiated features which bore, at all times, a powerful resemblance to those of Mrs. Lorimer, I had rushed to the brink of this terrible precipice!

Why did I linger on the verge? Why, thus perilously situated, did I not throw myself headlong? The steel was yet in my hand. A single blow would have pierced my heart, and shut out from my remembrance and foresight the past and the future?

The moment of insanity had gone by, and I was once more myself. Instead of regarding the act which I had meditated as the dictate of compassion or of justice, it only added to the sum of my ingratitude, and gave wings to the whirlwind that was sent to bear me to perdition.

Perhaps I was influenced by a sentiment which I had not leisure to distribute into parts. My understanding was, no doubt, bewildered in the maze of consequences which would spring from my act. How should I explain my coming hither in this murderous guise, my arm lifted to destroy the idol of my soul, and the darling child of my patroness? In what words should I unfold the tale of Wiatte, and enumerate the motives that terminated in the present scene? What penalty had not my infatuation and cruelty deserved? What could I less than turn the dagger's point against my own bosom?

A second time, the blow was thwarted and diverted. Once more this beneficent interposer held my arm from the perpetration of a new iniquity. Once more frustrated the instigations of that dæmon, of whose malice a mysterious destiny had consigned me to be the sport and the prey.

Every new moment added to the sum of my inexpiable guilt. Murder was succeeded, in an instant, by the more detestable enormity of suicide. She, to whom my ingratitude was flagrant in proportion to the benefits of which she was the author, had now added to her former acts, that of rescuing me from the last of mischiefs.

I threw the weapon on the floor. The zeal which prompted her to seize my arm, this action occasioned to subside, and to yield place to those emotions which this spectacle was calculated to excite. She watched me in silence, and with an air of ineffable solicitude. Clarice, governed by the instinct of modesty, wrapt her bosom and face in the bedclothes, and testified her horror by vehement, but scarcely articulate exclamations.

I moved forward, but my steps were random and tottering. My thoughts were fettered by reverie, and my gesticulations destitute of meaning. My tongue faltered without speaking, and I felt as if life and death were struggling within me for the mastery.

My will, indeed, was far from being neutral in this contest. To such as I, annihilation is the supreme good. To shake off the ills that fasten on us by shaking off existence, is a lot which the system of nature has denied to man. By escaping from life, I should be delivered from this scene, but should only rush into a world of retribution, and be immersed in new agonies.

I was yet to live. No instrument of my deliverance was within reach. I was powerless. To rush from the presence of these women, to hide me forever from their scrutiny, and their upbraiding, to snatch from their minds all traces of the existence of Clithero, was the scope of unutterable longings.

Urged to flight by every motive of which my nature was susceptible, I was yet rooted to the spot. Had the pause been only to be interrupted by me, it would have lasted forever.

At length, the lady, clasping her hands and lifting them, exclaimed, in a tone melting into pity and grief:

Clithero! what is this? How came you hither and why?

I struggled for utterance: I came to murder you. Your brother has perished by my hands. Fresh from the commission of this deed, I have hastened hither, to perpetrate the same crime upon you.

My brother! replied the lady, with new vehemence, O! say not so! I have just heard of his return from Sarsefield and that he lives.

He is dead, repeated I, with fierceness: I know it. It was I that killed him.

Dead! she faintly articulated, And by thee Clithero? O! cursed chance that hindered thee from killing me also! Dead! Then is the omen fulfilled! Then am I undone! Lost forever!

Her eyes now wandered from me, and her countenance sunk into a wild and rueful expression. Hope was utterly extinguished in her heart, and life forsook her at the same moment. She sunk upon the floor pallid and breathless. . . .

How she came into possession of this knowledge I know not. It is possible that Sarsefield had repented of concealment, and, in the interval that passed between our separation and my encounter with Wiatte, had returned, and informed her of the reappearance of this miscreant

Thus then was my fate consummated. I was rescued from destroying her by a dagger, only to behold her perish by the tidings which I brought. Thus was every omen of mischief and misery fulfilled. Thus was the enmity of Wiatte, rendered efficacious, and the instrument of his destruction, changed into the executioner of his revenge.

Such is the tale of my crimes. It is not for me to hope that the curtain of oblivion will ever shut out the dismal spectacle. It will haunt me forever. The torments that grow out of it, can terminate only with the thread of my existence, but that I know full well will never end. Death is but a shifting of the scene, and the endless progress of eternity, which, to the good, is merely the perfection of felicity, is, to the wicked, an accumulation of woe. The self-destroyer is his own enemy. this has ever been my opinion. Hitherto it has influenced my action. Now, though the belief continues, its influence on my conduct is annihilated. I am no stranger to the depth of that abyss, into which I shall plunge. No matter. Change is precious for its own sake.

Well: I was still to live. My abode must be somewhere fixed. My conduct was henceforth the result of a perverse and rebellious principle. I banished myself forever from my native soil. I vowed never more to behold the face of my Clarice, to abandon my friends, my books, all my wonted labours, and accustomed recreations.

I was neither ashamed nor afraid. I considered not in what way the justice of the country would affect me. It merely made no part of my contemplations. I was not embarrassed by the choice of expedients, for trammeling up[5] the visible consequences and for eluding suspicion. The idea of abjuring my country, and flying forever from the hateful scene, partook, to my apprehension, of the vast, the boundless, and strange: of plunging from the height of fortune to

5. Binding up.

obscurity and indigence, corresponded with my present state of mind. It was of a piece with the tremendous and wonderful events that had just happened.

These were the images that haunted me, while I stood speechlessly gazing at the ruin before me. I heard a noise from without, or imagined that I heard it. My reverie was broken, and my muscular power restored. I descended into the street, through doors of which I possessed one set of keys, and hurried by the shortest way beyond the precincts of the city. I had laid no plan. My conceptions, with regard to the future, were shapeless and confused. Successive incidents supplied me with a clue, and suggested, as they rose, the next step to be taken.

I threw off the garb of affluence, and assumed a beggar's attire. That I had money about me for the accomplishment of my purposes was wholly accidental. I travelled along the coast, and when I arrived at one town, knew not why I should go further; but my restlessness was unabated, and change was some relief. I at length arrived at Belfast. A vessel was preparing for America. I embraced eagerly the opportunity of passing into a new world. I arrived at Philadelphia. As soon as I landed I wandered hither, and was content to wear out my few remaining days in the service of Inglefield.

I have no friends. Why should I trust my story to another? I have no solicitude about concealment; but who is there who will derive pleasure or benefit from my rehearsal? And why should I expatiate on so hateful a theme? Yet now have I consented to this. I have confided in you the history of my disasters. I am not fearful of the use that you may be disposed to make of it. I shall quickly set myself beyond the reach of human tribunals. I shall relieve the ministers of law from the trouble of punishing. The recent events which induced you to summon me to this conference, have likewise determined me to make this disclosure.

I was not aware, for some time, of my perturbed sleep. No wonder that sleep cannot soothe miseries like mine: that I am alike infested by memory in wakefulness and slumber. Yet I was anew distressed at the discovery that my thoughts found their way to my lips, without my being conscious of it, and that my steps wandered forth unknowingly and without the guidance of my will.

The story you have told is not incredible. The disaster to which you allude did not fail to excite my regret. I can still weep over the untimely fall of youth and worth. I can no otherwise account for my frequenting this shade than by the distant resemblance which the death of this man bore to that of which I was the perpetrator. This resemblance occurred to me at first. If time were able to weaken the impression which was produced by my crime, this similitude was adapted to revive and inforce them.

The wilderness, and the cave to which you followed me, were familiar to my sunday rambles. Often have I indulged in audible griefs on the cliffs of that valley. Often have I brooded over my sorrows in the recesses of that cavern. This scene is adapted to my temper. Its mountainous asperities supply me with images of desolation and seclusion, and its headlong streams lull me into temporary forgetfulness of mankind.

I comprehend you. You suspect me of concern in the death of Waldegrave. You could not do otherwise. The conduct that you have witnessed was that of a murderer. I will not upbraid you for your suspicions, though I have bought exemption from them at an high price.

1799

American Literature
1820–1865

AN AMERICAN RENAISSANCE?

This volume of *The Norton Anthology of American Literature* presents works by Ralph Waldo Emerson, Edgar Allan Poe, Frederick Douglass, Nathaniel Hawthorne, Herman Melville, Walt Whitman, Emily Dickinson, Henry David Thoreau, Harriet Beecher Stowe, and their contemporaries—the writers generally regarded as central to our understanding of American literary traditions from the nineteenth century to the present day. The writers in this volume, particularly those who began publishing after 1830, are often celebrated as a group for having sparked a literary renaissance that helped American writing to achieve its first significant maturity. But the authors of this period were not always valued so highly by literary historians. In the early decades of the twentieth century, American literature was generally not taught in American universities, or else it was taught in subordinate relation to English literature, which was viewed as having an infinitely superior literary tradition. Among the important critical books that helped change this situation was F. O. Matthiessen's *American Renaissance: Art and Expression in the Age of Emerson and Whitman* (1941). Matthiessen gave American literature what had always been integral to the study of English literature: a Renaissance. England may have had Spenser, Shakespeare, and Donne, but America, Matthiessen argued, had Emerson, Thoreau, Hawthorne, Melville, and Whitman. According to the critics who helped to establish American literature as a field of study, the "Renaissance" was inspired during the 1830s by the writings of Emerson and came into its own in the 1850s with such

George Innes, *The Lackawanna Valley* (detail), 1855. For more information about this painting, see the color insert in this volume.

major works as Hawthorne's *The Scarlet Letter* (1850), Melville's *Moby-Dick* (1851), Thoreau's *Walden* (1854), and Whitman's *Leaves of Grass* (1855). These and other key texts have an important place in this anthology, which owes a large debt to mid-twentieth-century formulations of the literary significance of the antebellum period.

Nevertheless, over the past several decades, the idea of an American Renaissance has come under considerable challenge. For instance, critics have noted that Matthiessen and others tended to exclude the significant contributions of women and minority writers, especially African Americans, and consequently closed off considerations of the wide range of writing developing in the United States during this time. Up to the 1970s and 1980s, critics working in the field of American literary studies generally had little interest in popular authors of the period, such as the poets Lydia Sigourney and Henry Wadsworth Longfellow or the novelists Fanny Fern and Harriet Beecher Stowe, and little interest in publications outside of Massachusetts and New York. Critics have also faulted exponents of an American Renaissance for failing to attend to slavery, immigration, and other political and social contexts, all of which had a significant influence on the writing of the time, and for overemphasizing the separateness of English and American literary traditions, given that writers on both sides of the Atlantic were working in the same language and reading each other's works.

And yet, granting all of the shortcomings of the concept of an American Renaissance, one could say about the term what Benjamin Franklin in his *Autobiography* says about his efforts to subdue his pride: "Disguise it, struggle with it, beat it down, stifle it, mortify it as much as one pleases, it is still alive, and will every now and then peep out and show itself." For better or worse, the notion of an American Renaissance has continued to exert an enormous influence on the way that the literature of this period is understood, even though the idea of a literal renaissance (or rebirth) makes little sense in relation to a national literary tradition that was still in the process of coming into being.

The idea of an American Renaissance has been so influential in part because the literature of this period truly was crucial to the development of American literary traditions, at once building on writings that had preceded it and pointing to future possibilities. When this literature is viewed in much broader contexts and appreciated in its full complexity, its centrality to American literary history becomes even more evident. But the literature of the 1830s through the 1850s, and especially that of the 1850s, cannot be disconnected from the decades immediately preceding it, a time when many U.S. cultural commentators were calling on Americans to produce literary texts worthy of a great nation. The American literary renaissance could be viewed retrospectively as a fulfillment of the repeated calls, from the 1770s on, for such an exemplary literature, though it may also be said that early expressions of American literary nationalism reveal the conflicts and concerns attending the development of U.S. nationalism from the 1790s to the 1820s—conflicts and concerns that would continue to engage writers of the antebellum period. In fact, it was in the decade of the 1820s rather than the 1850s that critics of the time generally agreed that the United States *had* produced writers worthy of a great nation and agreed as well on the identity of the most important writers—namely, Washington Irving, William Cullen Bryant, James Fenimore Cooper, and Catharine Maria Sedgwick. No such consensus existed in the 1850s, as writers like Melville, Thoreau, and Whitman had very small readerships; Dickinson, who would publish just a small number of poems in newspapers and miscellanies, was basically unknown; and Hawthorne's most enthusiastic readers were limited to a relatively small number of people in the Northeast. The 1820s can be seen as the first great culmination of American literary nationalism, a decade that helped spawn the "Renaissance" to come.

AMERICAN LITERARY NATIONALISM AND THE 1820s

From the moment of the successful outcome of the American Revolution, literary nationalism had an important place in the emergent culture of the new nation. Convinced that a sign of a great nation was the existence of a great national literature, patriotic writers of the early republic attempted to produce "American" works as quickly as possible; such epic poems as Timothy Dwight's *The Conquest of Canaan* (1785) and Joel Barlow's *The Columbiad* (1807) can be regarded as simultaneously bombastic and impressive achievements along these lines. From a different but still highly nationalistic perspective, Charles Brockden Brown proclaimed in the preface to his 1799 novel *Edgar Huntly* that he would make use of native materials—"incidents of Indian hostility, and the perils of the western wilderness"—to show how the United States offers "themes to the moral painter" that "differ essentially from those which exist in Europe." But even as writers of the time boldly sought to produce distinctively American works, there was a sense during the 1790s and early 1800s—a period haunted by the French Revolution's Reign of Terror and the subsequent Napoleonic Wars—that American nationality was provisional, vulnerable, fragile. The War of 1812, which emerged from ongoing conflicts with England, can therefore be seen as a war that, at least in part, spoke to Americans' desires to put an end to national anxiety by in effect reenacting the American Revolution against England and winning a victory once and for all. In its own time, this war was labeled "The Second War with England." When English troops stormed the District of Columbia in 1814 and burned the Capitol and the White House, Americans' grim sense of vulnerability was underscored. But all that changed when Andrew Jackson's outnumbered troops defeated the English army at New Orleans in 1815, shortly after a peace treaty had officially ended the second major war between the two nations. From New Orleans there emerged a national mythology of the republican hero—the antiaristocratic, antimonarchical person from an obscure background—who incarnated the strengths and virtues of the U.S. nation. The immediate beneficiary of that mythology, Andrew Jackson, would achieve further acclaim among his white compatriots for fighting the Indians in the Floridas. When he was eventually elected president in 1828, he was regarded as the incarnation of the democratic spirit of the age. Jacksonian democratic energies and ideals would have an enormous impact on the writing that would emerge in the United States over the next several decades, both in its celebration of the capacities of ordinary people and its hostility to unearned social distinction and inherited wealth.

Well before 1828, however, the optimistic nationalism that found expression after the War of 1812 led to renewed efforts to develop a distinctively American literature worthy of a democratic republic that fully expected to take its place among the great nations of the world. Calls for a new American literature appeared regularly in the pages of the *North American Review*, an influential journal founded in Boston shortly after the war ended in 1815. In the journal's November 1815 issue, for instance, the critic Walter Channing urged his countrymen to produce "a literature of our own," even as he worried over the difficulties of developing such a literature in relation to English literary traditions. As the critic Edward Tyrell Channing remarked in an 1816 issue of the journal, a national literature "will have but feeble claims to excellence and distinction, when it stoops to put on foreign ornament and manner, and to adopt from other nations, images, allusions, and a metaphorical language, which are perfectly unmeaning and sickly out of their birth-place." Similarly, in his 1818 book, *An Essay on American Poetry*, the critic Solyman Brown asserted that Americans could not claim to have won the War of 1812 until that victory manifested itself in the production of a distinctively American literature: "The proudest freedom to which a nation can aspire, not excepting even political independence, is found in complete emancipation from literary thralldom." From the perspective of British literary nationalists, such emancipation would be slow in coming, given that, as they regularly maintained, American literature would always be overshadowed and subsumed by the long literary tradition of the parent country. Making just such an argument, the English critic Sydney Smith, in an oft-quoted attack on American literary nationalists, sarcastically demanded in an 1820 issue of the *Edinburgh Review*: "In the four quarters of the globe, who reads an American book?" As it turned out, Smith posed his question at an inopportune moment, for Americans could gloatingly respond that thousands of people in the United States and England were beginning to read American books. Not only were Charles Brockden Brown's novels of the 1790s achieving a new popularity in England but, right around the time of Smith's attack, the publication of Irving's *The Sketch Book* (1819–20), Bryant's *Poems* (1821), and Cooper's *The Spy* (1821) and *The Pioneers* (1823) suggested to many in the United States, England, and elsewhere that a worthy American literature *had* begun to take its place among the literatures of the more established nations.

It is worth underscoring, however, that during the 1820s Americans took pride in a literature that they regarded not necessarily as distinct from but rather in conversation with English literary traditions. Given the language that the countries shared, most American literary nationalists simply hoped that American writers could take their places alongside their British siblings or cousins. After all, literate Americans delighted in Spenser's *The Faerie Queen*, Shakespeare's plays, Milton's *Paradise Lost*, the essays of Joseph Addison and Richard Steele, and the poetry of Alexander Pope; and in the early decades of the nineteenth century they were reading the romantic poets Wordsworth and Byron (among others) and, beginning in 1814 with the publication of *Waverley*, the historical novels of Walter Scott. Moreover, Irving's *The Sketch Book* had important sources in the essays of Addison and Steele; Bryant's poetry had important sources in Wordsworth; and Cooper's novels had important sources in Scott. Cooper objected to being termed the "American Scott," but the label would ultimately have been viewed as testimony to his novelistic mastery. For the most part, American writers of this time had a sophisticated understanding of their relationship to British and other literary traditions and would have regarded as nonsense the idea that they were expected to create a completely separate American literature.

They would have also regarded as nonsense the idea that American literature should be uncritically patriotic. One of the more notable features of the acclaimed 1820s writings of Irving, Bryant, and Cooper (along with the writings of their contemporaries such as Sedgwick, Sigourney, and Lydia Maria Child) was just how critical these writings could be of early national culture. Much of Irving's *The Sketch Book* is set in Europe, and though an often playfully ironic narrative voice of the American traveler holds the volume together, that persona is generally reverential toward the European historical past while casting a skeptical eye on a boastful U.S. culture that seems to have little interest in art and history. In his historical fictions of that decade, Cooper is similarly skeptical of U.S. claims to progress, presenting a demythified vision of the American Revolution in *The Spy*, and in *The Pioneers* depicting democratic energies as sometimes a threat to orderly government and the natural environment. In Cooper, as in Bryant, Sedgwick, and other writers of the period, visions of historical progress are tempered by the notion, widely disseminated during the Enlightenment and beyond, that all mighty nations must eventually fall. At a time when Indian removal was becoming national policy on the basis that, as many Americans believed, the day of the Indian was over, Cooper and Bryant suggested in works like *The Last of the Mohicans* and "The Prairies" that the U.S. nation was equally subject to the historical cycle of rise and decline.

Adding to uncertainty about the future was the fact that the very shape, size, and demographic character of the nation were in flux. Jefferson's acquisition of the Louisiana Territory from France in 1803 doubled the size of the nation's total acreage, but its borders remained ill-defined, and the purchase soon raised difficult questions about how to balance the admission of new free states and new slave states in the expanding republic. The Missouri Compromises of 1820–21 appeared to resolve the political question by admitting Missouri as a slave state, Maine as a free state, and banning slavery in the northern reaches of the Louisiana Territory, but sectional conflict on slavery, states' rights, internal improvements, national tariffs, and other matters would continue to intensify in the wake of a compromise that was supposed to put an end to such conflicts. The assertion by South Carolina's legislature in 1832 of its right to "nullify" federal policies was one among many signs of the lack of national consensus during the two decades (1815–35) that have been celebrated by some historians as the era of good feelings.

Still, in the wake of the War of 1812, there was a shared belief among the major writers of the time that, as Brockden Brown had suggested back in the 1790s, the United States did have distinct materials with which to develop a distinctive (though not separate) national literature. Authors such as Irving, Cooper, and Bryant placed a special emphasis on the importance of the natural landscape for the development of national character, finding in the relatively unspoiled vast lands of the continent a nurturing ground for the spiritual growth of a nation that, they sometimes suggested, could possibly emerge as "better" than any of those of long-settled Europe. These writers shared the vision of the popular Hudson River landscape painters of the antebellum period, New Yorkers like Thomas Cole and Asher Durand, who regularly portrayed individuals dwarfed by mountains and forests in a vast

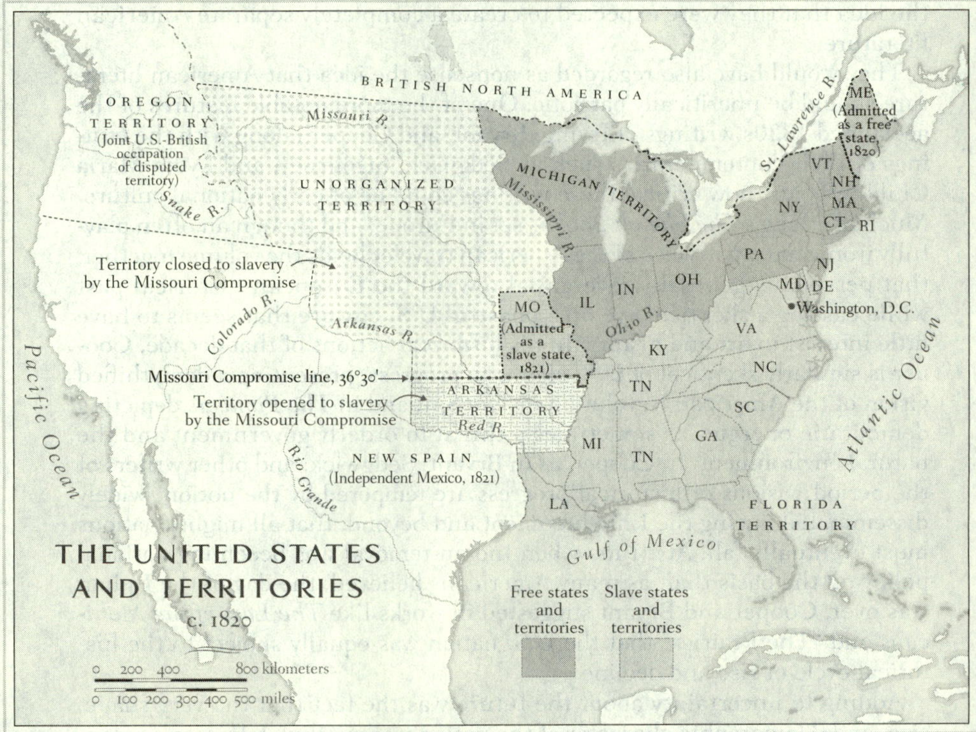

THE UNITED STATES
AND TERRITORIES
c. 1820

BRITISH NORTH AMERICA

OREGON
TERRITORY
(Joint U.S.-British
occupation
of disputed
territory)

Missouri R.

UNORGANIZED
TERRITORY

Snake R.

Territory closed to slavery
by the Missouri Compromise

Colorado R.

Arkansas R.

Missouri Compromise line, 36°30'

Territory opened to slavery
by the Missouri Compromise

ARKANSAS
TERRITORY
Red R.

NEW SPAIN
(Independent Mexico, 1821)

Rio Grande

MICHIGAN TERRITORY

Mississippi R.

MO
(Admitted
as a
slave state,
1821)

IL

IN

OH

Ohio R.

MI

TN

LA

Pacific Ocean

Pacific Ocean

ME
(Admitted
as a free
state,
1820)

St. Lawrence R.

VT
NH
NY   MA
CT   RI

PA

NJ
MD DE
•Washington, D.C.

VA

KY

TN

NC

SC

GA

FLORIDA
TERRITORY

Gulf of Mexico

Atlantic Ocean

Free states
and
territories

Slave states
and
territories

0   200   400   800 kilometers
0 100 200 300 400 500 miles

and unsettled nature where God's spirit could be apprehended. Cole may have identified republican decline as the ultimate historical reality (see his 1836 "The Course of Empire: Desolation," in the color insert to this volume), but most writers and artists of the period, including Cole, imagined that decline as hundreds, if not thousands, of years away. The American literary nationalism of the 1820s, like the American literary nationalism of the 1790s, explored difficult questions about the nation's future, about its strengths and vulnerabilities, and about its character and potential as a democratic republic. But the emergence of internationally acclaimed writers like Irving, Bryant, and Cooper also helped open up new literary opportunities for American writers, even as they would continue to have to compete with English writers for markets and prestige.

THE LITERARY MARKETPLACE IN AN
EXPANDING NATION

By the second decade of the nineteenth century, Americans had easy access to contemporary British literature and criticism. Crossing the Atlantic on sailing ships and by the late 1830s on steamers, books or magazines first published in London could be distributed or republished almost immediately in the larger coastal cities—Boston, New York, Philadelphia, and Charleston. Volumes of poetry by the Scottish poet Robert Burns and by the English Romantics (Wordsworth, Coleridge, Byron, Shelley, Keats, and others), then

Tennyson, and a little later Elizabeth Barrett Browning and Robert Browning were reprinted in the United States within months of their initial publication. Sir Walter Scott's historical novels were immensely popular in the United States (as a young man Hawthorne dreamed of becoming an American Scott), and during the 1840s and 1850s crowds of Charles Dickens fans would congregate at the docks to greet steamships arriving in New York City with the latest installment of one of his serialized novels.

Geography and modes of transportation bore directly on publishing practices in the United States during this period. In 1800 there were few publishing firms; writers who wanted to publish a book generally took the handwritten manuscript to a local printer. They paid job rates to have it printed and made their own arrangements for distribution and sales, frequently having signed up committed purchasers beforehand in what was then called the "subscription" system. By around 1820 publishing centers began to develop in the major seaports, which could receive the latest British books by the fastest ships; these publishers shipped hastily reprinted copies inland by river traffic. The leading publishing towns were New York and Philadelphia; the Erie Canal, completed in 1825, gave New York an advantage in distributing books west to Ohio. Boston remained peripheral to the publishing industry until railroad connections to the West developed during the 1840s. Despite the aggressive merchandizing techniques of a few firms, a national market for American literature was slow to develop.

Besides the technical problems of book distribution across the nation's huge expanse, economic interests of American publishers and booksellers were sometimes (but not always) antithetical to the interests of American writers. A national copyright law became effective in the United States in 1790, but not until 1891 did U.S. writers get international copyright protection and foreign writers receive similar protection in the United States. For most of the century, American publishers routinely pirated English writers, paying nothing to Scott, Dickens, and other popular writers for works sold widely in inexpensive editions throughout the United States. American readers benefited from the situation, but the availability to publishers of texts that they did not have to purchase or pay royalties on made it perpetually difficult for U.S. writers to be paid for their work in their home country. As a result, there were relatively few professional authors in the United States before the Civil War. Bryant supported himself as a newspaper editor; Hawthorne received various political appointments over his lifetime; Emerson lived on a legacy from his first wife and on his well-compensated lectures; the financially struggling Melville was forced to spend the last several decades of his life working in the New York custom house; for most of his career, Longfellow taught languages at Harvard.

To survive economically, some American writers attempted to line up contracts with British publishers. But Irving's apparent conquest of the British publishing system, by which he received large sums for *The Sketch Book* and succeeding volumes, proved to be a short-term solution that worked mostly for Irving. Cooper and others followed in Irving's path for a time and were paid by magnanimous British publishers under a system whereby works first printed in Great Britain were presumed to hold a British copyright. But this practice was ruled illegal by a British judge in 1849, making it even harder for American writers to stake a claim to the British market, though Melville and other writers continued to make the effort and occasionally met with success. Some of the American authors who did best in England were antislavery writers, for the English apparently could not get enough of works that held their former colony up to shame. Frederick Douglass and William Wells Brown found a significant audience in Great Britain (the first African American novel, Brown's *Clotel* [1853], was published *only* in England), and there were few writers more admired and widely read in England than Harriet Beecher Stowe.

Nevertheless, authorship and publishing were far from moribund in the antebellum United States. The period from 1820 to 1865 saw a dizzying growth in the nation's population and territorial reach; dramatic technological developments that would allow publishers to bring out works in ever-greater numbers at ever-greater profits; increasing urbanization (which helped enlarge readership in key profitable markets); and the expansion of railroads, canals, and other forms of transportation that would allow for more extensive and economical forms of distribution. The nation's population of approximately four million in 1790 jumped to thirty million by 1860, in part because of the massive emigration from Ireland and elsewhere in Europe that occurred during the 1840s and 1850s. Territorial space available to this burgeoning population dramatically increased following the war with Mexico (1846–48), which, as a result of the 1848 Treaty of Guadalupe Hidalgo, added 1.2 million square miles of land to the 1.8 million square miles that the nation held before the war; this is the area that would become Texas, California, Arizona, Nevada, and Utah, and parts of New Mexico, Colorado, and Wyoming. Beginning in the 1820s and continuing through the nineteenth century, there were ongoing efforts to connect and extend U.S. territory through the development of roads, canals, and railroads. Travel literature to the West (or what we now call the Midwest), such as Caroline Kirkland's *A New Home—Who'll Follow?* (1839) and Margaret Fuller's *Summer on the Lakes* (1843), became an increasingly popular genre. Richard Henry Dana in *Two Years before the Mast* (1840) and Francis Parkman in *The Oregon Trail* (1849) would write popular accounts of their respective travels to the Pacific Northwest. Dana's and Parkman's writings especially resonated with readers during the 1850s, the heyday of California immigration following the discovery of gold in California in the late 1840s.

There was also an increasing interest in urban writings, in large part because of the tremendous rise in the populations of Boston, Philadelphia, and New York brought about mostly by Irish immigration but also by an influx of native-born rural people to the cities from the farms, which suffered massive failures during the economic depression of the 1850s. Taken together, the growth of U.S. cities and the ongoing expansion of the nation's territorial reach contributed to one of the most significant developments of the time for those writers aspiring to professional authorship: the dramatic growth of newspaper and magazine publishing from the early years of the nineteenth century to the 1860s. Between 1800 and 1825, approximately four hundred newspapers were founded, and that number went into the thousands by 1860. Before 1825 there were approximately a hundred magazines published in the United States; by 1850 there were about six hundred. More than the typical U.S. book publisher, the proliferating newspapers and magazines provided writers with forums for their poetry and fiction, along with personal essays, travel writing, political reportage, and other writings suitable for daily, weekly, and monthly presses. Poe, Sigourney, Fuller, Hawthorne, Fern, and many other writers worked on their craft and developed their reputations with the help of their periodical publications.

Among the most popular magazines of the time were the mass-market *Graham's* and *Godey's Lady's Book*, both published in Philadelphia. Poe published stories and sketches in these journals, as did many women writers. The *Lady's Book*, in fact, though published by Louis A. Godey, was edited for some forty years by the novelist and essayist Sarah J. Hale, whose editorial role in one of the major journals of the day points to the key place of women in the antebellum literary marketplace. Despite traditional notions that imaginative literature and creative writing could be especially harmful to women by inflaming their imaginations and undermining their moral place in the private domain of the home, women found ways to enter the literary marketplace. For example, they could write at home and mail their manuscripts to magazines, thus retaining their status as domestic beings. Much writing by women of the antebellum period addressed questions of domesticity head-on, sometimes, as with Fuller, criticizing the idea of separate cultural spheres for men and women; but more often, as with Stowe, showing how women could have an effect on the culture from within the home. But even with her emphasis on the cultural power of domesticity, Stowe, like Fuller, fully embraced the public sphere of authorship. Just about all of the

"A Reading Party." Plate from *Godey's Lady's Book*, 1846.

women writers represented in this anthology made an important mark in the periodical culture of the time, and some used their connections to magazines and newspapers to develop as professional authors who were able to live on earnings from their writings. Child, Fuller, Fern, and Rebecca Harding Davis all had newspaper columns, and Fern was paid lavishly for hers. Kirkland edited the New York *Union* and wrote for other magazines; Child and Fuller also served as editors of journals; Stowe and Louisa May Alcott got their starts writing sketches and short stories for regional newspapers. In this context, the refusal of Emily Dickinson to follow any of the norms of female authorship, while remaining firmly enclosed in the home space and writing some of the great lyrics of the century, points to her recognition of and resistance to cultural ideals of female authorship in her day.

"RENAISSANCE," REFORM, CONFLICT

Various reform movements, such as antislavery, temperance, women's rights, and even nativist anti-Catholicism (an extreme manifestation of Protestant evangelical reform), contributed to the proliferation of print during the antebellum period. As a theme and focus of cultural debate, reform emerged as a crucial constituent of the antebellum writings traditionally associated with the American Renaissance. Recognizing the centrality of reform to his cultural moment, Emerson declared in "Man the Reformer" (1841) that "the doctrine of Reform had never such scope as at the present hour." Though the Transcendentalism for which he stood emphasized self-culture and personal reform rather than public initiatives, by the 1840s Emerson had begun to link himself to activist reform movements. In "Emancipation in the West Indies" (1844), for example, he called on the "great masses of men" to take a larger role in opposing slavery, and he would remain firmly committed to antislavery reform up to the time of the Civil War. He also offered occasional remarks on the value of temperance (one of the most popular reform movements of the antebellum period); in the spirit of Protestant reformers going back to the Reformation (when Protestant meant quite specifically a protest against Catholicism), he drew on anti-Catholic rhetoric in some essays attacking the hierarchies and deadness of established institutions; and in 1855 he addressed a women's rights convention in support of women's suffrage, which he would continue to endorse.

Emersonian reform also had a literary aspect to it, rejecting the American literary nationalism of the 1820s as imitative and timid. Emerson's "The American Scholar" (1837) is often referred to as the nation's "declaration of cultural independence," the essay that helped inspire many authors who have come to be associated with both traditional and more multicultural notions of an American Renaissance. First delivered as a lecture to Harvard's Phi Beta Kappa Society, "The American Scholar" called on those Americans with a "love of letters" to "lead in a new age" of men "inspired by the Divine Soul which also inspires all men." Trained as a Unitarian minister, Emerson had broken with the church by the time he began to deliver and publish his lectures, and in *Nature*, a short book of 1836, made it clear that he had absorbed some of the major ideas of the European romantics on the creative powers of the individual mind, the regenerative value of nature, the limits of historical associations and traditions, the stultifying effects of established institutions, and the mystical glories of a presocialized infancy. Ironically, in *Nature*, "The American Scholar," and his other writings of the time, Emerson drew on major philosophical and aesthetic ideas circulating in Europe to write as a literary reformer exhorting Americans to break their dependency on the "courtly muses of Europe." In this lecture and other writings of the 1830s and 1840s, Emerson underscored the parallels between Romantic ideas of infancy and the infancy of the new nation, invoked the regenerative and spiritual powers of the American landscape ("America is a poem in our eyes," he declared in "The Poet" [1844]), drew connections between self-reliance and Jacksonian democratic energies, and linked his celebration of nonconformity and resistance to the reform agenda of many Americans of the period.

Emerson's attacks on the Unitarian and other established churches for what he described as their refusal to honor the possibility of the miraculous in the here and now, and his affirmations of the near god-like powers of the creative imagination, helped popularize what many literary historians have termed the Transcendentalist movement. In various ways, Emersonian Transcendentalism (which was never really a formalized movement) inspired the writings of Fuller, Thoreau, and Whitman. Even more skeptical authors like Poe, Hawthorne, Melville, and Dickinson, through their resistance to Emerson's proclamations on the individual's ability to break from institutions and traditional Christian beliefs to become a kind of god, arguably exhibited the influence of Emerson, who himself could be skeptical of transcendental extremism (for the dark side of the ecstasies of *Nature*, see his "Experience" [1844], which presents the individual as forever skating on surfaces). In the wake of Emerson's important essays of the 1830s and 1840s, much writing of the antebellum period grappled with questions about the value of history, the ability of the individual to apprehend the godhead directly, the capacity of language to achieve and convey knowledge, and the difficulties of making sense of a universe in which meaning derives from individual creative insights rather than received authority. The fictional worlds of *The Scarlet Letter* and *Moby-Dick*, works that are obsessed with the problematics of interpretation, whether of the letter A or a whale, have a profoundly different feel from the more consensual, commonsensical fictional worlds of Irving, Sedgwick, and Cooper.

Antebellum writing taken as a whole is much too various and conflicted to be viewed simply through the lens of Emerson's New England–based reformism. But as Emerson himself helps us to understand, one of the impulses that holds together many of the writings of the period, including Emerson's, is reformism—the conviction that American literature and culture were not living up to their Revolutionary or democratic promises. But during this time there were also a variety of notions about what constituted reform. Proslavery, not just antislavery, could be regarded in a reform context; many southerners, for instance, looked back to the founding of the nation and believed that the Constitution favored states' rights over what they regarded as the encroaching authoritarianism of the federal government. Reformism, particularly in the context of an expanding nation with its multiple constituencies and agendas, could be as much a source of conflict as consensus.

Many of the antebellum reform movements based in the North were actively directed by Protestant elites concerned with maintaining their social power and authority during a time of increasing class and ethnic diversity. Desires to hold on to such power could be taken to an unattractive extreme in the period's pervasive anti-Catholic nativism. But concerns about the poor and working-class immigrants also had an important place in antebellum urban reform movements, as urban reformers such as Lydia Maria Child sought to expose readers to the plight of the impoverished in order to prompt philanthropic interventions. The fact that women had such a significant place in urban reform movements is not surprising, given that urban reform often centered on creating homelike, domestically attractive conditions for the poor, and that another major reform effort of the antebellum period centered on women's rights. In "The Great Lawsuit" (1843), Margaret Fuller drew on the Declaration of Independence and Emersonian transcendental reform, among numerous other sources, to make the case that women should have greater opportunities for education and participation in the public sphere, including the right to "represent themselves"—that is, to vote. In 1848, at the first women's rights convention in Seneca Falls, New York, Elizabeth Cady Stanton's resounding "Declaration of Sentiments" invoked Jefferson's Declaration, substituting male for British tyrannical authority to show how the nation's social institutions and legal codes mainly served the interests of America's white male citizenry. That same year, the New York State Legislature, in response to critics like Stanton, passed the nation's most liberalized married women's property act, which made it legal for women to maintain control over the property they brought to their marriages. But throughout the nineteenth century, in most states married women remained without any legal rights to property or earnings within marriage.

For good reason, then, a number of women writers of the period addressed questions of power: how to use power from within the domestic sphere, how to gain power in the public sphere, how to fend off the dangers of unchecked patriarchal power. The danger posed by patriarchal power was a central theme of both antislavery and temperance reform. Sigourney and Stowe were two of the most prominent antislavery writers who supported the temperance movement, as they saw drinking as a male activity that lured men away from their homes into the saloons and transformed them into drunken hooligans. In temperance writings of the period, women authors regularly depicted drunken husbands or fathers as men who became driven by their animal passions, to the point where these "slaves to the bottle" became slaves to their own bodies. Such imagery and cultural concerns informed Child's antislavery story "The Quadroons" (1842); Stowe's antislavery novels Uncle Tom's Cabin (1852) and Dred (1856), whose villains were drunkards; and the antislavery writer Frances Harper's short story "The Two Offers" (1859).

A number of writers of the antebellum period, male and female, took as one of their main subjects the anguishing paradox that the nation that boastfully presented itself as the most idealistic in the world—the bastion of freedom and equality—was implicated in ongoing national crimes: the near-genocide of the American Indians, the enslavement of black people, and an expansionism that ignored other national sovereignties, especially that of Mexico. Because the war with Mexico of 1846–48 came to be understood by many Americans as consistent with the nation's "Manifest Destiny" to expand across the continent, only a small minority of American writers voiced more than perfunctory opposition; the best known of these dissenters was Thoreau, who spent a night in the Concord jail in symbolic protest against being taxed to support a war that he believed was mainly intended to enlarge the domain of slavery. Emerson and Child were dissenters earlier, during the 1830s, when most writers were silent about the forced removal of southeastern Indian tribes from their homelands to territory west of the Mississippi River, as permitted by the Indian Removal Act of 1830. American destiny plainly required a little practical callousness, most whites felt, or if not callousness, then the worst kind of sympathy: a lament for "vanishing" Indians who were being killed off all the more quickly or at least without remorse because of such sentimental acquiescence. Native American spokespersons and authors like Black Hawk and William Apess questioned whites' constant interventions into Indian affairs. They were particularly critical of whites' deceptive treaties and land-grabbing policies, as were those grouped in the section in this anthology titled "Native Americans: Removal and Resistance." Of the major antebellum writers who were not Native American, only Child kept a critical eye over the decades on the white power, as opposed to the presumed providential inevitability, that was relentlessly working to shrink Indian lands and confuse extinction with extermination.

Most white Americans accepted what they thought of as the destined "extinction" of the Native Americans. There was much more conflict over the practice of slavery, which Melville called "man's foulest crime." The antislavery campaign stirred the consciences of a number of white writers, and, unsurprisingly, resistance to slavery and critiques of whites' antiblack racism were among the principal topics of antebellum African American writing. Describing his own enslavement, the fugitive Frederick Douglass displayed a powerful capacity to stir both readers and audiences in lecture halls, in large part through his ability to make whites sympathize with the situation of blacks. The reformist potential of sympathy is the crucial theme of his novella, "The Heroic Slave" (1853), and of Frances Harper's antislavery poetry. Harper and Douglass were both inspired by Stowe's *Uncle Tom's Cabin*, the best-selling novel of the antebellum period. Twentieth-century attacks on this novel for its supposed bad faith would have made little sense to Harper and Douglass. William Wells Brown may have been more skeptical of Stowe, as his ironically conceived novel *Clotel* suggests, but even he praised Stowe in the pages of William Lloyd Garrison's antislavery newspaper, the *Liberator*.

A politics of antislavery had an important place in the careers of a number of the writers represented in this anthology. (For further commentary on slavery, along with selections from some of the other most important antislavery writers of the period, see the section on "Slavery, Race, and the Making of American Literature.") When the Fugitive Slave Law of 1850 was enforced in Boston in 1851 (by Melville's father-in-law, Chief Justice Lemuel Shaw), Thoreau in his journals expressed his outrage that Massachusetts citizens were being compelled to return escaping slaves to their Southern masters; after another famous case in 1854, he wrote his most scathing speech, "Slavery in Massachusetts," for delivery at a Fourth of July counterceremony at which a copy of the Constitution was burned. In that speech he summed up the disillusionment that many of his generation shared, presenting Massachusetts as a type of hell. More obliquely than Thoreau, Melville explored slavery in "Benito Cereno" as an index to the white supremacism that he regarded as a stain on the national character. At his bitterest, he felt in the mid-1850s that "free Ameriky" was "intrepid, unprincipled, reckless, predatory, with boundless ambition, civilized in externals but a savage at heart." In response to antislavery criticism, Southerners passionately defended the institution of slavery in such works as George Fitzhugh's *Sociology for the South* (1854) and Caroline Lee Hentz's *The Planter's Northern Bride* (1854), one of several anti–*Uncle Tom's Cabin* novels published during the 1850s.

John Brown's violent raid on Harpers Ferry in 1859, a failed effort to initiate a slave rebellion in the South, drew eloquent defenses from Emerson, Thoreau, Douglass, Stowe, and Child, though most in the North and across the country condemned Brown as a radical who threatened to bring the nation into a bloody civil war. With the outbreak of the Civil War, Douglass, Wells Brown, Child, Stowe, and other major writers of the period sought to present the war as, in the spirit of John Brown, a holy war against slavery that might redeem the millennial promise of the nation, which is to say, as the fulfillment of the promise of reform going back to Emerson and, as Lincoln himself suggested in his "Address Delivered at the Dedication of the Cemetery at Gettysburg" (1863), to the principles of the Declaration of Independence itself. The idea of the United States as an exceptional nation because it had been set aside for an exceptional destiny proved almost impossible to overcome, even in moments when the country marched into bloody internal conflict. When the war began on April 12, 1861, with Confederate guns opening fire on Fort Sumter, in South Carolina's Charleston Harbor, few understood what lay ahead; Northerners and Southerners alike erroneously expected the war to last only a few months. Visiting Boston and Concord in 1862, fresh from the newly formed West Virginia (the portion of the slave state Virginia that had chosen to stay with the Union), Rebecca Harding Davis saw that Emerson had little notion of the suffering involved in the war. Shortly before he died, Hawthorne, who had remained committed to the Democrats' vision of Union even at the price of retaining slavery for the foreseeable future, published a negative account of the war, "Chiefly about War Matters," in the 1862 *Atlantic*; while mocking Lincoln as a leader, the essay nonetheless raised pointed questions about Americans' failure to anticipate that a war of this nature would bring unimagined bloodshed, eventually killing over six hundred thousand Americans before Robert E. Lee's surrender to Ulysses S. Grant at Appomattox, Virginia, on April 9, 1865.

Among the most notable literary responses to the Civil War from writers who had published during the antebellum period were two poetry collections: Whitman's *Drum-Taps* (1865) and Melville's *Battle-Pieces* (1866). (More privately at home, Dickinson was spurred to tragic lyricism by the deaths of young Amherst students she had known.) After a small run of his *Drum-Taps* had been sold, Whitman held back the edition for a sequel mainly consisting of newly written poems on the just-assassinated Lincoln, among them his great elegy, "When Lilacs Last in the Dooryard Bloom'd." Both Whitman and Melville looked ahead as well as backward, Whitman calling "reconciliation" the "word over all," and Melville urging in his "Supplement" to *Battle-Pieces* that the victorious North "be Christians toward our fellow-whites, as well as philanthropic toward the blacks, our fellow-men." But Melville's emphasis on Northern whites' responsibility to show charity and "kindliness" toward Southern whites, who he remarked "stand nearer to us

"Burial Trench at Gettysburg." Photograph by Timothy H. O'Sullivan (1840–1882).

in nature," was problematic, for it pointed to the racism that contributed to the nation's larger failure to follow through on the reformist potential of the Civil War. By the time she died, Child was lamenting Reconstruction's failure to educate and offer economic uplift to the the former slaves. In *Democratic Vistas* (1870), Whitman railed against the political corruption and materialism on display in the immediate wake of the Civil War. Though he worked for several Republican administrations, Douglass became disillusioned by the resurgence of segregationist practices and antiblack violence, most notably lynching, after the end of Reconstruction in 1877. A year before his death, in one of his greatest speeches, "The Lessons of the Hour" (1894), he called on the nation, as he had in "What to the Slave Is the Fourth of July?" (1852), to live up to its founding ideals of "human brotherhood and the self-evident truths of liberty and equality," proclaiming that if Americans were only willing to do that, "your problem will be solved" and "your Republic will stand and flourish forever." With his insistence on the unbounded potential of every individual and his critique of the racist and materialistic nation of the 1890s, Douglass re-articulated some of the same arguments that he had made in 1845 and that Emerson had made in the 1830s and 1840s. Viewed from this reformist perspective, the cultural work of the American Renaissance continues to remain in process.

THE SMALL AND LARGE WORLD OF AMERICAN WRITERS, 1820–1865

An anthology organized by a national literature, a specific time period, and an array of major authors presented in the chronological order of their birthdates might seem artificially closed off from literature of other eras and nations. But close attention to nation and chronology by no means cuts off conversations among the writers included here and those of other periods and nations. On the contrary, it provides a foundation for developing such complex conversations. Nevertheless, it is important to underscore that the era has a real existence of its own in literary terms: the authors in this anthology often *were* in conversation with one another; their world was relatively small and the number of instances of direct and indirect influences, counterinfluences, productive friendships, productive rejections of influences and friendships, and so on, are stunning. Sedgwick read Cooper's *Last of the Mohicans* and wrote a "response" in *Hope Leslie*, emphasizing the domestic and cross-racial possibilities in ways she thought Cooper did not. Whitman and Bryant were on friendly terms in New York City, even as Whitman was turning against the studied meditative verse of his compatriot; Child and John Greenleaf Whittier were long-time friends in the antislavery cause. Emerson was friends with Fuller and Thoreau, both of whom were influenced by his writings, and though he did not meet Whitman until after the publication of the first edition of *Leaves of Grass* (1855), Emerson's theorizing on poetry in "The Poet," which implicitly attacked Poe's ideas on poetry, had a pronounced influence not only on Whitman but also on Dickinson and a number of other American poets. While in Massachusetts during the early 1840s, Douglass imbibed the spirit of Emersonian self-reliance, and his *Narrative* presented his own variations on Emerson's notion of the divinity of self. Douglass inspired Stowe, who, while working on *Uncle Tom's Cabin*, wrote Douglass asking for more precise descriptions of a slave plantation and, after the publication of *Uncle Tom's Cabin*, met with him at her home in Andover and took pleasure in the fact that Douglass was one of her greatest champions. As much as Douglass admired *Uncle Tom's Cabin*, however, he pointed to problems with Stowe's conception of race in his novella of slave rebellion, "The Heroic Slave," which may have had an influence on Melville's novella of slave rebellion, "Benito Cereno." There is evidence that Douglass influenced Melville's conception of black music and dance in *Moby-Dick*; and it is worth noting that Douglass printed an excerpt from Melville's first novel, *Typee* (1846), in his newspaper the *North Star.*

Melville admired a number of American writers, championing Cooper in the late 1840s, writing several sketches in the mode of Irving, parodying Sedgwick, and responding both positively and negatively to Emerson. He called Emerson a "deep diver" and yet at times found him naively optimistic; in *Moby-Dick* he posits the specter of an indifferent and even hostile nature in which it would be next to impossible, even suicidal, for an individual to become what Emerson termed a "transparent eyeball." Melville dedicated *Moby-Dick* to Nathaniel Hawthorne, whom he met at a picnic in 1850 and idolized in the early 1850s, writing an essay on American literary nationalism in his honor, "Hawthorne and His Mosses" (1850); Hawthorne and Melville mutually influenced one another during the early 1850s. At around the same time, the African American writer William Wells Brown was reading the short stories of Lydia Maria Child and almost word for word used one of those stories, "The Quadroons," to establish the plot of his novel *Clotel*. Frances Harper knew Wells Brown and his work and also took inspiration from such popular poets as Sigourney, Longfellow, and Whittier, who wrote a number of powerful antislavery poems. Poe, who admired Sigourney, knew and attacked many of the celebrated writers of the day, such as Longfellow and Hawthorne, even as his poetry and criticism inspired some of Whitman's poetry, most notably "Out of the Cradle Endlessly Rocking" (1859), and his short stories influenced Hawthorne, whose fiction, much as Poe would have wanted to deny it, influenced his own: there are close connections between Hawthorne's "Young Goodman Brown" (1835), Poe's "The Fall of the House of Usher" (1839), and Hawthorne's *The House of the Seven Gables* (1851). Stowe thought highly of Hawthorne; and Harriet Jacobs, who may have known of Hawthorne's work, esteemed *Uncle Tom's Cabin* and wrote directly to Stowe asking for help in editing her autobiographical *Incidents in the Life of a Slave Girl* (1861). When Stowe refused, Jacobs got the editorial support of Child, whose fiction earlier had had an impact on Wells Brown. After escaping from slavery, Jacobs lived in New York City in the household of the brother of the best-selling writer Fanny Fern, Nathaniel Parker Willis, whom Fern satirized as "Hyacinth" in her most popular novel, *Ruth Hall*. Fern admired Whitman, Irving, and Hawthorne; and Hawthorne praised Fern in a letter to his editor and friend William Ticknor. Hawthorne also praised Rebecca Harding Davis, who claimed Hawthorne as one of her most important influences. After reading Davis's "Life in the Iron Mills" (1861), Hawthorne considered traveling to Wheeling, Virginia, to meet her, but was happy when she chose to visit him at his home in Concord, Massachusetts. Louisa May Alcott borrowed books from Emerson, got nature lessons from Thoreau, and read (and was influenced by) the fiction of her neighbor Nathaniel Hawthorne. Dickinson, whose family subscribed to numerous newspapers and magazines, and who ordered books by mail from Boston, read just about all of these authors and argued with them in many of her poems.

Most of the writers represented in this anthology also ranged beyond the borders of the United States. Washington Irving was in England when *The Sketch Book* was published, and he remained abroad for over a decade, serving as a U.S. diplomat in Spain; at the height of his early career, Cooper traveled to France in 1826 and remained in Europe for the next seven years. Two decades later, Margaret Fuller traveled to Italy and participated in the Roman Revolution of the late 1840s; and in the early 1850s Hawthorne became consul in Liverpool and remained in Europe for nearly eight years. Travel abroad was central to Poe's, Emerson's, and Longfellow's educations; Stowe made a grand tour of Europe during the 1850s; and Douglass, Wells Brown, Jacobs, and many other African Americans spent significant time in England. Melville toured England and later the Holy Land. All of these writers had friends abroad, regarded the literature of the United States as part of a larger world literature, and, accordingly, read widely, particularly in English and other European literatures.

A number of the U.S. authors from this period also had significant interests in the literatures of the southern Americas. Because of his fascination with Christopher Columbus, which culminated in his best-selling biography of 1828 and several other works about Spanish America, Irving was perhaps the most celebrated U.S. author to read widely in writings south of the national borders, but authors ranging from Hawthorne to Melville, Douglass to Whitman, Child to Wells Brown, exhibited a curiosity about the Caribbean and Central and South America. Douglass's "The Heroic Slave" and Melville's "Benito Cereno" are two compelling examples of works that look beyond the southern borders of the United States. Whitman also had a capacious hemispheric perspective on the Americas, and in the twentieth century he would find some of his most enthusiastic readers in Chile, Argentina, and Mexico.

As far as literary matters are concerned, all of the writers in this anthology were interested in much more than the contemporary. A glance at the footnotes in this volume will reveal the enormous influence of classics from ancient Greece and Rome, Greek and Roman myth, Indian and Asian religions (which is especially true for Thoreau), the English Renaissance (especially Shakespeare), Milton, English and German Romantics, the Bible, and a range of popular and classic literature from Scandinavian and numerous other countries. And yet even as many of these writers had a capacious vision that took them beyond national borders and the limits of any period chronology, they were aware that they resided in a relatively new nation lacking literary traditions, and that there was a burden on them to establish such traditions. Melville's essay "Hawthorne and His Mosses" is among the period's notable examples of such literary nationalist ambition, which was neither insular nor separatist. As Melville remarks when comparing Hawthorne to Shakespeare: "I do not say that Nathaniel of Salem is a greater than William of Avon, or as great. But the difference between the two men is by no means immeasurable." Melville, who resented British condescension toward American writers, aspired for parity between English and American literary traditions rather than a separation of American from English literature. With his emphasis on the democratic individual, Whitman was capable of a more hyperbolic American literary nationalism than any of the other writers in this volume, so it is ironic that the great majority of his most enthusiastic nineteenth-century readers lived in England.

In addition to making claims for an American literary nationalism, the writers in this anthology sought to *create* American literary traditions. They did so by looking back to earlier colonial literatures and claiming them as "American." Many of the colonial texts that we now read as canonical, such as works by John Winthrop and William Bradford, were first republished in the nineteenth century and owe some of their current status to their recovery by early national and antebellum writers. Linking their nineteenth-century writings to the colonial past, Sedgwick, Cooper, Hawthorne, Whittier, and many others created a sense of a continuously unfolding national history and literature that came to a fruition of sorts in the nineteenth century.

Crucial to this period of American literary history, then, was a pronounced sense among a number of its authors about their role not just in consolidating traditions but also in creating the traditions that would develop from their writings. Such an orientation is most pronounced in Whitman, whose poetry regularly imagines future readers and writers, but it is arguably a central impulse behind much of the literature of the period. In this respect, it should be kept in mind that a number of the writers represented in this anthology were somewhat neglected when they first began publishing, and that their greatest impact was not on writing of their own time but on writing to come. In addition to Whitman, who was generally neglected until the turn into the twentieth century, authors such as Thoreau, Melville, and Dickinson found their most enthusiastic readers in the twentieth century. Melville and Dickinson, for instance, weren't really "discovered" until the 1920s and 1930s, when they had an immediate impact on writers living then. Even those who were fairly well known during the antebellum period—Poe, Hawthorne, Douglass, and others—came to be much better known in the twentieth century (Douglass's 1845 *Narrative*, for instance, was not republished after the early 1850s until 1960) and in some ways exerted an influence on twentieth-century literature and culture more significant than what they exerted on their nineteenth-century contemporaries. The point that should be emphasized is that the diverse writings of the 1820–65 period continue to remain foundational to the study of American literature not only because of what they accomplished within their own antebellum moment but also because, as Whitman would say about himself, they ultimately cannot be contained within that moment and even within a national frame. The literature of this period encompasses multitudes and continues to write its (and our) literary futures.

AMERICAN LITERATURE 1820–1865

TEXTS	CONTEXTS
1815 Founding of the *North American Review*	**1815** Treaty of Ghent, ending the second war with England. Before news of the treaty reaches Andrew Jackson, he leads American troops to victory over the British at the Battle of New Orleans.
1817 William Cullen Bryant, "**Thanatopsis**"	
1820 Washington Irving, ***The Sketch Book***	**1820** Missouri Compromise admits Missouri as a slave state, Maine as a free state, and excludes slavery in the Louisiana Territory north of latitude 36° 30'
1821 Bryant, ***Poems***	**1821** Sequoyah (George Guess) invents syllabary in which Cherokee language can be written
1823 James Fenimore Cooper, *The Pioneers*	**1823** Monroe Doctrine warns all European powers not to establish new colonies on either American continent
	1825 Erie Canal opens, connecting Great Lakes region with the Atlantic
1826 Cooper, ***The Last of the Mohicans***	
1827 David Cusick, *Sketches Of Ancient History of the Six Nations* • Lydia Sigourney, *Poems* • Catharine Sedgwick, *Hope Leslie*	**1827** Baltimore & Ohio, first U.S. railroad
	1827–28 Cherokee Nation ratifies its new constitution • The newspaper *The Cherokee Phoenix* founded
1828–30 Cherokee Council composes **Memorials** to Congress	
1829 William Apess, *A Son of the Forest* • David Walker, **Appeal**	**1829–37** President Andrew Jackson encourages westward migration of white population
	1830 Congress passes Indian Removal Act, allowing Jackson to negotiate treaties with the eastern tribes for their relocation west of the Mississippi
	1831 William Lloyd Garrison starts *The Liberator*, antislavery journal • Nat Turner leads a slave rebellion in Southampton County, Virginia; approximately sixty whites are killed and two hundred blacks are killed in retaliation
1833 Black Hawk, *Life*	
1835 William Glmore Simms, *The Yemassee: A Romance of Carolina*	
1836 Ralph Waldo Emerson, ***Nature***	
1837 Nathaniel Hawthorne, ***Twice-Told Tales***	**1837** Financial panic: failures of numerous banks lead to severe unemployment that persists into the early 1840s

Boldface titles indicate works in the anthology.

TEXTS	CONTEXTS
	1838 Around this time, Underground Railroad begins aiding slaves escaping north, often to Canada
	1838–39 "Trail of Tears": Cherokees forced from their homelands by federal troops
1839 Caroline Stansbury Kirkland, *A New Home—Who'll Follow?*	
1840 Richard Henry Dana Jr., *Two Years before the Mast*	1840 Founding of the Washingtonian Temperance Society; temperance quickly emerges as one of the most popular social reform movements of the period
1843 Margaret Fuller, "**The Great Lawsuit**" • Lydia Maria Child, *Letters from New-York*	
	1844 Samuel Morse invents telegraph
1845 Edgar Allan Poe, "**The Raven**" • Frederick Douglass, ***Narrative of the Life of Frederick Douglass***	1845 United States annexes Texas
	1846 David Wilmot, a congressman from Pennsylvania, proposes in Congress that slavery be banned in territories gained from the Mexican War; his proviso is defeated
	1846–48 United States wages war against Mexico; Treaty of Guadalupe Hidalgo cedes entire Southwest to United States
1847 Henry Wadsworth Longfellow, *Evangeline*	1847 Brigham Young leads Mormons from Nauvoo, Illinois, to Salt Lake, Utah Territory
	1848 Seneca Falls Convention inaugurates campaign for women's rights
	1848–49 Beginning years of the California Gold Rush, which brings hundreds of thousands of new settlers to California
1850 Nathaniel Hawthorne, *The Scarlet Letter*	1850 Fugitive Slave Act of the Compromise of 1850 obliges free states to return escaped slaves to slaveholders
1851 Herman Melville, *Moby-Dick*	
1852 Harriet Beecher Stowe, ***Uncle Tom's Cabin***	
1853 William Wells Brown, *Clotel*	
1854 Henry David Thoreau, ***Walden*** • Frances Ellen Watkins Harper, ***Poems on Miscellaneous Subjects***	1854 Republican Party formed, consolidating antislavery factions • Kansas-Nebraska Act approved by Congress; the act repeals the Missouri Compromise, making it legal for the white voting residents of a territory to determine whether it should be admitted as a slave or free state

TEXTS	CONTEXTS
1855 Walt Whitman, *Leaves of Grass* • P. T. Barnum, *The Life of P.T. Barnum, Written by Himself*	
1857 Fanny Fern (Sarah Willis Parton), *Fresh Leaves*	**1857** Supreme Court *Dred Scott* decision denies citizenship to African Americans
1858 Abraham Lincoln, "A House Divided"	
1859 E.D.E.N. Southworth, *The Hidden Hand*	**1859** First successful U.S. oil well drilled, in Pennsylvania
1860–65 Emily Dickinson writes several hundred **poems**	**1860** Short-Lived Pony Express runs from Missouri to California
1861 Harriet Jacobs, *Incidents in the Life of a Slave Girl* • Rebecca Harding Davis, *Life in the Iron-Mills*	**1861** South Carolina batteries fire on U.S. fort, initiating the Civil War; Southern states secede from the Union and found the Confederate States of America
	1861–65 Civil War
1862 Elizabeth Stoddard, *The Morgesons*	
	1863 Emancipation Proclamation • Battle of Gettysburg
	1865 Thirteenth Amendment abolishes slavery in the United States
1866 John Greenleaf Whittier, *Snow-Bound: A Winter Idyl*	**1866** Completion of two successful transatlantic cables • Civil Rights Act
	1868 Fourteenth Amendment grants citizenship to those born or naturalized in the United States
1868–69 Louisa May Alcott, *Little Women*	
	1869 First transcontinental railroad completed; Central Pacific construction crews composed largely of Chinese laborers

WASHINGTON IRVING
1783–1859

Washington Irving had an unusually long and varied career, publishing his first satirical essays in 1802, when he was nineteen, and his last book, a five-volume life of George Washington, just a few months before he died at age seventy-six. Celebrated by Americans for his contributions to a burgeoning national literature, Irving also became the first American writer of the nineteenth century to achieve an international literary reputation. Although he was regarded as a genial and comic writer, Irving regularly addressed darker and more complex themes of historical transformation and personal dislocation. His innovative travel sketches blurred the line between the personal essay and fiction, and he is considered one of the "inventors" of the modern short story. During a time in which there were no international copyright agreements, he managed to secure simultaneous British and American copyrights for his work. His canny understanding of the literary marketplace helped him to become the first American who was able to support himself solely through his writing.

Irving was born in New York City on April 3, 1783, the last of eleven children of a Scottish-born father and English-born mother. He read widely in English literature at home, modeling his early prose on the *Spectator* papers by Joseph Addison and delighting in many other writers, including Shakespeare, Oliver Goldsmith, and Laurence Sterne. His brothers enjoyed writing poems and essays as companionable recreation, and, inspired by their example, he wrote a series of satirical essays on the theater and New York society under the pseudonym of Jonathan Oldstyle. Nine of these essays were published in his brother Peter's newspaper, the *Morning Chronicle*, during 1802–3.

When Irving showed signs of tuberculosis in 1804, his brothers sent him abroad for a two-year tour of Europe. On his return in 1806, he studied law with Judge Josiah Hoffman, and he was admitted to the bar shortly thereafter. More important for his literary career, he and his brother William (along with William's brother-in-law, James Kirke Paulding) started a satirical magazine, *Salmagundi* (the name of a spicy hash), which ran from 1807 to 1808 with poems, sketches, and essays on a range of topics. In 1808 Irving began work on *A History of New-York from the Beginning of the World to the End of the Dutch Dynasty*, at first conceiving it as a parody of Samuel Lathem Mitchell's *The Picture of New-York* (1807), then taking on a variety of satiric targets, including President Jefferson, whom he portrayed as an early Dutch governor of New Amsterdam, William the Testy. Narrated by the comical invented character Diedrich Knickerbocker, who dabbles in historical research, *A History of New-York* appeared in 1809 and brought Irving his first literary celebrity. That same year Judge Hoffman's daughter Matilda, to whom he had become engaged, died suddenly from consumption; Irving would remain a lifelong bachelor. Most biographers attribute Irving's bachelorhood to his grief at the death of Matilda. But her death did free him from the commitment he had made to her father to devote himself to the law, which he hated; and in the figure of his most famous fictional persona, the genial bachelor Geoffrey Crayon, and even in his most famous fictional creation, Rip Van Winkle, there are hints that the single life suited Irving just fine.

During the War of 1812 Irving was editor of the *Analectic Magazine*, which he filled mainly with writings from British periodicals, while also including his own timely series of patriotic biographical sketches of American naval heroes. Toward the end of the war he was made a colonel in the New York State militia. In May 1815, a major change occurred in his life: he left for Europe and stayed away for seventeen years. At first he worked in Liverpool with his brother Peter, an importer of English hardware, but in 1818, shortly after their mother died in New York, Peter went bankrupt. Grief-stricken, and yet grateful to be freed from the responsibilities of working for the family firm, Irving once again took up writing. He met Sir Walter Scott, an admirer of the Knickerbocker *History*, who directed him to the wealth of unused literary material in German folktales. There, as scholars have shown, Irving found the source for "Rip Van Winkle," some passages of which are close paraphrases of the original, J.C.C.N. Otmar's "Peter Klaus" (1800), which also depicts a protagonist sleeping for twenty years. Irving began sending sections of *The Sketch Book* to the United States for publication in what would turn out to be seven installments published from 1819 to 1820. When the two-volume complete *Sketch Book* was printed in England in 1820, it made Irving famous and brought him the friendship of many of the leading British writers of the time. As Irving knew, part of his success derived from British reviewers' pleasure that a book by an American, as Frances Jeffrey wrote in the *Edinburgh Review*, "should be written throughout with the greatest care and accuracy, and worked up to great purity and beauty of diction, on the model of the most elegant and polished of our native writers." Addison lay behind Irving's depiction of English country life, and Oliver Goldsmith influenced his sketch of Westminster Abbey. But among *The Sketch Book*'s graceful tributes to English scenes and characters were two immensely popular tales set in rural New York, "Rip Van Winkle" and "The Legend of Sleepy Hollow."

Irving's next two books, *Bracebridge Hall* (1822) and *Tales of a Traveller* (1824), were less successful, and in 1824 he accepted an invitation from the American minister to Spain to work with original manuscripts in Madrid to produce an account of Columbus's voyages. In 1828 he published *The Life and Voyages of Christopher Columbus*, which became the basis for standard schoolroom accounts of Columbus during the nineteenth and early twentieth century. Out of Irving's Spanish years came also *The Conquest of Granada* (1829), *Voyages and Discoveries of the Companions of Columbus* (1831), and *The Alhambra* (1832), which was soon known as "the Spanish *Sketch Book*."

In 1829 Irving was appointed secretary to the American legation in London. When he finally returned to the United States in 1832 after his long absence, critics wondered openly about whether this much admired "native" writer had become Europeanized. Setting out to reclaim his Americanness, Irving proclaimed his love for his country and headed west, taking a horseback journey into what is now Oklahoma. His travels and research resulted in three major works on the American West: *A Tour of the Prairies* (1835); *Astoria* (1836), an account of John Jacob Astor's fur-trading colony in Oregon; and *The Adventures of Captain Bonneville, U.S.A.* (1837), a narrative of explorations in the Rockies and the Far West.

In the late 1830s Irving bought and began refurbishing a house near Tarrytown, along the Hudson north of New York City. But before settling down, in 1842 he accepted an appointment as minister to Spain and returned to Europe, spending four years in Madrid. After his return to the United States in 1846, he arranged with G.P. Putnam to publish a collected edition of his writings; he also prepared a biography of Oliver Goldsmith (1849). Irving's main work after 1850 was his long-contemplated life of George Washington, which he himself regarded as his greatest literary accomplishment. He collapsed just after finishing the last of its five volumes, and he died a few months later, on November 28, 1859.

Cooper, Hawthorne, and many other American writers were inspired by the success of *The Sketch Book*. Although Melville, in his essay on Hawthorne's *Mosses from an Old Manse*, declared his preference for creative geniuses over adept imitators like Irving, he could not escape Irving's influence, which emerges both in his short stories and in a late poem, "Rip Van Winkle's Lilacs." From the beginning, many readers identified with Rip as a counterhero, an anti-Franklinian who made a success of failure; and subsequent generations have responded profoundly to Irving's pervasive theme of mutability, especially as localized in his portrayal of the bewildering rapidity of change in American life.

The Author's Account of *Himself*[1]

I am of this mind with Homer, that as the snaile that crept out of
her shel was turned eftsoones into a toad, and thereby was forced
to make a stoole to sit on; so the traveller that stragleth from his
owne country is in a short time transformed into so monstrous a
shape, that he is faine to alter his mansion with his manners, and
to live where he can, not where he would.

Lyly's Euphues.[2]

I was always fond of visiting new scenes, and observing strange characters
and manners. Even when a mere child I began my travels, and made many
tours of discovery into foreign parts and unknown regions of my native city,
to the frequent alarm of my parents, and the emolument of the town-crier.
As I grew into boyhood, I extended the range of my observations. My holiday
afternoons were spent in rambles about the surrounding country. I made
myself familiar with all its places famous in history or fable. I knew every spot
where a murder or robbery had been committed, or a ghost been seen. I visited the neighbouring villages, and added greatly to my stock of knowledge,
by noting their habits and customs, and conversing with their sages and great
men. I even journeyed one long summer's day to the summit of the most distant hill, from whence I stretched my eye over many a mile of terra incognita,[3] and was astonished to find how vast a globe I inhabited.

This rambling propensity strengthened with my years. Books of voyages
and travels became my passion, and in devouring their contents, I neglected
the regular exercises of the school. How wistfully would I wander about the
pier heads in fine weather, and watch the parting ships, bound to distant
climes—with what longing eyes would I gaze after their lessening sails, and
waft myself in imagination to the ends of the earth.

Farther reading and thinking, though they brought this vague inclination
into more reasonable bounds, only served to make it more decided. I visited
various parts of my own country; and had I been merely a lover of fine scenery, I should have felt little desire to seek elsewhere for its gratification: for
on no country have the charms of nature been more prodigally lavished. Her
mighty lakes, like oceans of liquid silver; her mountains, with their bright
aerial tints; her valleys, teeming with wild fertility; her tremendous cataracts,
thundering in their solitudes; her boundless plains, waving with spontaneous verdure; her broad deep rivers, rolling in solemn silence to the ocean;
her trackless forests, where vegetation puts forth all its magnificence; her
skies, kindling with the magic of summer clouds and glorious sunshine:—no,
never need an American look beyond his own country for the sublime and
beautiful of natural scenery.

But Europe held forth all the charms of storied and poetical association.
There were to be seen the masterpieces of art, the refinements of highly
cultivated society, the quaint peculiarities of ancient and local custom. My
native country was full of youthful promise; Europe was rich in the accumulated treasures of age. Her very ruins told the history of times gone by, and
every mouldering stone was a chronicle. I longed to wander over the scenes of

---

1. The text is taken from the May 1819 first
installment of *The Sketch Book of Geoffrey
Crayon, Gent.* (For *The Sketch Book* and some of
his subsequent essays and books, Irving adopted
the pseudonym of Geoffrey Crayon.)
2. From *Euphues and His England* (1580), by the
English writer John Lyly (1554–1606).
3. Unknown land (Latin).

renowned achievement—to tread, as it were, in the footsteps of antiquity—to loiter about the ruined castle—to meditate on the falling tower—to escape, in short, from the commonplace realities of the present, and lose myself among the shadowy grandeurs of the past.

I had, beside all this, an earnest desire to see the great men of the earth. We have, it is true, our great men in America: not a city but has an ample share of them. I have mingled among them in my time, and been almost withered by the shade into which they cast me; for there is nothing so baleful to a small man as the shade of a great one, particularly the great man of a city. But I was anxious to see the great men of Europe; for I had read in the works of various philosophers, that all animals degenerated in America, and man among the number.[4] A great man of Europe, therefore, thought I, must be as superior to a great man of America, as a peak of the Alps to a highland of the Hudson; and in this idea I was confirmed, by observing the comparative importance and swelling magnitude of many English travellers among us; who, I was assured, were very little people in their own country. I will visit this land of wonders, therefore, thought I, and see the gigantic race from which I am degenerated.

It has been either my good or evil lot to have my roving passion gratified. I have wandered through different countries, and witnessed many of the shifting scenes of life. I cannot say that I have studied them with the eye of a philosopher, but rather with the sauntering gaze with which humble lovers of the picturesque stroll from the window of one print shop to another; caught sometimes by the delineations of beauty, sometimes by the distortions of caricature, and sometimes by the loveliness of landscape. As it is the fashion for modern tourists to travel pencil in hand, and bring home their port folios filled with sketches, I am disposed to get up a few for the entertainment of my friends. When I look over, however, the hints and memorandums I have taken down for the purpose, my heart almost fails me to find how my idle humour has led me aside from the great objects studied by every regular traveller who would make a book. I fear I shall give equal disappointment with an unlucky landscape painter, who had travelled on the continent, but following the bent of his vagrant inclination, had sketched in nooks, and corners, and by-places. His sketch book was accordingly crowded with cottages, and landscapes, and obscure ruins; but he had neglected to paint St. Peter's, or the Coliseum; the cascade of Terni,[5] or the bay of Naples; and had not a single glacier or volcano in his whole collection.

1819

Rip Van Winkle[1]

The following Tale was found among the papers of the late Diedrich Knickerbocker, an old gentleman of New-York, who was very curious in the Dutch

4. In the late 18th century, some Europeans argued that the North American environment caused humans to degenerate physically. These arguments were made most forcefully by the French naturalist Georges-Louis Leclerc, Comte de Buffon (1707–1788). Thomas Jefferson refuted de Buffon in his 1787 *Notes on the State of Virginia*.

5. The locale of Mount Vesuvius and the ruins

of Pompeii. Other popular tourist sites listed here are St. Peter's Basilica (built 1506–1626) in Vatican City; the Roman Colosseum (built c. 70–86 C.E.); and the Cascata della Mamore, a man-made waterfall built near Terni (60 miles north of Rome) in 271 B.C.E.

1. "Rip Van Winkle" was the last of the sketches printed in the May 1819 first installment of *The Sketch Book*, the source of the present text.

history of the province, and the manners of the descendants from its primitive settlers. His historical researches, however, did not lay so much among books, as among men; for the former are lamentably scanty on his favourite topics; whereas he found the old burghers, and still more, their wives, rich in that legendary lore, so invaluable to true history. Whenever, therefore, he happened upon a genuine Dutch family, snugly shut up in its low-roofed farm house, under a spreading sycamore, he looked upon it as a little clasped volume of black-letter,[2] and studied it with the zeal of a bookworm.

The result of all these researches was a history of the province, during the reign of the Dutch governors, which he published some years since. There have been various opinions as to the literary character of his work, and, to tell the truth, it is not a whit better than it should be. Its chief merit is its scrupulous accuracy, which, indeed, was a little questioned, on its first appearance, but has since been completely established;[3] and it is now admitted into all historical collections, as a book of unquestionable authority.

The old gentleman died shortly after the publication of his work, and now, that he is dead and gone, it cannot do much harm to his memory, to say, that his time might have been much better employed in weightier labours. He, however, was apt to ride his hobby his own way; and though it did now and then kick up the dust a little in the eyes of his neighbours, and grieve the spirit of some friends, for whom he felt the truest deference and affection; yet his errors and follies are remembered "more in sorrow than in anger,"[4] and it begins to be suspected, that he never intended to injure or offend. But however his memory may be appreciated by critics, it is still held dear among many folk, whose good opinion is well worth having; particularly certain biscuit bakers, who have gone so far as to imprint his likeness on their new year cakes, and have thus given him a chance for immortality, almost equal to being stamped on a Waterloo medal, or a Queen Anne's farthing.[5]

Rip Van Winkle
A Posthumous Writing of Diedrich Knickerbocker

> By Woden, God of Saxons,
> From whence comes Wensday, that is Wodensday,
> Truth is a thing that ever I will keep
> Unto thylke day in which I creep into
> My sepulchre—
>
> —CARTWRIGHT[6]

Whoever has made a voyage up the Hudson, must remember the Kaatskill mountains.[7] They are a dismembered branch of the great Appalachian family, and are seen away to the west of the river, swelling up to a noble height, and lording it over the surrounding country. Every change of season, every change

2. Typeface in early printed books, resembling medieval script; such books, because of their value, were often equipped with clasps so they could be shut tightly and even locked.

3. A comical allusion to the deliberate inaccuracies of his 1809 Knickerbocker's *History of New-York*.

4. Shakespeare's *Hamlet* 1.2.231. To this quotation Irving appended the following footnote: "Vide [see] the excellent discourse of G. C. Verplanck, Esq. before the New-York Historical Society." If Irving's friend Gulian C. Verplanck ever made such an address about a fictional character,

it would have been in fun.

5. Waterloo medals were minted liberally after the defeat of Napoleon in 1815, whereas farthings (tiny coins) from the reign of Queen Anne of England (1702–14) were commonly, though wrongly, considered rare.

6. In this quotation from *The Ordinary*, 3.1.1050–54, a play by the English writer William Cartwright (1611–1643), the speaker is a pedant named Moth. "Woden": Old English for "Odin," the chief Norse god.

7. Catskill Mountains, a range in southeastern New York.

of weather, indeed, every hour of the day, produces some change in the magical hues and shapes of these mountains, and they are regarded by all the good wives, far and near, as perfect barometers. When the weather is fair and settled, they are clothed in blue and purple, and print their bold outlines on the clear evening sky; but some times, when the rest of the landscape is cloudless, they will gather a hood of gray vapours about their summits, which, in the last rays of the setting sun, will glow and light up like a crown of glory.

At the foot of these fairy mountains, the voyager may have descried the light smoke curling up from a village, whose shingle roofs gleam among the trees, just where the blue tints of the upland melt away into the fresh green of the nearer landscape. It is a little village of great antiquity, having been founded by some of the Dutch colonists, in the early times of the province, just about the beginning of the government of the good Peter Stuyvesant,[8] (may he rest in peace!) and there were some of the houses of the original settlers standing within a few years, with lattice windows, gable fronts surmounted with weathercocks, and built of small yellow bricks brought from Holland.

In that same village, and in one of these very houses, (which, to tell the precise truth, was sadly time worn and weather beaten,) there lived many years since, while the country was yet a province of Great Britain, a simple good natured fellow, of the name of Rip Van Winkle. He was a descendant of the Van Winkles who figured so gallantly in the chivalrous days of Peter Stuyvesant, and accompanied him to the siege of Fort Christina. He inherited, however, but little of the martial character of his ancestors. I have observed that he was a simple good natured man; he was moreover a kind neighbour, and an obedient, henpecked husband. Indeed, to the latter circumstance might be owing that meekness of spirit which gained him such universal popularity; for those men are most apt to be obsequious and conciliating abroad, who are under the discipline of shrews at home. Their tempers, doubtless, are rendered pliant and malleable in the fiery furnace of domestic tribulation, and a curtain lecture[9] is worth all the sermons in the world for teaching the virtues of patience and long suffering. A termagant wife may, therefore, in some respects, be considered a tolerable blessing; and if so, Rip Van Winkle was thrice blessed.

Certain it is, that he was a great favourite among all the good wives of the village, who, as usual with the amiable sex, took his part in all family squabbles, and never failed, whenever they talked those matters over in their evening gossippings, to lay all the blame on Dame Van Winkle. The children of the village, too, would shout with joy whenever he approached. He assisted at their sports, made their playthings, taught them to fly kites and shoot marbles, and told them long stories of ghosts, witches, and Indians. Whenever he went dodging about the village, he was surrounded by a troop of them, hanging on his skirts, clambering on his back, and playing a thousand tricks on him with impunity; and not a dog would bark at him throughout the neighbourhood.

The great error in Rip's composition was an insuperable aversion to all kinds of profitable labour. It could not be for the want of assiduity or perseverance; for he would sit on a wet rock, with a rod as long and heavy as a

---

8. Last governor of the Dutch province of New Netherlands (1592–1672); in 1655 (as mentioned in the next paragraph), his troops defeated Swedish colonists at Fort Christina, near what is now Wilmington, Delaware.

9. Archaic term for when a wife says no to her husband's sexual entreaties after the curtains around the four-poster bed have been drawn for the night.

Tartar's lance, and fish all day without a murmur, even though he should not be encouraged by a single nibble. He would carry a fowling piece on his shoulder, for hours together, trudging through woods and swamps, and up hill and down dale, to shoot a few squirrels or wild pigeons. He would never even refuse to assist a neighbour in the roughest toil, and was a foremost man at all country frolicks for husking Indian corn, or building stone fences; the women of the village, too, used to employ him to run their errands, and to do such little odd jobs as their less obliging husbands would not do for them;—in a word, Rip was ready to attend to any body's business but his own; but as to doing family duty, and keeping his farm in order, it was impossible.

In fact, he declared it was no use to work on his farm; it was the most pestilent little piece of ground in the whole country; every thing about it went wrong, and would go wrong, in spite of him. His fences were continually falling to pieces; his cow would either go astray, or get among the cabbages; weeds were sure to grow quicker in his fields than any where else; the rain always made a point of setting in just as he had some out-door work to do. So that though his patrimonial estate had dwindled away under his management, acre by acre, until there was little more left than a mere patch of Indian corn and potatoes, yet it was the worst conditioned farm in the neighbourhood.

His children, too, were as ragged and wild as if they belonged to nobody. His son Rip, an urchin begotten in his own likeness, promised to inherit the habits, with the old clothes of his father. He was generally seen trooping like a colt at his mother's heels, equipped in a pair of his father's cast-off galligaskins,[1] which he had much ado to hold up with one hand, as a fine lady does her train in bad weather.

Rip Van Winkle, however, was one of those happy mortals, of foolish, well-oiled dispositions, who take the world easy, eat white bread or brown, which ever can be got with least thought or trouble, and would rather starve on a penny than work for a pound. If left to himself, he would have whistled life away, in perfect contentment; but his wife kept continually dinning in his ears about his idleness, his carelessness, and the ruin he was bringing on his family. Morning, noon, and night, her tongue was incessantly going, and every thing he said or did was sure to produce a torrent of household eloquence. Rip had but one way of replying to all lectures of the kind, and that, by frequent use, had grown into a habit. He shrugged his shoulders, shook his head, cast up his eyes, but said nothing. This, however, always provoked a fresh volley from his wife, so that he was fain to draw off his forces, and take to the outside of the house—the only side which, in truth, belongs to a henpecked husband.

Rip's sole domestic adherent was his dog Wolf, who was as much henpecked as his master; for Dame Van Winkle regarded them as companions in idleness, and even looked upon Wolf with an evil eye, as the cause of his master's so often going astray. True it is, in all points of spirit befitting an honourable dog, he was as courageous an animal as ever scoured the woods—but what courage can withstand the ever-during and all-besetting terrors of a woman's tongue? The moment Wolf entered the house, his crest fell, his tail drooped to the ground, or curled between his legs, he sneaked about with a gallows air, casting many a sidelong glance at Dame Van Winkle, and at the

1. Loose, wide trousers.

least flourish of a broomstick or ladle, would fly to the door with yelping precipitation.

Times grew worse and worse with Rip Van Winkle as years of matrimony rolled on; a tart temper never mellows with age, and a sharp tongue is the only edge tool that grows keener by constant use. For a long while he used to console himself, when driven from home, by frequenting a kind of perpetual club of the sages, philosophers, and other idle personages of the village, that held its sessions on a bench before a small inn, designated by a rubicund portrait of his majesty George the Third. Here they used to sit in the shade, of a long lazy summer's day, talk listlessly over village gossip, or tell endless sleepy stories about nothing. But it would have been worth any statesman's money to have heard the profound discussions that sometimes took place, when by chance an old newspaper fell into their hands, from some passing traveller. How solemnly they would listen to the contents, as drawled out by Derrick Van Bummel, the schoolmaster, a dapper learned little man, who was not to be daunted by the most gigantic word in the dictionary; and how sagely they would deliberate upon public events some months after they had taken place.

The opinions of this junto[2] were completely controlled by Nicholas Vedder, a patriarch of the village, and landlord of the inn, at the door of which he took his seat from morning till night, just moving sufficiently to avoid the sun, and keep in the shade of a large tree; so that the neighbours could tell the hour by his movements as accurately as by a sun dial. It is true, he was rarely heard to speak, but smoked his pipe incessantly. His adherents, however, (for every great man has his adherents,) perfectly understood him, and knew how to gather his opinions. When any thing that was read or related displeased him, he was observed to smoke his pipe vehemently, and send forth short, frequent, and angry puffs; but when pleased, he would inhale the smoke slowly and tranquilly, and emit it in light and placid clouds, and sometimes taking the pipe from his mouth, and letting the fragrant vapour curl about his nose, would gravely nod his head in token of perfect approbation.

From even this strong hold the unlucky Rip was at length routed by his termagant wife, who would suddenly break in upon the tranquillity of the assemblage, call the members all to nought, nor was that august personage, Nicholas Vedder himself, sacred from the daring tongue of this terrible virago, who charged him outright with encouraging her husband in habits of idleness.

Poor Rip was at last reduced almost to despair; and his only alternative to escape from the labour of the farm and the clamour of his wife, was to take gun in hand, and stroll away into the woods. Here he would sometimes seat himself at the foot of a tree, and share the contents of his wallet[3] with Wolf, with whom he sympathised as a fellow sufferer in persecution. "Poor Wolf," he would say, "thy mistress leads thee a dogs' life of it; but never mind, my lad, while I live thou shalt never want a friend to stand by thee!" Wolf would wag his tail, look wistfully in his master's face, and if dogs can feel pity, I verily believe he reciprocated the sentiment with all his heart.

In a long ramble of the kind on a fine autumnal day, Rip had unconsciously scrambled to one of the highest parts of the Kaatskill mountains. He was after his favourite sport of squirrel shooting, and the still solitudes had

2. Ruling committee (Spanish).   3. Knapsack.

echoed and re-echoed with the reports of his gun. Panting and fatigued, he threw himself, late in the afternoon, on a green knoll, covered with mountain herbage, that crowned the brow of a precipice. From an opening between the trees, he could overlook all the lower country for many a mile of rich woodland. He saw at a distance the lordly Hudson, far, far below him, moving on its silent but majestic course, the reflection of a purple cloud, or the sail of a lagging bark, here and there sleeping on its glassy bosom, and at last losing itself in the blue highlands.

On the other side he looked down into a deep mountain glen, wild, lonely, and shagged, the bottom filled with fragments from the impending cliffs, and scarcely lighted by the reflected rays of the setting sun. For some time Rip lay musing on this scene, evening was gradually advancing, the mountains began to throw their long blue shadows over the valleys, he saw that it would be dark long before he could reach the village, and he heaved a heavy sigh when he thought of encountering the terrors of Dame Van Winkle.

As he was about to descend, he heard a voice from a distance, hallooing, "Rip Van Winkle! Rip Van Winkle!" He looked around, but could see nothing but a crow winging its solitary flight across the mountain. He thought his fancy must have deceived him, and turned again to descend, when he heard the same cry ring through the still evening air; "Rip Van Winkle! Rip Van Winkle!"—at the same time Wolf bristled up his back, and giving a low growl, skulked to his master's side, looking fearfully down into the glen. Rip now felt a vague apprehension stealing over him; he looked anxiously in the same direction, and perceived a strange figure slowly toiling up the rocks, and bending under the weight of something he carried on his back. He was surprised to see any human being in this lonely and unfrequented place, but supposing it to be some one of the neighbourhood in need of his assistance, he hastened down to yield it.

On nearer approach, he was still more surprised at the singularity of the stranger's appearance. He was a short square built old fellow, with thick bushy hair, and a grizzled beard. His dress was of the antique Dutch fashion—a cloth jerkin[4] strapped round the waist—several pair of breeches, the outer one of ample volume, decorated with rows of buttons down the sides, and bunches at the knees. He bore on his shoulder a stout keg, that seemed full of liquor, and made signs for Rip to approach and assist him with the load. Though rather shy and distrustful of this new acquaintance, Rip complied with his usual alacrity, and mutually relieving each other, they clambered up a narrow gully, apparently the dry bed of a mountain torrent. As they ascended, Rip every now and then heard long rolling peals, like distant thunder, that seemed to issue out of a deep ravine, or rather cleft between lofty rocks, toward which their rugged path conducted. He paused for an instant, but supposing it to be the muttering of one of those transient thunder showers which often take place in mountain heights, he proceeded. Passing through the ravine, they came to a hollow, like a small amphitheatre, surrounded by perpendicular precipices, over the brinks of which impending trees shot their branches, so that you only caught glimpses of the azure sky, and the bright evening cloud. During the whole time, Rip and his companion had laboured on in silence; for though the former marvelled greatly what could be the object of carrying a keg of liquor up this wild mountain, yet

4. Jacket fitted tightly at the waist.

there was something strange and incomprehensible about the unknown, that inspired awe, and checked familiarity.

On entering the amphitheatre, new objects of wonder presented themselves. On a level spot in the centre was a company of odd-looking personages playing at nine-pins. They were dressed in a quaint, outlandish fashion: some wore short doublets,[5] others jerkins, with long knives in their belts, and most had enormous breeches, of similar style with that of the guide's. Their visages, too, were peculiar: one had a large head, broad face, and small piggish eyes; the face of another seemed to consist entirely of nose, and was surmounted by a white sugarloaf hat, set off with a little red cockstail. They all had beards, of various shapes and colours. There was one who seemed to be the commander. He was a stout old gentleman, with a weather-beaten countenance; he wore a laced doublet, broad belt and hanger,[6] high crowned hat and feather, red stockings, and high heeled shoes, with roses in them. The whole group reminded Rip of the figures in an old Flemish painting, in the parlour of Dominie[7] Van Schaick, the village parson, and which had been brought over from Holland at the time of the settlement.

What seemed particularly odd to Rip, was, that though these folks were evidently amusing themselves, yet they maintained the gravest faces, the most mysterious silence, and were, withal, the most melancholy party of pleasure he had ever witnessed. Nothing interrupted the stillness of the scene, but the noise of the balls, which, whenever they were rolled, echoed along the mountains like rumbling peals of thunder.

As Rip and his companion approached them, they suddenly desisted from their play, and stared at him with such fixed statue-like gaze, and such strange, uncouth, lack lustre countenances, that his heart turned within him, and his knees smote together. His companion now emptied the contents of the keg into large flagons, and made signs to him to wait upon the company. He obeyed with fear and trembling; they quaffed the liquor in profound silence, and then returned to their game.

By degrees, Rip's awe and apprehension subsided. He even ventured, when no eye was fixed upon him, to taste the beverage, which he found had much of the flavour of excellent Hollands.[8] He was naturally a thirsty soul, and was soon tempted to repeat the draught. One taste provoked another, and he reiterated his visits to the flagon so often, that at length his senses were overpowered, his eyes swam in his head, his head gradually declined, and he fell into a deep sleep.

On awaking, he found himself on the green knoll from whence he had first seen the old man of the glen. He rubbed his eyes—it was a bright sunny morning. The birds were hopping and twittering among the bushes, and the eagle was wheeling aloft, and breasting the pure mountain breeze. "Surely," thought Rip, "I have not slept here all night." He recalled the occurrences before he fell asleep. The strange man with the keg of liquor—the mountain ravine—the wild retreat among the rocks—the wo-begone party at nine-pins—the flagon—"Oh! that flagon! that wicked flagon!" thought Rip—"what excuse shall I make to Dame Van Winkle?"

5. Male jacket covering from neck to upper thighs, where it hooked to hose.
6. Short, curved sword.
7. Minister.
8. Gin made in Holland.

He looked round for his gun, but in place of the clean well-oiled fowling-piece, he found an old firelock lying by him, the barrel encrusted with rust, the lock falling off, and the stock worm-eaten. He now suspected that the grave roysters[9] of the mountain had put a trick upon him, and having dosed him with liquor, had robbed him of his gun. Wolf, too, had disappeared, but he might have strayed away after a squirrel or partridge. He whistled after him, shouted his name, but all in vain; the echoes repeated his whistle and shout, but no dog was to be seen.

He determined to revisit the scene of the last evening's gambol, and if he met with any of the party, to demand his dog and gun. As he arose to walk he found himself stiff in the joints, and wanting in his usual activity. "These mountain beds do not agree with me," thought Rip, "and if this frolick should lay me up with a fit of the rheumatism, I shall have a blessed time with Dame Van Winkle." With some difficulty he got down into the glen: he found the gully up which he and his companion had ascended the preceding evening, but to his astonishment a mountain stream was now foaming down it, leaping from rock to rock, and filling the glen with babbling murmurs. He, however, made shift to scramble up its sides, working his toilsome way through thickets of birch, sassafras, and witch hazle, and sometimes tripped up or entangled by the wild grape vines that twisted their coils and tendrils from tree to tree, and spread a kind of network in his path.

At length he reached to where the ravine had opened through the cliffs, to the amphitheatre; but no traces of such opening remained. The rocks presented a high impenetrable wall, over which the torrent came tumbling in a sheet of feathery foam, and fell into a broad deep basin, black from the shadows of the surrounding forest. Here, then, poor Rip was brought to a stand. He again called and whistled after his dog; he was only answered by the cawing of a flock of idle crows, sporting high in air about a dry tree that overhung a sunny precipice; and who, secure in their elevation, seemed to look down and scoff at the poor man's perplexities. What was to be done? the morning was passing away, and Rip felt famished for his breakfast. He grieved to give up his dog and gun; he dreaded to meet his wife; but it would not do to starve among the mountains. He shook his head, shouldered the rusty firelock, and, with a heart full of trouble and anxiety, turned his steps homeward.

As he approached the village, he met a number of people, but none that he knew, which somewhat surprised him, for he had thought himself acquainted with every one in the country round. Their dress, too, was of a different fashion from that to which he was accustomed. They all stared at him with equal marks of surprise, and whenever they cast eyes upon him, invariably stroked their chins. The constant recurrence of this gesture, induced Rip, involuntarily, to do the same, when, to his astonishment, he found his beard had grown a foot long!

He had now entered the skirts of the village. A troop of strange children ran at his heels, hooting after him, and pointing at his gray beard. The dogs, too, not one of which he recognized for his old acquaintances, barked at him as he passed. The very village seemed altered: it was larger and more populous. There were rows of houses which he had never seen before, and those which had been his familiar haunts had disappeared. Strange names were

9. Revelers.

over the doors—strange faces at the windows—every thing was strange. His mind now began to misgive him, that both he and the world around him were bewitched. Surely this was his native village, which he had left but the day before. There stood the Kaatskill mountains—there ran the silver Hudson at a distance—there was every hill and dale precisely as it had always been— Rip was sorely perplexed—"That flagon last night," thought he, "has addled my poor head sadly!"

It was with some difficulty he found the way to his own house, which he approached with silent awe, expecting every moment to hear the shrill voice of Dame Van Winkle. He found the house gone to decay—the roof fallen in, the windows shattered, and the doors off the hinges. A half starved dog, that looked like Wolf, was skulking about it. Rip called him by name, but the cur snarled, showed his teeth, and passed on. This was an unkind cut indeed— "My very dog," sighed poor Rip, "has forgotten me!"

He entered the house, which, to tell the truth, Dame Van Winkle had always kept in neat order. It was empty, forlorn, and apparently abandoned. This desolateness overcame all his connubial fears—he called loudly for his wife and children—the lonely chambers rung for a moment with his voice, and then all again was silence.

He now hurried forth, and hastened to his old resort, the little village inn—but it too was gone. A large rickety wooden building stood in its place, with great gaping windows, some of them broken, and mended with old hats and petticoats, and over the door was painted, "The Union Hotel, by Jonathan Doolittle." Instead of the great tree that used to shelter the quiet little Dutch inn of yore, there now was reared a tall naked pole, with something on top that looked like a red night cap,[1] and from it was fluttering a flag, on which was a singular assemblage of stars and stripes—all this was strange and incomprehensible. He recognised on the sign, however, the ruby face of King George, under which he had smoked so many a peaceful pipe, but even this was singularly metamorphosed. The red coat was changed for one of blue and buff,[2] a sword was stuck in the hand instead of a sceptre, the head was decorated with a cocked hat, and underneath was painted in large characters, GENERAL WASHINGTON.

There was, as usual, a crowd of folk about the door, but none that Rip recollected. The very character of the people seemed changed. There was a busy, bustling, disputatious tone about it, instead of the accustomed phlegm and drowsy tranquillity. He looked in vain for the sage Nicholas Vedder, with his broad face, double chin, and fair long pipe, uttering clouds of tobacco smoke instead of idle speeches; or Van Bummel, the schoolmaster, doling forth the contents of an ancient newspaper. In place of these, a lean bilious looking fellow, with his pockets full of handbills, was haranguing vehemently about rights of citizens—election—members of congress—liberty—Bunker's hill— heroes of seventy-six—and other words, that were a perfect Babylonish jargon[3] to the bewildered Van Winkle.

The appearance of Rip, with his long grizzled beard, his rusty fowling piece, his uncouth dress, and the army of women and children that had gathered at his heels, soon attracted the attention of the tavern politicians. They

1. Limp, close-fitting cap adopted during the French Revolution as a symbol of liberty (such caps were worn by freed slaves in ancient Rome). The pole is a "liberty pole"—i.e., a tall flagstaff topped by a liberty cap.
2. Colors of the Revolutionary uniform.
3. Cf. Genesis 11.1–9, Babel being confused with Babylon.

crowded around him, eyeing him from head to foot, with great curiosity.[4] The orator bustled up to him, and drawing him partly aside, inquired "which side he voted?" Rip stared in vacant stupidity. Another short but busy little fellow pulled him by the arm, and raising on tiptoe, inquired in his ear, "whether he was Federal or Democrat."[5] Rip was equally at a loss to comprehend the question; when a knowing, self-important old gentleman, in a sharp cocked hat, made his way through the crowd, putting them to the right and left with his elbows as he passed, and planting himself before Van Winkle, with one arm akimbo, the other resting on his cane, his keen eyes and sharp hat penetrating, as it were, into his very soul, demanded, in an austere tone, "what brought him to the election with a gun on his shoulder, and a mob at his heels, and whether he meant to breed a riot in the village?" "Alas! gentlemen," cried Rip, somewhat dismayed, "I am a poor quiet man, a native of the place, and a loyal subject of the King, God bless him!"

Here a general shout burst from the bystanders—"A tory! a tory! a spy! a refugee! hustle him! away with him!" It was with great difficulty that the self-important man in the cocked hat restored order; and having assumed a tenfold austerity of brow, demanded again of the unknown culprit, what he came there for, and whom he was seeking. The poor man humbly assured them that he meant no harm; but merely came there in search of some of his neighbours, who used to keep about the tavern.

"Well—who are they?—name them."

Rip bethought himself a moment, and inquired, "where's Nicholas Vedder?"

There was a silence for a little while, when an old man replied, in a thin piping voice, "Nicholas Vedder? why he is dead and gone these eighteen years! There was a wooden tombstone in the church yard that used to tell all about him, but that's rotted and gone too."

"Where's Brom Dutcher?"

"Oh he went off to the army in the beginning of the war; some say he was killed at the battle of Stoney-Point—others say he was drowned in a squall, at the foot of Antony's Nose.[6] I don't know—he never came back again."

"Where's Van Bummel, the schoolmaster?"

"He went off to the wars too, was a great militia general, and is now in Congress."

Rip's heart died away, at hearing of these sad changes in his home and friends, and finding himself thus alone in the world. Every answer puzzled him, too, by treating of such enormous lapses of time, and of matters which he could not understand: war—congress—Stoney-Point;—he had no courage to ask after any more friends, but cried out in despair, "does nobody here know Rip Van Winkle?"

"Oh, Rip Van Winkle!" exclaimed two or three, "Oh, to be sure! that's Rip Van Winkle yonder, leaning against the tree."

Rip looked, and beheld a precise counterpart of himself, as he went up the mountain: apparently as lazy, and certainly as ragged. The poor fellow was now completely confounded. He doubted his own identity, and whether

4. For a contemporary painting depicting Rip Van Winkle's appearance in his village, see John Quidor's *The Return of Rip Van Winkle* (1829) in the color plates section of this volume.
5. Political parties that developed in the Washington administration (1789–97), with Alexander Hamilton (1755–1804) leading the Federalists and Thomas Jefferson (1743–1826), the Democrats.
6. A mountain near West Point. Stoney Point, a British fort, was captured by General Anthony Wayne (1745–1796) during the Revolution.

he was himself or another man. In the midst of his bewilderment, the man in the cocked hat demanded who he was, and what was his name?

"God knows," exclaimed he, at his wit's end; "I'm not myself—I'm somebody else—that's me yonder—no—that's somebody else, got into my shoes—I was myself last night, but I fell asleep on the mountain, and they've changed my gun, and every thing's changed, and I'm changed, and I can't tell what's my name, or who I am!"

The bystanders began now to look at each other, nod, wink significantly, and tap their fingers against their foreheads. There was a whisper, also, about securing the gun, and keeping the old fellow from doing mischief. At the very suggestion of which, the self-important man in the cocked hat retired with some precipitation. At this critical moment a fresh likely woman pressed through the throng to get a peep at the graybearded man. She had a chubby child in her arms, which, frightened at his looks, began to cry. "Hush, Rip," cried she, "hush, you little fool, the old man wont hurt you." The name of the child, the air of the mother, the tone of her voice, all awakened a train of recollections in his mind.

"What is your name, my good woman?" asked he.

"Judith Gardenier."

"And your father's name?"

"Ah, poor man, his name was Rip Van Winkle; it's twenty years since he went away from home with his gun, and never has been heard of since—his dog came home without him; but whether he shot himself, or was carried away by the Indians, nobody can tell. I was then but a little girl."

Rip had but one question more to ask; but he put it with a faltering voice:

"Where's your mother?"

Oh, she too had died but a short time since; she broke a blood vessel in a fit of passion at a New-England pedlar.

There was a drop of comfort, at least, in this intelligence. The honest man could contain himself no longer.—He caught his daughter and her child in his arms.—"I am your father!" cried he—"Young Rip Van Winkle once—old Rip Van Winkle now!—Does nobody know poor Rip Van Winkle!"

All stood amazed, until an old woman, tottering out from among the crowd, put her hand to her brow, and peering under it in his face for a moment, exclaimed, "Sure enough! it is Rip Van Winkle—it is himself. Welcome home again, old neighbour—Why, where have you been these twenty long years?"

Rip's story was soon told, for the whole twenty years had been to him but as one night. The neighbours stared when they heard it; some were seen to wink at each other, and put their tongues in their cheeks; and the self-important man in the cocked hat, who, when the alarm was over, had returned to the field, screwed down the corners of his mouth, and shook his head—upon which there was a general shaking of the head throughout the assemblage.

It was determined, however, to take the opinion of old Peter Vanderdonk, who was seen slowly advancing up the road. He was a descendant of the historian of that name,[7] who wrote one of the earliest accounts of the province. Peter was the most ancient inhabitant of the village, and well versed

7. Adriaen Van der Donck (1620–1655?) wrote a history of New Netherlands (1655).

in all the wonderful events and traditions of the neighbourhood. He recollected Rip at once, and corroborated his story in the most satisfactory manner. He assured the company that it was a fact, handed down from his ancestor the historian, that the Kaatskill mountains had always been haunted by strange beings. That it was affirmed that the great Hendrick Hudson, the first discoverer of the river and country, kept a kind of vigil there every twenty years, with his crew of the Half-moon, being permitted in this way to revisit the scenes of his enterprize, and keep a guardian eye upon the river, and the great city[8] called by his name. That his father had once seen them in their old Dutch dresses playing at nine pins in a hollow of the mountain; and that he himself had heard, one summer afternoon, the sound of their balls, like long peals of thunder.

To make a long story short, the company broke up, and returned to the more important concerns of the election. Rip's daughter took him home to live with her; she had a snug, well-furnished house, and a stout cheery farmer for a husband, whom Rip recollected for one of the urchins that used to climb upon his back. As to Rip's son and heir, who was the ditto of himself, seen leaning against the tree, he was employed to work on the farm; but evinced an hereditary disposition to attend to any thing else but his business.

Rip now resumed his old walks and habits; he soon found many of his former cronies, though all rather the worse for the wear and tear of time; and preferred making friends among the rising generation, with whom he soon grew into great favour.

Having nothing to do at home, and being arrived at that happy age when a man can do nothing with impunity, he took his place once more on the bench, at the inn door, and was reverenced as one of the patriarchs of the village, and a chronicle of the old times "before the war." It was some time before he could get into the regular track of gossip, or could be made to comprehend the strange events that had taken place during his torpor. How that there had been a revolutionary war—that the country had thrown off the yoke of old England—and that, instead of being a subject of his Majesty George the Third, he was now a free citizen of the United States. Rip, in fact, was no politician; the changes of states and empires made but little impression on him. But there was one species of despotism under which he had long groaned, and that was—petticoat government. Happily, that was at an end; he had got his neck out of the yoke of matrimony, and could go in and out whenever he pleased, without dreading the tyranny of Dame Van Winkle. Whenever her name was mentioned, however, he shook his head, shrugged his shoulders, and cast up his eyes; which might pass either for an expression of resignation to his fate, or joy at his deliverance.

He used to tell his story to every stranger that arrived at Mr. Doolittle's hotel. He was observed, at first, to vary on some points every time he told it, which was, doubtless, owing to his having so recently awaked. It at last settled down precisely to the tale I have related, and not a man, woman, or child in the neighbourhood, but knew it by heart. Some always pretended to doubt the reality of it, and insisted that Rip had been out of his head, and that this was one point on which he always remained flighty. The old Dutch inhabitants, however, almost universally gave it full credit. Even to this day they never hear a thunder storm of a summer afternoon, about the Kaatskill, but they say Hendrick Hudson and his crew are at their game of nine pins; and it is a common wish of all henpecked husbands in the neighbourhood, when life hangs heavy on their hands, that they might have a quieting draught out of Rip Van Winkle's flagon.

NOTE

The foregoing tale, one would suspect, had been suggested to Mr. Knickerbocker by a little German superstition about Charles V.[9] and the Kypphauser mountain; the subjoined note, however, which he had appended to the tale, shows that it is an absolute fact, narrated with his usual fidelity:

"The story of Rip Van Winkle may seem incredible to many, but nevertheless I give it my full belief, for I know the vicinity of our old Dutch settlements to have been very subject to marvellous events and appearances. Indeed, I have heard many stranger stories than this, in the villages along the Hudson; all of which were too well authenticated to admit of a doubt. I have even talked with Rip Van Winkle myself, who, when last I saw him, was a very venerable old man, and so perfectly rational and consistent on every other point, that I think no conscientious person could refuse to take this into the bargain; nay, I have seen a certificate on the subject taken before a country justice, and signed with a cross, in the justice's own hand writing. The story, therefore, is beyond the possibility of doubt.   D.K."

1819

9. Later Irving changed "Charles V." (Holy Roman emperor, 1519–56) to "The Emperor Frederick *der Rothbart*" (i.e., Frederick Barbarossa; Holy Roman emperor, 1152–90). ("Rothbart" and "Barbarossa" both mean "redbeard.") In either form, the allusion is to a source other than the actual one, the story of Peter Klaus in the folktales of J.C.C.N. Otmar (1800).

JAMES FENIMORE COOPER
1789–1851

The author of thirty-two novels, a history of the American navy, five travel books, and two major works of social criticism, James Fenimore Cooper was among the most important writers of his time—a writer who helped chart the future course of American fiction. He wrote novels of manners, transatlantic and European fiction, and several historical novels on the American Revolution. A pioneering author of sea fiction, he had a significant influence on Herman Melville. But Cooper remains best known for the five historical novels of the Leatherstocking series, which are set between 1740 and the early 1800s. These novels—*The Pioneers* (1823), *The Last of the Mohicans* (1826), *The Prairie* (1827), *The Pathfinder* (1840), and *The Deerslayer* (1841)—explore the imperial, racial, and social conflicts central to the emergence of the United States; and their evocative portrayals of the frontiersman Natty Bumppo and his Indian friend Chingachgook helped to develop what the British novelist and critic D. H. Lawrence influentially called "the myth of America." Central to that myth is the image of a nation founded through conflict and dispossession that nonetheless managed to sustain belief in its youthful innocence.

Cooper was born on September 15, 1789, in Burlington, New Jersey, and in 1790 moved with his parents to Cooperstown, on Otsego Lake in central New York, a town founded and developed by his father, Judge William Cooper. A two-term member of Congress known for his energetic entrepreneurship and ardent Federalism, the judge hoped to educate his son to manage the family settlements, sending him first to an academy in Albany and then to Yale, where the thirteen-year-old Cooper became known as a prankster. Expelled from Yale because of misconduct in 1805, Cooper (at his father's insistence) became a sailor in 1806 and was commissioned as a midshipman in the U.S. Navy in 1808. One year later, when Judge Cooper unexpectedly died, leaving behind an apparently large fortune for his heirs, the twenty-year-old Cooper seemed set for life. He resigned from the navy and, in 1811, married Susan DeLancey, whose prominent New York State family had lost considerable possessions by siding with the British during the Revolution but still owned lands in Westchester County. For several years Cooper oversaw properties in Westchester County and Cooperstown. But the family fortunes steadily diminished. In 1819, with the death of an older brother, Cooper became the person primarily responsible for the debt-ridden Cooper estate. A failure at managing the "real" Cooperstown, Cooper through his authorship of the Leatherstocking novels may well have sought to take imaginative possession of the New York lands he could never oversee with the skill of his father.

Cooper began his writing career in 1820, in large part in an effort to earn enough money to pay his debts. According to family lore, he bet his wife that he could write a better novel than the British novel of manners the two had been reading together. The result was *Precaution* (1820), a leaden novel of British high society modeled on Jane Austen's *Persuasion* (1818). Following that insignificant start, Cooper turned to the historical romance as popularized by the Scottish writer Sir Walter Scott, and produced *The Spy* (1821), the first important novel about the American Revolution. Its success led him to move to New York City and embark on a successful literary career. He founded a literary society there, the Bread and Cheese Club, and became the center of a circle that included notable painters of the Hudson River School as well as writers (William Cullen Bryant among them) and professionals. In 1823 he published *The Pioneers*, the first of the Leatherstocking novels featuring Natty Bumppo. Cooper had not written *The Pioneers* with the intention of inaugurating a series, but response to Natty Bumppo was so positive that he returned to him three years later with *The Last of the Mohicans*, consolidating his creation of one of the most popular characters in world literature. With his previous novels, Cooper had assumed the financial risk of paying printers and doing the bulk of the promotion. *Mohicans* was the first of his novels published by the Philadelphia firm of Carey and Lea, which paid him $5,000 (around $85,000 in today's value) for the novel. Although Cooper was never financially secure, this new arrangement helped him to pay off his family's debts.

In 1826, at the height of his fame, Cooper sailed for Europe with his wife and their five children. In Paris, where he became intimate with the aged Lafayette, he wrote *The Prairie* (1827) and *Notions of the Americans* (1828), a defense of the United States against criticism by European travelers. Smarting under the half-complimentary, half-patronizing epithet of "The American Scott," he wrote three historical novels set in medieval Europe—*The Bravo* (1831), *The Heidenmauer* (1832), and *The Headsman* (1833)—as a realistic corrective to what he regarded as Sir Walter Scott's glorifications of the past. On his return to the United States in 1833, Cooper was so angered by the negative reception of these novels that he renounced novel writing in *Letter to His Countrymen* (1834). Subsequently, at Cooperstown he gave notice that a point of land on Otsego Lake where the townspeople had been picnicking was private property and not to be used without his permission. Newspapers began attacking him as a would-be aristocrat poisoned by his residence abroad, and for years Cooper embroiled himself in lawsuits designed not to gain damages for libels but to tame the vitriolic press. Even while pursuing these legal efforts, Cooper continued to write book after book—social and political satires growing out of his experiences with the press, a political primer on the dangers of an unchecked, demagogic democracy (*The American Democrat* [1838]), and (silently retracting his 1834 renunciation of fiction writing) a series of sociopolitical novels and two additional Leatherstocking novels: *The Pathfinder* (1840) and *The Deerslayer* (1841). His monumental *History of the Navy of the United States of America* (1839) became the focus of new quarrels and a new lawsuit, and controversy continued to surround Cooper when he published his "Littlepage" novels—*Satanstoe* (1845), *The Chainbearer* (1845), and *The Redskins* (1846)—which supported landowners over tenants in the controversy known as the Anti-Rent War, and his anti-utopian novel *The Crater* (1847), which imagined the demise of the American republic as a result of demagogues' assaults on the Constitution. When Herman Melville reviewed Cooper's last great sea novel, *The Sea Lions* (1849), in the April 1849 issue of the *Literary World*, he lambasted "those who more for fashion's sake than anything else, have of late joined in decrying our national novelist" and concluded by warmly recommending what he termed one of Cooper's "happiest" novels.

A lifelong defender of American democracy against European aristocracy and home-grown demagoguery, Cooper had become out of step with some of his countrypeople. When Cooper died on September 14, 1851, a day before his sixty-second birthday, his detractors—who spoke of him as a reactionary prig—were vastly outnumbered by his admirers. At a memorial commemoration on February 25, 1852, Washington Irving declared that the death of Cooper "left a space in our literature which will not be easily supplied"; Emerson spoke of "an old debt to him of happy days, on the first appearance of the *Pioneers*"; and the historian Francis Parkman proclaimed that of "all American writers, Cooper is the most original and the most thoroughly national." Throughout the century and into the next, Cooper's Leatherstocking novels had an incalculable vogue in the United States and abroad. Major European writers as diverse as Honoré de Balzac and Leo Tolstoy were profoundly moved by *The Pioneers* and the subsequent Natty Bumppo novels, while the novelist Joseph Conrad proclaimed that Cooper "wrote as well as any novelist of the time." Dissenting from such adulation, Mark Twain asserted in his classic essay "Fenimore Cooper's Literary Offenses" (1895) that Cooper's English is "a crime against the language." Nevertheless, the Leatherstocking novels are probably the books that most influenced Twain's own *Huckleberry Finn* and many other frontier and western novels published after the appearance of *Mohicans* in 1826. Twain's account of Huck's flight from society and his friendship with the runaway slave Jim drew on what continues to appeal to modern readers of Cooper: the profound dramatizations of such key American conflicts as natural rights versus legal rights, order versus change, wilderness versus established society, and—especially—the possibilities of democratic freedom and interracial friendship as exemplified by the enduring image of Natty Bumppo and Chingachgook on the vanishing frontier.

The Last of the Mohicans

The second novel in the Leatherstocking series, *The Last of the Mohicans; A Narrative of 1757* (1826), depicts Natty Bumppo, also known as Hawk-eye, as a wilderness scout in the British colony of New York at the time of the French and Indian War (1754–63). At the center of the novel is a fictionalized account of the August 10, 1757, massacre at Fort William Henry, in which perhaps hundreds of British colonists were killed or injured by the Huron Indians and other tribes allied with the French general Montcalm. According to Cooper, the ineptness of the British general Webb left the colonists vulnerable to the retaliatory violence of the Indians. By drawing on this historical incident, Cooper suggests that the colonists' progress toward independence required the departure from North America of both the French and the British military as well as any other European power aspiring to rule the continent. Published a few years before

President Andrew Jackson initiated his Indian removal policies, the novel at first glance seems to reinforce the idea that progress required the "extinction" or expulsion of the Indians. But at the heart of the novel is a poignant interracial friendship between the white man, Natty Bumppo, and the Mohican, Chingachgook, suggestive of Cooper's unhappiness with the brutalities that would eventually result in the death of Chingachgook's heroic son Uncas, "the last of the Mohicans." In Cooper's complex historical vision, progress always comes at a price, and the overall novel laments the sufferings of the Mohicans, whom Cooper presents as committed to the highest moral and ethical standards.

The chapter reprinted here comes from the beginning of the novel. Major Duncan Hayward is escorting the daughters of the British Lieutenant Colonel Munro, Alice and Cora, to Fort William Henry, which at the time is under the command of Munro himself. Unbeknownst to Hayward and the daughters, the Huron Magua, who

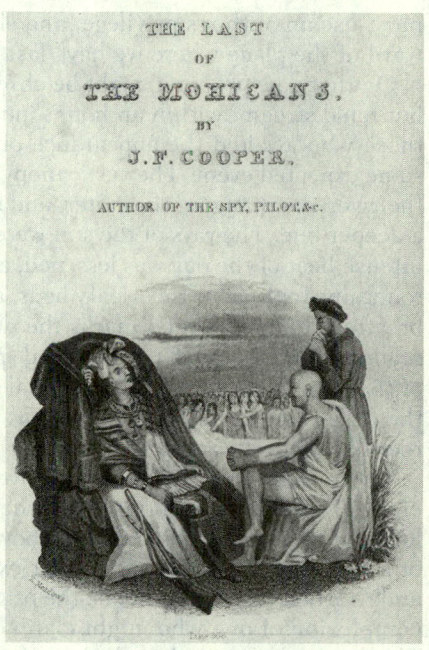

The cover of an 1836 British printing of *The Last of the Mohicans* (1826).

offers himself as a guide in the wilderness, had once been flogged by Munro, and now vengefully wishes to capture the daughters. Natty, Chingachgook, and Uncas will eventually help the daughters reunite with their father. At this early point in the novel, however, before they have even met the Munro party, the friends Natty and Chingachgook discuss the colonial history of the Americas and convey the differing historical perspectives of the English and the Native Americans.

From The Last of the Mohicans

From Volume I

Chapter III

[NATTY BUMPPO AND CHINGACHGOOK; STORIES OF THE FATHERS]

> Before these fields were shorn and tilled,
>   Full to the brim our rivers flowed;
> The melody of waters filled
>   The fresh and boundless wood;
> And torrents dashed, and rivulets played,
>   And fountains spouted in the shade.
> *Bryant*[1]

Leaving the unsuspecting Heyward, and his confiding companions, to penetrate still deeper into a forest that contained such treacherous inmates, we

1. From "An Indian at the Burial-Place of His Fathers" (1824), by William Cullen Bryant (1794–1878).

must use an author's privilege, and shift the scene a few miles to the west-ward of the place where we have last seen them.

On that day, two men might be observed, lingering on the banks of a small but rapid stream, within an hour's journey of the encampment of Webb, like those who awaited the appearance of an absent person, or the approach of some expected event. The vast canopy of woods spread itself to the margin of the river, overhanging the water, and shadowing its dark glassy current with a deeper hue. The rays of the sun were beginning to grow less fierce, and the intense heat of the day was lessened, as the cooler vapours of the springs and fountains rose above their leafy beds, and rested in the atmosphere. Still that breathing silence, which marks the drowsy sultriness of an American land-scape in July, pervaded the secluded spot, interrupted, only, by the low voices of the men in question, an occasional and lazy tap of a reviving wood-pecker, the discordant cry of some gaudy jay, or a swelling on the ear, from the dull roar of a distant water-fall.

These feeble and broken sounds were, however, too familiar to the forest-ers, to draw their attention from the more interesting matter of their dia-logue. While one of these loiterers showed the red skin and wild accoutrements of a native of the woods, the other exhibited, through the mask of his rude and nearly savage equipments, the brighter, though sun-burnt and long-faded complexion of one who might claim descent from an European parentage. The former was seated on the end of a mossy log, in a posture that permitted him to heighten the effect of his earnest language, by the calm but expressive gestures of an Indian, engaged in debate. His body, which was nearly naked, presented a terrific emblem of death, drawn in intermingled colours of white and black. His closely shaved head, on which no other hair than the well known and chivalrous scalping tuft was preserved, was without ornament of any kind, with the exception of a solitary Eagle's plume, that crossed his crown, and depended[2] over the left shoulder. A tomahawk and scalping-knife, of English manufacture, were in his girdle; while a short military rifle, of that sort with which the policy of the whites armed their savage allies, lay care-lessly across his bare and sinewy knee. The expanded chest, full-formed limbs, and grave countenance of this warrior, would denote that he had reached the vigour of his days, though no symptoms of decay appeared to have yet weakened his manhood.

The frame of the white man, judging by such parts as were not concealed by his clothes, was like that of one who had known hardships and exertion from his earliest youth. His person, though muscular, was rather attenuated than full; but every nerve and muscle appeared strung and indurated,[3] by unremitted exposure and toil. He wore a hunting-shirt of forest-green, fringed with faded yellow, and a summer cap, of skins which had been shorn of their fur. He also bore a knife in a girdle of wampum, like that which confined the scanty garments of the Indian, but no tomahawk. His moccasins were orna-mented after the gay fashion of the natives, while the only part of his under dress which appeared below the hunting-frock, was a pair of buckskin leg-

<hr>

2. Hung down. "Scalping tuft": Cooper supplied the following note to the 1831 edition of *Mohi-cans*: "The North American warrior caused the hair to be plucked from his whole body; a small tuft, only, was left on the crown of his head, in order that his enemy might avail himself of it, in wrenching the scalp in the event of his fall. The scalp was the only admissible trophy of victory. Thus, it was deemed more important to obtain the scalp than to kill the man. . . ."
3. Hardened.

gings, that laced at the sides, and were gartered above the knees, with the sinews of a deer. A pouch and horn completed his personal accoutrements, though a rifle of a great length, which the theory of the more ingenious whites had taught them, was the most dangerous of all fire-arms, leaned against a neighbouring sapling. The eye of the hunter, or scout, whichever he might be, was small, quick, keen, and restless, roving while he spoke, on every side of him, as if in quest of game, or distrusting the sudden approach of some lurking enemy. Notwithstanding these symptoms of habitual suspicion, his countenance was not only without guile, but at the moment at which he is introduced was charged with an expression of sturdy honesty.

"Even your traditions make the case in my favour, Chingachgook," he said, speaking in the tongue which was known to all the natives who formerly inhabited the country between the Hudson and the Potomack,[4] and of which we shall give a free translation for the benefit of the reader; endeavouring, at the same time, to preserve some of the peculiarities, both of the individual and of the language. "Your fathers came from the setting sun, crossed the big river,[5] fought the people of the country, and took the land; and mine came from the red sky of the morning, over the salt lake, and did their work much after the fashion that had been set them by yours; then let God judge the matter between us, and friends, spare their words!"

"My fathers fought with the naked red-man!" returned the Indian, sternly, in the same language. "Is there no difference, Hawk-eye, between the stone-headed arrow of the warrior, and the leaden bullet with which you kill?"

"There is reason in an Indian, though nature has made him with a red skin!" said the white man, shaking his head, like one on whom such an appeal to his justice was not thrown away. For a moment he appeared to be conscious of having the worst of the argument, then rallying again, he answered to the objection of his antagonist in the best manner his limited information would allow: "I am no scholar, and I care not who knows it; but judging from what I have seen at deer chaces, and squirrel hunts, of the sparks below, I should think a rifle in the hands of their grandfathers, was not so dangerous as a hickory bow, and a good flint-head might be, if drawn with Indian judgment, and sent by an Indian eye."

"You have the story told by your fathers," returned the other, coldly waving his hand, in proud disdain. "What say your old men? do they tell the young warriors, that the pale-faces met the red-men, painted for war and armed with the stone hatchet or wooden gun?"

"I am not a prejudiced man, nor one who vaunts himself on his natural privileges, though the worst enemy I have on earth, and he is an Iroquois, daren't deny that I am genuine white," the scout replied, surveying, with secret satisfaction, the faded colour of his bony and sinewy hand; "and I am willing to own that my people have many ways, of which, as an honest man, I can't approve. It is one of their customs to write in books what they have done and seen, instead of telling them in their villages, where the lie can be given to the face of a cowardly boaster, and the brave soldier can call on his

---

4. Potomac; river flowing from the Alleghenies to the Chesapeake Bay.
5. Cooper supplied the following note to the 1831 edition of *Mohicans*: "The Mississippi. The scout alludes to a tradition which is very popular among the tribes of the Atlantic states. Evidence of their Asiatic origin is deduced from the circumstance, though great uncertainty hangs over the whole history of the Indians."

comrades to witness for the truth of his words. In consequence of this bad fashion, a man who is too conscientious to misspend his days among the women, in learning the names of black marks, may never hear of the deeds of his fathers, nor feel a pride in striving to outdo them. For myself, I conclude all the Bumppos could shoot; for I have a natural turn with a rifle, which must have been handed down from generation to generation, as our holy commandments tell us, all good and evil gifts are bestowed; though I should be loth to answer for other people in such a matter. But every story has its two sides; so I ask you, Chingachgook, what passed when our fathers first met?"

A silence of a minute succeeded, during which the Indian sat mute; then, full of the dignity of his office, he commenced his brief tale, with a solemnity that served to heighten its appearance of truth.

"Listen, Hawk-eye, and your ears shall drink no lies. 'Tis what my fathers have said, and what the Mohicans have done." He hesitated a single instant, and bending a cautious glance towards his companion, he continued in a manner that was divided between interrogation and assertion—"does not this stream at our feet, run towards the summer, until its waters grow salt, and the current flows upward!"

"It can't be denied, that your traditions tell you true in both these matters," said the white man; "for I have been there, and have seen them; though, why water, which is so sweet in the shade, should become bitter in the sun, is an alteration for which I have never been able to account."

"And the current!" demanded the Indian, who expected his reply with that sort of interest that a man feels in the confirmation of testimony, at which he marvels even while he respects it; "the fathers of Chingachgook have not lied!"

"The Holy Bible is not more true, and that is the truest thing in nature. They call this up-stream current the tide, which is a thing soon explained, and clear enough. Six hours the waters run in, and six hours they run out, and the reason is this; when there is higher water in the sea than in the river, it runs in, until the river gets to be highest, and then it runs out again."

"The waters in the woods, and on the great lakes, run downward until they lie like my hand," said the Indian, stretching the limb horizontally before him, "and then they run no more."

"No honest man will deny it," said the scout, a little nettled at the implied distrust of his explanation of the mystery of the tides; "and I grant that it is true on the small scale, and where the land is level. But every thing depends on what scale you look at things. Now, on the small scale, the 'arth is level; but on the large scale it is round. In this manner, pools and ponds, and even the great fresh water lakes, may be stagnant, as you and I both know they are, having seen them; but when you come to spread water over a great tract, like the sea, where the earth is round, how in reason can the water be quiet? You might as well expect the river to lie still on the brink of those black rocks a mile above us, though your own ears tell you that it is tumbling over them at this very moment!"

If unsatisfied by the philosophy of his companion, the Indian was far too dignified to betray his unbelief. He listened like one who was convinced, and resumed his narrative in his former solemn manner.

"We came from the place where the sun is hid at night, over great plains where the buffaloes live, until we reached the big river. There we fought the Alligewi,[6] till the ground was red with their blood. From the banks of the big river to the shores of the salt lake, there were none to meet us. The Maquas[7] followed at a distance. We said the country should be ours from the place where the water runs up no longer, on this stream, to a river, twenty suns' journey toward the summer. The land we had taken like warriors, we kept like men. We drove the Maquas into the woods with the bears. They only tasted salt at the licks; they drew no fish from the great lake: we threw them the bones."

"All this I have heard and believe," said the white man, observing that the Indian paused; "but it was long before the English came into the country."

"A pine grew then, where this chestnut now stands. The first pale faces who came among us spoke no English. They came in a large canoe, when my fathers had buried the tomahawk with the red men around them. Then, Hawk-eye," he continued, betraying his deep emotion, only by permitting his voice to fall to those low, guttural tones, which render his language, as spoken at times, so very musical; "then, Hawk-eye, we were one people, and we were happy. The salt lake gave us its fish, the wood its deer, and the air its birds. We took wives who bore us children; we worshipped the Great Spirit; and we kept the Maquas beyond the sound of our songs of triumph!"

"Know you any thing of your own family, at that time?" demanded the white. "But you are a just man for an Indian! and as I suppose you hold their gifts, your fathers must have been brave warriors, and wise men at the council fire."

"My tribe is the grandfather of nations," said the native, "but I am an unmixed man. The blood of chiefs is in my veins, where it must stay for ever. The Dutch landed, and gave my people the fire-water;[8] they drank until the heavens and the earth seemed to meet, and they foolishly thought they had found the Great Spirit. Then they parted with their land. Foot by foot, they were driven back from the shores, until I, that am a chief and a Sagamore,[9] have never seen the sun shine but through the trees, and have never visited the graves of my fathers."

"Graves bring solemn feelings over the mind," returned the scout, a good deal touched at the calm suffering of his companion; "and often aid a man in his good intentions, though, for myself, I expect to leave my own bones unburied, to bleach in the woods, or to be torn asunder by the wolves. But where are to be found your race, which came to their kin in the Delaware country, so many summers since?"

"Where are the blossoms of those summers!—fallen, one by one: so all of my family departed, each in his turn, to the land of spirits. I am on the hilltop, and must go down into the valley; and when Uncas follows in my footsteps, there will no longer be any of the blood of the Sagamores, for my boy is the last of the Mohicans."

"Uncas is here!" said another voice, in the same soft, guttural tones, near his elbow; "who wishes Uncas?"

The white man loosened his knife in its leathern sheath, and made an involuntary movement of the hand towards his rifle, at this sudden interruption, but the Indian sat composed, and without turning his head at the unexpected sounds.

---

6. Alleghanys, who, according to the Mohicans' tradition, were identical with the Cherokees.
7. Iroquois.

8. Alcoholic beverages.
9. Leader among chiefs.

At the next instant, a youthful warrior passed between them, with a noiseless step, and seated himself on the bank of the rapid stream. No exclamation of surprise escaped the father, nor was any question made or reply given for several minutes, each appearing to await the moment, when he might speak, without betraying a womanish curiosity or childish impatience. The white man seemed to take counsel from their customs, and relinquishing his grasp of the rifle, he also remained silent and reserved. At length Chingachgook turned his eyes slowly towards his son, and demanded—

"Do the Maquas dare to leave the print of their moccasins in these woods?"

"I have been on their trail," replied the young Indian, "and know that they number as many as the fingers of my two hands; but they lie hid like cowards."

"The thieves are outlying for scalps and plunder!" said the white man, whom we shall call Hawk-eye, after the manner of his companions. "That busy Frenchman, Montcalm, will send his spies into our very camp, but he will know what road we travel!"

"'Tis enough!" returned the father, glancing his eye towards the setting sun; "they shall be driven like deer from their bushes. Hawk-eye, let us eat to-night, and show the Maquas that we are men tomorrow."

"I am as ready to do the one as the other," replied the scout; "but to fight the Iroquois,'tis necessary to find the skulkers; and to eat,'tis necessary to get the game—talk of the devil and he will come; there is a pair of the biggest antlers I have seen this season, moving the bushes below the hill! Now, Uncas," he continued in a half whisper, and laughing with a kind of inward sound, like one who had learnt to be watchful, "I will bet my charger three times full of powder, against a foot of wampum,[1] that I take him atwixt the eyes, and nearer to the right than to the left."

"It cannot be!" said the young Indian, springing to his feet with youthful eagerness; "all but the tips of his horns are hid!"

"He's a boy!" said the white man, shaking his head while he spoke, and addressing the father. "Does he think when a hunter sees a part of the creature, he can't tell where the rest of him should be!"

Adjusting his rifle, he was about to make an exhibition of that skill, on which he so much valued himself, when the warrior struck up the piece with his hand, saying,

"Hawk-eye! will you fight the Maquas?"

"These Indians know the nature of the woods, as it might be by instinct!" returned the scout, dropping his rifle, and turning away like a man who was convinced of his error. "I must leave the buck to your arrow, Uncas, or we may kill a deer for them thieves, the Iroquois, to eat."

The instant the father seconded this intimation by an expressive gesture of the hand, Uncas threw himself on the ground, and approached the animal with wary movements. When, within a few yards of the cover, he fitted an arrow to his bow with the utmost care, while the antlers moved, as if their owner snuffed an enemy in the tainted air. In another moment the twang of the bow was heard, a white streak was seen glancing into the bushes, and the wounded buck plunged from the cover, to the very feet of his hidden enemy. Avoiding the horns of the infuriated animal, Uncas darted to his side, and passed his knife across the throat, when bounding to the edge of the river, it fell, dying the waters with its blood to a great distance.

1. Beads or other articles used as currency.

"'Twas done with Indian skill," said the scout, laughing inwardly, but with vast satisfaction; "and was a pretty sight to behold! Though an arrow is a near shot, and needs a knife to finish the work."

"Hugh!" ejaculated his companion, turning quickly, like a hound who scented his game.

"By the Lord, there is a drove of them!" exclaimed the hunting scout, whose eyes began to glisten with the ardour of his usual occupation; "if they come within range of a bullet, I will drop one, though the whole Six Nations[2] should be lurking within sound! What do you hear, Chingachgook? for to my ears the woods are dumb."

"There is but one deer, and he is dead," said the Indian, bending his body, till his ear nearly touched the earth. "I hear the sounds of feet!"

"Perhaps the wolves have driven that buck to shelter, and are following in his trail."

"No. The horses of white men are coming!" returned the other, raising himself with dignity, and resuming his seat on the log with all his former composure. "Hawk-eye, they are your brothers; speak to them."

"That will I, and in English that the king needn't be ashamed to answer," returned the hunter, speaking in the language of which he boasted; "but I see nothing, nor do I hear the sounds of man or beast; 'tis strange that an Indian should understand white sounds better than a man, who, his very enemies will own, has no cross[3] in his blood, although he may have lived with the red skins long enough to be suspected! Ha! there goes something like the cracking of a dry stick, too—now I hear the bushes move—yes, yes, there is a tramping that I mistook for the falls—and—but here they come themselves; God keep them from the Iroquois!"

1826

2. A formal tribal alliance, also known as the Iroquois Confederacy, of the Mohawks, Oneidas, Onondagas, Cayugas, Senecas, and Tuscaroras in the area of what is now upstate New York.

3. In this and other novels of the Leatherstocking series, Natty Bumppo insists on his pure whiteness.

WILLIAM CULLEN BRYANT
1794–1878

William Cullen Bryant made his mark on American poetry in 1821 with the publication of a slim volume, *Poems*, whose lyrical meditations on nature and death brought him international recognition as a poet worthy of being considered alongside William Wordsworth. He continued to publish poetry in miscellanies and newspapers, while bringing out volumes of his new and collected poems throughout his long lifetime. Though he never again received the critical acclaim that he had in 1821, he became increasingly popular and had many admirers. In an 1846 issue of the *Brooklyn Eagle*, for instance, Walt Whitman criticized the "literary quacks" who failed to appreciate "this beautiful poet," describing him as "a poet who, to our mind, stands among the first in the world." That same year, Poe proclaimed in the widely read *Godey's Lady's Book* that "Mr. Bryant has genius, and that of a marked character" and lamented that his talent "has been overlooked by modern schools."

In part Bryant was overlooked because he refused to promote himself. Unlike Poe, Emerson, and Whitman, who all wrote poetic manifestos celebrating their own approaches to poetry, Bryant quietly published his work without making large claims for its importance. For much of his adult life he worked as a newspaper editor committed first to the Jacksonian Democratic party and then to the Free Soil and Republican parties. The poetry he continued to write and publish took on an increasingly public aspect, adding political topics of the day to his subject matter.

Bryant was born in the rural town of Cummington, Massachusetts. Encouraged by his parents, he learned Greek and Latin as a child. In 1807, when he was twelve, he published his first poem in the *Hampshire Gazette* in Northampton, Massachusetts; in 1808, he wrote a long anti-Jefferson poem, *The Embargo; or, Sketches of the Times: A Satire by a Youth of Thirteen*, which his Federalist father printed as a pamphlet. Bryant entered Williams College in 1810, but left after seven months with the hope of transferring to Yale. When his father revealed that he could no longer afford Bryant's college expenses, he continued to write poetry while preparing for a legal career by working in the law office of a family friend. He was admitted to the bar in 1815.

In July 1815, Bryant wrote "To a Waterfowl" and soon after wrote the first, shorter version of "Thanatopsis," the poem that established his reputation. Bryant's mother had taught him a harsh Calvinism, emphasizing that with Adam and Eve's sin, God withdrew from nature as He withdrew from humankind. "Thanatopsis," however, conveys a pantheistic view of God in nature indicative of the increasing influence of liberal Protestantism, particularly Unitarianism, on Bryant's imagination. In his early teens Bryant was attracted to the pensive gloom of such eighteenth-century British graveyard poets as Robert Blair ("The Grave" [1743]) and Thomas Gray ("Elegy Written in a Country Churchyard" [1750]). His reading of Wordsworth's *Lyrical Ballads* (1798) influenced his prosody and inspired his own continuing development from a neoclassical to a Romantic poet who discerned moral lessons and a divine presence in the American landscape. Bryant's ever-supportive father sponsored the publication of the early version of "Thanatopsis" in the 1817 *North American Review*; the 1821 version concludes with a fervent injunction to trust in self and nature, thereby anticipating (and perhaps helping to inspire) Emerson's writings of the 1830s and 1840s.

Bryant would have liked to support himself as a poet, but this was impossible at the time, so in 1816 he opened a law partnership; he worked as a lawyer into the mid-1820s. In 1821 he married Frances Fairchild; the couple had two daughters. That same year he was invited to deliver the Phi Beta Kappa poem at Harvard College's commencement. He read a long poem on the progress of liberty, "The Ages," whose favorable reception induced him to publish his *Poems* later that year. Buoyed by the book's success, Bryant, who found the practice of law uncongenial, embarked on a practical kind of literary career by moving to New York City to edit the *New-York Review and Atheneum Magazine*. Welcomed as a celebrity, he embraced metropolitan life, becoming an early member of James Fenimore Cooper's Bread and Cheese Club and developing a close friendship with Catharine Sedgwick. She dedicated her second novel, *Redwood* (1823), to him and he favorably reviewed it in the April 1825 *North American Review*. Though the *New-York Review* failed, Bryant stayed in New York as an editorial assistant on the New York *Evening Post*. By 1829 he was the newspaper's part owner and editor-in-chief, a position he would keep for nearly fifty years. Over the decades he made the *Evening Post* one of the most respected, widely read, and profitable newspapers in the country. By then a deeply committed Jacksonian Democrat, he championed the rights of labor unions, the virtues of free trade, prison reform, the importance of international copyright protection for authors, and antislavery. Bryant's loathing of slavery eventually prompted him to lead the antislavery Free-Soil movement within the Democratic Party, and then leave the party altogether. In the mid-1850s he helped form the Republican Party and in 1860 was an influential supporter of Abraham Lincoln.

As he and his newspaper prospered, Bryant traveled widely in the United States and abroad. In 1834, on his first trip to Europe, he sent back travel essays that were published in his newspaper. After continuing to publish similar essays during the 1830s and 1840s, in 1850 he brought out *Letters of a Traveller*, the first of three collections of his travel writings. He also published more than ten volumes of poetry between 1832 and 1876. His best known public poem was "The Death of Lincoln," which he wrote shortly after the assassination; it was read to thousands gathered at New York City's Union Square the day before Lincoln's body arrived for a viewing. Bryant's wife, Frances, died in 1866, but he held on to his editorship at the *Evening Post*. In his seventies he began the remarkably ambitious project of translating Homer. His blank-verse version of the *Iliad* appeared in 1870 and his *Odyssey* followed in 1872. The 1876 publication of his collected *Poems* crowned his career. Two years later, he died of the consequences of a fall after he gave a speech at the unveiling of a statue of the Italian patriot and revolutionary Giuseppe Mazzini in Central Park. In New York City flags were lowered to half-staff, and Bryant was mourned as a great poet and editor.

Thanatopsis[1]

To him who in the love of Nature holds
Communion with her visible forms, she speaks
A various language; for his gayer hours
She has a voice of gladness, and a smile
And eloquence of beauty, and she glides   5
Into his darker musings, with a mild
And gentle sympathy, that steals away
Their sharpness, ere he is aware. When thoughts
Of the last bitter hour come like a blight
Over thy spirit, and sad images   10
Of the stern agony, and shroud, and pall,
And breathless darkness, and the narrow house,
Make thee to shudder, and grow sick at heart;—
Go forth under the open sky, and list[2]
To Nature's teachings, while from all around—   15
Earth and her waters, and the depths of air,—
Comes a still voice—Yet a few days, and thee
The all-beholding sun shall see no more
In all his course; nor yet in the cold ground,
Where thy pale form was laid, with many tears,   20
Nor in the embrace of ocean shall exist
Thy image. Earth, that nourished thee, shall claim
Thy growth, to be resolv'd to earth again;
And, lost each human trace, surrend'ring up
Thine individual being, shalt thou go   25
To mix forever with the elements,
To be a brother to th' insensible rock
And to the sluggish clod, which the rude swain
Turns with his share,[3] and treads upon. The oak
Shall send his roots abroad, and pierce thy mould.   30
Yet not to thy eternal resting place
Shalt thou retire alone—nor couldst thou wish

---

1. From *Poems* (1821); a shorter version appeared in the September 1817 issue of the *North American Review*.
2. Listen.
3. Plowshare. "Swain": farmer.

Couch more magnificent. Thou shalt lie down
With patriarchs of the infant world—with kings,
The powerful of the earth—the wise, the good,   35
Fair forms, and hoary seers of ages past,
All in one mighty sepulchre.—The hills
Rock-ribb'd and ancient as the sun,—the vales
Stretching in pensive quietness between;
The venerable woods—rivers that move   40
In majesty, and the complaining brooks
That make the meadows green; and pour'd round all,
Old ocean's grey and melancholy waste,—
Are but the solemn decorations all
Of the great tomb of man. The golden sun,   45
The planets, all the infinite host of heaven,
Are shining on the sad abodes of death,
Through the still lapse of ages. All that tread
The globe are but a handful to the tribes
That slumber in its bosom.—Take the wings   50
Of morning—and the Barcan desert[4] pierce,
Or lose thyself in the continuous woods
Where rolls the Oregan,[5] and hears no sound,
Save his own dashings—yet—the dead are there,
And millions in those solitudes, since first   55
The flight of years began, have laid them down
In their last sleep—the dead reign there alone.—
So shalt thou rest—and what if thou shalt fall
Unnoticed by the living—and no friend
Take note of thy departure? All that breathe   60
Will share thy destiny. The gay will laugh
When thou art gone, the solemn brood of care
Plod on, and each one as before will chase
His favourite phantom; yet all these shall leave
Their mirth and their employments, and shall come,   65
And make their bed with thee. As the long train
Of ages glide away, the sons of men,
The youth in life's green spring, and he who goes
In the full strength of years, matron, and maid,
The bow'd with age, the infant in the smiles   70
And beauty of its innocent age cut off,—
Shall one by one be gathered to thy side,
By those, who in their turn shall follow them.
So live, that when thy summons comes to join
The innumerable caravan, that moves   75
To the pale realms of shade, where each shall take
His chamber in the silent halls of death,
Thou go not, like the quarry-slave at night,
Scourged to his dungeon, but sustain'd and sooth'd
By an unfaltering trust, approach thy grave,   80
Like one who wraps the drapery of his couch
About him, and lies down to pleasant dreams.

1817   1821

---

4. In Barca (northeast Libya).
5. An early variant spelling of Oregon; now the Columbia River.

To a Waterfowl[1]

Whither, 'midst falling dew,
While glow the heavens with the last steps of day,
Far, through their rosy depths, dost thou pursue
    Thy solitary way?

Vainly the fowler's eye   5
Might mark thy distant flight to do thee wrong,
As, darkly painted on the crimson sky,
    Thy figure floats along.

Seek'st thou the plashy[2] brink
Of weedy lake, or marge of river wide,   10
Or where the rocking billows rise and sink
    On the chafed ocean side?

There is a Power whose care
Teaches thy way along that pathless coast,—
The desert and illimitable air,—   15
    Lone wandering, but not lost.

All day thy wings have fann'd
At that far height, the cold thin atmosphere:
Yet stoop not, weary, to the welcome land,
    Though the dark night is near.   20

And soon that toil shall end,
Soon shalt thou find a summer home, and rest,
And scream among thy fellows; reeds shall bend
    Soon o'er thy sheltered nest.

Thou'rt gone, the abyss of heaven   25
Hath swallowed up thy form; yet, on my heart
Deeply hath sunk the lesson thou hast given,
    And shall not soon depart.

He, who, from zone to zone,
Guides through the boundless sky thy certain flight,   30
In the long way that I must tread alone,
    Will lead my steps aright.

1818   1821

The Prairies[1]

These are the Gardens of the Desert, these
The unshorn fields, boundless and beautiful,

---

1. From *Poems* (1821); an earlier version appeared in the May 1818 issue of the *North American Review*.
2. Marshy.

1. From the first printing in *Poems* (1834). Bryant wrote the poem over a year after visiting his brothers in Illinois during 1832.

And fresh as the young earth, ere man had sinned—
The Prairies. I behold them for the first,
And my heart swells, while the dilated sight   5
Takes in the encircling vastness. Lo! they stretch
In airy undulations, far away,
As if the ocean, in his gentlest swell,
Stood still, with all his rounded billows fixed,
And motionless for ever.—Motionless?—   10
No—they are all unchained again. The clouds
Sweep over with their shadows, and beneath
The surface rolls and fluctuates to the eye;
Dark hollows seem to glide along and chase
The sunny ridges. Breezes of the South!   15
Who toss the golden and the flame-like flowers,
And pass the prairie-hawk that, poised on high,
Flaps his broad wings, yet moves not—ye have played
Among the palms of Mexico and vines
Of Texas, and have crisped the limpid brooks   20
That from the fountains of Sonora[2] glide
Into the calm Pacific—have ye fanned
A nobler or a lovelier scene than this?
Man hath no part in all this glorious work:
The hand that built the firmament hath heaved   25
And smoothed these verdant swells, and sown their slopes
With herbage, planted them with island groves,
And hedged them round with forests. Fitting floor
For this magnificent temple of the sky—
With flowers whose glory and whose multitude   30
Rival the constellations! The great heavens
Seem to stoop down upon the scene in love,—
A nearer vault, and of a tenderer blue,
Than that which bends above the eastern hills.
    As o'er the verdant waste I guide my steed,   35
Among the high rank grass that sweeps his sides,
The hollow beating of his footstep seems
A sacrilegious sound. I think of those
Upon whose rest he tramples. Are they here—
The dead of other days!—and did the dust   40
Of these fair solitudes once stir with life
And burn with passion? Let the mighty mounds[3]
That overlook the rivers, or that rise
In the dim forest crowded with old oaks,
Answer. A race, that long has passed away,   45
Built them;—a disciplined and populous race
Heaped, with long toil, the earth, while yet the Greek
Was hewing the Pentelicus[4] to forms
Of symmetry, and rearing on its rock
The glittering Parthenon. These ample fields   50

---

2. River in northwest Mexico.
3. The burial mounds common in Illinois. Bryant
follows a contemporary theory that they were built
by a culture older than the American Indians.

4. Greek mountain from which a fine white marble was quarried, including that used in building
the Parthenon, the temple of Athena on the
Acropolis in Athens.

Nourished their harvests, here their herds were fed,
When haply by their stalls the bison lowed,
And bowed his maned shoulder to the yoke.
All day this desert murmured with their toils,
Till twilight blushed and lovers walked, and wooed   55
In a forgotten language, and old tunes,
From instruments of unremembered form,
Gave the soft winds a voice. The red man came—
The roaming hunter tribes, warlike and fierce,
And the mound-builders vanished from the earth.   60
The solitude of centuries untold
Has settled where they dwelt. The prairie wolf
Hunts in their meadows, and his fresh dug den
Yawns by my path. The gopher mines the ground
Where stood their swarming cities. All is gone—   65
All—save the piles of earth that hold their bones—
The platforms where they worshipped unknown gods—
The barriers which they builded from the soil
To keep the foe at bay—till o'er the walls
The wild beleaguerers broke, and, one by one,   70
The strong holds of the plain were forced, and heaped
With corpses. The brown vultures of the wood
Flocked to those vast uncovered sepulchres,
And sat, unscared and silent, at their feast.
Haply some solitary fugitive,   75
Lurking in marsh and forest, till the sense
Of desolation and of fear became
Bitterer than death, yielded himself to die.
Man's better nature triumphed. Kindly words
Welcomed and soothed him; the rude conquerors   80
Seated the captive with their chiefs. He chose
A bride among their maidens. And at length
Seemed to forget,—yet ne'er forgot,—the wife
Of his first love, and her sweet little ones
Butchered, amid their shrieks, with all his race.   85
    Thus change the forms of being. Thus arise
Races of living things, glorious in strength,
And perish, as the quickening breath of God
Fills them, or is withdrawn. The red man too—
Has left the blooming wilds he ranged so long,   90
And, nearer to the Rocky Mountains, sought
A wider hunting ground. The beaver builds
No longer by these streams, but far away,
On waters whose blue surface ne'er gave back
The white man's face—among Missouri's springs,   95
And pools whose issues swell the Oregan,[5]
He rears his little Venice.[6] In these plains
The bison feeds no more. Twice twenty leagues
Beyond remotest smoke of hunter's camp,
Roams the majestic brute, in herds that shake   100
The earth with thundering steps—yet here I meet

---

5. The Columbia River.   6. I.e., builds a city in the water.

His ancient footprints stamped beside the pool.
   Still this great solitude is quick with life.
Myriads of insects, gaudy as the flowers
They flutter over, gentle quadrupeds,   105
And birds, that scarce have learned the fear of man
Are here, and sliding reptiles of the ground,
Startlingly beautiful. The graceful deer
Bounds to the wood at my approach. The bee,
A more adventurous colonist than man,   110
With whom he came across the eastern deep,
Fills the savannas with his murmurings,
And hides his sweets, as in the golden age,
Within the hollow oak. I listen long
To his domestic hum, and think I hear   115
The sound of that advancing multitude
Which soon shall fill these deserts. From the ground
Comes up the laugh of children, the soft voice
Of maidens, and the sweet and solemn hymn
Of Sabbath worshippers. The low of herds   120
Blends with the rustling of the heavy grain
Over the dark-brown furrows. All at once
A fresher wind sweeps by, and breaks my dream,
And I am in the wilderness alone.

1834

WILLIAM APESS
1798–1839

Little is known of William Apess's life other than what he tells us in *A Son of the Forest* (1829), the first extensive autobiography published by a Native American. His grandfather, says Apess, was a white man who married the granddaughter of the Wampanoag leader King Philip, or Metacom, the loser, in 1676, of King Philip's War. Philip increasingly occupied Apess's thoughts during his lifetime, serving as the subject of his last published work. Apess's father, although of mixed blood, joined the Pequot tribe and married an Indian woman who may have been part African American. Born in Colrain, Massachusetts, Apess drops from public record after 1838. He died in New York on April 10, 1839, of what was described as "apoplexy."

In *A Son of the Forest*, Apess details the pains of his early life: at three he was taken into the home of his poor, alcoholic maternal grandparents; he was severely beaten and, at four or five, sold as an indentured laborer. His first master allowed him to attend school for six years, which constituted his entire formal education; he also introduced Apess to Christianity. Apess served as a soldier in the abortive American attack on Montreal in the War of 1812 and converted to evangelical Methodism after leaving the army. At the conclusion of *A Son of the Forest*, Apess writes that he achieved an "exhorter's" license from his church, enabling him to earn a living as an itinerant preacher; only later would he realize his goal of ordination as a Methodist minister.

A fervent Christian, Apess early understood Christianity as incompatible with any form of race prejudice, sounding a note that presages Christian abolitionists later in the nineteenth century. In 1833, Apess went to preach at Mashpee, the only remaining Indian town in Massachusetts. There he became involved in the Mashpees' struggle to preserve their resources and rights, which were threatened by the overseers imposed on them by the Commonwealth of Massachusetts. The Mashpee eventually drew up petitions, probably composed by Apess, requiring that no whites cut wood or hay on Mashpee lands without the Indians' consent for "we, as a tribe, will rule ourselves, and have the right to do so; for all men are born free and equal, says the Constitution of the Country." Such unprecedented assertiveness on the part of the Indians alarmed the governor of Massachusetts, who announced his readiness to put down the unrest with troops. Apess's version of the controversy appears in his *Indian Nullification of the Unconstitutional Laws of Massachusetts, Relative to the Marshpee* [sic] *Tribe; or, The Pretended Riot Explained* (1835). A year before the book appeared, its case was won when the state legislature granted the Mashpee the same rights of self-governance that other Massachusetts townships possessed.

Apess's career as a preacher and an author comes to a close with his "Eulogy on King Philip," delivered in 1836 at the Odeon in Boston, one of the city's largest public lecture halls, and published that same year. In the "Eulogy" Apess meditates on his distant relation, naming Philip the foremost man that America had thus far produced. He reminds his audience, descendants of the Pilgrims, of the crimes of their ancestors, although "you and I have to rejoice that we have not to answer for our fathers' crimes; neither shall we do right to charge them one to another." Nonetheless, he notes, "in vain have I looked for the Christian to take me by the hand and bid me welcome to his cabin, as my fathers did them [the Christians], before we were born." Apess concludes that a "different course must be pursued. . . . And while you ask yourselves, 'What do they, the Indians, want?' you have only to look at the unjust laws made for them and say, 'They want what I want'": justice and Christian fellowship.

The selection here is from *The Experiences of Five Christian Indians of the Pequot Tribe*, published in 1833, the year Apess came to Mashpee. The first of these "experiences" is Apess's own, an account of his life and conversion that repeats some of the material in *A Son of the Forest* but intensifies considerably the condemnation of Euro-American treatment of Native peoples. Apess concludes this book with the text included here, "An Indian's Looking-Glass for the White Man," a searing indictment of race prejudice against people of color generally and Native Americans particularly. Apess's probing, ironic voice, with its direct address to the reader, may well have influenced that later speaker on behalf of racial justice, Henry David Thoreau. There is also a good deal of evidence suggesting that Apess's work may have been known to Herman Melville and Frederick Douglass.

An Indian's Looking-Glass for the White Man[1]

Having a desire to place a few things before my fellow creatures who are traveling with me to the grave, and to that God who is the maker and preserver both of the white man and the Indian, whose abilities are the same and who are to be judged by one God, who will show no favor to outward appearances but will judge righteousness. Now I ask if degradation has not been heaped long enough upon the Indians? And if so, can there not be a compromise? Is it right to hold and promote prejudices? If not, why not put them all away? I mean here, among those who are civilized. It may be that many are ignorant of the situation of many of my brethren within

1. The text is from *The Experiences of Five Christian Indians of the Pequot Tribe* (1833), reprinted in *On Our Own Ground: The Complete Writings of William Apess, a Pequot*, ed. Barry O'Connell (1992).

the limits of New England. Let me for a few moments turn your attention to the reservations in the different states of New England, and, with but few exceptions, we shall find them as follows: the most mean, abject, miserable race of beings in the world—a complete place of prodigality and prostitution.

Let a gentleman and lady of integrity and respectability visit these places, and they would be surprised; as they wandered from one hut to the other they would view, with the females who are left alone, children half-starved and some almost as naked as they came into the world. And it is a fact that I have seen them as much so—while the females are left without protection, and are seduced by white men, and are finally left to be common prostitutes for them and to be destroyed by that burning, fiery curse, that has swept millions, both of red and white men, into the grave with sorrow and disgrace— rum. One reason why they are left so is because their most sensible and active men are absent at sea. Another reason is because they are made to believe they are minors and have not the abilities given them from God to take care of themselves, without it is to see to a few little articles, such as baskets and brooms. Their land is in common stock, and they have nothing to make them enterprising.

Another reason is because those men who are Agents,[2] many of them are unfaithful and care not whether the Indians live or die; they are much imposed upon by their neighbors, who have no principle. They would think it no crime to go upon Indian lands and cut and carry off their most valuable timber, or anything else they chose; and I doubt not but they think it clear gain. Another reason is because they have no education to take care of themselves; if they had, I would risk them to take care of their own property.

Now I will ask if the Indians are not called the most ingenious people among us. And are they not said to be men of talents? And I would ask: Could there be a more efficient way to distress and murder them by inches than the way they have taken? And there is no people in the world but who may be destroyed in the same way. Now, if these people are what they are held up in our view to be, I would take the liberty to ask why they are not brought forward and pains taken to educate them, to give them all a common education, and those of the brightest and first-rate talents put forward and held up to office. Perhaps some unholy, unprincipled men would cry out, "The skin was not good enough"; but stop, friends—I am not talking about the skin but about principles. I would ask if there cannot be as good feelings and principles under a red skin as there can be under a white. And let me ask: Is it not on the account of a bad principle that we who are red children have had to suffer so much as we have? And let me ask: Did not this bad principle proceed from the whites or their forefathers? And I would ask: Is it worthwhile to nourish it any longer? If not, then let us have a change, although some men no doubt will spout their corrupt principles against it, that are in the halls of legislation and elsewhere. But I presume this kind of talk will seem surprising and horrible. I do not see why it should so long as they (the whites) say that they think as much of us as they do of themselves.

2. Those appointed by the Commonwealth of Massachusetts to oversee Indian affairs in such towns as Mashpee.

This I have heard repeatedly, from the most respectable gentlemen and ladies—and having heard so much precept, I should now wish to see the example. And I would ask who has a better right to look for these things than the naturalist[3] himself—the candid man would say none.

I know that many say that they are willing, perhaps the majority of the people, that we should enjoy our rights and privileges as they do. If so, I would ask, Why are not we protected in our persons and property throughout the Union? Is it not because there reigns in the breast of many who are leaders a most unrighteous, unbecoming, and impure black principle, and as corrupt and unholy as it can be—while these very same unfeeling, self-esteemed characters pretend to take the skin as a pretext to keep us from our unalienable and lawful rights? I would ask you if you would like to be disfranchised from all your rights, merely because your skin is white, and for no other crime. I'll venture to say, these very characters who hold the skin to be such a barrier in the way would be the first to cry out, "Injustice! awful injustice!"

But, reader, I acknowledge that this is a confused world, and I am not seeking for office, but merely placing before you the black inconsistency that you place before me—which is ten times blacker than any skin that you will find in the universe. And now let me exhort you to do away that principle, as it appears ten times worse in the sight of God and candid men than skins of color—more disgraceful than all the skins that Jehovah ever made. If black or red skins or any other skin of color is disgraceful to God, it appears that he has disgraced himself a great deal—for he has made fifteen colored people to one white and placed them here upon this earth.

Now let me ask you, white man, if it is a disgrace for to eat, drink, and sleep with the image of God, or sit, or walk and talk with them. Or have you the folly to think that the white man, being one in fifteen or sixteen, are the only beloved images of God? Assemble all nations together in your imagination, and then let the whites be seated among them, and then let us look for the whites, and I doubt not it would be hard finding them; for to the rest of the nations, they are still but a handful. Now suppose these skins were put together, and each skin had its national crimes written upon it—which skin do you think would have the greatest? I will ask one question more. Can you charge the Indians with robbing a nation almost of their whole continent, and murdering their women and children, and then depriving the remainder of their lawful rights, that nature and God require them to have? And to cap the climax, rob another nation to till their grounds and welter out their days under the lash with hunger and fatigue under the scorching rays of a burning sun?[4] I should look at all the skins, and I know that when I cast my eye upon that white skin, and if I saw those crimes written upon it, I should enter my protest against it immediately and cleave to that which is more honorable. And I can tell you that I am satisfied with the manner of my creation, fully—whether others are or not.

But we will strive to penetrate more fully into the conduct of those who profess to have pure principles and who tell us to follow Jesus Christ and imitate him and have his Spirit. Let us see if they come anywhere near him and his ancient disciples. The first thing we are to look at are his precepts, of which we will mention a few. "Thou shalt love the Lord thy God with all

3. I.e., the American Indian; a play on the view of Indians as children of nature or "sons of the forest".

4. The reference is to the "nation" of Africa, many of whose people were brought to the United States as slaves.

thy heart, with all thy soul, with all thy mind, and with all thy strength. The second is like unto it. Thou shalt love thy neighbor as thyself. On these two precepts hang all the law and the prophets" (Matthew 22.37, 38, 39, 40). "By this shall all men know that they are my disciples, if ye have love one to another" (John 13.35). Our Lord left this special command with his followers, that they should love one another.

Again, John in his Epistles says, "He who loveth God loveth his brother also" (1 John 4.21). "Let us not love in word but in deed" (1 John 3.18). "Let your love be without dissimulation. See that ye love one another with a pure heart fervently" (1 Peter 1.22). "If any man say, I love God, and hateth his brother, he is a liar" (1 John 4.20). "Whosoever hateth his brother is a murderer, and no murderer hath eternal life abiding in him" (1 John 3.15). The first thing that takes our attention is the saying of Jesus, "Thou shalt love," etc. The first question I would ask my brethren in the ministry, as well as that of the membership: What is love, or its effects? Now, if they who teach are not essentially affected with pure love, the love of God, how can they teach as they ought? Again, the holy teachers of old said, "Now if any man have not the spirit of Christ, he is none of his" (Romans 8.9). Now, my brethren in the ministry, let me ask you a few sincere questions. Did you ever hear or read of Christ teaching his disciples that they ought to despise one because his skin was different from theirs? Jesus Christ being a Jew, and those of his Apostles certainly were not whites—and did not he who completed the plan of salvation complete it for the whites as well as for the Jews, and others? And were not the whites the most degraded people on the earth at that time? And none were more so, for they sacrificed their children to dumb idols![5] And did not St. Paul labor more abundantly for building up a Christian nation among you than any of the Apostles? And you know as well as I that you are not indebted to a principle beneath a white skin for your religious services but to a colored one.

What then is the matter now? Is not religion the same now under a colored skin as it ever was? If so, I would ask, why is not a man of color respected? You may say, as many say, we have white men enough. But was this the spirit of Christ and his Apostles? If it had been, there would not have been one white preacher in the world—for Jesus Christ never would have imparted his grace or word to them, for he could forever have withheld it from them. But we find that Jesus Christ and his Apostles never looked at the outward appearances. Jesus in particular looked at the hearts, and his Apostles through him, being discerners of the spirit, looked at their fruit without any regard to the skin, color, or nation; as St. Paul himself speaks, "Where there is neither Greek nor Jew, circumcision nor uncircumcision, Barbarian nor Scythian, bond nor free—but Christ is all, and in all" (Colossians 3.11). If you can find a spirit like Jesus Christ and his Apostles prevailing now in any of the white congregations, I should like to know it. I ask: Is it not the case that everybody that is not white is treated with contempt and counted as barbarians? And I ask if the word of God justifies the white man in so doing. When the prophets prophesied, of whom did they speak? When they spoke of heathens, was it not the whites and others who were counted Gentiles? And I ask if all nations with the exception of the Jews were not

---

5. The ancient Hebrews considered various Middle Eastern peoples idolators whose practices presumably included child sacrifice.

counted heathens. And according to the writings of some, it could not mean the Indians, for they are counted Jews.[6] And now I would ask: Why is all this distinction made among these Christian societies? I would ask: What is all this ado about missionary societies, if it be not to Christianize those who are not Christians? And what is it for? To degrade them worse, to bring them into society where they must welter out their days in disgrace merely because their skin is of a different complexion. What folly it is to try to make the state of human society worse than it is. How astonished some may be at this—but let me ask: Is it not so? Let me refer you to the churches only. And, my brethren, is there any agreement? Do brethren and sisters love one another? Do they not rather hate one another? Outward forms and ceremonies, the lusts of the flesh, the lusts of the eye, and pride of life is of more value to many professors[7] than the love of God shed abroad in their hearts, or an attachment to his altar, to his ordinances, or to his children. But you may ask: Who are the children of God? Perhaps you may say, none but white. If so, the word of the Lord is not true.

I will refer you to St. Peter's precepts (Acts 10): "God is no respecter of persons," etc. Now if this is the case, my white brother, what better are you than God? And if no better, why do you, who profess his Gospel and to have his spirit, act so contrary to it? Let me ask why the men of a different skin are so despised. Why are not they educated and placed in your pulpits? I ask if his services well performed are not as good as if a white man performed them. I ask if a marriage or a funeral ceremony or the ordinance of the Lord's house would not be as acceptable in the sight of God as though he was white. And if so, why is it not to you? I ask again: Why is it not as acceptable to have men to exercise their office in one place as well as in another? Perhaps you will say that if we admit you to all of these privileges you will want more. I expect that I can guess what that is—Why, say you, there would be intermarriages. How that would be I am not able to say— and if it should be, it would be nothing strange or new to me; for I can assure you that I know a great many that have intermarried, both of the whites and the Indians—and many are their sons and daughters and people, too, of the first respectability. And I could point to some in the famous city of Boston and elsewhere. You may look now at the disgraceful act in the statute law passed by the legislature of Massachusetts, and behold the fifty-pound fine levied upon any clergyman or justice of the peace that dare to encourage the laws of God and nature by a legitimate union in holy wedlock between the Indians and whites. I would ask how this looks to your lawmakers. I would ask if this corresponds with your sayings—that you think as much of the Indians as you do of the whites. I do not wonder that you blush, many of you, while you read; for many have broken the ill-fated laws made by man to hedge up the laws of God and nature. I would ask if they who have made the law have not broken it—but there is no other state in New England that has this law but Massachusetts; and I think, as many of you do not, that you have done yourselves no credit.

But as I am not looking for a wife, having one of the finest cast, as you no doubt would understand while you read her experience and travail of soul in the way to heaven, you will see that it is not my object. And if I had none,

6. A reference to the (mistaken) notion that Native Americans were descended from the ten lost tribes of Israel.

7. I.e., those who profess the Christian faith.

I should not want anyone to take my right from me and choose a wife for me; for I think that I or any of my brethren have a right to choose a wife for themselves as well as the whites—and as the whites have taken the liberty to choose my brethren, the Indians, hundreds and thousands of them, as partners in life, I believe the Indians have as much right to choose their partners among the whites if they wish. I would ask you if you can see anything inconsistent in your conduct and talk about the Indians. And if you do, I hope you will try to become more consistent. Now, if the Lord Jesus Christ, who is counted by all to be a Jew—and it is well known that the Jews are a colored people,[8] especially those living in the East, where Christ was born—and if he should appear among us, would he not be shut out of doors by many, very quickly? And by those too who profess religion?

By what you read, you may learn how deep your principles are. I should say they were skin-deep. I should not wonder if some of the most selfish and ignorant would spout a charge of their principles now and then at me. But I would ask: How are you to love your neighbors as yourself? Is it to cheat them? Is it to wrong them in anything? Now, to cheat them out of any of their rights is robbery. And I ask: Can you deny that you are not robbing the Indians daily, and many others? But at last you may think I am what is called a hard and uncharitable man. But not so. I believe there are many who would not hesitate to advocate our cause; and those too who are men of fame and respectability—as well as ladies of honor and virtue. There is a Webster, an Everett, and a Wirt,[9] and many others who are distinguished characters—besides a host of my fellow citizens, who advocate our cause daily. And how I congratulate such noble spirits—how they are to be prized and valued; for they are well calculated to promote the happiness of mankind. They well know that man was made for society, and not for hissing-stocks[1] and outcasts. And when such a principle as this lies within the hearts of men, how much it is like its God—and how it honors its Maker—and how it imitates the feelings of the Good Samaritan, that had his wounds bound up, who had been among thieves and robbers.

Do not get tired, ye noble-hearted—only think how many poor Indians want their wounds done up daily; the Lord will reward you, and pray you stop not till this tree of distinction shall be leveled to the earth, and the mantle of prejudice torn from every American heart—then shall peace pervade the Union.

1833

8. Referring to the belief that Moses and the biblical Hebrews, including Jesus, were people of color.
9. William Wirt (1772–1834), lawyer, politician, orator, and writer; he served as attorney general under President James Monroe and was nominated by the Whig Party for president. Daniel Webster (1782–1852), orator, legislator, statesman, and interpreter of the Constitution; he served as congressman from New Hampshire, senator from Massachusetts, and secretary of state under President William Henry Harrison. Edward Everett (1794–1865), the first Eliot Professor of Greek at Harvard and the editor of the prestigious North American Review; he served in Congress and as governor of Massachusetts.
1. Those who are laughed at or hissed at (i.e., laughingstocks).

RALPH WALDO EMERSON
1803–1882

Ralph Waldo Emerson is arguably the most influential American writer of the nineteenth century—the writer with whom numerous other significant writers of the time sought to come to terms. Without Emerson's inspirational essays on nonconformity, self-reliance, and anti-institutionalism, Henry David Thoreau's and Margaret Fuller's careers may have followed different paths; and without Emerson's call for an American bard whose poetry "speaks somewhat wildly" in addressing the nation's "ample geography," Whitman's great poetry might never have been written. Though Melville rejected Emerson's optimism, satirizing him in *The Confidence-Man* (1857) as a philosophical con man, he termed him a "deep diver" as well; Emerson's conception of nature as a sign of spirit permeates Melville's dynamic representations of the whale and the natural world in *Moby-Dick* (1851). Emerson's persisting influence on late-nineteenth- and twentieth-century American writers is evident in astonishing permutations, on figures as diverse as Emily Dickinson, Louisa May Alcott, William James, Theodore Dreiser, Robert Frost, John Dewey, and his namesake Ralph Waldo Ellison.

Emerson was born in Boston on May 25, 1803, the son of a Unitarian minister and the second of five surviving boys. He was eight years old when his father died. Determined to send as many sons as she could to Harvard—the traditional route for ministers-in-training—Emerson's mother kept a succession of boardinghouses. Around this time, Emerson's brilliant, eccentric aunt, Mary Moody Emerson (1774–1863), stepped in to become his principal educator and inspiration, guiding his reading and challenging his thinking over the next several decades. In the more conventional setting of Boston Public Latin School, where he was sent at age nine, and Harvard College, which he attended from 1817 to 1821, Emerson showed no particular promise. Graduating from Harvard thirtieth in a class of fifty-nine, Emerson served, as he put it, as "a hopeless Schoolmaster" in several Boston-area schools. Turning to the study of theology in 1825 at Harvard's Divinity School, he began preaching as a Unitarian in October 1826, and early in 1829 he was ordained by the Unitarians as a junior pastor at Boston's Second Church. In July of that year, he was promoted to pastor.

Boston Unitarianism, led in the 1820s by William Ellery Channing (1780–1842), accepted the Bible as the revelation of God's intentions but no longer held that human beings were innately depraved; some Unitarians, like Channing, came close to suggesting that Jesus was not a god but rather the highest expression of humanity. Emerson was deeply influenced by Channing, and his skepticism toward historical Christianity was strengthened by his exposure to the German "higher criticism," which regarded the Judeo-Christian Bible as a document produced in a specific historical time, rather than as the direct word of God, and interpreted biblical miracles as stories comparable to the myths of other cultures. Emerson was gradually developing a greater faith in individual moral sentiment and intuition than in revealed religion.

In 1831 Emerson faced a personal crisis: his wife, Ellen Tucker Emerson, whom he had married in 1829, died of tuberculosis on February 8, at the age of nineteen. Grief-stricken, Emerson wrote his aunt Mary: "My angel is gone to heaven this morning & I am alone in the world." Emerson also faced a spiritual crisis, perhaps precipitated by the death of Ellen, as his thinking developed into a full-fledged disillusionment with his position as pastor and with Unitarianism itself. Early in 1832 Emerson notified his church that he had become so skeptical of the validity of the Lord's Supper that he could no longer administer the sacrament, regarding it, as he remarked in his journal, as "worship in the dead forms of our forefathers." He resigned his pastorate on December 22, 1832, and on Christmas Day sailed for Europe, where he would remain until October 1833. During his European tour, he called on a number of well-known writers, in Italy meeting Walter Savage Landor, in England Samuel Coleridge and William Wordsworth, and in Scotland Thomas Carlyle, with whom he began a lifelong intellectual friendship.

Shortly after his return from Europe in late 1833, Emerson settled a legal dispute with the Tucker family and received the first installment of his wife's legacy. Soon he was assured of more than a thousand dollars annually, a considerable sum for that time. Without the need to produce a constant income, he began a new careeer as a lecturer, speaking around New England in the lyceums—public halls that brought a variety of speakers and performers to cities and smaller towns. In 1835, after a ten-month courtship, he married Lydia Jackson of Plymouth, and they moved to rural Concord, Massachusetts, where the Emerson family had property. There, Emerson completed his first book, *Nature*, which was published anonymously and at Emerson's own expense in 1836. This little book did not immediately establish Emerson as an important American writer, but, even with its philosophical complexities, it did confirm his future as a prose writer. As the reviewers understood, *Nature* was not a Christian book but one influenced by a range of idealistic philosophies, ancient and modern, Transcendentalism being merely the latest name for a way of thinking going back to Plato and more recently refashioned by a number of European romantics.

Although the favorable reception of *Nature* in England encouraged some American journalists to take Emerson seriously as an intellectual force, Emerson's immediate reward was having the book become the unofficial manifesto for a number of his like-minded friends, who, over the next eight years, would meet irregularly and informally in Emerson's study and elsewhere. Termed "Transcendentalists" by mocking outsiders, the group was composed mainly of ministers who rejected the view of the philosopher John Locke (1643–1704) that the mind was a merely passive receptor of sense impressions, endorsing Samuel Coleridge's and other romantics' alternative conception of the mind as actively intuitive and creative. Participants included the educators Bronson Alcott (1799–1888) and Elizabeth Palmer Peabody (1804–1894), the abolitionist and Unitarian minister Theodore Parker (1810–1860), the Unitarian minister (later an influential American Catholic) Orestes A. Brownson (1803–1876), Margaret Fuller, and Henry David Thoreau. The group began its own journal, *The Dial* (1840–44), edited for the most part by Emerson, Fuller, and Thoreau.

Nature reached a smaller audience than did many of Emerson's lectures, which were often written up in newspapers; his formal Harvard addresses to the Phi Beta Kappa Society in 1837 on the American scholar and to the Divinity School graduates in 1838 on the state of Christianity were both printed as pamphlets. Conservative ministers attacked "The Divinity School Adress" for its rejection of historical Christianity and its bold questioning of the claims made for Christ as a divine savior. But with the publication of *Essays* (1841), Emerson's lasting reputation began to take shape. Far more than *Nature*, this book was directed to a popular audience. The twelve essays in the volume had been tried out, in whole or in part, in his lectures, so that their final form was shaped by the responses of his many audiences.

Early in 1842 Emerson's first son, Waldo, died at the age of five, a loss from which Emerson never fully recovered. Writing in his journal the day after Waldo's death, he expressed his grief and confusion: "Sorrow makes us all children again[,] destroys all differences of intellect[.] The wisest know nothing[.]" For the philosopher of idealism who had argued that the world can be apprehended mainly through intuition, the death of a beloved son pushed him toward the skepticism expressed most powerfully in "Experience" (1844), an essay presenting individuals as perpetually skating on surfaces. At the conclusion of the essay, however, Emerson, in an anticipation of the American school of pragmatism that he would profoundly influence, insisted on the importance of continuing to act in the world, however elusive and tragic that world might be.

Emerson continued to work steadily on essays derived from his extensive journals and his lecturing. In 1844 he brought out a second series of essays, including his influential "The Poet," which grappled with aesthetic issues of form and meter and foretold—indeed provided the blueprints for—the style and subject matter of some of the great national poets to come. Meter does not make the argument, he wrote, in striking contrast to his contemporary Edgar Allan Poe, but the argument (or poetic idea or vision) makes its own meter; thus he inspired Whitman to break with poetic tradition by introducing the idea of "open form" poetry. Emerson lectured in Boston, across the Northeast, in the South, and even (after the completion of the transcontinental railroad in 1869) in California, giving more than fifteen hundred lectures over the course of his career. These as much as his essays helped develop his reputation.

As Emerson's reputation continued to grow, he gained modest recognition for his own poems, which he collected at the end of 1846. In 1847–48 he took a second trip to Europe, delivering approximately seventy lectures in England and Scotland. One eventual result of that tour was the publication in 1856 of *English Traits*, an inquiry into the supposed racial, historical, and cultural characteristics of Anglo-Saxonism. (Like many thinkers of the time, Emerson accepted the idea of racial differences and hierarchies.) Two other books emerged from his lectures: *Representative Men* (1850), which examined exemplary intellectual and cultural figures, such as Shakespeare and Napoleon; and *The Conduct of Life* (1860), which examined tensions between thought and delimiting worldly forces, even as Emerson reaffirmed the power of self-culture and the individual mind.

Precisely because he so valued individual self-culture, Emerson was skeptical of social reforms that required group participation. In the early 1840s he refused to participate in the reformist, socialistic community Brook Farm in West Roxbury, Massachusetts, which drew a number of the Transcendentalists associated with *The Dial*. Abolitionism did engage his attention, however, and in 1844 he delivered a passionate antislavery address, "Emancipation of the Negroes in the British West Indies," at the Concord Court House on August 1, 1844. Appalled by the Fugitive Slave Law of 1850, Emerson became more fervent in his views during the 1850s, offering scathing attacks on Northern supporters of what he termed "this filthy law." In his 1855 "Lecture on Slavery," presented before the Massachusetts Anti-Slavery Society at the Tremont Temple in Boston, Emerson declaimed against the "outrage of giving back a stolen and plundered man to his thieves." Valuing individual rights and believing in the individual mind (or soul) as divine, Emerson regarded slavery as abhorrent. He also argued in favor of women's rights. In 1855, the same year he attacked slavery at Boston's Tremont Temple, he spoke before a women's rights convention to support women's right to vote, to "hold their property as men do theirs," and to "enter a school as freely as a church." Although Emerson never achieved national prominence as a social reformer, his lectures and essays motivated many of his admirers to become political and social activists.

Emerson's contemporary reputation rested on his lectures and essays, but all along he had been producing another major body of writings, his journals, which he called his "savings bank." The journals were not published in full until the late twentieth century, under the title *Journals and Miscellaneous Notebooks*. A historical record of responses to people and events, the journals, as critics are increasingly recognizing, are among the best accounts of the intellectual and spiritual life of a nineteenth-century American writer. Following the Civil War, Emerson cut back on his writing, partly for health reasons (as he aged he began to display the symptoms of senility). But he had his vigorous moments. In 1871 he traveled to California, and in late 1872 and into 1873, following a fire that severely damaged his house, he traveled to Europe and Egypt with his daughter Ellen and met with Carlyle one last time. Upon his return to Concord, he lectured occasionally in Boston and Concord. He died on April 27, 1882, and was buried in Concord's Sleepy Hollow Cemetery.

In a journal entry of 1836, Emerson wrote: "There is creative reading as well as creative writing." As a creative writer, Emerson attempted to get his whole philosophy into every essay, and even into single sentences. At the same time, he was skeptical of the capacity of language to embody truths, so he presented his essays as epistemological quests of sorts that, in the twistings and turnings and circlings of his thought, made enormous demands on his readers. Emerson's language can be elliptical and sometimes maddeningly abstract, but there is no American writer who placed greater importance on the reader's active interpretive role in generating new meanings and new ways of seeing the world. Emerson's respect for the independent spirit of his readers, his prompting of readers to trust their ideas and take them in new and even different directions—the main point of "Self Reliance," perhaps his most famous essay—may in fact be the key to his broad literary and cultural influence.

Nature[1]

"Nature is but an image or imitation of wisdom, the last thing of the soul; nature being a thing which doth only do, but not know."
—PLOTINUS[2]

Introduction

Our age is retrospective. It builds the sepulchres of the fathers. It writes biographies, histories, and criticism. The foregoing generations beheld God and nature face to face; we, through their eyes. Why should not we also enjoy an original relation to the universe? Why should not we have a poetry and philosophy of insight and not of tradition, and a religion by revelation to us, and not the history of theirs? Embosomed for a season in nature, whose floods of life stream around and through us, and invite us by the powers they supply, to action proportioned to nature, why should we grope among the dry bones of the past,[3] or put the living generation into masquerade out of its faded wardrobe? The sun shines to-day also. There is more wool and flax in the fields. There are new lands, new men, new thoughts. Let us demand our own works and laws and worship.

Undoubtedly we have no questions to ask which are unanswerable. We must trust the perfection of the creation so far, as to believe that whatever curiosity the order of things has awakened in our minds, the order of things can satisfy. Every man's condition is a solution in hieroglyphic to those inquiries he would put. He acts it as life, before he apprehends it as truth. In like manner, nature is already, in its forms and tendencies, describing its own design. Let us interrogate the great apparition, that shines so peacefully around us. Let us inquire, to what end is nature?

---

1. *Nature* was published anonymously in 1836 by James Monroe and Company of Boston, paid for by Emerson himself (the company published a thousand copies for Emerson's approximately one-hundred-dollar payment). Emerson gave copies to friends, and the book was also advertised in local newspapers. The text used here is that of the first 1836 edition. A few obvious typographical errors have been corrected; and the changes that Emerson himself made in presentation copies to the opening of Chapter 4 have been adopted. Otherwise, the occasional oddities of punctuation, spelling, and subject–verb agreements that appeared in the 1836 text remain in this reprinting.
2. Emerson found the motto from the Roman philosopher Plotinus (205?–270?) in his copy of Ralph Cudworth's *The True Intellectual System of the Universe* (1820).
3. An echo of Ezekiel 37.1–14, especially 37.4, where God tells Ezekiel to "Prophesy upon these bones, and say unto them, O ye dry bones, hear the word of the Lord."

All science has one aim, namely, to find a theory of nature. We have theories of races and of functions, but scarcely yet a remote approximation to an idea of creation. We are now so far from the road to truth, that religious teachers dispute and hate each other, and speculative men are esteemed unsound and frivolous. But to a sound judgment, the most abstract truth is the most practical. Whenever a true theory appears, it will be its own evidence. Its test is, that it will explain all phenomena. Now many are thought not only unexplained but inexplicable; as language, sleep, dreams, beasts, sex.

Philosophically considered, the universe is composed of Nature and the Soul. Strictly speaking, therefore, all that is separate from us, all which Philosophy distinguishes as the NOT ME,[4] that is, both nature and art, all other men and my own body, must be ranked under this name, NATURE. In enumerating the values of nature and casting up their sum, I shall use the word in both senses;—in its common and in its philosophical import. In inquiries so general as our present one, the inaccuracy is not material; no confusion of thought will occur. *Nature*, in the common sense, refers to essences unchanged by man; space, the air, the river, the leaf. *Art* is applied to the mixture of his will with the same things, as in a house, a canal, a statue, a picture. But his operations taken together are so insignificant, a little chipping, baking, patching, and washing, that in an impression so grand as that of the world on the human mind, they do not vary the result.

Chapter I. Nature

To go into solitude, a man needs to retire as much from his chamber as from society. I am not solitary whilst I read and write, though nobody is with me. But if a man would be alone, let him look at the stars. The rays that come from those heavenly worlds, will separate between him and vulgar things. One might think the atmosphere was made transparent with this design, to give man, in the heavenly bodies, the perpetual presence of the sublime. Seen in the streets of cities, how great they are! If the stars should appear one night in a thousand years, how would men believe and adore; and preserve for many generations the remembrance of the city of God which had been shown! But every night come out these preachers of beauty, and light the universe with their admonishing smile.

The stars awaken a certain reverence, because though always present, they are always inaccessible; but all natural objects make a kindred impression, when the mind is open to their influence. Nature never wears a mean appearance. Neither does the wisest man extort all her secret, and lose his curiosity by finding out all her perfection. Nature never became a toy to a wise spirit. The flowers, the animals, the mountains, reflected all the wisdom of his best hour, as much as they had delighted the simplicity of his childhood.

When we speak of nature in this manner, we have a distinct but most poetical sense in the mind. We mean the integrity of impression made by manifold natural objects. It is this which distinguishes the stick of timber of the wood-cutter, from the tree of the poet. The charming landscape which I saw this morning, is indubitably made up of some twenty or thirty farms. Miller owns this field, Locke that, and Manning the woodland beyond. But

---

4. Emerson draws on Thomas Carlyle's *Sartor Resartus* (1833–34) for his idea of "NOT ME," which Carlyle presents as similar to the German philosophical concept of "everything but the self."

Shortly after the publication of *Nature*, Emerson's friend, the artist
and poet Christopher Cranch (1813–1893), depicted him as a
"transparent eye-ball" in "Illustrations of the New Philosophy"
(c. 1836).

none of them owns the landscape. There is a property in the horizon which
no man has but he whose eye can integrate all the parts, that is, the poet.
This is the best part of these men's farms, yet to this their land-deeds give
them no title.

To speak truly, few adult persons can see nature. Most persons do not see
the sun. At least they have a very superficial seeing. The sun illuminates
only the eye of the man, but shines into the eye and the heart of the child.
The lover of nature is he whose inward and outward senses are still truly
adjusted to each other; who has retained the spirit of infancy even into the
era of manhood.[5] His intercourse with heaven and earth, becomes part of
his daily food. In the presence of nature, a wild delight runs through the
man, in spite of real sorrows. Nature says,—he is my creature, and maugre[6]
all his impertinent griefs, he shall be glad with me. Not the sun or the summer alone, but every hour and season yields its tribute of delight; for every
hour and change corresponds to and authorizes a different state of the
mind, from breathless noon to grimmest midnight. Nature is a setting that

5. An echo of Samuel Taylor Coleridge's *Bio-*
graphia Literaria (1817), ch. 4, in which Coleridge
defines the character and privilege of genius as

the ability to carry the feelings of childhood into
adulthood.
6. Despite (archaic).

fits equally well a comic or a mourning piece. In good health, the air is a cordial of incredible virtue. Crossing a bare common, in snow puddles, at twilight, under a clouded sky, without having in my thoughts any occurrence of special good fortune, I have enjoyed a perfect exhilaration. Almost I fear to think how glad I am. In the woods too, a man casts off his years, as the snake his slough, and at what period soever of life, is always a child. In the woods, is perpetual youth. Within these plantations of God, a decorum and sanctity reign, a perennial festival is dressed, and the guest sees not how he should tire of them in a thousand years. In the woods, we return to reason and faith. There I feel that nothing can befal me in life,—no disgrace, no calamity, (leaving me my eyes,) which nature cannot repair. Standing on the bare ground,—my head bathed by the blithe air, and uplifted into infinite space,—all mean egotism vanishes. I become a transparent eye-ball. I am nothing. I see all. The currents of the Universal Being circulate through me; I am part or particle of God. The name of the nearest friend sounds then foreign and accidental. To be brothers, to be acquaintances,—master or servant, is then a trifle and a disturbance. I am the lover of uncontained and immortal beauty. In the wilderness, I find something more dear and connate[7] than in streets or villages. In the tranquil landscape, and especially in the distant line of the horizon, man beholds somewhat as beautiful as his own nature.

The greatest delight which the fields and woods minister, is the suggestion of an occult relation between man and the vegetable. I am not alone and unacknowledged. They nod to me and I to them. The waving of the boughs in the storm, is new to me and old. It takes me by surprise, and yet is not unknown. Its effect is like that of a higher thought or a better emotion coming over me, when I deemed I was thinking justly or doing right.

Yet it is certain that the power to produce this delight, does not reside in nature, but in man, or in a harmony of both. It is necessary to use these pleasures with great temperance. For, nature is not always tricked in holiday attire, but the same scene which yesterday breathed perfume and glittered as for the frolic of the nymphs, is overspread with melancholy today. Nature always wears the colors of the spirit. To a man laboring under calamity, the heat of his own fire hath sadness in it. Then, there is a kind of contempt of the landscape felt by him who has just lost by death a dear friend. The sky is less grand as it shuts down over less worth in the population.

Chapter II. Commodity

Whoever considers the final cause[8] of the world, will discern a multitude of uses that enter as parts into that result. They all admit of being thrown into one of the following classes; Commodity; Beauty; Language; and Discipline.

Under the general name of Commodity, I rank all those advantages which our senses owe to nature. This, of course, is a benefit which is temporary and mediate, not ultimate, like its service to the soul. Yet although low, it is perfect in its kind, and is the only use of nature which all men apprehend. The misery of man appears like childish petulance, when we explore the steady and prodigal provision that has been made for his support and delight

---

7. Related.   8. In the sense of "purpose."

on this green ball which floats him through the heavens. What angels invented these splendid ornaments, these rich conveniences, this ocean of air above, this ocean of water beneath, this firmament of earth between? this zodiac of lights, this tent of dropping clouds, this striped coat of climates, this fourfold year? Beasts, fire, water, stones, and corn serve him. The field is at once his floor, his work-yard, his play-ground, his garden, and his bed.

> "More servants wait on man
> Than he'll take notice of."————[9]

Nature, in its ministry to man, is not only the material, but is also the process and the result. All the parts incessantly work into each other's hands for the profit of man. The wind sows the seed; the sun evaporates the sea; the wind blows the vapor to the field; the ice, on the other side of the planet, condenses rain on this; the rain feeds the plant; the plant feeds the animal; and thus the endless circulations of the divine charity nourish man.

The useful arts are but reproductions or new combinations by the wit of man, of the same natural benefactors. He no longer waits for favoring gales, but by means of steam, he realizes the fable of Æolus's bag,[1] and carries the two and thirty winds in the boiler of his boat. To diminish friction, he paves the road with iron bars, and, mounting a coach with a ship-load of men, animals, and merchandise behind him, he darts through the country, from town to town, like an eagle or a swallow through the air. By the aggregate of these aids, how is the face of the world changed, from the era of Noah to that of Napoleon! The private poor man hath cities, ships, canals, bridges, built for him. He goes to the post-office, and the human race run on his errands; to the book-shop, and the human race read and write of all that happens, for him; to the court-house, and nations repair his wrongs. He sets his house upon the road, and the human race go forth every morning, and shovel out the snow, and cut a path for him.

But there is no need of specifying particulars in this class of uses. The catalogue is endless, and the examples so obvious, that I shall leave them to the reader's reflection, with the general remark, that this mercenary benefit is one which has respect to a farther good. A man is fed, not that he may be fed, but that he may work.

Chapter III. Beauty

A nobler want of man is served by nature, namely, the love of Beauty.

The ancient Greeks called the world κόσμος[2] beauty. Such is the constitution of all things, or such the plastic[3] power of the human eye, that the primary forms, as the sky, the mountain, the tree, the animal, give us a delight *in and for themselves*; a pleasure arising from outline, color, motion, and grouping. This seems partly owing to the eye itself. The eye is the best of artists. By the mutual action of its structure and of the laws of light, perspective is produced, which integrates every mass of objects, of what character soever, into a well colored and shaded globe, so that where the

---

9. From "Man" (1633), by the English poet George Herbert (1593–1633), quoted at length in chapter VIII, "Prospects."
1. In Homer's *Odyssey* 10, Aeolus, the god of winds, gives Odysseus a bag containing favor-able winds, but they create a storm when his unwary sailors let them all out at once. "Realizes": brings into real existence.
2. Cosmos, or order (Greek).
3. Creative.

particular objects are mean and unaffecting, the landscape which they compose, is round and symmetrical. And as the eye is the best composer, so light is the first of painters. There is no object so foul that intense light will not make beautiful. And the stimulus it affords to the sense, and a sort of infinitude which it hath, like space and time, make all matter gay. Even the corpse hath its own beauty. But beside this general grace diffused over nature, almost all the individual forms are agreeable to the eye, as is proved by our endless imitations[4] of some of them, as the acorn, the grape, the pine-cone, the wheat-ear, the egg, the wings and forms of most birds, the lion's claw, the serpent, the butterfly, sea-shells, flames, clouds, buds, leaves, and the forms of many trees, as the palm.

For better consideration, we may distribute the aspects of Beauty in a threefold manner.

1. First, the simple perception of natural forms is a delight. The influence of the forms and actions in nature, is so needful to man, that, in its lowest functions, it seems to lie on the confines of commodity and beauty. To the body and mind which have been cramped by noxious work or company, nature is medicinal and restores their tone. The tradesman, the attorney comes out of the din and craft[5] of the street, and sees the sky and the woods, and is a man again. In their eternal calm, he finds himself. The health of the eye seems to demand a horizon. We are never tired, so long as we can see far enough.

But in other hours, Nature satisfies the soul purely by its loveliness, and without any mixture of corporeal benefit. I have seen the spectacle of morning from the hill-top over against my house, from day-break to sun-rise, with emotions which an angel might share. The long slender bars of cloud float like fishes in the sea of crimson light. From the earth, as a shore, I look out into that silent sea. I seem to partake its rapid transformations: the active enchantment reaches my dust, and I dilate and conspire with[6] the morning wind. How does Nature deify us with a few and cheap elements! Give me health and a day, and I will make the pomp of emperors ridiculous. The dawn is my Assyria; the sun-set and moon-rise my Paphos, and unimaginable realms of faerie, broad noon shall be my England of the senses and the understanding; the night shall be my Germany of mystic philosophy and dreams.[7]

Not less excellent, except for our less susceptibility in the afternoon, was the charm, last evening, of a January sunset. The western clouds divided and subdivided themselves into pink flakes modulated with tints of unspeakable softness; and the air had so much life and sweetness, that it was a pain to come within doors. What was it that nature would say? Was there no meaning in the live repose of the valley behind the mill, and which Homer or Shakspeare could not re-form for me in words? The leafless trees become spires of flame in the sunset, with the blue east for their background, and the stars of the dead calices of flowers, and every withered stem and stubble rimed[8] with frost, contribute something to the mute music.

The inhabitants of cities suppose that the country landscape is pleasant only half the year. I please myself with observing the graces of the winter

4. As in architectural and furniture design and decoration.
5. Craftiness, materialism.
6. Breathe with.
7. Emerson is contrasting the rational empiricism of Scottish Common Sense philosophy with the mystical idealism of post-Kantian German philosophy. "Assyria": an ancient Near Eastern empire. "Paphos": an ancient city in Cyprus (site of worship of Aphrodite).
8. Coated. "Calices": i.e., calyxes; the outer whorls of leaves or sepals at the bases of flowers.

scenery, and believe that we are as much touched by it as by the genial influences of summer. To the attentive eye, each moment of the year has its own beauty, and in the same field, it beholds, every hour, a picture which was never seen before, and which shall never be seen again. The heavens change every moment, and reflect their glory or gloom on the plains beneath. The state of the crop in the surrounding farms alters the expression of the earth from week to week. The succession of native plants in the pastures and roadsides, which make the silent clock by which time tells the summer hours, will make even the divisions of the day sensible to a keen observer. The tribes of birds and insects, like the plants punctual to their time, follow each other, and the year has room for all. By water-courses, the variety is greater. In July, the blue pontederia or pickerel-weed blooms in large beds in the shallow parts of our pleasant river,[9] and swarms with yellow butterflies in continual motion. Art cannot rival this pomp of purple and gold. Indeed the river is a perpetual gala, and boasts each month a new ornament.

But this beauty of Nature which is seen and felt as beauty, is the least part. The shows of day, the dewy morning, the rainbow, mountains, orchards in blossom, stars, moonlight, shadows in still water, and the like, if too eagerly hunted, become shows merely, and mock us with their unreality. Go out of the house to see the moon, and 't is mere tinsel; it will not please as when its light shines upon your necessary journey. The beauty that shimmers in the yellow afternoons of October, who ever could clutch it? Go forth to find it, and it is gone: 't is only a mirage as you look from the windows of the diligence.

2. The presence of a higher, namely, of the spiritual element is essential to its perfection. The high and divine beauty which can be loved without effeminacy, is that which is found in combination with the human will, and never separate. Beauty is the mark God sets upon virtue. Every natural action is graceful. Every heroic act is also decent,[1] and causes the place and the bystanders to shine. We are taught by great actions that the universe is the property of every individual in it. Every rational creature has all nature for his dowry and estate. It is his, if he will. He may divest himself of it; he may creep into a corner, and abdicate his kingdom, as most men do, but he is entitled to the world by his constitution. In proportion to the energy of his thought and will, he takes up the world into himself. "All those things for which men plough, build, or sail, obey virtue;" said an ancient historian.[2] "The winds and waves," said Gibbon,[3] "are always on the side of the ablest navigators." So are the sun and moon and all the stars of heaven. When a noble act is done,—perchance in a scene of great natural beauty; when Leonidas and his three hundred martyrs consume one day in dying, and the sun and moon come each and look at them once in the steep defile of Thermopylæ; when Arnold Winkelried,[4] in the high Alps, under the shadow of the avalanche, gathers in his side a sheaf of Austrian spears to break the line for his comrades; are not these heroes entitled to add the beauty of the scene to the beauty of the deed? When the bark of Columbus nears the shore of

9. The Concord River.
1. Beautiful.
2. Sallust (1st century B.C.E.), Roman historian, in "The Conspiracy of Cataline," ch. 2.
3. Edward Gibbon (1737–1794), English historian, from The Decline and Fall of the Roman

Empire, ch. 68.
4. Arnold von Winkelried, a Swiss hero, was killed (1386) in a battle against the Austrians at Sempach. Leonidas, king of Sparta, was killed (c. 480 B.C.E.) defending the pass at Thermopylae against the Persian army led by Xerxes.

America;—before it, the beach lined with savages, fleeing out of all their huts of cane; the sea behind; and the purple mountains of the Indian Archipelago around, can we separate the man from the living picture? Does not the New World clothe his form with her palm-groves and savannahs as fit drapery? Ever does natural beauty steal in like air, and envelope great actions. When Sir Harry Vane[5] was dragged up the Tower-hill, sitting on a sled, to suffer death, as the champion of the English laws, one of the multitude cried out to him, "You never sate on so glorious a seat." Charles II., to intimidate the citizens of London, caused the patriot Lord Russel[6] to be drawn in an open coach, through the principal streets of the city, on his way to the scaffold. "But," to use the simple narrative of his biographer, "the multitude imagined they saw liberty and virtue sitting by his side." In private places, among sordid objects, an act of truth or heroism seems at once to draw to itself the sky as its temple, the sun as its candle. Nature stretcheth out her arms to embrace man, only let his thoughts be of equal greatness. Willingly does she follow his steps with the rose and the violet, and bend her lines of grandeur and grace to the decoration of her darling child. Only let his thoughts be of equal scope, and the frame will suit the picture. A virtuous man, is in unison with her works, and makes the central figure of the visible sphere. Homer, Pindar, Socrates, Phocion,[7] associate themselves fitly in our memory with the whole geography and climate of Greece. The visible heavens and earth sympathize with Jesus. And in common life, whosoever has seen a person of powerful character and happy genius, will have remarked how easily he took all things along with him,—the persons, the opinions, and the day, and nature became ancillary to a man.

3. There is still another aspect under which the beauty of the world may be viewed, namely, as it becomes an object of the intellect. Beside the relation of things to virtue, they have a relation to thought. The intellect searches out the absolute order of things as they stand in the mind of God, and without the colors of affection. The intellectual and the active powers seem to succeed each other in man, and the exclusive activity of the one, generates the exclusive activity of the other. There is something unfriendly in each to the other, but they are like the alternate periods of feeding and working in animals; each prepares and certainly will be followed by the other. Therefore does beauty, which, in relation to actions, as we have seen comes unsought, and comes because it is unsought, remain for the apprehension and pursuit of the intellect; and then again, in its turn, of the active power. Nothing divine dies. All good is eternally reproductive. The beauty of nature reforms itself in the mind, and not for barren contemplation, but for new creation.

All men are in some degree impressed by the face of the world. Some men even to delight. This love of beauty is Taste. Others have the same love in such excess, that, not content with admiring, they seek to embody it in new forms. The creation of beauty is Art.

The production of a work of art throws a light upon the mystery of humanity. A work of art is an abstract or epitome of the world. It is the result or

---

5. English Puritan leader (1613–1662) who was executed for treason by the Restoration government because he was suspected of conspiring against King Charles II (1630–1685).
6. William Lord Russel (1639–1683) was executed by English authorities for allegedly plot-

ting to kill Charles II.
7. Athenian statesman and general of the 4th century B.C.E. Emerson knew of him from Plutarch's *Lives*. Pindar was a Greek lyric poet of the 5th and 6th centuries B.C.E. Socrates was a Greek philosopher of the 5th century B.C.E.

expression of nature, in miniature. For although the works of nature are innumerable and all different, the result or the expression of them all is similar and single. Nature is a sea of forms radically alike and even unique. A leaf, a sun-beam, a landscape, the ocean, make an analogous impression on the mind. What is common to them all,—that perfectness and harmony, is beauty. Therefore the standard of beauty, is the entire circuit of natural forms,—the totality of nature; which the Italians expressed by defining beauty "il piu nell' uno."[8] Nothing is quite beautiful alone: nothing but is beautiful in the whole. A single object is only so far beautiful as it suggests this universal grace. The poet, the painter, the sculptor, the musician, the architect seek each to concentrate this radiance of the world on one point, and each in his several work to satisfy the love of beauty which stimulates him to produce. Thus is Art, a nature passed through the alembic[9] of man. Thus in art, does nature work through the will of a man filled with the beauty of her first works.

The world thus exists to the soul to satisfy the desire of beauty. Extend this element to the uttermost, and I call it an ultimate end. No reason can be asked or given why the soul seeks beauty. Beauty, in its largest and profoundest sense, is one expression for the universe. God is the all-fair. Truth, and goodness, and beauty, are but different faces of the same All. But beauty in nature is not ultimate. It is the herald of inward and eternal beauty, and is not alone a solid and satisfactory good. It must therefore stand as a part and not as yet the last or highest expression of the final cause of Nature.

Chapter IV. Language

A third use which Nature subserves to man is that of Language. Nature is the vehicle of thought, and in a simple, double, and threefold degree.

1. Words are signs of natural facts.
2. Particular natural facts are symbols of particular spiritual facts.
3. Nature is the symbol of spirit.

1. Words are signs of natural facts. The use of natural history is to give us aid in supernatural history. The use of the outer creation is to give us language for the beings and changes of the inward creation. Every word which is used to express a moral or intellectual fact, if traced to its root, is found to be borrowed from some material appearance. *Right* originally means *straight*; *wrong* means *twisted*. *Spirit* primarily means *wind*; *transgression*, the crossing of a *line*; *supercilious*, the *raising of the eye-brow*. We say the *heart* to express emotion, the *head* to denote thought; and *thought* and *emotion* are, in their turn, words borrowed from sensible things, and now appropriated to spiritual nature. Most of the process by which this transformation is made, is hidden from us in the remote time when language was framed; but the same tendency may be daily observed in children. Children and savages use only nouns or names of things, which they continually convert into verbs, and apply to analogous mental acts.

2. But this origin of all words that convey a spiritual import,—so conspicuous a fact in the history of language,—is our least debt to nature. It is not words only that are emblematic; it is things which are emblematic.

---

8. The many in one (Italian); a borrowing from Coleridge.

9. A distilling apparatus.

Every natural fact is a symbol of some spiritual fact.[1] Every appearance in nature corresponds to some state of the mind, and that state of the mind can only be described by presenting that natural appearance as its picture. An enraged man is a lion, a cunning man is a fox, a firm man is a rock, a learned man is a torch. A lamb is innocence; a snake is subtle spite; flowers express to us the delicate affections. Light and darkness are our familiar expression for knowledge and ignorance; and heat for love. Visible distance behind and before us, is respectively our image of memory and hope.

Who looks upon a river in a meditative hour, and is not reminded of the flux of all things? Throw a stone into the stream, and the circles that propagate themselves are the beautiful type of all influence. Man is conscious of a universal soul within or behind his individual life, wherein, as in a firmament, the natures of Justice, Truth, Love, Freedom, arise and shine. This universal soul, he calls Reason: it is not mine or thine or his, but we are its; we are its property and men.[2] And the blue sky in which the private earth is buried, the sky with its eternal calm, and full of everlasting orbs, is the type of Reason. That which, intellectually considered, we call Reason, considered in relation to nature, we call Spirit. Spirit is the Creator. Spirit hath life in itself. And man in all ages and countries, embodies it in his language, as the FATHER.

It is easily seen that there is nothing lucky or capricious in these analogies, but that they are constant, and pervade nature. These are not the dreams of a few poets, here and there, but man is an analogist, and studies relations in all objects. He is placed in the centre of beings, and a ray of relation passes from every other being to him. And neither can man be understood without these objects, nor these objects without man. All the facts in natural history taken by themselves, have no value, but are barren like a single sex. But marry it to human history, and it is full of life. Whole Floras, all Linnæus' and Buffon's[3] volume, are but dry catalogues of facts; but the most trivial of these facts, the habit of a plant, the organs, or work, or noise of an insect, applied to the illustration of a fact in intellectual philosophy, or, in any way associated to human nature, affects us in the most lively and agreeable manner. The seed of a plant,—to what affecting analogies in the nature of man, is that little fruit made use of, in all discourse, up to the voice of Paul, who calls the human corpse a seed,—"It is sown a natural body; it is raised a spiritual body."[4] The motion of the earth round its axis, and round the sun, makes the day, and the year. These are certain amounts of brute light and heat. But is there no intent of an analogy between man's life and the seasons? And do the seasons gain no grandeur or pathos from that analogy? The instincts of the ant are very unimportant considered as the ant's; but the moment a ray of relation is seen to extend from it to man, and the little drudge is seen to be a monitor, a little body with a mighty heart, then all its habits, even that said to be recently observed, that it never sleeps, become sublime.

1. This passage invokes the doctrine of correspondences between the spiritual and natural worlds developed by the Swedish theologian and mystic Emanuel Swedenborg (1688–1772).
2. By *reason*, Emerson means something like the intuitive powers of the mind; by *understanding*, he means logical and empirical reasoning. For Emerson, a suprarational reason is the higher faculty. Emerson probably derived these Kantian terms from Samuel Taylor Coleridge's *Biographia Literaria* (1817).
3. French naturalist (1707–1788). Linnæus was Carl von Linné (1707–1778), Swedish botanist. Both were developing systems of classification for natural objects.
4. 1 Corinthians 15.44.

Because of this radical[5] correspondence between visible things and human thoughts, savages, who have only what is necessary, converse in figures. As we go back in history, language becomes more picturesque, until its infancy, when it is all poetry; or, all spiritual facts are represented by natural symbols. The same symbols are found to make the original elements of all languages. It has moreover been observed, that the idioms of all languages approach each other in passages of the greatest eloquence and power. And as this is the first language, so is it the last. This immediate dependence of language upon nature, this conversion of an outward phenomenon into a type of somewhat in human life, never loses its power to affect us. It is this which gives that piquancy to the conversation of a strong-natured farmer or back-woodsman, which all men relish.

Thus is nature an interpreter, by whose means man converses with his fellow men. A man's power to connect his thought with its proper symbol, and so utter it, depends on the simplicity of his character, that is, upon his love of truth and his desire to communicate it without loss. The corruption of man is followed by the corruption of language. When simplicity of character and the sovereignty of ideas is broken up by the prevalence of secondary desires, the desire of riches, the desire of pleasure, the desire of power, the desire of praise,—and duplicity and falsehood take place of simplicity and truth, the power over nature as an interpreter of the will, is in a degree lost; new imagery ceases to be created, and old words are perverted to stand for things which are not; a paper currency is employed when there is no bullion in the vaults. In due time, the fraud is manifest, and words lose all power to stimulate the understanding or the affections. Hundreds of writers may be found in every long-civilized nation, who for a short time believe, and make others believe, that they see and utter truths, who do not of themselves clothe one thought in its natural garment, but who feed unconsciously upon the language created by the primary writers of the country, those, namely, who hold primarily on nature.

But wise men pierce this rotten diction and fasten words again to visible things; so that picturesque language is at once a commanding certificate that he who employs it, is a man in alliance with truth and God. The moment our discourse rises above the ground line of familiar facts, and is inflamed with passion or exalted by thought, it clothes itself in images. A man conversing in earnest, if he watch his intellectual processes, will find that always a material image, more or less luminous, arises in his mind, contemporaneous with every thought, which furnishes the vestment of the thought. Hence, good writing and brilliant discourse are perpetual allegories. This imagery is spontaneous. It is the blending of experience with the present action of the mind. It is proper creation. It is the working of the Original Cause through the instruments he has already made.

These facts may suggest the advantage which the country-life possesses for a powerful mind, over the artificial and curtailed life of cities. We know more from nature than we can at will communicate. Its light flows into the mind evermore, and we forget its presence. The poet, the orator, bred in the woods, whose scenes have been nourished by their fair and appeasing changes, year after year, without design and without heed,—shall not lose their lesson altogether, in the roar of cities or the broil of politics. Long

5. Fundamental (literally "from the root").

hereafter, amidst agitation and terror in national councils,—in the hour of revolution,—these solemn images shall reappear in their morning lustre, as fit symbols and words of the thoughts which the passing events shall awaken. At the call of a noble sentiment, again the woods wave, the pines murmur, the river rolls and shines, and the cattle low upon the mountains, as he saw and heard them in his infancy. And with these forms, the spells of persuasion, the keys of power are put into his hands.

3. We are thus assisted by natural objects in the expression of particular meanings. But how great a language to convey such pepper-corn[6] informations! Did it need such noble races of creatures, this profusion of forms, this host of orbs in heaven, to furnish man with the dictionary and grammar of his municipal speech? Whilst we use this grand cipher to expedite the affairs of our pot and kettle, we feel that we have not yet put it to its use, neither are able. We are like travellers using the cinders of a volcano to roast their eggs. Whilst we see that it always stands ready to clothe what we would say, we cannot avoid the question, whether the characters are not significant of themselves. Have mountains, and waves, and skies, no significance but what we consciously give them, when we employ them as emblems of our thoughts? The world is emblematic. Parts of speech are metaphors because the whole of nature is a metaphor of the human mind. The laws of moral nature answer to those of matter as face to face in a glass. "The visible world and the relation of its parts, is the dial plate of the invisible."[7] The axioms of physics translate the laws of ethics.[8] Thus, "the whole is greater than its part;" "reaction is equal to action;" "the smallest weight may be made to lift the greatest, the difference of weight being compensated by time;" and many the like propositions, which have an ethical as well as physical sense. These propositions have a much more extensive and universal sense when applied to human life, than when confined to technical use.

In like manner, the memorable words of history, and the proverbs of nations, consist usually of a natural fact, selected as a picture or parable of a moral truth. Thus; A rolling stone gathers no moss; A bird in the hand is worth two in the bush; A cripple in the right way, will beat a racer in the wrong; Make hay whilst the sun shines; 'T is hard to carry a full cup even; Vinegar is the son of wine; The last ounce broke the camel's back; Long-lived trees make roots first;—and the like.[9] In their primary sense these are trivial facts, but we repeat them for the value of their analogical import. What is true of proverbs, is true of all fables, parables, and allegories.

This relation between the mind and matter is not fancied by some poet, but stands in the will of God, and so is free to be known by all men. It appears to men, or it does not appear. When in fortunate hours we ponder this miracle, the wise man doubts, if, at all other times, he is not blind and deaf;

> ——"Can these things be,
> And overcome us like a summer's cloud,
> Without our special wonder?"[1]

---

6. Ordinary, everyday.
7. Emerson copied the Swedenborg quotation from the *New Jerusalem Magazine* (July 1832).
8. Adapted from Mme. De Staël's "Germany" (1813): "Even a mathematical axiom is a moral rule."

9. Proverbs drawn from several writers, including Francis Bacon, *The Advancement of Learning* (1605), and Scottish theologian Robert Leighton (1611–1684), *Select Works* (1832).
1. Shakespeare's *Macbeth* 3.4.110–12.

for the universe becomes transparent, and the light of higher laws than its own, shines through it. It is the standing problem which has exercised the wonder and the study of every fine genius since the world began; from the era of the Egyptians and the Brahmins, to that of Pythagoras, of Plato, of Bacon, of Leibnitz,[2] of Swedenborg. There sits the Sphinx at the road-side, and from age to age, as each prophet comes by, he tries his fortune at reading her riddle.[3] There seems to be a necessity in spirit to manifest itself in material forms; and day and night, river and storm, beast and bird, acid and alkali, preëxist in necessary Ideas in the mind of God, and are what they are by virtue of preceding affections, in the world of spirit. A Fact is the end or last issue of spirit. The visible creation is the terminus or the circumference of the invisible world. "Material objects," said a French philosopher, "are necessarily kinds of *scoriæ* of the substantial thoughts of the Creator, which must always preserve an exact relation to their first origin; in other words, visible nature must have a spiritual and moral side."[4]

This doctrine is abstruse, and though the images of "garment," "scoriæ," "mirror," &c., may stimulate the fancy, we must summon the aid of subtler and more vital expositors to make it plain. "Every scripture is to be interpreted by the same spirit which gave it forth,"—is the fundamental law of criticism.[5] A life in harmony with nature, the love of truth and of virtue, will purge the eyes to understand her text. By degrees we may come to know the primitive sense of the permanent objects of nature, so that the world shall be to us an open book, and every form significant of its hidden life and final cause.

A new interest surprises us, whilst, under the view now suggested, we contemplate the fearful extent and multitude of objects; since "every object rightly seen, unlocks a new faculty of the soul."[6] That which was unconscious truth, becomes, when interpreted and defined in an object, a part of the domain of knowledge,—a new amount to the magazine[7] of power.

Chapter V. Discipline

In view of this significance of nature, we arrive at once at a new fact, that nature is a discipline. This use of the world includes the preceding uses, as parts of itself.

Space, time, society, labor, climate, food, locomotion, the animals, the mechanical forces, give us sincerest lessons, day by day, whose meaning is unlimited. They educate both the Understanding and the Reason. Every property of matter is a school for the understanding,—its solidity or resis-

2. Gottfried Wilhelm Leibnitz (1646–1716), German mathematician who championed philosophical idealism and symbolic logic. Pythagorus (c. 582–ca. 507 B.C.E.), Greek philosopher who believed in the transmigration of souls. Plato (c. 427–347 B.C.E.), Greek philosopher who was the founder of philosophical idealism. Sir Francis Bacon (1561–1626), English philosopher who developed inductive and empirical approaches to science.
3. In Greek mythology, a winged monster with a lion's body and head of a woman, who challenged those entering Thebes with a riddle; when they answered incorrectly, she killed them. But when Oedipus answered correctly, the Sphinx was so distraught that she killed herself,

much to the delight of the Theban people, who named Oedipus their king.
4. From the French Swedenborgian Guillaume Oegger's "The True Messiah" (1829), which Emerson had seen in a manuscript translation, perhaps by Elizabeth Peabody. Scoriæ: i.e., scoria; slag or refuse left after metal has been smelted from ore.
5. From the English Quaker George Fox (1624–1691). Emerson's probable source for this quote is William Sewel's *History of the Rise, Increase, and Progress of the Christian People called Quakers* (1722).
6. From Coleridge's *Aids to Reflection* (1829).
7. Storehouse.

tance, its inertia, its extension, its figure, its divisibility. The understanding adds, divides, combines, measures, and finds everlasting nutriment and room for its activity in this worthy scene. Meantime, Reason transfers all these lessons into its own world of thought, by perceiving the analogy that marries Matter and Mind.

1. Nature is a discipline of the understanding in intellectual truths. Our dealing with sensible objects is a constant exercise in the necessary lessons of difference, of likeness, of order, of being and seeming, of progressive arrangement; of ascent from particular to general; of combination to one end of manifold forces. Proportioned to the importance of the organ to be formed, is the extreme care with which its tuition is provided,—a care pretermitted[8] in no single case. What tedious training, day after day, year after year, never ending, to form the common sense; what continual reproduction of annoyances, inconveniences, dilemmas; what rejoicing over us of little men; what disputing of prices, what reckonings of interest,—and all to form the Hand of the mind;—to instruct us that "good thoughts are no better than good dreams, unless they be executed!"[9]

The same good office is performed by Property and its filial systems of debt and credit. Debt, grinding debt, whose iron face the widow, the orphan, and the sons of genius fear and hate;—debt, which consumes so much time, which so cripples and disheartens a great spirit with cares that seem so base, is a preceptor whose lessons cannot be foregone, and is needed most by those who suffer from it most. Moreover, property, which has been well compared to snow,—"if it fall level to-day, it will be blown into drifts tomorrow,"—is merely the surface action of internal machinery, like the index on the face of a clock. Whilst now it is the gymnastics of the understanding, it is hiving in the foresight of the spirit, experience in profounder laws.

The whole character and fortune of the individual is affected by the least inequalities in the culture of the understanding; for example, in the perception of differences. Therefore is Space, and therefore Time, that man may know that things are not huddled and lumped, but sundered and individual. A bell and a plough have each their use, and neither can do the office of the other. Water is good to drink, coal to burn, wool to wear; but wool cannot be drunk, nor water spun, nor coal eaten. The wise man shows his wisdom in separation, in gradation, and his scale of creatures and of merits, is as wide as nature. The foolish have no range in their scale, but suppose every man is as every other man. What is not good they call the worst, and what is not hateful, they call the best.

In like manner, what good heed, nature forms in us! She pardons no mistakes. Her yea is yea, and her nay, nay.

The first steps in Agriculture, Astronomy, Zoölogy, (those first steps which the farmer, the hunter, and the sailor take,) teach that nature's dice are always loaded; that in her heaps and rubbish are concealed sure and useful results.

How calmly and genially the mind apprehends one after another the laws of physics! What noble emotions dilate the mortal as he enters into the counsels of the creation, and feels by knowledge the privilege to BE! His insight refines him. The beauty of nature shines in his own breast. Man is

8. Neglected. "Tuition": guardianship.
9. Adapted from Bacon's "Of Great Place," in *Essays* (1625).

greater that he can see this, and the universe less, because Time and Space relations vanish as laws are known.

Here again we are impressed and even daunted by the immense Universe to be explored. 'What we know, is a point to what we do not know.'[1] Open any recent journal of science, and weigh the problems suggested concerning Light, Heat, Electricity, Magnetism, Physiology, Geology, and judge whether the interest of natural science is likely to be soon exhausted.

Passing by many particulars of the discipline of nature we must not omit to specify two.

The exercise of the Will or the lesson of power is taught in every event. From the child's successive possession of his several senses up to the hour when he saith, "thy will be done!"[2] he is learning the secret, that he can reduce under his will, not only particular events, but great classes, nay the whole series of events, and so conform all facts to his character. Nature is thoroughly mediate. It is made to serve. It receives the dominion of man as meekly as the ass on which the Saviour rode.[3] It offers all its kingdoms to man as the raw material which he may mould into what is useful. Man is never weary of working it up. He forges the subtile and delicate air into wise and melodious words, and gives them wing as angels of persuasion and command. More and more, with every thought, does his kingdom stretch over things, until the world becomes, at last, only a realized will,—the double of the man.

2. Sensible objects conform to the premonitions of Reason and reflect the conscience. All things are moral; and in their boundless changes have an unceasing reference to spiritual nature. Therefore is nature glorious with form, color, and motion, that every globe in the remotest heaven; every chemical change from the rudest crystal up to the laws of life; every change of vegetation from the first principle of growth in the eye of a leaf, to the tropical forest and antediluvian[4] coal-mine; every animal function from the sponge up to Hercules,[5] shall hint or thunder to man the laws of right and wrong, and echo the Ten Commandments. Therefore is nature always the ally of Religion: lends all her pomp and riches to the religious sentiment. Prophet and priest, David, Isaiah,[6] Jesus, have drawn deeply from this source.

This ethical character so penetrates the bone and marrow of nature, as to seem the end for which it was made. Whatever private purpose is answered by any member or part, this is its public and universal function, and is never omitted. Nothing in nature is exhausted in its first use. When a thing has served an end to the uttermost, it is wholly new for an ulterior service. In God, every end is converted into a new means. Thus the use of Commodity, regarded by itself, is mean and squalid. But it is to the mind an education in the great doctrine of Use, namely, that a thing is good only so far as it serves; that a conspiring of parts and efforts to the production of an end, is essential to any being. The first and gross manifestation of this truth, is our inevitable and hated training in values and wants, in corn and meat.

It has already been illustrated, in treating of the significance of material things, that every natural process is but a version of a moral sentence. The

1. A saying ascribed both to Sir Isaac Newton (1642–1727), English mathematician and philosopher, and to Bishop Joseph Butler (1692–1752), English moralist.
2. Matthew 6.10 and 26.42.
3. Matthew 21.5.

4. Before the Flood, which destroyed all living creatures not in Noah's ark (Genesis 6–9).
5. Roman name for the Greek mythological hero Heracles, renowned for feats of strength.
6. Old Testament prophet. David was the second king of Israel.

moral law lies at the centre of nature and radiates to the circumference. It is the pith and marrow of every substance, every relation, and every process. All things with which we deal, preach to us. What is a farm but a mute gospel? The chaff and the wheat, weeds and plants, blight, rain, insects, sun,—it is a sacred emblem from the first furrow of spring to the last stack which the snow of winter overtakes in the fields. But the sailor, the shepherd, the miner, the merchant, in their several resorts, have each an experience precisely parallel and leading to the same conclusions. Because all organizations are radically alike. Nor can it be doubted that this moral sentiment which thus scents the air, and grows in the grain, and impregnates the waters of the world, is caught by man and sinks into his soul. The moral influence of nature upon every individual is that amount of truth which it illustrates to him. Who can estimate this? Who can guess how much firmness the sea-beaten rock has taught the fisherman? how much tranquillity has been reflected to man from the azure sky, over whose unspotted deeps the winds forevermore drive flocks of stormy clouds, and leave no wrinkle or stain? how much industry and providence and affection we have caught from the pantomime of brutes? What a searching preacher of self-command is the varying phenomenon of Health!

Herein is especially apprehended the Unity of Nature,—the Unity in Variety,—which meets us everywhere. All the endless variety of things make a unique, an identical impression. Xenophanes[7] complained in his old age, that, look where he would, all things hastened back to Unity. He was weary of seeing the same entity in the tedious variety of forms. The fable of Proteus has a cordial[8] truth. Every particular in nature, a leaf, a drop, a crystal, a moment of time is related to the whole, and partakes of the perfection of the whole. Each particle is a microcosm, and faithfully renders the likeness of the world.

Not only resemblances exist in things whose analogy is obvious, as when we detect the type of the human hand in the flipper of the fossil saurus, but also in objects wherein there is great superficial unlikeness. Thus architecture is called 'frozen music,' by De Stael and Goethe.[9] 'A Gothic church,' said Coleridge,[1] 'is a petrified religion.' Michael Angelo maintained, that, to an architect, a knowledge of anatomy is essential.[2] In Haydn's[3] oratorios, the notes present to the imagination not only motions, as, of the snake, the stag, and the elephant, but colors also; as the green grass. The granite is differenced in its laws only by the more or less of heat, from the river that wears it away. The river, as it flows, resembles the air that flows over it; the air resembles the light which traverses it with more subtile currents; the light resembles the heat which rides with it through Space. Each creature is only a modification of the other; the likeness in them is more than the difference, and their radical law is one and the same. Hence it is, that a rule of one art, or a law of one organization, holds true throughout nature. So intimate is this Unity, that, it is easily seen, it lies under the undermost garment of nature, and betrays its source in universal Spirit. For, it pervades

7. Greek philosopher of 5th and 6th centuries B.C.E. who taught the unity of all existence.
8. Vital, heartwarming. Proteus was a sea god who could change his shape to evade any captor.
9. Johann Wolfgang von Goethe (1749–1832), in his *Conversations with Eckermann*. Mme. de Staël (1766–1817), in *Corinne*, book 4, chapter 3.

1. In his "Lecture on the General Character of the Gothic Mind in the Middle Ages" (1836).
2. From the sketch of Michelangelo (1475–1564) in *Lives of Eminent Persons* (1833).
3. Joseph Haydn (1732–1809), Austrian composer.

Thought also. Every universal truth which we express in words, implies or supposes every other truth. *Omne verum vero consonat.*[4] It is like a great circle on a sphere, comprising all possible circles; which, however, may be drawn, and comprise it, in like manner. Every such truth is the absolute Ens[5] seen from one side. But it has innumerable sides.

The same central Unity is still more conspicuous in actions. Words are finite organs of the infinite mind. They cannot cover the dimensions of what is in truth. They break, chop, and impoverish it. An action is the perfection and publication of thought. A right action seems to fill the eye, and to be related to all nature. "The wise man, in doing one thing, does all; or, in the one thing he does rightly, he sees the likeness of all which is done rightly."[6]

Words and actions are not the attributes of mute and brute nature. They introduce us to that singular form which predominates over all other forms. This is the human. All other organizations appear to be degradations of the human form. When this organization appears among so many that surround it, the spirit prefers it to all others. It says, 'From such as this, have I drawn joy and knowledge. In such as this, have I found and beheld myself. I will speak to it. It can speak again. It can yield me thought already formed and alive.' In fact, the eye,—the mind,—is always accompanied by these forms, male and female; and these are incomparably the richest informations[7] of the power and order that lie at the heart of things. Unfortunately, every one of them bears the marks as of some injury; is marred and superficially defective. Nevertheless, far different from the deaf and dumb nature around them, these all rest like fountain-pipes on the unfathomed sea of thought and virtue whereto they alone, of all organizations, are the entrances.

It were a pleasant inquiry to follow into detail their ministry to our education, but where would it stop? We are associated in adolescent and adult life with some friends, who, like skies and waters, are coextensive with our idea; who, answering each to a certain affection of the soul, satisfy our desire on that side; whom we lack power to put at such focal distance from us, that we can mend or even analyze them. We cannot chuse but love them. When much intercourse with a friend has supplied us with a standard of excellence, and has increased our respect for the resources of God who thus sends a real person to outgo our ideal; when he has, moreover, become an object of thought, and, whilst his character retains all its unconscious effect, is converted in the mind into solid and sweet wisdom,—it is a sign to us that his office is closing, and he is commonly withdrawn from our sight in a short time.

Chapter VI. Idealism

Thus is the unspeakable but intelligible and practicable meaning of the world conveyed to man, the immortal pupil, in every object of sense. To this one end of Discipline, all parts of nature conspire.

A noble doubt perpetually suggests itself, whether this end be not the Final Cause of the Universe; and whether nature outwardly exists. It is a sufficient account of that Appearance we call the World, that God will teach a human mind, and so makes it the receiver of a certain number of

---

4. Every truth is consonant with every other truth (Latin).
5. Abstract being (Latin).

6. Paraphrase of Goethe's *Wilhelm Meister* (1795–96).
7. Products of the inward, form-giving capacity.

congruent sensations, which we call sun and moon, man and woman, house and trade. In my utter impotence to test the authenticity of the report of my senses, to know whether the impressions they make on me correspond with outlying objects, what difference does it make, whether Orion[8] is up there in heaven, or some god paints the image in the firmament of the soul? The relations of parts and the end of the whole remaining the same, what is the difference, whether land and sea interact, and worlds revolve and intermingle without number or end,—deep yawning under deep,[9] and galaxy balancing galaxy, throughout absolute space, or, whether, without relations of time and space, the same appearances are inscribed in the constant faith of man. Whether nature enjoy a substantial existence without, or is only in the apocalypse[1] of the mind, it is alike useful and alike venerable to me. Be it what it may, it is ideal to me, so long as I cannot try the accuracy of my senses.

The frivolous make themselves merry with the Ideal theory,[2] as if its consequences were burlesque; as if it affected the stability of nature. It surely does not. God never jests with us, and will not compromise the end of nature, by permitting any inconsequence in its procession. Any distrust of the permanence of laws, would paralyze the faculties of man. Their permanence is sacredly respected, and his faith therein is perfect. The wheels and springs of man are all set to the hypothesis of the permanence of nature. We are not built like a ship to be tossed, but like a house to stand. It is a natural consequence of this structure, that, so long as the active powers predominate over the reflective, we resist with indignation any hint that nature is more short-lived or mutable than spirit. The broker, the wheelwright, the carpenter, the tollman, are much displeased at the intimation.

But whilst we acquiesce entirely in the permanence of natural laws, the question of the absolute existence of nature, still remains open. It is the uniform effect of culture on the human mind, not to shake our faith in the stability of particular phenomena, as of heat, water, azote;[3] but to lead us to regard nature as a phenomenon, not a substance; to attribute necessary existence to spirit; to esteem nature as an accident and an effect.

To the senses and the unrenewed understanding, belongs a sort of instinctive belief in the absolute existence of nature. In their view, man and nature are indissolubly joined. Things are ultimates, and they never look beyond their sphere. The presence of Reason mars this faith. The first effort of thought tends to relax this despotism of the senses, which binds us to nature as if we were a part of it, and shows us nature aloof, and, as it were, afloat. Until this higher agency intervened, the animal eye sees, with wonderful accuracy, sharp outlines and colored surfaces. When the eye of Reason opens, to outline and surface are at once added, grace and expression. These proceed from imagination and affection, and abate somewhat of the angular distinctness of objects. If the Reason be stimulated to more earnest vision, outlines and surfaces become transparent, and are no longer seen; causes and spirits are seen through them. The best, the happiest moments of life,

8. Constellation named for the mythical Greek hunter.
9. From Psalm 42.7: "Deep calleth unto deep at the noise of thy waterspouts: all thy waves and thy billows are gone over me."
1. Revelation (Greek).

2. The idea that the mind cannot know anything except its own ideas and thus cannot know material things in themselves is associated with Bishop George Berkeley (1685–1753), whose writings were an important influence on Emerson.
3. Nitrogen.

are these delicious awakenings of the higher powers, and the reverential withdrawing of nature before its God.

Let us proceed to indicate the effects of culture. 1. Our first institution[4] in the Ideal philosophy is a hint from nature herself.

Nature is made to conspire with spirit to emancipate us. Certain mechanical changes, a small alteration in our local position apprizes us of a dualism. We are strangely affected by seeing the shore from a moving ship, from a balloon, or through the tints of an unusual sky. The least change in our point of view, gives the whole world a pictorial air. A man who seldom rides, needs only to get into a coach and traverse his own town, to turn the street into a puppet-show. The men, the women,—talking, running, bartering, fighting,—the earnest mechanic, the lounger, the beggar, the boys, the dogs, are unrealized[5] at once, or, at least, wholly detached from all relation to the observer, and seen as apparent, not substantial beings. What new thoughts are suggested by seeing a face of country quite familiar, in the rapid movement of the railroad car! Nay, the most wonted objects, (make a very slight change in the point of vision,) please us most. In a camera obscura,[6] the butcher's cart, and the figure of one of our own family amuse us. So a portrait of a well-known face gratifies us. Turn the eyes upside down, by looking at the landscape through your legs, and how agreeable is the picture, though you have seen it any time these twenty years!

In these cases, by mechanical means, is suggested the difference between the observer and the spectacle,—between man and nature. Hence arises a pleasure mixed with awe; I may say, a low degree of the sublime is felt from the fact, probably, that man is hereby apprized, that, whilst the world is a spectacle, something in himself is stable.

2. In a higher manner, the poet communicates the same pleasure. By a few strokes he delineates, as on air, the sun, the mountain, the camp, the city, the hero, the maiden, not different from what we know them, but only lifted from the ground and float before the eye. He unfixes the land and the sea, makes them revolve around the axis of his primary thought, and disposes them anew. Possessed himself by a heroic passion, he uses matter as symbols of it. The sensual man conforms thoughts to things; the poet conforms things to his thoughts.[7] The one esteems nature as rooted and fast; the other, as fluid, and impresses his being thereon. To him, the refractory world is ductile and flexible; he invests dusts and stones with humanity and makes them the words of the Reason. The imagination may be defined to be, the use which the Reason makes of the material world. Shakspeare possesses the power of subordinating nature for the purposes of expression, beyond all poets. His imperial muse tosses the creation like a bauble from hand to hand, to embody any capricious shade of thought that is uppermost in his mind. The remotest spaces of nature are visited, and the farthest sundered things are brought together, by a subtile spiritual connexion. We are made aware that magnitude of material things is merely relative, and all objects shrink and expand to serve the passion of the poet. Thus, in his sonnets, the lays of birds, the scents and dyes of flowers, he finds to be the

---

4. Instruction. "Effects of culture": in the sense of the effects of awakening thought.
5. Made unsubstantial. "Mechanic": manual laborer.
6. Dark chamber or box with a lens or opening through which an image is projected in natural colors onto an opposite surface.
7. From Bacon's "The Advancement of Learning" (2.4.2), but more directly from William Hazlitt's adaptation.

shadow of his beloved; time, which keeps her from him, is his *chest*; the suspicion she has awakened, is her *ornament*;[8]

> The ornament of beauty is Suspect,
> A crow which flies in heaven's sweetest air.[9]

His passion is not the fruit of chance; it swells, as he speaks, to a city, or a state.

> No, it was builded far from accident;
> It suffers not in smiling pomp, nor falls
> Under the brow of thralling discontent;
> It fears not policy, that heretic,
> That works on leases of short numbered hours,
> But all alone stands hugely politic.[1]

In the strength of his constancy, the Pyramids[2] seem to him recent and transitory. And the freshness of youth and love dazzles him with its resemblance to morning.

> Take those lips away
> Which so sweetly were forsworn;
> And those eyes,—the break of day,
> Lights that do mislead the morn.[3]

The wild beauty of this hyperbole, I may say, in passing, it would not be easy to match in literature.

This transfiguration which all material objects undergo through the passion of the poet,—this power which he exerts, at any moment, to magnify the small, to micrify the great,—might be illustrated by a thousand examples from his Plays. I have before me the Tempest, and will cite only these few lines.

> PROSPERO.   The strong based promontory
> Have I made shake, and by the spurs plucked up
> The pine and cedar.[4]

Prospero calls for music to sooth the frantic Alonzo, and his companions;

> A solemn air, and the best comforter
> To an unsettled fancy, cure thy brains
> Now useless, boiled within thy skull.

Again;

> The charm dissolves space
> And, as the morning steals upon the night,
> Melting the darkness, so their rising senses
> Begin to chase the ignorant fumes that mantle
> Their clearer reason.

---

8. Emerson summarizes Shakespeare's Sonnet 98 and refers to Sonnet 65 ("Shall Time's best jewel from Time's chest lie hid?").
9. Shakespeare's Sonnet 70.
1. Shakespeare's Sonnet 124.
2. Shakespeare's Sonnet 123: "No, Time, thou shalt not boast that I do change: / Thy pyramids built up with newer might / To me are nothing

novel, nothing strange: / They are but dressings of a former sight."
3. From Shakespeare's *Measure for Measure* 5.1.1–4.
4. Shakespeare's *The Tempest* 5.1.46–48; later quotations are from 5.1.58–60, 64–68, and 79–82.

> Their understanding
> Begins to swell: and the approaching tide
> Will shortly fill the reasonable shores
> That now lie foul and muddy.

The perception of real affinities between events, (that is to say, of *ideal* affinities, for those only are real,) enables the poet thus to make free with the most imposing forms and phenomena of the world, and to assert the predominance of the soul.

3. Whilst thus the poet delights us by animating[5] nature like a creator, with his own thoughts, he differs from the philosopher only herein, that the one proposes Beauty as his main end; the other Truth. But, the philosopher, not less than the poet, postpones the apparent order and relations of things to the empire of thought. "The problem of philosophy," according to Plato, "is, for all that exists conditionally, to find a ground unconditioned and absolute."[6] It proceeds on the faith that a law determines all phenomena, which being known, the phenomena can be predicted. That law, when in the mind, is an idea. Its beauty is infinite. The true philosopher and the true poet are one, and a beauty, which is truth, and a truth, which is beauty, is the aim of both. Is not the charm of one of Plato's or Aristotle's definitions, strictly like that of the Antigone of Sophocles?[7] It is, in both cases, that a spiritual life has been imparted to nature; that the solid seeming block of matter has been pervaded and dissolved by a thought; that this feeble human being has penetrated the vast masses of nature with an informing soul, and recognised itself in their harmony, that is, seized their law. In physics, when this is attained, the memory disburthens itself of its cumbrous catalogues of particulars, and carries centuries of observation in a single formula.

Thus even in physics, the material is ever degraded before the spiritual. The astronomer, the geometer, rely on their irrefragable analysis, and disdain the results of observation. The sublime remark of Euler[8] on his law of arches, "This will be found contrary to all experience, yet it is true;" had already transferred nature into the mind, and left matter like an outcast corpse.

4. Intellectual science has been observed to beget invariably a doubt of the existence of matter. Turgot[9] said, "He that has never doubted the existence of matter, may be assured he has no aptitude for metaphysical inquiries." It fastens the attention upon immortal necessary uncreated natures, that is, upon Ideas; and in their beautiful and majestic presence, we feel that our outward being is a dream and a shade. Whilst we wait in this Olympus of gods, we think of nature as an appendix to the soul. We ascend into their region, and know that these are the thoughts of the Supreme Being. "These are they who were set up from everlasting, from the beginning, or ever the earth was. When he prepared the heavens, they were there; when he established the clouds above, when he strengthened the fountains of the deep. Then they were by him, as one brought up with him. Of them took he counsel."[1]

---

5. Giving life to.

6. Emerson draws this quotation from Coleridge's "The Friend" (1818).

7. Greek dramatist of the 5th century B.C.E.; in his tragedy *Antigone* the title character chooses death rather than violate her sacred duty to perform funeral rites for her slain brother.

8. Leonhard Euler (1707–1783), Swiss mathematician and physicist. Emerson took the quotation from Coleridge's *Aids to Reflection* (1829).

9. Anne Robert Jacques Turgot (1727–1781), French economist and author of a book on proofs of the existence of God.

1. Cf. Proverbs 8.23–30.

Their influence is proportionate. As objects of science, they are accessible to few men. Yet all men are capable of being raised by piety or by passion, into their region. And no man touches these divine natures, without becoming, in some degree, himself divine. Like a new soul, they renew the body. We become physically nimble and lightsome; we tread on air; life is no longer irksome, and we think it will never be so. No man fears age or misfortune or death, in their serene company, for he is transported out of the district of change. Whilst we behold unveiled the nature of Justice and Truth, we learn the difference between the absolute and the conditional or relative. We apprehend the absolute. As it were, for the first time, *we exist*. We become immortal, for we learn that time and space are relations of matter; that, with a perception of truth, or a virtuous will, they have no affinity.

5. Finally, religion and ethics, which may be fitly called,—the practice of ideas, or the introduction of ideas into life,—have an analogous effect with all lower culture, in degrading nature and suggesting its dependence on spirit. Ethics and religion differ herein; that the one is the system of human duties commencing from man; the other, from God. Religion includes the personality of God; Ethics does not. They are one to our present design. They both put nature under foot. The first and last lesson of religion is, "The things that are seen, are temporal; the things that are unseen are eternal."[2] It puts an affront upon nature. It does that for the unschooled, which philosophy does for Berkeley and Viasa.[3] The uniform language that may be heard in the churches of the most ignorant sects, is,—'Contemn the unsubstantial shows of the world; they are vanities, dreams, shadows, unrealities; seek the realities of religion.' The devotee flouts nature. Some theosophists[4] have arrived at a certain hostility and indignation towards matter, as the Manichean and Plotinus. They distrusted in themselves any looking back to these flesh-pots of Egypt. Plotinus was ashamed of his body.[5] In short, they might all better say of matter, what Michael Angelo said of external beauty, "it is the frail and weary weed, in which God dresses the soul, which he has called into time."[6]

It appears that motion, poetry, physical and intellectual science, and religion, all tend to affect our convictions of the reality of the external world. But I own there is something ungrateful in expanding too curiously the particulars of the general proposition, that all culture tends to imbue us with idealism. I have no hostility to nature, but a child's love to it. I expand and live in the warm day like corn and melons. Let us speak her fair. I do not wish to fling stones at my beautiful mother, nor soil my gentle nest. I only wish to indicate the true position of nature in regard to man, wherein to establish man, all right education tends; as the ground which to attain is the object of human life, that is, of man's connexion with nature. Culture inverts the vulgar views of nature, and brings the mind to call that apparent, which it uses to call real, and that real, which it uses to call visionary. Children, it is true, believe in the external world. The belief that it appears only, is an afterthought, but with culture, this faith will as surely arise on the mind as did the first.

2. 2 Corinthians 4.18.
3. Reputed author of the Vedas, the ancient sacred literature of Hinduism. George Berkeley (1685–1753), Irish idealist philosopher.
4. In the broad sense of those who attempt to establish direct contact with divine principle through contemplation and revelation.
5. Plotinus was associated with Neoplatonism, a doctrine merging features from Greek philosophies with those of Judaism and Christianity.
6. Michelangelo's Sonnet 51 (c. 1530).

The advantage of the ideal theory over the popular faith, is this, that it presents the world in precisely that view which is most desirable to the mind. It is, in fact, the view which Reason, both speculative and practical, that is, philosophy and virtue, take. For, seen in the light of thought, the world always is phenomenal;[7] and virtue subordinates it to the mind. Idealism sees the world in God. It beholds the whole circle of persons and things, of actions and events, of country and religion, not as painfully accumulated, atom after atom, act after act, in an aged creeping Past, but as one vast picture, which God paints on the instant eternity, for the contemplation of the soul. Therefore the soul holds itself off from a too trivial and microscopic study of the universal tablet. It respects the end too much, to immerse itself in the means. It sees something more important in Christianity, than the scandals of ecclesiastical history or the niceties of criticism; and, very incurious concerning persons or miracles, and not at all disturbed by chasms of historical evidence, it accepts from God the phenomenon, as it finds it, as the pure and awful form of religion in the world. It is not hot and passionate at the appearance of what it calls its own good or bad fortune, at the union or opposition of other persons. No man is its enemy. It accepts whatsoever befalls, as part of its lesson. It is a watcher more than a doer, and it is a doer, only that it may the better watch.

Chapter VII. Spirit

It is essential to a true theory of nature and of man, that it should contain somewhat progressive. Uses that are exhausted or that may be, and facts that end in the statement, cannot be all that is true of this brave lodging wherein man is harbored, and wherein all his faculties find appropriate and endless exercise. And all the uses of nature admit of being summed in one, which yields the activity of man an infinite scope. Through all its kingdoms, to the suburbs and outskirts of things, it is faithful to the cause whence it had its origin. It always speaks of Spirit. It suggests the absolute. It is a perpetual effect. It is a great shadow pointing always to the sun behind us.

The aspect of nature is devout. Like the figure of Jesus, she stands with bended head, and hands folded upon the breast. The happiest man is he who learns from nature the lesson of worship.

Of that ineffable essence which we call Spirit, he that thinks most, will say least. We can foresee God in the coarse and, as it were, distant phenomena of matter; but when we try to define and describe himself, both language and thought desert us, and we are as helpless as fools and savages. That essence refuses to be recorded in propositions, but when man has worshipped him intellectually, the noblest ministry of nature is to stand as the apparition[8] of God. It is the great organ through which the universal spirit speaks to the individual, and strives to lead back the individual to it.

When we consider Spirit, we see that the views already presented do not include the whole circumference of man. We must add some related thoughts.

Three problems are put by nature to the mind; What is matter? Whence is it? and Whereto? The first of these questions only, the ideal theory answers. Idealism saith: matter is a phenomenon, not a substance. Idealism acquaints us with the total disparity between the evidence of our own being, and the

---

7. Only an appearance.   8. Visible state.

evidence of the world's being. The one is perfect, the other, incapable of any assurance; the mind is a part of the nature of things; the world is a divine dream, from which we may presently awake to the glories and certainties of day. Idealism is a hypothesis to account for nature by other principles than those of carpentry and chemistry. Yet, if it only deny the existence of matter, it does not satisfy the demands of the spirit. It leaves God out of me. It leaves me in the splendid labyrinth of my perceptions, to wander without end. Then the heart resists it, because it baulks the affections in denying substantive being to men and women. Nature is so pervaded with human life, that there is something of humanity in all, and in every particular. But this theory makes nature foreign to me, and does not account for that consanguinity which we acknowledge to it.

Let it stand then, in the present state of our knowledge, merely as a useful introductory hypothesis, serving to apprize us of the eternal distinction between the soul and the world.

But when, following the invisible steps of thought, we come to inquire, Whence is matter? and Whereto? many truths arise to us out of the recesses of consciousness. We learn that the highest is present to the soul of man, that the dread universal essence, which is not wisdom, or love, or beauty, or power, but all in one, and each entirely, is that for which all things exist, and that by which they are; that spirit creates; that behind nature, throughout nature, spirit is present; that spirit is one and not compound; that spirit does not act upon us from without, that is, in space and time, but spiritually, or through ourselves. Therefore, that spirit, that is, the Supreme Being, does not build up nature around us, but puts it forth through us, as the life of the tree puts forth new branches and leaves through the pores of the old. As a plant upon the earth, so a man rests upon the bosom of God: he is nourished by unfailing fountains, and draws, at his need, inexhaustible power. Who can set bounds to the possibilities of man? Once inspire the infinite, by being admitted to behold the absolute natures of justice and truth, and we learn that man has access to the entire mind of the Creator, is himself the creator in the finite. This view, which admonishes me where the sources of wisdom and power lie, and points to virtue as to

> "The golden key
> Which opes the palace of eternity,"[9]

carries upon its face the highest certificate of truth, because it animates me to create my own world through the purification of my soul.

The world proceeds from the same spirit as the body of man. It is a remoter and inferior incarnation of God, a projection of God in the unconscious. But it differs from the body in one important respect. It is not, like that, now subjected to the human will. Its serene order is inviolable by us. It is therefore, to us, the present expositor of the divine mind. It is a fixed point whereby we may measure our departure. As we degenerate, the contrast between us and our house is more evident. We are as much strangers in nature, as we are aliens from God. We do not understand the notes of the birds. The fox and the deer run away from us; the bear and tiger rend us. We do not know the uses of more than a few plants, as corn and the apple, the potato and the vine. Is not the landscape, every glimpse of which hath

---

9. From Milton's *Comus* 13–14.

a grandeur, a face of him? Yet this may show us what discord is between man and nature, for you cannot freely admire a noble landscape, if laborers are digging in the field hard by. The poet finds something ridiculous in his delight, until he is out of the sight of men.

Chapter VIII. Prospects

In inquiries respecting the laws of the world and the frame of things, the highest reason is always the truest. That which seems faintly possible—it is so refined, is often faint and dim because it is deepest seated in the mind among the eternal verities. Empirical science is apt to cloud the sight, and, by the very knowledge of functions and processes, to bereave the student of the manly contemplation of the whole. The savant[1] becomes unpoetic. But the best read naturalist who lends an entire and devout attention to truth, will see that there remains much to learn of his relation to the world, and that it is not to be learned by any addition or subtraction or other comparison of known quantities, but is arrived at by untaught sallies of the spirit, by a continual self-recovery, and by entire humility. He will perceive that there are far more excellent qualities in the student than preciseness and infallibility; that a guess is often more fruitful than an indisputable affirmation, and that a dream may let us deeper into the secret of nature than a hundred concerted experiments.

For, the problems to be solved are precisely those which the physiologist and the naturalist omit to state. It is not so pertinent to man to know all the individuals of the animal kingdom, as it is to know whence and whereto is this tyrannizing unity in his constitution, which evermore separates and classifies things, endeavouring to reduce the most diverse to one form. When I behold a rich landscape, it is less to my purpose to recite correctly the order and super-position of the strata, than to know why all thought of multitude is lost in a tranquil sense of unity. I cannot greatly honor minuteness in details, so long as there is no hint to explain the relation between things and thoughts; no ray upon the *metaphysics* of conchology, of botany, of the arts, to show the relation of the forms of flowers, shells, animals, architecture, to the mind, and build science upon ideas. In a cabinet[2] of natural history, we become sensible of a certain occult recognition and sympathy in regard to the most bizarre forms of beast, fish, and insect. The American who has been confined, in his own country, to the sight of buildings designed after foreign models, is surprised on entering York Minster or St. Peter's at Rome, by the feeling that these structures are imitations also,— faint copies of an invisible archetype. Nor has science sufficient humanity, so long as the naturalist overlooks that wonderful congruity which subsists between man and the world; of which he is lord, not because he is the most subtile inhabitant, but because he is its head and heart, and finds something of himself in every great and small thing, in every mountain stratum, in every new law of color, fact of astronomy, or atmospheric influence which observation or analysis lay open. A perception of this mystery inspires the muse of George Herbert, the beautiful psalmist of the seventeenth century. The following lines are part of his little poem on Man.[3]

1. Learned person.
2. Display case, or room containing many display cases.
3. Stanzas 1–4 and 6 of "Man" (1633).

"Man is all symmetry,
Full of proportions, one limb to another,
    And to all the world besides.
    Each part may call the farthest, brother;
For head with foot hath private amity,
    And both with moons and tides.

"Nothing hath got so far
But man hath caught and kept it as his prey;
    His eyes dismount the highest star;
    He is in little all the sphere.
Herbs gladly cure our flesh, because that they
    Find their acquaintance there.

"For us, the winds do blow.
The earth doth rest, heaven move, and fountains flow;
    Nothing we see, but means our good,
    As our delight, or as our treasure;
The whole is either our cupboard of food,
    Or cabinet of pleasure.

"The stars have us to bed;
Night draws the curtain; which the sun withdraws.
    Music and light attend our head.
    All things unto our flesh are kind,
In their descent and being; to our mind,
    In their ascent and cause.

"More servants wait on man
Than he'll take notice of. In every path,
    He treads down that which doth befriend him
    When sickness makes him pale and wan.
Oh mighty love! Man is one world, and hath
    Another to attend him."

The perception of this class of truths makes the eternal attraction which draws men to science, but the end is lost sight of in attention to the means. In view of this half-sight of science, we accept the sentence of Plato, that, "poetry comes nearer to vital truth than history."[4] Every surmise and vaticination[5] of the mind is entitled to a certain respect, and we learn to prefer imperfect theories, and sentences, which contain glimpses of truth, to digested systems which have no one valuable suggestion. A wise writer will feel that the ends of study and composition are best answered by announcing undiscovered regions of thought, and so communicating, through hope, new activity to the torpid spirit.

I shall therefore conclude this essay with some traditions of man and nature, which a certain poet[6] sang to me; and which, as they have always

4. In copying two quotations from the *Edinburgh Review* Emerson blurred the attributions; here he quotes not from Plato, but from section 9 of Aristotle's *Poetics*.
5. Foretelling, prophesying.

6. Perhaps a joking reference to Bronson Alcott (1799–1888), Emerson's neighbor and Trancendentalist friend, who authored his own "Orphic Sayings" (though these poetic passages are by Emerson).

been in the world, and perhaps reappear to every bard, may be both history and prophecy.

'The foundations of man are not in matter, but in spirit. But the element of spirit is eternity. To it, therefore, the longest series of events, the oldest chronologies are young and recent. In the cycle of the universal man, from whom the known individuals proceed, centuries are points, and all history is but the epoch of one degradation.

'We distrust and deny inwardly our sympathy with nature. We own and disown our relation to it, by turns. We are, like Nebuchadnezzar, dethroned, bereft of reason, and eating grass like an ox.[7] But who can set limits to the remedial force of spirit?

'A man is a god in ruins. When men are innocent, life shall be longer, and shall pass into the immortal, as gently as we awake from dreams. Now, the world would be insane and rabid, if these disorganizations should last for hundreds of years. It is kept in check by death and infancy. Infancy is the perpetual Messiah, which comes into the arms of fallen men, and pleads with them to return to paradise.

'Man is the dwarf of himself. Once he was permeated and dissolved by spirit. He filled nature with his overflowing currents. Out from him sprang the sun and moon; from man, the sun; from woman, the moon. The laws of his mind, the periods of his actions externized themselves into day and night, into the year and the seasons. But, having made for himself this huge shell, his waters retired; he no longer fills the veins and veinlets; he is shrunk to a drop. He sees, that the structure still fits him, but fits him colossally. Say, rather, once it fitted him, now it corresponds to him from far and on high. He adores timidly his own work. Now is man the follower of the sun, and woman the follower of the moon. Yet sometimes he starts in his slumber, and wonders at himself and his house, and muses strangely at the resemblance betwixt him and it. He perceives that if his law is still paramount, if still he have elemental power, "if his word is sterling yet in nature," it is not conscious power, it is not inferior but superior to his will. It is Instinct.' Thus my Orphic poet sang.

At present, man applies to nature but half his force. He works on the world with his understanding alone. He lives in it, and masters it by a penny-wisdom; and he that works most in it, is but a half-man and whilst his arms are strong and his digestion good, his mind is imbruted and he is a selfish savage. His relation to nature, his power over it, is through the understanding; as by manure; the economic use of fire, wind, water, and the mariner's needle; steam, coal, chemical agriculture; the repairs of the human body by the dentist and the surgeon. This is such a resumption of power, as if a banished king should buy his territories inch by inch, instead of vaulting at once into his throne. Meantime, in the thick darkness, there are not wanting gleams of a better light,—occasional examples of the action of man upon nature with his entire force,—with reason as well as understanding. Such examples are; the traditions of miracles in the earliest antiquity of all nations; the history of Jesus Christ; the achievements of a principle, as in religious and political revolutions, and in the abolition of the Slave-trade; the miracles of enthusiasm,[8] as those reported of Swedenborg, Hohenlohe, and the

---

7. The Babylonian king Nebuchadnezzar (d. 562 B.C.E.) "was driven from men, and did eat grass as oxen" (Daniel 4.33).

8. State of supernatural ecstasy or possession.

Shakers;[9] many obscure and yet contested facts, now arranged under the name of Animal Magnetism;[1] prayer; eloquence, self-healing; and the wisdom of children. These are examples of Reason's momentary grasp of the sceptre, the exertions of a power which exists not in time or space, but an instantaneous in-streaming causing power. The difference between the actual and the ideal force of man is happily figured by the schoolmen,[2] in saying, that the knowledge of man is an evening knowledge, *vespertina cognitio*, but that of God is a morning knowledge, *matutina cognitio*.

The problem of restoring to the world original and eternal beauty, is solved by the redemption of the soul. The ruin or the blank, that we see when we look at nature, is in our own eye. The axis of vision is not coincident with the axis of things, and so they appear not transparent but opake. The reason why the world lacks unity, and lies broken and in heaps, is, because man is disunited with himself. He cannot be a naturalist, until he satisfies all the demands of the spirit. Love is as much its demand, as perception. Indeed, neither can be perfect without the other. In the uttermost meaning of the words, thought is devout, and devotion is thought. Deep calls unto deep.[3] But in actual life, the marriage is not celebrated. There are innocent men who worship God after the tradition of their fathers, but their sense of duty has not yet extended to the use of all their faculties. And there are patient naturalists, but they freeze their subject under the wintry light of the understanding. Is not prayer also a study of truth,—a sally of the soul into the unfound infinite? No man ever prayed heartily, without learning something. But when a faithful thinker, resolute to detach every object from personal relations, and see it in the light of thought, shall, at the same time, kindle science with the fire of the holiest affections, then will God go forth anew into the creation.

It will not need, when the mind is prepared for study, to search for objects. The invariable mark of wisdom is to see the miraculous in the common. What is a day? What is a year? What is summer? What is woman? What is a child? What is sleep? To our blindness, these things seem unaffecting. We make fables to hide the baldness of the fact and conform it, as we say, to the higher law of the mind. But when the fact is seen under the light of an idea, the gaudy fable fades and shrivels. We behold the real higher law. To the wise, therefore, a fact is true poetry, and the most beautiful of fables. These wonders are brought to our own door. You also are a man. Man and woman, and their social life, poverty, labor, sleep, fear, fortune, are known to you. Learn that none of these things is superficial, but that each phenomenon hath its roots in the faculties and affections of the mind. Whilst the abstract question occupies your intellect, nature brings it in the concrete to be solved by your hands. It were a wise inquiry for the closet,[4] to compare, point by point, especially at remarkable crises in life, our daily history, with the rise and progress of ideas in the mind.

So shall we come to look at the world with new eyes. It shall answer the endless inquiry of the intellect,—What is truth? and of the affections,—

9. A Protestant millenarian sect known for its commitments to sexual equality and celibacy, the Shakers were founded in England in 1747 and moved to America in 1774; like the Quakers, they preached the importance of attending to one's inner light. Leopold Franz Emmerich, prince of Hohenlohe (1794–1849), reputed miracle healer.
1. Hypnotism.
2. Medieval scholastic philosophers.
3. Psalm 42.7.
4. The scholar's private workroom.

What is good? by yielding itself passive to the educated Will. Then shall come to pass what my poet said; 'Nature is not fixed but fluid. Spirit alters, moulds, makes it. The immobility or bruteness of nature, is the absence of spirit; to pure spirit, it is fluid, it is volatile, it is obedient. Every spirit builds itself a house; and beyond its house, a world; and beyond its world, a heaven. Know then, that the world exists for you. For you is the phenomenon perfect. What we are, that only can we see. All that Adam had, all that Cæsar could, you have and can do. Adam called his house, heaven and earth; Cæsar called his house, Rome; you perhaps call yours, a cobler's trade; a hundred acres of ploughed land; or a scholar's garret. Yet line for line and point for point, your dominion is as great as theirs, though without fine names. Build, therefore your own world. As fast as you can conform your life to the pure idea in your mind, that will unfold its great proportions. A correspondent revolution in things will attend the influx of the spirit. So fast will disagreeable appearances, swine, spiders, snakes, pests, mad-houses, prisons, enemies, vanish; they are temporary and shall be no more seen. The sordor and filths of nature, the sun shall dry up, and the wind exhale. As when the summer comes from the south, the snow-banks melt, and the face of the earth becomes green before it, so shall the advancing spirit create its ornaments along its path, and carry with it the beauty it visits, and the song which enchants it; it shall draw beautiful faces, and warm hearts, and wise discourse, and heroic acts, around its way, until evil is no more seen. The kingdom of man over nature, which cometh not with observation,[5]—a dominion such as now is beyond his dream of God,—he shall enter without more wonder than the blind man feels who is gradually restored to perfect sight.'

1836

The American Scholar[1]

Mr. President, and Gentlemen,

I greet you on the re-commencement of our literary year.[2] Our anniversary is one of hope, and, perhaps, not enough of labor. We do not meet for games of strength or skill, for the recitation of histories, tragedies and odes, like the ancient Greeks; for parliaments of love and poesy, like the Troubadours;[3] nor for the advancement of science, like our cotemporaries in the British and European capitals. Thus far, our holiday has been simply a friendly sign of the survival of the love of letters amongst a people too busy to give to letters any more. As such, it is precious as the sign of an indestructible instinct. Perhaps the time is already come, when it ought to be, and will be something else; when the sluggard intellect of this continent will look from under its iron lids and fill the postponed expectation of the world with something better than the exertions of mechanical skill. Our day of dependence, our long appren-

5. Luke 17.20.
1. The text printed here is that of the first publication (1837) as a pamphlet titled *An Oration, Delivered before the Phi Beta Kappa Society at Cambridge, August 31, 1837*. By changing the title to "The American Scholar" when he republished it in *Nature, Addresses, and Lectures* (1849), Emerson made clear that he was addressing a larger audience than this first group.
2. Also a reference to the academic year traditionally beginning in September.
3. Poets of southern France, especially Provence, in the 12th and 13th centuries.

ticeship to the learning of other lands, draws to a close. The millions that around us are rushing into life, cannot always be fed on the sere remains of foreign harvests. Events, actions arise, that must be sung, that will sing themselves. Who can doubt that poetry will revive and lead in a new age, as the star in the constellation Harp which now flames in our zenith, astronomers announce, shall one day be the pole-star[4] for a thousand years.

In the light of this hope, I accept the topic which not only usage, but the nature of our association, seem to prescribe to this day,—the AMERICAN SCHOLAR. Year by year, we come up hither to read one more chapter of his biography. Let us inquire what new lights, new events and more days have thrown on his character, his duties and his hopes.

It is one of those fables, which out of an unknown antiquity, convey an unlooked for wisdom, that the gods, in the beginning, divided Man into men, that he might be more helpful to himself;[5] just as the hand was divided into fingers, the better to answer its end.

The old fable covers a doctrine ever new and sublime; that there is One Man,—present to all particular men only partially, or through one faculty; and that you must take the whole society to find the whole man. Man is not a farmer, or a professor, or an engineer, but he is all. Man is priest, and scholar, and statesman, and producer, and soldier. In the *divided* or social state, these functions are parcelled out to individuals, each of whom aims to do his stint of the joint work, whilst each other performs his. The fable implies that the individual to possess himself, must sometimes return from his own labor to embrace all the other laborers. But unfortunately, this original unit, this fountain of power, has been so distributed to multitudes, has been so minutely subdivided and peddled out, that it is spilled into drops, and cannot be gathered. The state of society is one in which the members have suffered amputation from the trunk, and strut about so many walking monsters,—a good finger, a neck, a stomach, an elbow, but never a man.

Man is thus metamorphosed into a thing, into many things. The planter, who is Man sent out into the field to gather food, is seldom cheered by any idea of the true dignity of his ministry. He sees his bushel and his cart, and nothing beyond, and sinks into the farmer, instead of Man on the farm. The tradesman scarcely ever gives an ideal worth to his work, but is ridden by the routine of his craft, and the soul is subject to dollars. The priest becomes a form; the attorney, a statute-book; the mechanic, a machine; the sailor, a rope of a ship.

In this distribution of functions, the scholar is the delegated intellect. In the right state, he is, *Man Thinking*. In the degenerate state, when the victim of society, he tends to become a mere thinker, or, still worse, the parrot of other men's thinking.

In this view of him, as Man Thinking, the whole theory of his office[6] is contained. Him nature solicits, with all her placid, all her monitory pictures. Him the past instructs. Him the future invites. Is not, indeed, every man a student, and do not all things exist for the student's behoof? And, finally, is not the true scholar the only true master? But, as the old oracle said, "All things have two handles. Beware of the wrong one."[7] In life, too often, the

---

4. The North Star. "Harp": Lyra, a northern constellation, which includes the bright star Vega.
5. Emerson knew one such fable from Plato's *Symposium*.

6. Function.
7. From the Greek philosopher Epictetus (c. 50–c. 138 C.E.), who taught that the true good is within oneself.

scholar errs with mankind and forfeits his privilege. Let us see him in his school, and consider him in reference to the main influences he receives.

I. The first in time and the first in importance of the influences upon the mind is that of nature. Every day, the sun; and, after sunset, night and her stars. Ever the winds blow; ever the grass grows. Every day, men and women, conversing, beholding and beholden. The scholar must needs stand wistful and admiring before this great spectacle. He must settle its value in his mind. What is nature to him? There is never a beginning, there is never an end to the inexplicable continuity of this web of God, but always circular power returning into itself. Therein it resembles his own spirit, whose beginning, whose ending he never can find—so entire, so boundless. Far, too, as her splendors shine, system on system shooting like rays, upward, downward, without centre, without circumference,—in the mass and in the particle nature hastens to render account of herself to the mind. Classification begins. To the young mind, every thing is individual, stands by itself. By and by, it finds how to join two things, and see in them one nature; then three, then three thousand; and so, tyrannized over by its own unifying instinct, it goes on tying things together, diminishing anomalies, discovering roots running under ground, whereby contrary and remote things cohere, and flower out from one stem. It presently learns, that, since the dawn of history, there has been a constant accumulation and classifying of facts. But what is classification but the perceiving that these objects are not chaotic, and are not foreign, but have a law which is also a law of the human mind? The astronomer discovers that geometry, a pure abstraction of the human mind, is the measure of planetary motion. The chemist finds proportions and intelligible method throughout matter: and science is nothing but the finding of analogy, identity in the most remote parts. The ambitious soul sits down before each refractory fact; one after another, reduces all strange constitutions, all new powers, to their class and their law, and goes on forever to animate the last fibre of organization, the outskirts of nature, by insight.

Thus to him, to this school-boy under the bending dome of day, is suggested, that he and it proceed from one root; one is leaf and one is flower; relation, sympathy, stirring in every vein. And what is that Root? Is not that the soul of his soul?—A thought too bold—a dream too wild. Yet when this spiritual light shall have revealed the law of more earthly natures,—when he has learned to worship the soul, and to see that the natural philosophy that now is, is only the first gropings of its gigantic hand, he shall look forward to an ever expanding knowledge as to a becoming creator. He shall see that nature is the opposite of the soul, answering to it part for part. One is seal, and one is print. Its beauty is the beauty of his own mind. Its laws are the laws of his own mind. Nature then becomes to him the measure of his attainments. So much of nature as he is ignorant of, so much of his own mind does he not yet possess. And, in fine, the ancient precept, "Know thyself," and the modern precept, "Study nature," become at last one maxim.

II. The next great influence[8] into the spirit of the scholar, is, the mind of the Past,—in whatever form, whether of literature, of art, of institutions, that mind is inscribed. Books are the best type of the influence of the past, and perhaps we shall get at the truth—learn the amount of this influence more conveniently—by considering their value alone.

8. Inflowing.

The theory of books is noble. The scholar of the first age received into him the world around; brooded thereon; gave it the new arrangement of his own mind, and uttered it again. It came into him—life; it went out from him—truth. It came to him—short-lived actions; it went out from him—immortal thoughts. It came to him—business; it went from him—poetry. It was—dead fact; now, it is quick[9] thought. It can stand, and it can go. It now endures, it now flies, it now inspires.[1] Precisely in proportion to the depth of mind from which it issued, so high does it soar, so long does it sing.

Or, I might say, it depends on how far the process had gone, of transmuting life into truth. In proportion to the completeness of the distillation, so will the purity and imperishableness of the product be. But none is quite perfect. As no air-pump can by any means make a perfect vacuum, so neither can any artist entirely exclude the conventional, the local, the perishable from his book, or write a book of pure thought that shall be as efficient, in all respects, to a remote posterity, as to cotemporaries, or rather to the second age. Each age, it is found, must write its own books; or rather, each generation for the next succeeding. The books of an older period will not fit this.

Yet hence arises a grave mischief. The sacredness which attaches to the act of creation,—the act of thought,—is instantly transferred to the record. The poet chanting, was felt to be a divine man. Henceforth the chant is divine also. The writer was a just and wise spirit. Henceforward it is settled, the book is perfect; as love of the hero corrupts into worship of his statue. Instantly, the book becomes noxious. The guide is a tyrant. We sought a brother, and lo, a governor. The sluggish and perverted mind of the multitude, always slow to open to the incursions of Reason, having once so opened, having once received this book, stands upon it, and makes an outcry, if it is disparaged. Colleges are built on it. Books are written on it by thinkers, not by Man Thinking; by men of talent, that is, who start wrong, who set out from accepted dogmas, not from their own sight of principles. Meek young men grow up in libraries, believing it their duty to accept the views which Cicero, which Locke, which Bacon have given, forgetful that Cicero, Locke and Bacon were only young men in libraries when they wrote these books.[2]

Hence, instead of Man Thinking, we have the bookworm. Hence, the book-learned class, who value books, as such; not as related to nature and the human constitution, but as making a sort of Third Estate[3] with the world and the soul. Hence, the restorers of readings, the emendators, the bibliomaniacs of all degrees.

This is bad; this is worse than it seems. Books are the best of things, well used; abused, among the worst. What is the right use? What is the one end which all means go to effect? They are for nothing but to inspire. I had better never see a book than to be warped by its attraction clean out of my own orbit, and made a satellite instead of a system. The one thing in the world of value, is, the active soul,—the soul, free, sovereign, active. This every man is

---

9. Living. "Business": busyness, activity.
1. Breathes in. "Go": walk.
2. As a young man Marcus Tullius Cicero (106–143 B.C.E.), Roman statesman, was renowned for his oratory. John Locke (1632–1704), English philosopher and political thinker, wrote *Essay Concerning Human Understanding* (1690) before he

was forty. Sir Francis Bacon (1561–1626), English statesman and philosopher, is best known for his essays.
3. The term "Third Estate" is based on an obsolete social classification: first the clergy, second the nobility, third the common people.

entitled to; this every man contains within him, although in almost all men, obstructed, and as yet unborn. The soul active sees absolute truth; and utters truth, or creates. In this action, it is genius; not the privilege of here and there a favorite, but the sound estate of every man. In its essence, it is progressive. The book, the college, the school of art, the institution of any kind, stop with some past utterance of genius. This is good, say they,—let us hold by this. They pin me down. They look backward and not forward. But genius always looks forward. The eyes of man are set in his forehead, not in his hindhead. Man hopes. Genius creates. To create,—to create,—is the proof of a divine presence. Whatever talents may be, if the man create not, the pure efflux[4] of the Deity is not his:—cinders and smoke, there may be, but not yet flame. There are creative manners, there are creative actions, and creative words; manners, actions, words, that is, indicative of no custom or authority, but springing spontaneous from the mind's own sense of good and fair.

On the other part, instead of being its own seer, let it receive always from another mind its truth, though it were in torrents of light, without periods of solitude, inquest and self-recovery, and a fatal disservice is done. Genius is always sufficiently the enemy of genius by over-influence. The literature of every nation bear me witness. The English dramatic poets have Shakspearized now for two hundred years.

Undoubtedly, there is a right way of reading,—so it be sternly subordinated. Man Thinking must not be subdued by his instruments. Books are for the scholar's idle times. When he can read God directly, the hour is too precious to be wasted in other men's transcripts of their readings. But when the intervals of darkness come, as come they must,—when the soul seeth not, when the sun is hid, and the stars withdraw their shining,—we repair to the lamps which were kindled by their ray to guide our steps to the East again, where the dawn is. We hear that we may speak. The Arabian proverb says, "A fig tree looking on a fig tree, becometh fruitful."

It is remarkable, the character of the pleasure we derive from the best books. They impress us ever with the conviction that one nature wrote and the same reads. We read the verses of one of the great English poets, of Chaucer, of Marvell, of Dryden,[5] with the most modern joy,—with a pleasure, I mean, which is in great part caused by the abstraction of all *time* from their verses. There is some awe mixed with the joy of our surprise, when this poet, who lived in some past world, two or three hundred years ago, says that which lies close to my own soul, that which I also had well nigh thought and said. But for the evidence thence afforded to the philosophical doctrine of the identity of all minds, we should suppose some pre-established harmony, some foresight of souls that were to be, and some preparation of stores for their future wants, like the fact observed in insects, who lay up food before death for the young grub they shall never see.

I would not be hurried by any love of system, by any exaggeration of instincts, to underrate the Book. We all know, that as the human body can be nourished on any food, though it were boiled grass and the broth of shoes, so the human mind can be fed by any knowledge. And great and heroic men have existed, who had almost no other information than by the printed page. I only would say, that it needs a strong head to bear that diet. One must be

---

4. Flowing forth.
5. English poets: Geoffrey Chaucer (1340–

1400), Andrew Marvell (1621–1678), and John Dryden (1631–1700).

an inventor to read well. As the proverb says, "He that would bring home the wealth of the Indies, must carry out the wealth of the Indies." There is then creative reading, as well as creative writing. When the mind is braced by labor and invention, the page of whatever book we read becomes luminous with manifold allusion. Every sentence is doubly significant, and the sense of our author is as broad as the world. We then see, what is always true, that as the seer's hour of vision is short and rare among heavy days and months, so is its record, perchance, the least part of his volume. The discerning will read in his Plato or Shakspeare, only that least part,—only the authentic utterances of the oracle,—and all the rest he rejects, were it never so many times Plato's and Shakspeare's.

Of course, there is a portion of reading quite indispensable to a wise man. History and exact science he must learn by laborious reading. Colleges, in like manner, have their indispensable office,—to teach elements. But they can only highly serve us, when they aim not to drill, but to create; when they gather from far every ray of various genius to their hospitable halls, and, by the concentrated fires, set the hearts of their youth on flame. Thought and knowledge are natures in which apparatus and pretension avail nothing. Gowns, and pecuniary foundations, though of towns of gold, can never countervail the least sentence or syllable of wit.[6] Forget this, and our American colleges will recede in their public importance whilst they grow richer every year.

III. There goes in the world a notion that the scholar should be a recluse, a valetudinarian,[7]—as unfit for any handiwork or public labor, as a penknife for an axe. The so called "practical men" sneer at speculative men, as if, because they speculate or *see*, they could do nothing. I have heard it said that the clergy,—who are always more universally than any other class, the scholars of their day,—are addressed as women: that the rough, spontaneous conversation of men they do not hear, but only a mincing and diluted speech. They are often virtually disfranchised; and, indeed, there are advocates for their celibacy. As far as this is true of the studious classes, it is not just and wise. Action is with the scholar subordinate, but it is essential. Without it, he is not yet man. Without it, thought can never ripen into truth. Whilst the world hangs before the eye as a cloud of beauty, we can not even see its beauty. Inaction is cowardice, but there can be no scholar without the heroic mind. The preamble of thought, the transition through which it passes from the unconscious to the conscious, is action. Only so much do I know, as I have lived. Instantly, we know whose words are loaded with life, and whose not.

The world,—this shadow of the soul, or *other me*, lies wide around. Its attractions are the keys which unlock my thoughts and make me acquainted with myself. I launch eagerly into this resounding tumult. I grasp the hands of those next me, and take my place in the ring to suffer and to work, taught by an instinct that so shall the dumb abyss be vocal with speech. I pierce its order; I dissipate its fear; I dispose of it within the circuit of my expanding life. So much only of life as I know by experience, so much of the wilderness have I vanquished and planted, or so far have I extended my being, my dominion. I do not see how any man can afford, for the sake of his nerves and his nap, to spare any action in which he can partake. It is pearls and rubies

6. Intelligence. "Gowns": academic robes.   7. Invalid.

to his discourse. Drudgery, calamity, exasperation, want, are instructers in eloquence and wisdom. The true scholar grudges every opportunity of action past by, as a loss of power.

It is the raw material out of which the intellect moulds her splendid products. A strange process too, this, by which experience is converted into thought, as a mulberry leaf is converted into satin.[8] The manufacture goes forward at all hours.

The actions and events of our childhood and youth are now matters of calmest observation. They lie like fair pictures in the air. Not so with our recent actions,—with the business which we now have in hand. On this we are quite unable to speculate. Our affections as yet circulate through it. We no more feel or know it, than we feel the feet, or the hand, or the brain of our body. The new deed is yet a part of life,—remains for a time immersed in our unconscious life. In some contemplative hour, it detaches itself from the life like a ripe fruit, to become a thought of the mind. Instantly, it is raised, transfigured; the corruptible has put on incorruption.[9] Always now it is an object of beauty, however base its origin and neighborhood. Observe, too, the impossibility of antedating this act. In its grub state, it cannot fly, it cannot shine,—it is a dull grub. But suddenly, without observation, the selfsame thing unfurls beautiful wings, and is an angel of wisdom. So is there no fact, no event, in our private history, which shall not, sooner or later, lose its adhesive inert form, and astonish us by soaring from our body into the empyrean.[1] Cradle and infancy, school and playground, the fear of boys, and dogs, and ferules,[2] the love of little maids and berries, and many another fact that once filled the whole sky, are gone already; friend and relative, profession and party, town and country, nation and world, must also soar and sing.

Of course, he who has put forth his total strength in fit actions, has the richest return of wisdom. I will not shut myself out of this globe of action and transplant an oak into a flower pot, there to hunger and pine; nor trust the revenue of some single faculty, and exhaust one vein of thought, much like those Savoyards,[3] who, getting their livelihood by carving shepherds, shepherdesses, and smoking Dutchmen, for all Europe, went out one day to the mountain to find stock, and discovered that they had whittled up the last of their pine trees. Authors we have in numbers, who have written out their vein, and who, moved by a commendable prudence, sail for Greece or Palestine, follow the trapper into the prairie, or ramble round Algiers to replenish their merchantable stock.[4]

If it were only for a vocabulary the scholar would be covetous of action. Life is our dictionary. Years are well spent in country labors; in town—in the insight into trades and manufactures; in frank intercourse with many men and women; in science; in art; to the one end of mastering in all their facts a language, by which to illustrate and embody our perceptions. I learn immediately from any speaker how much he has already lived, through the

8. A form of silk produced by silkworms, which feed on mulberry leaves.
9. "For this corruptible must put on incorruption, and this mortal must put on immortality" (I Corinthians 15.53).
1. The highest reaches of heaven.
2. Rods used for punishing children.
3. Savoy is in the western Alps, where France,

Italy, and Switzerland converge.
4. Likely references to Emerson's contemporaries: Nathaniel Parker Willis (1806–1867), editor and travel writer; Washington Irving, whose A Tour on the Prairies appeared in 1835; and James Fenimore Cooper, whose The Prairie was published in 1827.

poverty or the splendor of his speech. Life lies behind us as the quarry from whence we get tiles and copestones for the masonry of to-day. This is the way to learn grammar. Colleges and books only copy the language which the field and the workyard made.

But the final value of action, like that of books, and better than books, is, that it is a resource. That great principle of Undulation in nature, that shows itself in the inspiring and expiring of the breath; in desire and satiety; in the ebb and flow of the sea, in day and night, in heat and cold, and as yet more deeply ingrained in every atom and every fluid, is known to us under the name of Polarity,—these "fits of easy transmission and reflection," as Newton[5] called them, are the law of nature because they are the law of spirit.

The mind now thinks; now acts; and each fit reproduces the other. When the artist has exhausted his materials, when the fancy no longer paints, when thoughts are no longer apprehended, and books are a weariness,—he has always the resource to *live*. Character is higher than intellect. Thinking is the function. Living is the functionary. The stream retreats to its source. A great soul will be strong to live, as well as strong to think. Does he lack organ or medium to impart his truths? He can still fall back on this elemental force of living them. This is a total act. Thinking is a partial act. Let the grandeur of justice shine in his affairs. Let the beauty of affection cheer his lowly roof. Those "far from fame" who dwell and act with him, will feel the force of his constitution in the doings and passages of the day better than it can be measured by any public and designed display. Time shall teach him that the scholar loses no hour which the man lives. Herein he unfolds the sacred germ of his instinct screened from influence. What is lost in seemliness is gained in strength. Not out of those on whom systems of education have exhausted their culture, comes the helpful giant to destroy the old or to build the new, but out of unhandselled[6] savage nature, out of terrible Druids and Berserkirs, come at last Alfred[7] and Shakspear.

I hear therefore with joy whatever is beginning to be said of the dignity and necessity of labor to every citizen. There is virtue yet in the hoe and the spade, for learned as well as for unlearned hands. And labor is every where welcome; always we are invited to work; only be this limitation observed, that a man shall not for the sake of wider activity sacrifice any opinion to the popular judgments and modes of action.

I have now spoken of the education of the scholar by nature, by books, and by action. It remains to say somewhat of his duties.

They are such as become Man Thinking. They may all be comprised in self-trust. The office of the scholar is to cheer, to raise, and to guide men by showing them facts amidst appearances. He plies the slow, unhonored, and unpaid task of observation. Flamsteed and Herschel, in their glazed[8] observatory, may catalogue the stars with the praise of all men, and the results being splendid and useful, honor is sure. But he, in his private observatory, cataloguing obscure and nebulous stars of the human mind, which as yet

5. From the *Optics* (1704) of Sir Isaac Newton (1642–1727), English scientist and mathematician.
6. A handsel is a gift to express good wishes at the outset of some enterprise; apparently Emerson uses "unhandselled" to mean something like unauspicious.

7. The enlightened 9th-century king of the West Saxons. "Terrible Druids and Berserkirs": uncivilized Celts and Anglo-Saxons.
8. Glass-roofed. John Flamsteed (1646–1719), English astronomer, first royal astronomer at Greenwich Observatory. Sir William Herschel (1738–1822), German-born English astronomer.

no man has thought of as such,—watching days and months, sometimes, for a few facts; correcting still his old records;—must relinquish display and immediate fame. In the long period of his preparation, he must betray often an ignorance and shiftlessness in popular arts, incurring the disdain of the able who shoulder him aside. Long he must stammer in his speech; often forego the living for the dead. Worse yet, he must accept—how often! poverty and solitude. For the ease and pleasure of treading the old road, accepting the fashions, the education, the religion of society, he takes the cross of making his own, and, of course, the self accusation, the faint heart, the frequent uncertainty and loss of time which are the nettles and tangling vines in the way of the self-relying and self-directed; and the state of virtual hostility in which he seems to stand to society, and especially to educated society. For all this loss and scorn, what offset? He is to find consolation in exercising the highest functions of human nature. He is one who raises himself from private considerations, and breathes and lives on public and illustrious thoughts. He is the world's eye. He is the world's heart. He is to resist the vulgar prosperity that retrogrades ever to barbarism, by preserving and communicating heroic sentiments, noble biographies, melodious verse, and the conclusions of history. Whatsoever oracles the human heart in all emergencies, in all solemn hours has uttered as its commentary on the world of actions,—these he shall receive and impart. And whatsoever new verdict Reason from her inviolable seat pronounces on the passing men and events of to-day,—this he shall hear and promulgate.

These being his functions, it becomes him to feel all confidence in himself, and to defer never to the popular cry. He and he only knows the world. The world of any moment is the merest appearance. Some great decorum, some fetish of a government, some ephemeral trade, or war, or man, is cried up by half mankind and cried down by the other half, as if all depended on this particular up or down. The odds are that the whole question is not worth the poorest thought which the scholar has lost in listening to the controversy. Let him not quit his belief that a popgun is a popgun, though the ancient and honorable of the earth affirm it to be the crack of doom. In silence, in steadiness, in severe abstraction, let him hold by himself; add observation to observation; patient of neglect, patient of reproach, and bide his own time,—happy enough if he can satisfy himself alone that this day he has seen something truly. Success treads on every right step. For the instinct is sure that prompts him to tell his brother what he thinks. He then learns that in going down into the secrets of his own mind, he has descended into the secrets of all minds. He learns that he who has mastered any law in his private thoughts, is master to that extent of all men whose language he speaks, and of all into whose language his own can be translated. The poet in utter solitude remembering his spontaneous thoughts and recording them, is found to have recorded that which men in "cities vast" find true for them also. The orator distrusts at first the fitness of his frank confessions,—his want of knowledge of the persons he addresses,—until he finds that he is the complement of his hearers;—that they drink his words because he fulfils for them their own nature; the deeper he dives into his privatest secretest presentiment,—to his wonder he finds, this is the most acceptable, most public, and universally true. The people delight in it; the better part of every man feels, This is my music: this is myself.

In self-trust, all the virtues are comprehended. Free should the scholar be,—free and brave. Free even to the definition of freedom, "without any hindrance that does not arise out of his own constitution." Brave; for fear is a thing which a scholar by his very function puts behind him. Fear always springs from ignorance. It is a shame to him if his tranquillity, amid dangerous times, arise from the presumption that like children and women, his is a protected class; or if he seek a temporary peace by the diversion of his thoughts from politics or vexed questions, hiding his head like an ostrich in the flowering bushes, peeping into microscopes, and turning rhymes, as a boy whistles to keep his courage up. So is the danger a danger still: so is the fear worse. Manlike let him turn and face it. Let him look into its eye and search its nature, inspect its origin—see the whelping of this lion,—which lies no great way back; he will then find in himself a perfect comprehension of its nature and extent; he will have made his hands meet on the other side, and can henceforth defy it, and pass on superior. The world is his who can see through its pretension. What deafness, what stone-blind custom, what overgrown error you behold, is there only by sufferance,—by your sufferance. See it to be a lie, and you have already dealt it its mortal blow.

Yes, we are the cowed,—we the trustless. It is a mischievous notion that we are come late into nature; that the world was finished a long time ago. As the world was plastic and fluid in the hands of God, so it is ever to so much of his attributes as we bring to it. To ignorance and sin, it is flint. They adapt themselves to it as they may; but in proportion as a man has anything in him divine, the firmament flows before him, and takes his signet[9] and form. Not he is great who can alter matter, but he who can alter my state of mind. They are the kings of the world who give the color of their present thought to all nature and all art, and persuade men by the cheerful serenity of their carrying the matter, that this thing which they do, is the apple which the ages have desired to pluck, now at last ripe, and inviting nations to the harvest. The great man makes the great thing. Wherever Macdonald sits, there is the head of the table.[1] Linnæus makes botany the most alluring of studies and wins it from the farmer and the herb-woman. Davy, chemistry: and Cuvier,[2] fossils. The day is always his, who works in it with serenity and great aims. The unstable estimates of men crowd to him whose mind is filled with a truth, as the heaped waves of the Atlantic follow the moon.

For this self-trust, the reason is deeper than can be fathomed,—darker than can be enlightened. I might not carry with me the feeling of my audience in stating my own belief. But I have already shown the ground of my hope, in adverting to the doctrine that man is one. I believe man has been wronged: he has wronged himself. He has almost lost the light that can lead him back to his prerogatives. Men are become of no account. Men in history, men in the world of to-day are bugs, are spawn, and are called "the mass" and "the herd." In a century, in a millennium, one or two men; that is to say—one or two approximations to the right state of every man. All the rest behold in the hero or the poet their own green and crude being—ripened; yes, and are content to be less, so *that* may attain to its full stature. What a testimony—full of grandeur, full of pity, is borne to the demands of his own nature, by the poor clansman, the poor partisan, who rejoices in the glory of his chief. The poor and the low find some amends to their immense

9. Seal.
1. An old proverb says, "Where Macgregor sits, there is the head of the table"; Emerson substitutes another typical name for a Scottish chief.
2. Georges Cuvier (1769–1832), French pioneer

in comparative anatomy and paleontology. Carl von Linné ("Linnæus") (1707–1778), Swedish botanist. Sir Humphry Davy (1778–1829), English chemist.

moral capacity, for their acquiescence in a political and social inferiority. They are content to be brushed like flies from the path of a great person, so that justice shall be done by him to that common nature which it is the dearest desire of all to see enlarged and glorified. They sun themselves in the great man's light, and feel it to be their own element. They cast the dignity of man from their downtrod selves upon the shoulders of a hero, and will perish to add one drop of blood to make that great heart beat, those giant sinews combat and conquer. He lives for us, and we live in him.

Men such as they are, very naturally seek money or power; and power because it is as good as money,—the "spoils," so called, "of office." And why not? for they aspire to the highest, and this, in their sleep-walking, they dream is highest. Wake them, and they shall quit the false good and leap to the true, and leave government to clerks and desks. This revolution is to be wrought by the gradual domestication of the idea of Culture. The main enterprise of the world for splendor, for extent, is the upbuilding of a man. Here are the materials strown along the ground. The private life of one man shall be a more illustrious monarchy,—more formidable to its enemy, more sweet and serene in its influence to its friend, than any kingdom in history. For a man, rightly viewed, comprehendeth the particular natures of all men. Each philosopher, each bard, each actor, has only done for me, as by a delegate, what one day I can do for myself. The books which once we valued more than the apple of the eye, we have quite exhausted. What is that but saying that we have come up with the point of view which the universal mind took through the eyes of that one scribe; we have been that man, and have passed on. First, one; then another; we drain all cisterns, and waxing greater by all these supplies, we crave a better and more abundant food. The man has never lived that can feed us ever. The human mind cannot be enshrined in a person who shall set a barrier on any one side to this unbounded, unboundable empire. It is one central fire which flaming now out of the lips of Etna, lightens the capes of Sicily; and now out of the throat of Vesuvius,[3] illuminates the towers and vineyards of Naples. It is one light which beams out of a thousand stars. It is one soul which animates all men.

But I have dwelt perhaps tediously upon this abstraction of the Scholar. I ought not to delay longer to add what I have to say, of nearer reference to the time and to this country.

Historically, there is thought to be a difference in the ideas which predominate over successive epochs, and there are data for marking the genius of the Classic, of the Romantic, and now of the Reflective or Philosophical age. With the views I have intimated of the oneness or the identity of the mind through all individuals, I do not much dwell on these differences. In fact, I believe each individual passes through all three. The boy is a Greek; the youth, romantic; the adult, reflective. I deny not, however, that a revolution in the leading idea may be distinctly enough traced.

Our age is bewailed as the age of Introversion. Must that needs be evil? We, it seems, are critical. We are embarrassed with second thoughts. We cannot enjoy any thing for hankering to know whereof the pleasure consists. We are lined with eyes. We see with our feet. The time is infected with Hamlet's unhappiness,—

---

3. Active volcanoes in eastern Sicily and southern Italy.

"Sicklied o'er with the pale cast of thought."[4]

Is it so bad then? Sight is the last thing to be pitied. Would we be blind? Do we fear lest we should outsee nature and God, and drink truth dry? I look upon the discontent of the literary class as a mere announcement of the fact that they find themselves not in the state of mind of their fathers, and regret the coming state as untried; as a boy dreads the water before he has learned that he can swim. If there is any period one would desire to be born in,—is it not the age of Revolution; when the old and the new stand side by side, and admit of being compared; when the energies of all men are searched by fear and by hope; when the historic glories of the old, can be compensated by the rich possibilities of the new era? This time, like all times, is a very good one, if we but know what to do with it.

I read with joy some of the auspicious signs of the coming days as they glimmer already through poetry and art, through philosophy and science, through church and state.

One of these signs is the fact that the same movement which effected the elevation of what was called the lowest class in the state, assumed in literature a very marked and as benign an aspect. Instead of the sublime and beautiful, the near, the low, the common, was explored and poetised. That which had been negligently trodden under foot by those who were harnessing and provisioning themselves for long journies into far countries, is suddenly found to be richer than all foreign parts. The literature of the poor, the feelings of the child, the philosophy of the street, the meaning of household life, are the topics of the time. It is a great stride. It is a sign—is it not? of new vigor, when the extremities are made active, when currents of warm life run into the hands and the feet. I ask not for the great, the remote, the romantic; what is doing in Italy or Arabia; what is Greek art, or Provençal Minstrelsy;[5] I embrace the common, I explore and sit at the feet of the familiar, the low. Give me insight into to-day, and you may have the antique and future worlds. What would we really know the meaning of? The meal in the firkin;[6] the milk in the pan; the ballad in the street; the news of the boat; the glance of the eye; the form and the gait of the body;— show me the ultimate reason of these matters;—show me the sublime presence of the highest spiritual cause lurking, as always it does lurk, in these suburbs and extremities of nature; let me see every trifle bristling with the polarity that ranges it instantly on an eternal law; and the shop, the plough, and the ledger, referred to the like cause by which light undulates and poets sing;—and the world lies no longer a dull miscellany and lumber room,[7] but has form and order; there is no trifle; there is no puzzle; but one design unites and animates the farthest pinnacle and the lowest trench.

This idea has inspired the genius of Goldsmith, Burns, Cowper, and in a newer time, of Goethe, Wordsworth, and Carlyle.[8] This idea they have differently followed and with various success. In contrast with their writing, the style of Pope, of Johnson, of Gibbon,[9] looks cold and pedantic. This writing is

---

4. Shakespeare's *Hamlet* 3.1.85.
5. Music of the medieval troubadours of Provence, in southeastern France.
6. Small wooden vessel.
7. Junk room.
8. Emerson contrasts the so-called pre-Romantics Oliver Goldsmith (1730–1794), Robert Burns (1759–1796), and William Cowper (1731–1800) with the Romantics Johann Wolfgang von Goethe (1749–1832), William Wordsworth (1770–1850), and Thomas Carlyle (1795–1881).
9. The 18th-century British writers Alexander Pope (1688–1744), Samuel Johnson (1709–1784), and Edward Gibbon (1737–1794).

blood-warm. Man is surprised to find that things near are not less beautiful and wondrous than things remote. The near explains the far. The drop is a small ocean. A man is related to all nature. This perception of the worth of the vulgar, is fruitful in discoveries. Goethe, in this very thing the most modern of the moderns, has shown us, as none ever did, the genius of the ancients.

There is one man of genius who has done much for this philosophy of life, whose literary value has never yet been rightly estimated;—I mean Emanuel Swedenborg.[1] The most imaginative of men, yet writing with the precision of a mathematician, he endeavored to engraft a purely philosophical Ethics on the popular Christianity of his time. Such an attempt, of course, must have difficulty which no genius could surmount. But he saw and showed the connexion between nature and the affections of the soul. He pierced the emblematic or spiritual character of the visible, audible, tangible world. Especially did his shade-loving muse hover over and interpret the lower parts of nature; he showed the mysterious bond that allies moral evil to the foul material forms, and has given in epical parables a theory of insanity, of beasts, of unclean and fearful things.

Another sign of our times, also marked by an analogous political movement is, the new importance given to the single person. Every thing that tends to insulate the individual,—to surround him with barriers of natural respect, so that each man shall feel the world is his, and man shall treat with man as a sovereign state with a sovereign state;—tends to true union as well as greatness. "I learned," said the melancholy Pestalozzi,[2] "that no man in God's wide earth is either willing or able to help any other man." Help must come from the bosom alone. The scholar is that man who must take up into himself all the ability of the time, all the contributions of the past, all the hopes of the future. He must be an university of knowledges. If there be one lesson more than another which should pierce his ear, it is, The world is nothing, the man is all; in yourself is the law of all nature, and you know not yet how a globule of sap ascends; in yourself slumbers the whole of Reason; it is for you to know all, it is for you to dare all. Mr. President and Gentlemen, this confidence in the unsearched might of man, belongs by all motives, by all prophecy, by all preparation, to the American Scholar. We have listened too long to the courtly muses of Europe. The spirit of the American freeman is already suspected to be timid, imitative, tame. Public and private avarice make the air we breathe thick and fat. The scholar is decent, indolent, complaisant. See already the tragic consequence. The mind of this country taught to aim at low objects, eats upon itself. There is no work for any but the decorous and the complaisant. Young men of the fairest promise, who begin life upon our shores, inflated by the mountain winds, shined upon by all the stars of God, find the earth below not in unison with these,—but are hindered from action by the disgust which the principles on which business is managed inspire, and turn drudges, or die of disgust,—some of them suicides. What is the remedy? They did not yet see, and thousands of young men as hopeful now crowding to the barriers for the career, do not yet see, that if the single man plant himself indomitably on his instincts, and there abide, the huge world will come round to him.

1. Swedish scientist, theologian, and mystic (1688–1772). Emerson was inspired by Swedenborg's notion of the correspondence between the natural and spiritual worlds.

2. Johann Heinrich Pestalozzi (1746–1827), Swiss educator who was an early advocate of kindergarten education. His theories influenced several of Emerson's friends.

Patience—patience;—with the shades of all the good and great for company; and for solace, the perspective of your own infinite life; and for work, the study and the communication of principles, the making those instincts prevalent, the conversion of the world. Is it not the chief disgrace in the world, not to be an unit;—not to be reckoned one character;—not to yield that peculiar fruit which each man was created to bear, but to be reckoned in the gross, in the hundred, or the thousand, of the party, the section, to which we belong; and our opinion predicted geographically, as the north, or the south. Not so, brothers and friends,—please God, ours shall not be so. We will walk on our own feet; we will work with our own hands; we will speak our own minds. Then shall man be no longer a name for pity, for doubt, and for sensual indulgence. The dread of man and the love of man shall be a wall of defence and a wreath of love around all. A nation of men will for the first time exist, because each believes himself inspired by the Divine Soul which also inspires all men.

1837

Self-Reliance[1]

Ne te quæsiveris extra.[2]

> "Man is his own star, and the soul that can
> Render an honest and a perfect man,
> Command all light, all influence, all fate,
> Nothing to him falls early or too late.
> Our acts our angels are, or good or ill,
> Our fatal shadows that walk by us still."
> —Epilogue to Beaumont and Fletcher's
> *Honest Man's Fortune*[3]

> Cast the bantling[4] on the rocks,
> Suckle him with the she-wolf's teat:
> Wintered with the hawk and fox,
> Power and speed be hands and feet.

I read the other day some verses written by an eminent painter[5] which were original and not conventional. Always the soul hears an admonition in such lines, let the subject be what it may. The sentiment they instil is of more value than any thought they may contain. To believe your own thought, to believe that what is true for you in your private heart, is true for all men,— that is genius. Speak your latent conviction and it shall be the universal sense; for always the inmost becomes the outmost,—and our first thought is rendered back to us by the trumpets of the Last Judgment. Familiar as the voice of the mind is to each, the highest merit we ascribe to Moses, Plato, and Milton, is that they set at naught books and traditions, and spoke not what men but what they thought. A man should learn to detect and watch

1. First published in *Essays* (1841), the source of the present text.
2. The Roman poet Persius (34–62 C.E.), *Satire* 1.7: "Do not search outside yourself" (Latin), i.e., do not imitate.
3. Published in 1647, the play by the Jacobean dramatists Francis Beaumont (1584–1616) and John Fletcher (1579–1625) was written in 1613.
4. Baby. The stanza is Emerson's.
5. Probably the American painter Washington Alston (1779–1847), whose poetry Emerson praised in a journal entry of September 20, 1837.

that gleam of light which flashes across his mind from within, more than the lustre of the firmament of bards and sages. Yet he dismisses without notice his thought, because it is his. In every work of genius we recognize our own rejected thoughts: they come back to us with a certain alienated majesty. Great works of art have no more affecting lesson for us than this. They teach us to abide by our spontaneous impression with good humored inflexibility then most when the whole cry of voices is on the other side. Else, to-morrow a stranger will say with masterly good sense precisely what we have thought and felt all the time, and we shall be forced to take with shame our own opinion from another.

There is a time in every man's education when he arrives at the conviction that envy is ignorance; that imitation is suicide; that he must take himself for better, for worse, as his portion; that though the wide universe is full of good, no kernel of nourishing corn can come to him but through his toil bestowed on that plot of ground which is given to him to till. The power which resides in him is new in nature, and none but he knows what that is which he can do, nor does he know until he has tried. Not for nothing one face, one character, one fact makes much impression on him, and another none. It is not without preëstablished harmony, this sculpture in the memory. The eye was placed where one ray should fall, that it might testify of that particular ray. Bravely let him speak the utmost syllable of his confession. We but half express ourselves, and are ashamed of that divine idea which each of us represents. It may be safely trusted as proportionate and of good issues, so it be faithfully imparted, but God will not have his work made manifest by cowards. It needs a divine man to exhibit any thing divine. A man is relieved and gay when he has put his heart into his work and done his best; but what he has said or done otherwise, shall give him no peace. It is a deliverance which does not deliver. In the attempt his genius deserts him; no muse befriends; no invention, no hope.

Trust thyself: every heart vibrates to that iron string. Accept the place the divine Providence has found for you; the society of your contemporaries, the connexion of events. Great men have always done so and confided themselves childlike to the genius of their age, betraying their perception that the Eternal was stirring at their heart, working through their hands, predominating in all their being. And we are now men, and must accept in the highest mind the same transcendent destiny; and not pinched in a corner, not cowards fleeing before a revolution, but redeemers and benefactors, pious aspirants to be noble clay plastic under the Almighty effort, let us advance and advance on Chaos and the Dark.

What pretty oracles nature yields us on this text in the face and behavior of children, babes and even brutes. That divided and rebel mind, that distrust of a sentiment because our arithmetic has computed the strength and means opposed to our purpose, these have not. Their mind being whole, their eye is as yet unconquered, and when we look in their faces, we are disconcerted. Infancy conforms to nobody: all conform to it, so that one babe commonly makes four or five out of the adults who prattle and play to it. So God has armed youth and puberty and manhood no less with its own piquancy and charm, and made it enviable and gracious and its claims not to be put by, if it will stand by itself. Do not think the youth has no force because he cannot speak to you and me. Hark! in the next room, who spoke so clear and emphatic? Good Heaven! it is he! it is that very lump of bashfulness and phlegm which for weeks has done nothing but eat when you were by, that now rolls out these words like bell-strokes. It seems he knows how to speak to his contemporaries. Bashful or bold, then, he will know how to make us seniors very unnecessary.

The nonchalance of boys who are sure of a dinner, and would disdain as much as a lord to do or say aught to conciliate one, is the healthy attitude of human nature. How is a boy the master of society; independent, irresponsible, looking out from his corner on such people and facts as pass by, he tries and sentences them on their merits, in the swift summary way of boys, as good, bad, interesting, silly, eloquent, troublesome. He cumbers himself never about consequences, about interests: he gives an independent, genuine verdict. You must court him: he does not court you. But the man is, as it were, clapped into jail by his consciousness. As soon as he has once acted or spoken with eclat, he is a committed person, watched by the sympathy or the hatred of hundreds whose affections must now enter into his account. There is no Lethe[6] for this. Ah, that he could pass again into his neutral, godlike independence! Who can thus lose all pledge, and having observed, observe again from the same unaffected, unbiased, unbribable, unaffrighted innocence, must always be formidable, must always engage the poet's and the man's regards. Of such an immortal youth the force would be felt. He would utter opinions on all passing affairs, which being seen to be not private but necessary, would sink like darts into the ear of men, and put them in fear.

These are the voices which we hear in solitude, but they grow faint and inaudible as we enter into the world. Society everywhere is in conspiracy against the manhood of every one of its members. Society is a joint-stock company[7] in which the members agree for the better securing of his bread to each shareholder, to surrender the liberty and culture of the eater. The virtue in most request is conformity. Self-reliance is its aversion. It loves not realities and creators, but names and customs.

Whoso would be a man must be a nonconformist. He who would gather immortal palms[8] must not be hindered by the name of goodness, but must explore if it be goodness. Nothing is at last sacred but the integrity of our own mind. Absolve you to yourself, and you shall have the suffrage of the world. I remember an answer which when quite young I was prompted to make to a valued adviser who was wont to importune me with the dear old doctrines of the church. On my saying, What have I to do with the sacredness of traditions, if I live wholly from within? my friend suggested—"But these impulses may be from below, not from above." I replied, 'They do not seem to me to be such; but if I am the devil's child, I will live then from the devil.' No law can be sacred to me but that of my nature. Good and bad are but names very readily transferable to that or this; the only right is what is after my constitution, the only wrong what is against it. A man is to carry himself in the presence of all opposition as if every thing were titular and ephemeral but he. I am ashamed to think how easily we capitulate to badges and names, to large societies and dead institutions. Every decent and well-spoken individual affects and sways me more than is right. I ought to go upright and vital, and speak the rude truth in all ways. If malice and vanity wear the coat of philanthropy, shall that pass? If an angry bigot assumes this bountiful cause of

6. Oblivion-producing water from the river of the underworld in Greek mythology.
7. Business for which the capital is held by its joint owners in transferable shares.
8. Great honors.

Abolition, and comes to me with his last news from Barbadoes,[9] why should I not say to him, 'Go love thy infant; love thy wood-chopper: be good-natured and modest: have that grace; and never varnish your hard, uncharitable ambition with this incredible tenderness for black folk a thousand miles off. Thy love afar is spite at home.' Rough and graceless would be such greeting, but truth is handsomer than the affectation of love. Your goodness must have some edge to it—else it is none. The doctrine of hatred must be preached as the counteraction of the doctrine of love when that pules[1] and whines. I shun father and mother and wife and brother, when my genius calls me.[2] I would write on the lintels of the door-post, *Whim*.[3] I hope it is somewhat better than whim at last, but we cannot spend the day in explanation. Expect me not to show cause why I seek or why I exclude company. Then, again, do not tell me, as a good man did to-day, of my obligation to put all poor men in good situations. Are they *my* poor? I tell thee, thou foolish philanthropist, that I grudge the dollar, the dime, the cent I give to such men as do not belong to me and to whom I do not belong. There is a class of persons to whom by all spiritual affinity I am bought and sold; for them I will go to prison, if need be; but your miscellaneous popular charities; the education at college of fools; the building of meeting-houses to the vain end to which many now stand; alms to sots; and the thousandfold Relief Societies;—though I confess with shame I sometimes succumb and give the dollar, it is a wicked dollar which by-and-by I shall have the manhood to withhold.

Virtues are in the popular estimate rather the exception than the rule. There is the man *and* his virtues. Men do what is called a good action, as some piece of courage or charity, much as they would pay a fine in expiation of daily non-appearance on parade. Their works are done as an apology or extenuation of their living in the world,—as invalids and the insane pay a high board. Their virtues are penances. I do not wish to expiate, but to live. My life is not an apology, but a life. It is for itself and not for a spectacle. I much prefer that it should be of a lower strain, so it be genuine and equal, than that it should be glittering and unsteady. I wish it to be sound and sweet, and not to need diet and bleeding.[4] My life should be unique; it should be an alms, a battle, a conquest, a medicine. I ask primary evidence that you are a man, and refuse this appeal from the man to his actions. I know that for myself it makes no difference whether I do or forbear those actions which are reckoned excellent. I cannot consent to pay for a privilege where I have intrinsic right. Few and mean as my gifts may be, I actually am, and do not need for my own assurance or the assurance of my fellows any secondary testimony.

What I must do, is all that concerns me, not what the people think. This rule, equally arduous in actual and in intellectual life, may serve for the whole distinction between greatness and meanness. It is the harder, because you will always find those who think they know what is your duty better than you know it. It is easy in the world to live after the world's opinion; it is easy

---

9. Island in the eastern Caribbean where slavery was officially abolished in 1834. Despite his apparent skepticism here, Emerson became increasingly committed to abolitionism during the 1840s.
1. Whimpers.
2. For shunning family to obey a divine command, see Matthew 10.34–37.

3. See Exodus 12 for God's instructions to Moses on marking with blood the "two side posts" and the "upper door post" (or lintel) of houses so that God would spare those within when He came to "smite all the firstborn in the land of Egypt, both man and beast."
4. The old medical treatment of bloodletting.

in solitude to live after our own; but the great man is he who in the midst of the crowd keeps with perfect sweetness the independence of solitude.

The objection to conforming to usages that have become dead to you, is, that it scatters your force. It loses your time and blurs the impression of your character. If you maintain a dead church, contribute to a dead Bible-Society, vote with a great party either for the Government or against it, spread your table like base housekeepers,—under all these screens, I have difficulty to detect the precise man you are. And, of course, so much force is withdrawn from your proper life. But do your thing, and I shall know you. Do your work, and you shall reinforce yourself. A man must consider what a blindman's-bluff is this game of conformity. If I know your sect, I anticipate your argument. I hear a preacher announce for his text and topic the expediency of one of the institutions of his church. Do I not know beforehand that not possibly can he say a new and spontaneous word? Do I not know that with all this ostentation of examining the grounds of the institution, he will do no such thing? Do I not know that he is pledged to himself not to look but at one side; the permitted side, not as a man, but as a parish minister? He is a retained attorney, and these airs of the bench are the emptiest affectation. Well, most men have bound their eyes with one or another handkerchief, and attached themselves to some one of these communities of opinion. This conformity makes them not false in a few particulars, authors of a few lies, but false in all particulars. Their every truth is not quite true. Their two is not the real two, their four not the real four: so that every word they say chagrins us, and we know not where to begin to set them right. Meantime nature is not slow to equip us in the prison-uniform of the party to which we adhere. We come to wear one cut of face and figure, and acquire by degrees the gentlest asinine expression. There is a mortifying experience in particular which does not fail to wreak itself also in the general history; I mean, "the foolish face of praise,"[5] the forced smile which we put on in company where we do not feel at ease in answer to conversation which does not interest us. The muscles, not spontaneously moved, but moved by a low usurping wilfulness, grow tight about the outline of the face and make the most disagreeable sensation, a sensation of rebuke and warning which no brave young man will suffer twice.

For non-conformity the world whips you with its displeasure. And therefore a man must know how to estimate a sour face. The bystanders look askance on him in the public street or in the friend's parlor. If this aversation had its origin in contempt and resistance like his own, he might well go home with a sad countenance; but the sour faces of the multitude, like their sweet faces, have no deep cause,—disguise no god, but are put on and off as the wind blows, and a newspaper directs. Yet is the discontent of the multitude more formidable than that of the senate and the college. It is easy enough for a firm man who knows the world to brook the rage of the cultivated classes. Their rage is decorous and prudent, for they are timid as being very vulnerable themselves. But when to their feminine rage the indignation of the people is added, when the ignorant and the poor are aroused, when the unintelligent brute force that lies at the bottom of society is made to growl and mow,[6] it needs the habit of magnanimity and religion to treat it godlike as a trifle of no concernment.

5. Alexander Pope's "Epistle to Dr. Arbuthnot" (1735), line 212.   6. Grimace.

The other terror that scares us from self-trust is our consistency; a reverence for our past act or word, because the eyes of others have no other data for computing our orbit than our past acts, and we are loath to disappoint them.

But why should you keep your head over your shoulder? Why drag about this monstrous corpse of your memory, lest you contradict somewhat you have stated in this or that public place? Suppose you should contradict yourself; what then? It seems to be a rule of wisdom never to rely on your memory alone, scarcely even in acts of pure memory, but bring the past for judgment into the thousand-eyed present, and live ever in a new day. Trust your emotion. In your metaphysics you have denied personality to the Deity: yet when the devout motions of the soul come, yield to them heart and life, though they should clothe God with shape and color. Leave your theory as Joseph his coat in the hand of the harlot, and flee.[7]

A foolish consistency is the hobgoblin of little minds, adored by little statesmen and philosophers and divines. With consistency a great soul has simply nothing to do. He may as well concern himself with his shadow on the wall. Out upon your guarded lips! Sew them up with packthread, do. Else, if you would be a man, speak what you think to-day in words as hard as cannon balls, and to-morrow speak what to-morrow thinks in hard words again, though it contradict every thing you said to-day. Ah, then, exclaim the aged ladies, you shall be sure to be misunderstood. Misunderstood! It is a right fool's word. Is it so bad then to be misunderstood? Pythagoras was misunderstood, and Socrates, and Jesus, and Luther, and Copernicus, and Galileo, and Newton,[8] and every pure and wise spirit that ever took flesh. To be great is to be misunderstood.

I suppose no man can violate his nature. All the sallies of his will are rounded in by the law of his being as the inequalities of Andes and Himmaleh[9] are insignificant in the curve of the sphere. Nor does it matter how you gauge and try him. A character is like an acrostic or Alexandrian stanza;[1]—read it forward, backward, or across, it still spells the same thing. In this pleasing contrite wood-life which God allows me, let me record day by day my honest thought without prospect or retrospect, and, I cannot doubt, it will be found symmetrical, though I mean it not, and see it not. My book should smell of pines and resound with the hum of insects. The swallow over my window should interweave that thread or straw he carries in his bill into my web also. We pass for what we are. Character teaches above our wills. Men imagine that they communicate their virtue or vice only by overt actions and do not see that virtue or vice emit a breath every moment.

Fear never but you shall be consistent in whatever variety of actions, so they be each honest and natural in their hour. For of one will, the actions will be harmonious, however unlike they seem. These varieties are lost sight of when seen at a little distance, at a little height of thought. One tendency

7. When Potiphar's wife demanded that Joseph sleep with her, "he left his garment in her hand, and fled" (Genesis 39.12).
8. Sir Isaac Newton (1642–1727), English mathematician and scientist who developed the laws of gravity and motion. Pythagorus (c. 582–c. 507 B.C.E.), Greek philosopher and mathematician who elaborated a theory of numbers. Martin Luther (1483–1546), German leader of the Protestant Reformation. Nicholas Copernicus (1473–

1543), Polish astronomer who argued that the planets revolve around a stationary sun. Galileo Galilei (1564–1662), Italian astronomer, mathematician, and physicist who supported the Copernican system and laid the foundations for modern science.
9. Mountain ranges in South America and Asia.
1. A palindrome, reading the same backward as forward.

unites them all. The voyage of the best ship is a zigzag line of a hundred tacks. This is only microscopic criticism. See the line from a sufficient distance, and it straightens itself to the average tendency. Your genuine action will explain itself and will explain your other genuine actions. Your conformity explains nothing. Act singly, and what you have already done singly, will justify you now. Greatness always appeals to the future. If I can be great enough now to do right and scorn eyes, I must have done so much right before, as to defend me now. Be it how it will, do right now. Always scorn appearances, and you always may. The force of character is cumulative. All the foregone days of virtue work their health into this. What makes the majesty of the heroes of the senate and the field, which so fills the imagination? The consciousness of a train of great days and victories behind. There they all stand and shed an united light on the advancing actor. He is attended as by a visible escort of angels to every man's eye. That is it which throws thunder into Chatham's voice, and dignity into Washington's port, and America into Adams's[2] eye. Honor is venerable to us because it is no ephemeris. It is always ancient virtue. We worship it to-day, because it is not of to-day. We love it and pay it homage, because it is not a trap for our love and homage, but is self-dependent, self-derived, and therefore of an old immaculate pedigree, even if shown in a young person.

I hope in these days we have heard the last of conformity and consistency. Let the words be gazetted[3] and ridiculous henceforward. Instead of the gong for dinner, let us hear a whistle from the Spartan fife.[4] Let us bow and apologize never more. A great man is coming to eat at my house. I do not wish to please him: I wish that he should wish to please me. I will stand here for humanity, and though I would make it kind, I would make it true. Let us affront and reprimand the smooth mediocrity and squalid contentment of the times, and hurl in the face of custom, and trade, and office, the fact which is the upshot of all history, that there is a great responsible Thinker and Actor moving wherever moves a man; that a true man belongs to no other time or place, but is the centre of things. Where he is, there is nature. He measures you, and all men, and all events. You are constrained to accept his standard. Ordinarily every body in society reminds us of somewhat else or of some other person. Character, reality, reminds you of nothing else. It takes place of the whole creation. The man must be so much that he must make all circumstances indifferent,—put all means into the shade. This all great men are and do. Every true man is a cause, a country, and an age; requires infinite spaces and numbers and time fully to accomplish his thought;—and posterity seem to follow his steps as a procession. A man Cæsar is born, and for ages after, we have a Roman Empire. Christ is born, and millions of minds so grow and cleave to his genius, that he is confounded with virtue and the possible of man. An institution is the lengthened shadow of one man; as, the Reformation, of Luther; Quakerism, of Fox; Methodism, of Wesley; Abolition, of Clarkson.[5] Scipio,[6] Milton called "the height of Rome;" and all history

2. Probably John Quincy Adams (1767–1848), sixth president of the United States and, afterward, long-time member of the House of Representatives, known as "Old Man Eloquence." William Pitt, first Earl of Chatham (1708–1778), English statesman and great orator. George Washington (1732–1799), first president of the United States. "Port": carriage or physical bearing.

3. Printed in a newspaper or other public forum.

4. The Spartans were known for their military discipline and willingness to endure physical hardships.

5. These founders are George Fox (1624–1691), John Wesley (1703–1791), and Thomas Clarkson (1760–1846).

6. Scipio Africanus (237–183 B.C.E.), the conqueror of Carthage.

resolves itself very easily into the biography of a few stout and earnest persons.

Let a man then know his worth, and keep things under his feet. Let him not peep or steal, or skulk up and down with the air of a charity-boy, a bastard, or an interloper, in the world which exists for him. But the man in the street finding no worth in himself which corresponds to the force which built a tower or sculptured a marble god, feels poor when he looks on these. To him a palace, a statue, or a costly book have an alien and forbidding air, much like a gay equipage, and seem to say like that, 'Who are you, sir?' Yet they all are his, suitors for his notice, petitioners to his faculties that they will come out and take possession. The picture waits for my verdict: it is not to command me, but I am to settle its claims to praise. That popular fable of the sot who was picked up dead drunk in the street, carried to the duke's house, washed and dressed and laid in the duke's bed, and, on his waking, treated with all obsequious ceremony like the duke, and assured that he had been insane,[7]—owes its popularity to the fact, that it symbolizes so well the state of man, who is in the world a sort of sot, but now and then wakes up, exercises his reason, and finds himself a true prince.

Our reading is mendicant and sycophantic. In history, our imagination makes fools of us, plays us false. Kingdom and lordship, power and estate are a gaudier vocabulary than private John and Edward in a small house and common day's work: but the things of life are the same to both: the sum total of both is the same. Why all this deference to Alfred, and Scanderbeg, and Gustavus?[8] Suppose they were virtuous: did they wear out virtue? As great a stake depends on your private act to-day, as followed their public and renowned steps. When private men shall act with vast views, the lustre will be transferred from the actions of kings to those of gentlemen.

The world has indeed been instructed by its kings, who have so magnetized the eyes of nations. It has been taught by this colossal symbol the mutual reverence that is due from man to man. The joyful loyalty with which men have every where suffered the king, the noble, or the great proprietor to walk among them by a law of his own, make his own scale of men and things, and reverse theirs, pay for benefits not with money but with honor, and represent the Law in his person, was the hieroglyphic by which they obscurely signified their consciousness of their own right and comeliness, the right of every man.

The magnetism which all original action exerts is explained when we inquire the reason of self-trust. Who is the Trustee? What is the aboriginal Self on which a universal reliance may be grounded? What is the nature and power of that science-baffling star, without parallax,[9] without calculable elements, which shoots a ray of beauty even into trivial and impure actions, if the least mark of independence appear? The inquiry leads us to that source, at once the essence of genius, the essence of virtue, and the essence of life, which we call Spontaneity or Instinct. We denote this primary wisdom as Intuition, whilst all later teachings are tuitions. In that deep force, the last fact behind which analysis cannot go, all things find their common origin.

7. See the "Induction" to Shakespeare's *The Taming of the Shrew*.

8. National heroes: Alfred (849–899), of England; Scanderbeg (1404?–1468), of Albania; and Gustavus (1594–1632), of Sweden.

9. An apparent change in the direction of an object caused by a change in the position from which it is observed. Emerson means without an observational position.

For the sense of being which in calm hours rises, we know not how, in the soul, is not diverse from things, from space, from light, from time, from man, but one with them, and proceedeth obviously from the same source whence their life and being also proceedeth. We first share the life by which things exist, and afterwards see them as appearances in nature, and forget that we have shared their cause. Here is the fountain of action and the fountain of thought. Here are the lungs of that inspiration which giveth man wisdom, of that inspiration of man which cannot be denied without impiety and atheism. We lie in the lap of immense intelligence, which makes us organs of its activity and receivers of its truth. When we discern justice, when we discern truth, we do nothing of ourselves, but allow a passage to its beams. If we ask whence this comes, if we seek to pry into the soul that causes,—all metaphysics, all philosophy is at fault. Its presence or its absence is all we can affirm. Every man discerns between the voluntary acts of his mind, and his involuntary perceptions. And to his involuntary perceptions, he knows a perfect respect is due. He may err in the expression of them, but he knows that these things are so, like day and night, not to be disputed. All my wilful actions and acquisitions are but roving;—the most trivial reverie, the faintest native emotion are domestic and divine. Thoughtless people contradict as readily the statement of perceptions as of opinions, or rather much more readily; for, they do not distinguish between perception and notion. They fancy that I choose to see this or that thing. But perception is not whimsical, but fatal. If I see a trait, my children will see it after me, and in course of time, all mankind,—although it may chance that no one has seen it before me. For my perception of it is as much a fact as the sun.

The relations of the soul to the divine spirit are so pure that it is profane to seek to interpose helps. It must be that when God speaketh, he should communicate not one thing, but all things; should fill the world with his voice; should scatter forth light, nature, time, souls from the centre of the present thought; and new date and new create the whole. Whenever a mind is simple, and receives a divine wisdom, then old things pass away,—means, teachers, texts, temples fall; it lives now and absorbs past and future into the present hour. All things are made sacred by relation to it,—one thing as much as another. All things are dissolved to their centre by their cause, and in the universal miracle petty and particular miracles disappear. This is and must be. If, therefore, a man claims to know and speak of God, and carries you backward to the phraseology of some old mouldered nation in another country, in another world, believe him not. Is the acorn better than the oak which is its fulness and completion? Is the parent better than the child into whom he has cast his ripened being? Whence then this worship of the past? The centuries are conspirators against the sanity and majesty of the soul. Time and space are but physiological colors which the eye maketh, but the soul is light; where it is, is day; where it was, is night; and history is an impertinence and an injury, if it be anything more than a cheerful apologue or parable of my being and becoming.

Man is timid and apologetic. He is no longer upright. He dares not say 'I think,' 'I am,' but quotes some saint or sage. He is ashamed before the blade of grass or the blowing rose. These roses under my window make no reference to former roses or to better ones; they are for what they are; they exist with God to-day. There is no time to them. There is simply the rose; it is perfect in every moment of its existence. Before a leaf-bud has burst, its whole life acts; in the full-blown flower, there is no more; in the leafless root, there is no less. Its nature is satisfied, and it satisfies nature, in all moments alike. There is no time to it. But man postpones or remembers; he does not live in the present, but with reverted eye laments the past, or, heedless of the riches that surround him, stands on tiptoe to foresee the future. He cannot be happy and strong until he too lives with nature in the present, above time.

This should be plain enough. Yet see what strong intellects dare not yet hear God himself, unless he speak the phraseology of I know not what David, or Jeremiah, or Paul.[1] We shall not always set so great a price on a few texts, on a few lines. We are like children who repeat by rote the sentences of grandames and tutors, and, as they grow older, of the men of talents and character they chance to see,—painfully recollecting the exact words they spoke; afterwards, when they come into the point of view which those had who uttered these sayings, they understand them, and are willing to let the words go; for, at any time, they can use words as good, when occasion comes. So was it with us, so will it be, if we proceed. If we live truly, we shall see truly. It is as easy for the strong man to be strong, as it is for the weak to be weak. When we have new perception, we shall gladly disburthen the memory of its hoarded treasures as old rubbish. When a man lives with God, his voice shall be as sweet as the murmur of the brook and the rustle of the corn.

And now at last the highest truth on this subject remains unsaid; probably, cannot be said; for all that we say is the far off remembering of the intuition. That thought, by what I can now nearest approach to say it, is this. When good is near you, when you have life in yourself,—it is not by any known or appointed way; you shall not discern the foot-prints of any other; you shall not see the face of man; you shall not hear any name;—the way, the thought, the good shall be wholly strange and new. It shall exclude all other being. You take the way from man not to man. All persons that ever existed are its fugitive ministers. There shall be no fear in it. Fear and hope are alike beneath it. It asks nothing. There is somewhat low even in hope. We are then in vision. There is nothing that can be called gratitude nor properly joy. The soul is raised over passion. It seeth identity and eternal causation. It is a perceiving that Truth and Right are. Hence it becomes a Tranquillity out of the knowing that all things go well. Vast spaces of nature; the Atlantic Ocean, the South Sea; vast intervals of time, years, centuries, are of no account. This which I think and feel, underlay that former state of life and circumstances, as it does underlie my present, and will always all circumstance, and what is called life, and what is called death.

Life only avails, not the having lived. Power ceases in the instant of repose; it resides in the moment of transition from a past to a new state; in the shooting of the gulf; in the darting to an aim. This one fact the world hates, that the soul *becomes*; for, that forever degrades the past; turns all riches to poverty; all reputation to a shame; confounds the saint with the rogue; shoves Jesus and Judas equally aside. Why then do we prate of self-reliance? Inasmuch as the soul is present, there will be power not confident but agent. To talk of reliance, is a poor external way of speaking. Speak rather of that which relies, because it works and is. Who has more soul than I, masters me, though he should not raise his finger. Round him I must revolve by the gravi-

---

1. Biblical authors of the Book of Psalms, the Book of Jeremiah, and various New Testament Epistles, respectively.

tation of spirits; who has less, I rule with like facility. We fancy it rhetoric when we speak of eminent virtue. We do not yet see that virtue is Height, and that a man or a company of men plastic and permeable to principles, by the law of nature must overpower and ride all cities, nations, kings, rich men, poets, who are not.

This is the ultimate fact which we so quickly reach on this as on every topic, the resolution of all into the ever blessed ONE. Virtue is the governor, the creator, the reality. All things real are so by so much of virtue as they contain. Hardship, husbandry, hunting, whaling, war, eloquence, personal weight, are somewhat, and engage my respect as examples of the soul's presence and impure action. I see the same law working in the nature for conservation and growth. The poise of a planet, the bended tree recovering itself from the strong wind, the vital resources of every vegetable and animal, are also demonstrations of the self-sufficing, and therefore self-relying soul. All history from its highest to its trivial passages is the various record of this power.

Thus all concentrates; let us not rove; let us sit at home with the cause. Let us stun and astonish the intruding rabble of men and books and institutions by a simple declaration of the divine fact. Bid them take the shoes from off their feet,[2] for God is here within. Let our simplicity judge them, and our docility to our own law demonstrate the poverty of nature and fortune beside our native riches.

But now we are a mob. Man does not stand in awe of man, nor is the soul admonished to stay at home, to put itself in communication with the internal ocean, but it goes abroad to beg a cup of water of the urns of men. We must go alone. Isolation must precede true society. I like the silent church before the service begins, better than any preaching. How far off, how cool, how chaste the persons look, begirt each one with a precinct or sanctuary. So let us always sit. Why should we assume the faults of our friend, or wife, or father, or child, because they sit around our hearth, or are said to have the same blood? All men have my blood, and I have all men's. Not for that will I adopt their petulance or folly, even to the extent of being ashamed of it. But your isolation must not be mechanical, but spiritual, that is, must be elevation. At times the whole world seems to be in conspiracy to importune you with emphatic trifles. Friend, client, child, sickness, fear, want, charity, all knock at once at thy closet door and say, 'Come out unto us.'—Do not spill thy soul; do not all descend; keep thy state; stay at home in thine own heaven; come not for a moment into their facts, into their hubbub of conflicting appearances, but let in the light of thy law on their confusion. The power men possess to annoy me, I give them by a weak curiosity. No man can come near me but through my act. "What we love that we have, but by desire we bereave ourselves of the love."[3]

If we cannot at once rise to the sanctities of obedience and faith, let us at least resist our temptations, let us enter into the state of war, and wake Thor and Woden,[4] courage and constancy in our Saxon breasts. This is to be done in our smooth times by speaking the truth. Check this lying hospitality and

---

2. In Exodus 3.5, God commands Moses "to put off thy shoes from off thy feet, for the place whereon thou standest is holy ground."
3. In his notebook, Emerson attributed this quotation to the German poet and dramatist Fried-

rich Schiller (1759–1805).
4. Norse gods, here taken as ancestral gods of the Anglo-Saxon as well, associated respectively with courage and endurance.

lying affection. Live no longer to the expectation of these deceived and deceiving people with whom we converse. Say to them, O father, O mother, O wife, O brother, O friend, I have lived with you after appearances hitherto. Henceforward I am the truth's. Be it known unto you that henceforward I obey no law less than the eternal law. I will have no covenants but proximities. I shall endeavor to nourish my parents, to support my family, to be the chaste husband of one wife,—but these relations I must fill after a new and unprecedented way. I appeal from your customs. I must be myself. I cannot break myself any longer for you, or you. If you can love me for what I am, we shall be the happier. If you cannot, I will still seek to deserve that you should. I must be myself. I will not hide my tastes or aversions. I will so trust that what is deep is holy, that I will do strongly before the sun and moon whatever inly rejoices me, and the heart appoints. If you are noble, I will love you; if you are not, I will not hurt you and myself by hypocritical attentions. If you are true, but not in the same truth with me, cleave to your companions; I will seek my own. I do this not selfishly, but humbly and truly. It is alike your interest and mine and all men's, however long we have dwelt in lies, to live in truth. Does this sound harsh to-day? You will soon love what is dictated by your nature as well as mine, and if we follow the truth, it will bring us out safe at last.—But so you may give these friends pain. Yes, but I cannot sell my liberty and my power, to save their sensibility. Besides, all persons have their moments of reason when they look out into the region of absolute truth; then will they justify me and do the same thing.

The populace think that your rejection of popular standards is a rejection of all standard, and mere antinomianism;[5] and the bold sensualist will use the name of philosophy to gild his crimes. But the law of consciousness abides. There are two confessionals, in one or the other of which we must be shriven. You may fulfil your round of duties by clearing yourself in the *direct*, or, in the *reflex* way. Consider whether you have satisfied your relations to father, mother, cousin, neighbor, town, cat, and dog; whether any of these can upbraid you. But I may also neglect this reflex standard, and absolve me to myself. I have my own stern claims and perfect circle. It denies the name of duty to many offices that are called duties. But if I can discharge its debts, it enables me to dispense with the popular code. If any one imagines that this law is lax, let him keep its commandment one day.

And truly it demands something godlike in him who has cast off the common motives of humanity, and has ventured to trust himself for a taskmaster. High be his heart, faithful his will, clear his sight, that he may in good earnest be doctrine, society, law to himself, that a simple purpose may be to him as strong as iron necessity is to others.

If any man consider the present aspects of what is called by distinction *society*, he will see the need of these ethics. The sinew and heart of man seem to be drawn out, and we are become timorous desponding whimperers. We are afraid of truth, afraid of fortune, afraid of death, and afraid of each other. Our age yields no great and perfect persons. We want men and women who shall renovate life and our social state, but we see that most natures are insolvent; cannot satisfy their own wants, have an ambition out of all proportion to their practical force, and so do lean and beg day and night continually. Our

5. Doctrine of salvation by faith alone.

housekeeping is mendicant, our arts, our occupations, our marriages, our religion we have not chosen, but society has chosen for us. We are parlor soldiers. The rugged battle of fate, where strength is born, we shun.

If our young men miscarry in their first enterprizes, they lose all heart. If the young merchant fails, men say he is *ruined*. If the finest genius studies at one of our colleges, and is not installed in an office within one year afterwards in the cities or suburbs of Boston or New York, it seems to his friends and to himself that he is right in being disheartened and in complaining the rest of his life. A sturdy lad from New Hampshire or Vermont, who in turn tries all the professions, who *teams it*, *farms it*, *peddles*, keeps a school, preaches, edits a newspaper, goes to Congress, buys a township, and so forth, in successive years, and always, like a cat, falls on his feet, is worth a hundred of these city dolls. He walks abreast with his days, and feels no shame in not 'studying a profession,' for he does not postpone his life, but lives already. He has not one chance, but a hundred chances. Let a stoic arise who shall reveal the resources of man, and tell men they are not leaning willows, but can and must detach themselves; that with the exercise of self-trust, new powers shall appear; that a man is the word made flesh, born to shed healing to the nations, that he should be ashamed of our compassion, and that the moment he acts from himself, tossing the laws, the books, idolatries, and customs out of the window,—we pity him no more but thank and revere him,—and that teacher shall restore the life of man to splendor, and make his name dear to all History.

It is easy to see that a greater self-reliance,—a new respect for the divinity in man,—must work a revolution in all the offices and relations of men; in their religion; in their education; in their pursuits; their modes of living; their association; in their property; in their speculative views.

1. In what prayers do men allow themselves! That which they call a holy office, is not so much as brave and manly. Prayer looks abroad and asks for some foreign addition to come through some foreign virtue, and loses itself in endless mazes of natural and supernatural, and mediatorial and miraculous. Prayer that craves a particular commodity—any thing less than all good, is vicious. Prayer is the contemplation of the facts of life from the highest point of view. It is the soliloquy of a beholding and jubilant soul. It is the spirit of God pronouncing his works good. But prayer as a means to effect a private end, is theft and meanness. It supposes dualism and not unity in nature and consciousness. As soon as the man is at one with God, he will not beg. He will then see prayer in all action. The prayer of the farmer kneeling in his field to weed it, the prayer of the rower kneeling with the stroke of his oar, are true prayers heard throughout nature, though for cheap ends. Caratach, in Fletcher's Bonduca, when admonished to inquire the mind of the god Audate, replies,

> "His hidden meaning lies in our endeavors,
> Our valors are our best gods."[6]

Another sort of false prayers are our regrets. Discontent is the want of self-reliance; it is infirmity of will. Regret calamities, if you can thereby help the sufferer; if not, attend your own work, and already the evil begins to be

6. Lines 1294–95; the play by the English playwright John Fletcher (1579–1625) was produced around 1614.

repaired. Our sympathy is just as base. We come to them who weep foolishly, and sit down and cry for company, instead of imparting to them truth and health in rough electric shocks, putting them once more in communication with the soul. The secret of fortune is joy in our hands. Welcome evermore to gods and men is the self-helping man. For him all doors are flung wide. Him all tongues greet, all honors crown, all eyes follow with desire. Our love goes out to him and embraces him, because he did not need it. We solicitously and apologetically caress and celebrate him, because he held on his way and scorned our disapprobation. The gods love him because men hated him. "To the persevering mortal," said Zoroaster,[7] "the blessed Immortals are swift."

As men's prayers are a disease of the will, so are their creeds a disease of the intellect. They say with those foolish Israelites, 'Let not God speak to us, lest we die. Speak thou, speak any man with us, and we will obey.'[8] Everywhere I am bereaved of meeting God in my brother, because he has shut his own temple doors, and recites fables merely of his brother's, or his brother's brother's God. Every new mind is a new classification. If it prove a mind of uncommon activity and power, a Locke, a Lavoisier, a Hutton, a Bentham, a Spurzheim,[9] it imposes its classification on other men, and lo! a new system. In proportion always to the depth of the thought, and so to the number of the objects it touches and brings within reach of the pupil, is his complacency. But chiefly is this apparent in creeds and churches, which are also classifications of some powerful mind acting on the great elemental thought of Duty, and man's relation to the Highest. Such is Calvinism, Quakerism, Swedenborgianism.[1] The pupil takes the same delight in subordinating every thing to the new terminology that a girl does who has just learned botany, in seeing a new earth and new seasons thereby. It will happen for a time, that the pupil will feel a real debt to the teacher,—will find his intellectual power has grown by the study of his writings. This will continue until he has exhausted his master's mind. But in all unbalanced minds, the classification is idolized, passes for the end, and not for a speedily exhaustible means, so that the walls of the system blend to their eye in the remote horizon with the walls of the universe; the luminaries of heaven seem to them hung on the arch their master built. They cannot imagine how you aliens have any right to see,—how you can see; 'It must be somehow that you stole the light from us.' They do not yet perceive, that, light unsystematic, indomitable, will break into any cabin, even into theirs. Let them chirp awhile and call it their own. If they are honest and do well, presently their neat new pinfold[2] will be too strait and low, will crack, will lean, will rot and vanish, and the immortal light, all young and joyful, million-orbed, million-colored, will beam over the universe as on the first morning.

2. It is for want of self-culture that the idol of Travelling, the idol of Italy, of England, of Egypt, remains for all educated Americans. They who made

<hr />

7. Religious prophet of ancient Persia.
8. See the fearful words of the Hebrews after God gave Moses the Ten Commandments, Exodus 20.19: "And they said unto Moses, Speak thou with us, and we will hear: but let not God speak with us, lest we die."
9. These innovators are John Locke (1632–1704), English philosopher; Antoine Lavoisier (1743–1797), French chemist; James Hutton (1726–1797), Scottish geologist; Jeremy Bentham (1748–1832), English philosopher; and Johann

Kaspar Spurzheim (1776–1832), German physician whose work led to the pseudoscience of phrenology, assessing character by interpreting the bumps on the skull.
1. Three widely varying religious movements founded by or based on the teachings of, respectively, John Calvin (1509–1564), French theologian; George Fox (1624–1691), English clergyman; and Emanuel Swedenborg (1688–1772), Swedish scientist and theologian.
2. Enclosure for animals.

England, Italy, or Greece venerable in the imagination, did so not by rambling round creation as a moth round a lamp, but by sticking fast where they were, like an axis of the earth. In manly hours, we feel that duty is our place, and that the merrymen of circumstance should follow as they may. The soul is no traveller: the wise man stays at home with the soul, and when his necessities, his duties, on any occasion call him from his house, or into foreign lands, he is at home still, and is not gadding abroad from himself, and shall make men sensible by the expression of his countenance, that he goes the missionary of wisdom and virtue, and visits cities and men like a sovereign, and not like an interloper or a valet.

I have no churlish objection to the circumnavigation of the globe, for the purposes of art, of study, and benevolence, so that the man is first domesticated, or does not go abroad with the hope of finding somewhat greater than he knows. He who travels to be amused, or to get somewhat which he does not carry, travels away from himself, and grows old even in youth among old things. In Thebes, in Palmyra,[3] his will and mind have become old and dilapidated as they. He carries ruins to ruins.

Travelling is a fool's paradise. We owe to our first journeys the discovery that place is nothing. At home I dream that at Naples, at Rome, I can be intoxicated with beauty, and lose my sadness. I pack my trunk, embrace my friends, embark on the sea, and at last wake up in Naples, and there beside me is the stern Fact, the sad self, unrelenting, identical, that I fled from. I seek the Vatican, and the palaces. I affect to be intoxicated with sights and suggestions, but I am not intoxicated. My giant goes with me wherever I go.

3. But the rage of travelling is itself only a symptom of a deeper unsoundness affecting the whole intellectual action. The intellect is vagabond, and the universal system of education fosters restlessness. Our minds travel when our bodies are forced to stay at home. We imitate; and what is imitation but the travelling of the mind? Our houses are built with foreign taste; our shelves are garnished with foreign ornaments; our opinions, our tastes, our whole minds lean, and follow the Past and the Distant, as the eyes of a maid follow her mistress. The soul created the arts wherever they have flourished. It was in his own mind that the artist sought his model. It was an application of his own thought to the thing to be done and the conditions to be observed. And why need we copy the Doric or the Gothic model?[4] Beauty, convenience, grandeur of thought, and quaint expression are as near to us as to any, and if the American artist will study with hope and love the precise thing to be done by him, considering the climate, the soil, the length of the day, the wants of the people, the habit and form of the government, he will create a house in which all these will find themselves fitted, and taste and sentiment will be satisfied also.

Insist on yourself; never imitate. Your own gift you can present every moment with the cumulative force of a whole life's cultivation; but of the adopted talent of another, you have only an extemporaneous, half possession. That which each can do best, none but his Maker can teach him. No man yet knows what it is, nor can, till that person has exhibited it. Where is the master who could have taught Shakspeare? Where is the master who could have instructed Franklin, or Washington, or Bacon, or Newton? Every great man

---

3. Ruins of ancient cities in Egypt and Syria, respectively.

4. I.e., ancient Greek or medieval European architecture.

is an unique. The Scipionism[5] of Scipio is precisely that part he could not borrow. If any body will tell me whom the great man imitates in the original crisis when he performs a great act, I will tell him who else than himself can teach him. Shakspeare will never be made by the study of Shakspeare. Do that which is assigned thee, and thou canst not hope too much or dare too much. There is at this moment, there is for me an utterance bare and grand as that of the colossal chisel of Phidias,[6] or trowel of the Egyptians, or the pen of Moses, or Dante, but different from all these. Now possibly will the soul all rich, all eloquent, with thousand-cloven tongue, deign to repeat itself; but if I can hear what these patriarchs say, surely I can reply to them in the same pitch of voice: for the ear and the tongue are two organs of one nature. Dwell up there in the simple and noble regions of thy life, obey thy heart, and thou shalt reproduce the Foreworld again.

4. As our Religion, our Education, our Art look abroad, so does our spirit of society. All men plume themselves on the improvement of society, and no man improves.

Society never advances. It recedes as fast on one side as it gains on the other. Its progress is only apparent, like the workers of a treadmill. It undergoes continual changes: it is barbarous, it is civilized, it is christianized, it is rich, it is scientific; but this change is not amelioration. For every thing that is given, something is taken. Society acquires new arts and loses old instincts. What a contrast between the well-clad, reading, writing, thinking American, with a watch, a pencil, and a bill of exchange in his pocket, and the naked New Zealander, whose property is a club, a spear, a mat, and an undivided twentieth of a shed to sleep under. But compare the health of the two men, and you shall see that his aboriginal strength the white man has lost. If the traveller tell us truly, strike the savage with a broad axe, and in a day or two the flesh shall unite and heal as if you struck the blow into soft pitch, and the same blow shall send the white to his grave.

The civilized man has built a coach, but has lost the use of his feet. He is supported on crutches, but loses so much support of muscle. He has got a fine Geneva watch, but he has lost the skill to tell the hour by the sun. A Greenwich nautical almanac he has, and so being sure of the information when he wants it, the man in the street does not know a star in the sky. The solstice he does not observe; the equinox he knows as little; and the whole bright calendar of the year is without a dial in his mind. His notebooks impair his memory; his libraries overload his wit; the insurance office increases the number of accidents; and it may be a question whether machinery does not encumber; whether we have not lost by refinement some energy, by a christianity entrenched in establishments and forms, some vigor of wild virtue. For every stoic was a stoic;[7] but in Christendom where is the Christian?

There is no more deviation in the moral standard than in the standard of height or bulk. No greater men are now than ever were. A singular equality may be observed between the great men of the first and of the last ages; nor can all the science, art, religion and philosophy of the nineteenth century avail to educate greater men than Plutarch's heroes,[8] three or four and twenty centuries ago. Not in time is the race progressive. Phocion,

5. I.e., the essence of the man.
6. Greek sculptor of the 5th century B.C.E.
7. Emerson refers particularly to the Stoics, members of the Greek school of philosophy founded by Zeno about 308 B.C.E. It taught the ideal of a calm, self-controlled existence in which every occurrence is accepted as fated.
8. The lives of famous Greeks and Romans written by Plutarch (46?–120? C.E.), Greek biographer.

Socrates, Anaxagoras, Diogenes,[9] are great men, but they leave no class. He who is really of their class will not be called by their name, but be wholly his own man, and, in his turn the founder of a sect. The arts and inventions of each period are only its costume, and do not invigorate men. The harm of the improved machinery may compensate its good. Hudson and Behring[1] accomplished so much in their fishing-boats, as to astonish Parry and Franklin,[2] whose equipment exhausted the resources of science and art. Galileo, with an opera-glass, discovered a more splendid series of facts than any one since. Columbus found the New World in an undecked boat. It is curious to see the periodical disuse and perishing of means and machinery which were introduced with loud laudation, a few years or centuries before. The great genius returns to essential man. We reckoned the improvements of the art of war among the triumphs of science, and yet Napoleon conquered Europe by the Bivouac,[3] which consisted of falling back on naked valor, and disencumbering it of all aids. The Emperor held it impossible to make a perfect army, says Las Cases,[4] "without abolishing our arms, magazines, commissaries, and carriages, until in imitation of the Roman custom, the soldier should receive his supply of corn, grind it in his hand-mill, and bake his bread himself."

Society is a wave. The wave moves onward, but the water of which it is composed, does not. The same particle does not rise from the valley to the ridge. Its unity is only phenomenal. The persons who make up a nation today, next year die, and their experience with them.

And so the reliance on Property, including the reliance on governments which protect it, is the want of self-reliance. Men have looked away from themselves and at things so long, that they have come to esteem what they call the soul's progress, namely, the religious, learned, and civil institutions, as guards of property, and they deprecate assaults on these, because they feel them to be assaults on property. They measure their esteem of each other, by what each has, and not by what each is. But a cultivated man becomes ashamed of his property, ashamed of what he has, out of new respect for his being. Especially, he hates what he has, if he see that it is accidental,—came to him by inheritance, or gift, or crime; then he feels that it is not having; it does not belong to him, has no root in him, and merely lies there, because no revolution or no robber takes it away. But that which a man is, does always by necessity acquire, and what the man acquires is permanent and living property, which does not wait the beck of rulers, or mobs, or revolutions, or fire, or storm, or bankruptcies, but perpetually renews itself wherever the man is put. "Thy lot or portion of life," said the Caliph Ali,[5] "is seeking after thee; therefore be at rest from seeking after it." Our dependence on these foreign goods leads us to our slavish respect for numbers. The political parties meet in numerous conventions; the greater the concourse, and with each new uproar of announcement, The delegation from Essex![6] The Democrats from New Hampshire! The Whigs of Maine! the young patriot feels himself stronger than before by a new thousand of eyes and arms. In like manner the

9. Four Greek philosophers: Phocion (402?–317 B.C.E.), Socrates (470?–399 B.C.E.), Anaxagoras (500?–428 B.C.E.), and Diogenes (412?–323 B.C.E.).
1. Vitus Jonassen Bering (1680–1741), Danish navigator who explored the northern Pacific Ocean. Henry Hudson (d. 1611), English navigator (sometimes in service of the Dutch).
2. Sir William Edward Perry (1790–1855) and Sir

John Franklin (1786–1847), English explorers of the Arctic.
3. Temporary military camp.
4. Comte Emmanuel de Las Cases (1766–1842), author of a book recording his conversations with the exiled Napoleon at St. Helena.
5. Fourth Muslim caliph of Mecca (602?–661).
6. County in Massachusetts.

reformers summon conventions, and vote and resolve in multitude. But not so, O friends! will the God deign to enter and inhabit you, but by a method precisely the reverse. It is only as a man puts off from himself all external support, and stands alone, that I see him to be strong and to prevail. He is weaker by every recruit to his banner. Is not a man better than a town? Ask nothing of men, and in the endless mutation, thou only firm column must presently appear the upholder of all that surrounds thee. He who knows that power is in the soul, that he is weak only because he has looked for good out of him and elsewhere, and so perceiving, throws himself unhesitatingly on his thought, instantly rights himself, stands in the erect position, commands his limbs, works miracles; just as a man who stands on his feet is stronger than a man who stands on his head.

So use all that is called Fortune. Most men gamble with her, and gain all, and lose all, as her wheel rolls. But do thou leave as unlawful these winnings, and deal with Cause and Effect, the chancellors of God. In the Will work and acquire, and thou hast chained the wheel of Chance, and shalt always drag her after thee. A political victory, a rise of rents, the recovery of your sick, or the return of your absent friend, or some other quite external event, raises your spirits, and you think good days are preparing for you. Do not believe it. It can never be so. Nothing can bring you peace but yourself. Nothing can bring you peace but the triumph of principles.

1841

The Poet[1]

A moody child and wildly wise
Pursued the game with joyful eyes,
Which chose, like meteors, their way,
And rived the dark with private ray:
They overleapt the horizon's edge,
Searched with Apollo's privilege;
Through man, and woman, and sea, and star,
Saw the dance of nature forward far;
Through worlds, and races, and terms, and times,
Saw musical order, and pairing rhymes.

Olympian bards who sung
Divine ideas below,
Which always find us young,
And always keep us so.

Those who are esteemed umpires of taste, are often persons who have acquired some knowledge of admired pictures or sculptures, and have an inclination for whatever is elegant; but if you inquire whether they are beautiful souls, and whether their own acts are like fair pictures, you learn that they are selfish and sensual. Their cultivation is local, as if you should rub a log of dry wood in one spot to produce fire, all the rest remaining cold. Their knowledge of the fine arts is some study of rules and particulars, or

---

1. First published in *Essays, Second Series* (1844), the source of the present text, "The Poet" contains the fullest elaboration of Emerson's aesthetic ideas and his most incisive comments on contemporary poetry and criticism. The first prefatory poem is from one of Emerson's uncompleted poems, and the second is from his "Ode to Beauty" (1843).

some limited judgment of color or form, which is exercised for amusement or for show. It is a proof of the shallowness of the doctrine of beauty, as it lies in the minds of our amateurs, that men seem to have lost the perception of the instant dependence of form upon soul. There is no doctrine of forms in our philosophy. We were put into our bodies, as fire is put into a pan, to be carried about; but there is no accurate adjustment between the spirit and the organ, much less is the latter the germination of the former. So in regard to other forms, the intellectual men do not believe in any essential dependence of the material world on thought and volition. Theologians think it a pretty air-castle to talk of the spiritual meaning of a ship or a cloud, of a city or a contract, but they prefer to come again to the solid ground of historical evidence; and even the poets are contented with a civil and conformed manner of living, and to write poems from the fancy, at a safe distance from their own experience. But the highest minds of the world have never ceased to explore the double meaning, or, shall I say, the quadruple, or the centuple, or much more manifold meaning, of every sensuous fact: Orpheus, Empedocles, Heraclitus, Plato, Plutarch, Dante, Swedenborg,[2] and the masters of sculpture, picture, and poetry. For we are not pans and barrows, nor even porters of the fire and torchbearers, but children of the fire, made of it, and only the same divinity transmuted, and at two or three removes, when we know least about it. And this hidden truth, that the foundations whence all this river of Time, and its creatures, floweth, are intrinsically ideal and beautiful, draws us to the consideration of the nature and functions of the Poet, or the man of Beauty, to the means and materials he uses, and to the general aspect of the art in the present time.

The breadth of the problem is great, for the poet is representative. He stands among partial men for the complete man, and apprises us not of his wealth, but of the commonwealth. The young man reveres men of genius, because, to speak truly, they are more himself than he is. They receive of the soul as he also receives, but they more. Nature enhances her beauty, to the eye of loving men, from their belief that the poet is beholding her shows at the same time. He is isolated among his contemporaries, by truth and by his art, but with this consolation in his pursuits, that they will draw all men sooner or later. For all men live by truth, and stand in need of expression. In love, in art, in avarice, in politics, in labor, in games, we study to utter our painful secret. The man is only half himself, the other half is his expression.

Notwithstanding this necessity to be published, adequate expression is rare. I know not how it is that we need an interpreter; but the great majority of men seem to be minors, who have not yet come into possession of their own, or mutes, who cannot report the conversation they have had with nature. There is no man who does not anticipate a supersensual utility in the sun, and stars, earth, and water. These stand and wait to render him a peculiar service. But there is some obstruction, or some excess of phlegm in our constitution, which does not suffer them to yield the due effect. Too feeble fall the impressions of nature on us to make us artists. Every touch should thrill. Every man should be so much an artist, that he could report in conversation what had befallen him. Yet, in our experience, the rays or appulses[3]

2. Emanuel Swedenborg (1688–1772), Swedish scientist and mystic. Orpheus, a legendary Greek poet. Empedocles (5th century B.C.E.), Heraclitus (6th century B.C.E.), and Plato (4th century B.C.E.) were Greek philosophers. Plutarch (1st century), Greek biographer. Dante (1265–1321), Italian poet.
3. Energies.

have sufficient force to arrive at the senses, but not enough to reach the quick, and compel the reproduction of themselves in speech. The poet is the person in whom these powers are in balance, the man without impediment, who sees and handles that which others dream of, traverses the whole scale of experience, and is representative of man, in virtue of being the largest power to receive and to impart.

For the Universe has three children, born at one time, which reappear, under different names, in every system of thought, whether they be called cause, operation, and effect; or, more poetically, Jove, Pluto, Neptune;[4] or, theologically, the Father, the Spirit, and the Son; but which we will call here, the Knower, the Doer, and the Sayer. These stand respectively for the love of truth, for the love of good, and for the love of beauty. These three are equal. Each is that which he is essentially, so that he cannot be surmounted or analyzed, and each of these three has the power of the others latent in him, and his own patent.

The poet is the sayer, the namer, and represents beauty. He is a sovereign, and stands on the centre. For the world is not painted or adorned, but is from the beginning beautiful; and God has not made some beautiful things, but Beauty is the creator of the universe. Therefore the poet is not any permissive potentate, but is emperor in his own right. Criticism is infested with a cant of materialism, which assumes that manual skill and activity is the first merit of all men, and disparages such as say and do not, overlooking the fact that some men, namely, poets, are natural sayers, sent into the world to the end of expression, and confounds them with those whose province is action, but who quit it to imitate the sayers. But Homer's words are as costly and admirable to Homer, as Agamemnon's victories are to Agamemnon.[5] The poet does not wait for the hero or the sage, but, as they act and think primarily, so he writes primarily what will and must be spoken, reckoning the others, though primaries also, yet, in respect to him, secondaries and servants; as sitters or models in the studio of a painter, or as assistants who bring building materials to an architect.

For poetry was all written before time was, and whenever we are so finely organized that we can penetrate into that region where the air is music, we hear those primal warblings, and attempt to write them down, but we lose ever and anon a word, or a verse, and substitute something of our own, and thus miswrite the poem. The men of more delicate ear write down these cadences more faithfully, and these transcripts, though imperfect, become the songs of the nations. For nature is as truly beautiful as it is good, or as it is reasonable, and must as much appear, as it must be done, or be known. Words and deeds are quite indifferent modes of the divine energy. Words are also actions, and actions are a kind of words.

The sign and credentials of the poet are, that he announces that which no man foretold. He is the true and only doctor;[6] he knows and tells; he is the only teller of news, for he was present and privy to the appearance which he describes. He is a beholder of ideas, and an utterer of the necessary and causal. For we do not speak now of men of poetical talents, or of industry and skill in metre, but of the true poet. I took part in a conversation the

4. In Roman mythology, the supreme god, god of the underworld, and god of the sea, respectively.
5. Emerson is comparing the author (Homer) with his character (Agamemnon, in *The Iliad*).
6. Teacher and healer.

other day, concerning a recent writer of lyrics, a man of subtle mind, whose head appeared to be a music-box of delicate tunes and rhythms, and whose skill, and command of language, we could not sufficiently praise. But when the question arose, whether he was not only a lyrist, but a poet, we were obliged to confess that he is plainly a contemporary, not an eternal man. He does not stand out of our low limitations, like a Chimborazo under the line,[7] running up from the torrid base through all the climates of the globe, with belts of the herbage of every latitude on its high and mottled sides; but this genius is the landscape-garden of a modern house, adorned with fountains and statues, with well-bred men and women standing and sitting in the walks and terraces. We hear, through all the varied music, the ground-tone of conventional life. Our poets are men of talents who sing, and not the children of music. The argument is secondary, the finish of the versus is primary.

For it is not metres, but a metre-making argument, that makes a poem,— a thought so passionate and alive, that, like the spirit of a plant or an animal, it has an architecture of its own, and adorns nature with a new thing. The thought and the form are equal in the order of time, but in the order of genesis the thought is prior to the form. The poet has a new thought: he has a whole new experience to unfold; he will tell us how it was with him, and all men will be the richer in his fortune. For, the experience of each new age requires a new confession, and the world seems always waiting for its poet. I remember, when I was young, how much I was moved one morning by tidings that genius had appeared in a youth who sat near me at table. He had left his work, and gone rambling none knew whither, and had written hundreds of lines, but could not tell whether that which was in him was therein told: he could tell nothing but that all was changed,—man, beast, heaven, earth, and sea. How gladly we listened! how credulous! Society seemed to be compromised. We sat in the aurora of a sunrise which was to put out all the stars. Boston seemed to be at twice the distance it had the night before, or was much farther than that. Rome,—what was Rome! Plutarch and Shakspeare were in the yellow leaf, and Homer no more should be heard of. It is much to know that poetry has been written this very day, under this very roof, by your side. What! that wonderful spirit has not expired! these stony moments are still sparkling and animated! I had fancied that the oracles were all silent, and nature had spent her fires, and behold! all night, from every pore, these fine auroras have been streaming. Every one has some interest in the advent of the poet, and no one knows how much it may concern him. We know that the secret of the world is profound, but who or what shall be our interpreter, we know not. A mountain ramble, a new style of face, a new person, may put the key into our hands. Of course, the value of genius to us is in the veracity of its report. Talent may frolic and juggle; genius realizes and adds. Mankind, in good earnest, have availed so far in understanding themselves and their work, that the foremost watchman on the peak announces his news. It is the truest word ever spoken, and the phrase will be the fittest, most musical, and the unerring voice of the world for that time.

All that we call sacred history attests that the birth of a poet is the principal event in chronology. Man, never so often deceived, still watches for the arrival of a brother who can hold him steady to a truth, until he has

---

7. Equator. Chimborazo is a mountain in Ecuador.

made it his own. With what joy I begin to read a poem, which I confide in as an inspiration! And now my chains are to be broken; I shall mount above these clouds and opaque airs in which I live,—opaque, though they seem transparent,—and from the heaven of truth I shall see and comprehend my relations. That will reconcile me to life, and renovate nature, to see trifles animated by a tendency, and to know what I am doing. Life will no more be a noise; now I shall see men and women, and know the signs by which they may be discerned from fools and satans. This day shall be better than my birth-day: then I became an animal: now I am invited into the science of the real. Such is the hope, but the fruition is postponed. Oftener it falls, that this winged man, who will carry me into the heaven, whirls me into the clouds, then leaps and frisks about with me from cloud to cloud, still affirming that he is bound heavenward; and I, being myself a novice, am slow in perceiving that he does not know the way into the heavens, and is merely bent that I should admire his skill to rise, like a fowl or a flying fish, a little way from the ground or the water; but the all-piercing, all-feeding, and ocular[8] air of heaven, that man shall never inhabit. I tumble down again soon into my old nooks, and lead the life of exaggerations as before, and have lost my faith in the possibility of any guide who can lead me thither where I would be.

But leaving these victims of vanity, let us, with new hope, observe how nature, by worthier impulses, has ensured the poet's fidelity to his office of announcement and affirming, namely, by the beauty of things, which becomes a new, and higher beauty, when expressed. Nature offers all her creatures to him as a picture-language. Being used as a type, a second wonderful value appears in the object, far better than its old value, as the carpenter's stretched cord, if you hold your ear close enough, is musical in the breeze. "Things more excellent than every image," says Jamblichus,[9] "are expressed through images." Things admit of being used as symbols, because nature is a symbol, in the whole, and in every part. Every line we can draw in the sand, has expression; and there is no body without its spirit or genius. All form is an effect of character; all condition, of the quality of the life; all harmony, of health; (and, for this reason, a perception of beauty should be sympathetic, or proper only to the good.) The beautiful rests on the foundations of the necessary. The soul makes the body, as the wise Spenser teaches:—

> "So every spirit, as it is most pure,
> And hath in it the more of heavenly light,
> So it the fairer body doth procure
> To habit in, and it more fairly dight,
> With cheerful grace and amiable sight.
> For, of the soul, the body form doth take,
> For soul is form, and doth the body make."[1]

Here we find ourselves, suddenly, not in a critical speculation, but in a holy place, and should go very warily and reverently. We stand before the secret of the world, there where Being passes into Appearance, and Unity into Variety.

The Universe is the externisation of the soul. Wherever the life is, that bursts into appearance around it. Our science is sensual, and therefore

---

8. Visible.
9. Neoplatonic philosopher of the 4th century C.E. (Neoplatonism is a mystical religious system combining features of Platonic and other Greek philosophies with features of Judaism and Christianity.)
1. "An Hymn in Honour of Beauty" (1596), by the English poet Edmund Spenser (1552–1599).

superficial. The earth, and the heavenly bodies, physics, and chemistry, we sensually treat, as if they were self-existent; but these are the retinue of that Being we have. "The mighty heaven," said Proclus,[2] "exhibits, in its trans-figurations, clear images of the splendor of intellectual perceptions; being moved in conjunction with the unapparent periods of intellectual natures." Therefore, science always goes abreast with the just elevation of the man, keeping step with religion and metaphysics; or, the state of science is an index of our self-knowledge. Since everything in nature answers to a moral power, if any phenomenon remains brute and dark, it is that the corresponding faculty in the observer is not yet active.

No wonder, then, if these waters be so deep, that we hover over them with a religious regard. The beauty of the fable proves the importance of the sense; to the poet, and to all others; or, if you please, every man is so far a poet as to be susceptible of these enchantments of nature: for all men have the thoughts whereof the universe is the celebration. I find that the fascination resides in the symbol. Who loves nature? Who does not? Is it only poets, and men of leisure and cultivation, who live with her? No; but also hunters, farmers, grooms, and butchers, though they express their affection in their choice of life, and not in their choice of words. The writer wonders what the coachman or the hunter values in riding, in horses, and dogs. It is not superficial qualities. When you talk with him, he holds these at as slight a rate as you. His worship is sympathetic; he has no definitions, but he is commanded in nature, by the living power which he feels to be there present. No imitation, or playing of these things, would content him; he loves the earnest of the northwind, of rain, of stone, and wood, and iron. A beauty not explicable, is dearer than a beauty which we can see to the end of. It is nature the symbol, nature certifying the supernatural, body overflowed by life, which he worships, with coarse, but sincere rites.

The inwardness, and mystery, of this attachment, drives men of every class to the use of emblems. The schools of poets, and philosophers, are not more intoxicated with their symbols, than the populace with theirs. In our political parties, compute the power of badges and emblems. See the great ball which they roll from Baltimore to Bunker hill! In the political processions, Lowell goes in a loom, and Lynn in a shoe, and Salem in a ship.[3] Witness the ciderbarrel, the log-cabin, the hickory-stick, the palmetto,[4] and all the cognizances of party. See the power of national emblems. Some stars, lilies, leopards, a crescent, a lion, an eagle, or other figure, which came into credit God knows how, on an old rag of bunting, blowing in the wind, on a fort, at the ends of the earth, shall make the blood tingle under the rudest, or the most conventional exterior. The people fancy they hate poetry, and they are all poets and mystics!

Beyond this universality of the symbolic language, we are apprised of the divineness of this superior use of things, whereby the world is a temple, whose walls are covered with emblems, pictures, and commandments of the Deity, in this, that there is no fact in nature which does not carry the whole

---

2. Greek Neoplatonic philosopher (411–485).
3. Towns are symbolized by major products. "The great ball": as a campaign stunt, William Henry Harrison's supporters during the 1840 presidential campaign rolled huge balls at rallies to cries of "Keep the ball a-rolling."
4. Allusions to the 1840 presidential election.

Harrison's "Log Cabin and Hard Cider" campaign, which emphasized the candidate's humble roots while offering free alcohol to his supporters, helped him defeat Martin Van Buren. South Carolina, nicknamed the Palmetto State for its palm-like trees, claimed to be the birthplace of Andrew Jackson ("Old Hickory").

sense of nature; and the distinctions which we make in events, and in affairs, of low and high, honest and base, disappear when nature is used as a symbol. Thought makes every thing fit for use. The vocabulary of an omniscient man would embrace words and images excluded from polite conversation. What would be base, or even obscene, to the obscene, becomes illustrious, spoken in a new connexion of thought. The piety of the Hebrew prophets purges their grossness. The circumcision is an example of the power of poetry to raise the low and offensive. Small and mean things serve as well as great symbols. The meaner the type by which a law is expressed, the more pungent it is, and the more lasting in the memories of men: just as we choose the smallest box, or case, in which any needful utensil can be carried. Bare lists of words are found suggestive, to an imaginative and excited mind; as it is related of Lord Chatham, that he was accustomed to read in Bailey's Dictionary,[5] when he was preparing to speak in Parliament. The poorest experience is rich enough for all the purposes of expressing thought. Why covet a knowledge of new facts? Day and night, house and garden, a few books, a few actions, serve us as well as would all trades and all spectacles. We are far from having exhausted the significance of the few symbols we use. We can come to use them yet with a terrible simplicity. It does not need that a poem should be long. Every word was once a poem. Every new relation is a new word. Also, we use defects and deformaties to a sacred purpose, so expressing our sense that the evils of the world are such only to the evil eye. In the old mythology, mythologists observe, defects are ascribed to divine natures, as lameness to Vulcan, blindness to Cupid, and the like, to signify exuberances.

For, as it is dislocation and detachment from the life of God, that makes things ugly, the poet, who re-attaches things to nature and the Whole,— re-attaching even artificial things, and violations of nature, to nature, by a deeper insight,—disposes very easily of the most disagreeable facts. Readers of poetry see the factory-village, and the railway, and fancy that the poetry of the landscape is broken up by these; for these works of art are not yet consecrated in their reading; but the poet sees them fall within the great Order not less than the bee-hive, or the spider's geometrical web. Nature adopts them very fast into her vital circles, and the gliding train of cars she loves like her own. Besides, in a centred mind, it signifies nothing how many mechanical inventions you exhibit. Though you add millions, and never so surprising, the fact of mechanics has not gained a grain's weight. The spiritual fact remains unalterable, by many or by few particulars; as no mountain is of any appreciable height to break the curve of the sphere. A shrewd country-boy goes to the city for the first time, and the complacent citizen is not satisfied with his little wonder. It is not that he does not see all the fine houses, and know that he never saw such before, but he disposes of them as easily as the poet finds place for the railway. The chief value of the new fact, is to enhance the great and constant fact of Life, which can dwarf any and every circumstance, and to which the belt of wampum, and the commerce of America, are alike.

The world being thus put under the mind for verb and noun, the poet is he who can articulate it. For, though life is great, and fascinates, and

---

5. Nathan (or Nathaniel) Bailey (d. 1742) published *An Universal Etymological English Dictionary* (1721), which ran through many editions. Lord Chatham was William Pitt (1708–1778), English statesman famous for his oratory.

absorbs,—and though all men are intelligent of the symbols through which it is named,—yet they cannot originally use them. We are symbols, and inhabit symbols; workmen, work, and tools, words and things, birth and death, all are emblems; but we sympathize with the symbols, and, being infatuated with the economical uses of things, we do not know that they are thoughts. The poet, by an ulterior intellectual perception, gives them a power which makes their old use forgotten, and puts eyes, and a tongue, into every dumb and inanimate object. He perceives the independence of the thought on the symbol, the stability of the thought, the accidency and fugacity of the symbol. As the eyes of Lyncæus[6] were said to see through the earth, so the poet turns the world to glass, and shows us all things in their right series and procession. For, through that better perception, he stands one step nearer to things, and sees the flowing or metamorphosis; perceives that thought is multiform; that within the form of every creature is a force impelling it to ascend into a higher form; and, following with his eyes the life, uses the forms which express that life, and so his speech flows with the flowing of nature. All the facts of the animal economy, sex, nutriment, gestation, birth, growth, are symbols of the passage of the world into the soul of man, to suffer there a change, and re-appear a new and higher fact. He uses forms according to the life, and not according to the form. This is true science. The poet alone knows astronomy, chemistry, vegetation, and animation, for he does not stop at these facts, but employs them as signs. He knows why the plain, or meadow of space, was strown with these flowers we call suns, and moons, and stars; why the great deep is adorned with animals, with men, and gods; for, in every word he speaks he rides on them as the horses of thought.

By virtue of this science the poet is the Namer, or Language-maker, naming things sometimes after their appearance, sometimes after their essence, and giving to every one its own name and not another's, thereby rejoicing the intellect, which delights in detachment or boundary. The poets made all the words, and therefore language is the archives of history, and, if we must say it, a sort of tomb of the muses. For, though the origin of most of our words is forgotten, each word was at first a stroke of genius, and obtained currency, because for the moment it symbolized the world to the first speaker and to the hearer. The etymologist finds the deadest word to have been once a brilliant picture. Language is fossil poetry. As the limestone of the continent consists of infinite masses of the shells of animalcules, so language is made up of images, or tropes, which now, in their secondary use, have long ceased to remind us of their poetic origin. But the poet names the thing because he sees it, or comes one step nearer to it than any other. This expression, or naming, is not art, but a second nature, grown out of the first, as a leaf out of a tree. What we call nature, is a certain self-regulated motion, or change; and nature does all things by her own hands, and does not leave another to baptise her, but baptises herself; and this through the metamorphosis again. I remember that a certain poet[7] described it to me thus:

> Genius is the activity which repairs the decays of things, whether wholly or partly of a material and finite kind. Nature, through all her kingdoms, insures herself. Nobody cares for planting the poor fungus: so

6. In Greek mythology, a keen-sighted crewman who sailed with Jason in search of the Golden Fleece.

7. A private joke: the poet is Emerson himself.

she shakes down from the gills of one agaric[8] countless spores, any one of which, being preserved, transmits new billions of spores to-morrow or next day. The new agaric of this hour has a chance which the old one had not. This atom of seed is thrown into a new place, not subject to the accidents which destroyed its parent two rods off. She makes a man; and having brought him to ripe age, she will no longer run the risk of losing this wonder at a blow, but she detaches from him a new self, that the kind may be safe from accidents to which the individual is exposed. So when the soul of the poet has come to ripeness of thought, she detaches and sends away from it its poems or songs,—a fearless, sleepless, deathless progeny, which is not exposed to the accidents of the weary kingdom of time: a fearless, vivacious offspring, clad with wings (such was the virtue of the soul out of which they came), which carry them fast and far, and infix them irrecoverably into the hearts of men. These wings are the beauty of the poet's soul. The songs, thus flying immortal from their mortal parent, are pursued by clamorous flights of censures, which swarm in far greater numbers, and threaten to devour them; but these last are not winged. At the end of a very short leap they fall plump down, and rot, having received from the souls out of which they came no beautiful wings. But the melodies of the poet ascend, and leap, and pierce into the deeps of infinite time.

So far the bard taught me, using his freer speech. But nature has a higher end, in the production of new individuals, than security, namely, *ascension*, or, the passage of the soul into higher forms. I knew, in my younger days, the sculptor who made the statue of the youth which stands in the public garden. He was, as I remember, unable to tell directly, what made him happy, or unhappy, but by wonderful indirections he could tell. He rose one day, according to his habit, before the dawn, and saw the morning break, grand as the eternity out of which it came, and, for many days after, he strove to express this tranquillity, and, lo! his chisel had fashioned out of marble the form of a beautiful youth, Phosphorus,[9] whose aspect is such, that, it is said, all persons who look on it become silent. The poet also resigns himself to his mood, and that thought which agitated him is expressed, but *alter idem*,[1] in a manner totally new. The expression is organic, or, the new type which things themselves take when liberated. As, in the sun, objects paint their images on the retina of the eye, so they, sharing the aspiration of the whole universe, tend to paint a far more delicate copy of their essence in his mind. Like the metamorphosis of things into higher organic forms, is their change into melodies. Over everything stands its dæmon, or soul, and, as the form of the thing is reflected by the eye, so the soul of the thing is reflected by a melody. The sea, the mountain-ridge, Niagara, and every flower-bed, pre-exist, or super-exist, in pre-cantations,[2] which sail like odors in the air, and when any man goes by with an ear sufficiently fine, he overhears them, and endeavors to write down the notes, without diluting or depraving them. And herein is the legitimation of criticism, in the mind's faith, that the poems are a corrupt version of some text in nature, with which they ought to be made to tally. A rhyme in one of our sonnets should not be less pleasing than the iterated nodes of a seashell, or the resembling difference of a group

---

8. Fungus, such as a mushroom.
9. Greek god associated with the morning star.

1. The same yet different (Latin).
2. Prophetic incantations or spells.

of flowers. The pairing of the birds is an idyl, not tedious as our idyls are; a tempest is a rough ode, without falsehood or rant: a summer, with its harvest sown, reaped, and stored, is an epic song, subordinating how many admirably executed parts. Why should not the symmetry and truth that modulate these, glide into our spirits, and we participate the invention of nature?

This insight, which expresses itself by what is called Imagination, is a very high sort of seeing, which does not come by study, but by the intellect being where and what it sees, by sharing the path, or circuit of things through forms, and so making them translucid to others. The path of things is silent. Will they suffer a speaker to go with them? A spy they will not suffer; a lover, a poet, is the transcendency of their own nature,—him they will suffer. The condition of true naming, on the poet's part, is his resigning himself to the divine *aura*[3] which breathes through forms, and accompanying that.

It is a secret which every intellectual man quickly learns, that, beyond the energy of his possessed and conscious intellect, he is capable of a new energy (as of an intellect doubled on itself), by abandonment to the nature of things; that, beside his privacy of power as an individual man, there is a great public power, on which he can draw, by unlocking, at all risks, his human doors, and suffering the ethereal tides to roll and circulate through him: then he is caught up into the life of the Universe, his speech is thunder, his thought is law, and his words are universally intelligible as the plants and animals. The poet knows that he speaks adequately, then, only when he speaks somewhat wildly, or, "with the flower of the mind;" not with the intellect, used as an organ, but with the intellect released from all service, and suffered to take its direction from its celestial life; or, as the ancients were wont to express themselves, not with intellect alone, but with the intellect inebriated by nectar. As the traveller who has lost his way, throws his reins on his horse's neck, and trusts to the instinct of the animal to find his road, so must we do with the divine animal who carries us through this world. For if in any manner we can stimulate this instinct, new passages are opened for us into nature, the mind flows into and through things hardest and highest, and the metamorphosis is possible.

This is the reason why bards love wine, mead,[4] narcotics, coffee, tea, opium, the fumes of sandal-wood and tobacco, or whatever other species of animal exhilaration. All men avail themselves of such means as they can, to add this extraordinary power to their normal powers; and to this end they prize conversation, music, pictures, sculpture, dancing, theatres, travelling, war, mobs, fires, gaming, politics, or love, or science, or animal intoxication, which are several coarser or finer *quasi*-mechanical substitutes for the true nectar, which is the ravishment of the intellect by coming nearer to the fact. These are auxiliaries to the centrifugal tendency of a man, to his passage out into free space, and they help him to escape the custody of that body in which he is pent up, and of that jail-yard of individual relations in which he is enclosed. Hence a great number of such as were professionally expressors of Beauty, as painters, poets, musicians, and actors, have been more than others wont to lead a life of pleasure and indulgence; all but the few who received the true nectar; and, as it was a spurious mode of attaining freedom,

3. I.e., all-pervading spirit.
4. A beverage made from fermented honey, malt, yeast, and water.

as it was an emancipation not into the heavens, but into the freedom of baser places, they were punished for that advantage they won, by a dissipation and deterioration. But never can any advantage be taken of nature by a trick. The spirit of the world, the great calm presence of the creator, comes not forth to the sorceries of opium or of wine. The sublime vision comes to the pure and simple soul in a clean and chaste body. That is not an inspiration which we owe to narcotics, but some counterfeit excitement and fury. Milton says, that the lyric poet may drink wine and live generously, but the epic poet, he who shall sing of the gods, and their descent unto men, must drink water out of a wooden bowl.[5] For poetry is not 'Devil's wine,' but God's wine. It is with this as it is with toys. We fill the hands and nurseries of our children with all manner of dolls, drums, and horses, withdrawing their eyes from the plain face and sufficing objects of nature, the sun, and moon, the animals, the water, and stones, which should be their toys. So the poet's habit of living should be set on a key so low and plain, that the common influences should delight him. His cheerfulness should be the gift of the sunlight; the air should suffice for his inspiration, and he should be tipsy with water. That spirit which suffices quiet hearts, which seems to come forth to such from every dry knoll of sere grass, from every pine-stump, and half-imbedded stone, on which the dull March sun shines, comes forth to the poor and hungry, and such as are of simple taste. If thou fill thy brain with Boston and New York, with fashion and covetousness, and wilt stimulate thy jaded senses with wine and French coffee, thou shalt find no radiance of wisdom in the lonely waste of the pinewoods.

If the imagination intoxicates the poet, it is not inactive in other men. The metamorphosis excites in the beholder an emotion of joy. The use of symbols has a certain power of emancipation and exhilaration for all men. We seem to be touched by a wand, which makes us dance and run about happily, like children. We are like persons who come out of a cave or cellar into the open air. This is the effect on us of tropes,[6] fables, oracles, and all poetic forms. Poets are thus liberating gods. Men have really got a new sense, and found within their world, another world, or nest of worlds; for, the meta-morphosis once seen, we divine that it does not stop. I will not now consider how much this makes the charm of algebra and the mathematics, which also have their tropes, but it is felt in every definition; as, when Aristotle defines *space* to be an immovable vessel, in which things are contained;—or, when Plato defines a *line* to be a flowing point; or, *figure* to be a bound of solid; and many the like. What a joyful sense of freedom we have, when Vitruvius announces the old opinion of artists, that no architect can build any house well, who does not know something of anatomy. When Socrates, in Charmi-des, tells us that the soul is cured of its maladies by certain incantations, and that these incantations are beautiful reasons, from which temperance is generated in souls; when Plato calls the world an animal; and Timæus affirms that the plants also are animals; or affirms a man to be a heavenly tree, growing with his root, which is his head, upward; and, as George Chapman, following him, writes,—

> "So in our tree of man, whose nervie root
> Springs in his top;"

---

5. In Milton's "Sixth Latin Elegy" (1629). 6. Figures of speech.

when Orpheus speaks of hoariness as "that white flower which marks extreme old age;" when Proclus calls the universe the statue of the intellect; when Chaucer, in his praise of 'Gentilesse,' compares good blood in mean condition to fire, which, though carried to the darkest house betwixt this and the mount of Caucasus, will yet hold its natural office, and burn as bright as if twenty thousand men did it behold; when John saw, in the apocalypse, the ruin of the world through evil, and the stars fall from heaven, as the figtree casteth her untimely fruit; when Æsop reports the whole catalogue of common daily relations through the masquerade of birds and beasts;—we take the cheerful hint of the immortality of our essence, and its versatile habit and escapes, as when the gypsies say, "it is in vain to hang them, they cannot die."[7]

The poets are thus liberating gods. The ancient British bards had for the title of their order, "Those who are free throughout the world." They are free, and they make free. An imaginative book renders us much more service at first, by stimulating us through its tropes, than afterward, when we arrive at the precise sense of the author. I think nothing is of any value in books, excepting the transcendental and extraordinary. If a man is inflamed and carried away by his thought, to that degree that he forgets the authors and the public, and heeds only this one dream, which holds him like an insanity, let me read his paper, and you may have all the arguments and histories and criticism. All the value which attaches to Pythagoras, Paracelsus, Cornelius Agrippa, Cardan, Kepler, Swedenborg, Schelling, Oken,[8] or any other who introduces questionable facts into his cosmogony, as angels, devils, magic, astrology, palmistry, mesmerism,[9] and so on, is the certificate we have of departure from routine, and that here is a new witness. That also is the best success in conversation, the magic of liberty, which puts the world, like a ball, in our hands. How cheap even the liberty then seems; how mean to study, when an emotion communicates to the intellect the power to sap and upheave nature; how great the perspective! nations, times, systems, enter and disappear, like threads in tapestry of large figure and many colors; dream delivers us to dream, and, while the drunkenness lasts, we will sell our bed, our philosophy, our religion, in our opulence.

There is good reason why we should prize this liberation. The fate of the poor shepherd, who, blinded and lost in the snowstorm, perishes in a drift within a few feet of his cottage door, is an emblem of the state of man. On the brink of the waters of life and truth, we are miserably dying. The inaccessibleness of every thought but that we are in, is wonderful. What if you come near to it,—you are as remote, when you are nearest, as when you are farthest. Every thought is also a prison; every heaven is also a prison. Therefore we love the poet, the inventor, who in any form, whether in an ode, or in an

7. Vitruvius Pollio (50?–26 B.C.E.), Roman writer on architecture. *Charmides* and *Timaeus* are two of Plato's Dialogues. The Chapman quotation is from his dedication to his translation of Homer. Chaucer's praise of "gentilesse" is in "The Wife of Bath's Tale." John's vision is in Revelation 6.13. The Greek Aesop in the 6th century B.C.E. wrote beast fables that commented on human foibles. The saying attributed to gypsies comes from the English travel writer George Borrow's *The Zincali* (1841).

8. Lorenz Oken (1779–1851), German naturalist. Pythagoras (6th century B.C.E.), Greek mathematician and mystic philosopher. Paracelsus (1493–1541), German alchemist. Agrippa (1486–1535), German physician. Girolamo Cardano (1501–1576), Italian mathematician. Johannes Kepler (1571–1630), German astronomer. Swedenborg, see n. 2, p. 567. Friedrich Wilhelm Joseph von Schelling (1775–1854), German philosopher.
9. Hypnotism.

action, or in looks and behavior, has yielded us a new thought. He unlocks our chains, and admits us to a new scene.

This emancipation is dear to all men, and the power to impart it, as it must come from greater depth and scope of thought, is a measure of intellect. Therefore all books of the imagination endure, all which ascend to that truth, that the writer sees nature beneath him, and uses it as his exponent.[1] Every verse or sentence, possessing this virtue, will take care of its own immortality. The religions of the world are the ejaculations[2] of a few imaginative men.

But the quality of the imagination is to flow, and not to freeze. The poet did not stop at the color, or the form, but read their meaning; neither may he rest in this meaning, but he makes the same objects exponents of his new thought. Here is the difference betwixt the poet and the mystic, that the last nails a symbol to one sense, which was a true sense for a moment, but soon becomes old and false. For all symbols are fluxional; all language is vehicular and transitive, and is good, as ferries and horses are, for conveyance, not as farms and houses are, for homestead. Mysticism consists in the mistake of an accidental and individual symbol for an universal one. The morning-redness happens to be the favorite meteor to the eyes of Jacob Behmen,[3] and comes to stand to him for truth and faith; and he believes should stand for the same realities to every reader. But the first reader prefers as naturally the symbol of a mother and child, or a gardener and his bulb, or a jeweller polishing a gem. Either of these, or of a myriad more, are equally good to the person to whom they are significant. Only they must be held lightly, and be very willingly translated into the equivalent terms which others use. And the mystic must be steadily told,—All that you say is just as true without the tedious use of that symbol as with it. Let us have a little algebra, instead of this trite rhetoric,—universal signs, instead of these village symbols,—and we shall both be gainers. The history of hierarchies seems to show, that all religious error consisted in making the symbol too stark and solid, and, at last, nothing but an excess of the organ of language.

Swedenborg, of all men in the recent ages, stands eminently for the translator of nature into thought. I do not know the man in history to whom things stood so uniformly for words. Before him the metamorphosis continually plays. Everything on which his eye rests, obeys the impulses of moral nature. The figs become grapes whilst he eats them. When some of his angels affirmed a truth, the laurel twig which they held blossomed in their hands. The noise which, at a distance, appeared like gnashing and thumping, on coming nearer was found to be the voice of disputants. The men, in one of his visions, seen in heavenly light, appeared like dragons, and seemed in darkness: but, to each other, they appeared as men, and, when the light from heaven shone into their cabin, they complained of the darkness, and were compelled to shut the window that they might see.

There was this perception in him, which makes the poet or seer, an object of awe and terror, namely, that the same man, or society of men, may wear one aspect to themselves and their companions, and a different aspect to higher intelligences. Certain priests, whom he describes as conversing very learnedly together, appeared to the children, who were at some distance,

---

1. Means of expounding his beliefs.
2. Throwings forth.

3. German mystic (1575–1624).

like dead horses: and many the like misappearances. And instantly the mind inquires, whether these fishes under the bridge, yonder oxen in the pasture, those dogs in the yard, are immutably fishes, oxen, and dogs, or only so appear to me, and perchance to themselves appear upright men; and whether I appear as a man to all eyes. The Brahmins[4] and Pythagoras propounded the same question, and if any poet has witnessed the transformation, he doubtless found it in harmony with various experiences. We have all seen changes as considerable in wheat and caterpillars. He is the poet, and shall draw us with love and terror, who sees, through the flowing vest, the firm nature, and can declare it.

I look in vain for the poet whom I describe. We do not, with sufficient plainness, or sufficient profoundness, address ourselves to life, nor dare we chaunt our own times and social circumstance. If we filled the day with bravery, we should not shrink from celebrating it. Time and nature yield us many gifts, but not yet the timely man, the new religion, the reconciler, whom all things await. Dante's praise is, that he dared to write his autobiography in colossal cipher, or into universality. We have yet had no genius in America, with tyrannous eye, which knew the value of our incomparable materials, and saw, in the barbarism and materialism of the times, another carnival of the same gods whose picture he so much admires in Homer; then in the middle age; then in Calvinism. Banks and tariffs, the newspaper and caucus, methodism and unitarianism, are flat and dull to dull people, but rest on the same foundations of wonder as the town of Troy, and the temple of Delphos,[5] and are as swiftly passing away. Our logrolling, our stumps and their politics, our fisheries, our Negroes, and Indians, our boasts,[6] and our repudiations, the wrath of rogues, and the pusillanimity of honest men, the northern trade, the southern planting, the western clearing, Oregon, and Texas, are yet unsung. Yet America is a poem in our eyes; its ample geography dazzles the imagination, and it will not wait long for metres. If I have not found that excellent combination of gifts in my countrymen which I seek, neither could I aid myself to fix the idea of the poet by reading now and then in Chalmers's collection of five centuries of English poets.[7] These are wits, more than poets, though there have been poets among them. But when we adhere to the ideal of the poet, we have our difficulties even with Milton and Homer. Milton is too literary, and Homer too literal and historical.

But I am not wise enough for a national criticism, and must use the old largeness a little longer, to discharge my errand from the muse to the poet concerning his art.

Art is the path of the creator to his work. The paths, or methods, are ideal and eternal, though few men ever see them, not the artist himself for years, or for a lifetime, unless he comes into the conditions. The painter, the sculptor, the composer, the epic rhapsodist, the orator, all partake one desire, namely, to express themselves symmetrically and abundantly, not dwarfishly and fragmentarily. They found or put themselves in certain conditions, as, the painter and sculptor before some impressive human figures; the orator,

4. The highest social caste in Hindu culture, from which all priests are drawn.
5. The home of the Delphic oracle, or prophetess, in Greece. Troy is the site of the Trojan War in Asia Minor.
6. The common correction for the 1st edition's "boats." "Logrolling" seems to be used in the metaphorical sense of exchanging political favors. "Stumps" refers to the practice political orators had of addressing audiences from any makeshift platform, even a tree stump.
7. A popular collection of poetry compiled by Alexander Chalmers (1759–1834), Scottish journalist and biographer.

into the assembly of the people; and the others, in such scenes as each has found exciting to his intellect; and each presently feels the new desire. He hears a voice, he sees a beckoning. Then he is apprised, with wonder, what herds of dæmons hem him in. He can no more rest; he says, with the old painter, "By God, it is in me, and must go forth of me." He pursues a beauty, half seen, which flies before him. The poet pours out verses in every solitude. Most of the things he says are conventional, no doubt; but by and by he says something which is original and beautiful. That charms him. He would say nothing else but such things. In our way of talking, we say, "That is yours, this is mine;" but the poet knows well that it is not his; that it is as strange and beautiful to him as to you; he would fain hear the like eloquence at length. Once having tasted this immortal ichor,[8] he cannot have enough of it, and, as an admirable creative power exists in these intellections, it is of the last importance that these things get spoken. What a little of all we know is said! What drops of all the sea of our science are bailed up! and by what accident it is that these are exposed, when so many secrets sleep in nature! Hence the necessity of speech and song; hence these throbs and heart-beatings in the orator, at the door of the assembly, to the end, namely, that thought may be ejaculated as Logos, or Word.

Doubt not, O Poet, but persist. Say, "It is in me, and shall out." Stand there, baulked and dumb, stuttering and stammering, hissed and hooted, stand and strive, until, at last, rage draw out of thee that *dream*-power which every night shows thee is thine own; a power transcending all limit and privacy, and by virtue of which a man is the conductor of the whole river of electricity. Nothing walks, or creeps, or grows, or exists, which must not in turn arise and walk before him as exponent of his meaning. Comes he to that power, his genius is no longer exhaustible. All the creatures, by pairs and by tribes, pour into his mind as into a Noah's ark, to come forth again to people a new world. This is like the stock of air for our respiration, or for the combustion of our fireplace, not a measure of gallons, but the entire atmosphere if wanted. And therefore the rich poets, as Homer, Chaucer, Shakspeare, and Raphael,[9] have obviously no limits to their works, except the limits of their lifetime, and resemble a mirror carried through the street, ready to render an image of every created thing.

O poet! a new nobility is conferred in groves and pastures, and not in castles, or by the sword-blade, any longer. The conditions are hard, but equal. Thou shalt leave the world, and know the muse only. Thou shalt not know any longer the times, customs, graces, politics, or opinions of men, but shalt take all from the muse. For the time of towns is tolled from the world by funereal chimes, but in nature the universal hours are counted by succeeding tribes of animals and plants, and by growth of joy on joy. God wills also that thou abdicate a manifold and duplex life, and that thou be content that others speak for thee. Others shall be thy gentlemen, and shall represent all courtesy and worldly life for thee; others shall do the great and resounding actions also. Thou shalt lie close hid with nature, and canst not be afforded to the Capitol or the Exchange.[1] The world is full of renunciations and apprenticeships, and this is thine: thou must pass for a fool and a churl for a

8. In Greek myth, blood of the gods, but Emerson may mean nectar, the drink of the gods.
9. Raphael Sanzio (1483–1520), renowned painter of the Italian Renaissance.
1. Stock exchange.

long season. This is the screen and sheath in which Pan[2] has protected his well-beloved flower, and thou shalt be known only to thine own, and they shall console thee with tenderest love. And thou shalt not be able to rehearse the names of thy friends in thy verse, for an old shame before the holy ideal. And this is the reward: that the ideal shall be real to thee; and the impressions of the actual world shall fall like summer rain, copious, but not troublesome, to thy invulnerable essence. Thou shalt have the whole land for thy park and manor, the sea for thy bath and navigation, without tax and without envy; the woods and the rivers thou shalt own; and thou shalt possess that wherein others are only tenants and boarders. Thou true land-lord! sea-lord! air-lord! Wherever snow falls, or water flows, or birds fly, wherever day and night meet in twilight, wherever the blue heaven is hung by clouds, or sown with stars, wherever are forms with transparent boundaries, wherever are outlets into celestial space, wherever is danger, and awe, and love, there is Beauty, plenteous as rain, shed for thee, and though thou shouldest walk the world over, thou shalt not be able to find a condition inopportune or ignoble.

1844

Each and All[1]

Little thinks, in the field, yon red-cloaked clown[2]
Of thee from the hill-top looking down;
The heifer that lows in the upland farm,
Far-heard, lows not thine ear to charm;
The sexton, tolling his bell at noon   5
Deems not that great Napoleon
Stops his horse, and lists with delight,
Whilst his files sweep round yon Alpine height;
Nor knowest thou what argument
Thy life to thy neighbor's creed has lent.   10
All are needed by each one;
Nothing is fair or good alone.
I thought the sparrow's note from heaven,
Singing at dawn on the alder bough;
I brought him home, in his nest at even;[3]   15
He sings the song, but it cheers not now,
For I did not bring home the river and sky;—
He sang to my ear,—they sang to my eye,
The delicate shells lay on the shore;
The bubbles of the latest wave   20
Fresh pearls to their enamel gave;
And the bellowing of the savage sea
Greeted their safe escape to me.
I wiped away the weeds and foam,

---

2. In Greek myth, the god of woods and fields, represented with goat's legs, horns, and ears.
1. First published in *Western Messenger* (February 1839) as "Each in All." The text is from Emerson's *Poems* (1847).
2. Rustic.
3. Evening.

I fetched my sea-born treasures home;   25
But the poor, unsightly, noisome[4] things
Had left their beauty on the shore;
With the sun, and the sand, and the wild uproar.
The lover watched his graceful maid,
As 'mid the virgin train she strayed,   30
Nor knew her beauty's best attire
Was woven still by the snow-white choir.
At last she came to his hermitage,
Like the bird from the woodlands to the cage;—
The gay enchantment was undone,   35
A gentle wife, but fairy none.
Then I said, 'I covet truth;
Beauty is unripe childhood's cheat;
I leave it behind with the games of youth.'—
As I spoke, beneath my feet   40
The ground-pine curled its pretty wreath,
Running over the club-moss burrs;
I inhaled the violet's breath;
Around me stood the oaks and firs;
Pine-cones and acorns lay on the ground;   45
Over me soared the eternal sky,
Full of light and of deity;
Again I saw, again I heard,
The rolling river, the morning bird;—
Beauty through my senses stole;   50
I yielded myself to the perfect whole.

                                                        1839, 1847

Brahma[1]

If the red slayer think he slays,
    Or if the slain think he is slain,
They know not well the subtle ways
    I keep, and pass, and turn again.

Far or forgot to me is near;   5
    Shadow and sunlight are the same;
The vanished gods to me appear;
    And one to me are shame and fame.

They reckon ill who leave me out;
    When me they fly, I am the wings;   10
I am the doubter and the doubt,
    And I the hymn the Brahmin[2] sings.

---

4. Having an offensive smell.
1. The text is from the November 1857 *Atlantic Monthly*. "Brahma": the creator god of sacred Hindu texts.

2. Members of the highest Hindu caste; originally the priests responsible for officiating at religious rites.

The strong gods pine for my abode,
   And pine in vain the sacred Seven;[3]
But thou, meek lover of the good!   15
   Find me, and turn thy back on heaven.

1857

---

3. Seers or saints of ancient Hindu poetry.

Native Americans:
Removal and Resistance

Just as the great majority of Native American peoples had fought on the side of the British during the Revolutionary War, so too did many Native peoples take the British side in the War of 1812. The reason, at base, was straightforward: Native Americans risked losing much more of their land and their autonomy at the hands of the colonials (1776), later the Americans (1812), than they did at the hands of the British. When the treaty of Ghent ending the war with Britain was signed in 1814, the United States could at last feel no longer threatened by any European nation; but the American threat to Native nations was substantially increased.

If President James Monroe invited Indian people to the White House in 1822, things were to be different under his successor, Andrew Jackson. Jackson, who had fought against the Seminoles and Creeks in Florida, was elected president in 1828. "Indian removal"—the relocation of the southeastern tribes to lands west of the Mississippi—was an important part of his agenda. The Cherokees of Georgia were a major target for removal. By the time of Jackson's election, the Cherokees had a written language, a constitution modeled after that of the United States, and the first newspaper, the Cherokee *Phoenix*, to publish both in an indigenous language and in English. Although the Cherokees, in "memorials" to Congress and in editorials and articles in their newspaper, spoke out strongly against Jackson's removal policy, Congress nonetheless passed the Indian Removal Act in 1830, granting the president the authority to enter into treaties with the eastern tribes for their removal west of the Mississippi River. Finally, in 1838—in spite of frantic protest by many, including Ralph Waldo Emerson—the Cherokees were indeed forcibly removed by federal troops under General Winfield Scott. They were sent on what would be called the Trail of Tears to "Indian Country," present-day Oklahoma, a march in winter during which some four thousand people died, out of a population of about thirteen thousand.

Between the passage of the Removal Act and the Trail of Tears came the removal under different auspices of Black Hawk's Sauk people, the consequence of the so-called Black Hawk War of 1832, the last Indian war fought (for the most part) east of the Mississippi. Black Hawk's account of some of these matters, documenting removal and resistance, is included here.

BLACK HAWK

A member of the Sauk nation, Black Hawk (1767?–1838) was born at Saukenuk on the Rock River in western Illinois. The town was destroyed by American militiamen during the Revolutionary War, and this act may well have initiated Black Hawk's lifelong distrust of and distaste for the Americans. In 1804, when the United States took control of the Louisiana Purchase from France, the Sauk chief Quashquame and some few others were persuaded to sign a treaty at St. Louis ceding Sauk lands east of the Mississippi to the federal government. The signers of the treaty believed that they would be permitted to remain on their lands forever in spite of the sale. They did not understand that the document they had signed permitted them to remain only until the government sold or otherwise disposed of those lands. In 1816 Black Hawk and other Sauk chiefs signed another treaty, this one confirming the provisions of the 1804 treaty, but again, as Black Hawk insists, they had no clear idea of what was involved.

By the 1820s, settlers had begun to press into Sauk territory on the Rock River, and by 1829, submitting to the pressures put on them by the advancing Americans, many Sauk agreed to remove west of the Mississippi. The few who remained were forced west by U.S. troops under the command of General Edmund Gaines. Nonetheless, in 1832 Black Hawk led a party back to the Rock River, surely knowing that American opposition would ensue, yet determined to reestablish his people on their traditional homelands. His hopes in this endeavor were strengthened by a half-Sauk, half-Winnebago man named Wabokieshiek or White Cloud, known as the Winnebago Prophet, who had told Black Hawk that the return would be supported by Pottawatomi allies as well as by some English from Canada. This was not at all the case.

Governor John Reynolds of Illinois proclaimed Black Hawk's return "an invasion of the state" and called up five brigades of volunteers (the young Abraham Lincoln was among them) to join General Gaines, who had orders to force Black Hawk and his people back across the Mississippi. The federal and Illinois troops pursued Black Hawk and his people from the end of June until August 1832. They caught up with them as they were attempting a retreat to the western shore of the Mississippi. The Steamboat *Warrior*, chartered by the U.S. Army, fired on Black Hawk's party as they attempted to cross the river, continuing to fire even as Black Hawk himself waved a white flag of surrender. Finally, on August 2, at Bad Axe, a junction of the Mississippi and the Bad Axe River in what is today Wisconsin, the remaining Sauk were attacked in a battle that turned into a massacre, with some three hundred of Black Hawk's band—many of them women and children—killed, and hundreds taken prisoner. Eight American soldiers died.

Black Hawk was imprisoned and taken east, where he twice met President Jackson. Returned, finally, to his people, he participated in the production of the *Life of Ma-ka-tai-me-she-kia-kiak, or Black Hawk . . . with an account of the cause and general history of the late war . . . dictated by himself*, a narrative of his life published in Cincinnati in 1833. It is not clear whether Black Hawk himself initiated the project—if he did, it was probably at the urging of many who had spoken with him in the East—or whether the initiator was John Barton Patterson, a young and ambitious local newspaper editor. Also involved in the making of Black Hawk's autobiography was Antoine LeClaire, part Pottawatomi, part French, who served as Black Hawk's interpreter. Upon the autobiography's publication, there was a predictable questioning of its authenticity. Roger Nichols's work convincingly makes the case that Black Hawk did indeed narrate the greater part of what we have, even managing, despite the cumbersome division of labor, to produce what Neil Schmitz has called "a Sauk history advocating a Sauk politics."

The selection printed here, from the 1833 text, published in Donald Jackson's edition, *Black Hawk: An Autobiography* (1964), presents Black Hawk's strong sense of himself, his ties to his people, and his broad critique of the Americans.

From Life of Ma-ka-tai-me-she-kia-kiak, or Black Hawk

* * *

The great chief[1] at St. Louis having sent word for us to go down and confirm the treaty of peace, we did not hesitate, but started immediately, that

1. William Clark [Jackson's note].

we might smoke the *peace-pipe* with him. On our arrival, we met the great chiefs in council. They explained to us the words of our Great Father at Washington, accusing us of heinous crimes and divers misdemeanors, particularly in not coming down when first invited. We knew very well that our *Great Father had deceived us*, and thereby *forced* us to join the British, and could not believe that he had put this speech into the mouths of these chiefs to deliver to us. I was not a civil chief, and consequently made no reply: but our chiefs told the commissioners that "what they had said was a *lie!*—that our Great Father had sent no such speech, he knowing the situation in which we had been placed had been *caused by him!*" The white chiefs appeared very angry at this reply, and said they "would break off the treaty with us, and *go to war*, as they would not be insulted."

Our chiefs had no intention of insulting them, and told them so—"that they merely wished to explain to them that *they had told a lie*, without making them angry; in the same manner that the whites do, when they do not believe what is told them!" The council then proceeded, and the pipe of peace was smoked.

Here, for the first time, I touched the goose quill to the treaty—not knowing, however, that, by that act, I consented to give away my village. Had that been explained to me, I should have opposed it, and never would have signed their treaty, as my recent conduct will clearly prove.[2]

What do we know of the manner of the laws and customs of the white people? They might buy our bodies for dissection, and we would touch the goose quill to confirm it, without knowing what we are doing. This was the case with myself and people in touching the goose quill the first time.

* * *

I returned to my hunting ground, after an absence of one moon. * * * In a short time we came up to our village, and found that the whites had not left it—but that others had come, and that the greater part of our corn-fields had been enclosed. When we landed, the whites appeared displeased because we had come back. We repaired the lodges that had been left standing, and built others. Ke-o-kuck came to the village; but his object was to persuade others to follow him to the Ioway. He had accomplished nothing towards making arrangements for us to remain, or to exchange other lands for our village. There was no more friendship existing between us. I looked upon him as a coward, and no brave, to abandon his village to be occupied by strangers. What *right* had these people to our village, and our fields, which the Great Spirit had given us to live upon?

My reason teaches me that *land cannot be sold*. The Great Spirit gave it to his children to live upon, and cultivate, as far as is necessary for their subsistence; and so long as they occupy and cultivate it, they have the right to the soil—but if they voluntarily leave it, then any other people have a right to settle upon it. Nothing can be sold, but such things as can be carried away.

In consequence of the improvements of the intruders on our fields, we found considerable difficulty to get ground to plant a little corn. Some of the whites permitted us to plant small patches in the fields they had fenced, keeping all the best ground for themselves. Our women had great difficulty

2. This was the treaty of May 13, 1816, in which the Sauk of the Rock River unconditionally assented to and confirmed the treaty of 1804—as the Missouri Sauk and the Fox had done the year before. And once more there was misunderstanding, as shown by Black Hawk's account [Jackson's note].

in climbing their fences, (being unaccustomed to the kind,) and were ill-treated if they left a rail down.

One of my old friends thought he was safe. His corn-field was on a small island of Rock river. He planted his corn; it came up well—but the white man saw it!—he wanted the island, and took his team over, ploughed up the corn, and re-planted it for himself! The old man shed tears; not for himself, but the distress his family would be in if they raised no corn.

The white people brought whisky into our village, made our people drunk, and cheated them out of their horses, guns, and traps! This fraudulent system was carried to such an extent that I apprehended serious difficulties might take place, unless a stop was put to it. Consequently, I visited all the whites and begged them not to sell whisky to my people. One of them continued the practice openly. I took a party of my young men, went to his house, and took out his barrel and broke in the head and turned out the whisky. I did this for fear some of the whites might be killed by my people when drunk.

Our people were treated badly by the whites on many occasions. At one time, a white man beat one of our women cruelly, for pulling a few suckers of corn out of his field, to suck, when hungry! At another time, one of our young men was beat with clubs by two white men for opening a fence which crossed our road, to take his horse through. His shoulder blade was broken, and his body badly bruised, from which he soon after *died!*

Bad, and cruel, as our people were treated by the whites, not one of them was hurt or molested by any of my band. I hope this will prove that we are a peaceable people—having permitted ten men to take possession of our corn-fields; prevent us from planting corn; burn and destroy our lodges; ill-treat our women; and *beat to death* our men, without offering resistance to their barbarous cruelties. This is a lesson worthy for the white man to learn: to use forbearance when injured.

We acquainted our agent daily with our situation, and through him, the great chief at St. Louis—and hoped that something would be done for us. The whites were *complaining* at the same time that *we* were *intruding* upon *their rights!* THEY made themselves out the *injured* party, and *we* the *intruders!* and called loudly to the great war chief to protect *their* property!

How smooth must be the language of the whites, when they can make right look like wrong, and wrong like right.

During this summer, I happened at Rock Island, when a great chief arrived, (whom I had known as the great chief of Illinois, [governor Cole,] in company with another chief, who, I have been told, is a great writer, [judge Jas. Hall.] I called upon them and begged to explain to them the grievances under which me and my people were laboring, hoping that they could do something for us. The great chief, however, did not seem disposed to council with me. He said he was no longer the great chief of Illinois—that his children had selected another father in his stead, and that he now only ranked as they did. I was surprised at this talk, as I had always heard that he was a good, brave, and great chief. But the white people never appear to be satisfied. When they get a good father, they hold councils, (at the suggestion of some bad, ambitious man, who wants the place himself,) and conclude, among themselves, that this man, or some other equally ambitious, would make a better father than they have, and nine times out of ten they don't get as good a one again.

I insisted on explaining to these two chiefs the true situation of my people. They gave their assent: I rose and made a speech, in which I explained to them the treaty made by Quàsh-quà-me, and three of our braves, according to the manner the trader and others had explained it to me. I then told them that Quàsh-quà-me and his party *denied*, positively, having ever sold my village; and that, as I had never known them to *lie*, I was determined to keep it in possession.

I told them that the white people had already entered our village, *burnt our lodges, destroyed our fences, ploughed up our corn, and beat our people*: that they had brought *whisky* into our country, *made our people drunk*, and taken from them their *horses, guns*, and *traps*; and that I had borne all this injury, without suffering any of my braves to raise a hand against the whites.

My object in holding this council, was to get the opinion of these two chiefs, as to the best course for me to pursue. I had appealed in vain, time after time, to our agent, who regularly represented our situation to the great chief at St. Louis, whose duty it was to call upon our Great Father to have justice done to us; but instead of this, we are told *that the white people want our country, and we must leave it to them!*

I did not think it possible that our Great Father wished us to leave our village, where we had lived so long, and where the bones of so many of our people had been laid. The great chief said that, as he was no longer a chief, he could do nothing for us; and felt sorry that it was not in his power to aid us—nor did he know how to advise us. Neither of them could do any thing for us; but both evidently appeared very sorry. It would give me great pleasure, at all times, to take these two chiefs by the hand.

That fall I paid a visit to the agent, before we started to our hunting grounds, to hear if he had any good news for me. He had news! He said that the land on which our village stood was now ordered to be sold to individuals; and that, when sold, *our right* to remain, by treaty, would be at an end, and that if we returned next spring, we would be *forced* to remove!

1833

PETALESHARO

Petalesharo (1797?–1874)—the name means "generous chief" or "man chief"—was a Skidi (also called Loup) Pawnee, one of four bands of the Pawnee nation, which occupied lands in the old Missouri Territory. From October 1821 until March 1822, he was one of several Native people brought to Washington for an extended visit. During that time, the *National Daily Intelligencer* published an article called "Anecdote of a Pawnee Chief," which told of Petalesharo's successful efforts, in 1817 and 1820, to prevent young women captured from other tribes from being sacrificed in the Morning Star Ceremony. (The Skidi Pawnees were one of the very few tribes north of what is now the Mexican border to practice human sacrifice.) This account made him a most sought-after person. Petalesharo was one of the first Native people to be painted by Charles Bird King for the McKenney-Hall Indian Gallery (the paintings were reproduced in the gallery's *History of the Indian Tribes of North America* published in 1838–44); he was also painted by Samuel F.B. Morse, better known for his invention of Morse Code.

The speeches printed here were delivered on February 4, 1822, at a conference attended by President James Monroe. They were first published by James Buchanan,

British consul for the state of New York, in his *Sketches of the North American Indians* (1824). The first, which is identified as having been delivered by "The Pawnee Chief," is the speech usually referred to as "Petalesharo's Speech." But it is followed in Buchanan by a speech assigned to a "Pawnee Loup Chief," a more likely designation for Petalesharo. Although the date and the occasion for both of these are certain, it is not clear who translated and transcribed the speeches—and, it should be stressed, we do not know whether "Petalesharo's speech" was in fact delivered by him or by an unnamed "Pawnee Chief." The speaker, whoever he may be, like Red Jacket (and others) before him, offers a "separatist" view of religion and culture, asserting that while the Great Father of the whites may be fine for them, "there is still *another* Great Father . . . *the Father of us all*," and it is to him that Native peoples continue to adhere. The second speech combines what is probably intended simply as good advice for the whites with a warrior's brief statement of his prowess.

The text is from Buchanan's *Sketches of the North American Indians* (1824).

Speech of the Pawnee Chief

My Great Father:—I have travelled a great distance to see you—I have seen you and my heart rejoices. I have heard your words—they have entered one ear and shall not escape the other, and I will carry them to my people as pure as they came from your mouth.

My Great Father:—I am going to speak the truth. The Great Spirit looks down upon us, and I call *Him* to witness all that may pass between us on this occasion. If I am here now and have seen your people, your houses, your vessels on the big lake, and a great many wonderful things far beyond my comprehension, which appear to have been made by the Great Spirit and placed in your hands, I am indebted to my Father here, who invited me from home, under whose wings I have been protected.[1] Yes, my Great Father, I have travelled with your chief; I have followed him, and trod in his tracks; but there is still *another* Great Father *to whom I am much indebted—it is the Father of us all.* Him who made us and placed us on this earth. I feel grateful to the Great Spirit for strengthening my heart for such an undertaking, and for preserving the life which he gave me. The Great Spirit made us all—he made my skin red, and yours white; he placed us on this earth, and intended that we should live differently from each other.

He made the whites to cultivate the earth, and feed on domestic animals; but he made us, red skins, to rove through the uncultivated woods and plains; to feed on wild animals; and to dress with their skins. He also intended that we should go to war—to take scalps—*steal horses from* and triumph over our enemies—cultivate peace at home, and promote the happiness of each other. I believe there are no people of any colour on this earth who do not believe in the Great Spirit—in rewards, and in punishments. We worship him, but we worship him not as you do. We differ from you in appearance and manners as well as in our customs; and we differ from you in our religion; we have no large houses as you have to worship the Great Spirit in; if we had them to-day, we should want others to-morrow, for we have not, like you, a fixed habitation—we have no settled home except our villages, where we remain but two moons in twelve. We, like animals, rove through the country, whilst you whites reside between us and heaven but still, my Great Father,

1. Pointing to Major O'Fallon [Buchanan's note].

we love the Great Spirit—we acknowledge his supreme power—our peace, our health, and our happiness depend upon him, and our lives belong to him—he made us and he can destroy us.

My Great Father:—Some of your good chiefs, as they are called (missionaries,) have proposed to send some of their good people among us to change our habits, to make us work and live like the white people. I will not tell a lie—I am going to tell the truth. You love your country—you love your people—you love the manner in which they live, and you think your people brave.—I am like you, my Great Father, I love my country—I love my people—I love the manner in which we live, and think myself and warriors brave. Spare me then, my Father; let me enjoy my country, and pursue the buffalo, and the beaver, and the other wild animals of our country, and I will trade their skins with your people. I have grown up, and lived thus long without work—I am in hopes you will suffer me to die without it. We have plenty of buffalo, beaver, deer and other wild animals—we have also an abundance of horses—we have every thing we want—we have plenty of land, if you will keep your people off of it. My father has a piece on which he lives (Council Bluffs) and we wish him to enjoy it—we have enough without it—but we wish him to live near us to give us good counsel—to keep our ears and eyes open that we may continue to pursue the right road—the road to happiness. He settles all differences between us and the whites, between the red skins themselves—he makes the whites do justice to the red skins, and he makes the red skins do justice to the whites. He saves the effusion of human blood, and restores peace and happiness on the land. You have already sent us a father; it is enough he knows us and we know him—we have confidence in him—we keep our eye constantly upon him, and since we have heard your words, we will listen more attentively to *his*.

It is too soon, my Great Father, to send those good men among us. *We are not starving yet*—we wish you to permit us to enjoy the chase until the game of our country is exhausted—until the wild animals become extinct. Let us exhaust our present resources before you make us toil and interrupt our happiness—let me continue to live as I have done, and after I have passed to the Good or Evil Spirit from off the wilderness of my present life, the subsistence of my children may become so precarious as to need and embrace the assistance of those good people.

There was a time when we did not know the whites—our wants were then fewer than they are now. They were always within our controul—we had then seen nothing which we could not get. Before our intercourse with the *whites* (who have caused such a destruction in our game,) we could lie down to sleep, and when we awoke we would find the buffalo feeding around our camp—but now we are killing them for their skins, and feeding the wolves with their flesh, to make our children cry over their bones.

Here, My Great Father, is a pipe which I present you, as I am accustomed to present pipes to all the red skins in peace with us. It is filled with such tobacco as we were accustomed to smoke before we knew the white people. It is pleasant, and the spontaneous growth of the most remote parts of our country. I know that the robes, leggins, mockasins, bear-claws, &c., are of little value to you, but we wish you to have them deposited and preserved in some conspicuous part of your lodge, so that when we are gone and the sod turned over our bones, if our children should visit this place, as we do now, they may see and recognize with pleasure the deposites of their fathers; and reflect on the times that are past.

Speech of the Pawnee Loup Chief

My Great Father:—Whenever I see a white man amongst us without a protector, I tremble for him. I am aware of the ungovernable disposition of some of our young men, and when I see an inexperienced white man, I am always afraid they will make me cry. I now begin to love your people, and, as I love my own people too, I am unwilling that any blood should be spilt between us. You are unacquainted with our fashions, and we are unacquainted with yours; and when any of your people come among us, I am always afraid that they will be struck on the head like dogs, as we should be here amongst you, but for our father in whose tracks we tread. When your people come among us, they should come as we come among you, with some one to protect them, whom we know and who knows us. Until this chief came amongst us, three winters since, we roved through the plains only thirsting for each other's blood—we were blind—we could not see the right road, and we hunted to destroy each other. We were always feeling for obstacles, and every thing we felt we thought one. Our warriors were always going to and coming from war. I myself have killed and scalped in every direction. I have often triumphed over my enemies.

ELIAS BOUDINOT

Elias Boudinot (1804?–1839) was born at Oothcaloga, a Cherokee "progressive" town, in northwestern Georgia. His birth name was Gallegina, and he was also called Buck Watie. His father, Oo'watie, or David Watie, sent him at the age of six to a nearby Moravian Mission School, where he continued until he was seventeen, at which time he set out north for another mission school, this one in Cornwall, Connecticut. It was on this trip that Buck Watie met the elderly Elias Boudinot, who had been a member of the Continental Congress and was at the time president of the American Bible Society. Consistent with an old Cherokee practice of changing names and with a newer Cherokee practice of adopting the names of prominent whites, Buck Watie became Elias Boudinot.

Although his family was staunchly progressive—his uncle was Major Ridge, whose picture says a good deal about him (see the color insert to this volume), and his younger brother, Stand Watie, joined white southerners to become the last Confederate general to surrender to the North in the Civil War (that both Buck and Stand took their father's surname indicates a movement away from traditional Cherokee matrilineal practice)—Boudinot opposed removal until some time in 1832. In what is probably his best-known work, "An Address to the Whites," delivered in Philadelphia in 1826, Boudinot makes the same case that the "Memorial" of the Cherokee Council would make to Congress opposing removal: he insists that not only are his people able to attain Christianity and "civilization" but that they are well on the way to those attainments. About two years after the passage of the Indian Removal Act in 1830 and, in particular, once Georgia had instituted a lottery to dispose of Cherokee lands to white citizens of the state, Boudinot concluded that further resistance to removal was hopeless.

In 1835, he, his uncle Major Ridge, and a small number of wealthy Cherokee planters met at New Echota, where, on December 29, they signed the Treaty of New Echota, agreeing to exchange Cherokee lands in the southeast for land in Indian

Country, present-day Oklahoma. Boudinot and his family went west before the Trail of Tears and so were already established when the last of the Cherokee people to survive the forced march arrived in Indian Country in early spring 1839. In June of that year, several Cherokees came to Boudinot to ask for medicine. Two followed him as he led them to the mission dispensary and then attacked him with a knife and a tomahawk, leaving him to die. That same day, his relatives Major Ridge and John Ridge were also killed for their part in signing the treaty. The murderers very likely acted in accord with a traditional practice of vengeance, taking lives in recompense for the lives of those who had died on the trail, and also in accord with a law passed by the Cherokee Council in 1829 making it a capital crime to cede Cherokee lands.

The selection printed here is from the first issue of the *Cherokee Phoenix*, dated February 21, 1828, as it appears in *Cherokee Editor: The Writings of Elias Boudinot* (1996), edited by Theda Purdue. Boudinot edited the paper until 1832, when the Cherokee Council asked him to withdraw because of his support for removal. The *Phoenix* was the first American newspaper to print an Indian language (in the syllabary Sequoyah had invented in 1821); it also printed articles in English. Boudinot alerts his readers, white and Indian, to the fact that "the design of this paper . . . is [for] the benefit of the Cherokees."

From the Cherokee Phoenix

To the Public

FEBRUARY 21, 1828

We are happy in being able, at length, to issue the first number of our paper, although after a longer delay than we anticipated. This delay has been owing to unavoidable circumstances, which, we think, will be sufficient to acquit us, and though our readers and patrons may be wearied in the expectation of gratifying their eyes on this paper of no ordinary novelty, yet we hope their patience will not be so exhausted, but that they will give it a calm perusal and pass upon it a candid judgment. It is far from our expectation that it will meet with entire and universal approbation, particularly from those who consider learning and science necessary to the merits of newspapers. Such must not expect to be gratified here, for the merits, (if merits they can be called,) on which our paper is expected to exist, are not alike with those which keep alive the political and religious papers of the day. We lay no claim to extensive information; and we sincerely hope, this public disclosure will save us from the severe criticisms, to which our ignorance of many things, will frequently expose us, in the future of our editorial labors.— Let the public but consider our motives, and the design of this paper, which is, the benefit of the Cherokees, and we are sure, those who wish well to the Indian race, will keep out of view all failings and deficiencies of the Editor, and give a prompt support to the first paper ever published in an Indian country, and under the direction of some remnants of those, who by the most mysterious course of providence, have dwindled into oblivion. To prevent us from the like destiny, is certainly a laudable undertaking, which the Christian, the Patriot, and the Philanthropist will not be ashamed to aid. Many are now engaged, by various means and with various success, in attempting to rescue, not only us, but all our kindred tribes, from the impending danger which has been so fatal to our forefathers; and we are happy to be in a situation to tender them our public acknowledgments for their unwearied efforts. Our present undertaking is intended to be nothing more than a feeble auxiliary to these efforts.

The masthead of the **Cherokee Phoenix**, the first newspaper in both a Native language and English, illustrates the complex cultural and political situation of the Cherokee Nation at the time. The two words on either side of the phoenix are in the Cherokee syllabary invented by Sequoyah (George Guess). They are pronounced roughly *Tsa-la-gi Tsi-le-hi-sa-ni*. The first word means "Cherokee"—as in the English below it—but the second word—unlike the English below it—does not mean "Phoenix" (there is no word in Cherokee for the Phoenix, but, rather, "I was down and I have risen" or "I will rise again" (the latter invokes both the Phoenix *and* Christ). In putting the word PROTECTION between the bird's wings, the Cherokees mean to remind the federal government of its responsibility to protect them from the threats of the state of Georgia.

Those therefore, who are engaged for the good of the Indians of every tribe, and who pray that salvation, peace, and the comforts of civilized life may be extended to every Indian fire side on this continent, will consider us as co-workers together in their benevolent labors. To them we make our appeal for patronage, and pledge ourselves to encourage and assist them, in whatever appears to be for the benefit of the Aborigines.

In the commencement of our labours, it is due to our readers that we should acquaint them with the general principles, which we have prescribed to ourselves as rules in conducting this paper. These principles we shall accordingly state briefly. It may, however, be proper to observe that the establishment which has been lately purchased, principally with the charities of our white brethren, is the property of the Nation, and that the paper, which is now offered to the public, is patronized by, and under the direction of, the Cherokee Legislature, as will be seen in the Prospectus already before the public. As servants, we are bound to that body, from which, however, we have not received any instructions, but are left at liberty to form such regulations for our conduct as will appear to us most conducive to the interests of the people, for whose benefit, this paper has been established.

As the Phoenix is a national newspaper, we shall feel ourselves bound to devote it to national purposes. "The laws and public documents of the Nation," and matters relating to the welfare and condition of the Cherokees as a people, will be faithfully published in English and Cherokee.

As the liberty of the press is so essential to the improvement of the mind, we shall consider our paper, a *free paper*, with, however, proper and usual restrictions. We shall reserve to ourselves the liberty of rejecting such communications as tend to evil, and such as are too intemperate and too personal. But the columns of this paper shall always be open to free and temperate discussions on matters of politics, religion, &c.

We shall avoid as much as possible, controversy on disputed doctrinal points in religion. Though we have our particular belief on this important subject, and perhaps are as strenuous upon it, as some of our brethren of a different faith, yet we conscientiously think, & in this thought we are supported by men of judgment that it would be injudicious, perhaps highly pernicious, to introduce to this people, the various minor differences of Christians. Our object is not sectarian, and if we had a wish to support, in our paper, the denomination with which we have the honor and privilege of being connected, yet we know our incompetency for the task.

We will not unnecessarily intermeddle with the politics and affairs of our neighbors. As we have no particular interest in the concerns of the surrounding states, we shall only expose ourselves to contempt and ridicule by improper intrusion. And though at times, we should do ourselves injustice, to be silent, on matters of great interest to the Cherokees, yet we will not return railing for railing, but consult mildness, for we have been taught to believe, that "A soft answer turneth away wrath; but grievous words stir up anger." The unpleasant controversy existing with the state of Georgia, of which, many of our readers are aware, will frequently make our situation trying, by having hard sayings and threatenings thrown out against us, a specimen of which will be found in our next. We pray God that we may be delivered from such spirit.

In regard to the controversy with Georgia, and the present policy of the General Government, in removing, and concentrating the Indians, out of the limits of any state, which, by the way, appears to be gaining strength, we will invariably and faithfully state the feelings of the majority of our people. Our views, as a people, on this subject, have been sadly misrepresented. These views we do not wish to conceal, but are willing that the public should know what we think of this policy, which, in our opinion, if carried into effect, will prove pernicious to us.

* * *

In fine, we shall pay a sacred regard to truth, and avoid, as much as possible, that partiality to which we shall be exposed. In relating facts of a local nature, whether political, moral, or religious, we shall take care that exaggeration shall not be our crime. We shall also feel ourselves bound to correct all mistatements, relating to the present condition of the Cherokees.

How far we shall be successful in advancing the improvement of our people, is not now for us to decide. We hope, however, our efforts will not be altogether in vain.—Now is the moment when mere speculation on the practicability of civilizing us is out of the question. Sufficient and repeated evidence has been given, that Indians can be reclaimed from a savage state, and that with proper advantages, they are as capable of improvement in mind as any other people; and let it be remembered, notwithstanding the assertions of those who talk to the contrary, that this improvement can be made, not only by the Cherokees, but by all the Indians, *in their present locations*. We are rendered bold in making this assertion, by considering the history of our people within the last fifteen years. There was a time within our remembrance, when darkness was sadly prevalent, and ignorance abounded amongst us—when strong and deep rooted prejudices were directed against many things relating to civilized life—and when it was thought a disgrace, for a

Cherokee to appear in the costume of a white man. We mention these things not by way of boasting, but to shew our readers that it is not a visionary thing to attempt to civilize and christianize all the Indians, but highly practicable.

* * *

We would now commit our feeble efforts to the good will and indulgence of the public, praying that God will attend them with his blessings, and hoping for that happy period, when all the Indian tribes of America shall arise, Phoenix like, from their ashes, and when the terms, "Indian depredation," "war-whoop," "scalping knife" and the like, shall become obsolete, and for ever be "buried deep under ground."

THE CHEROKEE MEMORIALS

I n 1828, Andrew Jackson, largely on his reputation as an Indian fighter, was elected president of the United States. In 1829, gold was discovered in Dahlonega on the western boundary of the Cherokee Nation in the state of Georgia. Georgia had for some time wished to rid itself of its Indian population, and the time seemed right to press the issue. Bills for the removal of the eastern Indians were introduced in both houses of Congress early in 1830; debate on the Removal Bill had begun in the House on February 24.

Anticipating these developments, the Cherokee Council had prepared a "memorial"—essentially a petition to Congress—as early as November 1829, which was received by the House in February of the following year, shortly before the official debate began. The memorial was probably authored for the most part by the clerk of the council, John Ridge, who had not yet broken with the "traditionalist" Cherokees, led by the principal chief John Ross, who were firmly opposed to removal. The memorial begins with what must be an intentional, although unstated reference to the Declaration of Independence. Whereas the Declaration made known to the world the "long rain of abuses and usurpations" for which the British king George III was responsible, the Cherokee memorial establishes the wrongs done by his namesake state, Georgia, petitioning the Congress of the United States—the same body that had adopted the Declaration—for redress of grievances. Although the American colonists had had to *declare* their independence, the Cherokees instead *affirm* theirs. As they demonstrate, they have always been treated by the American colonials and the United States as a sovereign nation.

Acknowledging that Georgia and the president have the power to force them to unfamiliar land west of the Mississippi, the Cherokee Council insists that the use of such power would lead to an unjust and unhappy fate for the Cherokee Nation. In the florid language of the period, the council offers its vision of Cherokee advancement "in civilized life . . . science and Christian knowledge," on the lands they have for long occupied.

This vision did not prevail. Basing his authority on the Treaty of New Echota—signed in 1835 by a minority of Cherokees—Jackson ordered the Cherokees to remove by the spring of 1838. Some moved west before that date. But the vast majority of the eastern Cherokee Nation refused to leave their homes. Thus it was that federal troops under the command of General Winfield Scott came to enforce the treaty. In the fall and winter of 1838–39, some thirteen thousand Cherokees were driven westward on what has come to be known as the Trail of Tears. Roughly one-third of them, about four thousand people, died en route. The survivors reached Indian Country, in what would eventually become Oklahoma, in the early spring of 1839.

Memorial of the Cherokee Council, November 5, 1829

To the Honorable Senate and House of Representatives of the United States of America in Congress assembled:

We, the representatives of the people of the Cherokee nation, in general council convened, compelled by a sense of duty we owe to ourselves and nation, and confiding in the justice of your honorable bodies, address and make known to you the grievances which disturb the quiet repose and harmony of our citizens, and the dangers by which we are surrounded. Extraordinary as this course may appear to you, the circumstances that have imposed upon us this duty we deem sufficient to justify the measure; and our safety as individuals, and as a nation, require that we should be heard by the immediate representatives of the people of the United States, whose humanity and magnanimity, by permission and will of Heaven, may yet preserve us from ruin and extinction.

The authorities of Georgia have recently and unexpectedly assumed a doctrine, horrid in its aspect, and fatal in its consequences to us, and utterly at variance with the laws of nations, of the United States, and the subsisting treaties between us, and the known history of said State, of this nation, and of the United States. She claims the exercise of sovereignty over this nation; and has threatened and decreed the extension of her jurisdictional limits over our people. The Executive of the United States, through the Secretary of War,[1] in a letter to our delegation of the 18th April last, has recognised this right to be abiding in, and possessed by, the State of Georgia; by the Declaration of Independence, and the treaty of peace concluded between the United States and Great Britain in 1783; and which it is urged vested in her all the rights of sovereignty pertaining to Great Britain, and which, in time previously, she claimed and exercised, within the limits of what constituted the "thirteen United States." It is a subject of vast importance to know whether the power of self-government abided in the Cherokee nation at the discovery of America, three hundred and thirty-seven years ago; and whether it was in any manner affected or destroyed by the charters of European potentates. It is evident from facts deducible from known history, that the Indians were found here by the white man, in the enjoyment of plenty and peace, and all the rights of soil and domain, inherited from their ancestors from time immemorial, well furnished with kings, chiefs, and warriors, the bulwarks of liberty, and the pride of their race. Great Britain established with them relationships of friendship and alliance, and at no time did she treat them as subjects, and as tenants at will, to her power. In war she fought them as a separate people, and they resisted her as a nation. In peace, she spoke the language of friendship, and they replied in the voice of independence, and frequently assisted her as allies, at their choice to fight her enemies in their own way and discipline, subject to the control of their own chiefs, and unaccountable to European officers and military law. Such was the connexion of this nation to Great Britain, to wit, that of friendship, and not allegiance, to the period of the declaration of

---

1. I.e., John Eaton. President Andrew Jackson (the "Executive of the United States") believed that treating the Indians as sovereign nations was a mistake and that Indian occupancy of lands within the United States was simply owing to the generosity and goodwill of the federal government and the states in question.

Independence by the United States, and during the Revolutionary contest, down to the treaty of peace between the United States and Great Britain, forty-six years ago, when she abandoned all hopes of conquest, and at the same time abandoned her Cherokee allies to the difficulties in which they had been involved, either to continue the war, or procure peace on the best terms they could, and close the scenes of carnage and blood, that had so long been witnessed and experienced by both parties. Peace was at last concluded at Hopewell, in '85, under the administration of Washington, by "the Commissioners, Plenipotentiaries of the United States in Congress assembled"; and the Cherokees were received "into the favor and protection of the United States of America." It remains to be proved, under a view of all these circumstances, and the knowledge we have of history, how our right to self-government was affected and destroyed by the Declaration of Independence, which never noticed the subject of Cherokee sovereignty; and the treaty of peace, in '83, between Great Britain and the United States, to which the Cherokees were not a party; but maintained hostilities on their part to the treaty of Hopewell, afterwards concluded. If, as it is stated by the Hon. Secretary of War, that the Cherokees were mere tenants at will,[2] and only permitted to enjoy possession of the soil to pursue game; and if the States of North Carolina and Georgia were sovereigns in truth and in right over us; why did President Washington send "Commissioners Plenipotentiaries" to treat with the subjects of those States? Why did they permit the chiefs and warriors to enter into treaty, when, if they were subjects, they had grossly rebelled and revolted from their allegiance? And why did not those sovereigns make their lives pay the forfeit of their guilt, agreeably to the laws of said States? The answer must be plain—they were not subjects, but a distinct nation, and in that light viewed by Washington, and by all the people of the Union, at that period. In the first and second articles of the Hopewell treaty, and the third article of the Holston treaty,[3] the United States and the Cherokee nation were bound to a mutual exchange of prisoners taken during the war; which incontrovertibly proves the possession of sovereignty by *both* contracting parties. It ought to be remembered too, in the conclusions of the treaties to which we have referred, and most of the treaties subsisting between the United States and this nation, that the phraseology, composition, etc. was always written by the Commissioners, on the part of the United States, for obvious reasons: as the Cherokees were unacquainted with letters. Again, in the Holston treaty, eleventh article, the following remarkable evidence is contained that our nation is not under the jurisdiction of any State: "If any citizen or inhabitant of the United States, or of either of the territorial districts of the United States, shall

2. I.e., the will of the states and the federal government "to allow" the Cherokees to live on their own ancestral lands. These lands came into the possession of the United States as a result of the Declaration of Independence and victory in the Revolutionary War. The Treaty of Hopewell, signed November 28, 1785, was the first treaty between the Cherokees and the United States enacted after the Revolutionary War. It established the boundaries of Cherokee lands and was negotiated as an agreement between two sovereign nations. The Cherokees refer to the treaty to show that they were formerly recognized as an independent nation and should still be treated as

such. This argument remains in force today.
3. Signed July 2, 1791, this treaty gave the federal government (not the states) exclusive right to regulate all citizens' trade with the Cherokees and redrew the boundaries, much encroached on by the settlers, of Cherokee lands. It also affirmed "Perpetual peace between the United States and the Cherokee Nation," and forbade non-Cherokee persons from hunting on or traversing Cherokee lands without a passport issued by the federal government. The Cherokees cite this as further evidence of their having been treated as a sovereign nation in the past.

go into any town, settlement, or territory, belonging to the Cherokees, and shall there commit any crime upon, or trespass against, the person or property of any peaceable and friendly Indian or Indians, which, *if committed within the jurisdiction of any State, or within the jurisdiction of either of the said districts*, against a citizen or any white inhabitant thereof, would be punishable by the laws of such State or district, such offender or offenders shall be proceeded against in the same manner as if the offence had been committed *within the jurisdiction of the State or district* to which he or they may belong, against a citizen or white inhabitant thereof." The power of a State may put our national existence under its feet, and coerce us into her jurisdiction; but it would be contrary to legal right, and the plighted faith of the United States' Government. It is said by Georgia and the Honorable Secretary of War, that one sovereignty cannot exist within another, and, therefore, we must yield to the stronger power; but is not this doctrine favorable to our Government, which does not interfere with that of any other? Our sovereignty and right of enforcing legal enactments, extend no further than our territorial limits, and that of Georgia is, and has always terminated at, her limits. The constitution of the United States (article 6) contains these words: "All treaties made under the authority of the United States shall be the supreme law of the land, and the judges in every State shall be bound thereby, any thing in the laws or constitution of any State to the contrary notwithstanding." The sacredness of treaties, made under the authority of the United States, is paramount and supreme, stronger than the laws and constitution of any State. The jurisdiction, then, of our nation over its soil is settled by the laws, treaties, and constitution of the United States, and has been exercised from time out of memory.

Georgia has objected to the adoption, on our part, of a constitutional form of government, and which has in no wise violated the intercourse and connexion which bind us to the United States, its constitution, and the treaties thereupon founded, and in existence between us. As a distinct nation, notwithstanding any unpleasant feelings it might have created to a neighboring State, we had a right to improve our Government, suitable to the moral, civil, and intellectual advancement of our people; and had we anticipated any notice of it, it was the voice of encouragement by an approving world. We would, also, while on this subject, refer your attention to the memorial and protest submitted before your honorable bodies, during the last session of Congress, by our delegation then at Washington.

Permit us, also, to make known to you the aggrieved and unpleasant situation under which we are placed by the claim which Georgia has set up to a large portion of our territory, under the treaty of the Indian Springs concluded with the late General M'Intosh[4] and his party; and which was declared void, and of no effect, by a subsequent treaty between the Creek Nation and the United States, at Washington City. The President of the United States, through the Secretary of War, assured our delegation, that, so far as he understood the Cherokees had rights, protection should be

---

4. General William McIntosh was a Creek Indian leader who signed the Treaty of Indian Springs on February 12, 1785. The treaty ceded Creek lands to the state of Georgia and agreed to the removal of the Creeks to west of the Mississippi. But the Creeks had earlier denied McIntosh's right to act on their behalf and did not honor the treaty. McIntosh was assassinated, and John Ridge and David Vann were engaged to negotiate a new treaty, the "subsequent treaty" referred to later in the sentence.

afforded; and, respecting the intrusions on our lands, he had been advised, "and instructions had been forwarded to the agent of the Cherokees, directing him to cause their removal; and earnestly hoped, that, on this matter, all cause for future complaint would cease, and the order prove effectual." In consequence of the agent's neglecting to comply with the instructions, and a suspension of the order made by the Secretary afterwards, our border citizens are at this time placed under the most unfortunate circumstances, by the intrusions of citizens of the United States, and which are almost daily increasing, in consequence of the suspension of the once contemplated "effectual order." Many of our people are experiencing all the evils of personal insult, and, in some instances, expulsion from their homes, and loss of property, from the unrestrained intruders let loose upon us, and the encouragement they are allowed to enjoy, under the last order to the agent for this nation, which amounts to a suspension of the force of treaties, and the wholesome operation of the intercourse laws[5] of the United States. The reason alleged by the War Department for this suspension is, that it had been requested so to do, until the claim the State of Georgia has made to a portion of the Cherokee country be determined; and the intruders are to remain unmolested within the border limits of this nation. We beg leave to protest against this unprecedented procedure. If the State of Georgia has a claim to any portion of our lands, and is entitled by law and justice to them, let her seek through a legal channel to establish it; and we do hope that the United States will not suffer her to take possession of them forcibly, and investigate her claim afterwards.

Arguments to effect the emigration of our people, and to escape the troubles and disquietudes incident to a residence contiguous to the whites, have been urged upon us, and the arm of protection has been withheld, that we may experience still deeper and ampler proofs of the correctness of the doctrine; but we still adhere to what is right and agreeable to ourselves; and our attachment to the soil of our ancestors is too strong to be shaken. We have been invited to a retrospective view of the past history of Indians, who have melted away before the light of civilization, and the mountains of difficulties that have opposed our race in their advancement in civilized life. We have done so; and, while we deplore the fate of thousands of our complexion and kind, we rejoice that our nation stands and grows a lasting monument of God's mercy, and a durable contradiction to the misconceived opinion that the aborigines are incapable of civilization. The opposing mountains, that cast fearful shadows in the road of Cherokee improvement, have dispersed into vernal clouds; and our people stand adorned with the flowers of achievement flourishing around them, and are encouraged to secure the attainment of all that is useful in science and Christian knowledge.

Under the fostering care of the United States we have thus prospered; and shall we expect approbation, or shall we sink under the displeasure and rebukes of our enemies?

We now look with earnest expectation to your honorable bodies for redress, and that our national existence may not be extinguished before a prompt and effectual interposition is afforded in our behalf. The faith of your Government is solemnly pledged for our protection against all illegal oppressions, so long as we remain firm to our treaties; and that we have, for

5. Laws regulating trade.

a long series of years, proved to be true and loyal friends, the known history of past events abundantly proves. Your Chief Magistrate himself[6] has borne testimony of our devotedness in supporting the cause of the United States, during their late conflict with a foreign foe. It is with reluctant and painful feelings that circumstances have at length compelled us to seek from you the promised protection, for the preservation of our rights and privileges. This resort to us is a last one, and nothing short of the threatening evils and dangers that beset us could have forced it upon the nation but it is a right we surely have, and in which we cannot be mistaken—that of appealing for justice and humanity to the United States, under whose kind and fostering care we have been led to the present degree of civilization, and the enjoyment of its consequent blessings. Having said thus much, with patience we shall await the final issue of your wise deliberations.

6. John Marshall, chief justice of the Supreme Court.

RALPH WALDO EMERSON

Ralph Waldo Emerson (1803–1882) was perhaps the most important American thinker of the first half of the nineteenth century and a strong influence on Thoreau and Walt Whitman, among others. Although he knew some of the New England abolitionists, he did not himself become active in the cause until the 1850s. In regard to the American Indians, Emerson seems to have shared the general eastern distaste for President Andrew Jackson's removal policies, although it is only in his letter to Jackson's successor, Martin Van Buren, reprinted here, that he committed himself publicly to the Cherokees' cause.

Emerson seems to have learned of the imminent removal of the Cherokees only on April 19, 1838, writing in his journal, "I can do nothing. Why shriek? Why strike ineffectual blows?" Yet the following day he composed the first draft of his letter to Van Buren, noting in his journal, "The amount of [it], [to] be sure, is merely a Scream but sometimes a scream is better than a thesis." The following day he recorded his sense that this was "A deliverance that does not deliver the soul." Clearly, writing this letter was not an easy thing for him to do.

The letter does not seem ever to have been sent directly to Van Buren. Under the heading of "Communication," it was published, "with some reluctance" on the part of the proprietors of the *National Daily Intelligencer*, in the issue of May 14, 1838, next appearing on May 19 in the *Yeoman's Gazette* in Concord. The earliest version we have been able to find is from the *New Bedford Mercury* of May 25, 1838, the source of the text below.

Letter to Martin Van Buren

President of the United States

CONCORD, Mass. 23d April, 1838.

Sir—The seat you fill, places you in a relation of credit and dearness to every citizen. By right, and natural position, every citizen is your friend. Before any acts contrary to his own judgement or interest have repelled the affections of any man, each may look with trust and loving anticipations to your government. Each has the highest right to call your attention to such subjects as are of a public nature and properly belong to the chief magistrate; and the good magistrate will feel a joy in meeting such confidence. In this belief, and at the instance of a few of my friends and neighbors, I crave of your patience a short hearing for their sentiments and my own; and the circumstance that my name will be utterly unknown to you, will only give the fairer chance to your equitable construction of what I have to say.

Sir, my communication respects the sinister rumours that fill this part of the country concerning the Cherokee people. The interest always felt in the Aboriginal Population—an interest naturally growing as that decays—has been heightened in regard to this tribe. Even in our distant state, some good rumor of their worth and civility has arrived. We have learned with joy their improvement in social arts. We have read their newspapers. We have seen some of them in our schools and colleges. In common with the great body of the American people we have witnessed with sympathy the painful labors of these red men to redeem their own race from the doom of eternal inferiority, and to borrow and domesticate in the tribe, the arts and customs of the caucasian race. And notwithstanding the unaccountable apathy with which of late years the Indians have been sometimes abandoned to their enemies, it is not to be doubted that it is the good pleasure and the understanding of all humane persons in the republic—of the men and the matrons sitting in the thriving independent families all over the land, that they shall be duly cared for, that they shall taste justice and love from all to whom we have delegated the office of dealing with them.

The newspapers now inform us, that, in December 1835, a treaty contracting for the exchange of all the Cherokee territory, was pretended to be made by an agent on the part of the United States with some persons appearing on the part of the Cherokees; that the fact afterwards transpired that these deputies did by no means represent the will of the nation, and that out of eighteen thousand souls composing the nation, fifteen thousand six hundred and sixty eight have protested against the so called Treaty. It now appears that the Government of the United States choose to hold the Cherokees to this sham treaty, and are proceeding to execute the same. Almost the entire Cherokee nation stand up and say, "This is not our act. Behold us. Here are we. Do not mistake that handful of deserters for us," and the American President and his Cabinet, the Senate and the House of Representatives neither hear these men nor see them, and are contracting to put this nation into carts and boats and to drag them over mountains and rivers to a wilderness at a vast distance beyond the Mississippi.—And a paper purporting to be an army order, taxes a month from this day, as the hour for this doleful removal.

In the name of God, Sir, we ask you if this be so? Do the newspapers rightly inform us? Men and women with pale and perplexed faces meet one another in streets and churches here, and ask if this be so? We have inquired if this be a gross misrepresentation from the party opposed to the Government and anxious to blacken it with the people. We have looked in newspapers of different parties, and find a horrid confirmation of the tale. We are slow to believe it. We hoped the Indians were misinformed and their remonstrance was premature, and will turn out to be a needless act of terror. The piety, the principle that is left in these United States,—if only its coarsest form, a regard to the speech of men, forbid us to entertain it as a fact. Such a dereliction of all faith and virtue, such a denial of justice and such deafness to screams for mercy, were never heard of in times of peace, and in the dealing of a nation with its own allies and wards, since the earth was made. Sir, does this Government think that the people of the United States are become savage and mad? From their mind are the sentiments of love and of a good nature nature wiped clean out? The soul of man, the justice the mercy, that is the heart's heart in all men from Maine to Georgia, does abhor this business.

In speaking thus the sentiments of my neighbors and my own, perhaps I overstep the bounds of decorum. But would it not be a higher indecorum, coldly to argue a matter like this? We only state the fact that a crime is projected that confounds our understandings by its magnitude,—a crime that really deprives us as well as the Cherokees of a country, for how could we call the conspiracy that should crush these poor Indians, our Government, or the land that was cursed by their parting and dying imprecations, our country, any more? You, Sir, will bring down that renowned chair in which you sit into infamy, if your seal is set to this instrument of perfidy, and the name of this nation, hitherto the sweet omen of religion and liberty, will stink to the world.

You will not do us the injustice of connecting this remonstrance with any sectional or party feeling.—It is in our hearts the simplest commandment of brotherly love. We will not have this great and solemn claim upon national and human justice huddled aside under the flimsy plea of its being a party act. Sir, to us the questions upon which the government and the people have been agitated during the past year touching the prostration of the currency and of trade, seem but motes in comparison. The hard times, it is true, have brought this discussion home to every farmhouse and poor man's house in this town; but it is the chirping of grasshoppers beside the immortal question whether justice shall be done by the race of civilized, to the race of savage man; whether all the attributes of reason, of civility, of justice, and even of mercy, shall be put off by the American people, and so vast an outrage upon the Cherokee nation, and upon human nature, shall be consummated.

One circumstance lessens the reluctance with which I intrude at this time on your attention, my conviction that the government ought to be admonished of a new historical fact which the discussion of this question has disclosed, namely that there exists in a great part of the northern people, a gloomy diffidence in the *moral* character of the government. On the broaching of this question, a general expression of despondency,—of disbelief that any good will accrue from a remonstrance on an act of fraud and robbery—appeared in those men to whom we naturally turn for aid and counsel. Will the American Government steal? Will it lie? Will it kill?—we ask triumphantly. Our wise men shake their heads dubiously. Our counsellers and old statesmen here, say, that ten years ago, they would have staked their life on the affirmation that the proposed Indian measures could not be executed, that the unanimous country would put them down. And now the steps of this crime follow each other so fast,—at such fatally quick time,—that the millions of virtuous citizens, whose agents the Government are, have no place to interpose, and must shut their eyes until the last howl and wailing of these poor tormented villages and tribes shall afflict the ear of the world.

I will not hide from you as an indication of this alarming distrust that a letter addressed as mine is, and suggesting to the mind of the Executive the plain obligations of man, has a burlesque character in the apprehension of some of my friends. I, sir, will not beforehand treat you with contumely of this distrust. I will at least state to you this fact and show you how plain and humane people whose love would be honor, regard the policy of the Government, and what injurious inferences they draw as to the mind of the Governors. A man with your experience in affairs must have seen cause to appreciate the futility of opposition to the moral sentiment. However feeble the sufferer, and however great the oppressor, it is in the nature of things that the blow should recoil on the aggressor. For God is in the sentiment, and it cannot be withstood. The potentate and the people perish before it; but with it, and as its executors, they are omnipotent.

I write thus, Sir, to inform you of the state of mind these Indian tidings have awakened here, and to pray with one voice more that you whose hands are strong with the delegated power of fifteen millions of men will avert with that might the terrific injury which threatens the Cherokee tribe.

With great respect, Sir,
I am your fellow-citizen,
Ralph Waldo Emerson

NATHANIEL HAWTHORNE
1804–1864

In 1879, the author Henry James called Nathaniel Hawthorne "the most valuable example of American genius," expressing the widely held belief that he was the most significant fiction writer of the antebellum period. Readers continue to celebrate Hawthorne for his prose style, his perceptive renderings of New England history, his psychological acuity, and his vivid characterizations—especially of female characters. Still, for many, he remains tantalizingly elusive, a writer who—as he remarked in the "Custom-House" introduction to *The Scarlet Letter*—wished to keep "the inmost Me behind its veil." He was, to be sure, a deeply private man, but the elusiveness of his fiction stems from a deliberate aesthetic of ambiguity, a refusal to "stick a pin through a butterfly" (as he put it in the preface to *The House of the Seven Gables*) by imposing a single moral on a story. Withholding interpretation—or offering multiple and conflicting interpretations—Hawthorne not only makes readers do their own interpretive work but also shows how interpretation is often a form of self-expression.

Hawthorne was born on July 4, 1804, in Salem, Massachusetts. His prominent Puritan ancestors on the Hawthorne side of the family were among the first settlers of Massachusetts and included a judge in the Salem witchcraft trials of 1692. The men in his mother's family, the Mannings, were tradesmen and businessmen. When Hawthorne's sea-captain father died in Surinam of yellow fever in 1808, his mother, Elizabeth Manning Hawthorne, moved with her three children into the Manning family's commodious house in Salem. There, with his mother, sisters, grandparents, two aunts, and five uncles, Hawthorne discovered his love of reading, displaying particular interest as a boy in John Bunyan's Puritan allegory *The Pilgrim's Progress*. In 1813 he injured his foot in an accident, was fitted with a protective boot and crutches and, while remaining home from school during the long recuperation period, continued to read extensively. By his midteens he was reading the British novelists Henry Fielding, Tobias Smollet, William Godwin, and Sir Walter Scott, while forming an ambition, as he wrote his sister Elizabeth when he was sixteen, of "becoming an Author, and relying for support upon my pen." Hawthorne enjoyed long visits to the Manning properties at Sebago Lake, Maine, and at age seventeen enrolled at Bowdoin College in Brunswick, Maine. At Bowdoin he developed what would become lifelong friendships with Horatio Bridge, Franklin Pierce, and other members of the nascent Democratic Party. These friends would later help further his literary career by providing him with patronage jobs and funds. Henry Wadsworth Longfellow, another Bowdoin classmate, belonged to the more conservative Federalist Society. At the graduation ceremonies in 1825, Longfellow spoke of the possibility that "Our Native Writers" could achieve lasting fame; and twelve years later he would enthusiastically review Hawthorne's *Twice-Told Tales* in the prestigious *North American Review*, calling the collection of tales and sketches a "sweet, sweet book."

During the years between Hawthorne's graduation from Bowdoin in 1825 and the publication of *Twice-Told Tales* in 1837, Hawthorne seems to have lived quietly at home in Salem with his mother and sisters. He read extensively in colonial histories and documents, which would become important sources for such historical tales as "My Kinsman, Major Molineaux" (1832) and "Young Goodman Brown" (1835), while keeping a close eye on his contemporary world, which would supply him with material for such popular sketches as "Little Annie's Ramble" (1835) and "A Rill from the Town Pump" (1835). In 1828 Hawthorne published his first novel, *Fanshawe*, at his own expense. Set at a college resembling Bowdoin, the novel was reviewed so negatively that he attempted to suppress its distribution. Over the next several years Hawthorne tried unsuccessfully to find a publisher for collections of the tales he was writing. He may have destroyed one collection, "Seven Tales of My Native Land"; in 1829 he failed to find a publisher for a volume called "Provincial Tales," which included "The Gentle Boy" and perhaps "My Kinsman, Major Molineaux." A proposed third volume called "The Story Teller," in which the title character wandered about New England telling his stories in dramatic settings and circumstances, also foundered.

During the early 1830s, however, Hawthorne managed to publish many of these early tales and sketches in the literary annuals that were issued every fall as Christmas gifts. Still, he received only a few dollars for each tale and no recognition, since publication in the annuals was anonymous. In 1836 he edited the *American Magazine of Useful and Entertaining Knowledge*, a job he secured through the Boston publisher Samuel Goodrich, whose annual, *The Token*, regularly published his tales. That same year, with the help of his sister Elizabeth, he wrote a children's reference work for Goodrich, *Peter Parley's Universal History on the Basis of Geography*. Unbeknownst to Hawthorne, his Bowdoin friend Horatio Bridge persuaded Goodrich to publish a collection of Hawthorne's tales by promising to repay any losses. This volume, *Twice-Told Tales*, appeared in March 1837 and was favorably reviewed in England as well as the United States. A notebook entry written sometime in 1836 was only a little premature: "In this dismal and sordid chamber FAME was won."

There is considerable uncertainty about Hawthorne's private affairs around the time of the publication of *Twice-Told Tales*. According to family lore, he may have challenged the future editor of the *Democratic Review*, John O'Sullivan, to a duel over Mary Silsbee of Salem. (During the 1840s O'Sullivan would publish over twenty of Hawthorne's stories in his journal.) Hawthorne may have also been enamored of Elizabeth Peabody, a Salemite who would become a major force in American educational reform as well as other progressive causes, and to whom he presented a copy of *Twice-Told Tales* in the fall of 1837. Sometime in late 1837 or 1838 Hawthorne met Elizabeth's youngest sister, Sophia Peabody, a painter whose migraine headaches often made her a virtual invalid; they were secretly engaged within a few months of the meeting. To save money for married life, Hawthorne accepted a patronage appointment as salt and coal measurer at the Boston Custom House during 1839 and 1840, and then invested some of his limited funds in the utopian community Brook Farm, located in West Roxbury, Massachusetts, where he spent seven months in 1841. During this period he published several children's books on colonial and revolutionary history—*Grandfather's Chair* (1841), *Famous Old People* (1841), *Liberty Tree* (1841), and *Biographical Stories for Children* (1842)—along with a revised and expanded edition of *Twice-Told Tales* (1842). He and Sophia Peabody were married in 1842; the couple rented a house in Concord named the "Old Manse" (owned by Emerson's family) and became friends with the notable writers and intellectuals of the area—Emerson, Thoreau, Margaret Fuller, and Ellery Channing, among others. The Hawthornes' first child, Una, was born in 1844. While a hoped-for novel failed to materialize, Hawthorne continued to publish sketches and tales. In 1845, he edited his friend Bridge's *Journal of an African Cruiser*, but little money came of this enterprise, and Hawthorne had to move his family back to Salem to live with his mother and sisters. The following year he published *Mosses from an Old Manse*, which added a number of his recent periodical publications to some earlier work.

The Hawthornes' second child, Julian, was born in 1846. Desperately in need of money, Hawthorne turned to his Democratic friends. The Democrats' local party leader, the historian George Bancroft, found work for Hawthorne as surveyor of the Salem Custom House, a position that Hawthorne assumed in April 1846. The work was not demanding, but the routine stifled Hawthorne's creative energies. Even though he wrote little in these years, Hawthorne resented being thrown out of office by the new Whig administration in June 1849 and was pleased that his ouster led to a furious controversy in the newspapers. He then spent a summer of "great diversity and severity of emotion" (as he wrote in a journal entry of 1855), climaxed by his mother's death on July 31. In September he was at work on *The Scarlet Letter*, which he planned as a long tale to make up half a volume called "Old Time Legends; together with Sketches, Experimental and Ideal." Besides the long introduction, "The Custom-House," which was Hawthorne's means of revenging himself on the Salem Whigs who had "decapitated" him, he planned to include several tales. On the lookout for New England novelistic talent, James Fields, the young associate of the publisher William D. Ticknor, persuaded Hawthorne to drop the stories. The novel was published by the Boston house of Ticknor, Reed, and Fields in 1850.

Although some reviewers denounced *The Scarlet Letter* as licentious or morbid for its treatment of adultery, the novel was nevertheless a literary success in the United States and Great Britain, and Hawthorne was celebrated for his brilliant prose style and uncanny ability to recreate the past. Hawthorne used the setting of Puritan Boston to address the politics of revolution, community, and government central to the emerging nation; he also used the setting to explore matters of sexuality, gender, and psychology in their historical complexity. In this dark novel of love and revenge, Hawthorne evokes emotional sympathy for the heroine, Hester Prynne, even as he appears to condemn her actions. Despite the appearance of condemnation, Hester, for many readers over the years, has emerged as more vibrantly alive and appealing than the male characters of the novel. Hester's status as heroine was apparent from the beginning; as the feminist-abolitionist Jane Swisshelm observed in her 1850 review of the novel, if Hawthorne wanted to teach a lesson about the putative sins of Hester, "he had better try again. For our part if we knew there was such another woman as Hester Prynne in Boston now, we should travel all the way there to pay our respects." Strong women characters—Hepzibah in *The House of the Seven Gables* (1851), Zenobia (modeled on Margaret Fuller) in *The Blithedale Romance* (1852), and Miriam in *The Marble Faun* (1860)—would remain central to Hawthorne's long fictions. Though some recent commentators have reviled Hawthorne for his 1855 complaint to his publisher Ticknor about the "d——d mob of scribbling women," the fact is that, as evidenced by such stories as "The Birthmark" and "Rappaccinni's Daughter" and all of the novels, few writers of the mid-nineteenth century were more insightful about the damage patriarchal culture can do to women.

Following the publication of *The Scarlet Letter*, the Hawthornes moved to Lenox, Massachusetts, in the Berkshire Mountains, in part to escape from the controversy surrounding the satirical "Custom-House" sketch, which had angered many in Salem. During a year and a half in Lenox, Hawthorne developed a complicated friendship with Herman Melville, who championed Hawthorne as a great American writer in his 1850 "Hawthorne and His Mosses" and dedicated *Moby-Dick* to him. Hawthorne, over time, pulled back from Melville, and their paths seldom crossed after 1852, when the Hawthornes moved to West Newton and then back to Concord. Hawthorne was especially productive during the early 1850s, publishing *The House of the Seven Gables*, a romance with a contemporary Salem setting, and *The Blithedale Romance*, which drew on Hawthorne's experiences at Brook Farm. Hawthorne also published *The Snow-Image and other Twice-Told Tales* (1852), two books of tales and myths for children (*A Wonder-Book* [1852] and *The Tanglewood Tales* [1853]), and *The Life of Franklin Pierce*, a presidential campaign biography for his Bowdoin friend. The victorious Pierce appointed Hawthorne American consul at Liverpool, a job that again pulled Hawthorne away from his writing but that helped him support a family augmented by the birth of a third child in 1850, his daughter Rose.

At Liverpool (1853–57) Hawthorne, an industrious consul, was particularly concerned to gain greater protections for American sailors from abusive officers. Hawthorne resigned the position early in 1857 after Pierce failed to gain the Democrats' nomination for a second term, and remained in Europe to travel with his family. A stay in Italy—starting in the miserably cold early months of 1858—turned into a nightmare when malaria nearly killed his daughter Una. Hawthorne kept a minutely detailed tourist's account of his travels in Italy, and he drew on these notebooks for the romance he began in Florence in 1858 and finished late in 1859 after his return to England. This novel, inspired by the statue of a faun attributed to the classical Greek sculptor Praxiteles, was published in London in February 1860 as *Transformation* and one month later in the United States under Hawthorne's preferred title, *The Marble Faun*. Acclaimed by reviewers, the novel proved to be especially popular with American travelers to Rome later in the nineteenth century, who enjoyed using it as a guidebook.

The Hawthornes returned to their Concord home, which Hawthorne had named The Wayside, in June 1860. Hawthorne's final years in the United States were an unhappy time for him. Una remained sickly, and Hawthorne's own health began to decline. Increasingly depressed, he began a romance about an American claimant to an ancestral English estate, then put it aside to begin a romance about the search for an elixir of life, and then put that one aside as well to start another. Meanwhile, the Jacksonian Democrat Hawthorne was baffled and disturbed by the coming of the Civil War, regarding the Northern declaration of war not as an idealistic campaign to bring about the end of slavery, which he viewed as an evil, but as a frenzied form of aggression. Following a visit to Washington, D.C., in which he met Abraham Lincoln, Hawthorne published "Chiefly about War-Matters" in the July 1862 issue of the *Atlantic*; the essay satirized Lincoln and conveyed Hawthorne's critique of a nation gone mad with war. Fields, the editor of the *Atlantic*, paid well for this and other of Hawthorne's contributions, but Hawthorne was increasingly unable to respond to Fields's demands. In 1863 Hawthorne published *Our Old Home*, a collection of his English sketches, which he loyally dedicated to Franklin Pierce, who, because of his Southern sympathies, was now anathema to many Northerners. Harriet Beecher Stowe expressed disbelief that Hawthorne would dedicate a book to "that arch-traitor Pierce"; and according to Annie Fields, the wife of Hawthorne's publisher, Emerson and many others who received complimentary copies of the book reported that they had cut out the dedication page. Suffering from health problems, a frail and somewhat isolated Hawthorne embarked on a trip to New Hampshire with his old friend Pierce early in May 1864, and died in his sleep, at a hotel, later that month. He was buried in the Sleepy Hollow Cemetery at Concord. Emerson, Longfellow, Fields, James Russell Lowell, and Oliver Wendell Holmes were among his pallbearers.

My Kinsman, Major Molineux[1]

After the kings of Great Britain had assumed the right of appointing the colonial governors,[2] the measures of the latter seldom met with the ready and general approbation, which had been paid to those of their predecessors, under the original charters. The people looked with most jealous scrutiny to the exercise of power, which did not emanate from themselves, and they usually rewarded the rulers with slender gratitude, for the compliances, by which, in softening their instructions from beyond the sea, they had incurred the reprehension of those who gave them. The annals of Massachusetts Bay will inform us, that of six governors, in the space of about forty years from the surrender of the old charter, under James II, two were imprisoned by a popular insurrection; a third, as Hutchinson[3] inclines to believe, was driven from the province by the whizzing of a musket ball; a fourth, in the opinion of the same historian, was hastened to his grave by continual bickerings with the house of representatives; and the remaining two, as well as their successors, till the Revolution, were favored with few and brief intervals of peaceful sway. The inferior members of the court party,[4] in times of high political excitement, led scarcely a more desirable life. These remarks may serve as preface to the following adventures, which chanced upon a summer night, not far from a hundred years ago. The reader, in order to avoid a long and dry detail of colonial affairs, is requested to dispense with an account of the train of circumstances, that had caused much temporary inflammation of the popular mind.

It was near nine o'clock of a moonlight evening, when a boat crossed the ferry with a single passenger, who had obtained his conveyance, at that unusual hour, by the promise of an extra fare. While he stood on the landing-place, searching in either pocket for the means of fulfilling his agreement, the ferryman lifted a lantern, by the aid of which, and the newly risen moon, he took a very accurate survey of the stranger's figure. He was a youth of barely eighteen years, evidently country-bred, and now, as it should seem, upon his first visit to town. He was clad in a coarse grey coat, well worn, but in excellent repair; his under garments[5] were durably constructed of leather, and sat tight to a pair of serviceable and well-shaped limbs; his stockings of blue yarn, were the incontrovertible handiwork of a mother or a sister; and on his head was a three-cornered hat, which in its better days had perhaps sheltered the graver brow of the lad's father. Under his left arm was a heavy cudgel, formed of an oak sapling, and retaining a part of the hardened root; and his equipment was completed by a wallet,[6] not so abundantly stocked as to incommode the vigorous shoulders on which it hung. Brown, curly hair, well-shaped features, and bright, cheerful eyes, were nature's gifts, and worth all that art could have done for his adornment.

1. The text is that of the first printing in *The Token* (1832).
2. In 1684 King Charles II (r. 1660–85) annulled the original Massachusetts Charter, which had allowed the colony to elect its own governor. King James II (r. 1685–88) appointed the colony's first royal governor in 1685.
3. Thomas Hutchinson (1711–1780), the last royal governor. The particular annals, or year-by-year histories, that Hawthorne has in mind are *The History of the Colony and Province of Massachusetts-Bay* (1764, 1767) by Hutchinson. James II (1633–1701) reigned briefly (1685–88) before being exiled to France in the Glorious Revolution.
4. The pro-Crown party.
5. Clothes worn on the lower part of the body.
6. Knapsack.

The youth, one of whose names was Robin, finally drew from his pocket the half of a little province-bill[7] of five shillings, which, in the depreciation of that sort of currency, did but satisfy the ferryman's demand, with the surplus of a sexangular piece of parchment valued at three pence. He then walked forward into the town, with as light a step, as if his day's journey had not already exceeded thirty miles, and with as eager an eye, as if he were entering London city, instead of the little metropolis of a New England colony. Before Robin had proceeded far, however, it occurred to him, that he knew not whither to direct his steps; so he paused, and looked up and down the narrow street, scrutinizing the small and mean wooden buildings, that were scattered on either side.

'This low hovel cannot be my kinsman's dwelling,' thought he, 'nor yonder old house, where the moonlight enters at the broken casement; and truly I see none hereabouts that might be worthy of him. It would have been wise to inquire my way of the ferryman, and doubtless he would have gone with me, and earned a shilling from the Major for his pains. But the next man I meet will do as well.'

He resumed his walk, and was glad to perceive that the street now became wider, and the houses more respectable in their appearance. He soon discerned a figure moving on moderately in advance, and hastened his steps to overtake it. As Robin drew nigh, he saw that the passenger was a man in years, with a full periwig of grey hair, a wide-skirted coat of dark cloth, and silk stockings rolled about his knees. He carried a long and polished cane, which he struck down perpendicularly before him, at every step; and at regular intervals he uttered two successive hems, of a peculiarly solemn and sepulchral intonation. Having made these observations, Robin laid hold of the skirt of the old man's coat, just when the light from the open door and windows of a barber's shop, fell upon both their figures.

'Good evening to you, honored Sir,' said he, making a low bow, and still retaining his hold of the skirt. 'I pray you to tell me whereabouts is the dwelling of my kinsman, Major Molineux?'

The youth's question was uttered very loudly; and one of the barbers, whose razor was descending on a well-soaped chin, and another who was dressing a Ramillies wig,[8] left their occupations, and came to the door. The citizen, in the meantime, turned a long favored countenance upon Robin, and answered him in a tone of excessive anger and annoyance. His two sepulchral hems, however, broke into the very centre of his rebuke, with most singular effect, like a thought of the cold grave obtruding among wrathful passions.

'Let go my garment, fellow! I tell you. I know not the man you speak of. What! I have authority, I have—hem, hem—authority; and if this be the respect you show your betters, your feet shall be brought acquainted with the stocks,[9] by daylight, tomorrow morning!'

Robin released the old man's skirt, and hastened away, pursued by an ill-mannered roar of laughter from the barber's shop. He was at first considerably surprised by the result of his question, but, being a shrewd youth, soon thought himself able to account for the mystery.

7. Local paper money.
8. Elaborately braided wig named for Ramillies, Belgium.
9. Wood-framed instrument of punishment with holes for confining the ankles and sometimes the wrists as well.

'This is some country representative,' was his conclusion, 'who has never seen the inside of my kinsman's door, and lacks the breeding to answer a stranger civilly. The man is old, or verily—I might be tempted to turn back and smite him on the nose. Ah, Robin, Robin! even the barber's boys laugh at you, for choosing such a guide! You will be wiser in time, friend Robin.'

He now became entangled in a succession of crooked and narrow streets, which crossed each other, and meandered at no great distance from the water-side. The smell of tar was obvious to his nostrils, the masts of vessels pierced the moonlight above the tops of the buildings, and the numerous signs, which Robin paused to read, informed him that he was near the centre of business. But the streets were empty, the shops were closed, and lights were visible only in the second stories of a few dwelling-houses. At length, on the corner of a narrow lane, through which he was passing, he beheld the broad countenance of a British hero swinging before the door of an inn, whence proceeded the voices of many guests. The casement of one of the lower windows was thrown back, and a very thin curtain permitted Robin to distinguish a party at supper, round a well-furnished table. The fragrance of good cheer steamed forth into the outer air, and the youth could not fail to recollect, that the last remnant of his travelling stock of provision had yielded to his morning appetite, and that noon had found, and left him, dinnerless.

'Oh, that a parchment three-penny might give me a right to sit down at yonder table,' said Robin, with a sigh. 'But the Major will make me welcome to the best of his victuals; so I will even step boldly in, and inquire my way to his dwelling.'

He entered the tavern, and was guided by the murmur of voices, and fumes of tobacco, to the public room. It was a long and low apartment, with oaken walls, grown dark in the continual smoke, and a floor, which was thickly sanded, but of no immaculate purity. A number of persons, the larger part of whom appeared to be mariners, or in some way connected with the sea, occupied the wooden benches, or leather-bottomed chairs, conversing on various matters, and occasionally lending their attention to some topic of general interest. Three or four little groups were draining as many bowls of punch, which the great West India trade[1] had long since made a familiar drink in the colony. Others, who had the aspect of men who lived by regular and laborious handicraft, preferred the insulated bliss of an unshared potation, and became more taciturn under its influence. Nearly all, in short, evinced a predilection for the Good Creature in some of its various shapes, for this is a vice, to which, as the Fast-day[2] sermons of a hundred years ago will testify, we have a long hereditary claim. The only guests to whom Robin's sympathies inclined him, were two or three sheepish countrymen, who were using the inn somewhat after the fashion of a Turkish Caravansary; they had gotten themselves into the darkest corner of the room, and, heedless of the Nicotian[3] atmosphere, were supping on the bread of their own ovens, and the bacon cured in their own chimney-smoke. But though Robin felt a sort of brotherhood with these strangers, his eyes were attracted from them, to a person who stood near the

---

1. West Indian molasses was shipped to New England and there made into rum.
2. Days set apart for public penitence. "Good Creature": rum. Hawthorne is alluding to 1 Timothy 4.4: "For every creature of God is good, and

nothing to be refused, if it be received with thanksgiving."
3. Synonym for nicotine. "Caravansary": an inn built around a court for accommodating caravans.

door, holding whispered conversation with a group of ill-dressed associates. His features were separately striking almost to grotesqueness, and the whole face left a deep impression in the memory. The forehead bulged out into a double prominence, with a vale between; the nose came boldly forth in an irregular curve, and its bridge was of more than a finger's breadth; the eyebrows were deep and shaggy, and the eyes glowed beneath them like fire in a cave.

While Robin deliberated of whom to inquire respecting his kinsman's dwelling, he was accosted by the innkeeper, a little man in a stained white apron, who had come to pay his professional welcome to the stranger. Being in the second generation from a French protestant, he seemed to have inherited the courtesy of his parent nation; but no variety of circumstance was ever known to change his voice from the one shrill note in which he now addressed Robin.

'From the country, I presume, Sir?' said he, with a profound bow. 'Beg to congratulate you on your arrival, and trust you intend a long stay with us. Fine town here, Sir, beautiful buildings, and much that may interest a stranger. May I hope for the honor of your commands in respect to supper?'

'The man sees a family likeness! the rogue has guessed that I am related to the Major!' thought Robin, who had hitherto experienced little superfluous civility.

All eyes were now turned on the country lad, standing at the door, in his worn three-cornered hat, grey coat, leather breeches, and blue yarn stockings, leaning on an oaken cudgel, and bearing a wallet on his back. Robin replied to the courteous innkeeper, with such an assumption of consequence, as befitted the Major's relative.

'My honest friend,' he said, 'I shall make it a point to patronise your house on some occasion, when—' here he could not help lowering his voice— 'I may have more than a parchment three-pence in my pocket. My present business,' continued he, speaking with lofty confidence, 'is merely to inquire the way to the dwelling of my kinsman, Major Molineux.'

There was a sudden and general movement in the room, which Robin interpreted as expressing the eagerness of each individual to become his guide. But the innkeeper turned his eyes to a written paper on the wall, which he read, or seemed to read, with occasional recurrences to the young man's figure.

'What have we here?' said he, breaking his speech into little dry fragments, "Left the house of the subscriber, bounden servant,[4] Hezekiah Mudge—had on when he went away, grey coat, leather breeches, master's third best hat. One pound currency reward to whoever shall lodge him in any jail in the province." 'Better trudge, boy, better trudge.'

Robin had begun to draw his hand towards the lighter end of the oak cudgel, but a strange hostility in every countenance, induced him to relinquish his purpose of breaking the courteous innkeeper's head. As he turned to leave the room, he encountered a sneering glance from the bold-featured personage whom he had before noticed; and no sooner was he beyond the door, than he heard a general laugh, in which the innkeeper's voice might be distinguished, like the dropping of small stones in a kettle.

---

4. A person bound, or "indentured," by contract to servitude for seven years (or another set period), usually in repayment for transportation to the colonies.

'Now is it not strange,' thought Robin, with his usual shrewdness, 'is it not strange, that the confession of an empty pocket, should outweigh the name of my kinsman, Major Molineux? Oh, if I had one of these grinning rascals in the woods, where I and my oak sapling grew up together, I would teach him that my arm is heavy, though my purse be light!'

On turning the corner of the narrow lane, Robin found himself in a spacious street, with an unbroken line of lofty houses on each side, and a steepled building at the upper end, whence the ringing of a bell announced the hour of nine. The light of the moon, and the lamps from numerous shop windows, discovered people promenading on the pavement, and amongst them, Robin hoped to recognise his hitherto inscrutable relative. The result of his former inquiries made him unwilling to hazard another, in a scene of such publicity, and he determined to walk slowly and silently up the street, thrusting his face close to that of every elderly gentleman, in search of the Major's lineaments. In his progress, Robin encountered many gay and gallant figures. Embroidered garments, of showy colors, enormous periwigs, gold-laced hats, and silver hilted swords, glided past him and dazzled his optics. Travelled youths, imitators of the European fine gentlemen of the period, trod jauntily along, half-dancing to the fashionable tunes which they hummed, and making poor Robin ashamed of his quiet and natural gait. At length, after many pauses to examine the gorgeous display of goods in the shop windows, and after suffering some rebukes for the impertinence of his scrutiny into people's faces, the Major's kinsman found himself near the steepled building, still unsuccessful in his search. As yet, however, he had seen only one side of the thronged street; so Robin crossed, and continued the same sort of inquisition down the opposite pavement, with stronger hopes than the philosopher seeking an honest man,[5] but with no better fortune. He had arrived about midway towards the lower end, from which his course began, when he overheard the approach of some one, who struck down a cane on the flag-stones at every step, uttering, at regular intervals, two sepulchral hems.

'Mercy on us!' quoth Robin, recognising the sound.

Turning a corner, which chanced to be close at his right hand, he hastened to pursue his researches, in some other part of the town. His patience was now wearing low, and he seemed to feel more fatigue from his rambles since he crossed the ferry, than from his journey of several days on the other side. Hunger also pleaded loudly within him, and Robin began to balance the propriety of demanding, violently and with lifted cudgel, the necessary guidance from the first solitary passenger, whom he should meet. While a resolution to this effect was gaining strength, he entered a street of mean appearance, on either side of which, a row of ill-built houses was straggling towards the harbor. The moonlight fell upon no passenger along the whole extent, but in the third domicile which Robin passed, there was a half-opened door, and his keen glance detected a woman's garment within.

'My luck may be better here,' said he to himself.

Accordingly, he approached the door, and beheld it shut closer as he did so; yet an open space remained, sufficing for the fair occupant to observe the stranger, without a corresponding display on her part. All that Robin

---

5. Diogenes, the Greek philosopher (412?–323 B.C.E.), carried a lantern about in daytime in his search for an honest man.

could discern was a strip of scarlet petticoat, and the occasional sparkle of an eye, as if the moonbeams were trembling on some bright thing.

'Pretty mistress,'—for I may call her so with a good conscience, thought the shrewd youth, since I know nothing to the contrary—'my sweet pretty mistress, will you be kind enough to tell me whereabouts I must seek the dwelling of my kinsman, Major Molineux?'

Robin's voice was plaintive and winning, and the female, seeing nothing to be shunned in the handsome country youth, thrust open the door, and came forth into the moonlight. She was a dainty little figure, with a white neck, round arms, and a slender waist, at the extremity of which her scarlet petticoat jutted out over a hoop, as if she were standing in a balloon. Moreover, her face was oval and pretty, her hair dark beneath the little cap, and her bright eyes possessed a sly freedom, which triumphed over those of Robin.

'Major Molineux dwells here,' said this fair woman.

Now her voice was the sweetest Robin had heard that night, the airy counterpart of a stream of melted silver; yet he could not help doubting whether that sweet voice spoke gospel truth. He looked up and down the mean street, and then surveyed the house before which they stood. It was a small, dark edifice of two stories, the second of which projected over the lower floor; and the front apartment had the aspect of a shop for petty commodities.

'Now truly I am in luck,' replied Robin, cunningly, 'and so indeed is my kinsman, the Major, in having so pretty a housekeeper. But I prithee trouble him to step to the door; I will deliver him a message from his friends in the country, and then go back to my lodgings at the inn.'

'Nay, the Major has been a-bed this hour or more, said the lady of the scarlet petticoat; 'and it would be to little purpose to disturb him to night, seeing his evening draught was of the strongest. But he is a kind-hearted man, and it would be as much as my life's worth, to let a kinsman of his turn away from the door. You are the good old gentleman's very picture, and I could swear that was his rainy-weather hat. Also, he has garments very much resembling those leather—But come in, I pray, for I bid you hearty welcome in his name.'

So saying, the fair and hospitable dame took our hero by the hand; and though the touch was light, and the force was gentleness, and though Robin read in her eyes what he did not hear in her words, yet the slender waisted woman, in the scarlet petticoat, proved stronger than the athletic country youth. She had drawn his half-willing footsteps nearly to the threshold, when the opening of a door in the neighborhood, startled the Major's housekeeper, and, leaving the Major's kinsman, she vanished speedily into her own domicile. A heavy yawn preceded the appearance of a man, who, like the Moonshine of Pyramus and Thisbe, carried a lantern,[6] needlessly aiding his sister luminary in the heavens. As he walked sleepily up the street, he turned his broad, dull face on Robin, and displayed a long staff, spiked at the end.

'Home, vagabond, home!' said the watchman, in accents that seemed to fall asleep as soon as they were uttered. 'Home, or we'll set you in the stocks by peep of day!'

'This is the second hint of the kind,' thought Robin. 'I wish they would end my difficulties, by setting me there to-night.'

---

6. In the play-within-a-play in Shakespeare's *Midsummer Night's Dream* 5.1, the character Moonshine carries a lantern representing the moonlight that shines on the lovers Pyramus and Thisbe.

Nevertheless, the youth felt an instinctive antipathy towards the guardian of midnight order, which at first prevented him from asking his usual question. But just when the man was about to vanish behind the corner, Robin resolved not to lose the opportunity, and shouted lustily after him—

'I say, friend! will you guide me to the house of my kinsman, Major Molineux?'

The watchman made no reply, but turned the corner and was gone; yet Robin seemed to hear the sound of drowsy laughter stealing along the solitary street. At that moment, also, a pleasant titter saluted him from the open window above his head; he looked up, and caught the sparkle of a saucy eye; a round arm beckoned to him, and next he heard light footsteps descending the staircase within. But Robin, being of the household of a New England clergyman, was a good youth, as well as a shrewd one; so he resisted temptation, and fled away.

He now roamed desperately, and at random, through the town, almost ready to believe that a spell was on him, like that, by which a wizard of his country, had once kept three pursuers wandering, a whole winter night, within twenty paces of the cottage which they sought. The streets lay before him, strange and desolate, and the lights were extinguished in almost every house. Twice, however, little parties of men, among whom Robin distinguished individuals in outlandish attire, came hurrying along, but though on both occasions they paused to address him, such intercourse did not at all enlighten his perplexity. They did but utter a few words in some language of which Robin knew nothing, and perceiving his inability to answer, bestowed a curse upon him in plain English, and hastened away. Finally, the lad determined to knock at the door of every mansion that might appear worthy to be occupied by his kinsman, trusting that perseverance would overcome the fatality which had hitherto thwarted him. Firm in this resolve, he was passing beneath the walls of a church, which formed the corner of two streets, when, as he turned into the shade of its steeple, he encountered a bulky stranger, muffled in a cloak. The man was proceeding with the speed of earnest business, but Robin planted himself full before him, holding the oak cudgel with both hands across his body, as a bar to further passage.

'Halt, honest man, and answer me a question,' said he, very resolutely, 'Tell me, this instant, whereabouts is the dwelling of my kinsman, Major Molineux?'

'Keep your tongue between your teeth, fool, and let me pass,' said a deep, gruff voice, which Robin partly remembered. 'Let me pass, I say, or I'll strike you to the earth!'

'No, no, neighbor!' cried Robin, flourishing his cudgel, and then thrusting its larger end close to the man's muffled face. 'No, no, I'm not the fool you take me for, nor do you pass, till I have an answer to my question. Whereabouts is the dwelling of my kinsman, Major Molineux?'

The stranger, instead of attempting to force his passage, stept back into the moonlight, unmuffled his own face and stared full into that of Robin.

'Watch here an hour, and Major Molineux will pass by,' said he.

Robin gazed with dismay and astonishment, on the unprecedented physiognomy of the speaker. The forehead with its double prominence, the broad-hooked nose, the shaggy eyebrows, and fiery eyes, were those which he had noticed at the inn, but the man's complexion had undergone a singular, or more properly, a two-fold change. One side of the face blazed of an intense red, while the other was black as midnight, the division line being in the broad bridge of the nose; and a mouth, which seemed to extend from ear to ear, was black or red, in contrast to the color of the cheek. The effect was as if two individual devils, a fiend of fire and a fiend of darkness, had united themselves to form this infernal visage. The stranger grinned in Robin's face, muffled his party-colored features, and was out of sight in a moment.

'Strange things we travellers see!' ejaculated Robin.

He seated himself, however, upon the steps of the church-door, resolving to wait the appointed time for his kinsman's appearance. A few moments were consumed in philosophical speculations, upon the species of the *genus homo*, who had just left him, but having settled this point shrewdly, rationally, and satisfactorily, he was compelled to look elsewhere for amusement. And first he threw his eyes along the street; it was of more respectable appearance than most of those into which he had wandered, and the moon, 'creating, like the imaginative power, a beautiful strangeness in familiar objects,' gave something of romance to a scene, that might not have possessed it in the light of day. The irregular, and often quaint architecture of the houses, some of whose roofs were broken into numerous little peaks; while others ascended, steep and narrow, into a single point; and others again were square; the pure milk-white of some of their complexions, the aged darkness of others, and the thousand sparklings, reflected from bright substances in the plastered walls of many; these matters engaged Robin's attention for awhile, and then began to grow wearisome. Next he endeavored to define the forms of distant objects, starting away with almost ghostly indistinctness, just as his eye appeared to grasp them; and finally he took a minute survey of an edifice, which stood on the opposite side of the street, directly in front of the church-door, where he was stationed. It was a large square mansion, distinguished from its neighbors by a balcony, which rested on tall pillars, and by an elaborate gothic window, communicating therewith.

'Perhaps this is the very house I have been seeking,' thought Robin.

Then he strove to speed away the time, by listening to a murmur, which swept continually along the street, yet was scarcely audible, except to an unaccustomed ear like his; it was a low, dull, dreamy sound, compounded of many noises, each of which was at too great a distance to be separately heard. Robin marvelled at this snore of a sleeping town, and marvelled more, whenever its continuity was broken, by now and then a distant shout, apparently loud where it originated. But altogether it was a sleep-inspiring sound, and to shake off its drowsy influence, Robin arose, and climbed a window-frame, that he might view the interior of the church. There the moonbeams came trembling in, and fell down upon the deserted pews, and extended along the quiet aisles. A fainter, yet more awful radiance, was hovering round the pulpit, and one solitary ray had dared to rest upon the opened page of the great bible. Had Nature, in that deep hour, become a worshipper in the house, which man had builded? Or was that heavenly light the visible sanctity of this place, visible because no earthly and impure feet were within the walls? The scene made Robin's heart shiver with a sensation of loneliness, stronger than he had ever felt in the remotest depths of his native woods; so he turned away, and sat down again before the door. There were graves around the church, and now an uneasy thought obtruded into Robin's breast. What if the object of his search, which had been so often and so strangely thwarted, were all the time mouldering in his shroud? What if his kinsman should glide through yonder gate, and nod and smile to him in passing dimly by?

'Oh, that any breathing thing were here with me!' said Robin.

Recalling his thoughts from this uncomfortable track, he sent them over forest, hill, and stream, and attempted to imagine how that evening of ambiguity and weariness, had been spent by his father's household. He pictured them assembled at the door, beneath the tree, the great old tree, which had been spared for its huge twisted trunk, and venerable shade, when a thousand leafy brethren fell. There, at the going down of the summer sun, it was his father's custom to perform domestic worship, that the neighbors might come and join with him like brothers of the family, and that the wayfaring man might pause to drink at that fountain, and keep his heart pure by freshening the memory of home. Robin distinguished the seat of every individual of the little audience; he saw the good man in the midst, holding the scriptures in the golden light that shone from the western clouds; he beheld him close the book, and all rise up to pray. He heard the old thanksgivings for daily mercies, the old supplications for their continuance, to which he had so often listened in weariness, but which were now among his dear remembrances. He perceived the slight inequality of his father's voice when he came to speak of the Absent One; he noted how his mother turned her face to the broad and knotted trunk, how his elder brother scorned, because the beard was rough upon his upper lip, to permit his features to be moved; how his younger sister drew down a low hanging branch before her eyes; and how the little one of all, whose sports had hitherto broken the decorum of the scene, understood the prayer for her playmate, and burst into clamorous grief. Then he saw them go in at the door; and when Robin would have entered also, the latch tinkled into its place, and he was excluded from his home.

'Am I here, or there?' cried Robin, starting; for all at once, when his thoughts had become visible and audible in a dream, the long, wide, solitary street shone out before him.

He aroused himself, and endeavored to fix his attention steadily upon the large edifice which he had surveyed before. But still his mind kept vibrating between fancy and reality; by turns, the pillars of the balcony lengthened into the tall, bare stems of pines, dwindled down to human figures, settled again in their true shape and size, and then commenced a new succession of changes. For a single moment, when he deemed himself awake, he could have sworn that a visage, one which he seemed to remember, yet could not absolutely name as his kinsman's, was looking towards him from the Gothic window. A deeper sleep wrestled with, and nearly overcame him, but fled at the sound of footsteps along the opposite pavement. Robin rubbed his eyes, discerned a man passing at the foot of the balcony, and addressed him in a loud, peevish, and lamentable cry.

'Halloo, friend! must I wait here all night for my kinsman, Major Molineux?'

The sleeping echoes awoke, and answered the voice; and the passenger, barely able to discern a figure sitting in the oblique shade of the steeple, traversed the street to obtain a nearer view. He was himself a gentleman in his prime, of open, intelligent, cheerful and altogether prepossessing countenance. Perceiving a country youth, apparently homeless and without friends, he accosted him in a tone of real kindness, which had become strange to Robin's ears.

'Well, my good lad, why are you sitting here?' inquired he. 'Can I be of service to you in any way?'

'I am afraid not, Sir,' replied Robin, despondingly; 'yet I shall take it kindly, if you'll answer me a single question. I've been searching half the night for one Major Molineux; now, Sir, is there really such a person in these parts, or am I dreaming?'

'Major Molineux! The name is not altogether strange to me,' said the gentleman smiling. 'Have you any objection to telling me the nature of your business with him?'

Then Robin briefly related that his father was a clergyman, settled on a small salary, at a long distance back in the country, and that he and Major Molineux were brothers' children. The Major, having inherited riches, and acquired civil and military rank, had visited his cousin in great pomp a year or two before; had manifested much interest in Robin and an elder brother, and, being childless himself, had thrown out hints respecting the future establishment of one of them in life. The elder brother was destined to succeed to the farm, which his father cultivated, in the interval of sacred duties; it was therefore determined that Robin should profit by his kinsman's generous intentions, especially as he had seemed to be rather the favorite, and was thought to possess other necessary endowments.

'For I have the name of being a shrewd youth,' observed Robin, in this part of his story.

'I doubt not you deserve it,' replied his new friend, good naturedly; 'but pray proceed.'

'Well, Sir, being nearly eighteen years old, and well grown, as you see,' continued Robin, raising himself to his full height, 'I thought it high time to begin the world. So my mother and sister put me in handsome trim, and my father gave me half the remnant of his last year's salary, and five days ago I started for this place, to pay the Major a visit. But would you believe it, Sir? I crossed the ferry a little after dusk, and have yet found nobody that would show me the way to his dwelling; only an hour or two since, I was told to wait here, and Major Molineux would pass by.'

'Can you describe the man who told you this?' inquired the gentleman.

'Oh, he was a very ill-favored fellow, Sir,' replied Robin, 'with two great bumps on his forehead, a hook nose, fiery eyes, and, what struck me as the strangest, his face was of two different colors. Do you happen to know such a man, Sir?'

'Not intimately,' answered the stranger, 'but I chanced to meet him a little time previous to your stopping me. I believe you may trust his word, and that the Major will very shortly pass through this street. In the mean time, as I have a singular curiosity to witness your meeting, I will sit down here upon the steps, and bear you company.'

He seated himself accordingly, and soon engaged his companion in animated discourse. It was but of brief continuance, however, for a noise of shouting, which had long been remotely audible, drew so much nearer, that Robin inquired its cause.

'What may be the meaning of this uproar?' asked he. 'Truly, if your town be always as noisy, I shall find little sleep, while I am an inhabitant.'

'Why, indeed, friend Robin, there do appear to be three or four riotous fellows abroad to-night,' replied the gentleman. 'You must not expect all the stillness of your native woods, here in our streets. But the watch will shortly be at the heels of these lads, and—'

'Aye, and set them in the stocks by peep of day,' interrupted Robin, recollecting his own encounter with the drowsy lantern-bearer. 'But, dear Sir, if I may trust my ears, an army of watchmen would never make head against such a multitude of rioters. There were at least a thousand voices went to make up that one shout.'

'May not one man have several voices, Robin, as well as two complexions?' said his friend.

'Perhaps a man may; but heaven forbid that a woman should!' responded the shrewd youth, thinking of the seductive tones of the Major's housekeeper.

The sounds of a trumpet in some neighboring street, now became so evident and continual, that Robin's curiosity was strongly excited. In addition to the shouts, he heard frequent bursts from many instruments of discord, and a wild and confused laughter filled up the intervals. Robin rose from the steps, and looked wistfully towards a point, whither several people seemed to be hastening.

'Surely some prodigious merrymaking is going on,' exclaimed he. 'I have laughed very little since I left home, Sir, and should be sorry to lose an opportunity. Shall we just step round the corner by that darkish house, and take our share of the fun?'

'Sit down again, sit down, good Robin,' replied the gentleman, laying his hand on the skirt of the grey coat. 'You forget that we must wait here for your kinsman; and there is reason to believe that he will pass by, in the course of a very few moments.'

The near approach of the uproar had now disturbed the neighborhood; windows flew open on all sides; and many heads, in the attire of the pillow, and confused by sleep suddenly broken, were protruded to the gaze of whoever had leisure to observe them. Eager voices hailed each other from house to house, all demanding the explanation, which not a soul could give. Half-dressed men hurried towards the unknown commotion, stumbling as they went over the stone steps, that thrust themselves into the narrow foot-walk. The shouts, the laughter, and the tuneless bray, the antipodes of music, came onward with increasing din, till scattered individuals, and then denser bodies, began to appear round a corner, at a distance of a hundred yards.

'Will you recognise your kinsman, Robin, if he passes in this crowd?' inquired the gentleman.

'Indeed, I can't warrant it, Sir; but I'll take my stand here, and keep a bright look out,' answered Robin, descending to the outer edge of the pavement.

A mighty stream of people now emptied into the street, and came rolling slowly towards the church. A single horseman wheeled the corner in the midst of them, and close behind him came a band of fearful wind-instruments, sending forth a fresher discord, now that no intervening buildings kept it from the ear. Then a redder light disturbed the moonbeams, and a dense multitude of torches shone along the street, concealing by their glare whatever object they illuminated. The single horseman, clad in a military dress, and bearing a drawn sword, rode onward as the leader, and, by his fierce and variegated countenance, appeared like war personified; the red of one cheek was an emblem of fire and sword; the blackness of the other betokened the mourning which attends them. In his train, were wild figures in the Indian dress, and many fantastic shapes without a model, giving the whole march a visionary air, as if a dream had broken forth from some feverish brain, and were sweeping visibly through the midnight streets. A mass of people, inactive, except as applauding spectators, hemmed the procession in, and several women ran along the sidewalks, piercing the confusion of heavier sounds, with their shrill voices of mirth or terror.[7]

'The double-faced fellow has his eye upon me,' muttered Robin, with an indefinite but uncomfortable idea, that he was himself to bear a part in the pageantry.

The leader turned himself in the saddle, and fixed his glance full upon the country youth, as the steed went slowly by. When Robin had freed his eyes from those fiery ones, the musicians were passing before him, and the torches were close at hand; but the unsteady brightness of the latter formed a veil which he could not penetrate. The rattling of wheels over the stones sometimes found its way to his ear, and confused traces of a human form appeared at intervals, and then melted into the vivid light. A moment more, and the leader thundered a command to halt; the trumpets vomited a horrid breath, and held their peace; the shouts and laughter of the people died away, and there remained only an universal hum, nearly allied to silence. Right before Robin's eyes was an uncovered cart. There the torches blazed the brightest, there the moon shone out like day, and there, in tar-and-feathery dignity, sate his kinsman, Major Molineux!

He was an elderly man, of large and majestic person, and strong, square features, betokening a steady soul; but steady as it was, his enemies had found the means to shake it. His face was pale as death, and far more ghastly; the broad forehead was contracted in his agony, so that the eyebrows formed one dark grey line; his eyes were red and wild, and the foam hung white upon his quivering lip. His whole frame was agitated by a quick, and continual tremor, which his pride strove to quell, even in those circumstances of overwhelming humiliation. But perhaps the bitterest pang of all was when his eyes met those of Robin; for he evidently knew him on the instant, as the youth stood witnessing the foul disgrace of a head that had grown grey in honor. They stared at each other in silence, and Robin's knees shook, and his hair bristled, with a mixture of pity and terror. Soon, however, a bewildering excitement began to seize upon his mind; the preceding adventures of the night, the unexpected appearance of the crowd, the torches, the confused din, and the hush that followed, the spectre of his kinsman reviled by that great multitude, all this, and more than all, a perception of tremendous ridicule in the whole scene, affected him with a sort of mental inebriety. At that moment a voice of sluggish merriment saluted Robin's ears; he turned instinctively, and just behind the corner of the church stood the lantern-bearer, rubbing his eyes, and drowsily enjoying the lad's amazement. Then he heard a peal of laughter like the ringing of silvery bells; a woman twitched his arm, a saucy eye met his, and he saw the lady of the scarlet petticoat. A sharp, dry cachinnation appealed to his memory, and, standing on tiptoe in the crowd, with his white apron over his head, he beheld the courteous little innkeeper. And lastly, there sailed over the heads of the multitude a great, broad laugh, broken in the midst by two deep sepulchral hems; thus—

'Haw, haw, haw—hem, hem—haw, haw, haw, haw!'

The sound proceeded from the balcony of the opposite edifice, and thither Robin turned his eyes. In front of the Gothic window stood the old citizen, wrapped in a wide gown, his grey periwig exchanged for a nightcap, which

---

7. Though set during the 1730s, the actions of the mob resemble those of the Boston Sons of Liberty during the Stamp Act crisis in 1765.

was thrust back from his forehead, and his silk stockings hanging down about his legs. He supported himself on his polished cane in a fit of convulsive merriment, which manifested itself on his solemn old features, like a funny inscription on a tomb-stone. Then Robin seemed to hear the voices of the barbers; of the guests of the inn; and of all who had made sport of him that night. The contagion was spreading among the multitude, when, all at once, it seized upon Robin, and he sent forth a shout of laughter that echoed through the street; every man shook his sides, every man emptied his lungs, but Robin's shout was the loudest there. The cloud-spirits peeped from their silvery islands, as the congregated mirth went roaring up the sky! The Man in the Moon heard the far bellow; 'Oho,' quoth he, 'the old Earth is frolicsome to-night!'

When there was a momentary calm in that tempestuous sea of sound, the leader gave the sign, and the procession resumed its march. On they went, like fiends that throng in mockery round some dead potentate, mighty no more, but majestic still in his agony. On they went, in counterfeited pomp, in senseless uproar, in frenzied merriment, trampling all on an old man's heart. On swept the tumult, and left a silent street behind.

• • • • •

'Well, Robin, are you dreaming?' inquired the gentleman, laying his hand on the youth's shoulder.

Robin started, and withdrew his arm from the stone post, to which he had instinctively clung, while the living stream rolled by him. His cheek was somewhat pale, and his eye not quite so lively as in the earlier part of the evening.

'Will you be kind enough to show me the way to the Ferry?' said he, after a moment's pause.

'You have then adopted a new subject of inquiry?' observed his companion, with a smile.

'Why, yes, Sir,' replied Robin, rather dryly. 'Thanks to you, and to my other friends, I have at last met my kinsman, and he will scarce desire to see my face again. I begin to grow weary of a town life, Sir. Will you show me the way to the Ferry?'

'No, my good friend Robin, not to-night, at least,' said the gentleman. 'Some few days hence, if you continue to wish it, I will speed you on your journey. Or, if you prefer to remain with us, perhaps, as you are a shrewd youth, you may rise in the world, without the help of your kinsman, Major Molineux.'

1832

Young Goodman Brown[1]

Young goodman Brown came forth, at sunset, into the street of Salem village,[2] but put his head back, after crossing the threshold, to exchange a parting kiss with his young wife. And Faith, as the wife was aptly named,

---

1. The text is that of the first publication in the *New-England Magazine* (April 1835). "Goodman": title used to address a man of humble birth.

2. In Massachusetts; the site of the witchcraft trials and executions of 1692.

thrust her own pretty head into the street, letting the wind play with the pink ribbons of her cap, while she called to goodman Brown.

'Dearest heart,' whispered she, softly and rather sadly, when her lips were close to his ear, 'pr'y thee, put off your journey until sunrise, and sleep in your own bed to-night. A lone woman is troubled with such dreams and such thoughts, that she's afeard of herself, sometimes. Pray, tarry with me this night, dear husband, of all nights in the year!'

'My love and my Faith,' replied young goodman Brown, 'of all nights in the year, this one night must I tarry away from thee. My journey, as thou callest it, forth and back again, must needs be done 'twixt now and sunrise. What, my sweet, pretty wife, dost thou doubt me already, and we but three months married!'

'Then, God bless you!' said Faith, with the pink ribbons, 'and may you find all well, when you come back.'

'Amen!' cried goodman Brown. 'Say thy prayers, dear Faith, and go to bed at dusk, and no harm will come to thee.'

So they parted; and the young man pursued his way, until, being about to turn the corner by the meeting-house, he looked back, and saw the head of Faith still peeping after him, with a melancholy air, in spite of her pink ribbons.

'Poor little Faith!' thought he, for his heart smote him. 'What a wretch am I, to leave her on such an errand! She talks of dreams, too. Methought, as she spoke, there was trouble in her face, as if a dream had warned her what work is to be done to-night. But, no, no! 't would kill her to think it. Well; she's a blessed angel on earth; and after this one night, I'll cling to her skirts and follow her to Heaven.'

With this excellent resolve for the future, goodman Brown felt himself justified in making more haste on his present evil purpose. He had taken a dreary road, darkened by all the gloomiest trees of the forest, which barely stood aside to let the narrow path creep through, and closed immediately behind. It was all as lonely as could be; and there is this peculiarity in such a solitude, that the traveler knows not who may be concealed by the innumerable trunks and the thick boughs overhead; so that, with lonely footsteps, he may yet be passing through an unseen multitude.

'There may be a devilish Indian behind every tree,' said goodman Brown, to himself; and he glanced fearfully behind him, as he added, 'What if the devil himself should be at my very elbow!'

His head being turned back, he passed a crook of the road, and looking forward again, beheld the figure of a man, in grave and decent attire, seated at the foot of an old tree. He arose, at goodman Brown's approach, and walked onward, side by side with him.

'You are late, goodman Brown,' said he. 'The clock of the Old South was striking as I came through Boston; and that is full fifteen minutes agone.'[3]

'Faith kept me back awhile,' replied the young man, with a tremor in his voice, caused by the sudden appearance of his companion, though not wholly unexpected.

It was now deep dusk in the forest, and deepest in that part of it where these two were journeying. As nearly as could be discerned, the second

---

3. Boston's Old South Church, built in 1669, was approximately sixteen miles from Salem. That the "figure" could make the journey from Old South to Salem in fifteen minutes signifies supernatural powers.

traveler was about fifty years old, apparently in the same rank of life as goodman Brown, and bearing a considerable resemblance to him, though perhaps more in expression than features. Still, they might have been taken for
father and son. And yet, though the elder person was as simply clad as the
younger, and as simple in manner too, he had an indescribable air of one who
knew the world, and would not have felt abashed at the governor's dinner-
table, or in king William's[4] court, were it possible that his affairs should
call him thither. But the only thing about him, that could be fixed upon as
remarkable, was his staff, which bore the likeness of a great black snake, so
curiously wrought, that it might almost be seen to twist and wriggle itself,
like a living serpent. This, of course, must have been an ocular deception,
assisted by the uncertain light.

'Come, goodman Brown!' cried his fellow-traveler, 'this is a dull pace for
the beginning of a journey. Take my staff, if you are so soon weary.'

'Friend,' said the other, exchanging his slow pace for a full stop, 'having
kept covenant by meeting thee here, it is my purpose now to return whence
I came. I have scruples, touching the matter thou wot'st[5] of.'

'Sayest thou so?' replied he of the serpent, smiling apart. 'Let us walk on,
nevertheless, reasoning as we go, and if I convince thee not, thou shalt turn
back. We are but a little way in the forest, yet.'

'Too far, too far!' exclaimed the goodman, unconsciously resuming his
walk. 'My father never went into the woods on such an errand, nor his
father before him. We have been a race of honest men and good Christians,
since the days of the martyrs.[6] And shall I be the first of the name of Brown,
that ever took this path, and kept'—

'Such company, thou wouldst say,' observed the elder person, interpreting
his pause. 'Good, goodman Brown! I have been as well acquainted with
your family as with ever a one among the Puritans; and that's no trifle to
say. I helped your grandfather, the constable, when he lashed the Quaker
woman so smartly through the streets of Salem.[7] And it was I that brought
your father a pitch-pine knot, kindled at my own hearth, to set fire to an
Indian village, in king Philip's[8] war. They were my good friends, both; and
many a pleasant walk have we had along this path, and returned merrily
after midnight. I would fain be friends with you, for their sake.'

'If it be as thou sayest,' replied goodman Brown, 'I marvel they never
spoke of these matters. Or, verily, I marvel not, seeing that the least rumor
of the sort would have driven them from New-England. We are a people of
prayer, and good works, to boot, and abide no such wickedness.'

'Wickedness or not,' said the traveler with the twisted staff, 'I have a very
general acquaintance here in New-England. The deacons of many a church
have drunk the communion wine with me; the selectmen, of divers towns,
make me their chairman; and a majority of the Great and General Court[9] are

---

4. Beginning in 1689, King William III (1650–
1702) ruled England with his wife, Queen Mary
II, until her death in 1694.
5. Wotest; to know (archaic).
6. I.e., during the reign of the Catholic Mary
Tudor of England (r. 1553–58), called "Bloody
Mary" for her persecution of Protestants. Common reading in New England was John Foxe's
Acts and Monuments (1563), soon known as
the *Book of Martyrs*; it concluded with detailed
accounts of martyrdom under Mary.

7. Hawthorne's paternal great-great-grandfather,
William Hathorne (1606–1681), had ordered the
whipping of a Quaker woman in Salem. Hawthorne mentions this incident in "The Custom-
House" preface to *The Scarlet Letter*.
8. Leader of the Wampanoag Indians, Metacomet (d. 1676), called Philip by the English, led
a bloody and ultimately unsuccessful war (1675–
76) against the New England colonists.
9. The legislature.

firm supporters of my interest. The governor and I, too—but these are state-secrets.'

'Can this be so!' cried goodman Brown, with a stare of amazement at his undisturbed companion. 'Howbeit, I have nothing to do with the governor and council; they have their own ways, and are no rule for a simple husband-man,[1] like me. But, were I to go on with thee, how should I meet the eye of that good old man, our minister, at Salem village? Oh, his voice would make me tremble, both Sabbath-day and lecture-day!'[2]

Thus far, the elder traveler had listened with due gravity, but now burst into a fit of irrepressible mirth, shaking himself so violently, that his snake-like staff actually seemed to wriggle in sympathy.

'Ha! ha! ha!' shouted he, again and again; then composing himself, 'Well, go on, goodman Brown, go on; but, pr'y thee, don't kill me with laughing!'

'Well, then, to end the matter at once,' said goodman Brown, consider-ably nettled, 'there is my wife, Faith. It would break her dear little heart; and I'd rather break my own!'

'Nay, if that be the case,' answered the other, 'e'en go thy ways, goodman Brown. I would not, for twenty old women like the one hobbling before us, that Faith should come to any harm.'

As he spoke, he pointed his staff at a female figure on the path, in whom goodman Brown recognized a very pious and exemplary dame, who had taught him his catechism, in youth, and was still his moral and spiritual adviser, jointly with the minister and deacon Gookin.[3]

'A marvel, truly, that goody Cloyse[4] should be so far in the wilderness, at night-fall!' said he. 'But, with your leave, friend, I shall take a cut through the woods, until we have left this Christian woman behind. Being a stranger to you, she might ask whom I was consorting with, and whither I was going.'

'Be it so,' said his fellow-traveler. 'Betake you to the woods, and let me keep the path.'

Accordingly, the young man turned aside, but took care to watch his com-panion, who advanced softly along the road, until he had come within a staff's length of the old dame. She, meanwhile, was making the best of her way, with singular speed for so aged a woman, and mumbling some indistinct words, a prayer, doubtless, as she went. The traveler put forth his staff, and touched her withered neck with what seemed the serpent's tail.

'The devil!' screamed the pious old lady.

'Then goody Cloyse knows her old friend?' observed the traveler, con-fronting her, and leaning on his writhing stick.

'Ah, forsooth, and is it your worship, indeed?' cried the good dame. 'Yea, truly is it, and in the very image of my old gossip, goodman Brown, the grand-father of the silly fellow that now is. But, would your worship believe it? my broomstick hath strangely disappeared, stolen, as I suspect, by that unhanged witch, goody Cory,[5] and that, too, when I was all anointed with the juice of smallage and cinque-foil and wolf's-bane'[6]—

---

1. Usually, farmer; here, man of ordinary status.
2. Midweek sermon day, Wednesday or Thursday.
3. Daniel Gookin (1612–1687), colonial magis-trate who looked after Indian affairs. Through-out the story Hawthorne uses historical names associated with Salem and the witchcraft trial.
4. Sarah Cloyce was accused of witchcraft and imprisoned during the Salem witch trials; she was released when the trials were suspended.

"Goody": i.e., goodwife; the polite title for a mar-ried woman of humble rank.
5. A woman named Martha Cory was hanged for witchcraft on September 22, 1692.
6. Plants associated with witchcraft. "Smallage": wild celery or parsley. "Cinque-foil": a five-lobed plant of the rose family (from the Latin for "five fingers"). "Wolf's-bane": hooded, poisonous plant known as monkshood (bane means "poison").

'Mingled with fine wheat and the fat of a new-born babe,' said the shape of old goodman Brown.

'Ah, your worship knows the receipt,'[7] cried the old lady, cackling aloud. 'So, as I was saying, being all ready for the meeting, and no horse to ride on, I made up my mind to foot it; for they tell me, there is a nice young man to be taken into communion to-night. But now your good worship will lend me your arm, and we shall be there in a twinkling.'

'That can hardly be,' answered her friend. 'I may not spare you my arm, goody Cloyse, but here is my staff, if you will.'

So saying, he threw it down at her feet, where, perhaps, it assumed life, being one of the rods which its owner had formerly lent to the Egyptian Magi.[8] Of this fact, however, goodman Brown could not take cognizance. He had cast up his eyes in astonishment, and looking down again, beheld neither goody Cloyse nor the serpentine staff, but his fellow-traveler alone, who waited for him as calmly as if nothing had happened.

'That old woman taught me my catechism!' said the young man; and there was a world of meaning in this simple comment.

They continued to walk onward, while the elder traveler exhorted his companion to make good speed and persevere in the path, discoursing so aptly, that his arguments seemed rather to spring up in the bosom of his auditor, than to be suggested by himself. As they went, he plucked a branch of maple, to serve for a walking-stick, and began to strip it of the twigs and little boughs, which were wet with evening dew. The moment his fingers touched them, they became strangely withered and dried up, as with a week's sunshine. Thus the pair proceeded, at a good free pace, until suddenly, in a gloomy hollow of the road, goodman Brown sat himself down on the stump of a tree, and refused to go any farther.

'Friend,' said he, stubbornly, 'my mind is made up. Not another step will I budge on this errand. What if a wretched old woman do choose to go to the devil, when I thought she was going to Heaven! Is that any reason why I should quit my dear Faith, and go after her?'

'You will think better of this, by-and-by,' said his acquaintance, composedly. 'Sit here and rest yourself awhile; and when you feel like moving again, there is my staff to help you along.'

Without more words, he threw his companion the maple stick, and was as speedily out of sight, as if he had vanished into the deepening gloom. The young man sat a few moments, by the roadside, applauding himself greatly, and thinking with how clear a conscience he should meet the minister, in his morning-walk, nor shrink from the eye of good old deacon Gookin. And what calm sleep would be his, that very night, which was to have been spent so wickedly, but purely and sweetly now, in the arms of Faith! Amidst these pleasant and praiseworthy meditations, goodman Brown heard the tramp of horses along the road, and deemed it advisable to conceal himself within the verge of the forest, conscious of the guilty purpose that had brought him thither, though now so happily turned from it.

On came the hoof-tramps and the voices of the riders, two grave old voices, conversing soberly as they drew near. These mingled sounds

---

7. Recipe.
8. Exodus 7.11 describes the magicians of Egypt who duplicated Aaron's feat of casting down his rod before Pharaoh and making it turn into a serpent.

appeared to pass along the road, within a few yards of the young man's hiding-place; but owing, doubtless, to the depth of the gloom, at that partic- ular spot, neither the travelers nor their steeds were visible. Though their figures brushed the small boughs by the way-side, it could not be seen that they intercepted, even for a moment, the faint gleam from the strip of bright sky, athwart which they must have passed. Goodman Brown alter- nately crouched and stood on tip-toe, pulling aside the branches, and thrusting forth his head as far as he durst, without discerning so much as a shadow. It vexed him the more, because he could have sworn, were such a thing possible, that he recognized the voices of the minister and deacon Gookin, jogging along quietly, as they were wont to do, when bound to some ordination or ecclesiastical council. While yet within hearing, one of the riders stopped to pluck a switch.

'Of the two, reverend Sir,' said the voice like the deacon's, 'I had rather miss an ordination-dinner than to-night's meeting. They tell me that some of our community are to be here from Falmouth and beyond, and others from Connecticut and Rhode-Island; besides several of the Indian powows,[9] who, after their fashion, know almost as much deviltry as the best of us. Moreover, there is a goodly young woman to be taken into communion.'

'Mighty well, deacon Gookin!' replied the solemn old tones of the minister. 'Spur up, or we shall be late. Nothing can be done, you know, until I get on the ground.'

The hoofs clattered again, and the voices, talking so strangely in the empty air, passed on through the forest, where no church had ever been gathered, nor solitary Christian prayed. Whither, then, could these holy men be jour- neying, so deep into the heathen wilderness? Young goodman Brown caught hold of a tree, for support, being ready to sink down on the ground, faint and overburthened with the heavy sickness of his heart. He looked up to the sky, doubting whether there really was a Heaven above him. Yet, there was the blue arch, and the stars brightening in it.

'With Heaven above, and Faith below, I will yet stand firm against the devil!' cried goodman Brown.

While he still gazed upward, into the deep arch of the firmament, and had lifted his hands to pray, a cloud, though no wind was stirring, hurried across the zenith, and hid the brightening stars. The blue sky was still visible, except directly overhead, where this black mass of cloud was sweeping swiftly northward. Aloft in the air, as if from the depths of the cloud, came a con- fused and doubtful sound of voices. Once, the listener fancied that he could distinguish the accents of town's-people of his own, men and women, both pious and ungodly, many of whom he had met at the communion-table, and had seen others rioting at the tavern. The next moment, so indistinct were the sounds, he doubted whether he had heard aught but the murmur of the old forest, whispering without a wind. Then came a stronger swell of those familiar tones, heard daily in the sunshine, at Salem village, but never, until now, from a cloud of night. There was one voice, of a young woman, uttering lamentations, yet with an uncertain sorrow, and entreating for some favor, which, perhaps, it would grieve her to obtain. And all the unseen mul- titude, both saints and sinners, seemed to encourage her onward.

9. Medicine men; usually spelled "pow-wow" and later used to refer to any conference or gathering. Falmouth is a town on Cape Cod, about seventy miles from Salem.

'Faith!' shouted goodman Brown, in a voice of agony and desperation; and the echoes of the forest mocked him, crying—'Faith! Faith!' as if bewildered wretches were seeking her, all through the wilderness.

The cry of grief, rage, and terror, was yet piercing the night, when the unhappy husband held his breath for a response. There was a scream, drowned immediately in a louder murmur of voices, fading into far-off laughter, as the dark cloud swept away, leaving the clear and silent sky above goodman Brown. But something fluttered lightly down through the air, and caught on the branch of a tree. The young man seized it, and beheld a pink ribbon.

'My Faith is gone!' cried he, after one stupefied moment. 'There is no good on earth; and sin is but a name. Come, devil! for to thee is this world given.'

And maddened with despair, so that he laughed loud and long, did goodman Brown grasp his staff and set forth again, at such a rate, that he seemed to fly along the forest-path, rather than to walk or run. The road grew wilder and drearier, and more faintly traced, and vanished at length, leaving him in the heart of the dark wilderness, still rushing onward, with the instinct that guides mortal man to evil. The whole forest was peopled with frightful sounds; the creaking of the trees, the howling of wild beasts, and the yell of Indians; while, sometimes, the wind tolled like a distant church-bell, and sometimes gave a broad roar around the traveler, as if all Nature were laughing him to scorn. But he was himself the chief horror of the scene, and shrank not from its other horrors.

'Ha! ha! ha!' roared goodman Brown, when the wind laughed at him. 'Let us hear which will laugh loudest! Think not to frighten me with your dev-iltry! Come witch, come wizard, come Indian powow, come devil himself! and here comes goodman Brown. You may as well fear him as he fear you!'

In truth, all through the haunted forest, there could be nothing more frightful than the figure of goodman Brown. On he flew, among the black pines, brandishing his staff with frenzied gestures, now giving vent to an inspiration of horrid blasphemy, and now shouting forth such laughter, as set all the echoes of the forest laughing like demons around him. The fiend in his own shape is less hideous, than when he rages in the breast of man. Thus sped the demoniac on his course, until, quivering among the trees, he saw a red light before him, as when the felled trunks and branches of a clearing have been set on fire, and throw up their lurid blaze against the sky, at the hour of midnight. He paused, in a lull of the tempest that had driven him onward, and heard the swell of what seemed a hymn, rolling solemnly from a distance, with the weight of many voices. He knew the tune; it was a familiar one in the choir of the village meeting-house. The verse died heavily away, and was lengthened by a chorus, not of human voices, but of all the sounds of the benighted wilderness, pealing in awful harmony together. Goodman Brown cried out; and his cry was lost to his own ear, by its unison with the cry of the desert.

In the interval of silence, he stole forward, until the light glared full upon his eyes. At one extremity of an open space, hemmed in by the dark wall of the forest, arose a rock, bearing some rude, natural resemblance either to an altar or a pulpit, and surrounded by four blazing pines, their tops a flame, their stems untouched, like candles at an evening meeting. The mass of foliage, that had overgrown the summit of the rock, was all on fire, blazing high into the night, and fitfully illuminating the whole field. Each pendent twig and leafy festoon was in a blaze. As the red light arose and fell, a numerous congregation alternately shone forth, then disappeared in shadow, and again grew, as it were, out of the darkness, peopling the heart of the solitary woods at once.

'A grave and dark-clad company!' quoth goodman Brown.

In truth, they were such. Among them, quivering to-and-fro, between gloom and splendor, appeared faces that would be seen, next day, at the council-board of the province, and others which, Sabbath after Sabbath, looked devoutly heavenward, and benignantly over the crowded pews, from the holiest pulpits in the land. Some affirm, that the lady of the governor was there. At least, there were high dames well known to her, and wives of honored husbands, and widows, a great multitude, and ancient maidens, all of excellent repute, and fair young girls, who trembled, lest their mothers should espy them. Either the sudden gleams of light, flashing over the obscure field, bedazzled goodman Brown, or he recognized a score of the church-members of Salem village, famous for their especial sanctity. Good old deacon Gookin had arrived, and waited at the skirts of that venerable saint, his revered pastor. But, irreverently consorting with these grave, reputable, and pious people, these elders of the church, these chaste dames and dewy virgins, there were men of dissolute lives and women of spotted fame, wretches given over to all mean and filthy vice, and suspected even of horrid crimes. It was strange to see, that the good shrank not from the wicked, nor were the sinners abashed by the saints. Scattered, also, among their pale-faced enemies, were the Indian priests, or powows, who had often scared their native forest with more hideous incantations than any known to English witchcraft.

'But, where is Faith?' thought goodman Brown; and, as hope came into his heart, he trembled.

Another verse of the hymn arose, a slow and solemn strain, such as the pious love, but joined to words which expressed all that our nature can conceive of sin, and darkly hinted at far more. Unfathomable to mere mortals is the lore of fiends. Verse after verse was sung, and still the chorus of the desert swelled between, like the deepest tone of a mighty organ. And, with the final peal of that dreadful anthem, there came a sound, as if the roaring wind, the rushing streams, the howling beasts, and every other voice of the unconverted wilderness, were mingling and according with the voice of guilty man, in homage to the prince of all. The four blazing pines threw up a loftier flame, and obscurely discovered shapes and visages of horror on the smoke-wreaths, above the impious assembly. At the same moment, the fire on the rock shot redly forth, and formed a glowing arch above its base, where now appeared a figure. With reverence be it spoken, the apparition bore no slight similitude, both in garb and manner, to some grave divine of the New-England churches.

'Bring forth the converts!' cried a voice, that echoed through the field and rolled into the forest.

At the word, goodman Brown stept forth from the shadow of the trees, and approached the congregation, with whom he felt a loathful brotherhood, by the sympathy of all that was wicked in his heart. He could have well nigh sworn, that the shape of his own dead father[1] beckoned him to advance,

---

1. The Salem witch trials came to focus on the question of "specter evidence"—whether the devil could take on the "shape" of innocent people. If he could, then many supposed appearances of the accused might have been impersonations. An increasing suspicion of the value of spectral evidence was among the factors leading to the suspension of the trials.

looking downward from a smoke-wreath, while a woman, with dim features of despair, threw out her hand to warn him back. Was it his mother? But he had no power to retreat one step, nor to resist, even in thought, when the minister and good old deacon Gookin, seized his arms, and led him to the blazing rock. Thither came also the slender form of a veiled female, led between goody Cloyse, that pious teacher of the catechism, and Martha Carrier, who had received the devil's promise to be queen of hell.[2] A rampant hag was she! And there stood the proselytes, beneath the canopy of fire.

'Welcome, my children,' said the dark figure, 'to the communion of your race![3] Ye have found, thus young, your nature and your destiny. My children, look behind you!'

They turned; and flashing forth, as it were, in a sheet of flame, the fiend-worshippers were seen; the smile of welcome gleamed darkly on every visage.

'There,' resumed the sable form, 'are all whom ye have reverenced from youth. Ye deemed them holier than yourselves, and shrank from your own sin, contrasting it with their lives of righteousness, and prayerful aspirations heavenward. Yet, here are they all, in my worshipping assembly! This night it shall be granted you to know their secret deeds; how hoary-bearded elders of the church have whispered wanton words to the young maids of their households; how many a woman, eager for widow's weeds, has given her husband a drink at bed-time, and let him sleep his last sleep in her bosom; how beardless youths have made haste to inherit their fathers' wealth; and how fair damsels—blush not, sweet ones!—have dug little graves in the garden, and bidden me, the sole guest, to an infant's funeral. By the sympathy of your human hearts for sin, ye shall scent out all the places—whether in church, bed-chamber, street, field, or forest—where crime has been committed, and shall exult to behold the whole earth one stain of guilt, one mighty blood-spot. Far more than this! It shall be yours to penetrate, in every bosom, the deep mystery of sin, the fountain of all wicked arts, and which, inexhaustibly supplies more evil impulses than human power—than my power, at its utmost!—can make manifest in deeds. And now, my children, look upon each other.'

They did so; and, by the blaze of the hell-kindled torches, the wretched man beheld his Faith, and the wife her husband, trembling before that unhallowed altar.

'Lo! there ye stand, my children,' said the figure, in a deep and solemn tone, almost sad, with its despairing awfulness, as if his once angelic nature could yet mourn for our miserable race. 'Depending upon one another's hearts, ye had still hoped, that virtue were not all a dream. Now are ye undeceived! Evil is the nature of mankind. Evil must be your only happiness. Welcome, again, my children, to the communion of your race!'

'Welcome!' repeated the fiend-worshippers, in one cry of despair and triumph.

And there they stood, the only pair, as it seemed, who were yet hesitating on the verge of wickedness, in this dark world. A basin was hollowed, naturally, in the rock. Did it contain water, reddened by the lurid light? or was it blood? or, perchance, a liquid flame? Herein did the Shape of Evil dip his

2. During her trial, the historical Martha Carrier told of how the devil promised that she could become the queen of hell; she was convicted and hanged for witchcraft on August 19, 1692.

3. The *New-England Magazine* erroneously printed "grave," corrected to "race" in *Mosses from an Old Manse* (1846).

hand, and prepare to lay the mark of baptism upon their foreheads, that they might be partakers of the mystery of sin, more conscious of the secret guilt of others, both in deed and thought, than they could now be of their own. The husband cast one look at his pale wife, and Faith at him. What polluted wretches would the next glance shew them to each other, shuddering alike at what they disclosed and what they saw!

'Faith! Faith!' cried the husband. 'Look up to Heaven, and resist the Wicked One!'

Whether Faith obeyed, he knew not. Hardly had he spoken, when he found himself amid calm night and solitude, listening to a roar of the wind, which died heavily away through the forest. He staggered against the rock and felt it chill and damp, while a hanging twig, that had been all on fire, besprinkled his cheek with the coldest dew.

The next morning, young goodman Brown came slowly into the street of Salem village, staring around him like a bewildered man. The good old minister was taking a walk along the graveyard, to get an appetite for breakfast and meditate his sermon, and bestowed a blessing, as he passed, on goodman Brown. He shrank from the venerable saint, as if to avoid an anathema. Old deacon Gookin was at domestic worship, and the holy words of his prayer were heard through the open window. 'What God doth the wizard pray to?' quoth goodman Brown. Goody Cloyse, that excellent old Christian, stood in the early sunshine, at her own lattice, catechising a little girl, who had brought her a pint of morning's milk. Goodman Brown snatched away the child, as from the grasp of the fiend himself. Turning the corner by the meeting-house, he spied the head of Faith, with the pink ribbons, gazing anxiously forth, and bursting into such joy at sight of him, that she skipt along the street, and almost kissed her husband before the whole village. But, goodman Brown looked sternly and sadly into her face, and passed on without a greeting.

Had goodman Brown fallen asleep in the forest, and only dreamed a wild dream of a witch-meeting?

Be it so, if you will. But, alas! it was a dream of evil omen for young goodman Brown. A stern, a sad, a darkly meditative, a distrustful, if not a desperate man, did he become, from the night of that fearful dream. On the Sabbath-day, when the congregation were singing a holy psalm, he could not listen, because an anthem of sin rushed loudly upon his ear, and drowned all the blessed strain. When the minister spoke from the pulpit, with power and fervid eloquence, and, with his hand on the open bible, of the sacred truths of our religion, and of saint-like lives and triumphant deaths, and of future bliss or misery unutterable, then did goodman Brown turn pale, dreading, lest the roof should thunder down upon the gray blasphemer and his hearers. Often, awakening suddenly at midnight, he shrank from the bosom of Faith, and at morning or eventide, when the family knelt down at prayer, he scowled, and muttered to himself, and gazed sternly at his wife, and turned away. And when he had lived long, and was borne to his grave, a hoary corpse, followed by Faith, an aged woman, and children and grandchildren, a goodly procession, besides neighbors, not a few, they carved no hopeful verse upon his tomb-stone; for his dying hour was gloom.

1835

The May-Pole of Merry Mount[1]

> There is an admirable foundation for a philosophic romance, in the curious history of the early settlement of Mount Wallaston, or Merry Mount. In the slight sketch here attempted, the facts, recorded on the grave pages of our New England annalists, have wrought themselves, almost spontaneously, into a sort of allegory. The masques, mummeries, and festive customs, described in the text, are in accordance with the manners of the age. Authority, on these points may be found in Strutt's Book of English Sports and Pastimes.[2]

Bright were the days at Merry Mount, when the May-Pole was the banner-staff of that gay colony! They who reared it, should their banner be triumphant, were to pour sun-shine over New England's rugged hills, and scatter flower-seeds throughout the soil. Jollity and gloom were contending for an empire. Midsummer eve[3] had come, bringing deep verdure to the forest, and roses in her lap, of a more vivid hue than the tender buds of Spring. But May, or her mirthful spirit, dwelt all the year round at Merry Mount, sporting with the Summer months, and revelling with Autumn, and basking in the glow of Winter's fireside. Through a world of toil and care, she flitted with a dreamlike smile, and came hither to find a home among the lightsome hearts of Merry Mount.

Never had the May-Pole been so gaily decked as at sunset on mid-summer eve. This venerated emblem was a pine tree, which had preserved the slender grace of youth, while it equalled the loftiest height of the old wood monarchs. From its top streamed a silken banner, colored like the rainbow. Down nearly to the ground, the pole was dressed with birchen boughs, and others of the liveliest green, and some with silvery leaves, fastened by ribbons that fluttered in fantastic knots of twenty different colors, but no sad ones. Garden flowers, and blossoms of the wilderness, laughed gladly forth amid the verdure, so fresh and dewy, that they must have grown by magic on that happy pine tree. Where this green and flowery splendor terminated, the shaft of the May-Pole was stained with the seven brilliant hues of the banner at its top. On the lowest green bough hung an abundant wreath of roses, some that had been gathered in the sunniest spots of the forest, and others, of still richer blush, which the colonists had reared from English seed. Oh, people of the Golden Age, the chief of your husbandry, was to raise flowers!

But what was the wild throng that stood hand in hand about the May-Pole? It could not be, that the Fauns and Nymphs, when driven from their classic groves and homes of ancient fable, had sought refuge, as all the persecuted

---

1. The text is that of the first printing in *The Token* (1836). "May-pole": in English tradition, the tall pole placed in a village around which flower-bedecked people danced to celebrate May Day (the coming of spring). Puritans condemned the custom as pagan.
2. Joseph Strutt, *The Sports and Pastimes of the People of England* (1801). Hawthorne also knew Nathaniel Morton's *New England Memorial* (1669), which drew on William Bradford's manuscript history *Of Plymouth Plantation*. Hawthorne's tale works loosely with the historical conflict between the colony of fur traders at Mount Wollaston, now Quincy, Massachusetts,

and the religious leaders of Plymouth and Salem from 1625 to 1630. Thomas Morton (ca. 1579–1647), one of the traders, had dubbed Mount Wollaston "Merry Mount" and in 1627 encouraged the use of the maypole. In 1628 John Endicott (1589?–1665), the governor of the Massachusetts Colony, led an expedition that cut down the maypole shortly after Morton was deported to England for trafficking firearms to the Indians. Morton presents his side of the conflict in *New English Canaan* (1637).
3. June 20, the day before the longest day of the year.

did, in the fresh woods of the West. These were Gothic monsters, though perhaps of Grecian ancestry. On the shoulders of a comely youth, uprose the head and branching antlers of a stag; a second, human in all other points, had the grim visage of a wolf; a third, still with the trunk and limbs of a mortal man, showed the beard and horns of a venerable he-goat. There was the likeness of a bear erect, brute in all but his hind legs, which were adorned with pink silk stockings. And here again, almost as wondrous, stood a real bear of the dark forest, lending each of his fore paws to the grasp of a human hand, and as ready for the dance as any in that circle. This inferior nature rose half-way, to meet his companions as they stooped. Other faces wore the similitude of man or woman, but distorted or extravagant, with red noses pendulous before their mouths, which seemed of awful depth, and stretched from ear to ear in an eternal fit of laughter. Here might be seen the Salvage Man,[4] well known in heraldry, hairy as a baboon, and girdled with green leaves. By his side, a nobler figure, but still a counterfeit, appeared an Indian hunter, with feathery crest and wampum belt. Many of this strange company wore fools-caps, and had little bells appended to their garments, tinkling with a silvery sound, responsive to the inaudible music of their gleesome spirits. Some youths and maidens were of soberer garb, yet well maintained their places in the irregular throng, by the expression of wild revelry upon their features. Such were the colonists of Merry Mount, as they stood in the broad smile of sunset, round their venerated May-Pole.

Had a wanderer, bewildered in the melancholy forest, heard their mirth, and stolen a half-affrighted glance, he might have fancied them the crew of Comus,[5] some already transformed to brutes, some midway between man and beast, and the others rioting in the flow of tipsey jollity that foreran the change. But a band of Puritans, who watched the scene, invisible themselves, compared the masques to those devils and ruined souls, with whom their superstition peopled the black wilderness.

Within the ring of monsters, appeared the two airiest forms, that had ever trodden on any more solid footing than a purple and golden cloud. One was a youth, in glistening apparel, with a scarf of the rainbow pattern crosswise on his breast. His right hand held a gilded staff, the ensign[6] of high dignity among the revellous, and his left grasped the slender fingers of a fair maiden, not less gaily decorated than himself. Bright roses glowed in contrast with the dark and glossy curls of each, and were scattered round their feet, or had sprung up spontaneously there. Behind this lightsome couple, so close to the May-Pole that its boughs shaded his jovial face, stood the figure of an English priest, canonically dressed, yet decked with flowers, in Heathen fashion, and wearing a chaplet of the native vine leaves. By the riot of his rolling eye, and the pagan decorations of his holy garb, he seemed the wildest monster there, and the very Comus of the crew.

'Votaries of the May-Pole,' cried the flower-decked priest, 'merrily, all day long, have the woods echoed to your mirth. But be this your merriest hour, my hearts! Lo, here stand the Lord and Lady of the May, whom I, a clerk[7] of Oxford, and high priest of Merry Mount, am presently to join in holy mat-

---

4. Person clad in foliage to represent a savage, as in medieval and Renaissance pageantry.
5. The god of revelry, here associated with Milton's *Comus* (1634), whose magical potions turn unsuspecting travelers in the woods into mon-

strous figures who join his crew.
6. Sign, token.
7. In Anglican usage, lay minister who assists the parish clergyman.

rimony. Up with your nimble spirits, ye morrice-dancers, green-men, and glee-maidens,[8] bears and wolves, and horned gentlemen! Come; a chorus now, rich with the old mirth of Merry England, and the wilder glee of this fresh forest; and then a dance, to show the youthful pair what life is made of, and how airily they should go through it! All ye that love the May-Pole, lend your voices to the nuptial song of the Lord and Lady of the May!'

This wedlock was more serious than most affairs of Merry Mount, where jest and delusion, trick and fantasy, kept up a continual carnival. The Lord and Lady of the May, though their titles must be laid down at sunset, were really and truly to be partners for the dance of life, beginning the measure that same bright eve. The wreath of roses, that hung from the lowest green bough of the May-Pole, had been twined for them, and would be thrown over both their heads, in symbol of their flowery union. When the priest had spoken, therefore, a riotous uproar burst from the rout of monstrous figures.

'Begin you the stave,[9] reverend Sir,' cried they all; 'and never did the woods ring to such a merry peal, as we of the May-Pole shall send up!'

Immediately a prelude of pipe, cittern,[1] and viol, touched with practised minstrelsy, began to play from a neighboring thicket, in such a mirthful cadence, that the boughs of the May-Pole quivered to the sound. But the May Lord, he of the gilded staff, chancing to look into his Lady's eyes, was wonderstruck at the almost pensive glance that met his own.

'Edith, sweet Lady of the May,' whispered he, reproachfully, 'is your wreath of roses a garland to hang above our graves, that you look so sad? Oh, Edith, this is our golden time! Tarnish it not by any pensive shadow of the mind; for it may be, that nothing of futurity will be brighter than the mere remembrance of what is now passing.'

'That was the very thought that saddened me! How came it in your mind too?' said Edith, in a still lower tone than he; for it was high treason to be sad at Merry Mount. 'Therefore do I sigh amid this festive music. And besides, dear Edgar, I struggle as with a dream, and fancy that these shapes of our jovial friends are visionary, and their mirth unreal, and that we are no true Lord and Lady of the May. What is the mystery in my heart?'

Just then, as if a spell had loosened them, down came a little shower of withering rose leaves from the May-Pole. Alas, for the young lovers! No sooner had their hearts glowed with real passion, than they were sensible of something vague and unsubstantial in their former pleasures, and felt a dreary presentiment of inevitable change. From the moment that they truly loved, they had subjected themselves to earth's doom of care, and sorrow, and troubled joy, and had no more a home at Merry Mount. That was Edith's mystery. Now leave we the priest to marry them, and the masquers to sport round the May-Pole, till the last sunbeam be withdrawn from its summit, and the shadows of the forest mingle gloomily in the dance. Meanwhile, we may discover who these gay people were.

Two hundred years ago, and more, the old world and its inhabitants became mutually weary of each other. Men voyaged by thousands to the West; some to barter glass beads, and such like jewels, for the furs of the Indian hunter; some to conquer virgin empires; and one stern band to pray. But none of

---

8. Women singers. "Morrice-dancers": participants in an English folk dance, originally "Moorish dance." "Green-men": men bedecked in greenery.

9. Stanza or verse.
1. Guitar with pear-shaped body.

these motives had much weight with the colonists of Merry Mount. Their leaders were men who had sported so long with life, that when Thought and Wisdom came, even these unwelcome guests were led astray, by the crowd of vanities which they should have put to flight. Erring Thought and perverted Wisdom were made to put on masques, and play the fool. The men of whom we speak, after losing the heart's fresh gaiety, imagined a wild philosophy of pleasure, and came hither to act out their latest day-dream. They gathered followers from all that giddy tribe, whose whole life is like the festal days of soberer men. In their train were minstrels, not unknown in London streets; wandering players, whose theatres had been the halls of noblemen; mummeries, rope-dancers, and mountebanks,[2] who would long be missed at wakes, church-ales, and fairs; in a word, mirth-makers of every sort, such as abounded in that age, but now began to be discountenanced by the rapid growth of Puritanism. Light had their footsteps been on land, and as lightly they came across the sea. Many had been maddened by their previous troubles into a gay despair; others were as madly gay in the flush of youth, like the May Lord and his Lady; but whatever might be the quality of their mirth, old and young were gay at Merry Mount. The young deemed themselves happy. The elder spirits, if they knew that mirth was but the counterfeit of happiness, yet followed the false shadow wilfully, because at least her garments glittered brightest. Sworn triflers of a life-time, they would not venture among the sober truths of life, not even to be truly blest.

All the hereditary pastimes of Old England were transplanted hither. The King of Christmas was duly crowned, and the Lord of Misrule[3] bore potent sway. On the eve of Saint John,[4] they felled whole acres of the forest to make bonfires, and danced by the blaze all night, crowned with garlands, and throwing flowers into the flame. At harvest time, though their crop was of the smallest, they made an image with the sheaves of Indian corn, and wreathed it with autumnal garlands, and bore it home triumphantly. But what chiefly characterized the colonists of Merry Mount, was their veneration for the May-Pole. It has made their true history a poet's tale. Spring decked the hallowed emblem with young blossoms and fresh green boughs; Summer brought roses of the deepest blush, and the perfected foliage of the forest; Autumn enriched it with that red and yellow gorgeousness, which converts each wildwood leaf into a painted flower; and Winter silvered it with sleet, and hung it round with icicles, till it flashed in the cold sunshine, itself a frozen sunbeam. Thus each alternate season did homage to the May-Pole, and paid it a tribute of its own richest splendor. Its votaries danced round it, once, at least, in every month; sometimes they called it their religion, or their altar; but always, it was the banner-staff of Merry Mount.

Unfortunately, there were men in the new world, of a sterner faith than these May-Pole worshippers. Not far from Merry Mount was a settlement of Puritans, most dismal wretches, who said their prayers before daylight, and then wrought in the forest or the cornfield, till evening made it prayer time again. Their weapons were always at hand, to shoot down the straggling savage. When they met in conclave, it was never to keep up the old English

---

2. Showmen who "mount benches" to sell medicines or (as here) to tell stories or do tricks. "Mummeries": masked actors. "Rope-dancers": tightrope walkers.

3. Person appointed to preside over the traditional Christmas revelry.
4. Midsummer eve.

mirth, but to hear sermons three hours long, or to proclaim bounties on the heads of wolves and the scalps of Indians. Their festivals were fast-days, and their chief pastime the singing of psalms. Woe to the youth or maiden, who did but dream of a dance! The selectman nodded to the constable; and there sat the light-heeled reprobate in the stocks; or if he danced, it was round the whipping-post, which might be termed the Puritan May-Pole.

A party of these grim Puritans, toiling through the difficult woods, each with a horse-load of iron armor to burthen his footsteps, would sometimes draw near the sunny precincts of Merry Mount. There were the silken colonists, sporting round their May-Pole; perhaps teaching a bear to dance, or striving to communicate their mirth to the grave Indian; or masquerading in the skins of deer and wolves, which they had hunted for that especial purpose. Often, the whole colony were playing at blindman's bluff, magistrates and all with their eyes bandaged, except a single scape-goat, whom the blinded sinners pursued by the tinkling of the bells at his garments. Once, it is said, they were seen following a flower-decked corpse, with merriment and festive music, to his grave. But did the dead man laugh? In their quietest times, they sang ballads and told tales, for the edification of their pious visiters; or perplexed them with juggling tricks; or grinned at them through horse-collars; and when sport itself grew wearisome, they made game of their own stupidity, and began a yawning match. At the very least of these enormities, the men of iron shook their heads and frowned so darkly, that the revellers looked up, imagining that a momentary cloud had overcast the sunshine, which was to be perpetual there. On the other hand, the Puritans affirmed, that, when a psalm was pealing from their place of worship, the echo, which the forest sent them back, seemed often like the chorus of a jolly catch, closing with a roar of laughter. Who but the fiend, and his fond slaves, the crew of Merry Mount, had thus disturbed them! In due time, a feud arose, stern and bitter on one side, and as serious on the other as any thing could be, among such light spirits as had sworn allegiance to the May-Pole. The future complexion of New England was involved in this important quarrel. Should the grisly saints establish their jurisdiction over the gay sinners, then would their spirits darken all the clime, and make it a land of clouded visages, of hard toil, of sermon and psalm, forever. But should the banner-staff of Merry Mount be fortunate, sunshine would break upon the hills, and flowers would beautify the forest, and late posterity do homage to the May-Pole!

After these authentic passages from history, we return to the nuptials of the Lord and Lady of the May. Alas! we have delayed too long, and must darken our tale too suddenly. As we glanced again at the May-Pole, a solitary sun-beam is fading from the summit, and leaves only a faint golden tinge, blended with the hues of the rainbow banner. Even that dim light is now withdrawn, relinquishing the whole domain of Merry Mount to the evening gloom, which has rushed so instantaneously from the black surrounding woods. But some of these black shadows have rushed forth in human shape.

Yes: with the setting sun, the last day of mirth had passed from Merry Mount. The ring of gay masquers was disordered and broken; the stag lowered his antlers in dismay; the wolf grew weaker than a lamb; the bells of the morrice-dancers tinkled with tremulous affright. The Puritans had played a characteristic part in the May-Pole mummeries. Their darksome figures were intermixed with the wild shapes of their foes, and made the scene a picture of the moment, when waking thoughts start up amid the scattered fantasies of a dream. The leader of the hostile party stood in the centre of the circle, while the rout of monsters cowered around him, like evil spirits in the presence of a dread magician. No fantastic foolery could look him in the face. So stern was the energy of his aspect, that the whole man, visage, frame, and soul, seemed wrought of iron, gifted with life and thought, yet all of one substance with his head-piece and breast-plate. It was the Puritan of Puritans; it was Endicott himself!

'Stand off, priest of Baal!'[5] said he, with a grim frown, and laying no reverent hand upon the surplice. 'I know thee, Claxton![6] Thou art the man, who couldst not abide the rule even of thine own corrupted church,[7] and hast come hither to preach iniquity, and to give example of it in thy life. But now shall it be seen that the Lord hath sanctified this wilderness for his peculiar people. Woe unto them that would defile it! And first for this flower-decked abomination, the altar of thy worship!'

And with his keen sword, Endicott assaulted the hallowed May-Pole. Nor long did it resist his arm. It groaned with a dismal sound; it showered leaves and rose-buds upon the remorseless enthusiast; and finally, with all its green boughs, and ribbons, and flowers, symbolic of departed pleasures, down fell the banner-staff of Merry Mount. As it sank, tradition says, the evening sky grew darker, and the woods threw forth a more sombre shadow.

'There,' cried Endicott, looking triumphantly on his work, 'there lies the only May-Pole in New England! The thought is strong within me, that, by its fall, is shadowed forth the fate of light and idle mirth-makers, amongst us and our posterity. Amen, saith John Endicott!'

'Amen!' echoed his followers.

But the votaries of the May-Pole gave one groan for their idol. At the sound, the Puritan leader glanced at the crew of Comus, each a figure of broad mirth, yet, at this moment, strangely expressive of sorrow and dismay.

'Valiant captain,' quoth Peter Palfrey, the Ancient[8] of the band, 'what order shall be taken with the prisoners?'

'I thought not to repent me of cutting down a May-Pole,' replied Endicott, 'yet now I could find in my heart to plant it again, and give each of these bestial pagans one other dance round their idol. It would have served rarely for a whipping-post!'

'But there are pine trees enow,' suggested the lieutenant.

'True, good Ancient,' said the leader. 'Wherefore, bind the heathen crew, and bestow on them a small matter of stripes apiece, as earnest[9] of our future justice. Set some of the rogues in the stocks to rest themselves, so soon as Providence shall bring us to one of our own well-ordered settlements, where such accommodations may be found. Further penalties, such as branding and cropping of ears, shall be thought of hereafter.'

'How many stripes for the priest?' inquired Ancient Palfrey.

'None as yet,' answered Endicott, bending his iron frown upon the culprit. 'It must be for the Great and General Court[1] to determine, whether stripes and long imprisonment, and other grievous penalty, may atone for

5. The slaying of the prophets of the fertility god Baal is described in 1 Kings 18.
6. "Did Governor Endicott speak less positively, we should suspect a mistake here. The Reverend Mr. Claxton, though an eccentric, is not known to have been an immoral man. We rather doubt his identity with the priest of Merry Mount" [Hawthorne's note]. An eccentric clergyman, William Blackstone was known for quarreling with both

the Merry Mounters and the Puritans.
7. The Anglican Church.
8. Lieutenant or standard bearer. Palfrey (d. 1663), one of the first English settlers of Salem, which had broken away from the Plymouth Colony in 1629.
9. Pledge.
1. Massachusetts legislature.

his transgressions. Let him look to himself! For such as violate our civil order, it may be permitted us to show mercy. But woe to the wretch that troubleth our religion!'

'And this dancing bear,' resumed the officer. 'Must he share the stripes of his fellows?'

'Shoot him through the head!' said the energetic Puritan. 'I suspect witchcraft in the beast.'

'Here be a couple of shining ones,' continued Peter Palfrey, pointing his weapon at the Lord and Lady of the May. 'They seem to be of high station among these mis-doers. Methinks their dignity will not be fitted with less than a double share of stripes.'

Endicott rested on his sword, and closely surveyed the dress and aspect of the hapless pair. There they stood, pale, downcast, and apprehensive. Yet there was an air of mutual support, and of pure affection, seeking aid and giving it, that showed them to be man and wife, with the sanction of a priest upon their love. The youth, in the peril of the moment, had dropped his gilded staff, and thrown his arm about the Lady of the May, who leaned against his breast, too lightly to burthen him, but with weight enough to express that their destinies were linked together, for good or evil. They looked first at each other, and then into the grim captain's face. There they stood, in the first hour of wedlock, while the idle pleasures, of which their companions were the emblems, had given place to the sternest cares of life, personified by the dark Puritans. But never had their youthful beauty seemed so pure and high, as when its glow was chastened by adversity.

'Youth,' said Endicott, 'ye stand in an evil case, thou and thy maiden wife. Make ready presently; for I am minded that ye shall both have a token to remember your wedding-day!'

'Stern man,' exclaimed the May Lord, 'How can I move thee? Were the means at hand, I would resist to the death. Being powerless, I entreat! Do with me as thou wilt; but let Edith go untouched!'

'Not so,' replied the immitigable zealot. 'We are not wont to show an idle courtesy to that sex, which requireth the stricter discipline. What sayest thou, maid? Shall thy silken bridegroom suffer thy share of the penalty, besides his own?'

'Be it death,' said Edith, 'and lay it all on me!'

Truly, as Endicott had said, the poor lovers stood in a woeful case. Their foes were triumphant, their friends captive and abased, their home desolate, the benighted wilderness around them, and a rigorous destiny, in the shape of the Puritan leader, their only guide. Yet the deepening twilight could not altogether conceal, that the iron man was softened; he smiled, at the fair spectacle of early love; he almost sighed, for the inevitable blight of early hopes.

'The troubles of life have come hastily on this young couple,' observed Endicott. 'We will see how they comport themselves under their present trials, ere we burthen them with greater. If, among the spoil, there be any garments of a more decent fashion, let them be put upon this May Lord and his Lady, instead of their glistening vanities. Look to it, some of you.'

'And shall not the youth's hair be cut?' asked Peter Palfrey, looking with abhorrence at the love-lock and long glossy curls of the young man.

'Crop it forthwith, and that in the true pumpkin shell fashion,'[2] answered the captain. 'Then bring them along with us, but more gently than their

2. Roundhead style; relatively close-cropped in Puritan fashion.

fellows. There be qualities in the youth, which may make him valiant to fight, and sober to toil, and pious to pray; and in the maiden, that may fit her to become a mother in our Israel,[3] bringing up babes in better nurture than her own hath been. Nor think ye, young ones, that they are the happiest, even in our lifetime of a moment, who misspend it in dancing round a May-Pole!'

And Endicott, the severest Puritan of all who laid the rock-foundation of New England, lifted the wreath of roses from the ruin of the May-Pole, and threw it, with his own gauntleted hand, over the heads of the Lord and Lady of the May. It was a deed of prophecy. As the moral gloom of the world overpowers all systematic gaiety, even so was their home of wild mirth made desolate amid the sad forest. They returned to it no more. But, as their flowery garland was wreathed of the brightest roses that had grown there, so, in the tie that united them, were intertwined all the purest and best of their early joys. They went heavenward, supporting each other along the difficult path which it was their lot to tread, and never wasted one regretful thought on the vanities of Merry Mount.

1835

The Minister's Black Veil[1]

A Parable[2]

BY THE AUTHOR OF 'SIGHTS FROM A STEEPLE'

The sexton stood in the porch of Milford[3] meeting-house, pulling lustily at the bell-rope. The old people of the village came stooping along the street. Children, with bright faces, tript merrily beside their parents, or mimicked a graver gait, in the conscious dignity of their sunday clothes. Spruce bachelors looked sidelong at the pretty maidens, and fancied that the sabbath sunshine made them prettier than on week-days. When the throng had mostly streamed into the porch, the sexton began to toll the bell, keeping his eye on the Reverend Mr. Hooper's door. The first glimpse of the clergyman's figure was the signal for the bell to cease its summons.

'But what has good Parson Hooper got upon his face?' cried the sexton in astonishment.

All within hearing immediately turned about, and beheld the semblance of Mr. Hooper, pacing slowly his meditative way towards the meeting-house. With one accord they started, expressing more wonder than if some strange minister were coming to dust the cushions of Mr. Hooper's pulpit.

'Are you sure it is our parson?' inquired Goodman Gray of the sexton.

'Of a certainty it is good Mr. Hooper,' replied the sexton. 'He was to have exchanged pulpits with Parson Shute of Westbury; but Parson Shute sent to excuse himself yesterday, being to preach a funeral sermon.'

3. Endicott makes the standard 17th-century Puritan identification of the New England settlers with the Jews, whom he regarded as another persecuted, God-chosen group.
1. The text is that of the first printing in The Token (1836).
2. Another clergyman in New-England, Mr. Joseph Moody, of York, Maine, who died about eighty years since, made himself remarkable by the same eccentricity that is here related of the Reverend Mr. Hooper. In his case, however, the symbol had a different import. In early life he had accidentally killed a beloved friend; and from that day till the hour of his own death, he hid his face from men [Hawthorne's note].
3. Town southwest of Boston.

THE MINISTER'S BLACK VEIL | 637

The cause of so much amazement may appear sufficiently slight. Mr. Hooper, a gentlemanly person of about thirty, though still a bachelor, was dressed with due clerical neatness, as if a careful wife had starched his band,[4] and brushed the weekly dust from his Sunday's garb. There was but one thing remarkable in his appearance. Swathed about his forehead, and hanging down over his face, so low as to be shaken by his breath, Mr. Hooper had on a black veil. On a nearer view, it seemed to consist of two folds of crape,[5] which entirely concealed his features, except the mouth and chin, but probably did not intercept his sight, farther than to give a darkened aspect to all living and inanimate things. With this gloomy shade before him, good Mr. Hooper walked onward, at a slow and quiet pace, stooping somewhat and looking on the ground, as is customary with abstracted men, yet nodding kindly to those of his parishioners who still waited on the meeting-house steps. But so wonder-struck were they, that his greeting hardly met with a return.

'I can't really feel as if good Mr. Hooper's face was behind that piece of crape,' said the sexton.

'I don't like it,' muttered an old woman, as she hobbled into the meeting-house. 'He has changed himself into something awful, only by hiding his face.'

'Our parson has gone mad!' cried Goodman Gray, following him across the threshold.

A rumor of some unaccountable phenomenon had preceded Mr. Hooper into the meeting-house, and set all the congregation astir. Few could refrain from twisting their heads towards the door; many stood upright, and turned directly about; while several little boys clambered upon the seats, and came down again with a terrible racket. There was a general bustle, a rustling of the women's gowns and shuffling of the men's feet, greatly at variance with that hushed repose which should attend the entrance of the minister. But Mr. Hooper appeared not to notice the perturbation of his people. He entered with an almost noiseless step, bent his head mildly to the pews on each side, and bowed as he passed his oldest parishioner, a white-haired great-grandsire, who occupied an arm-chair in the centre of the aisle. It was strange to observe, how slowly this venerable man became conscious of something singular in the appearance of his pastor. He seemed not fully to partake of the prevailing wonder, till Mr. Hooper had ascended the stairs, and showed himself in the pulpit, face to face with his congregation, except for the black veil. That mysterious emblem was never once withdrawn. It shook with his measured breath as he gave out the psalm; it threw its obscurity between him and the holy page, as he read the Scriptures; and while he prayed, the veil lay heavily on his uplifted countenance. Did he seek to hide it from the dread Being whom he was addressing?

Such was the effect of this simple piece of crape, that more than one woman of delicate nerves was forced to leave the meeting-house. Yet perhaps the pale-faced congregation was almost as fearful a sight to the minister, as his black veil to them.

Mr. Hooper had the reputation of a good preacher, but not an energetic one: he strove to win his people heavenward, by mild persuasive influences, rather than to drive them thither, by the thunders of the Word. The sermon which he now delivered, was marked by the same characteristics of style and manner, as the general series of his pulpit oratory. But there was something,

4. Collar of a clerical gown.   5. Crepe; a light, semitransparent fabric.

either in the sentiment of the discourse itself, or in the imagination of the auditors, which made it greatly the most powerful effort that they had ever heard from their pastor's lips. It was tinged, rather more darkly than usual, with the gentle gloom of Mr. Hooper's temperament. The subject had reference to secret sin, and those sad mysteries which we hide from our nearest and dearest, and would fain conceal from our own consciousness, even forgetting that the Omniscient can detect them. A subtle power was breathed into his words. Each member of the congregation, the most innocent girl, and the man of hardened breast, felt as if the preacher had crept upon them, behind his awful veil, and discovered their hoarded iniquity of deed or thought. Many spread their clasped hands on their bosoms. There was nothing terrible in what Mr. Hooper said; at least, no violence; and yet, with every tremor of his melancholy voice, the hearers quaked. An unsought pathos came hand in hand with awe. So sensible were the audience of some unwonted attribute in their minister, that they longed for a breath of wind to blow aside the veil, almost believing that a stranger's visage would be discovered, though the form, gesture, and voice were those of Mr. Hooper.

At the close of the services, the people hurried out with indecorous confusion, eager to communicate their pent-up amazement, and conscious of lighter spirits, the moment they lost sight of the black veil. Some gathered in little circles, huddled closely together, with their mouths all whispering in the centre; some went homeward alone, wrapt in silent meditation; some talked loudly, and profaned the Sabbath-day with ostentatious laughter. A few shook their sagacious heads, intimating that they could penetrate the mystery; while one or two affirmed that there was no mystery at all, but only that Mr. Hooper's eyes were so weakened by the midnight lamp, as to require a shade. After a brief interval, forth came good Mr. Hooper also, in the rear of his flock. Turning his veiled face from one group to another, he paid due reverence to the hoary heads, saluted the middle-aged with kind dignity, as their friend and spiritual guide, greeted the young with mingled authority and love, and laid his hands on the little children's heads to bless them. Such was always his custom on the Sabbath-day. Strange and bewildered looks repaid him for his courtesy. None, as on former occasions, aspired to the honor of walking by their pastor's side. Old Squire Saunders, doubtless by an accidental lapse of memory, neglected to invite Mr. Hooper to his table, where the good clergyman had been wont to bless the food, almost every Sunday since his settlement. He returned, therefore, to the parsonage, and, at the moment of closing the door, was observed to look back upon the people, all of whom had their eyes fixed upon the minister. A sad smile gleamed faintly from beneath the black veil, and flickered about his mouth, glimmering as he disappeared.

'How strange,' said a lady, 'that a simple black veil, such as any woman might wear on her bonnet, should become such a terrible thing on Mr. Hooper's face!'

'Something must surely be amiss with Mr. Hooper's intellects,' observed her husband, the physician of the village. 'But the strangest part of the affair is the effect of this vagary, even on a sober-minded man like myself. The black veil, though it covers only our pastor's face, throws its influence over his whole person, and makes him ghost-like from head to foot. Do you not feel it so?'

'Truly do I,' replied the lady; 'and I would not be alone with him for the world. I wonder he is not afraid to be alone with himself!'

'Men sometimes are so,' said her husband.

The afternoon service was attended with similar circumstances. At its conclusion, the bell tolled for the funeral of a young lady. The relatives and friends were assembled in the house, and the more distant acquaintances stood about the door, speaking of the good qualities of the deceased, when their talk was interrupted by the appearance of Mr. Hooper, still covered with his black veil. It was now an appropriate emblem. The clergyman stepped into the room where the corpse was laid, and bent over the coffin, to take a last farewell of his deceased parishioner. As he stooped, the veil hung straight down from his forehead, so that, if her eye-lids had not been closed for ever, the dead maiden might have seen his face. Could Mr. Hooper be fearful of her glance, that he so hastily caught back the black veil? A person, who watched the interview between the dead and living, scrupled not to affirm, that, at the instant when the clergyman's features were disclosed, the corpse had slightly shuddered, rustling the shroud and muslin cap, though the countenance retained the composure of death. A superstitious old woman was the only witness of this prodigy. From the coffin, Mr. Hooper passed into the chambers of the mourners, and thence to the head of the staircase, to make the funeral prayer. It was a tender and heart-dissolving prayer, full of sorrow, yet so imbued with celestial hopes, that the music of a heavenly harp, swept by the fingers of the dead, seemed faintly to be heard among the saddest accents of the minister. The people trembled, though they but darkly understood him, when he prayed that they, and himself, and all of mortal race, might be ready, as he trusted this young maiden had been, for the dreadful hour that should snatch the veil from their faces. The bearers went heavily forth, and the mourners followed, saddening all the street, with the dead before them, and Mr. Hooper in his black veil behind.

'Why do you look back?' said one in the procession to his partner.

'I had a fancy,' replied she, 'that the minister and the maiden's spirit were walking hand in hand.'

'And so had I, at the same moment,' said the other.

That night, the handsomest couple in Milford village were to be joined in wedlock. Though reckoned a melancholy man, Mr. Hooper had a placid cheerfulness for such occasions, which often excited a sympathetic smile, where livelier merriment would have been thrown away. There was no quality of his disposition which made him more beloved than this. The company at the wedding awaited his arrival with impatience, trusting that the strange awe, which had gathered over him throughout the day, would now be dispelled. But such was not the result. When Mr. Hooper came, the first thing that their eyes rested on was the same horrible black veil, which had added deeper gloom to the funeral, and could portend nothing but evil to the wedding. Such was its immediate effect on the guests, that a cloud seemed to have rolled duskily from beneath the black crape, and dimmed the light of the candles. The bridal pair stood up before the minister. But the bride's cold fingers quivered in the tremulous hand of the bridegroom, and her death-like paleness caused a whisper, that the maiden who had been buried a few hours before, was come from her grave to be married. If ever another wedding were so dismal, it was that famous one, where they tolled the wedding-knell.[6] After performing the ceremony, Mr. Hooper raised a glass of wine to his

6. A reference to Hawthorne's "The Wedding Knell," which appeared in *The Token* for 1836 along with this story.

lips, wishing happiness to the new-married couple, in a strain of mild pleas-antry that ought to have brightened the features of the guests, like a cheer-ful gleam from the hearth. At that instant, catching a glimpse of his figure in the looking-glass, the black veil involved his own spirit in the horror with which it overwhelmed all others. His frame shuddered—his lips grew white—he spilt the untasted wine upon the carpet—and rushed forth into the darkness. For the Earth, too, had on her Black Veil.

The next day, the whole village of Milford talked of little else than Parson Hooper's black veil. That, and the mystery concealed behind it, supplied a topic for discussion between acquaintances meeting in the street, and good women gossiping at their open windows. It was the first item of news that the tavern-keeper told to his guests. The children babbled of it on their way to school. One imitative little imp covered his face with an old black hand-kerchief, thereby so affrighting his playmates, that the panic seized him-self, and he well nigh lost his wits by his own waggery.

It was remarkable, that, of all the busy-bodies and impertinent people in the parish, not one ventured to put the plain question to Mr. Hooper, where-fore he did this thing. Hitherto, whenever there appeared the slightest call for such interference, he had never lacked advisers, nor shown himself averse to be guided by their judgment. If he erred at all, it was by so painful a degree of self-distrust, that even the mildest censure would lead him to consider an indifferent action as a crime. Yet, though so well acquainted with this amiable weakness, no individual among his parishioners chose to make the black veil a subject of friendly remonstrance. There was a feeling of dread, neither plainly confessed nor carefully concealed, which caused each to shift the responsibility upon another, till at length it was found expedient to send a deputation of the church, in order to deal with Mr. Hooper about the mystery, before it should grow into a scandal. Never did an embassy so ill discharge its duties. The minister received them with friendly courtesy, but became silent, after they were seated, leaving to his visitors the whole burthen[7] of introducing their important business. The topic, it might be supposed, was obvious enough. There was the black veil, swathed round Mr. Hooper's forehead, and concealing every feature above his placid mouth, on which, at times, they could perceive the glimmering of a melancholy smile. But that piece of crape, to their imagination, seemed to hang down before his heart, the symbol of a fearful secret between him and them. Were the veil but cast aside, they might speak freely of it, but not till then. Thus they sat a considerable time, speechless, confused, and shrinking uneasily from Mr. Hooper's eye, which they felt to be fixed upon them with an invisible glance. Finally, the deputies returned abashed to their constituents, pronouncing the matter too weighty to be handled, except by a council of the churches, if, indeed, it might not require a general synod.

But there was one person in the village, unappalled by the awe with which the black veil had impressed all beside herself. When the deputies returned without an explanation, or even venturing to demand one, she, with the calm energy of her character, determined to chase away the strange cloud that appeared to be settling round Mr. Hooper, every moment more darkly than before. As his plighted wife, it should be her privilege to know what the black veil concealed. At the minister's first visit, therefore, she entered upon

7. Burden.

the subject, with a direct simplicity, which made the task easier both for him and her. After he had seated himself, she fixed her eyes steadfastly upon the veil, but could discern nothing of the dreadful gloom that had so over-awed the multitude: it was but a double fold of crape, hanging down from his forehead to his mouth, and slightly stirring with his breath.

'No,' said she aloud, and smiling, 'there is nothing terrible in this piece of crape, except that it hides a face which I am always glad to look upon. Come, good sir, let the sun shine from behind the cloud. First lay aside your black veil: then tell me why you put it on.'

Mr. Hooper's smile glimmered faintly.

'There is an hour to come,' said he, 'when all of us shall cast aside our veils. Take it not amiss, beloved friend, if I wear this piece of crape till then.'

'Your words are a mystery too,' returned the young lady. 'Take away the veil from them, at least.'

'Elizabeth, I will,' said he, 'so far as my vow may suffer me. Know, then, this veil is a type[8] and a symbol, and I am bound to wear it ever, both in light and darkness, in solitude and before the gaze of multitudes, and as with strangers, so with my familiar friends. No mortal eye will see it withdrawn. This dismal shade must separate me from the world: even you, Elizabeth, can never come behind it!'

'What grievous affliction hath befallen you,' she earnestly inquired, 'that you should thus darken your eyes for ever?'

'If it be a sign of mourning,' replied Mr. Hooper, 'I, perhaps, like most other mortals, have sorrows dark enough to be typified by a black veil.'

'But what if the world will not believe that it is the type of an innocent sorrow?' urged Elizabeth. 'Beloved and respected as you are, there may be whispers, that you hide your face under the consciousness of secret sin. For the sake of your holy office, do away this scandal!'

The color rose into her cheeks, as she intimated the nature of the rumors that were already abroad in the village. But Mr. Hooper's mildness did not forsake him. He even smiled again—that same sad smile, which always appeared like a faint glimmering of light, proceeding from the obscurity beneath the veil.

'If I hide my face for sorrow, there is cause enough,' he merely replied; 'and if I cover it for secret sin, what mortal might not do the same?'

And with this gentle, but unconquerable obstinacy, did he resist all her entreaties. At length Elizabeth sat silent. For a few moments she appeared lost in thought, considering, probably, what new methods might be tried, to withdraw her lover from so dark a fantasy, which, if it had no other mean-ing, was perhaps a symptom of mental disease. Though of a firmer charac-ter than his own, the tears rolled down her cheeks. But, in an instant, as it were, a new feeling took the place of sorrow: her eyes were fixed insensibly on the black veil, when, like a sudden twilight in the air, its terrors fell around her. She arose, and stood trembling before him.

'And do you feel it then at last?' said he mournfully.

She made no reply, but covered her eyes with her hand, and turned to leave the room. He rushed forward and caught her arm.

'Have patience with me, Elizabeth!' cried he passionately. 'Do not desert me, though this veil must be between us here on earth. Be mine, and here-

8. Object that symbolically embodies or reveals a religious idea.

after there shall be no veil over my face, no darkness between our souls! It is but a mortal veil—it is not for eternity! Oh, you know not how lonely I am and how frightened to be alone behind my black veil. Do not leave me in this miserable obscurity for ever!'

'Lift the veil but once, and look me in the face,' said she.

'Never! It cannot be!' replied Mr. Hooper.

'Then, farewell!' said Elizabeth.

She withrew her arm from his grasp, and slowly departed, pausing at the door, to give one long, shuddering gaze, that seemed almost to penetrate the mystery of the black veil. But, even amid his grief, Mr. Hooper smiled to think that only a material emblem had separated him from happiness, though the horrors which it shadowed forth, must be drawn darkly between the fondest of lovers.

From that time no attempts were made to remove Mr. Hooper's black veil, or, by a direct appeal, to discover the secret which it was supposed to hide. By persons who claimed a superiority to popular prejudice, it was reckoned merely an eccentric whim, such as often mingles with the sober actions of men otherwise rational, and tinges them all with its own semblance of insanity. But with the multitude, good Mr. Hooper was irreparably a bugbear.[9] He could not walk the street with any peace of mind, so conscious was he that the gentle and timid would turn aside to avoid him, and that others would make it a point of hardihood to throw themselves in his way. The impertinence of the latter class compelled him to give up his customary walk, at sunset, to the burial ground; for when he leaned pensively over the gate, there would always be faces behind the grave-stones, peeping at his black veil. A fable went the rounds, that the stare of the dead people drove him thence. It grieved him, to the very depth of his kind heart, to observe how the children fled from his approach, breaking up their merriest sports, while his melancholy figure was yet afar off. Their instinctive dread caused him to feel, more strongly than aught else, that a preternatural horror was interwoven with the threads of the black crape. In truth, his own antipathy to the veil was known to be so great, that he never willingly passed before a mirror, nor stooped to drink at a still fountain, lest, in its peaceful bosom, he should be affrighted by himself. This was what gave plausibility to the whispers, that Mr. Hooper's conscience tortured him for some great crime, too horrible to be entirely concealed, or otherwise than so obscurely intimated. Thus, from beneath the black veil, there rolled a cloud into the sunshine, an ambiguity of sin or sorrow, which enveloped the poor minister, so that love or sympathy could never reach him. It was said, that ghost and fiend consorted with him there. With self-shudderings and outward terrors, he walked continually in its shadow, groping darkly within his own soul, or gazing through a medium that saddened the whole world. Even the lawless wind, it was believed, respected his dreadful secret, and never blew aside the veil. But still good Mr. Hooper sadly smiled, at the pale visages of the worldly throng as he passed by.

Among all its bad influences, the black veil had the one desirable effect, of making its wearer a very efficient clergyman. By the aid of his mysterious emblem—for there was no other apparent cause—he became a man of awful power, over souls that were in agony for sin. His converts always

9. Object of dread.

regarded him with a dread peculiar to themselves, affirming, though but figuratively, that, before he brought them to celestial light, they had been with him behind the black veil. Its gloom, indeed, enabled him to sympathize with all dark affections. Dying sinners cried aloud for Mr. Hooper, and would not yield their breath till he appeared; though ever, as he stooped to whisper consolation, they shuddered at the veiled face so near their own. Such were the terrors of the black veil, even when death had bared his visage! Strangers came long distances to attend service at his church, with the mere idle purpose of gazing at his figure, because it was forbidden them to behold his face. But many were made to quake ere they departed! Once, during Governor Belcher's administration, Mr. Hooper was appointed to preach the election sermon.[1] Covered with his black veil, he stood before the chief magistrate, the council, and the representatives, and wrought so deep an impression, that the legislative measures of that year, were characterized by all the gloom and piety of our earliest ancestral sway.

In this manner Mr. Hooper spent a long life, irreproachable in outward act, yet shrouded in dismal suspicions; kind and loving, though unloved, and dimly feared; a man apart from men, shunned in their health and joy, but ever summoned to their aid in mortal anguish. As years wore on, shedding their snows above his sable veil, he acquired a name throughout the New-England churches, and they called him Father Hooper. Nearly all his parishioners, who were of mature age when he was settled, had been borne away by many a funeral: he had one congregation in the church, and a more crowded one in the church-yard; and having wrought so late into the evening, and done his work so well, it was now good Father Hooper's turn to rest.

Several persons were visible by the shaded candlelight, in the death-chamber of the old clergyman. Natural connections he had none. But there was the decorously grave, though unmoved physician, seeking only to mitigate the last pangs of the patient whom he could not save. There were the deacons, and other eminently pious members of his church. There, also, was the Reverend Mr. Clark, of Westbury, a young and zealous divine, who had ridden in haste to pray by the bed-side of the expiring minister. There was the nurse, no hired handmaiden of death, but one whose calm affection had endured thus long, in secrecy, in solitude, amid the chill of age, and would not perish, even at the dying hour. Who, but Elizabeth! And there lay the hoary head of good Father Hooper upon the death-pillow, with the black veil still swathed about his brow and reaching down over his face, so that each more difficult gasp of his faint breath caused it to stir. All through life that piece of crape had hung between him and the world: it had separated him from cheerful brotherhood and woman's love, and kept him in that saddest of all prisons, his own heart; and still it lay upon his face, as if to deepen the gloom of his darksome chamber, and shade him from the sunshine of eternity.

For some time previous, his mind had been confused, wavering doubtfully between the past and the present, and hovering forward, as it were, at intervals, into the indistinctness of the world to come. There had been feverish turns, which tossed him from side to side, and wore away what little strength he had. But in his most convulsive struggles, and in the wildest vagaries of his

---

1. Sermon preached at the start of a governor's term. Jonathan Belcher (1682–1757) was governor of Massachusetts and New Hampshire (1730–41).

intellect, when no other thought retained its sober influence, he still showed an awful solicitude lest the black veil should slip aside. Even if his bewildered soul could have forgotten, there was a faithful woman at his pillow, who, with averted eyes, would have covered that aged face, which she had last beheld in the comeliness of manhood. At length the death-stricken old man lay quietly in the torpor of mental and bodily exhaustion, with an imperceptible pulse, and breath that grew fainter and fainter, except when a long, deep, and irregular inspiration seemed to prelude the flight of his spirit.

The minister of Westbury approached the bedside.

'Venerable Father Hooper,' said he, 'the moment of your release is at hand. Are you ready for the lifting of the veil, that shuts in time from eternity?'

Father Hooper at first replied merely by a feeble motion of his head; then, apprehensive, perhaps, that his meaning might be doubtful, he exerted himself to speak.

'Yea,' said he, in faint accents, 'my soul hath a patient weariness until that veil be lifted.'

'And is it fitting,' resumed the Reverend Mr. Clark, 'that a man so given to prayer, of such a blameless example, holy in deed and thought, so far as mortal judgment may pronounce; is it fitting that a father in the church should leave a shadow on his memory, that may seem to blacken a life so pure? I pray you, my venerable brother, let not this thing be! Suffer us to be gladdened by your triumphant aspect, as you go to your reward. Before the veil of eternity be lifted, let me cast aside this black veil from your face!'

And thus speaking, the reverend Mr. Clark bent forward to reveal the mystery of so many years. But, exerting a sudden energy, that made all the beholders stand aghast, Father Hooper snatched both his hands from beneath the bed-clothes, and pressed them strongly on the black veil, resolute to struggle, if the minister of Westbury would contend with a dying man.

'Never!' cried the veiled clergyman. 'On earth, never!'

'Dark old man!' exclaimed the affrighted minister, 'with what horrible crime upon your soul are you now passing to the judgment?'

Father Hooper's breath heaved; it rattled in his throat; but, with a mighty effort, grasping forward with his hands, he caught hold of life, and held it back till he should speak. He even raised himself in bed; and there he sat, shivering with the arms of death around him, while the black veil hung down, awful, at that last moment, in the gathered terrors of a life-time. And yet the faint, sad smile, so often there, now seemed to glimmer from its obscurity, and linger on Father Hooper's lips.

'Why do you tremble at me alone?' cried he, turning his veiled face round the circle of pale spectators. 'Tremble also at each other! Have men avoided me, and women shown no pity, and children screamed and fled, only for my black veil? What, but the mystery which it obscurely typifies, has made this piece of crape so awful? When the friend shows his inmost heart to his friend; the lover to his best-beloved; when man does not vainly shrink from the eye of his Creator, loathsomely treasuring up the secret of his sin; then deem me a monster, for the symbol beneath which I have lived, and die! I look around me, and lo! on every visage a black veil!'

While his auditors shrank from one another, in mutual affright, Father Hooper fell back upon his pillow, a veiled corpse, with a faint smile lingering on the lips. Still veiled, they laid him in his coffin, and a veiled corpse they bore him to the grave. The grass of many years has sprung up and withered on that grave, the burial-stone is moss-grown, and good Mr. Hooper's face is dust; but awful is still the thought, that it mouldered beneath the black veil!

1836

The Birth-Mark[1]

In the latter part of the last century, there lived a man of science—an eminent proficient in every branch of natural philosophy—who, not long before our story opens, had made experience of a spiritual affinity, more attractive than any chemical one. He had left his laboratory to the care of an assistant, cleared his fine countenance from the furnace-smoke, washed the stain of acids from his fingers, and persuaded a beautiful woman to become his wife. In those days, when the comparatively recent discovery of electricity, and other kindred mysteries of nature, seemed to open paths into the region of miracle, it was not unusual for the love of science to rival the love of woman, in its depth and absorbing energy. The higher intellect, the imagination, the spirit, and even the heart, might all find their congenial aliment in pursuits which, as some of their ardent votaries[2] believed, would ascend from one step of powerful intelligence to another, until the philosopher should lay his hand on the secret of creative force, and perhaps make new worlds for himself. We know not whether Aylmer possessed this degree of faith in man's ultimate control over nature. He had devoted himself, however, too unreservedly to scientific studies, ever to be weaned from them by any second passion. His love for his young wife might prove the stronger of the two; but it could only be by intertwining itself with his love of science, and uniting the strength of the latter to its own.

Such a union accordingly took place, and was attended with truly remarkable consequences, and a deeply impressive moral. One day, very soon after their marriage, Aylmer sat gazing at his wife, with a trouble in his countenance that grew stronger, until he spoke.

"Georgiana," said he, "has it never occurred to you that the mark upon your cheek might be removed?"

"No, indeed," said she, smiling; but perceiving the seriousness of his manner, she blushed deeply. "To tell you the truth, it has been so often called a charm, that I was simple enough to imagine it might be so."

"Ah, upon another face, perhaps it might," replied her husband. "But never on yours! No, dearest Georgiana, you came so nearly perfect from the hand of Nature, that this slightest possible defect—which we hesitate whether to term a defect or a beauty—shocks me, as being the visible mark of earthly imperfection."

"Shocks you, my husband!" cried Georgiana, deeply hurt; at first reddening with momentary anger, but then bursting into tears. "Then why did you take me from my mother's side? You cannot love what shocks you!"

---

1. First published in the *Pioneer* (March 1843), the source of the present text; the reprinting in *Mosses from an Old Manse* (1846) contains a few variants as well as two corrections (adopted and noted here).
2. Devoted admirers. "Aliment": nourishment.

To explain this conversation, it must be mentioned, that, in the centre of Georgiana's left cheek, there was a singular mark, deeply interwoven, as it were, with the texture and substance of her face. In the usual state of her complexion,—a healthy, though delicate bloom,—the mark wore a tint of deeper crimson, which imperfectly defined its shape amid the surrounding rosiness. When she blushed, it gradually became more indistinct, and finally vanished amid the triumphant rush of blood, that bathed the whole cheek with its brilliant glow. But, if any shifting emotion caused her to turn pale, there was the mark again, a crimson stain upon the snow, in what Aylmer sometimes deemed an almost fearful distinctness. Its shape bore not a little similarity to the human hand, though of the smallest pigmy size. Georgiana's lovers were wont to say, that some fairy, at her birth-hour, had laid her tiny hand upon the infant's cheek, and left this impress there, in token of the magic endowments that were to give her such sway over all hearts. Many a desperate swain would have risked life for the privilege of pressing his lips to the mysterious hand. It must not be concealed, however, that the impression wrought by this fairy sign-manual varied exceedingly; according to the difference of temperament in the beholders. Some fastidious persons—but they were exclusively of her own sex—affirmed that the Bloody Hand, as they chose to call it, quite destroyed the effect of Georgiana's beauty, and rendered her countenance even hideous. But it would be as reasonable to say, that one of those small blue stains, which sometimes occur in the purest statuary marble, would convert the Eve of Powers[3] to a monster. Masculine observers, if the birth-mark did not heighten their admiration, contented themselves with wishing it away, that the world might possess one living specimen of ideal loveliness, without the semblance of a flaw. After his marriage—for he thought little or nothing of the matter before—Aylmer discovered that this was the case with himself.

Had she been less beautiful—if Envy's self could have found aught else to sneer at—he might have felt his affection heightened by the prettiness of this mimic hand, now vaguely portrayed, now lost, now stealing forth again, and glimmering to-and-fro with every pulse of emotion that throbbed within her heart. But, seeing her otherwise so perfect, he found this one defect grow more and more intolerable, with every moment of their united lives. It was the fatal flaw of humanity, which Nature, in one shape or another, stamps ineffaceably on all her productions, either to imply that they are temporary and finite, or that their perfection must be wrought by toil and pain. The Crimson Hand expressed the ineludible gripe,[4] in which mortality clutches the highest and purest of earthly mould, degrading them into kindred with the lowest, and even with the very brutes, like whom their visible frames return to dust. In this manner, selecting it as the symbol of his wife's liability to sin, sorrow, decay, and death, Aylmer's sombre imagination was not long in rendering the birth-mark a frightful object, causing him more trouble and horror than ever Georgiana's beauty, whether of soul or sense, had given him delight.

At all the seasons which should have been their happiest, he invariably, and without intending it—nay, in spite of a purpose to the contrary—reverted to this one disastrous topic. Trifling as it at first appeared, it so connected

3. *Eve before the Fall*, a sculpture by the American Hiram Powers (1805–1873).

4. Grip (variant spelling).

itself with innumerable trains of thought, and modes of feeling, that it became the central point of all. With the morning twilight, Aylmer opened his eyes upon his wife's face, and recognised the symbol of imperfection; and when they sat together at the evening hearth, his eyes wandered stealthily to her cheek, and beheld, flickering with the blaze of the wood fire, the spectral Hand that wrote mortality, where he would fain have worshipped. Georgiana soon learned to shudder at his gaze. It needed but a glance, with the peculiar expression that his face often wore, to change the roses of her cheek into a deathlike paleness, amid which the Crimson Hand was brought strongly out, like a bas-relief[5] of ruby on the whitest marble.

Late, one night, when the lights were growing dim, so as hardly to betray the stain on the poor wife's cheek, she herself, for the first time, voluntarily took up the subject.

"Do you remember, my dear Aylmer," said she, with a feeble attempt at a smile—"have you any recollection of a dream, last night, about this odious Hand?"

"None!—none whatever!" replied Aylmer, starting; but then he added in a dry, cold tone, affected for the sake of concealing the real depth of his emotion:—"I might well dream of it; for, before I fell asleep, it had taken a pretty firm hold of my fancy."

"And you did dream of it," continued Georgiana, hastily; for she dreaded lest a gush of tears should interrupt what she had to say—"A terrible dream! I wonder that you can forget it. Is it possible to forget this one expression?— 'It is in her heart now—we must have it out!'—Reflect, my husband; for by all means I would have you recall that dream."

The mind is in a sad state, when Sleep, the all-involving, cannot confine her spectres within the dim region of her sway, but suffers them to break forth, affrighting this actual life with secrets that perchance belong to a deeper one. Aylmer now remembered his dream. He had fancied himself, with his servant Aminidab, attempting an operation for the removal of the birth-mark. But the deeper went the knife, the deeper sank the Hand, until at length its tiny grasp appeared to have caught hold of Georgiana's heart; whence, however, her husband was inexorably resolved to cut or wrench it away.

When the dream had shaped itself perfectly in his memory, Aylmer sat in his wife's presence with a guilty feeling. Truth often finds its way to the mind close-muffled in robes of sleep, and then speaks with uncompromising directness of matters in regard to which we practise an unconscious self-deception, during our waking moments. Until now, he had not been aware of the tyrannizing influence acquired by one idea over his mind, and of the lengths which he might find in his heart to go, for the sake of giving himself peace.

"Aylmer," resumed Georgiana, solemnly, "I know not what may be the cost to both of us, to rid me of this fatal birth-mark. Perhaps its removal may cause cureless deformity. Or, it may be, the stain goes as deep as life itself. Again, do we know that there is a possibility, on any terms, of unclasping the firm gripe of this little Hand, which was laid upon me before I came into the world?"

5. Low-relief; slightly raised.

"Dearest Georgiana, I have spent much thought upon the subject," hastily interrupted Aylmer—"I am convinced of the perfect practicability of its removal."

"If there be the remotest possibility of it," continued Georgiana, "let the attempt be made, at whatever risk. Danger is nothing to me; for life—while this hateful mark makes me the object of your horror and disgust—life is a burthen[6] which I would fling down with joy. Either remove this dreadful Hand, or take my wretched life! You have deep science! All the world bears witness of it. You have achieved great wonders! Cannot you remove this little, little mark, which I cover with the tips of two small fingers? Is this beyond your power, for the sake of your own peace, and to save your poor wife from madness?"

"Noblest—dearest—tenderest wife!" cried Aylmer, rapturously. "Doubt not my power. I have already given this matter the deepest thought—thought which might almost have enlightened me to create a being less perfect than yourself. Georgiana, you have led me deeper than ever into the heart of science. I feel myself fully competent to render this dear cheek as faultless as its fellow; and then, most beloved, what will be my triumph, when I shall have corrected what Nature left imperfect, in her fairest work! Even Pygmalion,[7] when his sculptured woman assumed life, felt not greater ecstasy than mine will be."

"It is resolved, then," said Georgiana, faintly smiling,—"And, Aylmer, spare me not, though you should find the birth-mark take refuge in my heart at last."

Her husband tenderly kissed her cheek—her right cheek—not that which bore the impress of the Crimson Hand.

The next day, Aylmer apprized his wife of a plan that he had formed, whereby he might have opportunity for the intense thought and constant watchfulness, which the proposed operation would require; while Georgiana, likewise, would enjoy the perfect repose essential to its success. They were to seclude themselves in the extensive apartments occupied by Aylmer as a laboratory, and where, during his toilsome youth, he had made discoveries in the elemental powers of nature, that had roused the admiration of all the learned societies in Europe. Seated calmly in this laboratory, the pale philosopher had investigated the secrets of the highest cloud-region, and of the profoundest mines; he had satisfied himself of the causes that kindled and kept alive the fires of the volcano; and had explained the mystery of fountains, and how it is that they gush forth, some so bright and pure, and others with such rich medicinal[8] virtues, from the dark bosom of the earth. Here, too, at an earlier period, he had studied the wonders of the human frame, and attempted to fathom the very process by which Nature assimilates all her precious influences from earth and air, and from the spiritual world, to create and foster Man, her masterpiece. The latter pursuit, however, Aylmer had long laid aside, in unwilling recognition of the truth, against which all seekers sooner or later stumble, that our great creative Mother, while she amuses us with apparently working in the broadest sunshine, is yet severely careful to keep her own secrets, and, in spite of her pretended openness, shows us nothing but results. She permits us, indeed, to mar, but seldom to

6. Burden.
7. In Greek myth, a king and sculptor who fell so deeply in love with his statue that Aphrodite granted his prayers and gave it life.
8. This 1846 reading replaces the 1843 *medical*.

mend, and, like a jealous patentee, on no account to make. Now, however, Aylmer resumed these half-forgotten investigations; not, of course, with such hopes or wishes as first suggested them; but because they involved much physiological truth, and lay in the path of his proposed scheme for the treatment of Georgiana.

As he led her over the threshold of the laboratory, Georgiana was cold and tremulous. Aylmer looked cheerfully into her face, with intent to reassure her, but was so startled with the intense glow of the birth-mark upon the whiteness of her cheek, that he could not restrain a strong convulsive shudder. His wife fainted.

"Aminidab! Aminidab!" shouted Aylmer, stamping violently on the floor.

Forthwith, there issued from an inner apartment a man of low stature, but bulky frame, with shaggy hair hanging about his visage, which was grimed with the vapors of the furnace. This personage had been Aylmer's under-worker during his whole scientific career, and was admirably fitted for that office by his great mechanical readiness, and the skill with which, while incapable of comprehending a single principle, he executed all the practical details of his master's experiments. With his vast strength, his shaggy hair, his smoky aspect, and the indescribable earthiness that incrusted him, he seemed to represent man's physical nature; while Aylmer's slender figure, and pale, intellectual face, were no less apt a type of the spiritual element.

"Throw open the door of the boudoir, Aminidab," said Aylmer, "and burn a pastille."[9]

"Yes, master," answered Aminidab, looking intently at the lifeless form of Georgiana; and then he muttered to himself;—"If she were my wife, I'd never part with that birth-mark."

When Georgiana recovered consciousness, she found herself breathing an atmosphere of penetrating fragrance, the gentle potency of which had recalled her from her deathlike faintness. The scene around her looked like enchantment. Aylmer had converted those smoky, dingy, sombre rooms, where he had spent his brightest years in recondite pursuits, into a series of beautiful apartments, not unfit to be the secluded abode of a lovely woman. The walls were hung with gorgeous curtains, which imparted the combination of grandeur and grace, that no other species of adornment can achieve; and as they fell from the ceiling to the floor, their rich and ponderous folds, concealing all angles and straight lines, appeared to shut in the scene from infinite space. For aught Georgiana knew, it might be a pavilion among the clouds. And Aylmer, excluding the sunshine, which would have interfered with his chemical processes, had supplied its place with perfumed lamps, emitting flames of various hue, but all uniting in a soft, empurpled radiance. He now knelt by his wife's side, watching her earnestly, but without alarm; for he was confident in his science, and felt that he could draw a magic circle round her, within which no evil might intrude.

"Where am I?—Ah, I remember!" said Georgiana, faintly; and she placed her hand over her cheek, to hide the terrible mark from her husband's eyes.

"Fear not, dearest!" exclaimed he, "Do not shrink from me! Believe me, Georgiana, I even rejoice in this single imperfection, since it will be such rapture to remove it."

9. A tablet burned to perfume the air.

"Oh, spare me!" sadly replied his wife—"Pray do not look at it again. I never can forget that convulsive shudder."

In order to soothe Georgiana, and, as it were, to release her mind from the burthen of actual things, Aylmer now put in practice some of the light and playful secrets, which science had taught him among its profounder lore. Airy figures, absolutely bodiless ideas, and forms of unsubstantial beauty, came and danced before her, imprinting their momentary footsteps on beams of light. Though she had some indistinct idea of the method of these optical phenomena, still the illusion was almost perfect enough to warrant the belief, that her husband possessed sway over the spiritual world. Then again, when she felt a wish to look forth from her seclusion, immediately, as if her thoughts were answered, the procession of external existence flitted across a screen. The scenery and the figures of actual life were perfectly represented, but with that bewitching, yet indescribable difference, which always makes a picture, an image, or a shadow, so much more attractive than the original. When wearied of this, Aylmer bade her cast her eyes upon a vessel, containing a quantity of earth. She did so, with little interest at first, but was soon startled, to perceive the germ of a plant, shooting upward from the soil. Then came the slender stalk—the leaves gradually unfolded themselves—and amid them was a perfect and lovely flower.

"It is magical!" cried Georgiana, "I dare not touch it."

"Nay, pluck it," answered Aylmer, "pluck it, and inhale its brief perfume while you may. The flower will wither in a few moments, and leave nothing save its brown seed-vessels—but thence may be perpetuated a race as ephemeral as itself."

But Georgiana had no sooner touched the flower than the whole plant suffered a blight, its leaves turning coal-black, as if by the agency of fire.

"There was too powerful a stimulus," said Aylmer thoughtfully.

To make up for this abortive experiment, he proposed to take her portrait by a scientific process of his own invention. It was to be effected by rays of light striking upon a polished plate of metal. Georgiana assented—but, on looking at the result, was affrighted to find the features of the portrait blurred and indefinable; while the minute figure of a hand appeared where the cheek should have been. Aylmer snatched the metallic plate, and threw it into a jar of corrosive acid.

Soon, however, he forgot these mortifying failures. In the intervals of study and chemical experiment, he came to her, flushed and exhausted, but seemed invigorated by her presence, and spoke in glowing language of the resources of his art. He gave a history of the long dynasty of the Alchemists, who spent so many ages in quest of the universal solvent, by which the Golden Principle might be elicited from all things vile and base.[1] Aylmer appeared to believe, that, by the plainest scientific logic, it was altogether within the limits of possibility to discover this long-sought medium; but, he added, a philosopher who should go deep enough to acquire the power, would attain too lofty a wisdom to stoop to the exercise of it. Not less singular were his opinions in regard to the Elixir Vitæ.[2] He more than intimated, that it was at his option to concoct a liquid that should prolong life for years—perhaps interminably—

1. The goal of many alchemists was to turn base metal into gold.

2. Elixir of life (Latin); a potion with the power to prolong life indefinitely.

but that it would produce a discord in nature, which all the world, and chiefly the quaffer of the immortal nostrum, would find cause to curse.

"Aylmer, are you in earnest?" asked Georgiana, looking at him with amazement and fear; "it is terrible to possess such power, or even to dream of possessing it!"

"Oh, do not tremble, my love!" said her husband, "I would not wrong either you or myself, by working such inharmonious effects upon our lives. But I would have you consider how trifling, in comparison, is the skill requisite to remove this little Hand."

At the mention of the birth-mark, Georgiana, as usual, shrank, as if a red-hot iron had touched her cheek.

Again Aylmer applied himself to his labors. She could hear his voice in the distant furnace-room, giving directions to Aminidab, whose harsh, uncouth, misshapen tones were audible in response, more like the grunt or growl of a brute than human speech. After hours of absence, Aylmer re-appeared, and proposed that she should now examine his cabinet of chemical products, and natural treasures of the earth. Among the former he showed her a small vial, in which, he remarked, was contained a gentle, yet most powerful fragrance, capable of impregnating all the breezes that blow across a kingdom. They were of inestimable value, the contents of that little vial; and, as he said so, he threw some of the perfume into the air, and filled the room with piercing and invigorating delight.

"And what is this?" asked Georgiana, pointing to a small crystal globe, containing a gold-colored liquid. "It is so beautiful to the eye, that I could imagine it the Elixir of Life."

"In one sense it is," replied Aylmer, "or rather the Elixir of Immortality. It is the most precious poison that ever was concocted in this world. By its aid, I could apportion the lifetime of any mortal at whom you might point your finger. The strength of the dose would determine whether he were to linger out years, or drop dead in the midst of a breath. No king, on his guarded throne, could keep his life, if I, in my private station, should deem that the welfare of millions justified me in depriving him of it."

"Why do you keep such a terrific drug?" inquired Georgiana in horror.

"Do not mistrust me, dearest!" said her husband, smiling; "its virtuous potency is yet greater than its harmful one. But, see! here is a powerful cosmetic. With a few drops of this, in a vase of water, freckles may be washed away as easily as the hands are cleansed. A stronger infusion would take the blood out of the cheek, and leave the rosiest beauty a pale ghost."

"Is it with this lotion that you intend to bathe my cheek?" asked Georgiana anxiously.

"Oh, no!" hastily replied her husband—"this is merely superficial. Your case demands a remedy that shall go deeper."

In his interviews with Georgiana, Aylmer generally made minute inquiries as to her sensations, and whether the confinement of the rooms, and the temperature of the atmosphere, agreed with her. These questions had such a particular drift, that Georgiana began to conjecture that she was already subjected to certain physical influences, either breathed in with the fragrant air, or taken with her food. She fancied, likewise—but it might be altogether fancy—that there was a stirring up of her system,—a strange, indefinite sensation creeping through her veins, and tingling, half painfully, half pleasurably, at her heart. Still, whenever she dared to look into the mirror, there she beheld herself, pale as a white rose, and with the crimson birth-mark stamped upon her cheek. Not even Aylmer now hated it so much as she.

To dispel the tedium of the hours which her husband found it necessary to devote to the processes of combination and analysis, Georgiana turned over the volumes of his scientific library. In many dark old tomes, she met with chapters full of romance and poetry. They were the works of the philosophers of the middle ages, such as Albertus Magnus, Cornelius Agrippa, Paracelsus, and the famous friar who created the prophetic Brazen Head.[3] All these antique naturalists stood in advance of their centuries, yet were imbued with some of their[4] credulity, and therefore were believed, and perhaps imagined themselves, to have acquired from the investigation of nature a power above nature, and from physics a sway over the spiritual world. Hardly less curious and imaginative were the early volumes of the Transactions of the Royal Society,[5] in which the members, knowing little of the limits of natural possibility, were continually recording wonders, or proposing methods whereby wonders might be wrought.

But, to Georgiana, the most engrossing volume was a large folio from her husband's own hand, in which he had recorded every experiment of his scientific career, with its original aim, the methods adopted for its development, and its final success or failure, with the circumstances to which either event was attributable. The book, in truth, was both the history and emblem of his ardent, ambitious, imaginative, yet practical and laborious, life. He handled physical details, as if there were nothing beyond them; yet spiritualized them all, and redeemed himself from materialism, by his strong and eager aspiration towards the infinite. In his grasp, the veriest clod of earth assumed a soul. Georgiana, as she read, reverenced Aylmer, and loved him more profoundly than ever, but with a less entire dependence on his judgment than heretofore. Much as he had accomplished, she could not but observe that his most splendid successes were almost invariably failures, if compared with the ideal at which he aimed. His brightest diamonds were the merest pebbles, and felt to be so by himself, in comparison with the inestimable gems which lay hidden beyond his reach. The volume, rich with achievements that had won renown for its author, was yet as melancholy a record as ever mortal hand had penned. It was the sad confession, and continual exemplification, of the short-comings of the composite man—the spirit burthened with clay and working in matter—and of the despair that assails the higher nature, at finding itself so miserably thwarted by the earthly part. Perhaps every man of genius, in whatever sphere, might recognise the image of his own experience in Aylmer's journal.

So deeply did these reflections affect Georgiana, that she laid her face upon the open volume, and burst into tears. In this situation she was found by her husband.

"It is dangerous to read in a sorcerer's books," said he, with a smile, though his countenance was uneasy and displeased. "Georgiana, there are pages in

---

3. I.e., Roger Bacon (1214?–1294), English Franciscan monk interested in science and alchemy, who fashioned a head of bronze said to predict changes in climate and health. Magnus (1206?–1280), German theologian and alchemist. Agrippa (1486–1535), German theologian and writer. Philippus Aureolus Paracelsus (1493–1541), Swiss alchemist and physician.
4. This 1846 reading replaces the 1843 *its*.
5. The Royal Society of London, chartered in 1662 to advance scientific inquiry.

that volume, which I can scarcely glance over and keep my senses. Take heed lest it prove as detrimental to you!"

"It has made me worship you more than ever," said she.

"Ah! wait for this one success," rejoined he, "then worship me if you will. I shall deem myself hardly unworthy of it. But, come! I have sought you for the luxury of your voice. Sing to me, dearest!"

So she poured out the liquid music of her voice to quench the thirst of his spirit. He then took his leave, with a boyish exuberance of gaiety, assuring her that her seclusion would endure but a little longer, and that the result was already certain. Scarcely had he departed, when Georgiana felt irresistibly impelled to follow him. She had forgotten to inform Aylmer of a symptom, which, for two or three hours past, had begun to excite her attention. It was a sensation in the fatal birth-mark, not painful, but which induced a restlessness throughout her system. Hastening after her husband, she intruded, for the first time, into the laboratory.

The first thing that struck her eye was the furnace, that hot and feverish worker, with the intense glow of its fire, which, by the quantities of soot clustered above it, seemed to have been burning for ages. There was a distilling apparatus in full operation. Around the room were retorts,[6] tubes, cylinders, crucibles, and other apparatus of chemical research. An electrical machine stood ready for immediate use. The atmosphere felt oppressively close, and was tainted with gaseous odors, which had been tormented forth by the processes of science. The severe and homely simplicity of the apartment, with its naked walls and brick pavement, looked strange, accustomed as Georgiana had become to the fantastic elegance of her boudoir. But what chiefly, indeed almost solely, drew her attention, was the aspect of Aylmer himself.

He was pale as death, anxious, and absorbed, and hung over the furnace as if it depended upon his utmost watchfulness whether the liquid, which it was distilling, should be the draught of immortal happiness or misery. How different from the sanguine and joyous mien that he had assumed for Georgiana's encouragement!

"Carefully now, Aminidab! Carefully, thou human machine! Carefully, thou man of clay!" muttered Aylmer, more to himself than his assistant. "Now, if there be a thought too much or too little, it is all over!"

"Hoh! hoh!" mumbled Aminidab—"look, master, look!"

Aylmer raised his eyes hastily, and at first reddened, then grew paler than ever, on beholding Georgiana. He rushed towards her, and seized her arm with a gripe that left the print of his fingers upon it.

"Why do you come hither? Have you no trust in your husband?" cried he impetuously. "Would you throw the blight of that fatal birth-mark over my labors? It is not well done. Go, prying woman, go!"

"Nay, Aylmer," said Georgiana, with the firmness of which she possessed no stinted endowment, "it is not you that have a right to complain. You mistrust your wife! You have concealed the anxiety with which you watch the development of this experiment. Think not so unworthily of me, my husband! Tell me all the risk we run; and fear not that I shall shrink, for my share in it is far less than your own!"

"No, no, Georgiana!" said Aylmer impatiently, "it must not be."

---

6. Glass vessels used for distillation.

"I submit," replied she, calmly. "And, Aylmer, I shall quaff whatever draught you bring me; but it will be on the same principle that would induce me to take a dose of poison, if offered by your hand."

"My noble wife," said Aylmer, deeply moved, "I knew not the height and depth of your nature, until now: Nothing shall be concealed. Know, then, that this Crimson Hand, superficial as it seems, has clutched its grasp, into your being, with a strength of which I had no previous conception. I have already administered agents powerful enough to do aught except to change your entire physical system. Only one thing remains to be tried. If that fail us, we are ruined!"

"Why did you hesitate to tell me this?" asked she.

"Because, Georgiana," said Aylmer, in a low voice, "there is danger!"

"Danger? There is but one danger—that this horrible stigma shall be left upon my cheek!" cried Georgiana. "Remove it! remove it!—whatever be the cost—or we shall both go mad!"

"Heaven knows, your words are too true," said Aylmer, sadly. "And now, dearest, return to your boudoir. In a little while, all will be tested."

He conducted her back, and took leave of her with a solemn tenderness, which spoke far more than his words how much was now at stake. After his departure, Georgiana became wrapt in musings. She considered the character of Aylmer, and did it completer justice than at any previous moment. Her heart exulted, while it trembled, at his honorable love, so pure and lofty that it would accept nothing less than perfection, nor miserably make itself contented with an earthlier nature than he had dreamed of. She felt how much more precious was such a sentiment, than that meaner kind which would have borne with the imperfection for her sake, and have been guilty of treason to holy love, by degrading its perfect idea to the level of the actual. And, with her whole spirit, she prayed, that, for a single moment, she might satisfy his highest and deepest conception. Longer than one moment, she well knew, it could not be; for his spirit was ever on the march—ever ascending—and each instant required something that was beyond the scope of the instant before.

The sound of her husband's footsteps aroused her. He bore a crystal goblet, containing a liquor colorless as water, but bright enough to be the draught of immortality. Aylmer was pale; but it seemed rather the consequence of a highly wrought state of mind, and tension of spirit, than of fear or doubt.

"The concoction of the draught has been perfect," said he, in answer to Georgiana's look. "Unless all my science have deceived me, it cannot fail."

"Save on your account, my dearest Aylmer," observed his wife, "I might wish to put off this birth-mark of mortality by relinquishing mortality itself, in preference to any other mode. Life is but a sad possession to those who have attained precisely the degree of moral advancement at which I stand. Were I weaker and blinder, it might be happiness. Were I stronger, it might be endured hopefully. But, being what I find myself, methinks I am of all mortals the most fit to die."

"You are fit for heaven without tasting death!" replied her husband. "But why do we speak of dying? The draught cannot fail. Behold its effect upon this plant!"

On the window-seat there stood a geranium, diseased with yellow blotches, which had overspread all its leaves. Aylmer poured a small quantity of the liquid upon the soil in which it grew. In a little time, when the roots of the

plant had taken up the moisture, the unsightly blotches began to be extinguished in a living verdure.

"There needed no proof," said Georgiana, quietly. "Give me the goblet. I
joyfully stake all upon your word."

"Drink, then, thou lofty creature!" exclaimed Aylmer, with fervid admiration. "There is no taint of imperfection on thy spirit. Thy sensible frame,
too, shall soon be all perfect!"

She quaffed the liquid, and returned the goblet to his hand.

"It is grateful," said she with a placid smile. "Methinks it is like water
from a heavenly fountain; for it contains I know not what of unobtrusive
fragrance and deliciousness. It allays a feverish thirst, that had parched me
for many days. Now, dearest, let me sleep. My earthly senses are closing over
my spirit, like the leaves round the heart of a rose, at sunset."

She spoke the last words with a gentle reluctance, as if it required almost
more energy than she could command to pronounce the faint and lingering
syllables. Scarcely had they loitered through her lips, ere she was lost in slumber. Aylmer sat by her side, watching her aspect with the emotions proper to
a man, the whole value of whose existence was involved in the process now to
be tested. Mingled with this mood, however, was the philosophic investigation, characteristic of the man of science. Not the minutest symptom escaped
him. A heightened flush of the cheek—a slight irregularity of breath—a quiver
of the eye-lid—a hardly perceptible tremor through the frame—such were
the details which, as the moments passed, he wrote down in his folio volume.
Intense thought had set its stamp upon every previous page of that volume;
but the thoughts of years were all concentrated upon the last.

While thus employed, he failed not to gaze often at the fatal Hand, and
not without a shudder. Yet once, by a strange and unaccountable impulse,
he pressed it with his lips. His spirit recoiled, however, in the very act, and
Georgiana, out of the midst of her deep sleep, moved uneasily and murmured, as if in remonstrance. Again, Aylmer resumed his watch. Nor was it
without avail. The Crimson Hand, which at first had been strongly visible
upon the marble paleness of Georgiana's cheek, now grew more faintly outlined. She remained not less pale than ever; but the birth-mark, with every
breath that came and went, lost somewhat of its former distinctness. Its presence had been awful; its departure was more awful still. Watch the stain of
the rainbow fading out of the sky; and you will know how that mysterious
symbol passed away.

"By Heaven, it is well nigh gone!" said Aylmer to himself, in almost irrepressible ecstasy. "I can scarcely trace it now. Success! Success! And now it
is like the faintest rose-color. The slightest flush of blood across her cheek
would overcome it. But she is so pale!"

He drew aside the window-curtain, and suffered the light of natural day
to fall into the room, and rest upon her cheek. At the same time, he heard
a gross, hoarse chuckle, which he had long known as his servant Aminidab's expression of delight.

"Ah, clod! Ah, earthly mass!" cried Aylmer, laughing in a sort of frenzy.
"You have served me well! Matter and Spirit—Earth and Heaven—have
both done their part in this! Laugh, thing of the senses! You have earned
the right to laugh."

These exclamations broke Georgiana's sleep. She slowly unclosed her
eyes, and gazed into the mirror, which her husband had arranged for that

purpose. A faint smile flitted over her lips, when she recognised how barely perceptible was now that Crimson Hand, which had once blazed forth with such disastrous brilliancy as to scare away all their happiness. But then her eyes sought Aylmer's face, with a trouble and anxiety that he could by no means account for.

"My poor Aylmer!" murmured she.

"Poor? Nay, richest! Happiest! Most favored!" exclaimed he. "My peerless bride, it is successful! You are perfect!"

"My poor Aylmer!" she repeated, with a more than human tenderness. "You have aimed loftily!—you have done nobly! Do not repent, that, with so high and pure a feeling, you have rejected the best that earth could offer. Aylmer—dearest Aylmer—I am dying!"

Alas, it was too true! The fatal Hand had grappled with the mystery of life, and was the bond by which an angelic spirit kept itself in union with a mortal frame. As the last crimson tint of the birth-mark—that sole token of human imperfection—faded from her cheek, the parting breath of the now perfect woman passed into the atmosphere, and her soul, lingering a moment near her husband, took its heavenward flight. Then a hoarse, chuckling laugh was heard again! Thus ever does the gross Fatality of Earth exult in its invariable triumph over the immortal essence, which, in this dim sphere of half-development, demands the completeness of a higher state. Yet, had Aylmer reached a profounder wisdom, he need not thus have flung away the happiness, which would have woven his mortal life of the self-same texture with the celestial. The momentary circumstance was too strong for him; he failed to look beyond the shadowy scope of Time, and living once for all in Eternity, to find the perfect Future in the present.

1843, 1846

HENRY WADSWORTH LONGFELLOW
1807–1882

Henry Wadsworth Longfellow was the most beloved American poet of the nineteenth century. His narrative poems *Evangeline* (1847), *The Song of Hiawatha* (1855), and *The Courtship of Miles Standish* (1858) went through numerous editions, and his collections of lyrics—*The Seaside and the Fireside* (1850), *Tales of a Wayside Inn* (1863), and many others—were also enormously popular. In Great Britain, Longfellow outsold England's poet laureate Alfred, Lord Tennyson; and shortly after Longfellow's death in 1882, he became the first American-born poet enshrined in Westminster Abbey's famed Poets' Corner. As literary modernism took hold in the twentieth century, Longfellow came to be seen as an unadventurous, timid poet; but such an assessment unfairly diminishes the achievement of a writer who saw value in working with (rather than against) established forms and traditions. Viewed in relation to his own culture and his own poetic aspirations, Longfellow exhibited a metrical complexity, a mastery of sound and atmosphere, a progressive social conscience, and a melancholy outlook for which his soothing words were especially appropriate, as though the poet were comforting himself as well as his audience.

Longfellow was born in Portland, Maine (then still a part of Massachusetts), on February 27, 1807, the second of eight children. Both of his parents encouraged his early interest in reading and writing, but when he was sent to Bowdoin College in 1821, the expectation was that the fourteen-year-old Longfellow would eventually become a lawyer like his father. Graduating at age eighteen in the class of 1825, which also included Nathaniel Hawthorne and the future president Franklin Pierce, Longfellow made the risky vocational decision to pursue his interest in literature. He was aided in this ambition by a college trustee who donated money to Bowdoin to hire Longfellow as a professor of modern languages, provided that Longfellow agreed to use his own funds to study languages in Europe. Supported by his father, Longfellow spent three years abroad, traveling in Germany, Italy, France, and Spain (where he met Washington Irving, the American writer he most admired). Returning to the United States in 1829 with a new fluency in four languages, the twenty-two-year-old Longfellow assumed the professorship at Bowdoin. In 1831 he married Mary Storer Potter; four years later he was appointed the Smith Professor of Modern Languages and Belles Lettres at Harvard University, with the understanding that he would need to improve his skills in Germanic languages. To that end, he traveled to Europe with his wife in 1835; while in Holland, Mary died of complications from a miscarriage. Just before returning to the United States in 1836, Longfellow toured Switzerland and Austria, meeting and falling in love with Fanny Appleton, the daughter of the wealthy Boston industrialist Nathan Appleton. After a seven-year courtship, they married in 1843. As a wedding gift, Longfellow's father-in-law bought the couple Craigie House in Cambridge, a mansion abutting Harvard Yard where Longfellow himself had been renting rooms.

Longfellow's first published poem appeared in Maine's *Portland Gazette* on November 17, 1820, when he was thirteen years old. He published poems and prose while in college, but in his initial years as a professor he focused on publishing scholarly articles in the *North American Review*, along with language textbooks and translations of European poetry. But he soon returned to his principal interest, which was writing his own poetry, publishing his first volume, *Voices of the Night*, in 1839. Other poetic volumes quickly followed, including *Ballads and Other Poems* (1841), *Poems on Slavery* (1842), and *The Belfrey of Bruges and Other Poems* (1846). Longfellow's great commercial breakthrough came with the publication of his 1847 narrative poem *Evangeline*, which went through six printings in nine weeks. *Evangeline* weaves a tragic love story into a poetic narrative of the British dispossession of an Acadian French settlement in Nova Scotia during the French and Indian War (1756–63). At a time of increasing modernization, Longfellow tapped into the cultural nostalgia for times past that would also come to inform his popular Indian poetic narrative, *Hiawatha*. During these years Longfellow also published short and long prose pieces. Inspired by Irving's *Sketch-Book*, he brought out a collection of travel sketches, *Outre-Mer*, in 1835. In 1839 he published a two-volume prose romance, *Hyperion*; another prose romance, *Kavanagh*, appeared in 1849.

As a poet and a teacher, Longfellow took pride in his cosmopolitanism and transatlanticism. Rejecting the call by American literary nationalists for writing that drew mainly on native sources, Longfellow in his poetry worked with a wide range of sources—Homer and Virgil, for instance, for the hexameters of *Evangeline*, and Finnish mythologies and folk meter for *Hiawatha*. At Harvard, he taught European literatures of many periods and nationalities; he also published *The Poets and Poetry of Europe* (1845; rev. ed. 1871), a book of translations for the general reading public.

In 1854, Longfellow resigned from Harvard to devote himself completely to writing, editing, and translating. When he published *Hiawatha* one year after his resignation, the excellent sales (around thirty thousand copies in the first six months of publication) earned him his annual Harvard salary ($1,800) many times over. His 1858 *The Courtship of Miles Standish and Other Poems* sold twenty-five thousand copies in the United States over the first two months of publication, and ten thousand copies in London on its first day of publication. By the 1870s Longfellow's annual income from his writing was around $15,000, an enormous sum at that time and over $100,000 at today's value.

As with his first marriage, tragedy struck unexpectedly. In 1861 Fanny Longfellow burned to death when her dress caught fire while she was melting wax to preserve locks of her daughters' hair. Longfellow himself nearly died when he tried to smother the flames. In his grief Longfellow turned to translating the *Divine Comedy* of Dante, making the labor the occasion for regular meetings with friends such as James Russell Lowell and the young William Dean Howells; the volumes were published between 1865 and 1871. Longfellow made one last visit to Europe in 1868–69, during which Queen Victoria gave him a private audience and Oxford awarded him an honorary doctoral degree. On his return, he continued with his various writing and editing projects. His long religious poem *Christus: A Mystery*, the labor of many years, was published in 1872, and a number of other poetic volumes followed over the next decade, including a thirty-one-volume anthology, *Poems of Place* (1877–79). Longfellow died a month after his seventy-fifth birthday on March 24, 1882. At the time he was working on a long poem about Michelangelo; *Michael Angelo: A Fragment* was published posthumously in 1883. One year later his bust was unveiled in Poets' Corner.

A Psalm of Life[1]

'Life that shall send
A challenge to its end,
And when it comes, say, 'Welcome, friend.'[2]

What the Heart of the Young Man Said to the Psalmist

I

Tell me not, in mournful numbers,[3]
  Life is but an empty dream!
For the soul is dead that slumbers,
  And things are not what they seem.

II

Life is real—life is earnest—   5
  And the grave is not its goal:
Dust thou art, to dust returnest,
  Was not spoken of the soul.

III

Not enjoyment, and not sorrow,
  Is our destin'd end or way;   10
But to *act*, that each to-morrow
  Find us farther than to-day.

---

1. The text is that of the first publication, in the *Knickerbocker or New-York Monthly Magazine* (September 1838). The poem was collected in *Voices of the Night* (1839).

2. Adapted from "Wishes to His Supposed Mistress" by the English poet Richard Crashaw (c. 1613–1649).
3. Meters, rhythms.

IV

Art is long, and time is fleeting,
   And our hearts, though stout and brave,
Still, like muffled drums, are beating   15
   Funeral marches to the grave.

V

In the world's broad field of battle,
   In the bivouac of Life,
Be not like dumb, driven cattle!
   Be a hero in the strife!   20

VI

Trust no Future, howe'er pleasant!
   Let the dead Past bury its dead!
Act—act in the glorious Present!
   Heart within, and God o'er head!

VII

Lives of great men all remind us   25
   We can make *our* lives sublime,
And, departing, leave behind us
   Footsteps on the sands of time.

VIII

Footsteps, that, perhaps another,
   Sailing o'er life's solemn main,   30
A forlorn and shipwreck'd brother,
   Seeing, shall take heart again.

IX

Let us then be up and doing,
   With a heart for any fate;
Still achieving, still pursuing,   35
   Learn to labor and to wait.

                      1838, 1839

The Slave's Dream[1]

Beside the ungathered rice he lay,
   His sickle in his hand;

1. From the first printing, in *Poems on Slavery* (1842), a little volume that marked the high point of Longfellow's public concern over slavery in the United States. Longfellow's contemporaries reacted variously. Whittier thought the poems had been "of important service" to the cause of abolitionism, while a more objective observer found them "perfect dish water" compared with Whittier's own poems against slavery. The majority, North and South, deplored the publication of the poems.

His breast was bare, his matted hair
　　Was buried in the sand.
Again, in the mist and shadow of sleep,   5
　　He saw his Native Land.

Wide through the landscape of his dreams
　　The lordly Niger[2] flowed;
Beneath the palm-trees on the plain
　　Once more a king he strode;   10
And heard the tinkling caravans
　　Descend the mountain-road.

He saw once more his dark-eyed queen
　　Among her children stand;
They clasped his neck, they kissed his cheeks,   15
　　They held him by the hand!—
A tear burst from the sleeper's lids
　　And fell into the sand.

And then at furious speed he rode
　　Along the Niger's bank;   20
His bridle-reins were golden chains,
　　And, with a martial clank,
At each leap he could feel his scabbard of steel
　　Smiting his stallion's flank.

Before him, like a blood-red flag,   25
　　The bright flamingoes flew;
From morn till night he followed their flight,
　　O'er plains where the tamarind grew,
Till he saw the roofs of Caffre[3] huts,
　　And the ocean rose to view.   30

At night he heard the lion roar,
　　And the hyena scream,
And the river-horse,[4] as he crushed the reeds
　　Beside some hidden stream;
And it passed, like a glorious roll of drums,   35
　　Through the triumph of his dream.

The forests, with their myriad tongues,
　　Shouted of liberty;
And the Blast of the Desert cried aloud,
　　With a voice so wild and free,   40
That he started in his sleep and smiled
　　At their tempestuous glee.

He did not feel the driver's whip,
　　Nor the burning heat of day;
For Death had illumined the Land of Sleep,   45

2. Great African river.　　　　　　　Africans.
3. Kaffir, used here to mean non-Muslim　4. Hippopotamus.

And his lifeless body lay
A worn-out fetter, that the soul
Had broken and thrown away!

1842

The Jewish Cemetery at Newport[1]

How strange it seems! These Hebrews in their graves.
  Close by the street of this fair sea-port town;
Silent beside the never-silent waves,
  At rest in all this moving up and down!

The trees are white with dust, that o'er their sleep   5
  Wave their broad curtains in the south-wind's breath,
While underneath such leafy tents they keep
  The long, mysterious Exodus of Death.

And these sepulchral stones, so old and brown,
  That pave with level flags[2] their burial-place,   10
Are like the tablets of the Law, thrown down
  And broken by Moses at the mountain's base.[3]

The very names recorded here are strange,
  Of foreign accent, and of different climes;
Alvares and Rivera[4] interchange   15
  With Abraham and Jacob of old times.

"Blessed be God! for he created Death!"
  The mourners said: "and Death is rest and peace."
Then added, in the certainty of faith:
  "And giveth Life, that never more shall cease."   20

Closed are the portals of their Synagogue,
  No Psalms of David now the silence break,
No Rabbi reads the ancient Decalogue[5]
  In the grand dialect the Prophets spake.

Gone are the living, but the dead remain,   25
  And not neglected, for a hand unseen,
Scattering its bounty, like a summer rain,
  Still keeps their graves and their remembrance green.

---

1. First published in *Putnam's Monthly* (July 1854), the source of the present text. The first Jewish settlers arrived in Newport, Rhode Island, in 1658, encouraged by the relatively tolerant religious attitudes of local leaders. During the colonial period, Newport had the second largest Jewish community in North America. The Touro Synagogue, the oldest still standing in the United States, dates from 1763. Longfellow visited Newport's Jewish Cemetery in July 1852.
2. Flagstones.
3. "Moses' anger waxed hot, and he cast the tablets out of his hands, and brake them beneath the mount" (Exodus 32.19).
4. The Newport Jews were Sephardims, immigrants from Spain and Portugal, where they had acquired local names.
5. The Ten Commandments.

How came they here? What burst of Christian hate;
    What persecution, merciless, and blind,   30
Drove o'er the sea,—that desert, desolate—
    These Ishmaels and Hagars[6] of mankind?

They lived in narrow streets and lanes obscure,
    Ghetto or Judenstrass,[7] in mirk and mire;
Taught in the school of patience to endure   35
    The life of anguish and the death of fire.

All their lives long, with the unleavened bread
    And bitter herbs[8] of exile and its fears,
The wasting famine of the heart they fed,
    And slaked its thirst with marah[9] of their tears.   40

Anathema maranatha![1] was the cry
    That rang from town to town, from street to street;
At every gate the accursed Mordecai[2]
    Was mocked, and jeered, and spurned by Christian feet.

Pride and humiliation hand in hand   45
    Walked with them through the world, where'er they went;
Trampled and beaten were they as the sand,
    And yet unshaken as the continent.

For in the back-ground, figures vague and vast,
    Of patriarchs and of prophets rose sublime,   50
And all the great traditions of the Past
    They saw reflected in the coming time.

And thus for ever with reverted look,
    The mystic volume of the world they read,
Spelling it backward like a Hebrew book,[3]   55
    Till Life became a Legend of the Dead.

But ah! what once has been shall be no more!
    The groaning earth in travail and in pain
Brings forth its races, but does not restore,
    and the dead nations never rise again.   60

1854

---

6. Outcasts. From Genesis 21, where Hagar, the concubine of Abraham, and their son, Ishmael, are driven from his household at the instigation of his wife, Sarah, after the birth of their son, Isaac.
7. Street of the Jews (German). "Ghetto": a section of a city to which Jews were restricted.
8. Foods eaten at Passover in remembrance of the exodus from slavery in Egypt.
9. Bitter water; see Exodus 15.22–25, which describes how the Hebrews, after crossing the Red Sea, came to Marah, where they found the water too bitter to drink until God showed Moses how to sweeten it with a tree.
1. "If any man love not the Lord Jesus Christ, let him be Anathema Maranatha" (1 Corinthians 16.22).
2. A Jewish leader abused by the Persians (Esther 2.5–6).
3. Hebrew is read from right to left.

My Lost Youth[1]

Often I think of the beautiful town
   That is seated by the sea;
Often in thought go up and down
The pleasant streets of that dear old town,
   And my youth comes back to me.   5
     And a verse of a Lapland song
     Is haunting my memory still:
   "A boy's will is the wind's will,
And the thoughts of youth are long, long thoughts."[2]

I can see the shadowy lines of its trees,   10
   And catch, in sudden gleams,
The sheen of the far-surrounding seas,
And islands that were the Hesperides[3]
   Of all my boyish dreams.
     And the burden of that old song,   15
     It murmurs and whispers still:
   "A boy's will is the wind's will,
And the thoughts of youth are long, long thoughts."

I remember the black wharves and the slips,
   And the sea-tides tossing free;   20
And Spanish sailors with bearded lips,
And the beauty and mystery of the ships,
   And the magic of the sea.
     And the voice of that wayward song
     Is singing and saying still: 25
   "A boy's will is the wind's will,
And the thoughts of youth are long, long thoughts."

I remember the bulwarks by the shore,
   And the fort upon the hill;
The sun-rise gun, with its hollow roar,   30
The drum-beat repeated o'er and o'er,
   And the bugle wild and shrill.
     And the music of that old song
     Throbs in my memory still:
   "A boy's will is the wind's will,   35
And the thoughts of youth are long, long thoughts."

I remember the sea-fight far away,
   How it thundered o'er the tide![4]
And the dead captains, as they lay

---

1. Longfellow wrote this poem about his home-town of Portland, Maine, in March 1855, at Cambridge. The text is that of the first printing in *Putnam's Monthly Magazine* (August 1855). It was reprinted in *The Courtship of Miles Standish and Other Poems* (1858).
2. Longfellow derived the refrain from lines in the English writer John Scheffer's *The History of Lapland* (1674): "A Youth's desire is the desire of the wind." Lapland is the area of northern Europe populated by the Finnic people of northern Norway, Sweden, Finland, and other nearby regions.
3. In Greek mythology, islands where the golden apples grew.
4. The American *Enterprise* and the British *Boxer* fought near Portland in 1813. Both captains were killed and carried ashore for burial.

In their graves, o'erlooking the tranquil bay,   40
  Where they in battle died.
    And the sound of that mournful song
    Goes through me with a thrill:
  "A boy's will is the wind's will,
And the thoughts of youth are long, long thoughts."   45

I can see the breezy dome of groves,
  The shadows of Deering's Woods;[5]
And the friendships old and the early loves
Come back with a Sabbath sound, as of doves
  In quiet neighborhoods.   50
    And the verse of that sweet old song,
    It flutters and murmurs still:
  "A boy's will is the wind's will,
And the thoughts of youth are long, long thoughts."

I remember the gleams and glooms that dart   55
  Across the schoolboy's brain;
The song and the silence in the heart,
That in part are prophecies, and in part
  Are longings wild and vain.
    And the voice of that fitful song   60
    Sings on, and is never still:
  "A boy's will is the wind's will,
And the thoughts of youth are long, long thoughts."

There are things of which I may not speak;
  There are dreams that cannot die;   65
There are thoughts that make the strong heart weak,
And bring a pallor into the cheek,
  And a mist before the eye.
    And the words of that fatal song
    Come over me like a chill: 70
  "A boy's will is the wind's will,
And the thoughts of youth are long, long thoughts."

Strange to me now are the forms I meet
  When I visit the dear old town;
But the native air is pure and sweet,   75
And the trees that o'ershadow each well-known street,
  As they balance up and down,
    Are singing the beautiful song,
    Are sighing and whispering still:
  "A boy's will is the wind's will,   80
And the thoughts of youth are long, long thoughts."

And Deering's Woods are fresh and fair,
  And with joy that is almost pain
My heart goes back to wander there,
And among the dreams of the days that were,   85

5. Wooded area in Portland now called Deering Oaks.

I find my lost youth again.
 And the strange and beautiful song,
 The groves are repeating it still:
 "A boy's will is the wind's will,
And the thoughts of youth are long, long thoughts." 90

1855

JOHN GREENLEAF WHITTIER
1807–1892

John Greenleaf Whittier was born to a Quaker family on December 17, 1807, on a farm near Haverhill, Massachusetts. Although no longer persecuted in New England, Quakers were still a people apart, and Whittier grew up with a sense of being different from most of his neighbors. Labor on the debt-ridden farm overstrained his health in adolescence, and thereafter throughout his long life he suffered from intermittent physical collapses. At fourteen, having had only a meager education in a household suspicious of non-Quaker literature, he found in the Scottish poet Robert Burns (1759–1796) an initial source of inspiration. Like Burns, Whittier began writing poems that employed regional dialect, dealt with homely subjects, and displayed a democratic social conscience. His first poem was published in 1826 in a local newspaper run by another young man, William Lloyd Garrison (1805–1879), whose dedication to the antislavery movement was to affect Whittier's life profoundly. In 1827 Garrison helped persuade Whittier's father that the young poet deserved a formal education, and Whittier supported himself through two terms at Haverhill Academy. In 1836, six years after his father's death, Whittier and his mother and sisters moved from the farm to a house in nearby Amesbury, Massachusetts, which he owned until his death.

In his twenties Whittier became editor of various newspapers, some of regional importance. The turning point of his career came in 1833, when Garrison brought him into the abolitionist movement. In June 1833 Whittier published an antislavery pamphlet, *Justice and Expediency*, and later that year he helped found the American Anti-Slavery Society. In the tradition of such antislavery Quakers as Anthony Benezet (1713–1784) and John Woolman (1720–1793), Whittier believed that there was only one practicable and just scheme of emancipation: "Immediate abolition of slavery; an immediate acknowledgment of the great truth, that man cannot hold property in man; an immediate surrender of baneful prejudice to Christian love; an immediate practical obedience to the command of Jesus Christ: 'Whatsoever ye would that men should do unto you, do even so to them'" *Justice and Expediency*). In an effort to disseminate his views to the widest possible audience, Whittier published over a hundred antislavery poems and quickly emerged as the most popular poet of the abolitionist movement. His antislavery poetry was collected in 1837 in an unauthorized volume, *Poems Written during the Progress of the Abolition Question in the United States*, funded by abolitionists; one year later he oversaw the publication of *Poems* (1838), which included most of his antislavery poetry up to that time. That same year Whittier, in disguise, joined an antiabolitionist mob to save some of his papers as his office was being ransacked and burned.

From the 1830s through the 1850s, Whittier was a working editor and writer associated with abolitionist newspapers such as the Washington, D.C., weekly *National*

Era, which serialized Harriet Beecher Stowe's *Uncle Tom's Cabin* from 1851 to 1852. During this time he published several additional volumes of poetry, including *Lays of My Home* (1843) and *The Chapel of Hermits and Other Poems* (1853), along with a serialized novel about New England's colonial past, *Leaves from Margaret Smith's Journal* (*National Era*, 1848–49). Like Nathaniel Hawthorne, Whittier had a keen interest in New England history. His first book, *Legends of New England* (1831), had explored New England's past in sketches and verse. In 1847 he published a sequel of sorts, the prose work *The Supernaturalism of New England*, which Hawthorne reviewed favorably in the New York monthly *Literary World*, terming it "no unworthy contribution from a poet to that species of literature which only a poet should meddle with." The New England writings of Hawthorne, Whittier, Catharine Sedgwick, and Stowe would have an important influence on the emergence of local-color regionalism later in the century.

Despite his wide-ranging interests in poetry, prose, and editing, Whittier well into the 1850s was generally regarded (contemptuously by some) as simply an abolitionist poet. His reputation underwent a change in the late 1850s, when abolitionism had become more accepted in the North, and when his poetry and humorous folk legends began to appear in the new (and very popular) *Atlantic Monthly*. With the outbreak of the Civil War, the nonviolent Quaker Whittier, whose progressive antislavery poems had contributed to northern militancy, became increasingly troubled by the carnage on the battlefield and sought refuge in a domestic poetry that recaptured an idealized, harmonic past. Grief-stricken at the death of his younger sister Elizabeth in 1865, he began work on *Snow-Bound*, which James T. Fields published as a book in 1866. In the aftermath of the Civil War, at a time of national mourning, readers responded enthusiastically to Whittier's nostalgic evocation of a historical moment when houses were not divided and all was mostly well with the world. Suddenly the poet on the margins emerged, along with Longfellow, as one of the nation's most-beloved poets. Whittier earned over $10,000 from the sales of *Snow-Bound*, an enormous sum for that time, and his subsequent volume, *The Tent on the Beach* (1867), was even more enthusiastically received, selling out its first printing of twenty thousand copies within the first three weeks of publication. During the final decades of his life, Whittier was regaled with honors, and even had a college in Iowa and a town in California named after him. On the occasion of his seventieth birthday, Stowe declared that Whittier's "life had been a consecration, his songs an inspiration, to all that is highest and best." In 1888 he helped edit a seven-volume edition of his collected works; his last volume, *At Sundown* (1890), was privately printed for friends. He died from a stroke in Hampton Falls, New Hampshire, on September 7, 1892.

Snow-Bound: A Winter Idyl[1]

To the memory of the household it describes, this poem is dedicated by the author.

"As the Spirits of Darkness be stronger in the dark, so Good Spirits which be Angels of Light are augmented not only by the Divine light of the Sun, but also by our common Wood Fire: and

1. The text followed here is that of the 1st edition (1866). In a prefatory note to the 1891 edition, Whittier remarked that the "inmates of the family at the Whittier homestead who are referred to in the poem were my father, mother, my brother and two sisters, and my uncle and aunt, both unmarried. In addition, there was the district schoolmaster who boarded with us. The 'not unfeared, half-unwelcome guest' was Harriet Livermore, daughter of Judge Livermore, of New Hampshire, a young woman of fine natural ability, enthusiastic, eccentric." Harriet Livermore (1788–1868) became a well-known preacher, an unusual career for a woman at the time. A millenarian, she warned of a coming Apocalypse.

as the celestial Fire drives away dark spirits, so also this our Fire
of Wood doth the same."
　　　　　　—Cor. Agrippa, *Occult Philosophy*, Book I. chap. v.[2]

"Announced by all the trumpets of the sky,
Arrives the snow; and, driving o'er the fields,
Seems nowhere to alight; the whited air
Hides hills and woods, the river and the heaven,
And veils the farm-house at the garden's end.
The sled and traveller stopped, the courier's feet
Delayed, all friends shut out, the housemates sit
Around the radiant fireplace, enclosed
In a tumultuous privacy of storm."
　　　　　　—Emerson[3]

The sun that brief December day
Rose cheerless over hills of gray,
And, darkly circled, gave at noon
A sadder light than waning moon.

Slow tracing down the thickening sky　　　　　　　　　5
Its mute and ominous prophecy,
A portent seeming less than threat,
It sank from sight before it set.
A chill no coat, however stout,
Of homespun stuff could quite shut out,　　　　　　　10
A hard, dull bitterness of cold,
　　That checked, mid-vein, the circling race
　　Of life-blood in the sharpened face,
The coming of the snow-storm told.

The wind blew east: we heard the roar　　　　　　　15
Of Ocean on his wintry shore,
And felt the strong pulse throbbing there
Beat with low rhythm our inland air.

Meanwhile we did our nightly chores,—
Brought in the wood from out of doors,　　　　　　　20
Littered the stalls, and from the mows
Raked down the herd's-grass for the cows;
Heard the horse whinnying for his corn;
And, sharply clashing horn on horn,
Impatient down the stanchion rows　　　　　　　　25
The cattle shake their walnut bows;[4]
While, peering from his early perch
Upon the scaffold's pole of birch,
The cock his crested helmet bent
And down his querulous challenge sent.　　　　　　　30

---

2. Heinrich Cornelius Agrippa (1486–1525) was
a German physician and student of occult science. In his 1891 prefatory note, Whittier said
that his family owned a 1651 edition of Agrippa's
Three Books of Occult Philosophy (1532).
3. The opening of Emerson's "The Snow-Storm"
(1841).

4. Stanchions (here made of walnut and shaped
like a bow) are adjustable braces set a few inches
from stationary posts; they are pulled aside at the
top to let a cow's head pass, then fixed against the
neck so the cow cannot back out while being
milked or fed.

Unwarmed by any sunset light
The gray day darkened into night,
A night made hoary with the swarm
And whirl-dance of the blinding storm,
As zigzag wavering to and fro   35
Crossed and recrossed the wingéd snow:
And ere the early bed-time came
The white drift piled the window-frame,
And through the glass the clothes-line posts
Looked in like tall and sheeted ghosts.   40

So all night long the storm roared on:
The morning broke without a sun;
In tiny spherule traced with lines
Of Nature's geometric signs,
In starry flake, and pellicle,[5]   45
All day the hoary meteor fell;
And, when the second morning shone,
We looked upon a world unknown,
On nothing we could call our own.
Around the glistening wonder bent   50
The blue walls of the firmament,
No cloud above, no earth below,—
A universe of sky and snow!
The old familiar sights of ours
Took marvellous shapes; strange domes and towers   55
Rose up where sty or corn-crib stood,
Or garden wall, or belt of wood;
A smooth white mound the brush-pile showed,
A fenceless drift what once was road;
The bridle-post an old man sat   60
With loose-flung coat and high cocked hat;
The well-curb had a Chinese roof;
And even the long sweep,[6] high aloof,
In its slant splendor, seemed to tell
Of Pisa's leaning miracle.   65

A prompt, decisive man, no breath
Our father wasted: "Boys, a path!"
Well pleased, (for when did farmer boy
Count such a summons less than joy?)
Our buskins[7] on our feet we drew;   70
    With mittened hands, and caps drawn low,
    To guard our necks and ears from snow,
We cut the solid whiteness through.
And, where the drift was deepest, made
A tunnel walled and overlaid   75
With dazzling crystal: we had read
Of rare Aladdin's wondrous cave,
And to our own his name we gave,

5. A thin crust of crystals.
6. I.e., a well sweep; a pole attached to a pivot, with a bucket at one end for raising water.
7. High-cut shoes, like a half boot.

With many a wish the luck were ours
To test his lamp's supernal powers.   80
We reached the barn with merry din,
And roused the prisoned brutes within.
The old horse thrust his long head out,
And grave with wonder gazed about;
The cock his lusty greeting said,   85
And forth his speckled harem led;
The oxen lashed their tails, and hooked,
And mild reproach of hunger looked;
The hornéd patriarch of the sheep,
Like Egypt's Amun[8] roused from sleep,   90
Shook his sage head with gesture mute,
And emphasized with stamp of foot.

All day the gusty north-wind bore
The loosening drift its breath before;
Low circling round its southern zone,   95
The sun through dazzling snow-mist shone.
No bell the hush of silence broke,
No neighboring chimney's social smoke
Curled over woods of snow-hung oak.
A solitude made more intense   100
By dreary voicéd elements,
The shrieking of the mindless wind,
The moaning tree-boughs swaying blind,
And on the glass the unmeaning beat
Of ghostly finger-tips of sleet.   105
Beyond the circle of our hearth
No welcome sound of toil or mirth
Unbound the spell, and testified
Of human life and thought outside.
We minded that the sharpest ear   110
The buried brooklet could not hear,
The music of whose liquid lip
Had been to us companionship,
And, in our lonely life, had grown
To have an almost human tone.   115

As night drew on, and, from the crest
Of wooded knolls that ridged the west,
The sun, a snow-blown traveller, sank
From sight beneath the smothering bank,
We piled, with care, our nightly stack   120
Of wood against the chimney-back,—
The oaken log, green, huge, and thick,
And on its top the stout back-stick;
The knotty forestick laid apart,
And filled between with curious art   125
The ragged brush; then, hovering near,

8. Egyptian god with a ram's head.

We watched the first red blaze appear,
Heard the sharp crackle, caught the gleam
On whitewashed wall and sagging beam,
Until the old, rude-furnished room   130
Burst, flower-like, into rosy bloom;
While radiant with a mimic flame
Outside the sparkling drift became,
And through the bare-boughed lilac-tree
Our own warm hearth seemed blazing free.   135
The crane and pendent trammels[9] showed,
The Turks' heads[1] on the andirons glowed;
While childish fancy, prompt to tell
The meaning of the miracle,
Whispered the old rhyme: *"Under the tree,*   140
When fire outdoors burns merrily,
There the witches are making tea."
The moon above the eastern wood
Shone at its full; the hill-range stood
Transfigured in the silver flood,   145
Its blown snows flashing cold and keen,
Dead white, save where some sharp ravine
Took shadow, or the sombre green
Of hemlocks turned to pitchy black
Against the whiteness at their back.   150
For such a world and such a night
Most fitting that unwarming light,
Which only seemed where'er it fell
To make the coldness visible.

Shut in from all the world without,   155
We sat the clean-winged hearth about.
Content to let the north-wind roar
In baffled rage at pane and door,
While the red logs before us beat
The frost-line back with tropic heat;   160
And ever, when a louder blast
Shook beam and rafter as it passed,
The merrier up its roaring draught
The great throat of the chimney laughed.
The house-dog on his paws outspread   165
Laid to the fire his drowsy head,
The cat's dark silhouette on the wall
A couchant[2] tiger's seemed to fall;
And, for the winter fireside meet,
Between the andirons' straddling feet,   170
The mug of cider simmered slow,
The apples sputtered in a row,
And, close at hand, the basket stood
With nuts from brown October's wood.

9. Pot hooks hanging from the crane, or movable arm.
1. A favorite ornamentation, turbanlike knots in
wrought iron.
2. Lying on stomach with head raised.

What matter how the night behaved?   175
What matter how the north-wind raved?
Blow high, blow low, not all its snow
Could quench our hearth-fire's ruddy glow.
O Time and Change!—with hair as gray
As was my sire's that winter day,   180
How strange it seems, with so much gone
Of life and love, to still live on!
Ah, brother! only I and thou
Are left of all that circle now,—
The dear home faces whereupon   185
That fitful firelight paled and shone.
Henceforward, listen as we will,
The voices of that hearth are still;
Look where we may, the wide earth o'er,
Those lighted faces smile no more.   190
We tread the paths their feet have worn,
    We sit beneath their orchard-trees,
    We hear, like them, the hum of bees
And rustle of the bladed corn;
We turn the pages that they read,   195
    Their written words we linger o'er,
But in the sun they cast no shade,
No voice is heard, no sign is made,
    No step is on the conscious floor!
Yet Love will dream, and Faith will trust,   200
(Since He who knows our need is just,)
That somehow, somewhere, meet we must.
Alas for him who never sees
The stars shine through his cypress-trees!
Who, hopeless, lays his dead away,   205
Nor looks to see the breaking day
Across the mournful marbles[3] play!
Who hath not learned, in hours of faith,
    The truth to flesh and sense unknown,
That Life is ever lord of Death,   210
    And Love can never lose its own!

We sped the time with stories old,
Wrought puzzles out, and riddles told,
Or stammered from our school-book lore
"The Chief of Gambia's golden shore."[4]   215
How often since, when all the land
Was clay in Slavery's shaping hand,
As if a trumpet called, I've heard
Dame Mercy Warren's rousing word:
"*Does not the voice of reason cry,*   220
    Claim the first right which Nature gave,
From the red scourge of bondage fly,

3. I.e., the gravestones.
4. From "The African Chief," a widely reprinted antislavery poem by the Bostonian Sarah Wentworth Morton (1759–1846). In lines 220–23 Whittier quotes the poem but misidentifies the author as the Massachusetts historian Mercy Otis Warren (1728–1814).

      Nor deign to live a burdened slave!"
Our father rode again his ride
On Memphremagog's[5] wooded side;   225
Sat down again to moose and samp[6]
In trapper's hut and Indian camp;
Lived o'er the old idyllic ease
Beneath St. François'[7] hemlock-trees;
Again for him the moonlight shone   230
On Norman cap and bodiced zone;[8]
Again he heard the violin play
Which led the village dance away,
And mingled in its merry whirl
The grandam and the laughing girl.   235
Or, nearer home, our steps he led
Where Salisbury's[9] level marshes spread
    Mile-wide as flies the laden bee;
Where merry mowers, hale and strong,
Swept, scythe on scythe, their swaths along   240
    The low green prairies of the sea.
We shared the fishing off Boar's Head,
    And round the rocky Isles of Shoals[1]
    The hake-broil on the drift-wood coals;
The chowder on the sand-beach made,   245
Dipped by the hungry, steaming hot,
With spoons of clam-shell from the pot.
We heard the tales of witchcraft old,
And dream and sign and marvel told
To sleepy listeners as they lay   250
Stretched idly on the salted hay,
Adrift along the winding shores,
When favoring breezes deigned to blow
The square sail of the gundalow[2]
And idle lay the useless oars.   255

Our mother, while she turned her wheel
Or run the new-knit stocking-heel,
Told how the Indian hordes came down
At midnight on Cochecho[3] town,
And how her own great-uncle bore   260
His cruel scalp-mark to fourscore.
Recalling, in her fitting phrase,
    So rich and picturesque and free,
    (The common unrhymed poetry
Of simple life and country ways,)   265
The story of her early days,—
She made for us the sunset shine
Aslant the tall columnar pine;

---

5. A lake between Vermont and Quebec.
6. Cornmeal mush.
7. Village north of Lake Memphremagog.
8. Whittier's father is recalling the traditional clothes of women in French-Canadian settlements. (A "zone" is a belt or bodice.)

9. Nearby town in northeastern Massachusetts.
1. Off the New Hampshire coast.
2. Flat-bottomed boat.
3. Settlement near Dover, New Hampshire, on the Cochecho River.

The river at her father's door
Its rippled moanings whispered o'er;   270
We heard the hawks at twilight play,
The boat-horn on Piscataqua,[4]
The loon's weird laughter far away.
So well she gleaned from earth and sky
That harvest of the ear and eye,   275
We almost felt the gusty air
That swept her native wood-paths bare,
Heard the far thresher's rhythmic flail,
The flapping of the fisher's sail,
Or saw, in sheltered cove and bay,   280
The ducks' black squadron anchored lay,
Or heard the wild geese calling loud
Beneath the gray November cloud.

Then, haply, with a look more grave,
And soberer tone, some tale she gave   285
From painful Sewell's[5] ancient tome,
Beloved in every Quaker home,
Of faith fire-winged by martyrdom,
Or Chalkley's Journal,[6] old and quaint,—
Gentlest of skippers, rare sea-saint!—   290
Who, when the dreary calms prevailed,
And water-butt and bread-cask failed,
And cruel, hungry eyes pursued
His portly presence mad for food,
With dark hints muttered under breath   295
Of casting lots for life or death,
Offered, if Heaven withheld supplies,
To be himself the sacrifice.
Then, suddenly, as if to save
The good man from his living grave,   300
A ripple on the water grew,
A school of porpoise flashed in view.
"Take, eat," he said, "and be content;[7]
These fishes in my stead are sent
By Him who gave the tangled ram   305
To spare the child of Abraham."[8]
Our uncle, innocent of books,
But rich in lore of fields and brooks,
The ancient teachers never dumb
Of Nature's unhoused lyceum,[9]   310
In moons and tides and weather wise,
He read the clouds as prophecies,
And foul or fair could well divine,

---

4. I.e., foghorn on the Piscataqua River.
5. William Sewell or Sewel (1650–1725), author of a history of the Quakers. The history made painful reading because of the persecution and martyrdom many Quakers had suffered.
6. The *Journal* of the Quaker sea captain and preacher Thomas Chalkley (1675–1741) was published in 1747.
7. Matthew 26.26: "Take, eat: this is my body" (Jesus' words at Passover).
8. See Genesis 22.13.
9. Lecture hall.

By many an occult hint and sign,
Holding the cunning-warded[1] keys   315
To all the woodcraft mysteries;
Himself to Nature's heart so near
That all her voices in his ear
Of beast or bird had meanings clear,
Like Apollonius of old,   320
Who knew the tales the sparrows told,
Or Hermes,[2] who interpreted
What the sage cranes of Nilus[3] said;
A simple, guileless, childlike man,
Content to live where life began;   325
Strong only on his native grounds,
The little world of sights and sounds
Whose girdle was the parish bounds,
Whereof his fondly partial pride
The common features magnified,   330
As Surrey hills to mountains grew
In White of Selborne's[4] loving view,—
He told how teal and loon he shot,
And how the eagle's eggs he got,
The feats on pond and river done,   335
The prodigies of rod and gun;
Till, warming with the tales he told,
Forgotten was the outside cold,
The bitter wind unheeded blew,
From ripening corn the pigeons flew,   340
The partridge drummed i' the wood, the mink
Went fishing down the river-brink.
In fields with bean or clover gay,
The woodchuck, like a hermit gray,
Peered from the doorway of his cell;   345
The muskrat plied the mason's trade,
And tier by tier his mud-walls laid;
And from the shagbark overhead
The grizzled squirrel dropped his shell.

Next, the dear aunt, whose smile of cheer   350
And voice in dreams I see and hear,—
The sweetest woman ever Fate
Perverse denied a household mate,
Who, lonely, homeless, not the less
Found peace in love's unselfishness,   355
And welcome wheresoe'er she went,
A calm and gracious element,
Whose presence seemed the sweet income
And womanly atmosphere of home,—

1. Carefully guarded.
2. Hermes Trismegistus (3rd century C.E.), legendary author of Egyptian books of magic. Apollonius (1st century C.E.), Greek mystic.
3. Nile River.

4. Gilbert White (1720–1793), English naturalist
who lived in the county of Surrey, in southern
England, and wrote *The Natural History and
Antiquities of Selborne* (1789).

Called up her girlhood memories,   360
The huskings and the apple-bees,
The sleigh-rides and the summer sails,
Weaving through all the poor details
And homespun warp of circumstance
A golden woof-thread of romance.   365
For well she kept her genial mood
And simple faith of maidenhood;
Before her still a cloud-land lay,
The mirage loomed across her way;
The morning dew, that dries so soon   370
With others, glistened at her noon;
Through years of toil and soil and care
From glossy tress to thin gray hair,
All unprofaned she held apart
The virgin fancies of the heart.   375
Be shame to him of woman born
Who hath for such but thought of scorn.
There, too, our elder sister plied
Her evening task the stand beside;
A full, rich nature, free to trust,   380
Truthful and almost sternly just,
Impulsive, earnest, prompt to act,
And make her generous thought a fact,
Keeping with many a light disguise
The secret of self-sacrifice.   385
O heart sore-tried! thou hast the best
That Heaven itself could give thee,—rest,
Rest from all bitter thoughts and things!
     How many a poor one's blessing went
     With thee beneath the low green tent   390
Whose curtain never outward swings!

As one who held herself a part
Of all she saw, and let her heart
     Against the household bosom lean,
Upon the motley-braided mat   395
Our youngest and our dearest sat,
Lifting her large, sweet, asking eyes,
     Now bathed within the fadeless green
And holy peace of Paradise.
O, looking from some heavenly hill,   400
     Or from the shade of saintly palms,
     Or silver reach of river calms,
Do those large eyes behold me still?
With me one little year ago:—
The chill weight of the winter snow   405
     For months upon her grave has lain;
And now, when summer south-winds blow
     And brier and harebell bloom again,
I tread the pleasant paths we trod,
I see the violet-sprinkled sod   410
Whereon she leaned, too frail and weak

The hillside flowers she loved to seek,
Yet following me where'er I went
With dark eyes full of love's content.
The birds are glad; the brier-rose fills   415
The air with sweetness; all the hills
Stretch green to June's unclouded sky;
But still I wait with ear and eye
For something gone which should be nigh,
A loss in all familiar things,   420
In flower that blooms, and bird that sings.
And yet, dear heart! remembering thee,
   Am I not richer than of old?
Safe in thy immortality,
   What change can reach the wealth I hold?   425
   What chance can mar the pearl and gold
Thy love hath left in trust with me?
And while in life's late afternoon,
   Where cool and long the shadows grow,
I walk to meet the night that soon   430
   Shall shape and shadow overflow,
I cannot feel that thou art far,
Since near at need the angels are;
And when the sunset gates unbar,
   Shall I not see thee waiting stand,   435
And, white against the evening star,
   The welcome of thy beckoning hand?

Brisk wielder of the birch and rule,
The master of the district school
Held at the fire his favored place,   440
Its warm glow lit a laughing face
Fresh-hued and fair, where scarce appeared
The uncertain prophecy of beard.
He played the old and simple games
Our modern boyhood scarcely names,   445
Sang songs, and told us what befalls
In classic Dartmouth's college halls.
Born the wild Northern hills among,
From whence his yeoman father wrung
By patient toil subsistence scant,   450
Not competence and yet not want,
He early gained the power to pay
His cheerful, self-reliant way;
Could doff at ease his scholar's gown
To peddle wares from town to town;   455
Or through the long vacation's reach
In lonely lowland districts teach,
Where all the droll experience found
At stranger hearths in boarding round,
The moonlit skater's keen delight,   460
The sleigh-drive through the frosty night,
The rustic party, with its rough
Accompaniment of blind-man's-buff,

And whirling plate,[5] and forfeits paid,
His winter task a pastime made.   465
Happy the snow-locked homes wherein
He tuned his merry violin,
Or played the athlete in the barn,
Or held the good dame's winding yarn,
Or mirth-provoking versions told   470
Of classic legends rare and old,
Wherein the scenes of Greece and Rome
Had all the commonplace of home,
And little seemed at best the odds
'Twixt Yankee pedlers and old gods;   475
Where Pindus-born Araxes[6] took
The guise of any grist-mill brook,
And dread Olympus[7] at his will
Became a huckleberry hill.

A careless boy that night he seemed;   480
   But at his desk he had the look
And air of one who wisely schemed,
   And hostage from the future took
   In trainéd thought and lore of book.
Large-brained, clear-eyed,—of such as he   485
Shall Freedom's young apostles be,
Who, following in War's bloody trail,
Shall every lingering wrong assail;
All chains from limb and spirit strike,
Uplift the black and white alike;   490
Scatter before their swift advance
The darkness and the ignorance,
The pride, the lust, the squalid sloth,
Which nurtured Treason's monstrous growth,
Made murder pastime, and the hell   495
Of prison-torture possible;
The cruel lie of caste refute,
Old forms recast, and substitute
For Slavery's lash the freeman's will,
For blind routine, wise-handed skill;   500
A school-house plant on every hill,
Stretching in radiate nerve-lines thence
The quick wires of intelligence;[8]
Till North and South together brought
Shall own the same electric thought,   505
In peace a common flag salute,
And, side by side in labor's free
And unresentful rivalry,
Harvest the fields wherein they fought.

---

5. Children's game of keeping a plate spinning on edge for as long as possible. "Blind-man's-buff": variant name for blind man's bluff, another children's game.
6. A Greek river, "born" in the Pindus Mountains.
7. Mountain that was the home of the Gods in Greek mythology.
8. Information, communication (the imagery is from the telegraph, then still a recent development).

Another guest[9] that winter night   510
Flashed back from lustrous eyes the light.
Unmarked by time, and yet not young,
The honeyed music of her tongue
And words of meekness scarcely told
A nature passionate and bold,   515
Strong, self-concentred, spurning guide,
Its milder features dwarfed beside
Her unbent will's majestic pride.
She sat among us, at the best,
A not unfeared, half-welcome guest,   520
Rebuking with her cultured phrase
Our homeliness of words and ways.
A certain pard-like,[1] treacherous grace
    Swayed the lithe limbs and drooped the lash,
    Lent the white teeth their dazzling flash;   525
    And under low brows, black with night,
    Rayed out at times a dangerous light;
The sharp heat-lightnings of her face
Presaging ill to him whom Fate
Condemned to share her love or hate.   530
A woman tropical, intense
In thought and act, in soul and sense,
She blended in a like degree
The vixen and the devotee,
Revealing with each freak or feint   535
    The temper of Petruchio's Kate,[2]
The raptures of Siena's saint.[3]
Her tapering hand and rounded wrist
Had facile power to form a fist;
The warm, dark languish of her eyes   540
Was never safe from wrath's surprise.
Brows saintly calm and lips devout
Knew every change of scowl and pout;
And the sweet voice had notes more high
And shrill for social battle-cry.   545

Since then what old cathedral town
Has missed her pilgrim staff and gown,
What convent-gate has held its lock
Against the challenge of her knock!
Through Smyrna's[4] plague-husked thoroughfares,   550
Up sea-set Malta's rocky stairs,
Gray olive slopes of hills that hem
Thy tombs and shrines, Jerusalem,
Or startling on her desert throne
The crazy Queen of Lebanon[5]   555
With claims fantastic as her own,

9. The boarder Harriet Livermore.
1. Leopardlike.
2. The heroine of Shakespeare's *Taming of the Shrew*.
3. St. Catharine (1347–1380) of Siena, in Tus-

cany, Italy.
4. Now Izmir in Turkey.
5. Lady Hester Stanhope (1776–1839), an Englishwoman who in 1810 settled in Lebanon, where she attempted to rule like a dictator over a

Her tireless feet have held their way;
And still, unrestful, bowed, and gray,
She watches under Eastern skies,
    With hope each day renewed and fresh,   560
    The Lord's quick coming in the flesh,
Whereof she dreams and prophesies!

Where'er her troubled path may be,
    The Lord's sweet pity with her go!
The outward wayward life we see,   565
    The hidden springs we may not know.
Nor is it given us to discern
    What threads the fatal sisters[6] spun,
    Through what ancestral years has run
The sorrow with the woman born,   570
What forged her cruel chain of moods,
What set her feet in solitudes,
    And held the love within her mute,
What mingled madness in the blood,
    A life-long discord and annoy,   575
    Water of tears with oil of joy,
And hid within the folded bud
    Perversities of flower and fruit.
It is not ours to separate
The tangled skein of will and fate,   580
To show what metes and bounds should stand
Upon the soul's debatable land,
And between choice and Providence
Divide the circle of events;
But He who knows our frame is just,[7]   585
    Merciful, and compassionate,
And full of sweet assurances
And hope for all the language is,
That He remembereth we are dust!

At last the great logs, crumbling low,   590
Sent out a dull and duller glow,
The bull's-eye watch[8] that hung in view,
Ticking its weary circuit through,
Pointed with mutely-warning sign
Its black hand to the hour of nine.   595
That sign the pleasant circle broke:
My uncle ceased his pipe to smoke,
Knocked from its bowl the refuse gray
And laid it tenderly away,
Then roused himself to safely cover   600
The dull red brands with ashes over.
And while, with care, our mother laid

small area. Whittier remarked in his 1891 preface
to "Snow-Bound" that Harriet Livermore lived
with Stanhope for a while before they quarreled
over interpretations of Christ's Second Coming.
6. In Greek mythology the goddesses of destiny,
the Fates.
7. Psalm 103.14: "For he knoweth our frame; he
remembereth that we are dust."
8. Watch with a thick glass face.

The work aside, her steps she stayed
One moment, seeking to express
Her grateful sense of happiness   605
For food and shelter, warmth and health,
And love's contentment more than wealth,
With simple wishes (not the weak,
Vain prayers which no fulfilment seek,
But such as warm the generous heart,   610
O'er-prompt to do with Heaven its part)
That none might lack, that bitter night,
For bread and clothing, warmth and light.

Within our beds awhile we heard
The wind that round the gables roared,   615
With now and then a ruder shock,
Which made our very bedsteads rock.
We heard the loosened clapboards tost,
The board-nails snapping in the frost;
And on us, through the unplastered wall,   620
Felt the light sifted snow-flakes fall.
But sleep stole on, as sleep will do
When hearts are light and life is new;
Faint and more faint the murmurs grew,
Till in the summer-land of dreams   625
They softened to the sound of streams,
Low stir of leaves, and dip of oars,
And lapsing waves on quiet shores.

Next morn we wakened with the shout
Of merry voices high and clear;   630
And saw the teamsters[9] drawing near
To break the drifted highways out.
Down the long hillside treading slow
We saw the half-buried oxen go,
Shaking the snow from heads uptost,   635
Their straining nostrils white with frost.
Before our door the straggling train
Drew up, an added team to gain.
The elders threshed their hands a-cold,
    Passed, with the cider-mug, their jokes   640
    From lip to lip; the younger folks
Down the loose snow-banks, wrestling, rolled,
Then toiled again the cavalcade
    O'er windy hill, through clogged ravine,
    And woodland paths that wound between   645
Low drooping pine-boughs winter-weighed.
From every barn a team afoot,
At every house a new recruit,
Where, drawn by Nature's subtlest law,
Haply the watchful young men saw   650

9. Those driving teams of oxen to plow snow.

Sweet doorway pictures of the curls
And curious eyes of merry girls,
Lifting their hands in mock defence
Against the snow-ball's compliments,
And reading in each missive tost   655
The charm with Eden never lost.
We heard once more the sleigh-bells' sound;
    And, following where the teamsters led,
The wise old Doctor went his round,
Just pausing at our door to say,   660
In the brief autocratic way
Of one who, prompt at Duty's call,
Was free to urge her claim on all,
    That some poor neighbor sick abed
At night our mother's aid would need.   665
For, one in generous thought and deed,
    What mattered in the sufferer's sight
    The Quaker matron's inward light,
The Doctor's mail[1] of Calvin's creed?
All hearts confess the saints elect   670
    Who, twain in faith, in love agree,
And melt not in an acid sect
    The Christian pearl of charity!

So days went on: a week had passed
Since the great world was heard from last.   675
The Almanac we studied o'er,
Read and reread our little store,
Of books and pamphlets, scarce a score;
One harmless novel, mostly hid
From younger eyes, a book forbid,   680
And poetry, (or good or bad,
A single book was all we had,)
Where Ellwood's meek, drab-skirted Muse,
    A stranger to the heathen Nine,[2]
    Sang, with a somewhat nasal whine,   685
The wars of David and the Jews.
At last the floundering carrier bore
The village paper to our door.
Lo! broadening outward as we read,
To warmer zones the horizon spread;   690
In panoramic length unrolled
We saw the marvels that it told.
Before us passed the painted Creeks,[3]

1. Armor, with the suggestion that the French Protestant reformer John Calvin's (1509–1564) doctrines of predestination and Original Sin are less humane than the "whole armor of God" which Paul enjoins Christians to put on in Ephesians 6.11–17.
2. Thomas Ellwood (1639–1714), English Quaker, wrote the *Davideis* (1712). Whittier has an essay on him in *Old Portraits and Modern Sketches* (1850). Here, Ellwood's source of inspiration wears "drab" Quaker clothes made of brownish yellow homespun, and knows nothing of the nine Greek goddesses who traditionally inspire artists and scientists.
3. Tribe of American Indians from Alabama who were subdued by Andrew Jackson in the Creek War (1813–14) and forced to resettle in present-day Oklahoma.

And daft McGregor on his raids
    In dim Floridian everglades.[4]   695
And up Taygetos winding slow
Rode Ypsilanti's Mainote Greeks,
A Turk's head at each saddle-bow![5]
Welcome to us its week-old news,
Its corner for the rustic Muse,   700
    Its monthly gauge of snow and rain,
Its record, mingling in a breath
The wedding knell and dirge of death;
Jest, anecdote, and love-lorn tale,
The latest culprit sent to jail;   705
Its hue and cry of stolen and lost,
Its vendue[6] sales and goods at cost,
    And traffic calling loud for gain.
We felt the stir of hall and street,
The pulse of life that round us beat;   710
The chill embargo of the snow
Was melted in the genial glow;
Wide swung again our ice-locked door,
And all the world was ours once more!

Clasp, Angel of the backward look   715
    And folded wings of ashen gray
    And voice of echoes far away,
The brazen covers of thy book;
The weird palimpsest[7] old and vast,
Wherein thou hid'st the spectral past;   720
Where, closely mingling, pale and glow
The characters of joy and woe;
The monographs of outlived years,
Or smile-illumed or dim with tears,
    Green hills of life that slope to death,   725
And haunts of home, whose vistaed trees
Shade off to mournful cypresses
    With the white amaranths[8] underneath.
Even while I look, I can but heed
    The restless sands' incessant fall,   730
Importunate hours that hours succeed,
Each clamorous with its own sharp need,
    And duty keeping pace with all.
Shut down and clasp the heavy lids;
I hear again the voice that bids   735
The dreamer leave his dream midway
For larger hopes and graver fears:

---

4. The Scottish adventurer Gregor McGregor (1786–1845) fought alongside Simón Bolívar (1783–1830) for the liberation of Venezuela from Spain, then in 1817 took possession of the Spanish-owned Amelia Island, off the Florida coast.
5. The Greek Revolutionary patriot Alexander Ypsilanti (1792–1828) defeated the Turks at Mount Taygetos in 1820; his saddle ornaments are heads of Turkish soldiers.
6. Auction.
7. Parchment with earlier writing still visible beneath later writing.
8. Flowers associated with immortality.

Life greatens in these later years,
The century's aloe[9] flowers to-day!

Yet, haply, in some lull of life,   740
Some Truce of God which breaks its strife,
The worldling's eyes shall gather dew,
   Dreaming in throngful city ways
Of winter joys his boyhood knew;
And dear and early friends—the few   745
Who yet remain—shall pause to view
   These Flemish pictures[1] of old days;
Sit with me by the homestead hearth,
And stretch the hands of memory forth
   To warm them at the wood-fire's blaze!   750
And thanks untraced to lips unknown
Shall greet me like the odors blown
From unseen meadows newly mown,
Or lilies floating in some pond,
Wood-fringed, the wayside gaze beyond;   755
The traveller owns the grateful sense
Of sweetness near, he knows not whence,
And, pausing, takes with forehead bare
The benediction of the air.

1866

9. The century plant, fabled to bloom only once every hundred years.
1. Dutch (Flemish) painters from the 17th century were known for their realistic domestic scenes.

EDGAR ALLAN POE
1809–1849

The facts of Poe's life, the most melodramatic of any of the major American writers of his generation, have been hard to determine; lurid legends about him circulated even before he died, some spread by Poe himself. Two days after Poe's death his supposed friend Rufus Griswold, a prominent anthologizer of American literature to whom Poe had entrusted his literary papers, began a campaign of character assassination, writing a vicious obituary and rewriting Poe's correspondence so as to alienate the public as well as his friends. Griswold's false claims and forgeries, unexposed for many years, significantly shaped Poe's reputation for decades.

Yet biographers now possess much reliable information about Poe's life. His mother, Elizabeth Arnold, was a prominent actress, touring the eastern seaboard in a profession that was then considered disreputable. In 1806, as a teenage widow, she married David Poe Jr., another actor. Edgar, the couple's second of three children, was born in Boston on January 19, 1809; a year later, David Poe deserted the family. In December

Edgar Allan Poe. Daguerreotype, 1848.

1811, Elizabeth Poe died at twenty-four while performing in Richmond, Virginia; the evidence suggests that her husband died soon afterward at the age of twenty-seven.

The disruptions of Poe's first two years were followed by years of security after John Allan, a young Richmond tobacco merchant, and his wife, Frances, took him in; his siblings (William Henry, born 1807, and Rosalie, born 1810) were sent to different foster parents. The Allans, who were childless, renamed the boy Edgar Allan and raised him as their son, but they never adopted him legally. Poe accompanied the family to England in 1815, where he attended good schools until the collapse of the London tobacco market forced the Allans back to Richmond in 1820. In 1824 Allan's firm failed and hostilities developed between Poe and his foster father. Allan lost interest in supporting Poe financially; even after inheriting all the property of a wealthy bachelor uncle, including several slave plantations, he provided only minimal funds to Poe for studying at the University of Virginia in 1826. Poe was a good student and wrote poetry on the side, but he ran into debt and began to drink. He gambled to pay his debts, instead losing as much as $2,000 (around $30,000 in current value). Allan refused to honor the debt, and Poe had to leave the university before his first year was completed. In March 1827, after another quarrel between the two, Allan ordered Poe out of the house.

The eighteen-year-old outcast Poe went first to Baltimore, reuniting briefly with his brother, Henry, who would die of alcoholism and consumption in 1831; then he moved north to his birthplace, where he paid for the printing of *Tamerlane and Other Poems*, "By a Bostonian," in 1827. Even before its publication, "Edgar A. Perry" (he had changed his name to avoid creditors) had joined the army. Released from the army with the rank of sergeant major, Poe now sought Allan's influence to help him get into the military academy at West Point. While waiting for the appointment, Poe condensed *Tamerlane*, revised other poems, and added new ones to make up a second volume, *Al Aaraaf, Tamerlane, and Minor Poems*, published in Baltimore in December 1829. In a short but favorable review, the influential New England critic John Neal declared that Poe could become "*foremost* in the rank of *real* poets."

Admitted to West Point in June 1830, Poe quickly became known for his conviviality and skills in mathematics and French. Despite renewed conflict with Allan, he believed himself the heir to Allan's great fortune. But his expectations were dashed when Allan, less than two years after the death of Frances Allan, married the thirty-year-old Louisa Patterson in October 1830 and had a son in 1831 (in fact when Allan died in 1834, Poe was not mentioned in the will). The disillusioned Poe began to miss classes and roll calls and, as he anticipated, was expelled from school. Supportive friends among the cadets collected funds to publish his *Poems*, which appeared in May 1831. In this third book of his poetry Poe revised some earlier poems and for the first time included versions of both "To Helen" and "Israfel."

Poe's mature career—from his twenty-first year to his death in his fortieth year—was spent in four literary centers: Baltimore, Richmond, Philadelphia, and New York. The Baltimore years—mid-1831 to late 1835—were marked by hard work and comparative sobriety. Poe lived in poverty among his once-prosperous relatives, including his aunt Maria Poe Clemm and her daughter, Virginia. Poe's first story, "Metzengerstein," was published anonymously in the *Philadelphia Saturday Courier*, in January 1832; other stories appeared in the same paper throughout the year. Over the next two years, Poe placed stories and poems in the *Baltimore Saturday Visiter*. In January 1834 he made a significant breakthrough, publishing his tale "The Visionary" in *Godey's Lady's Book*, a popular Philadelphia monthly edited by Sarah J. Hale, for many years the nation's most prominent woman of letters. The writer and editor John P. Kennedy, who had read Poe's submissions to the *Saturday Visiter*, introduced the increasingly well-known Poe to Thomas W. White, publisher of the new Richmond-based *Southern Literary Messenger*. In August 1835, Poe became White's editorial assistant, moving back to Richmond where, for the next seventeen months, he played a significant role in the operations of the journal. Not only his stories and poems but also his often slashing reviews appeared in the *Messenger*, gaining him a reputation as the "Tomahawk Man," as White called him. Relations between Poe and White deteriorated when Poe resumed drinking. Returning to Baltimore briefly, Poe secretly married Virginia Clemm, and later publicly wed the thirteen-year-old Virginia in a May 1836 ceremony in Richmond. Thereafter, wherever he went, he lived with Virginia and her mother, whose loyalty to him was probably the only stable element in his tempestuous life.

Hoping to make the *Southern Literary Messenger* a nationally esteemed publication, Poe had to negotiate between the proslavery views of white Virginians and the growing opposition to such views in the free North. As a result, though the journal did occasionally print proslavery pieces (including an anonymous defense of slavery in a review of April 1836 that was long attributed to Poe but was almost certainly not written by him), it usually adopted a middle-of-the-road position linking slavery to states' rights rather than God's will. In Poe's writings overall, slavery and race remain highly problematical. Like many white writers of the time, Poe sometimes resorted to racial stereotypes, and he sometimes conveyed his fears of the possibilities of black violence. For the most part, however, the perverse killers of his tales are white men. Critics continue to debate Poe's views on slavery and race. Although he spent years in the South and even held hopes for inheriting the property of a slaveholder, the fact is that his relative silence on the political debate on slavery makes him notably different from most southern intellectuals of the time—William Gilmore Simms, Nathaniel Beverly Tucker, and many others—who went on record with their proslavery views.

White fired Poe early in 1837, citing Poe's drinking, his demands for a higher salary, and his regular clashes with White about the day-to-day operations of the journal. Poe then moved, with his aunt (now his mother-in-law as well) and his wife, to New York City, where Mrs. Clemm ran a boarding house to support them all. In Richmond he had written a short novel, *The Narrative of Arthur Gordon Pym*, of which White had run two installments in the *Messenger* early in 1837. *Harper's* published it in July 1838, but it earned him little money. In 1838 Poe moved to Philadelphia, where, despite extreme poverty, he continued writing. "Ligeia" appeared in the *Baltimore American Museum* in September 1838, where other stories and poems followed. In May 1839 he got his first steady job in more than two years, as co-editor of *Burton's Gentleman's Magazine*. There, in a job that paid him a small salary, he published book reviews and stories, including "The Fall of the House of Usher" and "William Wilson." Late in 1839, the Philadelphia firm of Lea and Blanchard published *Tales of the Grotesque and Arabesque*, a collection of the twenty-five stories Poe had written to that date. The mostly good reviews did not lead to good sales; the country was in the midst of a depression.

By the late 1830s, Poe was at the height of his powers as a writer of tales, though his personal and professional life continued to be unstable. William Burton fired him for drinking in May 1840 but recommended him to George Graham, who had bought out *Burton's* and created a new magazine called *Graham's*. Throughout 1841, Poe was with *Graham's* as a co-editor, courting subscribers by writing articles on cryptography—the art and science of code breaking. He also published "The Murders in the Rue Morgue," the first of what he termed his "tales of ratiocination" featuring detective August Dupin, a tale that many critics regard as the earliest example of detective fiction. In January 1842, Virginia Poe, not yet twenty, began hemorrhaging from her lungs while singing; she lived as a tubercular invalid only five more years. Poe continued reviewing for *Graham's*, but he resigned from the magazine in May 1842 after a dispute with Graham. His hope of his own journal—to be called *The Stylus*—was never realized.

In April 1844, Poe again moved his family to New York City, working as an editor on the *New York Evening Mirror*. Poe's most successful year was 1845. The February issue of *Graham's* contained an essay by James Russell Lowell declaring Poe a man of "*genius*"; and Poe's most popular work, "The Raven," appeared in the February *American Review* after advance publication in the *New York Evening Mirror*. One new literary acquaintance, the influential editor Evert A. Duyckinck, selected a dozen of Poe's stories for a collection brought out by Wiley & Putnam in June and arranged for the same firm to publish *The Raven and Other Poems* in November. Poe lectured on the poets of America and became a principal reviewer for a new weekly, the *Broadway Journal*, which also reprinted most of Poe's stories and poems. Still hoping to have his own magazine, in which he could be free of editorial interference, he purchased the *Broadway Journal* only to see it fail in January 1846.

While the tempo of Poe's life speeded up, with ever more literary feuds and drinking bouts, he maintained an undiminished commitment to his writing. During 1847, the year that Virginia died from tuberculosis, Poe was seriously ill himself. In 1848 he published *Eureka*, a philosophical prose work that presented God as the force behind all matter, and all matter as seeking a return to oneness. He also published "Ulalume," a poem inspired by his grief at the loss of Virginia. In 1848 he fell in love with the poet Sarah Helen Whitman, who refused his initial proposal, then agreed to a December 1848 marriage, and finally broke off the relationship. In his final year, during a two-month stay in Richmond, Poe joined a temperance society and got engaged to Elmira Royster Shelton, a widow whom he had known in his childhood. On a subsequent trip to Baltimore, Poe was found senseless near a polling place on Election Day (October 3). Taken to a hospital, he died on October 7, 1849, "of congestion of the brain." His poem "Annabel Lee" was published posthumously later that year.

Much of Poe's collected writings consists of his criticism, representing his abiding ambition to become a powerful critic and influence the course of American literary history. Just as he had modeled his poems and first tales on British examples (or British imitations of the German), he took his critical concepts from treatises on aesthetics by late-eighteenth-century Scottish Common Sense philosophers, who emphasized the aesthetic importance of moral sympathy. Later, he modified his approach with borrowings from A.W. Schlegel, Coleridge, and other Romantics, who emphasized the importance of intuitively conceived notions of the beautiful. But despite modulations in his theories, Poe's critical principles were consistent: he thought poetry should appeal only to the sense of beauty; informational poetry, poetry of ideas, or any sort of didactic poetry was, in his view, illegitimate. Holding that true poetic emotion was a vague sensory state inspired by the work of art itself, he set himself against realistic details in poetry, although the prose tale, with truth as one object, could profit from the discreet use of specifics. He believed that poems and tales should be short enough to be read in one sitting; otherwise the unity of effect would be dissipated. In his most famous artistic treatise, "The Philosophy of Composition," Poe makes clear that, unlike Emerson, he remains skeptical of the possibilities of transcendental vision untethered by the material realities of body and aesthetic form. In crucial ways, then, Poe split with Emerson and other transcendentalists in arguing that the vision that comes to the artist and reader is inextricably linked to the formal qualities of the work of art itself.

Poe's reputation today rests not on his criticism, however, but on his poetry—"The Raven," "Ulalume," and "To Helen" made him internationally famous even in his lifetime—and his tales. He has had immense influence on poets and prose writers both in the United States and abroad; among those who have followed his lead are such modernists as T.S. Eliot and William Faulkner. The tales have proven hard to classify—are they burlesque exaggerations of popular forms of fiction, or serious attempts to contribute to or alter those forms, or both of these at the same time? Poe's own comments deliberately obscured his intentions. Responding to a query from his literary admirer John P. Kennedy in 1836, who labeled his work as "seriotragicomic," he said that most of his tales "were *intended* for half banter, half satire—although I might not have fully acknowledged this to be their aim even to myself." At the core of this and other of Poe's comments on his fiction is the pragmatism of a professional writer who recognized the advent of a mass market and wanted to succeed in it. He worked hard at structuring his tales of aristocratic madmen, self-tormented murderers, neurasthenic necrophiliacs, and other deviant types so as to produce, as he wrote in "The Philosophy of Composition," the greatest possible *effect* on his readers. Poe, more than most, understood his audience—its distractedness, its fascination with the new and short-lived, its anomie and confusion—and sought ways to gain its attention for stories that, aside from their shock value, regularly addressed compelling philosophical, cultural, and psychological issues: the place of irrationality, violence, and repression in human consciousness and social institutions; the alienation and dislocations attending democratic mass culture and the modernizing forces of the time; the tug and pull of the material and corporeal; the absolutely terrifying dimensions of one's own mind. Seriously as he took the writing of his tales, Poe always put his highest stock in poetry, which he called a "passion" and not merely a "purpose." As he remarked in "The Philosophy of Composition," poetry, even more than fiction, provides the possibility of taking the reader out of body, in effect out of time, through "that intense and pure elevation of *soul*" which can come with "the contemplation of the beautiful." In a life that was often a tangled mess, the pursuit of the beautiful in works of art motivated Poe's writing to the very end.

The Raven[1]

By —— Quarles

[*The following lines from a correspondent—besides the deep quaint strain of the sentiment, and the curious introduction of some ludicrous touches amidst the serious and impressive, as was doubtless intended by the author—appear to us one of the most felicitous specimens of unique rhyming which has for some time met our eye. The resources of English rhythm for varieties of melody, measure, and sound, producing corresponding diversities of effect, have been thoroughly studied, much more perceived, by very few poets in the language. While the classic tongues, especially the Greek, possess, by power of accent, several advantages for versification over our own, chiefly through greater abundance of spondaic feet,[2] we have other and very great advantages of sound by the modern usage of rhyme. Alliteration is nearly the only effect of that kind which the ancients had in common with us. It will be seen that much of the melody of "The Raven" arises from alliteration, and the studious use of similar sounds in unusual places. In regard to its measure, it may be noted that if all the verses were like the second, they might properly be placed merely in short lines, producing a not uncommon form; but the presence in all the others of one line— mostly the second in the verse—which flows continuously, with only an aspirate pause in the middle, like that before the short line in the Sapphic Adonic,[3] while the fifth has at the middle pause no similarity of sound with any part besides, gives the versification an entirely different effect. We could wish the capacities of our noble language, in prosody, were better understood.*—Ed. Am. Rev.]

Once upon a midnight dreary, while I pondered, weak and weary,
Over many a quaint and curious volume of forgotten lore,
While I nodded, nearly napping, suddenly there came a tapping,
As of some one gently rapping, rapping at my chamber door.
"'Tis some visiter," I muttered, "tapping at my chamber door—   5
                 Only this, and nothing more."

Ah, distinctly I remember it was in the bleak December,
And each separate dying ember wrought its ghost upon the floor.
Eagerly I wished the morrow;—vainly I had tried to borrow
From my books surcease of sorrow—sorrow for the lost Lenore—   10
For the rare and radiant maiden whom the angels name Lenore—
                 Nameless here for evermore.

And the silken sad uncertain rustling of each purple curtain
Thrilled me—filled me with fantastic terrors never felt before;
So that now, to still the beating of my heart, I stood repeating   15
"'Tis some visiter entreating entrance at my chamber door—
Some late visiter entreating entrance at my chamber door;—
                 This it is, and nothing more."

---

1. This printing of Poe's most famous poem is taken from the *American Review: A Whig Journal of Politics, Literature, Art and Science* 1 (February 1845), where it was first set in type from Poe's manuscript; the New York *Evening Mirror* printed the poem on January 29, 1845, probably from the proof sheets of the *American Review*. The prefatory paragraph, signed as if it were by the editor of the *American Review*, is retained here because Poe most likely wrote some or all of it himself. Many minor variations appear in later texts.
2. A spondee is a metrical foot consisting of two stressed syllables.
3. A Greek lyric form. An adonic is a dactyl (a foot with one long syllable and two short ones) followed by a spondee.

Presently my soul grew stronger; hesitating then no longer,
"Sir," said I, "or Madam, truly your forgiveness I implore;   20
But the fact is I was napping, and so gently you came rapping,
And so faintly you came tapping, tapping at my chamber door,
That I scarce was sure I heard you"—here I opened wide the door;—
                              Darkness there, and nothing more.

Deep into that darkness peering, long I stood there wondering, fearing,   25
Doubting, dreaming dreams no mortal ever dared to dream before;
But the silence was unbroken, and the darkness gave no token,
And the only word there spoken was the whispered word, "Lenore!"
This *I* whispered, and an echo murmured back the word, "Lenore!"
                              Merely this, and nothing more.   30

Then into the chamber turning, all my soul within me burning,
Soon I heard again a tapping somewhat louder than before.
"Surely," said I, "surely that is something at my window lattice;
Let me see, then, what thereat is, and this mystery explore—
Let my heart be still a moment and this mystery explore;—   35
                              'Tis the wind, and nothing more!"

Open here I flung the shutter, when, with many a flirt and flutter,
In there stepped a stately raven of the saintly days of yore;
Not the least obeisance made he; not an instant stopped or stayed he;
But, with mien of lord or lady, perched above my chamber door—   40
Perched upon a bust of Pallas[4] just above my chamber door—
                              Perched, and sat, and nothing more.

Then this ebony bird beguiling my sad fancy into smiling,
By the grave and stern decorum of the countenance it wore,
"Though thy crest be shorn and shaven, thou," I said, "art sure no craven, 45
Ghastly grim and ancient raven wandering from the Nightly shore—
Tell me what thy lordly name is on the Night's Plutonian[5] shore!"
                              Quoth the raven, "Nevermore."

Much I marvelled this ungainly fowl to hear discourse so plainly,
Though its answer little meaning—little relevancy bore;   50
For we cannot help agreeing that no sublunary[6] being
Ever yet was blessed with seeing bird above his chamber door—
Bird or beast upon the sculptured bust above his chamber door,
                              With such name as "Nevermore."

But the raven, sitting lonely on the placid bust, spoke only   55
That one word, as if his soul in that one word he did outpour.
Nothing farther then he uttered—not a feather then he fluttered—
Till I scarcely more than muttered, "Other friends have flown before—
On the morrow *he* will leave me, as my hopes have flown before."
                              Quoth the raven, "Nevermore." 60

4. Athena, the Greek goddess of wisdom and the arts.
5. Black, as in the underworld ruled by Pluto in Greek mythology.
6. Earthly, beneath the moon.

Wondering at the stillness broken by reply so aptly spoken,
"Doubtless," said I, "what it utters is its only stock and store,
Caught from some unhappy master whom unmerciful Disaster
Followed fast and followed faster—so, when Hope he would adjure,
Stern Despair returned, instead of the sweet Hope he dared adjure—   65
                           That sad answer, "Nevermore!"[7]

But the raven still beguiling all my sad soul into smiling,
Straight I wheeled a cushioned seat in front of bird, and bust, and door;
Then upon the velvet sinking, I betook myself to linking
Fancy unto fancy, thinking what this ominous bird of yore—   70
What this grim, ungainly, ghastly, gaunt, and ominous bird of yore
                           Meant in croaking "Nevermore."

This I sat engaged in guessing, but no syllable expressing
To the fowl whose fiery eyes now burned into my bosom's core;
This and more I sat divining, with my head at ease reclining   75
On the cushion's velvet lining that the lamplight gloated o'er,
But whose velvet violet lining with the lamplight gloating o'er,
                         She shall press, ah, nevermore!

Then, methought, the air grew denser, perfumed from an unseen censer
Swung by angels whose faint foot-falls tinkled on the tufted floor.   80
"Wretch," I cried, "thy God hath lent thee—by these angels he hath sent thee
Respite—respite and Nepenthe[8] from thy memories of Lenore!
Let me quaff this kind Nepenthe and forget this lost Lenore!"
                         Quoth the raven, "Nevermore."

"Prophet!" said I, "thing of evil!—prophet still, if bird or devil!—   85
Whether Tempter sent, or whether tempest tossed thee here ashore,
Desolate, yet all undaunted, on this desert land enchanted—
On this home by Horror haunted—tell me truly, I implore—
Is there—*is* there balm in Gilead?[9]—tell me—tell me, I implore!"
                         Quoth the raven, "Nevermore."   90

"Prophet!" said I, "thing of evil!—prophet still, if bird or devil!
By that Heaven that bends above us—by that God we both adore—
Tell this soul with sorrow laden if, within the distant Aidenn,[1]
It shall clasp a sainted maiden whom the angels name Lenore—
Clasp a rare and radiant maiden whom the angels name Lenore."   95
                         Quoth the raven, "Nevermore."

"Be that word our sign of parting, bird or fiend!" I shrieked, upstarting—
"Get thee back into the tempest and the Night's Plutonian shore!
Leave no black plume as a token of that lie thy soul hath spoken!

7. This stanza concluded in the 1845 volume with these lines: "Followed faster till his songs one burden bore— / Till the dirges of his Hope that melancholy burden bore / Of 'Never—nevermore.'"
8. Drug that induces oblivion.
9. An echo of the ironic words in Jeremiah 8.22: "Is there no balm in Gilead; is there no physician there?" Gilead is a mountainous area east of the Jordan River between the Sea of Galilee and the Dead Sea; evergreens growing there were a source of medicinal resins.
1. One of Poe's vaguely evocative place names, designed to suggest Eden.

Leave my loneliness unbroken—quit the bust above my door!   100
Take thy beak from out my heart, and take thy form from off my door!"
                              Quoth the raven, "Nevermore."

And the raven, never flitting, still is sitting, still is sitting
On the pallid bust of Pallas just above my chamber door;
And his eyes have all the seeming of a demon that is dreaming,   105
And the lamp-light o'er him streaming throws his shadow on the floor;
And my soul from out that shadow that lies floating on the floor
                              Shall be lifted—nevermore!

                                                          1845

Annabel Lee[1]

It was many and many a year ago,
      In a kingdom by the sea
That a maiden there lived whom you may know
      By the name of ANNABEL LEE;
And this maiden she lived with no other thought   5
      Than to love and be loved by me.

I was a child and *she* was a child,
      In this kingdom by the sea;
But we loved with a love that was more than love—
      I and my ANNABEL LEE—   10
With a love that the wingèd seraphs of heaven
      Coveted her and me.

And this was the reason that, long ago,
      In this kingdom by the sea,
A wind blew out of a cloud, chilling   15
      My beautiful ANNABEL LEE;
So that her highborn kinsmen came
      And bore her away from me,
To shut her up in a sepulchre
      In this kingdom by the sea.   20

The angels, not half so happy in heaven,
      Went envying her and me—
Yes!—that was the reason (as all men know,
      In this kingdom by the sea)
That the wind came out of the cloud by night,   25
      Chilling and killing my ANNABEL LEE.

But our love it was stronger by far than the love
      Of those who were older than we—
      Of many far wiser than we—

---

1. The text is that of the first printing, in an article by Rufus Griswold in the *New York Tribune* (October 9, 1849), signed "Ludwig," which was printed two days after Poe's death.

And neither the angels in heaven above,   30
    Nor the demons down under the sea,
Can ever dissever my soul from the soul
    Of the beautiful ANNABEL LEE:

For the moon never beams, without bringing me dreams
    Of the beautiful ANNABEL LEE;   35
And the stars never rise, but I feel the bright eyes
    Of the beautiful ANNABEL LEE:
And so, all the night tide, I lie down by the side
Of my darling—my darling—my life and my bride,
    In her sepulchre there by the sea—   40
    In her tomb by the sounding sea.

1849

Ligeia[1]

*And the will therein lieth, which dieth not. Who knoweth the
mysteries of the will, with its vigour? For God is but a great will
pervading all things by nature of its intentness. Man doth not yield
himself to the angels, nor unto death utterly, save only through the
weakness of his feeble will.*

—Joseph Glanvill[2]

I cannot, for my soul, remember how, when, or even precisely where I first
became acquainted with the lady Ligeia. Long years have since elapsed, and
my memory is feeble through much suffering: or, perhaps, I cannot *now*
bring these points to mind, because, in truth, the character of my beloved,
her rare learning, her singular yet placid cast of beauty, and the thrilling and
enthralling eloquence of her low, musical language, made their way into my
heart by paces, so steadily and stealthily progressive, that they have been
unnoticed and unknown. Yet I know that I met her most frequently in some
large, old, decaying city near the Rhine. Of her family—I have surely heard
her speak—that they are of a remotely ancient date cannot be doubted. Ligeia!
Buried in studies of a nature, more than all else, adapted to deaden impressions of the outward world, it is by that sweet word alone—by Ligeia, that I
bring before mine eyes in fancy the image of her who is no more. And now,
while I write, a recollection flashes upon me that I have *never known* the
paternal name of her who was my friend and my betrothed, and who became
the partner of my studies, and eventually the wife of my bosom. Was it a
playful charge on the part of my Ligeia? or was it a test of my strength of
affection that I should institute no inquiries upon this point? or was it rather
a caprice of my own—a wildly romantic offering on the shrine of the most
passionate devotion? I but indistinctly recall the fact itself—what wonder
that I have utterly forgotten the circumstances which originated or attended

1. "Ligeia" was first published in the *American
Museum* 1 (September 1838), the source of the
present text. Poe later revised the tale slightly and
added to it the poem "The Conqueror Worm."

2. Like many of Poe's epigraphs (often added
after first publication), this one is fabricated.
Joseph Glanvill (1636–1680) was one of the Cambridge Platonists, 17th-century English religious

it? And indeed, if ever that spirit which is entitled *Romance*—if ever she, the wan, and the misty-winged *Ashtophet*[3] of idolatrous Egypt, presided, as they tell, over marriages ill-omened, then most surely she presided over mine.

There is one dear topic, however, on which my memory faileth me not. It is the person of Ligeia. In stature she was tall, somewhat slender, and in her latter days even emaciated. I would in vain attempt to pourtray the majesty, the quiet ease of her demeanour, or the incomprehensible lightness and elasticity of her footfall. She came and departed like a shadow. I was never made aware of her entrance into my closed study save by the dear music of her low sweet voice, as she placed her delicate hand upon my shoulder. In beauty of face no maiden ever equalled her. It was the radiance of an opium dream—an airy and spirit-lifting vision more wildly divine than the phantasies which hovered about the slumbering souls of the daughters of Delos.[4] Yet her features were not of that regular mould which we have been falsely taught to worship in the classical labors of the Heathen. "There is no exquisite[5] beauty," saith Verülam, Lord Bacon, speaking truly of all the forms and *genera* of beauty, "without some *strangeness* in the proportions." Yet, although I saw that the features of Ligeia were not of classic regularity, although I perceived that her loveliness was indeed "exquisite," and felt that there was much of "strangeness" pervading it, yet I have tried in vain to detect the irregularity, and to trace home my own perception of "the strange." I examined the contour of the lofty and pale forehead—it was faultless—how cold indeed that word when applied to a majesty so divine! The skin rivaling the purest ivory, the commanding breadth and repose, the gentle prominence of the regions above the temples, and then the raven-black, the glossy, the luxuriant and naturally-curling tresses, setting forth the full force of the Homeric epithet, "hyacinthine;"[6] I looked at the delicate outlines of the nose—and nowhere but in the graceful medallions of the Hebrews had I beheld a similar perfection. There was the same luxurious smoothness of surface, the same scarcely perceptible tendency to the aquiline, the same harmoniously curved nostril speaking the free spirit. I regarded the sweet mouth. Here was indeed the triumph of all things heavenly—the magnificent turn of the short upper lip—the soft, voluptuous repose of the under—the dimples which sported, and the colour which spoke—the teeth glancing back, with a brilliancy almost startling, every ray of the holy light which fell upon them in her serene, and placid, yet most exultingly radiant of all smiles. I scrutinized the formation of the chin—and here, too, I found the gentleness of breadth, the softness and the majesty, the fulness and the spirituality, of the Greek, the contour which the God Apollo revealed but in a dream to Cleomenes, the son of the Athenian.[7] And then I peered into the large eyes of Ligeia.

For eyes we have no models in the remotely antique. It might have been, too, that in these eyes of my beloved lay the secret to which Lord Verülam alludes. They were, I must believe, far larger than the ordinary eyes of our race. They were even far fuller than the fullest of the Gazelle eyes of the

philosophers who tried to reconcile Christianity and Renaissance science.

3. Variant of Ashtoreth, Phoenician goddess of fertility.

4. Probably the maidens attending Artemis, goddess of wild nature and the hunt; she was born on Delos, a Greek island in the Aegean Sea.

5. In his essay "Of Beauty" Francis Bacon, Baron Verulam (1561–1626), wrote "excellent," not "exquisite."

6. In the *Odyssey*, Homer compares Odysseus's curly hair to the flowering hyacinth plant.

7. Classical Greek sculptor whose name is affixed to the Venus de' Medici. The god Apollo was the patron of artists.

tribe of the valley of Nourjahad.[8] Yet it was only at intervals—in moments of intense excitement—that this peculiarity became more than slightly noticeable in Ligeia. And at such moments was her beauty—in my heated fancy thus it appeared perhaps—the beauty of beings either above or apart from the earth—the beauty of the fabulous Houri[9] of the Turk. The colour of the orbs was the most brilliant of black, and far over them hung jetty lashes of great length. The brows, slightly irregular in outline, had the same hue. The "strangeness," however, which I have found in the eyes of my Ligeia was of a nature distinct from the formation, or the colour, or the brilliancy of the feature, and must, after all, be referred to the *expression*. Ah, word of no meaning! behind whose vast latitude of mere sound we intrench our ignorance of so much of the spiritual. The expression of the eyes of Ligeia! How, for long hours have I pondered upon it! How have I, through the whole of a mid-summer night, struggled to fathom it! What was it—that something more profound than the well of Democritus[1]—which lay far within the pupils of my beloved? What *was* it? I was possessed with a passion to discover. Those eyes! those large, those shining, those divine orbs! they became to me twin stars of Leda,[2] and I to them devoutest of astrologers. Not for a moment was the unfathomable meaning of their glance, by day or by night, absent from my soul.

There is no point, among the many incomprehensible anomalies of the science of mind, more thrillingly exciting than the fact—never, I believe noticed in the schools—that in our endeavours to recall to memory something long forgotten we often find ourselves *upon the very verge* of remembrance without being able, in the end, to remember. And thus, how frequently, in my intense scrutiny of Ligeia's eyes, have I felt approaching the full knowledge of the secret of their expression—felt it approaching—yet not quite be mine—and so at length utterly depart. And (strange, oh strangest mystery of all!) I found, in the commonest objects of the universe, a circle of analogies to that expression. I mean to say that, subsequently to the period when Ligeia's beauty passed into my spirit, there dwelling as in a shrine, I derived from many existences in the material world, a sentiment, such as I felt always aroused within me by her large and luminous orbs. Yet not the more could I define that sentiment, or analyze, or even steadily view it. I recognized it, let me repeat, sometimes in the commonest objects of the universe. It has flashed upon me in the survey of a rapidly-growing vine—in the contemplation of a moth, a butterfly, a chrysalis, a stream of running water. I have felt it in the ocean, in the falling of a meteor. I have felt it in the glances of unusually aged people. And there are one or two stars in heaven—(one especially, a star of the sixth magnitude, double and changeable, to be found near the large star in Lyra)[3] in a telescopic scrutiny of which I have been made aware of the feeling. I have been filled with it by certain sounds from stringed instruments, and not unfrequently by passages from books. Among innumerable other instances, I well remember something in a volume of

8. From the Asian romance *The History of Nourjahad* (1767), by the English writer Frances Sheridan (1724–1766).
9. Beautiful maiden waiting in paradise for the devout Muslim.
1. Greek philosopher (5th century B.C.E.); one of his proverbs is "Truth lies at the bottom of a well."

2. Queen of Sparta whom Zeus, in the form of a swan, raped, thereby begetting Helen of Troy and (according to some versions) the twin sons Castor and Pollux, whom Zeus transformed into the constellation Gemini.
3. The lesser star is epsilon Lyrae, the large one Vega or alpha Lyrae.

Joseph Glanvill, which, perhaps merely from its quaintness—who shall say?
never failed to inspire me with the sentiment.—"And the will therein lieth,
which dieth not. Who knoweth the mysteries of the will, with its vigor? For
God is but a great will pervading all things by nature of its intentness. Man
doth not yield him to the angels, nor unto death utterly, but only through
the weakness of his feeble will."

Length of years, and subsequent reflection, have enabled me to trace,
indeed, some remote connexion between this passage in the old English moralist and a portion of the character of Ligeia. An *intensity* in thought, action,
or speech was possibly, in her, a result, or at least an index, of that gigantic
volition which, during our long intercourse, failed to give other and more
immediate evidence of its existence. Of all women whom I have ever known,
she, the outwardly calm, the ever placid Ligeia, was the most violently a prey
to the tumultuous vultures of stern passion. And of such passion I could form
no estimate, save by the miraculous expansion of those eyes which at once so
delighted and appalled me, by the almost magical melody, modulation, distinctness and placidity of her very low voice, and by the fierce energy, (rendered doubly effective by contrast with her manner of utterance) of the words
which she uttered.

I have spoken of the learning of Ligeia: it was immense—such as I have
never known in woman. In all the classical tongues was she deeply proficient, and as far as my own acquaintance extended in regard to the modern
dialects of Europe, I have never known her at fault. Indeed upon any theme
of the most admired, because simply the most abstruse, of the boasted erudition of the academy, have I *ever* found Ligeia at fault? How singularly, how
thrillingly, this one point in the nature of my wife has forced itself, at this late
period, only, upon my attention! I said her knowledge was such as I had never
known in woman. Where breathes the man who, like her, has traversed, and
successfully, *all* the wide areas of moral, natural, and mathematical science?
I saw not then what I now clearly perceive, that the acquisitions of Ligeia
were gigantic, were astounding—yet I was sufficiently aware of her infinite
supremacy to resign myself, with a childlike confidence, to her guidance
through the chaotic world of metaphysical investigation at which I was most
busily occupied during the earlier years of our marriage. With how vast a
triumph—with how vivid a delight—with how much of all that is ethereal in
hope—did I *feel*, as she bent over me, in studies but little sought for—but
less known that delicious vista by slow but very perceptible degrees expanding before me, down whose long, gorgeous, and all untrodden path I might
at length pass onward to the goal of a wisdom too divinely precious not to
be forbidden!

How poignant, then, must have been the grief with which, after some
years, I beheld my well-grounded expectations take wings to themselves and
flee away! Without Ligeia I was but as a child groping benighted. Her presence, her readings alone, rendered vividly luminous the many mysteries of
the transcendentalism in which we were immersed. Letters, lambent and
golden, grew duller than Saturnian[4] lead wanting the radiant lustre of her
eyes. And now those eyes shone less and less frequently upon the pages over
which I poured. Ligeia grew ill. The wild eye blazed with a too—too glorious effulgence; the pale fingers became of the transparent waxen hue of the

---

4. Sluggish; in alchemy *saturnus* is the name for lead.

grave—and the blue veins upon the lofty forehead swelled and sunk impetuously with the tides of the most gentle emotion. I saw that she must die—and I struggled desperately in spirit with the grim Azrael.[5] And the struggles of the passionate Ligeia were, to my astonishment, even more energetic than my own. There had been much in her stern nature to impress me with the belief that, to her, death would have come without its terrors—but not so. Words are impotent to convey any just idea of the fierceness of resistance with which Ligeia wrestled with the dark shadow. I groaned in anguish at the pitiable spectacle. I would have soothed—I would have reasoned; but in the intensity of her wild desire for life—for life—*but* for life, solace and reason were alike the uttermost of folly. Yet not for an instant, amid the most convulsive writhings of her fierce spirit, was shaken the external placidity of her demeanor. Her voice grew more gentle—grew more low—yet I would not wish to dwell upon the wild meaning of the quietly-uttered words. My brain reeled as I hearkened, entranced, to a melody more than mortal—to assumptions and aspirations which mortality had never before known.

That Ligeia loved me, I should not have doubted; and I might have been easily aware that, in a bosom such as hers, love would have reigned no ordinary passion. But in death only, was I fully impressed with the intensity of her affection. For long hours, detaining my hand, would she pour out before me the overflowings of a heart whose more than passionate devotion amounted to idolatry. How had I deserved to be so blessed by such confessions.—How had I deserved to be so cursed with the removal of my beloved in the hour of her making them? But upon this subject I cannot bear to dilate. Let me say only, that in Ligeia's more than womanly abandonment to a love, alas, all unmerited, all unworthily bestowed; I at length recognised the principle of her longing, with so wildly earnest a desire for the life which was now fleeing so rapidly away. It is this wild longing—it is this eager intensity of desire for life—*but* for life—that I have no power to pourtray—no utterance capable to express. Methinks I again behold the terrific struggles of her lofty, her nearly idealized nature, with the might and the terror, and the majesty of the great Shadow. But she perished. The giant *will* succumbed to a power more stern. And I thought, as I gazed upon the corpse, of the wild passage in Joseph Glanvill. "The will therein lieth, which dieth not. Who knoweth the mysteries of the will, with its vigor? For God is but a great will pervading all things by nature of its intentness. Man doth not yield him to the angels, *nor unto death utterly*, save only through the weakness of his feeble will."

She died—and I, crushed into the very dust with sorrow, could no longer endure the lonely desolation of my dwelling in the dim and decaying city by the Rhine. I had no lack of what the world terms wealth—Ligeia had brought me far more, very far more, than falls ordinarily to the lot of mortals. After a few months, therefore, of weary and aimless wandering, I purchased, and put in some repair, an abbey, which I shall not name, in one of the wildest and least frequented portions of fair England. The gloomy and dreary grandeur of the building, the almost savage aspect of the domain, the many melancholy and time-honored memories connected with both, had much in unison with the feelings of utter abandonment which had driven me into that

5. The Angel of Death (in Judaism and Islam).

remote and unsocial region of the country. Yet, although the external abbey, with its verdant decay hanging about it suffered but little alteration, I gave way with a child-like perversity, and perchance with a faint hope of alleviating my sorrows, to a display of more than regal magnificence within. For such follies even in childhood I had imbibed a taste, and now they came back to me as if in the dotage of grief. Alas, I now feel how much even of incipient madness might have been discovered in the gorgeous and fantastic draperies, in the solemn carvings of Egypt, in the wild cornices and furniture of Arabesque,[6] in the bedlam patterns of the carpets of tufted gold! I had become a bounden slave in the trammels of opium, and my labors and my orders had taken a colouring from my dreams. But these absurdities I must not pause to detail. Let me speak only of that one chamber, ever accursed, whither, in a moment of mental alienation, I led from the altar as my bride—as the successor of the unforgotten Ligeia—the fair-haired and blue-eyed lady Rowena Trevanion, of Tremaine.

There is not any individual portion of the architecture and decoration of that bridal chamber which is not now visibly before me. Where were the souls of the haughty family of the bride, when, through thirst of gold, they permitted to pass the threshold of an apartment so bedecked, a maiden and a daughter so beloved? I have said that I minutely remember the details of the chamber—yet I am sadly forgetful on topics of deep moment—and here there was no system, no keeping, in the fantastic display, to take hold upon the memory. The room lay in a high turret of the castellated abbey, was pentagonal in shape, and of capacious size. Occupying the whole southern face of the pentagon was the sole window—an immense sheet of unbroken glass from Venice—a single pane, and tinted of a leaden hue, so that the rays of either the sun or moon, passing through it, fell with a ghastly lustre upon the objects within. Over the upper portion of this huge window extended the open trellice-work of an aged vine which clambered up the massy walls of the turret. The ceiling, of gloomy-looking oak, was excessively lofty, vaulted, and elaborately fretted with the wildest and most grotesque specimens of a semi-Gothic, semi-druidical[7] device. From out the most central recess of this melancholy vaulting, depended, by a single chain of gold, with long links, a huge censer of the same metal, Arabesque in pattern, and with many perforations so contrived that there writhed in and out of them, as if endued with a serpent vitality, a continual succession of parti-coloured fires. Some few ottomans and golden candelabras of Eastern figure were in various stations about—and there was the couch, too, the bridal couch, of an Indian model, and low, and sculptured of solid ebony, with a canopy above. In each of the angles of the chamber, stood on end a gigantic sarcophagus of black granite, from the tombs of the kings over against Luxor,[8] with their aged lids full of immemorial sculpture. But in the draping of the apartment lay, alas! the chief phantasy of all. The lofty walls—gigantic in height—even unproportionally so, were hung from summit to foot, in vast folds with a heavy and massy looking tapestry—tapestry of a material which was found alike as a carpet on the floor, as a covering for the ottomans, and the ebony bed, as a canopy for the bed, and as the gorgeous volutes[9] of the curtains which

6. Ornamental style employing intricate patterns of lines and figures.
7. Druids are the legendary priests, or wizards, of ancient Britain and Ireland. "Fretted": ornamented with intersecting patterns.
8. In Egypt, near Thebes; site of famous ruins.
9. Scroll-like ornaments.

partially shaded the window. This material was the richest cloth of gold. It was spotted all over, at irregular intervals, with Arabesque figures, of about a foot in diameter, and wrought upon the cloth in patterns of the most jetty black. But these figures partook of the true character of the Arabesque only when regarded from a single point of view. By a contrivance now common, and indeed traceable to a very remote period of antiquity, they were made changeable in aspect. To one entering the room they bore the appearance of ideal monstrosities; but, upon a farther advance, this appearance suddenly departed; and, step by step, as the visitor moved his station in the chamber, he saw himself surrounded by an endless succession of the ghastly forms which belong to the superstition of the Northman, or arise in the guilty slumbers of the monk. The phantasmagoric effect was vastly heightened by the artificial introduction of a strong continual current of wind behind the draperies— giving a hideous and uneasy vitality to the whole.

In halls such as these—in a bridal chamber such as this, I passed, with the lady of Tremaine, the unhallowed hours of the first month of our marriage— passed them with but little disquietude. That my wife dreaded the fierce moodiness of my temper—that she shunned me, and loved me but little, I could not help perceiving—but it gave me rather pleasure than otherwise. I loathed her with a hatred belonging more to demon than to man. My memory flew back, (oh, with what intensity of regret!) to Ligeia, the beloved, the beau-tiful, the entombed. I revelled in recollections of her purity, of her wisdom, of her lofty, her ethereal nature, of her passionate, her idolatrous love. Now, then, did my spirit fully and freely burn with more than all the fires of her own. In the excitement of my opium dreams (for I was habitually fettered in the iron shackles of the drug)[1] I would call aloud upon her name, during the silence of the night, or among the sheltered recesses of the glens by day, as if, by the wild eagerness, the solemn passion, the consuming intensity of my longing for the departed Ligeia, I could restore the departed Ligeia to the pathways she had abandoned upon earth.

About the commencement of the second month of the marriage, the lady Rowena was attacked with sudden illness from which her recovery was slow. The fever which consumed her, rendered her nights uneasy, and, in her per-turbed state of half-slumber, she spoke of sounds, and of motions, in and about the chamber of the turret which had no origin save in the distemper of her fancy, or, perhaps, in the phantasmagoric influences of the chamber itself. She became at length convalescent—finally well. Yet but a brief period elapsed, ere a second more violent disorder again threw her upon a bed of suffering—and from this attack her frame, at all times feeble, never alto-gether recovered. Her illnesses were, after this period, of alarming charac-ter, and of more alarming recurrence, defying alike the knowledge and the great exertions of her medical men. With the increase of the chronic dis-ease which had thus, apparently, taken too sure hold upon her constitution to be eradicated by human means, I could not fail to observe a similar increase in the nervous irritability of her temperament, and in her excitability by trivial causes of fear. Indeed reason seemed fast tottering from her throne. She spoke again, and now more frequently and pertinaciously, of the sounds, of the slight sounds, and of the unusual motions among the tapestries, to

1. The *American Museum* has no punctuation after "dreams" or "drug" in this sentence; parentheses are added to the present text.

which she had formerly alluded. It was one night near the closing in of September, when she pressed this distressing subject with more than usual emphasis upon my attention. She had just awakened from a perturbed slumber, and I had been watching, with feelings half of anxiety, half of a vague terror, the workings of her emaciated countenance. I sat by the side of her ebony bed, upon one of the ottomans of India. She partly arose, and spoke, in an earnest low whisper, of sounds which she *then* heard, but which I could not hear, of motions which she *then* saw, but which I could not perceive. The wind was rushing hurriedly behind the tapestries, and I wished to show her (what, let me confess it, I could not *all* believe) that those faint, almost articulate, breathings, and the very gentle variations of the figures upon the wall, were but the natural effects of that customary rushing of the wind. But a deadly pallor overspreading her face, had proved to me that my exertions to re-assure her would be fruitless. She appeared to be fainting, and no attendants were within call. I remembered where was deposited a decanter of some light wine which had been ordered by her physicians, and hastened across the chamber to procure it. But, as I stepped beneath the light of the censer, two circumstances of a startling nature attracted my attention. I had felt that some palpable object had passed lightly by my person; and I saw that there lay a faint, indefinite shadow upon the golden carpet in the very middle of the rich lustre, thrown from the censer. But I was wild with the excitement of an immoderate dose of opium, and heeded these things but little, nor spoke of them to Rowena. Finding the wine, I re-crossed the chamber, and poured out a goblet-ful, which I held to the lips of the fainting lady. But she had now partially recovered, and took, herself, the vessel, while I sank upon the ottoman near me, with my eyes rivetted upon her person. It was then that I became distinctly aware of a gentle foot-fall upon the carpet, and near the couch; and, in a second thereafter, as Rowena was in the act of raising the wine to her lips, I saw, or may have dreamed that I saw, fall within the goblet, as if from some invisible spring in the atmosphere of the room, three or four large drops of a brilliant and ruby colored fluid. If this I saw—not so Rowena. She swallowed the wine unhesitatingly, and I forbore to speak to her of a circumstance which must, after all, I considered, have been but the suggestion of a vivid imagination, rendered morbidly active by the terror of the lady, by the opium, and by the hour.

Yet I cannot conceal it from myself, after this period, a rapid change for the worse took place in the disorder of my wife, so that, on the third subsequent night, the hands of her menials prepared her for the tomb, and on the fourth, I sat alone, with her shrouded body, in that fantastical chamber which had received her as my bride. Wild visions, opium engendered, flitted, shadow-like, before me. I gazed with unquiet eye upon the sarcophagi in the angles of the room, upon the varying figures of the drapery, and upon the writhing of the parti-colored fires in the censer overhead. My eyes then fell, as I called to mind the circumstances of a former night, to the spot beneath the glare of the censer where I had beheld the faint traces of the shadow. It was there, however, no longer, and, breathing with greater freedom, I turned my glances to the pallid and rigid figure upon the bed. Then rushed upon me a thousand memories of Ligeia—and then came back upon my heart, with the turbulent violence of a flood, the whole of that unutterable woe with which I had regarded *her* thus enshrouded. The night waned; and still, with a bosom full of bitter thoughts of the one only and supremely beloved, I remained with mine eyes rivetted upon the body of Rowena.

It might have been midnight, or perhaps earlier, or later, for I had taken no note of time, when a sob, low, gentle, but very distinct, startled me from my revery. I *felt* that it came from the bed of ebony—the bed of death. I listened in an agony of superstitious terror—but there was no repetition of the sound; I strained my vision to detect any motion in the corpse, but there was not the slightest perceptible. Yet I could not have been deceived. I had heard the noise, however faint, and my whole soul was awakened within me, as I resolutely and perseveringly kept my attention rivetted upon the body. Many minutes elapsed before any circumstance occurred tending to throw light upon the mystery. At length it became evident that a slight, a very faint, and barely noticeable tinge of colour had flushed up within the cheeks, and along the sunken small veins of the eyelids. Through a species of unutterable horror and awe, for which the language of mortality has no sufficiently energetic expression, I felt my brain reel, my heart cease to beat, my limbs grow rigid where I sat. Yet a sense of duty finally operated to restore my self-possession. I could no longer doubt that we had been precipitate in our preparations for interment—that Rowena still lived. It was necessary that some immediate exertion be made; yet the turret was altogether apart from the portion of the Abbey tenanted by the servants—there were none within call, and I had no means of summoning them to my aid without leaving the room for many minutes—and this I could not venture to do. I therefore struggled alone in my endeavors to call back the spirit still hovering. In a short period it became evident however, that a relapse had taken place; the color utterly disappeared from both eyelid and cheek, leaving a wanness even more than that of marble; the lips became doubly shrivelled and pinched up in the ghastly expression of death; a coldness surpassing that of ice, overspread rapidly the surface of the body, and all the usual rigorous stiffness immediately supervened. I fell back with a shudder upon the ottoman from which I had been so startlingly aroused, and again gave myself up to passionate waking visions of Ligeia.

An hour thus elapsed when, (could it be possible?) I was a second time aware of some vague sound issuing from the region of the bed. I listened—in extremity of horror. The sound came again—it was a sigh. Rushing to the corpse, I saw—distinctly saw—a tremor upon the lips. In a minute after they slightly relaxed, disclosing a bright line of the pearly teeth. Amazement now struggled in my bosom with the profound awe which had hitherto reigned therein alone. I felt that my vision grew dim, that my brain wandered, and it was only by a convulsive effort that I at length succeeded in nerving myself to the task which duty thus, once more, had pointed out. There was now a partial glow upon the forehead, upon the cheek and throat—a perceptible warmth pervaded the whole frame—there was even a slight pulsation at the heart. The lady lived; and with redoubled ardour I betook myself to the task of restoration. I chafed, and bathed the temples, and the hands, and used every exertion which experience, and no little medical reading, could suggest. But in vain. Suddenly, the colour fled, the pulsation ceased, the lips resumed the expression of the dead, and, in an instant afterwards, the whole body took upon itself the icy chillness, the livid hue, the intense rigidity, the sunken outline, and each and all of the loathsome peculiarities of that which has been, for many days, a tenant of the tomb.

And again I sunk into visions of Ligeia—and again (what marvel that I shudder while I write?) *again* there reached my ears a low sob from the region of the ebony bed. But why shall I minutely detail the unspeakable horrors of that night? Why shall I pause to relate how, time after time, until near the period of the grey dawn, this hideous drama of revivification was repeated, and how each terrific relapse was only into a sterner and apparently more irredeemable death? Let me hurry to a conclusion.

The greater part of the fearful night had worn away, and the corpse of Rowena once again stirred—and now more vigorously than hitherto, although arousing from a dissolution more appalling in its utter hopelessness than any. I had long ceased to struggle or to move, and remained sitting rigidly upon the ottoman, a helpless prey to a whirl of violent emotions, of which extreme awe was perhaps the least terrible, the least consuming. The corpse, I repeat, stirred, and now more vigorously than before. The hues of life flushed up with unwonted energy into the countenance—the limbs relaxed—and, save that the eyelids were yet pressed heavily together, and that the bandages and draperies of the grave still imparted their charnel character to the figure, I might have dreamed that Rowena had indeed shaken off, utterly, the fetters of Death. But if this idea was not, even then, altogether adopted, I could, at least, doubt no longer, when, arising from the bed, tottering, with feeble steps, with closed eyes, and with the air of one bewildered in a dream, the lady of Tremaine stood bodily and palpably before me.

I trembled not—I stirred not—for a crowd of unutterable fancies connected with the air, the demeanour of the figure, rushing hurriedly through my brain, sent the purple blood ebbing in torrents from the temples to the heart. I stirred not—but gazed upon her who was before me. There was a mad disorder in my thoughts—a tumult unappeasable. Could it, indeed, be the *living* Rowena who confronted me? Why, *why* should I doubt it? The bandage lay heavily about the mouth—but then it was the mouth of the breathing lady of Tremaine. And the cheeks—there were the roses as in her noon of health—yes, these were indeed the fair cheeks of the living lady of Tremaine. And the chin, with its dimples, as in health, was it not hers?—but—but *had she then grown taller since her malady?* What inexpressible madness seized me with that thought? One bound, and I had reached her feet! Shrinking from my touch, she let fall from her head, unloosened, the ghastly cerements[2] which had confined it, and there streamed forth, into the rushing atmosphere of the chamber, huge masses of long and dishevelled hair. *It was blacker than the raven wings of the midnight!* And now the eyes opened of the figure which stood before me. "Here then at least," I shrieked aloud, "can I never—can I never be mistaken—these are the full, and the black, and the wild eyes of the lady—of the lady Ligeia!"

1838

2. Shrouds.

The Fall of the House of Usher[1]

During the whole of a dull, dark, and soundless day in the autumn of the year, when the clouds hung oppressively low in the heavens, I had been passing alone, on horseback, through a singularly dreary tract of country; and at length found myself, as the shades of the evening drew on, within view of the melancholy House of Usher. I know not how it was—but, with the first glimpse of the building, a sense of insufferable gloom pervaded my spirit. I say insufferable; for the feeling was unrelieved by any of that half-pleasurable, because poetic, sentiment, with which the mind usually receives even the sternest natural images of the desolate or terrible. I looked upon the scene before me—upon the mere house, and the simple landscape features of the domain—upon the bleak walls—upon the vacant eye-like windows—upon a few rank sedges—and upon a few white trunks of decayed trees—with an utter depression of soul which I can compare to no earthly sensation more properly than to the after-dream of the reveller upon opium—the bitter lapse into common life—the hideous dropping off of the veil. There was an iciness, a sinking, a sickening of the heart—an unredeemed dreariness of thought which no goading of the imagination could torture into aught of the sublime. What was it—I paused to think—what was it that so unnerved me in the contemplation of the House of Usher? It was a mystery all insoluble; nor could I grapple with the shadowy fancies that crowded upon me as I pondered. I was forced to fall back upon the unsatisfactory conclusion, that while, beyond doubt, there *are* combinations of very simple natural objects which have the power of thus affecting us, still the reason, and the analysis, of this power, lie among considerations beyond our depth. It was possible, I reflected, that a mere different arrangement of the particulars of the scene, of the details of this picture, would be sufficient to modify, or perhaps to annihilate its capacity for sorrowful impression; and, acting upon this idea, I reined my horse to the precipitous brink of a black and lurid tarn[2] that lay in unruffled lustre by the dwelling, and gazed down—but with a shudder even more thrilling than before—upon the re-modelled and inverted images of the gray sedge, and the ghastly tree-stems, and the vacant and eye-like windows.

Nevertheless, in this mansion of gloom I now proposed to myself a sojourn of some weeks. Its proprietor, Roderick Usher, had been one of my boon companions in boyhood; but many years had elapsed since our last meeting. A letter, however, had lately reached me in a distant part of the country—a letter from him—which, in its wildly importunate nature, had admitted of no other than a personal reply. The MS. gave evidence of nervous agitation. The writer spoke of acute bodily illness—of a pitiable mental idiosyncrasy which oppressed him—and of an earnest desire to see me, as his best, and indeed, his only personal friend, with a view of attempting, by the cheerfulness of my society, some alleviation of his malady. It was the manner in which all this, and much more, was said—it was the apparent *heart* that went with his request—which allowed me no room for hesitation—and I accordingly obeyed, what I still considered a very singular summons, forthwith.

Although, as boys, we had been even intimate associates, yet I really knew little of my friend. His reserve had been always excessive and habitual. I was

1. The text is that of the first publication in *Burton's Gentleman's Magazine, and American* *Monthly Review* 5 (September 1839).
2. A small lake, usually in the mountains.

aware, however, that his very ancient family had been noted, time out of mind, for a peculiar sensibility of temperament, displaying itself, through long ages, in many works of exalted art, and manifested, of late, in repeated deeds of munificent yet unobtrusive charity, as well as in a passionate devotion to the intricacies, perhaps even more than to the orthodox and easily recognizable beauties, of musical science. I had learned, too, the very remarkable fact, that the stem of the Usher race, all time-honored as it was, had put forth, at no period, any enduring branch; in other words, that the entire family lay in the direct line of descent, and had always, with very trifling and very temporary variation, so lain. It was this deficiency, I considered, while running over in thought the perfect keeping of the character of the premises with the accredited character of the people, and while speculating upon the possible influence which the one, in the long lapse of centuries, might have exercised upon the other—it was this deficiency, perhaps, of collateral issue, and the consequent undeviating transmission, from sire to son, of the patrimony with the name, which had, at length, so identified the two as to merge the original title of the estate in the quaint and equivocal appellation of the "House of Usher"—an appellation which seemed to include, in the minds of the peasantry who used it, both the family and the family mansion.

I have said that the sole effect of my somewhat childish experiment, of looking down within the tarn, had been to deepen the first singular impression. There can be no doubt that the consciousness of the rapid increase of my superstition—for why should I not so term it?—served mainly to accelerate the increase itself. Such, I have long known, is the paradoxical law of all sentiments having terror as a basis. And it might have been for this reason only, that, when I again uplifted my eyes to the house itself, from its image in the pool, there grew in my mind a strange fancy—a fancy so ridiculous, indeed, that I but mention it to show the vivid force of the sensations which oppressed me. I had so worked upon my imagination as really to believe that around about the whole mansion and domain there hung an atmosphere peculiar to themselves and their immediate vicinity—an atmosphere which had no affinity with the air of heaven, but which had reeked up from the decayed trees, and the gray walls, and the silent tarn, in the form of an inelastic vapor or gas—dull, sluggish, faintly discernible, and leaden-hued. Shaking off from my spirit what *must* have been a dream, I scanned more narrowly the real aspect of the building. Its principal feature seemed to be that of an excessive antiquity. The discoloration of ages had been great. Minute fungi overspread the whole exterior, hanging in a fine tangled webwork from the eaves. Yet all this was apart from any extraordinary dilapidation. No portion of the masonry had fallen; and there appeared to be a wild inconsistency between its still perfect adaptation of parts, and the utterly porous, and evidently decayed condition of the individual stones. In this there was much that reminded me of the specious totality of old wood-work which has rotted for long years in some neglected vault, with no disturbance from the breath of the external air. Beyond this indication of extensive decay, however, the fabric gave little token of instability. Perhaps the eye of a scrutinizing observer might have discovered a barely perceptible fissure, which, extending from the roof of the building in front, made its way down the wall in a zigzag direction, until it became lost in the sullen waters of the tarn.

Noticing these things, I rode over a short causeway to the house. A servant in waiting took my horse, and I entered the Gothic archway of the hall. A valet, of stealthy step, thence conducted me, in silence, through many dark and intricate passages in my progress to the studio of his master. Much that I encountered on the way contributed, I know not how, to heighten the vague sentiments of which I have already spoken. While the objects around me—while the carvings of the ceilings, the sombre tapestries of the walls, the ebon blackness of the floors, and the phantasmagoric armorial trophies which rattled as I strode, were but matters to which, or to such as which, I had been accustomed from my infancy—while I hesitated not to acknowledge how familiar was all this—I still wondered to find how unfamiliar were the fancies which ordinary images were stirring up. On one of the staircases, I met the physician of the family. His countenance, I thought, wore a mingled expression of low cunning and perplexity. He accosted me with trepidation and passed on. The valet now threw open a door and ushered me into the presence of his master.

The room in which I found myself was very large and excessively lofty. The windows were long, narrow, and pointed, and at so vast a distance from the black oaken floor as to be altogether inaccessible from within. Feeble gleams of encrimsoned light made their way through the trelliced panes, and served to render sufficiently distinct the more prominent objects around; the eye, however, struggled in vain to reach the remoter angles of the chamber, or the recesses of the vaulted and fretted ceiling. Dark draperies hung upon the walls. The general furniture was profuse, comfortless, antique, and tattered. Many books and musical instruments lay scattered about, but failed to give any vitality to the scene. I felt that I breathed an atmosphere of sorrow. An air of stern, deep, and irredeemable gloom hung over and pervaded all.

Upon my entrance, Usher arose from a sofa upon which he had been lying at full length, and greeted me with a vivacious warmth which had much in it, I at first thought of an overdone cordiality—of the constrained effort of the ennuyé[3] man of the world. A glance, however, at his countenance convinced me of his perfect sincerity. We sat down; and for some moments, while he spoke not, I gazed upon him with a feeling half of pity, half of awe. Surely, man had never before so terribly altered, in so brief a period, as had Roderick Usher! It was with difficulty that I could bring myself to admit the identity of the wan being before me with the companion of my early boyhood. Yet the character of his face had been at all times remarkable. A cadaverousness of complexion; an eye large, liquid, and luminous beyond comparison; lips somewhat thin and very pallid, but of a surpassingly beautiful curve; a nose of a delicate Hebrew model, but with a breadth of nostril unusual in similar formations; a finely moulded chin, speaking, in its want of prominence, of a want of moral energy; hair of a more than web-like softness and tenuity; these features, with an inordinate expansion above the regions of the temple, made up altogether a countenance not easily to be forgotten. And now in the mere exaggeration of the prevailing character of these features, and of the expression they were wont to convey, lay so much of change that I doubted to whom I spoke. The now ghastly pallor of the skin, and the now miraculous lustre of the eye, above all things startled and even awed me. The silken hair, too, had been suffered to grow all unheeded, and as, in its wild gossamer tex-

3. Bored (French).

ture, it floated rather than fell about the face, I could not, even with effort, connect its arabesque expression with any idea of simple humanity.

In the manner of my friend I was at once struck with an incoherence—an inconsistency; and I soon found this to arise from a series of feeble and futile struggles to overcome an habitual trepidancy, an excessive nervous agitation. For something of this nature I had indeed been prepared, no less by his letter, than by reminiscences of certain boyish traits, and by conclusions deduced from his peculiar physical conformation and temperament. His action was alternately vivacious and sullen. His voice varied rapidly from a tremulous indecision (when the animal spirits seemed utterly in abeyance) to that species of energetic concision—that abrupt, weighty, unhurried, and hollow-sounding enunciation—that leaden, self-balanced and perfectly modulated guttural utterance, which may be observed in the moments of the intensest excitement of the lost drunkard, or the irreclaimable eater of opium.

It was thus that he spoke of the object of my visit, of his earnest desire to see me, and of the solace he expected me to afford him. He entered, at some length, into what he conceived to be the nature of his malady. It was, he said, a constitutional and a family evil, and one for which he despaired to find a remedy—a mere nervous affection, he immediately added, which would undoubtedly soon pass off. It displayed itself in a host of unnatural sensations. Some of these, as he detailed them, interested and bewildered me— although, perhaps, the terms, and the general manner of the narration had their weight. He suffered much from a morbid acuteness of the senses; the most insipid food was alone endurable; he could wear only garments of certain texture; the odors of all flowers were oppressive; his eyes were tortured by even a faint light; and there were but peculiar sounds, and these from stringed instruments, which did not inspire him with horror.

To an anomalous species of terror I found him a bounden slave. "I shall perish," said he, "I *must* perish in this deplorable folly. Thus, thus, and not otherwise, shall I be lost. I dread the events of the future, not in themselves, but in their results. I shudder at the thought of any, even the most trivial, incident, which may operate upon this intolerable agitation of soul. I have, indeed, no abhorrence of danger, except in its absolute effect—in terror. In this unnerved—in this pitiable condition—I feel that I must inevitably abandon life and reason together in my struggles with some fatal demon of fear."

I learned, moreover, at intervals, and through broken and equivocal hints, another singular feature of his mental condition. He was enchained by certain superstitious impressions in regard to the dwelling which he tenanted, and from which, for many years, he had never ventured forth—in regard to an influence whose supposititious force was conveyed in terms too shadowy here to be restated—an influence which some peculiarities in the mere form and substance of his family mansion, had, by dint of long sufferance, he said, obtained over his spirit—an effect which the *physique* of the gray walls and turrets, and of the dim tarn into which they all looked down, had, at length, brought about upon the *morale* of his existence.

He admitted, however, although with hesitation, that much of the peculiar gloom which thus afflicted him could be traced to a more natural and far more palpable origin—to the severe and long-continued illness—indeed to the evidently approaching dissolution—of a tenderly beloved sister; his sole companion for long years—his last and only relative on earth. "Her decease," he said, with a bitterness which I can never forget, "would leave him (him the hopeless and the frail) the last of the ancient race of the Ushers." As he spoke, the lady Madeline (for so was she called) passed slowly through a remote portion of the apartment, and, without having noticed my presence, disappeared. I regarded her with an utter astonishment not unmingled with dread. Her figure, her air, her features—all, in their very minutest development were those—were identically (I can use no other sufficient term) were identically those of the Roderick Usher who sat beside me. A feeling of stupor oppressed me, as my eyes followed her retreating steps. As a door, at length, closed upon her exit, my glance sought instinctively and eagerly the countenance of the brother—but he had buried his face in his hands, and I could only perceive that a far more than ordinary wanness had overspread the emaciated fingers through which trickled many passionate tears.

The disease of the lady Madeline had long baffled the skill of her physicians. A settled apathy, a gradual wasting away of the person, and frequent although transient affections of a partially cataleptical[4] character, were the unusual diagnosis. Hitherto she had steadily borne up against the pressure of her malady, and had not betaken herself finally to bed; but, on the closing in of the evening of my arrival at the house, she succumbed, as her brother told me at night with inexpressible agitation, to the prostrating power of the destroyer—and I learned that the glimpse I had obtained of her person would thus probably be the last I should obtain—that the lady, at least while living, would be seen by me no more.

For several days ensuing, her name was unmentioned by either Usher or myself; and, during this period, I was busied in earnest endeavors to alleviate the melancholy of my friend. We painted and read together—or I listened, as if in a dream, to the wild improvisations of his speaking guitar. And thus, as a closer and still closer intimacy admitted me more unreservedly into the recesses of his spirit, the more bitterly did I perceive the futility of all attempt at cheering a mind from which darkness, as if an inherent positive quality, poured forth upon all objects of the moral and physical universe, in one unceasing radiation of gloom.

I shall ever bear about me, as Moslemin their shrouds at Mecca, a memory of the many solemn hours I thus spent alone with the master of the House of Usher. Yet I should fail in any attempt to convey an idea of the exact character of the studies, or of the occupations, in which he involved me, or led me the way. An excited and highly distempered ideality threw a sulphurous lustre over all. His long improvised dirges will ring for ever in my ears. Among other things, I bear painfully in mind a certain singular perversion and amplification of the wild air of the last waltz of Von Weber.[5] From the paintings over which his elaborate fancy brooded, and which grew, touch by touch, into vaguenesses at which I shuddered the more thrillingly, because I shuddered knowing not why, from these paintings (vivid as their images now are before me) I would in vain endeavor to educe more than a small portion which should lie within the compass of merely written words. By the utter simplicity, by the nakedness, of his designs, he arrested and overawed attention. If ever mortal painted an idea, that mortal was Roderick Usher. For me at least—in the circumstances then surrounding me—there

---

4. A condition characterized by a loss of sensation and muscular paralysis.
5. Carl Maria von Weber (1786–1826), influential German composer of the Romantic school. "The Last Waltz of Von Weber" was composed by Carl Gottlieb Reissiger (1798–1859).

arose out of the pure abstractions which the hypochondriac contrived to throw upon his canvas, an intensity of intolerable awe, no shadow of which felt I ever yet in the contemplation of the certainly glowing yet too concrete reveries of Fuseli.[6]

One of the phantasmagoric conceptions of my friend, partaking not so rigidly of the spirit of abstraction, may be shadowed forth, although feebly, in words. A small picture presented the interior of an immensely long and rectangular vault or tunnel, with low walls, smooth, white, and without interruption or device. Certain accessory points of the design served well to convey the idea that this excavation lay at an exceeding depth below the surface of the earth. No outlet was observed in any portion of its vast extent, and no torch, or other artificial source of light was discernible—yet a flood of intense rays rolled throughout, and bathed the whole in a ghastly and inappropriate splendor.

I have just spoken of that morbid condition of the auditory nerve which rendered all music intolerable to the sufferer, with the exception of certain effects of stringed instruments. It was, perhaps, the narrow limits to which he thus confined himself upon the guitar, which gave birth, in great measure, to the fantastic character of his performances. But the fervid *facility* of his impromptus could not be so accounted for. They must have been, and were, in the notes, as well as in the words of his wild fantasias, (for he not unfrequently accompanied himself with rhymed verbal improvisations,) the result of that intense mental collectedness and concentration to which I have previously alluded as observable only in particular moments of the highest artificial excitement. The words of one of these rhapsodies I have easily borne away in memory. I was, perhaps, the more forcibly impressed with it, as he gave it, because, in the under or mystic current of its meaning, I fancied that I perceived, and for the first time, a full consciousness on the part of Usher, of the tottering of his lofty reason upon her throne. The verses, which were entitled "The Haunted Palace," ran very nearly, if not accurately, thus:[7]

I

In the greenest of our valleys,
　　By good angels tenanted,
Once a fair and stately palace—
　　Snow-white palace—reared its head.
In the monarch Thought's dominion—
　　It stood there!
Never seraph spread a pinion
　　Over fabric half so fair.

II

Banners yellow, glorious, golden,
　　On its roof did float and flow;
(This—all this—was in the olden
　　Time long ago)

And every gentle air that dallied,
    In that sweet day,
Along the ramparts plumed and pallid,
    A winged odor went away.

III

Wanderers in that happy valley
    Through two luminous windows saw
Spirits moving musically
    To a lute's well-tunéd law,
Round about a throne, where sitting
    (Porphyrogene!)[8]
In state his glory well befitting,
    The sovereign of the realm was seen.

IV

And all with pearl and ruby glowing
    Was the fair palace door,
Through which came flowing, flowing, flowing,
    And sparkling evermore,
A troop of Echoes whose sole duty
    Was but to sing,
In voices of surpassing beauty,
    The wit and wisdom of their king.

V

But evil things, in robes of sorrow,
    Assailed the monarch's high estate;
(Ah, let us mourn, for never morrow
    Shall dawn upon him, desolate!)
And, round about his home, the glory
    That blushed and bloomed
Is but a dim-remembered story
    Of the old time entombed.

VI

And travellers now within that valley,
    Through the red-litten windows, see
Vast forms that move fantastically
    To a discordant melody;
While, like a rapid ghastly river,
    Through the pale door,
A hideous throng rush out forever,
    And laugh—but smile no more.

    I well remember that suggestions arising from this ballad led us into a train of thought wherein there became manifest an opinion of Usher's which I mention not so much on account of its novelty, (for other men have thought thus,) as on account of the pertinacity with which he maintained it. This

8. Born to the purple, of royal birth.

opinion, in its general form, was that of the sentience of all vegetable things. But, in his disordered fancy, the idea had assumed a more daring character, and trespassed, under certain conditions, upon the kingdom of inorganization. I lack words to express the full extent, or the earnest *abandon* of his persuasion. The belief, however, was connected (as I have previously hinted) with the gray stones of the home of his forefathers. The condition of the sentience had been here, he imagined, fulfilled in the method of collocation of these stones—in the order of their arrangement, as well as in that of the many fungi which overspread them, and of the decayed trees which stood around—above all, in the long undisturbed endurance of this arrangement, and in its reduplication in the still waters of the tarn. Its evidence—the evidence of the sentience—was to be seen, he said, (and I here started as he spoke,) in *the gradual yet certain condensation of an atmosphere of their own about the waters and the walls.* The result was discoverable, he added, in that silent, yet importunate and terrible influence which for centuries had moulded the destinies of his family, and which made *him* what I now saw him—what he was. Such opinions need no comment, and I will make none.

Our books—the books which, for years, had formed no small portion of the mental existence of the invalid—were, as might be supposed, in strict keeping with this character of phantasm. We pored together over such works as the Ververt et Chartreuse of Gresset; the Belphegor of Machiavelli; the Selenography of Brewster; the Heaven and Hell of Swedenborg; the Subterranean Voyage of Nicholas Klimm de Holberg; the Chiromancy of Robert Flud, of Jean D'Indaginé, and of De la Chambre; the Journey into the Blue Distance of Tieck; and the City of the Sun of Campanella.[9] One favorite volume was a small octavo edition of the Directorium Inquisitorium, by the Dominican Eymeric de Gironne; and there were passages in Pomponius Mela, about the old African Satyrs and Œgipans, over which Usher would sit dreaming for hours. His chief delight, however, was found in the earnest and repeated perusal of an exceedingly rare and curious book in quarto Gothic—the manual of a forgotten church—the *Vigilae Mortuorum secundum Chorum Ecclesiae Maguntinae.*[1]

I could not help thinking of the wild ritual of this work, and of its probable influence upon the hypochondriac, when, one evening, having informed me abruptly that the lady Madeline was no more, he stated his intention of preserving her corpse for a fortnight, previously to its final interment, in one of the numerous vaults within the main walls of the building. The worldly reason, however, assigned for this singular proceeding, was one which I did not feel at liberty to dispute. The brother had been led to his resolution (so he told me) by considerations of the unusual character of the malady of the

---

9. *The City of the Sun* by the Italian Tommaso Campanella (1568–1639) is a famous utopian work. Jean Baptiste Gresset (1709–1777) wrote the anticlerical *Vairvert* and *Ma Chartreuse*. In *Belphegor*, by Niccolò Machiavelli (1469–1527), a demon comes to earth to prove that women damn men to hell. Sir David Brewster (1781–1868), Scottish physicist who studied optics and light. Emanuel Swedenborg (1688–1772), Swedish scientist and mystic. Ludwig Holberg (1684–1754), Danish dramatist and historian, described a voyage to the land of death and back. The English physician Robert Flud (1574–1637) and two Frenchmen, Jean D'Indaginé (fl. early 16th century) and Maria Cireau de la Chambre (1594–1669), all wrote on chiromancy (palm reading). The German Ludwig Tieck (1773–1853) wrote *Das Alte Buch; oder Reise ins Blaue hinein*, which narrates a journey to another world.
1. A book called *The Vigils of the Dead, According to the Church-Choir of Mayence* was printed in Switzerland around 1500. Nicholas Eymeric de Gerone, who was inquisitor-general for Castile in 1356, recorded procedures for torturing heretics. Pomponius Mela (1st century) was a Roman whose widely used book on geography (printed in Italy in 1471) described strange beasts ("œgipans" are African goat-men).

deceased, of certain obtrusive and eager inquiries on the part of her medical men, and of the remote and exposed situation of the burial ground of the family. I will not deny that when I called to mind the sinister countenance of the person whom I met upon the staircase, on the day of my arrival at the house, I had no desire to oppose what I regarded as at best but a harmless, and not by any means an unnatural precaution.[2]

At the request of Usher, I personally aided him in the arrangements for the temporary entombment. The body having been encoffined, we two alone bore it to its rest. The vault in which we placed it (and which had been so long unopened that our torches, half smothered in its oppressive atmosphere, gave us little opportunity for investigation) was small, damp, and utterly without means of admission for light; lying, at great depth, immediately beneath that portion of the building in which was my own sleeping apartment. It had been used, apparently, in remote feudal times, for the worst purposes of a donjon[3] keep, and, in later days, as a place of deposit for powder, or other highly combustible substance, as a portion of its floor, and the whole interior of a long archway through which we reached it, were carefully sheathed with copper. The door, of massive iron, had been, also, similarly protected. Its immense weight caused an unusually sharp grating sound, as it moved upon its hinges.

Having deposited our mournful burden upon tressels[4] within this region of horror, we partially turned aside the yet unscrewed lid of the coffin, and looked upon the face of the tenant. The exact similitude between the brother and sister even here again startled and confounded me. Usher, divining, perhaps, my thoughts, murmured out some few words from which I learned that the deceased and himself had been twins, and that sympathies of a scarcely intelligible nature had always existed between them. Our glances, however, rested not long upon the dead—for we could not regard her unawed. The disease which had thus entombed the lady in the maturity of youth, had left, as usual in all maladies of a strictly cataleptical character, the mockery of a faint blush upon the bosom and the face, and that suspiciously lingering smile upon the lip which is so terrible in death. We replaced and screwed down the lid, and, having secured the door of iron, made our way, with toil, into the scarcely less gloomy apartments of the upper portion of the house.

And now, some days of bitter grief having elapsed, an observable change came over the features of the mental disorder of my friend. His ordinary manner had vanished. His ordinary occupations were neglected or forgotten. He roamed from chamber to chamber with hurried, unequal, and objectless step. The pallor of his countenance had assumed, if possible, a more ghastly hue—but the luminousness of his eye had utterly gone out. The once occasional huskiness of his tone was heard no more; and a tremulous quaver, as if of extreme terror, habitually characterized his utterance.— There were times, indeed, when I thought his unceasingly agitated mind was laboring with an oppressive secret, to divulge which he struggled for the necessary courage. At times, again, I was obliged to resolve all into the mere inexplicable vagaries of madness, as I beheld him gazing upon vacancy for long hours, in an attitude of the profoundest attention, as if listening to

---

2. The shortage of corpses for dissection had led to the new profession of "resurrection men," who dug up fresh corpses and sold them to medical students and surgeons.
3. Dungeon.
4. Trestles; braced supports.

some imaginary sound. It was no wonder that his condition terrified—that it infected me. I felt creeping upon me, by slow yet certain degrees, the wild influences of his own fantastic yet impressive superstitions.

It was, most especially, upon retiring to bed late in the night of the seventh or eighth day after the entombment of the lady Madeline, that I experienced the full power of such feelings. Sleep came not near my couch—while the hours waned and waned away. I struggled to reason off the nervousness which had dominion over me. I endeavored to believe that much, if not all of what I felt, was due to the phantasmagoric influence of the gloomy furniture of the room—of the dark and tattered draperies, which, tortured into motion by the breath of a rising tempest, swayed fitfully to and fro upon the walls, and rustled uneasily about the decorations of the bed. But my efforts were fruitless. An irrepressible tremor gradually pervaded my frame; and, at length, there sat upon my very heart an incubus[5] of utterly causeless alarm. Shaking this off with a gasp and a struggle, I uplifted myself upon the pillows, and, peering earnestly within the intense darkness of the chamber, harkened—I know not why, except that an instinctive spirit prompted me—to certain low and indefinite sounds which came, through the pauses of the storm, at long intervals, I knew not whence. Overpowered by an intense sentiment of horror, unaccountable yet unendurable, I threw on my clothes with haste, for I felt that I should sleep no more during the night, and endeavored to arouse myself from the pitiable condition into which I had fallen, by pacing rapidly to and fro through the apartment.

I had taken but few turns in this manner, when a light step on an adjoining staircase arrested my attention. I presently recognized it as that of Usher. In an instant afterwards he rapped, with a gentle touch, at my door, and entered, bearing a lamp. His countenance was, as usual, cadaverously wan—but there was a species of mad hilarity in his eyes—an evidently restrained hysteria in his whole demeanor. His air appalled me—but any thing was preferable to the solitude which I had so long endured, and I even welcomed his presence as a relief.

"And you have not seen it?" he said abruptly, after having stared about him for some moments in silence—"you have not then seen it?—but, stay! you shall." Thus speaking, and having carefully shaded his lamp, he hurried to one of the gigantic casements, and threw it freely open to the storm.

The impetuous fury of the entering gust nearly lifted us from our feet. It was, indeed, a tempestuous yet sternly beautiful night, and one wildly singular in its terror and its beauty. A whirlwind had apparently collected its force in our vicinity; for there were frequent and violent alterations in the direction of the wind; and the exceeding density of the clouds (which hung so low as to press upon the turrets of the house) did not prevent our perceiving the life-like velocity with which they flew careering from all points against each other, without passing away into the distance. I say that even their exceeding density did not prevent our perceiving this—yet we had no glimpse of the moon or stars—nor was there any flashing forth of the lightning. But the under surfaces of the huge masses of agitated vapor, as well as all terrestrial objects immediately around us, were glowing in the unnatural light of a faintly luminous and distinctly visible gaseous exhalation which hung about and enshrouded the mansion.

---

5. An evil spirit supposed to lie upon people in their sleep.

"You must not—you shall not behold this!" said I, shudderingly, to Usher, as I led him, with a gentle violence, from the window to a seat. "These appearances, which bewilder you, are merely electrical phenomena not uncommon—or it may be that they have their ghastly origin in the rank miasma of the tarn. Let us close this casement—the air is chilling and dangerous to your frame. Here is one of your favorite romances. I will read, and you shall listen—and so we will pass away this terrible night together."

The antique volume which I had taken up was the "Mad Trist" of Sir Launcelot Canning[6]—but I had called it a favorite of Usher's more in sad jest than in earnest; for, in truth, there is little in its uncouth and unimaginative prolixity which could have had interest for the lofty and spiritual ideality of my friend. It was, however, the only book immediately at hand; and I indulged a vague hope that the excitement which now agitated the hypochondriac might find relief (for the history of mental disorder is full of similar anomalies) even in the extremeness of the folly which I should read. Could I have judged, indeed, by the wild, overstrained air of vivacity with which he harkened, or apparently harkened, to the words of the tale, I might have well congratulated myself upon the success of my design.

I had arrived at that well-known portion of the story where Ethelred, the hero of the Trist, having sought in vain for peaceable admission into the dwelling of the hermit, proceeds to make good an entrance by force. Here, it will be remembered, the words of the narrative run thus—

"And Ethelred, who was by nature of a doughty heart, and who was now mighty withal, on account of the powerfulness of the wine which he had drunken, waited no longer to hold parley with the hermit, who, in sooth, was of an obstinate and maliceful turn, but, feeling the rain upon his shoulders, and fearing the rising of the tempest, uplifted his mace outright, and, with blows, made quickly room in the plankings of the door for his gauntleted hand, and now pulling therewith sturdily, he so cracked, and ripped, and tore all asunder, that the noise of the dry and hollow-sounding wood alarummed and reverberated throughout the forest."

At the termination of this sentence I started, and, for a moment, paused; for it appeared to me (although I at once concluded that my excited fancy had deceived me)—it appeared to me that, from some very remote portion of the mansion or of its vicinity, there came, indistinctly, to my ears, what might have been, in its exact similarity of character, the echo (but a stifled and dull one certainly) of the very cracking and ripping sound which Sir Launcelot had so particularly described. It was, beyond doubt, the coincidence alone which had arrested my attention; for, amid the rattling of the sashes of the casements, and the ordinary commingled noises of the still increasing storm, the sound, in itself, had nothing, surely, which should have interested or disturbed me. I continued the story.

"But the good champion Ethelred, now entering within the door, was sore enraged and amazed to perceive no signal of the maliceful hermit; but, in the stead thereof, a dragon of scaly and prodigious demeanor, and of a fiery tongue, which sate in guard before a palace of gold, with a floor of silver; and upon the wall there hung a shield of shining brass with this legend enwritten—

---

6. Not a real book. "Trist" here means meeting, or prearranged or fated encounter.

> Who entereth herein, a conqueror hath bin,
> Who slayeth the dragon, the shield he shall win.

And Ethelred uplifted his mace, and struck upon the head of the dragon, which fell before him, and gave up his pesty breath, with a shriek so horrid and harsh, and withal so piercing, that Ethelred had fain to close his ears with his hands against the dreadful noise of it, the like whereof was never before heard."

Here again I paused abruptly, and now with a feeling of wild amazement—for there could be no doubt whatever that, in this instance, I did actually hear (although from what direction it proceeded I found it impossible to say) a low and apparently distant, but harsh, protracted, and most unusual screaming or grating sound—the exact counterpart of what my fancy had already conjured up as the sound of the dragon's unnatural shriek as described by the romancer.

Oppressed, as I certainly was, upon the occurrence of this second and most extraordinary coincidence, by a thousand conflicting sensations, in which wonder and extreme terror were predominant, I still retained sufficient presence of mind to avoid exciting, by any observation, the sensitive nervousness of my companion. I was by no means certain that he had noticed the sounds in question; although, assuredly, a strange alteration had, during the last few minutes, taken place in his demeanor. From a position fronting my own, he had gradually brought round his chair, so as to sit with his face to the door of the chamber, and thus I could but partially perceive his features, although I saw that his lips trembled as if he were murmuring inaudibly. His head had dropped upon his breast—yet I knew that he was not asleep, from the wide and rigid opening of the eye, as I caught a glance of it in profile. The motion of his body, too, was at variance with his idea—for he rocked from side to side with a gentle yet constant and uniform sway. Having rapidly taken notice of all this, I resumed the narrative of Sir Launcelot, which thus proceeded:—

"And now, the champion, having escaped from the terrible fury of the dragon, bethinking himself of the brazen shield, and of the breaking up of the enchantment which was upon it, removed the carcass from out of the way before him, and approached valorously over the silver pavement of the castle to where the shield was upon the wall; which in sooth tarried not for his full coming, but fell down at his feet upon the silver floor, with a mighty great and terrible ringing sound."

No sooner had these syllables passed my lips, than—as if a shield of brass had indeed, at the moment, fallen heavily upon a floor of silver—I became aware of a distinct, hollow, metallic, and clangorous, yet apparently muffled reverberation. Completely unnerved, I started convulsively to my feet, but the measured rocking movement of Usher was undisturbed. I rushed to the chair in which he sat. His eyes were bent fixedly before him, and throughout his whole countenance there reigned a more than stony rigidity. But, as I laid my hand upon his shoulder, there came a strong shudder over his frame; a sickly smile quivered about his lips; and I saw that he spoke in a low, hurried, and gibbering murmur, as if unconscious of my presence. Bending closely over his person, I at length drank in the hideous import of his words.

"Not hear it?—yes, I hear it, and *have* heard it. Long—long—long—many minutes, many hours, many days, have I heard it—yet I dared not—oh, pity me, miserable wretch that I am!—I dared not—I *dared* not speak! *We have put her living in the tomb!* Said I not that my senses were acute?—I *now* tell you that I heard her first feeble movements in the hollow coffin. I heard them—many, many days ago—yet I dared not—*I dared not speak!* And now—to-night—Ethelred—ha! ha!—the breaking of the hermit's door, and the death-cry of the dragon, and the clangor of the shield—say, rather, the rending of the coffin, and the grating of the iron hinges, and her struggles within the coppered archway of the vault! Oh whither shall I fly? Will she not be here anon? Is she not hurrying to upbraid me for my haste? Have I not heard her footsteps on the stair? Do I not distinguish that heavy and horrible beating of her heart? Madman!"—here he sprung violently to his feet, and shrieked out his syllables, as if in the effort he were giving up his soul—"Madman! *I tell you that she now stands without the door!*"

As if in the superhuman energy of his utterance there had been found the potency of a spell—the huge antique pannels to which the speaker pointed, threw slowly back, upon the instant, their ponderous and ebony jaws. It was the work of the rushing gust—but then without those doors there *did* stand the lofty and enshrouded figure of the lady Madeline of Usher. There was blood upon her white robes, and the evidence of some bitter struggle upon every portion of her emaciated frame. For a moment she remained trembling and reeling to and fro upon the threshold—then, with a low moaning cry, fell heavily inward upon the person of her brother, and in her horrible and now final death-agonies, bore him to the floor a corpse, and a victim to the terrors he had dreaded.

From that chamber, and from that mansion, I fled aghast. The storm was still abroad in all its wrath as I found myself crossing the old causeway. Suddenly there shot along the path a wild light, and I turned to see whence a gleam so unusual could have issued—for the vast house and its shadows were alone behind me. The radiance was that of the full, setting, and blood-red moon, which now shone vividly through that once barely-discernible fissure, of which I have before spoken, as extending from the roof of the building, in a zig-zag direction, to the base. While I gazed, this fissure rapidly widened—there came a fierce breath of the whirlwind—the entire orb of the satellite burst at once upon my sight—my brain reeled as I saw the mighty walls rushing asunder—there was a long tumultuous shouting sound like the voice of a thousand waters—and the deep and dank tarn at my feet closed sullenly and silently over the fragments of the *"House of Usher."*

1839

The Tell-Tale Heart[1]

Art is long and Time is fleeting,
    And our hearts, though stout and brave,
Still, like muffled drums, are beating
    Funeral marches to the grave.
                    —*Longfellow*[2]

---

1. First published in *The Pioneer* (January 1843), the source of the present text.

2. Henry Wadsworth Longfellow's "A Psalm of Life" (1838), lines 13–16.

True!—nervous—very, very dreadfully nervous I had been, and am; but why *will* you say that I am mad? The disease had sharpened my senses—not destroyed—not dulled them. Above all was the sense of hearing acute. I heard all things in the heaven and in the earth. I heard many things in hell. How, then, am I mad? Harken! and observe how healthily—how calmly I can tell you the whole story.

It is impossible to say how first the idea entered my brain; but, once conceived, it haunted me day and night. Object there was none. Passion there was none. I loved the old man. He had never wronged me. He had never given me insult. For his gold I had no desire. I think it was his eye!—yes, it was this! He had the eye of a vulture—a pale blue eye, with a film over it. Whenever it fell upon me, my blood ran cold; and so, by degrees—very gradually—I made up my mind to take the life of the old man, and thus rid myself of the eye forever.

Now this is the point. You fancy me mad. Madmen know nothing. But you should have seen *me*. You should have seen how wisely I proceeded—with what caution—with what foresight—with what dissimulation I went to work! I was never kinder to the old man than during the whole week before I killed him. And every night, about midnight, I turned the latch of his door and opened it—oh so gently! And then, when I had made an opening sufficient for my head, I first put in a dark lantern,[3] all closed, closed, so that no light shone out, and then I thrust in my head. Oh, you would have laughed to see how cunningly I thrust it in! I moved it slowly—very, very slowly, so that I might not disturb the old man's sleep. It took me an hour to place my whole head within the opening so far that I could see the old man as he lay upon his bed. Ha!—would a madman have been so wise as this? And then, when my head was well in the room, I undid the lantern cautiously—oh, so cautiously (for the hinges creaked)—I undid it just so much that a single thin ray fell upon the vulture eye. And this I did for seven long nights—every night just at midnight—but I found the eye always closed; and so it was impossible to do the work; for it was not the old man who vexed me, but his Evil Eye. And every morning, when the day broke, I went boldly into his chamber, and spoke courageously to him, calling him by name in a hearty tone, and inquiring how he had passed the night. So you see he would have been a very profound old man, indeed, to suspect that every night, just at twelve, I looked in upon him while he slept.

Upon the eighth night I was more than usually cautious in opening the door. A watch's minute-hand moves more quickly than did mine. Never, before that night, had I *felt* the extent of my own powers—of my sagacity. I could scarcely contain my feelings of triumph. To think that there I was, opening the door, little by little, and the old man not even to dream of my secret deeds or thoughts. I fairly chuckled at the idea. And perhaps the old man heard me; for he moved in the bed suddenly, as if startled. Now you may think that I drew back—but no. His room was as black as pitch with the thick darkness, (for the shutters were close fastened, through fear of robbers,) and so I knew that he could not see the opening of the door, and I kept on pushing it steadily, steadily.

---

3. Lantern with a single opening and sliding panel that can cut off the light.

I had got my head in, and was about to open the lantern, when my thumb slipped upon the tin fastening, and the old man sprang up in the bed, crying out—"Who's there?"

I kept quite still and said nothing. For another hour I did not move a muscle, and in the meantime I did not hear the old man lie down. He was still sitting up in the bed, listening;—just as I have done, night after night, hearkening to the death-watches[4] in the wall.

Presently I heard a slight groan, and I knew that it was the groan of mortal terror. It was not a groan of pain, or of grief—oh, no!—it was the low, stifled sound that arises from the bottom of the soul when overcharged with *awe*. I knew the sound well. Many a night, just at midnight, when all the world slept, it has welled up from my own bosom, deepening, with its dreadful echo, the terrors that distracted me. I say I knew it well. I knew what the old man felt, and pitied him, although I chuckled at heart. I knew that he had been lying awake ever since the first slight noise, when he had turned in the bed. His fears had been, ever since, growing upon him. He had been trying to fancy them causeless, but could not. He had been saying to himself—"It is nothing but the wind in the chimney—it is only a mouse crossing the floor," or "it is merely a cricket which has made a single chirp." Yes, he had been trying to comfort himself with these suppositions; but he had found all in vain. *All in vain*; because death, in approaching the old man, had stalked with his black shadow before him, and the shadow had now reached and enveloped the victim. And it was the mournful influence of the unperceived shadow that caused him to feel—although he neither saw nor heard me—to *feel* the presence of my head within the room.

When I had waited a long time, very patiently, without hearing the old man lie down, I resolved to open a little—a very, very little crevice in the lantern. So I opened it—you cannot imagine how stealthily, stealthily—until, at length, a single dim ray, like the thread of the spider, shot from out the crevice and fell full upon the vulture eye.

It was open—wide, wide open—and I grew furious as I gazed upon it. I saw it with perfect distinctness—all a dull blue, with a hideous veil over it that chilled the very marrow in my bones; but I could see nothing else of the old man's face or person; for I had directed the ray, as if by instinct, precisely upon the damned spot.

And now—have I not told you that what you mistake for madness is but over acuteness of the senses?—now, I say, there came to my ears *a low, dull, quick sound—much such a sound as a watch makes when enveloped in cotton*. I knew *that* sound well, too. It was the beating of the old man's heart. It increased my fury, as the beating of a drum stimulates the soldier into courage.

But even yet I refrained and kept still. I scarcely breathed. I held the lantern motionless. I tried how steadily I could maintain the ray upon the eye. Meantime the hellish tattoo[5] of the heart increased. It grew quicker, and louder and louder every instant. The old man's terror *must* have been extreme! It grew louder, I say, louder every moment:—do you mark me well? I have told you that I am nervous:—so I am. And now, at the dead hour of night, and amid the dreadful silence of that old house, so strange a noise as

---

4. Beetles that make a hollow clicking sound by striking their heads against the wood into which they burrow.
5. Drumbeat.

this excited me to uncontrollable wrath. Yet, for some minutes longer, I refrained and kept still. But the beating grew louder, *louder*! I thought the heart must burst! And now a new anxiety seized me—the sound would be heard by a neighbor! The old man's hour had come! With a loud yell, I threw open the lantern and leaped into the room. He shrieked once— once only. In an instant I dragged him to the floor, and pulled the heavy bed over him. I then sat upon the bed and smiled gaily, to find the deed so far done. But, for many minutes, the heart beat on, with a muffled sound. This, however, did not vex me; it would not be heard through the walls. At length it ceased. The old man was dead. I removed the bed and examined the corpse. Yes, he was stone, stone dead. I placed my hand upon the heart and held it there many minutes. There was no pulsation. The old man was stone dead. His eye would trouble *me* no more.

If, still, you think me mad, you will think so no longer when I describe the wise precautions I took for the concealment of the body. The night waned, and I worked hastily, but in silence. First of all I dismembered the corpse. I cut off the head and the arms and the legs. I then took up three planks from the flooring of the chamber, and deposited all between the scantlings.[6] I then replaced the boards so cleverly, so cunningly, that no human eye—not even *his*—could have detected anything wrong. There was nothing to wash out—no stain of any kind—no blood-spot whatever. I had been too wary for that. A tub had caught all—ha! ha!

When I had made an end of these labors, it was four o'clock—still dark as midnight. As the bell sounded the hour, there came a knocking at the street door. I went down to open it with a light heart,—for what had I *now* to fear? There entered three men, who introduced themselves, with perfect suavity, as officers of the police. A shriek had been heard by a neighbor during the night; suspicion of foul play had been aroused; information had been lodged at the police-office, and they (the officers) had been deputed to search the premises.

I smiled,—for *what* had I to fear? I bade the gentlemen welcome. The shriek, I said, was my own in a dream. The old man, I mentioned, was absent in the country. I took my visiters all over the house. I bade them search— search *well*. I led them, at length, to *his* chamber. I showed them his trea- sures, secure, undisturbed. In the enthusiasm of my confidence, I brought chairs into the room, and desired them *here* to rest from their fatigues; while I myself, in the wild audacity of my perfect triumph, placed my own seat upon the very spot beneath which reposed the corpse of the victim.

The officers were satisfied. My *manner* had convinced them. I was singu- larly at ease. They sat, and, while I answered cheerily, they chatted of famil- iar things. But, ere long, I felt myself getting pale and wished them gone. My head ached, and I fancied a ringing in my ears: but still they sat and still chatted. The ringing became more distinct: I talked more freely, to get rid of the feeling; but it continued and gained definitiveness—until, at length, I found that the noise was *not* within my ears.

No doubt I now grew *very* pale;—but I talked more fluently, and with a heightened voice. Yet the sound increased—and what could I do? It was *a low, dull, quick sound—much such a sound as a watch makes when enveloped*

---

6. Small planks.

in cotton. I gasped for breath—and yet the officers heard it not. I talked more quickly—more vehemently;—but the noise steadily increased. I arose, and argued about trifles, in a high key and with violent gesticulations;—but the noise steadily increased. Why *would* they not be gone? I paced the floor to and fro, with heavy strides, as if excited to fury by the observations of the men;—but the noise steadily increased. Oh God! what *could* I do? I foamed—I raved—I swore! I swung the chair upon which I had sat, and grated it upon the boards;—but the noise arose over all and continually increased. It grew louder—louder—*louder!* And still the men chatted pleasantly, and smiled. Was it possible they heard not? Almighty God! no, no! They heard!—they suspected!—they *knew!*—they were making a mockery of my horror!—this I thought, and this I think. But anything better than this agony! Anything was more tolerable than this derision! I could bear those hypocritical smiles no longer! I felt that I must scream or die!—and now—again!—hark! louder! louder! louder! *louder!*—

"Villains!" I shrieked, "dissemble no more! I admit the deed!—tear up the planks!—here, here!—it is the beating of his hideous heart!"

1843

The Black Cat[1]

For the most wild, yet most homely narrative which I am about to pen, I neither expect nor solicit belief. Mad indeed would I be to expect it, in a case where my very senses reject their own evidence. Yet, mad am I not—and very surely do I not dream. But to-morrow I die, and to-day I would unburthen my soul. My immediate purpose is to place before the world, plainly, succinctly, and without comment, a series of mere household events. In their consequences, these events have terrified—have tortured—have destroyed me. Yet I will not attempt to expound them. To me, they have presented little but Horror—to many they will seem less terrible than *barroques.*[2] Hereafter, perhaps, some intellect may be found which will reduce my phantasm to the commonplace—some intellect more calm, more logical, and far less excitable than my own, which will perceive, in the circumstances I detail with awe, nothing more than an ordinary succession of very natural causes and effects.

From my infancy I was noted for the docility and humanity of my disposition. My tenderness of heart was even so conspicuous as to make me the jest of my companions. I was especially fond of animals, and was indulged by my parents with a great variety of pets. With these I spent most of my time, and never was so happy as when feeding and caressing them. This peculiarity of character grew with my growth, and, in my manhood, I derived from it one of my principal sources of pleasure. To those who have cherished an affection for a faithful and sagacious dog, I need hardly be at the trouble of explaining the nature or the intensity of the gratification thus derivable. There is something in the unselfish and self-sacrificing love of a brute, which

---

1. First published in the August 1843 *United States Saturday Post*, a Philadelphia weekly, and reprinted here from *Tales* (1845).
2. Odd (French).

goes directly to the heart of him who has had frequent occasion to test the paltry friendship and gossamer fidelity of mere *Man*.

I married early, and was happy to find in my wife a disposition not uncongenial with my own. Observing my partiality for domestic pets, she lost no opportunity of procuring those of the most agreeable kind. We had birds, gold-fish, a fine dog, rabbits, a small monkey, and *a cat*.

This latter was a remarkably large and beautiful animal, entirely black, and sagacious to an astonishing degree. In speaking of his intelligence, my wife, who at heart was not a little tinctured with superstition, made frequent allusion to the ancient popular notion, which regarded all black cats as witches in disguise. Not that she was ever *serious* upon this point—and I mention the matter at all for no better reason than that it happens, just now, to be remembered.

Pluto[3]—this was the cat's name—was my favorite pet and playmate. I alone fed him, and he attended me wherever I went about the house. It was even with difficulty that I could prevent him from following me through the streets.

Our friendship lasted, in this manner, for several years, during which my general temperament and character—through the instrumentality of the Fiend Intemperance—had (I blush to confess it) experienced a radical alteration for the worse. I grew, day by day, more moody, more irritable, more regardless of the feelings of others. I suffered myself to use intemperate language to my wife. At length, I even offered her personal violence. My pets, of course, were made to feel the change in my disposition. I not only neglected, but ill-used them. For Pluto, however, I still retained sufficient regard to restrain me from maltreating him, as I made no scruple of maltreating the rabbits, the monkey, or even the dog, when by accident, or through affection, they came in my way. But my disease grew upon me—for what disease is like Alcohol!—and at length even Pluto, who was now becoming old, and consequently somewhat peevish—even Pluto began to experience the effects of my ill temper.

One night, returning home, much intoxicated, from one of my haunts about town, I fancied that the cat avoided my presence. I seized him; when, in his fright at my violence, he inflicted a slight wound upon my hand with his teeth. The fury of a demon instantly possessed me. I knew myself no longer. My original soul seemed, at once, to take its flight from my body; and a more than fiendish malevolence, gin-nurtured, thrilled every fibre of my frame. I took from my waistcoat-pocket a pen-knife, opened it, grasped the poor beast by the throat, and deliberately cut one of its eyes from the socket! I blush, I burn, I shudder, while I pen the damnable atrocity.

When reason returned with the morning—when I had slept off the fumes of the night's debauch—I experienced a sentiment half of horror, half of remorse, for the crime of which I had been guilty; but it was, at best, a feeble and equivocal feeling, and the soul remained untouched. I again plunged into excess, and soon drowned in wine all memory of the deed.

In the meantime the cat slowly recovered. The socket of the lost eye presented, it is true, a frightful appearance, but he no longer appeared to suffer any pain. He went about the house as usual, but, as might be expected, fled

---

3. In Roman mythology, god of the dead and ruler of the underworld.

in extreme terror at my approach. I had so much of my old heart left, as to be at first grieved by this evident dislike on the part of a creature which had once so loved me. But this feeling soon gave place to irritation. And then came, as if to my final and irrevocable overthrow, the spirit of PERVERSE-NESS. Of this spirit philosophy takes no account. Yet I am not more sure that my soul lives, than I am that perverseness is one of the primitive impulses of the human heart—one of the indivisible primary faculties, or sentiments, which give direction to the character of Man. Who has not, a hundred times, found himself committing a vile or a silly action, for no other reason than because he knows he should *not*? Have we not a perpetual inclination, in the teeth of our best judgment, to violate that which is *Law*, merely because we understand it to be such? This spirit of perverseness, I say, came to my final overthrow. It was this unfathomable longing of the soul *to vex itself*—to offer violence to its own nature—to do wrong for the wrong's sake only—that urged me to continue and finally to consummate the injury I had inflicted upon the unoffending brute. One morning, in cool blood, I slipped a noose about its neck and hung it to the limb of a tree;—hung it with the tears streaming from my eyes, and with the bitterest remorse at my heart;—hung it *because* I knew that it had loved me, and *because* I felt it had given me no reason of offence;—hung it *because* I knew that in so doing I was committing a sin—a deadly sin that would so jeopardize my immortal soul as to place it—if such a thing were possible—even beyond the reach of the infinite mercy of the Most Merciful and Most Terrible God.

On the night of the day on which this cruel deed was done, I was aroused from sleep by the cry of fire. The curtains of my bed were in flames. The whole house was blazing. It was with great difficulty that my wife, a servant, and myself, made our escape from the conflagration. The destruction was complete. My entire worldly wealth was swallowed up, and I resigned myself thenceforward to despair.

I am above the weakness of seeking to establish a sequence of cause and effect, between the disaster and the atrocity. But I am detailing a chain of facts—and wish not to leave even a possible link imperfect. On the day succeeding the fire, I visited the ruins. The walls, with one exception, had fallen in. This exception was found in a compartment wall, not very thick, which stood about the middle of the house, and against which had rested the head of my bed. The plastering had here, in great measure, resisted the action of the fire—a fact which I attributed to its having been recently spread. About this wall a dense crowd were collected, and many persons seemed to be examining a particular portion of it with very minute and eager attention. The words "strange!" "singular!" and other similar expressions, excited my curiosity. I approached and saw, as if graven in *bas relief*[4] upon the white surface, the figure of a gigantic *cat*. The impression was given with an accuracy truly marvellous. There was a rope about the animal's neck.

When I first beheld this apparition—for I could scarcely regard it as less—my wonder and my terror were extreme. But at length reflection came to my aid. The cat, I remembered, had been hung in a garden adjacent to the house. Upon the alarm of fire, this garden had been immediately filled by the crowd—by some one of whom the animal must have been cut from the

---

4. Low relief (French); the slight projection from a flat sculptural background.

tree and thrown, through an open window, into my chamber. This had probably been done with the view of arousing me from sleep. The falling of other
walls had compressed the victim of my cruelty into the substance of the
freshly-spread plaster; the lime of which, with the flames, and the *ammonia*
from the carcass, had then accomplished the portraiture as I saw it.

Although I thus readily accounted to my reason, if not altogether to my
conscience, for the startling fact just detailed, it did not the less fail to
make a deep impression upon my fancy. For months I could not rid myself
of the phantasm of the cat; and, during this period, there came back into
my spirit a half-sentiment that seemed, but was not, remorse. I went so far
as to regret the loss of the animal, and to look about me, among the vile
haunts which I now habitually frequented, for another pet of the same species, and of somewhat similar appearance, with which to supply its place.

One night as I sat, half stupified, in a den of more than infamy, my attention was suddenly drawn to some black object, reposing upon the head of one
of the immense hogsheads[5] of Gin, or of Rum, which constituted the chief
furniture of the apartment. I had been looking steadily at the top of this
hogshead for some minutes, and what now caused me surprise was the fact
that I had not sooner perceived the object thereupon. I approached it, and
touched it with my hand. It was a black cat—a very large one—fully as large
as Pluto, and closely resembling him in every respect but one. Pluto had not
a white hair upon any portion of his body; but this cat had a large, although
indefinite splotch of white, covering nearly the whole region of the breast.

Upon my touching him, he immediately arose, purred loudly, rubbed
against my hand, and appeared delighted with my notice. This, then, was
the very creature of which I was in search. I at once offered to purchase it
of the landlord; but this person made no claim to it—knew nothing of it—
had never seen it before.

I continued my caresses, and, when I prepared to go home, the animal
evinced a disposition to accompany me. I permitted it to do so; occasionally stooping and patting it as I proceeded. When it reached the house it
domesticated itself at once, and became immediately a great favorite with
my wife.

For my own part, I soon found a dislike to it arising within me. This was just
the reverse of what I had anticipated; but—I know not how or why it was—its
evident fondness for myself rather disgusted and annoyed. By slow degrees,
these feelings of disgust and annoyance rose into the bitterness of hatred. I
avoided the creature; a certain sense of shame, and the remembrance of my
former deed of cruelty, preventing me from physically abusing it. I did not, for
some weeks, strike, or otherwise violently ill use it; but gradually—very gradually—I came to look upon it with unutterable loathing, and to flee silently
from its odious presence, as from the breath of a pestilence.

What added, no doubt, to my hatred of the beast, was the discovery, on the
morning after I brought it home, that, like Pluto, it also had been deprived of
one of its eyes. This circumstance, however, only endeared it to my wife, who,
as I have already said, possessed, in a high degree, that humanity of feeling
which had once been my distinguishing trait, and the source of many of my
simplest and purest pleasures.

5. Large casks.

With my aversion to this cat, however, its partiality for myself seemed to increase. It followed my footsteps with a pertinacity which it would be difficult to make the reader comprehend. Whenever I sat, it would crouch beneath my chair, or spring upon my knees, covering me with its loathsome caresses. If I arose to walk it would get between my feet and thus nearly throw me down, or, fastening its long and sharp claws in my dress, clamber, in this manner, to my breast. At such times, although I longed to destroy it with a blow, I was yet withheld from so doing, partly by a memory of my former crime, but chiefly—let me confess it at once—by absolute *dread* of the beast.

This dread was not exactly a dread of physical evil—and yet I should be at a loss how otherwise to define it. I am almost ashamed to own—yes, even in this felon's cell, I am almost ashamed to own—that the terror and horror with which the animal inspired me, had been heightened by one of the merest chimæras[6] it would be possible to conceive. My wife had called my attention, more than once, to the character of the mark of white hair, of which I have spoken, and which constituted the sole visible difference between the strange beast and the one I had destroyed. The reader will remember that this mark, although large, had been originally very indefinite; but, by slow degrees—degrees nearly imperceptible, and which for a long time my Reason struggled to reject as fanciful—it had, at length, assumed a rigorous distinctness of outline. It was now the representation of an object that I shudder to name—and for this, above all, I loathed, and dreaded, and would have rid myself of the monster *had I dared*—it was now, I say, the image of a hideous—of a ghastly thing—of the GALLOWS!—oh, mournful and terrible engine of Horror and of Crime—of Agony and of Death!

And now was I indeed wretched beyond the wretchedness of mere Humanity. And *a brute beast*—whose fellow I had contemptuously destroyed—*a brute beast* to work out for *me*—for me a man, fashioned in the image of the High God—so much of insufferable wo! Alas! neither by day nor by night knew I the blessing of Rest any more! During the former the creature left me no moment alone; and, in the latter, I started, hourly, from dreams of unutterable fear, to find the hot breath of *the thing* upon my face, and its vast weight—an incarnate Night-Mare that I had no power to shake off—incumbent eternally upon my *heart*!

Beneath the pressure of torments such as these, the feeble remnant of the good within me succumbed. Evil thoughts became my sole intimates—the darkest and most evil of thoughts. The moodiness of my usual temper increased to hatred of all things and of all mankind; while, from the sudden, frequent, and ungovernable outbursts of a fury to which I now blindly abandoned myself, my uncomplaining wife, alas! was the most usual and the most patient of sufferers.

One day she accompanied me, upon some household errand, into the cellar of the old building which our poverty compelled us to inhabit. The cat followed me down the steep stairs, and, nearly throwing me headlong, exasperated me to madness. Uplifting an axe, and forgetting, in my wrath, the childish dread which had hitherto stayed my hand, I aimed a blow at the animal which, of course, would have proved instantly fatal had it descended

6. Illusions.

as I wished. But this blow was arrested by the hand of my wife. Goaded, by the interference, into a rage more than demoniacal, I withdrew my arm from her grasp and buried the axe in her brain. She fell dead upon the spot, without a groan.

This hideous murder accomplished, I set myself forthwith, and with entire deliberation, to the task of concealing the body. I knew that I could not remove it from the house, either by day or by night, without the risk of being observed by the neighbors. Many projects entered my mind. At one period I thought of cutting the corpse into minute fragments, and destroying them by fire. At another, I resolved to dig a grave for it in the floor of the cellar. Again, I deliberated about casting it in the well in the yard—about packing it in a box, as if merchandize, with the usual arrangements, and so getting a porter to take it from the house. Finally I hit upon what I considered a far better expedient than either of these. I determined to wall it up in the cellar—as the monks of the middle ages are recorded to have walled up their victims.

For a purpose such as this the cellar was well adapted. Its walls were loosely constructed, and had lately been plastered throughout with a rough plaster, which the dampness of the atmosphere had prevented from harden-ing. Moreover, in one of the walls was a projection, caused by a false chim-ney, or fireplace, that had been filled up, and made to resemble the rest of the cellar. I made no doubt that I could readily displace the bricks at this point, insert the corpse, and wall the whole up as before, so that no eye could detect any thing suspicious.

And in this calculation I was not deceived. By means of a crow-bar I easily dislodged the bricks, and, having carefully deposited the body against the inner wall, I propped it in that position, while, with little trouble, I re-laid the whole structure as it originally stood. Having procured mortar, sand, and hair, with every possible precaution, I prepared a plaster which could not be distinguished from the old, and with this I very carefully went over the new brick-work. When I had finished, I felt satisfied that all was right. The wall did not present the slightest appearance of having been disturbed. The rubbish on the floor was picked up with the minutest care. I looked around triumphantly, and said to myself—"Here at least, then, my labor has not been in vain."

My next step was to look for the beast which had been the cause of so much wretchedness; for I had, at length, firmly resolved to put it to death. Had I been able to meet with it, at the moment, there could have been no doubt of its fate; but it appeared that the crafty animal had been alarmed at the violence of my previous anger, and forebore to present itself in my pres-ent mood. It is impossible to describe, or to imagine, the deep, the blissful sense of relief which the absence of the detested creature occasioned in my bosom. It did not make its appearance during the night—and thus for one night at least, since its introduction into the house, I soundly and tranquilly slept; aye, *slept* even with the burden of murder upon my soul!

The second and the third day passed, and still my tormentor came not. Once again I breathed as a freeman. The monster, in terror, had fled the premises forever! I should behold it no more! My happiness was supreme! The guilt of my dark deed disturbed me but little. Some few inquiries had been made, but these had been readily answered. Even a search had been instituted—but of course nothing was to be discovered. I looked upon my future felicity as secured.

Upon the fourth day of the assassination, a party of the police came, very unexpectedly, into the house, and proceeded again to make rigorous investigation of the premises. Secure, however, in the inscrutability of my place of concealment, I felt no embarrassment whatever. The officers bade me accompany them in their search. They left no nook or corner unexplored. At length, for the third or fourth time, they descended into the cellar. I quivered not in a muscle. My heart beat calmly as that of one who slumbers in innocence. I walked the cellar from end to end. I folded my arms upon my bosom, and roamed easily to and fro. The police were thoroughly satisfied and prepared to depart. The glee at my heart was too strong to be restrained. I burned to say if but one word, by way of triumph, and to render doubly sure their assurance of my guiltlessness.

"Gentlemen," I said at last, as the party ascended the steps, "I delight to have allayed your suspicions. I wish you all health, and a little more courtesy. By the bye, gentlemen, this—this is a very well constructed house." [In the rabid desire to say something easily, I scarcely knew what I uttered at all.]—"I may say an *excellently* well constructed house. These walls—are you going, gentlemen?—these walls are solidly put together;" and here, through the mere phrenzy of bravado, I rapped heavily, with a cane which I held in my hand, upon that very portion of the brick-work behind which stood the corpse of the wife of my bosom.

But may God shield and deliver me from the fangs of the Arch-Fiend! No sooner had the reverberation of my blows sunk into silence, than I was answered by a voice from within the tomb!—by a cry, at first muffled and broken, like the sobbing of a child, and then quickly swelling into one long, loud, and continuous scream, utterly anomalous and inhuman—a howl—a wailing shriek, half of horror and half of triumph, such as might have arisen only out of hell, conjointly from the throats of the damned in their agony and of the demons that exult in the damnation.

Of my own thoughts it is folly to speak. Swooning, I staggered to the opposite wall. For one instant the party upon the stairs remained motionless, through extremity of terror and of awe. In the next, a dozen stout arms were toiling at the wall. It fell bodily. The corpse, already greatly decayed and clotted with gore, stood erect before the eyes of the spectators. Upon its head, with red extended mouth and solitary eye of fire, sat the hideous beast whose craft had seduced me into murder, and whose informing voice had consigned me to the hangman. I had walled the monster up within the tomb!

1843, 1845

The Purloined Letter[1]

At Paris, just after dark one gusty evening in the autumn of 18—, I was enjoying the twofold luxury of meditation and a meerschaum,[2] in company with my friend C. Auguste Dupin, in his little back library, or book-closet,

---

1. The text is that of the first publication in *The Gift*, a Philadelphia annual dated 1845 but for sale late in 1844. Historians of detective fiction usually cite Poe's three stories about C. Auguste Dupin as the first of the genre. This is the third

Dupin story, the others being "The Murders in the Rue Morgue" (1841) and "The Mystery of Marie Rôget" (1842).
2. Tobacco pipe.

au troisième,[3] *No. 33, Rue Dunôt, Faubourg St. Germain*. For one hour at least we had maintained a profound silence; while each, to any casual observer, might have seemed intently and exclusively occupied with the curling eddies of smoke that oppressed the atmosphere of the chamber. For myself, however, I was mentally discussing certain topics which had formed matter for conversation between us at an earlier period of the evening; I mean the affair of the Rue Morgue, and the mystery attending the murder of Marie Rogêt.[4] I looked upon it, therefore, as something of coincidence, when the door of our apartment was thrown open and admitted our old acquaintance, Monsieur G——, the Prefect of the Parisian police.

We gave him a hearty welcome; for there was nearly half as much of the entertaining as of the contemptible about the man, and we had not seen him for several years. We had been sitting in the dark, and Dupin now arose for the purpose of lighting a lamp, but sat down again, without doing so, upon G.'s saying that he had called to consult us, or rather to ask the opinion of my friend, about some official business which had occasioned a great deal of trouble.

"If it is any point requiring reflection," observed Dupin, as he forebore to enkindle the wick, "we shall examine it to better purpose in the dark."

"That is another of your odd notions," said the Prefect, who had a fashion of calling every thing "odd" that was beyond his comprehension, and thus lived amid an absolute legion of "oddities."

"Very true," said Dupin, as he supplied his visiter with a pipe, and rolled towards him a very comfortable chair.

"And what is the difficulty now?" I asked. "Nothing more in the assassination way, I hope?"

"Oh no; nothing of that nature. The fact is, the business is *very* simple indeed, and I make no doubt that we can manage it sufficiently well ourselves; but then I thought Dupin would like to hear the details of it, because it is so excessively *odd*."

"Simple and odd," said Dupin.

"Why, yes; and not exactly that, either. The fact is, we have all been a good deal puzzled because the affair *is* so simple, and yet baffles us altogether."

"Perhaps it is the very simplicity of the thing which puts you at fault," said my friend.

"What nonsense you *do* talk!" replied the Prefect, laughing heartily.

"Perhaps the mystery is a little *too* plain," said Dupin.

"Oh, good heavens! who ever heard of such an idea?"

"A little *too* self-evident."

"Ha! ha! ha!—ha! ha! ha!—ho! ho! ho!" roared out our visiter, profoundly amused, "oh, Dupin, you will be the death of me yet!"

"And what, after all, *is* the matter on hand?" I asked.

"Why, I will tell you," replied the Prefect, as he gave a long, steady, and contemplative puff, and settled himself in his chair. "I will tell you in a few words; but, before I begin, let me caution you that this is an affair demanding the greatest secrecy, and that I should most probably lose the position I now hold, were it known that I confided it to any one."

"Proceed," said I.

3. Actually the fourth floor (because the French do not count the first, the *rez-de-chaussée*).   4. The earlier cases solved by Dupin.

"Or not," said Dupin.

"Well, then; I have received personal information, from a very high quarter, that a certain document of the last importance, has been purloined from the royal apartments. The individual who purloined it is known; this beyond a doubt; he was seen to take it. It is known, also, that it still remains in his possession."

"How is this known?" asked Dupin.

"It is clearly inferred," replied the Prefect, "from the nature of the document, and from the non-appearance of certain results which would at once arise from its passing *out* of the robber's possession;—that is to say, from his employing it as he must design in the end to employ it."

"Be a little more explicit," I said.

"Well, I may venture so far as to say that the paper gives its holder a certain power in a certain quarter where such power is immensely valuable." The Prefect was fond of the cant of diplomacy.

"Still I do not quite understand," said Dupin.

"No? Well; the disclosure of the document to a third person, who shall be nameless, would bring in question the honour of a personage of most exalted station; and this fact gives the holder of the document an ascendancy over the illustrious personage whose honour and peace are so jeopardized."

"But this ascendancy," I interposed, "would depend upon the robber's knowledge of the loser's knowledge of the robber. Who would dare—"

"The thief," said G, "is the—Minister D——, who dares all things, those unbecoming as well as those becoming a man. The method of the theft was not less ingenious than bold. The document in question—a letter, to be frank—had been received by the personage robbed while alone in the royal *boudoir*. During its perusal she was suddenly interrupted by the entrance of the other exalted personage from whom especially it was her wish to conceal it. After a hurried and vain endeavour to thrust it in a drawer, she was forced to place it, open as it was, upon a table. The address, however, was uppermost, and the contents thus unexposed, the letter escaped notice. At this juncture enters the Minister D——. His lynx eye immediately perceives the paper, recognises the handwriting of the address, observes the confusion of the personage addressed, and fathoms her secret. After some business transactions, hurried through in his ordinary manner, he produces a letter somewhat similar to the one in question, opens it, pretends to read it, and then places it in close juxtaposition to the other. Again he converses, for some fifteen minutes, upon the public affairs. At length, in taking leave, he takes also from the table the letter to which he had no claim. Its rightful owner saw, but, of course, dared not call attention to the act, in the presence of the third personage who stood at her elbow. The minister decamped; leaving his own letter—one of no importance—upon the table."

"Here, then," said Dupin to me, "you have precisely what you demand to make the ascendancy complete—the robber's knowledge of the loser's knowledge of the robber."

"Yes," replied the Prefect; "and the power thus attained has, for some months past, been wielded, for political purposes, to a very dangerous extent. The personage robbed is more thoroughly convinced, every day, of the necessity of reclaiming her letter. But this, of course, cannot be done openly. In fine, driven to despair, she has committed the matter to me."

"Than whom," said Dupin, amid a perfect whirlwind of smoke, "no more sagacious agent could, I suppose, be desired, or even imagined."

"You flatter me," replied the Prefect; "but it is possible that some such opinion may have been entertained."

"It is clear," said I, "as you observe, that the letter is still in possession of the minister; since it is this possession, and not any employment, of the letter, which bestows the power. With the employment the power departs."

"True," said G——; "and upon this conviction I proceeded. My first care was to make thorough search of the minister's hotel; and here my chief embarrassment lay in the necessity of searching without his knowledge. Beyond all things, I have been warned of the danger which would result from giving him reason to suspect our design."

"But," said I, "you are quite *au fait*[5] in these investigations. The Parisian police have done this thing often before."

"O yes; and for this reason I did not despair. The habits of the minister gave me, too, a great advantage. He is frequently absent from home all night. His servants are by no means numerous. They sleep at a distance from their master's apartments, and, being chiefly Neapolitans, are readily made drunk. I have keys, as you know, with which I can open any chamber or cabinet in Paris. For three months a night has not passed, during the greater part of which I have not been engaged, personally, in ransacking the D——Hotel. My honour is interested, and, to mention a great secret, the reward is enormous. So I did not abandon the search until I had become fully satisfied that the thief is a more astute man than myself. I fancy that I have investigated every nook and corner of the premises in which it is possible that the paper can be concealed."

"But is it not possible," I suggested, "that although the letter may be in possession of the minister, as it unquestionably is, he may have concealed it elsewhere than upon his own premises?"

"This is barely possible," said Dupin. "The present peculiar condition of affairs at court, and especially of those intrigues in which D——is known to be involved, would render the instant availability of the document—its susceptibility of being produced at a moment's notice—a point of nearly equal importance with its possession."

"Its susceptibility of being produced?" said I.

"That is to say, of being *destroyed*," said Dupin.

"True," I observed; "the paper is clearly then upon the premises. As for its being upon the person of the minister, we may consider that as out of the question."

"Entirely," said the Prefect. "He has been twice waylaid, as if by footpads, and his person rigorously searched under my own inspection."

"You might have spared yourself this trouble," said Dupin. "D——, I presume, is not altogether a fool, and, if not, must have anticipated these waylayings, as a matter of course."

"Not *altogether* a fool," said G——, "but then he's a poet, which I take to be only one remove from a fool."

"True;" said Dupin, after a long and thoughtful whiff from his meerschaum, "although I have been guilty of certain doggerel myself."

5. Informed about (French).

"Suppose you detail," said I, "the particulars of your search."

"Why the fact is, we took our time, and we searched *every where*. I have had long experience in these affairs. I took the entire building, room by room; devoting the nights of a whole week to each. We examined, first, the furniture of each apartment. We opened every possible drawer; and I presume you know that, to a properly trained police agent, such a thing as a *secret* drawer is impossible. Any man is a dolt who permits a 'secret' drawer to escape him in a search of this kind. The thing is *so* plain. There is a certain amount of bulk—of space—to be accounted for in every cabinet. Then we have accurate rules. The fiftieth part of a line could not escape us. After the cabinets we took the chairs. The cushions we probed with the fine long needles you have seen me employ. From the tables we removed the tops."

"Why so?"

"Sometimes the top of a table, or other similarly arranged piece of furniture, is removed by the person wishing to conceal an article; then the leg is excavated, the article deposited within the cavity, and the top replaced. The bottoms and tops of bed-posts are employed in the same way."

"But could not the cavity be detected by sounding?" I asked.

"By no means, if, when the article is deposited, a sufficient wadding of cotton be placed around it. Besides, in our case, we were obliged to proceed without noise."

"But you could not have removed—you could not have taken to pieces *all* articles of furniture in which it would have been possible to make a deposit in the manner you mention. A letter may be compressed into a thin spiral roll, not differing much in shape or bulk from a large knitting-needle, and in this form it might be inserted into the rung of a chair, for example. You did not take to pieces all the chairs?"

"Certainly not; but we did better—we examined the rungs of every chair in the hotel, and, indeed, the jointings of every description of furniture, by the aid of a most powerful microscope.[6] Had there been any traces of recent disturbance we should not have failed to detect it *instanter*.[7] A single grain of gimlet-dust, or sawdust, for example, would have been as obvious as an apple. Any disorder in the glueing—any unusual gaping in the joints—would have sufficed to insure detection."

"Of course you looked to the mirrors, between the boards and the plates, and you probed the beds and the bed-clothes, as well as the curtains and carpets."

"That of course; and when we had absolutely completed every particle of the furniture in this way, then we examined the house itself. We divided its entire surface into compartments, which we numbered, so that none might be missed; then we scrutinized each individual square inch throughout the premises, including the two houses immediately adjoining, with the microscope, as before."

"The two houses adjoining!" I exclaimed; "you must have had a great deal of trouble."

"We had; but the reward offered is prodigious."

"You include the *grounds* about the houses?"

---

6. A powerful magnifying glass. 7. Instantly (Latin).

"All the grounds are paved with brick. They gave us comparatively little trouble. We examined the moss between the bricks, and found it undisturbed."

"And the roofs?"

"We surveyed every inch of the external surface, and probed carefully beneath every tile."

"You looked among D——'s papers, of course, and into the books of the library?"

"Certainly; we opened every package and parcel; we not only opened every book, but we turned over every leaf in each volume, not contenting ourselves with a mere shake, according to the fashion of some of our police officers. We also measured the thickness of every book-*cover*, with the most accurate admeasurement, and applied to them the most jealous scrutiny of the microscope. Had any of the bindings been recently meddled with, it would have been utterly impossible that the fact should have escaped observation. Some five or six volumes, just from the hands of the binder, we carefully probed, longitudinally, with the needles."

"You explored the floors beneath the carpets?"

"Beyond doubt. We removed every carpet, and examined the boards with the microscope."

"And the paper on the walls?"

"Yes."

"You looked into the cellars?"

"We did; and, as time and labour were no objects, we dug up every one of them to the depth of four feet."

"Then," I said, "you have been making a miscalculation, and the letter is *not* upon the premises, as you suppose."

"I fear you are right there," said the Prefect. "And now, Dupin, what would you advise me to do?"

"To make a thorough re-search of the premises."

"That is absolutely needless," replied G——. "I am not more sure that I breathe than I am that the letter is not at the Hotel."

"I have no better advice to give you," said Dupin. "You have, of course, an accurate description of the letter?"

"Oh yes!"—And here the Prefect, producing a memorandum-book, proceeded to read aloud a minute account of the internal, and especially of the external, appearance of the missing document. Soon after finishing the perusal of this description, he took his departure, more entirely depressed in spirits than I had ever known the good gentleman before.

In about a month afterwards he paid us another visit, and found us occupied very nearly as before. He took a pipe and a chair, and entered into some ordinary conversation. At length I said,—

"Well, but G——, what of the purloined letter? I presume you have at last made up your mind that there is no such thing as overreaching the Minister?"

"Confound him, say I—yes; I made the re-examination, however, as Dupin suggested—but it was all labour lost, as I knew it would be."

"How much was the reward offered, did you say?" asked Dupin.

"Why, a very great deal—a *very* liberal reward—I don't like to say how much, precisely; but one thing I *will* say, that I wouldn't mind giving my individual check for fifty thousand francs to any one who could obtain me that letter. The fact is, it is becoming of more and more importance every day; and the reward has been lately doubled. If it were trebled, however, I could do no more than I have done."

"Why, yes," said Dupin, drawlingly, between the whiffs of his meerschaum, "I really—think, G——, you have not exerted yourself—to the utmost in this matter. You might—do a little more, I think, eh?"

"How?—in what way?"

"Why—puff, puff—you might—puff, puff—employ counsel in the matter, eh?—puff, puff, puff. Do you remember the story they tell of Abernethy?"[8]

"No; hang Abernethy!"

"To be sure! hang him and welcome. But, once upon a time, a certain rich miser conceived the design of spunging upon this Abernethy for a medical opinion. Getting up, for this purpose, an ordinary conversation in a private company, he insinuated his case to the physician, as that of an imaginary individual.

"'We will suppose,' said the miser, 'that his symptoms are such and such; now, doctor, what would *you* have directed him to take?'

"'Take!' said Abernethy, 'why, take *advice*, to be sure.'"

"But," said the Prefect, a little discomposed, "I am *perfectly* willing to take advice, and to pay for it. I would *really* give fifty thousand francs, every *centime* of it, to any one who would aid me in the matter!"

"In that case," replied Dupin, opening a drawer, and producing a check-book, "you may as well fill me up a check for the amount mentioned. When you have signed it, I will hand you the letter."

I was astounded. The Prefect appeared absolutely thunder-stricken. For some minutes he remained speechless and motionless, looking incredulously at my friend with open mouth, and eyes that seemed starting from their sockets; then, apparently recovering himself in some measure, he seized a pen, and after several pauses and vacant stares, finally filled up and signed a check for fifty thousand francs, and handed it across the table to Dupin. The latter examined it carefully and deposited it in his pocket-book; then, unlocking an *escritoire*,[9] took thence a letter and gave it to the Prefect. This functionary grasped it in a perfect agony of joy; opened it with a trembling hand, cast a rapid glance at its contents, and then, scrambling and struggling to the door, rushed at length unceremoniously from the room and from the house, without having uttered a solitary syllable since Dupin had requested him to fill up the check.

When he had gone, my friend entered into some explanations.

"The Parisian police," he said, "are exceedingly able in their way. They are persevering, ingenious, cunning, and thoroughly versed in the knowledge which their duties seem chiefly to demand. Thus when G—— detailed to us his mode of searching the premises at the Hotel D——, I felt the entire confidence in his having made a satisfactory investigation—so far as his labours extended."

"So far as his labours extended?" said I.

"Yes," said Dupin. "The measures adopted were not only the best of their kind, but carried out to absolute perfection. Had the letter been deposited

8. Probably the English surgeon John Abernethy (1764–1831).　　9. Writing desk (French).

within the range of their search, these fellows would, beyond a question, have found it."

I merely laughed—but he seemed quite serious in all that he said.

"The measures, then," he continued, "were good in their kind, and well executed; their defect lay in their being inapplicable to the case, and to the man. A certain set of highly ingenious resources are, with the Prefect, a sort of Procrustean bed,[1] to which he forcibly adapts his designs. But he perpetually errs by being too deep or too shallow, for the matter in hand; and many a schoolboy is a better reasoner than he. I knew one about eight years of age, whose success at guessing in the game of 'even and odd' attracted universal admiration. This game is simple, and is played with marbles. One player holds in his hand a number of these toys; and demands of another whether that number is even or odd. If the guess is right, the guesser wins one; if wrong, he loses one. The boy to whom I allude won all the marbles of the school. Of course he had some principle of guessing; and this lay in mere observation and admeasurement of the astuteness of his opponents. For example, an arrant simpleton is his opponent, and, holding up his closed hand, asks, 'are they even or odd?' Our schoolboy replies 'odd,' and loses; but upon the second trial he wins, for he then says to himself, 'the simpleton had them even upon the first trial, and his amount of cunning is just sufficient to make him have them odd upon the second; I will therefore guess odd;'—he guesses odd, and wins. Now, with a simpleton a degree above the first, he would have reasoned thus: 'this fellow finds that in the first instance I guessed odd, and, in the second, he will propose to himself, upon the first impulse, a simple variation from even to odd, as did the first simpleton; but then a second thought will suggest that this is too simple a variation, and finally he will decide upon putting it even as before. I will therefore guess even;'—he guesses even, and wins. Now this mode of reasoning in the schoolboy, whom his fellows termed 'lucky,'—what, in its last analysis, is it?"

"It is merely," I said, "an identification of the reasoner's intellect with that of his opponent."

"It is," said Dupin; "and, upon inquiring of the boy by what means he effected the *thorough* identification in which his success consisted, I received answer as follows: 'When I wish to find out how wise, or how stupid, or how good, or how wicked is any one, or what are his thoughts at the moment, I fashion the expression of my face, as accurately as possible, in accordance with the expression of his, and then wait to see what thoughts or sentiments arise in my mind or heart, as if to match or correspond with the expression.' This response of the schoolboy lies at the bottom of all the spurious profundity which has been attributed to Rochefoucault, to La Bougive, to Machiavelli, and to Campanella."[2]

"And the identification," I said, "of the reasoner's intellect with that of his opponent, depends, if I understand you aright, upon the accuracy with which the opponent's intellect is admeasured."

---

1. Procrustes, legendary Greek bandit, made his victims fit the bed he bound them to, either by stretching them to the required length or by hacking off any surplus length in the feet and legs.
2. Philosophers of the 15th to 16th centuries who depicted human behavior as ultimately motivated by selfishness. Duc de la Rochefoucauld (1613–

1680) and Jean de la Bruyère (1645–1696), French moralists. Niccolò Macchiavelli (1469–1527) and Tommaso Campanella (1568–1639), Italian philosophers. Poe used a variant spelling for Rouchefoucauld, and his printer probably misread "La Bruyère" as "La Bougive."

"For its practical value it depends upon this," replied Dupin; "and the Prefect and his cohort fail so frequently, first, by default of this identification, and, secondly, by ill-admeasurement, or rather through non-admeasurement, of the intellect with which they are engaged. They consider only their *own* ideas of ingenuity; and, in searching for any thing hidden, advert only to the modes in which *they* would have hidden it. They are right in this much—that their own ingenuity is a faithful representative of that of *the mass;* but when the cunning of the individual felon is diverse in character from their own, the felon foils them, of course. This always happens when it is above their own, and very usually when it is below. They have no variation of principle in their investigations; at best, when urged by some unusual emergency—by some extraordinary reward—they extend or exaggerate their old modes of *practice,* without touching their principles. What, for example, in this case of D——, has been done to vary the principle of action? What is all this boring, and probing, and sounding, and scrutinizing with the microscope, and dividing the surface of the building into registered square inches—what is it all but an exaggeration *of the application* of the one principle or set of principles of search, which are based upon the one set of notions regarding human ingenuity, to which the Prefect, in the long routine of his duty, has been accustomed? Do you not see he has taken it for granted that *all* men proceed to conceal a letter,—not exactly in a gimlet-hole bored in a chair-leg—but, at least, in *some* out-of-the-way hole or corner suggested by the same tenor of thought which would urge a man to secrete a letter in a gimlet-hole bored in a chair-leg? And do you not see also, that such *recherchés*[3] nooks for concealment are adapted only for ordinary occasions, and would be adopted only by ordinary intellects; for, in all cases of concealment, a disposal of the article concealed—a disposal of it in this *recherché* manner,—is, in the very first instance, presumed and presumable; and thus its discovery depends, not at all upon the acumen, but altogether upon the mere care, patience, and determination of the seekers; and where the case is of importance—or, what amounts to the same thing in the policial eyes, when the reward is of magnitude, the qualities in question have *never* been known to fail. You will now understand what I meant in suggesting that, had the purloined letter been hidden any where within the limits of the Prefect's examination—in other words, had the principle of its concealment been comprehended within the principles of the Prefect—its discovery would have been a matter altogether beyond question. This functionary, however, has been thoroughly mystified; and the remote source of his defeat lies in the supposition that the Minister is a fool, because he has acquired renown as a poet. All fools are poets; this the Prefect *feels*; and he is merely guilty of a *non distributio medii*[4] in thence inferring that all poets are fools."

"But is this really the poet?" I asked. "There are two brothers, I know; and both have attained reputation in letters. The Minister I believe has written learnedly on the Differential Calculus. He is a mathematician, and no poet."

"You are mistaken; I know him well; he is both. As poet *and* mathematician, he would reason well; as poet, profoundly; as mere mathematician, he could not have reasoned at all, and thus would have been at the mercy of the Prefect."

---

3. Out of the ordinary, esoteric (French). 4. A logical fallacy.

"You surprise me," I said, "by these opinions, which have been contradicted by the voice of the world. You do not mean to set at naught the well-digested idea of centuries. The mathematical reason has been long regarded as *the* reason *par excellence*."

"'Il y a à parièr,' replied Dupin, quoting from Chamfort, 'que toute idée publique, toute convention reçue, est une sottise, car elle a convenue au plus grand nombre.'[5] The mathematicians, I grant you, have done their best to promulgate the popular error to which you allude, and which is none the less an error for its promulgation as truth. With an art worthy a better cause, for example, they have insinuated the term 'analysis' into application to algebra. The French are the originators of this particular deception; but if a term is of any importance—if words derive any value from applicability—then 'analysis' conveys 'algebra' about as much as, in Latin, *'ambitus'* implies 'ambition,' *'religio'* 'religion,' or *'homines honesti,'* a set of *honourable* men."

"You have a quarrel on hand, I see," said I, "with some of the algebraists of Paris; but proceed."

"I dispute the availability, and thus the value, of that reason which is cultivated in any especial form other than the abstractly logical. I dispute, in particular, the reason educed by mathematical study. The mathematics are the science of form and quantity; mathematical reasoning is merely logic applied to observation upon form and quantity. The great error lies in supposing that even the truths of what is called *pure* algebra, are abstract or general truths. And this error is so egregious that I am confounded at the universality with which it has been received. Mathematical axioms are *not* axioms of general truth. What is true of *relation*—of form and quantity—is often grossly false in regard to morals, for example. In this latter science it is very usually *un*true that the aggregated parts are equal to the whole. In chemistry also the axiom fails. In the consideration of motive it fails; for two motives, each of a given value, have not, necessarily, a value when united, equal to the sum of their values apart. There are numerous other mathematical truths which are only truths within the limits of *relation*. But the mathematician argues, from his *finite truths*, through habit, as if they were of absolutely general applicability—as the world indeed imagines them to be. Bryant,[6] in his very learned 'Mythology,' mentions an analogous source of error, when he says that 'although the Pagan fables are not believed, yet we forget ourselves continually, and make inferences from them as existing realities.' With the algebraist, however, who are Pagans themselves, the 'Pagan fables' *are* believed, and the inferences are made, not so much through lapse of memory, as through an unaccountable addling of the brains. In short, I never yet encountered the mere mathematician who could be trusted out of equal roots, or one who did not clandestinely hold it as a point of his faith $x^2 + px$ was absolutely and unconditionally equal to q. Say to one of these gentlemen, by way of experiment, if you please, that you believe occasions may occur where $x^2 + px$ is *not* altogether equal to q, and, having made him understand what you mean, get out of his reach as speedily as convenient, for, beyond doubt, he will endeavour to knock you down.

5. The odds are that every common notion, every accepted convention, is nonsense, because it has suited itself to the majority (French). Sébastian Roch Nicolas Chamfort (1741–1794), author of *Maximes et Pensées.*

6. Jacob Bryant (1715–1804), English scholar who wrote *A New System, or an Analysis of Antient Mythology* (1774–76).

"I mean to say," continued Dupin, while I merely laughed at his last observations, "that if the Minister had been no more than a mathematician, the Prefect would have been under no necessity of giving me this check. Had he been no more than a poet, I think it probable that he would have foiled us all. I knew him, however, as both mathematician and poet, and my measures were adapted to his capacity, with reference to the circumstances by which he was surrounded. I knew him as a courtier, too, and as a bold *intriguant*. Such a man, I considered, could not fail to be aware of the ordinary policial modes of action. He could not have failed to anticipate—and events have proved that he did not fail to anticipate—the waylayings to which he was subjected. He must have foreseen, I reflected, the secret investigations of his premises. His frequent absences from home at night, which were hailed by the Prefect as certain aids to his success, I regarded only as *ruses*, to afford opportunity for thorough search to the police, and thus the sooner to impress them with the conviction to which G——, in fact, did finally arrive—the conviction that the letter was not upon the premises. I felt, also, that the whole train of thought, which I was at some pains in detailing to you just now, concerning the invariable principle of policial action in searches for articles concealed—I felt that this whole train of thought would necessarily pass through the mind of the Minister. It would imperatively lead him to despise all the ordinary *nooks* of concealment. *He* could not, I reflected, be so weak as not to see that the most intricate and remote recess of his hotel would be as open as his commonest closets to the eyes, to the probes, to the gimlets, and to the microscopes of the Prefect. I saw, in fine, that he would be driven, as a matter of course, to *simplicity*, if not deliberately induced to it as a matter of choice. You will remember, perhaps how desperately the Prefect laughed when I suggested, upon our first interview, that it was just possible this mystery troubled him so much on account of its being so *very* self-evident."

"Yes," said I, "I remember his merriment well. I really thought he would have fallen into convulsions."

"The material world," continued Dupin, "abounds with very strict analogies to the immaterial; and thus some colour of truth has been given to the rhetorical dogma, that metaphor, or simile, may be made to strengthen an argument, as well as to embellish a description. The principle of the *vis inertiæ*,[7] for example, with the amount of *momentum* proportionate with it and consequent upon it, seems to be identical in physics and metaphysics. It is not more true in the former, that a large body is with more difficulty set in motion than a smaller one, and that its subsequent *impetus* is commensurate with this difficulty, than it is, in the latter, that intellects of the vaster capacity, while more forcible, more constant, and more eventful in their movements than those of inferior grade, are yet the less readily moved, and more embarrassed and full of hesitation in the first few steps of their progress. Again: have you ever noticed which of the street signs, over the shop-doors, are the most attractive of attention?"

"I have never given the matter a thought," I said.

"There is a game of puzzles," he resumed, "which is played upon a map. One party playing requires another to find a given word—the name of town,

7. The power of inertia (Latin).

river, state, or empire—any word, in short, upon the motley and perplexed surface of the chart. A novice in the game generally seeks to embarrass his opponents by giving them the most minutely lettered names; but the adept selects such words as stretch, in large characters, from one end of the chart to the other. These, like the over-largely lettered signs and placards of the street, escape observation by dint of being excessively obvious; and here the physical oversight is precisely analogous with the moral inapprehension by which the intellect suffers to pass unnoticed those considerations which are too obtrusively and too palpably self-evident. But this is a point, it appears, somewhat above or beneath the understanding of the Prefect. He never once thought it probable, or possible, that the Minister had deposited the letter immediately beneath the nose of the whole world, by way of best preventing any portion of that world from perceiving it.

"But the more I reflected upon the daring, dashing, and discriminating ingenuity of D——; upon the fact that the document must always have been *at hand*, if he intended to use it to good purpose; and upon the decisive evidence, obtained by the Prefect, that it was not hidden within the limits of that dignitary's ordinary search—the more satisfied I became that, to conceal this letter, the Minister had resorted to the comprehensive and sagacious expedient of not attempting to conceal it at all.

"Full of these ideas, I prepared myself with a pair of green spectacles, and called one fine morning, quite by accident, at the ministerial hotel. I found D—— at home, yawning, lounging, and dawdling as usual, and pretending to be in the last extremity of *ennui*.[8] He is, perhaps, the most really energetic human being now alive—but that is only when nobody sees him.

"To be even with him, I complained of my weak eyes, and lamented the necessity of the spectacles, under cover of which I cautiously and thoroughly surveyed the whole apartment, while seemingly intent only upon the conversation of my host.

"I paid especial attention to a large writing-table near which he sat, and upon which lay confusedly, some miscellanous letters and other papers, with one or two musical instruments and a few books. Here, however, after a long and very deliberate scrutiny, I saw nothing to excite particular suspicion.

"At length my eyes, in going the circuit of the room, fell upon a trumpery fillagree card-rack of pasteboard, that hung dangling by a dirty blue riband, from a little brass knob just beneath the middle of the mantel-piece. In this rack, which had three or four compartments, were five or six visiting-cards, and a solitary letter. This last was much soiled and crumpled. It was torn nearly in two, across the middle—as if a design, in the first instance, to tear it entirely up as worthless, had been altered, or stayed, in the second. It had a large black seal, bearing the D—— cipher *very* conspicuously, and was addressed, in a diminutive female hand, to D——, the minister himself. It was thrust carelessly, and even, as it seemed, contemptuously, into one of the uppermost divisions of the rack.

"No sooner had I glanced at this letter, than I concluded it to be that of which I was in search. To be sure, it was, to all appearance, radically different from the one of which the Prefect had read us so minute a description. Here the seal was large and black, with the D—— cipher; there, it was small

8. Boredom (French).

and red, with the ducal arms of the S—— family. Here, the address, to the minister, was diminutive and feminine; there, the superscription, to a certain royal personage, was markedly bold and decided; the size alone formed a point of correspondence. But, then, the *radicalness* of these differences, which was excessive; the dirt, the soiled and torn condition of the paper, so inconsistent with the *true* methodical habits of D——, and so suggestive of a design to delude the beholder into an idea of the worthlessness of the document; these things, together with the hyper-obtrusive situation of this document, full in the view of every visiter, and thus exactly in accordance with the conclusions to which I had previously arrived; these things, I say, were strongly corroborative of suspicion, in one who came with the intention to suspect.

"I protracted my visit as long as possible, and, while I maintained a most animated discussion with the minister, upon a topic which I knew well had never failed to interest and excite him, I kept my attention really riveted upon the letter. In this examination, I committed to memory its external appearance and arrangement in the rack; and also fell, at length, upon a discovery which set at rest whatever trivial doubt I might have entertained. In scrutinizing the edges of the paper, I observed them to be more *chafed* than seemed necessary. They presented the *broken* appearance which is manifested when a stiff paper, having been once folded and pressed with a folder, is refolded in a reversed direction, in the same creases or edges which had formed the original fold. This discovery was sufficient. It was clear to me that the letter had been turned, as a glove, inside out, re-directed, and re-sealed. I bade the minister good morning and took my departure at once, leaving a gold snuff-box upon the table.

"The next morning I called for the snuff-box, when we resumed, quite eagerly, the conversation of the preceding day. While thus engaged, however, a loud report, as if of a pistol, was heard immediately beneath the windows of the hotel, and was succeeded by a series of fearful screams, and the shoutings of a terrified mob. D—— rushed to a casement, threw it open, and looked out. In the meantime, I stepped to the card-rack, took the letter, put it in my pocket, and replaced it by a *fac-simile*, which I had carefully prepared at my lodgings—imitating the D—— cipher, very readily, by means of a seal formed of bread.

"The disturbance in the street had been occasioned by the frantic behaviour of a man with a musket. He had fired it among a crowd of women and children. It proved, however, to have been without ball, and the fellow was suffered to go his way as a lunatic or a drunkard. When he had gone, D——came from the window, whither I had followed him immediately upon securing the object in view. Soon afterwards I bade him farewell. The pretended lunatic was a man in my own pay."

"But what purpose had you," I asked, "in replacing the letter by a *fac-simile*? Would it not have been better, at the first visit, to have seized it openly, and departed?"

"D——," replied Dupin, "is a desperate man, and a man of nerve. His hotel, too, is not without attendants devoted to his interests. Had I made the wild attempt you suggest, I should never have left the ministerial presence alive. The good people of Paris would have heard of me no more. But I had an object apart from these considerations. You know my political prepossessions. In this matter, I act as a partisan of the lady concerned. For eighteen months the minister has had her in his power. She has now him in hers—since, being unaware that the letter is not in his possession, he will proceed with his exactions as if it was. Thus will he inevitably commit himself, at once, to his political destruction. His downfall, too, will not be more precipitate than awkward. It is all very well to talk about the *facilis descensus Averni*;[9] but in all kinds of climbing, as Catalini[1] said of singing, it is far more easy to get up than to come down. In the present instance I have no sympathy—at least no pity for him who descends. He is that *monstrum horrendum*,[2] an unprincipled man of genius. I confess, however, that I should like very well to know the precise character of his thoughts, when, being defied by her whom the Prefect terms 'a certain personage,' he is reduced to opening the letter which I left for him in the card-rack."

"How? did you put any thing particular in it?"

"Why—it did not seem altogether right to leave the interior blank—that would have been insulting. To be sure, D——, at Vienna once, did me an evil turn, which I told him, quite good-humouredly, that I should remember. So, as I knew he would feel some curiosity in regard to the identity of the person who had outwitted him, I thought it a pity not to give him a clue. He is well acquainted with my MS., and I just copied into the middle of the blank sheet the words—

"'—Un dessein si funeste,
S'il n'est digne d'Atrée, est digne de Thyeste.'

They are to be found in Crébillon's 'Atrée.'"[3]

1844

The Philosophy of Composition[1]

Charles Dickens, in a note[2] now lying before me, alluding to an examination I once made of the mechanism of "Barnaby Rudge," says—"By the way, are you aware that Godwin wrote his 'Caleb Williams' backwards? He first involved his hero in a web of difficulties, forming the second volume, and then, for the first, cast about him for some mode of accounting for what had been done."[3]

I cannot think this the *precise* mode of procedure on the part of Godwin—and indeed what he himself acknowledges, is not altogether in accordance with Mr. Dickens' idea—but the author of "Caleb Williams" was too good an

9. From Virgil's *Aeneid*, book 6: "The descent to Avernus [Hell] is easy."

1. Angelica Catalani (1780–1849), Italian singer.

2. "Dreadful monstrosity" (Virgil's epithet for Polyphemus, the one-eyed man-eating giant, in book 3 of the *Aeneid*).

3. Prosper Jolyot de Crébillon (1674–1762) wrote *Atrée et Thyeste* (1707), in which the Greek mythological figure Thyestes seduces the wife of his brother Atreus, the king of Mycenae; in revenge Atreus murders the three sons of Thyestes and cooks them up to serve to their father at a feast. The quotation reads: "So baneful a scheme, / if not worthy of Atreus, is worthy of Thyestes" (French).

1. Poe wrote this as a lecture in hopes of capitalizing on the success of "The Raven." Poe, an advocate of rational composition rather than romantic effusions, here presents an account of how he wrote "The Raven" that may or may not be factual. In a letter of August 9, 1846, Poe called the essay his "best specimen of analysis." The text here is that of the first printing, in *Graham's Magazine* (April 1846).

2. Letter dated March 6, 1842.

3. William Godwin makes this claim in his 1832 preface to *Caleb Williams* (first published in 1794). As *Barnaby Rudge* was being serialized in 1842, Poe published an analysis of the novel that identified the murderer and correctly predicted the ending.

artist not to perceive the advantage derivable from at least a somewhat similar process. Nothing is more clear than that every plot, worth the name, must be elaborated to its *dénouement*[4] before any thing be attempted with the pen. It is only with the *dénouement* constantly in view that we can give a plot its indispensable air of consequence, or causation, by making the incidents, and especially the tone at all points, tend to the development of the intention.

There is a radical error, I think, in the usual mode of constructing a story. Either history affords a thesis—or one is suggested by an incident of the day—or, at best, the author sets himself to work in the combination of striking events to form merely the basis of his narrative—designing, generally, to fill in with description, dialogue, or autorial comment, whatever crevices of fact, or action, may, from page to page, render themselves apparent.

I prefer commencing with the consideration of an *effect*. Keeping originality *always* in view—for he is false to himself who ventures to dispense with so obvious and so easily attainable a source of interest—I say to myself, in the first place, "Of the innumerable effects, or impressions, of which the heart, the intellect, or (more generally) the soul is susceptible, what one shall I, on the present occasion, select?" Having chosen a novel, first, and secondly a vivid effect, I consider whether it can best be wrought by incident or tone—whether by ordinary incidents and peculiar tone, or the converse, or by peculiarity both of incident and tone—afterward looking about me (or rather within) for such combinations of event, or tone, as shall best aid me in the construction of the effect.

I have often thought how interesting a magazine paper might be written by any author who would—that is to say, who could—detail, step by step, the processes by which any one of his compositions attained its ultimate point of completion. Why such a paper has never been given to the world, I am much at a loss to say—but, perhaps, the autorial vanity has had more to do with the omission than any one other cause. Most writers—poets in especial—prefer having it understood that they compose by a species of fine frenzy[5]—an ecstatic intuition—and would positively shudder at letting the public take a peep behind the scenes, at the elaborate and vacillating crudities of thought—at the true purposes seized only at the last moment—at the innumerable glimpses of idea that arrived not at the maturity of full view—at the fully matured fancies discarded in despair as unmanageable—at the cautious selections and rejections—at the painful erasures and interpolations—in a word, at the wheels and pinions—the tackle for scene-shifting—the step-ladders and demon-traps—the cock's feathers, the red paint and the black patches, which, in ninety-nine cases out of the hundred, constitute the properties of the literary *histrio*.[6]

I am aware, on the other hand, that the case is by no means common, in which an author is at all in condition to retrace the steps by which his conclusions have been attained. In general, suggestions, having arisen pell-mell, are pursued and forgotten in a similar manner.

---

4. The final revelation showing the outcome, or untying, of the plot. From *dénouer* (French), "to untie."
5. The character Theseus's description of the poet in Shakespeare's *Midsummer Night's Dream* 5.1.12: "The poet's eye, in a fine frenzy rolling, / Doth glance from heaven to earth, from earth to heaven / And as imagination bodies forth / The forms of things unknown, the poet's pen / Turns them to shapes, and gives to airy nothing / A local habitation and a name."
6. Artist (Latin).

For my own part, I have neither sympathy with the repugnance alluded to, nor, at any time, the least difficulty in recalling to mind the progressive steps of any of my compositions; and, since the interest of an analysis, or reconstruction, such as I have considered a *desideratum*,[7] is quite independent of any real or fancied interest in the thing analyzed, it will not be regarded as a breach of decorum on my part to show the *modus operandi*[8] by which some one of my own works was put together. I select "The Raven," as the most generally known. It is my design to render it manifest that no one point in its composition is referrible either to accident or intuition—that the work proceeded, step by step, to its completion with the precision and rigid consequence of a mathematical problem.

Let us dismiss, as irrelevant to the poem *per se*, the circumstance—or say the necessity—which, in the first place, gave rise to the intention of composing a poem that should suit at once the popular and the critical taste.

We commence, then, with this intention.

The initial consideration was that of extent. If any literary work is too long to be read at one sitting, we must be content to dispense with the immensely important effect derivable from unity of impression—for, if two sittings be required, the affairs of the world interfere, and every thing like totality is at once destroyed. But since, *ceteris paribus*,[9] no poet can afford to dispense with *any thing* that may advance his design, it but remains to be seen whether there is, in extent, any advantage to counterbalance the loss of unity which attends it. Here I say no, at once. What we term a long poem is, in fact, merely a succession of brief ones—that is to say, of brief poetical effects. It is needless to demonstrate that a poem is such, only inasmuch as it intensely excites, by elevating, the soul; and all intense excitements are, through a psychal necessity, brief. For this reason, at least one half of the "Paradise Lost"[1] is essentially prose—a succession of poetical excitements interspersed, *inevitably*, with corresponding depressions—the whole being deprived, through the extremeness of its length, of the vastly important artistic element, totality, or unity, of effect.

It appears evident, then, that there is a distinct limit, as regards length, to all works of literary art—the limit of a single sitting—and that, although in certain classes of prose composition, such as "Robinson Crusoe,"[2] (demanding no unity,) this limit may be advantageously overpassed, it can never properly be overpassed in a poem. Within this limit, the extent of a poem may be made to bear mathematical relation to its merit—in other words, to the excitement or elevation—again in other words, to the degree of the true poetical effect which it is capable of inducing; for it is clear that the brevity must be in direct ratio of the intensity of the intended effect:—this, with one proviso—that a certain degree of duration is absolutely requisite for the production of any effect at all.

Holding in view these considerations, as well as that degree of excitement which I deemed not above the popular, while not below the critical, taste, I reached at once what I conceived the proper *length* for my intended poem—a length of about one hundred lines. It is, in fact, a hundred and eight.

7. Something to be desired (Latin).
8. Method of procedure (Latin).
9. Other things being equal (Latin).
1. For Poe, John Milton's blank verse epic (1667)

of some 10,500 lines is much too long to be poetry all the way through.
2. Daniel Defoe's novel of shipwreck in the Caribbean (1719).

My next thought concerned the choice of an impression, or effect, to be conveyed: and here I may as well observe that, throughout the construction, I kept steadily in view the design of rendering the work *universally* appreciable. I should be carried too far out of my immediate topic were I to demonstrate a point upon which I have repeatedly insisted, and which, with the poetical, stands not in the slightest need of demonstration—the point, I mean, that Beauty is the sole legitimate province of the poem. A few words, however, in elucidation of my real meaning, which some of my friends have evinced a disposition to misrepresent. That pleasure which is at once the most intense, the most elevating, and the most pure, is, I believe, found in the contemplation of the beautiful. When, indeed, men speak of Beauty, they mean, precisely, not a quality, as is supposed, but an effect—they refer, in short, just to that intense and pure elevation of *soul—not* of intellect, or of heart—upon which I have commented, and which is experienced in consequence of contemplating "the beautiful." Now I designate Beauty as the province of the poem, merely because it is an obvious rule of Art that effects should be made to spring from direct causes—that objects should be attained through means best adapted for their attainment—no one as yet having been weak enough to deny that the peculiar elevation alluded to, is *most readily* attained in the poem. Now the object, Truth, or the satisfaction of the intellect, and the object, Passion, or the excitement of the heart, are, although attainable, to a certain extent, in poetry, far more readily attainable in prose. Truth, in fact, demands a precision, and Passion, a *homeliness* (the truly passionate will comprehend me) which are absolutely antagonistic to that Beauty which, I maintain, is the excitement, or pleasurable elevation, of the soul. It by no means follows from any thing here said, that passion, or even truth, may not be introduced, and even profitably introduced, into a poem—for they may serve in elucidation, or aid the general effect, as do discords in music, by contrast—but the true artist will always contrive, first, to tone them into proper subservience to the predominant aim, and, secondly, to enveil them, as far as possible, in that Beauty which is the atmosphere and the essence of the poem.

Regarding, then, Beauty as my province, my next question referred to the *tone* of its highest manifestation—and all experience has shown that this tone is one of *sadness*. Beauty of whatever kind, in its supreme development, invariably excites the sensitive soul to tears. Melancholy is thus the most legitimate of all the poetical tones.

The length, the province, and the tone, being thus determined, I betook myself to ordinary induction, with the view of obtaining some artistic piquancy which might serve me as a key-note in the construction of the poem—some pivot upon which the whole structure might turn. In carefully thinking over all the usual artistic effects—or more properly *points*, in the theatrical sense—I did not fail to perceive immediately that no one had been so universally employed as that of the *refrain*. The universality of its employment sufficed to assure me of its intrinsic value, and spared me the necessity of submitting it to analysis. I considered it, however, with regard to its susceptibility of improvement, and soon saw it to be in a primitive condition. As commonly used, the *refrain*, or burden, not only is limited to lyric verse, but depends for its impression upon the force of monotone—both in sound and thought. The pleasure is deduced solely from the sense of identity—of repetition. I resolved to diversify, and so vastly heighten, the effect, by adhering, in general, to the monotone of sound, while I continually varied that of thought: that is to say, I determined to produce continuously novel effects, by the variation *of the application* of the *refrain*—the *refrain* itself remaining, for the most part, unvaried.

These points being settled, I next bethought me of the *nature* of my *refrain*. Since its application was to be repeatedly varied, it was clear that the *refrain* itself must be brief, for there would have been an insurmountable difficulty in frequent variations of application in any sentence of length. In proportion to the brevity of the sentence, would, of course, be the facility of the variation. This led me at once to a single word as the best *refrain*.

The question now arose as to the *character* of the word. Having made up my mind to a *refrain*, the division of the poem into stanzas was, of course, a corollary: the *refrain* forming the close to each stanza. That such a close, to have force, must be sonorous and susceptible of protracted emphasis, admitted no doubt: and these considerations inevitably led me to the long *o* as the most sonorous vowel, in connection with *r* as the most producible consonant.

The sound of the *refrain* being thus determined, it became necessary to select a word embodying this sound, and at the same time in the fullest possible keeping with that melancholy which I had predetermined as the tone of the poem. In such a search it would have been absolutely impossible to overlook the word "Nevermore." In fact, it was the very first which presented itself.

The next *desideratum* was a pretext for the continuous use of the one word "nevermore." In observing the difficulty which I at once found in inventing a sufficiently plausible reason for its continuous repetition, I did not fail to perceive that this difficulty arose solely from the pre-assumption that the word was to be so continuously or monotonously spoken by *a human* being—I did not fail to perceive, in short, that the difficulty lay in the reconciliation of this monotony with the exercise of reason on the part of the creature repeating the word. Here, then, immediately arose the idea of a *non*-reasoning creature capable of speech; and, very naturally, a parrot, in the first instance, suggested itself, but was superseded forthwith by a Raven, as equally capable of speech, and infinitely more in keeping with the intended *tone*.

I had now gone so far as the conception of a Raven—the bird of ill omen—monotonously repeating the one word, "Nevermore," at the conclusion of each stanza, in a poem of melancholy tone, and in length about one hundred lines. Now, never losing sight of the object *supremeness*, or perfection, at all points, I asked myself—"Of all melancholy topics, what, according to the *universal* understanding of mankind, is the *most* melancholy?" Death—was the obvious reply. "And when," I said, "is this most melancholy of topics most poetical?" From what I have already explained at some length, the answer, here also, is obvious—"When it most closely allies itself to *Beauty*: the death, then, of a beautiful woman is, unquestionably, the most poetical topic in the world—and equally is it beyond doubt that the lips best suited for such topic are those of a bereaved lover."

I had now to combine the two ideas, of a lover lamenting his deceased mistress and a Raven continuously repeating the word "Nevermore"—I had to combine these, bearing in mind my design of varying, at every turn, the *application* of the word repeated; but the only intelligible model of such combination is that of imagining the Raven employing the word in answer to the queries of the lover. And here it was that I saw at once the opportunity afforded for the effect on which I had been depending—that is to say, the effect of the *variation of application*. I saw that I could make the first query propounded by the lover—the first query to which the Raven should reply "Nevermore"—that I could make this first query a commonplace one—the second less so—the third still less, and so on—until at length the lover, startled from his original *nonchalance* by the melancholy character of the word itself—by its frequent repetition—and by a consideration of the ominous reputation of the fowl that uttered it—is at length excited to superstition, and wildly propounds queries of a far different character—queries whose solution he has passionately at heart—propounds them half in superstition and half in that species of despair which delights in self-torture—propounds them not altogether because he believes in the prophetic or demoniac character of the bird (which, reason assures him, is merely repeating a lesson learned by rote) but because he experiences a phrenzied pleasure in so modeling his questions as to receive from the *expected* "Nevermore" the most delicious because the most intolerable of sorrow. Perceiving the opportunity thus afforded me—or, more strictly, thus forced upon me in the progress of the construction—I first established in mind the climax, or concluding query—that to which "Nevermore" should be in the last place an answer—that in reply to which this word "Nevermore" should involve the utmost conceivable amount of sorrow and despair.

Here then the poem may be said to have its beginning—at the end, where all works of art should begin—for it was here, at this point of my preconsiderations, that I first put pen to paper in the composition of the stanza:

> "Prophet," said I, "thing of evil! prophet still if bird or devil!
> By that heaven that bends above us—by that God we both adore,
> Tell this soul with sorrow laden, if within the distant Aidenn,
> It shall clasp a sainted maiden whom the angels name Lenore—
> Clasp a rare and radiant maiden whom the angels name Lenore."
> Quoth the raven "Nevermore."

I composed this stanza, at this point, first that, by establishing the climax, I might the better vary and graduate, as regards seriousness and importance, the preceding queries of the lover—and, secondly, that I might definitely settle the rhythm, the metre, and the length and general arrangement of the stanza—as well as graduate the stanzas which were to precede, so that none of them might surpass this in rhythmical effect. Had I been able, in the subsequent composition, to construct more vigorous stanzas, I should, without scruple, have purposely enfeebled them, so as not to interfere with the climacteric effect.

And here I may as well say a few words of the versification. My first object (as usual) was originality. The extent to which this has been neglected, in versification, is one of the most unaccountable things in the world. Admitting that there is little possibility of variety in mere *rhythm*, it is still clear that the possible varieties of metre and stanza are absolutely infinite—and yet, *for centuries, no man, in verse, has ever done, or ever seemed to think of doing, an original thing*. The fact is, originality (unless in minds of very unusual force) is by no means a matter, as some suppose, of impulse or intuition. In general, to be found, it must be elaborately sought, and although a positive merit of the highest class, demands in its attainment less of invention than negation.

Of course, I pretend to no originality in either the rhythm or metre of the "Raven." The former is trochaic—the latter is octameter acatalectic, alternating with heptameter catalectic repeated in the *refrain* of the fifth verse, and terminating with tetrameter catalectic. Less pedantically—the feet employed throughout (trochees) consist of a long syllable followed by a short: the first line of the stanza consists of eight of these feet—the second of seven and a half (in effect two-thirds)—the third of eight—the fourth of seven and a half—the fifth the same—the sixth three and a half. Now, each of these lines, taken individually, has been employed before, and what originality the "Raven" has, is in their *combination into stanza*; nothing even remotely approaching this combination has ever been attempted. The effect of this originality of combination is aided by other unusual, and some altogether novel effects, arising from an extension of the application of the principles of rhyme and alliteration.

The next point to be considered was the mode of bringing together the lover and the Raven—and the first branch of this consideration was the *locale*. For this the most natural suggestion might seem to be a forest, or the fields—but it has always appeared to me that a close *circumscription of space* is absolutely necessary to the effect of insulated incident:—it has the force of a frame to a picture. It has an indisputable moral power in keeping concentrated the attention, and, of course, must not be confounded with mere unity of place.

I determined, then, to place the lover in his chamber—in a chamber rendered sacred to him by memories of her who had frequented it. The room is represented as richly furnished—this in mere pursuance of the ideas I have already explained on the subject of Beauty, as the sole true poetical thesis.

The *locale* being thus determined, I had now to introduce the bird—and the thought of introducing him through the window, was inevitable. The idea of making the lover suppose, in the first instance, that the flapping of the wings of the bird against the shutter, is a "tapping" at the door, originated in a wish to increase, by prolonging, the reader's curiosity, and in a desire to admit the incidental effect arising from the lover's throwing open the door, finding all dark, and thence adopting the half-fancy that it was the spirit of his mistress that knocked.

I made the night tempestuous, first, to account for the Raven's seeking admission, and secondly, for the effect of contrast with the (physical) serenity within the chamber.

I made the bird alight on the bust of Pallas,[3] also for the effect of contrast between the marble and the plumage—it being understood that the bust was absolutely *suggested* by the bird—the bust of *Pallas* being chosen, first, as most in keeping with the scholarship of the lover, and, secondly, for the sonorousness of the word, Pallas, itself.

About the middle of the poem, also, I have availed myself of the force of contrast, with a view of deepening the ultimate impression. For example, an air of the fantastic—approaching as nearly to the ludicrous as was admissible—is given to the Raven's entrance. He comes in "with many a flirt and flutter."

Not the *least obeisance made he*—not a moment stopped or stayed he,
  But with mien of lord or lady, perched above my chamber door.

In the two stanzas which follow, the design is more obviously carried out:—

3. Pallas Athena, the Greek goddess of wisdom and the arts.

Then this ebony bird beguiling my sad fancy into smiling
By the *grave and stern decorum of the countenance it wore,*
"Though thy *crest be shorn and shaven* thou," I said, "art sure no craven,
Ghastly grim and ancient Raven wandering from the nightly shore—
Tell me what thy lordly name is on the Night's Plutonian shore!"
     Quoth the Raven "Nevermore."

———

Much I marvelled *this ungainly fowl* to hear discourse so plainly,
Though its answer little meaning—little relevancy bore;
For we cannot help agreeing that no living human being
Ever yet was blessed with seeing bird above his chamber door—
Bird or beast upon the sculptured bust above his chamber door,
     With such name as "Nevermore."

The effect of the *dénouement* being thus provided for, I immediately drop the fantastic for a tone of the most profound seriousness:—this tone commencing in the stanza directly following the one last quoted, with the line,

  But the Raven, sitting lonely on that placid bust, spoke only, etc.

From this epoch the lover no longer jests—no longer sees any thing even of the fantastic in the Raven's demeanor. He speaks of him as a "grim, ungainly, ghastly, gaunt, and ominous bird of yore," and feels the "fiery eyes" burning into his "bosom's core." This revolution of thought, or fancy, on the lover's part, is intended to induce a similar one on the part of the reader—to bring the mind into a proper frame for the *dénouement*—which is now brought about as rapidly and as *directly* as possible.

  With the *dénouement* proper—with the Raven's reply, "Nevermore," to the lover's final demand if he shall meet his mistress in another world—the poem, in its obvious phase, that of a simple narrative, may be said to have its completion. So far, every thing is within the limits of the accountable—of the real. A raven, having learned by rote the single word "Nevermore," and having escaped from the custody of its owner, is driven, at midnight, through the violence of a storm, to seek admission at a window from which a light still gleams—the chamber-window of a student, occupied half in poring over a volume, half in dreaming of a beloved mistress deceased. The casement being thrown open at the fluttering of the bird's wings, the bird itself perches on the most convenient seat out of the immediate reach of the student, who, amused by the incident and the oddity of the visiter's demeanor, demands of it, in jest and without looking for a reply, its name. The raven addressed, answers with its customary word, "Nevermore"—a word which finds immediate echo in the melancholy heart of the student, who, giving utterance aloud to certain thoughts suggested by the occasion, is again startled by the fowl's repetition of "Nevermore." The student now guesses the state of the case, but is impelled, as I have before explained, by the human thirst for self-torture, and in part by superstition, to propound such queries to the bird as will bring him, the lover, the most of the luxury of sorrow, through the anticipated answer "Nevermore." With the indulgence, to the utmost extreme, of this self-torture, the narration, in what I have termed its first or obvious phase, has a natural termination, and so far there has been no overstepping of the limits of the real.

But in subjects so handled, however skilfully, or with however vivid an array of incident, there is always a certain hardness or nakedness, which repels the artistical eye. Two things are invariably required—first, some amount of complexity, or more properly, adaptation; and, secondly, some amount of suggestiveness—some under current, however indefinite of meaning. It is this latter, in especial, which imparts to a work of art so much of that *richness* (to borrow from colloquy a forcible term) which we are too fond of confounding with *the ideal*. It is the *excess* of the suggested meaning—it is the rendering this the upper instead of the under current of the theme—which turns into prose (and that of the very flattest kind) the so called poetry of the so called transcendentalists.

Holding these opinions, I added the two concluding stanzas of the poem—their suggestiveness being thus made to pervade all the narrative which has preceded them. The under-current of meaning is rendered first apparent in the lines—

> "Take thy beak from out *my heart,* and take thy form from off my door!"
> Quoth the Raven "Nevermore!"

It will be observed that the words, "from out my heart," involve the first metaphorical expression in the poem. They, with the answer, "Nevermore," dispose the mind to seek a moral in all that has been previously narrated. The reader begins now to regard the Raven as emblematical—but it is not until the very last line of the very last stanza, that the intention of making him emblematical of *Mournful and Never-ending Remembrance* is permitted distinctly to be seen:

> And the Raven, never flitting, still is sitting, still is sitting,
> On the pallid bust of Pallas just above my chamber door;
> And his eyes have all the seeming of a demon's that is dreaming,
> And the lamplight o'er him streaming throws his shadow on the floor;
> And my soul *from out that shadow* that lies floating on the floor
>   Shall be lifted—nevermore.

1846

ABRAHAM LINCOLN
1809–1865

Abraham Lincoln, the sixteenth president of the United States (1861–65), presided over the bloodiest war in U.S. history—one that preserved the Union and ended slavery. He was also one of the era's great prose stylists. Drawing on his boyhood in Kentucky and Indiana and his young manhood in rural Illinois, he used American traditions of ordinary speech and backwoods humor to great political effect and, in so doing, placed these regional traits at the center of American discourse. At the same time, he was passionately committed to the egalitarian principles of the Declaration of Independence and the spiritual ideals of the Bible, and he would regularly invoke both the Declaration and the Bible when contesting slavery and thinking about the future of the United States. His vision of a national house divided by slavery was of a piece with Harriet Beecher Stowe's domestic and millennial vision, though in his late Civil War speeches, Lincoln was far more magnanimous toward the South than most antislavery writers. With his assassination in 1865, Lincoln, who had been reviled by many in the North and South, came to be regarded almost mystically as a Christ-like figure whose death held out the promise that the great bloodletting of the war would give birth to a redeemed nation.

Lincoln was born on February 12, 1809, in a cabin in Hardin County, Kentucky. His father, Thomas Lincoln, and his mother, Mary Hanks, were barely literate; Lincoln himself attended school only sporadically—probably for no more than a year altogether. Although his access to books was limited, his memory was remarkable; years later he was able to draw on his childhood reading of the King James Bible, Aesop's *Fables*, John Bunyan's *Pilgrim's Progress*, Daniel Defoe's *Robinson Crusoe*, and Mason Locke Weems's *Life of George Washington*. Lincoln never lost his love of reading, adding John Stuart Mill, Lord Byron, Robert Burns, and especially Shakespeare to his list of favorites.

Lincoln spent his impoverished youth in Kentucky and southern Indiana, where his father farmed for a living. His mother died when he was nine, but his stepmother, who soon joined the family with children of her own, seems to have singled him out for special affection; Lincoln later spoke of her as his "angel mother." In 1830 the family moved to Illinois. After trying various jobs, Lincoln decided in the early 1830s to prepare for a career in law. In 1834 he was elected to the first of four terms as an Illinois state legislator. He passed the state bar examination in 1836 and moved the next year to the new state capital in Springfield, where he prospered as a lawyer. In 1842 he married Mary Todd, from a wealthy Kentucky family then residing in Springfield. The couple had four sons, only one of whom survived to adulthood.

The political and historical developments of the 1840s and 1850s that would result in Lincoln's election were complicated, but the central issue was whether slavery would be permitted in the new territories, which eventually would become states. Lincoln was elected to the U.S. Congress in 1846; always concerned with mediating rather than inflaming disputes, he voted against abolitionist measures, which he believed might eventually threaten the Union. At the same time, recalling his own remarkable rise from poverty, he insisted that new territories be kept free as "places for poor people to go and better their condition." He also joined an unsuccessful vote to censure President Polk for engaging in the war against Mexico (1846–48), a war he and many of his legislative colleagues believed to be both unjustified and unconstitutional. He did not run for reelection and it appeared that his political career had come to an end.

By 1854 the two major political parties of the time—the Whigs (to which Lincoln belonged) and the Democrats—had compromised on the extension of slavery into new territories and states. Strong antislavery elements in both parties, however, established independent organizations; and when, in 1854, the Republican Party was organized, Lincoln soon joined it. His new party lost the presidential election of 1856 to the Democrats, but in 1858 Lincoln reentered political life as the Republican candidate in the Illinois senatorial election. He opposed the Democrat Stephen A. Douglas, who had earlier sponsored the Kansas-Nebraska Bill, which left it to new territories to establish their status as slave or free when they achieved statehood. Lincoln may have won the famous series of debates with Douglas, but he lost the election. More important for the future, though, he had gained national recognition for his principled opposition to the extension of slavery and found a theme commensurate with his rapidly intensifying powers of thought and expression. As the "House Divided" speech suggests, Lincoln now added to the often biting satirical humor, and to the logic and natural grace of his earlier utterances, a resonance and moral purpose that mark his emergence as a national political leader and as a master of language.

This reputation was enhanced by the Cooper Union Address in 1860, his first in the East, in which Lincoln disputed the idea that slavery was endorsed by the Founding Fathers; and at the Republican presidential convention he won nomination on the third ballot. Lincoln was elected president of the United States in November 1860; but before he took office on March 4, 1861, seven Southern states had seceded from the Union to form the Confederacy. Little more than a month after his inauguration, the Civil War had begun. True to his long-standing commitment, he devoted himself to the preservation of the Union. To do this he had to develop an overall war strategy, devise a workable command system, and find the right personnel to execute his plans. All of this he was to accomplish by trial and error in the early months of the war. As months turned to years, he had to garner popular support for his purposes by using his extraordinary political and oratorical skills in times of high passion and internal division; in two of his most famous speeches, the Gettysburg Address and the Second Inaugural, he offered an almost biblical vision of a divided, suffering nation that would one day reunite to bring forth "a new birth of freedom."

Lincoln committed himself by degrees to the elimination of slavery throughout the country. Initially, he wished only to contain it; next, he proceeded cautiously with the 1863 Emancipation Proclamation, which freed only the slaves of the seceded Southern states; finally, he took the leading role in the passage of the Thirteenth Amendment, which outlawed slavery everywhere and forever in the United States. Elected to a second term in 1864, he had served scarcely a month of his new term when he was assassinated, while attending a play, by the actor John Wilkes Booth. He died on April 15, 1865. In subsequent weeks, mournful crowds gathered at the various stops on Lincoln's funeral train to pay homage to their fallen leader. Whitman spoke for the multitudes when he eulogized him in "When Lilacs Last in the Dooryard Bloom'd" (1865) as "the sweetest, wisest soul of all my days and lands."

Address Delivered at the Dedication of the Cemetery at Gettysburg, November 19, 1863[1]

Four score and seven years ago our fathers brought forth on this continent, a new nation, conceived in Liberty, and dedicated to the proposition that all men are created equal.

Now we are engaged in a great civil war, testing whether that nation, or any nation so conceived and so dedicated, can long endure. We are met on a great battle-field of that war. We have come to dedicate a portion of that field, as a final resting place for those who here gave their lives that that nation might live. It is altogether fitting and proper that we should do this.

But, in a larger sense, we can not dedicate—we can not consecrate—we can not hallow—this ground. The brave men, living and dead, who struggled here, have consecrated it, far above our poor power to add or detract. The world will little note, nor long remember what we say here, but it can never forget what they did here. It is for us the living, rather, to be dedicated here

1. The source of the text printed here is the fac-simile reproduced in W.F. Barton's *Lincoln at Gettysburg* (1930). Lincoln delivered the address approximately four months after the three-day battle between Robert E. Lee, with seventy thousand Southern troops, and George Gordon Meade, with more than ninety thousand Northern troops. The North was victorious in a battle that left over six thousand dead and thousands injured. Lincoln spoke at Cemetery Hill, which held the Union dead.

to the unfinished work which they who fought here have thus far so nobly advanced. It is rather for us to be here dedicated to the great task remaining before us—that from these honored dead we take increased devotion to that cause for which they gave the last full measure of devotion—that we here highly resolve that these dead shall not have died in vain—that this nation, under God, shall have a new birth of freedom—and that government of the people, by the people, for the people, shall not perish from the earth.

ABRAHAM LINCOLN

1863

Second Inaugural Address, March 4, 1865[1]

At this second appearing to take the oath of the presidential office, there is less occasion for an extended address than there was at the first. Then a statement, somewhat in detail, of a course to be pursued, seemed fitting and proper. Now, at the expiration of four years, during which public declarations have been constantly called forth on every point and phase of the great contest which still absorbs the attention, and engrosses the energies of the nation, little that is new could be presented. The progress of our arms, upon which all else chiefly depends, is as well known to the public as to myself; and it is, I trust, reasonably satisfactory and encouraging to all. With high hope for the future, no prediction in regard to it is ventured.

On the occasion corresponding to this four years ago, all thoughts were anxiously directed to an impending civil war. All dreaded it—all sought to avert it. While the inaugural address was being delivered from this place, devoted altogether to *saving* the Union without war, insurgent agents were in the city seeking to *destroy* it without war—seeking to dissol[v]e the Union, and divide effects, by negotiation. Both parties deprecated war; but one of them would *make* war rather than let the nation survive; and the other would *accept* war rather than let it perish. And the war came.

One eighth of the whole population were colored slaves, not distributed generally over the Union, but localized in the Southern part of it. These slaves constituted a peculiar and powerful interest. All knew that this interest was, somehow, the cause of the war. To strengthen, perpetuate, and extend this interest was the object for which the insurgents would rend the Union, even by war; while the government claimed no right to do more than to restrict the territorial enlargement of it. Neither party expected for the war, the magnitude, or the duration, which it has already attained. Neither anticipated that the *cause* of the conflict might cease with, or even before, the conflict itself should cease. Each looked for an easier triumph, and a result less fundamental and astounding. Both read the same Bible, and pray to the same God; and each invokes His aid against the other. It may seem strange that any men should dare to ask a just God's assistance in wringing

---

1. The text is based on photostats of the original manuscript, owned by the Abraham Lincoln Association. A little more than a month after Lincoln delivered this address, the Civil War came to an end at Appomattox, Virginia, on April 9, when Robert E. Lee formally surrendered to Ulysses S. Grant. Shortly after that, on April 14, Lincoln was fatally shot while attending a play at Ford's Theater in Washington, D.C.

their bread from the sweat of other men's faces; but let us judge not that we be not judged. The prayers of both could not be answered; that of neither has been answered fully. The Almighty has his own purposes. "Woe unto the world because of offences! for it must needs be that offences come; but woe to that man by whom the offence cometh!"[2] If we shall suppose that American Slavery is one of those offences which, in the providence of God, must needs come, but which, having continued through His appointed time, He now wills to remove, and that He gives to both North and South, this terrible war, as the woe due to those by whom the offence came, shall we discern therein any departure from those divine attributes which the believers in a Living God always ascribe to Him? Fondly do we hope—fervently do we pray—that this mighty scourge of war may speedily pass away. Yet, if God wills that it continue, until all the wealth piled by the bond-man's two hundred and fifty years of unrequited toil shall be sunk, and until every drop of blood drawn with the lash, shall be paid by another drawn with the sword, as was said three thousand years ago, so still it must be said "the judgments of the Lord, are true and righteous altogether."[3]

With malice toward none; with charity for all; with firmness in the right, as God gives us to see the right, let us strive on to finish the work we are in; to bind up the nation's wounds; to care for him who shall have borne the battle, and for his widow, and his orphan—to do all which may achieve and cherish a just and lasting peace, among ourselves, and with all nations.

1865

2. Matthew 18.7. 3. Psalm 19.9.

MARGARET FULLER
1810–1850

In their six-volume *History of Woman Suffrage* (1881), the U.S. feminists Elizabeth Cady Stanton, Susan B. Anthony, and Matilda Joslyn Gage declared that Margaret Fuller "possessed more influence upon the thought of American women than any woman previous to her time." By the time of her relatively early death in a shipwreck at the age of forty, she had published approximately three hundred essays and reviews—emerging as one of the best literary critics of her day—as well as a major travel narrative, an important book on women's rights that predated the first women's suffrage convention by several years, and a collection of her writings. She had also edited the *Dial* (the semi-official journal of the Transcendentalists) and become one of the first female columnists and the first female overseas journalist for a U.S. daily newspaper, Horace Greeley's *New York Tribune*. She not only argued for the intellectual equality of women to men but, in her writings and personal life, presented herself as an example of women's abilities. At a time when no institutions of higher learning were open to women, her richly allusive writings displayed a knowledge of literary traditions, history, religion, and political and legal thought that one would associate with a university-educated scholar or teacher; and at a time when women were expected to remain within the domestic sphere—and never under any circumstances to compete with men—her activist public presence and confident persona troubled and fascinated her male friends. Influenced by Emerson's philosophy of self-culture and self-reliance, which she extended to women, Fuller continually challenged herself to move in new directions.

Sarah Margaret Fuller was born at Cambridgeport (now part of Cambridge), Massachusetts, on May 23, 1810, the first of the nine children of Margarett Crane and Timothy Fuller. Her father, a lawyer and four-term congressman, supervised her education, teaching her Latin, Greek, French, and Italian in a rigorous regime involving long hours of study and drill. In an autobiographical account written when she was thirty years old, Fuller complained of the nightmares and headaches that accompanied what she termed her "unnatural" childhood; but a few years later, in "The Great Lawsuit" (1843), she praised the father of "Miranda" (Fuller's fictionalized self-portrait in the essay) for regarding her "as a living mind" and thus freeing her from the culture's strictures against developing female intellect. By the time she was ten, she had read extensively in Virgil, Cicero, Tacitus, Shakespeare, and numerous other classic writers. In 1824, her parents sent her to Miss Susan Prescott's Young Ladies' Seminary in Groton, Massachusetts, a sort of finishing school, which she left after a year, returning to live with her family in Cambridge. During the late 1820s she began to read such influential European romantics as the French novelist and political theorist Germaine de Staël and the German novelist, dramatist, and poet Johann Wolfgang von Goethe. Timothy Fuller moved the family to a farm in Groton in 1833, thus removing Margaret from the Cambridge environment she had come to find so stimulating. She continued with her self-education, however, translating Goethe's drama *Torquato Tasso* and publishing her first essay, "In Defense of Brutus," in an 1834 issue of the *Boston Daily Advertiser & Patriot*.

Fuller wanted to become a full-time writer and translator—activities then opening up to women—but those plans had to be abandoned when her father died of cholera in October 1835. Her mother was sickly, and the bulk of the responsibility for financially supporting the family fell to Fuller. Setting aside her own ambitions, she turned to teaching, first at Bronson Alcott's progressive co-educational Temple School in Boston, and then at the prestigious Greene Street School in Providence, Rhode Island. In her little spare time, she continued her writing and translating, placing several reviews and essays in the *Western Messenger*, and publishing a translation of *Eckermann's Conversations with Goethe* in 1839. Realizing that she would not be able to devote herself to her literary interests while holding a full-time teaching job, she resigned from Greene Street School in 1839—by this time, her siblings were old enough to work—and moved back to Cambridge. To support herself, she established her "Conversations"—paid seminars for elite women of the Boston and Cambridge area in which dialogue, rather than rote learning or lecture, was the dominant pedagogy. These meetings anticipated the women's book-club movement of later in the century and were fondly remembered for years afterward by their participants. Over the next six years the group addressed such topics as Greek mythology, the fine arts, ethics, education, demonology, philosophical idealism, and the intellectual potential of women.

Margaret Fuller, from a daguerreotype made in July 1846. This is the only known photograph of Fuller.

A friend of Emerson's since she first sought him out in 1836, Fuller edited the *Dial* from its founding in 1840 to 1842, while continuing to translate works by and about Goethe. In 1842 she resigned her editorship but kept on with her "Conversations" and writing. She did her first significant traveling in 1843, spending four months with friends touring the Great Lakes, Illinois, and the Wisconsin Territory. Upon her return, she researched the history of the old Northwest territories, wrote over thirty poems, and in 1844 brought out her first full-length book, *Summer on the Lakes, in 1843*, a volume of historical meditations, poetry, and travel narrative, which Edgar Allan Poe hailed as "remarkable." The New York editor Horace Greeley was so impressed with the book that he offered Fuller the position of full-time literary editor of the *New York Tribune*.

Fuller moved to New York City in late 1844, and during the next two years published over two hundred essays in the *Tribune*, including influential reviews of Poe, Hawthorne, Melville, and Frederick Douglass. (She republished a number of these reviews in her 1846 *Papers on Literature and Art*.) She also wrote columns on public questions—what we would now call investigative reporting—addressing such matters as the condition of the blind, of the insane, and of the female prisoners she had visited in New York's Sing Sing prison in late 1844. In 1845 Greeley published her *Woman in the Nineteenth Century*, which expanded her 1843 *Dial* essay "The Great Lawsuit: Man *versus* Men. Woman *versus* Women" into a full-length book. Taken together, the essay and book meditate powerfully on the ways that cultural constructions of gender limited both female and male potential. Providing examples of strong heroines and goddesses from history, literature, and mythology, she sought to inspire women readers to imagine greater possibilities for themselves. She also linked the situation of white domestic women to the situation of the slave, thus developing an overlapping critique of slavery and patriarchy. Lydia Maria Child declared in an 1845 review of *Woman in the Nineteenth Century* that Fuller raised important questions about whether under current conditions love is "a mockery, and marriage a sham." By the late nineteenth century both the book and "The Great Lawsuit" had emerged as landmarks in the history of feminist thought in the United States.

In August 1846, Fuller sailed for Europe, having arranged with Greeley to send back regular dispatches at the rate of ten dollars per column. Arriving first in England, she met the writer and philosopher Thomas Carlyle, whom she had long admired but who disappointed her by his reactionary political views and his cold response to the Italian revolutionary Giuseppe Mazzini, then a political refugee in England. In Paris she met the French woman novelist George Sand, whom she found more satisfactory than Carlyle, and another political revolutionary, the exiled Polish poet Adam Mickiewicz. She next went to Italy, at the time not a unified country but a collection of states—some independent, some controlled by the pope, and some controlled by Austria. Soon after settling in Rome she became romantically involved with Giovanni Angelo Ossoli, a nobleman eleven years her junior who supported the revolutionary cause of Italian unification (Risorgimento) led by Giuseppe Garibaldi and Mazzini. Her dispatches to the *Tribune* recorded her increasing preoccupation with the developing Italian revolution, which she linked to American ideals of republicanism that harked back to the original Roman republic, long her political ideal.

In December of 1847 Fuller became pregnant, but as a Protestant her marriage to the Catholic Ossoli seemed out of the question because of the opposition of his family and the difficulties of getting permission in Italy for an interfaith marriage. Through a dismal rainy season, she covered political events for the *Tribune* and became intimate with the Princess Belgioioso, a leader of the anti-Austrian faction who drew her still more deeply into Italian politics. When cities of northern Italy revolted against the Austrians in March 1848, Fuller described to her New York readers the joyous response of the Roman citizens. Emerson wrote from England urging her to return home before war broke out, but she was not ready to tell her

Massachusetts connections about her pregnancy, and chose instead to wait for the child's birth in the countryside near Rome. Ossoli, who had become a member of the civic guard, was with her when their son, Angelo, was born on September 5. Leaving the baby with a wet nurse—a common practice for the era—Fuller returned to Rome late in November in time to cover the flight of the pope and, early in 1849, the arrival of the Italian nationalist Garibaldi, the proclamation of the Roman Republic, and Mazzini's arrival in Rome as well. The republic lasted less than a year: French troops entered Rome on June 30, 1849, and quickly restored the pope to power. During the bloody siege, Fuller served as the director of the Hospital of the Fate Bene Fratelli, doing heroic work for the wounded revolutionaries.

After the defeat of the republican forces, Fuller moved to Florence with Angelo and Ossoli and began to work on a history of the short-lived Roman Republic. She may have married Ossoli, as his sister later claimed and as she herself stated in some of her letters home. But there was doubt about this among her friends, who may have been just as alarmed by her marriage to a Catholic as by her having a sexual liaison as an unmarried woman. Convinced that she and Ossoli would have better economic prospects in the United States, Fuller arranged passage home, and on May 17, 1850, the three sailed for the United States. On July 19, two months and two days later—sailing ships took many weeks to cross the Atlantic—the ship was wrecked within sight of land off Fire Island, New York, and all three perished. Angelo's body washed ashore. A trunk containing some of Fuller's papers was later recovered, but not her history of Rome. Thoreau traveled to the site and sought vainly for her body; at home, Emerson wrote mournfully in his journal, "I have lost in her my audience." Hawthorne, who had been friends with Fuller during the 1840s, may have had her in mind when creating Hester in *The Scarlet Letter* (1850). Wishing to memorialize her career and yet confused about how to present this unconventional woman to a general audience, Fuller's male friends, who brought out *Memoirs of Margaret Fuller Ossoli* in 1852, emphasized her eccentricities, egotism, and aloofness. But if her refusal to stay within feminine bounds disturbed her male contemporaries, that very nonconformity—an instance of Emerson's own teachings, after all—had been crucial to her achievements as an intellectual and writer.

From The Great Lawsuit: Man *versus* Men. Woman *versus* Women[1]

[FOUR KINDS OF EQUALITY]

Where the thought of equality has become pervasive, it shows itself in four kinds.

The household partnership. In our country the woman looks for a "smart but kind" husband, the man for a "capable, sweet tempered" wife.

The man furnishes the house, the woman regulates it. Their relation is one of mutual esteem, mutual dependence. Their talk is of business, their affection shows itself by practical kindness. They know that life goes more smoothly and cheerfully to each for the other's aid; they are grateful and content. The wife praises her husband as a "good provider," the husband in return compliments her as a "capital housekeeper." This relation is good as far as it goes.

Next comes a closer tie which takes the two forms, either of intellectual companionship, or mutual idolatry. The last, we suppose, is to no one a pleas-

---

1. Reprinted from the *Boston Dial* (July 1843). In 1845 Fuller published a revised, expanded version of this work under the title *Woman in the Nineteenth Century*.

ing subject of contemplation. The parties weaken and narrow one another; they lock the gate against all the glories of the universe that they may live in a cell together. To themselves they seem the only wise, to all others steeped in infatuation, the gods smile as they look forward to the crisis of cure, to men the woman seems an unlovely syren, to women the man an effeminate boy.

The other form, of intellectual companionship, has become more and more frequent. Men engaged in public life, literary men, and artists have often found in their wives companions and confidants in thought no less than in feeling. And, as in the course of things the intellectual development of woman has spread wider and risen higher, they have, not unfrequently, shared the same employment. As in the case of Roland and his wife, who were friends in the household and the nation's councils, read together, regulated home affairs, or prepared public documents together indifferently.

It is very pleasant, in letters begun by Roland and finished by his wife, to see the harmony of mind and the difference of nature, one thought, but various ways of treating it.

This is one of the best instances of a marriage of friendship. It was only friendship, whose basis was esteem; probably neither party knew love, except by name.

Roland was a good man, worthy to esteem and be esteemed, his wife as deserving of admiration as able to do without it. Madame Roland is the fairest specimen we have yet of her class, as clear to discern her aim, as valiant to pursue it, as Spenser's Britomart,[2] austerely set apart from all that did not belong to her, whether as woman or as mind. She is a antetype of a class to which the coming time will afford a field, the Spartan[3] matron, brought by the culture of a book-furnishing age to intellectual consciousness and expansion.

Self-sufficing strength and clear-sightedness were in her combined with a power of deep and calm affection. The page of her life is one of unsullied dignity.

Her appeal to posterity is one against the injustice of those who committed such crimes in the name of liberty. She makes it in behalf of herself and her husband. I would put beside it on the shelf a little volume, containing a similar appeal from the verdict of contemporaries to that of mankind, that of Godwin in behalf of his wife, the celebrated, the by most men detested Mary Wolstonecraft.[4] In his view it was an appeal from the injustice of those who did such wrong in the name of virtue.

Were this little book interesting for no other cause, it would be so for the generous affection evinced under the peculiar circumstances. This man had courage to love and honor this woman in the face of the world's verdict, and of all that was repulsive in her own past history. He believed he saw of what soul she was, and that the thoughts she had struggled to act out were noble. He loved her and he defended her for the meaning and intensity of her inner life. It was a good fact.

Mary Wolstonecraft, like Madame Dudevant[5] (commonly known as George Sand) in our day, was a woman whose existence better proved the need of

2. In Spenser's *The Fairie Queene*, the female knight Britomart represents chastity.
3. Resembling the ancient Greeks known for their austerity and military valor.
4. *Memoirs of the Author of "A Vindication of the Rights of Woman"* (1798) by the English author William Godwin (1756–1836). Mary Wollstone-

craft (1759–1797) married Godwin shortly before her death in childbirth.
5. Amandine Aurore Lucile Dudevant (1804–1876), French Romantic novelist who adopted a male pen name, wore male clothing, and had a succession of male lovers.

some new interpretation of woman's rights, than anything she wrote. Such women as these, rich in genius, of most tender sympathies, and capable of high virtue and a chastened harmony, ought not to find themselves by birth in a place so narrow, that in breaking bonds they become outlaws. Were there as much room in the world for such, as in Spenser's poem for Britomart, they would not run their heads so wildly against its laws. They find their way at last to purer air, but the world will not take off the brand it has set upon them. The champion of the rights of woman found in Godwin one who pleads her own cause like a brother. George Sand smokes, wears male attire, wishes to be addressed as Mon frère;[6] perhaps, if she found those who were as brothers indeed, she would not care whether she were brother or sister.

We rejoice to see that she, who expresses such a painful contempt for men in most of her works, as shows she must have known great wrong from them, in La Roche Mauprat[7] depicting one raised, by the workings of love, from the depths of savage sensualism to a moral and intellectual life. It was love for a pure object, for a steadfast woman, one of those who, the Italian said, could make the stair to heaven.

Women like Sand will speak now, and cannot be silenced; their characters and their eloquence alike foretell an era when such as they shall easier learn to lead true lives. But though such forebode, not such shall be the parents of it. Those who would reform the world must show that they do not speak in the heat of wild impulse; their lives must be unstained by passionate error; they must be severe lawgivers to themselves. As to their transgressions and opinions, it may be observed, that the resolve of Eloisa to be only the mistress of Abelard, was that of one who saw the contract of marriage a seal of degradation.[8] Wherever abuses of this sort are seen, the timid will suffer, the bold protest. But society is in the right to outlaw them till she has revised her law, and she must be taught to do so, by one who speaks with authority, not in anger and haste.

If Godwin's choice of the calumniated authoress of the "Rights of Woman," for his honored wife, be a sign of a new era, no less so is an article of great learning and eloquence, published several years since in an English review, where the writer, in doing full justice to Eloisa, shows his bitter regret that she lives not now to love him, who might have known better how to prize her love than did the egotistical Abelard.

These marriages, these characters, with all their imperfections, express an onward tendency. They speak of aspiration of soul, of energy of mind, seeking clearness and freedom. Of a like promise are the tracts now publishing by Goodwyn Barmby[9] (the European Pariah as he calls himself) and his wife Catharine. Whatever we may think of their measures, we see them in wedlock, the two minds are wed by the only contract that can permanently avail, of a common faith, and a common purpose.

We might mention instances, nearer home, of minds, partners in work and in life, sharing together, on equal terms, public and private interests, and which have not on any side that aspect of offence which characterizes the attitude of the last named; persons who steer straight onward, and in

6. Old friend and colleague (French); literally, "my brother."
7. An 1837 drama by George Sand.
8. In her famous letters written in the 12th century, Eloisa steadfastly refused to marry Abelard, because marriage would force him to give up his teaching of theology within the Church.
9. English publisher (1820–1881) of socialist tracts who founded the London Communist Propaganda Society in 1841.

our freer life have not been obliged to run their heads against any wall. But the principles which guide them might, under petrified or oppressive institutions, have made them warlike, paradoxical, or, in some sense, Pariahs. The phenomenon is different, the last the same, in all these cases. Men and women have been obliged to build their house from the very foundation. If they found stone ready in the quarry, they took it peaceably, otherwise they alarmed the country by pulling down old towers to get materials.

These are all instances of marriage as intellectual companionship. The parties meet mind to mind, and a mutual trust is excited which can buckler them against a million. They work together for a common purpose, and, in all these instances, with the same implement, the pen.

A pleasing expression in this kind is afforded by the union in the names of the Howitts.[1] William and Mary Howitt we heard named together for years, supposing them to be brother and sister; the equality of labors and reputation, even so, was auspicious, more so, now we find them man and wife. In his late work on Germany, Howitt mentions his wife with pride, as one among the constellation of distinguished English women, and in a graceful, simple manner.

In naming these instances we do not mean to imply that community of employment is an essential to union of this sort, more than to the union of friendship. Harmony exists no less in difference than in likeness, if only the same key-note govern both parts. Woman the poem, man the poet; woman the heart, man the head; such divisions are only important when they are never to be transcended. If nature is never bound down, nor the voice of inspiration stifled, that is enough. We are pleased that women should write and speak, if they feel the need of it, from having something to tell; but silence for a hundred years would be as well, if that silence be from divine command, and not from man's tradition.

While Goetz von Berlichingen[2] rides to battle, his wife is busy in the kitchen; but difference of occupation does not prevent that community of life, that perfect esteem, with which he says,

"Whom God loves, to him gives he such a wife!"

Manzoni thus dedicates his Adelchi.[3]

"To his beloved and venerated wife, Enrichetta Luigia Blondel, who, with conjugal affections and maternal wisdom, has preserved a virgin mind, the author dedicates this Adelchi, grieving that he could not, by a more splendid and more durable monument, honor the dear name and the memory of so many virtues."

The relation could not be fairer, nor more equal, if she too had written poems. Yet the position of the parties might have been the reverse as well; the woman might have sung the deeds, given voice to the life of the man, and beauty would have been the result, as we see in pictures of Arcadia[4] the nymph singing to the shepherds, or the shepherd with his pipe allures the nymphs, either makes a good picture. The sounding lyre requires not mus-

---

1. William Howitt (1792–1879) and Mary Howitt (1799–1888), prolific British authors and translators.
2. German knight (1481–1562), a sort of Robin Hood, familiar to Fuller from Goethe's play *Göetz*

von Berlichingen (1773).
3. A tragedy (1822) by Alessandro Manzoni (1785–1873), Italian writer.
4. Pastoral district of the Peloponnesus in Greece, symbolic of rustic simplicity and contentment.

cular strength, but energy of soul to animate the hand which can control it. Nature seems to delight in varying her arrangements, as if to show that she will be fettered by no rule, and we must admit the same varieties that she admits.

I have not spoken of the higher grade of marriage union, the religious, which may be expressed as pilgrimage towards a common shrine. This includes the others; home sympathies, and household wisdom, for these pilgrims must know how to assist one another to carry their burdens along the dusty way; intellectual communion, for how sad it would be on such a journey to have a companion to whom you could not communicate thoughts and aspirations, as they sprang to life, who would have no feeling for the more and more glorious prospects that open as we advance, who would never see the flowers that may be gathered by the most industrious traveler. It must include all these. Such a fellow pilgrim Count Zinzendorf[5] seems to have found in his countess of whom he thus writes:

"Twenty-five years' experience has shown me that just the help-mate whom I have is the only one that could suit my vocation, Who else could have so carried through my family affairs? Who lived so spotlessly before the world? Who so wisely aided me in my rejection of a dry morality? Who so clearly set aside the Pharisaism[6] which, as years passed, threatened to creep in among us? Who so deeply discerned as to the spirits of delusion which sought to bewilder us? Who would have governed my whole economy so wisely, richly, and hospitably when circumstances commanded? Who have taken indifferently the part of servant or mistress, without on the one side affecting an especial spirituality, on the other being sullied by any worldly pride? Who, in a community where all ranks are eager to be on a level, would, from wise and real causes, have known how to maintain inward and outward distinctions? Who, without a murmur, have seen her husband encounter such dangers by land and sea? Who undertaken with him and sustained such astonishing pilgrimages? Who amid such difficulties always held up her head, and supported me? Who found so many hundred thousands and acquitted them on her own credit? And, finally, who, of all human beings, would so well understand and interpret to others my inner and outer being as this one, of such nobleness in her way of thinking, such great intellectual capacity, and free from the theological perplexities that enveloped me?"

An observer[7] adds this testimony.

"We may in many marriages regard it as the best arrangement, if the man has so much advantage over his wife that she can, without much thought of her own, be, by him, led and directed, as by a father. But it was not so with the Count and his consort. She was not made to be a

---

5. Nikolas Ludwig, Count von Zinzendorf (1700–1760), German leader of the Moravian Church, or the Bohemian Brethren, a Catholic heretical group founded in Bohemia around 1722, influential both in Europe and in the Moravian settlements in the American colonies, which he visited.
6. Self-righteous hypocrisy, from the Jewish sect whom Jesus condemned as whitened sepulchres (Matthew 23.27), "which indeed appear beautiful outward, but are within full of dead men's bones, and of all uncleanness."
7. Spangenberg [Fuller's note]. August Gotlieb Spangenberg (1704–1792), successor to Count von Zinzendorf. See above, n. 5.

copy; she was an original; and, while she loved and honored him, she thought for herself on all subjects with so much intelligence, that he could and did look on her as a sister and friend also."

Such a woman is the sister and friend of all beings, as the worthy man is their brother and helper.

[THE GREAT RADICAL DUALISM]

The especial genius of woman I believe to be electrical in movement, intuitive in function, spiritual in tendency. She is great not so easily in classification, or re-creation, as in an instinctive seizure of causes, and a simple breathing out of what she receives that has the singleness of life, rather than the selecting or energizing of art.

More native to her is it to be the living model of the artist, than to set apart from herself any one form in objective reality; more native to inspire and receive the poem than to create it. In so far as soul is in her completely developed, all soul is the same; but as far as it is modified in her as woman, it flows, it breathes, it sings, rather than deposits soil, or finishes work, and that which is especially feminine flushes in blossom the face of earth, and pervades like air and water all this seeming solid globe, daily renewing and purifying its life. Such may be the especially feminine element, spoken of as Femality. But it is no more the order of nature that it should be incarnated pure in any form, than that the masculine energy should exist unmingled with it in any form.

Male and female represent the two sides of the great radical dualism. But, in fact, they are perpetually passing into one another. Fluid hardens to solid, solid rushes to fluid. There is no wholly masculine man, no purely feminine woman.

History jeers at the attempts of physiologists to bind great original laws by the forms which flow from them. They make a rule; they say from observation what can and cannot be. In vain! Nature provides exceptions to every rule. She sends women to battle, and sets Hercules spinning;[8] she enables women to bear immense burdens, cold, and frost; she enables the man, who feels maternal love, to nourish his infant like a mother. Of late she plays still gayer pranks. Not only she deprives organizations, but organs, of a necessary end. She enables people to read with the top of the head, and see with the pit of the stomach. Presently she will make a female Newton, and a male Syren.[9]

Man partakes of the feminine in the Apollo, woman of the Masculine as Minerva.

Let us be wise and not impede the soul. Let her work as she will. Let us have one creative energy, one incessant revelation. Let it take what form it will, and let us not bind it by the past to man or woman, black or white. Jove sprang from Rhea, Pallas from Jove.[1] So let it be.

---

8. I.e., sets the strongest men to domestic tasks.
9. In this inversion of sexual stereotypes, a male would be as alluring as the Syrens (or Sirens), Greek sea nymphs who lured mariners into shipwreck on the rocks surrounding their island. Isaac Newton (1642–1727), English

mathematician.
1. In Greek mythology, Rhea, the sister and wife of Cronus, and mother of Zeus (known to the Romans as Jove). Pallas Athena sprang from Jove's skull, fully grown and fully armed.

If it has been the tendency of the past remarks to call woman rather to the Minerva side,—if I, unlike the more generous writer, have spoken from society no less than the soul,—let it be pardoned. It is love that has caused this, love for many incarcerated souls, that might be freed could the idea of religious self-dependence be established in them, could the weakening habit of dependence on others be broken up.

Every relation, every gradation of nature, is incalculably precious, but only to the soul which is poised upon itself, and to whom no loss, no change, can bring dull discord, for it is in harmony with the central soul.

If any individual live too much in relations, so that he becomes a stranger to the resources of his own nature, he falls after a while into a distraction, or imbecility, from which he can only be cured by a time of isolation, which gives the renovating fountains time to rise up. With a society it is the same. Many minds, deprived of the traditionary or instinctive means of passing a cheerful existence, must find help in self-impulse or perish. It is therefore that while any elevation, in the view of union, is to be hailed with joy, we shall not decline celibacy as the great fact of the time. It is one from which no vow, no arrangement, can at present save a thinking mind. For now the rowers are pausing on their oars, they wait a change before they can pull together. All tends to illustrate the thought of a wise contemporary. Union is only possible to those who are units. To be fit for relations in time, souls, whether of man or woman, must be able to do without them in the spirit.

It is therefore that I would have woman lay aside all thought, such as she habitually cherishes, of being taught and led by men. I would have her, like the Indian girl, dedicate herself to the Sun, the Sun of Truth, and go no where if his beams did not make clear the path. I would have her free from compromise, from complaisance, from helplessness, because I would have her good enough and strong enough to love one and all beings, from the fulness, not the poverty of being.

Men, as at present instructed, will not help this work, because they also are under the slavery of habit. I have seen with delight their poetic impulses. A sister is the fairest ideal, and how nobly Wordsworth, and even Byron, have written of a sister.[2]

There is no sweeter sight than to see a father with his little daughter. Very vulgar men become refined to the eye when leading a little girl by the hand. At that moment the right relation between the sexes seems established, and you feel as if the man would aid in the noblest purpose, if you ask him in behalf of his little daughter. Once two fine figures stood before me, thus. The father of very intellectual aspect, his falcon eye softened by affection as he looked down on his fair child, she the image of himself, only more graceful and brilliant in expression. I was reminded of Southey's Kehama,[3] when lo, the dream was rudely broken. They were talking of education, and he said.

"I shall not have Maria brought too forward. If she knows too much, she will never find a husband; superior women hardly ever can."

---

2. Fuller alludes to the various tributes by William Wordsworth to his sister Dorothy and Lord Byron to his half-sister Augusta Leigh.

3. *The Curse of Kehama* (1810), by the English writer Robert Southey (1774–1843).

"Surely," said his wife, with a blush, "you wish Maria to be as good and wise as she can, whether it will help her to marriage or not."

"No," he persisted, "I want her to have a sphere and a home, and some one to protect her when I am gone."

It was a trifling incident, but made a deep impression. I felt that the holiest relations fail to instruct the unprepared and perverted mind. If this man, indeed, would have looked at it on the other side, he was the last that would have been willing to have been taken himself for the home and protection he could give, but would have been much more likely to repeat the tale of Alcibiades[4] with his phials.

But men do *not* look at both sides, and women must leave off asking them and being influenced by them, but retire within themselves, and explore the groundwork of being till they find their peculiar secret. Then when they come forth again, renovated and baptized, they will know how to turn all dross to gold, and will be rich and free though they live in a hut, tranquil, if in a crowd. Then their sweet singing shall not be from passionate impulse, but the lyrical overflow of a divine rapture, and a new music shall be elucidated from this many-chorded world.

Grant her then for a while the armor and the javelin.[5] Let her put from her the press of other minds and meditate in virgin loneliness. The same idea shall reappear in due time as Muse, or Ceres,[6] the all-kindly, patient Earth-Spirit.

I tire every one with my Goethean illustrations. But it cannot be helped.

Goethe, the great mind which gave itself absolutely to the leadings of truth, and let rise through him the waves which are still advancing through the century, was its intellectual prophet. Those who know him, see, daily, his thought fulfilled more and more, and they must speak of it, till his name weary and even nauseate, as all great names have in their time. And I cannot spare the reader, if such there be, his wonderful sight as to the prospects and wants of women.

As his Wilhelm grows in life and advances in wisdom, he becomes acquainted with women of more and more character, rising from Mariana to Macaria.[7]

Macaria, bound with the heavenly bodies in fixed revolutions, the centre of all relations, herself unrelated, expresses the Minerva side.

Mignon, the electrical, inspired lyrical nature.

All these women, though we see them in relations, we can think of as unrelated. They all are very individual, yet seem nowhere restrained. They satisfy for the present, yet arouse an infinite expectation.

The economist Theresa, the benevolent Natalia, the fair Saint, have chosen a path, but their thoughts are not narrowed to it. The functions of life to them are not ends, but suggestions.

Thus to them all things are important, because none is necessary. Their different characters have fair play, and each is beautiful in its minute indications, for nothing is enforced or conventional, but everything, however slight, grows from the essential life of the being.

---

4. Athenian general (c. 450–404 B.C.E.), who was convicted for drunkenly imitating sacred rituals.
5. The weapons of Athena, Greek goddess of wisdom.
6. The Roman goddess of agriculture.

7. Feminine characters in Johann Wolfgang von Goethe's *Wilhelm Meister's Apprenticeship* (1796); other female characters from the same book are named just below.

Mignon and Theresa wear male attire when they like, and it is graceful for them to do so, while Macaria is confined to her arm chair behind the green curtain, and the Fair Saint could not bear a speck of dust on her robe.

All things are in their places in this little world because all is natural and free, just as "there is room for everything out of doors." Yet all is rounded in by natural harmony which will always arise where Truth and Love are sought in the light of freedom.

Goethe's book bodes an era of freedom like its own, of "extraordinary generous seeking," and new revelations. New individualities shall be developed in the actual world, which shall advance upon it as gently as the figures come out upon his canvass.

A profound thinker has said "no married woman can represent the female world, for she belongs to her husband. The idea of woman must be represented by a virgin."

But that is the very fault of marriage, and of the present relation between the sexes, that the woman does belong to the man, instead of forming a whole with him. Were it otherwise there would be no such limitation to the thought.

Woman, self-centred, would never be absorbed by any relation; it would be only an experience to her as to man. It is a vulgar error that love, *a* love to woman is her whole existence; she also is born for Truth and Love in their universal energy. Would she but assume her inheritance, Mary would not be the only Virgin Mother. Not Manzoni[8] alone would celebrate in his wife the virgin mind with the maternal wisdom and conjugal affections. The soul is ever young, ever virgin.

And will not she soon appear? The woman who shall vindicate their birthright for all women; who shall teach them what to claim, and how to use what they obtain? Shall not her name be for her era Victoria, for her country and her life Virginia?[9] Yet predictions are rash; she herself must teach us to give her the fitting name.

1843

---

8. Another allusion to the preface to Manzoni's *Adelchi*.
9. I.e., shall not her character include power (such us made Victoria so fit a name for a queen) and purity?

Slavery, Race, and the Making of American Literature

In 1820 the English critic Sidney Smith became exasperated by the boasting of American literary nationalists, and in the pages of the *Edinburgh Review* he famously asked: "In the four quarters of the globe, who reads an American book? or goes to an American play? or looks at an American picture or statue?" His questions about Americans' self-proclaimed literary, cultural, and national superiority culminated with the most withering question of all: "Finally, under which of the old tyrannical governments of Europe is every sixth man a Slave, whom his fellow-creatures may buy and sell and torture?" For Smith, the making of American literature and culture could not be separated from the making of the nation itself. The paradoxical fact that a nation founded on the principles of equality would develop into a slave-holding republic was not lost on writers of the early national and antebellum period. The vast majority of the writers in this volume of *The Norton Anthology of American Literature* confronted issues of slavery and race at some point during their careers. Whether central to their writings, as was the case with Douglass, early Harriet Beecher Stowe, William Wells Brown, and others, or of peripheral interest, as was true, say, for Sedgwick and Fern, slavery could not be ignored. Tensions between the realities of slavery and the ideals of freedom inform much writing of the period.

The selections on slavery and race offered here take off from Thomas Jefferson, author of the first draft of the Declaration of Independence, who coined many of its most memorable phrases. Jefferson's *Notes on the State of Virginia* celebrated the democratic ideals of the Declaration while making clear that he regarded those ideals as best realized by whites. In the classificatory and hierarchical mode of the Enlightenment period, he presents black people as inferior to white people. Though he leaves the question of race open to further empirical analysis, his observations nevertheless helped give rise to the racial ethnological "science" of the nineteenth century, which invariably presented whites as superior to blacks. African American writers regularly sought to counter such claims, and in his *Appeal*, David Walker directly responds, or talks back, to Jefferson. Much African American writing of the period, and indeed much antislavery writing of the period, as we can see from the selection by William Lloyd Garrison, sought to abolish slavery and challenge the hierarchical claims of the racial ethnologists by invoking (or reclaiming) the principles of the Declaration. These principles were also insisted on by writers such as Emerson, Melville, Thoreau, and Whitman as they prodded readers to comprehend their own "enslavement" to cultural conventions. As Ishmael remarks at the opening of *Moby-Dick*: "Who aint a slave?" For many women writers of the period, from Lydia Maria Child to Harriet Beecher Stowe, slavery also raised questions about patriarchy and women's rights. As the selections from Angelina Grimké and Sojourner Truth suggest, women reformers saw themselves as especially qualified to contest slavery, which they regarded both as a specific institution in the slave South and as one of many manifestations of patriarchal power.

The best-selling literary work of the antebellum period was Harriet Beecher Stowe's antislavery novel *Uncle Tom's Cabin*; published in 1852, it sold around one million copies by the end of the decade. Inspired by feminist-abolitionists like Angelina Grimké, Stowe emphasized the importance of women to antislavery reform. In the manner of David Walker, Frederick Douglass, and numerous other African American writers, she lamented the unfinished work of the American Revolution by having the rebellious slave George Harris invoke the ideals of the Declaration. Like many Americans of the time, Stowe, even in a novel attacking slavery, seemed to accept notions of racial difference, presenting whites as unduly aggressive and blacks as domestic and religious to an extreme. The novel polarized the nation, spawning numerous other antislavery works in the North, along with a number of proslavery, anti–*Uncle Tom's Cabin* writings in the South. The debates on slavery exerted an especially strong influence on the literature of the 1840s and 1850s. Melville wrote a novella, "Benito Cereno," about a slave rebellion; Whitman in "Song of Myself" imagined himself offering succor to a fugitive slave; and Thoreau in "Slavery in Massachusetts" conceived of a Massachusetts that supported the Fugitive Slave Law of 1850 as a version of hell. Race, too, infused writings of the period, even texts that may not seem to be overtly about race. If whiteness was the culture's default and "superior" category of human existence, then, for many white writers blackness posed the threat (and sometimes appeal) of a dangerous otherness. Thus Poe's "The Black Cat" or Hawthorne's presentation of the "black" Chillingworth and Mistress Hibbens in *The Scarlet Letter* may well be inflected by anxieties about race.

In 1857, the Supreme Court ruled in the case of *Dred Scott v. Sanford* that blacks could never become U.S. citizens and were inferior to whites. That ruling, which robbed Jefferson's Declaration of Independence of its ambiguities and potential, made clear that the debates on slavery and race were debates about the nation. In the final selection here, the black nationalist Martin R. Delany, as if anticipating the Dred Scott decision, argues in his 1854 "Political Destiny" that disenfranchised African Americans should consider leaving the United States. Similarly, in William Wells Brown's *Clotel*, the surviving black characters choose to live in Europe; in Frederick Douglass's "The Heroic Slave," the black rebel Madison Washington ends up in Nassau. And though Harriet Jacobs manages to escape from slavery to New York City, she presents herself at the end of *Incidents in the Life of a Slave Girl* as continuing to live in a "free" state that is not as hospitable to black people as England. Most African American leaders committed themselves to the Civil War effort, but the problems raised by slavery and racism in the antebellum period would continue to engage writers of the Reconstruction era and beyond.

THOMAS JEFFERSON

The Declaration of Independence, drafted in 1776 by the Virginian Thomas Jefferson (1743–1826), declared that "all men are created equal." Those resonant words helped inspire the American Revolution and the subsequent development of the nation's democratic institutions. Several years after drafting the Declaration, Jefferson explored the possibility of ending slavery in Virginia, and at various times in his life he wrote about slavery as an evil, remarking in his 1787 *Notes on the State of Virginia*, for example, that the "whole commerce between master and slave is a perpetual exercise of the most boisterous passions, the most unremitting despotism on the one part, and degrading submission on the other." Yet Jefferson, the nation's third president (1801–9), was a slaveowner who, recent DNA evidence suggests, had at least one child with his slave Sally Hemings; at his death, he manumitted only slaves in the Hemings family. Some therefore view him as a hypocrite who celebrated human liberty while defending Southerners' rights to enslave black people; others regard him as a visionary Founding Father who, despite being influenced by the racist ideologies current in his day, gave the nation's democratic ideals their most powerful written expression. At the time that he wrote *Notes on the State of Virginia*, a book intended primarily for European readers, Jefferson disapproved of slavery, but his antislavery views were grounded in beliefs in whites' superiority to blacks. In later life, as he became economically dependent on his slaves, he became more of a defender of the South's rights to own slaves, though he hoped for a national future in which slavery would come to an end and blacks would be colonized to other countries. As the subsequent selection from David Walker makes clear, the free blacks of the antebellum period were particularly troubled by Jefferson's writings, even as they sought to reinvigorate the principles of his Declaration. The selection from *Notes* is taken from *The Works of Thomas Jefferson* (1904), ed. Paul Leicester Ford.

From Notes on the State of Virginia

* * *

It will probably be asked, Why not retain and incorporate the blacks into the state, and thus save the expence of supplying by importation of white settlers, the vacancies they will leave?[1] Deep rooted prejudices entertained by the whites; ten thousand recollections, by the blacks, of the injuries they have sustained; new provocations; the real distinctions which nature has made; and many other circumstances will divide us into parties, and produce convulsions, which will probably never end but in the extermination of the one or the other race.—To these objections, which are political, may be added others, which are physical and moral. The first difference which strikes us is that of colour. Whether the black of the negro resides in the reticular membrane between the skin and scarfskin,[2] or in the scarfskin itself; whether it proceeds from the colour of the blood, the colour of the bile, or from that of some other secretion, the difference is fixed in nature, and is as real as if its seat and cause were better known to us. And is this difference of no importance? Is it not the foundation of a greater or less share of beauty in the two races? Are not the fine mixtures of red and white, the expressions of every passion by greater or less suffusions of colour in the one, preferable to that eternal monotony, which reigns in the countenances, that immovable veil of black which covers all the emotions of the other race? Add to these, flowing hair, a more elegant symmetry of form, their own judgment in favour of the whites, declared by their preference of them as uniformly as in the preference of the Oran ootan[3] for the black woman over those of his own species. The circumstance of superior beauty, is thought worthy attention in the propagation of our horses, dogs, and other domestic animals; why not in that of man? Besides those of colour, figure and hair, there are other physical distinctions proving a difference of race. They have less hair on the face and body. They secrete less by the kidnies, and more by the glands of the skin, which gives them a very strong and disagreeable odour. This greater degree of transpiration, renders them more tolerant of heat, and less so of cold than the whites. Perhaps too a difference of structure in

1. In the text, Jefferson had just proposed the possibility of emancipating some of the slaves and shipping them "to other parts of the world."

2. The outermost layer of skin.
3. Orangutan.

the pulmonary apparatus, which a late ingenious experimentalist[4] has discovered to be the principal regulator of animal heat, may have disabled them from extricating, in the act of inspiration, so much of that fluid from the outer air, or obliged them in expiration, to part with more of it. They seem to require less sleep. A black after hard labour through the day, will be induced by the slightest amusements to sit up till midnight or later, though knowing he must be out with the first dawn of the morning. They are at least as brave, and more adventuresome. But this may perhaps proceed from a want of forethought, which prevents their seeing a danger till it be present. When present, they do not go through it with more coolness or steadiness than the whites. They are more ardent after their female; but love seems with them to be an eager desire, than a tender delicate mixture of sentiment and sensation. Their griefs are transient. Those numberless afflictions, which render it doubtful whether heaven has given life to us in mercy or in wrath, are less felt, and sooner forgotten with them. In general, their existence appears to participate more of sensation than reflection. To this must be ascribed their disposition to sleep when abstracted from their diversions, and unemployed in labour. An animal whose body is at rest, and who does not reflect, must be disposed to sleep of course. Comparing them by their faculties of memory, reason, and imagination, it appears to me that in memory they are equal to the whites; in reason much inferior, as I think one could scarcely be found capable of tracing and comprehending the investigations of Euclid:[5] and that in imagination they are dull, tasteless, and anomalous. It would be unfair to follow them to Africa for this investigation. We will consider them here, on the same stage with the whites, and where the facts are not apochryphal on which a judgment is to be formed. It will be right to make great allowances for the difference of condition, of education, of conversation, of the sphere in which they move. Many millions of them have been brought to, and born in America. Most of them, indeed, have been confined to tillage, to their own homes, and their own society: yet many have been so situated, that they might have availed themselves of the conversation of their masters; many have been brought up to the handicraft arts, and from that circumstance have always been associated with the whites. Some have been liberally educated, and all have lived in countries where the arts and sciences are cultivated to a considerable degree, and have had before their eyes samples of the best works from abroad. The Indians, with no advantages of this kind, will often carve figures on their pipes not destitute of design and merit. They will crayon out an animal, a plant, or a country, so as to prove the existence of a germ in their minds which only wants cultivation. They astonish you with strokes of the most sublime oratory; such as prove their reason and sentiment strong, their imagination glowing and elevated. But never yet could I find that a black had uttered a thought above the level of plain narration; never seen even an elementary trait of painting or sculpture. In music they are more generally gifted than the whites, with accurate ears for tune and time, and they have been found capable of imagining a small catch.[6] Whether they will be equal to the composition of a more extensive

---

4. Adair Crawford (1748–1795), an English chemist best known for his *Experiments and Observations on Animal Heat* (1779).
5. Greek mathematician c. 300 B.C.E.
6. The instrument proper to them is the Banjar, which they brought hither from Africa, and which is the original of the guitar, its chords being precisely the four lower chords of the guitar [Jefferson's note].

run of melody, or of complicated harmony, is yet to be proved. Misery is often the parent of the most affecting touches in poetry.—Among the blacks is misery enough, God knows, but no poetry. Love is the peculiar œstrum[7] of the poet. Their love is ardent, but it kindles the senses only, not the imagination. Religion, indeed, has produced a Phyllis Whately;[8] but it could not produce a poet. The compositions published under her name are below the dignity of criticism.

* * *

To justify a general conclusion, requires many observations, even where the subject may be submitted to the Anatomical knife, to Optical glasses, to analysis by fire or by solvents. How much more then where it is a faculty, not a substance, we are examining; where it eludes the research of all the senses; where the conditions of its existence are various and variously combined; where the effects of those which are present or absent bid defiance to calculation; let me add too, as a circumstance of great tenderness, where our conclusion would degrade a whole race of men from the rank in the scale of beings which their Creator may perhaps have given them. To our reproach it must be said, that though for a century and a half we have had under our eyes the races of black and of red men, they have never yet been viewed by us as subjects of natural history. I advance it, therefore, as a suspicion only, that the blacks, whether originally a distinct race, or made distinct by time and circumstances, are inferior to the whites in the endowments both of body and mind. * * *

1785

7. Passionate impulse.
8. Jefferson refers to the African American poet Phillis Wheatley (1753–1784), whose *Poems* (1773) was popular in England, going through at least four printings.

DAVID WALKER

Central to the development of African American writing of the antebellum period was a willingness to critique national ideologies and practices. Frederick Douglass's "What to the Slave Is the Fourth of July?" (1852), for example, pointed to the failure of the nation to live up to the ideals of the Declaration of Independence. Two decades before Douglass's most famous speech, David Walker (c. 1790–1830), a free black in Boston, maintained that the nation failed to live up to those ideals because the author of the Declaration was a racist. In *David Walker's Appeal, in Four Articles, Together with a Preamble, to the Colored Citizens of the World, But in Particular, and Very Expressly to those of the United States of America* (1829), Walker argued for African Americans' rights to freedom and dignity in the United States; in developing his argument, he challenged assumptions about black inferiority, particularly as set forth in Jefferson's *Notes on the State of Virginia*. Though Jefferson had died three years before the publication of the *Appeal*, Walker structured much of his text as a debate with Jefferson, and he hoped to use his text to create black community in the North and the South. To that end, he attempted to smuggle the book into the South with the help of black sailors. The book became notorious for its militant assertion that blacks, when faced with possible enslavement, should "kill or be killed." While the volume appalled and terrified whites, it inspired black abolitionists such as Henry Highland Garnet (1815–1882), who in his 1843 "Address to the Slaves" exhorted the slaves to violently resist the masters. But the volume's main intention was not to push blacks into a race war (unless whites offered no other choice) but to argue for blacks' rights to U.S. citizenship. In 1848 the *Appeal* was republished as part of a volume titled *Walker's Appeal, With a Brief Sketch of His Life. By Henry Highland Garnet. And also Garnet's Address to the Slaves of the United States of America*, from which the selection below is taken.

From David Walker's Appeal in Four Articles

My beloved brethren: The Indians of North and of South America—the Greeks—the Irish subjected under the king of Great Britain—the Jews that ancient people of the Lord—the inhabitants of the islands of the sea—in fine, all the inhabitants of the earth, (except however, the sons of Africa) are called *men*, and of course are, and ought to be free. But *we*, (coloured people) and our children are *brutes!!* and of course are and ought to be SLAVES to the American people and their children forever! to dig their mines and work their farms; and thus go on enriching them, from one generation to another with our blood and our tears!!

I promised in a preceding page to demonstrate to the satisfaction of the most incredulous, that we, (coloured people of these United States of America) are the *most wretched*, *degraded* and abject set of beings that ever *lived* since the world began, and that the white Americans having reduced us to the wretched state of *slavery*, treat us in that condition *more cruel* (they being an enlightened and christian people) than any heathen nation did any people whom it had reduced to our condition. These affirmations are so well confirmed in the minds of all unprejudiced men who have taken the trouble to read histories, that they need no elucidation from me.

*   *   *

I have been for years troubling the pages of historians to find out what our fathers have done to the *white Christians of America*, to merit such condign punishment as they have inflicted on them, and do continue to inflict on us their children. But I must aver, that my researches have hitherto been to no effect. I have therefore come to the immovable conclusion, that they (Americans) have, and do continue to punish us for nothing else, but for enriching them and their country. For I cannot conceive of any thing else. Nor will I ever believe otherwise until the Lord shall convince me.

The world knows, that slavery as it existed among the Romans, (which was the primary cause of their destruction) was, comparatively speaking, no more than a *cypher*, when compared with ours under the Americans. Indeed, I should not have noticed the Roman slaves, had not the very learned and penetrating Mr. Jefferson said, "When a master was murdered, all his slaves in the same house or within hearing, were condemned to death."[1]—Here let me ask Mr. Jefferson, (but he is gone to answer at the bar of God, for the deeds done in his body while living,) I therefore ask the whole

---

1. See his notes on Virginia [Walker's note].

American people, had I not rather die, or be put to death than to be a slave to any tyrant, who takes not only my own, but my wife and children's lives by the inches? Yea, would I meet death with avidity far! far!! in preference to such *servile submission* to the murderous hands of tyrants. Mr. Jefferson's very severe remarks on us have been so extensively argued upon by men whose attainments in literature, I shall never be able to reach, that I would not have meddled with it, were it not to solicit each of my brethren, who has the spirit of a man, to buy a copy of Mr. Jefferson's "Notes on Virginia," and put it in the hand of his son. For let no one of us suppose that the refutations which have been written by our white friends are enough—they are *whites*—we are *blacks*. We, and the world wish to see the charges of Mr. Jefferson refuted by the blacks *themselves*, according to their chance: for we must remember that what the whites have written respecting this subject, is other men's labors and did not emanate from the blacks. I know well, that there are some talents and learning among the coloured people of this country, which we have not a chance to develope, in consequence of oppression; but our oppression ought not to hinder us from acquiring all we can.—For we will have a chance to develope them by and by. God will not suffer us, always to be oppressed. Our sufferings will come to an *end*, in spite of all the Americans this side of *eternity*. Then we will want all the learning and talents among ourselves, and perhaps more, to govern ourselves.—"Every dog must have its day,"[2] the American's is coming to an end.

But let us review Mr. Jefferson's remarks respecting us some further. Comparing our miserable fathers, with the learned philosophers of Greece, he says: "Yet notwithstanding these and other discouraging circumstances among the Romans, their slaves were often their rarest artists. They excelled too in science, insomuch as to be usually employed as tutors to their master's children; Epictetus, Terence and Phædrus, were slaves,—but they were of the race of whites. It is not their *condition* then, but *nature*, which has produced the distinction."[3] See this, my brethren!! Do you believe that this assertion is swallowed by millions of the whites? Do you know that Mr. Jefferson was one of as great characters as ever lived among the whites? See his writings for the world, and public labors for the United States of America. Do you believe that the assertions of such a man, will pass away into oblivion unobserved by this people and the world? If you do you are much mistaken—See how the American people treat us—have we souls in our bodies? are we men who have any spirits at all? I know that there are many *swell-bellied* fellows among us whose greatest object is to fill their stomachs. Such I do not mean—I am after those who know and feel, that we are MEN as well as other people; to them, I say, that unless we try to refute Mr. Jefferson's arguments respecting us, we will only establish them.

But the slaves among the Romans. Every body who has read history, knows, that as soon as a slave among the Romans obtained his freedom, he could rise to the greatest eminence in the State, and there was no law instituted to hinder a slave from buying his freedom. Have not the Americans instituted laws to hinder us from obtaining our freedom. Do any deny this charge? Read the laws of Virginia, North Carolina, &c. Further: have not the Americans instituted laws to prohibit a man of colour from obtaining and holding

2. Attributed to John Heywood (1497?–1580?), English writer of proverbs and epigrams. 3. See his notes on Virginia [Walker's note].

any office whatever, under the government of the United States of America? Now, Mr. Jefferson tells us that our condition is not so hard, as the slaves were under the Romans!!!!

It is time for me to bring this article to a close. But before I close it, I must observe to my brethren that at the close of the first Revolution in this country with Great Britain, there were but thirteen States in the Union, now there are twenty-four, most of which are slave-holding States, and the whites are dragging us around in chains and hand-cuffs to their new States and Territories to work their mines and farms, to enrich them and their children, and millions of them believing firmly that we being a little darker than they, were made by our creator to be an inheritance to them and their children forever—the same as a parcel of *brutes!!*

Are we MEN!!—I ask you, O my brethren! are we MEN? Did our creator make us to be slaves to dust and ashes like ourselves? Are they not dying worms as well as we? Have they not to make their appearance before the tribunal of heaven, to answer for the deeds done in the body, as well as we? Have we any other master but Jesus Christ alone? Is he not their master as well as ours?—What right then, have we to obey and call any other master, but Himself? How we could be so *submissive* to a gang of men, whom we cannot tell whether they are as *good* as ourselves or not, I never could conceive. However, this is shut up with the Lord and we cannot precisely tell—but I declare, we judge men by their works.

The whites have always been an unjust, jealous unmerciful, avaricious and blood thirsty set of beings, always seeking after power and authority.—We view them all over the confederacy of Greece, where they were first known to be any thing, (in consequence of education) we see them there, cutting each other's throats—trying to subject each other to wretchedness and misery, to effect which they used all kinds of deceitful, unfair and unmerciful means. We view them next in Rome, where the spirit of tyranny and deceit rated still higher.—We view them in Gaul, Spain and in Britain—in fine, we view them all over Europe, together with what were scattered about in Asia and Africa, as heathens, and we see them acting more like devils than accountable men. But some may ask, did not the blacks of Africa, and the mulattoes of Asia, go on in the same way as did the whites of Europe. I answer no—they never were half so avaricious, deceitful and unmerciful as the whites, according to their knowledge.

But we will leave the whites or Europeans as heathens and take a view of them as christians, in which capacity we see them as cruel, if not more so than ever. In fact, take them as a body, they are ten times more cruel, avaricious and unmerciful than ever they were; for while they were heathens they were bad enough it is true, but it is positively a fact that they were not quite so audacious as to go and take vessel loads of men, women and children, and in cold blood and through devilishness, throw them into the sea, and murder them in all kind of ways. While they were heathens, they were too ignorant for such barbarity. But being christians, enlightened and sensible, they are completely prepared for such hellish cruelties. Now suppose God were to give them more sense, what would they do. If it were possible would they not *dethrone* Jehovah and seat themselves upon his throne? I therefore, in the name and fear of the Lord God of heaven and of earth, divested of prejudice either on the side of my colour or that of the whites, advance my suspicion, whether they are *as good by nature* as we are or not. Their actions, since they were known as a people, have been the reverse, I do indeed suspect them, but this, as I before observed, is shut up with the Lord, we cannot exactly tell, it will be proved in succeeding generations.

* * *

1829

WILLIAM LLOYD GARRISON

B orn in Newburyport, Massachusetts, the white abolitionist William Lloyd Garrison (1805–1879) worked on the antislavery newspaper *The Genius of Universal Emancipation* during the late 1820s. In 1831 he established his own antislavery newspaper, the *Liberator*, which—published in Boston from January 1831 to December 1865—became the most influential antislavery newspaper of the time. The only near competitors were Frederick Douglass's the *North Star* and *Frederick Douglass' Paper*. In his newspaper editorials and other writings, Garrison advocated moral persuasion over violence, condemned the Constitution as a proslavery document, rejected union with slaveholders, and—most important—called for the immediate (not gradual) emancipation of the slaves. In 1833 he organized the American Anti-Slavery Society, which remained one of the most effective antislavery organizations of the period. Under its auspices, he published Douglass's *Narrative* in 1845; but Douglass broke with him around 1850 when he became convinced that Garrison's view of the Constitution as a proslavery document was incorrect. Garrison's antislavery activities, particularly the publication of his newspaper, infuriated Southerners and contributed to the increasingly heated sectional tensions of the antebellum period. That Nat Turner's bloody slave rebellion in Southampton, Virginia, occurred just months after Garrison began publishing the *Liberator* was not lost on his Southern critics, who called for the suppression of the newspaper and other antislavery publications. In the editorial "To the Public," which appeared in the January 1, 1831, inaugural issue of the *Liberator*, the source of the selection printed here, Garrison invokes the Declaration of Independence of the Southerner Jefferson to argue for the need to fulfill the mandate of the American Revolution by bringing equality to all.

To the Public

In the month of August, I issued proposals for publishing "THE LIBERATOR" in Washington city; but the enterprise, though hailed in different sections of the country, was palsied by public indifference. Since that time, the removal of the Genius of Universal Emancipation[1] to the Seat of Government has rendered less imperious the establishment of a similar periodical in that quarter.

---

1. An antislavery newspaper edited by Benjamin Lundy (1789–1839). Garrison served as an editor from 1829 to 1830.

During my recent tour for the purpose of exciting the minds of the people by a series of discourses on the subject of slavery, every place that I visited gave fresh evidence of the fact, that a greater revolution in public sentiment was to be effected in the free states—*and particularly in New-England*—than at the south. I found contempt more bitter, opposition more active, detraction more relentless, prejudice more stubborn, and apathy more frozen, than among slave owners themselves. Of course, there were individual exceptions to the contrary. This state of things afflicted, but did not dishearten me. I determined, at every hazard, to lift up the standard of emancipation in the eyes of the nation, *within sight of Bunker Hill*[2] *and in the birth place of liberty*. That standard is now unfurled; and long may it float unhurt by the spoliations of time or the missiles of a desperate foe—yea, till every chain be broken, and every bondman set free! Let southern oppressors tremble—let their secret abettors tremble—let their northern apologists tremble—let all the enemies of the persecuted blacks tremble.

I deem the publication of my original Prospectus unnecessary, as it has obtained a wide circulation. The principles therein inculcated will be steadily pursued in this paper, excepting that I shall not array myself as the political partisan of any man. In defending the great cause of human rights, I wish to derive the assistance of all religions and of all parties.

Assenting to the "self-evident truth" maintained in the American Declaration of Independence, "that all men are created equal, and endowed by their Creator with certain inalienable rights—among which are life, liberty and the pursuit of happiness," I shall strenuously contend for the immediate enfranchisement of our slave population. In Park-street Church, on the Fourth of July, 1829, in an address on slavery, I unreflectingly assented to the popular but pernicious doctrine of *gradual* abolition. I seize this opportunity to make a full and unequivocal recantation, and thus publicly to ask pardon of my God, of my country, and of my brethren the poor slaves, for having uttered a sentiment so full of timidity, injustice and absurdity. A similar recantation, from my pen, was published in the Genius of Universal Emancipation at Baltimore, in September, 1829. My conscience is now satisfied.

I am aware, that many object to the severity of my language; but is there not cause for severity? I *will be* as harsh as truth, and as uncompromising as justice. On this subject, I do not wish to think, or speak, or write, with moderation. No! no! Tell a man whose house is on fire, to give a moderate alarm; tell him to moderately rescue his wife from the hands of the ravisher; tell the mother to gradually extricate her babe from the fire into which it has fallen;—but urge me not to use moderation in a cause like the present. I am in earnest—I will not equivocate—I will not excuse—I will not retreat a single inch—AND I WILL BE HEARD. The apathy of the people is enough to make every statue leap from its pedestal, and to hasten the resurrection of the dead.

It is pretended, that I am retarding the cause of emancipation by the coarseness of my invective, and the precipitancy of my measures. *The charge is not true*. On this question my influence,—humble as it is,—is felt at this moment to a considerable extent, and shall be felt in coming years—not perniciously, but beneficially—not as a curse, but as a blessing; and posterity

2. The site of a famous Revolutionary War battle in Boston on June 17, 1775.

The Liberator. Detail from the masthead of Garrison's antislavery paper, May 28, 1831.

will bear testimony that I was right. I desire to thank God, that he enables me to disregard "the fear of man which bringeth a snare,"[3] and to speak his truth in its simplicity and power. And here I close with this fresh dedication:

> Oppression! I have seen thee, face to face,
> And met thy cruel eye and cloudy brow;
> But thy soul-withering glance I fear not now—
> For dread to prouder feelings doth give place
> Of deep abhorrence! Scorning the disgrace
> Of slavish knees that at thy footstool bow
> I also kneel—but with far other vow
> Do hail thee and thy hord of hirelings base:—
> I swear, while life-blood warms my throbbing veins,
> Still to oppose and thwart, with heart and hand,
> Thy brutalising sway—till Afric's chains
> Are burst, and Freedom rules the rescued land,—
> Trampling Oppression and his iron rod:
> *Such is the vow I take*—SO HELP ME GOD![4]

1831

3. Proverbs 29.25.

4. The poem is by Garrison.

ANGELINA E. GRIMKÉ

Born and raised in a slaveholding family in Charleston, South Carolina, Angelina E. Grimké (1805–1879) moved to Philadelphia in the 1820s and, by the 1830s, was a fervent supporter of Garrisonian abolitionism. At a time when women in her social class were expected to remain at home and embrace the private realm of domesticity, she was regarded as a particularly shocking cultural figure for her boldness in lecturing on abolitionism before mixed audiences of men and women. She found that her work in antislavery led her to champion women's rights as well. As she remarked in 1838: "The investigation of the rights of the slave has led me to a better understanding of my own." Other women writers of the period, such as Lydia

Maria Child and Margaret Fuller, also saw connections between the causes of anti-slavery and women's rights. In *Appeal to the Christian Women of the South* (1836), the source of the selection printed here, Grimké, somewhat in the manner of Harriet Beecher Stowe in *Uncle Tom's Cabin*, urges Southern women to use their influence within the home to help bring about the end of slavery. Challenging key tenets of the proslavery argument, including the notion that emancipation would lead to a racial war of extermination (an argument that Jefferson made in *Notes in the State of Virginia*), Grimké in effect calls on Southern women to rebel against their own "enslavement" to patriarchy.

From Appeal to the Christian Women of the South

* * *

I have thus, I think, clearly proved to you seven propositions, viz.: First, that slavery is contrary to the declaration of our independence. Second, that it is contrary to the first charter of human rights given to Adam, and renewed to Noah. Third, that the fact of slavery having been the subject of prophecy, furnishes *no* excuse whatever to slavedealers. Fourth, that no such system existed under the patriarchal dispensation. Fifth, that *slavery never* existed under the Jewish dispensation; but so far otherwise, that every servant was placed under the *protection of law*, and care taken not only to prevent all *involuntary* servitude, but all *voluntary perpetual* bondage. Sixth, that slavery in America reduces a *man* to a *thing*, a "chattel personal," *robs him* of *all* his rights as a *human being*, fetters both his mind and body, and protects the *master* in the most unnatural and unreasonable power, whilst it *throws him out* of the protection of law. Seventh, that slavery is contrary to the example and precepts of our holy and merciful Redeemer, and of his apostles.

But perhaps you will be ready to query, why appeal to *women* on this subject? *We* do not make the laws which perpetuate slavery. *No* legislative power is vested in *us*; *we* can do nothing to overthrow the system, even if we wished to do so. To this I reply, I know you do not make the laws, but I also know that *you are the wives and mothers, the sisters and daughters of those who do*; and if you really suppose *you* can do nothing to overthrow slavery, you are greatly mistaken. You can do much in every way: four things I will name. 1st. You can read on this subject. 2d. You can pray over this subject. 3d. You can speak on this subject. 4th You can *act* on this subject. I have not placed reading before praying, because I regard it more important, but because, in order to pray aright, we must understand what we are praying for; it is only then we can "pray with the understanding and the spirit also."

1. Read then on the subject of slavery. Search the Scriptures daily, whether the things I have told you are true. Other books and papers might be a great help to you in this investigation, but they are not necessary, and it is hardly probable that your Committees of Vigilance[1] will allow you to have any other. The *Bible* then is the book I want you to read in the spirit of inquiry, and the spirit of prayer. Even the enemies of Abolitionists, acknowledge that their doctrines are drawn from it. In the great mob in Boston,[2] last autumn, when the books and papers of the Anti-Slavery Society, were thrown out of

1. Groups of Southern whites who attempted to suppress abolitionist writings.
2. In October 1835, a mob attacked William Lloyd Garrison and the English abolitionist George Thompson (1804–1878).

"Am I not a Woman . . . ?" In the early nineteenth century, British antislavery advocates popularized the image of the kneeling slave, with the caption "Am I not a Man and a Brother?" This image from George Bourne's *Slavery Illustrated in Its Effects upon Women* (1837) suggests the increasing interconnections between antislavery and the campaign for women's rights.

the windows of their office, one individual laid hold of the Bible and was about tossing it out to the ground, when another reminded him that it was the Bible he had in his hand. "O! 'tis all one," he replied, and out went the sacred volume, along with the rest. We thank him for the acknowledgment. Yes, "it is all one," for our books and papers are mostly commentaries on the Bible, and the Declaration. Read the *Bible* then, it contains the words of Jesus, and they are spirit and life. Judge for yourselves whether *he sanctioned* such a system of oppression and crime.

2. Pray over this subject. When you have entered into your closets, and shut to the doors, then pray to your father, who seeth in secret, that he would open your eyes to see whether slavery is *sinful*, and if it is, that he would enable you to bear a faithful, open and unshrinking testimony against it, and to do whatsoever your hands find to do, leaving the consequences entirely to him, who still says to us whenever we try to reason away duty from the fear of consequences, "*What is that to thee, follow thou me.*"[3] Pray also for that poor slave, that he may be kept patient and submissive under his hard lot, until God is pleased to open the door of freedom to him without violence or bloodshed. Pray too for the master that his heart may be softened, and he made willing to acknowledge, as Joseph's brethren did, "Verily we are guilty concerning our brother," before he will be compelled to add in consequence of Divine judgment, "therefore is all this evil come upon us."[4] Pray also for all your brethren and sisters who are laboring in the righteous cause of Emancipation in the Northern States, England and the world. There is great encouragement for prayer in these words of our Lord. "Whatsoever ye shall ask the Father *in my name*, he *will give* it to you"[5]—Pray then without ceasing, in the closet and the social circle.

3. Speak on this subject. It is through the tongue, the pen, and the press, that truth is principally propagated. Speak then to your relatives, your friends, your acquaintances on the subject of slavery; be not afraid if you are conscientiously convinced it is *sinful*, to say so openly, but calmly, and to let your sentiments be known. If you are served by the slaves of others, try to

3. John 21.22.
4. Cf. Genesis 42.21.
5. John 16.23.

ameliorate their condition as much as possible; never aggravate their faults, and thus add fuel to the fire of anger already kindled, in a master and mistress's bosom; remember their extreme ignorance, and consider them as your Heavenly Father does the *less* culpable on this account, even when they do wrong things. Discountenance *all* cruelty to them, all starvation, all corporal chastisement; these may brutalize and *break* their spirits, but will never bend them to willing, cheerful obedience. If possible, see that they are comfortably and *seasonably* fed, whether in the house or the field; it is unreasonable and cruel to expect slaves to wait for their breakfast until eleven o'clock, when they rise at five or six. Do all you can, to induce their owners to clothe them well, and to allow them many little indulgences which would contribute to their comfort. Above all, try to persuade your husband, father, brothers and sons, that *slavery is a crime against God and man*, and that it is a great sin to keep *human beings* in such abject ignorance; to deny them the privilege of learning to read and write. The Catholics are universally condemned, for denying the Bible to the common people, but, *slaveholders must not* blame them, for *they* are doing the *very same thing*, and for the very same reason, neither of these systems can bear the light which bursts from the pages of that Holy Book. And lastly, endeavour to inculcate submission on the part of the slaves, but whilst doing this be faithful in pleading the cause of the oppressed.

> "Will *you* behold unheeding,
> Life's holiest feelings crushed,
> Where *woman's* heart is bleeding,
> Shall *woman's* voice be hushed?"[6]

4. Act on this subject. Some of you *own* slaves yourselves. If you believe slavery is *sinful*, set them at liberty, "undo the heavy burdens and let the oppressed go free."[7] If they wish to remain with you, pay them wages, if not let them leave you. Should they remain teach them, and have them taught the common branches of an English education; they have minds and those minds, *ought to be improved*. So precious a talent as intellect, never was given to be wrapt in a napkin and buried in the earth. It is the *duty* of all, as far as they can, to improve their own mental faculties, because we are commanded to love God with *all our minds*, as well as with all our hearts, and we commit a great sin, if we *forbid or prevent* that cultivation of the mind in others, which would enable them to perform this duty. * * *

1836

---

6. From "Think of Our Country's Glory," by Elizabeth Margaret Chandler (1807–1834), in *Poetical Works* (1836).
7. Isaiah 58.6.

SOJOURNER TRUTH

B orn a slave in Ulster County in Upstate New York, Sojourner Truth (1797–1883) emerged as one of the nation's most flamboyant advocates of the rights of African Americans and women. At least five of her children were sold into slavery before New York State abolished slavery in 1827, and though she never learned to read or write, she successfully sued for the return of one of her sons in 1829. In 1843 she had a visionary experience that left her convinced God wanted her to speak the truth about the evils of Americans' sins against blacks and women. Like Angelina Grimké, she regularly spoke before mixed audiences of men and women, presenting the causes of antislavery and women's rights as inextricably intertwined. With the publication of the *Narrative of Sojourner Truth* in 1850, a life history that she dictated to Oliver Gilbert, she gained even greater renown. Harriet Beecher Stowe regarded Truth an inspiring example of the black Christian woman as antipatriarchal reformer, and she was not alone in being influenced by newspaper reports of Truth's dramatic speeches. In the summer of 1851, Truth addressed a women's rights convention in Akron, Ohio. The account that follows is from the June 21, 1851, issue of the *Anti-Slavery Bugle*.

Speech to the Women's Rights Convention in Akron, Ohio, 1851

One of the most unique and interesting speeches of the Convention was made by Sojourner Truth, an emancipated slave. It is impossible to transfer it to paper, or convey any adequate idea of the effect it produced upon the audience. Those only can appreciate it who saw her powerful form, her whole-souled, earnest gestures, and listened to her strong and truthful tones. She came forward to the platform and addressing the President said with great simplicity:

May I say a few words? Receiving an affirmative answer, she proceeded: I want to say a few words about this matter. I am a woman's rights. I have as much muscle as any man, and can do as much work as any man. I have plowed and reaped and husked and chopped and mowed, and can any man do more than that? I have heard much about the sexes being equal; I can carry as much as any man, and can cut as much too, if I can get it. I am as strong as any man that is now. As for intellect, all I can say is, if woman have a pint and man a quart—why cant she have her little pint full? You need not be afraid to give us our rights for fear we will take too much,—for we cant take more than our pint'll hold. The poor men seem to be all in confusion, and dont know what to do. Why children, if you have woman's rights give it to her and you will feel better. You will have your own rights, and they wont be so much trouble. I cant read, but I can hear. I have heard the bible and have learned that Eve caused man to sin. Well if woman upset the world, do give her a chance to set it rightside up again. The Lady has spoken about Jesus, how he never spurned woman from him, and she was right. When

Lazarus[1] died, Mary and Martha came to him with faith and love and besought him to raise their brother. And Jesus wept—and Lazarus came forth. And how came Jesus into the world? Through God who created him and woman who bore him. Man, where is your part? But the women are coming up blessed be God and a few of the men are coming up with them. But man is in a tight place, the poor slave is on him, woman is coming on him, and he is surely between a hawk and a buzzard.

1851

1. Restored to life by Jesus (John 11.1–44).

MARTIN R. DELANY

During the antebellum period, a number of African American leaders argued that the United States would forever remain a nation of slavery and white supremacy and that beneath the contradictions in Jefferson's vision lay the reality that he and others among the nation's founders never intended for blacks to become citizens of the new republic. Angered and disillusioned by the Compromise of 1850, with its infamous Fugitive Slave Law requiring all citizens to assist in returning escaped slaves to their "owners," the black Pittsburgh leader Martin R. Delany (1812–1885) broke with his friend Frederick Douglass, with whom he had co-edited the antislavery newspaper the *North Star*, and began to call for African American emigration. In 1854 he convened a National Emigration Convention of Colored Men in Cleveland; his address at the convention, "Political Destiny," counseled African Americans to emigrate to Central or South America or to the Caribbean. His emigrationist vision inspired a number of African Americans, including William Wells Brown, who, in the wake of the Supreme Court's 1857 Dred Scott decision declaring that blacks could never become citizens of the United States, advocated African American emigration to Haiti. With the outbreak of the Civil War, however, most black emigrationists, including Delany and Brown, committed themselves to the Union cause, which they regarded as the cause of antislavery. Delany himself became the first black major in the Union Army. For the remainder of his life, however, he remained tempted by the prospect of black emigration to Africa. The text of his 1854 emigrationist speech is taken from *Proceedings of the National Emigration Convention of Colored People* (1854).

From Political Destiny of the Colored Race on the American Continent

Let it then be understood, as a great principle of political economy, that no people can be free who themselves do not constitute an essential part of the *ruling element* of the country in which they live. Whether this element be founded upon a true or false, a just or an unjust basis; this position in community is necessary to personal safety. The liberty of no man is secure, who controls not his own political destiny. What is true of an individual, is true of a family; and that which is true of a family, is also true concerning a whole people. To suppose otherwise, is that delusion which at once induces its victim, through a period of long suffering, patiently to submit to every species of wrong; trusting against probability, and hoping against all reasonable grounds of expectation, for the granting of privileges and enjoyment of rights, which never will be attained. This delusion reveals the true secret of the power which holds in peaceable subjection, all the oppressed in every part of the world.

A people, to be free, must necessarily be *their own rulers*: that is, *each individual* must, in himself, embody the *essential ingredient*—so to speak—of the *sovereign principle* which composes the *true basis* of his liberty. This principle, when not exercised by himself, may, at his pleasure, be delegated to another—his true representative.

Said a great French writer: "A free agent, in a free government, should be his own governor;"[1] that is, he must possess within himself the *acknowledged right to govern*: this constitutes him a *governor*, though he may delegate to another the power to govern himself.

No one, then, can delegate to another a power he never possessed; that is, he cannot *give an agency* in that which he never had a right. Consequently, the colored man in the United States, being deprived of the right of inherent sovereignty, cannot *confer* a suffrage, because he possesses none to confer. Therefore, where there is no suffrage, there can neither be *freedom* nor *safety* for the disfranchised. And it is a futile hope to suppose that the agent of another's concerns will take a proper interest in the affairs of those to whom he is under no obligations. Having no favors to ask or expect, he therefore has none to lose.

In other periods and parts of the world—as in Europe and Asia—the people being of one common, direct origin of race, though established on the presumption of difference by birth, or what was termed *blood*, yet the distinction between the superior classes and common people, could only be marked by the difference, in the dress and education of the two classes. To effect this, the interposition of government was necessary; consequently, the costume and education of the people became a subject of legal restriction, guarding carefully against the privileges of the common people.

In Rome, the Patrician and Plebeian were orders in the ranks of her people—all of whom were termed citizens (*cives*)—recognized by the laws of the country; their dress and education being determined by law, the better to fix the distinction. In different parts of Europe, at the present day, if not the same, the distinction among the people is similar, only on a modified—and in some kingdoms—probably more tolerant or deceptive policy.

In the United States, our degradation being once—as it has in a hundred instances been done—legally determined, our color is sufficient, independently of costume, education, or other distinguishing marks, to keep up that distinction.

In Europe, when an inferior is elevated to the rank of equality with the superior class, the law first comes to his aid, which, in its decrees, entirely destroys his identity as an inferior, leaving no trace of his former condition visible.

---

1. The most likely source is *Principles of Politics* (1815), by Benjamin Constant (1767–1830), French-Swiss political theorist.

In the United States, among the whites, their color is made, by law and custom, the mark of distinction and superiority; while the color of the blacks is a badge of degradation, acknowledged by statute, organic law, and the common consent of the people.

With this view of the case—which we hold to be correct—to elevate to equality the degraded subject of law and custom, it can only be done, as in Europe, by an entire destruction of the identity of the former condition of the applicant. Even were this desirable—which we by no means admit—with the deep seated prejudices engendered by oppression, with which we have to contend, ages incalculable might reasonably be expected to roll around, before this could honorably be accomplished; otherwise, we should encourage and at once commence an indiscriminate concubinage and immoral commerce, of our mothers, sisters, wives and daughters, revolting to think of, and a physical curse to humanity.

If this state of things be to succeed, then, as in Egypt, under the dread of the inscrutable approach of the destroying angel, to appease the hatred of our oppressors, as a license to the passions of every white, let the lintel of each door of every black man, be stained with the blood of virgin purity and unsullied matron fidelity. Let it be written along the cornice in capitals, "The *will* of the white man is the rule of my household."[2] Remove the protection to our chambers and nurseries, that the places once sacred may henceforth become the unrestrained resort of the vagrant and rabble, always provided that the licensed commissioner of lust shall wear the indisputable impress of a *white* skin.

But we have fully discovered and comprehended the great political disease with which we are affected, the cause of its origin and continuance; and what is now left for us to do is to discover and apply a sovereign remedy—a healing balm to a sorely diseased body—a wrecked but not entirely shattered system. We propose for this disease a remedy. That remedy is Emigration. This Emigration should be well advised, and like remedies applied to remove the disease from the physical system of man, skillfully and carefully applied, within the proper time, directed to operate on that part of the system, whose greatest tendency shall be, to benefit the whole.

1854

---

2. Exodus 12.21–23 describes Moses instructing the Israelites to put the blood of the lamb just above their doorposts so God would know not to smite them.

HARRIET BEECHER STOWE
1811–1896

The author of the best-selling novel of the pre–Civil War period, Harriet Beecher Stowe was born in Litchfield, Connecticut, the seventh child and fourth daughter of Lyman Beecher, an eminent evangelical Calvinist minister, and Roxana Foote Beecher. After bearing two more children, Roxana died when Harriet was four; typically for this era, Lyman remarried quickly. Harriet Beecher found her stepmother aloof and overly formal, and continued to grieve for her mother. The family eventually numbered thirteen children, among whom Harriet was especially close to her brothers Henry Ward (1813–1887) and Charles (1815–1900), her sister Catharine (1800–1878), and her half-sister Isabella (1822–1907). Profoundly influenced by Lyman Beecher's ambitions to shape the nation along the lines of his Protestant evangelical vision, many of the children grew up to take on leadership roles in the culture. The men became ministers; the women became writers, teachers, and reformers. Catharine was a pioneer in women's education and teacher training; Isabella turned to suffragism and women's rights; Harriet wrote the most effective antislavery novel in the nation's history.

Between 1819 and 1824, Harriet Beecher studied at Sarah Pierce's Litchfield Female Academy, one of the earliest schools in the nation to offer serious academic training to women. Pierce (1806–1863) believed that properly trained women were ultimately destined (as she phrased it in a commencement address) to "instruct and enlighten the world." In 1823, Catharine Beecher, who had also attended Pierce's school, joined with another sister, Mary, to found a girls' academy in Hartford, Connecticut. Harriet Beecher began to study there in 1824 and became a teacher at the academy in 1827.

In 1832 the Beecher family moved to Cincinnati, where Lyman Beecher assumed the presidency of the new Lane Theological Seminary, convinced of the importance of doing Protestant evangelical work in the western states. Working with her father and her sister Harriet, Catharine Beecher founded the Western Female Institute in order to train "Protestant young women" to teach the children of farmers and workers in the burgeoning schools of the Midwest. Although the Beechers regretted leaving their beloved New England, they became part of an active home-based cultural life (scholars call this a "parlor culture") in Cincinnati, at that time the largest city in the West. Harriet Beecher began to write short stories in 1834. That same year she became acutely aware of the controversy over slavery when a number of Lane students, including the soon to be prominent abolitionist Theodore Dwight Weld, rebelled against Lyman Beecher's lukewarm antislavery position—he supported shipping free American blacks to a colony in Africa—and withdrew from the seminary.

In 1836, a year that saw major antiabolitionist riots in Cincinnati, Harriet Beecher married Calvin Stowe, a professor of biblical literature at Lane who was one of the best Hebrew scholars of his day. Because his salary was small and the Stowes began to rear a large family very quickly—twin girls (Eliza and Harriet) were born in 1836, a son (Henry) in 1838—Harriet Beecher Stowe continued to write for money even though she found childbirth extremely debilitating. Her first book—a collection of stories titled *The Mayflower*—appeared in 1843. Her first antislavery sketch, "Immediate Emancipation," appeared in 1845. The death of her baby boy Samuel, who succumbed to cholera in 1849 before he was a year old, was a great blow and infused her writing with sympathy for people who were helpless in the face of great personal loss. Although she had little firsthand knowledge of slavery, she had become increasingly interested in the abolitionist cause; now her deep sorrow forged an emotional link with the oppressed that was to push *Uncle Tom's Cabin* far beyond the standard abolitionist tract.

In 1849 Calvin Stowe accepted a position at Bowdoin College, in Maine, and the Stowes moved to New England in 1850. (In 1851, when the family moved again, he went to Andover Theological Seminary in Massachusetts.) Passage of the Fugitive Slave Act in 1850—which made it a federal crime to assist an escaping slave—had outraged Harriet Beecher Stowe and many other Northerners, who regarded the new law as having further implicated the North in the practice of slavery. For, if it was now a crime to help escaping slaves anywhere in the nation, one could no longer see slavery as simply a Southern institution. Fired by this development, she began writing *Uncle Tom's Cabin*, which was serialized during 1851–52 in the Washington, D.C., weekly antislavery journal, the *National Era*. In this setting, the novel was well received, but its audience was limited to adherents of the abolitionist cause.

The novel had an entirely different effect when it appeared in book form in 1852. It sold around three thousand copies the day of publication and more than three hundred thousand copies by the end of the year. (Comparable figures for today's population would have to be more than ten times larger.) As a reviewer in the *Literary World* put it: "No literary work of any character or merit, whether of poetry or prose, or imagination or observation, fancy or fact, truth or fiction, that has ever been written since there have been writers or readers, has ever commanded so great a popular success." Between 1852 and 1860 it was reprinted in twenty-two languages. The novel helped push abolitionism from the margins to the mainstream, and thus moved the nation closer to Civil War—an outcome that, in fact, Stowe had hoped to avert by her depictions of slave suffering. Her aim had been to inspire voluntary emancipation by demonstrating the evil and unchristian nature of slavery.

Uncle Tom's Cabin made Stowe a national and international celebrity. When she traveled to Europe in 1853 she was entertained and feted wherever she went. As a means of authenticating aspects of *Uncle Tom's Cabin*, she had published the book-length *Key to Uncle Tom's Cabin* before setting sail. Over the next several years she met with a number of black abolitionists, including Frederick Douglass, and came to regret that the ending of *Uncle Tom's Cabin*, where a number of the novel's prominent black characters choose to emigrate to Africa, seemed to support colonization (the policy of relocating free blacks to Africa). In her next antislavery novel, *Dred; A Tale of the Great Dismal Swamp* (1856), she depicted slave rebels who, following the death of their leader, made their way to New York and Canada. Though not as popular as *Uncle Tom's Cabin*, the novel nonetheless sold several hundred thousand copies and was praised by the British novelist George Eliot as "rare in both its intensity and range of power."

As the Civil War approached, Stowe continued to write on behalf of abolitionism in the *New York Independent* while turning to novels focused on New England culture and history. She made a pioneering contribution to regional writing in such books as *The Minister's Wooing* (1859), *The Pearl of Orr's Island* (1862), *Oldtown Folks* (1869), and *Poganuc People* (1878). Much of the power of these novels derives from Stowe's profoundly ambivalent tributes to the old New England character and its ways of life in the prerailroad days. She deplored New England's doctrinal severity, yet admired the region's homogeneous community life, which she strove to depict in meticulous, nostalgic detail. These novels developed the figure of an innocent young woman whose religious intuitions resist the bookish theologies of male religious authorities. A historical novel, *Agnes of Sorrento* (1862), which drew on her travels in Italy, featured the same kind of heroine in a fifteenth-century setting.

In 1863 Calvin Stowe retired, and the Stowes moved to Hartford, Connecticut. In this same year she became an Episcopalian, abandoning the rigors of Calvinism with which she had struggled for so long. Her life contained many sorrows; only three of her seven children—the twins and the youngest child, Charles, born in 1850—

outlived her. Calvin Stowe died in 1886; in her last decade, Harriet Beecher Stowe suffered greatly from physical illness and mental exhaustion.

When the modernist movement championed a critical ethos of understatement and antisentimentality, denying that politics had any place in serious literature, *Uncle Tom's Cabin* became a target of critical abuse. Overtly emotional, fearlessly political, and appealing to the widest possible audience, it represented literary values that modernism abhorred. More recently the novel's racial politics have come under fire, as some have objected to the extent to which it draws on stereotypes. But if it had not been so much a part of its own time, *Uncle Tom's Cabin* could never have achieved its effects, and reconsideration of the novel has helped revive appreciation for literature that is politically engaged and popularly effective. Understanding the importance of this novel in American culture also reminds readers of how central women were to literary life before the Civil War, and how openly they engaged with topics that, supposedly, were outside their sphere.

The text is that of the first American edition of *Uncle Tom's Cabin* (1852).

From Uncle Tom's Cabin; or, Life among the Lowly[1]

Volume I

CHAPTER VII. THE MOTHER'S STRUGGLE[2]

It is impossible to conceive of a human creature more wholly desolate and forlorn than Eliza, when she turned her footsteps from Uncle Tom's cabin.

Her husband's suffering and dangers, and the danger of her child, all blended in her mind, with a confused and stunning sense of the risk she was running, in leaving the only home she had ever known, and cutting loose from the protection of a friend whom she loved and revered. Then there was the parting from every familiar object,—the place where she had grown up, the trees under which she had played, the groves where she had walked many an evening in happier days, by the side of her young husband,— everything, as it lay in the clear, frosty starlight, seemed to speak reproachfully to her, and ask her whither could she go from a home like that?

But stronger than all was maternal love, wrought into a paroxysm of frenzy by the near approach of a fearful danger. Her boy was old enough to have walked by her side, and, in an indifferent case, she would only have led him by the hand; but now the bare thought of putting him out of her arms made her shudder, and she strained him to her bosom with a convulsive grasp, as she went rapidly forward.

The frosty ground creaked beneath her feet, and she trembled at the sound; every quaking leaf and fluttering shadow sent the blood backward to her heart, and quickened her footsteps. She wondered within herself at the strength that seemed to be come upon her; for she felt the weight of her boy as if it had been a feather, and every flutter of fear seemed to increase the supernatural power that bore her on, while from her pale lips burst forth,

1. The novel follows the fortunes of two slaves from the Shelby plantation in Kentucky. The first plot concerns Tom, about thirty-five years old and a devout Christian; the second concerns Eliza, a young mother. "Uncle" does not mean an old person, but an honored person.

2. At this point in the novel, Eliza has decided to run away with her son, Harry, rather than let him be sold to Haley. She has alerted Tom to his impending sale; he chooses to remain and allow himself to be sold to protect the other slave families on the plantation. As he knows, others would be sold in his place if he escaped.

in frequent ejaculations, the prayer to a Friend above—"Lord, help! Lord, save me!"

If it were *your* Harry, mother, or your Willie, that were going to be torn from you by a brutal trader, to-morrow morning,—if you had seen the man, and heard that the papers were signed and delivered, and you had only from twelve o'clock till morning to make good your escape,—how fast could *you* walk? How many miles could you make in those few brief hours, with the darling at your bosom,—the little sleepy head on your shoulder,—the small, soft arms trustingly holding on to your neck?

For the child slept. At first, the novelty and alarm kept him waking; but his mother so hurriedly repressed every breath or sound, and so assured him that if he were only still she would certainly save him, that he clung quietly round her neck, only asking, as he found himself sinking to sleep,

"Mother, I don't need to keep awake, do I?"

"No, my darling; sleep, if you want to."

"But, mother, if I do get asleep, you won't let him get me?"

"No! so may God help me!" said his mother, with a paler cheek, and a brighter light in her large dark eyes.

"You're *sure*, an't you, mother?"

"Yes, *sure*!" said the mother, in a voice that startled herself; for it seemed to her to come from a spirit within, that was no part of her; and the boy dropped his little weary head on her shoulder, and was soon asleep. How the touch of those warm arms, the gentle breathings that came in her neck, seemed to add fire and spirit to her movements! It seemed to her as if strength poured into her in electric streams, from every gentle touch and movement of the sleeping, confiding child. Sublime is the dominion of the mind over the body, that, for a time, can make flesh and nerve impregnable, and string the sinews like steel, so that the weak become so mighty.

The boundaries of the farm, the grove, the wood-lot, passed by her dizzily, as she walked on; and still she went, leaving one familiar object after another, slacking not, pausing not, till reddening daylight found her many a long mile from all traces of any familiar objects upon the open highway.

She had often been, with her mistress, to visit some connections, in the little village of T——, not far from the Ohio river, and knew the road well. To go thither, to escape across the Ohio river, were the first hurried outlines of her plan of escape; beyond that, she could only hope in God.

When horses and vehicles began to move along the highway, with that alert perception peculiar to a state of excitement, and which seems to be a sort of inspiration, she became aware that her headlong pace and distracted air might bring on her remark and suspicion. She therefore put the boy on the ground, and, adjusting her dress and bonnet, she walked on at as rapid a pace as she thought consistent with the preservation of appearances. In her little bundle she had provided a store of cakes and apples, which she used as expedients for quickening the speed of the child, rolling the apple some yards before them, when the boy would run with all his might after it; and this ruse, often repeated, carried them over many a half-mile.

After a while, they came to a thick patch of woodland, through which murmured a clear brook. As the child complained of hunger and thirst, she climbed over the fence with him; and, sitting down behind a large rock which concealed them from the road, she gave him a breakfast out of her little package. The boy wondered and grieved that she could not eat; and when, putting his arms round her neck, he tried to wedge some of his cake into her mouth, it seemed to her that the rising in her throat would choke her.

"No, no, Harry darling! mother can't eat till you are safe! We must go on— on—till we come to the river!" And she hurried again into the road, and again constrained herself to walk regularly and composedly forward.

She was many miles past any neighborhood where she was personally known. If she should chance to meet any who knew her, she reflected that the well-known kindness of the family would be of itself a blind to suspicion, as making it an unlikely supposition that she could be a fugitive. As she was also so white as not to be known as of colored lineage, without a critical survey, and her child was white also, it was much easier for her to pass on unsuspected.

On this presumption, she stopped at noon at a neat farmhouse, to rest herself, and buy some dinner for her child and self; for, as the danger decreased with the distance, the supernatural tension of the nervous system lessened, and she found herself both weary and hungry.

The good woman, kindly and gossipping, seemed rather pleased than otherwise with having somebody come in to talk with; and accepted, without examination, Eliza's statement, that she "was going on a little piece, to spend a week with her friends,"—all which she hoped in her heart might prove strictly true.

An hour before sunset, she entered the village of T——, by the Ohio river, weary and foot-sore, but still strong in heart. Her first glance was at the river, which lay, like Jordan, between her and the Canaan[3] of liberty on the other side.

It was now early spring, and the river was swollen and turbulent; great cakes of floating ice were swinging heavily to and fro in the turbid waters. Owing to the peculiar form of the shore on the Kentucky side, the land bending far out into the water, the ice had been lodged and detained in great quantities, and the narrow channel which swept round the bend was full of ice, piled one cake over another, thus forming a temporary barrier to the descending ice, which lodged, and formed a great, undulating raft, filling up the whole river, and extending almost to the Kentucky shore.

Eliza stood, for a moment, contemplating this unfavorable aspect of things, which she saw at once must prevent the usual ferry-boat from running, and then turned into a small public house on the bank, to make a few inquiries.

The hostess, who was busy in various fizzing and stewing operations over the fire, preparatory to the evening meal, stopped, with a fork in her hand, as Eliza's sweet and plaintive voice arrested her.

"What is it?" she said.

"Isn't there any ferry or boat, that takes people over to B——, now?" she said.

"No, indeed!" said the woman; "the boats has stopped running."

Eliza's look of dismay and disappointment struck the woman, and she said, inquiringly,

"May be you're wanting to get over?—anybody sick? Ye seem mighty anxious?"

---

3. In the Bible, the promised land for the Israelites, who wandered in the desert for forty years. The Jordan is the river they had to cross to get there.

"I've got a child that's very dangerous,"[4] said Eliza. "I never heard of it till last night, and I've walked quite a piece to-day, in hopes to get to the ferry."

"Well, now, that's onlucky," said the woman, whose motherly sympathies were much aroused; "I'm re'lly consarned for ye. Solomon!" she called, from the window, towards a small back building. A man, in leather apron and very dirty hands, appeared at the door.

"I say, Sol," said the woman, "is that ar man going to tote them bar'ls over to-night?"

"He said he should try, if't was any way prudent," said the man.

"There's a man a piece down here, that's going over with some truck[5] this evening, if he durs'to; he'll be in here to supper to-night, so you'd better set down and wait. That's a sweet little fellow," added the woman, offering him a cake.

But the child, wholly exhausted, cried with weariness.

"Poor fellow! he isn't used to walking, and I've hurried him on so," said Eliza.

"Well, take him into this room," said the woman, opening into a small bed-room, where stood a comfortable bed. Eliza laid the weary boy upon it, and held his hands in hers till he was fast asleep. For her there was no rest. As a fire in her bones, the thought of the pursuer urged her on; and she gazed with longing eyes on the sullen, surging waters that lay between her and liberty.

Here we must take our leave of her for the present, to follow the course of her pursuers.

Though Mrs. Shelby had promised that the dinner should be hurried on table, yet it was soon seen, as the thing has often been seen before, that it required more than one to make a bargain. So, although the order was fairly given out in Haley's hearing, and carried to Aunt Chloe[6] by at least half a dozen juvenile messengers, that dignitary only gave certain very gruff snorts, and tosses of her head, and went on with every operation in an unusually leisurely and circumstantial manner.

For some singular reason, an impression seemed to reign among the servants generally that Missis would not be particularly disobliged by delay; and it was wonderful what a number of counter accidents occurred constantly, to retard the course of things. One luckless wight contrived to upset the gravy; and then gravy had to be got up *de novo,*[7] with due care and formality, Aunt Chloe watching and stirring with dogged precision, answering shortly, to all suggestions of haste, that she "warn't a going to have raw gravy on the table, to help nobody's catchings." One tumbled down with the water, and had to go to the spring for more; and another precipitated the butter into the path of events; and there was from time to time giggling news brought into the kitchen that "Mas'r Haley was mighty oneasy, and that he couldn't sit in his cheer no ways, but was a walkin' and stalkin' to the winders and through the porch."

---

4. I.e., dangerously ill.
5. Goods.
6. Tom's wife, the Shelbys' cook. The entire household works together to delay Haley's depar-

ture in pursuit of Eliza.
7. From the beginning (Latin). "Wight": serving person, slave.

"Sarves him right!" said Aunt Chloe, indignantly. "He'll get wus nor oneasy, one of these days, if he don't mend his ways. *His* master'll be sending for him, and then see how he'll look!"

"He'll go to torment, and no mistake," said little Jake.

"He desarves it!" said Aunt Chloe, grimly; "he's broke a many, many, many hearts,—I tell ye all!" she said, stopping, with a fork uplifted in her hands; "it's like what Mas'r George reads in Ravelations,[8]—souls a callin' under the altar! and a callin' on the Lord for vengeance on sich!—and by and by the Lord he'll hear 'em—so he will!"

Aunt Chloe, who was much revered in the kitchen, was listened to with open mouth; and, the dinner being now fairly sent in, the whole kitchen was at leisure to gossip with her, and to listen to her remarks.

"Sich 'll be burnt up forever, and no mistake; won't ther?" said Andy.

"I'd be glad to see it, I'll be boun'," said little Jake.

"Chil'en!" said a voice, that made them all start. It was Uncle Tom, who had come in, and stood listening to the conversation at the door.

"Chil'en!" he said, "I'm afeard you don't know what ye're sayin'. Forever is a *dre'ful* word, chil'en; it's awful to think on 't. You oughtenter wish that ar to any human crittur."

"We wouldn't to anybody but the soul-drivers,"[9] said Andy; "nobody can help wishing it to them, they's so awful wicked."

"Don't natur herself kinder cry out on em?" said Aunt Chloe. "Don't dey tear der suckin' baby right off his mother's breast, and sell him, and der little children as is crying and holding on by her clothes,—don't dey pull 'em off and sells em? Don't dey tear wife and husband apart?" said Aunt Chloe, beginning to cry, "when it's jest takin' the very life on 'em?—and all the while does they feel one bit,—don't dey drink and smoke, and take it oncommon easy? Lor, if the devil don't get them, what's he good for?" And Aunt Chloe covered her face with her checked apron, and began to sob in good earnest.

"Pray for them that 'spitefully use you, the good book says," says Tom.[1]

"Pray for 'em!" said Aunt Chloe; "Lor, it's too tough! I can't pray for 'em."

"It's natur, Chloe, and natur's strong," said Tom, "but the Lord's grace is stronger; besides, you oughter think what an awful state a poor crittur's soul's in that'll do them ar things,—you oughter thank God that you an't *like* him, Chloe. I'm sure I'd rather be sold, ten thousand times over, than to have all that ar poor crittur's got to answer for."

"So'd I, a heap," said Jake. "Lor, *shouldn't* we cotch it, Andy?"

Andy shrugged his shoulders, and gave an acquiescent whistle.

"I'm glad Mas'r didn't go off this morning, as he looked to," said Tom; "that ar hurt me more than sellin', it did. Mebbe it might have been natural for him, but 't would have come desp't hard on me, as has known him from a baby; but I've seen Mas'r, and I begin ter feel sort o' reconciled to the Lord's will now. Mas'r couldn't help hisself; he did right, but I'm feared things will be kinder goin' to rack, when I'm gone. Mas'r can't be spected to be a pryin' round everywhar, as I've done, a keepin' up all the ends. The boys all means well, but they's powerful car'less. That ar troubles me."

---

8. The Book of Revelation, which contains symbolic prophecies of the end of the world. George is the Shelbys' son, who in Chapter IV reads the Bible to the slaves.
9. Slave owners or traders.

1. From Matthew 5.44: "Love your enemies, bless them that curse you, do good to them that hate you, and pray for them which despitefully use you, and persecute you."

The bell here rang, and Tom was summoned to the parlor.

"Tom," said his master, kindly, "I want you to notice that I give this gentleman bonds to forfeit a thousand dollars if you are not on the spot when he wants you; he's going to-day to look after his other business, and you can have the day to yourself. Go anywhere you like, boy."

"Thank you, Mas'r," said Tom.

"And mind yerself," said the trader, "and don't come it over your master with any o' yer nigger tricks; for I'll take every cent out of him, if you an't thar. If he'd hear to me, he wouldn't trust any on ye—slippery as eels!"

"Mas'r," said Tom,—and he stood very straight,—"I was jist eight years old when ole Missis put you into my arms, and you wasn't a year old. 'Thar,' says she, 'Tom, that's to be *your* young Mas'r; take good care on him,' says she. And now I jist ask you, Mas'r, have I ever broke word to you, or gone contrary to you, 'specially since I was a Christian?"

Mr. Shelby was fairly overcome, and the tears rose to his eyes.

"My good boy," said he, "the Lord knows you say but the truth; and if I was able to help it, all the world shouldn't buy you."

"And sure as I am a Christian woman," said Mrs. Shelby, "you shall be redeemed as soon as I can any way bring together means. Sir," she said to Haley, "take good account of who you sell him to, and let me know."

"Lor, yes, for that matter," said the trader, "I may bring him up in a year, not much the wuss for wear, and trade him back."

"I'll trade with you then, and make it for your advantage," said Mrs. Shelby.

"Of course," said the trader, "all's equal with me; li'ves trade 'em up as down, so I does a good business. All I want is a livin', you know, ma'am; that's all any on us wants, I s'pose."

Mr. and Mrs. Shelby both felt annoyed and degraded by the familiar impudence of the trader, and yet both saw the absolute necessity of putting a constraint on their feelings. The more hopelessly sordid and insensible he appeared, the greater became Mrs. Shelby's dread of his succeeding in recapturing Eliza and her child, and of course the greater her motive for detaining him by every female artifice. She therefore graciously smiled, assented, chatted familiarly, and did all she could to make time pass imperceptibly.

At two o'clock Sam and Andy brought the horses up to the posts, apparently greatly refreshed and invigorated by the scamper of the morning.

Sam was there new oiled from dinner, with an abundance of zealous and ready officiousness. As Haley approached, he was boasting, in flourishing style, to Andy, of the evident and eminent success of the operation, now that he had "farly come to it."

"Your master, I s'pose, don't keep no dogs," said Haley, thoughtfully, as he prepared to mount.

"Heaps on 'em," said Sam, triumphantly; "thar's Bruno—he's a roarer! and, besides that, 'bout every nigger of us keeps a pup of some natur or uther."

"Poh!" said Haley,—and he said something else, too, with regard to the said dogs, at which Sam muttered,

"I don't see no use cussin' on 'em, no way."

"But your master don't keep no dogs (I pretty much know he don't) for trackin' out niggers."

Sam knew exactly what he meant, but he kept on a look of earnest and desperate simplicity.

"Our dogs all smells round considerable sharp. I spect they's the kind, though they han't never had no practice. They's *far*[2] dogs, though, at most anything, if you'd get 'em started. Here, Bruno," he called, whistling to the lumbering Newfoundland, who came pitching tumultuously toward them.

"You go hang!" said Haley, getting up. "Come, tumble up now."

Sam tumbled up accordingly, dexterously contriving to tickle Andy as he did so, which occasioned Andy to split out into a laugh, greatly to Haley's indignation, who made a cut at him with his riding-whip.

"I's 'stonished at yer, Andy," said Sam, with awful gravity. "This yer's a seris bisness, Andy. Yer mustn't be a makin' game. This yer an't no way to help Mas'r."

"I shall take the straight road to the river," said Haley, decidedly, after they had come to the boundaries of the estate. "I know the way of all of 'em,—they makes tracks for the underground."[3]

"Sartin," said Sam, "dat's de idee. Mas'r Haley hits de thing right in de middle. Now, der's two roads to de river,—de dirt road and der pike,—which Mas'r mean to take?"

Andy looked up innocently at Sam, surprised at hearing this new geographical fact, but instantly confirmed what he said, by a vehement reiteration.

"Cause," said Sam, "I'd rather be 'clined to 'magine that Lizy'd take de dirt road, bein' it 's the least travelled."

Haley, notwithstanding that he was a very old bird, and naturally inclined to be suspicious of chaff, was rather brought up by this view of the case.

"If yer warn't both on yer such cussed liars, now!" he said, contemplatively, as he pondered a moment.

The pensive, reflective tone in which this was spoken appeared to amuse Andy prodigiously, and he drew a little behind, and shook so as apparently to run a great risk of falling off his horse, while Sam's face was immovably composed into the most doleful gravity.

"Course," said Sam, "Mas'r can do as he 'd ruther; go de straight road, if Mas'r thinks best,—it's all one to us. Now, when I study 'pon it, I think de straight road do best, *deridedly*."

"She would naturally go a lonesome way," said Haley, thinking aloud, and not minding Sam's remark.

"Dar an't no sayin'," said Sam; "gals is pecular; they never does nothin' ye thinks they will; mose gen'lly the contrar. Gals is nat'lly made contrary; and so, if you thinks they've gone one road, it is sartin you'd better go t' other, and then you'll be sure to find 'em. Now, my private 'pinion is, Lizy took der dirt road; so I think we'd better take de straight one."

This profound generic view of the female sex did not seem to dispose Haley particularly to the straight road; and he announced decidedly that he should go the other, and asked Sam when they should come to it.

"A little piece ahead," said Sam, giving a wink to Andy with the eye which was on Andy's side of the head; and he added, gravely, "but I've studded on de matter, and I'm quite clar we ought not to go dat ar way. I nebber been

2. Fair.
3. The Underground Railroad; the informal, secretive network of individuals whose homes were used by slaves escaping from the South to Canada.

over it no way. It's despit lonesome, and we might lose our way,—whar we'd
come to, de Lord only knows."

"Nevertheless," said Haley, "I shall go that way."

"Now I think on 't, I think I hearn 'em tell that dat ar road was all fenced
up and down by der creek, and thar, an't it, Andy?"

Andy wasn't certain; he'd only "hearn tell" about that road, but never
been over it. In short, he was strictly noncommittal.

Haley, accustomed to strike the balance of probabilities between lies of
greater or lesser magnitude, thought that it lay in favor of the dirt road
aforesaid. The mention of the thing he thought he perceived was involuntary on Sam's part at first, and his confused attempts to dissuade him he set
down to a desperate lying on second thoughts, as being unwilling to impli-
cate Eliza.

When, therefore, Sam indicated the road, Haley plunged briskly into it,
followed by Sam and Andy.

Now, the road, in fact, was an old one, that had formerly been a thoroughfare to the river, but abandoned for many years after the laying of the new
pike. It was open for about an hour's ride, and after that it was cut across by
various farms and fences. Sam knew this fact perfectly well,—indeed, the
road had been so long closed up, that Andy had never heard of it. He therefore rode along with an air of dutiful submission, only groaning and vocifer-
ating occasionally that 't was "desp't rough, and bad for Jerry's foot."

"Now, I jest give yer warning," said Haley, "I know yer; yer won't get me to
turn off this yer road, with all yer fussin'—so you shet up!"

"Mas'r will go his own way!" said Sam, with rueful submission, at the
same time winking most portentously to Andy, whose delight was now very
near the explosive point.

Sam was in wonderful spirits,—professed to keep a very brisk look-out,—
at one time exclaiming that he saw "a gal's bonnet" on the top of some distant eminence, or calling to Andy "if that thar wasn't 'Lizy' down in the
hollow;" always making these exclamations in some rough or craggy part
of the road, where the sudden quickening of speed was a special inconvenience to all parties concerned, and thus keeping Haley in a state of constant commotion.

After riding about an hour in this way, the whole party made a precipitate
and tumultuous descent into a barn-yard belonging to a large farming establishment. Not a soul was in sight, all the hands being employed in the fields;
but, as the barn stood conspicuously and plainly square across the road, it was
evident that their journey in that direction had reached a decided finale.

"Wan't dat ar what I telled Mas'r?" said Sam, with an air of injured innocence. "How does strange gentleman spect to know more about a country
dan de natives born and raised?"

"You rascal!" said Haley, "you knew all about this."

"Didn't I tell yer I *know'd*, and yer wouldn't believe me? I telled Mas'r 't
was all shet up, and fenced up, and I didn't spect we could get through,—
Andy heard me."

It was all too true to be disputed, and the unlucky man had to pocket his
wrath with the best grace he was able, and all three faced to the right about,
and took up their line of march for the highway.

In consequence of all the various delays, it was about three-quarters of
an hour after Eliza had laid her child to sleep in the village tavern that the

party came riding into the same place. Eliza was standing by the window, looking out in another direction, when Sam's quick eye caught a glimpse of her. Haley and Andy were two yards behind. At this crisis, Sam contrived to have his hat blown off, and uttered a loud and characteristic ejaculation, which startled her at once; she drew suddenly back; the whole train swept by the window, round to the front door.

A thousand lives seemed to be concentrated in that one moment to Eliza. Her room opened by a side door to the river. She caught her child, and sprang down the steps towards it. The trader caught a full glimpse of her, just as she was disappearing down the bank; and throwing himself from his horse, and calling loudly on Sam and Andy, he was after her like a hound after a deer. In that dizzy moment her feet to her scarce seemed to touch the ground, and a moment brought her to the water's edge. Right on behind they came; and, nerved with strength such as God gives only to the desperate, with one wild cry and flying leap, she vaulted sheer over the turbid current by the shore, on to the raft of ice beyond. It was a desperate leap—impossible to anything but madness and despair; and Haley, Sam, and Andy, instinctively cried out, and lifted up their hands, as she did it.

The huge green fragment of ice on which she alighted pitched and creaked as her weight came on it, but she staid there not a moment. With wild cries and desperate energy she leaped to another and still another cake;—stumbling—leaping—slipping—springing upwards again! Her shoes are gone—her stockings cut from her feet—while blood marked every step; but she saw nothing, felt nothing, till dimly, as in a dream, she saw the Ohio side, and a man helping her up the bank.

"Yer a brave gal, now, whoever ye ar!" said the man, with an oath.

Eliza recognized the voice and face of a man who owned a farm not far from her old home.

"O, Mr. Symmes!—save me—do save me—do hide me!" said Eliza.

"Why, what's this?" said the man. "Why, if 'tan't Shelby's gal!"

"My child!—this boy!—he'd sold him! There is his Mas'r," said she, pointing to the Kentucky shore. "O, Mr. Symmes, you've got a little boy!"

"So I have," said the man, as he roughly, but kindly, drew her up the steep bank. "Besides, you're a right brave gal. I like grit, wherever I see it."

When they had gained the top of the bank, the man paused.

"I'd be glad to do something for ye," said he; "but then there's nowhar I could take ye. The best I can do is to tell ye to go *thar*," said he, pointing to a large white house which stood by itself, off the main street of the village. "Go thar; they're kind folks. Thar's no kind o' danger but they'll help you,—they're up to all that sort o' thing."

"The Lord bless you!" said Eliza, earnestly.

"No 'casion, no 'casion in the world," said the man. "What I've done's of no 'count."

"And, oh, surely, sir, you won't tell any one!"

"Go to thunder, gal! What do you take a feller for? In course not," said the man. "Come, now, go along like a likely, sensible gal, as you are. You've arnt your liberty, and you shall have it, for all me."

The woman folded her child to her bosom, and walked firmly and swiftly away. The man stood and looked after her.

"Shelby, now, mebbe won't think this yer the most neighborly thing in the world; but what's a feller to do? If he catches one of my gals in the same fix, he's welcome to pay back. Somehow I never could see no kind o' critter a strivin' and pantin', and trying to clar theirselves, with the dogs arter 'em, and go agin 'em. Besides, I don't see no kind of 'casion for me to be hunter and catcher for other folks, neither."

So spoke this poor, heathenish Kentuckian, who had not been instructed in his constitutional relations,[4] and consequently was betrayed into acting in a sort of Christianized manner, which, if he had been better situated and more enlightened, he would not have been left to do.

Haley had stood a perfectly amazed spectator of the scene, till Eliza had disappeared up the bank, when he turned a blank, inquiring look on Sam and Andy.

"That ar was a tolable fair stroke of business," said Sam.

"The gal's got seven devils in her, I believe!" said Haley. "How like a wildcat she jumped!"

"Wal, now," said Sam, scratching his head, "I hope Mas'r'll 'scuse us tryin' dat ar road. Don't think I feel spry enough for dat ar, no way!" and Sam gave a hoarse chuckle.

"You laugh!" said the trader, with a growl.

"Lord bless you, Mas'r, I couldn't help it, now," said Sam, giving way to the long pent-up delight of his soul. "She looked so curi's, a leapin' and springin'—ice a crackin'—and only to hear her,—plump! ker chunk! ker splash! Spring! Lord! how she goes it!" and Sam and Andy laughed till the tears rolled down their cheeks.

"I'll make ye laugh t'other side yer mouths!" said the trader, laying about their heads with his riding-whip.

Both ducked, and ran shouting up the bank, and were on their horses before he was up.

"Good-evening, Mas'r!" said Sam, with much gravity. "I berry much spect Missis be anxious 'bout Jerry. Mas'r Haley won't want us no longer. Missis wouldn't hear of our ridin' the critters over Lizy's bridge to-night;" and, with a facetious poke into Andy's ribs, he started off, followed by the latter, at full speed,—their shouts of laughter coming faintly on the wind.

* * *

CHAPTER IX. IN WHICH IT APPEARS THAT A SENATOR IS BUT A MAN

The light of the cheerful fire shone on the rug and carpet of a cosey parlor, and glittered on the sides of the tea-cups and well-brightened tea-pot, as Senator Bird[5] was drawing off his boots, preparatory to inserting his feet in a pair of new handsome slippers, which his wife had been working for him while away on his senatorial tour. Mrs. Bird, looking the very picture of delight, was superintending the arrangements of the table, ever and anon mingling admonitory remarks to a number of frolicsome juveniles, who were effervescing in all those modes of untold gambol and mischief that have astonished mothers ever since the flood.

"Tom, let the door-knob alone,—there's a man! Mary! Mary! don't pull the cat's tail,—poor pussy! Jim, you mustn't climb on that table,—no, no!—

4. Allusion to the Fugitive Slave Law, recently passed by Congress as part of the Compromise of 1850, which made it a federal crime to aid fugitive slaves.
5. An Ohio state senator, returning from a session in Columbus, the state capital.

You don't know, my dear, what a surprise it is to us all, to see you here to-night!" said she, at last, when she found a space to say something to her husband.

"Yes, yes, I thought I'd just make a run down, spend the night, and have a little comfort at home. I'm tired to death, and my head aches!"

Mrs. Bird cast a glance at a camphor-bottle,[6] which stood in the half-open closet, and appeared to meditate an approach to it, but her husband interposed.

"No, no, Mary, no doctoring! a cup of your good hot tea, and some of our good home living, is what I want. It's a tiresome business, this legislating!"

And the senator smiled, as if he rather liked the idea of considering himself a sacrifice to his country.

"Well," said his wife, after the business of the tea-table was getting rather slack, "and what have they been doing in the Senate?"

Now, it was a very unusual thing for gentle little Mrs. Bird ever to trouble her head with what was going on in the house of the state, very wisely considering that she had enough to do to mind her own. Mr. Bird, therefore, opened his eyes in surprise, and said,

"Not very much of importance."

"Well; but is it true that they have been passing a law forbidding people to give meat and drink to those poor colored folks that come along?[7] I heard they were talking of some such law, but I didn't think any Christian legislature would pass it!"

"Why, Mary, you are getting to be a politician, all at once."

"No, nonsense! I wouldn't give a fip for all your politics, generally, but I think this is something downright cruel and unchristian. I hope, my dear, no such law has been passed."

"There has been a law passed forbidding people to help off the slaves that come over from Kentucky, my dear; so much of that thing has been done by these reckless Abolitionists, that our brethren in Kentucky are very strongly excited, and it seems necessary, and no more than Christian and kind, that something should be done by our state to quiet the excitement."

"And what is the law? It don't forbid us to shelter these poor creatures a night, does it, and to give 'em something comfortable to eat, and a few old clothes, and send them quietly about their business?"

"Why, yes, my dear; that would be aiding and abetting, you know."

Mrs. Bird was a timid, blushing little woman, of about four feet in height, and with mild blue eyes, and a peach-blow[8] complexion, and the gentlest, sweetest voice in the world;—as for courage, a moderate-sized cock-turkey had been known to put her to rout at the very first gobble, and a stout house-dog, of moderate capacity, would bring her into subjection merely by a show of his teeth. Her husband and children were her entire world, and in these she ruled more by entreaty and persuasion than by command or argument. There was only one thing that was capable of arousing her, and that provocation came in on the side of her unusually gentle and sympathetic nature;—anything in the shape of cruelty would throw her into a passion, which was the more alarming and inexplicable in proportion to the general

6. During the 19th century, camphor, a compound from a tree of the same name, was used for pain relief.

7. Such a state law would have added force to the federal Fugitive Slave Law.
8. Peach blossom.

softness of her nature. Generally the most indulgent and easy to be entreated of all mothers, still her boys had a very reverent remembrance of a most vehement chastisement she once bestowed on them, because she found them leagued with several graceless boys of the neighborhood, stoning a defenceless kitten.

"I'll tell you what," Master Bill used to say, "I was scared that time. Mother came at me so that I thought she was crazy, and I was whipped and tumbled off to bed, without any supper, before I could get over wondering what had come about; and, after that, I heard mother crying outside the door, which made me feel worse than all the rest. I'll tell you what," he'd say, "we boys never stoned another kitten!"

On the present occasion, Mrs. Bird rose quickly, with very red cheeks, which quite improved her general appearance, and walked up to her husband, with quite a resolute air, and said, in a determined tone,

"Now, John, I want to know if you think such a law as that is right and Christian?"

"You won't shoot me, now, Mary, if I say I do!"

"I never could have thought it of you, John; you didn't vote for it?"

"Even so, my fair politician."

"You ought to be ashamed, John! Poor, homeless, houseless creatures! It's a shameful, wicked, abominable law, and I'll break it, for one, the first time I get a chance; and I hope I *shall* have a chance, I do! Things have got to a pretty pass, if a woman can't give a warm supper and a bed to poor, starving creatures, just because they are slaves, and have been abused and oppressed all their lives, poor things!"

"But, Mary, just listen to me. Your feelings are all quite right, dear, and interesting, and I love you for them; but, then, dear, we mustn't suffer our feelings to run away with our judgment; you must consider it's not a matter of private feeling,—there are great public interests involved,—there is such a state of public agitation rising, that we must put aside our private feelings."

"Now, John, I don't know anything about politics, but I can read my Bible; and there I see that I must feed the hungry, clothe the naked, and comfort the desolate; and that Bible I mean to follow."

"But in cases where your doing so would involve a great public evil—"

"Obeying God never brings on public evils. I know it can't. It's always safest, all round, to *do as He* bids us."

"Now, listen to me, Mary, and I can state to you a very clear argument, to show—"

"O, nonsense, John! you can talk all night, but you wouldn't do it. I put it to you, John,—would *you* now turn away a poor, shivering, hungry creature from your door, because he was a runaway? *Would* you, now?"

Now, if the truth must be told, our senator had the misfortune to be a man who had a particularly humane and accessible nature, and turning away anybody that was in trouble never had been his forte; and what was worse for him in this particular pinch of the argument was, that his wife knew it, and, of course, was making an assault on rather an indefensible point. So he had recourse to the usual means of gaining time for such cases made and provided; he said "ahem," and coughed several times, took out his pockethandkerchief, and began to wipe his glasses. Mrs. Bird, seeing the defenceless condition of the enemy's territory, had no more conscience than to push her advantage.

"I should like to see you doing that, John—I really should! Turning a woman out of doors in a snow-storm, for instance; or, may be you'd take her up and put her in jail, wouldn't you? You would make a great hand at that!"

"Of course, it would be a very painful duty," began Mr. Bird, in a moderate tone.

"Duty, John! don't use that word! You know it isn't a duty—it can't be a duty! If folks want to keep their slaves from running away, let 'em treat 'em well,—that's my doctrine. If I had slaves (as I hope I never shall have), I'd risk their wanting to run away from me, or you either, John. I tell you folks don't run away when they are happy; and when they do run, poor creatures! they suffer enough with cold and hunger and fear, without everybody's turning against them; and, law or no law, I never will, so help me God!"

"Mary! Mary! My dear, let me reason with you."

"I hate reasoning, John,—especially reasoning on such subjects. There's a way you political folks have of coming round and round a plain right thing; and you don't believe in it yourselves, when it comes to practice. I know *you* well enough, John. You don't believe it's right any more than I do; and you wouldn't do it any sooner than I."

At this critical juncture, old Cudjoe, the black man-of-all-work, put his head in at the door, and wished "Missis would come into the kitchen;" and our senator, tolerably relieved, looked after his little wife with a whimsical mixture of amusement and vexation, and, seating himself in the arm-chair, began to read the papers.

After a moment, his wife's voice was heard at the door, in a quick, earnest tone,—"John! John! I do wish you'd come here, a moment."

He laid down his paper, and went into the kitchen, and started, quite amazed at the sight that presented itself:—A young and slender woman, with garments torn and frozen, with one shoe gone, and the stocking torn away from the cut and bleeding foot, was laid back in a deadly swoon upon two chairs. There was the impress of the despised race on her face, yet none could help feeling its mournful and pathetic beauty, while its stony sharpness, its cold, fixed, deathly aspect, struck a solemn chill over him. He drew his breath short, and stood in silence. His wife, and their only colored domestic, old Aunt Dinah, were busily engaged in restorative measures; while old Cudjoe had got the boy on his knee, and was busy pulling off his shoes and stockings, and chafing his little cold feet.

"Sure, now, if she an't a sight to behold!" said old Dinah, compassionately; "'pears like 'twas the heat that made her faint. She was tol'able peart when she cum in, and asked if she couldn't warm herself here a spell; and I was just a askin' her where she cum from, and she fainted right down. Never done much hard work, guess, by the looks of her hands."

"Poor creature!" said Mrs. Bird, compassionately, as the woman slowly unclosed her large, dark eyes, and looked vacantly at her. Suddenly an expression of agony crossed her face, and she sprang up, saying, "O, my Harry! Have they got him?"

The boy, at this, jumped from Cudjoe's knee, and, running to her side, put up his arms. "O, he's here! he's here!" she exclaimed.

"O, ma'am!" said she, wildly, to Mrs. Bird, "do protect us! don't let them get him!"

"Nobody shall hurt you here, poor woman," said Mrs. Bird, encouragingly. "You are safe; don't be afraid."

"God bless you!" said the woman, covering her face and sobbing; while the little boy, seeing her crying, tried to get into her lap.

With many gentle and womanly offices, which none knew better how to render than Mrs. Bird, the poor woman was, in time, rendered more calm. A temporary bed was provided for her on the settle,[9] near the fire; and, after a short time, she fell into a heavy slumber, with the child, who seemed no less weary, soundly sleeping on her arm; for the mother resisted, with nervous anxiety, the kindest attempts to take him from her; and, even in sleep, her arm encircled him with an unrelaxing clasp, as if she could not even then be beguiled of her vigilant hold.

Mr. and Mrs. Bird had gone back to the parlor, where, strange as it may appear, no reference was made, on either side, to the preceding conversation; but Mrs. Bird busied herself with her knitting-work, and Mr. Bird pretended to be reading the paper.

"I wonder who and what she is!" said Mr. Bird, at last, as he laid it down.

"When she wakes up and feels a little rested, we will see," said Mrs. Bird.

"I say, wife!" said Mr. Bird, after musing in silence over his newspaper.

"Well, dear!"

"She couldn't wear one of your gowns, could she, by any letting down, or such matter? She seems to be rather larger than you are."

A quite perceptible smile glimmered on Mrs. Bird's face, as she answered, "We'll see."

Another pause, and Mr. Bird again broke out,

"I say, wife!"

"Well! What now?"

"Why, there's that old bombazin[1] cloak, that you keep on purpose to put over me when I take my afternoon's nap; you might as well give her that,— she needs clothes."

At this instant, Dinah looked in to say that the woman was awake, and wanted to see Missis.

Mr. and Mrs. Bird went into the kitchen, followed by the two eldest boys, the smaller fry having, by this time, been safely disposed of in bed.

The woman was now sitting up on the settle, by the fire. She was looking steadily into the blaze, with a calm, heartbroken expression, very different from her former agitated wildness.

"Did you want me?" said Mrs. Bird, in gentle tones. "I hope you feel better now, poor woman!"

A long-drawn, shivering sigh was the only answer; but she lifted her dark eyes, and fixed them on her with such a forlorn and imploring expression, that the tears came into the little woman's eyes.

"You needn't be afraid of anything; we are friends here, poor woman! Tell me where you came from, and what you want," said she.

"I came from Kentucky," said the woman.

"When?" said Mr. Bird, taking up the interrogatory.

"To-night."

"How did you come?"

"I crossed on the ice."

"Crossed on the ice!" said every one present.

---

9. A small sofa.   1. Fabric woven of silk and wool.

"Yes," said the woman, slowly, "I did. God helping me, I crossed on the ice; for they were behind me—right behind—and there was no other way!"

"Law, Missis," said Cudjoe, "the ice is all in broken-up blocks, a swinging and a tetering up and down in the water!"

"I know it was—I know it!" said she, wildly; "but I did it! I wouldn't have thought I could,—I didn't think I should get over, but I didn't care! I could but die, if I didn't. The Lord helped me; nobody knows how much the Lord can help 'em, till they try," said the woman, with a flashing eye.

"Were you a slave?" said Mr. Bird.

"Yes, sir; I belonged to a man in Kentucky."

"Was he unkind to you?"

"No, sir; he was a good master."

"And was your mistress unkind to you?"

"No, sir—no! my mistress was always good to me."

"What could induce you to leave a good home, then, and run away, and go through such dangers?"

The woman looked up at Mrs. Bird, with a keen, scrutinizing glance, and it did not escape her that she was dressed in deep mourning.

"Ma'am," she said, suddenly, "have you ever lost a child?"

The question was unexpected, and it was a thrust on a new wound; for it was only a month since a darling child of the family had been laid in the grave.

Mr. Bird turned around and walked to the window, and Mrs. Bird burst into tears; but, recovering her voice, she said,

"Why do you ask that? I have lost a little one."

"Then you will feel for me. I have lost two, one after another,—left 'em buried there when I came away; and I had only this one left. I never slept a night without him; he was all I had. He was my comfort and pride, day and night; and, ma'am, they were going to take him away from me,—to *sell* him,—sell him down south, ma'am, to go all alone,—a baby that had never been away from his mother in his life! I couldn't stand it, ma'am. I knew I never should be good for anything, if they did; and when I knew the papers were signed, and he was sold, I took him and came off in the night; and they chased me,—the man that bought him, and some of Mas'r's folks,—and they were coming down right behind me, and I heard 'em. I jumped right on to the ice; and how I got across, I don't know,—but, first I knew, a man was helping me up the bank."

The woman did not sob nor weep. She had gone to a place where tears are dry; but every one around her was, in some way characteristic of themselves, showing signs of hearty sympathy.

The two little boys, after a desperate rummaging in their pockets, in search of those pocket-handkerchiefs which mothers know are never to be found there, had thrown themselves disconsolately into the skirts of their mother's gown, where they were sobbing, and wiping their eyes and noses, to their hearts' content;—Mrs. Bird had her face fairly hidden in her pocket-handkerchief; and old Dinah, with tears streaming down her black, honest face, was ejaculating, "Lord have mercy on us!" with all the fervor of a camp-meeting;—while old Cudjoe, rubbing his eyes very hard with his cuffs, and making a most uncommon variety of wry faces, occasionally responded in the same key, with great fervor. Our senator was a statesman, and of course could not be expected to cry, like other mortals; and so he turned his back to the company, and looked out of the window, and seemed particularly busy in clearing his throat and wiping his spectacle-glasses, occasionally blowing his nose in a manner that was calculated to excite suspicion, had any one been in a state to observe critically.

"How came you to tell me you had a kind master?" he suddenly exclaimed, gulping down very resolutely some kind of rising in his throat, and turning suddenly round upon the woman.

"Because he *was* a kind master; I'll say that of him, any way;—and my mistress was kind; but they couldn't help themselves. They were owing money; and there was some way, I can't tell how, that a man had a hold on them, and they were obliged to give him his will. I listened, and heard him telling mistress that, and she begging and pleading for me,—and he told her he couldn't help himself, and that the papers were all drawn;—and then it was I took him and left my home, and came away. I knew 'twas no use of my trying to live, if they did it; for 't 'pears like this child is all I have."

"Have you no husband?"

"Yes, but he belongs to another man. His master is real hard to him, and won't let him come to see me, hardly ever; and he's grown harder and harder upon us, and he threatens to sell him down south;—it's like I'll never see *him* again!"

The quiet tone in which the woman pronounced these words might have led a superficial observer to think that she was entirely apathetic; but there was a calm, settled depth of anguish in her large, dark eye, that spoke of something far otherwise.

"And where do you mean to go, my poor woman?" said Mrs. Bird.

"To Canada, if I only knew where that was. Is it very far off, is Canada?" said she, looking up, with a simple, confiding air, to Mrs. Bird's face.

"Poor thing!" said Mrs. Bird, involuntarily.

"Is't a very great way off, think?" said the woman, earnestly.

"Much further than you think, poor child!" said Mrs. Bird; "but we will try to think what can be done for you. Here, Dinah, make her up a bed in your own room, close by the kitchen, and I'll think what to do for her in the morning. Meanwhile, never fear, poor woman; put your trust in God; he will protect you."

Mrs. Bird and her husband reentered the parlor. She sat down in her little rocking-chair before the fire, swaying thoughtfully to and fro. Mr. Bird strode up and down the room, grumbling to himself, "Pish! pshaw! confounded awkward business!" At length, striding up to his wife, he said,

"I say, wife, she'll have to get away from here, this very night. That fellow will be down on the scent bright and early to-morrow morning; if 'twas only the woman, she could lie quiet till it was over; but that little chap can't be kept still by a troop of horse and foot, I'll warrant me; he'll bring it all out, popping his head out of some window or door. A pretty kettle of fish it would be for me, too, to be caught with them both here, just now! No; they'll have to be got off to-night."

"To-night! How is it possible?—where to?"

"Well, I know pretty well where to," said the senator, beginning to put on his boots, with a reflective air; and, stopping when his leg was half in, he embraced his knee with both hands, and seemed to go off in deep meditation.

"It's a confounded awkward, ugly business," said he, at last, beginning to tug at his boot-straps again, "and that's a fact!" After one boot was fairly on, the senator sat with the other in his hand, profoundly studying the figure of the carpet. "It will have to be done, though, for aught I see,—hang it all!" and he drew the other boot anxiously on, and looked out of the window.

Now, little Mrs. Bird was a discreet woman,—a woman who never in her life said, "I told you so!" and, on the present occasion, though pretty well aware of the shape her husband's meditations were taking, she very prudently forbore to meddle with them, only sat very quietly in her chair, and looked quite ready to hear her liege lord's intentions, when he should think proper to utter them.

"You see," he said, "there's my old client, Van Trompe, has come over from Kentucky, and set all his slaves free; and he has bought a place seven miles up the creek, here, back in the woods, where nobody goes, unless they go on purpose; and it's a place that isn't found in a hurry. There she'd be safe enough; but the plague of the thing is, nobody could drive a carriage there to-night, but *me*."

"Why not? Cudjoe is an excellent driver."

"Ay, ay, but here it is. The creek has to be crossed twice; and the second crossing is quite dangerous, unless one knows it as I do. I have crossed it a hundred times on horseback, and know exactly the turns to take. And so, you see, there's no help for it. Cudjoe must put in the horses, as quietly as may be, about twelve o'clock, and I'll take her over; and then, to give color to the matter, he must carry me on to the next tavern, to take the stage[2] for Columbus, that comes by about three or four, and so it will look as if I had had the carriage only for that. I shall get into business bright and early in the morning. But I'm thinking I shall feel rather cheap there, after all that's been said and done; but, hang it, I can't help it!"

"Your heart is better than your head, in this case, John," said the wife, laying her little white hand on his. "Could I ever have loved you, had I not known you better than you know yourself?" And the little woman looked so handsome, with the tears sparkling in her eyes, that the senator thought he must be a decidedly clever fellow, to get such a pretty creature into such a passionate admiration of him; and so, what could he do but walk off soberly, to see about the carriage. At the door, however, he stopped a moment, and then coming back, he said, with some hesitation,

"Mary, I don't know how you'd feel about it, but there's that drawer full of things—of—of—poor little Henry's." So saying, he turned quickly on his heel, and shut the door after him.

His wife opened the little bed-room door adjoining her room, and, taking the candle, set it down on the top of a bureau there; then from a small recess she took a key, and put it thoughtfully in the lock of a drawer, and made a sudden pause, while two boys, who, boy like, had followed close on her heels, stood looking, with silent, significant glances, at their mother. And oh! mother that reads this, has there never been in your house a drawer, or a closet, the opening of which has been to you like the opening again of a little grave? Ah! happy mother that you are, if it has not been so.

Mrs. Bird slowly opened the drawer. There were little coats of many a form and pattern, piles of aprons, and rows of small stockings; and even a pair of little shoes, worn and rubbed at the toes, were peeping from the folds of a paper. There was a toy horse and wagon, a top, a ball,—memorials gathered

2. Stagecoach.

with many a tear and many a heart-break! She sat down by the drawer, and, leaning her head on her hands over it, wept till the tears fell through her fingers into the drawer; then suddenly raising her head, she began, with nervous haste, selecting the plainest and most substantial articles, and gathering them into a bundle.

"Mamma," said one of the boys, gently touching her arm, "are you going to give away *those* things?"

"My dear boys," she said, softly and earnestly, "if our dear, loving little Henry looks down from heaven, he would be glad to have us do this. I could not find it in my heart to give them away to any common person—to anybody that was happy; but I give them to a mother more heart-broken and sorrowful than I am; and I hope God will send his blessings with them!"

There are in this world blessed souls, whose sorrows all spring up into joys for others; whose earthly hopes, laid in the grave with many tears, are the seed from which spring healing flowers and balm for the desolate and the distressed. Among such was the delicate woman who sits there by the lamp, dropping slow tears, while she prepares the memorials of her own lost one for the outcast wanderer.

After a while, Mrs. Bird opened a wardrobe, and, taking from thence a plain, serviceable dress or two, she sat down busily to her work-table, and, with needle, scissors, and thimble, at hand, quietly commenced the "letting down" process which her husband had recommended, and continued busily at it till the old clock in the corner struck twelve, and she heard the low rattling of wheels at the door.

"Mary," said her husband, coming in, with his overcoat in his hand, "you must wake her up now; we must be off."

Mrs. Bird hastily deposited the various articles she had collected in a small plain trunk, and locking it, desired her husband to see it in the carriage, and then proceeded to call the woman. Soon, arrayed in a cloak, bonnet, and shawl, that had belonged to her benefactress, she appeared at the door with her child in her arms. Mr. Bird hurried her into the carriage, and Mrs. Bird pressed on after her to the carriage steps. Eliza leaned out of the carriage, and put out her hand,—a hand as soft and beautiful as was given in return. She fixed her large, dark eyes, full of earnest meaning, on Mrs. Bird's face, and seemed going to speak. Her lips moved,—she tried once or twice, but there was no sound,—and pointing upward, with a look never to be forgotten, she fell back in the seat, and covered her face. The door was shut, and the carriage drove on.

What a situation, now, for a patriotic senator, that had been all the week before spurring up the legislature of his native state to pass more stringent resolutions against escaping fugitives, their harborers and abettors!

Our good senator in his native state had not been exceeded by any of his brethren at Washington, in the sort of eloquence which has won for them immortal renown! How sublimely he had sat with his hands in his pockets, and scouted[3] all sentimental weakness of those who would put the welfare of a few miserable fugitives before great state interests!

He was as bold as a lion about it, and "mightily convinced" not only himself, but everybody that heard him;—but then his idea of a fugitive was only an idea of the letters that spell the word,—or, at the most, the image of a

3. Mocked.

little newspaper picture of a man with a stick and bundle, with "Ran away from the subscriber" under it. The magic of the real presence of distress,— the imploring human eye, the frail, trembling human hand, the despairing appeal of helpless agony,—these he had never tried. He had never thought that a fugitive might be a hapless mother, a defenceless child,—like that one which was now wearing his lost boy's little well-known cap; and so, as our poor senator was not stone or steel,—as he was a man, and a downright noblehearted one, too,—he was, as everybody must see, in a sad case for his patriotism. And you need not exult over him, good brother of the Southern States; for we have some inklings that many of you, under similar circumstances, would not do much better. We have reason to know, in Kentucky, as in Mississippi, are noble and generous hearts, to whom never was tale of suffering told in vain. Ah, good brother! is it fair for you to expect of us services which your own brave, honorable heart would not allow you to render, were you in our place?

Be that as it may, if our good senator was a political sinner, he was in a fair way to expiate it by his night's penance. There had been a long continuous period of rainy weather, and the soft, rich earth of Ohio, as every one knows, is admirably suited to the manufacture of mud,—and the road was an Ohio railroad of the good old times.

"And pray, what sort of a road may that be?" says some eastern traveller, who has been accustomed to connect no ideas with a railroad, but those of smoothness or speed.

Know, then, innocent eastern friend, that in benighted regions of the west, where the mud is of unfathomable and sublime depth, roads are made of round rough logs, arranged transversely side by side, and coated over in their pristine freshness with earth, turf, and whatsoever may come to hand, and then the rejoicing native calleth it a road, and straightway essayeth to ride thereupon. In process of time, the rains wash off all the turf and grass aforesaid, move the logs hither and thither, in picturesque positions, up, down and crosswise, with divers chasms and ruts of black mud intervening.

Over such a road as this our senator went stumbling along, making moral reflections as continuously as under the circumstances could be expected,— the carriage proceeding along much as follows,—bump! bump! bump! slush! down in the mud!—the senator, woman and child, reversing their positions so suddenly as to come, without any very accurate adjustment, against the windows of the down-hill side. Carriage sticks fast, while Cudjoe on the outside is heard making a great muster among the horses. After various ineffectual pullings and twitchings, just as the senator is losing all patience, the carriage suddenly rights itself with a bounce,—two front wheels go down into another abyss, and senator, woman, and child, all tumble promiscuously on to the front seat,—senator's hat is jammed over his eyes and nose quite unceremoniously, and he considers himself fairly extinguished;—child cries, and Cudjoe on the outside delivers animated addresses to the horses, who are kicking, and floundering, and straining, under repeated cracks of the whip. Carriage springs up, with another bounce,—down go the hind wheels,— senator, woman, and child, fly over on to the back seat, his elbows encountering her bonnet, and both her feet being jammed into his hat, which flies off in the concussion. After a few moments the "slough" is passed, and the horses stop, panting;—the senator finds his hat, the woman straightens her bonnet and hushes her child, and they brace themselves firmly for what is yet to come.

For a while only the continuous bump! bump! intermingled, just by way of variety, with divers side plunges and compound shakes; and they begin to flatter themselves that they are not so badly off, after all. At last, with a square plunge, which puts all on to their feet and then down into their seats with incredible quickness, the carriage stops,—and, after much outside commotion, Cudjoe appears at the door.

"Please, sir, it's powerful bad spot, this yer. I don't know how we's to get clar out. I'm a thinkin' we'll have to be a gettin' rails."[4]

The senator despairingly steps out, picking gingerly for some firm foothold; down goes one foot an immeasurable depth,—he tries to pull it up, loses his balance, and tumbles over into the mud, and is fished out, in a very despairing condition, by Cudjoe.

But we forbear, out of sympathy to our readers' bones. Western travellers, who have beguiled the midnight hour in the interesting process of pulling down rail fences, to pry their carriages out of mud holes, will have a respectful and mournful sympathy with our unfortunate hero. We beg them to drop a silent tear, and pass on.

It was full late in the night when the carriage emerged, dripping and bespattered, out of the creek, and stood at the door of a large farm-house.

It took no inconsiderable perseverance to arouse the inmates; but at last the respectable proprietor appeared, and undid the door. He was a great, tall, bristling Orson of a fellow,[5] full six feet and some inches in his stockings, and arrayed in a red flannel hunting-shirt. A very heavy *mat* of sandy hair, in a decidedly tousled condition, and a beard of some days' growth, gave the worthy man an appearance, to say the least, not particularly prepossessing. He stood for a few minutes holding the candle aloft, and blinking on our travellers with a dismal and mystified expression that was truly ludicrous. It cost some effort of our senator to induce him to comprehend the case fully; and while he is doing his best at that, we shall give him a little introduction to our readers.

Honest old John Van Trompe was once quite a considerable land-holder and slave-owner in the State of Kentucky. Having "nothing of the bear about him but the skin,"[6] and being gifted by nature with a great, honest, just heart, quite equal to his gigantic frame, he had been for some years witnessing with repressed uneasiness the workings of a system equally bad for oppressor and oppressed. At last, one day, John's great heart had swelled altogether too big to wear his bonds any longer; so he just took his pocket-book out of his desk, and went over into Ohio, and bought a quarter of a township of good, rich land, made out free papers for all his people,—men, women, and children,—packed them up in wagons, and sent them off to settle down; and then honest John turned his face up the creek, and sat quietly down on a snug, retired farm, to enjoy his conscience and his reflections.

---

4. A reference to the practice of removing boards from rail fences to make tracks to enable a carriage or cart to get out of the mud.
5. A strong, wild man; from the story of "Orson and Valentine," an early French romance that appeared in English around 1550. Orson is the lost son of a king; abandoned in the woods, he was

raised by a bear.
6. As recorded in James Boswell's *Life of Samuel Johnson* (1791), the Anglo-Irish author Oliver Goldsmith (1730–1794) proclaimed that the great English author and critic Johnson (1709–1784) "had nothing of the bear but his skin."

"Are you the man that will shelter a poor woman and child from slave-catchers?" said the senator, explicitly.

"I rather think I am," said honest John, with some considerable emphasis.

"I thought so," said the senator.

"If there's anybody comes," said the good man, stretching his tall, muscular form upward, "why here I'm ready for him: and I've got seven sons, each six foot high, and they'll be ready for 'em. Give our respects to 'em," said John; "tell 'em it's no matter how soon they call,—make no kinder difference to us," said John, running his fingers through the shock of hair that thatched his head, and bursting out into a great laugh.

Weary, jaded, and spiritless, Eliza dragged herself up to the door, with her child lying in a heavy sleep on her arm. The rough man held the candle to her face, and uttering a kind of compassionate grunt, opened the door of a small bedroom adjoining to the large kitchen where they were standing, and motioned her to go in. He took down a candle, and lighting it, set it upon the table, and then addressed himself to Eliza.

"Now, I say, gal, you needn't be a bit afeard, let who will come here. I'm up to all that sort o' thing," said he, pointing to two or three goodly rifles over the mantel-piece; "and most people that know me know that 't wouldn't be healthy to try to get anybody out o' my house when I'm agin it. So *now* you jist go to sleep now, as quiet as if yer mother was a rockin' ye," said he, as he shut the door.

"Why, this is an uncommon handsome un," he said to the senator. "Ah, well; handsome uns has the greatest cause to run, sometimes, if they has any kind o' feelin, such as decent women should. I know all about that."

The senator, in a few words, briefly explained Eliza's history.

"O! ou! aw! now, I want to know?" said the good man, pitifully; "sho! now sho! That's natur now, poor crittur! hunted down now like a deer,—hunted down, jest for havin' natural feelin's, and doin' what no kind o' mother could help a doin'! I tell ye what, these yer things make me come the nighest to swearin', now, o' most anything," said honest John, as he wiped his eyes with the back of a great, freckled, yellow hand. "I tell yer what, stranger, it was years and years before I'd jine the church, 'cause the ministers round in our parts used to preach that the Bible went in for these ere cuttings up,—and I couldn't be up to 'em with their Greek and Hebrew, and so I took up agin 'em, Bible and all. I never jined the church till I found a minister that was up to 'em all in Greek and all that, and he said right the contrary; and then I took right hold, and jined the church,—I did now, fact," said John, who had been all this time uncorking some very frisky bottled cider, which at this juncture he presented.

"Ye'd better jest put up here, now, till daylight," said he, heartily, "and I'll call up the old woman, and have a bed got ready for you in no time."

"Thank you, my good friend," said the senator, "I must be along, to take the night stage for Columbus."

"Ah! well, then, if you must, I'll go a piece with you, and show you a cross road that will take you there better than the road you came on. That road's mighty bad."

John equipped himself, and, with a lantern in hand, was soon seen guiding the senator's carriage towards a road that ran down in a hollow, back of his dwelling. When they parted, the senator put into his hand a ten-dollar bill.

"It's for her," he said, briefly.

"Ay, ay," said John, with equal conciseness.

They shook hands, and parted.

* * *

CHAPTER XII. SELECT INCIDENT OF LAWFUL TRADE

"In Ramah there was a voice heard,—weeping, and lamentation,
and great mourning; Rachel weeping for her children, and would
not be comforted."[7]

Mr. Haley and Tom jogged onward in their wagon, each, for a time, absorbed in his own reflections. Now, the reflections of two men sitting side by side are a curious thing,—seated on the same seat, having the same eyes, ears, hands and organs of all sorts, and having pass before their eyes the same objects,—it is wonderful what a variety we shall find in these same reflections!

As, for example, Mr. Haley: he thought first of Tom's length, and breadth, and height, and what he would sell for, if he was kept fat and in good case till he got him into market. He thought of how he should make out his gang; he thought of the respective market value of certain supposititious men and women and children who were to compose it, and other kindred topics of the business; then he thought of himself, and how humane he was, that whereas other men chained their "niggers" hand and foot both, he only put fetters on the feet, and left Tom the use of his hands, as long as he behaved well; and he sighed to think how ungrateful human nature was, so that there was even room to doubt whether Tom appreciated his mercies. He had been taken in so by "niggers" whom he had favored; but still he was astonished to consider how good-natured he yet remained!

As to Tom, he was thinking over some words of an unfashionable old book, which kept running through his head again and again, as follows: "We have here no continuing city, but we seek one to come; wherefore God himself is not ashamed to be called our God; for he hath prepared for us a city."[8] These words of an ancient volume, got up principally by "ignorant and unlearned men," have, through all time, kept up, somehow, a strange sort of power over the minds of poor, simple fellows, like Tom. They stir up the soul from its depths, and rouse, as with trumpet call, courage, energy, and enthusiasm, where before was only the blackness of despair.

Mr. Haley pulled out of his pocket sundry newspapers, and began looking over their advertisements, with absorbed interest. He was not a remarkably fluent reader, and was in the habit of reading in a sort of recitative half-aloud, by way of calling in his ears to verify the deductions of his eyes. In this tone he slowly recited the following paragraph:

"EXECUTOR'S SALE,—NEGROES!—Agreeably to order of court, will be sold, on Tuesday, February 20, before the Court-house door, in the town of Washington, Kentucky, the following negroes: Hagar, aged 60; John, aged 30; Ben, aged 21; Saul, aged 25; Albert, aged 14. Sold for the benefit of the creditors and heirs of the estate of Jesse Blutchford, Esq.

SAMUEL MORRIS,

THOMAS FLINT,

Executors."

7. Paraphrase of Jeremiah 31.15.

8. Amalgam of Hebrews 11.16 and Hebrews 13.14.

"This yer I must look at," said he to Tom, for want of somebody else to talk to.

"Ye see, I'm going to get up a prime gang to take down with ye, Tom; it'll make it sociable and pleasant like,—good company will, ye know. We must drive right to Washington[9] first and foremost, and then I'll clap you into jail, while I does the business."

Tom received this agreeable intelligence quite meekly; simply wondering, in his own heart, how many of these doomed men had wives and children, and whether they would feel as he did about leaving them. It is to be confessed, too, that the naïve, off-hand information that he was to be thrown into jail by no means produced an agreeable impression on a poor fellow who had always prided himself on a strictly honest and upright course of life. Yes, Tom, we must confess it, was rather proud of his honesty, poor fellow,— not having very much else to be proud of;—if he had belonged to some of the higher walks of society, he, perhaps, would never have been reduced to such straits. However, the day wore on, and the evening saw Haley and Tom comfortably accommodated in Washington,—the one in a tavern, and the other in a jail.

About eleven o'clock the next day, a mixed throng was gathered around the court-house steps,—smoking, chewing, spitting, swearing, and conversing, according to their respective tastes and turns,—waiting for the auction to commence. The men and women to be sold sat in a group apart, talking in a low tone to each other. The woman who had been advertised by the name of Hagar was a regular African in feature and figure. She might have been sixty, but was older than that by hard work and disease, was partially blind, and somewhat crippled with rheumatism. By her side stood her only remaining son, Albert, a bright-looking little fellow of fourteen years. The boy was the only survivor of a large family, who had been successively sold away from her to a southern market. The mother held on to him with both her shaking hands, and eyed with intense trepidation every one who walked up to examine him.

"Don't be feard, Aunt Hagar," said the oldest of the men, "I spoke to Mas'r Thomas 'bout it, and he thought he might manage to sell you in a lot both together."

"Dey needn't call me worn out yet," said she, lifting her shaking hands. "I can cook yet, and scrub, and scour,—I'm wuth a buying, if I do come cheap;—tell em dat ar,—you *tell* em," she added, earnestly.

Haley here forced his way into the group, walked up to the old man, pulled his mouth open and looked in, felt of his teeth, made him stand and straighten himself, bend his back, and perform various evolutions to show his muscles; and then passed on to the next, and put him through the same trial. Walking up last to the boy, he felt of his arms, straightened his hands, and looked at his fingers, and made him jump, to show his agility.

"He an't gwine to be sold widout me!" said the old woman, with passionate eagerness; "he and I goes in a lot together; I's rail strong yet, Mas'r, and can do heaps o' work,—heaps on it, Mas'r."

"On plantation?" said Haley, with a contemptuous glance. "Likely story!" and, as if satisfied with his examination, he walked out and looked, and stood with his hands in his pocket, his cigar in his mouth, and his hat cocked on one side, ready for action.

9. Washington, Kentucky; upriver from New Orleans.

"What think of 'em?" said a man who had been following Haley's examination, as if to make up his own mind from it.

"Wal," said Haley, spitting, "I shall put in, I think, for the youngerly ones and the boy."

"They want to sell the boy and the old woman together," said the man.

"Find it a tight pull;—why, she's an old rack o' bones,—not worth her salt."

"You wouldn't, then?" said the man.

"Anybody'd be a fool 't would. She's half blind, crooked with rheumatis, and foolish to boot."

"Some buys up these yer old critturs, and ses there's a sight more wear in 'em than a body'd think," said the man, reflectively.

"No go, 't all," said Haley; "wouldn't take her for a present,—fact,—I've *seen*, now."

"Wal, 'tis kinder pity, now, not to buy her with her son,—her heart seems so sot on him,—s'pose they fling her in cheap."

"Them that's got money to spend that ar way, it's all well enough. I shall bid off on that ar boy for a plantation-hand;—wouldn't be bothered with her, no way,—not if they'd give her to me," said Haley.

"She'll take on desp't," said the man.

"Nat'lly, she will," said the trader, coolly.

The conversation was here interrupted by a busy hum in the audience; and the auctioneer, a short, bustling, important fellow, elbowed his way into the crowd. The old woman drew in her breath, and caught instinctively at her son.

"Keep close to yer mammy, Albert,—close,—dey'll put us up togedder," she said.

"O, mammy, I'm feared they won't," said the boy.

"Dey must, child; I can't live, no ways, if they don't," said the old creature, vehemently.

The stentorian tones of the auctioneer, calling out to clear the way, now announced that the sale was about to commence. A place was cleared, and the bidding began. The different men on the list were soon knocked off at prices which showed a pretty brisk demand in the market; two of them fell to Haley.

"Come, now, young un," said the auctioneer, giving the boy a touch with his hammer, "be up and show your springs, now."

"Put us two up togedder, togedder,—do please, Mas'r," said the old woman, holding fast to her boy.

"Be off," said the man, gruffy, pushing her hands away; "you come last. Now, darkey, spring;" and, with the word, he pushed the boy toward the block, while a deep, heavy groan rose behind him. The boy paused, and looked back; but there was no time to stay, and, dashing the tears from his large, bright eyes, he was up in a moment.

His fine figure, alert limbs, and bright face, raised an instant competition, and half a dozen bids simultaneously met the ear of the auctioneer. Anxious, half-frightened, he looked from side to side, as he heard the clatter of contending bids,—now here, now there,—till the hammer fell. Haley had got him. He was pushed from the block toward his new master, but stopped one moment, and looked back, when his poor old mother, trembling in every limb, held out her shaking hands toward him.

"Buy me too, Mas'r, for de dear Lord's sake!—buy me,—I shall die if you don't!"

"You'll die if I do, that's the kink of it," said Haley,—"no!" And he turned on his heel.

The bidding for the poor old creature was summary. The man who had addressed Haley, and who seemed not destitute of compassion, bought her for a trifle, and the spectators began to disperse.

The poor victims of the sale, who had been brought up in one place together for years, gathered round the despairing old mother, whose agony was pitiful to see.

"Couldn't dey leave me one? Mas'r allers said I should have one,—he did," she repeated over and over, in heartbroken tones.

"Trust in the Lord, Aunt Hagar," said the oldest of the men, sorrowfully.

"What good will it do?" said she, sobbing passionately.

"Mother, mother,—don't! don't!" said the boy. "They say you's got a good master."

"I don't care,—I don't care. O, Albert! oh, my boy! you's my last baby. Lord, how ken I?"

"Come, take her off, can't some of ye?" said Haley, dryly; "don't do no good for her to go on that ar way."

The old men of the company, partly by persuasion and partly by force, loosed the poor creature's last despairing hold, and, as they led her off to her new master's wagon, strove to comfort her.

"Now!" said Haley, pushing his three purchases together, and producing a bundle of handcuffs, which he proceeded to put on their wrists; and fastening each handcuff to a long chain, he drove them before him to the jail.

A few days saw Haley, with his possessions, safely deposited on one of the Ohio boats. It was the commencement of his gang, to be augmented, as the boat moved on, by various other merchandise of the same kind, which he, or his agent, had stored for him in various points along shore.

The La Belle Rivière,[1] as brave and beautiful a boat as ever walked the waters of her namesake river, was floating gayly down the stream, under a brilliant sky, the stripes and stars of free America waving and fluttering over head; the guards crowded with well-dressed ladies and gentlemen walking and enjoying the delightful day. All was full of life, buoyant and rejoicing;— all but Haley's gang, who were stored, with other freight, on the lower deck, and who, somehow, did not seem to appreciate their various privileges, as they sat in a knot, talking to each other in low tones.

"Boys," said Haley, coming up, briskly, "I hope you keep up good heart, and are cheerful. Now, no sulks, ye see; keep stiff upper lip, boys; do well by me, and I'll do well by you."

The boys addressed responded the invariable "Yes, Mas'r," for ages the watchword of poor Africa; but it's to be owned they did not look particularly cheerful; they had their various little prejudices in favor of wives, mothers, sisters, and children, seen for the last time,—and though "they that wasted them required of them mirth,"[2] it was not instantly forthcoming.

"I've got a wife," spoke out the article enumerated as "John, aged thirty," and he laid his chained hand on Tom's knee,—"and she don't know a word about this, poor girl!"

"Where does she live?" said Tom.

1. The Beautiful River (French).   2. Paraphrase of Psalm 137.3.

"In a tavern a piece down here," said John; "I wish, now, I *could* see her once more in this world," he added.

Poor John! It *was* rather natural; and the tears that fell, as he spoke, came as naturally as if he had been a white man. Tom drew a long breath from a sore heart, and tried, in his poor way, to comfort him.

And over head, in the cabin, sat fathers and mothers, husbands and wives; and merry, dancing children moved round among them, like so many little butterflies, and everything was going on quite easy and comfortable.

"O, mamma," said a boy, who had just come up from below, "there's a negro trader on board, and he's brought four or five slaves down there."

"Poor creatures!" said the mother, in a tone between grief and indignation.

"What's that?" said another lady.

"Some poor slaves below," said the mother.

"And they've got chains on," said the boy.

"What a shame to our country that such sights are to be seen!" said another lady.

"O, there's a great deal to be said on both sides of the subject," said a genteel woman, who sat at her state-room door sewing, while her little girl and boy were playing round her. "I've been south, and I must say I think the negroes are better off than they would be to be free."

"In some respects, some of them are well off, I grant," said the lady to whose remark she had answered. "The most dreadful part of slavery, to my mind, is its outrages on the feelings and affections,—the separating of families, for example."

"That *is* a bad thing, certainly," said the other lady, holding up a baby's dress she had just completed, and looking intently on its trimmings; "but then, I fancy, it don't occur often."

"O, it does," said the first lady, eagerly; "I've lived many years in Kentucky and Virginia both, and I've seen enough to make any one's heart sick. Suppose, ma'am, your two children, there, should be taken from you, and sold?"

"We can't reason from our feelings to those of this class of persons," said the other lady, sorting out some worsteds on her lap.

"Indeed, ma'am, you can know nothing of them, if you say so," answered the first lady, warmly. "I was born and brought up among them. I know they *do* feel, just as keenly,—even more so, perhaps,—as we do."

The lady said "Indeed!" yawned, and looked out the cabin window, and finally repeated, for a finale, the remark with which she had begun,—"After all, I think they are better off than they would be to be free."

"It's undoubtedly the intention of Providence that the African race should be servants,—kept in a low condition," said a grave-looking gentleman in black, a clergyman, seated by the cabin door. "'Cursed be Canaan; a servant of servants shall he be,' the scripture says."[3]

"I say, stranger, is that ar what that text means?" said a tall man, standing by.

"Undoubtedly. It pleased Providence, for some inscrutable reason, to doom the race to bondage, ages ago; and we must not set up our opinion against that."

---

3. Genesis 9.25, from the story of Noah and his son Ham; a passage cited by proslavery writers to justify slavery on the assumption that Africans were Ham's descendants.

"Well, then, we'll all go ahead and buy up niggers," said the man, "if that's the way of Providence,—won't we, Squire?" said he, turning to Haley, who had been standing, with his hands in his pockets, by the stove, and intently listening to the conversation.

"Yes," continued the tall man, "we must all be resigned to the decrees of Providence. Niggers must be sold, and trucked round, and kept under; it's what they's made for. 'Pears like this yer view's quite refreshing, an't it, stranger?" said he to Haley.

"I never thought on 't," said Haley. "I couldn't have said as much, myself; I ha'nt no larning. I took up the trade just to make a living; if 't an't right, I calculated to 'pent on 't in time, ye know."

"And now you'll save yerself the trouble, won't ye?" said the tall man. "See what 't is, now, to know scripture. If ye'd only studied yer Bible, like this yer good man, ye might have know'd it before, and saved ye a heap o' trouble. Ye could jist have said, 'Cussed be'—what's his name?—'and 't would all have come right.'" And the stranger, who was no other than the honest drover whom we introduced to our readers in the Kentucky tavern,[4] sat down, and began smoking, with a curious smile on his long, dry face.

A tall, slender young man, with a face expressive of great feeling and intelligence, here broke in, and repeated the words, "'All things whatsoever ye would that men should do unto you, do ye even so unto them.'[5] I suppose," he added, "*that* is scripture, as much as 'Cursed be Canaan.'"

"Wal, it seems quite *as* plain a text, stranger," said John the drover, "to poor fellows like us, now;" and John smoked on like a volcano.

The young man paused, looked as if he was going to say more, when suddenly the boat stopped, and the company made the usual steamboat rush, to see where they were landing.

"Both them ar chaps parsons?" said John to one of the men, as they were going out.

The man nodded.

As the boat stopped, a black woman came running wildly up the plank, darted into the crowd, flew up to where the slave gang sat, and threw her arms round that unfortunate piece of merchandise before enumerated— "John, aged thirty," and with sobs and tears bemoaned him as her husband.

But what needs tell the story, told too oft,—every day told,—of heartstrings rent and broken,—the weak broken and torn for the profit and convenience of the strong! It needs not to be told;—every day is telling it,—telling it, too, in the ear of One who is not deaf, though he be long silent.

The young man who had spoken for the cause of humanity and God before stood with folded arms, looking on this scene. He turned, and Haley was standing at his side. "My friend," he said, speaking with thick utterance, "how can you, how dare you, carry on a trade like this? Look at those poor creatures! Here I am, rejoicing in my heart that I am going home to my wife and child; and the same bell which is a signal to carry me onward towards them will part this poor man and his wife forever. Depend upon it, God will bring you into judgment for this."

The trader turned away in silence.

4. Mr. Symmes was introduced at the end of Chapter III. "Drover": cattle driver, farmer.

5. From the Sermon on the Mount (Matthew 7.12).

"I say, now," said the drover, touching his elbow, "there's differences in parsons, an't there? 'Cussed be Canaan' don't seem to go down with this 'un, does it?"

Haley gave an uneasy growl.

"And that ar an't the worse on 't," said John; "mabbe it won't go down with the Lord, neither, when ye come to settle with Him, one o' these days, as all on us must, I reckon."

Haley walked reflectively to the other end of the boat.

"If I make pretty handsomely on one or two next gangs," he thought, "I reckon I'll stop off this yer; it's really getting dangerous." And he took out his pocket-book, and began adding over his accounts,—a process which many gentlemen besides Mr. Haley have found a specific[6] for an uneasy conscience.

The boat swept proudly away from the shore, and all went on merrily, as before. Men talked, and loafed, and read, and smoked. Women sewed, and children played, and the boat passed on her way.

One day, when she lay to for a while at a small town in Kentucky, Haley went up into the place on a little matter of business.

Tom, whose fetters did not prevent his taking a moderate circuit, had drawn near the side of the boat, and stood listlessly gazing over the railings. After a time, he saw the trader returning, with an alert step, in company with a colored woman, bearing in her arms a young child. She was dressed quite respectably, and a colored man followed her, bringing along a small trunk. The woman came cheerfully onward, talking, as she came, with the man who bore her trunk, and so passed up the plank into the boat. The bell rung, the steamer whizzed, the engine groaned and coughed, and away swept the boat down the river.

The woman walked forward among the boxes and bales of the lower deck, and, sitting down, busied herself with chirruping to her baby.

Haley made a turn or two about the boat, and then, coming up, seated himself near her, and began saying something to her in an indifferent undertone.

Tom soon noticed a heavy cloud passing over the woman's brow; and that she answered rapidly, and with great vehemence.

"I don't believe it,—I won't believe it!" he heard her say. "You're jist a foo-lin with me."

"If you won't believe it, look here!" said the man, drawing out a paper; "this yer's the bill of sale, and there's your master's name to it; and I paid down good solid cash for it, too, I can tell you,—so, now!"

"I don't believe Mas'r would cheat me so; it can't be true!" said the woman, with increasing agitation.

"You can ask any of these men here, that can read writing. Here!" he said, to a man that was passing by, "jist read this yer, won't you! This yer gal won't believe me, when I tell her what 't is."

"Why, it's a bill of sale, signed by John Fosdick," said the man, "making over to you the girl Lucy and her child. It's all straight enough, for aught I see."

The woman's passionate exclamations collected a crowd around her, and the trader briefly explained to them the cause of the agitation.

6. Healing tonic.

"He told me that I was going down to Louisville, to hire out as cook to the same tavern where my husband works,—that's what Mas'r told me, his own self; and I can't believe he'd lie to me," said the woman.

"But he has sold you, my poor woman, there's no doubt about it," said a good-natured looking man, who had been examining the papers; "he has done it, and no mistake."

"Then it's no account talking," said the woman, suddenly growing quite calm; and, clasping her child tighter in her arms, she sat down on her box, turned her back round, and gazed listlessly into the river.

"Going to take it easy, after all!" said the trader. "Gal's got grit, I see."

The woman looked calm, as the boat went on; and a beautiful soft summer breeze passed like a compassionate spirit over her head,—the gentle breeze, that never inquires whether the brow is dusky or fair that it fans. And she saw sunshine sparkling on the water, in golden ripples, and heard gay voices, full of ease and pleasure, talking around her everywhere; but her heart lay as if a great stone had fallen on it. Her baby raised himself up against her, and stroked her cheeks with his little hands; and, springing up and down, crowing and chatting, seemed determined to arouse her. She strained him suddenly and tightly in her arms, and slowly one tear after another fell on his wondering, unconscious face; and gradually she seemed, and little by little, to grow calmer, and busied herself with tending and nursing him.

The child, a boy of ten months, was uncommonly large and strong of his age, and very vigorous in his limbs. Never, for a moment, still, he kept his mother constantly busy in holding him, and guarding his springing activity.

"That's a fine chap!" said a man, suddenly stopping opposite to him, with his hands in his pockets. "How old is he?"

"Ten months and a half," said the mother.

The man whistled to the boy, and offered him part of a stick of candy, which he eagerly grabbed at, and very soon had it in a baby's general depository, to wit, his mouth.

"Rum fellow!" said the man. "Knows what's what!" and he whistled, and walked on. When he had got to the other side of the boat, he came across Haley, who was smoking on top of a pile of boxes.

The stranger produced a match, and lighted a cigar, saying, as he did so, "Decentish kind o' wench you've got round there, stranger."

"Why, I reckon she *is* tol'able fair," said Haley, blowing the smoke out of his mouth.

"Taking her down south?" said the man.

Haley nodded, and smoked on.

"Plantation hand?" said the man.

"Wal," said Haley, "I'm fillin' out an order for a plantation, and I think I shall put her in. They telled me she was a good cook; and they can use her for that, or set her at the cotton-picking. She's got the right fingers for that; I looked at 'em. Sell well, either way;" and Haley resumed his cigar.

"They won't want the young 'un on a plantation," said the man.

"I shall sell him, first chance I find," said Haley, lighting another cigar.

"S'pose you'd be selling him tol'able cheap," said the stranger, mounting the pile of boxes, and sitting down comfortably.

"Don't know 'bout that," said Haley; "he's a pretty smart young 'un,— straight, fat, strong; flesh as hard as a brick!"

"Very true, but then there's all the bother and expense of raisin'."

"Nonsense!" said Haley; "they is raised as easy as any kind of critter there is going; they an't a bit more trouble than pups. This yer chap will be running all round, in a month."

"I've got a good place for raisin', and I thought of takin' in a little more stock," said the man. "One cook lost a young 'un last week,—got drownded in a wash-tub, while she was a hangin' out clothes,—and I reckon it would be well enough to set her to raisin' this yer."

Haley and the stranger smoked a while in silence, neither seeming willing to broach the test question of the interview. At last the man resumed:

"You wouldn't think of wantin' more than ten dollars for that ar chap, seeing you *must* get him off yer hand, any how?"

Haley shook his head, and spit impressively.

"That won't do, no ways," he said, and began his smoking again.

"Well, stranger, what will you take?"

"Well, now," said Haley, "I *could* raise that ar chap myself, or get him raised; he's oncommon likely and healthy, and he'd fetch a hundred dollars, six months hence; and, in a year or two, he'd bring two hundred, if I had him in the right spot;—so I shan't take a cent less nor fifty for him now."

"O, stranger! that's rediculous, altogether," said the man.

"Fact!" said Haley, with a decisive nod of his head.

"I'll give thirty for him," said the stranger, "but not a cent more."

"Now, I'll tell ye what I will do," said Haley, spitting again, with renewed decision. "I'll split the difference, and say forty-five; and that's the most I will do."

"Well, agreed!" said the man, after an interval.

"Done!" said Haley. "Where do you land?"

"At Louisville," said the man.

"Louisville," said Haley. "Very fair, we get there about dusk. Chap will be asleep,—all fair,—get him off quietly, and no screaming,—happens beautiful,—I like to do everything quietly,—I hates all kind of agitation and fluster." And so, after a transfer of certain bills had passed from the man's pocket-book to the trader's, he resumed his cigar.

It was a bright, tranquil evening when the boat stopped at the wharf at Louisville. The woman had been sitting with her baby in her arms, now wrapped in a heavy sleep. When she heard the name of the place called out, she hastily laid the child down in a little cradle formed by the hollow among the boxes, first carefully spreading under it her cloak; and then she sprung to the side of the boat, in hopes that, among the various hotel-waiters who thronged the wharf, she might see her husband. In this hope, she pressed forward to the front rails, and, stretching far over them, strained her eyes intently on the moving heads on the shore, and the crowd pressed in between her and the child.

"Now's your time," said Haley, taking the sleeping child up, and handing him to the stranger. "Don't wake him up, and set him to crying, now; it would make a devil of a fuss with the gal." The man took the bundle carefully, and was soon lost in the crowd that went up the wharf.

When the boat, creaking, and groaning, and puffing, had loosed from the wharf, and was beginning slowly to strain herself along, the woman returned to her old seat. The trader was sitting there,—the child was gone!

"Why, why,—where?" she began, in bewildered surprise.

"Lucy," said the trader, "your child's gone; you may as well know it first as last. You see, I know'd you couldn't take him down south; and I got a chance to sell him to a first-rate family, that'll raise him better than you can."

The trader had arrived at that stage of Christian and political perfection which has been recommended by some preachers and politicians of the north, lately, in which he had completely overcome every humane weakness and prejudice. His heart was exactly where yours, sir, and mine could be brought, with proper effort and cultivation. The wild look of anguish and utter despair that the woman cast on him might have disturbed one less practised; but he was used to it. He had seen that same look hundreds of times. You can get used to such things, too, my friend; and it is the great object of recent efforts to make our whole northern community used to them, for the glory of the Union. So the trader only regarded the mortal anguish which he saw working in those dark features, those clenched hands, and suffocating breathings, as necessary incidents of the trade, and merely calculated whether she was going to scream, and get up a commotion on the boat; for, like other supporters of our peculiar institution, he decidedly disliked agitation.

But the woman did not scream. The shot had passed too straight and direct through the heart, for cry or tear.

Dizzily she sat down. Her slack hands fell lifeless by her side. Her eyes looked straight forward, but she saw nothing. All the noise and hum of the boat, the groaning of the machinery, mingled dreamily to her bewildered ear; and the poor, dumb-stricken heart had neither cry nor tear to show for its utter misery. She was quite calm.

The trader, who, considering his advantages, was almost as humane as some of our politicians, seemed to feel called on to administer such consolation as the case admitted of.

"I know this yer comes kinder hard, at first, Lucy," said he; "but such a smart, sensible gal as you are, won't give way to it. You see it's *necessary*, and can't be helped!"

"O! don't, Mas'r, don't!" said the woman, with a voice like one that is smothering.

"You're a smart wench, Lucy," he persisted; "I mean to do well by ye, and get ye a nice place down river; and you'll soon get another husband,—such a likely gal as you—"

"O! Mas'r, if you *only* won't talk to me now," said the woman, in a voice of such quick and living anguish that the trader felt that there was something at present in the case beyond his style of operation. He got up, and the woman turned away, and buried her head in her cloak.

The trader walked up and down for a time, and occasionally stopped and looked at her.

"Takes it hard, rather," he soliloquized, "but quiet, tho';—let her sweat a while; she'll come right, by and by!"

Tom had watched the whole transaction from first to last, and had a perfect understanding of its results. To him, it looked like something unutterably horrible and cruel, because, poor, ignorant black soul! he had not learned to generalize, and to take enlarged views. If he had only been instructed by certain ministers of Christianity, he might have thought better of it, and seen in it an every-day incident of a lawful trade; a trade which is the vital support of an institution which some American divines tell us has no evils but such as are inseparable from any other relations in social and domestic life. But Tom, as we see, being a poor, ignorant fellow, whose reading had been confined entirely to the New Testament, could not comfort and solace himself with views like these. His very soul bled within him for what seemed to him the *wrongs* of the poor suffering thing that lay like a crushed reed on the boxes; the feeling, living, bleeding, yet immortal *thing*, which American state law coolly classes with the bundles, and bales, and boxes, among which she is lying.

Tom drew near, and tried to say something; but she only groaned. Honestly, and with tears running down his own cheeks, he spoke of a heart of love in the skies, of a pitying Jesus, and an eternal home; but the ear was deaf with anguish, and the palsied heart could not feel.

Night came on,—night calm, unmoved, and glorious, shining down with her innumerable and solemn angel eyes, twinkling, beautiful, but silent. There was no speech nor language, no pitying voice nor helping hand, from that distant sky. One after another, the voices of business or pleasure died away; all on the boat were sleeping, and the ripples at the prow were plainly heard. Tom stretched himself out on a box, and there, as he lay, he heard, ever and anon, a smothered sob or cry from the prostate creature,—"O! what shall I do? O Lord! O good Lord, do help me!" and so, ever and anon, until the murmur died away in silence.

At midnight, Tom waked, with a sudden start. Something black passed quickly by him to the side of the boat, and he heard a splash in the water. No one else saw or heard anything. He raised his head,—the woman's place was vacant! He got up, and sought about him in vain. The poor bleeding heart was still, at last, and the river rippled and dimpled just as brightly as if it had not closed above it.

Patience! patience! ye whose hearts swell indignant at wrongs like these. Not one throb of anguish, not one tear of the oppressed, is forgotten by the Man of Sorrows, the Lord of Glory. In his patient, generous bosom he bears the anguish of a world. Bear thou, like him, in patience, and labor in love; for sure as he is God, "the year of his redeemed *shall* come."[7]

The trader waked up bright and early, and came out to see to his live stock. It was now his turn to look about in perplexity.

"Where alive is that gal?" he said to Tom.

Tom, who had learned the wisdom of keeping counsel, did not feel called on to state his observations and suspicions, but said he did not know.

"She surely couldn't have got off in the night at any of the landings, for I was awake, and on the look-out, whenever the boat stopped. I never trust these yer things to other folks."

This speech was addressed to Tom quite confidentially, as if it was something that would be specially interesting to him. Tom made no answer.

The trader searched the boat from stem to stern, among boxes, bales and barrels, around the machinery, by the chimneys, in vain.

"Now, I say, Tom, be fair about this yer," he said, when, after a fruitless search, he came where Tom was standing. "You know something about it, now. Don't tell me,—I know you do. I saw the gal stretched out here about ten o'clock, and ag'in at twelve, and ag'in between one and two; and then at

7. Paraphrase of Isaiah 63.4.

four she was gone, and you was sleeping right there all the time. Now, you know something,—you can't help it."

"Well, Mas'r," said Tom, "towards morning something brushed by me, and I kinder half woke; and then I hearn a great splash, and then I clare woke up, and the gal was gone. That's all I know on 't."

The trader was not shocked nor amazed; because, as we said before, he was used to a great many things that you are not used to. Even the awful presence of Death struck no solemn chill upon him. He had seen Death many times,—met him in the way of trade, and got acquainted with him,—and he only thought of him as a hard customer, that embarrassed his property operations very unfairly; and so he only swore that the gal was a baggage, and that he was devilish unlucky, and that, if things went on in this way, he should not make a cent on the trip. In short, he seemed to consider himself an ill-used man, decidedly; but there was no help for it, as the woman had escaped into a state which *never will* give up a fugitive,—not even at the demand of the whole glorious Union. The trader, therefore, sat discontentedly down, with his little account-book, and put down the missing body and soul under the head of *losses*!

"He's a shocking creature, isn't he,—this trader? so unfeeling! It's dreadful, really!"

"O, but nobody thinks anything of these traders! They are universally despised,—never received into any decent society."

But who, sir, makes the trader? Who is most to blame? The enlightened, cultivated, intelligent man, who supports the system of which the trader is the inevitable result, or the poor trader himself? You make the public sentiment that calls for his trade, that debauches and depraves him, till he feels no shame in it; and in what are you better than he?

Are you educated and he ignorant, you high and he low, you refined and he coarse, you talented and he simple?

In the day of a future Judgment, these very considerations may make it more tolerable for him than for you.

In concluding these little incidents of lawful trade, we must beg the world not to think that American legislators are entirely destitute of humanity, as might, perhaps, be unfairly inferred from the great efforts made in our national body to protect and perpetuate this species of traffic.

Who does not know how our great men are outdoing themselves, in declaiming against the *foreign* slave-trade. There are a perfect host of Clarksons[8] and Wilberforces risen up among us on that subject, most edifying to hear and behold. Trading negroes from Africa, dear reader, is so horrid! It is not to be thought of! But trading them from Kentucky,— that's quite another thing!

---

8. The English abolitionist Thomas Clarkson (1760–1846), who with his countryman William Wilberforce was an architect of the 1807 act of Parliament abolishing the slave trade. A similar act was passed by the U.S. Congress the same year; it prohibited importation of slaves from abroad, which allowed the trade to flourish within the United States.

Volume II

FROM CHAPTER XXVI. DEATH[9]

Weep not for those whom the veil of the tomb,
In life's early morning, hath bid from our eyes.[1]

* * *

"Mamma," said Eva, "I want to have some of my hair cut off,—a good deal of it."

"What for?" said Marie.

"Mamma, I want to give some away to my friends, while I am able to give it to them myself. Won't you ask aunty to come and cut it for me?"

Marie raised her voice, and called Miss Ophelia, from the other room.

The child half rose from her pillow as she came in, and, shaking down her long golden-brown curls, said, rather playfully, "Come, aunty, shear the sheep!"

"What's that?" said St. Clare, who just then entered with some fruit he had been out to get for her.

"Papa, I just want aunty to cut off some of my hair;—there's too much of it, and it makes my head hot. Besides, I want to give some of it away."

Miss Ophelia came, with her scissors.

"Take care,—don't spoil the looks of it!" said her father; "cut underneath, where it won't show. Eva's curls are my pride."

"O, papa!" said Eva, sadly.

"Yes, and I want them kept handsome against the time I take you up to your uncle's plantation, to see Cousin Henrique," said St. Clare, in a gay tone.

"I shall never go there, papa;—I am going to a better country. O, do believe me! Don't you see, papa, that I get weaker, every day?"

"Why do you insist that I shall believe such a cruel thing, Eva?" said her father.

"Only because it is *true*, papa: and, if you will believe it now, perhaps you will get to feel about it as I do."

St. Clare closed his lips, and stood gloomily eying the long, beautiful curls, which, as they were separated from the child's head, were laid, one by one, in her lap. She raised them up, looked earnestly at them, twined them around her thin fingers, and looked, from time to time, anxiously at her father.

"It's just what I've been foreboding!" said Marie; "it's just what has been preying on my health, from day to day, bringing me downward to the grave, though nobody regards it. I have seen this, long. St. Clare, you will see, after a while, that I was right."

"Which will afford you great consolation, no doubt!" said St. Clare, in a dry, bitter tone.

Marie lay back on a lounge, and covered her face with her cambric handkerchief.

Eva's clear blue eye looked earnestly from one to the other. It was the calm, comprehending gaze of a soul half loosed from its earthly bonds; it was evident she saw, felt, and appreciated, the difference between the two.

She beckoned with her hand to her father. He came, and sat down by her.

9. Two years have passed. To escape the hot New Orleans summer, St. Clare has brought his family and slaves to his villa at Lake Pontchartrain in southeastern Louisiana. Eva, who has been showing signs of serious illness, has declared to Tom that she would be happy to die if her death would bring an end to the sufferings of the slaves.
1. From "Weep Not for Those" (1816), by the Irish poet Thomas Moore (1779–1852).

"Papa, my strength fades away every day, and I know I must go. There are some things I want to say and do,—that I ought to do; and you are so unwilling to have me speak a word on this subject. But it must come; there's no putting it off. Do be willing I should speak now!"

"My child, I *am* willing!" said St. Clare, covering his eyes with one hand, and holding up Eva's hand with the other.

"Then, I want to see all our people together. I have some things I *must* say to them," said Eva.

"*Well*," said St. Clare, in a tone of dry endurance.

Miss Ophelia despatched a messenger, and soon the whole of the servants were convened in the room.

Eva lay back on her pillows; her hair hanging loosely about her face, her crimson cheeks contrasting painfully with the intense whiteness of her complexion and the thin contour of her limbs and features, and her large, soul-like eyes fixed earnestly on every one.

The servants were struck with a sudden emotion. The spiritual face, the long locks of hair cut off and lying by her, her father's averted face, and Marie's sobs, struck at once upon the feelings of a sensitive and impressible race; and, as they came in, they looked one on another, sighed, and shook their heads. There was a deep silence, like that of a funeral.

Eva raised herself, and looked long and earnestly round at every one. All looked sad and apprehensive. Many of the women hid their faces in their aprons.

"I sent for you all, my dear friends," said Eva, "because I love you. I love you all; and I have something to say to you, which I want you always to remember. . . . I am going to leave you. In a few more weeks, you will see me no more—"

Here the child was interrupted by bursts of groans, sobs, and lamentations, which broke from all present, and in which her slender voice was lost entirely. She waited a moment, and then, speaking in a tone that checked the sobs of all, she said,

"If you love me, you must not interrupt me so. Listen to what I say. I want to speak to you about your souls. . . . Many of you, I am afraid, are very careless. You are thinking only about this world. I want you to remember that there is a beautiful world, where Jesus is. I am going there, and you can go there. It is for you, as much as me. But, if you want to go there, you must not live idle, careless, thoughtless lives. You must be Christians. You must remember that each one of you can become angels, and be angels forever. . . . If you want to be Christians, Jesus will help you. You must pray to him; you must read—"

The child checked herself, looked piteously at them, and said, sorrowfully,

"O, dear! you *can't* read,—poor souls!" and she hid her face in the pillow and sobbed, while many a smothered sob from those she was addressing, who were kneeling on the floor, aroused her.

"Never mind," she said, raising her face and smiling brightly through her tears, "I have prayed for you; and I know Jesus will help you, even if you can't read. Try all to do the best you can; pray every day; ask Him to help you, and get the Bible read to you whenever you can; and I think I shall see you all in heaven."

"Amen," was the murmured response from the lips of Tom and Mammy, and some of the elder ones, who belonged to the Methodist church. The younger and more thoughtless ones, for the time completely overcome, were sobbing, with their heads bowed upon their knees.

"I know," said Eva, "you all love me."

"Yes; oh, yes! indeed we do! Lord bless her!" was the involuntary answer of all.

"Yes, I know you do! There isn't one of you that hasn't always been very kind to me; and I want to give you something that, when you look at, you shall always remember me. I'm going to give all of you a curl of my hair; and, when you look at it, think that I loved you and am gone to heaven, and that I want to see you all there."

It is impossible to describe the scene, as, with tears and sobs, they gathered round the little creature, and took from her hands what seemed to them a last mark of her love. They fell on their knees; they sobbed, and prayed, and kissed the hem of her garment; and the elder ones poured forth words of endearment, mingled in prayers and blessings, after the manner of their susceptible race.

As each one took their gift, Miss Ophelia, who was apprehensive for the effect of all this excitement on her little patient, signed to each one to pass out of the apartment.

At last, all were gone but Tom and Mammy.

"Here, Uncle Tom," said Eva, "is a beautiful one for you. O, I am so happy, Uncle Tom, to think I shall see you in heaven,—for I'm sure I shall; and Mammy,—dear, good, kind Mammy!" she said, fondly throwing her arms round her old nurse,—"I know you'll be there, too."

"O, Miss Eva, don't see how I can live without ye, no how!" said the faithful creature. "'Pears like it's just taking everything off the place to oncet!"[2] and Mammy gave way to a passion of grief.

Miss Ophelia pushed her and Tom gently from the apartment, and thought they were all gone; but, as she turned, Topsy was standing there.

"Where did you start up from?" she said, suddenly.

"I was here," said Topsy, wiping the tears from her eyes. "O, Miss Eva, I've been a bad girl; but won't you give *me* one, too?"

"Yes, poor Topsy! to be sure, I will. There—every time you look at that, think that I love you, and wanted you to be a good girl!"

"O, Miss Eva, I *is* tryin!" said Topsy, earnestly; "but, Lor, it's so hard to be good! 'Pears like I an't used to it, no ways!"

"Jesus knows it, Topsy; he is sorry for you; he will help you."

Topsy, with her eyes hid in her apron, was silently passed from the apartment by Miss Ophelia; but, as she went, she hid the precious curl in her bosom.

* * *

Eva had been unusually bright and cheerful, that afternoon, and had sat raised in her bed, and looked over all her little trinkets and precious things, and designated the friends to whom she would have them given; and her manner was more animated, and her voice more natural, than they had known it for weeks. Her father had been in, in the evening, and had said that Eva appeared more like her former self than ever she had done since her sickness; and when he kissed her for the night, he said to Miss Ophelia,—

2. At once (colloquial).

"Cousin, we may keep her with us, after all; she is certainly better;" and he had retired with a lighter heart in his bosom than he had had there for weeks.

But at midnight,—strange, mystic hour!—when the veil between the frail present and the eternal future grows thin,—then came the messenger!

There was a sound in that chamber, first of one who stepped quickly. It was Miss Ophelia, who had resolved to sit up all night with her little charge, and who, at the turn of the night, had discerned what experienced nurses significantly call "a change." The outer door was quickly opened, and Tom, who was watching outside, was on the alert, in a moment.

"Go for the doctor, Tom! lose not a moment," said Miss Ophelia; and, stepping across the room, she rapped at St. Clare's door.

"Cousin," she said, "I wish you would come."

Those words fell on his heart like clods upon a coffin. Why did they? He was up and in the room in an instant, and bending over Eva, who still slept.

What was it he saw that made his heart stand still? Why was no word spoken between the two? Thou canst say, who hast seen that same expression on the face dearest to thee;—that look indescribable, hopeless, unmistakable, that says to thee that thy beloved is no longer thine.

On the face of the child, however, there was no ghastly imprint,—only a high and almost sublime expression,—the overshadowing presence of spiritual natures, the dawning of immortal life in that childish soul.

They stood there so still, gazing upon her, that even the ticking of the watch seemed too loud. In a few moments, Tom returned, with the doctor. He entered, gave one look, and stood silent as the rest.

"When did this change take place?" said he, in a low whisper, to Miss Ophelia.

"About the turn of the night," was the reply.

Marie, roused by the entrance of the doctor, appeared, hurriedly, from the next room.

"Augustine! Cousin!—O!—what!" she hurriedly began.

"Hush!" said St. Clare, hoarsely; "*she is dying!*"

Mammy heard the words, and flew to awaken the servants. The house was soon roused,—lights were seen, footsteps heard, anxious faces thronged the verandah, and looked tearfully through the glass doors; but St. Clare heard and said nothing,—he saw only *that look* on the face of the little sleeper.

"O, if she would only wake, and speak once more!" he said; and, stooping over her, he spoke in her ear,—"Eva, darling!"

The large blue eyes unclosed,—a smile passed over her face;—she tried to raise her head, and to speak.

"Do you know me, Eva?"

"Dear papa," said the child, with a last effort, throwing her arms about his neck. In a moment they dropped again; and, as St. Clare raised his head, he saw a spasm of mortal agony pass over the face,—she struggled for breath, and threw up her little hands.

"O, God, this is dreadful!" he said, turning away in agony, and wringing Tom's hand, scarce conscious what he was doing. "O, Tom, my boy, it is killing me!"

Tom had his master's hands between his own; and, with tears streaming down his dark cheeks, looked up for help where he had always been used to look.

"Pray that this may be cut short!" said St. Clare,—"this wrings my heart."

"O, bless the Lord! it's over,—it's over, dear Master!" said Tom; "look at her."

The child lay panting on her pillows, as one exhausted,—the large clear eyes rolled up and fixed. Ah, what said those eyes, that spoke so much of heaven? Earth was past, and earthly pain; but so solemn, so mysterious, was the triumphant brightness of that face, that it checked even the sobs of sorrow. They pressed around her, in breathless stillness.

"Eva," said St. Clare, gently.

She did not hear.

"O, Eva, tell us what you see! What is it?" said her father.

A bright, a glorious smile passed over her face, and she said, brokenly,— "O! love,—joy,—peace!" gave one sigh, and passed from death unto life!

"Farewell, beloved child! the bright, eternal doors have closed after thee; we shall see thy sweet face no more. O, woe for them who watched thy entrance into heaven, when they shall wake and find only the cold gray sky of daily life, and thou gone forever!"

* * *

HARRIET JACOBS
c. 1813–1897

The first African American woman known to have authored a slave narrative in the United States, Harriet Jacobs was born into slavery in Edenton, North Carolina. Her father was a skilled carpenter who was permitted to hire himself out, and her parents were allowed to live together even though they had different masters; therefore, as a child Jacobs was unaware that she was a slave. Her mother's death and a change of owners for both Jacobs and her father brought her into the family of Dr. and Mrs. James Norcom in 1825. There, as she grew to adulthood, she was sexually threatened by the doctor and abused by his jealous wife. As a defense against this treatment, Jacobs became involved with an unmarried white attorney, Samuel Tredwell Sawyer, with whom she had two children: Joseph, born in 1829, and Louisa Matilda, born in 1833. When Norcom sent her to a country plantation in 1835, she escaped back to Edenton, hiding for perhaps seven years in an attic crawl space in the home of her maternal grandmother, who had been emancipated some years earlier. While Jacobs was in hiding, Sawyer purchased, but did not emancipate, their two children. Jacobs finally escaped to the North in 1842, and later both her children came north as well. Life in the North remained insecure and perilous, however, because slave catchers were constantly hunting down escaped slaves to return them to the South, which they could do more aggressively after 1850 with the Fugitive Slave Law on their side.

For much of the next two decades Jacobs worked in the family of Nathaniel Parker Willis (1806–1867), one of the era's most popular writers and editors (and the brother of the popular writer Fanny Fern). She took care of his children and became particularly close to his second wife, Cornelia Grinnell Willis, a staunch abolitionist. In 1852 Cornelia Willis arranged to purchase Jacobs from Norcom's daughter, Jacobs's legal owner; then she emancipated Jacobs, who continued to work for Willis after he became a widower.

Jacobs spent most of 1849 in Rochester, New York, working for the Anti-Slavery Office run by her younger brother, who had also escaped slavery. She read through a large body of antislavery writings and also came to know a number of abolitionists, including many white women, among them the Quaker Amy Post, who became a mentor to her and in whose house she lived for nine months while her brother was away on lecture tours. Jacobs wanted to contribute her life story to the abolitionist cause in a way that would capture the attention of Northern white women in particular, to show them how slavery debased and demoralized women, at once subjecting them to white male lust and also depriving them of the right to make homes for their families. Yet this topic was difficult to discuss in an era when extreme sexual prudery was the norm, when standards of female sexual "purity" could result in blaming the unmarried slave mother rather than the man whose victim she was. In *Incidents in the Life of a Slave Girl* Jacobs tried to do more than create sympathy for her plight; she sought to win the respect and admiration of her readers for the courage with which she forestalled abuse and for the independence with which she chose a lover rather than having one forced on her. Her description of hiding in the attic, her emphasis on family life and maternal values, and her account of the difficulties of fugitive slaves in the North differentiate the book from the numerous slave narratives produced in the twenty years before the Civil War.

Encouraged by the success of Harriet Beecher Stowe's *Uncle Tom's Cabin* (1852)—one of whose heroines is the slave concubine Cassy—Jacobs began work on her narrative around 1853 and finished it by 1858. She was not successful in finding a publisher for it, however, until Lydia Maria Child (1802–1880), the well-known woman of letters and abolitionist, agreed to write a preface for it. Child became interested in the project, putting much editorial work into the manuscript; and when the contracted publishers went bankrupt, she arranged for its publication. The book came out under the pseudonym Linda Brent in 1861; it was sold by antislavery societies in the Northeast, was published in England in 1862, and received several favorable reviews. The outbreak of the Civil War made its message less pressing, however; and it sank from notice until the 1980s, when renewed interest in writings by African-American women and superb biographical scholarship by Jean Fagin Yellin, establishing that this was an autobiographical narrative and not a novel, brought belated acclaim to the work.

During and after the war Jacobs worked with the Quakers in their efforts to help freed slaves with direct aid and by organizing schools, orphanages, and nursing homes. She ran a boardinghouse in Cambridge, Massachusetts, and later moved to Washington, D.C., with her daughter. She is buried in Mount Auburn Cemetery in Cambridge.

From Incidents in the Life of a Slave Girl[1]

I. Childhood

I was born a slave; but I never knew it till six years of happy childhood had passed away. My father was a carpenter, and considered so intelligent and skilful in his trade, that, when buildings out of the common line were to be erected, he was sent for from long distances, to be head workman. On condition of paying his mistress two hundred dollars a year, and supporting himself, he was allowed to work at his trade, and manage his own affairs. His

---

1. The text is that of the 1861 edition, edited by Jean Fagin Yellin (1987).

strongest wish was to purchase his children; but, though he several times offered his hard earnings for that purpose, he never succeeded. In complexion
my parents were a light shade of brownish yellow, and were termed mulattoes. They lived together in a comfortable home; and, though we were all
slaves, I was so fondly shielded that I never dreamed I was a piece of merchandise, trusted to them for safe keeping, and liable to be demanded of
them at any moment. I had one brother, William, who was two years younger
than myself—a bright, affectionate child. I had also a great treasure in
my maternal grandmother, who was a remarkable woman in many respects.
She was the daughter of a planter in South Carolina, who, at his death, left
her mother and his three children free, with money to go to St. Augustine,[2]
where they had relatives. It was during the Revolutionary War; and they were
captured on their passage, carried back, and sold to different purchasers.
Such was the story my grandmother used to tell me; but I do not remember
all the particulars. She was a little girl when she was captured and sold to
the keeper of a large hotel.[3] I have often heard her tell how hard she fared
during childhood. But as she grew older she evinced so much intelligence,
and was so faithful, that her master and mistress could not help seeing it
was for their interest to take care of such a valuable piece of property. She
became an indispensable personage in the household, officiating in all capacities, from cook and wet nurse to seamstress. She was much praised for
her cooking; and her nice crackers became so famous in the neighborhood
that many people were desirous of obtaining them. In consequence of numerous requests of this kind, she asked permission of her mistress to bake
crackers at night, after all the household work was done; and she obtained
leave to do it, provided she would clothe herself and her children from the
profits. Upon these terms, after working hard all day for her mistress, she
began her midnight bakings, assisted by her two oldest children. The business proved profitable; and each year she laid by a little, which was saved
for a fund to purchase her children. Her master died, and the property was
divided among his heirs. The widow had her dower[4] in the hotel, which she
continued to keep open. My grandmother remained in her service as a slave;
but her children were divided among her master's children. As she had five,
Benjamin, the youngest one, was sold, in order that each heir might have an
equal portion of dollars and cents. There was so little difference in our ages
that he seemed more like my brother than my uncle. He was a bright, handsome lad, nearly white; for he inherited the complexion my grandmother
had derived from Anglo-Saxon ancestors. Though only ten years old, seven
hundred and twenty dollars were paid for him. His sale was a terrible blow to
my grandmother; but she was naturally hopeful, and she went to work with
renewed energy, trusting in time to be able to purchase some of her children.
She had laid up three hundred dollars, which her mistress one day begged as
a loan, promising to pay her soon. The reader probably knows that no promise or writing given to a slave is legally binding; for, according to Southern
laws, a slave, *being* property, can *hold* no property. When my grandmother

2. During the Revolutionary War, a British port
town in what is now Florida.
3. John Horniblow, who ran the King's Arms
hotel in Edenton, North Carolina. Jacobs's grandmother's legal name was Margaret (Molly) Horniblow (c. 1771–1853); as was typical for the era,

Molly received the surname of her owner. *Incidents* never mentions a grandfather, and no information has been recovered relating to the paternal
parentage of Molly's children.
4. Inheritance from her husband's estate.

lent her hard earnings to her mistress, she trusted solely to her honor. The honor of a slaveholder to a slave!

To this good grandmother I was indebted for many comforts. My brother Willie and I often received portions of the crackers, cakes, and preserves, she made to sell; and after we ceased to be children we were indebted to her for many more important services.

Such were the unusually fortunate circumstances of my early childhood. When I was six years old, my mother died, and then, for the first time, I learned, by the talk around me, that I was a slave. My mother's mistress was the daughter of my grandmother's mistress. She was the foster sister of my mother; they were both nourished at my grandmother's breast. In fact, my mother had been weaned at three months old, that the babe of the mistress might obtain sufficient food. They played together as children; and, when they became women, my mother was a most faithful servant to her whiter foster sister. On her death-bed her mistress promised that her children should never suffer for any thing; and during her lifetime she kept her word. They all spoke kindly of my dead mother, who had been a slave merely in name, but in nature was noble and womanly. I grieved for her, and my young mind was troubled with the thought who would now take care of me and my little brother. I was told that my home was now to be with her mistress; and I found it a happy one. No toilsome or disagreeable duties were imposed upon me. My mistress was so kind to me that I was always glad to do her bidding, and proud to labor for her as much as my young years would permit. I would sit by her side for hours, sewing diligently, with a heart as free from care as that of any free-born white child. When she thought I was tired, she would send me out to run and jump; and away I bounded, to gather berries or flowers to decorate her room. Those were happy days—too happy to last. The slave child had no thought for the morrow; but there came that blight, which too surely waits on every human being born to be a chattel.

When I was nearly twelve years old, my kind mistress sickened and died. As I saw the cheek grow paler, and the eye more glassy, how earnestly I prayed in my heart that she might live! I loved her; for she had been almost like a mother to me. My prayers were not answered. She died, and they buried her in the little churchyard, where, day after day, my tears fell upon her grave.

I was sent to spend a week with my grandmother. I was now old enough to begin to think of the future; and again and again I asked myself what they would do with me. I felt sure I should never find another mistress so kind as the one who was gone. She had promised my dying mother that her children should never suffer for any thing; and when I remembered that, and recalled her many proofs of attachment to me, I could not help having some hopes that she had left me free. My friends were almost certain it would be so. They thought she would be sure to do it, on account of my mother's love and faithful service. But, alas! we all know that the memory of a faithful slave does not avail much to save her children from the auction block.

After a brief period of suspense, the will of my mistress was read, and we learned that she had bequeathed me to her sister's daughter, a child of five years old. So vanished our hopes. My mistress had taught me the precepts of God's Word: "Thou shalt love thy neighbor as thyself."[5] "Whatsoever ye

5. Mark 12.31.

would that men should do unto you, do ye even so unto them."[6] But I was her slave, and I suppose she did not recognize me as her neighbor. I would give much to blot out from my memory that one great wrong. As a child, I loved my mistress; and, looking back on the happy days I spent with her, I try to think with less bitterness of this act of injustice. While I was with her, she taught me to read and spell; and for this privilege, which so rarely falls to the lot of a slave, I bless her memory.

She possessed but few slaves; and at her death those were all distributed among her relatives. Five of them were my grandmother's children, and had shared the same milk that nourished her mother's children. Notwithstanding my grandmother's long and faithful service to her owners, not one of her children escaped the auction block. These God-breathing machines are no more, in the sight of their masters, than the cotton they plant, or the horses they tend.

* * *

VII. The Lover

Why does the slave ever love? Why allow the tendrils of the heart to twine around objects which may at any moment be wrenched away by the hand of violence? When separations come by the hand of death, the pious soul can bow in resignation, and say, "Not my will, but thine be done, O Lord!"[7] But when the ruthless hand of man strikes the blow, regardless of the misery he causes, it is hard to be submissive. I did not reason thus when I was a young girl. Youth will be youth. I loved, and I indulged the hope that the dark clouds around me would turn out a bright lining. I forgot that in the land of my birth the shadows are too dense for light to penetrate. A land

> "Where laughter is not mirth; nor thought the mind;
> Nor words a language; no e'en men mankind.
> Where cries reply to curses, shrieks to blows,
> And each is tortured in his separate hell."[8]

There was in the neighborhood a young colored carpenter; a free born man. We had been well acquainted in childhood, and frequently met together afterwards. We became mutually attached, and he proposed to marry me. I loved him with all the ardor of a young girl's first love. But when I reflected that I was a slave, and that the laws gave no sanction to the marriage of such, my heart sank within me. My lover wanted to buy me; but I knew that Dr. Flint was too wilful and arbitrary a man to consent to that arrangement. From him, I was sure of experiencing all sorts of opposition, and I had nothing to hope from my mistress.[9] She would have been delighted to have got rid of me, but not in that way. It would have relieved her mind of a burden if she could have seen me sold to some distant state, but if I was married near home I should be just as much in her husband's power as I had previously been,—for the husband of a slave has no power to protect her.[1] Moreover, my mistress, like many others, seemed to think that slaves

---

6. Matthew 7.12.
7. Matthew 26.39.
8. From *The Lament of Tasso* 4.7–10 (1817), by the English poet George Gordon, Lord Byron (1788–1824).
9. Dr. Flint is the father of Brent's owner, Emily

Flint, who is a child at this time, giving Flint and his wife (whom Brent refers to as her mistress) legal power.
1. Flint has been attempting to coerce Brent into sexual relations.

had no right to any family ties of their own; that they were created merely to wait upon the family of the mistress. I once heard her abuse a young slave girl, who told her that a colored man wanted to make her his wife. "I will have you peeled and pickled, my lady," said she, "if I ever hear you mention that subject again. Do you suppose that I will have you tending *my* children with the children of that nigger?" The girl to whom she said this had a mulatto child, of course not acknowledged by its father. The poor black man who loved her would have been proud to acknowledge his helpless offspring.

Many and anxious were the thoughts I revolved in my mind. I was at a loss what to do. Above all things, I was desirous to spare my lover the insults that had cut so deeply into my own soul. I talked with my grandmother about it, and partly told her my fears. I did not dare to tell her the worst. She had long suspected all was not right, and if I confirmed her suspicions I knew a storm would rise that would prove the overthrow of all my hopes.

This love-dream had been my support through many trials; and I could not bear to run the risk of having it suddenly dissipated. There was a lady in the neighborhood, a particular friend of Dr. Flint's, who often visited the house. I had a great respect for her, and she had always manifested a friendly interest in me. Grandmother thought she would have great influence with the doctor. I went to this lady, and told her my story. I told her I was aware that my lover's being a free-born man would prove a great objection; but he wanted to buy me; and if Dr. Flint would consent to that arrangement, I felt sure he would be willing to pay any reasonable price. She knew that Mrs. Flint disliked me; therefore, I ventured to suggest that perhaps my mistress would approve of my being sold, as that would rid her of me. The lady listened with kindly sympathy, and promised to do her utmost to promote my wishes. She had an interview with the doctor, and I believe she pleaded my cause earnestly; but it was all to no purpose.

How I dreaded my master now! Every minute I expected to be summoned to his presence; but the day passed, and I heard nothing from him. The next morning, a message was brought to me: "Master wants you in his study." I found the door ajar, and I stood a moment gazing at the hateful man who claimed a right to rule me, body and soul. I entered, and tried to appear calm. I did not want him to know how my heart was bleeding. He looked fixedly at me, with an expression which seemed to say, "I have half a mind to kill you on the spot." At last he broke the silence, and that was a relief to both of us.

"So you want to be married, do you?" said he, "and to a free nigger."

"Yes, sir."

"Well, I'll soon convince you whether I am your master, or the nigger fellow you honor so highly. If you *must* have a husband, you may take up with one of my slaves."

What a situation I should be in, as the wife of one of *his* slaves, even if my heart had been interested!

I replied, "Don't you suppose, sir, that a slave can have some preference about marrying? Do you suppose that all men are alike to her?"

"Do you love this nigger?" said he, abruptly.

"Yes, sir."

"How dare you tell me so!" he exclaimed, in great wrath. After a slight pause, he added, "I supposed you thought more of yourself; that you felt above the insults of such puppies."

I replied, "If he is a puppy I am a puppy, for we are both of the negro race. It is right and honorable for us to love each other. The man you call a puppy never insulted me, sir; and he would not love me if he did not believe me to be a virtuous woman."

He sprang upon me like a tiger, and gave me a stunning blow. It was the first time he had ever struck me; and fear did not enable me to control my anger. When I had recovered a little from the effects, I exclaimed, "You have struck me for answering you honestly. How I despise you!"

There was silence for some minutes. Perhaps he was deciding what should be my punishment; or, perhaps, he wanted to give me time to reflect on what I had said, and to whom I had said it. Finally, he asked, "Do you know what you have said?"

"Yes, sir; but your treatment drove me to it."

"Do you know that I have a right to do as I like with you,—that I can kill you, if I please?"

"You have tried to kill me, and I wish you had; but you have no right to do as you like with me."

"Silence!" he exclaimed, in a thundering voice. "By heavens, girl, you forget yourself too far! Are you mad? If you are, I will soon bring you to your senses. Do you think any other master would bear what I have borne from you this morning? Many masters would have killed you on the spot. How would you like to be sent to jail for your insolence?"

"I know I have been disrespectful, sir," I replied; "but you drove me to it; I couldn't help it. As for the jail, there would be more peace for me there than there is here."

"You deserve to go there," he said, "and to be under such treatment, that you would forget the meaning of the word *peace*. It would do you good. It would take some of your high notions out of you. But I am not ready to send you there yet, notwithstanding your ingratitude for all my kindness and forbearance. You have been the plague of my life. I have wanted to make you happy, and I have been repaid with the basest ingratitude; but though you have proved yourself incapable of appreciating my kindness, I will be lenient towards you, Linda. I will give you one more chance to redeem your character. If you behave yourself and do as I require, I will forgive you and treat you as I always have done; but if you disobey me, I will punish you as I would the meanest slave on my plantation. Never let me hear that fellow's name mentioned again. If I ever know of your speaking to him, I will cow-hide you both; and if I catch him lurking about my premises, I will shoot him as soon as I would a dog. Do you hear what I say? I'll teach you a lesson about marriage and free niggers! Now go, and let this be the last time I have occasion to speak to you on this subject."

Reader, did you ever hate? I hope not. I never did but once; and I trust I never shall again. Somebody has called it "the atmosphere of hell;" and I believe it is so.

For a fortnight the doctor did not speak to me. He thought to mortify me; to make me feel that I had disgraced myself by receiving the honorable addresses of a respectable colored man, in preference to the base propos-als of a white man. But though his lips disdained to address me, his eyes were very loquacious. No animal ever watched its prey more narrowly than he watched me. He knew that I could write, though he had failed to make me read his letters; and he was now troubled lest I should exchange letters with another man. After a while he became weary of silence; and I was sorry for it. One morning, as he passed through the hall, to leave the house, he contrived to thrust a note into my hand. I thought I had better read it, and spare myself the vexation of having him read it to me. It expressed regret for the blow he had given me, and reminded me that I myself was wholly to blame for it. He hoped I had become convinced of the injury I was doing myself by incurring his displeasure. He wrote that he had made up his mind to go to Louisiana; that he should take several slaves with him, and intended I should be one of the number. My mistress would remain where she was; therefore I should have nothing to fear from that quarter. If I merited kindness from him, he assured me that it would be lavishly bestowed. He begged me to think over the matter, and answer the following day.

The next morning I was called to carry a pair of scissors to his room. I laid them on the table, with the letter beside them. He thought it was my answer, and did not call me back. I went as usual to attend my young mistress to and from school. He met me in the street, and ordered me to stop at his office on my way back. When I entered, he showed me his letter, and asked me why I had not answered it. I replied, "I am your daughter's property, and it is in your power to send me, or take me, wherever you please." He said he was very glad to find me so willing to go, and that we should start early in the autumn. He had a large practice in the town, and I rather thought he had made up the story merely to frighten me. However that might be, I was determined that I would never go to Louisiana with him.

Summer passed away, and early in the autumn, Dr. Flint's eldest son was sent to Louisiana to examine the country, with a view to emigrating. That news did not disturb me. I knew very well that I should not be sent with *him*. That I had not been taken to the plantation before this time, was owing to the fact that his son was there. He was jealous of his son; and jealousy of the overseer had kept him from punishing me by sending me into the fields to work. Is it strange that I was not proud of these protectors? As for the overseer, he was a man for whom I had less respect than I had for a bloodhound.

Young Mr. Flint did not bring back a favorable report of Louisiana, and I heard no more of that scheme. Soon after this, my lover met me at the corner of the street, and I stopped to speak to him. Looking up, I saw my master watching us from his window. I hurried home, trembling with fear. I was sent for, immediately, to go to his room. He met me with a blow. "When is mistress to be married?" said he, in a sneering tone. A shower of oaths and imprecations followed. How thankful I was that my lover was a free man! that my tyrant had no power to flog him for speaking to me in the street!

Again and again I revolved in my mind how all this would end. There was no hope that the doctor would consent to sell me on any terms. He had an iron will, and was determined to keep me, and to conquer me. My lover was an intelligent and religious man. Even if he could have obtained permission to marry me while I was a slave, the marriage would give him no power to protect me from my master. It would have made him miserable to witness the insults I should have been subjected to. And then, if we had children, I knew they must "follow the condition of the mother."[2] What a terrible blight that would be on the heart of a free, intelligent father! For *his* sake, I felt that

2. In Southern law, the mother's legal status as slave or free determined the legal status of the child.

I ought not to link his fate with my own unhappy destiny. He was going to Savannah to see about a little property left him by an uncle; and hard as it was to bring my feelings to it, I earnestly entreated him not to come back. I advised him to go to the Free States, where his tongue would not be tied, and where his intelligence would be of more avail to him. He left me, still hoping the day would come when I could be bought. With me the lamp of hope had gone out. The dream of my girlhood was over. I felt lonely and desolate.

Still I was not stripped of all. I still had my good grandmother, and my affectionate brother. When he put his arms round my neck, and looked into my eyes, as if to read there the troubles I dared not tell, I felt that I still had something to love. But even that pleasant emotion was chilled by the reflection that he might be torn from me at any moment, by some sudden freak of my master. If he had known how we love each other, I think he would have exulted in separating us. We often planned together how we could get to the north. But, as William remarked, such things are easier said than done. My movements were very closely watched, and we had no means of getting any money to defray our expenses. As for grandmother, she was strongly opposed to her children's undertaking any such project. She had not forgotten poor Benjamin's sufferings[3] and she was afraid that if another child tried to escape, he would have a similar or a worse fate. To me, nothing seemed more dreadful than my present life. I said to myself, "William *must* be free. He shall go to the north, and I will follow him." Many a slave sister has formed the same plans.

*　*　*

X. *A Perilous Passage in the Slave Girl's Life*

After my lover went away, Dr. Flint contrived a new plan. He seemed to have an idea that my fear of my mistress was his greatest obstacle. In the blandest tones, he told me that he was going to build a small house for me, in a secluded place, four miles away from the town. I shuddered; but I was constrained to listen, while he talked of his intention to give me a home of my own, and to make a lady of me. Hitherto, I had escaped my dreaded fate, by being in the midst of people. My grandmother had already had high words with my master about me. She had told him pretty plainly what she thought of his character, and there was considerable gossip in the neighborhood about our affairs, to which the open-mouthed jealousy of Mrs. Flint contributed not a little. When my master said he was going to build a house for me, and that he could do it with little trouble and expense, I was in hopes something would happen to frustrate his scheme; but I soon heard that the house was actually begun. I vowed before my Maker that I would never enter it. I had rather toil on the plantation from dawn till dark; I had rather live and die in jail, than drag on, from day to day, through such a living death. I was determined that the master, whom I so hated and loathed, who had blighted the prospects of my youth, and made my life a desert, should not, after my long struggle with him, succeed at last in trampling his victim under his feet. I would do any thing, every thing, for the sake of defeating him. What *could* I do? I thought and thought, till I became desperate, and made a plunge into the abyss.

---

3. One of Brent's uncles, caught attempting to escape, was jailed for six months, then sold to a trader. He eventually escaped to New York City but never saw his mother again.

And now, reader, I come to a period in my unhappy life, which I would gladly forget if I could. The remembrance fills me with sorrow and shame. It pains me to tell you of it; but I have promised to tell you the truth, and I will do it honestly, let it cost me what it may. I will not try to screen myself behind the plea of compulsion from a master; for it was not so. Neither can I plead ignorance or thoughtlessness. For years, my master had done his utmost to pollute my mind with foul images, and to destroy the pure principles inculcated by my grandmother, and the good mistress of my childhood. The influences of slavery had had the same effect on me that they had on other young girls; they had made me prematurely knowing, concerning the evil ways of the world. I knew what I did, and I did it with deliberate calculation.

But, O, ye happy women, whose purity has been sheltered from childhood, who have been free to choose the objects of your affection, whose homes are protected by law, do not judge the poor desolate slave girl too severely! If slavery had been abolished, I, also, could have married the man of my choice; I could have had a home shielded by the laws; and I should have been spared the painful task of confessing what I am now about to relate; but all my prospects had been blighted by slavery. I wanted to keep myself pure; and, under the most adverse circumstances, I tried hard to preserve my self-respect; but I was struggling alone in the powerful grasp of the demon Slavery; and the monster proved too strong for me. I felt as if I was forsaken by God and man; as if all my efforts must be frustrated; and I became reckless in my despair.

I have told you that Dr. Flint's persecutions and his wife's jealousy had given rise to some gossip in the neighborhood. Among others, it chanced that a white unmarried gentleman had obtained some knowledge of the circumstances in which I was placed. He knew my grandmother, and often spoke to me in the street. He became interested for me, and asked questions about my master, which I answered in part. He expressed a great deal of sympathy, and a wish to aid me. He constantly sought opportunities to see me, and wrote to me frequently. I was a poor slave girl, only fifteen years old.

So much attention from a superior person was, of course, flattering; for human nature is the same in all. I also felt grateful for his sympathy, and encouraged by his kind words. It seemed to me a great thing to have such a friend. By degrees, a more tender feeling crept into my heart. He was an educated and eloquent gentleman; too eloquent, alas, for the poor slave girl who trusted in him. Of course I saw whither all this was tending. I knew the impassable gulf between us; but to be an object of interest to a man who is not married, and who is not her master, is agreeable to the pride and feelings of a slave, if her miserable situation has left her any pride or sentiment. It seems less degrading to give one's self, than to submit to compulsion. There is something akin to freedom in having a lover who has no control over you, except that which he gains by kindness and attachment. A master may treat you as rudely as he pleases, and you dare not speak; moreover, the wrong does not seem so great with an unmarried man, as with one who has a wife to be made unhappy. There may be sophistry in all this; but the condition of a slave confuses all principles of morality, and, in fact, renders the practice of them impossible.

When I found that my master had actually begun to build the lonely cottage, other feelings mixed with those I have described. Revenge, and calculations of interest, were added to flattered vanity and sincere gratitude for kindness. I knew nothing would enrage Dr. Flint so much as to know that I favored another; and it was something to triumph over my tyrant even in that small way. I thought he would revenge himself by selling me, and I was sure my friend, Mr. Sands, would buy me.[4] He was a man of more generosity and feeling than my master, and I thought my freedom could be easily obtained from him. The crisis of my fate now came so near that I was desperate. I shuddered to think of being the mother of children that should be owned by my old tyrant. I knew that as soon as a new fancy took him, his victims were sold far off to get rid of them; especially if they had children. I had seen several women sold, with his babies at the breast. He never allowed his offspring by slaves to remain long in sight of himself and his wife. Of a man who was not my master I could ask to have my children well supported; and in this case, I felt confident I should obtain the boon. I also felt quite sure that they would be made free. With all these thoughts revolving in my mind, and seeing no other way of escaping the doom I so much dreaded, I made a headlong plunge. Pity me, and pardon me, O virtuous reader! You never knew what it is to be a slave; to be entirely unprotected by law or custom; to have the laws reduce you to the condition of a chattel, entirely subject to the will of another. You never exhausted your ingenuity in avoiding the snares, and eluding the power of a hated tyrant; you never shuddered at the sound of his footsteps, and trembled within hearing of his voice. I know I did wrong. No one can feel it more sensibly than I do. The painful and humiliating memory will haunt me to my dying day. Still, in looking back, calmly, on the events of my life, I feel that the slave woman ought not to be judged by the same standard as others.

The months passed on. I had many unhappy hours. I secretly mourned over the sorrow I was bringing on my grandmother, who had so tried to shield me from harm. I knew that I was the greatest comfort of her old age, and that it was a source of pride to her that I had not degraded myself, like most of the slaves. I wanted to confess to her that I was no longer worthy of her love; but I could not utter the dreaded words.

As for Dr. Flint, I had a feeling of satisfaction and triumph in the thought of telling *him*. From time to time he told me of his intended arrangements, and I was silent. At last, he came and told me the cottage was completed, and ordered me to go to it. I told him I would never enter it. He said, "I have heard enough of such talk as that. You shall go, if you are carried by force; and you shall remain there."

I replied, "I will never go there. In a few months I shall be a mother."

He stood and looked at me in dumb amazement, and left the house without a word. I thought I should be happy in my triumph over him. But now that the truth was out, and my relatives would hear of it, I felt wretched. Humble as were their circumstances, they had pride in my good character. Now, how could I look them in the face? My self-respect was gone! I had resolved that I would be virtuous, though I was a slave. I had said, "Let the storm beat! I will brave it till I die." And now, how humiliated I felt!

I went to my grandmother. My lips moved to make confession, but the words stuck in my throat. I sat down in the shade of a tree at her door and began to sew. I think she saw something unusual was the matter with me. The mother of slaves is very watchful. She knows there is no security for her children. After they have entered their teens she lives in daily expectation of

---

4. Brent misjudged Flint, who becomes even more possessive when he learns of her relationship with Sands.

trouble. This leads to many questions. If the girl is of a sensitive nature, timidity keeps her from answering truthfully, and this well-meant course has a tendency to drive her from maternal counsels. Presently, in came my mistress, like a mad woman, and accused me concerning her husband. My grandmother, whose suspicions had been previously awakened, believed what she said. She exclaimed, "O Linda! has it come to this? I had rather see you dead than to see you as you now are. You are a disgrace to your dead mother." She tore from my fingers my mother's wedding ring and her silver thimble. "Go away!" she exclaimed, "and never come to my house, again." Her reproaches fell so hot and heavy, that they left me no chance to answer. Bitter tears, such as the eyes never shed but once, were my only answer. I rose from my seat, but fell back again, sobbing. She did not speak to me; but the tears were running down her furrowed cheeks, and they scorched me like fire. She had always been so kind to me! So kind! How I longed to throw myself at her feet, and tell her all the truth! But she had ordered me to go, and never to come there again. After a few minutes, I mustered strength, and started to obey her. With what feelings did I now close that little gate, which I used to open with such an eager hand in my childhood! It closed upon me with a sound I never heard before.

Where could I go? I was afraid to return to my master's. I walked on recklessly, not caring where I went, or what would become of me. When I had gone four or five miles, fatigue compelled me to stop. I sat down on the stump of an old tree. The stars were shining through the boughs above me. How they mocked me, with their bright, calm light! The hours passed by, and as I sat there alone a chilliness and deadly sickness came over me. I sank on the ground. My mind was full of horrid thoughts. I prayed to die; but the prayer was not answered. At last, with great effort I roused myself, and walked some distance further, to the house of a woman who had been a friend of my mother. When I told her why I was there, she spoke soothingly to me; but I could not be comforted. I thought I could bear my shame if I could only be reconciled to my grandmother. I longed to open my heart to her. I thought if she could know the real state of the case, and all I had been bearing for years, she would perhaps judge me less harshly. My friend advised me to send for her. I did so; but days of agonizing suspense passed before she came. Had she utterly forsaken me? No. She came at last. I knelt before her, and told her the things that had poisoned my life; how long I had been persecuted; that I saw no way of escape; and in an hour of extremity I had become desperate. She listened in silence. I told her I would bear any thing and do any thing, if in time I had hopes of obtaining her forgiveness. I begged of her to pity me, for my dead mother's sake. And she did pity me. She did not say, "I forgive you;" but she looked at me lovingly, with her eyes full of tears. She laid her old hand gently on my head, and murmured, "Poor child! Poor child!"

* * *

XIV. Another Link to Life

I had not returned to my master's house since the birth of my child. The old man raved to have me thus removed from his immediate power; but his wife vowed, by all that was good and great, she would kill me if I came back; and he did not doubt her word. Sometimes he would stay away for a season.

Then he would come and renew the old threadbare discourse about his forbearance and my ingratitude. He labored, most unnecessarily, to convince me that I had lowered myself. The venomous old reprobate had no need of descanting on that theme. I felt humiliated enough. My unconscious babe was the ever-present witness of my shame. I listened with silent contempt when he talked about my having forfeited *his* good opinion; but I shed bitter tears that I was no longer worthy of being respected by the good and pure. Alas! slavery still held me in its poisonous grasp. There was no chance for me to be respectable. There was no prospect of being able to lead a better life.

Sometimes, when my master found that I still refused to accept what he called his kind offers, he would threaten to sell my child. "Perhaps that will humble you," said he.

Humble *me*! Was I not already in the dust?[5] But his threat lacerated my heart. I knew the law gave him power to fulfill it; for slaveholders have been cunning enough to enact that "the child shall follow the condition of the *mother*," not of the *father*; thus taking care that licentiousness shall not interfere with avarice. This reflection made me clasp my innocent babe all the more firmly to my heart. Horrid visions passed through my mind when I thought of his liability to fall into the slave trader's hands. I wept over him, and said, "O my child! perhaps they will leave you in some cold cabin to die, and then throw you into a hole, as if you were a dog."

When Dr. Flint learned that I was again to be a mother, he was exasperated beyond measure. He rushed from the house, and returned with a pair of shears. I had a fine head of hair; and he often railed about my pride of arranging it nicely. He cut every hair close to my head, storming and swearing all the time. I replied to some of his abuse, and he struck me. Some months before, he had pitched me down stairs in a fit of passion; and the injury I received was so serious that I was unable to turn myself in bed for many days. He then said, "Linda, I swear by God I will never raise my hand against you again;" but I knew that he would forget his promise.

After he discovered my situation, he was like a restless spirit from the pit. He came every day; and I was subjected to such insults as no pen can describe. I would not describe them if I could; they were too low, too revolting. I tried to keep them from my grandmother's knowledge as much as I could. I knew she had enough to sadden her life, without having my troubles to bear. When she saw the doctor treat me with violence, and heard him utter oaths terrible enough to palsy a man's tongue, she could not always hold her peace. It was natural and motherlike that she should try to defend me; but it only made matters worse.

When they told me my new-born babe was a girl, my heart was heavier than it had ever been before. Slavery is terrible for men; but it is far more terrible for women. Superadded to the burden common to all, *they* have wrongs, and sufferings, and mortifications peculiarly their own.

Dr. Flint had sworn that he would make me suffer, to my last day, for this new crime against *him*, as he called it; and as long as he had me in his power he kept his word. On the fourth day after the birth of my babe, he entered my room suddenly, and commanded me to rise and bring my baby to him.

5. Job 42.6.

The nurse who took care of me had gone out of the room to prepare some nourishment, and I was alone. There was no alternative. I rose, took up my babe, and crossed the room to where he sat. "Now stand there," said he, "till I tell you to go back!" My child bore a strong resemblance to her father, and to the deceased Mrs. Sands, her grandmother. He noticed this; and while I stood before him, trembling with weakness, he heaped upon me and my little one every vile epithet he could think of. Even the grandmother in her grave did not escape his curses. In the midst of his vituperations I fainted at his feet. This recalled him to his senses. He took the baby from my arms, laid it on the bed, dashed cold water in my face, took me up, and shook me violently, to restore my consciousness before any one entered the room. Just then my grandmother came in, and he hurried out of the house. I suffered in consequence of this treatment; but I begged my friends to let me die, rather than send for the doctor. There was nothing I dreaded so much as his presence. My life was spared; and I was glad for the sake of my little ones. Had it not been for these ties to life, I should have been glad to be released by death, though I had lived only nineteen years.

Always it gave me a pang that my children had no lawful claim to a name. Their father offered his; but, if I had wished to accept the offer, I dared not while my master lived. Moreover, I knew it would not be accepted at their baptism. A Christian name they were at least entitled to; and we resolved to call my boy for our dear good Benjamin, who had gone far away from us.

My grandmother belonged to the church, and she was very desirous of having the children christened. I knew Dr. Flint would forbid it, and I did not venture to attempt it. But chance favored me. He was called to visit a patient out of town, and was obliged to be absent during Sunday. "Now is the time," said my grandmother; "we will take the children to church, and have them christened."

When I entered the church, recollections of my mother came over me, and I felt subdued in spirit. There she had presented me for baptism, without any reason to feel ashamed. She had been married, and had such legal rights as slavery allows a slave. The vows had at least been sacred to *her*, and she had never violated them. I was glad she was not alive, to know under what different circumstances her grandchildren were presented for baptism. Why had my lot been so different from my mother's? *Her* master had died when she was a child; and she remained with her mistress till she married. She was never in the power of any master; and thus she escaped one class of the evils that generally fall upon slaves.

When my baby was about to be christened, the former mistress of my father stepped up to me, and proposed to give it her Christian name. To this I added the surname of my father, who had himself no legal right to it; for my grandfather on the paternal side was a white gentleman. What tangled skeins are the genealogies of slavery![6] I loved my father; but it mortified me to be obliged to bestow his name on my children.

When we left the church, my father's old mistress invited me to go home with her. She clasped a gold chain around my baby's neck. I thanked her for this kindness; but I did not like the emblem. I wanted no chain to be fastened on my daughter, not even if its links were of gold. How earnestly I

---

6. Jacobs stresses her mixed-race parentage not to claim that she is really white but to show the arbitrariness and absurdity of racial distinctions.

prayed that she might never feel the weight of slavery's chain, whose iron entereth into the soul.

* * *

XXI. The Loophole of Retreat[7]

A small shed had been added to my grandmother's house years ago. Some boards were laid across the joists at the top, and between these boards and the roof was a very small garret, never occupied by any thing but rats and mice. It was a pent roof, covered with nothing but shingles, according to the southern custom for such buildings. The garret was only nine feet long and seven wide. The highest part was three feet high, and sloped down abruptly to the loose board floor. There was no admission for either light or air. My uncle Phillip, who was a carpenter, had very skilfully made a concealed trap-door, which communicated with the storeroom. He had been doing this while I was waiting in the swamp. The storeroom opened upon a piazza. To this hole I was conveyed as soon as I entered the house. The air was stifling; the darkness total. A bed had been spread on the floor. I could sleep quite comfortably on one side; but the slope was so sudden that I could not turn on the other without hitting the roof. The rats and mice ran over my bed; but I was weary, and I slept such sleep as the wretched may, when a tempest has passed over them. Morning came. I knew it only by the noises I heard; for in my small den day and night were all the same. I suffered for air even more than for light. But I was not comfortless. I heard the voices of my children. There was joy and there was sadness in the sound. It made my tears flow. How I longed to speak to them! I was eager to look on their faces; but there was no hole, no crack, through which I could peep. This continued darkness was oppressive. It seemed horrible to sit or lie in a cramped position day after day, without one gleam of light. Yet I would have chosen this, rather than my lot as a slave, though white people considered it an easy one; and it was so compared with the fate of others. I was never cruelly over-worked; I was never lacerated with the whip from head to foot; I was never so beaten and bruised that I could not turn from one side to the other; I never had my heel-strings cut to prevent my running away; I was never chained to a log and forced to drag it about, while I toiled in the fields from morning till night; I was never branded with hot iron, or torn by bloodhounds. On the contrary, I had always been kindly treated, and tenderly cared for, until I came into the hands of Dr. Flint. I had never wished for freedom till then. But though my life in slavery was comparatively devoid of hardships, God pity the woman who is compelled to lead such a life!

My food was passed up to me through the trap-door my uncle had contrived; and my grandmother, my uncle Phillip, and aunt Nancy would seize such opportunities as they could, to mount up there and chat with me at the opening. But of course this was not safe in the daytime. It must all be done in darkness. It was impossible for me to move in an erect position, but I crawled about my den for exercise. One day I hit my head against something, and found it was a gimlet.[8] My uncle had left it sticking there when he made the trap-door. I was as rejoiced as Robinson Crusoe[9] could have been at finding

---

7. From *The Task* 4.88–90, a popular long poem (1785) by the English poet William Cowper (1731–1800). By this point in the narrative Brent has escaped from the Flint household and is hiding in a crawl space beneath the roof of her grandmother's house. The account states that she

remains there for seven years.
8. Small tool for boring holes.
9. Hero of a novel of the same name (1719) by the English writer Daniel Defoe (1660–1731) about a man shipwrecked on a desert island.

such a treasure. It put a lucky thought into my head. I said to myself, "Now I will have some light. Now I will see my children." I did not dare to begin my work during the daytime, for fear of attracting attention. But I groped round; and having found the side next the street, where I could frequently see my children, I struck the gimlet in and waited for evening. I bored three rows of holes, one above another; then I bored out the interstices between. I thus succeeded in making one hole about an inch long and an inch broad. I sat by it till late into the night, to enjoy the little whiff of air that floated in. In the morning I watched for my children. The first person I saw in the street was Dr. Flint. I had a shuddering, superstitious feeling that it was a bad omen. Several familiar faces passed by. At last I heard the merry laugh of children, and presently two sweet little faces were looking up at me, as though they knew I was there, and were conscious of the joy they imparted. How I longed to *tell* them I was there!

My condition was now a little improved. But for weeks I was tormented by hundreds of little red insects, fine as a needle's point, that pierced through my skin, and produced an intolerable burning. The good grandmother gave me herb teas and cooling medicines, and finally I got rid of them. The heat of my den was intense, for nothing but thin shingles protected me from the scorching summer's sun. But I had my consolations. Through my peeping-hole I could watch the children, and when they were near enough, I could hear their talk. Aunt Nancy brought me all the news she could hear at Dr. Flint's. From her I learned that the doctor had written to New York to a colored woman, who had been born and raised in our neighborhood, and had breathed his contaminating atmosphere. He offered her a reward if she could find out any thing about me. I know not what was the nature of her reply; but he soon after started for New York in haste, saying to his family that he had business of importance to transact. I peeped at him as he passed on his way to the steamboat. It was a satisfaction to have miles of land and water between us, even for a little while; and it was a still greater satisfaction to know that he believed me to be in the Free States. My little den seemed less dreary than it had done. He returned, as he did from his former journey to New York, without obtaining any satisfactory information. When he passed our house next morning, Benny was standing at the gate. He had heard them say that he had gone to find me, and he called out, "Dr. Flint, did you bring my mother home? I want to see her." The doctor stamped his foot at him in a rage, and exclaimed, "Get out of the way, you little damned rascal! If you don't, I'll cut off your head."

Benny ran terrified into the house, saying, "You can't put me in jail again. I don't belong to you now." It was well that the wind carried the words away from the doctor's ear. I told my grandmother of it, when we had our next conference at the trap-door; and begged of her not to allow the children to be impertinent to the irascible old man.

Autumn came, with a pleasant abatement of heat. My eyes had become accustomed to the dim light, and by holding my book or work in a certain position near the aperture I contrived to read and sew. That was a great relief to the tedious monotony of my life. But when winter came, the cold penetrated through the thin shingle roof, and I was dreadfully chilled. The winters there are not so long, or so severe, as in northern latitudes; but the houses are not built to shelter from cold, and my little den was peculiarly comfortless. The kind grandmother brought me bed-clothes and warm drinks. Often I was obliged to lie in bed all day to keep comfortable; but with all my precautions, my shoulders and feet were frostbitten. O, those long, gloomy days, with no object for my eye to rest upon, and no thoughts to occupy my mind, except the dreary past and the uncertain future! I was thankful when there came a day sufficiently mild for me to wrap myself up and sit at the loophole to watch the passers by. Southerners have the habit of stopping and talking in the streets, and I heard many conversations not intended to meet my ears. I heard slave-hunters planning how to catch some poor fugitive. Several times I heard allusions to Dr. Flint, myself, and the history of my children, who, perhaps, were playing near the gate. One would say, "I wouldn't move my little finger to catch her, as old Flint's property." Another would say, "I'll catch *any* nigger for the reward. A man ought to have what belongs to him, if he *is* a damned brute." The opinion was often expressed that I was in the Free States. Very rarely did any one suggest that I might be in the vicinity. Had the least suspicion rested on my grandmother's house, it would have been burned to the ground. But it was the last place they thought of. Yet there was no place, where slavery existed, that could have afforded me so good a place of concealment.

Dr. Flint and his family repeatedly tried to coax and bribe my children to tell something they had heard said about me. One day the doctor took them into a shop, and offered them some bright little silver pieces and gay handkerchiefs if they would tell where their mother was. Ellen shrank away from him, and would not speak; but Benny spoke up, and said, "Dr. Flint, I don't know where my mother is. I guess she's in New York; and when you go there again, I wish you'd ask her to come home, for I want to see her; but if you put her in jail, or tell her you'll cut her head off, I'll tell her to go right back."

* * *

XLI. Free at Last[1]

Mrs. Bruce, and every member of her family, were exceedingly kind to me. I was thankful for the blessings of my lot, yet I could not always wear a cheerful countenance. I was doing harm to no one; on the contrary, I was doing all the good I could in my small way; yet I could never go out to breathe God's free air without trepidation at my heart. This seemed hard; and I could not think it was a right state of things in any civilized country.

From time to time I received news from my good old grandmother. She could not write; but she employed others to write for her. The following is an extract from one of her last letters:—

"Dear Daughter: I cannot hope to see you again on earth; but I pray to God to unite us above, where pain will no more rack this feeble body of mine; where sorrow and parting from my children will be no more.[2] God has promised these things if we are faithful unto the end. My age and feeble health deprive me of going to church now; but God is with me here at home. Thank your brother for his kindness. Give much love to him, and tell him to remember the Creator in the days of his youth,[3] and strive to meet me in the Father's kingdom. Love to Ellen and Ben-

1. This is the final chapter of *Incidents*. Having escaped from the South on a ship headed to Philadelphia, Brent finds employment with the Bruce family of New York City, but she remains in constant fear of being returned to the South under the provisions of the Fugitive Slave Act of 1793.
2. Paraphrase of Revelation 21.4.
3. Ecclesiastes 12.1.

jamin. Don't neglect him. Tell him for me, to be a good boy. Strive, my child, to train them for God's children. May he protect and provide for you, is the prayer of your loving old mother."

These letters both cheered and saddened me. I was always glad to have tidings from the kind, faithful old friend of my unhappy youth; but her messages of love made my heart yearn to see her before she died, and I mourned over the fact that it was impossible. Some months after I returned from my flight to New England, I received a letter from her, in which she wrote, "Dr. Flint is dead. He has left a distressed family. Poor old man! I hope he made his peace with God."

I remembered how he had defrauded my grandmother of the hard earnings she had loaned; how he had tried to cheat her out of the freedom her mistress had promised her, and how he had persecuted her children; and I thought to myself that she was a better Christian than I was, if she could entirely forgive him. I cannot say, with truth, that the news of my old master's death softened my feelings towards him. There are wrongs which even the grave does not bury. The man was odious to me while he lived, and his memory is odious now.

His departure from this world did not diminish my danger. He had threatened my grandmother that his heirs should hold me in slavery after he was gone; that I never should be free so long as a child of his survived. As for Mrs. Flint, I had seen her in deeper afflictions than I supposed the loss of her husband would be, for she had buried several children; yet I never saw any signs of softening in her heart. The doctor had died in embarrassed circumstances, and had little to will to his heirs, except such property as he was unable to grasp. I was well aware what I had to expect from the family of Flints; and my fears were confirmed by a letter from the south, warning me to be on my guard, because Mrs. Flint openly declared that her daughter could not afford to lose so valuable a slave as I was.

I kept close watch of the newspapers for arrivals; but one Saturday night, being much occupied, I forgot to examine the Evening Express as usual. I went down into the parlor for it, early in the morning, and found the boy about to kindle a fire with it. I took it from him and examined the list of arrivals. Reader, if you have never been a slave, you cannot imagine the acute sensation of suffering at my heart, when I read the names of Mr. and Mrs. Dodge,[4] at a hotel in Courtland Street. It was a third-rate hotel, and that circumstance convinced me of the truth of what I had heard, that they were short of funds and had need of my value, as *they* valued me; and that was by dollars and cents. I hastened with the paper to Mrs. Bruce. Her heart and hand were always open to every one in distress, and she always warmly sympathized with mine. It was impossible to tell how near the enemy was. He might have passed and repassed the house while we were sleeping. He might at that moment be waiting to pounce upon me if I ventured out of doors. I had never seen the husband of my young mistress, and therefore I could not distinguish him from any other stranger. A carriage was hastily ordered; and, closely veiled, I followed Mrs. Bruce, taking the baby again with me into exile. After various turnings and crossings, and returnings, the carriage stopped at the house of one of Mrs. Bruce's friends, where I was kindly received. Mrs.

---

4. Dodge is the married name of Emily Flint, Brent's legal owner.

Bruce returned immediately, to instruct the domestics what to say if any one came to inquire for me.

It was lucky for me that the evening paper was not burned up before I had a chance to examine the list of arrivals. It was not long after Mrs. Bruce's return to her house, before several people came to inquire for me. One inquired for me, another asked for my daughter Ellen, and another said he had a letter from my grandmother, which he was requested to deliver in person.

They were told, "She *has* lived here, but she has left."

"How long ago?"

"I don't know, sir."

"Do you know where she went?"

"I do not, sir." And the door was closed.

This Mr. Dodge, who claimed me as his property, was originally a Yankee pedler in the south; then he became a merchant, and finally a slaveholder. He managed to get introduced into what was called the first society, and married Miss Emily Flint. A quarrel arose between him and her brother, and the brother cowhided him. This led to a family feud, and he proposed to remove to Virginia. Dr. Flint left him no property, and his own means had become circumscribed, while a wife and children depended upon him for support. Under these circumstances, it was very natural that he should make an effort to put me into his pocket.

I had a colored friend, a man from my native place, in whom I had the most implicit confidence. I sent for him, and told him that Mr. and Mrs. Dodge had arrived in New York. I proposed that he should call upon them to make inquiries about his friends at the south, with whom Dr. Flint's family were well acquainted. He thought there was no impropriety in his doing so, and he consented. He went to the hotel, and knocked at the door of Mr. Dodge's room, which was opened by the gentleman himself, who gruffly inquired, "What brought you here? How came you to know I was in the city?"

"Your arrival was published in the evening papers, sir; and I called to ask Mrs. Dodge about my friends at home. I didn't suppose it would give any offence."

"Where's that negro girl, that belongs to my wife?"

"What girl, sir?"

"You know well enough. I mean Linda, that ran away from Dr. Flint's plantation, some years ago. I dare say you've seen her, and know where she is."

"Yes, sir, I've seen her, and know where she is. She is out of your reach, sir."

"Tell me where she is, or bring her to me, and I will give her a chance to buy her freedom."

"I don't think it would be of any use, sir. I have heard her say she would go to the ends of the earth, rather than pay any man or woman for her freedom, because she thinks she has a right to it. Besides, she couldn't do it, if she would, for she has spent her earnings to educate her children."

This made Mr. Dodge very angry, and some high words passed between them. My friend was afraid to come where I was; but in the course of the day I received a note from him. I supposed they had not come from the south, in the winter, for a pleasure excursion; and now the nature of their business was very plain.

Mrs. Bruce came to me and entreated me to leave the city the next morning. She said her house was watched, and it was possible that some clew to me might be obtained. I refused to take her advice. She pleaded with an earnest tenderness, that ought to have moved me; but I was in a bitter, disheartened mood. I was weary of flying from pillar to post. I had been chased during half my life, and it seemed as if the chase was never to end. There I sat, in that great city, guiltless of crime, yet not daring to worship God in any of the churches. I heard the bells ringing for afternoon service, and, with contemptuous sarcasm, I said, "Will the preachers take for their text, 'Proclaim liberty to the captive, and the opening of prison doors to them that are bound'?[5] or will they preach from the text, 'Do unto others as ye would they should do unto you'?"[6] Oppressed Poles and Hungarians could find a safe refuge in that city; John Mitchell[7] was free to proclaim in the City Hall his desire for "a plantation well stocked with slaves;" but there I sat, an oppressed American, not daring to show my face. God forgive the black and bitter thoughts I indulged on that Sabbath day! The Scripture says, "Oppression makes even a wise man mad;"[8] and I was not wise.

I had been told that Mr. Dodge said his wife had never signed away her right to my children, and if he could not get me, he would take them. This it was, more than any thing else, that roused such a tempest in my soul. Benjamin was with his uncle William in California, but my innocent young daughter had come to spend a vacation with me. I thought of what I had suffered in slavery at her age, and my heart was like a tiger's when a hunter tries to seize her young.

Dear Mrs. Bruce! I seem to see the expression of her face, as she turned away discouraged by my obstinate mood. Finding her expostulations unavailing, she sent Ellen to entreat me. When ten o'clock in the evening arrived and Ellen had not returned, this watchful and unwearied friend became anxious. She came to us in a carriage, bringing a well-filled trunk for my journey—trusting that by this time I would listen to reason. I yielded to her, as I ought to have done before.

The next day, baby and I set out in a heavy snow storm, bound for New England again. I received letters from the City of Iniquity,[9] addressed to me under an assumed name. In a few days one came from Mrs. Bruce, informing me that my new master was still searching for me, and that she intended to put an end to this persecution by buying my freedom. I felt grateful for the kindness that prompted this offer, but the idea was not so pleasant to me as might have been expected. The more my mind had become enlightened, the more difficult it was for me to consider myself an article of property; and to pay money to those who had so grievously oppressed me seemed like taking from my sufferings the glory of triumph. I wrote to Mrs. Bruce, thanking her, but saying that being sold from one owner to another seemed too much like slavery; that such a great obligation could not be easily cancelled; and that I preferred to go to my brother in California.

Without my knowledge, Mrs. Bruce employed a gentleman in New York to enter into negotiations with Mr. Dodge. He proposed to pay three hundred dollars down, if Mr. Dodge would sell me, and enter into obligations to relinquish all claim to me or my children forever after. He who called

5. Isaiah 61.1.
6. Matthew 7.12.
7. Irish American (1815–1875) who founded the proslavery New York newspaper *The Citizen* and who argued that free blacks would take the jobs of Irish workers. "Poles and Hungarians": following the failed European revolutions of 1848, many political refugees settled in New York City and New England.
8. Ecclesiastes 7.7.
9. New York City, because it was the center of activity for hunters of fugitive slaves.

himself my master said he scorned so small an offer for such a valuable servant. The gentleman replied, "You can do as you choose, sir. If you reject this offer you will never get any thing; for the woman has friends who will convey her and her children out of the country."

Mr. Dodge concluded that "half a loaf was better than no bread," and he agreed to the proffered terms. By the next mail I received this brief letter from Mrs. Bruce: "I am rejoiced to tell you that the money for your freedom has been paid to Mr. Dodge. Come home to-morrow. I long to see you and my sweet babe."

My brain reeled as I read these lines. A gentleman near me said, "It's true; I have seen the bill of sale." "The bill of sale!" Those words struck me like a blow. So I was *sold* at last! A human being *sold* in the free city of New York! The bill of sale is on record, and future generations will learn from it that women were articles of traffic in New York, late in the nineteenth century of the Christian religion. It may hereafter prove a useful document to antiquaries, who are seeking to measure the progress of civilization in the United States. I well know the value of that bit of paper; but much as I love freedom, I do not like to look upon it. I am deeply grateful to the generous friend who procured it, but I despise the miscreant who demanded payment for what never rightfully belonged to him or his.

I had objected to having my freedom bought, yet I must confess that when it was done I felt as if a heavy load had been lifted from my weary shoulders. When I rode home in the cars I was no longer afraid to unveil my face and look at people as they passed. I should have been glad to have met Daniel Dodge himself; to have had him seen me and known me, that he might have mourned over the untoward circumstances which compelled him to sell me for three hundred dollars.

When I reached home, the arms of my benefactress were thrown round me, and our tears mingled. As soon as she could speak, she said, "O Linda, I'm *so* glad it's all over! You wrote to me as if you thought you were going to be transferred from one owner to another. But I did not buy you for your services. I should have done just the same, if you had been going to sail for California to-morrow. I should, at least, have the satisfaction of knowing that you left me a free woman."

My heart was exceedingly full. I remembered how my poor father had tried to buy me, when I was a small child, and how he had been disappointed. I hoped his spirit was rejoicing over me now. I remembered how my good old grandmother had laid up her earnings to purchase me in later years, and how often her plans had been frustrated. How that faithful, loving old heart would leap for joy, if she could look on me and my children now that we were free! My relatives had been foiled in all their efforts, but God had raised me up a friend among strangers, who had bestowed on me the precious, long-desired boon. Friend! It is a common word, often lightly used. Like other good and beautiful things, it may be tarnished by careless handling; but when I speak of Mrs. Bruce as my friend, the word is sacred.

My grandmother lived to rejoice in my freedom; but not long after, a letter came with a black seal. She had gone "where the wicked cease from troubling, and the weary are at rest."[1]

1. Job 3.17.

Time passed on, and a paper came to me from the south, containing an obituary notice of my uncle Phillip. It was the only case I ever knew of such an honor conferred upon a colored person. It was written by one of his friends, and contained these words: "Now that death has laid him low, they call him a good man and a useful citizen; but what are eulogies to the black man, when the world has faded from his vision? It does not require man's praise to obtain rest in God's kingdom." So they called a colored man a *citizen!* Strange words to be uttered in that region![2]

Reader, my story ends with freedom; not in the usual way, with marriage.[3] I and my children are now free! We are as free from the power of slaveholders as are the white people of the north; and though that, according to my ideas, is not saying a great deal, it is a vast improvement in *my* condition. The dream of my life is not yet realized. I do not sit with my children in a home of my own. I still long for a hearthstone of my own, however humble. I wish it for my children's sake far more than for my own. But God so orders circumstances as to keep me with my friend Mrs. Bruce. Love, duty, gratitude, also bind me to her side. It is a privilege to serve her who pities my oppressed people, and who has bestowed the inestimable boon of freedom on me and my children.

It has been painful to me, in many ways, to recall the dreary years I passed in bondage. I would gladly forget them if I could. Yet the retrospection is not altogether without solace; for with those gloomy recollections come tender memories of my good old grandmother, like light, fleecy clouds floating over a dark and troubled sea.

1861

2. Free blacks in North Carolina did not have the legal status of citizens.

3. Allusion to the way popular novels of the period typically ended with a happy marriage.

HENRY DAVID THOREAU
1817–1862

Henry David Thoreau aspired to write great literature by adventuring at home, traveling, as he put it, a good deal in Concord, Massachusetts. "As travelers go around the world and report natural objects and phenomena, so let another stay at home and report the phenomena of his own life," he remarked in a journal entry of August 1851. Known by some of his Concord neighbors as the Harvard graduate who never lived up to his potential, Thoreau presented himself in *Walden* as an exemplary figure who—by virtue of his philosophical questionings, economic good sense, nonconformity, and appreciative observation of the natural world—could serve as a model for others. Thoreau infuriated and inspired his Massachusetts neighbors and audiences while he lived; since his death, his writings have continued to provoke generations of readers to contemplate their obligations to society, nature, and themselves.

The third of four children of Cynthia (Dunbar) and John Thoreau, a storekeeper who opened a pencil-making business in the early 1820s, Thoreau was born in Concord on July 12, 1817. His sister Helen, five years his senior, was an important teacher in his childhood years; his brother, John, two years his senior, was his closest friend until John's untimely death in 1842; and his sister Sophia, two years his junior, cared for him at the end of his life. By the age of ten, Thoreau, who reveled in reading, had memorized passages from Shakespeare, John Bunyan, Samuel Johnson, and other writers. In 1828, he and his brother were enrolled in the private Concord Academy, and because Henry was regarded as the more academically promising of the two, the family, which was struggling economically (his mother ran their home as a boardinghouse to produce additional income), decided that he would be the one son to attend Harvard. Thoreau began his studies there in 1833, excelling in languages but otherwise failing to distinguish himself. After his 1837 graduation he returned to Concord, where he taught briefly at a local elementary school before resigning in protest when he was instructed to flog some of his students. In 1838 he took a teaching and administrative position at the Concord Academy, where a year later John joined him as a teacher and co-director of the school. The brothers had to close the Concord Academy in 1841 because of John's poor health. Paralyzed by tetanus from a razor cut, John died in Thoreau's arms on January 1, 1842. The grief at the loss of his beloved brother would inspire his elegiac *A Week on the Concord and Merrimack Rivers* (1849), which memorialized a two-week boating trip that the brothers took in 1839.

Thoreau met his fellow Concordian, Ralph Waldo Emerson, in 1836. Emerson, fourteen years his senior, became the most important influence and friendship in his life. Thoreau attended the informal meetings of the New England Transcendentalists that convened irregularly in Emerson's study and there met such people as Margaret Fuller and the education reformers Elizabeth Peabody and Bronson Alcott (father of Louisa May). With Emerson's encouragement, Thoreau also began to keep a journal, which served him as a sourcebook for some of his published writings and lectures, eventually growing to nearly two million words. Like Emerson's own journal, Thoreau's has emerged as one of his greatest literary achievements. In 1840, Thoreau commenced his efforts to make a name for himself as a published writer. He placed a poem and an essay in the inaugural issue of the *Dial*, the journal founded by the Concord Transcendentalist circle and edited by Margaret Fuller (and at times by Thoreau himself); he would publish over thirty essays, poems, and translations in the journal before it ceased operations in 1844. He never stopped reading, although contemporary writers meant little to him except for Emerson and Thomas Carlyle, whom he regarded as one of the great prophets of the era. He steeped himself in the classics—Greek, Latin, and English—and read the sacred writings of the Hindus in translation; they are an enormous influence on the cosmic vision of *Walden*.

Much of Thoreau's reading and writing during this time took place in Emerson's house, for beginning in 1841 Thoreau lived there on and off as a handyman and general help to Emerson's wife, Lydia, when Emerson himself was off on lecture tours. Thoreau moved to Staten Island in May 1843 to work as a tutor for the sons of Emerson's brother William, but unhappy with that work, he returned to Concord six months later, moving back to his family home, all the while keeping up his association with Emerson. In the spring he typically earned money as a surveyor, helping reestablish the boundaries of farms whose fences and walls had been washed away by melting snows. He also helped his father make pencils. Early in 1844 he delivered his first series of lectures, "The Conservative and the Reformer," in Boston's Armory Hall. To his great embarrassment, during a camping trip in April of that year, he accidentally set fire to the Concord woods near Walden Pond, burning approximately three hundred acres. Shortly after the fire, Thoreau decided to begin what he termed his "experiment" at Walden, building a cabin on land that Emerson owned near the pond and taking up residence there on July 4, 1845—a symbolic moment of personal liberation aligned with the celebration of national freedom. One of Thoreau's major goals in moving to the pond was to write a book about his 1839 boating journey with his brother (which he completed before he left after two years, two months, and two days). Only a couple of miles from town, his cabin became the destination of many local visitors, and he often went back to Concord for meals and conversation. During his time at Walden, Thoreau also spent one night of 1846 in the local jail when, in protest against what he regarded as the proslavery agenda of the war against Mexico, he refused to pay his poll tax. That experience would inspire "Resistance to Civil Government" (1849), which in due time would become a world-famous essay on the relationship of the individual to the state. He never disguised the fact that he was in jail for only one night but made that experience symbolic, just as he did with his sojourn at Walden Pond.

In 1849 Thoreau published the book he had drafted at Walden as *A Week on the Concord and Merrimack Rivers*, a work that mixes naturalist meditations, personal reflections, poetry, and scripture. Barely noticed by reviewers and readers, it sold fewer than three hundred of the thousand copies printed. Thoreau had subsidized the publication through his royalties, and in 1853, when he received the unsold books, he wrote in his journal: "I have now a library of nearly nine hundred volumes, over seven hundred of which I wrote myself." Despite the critical and financial setback of *A Week*, Thoreau worked intensively on *Walden* between 1847 and its publication in 1854. The prestigious Boston firm of Ticknor and Fields published the book in a small print run of two thousand copies, and by 1859 most of these copies had been sold. Encouraged by the relatively good reviews and sales, Thoreau over the next few years attempted to work up books from his Cape Cod travels of 1849 and 1850 and his Maine travels of 1857, bringing out sections of the Cape Cod manuscript in the 1855 *Putnam's Monthly Magazine*. None of the other books that Thoreau published or projected has achieved the influence and reputation of *Walden*, where Thoreau's whole literary character emerges—his love of nature, his rhetorical inventiveness, his humor, his philosophical adventurousness, his everyday nonconformity. In it he becomes, in the highest sense, a fully employed public servant, offering readers the fruits of his experience, thought, and artistic dedication.

His writing and lectures brought Thoreau a small but widening circle of admirers. His earlier journals had combined naturalistic observations with moral commentary; in the 1850s they increasingly recorded his observations of nature without comment and in great detail as he sought to understand the daily and seasonal rhythms of nature. Inspired by his reading during the early 1850s of the German naturalist Alexander von Humboldt (1769–1859) and the English naturalist Charles Darwin (1809–1882), he made himself into what critic Laura Dassow Walls has called "a scientific seer, walking, recording, measuring, and weaving the details of nature into meaning." Professors at Harvard, such as the geologist Louis Agassiz, found his scientific vision of interest. At the same time, Thoreau emerged as one of the most outspoken abolitionists in the Concord area. In 1854, the year of *Walden*'s publication, he delivered his best known antislavery speech, "Slavery in Massachusetts," at a rally in Framingham, Massachusetts, protesting the arrest of the fugitive slave Anthony Burns. Thoreau achieved his greatest prominence as an antislavery speaker with his defense of John Brown immediately after Brown's arrest at Harpers Ferry in October 1859. Before large audiences in Concord, Boston, and Worcester, Thoreau honored Brown's revolutionary antislavery aims. He thus welcomed the Civil War, with its promise of ridding the nation of slavery, even as he faced the difficulties of declining health brought on by tuberculosis, the great nineteenth-century killer of young adults. (His sister Helen had died of the disease in 1849.) In May 1861 Thoreau traveled to Minnesota with the hope of recovering his health, and there he collected botanical specimens and observed the Sioux Indians of the region. His health continuing to deteriorate, he returned to Concord and worked with his sister Sophia to prepare what he recognized would be posthumously published writings. He was forty-four when he died at Concord on May 6, 1862. The little fame he had achieved was as a social experimenter who applied Emerson's theoretical transcendentalism to daily life, and as John Brown's champion.

Recognition of Thoreau as an important writer was slow in coming, though the publication of *Walden* did occasion comment in some of the most widely read newspapers and magazines of the time. In the January 1856 issue of the highly respected *Westminster Review*, for instance, the English novelist George Eliot celebrated Thoreau as a writer of "great beauty," and urged her readers to take note of that "theoretic independence of formulæ, which is peculiar to some of the finer American minds." No essay in Thoreau's canon more powerfully exemplifies his independence than "Resistance to Civil Government," but outside of Thoreau's immediate circle at Concord, what little attention it received when initially published was negative. Thoreau's radical insistence that "under a government that imprisons any man unjustly, the true place for a just man is prison" alarmed local conservatives. The *Boston Post*, for instance, called the essay "crazy," and the reviewer for the *Boston Courier* urged him to "take a trip to France, and preach his doctrine of '*Resistance to Civil Government*' to the red republicans." Thoreau's most widely read works published during his lifetime were "Slavery in Massachusetts" (printed in William Lloyd Garrison's abolitionist newspaper the *Liberator* and reprinted in the *New York Tribune*) and "A Plea for Captain John Brown" (printed in *Echoes of Harpers Ferry* in 1860).

Between June 1862, the month after Thoreau's death, and November 1863, the Boston-based *Atlantic Monthly* published the essays "Walking," "Autumn Tints," "Wild Apples," "Life without Principle," and "Night and Moonlight." In 1862 Ticknor and Fields reissued *A Week* and *Walden* (which never again went out of print) and attempted to capitalize on the growing interest in Thoreau by publishing five new books: *Excursions* (1863), *The Maine Woods* (1864), *Cape Cod* (1864), *Letters to Various Persons* (1865), and *A Yankee in Canada, with Anti-Slavery and Reform Papers* (1866). An expanded version of Emerson's eulogy for Thoreau, published in the *Atlantic Monthly* for August 1863, confirmed Thoreau's growing reputation. By the early twentieth century, Thoreau was becoming widely recognized as a social philosopher, naturalist, and writer with few peers. In 1906 his journals were published for the first time in chronological order, in fourteen volumes as part of a twenty-volume set of his complete works. That same year, Mahatma Ghandi, in his African exile, read "Resistance to Civil Government" and later acknowledged its important influence on his thinking about how best to achieve Indian independence. Later in the century, Martin Luther King Jr. would similarly attest to the crucial influence of Thoreau on his adoption of nonviolent civil disobedience as a key to the civil rights movement.

By the middle of the twentieth century, Thoreau's literary reputation equaled or surpassed Emerson's, with *Walden* regarded as one of the masterpieces of American literature. It is a work that powerfully affected environmentalists like John Muir and Aldo Leopold, who greatly admired Thoreau for his concerns about the natural habitat; contemporary writers like Edward Abbey and Annie Dillard also cite him frequently. As crucial as environmental concerns, and even antislavery, were to Thoreau, however, he always insisted that all principled action had to be undertaken by the individual rather than through groups. It is important to recall that Thoreau described *Walden* as an "experiment"—an account of one possible way of viewing, representing, and acting in the world. In *Walden*'s punning wordplay, richly allusive sentences, and (with its numerous references to a panoply of Eastern and Western texts) truly global textual vision, Thoreau more than anything else attempted to push his readers to think—to "wake . . . up," as he put it in the book's epigraph. Life is short and life is miraculous, Thoreau insists, and it is incumbent on each individual to figure out how best to respond to the circumstances of the moment. Though there are considerable differences between Thoreau and Emerson, the most provocative literary expression of Emerson's call for self-reliance may well be Thoreau's bragging, visionary, down-to-earth *Walden*.

Resistance to Civil Government[1]

I heartily accept the motto,—"That government is best which governs least;"[2] and I should like to see it acted up to more rapidly and systematically. Carried out, it finally amounts to this, which also I believe,—"That government is best which governs not at all;" and when men are prepared for it, that will be the kind of government which they will have. Government is at best but an expedient; but most governments are usually, and all governments are sometimes, inexpedient. The objections which have been brought against a standing army, and they are many and weighty, and deserve to prevail, may also at last be brought against a standing government. The standing army is only an arm of the standing government. The government itself, which is only the mode which the people have chosen to execute their will, is equally liable to be abused and perverted before the people can act through it. Witness the present Mexican war, the work of comparatively a few individuals using the standing government as their tool; for, in the outset, the people would not have consented to this measure.[3]

This American government,—what is it but a tradition, though a recent one, endeavoring to transmit itself unimpaired to posterity, but each instant losing some of its integrity? It has not the vitality and force of a single living man; for a single man can bend it to his will. It is a sort of wooden gun to the people themselves; and, if ever they should use it in earnest as a real one against each other, it will surely split. But it is not the less necessary for this; for the people must have some complicated machinery or other, and hear its din, to satisfy that idea of government which they have. Governments show thus how successfully men can be imposed on, even impose on themselves, for their own advantage. It is excellent, we must all allow; yet this government never of itself furthered any enterprise, but by the alacrity with which it got out of its way. It does not keep the country free. It does not settle the West. It does not educate. The character inherent in the American people has done all that has been accomplished; and it would have done somewhat more, if the government had not sometimes got in its way. For government is an expedient by which men would fain succeed in letting one another alone; and, as has been said, when it is most expedient, the governed are most let alone by it. Trade and commerce, if they were not made of India rubber, would never manage to bounce over the obstacles which legislators are continually putting in their way; and, if one were to judge these men wholly by the effects of their actions, and not partly by their intentions, they would deserve to be

---

1. "Resistance to Civil Government" is reprinted here from its first appearance, in *Aesthetic Papers* (1849), edited by the educational reformer Elizabeth Peabody (1804–1894). Thoreau had delivered a version of the essay as a lecture in January and again in February 1848 at the Concord Lyceum, under the title "The Rights and Duties of the Individual in Relation to Government." After his death it was reprinted in *A Yankee in Canada, with Anti-Slavery and Reform Papers* (1866) as "Civil Disobedience." That title, although commonly used, may not be authorial; the title of the first printing, as Thoreau indicates, was a play on "The Duty of Submission to Civil Government Explained," the title of one of the chapters in *Prin-*

ciples of Moral and Political Philosophy (1785), a book by English theologian and moralist William Paley (1743–1805), that was one of Thoreau's Harvard textbooks.
2. These words appeared on the masthead of the *Democratic Review*, the New York magazine that published two early Thoreau pieces in 1843.
3. The Mexican War (1846–48) was criticized by Whigs and some Democrats as an "executive's war" because President Polk commenced hostilities without a congressional declaration of war. Many New Englanders, including Thoreau, regarded the war as part of the South's effort to extend the territorial domain of slavery.

classed and punished with those mischievous persons who put obstructions on the railroads.

But, to speak practically and as a citizen, unlike those who call themselves no-government men, I ask for, not at once no government, but *at once* a better government. Let every man make known what kind of government would command his respect, and that will be one step toward obtaining it.

After all, the practical reason why, when the power is once in the hands of the people, a majority are permitted, and for a long period continue, to rule, is not because they are most likely to be in the right, nor because this seems fairest to the minority, but because they are physically the strongest. But a government in which the majority rule in all cases cannot be based on justice, even as far as men understand it. Can there not be a government in which majorities do not virtually decide right and wrong, but conscience?—in which majorities decide only those questions to which the rule of expediency is applicable? Must the citizen ever for a moment, or in the least degree, resign his conscience to the legislator? Why has every man a conscience, then? I think that we should be men first, and subjects afterward. It is not desirable to cultivate a respect for the law, so much as for the right. The only obligation which I have a right to assume, is to do at any time what I think right. It is truly enough said,[4] that a corporation has no conscience; but a corporation of conscientious men is a corporation *with* a conscience. Law never made men a whit more just; and, by means of their respect for it, even the well-disposed are daily made the agents of injustice. A common and natural result of an undue respect for law is, that you may see a file of soldiers, colonel, captain, corporal, privates, powder-monkeys and all, marching in admirable order over hill and dale to the wars, against their wills, aye, against their common sense and consciences, which makes it very steep marching indeed, and produces a palpitation of the heart. They have no doubt that it is a damnable business in which they are concerned; they are all peaceably inclined. Now, what are they? Men at all? or small moveable forts and magazines, at the service of some unscrupulous man in power? Visit the Navy Yard, and behold a marine, such a man as an American government can make, or such as it can make a man with its black arts, a mere shadow and reminiscence of humanity, a man laid out alive and standing, and already, as one may say, buried under arms with funeral accompaniments, though it may be

"Not a drum was heard, nor a funeral note,
    As his corse to the ramparts we hurried;
Not a soldier discharged his farewell shot
    O'er the grave where our hero we buried."[5]

The mass of men serve the State thus, not as men mainly, but as machines, with their bodies. They are the standing army, and the militia, jailers, constables, *posse comitatus*,[6] &c. In most cases there is no free exercise whatever of the judgment or of the moral sense; but they put themselves on a level with wood and earth and stones; and wooden men can perhaps be manufactured that will serve the purpose as well. Such command no more respect

4. By the English jurist Sir Edward Coke (1552–1634), in a famous legal decision of 1612.
5. From the Irish poet Charles Wolfe's "Burial of

Sir John Moore at Corunna" (1817), a song Thoreau liked to sing. "Corse": corpse.
6. Sheriff's posse (Latin).

than men of straw, or a lump of dirt. They have the same sort of worth only as horses and dogs. Yet such as these even are commonly esteemed good citizens. Others, as most legislators, politicians, lawyers, ministers, and office-holders, serve the State chiefly with their heads; and, as they rarely make any moral distinctions, they are as likely to serve the devil, without intending it, as God. A very few, as heroes, patriots, martyrs, reformers in the great sense, and *men*, serve the State with their consciences also, and so necessarily resist it for the most part; and they are commonly treated by it as enemies. A wise man will only be useful as a man, and will not submit to be "clay," and "stop a hole to keep the wind away,"[7] but leave that office to his dust at least:—

> "I am too high-born to be propertied,
> To be a secondary at control,
> Or useful serving-man and instrument
> To any sovereign state throughout the world."[8]

He who gives himself entirely to his fellow-men appears to them useless and selfish; but he who gives himself partially to them is pronounced a benefactor and philanthropist.

How does it become a man to behave toward this American government to-day? I answer that he cannot without disgrace be associated with it. I cannot for an instant recognize that political organization as *my* government which is the *slave's* government also.

All men recognize the right of revolution; that is, the right to refuse allegiance to and to resist the government, when its tyranny or its inefficiency are great and unendurable. But almost all say that such is not the case now. But such was the case, they think, in the Revolution of '75. If one were to tell me that this was a bad government because it taxed certain foreign commodities brought to its ports, it is most probable that I should not make an ado about it, for I can do without them: all machines have their friction; and possibly this does enough good to counterbalance the evil. At any rate, it is a great evil to make a stir about it. But when the friction comes to have its machine, and oppression and robbery are organized, I say, let us not have such a machine any longer. In other words, when a sixth of the population of a nation which has undertaken to be the refuge of liberty are slaves, and a whole country is unjustly overrun and conquered by a foreign army, and subjected to military law, I think that it is not too soon for honest men to rebel and revolutionize. What makes this duty the more urgent is the fact, that the country so overrun is not our own, but ours is the invading army.

Paley, a common authority with many on moral questions, in his chapter on the "Duty of Submission to Civil Government," resolves all civil obligation into expediency; and he proceeds to say, "that so long as the interest of the whole society requires it, that is, so long as the established government cannot be resisted or changed without public inconveniency, it is the will of God that the established government be obeyed, and no longer."—"This principle being admitted, the justice of every particular case of resistance is reduced to a computation of the quantity of the danger and grievance on the one side, and of the probability and expense of redressing it on the other." Of this, he says, every man shall judge for himself. But Paley appears never

---

7. Shakespeare's *Hamlet* 5.1.236–37.   8. Shakespeare's *King John* 5.1.79–82.

to have contemplated those cases to which the rule of expediency does not apply, in which a people, as well as an individual, must do justice, cost what it may. If I have unjustly wrested a plank from a drowning man, I must restore it to him though I drown myself.[9] This, according to Paley, would be inconvenient. But he that would save his life, in such a case, shall lose it.[1] This people must cease to hold slaves, and to make war on Mexico, though it cost them their existence as a people.

In their practice, nations agree with Paley; but does any one think that Massachusetts does exactly what is right at the present crisis?

> "A drab of state, a cloth-o'-silver slut,
> To have her train borne up, and her soul trail in the dirt."[2]

Practically speaking, the opponents to a reform in Massachusetts are not a hundred thousand politicians at the South, but a hundred thousand merchants and farmers here,[3] who are more interested in commerce and agriculture than they are in humanity, and are not prepared to do justice to the slave and to Mexico, *cost what it may.* I quarrel not with far-off foes, but with those who, near at home, co-operate with, and do the bidding of those far away, and without whom the latter would be harmless. We are accustomed to say, that the mass of men are unprepared; but improvement is slow, because the few are not materially wiser or better than the many. It is not so important that many should be as good as you, as that there be some absolute goodness somewhere; for that will leaven the whole lump.[4] There are thousands who are *in opinion* opposed to slavery and to the war, who yet in effect do nothing to put an end to them; who, esteeming themselves children of Washington and Franklin, sit down with their hands in their pockets, and say that they know not what to do, and do nothing; who even postpone the question of freedom to the question of free-trade, and quietly read the prices-current along with the latest advices[5] from Mexico, after dinner, and, it may be, fall asleep over them both. What is the price-current of an honest man and patriot to-day? They hesitate, and they regret, and sometimes they petition; but they do nothing in earnest and with effect. They will wait, well disposed, for others to remedy the evil, that they may no longer have it to regret. At most, they give only a cheap vote, and a feeble countenance and God-speed, to the right, as it goes by them. There are nine hundred and ninety-nine patrons of virtue to one virtuous man; but it is easier to deal with the real possessor of a thing than with the temporary guardian of it.

All voting is a sort of gaming, like chequers or backgammon, with a slight moral tinge to it, a playing with right and wrong, with moral questions; and betting naturally accompanies it. The character of the voters is not staked. I cast my vote, perchance, as I think right; but I am not vitally concerned that that right should prevail. I am willing to leave it to the majority. Its obligation, therefore, never exceeds that of expediency. Even voting *for the right* is *doing* nothing for it. It is only expressing to men feebly your desire that it should prevail. A wise man will not leave the right to the mercy of chance, nor wish

9. A problem in situational ethics cited by Cicero (106–43 B.C.E.) in *De Officiis* 3, which Thoreau had studied.
1. Matthew 10.39; Luke 9.24.
2. Cyril Tourneur (1575?–1626), *The Revenger's Tragedy* 3.4.
3. Thoreau refers to the economic alliance of Southern cotton growers with Northern shippers, farmers, and manufacturers.
4. 1 Corinthians 5.6: "Know ye not that a little leaven leaventh the whole lump?"
5. New dispatches. "Children of Washington and Franklin": i.e., patriotic Americans, children of rebels and revolutionaries.

it to prevail through the power of the majority. There is but little virtue in the action of masses of men. When the majority shall at length vote for the abolition of slavery, it will be because they are indifferent to slavery, or because there is but little slavery left to be abolished by their vote. *They* will then be the only slaves. Only *his* vote can hasten the abolition of slavery who asserts his own freedom by his vote.

I hear of a convention to be held at Baltimore,[6] or elsewhere, for the selection of a candidate for the Presidency, made up chiefly of editors, and men who are politicians by profession; but I think, what is it to any independent, intelligent, and respectable man what decision they may come to, shall we not have the advantage of his wisdom and honesty, nevertheless? Can we not count upon some independent votes? Are there not many individuals in the country who do not attend conventions? But no: I find that the respectable man, so called, has immediately drifted from his position, and despairs of his country, when his country has more reason to despair of him. He forthwith adopts one of the candidates thus selected as the only *available* one, thus proving that he is himself *available* for any purposes of the demagogue. His vote is of no more worth than that of any unprincipled foreigner or hireling native, who may have been bought. Oh for a man who is a *man*, and, as my neighbor says, has a bone in his back which you cannot pass your hand through! Our statistics are at fault: the population has been returned too large. How many *men* are there to a square thousand miles in this country? Hardly one. Does not America offer any inducement for men to settle here? The American has dwindled into an Odd Fellow,—one who may be known by the development of his organ of gregariousness, and a manifest lack of intellect and cheerful self-reliance; whose first and chief concern, on coming into the world, is to see that the alms-houses are in good repair; and, before yet he has lawfully donned the virile garb,[7] to collect a fund for the support of the widows and orphans that may be; who, in short, ventures to live only by the aid of the mutual insurance company, which has promised to bury him decently.

It is not a man's duty, as a matter of course, to devote himself to the eradication of any, even the most enormous wrong; he may still properly have other concerns to engage him; but it is his duty, at least, to wash his hands of it, and, if he gives it no thought longer, not to give it practically his support. If I devote myself to other pursuits and contemplations, I must first see, at least, that I do not pursue them sitting upon another man's shoulders. I must get off him first, that he may pursue his contemplations too. See what gross inconsistency is tolerated. I have heard some of my townsmen say, "I should like to have them order me out to help put down an insurrection of the slaves, or to march to Mexico,—see if I would go;" and yet these very men have each, directly by their allegiance, and so indirectly, at least, by their money, furnished a substitute. The soldier is applauded who refuses to serve in an unjust war by those who do not refuse to sustain the unjust government which makes the war; is applauded by those whose own act and authority he disregards and sets at nought; as if the State were penitent to that degree

6. The Democratic convention was held in Baltimore in May 1848.
7. Adult clothes allowed for a Roman boy on reaching the age of fourteen. The Independent Order of Odd Fellows, a benevolent fraternal organization, was chosen by Thoreau for the satirical value of its name; in his view the archetypal American is not the individualist, the genuine odd fellow, but the conformist.

that it hired one to scourge it while it sinned, but not to that degree that it left off sinning for a moment. Thus, under the name of order and civil government, we are all made at last to pay homage to and support our own meanness. After the first blush of sin, comes its indifference; and from immoral it becomes, as it were, *un*moral, and not quite unnecessary to that life which we have made.

The broadest and most prevalent error requires the most disinterested virtue to sustain it. The slight reproach to which the virtue of patriotism is commonly liable, the noble are most likely to incur. Those who, while they disapprove of the character and measures of a government, yield to it their allegiance and support, are undoubtedly its most conscientious supporters, and so frequently the most serious obstacles to reform. Some are petitioning the State to dissolve the Union, to disregard the requisitions of the President. Why do they not dissolve it themselves,—the union between themselves and the State,—and refuse to pay their quota into its treasury? Do not they stand in the same relation to the State, that the State does to the Union? And have not the same reasons prevented the State from resisting the Union, which have prevented them from resisting the State?

How can a man be satisfied to entertain an opinion merely, and enjoy *it*? Is there any enjoyment in it, if his opinion is that he is aggrieved? If you are cheated out of a single dollar by your neighbor, you do not rest satisfied with knowing that you are cheated, or with saying that you are cheated, or even with petitioning him to pay you your due; but you take effectual steps at once to obtain the full amount, and see that you are never cheated again. Action from principle,—the perception and the performance of right,—changes things and relations; it is essentially revolutionary, and does not consist wholly with any thing which was. It not only divides states and churches, it divides families; aye, it divides the *individual*, separating the diabolical in him from the divine.

Unjust laws exist: shall we be content to obey them, or shall we endeavor to amend them, and obey them until we have succeeded, or shall we transgress them at once? Men generally, under such a government as this, think that they ought to wait until they have persuaded the majority to alter them. They think that, if they should resist, the remedy would be worse than the evil. But it is the fault of the government itself that the remedy *is* worse than the evil. *It* makes it worse. Why is it not more apt to anticipate and provide for reform? Why does it not cherish its wise minority? Why does it cry and resist before it is hurt? Why does it not encourage its citizens to be on the alert to point out its faults, and *do* better than it would have them? Why does it always crucify Christ, and excommunicate Copernicus and Luther,[8] and pronounce Washington and Franklin rebels?

One would think, that a deliberate and practical denial of its authority was the only offence never contemplated by government; else, why has it not assigned its definite, its suitable and proportionate penalty? If a man who has no property refuses but once to earn nine shillings[9] for the State, he is put in

8. Thoreau cites as announcers of new truths Copernicus (1473–1543), the Polish astronomer who died too soon after the publication of his new system of astronomy to be excommunicated from the Catholic Church for writing it, and Martin Luther (1483–1546), the German leader of the Protestant Reformation who was excommunicated.

9. Because of sporadic coin shortages, the British shilling was still in use in parts of the United States during the 1840s; it was valued at approximately 20 U.S. cents. The amount of the tax, assessed on adult male citizens, was $1.50, approximately $30 in today's currency.

prison for a period unlimited by any law that I know, and determined only by the discretion of those who placed him there; but if he should steal ninety times nine shillings from the State, he is soon permitted to go at large again.

If the injustice is part of the necessary friction of the machine of government, let it go, let it go: perchance it will wear smooth,—certainly the machine will wear out. If the injustice has a spring, or a pulley, or a rope, or a crank, exclusively for itself, then perhaps you may consider whether the remedy will not be worse than the evil; but if it is of such a nature that it requires you to be the agent of injustice to another, then, I say, break the law. Let your life be a counter friction to stop the machine. What I have to do is to see, at any rate, that I do not lend myself to the wrong which I condemn.

As for adopting the ways which the State has provided for remedying the evil, I know not of such ways. They take too much time, and a man's life will be gone. I have other affairs to attend to. I came into this world, not chiefly to make this a good place to live in, but to live in it, be it good or bad. A man has not every thing to do, but something; and because he cannot do *every thing*, it is not necessary that he should do *something* wrong. It is not my business to be petitioning the governor or the legislature any more than it is theirs to petition me; and, if they should not hear my petition, what should I do then? But in this case the State has provided no way: its very Constitution is the evil. This may seem to be harsh and stubborn and unconciliatory; but it is to treat with the utmost kindness and consideration the only spirit that can appreciate or deserves it. So is all change for the better, like birth and death which convulse the body.

I do not hesitate to say, that those who call themselves abolitionists should at once effectually withdraw their support, both in person and property, from the government of Massachusetts, and not wait till they constitute a majority of one, before they suffer the right to prevail through them. I think that it is enough if they have God on their side, without waiting for that other one. Moreover, any man more right than his neighbors, constitutes a majority of one already.[1]

I meet this American government, or its representative the State government, directly, and face to face, once a year, no more, in the person of its tax-gatherer; this is the only mode in which a man situated as I am necessarily meets it; and it then says distinctly, Recognize me; and the simplest, the most effectual, and, in the present posture of affairs, the indispensablest mode of treating with it on this head, of expressing your little satisfaction with and love for it, is to deny it then. My civil neighbor, the tax-gatherer,[2] is the very man I have to deal with,—for it is, after all, with men and not with parchment that I quarrel,—and he has voluntarily chosen to be an agent of the government. How shall he ever know well what he is and does as an officer of the government, or as a man, until he is obliged to consider whether he shall treat me, his neighbor, for whom he has respect, as a neighbor and well-disposed man, or as a maniac and disturber of the peace, and see if he can get over this obstruction to his neighborliness without a ruder and more impetuous thought or speech corresponding with his action? I know this well, that if one thousand, if one hundred, if ten men whom I could

---

1. John Knox (1505?–1572), the Scottish religious reformer, said that "a man with God is always in the majority."

2. Sam Staples, who sometimes assisted Thoreau in his surveying.

name,—if ten *honest* men only,—aye, if *one* HONEST man, in this State of Massachusetts, *ceasing to hold slaves*, were actually to withdraw from this copartnership, and be locked up in the county jail therefor, it would be the abolition of slavery in America. For it matters not how small the beginning may seem to be: what is once well done is done for ever. But we love better to talk about it: that we say is our mission. Reform keeps many scores of newspapers in its service, but not one man. If my esteemed neighbor, the State's ambassador,[3] who will devote his days to the settlement of the question of human rights in the Council Chamber, instead of being threatened with the prisons of Carolina, were to sit down the prisoner of Massachusetts, that State which is so anxious to foist the sin of slavery upon her sister,—though at present she can discover only an act of inhospitality to be the ground of a quarrel with her,—the Legislature would not wholly waive the subject the following winter.

Under a government which imprisons any unjustly, the true place for a just man is also a prison. The proper place to-day, the only place which Massachusetts has provided for her freer and less desponding spirits, is in her prisons, to be put out and locked out of the State by her own act, as they have already put themselves out by their principles. It is there that the fugitive slave, and the Mexican prisoner on parole, and the Indian come to plead the wrongs of his race, should find them; on that separate, but more free and honorable ground, where the State places those who are not *with* her but *against* her,—the only house in a slave-state in which a free man can abide with honor. If any think that their influence would be lost there, and their voices no longer afflict the ear of the State, that they would not be as an enemy within its walls, they do not know by how much truth is stronger than error, nor how much more eloquently and effectively he can combat injustice who has experienced a little in his own person. Cast your whole vote, not a strip of paper merely, but your whole influence. A minority is powerless while it conforms to the majority; it is not even a minority then; but it is irresistible when it clogs by its whole weight. If the alternative is to keep all just men in prison, or give up war and slavery, the State will not hesitate which to choose. If a thousand men were not to pay their tax-bills this year, that would not be a violent and bloody measure, as it would be to pay them, and enable the State to commit violence and shed innocent blood. This is, in fact, the definition of a peaceable revolution, if any such is possible. If the tax-gatherer, or any other public officer, asks me, as one has done, "But what shall I do?" my answer is, "If you really wish to do any thing, resign your office." When the subject has refused allegiance, and the officer has resigned his office, then the revolution is accomplished. But even suppose blood should flow. Is there not a sort of blood shed when the conscience is wounded? Through this wound a man's real manhood and immortality flow out, and he bleeds to an everlasting death. I see this blood flowing now.

I have contemplated the imprisonment of the offender, rather than the seizure of his goods,—though both will serve the same purpose,—because they who assert the purest right, and consequently are most dangerous to a corrupt State, commonly have not spent much time in accumulating property. To such the State renders comparatively small service, and a slight tax

3. Samuel Hoar (1778–1856), local political fig-ure who as agent of the state of Massachusetts had been expelled from Charleston, South Car-olina, in 1844 while interceding on behalf of imprisoned black seamen from Massachusetts.

is wont to appear exorbitant, particularly if they are obliged to earn it by special labor with their hands. If there were one who lived wholly without the use of money, the State itself would hesitate to demand it of him. But the rich man—not to make any invidious comparison—is always sold to the institution which makes him rich. Absolutely speaking, the more money, the less virtue; for money comes between a man and his objects, and obtains them for him; and it was certainly no great virtue to obtain it. It puts to rest many questions which he would otherwise be taxed to answer; while the only new question which it puts is the hard but superfluous one, how to spend it. Thus his moral ground is taken from under his feet. The opportunities of living are diminished in proportion as what are called the "means" are increased. The best thing a man can do for his culture when he is rich is to endeavour to carry out those schemes which he entertained when he was poor. Christ answered the Herodians according to their condition. "Show me the tribute-money," said he;—and one took a penny out of his pocket;—If you use money which has the image of Cæsar on it, and which he has made current and valuable, that is, *if you are men of the State*, and gladly enjoy the advantages of Cæsar's government, then pay him back some of his own when he demands it: "Render therefore to Cæsar that which is Cæsar's, and to God those things which are God's,"[4]—leaving them no wiser than before as to which was which; for they did not wish to know.

When I converse with the freest of my neighbors, I perceive that, whatever they may say about the magnitude and seriousness of the question, and their regard for the public tranquillity, the long and the short of the matter is, that they cannot spare the protection of the existing government, and they dread the consequences of disobedience to it to their property and families. For my own part, I should not like to think that I ever rely on the protection of the State. But, if I deny the authority of the State when it presents its tax-bill, it will soon take and waste all my property, and so harass me and my children without end. This is hard. This makes it impossible for a man to live honestly and at the same time comfortably in outward respects. It will not be worth the while to accumulate property; that would be sure to go again. You must hire or squat somewhere, and raise but a small crop, and eat that soon. You must live within yourself, and depend upon yourself, always tucked up and ready for a start, and not have many affairs. A man may grow rich in Turkey even, if he will be in all respects a good subject of the Turkish government. Confucious said,—"If a State is governed by the principles of reason, poverty and misery are subjects of shame; if a State is not governed by the principles of reason, riches and honors are the subjects of shame."[5] No: until I want the protection of Massachusetts to be extended to me in some distant southern port, where my liberty is endangered, or until I am bent solely on building up an estate at home at peaceful enterprise, I can afford to refuse allegiance to Massachusetts, and her right to my property and life. It costs me less in every sense to incur the penalty of disobedience to the State, than it would to obey. I should feel as if I were worth less in that case.

Some years ago, the State met me in behalf of the church, and commanded me to pay a certain sum toward the support of a clergyman whose preaching

4. Matthew 22.16–21. In their attempt to entrap Jesus, the Pharisees (a Jewish sect that held to Mosaic law) were using secular government func-
tionaries of Herod, the king of Judea.
5. Confucius's *Analects* 8.13.

my father attended, but never I myself. "Pay it," it said, "or be locked up in the jail." I declined to pay. But, unfortunately, another man saw fit to pay it. I did not see why the schoolmaster should be taxed to support the priest, and not the priest the schoolmaster; for I was not the State's schoolmaster, but I supported myself by voluntary subscription. I did not see why the lyceum should not present its tax-bill, and have the State to back its demand, as well as the church. However, at the request of the selectmen, I condescended to make some such statement as this in writing:—"Know all men by these presents, that I, Henry Thoreau, do not wish to be regarded as a member of any incorporated society which I have not joined." This I gave to the town-clerk; and he has it. The State, having thus learned that I did not wish to be regarded as a member of that church, has never made a like demand on me since; though it said that it must adhere to its original presumption that time. If I had known how to name them, I should then have signed off in detail from all the societies which I never signed on to; but I did not know where to find a complete list.

I have paid no poll-tax for six years.[6] I was put into a jail[7] once on this account, for one night; and, as I stood considering the walls of solid stone, two or three feet thick, the door of wood and iron, a foot thick, and the iron grating which strained the light, I could not help being struck with the foolishness of that institution which treated me as if I were mere flesh and blood and bones, to be locked up. I wondered that it should have concluded at length that this was the best use it could put me to, and had never thought to avail itself of my services in some way. I saw that, if there was a wall of stone between me and my townsmen, there was a still more difficult one to climb or break through, before they could get to be as free as I was. I did not for a moment feel confined, and the walls seemed a great waste of stone and mortar. I felt as if I alone of all my townsmen had paid my tax. They plainly did not know how to treat me, but behaved like persons who are underbred. In every threat and in every compliment there was a blunder; for they thought that my chief desire was to stand the other side of that stone wall. I could not but smile to see how industriously they locked the door on my meditations, which followed them out again without let or hinderance, and *they* were really all that was dangerous. As they could not reach me, they had resolved to punish my body; just as boys, if they cannot come at some person against whom they have a spite, will abuse his dog. I saw that the State was half-witted, that it was timid as a lone woman with her silver spoons, and that it did not know its friends from its foes, and I lost all my remaining respect for it, and pitied it.

Thus the State never intentionally confronts a man's sense, intellectual or moral, but only his body, his senses. It is not armed with superior wit or honesty, but with superior physical strength. I was not born to be forced. I will breathe after my own fashion. Let us see who is the strongest. What force has a multitude? They only can force me who obey a higher law than I. They force me to become like themselves. I do not hear of *men* being *forced* to live this way or that by masses of men. What sort of life were that to live? When I meet a government which says to me, "Your money or your life," why should I be in haste to give it my money? It may be in a great

6. I.e., since 1840.
7. The Middlesex County jail in Concord, a large three-story building.

strait, and not know what to do: I cannot help that. It must help itself; do as I do. It is not worth the while to snivel about it. I am not responsible for the successful working of the machinery of society. I am not the son of the engineer. I perceive that, when an acorn and a chestnut fall side by side, the one does not remain inert to make way for the other, but both obey their own laws, and spring and grow and flourish as best they can, till one, perchance, overshadows and destroys the other. If a plant cannot live according to its nature, it dies; and so a man.

The night in prison was novel and interesting enough. The prisoners in their shirt-sleeves were enjoying a chat and the evening air in the door-way, when I entered. But the jailer said, "Come, boys, it is time to lock up;" and so they dispersed, and I heard the sound of their steps returning into the hollow apartments. My room-mate was introduced to me by the jailer, as "a first-rate fellow and a clever man." When the door was locked, he showed me where to hang my hat, and how he managed matters there. The rooms were whitewashed once a month; and this one, at least, was the whitest, most simply furnished, and probably the neatest apartment in the town. He naturally wanted to know where I came from, and what brought me there; and, when I had told him, I asked him in my turn how he came there, presuming him to be an honest man, of course; and, as the world goes, I believe he was. "Why," said he, "they accuse me of burning a barn; but I never did it." As near as I could discover, he had probably gone to bed in a barn when drunk, and smoked his pipe there; and so a barn was burnt. He had the reputation of being a clever man, had been there some three months waiting for his trial to come on, and would have to wait as much longer; but he was quite domesticated and contented since he got his board for nothing, and thought that he was well treated.

He occupied one window, and I the other; and I saw, that, if one stayed there long, his principal business would be to look out the window. I had soon read all the tracts that were left there, and examined where former prisoners had broken out, and where a grate had been sawed off, and heard the history of the various occupants of that room; for I found that even here there was a history and a gossip which never circulated beyond the walls of the jail. Probably this is the only house in the town where verses are composed, which are afterward printed in a circular form, but not published. I was shown quite a long list of verses which were composed by some young men who had been detected in an attempt to escape, who avenged themselves by singing them.

I pumped my fellow-prisoner as dry as I could, for fear I should never see him again; but at length he showed me which was my bed, and left me to blow out the lamp.

It was like travelling into a far country, such as I had never expected to behold, to lie there for one night. It seemed to me that I never had heard the town-clock strike before, nor the evening sounds of the village; for we slept with the windows open, which were inside the grating. It was to see my native village in the light of the middle ages, and our Concord was turned into a Rhine stream, and visions of knights and castles passed before me. They were the voices of old burghers that I heard in the streets. I was an involuntary spectator and auditor of whatever was done and said in the kitchen of the adjacent village-inn,—a wholly new and rare experience to me. It was a closer view of my native town. I was fairly inside of it. I never had seen its institutions before. This is one of its peculiar institutions; for it is a shire town.[8] I began to comprehend what its inhabitants were about.

In the morning, our breakfasts were put through the hole in the door, in small oblong-square tin pans, made to fit, and holding a pint of chocolate, with brown bread, and an iron spoon. When they called for the vessels again, I was green enough to return what bread I had left; but my comrade seized it, and said that I should lay that up for lunch or dinner. Soon after, he was let out to work at haying in a neighboring field, whither he went every day, and would not be back till noon; so he bade me good-day, saying that he doubted if he should see me again.

When I came out of prison,—for some one interfered, and paid the tax,[9]—I did not perceive that great changes had taken place on the common, such as he observed who went in a youth, and emerged a tottering and gray-headed man; and yet a change had to my eyes come over the scene,—the town, and State, and country,—greater than any that mere time could effect. I saw yet more distinctly the State in which I lived. I saw to what extent the people among whom I lived could be trusted as good neighbors and friends; that their friendship was for summer weather only; that they did not greatly purpose to do right; that they were a distinct race from me by their prejudices and superstitions, as the Chinamen and Malays are; that, in their sacrifices to humanity, they ran no risks, not even to their property; that, after all, they were not so noble but they treated the thief as he had treated them, and hoped, by a certain outward observance and a few prayers, and by walking in a particular straight though useless path from time to time, to save their souls. This may be to judge my neighbors harshly; for I believe that most of them are not aware that they have such an institution as the jail in their village.

It was formerly the custom in our village, when a poor debtor came out of jail, for his acquaintances to salute him, looking through their fingers, which were crossed to represent the grating of a jail window, "How do ye do?" My neighbors did not thus salute me, but first looked at me, and then at one another, as if I had returned from a long journey. I was put into jail as I was going to the shoemaker's to get a shoe which was mended. When I was let out the next morning, I proceeded to finish my errand, and, having put on my mended shoe, joined a huckleberry party, who were impatient to put themselves under my conduct; and in half an hour,—for the horse was soon tackled,[1]—was in the midst of a huckleberry field, on one of our highest hills, two miles off; and then the State was nowhere to be seen.

This is the whole history of "My Prisons."[2]

I have never declined paying the highway tax, because I am as desirous of being a good neighbor as I am of being a bad subject; and, as for supporting schools, I am doing my part to educate my fellow-countrymen now. It is for no particular item in the tax-bill that I refuse to pay it. I simply wish to

8. Comparable to county seat.
9. The identity of this person is unknown.
1. Harnessed.

2. An allusion to the title of a book (1832) by the Italian poet Silvio Pellico (1789–1854) describing his years of hard labor in Austrian prisons.

refuse allegiance to the State, to withdraw and stand aloof from it effectually. I do not care to trace the course of my dollar, if I could, till it buys a man, or a musket to shoot one with,—the dollar is innocent,—but I am concerned to trace the effects of my allegiance. In fact, I quietly declare war with the State, after my fashion, though I will still make what use and get what advantage of her I can, as is usual in such cases.

If others pay the tax which is demanded of me, from a sympathy with the State, they do but what they have already done in their own case, or rather they abet injustice to a greater extent than the State requires. If they pay the tax from a mistaken interest in the individual taxed, to save his property or prevent his going to jail, it is because they have not considered wisely how far they let their private feelings interfere with the public good.

This, then, is my position at present. But one cannot be too much on his guard in such a case, lest his action be biassed by obstinacy, or an undue regard for the opinions of men. Let him see that he does only what belongs to himself and to the hour.

I think sometimes, Why, this people mean well; they are only ignorant; they would do better if they knew how; why give your neighbors this pain to treat you as they are not inclined to? But I think, again, this is no reason why I should do as they do, or permit others to suffer much greater pain of a different kind. Again, I sometimes say to myself, When many millions of men, without heat, without ill-will, without personal feeling of any kind, demand of you a few shillings only, without the possibility, such is their constitution, of retracting or altering their present demand, and without the possibility, on your side, of appeal to any other millions, why expose yourself to this overwhelming brute force? You do not resist cold and hunger, the winds and the waves, thus obstinately; you quietly submit to a thousand similar necessities. You do not put your head into the fire. But just in proportion as I regard this as not wholly a brute force, but partly a human force, and consider that I have relations to those millions as to so many millions of men, and not of mere brute or inanimate things, I see that appeal is possible, first and instantaneously, from them to the Maker of them, and, secondly, from them to themselves. But, if I put my head deliberately into the fire, there is no appeal to fire or to the Maker of fire, and I have only myself to blame. If I could convince myself that I have any right to be satisfied with men as they are, and to treat them accordingly, and not according, in some respects, to my requisitions and expectations of what they and I ought to be, then, like a good Mussulman[3] and fatalist, I should endeavor to be satisfied with things as they are, and say it is the will of God. And, above all, there is this difference between resisting this and a purely brute or natural force, that I can resist this with some effect; but I cannot expect, like Orpheus,[4] to change the nature of the rocks and trees and beasts.

I do not wish to quarrel with any man or nation. I do not wish to split hairs, to make fine distinctions, or set myself up as better than my neighbors. I seek rather, I may say, even an excuse for conforming to the laws of the land. I am but too ready to conform to them. Indeed I have reason to suspect myself on this head; and each year, as the tax-gatherer comes round, I find myself disposed to review the acts and position of the general

---

3. Muslim.
4. In Greek mythology, Orpheus's singing and playing of the lyre charmed animals and moved even rocks and trees to dance.

and state governments, and the spirit of the people, to discover a pretext for conformity. I believe that the State will soon be able to take all my work of this sort out of my hands, and then I shall be no better a patriot than my fellow-countrymen. Seen from a lower point of view, the Constitution, with all its faults, is very good; the law and the courts are very respectable; even this State and this American government are, in many respects, very admirable and rare things, to be thankful for, such as a great many have described them; but seen from a point of view a little higher, they are what I have described them; seen from a higher still, and the highest, who shall say what they are, or that they are worth looking at or thinking of at all?

However, the government does not concern me much, and I shall bestow the fewest possible thoughts on it. It is not many moments that I live under a government, even in this world. If a man is thought-free, fancy-free, imagination-free, that which *is not* never for a long time appearing *to be* to him, unwise rulers or reformers cannot fatally interrupt him.

I know that most men think differently from myself; but those whose lives are by profession devoted to the study of these or kindred subjects, content me as little as any. Statesmen and legislators, standing so completely within the institution, never distinctly and nakedly behold it. They speak of moving society, but have no resting-place without it. They may be men of a certain experience and discrimination, and have no doubt invented ingenious and even useful systems, for which we sincerely thank them; but all their wit and usefulness lie within certain not very wide limits. They are wont to forget that the world is not governed by policy and expediency. Webster[5] never goes behind government, and so cannot speak with authority about it. His words are wisdom to those legislators who contemplate no essential reform in the existing government; but for thinkers, and those who legislate for all time, he never once glances at the subject. I know of those whose serene and wise speculations on this theme would soon reveal the limits of his mind's range and hospitality. Yet, compared with the cheap professions of most reformers, and the still cheaper wisdom and eloquence of politicians in general, his are almost the only sensible and valuable words, and we thank Heaven for him. Comparatively, he is always strong, original, and, above all, practical. Still his quality is not wisdom, but prudence. The lawyer's truth is not Truth, but consistency, or a consistent expediency. Truth is always in harmony with herself, and is not concerned chiefly to reveal the justice that may consist with wrong-doing. He well deserves to be called, as he has been called, the Defender of the Constitution. There are really no blows to be given by him but defensive ones. He is not a leader, but a follower. His leaders are the men of '87.[6] "I have never made an effort," he says, "and never propose to make an effort; I have never countenanced an effort, and never mean to countenance an effort, to disturb the arrangement as originally made, by which the various States came into the Union."[7] Still thinking of the sanction which the Constitution gives to slavery, he says, "Because it was a part of the original compact,—let it stand." Notwithstanding his special acuteness and ability, he is unable to take a fact out of its merely political relations, and behold it as it lies absolutely to be disposed of by the intellect,—what, for

5. Daniel Webster (1782–1852), prominent Massachusetts Whig politician of the second quarter of the 19th century.

6. The authors of the U.S. Constitution.
7. From Webster's speech "The Admission of Texas" (December 22, 1845).

instance, it behoves a man to do here in America to-day with regard to slavery, but ventures, or is driven, to make some such desperate answer as the following, while professing to speak absolutely, and as a private man,—from which what new and singular code of social duties might be inferred?—"The manner," says he, "in which the government of those States where slavery exists are to regulate it, is for their own consideration, under their responsibility to their constituents, to the general laws of propriety, humanity, and justice, and to God. Associations formed elsewhere, springing from a feeling of humanity, or any other cause, having nothing whatever to do with it. They have never received any encouragement from me, and they never will."[8]

They who know of no purer sources of truth, who have traced up its stream no higher, stand, and wisely stand, by the Bible and the Constitution, and drink at it there with reverence and humility; but they who behold where it comes trickling into this lake or that pool, gird up their loins once more, and continue their pilgrimage toward its fountain-head.

No man with a genius for legislation has appeared in America. They are rare in the history of the world. There are orators, politicians, and eloquent men, by the thousand; but the speaker has not yet opened his mouth to speak, who is capable of settling the much-vexed questions of the day. We love eloquence for its own sake, and not for any truth which it may utter, or any heroism it may inspire. Our legislators have not yet learned the comparative value of free-trade and of freedom, of union, and of rectitude, to a nation. They have no genius or talent for comparatively humble questions of taxation and finance, commerce and manufactures and agriculture. If we were left solely to the wordy wit of legislators in Congress for our guidance, uncorrected by the seasonable experience and the effectual complaints of the people, America would not long retain her rank among the nations. For eighteen hundred years, though perchance I have no right to say it, the New Testament has been written; yet where is the legislator who has wisdom and practical talent enough to avail himself of the light which it sheds on the science of legislation?

The authority of government, even such as I am willing to submit to,—for I will cheerfully obey those who know and can do better than I, and in many things even those who neither know nor can do so well,—is still an impure one: to be strictly just, it must have the sanction and consent of the governed. It can have no pure right over my person and property but what I concede to it. The progress from an absolute to a limited monarchy, from a limited monarchy to a democracy, is a progress toward a true respect for the individual. Is a democracy, such as we know it, the last improvement possible in government? Is it not possible to take a step further towards recognizing and organizing the rights of man? There will never be a really free and enlightened State, until the State comes to recognize the individual as a higher and independent power, from which all its own power and authority are derived, and treats him accordingly. I please myself with imagining a State at last which can afford to be just to all men, and to treat the individual with respect as a neighbor; which even would not think it inconsistent with its own repose, if a few were to live aloof from it, not meddling with it, nor embraced by it, who fulfilled all the duties of neighbors and fellow-men.

8. "These extracts have been inserted since the Lecture was read" [Thoreau's note]. He is referring to the quotation beginning "The manner."

A State which bore this kind of fruit, and suffered it to drop off as fast as it ripened, would prepare the way for a still more perfect and glorious State, which also I have imagined, but not yet anywhere seen.

1849, 1866

Walden, or Life in the Woods[1]

> I do not propose to write an ode to dejection, but to brag as lustily as chanticleer in the morning, standing on his roost, if only to wake my neighbors up.

1. Economy

When I wrote the following pages, or rather the bulk of them, I lived alone, in the woods, a mile from any neighbor, in a house which I had built myself, on the shore of Walden Pond, in Concord, Massachusetts, and earned my living by the labor of my hands only. I lived there two years and two months. At present I am a sojourner in civilized life again.

I should not obtrude my affairs so much on the notice of my readers if very particular inquiries had not been made by my townsmen concerning my mode of life, which some would call impertinent, though they do not appear to me at all impertinent, but, considering the circumstances, very natural and pertinent. Some have asked what I got to eat; if I did not feel lonesome; if I was not afraid; and the like. Others have been curious to learn what portion of my income I devoted to charitable purposes; and some, who have large families, how many poor children I maintained. I will therefore ask those of my readers who feel no particular interest in me to pardon me if I undertake to answer some of these questions in this book. In most books, the *I*, or first person, is omitted; in this it will be retained; that, in respect to egotism, is the main difference. We commonly do not remember that it is, after all, always the first person that is speaking. I should not talk so much about myself if there were any body else whom I knew as well. Unfortunately, I am confined to this theme by the narrowness of my experience. Moreover, I, on my side, require of every writer, first or last, a simple and sincere account of his own life, and not merely what he has heard of other men's lives; some such account as he would send to his kindred from a distant land; for if he has lived sincerely, it must have been in a distant land to me. Perhaps these pages are more particularly addressed to poor students. As for the rest of my readers, they will accept such portions as apply to them. I trust that none will stretch the seams in putting on the coat, for it may do good service to him whom it fits.

I would fain say something, not so much concerning the Chinese and Sandwich Islanders[2] as you who read these pages, who are said to live in New

1. Thoreau began writing *Walden* early in 1846, some months after he began living at Walden Pond, and by late 1847, when he moved back into the village of Concord, he had drafted roughly half the book. Between 1852 and 1854 he rewrote the manuscript several times and substantially enlarged it. The text printed here is that of the 1st edition (1854), with a few printer's errors corrected on the basis of Thoreau's set of marked proofs, his corrections in his copy of *Walden*, and scholars' comparisons of the printed book and the manuscript drafts.
2. Hawaiians.

WALDEN;

OR,

LIFE IN THE WOODS.

BY HENRY D. THOREAU,

AUTHOR OF "A WEEK ON THE CONCORD AND MERRIMACK RIVERS."

I do not propose to write an ode to dejection, but to brag as lustily as chanticleer in the morning, standing on his roost, if only to wake my neighbors up. — Page 92.

BOSTON:

TICKNOR AND FIELDS.

M DCCC LIV.

Walden. Title page of the first edition (1854); the drawing is by Thoreau's sister Sophia.

England; something about your condition, especially your outward condition or circumstances in this world, in this town, what it is, whether it is necessary that it be as bad as it is, whether it cannot be improved as well as not. I have travelled a good deal in Concord; and every where, in shops, and offices, and fields, the inhabitants have appeared to me to be doing penance in a thousand remarkable ways. What I have heard of Brahmins sitting exposed to four fires and looking in the face of the sun; or hanging suspended, with their heads downward, over flames; or looking at the heavens over their shoulders "until it becomes impossible for them to resume their natural position, while from the twist of the neck nothing but liquids can pass into the stomach;" or dwelling, chained for life, at the foot of a tree; or measuring with their bodies, like caterpillars, the breadth of vast empires; or standing on one leg on the tops of pillars,—even these forms of conscious penance are hardly more incredible and astonishing than the scenes which I daily witness.[3] The twelve labors of Hercules[4] were trifling in comparison with those which my neighbors have undertaken; for they were only twelve, and had an end; but I could never see that these men slew or captured any monster or finished any labor. They have no friend Iolas to burn with a hot iron the root of the hydra's head, but as soon as one head is crushed, two spring up.

I see young men, my townsmen, whose misfortune it is to have inherited farms, houses, barns, cattle, and farming tools; for these are more easily acquired than got rid of. Better if they had been born in the open pasture and suckled by a wolf,[5] that they might have seen with clearer eyes what field they were called to labor in. Who made them serfs of the soil? Why should they eat their sixty acres, when man is condemned to eat only his peck of dirt? Why should they begin digging their graves as soon as they are born? They have got to live a man's life, pushing all these things before them, and get on as well as they can. How many a poor immortal soul have I met well nigh crushed and smothered under its load, creeping down the road of life, pushing before it a barn seventy-five feet by forty, its Augean stables never cleansed, and one hundred acres of land, tillage, mowing, pasture, and wood-lot! The portionless, who struggle with no such unnecessary inherited encumbrances, find it labor enough to subdue and cultivate a few cubic feet of flesh.

But men labor under a mistake. The better part of the man is soon ploughed into the soil for compost. By a seeming fate, commonly called necessity, they are employed, as it says in an old book, laying up treasures which moth and rust will corrupt and thieves break through and steal.[6] It is a fool's life, as they will find when they get to the end of it, if not before. It is said that Deucalion and Pyrrha created men by throwing stones over their heads behind them:[7]—

3. For his information on religious self-torture among high-caste Hindus in India, Thoreau drew on *The History of India* (1817) by James Mill (1773–1836).
4. Son of Zeus and Alcmene, this half-mortal could become a god only by performing twelve labors, each apparently impossible. The second labor, the slaying of the Lernaean hydra, a many-headed sea monster, is referred to just below. (Hercules' friend Iolas helped by searing the stump each time Hercules cut off one of the heads, which otherwise would have regenerated.) The seventh labor, mentioned in the following paragraph, was the cleansing of Augeas's filthy stables in one day, a feat Hercules accomplished by diverting two nearby rivers through the stables.
5. Roman myth tells of how Romulus and Remus, the founders of Rome, were suckled by a wolf.
6. Matthew 6.19.
7. According to Greek mythology, Deucalion and Pyrrha repopulated the earth by throwing stones behind them over their shoulders. The stones thrown by Deucalion turned into men, and the stones thrown by Pyrrha turned into women.

> Inde genus durum sumus, experiensque laborum,
> Et documenta damus quâ simus origine nati.[8]

Or, as Raleigh rhymes it in his sonorous way,—

> "From thence our kind hard-hearted is, enduring pain and care,
> Approving that our bodies of a stony nature are."

So much for a blind obedience to a blundering oracle, throwing the stones over their heads behind them, and not seeing where they fell.

Most men, even in this comparatively free country, through mere ignorance and mistake, are so occupied with the factitious cares and superfluously coarse labors of life that its finer fruits cannot be plucked by them. Their fingers, from excessive toil, are too clumsy and tremble too much for that. Actually, the laboring man has not leisure for a true integrity day by day; he cannot afford to sustain the manliest relations to men; his labor would be depreciated in the market. He has no time to be any thing but a machine. How can he remember well his ignorance—which his growth requires—who has so often to use his knowledge? We should feed and clothe him gratuitously sometimes, and recruit him with our cordials, before we judge of him. The finest qualities of our nature, like the bloom on fruits, can be preserved only by the most delicate handling. Yet we do not treat ourselves nor one another thus tenderly.

Some of you, we all know, are poor, find it hard to live, are sometimes, as it were, gasping for breath. I have no doubt that some of you who read this book are unable to pay for all the dinners which you have actually eaten, or for the coats and shoes which are fast wearing or are already worn out, and have come to this page to spend borrowed or stolen time, robbing your creditors of an hour. It is very evident what mean and sneaking lives many of you live, for my sight has been whetted by experience; always on the limits, trying to get into business and trying to get out of debt, a very ancient slough, called by the Latins, *æs alienum*, another's brass, for some of their coins were made of brass; still living, and dying, and buried by this other's brass; always promising to pay, promising to pay, to-morrow, and dying to-day, insolvent; seeking to curry favor, to get custom, by how many modes, only not state-prison offences; lying, flattering, voting, contracting yourselves into a nutshell of civility, or dilating into an atmosphere of thin and vaporous generosity, that you may persuade your neighbor to let you make his shoes, or his hat, or his coat, or his carriage, or import his groceries for him; making yourselves sick, that you may lay up something against a sick day, something to be tucked away in an old chest, or in a stocking behind the plastering, or, more safely, in the brick bank; no matter where, no matter how much or how little.

I sometimes wonder that we can be so frivolous, I may almost say, as to attend to the gross but somewhat foreign form of servitude called Negro Slavery, there are so many keen and subtle masters that enslave both north and south. It is hard to have a southern overseer; it is worse to have a northern one; but worst of all when you are the slave-driver of yourself. Talk of a divinity in man! Look at the teamster on the highway, wending to market by day or night; does any divinity stir within him? His highest duty to fodder and water

---

8. From *Metamorphoses*, by the Roman poet Ovid (43 B.C.E.–18 C.E.), and translated by Sir Walter Raleigh (1554?–1618) in his *History of the World* (1614).

his horses! What is his destiny to him compared with the shipping interests? Does not he drive for Squire Make-a-stir?[9] How godlike, how immortal, is he? See how he cowers and sneaks, how vaguely all the day he fears, not being immortal nor divine, but the slave and prisoner of his own opinion of himself, a fame won by his own deeds. Public opinion is a weak tyrant compared with our own private opinion. What a man thinks of himself, that it is which determines, or rather indicates, his fate. Self-emancipation even in the West Indian provinces of the fancy and imagination,—what Wilberforce[1] is there to bring that about? Think, also, of the ladies of the land weaving toilet cushions against the last day, not to betray too green an interest in their fates! As if you could kill time without injuring eternity.

The mass of men lead lives of quiet desperation. What is called resignation is confirmed desperation. From the desperate city you go into the desperate country, and have to console yourself with the bravery of minks and muskrats. A stereotyped but unconscious despair is concealed even under what are called the games and amusements of mankind. There is no play in them, for this comes after work. But it is a characteristic of wisdom not to do desperate things.

When we consider what, to use the words of the catechism, is the chief end of man,[2] and what are the true necessaries and means of life, it appears as if men had deliberately chosen the common mode of living because they preferred it to any other. Yet they honestly think there is no choice left. But alert and healthy natures remember that the sun rose clear. It is never too late to give up our prejudices. No way of thinking or doing, however ancient, can be trusted without proof. What every body echoes or in silence passes by as true to-day may turn out to be falsehood to-morrow, mere smoke of opinion, which some had trusted for a cloud that would sprinkle fertilizing rain on their fields. What old people say you cannot do you try and find that you can. Old deeds for old people, and new deeds for new. Old people did not know enough once, perchance, to fetch fresh fuel to keep the fire a-going; new people put a little dry wood under a pot, and are whirled round the globe with the speed of birds, in a way to kill old people, as the phrase is. Age is no better, hardly so well, qualified for an instructor as youth, for it has not profited so much as it has lost. One may almost doubt if the wisest man has learned any thing of absolute value by living. Practically, the old have no very important advice to give the young, their own experience has been so partial, and their lives have been such miserable failures, for private reasons, as they must believe; and it may be that they have some faith left which belies that experience, and they are only less young than they were. I have lived some thirty years on this planet, and I have yet to hear the first syllable of valuable or even earnest advice from my seniors. They have told me nothing, and probably cannot tell me any thing, to the purpose. Here is life, an experiment to a great extent untried by me; but it does not avail me that they have tried it. If I have any experience which I think valuable, I am sure to reflect that this my Mentors[3] said nothing about.

---

9. An allegorical name modeled on those in John Bunyan's *Pilgrim's Progress* (1678, 1684).
1. William Wilberforce (1759–1833), English philanthropist, was instrumental in helping to abolish the slave trade (1807) and end slavery in the British Empire (1833).
2. From the Westminster Shorter Catechism in the *New England Primer*: "What is the chief end of man? Man's chief end is to glorify God and to enjoy him forever."
3. From Mentor, in Homer's *Odyssey*: the friend whom Odysseus entrusted with the education of his son, Telemachus.

One farmer says to me, "You cannot live on vegetable food solely, for it furnishes nothing to make bones with;" and so he religiously devotes a part of his day to supplying his system with the raw material of bones; walking all the while he talks behind his oxen, which, with vegetable-made bones, jerk him and his lumbering plough along in spite of every obstacle. Some things are really necessaries of life in some circles, the most helpless and diseased, which in others are luxuries merely, and in others still are entirely unknown.

The whole ground of human life seems to some to have been gone over by their predecessors, both the heights and the valleys, and all things to have been cared for. According to Evelyn, "the wise Solomon prescribed ordinances for the very distances of trees; and the Roman prætors have decided how often you may go into your neighbor's land to gather the acorns which fall on it without trespass, and what share belongs to that neighbor."[4] Hippocrates[5] has even left directions how we should cut our nails; that is, even with the ends of the fingers, neither shorter nor longer. Undoubtedly the very tedium and ennui which presume to have exhausted the variety and the joys of life are as old as Adam. But man's capacities have never been measured; nor are we to judge of what he can do by any precedents, so little has been tried. Whatever have been thy failures hitherto, "be not afflicted, my child, for who shall assign to thee what thou hast left undone?"[6]

We might try our lives by a thousand simple tests; as, for instance, that the same sun which ripens my beans illumines at once a system of earths like ours. If I had remembered this it would have prevented some mistakes. This was not the light in which I hoed them. The stars are the apexes of what wonderful triangles! What distant and different beings in the various mansions of the universe are contemplating the same one at the same moment! Nature and human life are as various as our several constitutions. Who shall say what prospect life offers to another? Could a greater miracle take place than for us to look through each other's eyes for an instant? We should live in all the ages of the world in an hour; ay, in all the worlds of the ages. History, Poetry, Mythology!—I know of no reading of another's experience so startling and informing as this would be.

The greater part of what my neighbors call good I believe in my soul to be bad, and if I repent of any thing, it is very likely to be my good behavior. What demon possessed me that I behaved so well? You may say the wisest thing you can old man,—you who have lived seventy years, not without honor of a kind,—I hear an irresistible voice which invites me away from all that. One generation abandons the enterprises of another like stranded vessels.

I think that we may safely trust a good deal more than we do. We may waive just so much care of ourselves as we honestly bestow elsewhere. Nature is as well adapted to our weakness as to our strength. The incessant anxiety and strain of some is a well nigh incurable form of disease. We are made to exaggerate the importance of what work we do; and yet how much is not done by us! or, what if we had been taken sick? How vigilant we are! determined not to live by faith if we can avoid it; all the day long on the alert, at night we

4. *Silva; or a Discourse of Forest-Trees* (1664), by the English writer John Evelyn (1620–1706), who called for the reforestation of lands cleared for estates. "Prætors": in the Roman Republic, high elected magistrates.
5. Influential Greek physician (460?–377? B.C.E.),

who emphasized the importance of doctors making an ethical commitment to the care of their patients (known as the "Hippocratic Oath").
6. From H. H. Wilson's translation of the *Vishnu Purana* (1840), a Hindu religious text.

unwillingly say our prayers and commit ourselves to uncertainties. So thoroughly and sincerely are we compelled to live, reverencing our life, and denying the possibility of change. This is the only way, we say; but there are as many ways as there can be drawn radii from one centre. All change is a miracle to contemplate; but it is a miracle which is taking place every instant. Confucius said, "To know that we know what we know, and that we do not know what we do not know, this is true knowledge."[7] When one man has reduced a fact of the imagination to be a fact to his understanding, I foresee that all men will at length establish their lives on that basis.

Let us consider for a moment what most of the trouble and anxiety which I have referred to is about, and how much it is necessary that we be troubled, or, at least, careful. It would be some advantage to live a primitive and frontier life, though in the midst of an outward civilization, if only to learn what are the gross necessaries of life and what methods have been taken to obtain them; or even to look over the old day-books of the merchants, to see what it was that men most commonly bought at the stores, what they stored, that is, what are the grossest groceries. For the improvements of ages have had but little influence on the essential laws of man's existence; as our skeletons, probably, are not to be distinguished from those of our ancestors.

By the words *necessary of life*, I mean whatever, of all that man obtains by his own exertions, has been from the first, or from long use has become, so important to human life that few, if any, whether from savageness, or poverty, or philosophy, ever attempt to do without it. To many creatures there is in this sense but one necessary of life, Food. To the bison of the prairie it is a few inches of palatable grass, with water to drink; unless he seeks the Shelter of the forest or the mountain's shadow. None of the brute creation requires more than Food and Shelter. The necessaries of life for man in this climate may, accurately enough, be distributed under the several heads of Food, Shelter, Clothing, and Fuel; for not till we have secured these are we prepared to entertain the true problems of life with freedom and a prospect of success. Man has invented, not only houses, but clothes and cooked food; and possibly from the accidental discovery of the warmth of fire, and the consequent use of it, at first a luxury, arose the present necessity to sit by it. We observe cats and dogs acquiring the same second nature. By proper Shelter and Clothing we legitimately retain our own internal heat; but with an excess of these, or of Fuel, that is, with an external heat greater than our own internal, may not cookery properly be said to begin? Darwin, the naturalist, says of the inhabitants of Tierra del Fuego, that while his own party, who were well clothed and sitting close to a fire, were far from too warm, these naked savages, who were farther off, were observed, to his great surprise, "to be streaming with perspiration at undergoing such a roasting."[8] So, we are told, the New Hollander[9] goes naked with impunity, while the European shivers in his clothes. Is it impossible to combine the hardiness of these savages with the intellectualness of the civilized man? According to Liebig,[1] man's body is a stove, and food the fuel which keeps up the internal combustion in the lungs. In cold weather we eat more, in warm less. The animal heat is the

7. From *Analects* 2:17, by the Chinese philosopher Confucius (551?–479 B.C.E.).
8. Charles Darwin (1809–1882), *Journal of Researches* (1839).

9. Australian aborigine.
1. Justus, Baron von Liebig (1803–1873), German chemist, author of *Organic Chemistry* (1840).

result of a slow combustion, and disease and death take place when this is too rapid; or for want of fuel, or from some defect in the draught, the fire goes out. Of course the vital heat is not to be confounded with fire; but so much for analogy. It appears, therefore, from the above list, that the expression, *animal life*, is nearly synonymous with the expression, *animal heat*; for while Food may be regarded as the Fuel which keeps up the fire within us,— and Fuel serves only to prepare that Food or to increase the warmth of our bodies by addition from without,—Shelter and Clothing also serve only to retain the *heat* thus generated and absorbed.

The grand necessity, then, for our bodies, is to keep warm, to keep the vital heat in us. What pains we accordingly take, not only with our Food, and Clothing, and Shelter, but with our beds, which are our night-clothes, robbing the nests and breasts of birds to prepare this shelter within a shelter, as the mole has its bed of grass and leaves at the end of its burrow! The poor man is wont to complain that this is a cold world; and to cold, no less physical than social, we refer directly a great part of our ails. The summer, in some climates, makes possible to man a sort of Elysian[2] life. Fuel, except to cook his Food, is then unnecessary; the sun is his fire, and many of the fruits are sufficiently cooked by its rays; while Food generally is more various, and more easily obtained, and Clothing and Shelter are wholly or half unnecessary. At the present day, and in this country, as I find by my own experience, a few implements, a knife, an axe, a spade, a wheelbarrow, &c., and for the studious, lamplight, stationery, and access to a few books, rank next to necessaries, and can all be obtained at a trifling cost. Yet some, not wise, go to the other side of the globe, to barbarous and unhealthy regions, and devote themselves to trade for ten or twenty years, in order that they may live,—that is, keep comfortably warm,—and die in New England at last. The luxuriously rich are not simply kept comfortably warm, but unnaturally hot; as I implied before, they are cooked, of course *à la mode*.[3]

Most of the luxuries, and many of the so called comforts of life, are not only not indispensable, but positive hinderances to the elevation of mankind. With respect to luxuries and comforts, the wisest have ever lived a more simple and meager life than the poor. The ancient philosophers, Chinese, Hindoo, Persian, and Greek, were a class than which none has been poorer in outward riches, none so rich in inward. We know not much about them. It is remarkable that *we* know so much of them as we do. The same is true of the more modern reformers and benefactors of their race. None can be an impartial or wise observer of human life but from the vantage ground of what *we* should call voluntary poverty. Of a life of luxury the fruit is luxury, whether in agriculture, or commerce, or literature, or art. There are nowadays professors of philosophy, but not philosophers. Yet it is admirable to profess because it was once admirable to live. To be a philosopher is not merely to have subtle thoughts, nor even to found a school, but so to love wisdom as to live according to its dictates, a life of simplicity, independence, magnanimity, and trust. It is to solve some of the problems of life, not only theoretically, but practically. The success of great scholars and thinkers is commonly a courtier-like success, not kingly, not manly. They make shift to live merely by conformity, practically as their fathers did, and are in no sense

2. In Greek mythology, Elysium is the home of the blessed after death. 3. According to the latest fashion (French).

the progenitors of a nobler race of men. But why do men degenerate ever? What makes families run out? What is the nature of the luxury which enervates and destroys nations? Are we sure that there is none of it in our own lives? The philosopher is in advance of his age even in the outward form of his life. He is not fed, sheltered, clothed, warmed, like his contemporaries. How can a man be a philosopher and not maintain his vital heat by better methods than other men?

When a man is warmed by the several modes which I have described, what does he want next? Surely not more warmth of the same kind, as more and richer food, larger and more splendid houses, finer and more abundant clothing, more numerous incessant and hotter fires, and the like. When he has obtained those things which are necessary to life, there is another alternative than to obtain the superfluities; and that is, to adventure on life now, his vacation from humbler toil having commenced. The soil, it appears, is suited to the seed, for it has sent its radicle downward, and it may now send its shoot upward also with confidence. Why has man rooted himself thus firmly in the earth, but that he may rise in the same proportion into the heavens above?—for the nobler plants are valued for the fruit they bear at last in the air and light, far from the ground, and are not treated like the humbler esculents,[4] which, though they may be biennials, are cultivated only till they have perfected their root, and often cut down at top for this purpose, so that most would not know them in their flowering season.

I do not mean to prescribe rules to strong and valiant natures, who will mind their own affairs whether in heaven or hell, and perchance build more magnificently and spend more lavishly than the richest, without ever impoverishing themselves, not knowing how they live,—if, indeed, there are any such, as has been dreamed; nor to those who find their encouragement and inspiration in precisely the present condition of things, and cherish it with the fondness and enthusiasm of lovers,—and, to some extent, I reckon myself in this number; I do not speak to those who are well employed, in whatever circumstances, and they know whether they are well employed or not;—but mainly to the mass of men who are discontented, and idly complaining of the hardness of their lot or of the times, when they might improve them. There are some who complain most energetically and inconsolably of any, because they are, as they say, doing their duty. I also have in my mind that seemingly wealthy, but most terribly impoverished class of all, who have accumulated dross, but know not how to use it, or get rid of it, and thus have forged their own golden or silver fetters.

If I should attempt to tell how I have desired to spend my life in years past, it would probably surprise those of my readers who are somewhat acquainted with its actual history; it would certainly astonish those who know nothing about it. I will only hint at some of the enterprises which I have cherished.

In any weather, at any hour of the day or night, I have been anxious to improve the nick of time, and notch it on my stick too;[5] to stand on the meeting of two eternities, the past and future, which is precisely the present moment; to toe that line. You will pardon some obscurities, for there are

---

4. Edibles.
5. Allusion to Daniel Defoe's *Robinson Crusoe*

(1719), a novel Thoreau much admired. Crusoe kept track of time by cutting notches on wood.

more secrets in my trade than in most men's, and yet not voluntarily kept, but inseparable from its very nature. I would gladly tell all that I know about it, and never paint "No Admittance" on my gate.

I long ago lost a hound, a bay horse, and a turtle-dove,[6] and am still on their trail. Many are the travellers I have spoken concerning them, describing their tracks and what calls they answered to. I have met one or two who had heard the hound, and the tramp of the horse, and even seen the dove disappear behind a cloud, and they seemed as anxious to recover them as if they had lost them themselves.

To anticipate, not the sunrise and the dawn merely, but, if possible, Nature herself! How many mornings, summer and winter, before yet any neighbor was stirring about his business, have I been about mine! No doubt, many of my townsmen have met me returning from this enterprise, farmers starting for Boston in the twilight, or woodchoppers going to their work. It is true, I never assisted the sun materially in his rising, but, doubt not, it was of the last importance only to be present at it.

So many autumn, ay, and winter days, spent outside the town, trying to hear what was in the wind, to hear and carry it express! I well-nigh sunk all my capital in it, and lost my own breath into the bargain, running in the face of it. If it had concerned either of the political parties, depend upon it, it would have appeared in the Gazette with the earliest intelligence.[7] At other times watching from the observatory of some cliff or tree, to telegraph any new arrival; or waiting at evening on the hill-tops for the sky to fall, that I might catch something, though I never caught much, and that, manna-wise,[8] would dissolve again in the sun.

For a long time I was reporter to a journal, of no very wide circulation, whose editor has never yet seen fit to print the bulk of my contributions, and, as is too common with writers, I got only my labor for my pains.[9] However, in this case my pains were their own reward.

For many years I was self-appointed inspector of snow storms and rain storms, and did my duty faithfully; surveyor, if not of highways, then of forest paths and all across-lot routes, keeping them open, and ravines bridged and passable at all seasons, where the public heel had testified to their utility.

I have looked after the wild stock of the town, which give a faithful herdsman a good deal of trouble by leaping fences; and I have had an eye to the unfrequented nooks and corners of the farm; though I did not always know whether Jonas or Solomon worked in a particular field to-day; that was none of my business. I have watered the red huckleberry, the sand cherry and the nettle tree, the red pine and the black ash, the white grape and the yellow violet, which might have withered else in dry seasons.

In short, I went on thus for a long time, I may say it without boasting, faithfully minding my business, till it became more and more evident that my townsmen would not after all admit me into the list of town officers, nor make my place a sinecure with a moderate allowance. My accounts, which

6. Symbols of elusive ideas, or ideals, whose exact meanings have not been determined.
7. News. "Gazette": newspaper.
8. In Exodus 16, manna is the bread that God rained from heaven so the Israelites could survive in the desert on their way from Egypt to the Promised Land.
9. Thoreau puns on the common usage of *journal* to mean a daily newspaper as well as a diary. Thoreau himself is the negligent or too demanding editor.

I can swear to have kept faithfully, I have, indeed, never got audited, still less accepted, still less paid and settled. However, I have not set my heart on that.

Not long since, a strolling Indian went to sell baskets at the house of a well-known lawyer in my neighborhood. "Do you wish to buy any baskets?" he asked. "No, we do not want any," was the reply. "What!" exclaimed the Indian as he went out the gate, "do you mean to starve us?" Having seen his industrious white neighbors so well off,—that the lawyer had only to weave arguments, and by some magic wealth and standing followed, he had said to himself; I will go into business; I will weave baskets; it is a thing which I can do. Thinking that when he had made the baskets he would have done his part, and then it would be the white man's to buy them. He had not discovered that it was necessary for him to make it worth the other's while to buy them, or at least make him think that it was so, or to make something else which it would be worth his while to buy. I too had woven a kind of basket of a delicate texture, but I had not made it worth any one's while to buy them.[1] Yet not the less, in my case, did I think it worth my while to weave them, and instead of studying how to make it worth men's while to buy my baskets, I studied rather how to avoid the necessity of selling them. The life which men praise and regard as successful is but one kind. Why should we exaggerate any one kind at the expense of the others?

Finding that my fellow-citizens were not likely to offer me any room in the court house, or any curacy or living[2] any where else, but I must shift for myself, I turned my face more exclusively than ever to the woods, where I was better known. I determined to go into business at once, and not wait to acquire the usual capital, using such slender means as I had already got. My purpose in going to Walden Pond was not to live cheaply nor to live dearly there, but to transact some private business with the fewest obstacles; to be hindered from accomplishing which for want of a little common sense, a little enterprise and business talent, appeared not so sad as foolish.

I have always endeavored to acquire strict business habits; they are indispensable to every man. If your trade is with the Celestial Empire,[3] then some small counting house on the coast, in some Salem harbor, will be fixture enough. You will export such articles as the country affords, purely native products, much ice and pine timber and a little granite, always in native bottoms. These will be good ventures. To oversee all the details yourself in person; to be at once pilot and captain, and owner and underwriter; to buy and sell and keep the accounts; to read every letter received, and write or read every letter sent; to superintend the discharge of imports night and day; to be upon many parts of the coast almost at the same time;—often the richest freight will be discharged upon a Jersey shore,[4]—to be your own telegraph, unweariedly sweeping the horizon, speaking all passing vessels bound coastwise; to keep up a steady despatch of commodities, for the supply of such a distant and exorbitant market; to keep yourself informed of the state of the markets, prospects of war and peace every where, and anticipate the tendencies of trade and civilization,—taking advantage of the results of all exploring expeditions, using new passages and all improvements in

1. A reference to Thoreau's poorly selling first book, *A Week on the Concord and Merrimack Rivers* (1849).
2. A church office with a fixed, steady income.

3. China, from the belief that the Chinese emperors were sons of heaven.
4. I.e., by shipwreck on the way to New York.

navigation;—charts to be studied, the position of reefs and new lights and buoys to be ascertained, and ever, and ever, the logarithmic tables to be corrected, for by the error of some calculator the vessel often splits upon a rock that should have reached a friendly pier,—there is the untold fate of La Perouse;—universal science to be kept pace with, studying the lives of all great discoverers and navigators, great adventurers and merchants from Hanno[5] and the Phœnicians down to our day; in fine, account of stock to be taken from time to time, to know how you stand. It is a labor to task the faculties of a man,—such problems of profit and loss, of interest, of tare and tret,[6] and gauging of all kinds in it, as demand a universal knowledge.

I have thought that Walden Pond would be a good place for business, not solely on account of the railroad and the ice trade; it offers advantages which it may not be good policy to divulge; it is a good port and a good foundation. No Neva[7] marshes to be filled; though you must every where build on piles of your own driving. It is said that a flood-tide, with a westerly wind, and ice in the Neva, would sweep St. Petersburg from the face of the earth.

As this business was to be entered into without the usual capital, it may not be easy to conjecture where those means, that will still be indispensable to every such undertaking, were to be obtained. As for Clothing, to come at once to the practical part of the question, perhaps we are led oftener by the love of novelty, and a regard for the opinions of men, in procuring it, than by a true utility. Let him who has work to do recollect that the object of clothing is, first, to retain the vital heat, and secondly, in this state of society, to cover nakedness, and he may judge how much of any necessary or important work may be accomplished without adding to his wardrobe. Kings and queens who wear a suit but once, though made by some tailor or dress-maker to their majesties, cannot know the comfort of wearing a suit that fits. They are no better than wooden horses to hang the clean clothes on. Every day our garments become more assimilated to ourselves, receiving the impress of the wearer's character, until we hesitate to lay them aside, without such delay and medical appliances and some such solemnity even as our bodies. No man ever stood the lower in my estimation for having a patch in his clothes; yet I am sure that there is greater anxiety, commonly, to have fashionable, or at least clean and unpatched clothes, than to have a sound conscience. But even if the rent is not mended, perhaps the worst vice betrayed is improvidence. I sometimes try my acquaintances by such tests as this;—who could wear a patch, or two extra seams only, over the knee? Most behave as if they believed that their prospects for life would be ruined if they should do it. It would be easier for them to hobble to town with a broken leg than with a broken pantaloon. Often if an accident happens to a gentleman's legs, they can be mended; but if a similar accident happens to the legs of his pantaloons, there is no help for it; for he considers, not what is truly respectable, but what is respected. We know but few men, a great many coats and breeches. Dress a scarecrow in your last shift, you standing shiftless by, who would not soonest salute the scarecrow? Passing a cornfield the other day,

5. Carthaginian navigator (6th–5th centuries B.C.E.), credited with opening the coast of west Africa to trade. Jean François de Galaup, Comte de la Pérouse (1741–1788), French explorer of the western Pacific.

6. Terms from shipping: "tare" is the deduction to the purchaser for the weight of the container; "tret" is the deduction for any damages.
7. A river in Russia.

close by a hat and coat on a stake, I recognized the owner of the farm. He was only a little more weather-beaten than when I saw him last. I have heard of a dog that barked at every stranger who approached his master's premises with clothes on, but was easily quieted by a naked thief. It is an interesting question how far men would retain their relative rank if they were divested of their clothes. Could you, in such a case, tell surely of any company of civilized men, which belonged to the most respected class? When Madam Pfeiffer, in her adventurous travels round the world, from east to west, had got so near home as Asiatic Russia, she says that she felt the necessity of wearing other than a travelling dress, when she went to meet the authorities, for she "was now in a civilized country, where———people are judged of by their clothes."[8] Even in our democratic New England towns the accidental possession of wealth, and its manifestation in dress and equipage alone, obtain for the possessor almost universal respect. But they who yield such respect, numerous as they are, are so far heathen, and need to have a missionary sent to them. Beside, clothes introduced sewing, a kind of work which you may call endless; a woman's dress, at least, is never done.

A man who has at length found something to do will not need to get a new suit to do it in; for him the old will do, that has lain dusty in the garret for an indeterminate period. Old shoes will serve a hero longer than they have served his valet,—if a hero ever has a valet,—bare feet are older than shoes, and he can make them do. Only they who go to soirées and legislative halls must have new coats, coats to change as often as the man changes in them. But if my jacket and trousers, my hat and shoes, are fit to worship God in, they will do; will they not? Who ever saw his old clothes,—his old coat, actually worn out, resolved into its primitive elements, so that it was not a deed of charity to bestow it on some poor boy, by him perchance to be bestowed on some poorer still, or shall we say richer, who could do with less? I say, beware of all enterprises that require new clothes, and not rather a new wearer of clothes. If there is not a new man, how can the new clothes be made to fit? If you have any enterprise before you, try it in your old clothes. All men want, not something to *do with*, but something to *do*, or rather something to *be*. Perhaps we should never procure a new suit, however ragged or dirty the old, until we have so conducted, so enterprised or sailed in some way, that we feel like new men in the old, and that to retain it would be like keeping new wine in old bottles.[9] Our moulting season, like that of the fowls, must be a crisis in our lives. The loon retires to solitary ponds to spend it. Thus also the snake casts its slough, and the caterpillar its wormy coat, by an internal industry and expansion; for clothes are but our outmost cuticle and mortal coil. Otherwise we shall be found sailing under false colors, and be inevitably cashiered[1] at last by our own opinion, as well as that of mankind.

We don garment after garment, as if we grew like exogenous plants by addition without. Our outside and often thin and fanciful clothes are our epidermis or false skin, which partakes not of our life, and may be stripped off here and there without fatal injury; our thicker garments, constantly worn, are our cellular integument, or cortex; but our shirts are our liber[2] or true bark, which

---

8. Ida Pfeiffer (1797–1858), *A Lady's Voyage round the World* (1852).
9. "Neither do men put new wine into old bottles: else the bottles break, and the wine runneth out, and the bottles perish: but they put new wine into new bottles, and both are preserved" (Matthew 9.17).
1. Fired.
2. Inner bark. "Integument, or cortex": an enveloping inner layer.

cannot be removed without girdling and so destroying the man. I believe that all races at some seasons wear something equivalent to the shirt. It is desirable that a man be clad so simply that he can lay his hands on himself in the dark, and that he live in all respects so compactly and preparedly, that, if an enemy take the town, he can, like the old philosopher, walk out the gate empty-handed without anxiety. While one thick garment is, for most purposes, as good as three thin ones, and cheap clothing can be obtained at prices really to suit customers; while a thick coat can be bought for five dollars, which will last as many years, thick pantaloons for two dollars, cowhide boots for a dollar and a half a pair, a summer hat for a quarter of a dollar, and a winter cap for sixty-two and a half cents, or a better be made at home at a nominal cost, where is he so poor that, clad in such a suit, *of his own earning,* there will not be found wise men to do him reverence?

When I ask for a garment of a particular form, my tailoress tells me gravely, "They do not make them so now," not emphasizing the "They" at all, as if she quoted an authority as impersonal as the Fates, and I find it difficult to get made what I want, simply because she cannot believe that I mean what I say, that I am so rash. When I hear this oracular sentence, I am for a moment absorbed in thought, emphasizing to myself each word separately that I may come at the meaning of it, that I may find out by what degree of consanguinity *They* are related to *me,* and what authority they may have in an affair which affects me so nearly; and, finally, I am inclined to answer her with equal mystery, and without any more emphasis of the "they,"—"It is true, they did not make them so recently, but they do now." Of what use this measuring of me if she does not measure my character, but only the breadth of my shoulders, as it were a peg to hang the coat on? We worship not the Graces, nor the Parcæ,[3] but Fashion. She spins and weaves and cuts with full authority. The head monkey at Paris puts on a traveller's cap, and all the monkeys in America do the same. I sometimes despair of getting any thing quite simple and honest done in this world by the help of men. They would have to be passed through a powerful press first, to squeeze their old notions out of them, so that they would not soon get upon their legs again, and then there would be some one in the company with a maggot in his head, hatched from an egg deposited there nobody knows when, for not even fire kills these things, and you would have lost your labor. Nevertheless, we will not forget that some Egyptian wheat is said to have been handed down to us by a mummy.[4]

On the whole, I think that it cannot be maintained that dressing has in this or any country risen to the dignity of an art. At present men make shift to wear what they can get. Like shipwrecked sailors, they put on what they can find on the beach, and at a little distance, whether of space or time, laugh at each other's masquerade. Every generation laughs at the old fashions, but follows religiously the new. We are amused at beholding the costume of Henry VIII, or Queen Elizabeth, as much as if it was that of the King and Queen of the Cannibal Islands. All costume off a man is pitiful or grotesque. It is only the serious eye peering from and the sincere life passed within it, which restrain laughter and consecrate the costume of any people. Let Harlequin[5]

---

3. In Roman mythology, the three Fates.
4. Thoreau refers to the popular notion that wheat could be grown from the seeds found in Egyptian tombs.

5. Comic servant in the Italian *commedia dell'arte,* typically dressed in a mask and many-colored tights.

be taken with a fit of the colic and his trappings will have to serve that mood too. When the soldier is hit by a cannon ball rags are as becoming as purple.

The childish and savage taste of men and women for new patterns keeps how many shaking and squinting through kaleidoscopes that they may discover the particular figure which this generation requires to-day. The manufacturers have learned that this taste is merely whimsical. Of two patterns which differ only by a few threads more or less of a particular color, the one will be sold readily, the other lie on the shelf, though it frequently happens that after the lapse of a season the latter becomes the most fashionable. Comparatively, tattooing is not the hideous custom which it is called. It is not barbarous merely because the printing is skin-deep and unalterable.

I cannot believe that our factory system is the best mode by which men may get clothing. The condition of the operatives is becoming every day more like that of the English; and it cannot be wondered at, since, as far as I have heard or observed, the principal object is, not that mankind may be well and honestly clad, but, unquestionably, that the corporations may be enriched. In the long run men hit only what they aim at. Therefore, though they should fail immediately, they had better aim at something high.

As for a Shelter, I will not deny that this is now a necessary of life, though there are instances of men having done without it for long periods in colder countries than this. Samuel Laing says that "The Laplander in his skin dress, and in a skin bag which he puts over his head and shoulders, will sleep night after night on the snow—in a degree of cold which would extinguish the life of one exposed to it in any woollen clothing." He had seen them asleep thus. Yet he adds, "They are not hardier than other people."[6] But, probably, man did not live long on the earth without discovering the convenience which there is in a house, the domestic comforts, which phrase may have originally signified the satisfactions of the house more than of the family; though these must be extremely partial and occasional in those climates where the house is associated in our thoughts with winter or the rainy season chiefly, and two thirds of the year, except for a parasol, is unnecessary. In our climate, in the summer, it was formerly almost solely a covering at night. In the Indian gazettes a wigwam was the symbol of a day's march, and a row of them cut or painted on the bark of a tree signified that so many times they had camped. Man was not made so large limbed and robust but that he must seek to narrow his world, and wall in a space such as fitted him. He was at first bare and out of doors; but though this was pleasant enough in serene and warm weather, by daylight, the rainy season and the winter, to say nothing of the torrid sun, would perhaps have nipped his race in the bud if he had not made haste to clothe himself with the shelter of a house. Adam and Eve, according to a fable, wore the bower before other clothes. Man wanted a home, a place of warmth, or comfort, first of physical warmth, then the warmth of the affections.

We may imagine a time when, in the infancy of the human race, some enterprising mortal crept into a hollow in a rock for shelter. Every child begins the world again, to some extent, and loves to stay out doors, even in wet and cold. It plays house, as well as horse, having an instinct for it. Who does not remember the interest with which when young he looked at shelving rocks, or any approach to a cave? It was the natural yearning of that portion of our

---

6. *Journal of a Residence in Norway* (1837), by the English writer Laing (1780–1868).

most primitive ancestor which still survived in us. From the cave we have advanced to roofs of palm leaves, of bark and boughs, of linen woven and stretched, of grass and straw, of boards and shingles, of stones and tiles. At last, we know not what it is to live in the open air, and our lives are domestic in more senses than we think. From the hearth to the field is a great distance. It would be well perhaps if we were to spend more of our days and nights without any obstruction between us and the celestial bodies, if the poet did not speak so much from under a roof, or the saint dwell there so long. Birds do not sing in caves, nor do doves cherish their innocence in dovecots.

However, if one designs to construct a dwelling house, it behooves him to exercise a little Yankee shrewdness, lest after all he find himself in a work-house, a labyrinth without a clew, a museum, an almshouse, a prison, or a splendid mausoleum instead. Consider first how slight a shelter is absolutely necessary. I have seen Penobscot Indians,[7] in this town, living in tents of thin cotton cloth, while the snow was nearly a foot deep around them, and I thought that they would be glad to have it deeper to keep out the wind. Formerly, when how to get my living honestly, with freedom left for my proper pursuits, was a question which vexed me even more than it does now, for unfortunately I am become somewhat callous, I used to see a large box by the railroad, six feet long by three wide, in which the laborers locked up their tools at night, and it suggested to me that every man who was hard pushed might get such a one for a dollar, and, having bored a few auger holes in it, to admit the air at least, get into it when it rained and at night, and hook down the lid, and so have freedom in his love, and in his soul be free. This did not appear the worst, nor by any means a despicable alternative. You could sit up as late as you pleased, and, whenever you got up, go abroad without any land-lord or house-lord dogging you for rent. Many a man is harassed to death to pay the rent of a larger and more luxurious box who would not have frozen to death in such a box as this. I am far from jesting. Economy is a subject which admits of being treated with levity, but it cannot so be disposed of. A comfortable house for a rude and hardy race, that lived mostly out of doors, was once made here almost entirely of such materials as Nature furnished ready to their hands. Gookin, who was superintendent of the Indians subject to the Massachusetts Colony, writing in 1674, says, "The best of their houses are covered very neatly, tight and warm, with barks of trees, slipped from their bodies at those seasons when the sap is up, and made into great flakes, with pressure of weighty timber, when they are green. . . . The meaner sort are covered with mats which they make of a kind of bulrush, and are also indifferently tight and warm, but not so good as the former. . . . Some I have seen, sixty or a hundred feet long and thirty feet broad. . . . I have often lodged in their wigwams, and found them as warm as the best English houses."[8] He adds, that they were commonly carpeted and lined within with well-wrought embroidered mats, and were furnished with various utensils. The Indians had advanced so far as to regulate the effect of the wind by a mat suspended over the hole in the roof and moved by a string. Such a lodge was in the first instance constructed in a day or two at most, and taken down and put up in a few hours; and every family owned one, or its apartment in one.

In the savage state every family owns a shelter as good as the best, and sufficient for its coarser and simpler wants; but I think that I speak within bounds

---

7. An Algonquin tribe from what is now Maine.
8. Daniel Gookin (1612–1687), *Historical Collections of the Indians in New England* (completed in 1674; first published in 1792).

when I say that, though the birds of the air have their nests, and the foxes their holes,[9] and the savages their wigwams, in modern civilized society not more than one half the families own a shelter. In the large towns and cities, where civilization especially prevails, the number of those who own a shelter is a very small fraction of the whole. The rest pay an annual tax for this outside garment of all, become indispensable summer and winter, which would buy a village of Indian wigwams, but now helps to keep them poor as long as they live. I do not mean to insist here on the disadvantage of hiring compared with owning, but it is evident that the savage owns his shelter because it costs so little, while the civilized man hires his commonly because he cannot afford to own it; nor can he, in the long run, any better afford to hire. But, answers one, by merely paying this tax the poor civilized man secures an abode which is a palace compared with the savage's. An annual rent of from twenty-five to a hundred dollars, these are the country rates, entitles him to the benefit of the improvements of centuries, spacious apartments, clean paint and paper, Rumford fireplace,[1] back plastering, Venetian blinds, copper pump, spring lock, a commodious cellar, and many other things. But how happens it that he who is said to enjoy these things is so commonly a *poor* civilized man, while the savage, who has them not, is rich as a savage? If it is asserted that civilization is a real advance in the condition of man,—and I think that it is, though only the wise improve their advantages,—it must be shown that it has produced better dwellings without making them more costly; and the cost of a thing is the amount of what I will call life which is required to be exchanged for it, immediately or in the long run. An average house in this neighborhood costs perhaps eight hundred dollars, and to lay up this sum will take from ten to fifteen years of the laborer's life, even if he is not encumbered with a family;—estimating the pecuniary value of every man's labor at one dollar a day, for if some receive more, others receive less;—so that he must have spent more than half his life commonly before *his* wigwam will be earned. If we suppose him to pay a rent instead, this is but a doubtful choice of evils. Would the savage have been wise to exchange his wigwam for a palace on these terms?

It may be guessed that I reduce almost the whole advantage of holding this superfluous property as a fund in store against the future, so far as the individual is concerned, mainly to the defraying of funeral expenses. But perhaps a man is not required to bury himself. Nevertheless this points to an important distinction between the civilized man and the savage; and, no doubt, they have designs on us for our benefit, in making the life of a civilized people an *institution*, in which the life of the individual is to a great extent absorbed, in order to preserve and perfect that of the race. But I wish to show at what a sacrifice this advantage is at present obtained, and to suggest that we may possibly so live as to secure all the advantage without suffering any of the disadvantage. What mean ye by saying that the poor ye have always with you, or that the fathers have eaten sour grapes, and the children's teeth are set on edge?[2]

---

9. "The foxes have holes, and the birds of the air have nests; but the Son of man hath not where to lay his head" (Matthew 8.20).
1. Benjamin Thompson, Count Rumford (1753–1814), devised a shelf inside the chimney to prevent smoke from being carried back into a room by downdrafts.
2. Thoreau draws on Jesus' words to his disciples

"For ye have the poor always with you; but me ye have not always" (Matthew 26.11) and God's reproof to Ezekiel for employing a self-defeating proverb: "What mean ye, that ye use this proverb concerning the land of Israel, saying, The fathers have eaten sour grapes, and the children's teeth are set on edge?" (Ezekiel 18.2).

"As I live, saith the Lord God, ye shall not have occasion any more to use this proverb in Israel."

"Behold all souls are mine; as the soul of the father, so also the soul of the son is mine: the soul that sinneth it shall die."[3]

When I consider my neighbors, the farmers of Concord, who are at least as well off as the other classes, I find that for the most part they have been toiling twenty, thirty, or forty years, that they may become the real owners of their farms, which commonly they have inherited with encumbrances, or else bought with hired money,—and we may regard one third of that toil as the cost of their houses,—but commonly they have not paid for them yet. It is true, the encumbrances sometimes outweigh the value of the farm, so that the farm itself becomes one great encumbrance, and still a man is found to inherit it, being well acquainted with it, as he says. On applying to the assessors, I am surprised to learn that they cannot at once name a dozen in the town who own their farms free and clear. If you would know the history of these homesteads, inquire at the bank where they are mortgaged. The man who has actually paid for his farm with labor on it is so rare that every neighbor can point to him. I doubt if there are three such men in Concord. What has been said of the merchants, that a very large majority, even ninety-seven in a hundred, are sure to fail, is equally true of the farmers. With regard to the merchants, however, one of them says pertinently that a great part of their failures are not genuine pecuniary failures, but merely failures to fulfil their engagements, because it is inconvenient; that is, it is the moral character that breaks down. But this puts an infinitely worse face on the matter, and suggests, beside, that probably not even the other three succeed in saving their souls, but are perchance bankrupt in a worse sense than they who fail honestly. Bankruptcy and repudiation are the spring-boards from which much of our civilization vaults and turns its somersets,[4] but the savage stands on the unelastic plank of famine. Yet the Middlesex Cattle Show goes off here with éclat annually, as if all the joints of the agricultural machine were suent.[5]

The farmer is endeavoring to solve the problem of a livelihood by a formula more complicated than the problem itself. To get his shoestrings he speculates in herds of cattle. With consummate skill he has set his trap with a hair spring to catch comfort and independence, and then, as he turned away, got his own leg into it. This is the reason he is poor; and for a similar reason we are all poor in respect to a thousand savage comforts, though surrounded by luxuries. As Chapman[6] sings,—

> "The false society of men—
> —for earthly greatness
> All heavenly comforts rarefies to air."

And when the farmer has got his house, he may not be the richer but the poorer for it, and it be the house that has got him. As I understand it, that was a valid objection urged by Momus against the house which Minerva[7] made, that she "had not made it movable, by which means a bad neighborhood might be avoided;" and it may still be urged, for our houses are such unwieldy

---

3. Ezekiel 18.3–4, which Thoreau abridges to convey his rejection of the idea that the sins of the fathers must be visited on their children.
4. Somersaults.
5. In good working order; broken in. "Éclat": brilliance (French).
6. From the play *Caesar and Pompey* 5.2, by the English writer George Chapman (1559?–1634).
7. In Greek mythology, the goddess of wisdom. Monus was the Greek god of mockery and blame.

property that we are often imprisoned rather than housed in them; and the bad neighborhood to be avoided is our own scurvy selves. I know one or two families, at least, in this town, who, for nearly a generation, have been wishing to sell their houses in the outskirts and move into the village, but have not been able to accomplish it, and only death will set them free.

Granted that the *majority* are able at last either to own or hire the modern house with all its improvements. While civilization has been improving our houses, it has not equally improved the men who are to inhabit them. It has created palaces, but it was not so easy to create noblemen and kings. And *if the civilized man's pursuits are no worthier than the savage's, if he is employed the greater part of his life in obtaining gross necessaries and comforts merely, why should he have a better dwelling than the former?*

But how do the poor *minority* fare? Perhaps it will be found, that just in proportion as some have been placed in outward circumstances above the savage, others have been degraded below him. The luxury of one class is counterbalanced by the indigence of another. On the one side is the palace, on the other are the almshouse and "silent poor."[8] The myriads who built the pyramids to be the tombs of the Pharaohs were fed on garlic, and it may be were not decently buried themselves. The mason who finishes the cornice of the palace returns at night perchance to a hut not so good as a wigwam. It is a mistake to suppose that, in a country where the usual evidences of civilization exist, the condition of a very large body of the inhabitants may not be as degraded as that of savages. I refer to the degraded poor, not now to the degraded rich. To know this I should not need to look farther than to the shanties which every where border our railroads, that last improvement in civilization; where I see in my daily walks human beings living in sties, and all winter with an open door, for the sake of light, without any visible, often imaginable, wood pile, and the forms of both old and young are permanently contracted by the long habit of shrinking from cold and misery, and the development of all their limbs and faculties is checked. It certainly is fair to look at that class by whose labor the works which distinguish the generation are accomplished. Such too, to a greater or less extent, is the condition of the operatives of every denomination in England, which is the great workhouse of the world. Or I could refer you to Ireland, which is marked as one of the white or enlightened spots on the map.[9] Contrast the physical condition of the Irish with that of the North American Indian, or the South Sea Islander, or any other savage race before it was degraded by contact with the civilized man. Yet I have no doubt that that people's rulers are as wise as the average of civilized rulers. Their condition only proves what squalidness may consist with civilization. I hardly need refer now to the laborers in our Southern States who produce the staple exports of this country, and are themselves a staple production of the South.[1] But to confine myself to those who are said to be in *moderate* circumstances.

Most men appear never to have considered what a house is, and are actually though needlessly poor all their lives because they think that they must have such a one as their neighbors have. As if one were to wear any sort of coat which the tailor might cut out for him, or, gradually leaving off palmleaf

---

8. Poor people who do not want to be identified as needing public charity.
9. Thoreau refers to the habit some mapmakers had of leaving unexplored terrain in a dark color; other cartographers left unexplored areas white.
1. A reference to the domestic slave trade.

hat or cap of woodchuck skin, complain of hard times because he could not afford to buy him a crown! It is possible to invent a house still more convenient and luxurious than we have, which yet all would admit that man could not afford to pay for. Shall we always study to obtain more of these things, and not sometimes to be content with less? Shall the respectable citizen thus gravely teach, by precept and example, the necessity of the young man's providing a certain number of superfluous glow-shoes,[2] and umbrellas, and empty guest chambers for empty guests, before he dies? Why should not our furniture be as simple as the Arab's or the Indian's? When I think of the benefactors of the race, whom we have apotheosized as messengers from heaven, bearers of divine gifts to man, I do not see in my mind any retinue at their heels, any car-load of fashionable furniture. Or what if I were to allow— would it not be a singular allowance?—that our furniture should be more complex than the Arab's, in proportion as we are morally and intellectually his superiors! At present our houses are cluttered and defiled with it, and a good housewife would sweep out the greater part into the dust hole, and not leave her morning's work undone. Morning work! By the blushes of Aurora and the music of Memnon,[3] what should be man's *morning work* in this world? I had three pieces of limestone on my desk, but I was terrified to find that they required to be dusted daily, when the furniture of my mind was all undusted still, and I threw them out the window in disgust. How, then, could I have a furnished house? I would rather sit in the open air, for no dust gathers on the grass, unless where man has broken ground.

It is the luxurious and dissipated who set the fashions which the herd so diligently follow. The traveller who stops at the best houses, so called, soon discovers this, for the publicans presume him to be a Sardanapalus,[4] and if he resigned himself to their tender mercies he would soon be completely emasculated. I think that in the railroad car we are inclined to spend more on luxury than on safety and convenience, and it threatens without attaining these to become no better than a modern drawing room, with its divans, and ottomans, and sunshades, and a hundred other oriental things, which we are taking west with us, invented for the ladies of the harem and the effeminate natives of the Celestial Empire, which Jonathan[5] should be ashamed to know the names of. I would rather sit on a pumpkin and have it all to myself, than be crowded on a velvet cushion. I would rather ride on earth in an ox cart with a free circulation, than go to heaven in the fancy car of an excursion train and breathe a *malaria* all the way.

The very simplicity and nakedness of man's life in the primitive ages imply this advantage at least, that they left him still but a sojourner in nature. When he was refreshed with food and sleep he contemplated his journey again. He dwelt, as it were, in a tent in this world, and was either threading the valleys, or crossing the plains, or climbing the mountain tops. But lo! men have become the tools of their tools. The man who independently plucked the fruits when he was hungry is become a farmer; and he who stood under a tree for shelter, a housekeeper. We now no longer camp as for a night, but have settled down on earth and forgotten heaven. We have adopted Christianity

2. Galoshes.
3. In Roman mythology, the goddess of the dawn and her son. Memnon is associated here with the Egyptian colossus near Thebes that was said to emit musical sounds at dawn.

4. Ruler of Assyria (9th century B.C.E.).
5. A name at first applied comically to New England farmers; then later (as here, or with the name "Brother Jonathan") to the inhabitants of the entire United States.

merely as an improved method of *agri*-culture. We have built for this world a family mansion, and for the next a family tomb. The best works of art are the expression of man's struggle to free himself from this condition, but the effect of our art is merely to make this low state comfortable and that higher state to be forgotten. There is actually no place in this village for a work of *fine* art, if any had come down to us, to stand, for our lives, our houses and streets, furnish no proper pedestal for it. There is not a nail to hang a picture on, nor a shelf to receive the bust of a hero or a saint. When I consider how our houses are built and paid for, or not paid for, and their internal economy managed and sustained, I wonder that the floor does not give way under the visitor while he is admiring the gewgaws upon the mantel-piece, and let him through into the cellar, to some solid and honest though earthy foundation. I cannot but perceive that this so called rich and refined life is a thing jumped at, and I do not get on in the enjoyment of the *fine* arts which adorn it, my attention being wholly occupied with the jump; for I remember that the greatest genuine leap, due to human muscles alone, on record, is that of certain wandering Arabs, who are said to have cleared twenty-five feet on level ground. Without factitious support, man is sure to come to earth again beyond that distance. The first question which I am tempted to put to the proprietor of such great impropriety is, Who bolsters you? Are you one of the ninety-seven who fail? or of the three who succeed? Answer me these questions, and then perhaps I may look at your bawbles and find them ornamental. The cart before the horse is neither beautiful nor useful. Before we can adorn our houses with beautiful objects the walls must be stripped, and our lives must be stripped, and beautiful housekeeping and beautiful living be laid for a foundation: now, a taste for the beautiful is most cultivated out of doors, where there is no house and no housekeeper.

Old Johnson, in his "Wonder-Working Providence," speaking of the first settlers of this town, with whom he was contemporary, tells us that "they burrow themselves in the earth for their first shelter under some hillside, and, casting the soil aloft upon timber, they make a smoky fire against the earth, at the highest side." They did not "provide them houses," says he, "till the earth, by the Lord's blessing, brought forth bread to feed them," and the first year's crop was so light that "they were forced to cut their bread very thin for a long season."[6] The secretary of the Province of New Netherland, writing in Dutch, in 1650, for the information of those who wished to take up land there, states more particularly, that "those in New Netherland, and especially in New England, who have no means to build farm houses at first according to their wishes, dig a square pit in the ground, cellar fashion, six or seven feet deep, as long and as broad as they think proper, case the earth inside with wood all round the wall, and line the wood with the bark of trees or something else to prevent the caving in of the earth; floor this cellar with plank, and wainscot it overhead for a ceiling, raise a roof of spars clear up, and cover the spars with bark or green sods, so that they can live dry and warm in these houses with their entire families for two, three, and four years, it being understood that partitions are run through those cellars which are adapted to the size of the family. The wealthy and principal men in New England, in the beginning of the colonies, commenced their first

6. Edward Johnson (1598–1672), *Wonder-working Providence of Sion's Saviour in New England* (1654).

dwelling houses in this fashion for two reasons; firstly, in order not to waste time in building, and not to want food the next season; secondly, in order not to discourage poor laboring people whom they brought over in numbers from Fatherland. In the course of three or four years, when the country became adapted to agriculture, they built themselves handsome houses, spending on them several thousands."[7]

In this course which our ancestors took there was a show of prudence at least, as if their principle were to satisfy the more pressing wants first. But are the more pressing wants satisfied now? When I think of acquiring for myself one of our luxurious dwellings, I am deterred, for, so to speak, the country is not yet adapted to *human* culture, and we are still forced to cut our *spiritual* bread far thinner than our forefathers did their wheaten. Not that all architectural ornament is to be neglected even in the rudest periods; but let our houses first be lined with beauty, where they come in contact with our lives, like the tenement of the shellfish, and not overlaid with it. But, alas! I have been inside one or two of them, and know what they are lined with.

Though we are not so degenerate but that we might possibly live in a cave or a wigwam or wear skins to-day, it certainly is better to accept the advantages, though so dearly bought, which the invention and industry of mankind offer. In such a neighborhood as this, boards and shingles, lime and bricks, are cheaper and more easily obtained than suitable caves, or whole logs, or bark in sufficient quantities, or even well-tempered clay or flat stones. I speak understandingly on this subject, for I have made myself acquainted with it both theoretically and practically. With a little more wit we might use these materials so as to become richer than the richest now are, and make our civilization a blessing. The civilized man is a more experienced and wiser savage. But to make haste to my own experiment.

Near the end of March, 1845, I borrowed an axe and went down to the woods by Walden Pond, nearest to where I intended to build my house, and began to cut down some tall arrowy white pines, still in their youth, for timber. It is difficult to begin without borrowing, but perhaps it is the most generous course thus to permit your fellow-men to have an interest in your enterprise. The owner of the axe, as he released his hold on it, said that it was the apple of his eye; but I returned it sharper than I received it. It was a pleasant hillside where I worked, covered with pine woods, through which I looked out on the pond, and a small open field in the woods where pines and hickories were springing up. The ice in the pond was not yet dissolved, though there were some open spaces, and it was all dark colored and saturated with water. There were some slight flurries of snow during the days that I worked there; but for the most part when I came out on to the railroad, on my way home, its yellow sand heap stretched away gleaming in the hazy atmosphere, and the rails shone in the spring sun, and I heard the lark and pewee and other birds already come to commence another year with us. They were pleasant spring days, in which the winter of man's discontent was thawing as well as the earth, and the life that had lain torpid began to stretch itself. One day, when my axe had come off and I had cut a green hickory for a wedge, driving it with a stone, and had placed the whole to soak in a pond hole in order to swell the wood, I saw a striped snake run

7. Edmund Bailey O'Callaghan (1797–1880), *Documentary History of the State of New-York* (1851).

into the water, and he lay on the bottom, apparently without inconvenience, as long as I staid there, or more than a quarter of an hour; perhaps because he had not yet fairly come out of the torpid state. It appeared to me that for a like reason men remain in their present low and primitive condition; but if they should feel the influence of the spring of springs arousing them, they would of necessity rise to a higher and more ethereal life. I had previously seen the snakes in frosty mornings in my path with portions of their bodies still numb and inflexible, waiting for the sun to thaw them. On the 1st of April it rained and melted the ice, and in the early part of the day, which was very foggy, I heard a stray goose groping about over the pond and cackling as if lost, or like the spirit of the fog.

So I went on for some days cutting and hewing timber, and also studs and rafters, all with my narrow axe, not having many communicable or scholar-like thoughts, singing to myself,—

> Men say they know many things;
> But lo! they have taken wings,—
> The arts and sciences,
> And a thousand appliances;
> The wind that blows
> Is all that any body knows.[8]

I hewed the main timbers six inches square, most of the studs on two sides only, and the rafters and floor timbers on one side, leaving the rest of the bark on, so that they were just as straight and much stronger than sawed ones. Each stick was carefully mortised or tenoned by its stump, for I had borrowed other tools by this time. My days in the woods were not very long ones; yet I usually carried my dinner of bread and butter, and read the newspaper in which it was wrapped, at noon, sitting amid the green pine boughs which I had cut off, and to my bread was imparted some of their fragrance, for my hands were covered with a thick coat of pitch. Before I had done I was more the friend than the foe of the pine tree, though I had cut down some of them, having become better acquainted with it. Sometimes a rambler in the wood was attracted by the sound of my axe, and we chatted pleasantly over the chips which I had made.

By the middle of April, for I made no haste in my work, but rather made the most of it, my house was framed and ready for the raising. I had already bought the shanty of James Collins, an Irishman who worked on the Fitchburg Railroad, for boards. James Collins' shanty was considered an uncommonly fine one. When I called to see it he was not at home. I walked about the outside, at first unobserved from within, the window was so deep and high. It was of small dimensions, with a peaked cottage roof, and not much else to be seen, the dirt being raised five feet all around as if it were a compost heap. The roof was the soundest part, though a good deal warped and made brittle by the sun. Door-sill there was none, but a perennial passage for the hens under the door board. Mrs. C. came to the door and asked me to view it from the inside. The hens were driven in by my approach. It was dark, and had a dirt floor for the most part, dank, clammy, and aguish, only here a board and there a board which would not bear removal. She lighted a lamp to show me the inside of the roof and the walls, and also that the board

---

8. Like other poems in *Walden* not enclosed in quotation marks, this poem is Thoreau's.

floor extended under the bed, warning me not to step into the cellar, a sort of dust hole two feet deep. In her own words, they were "good boards overhead, good boards all around, and a good window,"—of two whole squares originally, only the cat had passed out that way lately. There was a stove, a bed, and a place to sit, an infant in the house where it was born, a silk parasol, gilt-framed looking-glass, and a patent new coffee mill nailed to an oak sapling, all told. The bargain was soon concluded, for James had in the mean while returned. I to pay four dollars and twenty-five cents to-night, he to vacate at five to-morrow morning, selling to nobody else meanwhile: I to take possession at six. It were well, he said, to be there early, and anticipate certain indistinct but wholly unjust claims on the score of ground rent and fuel. This he assured me was the only encumbrance. At six I passed him and his family on the road. One large bundle held their all,—bed, coffee-mill, looking-glass, hens,—all but the cat, she took to the woods and became a wild cat, and, as I learned afterward, trod in a trap set for woodchucks, and so became a dead cat at last.

I took down this dwelling the same morning, drawing the nails, and removed it to the pond side by small cartloads, spreading the boards on the grass there to bleach and warp back again in the sun. One early thrush gave me a note or two as I drove along the woodland path. I was informed treacherously by a young Patrick that neighbor Seeley, an Irishman, in the intervals of the carting, transferred the still tolerable, straight, and drivable nails, staples, and spikes to his pocket, and then stood when I came back to pass the time of day, and look freshly up, unconcerned, with spring thoughts, at the devastation; there being a dearth of work, as he said. He was there to represent spectatordom, and help make this seemingly insignificant event one with the removal of the gods of Troy.[9]

I dug my cellar in the side of a hill sloping to the south, where a woodchuck had formerly dug his burrow, down through sumach and blackberry roots, and the lowest stain of vegetation, six feet square by seven deep, to a fine sand where potatoes would not freeze in any winter. The sides were left shelving, and not stoned; but the sun having never shone on them, the sand still keeps its place. It was but two hours' work. I took particular pleasure in this breaking of ground, for in almost all latitudes men dig into the earth for an equable temperature. Under the most splendid house in the city is still to be found the cellar where they store their roots as of old, and long after the superstructure has disappeared posterity remark its dent in the earth. The house is still but a sort of porch at the entrance of a burrow.

At length, in the beginning of May, with the help of some of my acquaintances, rather to improve so good an occasion for neighborliness than from any necessity, I set up the frame of my house. No man was ever more honored in the character of his raisers[1] than I. They are destined, I trust, to assist at the raising of loftier structures one day. I began to occupy my house on the 4th of July, as soon as it was boarded and roofed, for the boards were carefully feather-edged and lapped, so that it was perfectly impervious to rain; but before boarding I laid the foundation of a chimney at one end,

9. In Virgil's *Aeneid*, book 2, after the fall of Troy, Aeneas escapes with his father and son and his household gods.

1. These "raisers" included Emerson; Alcott; Ellery Channing; two young brothers who had participated in the Brook Farm reform community, Burrill and George William Curtis; and the Concord farmer Edmund Hosmer and his three sons.

bringing two cartloads of stones up the hill from the pond in my arms. I built the chimney after my hoeing in the fall, before a fire became necessary for warmth, doing my cooking in the mean while out of doors on the ground, early in the morning: which mode I still think is in some respects more convenient and agreeable than the usual one. When it stormed before my bread was baked, I fixed a few boards over the fire, and sat under them to watch my loaf, and passed some pleasant hours in that way. In those days, when my hands were much employed, I read but little, but the least scraps of paper which lay on the ground, my holder, or table-cloth, afforded me as much entertainment, in fact answered the same purpose as the Iliad.[2]

It would be worth the while to build still more deliberately than I did, considering, for instance, what foundation a door, a window, a cellar, a garret, have in the nature of man, and perchance never raising any superstructure until we found a better reason for it than our temporal necessities even. There is some of the same fitness in a man's building his own house that there is in a bird's building its own nest. Who knows but if men constructed their dwellings with their own hands, and provided food for themselves and families simply and honestly enough, the poetic faculty would be universally developed, as birds universally sing when they are so engaged? But alas! we do like cowbirds and cuckoos, which lay their eggs in nests which other birds have built, and cheer no traveller with their chattering and unmusical notes. Shall we forever resign the pleasure of construction to the carpenter? What does architecture amount to in the experience of the mass of men? I never in all my walks came across a man engaged in so simple and natural an occupation as building his house. We belong to the community. It is not the tailor alone who is the ninth part of a man; it is as much the preacher, and the merchant, and the farmer. Where is this division of labor to end? and what object does it finally serve? No doubt another *may* also think for me; but it is not therefore desirable that he should do so to the exclusion of my thinking for myself.

True, there are architects so called in this country, and I have heard of one at least possessed with the idea of making architectural ornaments have a core of truth, a necessity, and hence a beauty, as if it were a revelation to him.[3] All very well perhaps from his point of view, but only a little better than the common dilettantism. A sentimental reformer in architecture, he began at the cornice, not at the foundation. It was only how to put a core of truth within the ornaments, that every sugar plum in fact might have an almond or caraway seed in it,—though I hold that almonds are most wholesome without the sugar,—and not how the inhabitant, the indweller, might build truly within and without, and let the ornaments take care of themselves. What reasonable man ever supposed that ornaments were something outward and in the skin merely,—that the tortoise got his spotted shell, or the shellfish its mother-o'-pearl tints, by such a contract as the inhabitants of Broadway their Trinity Church?[4] But a man has no more to do with the style of architecture of his house than a tortoise with that of its shell: nor need the soldier be so idle as to try to paint the precise *color* of his virtue on his standard. The enemy will find it out. He may turn pale when the trial comes. This man

2. Greek epic traditionally attributed to Homer.
3. The sculptor Horatio Greenough (1805–1852), who insisted on the importance of function in architectural decoration.
4. A New York City church built in a Gothic style during the 1840s.

seemed to me to lean over the cornice and timidly whisper his half truth to the rude occupants who really knew it better than he. What of architectural beauty I now see, I know has gradually grown from within outward, out of the necessities and character of the indweller, who is the only builder,—out of some unconscious truthfulness, and nobleness, without ever a thought for the appearance; and whatever additional beauty of this kind is destined to be produced will be preceded by a like unconscious beauty of life. The most interesting dwellings in this country, as the painter knows, are the most unpretending, humble log huts and cottages of the poor commonly; it is the life of the inhabitants whose shells they are, and not any peculiarity in their surfaces merely, which makes them *picturesque;* and equally interesting will be the citizen's suburban box, when his life shall be as simple and as agreeable to the imagination, and there is as little straining after effect in the style of his dwelling. A great proportion of architectural ornaments are literally hollow, and a September gale would strip them off, like borrowed plumes, without injury to the substantials. They can do without *architecture* who have no olives nor wines in the cellar. What if an equal ado were made about the ornaments of style in literature, and the architects of our bibles spent as much time about their cornices as the architects of our churches do? So are made the *belles-lettres* and the *beaux-arts*[5] and their professors. Much it concerns a man, forsooth, how a few sticks are slanted over him or under him, and what colors are daubed upon his box. It would signify somewhat, if, in any earnest sense, *he* slanted them and daubed it; but the spirit having departed out of the tenant, it is of a piece with constructing his own coffin,—the architecture of the grave, and "carpenter" is but another name for "coffin-maker." One man says, in his despair or indifference to life, take up a handful of the earth at your feet, and paint your house that color. Is he thinking of his last and narrow house? Toss up a copper for it as well. What an abundance of leisure he must have! Why do you take up a handful of dirt? Better paint your house your own complexion; let it turn pale or blush for you. An enterprise to improve the style of cottage architecture! When you have got my ornaments ready I will wear them.

Before winter I built a chimney, and shingled the sides of my house, which were already impervious to rain, with imperfect and sappy shingles made of the first slice of the log, whose edges I was obliged to straighten with a plane.

I have thus a tight shingled and plastered house, ten feet wide by fifteen long, and eight-feet posts, with a garret and a closet, a large window on each side, two trap doors, one door at the end, and a brick fireplace opposite. The exact cost of my house, paying the usual price for such materials as I used, but not counting the work, all of which was done by myself, was as follows; and I give the details because very few are able to tell exactly what their houses cost, and fewer still, if any, the separate cost of the various materials which compose them:—

Boards,	$8 03½	Mostly shanty boards
Refuse shingles for roof and sides,	4 00	
Laths,	1 25	

5. Literature and fine arts (French).

Two second-hand		
windows with glass,	2 43	
One thousand old brick,	4 00	
Two casks of lime,	2 40	That was high
Hair,	0 31	More than I needed
Mantle-tree iron,	0 15	
Nails,	3 90	
Hinges and screws,	0 14	
Latch,	0 10	
Chalk,	0 01	
Transportation,	1 40	I carried a good part on my back
In all,	$28 12½	

These are all the materials excepting the timber stones and sand, which I claimed by squatter's right. I have also a small wood-shed adjoining, made chiefly of the stuff which was left after building the house.

I intend to build me a house which will surpass any on the main street in Concord in grandeur and luxury, as soon as it pleases me as much and will cost me no more than my present one.

I thus found that the student who wishes for a shelter can obtain one for a lifetime at an expense not greater than the rent which he now pays annually. If I seem to boast more than is becoming, my excuse is that I brag for humanity rather than for myself; and my shortcomings and inconsistencies do not affect the truth of my statement. Notwithstanding much cant and hypocrisy,—chaff which I find it difficult to separate from my wheat, but for which I am as sorry as any man,—I will breathe freely and stretch myself in this respect, it is such a relief to both the moral and physical system; and I am resolved that I will not through humility become the devil's attorney. I will endeavor to speak a good word for the truth. At Cambridge College[6] the mere rent of a student's room, which is only a little larger than my own, is thirty dollars each year, though the corporation had the advantage of building thirty-two side by side and under one roof, and the occupant suffers the inconvenience of many and noisy neighbors, and perhaps a residence in the fourth story. I cannot but think that if we had more true wisdom in these respects, not only less education would be needed, because, forsooth, more would already have been acquired, but the pecuniary expense of getting an education would in a great measure vanish. Those conveniences which the student requires at Cambridge or elsewhere cost him or somebody else ten times as great a sacrifice of life as they would with proper management on both sides. Those things for which the most money is demanded are never the things which the student most wants. Tuition, for instance, is an important item in the term bill, while for the far more valuable education which he gets by associating with the most cultivated of his contemporaries no charge is made. The mode of founding a college is, commonly, to get up a subscription of dollars and cents, and then following blindly the principles of a division of labor to its extreme, a principle which should never be followed but with circumspection,—to call in a contractor who makes this a subject of speculation, and he employs Irishmen or other operatives actually to lay the

6. Harvard College.

foundations, while the students that are to be are said to be fitting themselves for it; and for these oversights successive generations have to pay. I
think that it would be *better than this*, for the students, or those who desire
to be benefited by it, even to lay the foundation themselves. The student who
secures his coveted leisure and retirement by systematically shirking any
labor necessary to man obtains but an ignoble and unprofitable leisure,
defrauding himself of the experience which alone can make leisure fruitful.
"But," says one, "you do not mean that the students should go to work with
their hands instead of their heads?" I do not mean that exactly, but I mean
something which he might think a good deal like that; I mean that they
should not *play* life, or *study* it merely, while the community supports them
at this expensive game, but earnestly *live* it from beginning to end. How
could youths better learn to live than by at once trying the experiment of
living? Methinks this would exercise their minds as much as mathematics. If
I wished a boy to know something about the arts and sciences, for instance,
I would not pursue the common course, which is merely to send him into
the neighborhood of some professor, where any thing is professed and practised but the art of life;—to survey the world through a telescope or a microscope, and never with his natural eye; to study chemistry, and not learn how
his bread is made, or mechanics, and not learn how it is earned; to discover
new satellites to Neptune, and not detect the motes in his eyes, or to what
vagabond he is a satellite himself; or to be devoured by the monsters that
swarm all around him, while contemplating the monsters in a drop of vinegar. Which would have advanced the most at the end of the month,—the boy
who had made his own jack-knife from the ore which he had dug and
smelted, reading as much as would be necessary for this,—or the boy who
had attended the lectures on metallurgy at the Institute in the mean while,
and had received a Rodgers penknife[7] from his father? Which would be most
likely to cut his fingers?—To my astonishment I was informed on leaving
college that I had studied navigation!—why, if I had taken one turn down
the harbor I should have known more about it. Even the *poor* student studies
and is taught only *political* economy, while that economy of living which is
synonymous with philosophy is not even sincerely professed in our colleges.
The consequence is, that while he is reading Adam Smith, Ricardo, and
Say,[8] he runs his father in debt irretrievably.

As with our colleges, so with a hundred "modern improvements"; there
is an illusion about them; there is not always a positive advance. The devil
goes on exacting compound interest to the last for his early share and numerous succeeding investments in them. Our inventions are wont to be pretty
toys, which distract our attention from serious things. They are but improved
means to an unimproved end, an end which it was already but too easy to
arrive at; as railroads lead to Boston or New York. We are in great haste to
construct a magnetic telegraph from Maine to Texas; but Maine and Texas,
it may be, have nothing important to communicate. Either is in such a predicament as the man who was earnest to be introduced to a distinguished
deaf woman, but when he was presented, and one end of her ear trumpet
was put into his hand, had nothing to say. As if the main object were to talk

7. High-quality knife made by the English firm
of Joseph Rodgers and Sons.
8. Three European economists: Adam Smith

(1723–1790), David Ricardo (1772–1823), and
Jean Baptiste Say (1767–1832).

fast and not to talk sensibly. We are eager to tunnel under the Atlantic and bring the old world some weeks nearer to the new; but perchance the first news that will leak through into the broad, flapping American ear will be that the Princess Adelaide[9] has the whooping cough. After all, the man whose horse trots a mile in a minute does not carry the most important messages; he is not an evangelist, nor does he come round eating locusts and wild honey. I doubt if Flying Childers[1] ever carried a peck of corn to mill.

One says to me, "I wonder that you do not lay up money; you love to travel; you might take the cars and go to Fitchburg[2] to-day and see the country." But I am wiser than that. I have learned that the swiftest traveller is he that goes afoot. I say to my friend, Suppose we try who will get there first. The distance is thirty miles; the fare ninety cents. That is almost a day's wages. I remember when wages were sixty cents a day for laborers on this very road. Well, I start now on foot, and get there before night; I have travelled at that rate by the week together. You will in the mean while have earned your fare, and arrive there some time to-morrow, or possibly this evening, if you are lucky enough to get a job in season. Instead of going to Fitchburg, you will be working here the greater part of the day. And so, if the railroad reached round the world, I think that I should keep ahead of you; and as for seeing the country and getting experience of that kind, I should have to cut your acquaintance altogether.

Such is the universal law, which no man can ever outwit, and with regard to the railroad even we may say it is as broad as it is long. To make a railroad round the world available to all mankind is equivalent to grading the whole surface of the planet. Men have an indistinct notion that if they keep up this activity of joint stocks and spades long enough all will at length ride somewhere, in next to no time, and for nothing; but though a crowd rushes to the depot, and the conductor shouts "All aboard!" when the smoke is blown away and the vapor condensed, it will be perceived that a few are riding, but the rest are run over,—and it will be called, and will be, "A melancholy accident." No doubt they can ride at last who shall have earned their fare, that is, if they survive so long, but they will probably have lost their elasticity and desire to travel by that time. This spending of the best part of one's life earning money in order to enjoy a questionable liberty during the least valuable part of it, reminds me of the Englishman who went to India to make a fortune first, in order that he might return to England and live the life of a poet. He should have gone up garret at once. "What!" exclaim a million Irishmen starting up from all the shanties in the land, "is not this railroad which we have built a good thing?" Yes, I answer, *comparatively* good, that is, you might have done worse; but I wish, as you are brothers of mine, that you could have spent your time better than digging in this dirt.

Before I finished my house, wishing to earn ten or twelve dollars by some honest and agreeable method, in order to meet my unusual expenses, I planted about two acres and a half of light and sandy soil near it chiefly with beans, but also a small part with potatoes, corn, peas, and turnips.

9. Adelaide Louisa Theresa Caroline Amelia (1792–1849), sister of Louis-Philippe, king of France from 1830 to 1848.

1. A famous English racehorse (1714–1741).
2. Village near Concord, Massachusetts.

The whole lot contains eleven acres, mostly growing up to pines and hickories, and was sold the preceding season for eight dollars and eight cents an acre. One farmer said that it was "good for nothing but to raise cheeping squirrels on." I put no manure on this land, not being the owner, but merely a squatter, and not expecting to cultivate so much again, and I did not quite hoe it all once. I got out several cords of stumps in ploughing, which supplied me with fuel for a long time, and left small circles of virgin mould, easily distinguishable through the summer by the greater luxuriance of the beans there. The dead and for the most part unmerchantable wood behind my house, and the driftwood from the pond, have supplied the remainder of my fuel. I was obliged to hire a team and a man for the ploughing, though I held the plough myself. My farm outgoes for the first season were, for implements, seed, work, &c., $14 72½. The seed corn was given me. This never costs any thing to speak of, unless you plant more than enough. I got twelve bushels of beans, and eighteen bushels of potatoes, beside some peas and sweet corn. The yellow corn and turnips were too late to come to any thing. My whole income from the farm was

	$23 44.
Deducting the outgoes,	14 72½
there are left,	$ 8 71½,

beside produce consumed and on hand at the time this estimate was made of the value of $4 50,—the amount on hand much more than balancing a little grass which I did not raise. All things considered, that is, considering the importance of a man's soul and of to-day, notwithstanding the short time occupied by my experiment, nay, partly even because of its transient character, I believe that that was doing better than any farmer in Concord did that year.

The next year I did better still, for I spaded up all the land which I required, about a third of an acre, and I learned from the experience of both years, not being in the least awed by many celebrated works on husbandry, Arthur Young[3] among the rest, that if one would live simply and eat only the crop which he raised, and raise no more than he ate, and not exchange it for an insufficient quantity of more luxurious and expensive things, he would need to cultivate only a few rods of ground, and that it would be cheaper to spade up that than to use oxen to plough it, and to select a fresh spot from time to time than to manure the old, and he could do all his necessary farm work as it were with his left hand at odd hours in the summer; and thus he would not be tied to an ox, or horse, or cow, or pig, as at present. I desire to speak impartially on this point, and as one not interested in the success or failure of the present economical and social arrangements. I was more independent than any farmer in Concord, for I was not anchored to a house or farm, but could follow the bent of my genius, which is a very crooked one, every moment. Beside being better off than they already, if my house had been burned or my crops had failed, I should have been nearly as well off as before.

I am wont to think that men are not so much the keepers of herds as herds are the keepers of men, the former are so much the freer. Men and oxen

3. Author of *Rural Oeconomy, or Essays on the Practical Parts of Husbandry* (1773).

exchange work; but if we consider necessary work only, the oxen will be seen to have greatly the advantage, their farm is so much the larger. Man does some of his part of the exchange work in his six weeks of haying, and it is no boy's play. Certainly no nation that lived simply in all respects, that is, no nation of philosophers, would commit so great a blunder as to use the labor of animals. True, there never was and is not likely soon to be a nation of philosophers, nor am I certain it is desirable that there should be. However, *I* should never have broken a horse or bull and taken him to board for any work he might do for me, for fear I should become a horse-man or a herdsman merely; and if society seems to be the gainer by so doing, are we certain that what is one man's gain is not another's loss, and that the stable-boy has equal cause with his master to be satisfied? Granted that some public works would not have been constructed without this aid, and let man share the glory of such with the ox and horse; does it follow that he could not have accomplished works yet more worthy of himself in that case? When men begin to do, not merely unnecessary or artistic, but luxurious and idle work, with their assistance, it is inevitable that a few do all the exchange work with the oxen, or, in other words, become the slaves of the strongest. Man thus not only works for the animal within him, but, for a symbol of this, he works for the animal without him. Though we have many substantial houses of brick or stone, the prosperity of the farmer is still measured by the degree to which the barn overshadows the house. This town is said to have the largest houses for oxen cows and horses hereabouts, and it is not behindhand in its public buildings; but there are very few halls for free worship or free speech in this county. It should not be by their architecture, but why not even by their power of abstract thought, that nations should seek to commemorate themselves? How much more admirable the Bhagvat-Geeta[4] than all the ruins of the East! Towers and temples are the luxury of princes. A simple and independent mind does not toil at the bidding of any prince. Genius is not a retainer to any emperor, nor is its material silver, or gold, or marble, except to a trifling extent. To what end, pray, is so much stone hammered? In Arcadia,[5] when I was there, I did not see any hammering stone. Nations are possessed with an insane ambition to perpetuate the memory of themselves by the amount of hammered stone they leave. What if equal pains were taken to smooth and polish their manners? One piece of good sense would be more memorable than a monument as high as the moon. I love better to see stones in place. The grandeur of Thebes[6] was a vulgar grandeur. More sensible is a rod of stone wall that bounds an honest man's field than a hundred-gated Thebes that has wandered farther from the true end of life. The religion and civilization which are barbaric and heathenish build splendid temples; but what you might call Christianity does not. Most of the stone a nation hammers goes toward its tomb only. It buries itself alive. As for the Pyramids, there is nothing to wonder at in them so much as the fact that so many men could be found degraded enough to spend their lives constructing a tomb for some ambitious booby, whom it would have been wiser and manlier to have drowned in the Nile, and then given his body to the dogs. I might possibly invent some excuse for them and him, but I have no time for it. As for the religion and love of art of the builders, it is much the same all the world over, whether the building be an Egyptian temple or the United States Bank. It costs more than it comes to. The mainspring is vanity, assisted by the love of garlic and bread and butter. Mr. Balcom, a promising young architect, designs it on the back of his Vitruvius,[7] with hard pencil and ruler, and the job is let out to Dobson & Sons, stonecutters. When the thirty centuries begin to look down on it, mankind begin to look up at it. As for your high towers and monuments, there was a crazy fellow once in this town who undertook to dig through to China, and he got so far that, as he said, he heard the Chinese pots and kettles rattle; but I think that I shall not go out of my way to admire the hole which he made. Many are concerned about the monuments of the West and the East,—to know who built them. For my part, I should like to know who in those days did not build them,—who were above such trifling. But to proceed with my statistics.

By surveying, carpentry, and day-labor of various other kinds in the village in the mean while, for I have as many trades as fingers, I had earned $13 34. The expense of food for eight months, namely, from July 4th to March 1st, the time when these estimates were made, though I lived there more than two years,—not counting potatoes, a little green corn, and some peas, which I had raised, nor considering the value of what was on hand at the last date, was

Rice,	01 73½	
Molasses,	1 73	Cheapest form of the saccharine.
Rye meal,	1 04¾	
Indian meal,	0 99¾	Cheaper than rye.
Pork,	0 22	
Flour,	0 88 }	Costs more than Indian meal, both money and trouble.
Sugar,	0 80	
Lard,	0 65	
Apples,	0 25	
Dried apple,	0 22	
Sweet potatoes,	0 10	
One pumpkin,	0 6	
One watermelon,	0 2	
Salt,	0 3	

All experiments which failed.

Yes, I did eat $8 74, all told; but I should not thus unblushingly publish my guilt, if I did not know that most of my readers were equally guilty with myself, and that their deeds would look no better in print. The next year I sometimes caught a mess of fish for my dinner, and once I went so far as to slaughter a woodchuck which ravaged my bean-field,—effect his transmigration, as a Tartar[8] would say,—and devour him, partly for experiment's sake; but though it afforded me a momentary enjoyment, notwithstanding a musky flavor, I saw that the longest use would not make that a good practice, however it might seem to have your woodchucks ready dressed by the village butcher.

7. Vitruvius Pollio (c. 80–c. 15 B.C.E.), Roman architect during the reigns of Julius Caesar and Augustus, author of De Architectura.
8. An inhabitant of Tartary, a broad area of Central Asia, and believer in a form of reincarnation called the transmigration of souls (or metempsychosis).

Clothing and some incidental expenses within the same dates, though little can be inferred from this item, amounted to

$8 40¾

Oil and some household utensils, $2 00

So that all the pecuniary outgoes, excepting for washing and mending, which for the most part were done out of the house, and their bills have not yet been received,—and these are all and more than all the ways by which money necessarily goes out in this part of the world,—were

House,	$28	12½
Farm one year,	14	72½
Food eight months,	8	74
Clothing, &c., eight months,	8	40¾
Oil, &c., eight months,	2	00
In all,	61	99¾

I address myself now to those of my readers who have a living to get. And to meet this I have for farm produce sold

	$23	44
Earned by day-labor,	13	34
In all,	$36	78,

which subtracted from the sum of the outgoes leaves a balance of $25 21¾ on the one side,—this being very nearly the means with which I started, and the measure of expenses to be incurred,—and on the other, beside the leisure and independence and health thus secured, a comfortable house for me as long as I choose to occupy it.

These statistics, however accidental and therefore uninstructive they may appear, as they have a certain completeness, have a certain value also. Nothing was given me of which I have not rendered some account. It appears from the above estimate, that my food alone cost me in money about twenty-seven cents[9] a week. It was, for nearly two years after this, rye and Indian meal without yeast, potatoes, rice, a very little salt pork, molasses, and salt, and my drink water. It was fit that I should live on rice, mainly, who loved so well the philosophy of India. To meet the objections of some inveterate cavillers, I may as well state, that if I dined out occasionally, as I always had done, and I trust shall have opportunities to do again, it was frequently to the detriment of my domestic arrangements. But the dining out, being, as I have stated, a constant element, does not in the least affect a comparative statement like this.

I learned from my two years' experience that it would cost incredibly little trouble to obtain one's necessary food, even in this latitude; that a man may use as simple a diet as the animals, and yet retain health and strength. I have made a satisfactory dinner, satisfactory on several accounts, simply off a dish of purslane[1] (*Portulaca oleracea*) which I gathered in my corn-field, boiled and salted. I give the Latin on account of the savoriness of the

9. Approximately five dollars in today's currency. 1. A type of greens.

trivial name. And pray what more can a reasonable man desire, in peaceful times, in ordinary noons, than a sufficient number of ears of green sweet-corn boiled, with the addition of salt? Even the little variety which I used was a yielding to the demands of appetite, and not of health. Yet men have come to such a pass that they frequently starve, not for want of necessaries, but for want of luxuries; and I know a good woman who thinks that her son lost his life because he took to drinking water only.

The reader will perceive that I am treating the subject rather from an economic than a dietetic point of view, and he will not venture to put my abstemiousness to the test unless he has a well-stocked larder.

Bread I at first made of pure Indian meal and salt, genuine hoe-cakes, which I baked before my fire out of doors on a shingle or the end of a stick of timber sawed off in building my house; but it was wont to get smoked and to have a piny flavor. I tried flour also; but have at last found a mixture of rye and Indian meal most convenient and agreeable. In cold weather it was no little amusement to bake several small loaves of this in succession, tending and turning them as carefully as an Egyptian his hatching eggs.[2] They were a real cereal fruit which I ripened, and they had to my senses a fragrance like that of other noble fruits, which I kept in as long as possible by wrapping them in cloths. I made a study of the ancient and indispensable art of bread-making, consulting such authorities as offered, going back to the primitive days and first invention of the unleavened kind, when from the wildness of nuts and meats men first reached the mildness and refinement of this diet, and travelling gradually down in my studies through that accidental souring of the dough which, it is supposed, taught the leavening process, and through the various fermentations thereafter, till I came to "good, sweet, wholesome bread," the staff of life. Leaven, which some deem the soul of bread, the *spiritus* which fills its cellular tissue, which is religiously preserved like the vestal fire,—some precious bottle-full, I suppose, first brought over in the May-flower, did the business for America, and its influence is still rising, swelling, spreading, in cerealian billows over the land,—this seed I regularly and faithfully procured from the village, till at length one morning I forgot the rules, and scalded my yeast; by which accident I discovered that even this was not indispensable,—for my discoveries were not by the synthetic but analytic process,—and I have gladly omitted it since, though most housewives earnestly assured me that safe and wholesome bread without yeast might not be, and elderly people prophesied a speedy decay of the vital forces. Yet I find it not to be an essential ingredient, and after going without it for a year am still in the land of the living; and I am glad to escape the trivialness of carrying a bottle-full in my pocket, which would sometimes pop and discharge its contents to my discomfiture. It is simpler and more respectable to omit it. Man is an animal who more than any other can adapt himself to all climates and circumstances. Neither did I put any sal soda, or other acid or alkali, into my bread. It would seem that I made it according to the recipe which Marcus Porcius Cato gave about two centuries before Christ. "Panem depsticium sic facito. Manus mortariumque bene lavato. Farinam in mortarium indito, aquæ paulatim addito, subigitoque pulchre. Ubi bene subegeris, defingito, coquitoque sub testu."[3] Which I take to mean—"Make kneaded bread thus.

---

2. Egyptians had devised incubators.
3. From *De Agri Cultura*, by the Roman political leader Cato (234–149 B.C.E.), who celebrated the simplicity of country life.

Wash your hands and trough well. Put the meal into the trough, add water gradually, and knead it thoroughly. When you have kneaded it well, mould it, and bake it under a cover," that is, in a baking-kettle. Not a word about leaven. But I did not always use this staff of life. At one time, owing to the emptiness of my purse, I saw none of it for more than a month.

Every New Englander might easily raise all his own breadstuffs in this land of rye and Indian corn, and not depend on distant and fluctuating markets for them. Yet so far are we from simplicity and independence that, in Concord, fresh and sweet meal is rarely sold in the shops, and hominy and corn in a still coarser form are hardly used by any. For the most part the farmer gives to his cattle and hogs the grain of his own producing, and buys flour, which is at least no more wholesome, at a greater cost, at the store. I saw that I could easily raise my bushel or two of rye and Indian corn, for the former will grow on the poorest land, and the latter does not require the best, and grind them in a hand-mill, and so do without rice and pork; and if I must have some concentrated sweet, I found by experiment that I could make a very good molasses either of pumpkins or beets, and I knew that I needed only to set out a few maples to obtain it more easily still, and while these were growing I could use various substitutes beside those which I have named, "For," as the Forefathers sang,—

> "we can make liquor to sweeten our lips
> Of pumpkins and parsnips and walnut-tree chips."[4]

Finally, as for salt, that grossest of groceries, to obtain this might be a fit occasion for a visit to the seashore, or, if I did without it altogether, I should probably drink the less water. I do not learn that the Indians ever troubled themselves to go after it.

Thus I could avoid all trade and barter, so far as my food was concerned, and having a shelter already, it would only remain to get clothing and fuel. The pantaloons which I now wear were woven in a farmer's family,—thank Heaven there is so much virtue still in man; for I think the fall from the farmer to the operative as great and memorable as that from the man to the farmer;—and in a new country fuel is an encumbrance. As for a habitat, if I were not permitted still to squat, I might purchase one acre at the same price for which the land I cultivated was sold—namely, eight dollars and eight cents. But as it was, I considered that I enhanced the value of the land by squatting on it.

There is a certain class of unbelievers who sometimes ask me such questions as, if I think that I can live on vegetable food alone; and to strike at the root of the matter at once,—for the root is faith,—I am accustomed to answer such, that I can live on board nails. If they cannot understand that, they cannot understand much that I have to say. For my part, I am glad to hear of experiments of this kind being tried; as that a young man tried for a fortnight to live on hard raw corn on the ear, using his teeth for all mortar. The squirrel tribe tried the same and succeeded. The human race is interested in these experiments, though a few old women who are incapacitated for them, or who own their thirds in mills, may be alarmed.

My furniture, part of which I made myself, and the rest cost me nothing of which I have not rendered an account, consisted of a bed, a table, a desk,

---

4. From the American historian and engraver John Warner Barber's (1798–1885) *Historical Collections of Massachusetts* (1839).

three chairs, a looking-glass three inches in diameter, a pair of tongs and andirons, a kettle, a skillet, and a frying-pan, a dipper, a wash-bowl, two knives and forks, three plates, one cup, one spoon, a jug for oil, a jug for molasses, and a japanned[5] lamp. None is so poor that he need sit on a pumpkin. That is shiftlessness. There is a plenty of such chairs as I like best in the village garrets to be had for taking them away. Furniture! Thank God, I can sit and I can stand without the aid of a furniture warehouse. What man but a philosopher would not be ashamed to see his furniture packed in a cart and going up country exposed to the light of heaven and the eyes of men, a beggarly account of empty boxes? That is Spaulding's furniture.[6] I could never tell from inspecting such a load whether it belonged to a so called rich man or a poor one; the owner always seemed poverty-stricken. Indeed, the more you have of such things the poorer you are. Each load looks as if it contained the contents of a dozen shanties; and if one shanty is poor, this is a dozen times as poor. Pray, for what do we *move* ever but to get rid of our furniture, our *exuviæ*;[7] at last to go from this world to another newly furnished, and leave this to be burned? It is the same as if all these traps were buckled to a man's belt, and he could not move over the rough country where our lines are cast without dragging them,—dragging his trap. He was a lucky fox that left his tail in the trap. The muskrat will gnaw his third leg off to be free. No wonder man has lost his elasticity. How often he is at a dead set! "Sir, if I may be so bold, what do you mean by a dead set?" If you are a seer, whenever you meet a man you will see all that he owns, ay, and much that he pretends to disown, behind him, even to his kitchen furniture and all the trumpery which he saves and will not burn, and he will appear to be harnessed to it and making what headway he can. I think that the man is at a dead set who has got through a knot hole or gateway where his sledge load of furniture cannot follow him. I cannot but feel compassion when I hear some trig, compact-looking man, seemingly free, all girded and ready, speak of his "furniture," as whether it is insured or not. "But what shall I do with my furniture?" My gay butterfly is entangled in a spider's web then. Even those who seem for a long while not to have any, if you inquire more narrowly you will find have some stored in somebody's barn. I look upon England to-day as an old gentleman who is travelling with a great deal of baggage, trumpery which has accumulated from long housekeeping, which he has not the courage to burn; great trunk, little trunk, bandbox and bundle. Throw away the first three at least. It would surpass the powers of a well man nowadays to take up his bed and walk, and I should certainly advise a sick one to lay down his bed and run. When I have met an immigrant tottering under a bundle which contained his all,—looking like an enormous wen which had grown out of the nape of his neck,—I have pitied him, not because that was his all, but because he had all *that* to carry. If I have got to drag my trap, I will take care that it be a light one and do not nip me in a vital part. But perchance it would be wisest never to put one's paw into it.

I would observe, by the way, that it costs me nothing for curtains, for I have no gazers to shut out but the sun and moon, and I am willing that they should look in. The moon will not sour milk nor taint meat of mine, nor will the sun injure my furniture or fade my carpet, and if he is sometimes too warm a friend, I find it still better economy to retreat behind some curtain

---

5. Lacquered with decorative scenes in the Japanese manner.

6. Unidentified.

7. Discarded objects (Latin).

which nature has provided, than to add a single item to the details of housekeeping. A lady once offered me a mat, but as I had no room to spare within the house, nor time to spare within or without to shake it, I declined it, preferring to wipe my feet on the sod before my door. It is best to avoid the beginnings of evil.

Not long since I was present at the auction of a deacon's effects, for his life had not been ineffectual:—

"The evil that men do lives after them."[8]

As usual, a great proportion was trumpery which had begun to accumulate in his father's day. Among the rest was a dried tapeworm. And now, after lying half a century in his garret and other dust holes, these things were not burned; instead of a *bonfire*, or purifying destruction of them, there was an *auction*, or increasing of them.[9] The neighbors eagerly collected to view them, bought them all, and carefully transported them to their garrets and dust holes, to lie there till their estates are settled, when they will start again. When a man dies he kicks the dust.

The customs of some savage nations might, perchance, be profitably imitated by us, for they at least go through the semblance of casting their slough annually; they have the idea of the thing, whether they have the reality or not. Would it not be well if we were to celebrate such a "busk," or "feast of first fruits," as Bartram[1] describes to have been the custom of the Mucclasse Indians? "When a town celebrates the busk," says he, "having previously provided themselves with new clothes, new pots, pans, and other household utensils and furniture, they collect all their worn out clothes and other despicable things, sweep and cleanse their houses, squares, and the whole town, of their filth, which with all the remaining grain and other old provisions they cast together into one common heap, and consume it with fire. After having taken medicine, and fasted for three days, all the fire in the town is extinguished. During this fast they abstain from the gratification of every appetite and passion whatever. A general amnesty is proclaimed; all malefactors may return to their town.—"

"On the fourth morning, the high priest, by rubbing dry wood together, produces new fire in the public square, from whence every habitation in the town is supplied with the new and pure flame."

They then feast on the new corn and fruits and dance and sing for three days, "and the four following days they receive visits and rejoice with their friends from neighboring towns who have in like manner purified and prepared themselves."

The Mexicans also practised a similar purification at the end of every fifty-two years, in the belief that it was time for the world to come to an end.

I have scarcely heard of a truer sacrament, that is, as the dictionary defines it, "outward and visible sign of an inward and spiritual grace," than this, and I have no doubt that they were originally inspired directly from Heaven to do thus, though they have no biblical record of the revelation.

For more than five years I maintained myself thus solely by the labor of my hands, and I found, that by working about six weeks in a year, I could meet

---

8. From Antony's speech to the citizens, in Shakespeare's *Julius Caesar* 3.2.
9. Thoreau puns on the Latin root of *auction*, which means "to increase."
1. William Bartram (1739–1832), *Travels through North and South Carolina* (1791).

all the expenses of living. The whole of my winters, as well as most of my summers, I had free and clear for study. I have thoroughly tried school-keeping, and found that my expenses were in proportion, or rather out of proportion, to my income, for I was obliged to dress and train, not to say think and believe, accordingly, and I lost my time into the bargain. As I did not teach for the good of my fellow-men, but simply for a livelihood, this was a failure. I have tried trade; but I found that it would take ten years to get under way in that, and that then I should probably be on my way to the devil. I was actually afraid that I might by that time be doing what is called a good business. When formerly I was looking about to see what I could do for a living, some sad experience in conforming to the wishes of friends being fresh in my mind to tax my ingenuity, I thought often and seriously of picking huckleberries; that surely I could do, and its small profits might suffice,—for my greatest skill has been to want but little,—so little capital it required, so little distraction from my wonted moods, I foolishly thought. While my acquaintances went unhesitatingly into trade or the professions, I contemplated this occupation as most like theirs; ranging the hills all sum-mer to pick the berries which came in my way, and thereafter carelessly dispose of them; so, to keep the flocks of Admetus.[2] I also dreamed that I might gather the wild herbs, or carry evergreens to such villagers as loved to be reminded of the woods, even to the city, by hay-cart loads. But I have since learned that trade curses every thing it handles; and though you trade in messages from heaven, the whole curse of trade attaches to the business.

As I preferred some things to others, and especially valued my freedom, as I could fare hard and yet succeed well, I did not wish to spend my time in earning rich carpets or other fine furniture, or delicate cookery, or a house in the Grecian or the Gothic style just yet. If there are any to whom it is no interruption to acquire these things, and who know how to use them when acquired, I relinquish to them the pursuit. Some are "industrious," and appear to love labor for its own sake, or perhaps because it keeps them out of worse mischief; to such I have at present nothing to say. Those who would not know what to do with more leisure than they now enjoy, I might advise to work twice as hard as they do,—work till they pay for themselves, and get their free papers. For myself I found that the occupation of a day-laborer was the most independent of any, especially as it required only thirty or forty days in a year to support one. The laborer's day ends with the going down of the sun, and he is then free to devote himself to his chosen pursuit, independent of his labor; but his employer, who speculates from month to month, has no respite from one end of the year to the other.

In short, I am convinced, both by faith and experience, that to maintain one's self on this earth is not a hardship but a pastime, if we will live simply and wisely; as the pursuits of the simpler nations are still the sports of the more artificial. It is not necessary that a man should earn his living by the sweat of his brow, unless he sweats easier than I do.

One young man of my acquaintance, who has inherited some acres, told me that he thought he should live as I did, *if he had the means.* I would not have any one adopt *my* mode of living on any account; for, beside that before he has fairly learned it I may have found out another for myself, I desire that there may be as many different persons in the world as possible;

---

2. Apollo, Greek god of poetry, tended the flocks of Admetus while banished from Olympus.

but I would have each one be very careful to find out and pursue *his own* way, and not his father's or his mother's or his neighbor's instead. The youth may build or plant or sail, only let him not be hindered from doing that which he tells me he would like to do. It is by a mathematical point only that we are wise, as the sailor or the fugitive slave keeps the polestar in his eye; but that is sufficient guidance for all our life. We may not arrive at our port within a calculable period, but we would preserve the true course.

Undoubtedly, in this case, what is true for one is truer still for a thousand, as a large house is not more expensive than a small one in proportion to its size, since one roof may cover, one cellar underlie, and one wall separate several apartments. But for my part, I preferred the solitary dwelling. Moreover, it will commonly be cheaper to build the whole yourself than to convince another of the advantage of the common wall; and when you have done this, the common partition, to be much cheaper, must be a thin one, and that other may prove a bad neighbor, and also not keep his side in repair. The only coöperation which is commonly possible is exceedingly partial and superficial; and what little true coöperation there is, is as if it were not, being a harmony inaudible to men. If a man has faith he will coöperate with equal faith every where; if he has not faith, he will continue to live like the rest of the world, whatever company he is joined to. To coöperate, in the highest as well as the lowest sense, means *to get our living together*. I heard it proposed lately that two young men should travel together over the world, the one without money, earning his means as he went, before the mast and behind the plough, the other carrying a bill of exchange in his pocket. It was easy to see that they could not long be companions or coöperate, since one would not *operate* at all. They would part at the first interesting crisis in their adventures. Above all, as I have implied, the man who goes alone can start today; but he who travels with another must wait till that other is ready, and it may be a long time before they get off.

But all this is very selfish, I have heard some of my townsmen say. I confess that I have hitherto indulged very little in philanthropic enterprises. I have made some sacrifices to a sense of duty, and among others have sacrificed this pleasure also. There are those who have used all their arts to persuade me to undertake the support of some poor family in the town; and if I had nothing to do,—for the devil finds employment for the idle,—I might try my hand at some such pastime as that. However, when I have thought to indulge myself in this respect, and lay their Heaven under an obligation by maintaining certain poor persons in all respects as comfortably as I maintain myself, and have even ventured so far as to make them the offer, they have one and all unhesitatingly preferred to remain poor. While my townsmen and women are devoted in so many ways to the good of their fellows, I trust that one at least may be spared to other and less humane pursuits. You must have a genius for charity as well as for any thing else. As for Doing-good, that is one of the professions which are full. Moreover, I have tried it fairly, and, strange as it may seem, am satisfied that it does not agree with my constitution. Probably I should not consciously and deliberately forsake my particular calling to do the good which society demands of me, to save the universe from annihilation; and I believe that a like but infinitely greater steadfastness elsewhere is all that now preserves it. But I would not stand between any man and his genius; and to him who does this work, which I decline, with his whole heart and soul and life, I would say, Persevere, even if the world call it doing evil, as it is most likely they will.

I am far from supposing that my case is a peculiar one; no doubt many of my readers would make a similar defence. At doing something,—I will not engage that my neighbors shall pronounce it good,—I do not hesitate to say that I should be a capital fellow to hire; but what that is, it is for my employer to find out. What *good* I do, in the common sense of that word, must be aside from my main path, and for the most part wholly unintended. Men say, practically, Begin where you are and such as you are, without aiming mainly to become of more worth, and with kindness aforethought go about doing good. If I were to preach at all in this strain, I should say rather, Set about being good. As if the sun should stop when he had kindled his fires up to the splendor of a moon or a star of the sixth magnitude, and go about like a Robin Goodfellow,[3] peeping in at every cottage window, inspiring lunatics, and tainting meats, and making darkness visible, instead of steadily increasing his genial heat and beneficence till he is of such brightness that no mortal can look him in the face, and then, and in the mean while too, going about the world in his own orbit, doing it good, or rather, as a truer philosophy has discovered, the world going about him getting good. When Phaeton,[4] wishing to prove his heavenly birth by his beneficence, had the sun's chariot but one day, and drove out of the beaten track, he burned several blocks of houses in the lower streets of heaven, and scorched the surface of the earth, and dried up every spring, and made the great desert of Sahara, till at length Jupiter hurled him headlong to the earth with a thunderbolt, and the sun, through grief at his death, did not shine for a year.

There is no odor so bad as that which arises from goodness tainted. It is human, it is divine, carrion. If I knew for a certainty that a man was coming to my house with the conscious design of doing me good, I should run for my life, as from that dry and parching wind of the African deserts called the simoom, which fills the mouth and nose and ears and eyes with dust till you are suffocated, for fear that I should get some of his good done to me,—some of its virus mingled with my blood. No,—in this case I would rather suffer evil the natural way. A man is not a good *man* to me because he will feed me if I should be starving, or warm me if I should be freezing, or pull me out of a ditch if I should ever fall into one. I can find you a Newfoundland dog that will do as much. Philanthropy is not love for one's fellow-man in the broadest sense. Howard[5] was no doubt an exceedingly kind and worthy man in his way, and has his reward; but, comparatively speaking, what are a hundred Howards to *us*, if their philanthropy do not help *us* in our best estate, when we are most worthy to be helped? I never heard of a philanthropic meeting in which it was sincerely proposed to do any good to me, or the like of me.

The Jesuits[6] were quite balked by those Indians who, being burned at the stake, suggested new modes of torture to their tormentors. Being superior to physical suffering, it sometimes chanced that they were superior to any consolation which the missionaries could offer; and the law to do as you would be done by fell with less persuasiveness on the ears of those, who, for

3. Mischievous sprite, known as Puck in Shakespeare's *A Midsummer Night's Dream*.
4. In Greek mythology, the son of Helios. He attempted to drive his father's chariot, the sun.
5. John Howard (1726?–1790), English prison reformer.
6. Roman Catholic missionaries of the Society of Jesus who attempted to convert the Indians to Christianity.

their part, did not care how they were done by, who loved their enemies after a new fashion, and came very near freely forgiving them all they did.

Be sure that you give the poor the aid they most need, though it be your example which leaves them far behind. If you give money, spend yourself with it, and do not merely abandon it to them. We make curious mistakes sometimes. Often the poor man is not so cold and hungry as he is dirty and ragged and gross. It is partly his taste, and not merely his misfortune. If you give him money, he will perhaps buy more rags with it. I was wont to pity the clumsy Irish laborers who cut ice on the pond, in such mean and ragged clothes, while I shivered in my more tidy and somewhat more fashionable garments, till, one bitter cold day, one who had slipped into the water came to my house to warm him, and I saw him strip off three pairs of pants and two pairs of stockings ere he got down to the skin, though they were dirty and ragged enough, it is true, and that he could afford to refuse the *extra* garments which I offered him, he had so many *intra* ones. This ducking was the very thing he needed. Then I began to pity myself, and I saw that it would be a greater charity to bestow on me a flannel shirt than a whole slop-shop on him. There are a thousand hacking at the branches of evil to one who is striking at the root, and it may be that he who bestows the largest amount of time and money on the needy is doing the most by his mode of life to produce that misery which he strives in vain to relieve. It is the pious slave-breeder devoting the proceeds of every tenth slave to buy a Sunday's liberty for the rest. Some show their kindness to the poor by employing them in their kitchens. Would they not be kinder if they employed themselves there? You boast of spending a tenth part of your income in charity; may be you should spend the nine tenths so, and done with it. Society recovers only a tenth part of the property then. Is this owing to the generosity of him in whose possession it is found, or to the remissness of the officers of justice?

Philanthropy is almost the only virtue which is sufficiently appreciated by mankind. Nay, it is greatly overrated; and it is our selfishness which overrates it. A robust poor man, one sunny day here in Concord, praised a fellow-townsman to me, because, as he said, he was kind to the poor; meaning himself. The kind uncles and aunts of the race are more esteemed than its true spiritual fathers and mothers. I once heard a reverend lecturer on England, a man of learning and intelligence, after enumerating her scientific, literary, and political worthies, Shakspeare, Bacon, Cromwell, Milton, Newton, and others, speak next of her Christian heroes, whom, as if his profession required it of him, he elevated to a place far above all the rest, as the greatest of the great. They were Penn, Howard, and Mrs. Fry.[7] Every one must feel the falsehood and cant of this. The last were not England's best men and women; only, perhaps, her best philanthropists.

I would not subtract any thing from the praise that is due to philanthropy, but merely demand justice for all who by their lives and works are a blessing to mankind. I do not value chiefly a man's uprightness and benevolence, which are, as it were, his stem and leaves. Those plants of whose greenness withered we make herb tea for the sick, serve but a humble use, and are most employed by quacks. I want the flower and fruit of a man; that some fragrance be wafted over from him to me, and some ripeness flavor our intercourse.

7. Elizabeth Fry (1780–1845), English Quaker and prison reformer. William Penn (1644–1718), Quaker leader and proprietor of Pennsylvania.

His goodness must not be a partial and transitory act, but a constant super-fluity, which costs him nothing and of which he is unconscious. This is a charity that hides a multitude of sins. The philanthropist too often surrounds mankind with the remembrance of his own cast-off griefs as an atmosphere, and calls it sympathy. We should impart our courage, and not our despair, our health and ease, and not our disease, and take care that this does not spread by contagion. From what southern plains comes up the voice of wailing? Under what latitudes reside the heathen to whom we would send light? Who is that intemperate and brutal man whom we would redeem? If any thing ail a man, so that he does not perform his functions, if he have a pain in his bowels even,—for that is the seat of sympathy,—he forthwith sets about reforming—the world. Being a microcosm himself, he discovers, and it is a true discovery, and he is the man to make it,—that the world has been eating green apples; to his eyes, in fact, the globe itself is a great green apple, which there is danger awful to think of that the children of men will nibble before it is ripe; and straightway his drastic philanthropy seeks out the Esquimaux and the Patagonian,[8] and embraces the populous Indian and Chinese villages; and thus, by a few years of philanthropic activity, the pow-ers in the mean while using him for their own ends, no doubt, he cures himself of his dyspepsia, the globe acquires a faint blush on one or both of its cheeks, as if it were beginning to be ripe, and life loses its crudity and is once more sweet and wholesome to live. I never dreamed of any enormity greater than I have committed. I never knew, and never shall know, a worse man than myself.

I believe that what so saddens the reformer is not his sympathy with his fellows in distress, but, though he be the holiest son of God, is his private ail. Let this be righted, let the spring come to him, the morning rise over his couch, and he will forsake his generous companions without apology. My excuse for not lecturing against the use of tobacco is, that I never chewed it; that is a penalty which reformed tobacco-chewers have to pay; though there are things enough I have chewed, which I could lecture against. If you should ever be betrayed into any of these philanthropies, do not let your left hand know what your right hand does, for it is not worth knowing. Rescue the drowning and tie your shoe-strings. Take your time, and set about some free labor.

Our manners have been corrupted by communication with the saints. Our hymn-books resound with a melodious cursing of God and enduring him forever. One would say that even the prophets and redeemers had rather con-soled the fears than confirmed the hopes of man. There is nowhere recorded a simple and irrepressible satisfaction with the gift of life, any memorable praise of God. All health and success does me good, however far off and withdrawn it may appear; all disease and failure helps to make me sad and does me evil, however much sympathy it may have with me or I with it. If, then, we would indeed restore mankind by truly Indian, botanic, magnetic, or natural means, let us first be as simple and well as Nature ourselves, dispel the clouds which hang over our own brows, and take up a little life into our pores. Do not stay to be an overseer of the poor, but endeavor to become one of the worthies of the world.

8. Inhabitant of Patagonia, in southernmost South America.

I read in the Gulistan, or Flower Garden, of Sheik Sadi of Shiraz, that "They asked a wise man, saying; Of the many celebrated trees which the Most High God has created lofty and umbrageous, they call none azad, or free, excepting the cypress, which bears no fruit; what mystery is there in this? He replied; Each has its appropriate produce, and appointed season, during the continuance of which it is fresh and blooming, and during their absence dry and withered; to neither of which states is the cypress exposed, being always flourishing; and of this nature are the azads, or religious independents.—Fix not thy heart on that which is transitory; for the Dijlah, or Tigris, will continue to flow through Bagdad after the race of caliphs is extinct: if thy hand has plenty, be liberal as the date tree; but if it affords nothing to give away, be an azad, or free man, like the cypress."[9]

Complemental Verses[1]

THE PRETENSIONS OF POVERTY

"Thou dost presume too much, poor needy wretch,
To claim a station in the firmament,
Because thy humble cottage, or thy tub,
Nurses some lazy or pedantic virtue
In the cheap sunshine or by shady springs,
With roots and pot-herbs; where thy right hand,
Tearing those humane passions from the mind,
Upon whose stocks fair blooming virtues flourish,
Degradeth nature, and benumbeth sense,
And, Gorgon-like, turns active men to stone.[2]
We not require the dull society
Of your necessitated temperance,
Or that unnatural stupidity
That knows nor joy nor sorrow; nor your forc'd
Falsely exalted passive fortitude
Above the active. This low abject brood,
That fix their seats in mediocrity,
Become your servile minds; but we advance
Such virtues only as admit excess,
Brave, bounteous acts, regal magnificence,
All-seeing prudence, magnanimity
That knows no bound, and that heroic virtue
For which antiquity hath left no name,
But patterns only, such as Hercules,
Achilles, Theseus. Back to thy loath'd cell;
And when thou seest the new enlightened sphere,
Study to know but what those worthies were."

—T. CAREW

---

9. Muslih-ud-Din (Saadi) (1184?–1291), *The Gulistan or Rose Garden.*
1. From *Coelum Britannicum* by the English Cavalier poet Thomas Carew (1595?–1645?). The

title is Thoreau's invention.
2. In Greek mythology the Gorgons were three sisters, with snakes for hair and eyes, who turned any beholder into stone.

2. Where I Lived, and What I Lived For

At a certain season of our life we are accustomed to consider every spot as the possible site of a house. I have thus surveyed the country on every side within a dozen miles of where I live. In imagination I have bought all the farms in succession, for all were to be bought and I knew their price. I walked over each farmer's premises, tasted his wild apples, discoursed on husbandry with him, took his farm at his price, at any price, mortgaging it to him in my mind; even put a higher price on it,—took every thing but a deed of it,—took his word for his deed, for I dearly love to talk,—cultivated it, and him too to some extent, I trust, and withdrew when I had enjoyed it long enough, leaving him to carry it on. This experience entitled me to be regarded as a sort of real-estate broker by my friends. Wherever I sat, there I might live, and the landscape radiated from me accordingly. What is a house but a *sedes*, a seat?—better if a country seat. I discovered many a site for a house not likely to be soon improved, which some might have thought too far from the village, but to my eyes the village was too far from it. Well, there I might live, I said; and there I did live, for an hour, a summer and a winter life; saw how I could let the years run off, buffet the winter through, and see the spring come in. The future inhabitants of this region, wherever they may place their houses, may be sure that they have been anticipated. An afternoon sufficed to lay out the land into orchard woodlot and pasture, and to decide what fine oaks or pines should be left to stand before the door, and whence each blasted tree could be seen to the best advantage; and then I let it lie, fallow perchance, for a man is rich in proportion to the number of things which he can afford to let alone.

My imagination carried me so far that I even had the refusal of several farms,—the refusal was all I wanted,—but I never got my fingers burned by actual possession. The nearest that I came to actual possession was when I bought the Hollowell Place, and had begun to sort my seeds, and collected materials with which to make a wheelbarrow to carry it on or off with; but before the owner gave me a deed of it, his wife—every man has such a wife—changed her mind and wished to keep it, and he offered me ten dollars to release him. Now, to speak the truth, I had but ten cents in the world, and it surpassed my arithmetic to tell, if I was that man who had ten cents, or who had a farm, or ten dollars, or all together. However, I let him keep the ten dollars and the farm too, for I had carried it far enough; or rather, to be generous, I sold him the farm for just what I gave for it, and, as he was not a rich man, made him a present of ten dollars, and still had my ten cents, and seeds, and materials for a wheelbarrow left. I found thus that I had been a rich man without any damage to my poverty. But I retained the landscape, and I have since annually carried off what it yielded without a wheelbarrow. With respect to landscapes,—

> "I am monarch of all I *survey*,
> My right there is none to dispute."[3]

I have frequently seen a poet withdraw, having enjoyed the most valuable part of a farm, while the crusty farmer supposed that he had got a few wild

3. William Cowper (1731–1800), "Verses Supposed to Be Written by Alexander Selkirk," with the pun italicized. Selkirk (1676–1721) was Daniel Defoe's model for Robinson Crusoe.

apples only. Why, the owner does not know it for many years when a poet has put his farm in rhyme, the most admirable kind of invisible fence, has fairly impounded it, milked it, skimmed it, and got all the cream, and left the farmer only the skimmed milk.

The real attractions of the Hollowell farm, to me, were; its complete retirement, being about two miles from the village, half a mile from the nearest neighbor, and separated from the highway by a broad field; its bounding on the river, which the owner said protected it by its fogs from frosts in the spring, though that was nothing to me; the gray color and ruinous state of the house and barn, and the dilapidated fences, which put such an interval between me and the last occupant; the hollow and lichen-covered apple trees, gnawed by rabbits, showing what kind of neighbors I should have; but above all, the recollection I had of it from my earliest voyages up the river, when the house was concealed behind a dense grove of red maples, through which I heard the house-dog bark. I was in haste to buy it, before the proprietor finished getting out some rocks, cutting down the hollow apple trees, and grubbing up some young birches which had sprung up in the pasture, or, in short, had made any more of his improvements. To enjoy these advantages I was ready to carry it on; like Atlas,[4] to take the world on my shoulders,—I never heard what compensation he received for that,—and do all those things which had no other motive or excuse but that I might pay for it and be unmolested in my possession of it; for I knew all the while that it would yield the most abundant crop of the kind I wanted if I could only afford to let it alone. But it turned out as I have said.

All that I could say, then, with respect to farming on a large scale, (I have always cultivated a garden,) was, that I had had my seeds ready. Many think that seeds improve with age. I have no doubt that time discriminates between the good and the bad; and when at last I shall plant, I shall be less likely to be disappointed. But I would say to my fellows, once for all, As long as possible live free and uncommitted. It makes but little difference whether you are committed to a farm or the county jail.

Old Cato, whose "De Re Rusticâ" is my "Cultivator," says, and the only translation I have seen makes sheer nonsense of the passage, "When you think of getting a farm, turn it thus in your mind, not to buy greedily; nor spare your pains to look at it, and do not think it enough to go round it once. The oftener you go there the more it will please you, if it is good."[5] I think I shall not buy greedily, but go round and round it as long as I live, and be buried in it first, that it may please me the more at last.

The present was my next experiment of this kind, which I purpose to describe more at length; for convenience, putting the experience of two years into one. As I have said, I do not propose to write an ode to dejection, but to brag as lustily as chanticleer in the morning, standing on his roost, if only to wake my neighbors up.

When first I took up my abode in the woods, that is, began to spend my nights as well as days there, which, by accident, was on Independence Day, or the fourth of July, 1845, my house was not finished for winter, but was merely a defence against the rain, without plastering or chimney, the walls being of

---

4. A Titan whom Zeus forced to stand on the earth supporting the heavens as punishment for warring against the Olympian gods.
5. Cato's *De Agri Cultura* 1.1.

rough weather-stained boards, with wide chinks, which made it cool at night. The upright white hewn studs and freshly planed door and window casings gave it a clean and airy look, especially in the morning, when its timbers were saturated with dew, so that I fancied that by noon some sweet gum would exude from them. To my imagination it retained throughout the day more or less of this auroral character, reminding me of a certain house on a mountain which I had visited the year before. This was an airy and unplastered cabin, fit to entertain a travelling god, and where a goddess might trail her garments. The winds which passed over my dwelling were such as sweep over the ridges of mountains, bearing the broken strains, or celestial parts only, of terrestrial music. The morning wind forever blows, the poem of creation is uninterrupted; but few are the ears that hear it. Olympus[6] is but the outside of the earth every where.

The only house I had been the owner of before, if I except a boat, was a tent, which I used occasionally when making excursions in the summer, and this is still rolled up in my garret; but the boat, after passing from hand to hand, has gone down the stream of time. With this more substantial shelter about me, I had made some progress toward settling in the world. This frame, so slightly clad, was a sort of crystallization around me, and reacted on the builder. It was suggestive somewhat as a picture in outlines. I did not need to go out doors to take the air, for the atmosphere within had lost none of its freshness. It was not so much within doors as behind a door where I sat, even in the rainiest weather. The Harivansa[7] says, "An abode without birds is like a meat without seasoning." Such was not my abode, for I found myself suddenly neighbor to the birds; not by having imprisoned one, but having caged myself near them. I was not only nearer to some of those which commonly frequent the garden and the orchard, but to those wilder and more thrilling songsters of the forest which never, or rarely, serenade a villager,—the wood-thrush, the veery, the scarlet tanager, the field-sparrow, the whippoorwill, and many others.

I was seated by the shore of a small pond, about a mile and a half south of the village of Concord and somewhat higher than it, in the midst of an extensive wood between that town and Lincoln, and about two miles south of that our only field known to fame, Concord Battle Ground;[8] but I was so low in the woods that the opposite shore, half a mile off, like the rest, covered with wood, was my most distant horizon. For the first week, whenever I looked out on the pond it impressed me like a tarn[9] high up on the side of a mountain, its bottom far above the surface of other lakes, and, as the sun arose, I saw it throwing off its nightly clothing of mist, and here and there, by degrees, its soft ripples or its smooth reflecting surface was revealed, while the mists, like ghosts, were stealthily withdrawing in every direction into the woods, as at the breaking up of some nocturnal conventicle. The very dew seemed to hang upon the trees later into the day than usual, as on the sides of mountains.

This small lake was of most value as a neighbor in the intervals of a gentle rain storm in August, when, both air and water being perfectly still, but the sky overcast, mid-afternoon had all the serenity of evening, and the

6. In Greek mythology, home of the gods.
7. A Hindu epic poem.
8. The site of battle on the first day of the American Revolution, April 19, 1775.
9. A small lake.

wood-thrush sang around, and was heard from shore to shore. A lake like this is never smoother than at such a time; and the clear portion of the air above it being shallow and darkened by clouds, the water, full of light and reflections, becomes a lower heaven itself so much the more important. From a hill top near by, where the wood had been recently cut off, there was a pleasing vista southward across the pond, through a wide indentation in the hills which form the shore there, where their opposite sides sloping toward each other suggested a stream flowing out in that direction through a wooded valley, but stream there was none. That way I looked between and over the near green hills to some distant and higher ones in the horizon, tinged with blue. Indeed, by standing on tiptoe I could catch a glimpse of some of the peaks of the still bluer and more distant mountain ranges in the north-west, those true-blue coins from heaven's own mint, and also of some portion of the village. But in other directions, even from this point, I could not see over or beyond the woods which surrounded me. It is well to have some water in your neighborhood, to give buoyancy to and float the earth. One value even of the smallest well is, that when you look into it you see that earth is not continent but insular. This is as important as that it keeps butter cool. When I looked across the pond from this peak toward the Sudbury meadows, which in time of flood I distinguished elevated perhaps by a mirage in their seething valley, like a coin in a basin, all the earth beyond the pond appeared like a thin crust insulated and floated even by this small sheet of intervening water, and I was reminded that this on which I dwelt was but *dry land*.

Though the view from my door was still more contracted, I did not feel crowded or confined in the least. There was pasture enough for my imagination. The low shrub-oak plateau to which the opposite shore arose, stretched away toward the prairies of the West and the steppes of Tartary,[1] affording ample room for all the roving families of men. "There are none happy in the world but beings who enjoy freely a vast horizon,"—said Damodara,[2] when his herds required new and larger pastures.

Both place and time were changed, and I dwelt nearer to those parts of the universe and to those eras in history which had most attracted me. Where I lived was as far off as many a region viewed nightly by astronomers. We are wont to imagine rare and delectable places in some remote and more celestial corner of the system, behind the constellation of Cassiopeia's Chair, far from noise and disturbance. I discovered that my house actually had its site in such a withdrawn, but forever new and unprofaned, part of the universe. If it were worth the while to settle in those parts near to the Pleiades or the Hyades, to Aldebaran or Altair,[3] then I was really there, or at an equal remoteness from the life which I had left behind, dwindled and twinkling with as fine a ray to my nearest neighbor, and to be seen only in moonless nights by him. Such was that part of creation where I had squatted;—

> "There was a shepherd that did live,
>   And held his thoughts as high
> As were the mounts whereon his flocks
>   Did hourly feed him by."[4]

1. Grasslands and plains of Asiatic Russia.
2. Another name for Krishna, the eighth avatar of Vishnu in Hindu mythology; Thoreau translates from a French edition of *Harivansa*.
3. A star in the constellation Aquila. The Pleiades and the Hyades are constellations. Aldeba-
ran, in the constellation Taurus, is one of the brightest stars.
4. Anonymous Jacobean verse set to music in *The Muses Garden* (1611) and probably found by Thoreau in Thomas Evans's *Old Ballads* (1810).

What should we think of the shepherd's life if his flocks always wandered to higher pastures than his thoughts?

Every morning was a cheerful invitation to make my life of equal simplicity, and I may say innocence, with Nature herself. I have been as sincere a worshipper of Aurora as the Greeks. I got up early and bathed in the pond; that was a religious exercise, and one of the best things which I did. They say that characters were engraven on the bathing tub of king Tching-thang to this effect: "Renew thyself completely each day; do it again, and again, and forever again."[5] I can understand that. Morning brings back the heroic ages. I was as much affected by the faint hum of a mosquito making its invisible and unimaginable tour through my apartment at earliest dawn, when I was sitting with door and windows open, as I could be by any trumpet that ever sang of fame. It was Homer's requiem; itself an Iliad and Odyssey in the air, singing its own wrath and wanderings. There was something cosmical about it; a standing advertisement, till forbidden,[6] of the everlasting vigor and fertility of the world. The morning, which is the most memorable season of the day, is the awakening hour. Then there is least somnolence in us; and for an hour, at least, some part of us awakes which slumbers all the rest of the day and night. Little is to be expected of that day, if it can be called a day, to which we are not awakened by our Genius,[7] but by the mechanical nudgings of some servitor, are not awakened by our own newly-acquired force and aspirations from within, accompanied by the undulations of celestial music, instead of factory bells, and a fragrance filling the air—to a higher life than we fell asleep from; and thus the darkness bear its fruit, and prove itself to be good, no less than the light. That man who does not believe that each day contains an earlier, more sacred, and auroral hour than he has yet profaned, has despaired of life, and is pursuing a descending and darkening way. After a partial cessation of his sensuous life, the soul of man, or its organs rather, are reinvigorated each day, and his Genius tries again what noble life it can make. All memorable events, I should say, transpire in morning time and in a morning atmosphere. The Vedas[3] say, "All intelligences awake with the morning." Poetry and art, and the fairest and most memorable of the actions of men, date from such an hour. All poets and heroes, like Memnon, are the children of Aurora, and emit their music at sunrise.[9] To him whose elastic and vigorous thought keeps pace with the sun, the day is a perpetual morning. It matters not what the clocks say or the attitudes and labors of men. Morning is when I am awake and there is a dawn in me. Moral reform is the effort to throw off sleep. Why is it that men give so poor an account of their day if they have not been slumbering? They are not such poor calculators. If they had not been overcome with drowsiness they would have performed something. The millions are awake enough for physical labor; but only one in a million is awake enough for effective intellectual exertion, only one in a hundred millions to a poetic or divine life. To be awake is to be alive. I have never yet met a man who was quite awake. How could I have looked him in the face?

We must learn to reawaken and keep ourselves awake, not by mechanical aids, but by an infinite expectation of the dawn, which does not forsake us in our soundest sleep. I know of no more encouraging fact than the

5. Confucius, *The Great Learning*, ch. 1.
6. In newspaper advertisements "TF" signaled to the compositor that an item was to be repeated daily "till forbidden."
7. Personification of the intellect's insights and perceptions.
8. The Vedas are Hindu scriptures; the quotation has not been located.
9. See p. 877, n. 3.

unquestionable ability of man to elevate his life by a conscious endeavor. It is something to be able to paint a particular picture, or to carve a statue, and so to make a few objects beautiful; but it is far more glorious to carve and paint the very atmosphere and medium through which we look, which morally we can do. To affect the quality of the day, that is the highest of arts. Every man is tasked to make his life, even in its details, worthy of the contemplation of his most elevated and critical hour. If we refused, or rather used up, such paltry information as we get, the oracles would distinctly inform us how this might be done.

I went to the woods because I wished to live deliberately, to front only the essential facts of life, and see if I could not learn what it had to teach, and not, when I came to die, discover that I had not lived. I did not wish to live what was not life, living is so dear; nor did I wish to practise resignation, unless it was quite necessary. I wanted to live deep and suck out all the marrow of life, to live so sturdily and Spartan[1]-like as to put to rout all that was not life, to cut a broad swath and shave close, to drive life into a corner, and reduce it to its lowest terms, and, if it proved to be mean, why then to get the whole and genuine meanness of it, and publish its meanness to the world; or if it were sublime, to know it by experience, and be able to give a true account of it in my next excursion. For most men, it appears to me, are in a strange uncertainty about it, whether it is of the devil or of God, and have *somewhat hastily* concluded that it is the chief end of man here to "glorify God and enjoy him forever."[2]

Still we live meanly, like ants; though the fable tells us that we were long ago changed into men; like pygmies we fight with cranes;[3] it is error upon error, and clout upon clout, and our best virtue has for its occasion a superfluous and evitable wretchedness. Our life is frittered away by detail. An honest man has hardly need to count more than his ten fingers, or in extreme cases he may add his ten toes, and lump the rest. Simplicity, simplicity, simplicity! I say, let your affairs be as two or three, and not a hundred or a thousand; instead of a million count half a dozen, and keep your accounts on your thumb nail. In the midst of this chopping sea of civilized life, such are the clouds and storms and quicksands and thousand-and-one items to be allowed for, that a man has to live, if he would not founder and go to the bottom and not make his port at all, by dead reckoning, and he must be a great calculator indeed who succeeds. Simplify, simplify. Instead of three meals a day, if it be necessary eat but one; instead of a hundred dishes, five; and reduce other things in proportion. Our life is like a German Confederacy,[4] made up of petty states, with its boundary forever fluctuating, so that even a German cannot tell you how it is bounded at any moment. The nation itself, with all its so called internal improvements, which, by the way, are all external and superficial, is just such an unwieldy and overgrown establishment, cluttered with furniture and tripped up by its own traps, ruined by luxury and heedless expense, by want of calculation and a worthy aim, as the million households in the land; and the only cure for it as for them is in a rigid economy, a stern and more than Spartan simplicity of life and elevation of purpose. It lives too

1. Citizens of Sparta, an ancient Greek city-state, known for their discipline, austerity, and bravery.
2. From the Shorter Catechism in the *New England Primer*.
3. In book 3 of the *Iliad*, the Trojans are com-pared to cranes fighting with pygmies. A story in Greek mythology tells of how Aeacus persuaded Zeus to turn ants into men.
4. Germany was not yet a unified nation.

fast. Men think that it is essential that the *Nation* have commerce, and export ice, and talk through a telegraph, and ride thirty miles an hour, without a doubt, whether *they* do or not; but whether we should live like baboons or like men, is a little uncertain. If we do not get out sleepers,[5] and forge rails, and devote days and nights to the work, but go to tinkering upon our *lives* to improve *them*, who will build railroads? And if railroads are not built, how shall we get to heaven in season? But if we stay at home and mind our business, who will want railroads? We do not ride on the railroad; it rides upon us. Did you ever think what those sleepers are that underlie the railroad? Each one is a man, an Irish-man, or a Yankee man. The rails are laid on them, and they are covered with sand, and the cars run smoothly over them. They are sound sleepers, I assure you. And every few years a new lot is laid down and run over; so that, if some have the pleasure of riding on a rail, others have the misfortune to be ridden upon. And when they run over a man that is walking in his sleep, a supernumerary sleeper in the wrong position, and wake him up, they suddenly stop the cars, and make a hue and cry about it, as if this were an exception. I am glad to know that it takes a gang of men for every five miles to keep the sleepers down and level in their beds as it is, for this is a sign that they may sometime get up again.

Why should we live with such hurry and waste of life? We are determined to be starved before we are hungry. Men say that a stitch in time saves nine, and so they take a thousand stitches to-day to save nine to-morrow. As for *work*, we haven't any of any consequence. We have the Saint Vitus' dance,[6] and cannot possibly keep our heads still. If I should only give a few pulls at the parish bell-rope, as for a fire, that is, without setting the bell, there is hardly a man on his farm in the outskirts of Concord, notwithstanding that press of engagements which was his excuse so many times this morning, nor a boy, nor a woman, I might almost say, but would forsake all and follow that sound, not mainly to save property from the flames, but, if we will confess the truth, much more to see it burn, since burn it must, and we, be it known, did not set it on fire,—or to see it put out, and have a hand in it, if that is done as handsomely; yes, even if it were the parish church itself. Hardly a man takes a half hour's nap after dinner, but when he wakes he holds up his head and asks, "What's the news?" as if the rest of mankind had stood his sentinels. Some give directions to be waked every half hour, doubtless for no other purpose; and then, to pay for it, they tell what they have dreamed. After a night's sleep the news is as indispensable as the breakfast. "Pray tell me any thing new that has happened to a man any where on this globe",—and he reads it over his coffee and rolls, that a man had had his eyes gouged out this morning on the Wachito River; never dreaming the while that he lives in the dark unfathomed mammoth cave of this world, and has but the rudiment of an eye himself.[7]

For my part, I could easily do without the post-office. I think that there are very few important communications made through it. To speak critically, I never received more than one or two letters in my life—I wrote this some years ago—that were worth the postage. The penny-post is, commonly, an

5. Wooden railroad ties (another pun).
6. Chorea, a severe nervous disorder character-ized by jerky motions.
7. Sightless fish had been found in Kentucky's

Mammoth Cave. "Wachito": also spelled "Ouachita," river flowing from Arkansas into the Red River in Louisiana.

institution through which you seriously offer a man that penny for his thoughts which is so often safely offered in jest. And I am sure that I never read any memorable news in a newspaper. If we read of one man robbed, or murdered, or killed by accident, or one house burned, or one vessel wrecked, or one steamboat blown up, or one cow run over on the Western Railroad, or one mad dog killed, or one lot of grasshoppers in the winter,—we never need read of another. One is enough. If you are acquainted with the principle, what do you care for a myriad instances and applications? To a philosopher all *news*, as it is called, is gossip, and they who edit and read it are old women over their tea. Yet not a few are greedy after this gossip. There was such a rush, as I hear, the other day at one of the offices to learn the foreign news by the last arrival, that several large squares of plate glass belonging to the establishment were broken by the pressure,—news which I seriously think a ready wit might write a twelvemonth or twelve years beforehand with sufficient accuracy. As for Spain, for instance, if you know how to throw in Don Carlos and the Infanta, and Don Pedro and Seville and Granada, from time to time in the right proportions,—they may have changed the names a little since I saw the papers,—and serve up a bull-fight when other entertainments fail, it will be true to the letter, and give us as good an idea of the exact state or ruin of things in Spain as the most succinct and lucid reports under this head in the newspapers: and as for England, almost the last significant scrap of news from that quarter was the revolution of 1649;[8] and if you have learned the history of her crops for an average year, you never need attend to that thing again, unless your speculations are of a merely pecuniary character. If one may judge who rarely looks into the newspapers, nothing new does ever happen in foreign parts, a French revolution not excepted.

What news! how much more important to know what that is which was never old! "Kieou-pe-yu (great dignitary of the state of Wei) sent a man to Khoung-tseu to know his news. Khoung-tseu caused the messenger to be seated near him, and questioned him in these terms: What is your master doing? The messenger answered with respect: My master desires to diminish the number of his faults, but he cannot accomplish it. The messenger being gone, the philosopher remarked: What a worthy messenger! What a worthy messenger!"[9] The preacher, instead of vexing the ears of drowsy farmers on their day of rest at the end of the week,—for Sunday is the fit conclusion of an ill-spent week, and not the fresh and brave beginning of a new one,— with this one other draggle-tail of a sermon, should shout with thundering voice,—"Pause! Avast! Why so seeming fast, but deadly slow?"

Shams and delusions are esteemed for soundest truths, while reality is fabulous. If men would steadily observe realities only, and not allow themselves to be deluded, life, to compare it with such things as we know, would be like a fairy tale and the Arabian Nights' Entertainments. If we respected only what is inevitable and has a right to be, music and poetry would resound along the streets. When we are unhurried and wise, we perceive that only

---

8. The year the Puritan Commonwealth, under Oliver Cromwell (1599–1658), temporarily replaced the British monarchy—the culminating event of the English Civil War of 1642–49. During the 1830s and 1840s, King Ferdinand VII of Spain (1784–1833) and his brother Don Carlos (1788–1855) contested for power, and Ferdinand triumphed when his thirteen-year-old daughter, the Infanta, or princess (1830–1904), was crowned Queen Isabella II. In 1362, Don Pedro the Cruel of Seville (1334–1369) and his army killed Abu Said Muhammad VI of Granada.
9. Confucius's *Analects* 14.

great and worthy things have any permanent and absolute existence,—that petty fears and petty pleasures are but the shadow of the reality. This is always exhilarating and sublime. By closing the eyes and slumbering, and consenting to be deceived by shows, men establish and confirm their daily life of routine and habit every where, which still is built on purely illusory foundations. Children, who play life, discern its true law and relations more clearly than men, who fail to live it worthily, but who think that they are wiser by experience, that is, by failure. I have read in a Hindoo book, that "there was a king's son, who, being expelled in infancy from his native city, was brought up by a forester, and, growing up to maturity in that state, imagined himself to belong to the barbarous race with which he lived. One of his father's ministers having discovered him, revealed to him what he was, and the misconception of his character was removed, and he knew himself to be a prince. So soul," continues the Hindoo philosopher, "from the circumstances in which it is placed, mistakes its own character, until the truth is revealed to it by some holy teacher, and then it knows itself to be *Brahme*."[1] I perceive that we inhabitants of New England live this mean life that we do because our vision does not penetrate the surface of things. We think that that *is* which *appears* to be. If a man should walk through this town and see only the reality, where, think you, would the "Mill-dam"[2] go to? If he should give us an account of the realities he beheld there, we should not recognize the place in his description. Look at a meeting-house, or a court-house, or a jail, or a shop, or a dwelling-house, and say what that thing really is before a true gaze, and they would all go to pieces in your account of them. Men esteem truth remote, in the outskirts of the system, behind the farthest star, before Adam and after the last man. In eternity there is indeed something true and sublime. But all these times and places and occasions are now and here. God himself culminates in the present moment, and will never be more divine in the lapse of all the ages. And we are enabled to apprehend at all what is sublime and noble only by the perpetual instilling and drenching of the reality which surrounds us. The universe constantly and obediently answers to our conceptions; whether we travel fast or slow, the track is laid for us. Let us spend our lives in conceiving them. The poet or the artist never yet had so fair and noble a design but some of his posterity at least could accomplish it.

Let us spend one day as deliberately as Nature, and not be thrown off the track by every nutshell and mosquito's wing that falls on the rails. Let us rise early and fast, or break fast, gently and without perturbation; let company come and let company go, let the bells ring and the children cry,—determined to make a day of it. Why should we knock under and go with the stream? Let us not be upset and overwhelmed in that terrible rapid and whirlpool called a dinner, situated in the meridian shallows. Weather this danger and you are safe, for the rest of the way is down hill. With unrelaxed nerves, with morning vigor, sail by it, looking another way, tied to the mast like Ulysses.[3] If the engine whistles, let it whistle till it is hoarse for its pains. If the bell rings, why should we run? We will consider what kind of music they are like. Let us settle ourselves, and work and wedge our feet downward through the mud

1. In the Hindu triad, Brahma is the divine reality in the aspect of creator; Vishnu is the preserver; and Siva, the destroyer.
2. The business center of Concord.

3. In Homer's *Odyssey*, Ulysses (Odysseus) took such a precaution to keep himself from yielding to the call of the Sirens—sea nymphs whose singing lured men to destruction.

and slush of opinion, and prejudice, and tradition, and delusion, and appearance, that alluvion[4] which covers the globe, through Paris and London, through New York and Boston and Concord, through church and state, through poetry and philosophy and religion, till we come to a hard bottom and rocks in place, which we can call *reality*, and say, This is, and no mistake; and then begin, having a *point d'appui*, below freshet and frost and fire, a place where you might found a wall or a state, or set a lamp-post safely, or perhaps a gauge, not a Nilometer,[5] but a Realometer, that future ages might know how deep a freshet of shams and appearances had gathered from time to time. If you stand right fronting and face to face to a fact, you will see the sun glimmer on both its surfaces, as if it were a cimeter, and feel its sweet edge dividing you through the heart and marrow, and so you will happily conclude your mortal career. Be it life or death, we crave only reality. If we are really dying, let us hear the rattle in our throats and feel cold in the extremities; if we are alive, let us go about our business.

Time is but the stream I go a-fishing in. I drink at it; but while I drink I see the sandy bottom and detect how shallow it is. Its thin current slides away, but eternity remains. I would drink deeper; fish in the sky, whose bottom is pebbly with stars. I cannot count one. I know not the first letter of the alphabet. I have always been regretting that I was not as wise as the day I was born. The intellect is a cleaver; it discerns and rifts its way into the secret of things. I do not wish to be any more busy with my hands than is necessary. My head is hands and feet. I feel all my best faculties concentrated in it. My instinct tells me that my head is an organ for burrowing, as some creatures use their snout and fore-paws, and with it I would mine and burrow my way through these hills. I think that the richest vein is somewhere hereabouts; so by the divining rod and thin rising vapors I judge; and here I will begin to mine.

5. *Solitude*

This is a delicious evening, when the whole body is one sense, and imbibes delight through every pore. I go and come with a strange liberty in Nature, a part of herself. As I walk along the stony shore of the pond in my shirt sleeves, though it is cool as well as cloudy and windy, and I see nothing special to attract me, all the elements are unusually congenial to me. The bullfrogs trump to usher in the night, and the note of the whippoorwill is borne on the rippling wind from over the water. Sympathy with the fluttering alder and poplar leaves almost takes away my breath; yet, like the lake, my serenity is rippled but not ruffled. These small waves raised by the evening wind are as remote from the storm as the smooth reflecting surface. Though it is now dark, the wind still blows and roars in the wood, the waves still dash, and some creatures lull the rest with their notes. The repose is never complete. The wildest animals do not repose, but seek their prey now; the fox, and skunk, and rabbit, now roam the fields and woods without fear. They are Nature's watchmen,—links which connect the days of animated life.

When I return to my house I find that visitors have been there and left their cards, either a bunch of flowers, or a wreath of evergreen, or a name in pencil on a yellow walnut leaf or a chip. They who come rarely to the woods

---

4. Sediment deposited by flowing water along a shore or bank.
5. Gauge used by the ancient Egyptians for mea-suring the depth of the Nile. *"Point d'appui"*: point of support (French).

take some little piece of the forest into their hands to play with by the way, which they leave, either intentionally or accidentally. One has peeled a willow wand, woven it into a ring, and dropped it on my table. I could always tell if visitors had called in my absence, either by the bended twigs or grass, or the print of their shoes, and generally of what sex or age or quality they were by some slight trace left, as a flower dropped, or a bunch of grass plucked and thrown away, even as far off as the railroad, half a mile distant, or by the lingering odor of a cigar or pipe. Nay, I was frequently notified of the passage of a traveller along the highway sixty rods off by the scent of his pipe.

There is commonly sufficient space about us. Our horizon is never quite at our elbows. The thick wood is not just at our door, nor the pond, but somewhat is always clearing, familiar and worn by us, appropriated and fenced in some way, and reclaimed from Nature. For what reason have I this vast range and circuit, some square miles of unfrequented forest, for my privacy, abandoned to me by men? My nearest neighbor is a mile distant, and no house is visible from any place but the hill-tops within half a mile of my own. I have my horizon bounded by woods all to myself; a distant view of the railroad where it touches the pond on the one hand, and of the fence which skirts the woodland road on the other. But for the most part it is as solitary where I live as on the prairies. It is as much Asia or Africa as New England. I have, as it were, my own sun and moon and stars, and a little world all to myself. At night there was never a traveller passed my house, or knocked at my door, more than if I were the first or last man; unless it were in the spring, when at long intervals some came from the village to fish for pouts,—they plainly fished much more in the Walden Pond of their own natures, and baited their hooks with darkness,—but they soon retreated, usually with light baskets, and left "the world to darkness and to me,"[6] and the black kernel of the night was never profaned by any human neighborhood. I believe that men are generally still a little afraid of the dark, though the witches are all hung, and Christianity and candles have been introduced.

Yet I experienced sometimes that the most sweet and tender, the most innocent and encouraging society may be found in any natural object, even for the poor misanthrope and most melancholy man. There can be no very black melancholy to him who lives in the midst of Nature and has his senses still. There was never yet such a storm but it was Æolian[7] music to a healthy and innocent ear. Nothing can rightly compel a simple and brave man to a vulgar sadness. While I enjoy the friendship of the seasons I trust that nothing can make life a burden to me. The gentle rain which waters my beans and keeps me in the house to-day is not drear and melancholy, but good for me too. Though it prevents my hoeing them, it is of far more worth than my hoeing. If it should continue so long as to cause the seeds to rot in the ground and destroy the potatoes in the low lands, it would still be good for the grass on the uplands, and, being good for the grass, it would be good for me. Sometimes, when I compare myself with other men, it seems as if I were more favored by the gods than they, beyond any deserts that I am conscious of; as if I had a warrant and surety at their hands which my fellows have not, and were especially guided and guarded. I do not flatter

6. From "Elegy Written in a Country Church-yard" (1751), by the English poet Thomas Gray (1716–1771).
7. The Aeolian harp (named for Aeolus, Greek keeper of the winds) was commonly placed in the open air or near an open window so that the wind could cause it to make musical sounds.

myself, but if it be possible they flatter me. I have never felt lonesome, or in the least oppressed by a sense of solitude, but once, and that was a few weeks after I came to the woods, when, for an hour, I doubted if the near neighborhood of man was not essential to a serene and healthy life. To be alone was something unpleasant. But I was at the same time conscious of a slight insanity in my mood, and seemed to foresee my recovery. In the midst of a gentle rain while these thoughts prevailed, I was suddenly sensible of such sweet and beneficent society in Nature, in the very pattering of the drops, and in every sound and sight around my house, an infinite and unaccountable friendliness all at once like an atmosphere sustaining me, as made the fancied advantages of human neighborhood insignificant, and I have never thought of them since. Every little pine needle expanded and swelled with sympathy and befriended me. I was so distinctly made aware of the presence of something kindred to me, even in scenes which we are accustomed to call wild and dreary, and also that the nearest of blood to me and humanest was not a person nor a villager, that I thought no place could ever be strange to me again.—

> "Mourning untimely consumes the sad;
> Few are their days in the land of the living,
> Beautiful daughter of Toscar."[8]

Some of my pleasantest hours were during the long rain storms in the spring or fall, which confined me to the house for the afternoon as well as the forenoon, soothed by their ceaseless roar and pelting; when an early twilight ushered in a long evening in which many thoughts had time to take root and unfold themselves. In those driving north-east rains which tried the village houses so, when the maids stood ready with mop and pail in front entries to keep the deluge out, I sat behind my door in my little house, which was all entry, and thoroughly enjoyed its protection. In one heavy thunder shower the lightning struck a large pitch-pine across the pond, making a very conspicuous and perfectly regular spiral groove from top to bottom, an inch or more deep, and four or five inches wide, as you would groove a walking-stick. I passed it again the other day, and was struck with awe on looking up and beholding that mark, now more distinct than ever, where a terrific and resistless bolt came down out of the harmless sky eight years ago. Men frequently say to me, "I should think you would feel lonesome down there, and want to be nearer to folks, rainy and snowy days and nights especially." I am tempted to reply to such,—This whole earth which we inhabit is but a point in space. How far apart, think you, dwell the two most distant inhabitants of yonder star, the breadth of whose disk cannot be appreciated by our instruments? Why should I feel lonely? is not our planet in the Milky Way? This which you put seems to me not to be the most important question. What sort of space is that which separates a man from his fellows and makes him solitary? I have found that no exertion of the legs can bring two minds much nearer to one another. What do we want most to dwell near to? Not to many men surely, the depot, the post-office, the bar-room, the meeting-house, the school-house, the grocery, Beacon Hill, or the Five Points,[9] where men most congregate, but to the perennial source of our life, whence in all

8. From "Croma," in Patrick MacGregor's translation of *The Genuine Remains of Ossian* (1841).
9. District in lower Manhattan, notorious in Thoreau's time for its poverty and violence. The State House is on Boston's Beacon Hill.

our experience we have found that to issue; as the willow stands near the water and sends out its roots in that direction. This will vary with different natures, but this is the place where a wise man will dig his cellar. . . . I one evening overtook one of my townsmen, who has accumulated what is called "a handsome property",—though I never got a *fair* view of it,—on the Walden road, driving a pair of cattle to market, who inquired of me how I could bring my mind to give up so many of the comforts of life. I answered that I was very sure I liked it passably well; I was not joking. And so I went home to my bed, and left him to pick his way through the darkness and the mud to Brighton,—or Bright-town,—which place he would reach some time in the morning.

Any prospect of awakening or coming to life to a dead man makes indifferent all times and places. The place where that may occur is always the same, and indescribably pleasant to all our senses. For the most part we allow only outlying and transient circumstances to make our occasions. They are, in fact, the cause of our distraction. Nearest to all things is that power which fashions their being. *Next* to us the grandest laws are continually being executed. *Next* to us is not the workman whom we have hired, with whom we love so well to talk, but the workman whose work we are.

"How vast and profound is the influence of the subtile powers of Heaven and of Earth!"

"We seek to perceive them, and we do not see them; we seek to hear them, and we do not hear them; identified with the substance of things, they cannot be separated from them."

"They cause that in all the universe men purify and sanctify their hearts, and clothe themselves in their holiday garments to offer sacrifices and oblations to their ancestors. It is an ocean of subtile intelligences. They are every where, above us, on our left, on our right; they environ us on all sides."[1]

We are the subjects of an experiment which is not a little interesting to me. Can we not do without the society of our gossips a little while under these circumstances,—have our own thoughts to cheer us? Confucious says truly, "Virtue does not remain as an abandoned orphan; it must of necessity have neighbors."[2]

With thinking we may be beside ourselves in a sane sense. By a conscious effort of the mind we can stand aloof from actions and their consequences; and all things, good and bad, go by us like a torrent. We are not wholly involved in Nature. I may be either the drift-wood in the stream, or Indra[3] in the sky looking down on it. I *may* be affected by a theatrical exhibition; on the other hand, I *may not* be affected by an actual event which appears to concern me much more. I only know myself as a human entity; the scene, so to speak, of thoughts and affections; and am sensible of a certain doubleness by which I can stand as remote from myself as from another. However intense my experience, I am conscious of the presence and criticism of a part of me, which, as it were, is not a part of me, but spectator, sharing no experience, but taking note of it; and that is no more I than it is you. When the play, it may be the tragedy, of life is over, the spectator goes his way. It was a kind of fiction, a work of the imagination only, so far as he was con-

---

1. Confucius's *The Doctrine of the Mean* 14.
2. Confucius's *Analects* 4.
3. In the Vedas, the Hindu god of the air, associated with rain and thunder.

cerned. This doubleness may easily make us poor neighbors and friends sometimes.

I find it wholesome to be alone the greater part of the time. To be in company, even with the best, is soon wearisome and dissipating. I love to be alone. I never found the companion that was so companionable as solitude. We are for the most part more lonely when we go abroad among men than when we stay in our chambers. A man thinking or working is always alone, let him be where he will. Solitude is not measured by the miles of space that intervene between a man and his fellows. The really diligent student in one of the crowded hives of Cambridge College is as solitary as a dervish[4] in the desert. The farmer can work alone in the field or the woods all day, hoeing or chopping, and not feel lonesome, because he is employed; but when he comes home at night he cannot sit down in a room alone, at the mercy of his thoughts, but must be where he can "see the folks," and recreate, and as he thinks remunerate himself for his day's solitude; and hence he wonders how the student can sit alone in the house all night and most of the day without ennui and "the blues;" but he does not realize that the student, though in the house, is still at work in *his* field, and chopping in *his* woods, as the farmer in his, and in turn seeks the same recreation and society that the latter does, though it may be a more condensed form of it.

Society is commonly too cheap. We meet at very short intervals, not having had time to acquire any new value for each other. We meet at meals three times a day, and give each other a new taste of that old musty cheese that we are. We have had to agree on a certain set of rules, called etiquette and politeness, to make this frequent meeting tolerable, and that we need not come to open war. We meet at the post-office, and at the sociable, and about the fireside every night; we live thick and are in each other's way, and stumble over one another, and I think that we thus lose some respect for one another. Certainly less frequency would suffice for all important and hearty communications. Consider the girls in a factory,—never alone, hardly in their dreams. It would be better if there were but one inhabitant to a square mile, as where I live. The value of a man is not in his skin, that we should touch him.

I have heard of a man lost in the woods and dying of famine and exhaustion at the foot of a tree, whose loneliness was relieved by the grotesque visions with which, owing to bodily weakness, his diseased imagination surrounded him, and which he believed to be real. So also, owing to bodily and mental health and strength, we may be continually cheered by a like but more normal and natural society, and come to know that we are never alone.

I have a great deal of company in my house; especially in the morning, when nobody calls. Let me suggest a few comparisons, that some one may convey an idea of my situation. I am no more lonely than the loon in the pond that laughs so loud, or than Walden Pond itself. What company has that lonely lake, I pray? And yet it has not the blue devils, but the blue angels in it, in the azure tint of its waters. The sun is alone, except in thick weather, when there sometimes appear to be two, but one is a mock sun. God is alone,—but the devil, he is far from being alone; he sees a great deal of company; he is legion. I am no more lonely than a single mullein or dandelion in a pasture, or a bean leaf, or sorrel, or a horse-fly, or a humble-bee. I am no more lonely

4. Sufi Muslim who takes religious vows of poverty and austerity.

than the Mill Brook, or a weathercock, or the northstar, or the south wind, or an April shower, or a January thaw, or the first spider in a new house.

I have occasional visits in the long winter evenings, when the snow falls fast and the wind howls in the wood, from an old settler and original proprietor, who is reported to have dug Walden Pond, and stoned it, and fringed it with pine woods; who tells me stories of old time and of new eternity; and between us we manage to pass a cheerful evening with social mirth and pleasant views of things, even without apples or cider,—a most wise and humorous friend, whom I love much, who keeps himself more secret than ever did Goffe or Whalley;[5] and though he is thought to be dead, none can show where he is buried. An elderly dame,[6] too, dwells in my neighborhood, invisible to most persons, in whose odorous herb garden I love to stroll sometimes, gathering simples and listening to her fables; for she has a genius of unequalled fertility, and her memory runs back farther than mythology, and she can tell me the original of every fable, and on what fact every one is founded, for the incidents occurred when she was young. A ruddy and lusty old dame, who delights in all weathers and seasons, and is likely to outlive all her children yet.

The indescribable innocence and beneficence of Nature,—of sun and wind and rain, of summer and winter,—such health, such cheer, they afford forever! and such sympathy have they ever with our race, that all Nature would be affected, and the sun's brightness fade, and the winds would sigh humanely, and the clouds rain tears, and the woods shed their leaves and put on mourning in midsummer, if any man should ever for a just cause grieve. Shall I not have intelligence with the earth? Am I not partly leaves and vegetable mould myself?

What is the pill which will keep us well, serene, contented? Not my or thy great-grandfather's, but our great-grandmother Nature's universal, vegetable, botanic medicines, by which she has kept herself young always, outlived so many old Parrs[7] in her day, and fed her health with their decaying fatness. For my panacea, instead of one of those quack vials of a mixture dipped from Acheron[8] and the Dead Sea, which come out of those long shallow black-schooner looking wagons which we sometimes see made to carry bottles, let me have a draught of undiluted morning air. Morning air! If men will not drink of this at the fountain-head of the day, why, then, we must even bottle up some and sell it in the shops, for the benefit of those who have lost their subscription ticket to morning time in this world. But remember, it will not keep quite till noon-day even in the coolest cellar, but drive out the stopples long ere that and follow westward the steps of Aurora. I am no worshipper of Hygeia, who was the daughter of that old herb-doctor Æsculapius,[9] and who is represented on monuments holding a serpent in one hand, and in the other a cup out of which the serpent sometimes drinks; but rather of Hebe, cupbearer to Jupiter, who was the daughter of Juno and wild lettuce, and who had the power of restoring gods and men to the vigor of youth. She was probably the only thoroughly sound-conditioned,

---

5. English Puritans who supported the execution of Charles I of England in 1649 and later, when sought as regicides, hid in Connecticut and Massachusetts settlements. "Old settler": some sort of divine creative power.
6. Mother Nature.

7. An Englishman known as Old Tom Parr was said to have been alive during three centuries (1483–1635).
8. In Greek mythology a principal river in Hades.
9. Roman god of medicine. Hygeia was the Greek goddess of health.

healthy, and robust young lady that ever walked the globe, and wherever she came it was spring.

17. Spring

The opening of large tracts by the ice-cutters commonly causes a pond to break up earlier; for the water, agitated by the wind, even in cold weather, wears away the surrounding ice. But such was not the effect on Walden that year, for she had soon got a thick new garment to take the place of the old. This pond never breaks up so soon as the others in this neighborhood, on account both of its greater depth and its having no stream passing through it to melt or wear away the ice. I never knew it to open in the course of a winter, not excepting that of '52–3, which gave the ponds so severe a trial. It commonly opens about the first of April, a week or ten days later than Flint's Pond and Fair-Haven, beginning to melt on the north side and in the shallower parts where it began to freeze. It indicates better than any water hereabouts the absolute progress of the season, being least affected by transient changes of temperature. A severe cold of a few days' duration in March may very much retard the opening of the former ponds, while the temperature of Walden increases almost uninterruptedly. A thermometer thrust into the middle of Walden on the 6th of March, 1847, stood at 32°, or freezing point; near the shore at 33°; in the middle of Flint's Pond, the same day, at 32½°; at a dozen rods from the shore, in shallow water, under ice a foot thick, at 36°. This difference of three and a half degrees between the temperature of the deep water and the shallow in the latter pond, and the fact that a great proportion of it is comparatively shallow, show why it should break up so much sooner than Walden. The ice in the shallowest part was at this time several inches thinner than in the middle. In mid-winter the middle had been the warmest and the ice thinnest there. So, also, every one who has waded about the shores of a pond in summer must have perceived how much warmer the water is close to the shore, where only three or four inches deep, than a little distance out, and on the surface where it is deep, than near the bottom. In spring the sun not only exerts an influence through the increased temperature of the air and earth, but its heat passes through ice a foot or more thick, and is reflected from the bottom in shallow water, and so also warms the water and melts the under side of the ice, at the same time that it is melting it more directly above, making it uneven, and causing the air bubbles which it contains to extend themselves upward and downward until it is completely honey-combed, and at last disappears suddenly in a single spring rain. Ice has its grain as well as wood, and when a cake begins to rot or "comb," that is, assume the appearance of honey-comb, whatever may be its position, the air cells are at right angles with what was the water surface. Where there is a rock or a log rising near to the surface the ice over it is much thinner, and is frequently quite dissolved by this reflected heat; and I have been told that in the experiment at Cambridge to freeze water in a shallow wooden pond, though the cold air circulated underneath, and so had access to both sides, the reflection of the sun from the bottom more than counterbalanced this advantage. When a warm rain in the middle of the winter melts off the snow-ice from Walden, and leaves a hard dark or transparent ice on the middle, there will be a strip of rotten though thicker white ice, a rod or more wide, about the shores, created by this reflected heat. Also, as I have said, the bubbles themselves within the ice operate as burning glasses to melt the ice beneath.

The phenomena of the year take place every day in a pond on a small scale. Every morning, generally speaking, the shallow water is being warmed more rapidly than the deep, though it may not be made so warm after all, and every evening it is being cooled more rapidly until the morning. The day is an epitome of the year. The night is the winter, the morning and evening are the spring and fall, and the noon is the summer. The cracking and booming of the ice indicate a change of temperature. One pleasant morning after a cold night, February 24th, 1850, having gone to Flint's Pond to spend the day, I noticed with surprise, that when I struck the ice with the head of my axe, it resounded like a gong for many rods around, or as if I had struck on a tight drum-head. The pond began to boom about an hour after sunrise, when it felt the influence of the sun's rays slanted upon it from the hills; it stretched itself and yawned like a waking man with a gradually increasing tumult, which was kept up three or four hours. It took a short siesta at noon, and boomed once more toward night, as the sun was withdrawing his influence. In the right stage of the weather a pond fires its evening gun with great regularity. But in the middle of the day, being full of cracks, and the air also being less elastic, it had completely lost its resonance, and probably fishes and muskrats could not then have been stunned by a blow on it. The fishermen say that the "thundering of the pond" scares the fishes and prevents their biting. The pond does not thunder every evening, and I cannot tell surely when to expect its thundering; but though I may perceive no difference in the weather, it does. Who would have suspected so large and cold and thick-skinned a thing to be so sensitive? Yet it has its law to which it thunders obedience when it should as surely as the buds expand in the spring. The earth is all alive and covered with papillæ. The largest pond is as sensitive to atmospheric changes as the globule of mercury in its tube.

One attraction in coming to the woods to live was that I should have leisure and opportunity to see the spring come in. The ice in the pond at length begins to be honey-combed, and I can set my heel in it as I walk. Fogs and rains and warmer suns are gradually melting the snow; the days have grown sensibly longer; and I see how I shall get through the winter without adding to my wood-pile, for large fires are no longer necessary. I am on the alert for the first signs of spring, to hear the chance note of some arriving bird, or the striped squirrel's chirp, for his stores must be now nearly exhausted, or see the woodchuck venture out of his winter quarters. On the 13th of March, after I had heard the bluebird, song-sparrow, and red-wing, the ice was still nearly a foot thick. As the weather grew warmer, it was not sensibly worn away by the water, nor broken up and floated off as in rivers, but, though it was completely melted for half a rod in width about the shore, the middle was merely honey-combed and saturated with water, so that you could put your foot through it when six inches thick; but by the next day evening, perhaps, after a warm rain followed by fog, it would have wholly disappeared, all gone off with the fog, spirited away. One year I went across the middle only five days before it disappeared entirely. In 1845 Walden was first completely open on the 1st of April; in '46, the 25th of March; in '47, the 8th of April; in '51, the 28th of March; in '52, the 18th of April; in '53, the 23rd of March; in '54, about the 7th of April.

Every incident connected with the breaking up of the rivers and ponds and the settling of the weather is particularly interesting to us who live in a climate of so great extremes. When the warmer days come, they who dwell near the river hear the ice crack at night with a startling whoop as loud as artillery, as if its icy fetters were rent from end to end, and within a few days see it rapidly going out. So the alligator comes out of the mud with quakings of the earth. One old man, who has been a close observer of Nature, and seems as thoroughly wise in regard to all her operations as if she had been put upon the stocks when he was a boy, and he had helped to lay her keel,— who has come to his growth, and can hardly acquire more of natural lore if he should live to the age of Methuselah[1]—told me, and I was surprised to hear him express wonder at any of Nature's operations, for I thought that there were no secrets between them, that one spring day he took his gun and boat, and thought that he would have a little sport with the ducks. There was ice still on the meadows, but it was all gone out of the river, and he dropped down without obstruction from Sudbury, where he lived, to Fair-Haven Pond, which he found, unexpectedly, covered for the most part with a firm field of ice. It was a warm day, and he was surprised to see so great a body of ice remaining. Not seeing any ducks, he hid his boat on the north or back side of an island in the pond, and then concealed himself in the bushes on the south side, to await them. The ice was melted for three or four rods from the shore, and there was a smooth and warm sheet of water, with a muddy bottom, such as the ducks love, within, and he thought it likely that some would be along pretty soon. After he had lain still there about an hour he heard a low and seemingly very distant sound, but singularly grand and impressive, unlike any thing he had ever heard, gradually swelling and increasing as if it would have a universal and memorable ending, a sullen rush and roar, which seemed to him all at once like the sound of a vast body of fowl coming in to settle there, and, seizing his gun, he started up in haste and excited; but he found, to his surprise, that the whole body of the ice had started while he lay there, and drifted in to the shore, and the sound he had heard was made by its edge grating on the shore,—at first gently nibbled and crumbled off, but at length heaving up and scattering its wrecks along the island to a considerable height before it came to a stand still.

At length the sun's rays have attained the right angle, and warm winds blow up mist and rain and melt the snow banks, and the sun dispersing the mist smiles on a checkered landscape of russet and white smoking with incense, through which the traveller picks his way from islet to islet, cheered by the music of a thousand tinkling rills and rivulets whose veins are filled with the blood of winter which they are bearing off.

Few phenomena gave me more delight than to observe the forms which thawing sand and clay assume in flowing down the sides of a deep cut on the railroad through which I passed on my way to the village, a phenomenon not very common on so large a scale, though the number of freshly exposed banks of the right material must have been greatly multiplied since railroads were invented. The material was sand of every degree of fineness and of various rich colors, commonly mixed with a little clay. When the frost comes out in the spring, and even in a thawing day in the winter, the sand begins to flow

1. "And the days of Methuselah were nine hundred sixty and nine years: and he died" (Genesis 5.27).

down the slopes like lava, sometimes bursting out through the snow and overflowing it where no sand was to be seen before. Innumerable little streams overlap and interlace one with another, exhibiting a sort of hybrid product, which obeys half way the law of currents, and half way that of vegetation. As it flows it takes the forms of sappy leaves or vines, making heaps of pulpy sprays a foot or more in depth, and resembling, as you look down on them, the laciniated lobed and imbricated thalluses[2] of some lichens; or you are reminded of coral, of leopards' paws or birds' feet, of brains or lungs or bowels, and excrements of all kinds. It is a truly *grotesque* vegetation, whose forms and color we see imitated in bronze, a sort of architectural foliage more ancient and typical than acanthus, chiccory, ivy, vine, or any vegetable leaves; destined perhaps, under some circumstances, to become a puzzle to future geologists. The whole cut impressed me as if it were a cave with its stalactites laid open to the light. The various shades of the sand are singularly rich and agreeable, embracing the different iron colors, brown, gray, yellowish, and reddish. When the flowing mass reaches the drain at the foot of the bank it spreads out flatter into *strands*, the separate streams losing their semi-cylindrical form and gradually becoming more flat and broad, running together as they are more moist, till they form an almost flat *sand*, still variously and beautifully shaded, but in which you can trace the original forms of vegetation; till at length, in the water itself, they are converted into *banks*, like those formed off the mouths of rivers, and the forms of vegetation are lost in the ripple marks on the bottom.

The whole bank, which is from twenty to forty feet high, is sometimes overlaid with a mass of this kind of foliage, or sandy rupture, for a quarter of a mile on one or both sides, the produce of one spring day. What makes this sand foliage remarkable is its springing into existence thus suddenly. When I see on the one side the inert bank,—for the sun acts on one side first,—and on the other this luxuriant foliage, the creation of an hour, I am affected as if in a peculiar sense I stood in the laboratory of the Artist who made the world and me,—had come to where he was still at work, sporting on this bank, and with excess of energy strewing his fresh designs about. I feel as if I were nearer to the vitals of the globe, for this sandy overflow is something such a foliaceous mass as the vitals of the animal body. You find thus in the very sands an anticipation of the vegetable leaf. No wonder that the earth expresses itself outwardly in leaves, it so labors with the idea inwardly. The atoms have already learned this law, and are pregnant by it. The overhanging leaf sees here its prototype. *Internally*, whether in the globe or animal body, it is a moist thick *lobe*, a word especially applicable to the liver and lungs and the *leaves* of fat. (λέιβω, *labor, lapsus*, to flow or slip downward, a lapsing; λοβο., *globus*, lobe, globe; also lap, flap, and many other words,) *externally* a dry thin *leaf*, even as the *f* and *v* are a pressed and dried *b*. The radicals of lobe are *lb*, the soft mass of the *b* (single lobed, or B, double lobed,) with a liquid *l* behind it pressing it forward. In globe, *glb*, the guttural *g* adds to the meaning the capacity of the throat. The feathers and wings of birds are still drier and thinner leaves. Thus, also, you pass from the lumpish grub in the earth to the airy and fluttering butterfly. The very globe continually transcends and translates itself, and becomes winged in its orbit. Even

---

2. Plant shoots or organisms lapped over in regular order like roof tiles. "Laciniated": deeply, irregularly lobed.

ice begins with delicate crystal leaves, as if it had flowed into moulds which the fronds of water plants have impressed on the watery mirror. The whole tree itself is but one leaf, and rivers are still vaster leaves whose pulp is intervening earth, and towns and cities are the ova of insects in their axils.

When the sun withdraws the sand ceases to flow, but in the morning the streams will start once more and branch and branch again into a myriad of others. You here see perchance how blood vessels are formed. If you look closely you observe that first there pushes forward from the thawing mass a stream of softened sand with a drop-like point, like the ball of the finger, feeling its way slowly and blindly downward, until at last with more heat and moisture, as the sun gets higher, the moist fluid portion, in its effort to obey the law to which the most inert also yields, separates from the latter and forms for itself a meandering channel or artery within that, in which is seen a little silvery stream glancing like lightning from one stage of pulpy leaves or branches to another, and ever and anon swallowed up in the sand. It is wonderful how rapidly yet perfectly the sand organizes itself as it flows, using the best material its mass affords to form the sharp edges of its channel. Such are the sources of rivers. In the silicious matter which the water deposits is perhaps the bony system, and in the still finer soil and organic matter the fleshy fibre or cellular tissue. What is man but a mass of thawing clay? The ball of the human finger is but a drop congealed. The fingers and toes flow to their extent from the thawing mass of the body. Who knows what the human body would expand and flow out to under a more genial heaven? Is not the hand a spreading *palm* leaf with its lobes and veins? The ear may be regarded, fancifully, as a lichen, *umbilicaria*, on the side of the head, with its lobe or drop. The lip (*labium* from *labor* (?)) laps or lapses from the sides of the cavernous mouth. The nose is a manifest congealed drop or stalactite. The chin is a still larger drop, the confluent dripping of the face. The cheeks are a slide from the brows into the valley of the face, opposed and diffused by the cheek bones. Each rounded lobe of the vegetable leaf, too, is a thick and now loitering drop, larger or smaller; the lobes are the fingers of the leaf; and as many lobes as it has, in so many directions it tends to flow, and more heat or other genial influences would have caused it to flow yet farther.

Thus it seemed that this one hillside illustrated the principle of all the operations of Nature. The Maker of this earth but patented a leaf. What Champollion[3] will decipher this hieroglyphic for us, that we may turn over a new leaf at last? This phenomenon is more exhilarating to me than the luxuriance and fertility of vineyards. True, it is somewhat excrementitious in its character, and there is no end to the heaps of liver, lights[4] and bowels, as if the globe were turned wrong side outward; but this suggests at least that Nature has some bowels, and there again is mother of humanity. This is the frost coming out of the ground; this is Spring. It precedes the green and flowery spring, as mythology precedes regular poetry. I know of nothing more purgative of winter fumes and indigestions. It convinces me that Earth is still in her swaddling clothes, and stretches forth baby fingers on every side. Fresh curls spring from the baldest brow. There is nothing inorganic. These folia-

3. Jean François Champollion (1790–1832), French archaeologist whose deciphering of the hieroglyphic inscriptions on the Rosetta Stone fueled great popular interest in Egyptology. The stone dates from 196 B.C.E. and was discovered by French soldiers in 1799.
4. Lungs.

ceous heaps lie along the bank like the slag of a furnace, showing that Nature is "in full blast" within. The earth is not a mere fragment of dead history, stratum upon stratum like the leaves of a book, to be studied by geologists and antiquaries chiefly, but living poetry like the leaves of a tree, which precede flowers and fruit,—not a fossil earth, but a living earth; compared with whose great central life all animal and vegetable life is merely parasitic. Its throes will heave our exuviæ from their graves. You may melt your metals and cast them into the most beautiful moulds you can; they will never excite me like the forms which this molten earth flows out into. And not only it, but the institutions upon it, are plastic like clay in the hands of the potter.

Ere long, not only on these banks, but on every hill and plain and in every hollow, the frost comes out of the ground like a dormant quadruped from its burrow, and seeks the sea with music, or migrates to other climes in clouds. Thaw with his gentle persuasion is more powerful than Thor with his hammer. The one melts, the other but breaks in pieces.

When the ground was partially bare of snow, and a few warm days had dried its surface somewhat, it was pleasant to compare the first tender signs of the infant year just peeping forth with the stately beauty of the withered vegetation which had withstood the winter,—life-everlasting, golden-rods, pinweeds, and graceful wild grasses, more obvious and interesting frequently than in summer even, as if their beauty was not ripe till then; even cotton-grass, cat-tails, mulleins, johnswort, hard-hack, meadowsweet, and other strong stemmed plants, those unexhausted granaries which entertain the earliest birds,—decent weeds,[5] at least, which widowed Nature wears. I am particularly attracted by the arching and sheaflike top of the wool-grass; it brings back the summer to our winter memories, and is among the forms which art loves to copy, and which, in the vegetable kingdom, have the same relation to types already in the mind of man that astronomy has. It is an antique style older than Greek or Egyptian. Many of the phenomena of Winter are suggestive of an inexpressible tenderness and fragile delicacy. We are accustomed to hear this king described as a rude and boisterous tyrant; but with the gentleness of a lover he adorns the tresses of Summer.

At the approach of spring the red-squirrels got under my house, two at a time, directly under my feet as I sat reading or writing, and kept up the queerest chuckling and chirruping and vocal pirouetting and gurgling sounds that ever were heard; and when I stamped they only chirruped the louder, as if past all fear and respect in their mad pranks, defying humanity to stop them. No you don't—chickaree—chickaree. They were wholly deaf to my arguments, or failed to perceive their force, and fell into a strain of invective that was irresistible.

The first sparrow of spring! The year beginning with younger hope than ever! The faint silvery warblings heard over the partially bare and moist fields from the blue-bird, the song-sparrow, and the red-wing, as if the last flakes of winter tinkled as they fell! What at such a time are histories, chronologies, traditions, and all written revelations? The brooks sing carols and glees to the spring. The marsh-hawk sailing low over the meadow is already seeking the first slimy life that awakes. The sinking sound of melting snow is heard in all dells, and the ice dissolves apace in the ponds. The grass flames up on the

5. Mourning garments.

hillsides like a spring fire,—"et primitus oritur herba imbribus primoribus evocata,"[6]—as if the earth sent forth an inward heat to greet the returning sun; not yellow but green is the color of its flame;—the symbol of perpetual youth, the grass-blade, like a long green ribbon, streams from the sod into the summer, checked indeed by the frost, but anon pushing on again, lifting its spear of last year's hay with the fresh life below. It grows as steadily as the rill oozes out of the ground. It is almost identical with that, for in the growing days of June, when the rills are dry, the grass blades are their channels, and from year to year the herds drink at this perennial green stream, and the mower draws from it betimes their winter supply. So our human life but dies down to its roots, and still puts forth its green blade to eternity.

Walden is melting apace. There is a canal two rods wide along the northerly and westerly sides, and wider still at the east end. A great field of ice has cracked off from the main body. I hear a song-sparrow singing from the bushes on the shore,—olit, olit, olit,—chip, chip, chip, che char,—che wiss, wiss, wiss. He too is helping to crack it. How handsome the great sweeping curves in the edge of the ice, answering somewhat to those of the shore, but more regular! It is unusually hard, owing to the recent severe but transient cold, and all watered or waved like a palace floor. But the wind slides eastward over its opaque surface in vain, till it reaches the living surface beyond. It is glorious to behold this ribbon of water sparkling in the sun, the bare face of the pond full of glee and youth, as if it spoke the joy of the fishes within it, and of the sands on its shore,—a silvery sheen as from the scales of a leuciscus, as it were all one active fish. Such is the contrast between winter and spring. Walden was dead and is alive again. But this spring it broke up more steadily, as I have said.

The change from storm and winter to serene and mild weather, from dark and sluggish hours to bright and elastic ones, is a memorable crisis which all things proclaim. It is seemingly instantaneous at last. Suddenly an influx of light filled my house, though the evening was at hand, and the clouds of winter still overhung it, and the eaves were dripping with sleety rain. I looked out the window, and lo! where yesterday was cold gray ice there lay the transparent pond already calm and full of hope as on a summer evening, reflecting a summer evening sky in its bosom, though none was visible overhead, as if it had intelligence with some remote horizon. I heard a robin in the distance, the first I had heard for many a thousand years, methought, whose note I shall not forget for many a thousand more,—the same sweet and powerful song of yore. O the evening robin, at the end of a New England summer day! If I could ever find the twig he sits upon! I mean he; I mean the twig. This at least is not the Turdus migratorius.[7] The pitch-pines and shrub-oaks about my house, which had so long drooped, suddenly resumed their several characters, looked brighter, greener, and more erect and alive, as if effectually cleansed and restored by the rain. I knew that it would not rain any more. You may tell by looking at any twig of the forest, ay, at your very wood-pile, whether its winter is past or not. As it grew darker, I was startled by the honking of geese flying low over the woods, like weary travellers getting in late from southern lakes, and indulging at last in unrestrained complaint and mutual consolation. Standing at my door, I could hear the rush of their

6. Varro's Rerum Rusticarum 2.2.14; Thoreau goes on to translate.

7. American robin.

wings; when, driving toward my house, they suddenly spied my light, and with hushed clamor wheeled and settled in the pond. So I came in, and shut the door, and passed my first spring night in the woods.

In the morning I watched the geese from the door through the mist, sailing in the middle of the pond, fifty rods off, so large and tumultuous that Walden appeared like an aritifical pond for their amusement. But when I stood on the shore they at once rose up with a great flapping of wings at the signal of their commander, and when they had got into rank circled about over my head, twenty-nine of them, and then steered straight to Canada, with a regular *honk* from the leader at intervals, trusting to break their fast in muddier pools. A "plump" of ducks rose at the same time and took the route to the north in the wake of their noisier cousins.

For a week I heard the circling groping clangor of some solitary goose in the foggy mornings, seeking its companion, and still peopling the woods with the sound of a larger life than they could sustain. In April the pigeons were seen again flying express in small flocks, and in due time I heard the martins twittering over my clearing, though it had not seemed that the township contained so many that it could afford me any, and I fancied that they were peculiarly of the ancient race that dwelt in hollow trees ere white men came. In almost all climes the tortoise and the frog are among the precursors and heralds of this season, and birds fly with song and glancing plumage, and plants spring and bloom, and winds blow, to correct this slight oscillation of the poles and preserve the equilibrium of Nature.

As every season seems best to us in its turn, so the coming in of spring is like the creation of Cosmos out of Chaos and the realization of the Golden Age.—

> "Eurus ad Auroram, Nabathæaque regna recessit,
> Persidaque, et radiis juga subdita matutinis."

> "The East-Wind withdrew to Aurora and the Nabathæan kingdom,
> And the Persian, and the ridges placed under the morning rays.

> • • •

> Man was born. Whether that Artificer of things,
> The origin of a better world, made him from the divine seed;
> Or the earth being recent and lately sundered from the high
> Ether, retained some seeds of cognate heaven."[8]

A single gentle rain makes the grass many shades greener. So our prospects brighten on the influx of better thoughts. We should be blessed if we lived in the present always, and took advantage of every accident that befell us, like the grass which confesses the influence of the slightest dew that falls on it; and did not spend our time in atoning for the neglect of past opportunities, which we call doing our duty. We loiter in winter while it is already spring. In a pleasant spring morning all men's sins are forgiven. Such a day is a truce to vice. While such a sun holds out to burn, the vilest sinner may return. Through our own recovered innocence we discern the innocence of our neighbors. You may have known your neighbor yesterday for a thief, a drunkard, or a sensualist, and merely pitied or despised him, and despaired of the world; but the

---

8. Ovid's *Metamorphoses* 1.61–62, 78–81.

sun shines bright and warm this first spring morning, re-creating the world, and you meet him at some serene work, and see how his exhausted and debauched veins expand with still joy and bless the new day, feel the spring influence with the innocence of infancy, and all his faults are forgotten. There is not only an atmosphere of good will about him, but even a savor of holiness groping for expression, blindly and ineffectually perhaps, like a new-born instinct, and for a short hour the south hill-side echoes to no vulgar jest. You see some innocent fair shoots preparing to burst from his gnarled rind and try another year's life, tender and fresh as the youngest plant. Even he has entered into the joy of his Lord. Why the jailer does not leave open his prison doors,—why the judge does not dismiss his case,—why the preacher does not dismiss his congregation! It is because they do not obey the hint which God gives them, nor accept the pardon which he freely offers to all.

"A return to goodness produced each day in the tranquil and beneficent breath of the morning, causes that in respect to the love of virtue and the hatred of vice, one approaches a little the primitive nature of man, as the sprouts of the forest which has been felled. In like manner the evil which one does in the interval of a day prevents the germs of virtues which began to spring up again from developing themselves and destroys them.

"After the germs of virtue have thus been prevented many times from developing themselves, then the beneficent breath of evening does not suffice to preserve them. As soon as the breath of evening does not suffice longer to preserve them, then the nature of man does not differ much from that of the brute. Men seeing the nature of this man like that of the brute, think that he has never possessed the innate faculty of reason. Are those the true and natural sentiments of man?"[9]

> "The Golden Age was first created, which without any avenger
> Spontaneously without law cherished fidelity and rectitude.
> Punishment and fear were not; nor were threatening words read
> On suspended brass; nor did the suppliant crowd fear
> The words of their judge; but were safe without an avenger.
> Not yet the pine felled on its mountains had descended
> To the liquid waves that it might see a foreign world,
> And mortals knew no shore but their own.
>
> • • •
>
> There was eternal spring, and placid zephyrs with warm
> Blasts soothed the flowers born without seed."[1]

On the 29th of April, as I was fishing from the bank of the river near the Nine-Acre-Corner bridge, standing on the quaking grass and willow roots, where the muskrats lurk, I heard a singular rattling sound, somewhat like that of the sticks which boys play with their fingers, when, looking up, I observed a very slight and graceful hawk, like a night-hawk, alternately soaring like a ripple and tumbling a rod or two over and over, showing the underside of its wings, which gleamed like a satin ribbon in the sun, or like the pearly inside of a shell. This sight reminded me of falconry and what

9. Mencius's (Meng-tzu's) *Works* 6.1.   1. Ovid's *Metamorphoses* 1.89–96, 107–08.

nobleness and poetry are associated with that sport. The Merlin[2] it seemed to me it might be called: but I care not for its name. It was the most ethereal flight I had ever witnessed. It did not simply flutter like a butterfly, nor soar like the larger hawks, but it sported with proud reliance in the fields of air; mounting again and again with its strange chuckle, it repeated its free and beautiful fall, turning over and over like a kite, and then recovering from its lofty tumbling, as if it had never set its foot on *terra firma*. It appeared to have no companion in the universe,—sporting there alone,—and to need none but the morning and the ether with which it played. It was not lonely, but made all the earth lonely beneath it. Where was the parent which hatched it, its kindred, and its father in the heavens? The tenant of the air, it seemed related to the earth but by an egg hatched some time in the crevice of a crag;—or was its native nest made in the angle of a cloud, woven of the rainbow's trimmings and the sunset sky, and lined with some soft midsummer haze caught up from earth? Its eyry[3] now some cliffy cloud.

Beside this I got a rare mess of golden and silver and bright cupreous[4] fishes, which looked like a string of jewels. Ah! I have penetrated to those meadows on the morning of many a first spring day, jumping from hummock to hummock, from willow root to willow root, when the wild river valley and the woods were bathed in so pure and bright a light as would have waked the dead, if they had been slumbering in their graves, as some suppose. There needs no stronger proof of immortality. All things must live in such a light. O Death, where was thy sting? O Grave, where was thy victory, then?[5]

Our village life would stagnate if it were not for the unexplored forests and meadows which surround it. We need the tonic of wildness,—to wade sometimes in marshes where the bittern and the meadow-hen lurk, and hear the booming of the snipe; to smell the whispering sedge where only some wilder and more solitary fowl builds her nest, and the mink crawls with its belly close to the ground. At the same time that we are earnest to explore and learn all things, we require that all things be mysterious and unexplorable, that land and sea be infinitely wild, unsurveyed and unfathomed by us because unfathomable. We can never have enough of Nature. We must be refreshed by the sight of inexhaustible vigor, vast and Titanic features, the sea-coast with its wrecks, the wilderness with its living and its decaying trees, the thunder cloud, and the rain which lasts three weeks and produces freshets. We need to witness our own limits transgressed, and some life pasturing freely where we never wander. We are cheered when we observe the vulture feeding on the carrion which disgusts and disheartens us and deriving health and strength from the repast. There was a dead horse in the hollow by the path to my house, which compelled me sometimes to go out of my way, especially in the night when the air was heavy, but the assurance it gave me of the strong appetite and inviolable health of Nature was my compensation for this. I love to see that Nature is so rife with life that myriads can be afforded to be sacrificed and suffered to prey on one another; that tender organizations can be so serenely squashed out of existence like pulp,— tadpoles which herons gobble up, and tortoises and toads run over in the road; and that sometimes it has rained flesh and blood! With the liability to

2. Small falcon or pigeon hawk.
3. Aerie; bird's nest.
4. Coppery.

5. 1 Corinthians 15.55: "O death, where is thy sting? O grave, where is thy victory?"

accident, we must see how little account is to be made of it. The impression made on a wise man is that of universal innocence. Poison is not poisonous after all, nor are any wounds fatal. Compassion is a very untenable ground. It must be expeditious. Its pleadings will not bear to be stereotyped.

Early in May, the oaks, hickories, maples, and other trees, just putting out amidst the pine woods around the pond, imparted a brightness like sunshine to the landscape, especially in cloudy days, as if the sun were breaking through mists and shining faintly on the hill-sides here and there. On the third or fourth of May I saw a loon in the pond, and during the first week of the month I heard the whippoorwill, the brown-thrasher, the veery, the wood-pewee, the chewink, and other birds. I had heard the woodthrush long before. The phœbe had already come once more and looked in at my door and window, to see if my house was cavern-like enough for her, sustaining herself on humming wings with clinched talons, as if she held by the air, while she surveyed the premises. The sulphur-like pollen of the pitch-pine soon covered the pond and the stones and rotten wood along the shore, so that you could have collected a barrel-ful. This is the "sulphur showers" we hear of. Even in Calidas' drama of Sacontala, we read of "rills dyed yellow with the golden dust of the lotus."[6] And so the seasons went rolling on into summer, as one rambles into higher and higher grass.

Thus was my first year's life in the woods completed; and the second year was similar to it. I finally left Walden September 6th, 1847.

18. Conclusion

To the sick the doctors wisely recommend a change of air and scenery. Thank Heaven, here is not all the world. The buck-eye does not grow in New England, and the mocking-bird is rarely heard here. The wild-goose is more of a cosmopolite than we; he breaks his fast in Canada, takes a luncheon in the Ohio, and plumes himself for the night in a southern bayou. Even the bison, to some extent, keeps pace with the seasons, cropping the pastures of the Colorado only till a greener and sweeter grass awaits him by the Yellowstone. Yet we think that if rail-fences are pulled down, and stone-walls piled up on our farms, bounds are henceforth set to our lives and our fates decided. If you are chosen town-clerk, forsooth, you cannot go to Tierra del Fuego[7] this summer: but you may go to the land of infernal fire nevertheless. The universe is wider than our views of it.

Yet we should oftener look over the tafferel of our craft, like curious passengers, and not make the voyage like stupid sailors picking oakum.[8] The other side of the globe is but the home of our correspondent. Our voyaging is only great-circle sailing, and the doctors prescribe for diseases of the skin merely. One hastens to Southern Africa to chase the giraffe; but surely that is not the game he would be after. How long, pray, would a man hunt giraffes if he could? Snipes and woodcocks also may afford rare sport; but I trust it would be nobler game to shoot one's self.—

---

6. Sir William Jones's 18th-century translation of *Sacontalá*, act 5, by Cálidás (5th century), Hindu writer.
7. Thoreau puns on the meaning of the name of the archipelago at the southern tip of South America: land of fire (Spanish).
8. Picking old rope apart so the pieces of hemp could be tarred and used for caulking. "Tafferel": i.e., taffrail; guardrail at a ship's stern.

"Direct your eye sight inward, and you'll find
A thousand regions in your mind
Yet undiscovered. Travel them, and be
Expert in home-cosmography."[9]

What does Africa,—what does the West stand for? Is not our own interior white on the chart? black though it may prove, like the coast, when discovered. Is it the source of the Nile, or the Niger, or the Mississippi, or a North West Passage around this continent, that we would find? Are these the problems which most concern mankind? Is Franklin[1] the only man who is lost, that his wife should be so earnest to find him? Does Mr. Grinnell[2] know where he himself is? Be rather the Mungo Park, the Lewis and Clarke and Frobisher,[3] of your own streams and oceans; explore your own higher latitudes,—with shiploads of preserved meats to support you, if they be necessary; and pile the empty cans sky-high for a sign. Were preserved meats invented to preserve meat merely? Nay, be a Columbus to whole new continents and worlds within you, opening new channels, not of trade, but of thought. Every man is the lord of a realm beside which the earthly empire of the Czar is but a petty state, a hummock left by the ice. Yet some can be patriotic who have no *self*-respect, and sacrifice the greater to the less. They love the soil which makes their graves, but have no sympathy with the spirit which may still animate their clay. Patriotism is a maggot in their heads. What was the meaning of that South-Sea Exploring Expedition,[4] with all its parade and expense, but an indirect recognition of the fact, that there are continents and seas in the moral world, to which every man is an isthmus or an inlet, yet unexplored by him, but that it is easier to sail many thousand miles through cold and storm and cannibals, in a government ship, with five hundred men and boys to assist one, than it is to explore the private sea, the Atlantic and Pacific Ocean of one's being alone.—

"Erret, et extremos alter scrutetur Iberos.
Plus habet hic vitæ, plus habet ille viæ."[5]

Let them wander and scrutinize the outlandish Australians.
I have more of God, they more of the road.

It is not worth the while to go round the world to count the cats in Zanzibar.[6] Yet do this even till you can do better, and you may perhaps find some "Symmes' Hole"[7] by which to get at the inside at last. England and France, Spain and Portugal, Gold Coast and Slave Coast, all front on this private sea; but no bark from them has ventured out of sight of land, though it

9. William Habington (1605–1654), "To My Honoured Friend Sir Ed. P. Knight."
1. Sir John Franklin (1785–1847), lost on a British expedition to the Arctic.
2. Henry Grinnell (1799–1874), a rich New York whale-oil merchant from a New Bedford family who sponsored two attempts to rescue Sir Franklin, one in 1850 and another in 1853.
3. I.e., an explorer like Martin Frobisher (1535?–1594), English mariner. Mungo Park (1771–1806), Scottish explorer of Africa. Meriwether Lewis (1774–1809) and William Clark (1770–1838), leaders of the American expedition into the Louisiana Territory (1804–6).
4. The famous expedition to the Pacific Antarc-

tic led by Charles Wilkes (1798–1877) during 1838–42.
5. Thoreau's journal for May 10, 1841, begins: "A good warning to the restless tourists of these days is contained in the last verses of Claudian's 'Old Man of Verona.'" Claudius Claudianus was the last of the Latin classic poets (fl. 395 C.E.) and author of *Epigrammata*, where Thoreau found the passage he loosely translates here.
6. Thoreau had read Charles Pickering's *The Races of Man* (1851), which reports on the domestic cats in Zanzibar.
7. In 1818 Captain John Symmes (1780–1829) theorized that the earth was hollow with openings at both the North and South Poles.

is without doubt the direct way to India. If you would learn to speak all tongues and conform to the customs of all nations, if you would travel farther than all travellers, be naturalized in all climes, and cause the Sphinx to dash her head against a stone,[8] even obey the precept of the old philosopher, and Explore thyself. Herein are demanded the eye and the nerve. Only the defeated and deserters go to the wars, cowards that run away and enlist. Start now on that farthest western way, which does not pause at the Mississippi or the Pacific, nor conduct toward a worn-out China or Japan, but leads on direct a tangent to this sphere, summer and winter, day and night, sun down, moon down, and at last earth down too.

It is said that Mirabeau took to highway robbery "to ascertain what degree of resolution was necessary in order to place one's self in formal opposition to the most sacred laws of society." He declared that "a soldier who fights in the ranks does not require half so much courage as a foot-pad,"—"that honor and religion have never stood in the way of a well-considered and a firm resolve."[9] This was manly, as the world goes; and yet it was idle, if not desperate. A saner man would have found himself often enough "in formal opposition" to what are deemed "the most sacred laws of society," through obedience to yet more sacred laws, and so have tested his resolution without going out of his way. It is not for a man to put himself in such an attitude to society, but to maintain himself in whatever attitude he find himself through obedience to the laws of his being, which will never be one of opposition to a just government, if he should chance to meet with such.

I left the woods for as good a reason as I went there. Perhaps it seemed to me that I had several more lives to live, and could not spare any more time for that one. It is remarkable how easily and insensibly we fall into a particular route, and make a beaten track for ourselves. I had not lived there a week before my feet wore a path from my door to the pond-side; and though it is five or six years since I trod it, it is still quite distinct. It is true, I fear that others may have fallen into it, and so helped to keep it open. The surface of the earth is soft and impressible by the feet of men; and so with the paths which the mind travels. How worn and dusty, then, must be the highways of the world, how deep the ruts of tradition and conformity! I did not wish to take a cabin passage, but rather to go before the mast and on the deck of the world, for there I could best see the moonlight amid the mountains. I do not wish to go below now.

I learned this, at least, by my experiment; that if one advances confidently in the direction of his dreams, and endeavors to live the life which he has imagined, he will meet with a success unexpected in common hours. He will put some things behind, will pass an invisible boundary; new, universal, and more liberal laws will begin to establish themselves around and within him; or the old laws be expanded, and interpreted in his favor in a more liberal sense, and he will live with the license of a higher order of beings. In proportion as he simplifies his life, the laws of the universe will appear less complex, and solitude will not be solitude, nor poverty poverty, nor weakness weakness. If you have built castles in the air, your work need not be lost; that is where they should be. Now put the foundations under them.

8. As the Theban Sphinx did when Oedipus guessed her riddle. Thebes here is the ancient Greek city, not the Egyptian city Thoreau has previously referred to.

9. Thoreau encountered this passage by the French statesman Comte de Mirabeau (1749–1791) in *Harper's* 1 (1850).

It is a ridiculous demand which England and America make, that you shall speak so that they can understand you. Neither men nor toad-stools grow so. As if that were important, and there were not enough to understand you without them. As if Nature could support but one order of understandings, could not sustain birds as well as quadrupeds, flying as well as creeping things, and *hush* and *who*, which Bright[1] can understand, were the best English. As if there were safety in stupidity alone. I fear chiefly lest my expression may not be *extra-vagant*[2] enough, may not wander far enough beyond the narrow limits of my daily experience, so as to be adequate to the truth of which I have been convinced. *Extra vagance!* it depends on how you are yarded. The migrating buffalo, which seeks new pastures in another latitude, is not extravagant like the cow which kicks over the pail, leaps the cow-yard fence, and runs after her calf, in milking time. I desire to speak somewhere *without* bounds; like a man in a waking moment, to men in their waking moments; for I am convinced that I cannot exaggerate enough even to lay the foundation of a true expression. Who that has heard a strain of music feared then lest he should speak extravagantly any more forever? In view of the future or possible, we should live quite laxly and undefined in front, our outlines dim and misty on that side; as our shadows reveal an insensible perspiration toward the sun. The volatile truth of our words should continually betray the inadequacy of the residual statement. Their truth is instantly *translated*; its literal monument alone remains. The words which express our faith and piety are not definite; yet they are significant and fragrant like frankincense to superior natures.

Why level downward to our dullest perception always, and praise that as common sense? The commonest sense is the sense of men asleep, which they express by snoring. Sometimes we are inclined to class those who are once-and-a-half witted with the half-witted, because we appreciate only a third part of their wit. Some would find fault with the morning-red, if they ever got up early enough. "They pretend," as I hear, "that the verses of Kabir have four different senses; illusion, spirit, intellect, and the exoteric doctrine of the Vedas;"[3] but in this part of the world it is considered a ground for complaint if a man's writings admit of more than one interpretation. While England endeavors to cure the potato-rot, will not any endeavor to cure the brain-rot, which prevails so much more widely and fatally?

I do not suppose that I have attained to obscurity, but I should be proud if no more fatal fault were found with my pages on this score than was found with the Walden ice. Southern customers objected to its blue color, which is the evidence of its purity, as if it were muddy, and preferred the Cambridge ice, which is white, but tastes of weeds. The purity men love is like the mists which envelop the earth, and not like the azure ether beyond.

Some are dinning in our ears that we Americans, and moderns generally, are intellectual dwarfs compared with the ancients, or even the Elizabethan men. But what is that to the purpose? A living dog is better than a dead lion.[4] Shall a man go and hang himself because he belongs to the race of pygmies, and not be the biggest pygmy that he can? Let every one mind his own business, and endeavor to be what he was made.

---

1. Name for an ox.
2. Thoreau provides the hyphen to emphasize the word's Latin roots (*extra*, "outside"; *vagari*, "to wander").

3. M. Garcin de Tassy's *Histoire de la littérature hindoui* (1839).
4. Ecclesiastes 9.4.

Why should we be in such desperate haste to succeed, and in such desperate enterprises? If a man does not keep pace with his companions, perhaps it is because he hears a different drummer. Let him step to the music which he hears, however measured or far away. It is not important that he should mature as soon as an apple-tree or an oak. Shall he turn his spring into summer? If the condition of things which we were made for is not yet, what were any reality which we can substitute? We will not be shipwrecked on a vain reality. Shall we with pains erect a heaven of blue glass over ourselves, though when it is done we shall be sure to gaze still at the true ethereal heaven far above, as if the former were not?

There was an artist in the city of Kouroo[5] who was disposed to strive after perfection. One day it came into his mind to make a staff. Having considered that in an imperfect work time is an ingredient, but into a perfect work time does not enter, he said to himself, It shall be perfect in all respects, though I should do nothing else in my life. He proceeded instantly to the forest for wood, being resolved that it should not be made of unsuitable material; and as he searched for and rejected stick after stick, his friends gradually deserted him, for they grew old in their works and died, but he grew not older by a moment. His singleness of purpose and resolution, and his elevated piety, endowed him, without his knowledge, with perennial youth. As he made no compromise with Time, Time kept out of his way, and only sighed at a distance because he could not overcome him. Before he had found a stock in all respects suitable the city of Kouroo was a hoary ruin, and he sat on one of its mounds to peel the stick. Before he had given it the proper shape the dynasty of the Candahars was at an end, and with the point of the stick he wrote the name of the last of that race in the sand, and then resumed his work. By the time he had smoothed and polished the staff Kalpa was no longer the pole-star; and ere he had put on the ferule and the head adorned with precious stones, Brahma had awoke and slumbered many times. But why do I stay to mention these things? When the finishing stroke was put to his work, it suddenly expanded before the eyes of the astonished artist into the fairest of all the creations of Brahma. He had made a new system in making a staff, a world with full and fair proportions; in which, though the old cities and dynasties had passed away, fairer and more glorious ones had taken their places. And now he saw by the heap of shavings still fresh at his feet, that, for him and his work, the former lapse of time had been an illusion, and that no more time had elapsed than is required for a single scintillation from the brain of Brahma to fall on and inflame the tinder of a mortal brain. The material was pure, and his art was pure; how could the result be other than wonderful?

No face which we can give to a matter will stead us so well at last as the truth. This alone wears well. For the most part, we are not where we are, but in a false position. Through an infirmity of our natures, we suppose a case, and put ourselves into it, and hence are in two cases at the same time, and it is doubly difficult to get out. In sane moments we regard only the facts, the case that is. Say what you have to say, not what you ought. Any truth is better than make-believe. Tom Hyde, the tinker, standing on the gallows, was asked if he had any thing to say. "Tell the tailors," said he, "to

5. Thoreau in all likelihood invented this fable of artistry, though the reference to "Kouroo" invokes "Kuru," a legendary hero in India.

remember to make a knot in their thread before they take the first stitch."[6] His companion's prayer is forgotten.

However mean your life is, meet it and live it; do not shun it and call it hard names. It is not so bad as you are. It looks poorest when you are richest. The fault-finder will find faults even in paradise. Love your life, poor as it is. You may perhaps have some pleasant, thrilling, glorious hours, even in a poor-house. The setting sun is reflected from the windows of the alms-house as brightly as from the rich man's abode; the snow melts before its door as early in the spring. I do not see but a quiet mind may live as contentedly there, and have as cheering thoughts, as in a palace. The town's poor seem to me often to live the most independent lives of any. May be they are simply great enough to receive without misgiving. Most think that they are above being supported by the town; but it oftener happens that they are not above supporting themselves by dishonest means, which should be more disreputable. Cultivate poverty like a garden herb, like sage. Do not trouble yourself much to get new things, whether clothes or friends. Turn the old; return to them. Things do not change; we change. Sell your clothes and keep your thoughts. God will see that you do not want society. If I were confined to a corner of a garret all my days, like a spider, the world would be just as large to me while I had my thoughts about me. The philosopher said: "From an army of three divisions one can take away its general, and put it in disorder; from the man the most abject and vulgar one cannot take away his thought."[7] Do not seek so anxiously to be developed, to subject yourself to many influences to be played on; it is all dissipation. Humility like darkness reveals the heavenly lights. The shadows of poverty and mean-ness gather around us, "and lo! creation widens to our view."[8] We are often reminded that if there were bestowed on us the wealth of Crœsus,[9] our aims must still be the same, and our means essentially the same. Moreover, if you are restricted in your range by poverty, if you cannot buy books and newspapers, for instance, you are but confined to the most significant and vital experiences; you are compelled to deal with the material which yields the most sugar and the most starch. It is life near the bone where it is sweet-est. You are defended from being a trifler. No man loses ever on a lower level by magnanimity on a higher. Superfluous wealth can buy superfluities only. Money is not required to buy one necessary of the soul.

I live in the angle of a leaden wall, into whose composition was poured a little alloy of bell metal. Often, in the repose of my mid-day, there reaches my ears a confused *tintinnabulum*[1] from without. It is the noise of my contempo-raries. My neighbors tell me of their adventures with famous gentlemen and ladies, what notabilities they met at the dinner-table; but I am no more inter-ested in such things than in the contents of the Daily Times. The interest and the conversation are about costume and manners chiefly; but a goose is a goose still, dress it as you will. They tell me of California and Texas, of England and the Indies, of the Hon. Mr. ——— of Georgia or of Massachu-setts, all transient and fleeting phenomena, till I am ready to leap from their

6. Presumably a reference to the tailors who will sew Hyde's shroud. Thoreau may have invented this anecdote; scholars have been unable to identify a Tom Hyde who was executed.
7. Confucius's *Analects* 9.25.
8. From the sonnet "To Night" (1828) by the Spanish-born writer Joseph Blanco White (1775–1841), who emigrated to England in 1810.
9. King of Lydia (d. 546 B.C.E.), fabled as the richest man on earth.
1. Tinkling.

court-yard like the Mameluke bey.[2] I delight to come to my bearings,—not walk in procession with pomp and parade, in a conspicuous place, but to walk even with the Builder of the universe, if I may,—not to live in this restless, nervous, bustling, trivial Nineteenth Century, but stand or sit thoughtfully while it goes by. What are men celebrating? They are all on a committee of arrangements, and hourly expect a speech from somebody. God is only the president of the day, and Webster is his orator.[3] I love to weigh, to settle, to gravitate toward that which most strongly and rightfully attracts me;—not hang by the beam of the scale and try to weigh less,—not suppose a case, but take the case that is; to travel the only path I can, and that on which no power can resist me. It affords me no satisfaction to commence to spring an arch before I have got a solid foundation. Let us not play at kittlybenders.[4] There is a solid bottom every where. We read that the traveller asked the boy if the swamp before him had a hard bottom. The boy replied that it had. But presently the traveller's horse sank in up to the girths, and he observed to the boy, "I thought you said that this bog had a hard bottom." "So it has," answered the latter, "but you have not got half way to it yet." So it is with the bogs and quicksands of society; but he is an old boy that knows it. Only what is thought said or done at a certain rare coincidence is good. I would not be one of those who will foolishly drive a nail into mere lath and plastering; such a deed would keep me awake nights. Give me a hammer, and let me feel for the furring.[5] Do not depend on the putty. Drive a nail home and clinch it so faithfully that you can wake up in the night and think of your work with satisfaction,—a work at which you would not be ashamed to invoke the Muse. So will help you God, and so only. Every nail driven should be as another rivet in the machine of the universe, you carrying on the work.

Rather than love, than money, than fame, give me truth. I sat at a table where were rich food and wine in abundance, and obsequious attendance, but sincerity and truth were not; and I went away hungry from the inhospitable board. The hospitality was as cold as the ices. I thought that there was no need of ice to freeze them. They talked to me of the age of the wine and the fame of the vintage; but I thought of an older, a newer, and purer wine, of a more glorious vintage, which they had not got, and could not buy. The style, the house and grounds and "entertainment" pass for nothing with me. I called on the king, but he made me wait in his hall, and conducted like a man incapacitated for hospitality. There was a man in my neighborhood who lived in a hollow tree. His manners were truly regal. I should have done better had I called on him.

How long shall we sit in our porticoes practising idle and musty virtues, which any work would make impertinent? As if one were to begin the day with long-suffering, and hire a man to hoe his potatoes; and in the afternoon go forth to practise Christian meekness and charity with goodness aforethought! Consider the China[6] pride and stagnant self-complacency of

---

2. A famous romantic exploit: in 1811 the Egyptian Mehemet Ali Pasha attempted to massacre the Mameluke caste, but one bey, or officer, escaped by leaping from a wall onto his horse.
3. Political meetings then had "presidents" (because they presided). Thoreau plays on the saying from Islam, "There is no other God than Allah, and Mohammed is his prophet." Thoreau again expresses his contempt for Massachusetts

senator Daniel Webster.
4. A game of trying to skate or slide over thin ice without breaking through.
5. Narrow lumber nailed as backing for lath. The first edition reads "furrowing," and one manuscript draft reads "stud."
6. Thoreau and others of the time regarded China as complacent in its isolationism.

mankind. This generation reclines a little to congratulate itself on being the last of an illustrious line; and in Boston and London and Paris and Rome, thinking of its long descent, it speaks of its progress in art and science and literature with satisfaction. There are the Records of the Philosophical Societies, and the public Eulogies of *Great Men*! It is the good Adam contemplating his own virtue. "Yes, we have done great deeds, and sung divine songs, which shall never die,"—that is, as long as *we* can remember them. The learned societies and great men of Assyria,[7]—where are they? What youthful philosophers and experimentalists we are! There is not one of my readers who has yet lived a whole human life. These may be but the spring months in the life of the race. If we have had the seven-years' itch,[8] we have not seen the seventeen-year locust yet in Concord. We are acquainted with a mere pellicle[9] of the globe on which we live. Most have not delved six feet beneath the surface, nor leaped as many above it. We know not where we are. Beside, we are sound asleep nearly half our time. Yet we esteem ourselves wise, and have an established order on the surface. Truly, we are deep thinkers, we are ambitious spirits! As I stand over the insect crawling amid the pine needles on the forest floor, and endeavoring to conceal itself from my sight, and ask myself why it will cherish those humble thoughts, and hide its head from me who might perhaps be its benefactor, and impart to its race some cheering information, I am reminded of the greater Benefactor and Intelligence that stands over me the human insect.

There is an incessant influx of novelty into the world, and yet we tolerate incredible dulness. I need only suggest what kind of sermons are still listened to in the most enlightened countries. There are such words as joy and sorrow, but they are only the burden of a psalm, sung with a nasal twang, while we believe in the ordinary and mean. We think that we can change our clothes only. It is said that the British Empire is very large and respectable, and that the United States are a first-rate power. We do not believe that a tide rises and falls behind every man which can float the British Empire like a chip, if he should ever harbor it in his mind. Who knows what sort of seventeen-year locust will next come out of the ground? The government of the world I live in was not framed, like that of Britain, in after-dinner conversations over the wine.

The life in us is like the water in the river. It may rise this year higher than man has ever known it, and flood the parched uplands; even this may be the eventful year, which will drown out all our muskrats. It was not always dry land where we dwell. I see far inland the banks which the stream anciently washed, before science began to record its freshets. Every one has heard the story which has gone the rounds of New England, of a strong and beautiful bug which came out of the dry leaf of an old table of apple-tree wood, which had stood in a farmer's kitchen for sixty years, first in Connecticut, and afterward in Massachusetts,—from an egg deposited in the living tree many years earlier still, as appeared by counting the annual layers beyond it; which was heard gnawing out for several weeks, hatched perchance by the heat of an urn.[1] Who does not feel his faith in a resurrection and immortality strengthened by hearing of this? Who knows what beautiful and winged

---

7. Ancient empire in western Asia.
8. Painful skin irritation caused by mites.
9. Skin.

1. An account of the incident is in Timothy Dwight's *Travels in New England and New York* (1821), vol. 2.

life, whose egg has been buried for ages under many concentric layers of woodenness in the dead dry life of society, deposited at first in the alburnum[2] of the green and living tree, which has been gradually converted into the semblance of its well-seasoned tomb,—heard perchance gnawing out now for years by the astonished family of man, as they sat round the festive board,—may unexpectedly come forth from amidst society's most trivial and handselled furniture, to enjoy its perfect summer life at last!

I do not say that John or Jonathan[3] will realize all this; but such is the character of that morrow which mere lapse of time can never make to dawn. The light which puts out our eyes is darkness to us. Only that day dawns to which we are awake. There is more day to dawn. The sun is but a morning star.

THE END

1854

FREDERICK DOUGLASS
1818–1895

In the concluding chapter of his famous autobiography, *Narrative of the Life of Frederick Douglass, An American Slave, Written by Himself* (1845), Douglass describes the moment in 1841 when he first stepped forward to speak at an antislavery convention in Nantucket, Massachusetts. "It was a severe cross," he says, "and I took it up reluctantly." However reluctant he may have been, in the moments following the speech, the twenty-three-year-old fugitive slave "felt a degree of freedom" and, just as important, realized he had discovered his vocation. As he states at the end of the *Narrative*: "From that time until now, I have been engaged in pleading the cause of my brethren—with what success, and with what devotion, I leave those acquainted with my labors to decide." Douglass would continue to plead the cause of African Americans for over fifty years. He published three versions of his autobiography—the *Narrative* (1845), *My Bondage and My Freedom* (1855), *Life and Times of Frederick Douglass* (1881, rev. ed. 1892)—as well as a novella, "The Heroic Slave" (1853), and numerous essays and speeches. He also established and edited three African American newspapers—the *North Star* (1847–51), *Frederick Douglass' Paper* (1851–59), and *Douglass' Monthly* (1859–63)—and edited a fourth, the *New National Era* (1870–73). By the time of his death, Douglass was thought of, in the United States and abroad, as the most influential African American leader of the nineteenth century and as one of the greatest orators of the age. In the manner of Benjamin Franklin, whom he greatly admired, Douglass presented himself as a representative American whose rise to prominence spoke to the promises of the nation's egalitarian ideology. But he also had a clear-eyed understanding of the hurdles that slavery and racism placed in

2. Young, soft wood.
3. John Bull or Brother Jonathan, i.e., England or America.

the way of African Americans. Regularly invoking the principles of the Declaration of Independence, Douglass throughout his life challenged the nation to live up to its founding ideals. In "The Lessons of the Hour" (1894), one of his final speeches, Douglass condemned the rise of lynching with the passion and vigor of his early writing, seeing this latest outbreak of violence against black people as a threat to what he had devoted his life to achieving: a multiracial United States offering equal rights and justice for all.

Douglass was born into slavery as Frederick Augustus Washington Bailey in February 1818 at Holme Hill Farm in Talbot County, on the eastern shore of Maryland. His mother was Harriet Bailey; his father was a white man whose identity is still not known, although widely assumed to have been his mother's owner, Aaron Anthony. In 1826, about a year after the death of his mother and shortly after the death of Anthony, Douglass became the property of Thomas Auld and was sent to live with Thomas's brother Hugh Auld and his wife, Sophia, in Baltimore. According to the 1845 Narrative, Sophia began to teach Douglass how to read, but Hugh forbade her to continue because, he said, learning "would forever unfit him to be a slave." Nevertheless, as the autobiographies recount, Douglass cleverly found ways to learn how to read and write. During this first residence in Baltimore, Douglass acquired and pored over The Columbian Orator (1797), a popular school text, finding its many speeches denouncing oppression applicable to his own situation. He read about abolition as an organized movement in the Baltimore American and established a close relationship with the free black Charles Lawson, a lay preacher who became his spiritual mentor and told Douglass that he had been chosen to do "great work."

In 1833, after seven years in Baltimore, Douglass was returned to Thomas Auld's plantation, where he quickly became known for his rebellious attitude and was sent to work on the farm of Edward Covey, a specialist in "slave breaking." The account of his decline and reawakening at Covey's farm, culminating in a hand-to-hand battle between Covey and Douglass in August 1834, is the turning point of the Narrative. Following this confrontation, Douglass took on a greater leadership role among the slaves, conducting a Sabbath school at William Freeland's plantation in 1835 and, in 1836, organizing an escape attempt with a group of slaves. For his role in the failed plot, Douglass was briefly jailed in Easton, Maryland. He was then returned to the Aulds in Baltimore, where he learned the caulking trade in the shipyards. Though Hugh Auld kept most of the money Frederick earned, Douglass was able to save enough to develop a feasible plan of escape. In this plan he was helped both financially and emotionally by the free black Anna Murray, to whom he became engaged on September 3, 1838, the very day he boarded a train for New York disguised as a sailor and carrying the borrowed papers of a free black seaman. Douglass withheld information about his mode of escape until the third of his autobiographies, when disclosing it could no longer endanger the lives and plans of other fugitives from Baltimore. Within days of his escape Anna joined him in New York City, and they were married on September 15. They soon left for New Bedford, Massachusetts, where the likelihood of his being captured as a fugitive slave was reduced by his assuming the name "Douglass," which he took from Sir Walter Scott's poem Lady of the Lake (1810).

Though Douglass in the Narrative emphasizes the splendor of New Bedford compared to towns under slavery, life in New Bedford was not easy for the newly married couple. Douglass was discriminated against when he sought work as a caulker and had to piece together a living doing odd jobs. In 1839 he became a licensed preacher in the African Methodist Episcopal Zion Church; that same year the Douglasses' first child, Rosetta, was born. A son, Lewis, was born the following year, and the other three Douglass children—Frederick, Charles, and Annie— were born in 1842, 1844, and 1849, respectively. Soon after arriving in New Bedford, Douglass subscribed to the abolitionist William Lloyd Garrison's Liberator. Garrison was in the audience when Douglass delivered his first antislavery speech, and shortly thereafter he hired Douglass as a speaker in his Massachusetts Anti-Slavery Society. During 1841–43, Douglass delivered his antislavery message on behalf of Garrison's organization in a number of Northern states, and on one occasion in 1843, in Pendleton, Indiana, he was attacked by an anti-abolitionist mob and suffered a broken hand. Douglass began work on his narrative in 1844, and it was published in May 1845 by Garrison's Anti-Slavery Office in Boston. The *Narrative* sold some thirty thousand copies in its first five years, making it a bona fide best seller for the time and helping to establish Douglass as an international spokesperson for freedom and equality. Some earlier slave narratives had been ghostwritten or composed with the help of white editors, but the *Narrative*'s vivid detail and stylistic distinctiveness, combined with the reputation Douglass had earned as an eloquent speaker, left no doubt that Douglass had in fact written his own story in his own words.

Garrison's abolitionist principles—a commitment to an immediate end to slavery, an advocacy of moral persuasion over violence, and a belief that the Constitution was a proslavery document—inspired Douglass in the early to middle 1840s. When he went on an extended speaking tour in Great Britain during 1845–46 (in part to escape the fugitive slave hunters that he feared would track him down after the publication of the *Narrative*), he spoke as a Garrisonian abolitionist. But upon his return to the United States as a free man—British antislavery friends had purchased his freedom for $711 in 1846—Douglass became increasingly suspicious of Garrison, particularly when Garrison attempted to bully him into shutting down his newspaper, the *North Star*, which Douglass founded not in New Bedford, but in Rochester, New York, where Douglass resettled in part to escape the influence of Garrison. In the inaugural issue of December 3, 1847, Douglass declared that in the antislavery and antiracism struggle, African Americans "must be our own representatives and advocates, not exclusively, but peculiarly—not distinct from, but in connection with our white friends." Garrison, who wanted absolute loyalty and control of the movement, began to question Douglass's antislavery politics and even published unsubstantiated rumors in the *Liberator* about Douglass's romantic involvement with Julia Griffiths, a white Englishwoman living in the Douglass home and helping with editorial work on the *North Star*. But along with the personality clashes, there were ideological differences between the two. By 1851, after forming a friendship with the New York abolitionist Gerrit Smith, Douglass formally broke with Garrison, announcing his belief in a more pragmatic political abolitionism that regarded the Constitution as an antislavery document, that saw the value in steadily working toward the goals of antislavery, and that defended the strategic use of black violence as a response to the violence of slavery.

In 1855 Douglass published *My Bondage and My Freedom*, a revised and substantially longer version of his 1845 autobiography. In covering the ten years of his life since the *Narrative*, Douglass wrote about his encounters with racism in the North, his work as an abolitionist, and his break with Garrison. No longer willing to "leave the philosophy" of abolition to Garrison and other white abolitionists, Douglass asserted his intellectual and interpretive independence and also his deeper connections to black moral reformers and abolitionists. It is significant that the second autobiography was introduced not by white abolitionists (as with the *Narrative*) but by the black physician and abolitionist James McCune Smith (1813–1865), who celebrated Douglass as "a Representative American man—a type of his countrymen." Like the *Narrative, My Bondage and My Freedom* was widely read, selling eighteen thousand copies during its first two years.

Like all autobiographers, Douglass artistically shaped the facts of his life to underscore the particular truths that he wished to convey at the moment of composition. In the 1845 *Narrative*, he presented himself as relatively isolated from his fellow slaves, describing his fight with Covey as a heroic instance of individual rebellion; in the 1855 *My Bondage and My Freedom*, he depicted the fight as involving several other African Americans who came to his assistance. Similarly, in 1845 Douglass said little about the role of his mother in his life because he wanted to show his white readers how slavery divided mothers and children; in

1855, he celebrated the influence of his grandmother and mother. This new emphasis on the importance of black culture and family to his developing identity as an antislavery leader resonated with the rhetoric of sentiment associated with Harriet Beecher Stowe's *Uncle Tom's Cabin* (1852) and other works by popular mid-nineteenth-century women writers; it testified to Douglass's awareness that women were a powerful force within the abolitionist movement. Stowe's influence can also be felt on Douglass's only work of fiction, the novella "The Heroic Slave," which he published in 1853 in *Frederick Douglass' Paper* and in a fund-raising volume for his newspaper. Like Stowe, he represented sympathetic bonds between whites and blacks that could lead to united action against enslavers. Unlike Stowe in *Uncle Tom's Cabin*, he celebrated a dark-skinned man capable of using violence against whites, and showed blacks moving south to the Caribbean instead of north to Canada.

Following the Supreme Court's 1857 ruling in the Dred Scott case, which declared that blacks could never become citizens of the United States, Douglass became more militant in his writing. Though he refused to participate in John Brown's 1859 raid on the federal arsenal at Harpers Ferry, which he regarded as a suicidal action, he was obliged to flee to Canada and thence to England because of his known association with Brown. He returned in May 1860 after receiving news of the death of his daughter Annie. Once the Civil War began, Douglass took an active role in the campaign to make free black men eligible to serve the Union cause; he became a successful recruiter of black soldiers, whose ranks soon included his own sons. Having helped to enlist these men, Douglass subsequently protested directly to President Lincoln over blacks' unequal pay and treatment in the Union army.

After the war, Douglass criticized Lincoln's successors over what he believed was a tardy and unjust Reconstruction policy. He was particularly insistent in calling for the swift passage of the Fifteenth Amendment, guaranteeing suffrage to the newly emancipated male slaves. By the 1870s, Douglass was a significant

Douglass's *Narrative*. Frontispiece and title page of the first edition (1845).

figure in the Republican Party, taking on such positions as president of the Freedman's Bank, federal marshal, and recorder of deeds for the District of Columbia. Never satisfied with the grudging legal concessions the Civil War yielded, Douglass persistently objected to every sign of discrimination against blacks and other disenfranchised people, including women. At times his writings seem to celebrate black manhood, but Douglass had a longstanding interest in women's rights. Though he broke temporarily with women's rights supporters in 1868–69, when he championed the Fifteenth Amendment (which failed to offer suffrage to women), he had attended the first Women's Rights Convention in Seneca Falls, New York, in 1848, and he continued to attend women's rights conventions and to editorialize and lecture in favor of women's rights. His final speech, delivered just hours before he died of a heart attack on February 20, 1895, was at a women's rights rally.

Douglass published the third of his autobiographies, *Life and Times of Frederick Douglass*, in 1881, and he brought out an expanded version in 1892. This last memoir added much to the record of Douglass's post–Civil War years, but did not fare nearly as well in the marketplace as the earlier two autobiographies. Douglass was accused in the black press of betraying his race by marrying his white former secretary Helen Pitts in 1884 (Anna Douglass had died in 1882), and several years later, when he was the U.S. consul general to Haiti, he was accused in newspapers and journals of being overly sympathetic to black Haitians when the United States was attempting to gain a naval port in the island nation. In the final version of his life history, Douglass took on his critics and asserted in the strongest possible terms his commitment to a cosmopolitan vision of a world without invidious racial distinctions and prejudices. It would be difficult to exaggerate the importance for Americans across the color line of Douglass's exemplary career as a champion of human rights.

Narrative of the Life of Frederick Douglass, An American Slave, Written by Himself[1]

Preface[2]

In the month of August, 1841, I attended an anti-slavery convention in Nantucket, at which it was my happiness to become acquainted with FREDERICK DOUGLASS, the writer of the following Narrative. He was a stranger to nearly every member of that body; but, having recently made his escape from the southern prison-house of bondage, and feeling his curiosity excited to ascertain the principles and measures of the abolitionists,—of whom he had heard a somewhat vague description while he was a slave,—he was induced to give his attendance, on the occasion alluded to, though at that time a resident in New Bedford.[3]

Fortunate, most fortunate occurrence!—fortunate for the millions of his manacled brethren, yet panting for deliverance from their awful thraldom!—

1. First printed in May 1845 by the Anti-Slavery Office in Boston, the source of the present text. Punctuation and hyphenation have been slightly regularized and a few typographical emendations have also been made.
2. The preface is by William Lloyd Garrison (1805–1879), the most influential white abolitionist at that time. He edited the antislavery newspaper the *Liberator*, which he founded in 1831, and headed the American Anti-Slavery Society, which published Douglass's *Narrative*.

Garrison called for immediate emancipation and advocated nonviolent moral persuasion as the best way of achieving social reform. Most slave narratives of the period came with prefaces by white abolitionists attesting to the moral character and literacy of the black author.
3. Douglass escaped from slavery in Maryland in September 1838 and settled in New Bedford, Massachusetts, where he became active among the New Bedford abolitionists.

fortunate for the cause of negro emancipation, and of universal liberty!— fortunate for the land of his birth, which he has already done so much to save and bless!—fortunate for a large circle of friends and acquaintances, whose sympathy and affection he has strongly secured by the many sufferings he has endured, by his virtuous traits of character, by his ever-abiding remembrance of those who are in bonds, as being bound with them!—fortunate for the multitudes, in various parts of our republic, whose minds he has enlightened on the subject of slavery, and who have been melted to tears by his pathos, or roused to virtuous indignation by his stirring eloquence against the enslavers of men!—fortunate for himself, as it at once brought him into the field of public usefulness, "gave the world assurance of a MAN," quickened the slumbering energies of his soul, and consecrated him to the great work of breaking the rod of the oppressor, and letting the oppressed go free!

I shall never forget his first speech at the convention—the extraordinary emotion it excited in my own mind—the powerful impression it created upon a crowded auditory,[4] completely taken by surprise—the applause which followed from the beginning to the end of his felicitous remarks. I think I never hated slavery so intensely as at that moment; certainly, my perception of the enormous outrage which is inflicted by it, on the godlike nature of its victims, was rendered far more clear than ever. There stood one, in physical proportion and stature commanding and exact—in intellect richly endowed—in natural eloquence a prodigy—in soul manifestly "created but a little lower than the angels"[5]—yet a slave, ay, a fugitive slave,— trembling for his safety, hardly daring to believe that on the American soil, a single white person could be found who would befriend him at all hazards, for the love of God and humanity! Capable of high attainments as an intellectual and moral being—needing nothing but a comparatively small amount of cultivation to make him an ornament to society and a blessing to his race—by the law of the land, by the voice of the people, by the terms of the slave code, he was only a piece of property, a beast of burden, a chattel[6] personal, nevertheless!

A beloved friend[7] from New Bedford prevailed on Mr. DOUGLASS to address the convention. He came forward to the platform with a hesitancy and embarrassment, necessarily the attendants of a sensitive mind in such a novel position. After apologizing for his ignorance, and reminding the audience that slavery was a poor school for the human intellect and heart, he proceeded to narrate some of the facts in his own history as a slave, and in the course of his speech gave utterance to many noble thoughts and thrilling reflections. As soon as he had taken his seat, filled with hope and admiration, I rose, and declared that PATRICK HENRY,[8] of revolutionary fame, never made a speech more eloquent in the cause of liberty, than the one we had just listened to from the lips of that hunted fugitive. So I believed at that time—such is my belief now. I reminded the audience of the peril which surrounded this self-emancipated young man at the North,—even in Massachusetts, on the soil of the Pilgrim Fathers, among the descendants of revolutionary sires; and I appealed to them, whether they would ever allow

---

4. Auditorium (archaic).
5. God created people "a little lower than the angels" (Psalms 8.5); Paul declares that Christ was made "a little lower than the angels" (Hebrews 2.7, 9).
6. Property.

7. William C. Coffin (1816–?), a prominent New Bedford abolitionist.
8. U.S. patriot (1736–1799), famous for the words: "I know not what course others may take, but as for me, give me liberty or give me death."

him to be carried back into slavery,—law or no law, constitution or no constitution. The response was unanimous and in thunder-tones—"NO!" "Will you succor and protect him as a brother-man—a resident of the old Bay State."[9] "YES!" shouted the whole mass, with an energy so startling, that the ruthless tyrants south of Mason and Dixon's line[1] might almost have heard the mighty burst of feeling, and recognized it as the pledge of an invincible determination, on the part of those who gave it, never to betray him that wanders, but to hide the outcast, and firmly to abide the consequences.

It was at once deeply impressed upon my mind, that, if Mr. DOUGLASS could be persuaded to consecrate his time and talents to the promotion of the anti-slavery enterprise, a powerful impetus would be given to it, and a stunning blow at the same time inflicted on northern prejudice against a colored complexion. I therefore endeavored to instill hope and courage into his mind, in order that he might dare to engage in a vocation so anomalous and responsible for a person in his situation; and I was seconded in this effort by warm-hearted friends, especially by the late General Agent of the Massachusetts Anti-Slavery Society, Mr. JOHN A. COLLINS, whose judgment in this instance entirely coincided with my own. At first, he could give no encouragement; with unfeigned diffidence, he expressed his conviction that he was not adequate to the performance of so great a task; the path marked out was wholly an untrodden one; he was sincerely apprehensive that he should do more harm than good. After much deliberation, however, he consented to make a trial; and ever since that period, he has acted as a lecturing agent, under the auspices either of the American or the Massachusetts Anti-Slavery Society. In labors he has been most abundant; and his success in combating prejudice, in gaining proselytes, in agitating the public mind, has far surpassed the most sanguine expectations that were raised at the commencement of his brilliant career. He has borne himself with gentleness and meekness, yet with true manliness of character. As a public speaker, he excels in pathos, wit, comparison, imitation, strength of reasoning, and fluency of language. There is in him that union of head and heart, which is indispensable to an enlightenment of the heads and a winning of the hearts of others. May his strength continue to be equal to his day! May he continue to "grow in grace, and in the knowledge of God," that he may be increasingly serviceable in the cause of bleeding humanity, whether at home or abroad!

It is certainly a very remarkable fact, that one of the most efficient advocates of the slave population, now before the public, is a fugitive slave, in the person of FREDERICK DOUGLASS; and that the free colored population of the United States are as ably represented by one of their own number, in the person of CHARLES LENOX REMOND,[2] whose eloquent appeals have extorted the highest applause of multitudes on both sides of the Atlantic. Let the calumniators of the colored race despise themselves for their baseness and illiberality of spirit, and henceforth cease to talk of the natural inferiority of those who require nothing but time and opportunity to attain to the highest point of human excellence.

It may, perhaps, be fairly questioned, whether any other portion of the population of the earth could have endured the privations, sufferings and

9. Massachusetts.
1. Established by the British astronomers and surveyors Charles Mason and Jeremiah Dixon during the 1760s, the line separating Pennsylvania and Maryland came to signify the boundary between slave and free states.

2. A free-born African American (1810–1873) from Massachusetts who was the first black employed in the United States as an antislavery lecturer. He toured with Douglass for the Massachusetts Anti-Slavery Society in 1842.

horrors of slavery, without having become more degraded in the scale of humanity than the slaves of African descent. Nothing has been left undone to cripple their intellects, darken their minds, debase their moral nature, obliterate all traces of their relationship to mankind; and yet how wonderfully they have sustained the mighty load of a most frightful bondage, under which they have been groaning for centuries! To illustrate the effect of slavery on the white man,—to show that he has no powers of endurance, in such a condition, superior to those of his black brother,—DANIEL O'CONNELL,[3] the distinguished advocate of universal emancipation, and the mightiest champion of prostrate but not conquered Ireland, relates the following anecdote in a speech delivered by him in the Conciliation Hall, Dublin, before the Loyal National Repeal Association, March 31, 1845. "No matter," said Mr. O'CONNELL, "under what specious term it may disguise itself, slavery is still hideous. *It has a natural, an inevitable tendency to brutalize every noble faculty of man.* An American sailor, who was cast away on the shore of Africa, where he was kept in slavery for three years, was, at the expiration of that period, found to be imbruted and stultified—he had lost all reasoning power; and having forgotten his native language, could only utter some savage gibberish between Arabic and English, which nobody could understand, and which even he himself found difficulty in pronouncing. So much for the humanizing influence of THE DOMESTIC INSTITUTION!" Admitting this to have been an extraordinary case of mental deterioration, it proves at least that the white slave can sink as low in the scale of humanity as the black one.

Mr. DOUGLASS has very properly chosen to write his own Narrative, in his own style, and according to the best of his ability, rather than to employ some one else. It is, therefore, entirely his own production; and, considering how long and dark was the career he had to run as a slave,—how few have been his opportunities to improve his mind since he broke his iron fetters,—it is, in my judgment, highly creditable to his head and heart. He who can peruse it without a tearful eye, a heaving breast, an afflicted spirit,—without being filled with an unutterable abhorrence of slavery and all its abettors, and animated with a determination to seek the immediate overthrow of that execrable system,—without trembling for the fate of this country in the hands of a righteous God, who is ever on the side of the oppressed, and whose arm is not shortened that it cannot save,—must have a flinty heart, and be qualified to act the part of a trafficker "in slaves and the souls of men."[4] I am confident that it is essentially true in all its statements; that nothing has been set down in malice, nothing exaggerated, nothing drawn from the imagination; that it comes short of the reality, rather than overstates a single fact in regard to SLAVERY AS IT IS.[5] The experience of FREDERICK DOUGLASS, as a slave, was not a peculiar one; his lot was not especially a hard one; his case may be regarded as a very fair specimen of the treatment of slaves in Maryland, in which State it is conceded that they are better fed and less cruelly treated than in Georgia, Alabama, or Louisiana. Many have suffered incomparably more, while very few on the plantations have suffered less, than himself. Yet how deplorable was his situation! what terrible chastisements were inflicted upon his person! what still more shocking outrages were perpetrated upon his mind! with all his noble powers and sublime aspirations, how like a brute was he treated,

---

3. Irish statesman (1775–1847), called the "Liberator," who advocated Irish independence from England.

4. Revelation 18.13.

5. Probably an allusion to Theodore Weld's widely read antislavery compendium *Slavery as It Is* (1839).

even by those professing to have the same mind in them that was in Christ Jesus! to what dreadful liabilities was he continually subjected! how destitute of friendly counsel and aid, even in his greatest extremities! how heavy was the midnight of woe which shrouded in blackness the last ray of hope, and filled the future with terror and gloom! what longings after freedom took possession of his breast, and how his misery augmented, in proportion as he grew reflective and intelligent,—thus demonstrating that a happy slave is an extinct man! how he thought, reasoned, felt, under the lash of the driver, with the chains upon his limbs! what perils he encountered in his endeavors to escape from his horrible doom! and how signal have been his deliverance and preservation in the midst of a nation of pitiless enemies!

This Narrative contains many affecting incidents, many passages of great eloquence and power; but I think the most thrilling one of them all is the description DOUGLASS gives of his feelings, as he stood soliloquizing respecting his fate, and the chances of his one day being a freeman, on the banks of the Chesapeake Bay—view in the receding vessels as they flew with their white wings before the breeze, and apostrophizing them as animated by the living spirit of freedom. Who can read that passage, and be insensible to its pathos and sublimity? Compressed into it is a whole Alexandrian library[6] of thought, feeling, and sentiment—all that can, all that need be urged, in the form of expostulation, entreaty, rebuke, against that crime of crimes,— making man the property of his fellow-man! O, how accursed is that system, which entombs the godlike mind of man, defaces the divine image, reduces those who by creation were crowned with glory and honor to a level with four-footed beasts, and exalts the dealer in human flesh above all that is called God! Why should its existence be prolonged one hour? Is it not evil, only evil, and that continually? What does its presence imply but the absence of all fear of God, all regard for man, on the part of the people of the United States? Heaven speed its eternal overthrow!

So profoundly ignorant of the nature of slavery are many persons, that they are stubbornly incredulous whenever they read or listen to any recital of the cruelties which are daily inflicted on its victims. They do not deny that the slaves are held as property; but that terrible fact seems to convey to their minds no idea of injustice, exposure to outrage, or savage barbarity. Tell them of cruel scourgings, of mutilations and brandings, of scenes of pollution and blood, of the banishment of all light and knowledge, and they affect to be greatly indignant at such enormous exaggerations, such wholesale misstatements, such abominable libels on the character of the southern planters! As if all these direful outrages were not the natural results of slavery! As if it were less cruel to reduce a human being to the condition of a thing, than to give him a severe flagellation, or to deprive him of necessary food and clothing! As if whips, chains, thumb-screws, paddles, bloodhounds, overseers, drivers, patrols, were not all indispensable to keep the slaves down, and to give protection to their ruthless oppressors! As if, when the marriage institution is abolished, concubinage, adultery, and incest, must not necessarily abound; when all the rights of humanity are annihilated, any barrier remains to protect the victim from the fury of the spoiler; when absolute power is assumed over life and liberty, it will not be wielded with destructive sway! Skeptics of this character abound in society. In some few

6. Alexandria, in Egypt, home of the greatest library in the Greco-Roman world.

instances, their incredulity arises from a want of reflection; but, generally, it indicates a hatred of the light, a desire to shield slavery from the assaults of its foes, a contempt of the colored race, whether bond or free. Such will try to discredit the shocking tales of slaveholding cruelty which are recorded in this truthful Narrative; but they will labor in vain. Mr. DOUGLASS has frankly disclosed the place of his birth, the names of those who claimed ownership in his body and soul, and the names also of those who committed the crimes which he has alleged against them. His statements, therefore, may easily be disproved, if they are untrue.

In the course of his Narrative, he relates two instances of murderous cruelty,—in one of which a planter deliberately shot a slave belonging to a neighboring plantation, who had unintentionally gotten within his lordly domain in quest of fish; and in the other, an overseer blew out the brains of a slave who had fled to a stream of water to escape a bloody scourging. Mr. DOUGLASS states that in neither of these instances was any thing done by way of legal arrest or judicial investigation. The Baltimore American, of March 17, 1845, relates a similar case of atrocity, perpetrated with similar impunity—as follows:—"*Shooting a Slave.*—We learn, upon the authority of a letter from Charles county, Maryland, received by a gentleman of this city, that a young man, named Matthews, a nephew of General Matthews, and whose father, it is believed, holds an office at Washington, killed one of the slaves upon his father's farm by shooting him. The letter states that young Matthews had been left in charge of the farm; that he gave an order to the servant, which was disobeyed, when he proceeded to the house, *obtained a gun, and, returning, shot the servant.* He immediately, the letter continues, fled to his father's residence, where he still remains unmolested."—Let it never be forgotten, that no slaveholder or overseer can be convicted of any outrage perpetrated on the person of a slave, however diabolical it may be, on the testimony of colored witnesses, whether bond or free. By the slave code, they are adjudged to be as incompetent to testify against a white man, as though they were indeed a part of the brute creation. Hence, there is no legal protection in fact, whatever there may be in form, for the slave population; and any amount of cruelty may be inflicted on them with impunity. Is it possible for the human mind to conceive of a more horrible state of society?

The effect of a religious profession on the conduct of southern masters is vividly described in the following Narrative, and shown to be any thing but salutary. In the nature of the case, it must be in the highest degree pernicious. The testimony of Mr. DOUGLASS, on this point, is sustained by a cloud of witnesses, whose veracity is unimpeachable. "A slaveholder's profession of Christianity is a palpable imposture. He is a felon of the highest grade. He is a man-stealer. It is of no importance what you put in the other scale."

Reader! are you with the man-stealers in sympathy and purpose, or on the side of their down-trodden victims? If with the former, then are you the foe of God and man. If with the latter, what are you prepared to do and dare in their behalf? Be faithful, be vigilant, be untiring in your efforts to break every yoke, and let the oppressed go free. Come what may—cost what it may—inscribe on the banner which you unfurl to the breeze, as your religious and political motto—"No COMPROMISE WITH SLAVERY! No UNION WITH SLAVEHOLDERS!"

WM. LLOYD GARRISON

Boston, May 1, 1845.

Letter from Wendell Phillips, Esq.[7]

BOSTON, *April* 22, 1845.

My Dear Friend:

You remember the old fable of "The Man and the Lion" where the lion complained that he should not be so misrepresented "when the lions wrote history."

I am glad the time has come when the "lions write history." We have been left long enough to gather the character of slavery from the involuntary evidence of the masters. One might, indeed, rest sufficiently satisfied with what, it is evident, must be, in general, the results of such a relation, without seeking farther to find whether they have followed in every instance. Indeed, those who stare at the half-peck of corn a week, and love to count the lashes on the slave's back, are seldom the "stuff" out of which reformers and abolitionists are to be made. I remember that, in 1838, many were waiting for the results of the West India experiment,[8] before they could come into our ranks. Those "results" have come long ago; but, alas! few of that number have come with them, as converts. A man must be disposed to judge of emancipation by other tests than whether it has increased the produce of sugar,—and to hate slavery for other reasons than because it starves men and whips women,— before he is ready to lay the first stone of his anti-slavery life.

I was glad to learn, in your story, how early the most neglected of God's children waken to a sense of their rights, and of the injustice done them. Experience is a keen teacher; and long before you had mastered your A B C, or knew where the "white sails" of the Chesapeake were bound, you began, I see, to gauge the wretchedness of the slave, not by his hunger and want, not by his lashes and toil, but by the cruel and blighting death which gathers over his soul.

In connection with this, there is one circumstance which makes your recollections peculiarly valuable, and renders your early insight the more remarkable. You come from that part of the country where we are told slavery appears with its fairest features. Let us hear, then, what it is at its best estate—-gaze on its bright side, if it has one; and then imagination may task her powers to add dark lines to the picture, as she travels southward to that (for the colored man) Valley of the Shadow of Death,[9] where the Mississippi sweeps along.

Again, we have known you long, and can put the most entire confidence in your truth, candor, and sincerity. Every one who has heard you speak has felt, and, I am confident, every one who reads your book will feel, persuaded that you give them a fair specimen of the whole truth. No one-sided portrait,—no wholesale complaints,—but strict justice done, whenever individual kindliness has neutralized, for a moment, the deadly system with which it was strangely allied. You have been with us, too, some years, and can fairly compare the twilight of rights, which your race enjoy at the North, with that "noon of night" under which they labor south of Mason and Dix-

---

7. A prominent Massachusetts-based abolitionist (1811–1884).
8. On August 1, 1834, England formally abolished

slavery in the West Indies; by 1838 slavery had been abolished throughout the British Empire.
9. Psalms 23.4.

on's line. Tell us whether, after all, the half-free colored man of Massachusetts is worse off than the pampered slave of the rice swamps!

In reading your life, no one can say that we have unfairly picked out some rare specimens of cruelty. We know that the bitter drops, which even you have drained from the cup, are no incidental aggravations, no individual ills, but such as must mingle always and necessarily in the lot of every slave. They are the essential ingredients, not the occasional results, of the system.

After all, I shall read your book with trembling for you. Some years ago, when you were beginning to tell me your real name and birthplace, you may remember I stopped you, and preferred to remain ignorant of all. With the exception of a vague description, so I continued, till the other day, when you read me your memoirs. I hardly knew, at the time, whether to thank you or not for the sight of them, when I reflected that it was still dangerous, in Massachusetts, for honest men to tell their names! They say the fathers, in 1776, signed the Declaration of Independence with the halter about their necks. You, too, publish your declaration of freedom with danger compassing you around. In all the broad lands which the Constitution of the United States overshadows, there is no single spot,—however narrow or desolate,—where a fugitive slave can plant himself and say, "I am safe." The whole armory of Northern Law has no shield for you. I am free to say that, in your place, I should throw the MS. into the fire.

You, perhaps, may tell your story in safety, endeared as you are to so many warm hearts by rarer gifts, and a still rare devotion of them to the service of others. But it will be owing only to your labors, and the fearless efforts of those who, trampling the laws and Constitution of the country under their feet, are determined that they will "hide the outcast," and that their hearths shall be, spite of the law, an asylum for the oppressed, if, some time or other, the humblest may stand in our streets, and bear witness in safety against the cruelties which he has been the victim.

Yet it is sad to think, that these very throbbing hearts which welcome your story, and form your best safeguard in telling it, are all beating contrary to the "statute in such case made and provided." Go on, my dear friend, till you, and those who, like you, have been saved, so as by fire, from the dark prison-house, shall stereotype these free, illegal pulses into statutes; and New England, cutting loose from a blood-stained Union, shall glory in being the house of refuge for the oppressed;—till we no longer merely "*hide* the outcast," or make a merit of standing idly by while he is hunted in our midst; but, consecrating anew the soil of the Pilgrims as an asylum for the oppressed, proclaim our *welcome* to the slave so loudly, that the tones shall reach every hut in the Carolinas, and make the broken-hearted bondman leap up at the thought of old Massachusetts.

God speed the day!

Till then, and ever,
Yours truly,
WENDELL PHILLIPS
FREDERICK DOUGLASS.

Chapter I

I was born in Tuckahoe, near Hillsborough, and about twelve miles from Easton, in Talbot county, Maryland. I have no accurate knowledge of my age, never having seen any authentic record containing it. By far the larger part of the slaves know as little of their ages as horses know of theirs, and it is the wish of most masters within my knowledge to keep their slaves thus ignorant. I do not remember to have ever met a slave who could tell of his birthday. They seldom come nearer to it than planting-time, harvest-time, cherry-time, spring-time, or fall-time. A want of information concerning my own was a source of unhappiness to me even during childhood. The white children could tell their ages. I could not tell why I ought to be deprived of the same privilege. I was not allowed to make any inquiries of my master concerning it. He deemed all such inquiries on the part of a slave improper and impertinent, and evidence of a restless spirit. The nearest estimate I can give makes me now between twenty-seven and twenty-eight years of age. I come to this, from hearing my master say, some time during 1835, I was about seventeen years old.

My mother was named Harriet Bailey. She was the daughter of Isaac and Betsey Bailey, both colored, and quite dark. My mother was of a darker complexion than either my grandmother or grandfather.

My father was a white man. He was admitted to be such by all I ever heard speak of my parentage. The opinion was also whispered that my master was my father; but of the correctness of this opinion, I know nothing; the means of knowing was withheld from me. My mother and I were separated when I was but an infant—before I knew her as my mother. It is a common custom, in the part of Maryland from which I ran away, to part children from their mothers at a very early age. Frequently, before the child has reached its twelfth month, its mother is taken from it, and hired out on some farm a considerable distance off, and the child is placed under the care of an old woman, too old for field labor. For what this separation is done, I do not know, unless it be to hinder the development of the child's affection toward its mother, and to blunt and destroy the natural affection of the mother for the child. This is the inevitable result.

I never saw my mother, to know her as such, more than four or five times in my life; and each of these times was very short in duration, and at night. She was hired[1] by a Mr. Stewart, who lived about twelve miles from my home. She made her journeys to see me in the night, travelling the whole distance on foot, after the performance of her day's work. She was a field hand, and a whipping is the penalty of not being in the field at sunrise, unless a slave has special permission from his or her master to the contrary—a permission which they seldom get, and one that gives to him that gives it the proud name of being a kind master. I do not recollect of ever seeing my mother by the light of day. She was with me in the night. She would lie down with me, and get me to sleep, but long before I waked she was gone. Very little communication ever took place between us. Death soon ended what little we could have while she lived, and with it her hardships and suffering. She died when I was about seven years old, on one of my master's farms, near Lee's Mill. I was not allowed to be present during her illness, at her death, or burial. She was gone long before I knew any thing

---

1. Slaves who were "hired out" had their wages paid to their owners.

about it. Never having enjoyed, to any considerable extent, her soothing presence, her tender and watchful care, I received the tidings of her death with much the same emotions I should have probably felt at the death of a stranger.

Called thus suddenly away, she left me without the slightest intimation of who my father was. The whisper that my master was my father, may or may not be true; and, true or false, it is of but little consequence to my purpose whilst the fact remains, in all its glaring odiousness, that slaveholders have ordained, and by law established, that the children of slave women shall in all cases follow the condition of their mothers; and this is done too obviously to administer to their own lusts, and make a gratification of their wicked desires profitable as well as pleasurable; for by this cunning arrangement, the slaveholder, in cases not a few, sustains to his slaves the double relation of master and father.

I know of such cases; and it is worthy of remark that such slaves invariably suffer greater hardships, and have more to contend with, than others. They are, in the first place, a constant offence to their mistress. She is ever disposed to find fault with them; they can seldom do any thing to please her; she is never better pleased than when she sees them under the lash, especially when she suspects her husband of showing to his mulatto children favors which he withholds from his black slaves. The master is frequently compelled to sell this class of his slaves, out of deference to the feelings of his white wife; and, cruel as the deed may strike any one to be, for a man to sell his own children to human flesh-mongers, it is often the dictate of humanity for him to do so; for, unless he does this, he must not only whip them himself, but must stand by and see one white son tie up his brother, of but few shades darker complexion than himself, and ply the gory lash to his naked back; and if he lisp one word of disapproval, it is set down to his parental partiality, and only makes a bad matter worse, both for himself and the slave whom he would protect and defend.

Every year brings with it multitudes of this class of slaves. It was doubtless in consequence of a knowledge of this fact, that one great statesman of the south predicted the downfall of slavery by the inevitable laws of population. Whether this prophecy is ever fulfilled or not, it is nevertheless plain that a very different-looking class of people are springing up at the south, and are now held in slavery, from those originally brought to this country from Africa; and if their increase will do no other good, it will do away the force of the argument, that God cursed Ham, and therefore American slavery is right.[2] If the lineal descendants of Ham are alone to be scripturally enslaved, it is certain that slavery at the south must soon become unscriptural; for thousands are ushered into the world, annually, who, like myself, owe their existence to white fathers, and those fathers most frequently their own masters.

I have had two masters. My first master's name was Anthony. I do not remember his first name. He was generally called Captain Anthony—a title which, I presume, he acquired by sailing a craft on the Chesapeake Bay. He was not considered a rich slaveholder. He owned two or three farms, and about thirty slaves. His farms and slaves were under the care of an overseer.

2. Some proslavery writers interpreted Genesis 9.20–27, in which Noah curses his son Ham and condemns him to bondage to his brothers, as a biblical justification of slavery.

The overseer's name was Plummer. Mr. Plummer was a miserable drunkard, a profane swearer, and a savage monster. He always went armed with a cowskin[3] and a heavy cudgel. I have known him to cut and slash the women's heads so horribly, that even master would be enraged at his cruelty, and would threaten to whip him if he did not mind himself. Master, however, was not a humane slaveholder. It required extraordinary barbarity on the part of an overseer to affect him. He was a cruel man, hardened by a long life of slaveholding. He would at times seem to take great pleasure in whipping a slave. I have often been awakened at the dawn of day by the most heart-rending shrieks of an own aunt of mine, whom he used to tie up to a joist, and whip upon her naked back till she was literally covered with blood. No words, no tears, no prayers, from his gory victim, seemed to move his iron heart from its bloody purpose. The louder she screamed, the harder he whipped; and where the blood ran fastest, there he whipped longest. He would whip her to make her scream, and whip her to make her hush; and not until overcome by fatigue, would he cease to swing the blood-clotted cowskin. I remember the first time I ever witnessed this horrible exhibition. I was quite a child, but I well remember it. I never shall forget it whilst I remember any thing. It was the first of a long series of such outrages, of which I was doomed to be a witness and a participant. It struck me with awful force. It was the blood-stained gate, the entrance to the hell of slavery, through which I was about to pass. It was a most terrible spectacle. I wish I could commit to paper the feelings with which I beheld it.

This occurrence took place very soon after I went to live with my old master, and under the following circumstances. Aunt Hester went out one night,—where or for what I do not know,—and happened to be absent when my master desired her presence. He had ordered her not to go out evenings, and warned her that she must never let him catch her in company with a young man, who was paying attention to her, belonging to Colonel Lloyd. The young man's name was Ned Roberts, generally called Lloyd's Ned. Why master was so careful of her, may be safely left to conjecture. She was a woman of noble form, and of graceful proportions, having very few equals, and fewer superiors, in personal appearance, among the colored or white women of our neighborhood.

Aunt Hester had not only disobeyed his orders in going out, but had been found in company with Lloyd's Ned; which circumstance, I found, from what he said while whipping her, was the chief offence. Had he been a man of pure morals himself, he might have been thought interested in protecting the innocence of my aunt; but those who knew him will not suspect him of any such virtue. Before he commenced whipping Aunt Hester, he took her into the kitchen, and stripped her from neck to waist, leaving her neck, shoulders, and back, entirely naked. He then told her to cross her hands, calling her at the same time a d—d b—h. After crossing her hands, he tied them with a strong rope, and led her to a stool under a large hook in the joist, put in for the purpose. He made her get upon the stool, and tied her hands to the hook. She now stood fair for his infernal purpose. Her arms were stretched up at their full length, so that she stood upon the ends of her toes. He then said to her, "Now, you d—d b—h, I'll learn you how to disobey

---

3. A whip made of raw cowhide.

my orders!" and after rolling up his sleeves, he commenced to lay on the heavy cowskin, and soon the warm, red blood (amid heart-rending shrieks from her, and horrid oaths from him) came dripping to the floor. I was so terrified and horror-stricken at the sight, that I hid myself in a closet, and dared not venture out till long after the bloody transaction was over. I expected it would be my turn next. It was all new to me. I had never seen any thing like it before. I had always lived with my grandmother on the outskirts of the plantation, where she was put to raise the children of the younger women. I had therefore been, until now, out of the way of the bloody scenes that often occurred on the plantation.

Chapter II

My master's family consisted of two sons, Andrew and Richard; one daughter, Lucretia, and her husband, Captain Thomas Auld. They lived in one house, upon the home plantation of Colonel Edward Lloyd. My master was Colonel Lloyd's clerk and superintendent. He was what might be called the overseer of the overseers. I spent two years of childhood on this plantation in my old master's family. It was here that I witnessed the bloody transaction recorded in the first chapter; and as I received my first impressions of slavery on this plantation, I will give some description of it, and of slavery as it there existed. The plantation is about twelve miles north of Easton, in Talbot county, and is situated on the border of Miles River. The principal products raised upon it were tobacco, corn, and wheat. These were raised in great abundance; so that, with the products of this and the other farms belonging to him, he was able to keep in almost constant employment a large sloop, in carrying them to market at Baltimore. This sloop was named Sally Lloyd, in honor of one of the colonel's daughters. My master's son-in-law, Captain Auld, was master of the vessel; she was otherwise manned by the colonel's own slaves. Their names were Peter, Isaac, Rich, and Jake. These were esteemed very highly by the other slaves, and looked upon as the privileged ones of the plantation; for it was no small affair, in the eyes of the slaves, to be allowed to see Baltimore.

Colonel Lloyd kept from three to four hundred slaves on his home plantation, and owned a large number more on the neighboring farms belonging to him. The names of the farms nearest to the home plantation were Wye Town and New Design. "Wye Town" was under the overseership of a man named Noah Willis. New Design was under the overseership of a Mr. Townsend. The overseers of these, and all the rest of the farms, numbering over twenty, received advice and direction from the managers of the home plantation. This was the great business place. It was the seat of government for the whole twenty farms. All disputes among the overseers were settled here. If a slave was convicted of any high misdemeanor, became unmanageable, or evinced a determination to run away, he was brought immediately here, severely whipped, put on board the sloop, carried to Baltimore, and sold to Austin Woolfolk, or some other slave-trader, as a warning to the slaves remaining.

Here, too, the slaves of all the other farms received their monthly allowance of food, and their yearly clothing. The men and women slaves received, as their monthly allowance of food, eight pounds of pork, or its equivalent in fish, and one bushel of corn meal. Their yearly clothing consisted of two coarse linen shirts, one pair of linen trousers, like the shirts, one jacket, one pair of trousers for winter, made of coarse negro cloth, one pair of stockings, and one pair of shoes; the whole of which could not have cost more than seven dollars. The allowance of the slave children was given to their mothers, or the old women having the care of them. The children unable to work in the field had neither shoes, stockings, jackets, nor trousers, given to them; their clothing consisted of two coarse linen shirts per year. When these failed them, they went naked until the next allowance-day. Children from seven to ten years old, of both sexes, almost naked, might be seen at all seasons of the year.

There were no beds given the slaves, unless one coarse blanket be considered such, and none but the men and women had these. This, however, is not considered a very great privation. They find less difficulty from the want of beds, than from the want of time to sleep; for when their day's work in the field is done, the most of them having their washing, mending, and cooking to do, and having few or none of the ordinary facilities for doing either of these, very many of their sleeping hours are consumed in preparing for the field the coming day; and when this is done, old and young, male and female, married and single, drop down side by side, on one common bed,—the cold, damp floor,—each covering himself or herself with their miserable blankets; and here they sleep till they are summoned to the field by the driver's horn. At the sound of this, all must rise, and be off to the field. There must be no halting; every one must be at his or her post; and woe betides them who hear not this morning summons to the field; for if they are not awakened by the sense of hearing, they are by the sense of feeling: no age nor sex finds any favor. Mr. Severe, the overseer, used to stand by the door of the quarter, armed with a large hickory stick and heavy cowskin, ready to whip any one who was so unfortunate as not to hear, or, from any other cause, was prevented from being ready to start for the field at the sound of the horn.

Mr. Severe was rightly named: he was a cruel man. I have seen him whip a woman, causing the blood to run half an hour at the time; and this, too, in the midst of her crying children, pleading for their mother's release. He seemed to take pleasure in manifesting his fiendish barbarity. Added to his cruelty, he was a profane swearer. It was enough to chill the blood and stiffen the hair of an ordinary man to hear him talk. Scarce a sentence escaped him but that was commenced or concluded by some horrid oath. The field was the place to witness his cruelty and profanity. His presence made it both the field of blood and of blasphemy. From the rising till the going down of the sun, he was cursing, raving, cutting, and slashing among the slaves of the field, in the most frightful manner. His career was short. He died very soon after I went to Colonel Lloyd's; and he died as he lived, uttering, with his dying groans, bitter curses and horrid oaths. His death was regarded by the slaves as the result of a merciful providence.

Mr. Severe's place was filled by a Mr. Hopkins. He was a very different man. He was less cruel, less profane, and made less noise, than Mr. Severe. His course was characterized by no extraordinary demonstrations of cruelty. He whipped, but seemed to take no pleasure in it. He was called by the slaves a good overseer.

The home plantation of Colonel Lloyd wore the appearance of a country village. All the mechanical operations for all the farms were performed here. The shoemaking and mending, the blacksmithing, cartwrighting, coopering, weaving, and grain-grinding, were all performed by the slaves on the home plantation. The whole place wore a business-like aspect very unlike the neighboring farms. The number of houses, too, conspired to give it advantage over the neighboring farms. It was called by the slaves the *Great House Farm*. Few privileges were esteemed higher, by the slaves of the out-farms, than that of being selected to do errands at the Great House Farm. It was associated in their minds with greatness. A representative could not be prouder of his election to a seat in the American Congress, than a slave on one of the out-farms would be of his election to do errands at the Great House Farm. They regarded it as evidence of great confidence reposed in them by their overseers; and it was on this account, as well as a constant desire to be out of the field from under the driver's lash, that they esteemed it a high privilege, one worth careful living for. He was called the smartest and most trusty fellow, who had this honor conferred upon him the most frequently. The competitors for this office sought as diligently to please their overseers, as the office-seekers in the political parties seek to please and deceive the people. The same traits of character might be seen in Colonel Lloyd's slaves, as are seen in the slaves of the political parties.

The slaves selected to go to the Great House Farm, for the monthly allowance for themselves and their fellow-slaves, were peculiarly enthusiastic. While on their way, they would make the dense old woods, for miles around, reverberate with their wild songs, revealing at once the highest joy and the deepest sadness. They would compose and sing as they went along, consulting neither time nor tune. The thought that came up, came out—if not in the word, in the sound;—and as frequently in the one as in the other. They would sometimes sing the most pathetic sentiment in the most rapturous tone, and the most rapturous sentiment in the most pathetic tone. Into all of their songs they would manage to weave something of the Great House Farm. Especially would they do this, when leaving home. They would then sing most exultingly the following words:—

> "I am going away to the Great House Farm!
> O, yea! O, yea! O!"

This they would sing, as a chorus, to words which to many would seem unmeaning jargon, but which, nevertheless, were full of meaning to themselves. I have sometimes thought that the mere hearing of those songs would do more to impress some minds with the horrible character of slavery, than the reading of whole volumes of philosophy on the subject could do.

I did not, when a slave, understand the deep meaning of those rude and apparently incoherent songs. I was myself within the circle; so that I neither saw nor heard as those without might see and hear. They told a tale of woe which was then altogether beyond my feeble comprehension; they were tones loud, long, and deep; they breathed the prayer and complaint of souls boiling over with the bitterest anguish. Every tone was a testimony against slavery, and a prayer to God for deliverance from chains. The hearing of those wild notes always depressed my spirit, and filled me with ineffable sadness. I have frequently found myself in tears while hearing them. The mere recurrence to those songs, even now, afflicts me; and while I am writing these lines, an expression of feeling has already found its way down my cheek. To those songs I trace my first glimmering conception of the dehumanizing character of slavery. I can never get rid of that conception. Those songs still follow me, to deepen my hatred of slavery, and quicken my sympathies for my brethren in bonds. If any one wishes to be impressed with the soul-killing effects of slavery, let him go to Colonel Lloyd's plantation, and, on allowance-day, place himself in the deep pine woods, and there let him, in silence, analyze the sounds that shall pass through the chambers of his soul,—and if he is not thus impressed, it will only be because "there is no flesh in his obdurate heart."[4]

I have often been utterly astonished, since I came to the north, to find persons who could speak of the singing, among slaves, as evidence of their contentment and happiness. It is impossible to conceive of a greater mistake. Slaves sing most when they are most unhappy. The songs of the slave represent the sorrows of his heart; and he is relieved by them, only as an aching heart is relieved by its tears. At least, such is my experience. I have often sung to drown my sorrow, but seldom to express my happiness. Crying for joy, and singing for joy, were alike uncommon to me while in the jaws of slavery. The singing of a man cast away upon a desolate island might be as appropriately considered as evidence of contentment and happiness, as the singing of a slave; the songs of the one and of the other are prompted by the same emotion.

Chapter III

Colonel Lloyd kept a large and finely cultivated garden, which afforded almost constant employment for four men, besides the chief gardener, (Mr. M'Durmond.) This garden was probably the greatest attraction of the place. During the summer months, people came from far and near—from Baltimore, Easton, and Annapolis—to see it. It abounded in fruits of almost every description, from the hardy apple of the north to the delicate orange of the south. This garden was not the least source of trouble on the plantation. Its excellent fruit was quite a temptation to the hungry swarms of boys, as well as the older slaves, belonging to the colonel, few of whom had the virtue or the vice to resist it. Scarcely a day passed, during the summer, but that some slave had to take the lash for stealing fruit. The colonel had to resort to all kinds of stratagems to keep his slaves out of the garden. The last and most successful one was that of tarring his fence all around, after which, if a slave was caught with any tar upon his person, it was deemed sufficient proof that he had either been into the garden, or had tried to get in. In either case, he was severely whipped by the chief gardener. This plan worked well; the slaves became as fearful of tar as of the lash. They seemed to realize the impossibility of touching *tar* without being defiled.

The colonel also kept a splendid riding equipage. His stable and carriage-house presented the appearance of some of our large city livery establishments. His horses were of the finest form and noblest blood. His carriage-house contained three splendid coaches, three or four gigs, besides dearborns and barouches[5] of the most fashionable style.

This establishment was under the care of two slaves—old Barney and young Barney—father and son. To attend to this establishment was their sole work. But it was by no means an easy employment; for in nothing was

4. From William Cowper's popular poem *The Task* (1785).   5. Different kinds of carriages.

Colonel Lloyd more particular than in the management of his horses. The slightest inattention to these was unpardonable, and was visited upon those, under whose care they were placed, with the severest punishment; no excuse could shield them, if the colonel only suspected any want of attention to his horses—a supposition which he frequently indulged, and one which, of course, made the office of old and young Barney a very trying one. They never knew when they were safe from punishment. They were frequently whipped when least deserving, and escaped whipping when most deserving it. Every thing depended upon the looks of the horses, and the state of Colonel Lloyd's own mind when his horses were brought to him for use. If a horse did not move fast enough, or hold his head high enough, it was owing to some fault of his keepers. It was painful to stand near the stable-door, and hear the various complaints against the keepers when a horse was taken out for use. "This horse has not had proper attention. He has not been sufficiently rubbed and curried, or he has not been properly fed; his food was too wet or too dry; he got it too soon or too late; he was too hot or too cold; he had too much hay, and not enough of grain; or he had too much grain, and not enough of hay; instead of old Barney's attending to the horse, he had very improperly left it to his son." To all these complaints, no matter how unjust, the slave must answer never a word. Colonel Lloyd could not brook any contradiction from a slave. When he spoke, a slave must stand, listen, and tremble; and such was literally the case. I have seen Colonel Lloyd make old Barney, a man between fifty and sixty years of age, uncover his bald head, kneel down upon the cold, damp ground, and receive upon his naked and toil-worn shoulders more than thirty lashes at the time. Colonel Lloyd had three sons—Edward, Murray, and Daniel,—and three sons-in-law, Mr. Winder, Mr. Nicholson, and Mr. Lowndes. All of these lived at the Great House Farm, and enjoyed the luxury of whipping the servants when they pleased, from old Barney down to William Wilkes, the coach-driver. I have seen Winder make one of the house-servants stand off from him a suitable distance to be touched with the end of his whip, and at every stroke raise great ridges upon his back.

To describe the wealth of Colonel Lloyd would be almost equal to describing the riches of Job.[6] He kept from ten to fifteen house-servants. He was said to own a thousand slaves, and I think this estimate quite within the truth. Colonel Lloyd owned so many that he did not know them when he saw them; nor did all the slaves of the out-farms know him. It is reported of him, that, while riding along the road one day, he met a colored man, and addressed him in the usual manner of speaking to colored people on the public highways of the south: "Well, boy, whom do you belong to?" "To Colonel Lloyd," replied the slave. "Well, does the colonel treat you well?" "No, sir," was the ready reply. "What, does he work you too hard?" "Yes, sir." "Well, don't he give you enough to eat?" "Yes, sir, he gives me enough, such as it is."

The colonel, after ascertaining where the slave belonged, rode on; the man also went on about his business, not dreaming that he had been conversing with his master. He thought, said, and heard nothing more of the matter, until two or three weeks afterwards. The poor man was then informed by his overseer that, for having found fault with his master, he was

6. The biblical figure whose many misfortunes fail to shake his faith in God.

now to be sold to a Georgia trader. He was immediately chained and hand-cuffed; and thus, without a moment's warning, he was snatched away, and forever sundered, from his family and friends, by a hand more unrelenting than death. This is the penalty of telling the truth, of telling the simple truth, in answer to a series of plain questions.

It is partly in consequence of such facts, that slaves, when inquired of as to their condition and the character of their masters, almost universally say they are contented, and that their masters are kind. The slaveholders have been known to send in spies among their slaves, to ascertain their views and feel-ings in regard to their condition. The frequency of this has had the effect to establish among the slaves the maxim, that a still tongue makes a wise head. They suppress the truth rather than take the consequences of telling it, and in so doing prove themselves a part of the human family. If they have any thing to say of their masters, it is generally in their masters' favor, especially when speaking to an untried man. I have been frequently asked, when a slave, if I had a kind master, and do not remember ever to have given a nega-tive answer; nor did I, in pursuing this course, consider myself as uttering what was absolutely false; for I always measured the kindness of my master by the standard of kindness set up among slaveholders around us. Moreover, slaves are like other people, and imbibe prejudices quite common to others. They think their own better than that of others. Many, under the influence of this prejudice, think their own masters are better than the masters of other slaves; and this, too, in some cases, when the very reverse is true. Indeed, it is not uncommon for slaves even to fall out and quarrel among themselves about the relative goodness of their masters, each contending for the superior goodness of his own over that of the others. At the very same time, they mutually execrate their masters when viewed separately. It was so on our plantation. When Colonel Lloyd's slaves met the slaves of Jacob Jepson, they seldom parted without a quarrel about their masters; Colonel Lloyd's slaves contending that he was the richest, and Mr. Jepson's slaves that he was the smartest, and most of a man. Colonel Lloyd's slaves would boast his ability to buy and sell Jacob Jepson. Mr. Jepson's slaves would boast his ability to whip Colonel Lloyd. These quarrels would almost always end in a fight between the parties, and those that whipped were supposed to have gained the point at issue. They seemed to think that the greatness of their masters was trans-ferable to themselves. It was considered as being bad enough to be a slave; but to be a poor man's slave was deemed a disgrace indeed!

Chapter IV

Mr. Hopkins remained but a short time in the office of overseer. Why his career was so short, I do not know, but suppose he lacked the necessary severity to suit Colonel Lloyd. Mr. Hopkins was succeeded by Mr. Austin Gore, a man possessing, in an eminent degree, all those traits of character indispensable to what is called a first-rate overseer. Mr. Gore had served Colonel Lloyd, in the capacity of overseer, upon one of the out-farms, and had shown himself worthy of the high station of overseer upon the home or Great House Farm.

Mr. Gore was proud, ambitious, and persevering. He was artful, cruel, and obdurate. He was just the man for such a place, and it was just the place for such a man. It afforded scope for the full exercise of all his powers, and

he seemed to be perfectly at home in it. He was one of those who could torture the slightest look, word, or gesture, on the part of the slave, into impudence, and would treat it accordingly. There must be no answering back to
him; no explanation was allowed a slave, showing himself to have been
wrongfully accused. Mr. Gore acted fully up to the maxim laid down by
slaveholders,—"It is better that a dozen slaves suffer under the lash, than that
the overseer should be convicted, in the presence of the slaves, of having
been at fault." No matter how innocent a slave might be—it availed him
nothing, when accused by Mr. Gore of any misdemeanor. To be accused was
to be convicted, and to be convicted was to be punished; the one always following the other with immutable certainty. To escape punishment was to
escape accusation; and few slaves had the fortune to do either, under the
overseership of Mr. Gore. He was just proud enough to demand the most
debasing homage of the slave, and quite servile enough to crouch, himself,
at the feet of the master. He was ambitious enough to be contented with
nothing short of the highest rank of overseers, and persevering enough to
reach the height of his ambition. He was cruel enough to inflict the severest
punishment, artful enough to descend to the lowest trickery, and obdurate
enough to be insensible to the voice of a reproving conscience. He was, of all
the overseers, the most dreaded by the slaves. His presence was painful; his
eye flashed confusion; and seldom was his sharp, shrill voice heard, without
producing horror and trembling in their ranks.

Mr. Gore was a grave man, and, though a young man, he indulged in no
jokes, said no funny words, seldom smiled. His words were in perfect keeping
with his looks, and his looks were in perfect keeping with his words. Overseers will sometimes indulge in a witty word, even with the slaves; not so with
Mr. Gore. He spoke but to command, and commanded but to be obeyed; he
dealt sparingly with his words, and bountifully with his whip, never using the
former where the latter would answer as well. When he whipped, he seemed
to do so from a sense of duty, and feared no consequences. He did nothing
reluctantly, no matter how disagreeable; always at his post, never inconsistent. He never promised but to fulfil. He was, in a word, a man of the most
inflexible firmness and stone-like coolness.

His savage barbarity was equalled only by the consummate coolness with
which he committed the grossest and most savage deeds upon the slaves
under his charge. Mr. Gore once undertook to whip one of Colonel Lloyd's
slaves, by the name of Demby. He had given Demby but few stripes, when, to
get rid of the scourging, he ran and plunged himself into a creek, and stood
there at the depth of his shoulders, refusing to come out. Mr. Gore told
him that he would give him three calls, and that, if he did not come out at
the third call, he would shoot him. The first call was given. Demby made no
response, but stood his ground. The second and third calls were given with
the same result. Mr. Gore then, without consultation or deliberation with
any one, not even giving Demby an additional call, raised his musket to his
face, taking deadly aim at his standing victim, and in an instant poor Demby
was no more. His mangled body sank out of sight, and blood and brains
marked the water where he had stood.

A thrill of horror flashed through every soul upon the plantation, excepting
Mr. Gore. He alone seemed cool and collected. He was asked by Colonel
Lloyd and my old master, why he resorted to this extraordinary expedient. His
reply was, (as well as I can remember,) that Demby had become unmanageable.

He was setting a dangerous example to the other slaves,—one which, if suffered to pass without some such demonstration on his part, would finally lead to the total subversion of all rule and order upon the plantation. He argued that if one slave refused to be corrected, and escaped with his life, the other slaves would soon copy the example; the result of which would be, the freedom of the slaves, and the enslavement of the whites. Mr. Gore's defence was satisfactory. He was continued in his station as overseer upon the home plantation. His fame as an overseer went abroad. His horrid crime was not even submitted to judicial investigation. It was committed in the presence of slaves, and they of course could neither institute a suit, nor testify against him; and thus the guilty perpetrator of one of the bloodiest and most foul murders goes unwhipped of justice, and uncensured by the community in which he lives. Mr. Gore lived in St. Michael's, Talbot county, Maryland, when I left there; and if he is still alive, he very probably lives there now; and if so, he is now, as he was then, as highly esteemed and as much respected as though his guilty soul had not been stained with his brother's blood.

I speak advisedly when I say this,—that killing a slave, or any colored person, in Talbot county, Maryland, is not treated as a crime, either by the courts or the community. Mr. Thomas Lanman, of St. Michael's, killed two slaves, one of whom he killed with a hatchet, by knocking his brains out. He used to boast of the commission of the awful and bloody deed. I have heard him do so laughingly, saying, among other things, that he was the only benefactor of his country in the company, and that when others would do as much as he had done, we should be relieved of "the d——d niggers."

The wife of Mr. Giles Hick, living but a short distance from where I used to live, murdered my wife's cousin, a young girl between fifteen and sixteen years of age, mangling her person in the most horrible manner, breaking her nose and breastbone with a stick, so that the poor girl expired in a few hours afterward. She was immediately buried, but had not been in her untimely grave but a few hours before she was taken up and examined by the coroner, who decided that she had come to her death by severe beating. The offence for which this girl was thus murdered was this:—She had been set that night to mind Mrs. Hick's baby, and during the night she fell asleep, and the baby cried. She, having lost her rest for several nights previous, did not hear the crying. They were both in the room with Mrs. Hicks. Mrs. Hicks, finding the girl slow to move, jumped from her bed, seized an oak stick of wood by the fireplace, and with it broke the girl's nose and breastbone, and thus ended her life. I will not say that this most horrid murder produced no sensation in the community. It did produce sensation, but not enough to bring the murderess to punishment. There was a warrant issued for her arrest, but it was never served. Thus she escaped not only punishment, but even the pain of being arraigned before a court for her horrid crime.

Whilst I am detailing bloody deeds which took place during my stay on Colonel Lloyd's plantation, I will briefly narrate another, which occurred about the same time as the murder of Demby by Mr. Gore.

Colonel Lloyd's slaves were in the habit of spending a part of their nights and Sundays in fishing for oysters, and in this way made up the deficiency of their scanty allowance. An old man belonging to Colonel Lloyd, while thus engaged, happened to get beyond the limits of Colonel Lloyd's, and on the premises of Mr. Beal Bondly. At this trespass, Mr. Bondly took offence, and with his musket came down to the shore, and blew its deadly contents into the poor old man.

Mr. Bondly came over to see Colonel Lloyd the next day, whether to pay him for his property, or to justify himself in what he had done, I know not. At any rate, this whole fiendish transaction was soon hushed up. There was very little said about it at all, and nothing done. It was a common saying, even among little white boys, that it was worth a half-cent to kill a "nigger," and a half-cent to bury one.

Chapter V

As to my own treatment while I lived on Colonel Lloyd's plantation, it was very similar to that of the other slave children. I was not old enough to work in the field, and there being little else than field work to do, I had a great deal of leisure time. The most I had to do was to drive up the cows at evening, keep the fowls out of the garden, keep the front yard clean, and run of errands for my old master's daughter, Mrs. Lucretia Auld. The most of my leisure time I spent in helping Master Daniel Lloyd in finding his birds, after he had shot them. My connection with Master Daniel was of some advantage to me. He became quite attached to me, and was a sort of protector of me. He would not allow the older boys to impose upon me, and would divide his cakes with me.

I was seldom whipped by my old master, and suffered little from any thing else than hunger and cold. I suffered much from hunger, but much more from cold. In hottest summer and coldest winter, I was kept almost naked—no shoes, no stockings, no jacket, no trousers, nothing on but a coarse tow linen shirt, reaching only to my knees. I had no bed. I must have perished with cold, but that, the coldest nights, I used to steal a bag which was used for carrying corn to the mill. I would crawl into this bag, and there sleep on the cold, damp, clay floor, with my head in and feet out. My feet have been so cracked with the frost, that the pen with which I am writing might be laid in the gashes.

We were not regularly allowanced. Our food was coarse corn meal boiled. This was called *mush*. It was put into a large wooden tray or trough, and set down upon the ground. The children were then called, like so many pigs, and like so many pigs they would come and devour the mush; some with oyster-shells, others with pieces of shingle, some with naked hands, and none with spoons. He that ate fastest got most; he that was strongest secured the best place; and few left the trough satisfied.

I was probably between seven and eight years old when I left Colonel Lloyd's plantation. I left it with joy. I shall never forget the ecstasy with which I received the intelligence that my old master (Anthony) had determined to let me go to Baltimore, to live with Mr. Hugh Auld, brother to my old master's son-in-law, Captain Thomas Auld. I received this information about three days before my departure. They were three of the happiest days I ever enjoyed. I spent the most part of all these three days in the creek, washing off the plantation scurf, and preparing myself for my departure.

The pride of appearance which this would indicate was not my own. I spent the time in washing, not so much because I wished to, but because Mrs. Lucretia had told me I must get all the dead skin off my feet and knees before I could go to Baltimore; for the people of Baltimore were very cleanly, and would laugh at me if I looked dirty. Besides, she was going to give me a pair of trousers, which I should not put on unless I got all the dirt off me. The thought of owning a pair of trousers was great indeed! It was almost a sufficient motive, not only to make me take off what would be called by pig-drovers the mange, but the skin itself. I went at it in good earnest, working for the first time with the hope of reward.

The ties that ordinarily bind children to their homes were all suspended in my case. I found no severe trial in my departure. My home was charmless; it was not home to me; on parting from it, I could not feel that I was leaving any thing which I could have enjoyed by staying. My mother was dead, my grandmother lived far off, so that I seldom saw her. I had two sisters and one brother, that lived in the same house with me; but the early separation of us from our mother had well nigh blotted the fact of our relationship from our memories. I looked for home elsewhere, and was confident of finding none which I should relish less than the one which I was leaving. If, however, I found in my new home hardship, hunger, whipping, and nakedness, I had the consolation that I should not have escaped any one of them by staying. Having already had more than a taste of them in the house of my old master, and having endured them there, I very naturally inferred my ability to endure them elsewhere, and especially at Baltimore; for I had something of the feeling about Baltimore that is expressed in the proverb, that "being hanged in England is preferable to dying a natural death in Ireland." I had the strongest desire to see Baltimore. Cousin Tom, though not fluent in speech, had inspired me with that desire by his eloquent description of the place. I could never point out any thing at the Great House, no matter how beautiful or powerful, but that he had seen something at Baltimore far exceeding, both in beauty and strength, the object which I pointed out to him. Even the Great House itself, with all its pictures, was far inferior to many buildings in Baltimore. So strong was my desire, that I thought a gratification of it would fully compensate for whatever loss of comforts I should sustain by the exchange. I left without a regret, and with the highest hopes of future happiness.

We sailed out of Miles River for Baltimore on a Saturday morning. I remember only the day of the week, for at that time I had no knowledge of the days of the month, nor the months of the year. On setting sail, I walked aft, and gave to Colonel Lloyd's plantation what I hoped would be the last look. I then placed myself in the bows of the sloop, and there spent the remainder of the day in looking ahead, interesting myself in what was in the distance rather than in things near by or behind.

In the afternoon of that day, we reached Annapolis, the capital of the State. We stopped but a few moments, so that I had no time to go on shore. It was the first large town that I had ever seen, and though it would look small compared with some of our New England factory villages, I thought it a wonderful place for its size—more imposing even than the Great House Farm!

We arrived at Baltimore early on Sunday morning, landing at Smith's Wharf, not far from Bowley's Wharf. We had on board the sloop a large flock of sheep; and after aiding in driving them to the slaughterhouse of Mr. Curtis on Louden Slater's Hill, I was conducted by Rich, one of the hands belonging on board of the sloop, to my new home in Alliciana Street, near Mr. Gardner's ship-yard, on Fells Point.

Mr. and Mrs. Auld were both at home, and met me at the door with their little son Thomas, to take care of whom I had been given. And here I saw what I had never seen before; it was a white face beaming with the most kindly emotions; it was the face of my new mistress, Sophia Auld. I wish I could describe the rapture that flashed through my soul as I beheld it. It was a new and strange sight to me, brightening up my pathway with the light of happiness. Little Thomas was told, there was his Freddy,—and I was told to take care of little Thomas; and thus I entered upon the duties of my new home with the most cheering prospect ahead.

I look upon my departure from Colonel Lloyd's plantation as one of the most interesting events of my life. It is possible, and even quite probable, that but for the mere circumstance of being removed from that plantation to Baltimore, I should have to-day, instead of being here seated by my own table, in the enjoyment of freedom and the happiness of home, writing this Narrative, been confined in the galling chains of slavery. Going to live at Baltimore laid the foundation, and opened the gateway, to all my subsequent prosperity. I have ever regarded it as the first plain manifestation of that kind providence which has ever since attended me, and marked my life with so many favors. I regarded the selection of myself as being somewhat remarkable. There were a number of slave children that might have been sent from the plantation to Baltimore. There were those younger, those older, and those of the same age. I was chosen from among them all, and was the first, last, and only choice.

I may be deemed superstitious, and even egotistical, in regarding this event as a special interposition of divine Providence in my favor. But I should be false to the earliest sentiments of my soul, if I suppressed the opinion. I prefer to be true to myself, even at the hazard of incurring the ridicule of others, rather than to be false, and incur my own abhorrence. From my earliest recollection, I date the entertainment of a deep conviction that slavery would not always be able to hold me within its foul embrace; and in the darkest hours of my career in slavery, this living word of faith and spirit of hope departed not from me, but remained like ministering angels to cheer me through the gloom. This good spirit was from God, and to him I offer thanksgiving and praise.

Chapter VI

My new mistress proved to be all she appeared when I first met her at the door,—a woman of the kindest heart and finest feelings. She had never had a slave under her control previously to myself, and prior to her marriage she had been dependent upon her own industry for a living. She was by trade a weaver; and by constant application to her business, she had been in a good degree preserved from the blighting and dehumanizing effects of slavery. I was utterly astonished at her goodness. I scarcely knew how to behave towards her. She was entirely unlike any other white woman I had ever seen. I could not approach her as I was accustomed to approach other white ladies. My early instruction was all out of place. The crouching servility, usually so acceptable a quality in a slave, did not answer when manifested toward her. Her favor was not gained by it; she seemed to be disturbed by it. She did not deem it impudent or unmannerly for a slave to look her in the face. The meanest slave was put fully at ease in her presence, and none left without feeling better for having seen her. Her face was made of heavenly smiles, and her voice of tranquil music.

But, alas! this kind heart had but a short time to remain such. The fatal poison of irresponsible power was already in her hands, and soon commenced its infernal work. That cheerful eye, under the influence of slavery, soon became red with rage; that voice, made all of sweet accord, changed to one of harsh and horrid discord; and that angelic face gave place to that of a demon.

Very soon after I went to live with Mr. and Mrs. Auld, she very kindly commenced to teach me the A, B, C. After I had learned this, she assisted me in learning to spell words of three or four letters. Just at this point of my progress, Mr. Auld found out what was going on, and at once forbade Mrs. Auld to instruct me further, telling her, among other things, that it was unlawful, as well as unsafe, to teach a slave to read. To use his own words, further, he said, "If you give a nigger an inch, he will take an ell.[7] A nigger should know nothing but to obey his master—to do as he is told to do. Learning would *spoil* the best nigger in the world. Now," said he, "if you teach that nigger (speaking of myself) how to read, there would be no keeping him. It would forever unfit him to be a slave. He would at once become unmanageable, and of no value to his master. As to himself, it could do him no good, but a great deal of harm. It would make him discontented and unhappy." These words sank deep into my heart, stirred up sentiments within that lay slumbering, and called into existence an entirely new train of thought. It was a new and special revelation, explaining dark and mysterious things, with which my youthful understanding had struggled, but struggled in vain. I now understood what had been to me a most perplexing difficulty—to wit, the white man's power to enslave the black man. It was a grand achievement, and I prized it highly. From that moment, I understood the pathway from slavery to freedom. It was just what I wanted, and I got it at a time when I the least expected it. Whilst I was saddened by the thought of losing the aid of my kind mistress, I was gladdened by the invaluable instruction which, by the merest accident, I had gained from my master. Though conscious of the difficulty of learning without a teacher, I set out with high hope, and a fixed purpose, at whatever cost of trouble, to learn how to read. The very decided manner with which he spoke, and strove to impress his wife with the evil consequences of giving me instruction, served to convince me that he was deeply sensible of the truths he was uttering. It gave me the best assurance that I might rely with the utmost confidence on the results which, he said, would flow from teaching me to read. What he most dreaded, that I most desired. What he most loved, that I most hated. That which to him was a great evil, to be carefully shunned, was to me a great good, to be diligently sought; and the argument which he so warmly urged, against my learning to read, only served to inspire me with a desire and determination to learn. In learning to read, I owe almost as much to the bitter opposition of my master, as to the kindly aid of my mistress. I acknowledge the benefit of both.

I had resided but a short time in Baltimore before I observed a marked difference, in the treatment of slaves, from that which I had witnessed in the country. A city slave is almost a freeman, compared with a slave on the plantation. He is much better fed and clothed, and enjoys privileges altogether unknown to the slave on the plantation. There is a vestige of decency, a sense of shame, that does much to curb and check those outbreaks of atro-

---

7. Unit of measurement equal to forty-five inches.

cious cruelty so commonly enacted upon the plantation. He is a desperate slaveholder, who will shock the humanity of his non-slaveholding neighbors with the cries of his lacerated slave. Few are willing to incur the odium attaching to the reputation of being a cruel master; and above all things, they would not be known as not giving a slave enough to eat. Every city slaveholder is anxious to have it known of him, that he feeds his slaves well; and it is due to them to say, that most of them do give their slaves enough to eat. There are, however, some painful exceptions to this rule. Directly opposite to us, on Philpot Street, lived Mr. Thomas Hamilton. He owned two slaves. Their names were Henrietta and Mary. Henrietta was about twenty-two years of age, Mary was about fourteen; and of all the mangled and emaciated creatures I ever looked upon, these two were the most so. His heart must be harder than stone, that could look upon these unmoved. The head, neck, and shoulders of Mary were literally cut to pieces. I have frequently felt her head, and found it nearly covered with festering sores, caused by the lash of her cruel mistress. I do not know that her master ever whipped her, but I have been an eye-witness to the cruelty of Mrs. Hamilton. I used to be in Mr. Hamilton's house nearly every day. Mrs. Hamilton used to sit in a large chair in the middle of the room, with a heavy cowskin always by her side, and scarce an hour passed during the day but was marked by the blood of one of these slaves. The girls seldom passed her without her saying, "Move faster, you *black gip!*" at the same time giving them a blow with the cowskin over the head or shoulders, often drawing the blood. She would then say, "Take that, you *black gip!*"—continuing, "If you don't move faster, I'll move you!" Added to the cruel lashings to which these slaves were subjected, they were kept nearly half-starved. They seldom knew what it was to eat a full meal. I have seen Mary contending with the pigs for the offal thrown into the street. So much was Mary kicked and cut to pieces, that she was oftener called *"pecked"* than by her name.

Chapter VII

I lived in Master Hugh's family about seven years. During this time, I succeeded in learning to read and write. In accomplishing this, I was compelled to resort to various stratagems. I had no regular teacher. My mistress, who had kindly commenced to instruct me, had, in compliance with the advice and direction of her husband, not only ceased to instruct, but had set her face against my being instructed by any one else. It is due, however, to my mistress to say of her, that she did not adopt this course of treatment immediately. She at first lacked the depravity indispensable to shutting me up in mental darkness. It was at least necessary for her to have some training in the exercise of irresponsible power, to make her equal to the task of treating me as though I were a brute.

My mistress was, as I have said, a kind and tender-hearted woman; and in the simplicity of her soul she commenced, when I first went to live with her, to treat me as she supposed one human being ought to treat another. In entering upon the duties of a slaveholder, she did not seem to perceive that I sustained to her the relation of a mere chattel, and that for her to treat me as a human being was not only wrong, but dangerously so. Slavery proved as injurious to her as it did to me. When I went there, she was a pious, warm, and tender-hearted woman. There was no sorrow or suffering for which she had not a tear. She had bread for the hungry, clothes for the naked, and comfort for every mourner that came within her reach. Slavery soon proved its ability to divest her of these heavenly qualities. Under its influence, the tender heart became stone, and the lamblike disposition gave way to one of tigerlike fierceness. The first step in her downward course was in her ceasing to instruct me. She now commenced to practise her husband's precepts. She finally became even more violent in her opposition than her husband himself. She was not satisfied with simply doing as well as he had commanded; she seemed anxious to do better. Nothing seemed to make her more angry than to see me with a newspaper. She seemed to think that here lay the danger. I have had her rush at me with a face made all up of fury, and snatch from me a newspaper, in a manner that fully revealed her apprehension. She was an apt woman; and a little experience soon demonstrated, to her satisfaction, that education and slavery were incompatible with each other.

From this time I was most narrowly watched. If I was in a separate room any considerable length of time, I was sure to be suspected of having a book, and was at once called to give an account of myself. All this, however, was too late. The first step had been taken. Mistress, in teaching me the alphabet, had given me the *inch*, and no precaution could prevent me from taking the *ell*.

The plan which I adopted, and the one by which I was most successful, was that of making friends of all the little white boys whom I met in the street. As many of these as I could, I converted into teachers. With their kindly aid, obtained at different times and in different places, I finally succeeded in learning to read. When I was sent of errands, I always took my book with me, and by going one part of my errand quickly, I found time to get a lesson before my return. I used also to carry bread with me, enough of which was always in the house, and to which I was always welcome; for I was much better off in this regard than many of the poor white children in our neighborhood. This bread I used to bestow upon the hungry little urchins, who, in return, would give me that more valuable bread of knowledge. I am strongly tempted to give the names of two or three of those little boys, as a testimonial of the gratitude and affection I bear them; but prudence forbids;—not that it would injure me, but it might embarrass them; for it is almost an unpardonable offence to teach slaves to read in this Christian country. It is enough to say of the dear little fellows, that they lived on Philpot Street, very near Durgin and Bailey's shipyard. I used to talk this matter of slavery over with them. I would sometimes say to them, I wished I could be as free as they would be when they got to be men. "You will be free as soon as you are twenty-one, *but I am a slave for life!* Have not I as good a right to be free as you have?" These words used to trouble them; they would express for me the liveliest sympathy, and console me with the hope that something would occur by which I might be free.

I was now about twelve years old, and the thought of being *a slave for life* began to bear heavily upon my heart. Just about this time, I got hold of a book entitled "The Columbian Orator."[8] Every opportunity I got, I used to read this book. Among much of other interesting matter, I found in it a dialogue between a master and his slave. The slave was represented as having run away from his master three times. The dialogue represented the conver-

8. A popular anthology of pieces for recitation (1797) compiled by the Massachusetts teacher and writer Caleb Bingham (1757–1817).

sation which took place between them, when the slave was retaken the third time. In this dialogue, the whole argument in behalf of slavery was brought forward by the master, all of which was disposed of by the slave. The slave was made to say some very smart as well as impressive things in reply to his master—things which had the desired though unexpected effect; for the conversation resulted in the voluntary emancipation of the slave on the part of the master.

In the same book, I met with one of Sheridan's[9] mighty speeches on and in behalf of Catholic emancipation. These were choice documents to me. I read them over and over again with unabated interest. They gave tongue to interesting thoughts of my own soul, which had frequently flashed through my mind, and died away for want of utterance. The moral which I gained from the dialogue was the power of truth over the conscience of even a slaveholder. What I got from Sheridan was a bold denunciation of slavery, and a powerful vindication of human rights. The reading of these documents enabled me to utter my thoughts, and to meet the arguments brought forward to sustain slavery; but while they relieved me of one difficulty, they brought on another even more painful than the one of which I was relieved. The more I read, the more I was led to abhor and detest my enslavers. I could regard them in no other light than a band of successful robbers, who had left their homes, and gone to Africa, and stolen us from our homes, and in a strange land reduced us to slavery. I loathed them as being the meanest as well as the most wicked of men. As I read and contemplated the subject, behold! that very discontentment which Master Hugh had predicted would follow my learning to read had already come, to torment and sting my soul to unutterable anguish. As I writhed under it, I would at times feel that learning to read had been a curse rather than a blessing. It had given me a view of my wretched condition, without the remedy. It opened my eyes to the horrible pit, but to no ladder upon which to get out. In moments of agony, I envied my fellow-slaves for their stupidity. I have often wished myself a beast. I preferred the condition of the meanest reptile to my own. Any thing, no matter what, to get rid of thinking! It was this everlasting thinking of my condition that tormented me. There was no getting rid of it. It was pressed upon me by every object within sight or hearing, animate or inanimate. The silver trump of freedom had roused my soul to eternal wakefulness. Freedom now appeared, to disappear no more forever. It was heard in every sound, and seen in every thing. It was ever present to torment me with a sense of my wretched condition. I saw nothing without seeing it, I heard nothing without hearing it, and felt nothing without feeling it. It looked from every star, it smiled in every calm, breathed in every wind, and moved in every storm.

I often found myself regretting my own existence, and wishing myself dead; and but for the hope of being free, I have no doubt but that I should have killed myself, or done something for which I should have been killed. While in this state of mind, I was eager to hear any one speak of slavery. I was a ready listener. Every little while, I could hear something about the abolitionists. It was some time before I found what the word meant. It was always used in such connections as to make it an interesting word to me. If a slave ran away and succeeded in getting clear, or if a slave killed his mas-

9. Richard Brinsley Sheridan (1751–1816), Irish dramatist and political leader.

ter, set fire to a barn, or did any thing very wrong in the mind of a slave-holder, it was spoken of as the fruit of *abolition*. Hearing the word in this connection very often, I set about learning what it meant. The dictionary afforded me little or no help. I found it was "the act of abolishing;" but then I did not know what was to be abolished. Here I was perplexed. I did not dare to ask any one about its meaning, for I was satisfied that it was some-thing they wanted me to know very little about. After a patient waiting, I got one of our city papers, containing an account of the number of petitions from the north, praying for the abolition of slavery in the District of Colum-bia, and of the slave trade between the States. From this time I understood the words *abolition* and *abolitionist*, and always drew near when that word was spoken, expecting to hear something of importance to myself and fellow-slaves. The light broke in upon me by degrees. I went one day down on the wharf of Mr. Waters; and seeing two Irishmen unloading a scow of stone, I went, unasked, and helped them. When we had finished, one of them came to me and asked me if I were a slave. I told him I was. He asked, "Are ye a slave for life?" I told him that I was. The good Irishman seemed to be deeply affected by the statement. He said to the other that it was a pity so fine a little fellow as myself should be a slave for life. He said it was a shame to hold me. They both advised me to run away to the north; that I should find friends there, and that I should be free. I pretended not to be interested in what they said, and treated them as if I did not understand them; for I feared they might be treacherous. White men have been known to encourage slaves to escape, and then, to get the reward, catch them and return them to their masters. I was afraid that these seemingly good men might use me so; but I nevertheless remembered their advice, and from that time I resolved to run away. I looked forward to a time at which it would be safe for me to escape. I was too young to think of doing so immediately; besides, I wished to learn how to write, as I might have occasion to write my own pass. I consoled myself with the hope that I should one day find a good chance. Meanwhile, I would learn to write.

The idea as to how I might learn to write was suggested to me by being in Durgin and Bailey's ship-yard, and frequently seeing the ship carpenters, after hewing, and getting a piece of timber ready for use, write on the timber the name of that part of the ship for which it was intended. When a piece of timber was intended for the larboard side, it would be marked thus—"L." When a piece was for the starboard side, it would be marked thus—"S." A piece for the larboard side forward, would be marked thus—"L.F." When a piece was for starboard side forward, it would be marked thus—"S.F." For larboard aft, it would be marked thus—"L.A." For starboard aft, it would be marked thus—"S.A." I soon learned the names of these letters, and for what they were intended when placed upon a piece of timber in the ship-yard. I immediately commenced copying them, and in a short time was able to make the four letters named. After that, when I met with any boy who I knew could write, I would tell him I could write as well as he. The next word would be, "I don't believe you. Let me see you try it." I would then make the letters which I had been so fortunate as to learn, and ask him to beat that. In this way I got a good many lessons in writing, which it is quite possible I should never have gotten in any other way. During this time, my copy-book was the board fence, brick wall, and pavement; my pen and ink was a lump of chalk. With these, I learned mainly how to write. I then commenced and continued copying the Italics in Webster's Spelling Book,[1] until I could make them all without looking on the book. By this time, my little Master Thomas had gone to school, and learned how to write, and had written over a number of copy-books. These had been brought home, and shown to some of our near neighbors, and then laid aside. My mistress used to go to class meeting at the Wilk Street meetinghouse every Monday afternoon, and leave me to take care of the house. When left thus, I used to spend the time in writing in the spaces left in Master Thomas's copy-book, copying what he had written. I continued to do this until I could write a hand very similar to that of Master Thomas. Thus, after a long, tedious effort for years, I finally succeeded in learning how to write.

Chapter VIII

In a very short time after I went to live at Baltimore, my old master's youngest son Richard died; and in about three years and six months after his death, my old master, Captain Anthony, died, leaving only his son, Andrew, and daughter, Lucretia, to share his estate. He died while on a visit to see his daughter at Hillsborough. Cut off thus unexpectedly, he left no will as to the disposal of his property. It was therefore necessary to have a valuation of the property, that it might be equally divided between Mrs. Lucretia and Master Andrew. I was immediately sent for, to be valued with the other property. Here again my feelings rose up in detestation of slavery. I had now a new conception of my degraded condition. Prior to this, I had become, if not insensible to my lot, at least partly so. I left Baltimore with a young heart overborne with sadness, and a soul full of apprehension. I took passage with Captain Rowe, in the schooner Wild Cat, and, after a sail of about twenty-four hours, I found myself near the place of my birth. I had now been absent from it almost, if not quite, five years. I, however, remembered the place very well. I was only about five years old when I left it, to go and live with my old master on Colonel Lloyd's plantation; so that I was now between ten and eleven years old.

We were all ranked together at the valuation. Men and women, old and young, married and single, were ranked with horses, sheep, and swine. There were horses and men, cattle and women, pigs and children, all holding the same rank in the scale of being, and were all subjected to the same narrow examination. Silvery-headed age and sprightly youth, maids and matrons, had to undergo the same indelicate inspection. At this moment, I saw more clearly than ever the brutalizing effects of slavery upon both slave and slaveholder.

After the valuation, then came the division. I have no language to express the high excitement and deep anxiety which were felt among us poor slaves during this time. Our fate for life was now to be decided. We had no more voice in that decision than the brutes among whom we were ranked. A single word from the white men was enough—against all our wishes, prayers, and entreaties—to sunder forever the dearest friends, dearest kindred, and strongest ties known to human beings. In addition to the pain of separation, there was the horrid dread of falling into the hands of Master Andrew.

1. *The American Spelling Book* (1783), by Noah Webster (1758–1843).

He was known to us all as being a most cruel wretch,—a common drunkard, who had, by his reckless mismanagement and profligate dissipation, already wasted a large portion of his father's property. We all felt that we might as well be sold at once to the Georgia traders, as to pass into his hands; for we knew that that would be our inevitable condition,—a condition held by us all in the utmost horror and dread.

I suffered more anxiety than most of my fellow-slaves. I had known what it was to be kindly treated; they had known nothing of the kind. They had seen little or nothing of the world. They were in very deed men and women of sorrow, and acquainted with grief. Their backs had been made familiar with the bloody lash, so that they had become callous; mine was yet tender; for while at Baltimore I got few whippings, and few slaves could boast of a kinder master and mistress than myself; and the thought of passing out of their hands into those of Master Andrew—a man who, but a few days before, to give me a sample of his bloody disposition, took my little brother by the throat, threw him on the ground, and with the heel of his boot stamped upon his head till the blood gushed from his nose and ears—was well calculated to make me anxious as to my fate. After he had committed this savage outrage upon my brother, he turned to me, and said that was the way he meant to serve me one of these days,—meaning, I suppose, when I came into his possession.

Thanks to a kind Providence, I fell to the portion of Mrs. Lucretia, and was sent immediately back to Baltimore, to live again in the family of Master Hugh. Their joy at my return equalled their sorrow at my departure. It was a glad day to me. I had escaped a [fate] worse than lion's jaws. I was absent from Baltimore, for the purpose of valuation and division, just about one month, and it seemed to have been six.

Very soon after my return to Baltimore, my mistress, Lucretia, died, leaving her husband and one child, Amanda; and in a very short time after her death, Master Andrew died. Now all the property of my old master, slaves included, was in the hands of strangers,—strangers who had had nothing to do with accumulating it. Not a slave was left free. All remained slaves, from the youngest to the oldest. If any one thing in my experience, more than another, served to deepen my conviction of the infernal character of slavery, and to fill me with unutterable loathing of slaveholders, it was their base ingratitude to my poor old grandmother. She had served my old master faithfully from youth to old age. She had been the source of all his wealth; she had peopled his plantation with slaves; she had become a great grandmother in his service. She had rocked him in infancy, attended him in childhood, served him through life, and at his death wiped from his icy brow the cold death-sweat, and closed his eyes forever. She was nevertheless left a slave—a slave for life—a slave in the hands of strangers; and in their hands she saw her children, her grandchildren, and her great-grandchildren, divided, like so many sheep, without being gratified with the small privilege of a single word, as to their or her own destiny. And, to cap the climax of their base ingratitude and fiendish barbarity, my grandmother, who was now very old, having outlived my old master and all his children, having seen the beginning and end of all of them, and her present owners finding she was of but little value, her frame already racked with the pains of old age, and complete helplessness fast stealing over her once active limbs, they took her to the woods, built her a little hut, put up a little mud-chimney, and then made her welcome to the privilege of supporting herself there in perfect loneliness;

thus virtually turning her out to die! If my poor old grandmother now lives, she lives to suffer in utter loneliness; she lives to remember and mourn over the loss of children, the loss of grandchildren, and the loss of great-grandchildren. They are, in the language of the slave's poet, Whittier,[2]—

> "Gone, gone, sold and gone
> To the rice swamp dank and lone,
> Where the slave-whip ceaseless swings,
> Where the noisome insect stings,
> Where the fever-demon strews
> Poison with the falling dews,
> Where the sickly sunbeams glare
> Through the hot and misty air:—
> Gone, gone, sold and gone
> To the rice swamp dank and lone,
> From Virginia hills and waters—
> Woe is me, my stolen daughters!"

The hearth is desolate. The children, the unconscious children, who once sang and danced in her presence, are gone. She gropes her way, in the darkness of age, for a drink of water. Instead of the voices of her children, she hears by day the moans of the dove, and by night the screams of the hideous owl. All is gloom. The grave is at the door. And now, when weighed down by the pains and aches of old age, when the head inclines to the feet, when the beginning and ending of human existence meet, and helpless infancy and painful old age combine together—at this time, this most needful time, the time for the exercise of that tenderness and affection which children only can exercise toward a declining parent—my poor old grandmother, the devoted mother of twelve children, is left all alone, in yonder little hut, before a few dim embers. She stands—she sits—she staggers—she falls—she groans—she dies—and there are none of her children or grandchildren present, to wipe from her wrinkled brow the cold sweat of death, or to place beneath the sod her fallen remains. Will not a righteous God visit for these things?

In about two years after the death of Mrs. Lucretia, Master Thomas married his second wife. Her name was Rowena Hamilton. She was the eldest daughter of Mr. William Hamilton. Master now lived in St. Michael's. Not long after his marriage, a misunderstanding took place between himself and Master Hugh; and as a means of punishing his brother, he took me from him to live with himself at St. Michael's. Here I underwent another most painful separation. It, however, was not so severe as the one I dreaded at the division of property; for, during this interval, a great change had taken place in Master Hugh and his once kind and affectionate wife. The influence of brandy upon him, and of slavery upon her, had effected a disastrous change in the characters of both; so that, as far as they were concerned, I thought I had little to lose by the change. But it was not to them that I was attached. It was to those little Baltimore boys that I felt the strongest attachment. I had received many good lessons from them, and was still receiving them, and the thought of leaving them was painful indeed. I was leaving, too,

2. John Greenleaf Whittier (1807–1882), American poet and abolitionist. Douglass quotes from Whittier's antislavery poem "The Farewell: Of a Virginia Slave Mother to Her Daughter Sold into Southern Bondage" (1838).

without the hope of ever being allowed to return. Master Thomas had said he would never let me return again. The barrier betwixt himself and brother he considered impassable.

I then had to regret that I did not at least make the attempt to carry out my resolution to run away; for the chances of success are tenfold greater from the city than from the country.

I sailed from Baltimore for St. Michael's in the sloop Amanda, Captain Edward Dodson. On my passage, I paid particular attention to the direction which the steamboats took to go to Philadelphia. I found, instead of going down, on reaching North Point they went up the bay, in a north-easterly direction. I deemed this knowledge of the utmost importance. My determination to run away was again revived. I resolved to wait only so long as the offering of a favorable opportunity. When that came, I was determined to be off.

Chapter IX

I have now reached a period of my life when I can give dates. I left Baltimore, and went to live with Master Thomas Auld, at St. Michael's, in March, 1832. It was now more than seven years since I lived with him in the family of my old master, on Colonel Lloyd's plantation. We of course were now almost entire strangers to each other. He was to me a new master, and I to him a new slave. I was ignorant of his temper and disposition; he was equally so of mine. A very short time, however brought us into full acquaintance with each other. I was made acquainted with his wife not less than with himself. They were well matched, being equally mean and cruel. I was now, for the first time during a space of more than seven years, made to feel the painful gnawings of hunger—a something which I had not experienced before since I left Colonel Lloyd's plantation. It went hard enough with me then, when I could look back to no period at which I had enjoyed a sufficiency. It was tenfold harder after living in Master Hugh's family, where I had always had enough to eat, and of that which was good. I have said Master Thomas was a mean man. He was so. Not to give a slave enough to eat, is regarded as the most aggravated development of meanness even among slaveholders. The rule is, no matter how coarse the food, only let there be enough of it. This is the theory; and in the part of Maryland from which I came, it is the general practice,—though there are many exceptions. Master Thomas gave us enough of neither coarse nor fine food. There were four slaves of us in the kitchen—my sister Eliza, my aunt Priscilla, Henny, and myself; and we were allowed less than half of a bushel of cornmeal per week, and very little else, either in the shape of meat or vegetables. It was not enough for us to subsist upon. We were therefore reduced to the wretched necessity of living at the expense of our neighbors. This we did by begging and stealing, whichever came handy in the time of need, the one being considered as legitimate as the other. A great many times have we poor creatures been nearly perishing with hunger, when food in abundance lay mouldering in the safe and smoke-house,[3] and our pious mistress was aware of the fact; and yet that mistress and her husband would kneel every morning, and pray that God would bless them in basket and store!

---

3. Used both to cure and to store meat and fish. "Safe": a meat safe is a structure for preserving food.

Bad as all slaveholders are, we seldom meet one destitute of every element of character commanding respect. My master was one of this rare sort. I do not know of one single noble act ever performed by him. The leading trait in his character was meanness; and if there were any other element in his nature, it was made subject to this. He was mean; and, like most other mean men, he lacked the ability to conceal his meanness. Captain Auld was not born a slaveholder. He had been a poor man, master only of a Bay craft. He came into possession of all his slaves by marriage; and of all men, adopted slaveholders are the worst. He was cruel, but cowardly. He commanded without firmness. In the enforcement of his rules he was at times rigid, and at times lax. At times, he spoke to his slaves with the firmness of Napoleon and the fury of a demon; at other times, he might well be mistaken for an inquirer who had lost his way. He did nothing of himself. He might have passed for a lion, but for his ears.[4] In all things noble which he attempted, his own meanness shone most conspicuous. His airs, words, and actions, were the airs, words, and actions of born slaveholders, and, being assumed, were awkward enough. He was not even a good imitator. He possessed all the disposition to deceive, but wanted the power. Having no resources within himself, he was compelled to be the copyist of many, and being such, he was forever the victim of inconsistency; and of consequence he was an object of contempt, and was held as such even by his slaves. The luxury of having slaves of his own to wait upon him was something new and unprepared for. He was a slaveholder without the ability to hold slaves. He found himself incapable of managing his slaves either by force, fear, or fraud. We seldom called him "master;" we generally called him "Captain Auld," and were hardly disposed to title him at all. I doubt not that our conduct had much to do with making him appear awkward, and of consequence fretful. Our want of reverence for him must have perplexed him greatly. He wished to have us call him master, but lacked the firmness necessary to command us to do so. His wife used to insist upon our calling him so, but to no purpose. In August, 1832, my master attended a Methodist camp-meeting[5] held in the Bay-side, Talbot county, and there experienced religion. I indulged a faint hope that his conversion would lead him to emancipate his slaves, and that, if he did not do this, it would, at any rate, make him more kind and humane. I was disappointed in both these respects. It neither made him to be humane to his slaves, nor to emancipate them. If it had any effect on his character, it made him more cruel and hateful in all his ways; for I believe him to have been a much worse man after his conversion than before. Prior to his conversion, he relied upon his own depravity to shield and sustain him in his savage barbarity; but after his conversion, he found religious sanction and support for his slaveholding cruelty. He made the greatest pretensions to piety. His house was the house of prayer. He prayed morning, noon, and night. He very soon distinguished himself among his brethren, and was soon made a class-leader and exhorter. His activity in revivals was great, and he proved himself an instrument in the hands of the church in converting many souls. His house was the preachers' home. They used to take great pleasure in coming there to put up; for while he starved us, he stuffed them. We have had three or four preachers there at a time. The names of those who used to come most

---

4. The suggestion is that his ears reveal him to be a jackass and thus not as powerful as he pretends.

5. Evangelical religious gathering, usually held outdoors.

frequently while I lived there, were Mr. Storks, Mr. Ewery, Mr. Humphry, and Mr. Hickey. I have also seen Mr. George Cookman[6] at our house. We slaves loved Mr. Cookman. We believed him to be a good man. We thought him instrumental in getting Mr. Samuel Harrison, a very rich slaveholder, to emancipate his slaves; and by some means got the impression that he was laboring to effect the emancipation of all the slaves. When he was at our house, we were sure to be called in to prayers. When the others were there, we were sometimes called in and sometimes not. Mr. Cookman took more notice of us than either of the other ministers. He could not come among us with betraying his sympathy for us, and, stupid as we were, we had the sagacity to see it.

While I lived with my master in St. Michael's, there was a white young man, a Mr. Wilson, who proposed to keep a Sabbath school for the instruction of such slaves as might be disposed to learn to read the New Testament. We met but three times, when Mr. West and Mr. Fairbanks, both class-leaders, with many others, came upon us with sticks and other missiles, drove us off, and forbade us to meet again. Thus ended our little Sabbath school in the pious town of St. Michael's.

I have said my master found religious sanction for his cruelty. As an example, I will state one of many facts going to prove the charge. I have seen him tie up a lame young woman, and whip her with a heavy cowskin upon her naked shoulders, causing the warm red blood to drip; and, in justification of the bloody deed, he would quote this passage of Scripture—"He that knoweth his master's will, and doeth it not, shall be beaten with many stripes."[7]

Master would keep this lacerated young woman tied up in this horrid situation four or five hours at a time. I have known him to tie her up early in the morning, and whip her before breakfast; leave her, go to his store, return at dinner, and whip her again, cutting her in the places already made raw with his cruel lash. The secret of master's cruelty toward "Henny" is found in the fact of her being almost helpless. When quite a child, she fell into the fire, and burned herself horribly. Her hands were so burnt that she never got the use of them. She could do very little but bear heavy burdens. She was to master a bill of expense; and as he was a mean man, she was a constant offence to him. He seemed desirous of getting the poor girl out of existence. He gave her away once to his sister; but, being a poor gift, she was not disposed to keep her. Finally, my benevolent master, to use his own words, "set her adrift to take care of herself." Here was a recently-converted man, holding on upon the mother, and at the same time turning out her helpless child, to starve and die! Master Thomas was one of the many pious slaveholders who hold slaves for the very charitable purpose of taking care of them.

My master and myself had quite a number of differences. He found me unsuitable to his purpose. My city life, he said, had had a very pernicious effect upon me. It had almost ruined me for every good purpose, and fitted me for every thing which was bad. One of my greatest faults was that of letting his horse run away, and go down to his father-in-law's farm, which was about five miles from St. Michael's. I would then have to go after it. My reason for this kind of carelessness, or carefulness, was, that I could always get something to eat when I went there. Master William Hamilton, my master's father-in-law, always gave his slaves enough to eat. I never left there hungry, no matter how great the need of my speedy return. Master Thomas at length said he would stand it no longer. I had lived with him nine months, during which time he had given me a number of severe whippings, all to no good purpose. He resolved to put me out, as he said, to be broken; and, for this purpose, he let me for one year to a man named Edward Covey. Mr. Covey was a poor man, a farm-renter. He rented the place upon which he lived, as also the hands with which he tilled it. Mr. Covey had acquired a very high reputation for breaking young slaves, and this reputation was of immense value to him. It enabled him to get his farm tilled with much less expense to himself than he could have had it done without such a reputation. Some slaveholders thought it not much loss to allow Mr. Covey to have their slaves one year, for the sake of training to which they were subjected, without any other compensation. He could hire young help with great ease, in consequence of this reputation. Added to the natural good qualities of Mr. Covey, he was a professor of religion—a pious soul—a member and a class-leader in the Methodist church. All of this added weight to his reputation as a "nigger-breaker." I was aware of all the facts, having been made acquainted with them by a young man who had lived there. I nevertheless made the change gladly; for I was sure of getting enough to eat, which is not the smallest consideration to a hungry man.

Chapter X

I left Master Thomas's house, and went to live with Mr. Covey, on the 1st of January, 1833. I was now, for the first time in my life, a field hand. In my new employment, I found myself even more awkward than a country boy appeared to be in a large city. I had been at my new home but one week before Mr. Covey gave me a very severe whipping, cutting my back, causing the blood to run, and raising ridges on my flesh as large as my little finger. The details of this affair are as follows: Mr. Covey sent me, very early in the morning of one of our coldest days in the month of January, to the woods, to get a load of wood. He gave me a team of unbroken oxen. He told me which was the in-hand ox, and which the off-hand one.[8] He then tied the end of a large rope around the horns of the in-hand-ox, and gave me the other end of it, and told me, if the oxen started to run, that I must hold on upon the rope. I had never driven oxen before, and of course I was very awkward. I, however, succeeded in getting to the edge of the woods with little difficulty; but I had got a very few rods into the woods, when the oxen took fright, and started full tilt, carrying the cart against trees, and over stumps, in the most frightful manner. I expected every moment that my brains would be dashed out against the trees. After running thus for a considerable distance, they finally upset the cart, dashing it with great force against a tree, and threw themselves into a dense thicket. How I escaped death, I do not know. There I was, entirely alone, in a thick wood, in a place new to me. My cart was upset and shattered, my oxen were entangled among the young trees, and there was none to help me. After a long spell of effort, I succeeded in getting my cart righted, my oxen disentangled, and again yoked to the cart. I now

---

8. The ox on the right of a pair hitched to a wagon. "In-hand ox": the one to the left.

proceeded with my team to the place where I had, the day before, been chopping wood, and loaded my cart pretty heavily, thinking in this way to tame my oxen. I then proceeded on my way home. I had now consumed one half of the day. I got out of the woods safely, and now felt out of danger. I stopped my oxen to open the woods gate; and just as I did so, before I could get hold of my ox-rope, the oxen again started, rushed through the gate, catching it between the wheel and the body of the cart, tearing it to pieces, and coming within a few inches of crushing me against the gate-post. Thus twice, in one short day, I escaped death by the merest chance. On my return, I told Mr. Covey what had happened, and how it happened. He ordered me to return to the woods again immediately. I did so, and he followed on after me. Just as I got into the woods, he came up and told me to stop my cart, and that he would teach me how to trifle away my time, and break gates. He then went to a large gum-tree, and with his axe cut three large switches, and, after trimming them up neatly with his pocket-knife, he ordered me to take off my clothes. I made him no answer, but stood with my clothes on. He repeated his order. I still made him no answer, nor did I move to strip myself. Upon this he rushed at me with the fierceness of a tiger, tore off my clothes, and lashed me till he had worn out his switches, cutting me so savagely as to leave the marks visible for a long time after. This whipping was the first of a number just like it, and for similar offences.

I lived with Mr. Covey one year. During the first six months, of that year, scarce a week passed without his whipping me. I was seldom free from a sore back. My awkwardness was almost always his excuse for whipping me. We were worked fully up to the point of endurance. Long before day we were up, our horses fed, and by the first approach of day we were off to the field with our hoes and ploughing teams. Mr. Covey gave us enough to eat, but scarce time to eat it. We were often less than five minutes taking our meals. We were often in the field from the first approach of day till its last lingering ray had left us; and at saving-fodder time, midnight often caught us in the field binding blades.[9]

Covey would be out with us. The way he used to stand it, was this. He would spend the most of his afternoons in bed. He would then come out fresh in the evening, ready to urge us on with his words, example, and frequently with the whip. Mr. Covey was one of the few slaveholders who could and did work with his hands. He was a hard-working man. He knew by himself just what a man or a boy could do. There was no deceiving him. His work went on in his absence almost as well as in his presence; and he had the faculty of making us feel that he was ever present with us. This he did by surprising us. He seldom approached the spot where we were at work openly, if he could do it secretly. He always aimed at taking us by surprise. Such was his cunning, that we used to call him, among ourselves, "the snake." When we were at work in the cornfield, he would sometimes crawl on his hands and knees to avoid detection, and all at once he would rise nearly in our midst, and scream out, "Ha, ha! Come, come! Dash on, dash on!" This being his mode of attack, it was never safe to stop a single minute. His comings were like a thief in the night. He appeared to us as being ever at hand. He was under every tree, behind every stump, in every bush, and at every window, on the plantation. He would sometimes mount his horse, as if bound to St. Michael's, a distance of

---

9. I.e., of wheat or other plants. "Saving-fodder time": harvest time.

seven miles, and in half an hour afterwards you would see him coiled up in the corner of the wood-fence, watching every motion of the slaves. He would, for this purpose, leave his horse tied up in the woods. Again, he would sometimes walk up to us, and give us orders as though he was upon the point of starting on a long journey, turn his back upon us, and make as though he was going to the house to get ready; and, before he would get half way thither, he would turn short and crawl into a fence-corner, or behind some tree, and there watch us till the going down of the sun.

Mr. Covey's *forte*[1] consisted in his power to deceive. His life was devoted to planning and perpetrating the grossest deceptions. Every thing he possessed in the shape of learning or religion, he made conform to his disposition to deceive. He seemed to think himself equal to deceiving the Almighty. He would make a short prayer in the morning, and a long prayer at night; and, strange as it may seem, few men would at times appear more devotional than he. The exercises of his family devotions were always commenced with singing; and, as he was a very poor singer himself, the duty of raising the hymn generally came upon me. He would read his hymn, and nod at me to commence. I would at times do so; at others, I would not. My non-compliance would almost always produce much confusion. To show himself independent of me, he would start and stagger through with his hymn in the most discordant manner. In this state of mind, he prayed with more than ordinary spirit. Poor man! such was his disposition, and success at deceiving, I do verily believe that he sometimes deceived himself into the solemn belief, that he was a sincere worshiper of the most high God; and this, too, at a time when he may be said to have been guilty of compelling his woman slave to commit the sin of adultery. The facts in the case are these: Mr. Covey was a poor man; he was just commencing in life; he was only able to buy one slave; and, shocking as is the fact, he bought her, as he said, for *a breeder*. This woman was named Caroline. Mr. Covey bought her from Mr. Thomas Lowe, about six miles from St. Michael's. She was a large, able-bodied woman, about twenty years old. She had already given birth to one child, which proved her to be just what he wanted. After buying her, he hired a married man of Mr. Samuel Harrison, to live with him one year; and him he used to fasten up with her every night! The result was, that, at the end of the year, the miserable woman gave birth to twins. At this result Mr. Covey seemed to be highly pleased, both with the man and the wretched woman. Such was his joy, and that of his wife, that nothing they could do for Caroline during her confinement was too good, or too hard, to be done. The children were regarded as being quite an addition to his wealth.

If at any one time of my life more than another, I was made to drink the bitterest dregs of slavery, that time was during the first six months of my stay with Mr. Covey. We were worked in all weathers. It was never too hot or too cold; it could never rain, blow, hail, or snow, too hard for us to work in the field. Work, work, work, was scarcely more the order of the day than of the night. The longest days were too short for him, and the shortest nights too long for him. I was somewhat unmanageable when I first went there, but a few months of this discipline tamed me. Mr. Covey succeeded in breaking me. I was broken in body, soul, and spirit. My natural elasticity was crushed, my intellect languished, the disposition to read departed, the

1. Strong point (French).

cheerful spark that lingered about my eye died; the dark night of slavery closed in upon me; and behold a man transformed into a brute!

Sunday was my only leisure time. I spent this in a sort of beast-like stupor, between sleep and wake, under some large tree. At times I would rise up, a flash of energetic freedom would dart through my soul, accompanied with a faint beam of hope, that flickered for a moment, and then vanished. I sank down again, mourning over my wretched condition. I was sometimes prompted to take my life, and that of Covey, but was prevented by a combination of hope and fear. My sufferings on this plantation seem now like a dream rather than a stern reality.

Our house stood within a few rods of the Chesapeake Bay, whose broad bosom was ever white with sails from every quarter of the habitable globe. Those beautiful vessels, robed in purest white, so delightful to the eye of freemen, were to me so many shrouded ghosts, to terrify and torment me with thoughts of my wretched condition. I have often, in the deep stillness of a summer's Sabbath, stood all alone upon the lofty banks of that noble bay, and traced, with saddened heart and tearful eye, the countless number of sails moving off to the mighty ocean. The sight of these always affected me powerfully. My thoughts would compel utterance; and there, with no audience but the Almighty, I would pour out my soul's complaint, in my rude way, with an apostrophe to the moving multitude of ships:—

"You are loosed from your moorings, and are free; I am fast in my chains, and am a slave! You move merrily before the gentle gale, and I sadly before the bloody whip! You are freedom's swift-winged angels, that fly round the world; I am confined in bands of iron! O that I were free! Oh, that I were on one of your gallant decks, and under your protecting wing! Alas! betwixt me and you, the turbid waters roll. Go on, go on. O that I could also go! Could I but swim! If I could fly! O, why was I born a man, of whom to make a brute! The glad ship is gone; she hides in the dim distance. I am left in the hottest hell of unending slavery. O God, save me! God, deliver me! Let me be free! Is there any God? Why am I a slave? I will run away. I will not stand it. Get caught, or get clear, I'll try it. I had as well die with ague as the fever. I have only one life to lose. I had as well be killed running as die standing. Only think of it; one hundred miles straight north, and I am free! Try it? Yes! God helping me, I will. It cannot be that I shall live and die a slave. I will take to the water. This very bay shall yet bear me into freedom. The steamboats steered in a north-east course from North Point. I will do the same; and when I get to the head of the bay, I will turn my canoe adrift, and walk straight through Delaware into Pennsylvania. When I get there, I shall not be required to have a pass; I can travel without being disturbed. Let but the first opportunity offer, and, come what will, I am off. Meanwhile, I will try to bear up under the yoke. I am not the only slave in the world. Why should I fret? I can bear as much as any of them. Besides, I am but a boy, and all boys are bound to some one. It may be that my misery in slavery will only increase my happiness when I get free. There is a better day coming."

Thus I used to think, and thus I used to speak to myself; goaded almost to madness at one moment, and at the next reconciling myself to my wretched lot.

I have already intimated that my condition was much worse, during the first six months of my stay at Mr. Covey's, than in the last six. The circumstances leading to the change in Mr. Covey's course toward me form an epoch in my humble history. You have seen how a man was made a slave; you shall see how a slave was made a man. On one of the hottest days of the month of August, 1833, Bill Smith, William Hughes, a slave named Eli, and myself, were engaged in fanning wheat.[2] Hughes was clearing the fanned wheat from before the fan, Eli was turning, Smith was feeding, and I was carrying wheat to the fan. The work was simple, requiring strength rather than intellect; yet, to one entirely unused to such work, it came very hard. About three o'clock of that day, I broke down; my strength failed me; I was seized with a violent aching of the head, attended with extreme dizziness; I trembled in every limb. Finding what was coming, I nerved myself up, feeling it would never do to stop work. I stood as long as I could stagger to the hopper with grain. When I could stand no longer, I fell, and felt as if held down by an immense weight. The fan of course stopped; every one had his own work to do; and no one could do the work of the other, and have his own go on at the same time.

Mr. Covey was at the house, about one hundred yards from the treading-yard where we were fanning. On hearing the fan stop, he left immediately, and came to the spot where we were. He hastily inquired what the matter was. Bill answered that I was sick, and there was no one to bring wheat to the fan. I had by this time crawled away under the side of the post and rail-fence by which the yard was enclosed, hoping to find relief by getting out of the sun. He then asked where I was. He was told by one of the hands. He came to the spot, and, after looking at me awhile, asked me what was the matter. I told him as well as I could, for I scarce had strength to speak. He then gave me a savage kick in the side, and told me to get up. I tried to do so, but fell back in the attempt. He gave me another kick, and again told me to rise. I again tried, and succeeded in gaining my feet; but, stooping to get the tub with which I was feeding the fan, I again staggered and fell. While down in this situation, Mr. Covey took up the hickory slat with which Hughes had been striking off the half-bushel measure, and with it gave me a heavy blow upon the head, making a large wound, and the blood ran freely; and with this again told me to get up. I made no effort to comply, having now made up my mind to let him do his worst. In a short time after receiving this blow, my head grew better. Mr. Covey had now left me to my fate. At this moment I resolved, for the first time, to go to my master, enter a complaint, and ask his protection. In order to do this, I must that afternoon walk seven miles; and this, under the circumstances, was truly a severe undertaking. I was exceedingly feeble; made so as much by the kicks and blows which I received, as by the severe fit of sickness to which I had been subjected. I, however, watched my chance, while Covey was looking in an opposite direction, and started for St. Michael's. I succeeded in getting a considerable distance on my way to the woods, when Covey discovered me, and called after me to come back, threatening what he would do if I did not come. I disregarded both his calls and his threats, and made my way to the woods as fast as my feeble state would allow; and thinking I might be overhauled by him if I kept the road, I walked through the woods, keeping far enough from the road to avoid detection, and near enough to prevent losing my way. I had not gone far before my little strength again failed me. I could go no farther. I fell down, and lay for a considerable time. The blood

2. Separating the wheat from the chaff.

was yet oozing from the wound on my head. For a time I thought I should bleed to death; and think now that I should have done so, but that the blood so matted my hair as to stop the wound. After lying there about three quarters of an hour, I nerved myself up again, and started on my way, through bogs and briers, barefooted and bareheaded, tearing my feet sometimes at nearly every step; and after a journey of about seven miles, occupying some five hours to perform it, I arrived at master's store. I then presented an appearance enough to affect any but a heart of iron. From the crown of my head to my feet, I was covered with blood. My hair was all clotted with dust and blood; my shirt was stiff with blood. My legs and feet were torn in sundry places with briers and thorns, and were also covered with blood. I suppose I looked like a man who had escaped a den of wild beasts, and barely escaped them. In this state I appeared before my master, humbly entreating him to interpose his authority for my protection. I told him all the circumstances as well as I could, and it seemed, as I spoke, at times to affect him. He would then walk the floor, and seek to justify Covey by saying he expected I deserved it. He asked me what I wanted. I told him, to let me get a new home; that as sure as I lived with Mr. Covey again, I should live with but to die with him; that Covey would surely kill me; he was in a fair way for it. Master Thomas ridiculed the idea that there was any danger of Mr. Covey's killing me, and said that he knew Mr. Covey; that he was a good man, and that he could not think of taking me from him; that, should he do so, he would lose the whole year's wages; that I belonged to Mr. Covey for one year, and that I must go back to him, come what might; and that I must not trouble him with any more stories, or that he would himself *get hold of me*. After threatening me thus, he gave me a very large dose of salts, telling me that I might remain in St. Michael's that night, (it being quite late,) but that I must be off back to Mr. Covey's early in the morning; and that if I did not, he would *get hold of me*, which meant that he would whip me. I remained all night, and, according to his orders, I started off to Covey's in the morning, (Saturday morning), wearied in body and broken in spirit. I got no supper that night, or breakfast that morning. I reached Covey's about nine o'clock; and just as I was getting over the fence that divided Mrs. Kemp's fields from ours, out ran Covey with his cowskin, to give me another whipping. Before he could reach me, I succeeded in getting to the cornfield; and as the corn was very high, it afforded me the means of hiding. He seemed very angry, and searched for me a long time. My behavior was altogether unaccountable. He finally gave up the chase, thinking, I suppose, that I must come home for something to eat; he would give himself no further trouble in looking for me. I spent that day mostly in the woods, having the alternative before me,—to go home and be whipped to death, or stay in the woods and be starved to death. That night, I fell in with Sandy Jenkins, a slave with whom I was somewhat acquainted. Sandy had a free wife[3] who lived about four miles from Mr. Covey's; and it being Saturday, he was on his way to see her. I told him my circumstances, and he very kindly invited me to go home with him. I went home with him, and talked this whole matter over, and got his advice as to what course it was best for me to pursue. I found Sandy an old adviser. He told me, with great solemnity, I must go back to Covey; but that before I went, I must go with him into another part of the woods, where there was a certain *root*, which, if

3. I.e., his wife had been set free and was not legally a slave.

I would take some of it with me, carrying it *always on my right side*, would render it impossible for Mr. Covey, or any other white man, to whip me. He said he had carried it for years; and since he had done so, he had never received a blow, and never expected to while he carried it. I at first rejected the idea, that the simple carrying of a root in my pocket would have any such effect as he had said, and was not disposed to take it; but Sandy impressed the necessity with much earnestness, telling me it could do no harm, if it did no good. To please him, I at length took the root, and, according to his direction, carried it upon my right side. This was Sunday morning. I immediately started for home; and upon entering the yard gate, out came Mr. Covey on his way to meeting. He spoke to me very kindly, bade me drive the pigs from a lot near by, and passed on towards the church. Now, this singular conduct of Mr. Covey really made me begin to think that there was something in the *root* which Sandy had given me; and had it been on any other day than Sunday, I could have attributed the conduct to no other cause then the influence of that root; and as it was, I was half inclined to think the *root* to be something more than I at first had taken it to be. All went well till Monday morning. On this morning, the virtue of the *root* was fully tested. Long before daylight, I was called to go and rub, curry, and feed, the horses. I obeyed, and was glad to obey. But whilst thus engaged, whilst in the act of throwing down some blades from the loft, Mr. Covey entered the stable with a long rope; and just as I was half out of the loft, he caught hold of my legs, and was about tying me. As soon as I found what he was up to, I gave a sudden spring, and as I did so, he holding to my legs, I was brought sprawling on the stable floor. Mr. Covey seemed now to think he had me, and could do what he pleased; but at this moment—from whence came the spirit I don't know—I resolved to fight; and, suiting my action to the resolution, I seized Covey hard by the throat; and as I did so, I rose. He held on to me, and I to him. My resistance was so entirely unexpected, that Covey seemed taken all aback. He trembled like a leaf. This gave me assurance, and I held him uneasy, causing the blood to run where I touched him with the ends of my fingers. Mr. Covey soon called out to Hughes for help. Hughes came, and, while Covey held me, attempted to tie my right hand. While he was in the act of doing so, I watched my chance, and gave him a heavy kick close under the ribs. This kick fairly sickened Hughes, so that he left me in the hands of Mr. Covey. This kick had the effect of not only weakening Hughes, but Covey also. When he saw Hughes bending over with pain, his courage quailed. He asked me if I meant to persist in my resistance. I told him I did, come what might; that he had used me like a brute for six months, and that I was determined to be used so no longer. With that, he strove to drag me to a stick that was lying just out of the stable door. He meant to knock me down. But just as he was leaning over to get the stick, I seized him with both hands by his collar, and brought him by a sudden snatch to the ground. By this time, Bill came. Covey called upon him for assistance. Bill wanted to know what he could do. Covey said, "Take hold of him, take hold of him!" Bill said his master hired him out to work, and not to help to whip me; so he left Covey and myself to fight our own battle out. We were at it for nearly two hours. Covey at length let me go, puffing and blowing at a great rate, saying that if I had not resisted, he would not have whipped me half so much. The truth was, that he had not whipped me at all. I considered him as getting entirely the worst end of the bargain; for he had drawn no blood from me, but I had from him. The whole six months afterwards, that I spent with Mr. Covey, he never laid the weight of his finger upon me in anger. He would occasionally say, he didn't want to get hold of me again. "No," thought I, "you need not; for you will come off worse than you did before."

This battle with Mr. Covey was the turning-point in my career as a slave. It rekindled the few expiring embers of freedom, and revived within me a sense of my own manhood. It recalled the departed self-confidence, and inspired me again with a determination to be free. The gratification afforded by the triumph was a full compensation for whatever else might follow, even death itself. He only can understand the deep satisfaction which I experienced, who has himself repelled by force the bloody arm of slavery. I felt as I never felt before. It was a glorious resurrection, from the tomb of slavery, to the heaven of freedom. My long-crushed spirit rose, cowardice departed, bold defiance took its place; and I now resolved that, however long I might remain a slave in form, the day had passed forever when I could be a slave in fact. I did not hesitate to let it be known of me, that the white man who expected to succeed in whipping, must also succeed in killing me.

From this time I was never again what might be called fairly whipped, though I remained a slave four years afterwards. I had several fights, but was never whipped.

It was for a long time a matter of surprise to me why Mr. Covey did not immediately have me taken by the constable to the whipping-post, and there regularly whipped for the crime of raising my hand against a white man in defence of myself. And the only explanation I can now think of does not entirely satisfy me; but such as it is, I will give it. Mr. Covey enjoyed the most unbounded reputation for being a first-rate overseer and negro-breaker. It was of considerable importance to him. That reputation was at stake; and had he sent me—a boy about sixteen years old—to the public whipping-post, his reputation would have been lost; so, to save his reputation, he suffered me to go unpunished.

My term of actual service to Mr. Edward Covey ended on Christmas day, 1833. The days between Christmas and New Year's day are allowed as holidays; and, accordingly, we were not required to perform any labor, more than to feed and take care of the stock. This time we regarded as our own, by the grace of our masters; and we therefore used or abused it nearly as we pleased. Those of us who had families at a distance, were generally allowed to spend the whole six days in their society. This time, however, was spent in various ways. The staid, sober, thinking and industrious ones of our number would employ themselves in making corn-brooms, mats, horse-collars, and baskets; and another class of us would spend the time hunting opossums, hares, and coons. But by far the larger part engaged in such sports and merriments as playing ball, wrestling, running foot-races, fiddling, dancing, and drinking whisky; and this latter mode of spending the time was by far the most agreeable to the feelings of our master. A slave who would work during the holidays was considered by our masters as scarcely deserving them. He was regarded as one who rejected the favor of his master. It was deemed a disgrace not to get drunk at Christmas; and he was regarded as lazy indeed, who had not provided himself with the necessary means, during the year, to get whisky enough to last him through Christmas.

From what I know of the effect of these holidays upon the slave, I believe them to be among the most effective means in the hands of the slaveholder in keeping down the spirit of insurrection. Were the slaveholders at once to abandon this practice, I have not the slightest doubt it would lead to an immediate insurrection among the slaves. These holidays serve as conductors, or safety-valves, to carry off the rebellious spirit of enslaved humanity. But for these, the slave would be forced up to the wildest desperation; and woe betide the slaveholder, the day he ventures to remove or hinder the operation of those conductors! I warn him that, in such an event, a spirit will go forth in their midst, more to be dreaded than the most appalling earthquake.

The holidays are part and parcel of the gross fraud, wrong, and inhumanity of slavery. They are professedly a custom established by the benevolence of the slaveholders; but I undertake to say, it is the result of selfishness, and one of the grossest frauds committed upon the down-trodden slave. They do not give the slaves this time because they would not like to have their work during its continuance, but because they know it would be unsafe to deprive them of it. This will be seen by the fact, that the slaveholders like to have their slaves spend those days just in such a manner as to make them as glad of their ending as of their beginning. Their object seems to be, to disgust their slaves with freedom, by plunging them into the lowest depths of dissipation. For instance, the slaveholders not only like to see the slave drink of his own accord, but will adopt various plans to make him drunk. One plan is, to make bets on their slaves, as to who can drink the most whisky without getting drunk; and in this way they succeed in getting whole multitudes to drink to excess. Thus, when the slave asks for virtuous freedom, the cunning slaveholder, knowing his ignorance, cheats him with a dose of vicious dissipation, artfully labelled with the name of liberty. The most of us used to drink it down, and the result was just what might be supposed: many of us were led to think that there was little to choose between liberty and slavery. We felt, and very properly too, that we had almost as well be slaves to man as to rum. So, when the holidays ended, we staggered up from the filth of our wallowing, took a long breath, and marched to the field,—feeling, upon the whole, rather glad to go, from what our master had deceived us into a belief was freedom, back to the arms of slavery.

I have said that this mode of treatment is a part of the whole system of fraud and inhumanity of slavery. It is so. The mode here adopted to disgust the slave with freedom, by allowing him to see only the abuse of it, is carried out in other things. For instance, a slave loves molasses; he steals some. His master, in many cases, goes off to town, and buys a large quantity; he returns, takes his whip, and commands the slave to eat the molasses, until the poor fellow is made sick at the very mention of it. The same mode is sometimes adopted to make the slaves refrain from asking for more food than their regular allowance. A slave runs through his allowance, and applies for more. His master is enraged at him; but, not willing to send him off without food, gives him more than is necessary, and compels him to eat it within a given time. Then, if he complains that he cannot eat it, he is said to be satisfied neither full nor fasting, and is whipped for being hard to please! I have an abundance of such illustrations of the same principle, drawn from my own observation, but think the cases I have cited sufficient. The practice is a very common one.

On the first of January, 1834, I left Mr. Covey, and went to live with Mr. William Freeland, who lived about three miles from St. Michael's. I soon found Mr. Freeland a very different man from Mr. Covey. Though not rich, he was what would be called an educated southern gentleman. Mr. Covey, as I have shown, was a well-trained negro-breaker and slave-driver. The former (slaveholder though he was) seemed to possess some regard for honor, some reverence for justice, and some respect for humanity. The latter seemed totally insensible to all such sentiments. Mr. Freeland had many of the faults peculiar to slaveholders, such as being very passionate and fretful; but I must do him the justice to say, that he was exceedingly free from those degrading vices to which Mr. Covey was constantly addicted. The one was open and frank, and we always knew where to find him. The other was a most artful deceiver, and could be understood only by such as were skilful enough to detect his cunningly-devised frauds. Another advantage I gained in my new master was, he made no pretensions to, or profession of, religion; and this, in my opinion, was truly a great advantage. I assert most unhesitatingly, that the religion of the south is a mere covering for the most horrid crimes,—a justifier of the most appalling barbarity,—a sanctifier of the most hateful frauds,—and a dark shelter under which the darkest, foulest, grossest, and most infernal deeds of slaveholders find the strongest protection. Were I to be again reduced to the chains of slavery, next to that enslavement, I should regard being the slave of a religious master the greatest calamity that could befall me. For of all slaveholders with whom I have ever met, religious slaveholders are the worst. I have ever found them the meanest and basest, the most cruel and cowardly, of all others. It was my unhappy lot not only to belong to a religious slaveholder, but to live in a community of such religionists. Very near Mr. Freeland lived the Rev. Daniel Weeden, and in the same neighborhood lived the Rev. Rigby Hopkins. These were members and ministers in the Reformed Methodist Church. Mr. Weeden owned, among others, a woman slave, whose name I have forgotten. This woman's back, for weeks, was kept literally raw, made so by the lash of this merciless, *religious* wretch. He used to hire hands. His maxim was, Behave well or behave ill, it is the duty of a master occasionally to whip a slave, to remind him of his master's authority. Such was his theory, and such his practice.

Mr. Hopkins was even worse than Mr. Weeden. His chief boast was his ability to manage slaves. The peculiar feature of his government was that of whipping slaves in advance of deserving it. He always managed to have one or more of his slaves to whip every Monday morning. He did this to alarm their fears, and strike terror into those who escaped. His plan was to whip for the smallest offences, to prevent the commission of large ones. Mr. Hopkins could always find some excuse for whipping a slave. It would astonish one, unaccustomed to a slaveholding life, to see with what wonderful ease a slaveholder can find things, of which to make occasion to whip a slave. A mere look, word, or motion,—a mistake, accident, or want of power,—are all matters for which a slave may be whipped at any time. Does a slave look dissatisfied? It is said, he has the devil in him, and it must be whipped out. Does he speak loudly when spoken to by his master? Then he is getting high-minded, and should be taken down a button-hole lower. Does he forget to pull off his hat at the approach of a white person? Then he is wanting in reverence, and should be whipped for it. Does he ever venture to vindicate his conduct, when censured for it? Then he is guilty of impudence,—one of the greatest crimes of which a slave can be guilty. Does he ever venture to suggest a different mode of doing things from that pointed out by his master? He is indeed presumptuous, and getting above himself; and nothing less than a flogging will do for him. Does he, while ploughing, break a plough,—or, while hoeing, break a hoe? It is owing to his carelessness, and for it a slave must always be whipped. Mr. Hopkins could always find something of this sort to justify the use of the lash, and he seldom failed to embrace such opportunities. There was not a man in the whole county, with whom the slaves who had the getting their own home, would not prefer to live, rather than with this Rev. Mr. Hopkins. And yet there was not a man any where round, who made higher professions of religion, or was more active in revivals—more attentive to the class, love-feast, prayer and preaching meetings, or more devotional in his family,—that prayed earlier, later, louder, and longer,—than this same reverend slave-driver, Rigby Hopkins.

But to return to Mr. Freeland, and to my experience while in his employment. He, like Mr. Covey, gave us enough to eat; but unlike Mr. Covey, he also gave us sufficient time to take our meals. He worked us hard, but always between sunrise and sunset. He required a good deal of work to be done, but gave us good tools with which to work. His farm was large, but he employed hands enough to work it, and with ease, compared with many of his neighbors. My treatment, while in his employment, was heavenly, compared with what I experienced at the hands of Mr. Edward Covey.

Mr. Freeland was himself the owner of but two slaves. Their names were Henry Harris and John Harris. The rest of his hands he hired. These consisted of myself, Sandy Jenkins[4] and Handy Caldwell. Henry and John were quite intelligent, and in a very little while after I went there, I succeeded in creating in them a strong desire to learn how to read. This desire soon sprang up in the others also. They very soon mustered up some old spelling-books, and nothing would do but that I must keep a Sabbath school. I agreed to do so, and accordingly devoted my Sundays to teaching these my loved fellow-slaves how to read. Neither of them knew his letters when I went there. Some of the slaves of the neighboring farms found what was going on, and also availed themselves of this little opportunity to learn to read. It was understood, among all who came, that there must be as little display about it as possible. It was necessary to keep our religious masters at St. Michael's unacquainted with the fact, that, instead of spending the Sabbath in wrestling, boxing, and drinking whisky, we were trying to learn how to read the will of God; for they had much rather see us engaged in those degrading sports, than to see us behaving like intellectual, moral, and accountable beings. My blood boils as I think of the bloody manner in which Messrs. Wright Fairbanks and Garrison West, both class-leaders, in connection with many others, rushed in upon us with sticks and stones, and broke up our virtuous little Sabbath school, at St. Michael's—all calling themselves Christians! humble followers of the Lord Jesus Christ! But I am again digressing.

I held my Sabbath school at the house of a free colored man, whose name I deem it imprudent to mention; for should it be known, it might embarrass him greatly, though the crime of holding the school was committed ten years ago. I had at one time over forty scholars, and those of the right sort,

---

4. This is the same man who gave me the roots to prevent my being whipped by Mr. Covey. He was a "clever soul." We used frequently to talk about the fight with Covey, and as often as we did so, he would claim my success as the result of the roots he gave me. This superstition is very common among the more ignorant slaves. A slave seldom dies but that his death is attributed to trickery [Douglass's note].

ardently desiring to learn. They were of all ages, though mostly men and women. I look back to those Sundays with an amount of pleasure not to be expressed. They were great days to my soul. The work of instructing my dear fellow-slaves was the sweetest engagement with which I was ever blessed. We loved each other, and to leave them at the close of the Sabbath was a severe cross indeed. When I think that those precious souls are to-day shut up in the prison-house of slavery, my feelings overcome me, and I am almost ready to ask, "Does a righteous God govern the universe? and for what does he hold the thunders in his right hand, if not to smite the oppressor, and deliver the spoiled out of the hand of the spoiler?" These dear souls came not to Sabbath school because it was popular to do so, nor did I teach them because it was reputable to be thus engaged. Every moment they spent in that school, they were liable to be taken up, and given thirty-nine lashes. They came because they wished to learn. Their minds had been starved by their cruel masters. They had been shut up in mental darkness. I taught them, because it was the delight of my soul to be doing something that looked like bettering the condition of my race. I kept up my school nearly the whole year I lived with Mr. Freeland; and, beside my Sabbath school, I devoted three evenings in the week, during the winter, to teaching the slaves at home. And I have the happiness to know, that several of those who came to Sabbath school learned how to read; and that one, at least, is now free through my agency.

The year passed off smoothly. It seemed only about half as long as the year which preceded it. I went through it without receiving a single blow. I will give Mr. Freeland the credit of being the best master I ever had, *till I became my own master*. For the ease with which I passed the year, I was, however, somewhat indebted to the society of my fellow-slaves. They were noble souls; they not only possessed loving hearts, but brave ones. We were linked and interlinked with each other. I loved them with a love stronger than any thing I have experienced since. It is sometimes said that we slaves do not love and confide in each other. In answer to this assertion, I can say, I never loved any or confided in any people more than my fellow-slaves, and especially those with whom I lived at Mr. Freeland's. I believe we would have died for each other. We never undertook to do any thing, of any importance, without a mutual consultation. We never moved separately. We were one; and as much so by our tempers and dispositions, as by the mutual hardships to which we were necessarily subjected by our condition as slaves.

At the close of the year 1834, Mr. Freeland again hired me of my master, for the year 1835. But, by this time, I began to want to live *upon free land* as well as *with Freeland*; and I was no longer content, therefore, to live with him or any other slaveholder. I began, with the commencement of the year, to prepare myself for a final struggle, which should decide my fate one way or the other. My tendency was upward. I was fast approaching manhood, and year after year had passed, and I was still a slave. These thoughts roused me—I must do something. I therefore resolved that 1835 should not pass without witnessing an attempt, on my part, to secure my liberty. But I was not willing to cherish this determination alone. My fellow-slaves were dear to me. I was anxious to have them participate with me in this, my life-giving determination. I therefore, though with great prudence, commenced early to ascertain their views and feelings in regard to their condition, and to imbue their minds with thoughts of freedom. I bent myself to devising ways and means for our escape, and meanwhile strove, on all fitting occasions, to impress them with the gross fraud and inhumanity of slavery. I went first to Henry, next to John, then to the others. I found, in them all, warm hearts and noble spirits. They were ready to hear, and ready to act when a feasible plan should be proposed. This was what I wanted. I talked to them of our want of manhood, if we submitted to our enslavement without at least one noble effort to be free. We met often, and consulted frequently, and told our hopes and fears, recounted the difficulties, real and imagined, which we should be called on to meet. At times we were almost disposed to give up, and try to content ourselves with our wretched lot; at others, we were firm and unbending in our determination to go. Whenever we suggested any plan, there was shrinking—the odds were fearful. Our path was beset with the greatest obstacles; and if we succeeded in gaining the end of it, our right to be free was yet questionable—we were yet liable to be returned to bondage. We could see no spot, this side of the ocean, where we could be free. We knew nothing about Canada. Our knowledge of the north did not extend farther than New York; and to go there, and be forever harassed with the frightful liability of being returned to slavery—with the certainty of being treated tenfold worse than before—the thought was truly a horrible one, and one which it was not easy to overcome. The case sometimes stood thus: At every gate through which we were to pass, we saw a watchman—at every ferry a guard—on every bridge a sentinel—and in every wood a patrol. We were hemmed in upon every side. Here were the difficulties, real or imagined—the good to be sought, and the evil to be shunned. On the one hand, there stood slavery, a stern reality, glaring frightfully upon us,—its robes already crimsoned with the blood of millions, and even now feasting itself greedily upon our own flesh. On the other hand, away back in the dim distance, under the flickering light of the north star, behind some craggy hill or snow-covered mountain, stood a doubtful freedom—half frozen—beckoning us to come and share its hospitality. This in itself was sometimes enough to stagger us; but when we permitted ourselves to survey the road, we were frequently appalled. Upon either side we saw grim death, assuming the most horrid shapes. Now it was starvation, causing us to eat our own flesh;—now we were contending with the waves, and were drowned;—now we were overtaken, and torn to pieces by the fangs of the terrible bloodhound. We were stung by scorpions, chased by wild beasts, bitten by snakes, and finally, after having nearly reached the desired spot,—after swimming rivers, encountering wild beasts, sleeping in the woods, suffering hunger and nakedness,—we were overtaken by our pursuers, and in our resistance, we were shot dead upon the spot! I say, this picture sometimes appalled us, and made us

> "rather bear those ills we had,
> Than fly to others, that we knew not of."[5]

In coming to a fixed determination to run away, we did more than Patrick Henry, when he resolved upon liberty or death. With us it was a doubtful liberty at most, and almost certain death if we failed. For my part, I should prefer death to hopeless bondage.

Sandy, one of our number, gave up the notion, but still encouraged us. Our company then consisted of Henry Harris, John Harris, Henry Bailey, Charles Roberts, and myself. Henry Bailey was my uncle, and belonged to

5. Shakespeare's *Hamlet* 3.1.81–82.

my master. Charles married my aunt: he belonged to my master's father-in-law, Mr. William Hamilton.

The plan we finally concluded upon was, to get a large canoe belonging to Mr. Hamilton, and upon the Saturday night previous to Easter holidays, paddle directly up the Chesapeake Bay. On our arrival at the head of the bay, a distance of seventy or eighty miles from where we lived, it was our purpose to turn our canoe adrift, and follow the guidance of the north star till we got beyond the limits of Maryland. Our reason for taking the water route was, that we were less liable to be suspected as runaways; we hoped to be regarded as fishermen; whereas, if we should take the land route, we should be subjected to interruptions of almost every kind. Any one having a white face, and being so disposed, could stop us, and subject us to examination.

The week before our intended start, I wrote several protections, one for each of us. As well as I can remember, they were in the following words, to wit:—

> "This is to certify that I, the undersigned, have given the bearer, my servant, full liberty to go to Baltimore, and spend the Easter holidays. Written with mine own hand, etc., 1835.
>
> "WILLIAM HAMILTON,
> "Near St. Michael's, in Talbot county, Maryland."

We were not going to Baltimore; but, in going up the bay, we went toward Baltimore, and these protections were only intended to protect us while on the bay.

As the time drew near for our departure, our anxiety became more and more intense. It was truly a matter of life and death with us. The strength of our determination was about to be fully tested. At this time, I was very active in explaining every difficulty, removing every doubt, dispelling every fear, and inspiring all with the firmness indispensable to success in our undertaking; assuring them that half was gained the instant we made the move; we had talked long enough; we were now ready to move; if not now, we never should be; and if we did not intend to move now, we had as well fold our arms, sit down, and acknowledge ourselves fit only to be slaves. This, none of us were prepared to acknowledge. Every man stood firm; and at our last meeting, we pledged ourselves afresh, in the most solemn manner, that, at the time appointed, we would certainly start in pursuit of freedom. This was in the middle of the week, at the end of which we were to be off. We went, as usual, to our several fields of labor, but with bosoms highly agitated with thoughts of our truly hazardous undertaking. We tried to conceal our feelings as much as possible; and I think we succeeded very well.

After a painful waiting, the Saturday morning, whose night was to witness our departure, came. I hailed it with joy, bring what of sadness it might. Friday night was a sleepless one for me. I probably felt more anxious than the rest, because I was, by common consent, at the head of the whole affair. The responsibility of success or failure lay heavily upon me. The glory of the one, and the confusion of the other, were alike mine. The first two hours of that morning were such as I never experienced before, and hope never to again. Early in the morning, we went, as usual, to the field. We were spreading manure; and all at once, while thus engaged, I was overwhelmed with an indescribable feeling, in the fulness of which I turned to Sandy, who was near by, and said, "We are betrayed!" "Well," said he, "that thought has this moment struck me." We said no more. I was never more certain of any thing.

The horn was blown as usual, and we went up from the field to the house for breakfast. I went for the form, more than for want of any thing to eat that morning. Just as I got to the house, in looking out at the lane gate, I saw four white men, with two colored men. The white men were on horseback, and the colored ones were walking behind, as if tied. I watched them a few moments till they got up to our lane gate. Here they halted, and tied the colored men to the gate-post. I was not yet certain as to what the matter was. In a few moments, in rode Mr. Hamilton, with a speed betokening great excitement. He came to the door, and inquired if Master William was in. He was told he was at the barn. Mr. Hamilton, without dismounting, rode up to the barn with extraordinary speed. In a few moments, he and Mr. Freeland returned to the house. By this time, the three constables rode up, and in great haste dismounted, tied their horses, and met Master William and Mr. Hamilton returning from the barn; and after talking awhile, they all walked up to the kitchen door. There was no one in the kitchen but myself and John. Henry and Sandy were up at the barn. Mr. Freeland put his head in at the door, and called me by name, saying, there were some gentlemen at the door who wished to see me. I stepped to the door, and inquired what they wanted. They at once seized me, and, without giving me any satisfaction, tied me—lashing my hands closely together. I insisted upon knowing what the matter was. They at length said, that they had learned I had been in a "scrape," and that I was to be examined before my master; and if their information proved false, I should not be hurt.

In a few moments, they succeeded in tying John. They then turned to Henry, who had by this time returned, and commanded him to cross his hands. "I won't!" said Henry, in a firm tone, indicating his readiness to meet the consequences of his refusal. "Won't you?" said Tom Graham, the constable. "No, I won't!" said Henry, in a still stronger tone. With this, two of the constables pulled out their shining pistols, and swore, by their Creator, that they would make him cross his hands or kill him. Each cocked his pistol, and, with fingers on the trigger, walked up to Henry, saying, at the same time, if he did not cross his hands, they would blow his damned heart out. "Shoot me, shoot me!" said Henry; "you can't kill me but once. Shoot, shoot,—and be damned! *I won't be tied!*" This he said in a tone of loud defiance; and at the same time, with a motion as quick as lightning, he with one single stroke dashed the pistols from the hand of each constable. As he did this, all hands fell upon him, and, after beating him some time, they finally overpowered him, and got him tied.

During the scuffle, I managed, I know not how, to get my pass out, and, without being discovered, put it into the fire. We were all now tied; and just as we were to leave for Easton jail, Betsy Freeland, mother of William Freeland, came to the door with her hands full of biscuits, and divided them between Henry and John. She then delivered herself of a speech, to the following effect:—addressing herself to me, she said, "*You devil! You yellow devil!* it was you that put it into the heads of Henry and John to run away. But for you, you long-legged mulatto devil! Henry nor John would never have thought of such a thing." I made no reply, and was immediately hurried off towards St. Michael's. Just a moment previous to the scuffle with Henry, Mr. Hamilton suggested the propriety of making a search for the protections which he had understood Frederick had written for himself and the rest. But, just at the moment he was about carrying his proposal into effect, his aid was needed in helping to tie Henry; and the excitement attending the scuffle caused them either to forget, or to deem it unsafe, under the circumstances, to search. So we were not yet convicted of the intention to run away.

When we got about half way to St. Michael's, while the constables having us in charge were looking ahead, Henry inquired of me what he should do with his pass. I told him to eat it with his biscuit, and own nothing; and we passed the word around, *"Own nothing;"* and *"Own nothing!"* said we all. Our confidence in each other was unshaken. We were resolved to succeed or fail together, after the calamity had befallen us as much as before. We were now prepared for any thing. We were to be dragged that morning fifteen miles behind horses, and then to be placed in the Easton jail. When we reached St. Michael's, we underwent a sort of examination. We all denied that we ever intended to run away. We did this more to bring out the evidence against us, than from any hope of getting clear of being sold; for, as I have said, we were ready for that. The fact was, we cared but little where we went, so we went together. Our greatest concern was about separation. We dreaded that more than any thing this side of death. We found the evidence against us to be the testimony of one person; our master would not tell who it was; but we came to a unanimous decision among ourselves as to who their informant was. We were sent off to the jail at Easton. When we got there, we were delivered up to the sheriff, Mr. Joseph Graham, and by him placed in jail. Henry, John, and myself, were placed in one room together—Charles, and Henry Bailey, in another. Their object in separating us was to hinder concert.

We had been in jail scarcely twenty minutes, when a swarm of slave traders, and agents for slave traders, flocked into jail to look at us, and to ascertain if we were for sale. Such a set of beings I never saw before! I felt myself surrounded by so many fiends from perdition. A band of pirates never looked more like their father, the devil. They laughed and grinned over us, saying, "Ah, my boys! we have got you, haven't we?" And after taunting us in various ways, they one by one went into an examination of us, with intent to ascertain our value. They would impudently ask us if we would not like to have them for our masters. We would make them no answer, and leave them to find out as best they could. Then they would curse and swear at us, telling us that they could take the devil out of us in a very little while, if we were only in their hands.

While in jail, we found ourselves in much more comfortable quarters than we expected when we went there. We did not get much to eat, nor that which was very good; but we had a good clean room, from the windows of which we could see what was going on in the street, which was very much better than though we had been placed in one of the dark, damp cells. Upon the whole, we got along very well, so far as the jail and its keeper were concerned. Immediately after the holidays were over, contrary to all our expectations, Mr. Hamilton and Mr. Freeland came up to Easton, and took Charles, the two Henrys, and John, out of jail, and carried them home, leaving me alone. I regarded this separation as a final one. It caused me more pain than any thing else in the whole transaction. I was ready for any thing rather than separation. I supposed that they had consulted together, and had decided that, as I was the whole cause of the intention of the others to run away, it was hard to make the innocent suffer with the guilty; and that they had, therefore, concluded to take the others home, and sell me, as a warning to the others that remained. It is due to the noble Henry to say, he seemed almost as reluctant at leaving the prison as at leaving home to come to the prison. But we knew we should, in all probability, be separated, if we were sold; and since he was in their hands, he concluded to go peaceably home.

I was now left to my fate. I was all alone, and within the walls of a stone prison. But a few days before, and I was full of hope. I expected to have been safe in a land of freedom; but now I was covered with gloom, sunk down to the utmost despair. I thought the possibility of freedom was gone. I was kept in this way about one week, at the end of which, Captain Auld, my master, to my surprise and utter astonishment, came up, and took me out, with the intention of sending me, with a gentleman of his acquaintance, into Alabama. But, from some cause or other, he did not send me to Alabama, but concluded to send me back to Baltimore, to live again with his brother Hugh, and to learn a trade.

Thus, after an absence of three years and one month, I was once more permitted to return to my old home at Baltimore. My master sent me away, because there existed against me a very great prejudice in the community, and he feared I might be killed.

In a few weeks after I went to Baltimore, Master Hugh hired me to Mr. William Gardner, an extensive ship-builder, on Fell's Point. I was put there to learn how to calk.[6] It, however, proved a very unfavorable place for the accomplishment of this object. Mr. Gardner was engaged that spring in building two large man-of-war brigs, professedly for the Mexican government. The vessels were to be launched in the July of that year, and in failure thereof, Mr. Gardner was to lose a considerable sum; so that when I entered, all was hurry. There was no time to learn any thing. Every man had to do that which he knew how to do. In entering the ship-yard, my orders from Mr. Gardner were, to do whatever the carpenters commanded me to do. This was placing me at the beck and call of about seventy-five men. I was to regard all these as masters. Their word was to be my law. My situation was a most trying one. At times I needed a dozen pair of hands. I was called a dozen ways in the space of a single minute. Three or four voices would strike my ear at the same moment. It was—"Fred., come help me to cant this timber here."—"Fred., come carry this timber yonder."—"Fred., bring that roller here."—"Fred., go get a fresh can of water."—"Fred., come help saw off the end of this timber."—"Fred., go quick, and get the crowbar."—"Fred., hold on the end of this fall."[7]—"Fred., go to the blacksmith's shop, and get a new punch."—"Hurra, Fred.! run and bring me a cold chisel."—"I say, Fred., bear a hand, and get up a fire as quick as lightning under that steam-box."—"Halloo, nigger! come, turn this grindstone."—"Come, come! move, move! and *bowse*[8] this timber forward."—"I say, darky, blast your eyes, why don't you heat up some pitch?"— "Halloo! halloo! halloo!" (Three voices at the same time.) "Come here!—Go there!—Hold on where you are! Damn you, if you move, I'll knock your brains out!"

This was my school for eight months; and I might have remained there longer, but for a most horrid fight I had with four of the white apprentices, in which my left eye was nearly knocked out, and I was horribly mangled in other respects. The facts in the case were these: Until a very little while after

6. Caulk; to seal a boat's cracks and joints against leakage.
7. Nautical term for the free end of a rope of a tackle or hoisting device.
8. To haul the timber by pulling on the rope.

I went there, white and black ship-carpenters worked side by side, and no one seemed to see any impropriety in it. All hands seemed to be very well satisfied. Many of the black carpenters were freemen. Things seemed to be going on very well. All at once, the white carpenters knocked off, and said they would not work with free colored workmen. Their reason for this, as alleged, was, that if free colored carpenters were encouraged, they would soon take the trade into their own hands, and poor white men would be thrown out of employment. They therefore felt called upon at once to put a stop to it. And, taking advantage of Mr. Gardner's necessities, they broke off, swearing they would work no longer, unless he would discharge his black carpenters. Now, though this did not extend to me in form, it did reach me in fact. My fellow-apprentices very soon began to feel it degrading to them to work with me. They began to put on airs, and talk about the "niggers" taking the country, saying we all ought to be killed; and, being encouraged by the journeymen, they commenced making my condition as hard as they could, by hectoring me around, and sometimes striking me. I, of course, kept the vow I made after the fight with Mr. Covey, and struck back again, regardless of consequences; and while I kept them from combining, I succeeded very well; for I could whip the whole of them, taking them separately. They, however, at length combined, and came upon me, armed with sticks, stones, and heavy handspikes. One came in front with a half brick. There was one at each side of me, and one behind me. While I was attending to those in front, and on either side, the one behind ran up with the handspike, and struck me a heavy blow upon the head. It stunned me. I fell, and with this they all ran upon me, and fell to beating me with their fists. I let them lay on for a while, gathering strength. In an instant, I gave a sudden surge, and rose to my hands and knees. Just as I did that, one of their number gave me, with his heavy boot, a powerful kick in the left eye. My eyeball seemed to have burst. When they saw my eye closed, and badly swollen, they left me. With this I seized the handspike, and for a time pursued them. But here the carpenters interfered, and I thought I might as well give it up. It was impossible to stand my hand against so many. All this took place in sight of not less than fifty white ship-carpenters, and not one interposed a friendly word; but some cried, "Kill the damned nigger! Kill him! kill him! He struck a white person." I found my only chance for life was in flight. I succeeded in getting away without an additional blow, and barely so; for to strike a white man is death by Lynch law,[9]—and that was the law in Mr. Gardner's ship-yard; nor is there much of any other out of Mr. Gardner's ship-yard.

I went directly home, and told the story of my wrongs to Master Hugh; and I am happy to say of him, irreligious as he was, his conduct was heavenly, compared with that of his brother Thomas under similar circumstances. He listened attentively to my narration of the circumstances leading to the savage outrage, and gave many proofs of his strong indignation at it. The heart of my once overkind mistress was again melted into pity. My puffed-out eye and blood-covered face moved her to tears. She took a chair by me, washed the blood from my face, and, with a mother's tenderness, bound up my head, covering the wounded eye with a lean piece of fresh beef. It was almost compensation for my suffering to witness, once more, a manifestation of kindness from this, my once affectionate old mistress. Master Hugh was very much

9. To be subject to lynching, without benefit of legal procedures.

enraged. He gave expression to his feelings by pouring out curses upon the heads of those who did the deed. As soon as I got a little the better of my bruises, he took me with him to Esquire Watson's, on Bond Street, to see what could be done about the matter. Mr. Watson inquired who saw the assault committed. Master Hugh told him it was done in Mr. Gardner's ship-yard, at midday, where there were a large company of men at work. "As to that," he said, "the deed was done, and there was no question as to who did it." His answer was, he could do nothing in the case, unless some white man would come forward and testify. He could issue no warrant on my word. If I had been killed in the presence of a thousand colored people, their testimony combined would have been insufficient to have arrested one of the murder-ers. Master Hugh, for once, was compelled to say this state of things was too bad. Of course, it was impossible to get any white man to volunteer his testi-mony in my behalf, and against the white young men. Even those who may have sympathized with me were not prepared to do this. It required a degree of courage unknown to them to do so; for just at that time, the slightest mani-festation of humanity toward a colored person was denounced as abolition-ism, and that name subjected its bearer to frightful liabilities. The watchwords of the bloody-minded in that region, and in those days, were, "Damn the abolitionists!" and "Damn the niggers!" There was nothing done, and proba-bly nothing would have been done if I had been killed. Such was, and such remains, the state of things in the Christian city of Baltimore.

Master Hugh, finding he could get no redress, refused to let me go back again to Mr. Gardner. He kept me himself, and his wife dressed my wound till I was again restored to health. He then took me into the ship-yard of which he was foreman, in the employment of Mr. Walter Price. There I was immediately set to calking, and very soon learned the art of using my mallet and irons. In the course of one year from the time I left Mr. Gardner's, I was able to command the highest wages given to the most experienced calkers. I was now of some importance to my master. I was bringing him from six to seven dollars per week. I sometimes brought him nine dollars per week: my wages were a dollar and a half a day. After learning how to calk, I sought my own employment, made my own contracts, and collected the money which I earned. My pathway became much more smooth than before; my condition was now much more comfortable. When I could get no calking to do, I did nothing. During these leisure times, those old notions about freedom would steal over me again. When in Mr. Gardner's employment, I was kept in such a perpetual whirl of excitement, I could think of nothing, scarcely, but my life; and in thinking of my life, I almost forgot my liberty. I have observed this in my experience of slavery,—that whenever my condition was improved, instead of its increasing my contentment, it only increased my desire to be free, and set me to thinking of plans to gain my freedom. I have found that, to make a contented slave, it is necessary to make a thoughtless one. It is necessary to darken his moral and mental vision, and, as far as possible, to annihilate the power of reason. He must be able to detect no inconsistencies in slavery; he must be made to feel that slavery is right; and he can be brought to that only when he ceases to be a man.

I was now getting, as I have said, one dollar and fifty cents per day. I con-tracted for it; I earned it; it was paid to me; it was rightfully my own; yet, upon each returning Saturday night, I was compelled to deliver every cent of that money to Master Hugh. And why? Not because he earned it,—not because he had any hand in earning it,—not because I owed it to him,—nor because he possessed the slightest shadow of a right to it; but solely because he had the power to compel me to give it up. The right of the grim-visaged pirate upon the high seas is exactly the same.

Chapter XI

I now come to that part of my life during which I planned, and finally succeeded in making, my escape from slavery. But before narrating any of the peculiar circumstances, I deem it proper to make known my intention not to state all the facts connected with the transaction.[1] My reasons for pursuing this course may be understood from the following: First, were I to give a minute statement of all the facts, it is not only possible but quite probable, that others would thereby be involved in the most embarrassing difficulties. Secondly, such a statement would most undoubtedly induce greater vigilance on the part of slaveholders than has existed heretofore among them; which would, of course, be the means of guarding a door whereby some dear brother bondman might escape his galling chains. I deeply regret the necessity that impels me to suppress any thing of importance connected with my experience in slavery. It would afford me great pleasure indeed, as well as materially add to the interest of my narrative, were I at liberty to gratify a curiosity, which I know exists in the minds of many, by an accurate statement of all the facts pertaining to my most fortunate escape. But I must deprive myself of this pleasure, and the curious of the gratification which such a statement would afford. I would allow myself to suffer under the greatest imputations which evil-minded men might suggest, rather than exculpate myself, and thereby run the hazard of closing the slightest avenue by which a brother slave might clear himself of the chains and fetters of slavery.

I have never approved of the very public manner in which some of our western friends have conducted what they call the *underground railroad*,[2] but which, I think, by their own declarations, has been made most emphatically the *upperground railroad*. I honor those good men and women for their noble daring, and applaud them for willingly subjecting themselves to bloody persecution, by openly avowing their participation in the escape of slaves. I, however, can see very little good resulting from such a course, either to themselves or the slaves escaping; while, upon the other hand, I see and feel assured that those open declarations are a positive evil to the slaves remaining, who are seeking to escape. They do nothing towards enlightening the slave, whilst they do much towards enlightening the master. They stimulate him to greater watchfulness, and enhance his power to capture his slave. We owe something to the slaves south of the line as well as to those north of it; and in aiding the latter on their way to freedom, we should be careful to do nothing which would be likely to hinder the former from escaping from slavery. I would keep the merciless slaveholder profoundly ignorant of the means of flight adopted by the slave. I would leave him to imagine himself surrounded by myriads of

---

1. During this period, many free black men worked as sailors. One of these men loaned Douglass free papers and clothes, enabling Douglass to escape from slavery by train and boat. He described his escape in the third and last of his autobiographies, *Life and Times of Frederick Douglass* (1881; rev. ed. 1892).
2. The network of routes, guides, and safe houses by which many slaves escaped to the North, moving by night from one known stopping place to the next, often the homes of abolitionists.

invisible tormentors, ever ready to snatch from his infernal grasp his trembling prey. Let him be left to feel his way in the dark; let darkness commensurate with his crime hover over him; and let him feel that at every step he takes, in pursuit of the flying bondman, he is running the frightful risk of having his hot brains dashed out by an invisible agency. Let us render the tyrant no aid; let us not hold the light by which he can trace the footprints of our flying brother. But enough of this. I will now proceed to the statement of those facts, connected with my escape, for which I am alone responsible, and for which no one can be made to suffer but myself.

In the early part of the year 1838, I became quite restless. I could see no reason why I should, at the end of each week, pour the reward of my toil into the purse of my master. When I carried to him my weekly wages, he would, after counting the money, look me in the face with a robber-like fierceness, and say, "Is this all?" He was satisfied with nothing less than the last cent. He would, however, when I made him six dollars, sometimes give me six cents, to encourage me. It had the opposite effect. I regarded it as a sort of admission of my right to the whole. The fact that he gave me any part of my wages was proof, to my mind, that he believed me entitled to the whole of them. I always felt worse for having received any thing; for I feared that the giving me a few cents would ease his conscience, and make him feel himself to be a pretty honorable sort of robber. My discontent grew upon me. I was ever on the look-out for means of escape; and, finding no direct means, I determined to try to hire my time, with a view of getting money with which to make my escape. In the spring of 1838, when Master Thomas came to Baltimore to purchase his spring goods, I got an opportunity, and applied to him to allow me to hire my time. He unhesitatingly refused my request, and told me this was another stratagem by which to escape. He told me I could go nowhere but that he could get me; and that, in the event of my running away, he should spare no pains in his efforts to catch me. He exhorted me to content myself, and be obedient. He told me, if I would be happy, I must lay out no plans for the future. He said, if I behaved myself properly, he would take care of me. Indeed, he advised me to complete thoughtlessness of the future, and taught me to depend solely upon him for happiness. He seemed to see fully the pressing necessity of setting aside my intellectual nature, in order to [insure] contentment in slavery. But in spite of him, and even in spite of myself, I continued to think, and to think about the injustice of my enslavement, and the means of escape.

About two months after this, I applied to Master Hugh for the privilege of hiring my time. He was not acquainted with the fact that I had applied to Master Thomas, and had been refused. He too, at first, seemed disposed to refuse; but, after some reflection, he granted me the privilege, and proposed the following terms: I was to be allowed all my time, make all contracts with those for whom I worked, and find my own employment; and, in return for this liberty, I was to pay him three dollars at the end of each week; find myself in calking tools, and in board and clothing. My board was two dollars and a half per week. This, with the wear and tear of clothing and calking tools, made my regular expenses about six dollars per week. This amount I was compelled to make up, or relinquish the privilege of hiring my time. Rain or shine, work or no work, at the end of each week the money must be forthcoming, or I must give up my privilege. This arrangement, it will be perceived, was decidedly in my master's favor. It relieved him of all need of looking after me. His money was sure. He received all the benefits of slave-holding without its evils; while I endured all the evils of a slave, and suffered all the care and anxiety of a freeman. I found it a hard bargain. But, hard as it was, I thought it better than the old mode of getting along. It was a step towards freedom to be allowed to bear the responsibilities of a freeman, and I was determined to hold on upon it. I bent myself to the work of making money. I was ready to work at night as well as day, and by the most untiring perseverance and industry, I made enough to meet my expenses, and lay up a little money every week. I went on thus from May till August. Master Hugh then refused to allow me to hire my time longer. The ground for his refusal was a failure on my part, one Saturday night, to pay him for my week's time. This failure was occasioned by my attending a camp meeting about ten miles from Baltimore. During the week, I had entered into an engagement with a number of young friends to start from Baltimore to the camp ground early Saturday evening; and being detained by my employer, I was unable to get down to Master Hugh's without disappointing the company. I knew that Master Hugh was in no special need of the money that night. I therefore decided to go to camp meeting, and upon my return pay him the three dollars. I staid at the camp meeting one day longer than I intended when I left. But as soon as I returned, I called upon him to pay him what he considered his due. I found him very angry; he could scarce restrain his wrath. He said he had a great mind to give me a severe whipping. He wished to know how I dared go out of the city without asking his permission. I told him I hired my time, and while I paid him the price which he asked for it, I did not know that I was bound to ask him when and where I should go. This reply troubled him; and, after reflecting a few moments, he turned to me, and said I should hire my time no longer; that the next thing he should know of, I would be running away. Upon the same plea, he told me to bring my tools and clothing home forthwith. I did so; but instead of seeking work, as I had been accustomed to do previously to hiring my time, I spent the whole week without the performance of a single stroke of work. I did this in retaliation. Saturday night, he called upon me as usual for my week's wages. I told him I had no wages; I had done no work that week. Here we were upon the point of coming to blows. He raved, and swore his determination to get hold of me. I did not allow myself a single word; but was resolved, if he laid the weight of his hand upon me, it should be blow for blow. He did not strike me, but told me that he would find me in constant employment in future. I thought the matter over during the next day, Sunday, and finally resolved upon the third day of September, as the day upon which I would make a second attempt to secure my freedom. I now had three weeks during which to prepare for my journey. Early on Monday morning, before Master Hugh had time to make any engagement for me, I went out and got employment of Mr. Butler, at his ship-yard near the drawbridge, upon what is called the City Block, thus making it unnecessary for him to seek employment for me. At the end of the week, I brought him between eight and nine dollars. He seemed very well pleased, and asked me why I did not do the same the week before. He little knew what my plans were. My object in working steadily was to remove any suspicion he might entertain of my intent to run away; and in this I succeeded admirably. I suppose he thought I was never better satisfied with my condition than at the very time during which I was planning my escape. The second week passed, and again I carried him my full wages; and so well pleased was he, that he gave me twenty-five cents, (quite a large sum for a slaveholder to give a slave), and bade me to make a good use of it. I told him I would.

Things went on without very smoothly indeed, but within there was trouble. It is impossible for me to describe my feelings as the time of my contemplated start drew near. I had a number of warm-hearted friends in Baltimore,—friends that I loved almost as I did my life,—and the thought of being separated from them forever was painful beyond expression. It is my opinion that thousands would escape from slavery, who now remain, but for the strong cords of affection that bind them to their friends. The thought of leaving my friends was decidedly the most painful thought with which I had to contend. The love of them was my tender point, and shook my decision more than all things else. Besides the pain of separation, the dread and apprehension of a failure exceeded what I had experienced at my first attempt. The appalling defeat I then sustained returned to torment me. I felt assured that, if I failed in this attempt, my case would be a hopeless one—it would seal my fate as a slave forever. I could not hope to get off with any thing less than the severest punishment, and being placed beyond the means of escape. It required no very vivid imagination to depict the most frightful scenes through which I should have to pass, in case I failed. The wretchedness of slavery, and the blessedness of freedom, were perpetually before me. It was life and death with me. But I remained firm, and, according to my resolution, on the third day of September, 1838, I left my chains, and succeeded in reaching New York without the slightest interruption of any kind. How I did so,—what means I adopted,—what direction I travelled, and by what mode of conveyance,—I must leave unexplained, for the reasons before mentioned.

I have been frequently asked how I felt when I found myself in a free State. I have never been able to answer the question with any satisfaction to myself. It was a moment of the highest excitement I ever experienced. I suppose I felt as one may imagine the unarmed mariner to feel when he is rescued by a friendly man-of-war from the pursuit of a pirate. In writing to a dear friend, immediately after my arrival at New York, I said I felt like one who had escaped a den of hungry lions. This state of mind, however, very soon subsided; and I was again seized with a feeling of great insecurity and loneliness. I was yet liable to be taken back, and subjected to all the tortures of slavery. This in itself was enough to damp the ardor of my enthusiasm. But the loneliness overcame me. There I was in the midst of thousands, and yet a perfect stranger; without home and without friends, in the midst of thousands of my own brethren—children of a common Father, and yet I dared not to unfold to any one of them my sad condition. I was afraid to speak to any one for fear of speaking to the wrong one, and thereby falling into the hands of money-loving kidnappers, whose business it was to lie in wait for the panting fugitive, as the ferocious beasts of the forest lie in wait for their prey. The motto which I adopted when I started from slavery was this—"Trust no man!" I saw in every white man an enemy, and in almost every colored man cause for distrust. It was a most painful situation; and, to understand it, one must needs experience it, or imagine himself in similar circumstances. Let him be a fugitive slave in a strange land—a land given up to be the hunting-ground for slaveholders—whose inhabitants are legalized kidnappers—where he is every moment subjected to the terrible liability of being seized upon by his fellowmen, as the hideous crocodile seizes upon his prey!—I say, let him place himself in my situation—without home or friends—without money or credit—wanting shelter, and no one to give it—wanting bread, and no money to buy it,—and at the same time let him feel that he is pursued by merciless men-hunters, and in total darkness as to what to do, where to go, or where to stay,—perfectly helpless both as to the means of defence and means of escape,—in the midst of plenty, yet suffering the terrible gnawings of hunger,—in the midst of houses, yet having no home,—among fellow-men, yet feeling as if in the midst of wild beasts, whose greediness to swallow up the trembling and half-famished fugitive is only equalled by that with which the monsters of the deep swallow up the helpless fish upon which they subsist,—I say, let him be placed in this most trying situation,—the situation in which I was placed,—then, and not till then, will he fully appreciate the hardships of, and know how to sympathize with, the toil-worn and whip-scarred fugitive slave.

Thank Heaven, I remained but a short time in this distressed situation. I was relieved from it by the humane hand of MR. DAVID RUGGLES,[3] whose vigilance, kindness, and perseverance, I shall never forget. I am glad of an opportunity to express, as far as words can, the love and gratitude I bear him. Mr. Ruggles is now afflicted with blindness, and is himself in need of the same kind offices which he was once so forward in the performance of toward others. I had been in New York but a few days, when Mr. Ruggles sought me out, and very kindly took me to his boarding-house at the corner of Church and Lespenard Streets. Mr. Ruggles was then very deeply engaged in the memorable *Darg* case,[4] as well as attending to a number of other fugitive slaves; devising ways and means for their successful escape; and, though watched and hemmed in on almost every side, he seemed to be more than a match for his enemies.

Very soon after I went to Mr. Ruggles, he wished to know of me where I wanted to go; as he deemed it unsafe for me to remain in New York. I told him I was a calker, and should like to go where I could get work. I thought of going to Canada; but he decided against it, and in favor of my going to New Bedford, thinking I should be able to get work there at my trade. At this time, Anna,[5] my intended wife, came on; for I wrote to her immediately after my arrival at New York, (notwithstanding my homeless, houseless, and helpless condition,) informing her of my successful flight, and wishing her to come on forthwith. In a few days after her arrival, Mr. Ruggles called in the Rev. J.W.C. Pennington,[6] who, in the presence of Mr. Ruggles, Mrs. Michaels, and two or three others, performed the marriage ceremony, and gave us a certificate, of which the following is an exact copy:—

"This may certify, that I joined together in holy matrimony Frederick Johnson[7] and Anna Murray, as man and wife, in the presence of Mr. David Ruggles and Mrs. Michaels.

"JAMES W. C. PENNINGTON

"*New York, Sept. 15, 1838.*"

3. A black journalist and abolitionist (1810–1849) who aided Douglass in his escape from Maryland, and in whose house Douglass stayed on his way to New Bedford in 1838.
4. In 1839, Ruggles had been arrested for harboring a fugitive slave from the plantation of John P. Darg of Arkansas.
5. She was free [Douglass's note]. Anna Murray Douglass (1813–1882) worked as a domestic in Baltimore and had been a member of the East Baltimore Mental Improvement Society before moving to New York to marry Douglass.
6. Like Douglass, Pennington (1807–1890) escaped from slavery in the eastern shore of Maryland. He became an abolitionist and Presbyterian minister, telling his life history in *The Fugitive Blacksmith* (1850).
7. I had changed my name from Frederick *Bailey* to that of *Johnson* [Douglass's note].

Upon receiving this certificate, and a five-dollar bill from Mr. Ruggles, I shouldered one part of our baggage, and Anna took up the other, and we set out forthwith to take passage on board of the steamboat John W. Richmond for Newport, on our way to New Bedford. Mr. Ruggles gave me a letter to a Mr. Shaw in Newport, and told me, in case my money did not serve me to New Bedford, to stop in Newport and obtain further assistance; but upon our arrival at Newport, we were so anxious to get to a place of safety, that, notwithstanding we lacked the necessary money to pay our fare, we decided to take seats in the stage, and promise to pay when we got to New Bedford. We were encouraged to do this by two excellent gentlemen, residents of New Bedford, whose names I afterward ascertained to be Joseph Ricketson and William C. Taber. They seemed at once to understand our circumstances, and gave us such assurance of their friendliness as put us fully at ease in their presence. It was good indeed to meet with such friends, at such a time. Upon reaching New Bedford, we were directed to the house of Mr. Nathan Johnson, by whom we were kindly received, and hospitably provided for. Both Mr. and Mrs. Johnson took a deep and lively interest in our welfare. They proved themselves quite worthy of the name of abolitionists. When the stage-driver found us unable to pay our fare, he held on upon our baggage as security for the debt. I had but to mention the fact to Mr. Johnson, and he forthwith advanced the money.

We now began to feel a degree of safety, and to prepare ourselves for the duties and responsibilities of a life of freedom. On the morning after our arrival at New Bedford, while at the breakfast-table, the question arose as to what name I should be called by. The name given me by my mother was, "Frederick Augustus Washington Bailey." I, however, had dispensed with the two middle names long before I left Maryland so that I was generally known by the name of "Frederick Bailey." I started from Baltimore bearing the name of "Stanley." When I got to New York, I again changed my name to "Frederick Johnson," and thought that would be the last change. But when I got to New Bedford, I found it necessary again to change my name. The reason of this necessity was, that there were so many Johnsons in New Bedford, it was already quite difficult to distinguish between them. I gave Mr. Johnson the privilege of choosing me a name, but told him he must not take from me the name of "Frederick." I must hold on to that, to preserve a sense of my identity. Mr. Johnson had just been reading the "Lady of the Lake," and at once suggested that my name be "Douglass."[8] From that time until now I have been called "Frederick Douglass;" and as I am more widely known by that name than by either of the others, I shall continue to use it as my own.

I was quite disappointed at the general appearance of things in New Bedford. The impression which I had received respecting the character and condition of the people of the north, I found to be singularly erroneous. I had very strangely supposed, while in slavery, that few of the comforts, and scarcely any of the luxuries, of life were enjoyed at the north, compared with what were enjoyed by the slaveholders of the south. I probably came to this conclusion from the fact that northern people owned no slaves. I supposed that they were about upon a level with the non-slaveholding population of the south. I knew *they* were exceedingly poor, and I had been accustomed to

---

8. Sir Walter Scott's (1771–1832) poem *Lady of the Lake* (1810), a historical romance set in the Scottish highlands in the 16th century. The plot involves the banishment and redemption of the Scottish hero James of Douglas.

regard their poverty as the necessary consequence of their being non-slaveholders. I had somehow imbibed the opinion that, in the absence of slaves, there could be no wealth, and very little refinement. And upon coming to the north, I expected to meet with a rough, hard-handed, and uncultivated population, living in the most Spartanlike simplicity, knowing nothing of the ease, luxury, pomp, and grandeur of southern slaveholders. Such being my conjectures, any one acquainted with the appearance of New Bedford may very readily infer how palpably I must have seen my mistake.

In the afternoon of the day when I reached New Bedford, I visited the wharves, to take a view of the shipping. Here I found myself surrounded with the strongest proofs of wealth. Lying at the wharves, and riding in the stream, I saw many ships of the finest model, in the best order, and of the largest size. Upon the right and left, I was walled in by granite warehouses of the widest dimensions, stowed to their utmost capacity with the necessaries and comforts of life. Added to this, almost every body seemed to be at work, but noiselessly so, compared with what I had been accustomed to in Baltimore. There were no loud songs heard from those engaged in loading and unloading ships. I heard no deep oaths or horrid curses on the laborer. I saw no whipping of men; but all seemed to go smoothly on. Every man appeared to understand his work, and went at it with a sober, yet cheerful earnestness, which betokened the deep interest which he felt in what he was doing, as well as a sense of his own dignity as a man. To me this looked exceedingly strange. From the wharves I strolled around and over the town, gazing with wonder and admiration at the splendid churches, beautiful dwellings, and finely-cultivated gardens; evincing an amount of wealth, comfort, taste, and refinement, such as I had never seen in any part of slaveholding Maryland.

Every thing looked clean, new, and beautiful. I saw few or no dilapidated houses, with poverty-stricken inmates; no half-naked children and bare-footed women, such as I had been accustomed to see in Hillsborough, Easton, St. Michael's, and Baltimore. The people looked more able, stronger, healthier, and happier, than those of Maryland. I was for once made glad by a view of extreme wealth, without being saddened by seeing extreme poverty. But the most astonishing as well as the most interesting thing to me was the condition of the colored people, a great many of whom, like myself, had escaped thither as a refuge from the hunters of men. I found many, who had not been seven years out of their chains, living in finer houses, and evidently enjoying more of the comforts of life, than the average of slaveholders in Maryland. I will venture to assert that my friend Mr. Nathan Johnson (of whom I can say with a grateful heart, "I was hungry, and he gave me meat; I was thirsty, and he gave me drink; I was a stranger, and he took me in"[9]) lived in a neater house, dined at a better table; took, paid for, and read, more newspapers; better understood the moral, religious, and political character of the nation,—than nine tenths of the slaveholders in Talbot county Maryland. Yet Mr. Johnson was a working man. His hands were hardened by toil, and not his alone, but those also of Mrs. Johnson. I found the colored people much more spirited than I had supposed they would be. I found among them a determination to protect each other from the blood-thirsty kidnapper, at all hazards. Soon after my arrival, I was told of a circumstance which illustrated their spirit. A colored man and a fugitive slave were on unfriendly

9. Cf. Matthew 25.35.

terms. The former was heard to threaten the latter with informing his master of his whereabouts. Straightway a meeting was called among the colored people, under the stereotyped notice, "Business of importance!" The betrayer was invited to attend. The people came at the appointed hour, and organized the meeting by appointing a very religious old gentleman as president, who, I believe, made a prayer, after which he addressed the meeting as follows: *"Friends, we have got him here, and I would recommend that you young men just take him outside the door, and kill him!"* With this, a number of them bolted at him; but they were intercepted by some more timid than themselves, and the betrayer escaped their vengeance, and has not been seen in New Bedford since. I believe there have been no more such threats, and should there be hereafter, I doubt not that death would be the consequence.

I found employment, the third day after my arrival, in stowing a sloop with a load of oil. It was new, dirty, and hard work for me; but I went at it with a glad heart and a willing hand. I was now my own master. It was a happy moment, the rapture of which can be understood only by those who have been slaves. It was the first work, the reward of which was to be entirely my own. There was no Master Hugh standing ready, the moment I earned the money, to rob me of it. I worked that day with a pleasure I had never before experienced. I was at work for myself and newly-married wife. It was to me the starting-point of a new existence. When I got through with that job, I went in pursuit of a job of calking; but such was the strength of prejudice against color, among the white calkers, that they refused to work with me, and of course I could get no employment.[1] Finding my trade of no immediate benefit, I threw off my calking habiliments, and prepared myself to do any kind of work I could get to do. Mr. Johnson kindly let me have his wood-horse and saw, and I very soon found myself a plenty of work. There was no work too hard—none too dirty. I was ready to saw wood, shovel coal, carry the hod, sweep the chimney, or roll oil casks,—all of which I did for nearly three years in New Bedford, before I became known to the anti-slavery world.

In about four months after I went to New Bedford, there came a young man to me, and inquired if I did not wish to take the "Liberator."[2] I told him I did; but, just having made my escape from slavery, I remarked that I was unable to pay for it then. I, however, finally became a subscriber to it. The paper came, and I read it from week to week with such feelings as it would be quite idle for me to attempt to describe. The paper became my meat and my drink. My soul was set all on fire. Its sympathy for my brethren in bonds—its scathing denunciations of slaveholders—its faithful exposures of slavery—and its powerful attacks upon the upholders of the institution— sent a thrill of joy through my soul, such as I had never felt before!

I had not long been a reader of the "Liberator," before I got a pretty correct idea of the principles, measures and spirit of the anti-slavery reform. I took right hold of the cause. I could do but little; but what I could, I did with a joyful heart, and never felt happier than when in an anti-slavery meeting. I seldom had much to say at the meetings, because what I wanted to say was said so much better by others. But, while attending an anti-slavery convention at

---

1. I am told that colored persons can now get employment at calking in New Bedford—a result of anti-slavery effort [Douglass's note].
2. The first issue of Garrison's the *Liberator* appeared in January 1831. It became the most widely read abolitionist paper during its thirty-five years of publication.

Nantucket, on the 11th of August, 1841, I felt strongly moved to speak, and was at the same time much urged to do so by Mr. William C. Coffin, a gentleman who had heard me speak in the colored people's meeting at New Bedford.[3] It was a severe cross, and I took it up reluctantly. The truth was, I felt myself a slave, and the idea of speaking to white people weighed me down. I spoke but a few moments, when I felt a degree of freedom, and said what I desired with considerable ease. From that time until now, I have been engaged in pleading the cause of my brethren—with what success, and with what devotion, I leave those acquainted with my labors to decide.

Appendix

I find, since reading over the foregoing Narrative, that I have, in several instances, spoken in such a tone and manner, respecting religion, as may possibly lead those unacquainted with my religious views to suppose me an opponent of all religion. To remove the liability of such misapprehension, I deem it proper to append the following brief explanation. What I have said respecting and against religion, I mean strictly to apply to the *slaveholding religion* of this land, and with no possible reference to Christianity proper; for, between the Christianity of this land, and the Christianity of Christ, I recognize the widest possible difference—so wide, that to receive the one as good, pure, and holy, is of necessity to reject the other as bad, corrupt, and wicked. To be the friend of the one, is of necessity to be the enemy of the other. I love the pure, peaceable, and impartial Christianity of Christ: I therefore hate the corrupt, slaveholding, women-whipping, cradle-plundering, partial and hypocritical Christianity of this land. Indeed, I can see no reason, but the most deceitful one, for calling the religion of this land Christianity. I look upon it as the climax of all misnomers, the boldest of all frauds, and the grossest of all libels. Never was there a clearer case of "stealing the livery of the court of heaven to serve the devil in."[4] I am filled with unutterable loathing when I contemplate the religious pomp and show, together with the horrible inconsistencies, which every where surround me. We have men-stealers for ministers, women-whippers for missionaries, and cradle-plunderers for church members. The man who wields the blood-clotted cowskin during the week fills the pulpit on Sunday, and claims to be a minister of the meek and lowly Jesus. The man who robs me of my earnings at the end of each week meets me as a class-leader on Sunday morning, to show me the way of life, and the path of salvation. He who sells my sister, for purposes of prostitution, stands forth as the pious advocate of purity. He who proclaims it a religious duty to read the Bible denies me the right of learning to read the name of the God who made me. He who is the religious advocate of marriage robs whole millions of its sacred influence, and leaves them to the ravages of wholesale pollution. The warm defender of the sacredness of the family relation is the same that scatters whole families,—sundering husbands and wives, parents and children, sisters and brothers,—leaving the hut vacant, and the hearth desolate. We see the thief preaching against theft, and the adulterer against adultery. We have men sold to build churches, women sold to support the

---

3. Douglass had become a licensed preacher in the African Methodist Episcopal Zion Church in 1839.

4. From *The Course of Time* (1827), book 8, 616–18, a popular poem by the Scotsman Robert Pollok (1798–1827).

gospel, and babes sold to purchase Bibles for the *poor heathen! all for the glory of God and the good of souls!* The slave auctioneer's bell and the church-going bell chime in with each other, and the bitter cries of the heart-broken slave are drowned in the religious shouts of his pious master. Revivals of religion and revivals in the slave-trade go hand in hand together. The slave prison and the church stand near each other. The clanking of fetters and the rattling of chains in the prison, and the pious psalm and solemn prayer in the church, may be heard at the same time. The dealers in the bodies and souls of men erect their stand in the presence of the pulpit, and they mutually help each other. The dealer gives his blood-stained gold to support the pulpit, and the pulpit, in return, covers his infernal business with the garb of Christianity. Here we have religion and robbery the allies of each other—devils dressed in angels' robes, and hell presenting the semblance of paradise.

> "Just God! and these are they,
>   Who minister at thine altar, God of right!
> Men who their hands, with prayer and blessing, lay
>   On Israel's ark of light.[5]

> "What! preach, and kidnap men?
>   Give thanks, and rob thy own afflicted poor?
> Talk of thy glorious liberty, and then
>   Bolt hard the captive's door?

> "What! servants of thy own
>   Merciful Son, who came to seek and save
> The homeless and the outcast, fettering down
>   The tasked and plundered slave!

> "Pilate and Herod[6] friends!
>   Chief priests and rulers, as of old, combine!
> Just God and holy! is that church which lends
>   Strength to the spoiler thine?"[7]

The Christianity of America is a Christianity, of whose votaries it may be as truly said, as it was of the ancient scribes and Pharisees,[8] "They bind heavy burdens, and grievous to be borne, and lay them on men's shoulders, but they themselves will not move them with one of their fingers. All their works they do for to be seen of men.——They love the uppermost rooms at feasts, and the chief seats in the synagogues, ... and to be called of men, Rabbi, Rabbi.——But woe unto you, scribes and Pharisees, hypocrites! for ye shut up the kingdom of heaven against men; for ye neither go in yourselves, neither suffer ye them that are entering to go in. Ye devour widows' houses, and for a pretence make long prayers; therefore ye shall receive the greater damnation. Ye compass sea and land to make one proselyte, and when he is made, ye make him twofold more the child of hell than yourselves.——Woe unto you, scribes and Pharisees, hypocrites! for ye pay tithe of mint, and anise, and

---

5. The Holy Ark containing the Torah; by extension, the entire body of law as contained in the Old Testament and Talmud.
6. Herod Antipas, ruler of Galilee, ordered the execution of John the Baptist and participated in the trial of Christ. Pontius Pilate was the Roman authority who condemned Christ to death.
7. From Whittier's antislavery poem "Clerical

Oppressors" (1835).
8. Members of a Jewish group that insisted on strict observance of written and oral religious laws. The scribes were the Jewish scholars who taught Jewish law and edited and interpreted the Bible. Christ's denunciation of the scribes and Pharisees is reported in Matthew 23.

cumin, and have omitted the weightier matters of the law, judgment, mercy, and faith; these ought ye to have done, and not to leave the other undone. Ye blind guides! which strain at a gnat, and swallow a camel. Woe unto you, scribes and Pharisees, hypocrites! for ye make clean the outside of the cup and of the platter; but within, they are full of extortion and excess.——Woe unto you, scribes and Pharisees, hypocrites! for ye are like unto whited sepulchres, which indeed appear beautiful outward, but are within full of dead men's bones, and of all uncleanness. Even so ye also outwardly appear righteous unto men, but within ye are full of hypocrisy and iniquity."[9]

Dark and terrible as is this picture, I hold it to be strictly true of the overwhelming mass of professed Christians in America. They strain at a gnat, and swallow a camel. Could any thing be more true of our churches? They would be shocked at the proposition of fellowshipping a *sheep*-stealer; and at the same time they hug to their communion a *man*-stealer, and brand me with being an infidel, if I find fault with them for it. They attend with Pharisaical strictness to the outward forms of religion, and at the same time neglect the weightier matters of the law, judgment, mercy, and faith. They are always ready to sacrifice, but seldom to show mercy. They are they who are represented as professing to love God whom they have not seen, whilst they hate their brother whom they have seen. They love the heathen on the other side of the globe. They can pray for him, pay money to have the Bible put into his hand, and missionaries to instruct him; while they despise and totally neglect the heathen at their own doors.

Such is, very briefly, my view of the religion of this land; and to avoid any misunderstanding, growing out of the use of general terms, I mean, by the religion of this land, that which is revealed in the words, deeds, and actions, of those bodies, north and south, calling themselves Christian churches, and yet in union with slaveholders. It is against religion, as presented by these bodies, that I have felt it my duty to testify.

I conclude these remarks by copying the following portrait of the religion of the south, (which is, by communion and fellowship, the religion of the north,) which I soberly affirm is "true to the life," and without caricature or the slightest exaggeration. It is said to have been drawn, several years before the present anti-slavery agitation began, by a northern Methodist preacher, who, while residing at the south, had an opportunity to see slaveholding morals, manners, and piety, with his own eyes. "Shall I not visit for these things? saith the Lord. Shall not my soul be avenged on such a nation as this?"[1]

A PARODY[2]

"Come, saints and sinners, hear me tell
How pious priests whip Jack and Nell,
And women buy and children sell,
And preach all sinners down to hell,
    And sing of heavenly union.

"They'll bleat and baa, dona like goats,
Gorge down black sheep, and strain at motes,

9. Cf. Matthew 23.4–28.
1. Jeremiah's voicing of God's condemnation of the kingdom of Judah (Jeremiah 5.9).
2. Douglass is parodying "Heavenly Union," a hymn sung in Southern churches at the time.

Array their backs in fine black coats,
Then seize their negroes by their throats,
   And choke, for heavenly union.

"They'll church you if you sip a dram,
And damn you if you steal a lamb;
Yet rob old Tony, Doll, and Sam,
Of human rights, and bread and ham;
   Kidnapper's heavenly union.

"They'll loudly talk of Christ's reward,
And bind his image with a cord,
And scold, and swing the lash abhorred,
And sell their brother in the Lord
   To handcuffed heavenly union.

"They'll read and sing a sacred song,
And make a prayer both loud and long,
And teach the right and do the wrong,
Hailing the brother, sister throng,
   With words of heavenly union.

"We wonder how such saints can sing,
Or praise the Lord upon the wing,
Who roar, and scold, and whip, and sting,
And to their slaves and mammon cling,
   In guilty conscience union.

"They'll raise tobacco, corn, and rye,
And drive, and thieve, and cheat, and lie,
And lay up treasures in the sky,
By making switch and cowskin fly,
   In hope of heavenly union.

"They'll crack old Tony on the skull,
And preach and roar like Bashan[3] bull,
Or braying ass, of mischief full,
Then seize old Jacob by the wool,
   And pull for heavenly union.

"A roaring, ranting, sleek man-thief,
Who lived on mutton, veal, and beef,
Yet never would afford relief
To needy, sable sons of grief,
   Was big with heavenly union.

"'Love not the world,' the preacher said,
And winked his eye, and shook his head;
He seized on Tom, and Dick, and Ned,
Cut short their meat, and clothes, and bread,
   Yet still loved heavenly union.

"Another preacher whining spoke
Of One whose heart for sinners broke:

---

3. Strong bulls mentioned in the Old Testament.

> He tied old Nanny to an oak,
> And drew the blood at every stroke,
>   And prayed for heavenly union.
>
> "Two others oped their iron jaws,
> And waved their children-stealing paws;
> There sat their children in gewgaws;
> By stinting negroes' backs and maws,
>   They kept up heavenly union.
>
> "All good from Jack another takes,
> And entertains their flirts and rakes,
> Who dress as sleek as glossy snakes,
> And cram their mouths with sweetened cakes;
>   And this goes down for union."

Sincerely and earnestly hoping that this little book may do something toward throwing light on the American slave system, and hastening the glad day of deliverance to the millions of my brethren in bonds—faithfully relying upon the power of truth, love, and justice, for success in my humble efforts—and solemnly pledging my self anew to the sacred cause,—I subscribe myself,

FREDERICK DOUGLASS

LYNN, Mass., April 28, 1845.

1845

What to the Slave Is the Fourth of July?

Extract from an Oration, at Rochester, July 5, 1852[1]

Fellow Citizens—Pardon me, and allow me to ask, why am I called upon to speak here to-day? What have I, or those I represent, to do with your national independence? Are the great principles of political freedom and of natural justice, embodied in that Declaration of Independence, extended to us? and am I, therefore, called upon to bring our humble offering to the national altar, and to confess the benefits, and express devout gratitude for the blessings, resulting from your independence to us?

Would to God, both for your sakes and ours, that an affirmative answer could be truthfully returned to these questions! Then would my task be light, and my burden easy and delightful. For who is there so cold that a nation's sympathy could not warm him? Who so obdurate and dead to the claims of gratitude, that would not thankfully acknowledge such priceless benefits? Who so stolid and selfish, that would not give his voice to swell the hallelujahs of a nation's jubilee, when the chains of servitude had been torn from his limbs? I am not that man. In a case like that, the dumb might eloquently speak, and the "lame man leap as an hart."[2]

But, such is not the state of the case. I say it with a sad sense of the disparity between us. I am not included within the pale of this glorious anniversary!

---

1. Douglass delivered this Fourth of July address on July 5, 1852, in Rochester, New York, before a racially mixed audience of approximately six hundred people. Later that year he published it as a pamphlet. He first published the "Extract" (several key pages from the longer work) in the appendix to *My Bondage and My Freedom* (1855), the source of the present text.
2. Deer. The quotation is from Isaiah 35.6.

Your high independence only reveals the immeasurable distance between us. The blessings in which you this day rejoice, are not enjoyed in common. The rich inheritance of justice, liberty, prosperity, and independence, bequeathed by your fathers, is shared by you, not by me. The sunlight that brought life and healing to you, has brought stripes and death to me. This Fourth of July is *yours*, not *mine*. You may rejoice, *I* must mourn. To drag a man in fetters into the grand illuminated temple of liberty, and call upon him to join you in joyous anthems, were inhuman mockery and sacrilegious irony. Do you mean, citizens, to mock me, by asking me to speak to-day? If so, there is a parallel to your conduct. And let me warn you that it is dangerous to copy the example of a nation whose crimes, towering up to heaven, were thrown down by the breath of the Almighty, burying that nation in irrecoverable ruin! I can to-day take up the plaintive lament of a peeled and woe-smitten people.

"By the rivers of Babylon, there we sat down. Yea! we wept when we remembered Zion. We hanged our harps upon the willows in the midst thereof. For there, they that carried us away captive, required of us a song; and they who wasted us required of us mirth, saying, Sing us one of the songs of Zion. How can we sing the Lord's song in a strange land? If I forget thee, O Jerusalem, let my right hand forget her cunning. If I do not remember thee, let my tongue cleave to the roof of my mouth."[3]

Fellow-citizens, above your national, tumultuous joy, I hear the mournful wail of millions, whose chains, heavy and grievous yesterday, are to-day rendered more intolerable by the jubilant shouts that reach them. If I do forget, if I do not faithfully remember those bleeding children of sorrow this day, "may my right hand forget her cunning, and may my tongue cleave to the roof of my mouth!" To forget them, to pass lightly over their wrongs, and to chime in with the popular theme, would be treason most scandalous and shocking, and would make me a reproach before God and the world. My subject, then, fellow-citizens, is AMERICAN SLAVERY. I shall see this day and its popular characteristics from the slave's point of view. Standing there, identified with the American bondman, making his wrongs mine, I do not hesitate to declare, with all my soul, that the character and conduct of this nation never looked blacker to me than on this Fourth of July. Whether we turn to the declarations of the past, or to the professions of the present, the conduct of the nation seems equally hideous and revolting. America is false to the past, false to the present, and solemnly binds herself to be false to the future. Standing with God and the crushed and bleeding slave on this occasion, I will, in the name of humanity which is outraged, in the name of liberty which is fettered, in the name of the constitution and the bible, which are disregarded and trampled upon, dare to call in question and to denounce, with all the emphasis I can command, everything that serves to perpetuate slavery—the great sin and shame of America! "I will not equivocate; I will not excuse;"[4] I will use the severest language I can command; and yet not one word shall escape me that any man, whose judgment is not blinded by prejudice, or who is not at heart a slaveholder, shall not confess to be right and just.

But I fancy I hear some one of my audience say, it is just in this circumstance that you and your brother abolitionists fail to make a favorable impression on the public mind. Would you argue more, and denounce less, would you persuade more and rebuke less, your cause would be much more

---

3. Psalms 137.1–6.
4. From "To the Public," an editorial by William

Lloyd Garrison in the inaugural issue of his anti-slavery newspaper *The Liberator* (January 1, 1831).

likely to succeed. But, I submit, where all is plain there is nothing to be argued. What point in the anti-slavery creed would you have me argue? On what branch of the subject do the people of this country need light? Must I undertake to prove that the slave is a man? That point is conceded already. Nobody doubts it. The slaveholders themselves acknowledge it in the enactment of laws for their government. They acknowledge it when they punish disobedience on the part of the slave. There are seventy-two crimes in the state of Virginia, which, if committed by a black man, (no matter how ignorant he be,) subject him to the punishment of death; while only two of these same crimes will subject a white man to the like punishment. What is this but the acknowledgment that the slave is a moral, intellectual, and responsible being. The manhood of the slave is conceded. It is admitted in the fact that southern statute books are covered with enactments forbidding, under severe fines and penalties, the teaching of the slave to read or write. When you can point to any such laws, in reference to the beasts of the field, then I may consent to argue the manhood of the slave. When the dogs in your streets, when the fowls of the air, when the cattle on your hills, when the fish of the sea, and the reptiles that crawl, shall be unable to distinguish the slave from a brute, then will I argue with you that the slave is a man!

For the present, it is enough to affirm the equal manhood of the negro race. Is it not astonishing that, while we are plowing, planting, and reaping, using all kinds of mechanical tools, erecting houses, constructing bridges, building ships, working in metals of brass, iron, copper, silver, and gold; that, while we are reading, writing, and cyphering, acting as clerks, merchants, and secretaries, having among us lawyers, doctors, ministers, poets, authors, editors, orators, and teachers; that, while we are engaged in all manner of enterprises common to other men—digging gold in California, capturing the whale in the Pacific, feeding sheep and cattle on the hillside, living, moving, acting, thinking, planning, living in families as husbands, wives, and children, and, above all, confessing and worshiping the christian's God, and looking hopefully for life and immortality beyond the grave,—we are called upon to prove that we are men![5]

Would you have me argue that man is entitled to liberty? that he is the rightful owner of his own body? You have already declared it. Must I argue the wrongfulness of slavery? Is that a question for republicans? Is it to be settled by the rules of logic and argumentation, as a matter beset with great difficulty, involving a doubtful application of the principle of justice, hard to be understood? How should I look to-day in the presence of Americans, dividing and subdividing a discourse, to show that men have a natural right to freedom, speaking of it relatively and positively, negatively and affirmatively? To do so, would be to make myself ridiculous, and to offer an insult to your understanding. There is not a man beneath the canopy of heaven that does not know that slavery is wrong *for him*.

What! am I to argue that it is wrong to make men brutes, to rob them of their liberty, to work them without wages, to keep them ignorant of their relations to their fellow men, to beat them with sticks, to flay their flesh with the lash, to load their limbs with irons, to hunt them with dogs, to sell them at auction, to sunder their families, to knock out their teeth, to burn their flesh, to starve them into obedience and submission to their masters? Must I argue that a system, thus marked with blood and stained with pollution, is

---

5. As suggested by his reference to women and children, Douglass here uses "men" to mean "human."

wrong? No; I will not. I have better employment for my time and strength than such arguments would imply.

What, then, remains to be argued? Is it that slavery is not divine; that God did not establish it; that our doctors of divinity are mistaken? There is blasphemy in the thought. That which is inhuman cannot be divine. Who can reason on such a proposition! They that can, may; I cannot. The time for such argument is past.

At a time like this, scorching irony, not convincing argument, is needed. Oh! had I the ability, and could I reach the nation's ear, I would to-day pour out a fiery stream of biting ridicule, blasting reproach, withering sarcasm, and stern rebuke. For it is not light that is needed, but fire; it is not the gentle shower, but thunder. We need the storm, the whirlwind, and the earthquake. The feeling of the nation must be quickened; the conscience of the nation must be roused; the propriety of the nation must be startled; the hypocrisy of the nation must be exposed; and its crimes against God and man must be proclaimed and denounced.

What to the American slave is your Fourth of July? I answer, a day that reveals to him, more than all other days in the year, the gross injustice and cruelty to which he is the constant victim. To him, your celebration is a sham; your boasted liberty, an unholy license; your national greatness, swelling vanity; your sounds of rejoicing are empty and heartless; your denunciations of tyrants, brass-fronted impudence; your shouts of liberty and equality, hollow mockery; your prayers and hymns, your sermons and thanksgivings, with all your religious parade and solemnity, are to him mere bombast, fraud, deception, impiety, and hypocrisy—a thin veil to cover up crimes which would disgrace a nation of savages. There is not a nation on the earth guilty of practices more shocking and bloody, than are the people of these United States, at this very hour.

Go where you may, search where you will, roam through all the monarchies and despotisms of the old world, travel through South America, search out every abuse, and when you have found the last, lay your facts by the side of the every-day practices of this nation, and you will say with me, that, for revolting barbarity and shameless hypocrisy, America reigns without a rival.

1852, 1855

WALT WHITMAN
1819–1892

Walt Whitman revolutionized American poetry. Responding to Emerson's call in "The Poet" (1842) for an American bard who would address all "the facts of the animal economy, sex, nutriment, gestation, birth," Whitman put the living, breathing, sexual body at the center of much of his poetry, challenging conventions of the day. Responding to Emerson's call for a "metre-making argument," he rejected traditions of poetic scansion and elevated diction, improvising the form that has come to be known as free verse, while adopting a wide-ranging vocabulary opening new possibilities for poetic expression. A poet of democracy, Whitman celebrated the mystical, divine potential of the individual; a poet of the urban, he wrote about the sights, sounds, and energy of the modern metropolis. In his 1855 preface to *Leaves of Grass*, he declared that "the proof of a poet is that his country absorbs him as affectionately as he has absorbed it." On the evidence of his enormous influence on later poets—Hart Crane, Langston Hughes, Robert Lowell, Allen Ginsberg, Adrienne Rich, Cherrie Moraga, and countless others, including Spain's Federico Garcia Lorca and Chile's Pablo Neruda—Whitman not only was affectionately absorbed by his own country but remains a persistent presence in poetry throughout the world.

Whitman was born on May 31, 1819, in West Hills, Long Island (New York), the second of eight surviving children of the Quakers Louisa Van Velsor and Walter Whitman. In 1823, Whitman's father, a farmer turned carpenter, sought to take advantage of a building boom by moving the family to Brooklyn—then a town at the western and most urbanized part of Long Island. Whitman left school when he was eleven, and was soon employed in the printing office of a newspaper; when his family moved east on Long Island in 1833, he remained in Brooklyn on his own. In his midteens he contributed pieces to one of the best Manhattan papers, the *Mirror*, and often crossed the East River on the ferry from Brooklyn to Manhattan to attend debating societies and the theater. He was hired as a compositor in Manhattan in 1835, but two major fires later that year disrupted the printing industry, and he rejoined his family. For five years Whitman taught at country and small-town schools at East Norwich, Long Swamp, and other towns on Long Island, interrupting his teaching to start a newspaper of his own in 1838 and to work briefly on another Long Island paper. By early 1840 he had started the series "Sun-Down Papers from the Desk of a School-Master" for the Jamaica, New York, *Democrat* and was writing poems and fiction. One of his stories prophetically culminated with the dream of writing "a wonderful and ponderous book."

Just before he turned twenty-one Whitman stopped teaching, went back to Manhattan, began work at the literary weekly *New World*, and soon became editor of a Manhattan daily, the *Aurora*. He also began a political career by speaking at Democratic rallies and writing for the *Democratic Review*, the foremost magazine of the Democratic Party. He exulted in the extremes of the city, where street-gang violence was countered by the lectures of Emerson and where even a young editor could get to know the poet William Cullen Bryant, editor of the *Evening Post*. Fired from the *Aurora*, which publicly charged him with laziness, he wrote a temperance novel, *Franklin Evans, or the Inebriate*, for a one-issue extra of the *New World* late in 1842. After three years of various literary and political jobs, he returned to Brooklyn in 1845, becoming a special contributor to the *Long Island Star*, assigned to Manhattan events, including theatrical and musical performances. All through the 1840s he attended operas on his journalist's passes and he would later say that without the "emotions, raptures, uplifts" of opera he could never have written *Leaves of Grass*. Just before he was twenty-seven he took over the editorship of the *Brooklyn Eagle*, writing most of the literary reviews, which included books by Carlyle, Emerson, Melville, Fuller, and Goethe, among others. Like most Democrats, he was able to justify the Mexican War (1846–48) by hailing the great American mission of "peopling the New World with a noble race." Yet at the beginning of 1848 he was fired from the *Eagle* because, like Bryant, he had become a Free-Soiler, opposed to the acquisition of more territory for slavery. Whitman served as a delegate to the Buffalo Free-Soil convention and helped to found the Free-Soil newspaper the *Brooklyn Freeman*. Around this time he began writing poetry in a serious way, experimenting with form and prosody; he published several topical poems in 1850, including "Europe," which would later appear in *Leaves of Grass*.

Whitman's notebook fragments suggest that he began to invent the overall shape of his first volume of poetry during the period 1853–54. On May 15, 1855, he took out a copyright for *Leaves of Grass*, and he spent the spring and early summer seeing his book through the press, probably setting some of the type himself. Published in Brooklyn, New York, during the first week of July, the volume, bound

Leaves of Grass. Frontispiece and title page of the first edition (1855).

in dark green cloth with a sprig of grass in gilt on the cover, contained twelve untitled poems (including the initial version of "Song of Myself") along with an exuberant preface declaring his ambition to be the American bard. In the image of Whitman on the book's frontispiece, which was based on an 1854 daguerreotype, the bearded Whitman—rejecting the conventional suit jacket, buttoned-up shirt, and high collar of the formal studio portrait—stands with one arm akimbo, one hand in a pocket, workingman's hat on slightly cocked head, shirt unbuttoned at the collar, looking directly at the reader. (See the reproduction above.) The image, like the poetry itself, defied convention by aligning the poet with working people. The poems, with their absence of standard verse and stanza patterns (although strongly rhythmic and controlled by numerous poetic devices of repetition and variation), also introduced his use of "catalogs"—journalistic and encyclopedic listings—that were to become a hallmark of his style. Whitman sent out numerous presentation and review copies of his book, receiving an immediate response from Emerson, who greeted him "at the beginning of a great career," but otherwise attracting little notice. As weeks passed, Whitman chose to publish a few anonymous reviews himself, praising *Leaves of Grass* in the *American Phrenological Journal*, for instance, as one of "the most glorious triumphs, in the known history of literature." In October he let Horace Greeley's *New York Tribune* print Emerson's private letter of praise, and he put clippings of the letter in presentation copies to Longfellow, among others. Emerson termed Whitman's appropriation of the letter "a strange, rude thing," but he remained interested in meeting the poet. While Whitman was angling for reviews in England and working on expanding his book, Emerson visited him in December of 1855. Thoreau, who admired *Leaves of Grass* but found several of its poems "simply sensual," visited him later in 1856. That year also saw the appearance of the second edition of *Leaves of Grass*, now with thirty-three poems, including "Crossing Brooklyn Ferry" under its initial title "Sundown Poem."

Returning to miscellaneous journalism, Whitman edited the *Brooklyn Times* from 1857 to 1859 and published several pieces in the *Times* affirming his Free-Soiler hopes for a continued national expansion into the western territories that would not entail the expansion of slavery. In the third (1860) edition of *Leaves of Grass*, Whitman began to group his poems thematically. For a section called "Enfans d' Adam," later retitled "Children of Adam," he wrote fifteen poems focused on what he termed the "amative" love of man for woman, in contrast to the "adhesive" love of man for man. Adhesive love figured in forty-five poems in a section titled "Calamus." These two sections in the 1860 edition differ from the sections in the final 1891–92 edition, for in the intervening editions (1867, 1871, 1881) Whitman revised and regrouped some of the poems, as he would with numerous other poems in the expanded editions he would go on to publish.

With the outbreak of the Civil War, Whitman began to visit the wounded and eventually offered his services as a nurse. He started at New-York Hospital, but in early 1863, after visiting with his wounded brother George in an army camp in Virginia, he moved to Washington, D.C., and began to work at the huge open-air military hospitals there. Nursing gave Whitman a profound sense of vocation. As he wrote a friend in 1863: "I am very happy . . . I was never so beloved. I am running over with health, fat, red & sunburnt in face. I tell thee I am just the one to go to our sick boys." But ministering to tens of thousands of maimed and dying young men took its toll. He succinctly voiced his anguish in a notebook entry of 1864: "the dead, the dead, the dead, our dead." During this time he worked on a series of poems that conveyed his evolving view of the war from heroic celebration to despair at the horrifying carnage. He later wrote a chapter in his prose work *Specimen Days* (1882) titled "The Real War Will Never Get in the Books," but to incorporate the "real war" into a book of poetry became one of the dominant impulses of the *Drum-Taps* collection, which he published in 1865. After Lincoln's assassination, Whitman reissued the volume with a sequel including "O Captain! My Captain!" and "When Lilacs Last in the Dooryard Bloom'd," his famous elegy for the murdered president.

As he prepared *Drum-Taps and Sequel* for publication in late 1865, Whitman was also revising *Leaves of Grass* at his desk in the Department of the Interior, where he had obtained a position as clerk. The new secretary of the interior, James Harlan, read the annotated copy and fired Whitman for writing an obscene book, objecting to Whitman's frankness about bodily functions and heterosexual love. Whitman's friend, the poet William O'Connor, found him another clerical position in the attorney general's office; and in his rage at the firing, O'Connor wrote *The Good Gray Poet* (1866), identifying Whitman with Jesus and Harlan with the forces of evil. Whitman continued to rework *Leaves of Grass*, incorporating *Drum-Taps* into it in 1867, and with his friends' help continued to propagandize for its recognition as a landmark in the history of poetry. He also published essays in 1867 and 1868 numbers of the New York periodical *Galaxy*, which he expanded into *Democratic Vistas* (1870), a book conveying his sometimes sharply condemnatory appraisal of postwar democratic culture.

The Washington years came to an abrupt end in 1873 when Whitman suffered a paralytic stroke. His mother died a few months later, and Whitman joined his brother George's household in Camden, New Jersey, to recuperate. During the second year of his illness, the government ceased to hold his clerk job open for him, and he became dependent for a living on occasional publication in newspapers and magazines. The 1867 edition of *Leaves of Grass* had involved much reworking and rearrangement, and the fifth edition (1871) continued that process, adding a new section titled "Passage to India." In 1876 Whitman privately published a prose work, *Memoranda during the War*, and six years later he brought out *Specimen Days*, which has affinities with his early editorial accounts of strolls through the city but is even more intensely personal, the record of representative days in the life of a poet who had lived in the midst of great national events.

During the 1870s and early 1880s, Whitman was increasingly noticed by the leading writers of the time, especially in England. The English poet Algernon Swinburne sent him a poem, the poet laureate Alfred Lord Tennyson sent him an admiring letter, and both Longfellow and Oscar Wilde visited him in Camden. Despite his frail health, Whitman lectured on Thomas Paine in Philadelphia in 1877 and on Abraham Lincoln in New York in 1879 (he would continue to deliver occasional public lectures on Lincoln until 1890). Opposition to his poetry because of its supposed immorality began to dissipate, and readers, having become accustomed over time to Whitman's poetic devices, began to recognize the poet as an artist. Still, in 1881, when the reputable Boston firm of James R. Osgood & Co. printed the sixth edition of *Leaves of Grass*, the Boston district attorney threatened to prosecute on the grounds of obscenity. Ironically, when the Philadelphia firm of Rees Welsh and Company reprinted this edition in 1882, the publicity contributed to Whitman's greatest sales in his lifetime: he earned nearly $1,500 in royalties from that edition (around $25,000 in today's value), compared to the $25 he had earned from the Osgood edition before the publisher withdrew it.

In 1884, the still infirm Whitman moved to a cottage at 328 Mickle Street in Camden, which he purchased for $1,750. A year later friends and admirers, including Mark Twain and John Greenleaf Whittier, presented him with a horse and buggy for local travel. He had another stroke in 1888 and in 1890 made preparations for his death by signing a $4,000 contract for the construction in Camden's Harleigh Cemetery of a granite mausoleum, or what he termed a "burial house," suitable for a national bard. In 1891 he did the final editing of *Complete Prose Works* (1892) and oversaw the preparations of the "deathbed" edition of the now more than three hundred poems in *Leaves of Grass* (1891–92), which was in fact a reissue of the 1881 edition with the addition of two later groups of poems, "Sands at Seventy" and "Good-bye My Fancy." Whitman died in Camden on March 26, 1892, and was buried in Harleigh Cemetery in the mausoleum he had helped design.

Except for the sequence "Live Oak, with Moss" (not published in Whitman's lifetime), all the Whitman poems reprinted here, regardless of when they were first composed and printed, are given in their final form: that of the 1891–92 edition of *Leaves of Grass*.

Preface to *Leaves of Grass* (1855)[1]

America does not repel the past or what it has produced under its forms or amid other politics or the idea of castes or the old religions . . . accepts the lesson with calmness . . . is not so impatient as has been supposed that the slough still sticks to opinions and manners and literature while the life which served its requirements has passed into the new life of the new forms . . . perceives that the corpse is slowly borne from the eating and sleeping rooms of the house . . . perceives that it waits a little while in the door . . . that it was fittest for its days . . . that its action has descended to the stalwart and wellshaped heir who approaches . . . and that he shall be fittest for his days.

The Americans of all nations at any time upon the earth have probably the fullest poetical nature. The United States themselves are essentially the greatest poem. In the history of the earth hitherto the largest and most stirring appear tame and orderly to their ampler largeness and stir. Here at last

---

1. The first edition of *Leaves of Grass* contained twelve untitled poems, which were introduced by this manifesto-like preface. The preface was not reprinted in subsequent editions, though some of its ideas were incorporated into future poems. The spellings and ellipses are Whitman's.

is something in the doings of man that corresponds with the broadcast doings of the day and night. Here is not merely a nation but a teeming nation of nations. Here is action untied from strings necessarily blind to particulars and details magnificently moving in vast masses. Here is the hospitality which forever indicates heroes. . . . Here are the roughs and beards and space and ruggedness and nonchalance that the soul loves. Here the performance disdaining the trivial unapproached in the tremendous audacity of its crowds and groupings and the push of its perspective spreads with crampless and flowing breadth and showers its prolific and splendid extravagance. One sees it must indeed own the riches of the summer and winter, and need never be bankrupt while corn grows from the ground or the orchards drop apples or the bays contain fish or men beget children upon women.

Other states indicate themselves in their deputies . . . . but the genius of the United States is not best or most in its executives or legislatures, nor in its ambassadors or authors or colleges or churches or parlors, nor even in its newspapers or inventors . . . but always most in the common people. Their manners speech dress friendships—the freshness and candor of their physiognomy—the picturesque looseness of their carriage . . . their deathless attachment to freedom—their aversion to anything indecorous or soft or mean—the practical acknowledgment of the citizens of one state by the citizens of all other states—the fierceness of their roused resentment—their curiosity and welcome of novelty—their self-esteem and wonderful sympathy—their susceptibility to a slight—the air they have of persons who never knew how it felt to stand in the presence of superiors—the fluency of their speech—their delight in music, the sure symptom of manly tenderness and native elegance of soul . . . their good temper and openhandedness—the terrible significance of their elections—the President's taking off his hat to them not they to him—these too are unrhymed poetry. It awaits the gigantic and generous treatment worthy of it.

The largeness of nature or the nation were monstrous without a corresponding largeness and generosity of the spirit of the citizen. Not nature nor swarming states nor streets and steamships nor prosperous business nor farms nor capital nor learning may suffice for the ideal of man . . . nor suffice the poet. No reminiscences may suffice either. A live nation can always cut a deep mark and can have the best authority the cheapest . . . namely from its own soul. This is the sum of the profitable uses of individuals or states and of present action and grandeur and of the subjects of poets.—As if it were necessary to trot back generation after generation to the eastern records! As if the beauty and sacredness of the demonstrable must fall behind that of the mythical! As if men do not make their mark out of any times! As if the opening of the western continent by discovery and what has transpired since in North and South America were less than the small theatre of the antique or the aimless sleepwalking of the middle ages! The pride of the United States leaves the wealth and finesse of the cities and all returns of commerce and agriculture and all the magnitude of geography or shows of exterior victory to enjoy the breed of fullsized men or one fullsized man unconquerable and simple.

The American poets are to enclose old and new for America is the race of races. Of them a bard[2] is to be commensurate with a people. To him the other

2. The ideal national poet, usually linked to older heroic or epic traditions.

continents arrive as contributions . . . he gives them reception for their sake and his own sake. His spirit responds to his country's spirit . . . . he incarnates its geography and natural life and rivers and lakes. Mississippi with annual freshets and changing chutes, Missouri and Columbia and Ohio and Saint Lawrence with the falls and beautiful masculine Hudson, do not embouchure[3] where they spend themselves more than they embouchure into him. The blue breadth over the inland sea of Virginia and Maryland and the sea off Massachusetts and Maine and over Manhattan bay and over Champlain and Erie and over Ontario and Huron and Michigan and Superior, and over the Texan and Mexican and Floridian and Cuban seas and over the seas off California and Oregon, is not tallied by the blue breadth of the waters below more than the breadth of above and below is tallied by him. When the long Atlantic coast stretches longer and the Pacific coast stretches longer he easily stretches with them north or south. He spans between them also from east to west and reflects what is between them. On him rise solid growths that offset the growths of pine and cedar and hemlock and liveoak and locust and chestnut and cypress and hickory and limetree and cottonwood and tuliptree and cactus and wildvine and tamarind and persimmon . . . . and tangles as tangled as any canebrake or swamp . . . . and forests coated with transparent ice and icicles hanging from the boughs and crackling in the wind . . . . and sides and peaks of mountains . . . . and pasturage sweet and free as savannah or upland or prairie . . . . with flights and songs and screams that answer those of the wild pigeon and highhold and orchard-oriole and coot and surf-duck and redshouldered-hawk and fish-hawk and white-ibis and indian-hen and cat-owl and water-pheasant and qua-bird and piedsheldrake and blackbird and mockingbird and buzzard and condor and nightheron and eagle. To him the hereditary countenance descends both mother's and father's. To him enter the essences of the real things and past and present events—of the enormous diversity of temperature and agriculture and mines—the tribes of red aborigines—the weatherbeaten vessels entering new ports or making landings on rocky coasts—the first settlements north or south—the rapid stature and muscle—the haughty defiance of '76, and the war and peace and formation of the constitution . . . . the union always surrounded by blatherers and always calm and impregnable—the perpetual coming of immigrants—the wharf hem'd cities and superior marine—the unsurveyed interior—the loghouses and clearings and wild animals and hunters and trappers . . . . the free commerce—the fisheries and whaling and gold-digging—the endless gestation of new states—the convening of Congress every December, the members duly coming up from all climates and the uttermost parts . . . . the noble character of the young mechanics and of all free American workmen and workwomen . . . . the general ardor and friendliness and enterprise—the perfect equality of the female with the male . . . . the large amativeness—the fluid movement of the population—the factories and mercantile life and laborsaving machinery—the Yankee swap—the New-York firemen and the target excursion[4]—the southern plantation life—the character of the northeast and of the northwest and southwest—slavery and the tremulous spreading of hands to protect it, and the stern opposition to it which shall never cease till it ceases or the speaking of

3. Pour.
4. Shooting contest. "Every December": Before the adoption of the Twentieth Amendment in 1933, Congress convened on the first Monday in December, according to Article 1, Section 4, of the Constitution. "Amativeness": amorousness.

tongues and the moving of lips cease. For such the expression of the American poet is to be transcendant and new. It is to be indirect and not direct or descriptive or epic. Its quality goes through these to much more. Let the age and wars of other nations be chanted and their eras and characters be illustrated and that finish the verse. Not so the great psalm of the republic. Here the theme is creative and has vista. Here comes one among the wellbeloved stonecutters and plans with decision and science and sees the solid and beautiful forms of the future where there are now no solid forms.

Of all nations the United States with veins full of poetical stuff most need poets and will doubtless have the greatest and use them the greatest. Their Presidents shall not be their common referee so much as their poets shall. Of all mankind the great poet is the equable man. Not in him but off from him things are grotesque or eccentric or fail of their sanity. Nothing out of its place is good and nothing in its place is bad. He bestows on every object or quality its fit proportions neither more nor less. He is the arbiter of the diverse and he is the key. He is the equalizer of his age and land . . . . he supplies what wants supplying and checks what wants checking. If peace is the routine out of him speaks the spirit of peace, large, rich, thrifty, building vast and populous cities, encouraging agriculture and the arts and commerce—lighting the study of man, the soul, immortality—federal, state or municipal government, marriage, health, freetrade, intertravel by land and sea . . . . nothing too close, nothing too far off . . . the stars not too far off. In war he is the most deadly force of the war. Who recruits him recruits horse and foot . . . he fetches parks of artillery[5] the best that engineer ever knew. If the time becomes slothful and heavy he knows how to arouse it . . . he can make every word he speaks draw blood. Whatever stagnates in the flat of custom or obedience or legislation he never stagnates. Obedience does not master him, he masters it. High up out of reach he stands turning a concentrated light . . . he turns the pivot with his finger . . . he baffles the swiftest runners as he stands and easily overtakes and envelops them. The time straying toward infidelity and confections and persiflage[6] he withholds by his steady faith . . . he spreads out his dishes . . . he offers the sweet firmfibred meat that grows men and women. His brain is the ultimate brain. He is no arguer . . . he is judgment. He judges not as the judge judges but as the sun falling around a helpless thing. As he sees the farthest he has the most faith. His thoughts are the hymns of the praise of things. In the talk on the soul and eternity and God off of his equal plane he is silent. He sees eternity less like a play with a prologue and denouement . . . . he sees eternity in men and women . . . he does not see men and women as dreams or dots. Faith is the antiseptic of the soul . . . it pervades the common people and preserves them . . . they never give up believing and expecting and trusting. There is that indescribable freshness and unconsciousness about an illiterate person that humbles and mocks the power of the noblest expressive genius. The poet sees for a certainty how one not a great artist may be just as sacred and perfect as the greatest artist. . . . . . The power to destroy or remould is freely used by him but never the power of attack. What is past is past. If he does not expose superior models and prove himself by every step he takes he is not what is wanted. The presence of the greatest poet conquers . . . not

---

5. I.e., parks full of artillery—from the custom of drilling and parading in civic parks.   6. Bantering talk.

parleying or struggling or any prepared attempts. Now he has passed that way see after him! there is not left any vestige of despair or misanthropy or cunning or exclusiveness or the ignominy of a nativity or color or delusion of hell or the necessity of hell . . . . . . and no man thenceforward shall be degraded for ignorance or weakness or sin.

The greatest poet hardly knows pettiness or triviality. If he breathes into any thing that was before thought small it dilates with the grandeur and life of the universe. He is a seer . . . . he is individual . . . he is complete in himself . . . . the others are as good as he, only he sees it and they do not. He is not one of the chorus . . . . he does not stop for any regulation . . . he is the president of regulation. What the eyesight does to the rest he does to the rest. Who knows the curious mystery of the eyesight? The other senses corroborate themselves, but this is removed from any proof but its own and foreruns the identities of the spiritual world. A single glance of it mocks all the investigations of man and all the instruments and books of the earth and all reasoning. What is marvellous? what is unlikely? what is impossible or baseless or vague? after you have once just opened the space of a peachpit and given audience to far and near and to the sunset and had all things enter with electric swiftness softly and duly without confusion or jostling or jam.

The land and sea, the animals fishes and birds, the sky of heaven and the orbs, the forests mountains and rivers, are not small themes . . . but folks expect of the poet to indicate more than the beauty and dignity which always attach to dumb real objects . . . . they expect him to indicate the path between reality and their souls. Men and women perceive the beauty well enough . . probably as well as he. The passionate tenacity of hunters, woodmen, early risers, cultivators of gardens and orchards and fields, the love of healthy women for the manly form, sea-faring persons, drivers of horses, the passion for light and the open air, all is an old varied sign of the unfailing perception of beauty and of a residence of the poetic in outdoor people. They can never be assisted by poets to perceive . . . some may but they never can. The poetic quality is not marshalled in rhyme or uniformity or abstract addresses to things nor in melancholy complaints or good precepts, but is the life of these and much else and is in the soul. The profit of rhyme is that it drops seeds of a sweeter and more luxuriant rhyme, and of uniformity that it conveys itself into its own roots in the ground out of sight. The rhyme and uniformity of perfect poems show the free growth of metrical laws and bud from them as unerringly and loosely as lilacs or roses on a bush, and take shapes as compact as the shapes of chestnuts and oranges and melons and pears, and shed the perfume impalpable to form. The fluency and ornaments of the finest poems or music or orations or recitations are not independent but dependent. All beauty comes from beautiful blood and a beautiful brain. If the greatnesses are in conjunction in a man or woman it is enough . . . . the fact will prevail through the universe . . . . but the gaggery[7] and gilt of a million years will not prevail. Who troubles himself about his ornaments or fluency is lost. This is what you shall do: Love the earth and sun and the animals, despise riches, give alms to every one that asks, stand up for the stupid and crazy, devote your income and labor to others, hate tyrants, argue not concerning God, have patience and indulgence toward the people, take off your hat to nothing known or unknown or to any man or number of men,

---

7. Falseness.

go freely with powerful uneducated persons and with the young and with the mothers of families, read these leaves in the open air every season of every year of your life, reexamine all you have been told at school or church or in any book, dismiss whatever insults your own soul, and your very flesh shall be a great poem and have the richest fluency not only in its words but in the silent lines of its lips and face and between the lashes of your eyes and in every motion and joint of your body. . . . . The poet shall not spend his time in unneeded work. He shall know that the ground is always ready ploughed and manured . . . . others may not know it but he shall. He shall go directly to the creation. His trust shall master the trust of everything he touches . . . . and shall master all attachment.

The known universe has one complete lover and that is the greatest poet. He consumes an eternal passion and is indifferent which chance happens and which possible contingency of fortune or misfortune and persuades daily and hourly his delicious pay. What balks or breaks others is fuel for his burning progress to contact and amorous joy. Other proportions of the reception of pleasure dwindle to nothing to his proportions. All expected from heaven or from the highest he is rapport with in the sight of the daybreak or a scene of the winter woods or the presence of children playing or with his arm round the neck of a man or woman. His love above all love has leisure and expanse . . . . he leaves room ahead of himself. He is no irresolute or suspicious lover . . . he is sure . . . he scorns intervals. His experience and the showers and thrills are not for nothing. Nothing can jar him . . . . suffering and darkness cannot—death and fear cannot. To him complaint and jealousy and envy are corpses buried and rotten in the earth . . . . he saw them buried. The sea is not surer of the shore or the shore of the sea than he is of the fruition of his love and of all perfection and beauty.

The fruition of beauty is no chance of hit or miss . . . it is inevitable as life . . . . it is exact and plumb as gravitation. From the eyesight proceeds another eyesight and from the hearing proceeds another hearing and from the voice proceeds another voice eternally curious of the harmony of things with man. To these respond perfections not only in the committees that were supposed to stand for the rest but in the rest themselves just the same. These understand the law of perfection in masses and floods . . . that its finish is to each for itself and onward from itself . . . that it is profuse and impartial . . . that there is not a minute of the light or dark nor an acre of the earth or sea without it—nor any direction of the sky nor any trade or employment nor any turn of events. This is the reason that about the proper expression of beauty there is precision and balance . . . one part does not need to be thrust above another. The best singer is not the one who has the most lithe and powerful organ . . . the pleasure of poems is not in them that take the handsomest measure and similes and sound.

Without effort and without exposing in the least how it is done the greatest poet brings the spirit of any or all events and passions and scenes and persons some more and some less to bear on your individual character as you hear or read. To do this well is to compete with the laws that pursue and follow time. What is the purpose must surely be there and the clue of it must be there . . . . and the faintest indication is the indication of the best and then becomes the clearest indication. Past and present and future are not disjoined but joined. The greatest poet forms the consistence of what is to be from what has been and is. He drags the dead out of their coffins and stands them again on their feet . . . . he says to the past, Rise and walk before me that I may realize you. He learns the lesson . . . . he places himself where the future becomes present. The greatest poet does not only dazzle his rays over character and scenes and passions . . . he finally ascends and finishes all . . . he exhibits the pinnacles that no man can tell what they are for or what is beyond . . . . he glows a moment on the extremest verge. He is most wonderful in his last half-hidden smile or frown . . . by that flash of the moment of parting the one that sees it shall be encouraged or terrified afterward for many years. The greatest poet does not moralize or make applications of morals . . . he knows the soul. The soul has that measureless pride which consists in never acknowledging any lessons but its own. But it has sympathy as measureless as its pride and the one balances the other and neither can stretch too far while it stretches in company with the other. The inmost secrets of art sleep with the twain. The greatest poet has lain close betwixt both and they are vital in his style and thoughts.

The art of art, the glory of expression and the sunshine of the light of letters is simplicity. Nothing is better than simplicity . . . . nothing can make up for excess or for the lack of definiteness. To carry on the heave of impulse and pierce intellectual depths and give all subjects their articulations are powers neither common nor very uncommon. But to speak in literature with the perfect rectitude and insousiance of the movements of animals and the unimpeachableness of the sentiment of trees in the woods and grass by the roadside is the flawless triumph of art. If you have looked on him who has achieved it you have looked on one of the masters of the artists of all nations and times. You shall not contemplate the flight of the graygull over the bay or the mettlesome action of the blood horse or the tall leaning of sunflowers on their stalk or the appearance of the sun journeying through heaven or the appearance of the moon afterward with any more satisfaction than you shall contemplate him. The greatest poet has less a marked style and is more the channel of thoughts and things without increase or diminution, and is the free channel of himself. He swears to his art, I will not be meddlesome, I will not have in my writing any elegance or effect or originality to hang in the way between me and the rest like curtains. I will have nothing hang in the way, not the richest curtains. What I tell I tell for precisely what it is. Let who may exalt or startle or fascinate or sooth I will have purposes as health or heat or snow has and be as regardless of observation. What I experience or portray shall go from my composition without a shred of my composition. You shall stand by my side and look in the mirror with me.

The old red blood and stainless gentility of great poets will be proved by their unconstraint. A heroic person walks at his ease through and out of that custom or precedent or authority that suits him not. Of the traits of the brotherhood of writers savans[8] musicians inventors and artists nothing is finer than silent defiance advancing from new free forms. In the need of poems philosophy politics mechanism science behaviour, the craft of art, an appropriate native grand-opera, shipcraft, or any craft, he is greatest forever and forever who contributes the greatest original practical example. The cleanest expression is that which finds no sphere worthy of itself and makes one.

The messages of great poets to each man and woman are, Come to us on equal terms, Only then can you understand us, We are no better than you,

8. Learned persons, scientists.

What we enclose you enclose, What we enjoy you may enjoy. Did you suppose there could be only one Supreme? We affirm there can be unnumbered Supremes, and that one does not countervail another any more than one eyesight countervails another . . and that men can be good or grand only of the consciousness of their supremacy within them. What do you think is the grandeur of storms and dismemberments and the deadliest battles and wrecks and the wildest fury of the elements and the power of the sea and the motion of nature and of the throes of human desires and dignity and hate and love? It is that something in the soul which says, Rage on, Whirl on, I tread master here and everywhere, Master of the spasms of the sky and of the shatter of the sea, Master of nature and passion and death, And of all terror and all pain.

The American bards shall be marked for generosity and affection and for encouraging competitors . . They shall be kosmos . . without monopoly or secresy . . glad to pass any thing to any one . . . hungry for equals night and day. They shall not be careful of riches and privilege . . . . they shall be riches and privilege . . . . they shall perceive who the most affluent man is. The most affluent man is he that confronts all the shows he sees by equivalents out of the stronger wealth of himself. The American bard shall delineate no class of persons nor one or two out of the strata of interests nor love most nor truth most nor the soul most nor the body most . . . . and not be for the eastern states more than the western or the northern states more than the southern.

Exact science and its practical movements are no checks on the greatest poet but always his encouragement and support. The outset and remembrance are there . . there the arms that lifted him first and brace him best . . . . there he returns after all his goings and comings. The sailor and traveler . . the anatomist chemist astronomer geologist phrenologist spiritualist mathematician historian and lexicographer are not poets, but they are the lawgivers of poets and their construction underlies the structure of every perfect poem. No matter what rises or is uttered they sent the seed of the conception of it . . . of them and by them stand the visible proofs of souls . . . . . always of their fatherstuff must be begotten the sinewy races of bards. If there shall be love and content between the father and the son and if the greatness of the son is the exuding of the greatness of the father there shall be love between the poet and the man of demonstrable science. In the beauty of poems are the tuft and final applause of science.

Great is the faith of the flush of knowledge and of the investigation of the depths of qualities and things. Cleaving and circling here swells the soul of the poet yet is president of itself always. The depths are fathomless and therefore calm. The innocence and nakedness are resumed . . . they are neither modest nor immodest. The whole theory of the special and supernatural and all that was twined with it or educed out of it departs as a dream. What has ever happened . . . . what happens and whatever may or shall happen, the vital laws enclose all . . . . they are sufficient for any case and for all cases . . . none to be hurried or retarded . . . . any miracle of affairs or persons inadmissible in the vast clear scheme where every motion and every spear of grass and the frames and spirits of men and women and all that concerns them are unspeakably perfect miracles all referring to all and each distinct and in its place. It is also not consistent with the reality of the soul to admit that there is anything in the known universe more divine than men and women.

Men and women and the earth and all upon it are simply to be taken as they are, and the investigation of their past and present and future shall be unintermitted and shall be done with perfect candor. Upon this basis philosophy speculates ever looking toward the poet, ever regarding the eternal tendencies of all toward happiness never inconsistent with what is clear to the senses and to the soul. For the eternal tendencies of all toward happiness make the only point of sane philosophy. Whatever comprehends less than that . . . whatever is less than the laws of light and of astronomical motion . . . or less than the laws that follow the thief the liar the glutton and the drunkard through this life and doubtless afterward . . . . . . or less than vast stretches of time or the slow formation of density or the patient upheaving of strata—is of no account. Whatever would put God in a poem or system of philosophy as contending against some being or influence is also of no account. Sanity and ensemble characterise the great master . . . spoilt in one principle all is spoilt. The great master has nothing to do with miracles. He sees health for himself in being one of the mass . . . . he sees the hiatus in singular eminence. To the perfect shape comes common ground. To be under the general law is great for that is to correspond with it. The master knows that he is unspeakably great and that all are unspeakably great . . . . that nothing for instance is greater than to conceive children and bring them up well . . . that to be is just as great as to perceive or tell.

In the make of the great masters the idea of political liberty is indispensible. Liberty takes the adherence of heroes wherever men and women exist . . . . but never takes any adherence or welcome from the rest more than from poets. They are the voice and exposition of liberty. They out of ages are worthy the grand idea . . . . to them it is confided and they must sustain it. Nothing has precedence of it and nothing can warp or degrade it. The attitude of great poets is to cheer up slaves and horrify despots. The turn of their necks, the sound of their feet, the motions of their wrists, are full of hazard to the one and hope to the other. Come nigh them awhile and though they neither speak or advise you shall learn the faithful American lesson. Liberty is poorly served by men whose good intent is quelled from one failure or two failures or any number of failures, or from the casual indifference or ingratitude of the people, or from the sharp show of the tushes of power, or the bringing to bear soldiers and cannon or any penal statutes. Liberty relies upon itself, invites no one, promises nothing, sits in calmness and light, is positive and composed, and knows no discouragement. The battle rages with many a loud alarm and frequent advance and retreat . . . . the enemy triumphs . . . . the prison, the handcuffs, the iron necklace and anklet, the scaffold, garrote and leadballs do their work . . . . the cause is asleep . . . . the strong throats are choked with their own blood . . . . the young men drop their eyelashes toward the ground when they pass each other . . . . and is liberty gone out of that place? No never. When liberty goes it is not the first to go nor the second or third to go . . it waits for all the rest to go . . it is the last. . . When the memories of the old martyrs are faded utterly away . . . . when the large names of patriots are laughed at in the public halls from the lips of the orators . . . . when the boys are no more christened after the same but christened after tyrants and traitors instead . . . . when the laws of the free are grudgingly permitted and laws for informers and bloodmoney are sweet to the taste of the people . . . . when I and you walk abroad upon the earth stung with compassion at the sight of numberless brothers answering our equal friendship and calling no man master—and when we are elated with noble joy at the sight of slaves . . . . when the soul retires in the cool communion of the night and surveys its experience and has much extasy over the word and deed that put back a helpless innocent person into the gripe of the gripers or into any cruel inferiority . . . . when those in all parts of these states who could easier realize the true American character but do not yet—when the swarms of cringers, suckers, doughfaces,[9] lice of politics, planners of sly involutions for their own preferment to city offices or state legislatures of the judiciary or congress or the presidency, obtain a response of love and natural deference from the people whether they get the offices or no . . . . when it is better to be a bound booby and rogue in office at a high salary than the poorest free mechanic or farmer with his hat unmoved from his head and firm eyes and a candid and generous heart . . . . and when servility by town or state or the federal government or any oppression on a large scale or small scale can be tried on without its own punishment following duly after in exact proportion against the smallest chance of escape . . . . or rather when all life and all the souls of men and women are discharged from any part of the earth—then only shall the instinct of liberty be discharged from that part of the earth.

As the attributes of the poets of the kosmos concentre in the real body and soul and in the pleasure of things they possess the superiority of genuineness over all fiction and romance. As they emit themselves facts are showered over with light . . . . the daylight is lit with more volatile light . . . . also the deep between the setting and rising sun goes deeper many fold. Each precise object or condition or combination or process exhibits a beauty . . . . the multiplication table its—old age its—the carpenter's trade its—the grand-opera its . . . . the hugehulled cheanshaped New-York clipper at sea under steam or full sail gleams with unmatched beauty . . . . the American circles and large harmonies of government gleam with theirs . . . . and the commonest definite intentions and actions with theirs. The poets of the kosmos advance through all interpositions and coverings and turmoils and strategems to first principles. They are of use . . . . they dissolve poverty from its need and riches from its conceit. You large proprietor they say shall not realize or perceive more than any one else. The owner of the library is not he who holds a legal title to it having bought and paid for it. Any one and every one is owner of the library who can read the same through all the varieties of tongues and subjects and styles, and in whom they enter with ease and take residence and force toward paternity and maternity, and make supple and powerful and rich and large. . . . . These American states strong and healthy and accomplished shall receive no pleasure from violations of natural models and must not permit them. In paintings or mouldings or carvings in mineral or wood, or in the illustrations of books or newspapers, or in any comic or tragic prints, or in the patterns of woven stuffs or any thing to beautify rooms or furniture or costumes, or to put upon cornices or monuments or on the prows or sterns of ships, or to put anywhere before the human eye indoors or out, that which distorts honest shapes or which creates unearthly beings or places or contingencies is a nuisance and revolt. Of the human form especially it is so great it must

9. Pliable politicians. The term was used at the time to refer to Northern politicians who supported Southern proslavery policies.

never be made ridiculous. Of ornaments to a work nothing outre[1] can be allowed . . but those ornaments can be allowed that conform to the perfect facts of the open air and that flow out of the nature of the work and come irrepressibly from it and are necessary to the completion of the work. Most works are most beautiful without ornament . . . Exaggerations will be revenged in human physiology. Clean and vigorous children are jetted and conceived only in those communities where the models of natural forms are public every day. . . . . Great genius and the people of these states must never be demeaned to romances. As soon as histories are properly told there is no more need of romances.

The great poets are also to be known by the absence in them of tricks and by the justification of perfect personal candor. Then folks echo a new cheap joy and a divine voice leaping from their brains: How beautiful is candor! All faults may be forgiven of him who has perfect candor. Henceforth let no man of us lie, for we have seen that openness wins the inner and outer world and that there is no single exception, and that never since our earth gathered itself in a mass have deceit or subterfuge or prevarication attracted its smallest particle or the faintest tinge of a shade—and that through the enveloping wealth and rank of a state or the whole republic of states a sneak or sly person shall be discovered and despised . . . . and that the soul has never been once fooled and never can be fooled . . . . and thrift without the loving nod of the soul is only a fœtid puff . . . . and there never grew up in any of the continents of the globe nor upon any planet or satellite or star, nor upon the asteroids, nor in any part of ethereal space, nor in the midst of density, nor under the fluid wet of the sea, nor in that condition which pre-cedes the birth of babes, nor at any time during the changes of life, nor in that condition that follows what we term death, nor in any stretch of abey-ance or action afterward of vitality, nor in any process of formation or ref-ormation anywhere, a being whose instinct hated the truth.

Extreme caution or prudence, the soundest organic health, large hope and comparison and fondness for women and children, large alimentiveness[2] and destructiveness and causality, with a perfect sense of the oneness of nature and the propriety of the same spirit applied to human affairs . . these are called up of the float of the brain of the world to be parts of the greatest poet from his birth out of his mother's womb and from her birth out of her mother's. Caution seldom goes far enough. It has been thought that the pru-dent citizen was the citizen who applied himself to solid gains and did well for himself and his family and completed a lawful life without debt or crime. The greatest poet sees and admits these economies as he sees the economies of food and sleep, but has higher notions of prudence than to think he gives much when he gives a few slight attentions at the latch of the gate. The prem-ises of the prudence of life are not the hospitality of it or the ripeness and harvest of it. Beyond the independence of a little sum laid aside for burial-money, and of a few clapboards around and shingles overhead on a lot of American soil owned, and the easy dollars that supply the year's plain cloth-ing and meals, the melancholy prudence of the abandonment of such a great being as a man is to the toss and pallor of years of moneymaking with all their scorching days and icy nights and all their stifling deceits and underhanded

1. Excessive, extravagant; from the French *outré*   2. Love of food.
(outrageous).

dodgings, or infinitessimals of parlors, or shameless stuffing while others starve . . and all the loss of the bloom and odor of the earth and of the flowers and atmosphere and of the sea and of the true taste of the women and men you pass or have to do with in youth or middle age, and the issuing sickness and desperate revolt at the close of a life without elevation or naivete, and the ghastly chatter of a death without serenity or majesty, is the great fraud upon modern civilization and forethought, blotching the surface and system which civilization undeniably drafts, and moistening with tears the immense features it spreads and spreads with such velocity before the reached kisses of the soul . . . Still the right explanation remains to be made about prudence. The prudence of the mere wealth and respectability of the most esteemed life appears too faint for the eye to observe at all when little and large alike drop quietly aside at the thought of the prudence suitable for immortality. What is wisdom that fills the thinness of a year or seventy or eighty years to wisdom spaced out by ages and coming back at a certain time with strong reinforcements and rich presents and the clear faces of wedding-guests as far as you can look in every direction running gaily toward you? Only the soul is of itself . . . . all else has reference to what ensues. All that a person does or thinks is of consequence. Not a move can a man or woman make that affects him or her in a day or a month or any part of the direct lifetime or the hour of death but the same affects him or her onward afterward through the indirect lifetime. The indirect is always as great and real as the direct. The spirit receives from the body just as much as it gives to the body. Not one name of word or deed . . not of venereal sores or discolorations . . not the privacy of the onanist[3] . . not of the putrid veins of gluttons or rumdrinkers . . . not peculation or cunning or betrayal or murder . . no serpentine poison of those that seduce women . . not the foolish yielding of women . . not prostitution . . not of any depravity of young men . . not of the attainment of gain by discreditable means . . not any nastiness of appetite . . not any harshness of officers to men or judges to prisoners or fathers to sons or sons to fathers or of husbands to wives or bosses to their boys . . not of greedy looks or malignant wishes . . . nor any of the wiles practised by people upon themselves . . . ever is or ever can be stamped on the programme but it is duly realized and returned, and that returned in further performances . . . and they returned again. Nor can the push of charity or personal force ever be any thing else than the profoundest reason, whether it brings arguments to hand or no. No specification is necessary . . to add or subtract or divide is in vain. Little or big, learned or unlearned, white or black, legal or illegal, sick or well, from the first inspiration down the windpipe to the last expiration out of it, all that a male or female does that is vigorous and benevolent and clean is so much sure profit to him or her in the unshakable order of the universe and through the whole scope of it forever. If the savage or felon is wise it is well . . . . if the greatest poet or savan is wise it is simply the same . . if the President or chief justice is wise it is the same . . . if the young mechanic or farmer is wise it is no more or less . . if the prostitute is wise it is no more nor less. The interest will come round . . all will come round. All the best actions of war and peace . . . all help given to relatives and strangers and the poor and old and sorrowful and young children and widows and the sick, and to all shunned persons . . all furtherance of fugitives and of the escape of slaves . . all the

---

3. Masturbator; from Onan, son of Judah, who "spilled *it* [his "seed"] on the ground" (Genesis 38.9).

self-denial that stood steady and aloof on wrecks and saw others take the seats of the boats . . . all offering of substance or life for the good old cause, or for a friend's sake or opinion's sake . . . all pains of enthusiasts scoffed at by their neighbors . . all the vast sweet love and precious suffering of mothers . . . all honest men baffled in strifes recorded or unrecorded . . . . all the grandeur and good of the few ancient nations whose fragments of annals we inherit . . and all the good of the hundreds of far mightier and more ancient nations unknown to us by name or date or location . . . . all that was ever manfully begun, whether it succeeded or no . . . . . all that has at any time been well suggested out of the divine heart of man or by the divinity of his mouth or by the shaping of his great hands . . and all that is well thought or done this day on any part of the surface of the globe . . or on any of the wandering stars or fixed stars by those there as we are here . . or that is henceforth to be well thought or done by you whoever you are, or by any one—these singly and wholly inured at their time and inure now and will inure always to the identities from which they sprung or shall spring. . . Did you guess any of them lived only its moment? The world does not so exist . . no parts palpable or impalpable so exist . . . no result exists now without being from its long antecedent result, and that from its antecedent, and so backward without the farthest mentionable spot coming a bit nearer the beginning than any other spot. . . . . Whatever satisfies the soul is truth. The prudence of the greatest poet answers at last the craving and glut of the soul, is not contemptuous of less ways of prudence if they conform to its ways, puts off nothing, permits no let-up for its own case or any case, has no particular sabbath or judgment-day, divides not the living from the dead or the righteous from the unrighteous, is satisfied with the present, matches every thought or act by its correlative, knows no possible forgiveness or deputed atonement . . knows that the young man who composedly periled his life and lost it has done exceeding well for himself, while the man who has not periled his life and retains it to old age in riches and ease has perhaps achieved nothing for himself worth mentioning . . and that only that person has no great prudence to learn who has learnt to prefer real longlived things, and favors body and soul the same, and perceives the indirect assuredly following the direct, and what evil or good he does leaping onward and waiting to meet him again—and who in his spirit in any emergency whatever neither hurries or avoids death.

The direct trial of him who would be the greatest poet is today. If he does not flood himself with the immediate age as with vast oceanic tides . . . . . and if he does not attract his own land body and soul to himself and hang on its neck with incomparable love and plunge his semitic[4] muscle into its merits and demerits . . . and if he be not himself the age transfigured . . . . and if to him is not opened the eternity which gives similitude to all periods and locations and processes and animate and inanimate forms, and which is the bond of time, and rises up from its inconceivable vagueness and infiniteness in the swimming shape of today, and is held by the ductile anchors of life, and makes the present spot the passage from what was to what shall be, and commits itself to the representation of this wave of an hour and this one of the sixty beautiful children of the wave—let him merge in the general run and wait his development. . . . . Still the final test of poems or any character or work remains. The prescient poet projects himself centuries ahead

4. A coinage for penis, derived from the Latin semen (seed).

and judges performer or performance after the changes of time. Does it live through them? Does it still hold on untired? Will the same style and the direction of genius to similar points be satisfactory now? Has no new discovery in science or arrival at superior planes of thought and judgment and behaviour fixed him or his so that either can be looked down upon? Have the marches of tens and hundreds and thousands of years made willing detours to the right hand and the left hand for his sake? Is he beloved long and long after he is buried? Does the young man think often of him? and the young woman think often of him? and do the middleaged and the old think of him?

A great poem is for ages and ages in common and for all degrees and complexions and all departments and sects and for a woman as much as a man and a man as much as a woman. A great poem is no finish to a man or woman but rather a beginning. Has any one fancied he could sit at last under some due authority and rest satisfied with explanations and realize and be content and full? To no such terminus does the greatest poet bring . . . he brings neither cessation or sheltered fatness and ease. The touch of him tells in action. Whom he takes he takes with firm sure grasp into live regions previously unattained . . . . thenceforward is no rest . . . . they see the space and ineffable sheen that turn the old spots and lights into dead vacuums. The companion of him beholds the birth and progress of stars and learns one of the meanings. Now there shall be a man cohered out of tumult and chaos . . . . the elder encourages the younger and shows him how . . . they two shall launch off fearlessly together till the new world fits an orbit for itself and looks unabashed on the lesser orbits of the stars and sweeps through the ceaseless rings and shall never be quiet again.

There will soon be no more priests. Their work is done. They may wait awhile . . perhaps a generation or two . . dropping off by degrees. A superior breed shall take their place . . . . the gangs of kosmos and prophets en masse shall take their place. A new order shall arise and they shall be the priests of man, and every man shall be his own priest. The churches built under their umbrage[5] shall be the churches of men and women. Through the divinity of themselves shall the kosmos and the new breed of poets be interpreters of men and women and of all events and things. They shall find their inspiration in real objects today, symptoms of the past and future . . . . They shall not deign to defend immortality or God or the perfection of things or liberty or the exquisite beauty and reality of the soul. They shall arise in America and be responded to from the remainder of the earth.

The English language befriends the grand American expression . . . . it is brawny enough and limber and full enough. On the tough stock of a race who through all change of circumstance was never without the idea of political liberty, which is the animus of all liberty, it has attracted the terms of daintier and gayer and subtler and more elegant tongues. It is the powerful language of resistance . . . it is the dialect of common sense. It is the speech of the proud and melancholy races and of all who aspire. It is the chosen tongue to express growth faith self-esteem freedom justice equality friendliness amplitude prudence decision and courage. It is the medium that shall well nigh express the inexpressible.

5. Shadow, protection.

No great literature nor any like style of behaviour or oratory or social inter-course or household arrangements or public institutions or the treatment by bosses of employed people, nor executive detail or detail of the army or navy, nor spirit of legislation or courts or police or tuition or architecture or songs or amusements or the costumes of young men, can long elude the jealous and passionate instinct of American standards. Whether or no the sign appears from the mouths of the people, it throbs a live interrogation in every freeman's and freewoman's heart after that which passes by or this built to remain. Is it uniform with my country? Are its disposals without ignominious distinc-tions? Is it for the evergrowing communes of brothers and lovers, large, well-united, proud beyond the old models, generous beyond all models? Is it something grown fresh out of the fields or drawn from the sea for use to me today here? I know that what answers for me an American must answer for any individual or nation that serves for a part of my materials. Does this answer? or is it without reference to universal needs? or sprung of the needs of the less developed society of special ranks? or old needs of pleasure over-laid by modern science and forms? Does this acknowledge liberty with audi-ble and absolute acknowledgement, and set slavery at nought for life and death? Will it help breed one goodshaped and wellhung man, and a woman to be his perfect and independent mate? Does it improve manners? Is it for the nursing of the young of the republic? Does it solve[6] readily with the sweet milk of the nipples of the breasts of the mother of many children? Has it too the old ever-fresh forbearance and impartiality? Does it look with the same love on the last born on those hardening toward stature, and on the errant, and on those who disdain all strength of assault outside of their own?

The poems distilled from other poems will probably pass away. The cow-ard will surely pass away. The expectation of the vital and great can only be satisfied by the demeanor of the vital and great. The swarms of the polished deprecating and reflectors and the polite float off and leave no remembrance. America prepares with composure and goodwill for the visi-tors that have sent word. It is not intellect that is to be their warrant and welcome. The talented, the artist, the ingenious, the editor, the statesman, the erudite . . they are not unappreciated . . they fall in their place and do their work. The soul of the nation also does its work. No disguise can pass on it . . no disguise can conceal from it. It rejects none, it permits all. Only toward as good as itself and toward the like of itself will it advance half-way. An individual is as superb as a nation when he has the qualities which make a superb nation. The soul of the largest and wealthiest and proudest nation may well go half-way to meet that of its poets. The signs are effec-tual. There is no fear of mistake. If the one is true the other is true. The proof of a poet is that his country absorbs him as affectionately as he has absorbed it.

1855

6. Dissolve.

From Inscriptions[1]

One's-Self I Sing

One's-Self I sing, a simple separate person,
Yet utter the word Democratic, the word En-Masse.

Of physiology from top to toe I sing,
Not physiognomy[2] alone nor brain alone is worthy for the Muse, I
    say the Form complete is worthier far,
The Female equally with the Male I sing.   5

Of Life immense in passion, pulse, and power,
Cheerful, for freest action form'd under the laws divine,
The Modern Man I sing.

                                             1867, 1871

Shut Not Your Doors

Shut not your doors to me proud libraries,
For that which was lacking on all your well-fill'd shelves, yet
    needed most, I bring,
Forth from the war emerging, a book I have made,
The words of my book nothing, the drift of it every thing,
A book separate, not link'd with the rest nor felt by the intellect,   5
But you ye untold latencies will thrill to every page.

                                             1865, 1881

Song of Myself[1]

1

I celebrate myself, and sing myself,
And what I assume you shall assume,
For every atom belonging to me as good belongs to you.

I loafe and invite my soul,
I lean and loafe at my ease observing a spear of summer grass.   5

My tongue, every atom of my blood, form'd from this soil, this air,
Born here of parents born here from parents the same, and their parents
    the same,

1. This title was first used for the opening poems of *Leaves of Grass* in 1871; in 1881 the number of poems was increased from nine to twenty-four.
2. The practice of judging or interpreting human character from facial features.
1. In the 1855 first edition of *Leaves of Grass*, the poem later called "Song of Myself" appeared without a title and without numbered sections or stanzas. For the 1856 edition, Whitman titled it "Poem of Walt Whitman, an American," and in the 1860 edition he titled it "Walt Whitman"; it retained that title in the 1867 and 1871 editions, and in the 1881 edition was named "Song of Myself." Whitman made numerous other changes to the poem from the first 1855 printing to the 1881 final version.

I, now thirty-seven years old in perfect health begin,
Hoping to cease not till death.

Creeds and schools in abeyance, 10
Retiring back a while sufficed at what they are, but never forgotten,
I harbor for good or bad, I permit to speak at every hazard,
Nature without check with original energy.

2

Houses and rooms are full of perfumes, the shelves are crowded with
    perfumes,
I breathe the fragrance myself and know it and like it,
The distillation would intoxicate me also, but I shall not let it. 15

The atmosphere is not a perfume, it has no taste of the distillation, it is
    odorless,
It is for my mouth forever, I am in love with it,
I will go to the bank by the wood and become undisguised and naked,
I am mad for it to be in contact with me. 20

The smoke of my own breath,
Echoes, ripples, buzz'd whispers, love-root, silk-thread, crotch and
    vine,
My respiration and inspiration, the beating of my heart, the passing of
    blood and air through my lungs,
The sniff of green leaves and dry leaves, and of the shore and dark-color'd
    sea-rocks, and of hay in the barn,
The sound of the belch'd words of my voice loos'd to the eddies of the
    wind, 25
A few light kisses, a few embraces, a reaching around of arms,
The play of shine and shade on the trees as the supple boughs wag,
The delight alone or in the rush of the streets, or along the fields and
    hillsides,
The feeling of health, the full-noon trill, the song of me rising from bed
    and meeting the sun.

Have you reckon'd a thousand acres much? have you reckon'd the earth
    much? 30
Have you practis'd so long to learn to read?
Have you felt so proud to get at the meaning of poems?

Stop this day and night with me and you shall possess the origin of all
    poems,
You shall possess the good of the earth and sun, (there are millions of
    suns left,)
You shall no longer take things at second or third hand, nor look through
    the eyes of the dead, nor feed on the spectres in books, 35
You shall not look through my eyes either, nor take things from me,
You shall listen to all sides and filter them from your self.

3

I have heard what the talkers were talking, the talk of the beginning and
    the end,
But I do not talk of the beginning or the end.

There was never any more inception than there is now,   40
Nor any more youth or age than there is now,
And will never be any more perfection than there is now,
Nor any more heaven or hell than there is now.

Urge and urge and urge,
Always the procreant urge of the world.   45

Out of the dimness opposite equals advance, always substance and
    increase, always sex,
Always a knit of identity, always distinction, always a breed of life.

To elaborate is no avail, learn'd and unlearn'd feel that it is so.

Sure as the most certain sure, plumb in the uprights, well entretied,[2]
    braced in the beams,
Stout as a horse, affectionate, haughty, electrical,   50
I and this mystery here we stand.

Clear and sweet is my soul, and clear and sweet is all that is not my soul.

Lack one lacks both, and the unseen is proved by the seen,
Till that becomes unseen and receives proof in its turn.

Showing the best and dividing it from the worst age vexes age,   55
Knowing the perfect fitness and equanimity of things, while they discuss
    I am silent, and go bathe and admire myself.

Welcome is every organ and attribute of me, and of any man hearty and
    clean,
Not an inch nor a particle of an inch is vile, and none shall be less familiar
    than the rest.

I am satisfied—I see, dance, laugh, sing;
As the hugging and loving bed-fellow sleeps at my side through the night,
    and withdraws at the peep of the day with stealthy tread,   60
Leaving me baskets cover'd with white towels swelling the house with
    their plenty,
Shall I postpone my acceptation and realization and scream at my eyes,
That they turn from gazing after and down the road,
And forthwith cipher[3] and show me to a cent,
Exactly the value of one and exactly the value of two, and which is ahead?   65

2. Cross-braced; reinforced.   3. Calculate.

4

Trippers and askers surround me,
People I meet, the effect upon me of my early life or the ward and city I
    live in, or the nation,
The latest dates, discoveries, inventions, societies, authors old and new,
My dinner, dress, associates, looks, compliments, dues,
The real or fancied indifference of some man or woman I love,   70
The sickness of one of my folks or of myself, or ill-doing or loss or lack
    of money, or depressions or exaltations,
Battles, the horrors of fratricidal war, the fever of doubtful news, the fitful
    events;
These come to me days and nights and go from me again,
But they are not the Me myself.

Apart from the pulling and hauling stands what I am,   75
Stands amused, complacent, compassionating, idle, unitary,
Looks down, is erect, or bends an arm on an impalpable certain rest,
Looking with side-curved head curious what will come next,
Both in and out of the game and watching and wondering at it.

Backward I see in my own days where I sweated through fog with
    linguists and contenders,   80
I have no mockings or arguments, I witness and wait.

5

I believe in you my soul, the other I am must not abase itself to you,
And you must not be abased to the other.

Loafe with me on the grass, loose the stop from your throat,
Not words, not music or rhyme I want, not custom or lecture, not even
    the best,   85
Only the lull I like, the hum of your valvèd voice.

I mind how once we lay such a transparent summer morning,
How you settled your head athwart my hips and gently turn'd over upon me,
And parted the shirt from my bosom-bone, and plunged your tongue to
    my bare-stript heart,
And reach'd till you felt my beard, and reach'd till you held my feet.   90

Swiftly arose and spread around me the peace and knowledge that pass
    all the argument of the earth,
And I know that the hand of God is the promise of my own,
And I know that the spirit of God is the brother of my own,
And that all the men ever born are also my brothers, and the women my
    sisters and lovers,
And that a kelson[4] of the creation is love,   95
And limitless are leaves stiff or drooping in the fields,
And brown ants in the little wells beneath them,
And mossy scabs of the worm fence,[5] heap'd stones, elder, mullein and
    poke-weed.

---

4. A basic structural unit; a reinforcing timber bolted to the keel (backbone) of a ship.

5. Fence built of interlocking rails in a zigzag pattern.

6

A child said *What is the grass?* fetching it to me with full hands;
How could I answer the child? I do not know what it is any more than
    he.   100

I guess it must be the flag of my disposition, out of hopeful green stuff
    woven.

Or I guess it is the handkerchief of the Lord,
A scented gift and remembrancer designedly dropt,
Bearing the owner's name someway in the corners, that we may see and
    remark, and say *Whose?*

Or I guess the grass is itself a child, the produced babe of the vegetation. 105

Or I guess it is a uniform hieroglyphic,
And it means, Sprouting alike in broad zones and narrow zones,
Growing among black folks as among white,
Kanuck, Tuckahoe, Congressman, Cuff,[6] I give them the same, I receive
    them the same.

And now it seems to me the beautiful uncut hair of graves.   110

Tenderly will I use you curling grass,
It may be you transpire from the breasts of young men,
It may be if I had known them I would have loved them,
It may be you are from old people, or from offspring taken soon out of
    their mothers' laps,
And here you are the mothers' laps.   115

This grass is very dark to be from the white heads of old mothers,
Darker than the colorless beards of old men,
Dark to come from under the faint red roofs of mouths.

O I perceive after all so many uttering tongues,
And I perceive they do not come from the roofs of mouths for nothing.   120

I wish I could translate the hints about the dead young men and women,
And the hints about old men and mothers, and the offspring taken soon
    out of their laps.

What do you think has become of the young and old men?
And what do you think has become of the women and children?

They are alive and well somewhere,   125
The smallest sprout shows there is really no death,
And if ever there was it led forward life, and does not wait at the end to
    arrest it,
And ceas'd the moment life appear'd.

---

6. From the African word *cuffee* (name for black male born on a Friday). "Kanuck": French Canadian (now sometimes considered pejorative). "Tuckahoe": Virginian, from eaters of the American Indian food plant Tuckahoe.

All goes onward and outward, nothing collapses,
And to die is different from what any one supposed, and luckier.   130

7

Has any one supposed it lucky to be born?
I hasten to inform him or her it is just as lucky to die, and I know it.

I pass death with the dying and birth with the new-wash'd babe, and
    am not contain'd between my hat and boots,
And peruse manifold objects, no two alike and every one good,
The earth good and the stars good, and their adjuncts all good.   135

I am not an earth nor an adjunct of an earth,
I am the mate and companion of people, all just as immortal and
    fathomless as myself,
(They do not know how immortal, but I know.)

Every kind for itself and its own, for me mine male and female,
For me those that have been boys and that love women,   140
For me the man that is proud and feels how it stings to be slighted,
For me the sweet-heart and the old maid, for me mothers and the mothers
    of mothers,
For me lips that have smiled, eyes that have shed tears,
For me children and the begetters of children.

Undrape! you are not guilty to me, nor stale nor discarded,   145
I see through the broadcloth and gingham whether or no,
And am around, tenacious, acquisitive, tireless, and cannot be shaken
    away.

8

The little one sleeps in its cradle,
I lift the gauze and look a long time, and silently brush away flies with
    my hand.

The youngster and the red-faced girl turn aside up the bushy hill,   150
I peeringly view them from the top.

The suicide sprawls on the bloody floor of the bedroom,
I witness the corpse with its dabbled hair, I note where the pistol has fallen.

The blab of the pave, tires of carts, sluff of boot-soles, talk of the
    promenaders,
The heavy omnibus, the driver with his interrogating thumb, the clank
    of the shod horses on the granite floor,   155
The snow-sleighs, clinking, shouted jokes, pelts of snow-balls,
The hurrahs for popular favorites, the fury of rous'd mobs,
The flap of the curtain'd litter, a sick man inside borne to the hospital,
The meeting of enemies, the sudden oath, the blows and fall,
The excited crowd, the policeman with his star quickly working his
    passage to the centre of the crowd,   160

The impassive stones that receive and return so many echoes,
What groans of over-fed or half-starv'd who fall sunstruck or in fits,
What exclamations of women taken suddenly who hurry home and
　　give birth to babes,
What living and buried speech is always vibrating here, what howls
　　restrain'd by decorum,
Arrests of criminals, slights, adulterous offers made, acceptances,
　　rejections with convex lips,   165
I mind them or the show or resonance of them—I come and I depart.

9

The big doors of the country barn stand open and ready,
The dried grass of the harvest-time loads the slow-drawn wagon,
The clear light plays on the brown gray and green intertinged,
The armfuls are pack'd to the sagging mow.   170

I am there, I help, I came stretch'd atop of the load,
I felt its soft jolts, one leg reclined on the other,
I jump from the cross-beams and sieze the clover and timothy,
And roll head over heels and tangle my hair full of wisps.

10

Alone far in the wilds and mountains I hunt,   175
Wandering amazed at my own lightness and glee,
In the late afternoon choosing a safe spot to pass the night,
Kindling a fire and broiling the fresh-kill'd game,
Falling asleep on the gather'd leaves with my dog and gun by my side.

The Yankee clipper is under her sky-sails, she cuts the sparkle and scud, 180
My eyes settle the land, I bend at her prow or shout joyously from the deck.

The boatmen and clam-diggers arose early and stopt for me,
I tuck'd my trowser-ends in my boots and went and had a good time;
You should have been with us that day round the chowder-kettle.

I saw the marriage of the trapper in the open air in the far west, the bride
　　was a red girl,   185
Her father and his friends sat near cross-legged and dumbly smoking,
　　they had moccasins to their feet and large thick blankets hanging from
　　their shoulders,
On a bank lounged the trapper, he was drest mostly in skins, his luxuriant
　　beard and curls protected his neck, he held his bride by the hand,
She had long eyelashes, her head was bare, her coarse straight locks
　　descended upon her voluptuous limbs and reach'd to her feet.

The runaway slave came to my house and stopt outside,
I heard his motions crackling the twigs of the woodpile,   190
Through the swung half-door of the kitchen I saw him limpsy[7] and weak,
And went where he sat on a log and led him in and assured him,
And brought water and fill'd a tub for his sweated body and bruis'd feet,

---

7. Limping or swaying.

And gave him a room that enter'd from my own, and gave him some coarse
    clean clothes,
And remember perfectly well his revolving eyes and his awkwardness,   195
And remember putting plasters on the galls of his neck and ankles;
He staid with me a week before he was recuperated and pass'd north,
I had him sit next me at table, my fire-lock lean'd in the corner.

11

Twenty-eight young men bathe by the shore,
Twenty-eight young men and all so friendly;   200
Twenty-eight years of womanly life and all so lonesome.

She owns the fine house by the rise of the bank,
She hides handsome and richly drest aft the blinds of the window.

Which of the young men does she like the best?
Ah the homeliest of them is beautiful to her.   205

Where are you off to, lady? for I see you,
You splash in the water there, yet stay stock still in your room.   *Others*

Dancing and laughing along the beach came the twenty-ninth bather,
The rest did not see her, but she saw them and loved them.

The beards of the young men glisten'd with wet, it ran from their long
    hair,   210
Little streams pass'd over their bodies.

An unseen hand also pass'd over their bodies,
It descended tremblingly from their temples and ribs.

The young men float on their backs, their white bellies bulge to the sun,
    they do not ask who seizes fast to them,
They do not know who puffs and declines with pendant and bending
    arch,   215
They do not think whom they souse with spray.

12

The butcher-boy puts off his killing-clothes, or sharpens his knife
    at the stall in the market,
I loiter enjoying his repartee and his shuffle and break-down.[8]
Blacksmiths with grimed and hairy chests environ the anvil,
Each has his main-sledge, they are all out, there is a great heat in the
    fire.   220

From the cinder-strew'd threshold I follow their movements,   *Others*
The lithe sheer of their waists plays even with their massive arms,
Overhand the hammers swing, overhand so slow, overhand so sure,
They do not hasten, each man hits in his place.

---

8. Dances familiar in popular entertainment and minstrelsy. The "shuffle" involves the sliding of feet
across the floor, and the "break-down" is faster and noisier.

13

The negro holds firmly the reins of his four horses, the block swags
    underneath on its tied-over chain,   225
The negro that drives the long dray of the stone-yard, steady and tall he
    stands pois'd on one leg on the string-piece,[9]
His blue shirt exposes his ample neck and breast and loosens over his
    hip-band,
His glance is calm and commanding, he tosses the slouch of his hat away
    from his forehead,
The sun falls on his crispy hair and mustache, falls on the black of his
    polish'd and perfect limbs.

I behold the picturesque giant and love him, and I do not stop there,   230
I go with the team also.

In me the caresser of life wherever moving, backward as well as forward
    sluing,[1]
To niches aside and junior[2] bending, not a person or object missing,
Absorbing all to myself and for this song.

Oxen that rattle the yoke and chain or halt in the leafy shade, what is
    that you express in your eyes?   235
It seems to me more than all the print I have read in my life.

My tread scares the wood-drake and wood-duck on my distant and
    day-long ramble.
They rise together, they slowly circle around.

I believe in those wing'd purposes,
And acknowledge red, yellow, white, playing within me,   240
And consider green and violet and the tufted crown intentional,
And do not call the tortoise unworthy because she is not something
    else,
And the jay in the woods never studied the gamut,[3] yet trills pretty well
    to me,
And the look of the bay mare shames silliness out of me.

14

The wild gander leads his flock through the cool night,   245
Ya-honk he says, and sounds it down to me like an invitation,
The pert may suppose it meaningless, but I listening close,
Find its purpose and place up there toward the wintry sky.

The sharp-hoof'd moose of the north, the cat on the house-sill, the
    chickadee, the prairie-dog,
The litter of the grunting sow as they tug at her teats,   250
The brood of the turkey-hen and she with her half-spread wings,

9. Long, heavy timber used to keep a load in
place.
1. Twisting.

2. Smaller.
3. Notes of the musical scale.

I see in them and myself the same old law.
The press of my foot to the earth springs a hundred affections,
They scorn the best I can do to relate them.

I am enamour'd of growing out-doors,   255
Of men that live among cattle or taste of the ocean or woods,
Of the builders and steerers of ships and the wielders of axes and mauls,
     and the drivers of horses,
I can eat and sleep with them week in and week out.

What is commonest, cheapest, nearest, easiest, is Me,
Me going in for my chances, spending for vast returns,   260
Adorning myself to bestow myself on the first that will take me,
Not asking the sky to come down to my good will,
Scattering it freely forever.

15

The pure contralto sings in the organ loft,
The carpenter dresses his plank, the tongue of his foreplane whistles
     its wild ascending lisp,   265
The married and unmarried children ride home to their Thanksgiving
     dinner,
The pilot seizes the king-pin,[4] he heaves down with a strong arm,
The mate stands braced in the whale-boat, lance and harpoon are ready,
The duck-shooter walks by silent and cautious stretches,
The deacons are ordain'd with cross'd hands at the altar,   270
The spinning-girl retreats and advances to the hum of the big wheel,
The farmer stops by the bars as he walks on a First-day[5] loafe and looks
     at the oats and rye,
The lunatic is carried at last to the asylum a confirm'd case,
(He will never sleep any more as he did in the cot in his mother's
     bed-room;)
The jour printer[6] with gray head and gaunt jaws works at his case,   275
He turns his quid of tobacco while his eyes blurr with the manuscript;
The malform'd limbs are tied to the surgeon's table,
What is removed drops horribly in a pail;
The quadroon[7] girl is sold at the auction-stand, the drunkard nods by the
     bar-room stove,
The machinist rolls up his sleeves, the policeman travels his beat, the
     gate-keeper marks who pass,   280
The young fellow drives the express-wagon, (I love him, though I do not
     know him;)
The half-breed straps on his light boots to compete in the race,
The western turkey-shooting draws old and young, some lean on their
     rifles, some sit on logs,
Out from the crowd steps the marksman, takes his position, levels his piece;

---

4. The extended spoke of the pilot wheel, used to maintain leverage during storms.
5. Sunday. Whitman frequently uses the numerical Quaker designations for the names of days and months. "Bars": i.e., of a rail fence.
6. I.e., a journeyman printer, or one who has passed an apprenticeship and is fully qualified for all professional work.
7. Term used at the time (often in reference to slaves) to refer to light-complected people thought to be one-fourth black.

The groups of newly-come immigrants cover the wharf or levee,   285
As the woolly-pates[8] hoe in the sugar-field, the overseer views them
    from his saddle,
The bugle calls in the ball-room, the gentlemen run for their partners,
    the dancers bow to each other,
The youth lies awake in the cedar-roof'd garret and harks to the musical
    rain,
The Wolverine[9] sets traps on the creek that helps fill the Huron,
The squaw wrapt in her yellow-hemm'd cloth is offering moccasins and
    bead-bags for sale,   290
The connoisseur peers along the exhibition-gallery with half-shut eyes
    bent sideways,
As the deck-hands make fast the steamboat the plank is thrown for the
    shore-going passengers,
The young sister holds out the skein while the elder sister winds it off
    in a ball, and stops now and then for the knots,
The one-year wife is recovering and happy having a week ago borne her
    first child,
The clean-hair'd Yankee girl works with her sewing-machine or in the
    factory or mill,   295
The paving-man[1] leans on his two-handed rammer, the reporter's lead
    flies swiftly over the note-book, the sign-painter is lettering with blue
    and gold,
The canal boy trots on the tow-path, the book-keeper counts at his desk,
    the shoemaker waxes his thread,
The conductor beats time for the band and all the performers follow him,
The child is baptized, the convert is making his first professions,
The regatta is spread on the bay, the race is begun, (how the white sails
    sparkle!)   300
The drover watching his drove sings out to them that would stray,
The pedler sweats with his pack on his back, (the purchaser higgling
    about the odd cent;)
The bride unrumples her white dress, the minute-hand of the clock
    moves slowly,
The opium-eater reclines with rigid head and just-open'd lips,
The prostitute draggles her shawl, her bonnet bobs on her tipsy and
    pimpled neck,   305
The crowd laugh at her blackguard oaths, the men jeer and wink to each
    other,
(Miserable! I do not laugh at your oaths nor jeer you;)
The President holding a cabinet council is surrounded by the great
    Secretaries,
On the piazza walk three matrons stately and friendly with twined arms,
The crew of the fish-smack pack repeated layers of halibut in the hold,   310
The Missourian crosses the plains toting his wares and his cattle,
As the fare-collector goes through the train he gives notice by the jingling
    of loose change,
The floor-men are laying the floor, the tinners are tinning the roof, the
    masons are calling for mortar,
In single file each shouldering his hod pass onward the laborers;

---

8. Black slaves (with stereotypical emphasis on
"woolly" hair).

9. Inhabitant of Michigan.
1. Man building or repairing streets.

Seasons pursuing each other the indescribable crowd is gather'd, it is the
    fourth of Seventh-month,[2] (what salutes of cannon and small arms!) 315
Seasons pursuing each other the plougher ploughs, the mower mows,
    and the winter-grain falls in the ground;
Off on the lakes the pike-fisher watches and waits by the hole in the
    frozen surface,
The stumps stand thick round the clearing, the squatter strikes deep
    with his axe,
Flatboatmen make fast towards dusk near the cotton-wood or pecan-trees,
Coon-seekers go through the regions of the Red river or through those
    drain'd by the Tennessee, or through those of the Arkansas, 320
Torches shine in the dark that hangs on the Chattahooch or Altamahaw,[3]
Patriarchs sit at supper with sons and grandsons and great-grandsons
    around them,
In walls of adobie, in canvas tents, rest hunters and trappers after their
    day's sport,
The city sleeps and the country sleeps,
The living sleep for their time, the dead sleep for their time, 325
The old husband sleeps by his wife and the young husband sleeps by his
    wife;
And these tend inward to me, and I tend outward to them,
And such as it is to be of these more or less I am,
And of these one and all I weave the song of myself.

16

I am of old and young, of the foolish as much as the wise, 330
Regardless of others, ever regardful of others,
Maternal as well as paternal, a child as well as a man,
Stuff'd with the stuff that is coarse and stuff'd with the stuff that is fine,
One of the Nation of many nations, the smallest the same and the largest
    the same,
A Southerner soon as a Northerner, a planter nonchalant and hospitable
    down by the Oconee[4] I live, 335
A Yankee bound my own way ready for trade, my joints the limberest joints
    on earth and the sternest joints on earth,
A Kentuckian walking the vale of the Elkhorn[5] in my deer-skin leggings, a
    Louisianian or Georgian,
A boatman over lakes or bays or along coasts, a Hoosier, Badger, Buckeye;[6]
At home on Kanadian[7] snow-shoes or up in the bush, or with fishermen
    off Newfoundland,
At home in the fleet of ice-boats, sailing with the rest and tacking, 340
At home on the hills of Vermont or in the woods of Maine, or the Texan
    ranch,
Comrade of Californians, comrade of free North-Westerners, (loving their
    big proportions,)
Comrade of raftsmen and coalmen, comrade of all who shake hands and
    welcome to drink and meat,

2. I.e., the Fourth of July.
3. Georgia rivers.
4. River in central Georgia.
5. River in Nebraska.

6. Inhabitants of Indiana, Wisconsin, and Ohio,
respectively.
7. Canadian.

A learner with the simplest, a teacher of the thoughtfullest,
A novice beginning yet experient of myriads of seasons,   345
Of every hue and caste am I, of every rank and religion,
A farmer, mechanic, artist, gentleman, sailor, quaker,
Prisoner, fancy-man, rowdy, lawyer, physician, priest.

I resist any thing better than my own diversity,
Breathe the air but leave plenty after me,   350
And am not stuck up, and am in my place.

(The moth and the fish-eggs are in their place,
The bright suns I see and the dark suns I cannot see are in their place,
The palpable is in its place and the impalpable is in its place.)

17

These are really the thoughts of all men in all ages and lands, they are
    not original with me,   355
If they are not yours as much as mine they are nothing, or next to nothing,
If they are not the riddle and the untying of the riddle they are nothing,
If they are not just as close as they are distant they are nothing.

This is the grass that grows wherever the land is and the water is,
This the common air that bathes the globe.   360

18

With music strong I come, with my cornets and my drums,
I play not marches for accepted victors only, I play marches for conquer'd
    and slain persons.

Have you heard that it was good to gain the day?
I also say it is good to fall, battles are lost in the same spirit in which they
    are won.

I beat and pound for the dead,   365
I blow through my embouchures[8] my loudest and gayest for them.

Vivas to those who have fail'd!
And to those whose war-vessels sank in the sea!

And to those themselves who sank in the sea!
And to all generals that lost engagements, and all overcome heroes!   370
And the numberless unknown heroes equal to the greatest heroes known!

19

This is the meal equally set, this the meat for natural hunger,
It is for the wicked just the same as the righteous, I make appointments
    with all,

---

8. Mouthpieces of musical instruments such as the cornet.

I will not have a single person slighted or left away,
The kept-woman, sponger, thief, are hereby invited,   375
The heavy-lipp'd slave is invited, the venerealee[9] is invited;
There shall be no difference between them and the rest.

This is the press of a bashful hand, this the float and odor of hair,
This is the touch of my lips to yours, this the murmur of yearning,
This the far-off depth and height reflecting my own face,   380
This the thoughtful merge of myself, and the outlet again.

Do you guess I have some intricate purpose?
Well I have, for the Fourth-month showers have, and the mica on the
    side of a rock has.

Do you take it I would astonish?
Does the daylight astonish? does the early redstart twittering through
    the woods?   385
Do I astonish more than they?

This hour I tell things in confidence,
I might not tell everybody, but I will tell you.

20

Who goes there? hankering, gross, mystical, nude;
How is it I extract strength from the beef I eat?   390

What is a man anyhow? what am I? what are you?

All I mark as my own you shall offset it with your own,
Else it were time lost listening to me.

I do not snivel that snivel the world over,
That months are vacuums and the ground but wallow and filth.   395

Whimpering and truckling fold with powders for invalids, conformity
    goes to the fourth-remov'd,[1]
I wear my hat as I please indoors or out.

Why should I pray? why should I venerate and be ceremonious?

Having pried through the strata, analyzed to a hair, counsel'd with
    doctors and calculated close,
I find no sweeter fat than sticks to my bones.   400

In all people I see myself, none more and not one a barley-corn[2] less,
And the good or bad I say of myself I say of them.

---

9. Someone afflicted with a venereal (sexually
transmitted) disease.
1. Those remote in relationship, such as "third
cousin, fourth removed." "Fold with powders": a
reference to the custom of wrapping a dose of
medicine in a piece of paper.
2. The seed or grain of barley, but also a unit of
measure equal to about one-third of an inch.

I know I am solid and sound,
To me the converging objects of the universe perpetually flow,
All are written to me, and I must get what the writing means.   405

I know I am deathless,
I know this orbit of mine cannot be swept by a carpenter's compass,
I know I shall not pass like a child's carlacue[3] cut with a burnt stick at
    night.

I know I am august,
I do not trouble my spirit to vindicate itself or be understood,   410
I see that the elementary laws never apologize,
(I reckon I behave no prouder than the level I plant my house by, after all.)

I exist as I am, that is enough,
If no other in the world be aware I sit content,
And if each and all be aware I sit content.   415

One world is aware and by far the largest to me, and that is myself,
And whether I come to my own to-day or in ten thousand or ten million
    years,
I can cheerfully take it now, or with equal cheerfulness I can wait.

My foothold is tenon'd and mortis'd[4] in granite,
I laugh at what you call dissolution,   420
And I know the amplitude of time.

21

I am the poet of the Body and I am the poet of the Soul,
The pleasures of heaven are with me and the pains of hell are with me,
The first I graft and increase upon myself, the latter I translate into a
    new tongue.

I am the poet of the woman the same as the man,   425
And I say it is as great to be a woman as to be a man,
And I say there is nothing greater than the mother of men.

I chant the chant of dilation or pride,
We have had ducking and deprecating about enough,
I show that size is only development.   430

Have you outstript the rest? are you the President?
It is a trifle, they will more than arrive there every one, and still
    pass on.

I am he that walks with the tender and growing night,
I call to the earth and sea half-held by the night.

---

3. Or *curlicue*, a fancy flourish made with a writing implement, here made in the dark with a lighted stick.
4. Here, mason's terms for a particular way of joining two stones together. A mortise is a cavity in a stone into which is placed the projection (tenon) from another stone.

Press close bare-bosom'd night—press close magnetic nourishing night!   435
Night of south winds—night of the large few stars!
Still nodding night—mad naked summer night.

Smile O voluptuous cool-breath'd earth!
Earth of the slumbering and liquid trees!
Earth of departed sunset—earth of the mountains misty-topt!   440
Earth of the vitreous pour of the full moon just tinged with blue!
Earth of shine and dark mottling the tide of the river!
Earth of the limpid gray of clouds brighter and clearer for my sake!
Far-swooping elbow'd earth—rich apple-blossom'd earth!
Smile, for your lover comes.   445

Prodigal, you have given me love—therefore I to you give love!
O unspeakable passionate love.

22

You sea! I resign myself to you also—I guess what you mean,
I behold from the beach your crooked inviting fingers,
I believe you refuse to go back without feeling of me,   450
We must have a turn together, I undress, hurry me out of sight of the land,
Cushion me soft, rock me in billowy drowse,
Dash me with amorous wet, I can repay you.

Sea of stretch'd ground-swells,
Sea breathing broad and convulsive breaths,   455
Sea of the brine of life and of unshovell'd yet always-ready graves,
Howler and scooper of storms, capricious and dainty sea,
I am integral with you, I too am of one phase and of all phases.

Partaker of influx and efflux I, extoller of hate and conciliation,
Extoller of amies[5] and those that sleep in each others' arms.   460

I am he attesting sympathy,
(Shall I make my list of things in the house and skip the house that
    supports them?)

I am not the poet of goodness only, I do not decline to be the poet of
    wickedness also.

What blurt is this about virtue and about vice?
Evil propels me and reform of evil propels me, I stand indifferent,   465
My gait is no fault-finder's or rejecter's gait,
I moisten the roots of all that has grown.

Did you fear some scrofula[6] out of the unflagging pregnancy?
Did you guess the celestial laws are yet to be work'd over and rectified?

I find one side a balance and the antipodal side a balance,   470
Soft doctrine as steady help as stable doctrine,
Thoughts and deeds of the present our rouse and early start.

---

5. Friends (French).
6. Form of tuberculosis characterized by swell-   ing of the lymph glands.

This minute that comes to me over the past decillions,[7]
There is no better than it and now.
What behaved well in the past or behaves well to-day is not such a
    wonder,   475
The wonder is always and always how there can be a mean man or an
    infidel.

23

Endless unfolding of words of ages!
And mine a word of the modern, the word En-Masse.

A word of the faith that never balks,
Here or henceforward it is all the same to me, I accept Time absolutely. 480

It alone is without flaw, it alone rounds and completes all,
That mystic baffling wonder alone completes all.

I accept Reality and dare not question it.
Materialism first and last imbuing.

Hurrah for positive science! long live exact demonstration!   485
Fetch stonecrop mixt with cedar and branches of lilac,
This is the lexicographer, this the chemist, this made a grammar of the
    old cartouches,[8]
These mariners put the ship through dangerous unknown seas,
This is the geologist, this works with the scalpel, and this is a
    mathematician.

Gentlemen, to you the first honors always!   490
Your facts are useful, and yet they are not my dwelling,
I but enter by them to an area of my dwelling.

Less the reminders of properties told my words,
And more the reminders they of life untold, and of freedom and extrication,
And make short account of neuters and geldings, and favor men and
    women fully equipt,   495
And beat the gong of revolt, and stop with fugitives and them that plot and
    conspire.

24

Walt Whitman, a kosmos, of Manhattan the son,
Turbulent, fleshy, sensual, eating, drinking and breeding,
No sentimentalist, no stander above men and women or apart from them,
No more modest than immodest.   500

Unscrew the locks from the doors!
Unscrew the doors themselves from their jambs!

---

7. The number one followed by thirty-three
zeroes.
8. On tablets of Egyptian hieroglyphics, the
ornamental area noting the name of a ruler or
deity. "Stonecrop": a fleshy-leafed plant.

Whoever degrades another degrades me,
And whatever is done or said returns at last to me.

Through me the afflatus[9] surging and surging, through me the current
    and index.   505

I speak the pass-word primeval, I give the sign of democracy,
By God! I will accept nothing which all cannot have their counterpart of
    on the same terms.

Through me many long dumb voices,
Voices of the interminable generations of prisoners and slaves,
Voices of the diseas'd and despairing and of thieves and dwarfs,   510

Voices of cycles of preparation and accretion,
And of the threads that connect the stars, and of wombs and of the
    fatherstuff,
And of the rights of them the others are down upon,
Of the deform'd, trivial, flat, foolish, despised,
Fog in the air, beetles rolling balls of dung.   515

Through me forbidden voices,
Voices of sexes and lusts, voices veil'd and I remove the veil,
Voices indecent by me clarified and transfigur'd.

I do not press my fingers across my mouth,
I keep as delicate around the bowels as around the head and heart,   520
Copulation is no more rank to me than death is.

I believe in the flesh and the appetites,
Seeing, hearing, feeling, are miracles, and each part and tag of me is a
    miracle.

Divine am I inside and out, and I make holy whatever I touch or am
    touch'd from,
The scent of these arm-pits aroma finer than prayer,   525
This head more than churches, bibles, and all the creeds.

If I worship one thing more than another it shall be the spread of my own
    body, or any part of it,
Translucent mould of me it shall be you!
Shaded ledges and rests it shall be you!
Firm masculine colter[1] it shall be you!   530
Whatever goes to the tilth[2] of me it shall be you!
You my rich blood! your milky stream pale strippings of my life!
Breast that presses against other breasts it shall be you!
My brain it shall be your occult convolutions!
Root of wash'd sweet-flag! timorous pond-snipe! nest of guarded duplicate
    eggs! it shall be you!   535
Mix'd tussled hay of head, beard, brawn, it shall be you!
Trickling sap of maple, fibre of manly wheat, it shall be you!
Sun so generous it shall be you!

9. Divine wind or spirit.   2. Cultivation or tillage of the soil.
1. The blade at the front of a plow.

Vapors lighting and shading my face it shall be you!
You sweaty brooks and dews it shall be you!   540
Winds whose soft-tickling genitals rub against me it shall be you!
Broad muscular fields, branches of live oak, loving lounger in my winding
    paths, it shall be you!
Hands I have taken, face I have kiss'd, mortal I have ever touch'd, it shall
    be you.

I dote on myself, there is that lot of me and all so luscious,
Each moment and whatever happens thrills me with joy,   545
I cannot tell how my ankles bend, nor whence the cause of my faintest
    wish,
Nor the cause of the friendship I emit, nor the cause of the friendship I
    take again.

That I walk up my stoop, I pause to consider if it really be,
A morning-glory at my window satisfies me more than the metaphysics of
    books.

To behold the day-break!   550
The little light fades the immense and diaphanous shadows,
The air tastes good to my palate.

Hefts[3] of the moving world at innocent gambols silently rising freshly
    exuding,
Scooting obliquely high and low.

Something I cannot see puts upward libidinous prongs,   555
Seas of bright juice suffuse heaven.

The earth by the sky staid with, the daily close of their junction,
The heav'd challenge from the east that moment over my head,
The mocking taunt, See then whether you shall be master!

25

Dazzling and tremendous how quick the sun-rise would kill me,   560
If I could not now and always send sun-rise out of me.

We also ascend dazzling and tremendous as the sun,
We found our own O my soul in the calm and cool of the day-break.

My voice goes after what my eyes cannot reach,
With the twirl of my tongue I encompass worlds and volumes of worlds.   565

Speech is the twin of my vision, it is unequal to measure itself,
It provokes me forever, it says sarcastically,
Walt you contain enough, why don't you let it out then?

Come now I will not be tantalized, you conceive too much of articulation,
Do you not know O speech how the buds beneath you are folded?   570

3. Something being heaved or raised upward.

Waiting in gloom, protected by frost,
The dirt receding before my prophetical screams,
I underlying causes to balance them at last,
My knowledge my live parts, it keeping tally with the meaning of all things,
Happiness, (which whoever hears me let him or her set out in search of
    this day.)   575

My final merit I refuse you, I refuse putting from me what I really am,
Encompass worlds, but never try to encompass me.
I crowd your sleekest and best by simply looking toward you.

Writing and talk do not prove me,
I carry the plenum[4] of proof and every thing else in my face,   580
With the hush of my lips I wholly confound the skeptic.

26

Now I will do nothing but listen,
To accrue what I hear into this song, to let sounds contribute toward it.

I hear bravuras of birds, bustle of growing wheat, gossip of flames, clack
    of sticks cooking my meals,
I hear the sound I love, the sound of the human voice,   585
I hear all sounds running together, combined, fused or following,
Sounds of the city and sounds out of the city, sounds of the day and
    night,
Talkative young ones to those that like them, the loud laugh of work-people
    at their meals,
The angry base of disjointed friendship, the faint tones of the sick,
The judge with hands tight to the desk, his pallid lips pronouncing a
    death-sentence,   590
The heave'e'yo of stevedores unlading ships by the wharves, the refrain
    of the anchor-lifters,
The ring of alarm-bells, the cry of fire, the whirr of swift-streaking engines
    and hose-carts with premonitory tinkles and color'd lights,
The steam-whistle, the solid roll of the train of approaching cars,
The slow march play'd at the head of the association marching two and
    two,
(They go to guard some corpse, the flag-tops are draped with black
    muslin.)   595

I hear the violoncello ('tis the young man's heart's complaint,)
I hear the key'd cornet, it glides quickly in through my ears,
It shakes mad-sweet pangs through my belly and breast.

I hear the chorus, it is a grand opera,
Ah this indeed is music—this suits me.   600

A tenor large and fresh as the creation fills me,
The orbic flex of his mouth is pouring and filling me full.

4. Fullness.

I hear the train'd soprano (what work with hers is this?)
The orchestra whirls me wider than Uranus[5] flies,
It wrenches such ardors from me I did not know I possess'd them,   605
It sails me, I dab with bare feet, they are lick'd by the indolent waves,
I am cut by bitter and angry hail, I lose my breath,
Steep'd amid honey'd morphine, my windpipe throttled in fakes[6] of death,
At length let up again to feel the puzzle of puzzles,
And that we call Being.   610

27

To be in any form, what is that?
(Round and round we go, all of us, and ever come back thither,)
If nothing lay more develop'd the quahaug[7] in its callous shell were
     enough.

Mine is no callous shell,
I have instant conductors all over me whether I pass or stop,   615
They seize every object and lead it harmlessly through me.

I merely stir, press, feel with my fingers, and am happy,
To touch my person to some one else's is about as much as I can stand.

28

Is this then a touch? quivering me to a new identity,
Flames and ether making a rush for my veins,   620
Treacherous tip of me reaching and crowding to help them,
My flesh and blood playing out lightning to strike what is hardly different
     from myself,
On all sides prurient provokers stiffening my limbs,
Straining the udder of my heart for its withheld drip,
Behaving licentious toward me, taking no denial,   625
Depriving me of my best as for a purpose,
Unbuttoning my clothes, holding me by the bare waist,
Deluding my confusion with the calm of the sunlight and pasture-fields,
Immodestly sliding the fellow-senses away,
They bribed to swap off with touch and go and graze at the edges of me,   630
No consideration, no regard for my draining strength or my anger,
Fetching the rest of the herd around to enjoy them a while,
Then all uniting to stand on a headland and worry me.

The sentries desert every other part of me,
They have left me helpless to a red marauder,   635
They all come to the headland to witness and assist against me.

I am given up by traitors,
I talk wildly, I have lost my wits, I and nobody else am the greatest traitor,
I went myself first to the headland, my own hands carried me there.

---

5. Seventh planet from the sun, thought at the
time to be the outermost limit of the solar
system.

6. Coils of rope.
7. Edible clam of the Atlantic coast.

You villain touch! what are you doing? my breath is tight in its throat,   640
Unclench your floodgates, you are too much for me.

29

Blind loving wrestling touch, sheath'd hooded sharp-tooth'd touch!
Did it make you ache so, leaving me?

Parting track'd by arriving, perpetual payment of perpetual loan,
Rich showering rain, and recompense richer afterward.   645

Sprouts take and accumulate, stand by the curb prolific and vital,
Landscapes projected masculine, full-sized and golden.

30

All truths wait in all things,
They neither hasten their own delivery nor resist it,
They do not need the obstetric forceps of the surgeon,   650
The insignificant is as big to me as any,
(What is less or more than a touch?)

Logic and sermons never convince,
The damp of the night drives deeper into my soul.

(Only what proves itself to every man and woman is so,   655
Only what nobody denies is so.)

A minute and a drop of me settle my brain,
I believe the soggy clods shall become lovers and lamps,
And a compend[8] of compends is the meat of a man or woman,
And a summit and flower there is the feeling they have for each other,   660
And they are to branch boundlessly out of that lesson until it becomes
    omnific,[9]
And until one and all shall delight us, and we them.

31

I believe a leaf of grass is no less than the journey-work of the stars,
And the pismire[1] is equally perfect, and a grain of sand, and the egg of
    the wren,
And the tree-toad is a chief-d'œuvre for the highest,   665
And the running blackberry would adorn the parlors of heaven,
And the narrowest hinge in my hand puts to scorn all machinery,
And the cow crunching with depress'd head surpasses any statue,
And a mouse is miracle enough to stagger sextillions of infidels.

---

8. I.e., a compendium, where something is
reduced to a short, essential summary.

9. All-encompassing.
1. Ant.

I find I incorporate gneiss,[2] coal, long-threaded moss, fruits, grains,
    esculent roots,   670
And am stucco'd with quadrupeds and birds all over,
And have distanced what is behind me for good reasons,
But call any thing back again when I desire it.
In vain the speeding or shyness,
In vain the plutonic rocks[3] send their old heat against my approach,   675
In vain the mastodon retreats beneath its own powder'd bones,
In vain objects stand leagues off and assume manifold shapes,
In vain the ocean settling in hollows and the great monsters lying low,
In vain the buzzard houses herself with the sky,
In vain the snake slides through the creepers and logs,   680
In vain the elk takes to the inner passes of the woods,
In vain the razor-bill'd auk sails far north to Labrador,
I follow quickly, I ascend to the nest in the fissure of the cliff.

32

I think I could turn and live with animals, they are so placid and
    self-contain'd,
I stand and look at them long and long.   685

They do not sweat and whine about their condition,
They do not lie awake in the dark and weep for their sins,
They do not make me sick discussing their duty to God,
Not one is dissatisfied, not one is demented with the mania of owning
    things,
Not one kneels to another, nor to his kind that lived thousands of
    years ago,   690
Not one is respectable or unhappy over the whole earth.

So they show their relations to me and I accept them,
They bring me tokens of myself, they evince them plainly in their
    possession.

I wonder where they get those tokens,
Did I pass that way huge times ago and negligently drop them?   695

Myself moving forward then and now and forever,
Gathering and showing more always and with velocity,
Infinite and omnigenous,[4] and the like of these among them,
Not too exclusive toward the reachers of my remembrancers,
Picking out here one that I love, and now go with him on brotherly
    terms.   700

A gigantic beauty of a stallion, fresh and responsive to my caresses,
Head high in the forehead, wide between the ears,
Limbs glossy and supple, tail dusting the ground,
Eyes full of sparkling wickedness, ears finely cut, flexibly moving.

---

2. Metamorphic rock in which minerals are arranged in layers.
3. Rock of igneus (fire-created) or magmatic (mol-ten) origin; from Pluto, ruler of infernal regions.
4. Belonging to every form of life.

His nostrils dilate as my heels embrace him,   705
His well-built limbs tremble with pleasure as we race around and return.

I but use you a minute, then I resign you, stallion,
Why do I need your paces when I myself out-gallop them?
Even as I stand or sit passing faster than you.

33

Space and Time! now I see it is true, what I guess'd at,   710
What I guess'd when I loaf'd on the grass,
What I guess'd while I lay alone in my bed,
And again as I walk'd the beach under the paling stars of the morning.

My ties and ballasts leave me, my elbows rest in sea-gaps,[5]
I skirt sierras, my palms cover continents,   715
I am afoot with my vision.

By the city's quadrangular houses—in log huts, camping with lumbermen,
Along the ruts of the turnpike, along the dry gulch and rivulet bed,
Weeding my onion-patch or hoeing rows of carrots and parsnips, crossing
    savannas,[6] trailing in forests,
Prospecting, gold-digging, girdling the trees of a new purchase,   720
Scorch'd ankle-deep by the hot sand, hauling my boat down the shallow
    river,
Where the panther walks to and fro on a limb overhead, where the buck
    turns furiously at the hunter,
Where the rattlesnake suns his flabby length on a rock, where the otter is
    feeding on fish,
Where the alligator in his tough pimples sleeps by the bayou,
Where the black bear is searching for roots or honey, where the beaver
    pats the mud with his paddle-shaped tail;   725
Over the growing sugar, over the yellow-flower'd cotton plant, over the rice
    in its low moist field,
Over the sharp-peak'd farm house, with its scallop'd scum and slender
    shoots from the gutters,[7]

Over the western persimmon, over the long-leav'd corn, over the delicate
    blue-flower'd flax,
Over the white and brown buckwheat, a hummer and buzzer there with
    the rest,
Over the dusky green of the rye as it ripples and shades in the breeze;   730
Scaling mountains, pulling myself cautiously up, holding on by low
    scragged limbs,
Walking the path worn in the grass and beat through the leaves of the
    brush,
Where the quail is whistling betwixt the woods and the wheat-lot,
Where the bat flies in the Seventh-month eve, where the great gold-bug[8]
    drops through the dark,

---

5. Estuaries or bays.
6. Grasslands.
7. Plants growing from soil lodged in house gutters and drain pipes. "Scallop'd scum": rain-
washed and sometimes weedy sediment on the
roofs of old farmhouses.
8. Beetle.

Where the brook puts out of the roots of the old tree and flows to the
    meadow,   735
Where cattle stand and shake away flies with the tremulous shuddering
    of their hides,
Where the cheese-cloth hangs in the kitchen, where andirons straddle the
    hearth-slab, where cobwebs fall in festoons from the rafters;
Where trip-hammers crash, where the press is whirling its cylinders,
Wherever the human heart beats with terrible throes under its ribs,
Where the pear-shaped balloon is floating aloft, (floating in it myself and
    looking composedly down,)   740
Where the life-car[9] is drawn on the slip-noose, where the heat hatches
    pale-green eggs in the dented sand,
Where the she-whale swims with her calf and never forsakes it,
Where the steam-ship trails hind-ways its long pennant of smoke,
Where the fin of the shark cuts like a black chip out of the water,
Where the half-burn'd brig is riding on unknown currents,   745
Where shells grow to her slimy deck, where the dead are corrupting below;
Where the dense-star'd flag is borne at the head of the regiments,
Approaching Manhattan up by the long-stretching island,
Under Niagara, the cataract falling like a veil over my countenance,
Upon a door-step, upon the horse-block of hard wood outside,   750
Upon the race-course, or enjoying picnics or jigs or a good game of
    baseball,
At he-festivals, with blackguard gibes, ironical license, bull-dances,[1]
    drinking, laughter,
At the cider-mill tasting the sweets of the brown mash, sucking the juice
    through a straw,
At apple-peelings wanting kisses for all the red fruit I find,
At musters, beach-parties, friendly bees,[2] huskings, house-raisings;   755
Where the mocking-bird sounds his delicious gurgles, cackles, screams,
    weeps,
Where the hay-rick[3] stands in the barn-yard, where the dry-stalks are
    scatter'd, where the brood-cow waits in the hovel,
Where the bull advances to do his masculine work, where the stud to the
    mare, where the cock is treading the hen,
Where the heifers browse, where geese nip their food with short jerks,
Where sun-down shadows lengthen over the limitless and lonesome
    prairie,   760
Where herds of buffalo make a crawling spread of the square miles far
    and near,
Where the humming-bird shimmers, where the neck of the long-lived
    swan is curving and winding,
Where the laughing-gull scoots by the shore, where she laughs her
    near-human laugh,
Where bee-hives range on a gray bench in the garden half hid by the high
    weeds,
Where band-neck'd partridges roost in a ring on the ground with their
    heads out,   765

9. Watertight compartment for lowering passengers from a ship when emergency evacuation is
required.
1. Rowdy backwoods dances for which men took
male partners.

2. Gatherings where people work while socializ-
ing with their neighbors. "Musters": assemblages
of people, particularly gatherings of military
troops for drill.
3. Hayrack, from which livestock eat hay.

Where burial coaches enter the arch'd gates of a cemetery,
Where winter wolves bark amid wastes of snow and icicled trees,
Where the yellow-crown'd heron comes to the edge of the marsh at night
    and feeds upon small crabs,
Where the splash of swimmers and divers cools the warm noon,
Where the katy-did works her chromatic[4] reed on the walnut-tree over
    the well,   770
Through patches of citrons[5] and cucumbers with silver-wired leaves,
Through the salt-lick or orange glade, or under conical firs,
Through the gymnasium, through the curtain'd saloon, through the office
    or public hall;
Pleas'd with the native and pleas'd with the foreign, pleas'd with the new
    and old,
Pleas'd with the homely woman as well as the handsome,   775
Pleas'd with the quakeress as she puts off her bonnet and talks melodiously,
Pleas'd with the tune of the choir of the whitewash'd church,
Pleas'd with the earnest words of the sweating Methodist preacher,
    impress'd seriously at the camp-meeting;
Looking in at the shop-windows of Broadway the whole forenoon, flatting
    the flesh of my nose on the thick plate glass,
Wandering the same afternoon with my face turn'd up to the clouds, or
    down a lane or along the beach,   780
My right and left arms round the sides of two friends, and I in the middle;
Coming home with the silent and dark-cheek'd bush-boy, (behind me he
    rides at the drape of the day,)
Far from the settlements studying the print of animals' feet, or the
    moccasin print,
By the cot in the hospital reaching lemonade to a feverish patient,
Nigh the coffin'd corpse when all is still, examining with a candle;   785
Voyaging to every port to dicker and adventure,
Hurrying with the modern crowd as eager and fickle as any,
Hot toward one I hate, ready in my madness to knife him,
Solitary at midnight in my back yard, my thoughts gone from me a long
    while,
Walking the old hills of Judæa with the beautiful gentle God by my side, 790
Speeding through space, speeding through heaven and the stars,
Speeding amid the seven satellites[6] and the broad ring, and the diameter
    of eighty thousand miles,
Speeding with tail'd meteors, throwing fire-balls like the rest,
Carrying the crescent child that carries its own full mother in its belly,[7]
Storming, enjoying, planning, loving, cautioning,   795
Backing and filling, appearing and disappearing,
I tread day and night such roads.

I visit the orchards of spheres and look at the product,
And look at quintillions ripen'd and look at quintillions green.

I fly those flights of a fluid and swallowing soul,   800
My course runs below the soundings of plummets.

4. Full tonal range.
5. Here, small, hard-skinned watermelons.
6. The then known moons of Saturn.

7. A crescent moon, with the full moon also palely visible.

I help myself to material and immaterial,
No guard can shut me off, no law prevent me.

I anchor my ship for a little while only,
My messengers continually cruise away or bring their returns to me.   805

I go hunting polar furs and the seal, leaping chasms with a pike-pointed
  staff, clinging to topples of brittle and blue.[8]

I ascend to the foretruck,[9]
I take my place late at night in the crow's-nest,
We sail the arctic sea, it is plenty light enough,
Through the clear atmosphere I stretch around on the wonderful beauty, 810
The enormous masses of ice pass me and I pass them, the scenery is
  plain in all directions,
The white-topt mountains show in the distance, I fling out my fancies
  toward them,
We are approaching some great battle-field in which we are soon to be
  engaged,
We pass the colossal outposts of the encampment, we pass with still feet
  and caution,
Or we are entering by the suburbs some vast and ruin'd city,   815
The blocks and fallen architecture more than all the living cities of the
  globe.

I am a free companion, I bivouac by invading watchfires,
I turn the bridegroom out of bed and stay with the bride myself,
I tighten her all night to my thighs and lips.

My voice is the wife's voice, the screech by the rail of the stairs,   820
They fetch my man's body up dripping and drown'd.

I understand the large hearts of heroes,
The courage of present times and all times,
How the skipper saw the crowded and rudderless wreck of the steam-ship,
  and Death chasing it up and down the storm,
How he knuckled tight and gave not back an inch, and was faithful of days
  and faithful of nights,   825
And chalk'd in large letters on a board, *Be of good cheer, we will not desert
  you;*
How he follow'd with them and tack'd with them three days and would not
  give it up,
How he saved the drifting company at last,
How the lank loose-gown'd women look'd when boated from the side of
  their prepared graves,
How the silent old-faced infants and the lifted sick, and the sharp-lipp'd
  unshaved men;   830
All this I swallow, it tastes good, I like it well, it becomes mine,
I am the man, I suffer'd, I was there.[1]

8. Toppled pieces of ice.
9. Highest platform of a foremast.
1. Whitman describes the wreck of the *San Francisco*, which sailed from New York on December
22, 1853, bound for South America, and was

caught in a storm a day later. The ship drifted
helplessly until early January. Over 150 died in
the disaster, which was reported widely in the
New York papers.

The disdain and calmness of martyrs,
The mother of old, condemn'd for a witch, burnt with dry wood, her
    children gazing on,
The hounded slave that flags in the race, leans by the fence, blowing,
    cover'd with sweat,   835
The twinges that sting like needles his legs and neck, the murderous
    buckshot and the bullets,
All these I feel or am.

I am the hounded slave, I wince at the bite of the dogs,
Hell and despair are upon me, crack and again crack the marksmen,
I clutch the rails of the fence, my gore dribs, thinn'd with the ooze of
    my skin,[2]   840
I fall on the weeds and stones,
The riders spur their unwilling horses, haul close,
Taunt my dizzy ears and beat me violently over the head with
    whip-stocks.

Agonies are one of my changes of garments,
I do not ask the wounded person how he feels, I myself become the
    wounded person,   845
My hurts turn livid upon me as I lean on a cane and observe.

I am the mash'd fireman with breast-bone broken,
Tumbling walls buried me in their debris,
Heat and smoke I inspired, I heard the yelling shouts of my comrades,
I heard the distant click of their picks and shovels,   850
They have clear'd the beams away, they tenderly lift me forth.

I lie in the night air in my red shirt, the pervading hush is for my sake,
Painless after all I lie exhausted but not so unhappy,
White and beautiful are the faces around me, the heads are bared of
    their fire-caps,
The kneeling crowd fades with the light of the torches.   855

Distant and dead resuscitate,
They show as the dial or move as the hands of me, I am the clock myself.

I am an old artillerist, I tell of my fort's bombardment,
I am there again.

Again the long roll of the drummers,   860
Again the attacking cannon, mortars,
Again to my listening ears the cannon responsive.

I take part, I see and hear the whole,
The cries, curses, roar, the plaudits of well-aim'd shots,
The ambulanza slowly passing trailing its red drip,   865
Workmen searching after damages, making indispensable repairs,
The fall of grenades through the rent roof, the fan-shaped explosion,
The whizz of limbs, heads, stone, wood, iron, high in the air.

2. Dribbles down, diluted with sweat.

Again gurgles the mouth of my dying general, he furiously waves with
    his hand,
He gasps through the clot *Mind not me—mind—the entrenchments.*   870

34

Now I tell what I knew in Texas in my early youth,
(I tell not the fall of Alamo,[3]
Not one escaped to tell the fall of Alamo,
The hundred and fifty are dumb yet at Alamo,)
'Tis the tale of the murder in cold blood of four hundred and twelve
    young men.   875

Retreating they had form'd in a hollow square with their baggage for
    breastworks,
Nine hundred lives out of the surrounding enemy's, nine times their
    number, was the price they took in advance,
Their colonel was wounded and their ammunition gone,
They treated for an honorable capitulation, receiv'd writing and seal,
    gave up their arms and march'd back prisoners of war.

They were the glory of the race of rangers,   880
Matchless with horse, rifle, song, supper, courtship,
Large, turbulent, generous, handsome, proud, and affectionate,
Bearded, sunburnt, drest in the free costume of hunters,
Not a single one over thirty years of age.

The second First-day morning they were brought out in squads and
    massacred, it was beautiful early summer,   885
The work commenced about five o'clock and was over by eight.

None obey'd the command to kneel,
Some made a mad and helpless rush, some stood stark and straight,
A few fell at once, shot in the temple or heart, the living and dead lay
    together,
The maim'd and mangled dug in the dirt, the new-comers saw them
    there,   890
Some half-kill'd attempted to crawl away,
These were despatch'd with bayonets or batter'd with the blunts of
    muskets,
A youth not seventeen years old seiz'd his assassin till two more came to
    release him,
The three were all torn and cover'd with the boy's blood.

At eleven o'clock began the burning of the bodies;   895
That is the tale of the murder of the four hundred and twelve young men.

---

3. During the Texas Revolution of 1835–36, emigrants from the United States to Texas—at the time part of Mexico—attempted to make Texas into a separate republic. Among battles fought in what is now the state of Texas were the battle of the Alamo—the Alamo fell on March 6, 1836, after a siege by Mexican forces beginning on February 23, when around two hundred men were killed—and the battle of Goliad, when some four hundred secessionist troops were killed after surrendering to the Mexicans on March 19 of the same year.

35

Would you hear of an old-time sea-fight?[4]
Would you learn who won by the light of the moon and stars?
List to the yarn, as my grandmother's father the sailor told it to me.

Our foe was no skulk in his ship I tell you, (said he,)   900
His was the surly English pluck, and there is no tougher or truer, and
    never was, and never will be;
Along the lower'd eve he came horribly raking us.

We closed with him, the yards entangled, the cannon touch'd,
My captain lash'd fast with his own hands.

We had receiv'd some eighteen pound shots under the water,   905
On our lower-gun-deck two large pieces had burst at the first fire, killing
    all around and blowing up overhead.

Fighting at sun-down, fighting at dark,
Ten o'clock at night, the full moon well up, our leaks on the gain, and five
    feet of water reported,
The master-at-arms loosing the prisoners confined in the after-hold to give
    them a chance for themselves.

The transit to and from the magazine[5] is now stopt by the sentinels,   910
They see so many strange faces they do not know whom to trust.

Our frigate takes fire,
The other asks if we demand quarter?
If our colors are struck and the fighting done?

Now I laugh content, for I hear the voice of my little captain,   915
We have not struck, he composedly cries, *we have just begun our part of
    the fighting.*

Only three guns are in use,
One is directed by the captain himself against the enemy's mainmast,
Two well serv'd with grape and canister[6] silence his musketry and clear
    his decks.

The tops[7] alone second the fire of this little battery, especially the
    main-top,   920
They hold out bravely during the whole of the action.

Not a moment's cease,
The leaks gain fast on the pumps, the fire eats toward the
    powder-magazine.

4. The famous Revolutionary War sea battle on September 23, 1779, between the American *Bon-Homme Richard,* commanded by John Paul Jones (1747–1792), and the British *Serapis* off the coast of northern England. When Jones was asked to surrender, he famously declared, "I have not yet begun to fight." He eventually defeated the *Serapis.*

5. Storeroom for ammunition.
6. Grapeshot ("grape"), clusters of small iron balls, was packed inside a metal cylinder ("canister") and used to charge a cannon.
7. Platforms enclosing the heads of each mast; here, the sailors manning the tops.

One of the pumps has been shot away, it is generally thought we are
    sinking.

Serene stands the little captain, 925
He is not hurried, his voice is neither high nor low,
His eyes give more light to us than our battle-lanterns.

Toward twelve there in the beams of the moon they surrender to us.

36

Stretch'd and still lies the midnight,
Two great hulls motionless on the breast of the darkness, 930
Our vessel riddled and slowly sinking, preparations to pass to the one
    we have conquer'd,
The captain on the quarter-deck coldly giving his orders through a
    countenance white as a sheet,
Near by the corpse of the child that serv'd in the cabin,
The dead face of an old salt with long white hair and carefully curl'd
    whiskers,
The flames spite of all that can be done flickering aloft and below, 935
The husky voices of the two or three officers yet fit for duty,
Formless stacks of bodies and bodies by themselves, dabs of flesh upon
    the masts and spars,
Cut of cordage, dangle of rigging, slight shock of the soothe of waves,
Black and impassive guns, litter of powder-parcels, strong scent,
A few large stars overhead, silent and mournful shining, 940
Delicate sniffs of sea-breeze, smells of sedgy grass and fields by the shore,
    death-messages given in charge to survivors,
The hiss of the surgeon's knife, the gnawing teeth of his saw,
Wheeze, cluck, swash of falling blood, short wild scream, and long, dull,
    tapering groan,
These so, these irretrievable.

37

You laggards there on guard! look to your arms! 945
In at the conquer'd doors they crowd! I am possess'd!
Embody all presences outlaw'd or suffering,
See myself in prison shaped like another man,
And feel the dull unintermitted pain.

For me the keepers of convicts shoulder their carbines and keep
    watch,
It is I let out in the morning and barr'd at night. 950

Not a mutineer walks handcuff'd to jail but I am handcuff'd to him and
    walk by his side,
(I am less the jolly one there, and more the silent one with sweat on my
    twitching lips.)

Not a youngster is taken for larceny but I go up too, and am tried and
    sentenced.

Not a cholera patient lies at the last gasp but I also lie at the last
    gasp,   955
My face is ash-color'd, my sinews gnarl, away from me people retreat.

Askers embody themselves in me and I am embodied in them,
I project my hat, sit shame-faced, and beg.

38

Enough! enough! enough!
Somehow I have been stunn'd. Stand back!   960
Give me a little time beyond my cuff'd head, slumbers, dreams, gaping,
I discover myself on the verge of a usual mistake.

That I could forget the mockers and insults!
That I could forget the trickling tears and the blows of the bludgeons
    and hammers!
That I could look with a separate look on my own crucifixion and bloody
    crowning.   965

I remember now,
I resume the overstaid fraction,
The grave of rock multiplies what has been confided to it, or to any graves,
Corpses rise, gashes heal, fastenings roll from me.

I troop forth replenish'd with supreme power, one of an average unending
    procession,   970
Inland and sea-coast we go, and pass all boundary lines,
Our swift ordinances on their way over the whole earth,
The blossoms we wear in our hats the growth of thousands of years.

Eleves,[8] I salute you! come forward!
Continue your annotations, continue your questionings.   975

39

The friendly and flowing savage, who is he?
Is he waiting for civilization, or past it and mastering it?

Is he some Southwesterner rais'd out-doors? is he Kanadian?
Is he from the Mississippi country? Iowa, Oregon, California?
The mountains? prairie-life, bush-life? or sailor from the sea?   980

Wherever he goes men and women accept and desire him,
They desire he should like them, touch them, speak to them, stay with
    them.

Behavior lawless as snow-flakes, words simple as grass, uncomb'd head,
    laughter, and naiveté,
Slow-stepping feet, common features, common modes and emanations,
They descend in new forms from the tips of his fingers,   985

8. Students (French).

They are wafted with the odor of his body or breath, they fly out of the
    glance of his eyes.

40

Flaunt of the sunshine I need not your bask—lie over!
You light surfaces only, I force surfaces and depths also.

Earth! you seem to look for something at my hands,
Say, old top-knot,[9] what do you want?   990

Man or woman, I might tell how I like you, but cannot,
And might tell what it is in me and what it is in you, but cannot,
And might tell that pining I have, that pulse of my nights and days.

Behold, I do not give lectures or a little charity,
When I give I give myself.   995

You there, impotent, loose in the knees,
Open your scarf'd chops till I blow grit[1] within you,
Spread your palms and lift the flaps of your pockets,
I am not to be denied, I compel, I have stores plenty and to spare,
And any thing I have I bestow.   1000

I do not ask who you are, that is not important to me,
You can do nothing and be nothing but what I will infold you.

To cotton-field drudge or cleaner of privies I lean,
On his right cheek I put the family kiss,
And in my soul I swear I never will deny him.   1005

On women fit for conception I start bigger and nimbler babes,
(This day I am jetting the stuff of far more arrogant republics.)

To any one dying, thither I speed and twist the knob of the door,
Turn the bed-clothes toward the foot of the bed,
Let the physician and the priest go home.   1010

I seize the descending man and raise him with resistless will,
O despairer, here is my neck,
By God, you shall not go down! hang your whole weight upon me.

I dilate you with tremendous breath, I buoy you up,
Every room of the house do I fill with an arm'd force,   1015
Lovers of me, bafflers of graves.

Sleep—I and they keep guard all night,
Not doubt, not decease shall dare to lay finger upon you,

---

9. An epithet common in frontier humor, deriving from the fact that some Native Americans gathered their hair into tufts at the top of the head. The poet seems to be addressing an older Indian, perhaps picking up on the reference to "the friendly and flowing savage" of the previous stanza.

1. Courage. "Scarf'd chops": lined, worn-down jaw or face.

I have embraced you, and henceforth possess you to myself,
And when you rise in the morning you will find what I tell you is so.   1020

41

I am he bringing help for the sick as they pant on their backs,
And for strong upright men I bring yet more needed help.

I heard what was said of the universe,
Heard it and heard it of several thousand years;
It is middling well as far as it goes—but is that all?   1025

Magnifying and applying come I,
Outbidding at the start the old cautious hucksters,
Taking myself the exact dimensions of Jehovah,[2]
Lithographing Kronos, Zeus his son, and Hercules[3] his grandson,
Buying drafts of Osiris, Isis, Belus, Brahma, Buddha,[4]   1030
In my portfolio placing Manito loose, Allah[5] on a leaf, the crucifix
     engraved,
With Odin and the hideous-faced Mexitli[6] and every idol and image,
Taking them all for what they are worth and not a cent more,
Admitting they were alive and did the work of their days,
(They bore mites as for unfledg'd birds who have now to rise and fly and
     sing for themselves,)   1035
Accepting the rough deific sketches to fill out better in myself, bestowing
     them freely on each man and woman I see,
Discovering as much or more in a framer framing a house,
Putting higher claims for him there with his roll'd-up sleeves driving the
     mallet and chisel,
Not objecting to special revelations, considering a curl of smoke or a hair
     on the back of my hand just as curious as any revelation,
Lads ahold of fire-engines and hook-and-ladder ropes no less to me than
     the gods of the antique wars,   1040
Minding their voices peal through the crash of destruction,
Their brawny limbs passing safe over charr'd laths, their white foreheads
     whole and unhurt out of the flames;
By the mechanic's wife with her babe at her nipple interceding for every
     person born,
Three scythes at harvest whizzing in a row from three lusty angels with
     shirts bagg'd out at their waists,
The snag-tooth'd hostler with red hair redeeming sins past and to come,   1045
Selling all he possesses, traveling on foot to fee lawyers for his brother
     and sit by him while he is tried for forgery;
What was strewn in the amplest strewing the square rod about me, and
     not filling the square rod then,

---

2. God of the Jews and Christians.
3. Son of Zeus and the mortal Alcmene, won immortality by performing twelve supposedly impossible feats. Kronos (or Cronus), in Greek mythology, was the Titan who ruled the universe until dethroned by Zeus, his son, the chief of the Olympian gods.
4. The Indian philosopher Siddhartha Gautama (known as the "Buddha"), founder of Buddhism. Osiris was the Egyptian god who annually died and was reborn, symbolizing the fertility of nature. Isis was the Egyptian goddess of fertility and the sister and wife of Osiris. Belus was a legendary god-king of Assyria. Brahma, in Hinduism, is the divine reality in the role of creator.
5. Arabic word for God, the supreme being in Islam. Manito was the nature god of the Algonquian Indians.
6. An Aztec war god. Odin was the chief Norse god.

The bull and the bug never worshipp'd half enough,[7]
Dung and dirt more admirable than was dream'd,
The supernatural of no account, myself waiting my time to be one of the
    supremes,   1050
The day getting ready for me when I shall do as much good as the best,
    and be as prodigious;
By my life-lumps![8] becoming already a creator,
Putting myself here and now to the ambush'd womb of the shadows.

42

A call in the midst of the crowd,
My own voice, orotund sweeping and final.   1055

Come my children,
Come my boys and girls, my women, household and intimates,
Now the performer launches his nerve, he has pass'd his prelude on the
    reeds within.

Easily written loose-finger'd chords—I feel the thrum of your climax and
    close.

My head slues round on my neck,   1060
Music rolls, but not from the organ,
Folks are around me, but they are no household of mine.

Ever the hard unsunk ground,
Ever the eaters and drinkers, ever the upward and downward sun, ever
    the air and the ceaseless tides,
Ever myself and my neighbors, refreshing, wicked, real,   1065
Ever the old inexplicable query, ever that thorn'd thumb, that breath of
    itches and thirsts,
Ever the vexer's *hoot! hoot!* till we find where the sly one hides and bring
    him forth,
Ever love, ever the sobbing liquid of life,
Ever the bandage under the chin, ever the trestles[9] of death.

Here and there with dimes on the eyes[1] walking,   1070
To feed the greed of the belly the brains liberally spooning,
Tickets buying, taking, selling, but in to the feast never once going,
Many sweating, ploughing, thrashing, and then the chaff for payment
    receiving,
A few idly owning, and they the wheat continually claiming.

This is the city and I am one of the citizens,   1075
Whatever interests the rest interests me, politics, wars, markets,
    newspapers, schools,

---

7. As Whitman implies, the bull and the bug had been worshiped in earlier religions, the bull in several, the scarab beetle as an Egyptian symbol of the soul.
8. Testicles.

9. Sawhorses or similar supports holding up a coffin.
1. Coins were placed on eyelids to hold them closed until burial.

The mayor and councils, banks, tariffs, steamships, factories, stocks,
    stores, real estate and personal estate.

The little plentiful manikins skipping around in collars and tail'd coats,
I am aware who they are, (they are positively not worms or fleas,)
I acknowledge the duplicates of myself, the weakest and shallowest is
    deathless with me,   1080
What I do and say the same waits for them,
Every thought that flounders in me the same flounders in them.

I know perfectly well my own egotism,
Know my omnivorous lines and must not write any less,
And would fetch you whoever you are flush with myself.   1085
Not words of routine this song of mine,
But abruptly to question, to leap beyond yet nearer bring;
This printed and bound book—but the printer and the printing-office boy?
The well-taken photographs—but your wife or friend close and solid in
    your arms?
The black ship mail'd with iron, her mighty guns in her turrets—but the
    pluck of the captain and engineers?   1090
In the houses the dishes and fare and furniture—but the host and
    hostess, and the look out of their eyes?
The sky up there—yet here or next door, or across the way?
The saints and sages in history—but you yourself?
Sermons, creeds, theology—but the fathomless human brain,
And what is reason? and what is love? and what is life?   1095

43

I do not despise you priests, all time, the world over,
My faith is the greatest of faiths and the least of faiths,
Enclosing worship ancient and modern and all between ancient and
    modern,
Believing I shall come again upon the earth after five thousand years,
Waiting responses from oracles, honoring the gods, saluting the sun,   1100
Making a fetich of the first rock or stump, powowing with sticks in the
    circle of obis.[2]
Helping the llama or brahmin[3] as he trims the lamps of the idols,
Dancing yet through the streets in a phallic procession, rapt and austere
    in the woods a gymnosophist,[4]
Drinking mead from the skull-cup, to Shastas and Vedas admirant,
    minding the Koran,[5]
Walking the teokallis,[6] spotted with gore from the stone and knife,
    beating the serpent-skin drum,   1105
Accepting the Gospels,[7] accepting him that was crucified, knowing
    assuredly that he is divine,

2. Magical charms, such as shells, used in African and West Indian religious practices. "Fetich": i.e., fetish; object of worship.
3. Here, also a Buddhist priest. "Llama": i.e., lama; a Buddhist monk of Tibet or Mongolia.
4. Members of an ancient Hindu ascetic sect.
5. The other worshipers include ancient warriors drinking mead (an alcoholic beverage made of fermented honey) from the skulls of defeated enemies; admiring or wondering readers of the sastras (or shastras or shasters, books of Hindu law) or of the Vedas (the oldest sacred writings of Hinduism); and those attentive to the Koran (the sacred book of Islam, containing Allah's revelations to Muhammad).
6. An ancient Central American temple built on a pyramidal mound.
7. Of the New Testament of the Bible.

To the mass kneeling or the puritan's prayer rising, or sitting patiently
    in a pew,
Ranting and frothing in my insane crisis, or waiting dead-like till my spirit
    arouses me,
Looking forth on pavement and land, or outside of pavement and land,
Belonging to the winders of the circuit of circuits.   1110

One of that centripetal and centrifugal gang I turn and talk like a man
    leaving charges before a journey.

Down-hearted doubters dull and excluded,
Frivolous, sullen, moping, angry, affected, dishearten'd, atheistical,
I know every one of you, I know the sea of torment, doubt, despair and
    unbelief.

How the flukes[8] splash!   1115
How they contort rapid as lightning, with spasms and spouts of blood!

Be at peace bloody flukes of doubters and sullen mopers,
I take my place among you as much as among any,
The past is the push of you, me, all, precisely the same,
And what is yet untried and afterward is for you, me, all, precisely the
    same.   1120

I do not know what is untried and afterward,
But I know it will in its turn prove sufficient, and cannot fail.

Each who passes is consider'd, each who stops is consider'd, not a single
    one can it fail.

It cannot fail the young man who died and was buried,
Nor the young woman who died and was put by his side,   1125
Nor the little child that peep'd in at the door, and then drew back and
    was never seen again,
Nor the old man who has lived without purpose, and feels it with
    bitterness worse than gall,
Nor him in the poor house tubercled by rum and the bad disorder,[9]

Nor the numberless slaughter'd and wreck'd, nor the brutish koboo[1]
    call'd the ordure of humanity,
Nor the sacs merely floating with open mouths for food to slip in,   1130
Nor any thing in the earth, or down in the oldest graves of the earth,
Nor any thing in the myriads of spheres, nor the myriads of myriads
    that inhabit them,
Nor the present, nor the least wisp that is known.

44

It is time to explain myself—let us stand up.

What is known I strip away,   1135
I launch all men and women forward with me into the Unknown.

---

8. The flat parts on either side of a whale's tail;   9. Syphilis.
here used figuratively.   1. Native of Sumatra.

The clock indicates the moment—but what does eternity indicate?

We have thus far exhausted trillions of winters and summers,
There are trillions ahead, and trillions ahead of them.

Births have brought us richness and variety,   1140
And other births will bring us richness and variety.

I do not call one greater and one smaller,
That which fills its period and place is equal to any.

Were mankind murderous or jealous upon you, my brother,
        my sister?
I am sorry for you, they are not murderous or jealous upon me,   1145
All has been gentle with me, I keep no account with lamentation,
(What have I to do with lamentation?)

I am an acme of things accomplish'd, and I an encloser of things to be.

My feet strike an apex of the apices[2] of the stairs,
On every step bunches of ages, and larger bunches between the steps,   1150
All below duly travel'd, and still I mount and mount.

Rise after rise bow the phantoms behind me,
Afar down I see the huge first Nothing, I know I was even there,
I waited unseen and always, and slept through the lethargic mist,
And took my time, and took no hurt from the fetid carbon.[3]   1155

Long I was hugg'd close—long and long.

Immense have been the preparations for me,
Faithful and friendly the arms that have help'd me.

Cycles[4] ferried my cradle, rowing and rowing like cheerful boatmen,
For room to me stars kept aside in their own rings,   1160
They sent influences to look after what was to hold me.

Before I was born out of my mother generations guided me,
My embryo has never been torpid, nothing could overlay it.

For it the nebula cohered to an orb,
The long slow strata piled to rest it on,   1165
Vast vegetables gave it sustenance,
Monstrous sauroids[5] transported it in their mouths and deposited it with
        care.

All forces have been steadily employ'd to complete and delight me,
Now on this spot I stand with my robust soul.

2. The highest points (variant plural of *apex*).   4. Centuries.
3. The "lethargic mist" (line 1154) and "fetid   5. Prehistoric large reptiles or dinosaurs, thought
carbon" suggest a time before the appearance of   to have carried their eggs in their mouths.
human beings on earth.

45

O span of youth! ever-push'd elasticity!   1170
O manhood, balanced, florid and full.

My lovers suffocate me,
Crowding my lips, thick in the pores of my skin,
Jostling me through streets and public halls, coming naked to me at night,
Crying by day *Ahoy!* from the rocks of the river, swinging and chirping
    over my head,   1175
Calling my name from flower-beds, vines, tangled underbrush,
Lighting on every moment of my life,
Bussing[6] my body with soft balsamic busses,
Noiselessly passing handfuls out of their hearts and giving them to be
    mine.

Old age superbly rising! O welcome, ineffable grace of dying days!   1180

Every condition promulges[7] not only itself, it promulges what grows after
    and out of itself,
And the dark hush promulges as much as any.

I open my scuttle[8] at night and see the far-sprinkled systems,
And all I see multiplied as high as I can cipher edge but the rim of the
    farther systems.

Wider and wider they spread, expanding, always expanding,   1185
Outward and outward and forever outward.

My sun has his sun and round him obediently wheels,
He joins with his partners a group of superior circuit,
And greater sets follow, making specks of the greatest inside them.

There is no stoppage and never can be stoppage,   1190
If I, you, and the worlds, and all beneath or upon their surfaces, were
    this moment reduced back to a pallid float,[9] it would not avail in the
    long run,
We should surely bring up again where we now stand,
And surely go as much farther, and then farther and farther.

A few quadrillions of eras, a few octillions of cubic leagues, do not hazard[1]
    the span or make it impatient,
They are but parts, any thing is but a part.   1195

See ever so far, there is limitless space outside of that,
Count ever so much, there is limitless time around that.

My rendezvous is appointed, it is certain,
The Lord will be there and wait till I come on perfect terms,
The great Camerado, the lover true for whom I pine will be there.   1200

---

6. Kissing.
7. Promulgates, officially announces.
8. Roof hatch.

9. Era before the formation of the solar system.
1. Imperil, make hazardous.

46

I know I have the best of time and space, and was never measured and
    never will be measured.

I tramp a perpetual journey, (come listen all!)
My signs are a rain-proof coat, good shoes, and a staff cut from the woods,
No friend of mine takes his ease in my chair,
I have no chair, no church, no philosophy,   1205
I lead no man to a dinner-table, library, exchange,²
But each man and each woman of you I lead upon a knoll,
My left hand hooking you round the waist,
My right hand pointing to landscapes of continents and the public road.

Not I, not any one else can travel that road for you,   1210
You must travel it for yourself.

It is not far, it is within reach,
Perhaps you have been on it since you were born and did not know,
Perhaps it is everywhere on water and on land.

Shoulder your duds dear son, and I will mine, and let us hasten forth, 1215
Wonderful cities and free nations we shall fetch as we go.

If you tire, give me both burdens, and rest the chuff³ of your hand on
    my hip,
And in due time you shall repay the same service to me,
For after we start we never lie by again.

This day before dawn I ascended a hill and look'd at the crowded
    heaven,   1220
And I said to my spirit *When we become the enfolders of those orbs, and
    the pleasure and knowledge of every thing in them, shall we be fill'd
    and satisfied then?*
And my spirit said *No, we but level that lift to pass and continue beyond.*

You are also asking me questions and I hear you,
I answer that I cannot answer, you must find out for yourself.

Sit a while dear son,   1225
Here are biscuits to eat and here is milk to drink,
But as soon as you sleep and renew yourself in sweet clothes, I kiss you
    with a good-by kiss and open the gate for your egress hence.

Long enough have you dream'd contemptible dreams,
Now I wash the gum from your eyes,
You must habit yourself to the dazzle of the light and of every moment
    of your life.   1230

Long have you timidly waded holding a plank by the shore,
Now I will you to be a bold swimmer,

---

2. Stock exchange.   3. The fleshy part of the palm.

To jump off in the midst of the sea, rise again, nod to me, shout, and
    laughingly dash with your hair.

47

I am the teacher of athletes,
He that by me spreads a wider breast than my own proves the width of
    my own,   1235
He most honors my style who learns under it to destroy the teacher.

The boy I love, the same becomes a man not through derived power, but
    in his own right,
Wicked rather than virtuous out of conformity or fear,
Fond of his sweetheart, relishing well his steak,
Unrequited love or a slight cutting him worse than sharp steel cuts,   1240
First-rate to ride, to fight, to hit the bull's eye, to sail a skiff, to sing a
    song or play on the banjo,
Preferring scars and the beard and faces pitted with small-pox over all
    latherers,
And those well-tann'd to those that keep out of the sun.

I teach straying from me, yet who can stray from me?
I follow you whoever you are from the present hour,   1245
My words itch at your ears till you understand them.

I do not say these things for a dollar or to fill up the time while I wait for
    a boat,
(It is you talking just as much as myself, I act as the tongue of you,
Tied in your mouth, in mine it begins to be loosen'd.)

I swear I will never again mention love or death inside a house,   1250
And I swear I will never translate myself at all, only to him or her who
    privately stays with me in the open air.

If you would understand me go to the heights or water-shore,
The nearest gnat is an explanation, and a drop or motion of waves a key,
The maul, the oar, the hand-saw, second my words.

No shutter'd room or school can commune with me,   1255
But roughs and little children better than they.

The young mechanic is closest to me, he knows me well,
The woodman that takes his axe and jug with him shall take me with him
    all day,
The farm-boy ploughing in the field feels good at the sound of my voice,
In vessels that sail my words sail, I go with fishermen and seamen and
    love them.   1260

The soldier camp'd or upon the march is mine,
On the night ere the pending battle many seek me, and I do not fail
    them,
On that solemn night (it may be their last) those that know me seek me.

My face rubs to the hunter's face when he lies down alone in his blanket,

The driver thinking of me does not mind the jolt of his wagon,   1265
The young mother and old mother comprehend me,
The girl and the wife rest the needle a moment and forget where they are,
They and all would resume what I have told them.

48

I have said that the soul is not more than the body,
And I have said that the body is not more than the soul,   1270
And nothing, not God, is greater to one than one's self is,
And whoever walks a furlong without sympathy walks to his own funeral
    drest in his shroud,
And I or you pocketless of a dime may purchase the pick of the earth,
And to glance with an eye or show a bean in its pod confounds the
    learning of all times,
And there is no trade or employment but the young man following it
    may become a hero,   1275
And there is no object so soft but it makes a hub for the wheel'd
    universe,
And I say to any man or woman, Let your soul stand cool and composed
    before a million universes.

And I say to mankind, Be not curious about God,
For I who am curious about each am not curious about God,
(No array of terms can say how much I am at peace about God and
    about death.)   1280

I hear and behold God in every object, yet understand God not in the least,
Nor do I understand who there can be more wonderful than myself.

Why should I wish to see God better than this day?
I see something of God each hour of the twenty-four, and each moment
    then,
In the faces of men and women I see God, and in my own face in the
    glass,   1285
I find letters from God dropt in the street, and every one is sign'd by
    God's name,
And I leave them where they are, for I know that wheresoe'er I go,
Others will punctually come for ever and ever.

49

And as to you Death, and you bitter hug of mortality, it is idle to try to
    alarm me.

To his work without flinching the accoucheur[4] comes,   1290
I see the elder-hand pressing receiving supporting,
I recline by the sills of the exquisite flexible doors,
And mark the outlet, and mark the relief and escape.

And as to you Corpse I think you are good manure, but that does not
    offend me,

4. Midwife.

I smell the white roses sweet-scented and growing,   1295
I reach to the leafy lips, I reach to the polish'd breasts of melons.

And as to you Life I reckon you are the leavings of many deaths,
(No doubt I have died myself ten thousand times before.)

I hear you whispering there O stars of heaven,
O suns—O grass of graves—O perpetual transfers and promotions,   1300
If you do not say any thing how can I say any thing?
Of the turbid pool that lies in the autumn forest,
Of the moon that descends the steeps of the soughing twilight,
Toss, sparkles of day and dusk—toss on the black stems that decay in
     the muck,
Toss to the moaning gibberish of the dry limbs.   1305

I ascend from the moon, I ascend from the night,
I perceive that the ghastly glimmer is noonday sunbeams reflected,
And debouch[5] to the steady and central from the offspring great or small.

50

There is that in me—I do not know what it is—but I know it is in me.

Wrench'd and sweaty—calm and cool then my body becomes,
     I sleep—I sleep long.   1310

I do not know it—it is without name—it is a word unsaid,
It is not in any dictionary, utterance, symbol.

Something it swings on more than the earth I swing on,
To it the creation is the friend whose embracing awakes me.

Perhaps I might tell more. Outlines! I plead for my brothers and
     sisters.   1315
Do you see O my brothers and sisters?
It is not chaos or death—it is form, union, plan—it is eternal life—it is
     Happiness.

51

The past and present wilt—I have fill'd them, emptied them,
And proceed to fill my next fold of the future.

Listener up there! what have you to confide to me?   1320
Look in my face while I snuff the sidle[6] of evening,
(Talk honestly, no one else hears you, and I stay only a minute longer.)

Do I contradict myself?
Very well then I contradict myself,
(I am large, I contain multitudes.)   1325

5. Pour forth.
6. To snuff out or extinguish a light, here the last glimmers of evening.

I concentrate toward them that are nigh, I wait on the door-slab.

Who has done his day's work? who will soonest be through with his supper?
Who wishes to walk with me?

Will you speak before I am gone? will you prove already too late?

52

The spotted hawk swoops by and accuses me, he complains of my gab
    and my loitering.   1330

I too am not a bit tamed, I too am untranslatable.
I sound my barbaric yawp over the roofs of the world.

The last scud of day[7] holds back for me,
It flings my likeness after the rest and true as any on the shadow'd wilds,
It coaxes me to the vapor and the dusk.   1335

I depart as air, I shake my white locks at the runaway sun,
I effuse my flesh in eddies,[8] and drift it in lacy jags.

I bequeath myself to the dirt to grow from the grass I love,
If you want me again look for me under your boot-soles.

You will hardly know who I am or what I mean,   1340
But I shall be good health to you nevertheless,
And filter and fibre your blood.

Failing to fetch me at first keep encouraged,
Missing me one place search another,
I stop somewhere waiting for you.   1345

1855, 1881

FROM CHILDREN OF ADAM[1]

Spontaneous Me

Spontaneous me, Nature,
The loving day, the mounting sun, the friend I am happy with,
The arm of my friend hanging idly over my shoulder,

---

7. Wind-driven clouds, or the last rays of the sun.
8. Air currents. "Effuse": pour forth.
1. This group of poems first appeared in the 1860 edition of *Leaves of Grass* as *Enfans d'Adam*; later the contents and order were slightly altered until they reached final form in 1871. In a notebook entry Whitman identifies the relationship of this group to the *Calamus* poems: "Theory of a Cluster of Poems the same *to the passion of Woman-Love* as the 'Calamus-Leaves' are to adhesiveness,

manly love. Full of animal-fire, tender, burning, the tremulous ache, delicious, yet such a torment. The swelling elate and vehement, that will not be denied. Adam, as a central figure and type. One piece presenting a vivid picture (in connection with the spirit) of a fully complete, well-developed man, eld, bearded, swart, fiery, as a more than rival of the youthful type-hero of novels and love poems."

The hillside whiten'd with blossoms of the mountain ash,
The same late in autumn, the hues of red, yellow, drab, purple, and
    light and dark green,   5
The rich coverlet of the grass, animals and birds, the private untrimm'd
    bank, the primitive apples, the pebble-stones,
Beautiful dripping fragments, the negligent list of one after another as I
    happen to call them to me or think of them,
The real poems, (what we call poems being merely pictures,)
The poems of the privacy of the night, and of men like me,
This poem drooping shy and unseen that I always carry, and that all
    men carry,   10
(Know once for all, avow'd on purpose, wherever are men like me, are
    our lusty lurking masculine poems,)
Love-thoughts, love-juice, love-odor, love-yielding, love-climbers, and
    the climbing sap,
Arms and hands of love, lips of love, phallic thumb of love, breasts of love,
    bellies press'd and glued together with love,
Earth of chaste love, life that is only life after love,
The body of my love, the body of the woman I love, the body of the man,
    the body of the earth,   15
Soft forenoon airs that blow from the south-west,
The hairy wild-bee that murmurs and hankers up and down, that gripes
    the full-grown lady-flower, curves upon her with amorous firm legs,
    takes his will of her, and holds himself tremulous and tight till he is
    satisfied;
The wet of woods through the early hours,
Two sleepers at night lying close together as they sleep, one with an arm
    slanting down across and below the waist of the other,
The smell of apples, aromas from crush'd sage-plant, mint, birch-bark,   20
The boy's longings, the glow and pressure as he confides to me what he
    was dreaming,
The dead leaf whirling its spiral whirl and falling still and content to the
    ground,
The no-form'd stings that sights, people, objects, sting me with,
The hubb'd sting of myself, stinging me as much as it ever can any one,
The sensitive, orbic, underlapp'd brothers, that only privileged feelers
    may be intimate where they are,   25
The curious roamer the hand roaming all over the body, the bashful
    withdrawing of flesh where the fingers soothingly pause and edge
    themselves,
The limpid liquid within the young man,
The vex'd corrosion so pensive and so painful,
The torment, the irritable tide that will not be at rest,
The like of the same I feel, the like of the same in others,   30
The young man that flushes and flushes, and the young woman that
    flushes and flushes,
The young man that wakes deep at night, the hot hand seeking to repress
    what would master him,
The mystic amorous night, the strange half-welcome pangs, visions,
    sweats,
The pulse pounding through palms and trembling encircling fingers, the
    young man all color'd, red, ashamed, angry;
The souse upon me of my lover the sea, as I lie willing and naked,   35

The merriment of the twin babes that crawl over the grass in the sun,
    the mother never turning her vigilant eyes from them,
The walnut-trunk, the walnut-husks, and the ripening or ripen'd long-
    round walnuts,
The continence of vegetables, birds, animals,
The consequent meanness of me should I skulk or find myself indecent,
    while birds and animals never once skulk or find themselves indecent,
The great chastity of paternity, to match the great chastity of maternity,   40
The oath of procreation I have sworn, my Adamic and fresh daughters,
The greed that eats me day and night with hungry gnaw, till I saturate
    what shall produce boys to fill my place when I am through,
The wholesome relief, repose, content,
And this bunch pluck'd at random from myself,
It has done its work—I toss it carelessly to fall where it may.   45

1856, 1867

Facing West from California's Shores

Facing west from California's shores,
Inquiring, tireless, seeking what is yet unfound,
I, a child, very old, over waves, towards the house of maternity,[1] the land
    of migrations, look afar,
Look off the shores of my Western sea, the circle almost circled;
For starting westward from Hindustan, from the vales of Kashmere,[2]   5
From Asia, from the north, from the God, the sage, and the hero,
From the south, from the flowery peninsulas and the spice islands,[3]
Long having wander'd since, round the earth having wander'd,
Now I face home again, very pleas'd and joyous,
(But where is what I started for so long ago?   10
And why is it yet unfound?)

1860, 1867

Crossing Brooklyn Ferry[1]

1

Flood-tide below me! I see you face to face!
Clouds of the west—sun there half an hour high—I see you also face to
    face.

Crowds of men and women attired in the usual costumes, how curious
    you are to me!

---

1. Asia, at the time believed to be the birthplace
of civilization.
2. Mountainous region adjacent to India, Paki-
stan, western China, and Tibet. "Hindustan":
India.

3. Indonesia.
1. First published as "Sun-Down Poem" in the
2nd edition of Leaves of Grass (1856), "Crossing
Brooklyn Ferry" was given its final title in 1860.

On the ferry-boats the hundreds and hundreds that cross, returning home,
    are more curious to me than you suppose,
And you that shall cross from shore to shore years hence are more to me,
    and more in my meditations, than you might suppose.   5

2

The impalpable sustenance of me from all things at all hours of the day,
The simple, compact, well-join'd scheme, myself disintegrated, every one
    disintegrated yet part of the scheme,
The similitudes of the past and those of the future,
The glories strung like beads on my smallest sights and hearings, on the
    walk in the street and the passage over the river,
The current rushing so swiftly and swimming with me far away,   10
The others that are to follow me, the ties between me and them,
The certainty of others, the life, love, sight, hearing of others.

Others will enter the gates of the ferry and cross from shore to shore,
Others will watch the run of the flood-tide,
Others will see the shipping of Manhattan north and west, and the
    heights of Brooklyn to the south and east,   15
Others will see the islands large and small;
Fifty years hence, others will see them as they cross, the sun half an hour
    high,
A hundred years hence, or ever so many hundred years hence, others will
    see them,
Will enjoy the sunset, the pouring-in of the flood-tide, the falling-back to
    the sea of the ebb-tide.

3

It avails not, time nor place—distance avails not,   20
I am with you, you men and women of a generation, or ever so many
    generations hence,
Just as you feel when you look on the river and sky, so I felt,
Just as any of you is one of a living crowd, I was one of a crowd,
Just as you are refresh'd by the gladness of the river and the bright flow, I
    was refresh'd,
Just as you stand and lean on the rail, yet hurry with the swift current, I
    stood yet was hurried,   25
Just as you look on the numberless masts of ships and the thick-stemm'd
    pipes of steamboats, I look'd.

I too many and many a time cross'd the river of old,
Watched the Twelfth-month[2] sea-gulls, saw them high in the air floating
    with motionless wings, oscillating their bodies,
Saw how the glistening yellow lit up parts of their bodies and left the rest
    in strong shadow,
Saw the slow-wheeling circles and the gradual edging toward the south,   30
Saw the reflection of the summer sky in the water,

2. December.

Had my eyes dazzled by the shimmering track of beams,
Look'd at the fine centrifugal spokes of light round the shape of my head
    in the sunlit water,
Look'd on the haze on the hills southward and south-westward,
Look'd on the vapor as it flew in fleeces tinged with violet,   35
Look'd toward the lower bay to notice the vessels arriving,
Saw their approach, saw aboard those that were near me,
Saw the white sails of schooners and sloops, saw the ships at anchor,
The sailors at work in the rigging or out astride the spars,
The round masts, the swinging motion of the hulls, the slender
    serpentine pennants,   40
The large and small steamers in motion, the pilots in their pilot-houses,
The white wake left by the passage, the quick tremulous whirl of the wheels,
The flags of all nations, the falling of them at sunset.
The scallop-edged waves in the twilight, the ladled cups, the frolicsome
    crests and glistening,
The stretch afar growing dimmer and dimmer, the gray walls of the
    granite storehouses by the docks,   45
On the river the shadowy group, the big steam-tug closely flank'd on
    each side by the barges, the hay-boat, the belated lighter,[3]
On the neighboring shore the fires from the foundry chimneys burning
    high and glaringly into the night,
Casting their flicker of black contrasted with wild red and yellow light
    over the tops of houses, and down into the clefts of streets.

4

These and all else were to me the same as they are to you,
I loved well those cities, loved well the stately and rapid river,
The men and women I saw were all near to me,   50
Others the same—others who looked back on me because I look'd
    forward to them,
(The time will come, though I stop here to-day and to-night.)

5

What is it then between us?
What is the count of the scores or hundreds of years between us?   55

Whatever it is, it avails not—distance avails not, and place avails not,
I too lived, Brooklyn of ample hills was mine,
I too walk'd the streets of Manhattan island, and bathed in the waters
    around it,
I too felt the curious abrupt questionings stir within me,
In the day among crowds of people sometimes they came upon me,   60
In my walks home late at night or as I lay in my bed they came upon me,
I too had been struck from the float forever held in solution,
I too had receiv'd identity by my body,
That I was I knew was of my body, and what I should be I knew I should
    be of my body.

3. Barge used to load or unload a cargo ship.

6

It is not upon you alone the dark patches fall,   65
The dark threw its patches down upon me also,
The best I had done seem'd to me blank and suspicious,
My great thoughts as I supposed them, were they not in reality meagre?
Nor is it you alone who know what it is to be evil,
I am he who knew what it was to be evil,   70
I too knitted the old knot of contrariety,
Blabb'd, blush'd, resented, lied, stole, grudg'd,
Had guile, anger, lust, hot wishes I dared not speak,
Was wayward, vain, greedy, shallow, sly, cowardly, malignant,
The wolf, the snake, the hog, not wanting in me,   75
The cheating look, the frivolous word, the adulterous wish, not wanting,
Refusals, hates, postponements, meanness, laziness, none of these
    wanting,
Was one with the rest, the days and haps of the rest,
Was call'd by my nighest name by clear loud voices of young men as they
    saw me approaching or passing,
Felt their arms on my neck as I stood, or the negligent leaning of their
    flesh against me as I sat,   80
Saw many I loved in the street or ferry-boat or public assembly, yet never
    told them a word,
Lived the same life with the rest, the same old laughing, gnawing,
    sleeping,
Play'd the part that still looks back on the actor or actress,
The same old role, the role that is what we make it, as great as we like,
Or as small as we like, or both great and small.   85

7

Closer yet I approach you,
What thought you have of me now, I had as much of you—I laid in my
    stores in advance,
I consider'd long and seriously of you before you were born.

Who was to know what should come home to me?
Who knows but I am enjoying this?   90
Who knows, for all the distance, but I am as good as looking at you now,
    for all you cannot see me?

8

Ah, what can ever be more stately and admirable to me than mast-hemm'd
    Manhattan?
River and sunset and scallop-edg'd waves of flood-tide?
The sea-gulls oscillating their bodies, the hay-boat in the twilight, and
    the belated lighter?
What gods can exceed these that clasp me by the hand, and with
    voices I love call me promptly and loudly by my nighest name as
    I approach?   95
What is more subtle than this which ties me to the woman or man that
    looks in my face?
Which fuses me into you now, and pours my meaning into you?

We understand then do we not?
What I promis'd without mentioning it, have you not accepted?
What the study could not teach—what the preaching could not
　　accomplish is accomplish'd, is it not?　　　　　　　　　100

9

Flow on, river! flow with the flood-tide, and ebb with the ebb-tide!
Frolic on, crested and scallop-edg'd waves!
Gorgeous clouds of the sunset! drench with your splendor me, or the
　　men and women generations after me!
Cross from shore to shore, countless crowds of passengers!
Stand up, tall masts of Mannahatta![4] stand up, beautiful hills of
　　Brooklyn!　　　　　　　　　　　　　　　　　105
Throb, baffled and curious brain! throw out questions and answers!
Suspend here and everywhere, eternal float of solution!
Gaze, loving and thirsting eyes, in the house or street or public assembly!
Sound out, voices of young men! loudly and musically call me by my
　　nighest name!
Live, old life! play the part that looks back on the actor or actress!　　110
Play the old role, the role that is great or small according as one makes it!
Consider, you who peruse me, whether I may not in unknown ways be
　　looking upon you;
Be firm, rail over the river, to support those who lean idly, yet haste with
　　the hasting current;
Fly on, sea-birds! fly sideways, or wheel in large circles high in the air;
Receive the summer sky, you water, and faithfully hold it till all downcast
　　eyes have time to take it from you!　　　　　　　　115
Diverge, fine spokes of light, from the shape of my head, or any one's
　　head, in the sunlit water!
Come on, ships from the lower bay! pass up or down, white-sail'd
　　schooners, sloops, lighters!
Flaunt away, flags of all nations! be duly lower'd at sunset!
Burn high your fires, foundry chimneys! cast black shadows at nightfall!
　　cast red and yellow light over the tops of the houses!
Appearances, now or henceforth, indicate what you are,　　　　120
You necessary film, continue to envelop the soul,
About my body for me, and your body for you, be hung our divinest aromas,
Thrive, cities—bring your freight, bring your shows, ample and sufficient
　　rivers,
Expand, being than which none else is perhaps more spiritual,
Keep your places, objects than which none else is more lasting.　　125

You have waited, you always wait, you dumb, beautiful ministers,
We receive you with free sense at last, and are insatiate henceforward,
Not you any more shall be able to foil us, or withhold yourselves from us,
We use you, and do not cast you aside—we plant you permanently within us,
We fathom you not—we love you—there is perfection in you also,　　130
You furnish your parts toward eternity,
Great or small, you furnish your parts toward the soul.

1856, 1881

4. Variant of Manhattan.

FROM SEA-DRIFT[1]

Out of the Cradle Endlessly Rocking[2]

Out of the cradle endlessly rocking,
Out of the mocking-bird's throat, the musical shuttle,
Out of the Ninth-month midnight,
Over the sterile sands and the fields beyond, where the child leaving his
    bed wander'd alone, bareheaded, barefoot,
Down from the shower'd halo,   5
Up from the mystic play of shadows twining and twisting as if they were
    alive,
Out from the patches of briers and blackberries,
From the memories of the bird that chanted to me,
From your memories sad brother, from the fitful risings and fallings I
    heard,
From under that yellow half-moon late-risen and swollen as if with tears,   10
From those beginning notes of yearning and love there in the mist,
From the thousand responses of my heart never to cease,
From the myriad thence-arous'd words,
From the word stronger and more delicious than any,
From such as now they start the scene revisiting,   15
As a flock, twittering, rising, or overhead passing,
Borne hither, ere all eludes me, hurriedly,
A man, yet by these tears a little boy again,
Throwing myself on the sand, confronting the waves,
I, chanter of pains and joys, uniter of here and hereafter,   20
Taking all hints to use them, but swiftly leaping beyond them,
A reminiscence sing.

Once Paumanok,[3]
When the lilac-scent was in the air and Fifth-month grass was growing,
Up this seashore in some briers,   25
Two feather'd guests from Alabama, two together,

And their nest, and four light-green eggs spotted with brown,
And every day the he-bird to and fro near at hand,
And every day the she-bird crouch'd on her nest, silent, with bright
    eyes,
And every day I, a curious boy, never too close, never disturbing them,   30
Cautiously peering, absorbing, translating.

Shine! shine! shine!
Pour down your warmth, great sun!
While we bask, we two together.

---

1. The *Sea-Drift* section of the 1881 edition of
Leaves of Grass was made up of two new poems,
seven poems from *Sea-Shore Memories* in the
1871 *Passage to India* section, and two poems
from the 1876 *Two Rivulets* section.
2. First published as "A Child's Reminiscence" in
the *New York Saturday Press* of December 24, 1859,

this poem was incorporated into the 1860 *Leaves of
Grass* as "A Word Out of the Sea." Whitman continued to revise it until it reached the present form
in the *Sea-Drift* section of the 1881 edition. "Out
of the Cradle Endlessly Rocking" had been the first
of the *Sea-Shore Memories* group.
3. Long Island.

Two together! 35
Winds blow south, or winds blow north,
Day come white, or night come black,
Home, or rivers and mountains from home,
Singing all time, minding no time,
While we two keep together. 40

Till of a sudden,
May-be kill'd, unknown to her mate,
One forenoon the she-bird crouch'd not on the nest,
Nor return'd that afternoon, nor the next
Nor ever appear'd again. 45

And thenceforward all summer in the sound of the sea,
And at night under the full of the moon in calmer weather,
Over the hoarse surging of the sea,
Or flitting from brier to brier by day,
I saw, I heard at intervals the remaining one, the he-bird, 50
The solitary guest from Alabama.

Blow! blow! blow!
Blow up sea-winds along Paumanok's shore;
I wait and I wait till you blow my mate to me.

Yes, when the stars glisten'd, 55
All night long on the prong of a moss-scallop'd stake,
Down almost amid the slapping waves,
Sat the lone singer wonderful causing tears.

He call'd on his mate,
He pour'd forth the meanings which I of all men know. 60

Yes my brother I know,
The rest might not, but I have treasur'd every note,
For more than once dimly down to the beach gliding,
Silent, avoiding the moonbeams, blending myself with the shadows,
Recalling now the obscure shapes, the echoes, the sounds and sights
    after their sorts, 65
The white arms out in the breakers tirelessly tossing,
I, with bare feet, a child, the wind wafting my hair,
Listen'd long and long.

Listen'd to keep, to sing, now translating the notes.
Following you my brother. 70

Soothe! soothe! soothe!
Close on its wave soothes the wave behind,
And again another behind embracing and lapping, every one close,
But my love soothes not me, not me.

Low hangs the moon, it rose late, 75
It is lagging—O I think it is heavy with love, with love.

O madly the sea pushes upon the land,
With love, with love.

O night! do I not see my love fluttering out among the breakers?
What is that little black thing I see there in the white?   80

Loud! loud! loud!
Loud I call to you, my love!

High and clear I shoot my voice over the waves,
Surely you must know who is here, is here,
You must know who I am, my love.   85

Low-hanging moon!
What is that dusky spot in your brown yellow?
O it is the shape, the shape of my mate!
O moon do not keep her from me any longer.

Land! land! O land!   90
Whichever way I turn, O I think you could give me my mate back again
         if you only would,
For I am almost sure I see her dimly whichever way I look.

O rising stars!
Perhaps the one I want so much will rise, will rise with some of you.

O throat! O trembling throat!   95
Sound clearer through the atmosphere!
Pierce the woods, the earth,
Somewhere listening to catch you must be the one I want.

Shake out carols!
Solitary here, the night's carols!   100
Carols of lonesome love! death's carols!
Carols under that lagging, yellow, waning moon!
O under that moon where she droops almost down into the sea!
O reckless despairing carols.

But soft! sink low!   105
Soft! let me just murmur,
And do you wait a moment you husky-nois'd sea,
For somewhere I believe I heard my mate responding to me,
So faint, I must be still, be still to listen,
But not altogether still, for then she might not come immediately to me.   110

Hither my love!
Here I am! here!
With this just-sustain'd note I announce myself to you,
This gentle call is for you my love, for you.

Do not be decoy'd elsewhere,   115
That is the whistle of the wind, it is not my voice,
That is the fluttering, the fluttering of the spray,
Those are the shadows of leaves.

O darkness! O in vain!
O I am very sick and sorrowful.   120

O brown halo in the sky near the moon, drooping upon the sea!
O troubled reflection in the sea!
O throat! O throbbing heart!
And I singing uselessly, uselessly all the night.

O past! O happy life! O songs of joy!   125
In the air, in the woods, over fields,
Loved! loved! loved! loved! loved!
But my mate no more, no more with me!
We two together no more.

The aria sinking,   130
All else continuing, the stars shining,
The winds blowing, the notes of the bird continuous echoing,
With angry moans the fierce old mother incessantly moaning,
On the sands of Paumanok's shore gray and rustling,
The yellow half-moon enlarged, sagging down, drooping, the face of the
    sea almost touching,   135
The boy ecstatic, with his bare feet the waves, with his hair the
    atmosphere dallying,
The love in the heart long pent, now loose, now at last tumultuously
    bursting,
The aria's meaning, the ears, the soul, swiftly depositing,
The strange tears down the cheeks coursing,
The colloquy there, the trio, each uttering,   140
The undertone, the savage old mother incessantly crying,
To the boy's soul's questions sullenly timing, some drown'd secret hissing,
To the outsetting bard.

Demon or bird! (said the boy's soul,)
Is it indeed toward your mate you sing? or is it really to me?   145
For I, that was a child, my tongue's use sleeping, now I have heard you,
Now in a moment I know what I am for, I awake,
And already a thousand singers, a thousand songs, clearer, louder and
    more sorrowful than yours,
A thousand warbling echoes have started to life within me, never to die.

O you singer solitary, singing by yourself, projecting me,   150
O solitary me listening, never more shall I cease perpetuating you,
Never more shall I escape, never more the reverberations,
Never more the cries of unsatisfied love be absent from me,
Never again leave me to be the peaceful child I was before what there in
    the night,
By the sea under the yellow and sagging moon,   155
The messenger there arous'd, the fire, the sweet hell within,
The unknown want, the destiny of me.

O give me the clew! (it lurks in the night here somewhere,)
O if I am to have so much, let me have more!

A word then, (for I will conquer it,)   160
The word final, superior to all,

Subtle, sent up—what is it?—I listen;
Are you whispering it, and have been all the time, you sea-waves?
Is that it from your liquid rims and wet sands?

Whereto answering, the sea,   165
Delaying not, hurrying not,
Whisper'd me through the night, and very plainly before daybreak,
Lisp'd to me the low and delicious word death,
And again death, death, death, death,
Hissing melodious, neither like the bird nor like my arous'd child's heart,   170
But edging near as privately for me rustling at my feet,
Creeping thence steadily up to my ears and laving me softly all over,
Death, death, death, death, death.

Which I do not forget,
But fuse the song of my dusky demon and brother,   175
That he sang to me in the moonlight on Paumanok's gray beach,
With the thousand responsive songs at random,
My own songs awaked from that hour,
And with them the key, the word up from the waves,
The word of the sweetest song and all songs,   180
That strong and delicious word which, creeping to my feet,
(Or like some old crone rocking the cradle, swathed in sweet garments,
        bending aside,)
The sea whisper'd me.

                                                            1859, 1881

From By the Roadside[1]

When I Heard the Learn'd Astronomer

When I heard the learn'd astronomer,
When the proofs, the figures, were ranged in columns before me,
When I was shown the charts and diagrams, to add, divide, and measure
        them,
When I sitting heard the astronomer where he lectured with much
        applause in the lecture-room,
How soon unaccountable I became tired and sick,   5
Till rising and gliding out I wander'd off by myself,
In the mystical moist night-air, and from time to time,
Look'd up in perfect silence at the stars.

                                                                 1865

---

1. *By the Roadside* is the 1881 section title for around two dozen short poems of roadside obser- vation, most of which first appeared in the 1860 edition of *Leaves of Grass*.

The Dalliance of the Eagles

Skirting the river road, (my forenoon walk, my rest,)
Skyward in air a sudden muffled sound, the dalliance of the eagles,
The rushing amorous contact high in space together,
The clinching interlocking claws, a living, fierce, gyrating wheel,
Four beating wings, two beaks, a swirling mass tight grappling,   5
In tumbling turning clustering loops, straight downward falling,
Till o'er the river pois'd, the twain yet one, a moment's lull,
A motionless still balance in the air, then parting, talons loosing,
Upward again on slow-firm pinions slanting, their separate diverse flight,
She hers, he his, pursuing.   10

                                                    1880, 1881

FROM DRUM-TAPS[1]

Beat! Beat! Drums!

Beat! beat! drums!—blow! bugles! blow!
Through the windows—through doors—burst like a ruthless force,
Into the solemn church, and scatter the congregation,
Into the school where the scholar is studying;
Leave not the bridegroom quiet—no happiness must he have now with
     his bride,   5
Nor the peaceful farmer any peace, ploughing his field or gathering his grain,
So fierce you whirr and pound you drums—so shrill you bugles blow.

Beat! beat! drums!—blow! bugles! blow!
Over the traffic of cities—over the rumble of wheels in the streets;
Are beds prepared for sleepers at night in the houses? no sleepers must
     sleep in those beds,   10
No bargainers' bargains by day—no brokers or speculators—would they
     continue?
Would the talkers be talking? would the singer attempt to sing?
Would the lawyer rise in the court to state his case before the judge?
Then rattle quicker, heavier drums—you bugles wilder blow.

Beat! beat! drums!—blow! bugles! blow!
Make no parley—stop for no expostulation,   15

1. The contents of the original *Drum-Taps* (first printed in 1865 as a little book) differed considerably from the contents of the *Drum-Taps* section finally arrived at in the 1881 *Leaves of Grass*. In the final arrangement the poetic purpose shifts throughout, roughly reflecting the chronology of the Civil War and the chronology of the composition of the poems. Whitman's initial aim was propagandistic. Indeed, "Beat! Beat! Drums!" served as a kind of recruiting poem when it was first printed in September 1861 issues of *Harper's Weekly* and the *New York Leader*, having been composed after the Southern victory at the first battle of Bull Run. The dominant impulse of most of the later poems is realistic—a determination to record the war the way it was, and in the best of the poems the realism is achieved through elaborate technical subtleties. The stages of Whitman's own attitudes toward the war are well stated in the epigraph he gave the *Drum-Taps* group in 1871 and then inserted parenthetically into "The Wound Dresser" in the 1881 edition: "Arous'd and angry, / I'd thought to beat the alarum, and urge relentless war, / But soon my fingers fail'd me, my face droop'd and I resign'd myself / To sit by the wounded and soothe them, or silently watch the dead."

Mind not the timid—mind not the weeper or prayer,
Mind not the old man beseeching the young man,
Let not the child's voice be heard, nor the mother's entreaties,
Make even the trestles to shake the dead where they lie awaiting the
    hearses,   20
So strong you thump O terrible drums—so loud you bugles blow.

                                    1861, 1867

Cavalry Crossing a Ford

A line in long array where they wind betwixt green islands,
They take a serpentine course, their arms flash in the sun—hark to the
    musical clank,
Behold the silvery river, in it the splashing horses loitering stop to drink,
Behold the brown-faced men, each group, each person a picture, the
    negligent rest on the saddles,
Some emerge on the opposite bank, others are just entering the ford—
    while,   5
Scarlet and blue and snowy white,
The guidon flags[1] flutter gayly in the wind.

                                    1865, 1871

The Wound-Dresser

1

An old man bending I come among new faces,
Years looking backward resuming in answer to children,
Come tell us old man, as from young men and maidens that love me,
(Arous'd and angry, I'd thought to beat the alarum, and urge relentless war,
But soon my fingers fail'd me, my face droop'd and I resign'd myself,   5
To sit by the wounded and soothe them, or silently watch the dead;)
Years hence of these scenes, of these furious passions, these chances,
Of unsurpass'd heroes, (was one side so brave? the other was equally
    brave;)
Now be witness again, paint the mightiest armies of earth,
Of those armies so rapid so wondrous what saw you to tell us?   10
What stays with you latest and deepest? of curious panics,
Of hard-fought engagements or sieges tremendous what deepest remains?

2

O maidens and young men I love and that love me,
What you ask of my days those the strangest and sudden your talking
    recalls,
Soldier alert I arrive after a long march cover'd with sweat and dust,   15

---

1. Small military flags carried by soldiers for signaling and identification at a distance.

In the nick of time I come, plunge in the fight, loudly shout in the rush
 of successful charge,
Enter the captur'd works[1]—yet lo, like a swift-running river they fade,
Pass and are gone they fade—I dwell not on soldiers' perils or soldiers' joys,
(Both I remember well—many the hardships, few the joys, yet I was
 content.)

But in silence in dreams' projections,   20
While the world of gain and appearance and mirth goes on,
So soon what is over forgotten, and waves wash the imprints off the sand,
With hinged knees returning I enter the doors, (while for you up there,
Whoever you are, follow without noise and be of strong heart.)

Bearing the bandages, water and sponge,   25
Straight and swift to my wounded I go,
Where they lie on the ground after the battle brought in,
Where their priceless blood reddens the grass the ground,
Or to the rows of the hospital tent, or under the roof'd hospital,

To the long rows of cots up and down each side I return,   30
To each and all one after another I draw near, not one do I miss,
An attendant follows holding a tray, he carries a refuse pail,
Soon to be fill'd with clotted rags and blood, emptied, and fill'd again.

I onward go, I stop,
With hinged knees and steady hand to dress wounds,   35
I am firm with each, the pangs are sharp yet unavoidable,
One turns to me his appealing eyes—poor boy! I never knew you,
Yet I think I could not refuse this moment to die for you, if that would
 save you.

3

On, on I go, (open doors of time! open hospital doors!)
The crush'd head I dress, (poor crazed hand tear not the bandage away,)   40
The neck of the cavalry-man with the bullet through and through I
 examine,
Hard the breathing rattles, quite glazed already the eye, yet life struggles
 hard,
(Come sweet death! be persuaded O beautiful death!
In mercy come quickly.)

From the stump of the arm, the amputated hand,   45
I undo the clotted lint, remove the slough, wash off the matter and blood,
Back on his pillow the soldier bends with curv'd neck and side-falling head,
His eyes are closed, his face is pale, he dares not look on the bloody stump,
And has not yet look'd on it.

I dress a wound in the side, deep, deep,   50
But a day or two more, for see the frame all wasted and sinking,
And the yellow-blue countenance see.

1. Fortified earthworks.

I dress the perforated shoulder, the foot with the bullet-wound,
Cleanse the one with a gnawing and putrid gangrene, so sickening, so
    offensive,
While the attendant stands behind aside me holding the tray and pail.   55

I am faithful, I do not give out,
The fractur'd thigh, the knee, the wound in the abdomen,
These and more I dress with impassive hand, (yet deep in my breast a fire,
    a burning flame.)

4

Thus in silence in dreams' projections,
Returning, resuming, I thread my way through the hospitals,   60
The hurt and wounded I pacify with soothing hand,
I sit by the restless all the dark night, some are so young,
Some suffer so much, I recall the experience sweet and sad,
(Many a soldier's loving arms about this neck have cross'd and rested,
Many a soldier's kiss dwells on these bearded lips.)   65

        1865, 1881

FROM MEMORIES OF PRESIDENT LINCOLN[1]

When Lilacs Last in the Dooryard Bloom'd

1

When lilacs last in the dooryard bloom'd,
And the great star[2] early droop'd in the western sky in the night,
I mourn'd, and yet shall mourn with ever-returning spring.

Ever-returning spring, trinity sure to me you bring,
Lilac blooming perennial and drooping star in the west,   5
And thought of him I love.

2

O powerful western fallen star!
O shades of night—O moody, tearful night!
O great star disappear'd—O the black murk that hides the star!
O cruel hands that hold me powerless—O helpless soul of me!   10
O harsh surrounding cloud that will not free my soul.

---

1. Composed in the months following Lincoln's assassination on April 14, 1865, this elegy was printed in the fall of that year as an appendix to the recently published *Drum-Taps* volume. In the 1881 edition of *Leaves of Grass* it and three shorter poems were joined to make up the section *Memories of President Lincoln*.
2. Literally Venus, although it becomes associated with Lincoln himself.

3

In the dooryard fronting an old farm-house near the white-wash'd palings,
Stands the lilac-bush tall-growing with heart-shaped leaves of rich green,
With many a pointed blossom rising delicate, with the perfume strong I
     love,
With every leaf a miracle—and from this bush in the dooryard,   15
With delicate-color'd blossoms and heart-shaped leaves of rich green,
A sprig with its flower I break.

4

In the swamp in secluded recesses,
A shy and hidden bird is warbling a song.

Solitary the thrush,   20
The hermit withdrawn to himself, avoiding the settlements,
Sings by himself a song.
Song of the bleeding throat,
Death's outlet song of life, (for well dear brother I know,
If thou wast not granted to sing thou would'st surely die.)   25

5

Over the breast of the spring, the land, amid cities,
Amid lanes and through old woods, where lately the violets peep'd from
     the ground, spotting the gray debris,
Amid the grass in the fields each side of the lanes, passing the endless
     grass,
Passing the yellow-spear'd wheat, every grain from its shroud in the dark-
     brown fields uprisen,
Passing the apple-tree blows[3] of white and pink in the orchards,   30
Carrying a corpse to where it shall rest in the grave,
Night and day journeys a coffin.[4]

6

Coffin that passes through lanes and streets,
Through day and night with the great cloud darkening the land,
With the pomp of the inloop'd flags with the cities draped in black,   35
With the show of the States themselves as of crape-veil'd women standing,
With processions long and winding and the flambeaus[5] of the night,
With the countless torches lit, with the silent sea of faces and the
     unbared heads,
With the waiting depot, the arriving coffin, and the sombre faces,
With dirges through the night, with the thousand voices rising strong
     and solemn,   40
With all the mournful voices of the dirges pour'd around the coffin,
The dim-lit churches and the shuddering organs—where amid these you
     journey,

3. Blossoms.   Illinois.
4. The train carrying Lincoln's body for burial   5. Torches.
traveled from Washington, D.C., to Springfield,

With the tolling tolling bells' perpetual clang,
Here, coffin that slowly passes,
I give you my sprig of lilac.   45

                                    7

(Nor for you, for one alone,
Blossoms and branches green to coffins all I bring,
For fresh as the morning, thus would I chant a song for you O sane and
     sacred death.

All over bouquets of roses,
O death, I cover you over with roses and early lilies,   50
But mostly and now the lilac that blooms the first,
Copious I break, I break the sprigs from the bushes,
With loaded arms I come, pouring for you,
For you and the coffins all of you O death.)

                                    8

O western orb sailing the heaven,   55
Now I know what you must have meant as a month since I walk'd,
As I walk'd in silence the transparent shadowy night,
As I saw you had something to tell as you bent to me night after night,
As you droop'd from the sky low down as if to my side, (while the other
     stars all look'd on,)
As we wander'd together the solemn night, (for something I know not
     what kept me from sleep,)   60
As the night advanced, and I saw on the rim of the west how full you
     were of woe,
As I stood on the rising ground in the breeze in the cool transparent night,
As I watch'd where you pass'd and was lost in the netherward black of the
     night,
As my soul in its trouble dissatisfied sank, as where you sad orb,
Concluded, dropt in the night, and was gone.   65

                                    9

Sing on there in the swamp,
O singer bashful and tender, I hear your notes, I hear your call,
I hear, I come presently, I understand you,
But a moment I linger, for the lustrous star has detain'd me,
The star my departing comrade holds and detains me.   70

                                    10

O how shall I warble myself for the dead one there I loved?
And how shall I deck my song for the large sweet soul that has gone?
And what shall my perfume be for the grave of him I love?

Sea-winds blown from east and west,
Blown from the Eastern sea and blown from the Western sea, till there
     on the prairies meeting,   75

These and with these and the breath of my chant,
I'll perfume the grave of him I love.

11

O what shall I hang on the chamber walls?
And what shall the pictures be that I hang on the walls,
To adorn the burial-house of him I love?   80

Pictures of growing spring and farms and homes,
With the Fourth-month[6] eve at sundown, and the gray smoke lucid and
    bright,
With floods of the yellow gold of the gorgeous, indolent, sinking sun,
    burning, expanding the air,
With the fresh sweet herbage under foot, and the pale green leaves of the
    trees prolific,
In the distance the flowing glaze, the breast of the river, with a
    wind-dapple here and there,   85
With ranging hills on the banks, with many a line against the sky, and
    shadows,
And the city at hand with dwellings so dense, and stacks of chimneys,
And all the scenes of life and the workshops, and the workmen homeward
    returning.

12

Lo, body and soul—this land,
My own Manhattan with spires, and the sparkling and hurrying tides,
    and the ships,   90
The varied and ample land, the South and the North in the light, Ohio's
    shores and flashing Missouri,
And ever the far-spreading prairies cover'd with grass and corn.

Lo, the most excellent sun so calm and haughty,
The violet and purple morn with just-felt breezes,
The gentle soft-born measureless light,   95
The miracle spreading bathing all, the fulfill'd noon,
The coming eve delicious, the welcome night and the stars,
Over my cities shining all, enveloping man and land.

13

Sing on, sing on you gray-brown bird,
Sing from the swamps, the recesses, pour your chant from the bushes,   100
Limitless out of the dusk, out of the cedars and pines.

Sing on dearest brother, warble your reedy song,
Loud human song, with voice of uttermost woe.

O liquid and free and tender!
O wild and loose to my soul!—O wondrous singer!   105

6. April.

You only I hear—yet the star holds me, (but will soon depart,)
Yet the lilac with mastering odor holds me.

14

Now while I sat in the day and look'd forth,
In the close of the day with its light and the fields of spring, and the
    farmers preparing their crops,
In the large unconscious scenery of my land with its lakes and
    forests,   110
In the heavenly aerial beauty, (after the perturb'd winds and the storms,)
Under the arching heavens of the afternoon swift passing, and the voices
    of children and women,
The many-moving sea-tides, and I saw the ships how they sail'd,
And the summer approaching with richness, and the fields all busy with
    labor,
And the infinite separate houses, how they all went on, each with its
    meals and minutia of daily usages,   115
And the streets how their throbbings throbb'd, and the cities pent—lo,
    then and there,
Falling upon them all and among them all, enveloping me with the rest,
Appear'd the cloud, appear'd the long black trail,
And I knew death, its thought, and the sacred knowledge of death.

Then with the knowledge of death as walking one side of me,   120
And the thought of death close-walking the other side of me,
And I in the middle as with companions, and as holding the hands of
    companions,
I fled forth to the hiding receiving night that talks not,
Down to the shores of the water, the path by the swamp in the dimness,
To the solemn shadowy cedars and ghostly pines so still.   125

And the singer so shy to the rest receiv'd me,
The gray-brown bird I know receiv'd us comrades three,
And he sang the carol of death, and a verse for him I love.

From deep secluded recesses,
From the fragrant cedars and the ghostly pines so still,   130
Came the carol of the bird.

And the charm of the carol rapt me,
As I held as if by their hands my comrades in the night,
And the voice of my spirit tallied the song of the bird.

Come lovely and soothing death,   135
Undulate round the world, serenely arriving, arriving,
In the day, in the night, to all, to each,
Sooner or later delicate death.

Prais'd be the fathomless universe,
For life and joy, and for objects and knowledge curious,   140
And for love, sweet love—but praise! praise! praise!
For the sure-enwinding arms of cool-enfolding death.

Dark mother always gliding near with soft feet,
Have none chanted for thee a chant of fullest welcome?
Then I chant it for thee, I glorify thee above all,   145
I bring thee a song that when thou must indeed come, come unfalteringly.

Approach strong deliveress,
When it is so, when thou hast taken them I joyously sing the dead,
Lost in the loving floating ocean of thee,
Laved in the flood of thy bliss O death.   150

From me to thee glad serenades,
Dances for thee I propose saluting thee, adornments and feastings for thee,
And the sights of the open landscape and the high-spread sky are fitting,
And life and the fields, and the huge and thoughtful night.

The night in silence under many a star,   155
The ocean shore and the husky whispering wave whose voice I know,
And the soul turning to thee O vast and well-veil'd death,
And the body gratefully nestling close to thee.

Over the tree-tops I float thee a song,
Over the rising and sinking waves, over the myriad fields and the prairies
    wide,
                                                                       160
Over the dense-pack'd cities all and the teeming wharves and ways,
I float this carol with joy, with joy to thee O death.

15

To the tally of my soul,
Loud and strong kept up the gray-brown bird,
With pure deliberate notes spreading filling the night.   165

Loud in the pines and cedars dim,
Clear in the freshness moist and the swamp-perfume,
And I with my comrades there in the night.

While my sight that was bound in my eyes unclosed,
As to long panoramas of visions.   170

And I saw askant[7] the armies,
I saw as in noiseless dreams hundreds of battle-flags,
Borne through the smoke of the battles and pierc'd with missiles I saw
    them,
And carried hither and yon through the smoke, and torn and bloody,
And at last but a few shreds left on the staffs, (and all in silence,) 175
And the staffs all splinter'd and broken.

I saw battle-corpses, myriads of them,
And the white skeletons of young men, I saw them,
I saw the debris and debris of all the slain soldiers of the war,
But I saw they were not as was thought,   180

---

7. Sideways, aslant.

They themselves were fully at rest, they suffer'd not,
The living remain'd and suffer'd, the mother suffer'd,
And the wife and the child and the musing comrade suffer'd,
And the armies that remain'd suffer'd.

16

Passing the visions, passing the night,   185
Passing, unloosing the hold of my comrades' hands,
Passing the song of the hermit bird and the tallying song of my soul,
Victorious song, death's outlet song, yet varying ever-altering song,
As low and wailing, yet clear the notes, rising and falling, flooding the night,
Sadly sinking and fainting, as warning and warning, and yet again
     bursting with joy,   190
Covering the earth and filling the spread of the heaven,
As that powerful psalm in the night I heard from recesses,
Passing, I leave thee lilac with heart-shaped leaves,
I leave thee there in the door-yard, blooming, returning with spring.

I cease from my song for thee,   195
From my gaze on thee in the west, fronting the west, communing with thee,
O comrade lustrous with silver face in the night.

Yet each to keep and all, retrievements out of the night,
The song, the wondrous chant of the gray-brown bird,
And the tallying chant, the echo arous'd in my soul,   200
With the lustrous and drooping star with the countenance full of woe,
With the holders holding my hand nearing the call of the bird,
Comrades mine and I in the midst, and their memory ever to keep, for
     the dead I loved so well,
For the sweetest, wisest soul of all my days and lands—and this for his
     dear sake,
Lilac and star and bird twined with the chant of my soul,   205
There in the fragrant pines and the cedars dusk and dim.

1865–66, 1881

Letter to Ralph Waldo Emerson[1]

Brooklyn, August, 1856.

Here are thirty-two Poems, which I send you, dear Friend and Master, not
having found how I could satisfy myself with sending any usual acknowledgment of your letter. The first edition, on which you mailed me that till
now unanswered letter, was twelve poems—I printed a thousand copies,

---

1. In July 21, 1855, Emerson sent Whitman a letter praising the first edition of *Leaves of Grass*.
Having already "allowed" the *New York Tribune* to
print the letter in a November issue, Whitman
embellished the spine of the 1856 edition of
Leaves of Grass with these words lettered in gold
taken from the letter: "I Greet You at the / Beginning of A / Great Career / R.W. Emerson." In the
back of the 1856 edition Whitman reprinted

Emerson's letter in full and followed it by this
"Letter to Ralph Waldo Emerson," dated Brooklyn, August 1856. Emerson's annoyance at Whitman's unauthorized use of his letter has obscured
the extraordinary virtues of Whitman's 1856
"reply," which can be read, in part, as a preface to
the 1856 edition, despite its placement at the back
of the volume.

and they readily sold; these thirty-two Poems I stereotype,[2] to print several thousand copies of. I much enjoy making poems. Other work I have set for myself to do, to meet people and The States face to face, to confront them with an American rude tongue; but the work of my life is making poems. I keep on till I make a hundred, and then several hundred—perhaps a thousand. The way is clear to me. A few years, and the average annual call for my Poems is ten or twenty thousand copies—more, quite likely. Why should I hurry or compromise? In poems or in speeches I say the word or two that has got to be said, adhere to the body, step with the countless common footsteps, and remind every man and woman of something.

Master, I am a man who has perfect faith. Master, we have not come through centuries, caste, heroisms, fables, to halt in this land today. Or I think it is to collect a ten-fold impetus that any halt is made. As nature, inexorable, onward, resistless, impassive amid the threats and screams of disputants, so America. Let all defer. Let all attend respectfully the leisure of These States, their politics, poems, literature, manners, and their free-handed modes of training their own offspring. Their own comes, just matured, certain, numerous and capable enough, with egotistical tongues, with sinewed wrists, seizing openly what belongs to them. They resume Personality, too long left out of mind. Their shadows are projected in employments, in books, in the cities, in trade; their feet are on the flights of the steps of the Capitol; they dilate, a large brawnier, more candid, more democratic, lawless, positive native to The States, sweet-bodied, completer, dauntless, flowing, masterful, beard-faced, new race of men.

Swiftly, on limitless foundations, the United States too are founding a literature. It is all as well done, in my opinion, as could be practicable. Each element here is in condition. Every day I go among the people of Manhattan Island, Brooklyn, and other cities, and among the young men, to discover the spirit of them, and to refresh myself. These are to be attended to; I am myself more drawn here than to those authors, publishers, importations, reprints, and so forth. I pass coolly through those, understanding them perfectly well, and that they do the indispensable service, outside of men like me, which nothing else could do. In poems, the young men of The States shall be represented, for they out-rival the best of the rest of the earth.

The lists of ready-made literature which America inherits by the mighty inheritance of the English language—all the rich repertoire of traditions, poems, histories, metaphysics, plays, classics, translations, have made, and still continue, magnificent preparations for that other plainly significant literature, to be our own, to be electric, fresh, lusty, to express the full-sized body, male and female—to give the modern meanings of things, to grow up beautiful, lasting, commensurate with America, with all the passions of home, with the inimitable sympathies of having been boys and girls together, and of parents who were with our parents.

What else can happen The States,[3] even in their own despite? That huge English flow, so sweet, so undeniable, has done incalculable good here, and

---

2. A printer's term before it became metaphorical, to stereotype was to make a mold of standing type, which could then be reused, while later printings could be made from the stereotyped plates. To go to the cost of stereotyping was evidence of optimism that future printings would be needed. In all likelihood, Whitman exaggerates press runs and sales here. The rarity of the 1856 edition of *Leaves of Grass*, for instance, argues against a publication run of several thousand copies.

3. Presumably, "to The States."

is to be spoken of for its own sake with generous praise and with gratitude. Yet the price The States have had to lie under for the same has not been a small price. Payment prevails; a nation can never take the issues of the needs of other nations for nothing. America, grandest of lands in the theory of its politics, in popular reading, in hospitality, breadth, animal beauty, cities, ships, machines, money, credit, collapses quick as lightning at the repeated, admonishing, stern words. Where are any mental expressions from you, beyond what you have copied or stolen? Where the born throngs of poets, literats, orators, you promised? Will you but tag after other nations? They struggled long for their literature, painfully working their way, some with deficient languages, some with priest-craft, some in the endeavor just to live— yet achieved for their times, works, poems, perhaps the only solid consolation left to them through ages afterward of shame and decay. You are young, have the perfectest of dialects, a free press, a free government, the world forwarding its best to be with you. As justice has been strictly done to you, from this hour do strict justice to yourself. Strangle the singers who will not sing you loud and strong. Open the doors of The West. Call for new great masters to comprehend new arts, new perfections, new wants. Submit to the most robust bard till he remedy your barrenness. Then you will not need to adopt the heirs of others; you will have true heirs, begotten of yourself, blooded with your own blood.

With composure I see such propositions, seeing more and more every day of the answers that serve. Expressions do not yet serve, for sufficient reasons; but that is getting ready, beyond what the earth has hitherto known, to take home the expressions when they come, and to identify them with the populace of The States, which is the schooling cheaply procured by any outlay any number of years. Such schooling The States extract from the swarms of reprints, and from the current authors and editors. Such service and extract are done after enormous, reckless, free modes, characteristic of The States. Here are to be attained results never elsewhere thought possible; the modes are very grand too. The instincts of the American people are all perfect, and tend to make heroes. It is a rare thing in a man here to understand The States.

All current nourishments to literature serve. Of authors and editors I do not know how many there are in The States, but there are thousands, each one building his or her step to the stairs by which giants shall mount. Of the twenty-four modern mammoth two-double, three-double, and four-double cylinder presses now in the world, printing by steam, twenty-one of them are in These States. The twelve thousand large and small shops for dispensing books and newspapers—the same number of public libraries, any one of which has all the reading wanted to equip a man or woman for American reading—the three thousand different newspapers, the nutriment of the imperfect ones coming in just as usefully as any—the story papers, various, full of strong-flavored romances, widely circulated—the one cent and two-cent journals—the political ones, no matter what side—the weeklies in the country—the sporting and pictorial papers—the monthly magazines, with plentiful imported feed—the sentimental novels, numberless copies of them—the low-priced flaring tales, adventures, biographies—all are prophetic; all waft rapidly on. I see that they swell wide, for reasons. I am not troubled at the movement of them, but greatly pleased. I see plying shuttles, the active ephemeral myriads of books also, faithfully weaving the garments of a generation of men, and a generation of women, they do not perceive or know. What a progress popular reading and writing has made in fifty years! What a progress fifty years hence! The time is at hand when inherent literature will be a main part of These States, as general and real as steam-power, iron, corn, beef, fish. First-rate American persons are to be supplied. Our perennial materials for fresh thoughts, histories, poems, music, orations, religions, recitations, amusements, will then not be disregarded, any more than our perennial fields, mines, rivers, seas. Certain things are established, and are immovable; in those things millions of years stand justified. The mothers and fathers of whom modern centuries have come, have not existed for nothing; they too had brains and hearts. Of course all literature, in all nations and years, will share marked attributes in common, as we all, of all ages, share the common human attributes. America is to be kept coarse and broad. What is to be done is to withdraw from precedents, and be directed to men and women— also to The States in their federalness; for the union of the parts of the body is not more necessary to their life than the union of These States is to their life.

A profound person can easily know more of the people than they know of themselves. Always waiting untold in the souls of the armies of common people, is stuff better than anything that can possibly appear in the leadership of the same. That gives final verdicts. In every department of These States, he who travels with a coterie, or with selected persons, or with imitators, or with infidels, or with the owners of slaves, or with that which is ashamed of the body of a man, or with that which is ashamed of the body of a woman, or with any thing less than the bravest and the openest, travels straight for the slopes of dissolution. The genius of all foreign literature is clipped and cut small, compared to our genius, and is essentially insulting to our usages, and to the organic compacts of These States. Old forms, old poems, majestic and proper in their own lands here in this land are exiles; the air here is very strong. Much that stands well and has a little enough place provided for it in the small scales of European kingdoms, empires, and the like, here stands haggard, dwarfed, ludicrous, or has no place little enough provided for it. Authorities, poems, models, laws, names, imported into America, are useful to America today to destroy them, and so move disencumbered to great works, great days.

Just so long, in our country or any country, as no revolutionists advance, and are backed by the people, sweeping off the swarms of routine representatives, officers in power, book-makers, teachers, ecclesiastics; politicians, just so long, I perceive, do they who are in power fairly represent that country, and remain of use, probably of very great use. To supersede them, when it is the pleasure of These States, full provision is made; and I say the time has arrived to use it with a strong hand. Here also the souls of the armies have not only overtaken the souls of the officers, but passed on, and left the souls of the officers behind out of sight many weeks' journey; and the souls of the armies now go en-masse without officers. Here also formulas, glosses, blanks, minutiæ, are choking the throats of the spokesmen to death. Those things most listened for, certainly those are the things least said. There is not a single History of the World. There is not one of America, or of the organic compacts of These States, or of Washington, or of Jefferson, nor of Language, nor any Dictionary of the English Language. There is no great author; every one has demeaned himself to some etiquette or some impotence. There is no manhood or life-power in poems; there are shoats and geldings more like. Or literature will be dressed up, a fine gentleman, distasteful to our instincts, foreign to our soil. Its neck bends right and left wherever it goes. Its costumes and jewelry prove how little it knows Nature. Its flesh is soft; it shows less and less of the indefinable hard something that is Nature. Where is any thing but the shaved Nature of synods and schools? Where is a savage and luxuriant man? Where is an overseer? In lives, in poems, in codes of law, in Congress, in tuitions, theatres, conversations, argumentations, not a single head lifts itself clean out, with proof that it is their master, and has subordinated them to itself, and is ready to try their superiors. None believes in These States, boldly illustrating them in himself. Not a man faces round at the rest with terrible negative voice, refusing all terms to be bought off from his own eye-sight, or from the soul that he is, or from friendship, or from the body that he is, or from the soil and sea. To creeds, literature, art, the army, the navy, the executive, life is hardly proposed, but the sick and dying are proposed to cure the sick and dying. The churches are one vast lie; the people do not believe them, and they do not believe themselves; the priests are continually telling what they know well enough is not so, and keeping back what they know is so. The spectacle is a pitiful one. I think there can never be again upon the festive earth more bad-disordered persons deliberately taking seats, as of late in These States, at the heads of the public tables—such corpses' eyes for judges—such a rascal and thief in the Presidency.[4]

Up to the present, as helps best, the people, like a lot of large boys, have no determined tastes, are quite unaware of the grandeur of themselves, and of their destiny, and of their immense strides—accept with voracity whatever is presented them in novels, histories, newspapers, poems, schools, lectures, every thing. Pretty soon, through these and other means, their development makes the fibre that is capable of itself, and will assume determined tastes. The young men will be clear what they want, and will have it. They will follow none except him whose spirit leads them in the like spirit with themselves. Any such man will be welcome as the flowers of May. Others will be put out without ceremony. How much is there anyhow, to the young men of These States, in a parcel of helpless dandies, who can neither fight, work, shoot, ride, run, command—some of them devout, some quite insane, some castrated—all second-hand, or third, fourth, or fifth hand—waited upon by waiters, putting not this land first, but always other lands first, talking of art, doing the most ridiculous things for fear of being called ridiculous, smirking and skipping along, continually taking off their hats—no one behaving, dressing, writing, talking, loving, out of any natural and manly tastes of his own, but each one looking cautiously to see how the rest behave, dress, write, talk, love—pressing the noses of dead books upon themselves and upon their country—favoring no poets, philosophs, literats here, but dog-like danglers at the heels of the poets, philosophs, literats of enemies' lands—favoring mental expressions, models of gentlemen and ladies, social habitudes in These States, to grow up in sneaking defiance of the popular substratums of The States? Of course they and the likes of them can never justify the strong poems of America. Of course no feed of theirs is to stop and be made welcome to muscle the bodies, male and female, for Manhattan Island, Brooklyn, Boston, Worcester, Hartford, Portland, Montreal, Detroit, Buffalo, Cleaveland, Milwaukee, St. Louis, Indianapolis, Chicago, Cincinnati, Iowa City, Phila-

4. The proslavery sympathizer Franklin Pierce (U.S. president 1853–57).

delphia, Baltimore, Raleigh, Savannah, Charleston, Mobile, New Orleans, Galveston, Brownsville, San Francisco, Havana, and a thousand equal cities, present and to come. Of course what they and the likes of them have been used for, draws toward its close, after which they will all be discharged, and not one of them will ever be heard of any more.

America, having duly conceived, bears out of herself offspring of her own to do the workmanship wanted. To freedom, to strength, to poems, to personal greatness, it is never permitted to rest, not a generation or part of a generation. To be ripe beyond further increase is to prepare to die. The architects of These States laid their foundations, and passed to further spheres. What they laid is a work done; as much more remains. Now are needed other architects, whose duty is not less difficult, but perhaps more difficult. Each age forever needs architects. America is not finished, perhaps never will be; now America is a divine true sketch. There are Thirty-Two States sketched— the population thirty millions. In a few years there will be Fifty States. Again in a few years there will be A Hundred States, the population hundreds of millions, the freshest and freest of men. Of course such men stand to nothing less than the freshest and freest expression.

Poets here, literats here, are to rest on organic different bases from other countries; not a class set apart, circling only in the circle of themselves, modest and pretty, desperately scratching for rhymes, pallid with white paper, shut off, aware of the old pictures and traditions of the race, but unaware of the actual race around them—not breeding in and in among each other till they all have the scrofula. Lands of ensemble, bards of ensemble! Walking freely out from the old traditions, as our politics has walked out, American poets and literats recognize nothing behind them superior to what is present with them—recognize with joy the sturdy living forms of men and women of These States, the divinity of sex, the perfect eligibility of the female with the male, all The States, liberty and equality, real articles, the different trades, mechanics, the young fellows of Manhattan Island, customs, instincts, slang, Wisconsin, Georgia, the noble Southern heart, the hot blood, the spirit that will be nothing less than master, the filibuster[5] spirit, the Western man, native-born perceptions, the eye for forms, the perfect models of made things, the wild smack of freedom, California, money, electric-telegraphs, free-trade, iron and the iron mines—recognize without demur those splendid resistless black poems, the steam-ships of the sea-board states, and those other resistless splendid poems, the locomotives, followed through the interior states by trains of rail-road cars.

A word remains to be said, as of one ever present, not yet permitted to be acknowledged, discarded or made dumb by literature, and the results apparent. To the lack of an avowed, empowered, unabashed development of sex, (the only salvation for the same,) and to the fact of speakers and writers fraudulently assuming as always dead what every one knows to be always alive, is attributable the remarkable non-personality and indistinctness of modern productions in books, art, talk; also that in the scanned lives of men and women most of them appear to have been for some time past of the neuter gender; and also the stinging fact that in orthodox society today, if the dresses were changed, the men might easily pass for women and the women for men.

---

5. During the 1850s, *filibuster* referred to those who led privately funded armed expeditions against Cuba, Mexico, and countries in Central and South America.

Infidelism usurps most with fœtid polite face; among the rest infidelism about sex. By silence or obedience the pens of savans, poets, historians, biographers, and the rest, have long connived at the filthy law, and books enslaved to it, that what makes the manhood of a man, that sex, womanhood, maternity, desires, lusty animations, organs, acts, are unmentionable and to be ashamed of, to be driven to skulk out of literature with whatever belongs to them. This filthy law has to be repealed—it stands in the way of great reforms. Of women just as much as men, it is the interest that there should not be infidelism about sex, but perfect faith. Women in These States approach the day of that organic equality with men, without which, I see, men cannot have organic equality among themselves. This empty dish, gallantry, will then be filled with something. This tepid wash, this diluted deferential love, as in songs, fictions, and so forth, is enough to make a man vomit; as to manly friendship, everywhere observed in The States, there is not the first breath of it to be observed in print. I say that the body of a man or woman, the main matter, is so far quite unexpressed in poems; but that the body is to be expressed, and sex is. Of bards for These States, if it come to a question, it is whether they shall celebrate in poems the eternal decency of the amativeness of Nature, the motherhood of all, or whether they shall be the bards of the fashionable delusion of the inherent nastiness of sex, and of the feeble and querulous modesty of deprivation. This is important in poems, because the whole of the other expressions of a nation are but flanges out of its great poems. To me, henceforth, that theory of any thing, no matter what, stagnates in its vitals, cowardly and rotten, while it cannot publicly accept, and publicly name, with specific words, the things on which all existence, all souls, all realization, all decency, all health, all that is worth being here for, all of woman and of man, all beauty, all purity, all sweetness, all friendship, all strength, all life, all immortality depend. The courageous soul, for a year or two to come, may be proved by faith in sex, and by disdaining concessions.

To poets and literats—to every woman and man, today or any day, the conditions of the present, needs, dangers, prejudices, and the like, are the perfect conditions on which we are here, and the conditions for wording the future with undissuadable words. These States, receivers of the stamina of past ages and lands, initiate the outlines of repayment a thousand fold. They fetch the American great masters, waited for by old words and new, who accept evil as well as good, ignorance as well as erudition, black as soon as white, foreign-born materials as well as home-born, reject none, force discrepancies into range, surround the whole, concentrate them on present periods and places, show the application to each and any one's body and soul, and show the true use of precedents. Always America will be agitated and turbulent. This day it is taking shape, not to be less so, but to be more so, stormily, capriciously, on native principles, with such vast proportions of parts! As for me, I love screaming, wrestling, boiling-hot days.

Of course, we shall have a national character, an identity. As it ought to be, and as soon as it ought to be, it will be. That, with much else, takes care of itself, is a result, and the cause of greater results. With Ohio, Illinois, Missouri, Oregon—with the states around the Mexican sea—with cheerfully welcomed immigrants from Europe, Asia, Africa—with Connecticut, Vermont, New Hampshire, Rhode Island—with all varied interests, facts, beliefs, parties, genesis—there is being fused a determined character, fit for the broadest use for the freewomen and freemen of The States, accomplished and to be accomplished, without any exception whatever—each indeed free, each idiomatic, as becomes live states and men, but each adhering to one enclosing general form of politics, manners, talk, personal style, as the plenteous varieties of the race adhere to one physical form. Such character is the brain and spine to all, including literature, including poems. Such character, strong, limber, just, open-mouthed, American-blooded, full of pride, full of ease, of passionate friendliness, is to stand compact upon that vast basis of the supremacy of Individuality—that new moral American continent without which, I see, the physical continent remained incomplete, may-be a carcass, a bloat—that newer America, answering face to face with The States, with ever-satisfying and ever-unsurveyable seas and shores.

Those shores you found. I say you have led The States there—have led Me there. I say that none has ever done, or ever can do, a greater deed for The States, than your deed. Others may line out the lines, build cities, work mines, break up farms; it is yours to have been the original true Captain who put to sea, intuitive, positive, rendering the first report, to be told less by any report, and more by the mariners of a thousand bays, in each tack of their arriving and departing, many years after you.

Receive, dear Master, these statements and assurances through me, for all the young men, and for an earnest that we know none before you, but the best following you; and that we demand to take your name into our keeping, and that we understand what you have indicated, and find the same indicated in ourselves, and that we will stick to it and enlarge upon it through These States.

WALT WHITMAN.

1856

Live Oak, with Moss[1]

I.

Not the heat flames up and consumes,
Not the sea-waves hurry in and out,
Not the air, delicious and dry, the air of the ripe summer, bears lightly along
   white down-balls of myriads of seeds, wafted, sailing gracefully, to drop
   where they may,
Not these—O none of these, more than the flames of me, consuming,
   burning for his love whom I love—O none, more than I, hurrying in
   and out;
Does the tide hurry, seeking something, and never give up?—O I, the
   same, to seek my life-long lover;   5
O nor down-balls, nor perfumes, nor the high rain-emitting clouds, are
   borne through the open air, more than my copious soul is borne
   through the open air, wafted in all directions, for friendship, for love.—

---

1. The *Live Oak, with Moss* sequence, composed in the late 1850s, is Whitman's most direct and coherent narrative of "manly love." Whitman included all twelve of the *Live Oak* poems in the forty-five-poem *Calamus* section of the 1860 edition of *Leaves of Grass*, but reordered the sequence in a way that obscured the narrative progression. Fredson Bowers first printed the original sequence in *Studies in Bibliography* (1953) from the manuscript in the Valentine Collection from the Library of Clifton Waller Barrett at the University of Virginia; its first textbook appearance was the 4th edition (1994) of this anthology. On scholarly debate about whether Whitman intended to publish these poems as a sequence, see Robert J. Scholnick in *Walt Whitman Quarterly Review* (2004).

II.

I saw in Louisiana a live-oak growing,
All alone stood it, and the moss hung down from the branches,
Without any companion it grew there, glistening out joyous leaves of
    dark green,
And its look, rude, unbending, lusty, made me think of myself;   10
But I wondered how it could utter joyous leaves, standing alone there
    without its friend, its lover—For I knew I could not;
And I plucked a twig with a certain number of leaves upon it, and twined
    around it a little moss, and brought it away—And I have placed it in
    sight in my room,
It is not needed to remind me as of my friends, (for I believe lately I think
    of little else than of them,)
Yet it remains to me a curious token—I write these pieces, and name them
    after it,
For all that, and though the live oak glistens there in Louisiana, solitary in
    a wide flat space, uttering joyous leaves all its life, without a friend, a
    lover, near—I know very well I could not.   15

III.

When I heard at the close of the day how I had been praised in the Capitol,
    still it was not a happy night for me that followed;
Nor when I caroused—Nor when my favorite plans were accomplished—
    was I really happy,
But that day I rose at dawn from the bed of perfect health, electric,
    inhaling sweet breath,
When I saw the full moon in the west grow pale and disappear in the
    morning light,
When I wandered alone over the beach, and undressing, bathed, laughing
    with the waters, and saw the sun rise,   20
And when I thought how my friend, my lover, was coming, then O I was
    happy;
Each breath tasted sweeter—and all that day my food nourished me
    more—And the beautiful day passed well,
And the next came with equal joy—And with the next, at evening, came
    my friend,
And that night, while all was still, I heard the waters roll slowly continually
    up the shores,
I heard the hissing rustle of the liquid and sands, as directed to me,
    whispering to congratulate me,—For the friend I love lay sleeping by
    my side,   25
In the stillness his face was inclined towards me, while the moon's clear
    beams shone,
And his arm lay lightly over my breast—And that night I was happy.

IV.

This moment as I sit alone, yearning and pensive, it seems to me there are
    other men, in other lands, yearning and pensive.
It seems to me I can look over and behold them, in Germany, France,
    Spain—Or far away in China, India, or Russia—talking other
    dialects,

And it seems to me if I could know those men I should love them as I love
    men in my own lands,   30
It seems to me they are as wise, beautiful, benevolent, as any in my own
    lands;
O I think we should be brethren—I think I should be happy with them.

V.

Long I thought that knowledge alone would suffice me—O if I could but
    obtain knowledge!
Then the Land of the Prairies engrossed me—the south savannas
    engrossed me—For them I would live—I would be their orator;
Then I met the examples of old and new heroes—I heard of warriors,
    sailors, and all dauntless persons—And it seemed to me I too had it
    in me to be as dauntless as any, and would be so;   35
And then to finish all, it came to me to strike up the songs of the New
    World—And then I believed my life must be spent in singing;
But now take notice, Land of the prairies, Land of the south savannas,
    Ohio's land,
Take notice, you Kanuck woods—and you, Lake Huron—and all that with
    you roll toward Niagara—and you Niagara also,
And you, Californian mountains—that you all find some one else that he
    be your singer of songs,
For I can be your singer of songs no longer—I have ceased to enjoy them.   40
I have found him who loves me, as I him, in perfect love,
With the rest I dispense—I sever from all that I thought would suffice me,
    for it does not—it is now empty and tasteless to me,
I heed knowledge, and the grandeur of The States, and the examples of
    heroes, no more,
I am indifferent to my own songs—I am to go with him I love, and he is to
    go with me,
It is to be enough for each of us that we are together—We never separate
    again.—   45

VI.

What think you I have taken my pen to record?
Not the battle-ship, perfect-model'd, majestic, that I saw to day arrive in
    the offing, under full sail,
Nor the splendors of the past day—nor the splendors of the night that
    envelopes me—Nor the glory and growth of the great city spread
    around me,
But the two men I saw to-day on the pier, parting the parting of dear
    friends.
The one to remain hung on the other's neck and passionately kissed him—
    while the one to depart tightly prest the one to remain in his arms.   50

VII.

You bards of ages hence! when you refer to me, mind not so much my poems,
Nor speak of me that I prophesied of The States and led them the way of
    their glories,
But come, I will inform you who I was underneath that impassive
    exterior—I will tell you what to say of me,

Publish my name and hang up my picture as that of the tenderest lover,
The friend, the lover's portrait, of whom his friend, his lover, was fondest, 55
Who was not proud of his songs, but of the measureless ocean of love
    within him—and freely poured it forth,
Who often walked lonesome walks thinking of his dearest friends, his
    lovers,
Who pensive, away from one he loved, often lay sleepless and dissatisfied
    at night,
Who, dreading lest the one he loved might after all be indifferent to him,
    felt the sick feeling—O sick! sick!
Whose happiest days were those, far away through fields, in woods, on
    hills, he and another, wandering hand in hand, they twain, apart
    from other men. 60
Who ever, as he sauntered the streets, curved with his arm the manly
    shoulder of his friend—while the curving arm of his friend rested
    upon him also.

VIII.

Hours continuing long, sore and heavy-hearted,
Hours of the dusk, when I withdraw to a lonesome and unfrequented spot,
    seating myself, leaning my face in my hands,
Hours sleepless, deep in the night, when I go forth, speeding swiftly the
    country roads, or through the city streets, or pacing miles and miles,
    stifling plaintive cries,
Hours discouraged, distracted,—For he, the one I cannot content myself
    without—soon I saw him content himself without me, 65
Hours when I am forgotten—(O weeks and months are passing, but I
    believe I am never to forget!)
Sullen and suffering hours—(I am ashamed—but it is useless—I am what
    I am;)
Hours of torment—I wonder if other men ever have the like, out of the
    like feelings?
Is there even one other like me—distracted—his friend, his lover, lost to
    him?
Is he too as I am now? Does he still rise in the morning, dejected,
    thinking who is lost to him? 70
And at night, awaking, think who is lost?
Does he too harbor his friendship silent and endless? Harbor his anguish
    and passion?
Does some stray reminder, or the casual mention of a name, bring the fit
    back upon him, taciturn and deprest?
Does he see himself reflected in me? In these hours does he see the face
    of his hours reflected?

IX.

I dreamed in a dream of a city where all the men were like brothers, 75
O I saw them tenderly love each other—I often saw them, in numbers,
    walking hand in hand;
I dreamed that was the city of robust friends—Nothing was greater there
    than manly love—it led the rest,
It was seen every hour in the actions of the men of that city, and in all
    their looks and words.—

X.

O you whom I often and silently come where you are, that I may be with
    you,
As I walk by your side, or sit near, or remain in the same room with you,   80
Little you know the subtle electric fire that for your sake is playing
    within me.—

XI.

Earth! Though you look so impassive, ample and spheric there—I now
    suspect that is not all,
I now suspect there is something terrible in you, ready to break forth,
For an athlete loves me,—and I him—But toward him there is something
    fierce and terrible in me,
I dare not tell it in words—not even in these songs.   85

XII.

To the young man, many things to absorb, to engraft, to develop, I teach,
    that he be my eleve,[2]
But if through him speed not the blood of friendship, hot and red—If he
    be not silently selected by lovers, and do not silently select lovers—
    of what use were it for him to seek to become eleve of mine?

1858–59   1953

2. Student (French).

HERMAN MELVILLE
1819–1891

Herman Melville was born in New York City in 1819, the third of eight children of Allan Melvill, a dry-goods merchant, and Maria Gansevoort, daughter of American Revolutionary hero General Peter Gansevoort. Melville's father incurred massive debt before dying suddenly and in delirium in 1832, and his wife and children, then living in Albany, became dependent on the Gansevoorts. Taken out of school when he was twelve, Melville (the *e* was added in the 1830s) held a succession of jobs: at a bank, at his brother Gansevoort's fur-cap store in Albany, at his uncle Thomas Melvill's farm in Pittsfield, Massachusetts, and at a country school near Pittsfield. In 1839 he voyaged to and from Liverpool as a cabin boy, but uncertainties about employment continued on his return. At age twenty-one, in January 1841, he sailed on a whaler for the South Seas. After over a year at sea, Melville and a shipmate, Toby Greene, jumped ship at the Marquesas Islands, approximately one thousand miles northeast of Tahiti, and for a few weeks in the summer of 1842 the two lived among the supposedly cannibalistic islanders of Tapai Valley. Picked up by an Australian whaler less than a month after he deserted, Melville signed on as an ordinary seaman with the naval frigate *United States*, cruised the Pacific, and arrived at Boston in October 1844.

Melville was twenty-five; he later said that from that year he dated the beginning of his life. He apparently did not look for a job after his discharge from the navy; he stayed with his brothers in New York City and began writing *Typee*, which drew on his experiences in the Marquesas. The book, published in 1846 in England and the United States, made a great sensation, capturing the imagination of readers with its combination of anthropological novelty and adventure. Shortly after its publication, Melville began writing a second novel, *Omoo*, which also drew on his experiences in the South Sea islands. Published in 1847, it was another best seller. Three days after his twenty-eighth birthday and in the flush of his success, Melville married Elizabeth Knapp Shaw on August 4, 1847. Her father, Lemuel Shaw, the chief justice of the Massachusetts Supreme Court, had been a school friend of Alan Melvill's. After the marriage Shaw provided several advances against his daughter's inheritance, allowing Melville to establish himself in Manhattan with his bride, his younger brother Allan, Allan's wife, his mother, his four sisters, and his new manuscript. But instead of supplying his publisher with yet another commercially promising tale of a Polynesian adventure, Melville attempted to elevate the travel-narrative genre to the level of spiritual and political allegory. In this third novel, *Mardi*, which was published in April 1849, Melville presented travel (as he would in *Moby-Dick*) as a philosophical journey. It is his longest novel and remains a difficult text for most readers. When first published, it sold poorly and received generally unfavorable reviews. After the birth of his first son, Malcolm, in 1849, Melville, seeking to regain his reputation, rapidly wrote the more accessible *Redburn* (1849), which drew on his travels to Liverpool, and *White-Jacket* (1850), based on his experiences on the man-of-war *United States*. Both novels were received enthusiastically in England and America.

In a buoyant mood, Melville began his whaling novel, *Moby-Dick*. Like *Mardi*, *Moby-Dick* was an enormously ambitious undertaking. There is compelling textual and biographical evidence that Melville wrote the book in stages, radically altering his conception of the novel from a relatively straightforward whaling narrative to something that aspired to be a "Gospels in this century" (as he termed the novel in an 1851 letter to Nathaniel Hawthorne). While composing the novel, Melville came under the spell of Shakespeare, Milton, Emerson, and numerous other writers. Melville was also inspired by his new literary friendship with Hawthorne, whom he had met at an August 1850 picnic in Pittsfield, Massachusetts. Immediately after their meeting, he read Hawthorne's *Mosses from an Old Manse* (1846) and wrote a belated review in which he expressed his thoughts about the challenges facing American writers. Convinced that the day had come when American writers could rival Shakespeare, Melville, in praising Hawthorne's achievements, honored what he believed infused the book he was writing: dark "Shakespearean" truths about human nature and the universe that, "in this world of lies," can be told only "covertly" and "by snatches."

As he continued to work on *Moby-Dick* and struggle with his finances, Melville late in 1850 moved his family to a farm near Pittsfield, where he was able to keep up his friendship with Hawthorne, who was living in nearby Lenox. In May 1851, Melville borrowed $2,050 from an old acquaintance; and as he anticipated doing final work on the galleys of *Moby-Dick*, he painfully defined his literary-economic dilemma to Hawthorne: "What I feel most moved to write, that is banned,—it will not pay. Yet, altogether, write the other way I cannot. So the product is a final hash, and all my books are botches." When *Moby-Dick* was published in late 1851, a reviewer for the *London Britannia* declared it "a most extraordinary work"; and a reviewer in the *New York Tribune* proclaimed that it was "the best production which has yet come from that seething brain, and . . . it gives us a higher opinion of the author's originality and power than even the favorite and fragrant first-fruits of his genius, the never-to-be-forgotten *Typee*." Still, there were a number of negative reviews from critics unhappy with the novel's length, philosophical abstractness, and mixing of genres, and the novel quickly vanished from the literary scene without bringing Melville the critical admiration that he had expected.

But Melville was not totally discouraged. Shortly after publishing *Moby-Dick*, he began *Pierre*, thinking he could express the agonies of the growth of a human psyche in a domestic novel focusing on the romantic, ethical, and intellectual perplexities attending Pierre Glendinning's coming into manhood. As he worked on this novel, reviews of *Moby-Dick* continued to appear. Disturbed by the mixed and sometimes hostile responses (the January 1852 *Southern Quarterly Review*, for instance, said a "writ de lunatic" was justified against Melville and his characters), Melville folded into his novel-in-progress a satirical account of the U.S. literary scene in which the timid and genteel succeed and the boldly adventurous fail. With its depictions of clerical hypocrisy, family dishonesty, and seemingly incestuous sexuality, Melville's wildly inventive and parodic novel was greeted—by those who bothered to take notice of it—as the work of a maniac, and it further hurt his chances for a commercially successful literary career. The novel, published in 1852, was widely denounced as immoral, and one *Pierre*-inspired account of the author was captioned: "HERMAN MELVILLE CRAZY." In a panic, family and friends attempted to get Melville a government job, but nothing came of their efforts.

Melville stayed on at the Pittsfield farm with his expanding household (his second son, Stanwix, was born in 1851, and two daughters, Elizabeth and Frances, were born in 1853 and 1855) and began a new career as a writer of short stories and novellas for two major American monthlies, *Harper's* and *Putnam's*. Paid at modest rates for fiction that was published anonymously, Melville, in works like "Bartleby, the Scrivener," "The Paradise of Bachelors and the Tartarus of Maids," and "Benito Cereno," took on such vexing issues of antebellum culture as racial and gender inequities, the social transformations caused by emerging industrial capitalism, and slavery. Some critics regard these works as among Melville's most socially progressive writings; others argue that Melville's choice of topical subjects should not obscure his metaphysical interest in the situation of individuals who exist, as the narrator of "Bartleby" puts it, "alone, absolutely alone in the universe. A bit of wreck in the mid Atlantic." In these enigmatic fictions, Melville seems more intent on exploring and engaging the ideological discourses of his time than on arguing for any particular reforms. For instance, although there may be no shrewder investigation of white racism and the evils of slavery than "Benito Cereno" (1855), which partly entraps readers in the stereotypical racist assumptions of the sea captain Amasa Delano, the novella is not an obvious attack on slavery as such, and it was ignored by the abolitionist press.

In 1855 Melville published *Israel Potter*, a tale of the American Revolution which had been serialized in *Putnam's*; and in 1856 he collected his stories in a volume titled *The Piazza Tales*. One year later he published *The Confidence-Man*, an indictment of the selfishness and duplicities of his contemporary world in the form of a metaphysical satire, allegory, and low comedy set on a Mississippi steamship. The novel went almost unread in the United States; in England the reviews were admiring but sales were disappointing. Deeply depressed by his struggles as a writer, Melville took an extended trip to Europe and the Levant, from October 1856 to May 1857, with funds supplied by his father-in-law, who hoped that the trip would lighten Melville's mood. But in England Melville confessed to Hawthorne (at the time U.S. consul at Liverpool) that he did not expect to enjoy his travels because "the spirit of adventure" had gone out of him. Upon his return he told a Gansevoort relative that he was "not going to write any more at the present." Instead, he lectured for small fees in eastern and midwestern states on "Statues in Rome" (1857), "The South Sea" (1858), and "Travel" (1859).

After the death of Judge Shaw in 1861, the Melvilles inherited funds that eased their economic pressures, and by October 1863 they were living in Manhattan. In 1864 Melville and his brother Allan made a trip to the Virginia battlefields looking for a Gansevoort cousin and (as Allan put it) hoping to "have opportunities to see that they may describe." Some of those opportunities proved fruitful for *Battle-Pieces* (1866), Melville's volume of Civil War poems, which was barely noticed by reviewers. Highly allusive, tightly formal, and marked by a seemingly Olympian detachment, *Battle-Pieces* is now regarded by many critics, along with Whitman's *Drum-Taps* (1865), as among the best volumes of poetry to have come out of the war. In the same year that he published *Battle-Pieces*, Melville at last obtained a political job as a deputy inspector of customs in New York City. When he had time to write, he worked mostly on his poetry.

These were dreary years for Melville. His job was dull and paid poorly, he had little ability to manage finances, and he was prone to anger and depression. His wife's half-brothers even considered him a danger to their sister, and by early 1867 Elizabeth may have begun to believe that he was insane. Her loyalty to him and her horror of gossip, however, kept her from acting on her minister's suggestion that she seek refuge with her family in Boston. Adding to the misery of the period, Malcolm killed himself late in 1867 at the age of eighteen. In the aftermath of the suicide, Melville began working on a poem about a diverse group of American and European pilgrims—and tourists—who talked their way through some of the same Palestinian scenes he had visited in 1857. This poem, *Clarel*, grew to eighteen thousand lines and appeared in 1876, paid for by a bequest from Elizabeth's uncle Peter Gansevoort. Addressing the conflict between religious faith and Darwinian skepticism that obsessed English contemporaries such as Matthew Arnold, the poem found few readers during the nineteenth century and remains one of Melville's understudied works.

A series of legacies came to the Melvilles in their last years, allowing Melville to retire from the customhouse at the beginning of 1886. During the late 1880s Melville and his wife drew closer together, in part out of their grief at the death of their second son, Stanwix, who was found dead in a San Francisco hotel in 1886. Around that time Melville once again began to devote himself to writing and publishing. He put together two volumes of poems, which he published with his own funds. In the mid-1880s a poem he was working on about a British sailor led him to compose a fictional narrative that was left nearly finished at Melville's death as *Billy Budd, Sailor*, his final study of the tense and ambiguous conflicts between the individual and various forms of authority.

Famously known during the 1840s as the "man who lived among the cannibals," Melville was neglected in the post–Civil War literary world. Shortly before his death in 1891, however, a revival of interest began, especially in England. The true Melville revival, however, took off with essays published on the occasion of Melville's centennial in 1919 and was given added momentum by the posthumous publication of *Billy Budd* in 1924. In one of the most curious phenomena of American literary history, the neglected Melville suddenly came to be regarded in the rarefied company of Shakespeare as a writer who, as Melville said of Shakespeare and Hawthorne, had mastered "the great Art of Telling the Truth" through the dazzling plentitude and sly indirections of his language.

Bartleby, the Scrivener[1]

A Story of Wall-Street

I am a rather elderly man. The nature of my avocations for the last thirty years has brought me into more than ordinary contact with what would seem an interesting and somewhat singular set of men, of whom as yet

---

1. The text of *Bartleby, the Scrivener* is from the first printing in the November and December 1853 issues of *Putnam's Monthly Magazine*.

"Scrivener": copyist or writer; in this story employed to make multiple copies of legal documents with pen and ink.

nothing that I know of has ever been written:—I mean the law-copyists or scriveners. I have known very many of them, professionally and privately, and if I pleased, could relate divers histories, at which good-natured gentlemen might smile, and sentimental souls might weep. But I waive the biographies of all other scriveners for a few passages in the life of Bartleby, who was a scrivener the strangest I ever saw or heard of. While of other law-copyists I might write the complete life, of Bartleby nothing of that sort can be done. I believe that no materials exist for a full and satisfactory biography of this man. It is an irreparable loss to literature. Bartleby was one of those beings of whom nothing is ascertainable, except from the original sources, and in his case those are very small. What my own astonished eyes saw of Bartleby, *that* is all I know of him, except, indeed, one vague report which will appear in the sequel.

Ere introducing the scrivener, as he first appeared to me, it is fit I make some mention of myself, my *employées*, my business, my chambers, and general surroundings; because some such description is indispensable to an adequate understanding of the chief character about to be presented.

Imprimis:[2] I am a man who, from his youth upwards, has been filled with a profound conviction that the easiest way of life is the best. Hence, though I belong to a profession proverbially energetic and nervous, even to turbulence, at times, yet nothing of that sort have I ever suffered to invade my peace. I am one of those unambitious lawyers who never addresses a jury, or in any way draws down public applause; but in the cool tranquillity of a snug retreat, do a snug business among rich men's bonds and mortgages and title-deeds. All who know me, consider me an eminently *safe* man. The late John Jacob Astor,[3] a personage little given to poetic enthusiasm, had no hesitation in pronouncing my first grand point to be prudence; my next, method. I do not speak it in vanity, but simply record the fact, that I was not unemployed in my profession by the late John Jacob Astor; a name which, I admit, I love to repeat, for it hath a rounded and orbicular sound to it, and rings like unto bullion. I will freely add, that I was not insensible to the late John Jacob Astor's good opinion.

Some time prior to the period at which this little history begins, my avocations had been largely increased. The good old office, now extinct in the State of New-York, of a Master in Chancery, had been conferred upon me. It was not a very arduous office, but very pleasantly remunerative. I seldom lose my temper; much more seldom indulge in dangerous indignation at wrongs and outrages; but I must be permitted to be rash here and declare, that I consider the sudden and violent abrogation of the office of Master in Chancery, by the new Constitution,[4] as a——premature act; inasmuch as I had counted upon a life-lease of the profits, whereas I only received those of a few short years. But this is by the way.

My chambers were up stairs at No.—Wall-street. At one end they looked upon the white wall of the interior of a spacious sky-light shaft, penetrating the building from top to bottom. This view might have been considered rather tame than otherwise, deficient in what landscape painters call "life."

2. In the first place (Latin).
3. Astor (1763–1848), a New Yorker, had made one of the largest fortunes of his era, first in fur trading and then in real estate and finance.

4. New York had adopted a "new Constitution" in 1846. *Chancery*: cases involving equity law that do not require a jury.

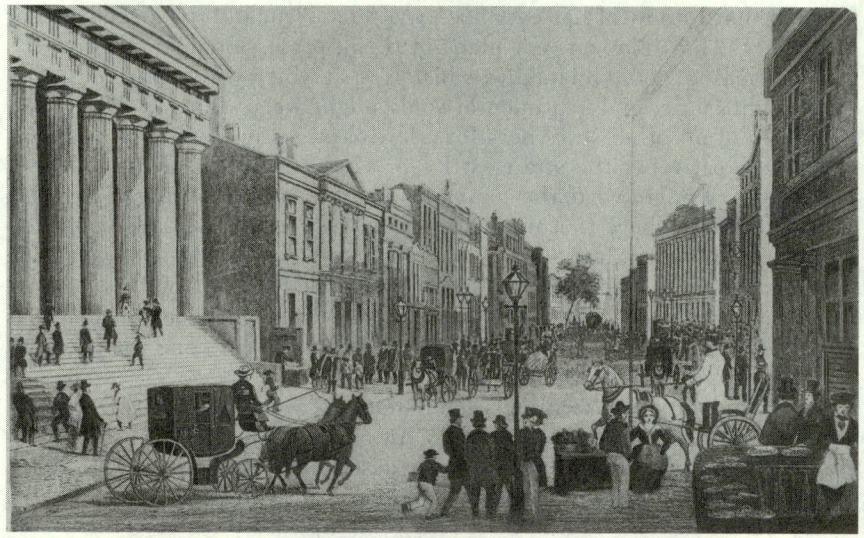

Wall Street, viewed from the corner of Broad Street, New York City, c. 1846.

But if so, the view from the other end of my chambers offered, at least, a contrast, if nothing more. In that direction my windows commanded an unobstructed view of a lofty brick wall, black by age and everlasting shade; which wall required no spy-glass to bring out its lurking beauties, but for the benefit of all near-sighted spectators, was pushed up to within ten feet of my window panes. Owing to the great height of the surrounding buildings, and my chambers being on the second floor, the interval between this wall and mine not a little resembled a huge square cistern.

At the period just preceding the advent of Bartleby, I had two persons as copyists in my employment, and a promising lad as an office-boy. First, Turkey; second, Nippers; third, Ginger Nut. These may seem names, the like of which are not usually found in the Directory. In truth they were nicknames, mutually conferred upon each other by my three clerks, and were deemed expressive of their respective persons or characters. Turkey was a short, pursy[5] Englishman of about my own age, that is, somewhere not far from sixty. In the morning, one might say, his face was of a fine florid hue, but after twelve o'clock, meridian—his dinner hour—it blazed like a grate full of Christmas coals; and continued blazing—but, as it were, with a gradual wane—till 6 o'clock, P.M. or thereabouts, after which I saw no more of the proprietor of the face, which gaining its meridian with the sun, seemed to set with it, to rise, culminate, and decline the following day, with the like regularity and undiminished glory. There are many singular coincidences I have known in the course of my life, not the least among which was the fact, that exactly when Turkey displayed his fullest beams from his red and radiant countenance, just then, too, at that critical moment, began the daily period when I considered his business capacities as seriously disturbed for the remainder of the twenty-four hours. Not that he was absolutely idle,

5. Shortwinded from obesity.

or averse to business then; far from it. The difficulty was, he was apt to be altogether too energetic. There was a strange, inflamed, flurried, flighty recklessness of activity about him. He would be incautious in dipping his pen into his inkstand. All his blots upon my documents, were dropped there after twelve o'clock, meridian. Indeed, not only would he be reckless and sadly given to making blots in the afternoon, but some days he went further, and was rather noisy. At such times, too, his face flamed with augmented blazonry, as if cannel coal had been heaped on anthracite.[6] He made an unpleasant racket with his chair; spilled his sand-box;[7] in mending his pens, impatiently split them all to pieces, and threw them on the floor in a sudden passion; stood up and leaned over his table, boxing his papers about in a most indecorous manner, very sad to behold in an elderly man like him. Nevertheless, as he was in many ways a most valuable person to me, and all the time before twelve o'clock, meridian, was the quickest, steadiest creature too, accomplishing a great deal of work in a style not easy to be matched—for these reasons, I was willing to overlook his eccentricities, though indeed, occasionally, I remonstrated with him. I did this very gently, however, because, though the civilest, nay, the blandest and most reverential of men in the morning, yet in the afternoon he was disposed, upon provocation, to be slightly rash with his tongue, in fact, insolent. Now, valuing his morning services as I did, and resolved not to lose them; yet, at the same time made uncomfortable by his inflamed ways after twelve o'clock; and being a man of peace, unwilling by my admonitions to call forth unseemly retorts from him; I took upon me, one Saturday noon (he was always worse on Saturdays), to hint to him, very kindly, that perhaps now that he was growing old, it might be well to abridge his labors; in short, he need not come to my chambers after twelve o'clock, but, dinner over, had best go home to his lodgings and rest himself till tea-time. But no; he insisted upon his afternoon devotions. His countenance became intolerably fervid, as he oratorically assured me—gesticulating with a long ruler at the other end of the room— that if his services in the morning were useful, how indispensable, then, in the afternoon?

"With submission, sir," said Turkey on this occasion, "I consider myself your right-hand man. In the morning I but marshal and deploy my columns; but in the afternoon I put myself at their head, and gallantly charge the foe, thus!"—and he made a violent thrust with the ruler.

"But the blots, Turkey," intimated I.

"True,—but, with submission, sir, behold these hairs! I am getting old. Surely, sir, a blot or two of a warm afternoon is not to be severely urged against gray hairs. Old age—even if it blot the page—is honorable. With submission, sir, we *both* are getting old."

This appeal to my fellow-feeling was hardly to be resisted. At all events, I saw that go he would not. So I made up my mind to let him stay, resolving, nevertheless, to see to it, that during the afternoon he had to do with my less important papers.

Nippers, the second on my list, was a whiskered, sallow, and, upon the whole, rather piratical-looking young man of about five and twenty. I always deemed him the victim of two evil powers—ambition and indigestion. The

---

6. The combination of "cannel coal," which burns quickly, and "anthracite," which burns slowly, pro- duces a high, bright flame.
7. Sand for blotting ink.

ambition was evinced by a certain impatience of the duties of a mere copyist, an unwarrantable usurpation of strictly professional affairs, such as the
original drawing up of legal documents. The indigestion seemed betokened
in an occasional nervous testiness and grinning irritability, causing the
teeth to audibly grind together over mistakes committed in copying; unnecessary maledictions, hissed, rather than spoken, in the heat of business; and
especially by a continual discontent with the height of the table where he
worked. Though of a very ingenious mechanical turn, Nippers could never
get this table to suit him. He put chips under it, blocks of various sorts, bits
of pasteboard, and at last went so far as to attempt an exquisite adjustment
by final pieces of folded blotting paper. But no invention would answer. If,
for the sake of easing his back, he brought the table lid at a sharp angle well
up towards his chin, and wrote there like a man using the steep roof of a
Dutch house for his desk:—then he declared that it stopped the circulation
in his arms. If now he lowered the table to his waistbands, and stooped over
it in writing, then there was a sore aching in his back. In short, the truth
of the matter was, Nippers knew not what he wanted. Or, if he wanted any
thing, it was to be rid of a scrivener's table altogether. Among the manifestations of his diseased ambition was a fondness he had for receiving visits from
certain ambiguous-looking fellows in seedy coats, whom he called his clients.
Indeed I was aware that not only was he, at times, considerable of a ward-
politician, but he occasionally did a little business at the Justices' courts, and
was not unknown on the steps of the Tombs.[8] I have good reason to believe,
however, that one individual who called upon him at my chambers, and who,
with a grand air, he insisted was his client, was no other than a dun, and the
alleged title-deed, a bill. But with all his failings, and the annoyances he
caused me, Nippers, like his compatriot Turkey, was a very useful man to me;
wrote a neat, swift hand; and, when he chose, was not deficient in a gentlemanly sort of deportment. Added to this, he always dressed in a gentlemanly
sort of way; and so, incidentally, reflected credit upon my chambers. Whereas
with respect to Turkey, I had much ado to keep him from being a reproach to
me. His clothes were apt to look oily and smell of eating-houses. He wore
his pantaloons very loose and baggy in summer. His coats were execrable;
his hat not to be handled. But while the hat was a thing of indifference to me,
inasmuch as his natural civility and deference, as a dependent Englishman,
always led him to doff it the moment he entered the room, yet his coat was
another matter. Concerning his coats, I reasoned with him; but with no
effect. The truth was, I suppose, that a man with so small an income, could
not afford to sport such a lustrous face and a lustrous coat at one and the
same time. As Nippers once observed, Turkey's money went chiefly for red
ink. One winter day I presented Turkey with a highly-respectable looking
coat of my own, a padded gray coat, of a most comfortable warmth, and
which buttoned straight up from the knee to the neck. I thought Turkey
would appreciate the favor, and abate his rashness and obstreperousness of
afternoons. But no. I verily believe that buttoning himself up in so downy
and blanket-like a coat had a pernicious effect upon him; upon the same
principle that too much oats are bad for horses. In fact, precisely as a rash,
restive horse is said to feel his oats, so Turkey felt his coat. It made him insolent. He was a man whom prosperity harmed.

8. The New York City prison, built in 1839 in the spirit of the Egyptian revival architecture of the time.

Though concerning the self-indulgent habits of Turkey I had my own private surmises, yet touching Nippers I was well persuaded that whatever might be his faults in other respects, he was, at least, a temperate young man. But indeed, nature herself seemed to have been his vintner, and at his birth charged him so thoroughly with an irritable, brandy-like disposition, that all subsequent potations were needless. When I consider how, amid the stillness of my chambers, Nippers would sometimes impatiently rise from his seat, and stooping over his table, spread his arms wide apart, seize the whole desk, and move it, and jerk it, with a grim, grinding motion on the floor, as if the table were a perverse voluntary agent, intent on thwarting and vexing him; I plainly perceive that for Nippers, brandy and water were altogether superfluous.

It was fortunate for me that, owing to its peculiar cause—indigestion—the irritability and consequent nervousness of Nippers, were mainly observable in the morning, while in the afternoon he was comparatively mild. So that Turkey's paroxysms only coming on about twelve o'clock, I never had to do with their eccentricities at one time. Their fits relieved each other like guards. When Nippers' was on, Turkey's was off; and *vice versa*. This was a good natural arrangement under the circumstances.

Ginger Nut, the third on my list, was a lad some twelve years old. His father was a carman,[9] ambitious of seeing his son on the bench instead of a cart, before he died. So he sent him to my office as student at law, errand boy, and cleaner and sweeper, at the rate of one dollar a week. He had a little desk to himself, but he did not use it much. Upon inspection, the drawer exhibited a great array of the shells of various sorts of nuts. Indeed, to this quick-witted youth the whole noble science of the law was contained in a nut-shell. Not the least among the employments of Ginger Nut, as well as one which he discharged with the most alacrity, was his duty as cake and apple purveyor for Turkey and Nippers. Copying law papers being proverbially a dry, husky sort of business, my two scriveners were fain to moisten their mouths very often with Spitzenbergs[1] to be had at the numerous stalls nigh the Custom House and Post Office. Also, they sent Ginger Nut very frequently for that peculiar cake—small, flat, round, and very spicy—after which he had been named by them. Of a cold morning when business was but dull, Turkey would gobble up scores of these cakes, as if they were mere wafers—indeed they sell them at the rate of six or eight for a penny—the scrape of his pen blending with the crunching of the crisp particles in his mouth. Of all the fiery afternoon blunders and flurried rashnesses of Turkey, was his once moistening a ginger-cake between his lips, and clapping it on to a mortgage for a seal.[2] I came within an ace of dismissing him then. But he mollified me by making an oriental bow, and saying—"With submission, sir, it was generous of me to find you in stationery on my own account."

Now my original business—that of a conveyancer and title hunter,[3] and drawer-up of recondite documents of all sorts—was considerably increased by receiving the master's office. There was now great work for scriveners. Not only must I push the clerks already with me, but I must have additional

---

9. Driver, teamster.
1. Red-and-yellow New York apples.
2. The narrator is playing on the resemblance between thin cookies and wax wafers used for sealing documents.

3. Someone who checks records to be sure there are no encumbrances on the title of property to be transferred. "Conveyancer": someone who draws up deeds for transferring title to property.

help. In answer to my advertisement, a motionless young man one morning, stood upon my office threshold, the door being open, for it was summer. I can see that figure now—pallidly neat, pitiably respectable, incurably forlorn! It was Bartleby.

After a few words touching his qualifications, I engaged him, glad to have among my corps of copyists a man of so singularly sedate an aspect, which I thought might operate beneficially upon the flighty temper of Turkey, and the fiery one of Nippers.

I should have stated before that ground glass folding-doors divided my premises into two parts, one of which was occupied by my scriveners, the other by myself. According to my humor I threw open these doors, or closed them. I resolved to assign Bartleby a corner by the folding-doors, but on my side of them, so as to have this quiet man within easy call, in case any trifling thing was to be done. I placed his desk close up to a small side-window in that part of the room, a window which originally had afforded a lateral view of certain grimy back-yards and bricks, but which, owing to subsequent erections, commanded at present no view at all, though it gave some light. Within three feet of the panes was a wall, and the light came down from far above, between two lofty buildings, as from a very small opening in a dome. Still further to a satisfactory arrangement, I procured a high green folding screen, which might entirely isolate Bartleby from my sight, though not remove him from my voice. And thus, in a manner, privacy and society were conjoined.

At first Bartleby did an extraordinary quantity of writing. As if long famishing for something to copy, he seemed to gorge himself on my documents. There was no pause for digestion. He ran a day and night line, copying by sun-light and by candle-light. I should have been quite delighted with his application, had he been cheerfully industrious. But he wrote on silently, palely, mechanically.

It is, of course, an indispensable part of a scrivener's business to verify the accuracy of his copy, word by word. Where there are two or more scriveners in an office, they assist each other in this examination, one reading from the copy, the other holding the original. It is a very dull, wearisome, and lethargic affair. I can readily imagine that to some sanguine temperaments it would be altogether intolerable. For example, I cannot credit that the mettlesome poet Byron would have contentedly sat down with Bartleby to examine a law document of, say five hundred pages, closely written in a crimpy hand.

Now and then, in the haste of business, it had been my habit to assist in comparing some brief document myself, calling Turkey or Nippers for this purpose. One object I had in placing Bartleby so handy to me behind the screen, was to avail myself of his services on such trivial occasions. It was on the third day, I think, of his being with me, and before any necessity had arisen for having his own writing examined, that, being much hurried to complete a small affair I had in hand, I abruptly called to Bartleby. In my haste and natural expectancy of instant compliance, I sat with my head bent over the original on my desk, and my right hand sideways, and somewhat nervously extended with the copy, so that immediately upon emerging from his retreat, Bartleby might snatch it and proceed to business without the least delay.

In this very attitude did I sit when I called to him, rapidly stating what it was I wanted him to do—namely, to examine a small paper with me. Imagine my surprise, nay, my consternation, when without moving from his privacy, Bartleby in a singularly mild, firm voice, replied, "I would prefer not to."

I sat awhile in perfect silence, rallying my stunned faculties. Immediately it occurred to me that my ears had deceived me, or Bartleby had entirely misunderstood my meaning. I repeated my request in the clearest tone I could assume. But in quite as clear a one came the previous reply, "I would prefer not to."

"Prefer not to," echoed I, rising in high excitement, and crossing the room with a stride. "What do you mean? Are you moon-struck? I want you to help me compare this sheet here—take it," and I thrust it towards him.

"I would prefer not to," said he.

I looked at him steadfastly. His face was leanly composed; his gray eye dimly calm. Not a wrinkle of agitation rippled him. Had there been the least uneasiness, anger, impatience or impertinence in his manner; in other words, had there been any thing ordinarily human about him, doubtless I should have violently dismissed him from the premises. But as it was, I should have as soon thought of turning my pale plaster-of-paris bust of Cicero[4] out of doors. I stood gazing at him awhile, as he went on with his own writing, and then reseated myself at my desk. This is very strange, thought I. What had one best do? But my business hurried me. I concluded to forget the matter for the present, reserving it for my future leisure. So calling Nippers from the other room, the paper was speedily examined.

A few days after this, Bartleby concluded four lengthy documents, being quadruplicates of a week's testimony taken before me in my High Court of Chancery. It became necessary to examine them. It was an important suit, and great accuracy was imperative. Having all things arranged I called Turkey, Nippers and Ginger Nut from the next room, meaning to place the four copies in the hands of my four clerks, while I should read from the original. Accordingly Turkey, Nippers and Ginger Nut had taken their seats in a row, each with his document in hand, when I called to Bartleby to join this interesting group.

"Bartleby! quick, I am waiting."

I heard a slow scrape of his chair legs on the uncarpeted floor, and soon he appeared standing at the entrance of his hermitage.

"What is wanted?" said he mildly.

"The copies, the copies," said I hurriedly. "We are going to examine them. There"—and I held towards him the fourth quadruplicate.

"I would prefer not to," he said, and gently disappeared behind the screen.

For a few moments I was turned into a pillar of salt,[5] standing at the head of my seated column of clerks. Recovering myself, I advanced towards the screen, and demanded the reason for such extraordinary conduct.

"*Why* do you refuse?"

"I would prefer not to."

With any other man I should have flown outright into a dreadful passion, scorned all further words, and thrust him ignominiously from my presence. But there was something about Bartleby that not only strangely disarmed me, but in a wonderful manner touched and disconcerted me. I began to reason with him.

"These are your own copies we are about to examine. It is labor saving to you, because one examination will answer for your four papers. It is common

4. Roman orator and statesman (106–42 B.C.E.).
5. The punishment of Lot's disobedient wife (Genesis 19.26).

usage. Every copyist is bound to help examine his copy. Is it not so? Will you not speak? Answer!"

"I prefer not to," he replied in a flute-like tone. It seemed to me that while I had been addressing him, he carefully revolved every statement that I made; fully comprehended the meaning; could not gainsay the irresistible conclusion; but, at the same time, some paramount consideration prevailed with him to reply as he did.

"You are decided, then, not to comply with my request—a request made according to common usage and common sense?"

He briefly gave me to understand that on that point my judgment was sound. Yes: his decision was irreversible.

It is not seldom the case that when a man is browbeaten in some unprecedented and violently unreasonable way, he begins to stagger in his own plainest faith. He begins, as it were, vaguely to surmise that, wonderful as it may be, all the justice and all the reason is on the other side. Accordingly, if any disinterested persons are present, he turns to them for some reinforcement for his own faltering mind.

"Turkey," said I, "what do you think of this? Am I not right?"

"With submission, sir," said Turkey, with his blandest tone, "I think that you are."

"Nippers," said I, "what do *you* think of it?"

"I think I should kick him out of the office."

(The reader of nice perceptions will here perceive that, it being morning, Turkey's answer is couched in polite and tranquil terms, but Nippers replies in ill-tempered ones. Or, to repeat a previous sentence, Nippers's ugly mood was on duty, and Turkey's off.)

"Ginger Nut," said I, willing to enlist the smallest suffrage in my behalf, "what do *you* think of it?"

"I think, sir, he's a little *luny*," replied Ginger Nut, with a grin.

"You hear what they say," said I, turning towards the screen, "come forth and do your duty."

But he vouchsafed no reply. I pondered a moment in sore perplexity. But once more business hurried me. I determined again to postpone the consideration of this dilemma to my future leisure. With a little trouble we made out to examine the papers without Bartleby, though at every page or two, Turkey deferentially dropped his opinion that this proceeding was quite out of the common; while Nippers, twitching in his chair with a dyspeptic nervousness, ground out between his set teeth occasional hissing maledictions against the stubborn oaf behind the screen. And for his (Nippers's) part, this was the first and the last time he would do another man's business without pay.

Meanwhile Bartleby sat in his hermitage, oblivious to every thing but his own peculiar business there.

Some days passed, the scrivener being employed upon another lengthy work. His late remarkable conduct led me to regard his ways narrowly. I observed that he never went to dinner; indeed that he never went any where. As yet I had never of my personal knowledge known him to be outside of my office. He was a perpetual sentry in the corner. At about eleven o'clock though, in the morning, I noticed that Ginger Nut would advance toward the opening in Bartleby's screen, as if silently beckoned thither by a gesture invisible to me where I sat. The boy would then leave the office jingling a few pence, and reappear with a handful of ginger-nuts which he delivered in the hermitage, receiving two of the cakes for his trouble.

He lives, then, on ginger-nuts, thought I; never eats a dinner, properly speaking; he must be a vegetarian then; but no; he never eats even vegetables, he eats nothing but ginger-nuts. My mind then ran on in reveries concerning the probable effects upon the human constitution of living entirely on ginger-nuts. Ginger-nuts are so called because they contain ginger as one of their peculiar constituents, and the final flavoring one. Now what was ginger? A hot, spicy thing. Was Bartleby hot and spicy? Not at all. Ginger, then, had no effect upon Bartleby. Probably he preferred it should have none.

Nothing so aggravates an earnest person as a passive resistance. If the individual so resisted be of a not inhuman temper, and the resisting one perfectly harmless in his passivity; then, in the better moods of the former, he will endeavor charitably to construe to his imagination what proves impossible to be solved by his judgment. Even so, for the most part, I regarded Bartleby and his ways. Poor fellow! thought I, he means no mischief; it is plain he intends no insolence; his aspect sufficiently evinces that his eccentricities are involuntary. He is useful to me. I can get along with him. If I turn him away, the chances are he will fall in with some less indulgent employer, and then he will be rudely treated, and perhaps driven forth miserably to starve. Yes. Here I can cheaply purchase a delicious self-approval. To befriend Bartleby; to humor him in his strange wilfulness, will cost me little or nothing, while I lay up in my soul what will eventually prove a sweet morsel for my conscience. But this mood was not invariable with me. The passiveness of Bartleby sometimes irritated me. I felt strangely goaded on to encounter him in new opposition, to elicit some angry spark from him answerable to my own. But indeed I might as well have essayed to strike fire with my knuckles against a bit of Windsor soap.[6] But one afternoon the evil impulse in me mastered me, and the following little scene ensued:

"Bartleby," said I, "when those papers are all copied, I will compare them with you."

"I would prefer not to."

"How? Surely you do not mean to persist in that mulish vagary?"

No answer.

I threw open the folding-doors near by, and turning upon Turkey and Nippers, exclaimed in an excited manner—

"He says, a second time, he won't examine his papers. What do you think of it, Turkey?"

It was afternoon, be it remembered. Turkey sat glowing like a brass boiler, his bald head steaming, his hands reeling among his blotted papers.

"Think of it?" roared Turkey; "I think I'll just step behind his screen, and black his eyes for him!"

So saying, Turkey rose to his feet and threw his arms into a pugilistic position. He was hurrying away to make good his promise, when I detained him, alarmed at the effect of incautiously rousing Turkey's combativeness after dinner.

"Sit down, Turkey," said I, "and hear what Nippers has to say. What do you think of it, Nippers? Would I not be justified in immediately dismissing Bartleby?"

6. Brown hand soap.

"Excuse me, that is for you to decide, sir. I think his conduct quite unusual, and indeed unjust, as regards Turkey and myself. But it may only be a passing whim."

"Ah," exclaimed I, "you have strangely changed your mind then—you speak very gently of him now."

"All beer," cried Turkey; "gentleness is effects of beer—Nippers and I dined together to-day. You see how gentle *I* am, sir. Shall I go and black his eyes?"

"You refer to Bartleby, I suppose. No, not to-day, Turkey," I replied; "pray, put up your fists."

I closed the doors, and again advanced towards Bartleby. I felt additional incentives tempting me to my fate. I burned to be rebelled against again. I remembered that Bartleby never left the office.

"Bartleby," said I, "Ginger Nut is away; just step round to the Post Office, won't you? (it was but a three minutes' walk,) and see if there is any thing for me."

"I would prefer not to."

"You *will* not?"

"I *prefer* not."

I staggered to my desk, and sat there in a deep study. My blind inveteracy returned. Was there any other thing in which I could procure myself to be ignominiously repulsed by this lean, penniless wight?—my hired clerk? What added thing is there, perfectly reasonable, that he will be sure to refuse to do?

"Bartleby!"

No answer.

"Bartleby," in a louder tone.

No answer.

"Bartleby," I roared.

Like a very ghost, agreeably to the laws of magical invocation, at the third summons, he appeared at the entrance of his hermitage.

"Go to the next room, and tell Nippers to come to me."

"I prefer not to," he respectfully and slowly said, and mildly disappeared.

"Very good, Bartleby," said I, in a quiet sort of serenely severe self-possessed tone, intimating the unalterable purpose of some terrible retribution very close at hand. At the moment I half intended something of the kind. But upon the whole, as it was drawing towards my dinner-hour, I thought it best to put on my hat and walk home for the day, suffering much from perplexity and distress of mind.

Shall I acknowledge it? The conclusion of this whole business was, that it soon became a fixed fact of my chambers, that a pale young scrivener, by the name of Bartleby, had a desk there; that he copied for me at the usual rate of four cents a folio (one hundred words); but he was permanently exempt from examining the work done by him, that duty being transferred to Turkey and Nippers, out of compliment doubtless to their superior acuteness; more-over, said Bartleby was never on any account to be dispatched on the most trivial errand of any sort; and that even if entreated to take upon him such a matter, it was generally understood that he would prefer not to—in other words, that he would refuse point-blank.

As days passed on, I became considerably reconciled to Bartleby. His steadiness, his freedom from all dissipation, his incessant industry (except when he chose to throw himself into a standing revery behind his screen), his great stillness, his unalterableness of demeanor under all circumstances, made him a valuable acquisition. One prime thing was this,—*he was always there*;—first in the morning, continually through the day, and the last at night. I had a singular confidence in his honesty. I felt my most precious papers perfectly safe in his hands. Sometimes to be sure I could not, for the very soul of me, avoid falling into sudden spasmodic passions with him. For it was exceeding difficult to bear in mind all the time those strange peculiarities, privileges, and unheard of exemptions, forming the tacit stipulations on Bartleby's part under which he remained in my office. Now and then, in the eagerness of dispatching pressing business, I would inadvertently summon Bartleby, in a short, rapid tone, to put his finger, say, on the incipient tie of a bit of red tape with which I was about compressing some papers. Of course, from behind the screen the usual answer, "I prefer not to," was sure to come; and then, how could a human creature with common infirmities of our nature, refrain from bitterly exclaiming upon such perverseness—such unreasonableness. However, every added repulse of this sort which I received only tended to lessen the probability of my repeating the inadvertence.

Here it must be said, that according to the customs of most legal gentlemen occupying chambers in densely-populated law buildings, there were several keys to my door. One was kept by a woman residing in the attic, which person weekly scrubbed and daily swept and dusted my apartments. Another was kept by Turkey for convenience sake. The third I sometimes carried in my own pocket. The fourth I knew not who had.

Now, one Sunday morning I happened to go to Trinity Church, to hear a celebrated preacher, and finding myself rather early on the ground, I thought I would walk round to my chambers for a while. Luckily I had my key with me; but upon applying it to the lock, I found it resisted by something inserted from the inside. Quite surprised, I called out; when to my consternation a key was turned from within; and thrusting his lean visage at me, and holding the door ajar, the apparition of Bartleby appeared, in his shirt sleeves, and otherwise in a strangely tattered dishabille, saying quietly that he was sorry, but he was deeply engaged just then, and—preferred not admitting me at present. In a brief word or two, he moreover added, that perhaps I had better walk round the block two or three times, and by that time he would probably have concluded his affairs.

Now, the utterly unsurmised appearance of Bartleby, tenanting my lawchambers of a Sunday morning, with his cadaverously gentlemanly *nonchalance*, yet withal firm and self-possessed, had such a strange effect upon me, that incontinently I slunk away from my own door, and did as desired. But not without sundry twinges of impotent rebellion against the mild effrontery of this unaccountable scrivener. Indeed, it was his wonderful mildness chiefly, which not only disarmed me, but unmanned me, as it were. For I consider that one, for the time, is a sort of unmanned when he tranquilly permits his hired clerk to dictate to him, and order him away from his own premises. Furthermore, I was full of uneasiness as to what Bartleby could possibly be doing in my office in his shirt sleeves, and in an otherwise dismantled condition of a Sunday morning. Was any thing amiss going on? Nay, that was out of the question. It was not to be thought of for a moment that Bartleby was an immoral person. But what could he be doing there?— copying? Nay again, whatever might be his eccentricities, Bartleby was an eminently decorous person. He would be the last man to sit down to his desk in any state approaching to nudity. Besides, it was Sunday; and there was something about Bartleby that forbade the supposition that he would by any secular occupation violate the proprieties of the day.

Nevertheless, my mind was not pacified; and full of a restless curiosity, at last I returned to the door. Without hindrance I inserted my key, opened it, and entered. Bartleby was not to be seen. I looked round anxiously, peeped behind his screen; but it was very plain that he was gone. Upon more closely examining the place, I surmised that for an indefinite period Bartleby must have ate, dressed, and slept in my office, and that too without plate, mirror, or bed. The cushioned seat of a ricketty old sofa in one corner bore the faint impress of a lean, reclining form. Rolled away under his desk, I found a blanket; under the empty grate, a blacking box and brush; on a chair, a tin basin, with soap and a ragged towel; in a newspaper a few crumbs of ginger-nuts and a morsel of cheese. Yes, thought I, it is evident enough that Bartleby has been making his home here, keeping bachelor's hall all by himself. Immediately then the thought came sweeping across me, What miserable friendlessness and loneliness are here revealed! His poverty is great; but his solitude, how horrible! Think of it. Of a Sunday, Wall-street is deserted as Petra;[7] and every night of every day it is an emptiness. This building too, which of week-days hums with industry and life, at nightfall echoes with sheer vacancy, and all through Sunday is forlorn. And here Bartleby makes his home; sole spectator of a solitude which he has seen all populous—a sort of innocent and transformed Marius[8] brooding among the ruins of Carthage!

For the first time in my life a feeling of overpowering stinging melancholy seized me. Before, I had never experienced aught but a not-unpleasing sadness. The bond of a common humanity now drew me irresistibly to gloom. A fraternal melancholy! For both I and Bartleby were sons of Adam. I remembered the bright silks and sparkling faces I had seen that day, in gala trim, swan-like sailing down the Mississippi of Broadway; and I contrasted them with the pallid copyist, and thought to myself, Ah, happiness courts the light, so we deem the world is gay; but misery hides aloof, so we deem that misery there is none. These sad fancyings—chimeras, doubtless, of a sick and silly brain—led on to other and more special thoughts, concerning the eccentricities of Bartleby. Presentiments of strange discoveries hovered round me. The scrivener's pale form appeared to me laid out, among uncaring strangers, in its shivering winding sheet.

Suddenly I was attracted by Bartleby's closed desk, the key in open sight left in the lock.

I mean no mischief, seek the gratification of no heartless curiosity, thought I; besides, the desk is mine, and its contents too, so I will make bold to look within. Every thing was methodically arranged, the papers smoothly placed. The pigeon holes were deep, and removing the files of documents, I groped into their recesses. Presently I felt something there, and dragged it out. It was an old bandanna handkerchief, heavy and knotted. I opened it, and saw it was a saving's bank.

I now recalled all the quiet mysteries which I had noted in the man. I remembered that he never spoke but to answer; that though at intervals he had considerable time to himself, yet I had never seen him reading—no,

7. Ancient city whose ruins are in Jordan, on a slope of Mount Hor.

8. Gaius Marius (157–86 B.C.E.), Roman general who returned to power after exile.

not even a newspaper; that for long periods he would stand looking out, at his pale window behind the screen, upon the dead brick wall; I was quite sure he never visited any refectory or eating house; while his pale face clearly indicated that he never drank beer like Turkey, or tea and coffee even, like other men; that he never went any where in particular that I could learn; never went out for a walk, unless indeed that was the case at present; that he had declined telling who he was, or whence he came, or whether he had any relatives in the world; that though so thin and pale, he never complained of ill health. And more than all, I remembered a certain unconscious air of pallid—how shall I call it?—of pallid haughtiness, say, or rather an austere reserve about him, which had positively awed me into my tame compliance with his eccentricities, when I had feared to ask him to do the slightest incidental thing for me, even though I might know, from his long-continued motionlessness, that behind his screen he must be standing in one of those dead-wall reveries of his.

Revolving all these things, and coupling them with the recently discovered fact that he made my office his constant abiding place and home, and not forgetful of his morbid moodiness; revolving all these things, a prudential feeling began to steal over me. My first emotions had been those of pure melancholy and sincerest pity; but just in proportion as the forlornness of Bartleby grew and grew to my imagination, did that same melancholy merge into fear, that pity into repulsion. So true it is, and so terrible too, that up to a certain point the thought or sight of misery enlists our best affections; but, in certain special cases, beyond that point it does not. They err who would assert that invariably this is owing to the inherent selfishness of the human heart. It rather proceeds from a certain hopelessness of remedying excessive and organic ill. To a sensitive being, pity is not seldom pain. And when at last it is perceived that such pity cannot lead to effectual succor, common sense bids the soul be rid of it. What I saw that morning persuaded me that the scrivener was the victim of innate and incurable disorder. I might give alms to his body; but his body did not pain him; it was his soul that suffered, and his soul I could not reach.

I did not accomplish the purpose of going to Trinity Church that morning. Somehow, the things I had seen disqualified me for the time from church-going. I walked homeward, thinking what I would do with Bartleby. Finally, I resolved upon this;—I would put certain calm questions to him the next morning, touching his history, &c., and if he declined to answer them openly and unreservedly (and I supposed he would prefer not), then to give him a twenty dollar bill over and above whatever I might owe him, and tell him his services were no longer required; but that if in any other way I could assist him, I would be happy to do so, especially if he desired to return to his native place, wherever that might be, I would willingly help to defray the expenses. Moreover, if, after reaching home, he found himself at any time in want of aid, a letter from him would be sure of a reply.

The next morning came.

"Bartleby," said I, gently calling to him behind his screen.

No reply.

"Bartleby," said I, in a still gentler tone, "come here; I am not going to ask you to do any thing you would prefer not to do—I simply wish to speak to you."

Upon this he noiselessly slid into view.

"Will you tell me, Bartleby, where you were born?"

"I would prefer not to."

"Will you tell me *any thing* about yourself?"

"I would prefer not to."

"But what reasonable objection can you have to speak to me? I feel friendly towards you."

He did not look at me while I spoke, but kept his glance fixed upon my bust of Cicero, which as I then sat, was directly behind me, some six inches above my head.

"What is your answer, Bartleby?" said I, after waiting a considerable time for a reply, during which his countenance remained immovable, only there was the faintest conceivable tremor of the white attenuated mouth.

"At present I prefer to give no answer," he said, and retired into his hermitage.

It was rather weak in me I confess, but his manner on this occasion nettled me. Not only did there seem to lurk in it a certain calm disdain, but his perverseness seemed ungrateful, considering the undeniable good usage and indulgence he had received from me.

Again I sat ruminating what I should do. Mortified as I was at his behavior, and resolved as I had been to dismiss him when I entered my office, nevertheless I strangely felt something superstitious knocking at my heart, and forbidding me to carry out my purpose, and denouncing me for a villain if I dared to breathe one bitter word against this forlornest of mankind. At last, familiarly drawing my chair behind his screen, I sat down and said: "Bartleby, never mind then about revealing your history; but let me entreat you, as a friend, to comply as far as may be with the usages of this office. Say now you will help to examine papers to-morrow or next day: in short, say now that in a day or two you will begin to be a little reasonable:—say so, Bartleby."

"At present I would prefer not to be a little reasonable," was his mildly cadaverous reply.

Just then the folding-doors opened, and Nippers approached. He seemed suffering from an unusually bad night's rest, induced by severer indigestion than common. He overheard those final words of Bartleby.

"*Prefer not*, eh?" gritted Nippers—"I'd *prefer* him, if I were you, sir," addressing me—"I'd *prefer* him; I'd give him preferences, the stubborn mule! What is it, sir, pray, that he *prefers* not to do now?"

Bartleby moved not a limb.

"Mr. Nippers," said I, "I'd prefer that you would withdraw for the present."

Somehow, of late I had got into the way of involuntarily using this word "prefer" upon all sorts of not exactly suitable occasions. And I trembled to think that my contact with the scrivener had already and seriously affected me in a mental way. And what further and deeper aberration might it not yet produce? This apprehension had not been without efficacy in determining me to summary means.

As Nippers, looking very sour and sulky, was departing, Turkey blandly and deferentially approached.

"With submission, sir," said he, "yesterday I was thinking about Bartleby here, and I think that if he would but prefer to take a quart of good ale every day, it would do much towards mending him, and enabling him to assist in examining his papers."

"So you have got the word too," said I, slightly excited.

"With submission, what word, sir," asked Turkey, respectfully crowding himself into the contracted space behind the screen, and by so doing, making me jostle the scrivener. "What word, sir?"

"I would prefer to be left alone here," said Bartleby, as if offended at being mobbed in his privacy.

"*That's* the word, Turkey," said I—"*that's* it."

"Oh, *prefer?* oh yes—queer word. I never use it myself. But, sir, as I was saying, if he would but prefer—"

"Turkey," interrupted I, "you will please withdraw."

"Oh certainly, sir, if you prefer that I should."

As he opened the folding-door to retire, Nippers at his desk caught a glimpse of me, and asked whether I would prefer to have a certain paper copied on blue paper or white. He did not in the least roguishly accent the word prefer. It was plain that it involuntarily rolled from his tongue. I thought to myself, surely I must get rid of a demented man, who already has in some degree turned the tongues, if not the heads of myself and clerks. But I thought it prudent not to break the dismission at once.

The next day I noticed that Bartleby did nothing but stand at his window in his dead-wall revery. Upon asking him why he did not write, he said that he had decided upon doing no more writing.

"Why, how now? what next?" exclaimed I, "do no more writing?"

"No more."

"And what is the reason?"

"Do you not see the reason for yourself," he indifferently replied.

I looked steadfastly at him, and perceived that his eyes looked dull and glazed. Instantly it occurred to me, that his unexampled diligence in copying by his dim window for the first few weeks of his stay with me might have temporarily impaired his vision.

I was touched. I said something in condolence with him. I hinted that of course he did wisely in abstaining from writing for a while; and urged him to embrace that opportunity of taking wholesome exercise in the open air. This, however, he did not do. A few days after this, my other clerks being absent, and being in a great hurry to dispatch certain letters by the mail, I thought that, having nothing else earthly to do, Bartleby would surely be less inflexible than usual, and carry these letters to the post-office. But he blankly declined. So, much to my inconvenience, I went myself.

Still added days went by. Whether Bartleby's eyes improved or not, I could not say. To all appearance, I thought they did. But when I asked him if they did, he vouchsafed no answer. At all events, he would do no copying. At last, in reply to my urgings, he informed me that he had permanently given up copying.

"What!" exclaimed I; "suppose your eyes should get entirely well—better than ever before—would you not copy then?"

"I have given up copying," he answered, and slid aside.

He remained as ever, a fixture in my chamber. Nay—if that were possible—he became still more of a fixture than before. What was to be done? He would do nothing in the office: why should he stay there? In plain fact, he had now become a millstone to me, not only useless as a necklace, but afflictive to bear. Yet I was sorry for him. I speak less than truth when I say that, on his own account, he occasioned me uneasiness. If he would but have named a single relative or friend, I would instantly have written, and urged their taking the poor fellow away to some convenient retreat. But he seemed alone, absolutely alone in the universe. A bit of wreck in the mid Atlantic. At length, necessities connected with my business tyrannized over all other considerations. Decently as I could, I told Bartleby that in six days' time he must unconditionally leave the office. I warned him to take measures, in the interval, for procuring some other abode. I offered to assist him in this endeavor, if he himself would but take the first step towards a removal. "And when you finally quit me, Bartleby," added I, "I shall see that you go not away entirely unprovided. Six days from this hour, remember."

At the expiration of that period, I peeped behind the screen, and lo! Bartleby was there.

I buttoned up my coat, balanced myself; advanced slowly towards him, touched his shoulder, and said, "The time has come; you must quit this place; I am sorry for you; here is money; but you must go."

"I would prefer not," he replied, with his back still towards me.

"You *must*."

He remained silent.

Now I had an unbounded confidence in this man's common honesty. He had frequently restored to me sixpences and shillings carelessly dropped upon the floor, for I am apt to be very reckless in such shirt-button affairs. The proceeding then which followed will not be deemed extraordinary.

"Bartleby," said I, "I owe you twelve dollars on account; here are thirty-two; the odd twenty are yours.—Will you take it?" and I handed the bills towards him.

But he made no motion.

"I will leave them here then," putting them under a weight on the table. Then taking my hat and cane and going to the door I tranquilly turned and added—"After you have removed your things from these offices, Bartleby, you will of course lock the door—since every one is now gone for the day but you—and if you please, slip your key underneath the mat, so that I may have it in the morning. I shall not see you again; so good-bye to you. If hereafter in your new place of abode I can be of any service to you, do not fail to advise me by letter. Good-bye, Bartleby, and fare you well."

But he answered not a word; like the last column of some ruined temple, he remained standing mute and solitary in the middle of the otherwise deserted room.

As I walked home in a pensive mood, my vanity got the better of my pity. I could not but highly plume myself on my masterly management in getting rid of Bartleby. Masterly I call it, and such it must appear to any dispassionate thinker. The beauty of my procedure seemed to consist in its perfect quietness. There was no vulgar bullying, no bravado of any sort, no choleric hectoring, and striding to and fro across the apartment, jerking out vehement commands for Bartleby to bundle himself off with his beggarly traps. Nothing of the kind. Without loudly bidding Bartleby depart—as an inferior genius might have done—I *assumed* the ground that depart he must; and upon that assumption built all I had to say. The more I thought over my procedure, the more I was charmed with it. Nevertheless, next morning, upon awakening, I had my doubts,—I had somehow slept off the fumes of vanity. One of the coolest and wisest hours a man has, is just after he awakes in the morning. My procedure seemed as sagacious as ever,—but only in theory. How it would prove in practice—there was the rub. It was truly a beautiful thought to have assumed Bartleby's departure; but, after all, that assumption was simply my own, and none of Bartleby's. The great point was, not whether I had assumed that he would quit me, but whether he would prefer so to do. He was more a man of preferences than assumptions.

After breakfast, I walked down town, arguing the probabilities *pro* and *con*. One moment I thought it would prove a miserable failure, and Bartleby would be found all alive at my office as usual; the next moment it seemed certain that I should see his chair empty. And so I kept veering about. At the corner of Broadway and Canal-street, I saw quite an excited group of people standing in earnest conversation.

"I'll take odds he doesn't," said a voice as I passed.

"Doesn't go?—done!" said I, "put up your money."

I was instinctively putting my hand in my pocket to produce my own, when I remembered that this was an election day. The words I had overheard bore no reference to Bartleby, but to the success or non-success of some candidate for the mayoralty. In my intent frame of mind, I had, as it were, imagined that all Broadway shared in my excitement, and were debating the same question with me. I passed on, very thankful that the uproar of the street screened my momentary absent-mindedness.

As I had intended, I was earlier than usual at my office door. I stood listening for a moment. All was still. He must be gone. I tried the knob. The door was locked. Yes, my procedure had worked to a charm; he indeed must be vanished. Yet a certain melancholy mixed with this: I was almost sorry for my brilliant success. I was fumbling under the door mat for the key, which Bartleby was to have left there for me, when accidentally my knee knocked against a panel, producing a summoning sound, and in response a voice came to me from within—"Not yet; I am occupied."

It was Bartleby.

I was thunderstruck. For an instant I stood like the man who, pipe in mouth, was killed one cloudless afternoon long ago in Virginia, by summer lightning; at his own warm open window he was killed, and remained leaning out there upon the dreamy afternoon, till some one touched him, when he fell.

"Not gone!" I murmured at last. But again obeying that wondrous ascendancy which the inscrutable scrivener had over me, and from which ascendancy, for all my chafing, I could not completely escape, I slowly went down stairs and out into the street, and while walking round the block, considered what I should next do in this unheard-of perplexity. Turn the man out by an actual thrusting I could not; to drive him away by calling him hard names would not do; calling in the police was an unpleasant idea; and yet, permit him to enjoy his cadaverous triumph over me,—this too I could not think of. What was to be done? or, if nothing could be done, was there any thing further that I could *assume* in the matter? Yes, as before I had prospectively assumed that Bartleby would depart, so now I might retrospectively assume that departed he was. In the legitimate carrying out of this assumption, I might enter my office in a great hurry, and pretending not to see Bartleby at all, walk straight against him as if he were air. Such a proceeding would in a singular degree have the appearance of a home-thrust. It was hardly possible that Bartleby could withstand such an application of the doctrine of assumptions. But upon second thoughts the success of the plan seemed rather dubious. I resolved to argue the matter over with him again.

"Bartleby," said I, entering the office, with a quietly severe expression, "I am seriously displeased. I am pained, Bartleby. I had thought better of you. I had imagined you of such a gentlemanly organization, that in any delicate dilemma a slight hint would suffice—in short, an assumption. But it appears I am deceived. Why," I added, unaffectedly starting, "you have not even touched that money yet," pointing to it, just where I had left it the evening previous.

He answered nothing.

"Will you, or will you not, quit me?" I now demanded in a sudden passion, advancing close to him.

"I would prefer *not* to quit you," he replied, gently emphasizing the *not*.

"What earthly right have you to stay here? Do you pay any rent? Do you pay my taxes? Or is this property yours?"

He answered nothing.

"Are you ready to go on and write now? Are your eyes recovered? Could you copy a small paper for me this morning? or help examine a few lines? or step round to the post-office? In a word, will you do any thing at all, to give a coloring to your refusal to depart the premises?"

He silently retired into his hermitage.

I was now in such a state of nervous resentment that I thought it but prudent to check myself at present from further demonstrations. Bartleby and I were alone. I remembered the tragedy of the unfortunate Adams and the still more unfortunate Colt in the solitary office of the latter; and how poor Colt, being dreadfully incensed by Adams,[9] and imprudently permitting himself to get wildly excited, was at unawares hurried into his fatal act—an act which certainly no man could possibly deplore more than the actor himself. Often it had occurred to me in my ponderings upon the subject, that had that altercation taken place in the public street, or at a private residence, it would not have terminated as it did. It was the circumstance of being alone in a solitary office, up stairs, of a building entirely unhallowed by humanizing domestic associations—an uncarpeted office, doubtless, of a dusty, haggard sort of appearance;—this it must have been, which greatly helped to enhance the irritable desperation of the hapless Colt.

But when this old Adam of resentment rose in me and tempted me concerning Bartleby, I grappled him and threw him. How? Why, simply by recalling the divine injunction: "A new commandment give I unto you, that ye love one another."[1] Yes, this it was that saved me. Aside from higher considerations, charity often operates as a vastly wise and prudent principle—a great safeguard to its possessor. Men have committed murder for jealousy's sake, and anger's sake, and hatred's sake, and selfishness' sake, and spiritual pride's sake; but no man that ever I heard of, ever committed a diabolical murder for sweet charity's sake. Mere self-interest, then, if no better motive can be enlisted, should, especially with high-tempered men, prompt all beings to charity and philanthropy. At any rate, upon the occasion in question, I strove to drown my exasperated feelings towards the scrivener by benevolently con-

9. Notorious murder case that occurred while Melville was in the South Seas. In 1841 Samuel Adams, a printer, called on John C. Colt (brother of the inventor of the revolver) at Broadway and Chambers Street in lower Manhattan to collect a debt. Colt murdered Adams with a hatchet and crated the corpse for shipment to New Orleans. The body was found, and Colt was soon arrested. Despite his pleas of self-defense Colt was convicted the next year, amid continuing newspaper publicity, and stabbed himself to death just before he was to be hanged. The setting of "Bartleby" is not far from the scene of the murder.
1. John 13.34.

structing his conduct. Poor fellow, poor fellow! thought I, he don't mean any thing; and besides, he has seen hard times, and ought to be indulged.

I endeavored also immediately to occupy myself, and at the same time to comfort my despondency. I tried to fancy that in the course of the morning, at such time as might prove agreeable to him, Bartleby, of his own free accord, would emerge from his hermitage, and take up some decided line of march in the direction of the door. But no. Half-past twelve o'clock came; Turkey began to glow in the face, overturn his inkstand, and become generally obstreperous; Nippers abated down into quietude and courtesy; Ginger Nut munched his noon apple; and Bartleby remained standing at his window in one of his profoundest dead-wall reveries. Will it be credited? Ought I to acknowledge it? That afternoon I left the office without saying one further word to him.

Some days now passed, during which, at leisure intervals I looked a little into "Edwards on the Will," and "Priestley on Necessity."[2] Under the circumstances, those books induced a salutary feeling. Gradually I slid into the persuasion that these troubles of mine touching the scrivener, had been all predestinated from eternity, and Bartleby was billeted upon me for some mysterious purpose of an all-wise Providence, which it was not for a mere mortal like me to fathom. Yes, Bartleby, stay there behind your screen, thought I; I shall persecute you no more; you are harmless and noiseless as any of these old chairs; in short, I never feel so private as when I know you are here. At last I see it, I feel it; I penetrate to the predestinated purpose of my life. I am content. Others may have loftier parts to enact; but my mission in this world, Bartleby, is to furnish you with office-room for such period as you may see fit to remain.

I believe that this wise and blessed frame of mind would have continued with me, had it not been for the unsolicited and uncharitable remarks obtruded upon me by my professional friends who visited the rooms. But thus it often is, that the constant friction of illiberal minds wears out at last the best resolves of the more generous. Though to be sure, when I reflected upon it, it was not strange that people entering my office should be struck by the peculiar aspect of the unaccountable Bartleby, and so be tempted to throw out some sinister observations concerning him. Sometimes an attorney having business with me, and calling at my office, and finding no one but the scrivener there, would undertake to obtain some sort of precise information from him touching my whereabouts; but without heeding his idle talk, Bartleby would remain standing immovable in the middle of the room. So after contemplating him in that position for a time, the attorney would depart, no wiser than he came.

Also, when a Reference[3] was going on, and the room full of lawyers and witnesses and business was driving fast; some deeply occupied legal gentleman present, seeing Bartleby wholly unemployed, would request him to run round to his (the legal gentleman's) office and fetch some papers for him.

---

2. *Freedom of the Will*, by colonial minister Jonathan Edwards (1703–1754), and *Doctrine of Philosophical Necessity Illustrated*, by English theologian and scientist Joseph Priestley (1733–1804). Both concluded that the will is not free, though from different perspectives. Whereas Edwards believed that God before the beginning of time had decided who should be saved and who should be damned (the Calvinist doctrine of predestination), Priestley rejected Calvinism and believed that benevolent divine forces in the material universe constrained individual free will in order to guide humankind towards a higher perfection.
3. The act of referring a disputed matter to referees.

Thereupon, Bartleby would tranquilly decline, and yet remain idle as before. Then the lawyer would give a great stare, and turn to me. And what could I say? At last I was made aware that all through the circle of my professional acquaintance, a whisper of wonder was running round, having reference to the strange creature I kept at my office. This worried me very much. And as the idea came upon me of his possibly turning out a long-lived man, and keep occupying my chambers, and denying my authority; and perplexing my visitors; and scandalizing my professional reputation; and casting a general gloom over the premises; keeping soul and body together to the last upon his savings (for doubtless he spent but half a dime a day), and in the end perhaps outlive me, and claim possession of my office by right of his perpetual occupancy: as all these dark anticipations crowded upon me more and more, and my friends continually intruded their relentless remarks upon the apparition in my room; a great change was wrought in me. I resolved to gather all my faculties together, and for ever rid me of this intolerable incubus.

Ere revolving any complicated project, however, adapted to this end, I first simply suggested to Bartleby the propriety of his permanent departure. In a calm and serious tone, I commended the idea to his careful and mature consideration. But having taken three days to meditate upon it, he apprised me that his original determination remained the same; in short, that he still preferred to abide with me.

What shall I do? I now said to myself, buttoning up my coat to the last button. What shall I do? what ought I to do? what does conscience say I *should* do with this man, or rather ghost. Rid myself of him, I must; go, he shall. But how? You will not thrust him, the poor, pale, passive mortal,—you will not thrust such a helpless creature out of your door? you will not dishonor yourself by such cruelty? No, I will not, I cannot do that. Rather would I let him live and die here, and then mason up his remains in the wall. What then will you do? For all your coaxing, he will not budge. Bribes he leaves under your own paper-weight on your table; in short, it is quite plain that he prefers to cling to you.

Then something severe, something unusual must be done. What! surely you will not have him collared by a constable, and commit his innocent pallor to the common jail? And upon what ground could you procure such a thing to be done?—a vagrant, is he? What! he a vagrant, a wanderer, who refuses to budge? It is because he will *not* be a vagrant, then, that you seek to count him *as* a vagrant. That is too absurd. No visible means of support: there I have him. Wrong again: for indubitably he *does* support himself, and that is the only unanswerable proof that any man can show of his possessing the means so to do. No more then. Since he will not quit me, I must quit him. I will change my offices; I will move elsewhere; and give him fair notice, that if I find him on my new premises I will then proceed against him as a common trespasser.

Acting accordingly, next day I thus addressed him: "I find these chambers too far from the City Hall; the air is unwholesome. In a word, I propose to remove my offices next week, and shall no longer require your services. I tell you this now, in order that you may seek another place."

He made no reply, and nothing more was said.

On the appointed day I engaged carts and men, proceeded to my chambers, and having but little furniture, every thing was removed in a few hours. Throughout, the scrivener remained standing behind the screen, which I directed to be removed the last thing. It was withdrawn; and being folded up like a huge folio, left him the motionless occupant of a naked room. I stood in the entry watching him a moment, while something from within me upbraided me.

I re-entered, with my hand in my pocket—and—and my heart in my mouth.

"Good-bye, Bartleby; I am going—good-bye, and God some way bless you; and take that," slipping something in his hand. But it dropped upon the floor, and then,—strange to say—I tore myself from him whom I had so longed to be rid of.

Established in my new quarters, for a day or two I kept the door locked, and started at every footfall in the passages. When I returned to my rooms after any little absence, I would pause at the threshold for an instant, and attentively listen, ere applying my key. But these fears were needless. Bartleby never came nigh me.

I thought all was going well, when a perturbed looking stranger visited me, inquiring whether I was the person who had recently occupied rooms at No.—Wall-street.

Full of forebodings, I replied that I was.

"Then sir," said the stranger, who proved a lawyer, "you are responsible for the man you left there. He refuses to do any copying; he refuses to do any thing; he says he prefers not to; and he refuses to quit the premises."

"I am very sorry, sir," said I, with assumed tranquillity, but an inward tremor, "but, really, the man you allude to is nothing to me—he is no relation or apprentice of mine, that you should hold me responsible for him."

"In mercy's name, who is he?"

"I certainly cannot inform you. I know nothing about him. Formerly I employed him as a copyist; but he has done nothing for me now for some time past."

"I shall settle him then,—good morning, sir."

Several days passed, and I heard nothing more; and though I often felt a charitable prompting to call at the place and see poor Bartleby, yet a certain squeamishness of I know not what withheld me.

All is over with him, by this time, thought I at last, when through another week no further intelligence reached me. But coming to my room the day after, I found several persons waiting at my door in a high state of nervous excitement.

"That's the man—here he comes," cried the foremost one, whom I recognized as the lawyer who had previously called upon me alone.

"You must take him away, sir, at once," cried a portly person among them, advancing upon me, and whom I knew to be the landlord of No.—Wall-street. "These gentlemen, my tenants, cannot stand it any longer; Mr. B——" pointing to the lawyer, "has turned him out of his room, and he now persists in haunting the building generally, sitting upon the banisters of the stairs by day, and sleeping in the entry by night. Every body is concerned; clients are leaving the offices; some fears are entertained of a mob; something you must do, and that without delay."

Aghast at this torrent, I fell back before it, and would fain have locked myself in my new quarters. In vain I persisted that Bartleby was nothing to me—no more than to any one else. In vain:—I was the last person known to have any thing to do with him, and they held me to the terrible account.

Fearful then of being exposed in the papers (as one person present obscurely threatened) I considered the matter, and at length said, that if the lawyer would give me a confidential interview with the scrivener, in his (the lawyer's) own room, I would that afternoon strive my best to rid them of the nuisance they complained of.

Going up stairs to my old haunt, there was Bartleby silently sitting upon the banister at the landing.

"What are you doing here, Bartleby?" said I.

"Sitting upon the banister," he mildly replied.

I motioned him into the lawyer's room, who then left us.

"Bartleby," said I, "are you aware that you are the cause of great tribulation to me, by persisting in occupying the entry after being dismissed from the office?"

No answer.

"Now one of two things must take place. Either you must do something, or something must be done to you. Now what sort of business would you like to engage in? Would you like to re-engage in copying for some one?"

"No; I would prefer not to make any change."

"Would you like a clerkship in a dry-goods store?"

"There is too much confinement about that. No, I would not like a clerk-ship; but I am not particular."

"Too much confinement," I cried, "why you keep yourself confined all the time!"

"I would prefer not to take a clerkship," he rejoined, as if to settle that little item at once.

"How would a bar-tender's business suit you? There is no trying of the eyesight in that."

"I would not like it at all; though, as I said before, I am not particular."

His unwonted wordiness inspirited me. I returned to the charge.

"Well then, would you like to travel through the country collecting bills for the merchants? That would improve your health."

"No, I would prefer to be doing something else."

"How then would going as a companion to Europe, to entertain some young gentleman with your conversation,—how would that suit you?"

"Not at all. It does not strike me that there is any thing definite about that. I like to be stationary. But I am not particular."

"Stationary you shall be then," I cried, now losing all patience, and for the first time in all my exasperating connection with him fairly flying into a passion. "If you do not go away from these premises before night, I shall feel bound—indeed I *am* bound—to—to—to quit the premises myself!" I rather absurdly concluded, knowing not with what possible threat to try to frighten his immobility into compliance. Despairing of all further efforts, I was precipitately leaving him, when a final thought occurred to me—one which had not been wholly unindulged before.

"Bartleby," said I, in the kindest tone I could assume under such exciting circumstances, "will you go home with me now—not to my office, but my dwelling—and remain there till we can conclude upon some convenient arrangement for you at our leisure? Come, let us start now, right away."

"No: at present I would prefer not to make any change at all."

I answered nothing; but effectually dodging every one by the suddenness and rapidity of my flight, rushed from the building, ran up Wall-street towards Broadway, and jumping into the first omnibus was soon removed from pursuit. As soon as tranquillity returned I distinctly perceived that I had now done all that I possibly could, both in respect to the demands of the landlord and his tenants, and with regard to my own desire and sense of duty, to benefit Bartleby, and shield him from rude persecution. I now strove to be entirely care-free and quiescent; and my conscience justified me in the attempt; though indeed it was not so successful as I could have wished. So fearful was I of being again hunted out by the incensed landlord and his exasperated tenants, that, surrendering my business to Nippers, for a few days I drove about the upper part of the town and through the sub-urbs, in my rockaway; crossed over to Jersey City and Hoboken, and paid fugitive visits to Manhattanville and Astoria.[4] In fact I almost lived in my rockaway for the time.

When again I entered my office, lo, a note from the landlord lay upon the desk. I opened it with trembling hands. It informed me that the writer had sent to the police, and had Bartleby removed to the Tombs as a vagrant. More-over, since I knew more about him than any one else, he wished me to appear at that place, and make a suitable statement of the facts. These tidings had a conflicting effect upon me. At first I was indignant; but at last almost approved. The landlord's energetic, summary disposition, had led him to adopt a proce-dure which I do not think I would have decided upon myself; and yet as a last resort, under such peculiar circumstances, it seemed the only plan.

As I afterwards learned, the poor scrivener, when told that he must be conducted to the Tombs, offered not the slightest obstacle, but in his pale unmoving way, silently acquiesced.

Some of the compassionate and curious bystanders joined the party; and headed by one of the constables arm in arm with Bartleby, the silent pro-cession filed its way through all the noise, and heat, and joy of the roaring thoroughfares at noon.

The same day I received the note I went to the Tombs, or to speak more properly, the Halls of Justice. Seeking the right officer, I stated the purpose of my call, and was informed that the individual I described was indeed within. I then assured the functionary that Bartleby was a perfectly honest man, and greatly to be compassionated, however unaccountably eccentric. I narrated all I knew, and closed by suggesting the idea of letting him remain in as indulgent confinement as possible till something less harsh might be done—though indeed I hardly knew what. At all events, if nothing else could be decided upon, the alms-house must receive him. I then begged to have an interview.

Being under no disgraceful charge, and quite serene and harmless in all his ways, they had permitted him freely to wander about the prison, and especially in the inclosed grass-platted yards thereof. And so I found him there, standing all alone in the quietest of the yards, his face towards a high wall, while all around, from the narrow slits of the jail windows, I thought I saw peering out upon him the eyes of murderers and thieves.

"Bartleby!"

"I know you," he said, without looking round,—"and I want nothing to say to you."

---

4. The narrator crossed the Hudson River to Jer-sey City and Hoboken, then drove far up Manhat-tan Island to the community of Manhattanville (Grant's Tomb is in what was Manhattanville), and finally crossed the East River to Astoria, on Long Island. "Rockaway": light open-sided carriage.

"It was not I that brought you here, Bartleby," said I, keenly pained at his implied suspicion. "And to you, this should not be so vile a place. Nothing reproachful attaches to you by being here. And see, it is not so sad a place as one might think. Look, there is the sky, and here is the grass."

"I know where I am," he replied, but would say nothing more, and so I left him.

As I entered the corridor again, a broad meat-like man, in an apron, accosted me, and jerking his thumb over his shoulder said—"Is that your friend?"

"Yes."

"Does he want to starve? If he does, let him live on the prison fare, that's all."

"Who are you?" asked I, not knowing what to make of such an unofficially speaking person in such a place.

"I am the grub-man. Such gentlemen as have friends here, hire me to provide them with something good to eat."

"Is this so?" said I, turning to the turnkey.

He said it was.

"Well then," said I, slipping some silver into the grub-man's hands (for so they called him). "I want you to give particular attention to my friend there; let him have the best dinner you can get. And you must be as polite to him as possible."

"Introduce me, will you?" said the grub-man, looking at me with an expression which seemed to say he was all impatience for an opportunity to give a specimen of his breeding.

Thinking it would prove of benefit to the scrivener, I acquiesced; and asking the grub-man his name, went up with him to Bartleby.

"Bartleby, this is Mr. Cutlets; you will find him very useful to you."

"Your sarvant, sir, your sarvant," said the grub-man, making a low salutation behind his apron. "Hope you find it pleasant here, sir;—spacious grounds—cool apartments, sir—hope you'll stay with us some time—try to make it agreeable. May Mrs. Cutlets and I have the pleasure of your company to dinner, sir, in Mrs. Cutlets' private room?"

"I prefer not to dine to-day," said Bartleby, turning away. "It would disagree with me; I am unused to dinners." So saying he slowly moved to the other side of the inclosure, and took up a position fronting the dead-wall.

"How's this?" said the grub-man, addressing me with a stare of astonishment. "He's odd, aint he?"

"I think he is a little deranged," said I, sadly.

"Deranged? deranged is it? Well now, upon my word, I thought that friend of yourn was a gentleman forger; they are always pale and genteel-like, them forgers. I can't help pity 'em—can't help it, sir. Did you know Monroe Edwards?"[5] he added touchingly, and paused. Then, laying his hand pityingly on my shoulder, sighed, "he died of consumption at Sing-Sing.[6] So you weren't acquainted with Monroe?"

"No, I was never socially acquainted with any forgers. But I cannot stop longer. Look to my friend yonder. You will not lose by it. I will see you again."

Some few days after this, I again obtained admission to the Tombs, and went through the corridors in quest of Bartleby; but without finding him.

5. The much-publicized trial of Colonel Edwards (1808–1847), accused of swindling two firms, was held in New York City in 1842 and ended in his conviction.
6. Prison at Ossining, New York, approximately thirty-five miles north of lower Manhattan.

"I saw him coming from his cell not long ago," said a turnkey, "may be he's gone to loiter in the yards."

So I went in that direction.

"Are you looking for the silent man?" said another turnkey passing me. "Yonder he lies—sleeping in the yard there. 'Tis not twenty minutes since I saw him lie down."

The yard was entirely quiet. It was not accessible to the common prisoners. The surrounding walls, of amazing thickness, kept off all sounds behind them. The Egyptian character of the masonry weighed upon me with its gloom. But a soft imprisoned turf grew under foot. The heart of the eternal pyramids, it seemed, wherein, by some strange magic, through the clefts, grass-seed, dropped by birds, had sprung.

Strangely huddled at the base of the wall, his knees drawn up, and lying on his side, his head touching the cold stones, I saw the wasted Bartleby. But nothing stirred. I paused; then went close up to him; stooped over, and saw that his dim eyes were open; otherwise he seemed profoundly sleeping. Something prompted me to touch him. I felt his hand, when a tingling shiver ran up my arm and down my spine to my feet.

The round face of the grub-man peered upon me now. "His dinner is ready. Won't he dine to-day, either? Or does he live without dining?"

"Lives without dining," said I, and closed the eyes.

"Eh!—He's asleep, aint he?"

"With kings and counsellors."[7] murmured I.

———————

There would seem little need for proceeding further in this history. Imagination will readily supply the meagre recital of poor Bartleby's interment. But ere parting with the reader, let me say, that if this little narrative has sufficiently interested him, to awaken curiosity as to who Bartleby was, and what manner of life he led prior to the present narrator's making his acquaintance, I can only reply, that in such curiosity I fully share, but am wholly unable to gratify it. Yet here I hardly know whether I should divulge one little item of rumor, which came to my ear a few months after the scrivener's decease. Upon what basis it rested, I could never ascertain; and hence, how true it is I cannot now tell. But inasmuch as this vague report has not been without a certain strange suggestive interest to me, however sad, it may prove the same with some others; and so I will briefly mention it. The report was this: that Bartleby had been a subordinate clerk in the Dead Letter Office at Washington, from which he had been suddenly removed by a change in the administration. When I think over this rumor, I cannot adequately express the emotions which seize me. Dead letters! does it not sound like dead men? Conceive a man by nature and misfortune prone to a pallid hopelessness, can any business seem more fitted to heighten it than that of continually handling these dead letters, and assorting them for the flames? For by the cart-load they are annually burned. Sometimes from out the folded paper the pale clerk takes a ring:—the finger it was meant for, perhaps, moulders in the grave; a bank-note sent in swiftest charity:—he whom it would relieve, nor eats nor hungers any more; pardon for those who died despairing; hope for those who died unhoping; good tidings for those who

7. Job 3.14.

died stifled by unrelieved calamities. On errands of life, these letters speed to death.

Ah Bartleby! Ah humanity!

1853

Benito Cereno[1]

In the year 1799, Captain Amasa Delano, of Duxbury, in Massachusetts, commanding a large sealer and general trader, lay at anchor, with a valuable cargo, in the harbor of St. Maria—a small, desert, uninhabited island toward the southern extremity of the long coast of Chili. There he had touched for water.

On the second day, not long after dawn, while lying in his berth, his mate came below, informing him that a strange sail was coming into the bay. Ships were then not so plenty in those waters as now. He rose, dressed, and went on deck.

The morning was one peculiar to that coast. Everything was mute and calm; everything gray. The sea, though undulated into long roods of swells, seemed fixed, and was sleeked at the surface like waved lead that has cooled and set in the smelter's mold. The sky seemed a gray surtout.[2] Flights of troubled gray fowl, kith and kin with flights of troubled gray vapors among which they were mixed, skimmed low and fitfully over the waters, as swallows over meadows before storms. Shadows present, foreshadowing deeper shadows to come.

To Captain Delano's surprise, the stranger, viewed through the glass,[3] showed no colors; though to do so upon entering a haven, however uninhabited in its shores, where but a single other ship might be lying, was the custom among peaceful seamen of all nations. Considering the lawlessness and loneliness of the spot, and the sort of stories, at that day, associated with those seas, Captain Delano's surprise might have deepened into some uneasiness had he not been a person of a singularly undistrustful good nature, not liable, except on extraordinary and repeated incentives, and hardly then, to indulge in personal alarms, any way involving the imputation of malign evil in man. Whether, in view of what humanity is capable, such a trait implies, along with a benevolent heart, more than ordinary quickness and accuracy of intellectual perception, may be left to the wise to determine.

But whatever misgivings might have obtruded on first seeing the stranger, would almost, in any seaman's mind, have been dissipated by observing that, the ship, in navigating into the harbor, was drawing too near the land; a sunken reef making out off her bow. This seemed to prove her a stranger, indeed, not only to the sealer, but the island; consequently, she could be no

---

1. This text is based on the first printing, in *Putnam's Monthly* for October, November, and December 1855, but it also incorporates the many small revisions Melville made for its 1856 republication in *The Piazza Tales*. Melville based his plot on a few narrative pages in ch. 18 of Captain Amasa Delano's *Narrative of Voyages and Travels in the Northern and Southern Hemispheres* (1817).

Melville's "deposition" near the end of *Benito Cereno* is roughly half from Delano's much longer section of documents, half his own writing. (A later relative of the real Delano [1763–1823] was Franklin Delano Roosevelt.)

2. Long overcoat.
3. Spyglass or telescope.

wonted freebooter[4] on that ocean. With no small interest, Captain Delano continued to watch her—a proceeding not much facilitated by the vapors partly mantling the hull, through which the far matin light from her cabin streamed equivocally enough; much like the sun—by this time hemisphered on the rim of the horizon, and apparently, in company with the strange ship, entering the harbor—which, wimpled by the same low, creeping clouds, showed not unlike a Lima intriguante's one sinister eye peering across the Plaza from the Indian loop-hole of her dusk *saya-y-manta*.[5]

It might have been but a deception of the vapors, but, the longer the stranger was watched, the more singular appeared her maneuvers. Ere long it seemed hard to decide whether she meant to come in or no—what she wanted, or what she was about. The wind, which had breezed up a little during the night, was now extremely light and baffling, which the more increased the apparent uncertainty of her movements.

Surmising, at last, that it might be a ship in distress, Captain Delano ordered his whale-boat to be dropped, and, much to the wary opposition of his mate, prepared to board her, and, at the least, pilot her in. On the night previous, a fishing-party of the seamen had gone a long distance to some detached rocks out of sight from the sealer, and, an hour or two before daybreak, had returned, having met with no small success. Presuming that the stranger might have been long off soundings, the good captain put several baskets of the fish, for presents, into his boat, and so pulled away. From her continuing too near the sunken reef, deeming her in danger, calling to his men, he made all haste to apprise those on board of their situation. But, some time ere the boat came up, the wind, light though it was, having shifted, had headed the vessel off, as well as partly broken the vapors from about her.

Upon gaining a less remote view, the ship, when made signally visible on the verge of the leaden-hued swells, with the shreds of fog here and there raggedly furring her, appeared like a white-washed monastery after a thunderstorm, seen perched upon some dun cliff among the Pyrenees. But it was no purely fanciful resemblance which now, for a moment, almost led Captain Delano to think that nothing less than a ship-load of monks was before him. Peering over the bulwarks were what really seemed, in the hazy distance, throngs of dark cowls; while, fitfully revealed through the open port-holes, other dark moving figures were dimly descried, as of Black Friars[6] pacing the cloisters.

Upon a still nigher approach, this appearance was modified, and the true character of the vessel was plain—a Spanish merchantman of the first class; carrying negro slaves, amongst other valuable freight, from one colonial port to another. A very large, and, in its time, a very fine vessel, such as in those days were at intervals encountered along that main; sometimes superseded Acapulco treasure-ships, or retired frigates of the Spanish king's navy, which, like superannuated Italian palaces, still, under a decline of masters, preserved signs of former state.

As the whale-boat drew more and more nigh, the cause of the peculiar pipe-clayed[7] aspect of the stranger was seen in the slovenly neglect pervading her. The spars, ropes, and great part of the bulwarks, looked woolly,

---

4. Pirate.
5. Skirt-and-cloak combination, the shawl part of which could be drawn about the face so that little more than an eye would show. "Matin": early

morning. "Wimpled": veiled.
6. Dominicans; an order of monks who wore black robes, including hoods.
7. Whitened.

from long unacquaintance with the scraper, tar, and the brush. Her keel seemed laid, her ribs put together, and she launched, from Ezekiel's Valley of Dry Bones.[8]

In the present business in which she was engaged, the ship's general model and rig appeared to have undergone no material change from their original war-like and Froissart pattern.[9] However, no guns were seen.

The tops were large, and were railed about with what had once been octagonal net-work, all now in sad disrepair. These tops hung overhead like three ruinous aviaries, in one of which was seen perched, on a ratlin, a white noddy,[1] strange fowl, so called from its lethargic, somnambulistic character, being frequently caught by hand at sea. Battered and mouldy, the castellated forecastle seemed some ancient turret, long ago taken by assault, and then left to decay. Toward the stern, two high-raised quarter galleries—the balustrades here and there covered with dry, tindery sea-moss—opening out from the unoccupied state-cabin, whose dead lights, for all the mild weather, were hermetically closed and calked—these tenantless balconies hung over the sea as if it were the grand Venetian canal. But the principal relic of faded grandeur was the ample oval of the shield-like stern-piece, intricately carved with the arms of Castile and Leon,[2] medallioned about by groups of mythological or symbolical devices; uppermost and central of which was a dark satyr in a mask, holding his foot on the prostrate neck of a writhing figure, likewise masked.

Whether the ship had a figure-head, or only a plain beak, was not quite certain, owing to canvas wrapped about that part, either to protect it while undergoing a re-furbishing, or else decently to hide its decay. Rudely painted or chalked, as in a sailor freak, along the forward side of a sort of pedestal below the canvas, was the sentence, "*Seguid vuestro jefe,*" (follow your leader); while upon the tarnished head-boards, near by, appeared, in stately capitals, once gilt, the ship's name, "SAN DOMINICK," each letter streakingly corroded with tricklings of copper-spike rust; while, like mourning weeds, dark festoons of sea-grass slimily swept to and fro over the name, with every hearse-like roll of the hull.

As at last the boat was hooked from the bow along toward the gangway amidship, its keel, while yet some inches separated from the hull, harshly grated as on a sunken coral reef. It proved a huge bunch of conglobated barnacles adhering below the water to the side like a wen;[3] a token of baffling airs and long calms passed somewhere in those seas.

Climbing the side, the visitor was at once surrounded by a clamorous throng of whites and blacks, but the latter outnumbering the former more than could have been expected, negro transportation-ship as the stranger in port was. But, in one language, and as with one voice, all poured out a common tale of suffering; in which the negresses, of whom there were not a few, exceeded the others in their dolorous vehemence. The scurvy, together with a fever, had swept off a great part of their number, more especially the Spaniards. Off Cape Horn,[4] they had narrowly escaped shipwreck; then, for days together, they had lain tranced without wind; their provisions were low; their water next to none; their lips that moment were baked.

8. Ezekiel 37.1.
9. Medieval; from Jean Froissart (1337–1410), historian of wars of England and France.
1. Seabird, usually black or brown. "Ratlin": small rope attached to the shrouds of a ship and forming a step of a rope ladder.
2. Old kingdoms of Spain; the arms would include a castle for Castile and a lion for León.
3. Cyst. "Conglobated": ball-like.
4. At the southern tip of South America.

While Captain Delano was thus made the mark of all eager tongues, his one eager glance took in all the faces, with every other object about him.

Always upon first boarding a large and populous ship at sea, especially a foreign one, with a nondescript crew such as Lascars or Manilla men,[5] the impression varies in a peculiar way from that produced by first entering a strange house with strange inmates in a strange land. Both house and ship, the one by its walls and blinds, the other by its high bulwarks like ramparts, hoard from view their interiors till the last moment; but in the case of the ship there is this addition; that the living spectacle it contains, upon its sudden and complete disclosure, has, in contrast with the blank ocean which zones it, something of the effect of enchantment. The ship seems unreal; these strange costumes, gestures, and faces, but a shadowy tableau just emerged from the deep, which directly must receive back what it gave.

Perhaps it was some such influence as above is attempted to be described, which, in Captain Delano's mind, hightened whatever, upon a staid scrutiny, might have seemed unusual; especially the conspicuous figures of four elderly grizzled negroes, their heads like black, doddered willow tops, who, in venerable contrast to the tumult below them, were couched sphynx-like, one on the starboard cat-head,[6] another on the larboard, and the remaining pair face to face on the opposite bulwarks above the main-chains. They each had bits of unstranded old junk in their hands, and, with a sort of stoical self-content, were picking the junk into oakum,[7] a small heap of which lay by their sides. They accompanied the task with a continuous, low, monotonous chant; droning and druling[8] away like so many gray-headed bag-pipers playing a funeral march.

The quarter-deck rose into an ample elevated poop, upon the forward verge of which, lifted, like the oakum-pickers, some eight feet above the general throng, sat along in a row, separated by regular spaces, the cross-legged figures of six other blacks; each with a rusty hatchet in his hand, which, with a bit of brick and a rag, he was engaged like a scullion in scouring; while between each two was a small stack of hatchets, their rusted edges turned forward awaiting a like operation. Though occasionally the four oakum-pickers would briefly address some person or persons in the crowd below, yet the six hatchet-polishers neither spoke to others, nor breathed a whisper among themselves, but sat intent upon their task, except at intervals, when, with the peculiar love in negroes of uniting industry with pastime, two and two they sideways clashed their hatchets together, like cymbals, with a barbarous din. All six, unlike the generality, had the raw aspect of unsophisticated Africans.

But that first comprehensive glance which took in those ten figures, with scores less conspicuous, rested but an instant upon them, as, impatient of the hubbub of voices, the visitor turned in quest of whomsoever it might be that commanded the ship.

But as if not unwilling to let nature make known her own case among his suffering charge, or else in despair of restraining it for the time, the Spanish captain, a gentlemanly, reserved-looking, and rather young man to a stranger's eye, dressed with singular richness, but bearing plain traces of recent

---

5. From East India or the Philippines, respectively.
6. Projecting piece of timber near the bow (to which the anchor is hoisted and secured).

7. Loose fiber from pieces of rope, used as waterproof sealant. "Old junk": worn-out rope.
8. Moaning.

sleepless cares and disquietudes, stood passively by, leaning against the main-mast, at one moment casting a dreary, spiritless look upon his excited people, at the next an unhappy glance toward his visitor. By his side stood a black of small stature, in whose rude face, as occasionally, like a shepherd's dog, he mutely turned it up into the Spaniard's, sorrow and affection were equally blended.

Struggling through the throng, the American advanced to the Spaniard, assuring him of his sympathies, and offering to render whatever assistance might be in his power. To which the Spaniard returned, for the present, but grave and ceremonious acknowledgments, his national formality dusked by the saturnine mood of ill health.

But losing no time in mere compliments, Captain Delano returning to the gangway, had his baskets of fish brought up; and as the wind still continued light, so that some hours at least must elapse ere the ship could be brought to the anchorage, he bade his men return to the sealer, and fetch back as much water as the whale-boat could carry, with whatever soft bread the steward might have, all the remaining pumpkins on board, with a box of sugar, and a dozen of his private bottles of cider.

Not many minutes after the boat's pushing off, to the vexation of all, the wind entirely died away, and the tide turning, began drifting back the ship helplessly seaward. But trusting this would not long last, Captain Delano sought with good hopes to cheer up the strangers, feeling no small satisfaction that, with persons in their condition he could—thanks to his frequent voyages along the Spanish main[9]—converse with some freedom in their native tongue.

While left alone with them, he was not long in observing some things tending to heighten his first impressions; but surprise was lost in pity, both for the Spaniards and blacks, alike evidently reduced from scarcity of water and provisions; while long-continued suffering seemed to have brought out the less good-natured qualities of the negroes, besides, at the same time, impairing the Spaniard's authority over them. But, under the circumstances, precisely this condition of things was to have been anticipated. In armies, navies, cities, or families, in nature herself, nothing more relaxes good order than misery. Still, Captain Delano was not without the idea, that had Benito Cereno been a man of greater energy, misrule would hardly have come to the present pass. But the debility, constitutional or induced by the hardships, bodily and mental, of the Spanish captain, was too obvious to be overlooked. A prey to settled dejection, as if long mocked with hope he would not now indulge it, even when it had ceased to be a mock, the prospect of that day or evening at furthest, lying at anchor, with plenty of water for his people, and a brother captain to counsel and befriend, seemed in no perceptible degree to encourage him. His mind appeared unstrung, if not still more seriously affected. Shut up in these oaken walls, chained to one dull round of command, whose unconditionality cloyed him, like some hypochondriac abbot he moved slowly about, at times suddenly pausing, starting, or staring, biting his lip, biting his finger-nail, flushing, paling, twitching his beard, with other symptoms of an absent or moody mind. This distempered spirit was lodged, as before hinted, in as distempered a frame. He was rather tall, but seemed

---

9. Sometimes used for the Caribbean Sea, but here the Atlantic and Pacific coasts of South America (mainland as opposed to islands).

never to have been robust, and now with nervous suffering was almost worn to a skeleton. A tendency to some pulmonary complaint appeared to have been lately confirmed. His voice was like that of one with lungs half gone, hoarsely suppressed, a husky whisper. No wonder that, as in this state he tottered about, his private servant apprehensively followed him. Sometimes the negro gave his master his arm, or took his handkerchief out of his pocket for him; performing these and similar offices with that affectionate zeal which transmutes into something filial or fraternal acts in themselves but menial; and which has gained for the negro the repute of making the most pleasing body servant in the world; one, too, whom a master need be on no stiffly superior terms with, but may treat with familiar trust; less a servant than a devoted companion.

Marking the noisy indocility of the blacks in general, as well as what seemed the sullen inefficiency of the whites, it was not without humane satisfaction that Captain Delano witnessed the steady good conduct of Babo.

But the good conduct of Babo, hardly more than the ill-behavior of others, seemed to withdraw the half-lunatic Don Benito from his cloudy langour. Not that such precisely was the impression made by the Spaniard on the mind of his visitor. The Spaniard's individual unrest was, for the present, but noted as a conspicuous feature in the ship's general affliction. Still, Captain Delano was not a little concerned at what he could not help taking for the time to be Don Benito's unfriendly indifference towards himself. The Spaniard's manner, too, conveyed a sort of sour and gloomy disdain, which he seemed at no pains to disguise. But this the American in charity ascribed to the harassing effects of sickness, since, in former instances, he had noted that there are peculiar natures on whom prolonged physical suffering seems to cancel every social instinct of kindness; as if forced to black bread themselves, they deemed it but equity that each person coming nigh them should, indirectly, by some slight or affront, be made to partake of their fare.

But ere long Captain Delano bethought him that, indulgent as he was at the first, in judging the Spaniard, he might not, after all, have exercised charity enough. At bottom it was Don Benito's reserve which displeased him; but the same reserve was shown towards all but his faithful personal attendant. Even the formal reports which, according to sea-usage, were, at stated times, made to him by some petty underling, either a white, mulatto or black, he hardly had patience enough to listen to, without betraying contemptuous aversion. His manner upon such occasions was, in its degree, not unlike that which might be supposed to have been his imperial countryman's, Charles V.,[1] just previous to the anchoritish retirement of that monarch from the throne.

This splenetic disrelish of his place was evinced in almost every function pertaining to it. Proud as he was moody, he condescended to no personal mandate. Whatever special orders were necessary, their delivery was delegated to his body-servant, who in turn transferred them to their ultimate destination, through runners, alert Spanish boys or slave boys, like pages or pilot-fish[2] within easy call continually hovering round Don Benito. So that to have beheld this undemonstrative invalid gliding about, apathetic and

---

1. King of Spain and Holy Roman emperor (1500–1558) who spent his last years in a monastery (without, however, relinquishing all political power and material possessions).
2. Fish often swimming in the company of a shark, therefore thought to pilot it.

mute, no landsman could have dreamed that in him was lodged a dictator-ship beyond which, while at sea, there was no earthly appeal.

Thus, the Spaniard, regarded in his reserve, seemed as the involuntary victim of mental disorder. But, in fact, his reserve might, in some degree, have proceeded from design. If so, then here was evinced the unhealthy climax of that icy though conscientious policy, more or less adopted by all commanders of large ships, which, except in signal emergencies, obliterates alike the manifestation of sway with every trace of sociality; transforming the man into a block, or rather into a loaded cannon, which, until there is call for thunder, has nothing to say.

Viewing him in this light, it seemed but a natural token of the perverse habit induced by a long course of such hard self-restraint, that, notwithstanding the present condition of his ship, the Spaniard should still persist in a demeanor, which, however harmless, or, it may be, appropriate, in a well appointed vessel, such as the San Dominick might have been at the outset of the voyage, was anything but judicious now. But the Spaniard perhaps thought that it was with captains as with gods: reserve, under all events, must still be their cue. But more probably this appearance of slumbering dominion might have been but an attempted disguise to conscious imbecility—not deep policy, but shallow device. But be all this as it might, whether Don Benito's manner was designed or not, the more Captain Delano noted its pervading reserve, the less he felt uneasiness at any particular manifestation of that reserve towards himself.

Neither were his thoughts taken up by the captain alone. Wonted to the quiet orderliness of the sealer's comfortable family of a crew, the noisy confusion of the San Dominick's suffering host repeatedly challenged his eye. Some prominent breaches not only of discipline but of decency were observed. These Captain Delano could not but ascribe, in the main, to the absence of those subordinate deck-officers to whom, along with higher duties, is entrusted what may be styled the police department of a populous ship. True, the old oakum-pickers appeared at times to act the part of monitorial constables to their countrymen, the blacks; but though occasionally succeeding in allaying trifling outbreaks now and then between man and man, they could do little or nothing toward establishing general quiet. The San Dominick was in the condition of a transatlantic emigrant ship, among whose multitude of living freight are some individuals, doubtless, as little troublesome as crates and bales; but the friendly remonstrances of such with their ruder companions are of not so much avail as the unfriendly arm of the mate. What the San Dominick wanted was, what the emigrant ship has, stern superior officers. But on these decks not so much as a fourth mate was to be seen.

The visitor's curiosity was roused to learn the particulars of those mishaps which had brought about such absenteeism, with its consequences; because, though deriving some inkling of the voyage from the wails which at the first moment had greeted him, yet of the details no clear understanding had been had. The best account would, doubtless, be given by the captain. Yet at first the visitor was loth to ask it, unwilling to provoke some distant rebuff. But plucking up courage, he at last accosted Don Benito, renewing the expression of his benevolent interest, adding, that did he (Captain Delano) but know the particulars of the ship's misfortunes, he would, perhaps, be better able in the end to relieve them. Would Don Benito favor him with the whole story?

Don Benito faltered; then, like some somnambulist suddenly interfered with, vacantly stared at his visitor, and ended by looking down on the deck. He maintained this posture so long, that Captain Delano, almost equally disconcerted, and involuntarily almost as rude, turned suddenly from him, walking forward to accost one of the Spanish seamen for the desired information. But he had hardly gone five paces, when with a sort of eagerness Don Benito invited him back, regretting his momentary absence of mind, and professing readiness to gratify him.

While most part of the story was being given, the two captains stood on the after part of the main-deck, a privileged spot, no one being near but the servant.

"It is now a hundred and ninety days," began the Spaniard, in his husky whisper, "that this ship, well officered and well manned, with several cabin passengers—some fifty Spaniards in all—sailed from Buenos Ayres bound to Lima, with a general cargo, hardware, Paraguay tea and the like—and," pointing forward, "that parcel of negroes, now not more than a hundred and fifty, as you see, but then numbering over three hundred souls. Off Cape Horn we had heavy gales. In one moment, by night, three of my best officers, with fifteen sailors, were lost, with the main-yard; the spar snapping under them in the slings, as they sought, with heavers,[3] to beat down the icy sail. To lighten the hull, the heavier sacks of mata were thrown into the sea, with most of the water-pipes[4] lashed on deck at the time. And this last necessity it was, combined with the prolonged detentions afterwards experienced, which eventually brought about our chief causes of suffering. When——"

Here there was a sudden fainting attack of his cough, brought on, no doubt, by his mental distress. His servant sustained him, and drawing a cordial from his pocket placed it to his lips. He a little revived. But unwilling to leave him unsupported while yet imperfectly restored, the black with one arm still encircled his master, at the same time keeping his eye fixed on his face, as if to watch for the first sign of complete restoration, or relapse, as the event might prove.

The Spaniard proceeded, but brokenly and obscurely, as one in a dream.

——"Oh, my God! rather than pass through what I have, with joy I would have hailed the most terrible gales; but——"

His cough returned and with increased violence; this subsiding, with reddened lips and closed eyes he fell heavily against his supporter.

"His mind wanders. He was thinking of the plague that followed the gales," plaintively sighed the servant; "my poor, poor master!" wringing one hand, and with the other wiping the mouth. "But be patient, Señor," again turning to Captain Delano, "these fits do not last long; master will soon be himself."

Don Benito reviving, went on; but as this portion of the story was very brokenly delivered, the substance only will here be set down.

It appeared that after the ship had been many days tossed in storms off the Cape, the scurvy broke out, carrying off numbers of the whites and blacks. When at last they had worked round into the Pacific, their spars and sails were so damaged, and so inadequately handled by the surviving mariners, most of whom were become invalids, that, unable to lay her northerly

---

3. Bars, most often used as levers.   4. Kegs of water. "Mata": Brazilian cotton.

course by the wind, which was powerful, the unmanageable ship for successive days and nights was blown northwestward, where the breeze suddenly deserted her, in unknown waters, to sultry calms. The absence of the water-pipes now proved as fatal to life as before their presence had menaced it. Induced, or at least aggravated, by the less than scanty allowance of water, a malignant fever followed the scurvy; with the excessive heat of the lengthened calm, making such short work of it as to sweep away, as by billows, whole families of the Africans, and a yet larger number, proportionably, of the Spaniards, including, by a luckless fatality, every remaining officer on board. Consequently, in the smart west winds eventually following the calm, the already rent sails having to be simply dropped, not furled, at need, had been gradually reduced to the beggar's rags they were now. To procure substitutes for his lost sailors, as well as supplies of water and sails, the captain at the earliest opportunity had made for Baldivia, the southernmost civilized port of Chili and South America; but upon nearing the coast the thick weather had prevented him from so much as sighting that harbor. Since which period, almost without a crew, and almost without canvas and almost without water, and at intervals giving its added dead to the sea, the San Dominick had been battle-dored[5] about by contrary winds, inveigled by currents, or grown weedy in calms. Like a man lost in woods, more than once she had doubled upon her own track.

"But throughout these calamities," huskily continued Don Benito, painfully turning in the half embrace of his servant, "I have to thank those negroes you see, who, though to your inexperienced eyes appearing unruly, have, indeed, conducted themselves with less of restlessness than even their owner could have thought possible under such circumstances."

Here he again fell faintly back. Again his mind wandered: but he rallied, and less obscurely proceeded.

"Yes, their owner was quite right in assuring me that no fetters would be needed with his blacks; so that while, as is wont in this transportation, those negroes have always remained upon deck—not thrust below, as in the Guineamen[6]—they have, also, from the beginning, been freely permitted to range within given bounds at their pleasure."

Once more the faintness returned—his mind roved—but, recovering, he resumed:

"But it is Babo here to whom, under God, I owe not only my own preservation, but likewise to him, chiefly, the merit is due, of pacifying his more ignorant brethren, when at intervals tempted to murmurings."

"Ah, master," sighed the black, bowing his face, "don't speak of me; Babo is nothing; what Babo has done was but duty."

"Faithful fellow!" cried Capt. Delano. "Don Benito, I envy you such a friend; slave I cannot call him."

As master and man stood before him, the black upholding the white, Captain Delano could not but bethink him of the beauty of that relationship which could present such a spectacle of fidelity on the one hand and confidence on the other. The scene was hightened by the contrast in dress, denoting their relative positions. The Spaniard wore a loose Chili jacket of dark velvet; white small clothes and stockings, with silver buckles at the knee and instep; a high-crowned sombrero, of fine grass; a slender sword, silver

5. Tossed back and forth, as a shuttlecock is hit back and forth by a pair of battledores (or paddles).

6. Ships transporting slaves from Guinea in West Africa.

mounted, hung from a knot in his sash; the last being an almost invariable adjunct, more for ornament than utility, of a South American gentleman's dress to this hour. Excepting when his occasional nervous contortions brought about disarray, there was a certain precision in his attire, curiously at variance with the unsightly disorder around; especially in the belittered Ghetto, forward of the main-mast, wholly occupied by the blacks.

The servant wore nothing but wide trowsers, apparently, from their coarseness and patches, made out of some old topsail; they were clean, and confined at the waist by a bit of unstranded rope, which, with his composed, deprecatory air at times, made him look something like a begging friar of St. Francis.

However unsuitable for the time and place, at least in the blunt-thinking American's eyes, and however strangely surviving in the midst of all his afflictions, the toilette of Don Benito might not, in fashion at least, have gone beyond the style of the day among South Americans of his class. Though on the present voyage sailing from Buenos Ayres, he had avowed himself a native and resident of Chili, whose inhabitants had not so generally adopted the plain coat and once plebeian pantaloons; but, with a becoming modification, adhered to their provincial costume, picturesque as any in the world. Still, relatively to the pale history of the voyage, and his own pale face, there seemed something so incongruous in the Spaniard's apparel, as almost to suggest the image of an invalid courtier tottering about London streets in the time of the plague.

The portion of the narrative which, perhaps, most excited interest, as well as some surprise, considering the latitudes in question, was the long calms spoken of, and more particularly the ship's so long drifting about. Without communicating the opinion, of course, the American could not but impute at least part of the detentions both to clumsy seamanship and faulty navigation. Eying Don Benito's small, yellow hands, he easily inferred that the young captain had not got into command at the hawse-hole,[7] but the cabin-window; and if so, why wonder at incompetence, in youth, sickness, and gentility united?

But drowning criticism in compassion, after a fresh repetition of his sympathies, Captain Delano having heard out his story, not only engaged, as in the first place, to see Don Benito and his people supplied in their immediate bodily needs, but, also, now further promised to assist him in procuring a large permanent supply of water, as well as some sails and rigging; and, though it would involve no small embarrassment to himself, yet he would spare three of his best seamen for temporary deck officers; so that without delay the ship might proceed to Conception,[8] there fully to refit for Lima, her destined port.

Such generosity was not without its effect, even upon the invalid. His face lighted up; eager and hectic, he met the honest glance of his visitor. With gratitude he seemed overcome.

"This excitement is bad for master," whispered the servant, taking his arm, and with soothing words gently drawing him aside.

When Don Benito returned, the American was pained to observe that his hopefulness, like the sudden kindling in his cheek, was but febrile and transient.

---

7. Metal-lined hole in the bow of a ship, through which a cable passes; the expression here means to begin a career as an ordinary seaman and not as an officer.

8. Concepción, Chile.

Ere long, with a joyless mien, looking up towards the poop, the host invited his guest to accompany him there, for the benefit of what little breath of wind might be stirring.

As during the telling of the story, Captain Delano had once or twice started at the occasional cymballing of the hatchet-polishers, wondering why such an interruption should be allowed, especially in that part of the ship, and in the ears of an invalid; and moreover, as the hatchets had anything but an attractive look, and the handlers of them still less so, it was, therefore, to tell the truth, not without some lurking reluctance, or even shrinking, it may be, that Captain Delano, with apparent complaisance, acquiesced in his host's invitation. The more so, since with an untimely caprice of punctilio, rendered distressing by his cadaverous aspect, Don Benito, with Castilian bows, solemnly insisted upon his guest's preceding him up the ladder leading to the elevation; where, one on each side of the last step, sat for armorial supporters and sentries two of the ominous file. Gingerly enough stepped good Captain Delano between them, and in the instant of leaving them behind, like one running the gauntlet, he felt an apprehensive twitch in the calves of his legs.

But when, facing about, he saw the whole file, like so many organ-grinders, still stupidly intent on their work, unmindful of everything beside, he could not but smile at his late fidgety panic.

Presently, while standing with his host, looking forward upon the decks below, he was struck by one of those instances of insubordination previously alluded to. Three black boys, with two Spanish boys, were sitting together on the hatches, scraping a rude wooden platter, in which some scanty mess had recently been cooked. Suddenly, one of the black boys, enraged at a word dropped by one of his white companions, seized a knife, and though called to forbear by one of the oakum-pickers, struck the lad over the head, inflicting a gash from which blood flowed.

In amazement, Captain Delano inquired what this meant. To which the pale Don Benito dully muttered, that it was merely the sport of the lad.

"Pretty serious sport, truly," rejoined Captain Delano. "Had such a thing happened on board the Bachelor's Delight, instant punishment would have followed."

At these words the Spaniard turned upon the American one of his sudden, staring, half-lunatic looks; then relapsing into his torpor, answered, "Doubtless, doubtless, Señor."

Is it, thought Captain Delano, that this hapless man is one of those paper captains I've known, who by policy wink at what by power they cannot put down? I know no sadder sight than a commander who has little of command but the name.

"I should think, Don Benito," he now said, glancing towards the oakum-picker who had sought to interfere with the boys, "that you would find it advantageous to keep all your blacks employed, especially the younger ones, no matter at what useless task, and no matter what happens to the ship. Why, even with my little band, I find such a course indispensable. I once kept a crew on my quarter-deck thrumming[9] mats for my cabin, when, for three days, I had given up my ship—mats, men, and all—for a speedy loss,

9. To "thrum" is to insert pieces of rope yarn into canvas, thus making a rough surface or mat (usu- ally for keeping ropes from chafing against wood or metal).

owing to the violence of a gale, in which we could do nothing but helplessly drive before it."

"Doubtless, doubtless," muttered Don Benito.

"But," continued Captain Delano, again glancing upon the oakum-pickers and then at the hatchet-polishers, near by. "I see you keep some at least of your host employed."

"Yes," was again the vacant response.

"Those old men there, shaking their pows[1] from their pulpits," continued Captain Delano, pointing to the oakum-pickers, "seem to act the part of old dominies to the rest, little heeded as their admonitions are at times. Is this voluntary on their part, Don Benito, or have you appointed them shepherds to your flock of black sheep?"

"What posts they fill, I appointed them," rejoined the Spaniard, in an acrid tone, as if resenting some supposed satiric reflection.

"And these others, these Ashantee[2] conjurors here," continued Captain Delano, rather uneasily eying the brandished steel of the hatchet-polishers, where in spots it had been brought to a shine, "this seems a curious business they are at, Don Benito?"

"In the gales we met," answered the Spaniard, "what of our general cargo was not thrown overboard was much damaged by the brine. Since coming into calm weather, I have had several cases of knives and hatchets daily brought up for overhauling and cleaning."

"A prudent idea, Don Benito. You are part owner of ship and cargo, I presume; but not of the slaves, perhaps?"

"I am owner of all you see," impatiently returned Don Benito, "except the main company of blacks, who belonged to my late friend, Alexandro Aranda."

As he mentioned this name, his air was heart-broken; his knees shook; his servant supported him.

Thinking he divined the cause of such unusual emotion, to confirm his surmise, Captain Delano, after a pause, said "And may I ask, Don Benito, whether—since awhile ago you spoke of some cabin passengers—the friend, whose loss so afflicts you at the outset of the voyage accompanied his blacks?"

"Yes."

"But died of the fever?"

"Died of the fever.—Oh, could I but—"

Again quivering, the Spaniard paused.

"Pardon me," said Captain Delano lowly, "but I think that, by a sympathetic experience, I conjecture, Don Benito, what it is that gives the keener edge to your grief. It was once my hard fortune to lose at sea a dear friend, my own brother, then supercargo.[3] Assured of the welfare of his spirit, its departure I could have borne like a man; but that honest eye, that honest hand—both of which had so often met mine—and that warm heart; all, all—like scraps to the dogs—to throw all to the sharks! It was then I vowed never to have for fellow-voyager a man I loved, unless, unbeknown to him, I had provided every requisite, in case of a fatality, for embalming his mortal part for interment on shore. Were your friend's remains now on board this ship, Don Benito, not thus strangely would the mention of his name affect you."

1. Heads.
2. West African peoples.

3. The officer responsible for the commercial affairs of the ship's voyage.

"On board this ship?" echoed the Spaniard. Then, with horrified gestures, as directed against some specter, he unconsciously fell into the ready arms of his attendant, who, with a silent appeal toward Captain Delano, seemed beseeching him not again to broach a theme so unspeakably distressing to his master.

This poor fellow now, thought the pained American, is the victim of that sad superstition which associates goblins with the deserted body of man, as ghosts with an abandoned house. How unlike are we made! What to me, in like case, would have been a solemn satisfaction, the bare suggestion, even, terrifies the Spaniard into this trance. Poor Alexandro Aranda! what would you say could you here see your friend—who, on former voyages, when you for months were left behind, has, I dare say, often longed, and longed, for one peep at you—now transported with terror at the least thought of having you anyway nigh him.

At this moment, with a dreary graveyard toll, betokening a flaw, the ship's forecastle bell, smote by one of the grizzled oakum-pickers, proclaimed ten o'clock through the leaden calm; when Captain Delano's attention was caught by the moving figure of a gigantic black, emerging from the general crowd below, and slowly advancing towards the elevated poop. An iron collar was about his neck, from which depended a chain, thrice wound round his body; the terminating links padlocked together at a broad band of iron, his girdle.

"How like a mute Atufal moves," murmured the servant.

The black mounted the steps of the poop, and, like a brave prisoner, brought up to receive sentence, stood in unquailing muteness before Don Benito, now recovered from his attack.

At the first glimpse of his approach, Don Benito had started, a resentful shadow swept over his face; and, as with the sudden memory of bootless rage, his white lips glued together.

This is some mulish mutineer, thought Captain Delano, surveying, not without a mixture of admiration, the colossal form of the negro.

"See, he waits your question, master," said the servant.

Thus reminded, Don Benito, nervously averting his glance, as if shunning, by anticipation, some rebellious response, in a disconcerted voice, thus spoke:—

"Atufal, will you ask my pardon now?"

The black was silent.

"Again, master," murmured the servant, with bitter upbraiding eying his countryman, "Again, master; he will bend to master yet."

"Answer," said Don Benito, still averting his glance, "say but the one word *pardon*, and your chains shall be off."

Upon this, the black, slowly raising both arms, let them lifelessly fall, his links clanking, his head bowed; as much as to say, "no, I am content."

"Go," said Don Benito, with inkept and unknown emotion.

Deliberately as he had come, the black obeyed.

"Excuse me, Don Benito," said Captain Delano, "but this scene surprises me; what means it, pray?"

"It means that that negro alone, of all the band, has given me peculiar cause of offense. I have put him in chains; I——"

Here he paused; his hand to his head, as if there were a swimming there, or a sudden bewilderment of memory had come over him; but meeting his servant's kindly glance seemed reassured, and proceeded:—

"I could not scourge such a form. But I told him he must ask my pardon. As yet he has not. At my command, every two hours he stands before me."

"And how long has this been?"

"Some sixty days."

"And obedient in all else? And respectful?"

"Yes."

"Upon my conscience, then," exclaimed Captain Delano, impulsively, "he has a royal spirit in him, this fellow."

"He may have some right to it," bitterly returned Don Benito, "he says he was king in his own land."

"Yes," said the servant, entering a word, "those slits in Atufal's ears once held wedges of gold; but poor Babo here, in his own land, was only a poor slave; a black man's slave was Babo, who now is the white's."

Somewhat annoyed by these conversational familiarities, Captain Delano turned curiously upon the attendant, then glanced inquiringly at his master; but, as if long wonted to these little informalities, neither master nor man seemed to understand him.

"What, pray, was Atufal's offense, Don Benito?" asked Captain Delano; "if it was not something very serious, take a fool's advice, and, in view of his general docility, as well as in some natural respect for his spirit, remit him his penalty."

"No, no, master never will do that," here murmured the servant to himself, "proud Atufal must first ask master's pardon. The slave there carries the padlock, but master here carries the key."

His attention thus directed, Captain Delano now noticed for the first time that, suspended by a slender silken cord, from Don Benito's neck hung a key. At once, from the servant's muttered syllables divining the key's purpose, he smiled and said:—"So, Don Benito—padlock and key—significant symbols, truly."

Biting his lip, Don Benito faltered.

Though the remark of Captain Delano, a man of such native simplicity as to be incapable of satire or irony, had been dropped in playful allusion to the Spaniard's singularly evidenced lordship over the black; yet the hypochondriac seemed in some way to have taken it as a malicious reflection upon his confessed inability thus far to break down, at least, on a verbal summons, the entrenched will of the slave. Deploring this supposed misconception, yet despairing of correcting it, Captain Delano shifted the subject; but finding his companion more than ever withdrawn, as if still sourly digesting the lees of the presumed affront above-mentioned, by-and-by Captain Delano likewise became less talkative, oppressed, against his own will, by what seemed the secret vindictiveness of the morbidly sensitive Spaniard. But the good sailor himself, of a quite contrary disposition, refrained, on his part, alike from the appearance as from the feeling of resentment, and if silent, was only so from contagion.

Presently the Spaniard, assisted by his servant, somewhat discourteously crossed over from his guest; a procedure which, sensibly enough, might have been allowed to pass for idle caprice of ill-humor, had not master and man, lingering round the corner of the elevated skylight, began whispering together in low voices. This was unpleasing. And more: the moody air of the Spaniard, which at times had not been without a sort of valetudinarian stateliness, now seemed anything but dignified; while the menial familiarity of the servant lost its original charm of simple-hearted attachment.

In his embarrassment, the visitor turned his face to the other side of the ship. By so doing, his glance accidentally fell on a young Spanish sailor, a coil of rope in his hand, just stepped from the deck to the first round of the mizzen-rigging. Perhaps the man would not have been particularly noticed, were it not that, during his ascent to one of the yards, he, with a sort of covert intentness, kept his eye fixed on Captain Delano, from whom, presently, it passed, as if by a natural sequence, to the two whisperers.

His own attention thus redirected to that quarter, Captain Delano gave a slight start. From something in Don Benito's manner just then, it seemed as if the visitor had, at least partly, been the subject of the withdrawn consultation going on—a conjecture as little agreeable to the guest as it was little flattering to the host.

The singular alternations of courtesy and ill-breeding in the Spanish captain were unaccountable, except on one of two suppositions—innocent lunacy, or wicked imposture.

But the first idea, though it might naturally have occurred to an indifferent observer, and, in some respect, had not hitherto been wholly a stranger to Captain Delano's mind, yet, now that, in an incipient way, he began to regard the stranger's conduct something in the light of an intentional affront, of course the idea of lunacy was virtually vacated. But if not a lunatic, what then? Under the circumstances, would a gentleman, nay, any honest boor, act the part now acted by his host? The man was an impostor. Some low-born adventurer, masquerading as an oceanic grandee; yet so ignorant of the first requisites of mere gentlemanhood as to be betrayed into the present remarkable indecorum. That strange ceremoniousness, too, at other times evinced, seemed not uncharacteristic of one playing a part above his real level. Benito Cereno—Don Benito Cereno—a sounding name. One, too, at that period, not unknown, in the surname, to supercargoes and sea captains trading along the Spanish Main, as belonging to one of the most enterprising and extensive mercantile families in all those provinces; several members of it having titles; a sort of Castilian Rothschild,[4] with a noble brother, or cousin, in every great trading town of South America. The alleged Don Benito was in early manhood, about twenty-nine or thirty. To assume a sort of roving cadetship[5] in the maritime affairs of such a house, what more likely scheme for a young knave of talent and spirit? But the Spaniard was a pale invalid. Never mind. For even to the degree of simulating mortal disease, the craft of some tricksters had been known to attain. To think that, under the aspect of infantile weakness, the most savage energies might be couched—those velvets of the Spaniard but the silky paw to his fangs.

From no train of thought did these fancies come; not from within, but from without; suddenly, too, and in one throng, like hoar frost; yet as soon to vanish as the mild sun of Captain Delano's good-nature regained its meridian.

Glancing over once more towards his host—whose side-face, revealed above the skylight, was now turned towards him—he was struck by the profile, whose clearness of cut was refined by the thinness incident to ill-health, as well as ennobled about the chin by the beard. Away with suspicion. He was a true off-shoot of a true hidalgo[6] Cereno.

---

4. Renowned German banking family.
5. Position of on-the-job training for a post of authority, appropriate for a younger or youngest son of an aristocratic family.
6. Spanish nobleman.

Relieved by these and other better thoughts, the visitor, lightly humming a tune, now began indifferently pacing the poop, so as not to betray to Don Benito that he had at all mistrusted incivility, much less duplicity; for such mistrust would yet be proved illusory, and by the event; though, for the present, the circumstance which had provoked that distrust remained unexplained. But when that little mystery should have been cleared up, Captain Delano thought he might extremely regret it, did he allow Don Benito to become aware that he had indulged in ungenerous surmises. In short, to the Spaniard's black-letter text, it was best, for awhile, to leave open margin.[7]

Presently, his pale face twitching and overcast, the Spaniard, still supported by his attendant, moved over towards his guest, when, with even more than his usual embarrassment, and a strange sort of intriguing intonation in his husky whisper, the following conversation began:—

"Señor, may I ask how long you have lain at this isle?"

"Oh, but a day or two, Don Benito."

"And from what port are you last?"

"Canton."[8]

"And there, Señor, you exchanged your seal-skins for teas and silks, I think you said?"

"Yes. Silks, mostly."

"And the balance you took in specie,[9] perhaps?"

Captain Delano, fidgeting a little, answered—

"Yes; some silver; not a very great deal, though."

"Ah—well. May I ask how many men have you, Señor?"

Captain Delano slightly started, but answered—

"About five-and-twenty, all told."

"And at present, Señor, all on board, I suppose?"

"All on board, Don Benito," replied the Captain, now with satisfaction.

"And will be to-night, Señor?"

At this last question, following so many pertinacious ones, for the soul of him Captain Delano could not but look very earnestly at the questioner, who, instead of meeting the glance, with every token of craven discomposure dropped his eyes to the deck; presenting an unworthy contrast to his servant, who, just then, was kneeling at his feet, adjusting a loose shoe-buckle; his disengaged face meantime, with humble curiosity, turned openly up into his master's downcast one.

The Spaniard, still with a guilty shuffle, repeated his question:—

"And—and will be to-night, Señor?"

"Yes, for aught I know," returned Captain Delano,—"but nay," rallying himself into fearless truth, "some of them talked of going off on another fishing party about midnight."

"Your ships generally go—go more or less armed, I believe, Señor?"

"Oh, a six-pounder or two, in case of emergency," was the intrepidly indifferent reply, "with a small stock of muskets, sealing-spears, and cutlasses, you know."

---

7. Without the elucidatory comments then often printed in margins as a gloss on the main text rather than printed at the bottom of the page as footnotes. Delano is deciding to reserve judgment. "Black-letter text": books printed in early type imitative of medieval script.
8. A port in China.
9. Coin, typically gold or silver.

As he thus responded, Captain Delano again glanced at Don Benito, but the latter's eyes were averted; while abruptly and awkwardly shifting the subject, he made some peevish allusion to the calm, and then, without apology, once more, with his attendant, withdrew to the opposite bulwarks, where the whispering was resumed.

At this moment, and ere Captain Delano could cast a cool thought upon what had just passed, the young Spanish sailor before mentioned was seen descending from the rigging. In act of stooping over to spring inboard to the deck, his voluminous, unconfined frock, or shirt, of coarse woollen, much spotted with tar, opened out far down the chest, revealing a soiled under garment of what seemed the finest linen, edged, about the neck, with a narrow blue ribbon, sadly faded and worn. At this moment the young sailor's eye was again fixed on the whisperers, and Captain Delano thought he observed a lurking significance in it, as if silent signs of some Freemason[1] sort had that instant been interchanged.

This once more impelled his own glance in the direction of Don Benito, and, as before, he could not but infer that himself formed the subject of the conference. He paused. The sound of the hatchet-polishing fell on his ears. He cast another swift side-look at the two. They had the air of conspirators. In connection with the late questionings and the incident of the young sailor, these things now begat such return of involuntary suspicion, that the singular guilelessness of the American could not endure it. Plucking up a gay and humorous expression, he crossed over to the two rapidly, saying:—"Ha, Don Benito, your black here seems high in your trust; a sort of privy-counselor, in fact."

Upon this, the servant looked up with a good-natured grin, but the master started as from a venomous bite. It was a moment or two before the Spaniard sufficiently recovered himself to reply; which he did, at last, with cold constraint:—"Yes, Señor, I have trust in Babo."

Here Babo, changing his previous grin of mere animal humor into an intelligent smile, not ungratefully eyed his master.

Finding that the Spaniard now stood silent and reserved, as if involuntarily, or purposely giving hint that his guest's proximity was inconvenient just then, Captain Delano, unwilling to appear uncivil even to incivility itself, made some trivial remark and moved off; again and again turning over in his mind the mysterious demeanor of Don Benito Cereno.

He had descended from the poop, and, wrapped in thought, was passing near a dark hatchway, leading down into the steerage, when, perceiving motion there, he looked to see what moved. The same instant there was a sparkle in the shadowy hatchway, and he saw one of the Spanish sailors prowling there hurriedly placing his hand in the bosom of his frock, as if hiding something. Before the man could have been certain who it was that was passing, he slunk below out of sight. But enough was seen of him to make it sure that he was the same young sailor before noticed in the rigging.

What was that which so sparkled? thought Captain Delano. It was no lamp—no match—no live coal. Could it have been a jewel? But how come sailors with jewels?—or with silk-trimmed under-shirts either? Has he been

---

1. A fraternal association founded early in the 18th century in Europe, characterized by local lodges whose members recognized each other by secret signs. It was politically active in New York in Melville's youth, associated in the public mind with atheism and revolution.

robbing the trunks of the dead cabin passengers? But if so, he would hardly wear one of the stolen articles on board ship here. Ah, ah—if now that was, indeed, a secret sign I saw passing between this suspicious fellow and his captain awhile since; if I could only be certain that in my uneasiness my senses did not deceive me, then—

Here, passing from one suspicious thing to another, his mind revolved the strange questions put to him concerning his ship.

By a curious coincidence, as each point was recalled, the black wizards of Ashantee would strike up with their hatchets, as in ominous comment on the white stranger's thoughts. Pressed by such enigmas and portents, it would have been almost against nature, had not, even into the least distrustful heart, some ugly misgivings obtruded.

Observing the ship now helplessly fallen into a current, with enchanted sails, drifting with increased rapidity seaward; and noting that, from a lately intercepted projection of the land, the sealer was hidden, the stout mariner began to quake at thoughts which he barely durst confess to himself. Above all, he began to feel a ghostly dread of Don Benito. And yet when he roused himself, dilated his chest, felt himself strong on his legs, and coolly considered it—what did all these phantoms amount to?

Had the Spaniard any sinister scheme, it must have reference not so much to him (Captain Delano) as to his ship (the Bachelor's Delight). Hence the present drifting away of the one ship from the other, instead of favoring any such possible scheme, was, for the time at least, opposed to it. Clearly any suspicion, combining such contradictions, must need be delusive. Beside, was it not absurd to think of a vessel in distress—a vessel by sickness almost dismanned of her crew—a vessel whose inmates were parched for water— was it not a thousand times absurd that such a craft should, at present, be of a piratical character; or her commander, either for himself or those under him, cherish any desire but for speedy relief and refreshment? But then, might not general distress, and thirst in particular, be affected? And might not that same undiminished Spanish crew, alleged to have perished off to a remnant, be at that very moment lurking in the hold? On heart-broken pretense of entreating a cup of cold water, fiends in human form had got into lonely dwellings, nor retired until a dark deed had been done. And among the Malay pirates, it was no unusual thing to lure ships after them into their treacherous harbors, or entice boarders from a declared enemy at sea, by the spectacle of thinly manned or vacant decks, beneath which prowled a hundred spears with yellow arms ready to upthrust them through the mats. Not that Captain Delano had entirely credited such things. He had heard of them—and now, as stories, they recurred. The present destination of the ship was the anchorage. There she would be near his own vessel. Upon gaining that vicinity, might not the San Dominick, like a slumbering volcano, suddenly let loose energies now hid?

He recalled the Spaniard's manner while telling his story. There was a gloomy hesitancy and subterfuge about it. It was just the manner of one making up his tale for evil purposes, as he goes. But if that story was not true, what was the truth? That the ship had unlawfully come into the Spaniard's possession? But in many of its details, especially in reference to the more calamitous parts, such as the fatalities among the seamen, the consequent prolonged beating about, the past sufferings from obstinate calms, and still continued suffering from thirst; in all these points, as well as others, Don

Benito's story had corroborated not only the wailing ejaculations of the indiscriminate multitude, white and black, but likewise—what seemed impossible to be counterfeit—by the very expression and play of every human feature, which Captain Delano saw. If Don Benito's story was throughout an invention, then every soul on board, down to the youngest negress, was his carefully drilled recruit in the plot: an incredible inference. And yet, if there was ground for mistrusting his veracity, that inference was a legitimate one.

But those questions of the Spaniard. There, indeed, one might pause. Did they not seem put with much the same object with which the burglar or assassin, by day-time, reconnoitres the walls of a house? But, with ill purposes, to solicit such information openly of the chief person endangered, and so, in effect, setting him on his guard; how unlikely a procedure was that? Absurd, then, to suppose that those questions had been prompted by evil designs. Thus, the same conduct, which, in this instance, had raised the alarm, served to dispel it. In short, scarce any suspicion or uneasiness, however apparently reasonable at the time, which was not now, with equal apparent reason, dismissed.

At last he began to laugh at his former forebodings; and laugh at the strange ship for, in its aspect someway siding with them, as it were; and laugh, too, at the odd-looking blacks, particularly those old scissors-grinders, the Ashantees; and those bed-ridden old knitting-women, the oakum-pickers; and almost at the dark Spaniard himself, the central hobglobin of all.

For the rest, whatever in a serious way seemed enigmatical, was now good-naturedly explained away by the thought that, for the most part, the poor invalid scarcely knew what he was about; either sulking in black vapors, or putting idle questions without sense or object. Evidently, for the present, the man was not fit to be entrusted with the ship. On some benevolent plea withdrawing the command from him, Captain Delano would yet have to send her to Conception, in charge of his second mate, a worthy person and good navigator—a plan not more convenient for the San Dominick than for Don Benito; for, relieved from all anxiety, keeping wholly to his cabin, the sick man, under the good nursing of his servant, would probably, by the end of the passage, be in a measure restored to health, and with that he should also be restored to authority.

Such were the American's thoughts. They were tranquilizing. There was a difference between the idea of Don Benito's darkly pre-ordaining Captain Delano's fate, and Captain Delano's lightly arranging Don Benito's. Nevertheless, it was not without something of relief that the good seaman presently perceived his whale-boat in the distance. Its absence had been prolonged by unexpected detention at the sealer's side, as well as its returning trip lengthened by the continual recession of the goal.

The advancing speck was observed by the blacks. Their shouts attracted the attention of Don Benito, who, with a return of courtesy, approaching Captain Delano, expressed satisfaction at the coming of some supplies, slight and temporary as they must necessarily prove.

Captain Delano responded; but while doing so, his attention was drawn to something passing on the deck below: among the crowd climbing the landward bulwarks, anxiously watching the coming boat, two blacks, to all appearances accidentally incommoded by one of the sailors, violently pushed him aside, which the sailor someway resenting, they dashed him to the deck, despite the earnest cries of the oakum-pickers.

"Don Benito," said Captain Delano quickly, "do you see what is going on there? Look!"

But, seized by his cough, the Spaniard staggered, with both hands to his face, on the point of falling. Captain Delano would have supported him, but the servant was more alert, who, with one hand sustaining his master, with the other applied the cordial. Don Benito restored, the black withdrew his support, slipping aside a little, but dutifully remaining within call of a whisper. Such discretion was here evinced as quite wiped away, in the visitor's eyes, any blemish of impropriety which might have attached to the attendant, from the indecorous conferences before mentioned; showing, too, that if the servant were to blame, it might be more the master's fault than his own, since when left to himself he could conduct thus well.

His glance called away from the spectacle of disorder to the more pleasing one before him, Captain Delano could not avoid again congratulating his host upon possessing such a servant, who, though perhaps a little too forward now and then, must upon the whole be invaluable to one in the invalid's situation.

"Tell me, Don Benito," he added, with a smile—"I should like to have your man here myself—what will you take for him? Would fifty doubloons be any object?"

"Master wouldn't part with Babo for a thousand doubloons," murmured the black, overhearing the offer, and taking it in earnest, and, with the strange vanity of a faithful slave appreciated by his master, scorning to hear so paltry a valuation put upon him by a stranger. But Don Benito, apparently hardly yet completely restored, and again interrupted by his cough, made but some broken reply.

Soon his physical distress became so great, affecting his mind, too, apparently, that, as if to screen the sad spectacle, the servant gently conducted his master below.

Left to himself, the American, to while away the time till his boat should arrive, would have pleasantly accosted some one of the few Spanish seamen he saw; but recalling something that Don Benito had said touching their ill conduct, he refrained, as a ship-master indisposed to countenance cowardice or unfaithfulness in seamen.

While, with these thoughts, standing with eye directed forward towards that handful of sailors, suddenly he thought that one or two of them returned the glance and with a sort of meaning. He rubbed his eyes, and looked again; but again seemed to see the same thing. Under a new form, but more obscure than any previous one, the old suspicions recurred, but, in the absence of Don Benito, with less of panic than before. Despite the bad account given of the sailors, Captain Delano resolved forthwith to accost one of them. Descending the poop, he made his way through the blacks, his movement drawing a queer cry from the oakum-pickers, prompted by whom, the negroes, twitching each other aside, divided before him; but, as if curious to see what was the object of this deliberate visit to their Ghetto, closing in behind, in tolerable order, followed the white stranger up. His progress thus proclaimed as by mounted kings-at-arms, and escorted as by a Caffre[2] guard of honor, Captain Delano, assuming a good humored, off-handed air, continued to advance; now and then saying a blithe word to the negroes, and his eye

---

2. Many 19th-century travelers to southern Africa referred admiringly to the Caffre tribe or tribes.

curiously surveying the white faces, here and there sparsely mixed in with the blacks, like stray white pawns venturously involved in the ranks of the chess-men opposed.

While thinking which of them to select for his purpose, he chanced to observe a sailor seated on the deck engaged in tarring the strap of a large block, with a circle of blacks squatted round him inquisitively eying the process.

The mean employment of the man was in contrast with something superior in his figure. His hand, black with continually thrusting it into the tar-pot held for him by a negro, seemed not naturally allied to his face, a face which would have been a very fine one but for its haggardness. Whether this haggardness had aught to do with criminality, could not be determined; since, as intense heat and cold, though unlike, produce like sensations, so innocence and guilt, when, through casual association with mental pain, stamping any visible impress, use one seal—a hacked one.

Not again that this reflection occurred to Captain Delano at the time, charitable man as he was. Rather another idea. Because observing so singular a haggardness combined with a dark eye, averted as in trouble and shame, and then again recalling Don Benito's confessed ill opinion of his crew, insensibly he was operated upon by certain general notions, which, while disconnecting pain and abashment from virtue, invariably link them with vice.

If, indeed, there be any wickedness on board this ship, thought Captain Delano, be sure that man there has fouled his hand in it, even as now he fouls it in the pitch. I don't like to accost him. I will speak to this other, this old Jack here on the windlass.[3]

He advanced to an old Barcelona tar, in ragged red breeches and dirty night-cap, cheeks trenched and bronzed, whiskers dense as thorn hedges. Seated between two sleepy-looking Africans, this mariner, like his younger shipmate, was employed upon some rigging—splicing a cable—the sleepy-looking blacks performing the inferior function of holding the outer parts of the ropes for him.

Upon Captain Delano's approach, the man at once hung his head below its previous level; the one necessary for business. It appeared as if he desired to be thought absorbed, with more than common fidelity, in his task. Being addressed, he glanced up, but with what seemed a furtive, diffident air, which sat strangely enough on his weather-beaten visage, much as if a grizzly bear, instead of growling and biting, should simper and cast sheep's eyes. He was asked several questions concerning the voyage, questions purposely referring to several particulars in Don Benito's narrative, not previously corroborated by those impulsive cries greeting the visitor on first coming on board. The questions were briefly answered, confirming all that remained to be confirmed of the story. The negroes about the windlass joined in with the old sailor, but, as they became talkative, he by degrees became mute, and at length quite glum, seemed morosely unwilling to answer more questions, and yet, all the while, this ursine air was somehow mixed with his sheepish one.

Despairing of getting into unembarrassed talk with such a centaur, Captain Delano, after glancing round for a more promising countenance, but

---

3. Mechanical device used for hoisting heavy objects or hauling up the anchor chain. "Jack": sailor.

seeing none, spoke pleasantly to the blacks to make way for him; and so, amid various grins and grimaces, returned to the poop, feeling a little strange at first, he could hardly tell why, but upon the whole with regained confidence in Benito Cereno.

How plainly, thought he, did that old whiskerando yonder betray a consciousness of ill-desert. No doubt, when he saw me coming, he dreaded lest I, apprised by his Captain of the crew's general misbehavior, came with sharp words for him, and so down with his head. And yet—and yet, now that I think of it, that very old fellow, if I err not, was one of those who seemed so earnestly eying me here awhile since. Ah, these currents spin one's head round almost as much as they do the ship. Ha, there now's a pleasant sort of sunny sight; quite sociable, too.

His attention had been drawn to a slumbering negress, partly disclosed through the lace-work of some rigging, lying, with youthful limbs carelessly disposed, under the lee of the bulwarks, like a doe in the shade of a woodland rock. Sprawling at her lapped breasts was her wide-awake fawn, stark naked, its black little body half lifted from the deck, crosswise with its dam's; its hands, like two paws, clambering upon her; its mouth and nose ineffectually rooting to get at the mark; and meantime giving a vexatious half-grunt, blending with the composed snore of the negress.

The uncommon vigor of the child at length roused the mother. She started up, at distance facing Captain Delano. But as if not at all concerned at the attitude in which she had been caught, delightedly she caught the child up, with maternal transports, covering it with kisses.

There's naked nature, now; pure tenderness and love, thought Captain Delano, well pleased.

This incident prompted him to remark the other negresses more particularly than before. He was gratified with their manners; like most uncivilized women, they seemed at once tender of heart and tough of constitution; equally ready to die for their infants or fight for them. Unsophisticated as leopardesses; loving as doves. Ah! thought Captain Delano, these perhaps are some of the very women whom Ledyard[4] saw in Africa, and gave such a noble account of.

These natural sights somehow insensibly deepened his confidence and ease. At last he looked to see how his boat was getting on; but it was still pretty remote. He turned to see if Don Benito had returned; but he had not.

To change the scene, as well as to please himself with a leisurely observation of the coming boat, stepping over into the mizzen-chains he clambered his way into the starboard quarter-gallery;[5] one of those abandoned Venetian-looking water-balconies previously mentioned; retreats cut off from the deck. As his foot pressed the half-damp, half-dry sea-mosses matting the place, and a chance phantom cats-paw[6]—an islet of breeze, unheralded, unfollowed—as this ghostly cats-paw came fanning his cheek, as his glance fell upon the row of small, round dead-lights, all closed like coppered eyes of the coffined, and the state-cabin door, once connecting with the gallery,

---

4. John Ledyard (1751–1789), American traveler, whose comment appeared in *Proceedings of the Association for Promoting the Discovery of the Interior Parts of Africa* (1790). In the *Putnam's* serialization, Melville attributed the passage to the Scottish traveler Mungo Park, who quoted it from Ledyard in his *Travels in the Interior of Africa* (1799); in *The Piazza Tales* Ledyard's name is properly restored.
5. Balcony or platform projecting from the stern of a ship.
6. Patch of open water visibly stirred by a puff of wind; also, the wind that produces a cat's-paw.

even as the dead-lights had once looked out upon it, but now calked fast like a sarcophagus lid, to a purple-black, tarred-over panel, threshold, and post; and he bethought him of the time, when that state-cabin and this state-balcony had heard the voices of the Spanish king's officers, and the forms of the Lima viceroy's daughters had perhaps leaned where he stood—as these and other images flitted through his mind, as the cats-paw through the calm, gradually he felt rising a dreamy inquietude, like that of one who alone on the prairie feels unrest from the repose of the noon.

He leaned against the carved balustrade, again looking off toward his boat; but found his eye falling upon the ribboned grass, trailing along the ship's water-line, straight as a border of green box; and parterres[7] of sea-weed, broad ovals and crescents, floating nigh and far, with what seemed long formal alleys between, crossing the terraces of swells, and sweeping round as if leading to the grottoes below. And overhanging all was the balustrade by his arm, which, partly stained with pitch and partly embossed with moss, seemed the charred ruin of some summer-house in a grand garden long running to waste.

Trying to break one charm, he was but becharmed anew. Though upon the wide sea, he seemed in some far inland country; prisoner in some deserted château, left to stare at empty grounds, and peer out at vague roads, where never wagon or wayfarer passed.

But these enchantments were a little disenchanted as his eye fell on the corroded main-chains. Of an ancient style, massy and rusty in link, shackle and bolt, they seemed even more fit for the ship's present business than the one for which she had been built.

Presently he thought something moved nigh the chains. He rubbed his eyes, and looked hard. Groves of rigging were about the chains; and there, peering from behind a great stay, like an Indian from behind a hemlock, a Spanish sailor, a marlingspike[8] in his hand, was seen, who made what seemed an imperfect gesture towards the balcony, but immediately, as if alarmed by some advancing step along the deck within, vanished into the recesses of the hempen forest, like a poacher.

What meant this? Something the man had sought to communicate, unbeknown to any one, even to his captain. Did the secret involve aught unfavorable to his captain? Were those previous misgivings of Captain Delano's about to be verified? Or, in his haunted mood at the moment, had some random, unintentional motion of the man, while busy with the stay, as if repairing it, been mistaken for a significant beckoning?

Not unbewildered, again he gazed off for his boat. But it was temporarily hidden by a rocky spur of the isle. As with some eagerness he bent forward, watching for the first shooting view of its beak, the balustrade gave way before him like charcoal. Had he not clutched an outreaching rope he would have fallen into the sea. The crash, though feeble, and the fall, though hollow, of the rotten fragments, must have been overheard. He glanced up. With sober curiosity peering down upon him was one of the old oakum-pickers, slipped from his perch to an outside boom; while below the old negro, and, invisible to him, reconnoitering from a port-hole like a fox from the mouth of its den, crouched the Spanish sailor again. From something

---

7. Ornamental arrangements, as of flower beds.
8. Pointed iron tool used to separate and splice

strands of rope.

suddenly suggested by the man's air, the mad idea now darted into Captain Delano's mind, that Don Benito's plea of indisposition, in withdrawing below, was but a pretense: that he was engaged there maturing his plot, of which the sailor, by some means gaining an inkling, had a mind to warn the stranger against; incited, it may be, by gratitude for a kind word on first boarding the ship. Was it from foreseeing some possible interference like this, that Don Benito had, beforehand, given such a bad character of his sailors, while praising the negroes; though, indeed, the former seemed as docile as the latter the contrary? The whites, too, by nature, were the shrewder race. A man with some evil design, would he not be likely to speak well of that stupidity which was blind to his depravity, and malign that intelligence from which it might not be hidden? Not unlikely, perhaps. But if the whites had dark secrets concerning Don Benito, could then Don Benito be any way in complicity with the blacks? But they were too stupid. Besides, who ever heard of a white so far a renegade as to apostatize[9] from his very species almost, by leaguing in against it with negroes? These difficulties recalled former ones. Lost in their mazes, Captain Delano, who had now regained the deck, was uneasily advancing along it, when he observed a new face; an aged sailor seated cross-legged near the main hatchway. His skin was shrunk up with wrinkles like a pelican's empty pouch; his hair frosted; his countenance grave and composed. His hands were full of ropes, which he was working into a large knot. Some blacks were about him obligingly dipping the strands for him, here and there, as the exigencies of the operation demanded.

Captain Delano crossed over to him, and stood in silence surveying the knot; his mind, by a not uncongenial transition, passing from its own entanglements to those of the hemp. For intricacy such a knot he had never seen in an American ship, or indeed any other. The old man looked like an Egyptian priest, making gordian knots for the temple of Ammon.[1] The knot seemed a combination of double-bowline-knot, treble-crown-knot, back-handed-well-knot, knot-in-and-out-knot, and jamming-knot.

At last, puzzled to comprehend the meaning of such a knot, Captain Delano addressed the knotter:—

"What are you knotting there, my man?"

"The knot," was the brief reply, without looking up.

"So it seems; but what is it for?"

"For some one else to undo," muttered back the old man, plying his fingers harder than ever, the knot being now nearly completed.

While Captain Delano stood watching him, suddenly the old man threw the knot towards him, saying in broken English,—the first heard in the ship,—something to this effect—"Undo it, cut it, quick." It was said lowly, but with such condensation of rapidity, that the long, slow words in Spanish, which had preceded and followed, almost operated as covers to the brief English between.

For a moment, knot in hand, and knot in head, Captain Delano stood mute; while, without further heeding him, the old man was now intent upon other ropes. Presently there was a slight stir behind Captain Delano. Turning,

9. To deny or renounce (typically said of religious faith).
1. In Egypt the oracle of Jupiter Ammon predicted to Alexander the Great (356–323 B.C.E.) that he would conquer the world. Later in Phrygia (in north-central Asia Minor), where the former King Gordius had foretold that whoever would untie his intricate knot would become master of Asia, Alexander cut the knot with his sword.

he saw the chained negro, Atufal, standing quietly there. The next moment the old sailor rose, muttering, and, followed by his subordinate negroes, removed to the forward part of the ship, where in the crowd he disappeared.

An elderly negro, in a clout[2] like an infant's, and with a pepper and salt head, and a kind of attorney air, now approached Captain Delano. In tolerable Spanish, and with a good-natured, knowing wink, he informed him that the old knotter was simple-witted, but harmless; often playing his odd tricks. The negro concluded by begging the knot, for of course the stranger would not care to be troubled with it. Unconsciously, it was handed to him. With a sort of congé,[3] the negro received it, and turning his back, ferreted into it like a detective Custom House officer after smuggled laces. Soon, with some African word, equivalent to pshaw, he tossed the knot overboard.

All this is very queer now, thought Captain Delano, with a qualmish sort of emotion; but as one feeling incipient sea-sickness, he strove, by ignoring the symptoms, to get rid of the malady. Once more he looked off for his boat. To his delight, it was now again in view, leaving the rocky spur astern.

The sensation here experienced, after at first relieving his uneasiness, with unforeseen efficacy, soon began to remove it. The less distant sight of that well-known boat—showing it, not as before, half blended with the haze, but with outline defined, so that its individuality, like a man's, was manifest; that boat, Rover by name, which, though now in strange seas, had often pressed the beach of Captain Delano's home, and, brought to its threshold for repairs, had familiarly lain there, as a Newfoundland dog; the sight of that household boat evoked a thousand trustful associations, which, contrasted with previous suspicions, filled him not only with lightsome confidence, but somehow with half humorous self-reproaches at his former lack of it.

"What, I, Amasa Delano—Jack of the Beach, as they called me when a lad—I, Amasa; the same that, duck-satchel in hand, used to paddle along the waterside to the school-house made from the old hulk;—I, little Jack of the Beach, that used to go berrying with cousin Nat and the rest; I to be murdered here at the ends of the earth, on board a haunted pirate-ship by a horrible Spaniard?—Too nonsensical to think of! Who would murder Amasa Delano? His conscience is clean. There is some one above. Fie, fie, Jack of the Beach! you are a child indeed; a child of the second childhood, old boy; you are beginning to dote and drule, I'm afraid."

Light of heart and foot, he stepped aft, and there was met by Don Benito's servant, who, with a pleasing expression, responsive to his own present feelings, informed him that his master had recovered from the effects of his coughing fit, and had just ordered him to go present his compliments to his good guest, Don Amasa, and say that he (Don Benito) would soon have the happiness to rejoin him.

There now, do you mark that? again thought Captain Delano, walking the poop. What a donkey I was. This kind gentleman who here sends me his kind compliments, he, but ten minutes ago, dark-lantern in hand, was dodging round some old grind-stone in the hold, sharpening a hatchet for me, I thought. Well, well; these long calms have a morbid effect on the mind, I've often heard, though I never believed it before. Ha! glancing towards the boat; there's Rover; good dog; a white bone in her mouth. A pretty big bone though,

---

2. Diaper; small piece of cloth. 3. Leave taking, signaled by a low bow.

seems to me.—What? Yes, she has fallen afoul of the bubbling tide-rip there. It sets her the other way, too, for the time. Patience.

It was now about noon, though, from the grayness of everything, it seemed to be getting towards dusk.

The calm was confirmed. In the far distance, away from the influence of land, the leaden ocean seemed laid out and leaded up, its course finished, soul gone, defunct. But the current from landward, where the ship was, increased; silently sweeping her further and further towards the tranced waters beyond.

Still, from his knowledge of those latitudes, cherishing hopes of a breeze, and a fair and fresh one, at any moment, Captain Delano, despite present prospects, buoyantly counted upon bringing the San Dominick safely to anchor ere night. The distance swept over was nothing; since, with a good wind, ten minutes' sailing would retrace more than sixty minutes' drifting. Meantime, one moment turning to mark "Rover" fighting the tide-rip, and the next to see Don Benito approaching, he continued walking the poop.

Gradually he felt a vexation arising from the delay of his boat; this soon merged into uneasiness; and at last, his eye falling continually, as from a stage-box into the pit, upon the strange crowd before and below him, and by and by recognising there the face—now composed to indifference—of the Spanish sailor who had seemed to beckon from the main chains, something of his old trepidations returned.

Ah, thought he—gravely enough—this is like the ague:[4] because it went off, it follows not that it won't come back.

Though ashamed of the relapse, he could not altogether subdue it; and so, exerting his good nature to the utmost, insensibly he came to a compromise.

Yes, this is a strange craft; a strange history, too, and strange folks on board. But—nothing more.

By way of keeping his mind out of mischief till the boat should arrive, he tried to occupy it with turning over and over, in a purely speculative sort of way, some lesser peculiarities of the captain and crew. Among others, four curious points recurred.

First, the affair of the Spanish lad assailed with a knife by the slave boy; an act winked at by Don Benito. Second, the tyranny in Don Benito's treatment of Atufal, the black; as if a child should lead a bull of the Nile by the ring in his nose. Third, the trampling of the sailor by the two negroes; a piece of insolence passed over without so much as a reprimand. Fourth, the cringing submission to their master of all the ship's underlings, mostly blacks; as if by the least inadvertence they feared to draw down his despotic displeasure.

Coupling these points, they seemed somewhat contradictory. But what then, thought Captain Delano, glancing towards his now nearing boat,—what then? Why, Don Benito is a very capricious commander. But he is not the first of the sort I have seen; though it's true he rather exceeds any other. But as a nation—continued he in his reveries—these Spaniards are all an odd set; the very word Spaniard has a curious, conspirator, Guy-Fawkish[5] twang to it. And yet, I dare say, Spaniards in the main are as good folks as any in Duxbury, Massachusetts. Ah good! At last "Rover" has come.

4. Fever with chills.
5. Guy Fawkes (1570–1606), Catholic conspira- tor executed for plotting to blow up the House of Lords.

As, with its welcome freight, the boat touched the side, the oakum-pickers, with venerable gestures, sought to restrain the blacks, who, at the sight of three gurried[6] water-casks in its bottom, and a pile of wilted pumpkins in its bow, hung over the bulwarks in disorderly raptures.

Don Benito with his servant now appeared; his coming, perhaps, hastened by hearing the noise. Of him Captain Delano sought permission to serve out the water, so that all might share alike, and none injure themselves by unfair excess. But sensible, and, on Don Benito's account, kind as this offer was, it was received with what seemed impatience; as if aware that he lacked energy as a commander, Don Benito, with the true jealousy of weakness, resented as an affront any interference. So, at least, Captain Delano inferred.

In another moment the casks were being hoisted in, when some of the eager negroes accidentally jostled Captain Delano, where he stood by the gangway; so that, unmindful of Don Benito, yielding to the impulse of the moment, with good-natured authority he bade the blacks stand back; to enforce his words making use of a half-mirthful, half-menacing gesture. Instantly the blacks paused, just where they were, each negro and negress suspended in his or her posture, exactly as the word had found them—for a few seconds continuing so—while, as between the responsive posts of a telegraph, an unknown syllable ran from man to man among the perched oakum-pickers. While the visitor's attention was fixed by this scene, suddenly the hatchet-polishers half rose, and a rapid cry came from Don Benito.

Thinking that at the signal of the Spaniard he was about to be massacred, Captain Delano would have sprung for his boat, but paused, as the oakum-pickers, dropping down into the crowd with earnest exclamations, forced every white and every negro back, at the same moment, with gestures friendly and familiar, almost jocose, bidding him, in substance, not be a fool. Simultaneously the hatchet-polishers resumed their seats, quietly as so many tailors, and at once, as if nothing had happened, the work of hoisting in the casks was resumed, whites and blacks singing at the tackle.

Captain Delano glanced towards Don Benito. As he saw his meager form in the act of recovering itself from reclining in the servant's arms, into which the agitated invalid had fallen, he could not but marvel at the panic by which himself had been surprised on the darting supposition that such a commander, who upon a legitimate occasion, so trivial, too, as it now appeared, could lose all self-command, was, with energetic iniquity, going to bring about his murder.

The casks being on deck, Captain Delano was handed a number of jars and cups by one of the steward's aids, who, in the name of his captain, entreated him to do as he had proposed: dole out the water. He complied, with republican impartiality as to this republican element, which always seeks one level, serving the oldest white no better than the youngest black; excepting, indeed, poor Don Benito, whose condition, if not rank, demanded an extra allowance. To him, in the first place, Captain Delano presented a fair pitcher of the fluid; but, thirsting as he was for it, the Spaniard quaffed not a drop until after several grave bows and salutes. A reciprocation of courtesies which the sight-loving Africans hailed with clapping of hands.

Two of the less wilted pumpkins being reserved for the cabin table, the residue were minced up on the spot for the general regalement. But the soft

6. Coated with slime, from "gurry," fish offal.

bread, sugar, and bottled cider, Captain Delano would have given the whites alone, and in chief Don Benito; but the latter objected; which disinterestedness not a little pleased the American; and so mouthfuls all around were given alike to whites and blacks; excepting one bottle of cider, which Babo insisted upon setting aside for his master.

Here it may be observed that as, on the first visit of the boat, the American had not permitted his men to board the ship, neither did he now; being unwilling to add to the confusion of the decks.

Not uninfluenced by the peculiar good humor at present prevailing, and for the time oblivious of any but benevolent thoughts, Captain Delano, who from recent indications counted upon a breeze within an hour or two at furthest, dispatched the boat back to the sealer with orders for all the hands that could be spared immediately to set about rafting casks to the watering-place and filling them. Likewise he bade word be carried to his chief officer, that if against present expectation the ship was not brought to anchor by sunset, he need be under no concern, for as there was to be a full moon that night, he (Captain Delano) would remain on board ready to play the pilot, come the wind soon or late.

As the two Captains stood together, observing the departing boat—the servant as it happened having just spied a spot on his master's velvet sleeve, and silently engaged rubbing it out—the American expressed his regrets that the San Dominick had no boats; none, at least, but the unseaworthy old hulk of the long-boat,[7] which, warped as a camel's skeleton in the desert, and almost as bleached, lay pot-wise inverted amidships, one side a little tipped, furnishing a subterraneous sort of den for family groups of the blacks, mostly women and small children; who, squatting on old mats below, or perched above in the dark dome, on the elevated seats, were descried, some distance within, like a social circle of bats, sheltering in some friendly cave; at intervals, ebon flights of naked boys and girls, three or four years old, darting in and out of the den's mouth.

"Had you three or four boats now, Don Benito," said Captain Delano, "I think that, by tugging at the oars, your negroes here might help along matters some.—Did you sail from port without boats, Don Benito?"

"They were stove in the gales, Señor."

"That was bad. Many men, too, you lost then. Boats and men.—Those must have been hard gales, Don Benito."

"Past all speech," cringed the Spaniard.

"Tell me, Don Benito," continued his companion with increased interest, "tell me, were these gales immediately off the pitch of Cape Horn?"

"Cape Horn?—who spoke of Cape Horn?"

"Yourself did, when giving me an account of your voyage," answered Captain Delano with almost equal astonishment at this eating of his own words, even as he ever seemed eating his own heart, on the part of the Spaniard. "You yourself, Don Benito, spoke of Cape Horn," he emphatically repeated.

The Spaniard turned, in a sort of stooping posture, pausing an instant, as one about to make a plunging exchange of elements, as from air to water.

At this moment a messenger-boy, a white, hurried by, in the regular performance of his function carrying the last expired half hour forward to the forecastle, from the cabin time-piece, to have it struck at the ship's large bell.

---

7. The largest rowboat stowed on the deck of a large ship.

"Master," said the servant, discontinuing his work on the coat sleeve, and addressing the rapt Spaniard with a sort of timid apprehensiveness, as one charged with a duty, the discharge of which, it was foreseen, would prove irksome to the very person who had imposed it, and for whose benefit it was intended, "master told me never mind where he was, or how engaged, always to remind him, to a minute, when shaving-time comes. Miguel has gone to strike the half-hour afternoon. It is *now*, master. Will master go into the cuddy?"[8]

"Ah—yes," answered the Spaniard, starting, somewhat as from dreams into realities; then turning upon Captain Delano, he said that ere long he would resume the conversation.

"Then if master means to talk more to Don Amasa," said the servant, "why not let Don Amasa sit by master in the cuddy, and master can talk, and Don Amasa can listen, while Babo here lathers and strops."

"Yes," said Captain Delano, not unpleased with this sociable plan, "yes, Don Benito, unless you had rather not, I will go with you."

"Be it so, Señor."

As the three passed aft, the American could not but think it another strange instance of his host's capriciousness, this being shaved with such uncommon punctuality in the middle of the day. But he deemed it more than likely that the servant's anxious fidelity had something to do with the matter; inasmuch as the timely interruption served to rally his master from the mood which had evidently been coming upon him.

The place called the cuddy was a light deck-cabin formed by the poop, a sort of attic to the large cabin below. Part of it had formerly been the quarters of the officers; but since their death all the partitionings had been thrown down, and the whole interior converted into one spacious and airy marine hall; for absence of fine furniture and picturesque disarray, of odd appurtenances, somewhat answering to the wide, cluttered hall of some eccentric bachelor-squire in the country, who hangs his shooting-jacket and tobacco-pouch on deer antlers, and keeps his fishing-rod, tongs, and walking-stick in the same corner.

The similitude was hightened, if not originally suggested, by glimpses of the surrounding sea; since, in one aspect, the country and the ocean seem cousins-german.[9]

The floor of the cuddy was matted. Overhead, four or five old muskets were stuck into horizontal holes along the beams. On one side was a claw-footed old table lashed to the deck; a thumbed missal on it, and over it a small, meager crucifix attached to the bulkhead. Under the table lay a dented cutlass or two, with a hacked harpoon, among some melancholy old rigging, like a heap of poor friars' girdles.[1] There were also two long, sharp-ribbed settees of malacca cane, black with age, and uncomfortable to look at as inquisitors' racks, with a large, misshapen arm-chair, which, furnished with a rude barber's crutch[2] at the back, working with a screw, seemed some grotesque engine of torment. A flag locker was in one corner, open, exposing various colored bunting, some rolled up, others half unrolled, still others tumbled. Opposite was a cumbrous washstand, of black mahogany, all of one block, with a pedestal, like a font, and over it a railed shelf, containing combs,

8. Small cabin on the deck of a ship or boat.
9. First cousins.

1. Rope belts.
2. Headrest.

brushes, and other implements of the toilet. A torn hammock of stained grass swung near; the sheets tossed, and the pillow wrinkled up like a brow, as if whoever slept here slept but illy, with alternate visitations of sad thoughts and bad dreams.

The further extremity of the cuddy, overhanging the ship's stern, was pierced with three openings, windows or port holes, according as men or cannon might peer, socially or unsocially, out of them. At present neither men nor cannon were seen, though huge ring-bolts and other rusty iron fixtures of the wood-work hinted of twenty-four-pounders.

Glancing towards the hammock as he entered, Captain Delano said, "You sleep here, Don Benito?"

"Yes, Señor, since we got into mild weather."

"This seems a sort of dormitory, sitting-room, sail-loft, chapel, armory, and private closet all together, Don Benito," added Captain Delano, looking round.

"Yes, Señor; events have not been favorable to much order in my arrangements."

Here the servant, napkin on arm, made a motion as if waiting his master's good pleasure. Don Benito signified his readiness, when, seating him in the malacca arm-chair, and for the guest's convenience drawing opposite it one of the settees, the servant commenced operations by throwing back his master's collar and loosening his cravat.

There is something in the negro which, in a peculiar way, fits him for avocations about one's person. Most negroes are natural valets and hairdressers; taking to the comb and brush congenially as to the castinets, and flourishing them apparently with almost equal satisfaction. There is, too, a smooth tact about them in this employment, with a marvelous, noiseless, gliding briskness, not ungraceful in its way, singularly pleasing to behold, and still more so to be the manipulated subject of. And above all is the great gift of good humor. Not the mere grin or laugh is here meant. Those were unsuitable. But a certain easy cheerfulness, harmonious in every glance and gesture; as though God had set the whole negro to some pleasant tune.

When to all this is added the docility arising from the unaspiring contentment of a limited mind, and that susceptibility of blind attachment sometimes inhering in indisputable inferiors, one readily perceives why those hypochondriacs, Johnson and Byron—it may be something like the hypochondriac, Benito Cereno—took to their hearts, almost to the exclusion of the entire white race, their serving men, the negroes, Barber and Fletcher.[3] But if there be that in the negro which exempts him from the inflicted sourness of the morbid or cynical mind, how, in his most prepossessing aspects, must he appear to a benevolent one? When at ease with respect to exterior things, Captain Delano's nature was not only benign, but familiarly and humorously so. At home, he had often taken rare satisfaction in sitting in his door, watching some free man of color at his work or play. If on a voyage he chanced to have a black sailor, invariably he was on chatty, and half-gamesome terms with him. In fact, like most men of a good, blithe heart, Captain Delano took to negroes, not philanthropically, but genially, just as other men to Newfoundland dogs.

3. William Fletcher, valet of Lord Byron (1788–1824), was a white Englishman, here confused with an American black servant of Edward Trelawny who accompanied Byron on some journeys.

Frank Barber worked for the English writer Samuel Johnson (1709–1784) for three decades; at his death in 1784 Johnson left Barber a large annuity.

Hitherto the circumstances in which he found the San Dominick had repressed the tendency. But in the cuddy, relieved from his former uneasiness, and, for various reasons, more sociably inclined than at any previous period of the day, and seeing the colored servant, napkin on arm, so debonair about his master, in a business so familiar as that of shaving, too, all his old weakness for negroes returned.

Among other things, he was amused with an odd instance of the African love of bright colors and fine shows, in the black's informally taking from the flag-locker a great piece of bunting of all hues, and lavishly tucking it under his master's chin for an apron.

The mode of shaving among the Spaniards is a little different from what it is with other nations. They have a basin, specifically called a barber's basin, which on one side is scooped out, so as accurately to receive the chin, against which it is closely held in lathering; which is done, not with a brush, but with soap dipped in the water of the basin and rubbed on the face.

In the present instance salt-water was used for lack of better; and the parts lathered were only the upper lip, and low down under the throat, all the rest being cultivated beard.

The preliminaries being somewhat novel to Captain Delano, he sat curiously eying them, so that no conversation took place, nor for the present did Don Benito appear disposed to renew any.

Setting down his basin, the negro searched among the razors, as for the sharpest, and having found it, gave it an additional edge by expertly strapping it on the firm, smooth, oily skin of his open palm; he then made a gesture as if to begin, but midway stood suspended for an instant, one hand elevating the razor, the other professionally dabbling among the bubbling suds on the Spaniard's lank neck. Not unaffected by the close sight of the gleaming steel, Don Benito nervously shuddered, his usual ghastliness was hightened by the lather, which lather, again, was intensified in its hue by the contrasting sootiness of the negro's body. Altogether the scene was somewhat peculiar, at least to Captain Delano, nor, as he saw the two thus postured, could he resist the vagary, that in the black he saw a headsman, and in the white, a man at the block. But this was one of those antic conceits, appearing and vanishing in a breath, from which, perhaps, the best regulated mind is not always free.

Meantime the agitation of the Spaniard had a little loosened the bunting from around him, so that one broad fold swept curtain-like over the chair-arm to the floor, revealing, amid a profusion of armorial bars and ground-colors—black, blue, and yellow—a closed castle in a blood-red field diagonal with a lion rampant in a white.

"The castle and the lion," exclaimed Captain Delano—"why, Don Benito, this is the flag of Spain you use here. It's well it's only I, and not the King, that sees this," he added with a smile, "but"—turning towards the black,— "it's all one, I suppose, so the colors be gay;" which playful remark did not fail somewhat to tickle the negro.

"Now, master," he said, readjusting the flag, and pressing the head gently further back into the crotch of the chair; "now master," and the steel glanced nigh the throat.

Again Don Benito faintly shuddered.

"You must not shake so, master.—See, Don Amasa, master always shakes when I shave him. And yet master knows I never yet have drawn blood, though it's true, if master will shake so, I may some of these times. Now master," he continued. "And now, Don Amasa, please go on with your talk about the gale, and all that, master can hear, and between times master can answer."

"Ah yes, these gales," said Captain Delano; "but the more I think of your voyage, Don Benito, the more I wonder, not at the gales, terrible as they must have been, but at the disastrous interval following them. For here, by your account, have you been these two months and more getting from Cape Horn to St. Maria, a distance which I myself, with a good wind, have sailed in a few days. True, you had calms, and long ones, but to be becalmed for two months, that is, at least, unusual. Why, Don Benito, had almost any other gentleman told me such a story, I should have been half disposed to a little incredulity."

Here an involuntary expression came over the Spaniard, similar to that just before on the deck, and whether it was the start he gave, or a sudden gawky roll of the hull in the calm, or a momentary unsteadiness of the servant's hand; however it was, just then the razor drew blood, spots of which stained the creamy lather under the throat; immediately the black barber drew back his steel, and remaining in his professional attitude, back to Captain Delano, and face to Don Benito, held up the trickling razor, saying, with a sort of half humorous sorrow, "See, master,—you shook so—here's Babo's first blood."

No sword drawn before James the First of England, no assassination in that timid King's presence,[4] could have produced a more terrified aspect than was now presented by Don Benito.

Poor fellow, thought Captain Delano, so nervous he can't even bear the sight of barber's blood; and this unstrung, sick man, is it credible that I should have imagined he meant to spill all my blood, who can't endure the sight of one little drop of his own? Surely, Amasa Delano, you have been beside yourself this day. Tell it not when you get home, sappy Amasa. Well, well, he looks like a murderer, doesn't he? More like as if himself were to be done for. Well, well, this day's experience shall be a good lesson.

Meantime, while these things were running through the honest seaman's mind, the servant had taken the napkin from his arm, and to Don Benito had said—"But answer Don Amasa, please, master, while I wipe this ugly stuff off the razor, and strop it again."

As he said the words, his face was turned half round, so as to be alike visible to the Spaniard and the American, and seemed by its expression to hint, that he was desirous, by getting his master to go on with the conversation, considerably to withdraw his attention from the recent annoying accident. As if glad to snatch the offered relief, Don Benito resumed, rehearsing to Captain Delano, that not only were the calms of unusual duration, but the ship had fallen in with obstinate currents; and other things he added, some of which were but repetitions of former statements, to explain how it came to pass that the passage from Cape Horn to St. Maria had been so exceedingly long, now and then mingling with his words, incidental praises, less qualified than before, to the blacks, for their general good conduct.

These particulars were not given consecutively, the servant at convenient times using his razor, and so, between the intervals of shaving, the story and panegyric went on with more than usual huskiness.

To Captain Delano's imagination, now again not wholly at rest, there was something so hollow in the Spaniard's manner, with apparently some

4. James I (1566–1625), king of Great Britain and Ireland (r. 1604–25), who lived in terror of assassination by Catholics, especially after the Gun- powder Plot (1605) and the assassination of King Henry IV of France in 1610.

reciprocal hollowness in the servant's dusky comment of silence, that the idea flashed across him, that possibly master and man, for some unknown purpose, were acting out, both in word and deed, nay, to the very tremor of Don Benito's limbs, some juggling play before him. Neither did the suspicion of collusion lack apparent support, from the fact of those whispered conferences before mentioned. But then, what could be the object of enacting this play of the barber before him? At last, regarding the notion as a whimsy, insensibly suggested, perhaps, by the theatrical aspect of Don Benito in his harlequin ensign,[5] Captain Delano speedily banished it.

The shaving over, the servant bestirred himself with a small bottle of scented waters, pouring a few drops on the head, and then diligently rubbing; the vehemence of the exercise causing the muscles of his face to twitch rather strangely.

His next operation was with comb, scissors and brush; going round and round, smoothing a curl here, clipping an unruly whisker-hair there, giving a graceful sweep to the temple-lock, with other impromptu touches evincing the hand of a master; while, like any resigned gentleman in barber's hands, Don Benito bore all, much less uneasily, at least, than he had done the razoring; indeed, he sat so pale and rigid now, that the negro seemed a Nubian[6] sculptor finishing off a white statue-head.

All being over at last, the standard of Spain removed, tumbled up, and tossed back into the flag-locker, the negro's warm breath blowing away any stray hair which might have lodged down his master's neck; collar and cravat readjusted; a speck of lint whisked off the velvet lapel; all this being done; backing off a little space, and pausing with an expression of subdued self-complacency, the servant for a moment surveyed his master, as, in toilet at least, the creature of his own tasteful hands.

Captain Delano playfully complimented him upon his achievement; at the same time congratulating Don Benito.

But neither sweet waters, nor shampooing, nor fidelity, nor sociality, delighted the Spaniard. Seeing him relapsing into forbidding gloom, and still remaining seated, Captain Delano, thinking that his presence was undesired just then, withdrew, on pretense of seeing whether, as he had prophecied, any signs of a breeze were visible.

Walking forward to the mainmast, he stood awhile thinking over the scene, and not without some undefined misgivings, when he heard a noise near the cuddy, and turning, saw the negro, his hand to his cheek. Advancing, Captain Delano perceived that the cheek was bleeding. He was about to ask the cause, when the negro's wailing soliloquy enlightened him.

"Ah, when will master get better from his sickness; only the sour heart that sour sickness breeds made him serve Babo so; cutting Babo with the razor, because, only by accident, Babo had given master one little scratch; and for the first time in so many a day, too. Ah, ah, ah," holding his hand to his face.

Is it possible, thought Captain Delano; was it to wreak in private his Spanish spite against this poor friend of his, that Don Benito, by his sullen manner, impelled me to withdraw? Ah, this slavery breeds ugly passions in man—Poor fellow!

He was about to speak in sympathy to the negro, but with a timid reluctance he now reëntered the cuddy.

---

5. Colorful Spanish flag.
6. Native of Nubia in East Africa, now part of Sudan.

Presently master and man came forth; Don Benito leaning on his servant as if nothing had happened.

But a sort of love-quarrel, after all, thought Captain Delano.

He accosted Don Benito, and they slowly walked together. They had gone but a few paces, when the steward—a tall, rajah-looking mulatto, orientally set off with a pagoda turban formed by three or four Madras handkerchiefs wound about his head, tier on tier—approaching with a saalam,[7] announced lunch in the cabin.

On their way thither, the two Captains were preceded by the mulatto, who, turning round as he advanced, with continual smiles and bows, ushered them on, a display of elegance which quite completed the insignificance of the small bare-headed Babo, who, as if not unconscious of inferiority, eyed askance the graceful steward. But in part, Captain Delano imputed his jealous watchfulness to that peculiar feeling which the full-blooded African entertains for the adulterated one. As for the steward, his manner, if not bespeaking much dignity of self-respect, yet evidenced his extreme desire to please; which is doubly meritorious, as at once Christian and Chesterfieldian.[8]

Captain Delano observed with interest that while the complexion of the mulatto was hybrid, his physiognomy was European; classically so.

"Don Benito," whispered he, "I am glad to see this usher-of the-golden-rod[9] of yours; the sight refutes an ugly remark once made to me by a Barbadoes planter; that when a mulatto has a regular European face, look out for him; he is a devil. But see, your steward here has features more regular than King George's of England; and yet there he nods, and bows, and smiles; a king, indeed—the king of kind hearts and polite fellows. What a pleasant voice he has, too?"

"He has, Señor."

"But, tell me, has he not, so far as you have known him, always proved a good, worthy fellow?" said Captain Delano, pausing, while with a final genuflexion the steward disappeared into the cabin; "come, for the reason just mentioned, I am curious to know."

"Francesco is a good man," a sort of sluggishly responded Don Benito, like a phlegmatic appreciator, who would neither find fault nor flatter.

"Ah, I thought so. For it were strange indeed, and not very creditable to us white-skins, if a little of our blood mixed with the African's, should, far from improving the latter's quality, have the sad effect of pouring vitriolic acid into black broth; improving the hue, perhaps, but not the wholesomeness."

"Doubtless, doubtless, Señor, but"—glancing at Babo—"not to speak of negroes, your planter's remark I have heard applied to the Spanish and Indian intermixtures in our provinces. But I know nothing about the matter," he listlessly added.

And here they entered the cabin.

The lunch was a frugal one. Some of Captain Delano's fresh fish and pumpkins, biscuit and salt beef, the reserved bottle of cider, and the San Dominick's last bottle of Canary.[1]

---

7. Literally, "health" (Arabic); a Muslim ceremonial greeting.

8. In his popular *Letters to His Son on the Art of Becoming a Man of the World and a Gentleman* (1747), Philip Stanhope, the fourth earl of Chesterfield (1694–1773), advocated a worldly code at variance with Jesus' absolute morality.

9. In this English usage, "usher" means an attendant charged with walking ceremoniously before a person of rank; certain ushers were known by the color of the rod or scepter they traditionally carried.

1. I.e., wine from the Canary Islands.

As they entered, Francesco, with two or three colored aids, was hovering over the table giving the last adjustments. Upon perceiving their master they withdrew, Francesco making a smiling congé, and the Spaniard, without condescending to notice it, fastidiously remarking to his companion that he relished not superfluous attendance.

Without companions, host and guest sat down, like a childless married couple, at opposite ends of the table, Don Benito waving Captain Delano to his place, and, weak as he was, insisting upon that gentleman being seated before himself.

The negro placed a rug under Don Benito's feet, and a cushion behind his back, and then stood behind, not his master's chair, but Captain Delano's. At first, this a little surprised the latter. But it was soon evident that, in taking his position, the black was still true to his master; since by facing him he could the more readily anticipate his slightest want.

"This is an uncommonly intelligent fellow of yours, Don Benito," whispered Captain Delano across the table.

"You say true, Señor."

During the repast, the guest again reverted to parts of Don Benito's story, begging further particulars here and there. He inquired how it was that the scurvy and fever should have committed such wholesale havoc upon the whites, while destroying less than half of the blacks. As if this question reproduced the whole scene of plague before the Spaniard's eyes, miserably reminding him of his solitude in a cabin where before he had had so many friends and officers round him, his hand shook, his face became hueless, broken words escaped; but directly the sane memory of the past seemed replaced by insane terrors of the present. With starting eyes he stared before him at vacancy. For nothing was to be seen but the hand of his servant pushing the Canary over towards him. At length a few sips served partially to restore him. He made random reference to the different constitution of races, enabling one to offer more resistance to certain maladies than another. The thought was new to his companion.

Presently Captain Delano, intending to say something to his host concerning the pecuniary part of the business he had undertaken for him, especially—since he was strictly accountable to his owners—with reference to the new suit of sails, and other things of that sort; and naturally preferring to conduct such affairs in private, was desirous that the servant should withdraw; imagining that Don Benito for a few minutes could dispense with his attendance. He, however, waited awhile; thinking that, as the conversation proceeded, Don Benito, without being prompted, would perceive the propriety of the step.

But it was otherwise. At last catching his host's eye, Captain Delano, with a slight backward gesture of his thumb, whispered, "Don Benito, pardon me, but there is an interference with the full expression of what I have to say to you."

Upon this the Spaniard changed countenance; which was imputed to his resenting the hint, as in some way a reflection upon his servant. After a moment's pause, he assured his guest that the black's remaining with them could be of no disservice; because since losing his officers he had made Babo (whose original office, it now appeared, had been captain of the slaves) not only his constant attendant and companion, but in all things his confidant.

After this, nothing more could be said; though, indeed, Captain Delano could hardly avoid some little tinge of irritation upon being left ungratified in so inconsiderable a wish, by one, too, for whom he intended such solid services. But it is only his querulousness, thought he; and so filling his glass he proceeded to business.

The price of the sails and other matters was fixed upon. But while this was being done, the American observed that, though his original offer of assistance had been hailed with hectic animation, yet now when it was reduced to a business transaction, indifference and apathy were betrayed. Don Benito, in fact, appeared to submit to hearing the details more out of regard to common propriety, than from any impression that weighty benefit to himself and his voyage was involved.

Soon, his manner became still more reserved. The effort was vain to seek to draw him into social talk. Gnawed by his splenetic mood, he sat twitching his beard, while to little purpose the hand of his servant, mute as that on the wall, slowly pushed over the Canary.

Lunch being over, they sat down on the cushioned transom; the servant placing a pillow behind his master. The long continuance of the calm had now affected the atmosphere. Don Benito sighed heavily, as if for breath.

"Why not adjourn to the cuddy," said Captain Delano; "there is more air there." But the host sat silent and motionless.

Meantime his servant knelt before him, with a large fan of feathers. And Francesco coming in on tiptoes, handed the negro a little cup of aromatic waters, with which at intervals he chafed his master's brow; smoothing the hair along the temples as a nurse does a child's. He spoke no word. He only rested his eye on his master's, as if, amid all Don Benito's distress, a little to refresh his spirit by the silent sight of fidelity.

Presently the ship's bell sounded two o'clock; and through the cabin-windows a slight rippling of the sea was discerned; and from the desired direction.

"There," exclaimed Captain Delano, "I told you so, Don Benito, look!"

He had risen to his feet, speaking in a very animated tone, with a view the more to rouse his companion. But though the crimson curtain of the stern-window near him that moment fluttered against his pale cheek, Don Benito seemed to have even less welcome for the breeze than the calm.

Poor fellow, thought Captain Delano, bitter experience has taught him that one ripple does not make a wind, any more than one swallow a summer. But he is mistaken for once. I will get his ship in for him, and prove it.

Briefly alluding to his weak condition, he urged his host to remain quietly where he was, since he (Captain Delano) would with pleasure take upon himself the responsibility of making the best use of the wind.

Upon gaining the deck, Captain Delano started at the unexpected figure of Atufal, monumentally fixed at the threshold, like one of those sculptured porters of black marble guarding the porches of Egyptian tombs.

But this time the start was, perhaps, purely physical. Atufal's presence, singularly attesting docility even in sullenness, was contrasted with that of the hatchet-polishers, who in patience evinced their industry; while both spectacles showed, that lax as Don Benito's general authority might be, still, whenever he chose to exert it, no man so savage or colossal but must, more or less, bow.

Snatching a trumpet which hung from the bulwarks, with a free step Captain Delano advanced to the forward edge of the poop, issuing his orders in his best Spanish. The few sailors and many negroes, all equally pleased, obediently set about heading the ship towards the harbor.

While giving some directions about setting a lower stu'n'-sail, suddenly Captain Delano heard a voice faithfully repeating his orders. Turning, he saw Babo, now for the time acting, under the pilot, his original part of captain of the slaves. This assistance proved valuable. Tattered sails and warped yards were soon brought into some trim. And no brace or halyard was pulled but to the blithe songs of the inspirited negroes.

Good fellows, thought Captain Delano, a little training would make fine sailors of them. Why see, the very women pull and sing too. These must be some of those Ashantee negresses that make such capital soldiers, I've heard. But who's at the helm. I must have a good hand there.

He went to see.

The San Dominick steered with a cumbrous tiller, with large horizontal pullies attached. At each pully-end stood a subordinate black, and between them, at the tiller-head, the responsible post, a Spanish seaman, whose countenance evinced his due share in the general hopefulness and confidence at the coming of the breeze.

He proved the same man who had behaved with so shame-faced an air on the windlass.

"Ah—it is you, my man," exclaimed Captain Delano—"well, no more sheep's-eyes now;—look straightforward and keep the ship so. Good hand, I trust? And want to get into the harbor, don't you?"

The man assented with an inward chuckle, grasping the tiller-head firmly. Upon this, unperceived by the American, the two blacks eyed the sailor intently.

Finding all right at the helm, the pilot went forward to the forecastle, to see how matters stood there.

The ship now had way enough to breast the current. With the approach of evening, the breeze would be sure to freshen.

Having done all that was needed for the present, Captain Delano, giving his last orders to the sailors, turned aft to report affairs to Don Benito in the cabin; perhaps additionally incited to rejoin him by the hope of snatching a moment's private chat while the servant was engaged upon deck.

From opposite sides, there were, beneath the poop, two approaches to the cabin; one further forward than the other, and consequently communicating with a longer passage. Marking the servant still above, Captain Delano, taking the nighest entrance—the one last named, and at whose porch Atufal still stood—hurried on his way, till, arrived at the cabin threshold, he paused an instant, a little to recover from his eagerness. Then, with the words of his intended business upon his lips, he entered. As he advanced toward the seated Spaniard, he heard another footstep, keeping time with his. From the opposite door, a salver in hand, the servant was likewise advancing.

"Confound the faithful fellow," thought Captain Delano; "what a vexatious coincidence."

Possibly, the vexation might have been something different, were it not for the brisk confidence inspired by the breeze. But even as it was, he felt a slight twinge, from a sudden indefinite association in his mind of Babo with Atufal.

"Don Benito," said he, "I give you joy; the breeze will hold, and will increase. By the way, your tall man and time-piece, Atufal, stands without. By your order, of course?"

Don Benito recoiled, as if at some bland satirical touch, delivered with such adroit garnish of apparent good-breeding as to present no handle for retort.

He is like one flayed alive, thought Captain Delano; where may one touch him without causing a shrink?

The servant moved before his master, adjusting a cushion; recalled to civility, the Spaniard stiffly replied: "You are right. The slave appears where you saw him, according to my command; which is, that if at the given hour I am below, he must take his stand and abide my coming."

"Ah now, pardon me, but that is treating the poor fellow like an ex-king indeed. Ah, Don Benito," smiling, "for all the license you permit in some things, I fear lest, at bottom, you are a bitter hard master."

Again Don Benito shrank; and this time, as the good sailor thought, from a genuine twinge of his conscience.

Again conversation became constrained. In vain Captain Delano called attention to the now perceptible motion of the keel gently cleaving the sea; with lack-lustre eye, Don Benito returned words few and reserved.

By-and-by, the wind having steadily risen, and still blowing right into the harbor, bore the San Dominick swiftly on. Rounding a point of land, the sealer at distance came into open view.

Meantime Captain Delano had again repaired to the deck, remaining there some time. Having at last altered the ship's course, so as to give the reef a wide berth, he returned for a few moments below.

I will cheer up my poor friend, this time, thought he.

"Better and better, Don Benito," he cried as he blithely reëntered; "there will soon be an end to your cares, at least for awhile. For when, after a long, sad voyage, you know, the anchor drops into the haven, all its vast weight seems lifted from the captain's heart. We are getting on famously, Don Benito. My ship is in sight. Look through this side-light here; there she is; all a-taunt-o! The Bachelor's Delight, my good friend. Ah, how this wind braces one up. Come, you must take a cup of coffee with me this evening. My old steward will give you as fine a cup as ever any sultan tasted. What say you, Don Benito, will you?"

At first, the Spaniard glanced feverishly up, casting a longing look towards the sealer, while with mute concern his servant gazed into his face. Suddenly the old ague of coldness returned, and dropping back to his cushions he was silent.

"You do not answer. Come, all day you have been my host; would you have hospitality all on one side?"

"I cannot go," was the response.

"What? it will not fatigue you. The ships will lie together as near as they can, without swinging foul. It will be little more than stepping from deck to deck; which is but as from room to room. Come, come, you must not refuse me."

"I cannot go," decisively and repulsively repeated Don Benito.

Renouncing all but the last appearance of courtesy, with a sort of cadaverous sullenness, and biting his thin nails to the quick, he glanced, almost glared, at his guest; as if impatient that a stranger's presence should interfere with the full indulgence of his morbid hour. Meantime the sound of the parted waters came more and more gurglingly and merrily in at the windows; as reproaching him for his dark spleen; as telling him that, sulk as he might, and go mad with it, nature cared not a jot; since, whose fault was it, pray?

But the foul mood was now at its depth, as the fair wind at its hight.

There was something in the man so far beyond any mere unsociality or sourness previously evinced, that even the forbearing good-nature of his guest could no longer endure it. Wholly at a loss to account for such demeanor, and deeming sickness with eccentricity, however extreme, no adequate excuse, well satisfied, too, that nothing in his own conduct could justify it, Captain Delano's pride began to be roused. Himself became reserved. But all seemed one to the Spaniard. Quitting him, therefore, Captain Delano once more went to the deck.

The ship was now within less than two miles of the sealer. The whale-boat was seen darting over the interval.

To be brief, the two vessels, thanks to the pilot's skill, ere long in neighborly style lay anchored together.

Before returning to his own vessel, Captain Delano had intended communicating to Don Benito the smaller details of the proposed services to be rendered. But, as it was, unwilling anew to subject himself to rebuffs, he resolved, now that he had seen the San Dominick safely moored, immediately to quit her, without further allusion to hospitality or business. Indefinitely postponing his ulterior plans, he would regulate his future actions according to future circumstances. His boat was ready to receive him; but his host still tarried below. Well, thought Captain Delano, if he has little breeding, the more need to show mine. He descended to the cabin to bid a ceremonious, and, it may be, tacitly rebukeful adieu. But to his great satisfaction, Don Benito, as if he began to feel the weight of that treatment with which his slighted guest had, not indecorously, retaliated upon him, now supported by his servant, rose to his feet, and grasping Captain Delano's hand, stood tremulous; too much agitated to speak. But the good augury hence drawn was suddenly dashed, by his resuming all his previous reserve, with augmented gloom, as, with half-averted eyes, he silently reseated himself on his cushions. With a corresponding return of his own chilled feelings, Captain Delano bowed and withdrew.

He was hardly midway in the narrow corridor, dim as a tunnel, leading from the cabin to the stairs, when a sound, as of the tolling for execution in some jail-yard, fell on his ears. It was the echo of the ship's flawed bell, striking the hour, drearily reverberated in this subterranean vault. Instantly, by a fatality not to be withstood, his mind, responsive to the portent, swarmed with superstitious suspicions. He paused. In images far swifter than these sentences, the minutest details of all his former distrusts swept through him.

Hitherto, credulous good-nature had been too ready to furnish excuses for reasonable fears. Why was the Spaniard, so superfluously punctilious at times, now heedless of common propriety in not accompanying to the side his departing guest? Did indisposition forbid? Indisposition had not forbidden more irksome exertion that day. His last equivocal demeanor recurred. He had risen to his feet, grasped his guest's hand, motioned toward his hat; then, in an instant, all was eclipsed in sinister muteness and gloom. Did this imply one brief, repentant relenting at the final moment, from some iniquitous plot, followed by remorseless return to it? His last glance seemed to express a calamitous, yet acquiescent farewell to Captain Delano forever. Why decline the invitation to visit the sealer that evening? Or was the Spaniard less hardened than the Jew, who refrained not from supping at the board of him whom the same night he meant to betray?[2] What imported all those day-long enigmas and contradictions, except they were intended to mystify, preliminary to some stealthy blow? Atufal, the pretended rebel, but punctual shadow, that moment lurked by the threshold without. He seemed a sentry, and more. Who, by his own confession, had stationed him there? Was the negro now lying in wait?

The Spaniard behind—his creature before: to rush from darkness to light was the involuntary choice.

The next moment, with clenched jaw and hand, he passed Atufal, and stood unharmed in the light. As he saw his trim ship lying peacefully at anchor, and almost within ordinary call; as he saw his household boat, with familiar faces in it, patiently rising and falling on the short waves by the San Dominick's side; and then, glancing about the decks where he stood, saw the oakum-pickers still gravely plying their fingers; and heard the low, buzzing whistle and industrious hum of the hatchet-polishers, still bestirring themselves over their endless occupation; and more than all, as he saw the benign aspect of nature, taking her innocent repose in the evening; the screened sun in the quiet camp of the west shining out like the mild light from Abraham's tent,[3] as charmed eye and ear took in all these, with the chained figure of the black, clenched jaw and hand relaxed. Once again he smiled at the phantoms which had mocked him, and felt something like a tinge of remorse, that, by harboring them even for a moment, he should, by implication, have betrayed an atheist doubt of the ever-watchful Providence above.

There was a few minutes' delay, while, in obedience to his orders, the boat was being hooked along to the gangway. During this interval, a sort of saddened satisfaction stole over Captain Delano, at thinking of the kindly offices he had that day discharged for a stranger. Ah, thought he, after good actions one's conscience is never ungrateful, however much so the benefited party may be.

Presently, his foot, in the first act of descent into the boat, pressed the first round of the side-ladder, his face presented inward upon the deck. In the same moment, he heard his name courteously sounded; and, to his pleased surprise, saw Don Benito advancing—an unwonted energy in his air, as if, at the last moment, intent upon making amends for his recent discourtesy. With instinctive good feeling, Captain Delano, withdrawing his foot, turned and reciprocally advanced. As he did so, the Spaniard's nervous eagerness increased, but his vital energy failed; so that, the better to support him, the servant, placing his master's hand on his naked shoulder, and gently holding it there, formed himself into a sort of crutch.

When the two captains met, the Spaniard again fervently took the hand of the American, at the same time casting an earnest glance into his eyes, but, as before, too much overcome to speak.

I have done him wrong, self-reproachfully thought Captain Delano; his apparent coldness has deceived me; in no instance has he meant to offend.

Meantime, as if fearful that the continuance of the scene might too much unstring his master, the servant seemed anxious to terminate it. And so, still presenting himself as a crutch, and walking between the two captains,

2. Judas Iscariot, who betrayed Christ after the Last Supper (Matthew 26).
3. The biblical patriarch Abraham, who pitched his tent in many places during his westward journey from Ur of the Chaldees to Canaan, on to Egypt, and then back to Canaan.

he advanced with them towards the gangway; while still, as if full of kindly contrition, Don Benito would not let go the hand of Captain Delano, but retained it in his, across the black's body.

Soon they were standing by the side, looking over into the boat, whose crew turned up their curious eyes. Waiting a moment for the Spaniard to relinquish his hold, the now embarrassed Captain Delano lifted his foot, to overstep the threshold of the open gangway; but still Don Benito would not let go his hand. And yet, with an agitated tone, he said, "I can go no further; here I must bid you adieu. Adieu, my dear, dear Don Amasa. Go—go!" suddenly tearing his hand loose, "go, and God guard you better than me, my best friend."

Not unaffected, Captain Delano would now have lingered; but catching the meekly admonitory eye of the servant, with a hasty farewell he descended into his boat, followed by the continual adieus of Don Benito, standing rooted in the gangway.

Seating himself in the stern, Captain Delano, making a last salute, ordered the boat shoved off. The crew had their oars on end. The bowsman pushed the boat a sufficient distance for the oars to be lengthwise dropped. The instant that was done, Don Benito sprang over the bulwarks, falling at the feet of Captain Delano; at the same time, calling towards his ship, but in tones so frenzied, that none in the boat could understand him. But, as if not equally obtuse, three sailors, from three different and distant parts of the ship, splashed into the sea, swimming after their captain, as if intent upon his rescue.

The dismayed officer of the boat eagerly asked what this meant. To which, Captain Delano, turning a disdainful smile upon the unaccountable Spaniard, answered that, for his part, he neither knew nor cared; but it seemed as if Don Benito had taken it into his head to produce the impression among his people that the boat wanted to kidnap him. "Or else—give way for your lives," he wildly added, starting at a clattering hubbub in the ship, above which rang the tocsin of the hatchet-polishers; and seizing Don Benito by the throat he added, "this plotting pirate means murder!" Here, in apparent verification of the words, the servant, a dagger in his hand, was seen on the rail overhead, poised in the act of leaping, as if with desperate fidelity to befriend his master to the last; while, seemingly to aid the black, the three white sailors were trying to clamber into the hampered bow. Meantime, the whole host of negroes, as if inflamed at the sight of their jeopardized captain, impended in one sooty avalanche over the bulwarks.

All this, with what preceded, and what followed, occurred with such involutions of rapidity, that past, present, and future seemed one.

Seeing the negro coming, Captain Delano had flung the Spaniard aside, almost in the very act of clutching him, and, by the unconscious recoil, shifting his place, with arms thrown up, so promptly grappled the servant in his descent, that with dagger presented at Captain Delano's heart, the black seemed of purpose to have leaped there as to his mark. But the weapon was wrenched away, and the assailant dashed down into the bottom of the boat, which now, with disentangled oars, began to speed through the sea.

At this juncture, the left hand of Captain Delano, on one side, again clutched the half-reclined Don Benito, heedless that he was in a speechless faint, while his right foot, on the other side, ground the prostrate negro; and his right arm pressed for added speed on the after oar, his eye bent forward, encouraging his men to their utmost.

But here, the officer of the boat, who had at last succeeded in beating off the towing sailors, and was now, with face turned aft, assisting the bowsman at his oar, suddenly called to Captain Delano, to see what the black was about; while a Portuguese oarsman shouted to him to give heed to what the Spaniard was saying.

Glancing down at his feet, Captain Delano saw the freed hand of the servant aiming with a second dagger—a small one, before concealed in his wool—with this he was snakishly writhing up from the boat's bottom, at the heart of his master, his countenance lividly vindictive, expressing the centred purpose of his soul, while the Spaniard, half-choked, was vainly shrinking away, with husky words, incoherent to all but the Portuguese.

That moment, across the long-benighted mind of Captain Delano, a flash of revelation swept, illuminating in unanticipated clearness, his host's whole mysterious demeanor, with every enigmatic event of the day, as well as the entire past voyage of the San Dominick. He smote Babo's hand down, but his own heart smote him harder. With infinite pity he withdrew his hold from Don Benito. Not Captain Delano, but Don Benito, the black, in leaping into the boat, had intended to stab.

Both the black's hands were held, as, glancing up towards the San Dominick, Captain Delano, now with scales dropped from his eyes, saw the negroes, not in misrule, not in tumult, not as if frantically concerned for Don Benito, but with mask torn away, flourishing hatchets and knives, in ferocious piratical revolt. Like delirious black dervishes, the six Ashantees danced on the poop. Prevented by their foes from springing into the water, the Spanish boys were hurrying up to the topmost spars, while such of the few Spanish sailors, not already in the sea, less alert, were descried, helplessly mixed in, on deck, with the blacks.

Meantime Captain Delano hailed his own vessel, ordering the ports up, and the guns run out. But by this time the cable of the San Dominick had been cut; and the fag-end, in lashing out, whipped away the canvas shroud about the beak, suddenly revealing, as the bleached hull swung round towards the open ocean, death for the figure-head, in a human skeleton; chalky comment on the chalked words below, *Follow your leader.*

At the sight, Don Benito, covering his face, wailed out: "'Tis he, Aranda! my murdered, unburied friend!"

Upon reaching the sealer, calling for ropes, Captain Delano bound the negro, who made no resistance, and had him hoisted to the deck. He would then have assisted the now almost helpless Don Benito up the side; but Don Benito, wan as he was, refused to move, or be moved, until the negro should have been first put below out of view. When, presently assured that it was done, he no more shrank from the ascent.

The boat was immediately dispatched back to pick up the three swimming sailors. Meantime, the guns were in readiness, though, owing to the San Dominick having glided somewhat astern of the sealer, only the aftermost one could be brought to bear. With this, they fired six times; thinking to cripple the fugitive ship by bringing down her spars. But only a few inconsiderable ropes were shot away. Soon the ship was beyond the guns' range, steering broad out of the bay; the blacks thickly clustering round the bowsprit,[4] one moment with taunting cries towards the whites, the next with

---

4. The large spar, such as the pole for a mast, extending from the foremost part of the ship.

upthrown gestures hailing the now dusky moors of ocean—cawing crows escaped from the hand of the fowler.

The first impulse was to slip the cables and give chase. But, upon second thoughts, to pursue with whale-boat and yawl seemed more promising.

Upon inquiring of Don Benito what fire arms they had on board the San Dominick, Captain Delano was answered that they had none that could be used; because, in the earlier stages of the mutiny, a cabin-passenger, since dead, had secretly put out of order the locks of what few muskets there were. But with all his remaining strength, Don Benito entreated the American not to give chase, either with ship or boat; for the negroes had already proved themselves such desperadoes, that, in case of a present assault, nothing but a total massacre of the whites could be looked for. But, regarding this warning as coming from one whose spirit had been crushed by misery, the American did not give up his design.

The boats were got ready and armed. Captain Delano ordered his men into them. He was going himself when Don Benito grasped his arm.

"What! have you saved my life, señor, and are you now going to throw away your own?"

The officers also, for reasons connected with their interests and those of the voyage, and a duty owing to the owners, strongly objected against their commander's going. Weighing their remonstrances a moment, Captain Delano felt bound to remain; appointing his chief mate—an athletic and resolute man, who had been a privateer's-man[5]—to head the party. The more to encourage the sailors, they were told, that the Spanish captain considered his ship good as lost; that she and her cargo, including some gold and silver, were worth more than a thousand doubloons. Take her, and no small part should be theirs. The sailors replied with a shout.

The fugitives had now almost gained an offing. It was nearly night; but the moon was rising. After hard, prolonged pulling, the boats came up on the ship's quarters, at a suitable distance laying upon their oars to discharge their muskets. Having no bullets to return, the negroes sent their yells. But, upon the second volley, Indian-like, they hurtled their hatchets. One took off a sailor's fingers. Another struck the whale-boat's bow, cutting off the rope there, and remaining stuck in the gunwale like a woodman's axe. Snatching it, quivering from its lodgment, the mate hurled it back. The returned gauntlet now stuck in the ship's broken quarter-gallery, and so remained.

The negroes giving too hot a reception, the whites kept a more respectful distance. Hovering now just out of reach of the hurtling hatchets, they, with a view to the close encounter which must soon come, sought to decoy the blacks into entirely disarming themselves of their most murderous weapons in a hand-to-hand fight, by foolishly flinging them, as missiles, short of the mark, into the sea. But ere long perceiving the stratagem, the negroes desisted, though not before many of them had to replace their lost hatchets with hand-spikes; an exchange which, as counted upon, proved in the end favorable to the assailants.

Meantime, with a strong wind, the ship still clove the water; the boats alternately falling behind, and pulling up, to discharge fresh volleys.

The fire was mostly directed towards the stern, since there, chiefly, the negroes, at present, were clustering. But to kill or maim the negroes was not

<hr>

5. Had served on a privateer—a ship commissioned by a government to prey on the shipping of other countries.

the object. To take them, with the ship, was the object. To do it, the ship must be boarded; which could not be done by boats while she was sailing so fast.

A thought now struck the mate. Observing the Spanish boys still aloft, high as they could get, he called to them to descend to the yards, and cut adrift the sails. It was done. About this time, owing to causes hereafter to be shown, two Spaniards, in the dress of sailors and conspicuously showing themselves, were killed; not by volleys, but by deliberate marksman's shots; while, as it afterwards appeared, by one of the general discharges, Atufal, the black, and the Spaniard at the helm likewise were killed. What now, with the loss of the sails, and loss of leaders, the ship became unmanageable to the negroes.

With creaking masts, she came heavily round to the wind; the prow slowly swinging, into view of the boats, its skeleton gleaming in the horizontal moonlight, and casting a gigantic ribbed shadow upon the water. One extended arm of the ghost seemed beckoning the whites to avenge it.

"Follow your leader!" cried the mate; and, one on each bow, the boats boarded. Sealing-spears and cutlasses crossed hatchets and hand-spikes. Huddled upon the long-boat amidships, the negresses raised a wailing chant, whose chorus was the clash of the steel.

For a time, the attack wavered; the negroes wedging themselves to beat it back; the half-repelled sailors, as yet unable to gain a footing, fighting as troopers in the saddle, one leg sideways flung over the bulwarks, and one without, plying their cutlasses like carters' whips. But in vain. They were almost overborne, when, rallying themselves into a squad as one man, with a huzza, they sprang inboard; where, entangled, they involuntarily separated again. For a few breaths' space, there was a vague, muffled, inner sound, as of submerged sword-fish rushing hither and thither through shoals of black-fish. Soon, in a reunited band, and joined by the Spanish seamen, the whites came to the surface, irresistibly driving the negroes toward the stern. But a barricade of casks and sacks, from side to side, had been thrown up by the mainmast. Here the negroes faced about, and though scorning peace or truce, yet fain would have had respite. But, without pause, overleaping the barrier, the unflagging sailors again closed. Exhausted, the blacks now fought in despair. Their red tongues lolled, wolf-like, from their black mouths. But the pale sailors' teeth were set; not a word was spoken; and, in five minutes more, the ship was won.

Nearly a score of the negroes were killed. Exclusive of those by the balls,[6] many were mangled; their wounds—mostly inflicted by the long-edged sealing-spears—resembling those shaven ones of the English at Preston Pans, made by the poled scythes of the Highlanders.[7] On the other side, none were killed, though several were wounded; some severely, including the mate. The surviving negroes were temporarily secured, and the ship, towed back into the harbor at midnight, once more lay anchored.

Omitting the incidents and arrangements ensuing, suffice it that, after two days spent in refitting, the ships sailed in company for Conception, in Chili, and thence for Lima, in Peru; where, before the vice-regal courts, the whole affair, from the beginning, underwent investigation.

Though, midway on the passage, the ill-fated Spaniard, relaxed from constraint, showed some signs of regaining health with free-will; yet, agreeably

6. Those killed by musketballs.
7. At the battle of Preston Pans (in East Lothian, Scotland) during 1745, Prince Charles Edward, grandson of James II, led Scottish Highlanders armed with scythes fastened to poles to victory over the royal forces.

to his own foreboding, shortly before arriving at Lima, he relapsed, finally becoming so reduced as to be carried ashore in arms. Hearing of his story and plight, one of the many religious institutions of the City of Kings opened an hospitable refuge to him, where both physician and priest were his nurses, and a member of the order volunteered to be his one special guardian and consoler, by night and by day.

The following extracts, translated from one of the official Spanish documents, will it is hoped, shed light on the preceding narrative, as well as, in the first place, reveal the true port of departure and true history of the San Dominick's voyage, down to the time of her touching at the island of St. Maria.

But, ere the extracts come, it may be well to preface them with a remark.

The document selected, from among many others, for partial translation, contains the deposition of Benito Cereno; the first taken in the case. Some disclosures therein were, at the time, held dubious for both learned and natural reasons. The tribunal inclined to the opinion that the deponent, not undisturbed in his mind by recent events, raved of some things which could never have happened. But subsequent depositions of the surviving sailors, bearing out the revelations of their captain in several of the strangest particulars, gave credence to the rest. So that the tribunal, in its final decision, rested its capital sentences upon statements which, had they lacked confirmation, it would have deemed it but duty to reject.

I, DON JOSE DE ABOS AND PADILLA, His Majesty's Notary for the Royal Revenue, and Register of this Province, and Notary Public of the Holy Crusade of this Bishopric, etc.

Do certify and declare, as much as is requisite in law, that, in the criminal cause commenced the twenty-fourth of the month of September, in the year seventeen hundred and ninety-nine, against the negroes of the ship San Dominick, the following declaration before me was made.

Declaration of the first witness, DON BENITO CERENO

The same day, and month, and year, His Honor, Doctor Juan Martinez de Rozas, Councilor of the Royal Audience of this Kingdom, and learned in the law of this Intendency, ordered the captain of the ship San Dominick, Don Benito Cereno, to appear; which he did in his litter, attended by the monk Infelez; of whom he received the oath, which he took by God, our Lord, and a sign of the Cross; under which he promised to tell the truth of whatever he should know and should be asked;—and being interrogated agreeably to the tenor of the act commencing the process, he said, that on the twentieth of May last, he set sail with his ship from the port of Valparaiso, bound to that of Callao; loaded with the produce of the country beside thirty cases of hardware and one hundred and sixty blacks, of both sexes, mostly belonging to Don Alexandro Aranda, gentleman, of the city of Mendoza;[8] that the crew of the ship consisted of thirty-six men, beside the persons who went as passengers; that the negroes were in part as follows:

---

8. City in Argentina. "Intendency": court district. "Litter": seat or chair in which a person can be carried. Callao is a city in Peru; Valparaiso is in Chile.

[*Here, in the original, follows a list of some fifty names, descriptions, and ages, compiled from certain recovered documents of Aranda's, and also from recollections of the deponent, from which portions only are extracted.*]

—One, from about eighteen to nineteen years, named José, and this was the man that waited upon his master, Don Alexandro, and who speaks well the Spanish, having served him four or five years; * * * a mulatto, named Francisco, the cabin steward, of a good person and voice, having sung in the Valparaiso churches, native of the province of Buenos Ayres, aged about thirty-five years. * * * A smart negro, named Dago, who had been for many years a grave-digger among the Spaniards, aged forty-six years. * * * Four old negroes, born in Africa, from sixty to seventy, but sound, calkers by trade, whose names are as follows:—the first was named Muri, and he was killed (as was also his son named Diamelo); the second, Nacta; the third, Yola, likewise killed; the fourth, Ghofan; and six full-grown negroes, aged from thirty to forty-five, all raw, and born among the Ashantees—Matiluqui, Yan, Lecbe, Mapenda, Yambaio, Akim; four of whom were killed; * * * a powerful negro named Atufal, who, being supposed to have been a chief in Africa, his owners set great store by him. * * * And a small negro of Senegal, but some years among the Spaniards, aged about thirty, which negro's name was Babo; * * * that he does not remember the names of the others, but that still expecting the residue of Don Alexandro's papers will be found, will then take due account of them all, and remit to the court; * * * and thirty-nine women and children of all ages.

[*The catalogue over, the deposition goes on:*]

* * * That all the negroes slept upon deck, as is customary in this navigation, and none wore fetters, because the owner, his friend Aranda, told him that they were all tractable; * * * that on the seventh day after leaving port, at three o'clock in the morning, all the Spaniards being asleep except the two officers on the watch, who were the boatswain, Juan Robles, and the carpenter, Juan Bautista Gayete, and the helmsman and his boy, the negroes revolted suddenly, wounded dangerously the boatswain and the carpenter, and successively killed eighteen men of those who were sleeping upon deck, some with hand-spikes and hatchets, and others by throwing them alive overboard, after tying them; that of the Spaniards upon deck, they left about seven, as he thinks, alive and tied, to manœuvre the ship, and three or four more who hid themselves, remained also alive. Although in the act of revolt the negroes made themselves masters of the hatchway, six or seven wounded went through it to the cockpit, without any hindrance on their part; that during the act of revolt, the mate and another person, whose name he does not recollect, attempted to come up through the hatchway, but being quickly wounded, were obliged to return to the cabin; that the deponent resolved at break of day to come up the companionway, where the negro Babo was, being the ringleader, and Atufal, who assisted him, and having spoken to them, exhorted them to cease committing such atrocities, asking them, at the same time, what they wanted and intended to do, offering, himself, to obey their commands; that, notwithstanding this, they threw, in his presence, three men, alive and tied, overboard; that they told the deponent to come up, and that they would not kill him; which having done, the negro

Babo asked him whether there were in those seas any negro countries where they might be carried, and he answered them, No; that the negro Babo afterwards told him to carry them to Senegal, or to the neighboring islands of St. Nicholas; and he answered, that this was impossible, on account of the great distance, the necessity involved of rounding Cape Horn, the bad condition of the vessel, the want of provisions, sails, and water; but that the negro Babo replied to him he must carry them in any way; that they would do and conform themselves to everything the deponent should require as to eating and drinking; that after a long conference, being absolutely compelled to please them, for they threatened him to kill all the whites if they were not, at all events, carried to Senegal, he told them that what was most wanting for the voyage was water; that they would go near the coast to take it, and thence they would proceed on their course; that the negro Babo agreed to it; and the deponent steered towards the intermediate ports, hoping to meet some Spanish or foreign vessel that would save them; that within ten or eleven days they saw the land, and continued their course by it in the vicinity of Nasca; that the deponent observed that the negroes were now restless and mutinous, because he did not effect the taking in of water, the negro Babo having required, with threats, that it should be done, without fail, the following day; he told him he saw plainly that the coast was steep, and the rivers designated in the maps were not to be found, with other reasons suitable to the circumstances; that the best way would be to go to the island of Santa Maria, where they might water easily, it being a solitary island, as the foreigners did; that the deponent did not go to Pisco, that was near, nor make any other port of the coast, because the negro Babo had intimated to him several times, that he would kill all the whites the very moment he should perceive any city, town, or settlement of any kind on the shores to which they should be carried; that having determined to go to the island of Santa Maria, as the deponent had planned, for the purpose of trying whether, on the passage or near the island itself, they could find any vessel that should favor them, or whether he could escape from it in a boat to the neighboring coast of Arruco;[9] to adopt the necessary means he immediately changed his course, steering for the island; that the negroes Babo and Atufal held daily conferences, in which they discussed what was necessary for their design of returning to Senegal, whether they were to kill all the Spaniards, and particularly the deponent; that eight days after parting from the coast of Nasca, the deponent being on the watch a little after day-break, and soon after the negroes had their meeting, the negro Babo came to the place where the deponent was, and told him that he had determined to kill his master, Don Alexandro Aranda, both because he and his companions could not otherwise be sure of their liberty, and that, to keep the seamen in subjection, he wanted to prepare a warning of what road they should be made to take did they or any of them oppose him; and that, by means of the death of Don Alexandro, that warning would best be given; but, that what this last meant, the deponent did not at the time comprehend, nor could not, further than that the death of Don Alexandro was intended; and moreover, the negro Babo proposed to the deponent to call the mate Raneds, who was sleeping in the cabin, before the thing was done, for fear, as the deponent understood it, that the mate, who was a good navigator, should be killed with Don Alexandro and the rest; that

9. I.e., Arica, Chile. Nasca and Pisco are both in Peru.

the deponent, who was the friend, from youth, of Don Alexandro, prayed and conjured, but all was useless; for the negro Babo answered him that the thing could not be prevented, and that all the Spaniards risked their death if they should attempt to frustrate his will in this matter or any other; that, in this conflict, the deponent called the mate, Raneds, who was forced to go apart, and immediately the negro Babo commanded the Ashantee Martinqui and the Ashantee Lecbe to go and commit the murder; that those two went down with hatchets to the berth of Don Alexandro; that, yet half alive and mangled, they dragged him on deck; that they were going to throw him overboard in that state, but the negro Babo stopped them, bidding the murder be completed on the deck before him, which was done, when, by his orders, the body was carried below, forward; that nothing more was seen of it by the deponent for three days; * * * that Don Alonzo Sidonia, an old man, long resident at Valparaiso, and lately appointed to a civil office in Peru, whither he had taken passage, was at the time sleeping in the berth opposite Don Alexandro's; that, awakening at his cries, surprised by them, and at the sight of the negroes with their bloody hatchets in their hands, he threw himself into the sea through a window which was near him, and was drowned, without it being in the power of the deponent to assist or take him up; * * * that, a short time after killing Aranda, they brought upon deck his germancousin, of middle-age, Don Francisco Masa, of Mendoza, and the young Don Joaquin, Marques de Aramboalaza, then lately from Spain, with his Spanish servant Ponce, and the three young clerks of Aranda, José Morairi, Lorenzo Bargas, and Hermenegildo Gandix, all of Cadiz; that Don Joaquin and Hermenegildo Gandix, the negro Babo for purposes hereafter to appear, preserved alive; but Don Francisco Masa, José Morairi, and Lorenzo Bargas, with Ponce the servant, beside the boatswain, Juan Robles, the boatswain's mates, Manuel Viscaya and Roderigo Hurta, and four of the sailors, the negro Babo ordered to be thrown alive into the sea, although they made no resistance, nor begged for anything else but mercy; that the boatswain, Juan Robles, who knew how to swim, kept the longest above water, making acts of contrition, and, in the last words he uttered, charged this deponent to cause mass to be said for his soul to our Lady of Succor; * * * that, during the three days which followed, the deponent, uncertain what fate had befallen the remains of Don Alexandro, frequently asked the negro Babo where they were, and if still on board, whether they were to be preserved for interment ashore, entreating him so to order it; that the negro Babo answered nothing till the fourth day, when at sunrise, the deponent coming on deck, the negro Babo showed him a skeleton, which had been substituted for the ship's proper figure-head, the image of Christopher Colon, the discoverer of the New World; that the negro Babo asked him whose skeleton that was, and whether, from its whiteness, he should not think it a white's; that, upon his covering his face, the negro Babo, coming close, said words to this effect: "Keep faith with the blacks from here to Senegal, or you shall in spirit, as now in body, follow your leader," pointing to the prow; * * * that the same morning the negro Babo took by succession each Spaniard forward, and asked him whose skeleton that was, and whether, from its whiteness, he should not think it a white's; that each Spaniard covered his face; that then to each the negro Babo repeated the words in the first place said to the deponent; * * * that they (the Spaniards), being then assembled aft, the negro Babo harangued them, saying that he had now done all; that the deponent (as navigator for the negroes) might pursue his course, warning him and all of them that they should, soul and body, go the way of Don Alexandro if he saw them (the Spaniards) speak or plot anything against them (the negroes)—a threat which was repeated every day; that, before the events last mentioned, they had tied the cook to throw him overboard, for it is not known what thing they heard him speak, but finally the negro Babo spared his life, at the request of the deponent; that a few days after, the deponent, endeavoring not to omit any means to preserve the lives of the remaining whites, spoke to the negroes peace and tranquillity, and agreed to draw up a paper, signed by the deponent and the sailors who could write, as also by the negro Babo, for himself and all the blacks, in which the deponent obliged himself to carry them to Senegal, and they not to kill any more, and he formally to make over to them the ship, with the cargo, with which they were for that time satisfied and quieted. * * * But the next day, the more surely to guard against the sailors' escape, the negro Babo commanded all the boats to be destroyed but the long-boat, which was unseaworthy, and another, a cutter in good condition, which, knowing it would yet be wanted for towing the water casks, he had lowered down into the hold.

*　*　*　*　*

[*Various particulars of the prolonged and perplexed navigation ensuing here follow, with incidents of a calamitous calm, from which portion one passage is extracted, to wit:*]

—That on the fifth day of the calm, all on board suffering much from the heat, and want of water, and five having died in fits, and mad, the negroes became irritable, and for a chance gesture, which they deemed suspicious—though it was harmless—made by the mate, Raneds, to the deponent, in the act of handing a quadrant, they killed him; but that for this they afterwards were sorry, the mate being the only remaining navigator on board, except the deponent.

*　*　*　*　*

—That omitting other events, which daily happened, and which can only serve uselessly to recall past misfortunes and conflicts, after seventy-three days' navigation, reckoned from the time they sailed from Nasca, during which they navigated under a scanty allowance of water, and were afflicted with the calms before mentioned, they at last arrived at the island of Santa Maria, on the seventeenth of the month of August, at about six o'clock in the afternoon, at which hour they cast anchor very near the American ship, Bachelor's Delight, which lay in the same bay, commanded by the generous Captain Amasa Delano; but at six o'clock in the morning, they had already descried the port, and the negroes became uneasy, as soon as at distance they saw the ship, not having expected to see one there; that the negro Babo pacified them, assuring them that no fear need be had; that straightway he ordered the figure on the bow to be covered with canvas, as for repairs, and had the decks a little set in order; that for a time the negro Babo and the negro Atufal conferred; that the negro Atufal was for sailing away, but the negro Babo would not, and, by himself, cast about what to do; that at last he came to the deponent, proposing to him to say and do all that the deponent declares to have said and done to the American captain; * * * * * that the negro Babo warned him that if he varied in the least, or uttered any word, or gave any look that should give the least intimation of the past events or present state, he would instantly kill him, with all his companions, showing a dagger, which he carried hid, saying something which, as he understood it, meant that that dagger would be alert as his eye; that the negro Babo then announced the plan to all his companions, which pleased them; that he then, the better to disguise the truth, devised many expedients, in some of them uniting deceit and defense; that of this sort was the device of the six Ashantees before named, who were his bravoes;[1] that them he stationed on the break of the poop, as if to clean certain hatchets (in cases, which were part of the cargo), but in reality to use them, and distribute them at need, and at a given word he told them that, among other devices, was the device of presenting Atufal, his right-hand man, as chained, though in a moment the chains could be dropped; that in every particular he informed the deponent what part he was expected to enact in every device, and what story he was to tell on every occasion, always threatening him with instant death if he varied in the least; that, conscious that many of the negroes would be turbulent, the negro Babo appointed the four aged negroes, who were calkers, to keep what domestic order they could on the decks; that again and again he harangued the Spaniards and his companions, informing them of his intent, and of his devices, and of the invented story that this deponent was to tell, charging them lest any of them varied from that story; that these arrangements were made and matured during the interval of two or three hours, between their first sighting the ship and the arrival on board of Captain Amasa Delano; that this happened about half-past seven o'clock in the morning, Captain Amasa Delano coming in his boat, and all gladly receiving him; that the deponent, as well as he could force himself, acting then the part of principal owner, and a free captain of the ship, told Captain Amasa Delano, when called upon, that he came from Buenos Ayres, bound to Lima, with three hundred negroes; that off Cape Horn, and in a subsequent fever, many negroes had died; that also, by similar casualties, all the sea officers and the greatest part of the crew had died.

* * * * *

[*And so the deposition goes on, circumstantially recounting the fictitious story dictated to the deponent by Babo, and through the deponent imposed upon Captain Delano; and also recounting the friendly offers of Captain Delano, with other things, but all of which is here omitted. After the fictitious story, etc., the deposition proceeds:*]

—that the generous Captain Amasa Delano remained on board all the day, till he left the ship anchored at six o'clock in the evening, deponent speaking to him always of his pretended misfortunes, under the forementioned principles, without having had it in his power to tell a single word, or give him the least hint, that he might know the truth and state of things; because the negro Babo, performing the office of an officious servant with all the appearance of submission of the humble slave, did not leave

1. Henchmen.

the deponent one moment; that this was in order to observe the deponent's actions and words, for the negro Babo understands well the Spanish; and besides, there were thereabout some others who were constantly on the watch, and likewise understood the Spanish; * * * that upon one occasion, while deponent was standing on the deck conversing with Amasa Delano, by a secret sign the negro Babo drew him (the deponent) aside, the act appearing as if originating with the deponent; that then, he being drawn aside, the negro Babo proposed to him to gain from Amasa Delano full particulars about his ship, and crew, and arms; that the deponent asked "For what?" that the negro Babo answered he might conceive; that, grieved at the prospect of what might overtake the generous Captain Amasa Delano, the deponent at first refused to ask the desired questions, and used every argument to induce the negro Babo to give up this new design; that the negro Babo showed the point of his dagger; that, after the information had been obtained, the negro Babo again drew him aside, telling him that that very night he (the deponent) would be captain of two ships, instead of one, for that, great part of the American's ship's crew being to be absent fishing, the six Ashantees, without any one else, would easily take it; that at this time he said other things to the same purpose; that no entreaties availed; that, before Amasa Delano's coming on board, no hint had been given touching the capture of the American ship; that to prevent this project the deponent was powerless; * * * —that in some things his memory is confused, he cannot distinctly recall every event; * * * —that as soon as they had cast anchor at six of the clock in the evening, as has before been stated, the American Captain took leave to return to his vessel; that upon a sudden impulse, which the deponent believes to have come from God and his angels, he, after the farewell had been said, followed the generous Captain Amasa Delano as far as the gunwale, where he stayed, under pretense of taking leave, until Amasa Delano should have been seated in his boat; that on shoving off, the deponent sprang from the gunwale into the boat, and fell into it, he knows not how, God guarding him; that—

* * * * *

[Here, in the original, follows the account of what further happened at the escape, and how the San Dominick was retaken, and of the passage to the coast; including in the recital many expressions of "eternal gratitude" to the "generous Captain Amasa Delano." The deposition then proceeds with recapitulatory remarks, and a partial renumeration of the negroes, making record of their individual part in the past events, with a view to furnishing, according to command of the court, the data whereon to found the criminal sentences to be pronounced. From this portion is the following:]

—That he believes that all the negroes, though not in the first place knowing to the design of revolt, when it was accomplished, approved it. * * * That the negro, José, eighteen years old, and in the personal service of Don Alexandro, was the one who communicated the information to the negro Babo, about the state of things in the cabin, before the revolt; that this is known, because, in the preceding midnight, he used to come from his berth, which was under his master's, in the cabin, to the deck where the ringleader and his associates were, and had secret conversations with the negro Babo, in which he was several times seen by the mate; that, one night, the mate drove him away twice; * * that this same negro José, was the one who, without being commanded to do so by the negro Babo, as Lecbe and Martinqui were, stabbed his master, Don Alexandro, after he had been dragged half-lifeless to the deck; * * that the mulatto steward, Francisco, was of the first band of revolters, that he was, in all things, the creature and tool of the negro Babo; that, to make his court, he just before a repast in the cabin, proposed, to the negro Babo, poisoning a dish for the generous Captain Amasa Delano; this is known and believed, because the negroes have said it; but that the negro Babo, having another design, forbade Francisco; * * that the Ashantee Lecbe was one of the worst of them; for that, on the day the ship was retaken, he assisted in the defense of her, with a hatchet in each hand, one of which he wounded, in the breast, the chief mate of Amasa Delano, in the first act of boarding; this all knew; that, in sight of the deponent, Lecbe struck, with a hatchet, Don Francisco Masa when, by the negro Babo's orders, he was carrying him to throw him overboard, alive; beside participating in the murder, before mentioned, of Don Alexandro Aranda, and others of the cabin-passengers; that, owing to the fury with which the Ashantees fought in the engagement with the boats, but this Lecbe and Yau survived; that Yau was bad as Lecbe; that Yau was the man who, by Babo's command, willingly prepared the skeleton of Don Alexandro, in a way the negroes afterwards told the deponent, but which he, so long as reason is left him, can never divulge; that Yau and Lecbe were the two who, in a calm by night, riveted the skeleton to the bow; this also the negroes told him; that the negro Babo was he who traced the inscription below it; that the negro Babo was the plotter from first to last; he ordered every murder, and was the helm and keel of the revolt; that Atufal was his lieutenant in all; but Atufal, with his own hand, committed no murder; nor did the negro Babo; * * that Atufal was shot, being killed in the fight with the boats, ere boarding; * * that the negresses, of age, were knowing to the revolt and testified themselves satisfied at the death of their master, Don Alexandro; that, had the negroes not restrained them, they would have tortured to death, instead of simply killing, the Spaniards slain by command of the negro Babo; that the negresses used their utmost influence to have the deponent made away with; that, in the various acts of murder, they sang songs and danced—not gaily, but solemnly; and before the engagement with the boats, as well as during the action, they sang melancholy songs to the negroes, and that this melancholy tone was more inflaming than a different one would have been, and was so intended; that all this is believed, because the negroes have said it.

—that of the thirty-six men of the crew exclusive of the passengers, (all of whom are now dead), which the deponent had knowledge of, six only remained alive, with four cabin-boys and ship-boys, not included with the crew; * * —that the negroes broke an arm of one of the cabin-boys and gave him strokes with hatchets.

[*Then follow various random disclosures referring to various periods of time. The following are extracted:*]

—That during the presence of Captain Amasa Delano on board, some attempts were made by the sailors, and one by Hermenegildo Gandix, to convey hints to him of the true state of affairs; but that these attempts were ineffectual, owing to fear of incurring death, and furthermore owing to the devices which offered contradictions to the true state of affairs; as well as owing to the generosity and piety of Amasa Delano incapable of sounding such wickedness; * * * that Luys Galgo, a sailor about sixty years of age, and formerly of the king's navy, was one of those who sought to convey tokens to Captain Amasa Delano; but his intent, though undiscovered, being suspected, he was, on a pretense, made to retire out of sight, and at last into the hold, and there was made away with. This the negroes have since said; * * * that one of the ship-boys feeling, from Captain Amasa Delano's presence, some hopes of release, and not having enough prudence, dropped some chance-word respecting his expectations, which being overheard and understood by a slave-boy with whom he was eating at the time, the latter struck him on the head with a knife, inflicting a bad wound, but of which the boy is now healing; that likewise, not long before the ship was brought to anchor, one of the seamen, steering at the time, endangered himself by letting the blacks remark some expression in his countenance, arising from a cause similar to the above; but this sailor, by his heedful after conduct, escaped; * * * that these statements are made to show the court that from the beginning to the end of the revolt, it was impossible for the deponent and his men to act otherwise than they did; * * * —that the third clerk, Hermenegildo Gandix, who before had been forced to live among the seamen, wearing a seaman's habit, and in all respects appearing to be one for the time; he, Gandix, was killed by a musket-ball fired through a mistake from the boats before boarding; having in his fright run up the mizzen-rigging, calling to the boats—"don't board," lest upon their boarding the negroes should kill him; that this inducing the Americans to believe he some way favored the cause of the negroes, they fired two balls at him, so that he fell wounded from the rigging, and was drowned in the sea; * * * —that the young Don Joaquin, Marques de Arambaolaza, like Hermenegildo Gandix, the third clerk, was degraded to the office and appearance of a common seaman; that upon one occasion when Don Joaquin shrank, the negro Babo commanded the Ashantee Lecbe to take tar and heat it, and pour it upon Don Joaquin's hands; * * * —that Don Joaquin was killed owing to another mistake of the Americans, but one impossible to be avoided, as upon the approach of the boats, Don Joaquin, with a hatchet tied edge out and upright to his hand, was made by the negroes to appear on the bulwarks; whereupon, seen with arms in his hands and in a questionable attitude, he was shot for a renegade seaman; * * * —that on the person of Don Joaquin was found secreted a jewel, which, by papers that were discovered, proved to have been meant for the shrine of our Lady of Mercy in Lima; a votive offering, beforehand prepared and guarded, to attest his gratitude, when he should have landed in Peru, his last destination, for the safe conclusion of his entire voyage from Spain; * * * —that the jewel, with the other effects of the late Don Joaquin, is in the custody of the brethren of the Hospital de Sacerdotes, awaiting the disposition of the honorable court; * * * —that, owing to the condition of the deponent, as well as the haste in which the boats departed for the attack, the Americans were not forewarned that there were, among the apparent crew, a passenger and one of the clerks disguised by the negro Babo; * * * —that, beside the negroes killed in the action, some were killed after the capture and re-anchoring at night, when shackled to the ring-bolts on deck; that these deaths were committed by the sailors, ere they could be prevented.

That so soon as informed of it, Captain Amasa Delano used all his authority, and, in particular with his own hand, struck down Martinez Gola, who, having found a razor in the pocket of an old jacket of his, which one of the shackled negroes had on, was aiming it at the negro's throat; that the noble Captain Amasa Delano also wrenched from the hand of Bartholomew Barlo, a dagger secreted at the time of the massacre of the whites, with which he was in the act of stabbing a shackled negro, who, the same day, with another negro, had thrown him down and jumped upon him; * * * —that, for all the events, befalling through so long a time, during which the ship was in the hands of the negro Babo, he cannot here give account; but that, what he had said is the most substantial of what occurs to him at present, and is the truth under the oath which he has taken; which declaration he affirmed and ratified, after hearing it read to him.

He said that he is twenty-nine years of age, and broken in body and mind; that when finally dismissed by the court, he shall not return home to Chili, but betake himself to the monastery on Mount Agonia without; and signed with his honor, and crossed himself, and, for the time, departed as he came, in his litter, with the monk Infelez, to the Hospital de Sacerdotes.

BENITO CERENO.
DOCTOR ROZAS.

If the Deposition have served as the key to fit into the lock of the complications which precede it, then, as a vault whose door has been flung back, the San Dominick's hull lies open to-day.

Hitherto the nature of this narrative, besides rendering the intricacies in the beginning unavoidable, has more or less required that many things, instead of being set down in the order of occurrence, should be retrospectively, or irregularly given; this last is the case with the following passages, which will conclude the account:

During the long, mild voyage to Lima, there was, as before hinted, a period during which the sufferer a little recovered his health, or, at least in some degree, his tranquillity. Ere the decided relapse which came, the two captains had many cordial conversations—their fraternal unreserve in singular contrast with former withdrawments.

Again and again, it was repeated, how hard it had been to enact the part forced on the Spaniard by Babo.

"Ah, my dear friend," Don Benito once said, "at those very times when you thought me so morose and ungrateful, nay, when, as you now admit, you half thought me plotting your murder, at those very times my heart was frozen; I could not look at you, thinking of what, both on board this ship and your own, hung, from other hands, over my kind benefactor. And as God lives, Don Amasa, I know not whether desire for my own safety alone could have nerved me to that leap into your boat, had it not been for the thought that, did you, unenlightened, return to your ship, you, my best friend, with all who might be with you, stolen upon, that night, in your hammocks, would never in this world have wakened again. Do but think how you walked this deck, how you sat in this cabin, every inch of ground mined into honeycombs under you. Had I dropped the least hint, made the least advance towards an understanding between us, death, explosive death—yours as mine—would have ended the scene."

"True, true," cried Captain Delano, starting, "you saved my life, Don Benito, more than I yours; saved it, too, against my knowledge and will."

"Nay, my friend," rejoined the Spaniard, courteous even to the point of religion, "God charmed your life, but you saved mine. To think of some things you did—those smilings and chattings, rash pointings and gesturings. For less than these, they slew my mate, Raneds; but you had the Prince of Heaven's safe conduct through all ambuscades."

"Yes, all is owing to Providence, I know; but the temper of my mind that morning was more than commonly pleasant, while the sight of so much suffering, more apparent than real, added to my good nature, compassion, and charity, happily interweaving the three. Had it been otherwise, doubtless, as you hint, some of my interferences might have ended unhappily enough. Besides, those feelings I spoke of enabled me to get the better of momentary distrust, at times when acuteness might have cost me my life, without saving another's. Only at the end did my suspicions get the better of me, and you know how wide of the mark they then proved."

"Wide, indeed," said Don Benito, sadly; "you were with me all day; stood with me, sat with me, talked with me, looked at me, ate with me, drank with me; and yet, your last act was to clutch for a monster, not only an innocent man, but the most pitiable of all men. To such degree may malign machinations and deceptions impose. So far may even the best man err, in judging the conduct of one with the recesses of whose condition he is not acquainted. But you were forced to it; and you were in time undeceived. Would that, in both respects, it was so ever, and with all men."

"You generalize, Don Benito; and mournfully enough. But the past is passed; why moralize upon it? Forget it. See, yon bright sun has forgotten it all, and the blue sea, and the blue sky; these have turned over new leaves."

"Because they have no memory," he dejectedly replied; "because they are not human."

"But these mild trades[2] that now fan your cheek, do they not come with a human-like healing to you? Warm friends, steadfast friends are the trades."

"With their steadfastness they but waft me to my tomb, señor," was the foreboding response.

"You are saved," cried Captain Delano, more and more astonished and pained; "you are saved; what has cast such a shadow upon you?"

"The negro."

There was silence, while the moody man sat, slowly and unconsciously gathering his mantle about him, as if it were a pall.

There was no more conversation that day.

But if the Spaniard's melancholy sometimes ended in muteness upon topics like the above, there were others upon which he never spoke at all; on which, indeed, all his old reserves were piled. Pass over the worst, and, only to elucidate, let an item or two of these be cited. The dress so precise and costly, worn by him on the day whose events have been narrated, had not willingly been put on. And that silver-mounted sword, apparent symbol of despotic command, was not, indeed, a sword, but the ghost of one. The scabbard, artificially stiffened, was empty.

As for the black—whose brain, not body, had schemed and led the revolt, with the plot—his slight frame, inadequate to that which it held, had at once

---

2. Trade winds; here, dependable winds blowing from southeast to northwest.

yielded to the superior muscular strength of his captor, in the boat. Seeing all was over, he uttered no sound, and could not be forced to. His aspect seemed to say, since I cannot do deeds, I will not speak words. Put in irons in the hold, with the rest, he was carried to Lima. During the passage Don Benito did not visit him. Nor then, nor at any time after, would he look at him. Before the tribunal he refused. When pressed by the judges he fainted. On the testimony of the sailors alone rested the legal identity of Babo.

Some months after, dragged to the gibbet at the tail of a mule, the black met his voiceless end. The body was burned to ashes; but for many days, the head, that hive of subtlety, fixed on a pole in the Plaza, met, unabashed, the gaze of the whites; and across the Plaza looked towards St. Bartholomew's church, in whose vaults slept then, as now, the recovered bones of Aranda; and across the Rimac bridge looked towards the monastery, on Mount Agonia without; where, three months after being dismissed by the court, Benito Cereno, borne on the bier, did, indeed, follow his leader.

1855, 1856

FROM BATTLE-PIECES[1]

The Portent

(1859)[2]

Hanging from the beam,
   Slowly swaying (such the law),
Gaunt the shadow on your green,
   Shenandoah!
The cut is on the crown[3]   5
   (Lo, John Brown),
And the stabs shall heal no more.

Hidden in the cap[4]
   Is the anguish none can draw;
So your future veils its face,
   Shenandoah!   10
But the streaming beard is shown
   (Weird John Brown),
The meteor of the war.

1866

1. *Battle-Pieces and Aspects of the War* was published by the Harpers in 1866, the source of the present text.
2. On October 16, 1859, John Brown (1800–1859) led twenty-one men, including five African Americans, in an attack on an unguarded federal arsenal at Harpers Ferry in western Virginia in an effort to secure arms for the slave revolt he hoped to inspire. Within two days his group was defeated by a force of American troops. Convicted of treason against the state of Virginia, he was hanged in the Shenandoah Valley, at Charlestown, Virginia, on December 2, 1859. Melville takes Brown's raid as a portent of the Civil War.
3. Brown received a head wound when captured.
4. Hood placed over the head at the time of execution.

FRANCES ELLEN WATKINS HARPER
1825–1911

Frances Ellen Watkins Harper was the most popular African American poet of the nineteenth century. The author of nine volumes of poetry, four novels, several short stories, and numerous essays and letters, she was also a strikingly effective lecturer, known for her ability to extemporize on such topics as antislavery, temperance, and black uplift. Born in Baltimore, Maryland, then a slave state, to free black parents who died when she was young, Harper was raised by her uncle William J. Watkins, a prominent educator, minister, and abolitionist. She taught school in Ohio and Pennsylvania, writing poetry in her spare time (she may have published a volume, *Forest Leaves*, in 1845, but no copies survive). In the early 1850s she left teaching to lecture for the Maine Anti-Slavery Society and other antislavery organizations. She also worked with the African American abolitionist William Still (1821–1902) to help fugitive slaves escape to Canada through the linked networks of sympathizers, known as the Underground Railroad, who offered refuge to fugitives as they traveled north. During this time she began publishing poems in antislavery periodicals and newspapers, bringing out *Poems on Miscellaneous Subjects* in 1854. Prefaced by the abolitionist William Lloyd Garrison, the collection included several poetic responses to Stowe's *Uncle Tom's Cabin* (a novel Harper greatly admired), along with poems on temperance, biblical stories, and the black experience in slavery. During its first four years in print, *Poems* sold approximately twelve thousand copies; she revised and enlarged it in 1857, and it was reprinted twenty times thereafter during her lifetime.

In her best poems of the antebellum period, such as "Bury Me in a Free Land" (1858), Harper wrote about the slaves' suffering with lyrical intensity; but she also conveyed the sense of blacks' powerful resistance to slavery, along with her hopes for an egalitarian, multiracial America. In her intriguing short story "The Two Offers" (1859), one of the first published short stories by an African American, Harper presents female characters whose conversations and lives illustrate the possibility that women can achieve happiness without marriage. The story also spoke to Harper's concerns (shared by a number of women reformers) about the threat that intemperance posed to women. Perhaps in an effort to convey a feminist vision that was not limited by race, Harper, who published the story in an African American journal, kept the racial identities of the characters unclear.

With the exception of "Learning to Read," the selections printed here draw from Harper's work during the antebellum period, when she was known as Frances Ellen Watkins, but she remained an actively publishing author and lecturer until around 1900. Though primarily motivated by her literary and political passions, Harper also needed to keep up with her writing and lecturing out of financial necessity. In 1860 she married Fenton Harper, a widower with three children, and when he died in 1864, virtually bankrupt, she took on the responsibility of supporting Fenton Harper's children, along with their own child, Mary. Harper worked as a paid lecturer for several reform organizations, even as she continued to publish her poetry, including *Moses: A Story of the Nile* (1869), a long poem in blank verse; *Poems* (1871), which sold approximately 50,000 copies over several printings; and *Sketches of Southern Life* (1872), poems that have at their center the feisty former slave Aunt Chloe. That volume, more than any of her other collections published after the Civil War, was informed by Harper's optimism that blacks could rise in the culture and become fully integrated into national life. Between 1869 and 1882, Harper serialized three novels in the *Christian Recorder*, the journal of the African Methodist Episcopal Church—*Minnie's Sacrifice* (1869), *Sowing and Reaping* (1876–77), and *Trial and Triumph* (1888–89). Her best-known work, in addition to her 1854 and 1871 poetry collections, is the 1892 novel *Iola Leroy; or, Shadows Uplifted*, a historical novel tracing the efforts of the light-skinned mulatta Iola Leroy as she attempts to reunite members of her formerly enslaved family after the Civil War. Crucially, at a key point near the end of the novel, Iola rejects the marriage proposal of a white doctor, who wants her to pass as white, choosing to remain close to her family and devote herself to the uplift of her race. In her fiercely determined feminism and race consciousness, Iola Leroy exemplified her author's commitment to black community. After the publication of *Iola Leroy*, Harper published five additional volumes of poetry; she also remained politically active, continuing her work for the Women's Christian Temperance Union and helping to found the National Association of Colored Women in 1896. She died of heart disease in Philadelphia on February 22, 1911.

Eliza Harris[1]

Like a fawn from the arrow, startled and wild,
A woman swept by us, bearing a child;
In her eye was the night of a settled despair,
And her brow was o'ershaded with anguish and care.

She was nearing the river—in reaching the brink,   5
She heeded no danger, she paused not to think!
For she is a mother—her child is a slave—
And she'll give him his freedom, or find him a grave!

'Twas a vision to haunt us, that innocent face—
So pale in its aspect, so fair in its grace;   10
As the tramp of the horse and the bay of the hound,
With the fetters that gall, were trailing the ground!

She was nerved by despair, and strengthen'd by woe,
As she leap'd o'er the chasms that yawn'd from below;
Death howl'd in the tempest, and rav'd in the blast,   15
But she heard not the sound till the danger was past.

Oh! how shall I speak of my proud country's shame?
Of the stains on her glory, how give them their name?
How say that her banner in mockery waves—
Her "star-spangled banner"—o'er millions of slaves?   20

How say that the lawless may torture and chase
A woman whose crime is the hue of her face?
How the depths of the forest may echo around
With the shrieks of despair, and the bay of the hound?

---

1. The text is from *Poems on Miscellaneous Subjects* (Boston, 1854). Earlier versions appeared in December 1853 issues of *Frederick Douglass' Paper* and the *Liberator*. In chap. 7 of Harriet Beecher Stowe's *Uncle Tom's Cabin* (1852), the slave Eliza Harris escapes to the North with her son by crossing the icy Ohio River (see p. 781).

With her step on the ice, and her arm on her child,   25
The danger was fearful, the pathway was wild;
But, aided by Heaven, she gained a free shore,
Where the friends of humanity open'd their door.

So fragile and lovely, so fearfully pale,
Like a lily that bends to the breath of the gale,   30
Save the heave of her breast, and the sway of her hair,
You'd have thought her a statue of fear and despair.

In agony close to her bosom she press'd
The life of her heart, the child of her breast:—
Oh! love from its tenderness gathering might,   35
Had strengthen'd her soul for the dangers of flight.

But she's free!—yes, free from the land where the slave
From the hand of oppression must rest in the grave;
Where bondage and torture, where scourges and chains
Have plac'd on our banner indelible stains.   40

The bloodhounds have miss'd the scent of her way;
The hunter is rifled and foil'd of his prey;
Fierce jargon and cursing, with clanking of chains,
Make sounds of strange discord on Liberty's plains.

With the rapture of love and fullness of bliss,   45
She plac'd on his brow a mother's fond kiss:—
Oh! poverty, danger and death she can brave,
For the child of her love is no longer a slave!

                                                          1853, 1854

Ethiopia[1]

Yes! Ethiopia yet shall stretch
    Her bleeding hands abroad;
Her cry of agony shall reach
    The burning throne of God.[2]

The tyrant's yoke from off her neck,   5
    His fetters from her soul,
The mighty hand of God shall break,
    And spurn the base control.

Redeemed from dust and freed from chains,
    Her sons shall lift their eyes;   10
From cloud-capt hills and verdant plains
    Shall shouts of triumph rise.

1. The text is from *Poems* (1854). In the 19th century the term *Ethiopia* was often used to designate Africa and Africans or people of African descent.

2. Allusion to Psalms 68.31: "Princes shall come out of Egypt; Ethiopia shall soon stretch out her hands unto God."

Upon her dark, despairing brow,
    Shall play a smile of peace;
For God shall bend unto her wo,   15
    And bid her sorrows cease.

'Neath sheltering vines and stately palms
    Shall laughing children play,
And aged sires with joyous psalms
    Shall gladden every day.   20

Secure by night, and blest by day,
    Shall pass her happy hours;
Nor human tigers hunt for prey
    Within her peaceful bowers.

Then, Ethiopia! stretch, oh! stretch   25
    Thy bleeding hands abroad;
Thy cry of agony shall reach
    And find redress from God.

1854

Bury Me in a Free Land[1]

You may make my grave wherever you will,
    In a lowly vale or a lofty hill;
You may make it among earth's humblest graves,
    But not in a land where men are slaves.

I could not sleep if around my grave   5
    I heard the steps of a trembling slave;
His shadow above my silent tomb
    Would make it a place of fearful gloom.

I could not rest if I heard the tread
    Of a coffle-gang to the shambles[2] led,   10
And the mother's shriek of wild despair
    Rise like a curse on the trembling air.

I could not rest if I heard the lash
    Drinking her blood at each fearful gash,
And I saw her babes torn from her breast   15
    Like trembling doves from their parent nest.

I'd shudder and start, if I heard the bay
    Of the bloodhounds seizing their human prey;
If I heard the captive plead in vain
    As they tightened afresh his galling[3] chain.   20

1. The text is from the November 20, 1858, issue of the *Anti-Slavery Bugle*, published in Salem, Ohio.
2. Slaughterhouse. "Coffle-gang": chained slaves.
3. Chafing.

If I saw young girls, from their mothers' arms
    Bartered and sold for their youthful charms
My eye would flash with a mournful flame,
    My death paled cheek grow red with shame.

I would sleep, dear friends, where bloated might   25
    Can rob no man of his dearest right;
My rest shall be calm in any grave
    Where none calls his brother a slave.

I ask no monument proud and high
    To arrest the gaze of passers by;   30
All that my spirit yearning craves,
    Is—bury me not in the land of slaves.

1858

Learning to Read[1]

Very soon the Yankee teachers
    Came down and set up school;
But, oh! how the Rebs[2] did hate it,—
    It was agin' their rule.

Our masters always tried to hide   5
    Book learning from our eyes;
Knowledge did'nt agree with slavery—
    'Twould make us all too wise.

But some of us would try to steal
    A little from the book,   10
And put the words together,
    And learn by hook or crook.

I remember Uncle Caldwell,
    Who took pot liquor[3] fat
And greased the pages of his book,   15
    And hid it in his hat.

And had his master ever seen
    The leaves upon his head,
He'd have thought them greasy papers,
    But nothing to be read.   20

And there was Mr. Turner's Ben,
    Who heard the children spell,
And picked the words right up by heart,
    And learned to read 'em well.

1. The text is from *Sketches from Southern Life* (1872). This is one of six poems in the volume in the voice of the former slave Aunt Chloe.
2. Rebels; Southerners are here linked to the Rebel or Confederate forces that fought during the Civil War.
3. The liquid left after cooking meat and vegetables together.

Well, the Northern folks kept sending   25
    The Yankee teachers down;
And they stood right up and helped us,
    Though Rebs did sneer and frown.

And, I longed to read my Bible,
    For precious words it said;   30
But when I begun to learn it,
    Folks just shook their heads,

And said there is no use trying,
    Oh! Chloe, you're too late;
But as I was rising sixty,   35
    I had no time to wait.

So I got a pair of glasses,
    And straight to work I went,
And never stopped till I could read
    The hymns and Testament.   40

Then I got a little cabin
    A place to call my own—
And I felt as independent
    As the queen upon her throne.

1872

EMILY DICKINSON
1830–1886

Emily Dickinson is recognized as one of the greatest American poets, a poet who continues to exert an enormous influence on the way writers think about the possibilities of poetic craft and vocation. Little known in her own lifetime, she was first publicized in almost mythic terms as a reclusive, eccentric, death-obsessed spinster who wrote in fits and starts as the spirit moved her—the image of the woman poet at her oddest. As with all myths, this one has some truth to it, but the reality is more interesting and complicated. Though she lived in her parents' homes for all but a year of her life, she was acutely aware of current events and drew on them for some of her poetry. Her dazzlingly complex lyrics—compressed statements abounding in startling imagery and marked by an extraordinary vocabulary— explore a wide range of subjects: psychic pain and joy, the relationship of self to nature, the intensely spiritual, and the intensely ordinary. Her poems about death confront its grim reality with honesty, humor, curiosity, and above all a refusal to be comforted. In her poems about religion, she expressed piety and hostility, and she was fully capable of moving within the same poem from religious consolation to a rejection of doctrinal piety and a querying of God's plans for the universe. Her many love poems seem to have emerged in part from close relationships with at least one woman and several men. It is sometimes possible to extract autobiography from her poems, but she was not a confessional poet; rather, she used personae—first-person speakers—to dramatize the various situations, moods, and perspectives she explored in her lyrics. Though each of her poems is individually short, when collected in one volume her nearly eighteen hundred surviving poems (she probably wrote hundreds more that were lost) have the feel of an epic produced by a person who devoted much of her life to her art.

Emily Elizabeth Dickinson was born on December 10, 1830, in Amherst, Massachusetts, the second child of Emily Norcross Dickinson and Edward Dickinson. Economically, politically, and intellectually, the Dickinsons were among Amherst's most prominent families. Edward Dickinson, a lawyer, served as a state representative and a state senator. He helped found Amherst College as a Calvinist alternative to the more liberal Harvard and Yale, and was its treasurer for thirty-six years. During his term in the U.S. House of Representatives (1853–54), Emily visited him in Washington, D.C., and stayed briefly in Philadelphia on her way home, but travel of any kind was unusual for her. She lived most of her life in the spacious Dickinson family house in Amherst called the Homestead. Among her closest friends and lifelong allies were her brother, Austin, a year and a half older than she, and her younger sister, Lavinia. In 1856, when her brother married Emily's close friend Susan Gilbert, the couple moved into what was called the Evergreens, a house next door to the Homestead, built for the newlyweds by Edward Dickinson. Neither Emily nor Lavinia married. The two women stayed with their parents, as was typical of unmarried middle- and upper-class women of the time. New England in this period had many more women than men in these groups, owing to the male population exodus during the California Gold Rush years (1849 and after) and the carnage of the Civil War. For Dickinson, home was a place of "Infinite power."

Dickinson attended Amherst Academy from 1840 through 1846, and then boarded at Mount Holyoke Female Seminary—located in South Hadley, some ten miles from Amherst—for less than a year, never completing the three-year course of study. The school, presided over by the devoutly Calvinist Mary Lyon, was especially interested in the students' religious development, and hoped that those needing to support themselves or their families would become missionaries. Students were regularly queried as to whether they "professed faith," had "hope," or were resigned to "no hope"; Dickinson remained adamantly among the small group of "no hopes." Arguably, her assertion of no hope was a matter of defiance, a refusal to capitulate to the demands of orthodoxy. A year after leaving Mount Holyoke, Dickinson, in a letter to a friend, described her failure to convert with darkly comic glee: "I am one of the lingering *bad* ones," she said. But she went on to assert that it was her very "failure" to conform to the conventional expectations of her evangelical culture that helped liberate her to think on her own—to "pause," as she put it, "and ponder, and ponder."

Once back at home, Dickinson embarked on a lifelong course of reading. Her deepest literary debts were to the Bible and classic English authors, such as Shakespeare and Milton. Through the national magazines the family subscribed to and books ordered from Boston, she encountered the full range of the English and American literature of her time, including among Americans Longfellow, Holmes, Lowell, Hawthorne, and Emerson. She read the novels of Charles Dickens as they appeared and knew the poems of Robert Browning and the poet laureate Tennyson. But the English contemporaries who mattered most to her were the Brontë sisters, George Eliot, and above all, as an example of a successful contemporary woman poet, Elizabeth Barrett Browning. Poem 627, suggests that Browning may have helped awaken Dickinson to her vocation when she was still "a somber Girl."

No one has persuasively traced the precise stages of Dickinson's artistic growth from this supposedly "somber Girl" to the young woman who, within a few years of her return from Mount Holyoke, began writing a new kind of poetry, with its distinctive voice, style, and transformation of traditional form. She found a paradoxical poetic freedom within the confines of the meter of the "fourteener"—seven-beat lines usually broken into stanzas alternating four and three beats—familiar to her from earliest childhood. This is the form of nursery rhymes, ballads, church hymns, and some classic English poetry—strongly rhythmical, easy to memorize and recite. But Dickinson veered sharply from this form's expectations. If Walt Whitman at this time was heeding Emerson's call for a "metre-making argument" by turning to an open form—as though rules did not exist—Dickinson made use of this and other familiar forms only to break their rules. She used dashes and syntactical fragments to convey her pursuit of a truth that could best be communicated indirectly; these fragments dispensed with prosy verbiage and went directly to the core. Her use of enjambment (the syntactical technique of running past the conventional stopping place of a line or a stanza break) forced her reader to learn where to pause to collect the sense before reading on, often creating dizzying ambiguities. She multiplied aural possibilities by making use of what later critics termed "off" or "slant" rhymes that, as with her metrical and syntactical experimentations, contributed to the expressive power of her poetry. In short, poetic forms thought to be simple, predictable, and safe were altered irrevocably by Dickinson's language experiments with the lyric. Along with its opposite, free verse, the compressed lyric flaunting its refusal to conform became a hallmark of modernist poetry in the twentieth century.

Writing about religion, science, music, nature, books, and contemporary events both national and local, Dickinson often presented her poetic ideas as terse, striking definitions or propositions, or dramatic narrative scenes, in a highly abstracted moment, or setting, often at the boundaries between life and death. The result was a poetry that, as is typical of the lyric tradition, focused on the speaker's response to a situation rather than the details of the situation itself. Her "nature" poems offer precise observations that are often as much about psychological and spiritual matters as about the specifics of nature. The sight of a familiar bird—the robin—in the poem beginning "A bird came down the walk" leads to a statement about nature's strangeness rather than the expected statement about friendly animals. Whitman generally seems intoxicated by his ability to appropriate nature for his own purposes; Dickinson's nature is much more resistant to human schemes, and the poet's experiences of nature range from a sense of its hostility to an ability to become an "Inebriate of Air" and "Debauchee of Dew." Openly expressive of sexual and romantic longings, her personae reject conventional gender roles. In one of her most famous poems, for instance, she imagines herself as a "Loaded Gun" with "the power to kill."

Dickinson's private letters, in particular three drafts of letters to an unidentified "Master," and dozens of love poems have convinced biographers that she fell in love a number of times; candidates include Benjamin Newton, a law clerk in her father's office; one or more married men; and, Susan Gilbert Dickinson, the friend who became her sister-in-law. The exact nature of any of these relationships is hard to determine, in part because Dickinson's letters and poems could just as easily be taken as poetic meditations on desire as writings directed to specific people. On the evidence of the approximately five hundred letters that Dickinson wrote Susan, many of which contained drafts or copies of her latest poems, that relationship melded love, friendship, intellectual exchange, and art. (See their letters on a Dickinson poem on p. 1215.) One of the men she was involved with was Samuel Bowles, editor of the Springfield *Republican*, whom Dickinson described (in a letter to Bowles himself) as having "the most triumphant face out of paradise"; another was the Reverend Charles Wadsworth, whom she met in Philadelphia in 1855 and who visited her in Amherst in 1860. Evidence suggests that she was upset by his decision to move to San Francisco in 1862, but none of her letters to Wadsworth survive.

Knowing her powers as a poet, Dickinson wanted to be published, but only around a dozen poems appeared during her lifetime. She sent many poems to Bowles, perhaps hoping he would publish them in the *Republican*. Although he did publish a few, he also edited them into more conventional shape. She also sent poems to editor Josiah Holland at *Scribner's*, who chose not to publish her. She sent four poems to Thomas Wentworth Higginson, a contributing editor at the *Atlantic Monthly*, after he printed "Letter to a Young Contributor" in the April 1862 issue. Her cover letter of April 15, 1862, asked him, "Are you too deeply occupied to say if my Verse is alive?" (See two Dickinson letters to Higginson on pp. 1218–19.) Higginson, like other editors, saw her formal innovations as imperfections. But he remained intrigued by Dickinson and in 1869 invited her to visit him in Boston. When she refused, he visited her in 1870. He would eventually become one of the editors of her posthumously published poetry.

But if Dickinson sought publication, she also regarded it as "the Auction / Of the Mind of Man," as she put it in poem 788; at the very least, she was unwilling to submit to the changes, which she called "surgery," imposed on her poems by editors. Some critics have argued that Dickinson's letters constituted a form of publication, for Dickinson included poems in many of her letters. Even more intriguing, beginning around 1858 Dickinson began to record her poems on white, unlined paper, in some cases marking moments of textual revision, and then folded and stacked the sheets and sewed groups of them together in what are called fascicles. She created thirty such fascicles, ranging in length from sixteen to twenty-four pages; and there is considerable evidence that she worked diligently at the groupings, thinking about chronology, subject matter, and specific thematic orderings within each. These fascicles were left for others to discover after her death, neatly stacked in a drawer. It can be speculated that Dickinson, realizing that her unconventional poetry would not be published in her own lifetime as written, became a sort of self-publisher. Critics remain uncertain, however, about just how self-conscious her arrangements were and argue over what is lost and gained by considering individual poems in the context of their fascicle placement. There is also debate about whether the posthumous publication of Dickinson's manuscript poetry violates the visual look of the poems—their inconsistent dashes and even some of the designs that Dickinson added to particular poems. The selections printed here include a photographic reproduction of poem 269, which can be compared to the now-standard printed version, also included here.

Dickinson's final decades were marked by health problems and a succession of losses. Beginning in the early 1860s she suffered from eye pain. She consulted with an ophthalmologist in Boston in 1864 and remained concerned about losing her vision. In 1874 her father died in a Boston hotel room after taking an injection of morphine for his pain, and one year later her mother had a stroke and would remain bedridden until her death in 1882. Her beloved eight-year-old nephew, Gilbert, died of typhoid fever in 1883, next door at the Evergreens; and in 1885, her close friend from childhood, Helen Hunt Jackson, who had asked to be Dickinson's literary executor, died suddenly in San Francisco. Dickinson's seclusion late in life may have been a response to her grief at these losses or a concern for her own health, but ultimately a focus on the supposed eccentricity of her desire for privacy draws attention away from the huge number of poems she wrote—she may well have secluded herself so that she could follow her vocation. Emily Dickinson died on May 15, 1886, perhaps from a kidney disorder called "Bright's Disease," the official diagnosis, but just as likely from hypertension.

In 1881 the astronomer David Todd, with his young wife, Mabel Loomis Todd, arrived in Amherst to direct the Amherst College Observatory. The next year, Austin Dickinson and Mabel Todd began an affair that lasted until Austin's death in 1895. Despite this turn of events, Mabel Todd and Emily Dickinson established a friendship without actually meeting (Todd saw Dickinson once, in her coffin), and Todd decided that the poet was "in many respects a genius." Soon after Dickinson's death, Mabel Todd (at Emily's sister Lavinia's invitation) painstakingly transcribed many of her poems. The subsequent preservation and publication of her poetry and letters were initiated and carried forth by Todd. She persuaded Higginson to help her see a posthumous collection of poems into print in 1890 and a second volume of poems in 1891; she went on to publish a collection of Dickinson's letters in 1894 and a third volume of poems in 1896. In the 1890s some critics reacted patronizingly toward what they saw as verse that violated the laws of meter, and even Todd and Higginson edited some of the poems to make them more conventional. The three volumes were popular, going through more than ten printings and selling over ten thousand copies.

During the 1890s, Susan Dickinson and her daughter, Martha Dickinson Bianchi, also published a few of Dickinson's poems in journals such as *The Century*. By 1900 or so, however, Dickinson's work had fallen out of favor, and had Martha Dickinson Bianchi not resumed publication of her aunt's poetry in 1914 (she published eight volumes of Dickinson's work between 1914 and 1937), Dickinson's writings might never have achieved the audience they have today. Taken together, the editorial labors of Todd, Higginson, Susan Dickinson, and Bianchi set in motion the critical and textual work that would help establish Dickinson as one of the great American poets. They also made her poetry available to the American modernists, poets such as Hart Crane and Marianne Moore; Dickinson and Whitman are the nineteenth-century poets who exerted the greatest influence on American poetry to come.

The texts of the poems, and the numbering, are from R.W. Franklin's one-volume edition, *The Poems of Emily Dickinson: Reading Edition* (1999), which draws on his three-volume variorum, *The Poems of Emily Dickinson* (1998). Bracketed numbers refer to the numbering of Thomas Johnson's *The Poems of Emily Dickinson* (1955), for many years the standard edition. The dating of Dickinson's poetry remains uncertain, though Franklin is more accurate than Johnson. The date following each poem corresponds to Franklin's estimate of Dickinson's first finished draft; if the poem was published in Dickinson's lifetime, that date is supplied as well.

39

[49]

I never lost as much but twice -
And that was in the sod.
Twice have I stood a beggar
Before the door of God!

Angels - twice descending   5
Reimbursed my store -
Burglar! Banker - Father!
I am poor once more!

1858

112[1]

[67]

Success is counted sweetest
By those who ne'er succeed.
To comprehend a nectar
Requires sorest need.

Not one of all the purple Host   5
Who took the Flag[2] today
Can tell the definition
So clear of Victory

---

1. Dickinson published a version of this poem in the *Brooklyn Daily Union*, April 27, 1864, and it was republished in *A Masque of Poets* (1878), edited by her friend Helen Hunt Jackson. When it was printed in *Masque*, most reviewers thought it was by Emerson.
2. Triumphed.

As he defeated - dying -
On whose forbidden ear   10
The distant strains of triumph
Burst agonized and clear!

                                          1859, 1864

122[1]

[130]

These are the days when Birds come back -
A very few - a Bird or two -
To take a backward look.

These are the days when skies resume
The old - old sophistries[2] of June -   5
A blue and gold mistake.

Oh fraud that cannot cheat the Bee.
Almost thy plausibility
Induces my belief,

Till ranks of seeds their witness bear -   10
And softly thro' the altered air
Hurries a timid leaf.

Oh sacrament of summer days,
Oh Last Communion[3] in the Haze -
Permit a child to join -   15

Thy sacred emblems to partake -
Thy consecrated bread to take
And thine immortal wine!

                                          1859, 1864

124[1]

[216]

Safe in their Alabaster[2] Chambers -
Untouched by Morning -
And untouched by noon -
Sleep the meek members of the Resurrection,
Rafter of Satin and Roof of Stone -   5

1. Dickinson published a version of this poem in
the *Drum Beat*, March 11, 1864.
2. Deceptively subtle reasonings.
3. The end of summer is compared to the death
of Christ commemorated by the Christian sacra-

ment of Communion.
1. Dickinson published a version of this poem in
the *Springfield Daily Republican*, March 1, 1862.
2. Translucent, white chalky material.

Grand go the Years,
In the Crescent above them -
Worlds scoop their Arcs -
And Firmaments - row -
Diadems - drop -   10
And Doges[3] - surrender -
Soundless as Dots,
On a Disc of Snow.[4]

1859, 1862

202

[185]

"Faith" is a fine invention
For Gentlemen who *see*!
But Microscopes are prudent
In an Emergency!

1861

207

[214]

I taste a liquor never brewed -
From Tankards scooped in Pearl -
Not all the Frankfort Berries
Yield such an Alcohol!

Inebriate of air - am I -   5
And Debauchee of Dew -
Reeling - thro' endless summer days -
From inns of molten Blue -

When "Landlords" turn the drunken Bee
Out of the Foxglove's door -   10
When Butterflies - renounce their "drams" -
I shall but drink the more!

Till Seraphs[1] swing their snowy Hats -
And Saints - to windows run -
To see the little Tippler   15
Leaning against the - Sun!

1861

---

3. Chief magistrates in the republics of Venice
and Genoa from the 11th through the 16th
centuries.

4. For Dickinson's other versions of this poem,
see pp. 1215–17.
1. Angels.

236

[324]

Some keep the Sabbath going to Church -
I keep it, staying at Home -
With a Bobolink for a Chorister -
And an Orchard, for a Dome -

Some keep the Sabbath in Surplice[1]   5
I, just wear my Wings -
And instead of tolling the Bell, for Church,
Our little Sexton[2] - sings.

God preaches, a noted Clergyman -
And the sermon is never long,   10
So instead of getting to Heaven, at last -
I'm going, all along.

1861

259

[287]

A Clock stopped -
Not the Mantel's -
Geneva's[1] farthest skill
Cant put the puppet bowing -
That just now dangled still -   5

An awe came on the Trinket!
The Figures hunched - with pain -
Then quivered out of Decimals -
Into Degreeless noon -

It will not stir for Doctor's -   10
This Pendulum of snow -
The Shopman importunes it -
While cool - concernless No -

Nods from the Gilded pointers -
Nods from the Seconds slim -   15
Decades of Arrogance between
The Dial life -
And Him -

1861

---

1. Open-sleeved ceremonial robe worn by
clergymen.

2. Church custodian.
1. A city in Switzerland famous for its clocks.

260

[288]

I'm Nobody! Who are you?
Are you - Nobody - too?
Then there's a pair of us!
Dont tell! they'd advertise - you know!

How dreary - to be - Somebody!   5
How public - like a Frog -
To tell one's name - the livelong June -
To an admiring Bog!

1861

269

[249]

Wild nights - Wild nights!
Were I with thee
Wild nights should be
Our luxury!

Futile - the winds -   5
To a Heart in port -
Done with the Compass -
Done with the Chart!

Rowing in Eden -
Ah - the Sea!   10
Might I but moor - tonight -
In thee!

1861

320

[258]

There's a certain Slant of light,
Winter Afternoons -
That oppresses, like the Heft
Of Cathedral Tunes -

Heavenly Hurt, it gives us -   5
We can find no scar,
But internal difference -
Where the Meanings, are -

Poem 269 [249] of Fascicle 11, from vol. 1 of *The Manuscript Books of Emily Dickinson* (1981), ed. R. W. Franklin, reproduced with the permission of Harvard University Press. Dickinson's handwriting, which changed over the years, can be dated by comparison with her letters.

None may teach it - Any -
'Tis the Seal Despair -   10
An imperial affliction
Sent us of the Air -

When it comes, the Landscape listens -
Shadows - hold their breath -
When it goes, 'tis like the Distance   15
On the look of Death -

1862

339

[241]

I like a look of Agony,
Because I know it's true -
Men do not sham Convulsion,
Nor simulate, a Throe -

The eyes glaze once - and that is Death -   5
Impossible to feign
The Beads opon the Forehead
By homely Anguish strung.

1862

340

[280]

I felt a Funeral, in my Brain,
And Mourners to and fro
Kept treading - treading - till it seemed
That Sense was breaking through -

And when they all were seated,   5
A Service, like a Drum -
Kept beating - beating - till I thought
My mind was going numb -

And then I heard them lift a Box
And creak across my Soul   10
With those same Boots of Lead, again,
Then Space - began to toll,

As all the Heavens were a Bell,
And Being, but an Ear,
And I, and Silence, some strange Race   15
Wrecked, solitary, here -

And then a Plank in Reason, broke,
And I dropped down, and down -
And hit a World, at every plunge,
And Finished knowing - then -   20

                                                 1862

347

[348]

I dreaded that first Robin, so,
But He is mastered, now,
I'm some accustomed to Him grown,
He hurts a little, though -

I thought if I could only live   5
Till that first Shout got by -
Not all Pianos in the Woods
Had power to mangle me -

I dared not meet the Daffodils -
For fear their Yellow Gown   10
Would pierce me with a fashion
So foreign to my own -

I wished the Grass would hurry -
So when 'twas time to see -
He'd be too tall, the tallest one   15
Could stretch to look at me -

I could not bear the Bees should come,
I wished they'd stay away
In those dim countries where they go,
What word had they, for me?   20

They're here, though; not a creature failed -
No Blossom stayed away
In gentle deference to me -
The Queen of Calvary[1] -

Each one salutes me, as he goes,   25
And I, my childish Plumes,
Lift, in bereaved acknowledgement
Of their unthinking Drums -

                                                 1862

---

1. Hill on which Jesus was crucified (Luke 23.33).

348

[505]

I would not paint - a picture -
I'd rather be the One
It's bright impossibility
To dwell - delicious - on -
And wonder how the fingers feel   5
Whose rare - celestial - stir -
Evokes so sweet a torment -
Such sumptuous - Despair -

I would not talk, like Cornets -
I'd rather be the One   10
Raised softly to the Ceilings -
And out, and easy on -
Through Villages of Ether -
Myself endued Balloon
By but a lip of Metal -   15
The pier to my Pontoon[1] -

Nor would I be a Poet -
It's finer - Own the Ear -
Enamored - impotent - content -
The License to revere,   20
A privilege so awful
What would the Dower be,
Had I the Art to stun myself
With Bolts - of Melody!

                                                1862

353

[508]

I'm ceded - I've stopped being Their's -
The name They dropped opon my face
With water, in the country church
Is finished using, now,
And They can put it with my Dolls,   5
My childhood, and the string of spools,
I've finished threading - too -

Baptized, before, without the choice,
But this time, consciously, Of Grace -
Unto supremest name -   10
Called to my Full - The Crescent dropped -
Existence's whole Arc, filled up,
With one - small Diadem -

---

1. Floating structure or boat.

My second Rank - too small the first -
Crowned - Crowing - on my Father's breast -   15
A half unconscious Queen -
But this time - Adequate - Erect,
With Will to choose,
Or to reject,
And I choose, just a Crown -   20

      1862

355

[510]

It was not Death, for I stood up,
And all the Dead, lie down -
It was not Night, for all the Bells
Put out their Tongues, for Noon.

It was not Frost, for on my Flesh   5
I felt Siroccos[1] - crawl -
Nor Fire - for just my marble feet
Could keep a Chancel,[2] cool -

And yet, it tasted, like them all,
The Figures I have seen   10
Set orderly, for Burial,
Reminded me, of mine -

As if my life were shaven,
And fitted to a frame,
And could not breathe without a key,   15
And 'twas like Midnight, some -

When everything that ticked - has stopped -
And space stares - all around -
Or Grisly frosts - first Autumn morns,
Repeal the Beating Ground -   20

But, most, like Chaos - Stopless - cool -
Without a Chance, or spar -
Or even a Report of Land -
To justify - Despair.

      1862

1. Hot winds from North Africa.
2. The part of the church that contains the choir and sanctuary.

359

[328]

A Bird, came down the Walk -
He did not know I saw -
He bit an Angle Worm in halves
And ate the fellow, raw,

And then, he drank a Dew   5
From a convenient Grass -
And then hopped sidewise to the Wall
To let a Beetle pass -

He glanced with rapid eyes,
That hurried all abroad -   10
They looked like frightened Beads, I thought,
He stirred his Velvet Head. -

Like one in danger, Cautious,
I offered him a Crumb,
And he unrolled his feathers,   15
And rowed him softer Home -

Than Oars divide the Ocean,
Too silver for a seam,
Or Butterflies, off Banks of Noon,
Leap, plashless[1] as they swim.   20

1862

365

[338]

I know that He exists.
Somewhere - in silence -
He has hid his rare life
From our gross eyes.

'Tis an instant's play-   5
'Tis a fond Ambush -
Just to make Bliss
Earn her own surprise!

But - should the play
Prove piercing earnest -   10
Should the glee - glaze -
In Death's - stiff - stare -

1. Splashless.

Would not the fun
Look too expensive!
Would not the jest -   15
Have crawled too far!

1862

372

[*341*]

After great pain, a formal feeling comes -
The Nerves sit ceremonious, like Tombs -
The stiff Heart questions 'was it He, that bore,'
And 'Yesterday, or Centuries before'?

The Feet, mechanical, go round -   5
A Wooden way
Of Ground, or Air, or Ought -
Regardless grown,
A Quartz contentment, like a stone -

This is the Hour of Lead -   10
Remembered, if outlived,
As Freezing persons, recollect the Snow -
First - Chill - then Stupor - then the letting go -

1862

373

[*501*]

This World is not conclusion.
A Species stands beyond -
Invisible, as Music -
But positive, as Sound -
It beckons, and it baffles -   5
Philosophy, dont know -
And through a Riddle, at the last -
Sagacity, must go -
To guess it, puzzles scholars -
To gain it, Men have borne   10
Contempt of Generations
And Crucifixion, shown -
Faith slips - and laughs, and rallies -
Blushes, if any see -
Plucks at a twig of Evidence -   15
And asks a Vane, the way -
Much Gesture, from the Pulpit -
Strong Hallelujahs roll -

Narcotics cannot still the Tooth
That nibbles at the soul -   20

1862

409

[303]

The Soul selects her own Society -
Then - shuts the Door -
To her divine Majority -
Present no more -

Unmoved - she notes the Chariots - pausing -   5
At her low Gate -
Unmoved - an Emperor be kneeling
Opon her Mat -

I've known her - from an ample nation -
Choose One -   10
Then - close the Valves of her attention -
Like Stone -

1862

411

[528]

Mine - by the Right of the White Election!
Mine - by the Royal Seal!
Mine - by the sign in the Scarlet prison -
Bars - cannot conceal!

Mine - here - in Vision - and in Veto!   5
Mine - by the Grave's Repeal -
Titled - Confirmed -
Delirious Charter!
Mine - long as Ages steal!

1862

446

[448]

This was a Poet -
It is That
Distills amazing sense

From Ordinary Meanings -
And Attar[1] so immense   5

From the familiar species
That perished by the Door -
We wonder it was not Ourselves
Arrested it - before -

Of Pictures, the Discloser -   10
The Poet - it is He -
Entitles Us - by Contrast -
To ceaseless Poverty -

Of Portion - so unconscious -
The Robbing - could not harm -   15
Himself - to Him - a Fortune -
Exterior - to Time -

                                                              1862

448

[449]

I died for Beauty - but was scarce
Adjusted in the Tomb
When One who died for Truth, was lain
In an adjoining Room -

He questioned softly "Why I failed"?   5
"For Beauty", I replied -
"And I - for Truth - Themself are One -
We Bretheren, are", He said -

And so, as Kinsmen, met a Night -
We talked between the Rooms -   10
Until the Moss had reached our lips -
And covered up - Our names -

                                                              1862

479

[712]

Because I could not stop for Death -
He kindly stopped for me -
The Carriage held but just Ourselves -
And Immortality.

1. Fragrance.

We slowly drove - He knew no haste 5
And I had put away
My labor and my leisure too,
For His Civility -

We passed the School, where Children strove
At Recess - in the Ring - 10
We passed the Fields of Gazing Grain -
We passed the Setting Sun -

Or rather - He passed Us -
The Dews drew quivering and Chill -
For only Gossamer,[1] my Gown - 15
My Tippet - only Tulle[2] -

We paused before a House that seemed
A Swelling of the Ground -
The Roof was scarcely visible -
The Cornice[3] - in the Ground - 20

Since then - 'tis Centuries - and yet
Feels shorter than the Day
I first surmised the Horses' Heads
Were toward Eternity -

1862

519

[441]

This is my letter to the World
That never wrote to Me -
The simple News that Nature told -
With tender Majesty

Her Message is committed 5
To Hands I cannot see -
For love of Her - Sweet - countrymen -
Judge tenderly - of Me

1863

591

[465]

I heard a Fly buzz - when I died -
The Stillness in the Room

1. Delicate, light fabric.
2. Thin silk. "Tippet": scarf for covering neck and shoulders.
3. Decorative molding beneath a roof.

Was like the Stillness in the Air -
Between the Heaves of Storm -

The Eyes around - had wrung them dry -   5
And Breaths were gathering firm
For that last Onset - when the King
Be witnessed - in the Room -

I willed my Keepsakes - Signed away
What portion of me be   10
Assignable - and then it was
There interposed a Fly -

With Blue - uncertain - stumbling Buzz -
Between the light - and me -
And then the Windows failed - and then   15
I could not see to see -

                                                    1863

598

[632]

The Brain - is wider than the Sky -
For - put them side by side -
The one the other will contain
With ease - and You - beside -

The Brain is deeper than the sea -   5
For - hold them - Blue to Blue -
The one the other will absorb -
As Sponges - Buckets - do -

The Brain is just the weight of God -
For - Heft them - Pound for Pound -   10
And they will differ - if they do -
As Syllable from Sound -

                                                    1863

620

[435]

Much Madness is divinest Sense -
To a discerning Eye -
Much Sense - the starkest Madness -
'Tis the Majority
In this, as all, prevail -   5
Assent - and you are sane -

Demur - you're straightway dangerous -
And handled with a Chain -

1863

656

[520]

I started Early - Took my Dog -
And visited the Sea -
The Mermaids in the Basement
Came out to look at me -

And Frigates - in the Upper Floor   5
Extended Hempen Hands -
Presuming Me to be a Mouse -
Aground - opon the Sands -

But no Man moved Me - till the Tide
Went past my simple Shoe -   10
And past my Apron - and my Belt
And past my Boddice - too -

And made as He would eat me up -
As wholly as a Dew
Opon a Dandelion's Sleeve -   15
And then - I started - too -

And He - He followed - close behind -
I felt His Silver Heel
Opon my Ancle - Then My Shoes
Would overflow with Pearl -   20

Until We met the Solid Town -
No One He seemed to know -
And bowing - with a Mighty look -
At me - The Sea withdrew -

1863

706

[640]

I cannot live with You -
It would be Life -
And Life is over there -
Behind the Shelf

The Sexton keeps the key to -   5
Putting up

Our Life - His Porcelain -
Like a Cup -

Discarded of the Housewife -
Quaint - or Broke -   10
A newer Sevres[1] pleases -
Old Ones crack -

I could not die - with You -
For One must wait
To shut the Other's Gaze down -   15
You - could not -

And I - Could I stand by
And see You - freeze -
Without my Right of Frost -
Death's privilege?   20

Nor could I rise - with You -
Because Your Face
Would put out Jesus' -
That New Grace

Glow plain - and foreign   25
On my homesick eye -
Except that You than He
Shone closer by -

They'd judge Us - How -
For You - served Heaven - You know,   30
Or sought to -
I could not -

Because You saturated sight -
And I had no more eyes
For sordid excellence   35
As Paradise

And were You lost, I would be -
Though my name
Rang loudest
On the Heavenly fame -   40

And were You - saved -
And I - condemned to be
Where You were not
That self - were Hell to me -

So we must meet apart -   45
You there - I - here -
With just the Door ajar

---

1. Porcelain china (French), usually elaborately decorated.

That Oceans are - and Prayer -
And that White Sustenance -
Despair -   50

1863

760

[650]

Pain - has an Element of Blank -
It cannot recollect
When it begun - Or if there were
A time when it was not -

It has no Future - but itself -   5
It's Infinite contain
It's Past - enlightened to perceive
New Periods - Of Pain.

1863

764

[754]

My Life had stood - a Loaded Gun -
In Corners - till a Day
The Owner passed - identified -
And carried Me away -

And now We roam in Sovreign Woods -   5
And now We hunt the Doe -
And every time I speak for Him
The Mountains straight reply -

And do I smile, such cordial light
Opon the Valley glow -   10
It is as a Vesuvian[1] face
Had let it's pleasure through -

And when at Night - Our good Day done -
I guard My Master's Head -
'Tis better than the Eider Duck's   15
Deep Pillow - to have shared -

To foe of His - I'm deadly foe -
None stir the second time -
On whom I lay a Yellow Eye -
Or an emphatic Thumb -   20

---

1. Reference to Mount Vesuvius, the volcano in southern Italy that destroyed Pompeii (79 C.E.).

Though I than He - may longer live
He longer must - than I -
For I have but the power to kill,
Without - the power to die -

1863

788

[709]

Publication - is the Auction
Of the Mind of Man -
Poverty - be justifying
For so foul a thing

Possibly - but We - would rather   5
From Our Garret go
White - unto the White Creator -
Than invest - Our Snow -

Thought belong to Him who gave it -
Then - to Him Who bear   10
It's Corporeal illustration - sell
The Royal Air -

In the Parcel - Be the Merchant
Of the Heavenly Grace -
But reduce no Human Spirit
To Disgrace of Price -

1863

1096[1]

[986]

A narrow Fellow in the Grass
Occasionally rides -
You may have met him? Did you not
His notice instant is -

The Grass divides as with a Comb -   5
A spotted Shaft is seen,
And then it closes at your Feet
And opens further on -

He likes a Boggy Acre -
A Floor too cool for Corn -   10

1. Dickinson published a version of this poem in the *Springfield Daily Republican*, February 14, 1866.

But when a Boy and Barefoot
I more than once at Noon

Have passed I thought a Whip Lash
Unbraiding in the Sun
When stooping to secure it   15
It wrinkled And was gone -

Several of Nature's People
I know and they know me
I feel for them a transport
Of Cordiality   20

But never met this Fellow
Attended or alone
Without a tighter Breathing
And Zero at the Bone.

                                      1865, 1866

1108

[1078]

The Bustle in a House
The Morning after Death
Is solemnest of industries
Enacted opon Earth -

The Sweeping up the Heart   5
And putting Love away
We shall not want to use again
Until Eternity -

                                               1865

1263

[1129]

Tell all the truth but tell it slant -
Success in Circuit lies
Too bright for our infirm Delight
The Truth's superb surprise
As Lightning to the Children eased   5
With explanation kind
The Truth must dazzle gradually
Or every man be blind -

                                               1872

1577

[1545]

The Bible is an antique Volume -
Written by faded Men
At the suggestion of Holy Spectres -
Subjects - Bethlehem -
Eden - the ancient Homestead -   5
Satan - the Brigadier -
Judas - the Great Defaulter -
David - the Troubadour -
Sin - a distinguished Precipice
Others must resist -   10
Boys that "believe" are very lonesome -
Other Boys are "lost" -
Had but the Tale a warbling Teller -
All the Boys would come -
Orpheu's Sermon[1] captivated -   15
It did not condemn -

                                                    1882

1668

[1624]

Apparently with no surprise
To any happy Flower
The Frost beheads it at it's play -
In accidental power -
The blonde Assassin passes on -   5
The Sun proceeds unmoved
To measure off another Day
For an Approving God -

                                                    1884

1773[1]

[1732]

My life closed twice before it's close;
It yet remains to see
If Immortality unveil
A third event to me,

So huge, so hopeless to conceive   5
As these that twice befell.

---

1. In Greek mythology, Orpheus played music
that would transfix wild beasts and still rivers.
1. Transcribed by Mabel Loomis Todd; there is

no surviving manuscript. As with poem 1715, it is
hard to determine a probable date of composition.

Parting is all we know of heaven,
And all we need of hell.

Letter Exchange with Susan Gilbert Dickinson
on Poem 124 [216][1]

The Sleeping[2]

Safe in their alabaster chambers,
Untouched by morning,
   And untouched by noon,
Sleep the meek members of the Resurrection,
   Rafter of satin, and roof of stone.   5

Light laughs the breeze
In her castle above them,
   Babbles the bee in a stolid ear,
Pipe the sweet birds in ignorant cadences:
   Ah! What sagacity perished here!   10
              Pelham Hill, June, 1861.

Emily Dickinson to Susan Gilbert Dickinson

Safe in their Alabaster Chambers,
Untouched by Morning -
And untouched by Noon -
Lie the meek members of
the Resurrection -
Rafter of Satin - and Roof of
Stone -
Grand go the Years - in the
Crescent - above them -
Worlds scoop their Arcs -
And Firmaments - row -
Diadems - drop - and Doges -
Surrender -
Soundless as dots - on a
Disc of Snow -

Perhaps this verse would
please you better - Sue -
              Emily'

1. Dickinson exchanged hundreds of letters with her friend and sister-in-law Susan Huntington Gilbert Dickinson (1850–1913). who married Emily's brother, Austin in 1856. The letters and poems printed here are from *Open Me Carefully: Emily Dickinson's Intimate Letters of Susan Huntington Dickinson* (1998), ed. Ellen Louise Hart and Martha Nell Smith, reprinted with the permission of Paris Press. The letters, which in manuscript appear to be letter-poems, were probably all written in 1861. Their focus is on Dickinson's poem 124 [216], which exists in multiple versions.
2. This version of poem 124 was published in the Springfield *Republican* on March 1, 1862. Dickinson had sent Susan a manuscript version of this poem sometime between 1859 and 1861, but the manuscript is not extant, nor is Susan's initial letter of response, which had criticized the second stanza.

Susan Gilbert Dickinson to Emily Dickinson

I am not suited
dear Emily with the second
verse - It is remarkable as the
chain lightening that blinds us
hot nights in the Southern sky
but it does not go with the
ghostly shimmer of the first verse
as well as the other one - It just
occurs to me that the first verse
is complete in itself it needs
no other, and can't be coupled -
Strange things always go alone - as
there is only one Gabriel and one
Sun -   You never made a peer
for that verse,[3] and I <u>guess</u> you[r]
kingdom doesn't hold one - I
always go to the fire and get warm
after thinking of it, but I never
<u>can</u> again - The flowers are sweet
and bright and look as if they
would kiss one - ah, they expect
a humming-bird - Thanks for
them of course - and not thanks
only recognition either - Did it
ever occur to you that is all there
is here after all - "Lord that I
may receive my sight"[4] -

  Susan is tired making <u>bibs</u> for
her bird - her ring-dove[5] - he will
paint my cheeks when I am old
to pay me -

      Sue -

Emily Dickinson to Susan Gilbert Dickinson

Is <u>this</u>, <u>frostier</u>?

Springs - shake the Sills -
But - the Echoes - stiffen -
Hoar - is the Window - and
numb - the Door -
Tribes of Eclipse - in Tents
of Marble -
 Staples of Ages - have
 buckled - there[6] -

---

3. Susan refers to Dickinson's poem 285 [673], which calls life on earth "but a filament" of the "diviner thing" that "smites the Tinder in the Sun" and "hinders Gabriel's wing."
4. In Luke 18.41–43, the blind man's faith in Jesus brings him sight.

5. Susan's son, Ned, who was born on July 19, 1861. Susan is imagining her grown son repaying all her attention by caring for her in old age.
6. Dickinson incorporated this stanza into a new version of the poem, which she bound into Fascicle 10.

Dear Sue -
   Your praise is good -
to me - because I <u>know</u>
it <u>knows</u> - and <u>suppose</u> -
it <u>means</u> -
Could I make you and
Austin - proud - sometime - a
great way off - 'twould give
me taller feet -
Here is a crumb - for the
"Ring dove" - and a spray'
for <u>his Nest</u>, a little while
ago - <u>just</u> - "<u>Sue</u>" -
      Emily'

From Fascicle 10[7]

Safe in their Alabaster chambers -
Untouched by Morning -
And untouched by Noon -
Lie the meek members of the Resurrection -
Rafter of Satin - and Roof of Stone!   5

Grand go the Years - in the Crescent - above them -
Worlds scoop their Arcs -
And Firmaments - row -
Diadems - drop - and Doges - surrender -
Soundless as dots - on a Disc of snow -   10

Springs - shake the sills -
But - the Echoes - stiffen -
Hoar - is the window -
And - numb - the door -
Tribes - of Eclipse - in Tents - of Marble -
Staples - of Ages - have buckled - there -

Springs - shake the seals -
But the silence - stiffens -
Frosts unhook - in the Northern Zones -
Icicles - crawl from polar Caverns -
Midnights in Marble -
Refutes - the Suns -

---

7. Dickinson wrote out a complete record of her attempts with poem 124 [216], as influenced by her exchanges with Susan Dickinson, and bound it into Fascicle 10. She first wrote a ten-line version of the entire poem and then beneath that version wrote two versions of a six-line stanza that she was considering as a substitution for the five-line second stanza. The fascicle version of poem 124 [216] suggests that many Dickinson poems were always in progress. The source here is *The Poems of Emily Dickinson: Variorum Edition* (1998), ed. R.W. Franklin, reprinted with the permission of Harvard University Press.

Letters to Thomas Wentworth Higginson[1]

15 April 1862

Mr Higginson,

Are you too deeply occupied to say if my Verse is alive?[2]

The Mind is so near itself – it cannot see, distinctly – and I have none to ask –

Should you think it breathed – and had you the leisure to tell me, I should feel quick gratitude –

If I make the mistake – that you dared to tell me – would give me sincerer honor – toward you –

I enclose my name – asking you, if you please – Sir – to tell me what is true?

That you will not betray me – it is needless to ask – since Honor is it's own pawn –[3]

25 April 1862

Mr Higginson,

Your kindness claimed earlier gratitude – but I was ill – and write today, from my pillow:

Thank you for the surgery – it was not so painful as I supposed. I bring you others – as you ask – though they might not differ –

While my thought is undressed – I can make the distinction, but when I put them in the Gown – they look alike, and numb.

You asked how old I was? I made no verse – but one or two – until this winter – Sir –

I had a terror – since September – I could tell to none – and so I sing, as the Boy does by the Burying Ground – because I am afraid – You inquire my Books – For Poets – I have Keats – and Mr and Mrs Browning. For Prose – Mr Ruskin - Sir Thomas Browne – and the Revelations.[4] I went to school – but in your manner of the phrase – had no education. When a little Girl, I had a friend, who taught me Immortality – but venturing too near, himself – he never returned – Soon after, my Tutor, died[5] – and for several years, my Lexicon – was my only companion – Then I found one more – but he was not contented I be his scholar – so he left the Land.[6]

---

1. Dickinson first wrote Higginson (1823–1911) on April 15, 1862, responding to his article "Letter to a Young Contributor," which he published in the *Atlantic Monthly* earlier in the month. A contributing editor at the magazine, and for the past decade a radical abolitionist, Higginson, who had trained at Harvard Divinity School, had recently resigned his ministry. As an editor, he was intrigued by Dickinson's poetry, but he never offered to publish her work. In her letter of April 25, 1862, Dickinson refers to the editorial "surgery" he did on the poems she sent him. Over the next twenty-four years, she sent him many letters (including one just before she died) and nearly 100 poems. He visited her twice at her Amherst home, in 1870 and 1873. When he helped to publish the first two volumes of her posthumously published poems, Higginson edited the poems, giving them more conventional rhyme and meter. Both letters are taken from *Emily Dickinson:* *Selected Letters* (1971), ed. Thomas H. Johnson.

2. Dickinson sent four poems with the letter, including 124 [216], "Safe in their Alabaster Chambers."

3. Instead of signing the letter, Dickinson enclosed a card with her signature.

4. Revelation is the concluding prophetic book of the New Testament. Dickinson refers to the English poets John Keats (1795–1821), Elizabeth Barrett Browning, and Robert Browning; the English art critic and social theorist John Ruskin (1819–1900); and the English physician and writer Sir Thomas Browne (1605–1682).

5. The friend and tutor was probably Benjamin Franklin Newton (1821–1853), who had studied law in her father's office during the 1840s.

6. Dickinson's friend the Reverend Charles Wadsworth (1814–1882) had recently accepted a pastorate in California.

You ask of my Companions Hills – Sir – and the Sundown – and a Dog – large as myself, that my Father bought me – They are better than Beings – because they know – but do not tell – and the noise in the Pool, at Noon – excels my Piano. I have a Brother and Sister – My Mother does not care for thought – and Father, too busy with his Briefs[7] – to notice what we do – He buys me many Books – but begs me not to read them – because he fears they joggle the Mind. They are religious – except me – and address an Eclipse, every morning – whom they call their "Father." But I fear my story fatigues you – I would like to learn – Could you tell me how to grow – or is it unconveyed – like Melody – or Witchcraft?

You speak of Mr Whitman – I never read his Book[8] – but was told that he was disgraceful –

I read Miss Prescott's "Circumstance,"[9] but it followed me, in the Dark – so I avoided her –

Two Editors of Journals[1] came to my Father's House, this winter – and asked me for my Mind – and when I asked them "Why," they said I was penurious – and they, would use it for the World –

I could not weigh myself – Myself –

My size felt small – to me – I read your Chapters in the Atlantic – and experienced honor for you – I was sure you would not reject a confiding question –

Is this – Sir – what you asked me to tell you?

Your friend,

E – Dickinson.

---

7. Legal statements.
8. The third edition of Whitman's *Leaves of Grass* was published in 1860.
9. Harriet Prescott Spofford's (1835–1921) short story "Circumstance" had appeared in the May

1860 *Atlantic*.
1. Possibly Samuel Bowles (1826–1878) and J. G. Holland (1819–1881), who were both associated with the *Springfield Daily Republican*.

REBECCA HARDING DAVIS
1831–1910

The author of over five hundred published works, including short stories, essays, sketches, novels, and children's writings, Rebecca Harding Davis is best known today for the pioneering realism of her first published story, "Life in the Iron-Mills." The story was a sensation when it appeared in the 1861 *Atlantic Monthly*, and while Davis's subsequent work never equaled it in power, her career was marked by success with both the highbrow readers of the *Atlantic* and the mass audiences that enjoyed her writings in the popular magazines and newspapers of the day.

Rebecca Harding was born in 1831 in Washington, Pennsylvania, her mother's hometown, and then taken to Florence, Alabama, where her father, a book-loving English emigrant, was in business. In 1836 the family moved to Wheeling, Virginia, a jumping-off place for the West as well as a prosperous manufacturing center, located in an anomalous fingerlike part of a slave state that reached far north between the free states of Ohio and Pennsylvania. Rebecca Harding at fourteen returned to her Pennsylvania birthplace, living with an aunt while attending a female seminary. After graduating as valedictorian in 1848, she returned to her family in Wheeling. By her late twenties she had read English reform novels such as those by Charles Kingsley and Elizabeth Gaskell and had begun to publish anonymous reviews of new books in local newspapers. During the election year 1860, she wrote "Life in the Iron-Mills," apparently the first story she completed, and sent it to the *Atlantic Monthly*, the most prestigious magazine in the country, published in Boston under the editorship of James T. Fields. The story appeared anonymously (by custom and by Harding's request) the month the Civil War broke out and Wheeling became capital of the new free state of West Virginia. With the author's name an open secret, the story's strength was recognized by many readers, including Emily Dickinson. Buoyed by Fields's enthusiastic request for additional contributions, Harding began a serialized novel in the October 1861 *Atlantic*—"A Story of Today"—which offered, in one of the characters' words, "a glimpse of the underlife in America." In the voice of her narrator, Harding offered a manifesto of realism before there was a literary movement so identified: "You want something . . . to lift you out of this crowded, tobacco-stained commonplace, to kindle and chafe and glow in you. I want you to dig into this commonplace, this vulgar American life, and see what is in it. Sometimes I think it has a raw and awful significance that we do not see." This work, which Fields published in book form as *Margret Howth* (1862), further explored the dire effects of industrial capitalism, while addressing as well, through her portrayal of the black woman Lois Yare, the racial injustice that helped bring about the Civil War.

As a literary celebrity, Harding journeyed to Boston in 1862 and was welcomed by the literary establishment. She met Oliver Wendell Holmes and Nathaniel Hawthorne (whose fiction had inspired her own work), and became good friends with Annie Fields, her hostess. She had received a fan letter from an apprentice lawyer in Philadelphia, L. Clarke Davis, a man literary enough himself to have a connection with *Peterson's Magazine*, one of the leading magazines of the day. She met him on her way home from Boston, and they married in 1863. She continued her career as a magazine writer even after her three children were born, creating an extensive body of work that alternated between formula romance and social realism. In the best of her later novels, *Waiting for the Verdict* (1868), Davis addressed the continuing injustices facing African Americans in the postemancipation United States. She also addressed questions of gender, and in *Earthen Pitchers* (1873–74) and the short story "The Wife's Story" (1864) paid particular attention to conflicts between motherhood and career aspirations, as she and many other women of her generation were experiencing them.

In 1892 Davis received favorable critical attention for a collection of short stories, *Silhouettes of American Life*. But well before her death in 1910, she had been overshadowed, first by the success of her husband as an editor and then by the astonishing success of her son, Richard Harding Davis (1864–1916), who became the most glamorous journalist and one of the most popular writers of his generation. Concerned that he might sacrifice his talent for money as perhaps she thought she herself had done, in 1890 she warned him about "beginning to do hack work for money . . . the beginning of decadence both in work and reputation for you. I know by my own and a thousand other people."

"Life in the Iron-Mills" remains a landmark in the development of literary realism in nineteenth-century America. The story achieved a renewed popularity—and brought Rebecca Harding Davis back into a prominent place in literary history—through its republication in 1972 in a Feminist Press volume edited by the fiction writer and essayist Tillie Olson. In "Life in the Iron-Mills," Davis compels her middle-class readers to confront the underside of American industrial prosperity, particularly the exploitation of immigrant laborers, while refusing to provide easy answers to the social problems she so powerfully represents.

Life in the Iron-Mills[1]

"Is this the end?
O Life, as futile, then, as frail!
What hope of answer or redress?"[2]

A cloudy day: do you know what that is in a town of iron-works?[3] The sky sank down before dawn, muddy, flat, immovable. The air is thick, clammy with the breath of crowded human beings. It stifles me. I open the window, and, looking out, can scarcely see through the rain the grocer's shop opposite, where a crowd of drunken Irishmen are puffing Lynchburg tobacco[4] in their pipes. I can detect the scent through all the foul smells ranging loose in the air.

The idiosyncrasy of this town is smoke. It rolls sullenly in slow folds from the great chimneys of the iron-foundries, and settles down in black, slimy pools on the muddy streets. Smoke on the wharves, smoke on the dingy boats, on the yellow river,—clinging in a coating of greasy soot to the house-front, the two faded poplars, the faces of the passers-by. The long train of mules, dragging masses of pig-iron[5] through the narrow street, have a foul vapor hanging to their reeking sides. Here, inside, is a little broken figure of an angel pointing upward from the mantel-shelf; but even its wings are covered with smoke, clotted and black. Smoke everywhere! A dirty canary chirps desolately in a cage beside me. Its dream of green fields and sunshine is a very old dream,—almost worn out, I think.

From the back-window I can see a narrow brick-yard sloping down to the river-side, strewed with rain-butts[6] and tubs. The river, dull and tawny-colored, (*la belle rivière!*)[7] drags itself sluggishly along, tired of the heavy weight of boats and coal-barges. What wonder? When I was a child, I used to fancy a look of weary, dumb appeal upon the face of the negro-like river slavishly bearing its burden day after day. Something of the same idle notion comes to me to-day, when from the street-window I look on the slow stream of human life creeping past, night and morning, to the great mills. Masses of men, with dull, besotted faces bent to the ground, sharpened here and there by pain or cunning; skin and muscle and flesh begrimed with smoke and ashes; stooping all night over boiling caldrons of metal, laired by day in dens of drunkenness and infamy; breathing from infancy to death an air saturated with fog and grease and soot, vileness for soul and body. What do you make of a case like that, amateur psychologist? You call it an altogether serious thing to be alive: to these men it is a drunken jest, a joke,—horrible to angels perhaps, to them commonplace enough. My fancy about the river was an idle one: it is no type of such a life. What if it be stagnant and slimy here? It knows that beyond there waits for it odorous sunlight,—quaint old gardens, dusky with soft, green foliage of apple-trees, and flushing crimson

---

1. The text is that of the first printing in the *Atlantic Monthly* (April 1861), except for two paragraphs on page 1725, the source of which is *Atlantic Tales* (1865).
2. Adapted from Alfred, Lord Tennyson's *In Memoriam A.H.H.* (1850), 12.4: "Is this the end of all my care?' . . . 'Is this the end? Is this the end?'" and from 56.7: "O Life as futile, then, as frail / O for thy voice to soothe and bless! / What hope of answer, or redress? / Behind the veil, behind the veil."

3. The town is not named, but is based on Harding's hometown, Wheeling, Virginia (now West Virginia), on the banks of the Ohio River.
4. A low-cost tobacco from south-central Virginia.
5. Oblong blocks of iron, hardened after being poured from a smelting furnace.
6. Large casks used to catch rainwater for household and industrial use.
7. The beautiful river (French).

with roses,—air, and fields, and mountains. The future of the Welsh puddler[8] passing just now is not so pleasant. To be stowed away, after his grimy work is done, in a hole in the muddy graveyard, and after that,——*not* air, nor green fields, nor curious roses.

Can you see how foggy the day is? As I stand here, idly tapping the window-pane, and looking out through the rain at the dirty back-yard and the coal-boats below, fragments of an old story float up before me,—a story of this house into which I happened to come to-day. You may think it a tiresome story enough, as foggy as the day, sharpened by no sudden flashes of pain or pleasure.—I know: only the outline of a dull life, that long since, with thousands of dull lives like its own, was vainly lived and lost: thousands of them,—massed, vile, slimy lives, like those of the torpid lizards in yonder stagnant water-butt.—Lost? There is a curious point for you to settle, my friend, who study psychology in a lazy, *dilettante* way. Stop a moment. I am going to be honest. This is what I want you to do. I want you to hide your disgust, take no heed to your clean clothes, and come right down with me,—here, into the thickest of the fog and mud and foul effluvia. I want you to hear this story. There is a secret down here, in this nightmare fog, that has lain dumb for centuries: I want to make it a real thing to you. You, Egoist, or Pantheist, or Arminian, busy in making straight paths[9] for your feet on the hills, do not see it clearly,—this terrible question which men here have gone mad and died trying to answer. I dare not put this secret into words. I told you it was dumb. These men, going by with drunken faces and brains full of unawakened power, do not ask it of Society or of God. Their lives ask it; their deaths ask it. There is no reply. I will tell you plainly that I have a great hope; and I bring it to you to be tested. It is this: that this terrible dumb question is its own reply; that it is not the sentence of death we think it, but, from the very extremity of its darkness, the most solemn prophecy which the world has known of the Hope to come. I dare make my meaning no clearer, but will only tell my story. It will, perhaps, seem to you as foul and dark as this thick vapor about us, and as pregnant with death; but if your eyes are free as mine are to look deeper, no perfume-tinted dawn will be so fair with promise of the day that shall surely come.

My story is very simple,—only what I remember of the life of one of these men,—a furnace-tender in one of Kirby & John's rolling-mills,—Hugh Wolfe. You know the mills? They took the great order for the lower Virginia railroads there last winter; run usually with about a thousand men. I cannot tell why I choose the half-forgotten story of this Wolfe more than that of myriads of these furnace-hands. Perhaps because there is a secret, underlying sympathy between that story and this day with its impure fog and thwarted sunshine,—or perhaps simply for the reason that this house is the one where the Wolfes lived. There were the father and son,—both hands, as I said, in one of Kirby & John's mills for making railroad-iron,—and Deborah, their cousin, a picker[1] in some of the cotton-mills. The house was rented then to half a dozen families. The Wolfes had two of the cellar-rooms. The old man,

8. Worker who stirs iron oxide into a molten vat of pig iron to make wrought iron or steel.
9. Echoes Hebrews 12.13: "And make straight paths for your feet, lest that which is lame be turned out of the way; but let it rather be healed." "Egoist": one acting only according to self-interest.

"Pantheist": one who identifies the deity with nature. "Arminian": follower of theologian Jacobus Arminius (1560–1607), who argued that salvation was freely available to all through good works.
1. Worker in a cotton mill who operates the machine that separates cotton fibers.

like many of the puddlers and feeders[2] of the mills, was Welsh,—had spent half of his life in the Cornish tin-mines. You may pick the Welsh emigrants, Cornish miners, out of the throng passing the windows, any day. They are a trifle more filthy; their muscles are not so brawny; they stoop more. When they are drunk, they neither yell, nor shout, nor stagger, but skulk along like beaten hounds. A pure, unmixed blood, I fancy: shows itself in the slight angular bodies and sharply-cut facial lines. It is nearly thirty years since the Wolfes lived here. Their lives were like those of their class: incessant labor, sleeping in kennel-like rooms, eating rank pork and molasses, drinking—God and the distillers only know what; with an occasional night in jail, to atone for some drunken excess. Is that all of their lives?—of the portion given to them and these their duplicates swarming the streets to-day?—nothing beneath?—all? So many a political reformer will tell you,—and many a private reformer, too, who has gone among them with a heart tender with Christ's charity, and come out outraged, hardened.

One rainy night, about eleven o'clock, a crowd of half-clothed women stopped outside of the cellar-door. They were going home from the cotton-mill.

"Good-night, Deb," said one, a mulatto, steadying herself against the gas-post. She needed the post to steady her. So did more than one of them.

"Dah's a ball to Miss Potts' to-night. Ye'd best come."

"Inteet, Deb, if hur'll come, hur'll hef fun," said a shrill Welsh voice in the crowd.

Two or three dirty hands were thrust out to catch the gown of the woman, who was groping for the latch of the door.

"No."

"No? Where's Kit Small, then?"

"Begorra! on the spools.[3] Alleys behint, though we helped her, we dud. An wid ye! Let Deb alone! It's ondacent frettin' a quite body. Be the powers, an' we'll have a night of it! there'll be lashin's o' drink,—the Vargent[4] be blessed and praised for 't!"

They went on, the mulatto inclining for a moment to show fight, and drag the woman Wolfe off with them; but, being pacified, she staggered away.

Deborah groped her way into the cellar, and, after considerable stumbling, kindled a match, and lighted a tallow dip, that sent a yellow glimmer over the room. It was low, damp,—the earthen floor covered with a green, slimy moss,—a fetid air smothering the breath. Old Wolfe lay asleep on a heap of straw, wrapped in a torn horse-blanket. He was a pale, meek little man, with a white face and red rabbit-eyes. The woman Deborah was like him; only her face was even more ghastly, her lips bluer, her eyes more watery. She wore a faded cotton gown and a slouching bonnet. When she walked, one could see that she was deformed, almost a hunchback. She trod softly, so as not to waken him, and went through into the room beyond. There she found by the half-extinguished fire an iron saucepan filled with cold boiled potatoes, which she put upon a broken chair with a pint-cup of ale. Placing the old candlestick beside this dainty repast, she untied her bonnet, which hung limp and wet over her face, and prepared to eat her supper. It was the first

---

2. Worker who feeds molten metal into the cast-ing form while the iron is hardening.
3. Spindles in the mill on which the cotton is stretched and wound by the spinning machine.

"Begorra!": a stereotypically Irish form of "By God!"
4. The Virgin Mary.

food that had touched her lips since morning. There was enough of it, how-ever: there is not always. She was hungry,—one could see that easily enough,—and not drunk, as most of her companions would have been found at this hour. She did not drink, this woman,—her face told that, too,—nothing stronger than ale. Perhaps the weak, flaccid wretch had some stimu-lant in her pale life to keep her up,—some love or hope, it might be, or urgent need. When that stimulant was gone, she would take to whiskey. Man cannot live by work alone. While she was skinning the potatoes, and munching them, a noise behind her made her stop.

"Janey!" she called, lifting the candle and peering into the darkness. "Janey, are you there?"

A heap of ragged coats was heaved up, and the face of a young girl emerged, staring sleepily at the woman.

"Deborah," she said, at last, "I'm here the night."

"Yes, child. Hur's welcome," she said, quietly eating on.

The girl's face was haggard and sickly; her eyes were heavy with sleep and hunger: real Milesian[5] eyes they were, dark, delicate blue, glooming out from black shadows with a pitiful fright.

"I was alone," she said, timidly.

"Where's the father?" asked Deborah, holding out a potato, which the girl greedily seized.

"He's beyant,—wid Haley,—in the stone house." (Did you ever hear the word *jail* from an Irish mouth?) "I came here. Hugh told me never to stay me-lone."

"Hugh?"

"Yes."

A vexed frown crossed her face. The girl saw it, and added quickly,—

"I have not seen Hugh the day, Deb. The old man says his watch[6] lasts till the mornin'."

The woman sprang up, and hastily began to arrange some bread and flitch[7] in a tin pail, and to pour her own measure of ale into a bottle. Tying on her bonnet, she blew out the candle.

"Lay ye down, Janey dear," she said, gently, covering her with the old rags. "Hur can eat the potatoes, if hur's hungry."

"Where are ye goin', Deb? The rain's sharp."

"To the mill, with Hugh's supper."

"Let him bide till th' morn. Sit ye down."

"No, no,"—sharply pushing her off. "The boy'll starve."

She hurried from the cellar, while the child wearily coiled herself up for sleep. The rain was falling heavily, as the woman, pail in hand, emerged from the mouth of the alley, and turned down the narrow street, that stretched out, long and black, miles before her. Here and there a flicker of gas lighted an uncertain space of muddy footwalk and gutter; the long rows of houses, except an occasional lager-bier shop, were closed; now and then she met a band of millhands skulking to or from their work.

Not many even of the inhabitants of a manufacturing town know the vast machinery of system by which the bodies of workmen are governed, that goes

5. Reference to the legendary Miletus, an ancient city on the Aegean whose people were thought by some to be the ancestors of the Irish.

6. Work shift.
7. Salt pork.

on unceasingly from year to year. The hands of each mill are divided into watches that relieve each other as regularly as the sentinels of an army. By night and day the work goes on, the unsleeping engines groan and shriek, the fiery pools of metal boil and surge. Only for a day in the week, in half-courtesy to public censure, the fires are partially veiled; but as soon as the clock strikes midnight, the great furnaces break forth with renewed fury, the clamor begins with fresh, breathless vigor, the engines sob and shriek like "gods in pain."

As Deborah hurried down through the heavy rain, the noise of these thousand engines sounded through the sleep and shadow of the city like far-off thunder. The mill to which she was going lay on the river, a mile below the city-limits. It was far, and she was weak, aching from standing twelve hours at the spools. Yet it was her almost nightly walk to take this man his supper, though at every square she sat down to rest, and she knew she should receive small word of thanks.

Perhaps, if she had possessed an artist's eye, the picturesque oddity of the scene might have made her step stagger less, and the path seem shorter; but to her the mills were only "summat deilish[8] to look at by night."

The road leading to the mills had been quarried from the solid rock, which rose abrupt and bare on one side of the cinder-covered road, while the river, sluggish and black, crept past on the other. The mills for rolling[9] iron are simply immense tent-like roofs, covering acres of ground, open on every side. Beneath these roofs Deborah looked in on a city of fires, that burned hot and fiercely in the night. Fire in every horrible form: pits of flame waving in the wind; liquid metal-flames writhing in tortuous streams through the sand; wide caldrons filled with boiling fire, over which bent ghastly wretches stirring the strange brewing; and through all, crowds of half-clad men, looking like revengeful ghosts in the red light, hurried, throwing masses of glittering fire. It was like a street in Hell. Even Deborah muttered, as she crept through, "'T looks like t' Devil's place!" It did,—in more ways than one.

She found the man she was looking for, at last, heaping coal on a furnace. He had not time to eat his supper; so she went behind the furnace, and waited. Only a few men were with him, and they noticed her only by a "Hyur comes t' hunchback, Wolfe."

Deborah was stupid with sleep; her back pained her sharply; and her teeth chattered with cold, with the rain that soaked her clothes and dripped from her at every step. She stood, however, patiently holding the pail, and waiting.

"Hout, woman! ye look like a drowned cat. Come near to the fire,"—said one of the men, approaching to scrape away the ashes.

She shook her head. Wolfe had forgotten her. He turned, hearing the man, and came closer.

"I did no' think; gi' me my supper, woman."

She watched him eat with a painful eagerness. With a woman's quick instinct, she saw that he was not hungry,—was eating to please her. Her pale, watery eyes began to gather a strange light.

"Is't good, Hugh? T' ale was a bit sour, I feared."

8. Devilish. 9. Process of producing sheet metal.

"No, good enough." He hesitated a moment. "Ye 're tired, poor lass! Bide here till I go. Lay down there on that heap of ash, and go to sleep."

He threw her an old coat for a pillow, and turned to his work. The heap was the refuse of the burnt iron, and was not a hard bed; the half-smothered warmth, too, penetrated her limbs, dulling their pain and cold shiver.

Miserable enough she looked, lying there on the ashes like a limp, dirty rag,—yet not an unfitting figure to crown the scene of hopeless discomfort and veiled crime: more fitting, if one looked deeper into the heart of things,—at her thwarted woman's form, her colorless life, her waking stupor that smothered pain and hunger,—even more fit to be a type of her class. Deeper yet if one could look, was there nothing worth reading in this wet, faded thing, halfcovered with ashes? no story of a soul filled with groping passionate love, heroic unselfishness, fierce jealousy? of years of weary try-ing to please the one human being whom she loved, to gain one look of real heart-kindness from him? If anything like this were hidden beneath the pale, bleared eyes, and dull, washed-out-looking face, no one had ever taken the trouble to read its faint signs: not the half-clothed furnace-tender, Wolfe, certainly. Yet he was kind to her: it was his nature to be kind, even to the very rats that swarmed in the cellar: kind to her in just the same way. She knew that. And it might be that very knowledge had given to her face its apathy and vacancy more than her low, torpid life. One sees that dead, vacant look steal sometimes over the rarest, finest of women's faces,—in the very midst, it may be, of their warmest summer's day; and then one can guess at the secret of intolerable solitude that lies hid beneath the delicate laces and brilliant smile. There was no warmth, no brilliancy, no summer for this woman; so the stupor and vacancy had time to gnaw into her face perpetually. She was young, too, though no one guessed it; so the gnawing was the fiercer.

She lay quiet in the dark corner, listening, through the monotonous din and uncertain glare of the works, to the dull plash of the rain in the far distance,—shrinking back whenever the man Wolfe happened to look towards her. She knew, in spite of all his kindness, that there was that in her face and form which made him loathe the sight of her. She felt by instinct, although she could not comprehend it, the finer nature of the man, which made him among his fellow-workmen something unique, set apart. She knew, that, down under all the vileness and coarseness of his life, there was a grop-ing passion for whatever was beautiful and pure,—that his soul sickened with disgust at her deformity, even when his words were kindest. Through this dull consciousness, which never left her, came, like a sting, the recollec-tion of the dark blue eyes and lithe figure of the little Irish girl she had left in the cellar. The recollection struck through even her stupid intellect with a vivid glow of beauty and of grace. Little Janey, timid, helpless, clinging to Hugh as her only friend: that was the sharp thought, the bitter thought, that drove into the glazed eyes a fierce light of pain. You laugh at it? Are pain and jealousy less savage realities down here in this place I am taking you to than in your own house or your own heart,—your heart, which they clutch at sometimes? The note is the same, I fancy, be the octave high or low.

If you could go into this mill where Deborah lay, and drag out from the hearts of these men the terrible tragedy of their lives, taking it as a symptom of the disease of their class, no ghost Horror would terrify you more. A real-ity of soul-starvation, of living death, that meets you every day under the besotted faces on the street,—I can paint nothing of this, only give you the outside outlines of a night, a crisis in the life of one man: whatever muddy depth of soul-history lies beneath you can read according to the eyes God has given you.

Wolfe, while Deborah watched him as a spaniel its master, bent over the furnace with his iron pole, unconscious of her scrutiny, only stopping to receive orders. Physically, Nature had promised the man but little. He had already lost the strength and instinct vigor of a man, his muscles were thin, his nerves weak, his face (a meek, woman's face) haggard, yellow with consumption. In the mill he was known as one of the girl-men: "Molly Wolfe" was his *sobriquet.*[1] He was never seen in the cockpit, did not own a terrier,[2] drank but seldom; when he did, desperately. He fought sometimes, but was always thrashed, pommelled to a jelly. The man was game enough, when his blood was up: but he was no favorite in the mill; he had the taint of school-learning on him,—not to a dangerous extent, only a quarter or so in the free-school in fact, but enough to ruin him as a good hand in a fight.

For other reasons, too, he was not popular. Not one of themselves, they felt that, though outwardly as filthy and ash-covered; silent, with foreign thoughts and longings breaking out through his quietness in innumerable curious ways: this one, for instance. In the neighboring furnace-buildings lay great heaps of the refuse from the ore after the pig-metal is run. *Korl* we call it here: a light, porous substance, of a delicate, waxen, flesh-colored tinge. Out of the blocks of this korl, Wolfe, in his off-hours from the furnace, had a habit of chipping and moulding figures,—hideous, fantastic enough, but sometimes strangely beautiful: even the mill-men saw that, while they jeered at him. It was a curious fancy in the man, almost a passion. The few hours for rest he spent hewing and hacking with his blunt knife, never speaking, until his watch came again,—working at one figure for months, and, when it was finished, breaking it to pieces perhaps, in a fit of disappointment. A morbid, gloomy man, untaught, unled, left to feed his soul in grossness and crime, and hard, grinding labor.

I want you to come down and look at this Wolfe, standing there among the lowest of his kind, and see him just as he is, that you may judge him justly when you hear the story of this night. I want you to look back, as he does every day, at his birth in vice, his starved infancy; to remember the heavy years he has groped through as boy and man,—the slow, heavy years of constant, hot work. So long ago he began, that he thinks sometimes he has worked there for ages. There is no hope that it will ever end. Think that God put into this man's soul a fierce thirst for beauty,—to know it, to create it; to *be*—something, he knows not what,—other than he is. There are moments when a passing cloud, the sun glinting on the purple thistles, a kindly smile, a child's face, will rouse him to a passion of pain,—when his nature starts up with a mad cry of rage against God, man, whoever it is that has forced this vile, slimy life upon him. With all this groping, this mad desire, a great blind intellect stumbling through wrong, a loving poet's heart, the man was by habit only a coarse, vulgar laborer, familiar with sights and words you would blush to name. Be just: when I tell you about this night, see him as he is. Be just,—not like man's law, which seizes on one isolated fact, but like

1. Nickname.
2. Dogs bred to hunt. "Cockpit": where fighting cocks are set against each other until one is severely injured or killed.

God's judging angel, whose clear, sad eye saw all the countless cankering days of this man's life, all the countless nights, when, sick with starving, his soul fainted in him, before it judged him for this night, the saddest of all.

I called this night the crisis of his life. If it was, it stole on him unawares. These great turning-days of life cast no shadow before, slip by unconsciously. Only a trifle, a little turn of the rudder, and the ship goes to heaven or hell.

Wolfe, while Deborah watched him, dug into the furnace of melting iron with his pole, dully thinking only how many rails the lump would yield. It was late,—nearly Sunday morning; another hour, and the heavy work would be done,—only the furnaces to replenish and cover for the next day. The workmen were growing more noisy, shouting, as they had to do, to be heard over the deep clamor of the mills. Suddenly they grew less boisterous,—at the far end, entirely silent. Something unusual had happened. After a moment, the silence came nearer; the men stopped their jeers and drunken choruses. Deborah, stupidly lifting up her head, saw the cause of the quiet. A group of five or six men were slowly approaching, stopping to examine each furnace as they came. Visitors often came to see the mills after night: except by growing less noisy, the men took no notice of them. The furnace where Wolfe worked was near the bounds of the works; they halted there hot and tired: a walk over one of these great foundries is no trifling task. The woman, drawing out of sight, turned over to sleep. Wolfe, seeing them stop, suddenly roused from his indifferent stupor, and watched them keenly. He knew some of them: the overseer, Clarke,—a son of Kirby, one of the mill-owners,—and a Doctor May, one of the town-physicians. The other two were strangers. Wolfe came closer. He seized eagerly every chance that brought him into contact with this mysterious class that shone down on him perpetually with the glamour of another order of being. What made the difference between them? That was the mystery of his life. He had a vague notion that perhaps to-night he could find it out. One of the strangers sat down on a pile of bricks, and beckoned young Kirby to his side.

"This *is* hot, with a vengeance. A match, please?"—lighting his cigar. "But the walk is worth the trouble. If it were not that you must have heard it so often, Kirby, I would tell you that your works look like Dante's Inferno."[3]

Kirby laughed.

"Yes. Yonder is Farinata himself[4] in the burning tomb,"—pointing to some figure in the shimmering shadows.

"Judging from some of the faces of your men," said the other, "they bid fair to try the reality of Dante's vision, some day."

Young Kirby looked curiously around, as if seeing the faces of his hands for the first time.

"They're bad enough, that's true. A desperate set, I fancy. Eh, Clarke?"

The overseer did not hear him. He was talking of net profits just then,—giving, in fact, a schedule of the annual business of the firm to a sharp peering little Yankee, who jotted down notes on a paper laid on the crown of his hat: a reporter for one of the city-papers, getting up a series of reviews of the leading manufactories. The other gentlemen had accompanied them merely for amusement. They were silent until the notes were finished, dry-

3. *Hell*, the first part of *The Divine Comedy* by the Italian poet Dante Alighieri (1265–1321).
4. In Canto 10 of the *Inferno*, Farinata degli Uberti is one of the heretics, a leader of the Florentine faction opposed to Dante's own family.

ing their feet at the furnaces, and sheltering their faces from the intolerable heat. At last the overseer concluded with—

"I believe that is a pretty fair estimate, Captain."

"Here, some of you men!" said Kirby, "bring up those boards. We may as well sit down, gentlemen, until the rain is over. It cannot last much longer at this rate."

"Pig-metal,"—mumbled the reporter,—"um!—coal facilities,—um!—hands employed, twelve hundred,—bitumen,—um!—all right, I believe, Mr. Clarke;—sinking-fund,—what did you say was your sinking-fund?"[5]

"Twelve hundred hands?" said the stranger, the young man who had first spoken. "Do you control their votes, Kirby?"

"Control? No." The young man smiled complacently. "But my father brought seven hundred votes to the polls for his candidate last November. No force-work, you understand,—only a speech or two, a hint to form themselves into a society, and a bit of red and blue bunting to make them a flag. The Invincible Roughs,—I believe that is their name. I forget the motto: 'Our country's hope,' I think."

There was a laugh. The young man talking to Kirby sat with an amused light in his cool gray eye, surveying critically the half-clothed figures of the puddlers, and the slow swing of their brawny muscles. He was a stranger in the city,—spending a couple of months in the borders of a Slave State,[6] to study the institutions of the South,—a brother-in-law of Kirby's,—Mitchell. He was an amateur gymnast,—hence his anatomical eye; a patron, in a *blasé* way, of the prize-ring; a man who sucked the essence out of a science or philosophy in an indifferent, gentlemanly way; who took Kant, Novalis, Humboldt,[7] for what they were worth in his own scales; accepting all, despising nothing, in heaven, earth, or hell, but one-idead men; with a temper yielding and brilliant as summer water, until his Self was touched, when it was ice, though brilliant still. Such men are not rare in the States.

As he knocked the ashes from his cigar, Wolfe caught with a quick pleasure the contour of the white hand, the blood-glow of a red ring he wore. His voice, too, and that of Kirby's, touched him like music,—low, even, with chording cadences. About this man Mitchell hung the impalpable atmosphere belonging to the thoroughbred gentleman. Wolfe, scraping away the ashes beside him, was conscious of it, did obeisance to it with his artist sense, unconscious that he did so.

The rain did not cease. Clarke and the reporter left the mills; the others, comfortably seated near the furnace, lingered, smoking and talking in a desultory way. Greek would not have been more unintelligible to the furnace-tenders, whose presence they soon forgot entirely. Kirby drew out a newspaper from his pocket and read aloud some article, which they discussed eagerly. At every sentence, Wolfe listened more and more like a dumb, hopeless animal, with a duller, more stolid look creeping over his face, glancing now and then at Mitchell, marking acutely every smallest sign of refinement, then back to himself, seeing as in a mirror his filthy body, his more stained soul.

5. Fund accumulated to pay off a corporate debt.
6. The story was written and set a few years before the northwest area of the slave state of Virginia broke off to become the free state of West Virginia (1863).

7. Alexander von Humboldt (1769–1859), German naturalist and explorer of South America and Asia. Immanuel Kant (1724–1804), German philosopher. Novalis, pseudonym of the German poet Friedrich von Hardenberg (1772–1801).

Never! He had no words for such a thought, but he knew now, in all the sharpness of the bitter certainty, that between them there was a great gulf[8] never to be passed. Never!

The bell of the mills rang for midnight. Sunday morning had dawned. Whatever hidden message lay in the tolling bells floated past these men unknown. Yet it was there. Veiled in the solemn music ushering the risen Saviour was a key-note to solve the darkest secrets of a world gone wrong,— even this social riddle which the brain of the grimy puddler grappled with madly to-night.

The men began to withdraw the metal from the caldrons. The mills were deserted on Sundays, except by the hands who fed the fires, and those who had no lodgings and slept usually on the ash-heaps. The three strangers sat still during the next hour, watching the men cover the furnaces, laughing now and then at some jest of Kirby's.

"Do you know," said Mitchell, "I like this view of the works better than when the glare was fiercest? These heavy shadows and the amphitheatre of smothered fires are ghostly, unreal. One could fancy these red smouldering lights to be the half-shut eyes of wild beasts, and the spectral figures their victims in the den."

Kirby laughed. "You are fanciful. Come, let us get out of the den. The spectral figures, as you call them, are a little too real for me to fancy a close proximity in the darkness,—unarmed, too."

The others rose, buttoning their overcoats, and lighting cigars.

"Raining, still," said Doctor May, "and hard. Where did we leave the coach, Mitchell?"

"At the other side of the works.—Kirby, what's that?"

Mitchell started back, half-frightened, as, suddenly turning a corner, the white figure of a woman faced him in the darkness,—a woman, white, of giant proportions, crouching on the ground, her arms flung out in some wild gesture of warning.

"Stop! Make that fire burn there!" cried Kirby, stopping short.

The flame burst out, flashing the gaunt figure into bold relief.

Mitchell drew a long breath.

"I thought it was alive," he said, going up curiously.

The others followed.

"Not marble, eh?" asked Kirby, touching it.

One of the lower overseers stopped.

"Korl, Sir."

"Who did it?"

"Can't say. Some of the hands; chipped it out in off-hours."

"Chipped to some purpose, I should say. What a flesh-tint the stuff has! Do you see, Mitchell?"

"I see."

He had stepped aside where the light fell boldest on the figure, looking at it in silence. There was not one line of beauty or grace in it: a nude woman's form, muscular, grown coarse with labor, the powerful limbs instinct with some one poignant longing. One idea: there it was in the tense, rigid muscles,

8. Words Jesus assigns to Abraham in the parable of the beggar Lazarus and the rich man (Luke 16.26): "And beside all this, between us and you there is a great gulf fixed"—the gulf between heaven, where Lazarus has found comfort, and hell, where the rich man is suffering.

the clutching hands, the wild, eager face, like that of a starving wolf's. Kirby and Doctor May walked around it, critical, curious. Mitchell stood aloof, silent. The figure touched him strangely.

"Not badly done," said Doctor May. "Where did the fellow learn that sweep of the muscles in the arm and hand? Look at them! They are groping,—do you see?—clutching: the peculiar action of a man dying of thirst."

"They have ample facilities for studying anatomy," sneered Kirby, glancing at the half-naked figures.

"Look," continued the Doctor, "at this bony wrist, and the strained sinews of the instep! A working-woman,—the very type of her class."

"God forbid!" muttered Mitchell.

"Why?" demanded May. "What does the fellow intend by the figure? I cannot catch the meaning."

"Ask him," said the other, dryly. "There he stands,"—pointing to Wolfe, who stood with a group of men, leaning on his ash-rake.

The Doctor beckoned him with the affable smile which kind-hearted men put on, when talking to these people.

"Mr. Mitchell has picked you out as the man who did this,—I'm sure I don't know why. But what did you mean by it?"

"She be hungry."

Wolfe's eyes answered Mitchell, not the Doctor.

"Oh-h! But what a mistake you have made, my fine fellow! You have given no sign of starvation to the body. It is strong,—terribly strong. It has the mad, half-despairing gesture of drowning."

Wolfe stammered, glanced appealingly at Mitchell, who saw the soul of the thing, he knew. But the cool, probing eyes were turned on himself now,—mocking, cruel, relentless.

"Not hungry for meat," the furnace-tender said at last.

"What then? Whiskey?" jeered Kirby, with a coarse laugh.

Wolfe was silent a moment, thinking.

"I dunno," he said, with a bewildered look. "It mebbe. Summat to make her live, I think,—like you. Whiskey ull do it, in a way."

The young man laughed again. Mitchell flashed a look of disgust somewhere,—not at Wolfe.

"May," he broke out impatiently, "are you blind? Look at that woman's face! It asks questions of God, and says, 'I have a right to know.' Good God, how hungry it is!"

They looked a moment; then May turned to the mill-owner:—

"Have you many such hands as this? What are you going to do with them? Keep them at puddling iron?"

Kirby shrugged his shoulders. Mitchell's look had irritated him.

"*Ce n'est pas mon affaire.*[9] I have no fancy for nursing infant geniuses. I suppose there are some stray gleams of mind and soul among these wretches. The Lord will take care of his own; or else they can work out their own salvation. I have heard you call our American system a ladder which any man can scale. Do you doubt it? Or perhaps you want to banish all social ladders, and put us all on a flat table-land,—eh, May?"

9. It's none of my business (French).

The Doctor looked vexed, puzzled. Some terrible problem lay hid in this woman's face, and troubled these men. Kirby waited for an answer, and, receiving none, went on, warming with his subject.

"I tell you, there's something wrong that no talk of 'Liberté' or 'Egalité'[1] will do away. If I had the making of men, these men who do the lowest part of the world's work should be machines,—nothing more,—hands. It would be kindness. God help them! What are taste, reason, to creatures who must live such lives as that?" He pointed to Deborah, sleeping on the ash-heap. "So many nerves to sting them to pain. What if God had put your brain, with all its agony of touch, into your fingers, and bid you work and strike with that?"

"You think you could govern the world better?" laughed the Doctor.

"I do not think at all."

"That is true philosophy. Drift with the stream, because you cannot dive deep enough to find bottom, eh?"

"Exactly," rejoined Kirby. "I do not think. I wash my hands of all social problems,—slavery, caste, white or black. My duty to my operatives has a narrow limit,—the pay-hour on Saturday night. Outside of that, if they cut korl, or cut each other's throats, (the more popular amusement of the two,) I am not responsible."

The Doctor sighed,—a good honest sigh, from the depths of his stomach.

"God help us! Who is responsible?"

"Not I, I tell you," said Kirby, testily. "What has the man who pays them money to do with their souls' concerns, more than the grocer or butcher who takes it?"

"And yet," said Mitchell's cynical voice, "look at her! How hungry she is!"

Kirby tapped his boot with his cane. No one spoke. Only the dumb face of the rough image looking into their faces with the awful question, "What shall we do to be saved?"[2] Only Wolfe's face, with its heavy weight of brain, its weak, uncertain mouth, its desperate eyes, out of which looked the soul of his class,—only Wolfe's face turned towards Kirby's. Mitchell laughed,—a cool, musical laugh.

"Money has spoken!" he said, seating himself lightly on a stone with the air of an amused spectator at a play. "Are you answered?"—turning to Wolfe his clear, magnetic face.

Bright and deep and cold as Arctic air, the soul of the man lay tranquil beneath. He looked at the furnace-tender as he had looked at a rare mosaic in the morning; only the man was the more amusing study of the two.

"Are you answered? Why, May, look at him! 'De profundis clamavi.'[3] Or, to quote in English, 'Hungry and thirsty, his soul faints in him.' And so Money sends back its answer into the depths through you, Kirby! Very clear the answer, too!—I think I remember reading the same words somewhere:—washing your hands in Eau de Cologne, and saying, 'I am innocent of the blood of this man. See ye to it!'"[4]

1. "Liberty" and "Equality," slogans of the French Revolution.
2. The keeper of the prison in Philippi implored Paul and Silas, after an earthquake had opened the prison doors and released the prisoners' bonds, "Sirs, what must I do to be saved?" (Acts 16.30).
3. The Latin version of Psalm 130.1: "Out of the depths have I cried unto thee, O Lord."
4. The Roman governor Pontius Pilate yielded to the mob's demand that Jesus be crucified but renounced responsibility for it: "When Pilate saw that he could prevail nothing, but that rather a tumult was made, he took water, and washed his hands before the multitude, saying, I am innocent of the blood of this just person: see ye to it" (Matthew 27.24).

Kirby flushed angrily.

"You quote Scripture freely."

"Do I not quote correctly? I think I remember another line, which may amend my meaning? 'Inasmuch as ye did it unto one of the least of these, ye did it unto me.' Deist?[5] Bless you, man, I was raised on the milk of the Word. Now, Doctor, the pocket of the world having uttered its voice, what has the heart to say? You are a philanthropist, in a small way,—*n'est ce pas?*[6] Here, boy, this gentleman can show you how to cut korl better,—or your destiny. Go on, May!"

"I think a mocking devil possesses you to-night," rejoined the Doctor, seriously.

He went to Wolfe and put his hand kindly on his arm. Something of a vague idea possessed the Doctor's brain that much good was to be done here by a friendly word or two: a latent genius to be warmed into life by a waited-for sunbeam. Here it was: he had brought it. So he went on complacently:—

"Do you know, boy, you have it in you to be a great sculptor, a great man?—do you understand?" (talking down to the capacity of his hearer: it is a way people have with children, and men like Wolfe,)—"to live a better, stronger life than I, or Mr. Kirby here? A man may make himself anything he chooses. God has given you stronger powers than many men,—me, for instance."

May stopped, heated, glowing with his own magnanimity. And it was magnanimous. The puddler had drunk in every word, looking through the Doctor's flurry, and generous heat, and self-approval, into his will, with those slow, absorbing eyes of his.

"Make yourself what you will. It is your right."

"I know," quietly. "Will you help me?"

Mitchell laughed again. The Doctor turned now, in a passion,—

"You know, Mitchell, I have not the means. You know, if I had, it is in my heart to take this boy and educate him for"—

"The glory of God, and the glory of John May."

May did not speak for a moment; then, controlled, he said,—

"Why should one be raised, when myriads are left?—I have not the money, boy," to Wolfe, shortly.

"Money?" He said it over slowly, as one repeats the guessed answer to a riddle, doubtfully. "That is it? Money?"

"Yes, money,—that is it," said Mitchell, rising, and drawing his furred coat about him. "You've found the cure for all the world's diseases.—Come, May, find your good-humor, and come home. This damp wind chills my very bones. Come and preach your Saint-Simonian doctrines[7] to-morrow to Kirby's hands. Let them have a clear idea of the rights of the soul, and I'll venture next week they'll strike for higher wages. That will be the end of it."

"Will you send the coach-driver to this side of the mills?" asked Kirby, turning to Wolfe.

He spoke kindly: it was his habit to do so. Deborah, seeing the puddler go, crept after him. The three men waited outside. Doctor May walked up and down, chafed. Suddenly he stopped.

---

5. One who believes in a God who created the world but thereafter leaves it alone. What Jesus says in Matthew 25.40: "Verily I say unto you, Inasmuch as ye have done it unto one of the least of these my brethren, ye have done it unto me."
6. Aren't you? (French).
7. Doctrines of Henri de Saint-Simon (1760–1825), founder of French socialism.

"Go back, Mitchell! You say the pocket and the heart of the world speak without meaning to these people. What has its head to say? Taste, culture, refinement? Go!"

Mitchell was leaning against a brick wall. He turned his head indolently, and looked into the mills. There hung about the place a thick, unclean odor. The slightest motion of his hand marked that he perceived it, and his insufferable disgust. That was all. May said nothing, only quickened his angry tramp.

"Besides," added Mitchell, giving a corollary to his answer, "it would be of no use. I am not one of them."

"You do not mean"—said May, facing him.

"Yes, I mean just that. Reform is born of need, not pity. No vital movement of the people's has worked down, for good or evil; fermented, instead, carried up the heaving, cloggy mass. Think back through history, and you will know it. What will this lowest deep—thieves, Magdalens, negroes—do with the light filtered through ponderous Church creeds, Baconian theories, Goethe schemes?[8] Some day, out of their bitter need will be thrown up their own light-bringer,—their Jean Paul, their Cromwell,[9] their Messiah."

"Bah!" was the Doctor's inward criticism. However, in practice, he adopted the theory; for, when, night and morning, afterwards, he prayed that power might be given these degraded souls to rise, he glowed at heart, recognizing an accomplished duty.

Wolfe and the woman had stood in the shadow of the works as the coach drove off. The Doctor had held out his hand in a frank, generous way, telling him to "take care of himself, and to remember it was his right to rise." Mitchell had simply touched his hat, as to an equal, with a quiet look of thorough recognition. Kirby had thrown Deborah some money, which she found, and clutched eagerly enough. They were gone now, all of them. The man sat down on the cinder-road, looking up into the murky sky.

"'T be late, Hugh. Wunnot hur come?"

He shook his head doggedly, and the woman crouched out of his sight against the wall. Do you remember rare moments when a sudden light flashed over yourself, your world, God? when you stood on a mountain-peak, seeing your life as it might have been, as it is? one quick instant, when custom lost its force and every-day usage? when your friend, wife, brother, stood in a new light? your soul was bared, and the grave,—a foretaste of the nakedness of the Judgment-Day? So it came before him, his life, that night. The slow tides of pain he had borne gathered themselves up and surged against his soul. His squalid daily life, the brutal coarseness eating into his brain, as the ashes into his skin: before, these things had been a dull aching into his consciousness; to-night, they were reality. He griped the filthy red shirt that clung, stiff with soot, about him, and tore it savagely from his arm. The flesh beneath was muddy with grease and ashes,—and the heart beneath that! And the soul? God knows.

8. Abstract or fanciful theories such as those the English essayist and statesman Francis Bacon (1561–1624) advanced in his *New Atlantis* (1627), or the visionary faith in technological progress revealed by the German writer Johann Wolfgang von Goethe (1749–1832) in *Wilhelm Meister's Travels* (1821–29). "Magdalens": whores; from Mary Magdalene, out of whom Jesus cast seven devils (Mark 16.9).

9. Oliver Cromwell (1599–1658), English military, political, and religious leader. Jean Paul Richter (1763–1825), German novelist, author of *The Titan* (1803).

Then flashed before his vivid poetic sense the man who had left him,—the pure face, the delicate, sinewy limbs, in harmony with all he knew of beauty or truth. In his cloudy fancy he had pictured a Something like this. He had found it in this Mitchell, even when he idly scoffed at his pain: a Man all-knowing, all-seeing, crowned by Nature, reigning,—the keen glance of his eye falling like a sceptre on other men. And yet his instinct taught him that he too—He! He looked at himself with sudden loathing, sick, wrung his hands with a cry, and then was silent. With all the phantoms of his heated, ignorant fancy, Wolfe had not been vague in his ambitions. They were practical, slowly built up before him out of his knowledge of what he could do. Through years he had day by day made this hope a real thing to himself,—a clear, projected figure of himself, as he might become.

Able to speak, to know what was best, to raise these men and women working at his side up with him: sometimes he forgot this defined hope in the frantic anguish to escape,—only to escape,—out of the wet, the pain, the ashes, somewhere, anywhere,—only for one moment of free air on a hillside, to lie down and let his sick soul throb itself out in the sunshine. But to-night he panted for life. The savage strength of his nature was roused; his cry was fierce to God for justice.

"Look at me!" he said to Deborah, with a low, bitter laugh, striking his puny chest savagely. "What am I worth, Deb? Is it my fault that I am no better? My fault? My fault?"

He stopped, stung with a sudden remorse, seeing her hunchback shape writhing with sobs. For Deborah was crying thankless tears, according to the fashion of women.

"God forgi' me, woman! Things go harder wi' you nor me. It's a worse share."

He got up and helped her to rise; and they went doggedly down the muddy street, side by side.

"It's all wrong," he muttered, slowly,—"all wrong! I dunnot understan'. But it'll end some day."

"Come home, Hugh!" she said, coaxingly; for he had stopped, looking around bewildered.

"Home,—and back to the mill!" He went on saying this over to himself, as if he would mutter down every pain in this dull despair.

She followed him through the fog, her blue lips chattering with cold. They reached the cellar at last. Old Wolfe had been drinking since she went out, and had crept nearer the door. The girl Janey slept heavily in the corner. He went up to her, touching softly the worn white arm with his fingers. Some bitterer thought stung him, as he stood there. He wiped the drops from his forehead, and went into the room beyond, livid, trembling. A hope, trifling, perhaps, but very dear, had died just then out of the poor puddler's life, as he looked at the sleeping, innocent girl,—some plan for the future, in which she had borne a part. He gave it up that moment, then and forever. Only a trifle, perhaps, to us: his face grew a shade paler,—that was all. But, somehow, the man's soul, as God and the angels looked down on it, never was the same afterwards.

Deborah followed him into the inner room. She carried a candle, which she placed on the floor, closing the door after her. She had seen the look on his face, as he turned away: her own grew deadly. Yet, as she came up to him, her eyes glowed. He was seated on an old chest, quiet, holding his face in his hands.

"Hugh!" she said, softly.

He did not speak.

"Hugh, did hur hear what the man said,—him with the clear voice? Did hur hear? Money, money,—that it wud do all?"

He pushed her away,—gently, but he was worn out; her rasping tone fretted him.

"Hugh!"

The candle flared a pale yellow light over the cobwebbed brick walls, and the woman standing there. He looked at her. She was young, in deadly earnest; her faded eyes, and wet, ragged figure caught from their frantic eagerness a power akin to beauty.

"Hugh, it is true! Money ull do it! Oh, Hugh, boy, listen till me! He said it true! It is money!"

"I know. Go back! I do not want you here."

"Hugh, it is t' last time. I'll never worrit hur again."

There were tears in her voice now, but she choked them back.

"Hear till me only to-night! If one of t' witch people wud come, them we heard of t' home, and gif hur all hur wants, what then? Say, Hugh!"

"What do you mean?"

"I mean money."

Her whisper shrilled through his brain.

"If one of t' witch dwarfs wud come from t' lane moors to-night, and gif hur money, to go out,—*out*, I say,—out, lad, where t' sun shines, and t' heath grows, and t' ladies walk in silken gownds, and God stays all t' time,—where t' man lives that talked to us to-night,—Hugh knows,—Hugh could walk there like a king!"

He thought the woman mad, tried to check her, but she went on, fierce in her eager haste.

"If *I* were t' witch dwarf, if I had t' money, wud hur thank me? Wud hur take me out o' this place wid hur and Janey? I wud not come into the gran' house hur wud build, to vex hur wid t' hunch,—only at night, when t' shadows were dark, stand far off to see hur."

Mad? Yes! Are many of us mad in this way?

"Poor Deb! poor Deb!" he said, soothingly.

"It is here," she said, suddenly, jerking into his hand a small roll. "I took it! I did it! Me, me!—not hur! I shall be hanged, I shall be burnt in hell, if anybody knows I took it! Out of his pocket, as he leaned against t' bricks. Hur knows?"

She thrust it into his hand, and then, her errand done, began to gather chips together to make a fire, choking down hysteric sobs.

"Has it come to this?"

That was all he said. The Welsh Wolfe blood was honest. The roll was a small green pocket-book containing one or two gold pieces, and a check for an incredible amount, as it seemed to the poor puddler. He laid it down, hiding his face again in his hands.

"Hugh, don't be angry wud me! It's only poor Deb,—hur knows?"

He took the long skinny fingers kindly in his.

"Angry? God help me, no! Let me sleep. I am tired."

He threw himself heavily down on the wooden bench, stunned with pain and weariness. She brought some old rags to cover him.

It was late on Sunday evening before he awoke. I tell God's truth, when I say he had then no thought of keeping this money. Deborah had hid it in his pocket. He found it there. She watched him eagerly, as he took it out.

"I must gif it to him," he said, reading her face.

"Hur knows," she said with a bitter sigh of disappointment. "But it is hur right to keep it."

His right! The word struck him. Doctor May had used the same. He washed himself, and went out to find this man Mitchell. His right! Why did this chance word cling to him so obstinately? Do you hear the fierce devils whisper in his ear, as he went slowly down the darkening street?

The evening came on, slow and calm. He seated himself at the end of an alley leading into one of the larger streets. His brain was clear to-night, keen, intent, mastering. It would not start back, cowardly, from any hellish temptation, but meet it face to face. Therefore the great temptation of his life came to him veiled by no sophistry,[1] but bold, defiant, owning its own vile name, trusting to one bold blow for victory.

He did not deceive himself. Theft! That was it. At first the word sickened him; then he grappled with it. Sitting there on a broken cart-wheel, the fading day, the noisy groups, the church-bells' tolling passed before him like a panorama,[2] while the sharp struggle went on within. This money! He took it out, and looked at it. If he gave it back, what then? He was going to be cool about it.

People going by to church saw only a sickly mill-boy watching them quietly at the alley's mouth. They did not know that he was mad, or they would not have gone by so quietly: mad with hunger; stretching out his hands to the world, that had given so much to them, for leave to live the life God meant him to live. His soul within him was smothering to death; he wanted so much, thought so much, and *knew*—nothing. There was nothing of which he was certain, except the mill and things there. Of God and heaven he had heard so little, that they were to him what fairy-land is to a child: something real, but not here; very far off. His brain, greedy, dwarfed, full of thwarted energy and unused powers, questioned these men and women going by, coldly, bitterly, that night. Was it not his right to live as they,—a pure life, a good, true-hearted life, full of beauty and kind words? He only wanted to know how to use the strength within him. His heart warmed, as he thought of it. He suffered himself to think of it longer. If he took the money?

Then he saw himself as he might be, strong, helpful, kindly. The night crept on, as this one image slowly evolved itself from the crowd of other thoughts and stood triumphant. He looked at it. As he might be! What wonder, if it blinded him to delirium,—the madness that underlies all revolution, all progress, and all fall?

You laugh at the shallow temptation? You see the error underlying its argument so clearly,—that to him a true life was one of full development rather than self-restraint? that he was deaf to the higher tone in a cry of voluntary suffering for truth's sake than in the fullest flow of spontaneous harmony? I do not plead his cause. I only want to show you the mote in my brother's eye: then you can see clearly to take it out.[3]

1. Subtly deceptive argumentation or reasoning.
2. Continuous scenes painted on a huge canvas and unrolled before audiences; attending a panorama was a popular mid-19th-century recreation.
3. Jesus' words in the Sermon on the Mount (Matthew 7.3–4): "And why beholdest thou the mote that is in thy brother's eye, but considerest not the beam that is in thine own eye? Or how wilt thou say to thy brother, Let me pull out the mote out of thine eye; and behold, a beam is in thine own eye?" (Here a mote is a speck of dust and a beam is the large timber used to support a roof.)

The money,—there it lay on his knee, a little blotted slip of paper, nothing in itself; used to raise him out of the pit, something straight from God's hand. A thief! Well, what was it to be a thief? He met the question at last, face to face, wiping the clammy drops of sweat from his forehead. God made this money—the fresh air, too—for his children's use. He never made the difference between poor and rich. The Something who looked down on him that moment through the cool gray sky had a kindly face, he knew,—loved his children alike. Oh, he knew that!

There were times when the soft floods of color in the crimson and purple flames, or the clear depth of amber in the water below the bridge, had somehow given him a glimpse of another world than this,—of an infinite depth of beauty and of quiet somewhere,—somewhere,—a depth of quiet and rest and love. Looking up now, it became strangely real. The sun had sunk quite below the hills, but his last rays struck upward, touching the zenith. The fog had risen, and the town and river were steeped in its thick, gray damp; but overhead, the sun-touched smoke-clouds opened like a cleft ocean,—shifting, rolling seas of crimson mist, waves of billowy silver veined with blood-scarlet, inner depths unfathomable of glancing light. Wolfe's artist-eye grew drunk with color. The gates of that other world! Fading, flashing before him now! What, in that world of Beauty, Content, and Right, were the petty laws, the mine and thine, of mill—owners and mill hands?

A consciousness of power stirred within him. He stood up. A man,—he thought, stretching out his hands,—free to work, to live, to love! Free! His right! He folded the scrap of paper in his hand. As his nervous fingers took it in, limp and blotted, so his soul took in the mean temptation, lapped it in fancied rights, in dreams of improved existences, drifting and endless as the cloud—seas of color. Clutching it, as if the tightness of his hold would strengthen his sense of possession, he went aimlessly down the street. It was his watch at the mill. He need not go, need never go again, thank God!—shaking off the thought with unspeakable loathing.

Shall I go over the history of the hours of that night? how the man wandered from one to another of his old haunts, with a half-consciousness of bidding them farewell,—lanes and alleys and back-yards where the mill-hands lodged,—noting, with a new eagerness, the filth and drunkenness, the pig-pens, the ash-heaps covered with potato-skins, the bloated, pimpled women at the doors,—with a new disgust, a new sense of sudden triumph, and, under all, a new, vague dread, unknown before, smothered down, kept under, but still there? It left him but once during the night, when, for the second time in his life, he entered a church. It was a sombre Gothic pile, where the stained light lost itself in far-retreating arches; built to meet the requirements and sympathies of a far other class than Wolfe's. Yet it touched, moved him uncontrollably. The distances, the shadows, the still, marble figures, the mass of silent kneeling worshippers, the mysterious music, thrilled, lifted his soul with a wonderful pain. Wolfe forgot himself, forgot the new life he was going to live, the mean terror gnawing underneath. The voice of the speaker strengthened the charm; it was clear, feeling, full, strong. An old man, who had lived much, suffered much; whose brain was keenly alive, dominant; whose heart was summer-warm with charity. He taught it to-night. He held up Humanity in its grand total; showed the great world-cancer to his people. Who could show it better? He was a Christian reformer; he had studied the age thoroughly; his outlook at man had been free, world-wide, over all time. His faith stood sublime upon the Rock of Ages; his fiery zeal guided vast schemes by which the Gospel was to be preached to all nations. How did he preach it to-night? In burning, light-laden words he painted Jesus, the incarnate Life, Love, the universal Man: words that became reality in the lives of these people,—that lived again in beautiful words and actions, trifling, but heroic. Sin, as he defined it, was a real foe to them; their trials, temptations, were his. His words passed far over the furnace-tender's grasp, toned to suit another class of culture; they sounded in his ears a very pleasant song in an unknown tongue. He meant to cure this world-cancer with a steady eye that had never glared with hunger, and a hand that neither poverty nor strychnine-whiskey[4] had taught to shake. In this morbid, distorted heart of the Welsh puddler he had failed.

Eighteen centuries ago, the Master of this man tried reform in the streets of a city as crowded and vile as this, and did not fail. His disciple, showing Him to-night to cultured hearers, showing the clearness of the God-power acting through Him, shrank back from one coarse fact; that in birth and habit the man Christ was thrown up from the lowest of the people: his flesh, their flesh; their blood, his blood; tempted like them, to brutalize day by day; to lie, to steal: the actual slime and want of their hourly life, and the wine-press he trod alone.

Yet, is there no meaning in this perpetually covered truth? If the son of the carpenter had stood in the church that night, as he stood with the fishermen and harlots by the sea of Galilee, before His Father and their Father, despised and rejected of men, without a place to lay His head, wounded for their iniquities, bruised for their transgressions, would not that hungry mill-boy at least, in the back seat, have "known the man"? That Jesus did not stand there.[5]

Wolfe rose at last, and turned from the church down the street. He looked up; the night had come on foggy, damp; the golden mists had vanished, and the sky lay dull and ash-colored. He wandered again aimlessly down the street, idly wondering what had become of the cloud-sea of crimson and scarlet. The trial-day of this man's life was over, and he had lost the victory. What followed was mere drifting circumstance,—a quicker walking over the path,—that was all. Do you want to hear the end of it? You wish me to make a tragic story out of it? Why, in the police-reports of the morning paper you can find a dozen such tragedies: hints of shipwrecks unlike any that ever befell on the high seas; hints that here a power was lost to heaven,—that there a soul went down where no tide can ebb or flow. Commonplace enough the hints are,—jocose sometimes, done up in rhyme.

Doctor May, a month after the night I have told you of, was reading to his wife at breakfast from this fourth column of the morning-paper: an unusual thing,—these police-reports not being, in general, choice reading for ladies; but it was only one item he read.

"Oh, my dear! You remember that man I told you of, that we saw at Kirby's mill?—that was arrested for robbing Mitchell? Here he is; just listen:—'Circuit Court. Judge Day. Hugh Wolfe, operative in Kirby & John's Loudon Mills. Charge, grand larceny. Sentence, nineteen years hard labor in

4. Whiskey full of impurities, sometimes poisonous.

5. This paragraph and the previous one are taken from the 1865 collection, *Atlantic Tales*, where the author was allowed to insert this in place of the passage censored from her manuscript. See Janice Milner Lasseter in the Davis entry in "Selected Bibliographies."

penitentiary.'—Scoundrel! Serves him right! After all our kindness that night! Picking Mitchell's pocket at the very time!"

His wife said something about the ingratitude of that kind of people, and then they began to talk of something else.

Nineteen years! How easy that was to read! What a simple word for Judge Day to utter! Nineteen years! Half a lifetime!

Hugh Wolfe sat on the window-ledge of his cell, looking out. His ankles were ironed. Not usual in such cases; but he had made two desperate efforts to escape. "Well," as Haley, the jailer, said, "small blame to him! Nineteen years' inprisonment was not a pleasant thing to look forward to." Haley was very good-natured about it, though Wolfe had fought him savagely.

"When he was first caught," the jailer said afterwards, in telling the story, "before the trial, the fellow was cut down at once,—laid there on that pallet like a dead man, with his hands over his eyes. Never saw a man so cut down in my life. Time of the trial, too, came the queerest dodge[6] of any customer I ever had. Would choose no lawyer. Judge gave him one, of course. Gibson it was. He tried to prove the fellow crazy; but it wouldn't go. Thing was plain as daylight: money found on him. 'T was a hard sentence,—all the law allows; but it was for 'xample's sake. These mill-hands are gettin' onbearable. When the sentence was read, he just looked up, and said the money was his by rights, and that all the world had gone wrong. That night, after the trial, a gentleman came to see him here, name of Mitchell,—him as he stole from. Talked to him for an hour. Thought he came for curiosity, like. After he was gone, thought Wolfe was remarkable quiet, and went into his cell. Found him very low; bed all bloody. Doctor said he had been bleeding at the lungs. He was as weak as a cat; yet if ye'll b'lieve me, he tried to get a-past me and get out. I just carried him like a baby, and threw him on the pallet. Three days after, he tried it again: that time reached the wall. Lord help you! he fought like a tiger,—giv' some terrible blows. Fightin' for life, you see; for he can't live long, shut up in the stone crib down yonder. Got a death-cough now. 'T took two of us to bring him down that day; so I just put the irons on his feet. There he sits, in there. Goin' to-morrow, with a batch more of 'em. That woman, hunchback, tried with him,—you remember?—she's only got three years. 'Complice. But *she's* a woman, you know. He's been quiet ever since I put on irons: giv' up, I suppose. Looks white, sick-lookin'. It acts different on 'em, bein' sentenced. Most of 'em gets reckless, devilish—like. Some prays awful, and sings them vile songs of the mills, all in a breath. That woman, now, she's desper't'. Been beggin' to see Hugh, as she calls him, for three days. I'm a-goin' to let her in. She don't go with him. Here she is in this next cell. I'm a-goin' now to let her in."

He let her in. Wolfe did not see her. She crept into a corner of the cell, and stood watching him. He was scratching the iron bars of the window with a piece of tin which he had picked up, with an idle, uncertain, vacant stare, just as a child or idiot would do.

"Tryin' to get out, old boy?" laughed Haley. "Them irons will need a crowbar beside your tin, before you can open 'em."

Wolfe laughed, too, in a senseless way.

"I think I'll get out," he said.

"I believe his brain's touched," said Haley, when he came out.

6. Trick, stratagem.

The puddler scraped away with the tin for half an hour. Still Deborah did not speak. At last she ventured nearer, and touched his arm.

"Blood?" she said, looking at some spots on his coat with a shudder.

He looked up at her. "Why, Deb!" he said, smiling,—such a bright, boyish smile, that it went to poor Deborah's heart directly, and she sobbed and cried out loud.

"Oh, Hugh, lad! Hugh! dunnot look at me, when it wur my fault! To think I brought hur to it! And I loved hur so! Oh lad, I dud!"

The confession, even in this wretch, came with the woman's blush through the sharp cry.

He did not seem to hear her,—scraping away diligently at the bars with the bit of tin.

Was he going mad? She peered closely into his face. Something she saw there made her draw suddenly back,—something which Haley had not seen, that lay beneath the pinched, vacant look it had caught since the trial, or the curious gray shadow that rested on it. That gray shadow,—yes, she knew what that meant. She had often seen it creeping over women's faces for months, who died at last of slow hunger or consumption. That meant death, distant, lingering: but this—Whatever it was the woman saw, or thought she saw, used as she was to crime and misery, seemed to make her sick with a new horror. Forgetting her fear of him, she caught his shoulders, and looked keenly, steadily, into his eyes.

"Hugh!" she cried, in a desperate whisper,—"oh, boy, not that! for God's sake, not *that*!"

The vacant laugh went off his face, and he answered her in a muttered word or two that drove her away. Yet the words were kindly enough. Sitting there on his pallet, she cried silently a hopeless sort of tears, but did not speak again. The man looked up furtively at her now and then. Whatever his own trouble was, her distress vexed him with a momentary sting.

It was market-day. The narrow window of the jail looked down directly on the carts and wagons drawn up in a long line, where they had unloaded. He could see, too, and hear distinctly the clink of money as it changed hands, the busy crowd of whites and blacks shoving, pushing one another, and the chaffering and swearing at the stalls. Somehow, the sound, more than anything else had done, wakened him up,—made the whole real to him. He was done with the world and the business of it. He let the tin fall, and looked out, pressing his face close to the rusty bars. How they crowded and pushed! And he,—he should never walk that pavement again! There came Neff Sanders, one of the feeders at the mill, with a basket on his arm. Sure enough, Neff was married the other week. He whistled, hoping he would look up; but he did not. He wondered if Neff remembered he was there,—if any of the boys thought of him up there, and thought that he never was to go down that old cinder-road again. Never again! He had not quite understood it before; but now he did. Not for days or years, but never!—that was it.

How clear the light fell on that stall in front of the market! and how like a picture it was, the dark-green heaps of corn, and the crimson beets, and golden melons! There was another with game: how the light flickered on that pheasant's breast, with the purplish blood dripping over the brown feathers! He could see the red shining of the drops, it was so near. In one minute he could be down there. It was just a step. So easy, as it seemed, so natural to go! Yet it could never be—not in all the thousands of years to come—that he should put his foot on that street again! He thought of himself with a sorrowful pity, as of some one else. There was a dog down in the market, walking after his master with such a stately, grave look!—only a dog, yet he could go backwards and forwards just as he pleased: he had good luck! Why, the very vilest cur, yelping there in the gutter, had not lived his life, had been free to act out whatever thought God had put into his brain; while he—No, he would not think of that! He tried to put the thought away, and to listen to a dispute between a countryman and a woman about some meat; but it would come back. He, what had he done to bear this?

Then came the sudden picture of what might have been, and now. He knew what it was to be in the penitentiary,—how it went with men there. He knew how in these long years he should slowly die, but not until soul and body had become corrupt and rotten,—how, when he came out, if he lived to come, even the lowest of the mill-hands would jeer him,—how his hands would be weak, and his brain senseless and stupid. He believed he was almost that now. He put his hand to his head, with a puzzled, weary look. It ached, his head, with thinking. He tried to quiet himself. It was only right, perhaps; he had done wrong. But was there right or wrong for such as he? What was right? And who had ever taught him? He thrust the whole matter away. A dark, cold quiet crept through his brain. It was all wrong; but let it be! It was nothing to him more than the others. Let it be!

The door grated, as Haley opened it.

"Come, my woman! Must lock up for t' night. Come, stir yerself!"

She went up and took Hugh's hand.

"Good—night, Deb," he said, carelessly.

She had not hoped he would say more; but the tired pain on her mouth just then was bitterer than death. She took his passive hand and kissed it.

"Hur'll never see Deb again!" she ventured, her lips growing colder and more bloodless.

What did she say that for? Did he not know it? Yet he would not be impatient with poor old Deb. She had trouble of her own, as well as he.

"No, never again," he said, trying to be cheerful.

She stood just a moment, looking at him. Do you laugh at her, standing there, with her hunchback, her rags, her bleared, withered face, and the great despised love tugging at her heart?

"Come, you!" called Haley, impatiently.

She did not move.

"Hugh!" she whispered.

It was to be her last word. What was it?

"Hugh, boy, not THAT!"

He did not answer. She wrung her hands, trying to be silent, looking in his face in an agony of entreaty. He smiled again, kindly.

"It is best, Deb. I cannot bear to be hurted any more."

"Hur knows," she said, humbly.

"Tell my father good-bye; and—and kiss little Janey."

She nodded, saying nothing, looked in his face again, and went out of the door. As she went, she staggered.

"Drinkin' to-day?" broke out Haley, pushing her before him. "Where the Devil did you get it? Here, in with ye!" and he shoved her into her cell, next to Wolfe's, and shut the door.

Along the wall of her cell there was a crack low down by the floor, through which she could see the light from Wolfe's. She had discovered it days before. She hurried in now, and, kneeling down by it, listened, hoping to hear some sound. Nothing but the rasping of the tin on the bars. He was at his old amusement again. Something in the noise jarred on her ear, for she shivered as she heard it. Hugh rasped away at the bars. A dull old bit of tin, not fit to cut korl with.

He looked out of the window again. People were leaving the market now. A tall mulatto girl, following her mistress, her basket on her head, crossed the street just below, and looked up. She was laughing; but, when she caught sight of the haggard face peering out through the bars, suddenly grew grave, and hurried by. A free, firm step, a clear-cut olive face, with a scarlet turban tied on one side, dark, shining eyes, and on the head the basket poised, filled with fruit and flowers, under which the scarlet turban and bright eyes looked out half-shadowed. The picture caught his eye. It was good to see a face like that. He would try to-morrow, and cut one like it. *To-morrow*! He threw down the tin, trembling, and covered his face with his hands. When he looked up again, the daylight was gone.

Deborah, crouching near by on the other side of the wall, heard no noise. He sat on the side of the low pallet, thinking. Whatever was the mystery which the woman had seen on his face, it came out now slowly, in the dark there, and became fixed,—a something never seen on his face before. The evening was darkening fast. The market had been over for an hour; the rumbling of the carts over the pavement grew more infrequent: he listened to each, as it passed, because he thought it was to be for the last time. For the same reason, it was, I suppose, that he strained his eyes to catch a glimpse of each passer-by, wondering who they were, what kind of homes they were going to, if they had children,—listening eagerly to every chance word in the street, as if—(God be merciful to the man! what strange fancy was this?)—as if he never should hear human voices again.

It was quite dark at last. The street was a lonely one. The last passenger, he thought, was gone. No,—there was a quick step: Joe Hill, lighting the lamps. Joe was a good old chap; never passed a fellow without some joke or other. He remembered once seeing the place where he lived with his wife. "Granny Hill" the boys called her. Bedridden she was; but so kind as Joe was to her! kept the room so clean!—and the old woman, when he was there, was laughing at "some of t' lad's foolishness." The step was far down the street; but he could see him place the ladder, run up, and light the gas. A longing seized him to be spoken to once more.

"Joe!" he called, out of the grating. "Good-bye, Joe!"

The old man stopped a moment, listening uncertainly; then hurried on. The prisoner thrust his hand out of the window, and called again, louder; but Joe was too far down the street. It was a little thing; but it hurt him,—this disappointment.

"Good-bye, Joe!" he called, sorrowfully enough.

"Be quiet!" said one of the jailers, passing the door, striking on it with his club.

Oh, that was the last, was it?

There was an inexpressible bitterness on his face, as he lay down on the bed, taking the bit of tin, which he had rasped to a tolerable degree of sharpness, in his hand,—to play with, it may be. He bared his arms, looking intently at their corded veins and sinews. Deborah, listening in the next cell, heard a slight clicking sound, often repeated. She shut her lips tightly, that she might not scream; the cold drops of sweat broke over her, in her dumb agony.

"Hur knows best," she muttered at last, fiercely clutching the boards where she lay.

If she could have seen Wolfe, there was nothing about him to frighten her. He lay quite still, his arms outstretched, looking at the pearly stream of moonlight coming into the window. I think in that one hour that came then he lived back over all the years that had gone before. I think that all the low, vile life, all his wrongs, all his starved hopes, came then, and stung him with a farewell poison that made him sick unto death. He made neither moan nor cry, only turned his worn face now and then to the pure light, that seemed so far off, as one that said, "How long, O Lord? how long?"

The hour was over at last. The moon, passing over her nightly path, slowly came nearer, and threw the light across his bed on his feet. He watched it steadily, as it crept up, inch by inch, slowly. It seemed to him to carry with it a great silence. He had been so hot and tired there always in the mills! The years had been so fierce and cruel! There was coming now quiet and coolness and sleep. His tense limbs relaxed, and settled in a calm languor. The blood ran fainter and slow from his heart. He did not think now with a savage anger of what might be and was not; he was conscious only of deep stillness creeping over him. At first he saw a sea of faces: the mill-men,—women he had known, drunken and bloated,—Janey's timid and pitiful—poor old Debs: then they floated together like a mist, and faded away, leaving only the clear, pearly moonlight.

Whether, as the pure light crept up the stretched-out figure, it brought with it calm and peace, who shall say? His dumb soul was alone with God in judgment. A Voice may have spoken for it from far-off Calvary, "Father, forgive them, for they know not what they do!"[7] Who dare say? Fainter and fainter the heart rose and fell, slower and slower the moon floated from behind a cloud, until, when at last its full tide of white splendor swept over the cell, it seemed to wrap and fold into a deeper stillness the dead figure that never should move again. Silence deeper than the Night! Nothing that moved, save the black, nauseous stream of blood dripping slowly from the pallet to the floor!

There was outcry and crowd enough in the cell the next day. The coroner and his jury, the local editors, Kirby himself, and boys with their hands thrust knowingly into their pockets and heads on one side, jammed into the corners. Coming and going all day. Only one woman. She came late, and outstayed them all. A Quaker, or Friend, as they call themselves. I think this woman was known by that name in heaven. A homely body, coarsely dressed in gray and white. Deborah (for Haley had let her in) took notice of her. She watched them all—sitting on the end of the pallet, holding his head in her arms—with the ferocity of a watch-dog, if any of them touched the body. There was no meekness, no sorrow, in her face; the stuff out of which murderers are made, instead. All the time Haley and the woman were laying straight the limbs and cleaning the cell, Deborah sat still, keenly watching the Quaker's face. Of all the crowd there that day, this woman alone had not spoken to her,—only once or twice had put some cordial to her lips. After

---

7. Luke 23.34: "Father, forgive them: for they know not what they do" (Jesus' words on the cross). Calvary was the site of the Crucifixion.

they all were gone, the woman, in the same still, gentle way, brought a vase of wood-leaves and berries, and placed it by the pallet, then opened the narrow window. The fresh air blew in, and swept the woody fragrance over the dead face. Deborah looked up with a quick wonder.

"Did hur know my boy wud like it? Did hur know Hugh?"

"I know Hugh now."

The white fingers passed in a slow, pitiful way over the dead, worn face. There was a heavy shadow in the quiet eyes.

"Did hur know where they'll bury Hugh?" said Deborah in a shrill tone, catching her arm.

This had been the question hanging on her lips all day.

"In t' town-yard? Under t' mud and ash? T' lad 'll smother, woman! He wur born in t' lane moor, where t' air is frick[8] and strong. Take hur out, for God's sake, take hur out where t' air blows!"

The Quaker hesitated, but only for a moment. She put her strong arm around Deborah and led her to the window.

"Thee sees the hills, friend, over the river? Thee sees how the light lies warm there, and the winds of God blow all the day? I live there,—where the blue smoke is, by the trees. Look at me." She turned Deborah's face to her own, clear and earnest. "Thee will believe me? I will take Hugh and bury him there to-morrow."

Deborah did not doubt her. As the evening wore on, she leaned against the iron bars, looking at the hills that rose far off, through the thick sodden clouds, like a bright, unattainable calm. As she looked, a shadow of their solemn repose fell on her face; its fierce discontent faded into a pitiful, humble quiet. Slow, solemn tears gathered in her eyes: the poor weak eyes turned so hopelessly to the place where Hugh was to rest, the grave heights looking higher and brighter and more solemn than ever before. The Quaker watched her keenly. She came to her at last, and touched her arm.

"When thee comes back," she said, in a low, sorrowful tone, like one who speaks from a strong heart deeply moved with remorse or pity, "thee shall begin thy life again,—there on the hills. I came too late; but not for thee,—by God's help, it may be."

Not too late. Three years after, the Quaker began her work. I end my story here. At evening-time it was light. There is no need to tire you with the long years of sunshine, and fresh air, and slow, patient Christ-love, needed to make healthy and hopeful this impure body and soul. There is a homely pine house, on one of these hills, whose windows overlook broad, wooded slopes and clover-crimsoned meadows,—niched into the very place where the light is warmest, the air freest. It is the Friends'[9] meeting-house. Once a week they sit there, in their grave, earnest way, waiting for the Spirit of Love to speak, opening their simple hearts to receive His words. There is a woman, old, deformed, who takes a humble place among them: waiting like them: in her gray dress, her worn face, pure and meek, turned now and then to the sky. A woman much loved by these silent, restful people; more silent than they, more humble, more loving. Waiting: with her eyes turned to hills higher and purer than these on which she lives,—dim and far off now, but to be reached some day. There may be in her heart some latent hope to meet there

8. Fresh.

9. Quakers.

the love denied her here,—that she shall find him whom she lost, and that then she will not be all-unworthy. Who blames her? Something is lost in the passage of every soul from one eternity to the other,—something pure and beautiful, which might have been and was not: a hope, a talent, a love, over which the soul mourns, like Esau deprived of his birthright.[1] What blame to the meek Quaker, if she took her lost hope to make the hills of heaven more fair?

Nothing remains to tell that the poor Welsh puddler once lived, but this figure of the mill-woman cut in korl. I have it here in a corner of my library. I keep it hid behind a curtain,—it is such a rough, ungainly thing. Yet there are about it touches, grand sweeps of outline, that show a master's hand. Sometimes,—to-night, for instance,—the curtain is accidentally drawn back, and I see a bare arm stretched out imploringly in the darkness, and an eager, wolfish face watching mine: a wan, woful face, through which the spirit of the dead korl-cutter looks out, with its thwarted life, its mighty hunger, its unfinished work. Its pale, vague lips seem to tremble with a terrible question. "Is this the End?" they say,—"nothing beyond?—no more?" Why, you tell me you have seen that look in the eyes of dumb brutes,—horses dying under the lash. I know.

The deep of the night is passing while I write. The gas-light wakens from the shadows here and there the objects which lie scattered through the room: only faintly, though; for they belong to the open sunlight. As I glance at them, they each recall some task or pleasure of the coming day. A half-moulded child's head; Aphrodite;[2] a bough of forest-leaves; music; work; homely fragments, in which lie the secrets of all eternal truth and beauty. Prophetic all! Only this dumb, woful face seems to belong to and end with the night. I turn to look at it. Has the power of its desperate need commanded the darkness away? While the room is yet steeped in heavy shadow, a cool, gray light suddenly touches its head like a blessing hand, and its groping arm points through the broken cloud to the far East, where, in the flickering, nebulous crimson, God has set the promise of the Dawn.

1861, 1865

---

1. Genesis 25 and 27 tell the story of Jacob's depriving his elder twin brother, Esau, of his   birthright.
2. Venus, the goddess of love.

LOUISA MAY ALCOTT
1832–1888

The author of the perennially popular novel *Little Women* (1868–69), Louisa May Alcott was the second of four daughters of the philosopher-teacher Amos Bronson Alcott and Abigail May Alcott. Born in Germantown, near Philadelphia, on November 29, 1832, she grew up in Boston and Concord and lived among the leading Massachusetts cultural figures of the time. Margaret Fuller taught in her father's school in Boston (which folded in 1839 after controversies over sex education and admitting black children); Ralph Waldo Emerson introduced her to Goethe's writings and encouraged her to borrow books from his library; Thoreau gave her informal lessons about the natural world, and later hosted her and her father while he was living at Walden Pond; Hawthorne for several years lived nearby. Her maternal uncle, Samuel May, was a leading Boston abolitionist, and she came to know William Lloyd Garrison, Theodore Parker, and other prominent abolitionists, joining with them in 1854 when they attempted to prevent the return of the fugitive slave Anthony Burns to Virginia. In "Recollections of My Childhood" (1888), Alcott gloried in having shared in the struggle "which put an end to a great wrong."

During Louisa May Alcott's youth, her father was well known and controversial, regarded by some as a great philosopher but by others as a half-crazed mystic, particularly after the first installment of his abstruse "Orphic Sayings" appeared in the 1840 *Dial,* the journal published by the informal group known as "transcendentalists." As an educator, he observed his first two daughters closely and took hundreds of pages of notes on their behavior. He believed self-contradictorily in a child's natural goodness and in the importance of instilling traits in a child that his Puritan ancestors would have approved, such as self-denial and self-criticism. When Louisa was two years old, he gave her an apple with instructions not to eat it; she ate the apple, while her older sister, to whom Bronson had given the same instructions, dutifully left it alone, an outcome that he interpreted as a sign of his second daughter's overly willful nature. Over time, Louisa, while remaining deeply attached to her father, increasingly resented his efforts to stifle her independence, and much of her writing would deal with young women struggling to express and value their individuality. Her mother more warmly encouraged her reading and writing. With her sisters, she wrote and staged plays for family entertainment. She kept a regular journal, wrote stories from a very early age, and was enamored of Sir Walter Scott's historical novels, John Bunyan's *Pilgrim's Progress,* and Charles Dickens's novels (which she read as they were being serialized), as well as works by Goethe, Hawthorne, the Brontës, and many other writers.

In 1843, when Louisa May Alcott was ten, her father founded Fruitlands, a vegetarian reform community near Concord that banned money and regarded participants as members of one large family. He moved his family there, but after several months of hardship in which, according to his wife's view, the men did nothing but think and the women did all the hard physical work, Abigail threatened to leave with her children, even if this meant severing her ties with her husband. He reluctantly gave up on the project early in 1844 and moved the family back to Concord. (Alcott would later satirize the community in her short story "Transcendental Wild Oats" [1873]). Because Bronson had invested all of his money in Fruitlands, for years afterward the Alcotts lived in poverty. After several years in Concord they moved to Boston, where Abigail tried to support the family by becoming a social worker—one of the earliest practitioners of this profession—and then by running an employment agency, while Bronson attempted to make money through holding "conversations" (symposia in which participants paid a small fee) on various philosophical topics. The family moved constantly in attempts to find rental situations they could afford. Writing about these years of economic struggle in her 1888 "Recollections," Alcott maintained that as a sixteen-year-old she made the following declaration: "I will do something by-and-by. Don't care what, teach, sew, act, write, anything to help the family; I'll be rich and famous and happy before I die, see if I won't."

Alcott did teach and sew; she also worked as a governess and took on other short-term jobs. But mainly she attempted to make money through her writing. Her first story, "The Rival Painters," for which she was paid the modest sum of five dollars, appeared in an 1852 issue of a weekly newspaper called the *Olive Branch,* while a collection of childrens' stories, *Flower Fables,* originally written for Emerson's daughter Ellen during the 1840s, was published in 1854, earning a total of thirty-five dollars. Although it would be some years before Alcott learned to demand proper payment for her work, she was gaining a reputation with her early publications. In 1860 her story "A Modern Cinderella" appeared in the *Atlantic Monthly,* the most prestigious literary magazine of the time.

Shortly before the Civil War, Alcott's younger sister Lizzie died of the aftereffects of scarlet fever, which Louisa managed to fight off. Her beloved neighbor Henry David Thoreau died in 1862. She was struggling with a novel, *Moods*, which she would eventually publish in 1864, but at this time her chief ambition was to contribute to the Civil War effort. Shortly after writing in her journal "I long to be a man; but as I can't fight, I will content myself with working for those who can," she volunteered for the nursing corps. Beginning in December 1862, she worked at the unsanitary and poorly run Union Hotel Hospital in Washington, D.C., overseeing amputations and comforting the many men who were dying. The work took its toll, and by late January of 1863 she was suffering from typhoid pneumonia and had to give up nursing. Although she survived the disease, she was badly damaged by the poisonous treatment—huge doses of mercury, at that time the normal therapy for many diseases—which left her with permanent fatigue and neuralgia over the remaining twenty-five years of her life.

Despite her health problems, Alcott began to write again after she recovered from pneumonia. In 1863 she published sketches about her hospital experience in the *Boston Commonwealth*, working with the persona of a feisty, ironic nurse named Tribulation Periwinkle, and the pieces were published as *Hospital Sketches* later in the year. She also published several short stories about the Civil War, including two, "M.L." and "My Contraband," about interracial sexuality. ("M.L." points to the possibility of love across the color line; "My Contraband" offers suggestions about such a possibility, while underscoring the hard truths of the sexual violation of black women on slave plantations.) Eager for money and desirous of experimenting with fiction that would allow her to write unconventionally, in a Gothic mode, about such topics as incest, suicide, drug addiction, sexual passion, and the supernatural, she began publishing melodramatic sensation stories under the name of A. M. Barnard, earning $100 (around $1200 in today's currency) for each story. Those stories, discovered by the critic Madeleine Stern during the 1980s and 1990s, helped transform critics' understanding of Alcott, who for over a century was known mainly as the author of *Little Women* (though Alcott does write about her surrogate Jo's turn to sensation fiction in *Little Women*).

In 1867 Alcott was offered the editorship of a children's magazine, *Mercury Museum*, and at the same time she was solicited by the editor Thomas Niles of Roberts Brothers to write a novel for girls. She was not initially enthusiastic about the novel, and Niles found the first twelve chapters dull. But his nieces loved what they read. Accordingly, Niles urged Alcott to persevere, and she wrote 400 manuscript pages during June and July of 1868. Part 1 of *Little Women*, appearing later in the year, quickly sold out its first printing; Part II appeared in 1869, and the novel has never gone out of print. A semiautobiographical story of her girlhood and young womanhood, the novel, which sanitized some of the misery of the Alcotts' poverty, brought together the four differently imperfect but sympathetic March sisters and their adored mother in a family portrait that focused on the girls' struggles and triumphs as three of the four (one dies tragically) grow into young womanhood. More adventurously, the novel explored questions of gender and power, focusing on Jo's dissatisfaction with the constraints of girlhood and her efforts to become a successful writer. There is an appealing neighbor, Laurie, who seems a likely candidate to marry Jo, but she declines his offer. By the end of the novel the successful author Jo chooses to marry the more fatherly Professor Bhaer, temporarily giving up writing to have children and assist her husband in running a school for boys. In Alcott's later novel *Jo's Boys* (1886), however, Jo resumes writing and helps to make the school coeducational.

The novel's success allowed Alcott to pay off her family's debts and support her mother and father. She published *An Old-Fashioned Girl* in 1870, *Little Men* in 1872, and *Work* (one of the finest nineteenth-century novels about women and labor) in 1873. As the physical act of writing became increasingly painful, she tried learning to write with her left hand. In 1874 she confided to her journal: "When I had youth I had no money; now that I have the money I have no time; and when I get the time, if I ever do, I shall have no health to enjoy life." Still, she continued to push on with her writing, returning to the mode of sensation fiction with the novel *A Modern Mephistopheles*, published in 1877 in Roberts Brothers' "No Name Series" (novels published anonymously by famous writers). By the late 1870s Alcott had become almost too ill to write, though she labored on with *Jo's Boys* and several other projects. Her beloved mother, Abigail, died in 1877; two years later, her youngest sister, May (the prototype for Amy in *Little Women*), died in childbirth in Paris, and Louisa adopted the child, Louisa May Nierker, in 1880. Three years later, her father suffered a paralytic stroke, and for a while Alcott was caring for her father and the young Louisa. In 1886, suffering from pain and exhaustion, she was admitted to Dr. Rhoda Lawrence's nursing home in West Roxbury, Massachusetts. She died on March 6, 1888, two days after the death of her father.

In recent decades much of Alcott's writing has been put back into print, allowing readers to appreciate the wide range of her children's fiction, her realistic novels and short stories, and her slyly comic melodramas and sensation fiction. Jo March's goals were not only to be independent and to help those she loved, but also to produce a literary work of enduring merit that "went to the hearts of those who read it." Alcott achieved that goal as the author of *Little Women* and many other works published during her approximately forty-year career as a writer.

My Contraband[1]

Doctor Franck came in as I sat sewing up the rents in an old shirt, that Tom might go tidily to his grave. New shirts were needed for the living, and there was no wife or mother to "dress him handsome when he went to meet the Lord," as one woman said, describing the fine funeral she had pinched[2] herself to give her son.

"Miss Dane, I'm in a quandary," began the Doctor, with that expression of countenance which says as plainly as words, "I want to ask a favor, but I wish you'd save me the trouble."

"Can I help you out of it?"

"Faith! I don't like to propose it, but you certainly can, if you please."

"Then name it, I beg."

"You see a Reb[3] has just been brought in crazy with typhoid; a bad case every way; a drunken, rascally little captain somebody took the trouble to capture, but whom nobody wants to take the trouble to cure. The wards are full, the ladies worked to death, and willing to be for our own boys, but rather slow to risk their lives for a Reb. Now, you've had the fever,[4] you like queer patients, your mate will see to your ward for a while, and I will find you a good attendant. The fellow won't last long, I fancy; but he can't die without some sort of care, you know. I've put him in the fourth story of the west wing, away from the rest. It is airy, quiet, and comfortable there. I'm on that ward, and will do my best for you in every way. Now, then, will you go?"

---

1. The story first appeared as "The Brothers" in the November 1863 *Atlantic Monthly*. Alcott objected to the title, which editor James T. Fields had insisted on, and she reprinted the story with her preferred title, along with other editorial changes, in *Hospital Sketches and Camp and Fireside Stories* (1869), the source of the text printed here. "Contraband": during the Civil War, the term referred to a slave who escaped to the Union side, or was taken by Union forces, and then was granted his or her freedom. The word also means "prohibited," which adds resonance to a title that could also refer to Nurse Dane's prohibited or forbidden thoughts.
2. Scrimped.
3. Short for "Rebel," term used by the Union side to describe Confederate soldiers.
4. I.e., to have immunities through antibodies.

"Of course I will, out of perversity, if not common charity; for some of these people think that because I'm an abolitionist I am also a heathen, and I should rather like to show them that, though I cannot quite love my enemies, I am willing to take care of them."

"Very good; I thought you'd go; and speaking of abolition reminds me that you can have a contraband for servant, if you like. It is that fine mulatto fellow who was found burying his rebel master after the fight, and, being badly cut over the head, our boys brought him along. Will you have him?"

"By all means,—for I'll stand to my guns on that point, as on the other; these black boys are far more faithful and handy than some of the white scamps given me to serve, instead of being served by. But is this man well enough?"

"Yes, for that sort of work, and I think you'll like him. He must have been a handsome fellow before he got his face slashed; not much darker than myself; his master's son, I dare say, and the white blood makes him rather high and haughty about some things. He was in a bad way when he came in, but vowed he'd die in the street rather than turn in with the black fellows below; so I put him up in the west wing, to be out of the way, and he's seen to the captain all the morning. When can you go up?"

"As soon as Tom is laid out, Skinner moved, Haywood washed, Marble dressed, Charley rubbed, Downs taken up, Upham laid down, and the whole forty fed."

We both laughed, though the Doctor was on his way to the dead-house and I held a shroud on my lap. But in a hospital one learns that cheerfulness is one's salvation; for, in an atmosphere of suffering and death, heaviness of heart would soon paralyze usefulness of hand, if the blessed gift of smiles had been denied us.

In an hour I took possession of my new charge, finding a dissipated-looking boy of nineteen or twenty raving in the solitary little room, with no one near him but the contraband in the room adjoining. Feeling decidedly more interest in the black man than in the white, yet remembering the Doctor's hint of his being "high and haughty," I glanced furtively at him as I scattered chloride of lime about the room to purify the air, and settled matters to suit myself. I had seen many contrabands, but never one so attractive as this. All colored men are called "boys," even if their heads are white; this boy was five-and-twenty at least, strong-limbed and manly, and had the look of one who never had been cowed by abuse or worn with oppressive labor. He sat on his bed doing nothing; no book, no pipe, no pen or paper anywhere appeared, yet anything less indolent or listless than his attitude and expression I never saw. Erect he sat, with a hand on either knee, and eyes fixed on the bare wall opposite, so rapt in some absorbing thought as to be unconscious of my presence, though the door stood wide open and my movements were by no means noiseless. His face was half averted, but I instantly approved the Doctor's taste, for the profile which I saw possessed all the attributes of comeliness belonging to his mixed race. He was more quadroon[5] than mulatto, with Saxon features, Spanish complexion darkened by exposure, color in lips and cheek, waving hair, and an eye full of the passionate melancholy which in such men always seems to utter a mute protest against the broken law

5. One-fourth black; a term used at the time to refer to a light-complected person of mixed racial ancestry.

that doomed them at their birth. What could he be thinking of? The sick boy cursed and raved, I rustled to and fro, steps passed the door, bells rang, and the steady rumble of army-wagons came up from the street, still he never stirred. I had seen colored people in what they call "the black sulks," when, for days, they neither smiled nor spoke, and scarcely ate. But this was something more than that; for the man was not dully brooding over some small grievance; he seemed to see an all-absorbing fact or fancy recorded on the wall, which was a blank to me. I wondered if it were some deep wrong or sorrow, kept alive by memory and impotent regret; if he mourned for the dead master to whom he had been faithful to the end; or if the liberty now his were robbed of half its sweetness by the knowledge that some one near and dear to him still languished in the hell from which he had escaped. My heart quite warmed to him at that idea; I wanted to know and comfort him; and, following the impulse of the moment, I went in and touched him on the shoulder.

In an instant the man vanished and the slave appeared. Freedom was too new a boon to have wrought its blessed changes yet; and as he started up, with his hand at his temple, and an obsequious "Yes, Missis," any romance that had gathered round him fled away, leaving the saddest of all sad facts in living guise before me. Not only did the manhood seem to die out of him, but the comeliness that first attracted me; for, as he turned, I saw the ghastly wound that had laid open cheek and forehead. Being partly healed, it was no longer bandaged, but held together with strips of that transparent plaster which I never see without a shiver, and swift recollections of the scenes with which it is associated in my mind. Part of his black hair had been shorn away, and one eye was nearly closed; pain so distorted, and the cruel sabre-cut so marred that portion of his face, that, when I saw it, I felt as if a fine medal had been suddenly reversed, showing me a far more striking type of human suffering and wrong than Michael Angelo's bronze prisoner.[6] By one of those inexplicable processes that often teach us how little we understand ourselves, my purpose was suddenly changed; and, though I went in to offer comfort as a friend, I merely gave an order as a mistress.

"Will you open these windows? this man needs more air."

He obeyed at once, and, as he slowly urged up the unruly sash, the handsome profile was again turned toward me, and again I was possessed by my first impression so strongly that I involuntarily said,—

"Thank you."

Perhaps it was fancy, but I thought that in the look of mingled surprise and something like reproach which he gave me, there was also a trace of grateful pleasure. But he said, in that tone of spiritless humility these poor souls learn so soon,—

"I isn't a white man, Missis, I'se a contraband."

"Yes, I know it; but a contraband is a free man, and I heartily congratulate you."

He liked that; his face shone, he squared his shoulders, lifted his head, and looked me full in the eye with a brisk,—

"Thank ye, Missis; anything more to do fer yer?"

"Doctor Franck thought you would help me with this man, as there are many patients and few nurses or attendants. Have you had the fever?"

6. "The Rebellious Slave," a sculpture by the Italian artist Michelangelo Buonarroti (1475–1564).

"No, Missis."

"They should have thought of that when they put him here; wounds and fevers should not be together. I'll try to get you moved."

He laughed a sudden laugh: if he had been a white man, I should have called it scornful; as he was a few shades darker than myself, I suppose it must be considered an insolent, or at least an unmannerly one.

"It don't matter, Missis. I'd rather be up here with the fever than down with those niggers; and there isn't no other place fer me."

Poor fellow! that was true. No ward in all the hospital would take him in to lie side by side with the most miserable white wreck there. Like the bat in Æsop's fable,[7] he belonged to neither race; and the pride of one and the helplessness of the other, kept him hovering alone in the twilight a great sin has brought to overshadow the whole land.

"You shall stay, then; for I would far rather have you than my lazy Jack. But are you well and strong enough?"

"I guess I'll do, Missis."

He spoke with a passive sort of acquiescence,—as if it did not much matter if he were not able, and no one would particularly rejoice if he were.

"Yes, I think you will. By what name shall I call you?"

"Bob, Missis."

Every woman has her pet whim; one of mine was to teach the men self-respect by treating them respectfully. Tom, Dick, and Harry would pass, when lads rejoiced in those familiar abbreviations; but to address men often old enough to be my father in that style did not suit my old-fashioned ideas of propriety. This "Bob" would never do; I should have found it as easy to call the chaplain "Gus" as my tragical-looking contraband by a title so strongly associated with the tail of a kite.[8]

"What is your other name?" I asked. "I like to call my attendants by their last names rather than by their first."

"I'se got no other, Missis; we has our masters' names, or do without. Mine's dead, and I won't have anything of his 'bout me."

"Well, I'll call you Robert, then, and you may fill this pitcher for me, if you will be so kind."

He went; but, through all the tame obedience years of servitude had taught him, I could see that the proud spirit his father gave him was not yet subdued, for the look and gesture with which he repudiated his master's name were a more effective declaration of independence than any Fourth-of-July orator could have prepared.

We spent a curious week together. Robert seldom left his room, except upon my errands; and I was a prisoner all day, often all night, by the bedside of the rebel. The fever burned itself rapidly away, for there seemed little vitality to feed it in the feeble frame of this old young man, whose life had been none of the most righteous, judging from the revelations made by his unconscious lips; since more than once Robert authoritatively silenced him, when my gentler hushings were of no avail, and blasphemous wanderings or ribald camp-songs made my cheeks burn and Robert's face assume an aspect of disgust. The captain was a gentleman in the world's eye, but the contra-

7. In a fable by the ancient Greek storyteller Aesop (c. 620–564 B.C.E.), during a war between birds and mammals, the bat takes turns fighting on either side and ends up an outcast.
8. The "bob" or weight on the kite tail provides balance.

band was the gentleman in mine;—I was a fanatic, and that accounts for such depravity of taste, I hope. I never asked Robert of himself, feeling that somewhere there was a spot still too sore to bear the lightest touch; but, from his language, manner, and intelligence, I inferred that his color had procured for him the few advantages within the reach of a quick-witted, kindly-treated slave. Silent, grave, and thoughtful, but most serviceable, was my contraband; glad of the books I brought him, faithful in the performance of the duties I assigned to him, grateful for the friendliness I could not but feel and show toward him. Often I longed to ask what purpose was so visibly altering his aspect with such daily deepening gloom. But I never dared, and no one else had either time or desire to pry into the past of this specimen of one branch of the chivalrous "F. F. Vs."[9]

On the seventh night, Dr. Franck suggested that it would be well for some one, besides the general watchman of the ward, to be with the captain, as it might be his last. Although the greater part of the two preceding nights had been spent there, of course I offered to remain,—for there is a strange fascination in these scenes, which renders one careless of fatigue and unconscious of fear until the crisis is past.

"Give him water as long as he can drink, and if he drops into a natural sleep, it may save him. I'll look in at midnight, when some change will probably take place. Nothing but sleep or a miracle will keep him now. Good-night."

Away went the Doctor; and, devouring a whole mouthful of grapes, I lowered the lamp, wet the captain's head, and sat down on a hard stool to begin my watch. The captain lay with his hot, haggard face turned toward me, filling the air with his poisonous breath, and feebly muttering, with lips and tongue so parched that the sanest speech would have been difficult to understand. Robert was stretched on his bed in the inner room, the door of which stood ajar, that a fresh draught from his open window might carry the fever-fumes away through mine. I could just see a long, dark figure, with the lighter outline of a face, and, having little else to do just then, I fell to thinking of this curious contraband, who evidently prized his freedom highly, yet seemed in no haste to enjoy it. Dr. Franck had offered to send him on to safer quarters, but he had said, "No, thank yer, sir, not yet," and then had gone away to fall into one of those black moods of his, which began to disturb me, because I had no power to lighten them. As I sat listening to the clocks from the steeples all about us, I amused myself with planning Robert's future, as I often did my own, and had dealt out to him a generous hand of trumps wherewith to play this game of life which hitherto had gone so cruelly against him, when a harsh choked voice called,—

"Lucy!"

It was the captain, and some new terror seemed to have gifted him with momentary strength.

"Yes, here's Lucy," I answered, hoping that by following the fancy I might quiet him,—for his face was damp with the clammy moisture, and his frame shaken with the nervous tremor that so often precedes death. His dull eye fixed upon me, dilating with a bewildered look of incredulity and wrath, till he broke out fiercely,—

9. First Families of Virginia (typically wealthy landowners, and usually descended from early settlers of the colony).

"That's a lie! she's dead,—and so's Bob, damn him!"

Finding speech a failure, I began to sing the quiet tune that had often soothed delirium like this; but hardly had the line,—

"See gentle patience smile on pain,"[1]

passed my lips, when he clutched me by the wrist, whispering like one in mortal fear,—

"Hush! she used to sing that way to Bob, but she never would to me. I swore I'd whip the devil out of her, and I did; but you know before she cut her throat she said she'd haunt me, and there she is!"

He pointed behind me with an aspect of such pale dismay, that I involuntarily glanced over my shoulder and started as if I had seen a veritable ghost; for, peering from the gloom of that inner room, I saw a shadowy face, with dark hair all about it, and a glimpse of scarlet at the throat. An instant showed me that it was only Robert leaning from his bed's foot, wrapped in a gray army-blanket, with his red shirt just visible above it, and his long hair disordered by sleep. But what a strange expression was on his face! The unmarred side was toward me, fixed and motionless as when I first observed it,—less absorbed now, but more intent. His eye glittered, his lips were apart like one who listened with every sense, and his whole aspect reminded me of a hound to which some wind had brought the scent of unsuspected prey.

"Do you know him, Robert? Does he mean you?"

"Laws, no, Missis; they all own half-a-dozen Bobs: but hearin' my name woke me; that's all."

He spoke quite naturally, and lay down again, while I returned to my charge, thinking that this paroxysm was probably his last. But by another hour I perceived a hopeful change; for the tremor had subsided, the cold dew was gone, his breathing was more regular, and Sleep, the healer, had descended to save or take him gently away. Doctor Franck looked in at midnight, bade me keep all cool and quiet, and not fail to administer a certain draught as soon as the captain woke. Very much relieved, I laid my head on my arms, uncomfortably folded on the little table, and fancied I was about to perform one of the feats which practice renders possible,—"sleeping with one eye open," as we say: a half-and-half doze, for all senses sleep but that of hearing; the faintest murmur, sigh, or motion will break it, and give one back one's wits much brightened by the brief permission to "stand at ease." On this night the experiment was a failure, for previous vigils, confinement, and much care had rendered naps a dangerous indulgence. Having roused half-a-dozen times in an hour to find all quiet, I dropped my heavy head on my arms, and, drowsily resolving to look up again in fifteen minutes, fell fast asleep.

The striking of a deep-voiced clock awoke me with a start. "That is one," thought I; but, to my dismay, two more strokes followed, and in remorseful haste I sprang up to see what harm my long oblivion had done. A strong hand put me back into my seat, and held me there. It was Robert. The instant my eye met his my heart began to beat, and all along my nerves tingled that electric flash which foretells a danger that we cannot see. He was very pale, his

---

1. From the song "See, Gentle Patience Smiles on Pain" (1835), words by the English poet Anne Steele (1716–1778) and arranged by Henry Kemble Oliver (1800–1885), from *The Boston Academy's Collection of Church Music* (1836).

mouth grim, and both eyes full of somber fire; for even the wounded one was open now, all the more sinister for the deep scar above and below. But his touch was steady, his voice quiet, as he said,—

"Sit still, Missis; I won't hurt yer, nor scare yer, ef I can help it, but yer waked too soon."

"Let me go, Robert,—the captain is stirring,—I must give him something."

"No, Missis, yer can't stir an inch. Look here!"

Holding me with one hand, with the other he took up the glass in which I had left the draught, and showed me it was empty.

"Has he taken it?" I asked, more and more bewildered.

"I flung it out o' winder, Missis; he'll have to do without."

"But why, Robert? why did you do it?"

"'Kase I hate him!"

Impossible to doubt the truth of that; his whole face showed it, as he spoke through his set teeth, and launched a fiery glance at the unconscious captain. I could only hold my breath and stare blankly at him, wondering what mad act was coming next. I suppose I shook and turned white, as women have a foolish habit of doing when sudden danger daunts them; for Robert released my arm, sat down upon the bedside just in front of me, and said, with the ominous quietude that made me cold to see and hear,—

"Don't yer be frightened, Missis; don't try to run away, fer the door's locked and the key in my pocket; don't yer cry out, fer yer'd have to scream a long while, with my hand on yer mouth, 'efore yer was heard. Be still, an' I'll tell yer what I'm gwine to do."

"Lord help us! he has taken the fever in some sudden, violent way, and is out of his head. I must humor him till some one comes"; in pursuance of which swift determination, I tried to say, quite composedly,—

"I will be still and hear you; but open the window. Why did you shut it?"

"I'm sorry I can't do it, Missis; but yer'd jump out, or call, if I did, an' I'm not ready yet. I shut it to make yer sleep, an' heat would do it quicker'n anything else I could do."

The captain moved, and feebly muttered "Water!" Instinctively I rose to give it to him, but the heavy hand came down upon my shoulder, and in the same decided tone Robert said,—

"The water went with the physic;[2] let him call."

"Do let me go to him! he'll die without care!"

"I mean he shall;—don't yer meddle, ef yer please, Missis."

In spite of his quiet tone and respectful manner, I saw murder in his eyes, and turned faint with fear; yet the fear excited me, and, hardly knowing what I did, I seized the hands that had seized me, crying,—

"No, no; you shall not kill him! It is base to hurt a helpless man. Why do you hate him? He is not your master."

"He's my brother."

I felt that answer from head to foot, and seemed to fathom what was coming, with a prescience vague, but unmistakable. One appeal was left to me, and I made it.

2. Medicine.

"Robert, tell me what it means? Do not commit a crime and make me accessory to it. There is a better way of righting wrong than by violence;— let me help you find it."

My voice trembled as I spoke, and I heard the frightened flutter of my heart; so did he, and if any little act of mine had ever won affection or respect from him, the memory of it served me then. He looked down, and seemed to put some question to himself; whatever it was, the answer was in my favor, for when his eyes rose again, they were gloomy, but not desperate.

"I *will* tell yer, Missis; but mind, this makes no difference; the boy is mine. I'll give the Lord a chance to take him fust: if He don't, I shall."

"Oh, no! remember he is your brother."

An unwise speech; I felt it as it passed my lips, for a black frown gathered on Robert's face, and his strong hands closed with an ugly sort of grip. But he did not touch the poor soul gasping there behind him, and seemed content to let the slow suffocation of that stifling room end his frail life.

"I'm not like to forget dat, Missis, when I've been thinkin' of it all this week. I knew him when they fetched him in, an' would 'a' done it long 'fore this, but I wanted to ask where Lucy was; he knows,—he told to-night,—an' now he's done for."

"Who is Lucy?" I asked hurriedly, intent on keeping his mind busy with any thought but murder.

With one of the swift transitions of a mixed temperament like this, at my question Robert's deep eyes filled, the clenched hands were spread before his face, and all I heard were the broken words,—

"My wife,—he took her——"

In that instant every thought of fear was swallowed up in burning indignation for the wrong, and a perfect passion of pity for the desperate man so tempted to avenge an injury for which there seemed no redress but this. He was no longer slave or contraband, no drop of black blood marred him in my sight, but an infinite compassion yearned to save, to help, to comfort him. Words seemed so powerless I offered none, only put my hand on his poor head, wounded, homeless, bowed down with grief for which I had no cure, and softly smoothed the long, neglected hair, pitifully wondering the while where was the wife who must have loved this tender-hearted man so well.

The captain moaned again, and faintly whispered, "Air!" but I never stirred. God forgive me! just then I hated him as only a woman thinking of a sister woman's wrong could hate. Robert looked up; his eyes were dry again, his mouth grim. I saw that, said, "Tell me more," and he did; for sympathy is a gift the poorest may give, the proudest stoop to receive.

"Yer see, Missis, his father,—I might say ours, ef I warn't ashamed of both of 'em,—his father died two years ago, an' left us all to Marster Ned,— that's him here, eighteen then. He always hated me, I looked so like old Marster: he don't,—only the light skin an' hair. Old Marster was kind to all of us, me 'specially, an' bought Lucy off the next plantation down there in South Car'lina, when he found I liked her. I married her, all I could;[3] it warn't much, but we was true to one another till Marster Ned come home a year after an' made hell fer both of us. He sent my old mother to be used up in his rice-swamp in Georgy; he found me with my pretty Lucy, an' though young

---

3. Southern states did not recognize slave marriages as having legal standing.

Miss cried, an' I prayed to him on my knees, an' Lucy run away, he wouldn't have no mercy; he brought her back, an'—took her."

"Oh, what did you do?" I cried, hot with helpless pain and passion.

How the man's outraged heart sent the blood flaming up into his face and deepened the tones of his impetuous voice, as he stretched his arm across the bed, saying, with a terribly expressive gesture,—

"I half murdered him, an' to-night I'll finish."

"Yes, yes,—but go on now; what came next?"

He gave me a look that showed no white man could have felt a deeper degradation in remembering and confessing these last acts of brotherly oppression.

"They whipped me till I couldn't stand, an' then they sold me further South. Yer thought I was a white man once,—look here!"

With a sudden wrench he tore the shirt from neck to waist, and on his strong, brown shoulders showed me furrows deeply ploughed, wounds which, though healed, were ghastlier to me than any in that house. I could not speak to him, and, with the pathetic dignity a great grief lends the humblest sufferer, he ended his brief tragedy by simply saying,—

"That's all, Missis. I'se never seen her since, an' now I never shall in this world,—maybe not in t'other."

"But, Robert, why think her dead? The captain was wandering when he said those sad things; perhaps he will retract them when he is sane. Don't despair; don't give up yet."

"No, Missis, I'spect he's right; she was too proud to bear that long. It's like her to kill herself. I told her to, if there was no other way; an' she always minded me, Lucy did. My poor girl! Oh, it warn't right! No, by God, it warn't!"

As the memory of this bitter wrong, this double bereavement, burned in his sore heart, the devil that lurks in every strong man's blood leaped up; he put his hand upon his brother's throat, and, watching the white face before him, muttered low between his teeth,—

"I'm lettin' him go too easy; there's no pain in this; we a'n't even yet. I wish he knew me. Marster Ned! it's Bob; where's Lucy?"

From the captain's lips there came a long faint sigh, and nothing but a flutter of the eyelids showed that he still lived. A strange stillness filled the room as the elder brother held the younger's life suspended in his hand, while wavering between a dim hope and a deadly hate. In the whirl of thoughts that went on in my brain, only one was clear enough to act upon. I must prevent murder, if I could,—but how? What could I do up there alone, locked in with a dying man and a lunatic?—for any mind yielded utterly to any unrighteous impulse is mad while the impulse rules it. Strength I had not, nor much courage, neither time nor wit for stratagem, and chance only could bring me help before it was too late. But one weapon I possessed,—a tongue,—often a woman's best defence; and sympathy, stronger than fear, gave me power to use it. What I said Heaven only knows, but surely Heaven helped me; words burned on my lips, tears streamed from my eyes, and some good angel prompted me to use the one name that had power to arrest my hearer's hand and touch his heart. For at that moment I heartily believed that Lucy lived, and this earnest faith roused in him a like belief.

He listened with the lowering look of one in whom brute instinct was sovereign for the time,—a look that makes the noblest countenance base. He was but a man,—a poor, untaught, outcast, outraged man. Life had few joys for him; the world offered him no honors, no success, no home, no love. What future would this crime mar? and why should he deny himself that sweet, yet bitter morsel called revenge? How many white men, with all New England's freedom, culture, Christianity, would not have felt as he felt then? Should I have reproached him for a human anguish, a human longing for redress, all now left him from the ruin of his few poor hopes? Who had taught him that self-control, self-sacrifice, are attributes that make men masters of the earth, and lift them nearer heaven? Should I have urged the beauty of forgiveness, the duty of devout submission? He had no religion, for he was no saintly "Uncle Tom,"[4] and Slavery's black shadow seemed to darken all the world to him, and shut out God. Should I have warned him of penalties, of judgments, and the potency of law? What did he know of justice, or the mercy that should temper that stern virtue, when every law, human and divine, had been broken on his hearthstone? Should I have tried to touch him by appeals to filial duty, to brotherly love? How had his appeals been answered? What memories had father and brother stored up in his heart to plead for either now? No,—all these influences, these associations, would have proved worse than useless, had I been calm enough to try them. I was not; but instinct, subtler than reason, showed me the one safe clue by which to lead this troubled soul from the labyrinth in which it groped and nearly fell. When I paused, breathless, Robert turned to me, asking, as if human assurances could strengthen his faith in Divine Omnipotence,—

"Do you believe, if I let Marster Ned live, the Lord will give me back my Lucy?"

"As surely as there is a Lord, you will find her here or in the beautiful hereafter, where there is no black or white, no master and no slave."

He took his hand from his brother's throat, lifted his eyes from my face to the wintry sky beyond, as if searching for that blessed country, happier even than the happy North. Alas, it was the darkest hour before the dawn!— there was no star above, no light below but the pale glimmer of the lamp that showed the brother who had made him desolate. Like a blind man who believes there is a sun, yet cannot see it, he shook his head, let his arms drop nervelessly upon his knees, and sat there dumbly asking that question which many a soul whose faith is firmer fixed than his has asked in hours less dark than this,—"Where is God?" I saw the tide had turned, and strenuously tried to keep this rudderless life-boat from slipping back into the whirlpool wherein it had been so nearly lost.

"I have listened to you, Robert; now hear me, and heed what I say, because my heart is full of pity for you, full of hope for your future, and a desire to help you now. I want you to go away from here, from the temptation of this place, and the sad thoughts that haunt it. You have conquered yourself once, and I honor you for it, because, the harder the battle, the more glorious the victory; but it is safer to put a greater distance between you and this man. I will write you letters, give you money, and send you to good old Massachu- setts to begin your new life a freeman,—yes, and a happy man; for when the captain is himself again, I will learn where Lucy is, and move heaven and earth to find and give her back to you. Will you do this, Robert?"

Slowly, very slowly, the answer came; for the purpose of a week, perhaps a year, was hard to relinquish in an hour.

---

4. Reference to the black Christian hero of Harriet Beecher Stowe's novel *Uncle Tom's Cabin* (1852).

"Yes, Missis, I will."

"Good! Now you are the man I thought you, and I'll work for you with all my heart. You need sleep, my poor fellow; go, and try to forget. The captain is alive, and as yet you are spared that sin. No, don't look there; I'll care for him. Come, Robert, for Lucy's sake."

Thank Heaven for the immortality of love! for when all other means of salvation failed, a spark of this vital fire softened the man's iron will, until a woman's hand could bend it. He let me take from him the key, let me draw him gently away, and lead him to the solitude which now was the most healing balm I could bestow. Once in his little room, he fell down on his bed and lay there, as if spent with the sharpest conflict of his life. I slipped the bolt across his door, and unlocked my own, flung up the window, steadied myself with a breath of air, then rushed to Doctor Franck. He came; and till dawn we worked together, saving one brother's life, and taking earnest thought how best to secure the other's liberty. When the sun came up as blithely as if it shone only upon happy homes, the Doctor went to Robert. For an hour I heard the murmur of their voices; once I caught the sound of heavy sobs, and for a time a reverent hush, as if in the silence that good man were ministering to soul as well as body. When he departed he took Robert with him, pausing to tell me he should get him off as soon as possible, but not before we met again.

Nothing more was seen of them all day; another surgeon came to see the captain, and another attendant came to fill the empty place. I tried to rest, but could not, with the thought of poor Lucy tugging at my heart, and was soon back at my post again, anxiously hoping that my contraband had not been too hastily spirited away. Just as night fell there came a tap, and, opening, I saw Robert literally "clothed, and in his right mind."[5] The Doctor had replaced the ragged suit with tidy garments, and no trace of that tempestuous night remained but deeper lines upon the forehead, and the docile look of a repentant child. He did not cross the threshold, did not offer me his hand,—only took off his cap, saying, with a traitorous falter in his voice,—

"God bless yer, Missis! I'm gwine."

I put out both my hands, and held his fast.

"Good-by, Robert! Keep up good heart, and when I come home to Massachusetts we'll meet in a happier place than this. Are you quite ready, quite comfortable for your journey?"

"Yes, Missis, yes; the Doctor's fixed everything; I'se gwine with a friend of his; my papers are all right, an' I'm as happy as I can be till I find"——

He stopped there; then went on, with a glance into the room,—

"I'm glad I didn't do it, an' I thank yer, Missis, fer hinderin' me,—thank yer hearty; but I'm afraid I hate him jest the same."

Of course he did; and so did I; for these faulty hearts of ours cannot turn perfect in a night, but need frost and fire, wind and rain, to ripen and make them ready for the great harvest-home. Wishing to divert his mind, I put my poor mite[6] into his hand, and, remembering the magic of a certain little book, I gave him mine, on whose dark cover whitely shone the Virgin Mother and the Child, the grand history of whose life the book contained. The money went into Robert's pocket with a grateful murmur, the book into his bosom, with a long look and a tremulous—

---

5. Refers to a follower of Jesus who had formerly been wild and demonical; see Mark 5.15.

6. Small amount of money.

"I never saw *my* baby, Missis."

I broke down then; and though my eyes were too dim to see, I felt the touch of lips upon my hands, heard the sound of departing feet, and knew my contraband was gone.

When one feels an intense dislike, the less one says about the subject of it the better; therefore I shall merely record that the captain lived,—in time was exchanged;[7] and that, whoever the other party was, I am convinced the Government got the best of the bargain. But long before this occurred, I had fulfilled my promise to Robert; for as soon as my patient recovered strength of memory enough to make his answer trustworthy, I asked, without any circumlocution,—

"Captain Fairfax, where is Lucy?"

And too feeble to be angry, surprised, or insincere, he straightway answered,—

"Dead, Miss Dane."

"And she killed herself when you sold Bob?"

"How the devil did you know that?" he muttered, with an expression half-remorseful, half-amazed; but I was satisfied, and said no more.

Of course this went to Robert, waiting far away there in a lonely home,— waiting, working, hoping for his Lucy. It almost broke my heart to do it; but delay was weak, deceit was wicked; so I sent the heavy tidings, and very soon the answer came,—only three lines; but I felt that the sustaining power of the man's life was gone.

"I tort I'd never see her any more; I'm glad to know she's out of trouble. I thank yer, Missis; an' if they let us, I'll fight fer yer till I'm killed, which I hope will be 'fore long."

Six months later he had his wish, and kept his word.

Every one knows the story of the attack on Fort Wagner; but we should not tire yet of recalling how our Fifty-Fourth,[8] spent with three sleepless nights, a day's fast, and a march under the July sun, stormed the fort as night fell, facing death in many shapes, following their brave leaders through a fiery rain of shot and shell, fighting valiantly for "God and Governor Andrew,"— how the regiment that went into action seven hundred strong, came out having had nearly half its number captured, killed, or wounded, leaving their young commander to be buried, like a chief of earlier times, with his body-guard around him, faithful to the death. Surely, the insult turns to honor, and the wide grave needs no monument but the heroism that consecrates it in our sight; surely, the hearts that held him nearest, see through their tears a noble victory in the seeming sad defeat; and surely, God's benediction was bestowed, when this loyal soul answered, as Death called the roll, "Lord, here am I, with the brothers Thou hast given me!"

The future must show how well that fight was fought; for though Fort Wagner once defied us, public prejudice is down; and through the cannon-smoke of that black night, the manhood of the colored race shines before many eyes that would not see, rings in many ears that would not hear, wins many hearts that would not hitherto believe.

7. The "exchange" would have been for a captured Union officer.
8. The Fifty-Fourth Massachusetts Voluntary Infantry, a black regiment led by the white captain Robert Gould Shaw (1837–1863), made a valiant but failed attack on Fort Wagner, near Charleston, South Carolina, in July 1863. Shaw and a number of the black soldiers were killed during the battle. The first black troops were organized with the help of abolitionist John Albion Andrew (1818–1867), governor of Massachusetts.

When the news came that we were needed, there was none so glad as I to leave teaching contrabands, the new work I had taken up, and go to nurse "our boys," as my dusky flock so proudly called the wounded of the Fifty-Fourth. Feeling more satisfaction, as I assumed my big apron and turned up my cuffs, than if dressing for the President's levee,[9] I fell to work in Hospital No. 10 at Beaufort.[1] The scene was most familiar, and yet strange; for only dark faces looked up at me from the pallets so thickly laid along the floor, and I missed the sharp accent of my Yankee boys in the slower, softer voices calling cheerily to one another, or answering my questions with a stout, "We'll never give it up, Missis, till the last Reb's dead," or, "If our people's free, we can afford to die."

Passing from bed to bed, intent on making one pair of hands do the work of three, at least, I gradually washed, fed, and bandaged my way down the long line of sable heroes, and coming to the very last, found that he was my contraband. So old, so worn, so deathly weak and wan, I never should have known him but for the deep scar on his cheek. That side lay uppermost, and caught my eye at once; but even then I doubted, such an awful change had come upon him, when, turning to the ticket just above his head, I saw the name, "Robert Dane." That both assured and touched me, for, remembering that he had no name, I knew that he had taken mine. I longed for him to speak to me, to tell how he had fared since I lost sight of him, and let me perform some little service for him in return for many he had done for me; but he seemed asleep; and as I stood re-living that strange night again, a bright lad, who lay next him softly waving an old fan across both beds, looked up and said,—

"I guess you know him, Missis?"

"You are right. Do you?"

"As much as any one was able to, Missis."

"Why do you say 'was,' as if the man were dead and gone?"

"I s'pose because I know he'll have to go. He's got a bad jab in the breast, an' is bleedin' inside, the Doctor says. He don't suffer any, only gets weaker 'n' weaker every minute. I've been fannin' him this long while, an' he's talked a little; but he don't know me now, so he's most gone, I guess."

There was so much sorrow and affection in the boy's face, that I remembered something, and asked, with redoubled interest,—

"Are you the one that brought him off? I was told about a boy who nearly lost his life in saving that of his mate."

I dare say the young fellow blushed, as any modest lad might have done; I could not see it, but I heard the chuckle of satisfaction that escaped him, as he glanced from his shattered arm and bandaged side to the pale figure opposite.

"Lord, Missis, that's nothin'; we boys always stan' by one another, an' I warn't goin' to leave him to be tormented any more by them cussed Rebs. He's been a slave once, though he don't look half so much like it as me, an' I was born in Boston."

He did not; for the speaker was as black as the ace of spades,—being a sturdy specimen, the knave of clubs would perhaps be a fitter representative,—but the dark freeman looked at the white slave with the pitiful, yet puzzled expression I have so often seen on the faces of our wisest men, when this tangled question of Slavery presented itself, asking to be cut or patiently undone.

"Tell me what you know of this man; for, even if he were awake, he is too weak to talk."

"I never saw him till I joined the regiment, an' no one 'peared to have got much out of him. He was a shut-up sort of feller, an' didn't seem to care for anything but gettin' at the Rebs. Some say he was the fust man of us that enlisted; I know he fretted till we were off, an' when we pitched into old Wagner, he fought like the devil."

"Were you with him when he was wounded? How was it?"

"Yes, Missis. There was somethin' queer about it; for he 'peared to know the chap that killed him, an' the chap knew him. I don't dare to ask, but I rather guess one owned the other some time; for, when they clinched, the chap sung out, 'Bob!' an' Dane, 'Marster Ned!'—then they went at it."

I sat down suddenly, for the old anger and compassion struggled in my heart, and I both longed and feared to hear what was to follow.

"You see, when the Colonel,—Lord keep an' send him back to us!—it a'n't certain yet, you know, Missis, though it's two days ago we lost him,—well, when the Colonel shouted, 'Rush on, boys, rush on!' Dane tore away as if he was goin' to take the fort alone; I was next him, an' kept close as we went through the ditch an' up the wall. Hi! warn't that a rusher!" and the boy flung up his well arm with a whoop, as if the mere memory of that stirring moment came over him in a gust of irrepressible excitement.

"Were you afraid?" I said, asking the question women often put, and receiving the answer they seldom fail to get.

"No, Missis!"—emphasis on the "Missis"—"I never thought of anything but the damn' Rebs, that scalp, slash, an' cut our ears off, when they git us. I was bound to let daylight into one of 'em at least, an' I did. Hope he liked it!"

"It is evident that you did. Now go on about Robert, for I should be at work."

"He was one of the fust up; I was just behind, an' though the whole thing happened in a minute, I remember how it was, for all I was yellin' an' knockin' round like mad. Just where we were, some sort of an officer was wavin' his sword an' cheerin' on his men; Dane saw him by a big flash that come by; he flung away his gun, give a leap, an' went at that feller as if he was Jeff, Beauregard, an' Lee, all in one.[2] I scrabbled after as quick as I could, but was only up in time to see him git the sword straight through him an' drop into the ditch. You needn't ask what I did next, Missis, for I don't quite know myself; all I'm clear about is, that I managed somehow to pitch that Reb into the fort as dead as Moses, git hold of Dane, an' bring him off. Poor old feller! we said we went in to live or die; he said he went in to die, an' he's done it."

I had been intently watching the excited speaker; but as he regretfully added those last words I turned again, and Robert's eyes met mine,—those melancholy eyes, so full of an intelligence that proved he had heard, remembered, and reflected with that preternatural power which often outlives all other faculties. He knew me, yet gave no greeting; was glad to see a woman's face, yet had no smile wherewith to welcome it; felt that he was dying, yet uttered no farewell. He was too far across the river to return or linger now;

---

2. Political and military leaders of the Confederacy: Jefferson Davis (1808–1889) was president of the Confederate States of America (1861–65), and P. G. T. Beauregard (1818–1893) and Robert E. Lee (1807–1870) were his key military commanders.

departing thought, strength, breath, were spent in one grateful look, one murmur of submission to the last pang he could ever feel. His lips moved, and, bending to them, a whisper chilled my cheek, as it shaped the broken words,—

"I'd 'a' done it,—but it's better so,—I'm satisfied."

Ah! well he might be,—for, as he turned his face from the shadow of the life that was, the sunshine of the life to be touched it with a beautiful content, and in the drawing of a breath my contraband found wife and home, eternal liberty and God.

1863   1869

American Literature
1865–1914

THE TRANSFORMATION OF A NATION

From the earliest moment of settlement in what would become the United States, the nation's borders were relentlessly pushed westward. Thomas Jefferson's Louisiana Purchase (1803) added a huge swath of territory west of the Alleghenies; the outcome of the Mexican War (1846–48) brought the entire Southwest, including California, into the nation; and the discovery of gold in California in 1848 increased the pace of westward movement beyond anything that could have been imagined even one year earlier. White Americans, mostly of English, Scottish, German, and French descent, settled across these regions, increasing the pace by which the U.S. government was forcibly relocating Native American tribes—the term was Removal and the practice had begun in the 1830s—from their homelands to places further west, and attempting to force Hispanic Americans south of the new border with Mexico. As these settlers moved into the extensive terrain west of the Mississippi River, they leveled vast stands of timber, exterminated the buffalo and other wild game in favor of cattle and sheep, and established farms, villages, cities and the railroads that linked them to markets in the Midwest and East. New technologies converted the country's immense natural resources into industrial products both for its own burgeoning population and for foreign consumers.

The Civil War (1861–65), the seemingly inevitable result of growing economic, political, social, and cultural divisions between North and South, cost some eight billion dollars and claimed more than six hundred thousand lives. Its savagery seems also to have left the country morally exhausted. Nevertheless, the country

Children Sleeping in Mulberry Street, 1890, Jacob Riis. For more information about this image, see the color insert in this volume.

Golden Spike Ceremony. Joining the tracks for the first transcontinental railroad, Promontory, Utah Territory, 1869.

prospered materially over the next five decades, as the war effort had stimulated innovations in methods of efficiently moving large numbers of people, raw materials, and goods. The first transcontinental railroad, completed in 1869 with the use of poorly paid laborers from China brought in through Western seaports—especially in San Francisco and Seattle—made it possible to cross the country quickly and inexpensively. The railroad also allowed for rapid, inexpensive shipments of goods, thereby moving the American economy itself into the industrial age, once and for all. The telegraph, introduced in the 1840s, now ran into small towns (many of them newly settled); electricity was introduced on a large scale; and around the end of the nineteenth century the telephone began to revolutionize daily life. Coal, oil, iron, gold, silver, and other kinds of mineral wealth were discovered and extracted, producing many individual fortunes that helped to capitalize further development. Such development required more people, preferably (from the point of view of employers) in numbers sufficient to keep down the cost of labor. Often lured by advertisements from railroad and land companies, immigrants arrived in the United States from the Scandinavian countries beginning in the 1870s and 1880s, and in the 1880s to the turn of the century and beyond, from eastern and southern European countries like Italy, Poland, Czechoslovakia, Lithuania, and Russia. Many European newcomers, taking advantage of the railroads, went to the plains to farm; but most became urban dwellers, causing enormous population growth in such cities as New York, Boston, and Chicago at the same time that Chinese and then Japanese immigrants hastened the growth of San Francisco and other Western cities.

The historian Frederick Jackson Turner declared in 1893 that the Western frontier, which he regarded as crucial to the formation of America's democratic character, no longer existed. He based his analysis on the census of

Ellis Island. Staff interviewing new immigrants, c. 1910. From 1892 to 1954,
New York's Ellis Island was the gateway for millions of immigrants to the United States.

1890, which found no place in the United States with fewer than two people
per square mile. (Native Americans were not counted in this estimate.) Now
the United States, eager to compete with European nations, attempted to
expand its influence beyond its continental borders, looking to gain the former Spanish possessions of Cuba, Puerto Rico, and the Philippines following
the Spanish-American War in 1898. U.S. colonization also included Hawaii,
annexed as a colony in 1898. The effects of American expansionism had long
been experienced by indigenous peoples. From the time of the earliest treaties with the United States, Native nations agreed to cede large tracts of land
with some territory specifically "reserved" for themselves. What we currently
think of as Indian reservations came about as a result of President Ulysses S.
Grant's policies of the late 1860s, which sought—and mostly forced—the
agreement of various Native nations to limit themselves to lands designated
by the federal government. Around this time, anthropologists (then known as
ethnologists) began to study tribal lifeways, especially of the Zuni and other
tribes of the Southwest. In 1883, two years after Helen Hunt Jackson's *A
Century of Dishonor* surveyed the history of whites' treaty-breaking behavior
with the Indians, an organization of eastern philanthropists calling itself
"Friends of the Indian" began to agitate in favor of assimilating Native Americans into the white mainstream. This organization meant well, but its methods inevitably devalued Native ways of life in favor of white schooling, white
patterns of town settlement and agriculture, and above all white religion.
Throughout this period, however, Native writers such as Zitkala Ša (Gertrude Simmons Bonnin), a Lakota woman, insisted on contributing to the
national discussion, speaking in their own voices in published texts as they
had been doing at least since the 1830s.

At the same time that the frontier came to be regarded as a crucial constituent of American identity, industrialization on a scale unprecedented

in Great Britain and Europe came to the fore in the United States. (Some historians believe that the frontier myth served to mask the reality of the industrial economy.) Between 1850 and 1880, capital invested in manufacturing more than quadrupled and factory employment nearly doubled. By 1885 four transcontinental railroad lines had been completed, using in their own construction and carrying to manufacturing centers in Cleveland and Detroit the nation's quintupled output of steel from Pittsburgh and Chicago. Major industries were consolidated into monopolies, allowing a small number of men to control such enormously profitable enterprises as steel, oil, railroads, meatpacking, banking, and finance, among them Jay Gould, Jim Hill, Leland Stanford, Cornelius Vanderbilt, Andrew Carnegie, J. P. Morgan, and John D. Rockefeller. Called "robber barons" by some and celebrated as captains of industry by others, these men squeezed out competitors and accumulated vast wealth and power. The new millionaires formed a wealthy class whose style of life, reported on in the mass media, offered a startling contrast to the lives of ordinary people.

But the ordinary was by the end of the century a quite different thing from what it had been before or shortly after the Civil War. In 1865 the United States, except for the manufacturing centers of the northeastern seaboard, was still a country of farms, villages, and small towns. Manufacturing was more a matter of workshops than factories. In 1870 the U.S. population was 38.5 million; by 1910, 92 million; by 1920, 123 million. This increase in population was due almost entirely to the arrival of immigrants from southern and eastern Europe: Russia, Poland, Italy, and the Balkan nations. The percentage of city versus country dwellers was reversed as cities like New York grew from half a million to nearly 3.5 million between 1865 and the turn of the twentieth century. Chicago, with a population of only 29,000 in 1850, had more than 2 million inhabitants by 1910. These immigrants and their descendants enabled the United States to become an urban, industrial, international, capitalist power while altering the ethnic composition of the still mostly white population and contributing immeasurably, albeit not without considerable conflict, to the democratization of the nation's cultural life. By 1890, New Englanders and their now-scattered descendants were no longer numerically dominant.

This transformation of the continent brought hardships for many. Farmers in the Midwest and High Plains depended on the railroads for transport of their crops but were squeezed off the land by the pricing policies of these very same railroads—what the novelist Frank Norris characterized as the giant "octopus" of corporate power wielded by the Southern Pacific and other railroads. Though the Homestead Act of 1862 promised free or cheap acreage to every individual or family who would settle and "improve" land according to a set formula, much of the available land was donated to railroads to encourage their growth. Speculators bought land as well. It is estimated that only 10 percent of the land opened by the Homestead Act actually went to would-be independent farmers. Buying at high prices, or forced to rent, such farmers were "under the lion's paw," as the midwestern writer Hamlin Garland put it, of land speculators and absentee landlords, or faced with mortgage payments they could not make. Large-scale farming took over from the family farm, increasing agricultural yields but displacing many farmers who joined the population of the cities. These cities were also, as the socialist novelists Jack London and Upton Sinclair argued—adapting the ideas of Darwin to the social field—"jungles" where only the strongest, most ruthless, and luckiest survived. Wages were low, and workers faced inhumane and dangerous working conditions; at this time there were few laws regulating safety and working hours. In addition, the 1890s saw severe economic depressions caused by changes to the gold standard, overspeculation by banks and investors in railroads, sporadic droughts, and foreign debts.

Neither farmers nor urban laborers organized effectively to pursue their own interests. Legislators usually favored business and industry, sometimes in the honest belief that a healthy economy required capitalism, sometimes via bribery and kickbacks—as in President Ulysses S. Grant's administration, or in the looting of the New York City treasury by William Marcy ("Boss") Tweed in the 1870s, or in municipal corruption cases exposed by the journalist Lincoln Steffens and other "muckrakers" including Stephen Crane and Frank Norris. Early attempts by labor to organize were often violent, and such groups as the terroristic "Molly Maguires," active in the 1870s and 1880s in the coal-mining area of northeastern Pennsylvania, bolstered the conviction of those who believed in open markets and free enterprise that labor organizations were un-American. Industrial workers had little political leverage before the 1880s, when the American Federation of Labor emerged as the first unified voice of workers. But not until collective bargaining legislation was enacted in the 1930s did labor acquire the right to strike. As for farmers, their organizing efforts involved experiments in cooperative farming and storage, which usually failed—partly for lack of funds but also because of the long tradition of independence among agricultural people. It was with the hope of owning one's own land that immigrants and native-born white people had moved to the prairies in the first place. On the other hand, individual ownership of land parcels was forced on many Native American nations through the Dawes Allotment Act of 1887—an outgrowth of "Friends of the Indian" policies. Whatever the intentions of the Dawes Act, it fragmented the collectively held Native lands and reduced the Native land base by some 90 million acres.

THE LITERARY MARKETPLACE

The rapid transcontinental settlement and new urban industrial conditions summarized above had a significant impact on the literature of the time. New themes, new forms, new subjects, new regions, new authors, and new audiences all emerged in the half century following the Civil War. In fiction, characters rarely represented before the Civil War became familiar figures: industrial workers and the rural poor, ambitious business leaders and vagrants, prostitutes and unheroic soldiers. Women from many social groups, African Americans, Native Americans, ethnic minorities, immigrants: all wrote for publication, and a rapidly burgeoning market for printed works helped establish authorship as a possible career for many.

Newspapers had been important to the political, social, and cultural life of America since colonial times, but after the Civil War their numbers and influence grew. Joseph Pulitzer established the St. Louis *Post-Dispatch* in 1878, and in 1883 he bought the New York *World;* both papers were hugely successful. William Randolph Hearst, a Californian who inherited a fortune from his mining entrepreneur father, made the San Francisco *Examiner* the dominant newspaper in California, then bought the New York *Journal* in 1895 to compete with Pulitzer's *World,* and gradually acquired newspapers across the country. In 1897 the *Jewish Daily Forward,* in Yiddish, was founded by Abraham Cahan; its circulation eventually reached 250,000, and it was read by three or four times that number. Many of the noted authors of the period started as newspaper journalists: Abraham Cahan, Ambrose Bierce, Stephen Crane, Theodore Dreiser, Jack London, Sui Sin Far, Joel Chandler Harris, William Dean Howells, Frank Norris, and Mark Twain among them. Perhaps of equal importance to the development of literary careers and literature as an American institution was the establishment of newspaper syndicates in the 1880s by Irving Bachellor and S. S. McClure. These syndicates distributed material to newspapers and magazines in all sections of the country, publishing humor, news, and serialized novels such as Crane's *The Red Badge of Courage.*

Magazines had become important in American life by the mid-eighteenth century, but they too increased in number and scope. New York City and Boston magazines such as *Harper's New Monthly Magazine* (1850), *Scribner's Monthly* (1870), *Century Illustrated Monthly Magazine* (1881), the *Atlantic Monthly* (1857), and the *Galaxy* (1866) published work by Kate Chopin, Sarah Orne Jewett, Henry James, William Dean Howells, Charles Chesnutt, Sui Sin Far, Zitkala Ša, and Mark Twain. In San Francisco, the *Overland Monthly* (1868) emerged as the leading western literary periodical with a regional focus; it published Bret Harte, Ambrose Bierce, Jack London, Mary Austin, Sui Sin Far, and Mark Twain among others. Without these periodicals, many writers would not have been able to support themselves; the income and audiences were crucial to the further formation of the complex literary tradition of a vast nation undergoing modernization.

Periodicals also contributed to the emergence of what the critic Warner Berthoff has called "the literature of argument"—writings in sociology, philosophy, and psychology impelled by the spirit of exposure and reform. It would be hard to exaggerate the influence—on other writers as well as on the educated public—of works such as Henry George's *Progress and Poverty* (1879), Henry Demarest Lloyd's *Wealth against Commonwealth* (1894), Charlotte Perkins Gilman's *Women and Economics* (1898), Thorstein Veblen's *The Theory of the Leisure Class* (1899), and William James's *The Varieties of Religious Experience* (1902). For many women writers, magazines provided an important public space for exploring new perspectives on gender and women's rights.

As the United States became an international political, economic, and military power during this half century, editors and readers welcomed (in translation) works by the leading European figures of the time, such as Russians Leo Tolstoy and Anton Chekhov, Norwegian playwright Henrik Ibsen, and French novelist Émile Zola. American writers during this period increasingly adopted the form of realism—itself a product of the interplay of historical forces and aesthetic developments early apparent in the French writer Gustave Flaubert's *Madame Bovary* (serialized in 1856, published as a book in 1857), which followed the mundane although ultimately tragic life of an ordinary housewife. Among the most critically praised American writers of the period were Mark Twain, William Dean Howells, Henry James, and Edith Wharton, who encompassed literary style from the comic vernacular through ordinary discourse to impressionistic subjectivity, while still under the sway of literary realism. These writers, two from the Midwest (Twain and Howells) and two from the East Coast (James and Wharton), recorded life on the vanishing frontier, in the village, small town, and turbulent metropolis, as well as in European resorts and capitals. They established the literary identity of distinctively American protagonists, specifically the vernacular boy hero and the "American Girl," the baffled and strained middle-class family, the businessman, and the psychologically complicated citizens of a new international culture. They set the example and charted the future course for the subjects, themes, techniques, and styles of the U.S. fiction we still call modern.

Developments in the literary marketplace and in the nation's preoccupations had the effect of greatly enhancing the reputation of prose fiction—the idea of a "great" American novel was first enunciated soon after the Civil War. But two of the most important American writers of their time and beyond, both of whom began working before the Civil War, were devoted to the idea that poetry was a crucial expression of the human spirit. In different ways each pointed towards the huge renaissance of poetry after World War I. Walt Whitman promulgated an expansive, gregarious open form fit for the "open road" of American life; Emily Dickinson's tight, elliptical verses reflect a sense of the psychological interior where meanings are made and unmade: "internal difference, where the meanings are."

FORMS OF REALISM AND NATURALISM

The two great literary movements of the late nineteenth century were realism and naturalism. The term *realism* refers to a movement in English, European, and American literature that gathered force from the 1830s to the end of the century. As defined by William Dean Howells, the magazine editor who was for some decades the chief American advocate of realist aesthetics as well as the author of over thirty novels, including *The Rise of Silas Lapham* (1885) and *A Hazard of New Fortunes* (1890), realism "is nothing more and nothing less than the truthful treatment of material." But truthful treatment of material depends on the material in question; Henry James spoke of the documentary value of Howells's work, thereby calling attention to realism's preoccupation with the observable surfaces of the world in which fictional characters lived, surfaces that made the world seem lifelike to readers. Characters in Howells's novels were "representative," that is, composites of the sort of people readers thought they already knew, people without fame or huge fortunes, without startling accomplishments or immense abilities.

By contrast, the realism practiced by Edith Wharton and Henry James focused on the interior moral and psychological lives of upper-class people, although always taking care in describing these people's surroundings. Wharton and James hoped to convince readers—most of whom were from the middle class—that the inner lives of the privileged were in accord with the truths of human nature. Wealthy people had what working people did not—time to develop and display their inner selves; they were just like everybody else, although more so. In novels such as *The House of Mirth* (1905), *The Custom of the Country* (1913), and *The Age of Innocence* (1920), Wharton depicts the intangibles of thwarted desire, self-betrayal, hostile emotion, and repressed voices. At times, her accounts of the struggles of individuals such as Lily Bart of *The House of Mirth* to survive in a seemingly pleasant but actually hostile society reflect an almost Darwinian view of upper-class life, a naturalistic vision of human struggle; this is not the pleasant world of Howells's well-meaning characters, but it is no less "realistic."

Realist writers believed in the power of language to represent reality in ways that were aesthetically satisfying and true to their sense of the world. But realism could never once and for all convey the real world through language; the world was always out there waiting for another writer to decide how to treat it. What they were trying to represent was always able to elude their desire to fix it in print; but that did not stop them from trying. Two of the most acclaimed artists of the era—Mark Twain and Henry James—understood that language was an interpretation of the real rather than the real thing itself. As a western writer, Twain worked within a tradition of vernacular tale-telling, which some later writers saw as the essence of a truly American style. Because this style was already an exaggeration, it could not truly be called "realistic" in the Howellsian sense; and Twain's later work is infused with pessimism and social critique well beyond the realistic norm. James, beginning with recognizably realistic fiction, using a large cast of individualized, although usually upper-class characters described by an all-knowing narrator, as in *The American* (1876), developed increasingly subtle metaphorical and proto-modernistic representations of the flow of a character's inner thought—the so-called "stream of consciousness"—as in *The Golden Bowl* (1904).

Naturalism can be thought of as a version of realism, or as an alternative to it. Literary naturalists, unlike the realists for whom human beings defined themselves within recognizable settings, wrote about human life as it was shaped by forces beyond human control. For them, their view was truly realistic, while Howellsian realism was a form of prettifying. Naturalism introduces characters from the fringes and depths of society, far from the middle class, whose lives really do spin out of control; their fates are seen to be the outcome of degenerate heredity, a sordid environment, and the bad luck that can often seem to control the lives of people without money or influence. Charles Darwin's *Origin of Species* (1859) and *Descent of Man* (1870) theorized that human beings had developed over the ages from nonhuman forms of life, successfully adapting to changing environmental conditions. Darwin was not interested in the social world, but in the 1870s, the English philosopher Herbert Spencer applied Darwin's evolutionary theory of the "survival of the fittest" to human groups. This idea was enthusiastically welcomed by many leading American businessmen. Andrew Carnegie, for example, argued that unrestrained competition was the equivalent of a law of nature designed to eliminate those unfit for the new economic order.

For the novelists, naturalism was thought to make their work scientific—thus truly realistic—rather than romantic. Émile Zola (1840–1902), the influential French theorist and novelist, wrote in his influential essay "The Experimental Novel" (1880):

> We must operate with characters, passions, human and social data as the chemist and the physicist work on inert bodies, as the physiologist works on living bodies. Determinism governs everything. It is scientific investigation; it is experimental reasoning that combats one by one the hypotheses of the idealists and will replace novels of pure imagination by novels of observation and experiment.

A number of American writers adopted aspects of Zola's form of naturalism, though each brought naturalism into his or her work in different ways, to different degrees, and combined with other perspectives. At some level they all understood that they were fabulists, not scientists, and ultimately none of them was willing to sacrifice some idea of human life as meaningful. Even the statement that life has no meaning is, after all, a meaningful statement; there is no escape from this paradox. Naturalists wanted to explore how biology, environment, and other material forces shaped lives—particularly the lives of lower-class people, who supposedly had less control over their lives than those who were better off. In this respect, naturalism is an intervention that strives to make lower-class lives comprehensible to the middle-class readers who comprised the main audience for fiction. Thus, Ambrose Bierce, Stephen Crane, Theodore Dreiser, Jack London, and Frank Norris all allowed in different degrees for the value of human beings, for their potential to make some measure of sense out of their experience, and for their capacity to act compassionately—even altruistically—under the most adverse circumstances. Even though, therefore, they were challenging conventional wisdom about human motivation and causality in the natural world, the bleakness and pessimism sometimes found in their fiction are not the same as despair and cynicism. Careful reading of such Ambrose Bierce stories as "Chicamauga" and "An Occurrence at Owl Creek Bridge" reveals his awareness of fiction as a tool to explore inner truths.

Stephen Crane, too, did not believe that environment counts for everything, though he said of *Maggie: A Girl of the Streets* (1893) that it does count for a great deal in determining human fate. Not every person born in a slum becomes a criminal, drunkard, or suicide; and Crane clearly depicts Maggie's final action in the novella as her considered choice. In "The Blue Hotel" the earth is described in one of the most famous passages in naturalistic fiction as a "whirling, fire-smote, ice-locked, disease-stricken, space-lost bulb." But questions of responsibility and agency are still alive at the end of the story. In Crane's Civil War novel *The Red Badge of Courage,* the main character Henry Fleming responds throughout to the world of chaos and violence that surrounds him with alternating surges of panic and self-congratulations, not as a man who has fully understood himself and his place in the world. And yet, Henry has learned something; Crane, like most naturalists, is more ambiguous, more accepting of paradoxes, than a simplified notion of naturalism would suggest.

Biology, environment, psychological drives, and chance play a large part in shaping human ends in Crane's fiction. But these thematic matters are inflected by his distinct literary style, which merges honest reportage with impressionistic literary techniques to present incomplete characters and a broken world—a world more random than scientifically predictable. We are also left, however, with the hardly pessimistic implications of "The Open Boat": that precisely because human beings are exposed to a savage world of chance where death is always imminent, they would do well to learn the art of sympathetic identification with others and how to practice solidarity, an art often learned at the price of death. After all, a belief in the meaning of deeply felt human connection is Crane's final sense of reality in this story.

Theodore Dreiser did not share Crane's tendency to use words and images as if he were a composer or painter. Like Crane, he tended to see men and women as victims of their destinies rather than creators of their lives. But his significance for readers lies in his cumulative technique that represents the solidity of the world in which his characters are entrapped. If Crane gave American readers a new sense of human consciousness under conditions of extreme pressure, Dreiser gave them in novels such as *Sister Carrie* (1900) and *Jennie Gerhardt* (1911) a sense of the fumbling, yearning, confused response to the simultaneously enchanting, exciting, ugly, and dangerous metropolis that had become home to such large numbers of Americans by the turn of the century. Like Dreiser, Abraham Cahan wrote about city dwellers, in particular about eastern European Jews who, starting in 1882, had been coming to the United States in large numbers. Many of these Yiddish-speaking immigrants settled in Manhattan's Lower East Side. Cahan's major novel *The Rise of David Levinsky* (1917) explores the tensions entailed in attempts to reconcile traditional values and ways of living with American modernity in an urban work that, in the manner of literary naturalists, puts into conflict individual agency with larger social and natural forces, while providing new perspectives on ethnicity. Cahan's stories also explore themes of immigrant assimilation.

In Jack London's most successful works, such as his novels *The Call of the Wild* (1903) and *The Sea-Wolf* (1904), along with most of his nearly two hundred short stories, there are currents of myth and romance. London was notoriously inconsistent—a socialist and an individualist, a believer in Anglo-Saxon superiority who attacked white racism and colonialism. Most of his short story "The Law of Life" (1901) recounts Old Koshkoosh's memories, especially his youthful encounter with a dying moose set upon by wolves. Koshkoosh himself, an imagined recreation of an indigenous person, has been left to die by his tribe as is customary, London suggests, when people reach extreme old age. He thinks: "Nature did not care. To life she set one task, gave one law. To perpetuate was the task of life, its law is death." This thought suggests a deterministic view of life, but what London underscores in the overall story is that acts of imagination and identification lend meaning and dignity to human existence.

In sum, despite conventional notions that insisted on humanity's elevated place in the universe and a middle-class readership that disliked ugliness and "immorality," urban America and the sparsely populated hinterlands proved to be fertile ground for realistic literary techniques and naturalistic ideas, though the ideas were often inconsistently applied and the documentary techniques usually interwoven with other literary strategies. Crucial to American writing during this period, realism and naturalism took on many forms and exposed readers to a wide range of subjects and perspectives.

REGIONAL WRITING

Regional writing, another expression of the realist impulse, resulted from the desire both to preserve a record of distinctive ways of life and to come to terms with the new world that seemed to be replacing these early and allegedly happier times. More practically, regional writing responded to the new market of mass magazines, for which the short story form was ideal, and for which variations of local habits could provide an endless source of narrative. By the end of the nineteenth century, virtually every region of the country had one or more "local colorists" dedicated to capturing its natural, social, and linguistic features. Though often suffused with nostalgia, the best work of the regionalists renders convincing details of a particular time and investigates psychological character traits from a broad perspective. Bret Harte's "The Luck of Roaring Camp," which made Harte a national celebrity in 1868, is sometimes treated as an example of local color, but it is more concerned with creating myths of the colorful West than it is in realism. Like other literary forms, it is a hybrid rather than a pure example of a strategy rigorously applied. Writers as diverse as Owen Wister, author of the popular novel *The Virginian* (1902), Mark Twain, Ambrose Bierce, Mary Austin, and Jack London all contributed to the work of depicting the West as a legendary region—or (as in the case of Twain and Bierce) to the work of debunking such a legend.

Hamlin Garland, rather than creating a myth of a region, set out to destroy one. Like many writers of the time, Garland was encouraged by Howells to write about what he knew best—in his case the farmers of the upper Midwest. As he later said, his purpose in his early stories was to show that the "mystic quality connected with free land . . . was a myth." Garland's farmers are not the vigorous and thoughtful yeomen of Hector St. John de Crèvecoeur's *Letters from an American Farmer* (1782), but bent, drab figures. In Garland's "Under the Lion's Paw," from the collection *Main-Travelled Roads* (1891), local color is not nostalgia but realism in the service of social protest—another indication that realism could never be only "realistic" but was always something more.

The places and the themes of regional writers assumed increasing importance in the twentieth century. Many women initially associated with regionalism expanded their interests to write about the world of women: Sarah Orne Jewett, Mary E. Wilkins Freeman, Sui Sin Far, Charlotte Perkins Gilman, Sarah Winnemucca, and others. Mary Austin was a self-declared feminist, and much of her writing, including her classic *Land of Little Rain* (1903), invites readers to see the world from a woman's perspective. But more important, in "The Land of Little Rain" and other sketches, she introduced the desert country of southern California to readers and showed how the characters who live in this inhospitable terrain are products of it. Stowe, Jewett, and Freeman do more than lament the postwar economic and spiritual decline of New England; their female characters suggest the capacity of human beings to live independently and with dignity in the face of community pressures, patriarchal power, and material deprivation.

Kate Chopin may be thought of as a regional writer interested in the customs, language, and landscapes of the northern Louisiana countryside and, downriver, New Orleans. But in addition to working with local color, Chopin wrote probing psychological fiction with intriguing female protagonists. Edna Pontellier of *The Awakening* (1899) looks back to Flaubert's *Madame Bovary* and forward to Virginia Woolf's *Mrs. Dalloway* (1925). Chopin began her writing career only after she returned to her native St. Louis from a long sojourn in Louisiana, and in her narratives she memorializes (and perhaps romanticizes) the relaxed and sensuous way of life of the local population. Though the lives she portrays seem less severe and repressed than those in the Protestant towns and villages of New England regionalism, Chopin nonetheless depicts—especially in *The Awakening*—the struggles of women in conservative Catholic communities. With its focus on the inner life of Edna Pontellier, *The Awakening* in particular, a novel that has served to crystallize many women's issues at the turn of the century and since, testifies to the fact that regionalism, despite its avowed focus on lives outside of the urban mainstream, is by no means a marginal genre.

From a very different perspective, Native Americans also described their lives and traditions—especially as these were imperiled by white advances into their territories. The oratory of Charlot and Smohalla, the Ghost Dance religion, and the writings of Zitkala Ša, Sarah Winnemucca, and Charles Alexander Eastman (Ohiyesa) all widened public appreciation of literary models outside the European tradition while also challenging the dominant culture's identification of the West with the imaginary line of the frontier.

REALISM AS ARGUMENT

Realism was an important spur to the development of nonfiction. Between the end of the Civil War and the outbreak of World War I, much nonfiction prose described, analyzed, and critiqued the social, economic, and political institutions that had emerged in this period of rapid growth and change. Women's rights, political corruption, the degradation of the natural world, economic inequity, business deceptions, the exploitation of labor, tenement housing—these became the subjects of articles and books by numerous journalists, historians, social critics, photographers, and economists. Much of this writing had literary ambition and is regarded as among the great literary achievements of the era. For example, in his autobiographical work of moral instruction and philosophy, *The Education of Henry Adams* (1918), Henry Adams registers through a literary sensibility a historian's sense of the disorientation that accompanies rapid and continuous change.

Of all the issues of the day, perhaps the most persistent and resistant to solution was the fact of racial inequality in the social arena. Several selections in this anthology address the long history of white injustices to black Americans, particularly as it became clear, with the end of Reconstruction and the withdrawal of federal troops from the southern states in 1877, and then with the subsequent shift to segregationist Jim Crow laws and the Supreme Court's "separate but equal" decision in the case of *Plessy v. Ferguson* (1896), that there had been considerable erosion of the Constitutional amendments promising to guarantee the civil rights of African Americans. Among the most significant and influential voices of the period were those of African Americans addressing such topics as race, black community, and continuing racial inequities. In their short fiction and novels, Charles Chesnutt, Pauline Hopkins, and James Weldon Johnson investigated the very nature of "race," pointing to its contradictions and (especially in the case of Hopkins) its promises for the regeneration of black community. Two works by black writers and leaders from the turn of the century have a special claim on our attention: the widely admired autobiography of Booker T. Washington, *Up from Slavery* (1900), and the richly imagined *The Souls of Black Folk* (1903) by W. E. B. Du Bois, with its powerfully argued rejection of Washington's assimilationist philosophy. The

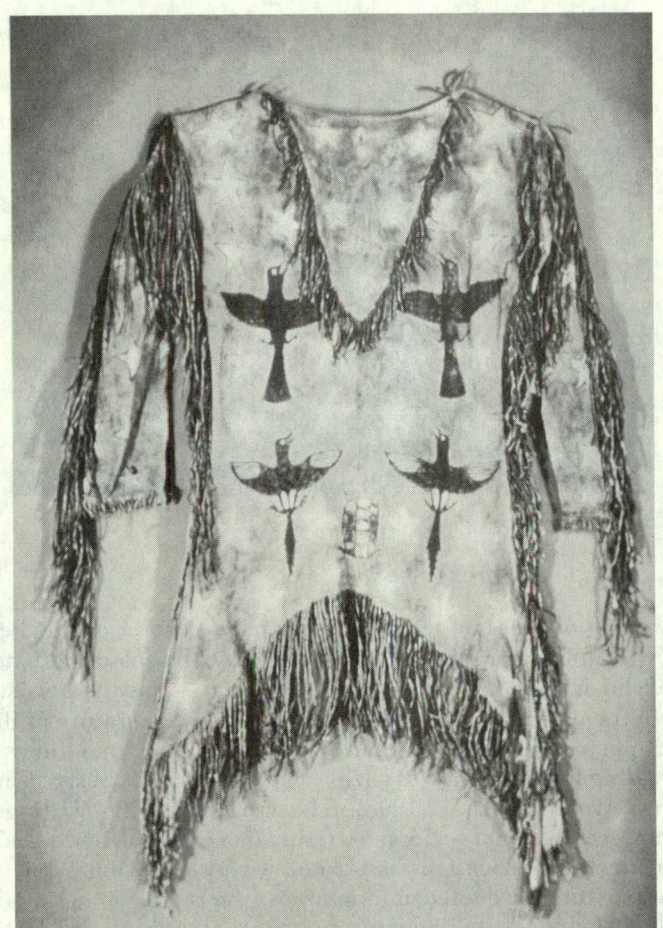

Arapaho Ghost Dance Shirt. After the emissaries sent to visit Wovoka, the prophet of the Ghost Dance, returned with glowing reports, the Arapahos became the first adherents of the Ghost Dance on the plains. Wovoka had described special shirts to be worn while performing the Dance, and this is one made by the Arapahos. It is unclear whether the shirts, as some said, were supposed to make the wearer impervious to bullets or only to enhance the power of the Dance.

Washington–Du Bois controversy set some of the key terms of the continuing debate among black leaders about which strategies would most effectively hasten educational, social, economic, and political equality for blacks in the United States. It is fair to say that in very different ways *Up from Slavery* and *The Souls of Black Folk*—admirable literary achievements in themselves—carried forward the antebellum traditions of such writers as David Walker, Frederick Douglass, and Harriet Jacobs and set some of the terms of the cultural debates that would become central to the Harlem Renaissance.

In the half century we have been considering, material, intellectual, social, and psychological changes in the lives of many Americans went forward at such extreme speed and on such a massive scale that the enormously

Jim Crow Railroad Car.

diverse writing of the time registers, at its core, degrees of shocked recognition of the human consequences of these radical transformations. Sometimes the shock is expressed in recoil and denial—thus the persistence, in the face of the ostensible triumph of realism, of the literature of diversion: nostalgic poetry, sentimental and melodramatic drama, and popular swashbuckling historical novels such as Charles Major's best-selling *When Knighthood Was in Flower* (1898). The more enduring writings of the period, however, attempt to come to terms imaginatively with the individual and collective dislocations associated with the closing of the frontier, urbanization, unprecedented immigration, the surge of national wealth unequally distributed, revised conceptions of human nature and destiny, racial inequality and the concept of race, the reordering of family and civil life, and the pervasive spread of mechanical and organizational technologies. Although change is, as Ralph Waldo Emerson remarked, "the law of life," in the half century after the Civil War, writers seemed more aware of turbulence and disruption than before, and attempted to generate new forms of literary art that could represent and make sense of a nation in flux.

AMERICAN LITERATURE 1865–1914

TEXTS	CONTEXTS
1855 Walt Whitman, *Leaves of Grass*	
1860–65 Emily Dickinson writes several hundred **poems**	**1860** Short-lived Pony Express runs from Missouri to California
	1861 South Carolina batteries fire on Fort Sumter, initiating the Civil War • Southern states secede from the Union and found the Confederate States of America
1865 Walt Whitman, *Drum-Taps*	**1865** Civil War ends • Reconstruction begins • Lincoln assassinated • Thirteenth Amendment ratified, prohibiting slavery
	1867 United States purchases Alaska from Russia • Jesse Chisholm maps out the Chisholm Trail, connecting Texas cattle ranches to railheads in Kansas City, Cheyenne, Dodge City, and Abilene
1868 Louisa May Alcott, *Little Women*	**1868** Fourteenth Amendment passed, guaranteeing citizenship to all peoples born in the United States (exclusive of Native peoples) • Congress institutes eight-hour workday for federal employees • sweatshops, using mostly immigrant labor, begin to proliferate in cities
	1869 First transcontinental railroad completed by construction crews composed largely of Chinese laborers • Susan B. Anthony elected president of American Equal Rights Association; Elizabeth Cady Stanton elected president of National Women's Suffrage Association
1870 Bret Harte, *The Luck of Roaring Camp and Other Sketches*	**1870** Fifteenth Amendment, giving African American men the right to vote, ratified
	1871 Indian Appropriation Act ends the practice of negotiating treaties with the tribes as sovereign nations
1872 Mark Twain, *Roughing It*	**1872** Yellowstone, first U.S. national park, established
	1873 Economic panic: financial depression lasts until 1879
	1874 Women's Christian Temperance Union founded in Cleveland • invention of barbed wire effectively ends the open range
1876 Charlot, "[He has filled graves with our bones]"	**1876** Custer's regiment defeated by the Sioux and Cheyenne at Little Big Horn River, Montana • Alexander Graham Bell invents the telephone
	1877 Reconstruction ends • segregationist Jim Crow laws begin

Boldface titles indicate works in the anthology.

TEXTS	CONTEXTS
1878 Henry James, *Daisy Miller*	
	1879 Thomas Edison invents the electric lightbulb • female lawyers permitted to argue before Supreme Court
1880 Joel Chandler Harris, *Uncle Remus: His Songs and Sayings*	**1880–1910** Massive immigration from Europe
1881 Helen Hunt Jackson, *A Century of Dishonor*	**1881** Tuskegee Institute founded
	1882 J. D. Rockefeller organizes Standard Oil Trust • Chinese Exclusion Act instituted
1883 Emma Lazarus, "The New Colossus"	
1884 Twain, *Adventures of Huckleberry Finn*	**1884** Tailors' strike in New York City brings national attention to sweatshops
1885 María Amparo Ruiz de Burton, *The Squatter and the Don*	
	1886 Statue of Liberty dedicated • Haymarket Square labor riot leaves eleven dead • American Federation of Labor organized
	1887 General Allotment Act or Dawes Act permits the president to divide tribally owned lands into individual allotments to be held in trust for twenty-five years, with "surplus" lands to be sold to non-Indians. This led the Indians to lose some 90 million acres of land by the time Dawes was repealed in 1934.
1889 Theodore Roosevelt, *The Winning of the West* • Hamlin Garland, "Under the Lion's Paw"	
1890 Ambrose Bierce, **"An Occurrence at Owl Creek Bridge"**	**1890** U.S. Bureau of the Census declares the "frontier" "to be closed." There is no more "free" or "unoccupied" land • Sitting Bull killed. Massacre of Big Foot's Minneconjou band by federal troops at Wounded Knee Creek ends the Ghost Dance among the Sioux • Ellis Island Immigration Station opens
1891 José Martí, "Our America" • Mary E. Wilkins Freeman, **"A New England Nun"**	
1892 Anna Julia Cooper, *A Voice from the South* • Charlotte Perkins Gilman, **"The Yellow Wall-paper"**	
1893 Stephen Crane, *Maggie: A Girl of the Streets* • Frederick Jackson Turner, *The Significance of the Frontier*	**1893** World's Columbian Exposition held in Chicago • Economic panic and depression, set off by the collapse of the Philadelphia and Reading Railroads
1895 Crane, *Black Riders* and *The Red Badge of Courage*	

TEXTS	CONTEXTS
1896 Paul Laurence Dunbar, *Lyrics of a Lowly Life* • James Mooney publishes *Ghost Dance Songs*	**1896** *Plessy v. Ferguson* upholds segregated transportation
1897 Crane, *The Open Boat and Other Tales of Adventure*	**1897–98** Klondike Gold Rush
1898 Abraham Cahan, *The Imported Bridegroom and Other Stories*	**1898** United States annexes Hawaii
	1898–99 Spanish-American War
1899 Charles Chesnutt, *The Conjure Woman* and *The Wife of His Youth and Other Stories of the Color Line* • Kate Chopin, *The Awakening* • Frank Norris, *McTeague*	
1900 Theodore Dreiser, *Sister Carrie* • Ida B. Wells-Barnett, *Mob-Rule in New Orleans* • Pauline Hopkins, *Contending Forces*	**1900** U.S. population exceeds seventy-five million
1901 Zitkala Ša, *Impressions of an Indian Childhood and The School Days of an Indian Girl* • Norris, *The Octopus* • London, "The Law of Life" • Booker T. Washington, *Up From Slavery*	**1901** J. P. Morgan founds U.S. Steel Corporation • first transatlantic radio • oil discovered in Spindletop, Texas
1903 W. E. B. Du Bois, *The Souls of Black Folk* • London, *The Call of the Wild* • Mary Austin, *The Land of Little Rain*	**1903** Henry Ford founds Ford Motor Co. • Wright brothers make the first successful airplane flight • *The Great Train Robbery* is first U.S. cinematic narrative
1904 Edith Wharton, "The Other Two"	**1904** National Child Labor Committee formed
1905 William Dean Howells, "Editha"	**1905** Industrial Workers of the World (the Wobblies) founded
1906 Upton Sinclair, *The Jungle*	**1906** April 18: San Francisco earthquake and fire
1907 Henry Adams, *The Education of Henry Adams*, privately printed	
	1909 National Association for the Advancement of Colored People (NAACP) founded
1910 Jane Addams, *Twenty Years at Hull-House* • Sui Sin Far, "Mrs. Spring Fragrance"	**1910** Mexican Revolution
1912 James Weldon Johnson • *The Autobiography of an Ex-Colored Man*	
	1914 U.S. Marines invade and occupy Vera Cruz, Mexico • Panama Canal opens

MARK TWAIN (SAMUEL L. CLEMENS)
1835–1910

Samuel Langhorne Clemens, the third of five children, was born on November 30, 1835, in the village of Florida, Missouri, and grew up in the somewhat larger Mississippi river town of Hannibal, Missouri, that place of idylls and also dangers he called St. Petersburg in his writings, home to his two most famous characters, Tom Sawyer and Huck Finn. Twain's father, a justice of the peace who had unsuccessfully tried to become a storekeeper, died when Twain was twelve, and from that time on Twain worked to support himself and the rest of the family. After his father's death, Twain was apprenticed to a printer, and in 1851, when his brother Orion became a publisher in Hannibal, Twain went to work for him. But he soon made an escape from his brother's print shop, as he was being paid virtually nothing for his work, often running the entire operation by himself. In 1853 he began three years of travel, stopping in St. Louis, New York, Philadelphia, Keokuk (Iowa), and Cincinnati, in each place working as an itinerant journeyman printer. In 1856 he left Cincinnati for New Orleans by steamboat, intending to go to the Amazon. He changed his plans, however, and instead apprenticed himself to Horace Bixby, a Mississippi riverboat pilot. After training for eighteen months, Twain became a pilot himself, and he practiced this lucrative and prestigious trade until 1861, when the Civil War virtually ended commercial river traffic. During this time he wrote humorous accounts of his activities for the Keokuk *Saturday Post*. But he soon left the Mississippi River Valley because the river was closed by Union blockades and because he was in danger of being drafted into the Union Navy for his skills.

Slavery was legal in Missouri, though the state did not join the Confederacy, and Twain may have seen brief service in a woefully unorganized Confederate militia, an experience that he later fictionalized in "The Private History of a Campaign That Failed" (1885). In 1861 he went west with his brother Orion, who had been appointed secretary of the Nevada Territorial government. This move started him on the path toward his life as a humorist, lecturer, journalist, and author. In *Roughing It* (1872), written a decade later, Twain fictionally elaborated the brothers' stagecoach adventures on the way to Carson City and recounted his unsuccessful schemes for making money (including mining the Comstock lode in Virginia City) once he got there. Throughout *Roughing It,* which also covers his stint in San Francisco as a reporter and his half-hearted gold-mining in the Sierras, as well as his trip to Hawaii, Twain debunked the idea of the West as a place where fortunes could be easily made and showed its disappointing and even brutal side. In this respect, Twain joined the group of writers who were trying to tell eastern readers what the West was really like, while exalting in the freedom and outright craziness of western startup towns and encampments, operating far from eastern laws, orthodoxies, and even common sense.

In the West, Twain began writing for newspapers, first the *Territorial Enterpr*ise in Virginia City and then, after 1864, the *Californian* in San Francisco. The fashion of the time called for a pen name, and so from a columnist for the New Orleans *Times-Picayune*, he borrowed "Mark Twain," which means in riverboat terms "two fathoms deep," or "safe water." His early writing was modeled on the humorous journalism of the day, especially that practiced by his friend and roommate in Nevada, who wrote under the pen name Dan De Quille. Also important to his development during these years were friendships with the western writer Bret Harte, the famous professional lecturer and comic Artemus Ward, and the obscure amateur raconteur Jim Gillis. Twain's reputation as a lecturer and his first success as a writer lay in his skillful retelling of a well-known tall tale, "The Notorious Jumping Frog of Calaveras County," first published in 1865.

In this same year Twain signed with the *Sacramento Union* to write a series of letters covering the newly opened steamboat passenger service between San Francisco and Honolulu. In these letters he used a fictitious character, Mr. Brown, to present inelegant ideas and unorthodox views, attitudes, and information, often in impolite language. This device allowed him to say just about anything he wanted, provided he could convincingly claim he was simply reporting what others said and did. The refinement of this deadpan technique made it a staple of his lectures. Twain's first book of this period, and still one of his most popular, was *Innocents Abroad* (1869), consisting of a revised form of the letters he wrote for the *Alta California* and *New York Tribune* during his 1867 excursion on the *Quaker City* to the Mediterranean and Holy Land. With his fare paid for by the *Alta California*, Twain, through letters to that San Francisco newspaper, provided a running account of the first great modern American tourist raid on the Old World. Twain wrote hilarious satires of his fellow passengers as well as the pretentious, decadent, and undemocratic Old World as viewed by a citizen of a young country on the rise. A characteristically impertinent note was sounded in a remark upon disembarking in New York: When Twain was asked for his impressions of the Holy Land, he said he knew for a fact there would be no Second Coming, for if Jesus had been there once he certainly wouldn't go back. Such scoffing drew angry editorials and speeches, publicity that helped make *Innocents Abroad* successful.

Twain's publishers sold *Innocents Abroad* and other of his books mainly by subscription, with door-to-door salespeople offering sometimes gaudy, always lavishly illustrated volumes of his books as diversion and entertainment. Though the trade was regarded as low, and though many books sold by subscription were not reviewed by the established literary and general interest magazines of the time, subscription houses accounted for nearly two-thirds of American bookselling in the 1870s. Twain's shrewd understanding of the dynamics of the publishing industry, including the importance of lining up first-rate illustrators, helped to establish him as a popular author during this time.

Twain's many travels, including later lecture tours around the globe, did not erase the rich material of his Missouri boyhood, which ran deep in his memory and imagination. To get to it, he had, in effect, to work chronologically backward and psychically inward. He tentatively probed this material as early as 1870 in an early version of *The Adventures of Tom Sawyer* called *A Boy's Manuscript*. In 1875 he wrote *Old Times on the Mississippi* in seven installments for the *Atlantic Monthly* (edited by his friend William Dean Howells, who tirelessly promoted Twain's career), arriving at the place that many critics see as his imaginative home. These sketches were later incorporated into *Life on the Mississippi* (1883), written after Twain took a monthlong steamboat trip on the Mississippi, stopping along the way to visit Hannibal. The added material—part history, part memoir, part travelogue—offers, among other things, a critique of the southern romanticism Twain believed had made the Civil War inevitable, a theme that would reappear in his masterpiece, *Adventures of Huckleberry Finn*.

Twain had married Olivia Langdon, daughter of a wealthy coal dealer from Buffalo, New York, in 1870. This entry into a higher stratum of society than he had previously known, along with his increasing fascination with wealth, created a constant struggle in his work between the conventional and the disruptive, which is typical of much of the best American humor. In the perennially popular *The Adventures of Tom Sawyer* (1876), the struggle emerges in the contrast between the entrepreneurial but entirely respectable Tom and his disreputable friend Huck. In this narrative, Twain also mingles childhood pleasures with childhood fears of the violence, terror, and death lurking at the edges of the village.

This book has long been recognized as an adult classic as well as a children's book, and its publication further consolidated Twain's status as a writer of popular fiction.

Twain began *Adventures of Huckleberry Finn* in 1876 as a sequel to *Tom Sawyer*, but he put the manuscript aside for several years and finished it in 1884, when his thinking about Huck and his story had changed and matured considerably. In recent years the racial (and racist) implications of *Huck Finn* have been the subjects of critical debate, as have questions about the racial beliefs of the author. (For more on the critical controversy, see the selections in "Race and the Ending of *Adventures of Huckleberry Finn*" immediately following the novel.) Similar questions have been raised about gender and sexuality in Twain's life and work. In Twain's own day *Huck Finn* was banned in many libraries and schools around the country and denounced in pulpits not for its racial content but for its supposedly encouraging boys to swear, smoke, and run away. Nevertheless, *Huck Finn* has enjoyed extraordinary popularity since its publication. It broke literary ground as a novel written in the vernacular and established the vernacular's capacity to result in high art. Its unpretentious, colloquial, yet poetic style, its wide-ranging humor, its embodiment of the enduring and widely shared dream of innocence and freedom, and its recording of a vanished way of life in the pre–Civil War Mississippi Valley have instructed and moved people of all ages and conditions all over the world. *Huck Finn* sold 51,000 copies in its first fourteen months, compared to *Tom Sawyer's* 25,000 in the same period. Ernest Hemingway once called it the source of "all modern American literature."

Twain wrote another successful and memorable book in this period, the bitter *A Connecticut Yankee in King Arthur's Court* (1889). The novel seems to be a satire on sixth-century Arthurian England seen through the eyes of a crafty "Yankee," Hank Morgan, who is transported back thirteen centuries and tries to "introduce," in Twain's words, the "great and beneficent civilization of the nineteenth century" into the chivalric and decidedly undemocratic world of Camelot. But Hank's "Gilded Age" schemes end in their own destruction and the massacre of thousands of knights. *The Tragedy of Pudd'nhead Wilson* (1894) similarly offers a dark and troubling view of nineteenth-century American values. Set in a Mississippi River town of the 1830s, the novel follows the tragic consequences of switching two babies at birth—one free, one slave, and both children of the same white, slave-owning father. The novel provides an intense, sometimes chaotic meditation on the absurdities of defining individuals in relation to race; on the impact on personality and fate of labels like "white" and "black"; and on biological, legal, and social descriptions of human identity.

In the decade after *Puddn'head Wilson* was published, Twain experienced a series of calamities. Suddenly, his health became bad; poor investments led to bankruptcy in the panic of 1893; his youngest daughter, Jean, was diagnosed as epileptic; his oldest daughter, Susy, died of meningitis while he was away; and his wife, Livy, began to decline into permanent invalidism. For several years writing was both agonized labor and necessary therapy. The results of these circumstances were a travel book, *Following the Equator* (1897), which records the round-the-world lecture tour that Twain undertook to pay off debts; a sardonically brilliant interrogation of middle-class American morality, "The Man That Corrupted Hadleyburg" (1900); an embittered treatise on humanity's foibles, follies, and venality, *What Is Man?* (1906); and the bleakly despairing *The Mysterious Stranger*, first published in an inaccurate and unauthorized version by Albert Bigelow Paine, Twain's first biographer, in 1916. Scholars continue to study the large bulk of Twain's unfinished or (until recently) unpublished writings and have called for reevaluation of his work from the decade after 1895. His late writings, most of which Twain declined to see published while he lived, reveal a darkening worldview and an upwelling of anger against orthodoxies of every sort, including organized religious belief and international capitalism and colonialism.

In his later years, Twain, by now world famous, found himself consulted by the press on every subject of general interest. Though his views on political, military, and social subjects were often acerbic, it was only to his best friends that he confessed the depth of his disillusionment. Much of this bitterness informs such published works as "To a Person Sitting in Darkness" (1901), "The United States of Lyncherdom" (1901), and "King Leopold's Soliloquy" (1905), as well as other writings unpublished in his lifetime, such as *Letters from the Earth,* in which he skewers religion from the skeptical and irreverent perspective of Satan.

Twain maintained his power with language throughout his career. What he said of one of his characters explains a large part of his permanent appeal: "He could curl his tongue around the bulliest words in the language when he was a mind to, and lay them before you without a jint [joint] started, anywheres" (*Life on the Mississippi* [1883], Chapter 3). Twain knew the nation's various regions and its history; he represented, expressed, and attacked the American character all at once. Humor was his way of bringing together these three approaches. As his friend Howells observed, Twain was unlike any of his contemporaries in American letters: "Emerson, Longfellow, Lowell, Holmes—I knew them all and all the rest of our sages, poets, seers, critics, humorists; they were like one another and like other literary men; but Clemens was sole, incomparable, the Lincoln of our literature."

The Notorious Jumping Frog of Calaveras County[1]

In compliance with the request of a friend of mine, who wrote me from the East, I called on good-natured, garrulous old Simon Wheeler, and inquired after my friend's friend, Leonidas W. Smiley, as requested to do, and I hereunto append the result. I have a lurking suspicion that *Leonidas W.* Smiley is a myth; that my friend never knew such a personage; and that he only conjectured that if I asked old Wheeler about him, it would remind him of his infamous *Jim* Smiley, and he would go to work and bore me to death with some exasperating reminiscence of him as long and as tedious as it should be useless to me. If that was the design, it succeeded.

I found Simon Wheeler dozing comfortably by the barroom stove of the dilapidated tavern in the decayed mining camp of Angel's, and I noticed that he was fat and bald-headed, and had an expression of winning gentleness and simplicity upon his tranquil countenance. He roused up, and gave me good-day. I told him a friend of mine had commissioned me to make some inquiries about a cherished companion of his boyhood named *Leonidas W.* Smiley—*Rev. Leonidas W.* Smiley, a young minister of the Gospel, who he had heard was at one time a resident of Angel's Camp. I added that if Mr. Wheeler could tell me anything about this Rev. Leonidas W. Smiley, I would feel under many obligations to him.

Simon Wheeler backed me into a corner and blockaded me there with his chair, and then sat down and reeled off the monotonous narrative which follows this paragraph. He never smiled, he never frowned, he never changed his voice from the gentle-flowing key to which he tuned his initial sentence, he never betrayed the slightest suspicion of enthusiasm; but all through the interminable narrative there ran a vein of impressive earnestness and sincerity,

---

1. The story first appeared in the *New York Saturday Press* of November 18, 1865, and was subsequently revised several times. The source of the text is the version published in *Mark Twain's* *Sketches, New and Old* (1875). In a note, Twain instructs his readers that "Calaveras" is pronounced *Cal-e-va'-ras.*

which showed me plainly that, so far from his imagining that there was any-thing ridiculous or funny about his story, he regarded it as a really important matter, and admired its two heroes as men of transcendent genius in *finesse*. I let him go on in his own way, and never interrupted him once.

Rev. Leonidas W. H'm, Reverend Le—well, there was a feller here once by the name of *Jim* Smiley, in the winter of '49—or may be it was the spring of '50—I don't recollect exactly, somehow, though what makes me think it was one or the other is because I remember the big flume warn't finished when he first come to the camp; but any way, he was the curiosest man about always betting on anything that turned up you ever see, if he could get anybody to bet on the other side; and if he couldn't he'd change sides. Any way that suited the other man would suit *him*—any way just so's he got a bet, *he* was satisfied. But still he was lucky, uncommon lucky; he most always come out winner. He was always ready and laying for a chance; there couldn't be no solit'ry thing mentioned but that feller'd offer to bet on it, and take ary side you please, as I was just telling you. If there was a horse-race, you'd find him flush or you'd find him busted at the end of it; if there was a dog-fight, he'd bet on it; if there was a cat-fight, he'd bet on it; if there was a chicken-fight, he'd bet on it; why, if there was two birds set-ting on a fence, he would bet you which one would fly first; or if there was a camp-meeting, he would be there reg'lar to bet on Parson Walker, which he judged to be the best exhorter about here, and so he was too, and a good man. If he even see a straddle-bug start to go anywheres, he would bet you how long it would take him to get to—to wherever he was going to, and if you took him up, he would foller that straddle-bug to Mexico but what he would find out where he was bound for and how long he was on the road. Lots of the boys here has seen that Smiley, and can tell you about him. Why, it never made no difference to *him*—he'd bet on *any* thing—the dan-gdest feller. Parson Walker's wife laid very sick once, for a good while, and it seemed as if they warn't going to save her; but one morning he come in, and Smiley up and asked him how she was, and he said she was considable better—thank the Lord for his inf'nite mercy—and coming on so smart that with the blessing of Prov'dence she'd get well yet; and Smiley, before he thought says, "Well, I'll resk two-and-a-half she don't anyway."

Thish-yer Smiley had a mare—the boys called her the fifteen-minute nag, but that was only in fun, you know, because of course she was faster than that—and he used to win money on that horse, for all she was so slow and always had the asthma, or the distemper, or the consumption, or something of that kind. They used to give her two or three hundred yards start, and then pass her under way; but always at the fag end of the race she'd get excited and desperate-like, and come cavorting and straddling up, and scattering her legs around limber, sometimes in the air, and sometimes out to one side among the fences, and kicking up m-o-r-e dust and raising m-o-r-e racket with her coughing and sneezing and blowing her nose—and *always* fetch up at the stand just about a neck ahead, as near as you could cipher it down.

And he had a little small bull-pup, that to look at him you'd think he warn't worth a cent but to set around and look ornery and lay for a chance to steal something. But as soon as money was up on him he was a different dog; his under-jaw'd begin to stick out like the fo'castle of a steamboat, and his teeth would uncover and shine like the furnaces. And a dog might tackle him and bully-rag him, and bite him, and throw him over his shoulder two or three times, and Andrew Jackson—which was the name of the pup—Andrew Jackson would never let on but what *he* was satisfied, and hadn't expected nothing else—and the bets being doubled and doubled on the other side all the time, till the money was all up; and then all of a sudden he would grab that other dog jest by the j'int of his hind leg and freeze to it—not chaw, you understand, but only just grip and hang on till they throwed up the sponge, if it was a year. Smiley always come out winner on that pup, till he harnessed a dog once that didn't have no hind legs, because they'd been sawed off in a circular saw, and when the thing had gone along far enough, and the money was all up, and he come to make a snatch for his pet holt, he see in a minute how he's been imposed on, and how the other dog had him in the door, so to speak, and he 'peared surprised, and then he looked sorter discouraged-like, and didn't try no more to win the fight, and so he got shucked out bad. He give Smiley a look, as much as to say his heart was broke, and it was *his* fault, for putting up a dog that hadn't no hind legs for him to take holt of, which was his main dependence in a fight, and then he limped off a piece and laid down and died. It was a good pup, was that Andrew Jackson, and would have made a name for hisself if he'd lived, for the stuff was in him and he had genius—I know it, because he hadn't no opportunities to speak of, and it don't stand to reason that a dog could make such a fight as he could under them circumstances if he hadn't no talent. It always makes me feel sorry when I think of that last fight of his'n, and the way it turned out.

Well, thish-yer Smiley had rat-tarriers, and chicken cocks, and tomcats and all them kind of things, till you couldn't rest, and you couldn't fetch nothing for him to bet on but he'd match you. He ketched a frog one day, and took him home, and said he cal'lated to educate him; and so he never done nothing for three months but set in his back yard and learn that frog to jump. And you bet you he *did* learn him, too. He'd give him a little punch behind, and the next minute you'd see that frog whirling in the air like a doughnut— see him turn one summerset, or may be a couple, if he got a good start, and come down flat-footed and all right, like a cat. He got him up so in the matter of ketching flies, and kep' him in practice so constant, that he'd nail a fly every time as fur as he could see him. Smiley said all a frog wanted was education, and he could do 'most anything—and I believe him. Why, I've seen him set Dan'l Webster down here on this floor—Dan'l Webster was the name of the frog—and sing out, "Flies, Dan'l, flies!" and quicker'n you could wink he'd spring straight up and snake a fly off'n the counter there, and flop down on the floor ag'in as solid as a gob of mud, and fall to scratching the side of his head with his hind foot as indifferent as if he hadn't no idea he'd been doin' any more'n any frog might do. You never see a frog so modest and straightfor'ard as he was, for all he was so gifted. And when it come to fair and square jumping on a dead level, he could get over more ground at one straddle than any animal of his breed you ever see. Jumping on a dead level was his strong suit, you understand; and when it come to that, Smiley would ante up money on him as long as he had a red. Smiley was monstrous proud of his frog, and well he might be, for fellers that had traveled and been everywheres all said he laid over any frog that ever *they* see.

Well, Smiley kep' the beast in a little lattice box, and he used to fetch him down town sometimes and lay for a bet. One day a feller—a stranger in the camp, he was—come acrost him with his box, and says:

"What might it be that you've got in the box?"

And Smiley says, sorter indifferent-like, "It might be a parrot, or it might be a canary, maybe, but it ain't—it's only just a frog."

And the feller took it, and looked at it careful, and turned it round this way and that, and says, "H'm—so 'tis. Well, what's *he* good for?"

"Well," Smiley says, easy and careless, "he's good enough for *one* thing, I should judge—he can outjump any frog in Calaveras county."

The feller took the box again, and took another long, particular look, and give it back to Smiley, and says, very deliberate, "Well," he says, "I don't see no p'ints about that frog that's any better'n any other frog."

"Maybe you don't," Smiley says. "Maybe you understand frogs and maybe you don't understand 'em; maybe you've had experience, and maybe you ain't only an amature, as it were. Anyways, I've got *my* opinion and I'll resk forty dollars that he can outjump any frog in Calaveras county."

And the feller studied a minute, and then says, kinder sad like, "Well, I'm only a stranger here, and I ain't got no frog; but if I had a frog, I'd bet you."

And then Smiley says, "That's all right—that's all right—if you'll hold my box a minute, I'll go and get you a frog." And so the feller took the box, and put up his forty dollars along with Smiley's, and set down to wait.

So he set there a good while thinking and thinking to hisself, and then he got the frog out and prized his mouth open and took a teaspoon and filled him full of quail shot—filled him pretty near up to his chin—and set him on the floor. Smiley he went to the swamp and slopped around in the mud for a long time, and finally he ketched a frog, and fetched him in, and give him to this feller, and says:

"Now, if you're ready, set him alongside of Dan'l, with his forepaws just even with Dan'l's, and I'll give the word." Then he says, "One—two—three-*git!*" and him and the feller touched up the frogs from behind, and the new frog hopped off lively, but Dan'l give a heave, and hysted up his shoulders—so— like a Frenchman, but it warn't no use—he couldn't budge; he was planted as solid as a church, and he couldn't no more stir than if he was anchored out. Smiley was a good deal surprised, and he was disgusted too, but he didn't have no idea what the matter was, of course.

The feller took the money and started away; and when he was going out at the door, he sorter jerked his thumb over his shoulder—so—at Dan'l, and says again, very deliberate, "Well," he says, "*I* don't see no p'ints about that frog that's any better'n any other frog."

Smiley he stood scratching his head and looking down at Dan'l a long time, and at last he says, "I do wonder what in the nation that frog throw'd off for—I wonder if there ain't something the matter with him—he 'pears to look mighty baggy, somehow." And he ketched Dan'l by the nap of the neck, and hefted him, and says, "Why blame my cats if he don't weigh five pound!" and turned him upside down and he belched out a double handful of shot. And then he see how it was, and he was the maddest man—he set the frog down and took out after that feller, but he never ketched him. And——"

[Here Simon Wheeler heard his name called from the front yard, and got up to see what was wanted.] And turning to me as he moved away, he said: "Just set where you are, stranger, and rest easy—I ain't going to be gone a second."

But, by your leave, I did not think that a continuation of the history of the enterprising vagabond *Jim* Smiley would be likely to afford me much information concerning the *Rev. Leonidas W.* Smiley, and so I started away.

At the door I met the sociable Wheeler returning, and he button-holed me and recommenced:

"Well, thish-yer Smiley had a yaller one-eyed cow that didn't have no tail, only jest a short stump like a bannanner, and——"

However, lacking both time and inclination, I did not wait to hear about the afflicted cow, but took my leave.

1865, 1867

ADVENTURES OF HUCKLEBERRY FINN[1]

(Tom Sawyer's Comrade)

Scene: The Mississippi Valley

Time: Forty to Fifty Years Ago[2]

NOTICE

Persons attempting to find a motive in this narrative will be prosecuted; persons attempting to find a moral in it will be banished; persons attempting to find a plot in it will be shot.

BY ORDER OF THE AUTHOR
PER G. G., CHIEF OF ORDNANCE.

Explanatory

In this book a number of dialects are used, to wit: the Missouri negro dialect; the extremest form of the backwoods South-Western dialect; the ordinary "Pike-County"[3] dialect; and four modified varieties of this last. The shadings have not been done in a hap-hazard fashion, or by guess-work; but pains-takingly, and with the trustworthy guidance and support of personal familiarity with these several forms of speech.

I make this explanation for the reason that without it many readers would suppose that all these characters were trying to talk alike and not succeeding.

THE AUTHOR

---

1. *Adventures of Huckleberry Finn* was first published in England in December 1884. The text printed here is a corrected version of the first American edition of 1885.

2. I.e., in 1835 or 1845—well before the Civil War.

3. Pike County, Missouri.

Chapter I

You don't know about me, without you have read a book by the name of "The Adventures of Tom Sawyer,"[4] but that ain't no matter. That book was made by Mr. Mark Twain, and he told the truth, mainly. There was things which he stretched, but mainly he told the truth. That is nothing. I never seen anybody but lied, one time or another, without it was Aunt Polly, or the widow, or maybe Mary. Aunt Polly—Tom's Aunt Polly, she is—and Mary, and the Widow Douglas, is all told about in that book—which is mostly a true book; with some stretchers, as I said before.

Now the way that the book winds up, is this: Tom and me found the money that the robbers hid in the cave, and it made us rich. We got six thousand dollars apiece—all gold. It was an awful sight of money when it was piled up. Well, Judge Thatcher, he took it and put it out at interest, and it fetched us a dollar a day apiece, all the year round—more than a body could tell what to do with. The Widow Douglas, she took me for her son, and allowed she would sivilize me; but it was rough living in the house all the time, considering how dismal regular and decent the widow was in all her ways; and so when I couldn't stand it no longer, I lit out. I got into my old rags, and my sugar-hogshead[5] again, and was free and satisfied. But Tom Sawyer, he hunted me up and said he was going to start a band of robbers, and I might join if I would go back to the widow and be respectable. So I went back.

The widow she cried over me, and called me a poor lost lamb, and she called me a lot of other names, too, but she never meant no harm by it. She put me in them new clothes again, and I couldn't do nothing but sweat and sweat, and feel all cramped up. Well, then, the old thing commenced again. The widow rung a bell for supper, and you had to come to time. When you got to the table you couldn't go right to eating, but you had to wait for the widow to tuck down her head and grumble a little over the victuals, though there warn't really anything the matter with them. That is, nothing only everything was cooked by itself. In a barrel of odds and ends it is different; things get mixed up, and the juice kind of swaps around, and the things go better.

After supper she got out her book and learned me about Moses and the Bulrushers;[6] and I was in a sweat to find out all about him; but by-and-by she let it out that Moses had been dead a considerable long time; so then I didn't care no more about him; because I don't take no stock in dead people.

Pretty soon I wanted to smoke, and asked the widow to let me. But she wouldn't. She said it was a mean practice and wasn't clean, and I must try to not do it any more. That is just the way with some people. They get down on a thing when they don't know nothing about it. Here she was a bothering about Moses, which was no kin to her, and no use to anybody, being gone, you see, yet finding a power of fault with me for doing a thing that had some good in it. And she took snuff too; of course that was all right, because she done it herself.

Her sister, Miss Watson, a tolerable slim old maid, with goggles on, had just come to live with her, and took a set at me now, with a spelling-book. She worked me middling hard for about an hour, and then the widow made

---

4. Published in 1876.
5. A large barrel.
6. Pharaoh's daughter discovered the infant

Moses floating in the Nile in a basket woven from bulrushes (Exodus 2). She adopted him into the royal family just as the widow has adopted Huck.

E.W. Kemble
·1884·

HUCKLEBERRY FINN

Huck. E. W. Kemble's illustration of Huckleberry
Finn on the frontispiece of the first edition (1884).

her ease up. I couldn't stood it much longer. Then for an hour it was deadly
dull, and I was fidgety. Miss Watson would say, "Don't put your feet up
there, Huckleberry"; and "don't scrunch up like that, Huckleberry—set up
straight"; and pretty soon she would say, "Don't gap and stretch like that,
Huckleberry—why don't you try to behave?" Then she told me all about the
bad place, and I said I wished I was there. She got mad, then, but I didn't
mean no harm. All I wanted was to go somewheres; all I wanted was a change,
I warn't particular. She said it was wicked to say what I said; said she wouldn't
say it for the whole world; *she* was going to live so as to go to the good place.
Well, I couldn't see no advantage in going where she was going, so I made up
my mind I wouldn't try for it. But I never said so, because it would only make
trouble, and wouldn't do no good.

Now she had got a start, and she went on and told me all about the good
place. She said all a body would have to do there was to go around all day
long with a harp and sing, forever and ever.[7] So I didn't think much of it.
But I never said so. I asked her if she reckoned Tom Sawyer would go there,
and, she said, not by a considerable sight. I was glad about that, because I
wanted him and me to be together.

7. Conventional conceptions of the Christian heaven were satirized early and late in Twain's
writings.

Miss Watson she kept pecking at me, and it got tiresome and lonesome. By-and-by they fetched the niggers[8] in and had prayers, and then everybody was off to bed. I went up to my room with a piece of candle and put it on the table. Then I set down in a chair by the window and tried to think of something cheerful, but it warn't no use. I felt so lonesome I most wished I was dead. The stars was shining, and the leaves rustled in the woods ever so mournful; and I heard an owl, away off, who-whooing about somebody that was dead, and a whippowill and a dog crying about somebody that was going to die; and the wind was trying to whisper something to me and I couldn't make out what it was, and so it made the cold shivers run over me. Then away out in the woods I heard that kind of a sound that a ghost makes when it wants to tell about something that's on its mind and can't make itself understood, and so can't rest easy in its grave and has to go about that way every night grieving. I got so down-hearted and scared, I did wish I had some company. Pretty soon a spider went crawling up my shoulder, and I flipped it off and it lit in the candle; and before I could budge it was all shriveled up. I didn't need anybody to tell me that that was an awful bad sign and would fetch me some bad luck, so I was scared and most shook the clothes off of me. I got up and turned around in my tracks three times and crossed my breast every time; and then I tied up a little lock of my hair with a thread to keep witches away. But I hadn't no confidence. You do that when you've lost a horse-shoe that you've found, instead of nailing it up over the door, but I hadn't ever heard anybody say it was any way to keep off bad luck when you'd killed a spider.

I set down again, a shaking all over, and got out my pipe for a smoke; for the house was all as still as death, now, and so the widow wouldn't know. Well, after a long time I heard the clock away off in the town go boom—boom—boom—twelve licks—and all still again—stiller than ever. Pretty soon I heard a twig snap, down in the dark amongst the trees—something was a stirring. I set still and listened. Directly I could just barely hear a *"me-yow! me-yow!"* down there. That was good! Says I, *"me-yow! me-yow!"* as soft as I could, and then I put out the light and scrambled out of the window onto the shed. Then I slipped down to the ground and crawled in amongst the trees, and sure enough there was Tom Sawyer waiting for me.

Chapter II

We went tip-toeing along a path amongst the trees back towards the end of the widow's garden, stooping down so as the branches wouldn't scrape our heads. When we was passing by the kitchen I fell over a root and made a noise. We scrouched down and laid still. Miss Watson's big nigger, named Jim, was setting in the kitchen door; we could see him pretty clear, because there was a light behind him. He got up and stretched his neck out about a minute, listening. Then he says,

"Who dah?"

8. This word is now unacceptable, but at the time of this novel's setting (before the Civil War) it was a more-or-less common term among whites without the powerfully negative connotations it has since acquired. Because Huck comes to see Jim as fully human, despite his participation in racial prejudices of his time and place, his use of the word highlights the change in his perceptions. For debate on the racial politics of *Huckleberry Finn*, see the selections in "Critical Controversy: Race and the Ending of *Adventures of Huckleberry Finn*," pp. 1466–80.

He listened some more; then he come tip-toeing down and stood right between us; we could a touched him, nearly. Well, likely it was minutes and minutes that there warn't a sound, and we all there so close together. There was a place on my ankle that got to itching; but I dasn't scratch it; and then my ear begun to itch; and next my back, right between my shoulders. Seemed like I'd die if I couldn't scratch. Well, I've noticed that thing plenty of times since. If you are with the quality, or at a funeral, or trying to go to sleep when you ain't sleepy—if you are anywheres where it won't do for you to scratch, why you will itch all over in upwards of a thousand places. Pretty soon Jim says:

"Say—who is you? Whar is you? Dog my cats ef I didn' hear sumf'n. Well, I knows what I's gwyne to do. I's gwyne to set down here and listen tell I hears it agin."

So he set down on the ground betwixt me and Tom. He leaned his back up against a tree, and stretched his legs out till one of them most touched one of mine. My nose begun to itch. It itched till the tears come into my eyes. But I dasn't scratch. Then it begun to itch on the inside. Next I got to itching underneath. I didn't know how I was going to set still. This miserableness went on as much as six or seven minutes; but it seemed a sight longer than that. I was itching in eleven different places now. I reckoned I couldn't stand it more'n a minute longer, but I set my teeth hard and got ready to try. Just then Jim begun to breathe heavy; next he begun to snore—and then I was pretty soon comfortable again.

Tom he made a sign to me—kind of a little noise with his mouth—and we went creeping away on our hands and knees. When we was ten foot off, Tom whispered to me and wanted to tie Jim to the tree for fun; but I said no; he might wake and make a disturbance, and then they'd find out I warn't in. Then Tom said he hadn't got candles enough, and he would slip in the kitchen and get some more. I didn't want him to try. I said Jim might wake up and come. But Tom wanted to resk it; so we slid in there and got three candles, and Tom laid five cents on the table for pay. Then we got out, and I was in a sweat to get away; but nothing would do Tom but he must crawl to where Jim was, on his hands and knees, and play something on him. I waited, and it seemed a good while, everything was so still and lonesome.

As soon as Tom was back, we cut along the path, around the garden fence, and by-and-by fetched up on the steep top of the hill the other side of the house. Tom said he slipped Jim's hat off of his head and hung it on a limb right over him, and Jim stirred a little, but he didn't wake. Afterwards Jim said the witches bewitched him and put him in a trance, and rode him all over the State, and then set him under the trees again and hung his hat on a limb to show who done it. And next time Jim told it he said they rode him down to New Orleans; and after that, every time he told it he spread it more and more, till by-and-by he said they rode him all over the world, and tired him most to death, and his back was all over saddle-boils. Jim was monstrous proud about it, and he got so he wouldn't hardly notice the other niggers. Niggers would come miles to hear Jim tell about it, and he was more looked up to than any nigger in that country. Strange niggers[9] would stand with their mouths open and look him all over, same as if he was a wonder. Niggers is always talking about witches in the dark by the kitchen fire; but

9. Those who did not live in the immediate area.

whenever one was talking and letting on to know all about such things, Jim would happen in and say, "Hm! What you know 'bout witches?" and that nigger was corked up and had to take a back seat. Jim always kept that five-center piece around his neck with a string and said it was a charm the devil give to him with his own hands and told him he could cure anybody with it and fetch witches whenever he wanted to, just by saying something to it; but he never told what it was he said to it. Niggers would come from all around there and give Jim anything they had, just for a sight of the five-center piece; but they wouldn't touch it, because the devil had had his hands on it. Jim was most ruined, for a servant, because he got so stuck up on account of having seen the devil and been rode by witches.

Well, when Tom and me got to the edge of the hill-top, we looked away down into the village[1] and could see three or four lights twinkling, where there was sick folks, may be; and the stars over us was sparkling ever so fine; and down by the village was the river, a whole mile broad, and awful still and grand. We went down the hill and found Jo Harper, and Ben Rogers, and two or three more of the boys, hid in the old tanyard. So we unhitched a skiff and pulled down the river two mile and a half, to the big scar on the hillside, and went ashore.

We went to a clump of bushes, and Tom made everybody swear to keep the secret, and then showed them a hole in the hill, right in the thickest part of the bushes. Then we lit the candles and crawled in on our hands and knees. We went about two hundred yards, and then the cave opened up. Tom poked about amongst the passages and pretty soon ducked under a wall where you wouldn't a noticed that there was a hole. We went along a narrow place and got into a kind of room, all damp and sweaty and cold, and there we stopped. Tom says:

"Now we'll start this band of robbers and call it Tom Sawyer's Gang. Everybody that wants to join has got to take an oath, and write his name in blood."

Everybody was willing. So Tom got out a sheet of paper that he had wrote the oath on, and read it. It swore every boy to stick to the band, and never tell any of the secrets; and if anybody done anything to any boy in the band, whichever boy was ordered to kill that person and his family must do it, and he mustn't eat and he mustn't sleep till he had killed them and hacked a cross in their breasts, which was the sign of the band. And nobody that didn't belong to the band could use that mark, and if he did he must be sued; and if he done it again he must be killed. And if anybody that belonged to the band told the secrets, he must have his throat cut, and then have his carcass burnt up and the ashes scattered all around, and his name blotted off of the list with blood and never mentioned again by the gang, but have a curse put on it and be forgot, forever.

Everybody said it was a real beautiful oath, and asked Tom if he got it out of his own head. He said, some of it, but the rest was out of pirate books, and robber books, and every gang that was high-toned had it.

Some thought it would be good to kill the *families* of boys that told the secrets. Tom said it was a good idea, so he took a pencil and wrote it in. Then Ben Rogers says:

"Here's Huck Finn, he hain't got no family—what you going to do 'bout him?"

---

1. The village, called St. Petersburg here and in *Tom Sawyer*, is modeled on Hannibal, Missouri.

"Well, hain't he got a father?" says Tom Sawyer.

"Yes, he's got a father, but you can't never find him, these days. He used to lay drunk with the hogs in the tanyard, but he hain't been seen in these parts for a year or more."

They talked it over, and they was going to rule me out, because they said every boy must have a family or somebody to kill, or else it wouldn't be fair and square for the others. Well, nobody could think of anything to do—everybody was stumped, and set still. I was most ready to cry; but all at once I thought of a way, and so I offered them Miss Watson—they could kill her. Everybody said:

"Oh, she'll do, she'll do. That's all right. Huck can come in."

Then they all stuck a pin in their fingers to get blood to sign with, and I made my mark on the paper.

"Now," says Ben Rogers, "what's the line of business of this Gang?"

"Nothing only robbery and murder," Tom said.

"But who are we going to rob? houses—or cattle—or—"

"Stuff! stealing cattle and such things ain't robbery, it's burglary," says Tom Sawyer. "We ain't burglars. That ain't no sort of style. We are highway-men. We stop stages and carriages on the road, with masks on, and kill the people and take their watches and money."

"Must we always kill the people?"

"Oh, certainly. It's best. Some authorities think different, but mostly it's considered best to kill them. Except some that you bring to the cave here and keep them till they're ransomed."

"Ransomed? What's that?"

"I don't know. But that's what they do. I've seen it in books; and so of course that's what we've got to do."

"But how can we do it if we don't know what it is?"

"Why blame it all, we've *got* to do it. Don't I tell you it's in the books? Do you want to go to doing different from what's in the books, and get things all muddled up?"

"Oh, that's all very fine to *say*, Tom Sawyer, but how in the nation[2] are these fellows going to be ransomed if we don't know how to do it to them? that's the thing I want to get at. Now what do you *reckon* it is?"

"Well I don't know. But per'aps if we keep them till they're ransomed, it means that we keep them till they're dead."

"Now, that's something *like*. That'll answer. Why couldn't you said that before? We'll keep them till they're ransomed to death—and a bothersome lot they'll be, too, eating up everything and always trying to get loose."

"How you talk, Ben Rogers. How can they get loose when there's a guard over them, ready to shoot them down if they move a peg?"

"A guard. Well, that *is* good. So somebody's got to set up all night and never get any sleep, just so as to watch them. I think that's foolishness. Why can't a body take a club and ransom them as soon as they get here?"

"Because it ain't in the books so—that's why. Now Ben Rogers, do you want to do things regular, or don't you?—that's the idea. Don't you reckon that the people that made the books knows what's the correct thing to do? Do you reckon *you* can learn 'em anything? Not by a good deal. No, sir, we'll just go on and ransom them in the regular way."

2. Damnation.

"All right. I don't mind; but I say it's a fool way, anyhow. Say—do we kill the women, too?"

"Well, Ben Rogers, if I was as ignorant as you I wouldn't let on. Kill the women? No—nobody ever saw anything in the books like that. You fetch them to the cave, and you're always as polite as pie to them; and by-and-by they fall in love with you and never want to go home any more."

"Well, if that's the way, I'm agreed, but I don't take no stock in it. Mighty soon we'll have the cave so cluttered up with women, and fellows waiting to be ransomed, that there won't be no place for the robbers. But go ahead, I ain't got nothing to say."

Little Tommy Barnes was asleep, now, and when they waked him up he was scared, and cried, and said he wanted to go home to his ma, and didn't want to be a robber any more.

So they all made fun of him, and called him cry-baby, and that made him mad, and he said he would go straight and tell all the secrets. But Tom give him five cents to keep quiet, and said we would all go home and meet next week and rob somebody and kill some people.

Ben Rogers said he couldn't get out much, only Sundays, and so he wanted to begin next Sunday; but all the boys said it would be wicked to do it on Sunday, and that settled the thing. They agreed to get together and fix a day as soon as they could, and then we elected Tom Sawyer first captain and Jo Harper second captain of the Gang, and so started home.

I clumb up the shed and crept into my window just before day was breaking. My new clothes was all greased up and clayey, and I was dog-tired.

Chapter III

Well, I got a good going-over in the morning, from old Miss Watson, on account of my clothes; but the widow she didn't scold, but only cleaned off the grease and clay and looked so sorry that I thought I would behave a while if I could. Then Miss Watson she took me in the closet[3] and prayed, but nothing come of it. She told me to pray every day, and whatever I asked for I would get it. But it warn't so. I tried it. Once I got a fish-line, but no hooks. It warn't any good to me without hooks. I tried for the hooks three or four times, but somehow I couldn't make it work. By-and-by, one day, I asked Miss Watson to try for me, but she said I was a fool. She never told me why, and I couldn't make it out no way.

I set down, one time, back in the woods, and had a long think about it. I says to myself, if a body can get anything they pray for, why don't Deacon Winn get back the money he lost on pork? Why can't the widow get back her silver snuff-box that was stole? Why can't Miss Watson fat up? No, says I to myself, there ain't nothing in it. I went and told the widow about it, and she said the thing a body could get by praying for it was "spiritual gifts." This was too many for me, but she told me what she meant—I must help other people, and do everything I could for other people, and look out for them all the time, and never think about myself. This was including Miss Watson, as I took it. I went out in the woods and turned it over in my mind a long time, but I couldn't see no advantage about it—except for the other people—so at

---

3. "But thou, when thou prayest, enter into thy closet" (Matthew 6.6) is apparently the admonition Miss Watson has in mind.

last I reckoned I wouldn't worry about it any more, but just let it go. Sometimes the widow would take me one side and talk about Providence in a way to make a boy's mouth water; but maybe next day Miss Watson would take hold and knock it all down again. I judged I could see that there was two Providences, and a poor chap would stand considerable show with the widow's Providence, but if Miss Watson's got him there warn't no help for him any more. I thought it all out, and reckoned I would belong to the widow's, if he wanted me, though I couldn't make out how he was agoing to be any better off then than what he was before, seeing I was so ignorant and so kind of low-down and ornery.

Pap he hadn't been seen for more than a year, and that was comfortable for me; I didn't want to see him no more. He used to always whale me when he was sober and could get his hands on me; though I used to take to the woods most of the time when he was around. Well, about this time he was found in the river drowned, about twelve mile above town, so people said. They judged it was him, anyway; said this drowned man was just his size, and was ragged, and had uncommon long hair—which was all like pap—but they couldn't make nothing out of the face, because it had been in the water so long it warn't much like a face at all. They said he was floating on his back in the water. They took him and buried him on the bank. But I warn't comfortable long, because I happened to think of something. I knowed mighty well that a drownded man don't float on his back, but on his face. So I knowed, then, that this warn't pap, but a woman dressed up in a man's clothes. So I was uncomfortable again. I judged the old man would turn up again by-and-by, though I wished he wouldn't.

We played robber now and then about a month, and then I resigned. All the boys did. We hadn't robbed nobody, we hadn't killed any people, but only just pretended. We used to hop out of the woods and go charging down on hog-drovers and women in carts taking garden stuff to market, but we never hived[4] any of them. Tom Sawyer called the hogs "ingots," and he called the turnips and stuff "julery" and we would go to the cave and pow-wow over what we had done and how many people we had killed and marked. But I couldn't see no profit in it. One time Tom sent a boy to run about town with a blazing stick, which he called a slogan (which was the sign for the Gang to get together), and then he said he had got secret news by his spies that next day a whole parcel of Spanish merchants and rich A-rabs was going to camp in Cave Hollow with two hundred elephants, and six hundred camels, and over a thousand "sumter" mules,[5] all loaded with di'monds, and they didn't have only a guard of four hundred soldiers, and so we would lay in ambuscade, as he called it, and kill the lot and scoop the things. He said we must slick up our swords and guns, and get ready. He never could go after even a turnip-cart but he must have the swords and guns all scoured up for it; though they was only lath and broom-sticks, and you might scour at them till you rotted and then they warn't worth a mouthful of ashes more than what they was before. I didn't believe we could lick such a crowd of Spaniards and A-rabs, but I wanted to see the camels and elephants, so I was on hand next day, Saturday, in the ambuscade; and when we got the word, we rushed out of the woods and down the hill. But there warn't no Spaniards and A-rabs, and

---

4. Captured, secured.   5. Pack mules.

there warn't no camels nor no elephants. It warn't anything but a Sunday-school picnic, and only a primer-class at that. We busted it up, and chased the children up the hollow; but we never got anything but some doughnuts and jam, though Ben Rogers got a rag doll, and Jo Harper got a hymn-book and a tract; and then the teacher charged in and made us drop everything and cut. I didn't see no di'monds, and I told Tom Sawyer so. He said there was loads of them there, anyway; and he said there was A-rabs there, too, and elephants and things. I said, why couldn't we see them, then? He said if I warn't so ignorant, but had read a book called "Don Quixote,"[6] I would know without asking. He said it was all done by enchantment. He said there was hundreds of soldiers there, and elephants and treasure, and so on, but we had enemies which he called magicians, and they had turned the whole thing into an infant Sunday school, just out of spite. I said, all right, then the thing for us to do was to go for the magicians. Tom Sawyer said I was a numskull.

"Why," says he, "a magician could call up a lot of genies, and they would hash you up like nothing before you could say Jack Robinson. They are as tall as a tree and as big around as a church."

"Well," I says, "s'pose we got some genies to help *us*—can't we lick the other crowd then?"

"How you going to get them?"

"I don't know. How do *they* get them?"

"Why they rub an old tin lamp or an iron ring, and then the genies come tearing in, with the thunder and lightning a-ripping around and the smoke a-rolling, and everything they're told to do they up and do it. They don't think nothing of pulling a shot tower[7] up by the roots, and belting a Sunday-school superintendent over the head with it—or any other man."

"Who makes them tear around so?"

"Why, whoever rubs the lamp or the ring. They belong to whoever rubs the lamp or the ring, and they've got to do whatever he says. If he tells them to build a palace forty miles long, out of di'monds, and fill it full of chewing gum, or whatever you want, and fetch an emperor's daughter from China for you to marry, they've got to do it—and they've got to do it before sun-up next morning, too. And more—they've got to waltz that palace around over the country whenever you want it, you understand."

"Well," says I, "I think they are a pack of flatheads for not keeping the palace themselves 'stead of fooling them away like that. And what's more—if I was one of them I would see a man in Jericho before I would drop my business and come to him for the rubbing of an old tin lamp."

"How you talk, Huck Finn. Why, you'd *have* to come when he rubbed it, whether you wanted to or not."

"What, and I as high as a tree and as big as a church? All right, then; I *would* come; but I lay I'd make that man climb the highest tree there was in the country."

"Shucks, it ain't no use to talk to you, Huck Finn. You don't seem to know anything, somehow—perfect sap-head."

I thought all this over for two or three days, and then I reckoned I would see if there was anything in it. I got an old tin lamp and an iron ring and

---

6. Tom is here alluding to stories in *The Arabian Nights Entertainments* (1838–41) and to the hero in Cervantes' *Don Quixote* (1605).

7. A device in which gunshot was formed by dripping molten lead into water.

went out in the woods and rubbed and rubbed till I sweat like an Injun, cal-culating to build a palace and sell it; but it warn't no use, none of the genies come. So then I judged that all that stuff was only just one of Tom Sawyer's lies. I reckoned he believed in the A-rabs and the elephants, but as for me I think different. It had all the marks of a Sunday school.

Chapter IV

Well, three or four months run along, and it was well into the winter, now. I had been to school most all the time, and could spell, and read, and write just a little, and could say the multiplication table up to six times seven is thirty-five, and I don't reckon I could ever get any further than that if I was to live forever. I don't take no stock in mathematics, anyway.

At first I hated the school, but by-and-by I got so I could stand it. Whenever I got uncommon tired I played hookey, and the hiding I got next day done me good and cheered me up. So the longer I went to school the easier it got to be. I was getting sort of used to the widow's ways, too, and they warn't so raspy on me. Living in a house, and sleeping in a bed, pulled on me pretty tight, mostly, but before the cold weather I used to slide out and sleep in the woods, sometimes, and so that was a rest to me. I liked the old ways best, but I was getting so I liked the new ones, too, a little bit. The widow said I was coming along slow but sure, and doing very satisfactory. She said she warn't ashamed of me.

One morning I happened to turn over the salt-cellar at breakfast. I reached for some of it as quick as I could, to throw over my left shoulder and keep off the bad luck, but Miss Watson was in ahead of me, and crossed me off. She says, "Take your hands away, Huckleberry—what a mess you are always mak-ing." The widow put in a good word for me, but that warn't going to keep off the bad luck, I knowed that well enough. I started out, after breakfast, feeling worried and shaky, and wondering where it was going to fall on me, and what it was going to be. There is ways to keep off some kinds of bad luck, but this wasn't one of them kind; so I never tried to do anything, but just poked along low-spirited and on the watch-out.

I went down the front garden and clumb over the stile,[8] where you go through the high board fence. There was an inch of new snow on the ground, and I seen somebody's tracks. They had come up from the quarry and stood around the stile a while, and then went on around the garden fence. It was funny they hadn't come in, after standing around so. I couldn't make it out. It was very curious, somehow. I was going to follow around, but I stooped down to look at the tracks first. I didn't notice anything at first, but next I did. There was a cross in the left boot-heel made with big nails, to keep off the devil.

I was up in a second and shinning down the hill. I looked over my shoul-der every now and then, but I didn't see nobody. I was at Judge Thatcher's as quick as I could get there. He said:

"Why, my boy, you are all out of breath. Did you come for your interest?"

"No sir," I says; "is there some for me?"

"Oh, yes, a half-yearly is in, last night. Over a hundred and fifty dollars. Quite a fortune for you. You better let me invest it along with your six thou-sand, because if you take it you'll spend it."

8. Steps that flank and straddle a fence.

"No sir," I says, "I don't want to spend it. I don't want it at all—nor the six thousand, nuther. I want you to take it; I want to give it to you—the six thousand and all."

He looked surprised. He couldn't seem to make it out. He says:

"Why, what can you mean, my boy?"

I says, "Don't you ask me no questions about it, please. You'll take it—won't you?"

He says:

"Well I'm puzzled. Is something the matter?"

"Please take it," says I, "and don't ask me nothing—then I won't have to tell no lies."

He studied a while, and then he says:

"Oho-o. I think I see. You want to *sell* all your property to me—not give it. That's the correct idea."

Then he wrote something on a paper and read it over, and says:

"There—you see it says 'for a consideration.' That means I have bought it of you and paid you for it. Here's a dollar for you. Now, you sign it."

So I signed it, and left.

Miss Watson's nigger, Jim, had a hair-ball[9] as big as your fist, which had been took out of the fourth stomach of an ox, and he used to do magic with it. He said there was a spirit inside of it, and it knowed everything. So I went to him that night and told him pap was here again, for I found his tracks in the snow. What I wanted to know, was, what he was going to do, and was he going to stay? Jim got out his hair-ball, and said something over it, and then he held it up and dropped it on the floor. It fell pretty solid, and only rolled about an inch. Jim tried it again, and then another time, and it acted just the same. Jim got down on his knees and put his ear against it and listened. But it warn't no use; he said it wouldn't talk. He said sometimes it wouldn't talk without money. I told him I had an old slick counterfeit quarter that warn't no good because the brass showed through the silver a little, and it wouldn't pass nohow, even if the brass didn't show, because it was so slick it felt greasy, and so that would tell on it every time. (I reckoned I wouldn't say nothing about the dollar I got from the judge.) I said it was pretty bad money, but maybe the hair-ball would take it, because maybe it wouldn't know the difference. Jim smelt it, and bit it, and rubbed it, and said he would manage so the hair-ball would think it was good. He said he would split open a raw Irish potato and stick the quarter in between and keep it there all night, and next morning you couldn't see no brass, and it wouldn't feel greasy no more, and so anybody in town would take it in a minute, let alone a hair-ball. Well, I knowed a potato would do that, before, but I had forgot it.

Jim put the quarter under the hair-ball and got down and listened again. This time he said the hair-ball was all right. He said it would tell my whole fortune if I wanted it to. I says, go on. So the hair-ball talked to Jim, and Jim told it to me. He says:

"Yo' ole father doan' know, yit, what he's a-gwyne to do. Sometimes he spec he'll go 'way, en den agin he spec he'll stay. De bes' way is to res' easy en let de ole man take his own way. Dey's two angels hoverin' roun' 'bout him. One uv 'em is white en shiny, en 'tother one is black. De white one gits him to go right, a little while, den de black one sail in en bust it all up. A body can't tell,

9. Clump of hair found in an animal's stomach; believed by Jim and Huck to have magical powers.

yit, which one gwyne to fetch him at de las'. But you is all right. You gwyne to have considable trouble in yo' life, en considable joy. Sometimes you gwyne to git hurt, en sometimes you gwyne to git sick; but every time you's gwyne to git well agin. Dey's two gals flyin' 'bout you in yo' life. One uv 'em's light en 'tother one is dark. One is rich en 'tother is po'. You's gwyne to marry de po' one fust en de rich one by-en-by. You wants to keep 'way fum de water as much as you kin, en don't run no resk, 'kase it's down in de bills dat you's gwyne to git hung."

When I lit my candle and went up to my room that night, there set pap, his own self!

Chapter V

I had shut the door to. Then I turned around, and there he was. I used to be scared of him all the time, he tanned me so much. I reckoned I was scared now, too; but in a minute I see I was mistaken. That is, after the first jolt, as you may say, when my breath sort of hitched—he being so unexpected; but right away after, I see I warn't scared of him worth bothering about.

He was most fifty, and he looked it. His hair was long and tangled and greasy, and hung down, and you could see his eyes shining through like he was behind vines. It was all black, no gray; so was his long, mixed-up whiskers. There warn't no color in his face, where his face showed; it was white; not like another man's white, but a white to make a body sick, a white to make a body's flesh crawl—a tree-toad white, a fish-belly white. As for his clothes—just rags, that was all. He had one ankle resting on 'tother knee; the boot on that foot was busted, and two of his toes stuck through, and he worked them now and then. His hat was laying on the floor; an old black slouch with the top caved in, like a lid.

I stood a-looking at him; he set there a-looking at me, with his chair tilted back a little. I set the candle down. I noticed the window was up; so he had clumb in by the shed. He kept a-looking me all over. By-and-by he says:

"Starchy clothes—very. You think you're a good deal of a big-bug, *don't* you?"

"Maybe I am, maybe I ain't," I says.

"Don't you give me none o' your lip," says he. "You've put on considerble many frills since I been away. I'll take you down a peg before I get done with you. You're educated, too, they say; can read and write. You think you're better'n your father, now, don't you, because he can't? *I'll* take it out of you. Who told you you might meddle with such hifalut'n foolishness, hey?—who told you you could?"

"The widow. She told me."

"The widow, hey?—and who told the widow she could put in her shovel about a thing that ain't none of her business?"

"Nobody never told her."

"Well, I'll learn her how to meddle. And looky here—you drop that school, you hear? I'll learn people to bring up a boy to put on airs over his own father and let on to be better'n what *he* is. You lemme catch you fooling around that school again, you hear? Your mother couldn't read, and she couldn't write, nuther, before she died. None of the family couldn't, before *they* died. *I* can't; and here you're a-swelling yourself up like this. I ain't the man to stand it—you hear? Say—lemme hear you read."

I took up a book and begun something about General Washington and the wars. When I'd read about a half a minute, he fetched the book a whack with his hand and knocked it across the house. He says:

"It's so. You can do it. I had my doubts when you told me. Now looky here; you stop that putting on frills. I won't have it. I'll lay for you, my smarty; and if I catch you about that school I'll tan you good. First you know you'll get religion, too. I never see such a son."

He took up a little blue and yaller picture of some cows and a boy, and says: "What's this?"

"It's something they give me for learning my lessons good."

He tore it up, and says—

"I'll give you something better—I'll give you a cowhide."[1]

He set there a-mumbling and a-growling a minute, and then he says—

"*Ain't* you a sweet-scented dandy, though? A bed; and bedclothes; and a look'n-glass; and a piece of carpet on the floor—and your own father got to sleep with the hogs in the tanyard. I never see such a son. I bet I'll take some o' these frills out o' you before I'm done with you. Why there ain't no end to your airs—they say you're rich. Hey?—how's that?"

"They lie—that's how."

"Looky here—mind how you talk to me; I'm a-standing about all I can stand, now—so don't gimme no sass. I've been in town two days, and I hain't heard nothing but about you bein' rich. I heard about it away down the river, too. That's why I come. You git me that money to-morrow—I want it."

"I hain't got no money."

"It's a lie. Judge Thatcher's got it. You git it. I want it."

"I hain't got no money, I tell you. You ask Judge Thatcher; he'll tell you the same."

"All right. I'll ask him; and I'll make him pungle,[2] too, or I'll know the reason why. Say—how much you got in your pocket? I want it."

"I hain't got only a dollar, and I want that to—"

"It don't make no difference what you want it for—you just shell it out."

He took it and bit it to see if it was good, and then he said he was going down town to get some whiskey; said he hadn't had a drink all day. When he had got out on the shed, he put his head in again, and cussed me for putting on frills and trying to be better than him; and when I reckoned he was gone, he come back and put his head in again, and told me to mind about that school, because he was going to lay for me and lick me if I didn't drop that.

Next day he was drunk, and he went to Judge Thatcher's and bullyragged him and tried to make him give up the money, but he couldn't, and then he swore he'd make the law force him.

The judge and the widow went to law to get the court to take me away from him and let one of them be my guardian; but it was a new judge that had just come, and he didn't know the old man; so he said courts mustn't interfere and separate families if they could help it; said he'd druther not take a child away from its father. So Judge Thatcher and the widow had to quit on the business.

That pleased the old man till he couldn't rest. He said he'd cowhide me till I was black and blue if I didn't raise some money for him. I borrowed three dollars from Judge Thatcher, and pap took it and got drunk and went a-blow-

---

1. A beating with a cowhide whip.   2. Pay.

ing around and cussing and whooping and carrying on; and he kept it up all over town, with a tin pan, till most midnight; then they jailed him, and next day they had him before court, and jailed him again for a week. But he said *he* was satisfied; said he was boss of his son, and he'd make it warm for *him*.

When he got out the new judge said he was agoing to make a man of him. So he took him to his own house, and dressed him up clean and nice, and had him to breakfast and dinner and supper with the family, and was just old pie to him, so to speak. And after supper he talked to him about temperance and such things till the old man cried, and said he'd been a fool, and fooled away his life; but now he was agoing to turn over a new leaf and be a man nobody wouldn't be ashamed of, and he hoped the judge would help him and not look down on him. The judge said he could hug him for them words; so *he* cried, and his wife she cried again; pap said he'd been a man that had always been misunderstood before, and the judge said he believed it. The old man said that what a man wanted that was down, was sympathy; and the judge said it was so; so they cried again. And when it was bedtime, the old man rose up and held out his hand, and says:

"Look at it gentlemen, and ladies all; take ahold of it; shake it. There's a hand that was the hand of a hog; but it ain't so no more; it's the hand of a man that's started in on a new life, and 'll die before he'll go back. You mark them words—don't forget I said them. It's a clean hand now; shake it—don't be afeard."

So they shook it, one after the other, all around, and cried. The judge's wife she kissed it. Then the old man he signed a pledge—made his mark. The judge said it was the holiest time on record, or something like that. Then they tucked the old man into a beautiful room, which was the spare room, and in the night sometime he got powerful thirsty and clumb out onto the porch-roof and slid down a stanchion and traded his new coat for a jug of forty-rod,[3] and clumb back again and had a good old time; and towards daylight he crawled out again, drunk as a fiddler, and rolled off the porch and broke his left arm in two places and was almost froze to death when somebody found him after sun-up. And when they come to look at that spare room, they had to take soundings before they could navigate it.

The judge he felt kind of sore. He said he reckoned a body could reform the ole man with a shot-gun, maybe, but he didn't know no other way.

Chapter VI

Well, pretty soon the old man was up and around again, and then he went for Judge Thatcher in the courts to make him give up that money, and he went for me, too, for not stopping school. He catched me a couple of times and thrashed me, but I went to school just the same, and dodged him or outrun him most of the time. I didn't want to go to school much, before, but I reckoned I'd go now to spite pap. That law trial was a slow business; appeared like they warn't ever going to get started on it; so every now and then I'd borrow two or three dollars off of the judge for him, to keep from getting a cowhiding. Every time he got money he got drunk; and every time he got drunk he raised Cain around town; and every time he raised Cain he got jailed. He was just suited—this kind of thing was right in his line.

3. Home-distilled whiskey strong enough to knock a person forty rods, or 220 yards.

He got to hanging around the widow's too much, and so she told him at last, that if he didn't quit using[4] around there she would make trouble for him. Well, *wasn't* he mad? He said he would show who was Huck Finn's boss. So he watched out for me one day in the spring, and catched me, and took me up the river about three mile, in a skiff, and crossed over to the Illinois shore where it was woody and there warn't no houses but an old log hut in a place where the timber was so thick you couldn't find it if you didn't know where it was.

He kept me with him all the time, and I never got a chance to run off. We lived in that old cabin, and he always locked the door and put the key under his head, nights. He had a gun which he had stole, I reckon, and we fished and hunted, and that was what we lived on. Every little while he locked me in and went down to the store, three miles, to the ferry, and traded fish and game for whisky and fetched it home and got drunk and had a good time, and licked me. The widow she found out where I was, by-and-by, and she sent a man over to try to get hold of me, but pap drove him off with the gun, and it warn't long after that till I was used to being where I was, and liked it, all but the cowhide part.

It was kind of lazy and jolly, laying off comfortable all day, smoking and fishing, and no books nor study. Two months or more run along, and my clothes got to be all rags and dirt, and I didn't see how I'd ever got to like it so well at the widow's, where you had to wash, and eat on a plate, and comb up, and go to bed and get up regular, and be forever bothering over a book and have old Miss Watson pecking at you all the time. I didn't want to go back no more. I had stopped cussing, because the widow didn't like it; but now I took to it again because pap hadn't no objections. It was pretty good times up in the woods there, take it all around.

But by-and-by pap got too handy with his hick'ry, and I couldn't stand it. I was all over welts. He got to going away so much, too, and locking me in. Once he locked me in and was gone three days. It was dreadful lonesome. I judged he had got drowned and I wasn't ever going to get out any more. I was scared. I made up my mind I would fix up some way to leave there. I had tried to get out of that cabin many a time, but I couldn't find no way. There warn't a window to it big enough for a dog to get through. I couldn't get up the chimbly, it was too narrow. The door was thick solid oak slabs. Pap was pretty careful not to leave a knife or anything in the cabin when he was away; I reckon I had hunted the place over as much as a hundred times; well, I was 'most all the time at it, because it was about the only way to put in the time. But this time I found something at last; I found an old rusty wood-saw without any handle; it was laid in between a rafter and the clapboards of the roof. I greased it up and went to work. There was an old horse-blanket nailed against the logs at the far end of the cabin behind the table, to keep the wind from blowing through the chinks and putting the candle out. I got under the table and raised the blanket and went to work to saw a section of the big bottom log out, big enough to let me through. Well, it was a good long job, but I was getting towards the end of it when I heard pap's gun in the woods. I got rid of the signs of my work, and dropped the blanket and hid my saw, and pretty soon pap come in.

4. Loitering.

Pap warn't in a good humor—so he was his natural self. He said he was down to town, and everything was going wrong. His lawyer said he reckoned he would win his lawsuit and get the money, if they ever got started on the trial; but then there was ways to put it off a long time, and Judge Thatcher knowed how to do it. And he said people allowed there'd be another trial to get me away from him and give me to the widow for my guardian, and they guessed it would win, this time. This shook me up considerable, because I didn't want to go back to the widow's any more and be so cramped up and sivilized, as they called it. Then the old man got to cussing, and cussed everything and everybody he could think of, and then cussed them all over again to make sure he hadn't skipped any, and after that he polished off with a kind of general cuss all round, including a considerable parcel of people which he didn't know the names of, and so called them what's-his-name, when he got to them, and went right along with his cussing.

He said he would like to see the widow get me. He said he would watch out, and if they tried to come any such game on him he knowed of a place six or seven mile off, to stow me in, where they might hunt till they dropped and they couldn't find me. That made me pretty uneasy again, but only for a minute; I reckoned I wouldn't stay on hand till he got that chance.

The old man made me go to the skiff and fetch the things he had got. There was a fifty-pound sack of corn meal, and a side of bacon, ammunition, and a four-gallon jug of whisky, and an old book and two newspapers for wadding, besides some tow.[5] I toted up a load, and went back and set down on the bow of the skiff to rest. I thought it all over, and I reckoned I would walk off with the gun and some lines, and take to the woods when I run away. I guessed I wouldn't stay in one place, but just tramp right across the country, mostly night times, and hunt and fish to keep alive, and so get so far away that the old man nor the widow couldn't ever find me any more. I judged I would saw out and leave that night if pap got drunk enough, and I reckoned he would. I got so full of it I didn't notice how long I was staying, till the old man hollered and asked me whether I was asleep or drownded.

I got the things all up to the cabin, and then it was about dark. While I was cooking supper the old man took a swig or two and got sort of warmed up, and went to ripping again. He had been drunk over in town, and laid in the gutter all night, and he was a sight to look at. A body would a thought he was Adam, he was just all mud.[6] Whenever his liquor begun to work, he most always went for the govment. This time he says:

"Call this a govment! why, just look at it and see what it's like. Here's the law a-standing ready to take a man's son away from him—a man's own son, which he has had all the trouble and all the anxiety and all the expense of raising. Yes, just as that man has got that son raised at last, and ready to go to work and begin to do suthin' for *him* and give him a rest, the law up and goes for him. And they call *that* govment! That ain't all, nuther. The law backs that old Judge Thatcher up and helps him to keep me out o' my property. Here's what the law does. The law takes a man worth six thousand dollars and upards, and jams him into an old trap of a cabin like this, and lets him go round in clothes that ain't fitten for a hog. They call that

---

5. Cheap rope. "Wadding": material (here paper) used to pack the gunpowder in a rifle.   6. God created Adam from earth in Genesis 2.7.

govment! A man can't get his rights in a govment like this. Sometimes I've a mighty notion to just leave the country for good and all. Yes, and I *told* 'em so: I told old Thatcher so to his face. Lots of 'em heard me, and can tell what I said. Says I, for two cents I'd leave the blamed country and never come anear it agin. Them's the very words. I says, look at my hat—if you call it a hat—but the lid raises up and the rest of it goes down till it's below my chin, and then it ain't rightly a hat at all, but more like my head was shoved up through a jint o' stove-pipe. Look at it, says I—such a hat for me to wear—one of the wealthiest men in this town, if I could git my rights.

"Oh, yes, this is a wonderful govment, wonderful. Why, looky here. There was a free nigger there, from Ohio; a mulatter,[7] most as white as a white man. He had the whitest shirt on you ever see, too, and the shiniest hat; and there ain't a man in that town that's got as fine clothes as what he had; and he had a gold watch and chain and a silver-headed cane—the awfulest old gray-headed nabob in the State. And what do you think? they said he was a p'fessor in a college, and could talk all kinds of languages, and knowed every thing. And that ain't the wust. They said he could *vote*, when he was at home. Well, that let me out. Thinks I, what is the country a-coming to? It was 'lection day, and I was just about to go and vote, myself, if I warn't too drunk to get there; but when they told me there was a State in this country where they'd let that nigger vote, I drawed out. I says I'll never vote agin. Them's the very words I said; they all heard me; and the country may rot for all me—I'll never vote agin as long as I live. And to see the cool way of that nigger—why, he wouldn't a give me the road if I hadn't shoved him out o' the way. I says to the people, why ain't this nigger put up at auction and sold?—that's what I want to know. And what do you reckon they said? Why, they said he couldn't be sold till he'd been in the State six months, and he hadn't been there that long yet. There, now—that's a specimen. They call that a govment that can't sell a free nigger till he's been in the State six months. Here's a govment that calls itself a govment, and lets on to be a govment, and thinks it is a govment, and yet's got to set stock-still for six whole months before it can take ahold of a prowling, thieving, infernal, white-shirted free nigger, and[8]—"

Pap was agoing on so, he never noticed where his old limber legs was taking him to, so he went head over heels over the tub of salt pork, and barked both shins, and the rest of his speech was all the hottest kind of language—mostly hove at the nigger and the govment, though he give the tub some, too, all along, here and there. He hopped around the cabin considerble, first on one leg and then on the other, holding first one shin and then the other one, and at last he let out with his left foot all of a sudden and fetched the tub a rattling kick. But it warn't good judgment, because that was the boot that had a couple of his toes leaking out of the front end of it; so now he raised a howl that fairly made a body's hair raise, and down he went in the dirt, and rolled there, and held his toes; and the cussing he done then laid over any thing he had ever done previous. He said so his own self, afterwards. He had heard old Sowberry Hagan in his best days, and he said it laid over him, too; but I reckon that was sort of piling it on, maybe.

7. Mulatto, of mixed white and black ancestry. Ohio was a free state.
8. Missouri's original constitution prohibited the entrance of freed slaves and mulattoes into the state, but the second Missouri Compromise of 1820 deleted the provision. In the 1830s and 1840s, however, increasingly strict antiblack laws were passed, and by 1850 a black person without freedom papers could be sold downriver with a mere sworn statement of ownership from a white man.

After supper pap took the jug, and said he had enough whisky there for two drunks and one delirium tremens. That was always his word. I judged he would be blind drunk in about an hour, an then I would steal the key, or saw myself out, one or 'tother. He drank, and drank, and tumbled down on his blankets, by-and-by; but luck didn't run my way. He didn't go sound asleep, but was uneasy. He groaned, and moaned, and thrashed around this way and that, for a long time. At last I got so sleepy I couldn't keep my eyes open, all I could do, and so before I knowed what I was about I was sound asleep, and the candle burning.

I don't know how long I was asleep, but all of a sudden there was an awful scream and I was up. There was pap, looking wild and skipping around every which way and yelling about snakes. He said they was crawling up his legs; and then he would give a jump and scream, and say one had bit him on the cheek—but I couldn't see no snakes. He started to run round and round the cabin, hollering "take him off! take him off! he's biting me on the neck!" I never see a man look so wild in the eyes. Pretty soon he was all fagged out, and fell down panting; then he rolled over and over, wonderful fast, kicking things every which way, and striking and grabbing at the air with his hands, and screaming, and saying there was devils ahold of him. He wore out, by-and-by, and laid still a while, moaning. Then he laid stiller, and didn't make a sound. I could hear the owls and the wolves, away off in the woods, and it seemed terrible still. He was laying over by the corner. By-and-by he raised up, part way, and listened, with his head to one side. He says very low:

"Tramp—tramp—tramp; that's the dead; tramp—tramp—tramp; they're coming after me; but I won't go—Oh, they're here! don't touch me—don't! hands off—they're cold; let go—Oh, let a poor devil alone!"

Then he went down on all fours and crawled off begging them to let him alone, and he rolled himself up in his blanket and wallowed in under the old pine table, still a-begging; and then he went to crying. I could hear him through the blanket.

By-and-by he rolled out and jumped up on his feet looking wild, and he see me and went for me. He chased me round and round the place, with a clasp-knife, calling me the Angel of Death and saying he would kill me and then I couldn't come for him no more. I begged, and told him I was only Huck, but he laughed *such* a screechy laugh, and roared and cussed, and kept on chasing me up. Once when I turned short and dodged under his arm he made a grab and got me by the jacket between my shoulders, and I thought I was gone; but I skid out of the jacket quick as lightning, and saved myself. Pretty soon he was all tired out, and dropped down with his back against the door, and said he would rest a minute and then kill me. He put his knife under him, and said he would sleep and get strong, and then he would see who was who.

So he dozed off, pretty soon. By-and-by I got the old split bottom[9] chair and clumb up, as easy as I could, not to make any noise, and got down the gun. I slipped the ramrod down it to make sure it was loaded, and then I laid it across the turnip barrel, pointing towards pap, and set down behind it to wait for him to stir. And how slow and still the time did drag along.

---

9. I.e., splint-bottom, made by interweaving thin strips of wood.

Chapter VII

"Git up! what you 'bout!"

I opened my eyes and looked around, trying to make out where I was. It was after sun-up, and I had been sound asleep. Pap was standing over me, looking sour—and sick, too. He says—

"What you doin' with this gun?"

I judged he didn't know nothing about what he had been doing, so I says:

"Somebody tried to get in, so I was laying for him."

"Why didn't you roust me out?"

"Well I tried to, but I couldn't; I couldn't budge you."

"Well, all right. Don't stand there palavering all day, but out with you and see if there's a fish on the lines for breakfast. I'll be along in a minute."

He unlocked the door and I cleared out, up the river bank. I noticed some pieces of limbs and such things floating down, and a sprinkling of bark; so I knowed the river had begun to rise. I reckoned I would have great times, now, if I was over at the town. The June rise used to be always luck for me; because as soon as that rise begins, here comes cord-wood floating down, and pieces of log rafts—sometimes a dozen logs together; so all you have to do is to catch them and sell them to the wood yards and the sawmill.

I went along up the bank with one eye out for pap and 'tother one out for what the rise might fetch along. Well, all at once, here comes a canoe; just a beauty, too, about thirteen or fourteen foot long, riding high like a duck. I shot head first off of the bank, like a frog, clothes and all on, and struck out for the canoe. I just expected there'd be somebody laying down in it, because people often done that to fool folks, and when a chap had pulled a skiff out most to it they'd raise up and laugh at him. But it warn't so this time. It was a drift-canoe, sure enough, and I clumb in and paddled her ashore. Thinks I, the old man will be glad when he sees this—she's worth ten dollars. But when I got to shore pap wasn't in sight yet, and as I was running her into a little creek like a gully, all hung over with vines and willows, I struck another idea; I judged I'd hide her good, and then, stead of taking to the woods when I run off, I'd go down the river about fifty mile and camp in one place for good, and not have such a rough time tramping on foot.

It was pretty close to the shanty, and I thought I heard the old man coming, all the time; but I got her hid; and then I out and looked around a bunch of willows, and there was the old man down the path apiece just drawing a bead on a bird with his gun. So he hadn't seen anything.

When he got along, I was hard at it taking up a "trot" line.[1] He abused me a little for being so slow, but I told him I fell in the river and that was what made me so long. I knowed he would see I was wet, and then he would be asking questions. We got five catfish off of the lines and went home.

While we laid off, after breakfast, to sleep up, both of us being about wore out, I got to thinking that if I could fix up some way to keep pap and the widow from trying to follow me, it would be a certainer thing than trusting to luck to get far enough off before they missed me; you see, all kinds of things might happen. Well, I didn't see no way for a while, but by-and-by pap raised up a minute, to drink another barrel of water, and he says:

---

1. A long fishing line fastened across a stream; to this line several shorter baited lines are attached.

"Another time a man comes a-prowling round here, you roust me out, you hear? That man warn't here for no good. I'd a shot him. Next time, you roust me out, you hear?"

Then he dropped down and went to sleep again—but what he had been saying give me the very idea I wanted. I says to myself, I can fix it now so nobody won't think of following me.

About twelve o'clock we turned out and went along up the bank. The river was coming up pretty fast, and lots of drift-wood going by on the rise. By-and-by, along comes part of a log raft—nine logs fast together. We went out with the skiff and towed it ashore. Then we had dinner. Anybody but pap would a waited and seen the day through, so as to catch more stuff; but that warn't pap's style. Nine logs was enough for one time; he must shove right over to town and sell. So he locked me in and took the skiff and started off towing the raft about half-past three. I judged he wouldn't come back that night. I waited till I reckoned he had got a good start, then I out with my saw and went to work on that log again. Before he was 'tother side of the river I was out of the hole; him and his raft was just a speck on the water away off yonder.

I took the sack of corn meal and took it to where the canoe was hid, and shoved the vines and branches apart and put it in; then I done the same with the side of bacon; then the whiskey jug; I took all the coffee and sugar there was, and all the ammunition; I took the wadding; I took the bucket and gourd, I took a dipper and a tin cup, and my old saw and two blankets, and the skillet and the coffee-pot. I took fish-lines and matches and other things—everything that was worth a cent. I cleaned out the place. I wanted an axe, but there wasn't any, only the one out at the wood pile, and I knowed why I was going to leave that. I fetched out the gun, and now I was done.

I had wore the ground a good deal, crawling out of the hole and dragging out so many things. So I fixed that as good as I could from the outside by scattering dust on the place, which covered up the smoothness and the saw-dust. Then I fixed the piece of log back into its place, and put two rocks under it and one against it to hold it there,—for it was bent up at the place, and didn't quite touch ground. If you stood four or five foot away and didn't know it was sawed, you wouldn't ever notice it; and besides, this was the back of the cabin and it warn't likely anybody would go fooling around there.

It was all grass clear to the canoe; so I hadn't left a track. I followed around to see. I stood on the bank and looked out over the river. All safe. So I took the gun and went up a piece into the woods and was hunting around for some birds, when I see a wild pig; hogs soon went wild in them bottoms after they had got away from the prairie farms. I shot this fellow and took him into camp.

I took the axe and smashed in the door—I beat it and hacked it consider-able, a-doing it. I fetched the pig in and took him back nearly to the table and hacked into his throat with the ax, and laid him down on the ground to bleed—I say ground, because it *was* ground—hard packed, and no boards. Well, next I took an old sack and put a lot of big rocks in it,—all I could drag—and I started it from the pig and dragged it to the door and through the woods down to the river and dumped it in, and down it sunk, out of sight. You could easy see that something had been dragged over the ground. I did wish Tom Sawyer was there, I knowed he would take an interest in this kind of business, and throw in the fancy touches. Nobody could spread himself like Tom Sawyer in such a thing as that.

Well, last I pulled out some of my hair, and bloodied the ax good, and stuck it on the back side, and slung the ax in the corner. Then I took up the pig and held him to my breast with my jacket (so he couldn't drip) till I got a good piece below the house and then dumped him into the river. Now I thought of something else. So I went and got the bag of meal and my old saw out of the canoe and fetched them to the house. I took the bag to where it used to stand, and ripped a hole in the bottom of it with the saw, for there warn't no knives and forks on the place—pap done everything with his clasp-knife, about the cooking. Then I carried the sack about a hundred yards across the grass and through the willows east of the house, to a shallow lake that was five mile wide and full of rushes—and ducks too, you might say, in the season. There was a slough or a creek leading out of it on the other side, that went miles away, I don't know where, but it didn't go to the river. The meal sifted out and made a little track all the way to the lake. I dropped pap's whetstone there too, so as to look like it had been done by accident. Then I tied up the rip in the meal sack with a string, so it wouldn't leak no more, and took it and my saw to the canoe again.

It was about dark, now; so I dropped the canoe down the river under some willows that hung over the bank, and waited for the moon to rise. I made fast to a willow; then I took a bite to eat, and by-and-by laid down in the canoe to smoke a pipe and lay out a plan. I says to myself, they'll follow the track of that sackful of rocks to the shore and then drag the river for me. And they'll follow that meal track to the lake and go browsing down the creek that leads out of it to find the robbers that killed me and took the things. They won't ever hunt the river for anything but my dead carcass. They'll soon get tired of that, and won't bother no more about me. All right; I can stop anywhere I want to. Jackson's Island[2] is good enough for me; I know that island pretty well, and nobody ever comes there. And then I can paddle over to town, nights, and slink around and pick up things I want. Jackson's Island's the place.

I was pretty tired, and the first thing I knowed, I was asleep. When I woke up I didn't know where I was, for a minute. I set up and looked around, a little scared. Then I remembered. The river looked miles and miles across. The moon was so bright I could a counted the drift logs that went a slipping along, black and still, hundreds of yards out from shore. Everything was dead quiet, and it looked late, and *smelt* late. You know what I mean—I don't know the words to put it in.

I took a good gap and a stretch, and was just going to unhitch and start, when I heard a sound away over the water. I listened. Pretty soon I made it out. It was that dull kind of a regular sound that comes from oars working in rowlocks when it's a still night. I peeped out through the willow branches, and there it was—a skiff, away across the water. I couldn't tell how many was in it. It kept a-coming, and when it was abreast of me I see there warn't but one man in it. Thinks I, maybe it's pap, though I warn't expecting him. He dropped below me, with the current, and by-and-by he come a-swinging up shore in the easy water, and he went by so close I could a reached out the gun and touched him. Well, it *was* pap, sure enough—and sober, too, by the way he laid to his oars.

I didn't lose no time. The next minute I was a-spinning down stream soft but quick in the shade of the bank. I made two mile and a half, and then struck out a quarter of a mile or more towards the middle of the river,

2. The same island that serves for an adventure in *Tom Sawyer* (Ch. 13).

because pretty soon I would be passing the ferry landing and people might see me and hail me. I got out amongst the drift-wood and then laid down in the bottom of the canoe and let her float. I laid there and had a good rest and a smoke out of my pipe, looking away into the sky, not a cloud in it. The sky looks ever so deep when you lay down on your back in the moonshine; I never knowed it before. And how far a body can hear on the water such nights! I heard people talking at the ferry landing. I heard what they said, too, every word of it. One man said it was getting towards the long days and the short nights, now. 'Tother one said *this* warn't one of the short ones, he reckoned—and then they laughed, and he said it over again and they laughed again; then they waked up another fellow and told him, and laughed, but he didn't laugh; he ripped out something brisk and said let him alone. The first fellow said he 'lowed to tell it to his old woman—she would think it was pretty good; but he said that warn't nothing to some things he had said in his time. I heard one man say it was nearly three o'clock, and he hoped daylight wouldn't wait more than about a week longer. After that, the talk got further and further away, and I couldn't make out the words any more, but I could hear the mumble; and now and then a laugh, too, but it seemed a long ways off.

I was away below the ferry now. I rose up and there was Jackson's Island, about two mile and a half down stream, heavy-timbered and standing up out of the middle of the river, big and dark and solid, like a steamboat without any lights. There warn't any signs of the bar at the head—it was all under water, now.

It didn't take me long to get there. I shot past the head at a ripping rate, the current was so swift, and then I got into the dead water and landed on the side towards the Illinois shore. I run the canoe into a deep dent in the bank that I knowed about; I had to part the willow branches to get in; and when I made fast nobody could a seen the canoe from the outside.

I went up and set down on a log at the head of the island and looked out on the big river and the black driftwood, and away over to the town, three mile away, where there was three or four lights twinkling. A monstrous big lumber raft was about a mile up stream, coming along down, with a lantern in the middle of it. I watched it come creeping down, and when it was most abreast of where I stood I heard a man say, "Stern oars, there! heave her head to stabboard!"[3] I heard that just as plain as if the man was by my side.

There was a little gray in the sky, now; so I stepped into the woods and laid down for a nap before breakfast.

Chapter VIII

The sun was up so high when I waked, that I judged it was after eight o'clock. I laid there in the grass and the cool shade, thinking about things and feeling rested and ruther comfortable and satisfied. I could see the sun out at one or two holes, but mostly it was big trees all about, and gloomy in there amongst them. There was freckled places on the ground where the light sifted down through the leaves, and the freckled places swapped about a little, showing there was a little breeze up there. A couple of squirrels set on a limb and jabbered at me very friendly.

I was powerful lazy and comfortable—didn't want to get up and cook breakfast. Well, I was dozing off again, when I thinks I hears a deep sound

---

3. Starboard, the right-hand side of a boat, facing forward.

of "boom!" away up the river. I rouses up and rests on my elbow and listens; pretty soon I hears it again. I hopped up and went and looked out at a hole in the leaves, and I see a bunch of smoke laying on the water a long ways up—about abreast the ferry. And there was the ferry-boat full of people, floating along down. I knowed what was the matter, now. "Boom!" I see the white smoke squirt out of the ferry-boat's side. You see, they was firing cannon over the water, trying to make my carcass come to the top.

I was pretty hungry, but it warn't going to do for me to start a fire, because they might see the smoke. So I set there and watched the cannon-smoke and listened to the boom. The river was a mile wide, there, and it always looks pretty on a summer morning—so I was having a good enough time seeing them hunt for my remainders, if I only had a bite to eat. Well, then I happened to think how they always put quicksilver in loaves of bread and float them off because they always go right to the drownded carcass and stop there. So says I, I'll keep a lookout, and if any of them's floating around after me, I'll give them a show. I changed to the Illinois edge of the island to see what luck I could have, and I warn't disappointed. A big double loaf come along, and I most got it, with a long stick, but my foot slipped and she floated out further. Of course I was where the current set in the closest to the shore—I knowed enough for that. But by-and-by along comes another one, and this time I won. I took out the plug and shook out the little dab of quicksilver, and set my teeth in. It was "baker's bread"—what the quality eat—none of your low-down corn-pone.[4]

I got a good place amongst the leaves, and set there on a log, munching the bread and watching the ferry-boat, and very well satisfied. And then something struck me. I says, now I reckon the widow or the parson or somebody prayed that this bread would find me, and here it has gone and done it. So there ain't no doubt but there is something in that thing. That is, there's something in it when a body like the widow or the parson prays, but it don't work for me, and I reckon it don't work for only just the right kind.

I lit a pipe and had a good long smoke and went on watching. The ferry-boat was floating with the current, and I allowed I'd have a chance to see who was aboard when she come along, because she would come in close, where the bread did. When she'd got pretty well along down towards me, I put out my pipe and went to where I fished out the bread, and laid down behind a log on the bank in a little open place. Where the log forked I could peep through.

By-and-by she came along, and she drifted in so close that they could a run out a plank and walked ashore. Most everybody was on the boat. Pap, and Judge Thatcher, and Bessie Thatcher, and Jo Harper, and Tom Sawyer, and his old Aunt Polly, and Sid and Mary, and plenty more. Everybody was talking about the murder, but the captain broke in and says:

"Look sharp, now; the current sets in the closest here, and maybe he's washed ashore and got tangled amongst the brush at the water's edge. I hope so, anyway."

I didn't hope so. They all crowded up and leaned over the rails, nearly in my face, and kept still, watching with all their might. I could see them first-rate, but they couldn't see me. Then the captain sung out:

"Stand away!" and the cannon let off such a blast right before me that it made me deef with the noise and pretty near blind with the smoke, and I

4. Corn bread.

judged I was gone. If they'd a had some bullets in, I reckon they'd a got the corpse they was after. Well, I see I warn't hurt, thanks to goodness. The boat floated on and went out of sight around the shoulder of the island. I could hear the booming, now and then, further and further off, and by-and-by after an hour, I didn't hear it no more. The island was three mile long. I judged they had got to the foot, and was giving it up. But they didn't yet a while. They turned around the foot of the island and started up the channel on the Missouri side, under steam, and booming once in a while as they went. I crossed over to that side and watched them. When they got abreast the head of the island they quit shooting and dropped over to the Missouri shore and went home to the town.

I knowed I was all right now. Nobody else would come a-hunting after me. I got my traps out of the canoe and made me a nice camp in the thick woods. I made a kind of a tent out of my blankets to put my things under so the rain couldn't get at them. I catched a cat fish and haggled him open with my saw, and towards sundown I started my camp fire and had supper. Then I set out a line to catch some fish for breakfast.

When it was dark I set by my camp fire smoking, and feeling pretty satisfied; but by-and-by it got sort of lonesome, and so I went and set on the bank and listened to the currents washing along, and counted the stars and drift-logs and rafts that come down, and then went to bed; there ain't no better way to put in time when you are lonesome; you can't stay so, you soon get over it.

And so for three days and nights. No difference—just the same thing. But the next day I went exploring around down through the island. I was boss of it; it all belonged to me, so to say, and I wanted to know all about it; but mainly I wanted to put in the time. I found plenty strawberries, ripe and prime; and green summer-grapes, and green razberries; and the green black-berries was just beginning to show. They would all come handy by-and-by, I judged.

Well, I went fooling along in the deep woods till I judged I warn't far from the foot of the island. I had my gun along, but I hadn't shot nothing; it was for protection; thought I would kill some game nigh home. About this time I mighty near stepped on a good sized snake, and it went sliding off through the grass and flowers, and I after it, trying to get a shot at it. I clipped along, and all of sudden I bounded right on to the ashes of a camp fire that was still smoking.

My heart jumped up amongst my lungs. I never waited for to look further, but uncocked my gun and went sneaking back on my tip-toes as fast as ever I could. Every now and then I stopped a second, amongst the thick leaves, and listened; but my breath come so hard I couldn't hear nothing else. I slunk along another piece further, then listened again; and so on, and so on; if I see a stump, I took it for a man; if I trod on a stick and broke it, it made me feel like a person had cut one of my breaths in two and I only got half, and the short half, too.

When I got to camp I warn't feeling very brash, there warn't much sand in my craw;[5] but I says, this ain't no time to be fooling around. So I got all my traps into my canoe again so as to have them out of sight, and I put out the fire and scattered the ashes around to look like an old last year's camp, and then clumb a tree.

5. Slang for not feeling very brave.

I reckon I was up in the tree two hours; but I didn't see nothing, I didn't hear nothing—I only *thought* I heard and seen as much as a thousand things. Well, I couldn't stay up there forever; so at last I got down, but I kept in the thick woods and on the lookout all the time. All I could get to eat was berries and what was left over from breakfast.

By the time it was night I was pretty hungry. So when it was good and dark, I slid out from shore before moonrise and paddled over to the Illinois bank—about a quarter of a mile. I went out in the woods and cooked a supper, and I had about made up my mind I would stay there all night, when I hear a *plunkety-plunk, plunkety-plunk,* and says to myself, horses coming; and next I hear people's voices. I got everything into the canoe as quick as I could, and then went creeping through the woods to see what I could find out. I hadn't got far when I hear a man say:

"We'd better camp here, if we can find a good place; the horses is about beat out. Let's look around."[6]

I didn't wait, but shoved out and paddled away easy. I tied up in the old place, and reckoned I would sleep in the canoe.

I didn't sleep much. I couldn't, somehow, for thinking. And every time I waked up I thought somebody had me by the neck. So the sleep didn't do me no good. By-and-by I says to myself, I can't live this way; I'm agoing to find out who it is that's here on the island with me; I'll find it out or bust. Well, I felt better, right off.

So I took my paddle and slid out from shore just a step or two, and then let the canoe drop along down amongst the shadows. The moon was shining, and outside of the shadows it made it most as light as day. I poked along well onto an hour, everything still as rocks and sound asleep. Well by this time I was most down to the foot of the island. A little ripply, cool breeze begun to blow, and that was as good as saying the night was about done. I give her a turn with the paddle and brung her nose to shore; then I got my gun and slipped out and into the edge of the woods. I set down there on a log and looked out through the leaves. I see the moon go off watch and the darkness begin to blanket the river. But in a little while I see a pale streak over the tree-tops, and knowed the day was coming. So I took my gun and slipped off towards where I had run across that camp fire, stopping every minute or two to listen. But I hadn't no luck, somehow; I couldn't seem to find the place. But by-and-by, sure enough, I catched a glimpse of fire, away through the trees. I went for it, cautious and slow. By-and-by I was close enough to have a look, and there laid a man on the ground. It most give me the fan-tods.[7] He had a blanket around his head, and his head was nearly in the fire. I set there behind a clump of bushes, in about six foot of him, and kept my eyes on him steady. It was getting gray daylight, now. Pretty soon he gapped, and stretched himself, and hove off the blanket, and it was Miss Watson's Jim! I bet I was glad to see him. I says:

"Hello, Jim!" and skipped out.

He bounced up and stared at me wild. Then he drops down on his knees, and puts his hands together and says:

"Doan' hurt me—don't! I hain't ever done no harm to a ghos'. I awluz liked dead people, en done all I could for 'em. You go en git in de river agin, whah you b'longs, en doan' do nuffn to Ole Jim, 'at 'uz awluz yo' fren'."

6. Apparently this episode is a vestige of an early conception of the novel involving Pap in a murder plot and court trial.

7. Slang for the hallucinatory state associated with delirium tremens, a condition that afflicts alcoholics.

Well, I warn't long making him understand I warn't dead. I was ever so glad to see Jim. I warn't lonesome, now. I told him I warn't afraid of *him* telling the people where I was. I talked along, but he only set there and looked at me; never said nothing. Then I says:

"It's good daylight. Let's get breakfast. Make up your camp fire good."

"What's de use er makin' up de camp fire to cook strawbries en sich truck? But you got a gun, hain't you? Den we kin git sumfn better den strawbries."

"Strawberries and such truck," I says. "Is that what you live on?"

"I couldn' git nuffn else," he says.

"Why, how long you been on the island, Jim?"

"I come heah de night arter you's killed."

"What, all that time?"

"Yes-indeedy."

"And ain't you had nothing but that kind of rubbage to eat?"

"No, sah—nuffn else."

"Well, you must be most starved, ain't you?"

"I reck'n I could eat a hoss. I think I could. How long you ben on de islan'?"

"Since the night I got killed."

"No! W'y, what has you lived on? But you got a gun. Oh, yes, you got a gun. Dat's good. Now you kill sumfn en I'll make up de fire."

So we went over to where the canoe was, and while he built a fire in a grassy open place amongst the trees, I fetched meal and bacon and coffee, and coffee-pot and frying-pan, and sugar and tin cups, and the nigger was set back considerable, because he reckoned it was all done with witchcraft. I catched a good big cat-fish, too, and Jim cleaned him with his knife, and fried him.

When breakfast was ready, we lolled on the grass and eat it smoking hot. Jim laid it in with all his might, for he was most about starved. Then when we had got pretty well stuffed, we laid off and lazied.

By-and-by Jim says:

"But looky here, Huck, who wuz it dat 'uz killed in dat shanty, ef it warn't you?"

Then I told him the whole thing, and he said it was smart. He said Tom Sawyer couldn't get up no better plan than what I had. Then I says:

"How do you come to be here, Jim, and how'd you get here?"

He looked pretty uneasy, and didn't say nothing for a minute. Then he says:

"Maybe I better not tell."

"Why, Jim?"

"Well, dey's reasons. But you wouldn' tell on me ef I 'uz to tell you, would you, Huck?"

"Blamed if I would, Jim."

"Well, I b'lieve you, Huck. I—I *run off.*"

"Jim!"

"But mind, you said you wouldn't tell—you know you said you wouldn't tell, Huck."

"Well, I did. I said I wouldn't, and I'll stick to it. Honest *injun* I will. People would call me a low down Ablitionist and despise me for keeping mum—but that don't make no difference. I ain't agoing to tell, and I ain't agoing back there anyways. So now, le's know all about it."

"Well, you see, it 'uz dis way. Ole Missus—dat's Miss Watson—she pecks on me all de time, en treats me pooty rough, but she awluz said she wouldn' sell me down to Orleans. But I noticed dey wuz a nigger trader roun' de place considerable, lately, en I begin to git oneasy. Well, one night I creeps to de do', pooty late, en de do' warn't quite shet, en I hear ole missus tell de widder she gwyne to sell me down to Orleans, but she didn' want to, but she could git eight hund'd dollars for me, en it 'uz sich a big stack o' money she couldn' resis'. De widder she try to git her to say she wouldn' do it, but I never waited to hear de res'. I lit out mighty quick, I tell you.

"I tuck out en shin down de hill en 'spec to steal a skift 'long de sho' som'ers 'bove de town, but dey wuz people a-stirrin' yit, so I hid in de ole tumbledown cooper shop on de bank to wait for everybody to go 'way. Well, I wuz dah all night. Dey wuz somebody roun' all de time. 'Long 'bout six in de mawnin', skifts begin to go by, en 'bout eight or nine every skift dat went 'long wuz talkin' 'bout how yo' pap come over to de town en say you's killed. Dese las' skifts wuz full o' ladies en genlmen agoin' over for to see de place. Sometimes dey'd pull up at de sho' en take a res' b'fo' dey started acrost, so by de talk I got to know all 'bout de killin'. I 'uz powerful sorry you's killed, Huck, but I ain't no mo', now.

"I laid dah under de shavins all day. I 'uz hungry, but I warn't afeared; bekase I knowed ole missus en de widder wuz goin' to start to de camp-meetn' right arter breakfas' en be gone all day, en dey knows I goes off wid de cattle 'bout daylight, so dey wouldn' 'spec to see me roun' de place, en so dey wouldn' miss me tell arter dark in de evenin'. De yuther servants wouldn' miss me, kase dey'd shin out en take holiday, soon as de ole folks 'uz out'n de way.

"Well, when it come dark I tuck out up de river road, en went 'bout two mile er more to whah dey warn't no houses. I'd made up my mind 'bout what I's agwyne to do. You see ef I kep' on tryin' to git away afoot, de dogs 'ud track me; ef I stole a skift to cross over, dey'd miss dat skift, you see, en dey'd know 'bout whah I'd lan' on de yuther side en whah to pick up my track. So I says, a raff is what I's arter; it doan' *make* no track.

"I see a light a-comin' roun' de p'int, bymeby, so I wade' in en shove' a log ahead o' me, en swum more'n half-way acrost de river, en got in 'mongst de drift-wood, en kep' my head down low, en kinder swum agin de current tell de raff come along. Den I swum to de stern uv it, en tuck aholt. It clouded up en 'uz pooty dark for a little while. So I clumb up en laid down on de planks. De men 'uz all 'way yonder in de middle, whah de lantern wuz. De river wuz arisin' en dey wuz a good current; so I reck'n'd 'at by fo' in de mawnin' I'd be twenty-five mile down de river, en den I'd slip in, jis' b'fo' daylight, en swim asho' en take to de woods on de Illinoi side.[8]

"But I didn' have no luck. When we 'uz mos' down to de head er de islan', a man begin to come aft wid de lantern. I see it warn't no use fer to wait, so I slid overboad, en struck out fer de islan'. Well, I had a notion I could lan' mos' anywhers, but I couldn'—bank too bluff. I 'uz mos' to de foot er de islan' b'fo' I foun' a good place. I went into de woods en jedged I wouldn' fool wid raffs no mo', long as dey move de lantern roun' so. I had my pipe en a plug er dog-leg,[9] en some matches in my cap, en dey warn't wet, so I 'uz all right."

"And so you ain't had no meat nor bread to eat all this time? Why didn't you get mud-turkles?"

8. Though Illinois was not a slave state, by state law any black person without freedom papers could be arrested and subjected to forced labor. Jim's chances for escape would be improved if he went down the Mississippi and then up the Ohio.
9. Cheap tobacco.

"How you gwyne to git'm? You can't slip up on um en grab um; en how's a body gwyne to hit um wid a rock? How could a body do it in de night? en I warn't gwyne to show myself on de bank in de daytime."

"Well, that's so. You've had to keep in the woods all the time, of course. Did you hear 'em shooting the cannon?"

"Oh, yes. I knowed dey was arter you. I see um go by heah; watched um thoo de bushes."

Some young birds come along, flying a yard or two at a time and lighting. Jim said it was a sign it was going to rain. He said it was a sign when young chickens flew that way, and so he reckoned it was the same way when young birds done it. I was going to catch some of them, but Jim wouldn't let me. He said it was death. He said his father laid mighty sick once, and some of them catched a bird, and his old granny said his father would die, and he did.

And Jim said you mustn't count the things you are going to cook for dinner, because that would bring bad luck. The same if you shook the table-cloth after sundown. And he said if a man owned a bee-hive, and that man died, the bees must be told about it before sun-up next morning, or else the bees would all weaken down and quit work and die. Jim said bees wouldn't sting idiots; but I didn't believe that, because I had tried them lots of times myself, and they wouldn't sting me.

I had heard about some of these things before, but not all of them. Jim knowed all kinds of signs. He said he knowed most everything. I said it looked to me like all the signs was about bad luck, and so I asked him if there warn't any good-luck signs. He says:

"Mighty few—an' *dey* ain' no use to a body. What you want to know when good luck's a-comin' for? want to keep it off?" And he said: "Ef you's got hairy arms en a hairy breas', it's a sign dat you's agwyne to be rich. Well, dey's some use in a sign like dat, 'kase it's so fur ahead. You see, maybe you's got to be po' a long time fust, en so you might git discourage' en kill yo'sef 'f you didn' know by de sign dat you gwyne to be rich bymeby."

"Have you got hairy arms and a hairy breast, Jim?"

"What's de use to ax dat question? don' you see I has?"

"Well, are you rich?"

"No, but I ben rich wunst, and gwyne to be rich agin. Wunst I had foteen dollars, but I tuck to specalat'n', en got busted out."

"What did you speculate in, Jim?"

"Well, fust I tackled stock."

"What kind of stock?"

"Why, live stock. Cattle, you know. I put ten dollars in a cow. But I ain't gwyne to resk no mo' money in stock. De cow up 'n' died on my han's."

"So you lost the ten dollars."

"No, I didn' lose it all. I on'y los' 'bout nine of it. I sole de hide en taller for a dollar en ten cents."

"You had five dollars and ten cents left. Did you speculate any more?"

"Yes. You know dat one-laigged nigger dat b'longs to old Misto Bradish? well, he sot up a bank, en say anybody dat put in a dollar would git fo' dollars mo' at de en' er de year. Well, all de niggers went in, but dey didn' have much. I wuz de on'y one dat had much. So I stuck out for mo' dan fo' dollars, en I said 'f I didn' git it I'd start a bank myself. Well o' course dat nigger want' to keep me out er de business, bekase he say dey warn't business 'nough for two banks, so he say I could put in my five dollars en he pay me thirty-five at de en' er de year.

"So I done it. Den I reck'n'd I'd inves' de thirty-five dollars right off en keep things a-movin'. Dey wuz a nigger name' Bob, dat had ketched a wood-flat,[1] en his marster didn' know it; en I bought it off'n him en told him to take de thirty-five dollars when de en' er de year come; but somebody stole de wood-flat dat night, en nex' day de one-laigged nigger say de bank 's busted. So dey didn' none uv us git no money."

"What did you do with the ten cents, Jim?"

"Well, I 'uz gwyne to spen' it, but I had a dream, en de dream tole me to give it to a nigger name' Balum—Balum's Ass[2] dey call him for short, he's one er dem chuckle-heads, you know. But he's lucky, dey say, en I see I warn't lucky. De dream say let Balum inves' de ten cents en he'd make a raise for me. Well, Balum he tuck de money, en when he wuz in church he hear de preacher say dat whoever give to de po' len' to de Lord, en boun' to git his money back a hund'd times. So Balum he tuck en give de ten cents to de po', en laid low to see what wuz gwyne to come of it."

"Well, what did come of it, Jim?"

"Nuffn never come of it. I couldn' manage to k'leck dat money no way; en Balum he couldn'. I ain' gwyne to len' no mo' money 'dout I see de security. Boun' to git yo' money back a hund'd times, de preacher says! Ef I could git de ten *cents* back, I'd call it squah, en be glad er de chanst."

"Well, it's all right anyway, Jim, long as you're going to be rich again some time or other."

"Yes—en I's rich now, come to look at it. I owns mysef, en I's wuth eight hund'd dollars. I wisht I had de money, I wouldn' want no mo'."

Chapter IX

I wanted to go and look at a place right about the middle of the island, that I'd found when I was exploring; so we started, and soon got to it, because the island was only three miles long and a quarter of a mile wide.

This place was a tolerable long steep hill or ridge, about forty foot high. We had a rough time getting to the top, the sides was so steep and the bushes so thick. We tramped and clumb around all over it, and by-and-by found a good big cavern in the rock, most up to the top on the side towards Illinois. The cavern was as big as two or three rooms bunched together, and Jim could stand up straight in it. It was cool in there. Jim was for putting our traps in there, right away, but I said we didn't want to be climbing up and down there all the time.

Jim said if we had the canoe hid in a good place, and had all the traps in the cavern, we could rush there if anybody was to come to the island, and they would never find us without dogs. And besides, he said them little birds had said it was going to rain, and did I want the things to get wet?

So we went back and got the canoe and paddled up abreast the cavern, and lugged all the traps up there. Then we hunted up a place close by to

---

1. A flat-bottomed boat used to transport timber.
2. Balaam, Old Testament prophet. God's avenging angel interrupted this prophet's journey to curse the Israelites by standing in the path of his progress. Balaam was blind to the angel's presence, but his donkey saw the angel clearly and swerved off the road (Numbers 22).

hide the canoe in, amongst the thick willows. We took some fish off of the lines and set them again, and begun to get ready for dinner.

The door of the cavern was big enough to roll a hogshead in, and on one side of the door the floor stuck out a little bit and was flat and a good place to build a fire on. So we built it there and cooked dinner.

We spread the blankets inside for a carpet, and eat our dinner in there. We put all the other things handy at the back of the cavern. Pretty soon it darkened up and begun to thunder and lighten; so the birds was right about it. Directly it begun to rain, and it rained like all fury, too, and I never see the wind blow so. It was one of these regular summer storms. It would get so dark that it looked all blue-black outside, and lovely; and the rain would thrash along by so thick that the trees off a little ways looked dim and spider-webby; and here would come a blast of wind that would bend the trees down and turn up the pale underside of the leaves; and then a perfect ripper of a gust would follow along and set the branches to tossing their arms as if they was just wild; and next, when it was just about the bluest and blackest—*fst!* it was as bright as glory and you'd have a little glimpse of tree-tops a-plung-ing about, away off yonder in the storm, hundreds of yards further than you could see before; dark as sin again in a second, and now you'd hear the thun-der let go with an awful crash and then go rumbling, grumbling, tumbling down the sky towards the under side of the world, like rolling empty barrels down stairs, where it's long stairs and they bounce a good deal, you know.

"Jim, this is nice," I says. "I wouldn't want to be nowhere else but here. Pass me along another hunk of fish and some hot cornbread."

"Well, you wouldn' a ben here, 'f it hadn' a ben for Jim. You'd a ben down dah in de woods widout any dinner, en gittn' mos' drownded, too, dat you would, honey. Chickens knows when its gwyne to rain, en so do de birds, chile."

The river went on raising and raising for ten or twelve days, till at last it was over the banks. The water was three or four foot deep on the island in the low places and on the Illinois bottom. On that side it was a good many miles wide; but on the Missouri side it was the same old distance across—a half a mile—because the Missouri shore was just a wall of high bluffs.

Daytimes we paddled all over the island in the canoe. It was mighty cool and shady in the deep woods even if the sun was blazing outside. We went winding in and out amongst the trees; and sometimes the vines hung so thick we had to back away and go some other way. Well, on every old broken-down tree, you could see rabbits, and snakes, and such things; and when the island had been overflowed a day or two, they got so tame, on account of being hungry, that you could paddle right up and put your hand on them if you wanted to; but not the snakes and turtles—they would slide off in the water. The ridge our cavern was in, was full of them. We could a had pets enough if we'd wanted them.

One night we catched a little section of a lumber raft—nice pine planks. It was twelve foot wide and about fifteen or sixteen foot long, and the top stood above water six or seven inches, a solid level floor. We could see saw-logs go by in the daylight, sometimes, but we let them go; we didn't show ourselves in daylight.

Another night, when we was up at the head of the island, just before day-light, here comes a frame house down, on the west side. She was a two-story, and tilted over, considerable. We paddled out and got aboard—clumb in at an up-stairs window. But it was too dark to see yet, so we made the canoe fast and set in her to wait for daylight.

The light begun to come before we got to the foot of the island. Then we looked in at the window. We could make out a bed, and a table, and two old chairs, and lots of things around about on the floor; and there was clothes hanging against the wall. There was something laying on the floor in the far corner that looked like a man. So Jim says.

"Hello, you!"

But it didn't budge. So I hollered again, and then Jim says:

"De man ain' asleep—he's dead. You hold still—I'll go en see."

He went and bent down and looked, and says:

"It's a dead man. Yes, indeedy; naked, too. He's ben shot in de back. I reck'n he's ben dead two er three days. Come in, Huck, but doan' look at his face—it's too gashly."

I didn't look at him at all. Jim throwed some old rags over him, but he needn't done it; I didn't want to see him. There was heaps of old greasy cards scattered around over the floor, and old whisky bottles, and a couple of masks made out of black cloth; and all over the walls was the ignorantest kind of words and pictures, made with charcoal. There was two old dirty calico dresses, and a sun-bonnet, and some women's under-clothes, hanging against the wall, and some men's clothing, too. We put the lot into the canoe; it might come good. There was a boy's old speckled straw hat on the floor; I took that too. And there was a bottle that had had milk in it; and it had a rag stopper for a baby to suck. We would a took the bottle, but it was broke. There was a seedy old chest, and an old hair trunk with the hinges broke. They stood open, but there warn't nothing left in them that was any account. The way things was scattered about, we reckoned the people left in a hurry and warn't fixed so as to carry off most of their stuff.

We got an old tin lantern, and a butcher-knife without any handle, and a bran-new Barlow knife[3] worth two bits in any store, and a lot of tallow candles, and a tin candlestick, and a gourd, and a tin cup, and a ratty old bed-quilt off the bed, and a reticule with needles and pins and beeswax and buttons and thread and all such truck in it, and a hatchet and some nails, and a fish-line as thick as my little finger, with some monstrous hooks on it, and a roll of buckskin, and a leather dog-collar, and a horse-shoe, and some vials of medicine that didn't have no label on them; and just as we was leaving I found a tolerable good curry-comb, and Jim he found a ratty old fiddle-bow, and a wooden leg. The straps was broke off of it, but barring that, it was a good enough leg, though it was too long for me and not long enough for Jim, and we couldn't find the other one, though we hunted all around.

And so, take it all around, we made a good haul. When we was ready to shove off, we was a quarter of a mile below the island, and it was pretty broad day; so I made Jim lay down in the canoe and cover up with the quilt, because if he set up, people could tell he was a nigger a good ways off. I paddled over to the Illinois shore, and drifted down most a half a mile doing it. I crept up the dead water under the bank, and hadn't no accidents and didn't see nobody. We got home all safe.

3. Pocketknife with one blade, named for the inventor.

Chapter X

After breakfast I wanted to talk about the dead man and guess out how he come to be killed, but Jim didn't want to. He said it would fetch bad luck; and besides, he said, he might come and ha'nt us; he said a man that warn't buried was more likely to go a-ha'nting around than one that was planted and comfortable. That sounded pretty reasonable, so I didn't say no more; but I couldn't keep from studying over it and wishing I knowed who shot the man, and what they done it for.

We rummaged the clothes we'd got, and found eight dollars in silver sewed up in the lining of an old blanket overcoat. Jim said he reckoned the people in that house stole the coat, because if they'd a knowed the money was there they wouldn't a left it. I said I reckoned they killed him, too; but Jim didn't want to talk about that. I says:

"Now, you think it's bad luck; but what did you say when I fetched in the snake-skin that I found on the top of the ridge day before yesterday? You said it was the worst bad luck in the world to touch a snake-skin with my hands. Well, here's your bad luck! We've raked in all this truck and eight dollars besides. I wish we could have some bad luck like this every day, Jim."

"Never you mind, honey, never you mind. Don't you git too peart.[4] It's a-comin'. Mind I tell you, it's a-comin'."

It did come, too. It was Tuesday that we had that talk. Well, after dinner Friday, we was laying around in the grass at the upper end of the ridge, and got out of tobacco. I went to the cavern to get some, and found a rattlesnake in there. I killed him, and curled him up on the foot of Jim's blanket, ever so natural, thinking there'd be some fun when Jim found him there. Well, by night I forgot all about the snake, and when Jim flung himself down on the blanket while I struck a light, the snake's mate was there, and bit him.

He jumped up yelling, and the first thing the light showed was the varmint curled up and ready for another spring. I laid him out in a second with a stick, and Jim grabbed pap's whisky jug and began to pour it down.

He was barefooted, and the snake bit him right on the heel. That all comes of my being such a fool as to not remember that whenever you leave a dead snake its mate always comes there and curls around it. Jim told me to chop off the snake's head and throw it away, and then skin the body and roast a piece of it. I done it, and he eat it and said it would help cure him. He made me take off the rattles and tie them around his wrist, too. He said that that would help. Then I slid out quiet and throwed the snakes clear away amongst the bushes; for I warn't going to let Jim find out it was all my fault, not if I could help it.

Jim sucked and sucked at the jug, and now and then he got out of his head and pitched around and yelled; but every time he come to himself he went to sucking at the jug again. His foot swelled up pretty big, and so did his leg; but by-and-by the drunk begun to come, and so I judged he was all right; but I'd druther been bit with a snake than pap's whiskey.

Jim was laid up for four days and nights. Then the swelling was all gone and he was around again. I made up my mind I wouldn't ever take aholt of a snake-skin again with my hands, now that I see what had come of it. Jim said he reckoned I would believe him next time. And he said that handling a snake-skin was such awful bad luck that maybe we hadn't got to the end of it yet. He said he druther see the new moon over his left shoulder as much as a thousand times than take up a snake-skin in his hand. Well, I was getting to feel that way myself, though I've always reckoned that looking at the new moon over your left shoulder is one of the carelessest and foolishest things a body can do. Old Hank Bunker done it once, and bragged about it; and in less than two years he got drunk and fell off of the shot tower and spread himself out so that he was just a kind of layer, as you may say; and they slid him edgeways between two barn doors for a coffin, and buried him so, so they say, but I didn't see it. Pap told me. But anyway, it all come of looking at the moon that way, like a fool.

Well, the days went along, and the river went down between its banks again; and about the first thing we done was to bait one of the big hooks with a skinned rabbit and set it and catch a cat-fish that was as big as a man, being six foot two inches long, and weighed over two hundred pounds. We couldn't handle him, of course; he would a flung us into Illinois. We just set there and watched him rip and tear around till he drowned. We found a brass button in his stomach, and a round ball, and lots of rubbage. We split the ball open with the hatchet, and there was a spool in it. Jim said he'd had it there a long time, to coat it over so and make a ball of it. It was as big a fish as was ever catched in the Mississippi, I reckon. Jim said he hadn't ever seen a bigger one. He would a been worth a good deal over at the village. They peddle out such a fish as that by the pound in the market house there; everybody buys some of him; his meat's as white as snow and makes a good fry.

Next morning I said it was getting slow and dull, and I wanted to get a stirring up, some way. I said I reckoned I would slip over the river and find out what was going on. Jim liked that notion; but he said I must go in the dark and look sharp. Then he studied it over and said, couldn't I put on some of them old things and dress up like a girl? That was a good notion, too. So we shortened up one of the calico gowns and I turned up my trowser-legs to my knees and got into it. Jim hitched it behind with the hooks, and it was a fair fit. I put on the sun-bonnet and tied it under my chin, and then for a body to look in and see my face was like looking down a joint of stove-pipe. Jim said nobody would know me, even in the daytime, hardly. I practiced around all day to get the hang of the things, and by-and-by I could do pretty well in them, only Jim said I didn't walk like a girl; and he said I must quit pulling up my gown to get at my britches pocket. I took notice, and done better.

I started up the Illinois shore in the canoe just after dark.

I started across to the town from a little below the ferry landing, and the drift of the current fetched me in at the bottom of the town. I tied up and started along the bank. There was a light burning in a little shanty that hadn't been lived in for a long time, and I wondered who had took up quarters there. I slipped up and peeped in at the window. There was a woman about forty year old in there, knitting by a candle that was on a pine table. I didn't know her face; she was a stranger, for you couldn't start a face in that town that I didn't know. Now this was lucky, because I was weakening; I was getting afraid I had come; people might know my voice and find me out. But if this woman had been in such a little town two days she could tell me all I wanted to know; so I knocked at the door, and made up my mind I wouldn't forget I was a girl.

Chapter XI

"Come in," says the woman, and I did. She says:

"Take a cheer."

I done it. She looked me all over with her little shiny eyes, and says:

"What might your name be?"

"Sarah Williams."

"Where 'bouts do you live? In this neighborhood?"

"No'm. In Hookerville, seven mile below. I've walked all the way and I'm all tired out."

"Hungry, too, I reckon. I'll find you something."

"No'm, I ain't hungry. I was so hungry I had to stop two mile below here at a farm; so I ain't hungry no more. It's what makes me so late. My mother's down sick, and out of money and everything, and I come to tell my uncle Abner Moore. He lives at the upper end of the town, she says. I hain't ever been here before. Do you know him?"

"No; but I don't know everybody yet. I haven't lived here quite two weeks. It's a considerable ways to the upper end of the town. You better stay here all night. Take off your bonnet."

"No," I says, "I'll rest a while, I reckon, and go on. I ain't afeard of the dark."

She said she wouldn't let me go by myself, but her husband would be in by-and-by, maybe in a hour and a half, and she'd send him along with me. Then she got to talking about her husband, and about her relations up the river, and her relations down the river, and how much better off they used to was, and how they didn't know but they'd made a mistake coming to our town, instead of letting well alone—and so on and so on, till I was afeard I had made a mistake coming to her to find out what was going on in the town; but by-and-by she dropped onto pap and the murder, and then I was pretty willing to let her clatter right along. She told about me and Tom Sawyer finding the six thousand dollars (only she got it ten) and all about pap and what a hard lot he was, and what a hard lot I was, and at last she got down to where I was murdered. I says:

"Who done it? We've heard considerable about these goings on, down in Hookerville, but we don't know who 'twas that killed Huck Finn."

"Well, I reckon there's a right smart chance of people *here* that'd like to know who killed him. Some thinks old Finn done it himself."

"No—is that so?"

"Most everybody thought it at first. He'll never know how nigh he come to getting lynched. But before night they changed around and judged it was done by a runaway nigger named Jim."

"Why *he*—"

I stopped. I reckoned I better keep still. She run on, and never noticed I had put in at all.

"The nigger run off the very night Huck Finn was killed. So there's a reward out for him—three hundred dollars. And there's a reward out for old Finn too—two hundred dollars. You see, he come to town the morning after the murder, and told about it, and was out with 'em on the ferry-boat hunt, and right away after he up and left. Before night they wanted to lynch him, but he was gone, you see. Well, next day they found out the nigger was gone; they found out he hadn't ben seen sence ten o'clock the night the murder was done. So then they put it on him, you see, and while they was full of it, next day back comes old Finn and went boohooing to Judge Thatcher to get money to hunt for the nigger all over Illinois with. The judge give him some, and that evening he got drunk and was around till after midnight with a couple of mighty hard looking strangers, and then went off with them. Well, he hain't come back sence, and they ain't looking for him back till this thing blows over a little, for people thinks now that he killed his boy and fixed things so folks would think robbers done it, and then he'd get Huck's money without having to bother a long time with a lawsuit. People do say he warn't any too good to do it. Oh, he's sly, I reckon. If he don't come back for a year, he'll be all right. You can't prove anything on him, you know; everything will be quieted down then, and he'll walk into Huck's money as easy as nothing."

"Yes, I reckon so, 'm. I don't see nothing in the way of it. Has everybody quit thinking the nigger done it?"

"Oh no, not everybody. A good many thinks he done it. But they'll get the nigger pretty soon, now, and maybe they can scare it out of him."

"Why, are they after him yet?"

"Well, you're innocent, ain't you! Does three hundred dollars lay round every day for people to pick up? Some folks thinks the nigger ain't far from here. I'm one of them—but I hain't talked it around. A few days ago I was talking with an old couple that lives next door in the log shanty, and they happened to say hardly anybody ever goes to that island over yonder that they call Jackson's Island. Don't anybody live there? says I. No, nobody, says they. I didn't say any more, but I done some thinking. I was pretty near certain I'd seen smoke over there, about the head of the island, a day or two before that, so I says to myself, like as not that nigger's hiding over there; anyway, says I, it's worth the trouble to give the place a hunt. I hain't seen any smoke sence, so I reckon maybe he's gone, if it was him; but husband's going over to see— him and another man. He was gone up the river; but he got back to-day and I told him as soon as he got here two hours ago."

I had got so uneasy I couldn't set still. I had to do something with my hands; so I took up a needle off of the table and went to threading it. My hands shook and I was making a bad job of it. When the woman stopped talking, I looked up, and she was looking at me pretty curious, and smiling a little. I put down the needle and thread and let on to be interested—and I was, too—and says:

"Three hundred dollars is a power of money. I wish my mother could get it. Is your husband going over there to-night?"

"Oh, yes. He went up town with the man I was telling you of, to get a boat and see if they could borrow another gun. They'll go over after midnight."

"Couldn't they see better if they was to wait till daytime?"

"Yes. And couldn't the nigger see better too? After midnight he'll likely be asleep, and they can slip around through the woods and hunt up his camp fire all the better for the dark, if he's got one."

"I didn't think of that."

The woman kept looking at me pretty curious, and I didn't feel a bit comfortable. Pretty soon she says:

"What did you say your name was, honey?"

"M—Mary Williams."

Somehow it didn't seem to me that I said it was Mary before, so I didn't look up; seemed to me I said it was Sarah; so I felt sort of cornered, and was afeared maybe I was looking it, too. I wished the woman would say something more; the longer she set still, the uneasier I was. But now she says:

"Honey, I thought you said it was Sarah when you first come in?"

"Oh, yes'm, I did. Sarah Mary Williams. Sarah's my first name. Some calls me Sarah, some calls me Mary."

"Oh, that's the way of it?"

"Yes'm."

I was feeling better, then, but I wished I was out of there, anyway. I couldn't look up yet.

Well, the woman fell to talking about how hard times was, and how poor they had to live, and how the rats was as free as if they owned the place, and so forth, and so on, and then I got easy again. She was right about the rats. You'd see one stick his nose out of a hole in the corner every little while. She said she had to have things handy to throw at them when she was alone, or they wouldn't give her no peace. She showed me a bar of lead, twisted up into a knot, and she said she was a good shot with it generly, but she'd wrenched her arm a day or two ago, and didn't know whether she could throw true, now. But she watched for a chance, and directly she banged away at a rat, but she missed him wide, and said "Ouch!" it hurt her arm so. Then she told me to try for the next one. I wanted to be getting away before the old man got back, but of course I didn't let on. I got the thing, and the first rat that showed his nose I let drive, and if he'd a stayed where he was he'd a been a tolerable sick rat. She said that that was first-rate, and she reckoned I would hive[5] the next one. She went and got the lump of lead and fetched it back and brought along a hank of yarn, which she wanted me to help her with. I held up my two hands and she put the hank over them and went on talking about her and her husband's matters. But she broke off to say:

"Keep your eye on the rats. You better have the lead in your lap, handy."

So she dropped the lump into my lap, just at that moment, and I clapped my legs together on it and she went on talking. But only about a minute. Then she took off the hank and looked me straight in the face, but very pleasant, and says:

"Come, now—what's your real name?"

"Wh-what, mum?"

"What's your real name? Is it Bill, or Tom, or Bob?—or what is it?"

I reckon I shook like a leaf, and I didn't know hardly what to do. But I says:

"Please to don't poke fun at a poor girl like me, mum. If I'm in the way, here I'll—"

"No, you won't. Set down and stay where you are. I ain't going to hurt you, and I ain't going to tell on you, nuther. You just tell me your secret, and trust me. I'll keep it; and what's more, I'll help you. So'll my old man, if you want him to. You see, you're a run-away 'prentice—that's all. It ain't anything. There ain't any harm in it. You've been treated bad, and you made up your mind to cut. Bless you, child, I wouldn't tell on you. Tell me all about it, now—that's a good boy.

So I said it wouldn't be no use to try to play it any longer, and I would just make a clean breast and tell her everything, but she mustn't go back on her promise. Then I told her my father and mother was dead, and the law had bound me out to a mean old farmer in the country thirty mile back from the river, and he treated me so bad I couldn't stand it no longer; he went away to be gone a couple of days, and so I took my chance and stole some of his

5. Hit or kill.

daughter's old clothes, and cleared out, and I had been three nights coming the thirty miles; I traveled nights, and hid daytimes and slept, and the bag of bread and meat I carried from home lasted me all the way and I had a plenty. I said I believed my uncle Abner Moore would take care of me, and so that was why I struck out for this town of Goshen.

"Goshen, child? This ain't Goshen. This is St. Petersburg. Goshen's ten mile further up the river. Who told you this was Goshen?"

"Why, a man I met at day-break this morning, just as I was going to turn into the woods for my regular sleep. He told me when the roads forked I must take the right hand, and five mile would fetch me to Goshen."

"He was drunk I reckon. He told you just exactly wrong."

"Well, he did act like he was drunk, but it ain't no matter now. I got to be moving along. I'll fetch Goshen before day-light."

"Hold on a minute. I'll put you up a snack to eat. You might want it."

So she put me up a snack, and says:

"Say—when a cow's laying down, which end of her gets up first? Answer up prompt, now—don't stop to study over it. Which end gets up first?"

"The hind end, mum."

"Well, then, a horse?"

"The for'rard end, mum."

"Which side of a tree does the most moss grow on?"

"North side."

"If fifteen cows is browsing on a hillside, how many of them eats with their heads pointed the same direction?"

"The whole fifteen, mum."

"Well, I reckon you *have* lived in the country. I thought maybe you was trying to hocus me again. What's your real name, now?"

"George Peters, mum."

"Well, try to remember it, George. Don't forget and tell me it's Elexander before you go, and then get out by saying it's George Elexander when I catch you. And don't go about women in that old calico. You do a girl tolerable poor, but you might fool men, maybe. Bless you, child, when you set out to thread a needle, don't hold the thread still and fetch the needle up to it; hold the needle still and poke the thread at it—that's the way a woman most always does; but a man always does 'tother way. And when you throw at a rat or anything, hitch yourself up a tip-toe, and fetch your hand up over your head as awkard as you can, and miss your rat about six or seven foot. Throw stiff-armed from the shoulder, like there was a pivot there for it to turn on—like a girl; not from the wrist and elbow, with your arm out to one side, like a boy. And mind you, when a girl tries to catch anything in her lap, she throws her knees apart; she don't clap them together, the way you did when you catched the lump of lead. Why, I spotted you for a boy when you was threading the needle; and I contrived the other things just to make certain. Now trot along to your uncle, Sarah Mary Williams George Elexander Peters, and if you get into trouble you send word to Mrs. Judith Loftus, which is me, and I'll do what I can to get you out of it. Keep the river road, all the way, and next time you tramp, take shoes and socks with you. The river road's a rocky one, and your feet 'll be in a condition when you get to Goshen, I reckon."

I went up the bank about fifty yards, and then I doubled on my tracks and slipped back to where my canoe was, a good piece below the house. I jumped in and was off in a hurry. I went up stream far enough to make the head of the island, and then started across. I took off the sun-bonnet, for I didn't want no blinders on, then. When I was about the middle, I hear the clock begin to strike; so I stops and listens; the sound come faint over the water, but clear—eleven. When I struck the head of the island I never waited to blow, though I was most winded, but I shoved right into the timber where my old camp used to be, and started a good fire there on a high-and-dry spot.

Then I jumped in the canoe and dug out for our place a mile and a half below, as hard as I could go. I landed, and slopped through the timber and up the ridge and into the cavern. There Jim laid, sound asleep on the ground. I roused him out and says:

"Git up and hump yourself, Jim! There ain't a minute to lose. They're after us!"

Jim never asked no questions, he never said a word; but the way he worked for the next half an hour showed about how he was scared. By that time everything we had in the world was on our raft and she was ready to be shoved out from the willow cove where she was hid. We put out the camp fire at the cavern the first thing, and didn't show a candle outside after that.

I took the canoe out from shore a little piece and took a look, but if there was a boat around I couldn't see it, for stars and shadows ain't good to see by. Then we got out the raft and slipped along down in the shade, past the foot of the island dead still, never saying a word.

Chapter XII

It must a been close onto one o'clock when we got below the island at last, and the raft did seem to go mighty slow. If a boat was to come along, we was going to take to the canoe and break for the Illinois shore; and it was well a boat didn't come, for we hadn't ever thought to put the gun into the canoe, or a fishing-line or anything to eat. We was in ruther too much of a sweat to think of so many things. It warn't good judgment to put *everything* on the raft.

If the men went to the island, I just expect they found the camp fire I built, and watched it all night for Jim to come. Anyways, they stayed away from us, and if my building the fire never fooled them it warn't no fault of mine. I played it as low-down on them as I could.

When the first streak of day begun to show, we tied up to a tow-head in a big bend on the Illinois side, and hacked off cotton-wood branches with the hatchet and covered up the raft with them so she looked like there had been a cave-in in the bank there. A tow-head is a sand-bar that has cotton-woods on it as thick as harrow-teeth.

We had mountains on the Missouri shore and heavy timber on the Illinois side, and the channel was down the Missouri shore at that place, so we warn't afraid of anybody running across us. We laid there all day and watched the rafts and steamboats spin down the Missouri shore, and up-bound steamboats fight the big river in the middle. I told Jim all about the time I had jabbering with that woman; and Jim said she was a smart one, and if she was to start after us herself *she* wouldn't set down and watch a camp fire—no, sir, she'd fetch a dog. Well, then, I said, why couldn't she tell her husband to fetch a dog? Jim said he bet she did think of it by the time the men was ready to start, and he believed they must a gone up town to get a dog and so they lost all that time, or else we wouldn't be here on a tow-head sixteen or seventeen mile below the village—no, indeedy, we would be in that same old town again. So I said I didn't care what was the reason they didn't get us, as long as they didn't.

When it was beginning to come on dark, we poked our heads out of the cottonwood thicket and looked up, and down, and across; nothing in sight; so Jim took up some of the top planks of the raft and built a snug wigwam to get under in blazing weather and rainy, and to keep the things dry. Jim made a floor for the wigwam, and raised it a foot or more above the level of the raft, so now the blankets and all the traps was out of the reach of steamboat waves. Right in the middle of the wigwam we made a layer of dirt about five or six inches deep with a frame around it for to hold it to its place; this was to build a fire on in sloppy weather or chilly; the wigwam would keep it from being seen. We made an extra steering oar, too, because one of the others might get broke, on a snag or something. We fixed up a short forked stick to hang the old lantern on; because we must always light the lantern whenever we see a steamboat coming down stream, to keep from getting run over; but we wouldn't have to light it up for upstream boats unless we see we was in what they call "crossing;" for the river was pretty high yet, very low banks being still a little under water; so up-bound boats didn't always run the channel, but hunted easy water.

This second night we run between seven and eight hours, with a current that was making over four mile an hour. We catched fish, and talked, and we took a swim now and then to keep off sleepiness. It was kind of solemn, drifting down the big still river, laying on our backs looking up at the stars, and we didn't ever feel like talking loud, and it warn't often that we laughed, only a little kind of a low chuckle. We had mighty good weather, as a general thing, and nothing ever happened to us at all, that night, nor the next, nor the next.

Every night we passed towns, some of them away up on black hillsides, nothing but just a shiny bed of lights, not a house could you see. The fifth night we passed St. Louis, and it was like the whole world lit up. In St. Petersburg they used to say there was twenty or thirty thousand people in St. Louis,[6] but I never believed it till I see that wonderful spread of lights at two o'clock that still night. There warn't a sound there; everybody was asleep.

Every night now, I used to slip ashore, towards ten o'clock, at some little village, and buy ten or fifteen cents' worth of meal or bacon or other stuff to eat; and sometimes I lifted a chicken that warn't roosting comfortable, and took him along. Pap always said, take a chicken when you get a chance, because if you don't want him yourself you can easy find somebody that does, and a good deed ain't ever forgot. I never see pap when he didn't want the chicken himself, but that is what he used to say, anyway.

Mornings, before daylight, I slipped into corn fields and borrowed a watermelon, or a mushmelon, or a punkin, or some new corn, or things of that kind. Pap always said it warn't no harm to borrow things, if you was meaning to pay them back, sometime; but the widow said it warn't anything but a soft name for stealing, and no decent body would do it. Jim said he reckoned the widow was partly right and pap was partly right; so the best way would be for us to pick out two or three things from the list and say we wouldn't borrow

---

6. St. Louis is 170 miles down the Mississippi from Hannibal.

them any more—then he reckoned it wouldn't be no harm to borrow the others. So we talked it over all one night, drifting along down the river, trying to make up our minds whether to drop the watermelons, or the cantelopes, or the mushmelons, or what. But towards daylight we got it all settled satisfactory, and concluded to drop crabapples and p'simmons. We warn't feeling just right, before that, but it was all comfortable now. I was glad the way it come out, too, because crabapples ain't ever good, and the p'simmons wouldn't be ripe for two or three months yet.

We shot a water-fowl, now and then, that got up too early in the morning or didn't go to bed early enough in the evening. Take it all around, we lived pretty high.

The fifth night below St. Louis we had a big storm after midnight, with a power of thunder and lightning, and the rain poured down in a solid sheet. We stayed in the wigwam and let the raft take care of itself. When the lightning glared out we could see a big straight river ahead, and high rocky bluffs on both sides. By-and-by says I, "Hel-*lo* Jim, looky yonder!" It was a steamboat that had killed herself on a rock. We was drifting straight down for her. The lightning showed her very distinct. She was leaning over, with part of her upper deck above water, and you could see every little chimbly-guy[7] clean and clear, and a chair by the big bell, with an old slouch hat hanging on the back of it when the flashes come.

Well, it being away in the night, and stormy, and all so mysterious-like, I felt just the way any other boy would a felt when I see that wreck laying there so mournful and lonesome in the middle of the river. I wanted to get aboard of her and slink around a little, and see what there was there. So I says:

"Le's land on her, Jim."

But Jim was dead against it, at first. He says:

"I doan' want to go fool'n 'long er no wrack. We's doin' blame' well, en we better let blame' well alone, as de good book says. Like as not dey's a watchman on dat wrack."

"Watchman your grandmother," I says; "there ain't nothing to watch but the texas[8] and the pilot-house; and do you reckon anybody's going to resk his life for a texas and a pilot-house such a night as this, when it's likely to break up and wash off down the river any minute?" Jim couldn't say nothing to that, so he didn't try. "And besides," I says, "we might borrow something worth having, out of the captain's stateroom. Seegars, *I* bet you—and cost five cents apiece, solid cash. Steamboat captains is always rich, and get sixty dollars a month, and *they* don't care a cent what a thing costs, you know, long as they want it. Stick a candle in your pocket; I can't rest, Jim, till we give her a rummaging. Do you reckon Tom Sawyer would ever go by this thing? Not for pie, he wouldn't. He'd call it an adventure—that's what he'd call it; and he'd land on that wreck if it was his last act. And wouldn't he throw style into it?—wouldn't he spread himself, nor nothing? Why, you'd think it was Christopher C'lumbus discovering Kingdom-Come. I wish Tom Sawyer *was* here."

Jim he grumbled a little, but give in. He said we mustn't talk any more than we could help, and then talk mighty low. The lightning showed us the wreck again, just in time, and we fetched the starboard derrick,[9] and made fast there.

---

7. Wires used to steady the chimney stacks.
8. The large cabin on the top deck located just behind or beneath the pilothouse; it serves as officers' quarters.
9. Boom for lifting cargo.

The deck was high out, here. We went sneaking down the slope of it to lab-board, in the dark, towards the texas, feeling our way slow with our feet, and spreading our hands out to fend off the guys, for it was so dark we couldn't see no sign of them. Pretty soon we struck the forward end of the skylight, and clumb onto it; and the next step fetched us in front of the captain's door, which was open, and by Jimminy, away down through the texas-hall we see a light! and all in the same second we seem to hear low voices in yonder!

Jim whispered and said he was feeling powerful sick, and told me to come along. I says, all right; and was going to start for the raft; but just then I heard a voice wail out and say:

"Oh, please don't, boys; I swear I won't ever tell!"

Another voice said, pretty loud:

"It's a lie, Jim Turner. You've acted this way before. You always want more'n your share of the truck and you've always got it, too, because you've swore 't if you didn't you'd tell. But this time you've said it jest one time too many. You're the meanest, treacherousest hound in this country."

By this time Jim was gone for the raft. I was just a-biling with curiosity; and I says to myself, Tom Sawyer wouldn't back out now, and so I won't either; I'm agoing to see what's going on here. So I dropped on my hands and knees, in the little passage, and crept aft in the dark, till there warn't but about one stateroom betwixt me and the cross-hall of the texas. Then, in there I see a man stretched on the floor and tied hand and foot, and two men standing over him, and one of them had a dim lantern in his hand, and the other one had a pistol. This one kept pointing the pistol at the man's head on the floor and saying—

"I'd *like* to! And I orter, too, a mean skunk!"

The man on the floor would shrivel up, and say: "Oh, please don't, Bill—I hain't ever goin' to tell."

And every time he said that, the man with the lantern would laugh and say:

"'Deed you *ain't!* You never said no truer thing 'n that, you bet you." And once he said, "Hear him beg! and yit if we hadn't got the best of him and tied him, he'd a killed us both. And what *for?* Jist for noth'n. Jist because we stood on our *rights*—that's what for. But I lay you ain't agoin' to threaten nobody any more, Jim Turner. Put *up* that pistol, Bill."

Bill says:

"I don't want to, Jake Packard. I'm for killin' him—and didn't he kill old Hatfield jist the same way—and don't he deserve it?"

"But I don't *want* him killed, and I've got my reasons for it."

"Bless yo' heart for them words, Jake Packard! I'll never forget you, long's I live!" says the man on the floor, sort of blubbering.

Packard didn't take no notice of that, but hung up his lantern on a nail, and started towards where I was, there in the dark, and motioned Bill to come. I crawfished[1] as fast as I could, about two yards, but the boat slanted so that I couldn't make very good time; so to keep from getting run over and catched I crawled into a stateroom on the upper side. The man come a-pawing along in the dark, and when Packard got to my stateroom, he says:

"Here—come in here."

And in he come, and Bill after him. But before they got in, I was up in the upper berth, cornered, and sorry I come. Then they stood there, with their

---

1. Crept backward on all fours.

hands on the ledge of the berth, and talked. I couldn't see them, but I could tell where they was, by the whisky they'd been having. I was glad I didn't drink whisky; but it wouldn't made much difference, anyway, because most of the time they couldn't a treed me because I didn't breathe. I was too scared. And besides, a body *couldn't* breathe, and hear such talk. They talked low and earnest. Bill wanted to kill Turner. He says:

"He's said he'll tell, and he will. If we was to give both our shares to him *now,* it wouldn't make no difference after the row, and the way we've served him. Shore's you're born, he'll turn State's evidence; now you hear *me.* I'm for putting him out of his troubles."

"So'm I," says Packard, very quiet.

"Blame it, I'd sorter begun to think you wasn't. Well, then, that's all right. Les' go and do it."

"Hold on a minute; I hain't had my say yit. You listen to me. Shooting's good, but there's quieter ways if the thing's *got* to be done. But what I say, is this; it ain't good sense to go court'n around after a halter,[2] if you can git at what you're up to in some way that's jist as good and at the same time don't bring you into no resks. Ain't that so?"

"You bet it is. But how you goin' to manage it this time?"

"Well, my idea is this: we'll rustle around and gether up whatever pickins we've overlooked in the staterooms, and shove for shore and hide the truck. Then we'll wait. Now I say it ain't agoin' to be more 'n two hours befo' this wrack breaks up and washes off down the river. See? He'll be drownded, and won't have nobody to blame for it but his own self. I reckon that's a considerble sight better'n killin' of him. I'm unfavorable to killin' a man as long as you can git around it; it ain't good sense, it ain't good morals. Ain't I right?"

"Yes—I reck'n you are. But s'pose she *don't* break up and wash off?"

"Well, we can wait the two hours, anyway, and see, can't we?"

"All right, then; come along."

So they started, and I lit out, all in a cold sweat, and scrambled forward. It was dark as pitch there; but I said in a kind of a coarse whisper, "Jim!" and he answered up, right at my elbow, with a sort of a moan, and I says:

"Quick, Jim, it ain't no time for fooling around and moaning; there's a gang of murderers in yonder, and if we don't hunt up their boat and set her drifting down the river so these fellows can't get away from the wreck, there's one of 'em going to be in a bad fix. But if we find their boat we can put *all* of 'em in a bad fix—for the Sheriff 'll get 'em. Quick—hurry! I'll hunt the labboard side, you hunt the stabboard. You start at the raft, and—"

"Oh, my lordy, lordy! *Raf'*? Dey ain' no raf' no mo', she done broke loose en gone!—'en here we is!"

Chapter XIII

Well, I catched my breath and most fainted. Shut up on a wreck with such a gang as that! But it warn't no time to be sentimentering. We'd *got* to find that boat, now—had to have it for ourselves. So we went a-quaking and down the stabboard side, and slow work it was, too—seemed a week before we got to the stern. No sign of a boat. Jim said he didn't believe he could go any further—so scared he hadn't hardly any strength left, he said. But I said

2. Hangman's noose.

come on, if we get left on this wreck, we are in a fix, sure. So on we prowled, again. We struck for the stern of the texas, and found it, and then scrabbled along forwards on the skylight, hanging on from shutter to shutter, for the edge of the skylight was in the water. When we got pretty close to the cross-hall door there was the skiff, sure enough! I could just barely see her. I felt ever so thankful. In another second I would a been aboard of her; but just then the door opened. One of the men stuck his head out, only about a couple of foot from me, and I thought I was gone; but he jerked it in again, and says:

"Heave that blame lantern out o' sight, Bill!"

He flung a bag of something into the boat, and then got in himself, and set down. It was Packard. Then Bill *he* come out and got in. Packard says, in a low voice:

"All ready—shove off!"

I couldn't hardly hang onto the shutters, I was so weak. But Bill says:

"Hold on—'d you go through him?"

"No. Didn't you?"

"No. So he's got his share o' the cash, yet."

"Well, then, come along—no use to take truck and leave money."

"Say—won't he suspicion what we're up to?"

"Maybe he won't. But we got to have it anyway. Come along." So they got out and went in.

The door slammed to, because it was on the careened side; and in a half second I was in the boat, and Jim come a tumbling after me. I out with my knife and cut the rope, and away we went!

We didn't touch an oar, and we didn't speak nor whisper, nor hardly even breathe. We went gliding swift along, dead silent, past the tip of the paddle-box, and past the stern; then in a second or two more we was a hundred yards below the wreck, and the darkness soaked her up, every last sign of her, and we was safe, and knowed it.

When we was three or four hundred yards down stream, we see the lantern show like a little spark at the texas door, for a second, and we knowed by that that the rascals had missed their boat, and was beginning to understand that they was in just as much trouble, now, as Jim Turner was.

Then Jim manned the oars, and we took out after our raft. Now was the first time that I begun to worry about the men—I reckon I hadn't had time to before. I begun to think how dreadful it was, even for murderers, to be in such a fix. I says to myself, there ain't no telling but I might come to be a murderer myself, yet, and then how would I like it? So says I to Jim:

"The first light we see, we'll land a hundred yards below it or above it, in a place where it's a good hiding-place for you and the skiff, and then I'll go and fix up some kind of a yarn, and get somebody to go for that gang and get them out of their scrape, so they can be hung when their time comes."

But that idea was a failure; for pretty soon it begun to storm again, and this time worse than ever. The rain poured down, and never a light showed; everybody in bed, I reckon. We boomed along down the river, watching for lights and watching for our raft. After a long time the rain let up, but the clouds staid, and the lightning kept whimpering, and by-and-by a flash showed us a black thing ahead, floating, and we made for it.

It was the raft, and mighty glad was we to get aboard of it again. We seen a light, now, away down to the right, on shore. So I said I would go for it. The skiff was half full of plunder which that gang had stole, there on the wreck.

We hustled it onto the raft in a pile, and I told Jim to float along down, and show a light when he judged he had gone about two mile, and keep it burning till I come; then I manned my oars and shoved for the light. As I got down towards it, three or four more showed—up on a hillside. It was a village. I closed in above the shore-light, and laid on my oars and floated. As I went by, I see it was a lantern hanging on the jackstaff of a double-hull ferry-boat. I skimmed around for the watchman, a-wondering whereabouts he slept; and by-and-by I found him roosting on the bitts,[3] forward, with his head down between his knees. I give his shoulder two or three little shoves, and begun to cry.

He stirred up, in a kind of startlish way; but when he see it was only me, he took a good gap and stretch, and then he says:

"Hello, what's up? Don't cry, bub. What's the trouble?"

I says:

"Pap, and mam, and sis, and—"

Then I broke down. He says:

"Oh, dang it, now, *don't* take on so, we all has to have our troubles and this'n 'll come out all right. What's the matter with 'em?"

"They're—they're—are you the watchman of the boat?"

"Yes," he says, kind of pretty-well-satisfied like. "I'm the captain and the owner, and the mate, and the pilot, and watchman, and head deck-hand; and sometimes I'm the freight and passengers. I ain't as rich as old Jim Hornback, and I can't be so blame' generous and good to Tom, Dick and Harry as what he is, and slam around money the way he does; but I've told him a many a time 't I wouldn't trade places with him; for, says I, a sailor's life's the life for me, and I'm derned if I'd live two mile out o' town, where there ain't nothing ever goin' on, not for all his spondulicks and as much more on top of it. Says I—"

I broke in and says:

"They're in an awful peck of trouble, and—"

"*Who* is?"

"Why, pap, and mam, and sis, and Miss Hooker; and if you'd take your ferry-boat and go up there—"

"Up where? Where are they?"

"On the wreck."

"What wreck?"

"Why, there ain't but one."

"What, you don't mean the *Walter Scott*?"[4]

"Yes."

"Good land! what are they doin' *there*, for gracious sakes?"

"Well, they didn't go there a-purpose."

"I bet they didn't! Why, great goodness, there ain't no chance for 'em if they don't git off mighty quick! Why, how in the nation did they ever git into such a scrape?"

"Easy enough. Miss Hooker was a-visiting, up there to the town—"

"Yes, Booth's Landing—go on."

---

3. Vertical wooden posts to which cables can be secured.
4. Twain blamed the feudalistic fantasies of the pre–Civil War South on the romantic novels of Sir Walter Scott (1771–1832). He expressed him-

self most vividly on this subject in *Life on the Mississippi* (Ch. 46), where he observes: "Sir Walter had so large a hand in making Southern character, as it existed before the war, that he is in great measure responsible for the war."

"She was a-visiting, there at Booth's Landing, and just in the edge of the evening she started over with her nigger woman in the horse-ferry, to stay all night at her friend's house, Miss What-you-may-call her, I disremember her name, and they lost their steering-oar, and swung around and went a-floating down, stern-first, about two mile, and saddle-baggsed[5] on the wreck, and the ferry man and the nigger woman and the horses was all lost, but Miss Hooker she made a grab and got aboard the wreck. Well, about an hour after dark, we come along down in our trading-scow, and it was so dark we didn't notice the wreck till we was right on it; and so *we* saddle-baggsed; but all of us was saved but Bill Whipple—and oh, he *was* the best cretur!—I most wish't it had been me, I do."

"My George! It's the beatenest thing I ever struck. And *then* what did you all do?"

"Well, we hollered and took on, but it's so wide there, we couldn't make nobody hear. So pap said somebody got to get ashore and get help somehow. I was the only one that could swim, so I made a dash for it, and Miss Hooker she said if I didn't strike help sooner, come here and hunt up her uncle, and he'd fix the thing. I made the land about a mile below, and been fooling along ever since, trying to get people to do something, but they said, 'What, in such a night and such a current? there ain't no sense in it; go for the steam-ferry.' Now if you'll go, and—"

"By Jackson, I'd *like* to, and blame it I don't know but I will; but who in the dingnation's agoin' to *pay* for it? Do you reckon your pap—"

"Why *that's* all right. Miss Hooker she told me, *particular,* that her uncle Hornback—"

"Great guns! is *he* her uncle? Look here, you break for that light over yonder-way, and turn out west when you git there, and about a quarter of a mile out you'll come to the tavern; tell 'em to dart you out to Jim Hornback's and he'll foot the bill. And don't you fool around any, because he'll want to know the news. Tell him I'll have his niece all safe before he can get to town. Hump yourself, now; I'm agoing up around the corner here, to roust out my engineer."

I struck for the light, but as soon as he turned the corner I went back and got into my skiff and bailed her out and then pulled up shore in the easy water about six hundred yards, and tucked myself in among some wood-boats; for I couldn't rest easy till I could see the ferry-boat start. But take it all around, I was feeling ruther comfortable on accounts of taking all this trouble for that gang, for not many would a done it. I wished the widow knowed about it. I judged she would be proud of me for helping these rapscallions, because rapscallions and dead beats is the kind the widow and good people takes the most interest in.

Well, before long, here comes the wreck, dim and dusky, sliding along down! A kind of cold shiver went through me, and then I struck out for her. She was very deep, and I see in a minute there warn't much chance for anybody being alive in her. I pulled all around her and hollered a little, but there wasn't any answer; all dead still. I felt a little bit heavy-hearted about the gang, but not much, for I reckoned if they could stand it, I could.

Then here comes the ferry-boat; so I shoved for the middle of the river on a long down-stream slant; and when I judged I was out of eye-reach, I laid on

---

5. Broken and doubled around the wreck.

my oars, and looked back and see her go and smell around the wreck for Miss Hooker's remainders, because the captain would know her uncle Hornback would want them; and then pretty soon the ferry-boat give it up and went for shore, and I laid into my work and went a-booming down the river.

It did seem a powerful long time before Jim's light showed up; and when it did show, it looked like it was a thousand mile off. By the time I got there the sky was beginning to get a little gray in the east; so we struck for an island, and hid the raft, and sunk the skiff, and turned in and slept like dead people.

Chapter XIV

By-and-by, when we got up, we turned over the truck the gang had stole off of the wreck, and found boots, and blankets, and clothes, and all sorts of other things, and a lot of books, and a spyglass, and three boxes of seegars. We hadn't ever been this rich before, in neither of our lives. The seegars was prime. We laid off all the afternoon in the woods talking, and me reading the books, and having a general good time. I told Jim all about what happened inside the wreck, and at the ferry-boat; and I said these kinds of things was adventures; but he said he didn't want no more adventures. He said that when I went in the texas and he crawled back to get on the raft and found her gone, he nearly died; because he judged it was all up with *him,* anyway it could be fixed; for if he didn't get saved he would get drownded; and if he did get saved, whoever saved him would send him back home so as to get the reward, and then Miss Watson would sell him South, sure. Well, he was right; he was most always right; he had an uncommon level head, for a nigger.

I read considerable to Jim about kings, and dukes, and earls, and such, and how gaudy they dressed, and how much style they put on, and called each other your majesty, and your grace, and your lordship, and so on, 'stead of mister; and Jim's eyes bugged out, and he was interested. He says:

"I didn't know dey was so many un um. I hain't hearn 'bout none un um, skasely, but ole King Sollermun, onless you counts dem kings dat's in a pack er k'yards. How much do a king git?"

"Get?" I says; "why, they get a thousand dollars a month if they want it; they can have just as much as they want; everything belongs to them."

"*Ain'* dat gay? En what dey got to do, Huck?"

"*They* don't do nothing! Why how you talk. They just set around."

"No—is dat so?"

"Of course it is. They just set around. Except maybe when there 's a war; then they go to the war. But other times they just lazy around; or go hawking—just hawking and sp—Sh!—d' you hear a noise?"

We skipped out and looked; but it warn't nothing but the flutter of a steamboat's wheel, away down coming around the point; so we come back.

"Yes," says I, "and other times, when things is dull, they fuss with the parlyment; and if everybody don't go just so he whacks their heads off. But mostly they hang round the harem."

"Roun' de which?"

"Harem."

"What's de harem?"

"The place where he keep his wives. Don't you know about the harem? Solomon had one; he had about a million wives."

"Why, yes, dat's so; I—I'd done forgot it. A harem's a bo'd'n-house, I reck'n. Mos' likely dey has rackety times in de nussery. En I reck'n de wives quarrels considable; en dat 'crease de racket. Yit dey say Sollermun de wises' man dat ever live.' I doan' take no stock in dat. Bekase why: would a wise man want to live in de mids' er sich a blimblammin' all de time? No—'deed he wouldn't. A wise man 'ud take en buil' a biler-factry; en den he could shet *down* de biler-factry when he want to res'."

"Well, but he *was* the wisest man, anyway; because the widow she told me so, her own self."

"I doan k'yer what de widder say, he *warn'* no wise man, nuther. He had some er de dad-fetchedes' ways I ever see. Does you know 'bout dat chile dat he 'uz gwyne to chop in two?"[6]

"Yes, the widow told me all about it."

"*Well,* den! Warn' dat de beatenes' notion in de worl'? You jes' take en look at it a minute. Dah's de stump, dah—dat's one er de women; heah's you—dat's de yuther one; I's Sollermun; en dish-yer dollar bill's de chile. Bofe un you claims it. What does I do? Does I shin aroun' mongs' de neighbors en fine out which un you de bill do b'long to, en han' it over to de right one, all safe en soun', de way dat anybody dat had any gumption would? No—I take en whack de bill in *two,* en give half un it to you, en de yuther half to de yuther woman. Dat's de way Sollermun was gwyne to do wid de chile. Now I want to ask you: what's de use er dat half a bill?—can't buy noth'n wid it. En what use is a half a chile? I wouldn' give a dern for a million un um."

"But hang it, Jim, you've clean missed the point—blame it, you've missed it a thousand mile."

"Who? Me? Go 'long. Doan' talk to *me* 'bout yo' pints. I reck'n I knows sense when I sees it; en dey ain' no sense in sich doin's as dat. De 'spute warn't 'bout a half a chile, de 'spute was 'bout a whole chile; en de man dat think he kin settle a 'spute 'bout a whole chile wid a half a chile, doan' know enough to come in out'n de rain. Doan' talk to me 'bout Sollermun, Huck, I knows him by de back."

"But I tell you you don't get the point."

"Blame de pint! I reck'n I knows what I knows. En mine you, de *real* pint is down furder—it's down deeper. It lays in de way Sollermun was raised. You take a man dat's got on'y one er two children; is dat man gwyne to be waseful o' chillen? No, he ain't; he can't 'ford it. *He* know how to value 'em. But you take a man dat's got 'bout five million chillen runnin' roun' de house, en it's diffunt. *He* as soon chop a chile in two as a cat. Dey's plenty mo'. A chile er two, mo' er less, warn't no consekens to Sollermun, dad fetch him!"

I never see such a nigger. If he got a notion in his head once, there warn't no getting it out again. He was the most down on Solomon of any nigger I ever see. So I went to talking about other kings, and let Solomon slide. I told about Louis Sixteenth that got his head cut off in France long time ago; and about his little boy the dolphin,[7] that would a been a king, but they took and shut him up in jail, and some say he died there.

---

6. In 1 Kings 3.16–28. When two women appeared before him claiming to be the mother of the same infant, Solomon ordered the child cut in two, expecting the real mother to object. The real mother pleaded with him to save the baby and to give it to the other woman, who had maliciously agreed to Solomon's original plan.
7. The Dauphin, Louis Charles, next in line of the succession to the throne, was eight years old when his father, Louis XVI, was beheaded (1793). Though the boy died in prison, probably in 1795, legends of his escape to America (and elsewhere) persisted, and Twain owned a book on the subject by Horace W. Fuller: *Imposters and Adventurers, Noted French Trials* (1882).

"Po' little chap."

"But some says he got out and got away, and come to America."

"Dat's good! But he'll be pooty lonesome—dey ain' no kings here, is dey, Huck?"

"No."

"Den he cain't git no situation. What he gwyne to do?"

"Well, I don't know. Some of them gets on the police, and some of them learns people how to talk French."

"Why, Huck, doan' de French people talk de same way we does?"

"No, Jim; you couldn't understand a word they said—not a single word."

"Well now, I be ding-busted! How do dat come?"

"I don't know; but it's so. I got some of their jabber out of a book. Spose a man was to come to you and say Polly-voo-franzy—what would you think?"

"I wouldn' think nuff'n; I'd take en bust him over de head. Dat is, if he warn't white. I wouldn't 'low no nigger to call me dat."

"Shucks, it ain't calling you anything. It's only saying do you know how to talk French?"

"Well, den, why couldn't he say it?"

"Why, he is a-saying it. That's a Frenchman's way of saying it."

"Well, it's a blame' ridicklous way, en I doan' want to hear no mo' 'bout it. Dey ain' no sense in it."

"Looky here, Jim; does a cat talk like we do?"

"No, a cat don't."

"Well, does a cow?"

"No, a cow don't, nuther."

"Does a cat talk like a cow, or a cow talk like a cat?"

"No, dey don't."

"It's natural and right for 'em to talk different from each other, ain't it?"

"'Course."

"And ain't it natural and right for a cat and a cow to talk different from us?"

"Why, mos' sholy it is."

"Well, then, why ain't it natural and right for a Frenchman to talk different from us? You answer me that."

"Is a cat a man, Huck?"

"No."

"Well, den, dey ain't no sense in a cat talkin' like a man. Is a cow a man?—er is a cow a cat?"

"No, she ain't either of them."

"Well, den, she ain' got no business to talk like either one er the yuther of 'em. Is a Frenchman a man?"

"Yes."

"Well, den! Dad blame it, why doan' he talk like a man? You answer me dat!"

I see it warn't no use wasting words—you can't learn a nigger to argue. So I quit.

Chapter XV

We judged that three nights more would fetch us to Cairo,[8] at the bottom of Illinois, where the Ohio River comes in, and that was what we was after.

8. Pronounced Cair-ō, the town is 364 miles from Hannibal, 194 miles from St. Louis.

We would sell the raft and get on a steamboat and go way up the Ohio amongst the free States, and then be out of trouble.[9]

Well, the second night a fog begun to come on, and we made for a tow-head to tie to, for it wouldn't do to try to run in fog; but when I paddled ahead in the canoe, with the line, to make fast, there warn't anything but little saplings to tie to. I passed the line around one of them right on the edge of the cut bank, but there was a stiff current, and the raft come booming down so lively she tore it out by the roots and away she went. I see the fog closing down, and it made me so sick and scared I couldn't budge for most a half a minute it seemed to me—and then there warn't no raft in sight; you couldn't see twenty yards. I jumped into the canoe and run back to the stern and grabbed the paddle and set her back a stroke. But she didn't come. I was in such a hurry I hadn't untied her. I got up and tried to untie her, but I was so excited my hands shook so I couldn't hardly do anything with them.

As soon as I got started I took out after the raft, hot and heavy, right down the tow-head. That was all right as far as it went, but the tow-head warn't sixty yards long, and the minute I flew by the foot of it I shot out into the solid white fog, and hadn't no more idea which way I was going than a dead man.

Thinks I, it won't do to paddle; first I know I'll run into the bank or a tow-head or something; I got to set still and float, and yet it's mighty fidgety business to have to hold your hands still at such a time. I whooped and listened. Away down there, somewheres, I hears a small whoop, and up comes my spirits. I went tearing after it, listening sharp to hear it again. The next time it come, I see I warn't heading for it but heading away to the right of it. And the next time, I was heading away to the left of it—and not gaining on it much, either, for I was flying around, this way and that and 'tother, but it was going straight ahead all the time.

I did wish the fool would think to beat a tin pan, and beat it all the time, but he never did, and it was the still places between the whoops that was making the trouble for me. Well, I fought along, and directly I hears the whoops *behind* me. I was tangled good, now. That was somebody's else's whoop, or else I was turned around.

I throwed the paddle down. I heard the whoop again; it was behind me yet, but in a different place; it kept coming, and kept changing its place, and I kept answering, till by-and-by it was in front of me again and I knowed the current had swung the canoe's head down stream and I was all right, if that was Jim and not some other raftsman hollering. I couldn't tell nothing about voices in a fog, for nothing don't look natural nor sound natural in a fog.

The whooping went on, and in about a minute I come a booming down on a cut bank[1] with smoky ghosts of big trees on it, and the current throwed me off to the left and shot by, amongst a lot of snags that fairly roared, the current was tearing by them so swift.

In another second or two it was solid white and still again. I set perfectly still, then, listening to my heart thump, and I reckon I didn't draw a breath while it thumped a hundred.

---

9. Southern Illinois was proslavery in sentiment. The state, moreover, had a system of indentured labor, not unlike slavery, to which a black person without proof of free status might be subjected. Although even in the "free" states there were sim-ilar dangers for Jim, the chances of his making his way to freedom and safety in Canada from Ohio or Pennsylvania would be much greater.

1. Steep bank carved out by the force of the current.

I just give up, then. I knowed what the matter was. That cut bank was an island, and Jim had gone down 'tother side of it. It warn't no tow-head, that you could float by in ten minutes. It had the big timber of a regular island; it might be five or six mile long and more than a half a mile wide.

I kept quiet, with my ears cocked, about fifteen minutes, I reckon. I was floating along, of course, four or five mile an hour; but you don't ever think of that. No, you *feel* like you are laying dead still on the water; and if a little glimpse of a snag slips by, you don't think to yourself how fast *you're* going, but you catch your breath and think, my! how that snag's tearing along. If you think it ain't dismal and lonesome out in a fog that way, by yourself, in the night, you try it once—you'll see.

Next, for about a half an hour, I whoops now and then; at last I hears the answer a long ways off, and tries to follow it, but I couldn't do it, and directly I judged I'd got into a nest of tow-heads, for I had little dim glimpses of them on both sides of me, sometimes just a narrow channel between; and some that I couldn't see, I knowed was there, because I'd hear the wash of the current against the old dead brush and trash that hung over the banks. Well, I warn't long losing the whoops, down amongst the tow-heads; and I only tried to chase them a little while, anyway, because it was worse than chasing a Jack-o-lantern. You never knowed a sound dodge around so, and swap places so quick and so much.

I had to claw away from the bank pretty lively, four or five times, to keep from knocking the islands out of the river; and so I judged the raft must be butting into the bank every now and then, or else it would get further ahead and clear out of hearing—it was floating a little faster than what I was.

Well, I seemed to be in the open river again, by-and-by, but I couldn't hear no sign of a whoop nowheres. I reckoned Jim had fetched up on a snag, maybe, and it was all up with him. I was good and tired, so I laid down in the canoe and said I wouldn't bother no more. I didn't want to go to sleep, of course; but I was so sleepy I couldn't help it; so I thought I would take just one little cat-nap.

But I reckon it was more than a cat-nap, for when I waked up the stars was shining bright, the fog was all gone, and I was spinning down a big bend stern first. First I didn't know where I was; I thought I was dreaming; and when things begun to come back to me, they seemed to come up dim out of last week.

It was a monstrous big river here, with the tallest and the thickest kind of timber on both banks; just a solid wall, as well as I could see, by the stars. I looked away down stream, and seen a black speck on the water. I took out after it; but when I got to it it warn't nothing but a couple of saw-logs made fast together. Then I see another speck, and chased that; then another, and this time I was right. It was the raft.

When I got to it Jim was setting there with his head down between his knees, asleep, with his right arm hanging over the steering oar. The other oar was smashed off, and the raft was littered up with leaves and branches and dirt. So she'd had a rough time.

I made fast and laid down under Jim's nose on the raft, and begun to gap, and stretch my fists out against Jim, and says:

"Hello, Jim, have I been asleep? Why didn't you stir me up?"

"Goodness gracious, is dat you, Huck? En you ain' dead—you ain' drownded—you's back agin? It's too good for true, honey, it's too good for true. Lemme look at you, chile, lemme feel o' you. No, you ain' dead? you's back agin, 'live en soun', jis de same ole Huck—de same ole Huck, thanks to goodness!"

"What's the matter with you, Jim? You been a drinking?"

"Drinkin'? Has I ben a drinkin'? Has I had a chance to be a drinkin'?"

"Well, then, what makes you talk so wild?"

"How does I talk wild?"

"*How?* why, haint you been talking about my coming back, and all that stuff, as if I'd been gone away?"

"Huck—Huck Finn, you look me in de eye; look me in de eye. *Hain't* you ben gone away?"

"Gone away? Why, what in the nation do you mean? *I* hain't been gone anywhere. Where would I go to?"

"Well, looky here, boss, dey's sumf'n wrong, dey is. Is I *me,* or who *is* I? Is I heah, or whah *is* I? Now dat's what I wants to know?"

"Well, I think you're here, plain enough, but I think you're a tangle-headed old fool, Jim."

"I is, is I? Well you answer me dis. Didn't you tote out de line in de canoe, fer to make fas' to de tow-head?"

"No, I didn't. What tow-head? I hain't seen no tow-head."

"You hain't seen no tow-head? Looky here—didn't de line pull loose en de raf' go a hummin' down de river, en leave you en de canoe behine in de fog?"

"What fog?"

"Why *de* fog. De fog dat's ben aroun' all night. En didn't you whoop, en didn't I whoop, tell we got mix' up in de islands en one un us got 'los' en 'tother one was jis' as good as los', 'kase he didn' know whah he wuz? En didn't I bust up agin a lot er dem islands en have a turrible time en mos' git drownded? Now ain' dat so, boss—ain't it so? You answer me dat."

"Well, this is too many for me, Jim. I hain't seen no fog, nor no islands, nor no troubles, nor nothing. I been setting here talking with you all night till you went to sleep about ten minutes ago, and I reckon I done the same. You couldn't a got drunk in that time, so of course you've been dreaming."

"Dad fetch it, how is I gwyne to dream all dat in ten minutes?"

"Well, hang it all, you did dream it, because there didn't any of it happen."

"But Huck, it's all jis' as plain to me as—"

"It don't make no difference how plain it is, there ain't nothing in it. I know, because I've been here all the time."

Jim didn't say nothing for about five minutes, but set there studying over it. Then he says:

"Well, den, I reck'n I did dream it, Huck; but dog my cats ef it ain't de powerfullest dream I ever see. En I hain't ever had no dream b'fo' dat's tired me like dis one."

"Oh, well, that's all right, because a dream does tire a body like everything, sometimes. But this one was a staving[2] dream—tell me all about it, Jim."

So Jim went to work and told me the whole thing right through, just as it happened, only he painted it up considerable. Then he said he must start in and "'terpret" it, because it was sent for a warning. He said the first tow-

2. Vivid, compelling.

head stood for a man that would try to do us some good, but the current was another man that would get us away from him. The whoops was warnings that would come to us every now and then, and if we didn't try hard to make out to understand them they'd just take us into bad luck, 'stead of keeping us out of it. The lot of tow-heads was troubles we was going to get into with quarrelsome people and all kinds of mean folks, but if we minded our business and didn't talk back and aggravate them, we would pull through and get out of the fog and into the big clear river, which was the free States, and wouldn't have no more trouble.

It had clouded up pretty dark just after I got onto the raft, but it was clearing up again, now.

"Oh, well, that's all interpreted well enough, as far as it goes, Jim," I says; "but what does *these* things stand for?"

It was the leaves and rubbish on the raft, and the smashed oar. You could see them first rate, now.

Jim looked at the trash, and then looked at me, and back at the trash again. He had got the dream fixed so strong in his head that he couldn't seem to shake it loose and get the facts back into its place again, right away. But when he did get the thing straightened around, he looked at me steady, without ever smiling, and says:

"What do dey stan' for? I's gwyne to tell you. When I got all wore out wid work, en wid de callin' for you, en went to sleep, my heart wuz mos' broke bekase you wuz los', en I didn' k'yer no mo' what become er me en de raf'. En when I wake up en fine you back agin', all safe en soun', de tears come en I could a got down on my knees en kiss' yo' foot I's so thankful. En all you wuz thinkin' 'bout wuz how you could make a fool uv ole Jim wid a lie. Dat truck dah is *trash*; en trash is what people is dat puts dirt on de head er dey fren's en makes 'em ashamed."

Then he got up slow, and walked to the wigwam, and went in there, without saying anything but that. But that was enough. It made me feel so mean I could almost kissed *his* foot to get him to take it back.

It was fifteen minutes before I could work myself up to go and humble myself to a nigger—but I done it, and I warn't ever sorry for it afterwards, neither. I didn't do him no more mean tricks, and I wouldn't done that one if I'd a knowed it would make him feel that way.

Chapter XVI

We slept most all day, and started out at night, a little ways behind a monstrous long raft that was as long going by as a procession. She had four long sweeps[3] at each end, so we judged she carried as many as thirty men, likely. She had five big wigwams aboard, wide apart, and an open camp fire in the middle, and a tall flagpole at each end. There was a power of style about her. It *amounted* to something being a raftsman on such a craft as that.

We went drifting down into a big bend, and the night clouded up and got hot. The river was very wide, and was walled with solid timber on both sides; you couldn't see a break in it hardly ever, or a light. We talked about Cairo, and wondered whether we would know it when we got to it. I said likely we wouldn't, because I had heard say there warn't but about a dozen houses

3. Long oars used chiefly for steering

there, and if they didn't happen to have them lit up, how was we going to know we was passing a town? Jim said if the two big rivers joined together there, that would show. But I said maybe we might think we was passing the foot of an island and coming into the same old river again. That disturbed Jim—and me too. So the question was, what to do? I said, paddle ashore the first time a light showed, and tell them pap was behind, coming along with a trading-scow, and was a green hand at the business, and wanted to know how far it was to Cairo. Jim thought it was a good idea, so we took a smoke on it and waited.

There warn't nothing to do, now, but to look out sharp for the town, and not pass it without seeing it. He said he'd be mighty sure to see it, because he'd be a free man the minute he seen it, but if he missed it he'd be in the slave country again and no more show for freedom. Every little while he jumps up and says:

"Dah she is!"

But it warn't. It was Jack-o-lanterns, or lightning-bugs; so he set down again, and went to watching, same as before. Jim said it made him all over trembly and feverish to be so close to freedom. Well, I can tell you it made me all over trembly and feverish, too, to hear him, because I begun to get it through my head that he *was* most free—and who was to blame for it? Why, *me*. I couldn't get that out of my conscience, no how nor no way. It got to troubling me so I couldn't rest; I couldn't stay still in one place. It hadn't ever come home to me before, what this thing was that I was doing. But now it did; and it staid with me, and scorched me more and more. I tried to make out to myself that *I* warn't to blame, because I didn't run Jim off from his rightful owner; but it warn't no use, conscience up and says, every time, "But you knowed he was running for his freedom, and you could a paddled ashore and told somebody." That was so—I couldn't get around that, noway. That was where it pinched. Conscience says to me, "What had poor Miss Watson done to you, that you could see her nigger go off right under your eyes and never say one single word? What did that poor old woman do to you, that you could treat her so mean? Why, she tried to learn you your book, she tried to learn you your manners, she tried to be good to you every way she knowed how. *That's* what she done."

I got to feeling so mean and so miserable I most wished I was dead. I fidgeted up and down the raft, abusing myself to myself, and Jim was fidgeting up and down past me. We neither of us could keep still. Every time he danced around and says, "Dah's Cairo!" it went through me like a shot, and I thought if it *was* Cairo I reckoned I would die of miserableness.

Jim talked out loud all the time while I was talking to myself. He was saying how the first thing he would do when he got to a free State he would go to saving up money and never spend a single cent, and when he got enough he would buy his wife, which was owned on a farm close to where Miss Watson lived; and then they would both work to buy the two children, and if their master wouldn't sell them, they'd get an Ab'litionist to go and steal them.

It most froze me to hear such talk. He wouldn't ever dared to talk such talk in his life before. Just see what a difference it made in him the minute he judged he was about free. It was according to the old saying, "give a nigger an inch and he'll take an ell." Thinks I, this is what comes of my not thinking. Here was this nigger which I had as good as helped to run away, coming right out flat-footed and saying he would steal his children—children that belonged to a man I didn't even know; a man that hadn't ever done me no harm.

I was sorry to hear Jim say that, it was such a lowering of him. My conscience got to stirring me up hotter than ever, until at last I says to it, "Let up on me—it ain't too late, yet—I'll paddle ashore at the first light, and tell." I felt easy, and happy, and light as a feather, right off. All my troubles was gone. I went to looking out sharp for a light, and sort of singing to myself. By-and-by one showed. Jim sings out:

"We's safe, Huck, we's safe! Jump up and crack yo' heels, dat's de good ole Cairo at las', I jis knows it!"

I says:

"I'll take the canoe and go see, Jim. It mightn't be, you know."

He jumped and got the canoe ready, and put his old coat in the bottom for me to set on, and give me the paddle; and as I shoved off, he says:

"Pooty soon I'll be a-shout'n for joy, en I'll say, it's all on accounts o' Huck; I's a free man, en I couldn't ever ben free ef it hadn' ben for Huck; Huck done it. Jim won't ever forgit you, Huck; you's de bes' fren' Jim's ever had; en you's de *only* fren' ole Jim's got now."

I was paddling off, all in a sweat to tell on him; but when he says this, it seemed to kind of take the tuck all out of me. I went along slow then, and I warn't right down certain whether I was glad I started or whether I warn't. When I was fifty yards off, Jim says:

"Dah you goes, de ole true Huck; de on'y white genlman dat ever kep' his promise to ole Jim."

Well, I just felt sick. But I says, I *got* to do it—I can't get *out* of it. Right then, along comes a skiff with two men in it, with guns, and they stopped and I stopped. One of them says:

"What's that, yonder?"

"A piece of raft," I says.

"Do you belong on it?"

"Yes, sir."

"Any men on it?"

"Only one, sir."

"Well, there's five niggers run off to-night, up yonder above the head of the bend. Is your man white or black?"

I didn't answer up prompt. I tried to, but the words wouldn't come. I tried, for a second or two, to brace up and out with it, but I warn't man enough—hadn't the spunk of a rabbit. I see I was weakening; so I just give up trying, and up and says—

"He's white."

"I reckon we'll go and see for ourselves."

"I wish you would," says I, "because it's pap that's there, and maybe you'd help me tow the raft ashore where the light is. He's sick—and so is mam and Mary Ann."

"Oh, the devil! we're in a hurry, boy. But I s'pose we've got to. Come—buckle to your paddle, and let's get along."

I buckled to my paddle and they laid to their oars. When we had made a stroke or two, I says:

"Pap'll be mighty much obleeged to you, I can tell you. Everybody goes away when I want them to help me tow the raft ashore, and I can't do it myself."

"Well, that's infernal mean. Odd, too. Say, boy, what's the matter with your father?"

"It's the—a—the—well, it ain't anything, much."

They stopped pulling. It warn't but a mighty little ways to the raft, now. One says:

"Boy, that's a lie. What *is* the matter with your pap? Answer up square, now, and it'll be the better for you."

"I will, sir, I will, honest—but don't leave us, please. It's the—the—gentlemen, if you'll only pull ahead, and let me heave you the head-line you won't have to come a-near the raft—please do."

"Set her back, John, set her back!" says one. They backed water. "Keep away, boy—keep to looard.[4] Confound it, I just expect the wind has blowed it to us. Your pap's got the small-pox,[5] and you know it precious well. Why didn't you come out and say so? Do you want to spread it all over?"

"Well," says I, a-blubbering, "I've told everybody before, and then they just went away and left us."

"Poor devil, there's something in that. We are right down sorry for you, but we—well, hang it, we don't want the small-pox, you see. Look here, I'll tell you what to do. Don't you try to land by yourself, or you'll smash everything to pieces. You float along down about twenty miles and you'll come to a town on the left-hand side of the river. It will be long after sun-up, then, and when you ask for help, you tell them your folks are all down with chills and fever. Don't be a fool again, and let people guess what is the matter. Now we're trying to do you a kindness; so you just put twenty miles between us, that's a good boy. It wouldn't do any good to land yonder where the light is—it's only a wood-yard. Say—I reckon your father's poor, and I'm bound to say he's in pretty hard luck. Here—I'll put a twenty dollar gold piece on this board, and you get it when it floats by. I feel mighty mean to leave you, but my kingdom! it won't do to fool with small-pox, don't you see?"

"Hold on, Parker," says the other man, "here's a twenty to put on the board for me. Good-bye boy, you do as Mr. Parker told you, and you'll be all right."

"That's so, my boy—good-bye, good-bye. If you see any runaway niggers, you get help and nab them, and you can make some money by it."

"Good-bye, sir," says I, "I won't let no runaway niggers get by me if I can help it."

They went off, and I got aboard the raft, feeling bad and low, because I knowed very well I had done wrong, and I see it warn't no use for me to try to learn to do right; a body that don't get *started* right when he's little, ain't got no show—when the pinch comes there ain't nothing to back him up and keep him to his work, and so he gets beat. Then I thought a minute, and says to myself, hold on,—s'pose you'd a done right and give Jim up; would you felt better than what you do now? No, says I, I'd feel bad—I'd feel just the same way I do now. Well, then, says I, what's the use you learning to do right, when it's troublesome to do right and ain't no trouble to do wrong, and the wages is just the same? I was stuck. I couldn't answer that. So I reckoned I wouldn't bother no more about it, but after this always do whichever come handiest at the time.

I went into the wigwam; Jim warn't there. I looked all around; he warn't anywhere. I says:

"Jim!"

"Here I is, Huck. Is dey out o' sight yit? Don't talk loud."

He was in the river, under the stern oar, with just his nose out. I told him they was out of sight, so he come aboard. He says:

"I was a-listenin' to all de talk, en I slips into de river en was gwyne to shove for sho' if dey come aboard. Den I was gwyne to swim to de raf' agin when dey was gone. But lawsy, how you did fool 'em, Huck! Dat *wuz* de smartes' dodge! I tell you, chile, I 'speck it save' ole Jim—ole Jim ain' gwyne to forgit you for dat, honey."

Then we talked about the money. It was a pretty good raise, twenty dollars apiece. Jim said we could take deck passage on a steamboat now, and the money would last us as far as we wanted to go in the free States. He said twenty mile more warn't far for the raft to go, but he wished we was already there.

Towards daybreak we tied up, and Jim was mighty particular about hiding the raft good. Then he worked all day fixing things in bundles, and getting all ready to quit rafting.

That night about ten we hove in sight of the lights of a town away down in a left-hand bend.

I went off in the canoe, to ask about it. Pretty soon I found a man out in the river with a skiff, setting a trot-line. I ranged up and says:

"Mister, is that town Cairo?"

"Cairo? no. You must be a blame' fool."

"What town is it, mister?"

"If you want to know, go and find out. If you stay here botherin' around me for about a half a minute longer, you'll get something you won't want."

I paddled to the raft. Jim was awful disappointed, but I said never mind, Cairo would be the next place, I reckoned.

We passed another town before daylight, and I was going out again; but it was high ground, so I didn't go. No high ground about Cairo, Jim said. I had forgot it. We laid up for the day, on a tow-head tolerable close to the left-hand bank. I begun to suspicion something. So did Jim. I says:

"Maybe we went by Cairo in the fog that night."

He says:

"Doan' less' talk about it, Huck. Po' niggers can't have no luck. I awluz 'spected dat rattle-snake skin warn't done wid it's work."

"I wish I'd never seen that snake-skin, Jim—I do wish I'd never laid eyes on it."

"It ain't yo' fault, Huck; you didn't know. Don't you blame yo'sef 'bout it."

When it was daylight, here was the clear Ohio water in shore, sure enough, and outside was the old regular Muddy! So it was all up with Cairo.[6]

We talked it all over. It wouldn't do to take to the shore; we couldn't take the raft up the stream, of course. There warn't no way but to wait for dark, and start back in the canoe and take the chances. So we slept all day amongst the cotton-wood thicket, so as to be fresh for the work, and when we went back to the raft about dark the canoe was gone!

We didn't say a word for a good while. There warn't anything to say. We both knowed well enough it was some more work of the rattle-snake skin;

6. Because Cairo is located at the confluence of the Ohio and Mississippi rivers, which in turn lies below the confluence of the Missouri (Big Muddy) and Mississippi, they know that they have passed Cairo and lost the opportunity to sell the raft and travel up the Ohio by steamboat to freedom.

so what was the use to talk about it? It would only look like we was finding fault, and that would be bound to fetch more bad luck—and keep on fetching it, too, till we knowed enough to keep still.

By-and-by we talked about what we better do, and found there warn't no way but just to go along down with the raft till we got a chance to buy a canoe to go back in. We warn't going to borrow it when there warn't anybody around, the way pap would do, for that might set people after us.

So we shoved out, after dark, on the raft.[7]

Anybody that don't believe yet, that it's foolishness to handle a snake-skin, after all that that snake-skin done for us, will believe it now, if they read on and see what more it done for us.

The place to buy canoes is off of rafts laying up at shore. But we didn't see no rafts laying up; so we went along during three hours and more. Well, the night got gray, and ruther thick, which is the next meanest thing to fog. You can't tell the shape of the river, and you can't see no distance. It got to be very late and still, and then along comes a steamboat up the river. We lit the lantern, and judged she would see it. Up-stream boats didn't generly come close to us; they go out and follow the bars and hunt for easy water under the reefs; but nights like this they bull right up the channel against the whole river.

We could hear her pounding along, but we didn't see her good till she was close. She aimed right for us. Often they do that and try to see how close they can come without touching; sometimes the wheel bites off a sweep, and then the pilot sticks his head out and laughs, and thinks he's mighty smart. Well, here she comes, and we said she was going to try to shave us; but she didn't seem to be sheering off a bit. She was a big one, and she was coming in a hurry, too, looking like a black cloud with rows of glow-worms around it; but all of a sudden she bulged out, big and scary, with a long row of wide-open furnace doors shining like red-hot teeth, and her monstrous bows and guards hanging right over us. There was a yell at us, and a jingling of bells to stop the engines, a pow-wow of cussing, and whistling of steam—and as Jim went overboard on one side and I on the other, she come smashing straight through the raft.

I dived—and I aimed to find the bottom, too, for a thirty-foot wheel had got to go over me, and I wanted it to have plenty of room. I could always stay under water a minute; this time I reckon I staid under water a minute and a half. Then I bounced for the top in a hurry, for I was nearly busting. I popped out to my arm-pits and blowed the water out of my nose, and puffed a bit. Of course there was a booming current; and of course that boat started her engines again ten seconds after she stopped them, for they never cared much for raftsmen; so now she was churning along up the river, out of sight in the thick weather, though I could hear her.

I sung out for Jim about a dozen times, but I didn't get any answer; so I grabbed a plank that touched me while I was "treading water," and struck out for shore, shoving it ahead of me. But I made out to see that the drift of the current was towards the left-hand shore,[8] which meant that I was in a crossing; so I changed off and went that way.

---

7. Twain was "stuck" at this point in the writing of the novel and put the 400-page manuscript aside for approximately three years. In the winter of 1879–80 he added the two chapters dealing with the feud (XVII and XVIII) and then the three chapters (XIX–XXI) in which the king and duke enter the story and for a time dominate the action. The novel was not completed until 1883, when Twain wrote the last half of it in a few months of concentrated work. As late as 1882, he was not confident he would ever complete the book.

8. Kentucky, where the feud in chapters XVII and XVIII is set.

It was one of these long, slanting, two-mile crossings; so I was a good long time in getting over. I made a safe landing, and clum up the bank. I couldn't see but a little ways, but I went poking along over rough ground for a quarter of a mile or more, and then I run across a big old-fashioned double log house before I noticed it. I was going to rush by and get away, but a lot of dogs jumped out and went to howling and barking at me, and I knowed better than to move another peg.

Chapter XVII

In about half a minute somebody spoke out of a window, without putting his head out, and says:

"Be done, boys! Who's there?"

I says:

"It's me."

"Who's me?"

"George Jackson, sir."

"What do you want?"

"I don't want nothing, sir. I only want to go along by, but the dogs won't let me."

"What are you prowling around here this time of night, for—hey?"

"I warn't prowling around, sir; I fell overboard off of the steamboat."

"Oh, you did, did you? Strike a light there, somebody. What did you say your name was?"

"George Jackson, sir. I'm only a boy."

"Look here; if you're telling the truth, you needn't be afraid—nobody'll hurt you. But don't try to budge; stand right where you are. Rouse our Bob and Tom, some of you, and fetch the guns. George Jackson, is there anybody with you?"

"No, sir, nobody."

I heard the people stirring around in the house, now, and see a light. The man sung out:

"Snatch that light away, Betsy, you old fool—ain't you got any sense? Put it on the floor behind the front door. Bob, if you and Tom are ready, take your places."

"All ready."

"Now, George Jackson, do you know the Shepherdsons?"

"No, sir—I never heard of them."

"Well, that may be so, and it mayn't. Now, all ready. Step forward, George Jackson. And mind, don't you hurry—come mighty slow. If there's anybody with you, let him keep back—if he shows himself he'll be shot. Come along, now. Come slow; push the door open, yourself—just enough to squeeze in, d' you hear?"

I didn't hurry, I couldn't if I'd a wanted to. I took one slow step at a time, and there warn't a sound, only I thought I could hear my heart. The dogs were as still as the humans, but they followed a little behind me. When I got to the three log door-steps, I heard them unlocking and unbarring and unbolting. I put my hand on the door and pushed it a little and a little more, till somebody said, "There, that's enough—put your head in." I done it, but I judged they would take it off.

The candle was on the floor, and there they all was, looking at me, and me at them, for about a quarter of a minute. Three big men with guns pointed at me, which made me wince, I tell you; the oldest, gray and about sixty, the other two thirty or more—all of them fine and handsome—and the sweetest old gray-headed lady, and back of her two young women which I couldn't see right well. The old gentleman says:

"There—I reckon it's all right. Come in."

As soon as I was in, the old gentleman he locked the door and barred it and bolted it, and told the young men to come in with their guns, and they all went in a big parlor that had a new rag carpet on the floor, and got together in a corner that was out of range of the front windows—there warn't none on the side. They held the candle, and took a good look at me, and all said, "Why *he* ain't a Shepherdson—no, there ain't any Shepherdson about him." Then the old man said he hoped I wouldn't mind being searched for arms, because he didn't mean no harm by it—it was only to make sure. So he didn't pry into my pockets, but only felt outside with his hands, and said it was all right. He told me to make myself easy and at home, and tell all about myself; but the old lady says:

"Why bless you, Saul, the poor thing's as wet as he can be; and don't you reckon it may be he's hungry?"

"True for you, Rachel—I forgot."

So the old lady says:

"Betsy" (this was a nigger woman), "you fly around and get him something to eat, as quick as you can, poor thing; and one of you girls go and wake up Buck and tell him—Oh, here he is himself. Buck, take this little stranger and get the wet clothes off from him and dress him up in some of yours that's dry."

Buck looked about as old as me—thirteen or fourteen[9] or along there, though he was a little bigger than me. He hadn't on anything but a shirt, and he was very frowsy-headed. He come in gaping and digging one fist into his eyes, and he was dragging a gun along with the other one. He says:

"Ain't they no Shepherdsons around?"

They said, no, 'twas a false alarm.

"Well," he says, "if they'd a ben some, I reckon I'd a got one."

They all laughed, and Bob says:

"Why, Buck, they might have scalped us all, you've been so slow in coming."

"Well, nobody come after me, and it ain't right. I'm always kep' down; I don't get no show."

"Never mind, Buck, my boy," says the old man, "you'll have show enough, all in good time, don't you fret about that. Go 'long with you now, and do as your mother told you."

When we got up stairs to his room, he got me a coarse shirt and a round-about[1] and pants of his, and I put them on. While I was at it he asked me what my name was, but before I could tell him, he started to telling me about a blue jay and a young rabbit he had catched in the woods day before yesterday, and he asked me where Moses was when the candle went out. I said I didn't know; I hadn't heard about it before, no way.

"Well, guess," he says.

"How'm I going to guess," says I, "when I never heard tell about it before?"

"But you can guess, can't you? It's just as easy."

"*Which* candle?" I says.

---

9. In a notebook entry, Twain identifies Huck as "a boy of 14."

1. Short, close-fitting jacket.

"Why, any candle," he says.

"I don't know where he was," says I; "where was he?"

"Why he was in the *dark!* That's where he was!"

"Well, if you knowed where he was, what did you ask me for?"

"Why, blame it, it's a riddle, don't you see? Say, how long are you going to stay here? You got to stay always. We can just have booming times—they don't have no school now. Do you own a dog? I've got a dog—and he'll go in the river and bring out chips that you throw in. Do you like to comb up, Sundays, and all that kind of foolishness? You bet I don't, but ma she makes me. Confound these ole britches, I reckon I'd better put 'em on, but I'd ruther not, it's so warm. Are you all ready? All right—come along, old hoss."

Cold corn-pone, cold corn-beef, butter and butter-milk—that is what they had for me down there, and there ain't nothing better that ever I've come across yet. Buck and his ma and all of them smoked cob pipes, except the nigger woman, which was gone, and the two young women. They all smoked and talked, and I eat and talked. The young women had quilts around them, and their hair down their backs. They all asked me questions, and I told them how pap and me and all the family was living on a little farm down at the bottom of Arkansaw, and my sister Mary Ann run off and got married and never was heard of no more, and Bill went to hunt them and he warn't heard of no more, and Tom and Mort died, and then there warn't nobody but just me and pap left, and he was just trimmed down to nothing, on account of his troubles; so when he died I took what there was left, because the farm didn't belong to us, and started up the river, deck passage, and fell overboard; and that was how I come to be here. So they said I could have a home there as long as I wanted it. Then it was most daylight, and everybody went to bed, and I went to bed with Buck, and when I waked up in the morning, drat it all, I had forgot what my name was. So I laid there about an hour trying to think and when Buck waked up, I says:

"Can you spell, Buck?"

"Yes," he says.

"I bet you can't spell my name," says I.

"I bet you what you dare I can," says he.

"All right," says I, "go ahead."

"G-o-r-g-e J-a-x-o-n—there now," he says.

"Well," says I, "you done it, but I didn't think you could. It ain't no slouch of a name to spell—right off without studying."

I set it down, private, because somebody might want *me* to spell it, next, and so I wanted to be handy with it and rattle it off like I was used to it.

It was a mighty nice family, and a mighty nice house, too. I hadn't seen no house out in the country before that was so nice and had so much style. It didn't have an iron latch on the front door, nor a wooden one with a buckskin string, but a brass knob to turn, the same as houses in a town. There warn't no bed in the parlor, not a sign of a bed; but heaps of parlors in towns has beds in them. There was a big fireplace that was bricked on the bottom, and the bricks was kept clean and red by pouring water on them and scrubbing them with another brick; sometimes they washed them over with red water-paint that they call Spanish-brown, same as they do in town. They had big brass dog-irons that could hold up a saw-log.[2] There was a clock on the middle of the mantel-piece, with a picture of a town painted on the bottom half of

2. A log large enough to be sawed into planks.

the glass front, and a round place in the middle of it for the sun, and you could see the pendulum swing behind it. It was beautiful to hear that clock tick; and sometimes when one of these peddlers had been along and scoured her up and got her in good shape, she would start in and strike a hundred and fifty before she got tuckered out. They wouldn't took any money for her.

Well, there was a big outlandish parrot on each side of the clock, made out of something like chalk, and painted up gaudy. By one of the parrots was a cat made of crockery, and a crockery dog by the other; and when you pressed down on them they squeaked, but didn't open their mouths nor look different nor interested. They squeaked through underneath. There was a couple of big wild-turkey-wing fans spread out behind those things. On a table in the middle of the room was a kind of a lovely crockery basket that had apples and oranges and peaches and grapes piled up in it which was much redder and yellower and prettier than real ones is, but they warn't real because you could see where pieces had got chipped off and showed the white chalk or whatever it was, underneath.

This table had a cover made out of beautiful oil-cloth, with a red and blue spread-eagle painted on it, and a painted border all around. It come all the way from Philadelphia, they said. There was some books too, piled up perfectly exact, on each corner of the table. One was a big family Bible, full of pictures. One was "Pilgrim's Progress," about a man that left his family it didn't say why. I read considerable in it now and then. The statements was interesting, but tough. Another was "Friendship's Offering," full of beautiful stuff and poetry; but I didn't read the poetry. Another was Henry Clay's Speeches, and another was Dr. Gunn's Family Medicine, which told you all about what to do if a body was sick or dead. There was a Hymn Book, and a lot of other books.[3] And there was nice split-bottom chairs, and perfectly sound, too—not bagged down in the middle and busted, like an old basket.

They had pictures hung on the walls—mainly Washingtons and Lafayettes, and battles, and Highland Marys, and one called "Signing the Declaration."[4] There was some that they called crayons, which one of the daughters which was dead made her own self when she was only fifteen years old. They was different from any pictures I ever see before; blacker, mostly, than is common. One was a woman in a slim black dress, belted small under the armpits, with bulges like a cabbage in the middle of the sleeves, and a large black scoop-shovel bonnet with a black veil, and white slim ankles crossed about with black tape, and very wee black slippers, like a chisel, and she was leaning pensive on a tombstone on her right elbow, under a weeping willow, and her other hand hanging down her side holding a white handkerchief and a reticule, and underneath the picture it said "Shall I Never See Thee More Alas." Another one was a young lady with her hair all combed up straight to the top of her head, and knotted there in front of a comb like a chair-back, and she was crying into a handkerchief and had a dead bird laying on its back in her other hand with its heels up, and underneath the picture it said

3. The neatly stacked, unread books are meant to define the values and tastes of the time and place. The Bible, John Bunyan's *Pilgrim's Progress* (1678), and the hymn book establish Calvinistic piety; the speeches of the Kentucky politician Henry Clay (1777–1852) convey political orthodoxy; Gunn's *Domestic Medicine* (1830) suggests popular notions of science and medical practice.

Friendship's Offering was a popular gift book.
4. Painting in the U.S. Capitol Rotunda by John Trumbull (1756–1843), completed in 1819 and widely reproduced during the antebellum period. "Highland Mary" depicts the Scottish poet Robert Burns's first love, who died a few months after they met. He memorialized her in several poems, especially "To Mary in Heaven" (1792).

"I Shall Never Hear Thy Sweet Chirrup More Alas." There was one where a young lady was at a window looking up at the moon, and tears running down her cheeks; and she had an open letter in one hand with black sealing-wax showing on one edge of it, and she was mashing a locket with a chain to it against her mouth, and underneath the picture it said "And Art Thou Gone Yes Thou Art Gone Alas." These was all nice pictures, I reckon, but I didn't somehow seem to take to them, because if ever I was down a little, they always give me the fan-tods. Everybody was sorry she died, because she had laid out a lot more of these pictures to do, and a body could see by what she had done what they had lost. But I reckoned, that with her disposition, she was having a better time in the graveyard. She was at work on what they said was her greatest picture when she took sick, and every day and every night it was her prayer to be allowed to live till she got it done, but she never got the chance. It was a picture of a young woman in a long white gown, standing on the rail of a bridge all ready to jump off, with her hair all down her back, and looking up to the moon, with the tears running down her face, and she had two arms folded across her breast, and two arms stretched out in front, and two more reaching up towards the moon—and the idea was, to see which pair would look best and then scratch out all the other arms; but, as I was saying, she died before she got her mind made up, and now they kept this picture over the head of the bed in her room, and every time her birthday come they hung flowers on it. Other times it was hid with a little curtain. The young woman in the picture had a kind of a nice sweet face, but there was so many arms it made her look too spidery, seemed to me.

This young girl kept a scrap-book when she was alive, and used to paste obituaries and accidents and cases of patient suffering in it out of the *Presbyterian Observer*, and write poetry after them out of her own head. It was very good poetry.[5] This is what she wrote about a boy by the name of Stephen Dowling Bots that fell down a well and was drownded:

ODE TO STEPHEN DOWLING BOTS, DEC'D

And did young Stephen sicken,
    And did young Stephen die?
And did the sad hearts thicken,
    And did the mourners cry?

No; such was not the fate of
    Young Stephen Dowling Bots;
Though sad hearts round him thickened,
    'Twas not from sickness' shots.

No whooping-cough did rack his frame,
    Nor measles drear, with spots;
Not these impaired the sacred name
    Of Stephen Dowling Bots.

5. This parody derives in particular from two poems by "The Sweet Singer of Michigan," Julia A. Moore (1847–1920), whose sentimental poetry was popular at the time Twain was writing *Huck Finn*. In one of the two poems, "Little Libbie," the heroine "was choken on a piece of beef." The graveyard and obituary (or "sadful") schools of popular poetry are much older and more widespread.

> Despised love struck not with woe
>   That head of curly knots,
> Nor stomach troubles laid him low,
>   Young Stephen Dowling Bots.
>
> O no. Then list with tearful eye,
>   Whilst I his fate do tell.
> His soul did from this cold world fly,
>   By falling down a well.
>
> They got him out and emptied him;
>   Alas it was too late;
> His spirit was gone for to sport aloft
>   In the realms of the good and great.

If Emmeline Grangerford could make poetry like that before she was fourteen, there ain't no telling what she could a done by-and-by. Buck said she could rattle off poetry like nothing. She didn't ever have to stop to think. He said she would slap down a line, and if she couldn't find anything to rhyme with it she would just scratch it out and slap down another one, and go ahead. She warn't particular, she could write about anything you choose to give her to write about, just so it was sadful. Every time a man died, or a woman died, or a child died, she would be on hand with her "tribute" before he was cold. She called them tributes. The neighbors said it was the doctor first, then Emmeline, then the undertaker—the undertaker never got in ahead of Emmeline but once, and then she hung fire on a rhyme for the dead person's name, which was Whistler. She warn't ever the same, after that; she never complained, but she kind of pined away and did not live long. Poor thing, many's the time I made myself go up to the little room that used to be hers and get out her poor old scrapbook and read in it when her pictures had been aggravating me and I had soured on her a little. I liked all the family, dead ones and all, and warn't going to let anything come between us. Poor Emmeline made poetry about all the dead people when she was alive, and it didn't seem right that there warn't nobody to make some about her, now she was gone; so I tried to sweat out a verse or two myself, but I couldn't seem to make it go, somehow. They kept Emmeline's room trim and nice and all the things fixed in it just the way she liked to have them when she was alive, and nobody ever slept there. The old lady took care of the room herself, though there was plenty of niggers, and she sewed there a good deal and read her Bible there, mostly.

Well, as I was saying about the parlor, there was beautiful curtains on the windows: white, with pictures painted on them, of castles with vines all down the walls, and cattle coming down to drink. There was a little old piano, too, that had tin pans in it, I reckon, and nothing was ever so lovely as to hear the young ladies sing, "The Last Link is Broken" and play "The Battle of Prague"[6] on it. The walls of all the rooms was plastered, and most had carpets on the floors, and the whole house was whitewashed on the outside.

It was a double house, and the big open place betwixt them was roofed and floored, and sometimes the table was set there in the middle of the day,

---

6. A bloody story told in clichéd style, written by the Czech composer Franz Kotswara (1750–1791) in about 1788; Twain first heard it in 1878. William Clifton's *The Last Link Is Broken* was published about 1840.

and it was a cool, comfortable place. Nothing couldn't be better. And warn't the cooking good, and just bushels of it too!

Chapter XVIII

Col. Grangerford was a gentleman, you see. He was a gentleman all over; and so was his family. He was well born, as the saying is, and that's worth as much in a man as it is in a horse, so the Widow Douglas said, and nobody ever denied that she was of the first aristocracy in our town; and pap he always said it, too, though he warn't no more quality than a mudcat,[7] himself. Col. Grangerford was very tall and very slim, and had a darkish-paly complexion, not a sign of red in it anywheres; he was clean-shaved every morning, all over his thin face, and he had the thinnest kind of lips, and the thinnest kind of nostrils, and a high nose, and heavy eyebrows, and the blackest kind of eyes, sunk so deep back that they seemed like they was looking out of caverns at you, as you may say. His forehead was high, and his hair was black and straight, and hung to his shoulders. His hands was long and thin, and every day of his life he put on a clean shirt and a full suit from head to foot made out of linen so white it hurt your eyes to look at it; and on Sundays he wore a blue tail-coat with brass buttons on it. He carried a mahogany cane with a silver head to it. There warn't no frivolishness about him, not a bit, and he warn't ever loud. He was as kind as he could be—you could feel that, you know, and so you had confidence. Sometimes he smiled, and it was good to see; but when he straightened himself up like a liberty-pole,[8] and the lightning begun to flicker out from under his eye-brows you wanted to climb a tree first, and find out what the matter was afterwards. He didn't ever have to tell anybody to mind their manners—everybody was always good mannered where he was. Everybody loved to have him around, too; he was sunshine most always—I mean he made it seem like good weather. When he turned into a cloud-bank it was awful dark for a half a minute and that was enough; there wouldn't nothing go wrong again for a week.

When him and the old lady come down in the morning, all the family got up out of their chairs and give them good-day, and didn't set down again till they had set down. Then Tom and Bob went to the sideboard where the decanters was, and mixed a glass of bitters and handed it to him, and he held it in his hand and waited till Tom's and Bob's was mixed, and then they bowed and said "Our duty to you, sir, and madam;" and *they* bowed the least bit in the world and said thank you, and so they drank, all three, and Bob and Tom poured a spoonful of water on the sugar and the mite of whisky or apple brandy in the bottom of their tumblers, and give it to me and Buck, and we drank to the old people too.

Bob was the oldest, and Tom next. Tall, beautiful men with very broad shoulders and brown faces, and long black hair and black eyes. They dressed in white linen from head to foot, like the old gentleman, and wore broad Panama hats.

Then there was Miss Charlotte, she was twenty-five, and tall and proud and grand, but as good as she could be, when she warn't stirred up; but

7. General term for a number of species of catfish; in this context the lowliest and least esteemed.
8. Flagpole.

when she was, she had a look that would make you wilt in your tracks, like her father. She was beautiful.

So was her sister, Miss Sophia, but it was a different kind. She was gentle and sweet, like a dove, and she was only twenty.

Each person had their own nigger to wait on them—Buck, too. My nigger had a monstrous easy time, because I warn't used to having anybody do anything for me, but Buck's was on the jump most of the time.

This was all there was of the family, now; but there used to be more— three sons; they got killed; and Emmeline that died.

The old gentleman owned a lot of farms, and over a hundred niggers. Sometimes a stack of people would come there, horseback, from ten or fifteen miles around, and stay five or six days, and have such junketings round about and on the river, and dances and picnics in the woods, day-times, and balls at the house, nights. These people was mostly kin-folks of the family. The men brought their guns with them. It was a handsome lot of quality, I tell you.

There was another clan of aristocracy around there—five or six families— mostly of the name of Shepherdson. They was as high-toned, and well born, and rich and grand, as the tribe of Grangerfords. The Shepherdsons and the Grangerfords used the same steamboat landing, which was about two mile above our house; so sometimes when I went up there with a lot of our folks I used to see a lot of Shepherdsons there, on their fine horses.

One day Buck and me was away out in the woods, hunting, and heard a horse coming. We was crossing the road. Buck says:

"Quick! Jump for the woods!"

We done it, and then peeped down the woods through the leaves. Pretty soon a splendid young man come galloping down the road, setting his horse easy and looking like a soldier. He had his gun across his pommel. I had seen him before. It was young Harney Shepherdson. I heard Buck's gun go off at my ear, and Harney's hat tumbled off from his head. He grabbed his gun and rode straight to the place where we was hid. But we didn't wait. We started through the woods on a run. The woods warn't thick, so I looked over my shoulder, to dodge the bullet, and twice I seen Harney cover Buck with his gun; and then he rode away the way he come—to get his hat, I reckon, but I couldn't see. We never stopped running till we got home. The old gentleman's eyes blazed a minute—'twas pleasure, mainly, I judged—then his face sort of smoothed down, and he says, kind of gentle:

"I don't like that shooting from behind a bush. Why didn't you step into the road, my boy?"

"The Shepherdsons don't, father. They always take advantage."

Miss Charlotte she held her head up like a queen while Buck was telling his tale, and her nostrils spread and her eyes snapped. The two young men looked dark, but never said nothing. Miss Sophia she turned pale, but the color come back when she found the man warn't hurt.

Soon as I could get Buck down by the corn-cribs under the trees by ourselves, I says:

"Did you want to kill him, Buck?"

"Well, I bet I did."

"What did he do to you?"

"Him? He never done nothing to me."

"Well, then, what did you want to kill him for?"

"Why nothing—only it's on account of the feud."

"What's a feud?"

"Why, where was you raised? Don't you know what a feud is?"

"Never heard of it before—tell me about it."

"Well," says Buck, "a feud is this way. A man has a quarrel with another man, and kills him; then that other man's brother kills *him*; then the other brothers, on both sides, goes for one another; then the *cousins* chip in—and by-and-by everybody's killed off, and there ain't no more feud. But it's kind of slow, and takes a long time."

"Has this one been going on long, Buck?"

"Well I should *reckon!* it started thirty year ago, or som'ers along there. There was trouble 'bout something and then a lawsuit to settle it; and the suit went agin one of the men, and so he up and shot the man that won the suit—which he would naturally do, of course. Anybody would."

"What was the trouble about, Buck?—land?"

"I reckon maybe—I don't know."

"Well, who done the shooting?—was it a Grangerford or a Shepherdson?"

"Laws, how do *I* know? it was so long ago."

"Don't anybody know?"

"Oh, yes, pa knows, I reckon, and some of the other old folks; but they don't know, now, what the row was about in the first place."

"Has there been many killed, Buck?"

"Yes—right smart chance of funerals. But they don't always kill. Pa's got a few buck-shot in him; but he don't mind it 'cuz he don't weigh much anyway. Bob's been carved up some with a bowie, and Tom's been hurt once or twice."

"Has anybody been killed this year, Buck?"

"Yes, we got one and they got one. 'Bout three months ago, my cousin Bud, fourteen year old, was riding through the woods, on t'other side of the river, and didn't have no weapon with him, which was blame' foolishness, and in a lonesome place he hears a horse a-coming behind him, and sees old Baldy Shepherdson a-linkin' after him with his gun in his hand and his white hair a-flying in the wind; and 'stead of jumping off and taking to the brush, Bud 'lowed he could outrun him; so they had it, nip and tuck, for five mile or more, the old man a-gaining all the time; so at last Bud seen it warn't any use, so he stopped and faced around so as to have the bullet holes in front, you know, and the old man he rode up and shot him down. But he didn't git much chance to enjoy his luck, for inside of a week our folks laid *him* out."

"I reckon that old man was a coward, Buck."

"I reckon he *warn't* a coward. Not by a blame' sight. There ain't a coward amongst them Shepherdsons—not a one. And there ain't no cowards amongst the Grangerfords, either. Why, that old man kep' up his end in a fight one day, for a half an hour, against three Grangerfords, and come out winner. They was all a-horseback; he lit off of his horse and got behind a little wood-pile, and kep' his horse before him to stop the bullets; but the Grangerfords staid on their horses and capered around the old man, and peppered away at him, and he peppered away at them. Him and his horse both went home pretty leaky and crippled, but the Grangerfords had to be *fetched* home—and one of 'em was dead, and another died the next day. No, sir, if a body's out hunting for cowards, he don't want to fool away any time amongst them Shepherdsons, becuz they don't breed any of that *kind*."

Next Sunday we all went to church, about three mile, everybody a-horse-back. The men took their guns along, so did Buck, and kept them between their knees or stood them handy against the wall. The Shepherdsons done the same. It was pretty ornery preaching—all about brotherly love, and such-like tiresomeness; but everybody said it was a good sermon, and they all talked it over going home, and had such a powerful lot to say about faith, and good works, and free grace, and preforeordestination,[9] and I don't know what all, that it did seem to me to be one of the roughest Sundays I had run across yet.

About an hour after dinner everybody was dozing around, some in their chairs and some in their rooms, and it got to be pretty dull. Buck and a dog was stretched out on the grass in the sun, sound asleep. I went up to our room, and judged I would take a nap myself. I found that sweet Miss Sophia standing in her door, which was next to ours, and she took me in her room and shut the door very soft, and asked me if I liked her, and I said I did; and she asked me if I would do something for her and not tell anybody, and I said I would. Then she said she'd forgot her Testament, and left it in the seat at church, between two other books and would I slip out quiet and go there and fetch it to her, and not say nothing to nobody. I said I would. So I slid out and slipped off up the road, and there warn't anybody at the church, except maybe a hog or two, for there warn't any lock on the door, and hogs like a puncheon floor[1] in summer-time because it's cool. If you notice, most folks don't go to church only when they've got to; but a hog is different.

Says I to myself something's up—it ain't natural for a girl to be in such a sweat about a Testament; so I give it a shake, and out drops a little piece of paper with *"Half-past two"* wrote on it with a pencil. I ransacked it, but couldn't find anything else. I couldn't make anything out of that, so I put the paper in the book again, and when I got home and up stairs, there was Miss Sophia in her door waiting for me. She pulled me in and shut the door; then she looked in the Testament till she found the paper, and as soon as she read it she looked glad; and before a body could think, she grabbed me and give me a squeeze, and said I was the best boy in the world, and not to tell anybody. She was mighty red in the face, for a minute, and her eyes lighted up and it made her powerful pretty. I was a good deal astonished, but when I got my breath I asked her what the paper was about, and she asked me if I had read it, and I said no, and she asked me if I could read writing, and I told her "no, only coarse-hand,"[2] and then she said the paper warn't anything but a book-mark to keep her place, and I might go and play now.

I went off down to the river, studying over this thing, and pretty soon I noticed that my nigger was following along behind. When we was out of sight of the house, he looked back and around a second, and then comes a-running, and says:

"Mars Jawge, if you'll come down into de swamp, I'll show you a whole stack o' water-moccasins."

Thinks I, that's mighty curious; he said that yesterday. He oughter know a body don't love water-moccasins enough to go around hunting for them. What is he up to anyway? So I says—

"All right, trot ahead."

I followed a half a mile, then he struck out over the swamp and waded ankle deep as much as another half mile. We come to a little flat piece of land which was dry and very thick with trees and bushes and vines, and he says—

9. Huck combines the closely related Presbyterian terms *predestination* and *foreordination*.
1. A crude floor made from log slabs in which the flat side is turned up and the rounded side is set in the dirt.
2. Block printing.

"You shove right in dah, jist a few steps, Mars Jawge, dah's whah dey is. I's seed 'm befo', I don't k'yer to see 'em no mo'."

Then he slopped right along and went away, and pretty soon the trees hid him. I poked into the place a-ways, and come to a little open patch as big as a bedroom, all hung around with vines, and found a man laying there asleep—and by jings it was my old Jim!

I waked him up, and I reckoned it was going to be a grand surprise to him to see me again, but it warn't. He nearly cried, he was so glad, but he warn't surprised. Said he swum along behind me, that night, and heard me yell every time, but dasn't answer, because he didn't want nobody to pick *him* up, and take him into slavery again. Says he—

"I got hurt a little, en couldn't swim fas', so I wuz a considable ways behine you, towards de las'; when you landed I reck'ned I could ketch up wid you on de lan' 'dout havin' to shout at you, but when I see dat house I begin to go slow. I 'uz off too fur to hear what dey say to you—I wuz 'fraid o' de dogs—but when it 'uz all quiet again, I knowed you's in de house, so I struck out for de woods to wait for day. Early in de mawnin' some er de niggers come along, gwyne to de fields, en dey tuck me en showed me dis place, whah de dogs can't track me on accounts o' de water, en dey brings me truck to eat every night, en tells me how you's a gitt'n along."

"Why didn't you tell my Jack to fetch me here sooner, Jim?"

"Well, 'twarn't no use to 'sturb you, Huck, tell we could do sumfn—but we's all right, now. I ben a-buyin' pots en pans en vittles, as I got a chanst, en a patchin' up de raf', nights, when—"

"*What* raft, Jim?"

"Our ole raf'."

"You mean to say our old raft warn't smashed all to flinders?"

"No, she warn't. She was tore up a good deal—one en' of her was—but dey warn't no great harm done, on'y our traps was mos' all los'. Ef we hadn' dive' so deep en swum so fur under water, en de night hadn' ben so dark, en we warn't so sk'yerd, en ben sich punkin-heads, as de sayin' is, we'd a seed de raf'. But it's jis' as well we didn't, 'kase now she's all fixed up agin mos' as good as new, en we's got a new lot o' stuff, too, in de place o' what 'uz los'."

"Why, how did you get hold of the raft again, Jim—did you catch her?"

"How I gwyne to ketch her, en I out in de woods? No, some er de niggers foun' her ketched on a snag, along heah in de ben', en dey hid her in a crick, 'mongst de willows, en dey wuz so much jawin' 'bout which un 'um she b'long to de mos', dat I come to heah 'bout it pooty soon, so I ups en settles de trouble by tellin' um she don't b'long to none uv um, but to you en me; en I ast 'm if dey gwyne to grab a young white genlman's propaty, en git a hid'n for it? Den I gin 'm ten cents apiece, en dey 'uz mighty well satisfied, en wisht some mo' raf's 'ud come along en make 'm rich agin. Dey's mighty good to me, dese niggers is, en whatever I wants 'm to do fur me, I doan' have to ast 'm twice, honey. Dat Jack's a good nigger, en pooty smart."

"Yes, he is. He ain't ever told me you was here; told me to come, and he'd show me a lot of water-moccasins. If anything happens, *he* ain't mixed up in it. He can say he never seen us together, and it'll be the truth."

I don't want to talk much about the next day. I reckon I'll cut it pretty short. I waked up about dawn, and was agoing to turn over and go to sleep again, when I noticed how still it was—didn't seem to be anybody stirring. That warn't usual. Next I noticed that Buck was up and gone. Well, I gets up, a-wondering, and goes down stairs—nobody around; everything as still as a mouse. Just the same outside; thinks I, what does it mean? Down by the wood-pile I comes across my Jack, and says:

"What's it all about?"

Says he:

"Don't you know, Mars Jawge?"

"No," says I, "I don't."

"Well, den, Miss Sophia's run off! 'deed she has. She run off in de night, sometime—nobody don't know jis' when—run off to git married to dat young Harney Shepherdson, you know—leastways, so dey 'spec. De fambly foun' it out, 'bout half an hour ago—maybe a little mo'—en' I *tell* you dey warn't no time los'. Sich another hurryin' up guns en hosses *you* never see! De women folks has gone for to stir up de relations, en ole Mars Saul en de boys tuck dey guns en rode up de river road for to try to ketch dat young man en kill him 'fo' he kin git acrost de river wid Miss Sophia. I reck'n dey's gwyne to be mighty rough times."

"Buck went off 'thout waking me up."

"Well I reck'n he *did!* Dey warn't gwyne to mix you up in it. Mars Buck he loaded up his gun en 'lowed he's gwyne to fetch home a Shepherdson or bust. Well, dey'll be plenty un 'm dah, I reck'n, en you bet you he'll fetch one ef he gits a chanst."

I took up the river road as hard as I could put. By-and-by I begin to hear guns a good ways off. When I come in sight of the log store and the wood-pile where the steamboats land, I worked along under the trees and brush till I got to a good place, and then I clumb up into the forks of a cotton-wood that was out of reach, and watched. There was a wood-rank four foot high,[3] a little ways in front of the tree, and first I was going to hide behind that; but maybe it was luckier I didn't.

There was four or five men cavorting around on their horses in the open place before the log store, cussing and yelling, and trying to get at a couple of young chaps that was behind the wood-rank alongside of the steamboat landing—but they couldn't come it. Every time one of them showed himself on the river side of the wood-pile he got shot at. The two boys was squatting back to back behind the pile, so they could watch both ways.

By-and-by the men stopped cavorting around and yelling. They started riding towards the store; then up gets one of the boys, draws a steady bead over the wood-rank, and drops one of them out of his saddle. All the men jumped off of their horses and grabbed the hurt one and started to carry him to the store; and that minute the two boys started on the run. They got half-way to the tree I was in before the men noticed. Then the men see them, and jumped on their horses and took out after them. They gained on the boys, but it didn't do no good, the boys had too good a start; they got to the wood-pile that was in front of my tree, and slipped in behind it, and so they had the bulge[4] on the men again. One of the boys was Buck, and the other was a slim young chap about nineteen years old.

The men ripped around awhile, and then rode away. As soon as they was out of sight, I sung out to Buck and told him. He didn't know what to make of my voice coming out of the tree, at first. He was awful surprised. He told me to watch out sharp and let him know when the men come in sight again; said

---

3. Half a cord of stacked firewood.   4. Upper hand.

they was up to some devilment or other—wouldn't be gone long. I wished I was out of that tree, but I dasn't come down. Buck began to cry and rip, and 'lowed that him and his cousin Joe (that was the other young chap) would make up for this day, yet. He said his father and his two brothers was killed, and two or three of the enemy. Said the Shepherdsons laid for them, in ambush. Buck said his father and brothers ought to waited for their relations—the Shepherdsons was too strong for them. I asked him what was become of young Harney and Miss Sophia. He said they'd got across the river and was safe. I was glad of that; but the way Buck did take on because he didn't manage to kill Harney that day he shot at him—I hain't ever heard anything like it.

All of a sudden, bang! bang! bang! goes three or four guns—the men had slipped around through the woods and come in from behind without their horses! The boys jumped for the river—both of them hurt—and as they swum down the current the men run along the bank shooting at them and singing out, "Kill them, kill them!" It made me so sick I most fell out of the tree. I ain't agoing to tell *all* that happened!—it would make me sick again if I was to do that. I wished I hadn't ever come ashore that night, to see such things. I ain't ever going to get shut of them—lots of times I dream about them.

I staid in the tree till it begun to get dark, afraid to come down. Sometimes I heard guns away off in the woods; and twice I seen little gangs of men gallop past the log store with guns; so I reckoned the trouble was still agoing on. I was mighty downhearted; so I made up my mind I wouldn't ever go anear that house again, because I reckoned I was to blame, somehow. I judged that that piece of paper meant that Miss Sophia was to meet Harney somewheres at half-past two and run off; and I judged I ought to told her father about that paper and the curious way she acted, and then maybe he would a locked her up and this awful mess wouldn't ever happened.

When I got down out of the tree, I crept along down the river bank a piece, and found the two bodies laying in the edge of the water, and tugged at them till I got them ashore; then I covered up their faces, and got away as quick as I could. I cried a little when I was covering up Buck's face, for he was mighty good to me.

It was just dark, now. I never went near the house, but struck through the woods and made for the swamp. Jim warn't on his island, so I tramped off in a hurry for the crick, and crowded through the willows, red-hot to jump aboard and get out of that awful country—the raft was gone! My souls, but I was scared! I couldn't get my breath for most a minute. Then I raised a yell. A voice not twenty-five foot from me, says—

"Good lan'! is dat you, honey? Doan' make no noise."

It was Jim's voice—nothing ever sounded so good before. I run along the bank a piece and got aboard, and Jim he grabbed me and hugged me, he was so glad to see me. He says—

"Laws bless you, chile, I 'uz right down sho' you's dead agin. Jack's been heah, he say he reck'n you's ben shot, kase you didn' come home no mo'; so I's jes' dis minute a startin' de raf' down towards de mouf er de crick, so's to be all ready for to shove out en leave soon as Jack comes agin en tells me for certain you *is* dead. Lawsy, I's mighty glad to git you back agin, honey."

I says—

"All right—that's mighty good; they won't find me, and they'll think I've been killed, and floated down the river—there's something up there that'll help them to think so—so don't you lose no time, Jim, but just shove off for the big water as fast as ever you can."

I never felt easy till the raft was two mile below there and out in the middle of the Mississippi. Then we hung up our signal lantern, and judged that we was free and safe once more. I hadn't had a bite to eat since yesterday; so Jim he got out some corn-dodgers[5] and buttermilk, and pork and cabbage, and greens—there ain't nothing in the world so good, when it's cooked right—and whilst I eat my supper we talked, and had a good time. I was powerful glad to get away from the feuds, and so was Jim to get away from the swamp. We said there warn't no home like a raft, after all. Other places do seem so cramped up and smothery, but a raft don't. You feel mighty free and easy and comfortable on a raft.

Chapter XIX

Two or three days and nights went by; I reckon I might say they swum by, they slid along so quiet and smooth and lovely. Here is the way we put in the time. It was a monstrous big river down there—sometimes a mile and a half wide; we run nights, and laid up and hid day-times; soon as night was most gone, we stopped navigating and tied up—nearly always in the dead water under a tow-head; and then cut young cottonwoods and willows and hid the raft with them. Then we set out the lines. Next we slid into the river and had a swim, so as to freshen up and cool off; then we set down on the sandy bottom where the water was about knee deep, and watched the daylight come. Not a sound, anywheres—perfectly still—just like the whole world was asleep, only sometimes the bull-frogs a-cluttering, maybe. The first thing to see, looking away over the water, was a kind of dull line—that was the woods on t'other side—you couldn't make nothing else out; then a pale place in the sky; then more paleness, spreading around; then the river softened up, away off, and warn't black any more, but gray; you could see little dark spots drifting along, ever so far away—trading scows, and such things; and long black streaks—rafts; sometimes you could hear a sweep screaking; or jumbled up voices, it was so still, and sounds come so far; and by-and-by you could see a streak on the water which you know by the look of the streak that there's a snag there in a swift current which breaks on it and makes that streak look that way; and you see the mist curl up off of the water, and the east reddens up, and the river, and you make out a log cabin in the edge of the woods, away on the bank on t'other side of the river, being a wood-yard, likely, and piled by them cheats so you can throw a dog through it anywheres;[6] then the nice breeze springs up, and comes fanning you from over there, so cool and fresh, and sweet to smell, on account of the woods and the flowers; but sometimes not that way, because they've left dead fish laying around, gars, and such, and they do get pretty rank; and next you've got the full day, and everything smiling in the sun, and the song-birds just going it!

A little smoke couldn't be noticed, now, so we would take some fish off of the lines, and cook up a hot breakfast. And afterwards we would watch the lonesomeness of the river, and kind of lazy along, and by-and-by lazy off to sleep. Wake up, by-and-by, and look to see what done it, and maybe see a

---

5. Hard cornmeal rolls or cakes.
6. Stacks of wood in this yard were sold by their volume, gaps and holes included.

steamboat coughing along up stream, so far off towards the other side you couldn't tell nothing about her only whether she was stern-wheel or side-wheel; then for about an hour there wouldn't be nothing to hear nor nothing to see—just solid lonesomeness. Next you'd see a raft sliding by, away off yonder, and maybe a galoot[7] on it chopping, because they're almost always doing it on a raft; you'd see the ax flash, and come down—you don't hear nothing; you see that ax go up again, and by the time it's above the man's head, then you hear the *k'chunk!*—it had took all that time to come over the water. So we would put in the day, lazying around, listening to the stillness. Once there was a thick fog, and the rafts and things that went by was beating tin pans so the steamboats wouldn't run over them. A scow or a raft went by so close we could hear them talking and cussing and laughing—heard them plain; but we couldn't see no sign of them; it made you feel crawly, it was like spirits carrying on that way in the air. Jim said he believed it was spirits; but I says:

"No, spirits wouldn't say, 'dern the dern fog.'"

Soon as it was night, out we shoved; when we got her out to about the middle, we let her alone, and let her float wherever the current wanted her to; then we lit the pipes, and dangled our legs in the water and talked about all kinds of things—we was always naked, day and night, whenever the mosquitoes would let us—the new clothes Buck's folks made for me was too good to be comfortable, and besides I didn't go much on clothes, nohow.

Sometimes we'd have that whole river all to ourselves for the longest time. Yonder was the banks and the islands, across the water; and maybe a spark—which was a candle in a cabin window—and sometimes on the water you could see a spark or two—on a raft or a scow, you know; and maybe you could hear a fiddle or a song coming over from one of them crafts. It's lovely to live on a raft. We had the sky, up there, all speckled with stars, and we used to lay on our backs and look up at them, and discuss about whether they was made, or only just happened—Jim he allowed they was made, but I allowed they happened; I judged it would have took too long to *make* so many. Jim said the moon could a *laid* them; well, that looked kind of reasonable, so I didn't say nothing against it, because I've seen a frog lay most as many, so of course it could be done. We used to watch the stars that fell, too, and see them streak down. Jim allowed they'd got spoiled and was hove out of the nest.

Once or twice of a night we would see a steamboat slipping along in the dark, and now and then she would belch a whole world of sparks up out of her chimbleys, and they would rain down in the river and look awful pretty; then she would turn a corner and her lights would wink out and her pow-wow shut off and leave the river still again; and by-and-by her waves would get to us, a long time after she was gone, and joggle the raft a bit, and after that you wouldn't hear nothing for you couldn't tell how long, except maybe frogs or something.

After midnight the people on shore went to bed, and then for two or three hours the shores was black—no more sparks in the cabin windows. These sparks was our clock—the first one that showed again meant morning was coming, so we hunted a place to hide and tie up, right away.

One morning about day-break, I found a canoe and crossed over a chute[8] to the main shore—it was only two hundred yards—and paddled about a mile

---

7. Awkward, ungainly person (slang).   8. A narrow channel with swift-flowing water.

up a crick amongst the cypress woods, to see if I couldn't get some berries. Just as I was passing a place where a kind of a cow-path crossed the crick, here comes a couple of men tearing up the path as tight as they could foot it. I thought I was a goner, for whenever anybody was after anybody I judged it was *me*—or maybe Jim. I was about to dig out from there in a hurry, but they was pretty close to me then, and sung out and begged me to save their lives— said they hadn't been doing nothing, and was being chased for it—said there was men and dogs a-coming. They wanted to jump right in, but I says—

"Don't you do it. I don't hear the dogs and horses yet; you've got time to crowd through the brush and get up the crick a little ways; then you take to the water and wade down to me and get in—that'll throw the dogs off the scent."

They done it, and soon as they was aboard I lit out for our tow-head, and in about five or ten minutes we heard the dogs and the men away off, shouting. We heard them come along towards the crick, but couldn't see them; they seemed to stop and fool around a while; then, as we got further and further away all the time, we couldn't hardly hear them at all; by the time we had left a mile of woods behind us and struck the river, everything was quiet, and we paddled over to the tow-head and hid in the cotton-woods and was safe.

One of these fellows was about seventy, or upwards, and had a bald head and very gray whiskers. He had an old battered-up slouch hat on, and a greasy blue woolen shirt, and ragged old blue jeans britches stuffed into his boot tops, and home-knit galluses[9]—no, he only had one. He had an old long-tailed blue jeans coat with slick brass buttons, flung over his arm, and both of them had big fat ratty-looking carpet-bags.

The other fellow was about thirty and dressed about as ornery. After breakfast we all laid off and talked, and the first thing that come out was that these chaps didn't know one another.

"What got you into trouble?" says the baldhead to t'other chap.

"Well, I'd been selling an article to take the tartar off the teeth—and it does take it off, too, and generly the enamel along with it—but I staid about one night longer than I ought to, and was just in the act of sliding out when I ran across you on the trail this side of town, and you told me they were coming, and begged me to help you to get off. So I told you I was expecting trouble myself and would scatter out *with* you. That's the whole yarn— what's yourn?"

"Well, I'd ben a-runnin' a little temperance revival thar, 'bout a week, and was the pet of the women-folks, big and little, for I was makin' it mighty warm for the rummies, I *tell* you, and takin' as much as five or six dollars a night— ten cents a head, children and niggers free—and business a growin' all the time; when somehow or another a little report got around, last night, that I had a way of puttin' in my time with a private jug, on the sly. A nigger rousted me out this mornin', and told me the people was getherin' on the quiet, with their dogs and horses, and they'd be along pretty soon and give me 'bout half an hour's start, and then run me down, if they could; and if they got me they'd tar and feather me and ride me on a rail, sure. I didn't wait for no breakfast—I warn't hungry."

"Old man," says the young one, "I reckon we might double-team it together; what do you think?"

9. Suspenders.

"I ain't undisposed. What's your line—mainly?"

"Jour printer,[1] by trade; do a little in patent medicines; theatre-actor—tragedy, you know; take a turn at mesmerism and phrenology,[2] when there's a chance; teach singing-geography school for a change; sling a lecture, sometimes—oh, I do lots of things—most anything that comes handy, so it ain't work. What's your lay?"[3]

"I've done considerable in the doctoring way in my time. Layin' on o' hands is my best holt—for cancer, and paralysis, and sich things; and I k'n tell a fortune pretty good, when I've got somebody along to find out the facts for me. Preachin's my line, too; and workin' camp-meetin's; and missionaryin' around."

Nobody never said anything for a while; then the young man hove a sigh and says—

"Alas!"

"What 're you alassin' about?" says the baldhead.

"To think I should have lived to be leading such a life, and be degraded down into such company." And he begun to wipe the corner of his eye with a rag.

"Dern your skin, ain't the company good enough for you?" says the baldhead, pretty pert and uppish.

"Yes, it *is* good enough for me; it's as good as I deserve; for who fetched me so low, when I was so high? *I* did myself. I don't blame *you*, gentlemen—far from it; I don't blame anybody. I deserve it all. Let the cold world do its worst; one thing I know—there's a grave somewhere for me. The world may go on just as its always done, and take everything from me—loved ones, property, everything—but it can't take that. Some day I'll lie down in it and forget it all, and my poor broken heart will be at rest." He went on a-wiping.

"Drot your pore broken heart," says the baldhead; "what are you heaving your pore broken heart at *us* f'r? *We* hain't done nothing."

"No, I know you haven't. I ain't blaming you, gentlemen. I brought myself down—yes, I did it myself. It's right I should suffer—perfectly right—I don't make any moan."

"Brought you down from whar? Whar was you brought down from?"

"Ah, you would not believe me; the world never believes—let it pass—'tis no matter. The secret of my birth—"

"The secret of your birth? Do you mean to say—"

"Gentlemen," says the young man, very solemn, "I will reveal it to you, for I feel I may have confidence in you. By rights I am a duke!"

Jim's eyes bugged out when he heard that; and I reckon mine did, too. Then the baldhead says: "No! you can't mean it?"

"Yes. My great-grandfather, eldest son of the Duke of Bridgewater, fled to this country about the end of the last century, to breathe the pure air of freedom; married here, and died, leaving a son, his own father dying about the same time. The second son of the late duke seized the title and estates—the infant real duke was ignored. I am the lineal descendant of that infant—I am the rightful Duke of Bridgewater; and here am I, forlorn, torn from my high estate, hunted of men, despised by the cold world, ragged, worn, heartbroken, and degraded to the companionship of felons on a raft!"

---

1. A journeyman printer, not yet a salaried master-printer, who worked by the day.
2. The study of the shape of the skull as an indi-
cator of intelligence and character. "Mesmerism": a form of hypnotism.
3. Work, in the sense here of hustle or scheme.

Jim pitied him ever so much, and so did I. We tried to comfort him, but he said it warn't much use, he couldn't be much comforted; said if we was a mind to acknowledge him, that would do him more good than most anything else; so we said we would, if he would tell us how. He said we ought to bow, when we spoke to him, and say "Your Grace," or "My Lord," or "Your Lordship"—and he wouldn't mind it if we called him plain "Bridgewater," which he said was a title, anyway, and not a name; and one of us ought to wait on him at dinner, and do any little thing for him he wanted done.

Well, that was all easy, so we done it. All through dinner Jim stood around and waited on him, and says, "Will yo' Grace have some o' dis, or some o' dat?" and so on, and a body could see it was mighty pleasing to him.

But the old man got pretty silent, by-and-by—didn't have much to say, and didn't look pretty comfortable over all that petting that was going on around that duke. He seemed to have something on his mind. So, along in the afternoon, he says:

"Looky here, Bilgewater," he says, "I'm nation sorry for you, but you ain't the only person that's had troubles like that."

"No?"

"No, you ain't. You ain't the only person that's ben snaked down wrongfully out'n a high place."

"Alas!"

"No, you ain't the only person that's had a secret of his birth." And by jings, *he* begins to cry.

"Hold! What do you mean?"

"Bilgewater, kin I trust you?" says the old man, still sort of sobbing.

"To the bitter death!" He took the old man by the hand and squeezed it, and says, "The secret of your being: speak!"

"Bilgewater, I am the late Dauphin!"[4]

You bet you Jim and me stared, this time. Then the duke says:

"You are what?"

"Yes, my friend, it is too true—your eyes is lookin' at this very moment on the pore disappeared Dauphin, Looy the Seventeen, son of Looy the Sixteen and Marry Antonette."

"You! At your age! No! You mean you're the late Charlemagne;[5] you must be six or seven hundred years old, at the very least."

"Trouble has done it, Bilgewater, trouble has done it; trouble has brung these gray hairs and this premature balditude. Yes, gentlemen, you see before you, in blue jeans and misery, the wanderin', exiled, trampled-on and sufferin' rightful King of France."

Well, he cried and took on so, that me and Jim didn't know hardly what to do, we was so sorry—and so glad and proud we'd got him with us, too. So we set in, like we done before with the duke, and tried to comfort *him*. But he said it warn't no use, nothing but to be dead and done with it all could do him any good; though he said it often made him feel easier and better for a while if people treated him according to his rights, and got down on one knee to speak to him, and always called him "Your Majesty," and waited on him first at meals, and didn't set down in his presence till he asked them. So Jim and me set to majestying him, and doing this and that and t'other for him,

---

4. The Dauphin, born in 1785, would have been in his mid-fifties or sixties had he survived.

5. Charlemagne (742–814), emperor of the West (800–814).

and standing up till he told us we might set down. This done him heaps of good, and so he got cheerful and comfortable. But the duke kind of soured on him, and didn't look a bit satisfied with the way things was going; still, the king acted real friendly towards him, and said the duke's great-grandfather and all the other Dukes of Bilgewater was a good deal thought of by *his* father and was allowed to come to the palace considerable; but the duke staid huffy a good while, till by-and-by the king says:

"Like as not we got to be together a blamed long time, on this h-yer raft, Bilgewater, and so what's the use o' your bein' sour? It'll only make things oncomfortable. It ain't my fault I warn't born a duke, it ain't your fault you warn't born a king—so what's the use to worry? Make the best o' things the way you find 'em, says I—that's my motto. This ain't no bad thing that we've struck here—plenty grub and an easy life—come, give us your hand, Duke, and less all be friends."

The duke done it, and Jim and me was pretty glad to see it. It took away all the uncomfortableness, and we felt mighty good over it, because it would a been a miserable business to have any unfriendliness on the raft; for what you want, above all things, on a raft, is for everybody to be satisfied, and feel right and kind towards the others.

It didn't take me long to make up my mind that these liars warn't no kings nor dukes, at all, but just low-down humbugs and frauds. But I never said nothing, never let on; kept it to myself; it's the best way; then you don't have no quarrels, and don't get into no trouble. If they wanted us to call them kings and dukes, I hadn't no objections, 'long as it would keep peace in the family; and it warn't no use to tell Jim, so I didn't tell him. If I never learnt nothing else out of pap, I learnt that the best way to get along with his kind of people is to let them have their own way.

Chapter XX

They asked us considerable many questions; wanted to know what we covered up the raft that way for, and laid by in the daytime instead of running—was Jim a runaway nigger? Says I—

"Goodness sakes, would a runaway nigger run *south?*"

No, they allowed he wouldn't. I had to account for things some way, so I says:

"My folks was living in Pike County, in Missouri, where I was born, and they all died off but me and pa and my brother Ike. Pa, he 'lowed he'd break up and go down and live with Uncle Ben, who's got a little one-horse place on the river, forty-four mile below Orleans. Pa was pretty poor, and had some debts; so when he'd squared up there warn't nothing left but sixteen dollars and our nigger, Jim. That warn't enough to take us fourteen hundred mile, deck passage nor no other way. Well, when the river rose, pa had a streak of luck one day; he ketched this piece of a raft; so we reckoned we'd go down to Orleans on it. Pa's luck didn't hold out; a steamboat run over the forrard corner of the raft, one night, and we all went overboard and dove under the wheel; Jim and me come up, all right, but pa was drunk, and Ike was only four years old, so they never come up no more. Well, for the next day or two we had considerable trouble, because people was always coming out in skiffs and trying to take Jim away from me, saying they believed he was a runaway nigger. We don't run day-times no more, now; nights they don't bother us."

The duke says—

"Leave me alone to cipher out a way so we can run in the daytime if we want to. I'll think the thing over—I'll invent a plan that'll fix it. We'll let it alone for to-day, because of course we don't want to go by that town yonder in daylight—it mightn't be healthy."

Towards night it begun to darken up and look like rain; the heat lightning was squirting around, low down in the sky, and the leaves was beginning to shiver—it was going to be pretty ugly, it was easy to see that. So the duke and the king went to overhauling our wigwam, to see what the beds was like. My bed was a straw tick[6]—better than Jim's, which was a corn-shuck tick; there's always cobs around about in a shuck tick, and they poke into you and hurt; and when you roll over, the dry shucks sound like you was rolling over in a pile of dead leaves; it makes such a rustling that you wake up. Well, the duke allowed he would take my bed; but the king allowed he wouldn't. He says—

"I should a reckoned the difference in rank would a sejested to you that a corn-shuck bed warn't just fitten for me to sleep on. Your Grace'll take the shuck bed yourself."

Jim and me was in a sweat again, for a minute, being afraid there was going to be some more trouble amongst them; so we was pretty glad when the duke says—

"'Tis my fate to be always ground into the mire under the iron heel of oppression. Misfortune has broken my once haughty spirit; I yield, I submit; 'tis my fate. I am alone in the world—let me suffer; I can bear it."

We got away as soon as it was good and dark. The king told us to stand well out towards the middle of the river, and not show a light till we got a long ways below the town. We come in sight of the little bunch of lights by-and-by—that was the town, you know—and slid by, about a half a mile out, all right. When we was three-quarters of a mile below, we hoisted up our signal lantern; and about ten o'clock it come on to rain and blow and thunder and lighten like everything; so the king told us to both stay on watch till the weather got better; then him and the duke crawled into the wigwam and turned in for the night. It was my watch below, till twelve, but I wouldn't a turned in, anyway, if I'd had a bed; because a body don't see such a storm as that every day in the week, not by a long sight. My souls, how the wind did scream along! And every second or two there'd come a glare that lit up the white-caps for a half a mile around, and you'd see the islands looking dusty through the rain, and the trees thrashing around in the wind; then comes a *h-wack!*—bum! bum! bumble-umble-um-bum-bum-bum-bum—and the thunder would go rumbling and grumbling away, and quit—and then *rip* comes another flash and another sock-dolager.[7] The waves most washed me off the raft, sometimes, but I hadn't any clothes on, and didn't mind. We didn't have no trouble about snags; the lightning was glaring and flittering around so constant that we could see them plenty soon enough to throw her head this way or that and miss them.

I had the middle watch, you know, but I was pretty sleepy by that time, so Jim he said he would stand the first half of it for me; he was always mighty good, that way, Jim was. I crawled into the wigwam, but the king and the duke had their legs sprawled around so there warn't no show for me; so I laid out-side—I didn't mind the rain, because it was warm, and the waves warn't run-

6. Mattress.
7. Something exceptionally strong or climactic (slang).

ning so high, now. About two they come up again, though, and Jim was going to call me, but he changed his mind because he reckoned they warn't high enough yet to do any harm; but he was mistaken about that, for pretty soon all of a sudden along comes a regular ripper, and washed me overboard. It most killed Jim a-laughing. He was the easiest nigger to laugh that ever was, anyway.

I took the watch, and Jim he laid down and snored away; and by-and-by the storm let up for good and all; and the first cabin-light that showed, I rousted him out and we slid the raft into hiding-quarters for the day.

The king got out an old ratty deck of cards, after breakfast, and him and the duke played seven-up a while, five cents a game. Then they got tired of it, and allowed they would "lay out a campaign," as they called it. The duke went down into his carpet-bag and fetched up a lot of little printed bills, and read them out loud. One bill said "The celebrated Dr. Armand de Montalban of Paris," would "lecture on the Science of Phrenology" at such and such a place, on the blank day of blank, at ten cents admission, and "furnish charts of character at twenty-five cents apiece." The duke said that was *him*. In another bill he was the "world renowned Shaksperean tragedian, Garrick the Younger,[8] of Drury Lane, London." In other bills he had a lot of other names and done other wonderful things, like finding water and gold with a "divining rod," "dissipating witch-spells," and so on. By-and-by he says—

"But the histrionic muse is the darling. Have you ever trod the boards, Royalty?"

"No," says the king.

"You shall, then, before you're three days older, Fallen Grandeur," says the duke. "The first good town we come to, we'll hire a hall and do the sword-fight in Richard III. and the balcony scene in Romeo and Juliet. How does that strike you?"

"I'm in, up to the hub, for anything that will pay, Bilgewater, but you see I don't know nothing about play-actn', and hain't ever seen much of it. I was too small when pap used to have 'em at the palace. Do you reckon you can learn me?"

"Easy!"

"All right. I'm jist a-freezn' for something fresh, anyway. Less commence, right away."

So the duke he told him all about who Romeo was, and who Juliet was, and said he was used to being Romeo, so the king could be Juliet.

"But if Juliet's such a young gal, Duke, my peeled head and my white whiskers is goin' to look oncommon odd on her, maybe."

"No, don't you worry—these country jakes won't ever think of that. Besides, you know, you'll be in costume, and that makes all the difference in the world; Juliet's in a balcony, enjoying the moonlight before she goes to bed, and she's got on her night-gown and her ruffled night-cap. Here are the costumes for the parts."

He got out two or three curtain-calico suits, which he said was meedyevil armor for Richard III. and t'other chap, and a long white cotton night-shirt and a ruffled night-cap to match. The king was satisfied; so the duke got out his book and read the parts over in the most splendid spread-eagle way,

8. David Garrick (1717–1779) was a famous tragedian at the Theatre Royal in Drury Lane, London.

prancing around and acting at the same time, to show how it had got to be done; then he give the book to the king and told him to get his part by heart.

There was a little one-horse town about three mile down the bend, and after dinner the duke said he had ciphered out his idea about how to run in daylight without it being dangersome for Jim; so he allowed he would go down to the town and fix that thing. The king allowed he would go too, and see if he couldn't strike something. We was out of coffee, so Jim said I better go along with them in the canoe and get some.

When we got there, there warn't nobody stirring; streets empty, and perfectly dead and still, like Sunday. We found a sick nigger sunning himself in a back yard, and he said everybody that warn't too young or too sick or too old, was gone to camp-meeting, about two mile back in the woods. The king got the directions, and allowed he'd go and work that camp-meeting for all it was worth, and I might go, too.[9]

The duke said what he was after was a printing office. We found it; a little bit of a concern, up over a carpenter shop—carpenters and printers all gone to the meeting, and no doors locked. It was a dirty, littered-up place, and had ink marks, and handbills with pictures of horses and runaway niggers on them, all over the walls. The duke shed his coat and said he was all right, now. So me and the king lit out for the camp-meeting.

We got there in about a half an hour, fairly dripping, for it was a most awful hot day. There was as much as a thousand people there, from twenty mile around. The woods was full of teams and wagons, hitched everywheres, feeding out of the wagon troughs and stomping to keep off the flies. There was sheds made out of poles and roofed over with branches, where they had lemonade and gingerbread to sell, and piles of watermelons and green corn and such-like truck.

The preaching was going on under the same kinds of sheds, only they was bigger and held crowds of people. The benches was made out of outside slabs of logs, with holes bored in the round side to drive sticks into for legs. They didn't have no backs. The preachers had high platforms to stand on, at one end of the sheds. The women had on sunbonnets; and some had linsey-woolsey frocks, some gingham ones, and a few of the young ones had on calico. Some of the young men was barefooted, and some of the children didn't have on any clothes but just a tow-linen[1] shirt. Some of the old women was knitting, and some of the young folks was courting on the sly.

The first shed we come to, the preacher was lining out a hymn. He lined out two lines, everybody sung it, and it was kind of grand to hear it, there was so many of them and they done it in such a rousing way; then he lined out two more for them to sing—and so on. The people woke up more and more, and sung louder and louder; and towards the end, some begun to groan, and some begun to shout. Then the preacher begun to preach; and begun in earnest, too; and went weaving first to one side of the platform and then the other, and then a leaning down over the front of it, with his arms and his body going all the time, and shouting his words out with all his might; and every now and then he would hold up his Bible and spread it open, and kind of pass it around this way and that, shouting, "It's the brazen

9. Notoriously easy pickings for confidence men, camp meetings are extended outdoor evangelical meetings.
1. Coarse linen cloth. "Linsey-woolsey": cheap, often homespun, unpatterned cloth composed of wool and flax. "Gingham" and "calico" are inexpensive, store-bought printed cotton.

serpent in the wilderness! Look upon it and live!" And people would shout out, "Glory!—*A-a-men!*" And so he went on, and the people groaning and crying and saying amen:

"Oh, come to the mourners' bench!² come, black with sin! (*amen!*) come, sick and sore! (*amen!*) come, lame and halt, and blind! (*amen!*) come, pore and needy, sunk in shame! (*a-a-men!*) come all that's worn, and soiled, and suffering!—come with a broken spirit! come with a contrite heart! come in your rags and sin and dirt! the waters that cleanse is free, the door of heaven stands open—oh, enter in and be at rest!" (*a-a-men! glory, glory hallelujah!*)

And so on. You couldn't make out what the preacher said, any more, on account of the shouting and crying. Folks got up, everywheres in the crowd, and worked their way, just by main strength, to the mourners' bench, with the tears running down their faces; and when all the mourners had got up there to the front benches in a crowd, they sung, and shouted, and flung themselves down on the straw, just crazy and wild.

Well, the first I knowed, the king got agoing; and you could hear him over everybody; and next he went a-charging up on to the platform and the preacher he begged him to speak to the people, and he done it. He told them he was a pirate—been a pirate for thirty years, out in the Indian Ocean, and his crew was thinned out considerable, last spring, in a fight, and he was home now, to take out some fresh men, and thanks to goodness he'd been robbed last night, and put ashore off of a steamboat without a cent, and he was glad of it, it was the blessedest thing that ever happened to him, because he was a changed man now, and happy for the first time in his life; and poor as he was, he was going to start right off and work his way back to the Indian Ocean and put in the rest of his life trying to turn the pirates into the true path; for he could do it better than anybody else, being acquainted with all the pirate crews in that ocean; and though it would take him a long time to get there, without money, he would get there anyway, and every time he convinced a pirate he would say to him, "Don't you thank me, don't you give me no credit, it all belongs to them dear people in Pokeville camp-meeting, natural brothers and benefactors of the race—and that dear preacher there, the truest friend a pirate ever had!"

And then he busted into tears, and so did everybody. Then somebody sings out, "Take up a collection for him, take up a collection!" Well, a half a dozen made a jump to do it, but somebody sings out, "Let *him* pass the hat around!" Then everybody said it, the preacher too.

So the king went all through the crowd with his hat, swabbing his eyes, and blessing the people and praising them and thanking them for being so good to the poor pirates away off there; and every little while the prettiest kind of girls, with the tears running down their cheeks, would up and ask him would he let them kiss him, for to remember him by; and he always done it; and some of them he hugged and kissed as many as five or six times—and he was invited to stay a week; and everybody wanted him to live in their houses, and said they'd think it was an honor; but he said as this was the last day of the camp-meeting he couldn't do no good, and besides he was in a sweat to get to the Indian Ocean right off and go to work on the pirates.

When we got back to the raft and he come to count up, he found he had collected eighty-seven dollars and seventy-five cents. And then he had fetched

---

2. Front-row pews filled by penitents.

away a three-gallon jug of whisky, too, that he found under a wagon when we was starting home through the woods. The king said, take it all around, it laid over any day he'd ever put in in the missionarying line. He said it warn't no use talking, heathens don't amount to shucks, alongside of pirates, to work a camp-meeting with.

The duke was thinking *he'd* been doing pretty well, till the king come to show up, but after that he didn't think so so much. He had set up and printed off two little jobs for farmers, in that printing office—horse bills— and took the money, four dollars. And he had got in ten dollars worth of advertisements for the paper, which he said he would put in for four dollars if they would pay in advance—so they done it. The price of the paper was two dollars a year, but he took in three subscriptions for half a dollar apiece on condition of them paying him in advance; they were going to pay in cord-wood and onions, as usual, but he said he had just bought the concern and knocked down the price as low as he could afford it, and was going to run it for cash. He set up a little piece of poetry, which he made, himself, out of his own head—three verses—kind of sweet and saddish—the name of it was, "Yes, crush, cold world, this breaking heart"—and he left that all set up and ready to print in the paper and didn't charge nothing for it. Well, he took in nine dollars and a half, and said he'd done a pretty square day's work for it.

Then he showed us another little job he'd printed and hadn't charged for, because it was for us. It had a picture of a runaway nigger, with a bundle on a stick, over his shoulder, and "$200 reward" under it. The reading was all about Jim, and just described him to a dot. It said he run away from St. Jacques' plantation, forty mile below New Orleans, last winter, and likely went north, and whoever would catch him and send him back, he could have the reward and expenses.

"Now," says the duke, "after to-night we can run in the daytime if we want to. Whenever we see anybody coming, we can tie Jim hand and foot with a rope, and lay him in the wigwam and show this handbill and say we captured him up the river, and were too poor to travel on a steamboat, so we got this little raft on credit from our friends and are going down to get the reward. Handcuffs and chains would look still better on Jim, but it wouldn't go well with the story of us being so poor. Too much like jewelry. Ropes are the correct thing—we must preserve the unities,[3] as we say on the boards."

We all said the duke was pretty smart, and there couldn't be no trouble about running daytimes. We judged we could make miles enough that night to get out of the reach of the pow-wow we reckoned the duke's work in the printing office was going to make in that little town—then we could boom right along, if we wanted to.

We laid low and kept still, and never shoved out till nearly ten o'clock; then we slid by, pretty wide away from the town, and didn't hoist our lantern till we was clear out of sight of it.

When Jim called me to take the watch at four in the morning, he says—

"Huck, does you reck'n we gwyne to run acrost any mo' kings on dis trip?"

"No," I says, "I reckon not."

---

3. Of time, place, and action in classical drama; here the duke is using the term to mean "consistent with the rest of our story."

"Well," says he, "dat's all right, den. I doan' mine one er two kings, but dat's enough. Dis one's powerful drunk, en de duke ain' much better."

I found Jim had been trying to get him to talk French, so he could hear what it was like; but he said he had been in this country so long, and had so much trouble, he'd forgot it.

Chapter XXI

It was after sun-up, now, but we went right on, and didn't tie up. The king and the duke turned out, by-and-by, looking pretty rusty; but after they'd jumped overboard and took a swim, it chippered them up a good deal. After breakfast the king he took a seat on a corner of the raft, and pulled off his boots and rolled up his britches, and let his legs dangle in the water, so as to be comfortable, and lit his pipe, and went to getting his Romeo and Juliet by heart. When he had got it pretty good, him and the duke begun to practice it together. The duke had to learn him over and over again, how to say every speech; and he made him sigh, and put his hand on his heart, and after while he said he done it pretty well; "only," he says, "you mustn't bellow out *Romeo!* that way, like a bull—you must say it soft, and sick, and languishy, so—R-o-o-meo! that is the idea; for Juliet's a dear sweet mere child of a girl, you know, and she don't bray like a jackass."

Well, next they got out a couple of long swords that the duke made out of oak laths, and begun to practice the sword-fight—the duke called himself Richard III.; and the way they laid on, and pranced around the raft was grand to see. But by-and-by the king tripped and fell overboard, and after that they took a rest, and had a talk about all kinds of adventures they'd had in other times along the river.

After dinner, the duke says:

"Well, Capet,[4] we'll want to make this a first-class show, you know, so I guess we'll add a little more to it. We want a little something to answer encores with, anyway."

"What's onkores, Bilgewater?"

The duke told him, and then says:

"I'll answer by doing the Highland fling or the sailor's hornpipe; and you—well, let me see—oh, I've got it—you can do Hamlet's soliloquy."

"Hamlet's which?"

"Hamlet's soliloquy, you know; the most celebrated thing in Shakespeare. Ah, it's sublime, sublime! Always fetches the house. I haven't got it in the book—I've only got one volume—but I reckon I can piece it out from memory. I'll just walk up and down a minute, and see if I can call it back from recollection's vaults."

So he went to marching up and down, thinking, and frowning horrible every now and then; then he would hoist up his eyebrows; next he would squeeze his hand on his forehead and stagger back and kind of moan; next he would sigh, and next he'd let on to drop a tear. It was beautiful to see him. By-and-by he got it. He told us to give attention. Then he strikes a most noble attitude, with one leg shoved forwards, and his arms stretched away up, and his head tilted back, looking up at the sky; and then he begins to rip and rave and grit his teeth; and after that, all through his speech he howled, and

---

4. The family name of Louis XVI, who was guillotined in 1793.

spread around, and swelled up his chest, and just knocked the spots out of any acting ever *I* see before. This is the speech—I learned it, easy enough, while he was learning it to the king:[5]

To be, or not to be; that is the bare bodkin
That makes calamity of so long life;
For who would fardels bear, till Birnam Wood do come to Dunsinane,
But that the fear of something after death
Murders the innocent sleep,
Great nature's second course,
And makes us rather sling the arrows of outrageous fortune
Than fly to others that we know not of.
There's the respect must give us pause:
Wake Duncan with thy knocking! I would thou couldst;
For who would bear the whips and scorns of time,
The oppressor's wrong, the proud man's contumely,
The law's delay, and the quietus which his pangs might take,
In the dead waste and middle of the night, when churchyards yawn
In customary suits of solemn black,
But that the undiscovered country from whose bourne no traveler returns,
Breathes forth contagion on the world,
And thus the native hue of resolution, like the poor cat i' the adage,
Is sicklied o'er with care,
And all the clouds that lowered o'er our housetops,
With this regard their currents turn awry,
And lose the name of action.
'Tis a consummation devoutly to be wished. But soft you, the fair Ophelia:
Ope not thy ponderous and marble jaws,
But get thee to a nunnery—go!

Well, the old man he liked that speech, and he mighty soon got it so he could do it first rate. It seemed like he was just born for it; and when he had his hand in and was excited, it was perfectly lovely the way he would rip and tear and rair up behind when he was getting it off.

The first chance we got, the duke he had some show bills printed; and after that, for two or three days as we floated along, the raft was a most uncommon lively place, for there warn't nothing but sword-fighting and rehearsing—as the duke called it—going on all the time. One morning, when we was pretty well down the State of Arkansaw, we come in sight of a little one-horse town in a big bend; so we tied up about three-quarters of a mile above it, in the mouth of a crick which was shut in like a tunnel by the cypress trees, and all of us but Jim took the canoe and went down there to see if there was any chance in that place for our show.

We struck it mighty lucky; there was going to be a circus there that afternoon, and the country people was already beginning to come in, in all kinds of old shackly wagons, and on horses. The circus would leave before night, so our show would have a pretty good chance. The duke he hired the court house, and we went around and stuck up our bills. They read like this:

---

5. The comical garbling of Shakespeare was another stock-in-trade of the southwestern humorists in whose tradition Twain follows. The soliloquy is composed chiefly of phrases from *Hamlet* and *Macbeth*, but Twain also draws on several other plays.

Shaksperean Revival!!!

Wonderful Attraction!

For One Night Only!

The world renowned tragedians,

David Garrick the younger, of Drury Lane Theatre, London,

and

Edmund Kean the elder,[6] of the Royal Haymarket Theatre, White-
chapel, Pudding Lane, Piccadilly, London, and the

Royal Continental Theatres, in their sublime

Shaksperean Spectacle entitled

The Balcony Scene

in

Romeo and Juliet!!!

Romeo . . . . Mr. Garrick.

Juliet . . . . Mr. Kean.

Assisted by the whole strength of the company!

New costumes, new scenery, new appointments!

Also:

The thrilling, masterly, and blood-curdling

Broad-sword conflict

In Richard III.!!!

Richard III . . . . Mr. Garrick.

Richmond . . . . Mr. Kean.

also:

(by special request,)

Hamlet's Immortal Soliloquy!!

By the Illustrious Kean!

Done by him 300 consecutive nights in Paris!

For One Night Only,

On account of imperative European engagements!

Admission 25 cents; children and servants, 10 cents.

Then we went loafing around the town. The stores and houses was most all old shackly dried-up frame concerns that hadn't ever been painted; they was set up three or four foot above ground on stilts, so as to be out of reach of the water when the river was overflowed. The houses had little gardens around them, but they didn't seem to raise hardly anything in them but jimpson weeds, and sunflowers, and ash-piles, and old curled-up boots and shoes, and pieces of bottles, and rags, and played-out tin-ware. The fences was made of different kinds of boards, nailed on at different times; and they leaned every which-way, and had gates that didn't generly have but one hinge—a leather one. Some of the fences had been whitewashed, some time or another, but the duke said it was in Clumbus's time, like enough. There was generly hogs in the garden, and people driving them out.

All the stores was along one street. They had white-domestic awnings[7] in front, and the country people hitched their horses to the awning-posts. There was empty dry-goods boxes under the awnings, and loafers roosting on them all day long, whittling them with their Barlow knives; and chawing tobacco,

6. Here, as elsewhere, the duke garbles the facts. Garrick, Edmund Kean (1787–1833), and Charles John Kean (1811–1868) were all famous tragedi-ans at the Theatre Royal in Drury Lane, London.

7. Awnings made from canvas.

and gaping and yawning and stretching—a mighty ornery lot. They generly had on yellow straw hats most as wide as an umbrella, but didn't wear no coats nor waistcoats; they called one another Bill, and Buck, and Hank, and Joe, and Andy, and talked lazy and drawly, and used considerable many cuss-words. There was as many as one loafer leaning up against every awning-post, and he most always had his hands in his britches pockets, except when he fetched them out to lend a chaw of tobacco or scratch. What a body was hearing amongst them, all the time was—

"Gimme a chaw 'v tobacker, Hank."

"Cain't—I hain't got but one chaw left. Ask Bill."

Maybe Bill he gives him a chaw; maybe he lies and says he ain't got none. Some of them kinds of loafers never has a cent in the world, nor a chaw of tobacco of their own. They get all their chawing by borrowing—they say to a fellow, "I wisht you'd len' me a chaw, Jack, I jist this minute give Ben Thompson the last chaw I had"—which is a lie, pretty much every time; it don't fool anybody but a stranger; but Jack ain't no stranger, so he says—

"*You* give him a chaw, did you? so did your sister's cat's grandmother. You pay me back the chaws you've awready borry'd off'n me, Lafe Buckner, then I'll loan you one or two ton of it, and won't charge you no back intrust, nuther."

"Well, I *did* pay you back some of it wunst."

"Yes, you did—'bout six chaws. You borry'd store tobacker and paid back nigger-head."

Store tobacco is flat black plug, but these fellows mostly chaws the natural leaf twisted. When they borrow a chaw, they don't generly cut it off with a knife, but they set the plug in between their teeth, and gnaw with their teeth and tug at the plug with their hands till they get it in two—then sometimes the one that owns the tobacco looks mournful at it when it's handed back, and says, sarcastic—

"Here, gimme the *chaw*, and you take the *plug*."

All the streets and lanes was just mud, they warn't nothing else *but* mud—as black as tar, and nigh about a foot deep in some places; and two or three inches deep in *all* the places. The hogs loafed and grunted around, everywheres. You'd see a muddy sow and a litter of pigs come lazying along the street and whollop herself right down in the way, where folks had to walk around her, and she'd stretch out, and shut her eyes, and wave her ears, whilst the pigs was milking her, and look as happy as if she was on salary. And pretty soon you'd hear a loafer sing out, "Hi! *so* boy! sick him, Tige!" and away the sow would go, squealing most horrible, with a dog or two swinging to each ear, and three or four dozen more a-coming; and then you would see all the loafers get up and watch the thing out of sight, and laugh at the fun and look grateful for the noise. Then they'd settle back again till there was a dog-fight. There couldn't anything wake them up all over, and make them happy all over, like a dog-fight—unless it might be putting turpentine on a stray dog and setting fire to him, or tying a tin pan to his tail and see him run himself to death.

On the river front some of the houses was sticking out over the bank, and they was bowed and bent, and about ready to tumble in. The people had moved out of them. The bank was caved away under one corner of some others, and that corner was hanging over. People lived in them yet, but it was dangersome, because sometimes a strip of land as wide as a house caves in at a time. Sometimes a belt of land a quarter of a mile deep will start in and cave along and cave along till it all caves into the river in one summer. Such a town as that has to be always moving back, and back, and back, because the river's always gnawing at it.

The nearer it got to noon that day, the thicker and thicker was the wagons and horses in the streets, and more coming all the time. Families fetched their dinners with them, from the country, and eat them in the wagons. There was considerable whisky drinking going on, and I seen three fights. By-and-by somebody sings out—

"Here comes old Boggs!—in from the country for his little old monthly drunk—here he comes, boys!"

All the loafers looked glad—I reckoned they was used to having fun out of Boggs. One of them says—

"Wonder who he's a gwyne to chaw up this time. If he'd a chawed up all the men he's ben a gwyne to chaw up in the last twenty year, he'd have considerable ruputation, now."

Another one says, "I wisht old Boggs'd threaten me, 'cuz then I'd know I warn't gwyne to die for a thousan' year."

Boggs comes a-tearing along on his horse, whooping and yelling like an Injun, and singing out—

"Cler the track, thar. I'm on the war-path, and the price uv coffins is a gwyne to raise."

He was drunk, and weaving about in his saddle; he was over fifty year old, and had a very red face. Everybody yelled at him, and laughed at him, and sassed him, and he sassed back, and said he'd attend to them and lay them out in their regular turns, but he couldn't wait now, because he'd come to town to kill old Colonel Sherburn, and his motto was, "meat first, and spoon vittles to top off on."

He see me, and rode up and says—

"Whar'd you come f'm, boy? You prepared to die?"

Then he rode on. I was scared; but a man says—

"He don't mean nothing; he's always a carryin' on like that, when he's drunk. He's the best-naturedest old fool in Arkansaw—never hurt nobody, drunk nor sober."

Boggs rode up before the biggest store in town and bent his head down so he could see under the curtain of the awning, and yells—

"Come out here, Sherburn! Come out and meet the man you've swindled. You're the houn' I'm after, and I'm a gwyne to have you, too!"

And so he went on, calling Sherburn everything he could lay his tongue to, and the whole street packed with people listening and laughing and going on. By-and-by a proud-looking man about fifty-five—and he was a heap the best dressed man in that town, too—steps out of the store, and the crowd drops back on each side to let him come. He says to Boggs, mighty ca'm and slow—he says:

"I'm tired of this; but I'll endure it till one o'clock. Till one o'clock, mind—no longer. If you open your mouth against me only once, after that time, you can't travel so far but I will find you."

Then he turns and goes in. The crowd looked mighty sober; nobody stirred, and there warn't no more laughing. Boggs rode off blackguarding Sherburn as loud as he could yell, all down the street; and pretty soon back he comes and stops before the store, still keeping it up. Some men crowded around him and tried to get him to shut up, but he wouldn't; they told him it would be one o'clock in about fifteen minutes, and so he *must* go home—he must go right away. But it didn't do no good. He cussed away, with all his might, and throwed his hat down in the mud and rode over it, and pretty soon away he went a-raging down the street again, with his gray hair a-flying. Everybody that could get a chance at him tried their best to coax him off of his horse so they could lock him up and get him sober; but it warn't no use—up the street he would tear again, and give Sherburn another cussing. By-and-by somebody says—

"Go for his daughter!—quick, go for his daughter; sometimes he'll listen to her. If anybody can persuade him, she can."

So somebody started on a run. I walked down street a ways, and stopped. In about five or ten minutes, here comes Boggs again—but not on his horse. He was a-reeling across the street towards me, bareheaded, with a friend on both sides of him aholt of his arms and hurrying him along. He was quiet, and looked uneasy; and he warn't hanging back any, but was doing some of the hurrying himself. Somebody sings out—

"Boggs!"

I looked over there to see who said it, and it was that Colonel Sherburn. He was standing perfectly still, in the street, and had a pistol raised in his right hand—not aiming it, but holding it out with the barrel tilted up towards the sky. The same second I see a young girl coming on the run, and two men with her. Boggs and the men turned round, to see who called him, and when they see the pistol the men jumped to one side, and the pistol barrel come down slow and steady to a level—both barrels cocked. Boggs throws up both of his hands, and says, "O Lord, don't shoot!" Bang! goes the first shot, and he staggers back clawing at the air—bang! goes the second one, and he tumbles backwards onto the ground, heavy and solid, with his arms spread out. That young girl screamed out, and comes rushing, and down she throws herself on her father, crying, and saying, "Oh, he's killed him, he's killed him!" The crowd closed up around them, and shouldered and jammed one another, with their necks stretched, trying to see, and people on the inside trying to shove them back, and shouting, "Back, back! give him air, give him air!"

Colonel Sherburn he tossed his pistol onto the ground, and turned around on his heels and walked off.

They took Boggs to a little drug store, the crowd pressing around, just the same, and the whole town following, and I rushed and got a good place at the window, where I was close to him and could see in. They laid him on the floor, and put one large Bible under his head, and opened another one and spread it on his breast—but they tore open his shirt first, and I seen where one of the bullets went in. He made about a dozen long gasps, his breast lifting the Bible up when he drawed in his breath, and letting it down again when he breathed it out—and after that he laid still; he was dead.[8] Then they pulled his daughter away from him, screaming and crying, and took her off. She was about sixteen, and very sweet and gentle-looking, but awful pale and scared.

Well, pretty soon the whole town was there, squirming and scrouging and pushing and shoving to get at the window and have a look, but people that

---

8. Twain had witnessed a shooting very much like this one when he was ten years old. His father was the presiding judge at the trial, which ended in acquittal.

had the places wouldn't give them up, and folks behind them was saying all the time, "Say, now, you've looked enough, you fellows; 'taint right and 'taint fair, for you to stay thar all the time, and never give nobody a chance; other folks has their rights as well as you."

There was considerable jawing back, so I slid out, thinking maybe there was going to be trouble. The streets was full, and everybody was excited. Everybody that seen the shooting was telling how it happened, and there was a big crowd packed around each one of these fellows, stretching their necks and listening. One long lanky man, with long hair and a big white fur stove-pipe hat on the back of his head, and a crooked-handled cane, marked out the places on the ground where Boggs stood, and where Sherburn stood, and the people following him around from one place to t'other and watching everything he done, and bobbing their heads to show they understood, and stooping a little and resting their hands on their thighs to watch him mark the places on the ground with his cane; and then he stood up straight and stiff where Sherburn had stood, frowning and having his hat-brim down over his eyes, and sung out, "Boggs!" and then fetched his cane down slow to a level, and says "Bang!" staggered backwards, says "Bang!" again, and fell down flat on his back. The people that had seen the thing said he done it perfect; said it was just exactly the way it all happened. Then as much as a dozen people got out their bottles and treated him.

Well, by-and-by somebody said Sherburn ought to be lynched. In about a minute everybody was saying it; so away they went, mad and yelling, and snatching down every clothes-line they come to, to do the hanging with.

Chapter XXII

They swarmed up the street towards Sherburn's house, a-whooping and yelling and raging like Injuns, and everything had to clear the way or get run over and tromped to mush, and it was awful to see. Children was heeling it ahead of the mob, screaming and trying to get out of the way; and every window along the road was full of women's heads, and there was nigger boys in every tree, and bucks and wenches looking over every fence; and as soon as the mob would get nearly to them they would break and skaddle back out of reach. Lots of the women and girls was crying and taking on, scared most to death.

They swarmed up in front of Sherburn's palings as thick as they could jam together, and you couldn't hear yourself think for the noise. It was a little twenty-foot yard. Some sung out "Tear down the fence! tear down the fence!" Then there was a racket of ripping and tearing and smashing, and down she goes, and the front wall of the crowd begins to roll in like a wave.

Just then Sherburn steps out on to the roof of his little front porch, with a double-barrel gun in his hand, and takes his stand, perfectly ca'm and deliberate, not saying a word. The racket stopped, and the wave sucked back.

Sherburn never said a word—just stood there, looking down. The stillness was awful creepy and uncomfortable. Sherburn run his eye slow along the crowd; and wherever it struck, the people tried a little to outgaze him, but they couldn't; they dropped their eyes and looked sneaky. Then pretty soon Sherburn sort of laughed; not the pleasant kind, but the kind that makes you feel like when you are eating bread that's got sand in it.

Then he says, slow and scornful:

"The idea of *you* lynching anybody! It's amusing. The idea of you think-ing you had pluck enough to lynch a *man!* Because you're brave enough to tar and feather poor friendless cast-out women that come along here, did that make you think you had grit enough to lay your hands on a *man?* Why, a *man's* safe in the hands of ten thousand of your kind—as long as it's day-time and you're not behind him.

"Do I know you? I know you clear through. I was born and raised in the South, and I've lived in the North; so I know the average all around. The average man's a coward. In the North he lets anybody walk over him that wants to, and goes home and prays for a humble spirit to bear it. In the South one man, all by himself, has stopped a stage full of men, in the day-time, and robbed the lot. Your newspapers call you a brave people so much that you think you *are* braver than any other people—whereas you're just *as* brave, and no braver. Why don't your juries hang murderers? Because they're afraid the man's friends will shoot them in the back, in the dark—and it's just what they *would* do.

"So they always acquit; and then a *man* goes in the night, with a hundred masked cowards at his back, and lynches the rascal. Your mistake is, that you didn't bring a man with you; that's one mistake, and the other is that you didn't come in the dark, and fetch your masks. You brought *part* of a man—Buck Harkness, there—and if you hadn't had him to start you, you'd a taken it out in blowing.

"You didn't want to come. The average man don't like trouble and danger. *You* don't like trouble and danger. But if only *half* a man—like Buck Hark-ness, there—shouts 'Lynch him, lynch him!' you're afraid to back down—afraid you'll be found out to be what you are—*cowards*—and so you raise a yell, and hang yourselves onto that half-a-man's coat tail, and come raging up here, swearing what big things you're going to do. The pitifulest thing out is a mob; that's what an army is—a mob; they don't fight with courage that's born in them, but with courage that's borrowed from their mass, and from their officers. But a mob without any *man* at the head of it, is *beneath* piti-fulness. Now the thing for *you* to do, is to droop your tails and go home and crawl in a hole. If any real lynching's going to be done, it will be done in the dark, Southern fashion; and when they come they'll bring their masks, and fetch a *man* along. Now *leave*—and take your half-a-man with you"—tossing his gun up across his left arm and cocking it, when he says this.

The crowd washed back sudden, and then broke all apart and went tearing off every which way, and Buck Harkness he heeled it after them, looking tolerable cheap. I could a staid, if I'd a wanted to, but I didn't want to.

I went to the circus, and loafed around the back side till the watchman went by, and then dived in under the tent. I had my twenty-dollar gold piece and some other money, but I reckoned I better save it, because there ain't no telling how soon you are going to need it, away from home and amongst strangers, that way. You can't be too careful. I ain't opposed to spending money on circuses, when there ain't no other way, but there ain't no use in *wasting* it on them.

It was a real bully circus. It was the splendidest sight that ever was, when they all come riding in, two and two, a gentleman and lady, side by side, the men just in their drawers and under-shirts, and no shoes nor stirrups, and resting their hands on their thighs, easy and comfortable—there must a' been twenty of them—and every lady with a lovely complexion, and perfectly beautiful, and looking just like a gang of real sure-enough queens, and dressed in clothes that cost millions of dollars, and just littered with diamonds. It was a powerful fine sight; I never see anything so lovely. And then one by one they got up and stood, and went a-weaving around the ring so gentle and wavy and graceful, the men looking ever so tall and airy and straight, with their heads bobbing and skimming along, away up there under the tent-roof, and every lady's rose-leafy dress flapping soft and silky around her hips, and she looking like the most loveliest parasol.

And then faster and faster they went, all of them dancing, first one foot stuck out in the air and then the other, the horses leaning more and more, and the ring-master going round and round the centre-pole, cracking his whip and shouting "hi!—hi!" and the clown cracking jokes behind him; and by-and-by all hands dropped the reins, and every lady put her knuckles on her hips and every gentlemen folded his arms, and then how the horses did lean over and hump themselves! And so, one after the other they all skipped off into the ring, and made the sweetest bow I ever see, and then scampered out, and everybody clapped their hands and went just about wild.

Well, all through the circus they done the most astonishing things; and all the time that clown carried on so it most killed the people. The ring-master couldn't ever say a word to him but he was back at him quick as a wink with the funniest things a body ever said; and how he ever *could* think of so many of them, and so sudden and so pat, was what I couldn't noway understand. Why, I couldn't a thought of them in a year. And by-and-by a drunk man tried to get into the ring—said he wanted to ride; said he could ride as well as anybody that ever was. They argued and tried to keep him out, but he wouldn't listen, and the whole show come to a standstill. Then the people begun to holler at him and make fun of him, and that made him mad, and he begun to rip and tear; so that stirred up the people, and a lot of men began to pile down off of the benches and swarm towards the ring, saying "Knock him down! throw him out!" and one or two women begun to scream. So, then, the ring-master he made a little speech, and said he hoped there wouldn't be no disturbance, and if the man would promise he wouldn't make no more trouble, he would let him ride, if he thought he could stay on the horse. So everybody laughed and said all right, and the man got on. The minute he was on, the horse begun to rip and tear and jump and cavort around, with two circus men hanging onto his bridle trying to hold him, and the drunk man hanging onto his neck, and his heels flying in the air every jump, and the whole crowd of people standing up shouting and laughing till the tears rolled down. And at last, sure enough, all the circus men could do, the horse broke loose, and away he went like the very nation, round and round the ring, with that sot laying down on him and hanging to his neck, with first one leg hanging most to the ground on one side, and then t'other one on t'other side, and the people just crazy. It warn't funny to me, though; I was all of a tremble to see his danger. But pretty soon he struggled up astraddle and grabbed the bridle, a-reeling this way and that; and the next minute he sprung up and dropped the bridle and stood! and the horse agoing like a house afire too. He just stood up there, a-sailing around as easy and comfortable as if he warn't ever drunk in his life—and then he begun to pull off his clothes and sling them. He shed them so thick they kind of clogged up the air, and altogether he shed seventeen suits. And then, there he was, slim and handsome, and dressed the gaudiest and prettiest you ever saw, and he lit into that horse with his whip and made him fairly hum—and finally skipped off, and made his bow and danced off to the dressing-room, and everybody just a-howling with pleasure and astonishment.

Then the ring-master he see how he had been fooled, and he *was* the sickest ring-master you ever see, I reckon. Why, it was one of his own men! He had got up that joke all out of his own head, and never let on to nobody. Well, I felt sheepish enough, to be took in so, but I wouldn't a been in that ring-master's place, not for a thousand dollars. I don't know; there may be bullier circuses than what that one was, but I never struck them yet. Anyways it was plenty good enough for *me*; and wherever I run across it, it can have all of *my* custom, everytime.

Well, that night we had *our* show; but there warn't only about twelve people there; just enough to pay expenses. And they laughed all the time, and that made the duke mad; and everybody left, anyway, before the show was over, but one boy which was asleep. So the duke said these Arkansaw lunkheads couldn't come up to Shakspeare; what they wanted was low comedy—and may be something ruther worse than low comedy, he reckoned. He said he could size their style. So next morning he got some big sheets of wrapping-paper and some black paint, and drawed off some hand-bills and stuck them up all over the village. The bills said:

AT THE COURT HOUSE!
FOR 3 NIGHTS ONLY!
The World-Renowned Tragedians
DAVID GARRICK THE YOUNGER
AND
EDMUND KEAN THE ELDER!
*Of the London and Continental
Theatres,*
In their Thrilling Tragedy of
THE KING'S CAMELOPARD[9]
OR
THE ROYAL NONESUCH!!!
Admission 50 cents.

Then at the bottom was the biggest line of all—which said:

LADIES AND CHILDREN NOT ADMITTED.

"There," says he, "if that line don't fetch them, I don't know Arkansaw!"

Chapter XXIII

Well, all day him and the king was hard at it, rigging up a stage, and a curtain, and a row of candles for footlights; and that night the house was jam full of men in no time. When the place couldn't hold no more, the duke he quit tending door and went around the back way and come onto the stage

---

9. An archaic name for a giraffe, but also describes a legendary spotted beast the size of a camel.

and stood up before the curtain, and made a little speech, and praised up
this tragedy, and said it was the most thrillingest one that ever was; and so he
went on a-bragging about the tragedy and about Edmund Kean the Elder,
which was to play the main principal part in it; and at last when he'd got
everybody's expectations up high enough, he rolled up the curtain, and the
next minute the king come a-prancing out on all fours, naked; and he was
painted all over, ring-streaked-and-striped, all sorts of colors, as splendid as
a rainbow. And—but never mind the rest of his outfit, it was just wild, but
it was awful funny. The people most killed themselves laughing; and when
the king got done capering, and capered off behind the scenes, they roared
and clapped and stormed and haw-hawed till he come back and done it over
again; and after that, they made him do it another time. Well, it would a
made a cow laugh to see the shines that old idiot cut.

Then the duke he lets the curtain down, and bows to the people, and
says the great tragedy will be performed only two nights more, on accounts
of pressing London engagements, where the seats is all sold aready for it
in Drury Lane; and then he makes them another bow, and says if he has
succeeded in pleasing them and instructing them, he will be deeply
obleeged if they will mention it to their friends and get them to come and
see it.

Twenty people sings out:

"What, is it over? Is that *all?*"

The duke says yes. Then there was a fine time. Everybody sings out "sold,"[1]
and rose up mad, and was agoing for that stage and them tragedians. But a
big fine-looking man jumps up on a bench, and shouts:

"Hold on! Just a word, gentlemen." They stopped to listen. "We are sold—
mighty badly sold. But we don't want to be the laughing-stock of this whole
town, I reckon, and never hear the last of this thing as long as we live. *No.*
What we want, is to go out of here quiet, and talk this show up, and sell the
rest of the town! Then we'll all be in the same boat. Ain't that sensible?"
("You bet it is!—the jedge is right!" everybody sings out.) "All right, then—
not a word about any sell. Go along home, and advise everybody to come
and see the tragedy."

Next day you couldn't hear nothing around that town but how splendid
that show was. House was jammed again, that night, and we sold this crowd
the same way. When me and the king and the duke got home to the raft, we
all had a supper; and by-and-by, about midnight, they made Jim and me
back her out and float her down the middle of the river and fetch her in and
hide her about two mile below town.

The third night the house was crammed again—and they warn't newcomers, this time, but people that was at the show the other two nights. I stood
by the duke at the door, and I see that every man that went in had his pockets
bulging, or something muffled up under his coat—and I see it warn't no per-
fumery neither, not by a long sight. I smelt sickly eggs by the barrel, and rotten
cabbages, and such things; and if I know the signs of a dead cat being around,
and I bet I do, there was sixty-four of them went in. I shoved in there for a minute, but it was too various for me, I couldn't stand it. Well, when the place
couldn't hold no more people, the duke he give a fellow a quarter and told him

1. Cheated.

to tend door for him a minute, and then he started around for the stage door, I after him; but the minute we turned the corner and was in the dark, he says:

"Walk fast, now, till you get away from the houses, and then shin for the raft like the dickens was after you!"

I done it, and he done the same. We struck the raft at the same time, and in less than two seconds we was gliding down stream, all dark and still, and edging towards the middle of the river, nobody saying a word. I reckoned the poor king was in for a gaudy time of it with the audience; but nothing of the sort; pretty soon he crawls out from under the wigwam, and says:

"Well, how'd the old thing pan out this time, Duke?"

He hadn't been up town at all.

We never showed a light till we was about ten mile below that village. Then we lit up and had a supper, and the king and the duke fairly laughed their bones loose over the way they'd served them people. The duke says:

"Greenhorns, flatheads! *I* knew the first house would keep mum and let the rest of the town get roped in; and I knew they'd lay for us the third night, and consider it was *their* turn now. Well, it *is* their turn, and I'd give something to know how much they'd take for it. I *would* just like to know how they're putting in their opportunity. They can turn it into a picnic, if they want to—they brought plenty provisions."

Them rapscallions took in four hundred and sixty-five dollars in that three nights. I never see money hauled in by the wagon-load like that, before.

By-and-by, when they was asleep and snoring, Jim says:

"Don't it 'sprise you, de way dem kings carries on, Huck?"

"No," I says, "it don't."

"Why don't it, Huck?"

"Well, it don't, because it's in the breed. I reckon they're all alike."

"But, Huck, dese kings o' ourn is reglar rapscallions; dat's jist what dey is; dey's reglar rapscallions."

"Well, that's what I'm a-saying; all kings is mostly rapscallions, as fur as I can make out."

"Is dat so?"

"You read about them once—you'll see. Look at Henry the Eight; this'n 's a Sunday-School Superintendent to *him.* And look at Charles Second, and Louis Fourteen, and Louis Fifteen, and James Second, and Edward Second, and Richard Third, and forty more; besides all them Saxon heptarchies that used to rip around so in old times and raise Cain. My, you ought to seen old Henry the Eight when he was in bloom. He *was* a blossom. He used to marry a new wife every day, and chop off her head next morning. And he would do it just as indifferent as if he was ordering up eggs. 'Fetch up Nell Gwynn,' he says. They fetch her up. Next morning, 'Chop off her head!' And they chop it off. 'Fetch up Jane Shore,' he says; and up she comes. Next morning 'Chop off her head'—and they chop it off. 'Ring up Fair Rosamun.' Fair Rosamun answers the bell. Next morning, 'Chop off her head.' And he made every one of them tell him a tale every night; and he kept that up till he had hogged a thousand and one tales that way, and then he put them all in a book, and called it Domesday Book—which was a good name and stated the case. You don't know kings, Jim, but I know them; and this old rip of ourn is one of the cleanest I've struck in history. Well, Henry he takes a notion he wants to get up some trouble with this country. How does he go at it—give notice?—give the country a show? No. All of sudden he heaves all the tea in Boston Harbor overboard, and whacks out a declaration of independence, and dares them to come on. That was *his* style—he never give anybody a chance. He had suspicions of his father, the Duke of Wellington. Well, what did he do?—ask him to show up? No—drownded him in a butt of mamsey, like a cat. Spose people left money laying around where he was—what did he do? He collared it. Spose he contracted to do a thing; and you paid him, and didn't set down there and see that he done it—what did he do? He always done the other thing. Spose he opened his mouth—what then? If he didn't shut it up powerful quick, he'd lose a lie, every time. That's the kind of a bug Henry was; and if we'd a had him along 'stead of our kings, he'd a fooled that town a heap worse than ourn done.[2] I don't say that ourn is lambs, because they ain't, when you come right down to the cold facts; but they ain't nothing to *that* old ram, anyway. All I say is, kings is kings, and you got to make allowances. Take them all around, they're a mighty ornery lot. It's the way they're raised."

"But dis one do *smell* so like de nation, Huck."

"Well, they all do, Jim. *We* can't help the way a king smells; history don't tell no way."

"Now de duke, he's a tolerable likely man, in some ways."

"Yes, a duke's different. But not very different. This one's a middling hard lot, for a duke. When he's drunk, there ain't no near-sighted man could tell him from a king."

"Well, anyways, I doan' hanker for no mo' un um, Huck. Dese is all I kin stan'."

"It's the way I feel, too, Jim. But we've got them on our hands, and we got to remember what they are, and make allowances. Sometimes I wish we could hear of a country that's out of kings."

What was the use to tell Jim these warn't real kings and dukes? It wouldn't a done no good; and besides, it was just as I said; you couldn't tell them from the real kind.

I went to sleep, and Jim didn't call me when it was my turn. He often done that. When I waked up, just at day-break, he was setting there with his head down betwixt his knees, moaning and mourning to himself. I didn't take notice, nor let on. I knowed what it was about. He was thinking about his wife and his children, away up yonder, and he was low and homesick; because he hadn't ever been away from home before in his life; and I do believe he cared just as much for his people as white folks does for their'n. It don't seem natural, but I reckon it's so. He was often moaning and mourning that way, nights, when he judged I was asleep, and saying "Po' little 'Lizabeth! po' little Johnny! its mighty hard; I spec' I ain't ever gwyne to see you no mo', no mo'!" He was a mighty good nigger, Jim was.

But this time I somehow got to talking to him about his wife and young ones; and by-and-by he says:

"What makes me feel so bad dis time, 'uz bekase I hear sumpn over yonder on de bank like a whack, er a slam, while ago, en it mine me er de time I treat my little 'Lizabeth so ornery. She warn't on'y 'bout fo' year ole, en she tuck de sk'yarlet-fever, en had a powful rough spell; but she got well, en one day she was a-stannin' aroun', en I says to her, I says:

"'Shet de do'.'

2. Huck's "history" of kingly behavior is a hodgepodge of fact and fiction, drawn from English and American history.

"She never done it; jis' stood dar, kiner smilin' up at me. It make me mad; en I says agin, mighty loud, I says:

"'Doan' you hear me?—shet de do'!'

"She jis' stood de same way, kiner smilin' up. I was a-bilin'! I says:

"'I lay I *make* you mine!'

"En wid dat I fetch' her a slap side de head dat sont her a-sprawlin'. Den I went into de yuther room, en 'uz gone 'bout ten minutes; en when I come back, dah was dat do' a-stannin' open *yit,* en dat chile stannin' mos' right in it, a-lookin' down and mournin', en de tears runnin' down. My, but I *wuz* mad, I was agwyne for de chile, but jis' den—it was a do' dat open innerds—jis' den, 'long come de wind en slam it to, behine de chile, *ker-blam!*—en my lan', de chile never move'! My breff mos' hop outer me; en I feel so—so—I doan' know *how* I feel. I crope out, all a-tremblin', en crope aroun' en open de do' easy en slow, en poke my head in behine de chile, sof' en still, en all uv a sudden, I says *pow!* jis' as loud as I could yell. *She never budge!* Oh, Huck, I bust out a-cryin' en grab her up in my arms, en say, 'Oh, de po' little thing! de Lord God Amighty fogive po' ole Jim, kaze he never gwyne to fogive hisself as long's he live!' Oh, she was plumb deef en dumb, Huck, plumb deef en dumb—en I'd ben a'treat'n her so!"

Chapter XXIV

Next day, towards night, we laid up under a little willow tow-head out in the middle, where there was a village on each side of the river, and the duke and the king begun to lay out a plan for working them towns. Jim he spoke to the duke, and said he hoped it wouldn't take but a few hours, because it got mighty heavy and tiresome to him when he had to lay all day in the wigwam tied with the rope. You see, when we left him all alone we had to tie him, because if anybody happened on him all by himself and not tied, it wouldn't look much like he was a runaway nigger, you know. So the duke said it *was* kind of hard to have to lay roped all day, and he'd cipher out some way to get around it.

He was uncommon bright, the duke was, and he soon struck it. He dressed Jim up in King Lear's outfit—it was a long curtain-calico gown, and a white horse-hair wig and whiskers; and then he took his theatre-paint and painted Jim's face and hands and ears and neck all over a dead bull solid blue, like a man that's been drownded nine days. Blamed if he warn't the horriblest look-ing outrage I ever see. Then the duke took and wrote out a sign on a shingle so—

Sick Arab—but harmless when not out of his head.

And he nailed that shingle to a lath, and stood the lath up four or five foot in front of the wigwam. Jim was satisfied. He said it was a sight better than laying tied a couple of years every day and trembling all over every time there was a sound. The duke told him to make himself free and easy, and if anybody ever come meddling around, he must hop out of the wigwam, and carry on a little, and fetch a howl or two like a wild beast, and he reckoned they would light out and leave him alone. Which was sound enough judgment; but you take the average man, and he wouldn't wait for him to howl. Why, he didn't only look like he was dead, he looked considerable more than that.

These rapscallions wanted to try the Nonesuch again, because there was so much money in it, but they judged it wouldn't be safe, because maybe the news might a worked along down by this time. They couldn't hit no project that suited, exactly; so at last the duke said he reckoned he'd lay off and work his brains an hour or two and see if he couldn't put up something on the Arkansaw village; and the king he allowed he would drop over to t'other village, without any plan, but just trust in Providence to lead him the profitable way—meaning the devil, I reckon. We had all bought store clothes where we stopped last; and now the king put his'n on, and he told me to put mine on. I done it, of course. The king's duds was all black, and he did look real swell and starchy. I never knowed how clothes could change a body before. Why, before, he looked like the orneriest old rip that ever was; but now, when he'd take off his new white beaver[3] and make a bow and do a smile, he looked that grand and good and pious that you'd say he had walked right out of the ark, and maybe was old Leviticus[4] himself. Jim cleaned up the canoe, and I got my paddle ready. There was a big steamboat laying at the shore away up under the point, about three mile above town—been there a couple of hours, taking on freight. Says the king:

"Seein' how I'm dressed, I reckon maybe I better arrive down from St. Louis or Cincinnati, or some other big place. Go for the steamboat, Huckleberry; we'll come down to the village on her."

I didn't have to be ordered twice, to go and take a steamboat ride. I fetched the shore a half a mile above the village, and then went scooting along the bluff bank in the easy water. Pretty soon we come to a nice innocent-looking young country jake setting on a log swabbing the sweat off of his face, for it was powerful warm weather; and he had a couple of big carpet-bags by him.

"Run her nose in shore," says the king. I done it. "Wher' you bound for, young man?"

"For the steamboat; going to Orleans."

"Git aboard," says the king. "Hold on a minute, my servant 'll he'p you with them bags. Jump out and he'p the gentleman, Adolphus"—meaning me, I see.

I done so, and then we all three started on again. The young chap was mighty thankful; said it was tough work toting his baggage such weather. He asked the king where he was going, and the king told him he'd come down the river and landed at the other village this morning, and now he was going up a few mile to see an old friend on a farm up there. The young fellow says:

"When I first see you, I says to myself, 'It's Mr. Wilks, sure, and he come mighty near getting here in time.' But then I says again, 'No, I reckon it ain't him, or else he wouldn't be paddling up the river.' You *ain't* him, are you?"

"No, my name's Blodgett—Elexander Blodgett—*Reverend* Elexander Blodgett, I spose I must say, as I'm one o' the Lord's poor servants. But still I'm jist as able to be sorry for Mr. Wilks for not arriving in time, all the same, if he's missed anything by it—which I hope he hasn't."

"Well, he don't miss any property by it, because he'll get that all right; but he's missed seeing his brother Peter die—which he mayn't mind, nobody can tell as to that—but his brother would a give anything in this world to see *him* before he died; never talked about nothing else all these three weeks; hadn't seen him since they was boys together—and hadn't ever seen his brother

---

3. Hat.
4. The third book of the Old Testament is here confused with Noah.

William at all—that's the deef and dumb one—William ain't more than thirty or thirty-five. Peter and George was the only ones that come out here; George was the married brother; him and his wife both died last year. Harvey and William's the only ones that's left now; and, as I was saying, they haven't got here in time."

"Did anybody send 'em word?"

"Oh, yes; a month or two ago, when Peter was first took; because Peter said then that he sorter felt like he warn't going to get well this time. You see, he was pretty old, and George's g'yirls was too young to be much company for him, except Mary Jane the red-headed one; and so he was kinder lonesome after George and his wife died, and didn't seem to care much to live. He most desperately wanted to see Harvey—and William too, for that matter—because he was one of them kind that can't bear to make a will. He left a letter behind for Harvey, and said he'd told in it where his money was hid, and how he wanted the rest of the property divided up so George's g'yirls would be all right—for George didn't leave nothing. And that letter was all they could get him to put a pen to."

"Why do you reckon Harvey don't come? Wher' does he live?"

"Oh, he lives in England—Sheffield—preaches there—hasn't ever been in this country. He hasn't had any too much time—and besides he mightn't a got the letter at all, you know."

"Too bad, too bad he couldn't a lived to see his brothers, poor soul. You going to Orleans, you say?"

"Yes, but that ain't only a part of it. I'm going in a ship, next Wednesday, for Ryo Janeero,[5] where my uncle lives."

"It's a pretty long journey. But it'll be lovely; I wisht I was agoing. Is Mary Jane the oldest? How old is the others?"

"Mary Jane's nineteen, Susan's fifteen, and Joanna's about fourteen—that's the one that gives herself to good works and has a hare-lip."

"Poor things! to be left alone in the cold world so."

"Well, they could be worse off. Old Peter had friends, and they ain't going to let them come to no harm. There's Hobson, the Babtis' preacher; and Deacon Lot Hovey, and Ben Rucker, and Abner Shackleford, and Levi Bell, the lawyer; and Dr. Robinson, and their wives, and the widow Bartley, and—well, there's a lot of them; but these are the ones that Peter was thickest with, and used to write about sometimes, when he wrote home; so Harvey'll know where to look for friends when he gets here."

Well, the old man he went on asking questions till he just fairly emptied that young fellow. Blamed if he didn't inquire about everybody and everything in that blessed town, and all about all the Wilkses; and about Peter's business—which was a tanner; and about George's—which was a carpenter; and about Harvey's—which was a dissentering[6] minister, and so on, and so on. Then he says:

"What did you want to walk all the way up to the steamboat for?"

"Because she's a big Orleans boat, and I was afeard she mightn't stop there. When they're deep they won't stop for a hail. A Cincinnati boat will, but this is a St. Louis one."

"Was Peter Wilks well off?"

---

5. Rio de Janeiro, Brazil.   6. Dissenting.

"Oh, yes, pretty well off. He had houses and land, and it's reckoned he left three or four thousand in cash hid up som'ers."

"When did you say he died?"

"I didn't say, but it was last night."

"Funeral to-morrow, likely?"

"Yes, 'bout the middle of the day."

"Well, it's all terrible sad; but we've all got to go, one time or another. So what we want to do is to be prepared; then we're all right."

"Yes, sir, it's the best way. Ma used to always say that."

When we struck the boat, she was about done loading, and pretty soon she got off. The king never said nothing about going aboard, so I lost my ride, after all. When the boat was gone, the king made me paddle up another mile to a lonesome place, and then he got ashore, and says:

"Now hustle back, right off, and fetch the duke up here, and the new carpet-bags. And if he's gone over to t'other side, go over there and git him. And tell him to git himself up regardless. Shove along, now."

I see what *he* was up to; but I never said nothing, of course. When I got back with the duke, we hid the canoe and then they set down on a log, and the king told him everything, just like the young fellow had said it—every last word of it. And all the time he was a doing it, he tried to talk like an Englishman; and he done it pretty well too, for a slouch. I can't imitate him, and so I ain't agoing to try to; but he really done it pretty good. Then he says:

"How are you on the deef and dumb, Bilgewater?"

The duke said, leave him alone for that; said he had played a deef and dumb person on the histrionic boards. So then they waited for a steamboat.

About the middle of the afternoon a couple of little boats come along, but they didn't come from high enough up the river; but at last there was a big one, and they hailed her. She sent out her yawl, and we went aboard, and she was from Cincinnati; and when they found we only wanted to go four or five mile, they was booming mad, and give us a cussing, and said they wouldn't land us. But the king was ca'm. He says:

"If gentlemen kin afford to pay a dollar a mile apiece, to be took on and put off in a yawl, a steamboat kin afford to carry 'em, can't it?"

So they softened down and said it was all right; and when we got to the village, they yawled us ashore. About two dozen men flocked down, when they see the yawl a coming; and when the king says—

"Kin any of you gentlemen tell me wher' Mr. Peter Wilks lives?" they give a glance at one another, and nodded their heads, as much as to say, "What d' I tell you?" Then one of them says, kind of soft and gentle:

"I'm sorry, sir, but the best we can do is to tell you where he *did* live yesterday evening."

Sudden as winking, the ornery old cretur went all to smash, and fell up against the man, and put his chin on his shoulder, and cried down his back, and says:

"Alas, alas, our poor brother—gone, and we never got to see him; oh, it's too, *too* hard!"

Then he turns around, blubbering, and makes a lot of idiotic signs to the duke on his hands, and blamed if *he* didn't drop a carpet-bag and bust out a-crying. If they warn't the beatenest lot, them two frauds, that ever I struck.

Well, the men gethered around, and sympathized with them, and said all sorts of kind things to them, and carried their carpet-bags up the hill for them, and let them lean on them and cry, and told the king all about his brother's last moments, and the king he told it all over again on his hands to the duke, and both of them took on about that dead tanner like they'd lost the twelve disciples. Well, if ever I struck anything like it, I'm a nigger. It was enough to make a body ashamed of the human race.

Chapter XXV

The news was all over town in two minutes, and you could see the people tearing down on the run, from every which way, some of them putting on their coats as they come. Pretty soon we was in the middle of a crowd, and the noise of the tramping was like a soldier-march. The windows and door-yards was full; and every minute somebody would say, over a fence:

"Is it *them!*"

And somebody trotting along with the gang would answer back and say:

"You bet it is."

When we got to the house, the street in front of it was packed, and the three girls was standing in the door. Mary Jane *was* red-headed, and that don't make no difference, she was most awful beautiful, and her face and her eyes was all lit up like glory, she was so glad her uncles was come. The king he spread his arms, and Mary Jane she jumped for them, and the hare-lip jumped for the duke, and there they *had* it! Everybody most, leastways women, cried for joy to see them meet again at last and have such good times.

Then the king he hunched the duke, private—I see him do it—and then he looked around and see the coffin, over in the corner on two chairs; so then, him and the duke, with a hand across each other's shoulder, and t'other hand to their eyes, walked slow and solemn over there, everybody dropping back to give them room, and all the talk and noise stopping, people saying "Sh!" and all the men taking their hats off and drooping their heads, so you could a heard a pin fall. And when they got there, they bent over and looked in the coffin, and took one sight, and then they bust out a crying so you could a heard them to Orleans, most; and then they put their arms around each other's necks, and hung their chins over each other's shoulders; and then for three minutes, or maybe four, I never see two men leak the way they done. And mind you, everybody was doing the same; and the place was that damp I never see anything like it. Then one of them got on one side of the coffin, and t'other on t'other side, and they kneeled down and rested their foreheads on the coffin, and let on to pray all to theirselves. Well, when it come to that, it worked the crowd like you never see anything like it, and so everybody broke down and went to sobbing right out loud—the poor girls, too; and every woman, nearly, went up to the girls, without saying a word, and kissed them, solemn, on the forehead, and then put their hand on their head, and looked up towards the sky, with the tears running down, and then busted out and went off sobbing and swabbing, and give the next woman a show. I never see anything so disgusting.

Well, by-and-by the king he gets up and comes forward a little, and works himself up and slobbers out a speech, all full of tears and flapdoodle about its being a sore trial for him and his poor brother to lose the diseased, and to miss seeing diseased alive, after the long journey of four thousand mile, but it's a trial that's sweetened and sanctified to us by this dear sympathy and these holy tears, and so he thanks them out of his heart and out of his brother's heart, because out of their mouths they can't, words being too weak and cold, and all that kind of rot and slush, till it was just sickening; and then he blubbers out a pious goody-goody Amen, and turns himself loose and goes to crying fit to bust.

And the minute the words was out of his mouth somebody over in the crowd struck up the doxolojer,[7] and everybody joined in with all their might, and it just warmed you up and made you feel as good as church letting out. Music *is* a good thing; and after all that soul-butter and hogwash, I never see it freshen up things so, and sound so honest and bully.

Then the king begins to work his jaw again, and says how him and his nieces would be glad if a few of the main principal friends of the family would take supper here with them this evening, and help set up with the ashes of the diseased; and says if his poor brother laying yonder could speak, he knows who he would name, for they was names that was very dear to him, and mentioned often in his letters; and so he will name the same, to-wit, as follows, vizz:—Rev. Mr. Hobson, and Deacon Lot Hovey, and Mr. Ben Rucker, and Abner Shackleford, and Levi Bell, and Dr. Robinson, and their wives, and the widow Bartley.

Rev. Hobson and Dr. Robinson was down to the end of the town, a-hunting together; that is, I mean the doctor was shipping a sick man to t'other world, and the preacher was pinting him right. Lawyer Bell was away up to Louisville on some business. But the rest was on hand, and so they all come and shook hands with the king and thanked him and talked to him; and then they shook hands with the duke, and didn't say nothing but just kept a-smiling and bobbing their heads like a passel of sapheads whilst he made all sorts of signs with his hands and said "Goo-goo—goo-goo-goo," all the time, like a baby that can't talk.

So the king he blatted along, and managed to inquire about pretty much everybody and dog in town, by his name, and mentioned all sorts of little things that happened one time or another in the town, or to George's family, or to Peter; and he always let on that Peter wrote him the things, but that was a lie, he got every blessed one of them out of that young flathead that we canoed up to the steamboat.

Then Mary Jane she fetched the letter her father left behind, and the king he read it out loud and cried over it. It give the dwelling-house and three thousand dollars, gold, to the girls; and it give the tanyard (which was doing a good business), along with some other houses and land (worth about seven thousand), and three thousand dollars in gold to Harvey and William, and told where the six thousand cash was hid, down cellar. So these two frauds said they'd go and fetch it up, and have everything square and above-board; and told me to come with a candle. We shut the cellar door behind us, and when they found the bag they spilt it out on the floor, and it was a lovely sight, all them yallerboys.[8] My, the way the king's eyes did shine! He slaps the duke on the shoulder, and says:

"Oh, *this* ain't bully, nor noth'n! Oh, no, I reckon not! Why, Biljy, it beats the Nonesuch, *don't* it!"

The duke allowed it did. They pawed the yaller-boys, and sifted them through their fingers and let them jingle down on the floor; and the king says:

---

7. I.e., doxology, or hymn of praise to God. The particular doxology referred to here begins "Praise God, from whom all blessings flow."
8. Gold coins.

"It ain't no use talkin'; bein' brothers to a rich dead man, and representatives of furrin heirs that's got left, is the line for you and me, Bilge. Thish-
yer comes of trust'n to Providence. It's the best way, in the long run. I've
tried 'em all, and ther' ain't no better way."

Most everybody would a been satisfied with the pile, and took it on trust;
but no, they must count it. So they counts it, and it comes out four hundred
and fifteen dollars short. Says the king:

"Dern him, I wonder what he done with that four hundred and fifteen
dollars?"

They worried over that a while, and ransacked all around for it. Then the
duke says:

"Well, he was a pretty sick man, and likely he made a mistake—I reckon
that's the way of it. The best way's to let it go, and keep still about it. We can
spare it."

"Oh, shucks, yes, we can *spare* it. I don't k'yer noth'n 'bout that—it's the
count I'm thinkin' about. We want to be awful square and open and above-
board, here, you know. We want to lug this h'yer money up stairs and count
it before everybody—then ther' ain't noth'n suspicious. But when the dead
man says ther's six thous'n dollars, you know, we don't want to—"

"Hold on," says the duke. "Less make up the deffisit"—and he begun to
haul out yallerboys out of his pocket.

"It's a most amaz'n good idea, duke—you *have* got a rattlin' clever head
on you," says the king. "Blest if the old Nonesuch ain't a heppin' us out
agin"—and *he* begun to haul out yallerjackets and stack them up.

It most busted them, but they made up the six thousand clean and clear.

"Say," says the duke, "I got another idea. Le's go up stairs and count this
money, and then take and *give it to the girls.*"

"Good land, duke, lemme hug you! It's the most dazzling idea 'at ever a
man struck. You have cert'nly got the most astonishin' head I ever see. Oh,
this is the boss dodge,[9] ther' ain't no mistake 'bout it. Let 'em fetch along
their suspicions now, if they want to—this'll lay 'em out."

When we got up stairs, everybody gathered around the table, and the king
he counted it and stacked it up, three hundred dollars in a pile—twenty elegant little piles. Everybody looked hungry at it, and licked their chops. Then
they raked it into the bag again, and I see the king begin to swell himself up
for another speech. He says:

"Friends all, my poor brother that lays yonder, has done generous by them
that's left behind in the vale of sorrers. He has done generous by these-yer
poor little lambs that he loved and sheltered, and that's left fatherless and
motherless. Yes, and we that knowed him, knows that he would a done *more*
generous by 'em if he hadn't been afeard o' woundin' his dear William and
me. Now, *wouldn't* he? Ther' ain't no question 'bout it, in *my* mind. Well,
then—what kind o' brothers would it be, that 'd stand in his way at sech a
time? And what kind o' uncles would it be that 'd rob—yes, *rob*—sech poor
sweet lambs as these 'at he loved so, at sech a time? If I know William—and
I *think* I do—he—well, I'll jest ask him." He turns around and begins to
make a lot of signs to the duke with his hands; and the duke he looks at him
stupid and leather-headed a while, then all of sudden he seems to catch his
meaning, and jumps for the king, goo-gooing with all his might for joy, and

9. Best confidence trick.

hugs him about fifteen times before he lets up. Then the king says, "I knowed it; I reckon *that* 'll convince anybody the way *he* feels about it. Here, Mary Jane, Susan, Joanner, take the money—take it *all*. It's the gift of him that lays yonder, cold but joyful."

Mary Jane she went for him, Susan and the hare-lip went for the duke, and then such another hugging and kissing I never see yet. And everybody crowded up with the tears in their eyes, and most shook the hands off of them frauds, saying all the time:

"You *dear* good souls!—how *lovely!*—how *could* you!"

Well, then, pretty soon all hands got to talking about the diseased again, and how good he was, and what a loss he was, and all that; and before long a big iron-jawed man worked himself in there from outside, and stood a listening and looking, and not saying anything; and nobody saying anything to him either, because the king was talking and they was all busy listening. The king was saying—in the middle of something he'd started in on—

"—they bein' partickler friends o' the diseased. That's why they're invited here this evenin'; but to-morrow we want *all* to come—everybody; for he respected everybody, he liked everybody, and so it's fitten that his funeral orgies sh'd be public."

And so he went a-mooning on and on, liking to hear himself talk, and every little while he fetched in his funeral orgies again, till the duke he couldn't stand it no more; so he writes on a little scrap of paper, *"obsequies,* you old fool," and folds it up and goes to goo-gooing and reaching it over people's heads to him. The king he reads it, and puts it in his pocket, and says:

"Poor William, afflicted as he is, his *heart's* aluz right. Asks me to invite everybody to come to the funeral—wants me to make 'em all welcome. But he needn't a worried—it was jest what I was at."

Then he weaves along again, perfectly ca'm, and goes to dropping in his funeral orgies again every now and then, just like he done before. And when he done it the third time, he says:

"I say orgies, not because it's the common term, because it ain't—obsequies bein' the common term—but because orgies is the right term. Obsequies ain't used in England no more, now—it's gone out. We say orgies now, in England. Orgies is better, because it means the thing you're after, more exact. It's a word that's made up out'n the Greek *orgo,* outside, open, abroad; and the Hebrew *jeesum,* to plant, cover up; hence *inter.* So, you see, funeral orgies is an open er public funeral."[1]

He was the *worst* I ever struck. Well, the iron-jawed man he laughed right in his face. Everybody was shocked. Everybody says, "Why *doctor!*" and Abner Shackleford says:

"Why, Robinson, hain't you heard the news? This is Harvey Wilks."

The king he smiled eager, and shoved out his flapper, and says:

"*Is* it my poor brother's dear good friend and physician? I—"

"Keep your hands off of me!" says the doctor. "*You* talk like an Englishman—*don't* you? It's the worse imitation I ever heard. *You* Peter Wilks's brother. You're a fraud, that's what you are!"

Well, how they all took on! They crowded around the doctor, and tried to quiet him down, and tried to explain to him, and tell him how Harvey'd

1. The comic etymology was a stock-in-trade of the southwestern humorists and is still popular in comedy routines.

showed in forty ways that he *was* Harvey, and knowed everybody by name, and the names of the very dogs, and begged and *begged* him not to hurt Harvey's feelings and the poor girls' feelings, and all that; but it warn't no use, he stormed right along, and said any man that pretended to be an Englishman and couldn't imitate the lingo no better than what he did, was a fraud and a liar. The poor girls was hanging to the king and crying; and all of a sudden the doctor ups and turns on *them*. He says:

"I was your father's friend, and I'm your friend; and I warn you *as* a friend, and an honest one, that wants to protect you and keep you out of harm and trouble, to turn your backs on that scoundrel, and have nothing to do with him, the ignorant tramp, with his idiotic Greek and Hebrew as he calls it. He is the thinnest kind of an impostor—has come here with a lot of empty names and facts which he has picked up somewheres, and you take them for *proofs,* and are helped to fool yourselves by these foolish friends here, who ought to know better. Mary Jane Wilks, you know me for your friend, and for your unselfish friend, too. Now listen to me; turn this pitiful rascal out—I *beg* you to do it. Will you?"

Mary Jane straightened herself up, and my, but she was handsome! She says:

"*Here* is my answer." She hove up the bag of money and put it in the king's hands, and says, "Take this six thousand dollars, and invest it for me and my sisters any way you want to, and don't give us no receipt for it."

Then she put her arm around the king on one side, and Susan and the hare-lip done the same on the other. Everybody clapped their hands and stomped on the floor like a perfect storm, whilst the king held up his head and smiled proud. The doctor says:

"All right, I wash *my* hands of the matter. But I warn you all that a time's coming when you're going to feel sick whenever you think of this day"—and away he went.

"All right, doctor," says the king, kinder mocking him, "we'll try and get 'em to send for you"—which made them all laugh, and they said it was a prime good hit.

Chapter XXVI

Well, when they was all gone, the king he asks Mary Jane how they was off for spare rooms, and she said she had one spare room, which would do for Uncle William, and she'd give her own room to Uncle Harvey, which was a little bigger, and she would turn into the room with her sisters and sleep on a cot; and up garret was a little cubby, with a pallet in it. The king said the cubby would do for his valley—meaning me.

So Mary Jane took us up, and she showed them their rooms, which was plain but nice. She said she'd have her frocks and a lot of other traps took out of her room if they was in Uncle Harvey's way, but he said they warn't. The frocks was hung along the wall, and before them was a curtain made out of calico that hung down to the floor. There was an old hair trunk in one corner, and a guitar box in another, and all sorts of little knickknacks and jimcracks around, like girls brisken up a room with. The king said it was all the more homely and more pleasanter for these fixings, and so don't disturb them. The duke's room was pretty small, but plenty good enough, and so was my cubby.

That night they had a big supper, and all them men and women was there, and I stood behind the king and the duke's chairs and waited on them, and the niggers waited on the rest. Mary Jane she set at the head of the table, with Susan along side of her, and said how bad the biscuits was, and how mean the preserves was, and how ornery and tough the fried chickens was—and all that kind of rot, the way women always do for to force out compliments; and the people all knowed everything was tip-top, and said so—said "How *do* you get biscuits to brown so nice?" and "Where, for the land's sake *did* you get these amaz'n pickles?" and all that kind of humbug talky-talk, just the way people always does at a supper, you know.

And when it was all done, me and the hare-lip had supper in the kitchen off of the leavings, whilst the others was helping the niggers clean up the things. The hare-lip she got to pumping me about England, and blest if I didn't think the ice was getting mighty thin, sometimes. She says:

"Did you ever see the king?"

"Who? William Fourth?[2] Well, I bet I have—he goes to our church." I knowed he was dead years ago, but I never let on. So when I says he goes to our church, she says:

"What—regular?"

"Yes—regular. His pew's right over opposite ourn—on 'tother side the pulpit."

"I thought he lived in London?"

"Well, he does. Where *would* he live?"

"But I thought *you* lived in Sheffield?"[3]

I see I was up a stump. I had to let on to get choked with a chicken bone, so as to get time to think how to get down again. Then I says:

"I mean he goes to our church regular when he's in Sheffield. That's only in the summer-time, when he comes there to take the sea baths."

"Why, how you talk—Sheffield ain't on the sea."

"Well, who said it was?"

"Why, you did."

"I *didn't*, nuther."

"You did!"

"I didn't."

"You did."

"I never said nothing of the kind."

"Well, what *did* you say, then?"

"Said he come to take the sea *baths*—that's what I said."

"Well, then! how's he going to take the sea baths if it ain't on the sea?"

"Looky here," I says, "did you ever see any Congress water?"[4]

"Yes."

"Well, did you have to go to Congress to get it?"

"Why, no."

"Well, neither does William Fourth have to go to the sea to get a sea bath."

"How does he get it, then?"

"Gets it the way people down here gets Congress water—in barrels. There in the palace at Sheffield they've got furnaces, and he wants his

2. William IV of England (1765–1837) became king in 1830.
3. Industrial city north of London and many miles from the sea.
4. Famous mineral water from the Congress Spring in Saratoga Springs, New York.

water hot. They can't bile that amount of water away off there at the sea. They haven't got no conveniences for it."

"Oh, I see, now. You might a said that in the first place and saved time."

When she said that, I see I was out of the woods again, and so I was comfortable and glad. Next, she says:

"Do you go to church, too?"

"Yes—regular."

"Where do you set?"

"Why, in our pew."

"*Whose* pew?"

"Why, *ourn*—your Uncle Harvey's."

"His'n? What does *he* want with a pew?"

"Wants it to set in. What did you *reckon* he wanted with it?"

"Why, I thought he'd be in the pulpit."

Rot him, I forgot he was a preacher. I see I was up a stump again, so I played another chicken bone and got another think. Then I says:

"Blame it, do you suppose there ain't but one preacher to a church?"

"Why, what do they want with more?"

"What!—to preach before a king? I never see such a girl as you. They don't have no less than seventeen."

"Seventeen! My land! Why, I wouldn't set out such a string as that, not if I *never* got to glory. It must take 'em a week."

"Shucks, they don't *all* of 'em preach the same day—only *one* of 'em."

"Well, then, what does the rest of 'em do?"

"Oh, nothing much. Loll around, pass the plate—and one thing or another. But mainly they don't do nothing."

"Well, then, what are they *for?*"

"Why, they're for *style*. Don't you know nothing?"

"Well, I don't *want* to know no such foolishness as that. How is servants treated in England? Do they treat 'em better 'n we treat our niggers?"

"*No!* A servant ain't nobody there. They treat them worse than dogs."

"Don't they give 'em holidays, the way we do, Christmas and New Year's week, and Fourth of July?"

"Oh, just listen! A body could tell *you* hain't ever been to England, by that. Why, Hare-l—why, Joanna, they never see a holiday from year's end to year's end; never go to the circus, nor theatre, nor nigger shows, nor nowheres."

"Nor church?"

"Nor church."

"But *you* always went to church."

Well, I was gone up again. I forgot I was the old man's servant. But next minute I whirled in on a kind of an explanation how a valley was different from a common servant, and *had* to go to church whether he wanted to or not, and set with the family, on account of it's being the law. But I didn't do it pretty good, and when I got done I see she warn't satisfied. She says:

"Honest injun, now, hain't you been telling me a lot of lies?"

"Honest injun," says I.

"None of it at all?"

"None of it at all. Not a lie in it," says I.

"Lay your hand on this book and say it."

I see it warn't nothing but a dictionary, so I laid my hand on it and said it. So then she looked a little better satisfied, and says:

"Well, then, I'll believe some of it; but I hope to gracious if I'll believe the rest."

"What is it you won't believe, Joe?" says Mary Jane, stepping in with Susan behind her. "It ain't right nor kind for you to talk so to him, and him a stranger and so far from his people. How would you like to be treated so?"

"That's always your way, Maim—always sailing in to help somebody before they're hurt. I hain't done nothing to him. He's told some stretchers, I reckon; and I said I wouldn't swallow it all; and that's every bit and grain I *did* say. I reckon he can stand a little thing like that, can't he?"

"I don't care whether 'twas little or whether 'twas big, he's here in our house and a stranger, and it wasn't good of you to say it. If you was in his place, it would make you feel ashamed; and so you ought'nt to say a thing to another person that will make *them* feel ashamed."

"Why, Maim, he said—"

"It don't make no difference what he *said*—that ain't the thing. The thing is for you to treat him *kind,* and not be saying things to make him remember he ain't in his own country and amongst his own folks."

I says to myself, *this* is a girl that I'm letting that old reptle rob her of her money!

Then Susan *she* waltzed in; and if you'll believe me, she did give Hare-lip hark from the tomb![5]

Says I to myself, And this is *another* one that I'm letting him rob her of her money!

Then Mary Jane she took another inning, and went in sweet and lovely again—which was her way—but when she got done there warn't hardly anything left o' poor Hare-lip. So she hollered.

"All right, then," says the other girls, "you just ask his pardon."

She done it, too. And she done it beautiful. She done it so beautiful it was good to hear; and I wished I could tell her a thousand lies, so she could do it again.

I says to myself, this is *another* one that I'm letting him rob her of her money. And when she got through, they all jest laid theirselves out to make me feel at home and know I was amongst friends. I felt so ornery and low down and mean, that I says to myself, My mind's made up; I'll hive that money for them or bust.

So then I lit out—for bed, I said, meaning some time or another. When I got by myself, I went to thinking the thing over. I says to myself, shall I go to that doctor, private, and blow on these frauds? No—that won't do. He might tell who told him; then the king and the duke would make it warm for me. Shall I go, private, and tell Mary Jane? No—I dasn't do it. Her face would give them a hint, sure; they've got the money, and they'd slide right out and get away with it. If she was to fetch in help, I'd get mixed up in the business, before it was done with, I judge. No, there ain't no good way but one. I got to steal that money, somehow; and I got to steal it some way that they won't suspicion that I done it. They've got a good thing, here; and they ain't agoing to leave till they've played this family and this town for all they're worth, so I'll find a chance time enough. I'll steal it, and hide it; and by-and-by, when I'm away down the river, I'll write a letter and tell Mary Jane where it's hid.

5. A scolding.

But I better hive it to-night, if I can, because the doctor maybe hasn't let up as much as he lets on he has; he might scare them out of here, yet.

So, thinks I, I'll go and search them rooms. Up stairs the hall was dark, but I found the duke's room, and started to paw around it with my hands; but I recollected it wouldn't be much like the king to let anybody else take care of that money but his own self; so then I went to his room and begun to paw around there. But I see I couldn't do nothing without a candle, and I dasn't light one, of course. So I judged I'd got to do the other thing—lay for them, and eavesdrop. About that time, I hears their footsteps coming, and was going to skip under the bed; I reached for it, but it wasn't where I thought it would be; but I touched the curtain that hid Mary Jane's frocks, so I jumped in behind that and snuggled in amongst the gowns, and stood there perfectly still.

They come in and shut the door; and the first thing the duke done was to get down and look under the bed. Then I was glad I hadn't found the bed when I wanted it. And yet, you know, it's kind of natural to hide under the bed when you are up to anything private. They sets down, then, and the king says:

"Well, what is it? and cut it middlin' short, because it's better for us to be down there a whoopin'-up the mournin', than up here givin' 'em a chance to talk us over."

"Well, this is it, Capet. I ain't easy; I ain't comfortable. That doctor lays on my mind. I wanted to know your plans. I've got a notion, and I think it's a sound one."

"What is it, duke?"

"That we better glide out of this, before three in the morning, and clip it down the river with what we've got. Specially, seeing we got it so easy—*given* back to us, flung at our heads, as you may say, when of course we allowed to have to steal it back. I'm for knocking off and lighting out."

That made me feel pretty bad. About an hour or two ago, it would a been a little different, but now it made me feel bad and disappointed. The king rips out and says:

"What! And not sell out the rest o' the property? March off like a passel o' fools and leave eight or nine thous'n dollars' worth o' property layin' around jest sufferin' to be scooped in?—and all good salable stuff, too."

The duke he grumbled; said the bag of gold was enough, and he didn't want to go no deeper—didn't want to rob a lot of orphans of *everything* they had.

"Why, how you talk!" says the king. "We shan't rob 'em of nothing at all but jest this money. The people that *buys* the property is the suff'rers; because as soon's it's found out 'at we didn't own it—which won't be long after we've slid—the sale won't be valid, and it'll all go back to the estate. These-yer orphans 'll git their house back agin, and that's enough for *them;* they're young and spry, and k'n easy earn a livin'. *They* ain't agoing to suffer. Why, jest think—there's thous'n's and thous'n's that ain't nigh so well off. Bless you, *they* ain't got noth'n to complain of."

Well, the king he talked him blind; so at last he give in, and said all right, but said he believed it was blame foolishness to stay, and that doctor hanging over them. But the king says:

"Cuss the doctor! What do we k'yer for *him?* Hain't we got all the fools in town on our side? and ain't that a big enough majority in any town?"

So they got ready to go down stairs again. The duke says:

"I don't think we put that money in a good place."

That cheered me up. I'd begun to think I warn't going to get a hint of no kind to help me. The king says:

"Why?"

"Because Mary Jane 'll be in mourning from this out; and first you know the nigger that does up the rooms will get an order to box these duds up and put 'em away; and do you reckon a nigger can run across money and not borrow some of it?"

"Your head's level, agin, duke," says the king; and he come a fumbling under the curtain two or three foot from where I was. I stuck tight to the wall, and kept mighty still, though quivery; and I wondered what them fellows would say to me if they catched me; and I tried to think what I'd better do if they did catch me. But the king he got the bag before I could think more than about a half a thought, and he never suspicioned I was around. They took and shoved the bag through a rip in the straw tick that was under the feather bed, and crammed it in a foot or two amongst the straw and said it was all right, now, because a nigger only makes up the feather bed, and don't turn over the straw tick only about twice a year, and so it warn't in no danger of getting stole, now.

But I knowed better. I had it out of there before they was halfway down stairs. I groped along up to my cubby, and hid it there till I could get a chance to do better. I judged I better hide it outside of the house somewheres, because if they missed it they would give the house a good ransacking. I knowed that very well. Then I turned in, with my clothes all on; but I couldn't a gone to sleep, if I'd a wanted to, I was in such a sweat to get through with the business. By-and-by I heard the king and the duke come up; so I rolled off of my pallet and laid with my chin at the top of my ladder and waited to see if anything was going to happen. But nothing did.

So I held on till all the late sounds had quit and the early ones hadn't begun, yet; and then I slipped down the ladder.

Chapter XXVII

I crept to their doors and listened; they was snoring, so I tip-toed along, and got down stairs all right. There warn't a sound anywheres. I peeped through a crack of the dining-room door, and see the men that was watching the corpse all sound asleep on their chairs. The door was open into the parlor, where the corpse was laying, and there was a candle in both rooms, I passed along, and the parlor door was open; but I see there warn't nobody in there but the remainders of Peter; so I shoved on by; but the front door was locked, and the key wasn't there. Just then I heard somebody coming down the stairs, back behind me. I run in the parlor, and took a swift look around, and the only place I see to hide the bag was in the coffin. The lid was shoved along about a foot, showing the dead man's face down in there, with a wet cloth over it, and his shroud on. I tucked the money-bag in under the lid, just down beyond where his hands was crossed, which made me creep, they was so cold, and then I run back across the room and in behind the door.

The person coming was Mary Jane. She went to the coffin, very soft, and kneeled down and looked in; then she put up her handkerchief and I see she begun to cry, though I couldn't hear her, and her back was to me. I slid out, and as I passed the dining-room I thought I'd make sure them watchers hadn't seen me; so I looked through the crack and everything was all right. They hadn't stirred.

I slipped up to bed, feeling ruther blue, on accounts of the thing playing out that way after I had took so much trouble and run so much resk about it. Says I, if it could stay where it is, all right; because when we get down the river a hundred mile or two, I could write back to Mary Jane, and she could dig him up again and get it; but that ain't the thing that's going to happen; the thing that's going to happen is, the money 'll be found when they come to screw on the lid. Then the king 'll get it again, and it 'll be a long day before he gives anybody another chance to smouch it from him. Of course I *wanted* to slide down and get it out of there, but I dasn't try it. Every minute it was getting earlier, now, and pretty soon some of them watchers would begin to stir, and I might get catched—catched with six thousand dollars in my hands that nobody hadn't hired me to take care of. I don't wish to be mixed up in no such business as that, I says to myself.

When I got down stairs in the morning, the parlor was shut up, and the watchers was gone. There warn't nobody around but the family and the widow Bartley and our tribe. I watched their faces to see if anything had been happening, but I couldn't tell.

Towards the middle of the day the undertaker come, with his man, and they set the coffin in the middle of the room on a couple of chairs, and then set all our chairs in rows, and borrowed more from the neighbors till the hall and the parlor and the dining-room was full. I see the coffin lid was the way it was before, but I dasn't go to look in under it, with folks around.

Then the people begun to flock in, and the beats and the girls took seats in the front row at the head of the coffin, and for a half an hour the people filed around slow, in single rank, and looked down at the dead man's face a minute, and some dropped in a tear, and it was all very still and solemn, only the girls and the beats holding handkerchiefs to their eyes and keeping their heads bent, and sobbing a little. There warn't no other sound but the scraping of the feet on the floor, and blowing noses—because people always blows them more at a funeral than they do at other places except church.

When the place was packed full, the undertaker he slid around in his black gloves with his softy soothering ways, putting on the last touches, and getting people and things all shipshape and comfortable, and making no more sound than a cat. He never spoke; he moved people around, he squeezed in late ones, he opened up passage-ways, and done it all with nods, and signs with his hands. Then he took his place over against the wall. He was the softest, glidingest, stealthiest man I ever see; and there warn't no more smile to him than there is to a ham.

They had borrowed a melodeum[6]—a sick one; and when everything was ready, a young woman set down and worked it, and it was pretty skreeky and colicky, and everybody joined in and sung, and Peter was the only one that had a good thing, according to my notion. Then the Reverend Hobson opened up, slow and solemn, and begun to talk; and straight off the most outrageous row busted out in the cellar a body ever heard; it was only one dog, but he made a most powerful racket, and he kept it up, right along; the parson he had to stand there, over the coffin, and wait—you couldn't hear yourself

6. A melodeon, small keyboard organ.

think. It was right down awkward, and nobody didn't seem to know what to do. But pretty soon they see that long-legged undertaker make a sign to the preacher as much as to say, "Don't you worry—just depend on me." Then he stooped down and begun to glide along the wall, just his shoulders showing over the people's heads. So he glided along, and the pow-wow and racket getting more and more outrageous all the time; and at last, when he had gone around two sides of the room, he disappears down cellar. Then, in about two seconds we heard a whack, and the dog he finished up with a most amazing howl or two, and then everything was dead still, and the parson begun his solemn talk where he left off. In a minute or two here comes this undertaker's back and shoulders gliding along the wall again; and so he glided, and glided, around three sides of the room, and then rose up, and shaded his mouth with his hands, and stretched his neck out towards the preacher, over the people's heads, and says, in a kind of a coarse whisper, *"He had a rat!"* Then he drooped down and glided along the wall again to his place. You could see it was a great satisfaction to the people, because naturally they wanted to know. A little thing like that don't cost nothing, and it's just the little things that makes a man to be looked up to and liked. There warn't no more popular man in town than what that undertaker was.

Well, the funeral sermon was very good, but pison long and tiresome; and then the king he shoved in and got off some of his usual rubbage, and at last the job was through, and the undertaker begun to sneak up on the coffin with his screw-driver. I was in a sweat then, and watched him pretty keen. But he never meddled at all; just slid the lid along, as soft as mush, and screwed it down tight and fast. So there I was! I didn't know whether the money was in there, or not. So, says I, spose somebody has hogged that bag on the sly?—now how do *I* know whether to write to Mary Jane or not? 'Spose she dug him up and didn't find nothing—what would she think of me? Blame it, I says, I might get hunted up and jailed; I'd better lay low and keep dark, and not write at all; the thing's awful mixed, now; trying to better it, I've worsened it a hundred times, and I wish to goodness I'd just let it alone, dad fetch the whole business!

They buried him, and we come back home, and I went to watching faces again—I couldn't help it, and I couldn't rest easy. But nothing come of it; the faces didn't tell me nothing.

The king he visited around, in the evening, and sweetened every body up, and made himself ever so friendly; and he give out the idea that his congregation over in England would be in a sweat about him, so he must hurry and settle up the estate right away, and leave for home. He was very sorry he was so pushed, and so was everybody; they wished he could stay longer, but they said they could see it couldn't be done. And he said of course him and William would take the girls home with them; and that pleased everybody too, because then the girls would be well fixed, and amongst their own relations; and it pleased the girls, too—tickled them so they clean forgot they ever had a trouble in the world; and told him to sell out as quick as he wanted to, they would be ready. Them poor things was that glad and happy it made my heart ache to see them getting fooled and lied to so, but I didn't see no safe way for me to chip in and change the general tune.

Well, blamed if the king didn't bill the house and the niggers and all the property for auction straight off—sale two days after the funeral; but anybody could buy private beforehand if they wanted to.

So the next day after the funeral, along about noontime, the girls' joy got the first jolt; a couple of nigger traders come along, and the king sold them the niggers reasonable, for three-day drafts[7] as they called it, and away they went, the two sons up the river to Memphis, and their mother down the river to Orleans. I thought them poor girls and them niggers would break their hearts for grief; they cried around each other, and took on so it most made me down sick to see it. The girls said they hadn't ever dreamed of seeing the family separated or sold away from the town. I can't ever get it out of my memory, the sight of them poor miserable girls and niggers hanging around each other's necks and crying; and I reckon I couldn't a stood it all but would a had to bust out and tell on our gang if I hadn't knowed the sale warn't no account and the niggers would be back home in a week or two.

The thing made a big stir in the town, too, and a good many come out flat-footed and said it was scandalous to separate the mother and the children that way. It injured the frauds some; but the old fool he bulled right along, spite of all the duke could say or do, and I tell you the duke was powerful uneasy.

Next day was auction day. About broad-day in the morning, the king and the duke come up in the garret and woke me up, and I see by their look that there was trouble. The king says:

"Was you in my room night before last?"

"No, your majesty"—which was the way I always called him when nobody but our gang warn't around.

"Was you in there yisterday er last night?"

"No, your majesty."

"Honor bright, now—no lies."

"Honor bright, your majesty, I'm telling you the truth. I hain't been anear your room since Miss Mary Jane took you and the duke and showed it to you."

The duke says:

"Have you seen anybody else go in there?"

"No, your grace, not as I remember, I believe."

"Stop and think."

I studied a while, and see my chance, then I says:

"Well, I see the niggers go in there several times."

Both of them give a little jump; and looked like they hadn't ever expected it, and then like they *had*. Then the duke says:

"What, *all* of them?"

"No—leastways not all at once. That is, I don't think I ever see them all come *out* at once but just one time."

"Hello—when was that?"

"It was the day we had the funeral. In the morning. It warn't early, because I overslept. I was just starting down the ladder, and I see them."

"Well, go on, *go on*—what did they do? How'd they act?"

"They didn't do nothing. And they didn't act anyway, much, as fur as I see. They tip-toed away; so I seen, easy enough, that they'd shoved in there to do up your majesty's room, or something, sposing you was up; and found you *warn't* up, and so they was hoping to slide out of the way of trouble without waking you up, if they hadn't already waked you up."

7. Bank drafts or checks payable three days later.

"Great guns, *this* is a go!" says the king; and both of them looked pretty sick, and tolerable silly. They stood there a thinking and scratching their heads, a minute, and then the duke he bust into a kind of a little raspy chuckle, and says:

"It does beat all, how neat the niggers played their hand. They let on to be *sorry* they was going out of this region! and I believed they *was* sorry. And so did you, and so did everybody. Don't ever tell *me* any more that a nigger ain't got any histrionic talent. Why, the way they played that thing, it would fool *anybody*. In my opinion there's a fortune in 'em. If I had capital and a theatre, I wouldn't want a better lay out than that—and here we've gone and sold 'em for a song. Yes, and ain't privileged to sing the song, yet. Say, where *is* that song?—that draft."

"In the bank for to be collected. Where *would* it be?"

"Well, *that's* all right then, thank goodness."

Says I, kind of timid-like:

"Is something gone wrong?"

The king whirls on me and rips out:

"None o' your business! You keep your head shet, and mind y'r own affairs—if you got any. Long as you're in this town, don't you forget *that,* you hear?" Then he says to the duke, "We got to jest swaller it, and say noth'n: mum's the word for *us*."

As they was starting down the ladder, the duke he chuckles again, and says:

"Quick sales *and* small profits! It's a good business—yes."

The king snarls around on him and says,

"I was trying to do for the best, in sellin' 'm out so quick. If the profits has turned out to be none, lackin' considable, and none to carry, is it my fault any more'n it's yourn?"

"Well, *they'd* be in this house yet, and we *wouldn't* if I could a got my advice listened to."

The king sassed back, as much as was safe for him, and then swapped around and lit into *me* again. He give me down the banks[8] for not coming and *telling* him I see the niggers come out of his room acting that way—said any fool would a *knowed* something was up. And then waltzed in and cussed *himself* a while; and said it all come of him not laying late and taking his natural rest that morning, and he'd be blamed if he'd ever do it again. So they went off a jawing; and I felt dreadful glad I'd worked it all off onto the niggers and yet hadn't done the niggers no harm by it.

Chapter XXVIII

By-and-by it was getting-up time; so I come down the ladder and started for down stairs, but as I come to the girls' room, the door was open, and I see Mary Jane setting by her old hair trunk, which was open and she'd been packing things in it—getting ready to go to England. But she had stopped now, with a folded gown in her lap, and had her face in her hands, crying. I felt awful bad to see it; of course anybody would. I went in there, and says:

"Miss Mary Jane, you can't abear to see people in trouble, and *I* can't—most always. Tell me about it."

8. To scream insults or criticism (slang).

So she done it. And it was the niggers—I just expected it. She said the beautiful trip to England was most about spoiled for her; she didn't know *how* she was ever going to be happy there, knowing the mother and the children warn't ever going to see each other no more—and then busted out bitterer than ever, and flung up her hands, and says:

"Oh, dear, dear, to think they ain't *ever* going to see each other any more!"

"But they *will*—and inside of two weeks—and I *know* it!" says I.

Laws it was out before I could think!—and before I could budge, she throws her arms around my neck, and told me to say it *again,* say it *again,* say it *again!*

I see I had spoke too sudden, and said too much, and was in a close place. I asked her to let me think a minute; and she set there, very impatient and excited, and handsome, but looking kind of happy and eased-up, like a person that's had a tooth pulled out. So I went to studying it out. I says to myself, I reckon a body that ups and tells the truth when he is in a tight place, is taking considerable many resks, though I ain't had no experience, and can't say for certain; but it looks so to me, anyway; and yet here's a case where I'm blest if it don't look to me like the truth is better, and actuly *safer,* than pa lie. I must lay it by in my mind, and think it over some time or other, it's so kind of strange and unregular. I never see nothing like it. Well, I says to myself at last, I'm agoing to chance it; I'll up and tell the truth this time, though it does seem most like setting down on a kag of powder and touching it off just to see where you'll go to. Then I says:

"Miss Mary Jane, is there any place out of town a little ways, where you could go and stay three or four days?"

"Yes—Mr. Lothrop's. Why?"

"Never mind why, yet. If I'll tell you how I know the niggers will see each other again—inside of two weeks—here in this house—and *prove* how I know it—will you go to Mr. Lothrop's and stay four days?"

"Four days!" she says; "I'll stay a year!"

"All right," I says, "I don't want nothing more out of *you* than just your word—I druther have it than another man's kiss-the-Bible." She smiled, and reddened up very sweet, and I says, "If you don't mind it, I'll shut the door—and bolt it."

Then I come back and set down again, and says:

"Don't you holler. Just set still, and take it like a man. I got to tell the truth, and you want to brace up, Miss Mary, because it's a bad kind, and going to be hard to take, but there ain't no help for it. These uncles of yourn ain't no uncles at all—they're a couple of frauds—regular dead-beats. There, now we're over the worst of it—you can stand the rest middling easy."

It jolted her up like everything, of course; but I was over the shoal water now, so I went right along, her eyes a blazing higher and higher all the time, and told her every blame thing, from where we first struck that young fool going up to the steamboat, clear through to where she flung herself onto the king's breast at the front door and he kissed her sixteen or seventeen times—and then up she jumps, with her face afire like sunset, and says:

"The brute! Come—don't waste a minute—not a *second*—we'll have them tarred and feathered, and flung in the river!"[9]

9. The victim of this fairly commonplace mob punishment was tied to a rail, smeared with hot tar, and covered with feathers. Then the victim would be ridden out of town on the rail to the jeers of the mob.

Says I;

"Cert'nly. But do you mean, *before* you go to Mr. Lothrop's, or—"

"Oh," she says, "what am I *thinking* about!" she says, and set right down again. "Don't mind what I said—please don't—you *won't,* now, *will* you?" Laying her silky hand on mine in that kind of a way that I said I would die first. "I never thought, I was so stirred up," she says; "now go on, and I won't do so any more. You tell me what to do, and whatever you say, I'll do it."

"Well," I says, "it's a rough gang, them two frauds, and I'm fixed so I got to travel with them a while longer, whether I want to or not—I druther not tell you why—and if you was to blow on them this town would get me out of their claws, and I'd be all right, but there'd be another person that you don't know about who'd be in big trouble. Well, we got to save *him,* hain't we? Of course. Well, then, we won't blow on them."

Saying them words put a good idea in my head. I see how maybe I could get me and Jim rid of the frauds; get them jailed here, and then leave. But I didn't want to run the raft in day-time, without anybody aboard to answer questions but me; so I didn't want the plan to begin working till pretty late to-night. I says:

"Miss Mary Jane, I'll tell you what we'll do—and you won't have to stay at Mr. Lothrop's so long, nuther. How fur is it?"

"A little short of four miles—right out in the country, back here."

"Well, that'll answer. Now you go along out there, and lay low till nine or half-past, to-night, and then get them to fetch you home again—tell them you've thought of something. If you get here before eleven, put a candle in this window, and if I don't turn up, wait *till* eleven, and *then* if I don't turn up it means I'm gone, and out of the way, and safe. Then you come out and spread the news around, and get these beats jailed."

"Good," she says, "I'll do it."

"And if it just happens so that I don't get away, but get took up along with them, you must up and say I told you the whole thing beforehand, and you must stand by me all you can."

"Stand by you, indeed I will. They sha'n't touch a hair of your head!" she says, and I see her nostrils spread and her eyes snap when she said it, too.

"If I get away, I sha'n't be here," I says, "to prove these rapscallions ain't your uncles, and I couldn't do it if I *was* here. I could swear they was beats and bummers, that's all; though that's worth something. Well, there's others can do that better than what I can—and they're people that ain't going to be doubted as quick as I'd be. I'll tell you how to find them. Gimme a pencil and a piece of paper. There—'*Royal Nonesuch, Bricksville.*' Put it away, and don't lose it. When the court wants to find out something about these two, let them send up to Bricksville and say they've got the men that played the Royal Nonesuch, and ask for some witnesses—why, you'll have that entire town down here before you can hardly wink, Miss Mary. And they'll come a-biling, too."

I judged we had got everything fixed about right, now. So I says:

"Just let the auction go right along, and don't worry. Nobody don't have to pay for the things they buy till a whole day after the auction, on accounts of the short notice, and they ain't going out of this till they get that money—and the way we've fixed it the sale ain't going to count, and they ain't going to *get* no money. It's just like the way it was with the niggers—it warn't no sale, and the niggers will be back before long. Why, they can't collect the money for the *niggers,* yet—they're in the worst kind of a fix, Miss Mary."

"Well," she says, "I'll run down to breakfast now, and then I'll start straight for Mr. Lothrop's."

"'Deed, *that* ain't the ticket, Miss Mary Jane," I says, "by no manner of means; go *before* breakfast."

"Why?"

"What did you reckon I wanted you to go at all for, Miss Mary?"

"Well, I never thought—and come to think, I don't know. What was it?"

"Why, it's because you ain't one of these leather-face people. I don't want no better book than what your face is. A body can set down and read it off like coarse paint. Do you reckon you can go and face your uncles, when they come to kiss you good-morning, and never—"

"There, there, don't! Yes, I'll go before breakfast—I'll be glad to. And leave my sisters with them?"

"Yes—never mind about them. They've got to stand it yet a while. They might suspicion something if all of you was to go. I don't want you to see them, nor your sisters, nor nobody in this town—if a neighbor was to ask how is your uncles this morning, your face would tell something. No, you go right along, Miss Mary Jane, and I'll fix it with all of them. I'll tell Miss Susan to give your love to your uncles and say you've went away for a few hours for to get a little rest and change, or to see a friend, and you'll be back to-night or early in the morning."

"Gone to see a friend is all right, but I won't have my love given to them."

"Well, then, it sha'n't be." It was well enough to tell *her* so—no harm in it. It was only a little thing to do, and no trouble; and it's the little things that smoothes people's roads the most, down here below; it would make Mary Jane comfortable, and it wouldn't cost nothing. Then I says: "There's one more thing—that bag of money."

"Well, they've got that; and it makes me feel pretty silly to think *how* they got it."

"No, you're out, there. They hain't got it."

"Why, who's got it?"

"I wish I knowed, but I don't. I *had* it, because I stole it from them: and I stole it to give to you; and I know where I hid it, but I'm afraid it ain't there no more. I'm awful sorry, Miss Mary Jane, I'm just as sorry as I can be; but I done the best I could; I did, honest. I come nigh getting caught, and I had to shove it into the first place I come to, and run—and it warn't a good place."

"Oh, stop blaming yourself—it's too bad to do it, and I won't allow it— you couldn't help it; it wasn't your fault. Where did you hide it?"

I didn't want to set her to thinking about her troubles again; and I couldn't seem to get my mouth to tell her what would make her see that corpse laying in the coffin with that bag of money on his stomach. So for a minute I didn't say nothing—then I says:

"I'd ruther not *tell* you where I put it, Miss Mary Jane, if you don't mind letting me off; but I'll write it for you on a piece of paper, and you can read it along the road to Mr. Lothrop's; if you want to. Do you reckon that'll do?"

"Oh, yes."

So I wrote: "I put it in the coffin. It was in there when you was crying there, away in the night. I was behind the door, and I was mighty sorry for you, Miss Mary Jane."

It made my eyes water a little, to remember her crying there all by herself in the night, and them devils laying there right under her own roof, shaming her and robbing her; and when I folded it up and give it to her, I see the water come into her eyes, too; and she shook me by the hand, hard, and says:

"Good-bye—I'm going to do everything just as you've told me; and if I don't ever see you again, I sha'n't ever forget you, and I'll think of you a many and a many a time, and I'll *pray* for you, too!"—and she was gone.

Pray for me! I reckoned if she knowed me she'd take a job that was more nearer her size. But I bet she done it, just the same—she was just that kind. She had the grit to pray for Judus if she took the notion—there warn't no backdown to her, I judge. You may say what you want to, but in my opinion she had more sand in her than any girl I ever see; in my opinion she was just full of sand.[1] It sounds like flattery, but it ain't no flattery. And when it comes to beauty—and goodness too—she lays over them all. I hain't ever seen her since that time that I see her go out of that door; no, I hain't ever seen her since, but I reckon I've thought of her a many and a many a million times, and of her saying she would pray for me; and if ever I'd a thought it would do any good for me to pray for *her*, blamed if I wouldn't a done it or bust.

Well, Mary Jane she lit out the back way, I reckon; because nobody see her go. When I struck Susan and the hare-lip, I says:

"What's the name of them people over on t'other side of the river that you all goes to see sometimes?"

They says:

"There's several; but it's the Proctors, mainly."

"That's the name," I says; "I most forgot it. Well, Miss Mary Jane she told me to tell you she's gone over there in a dreadful hurry—one of them's sick."

"Which one?"

"I don't know; leastways I kinder forget; but I think it's—"

"Sakes alive, I hope it ain't *Hanner?*"

"I'm sorry to say it," I says, "but Hanner's the very one."

"My goodness—and she so well only last week! Is she took bad?"

"It ain't no name for it. They set up with her all night, Miss Mary Jane said, and they don't think she'll last many hours."

"Only think of that, now! What's the matter with her!"

I couldn't think of anything reasonable, right off that way, so I says:

"Mumps."

"Mumps your granny! They don't set up with people that's got the mumps."

"They don't, don't they? You better bet they do with *these* mumps. These mumps is different. It's a new kind, Miss Mary Jane said."

"How's it a new kind?"

"Because it's mixed up with other things."

"What other things?"

"Well, measles, and whooping-cough, and erysiplas, and consumption, and yaller janders, and brain fever, and I don't know what all."

"My land! And they call it the *mumps?*"

"That's what Miss Mary Jane said."

"Well, what in the nation do they call it the *mumps* for?"

---

1. Courage.

"Why, because it *is* the mumps. That's what it starts with."

"Well, ther' ain't no sense in it. A body might stump his toe, and take pison, and fall down the well, and break his neck, and bust his brains out, and somebody come along and ask what killed him, and some numskull up and say, 'Why, he stumped his *toe*.' Would ther' be any sense in that? *No*. And ther' ain't no sense in *this*, nuther. Is it ketching?"

"Is it *ketching*? Why, how you talk. Is a *harrow* catching?—in the dark? If you don't hitch onto one tooth, you're bound to on another, ain't you? And you can't get away with that tooth without fetching the whole harrow along, can you? Well, these kind of mumps is a kind of a harrow, as you may say— and it ain't no slouch of a harrow, nuther, you come to get it hitched on good."

"Well, it's awful, *I* think," says the hare-lip. "I'll go to Uncle Harvey and—"

"Oh, yes," I says, "I *would*. Of *course* I would. I wouldn't lose no time."

"Well, why wouldn't you?"

"Just look at it a minute, and maybe you can see. Hain't your uncles obleeged to get along home to England as fast as they can? And do you reckon they'd be mean enough to go off and leave you to go all that journey by yourselves? *You* know they'll wait for you. So fur, so good. Your uncle Harvey's a preacher, ain't he? Very well, then; is a *preacher* going to deceive a steamboat clerk? is he going to deceive a *ship clerk?*—so as to get them to let Miss Mary Jane go aboard? Now *you* know he ain't. What *will* he do, then? Why, he'll say, 'It's a great pity, but my church matters has got to get along the best way they can; for my niece has been exposed to the dreadful pluribus-unum[2] mumps, and so it's my bounden duty to set down here and wait the three months it takes to show on her if she's got it.' But never mind, if you think it's best to tell your uncle Harvey—"

"Shucks, and stay fooling around here when we could all be having good times in England whilst we was waiting to find out whether Mary Jane's got it or not? Why, you talk like a muggins."[3]

"Well, anyway, maybe you better tell some of the neighbors."

"Listen at that, now. You do beat all, for natural stupidness. Can't you *see* that *they'd* go and tell? Ther' ain't no way but just to not tell anybody at *all*."

"Well, maybe you're right—yes, I judge you *are* right."

"But I reckon we ought to tell Uncle Harvey she's gone out a while, any-way, so he wont be uneasy about her?"

"Yes, Miss Mary Jane she wanted you to do that. She says, 'Tell them to give Uncle Harvey and William my love and a kiss, and say I've run over the river to see Mr.—Mr.—what *is* the name of that rich family your uncle Peter used to think so much of?—I mean the one that—"

"Why, you must mean the Apthorps, ain't it?"

"Of course; bother them kind of names, a body can't ever seem to remember them, half the time, somehow. Yes, she said, say she has run over for to ask the Apthorps to be sure and come to the auction and buy this house, because she allowed her uncle Peter would ruther they had it than anybody else; and she's going to stick to them till they say they'll come, and then, if she ain't too tired, she's coming home; and if she is, she'll be home in the morning anyway. She said, don't say nothing about the Proctors, but only

---

2. Huck reaches for the handiest Latin phrase he could be expected to know; meaning "out of many, one" (the motto of the United States).
3. A fool.

about the Apthorps—which'll be perfectly true, because she *is* going there to speak about their buying the house; I know it, because she told me so, herself."

"All right," they said, and cleared out to lay for their uncles, and give them the love and the kisses, and tell them the message.

Everything was all right now. The girls wouldn't say nothing because they wanted to go to England; and the king and the duke would ruther Mary Jane was off working for the auction than around in reach of Doctor Robinson. I felt very good; I judged I had done it pretty neat—I reckoned Tom Sawyer couldn't a done it no neater himself. Of course he would a throwed more style into it, but I can't do that very handy, not being brung up to it.

Well, they held the auction in the public square, along towards the end of the afternoon, and it strung along, and strung along, and the old man he was on hand and looking his level piousest, up there longside of the auctioneer, and chipping in a little Scripture, now and then, or a little goody-goody saying, of some kind, and the duke he was around goo-gooing for sympathy all he knowed how, and just spreading himself generly.

But by-and-by the thing dragged through, and everything was sold. Everything but a little old trifling lot in the graveyard. So they'd got to work *that* off—I never see such a girafft as the king was for wanting to swallow *everything*. Well, whilst they was at it, a steamboat landed, and in about two minutes up comes a crowd a whooping and yelling and laughing and carrying on, and singing out:

"*Here's* your opposition line! here's your two sets o' heirs to old Peter Wilks—and you pays your money and you takes your choice!"

Chapter XXIX

They was fetching a very nice looking old gentleman along, and a nice looking younger one, with his right arm in a sling. And my souls, how the people yelled, and laughed, and kept it up. But I didn't see no joke about it, and I judged it would strain the duke and the king some to see any. I reckoned they'd turn pale. But no, nary a pale did *they* turn. The duke he never let on he suspicioned what was up, but just went a goo-gooing around, happy and satisfied, like a jug that's googling out buttermilk; and as for the king, he just gazed and gazed down sorrowful on them newcomers like it give him the stomach-ache in his very heart to think there could be such frauds and rascals in the world. Oh, he done it admirable. Lots of the principal people gethered around the king, to let him see they was on his side. That old gentleman that had just come looked all puzzled to death. Pretty soon he begun to speak, and I see, straight off, he pronounced *like* an Englishman, not the king's way, though the king's *was* pretty good, for an imitation. I can't give the old gent's words, nor I can't imitate him; but he turned around to the crowd, and says, about like this:

"This is a surprise to me which I wasn't looking for; and I'll acknowledge, candid and frank, I ain't very well fixed to meet it and answer it; for my brother and me has had misfortunes, he's broke his arm, and our baggage got put off at a town above here, last night in the night by a mistake. I am Peter Wilks's brother Harvey, and this is his brother William, which can't hear nor speak—and can't even make signs to amount to much, now 't he's only got one hand to work them with. We are who we say we are; and in a day or two, when I get the baggage, I can prove it. But, up till then, I won't say nothing more, but go to the hotel and wait."

So him and the new dummy[4] started off; and the king he laughs, and blethers out:

"Broke his arm—*very* likely *ain't* it?—and very convenient, too, for a fraud that's got to make signs, and hain't learnt how. Lost their baggage! That's *mighty* good!—and mighty ingenious—under the *circumstances!"*

So he laughed again; and so did everybody else, except three or four, or maybe half a dozen. One of these was that doctor; another one was a sharp looking gentleman, with a carpet-bag of the old-fashioned kind made out of carpet-stuff, that had just come off of the steamboat and was talking to him in a low voice, and glancing towards the king now and then and nodding their heads—it was Levi Bell, the lawyer that was gone up to Louisville; and another one was a big rough husky that come along and listened to all the old gentleman said, and was listening to the king now. And when the king got done, this husky up and says:

"Say, looky here; if you are Harvey Wilks, when'd you come to this town?"

"The day before the funeral, friend," says the king.

"But what time o' day?"

"In the evenin'—'bout an hour er two before sundown."

"How'd you come?"

"I come down on the *Susan Powell,* from Cincinnati."

"Well, then, how'd you come to be up at the Pint in the *mornin'*—in a canoe?"

"I warn't up at the Pint in the mornin'."

"It's a lie."

Several of them jumped for him and begged him not to talk that way to an old man and a preacher.

"Preacher be hanged, he's a fraud and a lair. He was up at the Pint that mornin'. I live up there, don't I? Well, I was up there, and he was up there. I *see* him there. He come in a canoe, along with Tim Collins and a boy."

The doctor he up and says:

"Would you know the boy again if you was to see him, Hines?"

"I reckon I would, but I don't know. Why, yonder he is, now. I know him perfectly easy."

It was me he pointed at. The doctor says:

"Neighbors. I don't know whether the new couple is frauds or not; but if *these* two ain't frauds, I am an idiot, that's all. I think it's our duty to see that they don't get away from here till we've looked into this thing. Come along, Hines; come along, the rest of you. We'll take these fellows to the tavern and affront them with t'other couple, and I reckon we'll find out *something* before we get through."

It was nuts for the crowd, though maybe not for the king's friends; so we all started. It was about sundown. The doctor he led me along by the hand, and was plenty kind enough, but he never let *go* my hand.

We all got in a big room in the hotel, and lit up some candles, and fetched in the new couple. First, the doctor says:

"I don't wish to be too hard on these two men, but *I* think they're frauds, and they may have complices that we don't know nothing about. If they

4. A person who can't hear or speak.

have, won't the complices get away with that bag of gold Peter Wilks left? It ain't unlikely. If these men ain't frauds, they won't object to sending for that money and letting us keep it till they prove they're all right—ain't that so?"

Everybody agreed to that. So I judged they had our gang in a pretty tight place, right at the outstart. But the king he only looked sorrowful, and says:

"Gentlemen, I wish the money was there, for I ain't got no disposition to throw anything in the way of a fair, open, out-and-out investigation o' this misable business; but alas, the money ain't there; you k'n send and see, if you want to."

"Where is it, then?"

"Well, when my niece give it to me to keep for her, I took and hid it inside o' the straw tick o' my bed, not wishin' to bank it for the few days we'd be here, and considerin' the bed a safe place, we not bein' used to niggers, and suppos'n' 'em honest, like servants in England. The niggers stole it the very next mornin' after I had went down stairs; and when I sold 'em, I hadn't missed the money yit, so they got clean away with it. My servant here k'n tell you 'bout it gentlemen."

The doctor and several said "Shucks!" and I see nobody didn't altogether believe him. One man asked me if I see the niggers steal it. I said no, but I see them sneaking out of the room and hustling away, and I never thought nothing, only I reckoned they was afraid they had waked up my master and was trying to get away before he made trouble with them. That was all they asked me. Then the doctor whirls on me and says:

"Are *you* English too?"

I says yes; and him and some others laughed, and said, "Stuff!"

Well, then they sailed in on the general investigation, and there we had it, up and down, hour in, hour out, and nobody never said a word about supper, nor ever seemed to think about it—and so they kept it up, and kept it up; and it *was* the worst mixed-up thing you ever see. They made the king tell his yarn, and they made the old gentleman tell his'n; and anybody but a lot of prejudiced chuckleheads would a *seen* that the old gentleman was spinning truth and t'other one lies. And by-and-by they had me up to tell what I knowed. The king he give me a left-handed look out of the corner of his eye, and so I knowed enough to talk on the right side. I begun to tell about Sheffield, and how we lived there, and all about the English Wilkses, and so on; but I didn't get pretty fur till the doctor begun to laugh; and Levi Bell, the lawyer says:

"Set down, my boy, I wouldn't strain myself, if I was you. I reckon you ain't used to lying, it don't seem to come handy; what you want is practice. You do it pretty awkward."

I didn't care nothing for the compliment, but I was glad to be let off, anyway.

The doctor he started to say something, and turns and says:

"If you'd been in town at first, Levi Bell—"

The king broke in and reached out his hand, and says:

"Why, is this my poor dead brother's old friend that he's wrote so often about?"

The lawyer and him shook hands, and the lawyer smiled and looked pleased, and they talked right along a while, and then got to one side and talked low; and at last the lawyer speaks up and says:

"That'll fix it. I'll take the order and send it, along with your brother's, and then they'll know it's all right."

So they got some paper and a pen, and the king he set down and twisted his head to one side, and chawed his tongue, and scrawled off something; and then they give the pen to the duke—and then for the first time, the duke looked sick. But he took the pen and wrote. So then the lawyer turns to the new old gentleman and says:

"You and your brother please write a line or two and sign your names."

The old gentleman wrote, but nobody couldn't read it. The lawyer looked powerful astonished, and says:

"Well, it beats *me*"—and snaked a lot of old letters out of his pocket, and examined them, and then examined the old man's writing, and then *them* again; and then says: "These old letters is from Harvey Wilks; and here's *these* two's handwritings, and anybody can see *they* didn't write them" (the king and the duke looked sold and foolish, I tell you, to see how the lawyer had took them in), "and here's *this* old gentleman's handwriting, and anybody can tell, easy enough, *he* didn't write them—fact is, the scratches he makes ain't properly *writing*, at all. Now here's some letters from—"

The new old gentleman says:

"If you please, let me explain. Nobody can read my hand but my brother there—so he copies for me. It's *his* hand you've got there, not mine."

"*Well!*" says the lawyer, "this *is* a state of things. I've got some of William's letters too; so if you'll get him to write a line or so we can com—"

"He *can't* write with his left hand," says the old gentleman. "If he could use his right hand, you would see that he wrote his own letters and mine too. Look at both, please—they're by the same hand."

The lawyer done it, and says:

"I believe it's so—and if it ain't so, there's a heap stronger resemblance than I'd noticed before, anyway. Well, well, well! I thought we was right on the track of a slution, but it's gone to grass, partly. But anyway, *one* thing is proved—*these* two ain't either of 'em Wilkses"—and he wagged his head towards the king and the duke.

Well, what do you think?—that muleheaded old fool wouldn't give in *then!* Indeed he wouldn't. Said it warn't no fair test. Said his brother William was the cussedest joker in the world, and hadn't *tried* to write—*he* see William was going to play one of his jokes the minute he put the pen to paper. And so he warmed up and went warbling and warbling right along, till he was actuly beginning to believe what he was saying, *himself*—but pretty soon the new old gentleman broke in, and says:

"I've thought of something. Is there anybody here that helped to lay out my br—helped to lay out the late Peter Wilks for burying?"

"Yes," says somebody, "me and Ab Turner done it. We're both here."

Then the old man turns towards the king, and says:

"Peraps this gentleman can tell me what was tatooed on his breast?"

Blamed if the king didn't have to brace up mighty quick, or he'd a squshed down like a bluff bank that the river has cut under, it took him so sudden—and mind you, it was a thing that was calculated to make most *anybody* sqush to get fetched such a solid one as that without any notice—because how was *he* going to know what was tatooed on the man? He whitened a little; he couldn't help it; and it was mighty still in there, and everybody bending a little forwards and gazing at him. Says I to myself, *Now* he'll throw up the sponge—there ain't no more use. Well, did he? A body can't hardly believe it, but he didn't. I reckon he thought he'd keep the thing up till he tired them people out, so they'd thin out, and him and the duke could break loose and get away. Anyway, he set there, and pretty soon he begun to smile, and says:

"Mf! It's a *very* tough question, *ain't* it! *Yes,* sir, I k'n tell you what's tatooed on his breast. It's jest a small, thin, blue arrow—that's what it is; and if you don't look clost, you can't see it. *Now* what do you say—hey?"

Well, *I* never see anything like that old blister for clean out-and-out cheek.

The new old gentleman turns brisk towards Ab Turner and his pard, and his eye lights up like he judged he'd got the king *this* time, and says:

"There—you've heard what he said! Was there any such mark on Peter Wilks's breast?"

Both of them spoke up and says:

"We didn't see no such mark."

"Good!" says the old gentleman. "Now, what you *did* see on his breast was a small dim P, and a B (which is an initial he dropped when he was young), and a W, with dashes between them, so: P—B—W"—and he marked them that way on a piece of paper. "Come—ain't that what you saw?"

Both of them spoke up again, and says:

"No, we *didn't.* We never seen any marks at all."

Well, everybody *was* in a state of mind, now; and they sings out:

"The whole *bilin'* of 'm 's frauds! Le's duck 'em! le's drown 'em! le's ride 'em on a rail!" and everybody was whooping at once, and there was a rattling pow-wow. But the lawyer he jumps on the table and yells, and says:

"Gentlemen—gentle*men!* Hear me just a word—just a *single* word—if you PLEASE! There's one way yet—let's go and dig up the corpse and look."

That took them.

"Hooray!" they all shouted, and was starting right off; but the lawyer and the doctor sung out:

"Hold on, hold on! Collar all these four men and the boy, and fetch *them* along, too!"

"We'll do it!" they all shouted: "and if we don't find them marks we'll lynch the whole gang!"

I *was* scared, now, I tell you. But there warn't no getting away, you know. They gripped us all, and marched us right along, straight for the graveyard, which was a mile and a half down the river, and the whole town at our heels, for we made noise enough, and it was only nine in the evening.

As we went by our house I wished I hadn't sent Mary Jane out of town; because now if I could tip her the wink, she'd light out and save me, and blow on our dead-beats.

Well, we swarmed along down the river road, just carrying on like wildcats; and to make it more scary, the sky was darking up, and the lightning beginning to wink and flitter, and the wind to shiver amongst the leaves. This was the most awful trouble and most dangersome I ever was in; and I was kinder stunned; everything was going so different from what I had allowed for; stead of being fixed so I could take my own time, if I wanted to, and see all the fun, and have Mary Jane at my back to save me and set me free when the close-fit come, here was nothing in the world betwixt me and sudden death but just them tatoo-marks. If they didn't find them—

I couldn't bear to think about it; and yet, somehow, I couldn't think about nothing else. It got darker and darker, and it was a beautiful time to give the crowd the slip; but that big husky had me by the wrist—Hines—and a body might as well try to give Goliar[5] the slip. He dragged me right along, he was so excited; and I had to run to keep up.

When they got there they swarmed into the graveyard and washed over it like an overflow. And when they got to the grave, they found they had about a hundred times as many shovels as they wanted, but nobody hadn't thought to fetch a lantern. But they sailed into digging, anyway, by the flicker of the lightning, and sent a man to the nearest house a half a mile off, to borrow one.

So they dug and dug, like everything; and it got awful dark, and the rain started, and the wind swished and swushed along, and the lightning come brisker and brisker, and the thunder boomed; but them people never took no notice of it, they was so full of this business; and one minute you could see everything and every face in that big crowd, and the shovelfuls of dirt sailing up out of the grave, and the next second the dark wiped it all out, and you couldn't see nothing at all.

At last they got out the coffin, and begun to unscrew the lid, and then such another crowding, and shouldering, and shoving as there was, to scrouge in and get a sight, you never see; and in the dark, that way, it was awful. Hines he hurt my wrist dreadful, pulling and tugging so, and I reckon he clean forgot I was in the world, he was so excited and panting.

All of a sudden the lightning let go a perfect sluice of white glare, and somebody sings out:

"By the living jingo, here's the bag of gold on his breast!"

Hines let out a whoop, like everybody else, and dropped my wrist and give a big surge to bust his way in and get a look, and the way I lit out and shinned for the road in the dark, there ain't nobody can tell.

I had the road all to myself, and I fairly flew—leastways I had it all to myself except the solid dark, and the now-and-then glares, and the buzzing of the rain, and the thrashing of the wind, and the splitting of the thunder; and sure as you are born I did clip it along!

When I struck the town, I see there warn't nobody out in the storm, so I never hunted for no back streets, but humped it straight through the main one; and when I begun to get towards our house I aimed my eye and set it. No light there; the house all dark—which made me feel sorry and disappointed, I didn't know why. But at last, just as I was sailing by, *flash* comes the light in Mary Jane's window! and my heart swelled up sudden, like to bust; and the same second the house and all was behind me in the dark, and wasn't ever going to be before me no more in this world. She *was* the best girl I ever see, and had the most sand.

The minute I was far enough above the town to see I could make the towhead, I begun to look sharp for a boat to borrow; and the first time the lightning showed me one that wasn't chained, I snatched it and shoved. It was a canoe, and warn't fastened with nothing but a rope. The tow-head was a rattling big distance off, away out there in the middle of the river, but I didn't lose no time; and when I struck the raft at last, I was so fagged I would

5. Goliath, a Philistine giant who challenged the Israelites. David, a young shepherd, accepted his challenge and killed him with a stone thrown from a sling.

a just laid down to blow and gasp if I could afforded it. But I didn't. As I sprung aboard I sung out:

"Out with you Jim, and set her loose! Glory be to goodness, we're shut of them!"

Jim lit out, and was a coming for me with both arms spread, he was so full of joy; but when I glimpsed him in the lightning, my heart shot up in my mouth, and I went overboard backwards; for I forgot he was old King Lear and a drownded A-rab all in one, and it most scared the livers and lights out of me. But Jim fished me out, and was going to hug me and bless me, and so on, he was so glad I was back and we was shut of the king and the duke, but I says:

"Not now—have it for breakfast, have it for breakfast! Cut loose and let her slide!"

So, in two seconds, away we went, a sliding down the river, and it *did* seem so good to be free again and all by ourselves on the big river and nobody to bother us. I had to skip around a bit, and jump up and crack my heels a few times, I couldn't help it; but about the third crack, I noticed a sound that I knowed mighty well—and held my breath and listened and waited—and sure enough, when the next flash busted out over the water, here they come!—and just a laying to their oars and making their skiff hum! It was the king and the duke.

So I wilted right down onto the planks, then, and give up; and it was all I could do to keep from crying.

Chapter XXX

When they got aboard, the king went for me, and shook me by the collar, and says:

"Tryin' to give us the slip, was ye, you pup! Tired of our company—hey!"

I says:

"No, your majesty, we warn't—*please* don't, your majesty!"

"Quick, then, and tell us what *was* your idea, or I'll shake the insides out o' you!"

"Honest, I'll tell you everything, just as it happened, your majesty. The man that had aholt of me was very good to me, and kept saying he had a boy about as big as me that died last year, and he was sorry to see a boy in such a dangerous fix; and when they was all took by surprise by finding the gold, and made a rush for the coffin, he lets go of me and whispers, 'Heel it, now, or they'll hang ye, sure!' and I lit out. It didn't seem no good for *me* to stay—I couldn't do nothing, and I didn't want to be hung if I could get away. So I never stopped running till I found the canoe; and when I got here I told Jim to hurry, or they'd catch me and hang me yet, and said I was afeard you and the duke wasn't alive, now, and I was awful sorry, and so was Jim, and was awful glad when we see you coming, you may ask Jim if I didn't."

Jim said it was so; and the king told him to shut up, and said, "Oh, yes, it's *mighty* likely!" and shook me up again, and said he reckoned he'd drownded me. But the duke says:

"Leggo the boy, you old idiot! Would *you* a done any different? Did you inquire around for *him,* when you got loose? *I* don't remember it."

So the king let go of me, and begun to cuss that town and everybody in it. But the duke says:

"You better a blame sight give *yourself* a good cussing, for you're the one that's entitled to it most. You hain't done a thing, from the start, that had any sense in it, except coming out so cool and cheeky with that imaginary blue-arrow mark. That *was* bright—it was right down bully; and it was the thing that saved us. For if it hadn't been for that, they'd a jailed us till them Englishmen's baggage come—and then—the penitentiary, you bet! But that trick took 'em to the graveyard, and the gold done us a still bigger kindness; for if the excited fools hadn't let go all holts and made that rush to get a look, we'd a slept in our cravats[6] to-night—cravats warranted to *wear*, too—longer than *we'd* need 'em."

They was still a minute—thinking—then the king says, kind of absent-minded like:

"Mf! And we reckoned the *niggers* stole it!"

That made me squirm!

"Yes," says the duke, kinder slow, and deliberate, and sarcastic, "*We* did."

After about a half a minute, the king drawls out:

"Leastways—*I* did."

The duke says, the same way:

"On the contrary—*I* did."

The king kind of ruffles up, and says:

"Looky here, Bilgewater, what'r you referrin' to?"

The duke says, pretty brisk:

"When it comes to that, maybe you'll let me ask, what was *you* referring to?"

"Shucks!" says the king, very sarcastic; "but *I* don't know—maybe you was asleep, and didn't know what you was about."

The duke bristles right up, now, and says:

"Oh, let *up* on this cussed nonsense—do you take me for a blame' fool? Don't you reckon *I* know who hid that money in that coffin?"

"*Yes,* sir! I know you *do* know—because you done it yourself!"

"It's a lie!"—and the duke went for him. The king sings out:

"Take y'r hands off!—leggo my throat!—I take it all back!"

The duke says:

"Well, you just own up, first, that you *did* hide that money there, intending to give me the slip one of these days, and come back and dig it up, and have it all to yourself."

"Wait jest a minute, duke—answer me this one question, honest and fair; if you didn't put the money there, say it, and I'll b'lieve you, and take back everything I said."

"You old scoundrel, I didn't, and you know I didn't. There, now!"

"Well, then, I b'lieve you. But answer me only jest this one more—now *don't* git mad; didn't you have it in your *mind* to hook the money and hide it?"

The duke never said nothing for a little bit; then he says:

"Well—I don't care if I *did,* I didn't *do* it, anyway. But you not only had it in mind to do it, but you *done* it."

"I wisht I may never die if I done it, duke, and that's honest. I won't say I warn't *goin'* to do it, because I *was;* but you—I mean somebody—got in ahead o' me."

"It's a lie! You done it, and you got to *say* you done it, or—"

The king begun to gurgle, and then he gasps out:

6. Nooses from a hanging.

"'Nough!—I *own up!*"

I was very glad to hear him say that, it made me feel much more easier than what I was feeling before. So the duke took his hands off, and says:

"If you ever deny it again, I'll drown you. It's *well* for you to set there and blubber like a baby—it's fitten for you, after the way you've acted. I never see such an old ostrich for wanting to gobble everything—and I a trusting you all the time, like you was my own father. You ought to be ashamed of yourself to stand by and hear it saddled onto a lot of poor niggers and you never say a word for 'em. It makes me feel ridiculous to think I was soft enough to *believe* that rubbage. Cuss you, I can see, now, why you was so anxious to make up the deffesit—you wanted to get what money I'd got out of the Nonesuch and one thing or another, and scoop it *all!*"

The king says, timid, and still a snuffling:

"Why, duke, it was you that said make up the deffersit, it warn't me."

"Dry up! I don't want to hear no more *out* of you!" says the duke. "And *now* you see what you *got* by it. They've got all their own money back, and all of *ourn* but a shekel[7] or two, *besides*. G'long to bed—and don't you deffersit *me* no more deffersits, long 's *you* live!"

So the king sneaked into the wigwam, and took to his bottle for comfort; and before long the duke tackled *his* bottle; and so in about a half an hour they was as thick as thieves again, and the tighter they got, the lovinger they got; and went off a snoring in each other's arms. They both got powerful mellow, but I noticed the king didn't get mellow enough to forget to remember to not deny about hiding the money-bag again. That made me feel easy and satisfied. Of course when they got to snoring, we had a long gabble, and I told Jim everything.

Chapter XXXI

We dasn't stop again at any town, for days and days; kept right along down the river. We was down south in the warm weather, now, and a mighty long ways from home. We begun to come to trees with Spanish moss on them, hanging down from the limbs like long gray beards. It was the first I ever see it growing, and it made the woods look solemn and dismal. So now the frauds reckoned they was out of danger, and they begun to work the villages again.

First they done a lecture on temperance; but they didn't make enough for them both to get drunk on. Then in another village they started a dancing school; but they didn't know no more how to dance than a kangaroo does; so the first prance they made, the general public jumped in and pranced them out of town. Another time they tried a go at yellocution; but they didn't yellocute long till the audience got up and give them a solid good cussing and made them skip out. They tackled missionarying, and mesmerizering, and doctoring, and telling fortunes, and a little of everything; but they couldn't seem to have no luck. So at last they got just about dead broke, and laid around the raft, as she floated along, thinking, and thinking, and never saying nothing, by the half a day at a time, and dreadful blue and desperate.

And at last they took a change, and begun to lay their heads together in the wigwam and talk low and confidential two or three hours at a time. Jim

---

7. Ancient coin, used here colloquially to suggest a coin of low value.

and me got uneasy. We didn't like the look of it. We judged they was studying up some kind of worse deviltry than ever. We turned it over and over,
and at last we made up our minds they was going to break into somebody's
house or store, or was going into the counterfeit-money business, or something. So then we was pretty scared, and made up an agreement that we
wouldn't have nothing in the world to do with such actions, and if we ever
got the least show we would give them the cold shake, and clear out and
leave them behind. Well, early one morning we hid the raft in a good safe
place about two mile below a little bit of a shabby village, named Pikesville,
and the king he went ashore, and told us all to stay hid whilst he went up to
town and smelt around to see if anybody had got any wind of the Royal
Nonesuch there yet. ("House to rob, you *mean*," says I to myself; "and when
you get through robbing it you'll come back here and wonder what's become
of me and Jim and the raft—and you'll have to take it out in wondering.")
And he said if he warn't back by midday, the duke and me would know it
was all right, and we was to come along.

So we staid where we was. The duke he fretted and sweated around, and
was in a mighty sour way. He scolded us for everything, and we couldn't seem
to do nothing right; he found fault with every little thing. Something was
a-brewing, sure. I was good and glad when midday come and no king; we
could have a change, anyway—and maybe a chance for *the* change, on top of
it. So me and the duke went up to the village, and hunted around there for
the king, and by-and-by we found him in the back room of a little low doggery,[8] very tight, and a lot of loafers bullyragging him for sport, and he a cussing and threatening with all his might, and so tight he couldn't walk, and
couldn't do nothing to them. The duke he begun to abuse him for an old fool,
and the king begun to sass back; and the minute they was fairly at it, I lit out,
and shook the reefs out of my hind legs, and spun down the river road like a
deer—for I see our chance; and I made up my mind that it would be a long
day before they ever see me and Jim again. I got down there all out of breath
but loaded up with joy, and sung out—

"Set her loose, Jim, we're all right, now!"

But there warn't no answer, and nobody come out of the wigwam. Jim was
gone! I set up a shout—and then another—and then another one; and run
this way and that in the woods, whooping and screeching; but it warn't
no use—old Jim was gone. Then I set down and cried; I couldn't help it. But
I couldn't set still long. Pretty soon I went out on the road, trying to think
what I better do, and I run across a boy walking, and asked him if he'd seen
a strange nigger, dressed so and so, and he says:

"Yes."

"Whereabouts?" says I.

"Down to Silas Phelps's place, two mile below here. He's a runaway nigger, and they've got him. Was you looking for him?"

"You bet I ain't! I run across him in the woods about an hour or two ago,
and he said if I hollered he'd cut my livers out—and told me to lay down and
stay where I was; and I done it. Been there ever since; afeard to come out."

"Well," he says, "you needn't be afraid no more, becuz they've got him.
He run off f'm down South, som'ers."

"It's a good job they got him."

8. Cheap barroom.

"Well, I *reckon!* There's two hundred dollars reward on him. It's like picking up money out'n the road."

"Yes, it is—and *I* could a had it if I'd been big enough; I see him *first.* Who nailed him?"

"It was an old fellow—a stranger—and he sold out his chance in him for forty dollars, becuz he's got to go up the river and can't wait. Think o' that, now! You bet *I'd* wait, if it was seven year."

"That's me, every time," says I. "But maybe his chance ain't worth no more than that, if he'll sell it so cheap. Maybe there's something ain't straight about it."

"But it *is,* though—straight as a string. I see the handbill myself. It tells all about him, to a dot—paints him like a picture, and tells the plantation he's frum, below New*rleans.* No-siree-*bob,* they ain't no trouble 'bout *that* speculation, you bet you. Say, gimme a chaw tobacker, won't ye?"

I didn't have none, so he left. I went to the raft, and set down in the wigwam to think. But I couldn't come to nothing. I thought till I wore my head sore, but I couldn't see no way out of the trouble. After all this long journey, and after all we'd done for them scoundrels, here was it all come to nothing, everything all busted up and ruined, because they could have the heart to serve Jim such a trick as that, and make him a slave again all his life, and amongst strangers, too, for forty dirty dollars.

Once I said to myself it would be a thousand times better for Jim to be a slave at home where his family was, as long as he'd *got* to be a slave, and so I'd better write a letter to Tom Sawyer and tell him to tell Miss Watson where he was. But I soon give up that notion, for two things: she'd be mad and disgusted at his rascality and ungratefulness for leaving her, and so she'd sell him straight down the river again; and if she didn't, everybody naturally despises an ungrateful nigger, and they'd make Jim feel it all the time, and so he'd feel ornery and disgraced. And then think of *me!* It would get all around, that Huck Finn helped a nigger to get his freedom; and if I was to ever see anybody from that town again, I'd be ready to get down and lick his boots for shame. That's just the way: a person does a low-down thing, and then he don't want to take no consequences of it. Thinks as long as he can hide it, it ain't no disgrace. That was my fix exactly. The more I studied about this, the more my conscience went to grinding me, and the more wicked and low-down and ornery I got to feeling. And at last, when it hit me all of a sudden that here was the plain hand of Providence slapping me in the face and letting me know my wickedness was being watched all the time from up there in heaven, whilst I was stealing a poor old woman's nigger that hadn't ever done me no harm, and now was showing me there's One that's always on the lookout, and ain't agoing to allow no such miserable doings to go only just so fur and no further, I most dropped in my tracks I was so scared. Well, I tried the best I could to kinder soften it up somehow for myself, by saying I was brung up wicked, and so I warn't so much to blame; but something inside of me kept saying, "There was the Sunday school, you could a gone to it; and if you'd a done it they'd a learnt you, there, that people that acts as I'd been acting about the nigger goes to everlasting fire."

It made me shiver. And I about made up my mind to pray; and see if I couldn't try to quit being the kind of a boy I was, and be better. So I kneeled down. But the words wouldn't come. Why wouldn't they? It warn't no use to try and hide it from Him. Nor from *me,* neither. I knowed very well why they wouldn't come. It was because my heart warn't right; it was because I warn't square; it was because I was playing double. I was letting *on* to give up sin, but away inside of me I was holding on to the biggest one of all. I was trying to make my mouth *say* I would do the right thing and the clean thing, and go and write to that nigger's owner and tell where he was; but deep down in me I knowed it was a lie—and He knowed it. You can't pray a lie—I found that out.

So I was full of trouble, full as I could be; and didn't know what to do. At last I had an idea; and I says, I'll go and write the letter—and *then* see if I can pray. Why, it was astonishing, the way I felt as light as a feather, right straight off, and my troubles all gone. So I got a piece of paper and a pencil, all glad and excited, and set down and wrote:

> Miss Watson your runaway nigger Jim is down here two mile below Pikesville and Mr. Phelps has got him and he will give him up for the reward if you send.
>
> Huck Finn.

I felt good and all washed clean of sin for the first time I had ever felt so in my life, and I knowed I could pray now. But I didn't do it straight off, but laid the paper down and set there thinking—thinking how good it was all this happened so, and how near I come to being lost and going to hell. And went on thinking. And got to thinking over our trip down the river; and I see Jim before me, all the time, in the day, and in the night-time, sometimes moonlight, sometimes storms, and we a floating along, talking, and singing, and laughing. But somehow I couldn't seem to strike no places to harden me against him, but only the other kind. I'd see him standing my watch on top of his'n, stead of calling me, so I could go on sleeping; and see him how glad he was when I come back out of the fog; and when I come to him again in the swamp, up there where the feud was; and such-like times; and would always call me honey, and pet me, and do everything he could think of for me, and how good he always was; and at last I struck the time I saved him by telling the men we had small-pox aboard, and he was so grateful, and said I was the best friend old Jim ever had in the world, and the *only* one he's got now; and then I happened to look around, and see that paper.

It was a close place. I took it up, and held it in my hand. I was a trembling, because I'd got to decide, forever, betwixt two things, and I knowed it. I studied a minute, sort of holding my breath, and then says to myself:

"All right, then, I'll *go* to hell"—and tore it up.

It was awful thoughts, and awful words, but they was said. And I let them stay said; and never thought no more about reforming. I shoved the whole thing out of my head; and said I would take up wickedness again, which was in my line, being brung up to it, and the other warn't. And for a starter, I would go to work and steal Jim out of slavery again; and if I could think up anything worse, I would do that, too; because as long as I was in, and in for good, I might as well go the whole hog.

Then I set to thinking over how to get at it, and turned over considerable many ways in my mind; and at last fixed up a plan that suited me. So then I took the bearings of a woody island that was down the river a piece, and as soon as it was fairly dark I crept out with my raft and went for it, and hid it there, and then turned in. I slept the night through, and got up before it was light, and had my breakfast, and put on my store clothes, and tied up some others and one thing or another in a bundle, and took the canoe and cleared for shore. I landed below where I judged was Phelps's place, and hid my bundle in the woods, and then filled up the canoe with water, and loaded rocks into her and sunk her where I could find her again when I wanted her, about a quarter of a mile below a little steam sawmill that was on the bank.

Then I struck up the road, and when I passed the mill I see a sign on it, "Phelps's Sawmill," and when I come to the farmhouses, two or three hundred yards further along, I kept my eyes peeled, but didn't see nobody around, though it was good daylight, now. But I didn't mind, because I didn't want to see nobody just yet—I only wanted to get the lay of the land. According to my plan, I was going to turn up there from the village, not from below. So I just took a look, and shoved along, straight for town. Well, the very first man I see, when I got there, was the duke. He was sticking up a bill for the Royal Nonesuch—three-night performance—like that other time. *They* had the cheek, them frauds! I was right on him, before I could shirk. He looked astonished, and says:

"Hel-*lo!* Where'd *you* come from?" Then he says, kind of glad and eager, "Where's the raft?—got her in a good place?"

I says:

"Why, that's just what I was agoing to ask your grace."

Then he didn't look so joyful—and says:

"What was your idea for asking *me?*" he says.

"Well," I says, "when I see the king in that doggery yesterday, I says to myself, we can't get him home for hours, till he's soberer; so I went a loafing around town to put in the time, and wait. A man up and offered me ten cents to help him pull a skiff over the river and back to fetch a sheep, and so I went along; but when we was dragging him to the boat, and the man left me aholt of the rope and went behind him to shove him along, he was too strong for me, and jerked loose and run, and we after him. We didn't have no dog, and so we had to chase him all over the country till we tired him out. We never got him till dark, then we fetched him over, and I started down for the raft. When I got there and see it was gone, I says to myself, 'they've got into trouble and had to leave; and they've took my nigger, which is the only nigger I've got in the world, and now I'm in a strange country, and ain't got no property no more, nor nothing, and no way to make my living'; so I set down and cried. I slept in the woods all night. But what *did* become of the raft then?—and Jim, poor Jim!"

"Blamed if *I* know—that is, what's become of the raft. That old fool had made a trade and got forty dollars, and when we found him in the doggery the loafers had matched half dollars with him and got every cent but what he'd spent for whisky; and when I got him home late last night and found the raft gone, we said, 'That little rascal has stole our raft and shook us, and run off down the river.'"

"I wouldn't shake my *nigger*, would I?—the only nigger I had in the world, and the only property."

"We never thought of that. Fact is, I reckon we'd come to consider him *our* nigger; yes, we did consider him so—goodness knows we had trouble enough for him. So when we see the raft was gone, and we flat broke, there warn't anything for it but to try the Royal Nonesuch another shake. And I've pegged along ever since, dry as a powderhorn. Where's that ten cents? Give it here."

I had considerable money, so I give him ten cents, but begged him to spend it for something to eat, and give me some, because it was all the money I had, and I hadn't had nothing to eat since yesterday. He never said nothing. The next minute he whirls on me and says:

"Do you reckon that nigger would blow on us? We'd skin him if he done that!"

"How can he blow? Hain't he run off?"

"No! That old fool sold him, and never divided with me, and the money's gone."

"*Sold* him?" I says, and begun to cry; "why, he was *my* nigger, and that was my money. Where is he?—I want my nigger."

"Well, you can't *get* your nigger, that's all—so dry up your blubbering. Looky here—do you think *you'd* venture to blow on us? Blamed if I think I'd trust you. Why, if you *was* to blow on us—"

He stopped, but I never see the duke look so ugly out of his eyes before. I went on a-whimpering, and says:

"I don't want to blow on nobody; and I ain't got no time to blow, nohow. I got to turn out and find my nigger."

He looked kinder bothered, and stood there with his bills fluttering on his arm, thinking, and wrinkling up his forehead. At last he says:

"I'll tell you something. We got to be here three days. If you'll promise you won't blow, and won't let the nigger blow, I'll tell you where to find him."

So I promised, and he says:

"A farmer by the name of Silas Ph—" and then he stopped. You see he started to tell me the truth; but when he stopped, that way, and begun to study and think again, I reckoned he was changing his mind. And so he was. He wouldn't trust me; he wanted to make sure of having me out of the way the whole three days. So pretty soon he says: "The man that bought him is named Abram Foster—Abram G. Foster—and he lives forty mile back here in the country, on the road to Lafayette."

"All right," I says, "I can walk it in three days. And I'll start this very afternoon."

"No you won't, you'll start *now*; and don't you lose any time about it, neither, nor do any gabbling by the way. Just keep a tight tongue in your head and move right along, and then you won't get into trouble with *us*, d'ye hear?"

That was the order I wanted, and that was the one I played for. I wanted to be left free to work my plans.

"So clear out," he says; "and you can tell Mr. Foster whatever you want to. Maybe you can get him to believe that Jim *is* your nigger—some idiots don't require documents—leastways I've heard there's such down South here. And when you tell him the handbill and the reward's bogus, maybe he'll believe you when you explain to him what the idea was for getting 'em out. Go 'long, now, and tell him anything you want to; but mind you don't work your jaw any *between* here and there."

So I left, and struck for the back country. I didn't look around, but I kinder felt like he was watching me. But I knowed I could tire him out at that. I went straight out in the country as much as a mile, before I stopped; then I doubled back through the woods towards Phelps's. I reckoned I better start in on my plan straight off, without fooling around, because I wanted to stop Jim's mouth till these fellows could get away. I didn't want no trouble with their kind. I'd seen all I wanted to of them, and wanted to get entirely shut of them.

Chapter XXXII

When I got there it was all still and Sunday-like, and hot and sunshiny—the hands was gone to the fields; and there was them kind of faint dronings of bugs and flies in the air that makes it seem so lonesome and like everybody's dead and gone; and if a breeze fans along and quivers the leaves, it makes you feel mournful, because you feel like it's spirits whispering—spirits that's been dead ever so many years—and you always think they're talking about *you*. As a general thing it makes a body wish *he* was dead, too, and done with it all.

Phelps's was one of these little one-horse cotton plantations; and they all look alike. A rail fence round a two-acre yard; a stile, made out of logs sawed off and up-ended, in steps, like barrels of a different length, to climb over the fence with, and for the women to stand on when they are going to jump onto a horse; some sickly grass-patches in the big yard, but mostly it was bare and smooth, like an old hat with the nap rubbed off; big double log house for the white folks—hewed logs, with the chinks stopped up with mud or mortar, and these mud-stripes been whitewashed some time or another; round-log kitchen, with a big broad, open but roofed passage joining it to the house; log smoke-house back of the kitchen; three little log nigger-cabins in a row t'other side the smokehouse; one little hut all by itself away down against the back fence, and some outbuildings down a piece the other side; ash-hopper,[9] and big kettle to bile soap in, by the little hut; bench by the kitchen door, with bucket of water and a gourd; hound asleep there, in the sun; more hounds asleep, round about; about three shade-trees away off in a corner; some currant bushes and gooseberry bushes in one place by the fence; outside of the fence a garden and a water-melon patch; then the cotton fields begins; and after the fields, the woods.

I went around and clumb over the back stile by the ash-hopper, and started for the kitchen. When I got a little ways, I heard the dim hum of a spinning-wheel wailing along up and sinking along down again; and then I knowed for certain I wished I was dead—for that *is* the lonesomest sound in the whole world.

I went right along, not fixing up any particular plan, but just trusting to Providence to put the right words in my mouth when the time come; for I'd noticed that Providence always did put the right words in my mouth, if I left it alone.

When I got half-way, first one hound and then another got up and went for me, and of course I stopped and faced them, and kept still. And such another pow-wow as they made! In a quarter of a minute I was a kind of a hub of a wheel, as you may say—spokes made out of dogs—circle of fifteen of them packed together around me, with their necks and noses stretched up towards me, a barking and howling; and more a coming; you could see them sailing over fences and around corners from everywheres.

A nigger woman come tearing out of the kitchen with a rolling-pin in her hand, singing out, "Begone! *you* Tige! you Spot! begone, sah!" and she fetched first one and then another of them a clip and sent him howling, and then the rest followed; and the next second, half of them come back, wagging their tails around me and making friends with me. There ain't no harm in a hound, nohow.

---

9. A container for lye used in making soap.

And behind the woman comes a little nigger girl and two little nigger boys, without anything on but tow-linen shirts, and they hung onto their mother's gown, and peeped out from behind her at me, bashful, the way they always do. And here comes the white woman running from the house, about forty-five or fifty year old, bare-headed, and her spinning-stick in her hand; and behind her comes her little white children, acting the same way the little niggers was doing. She was smiling all over so she could hardly stand—and says:

"It's *you,* at last!—*ain't* it?"

I out with a "Yes'm," before I thought.

She grabbed me and hugged me tight; and then gripped me by both hands and shook and shook; and the tears come in her eyes, and run down over; and she couldn't seem to hug and shake enough, and kept saying, "You don't look as much like your mother as I reckoned you would, but law sakes, I don't care for that, I'm *so* glad to see you! Dear, dear, it does seem like I could eat you up! Children, it's your cousin Tom!—tell him howdy."

But they ducked their heads, and put their fingers in their mouths, and hid behind her. So she run on:

"Lize, hurry up and get him a hot breakfast, right away—or did you get your breakfast on the boat?"

I said I had got it on the boat. So then she started for the house, leading me by the hand, and the children tagging after. When we got there, she set me down in a split-bottomed chair, and set herself down on a little low stool in front of me, holding both of my hands, and says:

"Now I can have a *good* look at you; and laws-a-me, I've been hungry for it a many and a many a time, all these long years, and it's come at last! We been expecting you a couple of days and more. What's kep' you?—boat get aground?"

"Yes'm—she—"

"Don't say yes'm—say Aunt Sally. Where'd she get aground?"

I didn't rightly know what to say, because I didn't know whether the boat would be coming up the river or down. But I go a good deal on instinct; and my instinct said she would be coming up—from down toward Orleans. That didn't help me much, though; for I didn't know the names of bars down that way. I see I'd got to invent a bar, or forget the name of the one we got aground on—or—Now I struck an idea, and fetched it out:

"It warn't the grounding—that didn't keep us back but a little. We blowed out a cylinder-head."

"Good gracious! anybody hurt?"

"No'm. Killed a nigger."

"Well, it's lucky; because sometimes people do get hurt. Two years ago last Christmas, your uncle Silas was coming up from Newrleans on the old *Lally Rook,*[1] and she blowed out a cylinder-head and crippled a man. And I think he died afterwards. He was a Babtist. Your uncle Silas knowed a family in Baton Rouge that knowed his people very well. Yes, I remember, now he *did* die. Mortification[2] set in, and they had to amputate him. But it didn't save him. Yes, it was mortification—that was it. He turned blue all over, and died in the hope of a glorious resurrection. They say he was a sight to look at. Your uncle's been up to the town every day to fetch you. And he's gone again, not

1. "Lalla Rookh" (1817), a popular Romantic poem by the Irish poet Thomas Moore (1779–1852).
2. Gangrene.

more'n an hour ago; he'll be back any minute, now. You must a met him on the road, didn't you?—oldish man, with a—"

"No, I didn't see nobody, Aunt Sally. The boat landed just at daylight, and I left my baggage on the wharf-boat and went looking around the town and out a piece in the country, to put in the time and not get here too soon; and so I come down the back way."

"Who'd you give the baggage to?"

"Nobody."

"Why, child, it'll be stole!"

"Not where I hid it I reckon it won't," I says.

"How'd you get your breakfast so early on the boat?"

It was kinder thin ice, but I says:

"The captain see me standing around, and told me I better have something to eat before I went ashore; so he took me in the texas to the officers' lunch, and give me all I wanted."

I was getting so uneasy I couldn't listen good. I had my mind on the children all the time; I wanted to get them out to one side, and pump them a little, and find out who I was. But I couldn't get no show, Mrs. Phelps kept it up and run on so. Pretty soon she made the cold chills streak all down my back, because she says:

"But here we're a running on this way, and you hain't told me a word about Sis, nor any of them. Now I'll rest my works a little, and you start up yourn; just tell me *everything*—tell me all about 'm all—every one of 'm; and how they are, and what they're doing, and what they told you to tell me; and every last thing you can think of."

Well, I see I was up a stump—and up it good. Providence had stood by me this fur, all right, but I was hard and tight aground, now. I see it warn't a bit of use to try to go ahead—I'd *got* to throw up my hand. So I says to myself, here's another place where I got to resk the truth. I opened my mouth to begin; but she grabbed me and hustled me in behind the bed, and says:

"Here he comes! stick your head down lower—there, that'll do; you can't be seen, now. Don't you let on you're here. I'll play a joke on him. Children, don't you say a word."

I see I was in a fix, now. But it warn't no use to worry; there warn't nothing to do but just hold still, and try to be ready to stand from under when the lightning struck.

I had just one little glimpse of the old gentleman when he come in, then the bed hid him. Mrs. Phelps she jumps for him and says:

"Has he come?"

"No," says her husband.

"Good-*ness* gracious!" she says, "what in the world *can* have become of him?"

"I can't imagine," says the old gentleman; "and I must say, it makes me dreadful uneasy."

"Uneasy!" she says, "I'm ready to go distracted! He *must* a come; and you've missed him along the road. I *know* it's so—something *tells* me so."

"Why Sally, I *couldn't* miss him along the road—*you* know that."

"But oh, dear, dear, what *will* Sis say! He must a come! You must a missed him. He—"

"Oh, don't distress me any more'n I'm already distressed. I don't know what in the world to make of it. I'm at my wit's end, and I don't mind acknowledging 't I'm right down scared. But there's no hope that he's come; for he *couldn't* come and me miss him. Sally, it's terrible—just terrible—something's happened to the boat, sure!"

"Why, Silas! Look yonder!—up the road!—ain't that somebody coming?"

He sprung to the window at the head of the bed, and that give Mrs. Phelps the chance she wanted. She stooped down quick, at the foot of the bed, and give me a pull, and out I come; and when he turned back from the window, there she stood, a-beaming and a-smiling like a house afire, and I standing pretty meek and sweaty alongside. The old gentleman stared, and says:

"Why, who's that?"

"Who do you reckon 't is?"

"I hain't no idea. Who *is* it?"

"It's *Tom Sawyer!*"

By jings, I most slumped through the floor. But there warn't no time to swap knives;[3] the old man grabbed me by the hand and shook, and kept on shaking; and all the time, how the woman did dance around and laugh and cry; and then how they both did fire off questions about Sid, and Mary, and the rest of the tribe.

But if they was joyful, it warn't nothing to what I was; for it was like being born again, I was so glad to find out who I was. Well, they froze to me for two hours; and at last when my chin was so tired it couldn't hardly go, any more, I had told them more about my family—I mean the Sawyer family—than ever happened to any six Sawyer families. And I explained all about how we blowed out a cylinder-head at the mouth of the White River and it took us three days to fix it. Which was all right, and worked first rate; because *they* didn't know but what it would take three days to fix it. If I'd a called it a bolt-head it would a done just as well.

Now I was feeling pretty comfortable all down one side, and pretty uncomfortable all up the other. Being Tom Sawyer was easy and comfortable; and it stayed easy and comfortable till by-and-by I hear a steamboat coughing along down the river—then I says to myself, spose Tom Sawyer come down on that boat?—and spose he steps in here, any minute, and sings out my name before I can throw him a wink to keep quiet? Well, I couldn't *have* it that way—it wouldn't do at all. I must go up the road and waylay him. So I told the folks I reckoned I would go up to the town and fetch down my baggage. The old gentleman was for going along with me, but I said no, I could drive the horse myself, and I druther he wouldn't take no trouble about me.

Chapter XXXIII

So I started for town, in the wagon, and when I was half-way I see a wagon coming, and sure enough it was Tom Sawyer, and I stopped and waited till he come along. I says "Hold on!" and it stopped alongside, and his mouth opened up like a trunk, and staid so; and he swallowed two or three times like a person that's got a dry throat, and then says:

"I hain't ever done you no harm. You know that. So then, what you want to come back and ha'nt *me* for?"

I says:

"I hain't come back—I hain't been *gone*."

3. Change plans.

When he heard my voice, it righted him up some, but he warn't quite satisfied yet. He says:

"Don't you play nothing on me, because I wouldn't on you. Honest injun, now, you ain't a ghost?"

"Honest injun, I ain't," I says.

"Well—I—I—well, that ought to settle it, of course; but I can't somehow seem to understand it, no way. Looky here, warn't you ever murdered *at all?*"

"No. I warn't ever murdered at all—I played it on them. You come in here and feel of me if you don't believe me."

So he done it; and it satisfied him; and he was that glad to see me again, he didn't know what to do. And he wanted to know all about it right off; because it was a grand adventure, and mysterious, and so it hit him where he lived. But I said, leave it along till by-and-by; and told his driver to wait, and we drove off a little piece, and I told him the kind of a fix I was in, and what did he reckon we better do? He said, let him alone a minute, and don't disturb him. So he thought and thought, and pretty soon he says:

"It's all right, I've got it. Take my trunk in your wagon, and let on it's your'n; and you turn back and fool along slow, so as to get to the house about the time you ought to; and I'll go towards town a piece, and take a fresh start, and get there a quarter or a half an hour after you; and you needn't let on to know me, at first."

I says:

"All right; but wait a minute. There's one more thing—a thing that *nobody* don't know but me. And that is, there's a nigger here that I'm trying to steal out of slavery—and his name is *Jim*—old Miss Watson's Jim."

He says:

"What! Why Jim is—"

He stopped and went to studying. I says:

"*I* know what you'll say. You'll say it's dirty low-down business; but what if it is?—*I'm* low down; and I'm agoing to steal him, and I want you to keep mum and not let on. Will you?"

His eye lit up, and he says:

"I'll *help* you steal him!"

Well, I let go all holts then, like I was shot. It was the most astonishing speech I ever heard—and I'm bound to say Tom Sawyer fell, considerable, in my estimation. Only I couldn't believe it. Tom Sawyer a *nigger stealer!*

"Oh, shucks," I says, "you're joking."

"I ain't joking, either."

"Well, then," I says, "joking or no joking, if you hear anything said about a runaway nigger, don't forget to remember that *you* don't know nothing about him, and *I* don't know nothing about him."

Then we took the trunk and put it in my wagon, and he drove off his way, and I drove mine. But of course I forgot all about driving slow, on accounts of being glad and full of thinking; so I got home a heap too quick for that length of trip. The old gentleman was at the door, and he says:

"Why, this is wonderful. Who ever would a thought it was in that mare to do it. I wish we'd a timed her. And she hain't sweated a hair—not a hair. It's wonderful. Why, I wouldn't take a hundred dollars for that horse now; I wouldn't, honest; and yet I'd a sold her for fifteen before, and thought 'twas all she was worth."

That's all he said. He was the innocentest, best old soul I ever see. But it warn't surprising; because he warn't only just a farmer, he was a preacher, too, and had a little one-horse log church down back of the plantation, which he built it himself at his own expense, for a church and school-house, and never charged nothing for his preaching, and it was worth it, too. There was plenty other farmer-preachers like that, and done the same way, down South.

In about half an hour Tom's wagon drove up to the front stile, and Aunt Sally she see it through the window because it was only about fifty yards, and says:

"Why, there's somebody come! I wonder who 'tis? Why, I do believe it's a stranger. Jimmy" (that's one of the children), "run and tell Lize to put on another plate for dinner."

Everybody made a rush for the front door, because, of course, a stranger don't come *every* year, and so he lays over the yaller fever, for interest, when he does come. Tom was over the stile and starting for the house; the wagon was spinning up the road for the village, and we was all bunched in the front door. Tom had his store clothes on, and an audience—and that was always nuts for Tom Sawyer. In them circumstances it warn't no trouble to him to throw in an amount of style that was suitable. He warn't a boy to meeky along up that yard like a sheep; no, he come ca'm and important, like the ram. When he got afront of us, he lifts his hat ever so gracious and dainty, like it was the lid of a box that had butterflies asleep in it and he didn't want to disturb them, and says:

"Mr. Archibald Nichols, I presume?"

"No, my boy," says the old gentleman, "I'm sorry to say 't your driver has deceived you; Nichols's place is down a matter of three mile more. Come in, come in."

Tom he took a look back over his shoulder, and says, "Too late—he's out of sight."

"Yes, he's gone, my son, and you must come in and eat your dinner with us; and then we'll hitch up and take you down to Nichols's."

"Oh, I *can't* make you so much trouble; I couldn't think of it. I'll walk—I don't mind the distance."

"But we won't *let* you walk—it wouldn't be Southern hospitality to do it. Come right in."

"Oh, *do*," says Aunt Sally; "it ain't a bit of trouble to us, not a bit in the world. You *must* stay. It's a long, dusty three mile, and we *can't* let you walk. And besides, I've already told 'em to put on another plate, when I see you coming; so you mustn't disappoint us. Come right in, and make yourself at home."

So Tom he thanked them very hearty and handsome, and let himself be persuaded, and come in; and when he was in, he said he was a stranger from Hicksville, Ohio, and his name was William Thompson—and he made another bow.

Well, he run on, and on, and on, making up stuff about Hicksville and everybody in it he could invent, and I getting a little nervous, and wondering how this was going to help me out of my scrape; and at last, still talking along, he reached over and kissed Aunt Sally right on the mouth, and then settled back again in his chair, comfortable, and was going on talking; but she jumped up and wiped it off with the back of her hand, and says:

"You owdacious puppy!"

He looked kind of hurt, and says:

"I'm surprised at you, m'am."

"You're s'rp—Why, what do you reckon I am? I've a good notion to take and—say, what do you mean by kissing me?"

He looked kind of humble, and says:

"I didn't mean nothing, m'am. I didn't mean no harm. I—I—thought you'd like it."

"Why, you born fool!" She took up the spinning-stick, and it looked like it was all she could do to keep from giving him a crack with it. "What made you think I'd like it?"

"Well, I don't know. Only, they—they—told me you would."

"*They* told you I would. Whoever told you's *another* lunatic. I never heard the beat of it. Who's *they?*"

"Why—everybody. They all said so, m'am."

It was all she could do to hold in; and her eyes snapped, and her fingers worked like she wanted to scratch him; and she says:

"Who's everybody? Out with their names—or ther'll be an idiot short."

He got up and looked distressed, and fumbled his hat, and says:

"I'm sorry, and I warn't expecting it. They told me to. They all told me to. They all said kiss her; and said she'll like it. They all said it—every one of them. But I'm sorry, m'am, and I won't do it no more—I won't, honest."

"You won't, won't you? Well, I sh'd *reckon* you won't!"

"No'm, I'm honest about it; I won't ever do it again. Till you ask me."

"Till I *ask* you! Well, I never see the beat of it in my born days! I lay you'll be the Methusalem-numskull[4] of creation before ever *I* ask you—or the likes of you."

"Well," he says, "it does surprise me so. I can't make it out, somehow. They said you would, and I thought you would. But—" He stopped and looked around slow, like he wished he could run across a friendly eye, somewhere's; and fetched up on the old gentleman's, and says, "Didn't *you* think she'd like me to kiss her, sir?"

"Why, no, I—I—well, no, I b'lieve I didn't."

Then he looks on around, the same way, to me—and says:

"Tom, didn't *you* think Aunt Sally 'd open out her arms and say, 'Sid Sawyer—'"

"My land!" she says, breaking in and jumping for him, "you impudent young rascal, to fool a body so—" and was going to hug him, but he fended her off, and says:

"No, not till you've asked me, first."

So she didn't lose no time, but asked him; and hugged him and kissed him, over and over again, and then turned him over to the old man, and he took what was left. And after they got a little quiet again, she says:

"Why, dear me, I never see such a surprise. We warn't looking for *you,* at all, but only Tom. Sis never wrote to me about anybody coming but him."

"It's because it warn't *intended* for any of us to come but Tom," he says; "but I begged and begged, and at the last minute she let me come, too; so, coming down the river, me and Tom thought it would be a first-rate surprise for him to come here to the house first, and for me to by-and-by tag along

---

4. Methuselah was a biblical patriarch said to have lived 969 years.

and drop in and let on to be a stranger. But it was a mistake, Aunt Sally. This ain't no healthy place for a stranger to come."

"No—not impudent whelps, Sid. You ought to had your jaws boxed; I hain't been so put out since I don't know when. But I don't care, I don't mind the terms—I'd be willing to stand a thousand such jokes to have you here. Well, to think of that performance! I don't deny it, I was most putrified[5] with astonishment when you give me that smack."

We had dinner out in that broad open passage betwixt the house and the kitchen; and there was things enough on that table for seven families—and all hot, too; none of your flabby tough meat that's laid in a cupboard in a damp cellar all night and tastes like a hunk of old cold cannibal in the morning. Uncle Silas he asked a pretty long blessing over it, but it was worth it; and it didn't cool it a bit, neither, the way I've seen them kind of interruptions do, lots of times.

There was a considerable good deal of talk, all the afternoon, and me and Tom was on the lookout all the time, but it warn't no use, they didn't happen to say nothing about any runaway nigger, and we was afraid to try to work up to it. But at supper, at night, one of the little boys says:

"Pa, mayn't Tom and Sid and me go to the show?"

"No," says the old man, "I reckon there ain't going to be any; and you couldn't go if there was; because the runaway nigger told Burton and me all about that scandalous show, and Burton said he would tell the people; so I reckon they've drove the owdacious loafers out of town before this time."

So there it was!—but I couldn't help it. Tom and me was to sleep in the same room and bed; so, being tired, we bid good-night and went up to bed, right after supper, and clumb out of the window and down the lightning-rod, and shoved for the town; for I didn't believe anybody was going to give the king and the duke a hint, and so, if I didn't hurry up and give them one they'd get into trouble sure.

On the road Tom he told me all about how it was reckoned I was murdered, and how pap disappeared, pretty soon, and didn't come back no more, and what a stir there was when Jim run away; and I told Tom all about our Royal Nonesuch rapscallions, and as much of the raft-voyage as I had time to; and as we struck into the town and up through the middle of it—it was as much as half-after eight, then—here comes a raging rush of people, with torches, and an awful whooping and yelling, and banging tin pans and blowing horns; and we jumped to one side to let them go by; and as they went by, I see they had the king and the duke astraddle of a rail—that is, I knowed it *was* the king and the duke, though they was all over tar and feathers, and didn't look like nothing in the world that was human—just looked like a couple of monstrous big soldier-plumes. Well, it made me sick to see it; and I was sorry for them poor pitiful rascals, it seemed like I couldn't ever feel any hardness against them any more in the world. It was a dreadful thing to see. Human beings *can* be awful cruel to one another.

We see we was too late—couldn't do no good. We asked some stragglers about it, and they said everybody went to the show looking very innocent; and laid low and kept dark till the poor old king was in the middle of his cavortings on the stage; then somebody give a signal, and the house rose up and went for them.

---

5. Petrified or stunned.

So we poked along back home, and I warn't feeling so brash as I was before, but kind of ornery, and humble, and to blame, somehow—though *I* hadn't done anything. But that's always the way; it don't make no difference whether you do right or wrong, a person's conscience ain't got no sense, and just goes for him *anyway*. If I had a yaller dog that didn't know no more than a person's conscience does, I would pison him. It takes up more room than all the rest of a person's insides, and yet ain't no good, nohow. Tom Sawyer he says the same.

Chapter XXXIV

We stopped talking, and got to thinking. By-and-by Tom says:

"Looky here, Huck, what fools we are, to not think of it before! I bet I know where Jim is."

"No! Where?"

"In that hut down by the ash-hopper. Why, looky here. When we was at dinner, didn't you see a nigger man go in there with some vittles?"

"Yes."

"What did you think the vittles was for?"

"For a dog."

"So'd I. Well, it wasn't for a dog."

"Why?"

"Because part of it was watermelon."

"So it was—I noticed it. Well, it does beat all, that I never thought about a dog not eating watermelon. It shows how a body can see and don't see at the same time."

"Well, the nigger unlocked the padlock when he went in, and he locked it again when he come out. He fetched uncle a key, about the time we got up from table—same key, I bet. Watermelon shows man, lock shows prisoner; and it ain't likely there's two prisoners on such a little plantation, and where the people's all so kind and good. Jim's the prisoner. All right—I'm glad we found it out detective fashion; I wouldn't give shucks for any other way. Now you work your mind and study out a plan to steal Jim, and I will study out one, too; and we'll take the one we like the best."

What a head for just a boy to have! If I had Tom Sawyer's head, I wouldn't trade it off to be a duke, nor mate of a steamboat, nor clown in a circus, nor nothing I can think of. I went to thinking out a plan, but only just to be doing something; I knowed very well where the right plan was going to come from. Pretty soon, Tom says:

"Ready?"

"Yes," I says.

"All right—bring it out."

"My plan is this," I says. "We can easy find out if it's Jim in there. Then get up my canoe to-morrow night, and fetch my raft over from the island. Then the first dark night that comes, steal the key out of the old man's britches, after he goes to bed, and shove off down the river on the raft, with Jim, hiding daytimes and running nights, the way me and Jim used to do before. Wouldn't that plan work?"

"*Work?* Why cert'nly, it would work, like rats a fighting. But it's too blame' simple; there ain't nothing *to* it. What's the good of a plan that ain't no more trouble than that? It's as mild as goose-milk. Why, Huck, it wouldn't make no more talk than breaking into a soap factory."

I never said nothing, because I warn't expecting nothing different; but I knowed mighty well that whenever he got *his* plan ready it wouldn't have none of them objections to it.

And it didn't. He told me what it was, and I see in a minute it was worth fifteen of mine, for style, and would make Jim just as free a man as mine would, and maybe get us all killed besides. So I was satisfied, and said we would waltz in on it. I needn't tell what it was, here, because I knowed it wouldn't stay the way it was. I knowed he would be changing it around, every which way, as we went along, and heaving in new bullinesses wherever he got a chance. And that is what he done.

Well, one thing was dead sure; and that was, that Tom Sawyer was in earnest and was actuly going to help steal that nigger out of slavery. That was the thing that was too many for me. Here was a boy that was respectable, and well brung up; and had a character to lose; and folks at home that had characters; and he was bright and not leather-headed; and knowing and not ignorant; and not mean, but kind; and yet here he was, without any more pride, or rightness, or feeling, than to stoop to this business, and make himself a shame, and his family a shame, before everybody. I *couldn't* understand it, no way at all. It was outrageous, and I knowed I ought to just up and tell him so; and so be his true friend, and let him quit the thing right where he was, and save himself. And I *did* start to tell him; but he shut me up, and says:

"Don't you reckon I know what I'm about? Don't I generly know what I'm about?"

"Yes."

"Didn't I *say* I was going to help steal the nigger?"

"Yes."

"*Well* then."

That's all he said, and that's all I said. It warn't no use to say any more; because when he said he'd do a thing, he always done it. But *I* couldn't make out how he was willing to go into this thing; so I just let it go, and never bothered no more about it. If he was bound to have it so, I couldn't help it.

When we got home, the house was all dark and still; so we went on down to the hut by the ash-hopper, for to examine it. We went through the yard, so as to see what the hounds would do. They knowed us, and didn't make no more noise than country dogs is always doing when anything comes by in the night. When we got to the cabin, we took a look at the front and the two sides; and on the side I warn't acquainted with—which was the north side—we found a square window-hole, up tolerable high, with just one stout board nailed across it. I says:

"Here's the ticket. This hole's big enough for Jim to get through, if we wrench off the board."

Tom says:

"It's as simple as tit-tat-toe, three-in-a-row, and as easy as playing hooky. I should *hope* we can find a way that's a little more complicated than *that*, Huck Finn."

"Well, then," I says, "how'll it do to saw him out, the way I done before I was murdered, that time?"

"That's more *like*," he says, "It's real mysterious, and troublesome, and good," he says; "but I bet we can find a way that's twice as long. There ain't no hurry; le's keep on looking around."

Betwixt the hut and the fence, on the back side, was a lean-to, that joined the hut at the eaves, and was made out of plank. It was as long as the hut, but narrow—only about six foot wide. The door to it was at the south end, and was padlocked. Tom he went to the soap kettle, and searched around and fetched back the iron thing they lift the lid with; so he took it and prized out one of the staples. The chain fell down, and we opened the door and went in, and shut it, and struck a match, and see the shed was only built against the cabin and hadn't no connection with it; and there warn't no floor to the shed, nor nothing in it but some old rusty played-out hoes, and spades, and picks, and a crippled plow. The match went out, and so did we, and shoved in the staple again, and the door was locked as good as ever. Tom was joyful. He says:

"Now we're all right. We'll *dig* him out. It'll take about a week!"

Then we started for the house, and I went in the back door—you only have to pull a buckskin latch-string, they don't fasten the doors—but that warn't romantical enough for Tom Sawyer: no way would do him but he must climb up the lightning-rod. But after he got up half-way about three times, and missed fire and fell every time, and the last time most busted his brains out, he thought he'd got to give it up; but after he rested, he allowed he would give her one more turn for luck, and this time he made the trip.

In the morning we was up at break of day, and down to the nigger cabins to pet the dogs and make friends with the nigger that fed Jim—if it *was* Jim that was being fed. The niggers was just getting through breakfast and starting for the fields; and Jim's nigger was piling up a tin pan with bread and meat and things; and whilst the other was leaving, the key come from the house.

This nigger had a good-natured, chuckle-headed face, and his wool was all tied up in little bunches with thread. That was to keep witches off. He said the witches was pestering him awful, these nights, and making him see all kinds of strange things, and hear all kinds of strange words and noises, and he didn't believe he was ever witched so long, before, in his life. He got so worked up, and got to running on so about his troubles, he forgot all about what he'd been agoing to do. So Tom says:

"What's the vittles for? Going to feed the dogs?"

The nigger kind of smiled around graduly over his face, like when you heave a brickbat in a mud puddle, and he says:

"Yes, Mars Sid, *a* dog. Cur'us dog too. Does you want to go en look at 'im?"

"Yes."

I hunched Tom, and whispers:

"You going, right here in the day-break? *That* warn't the plan."

"No, it warn't—but it's the plan *now.*"

So, drat him, we went along, but I didn't like it much. When we got in, we couldn't hardly see anything, it was so dark; but Jim was there, sure enough, and could see us; and he sings out:

"Why, *Huck!* En good *lan'!* ain' dat Misto Tom?"

I just knowed how it would be; I just expected it. *I* didn't know nothing to do; and if I had, I couldn't done it; because that nigger busted in and says:

"Why, de gracious sakes! do he know you genlmen?"

We could see pretty well, now. Tom he looked at the nigger, steady and kind of wondering, and says:

"Does *who* know us?"

"Why, dish-yer runaway nigger."

"I don't reckon he does; but what put that into your head?"

"What *put* it dar? Didn' he jis' dis minute sing out like he knowed you?"

Tom says, in a puzzled-up kind of way:

"Well, that's mighty curious. *Who* sung out? *When* did he sing out? *What* did he sing out?" And turns to me, perfectly ca'm, and says, "Did *you* hear anybody sing out?"

Of course there warn't nothing to be said but the one thing; so I says:

"No; *I* ain't heard nobody say nothing."

Then he turns to Jim, and looks him over like he never see him before; and says:

"Did you sing out?"

"No, sah," says Jim; "*I* hain't said nothing, sah."

"Not a word?"

"No, sah, I hain't said a word."

"Did you ever see us before?"

"No, sah; not as *I* knows on."

So Tom turns to the nigger, which was looking wild and distressed, and says, kind of severe:

"What do you reckon's the matter with you, anyway? What made you think somebody sung out?"

"Oh, it's de dad-blame' witches, sah, en I wisht I was dead, I do. Dey's awluz at it, sah, en dey do mos' kill me, dey sk'yers me so. Please to don't tell nobody 'bout it sah, er old Mars Silas he'll scole me; 'kase he say dey *ain't* no witches. I jis' wish to goodness he was heah now—*den* what would he say! I jis' bet he couldn' fine no way to git aroun' it *dis* time. But it's awluz jis' so; people dat's *sot*, stays sot; dey won't look into nothn' en fine it out f'r dey-selves, en when *you* fine it out en tell um 'bout it, dey doan' b'lieve you."

Tom give him a dime, and said we wouldn't tell nobody; and told him to buy some more thread to tie up his wool with; and then looks at Jim, and says:

"I wonder if Uncle Silas is going to hang this nigger. If I was to catch a nigger that was ungrateful enough to run away, *I* wouldn't give him up, I'd hang him." And whilst the nigger stepped to the door to look at the dime and bite it to see if it was good, he whispers to Jim and says:

"Don't ever let on to know us. And if you hear any digging going on nights, it's us: we're going to set you free."

Jim only had time to grab us by the hand and squeeze it, then the nigger come back, and we said we'd come again some time if the nigger wanted us to; and he said he would, more particular if it was dark, because the witches went for him mostly in the dark, and it was good to have folks around then.

Chapter XXXV

It would be most an hour, yet, till breakfast, so we left, and struck down into the woods; because Tom said we got to have *some* light to see how to dig by, and a lantern makes too much, and might get us into trouble; what we must have was a lot of them rotten chunks that's called fox-fire[6] and just makes a soft kind of a glow when you lay them in a dark place. We fetched an armful and hid it in the weeds, and set down to rest, and Tom says, kind of dissatisfied:

"Blame it, this whole thing is just as easy and awkard as it can be. And so it makes it so rotten difficult to get up a difficult plan. There ain't no watch-

6. Phosphorescent glow of fungus on rotting wood.

man to be drugged—now there *ought* to be a watchman. There ain't even a dog to give a sleeping-mixture to. And there's Jim chained by one leg, with a ten-foot chain, to the leg of his bed; why, all you got to do is to lift up the bedstead and slip off the chain. And Uncle Silas he trusts everybody; sends the key to the punkin-headed nigger, and don't send nobody to watch the nigger. Jim could a got out of that window hole before this, only there wouldn't be no use trying to travel with a ten-foot chain on his leg. Why, drat it, Huck, it's the stupidest arrangement I ever see. You got to invent *all* the difficulties. Well, we can't help it, we got to do the best we can with the materials we've got. Anyhow, there's one thing—there's more honor in getting him out through a lot of difficulties and dangers, where there warn't one of them furnished to you by the people who it was their duty to furnish them, and you had to contrive them all out of your own head. Now look at just that one thing of the lantern. When you come down to the cold facts, we simply got to *let on* that a lantern's resky. Why, we could work with a torchlight procession if we wanted to, *I* believe. Now, whilst I think of it, we got to hunt up something to make a saw out of, the first chance we get."

"What do we want of a saw?"

"What do we *want* of it? Hain't we got to saw the leg of Jim's bed off, so as to get the chain loose?"

"Why, you just said a body could lift up the bedstead and slip the chain off."

"Well, if that ain't just like you, Huck Finn. You *can* get up the infant-schooliest ways of going at a thing. Why, hain't you ever read any books at all?—Baron Trenck, nor Casanova, nor Benvenuto Chelleeny, nor Henri IV.,[7] nor none of them heroes? Whoever heard of getting a prisoner loose in such an old-maidy way as that? No; the way all the best authorities does, is to saw the bedleg in two, and leave it just so, and swallow the sawdust, so it can't be found, and put some dirt and grease around the sawed place so the very keenest seneskal[8] can't see no sign of it's being sawed, and thinks the bed-leg is perfectly sound. Then, the night you're ready, fetch the leg a kick, down she goes; slip off your chain, and there you are. Nothing to do but hitch your rope-ladder to the battlements, shin down it, break your leg in the moat—because a rope-ladder is nineteen foot too short, you know—and there's your horses and your trusty vassles, and they scoop you up and fling you across a saddle and away you go, to your native Langudoc, or Navarre,[9] or wherever it is. It's gaudy, Huck. I wish there was a moat to this cabin. If we get time, the night of the escape, we'll dig one."

I says:

"What do we want of a moat, when we're going to snake him out from under the cabin?"

But he never heard me. He had forgot me and everything else. He had his chin in his hand, thinking. Pretty soon, he sighs, and shakes his head; then sighs again, and says:

"No, it wouldn't do—there ain't necessity enough for it."

"For what?" I says.

"Why, to saw Jim's leg off," he says.

7. Baron Friedrich von der Trenck (1726–1794), an Austrian soldier, and Henry IV of France (1553–1610), military heroes. Benvenuto Cellini (1500–1571), an artist, and Giovanni Jacopo Casanova (1725–1798) were both famous lovers. All four were involved in daring escape attempts. 8. Seneschal, powerful official in the service of medieval nobles. 9. Provinces in France and Spain, respectively.

"Good land!" I says, "why, there ain't *no* necessity for it. And what would you want to saw his leg off for, anyway?"

"Well, some of the best authorities has done it. They couldn't get the chain off, so they just cut their hand off, and shoved. And a leg would be better still. But we got to let that go. There ain't necessity enough in this case; and besides, Jim's a nigger and wouldn't understand the reasons for it, and how it's the custom in Europe, so we'll let it go. But there's one thing—he can have a rope-ladder; we can tear up our sheets and make him a rope-ladder easy enough. And we can send it to him in a pie; it's mostly done that way. And I've et worse pies."

"Why, Tom Sawyer, how you talk," I says; "Jim ain't got no use for a rope-ladder."

"He *has* got use for it. How *you* talk, you better say; you don't know nothing about it. He's *got* to have a rope ladder; they all do."

"What in the nation can he *do* with it?"

"*Do* with it? He can hide it in his bed, can't he? That's what they all do; and he's got to, too. Huck, you don't ever seem to want to do anything that's regular; you want to be starting something fresh all the time. Spose he *don't* do nothing with it? ain't it there in his bed, for a clew, after he's gone? and don't you reckon they'll want clews? Of course they will. And you wouldn't leave them any? That would be a *pretty* howdy-do *wouldn't* it! I never heard of such a thing."

"Well," I says, "if it's in the regulations, and he's got to have it, all right, let him have it; because I don't wish to go back on no regulations; but there's one thing, Tom Sawyer—if we go tearing up our sheets to make Jim a rope-ladder, we're going to get into trouble with Aunt Sally, just as sure as you're born. Now, the way I look at it, a hickry-bark ladder don't cost nothing, and don't waste nothing, and is just as good to load up a pie with, and hide in a straw tick, as any rag ladder you can start; and as for Jim, he hain't had no experience, and so *he* don't care what kind of a—"

"Oh, shucks, Huck Finn, if I was as ignorant as you, I'd keep still—that's what I'd do. Who ever heard of a state prisoner escaping by a hickry-bark ladder? Why, it's perfectly ridiculous."

"Well, all right, Tom, fix it your own way; but if you'll take my advice, you'll let me borrow a sheet off of the clothes-line."

He said that would do. And that give him another idea, and he says:

"Borrow a shirt, too."

"What do we want of a shirt, Tom?"

"Want it for Jim to keep a journal on."

"Journal your granny—*Jim* can't write."

"Spose he *can't* write—he can make marks on the shirt, can't he, if we make him a pen out of an old pewter spoon or a piece of an old iron barrel-hoop?"

"Why, Tom, we can pull a feather out of a goose and make him a better one; and quicker, too."

"*Prisoners* don't have geese running around the donjon-keep to pull pens out of, you muggins. They *always* make their pens out of the hardest, toughest, troublesomest piece of old brass candlestick or something like that they can get their hands on; and it takes them weeks and weeks, and months and months to file it out, too, because they've got to do it by rubbing it on the wall. *They* wouldn't use a goose-quill if they had it. It ain't regular."

"Well, then, what'll we make him the ink out of?"

"Many makes it out of iron-rust and tears; but that's the common sort and women; the best authorities uses their own blood. Jim can do that; and when he wants to send any little common ordinary mysterious message to let the world know where he's captivated, he can write it on the bottom of a tin plate with a fork and throw it out of the window. The Iron Mask[1] always done that, and it's a blame' good way, too."

"Jim ain't got no tin plates. They feed him in a pan."

"That ain't anything; we can get him some."

"Can't nobody *read* his plates."

"That ain't got nothing to *do* with it, Huck Finn. All *he's* got to do is to write on the plate and throw it out. You don't *have* to be able to read it. Why, half the time you can't read anything a prisoner writes on a tin plate, or anywhere else."

"Well, then, what's the sense in wasting the plates?"

"Why, blame it all, it ain't the *prisoner's* plates."

"But it's *somebody's* plates, ain't it?"

"Well, spos'n it is? What does the *prisoner* care whose—"

He broke off there, because we heard the breakfast-horn blowing. So we cleared out for the house.

Along during that morning I borrowed a sheet and a white shirt off of the clothes-line; and I found an old sack and put them in it, and we went down and got the fox-fire, and put that in too. I called it borrowing, because that was what pap always called it; but Tom said it warn't borrowing, it was stealing. He said we was representing prisoners; and prisoners don't care how they get a thing so they get it, and nobody don't blame them for it, either. It ain't no crime in a prisoner to steal the thing he needs to get away with, Tom said; it's his right; and so, as long as we was representing a prisoner, we had a perfect right to steal anything on this place we had the least use for, to get ourselves out of prison with. He said if we warn't prisoners it would be a very different thing, and nobody but a mean ornery person would steal when he warn't a prisoner. So we allowed we would steal everything there was that come handy. And yet he made a mighty fuss, one day, after that, when I stole a watermelon out of the nigger patch and eat it; and he made me go and give the niggers a dime, without telling them what it was for. Tom said that what he meant was, we could steal anything we *needed*. Well, I says, I needed the watermelon. But he said I didn't need it to get out of prison with, there's where the difference was. He said if I'd a wanted it to hide a knife in, and smuggle it to Jim to kill the seneskal with, it would a been all right. So I let it go at that, though I couldn't see no advantage in my representing a prisoner, if I got to set down and chaw over a lot of gold-leaf distinctions like that, every time I see a chance to hog a watermelon.

Well, as I was saying, we waited that morning till everybody was settled down to business, and nobody in sight around the yard; then Tom he carried the sack into the lean-to whilst I stood off a piece to keep watch. By-and-by he come out, and we went and set down on the wood-pile, to talk. He says:

"Everything's all right, now, except tools; and that's easy fixed."

"Tools?" I says.

---

1. The chief character in Alexandre Dumas's novel *Le Vicomte de Bragelonne* (1848–50), part of which was translated into English as *The Man in the Iron Mask*.

"Yes."

"Tools for what?"

"Why, to dig with. We ain't agoing to *gnaw* him out, are we?"

"Ain't them old crippled picks and things in there good enough to dig a nigger out with?" I says.

He turns on me looking pitying enough to make a body cry, and says:

"Huck Finn, did you *ever* hear of a prisoner having picks and shovels, and all the modern conveniences in his wardrobe to dig himself out with? Now I want to ask you—if you got any reasonableness in you at all—what kind of a show would *that* give him to be a hero? Why, they might as well lend him the key, and done with it. Picks and shovels—why they wouldn't furnish 'em to a king."

"Well, then," I says, "if we don't want the picks and shovels, what do we want?"

"A couple of case-knives."[2]

"To dig the foundations out from under that cabin with?"

"Yes."

"Confound it, it's foolish, Tom."

"It don't make no difference how foolish it is, it's the *right* way—and it's the regular way. And there ain't no *other* way, that ever *I* heard of, and I've read all the books that gives any information about these things. They always dig out with a case-knife—and not through dirt, mind you; generly it's through solid rock. And it takes them weeks and weeks and weeks, and for ever and ever. Why, look at one of them prisoners in the bottom dungeon of the Castle Deef,[3] in the harbor of Marseilles, that dug himself out that way; how long was *he* at it, you reckon?"

"I don't know."

"Well, guess."

"I don't know. A month and a half?"

"*Thirty-seven year*—and he come out in China. *That's* the kind. I wish the bottom of *this* fortress was solid rock."

"*Jim* don't know nobody in China."

"What's *that* got to do with it? Neither did that other fellow. But you're always a-wandering off on a side issue. Why can't you stick to the main point?"

"All right—*I* don't care where he comes out, so he *comes* out; and Jim don't, either, I reckon. But there's one thing, anyway—Jim's too old to be dug out with a case-knife. He won't last."

"Yes he will *last*, too. You don't reckon it's going to take thirty-seven years to dig out through a *dirt* foundation, do you?"

"How long will it take, Tom?"

"Well, we can't resk being as long as we ought to, because it mayn't take very long for Uncle Silas to hear from down there by New Orleans. He'll hear Jim ain't from there. Then his next move will be to advertise Jim, or something like that. So we can't resk being as long digging him out as we ought to. By rights I reckon we ought to be a couple of years; but we can't. Things being so uncertain, what I recommend is this: that we really dig right in, as quick as we can; and after that, we can *let on*, to ourselves, that

---

2. Ordinary kitchen knives.
3. The hero of Alexandre Dumas's popular Romantic novel *The Count of Monte Cristo* (1844) was held prisoner at the Château d'If, a castle built by Francis I in 1524 on a small island in Marseilles harbor and used for many years as a state prison.

we was at it thirty-seven years. Then we can snatch him out and rush him away the first time there's an alarm. Yes, I reckon that'll be the best way."

"Now, there's *sense* in that," I says. "Letting on don't cost nothing; letting on ain't no trouble; and if it's any object, I don't mind letting on we was at it a hundred and fifty year. It wouldn't strain me none, after I got my hand in. So I'll mosey along now, and smouch a couple of case-knives."

"Smouch three," he says; "we want one to make a saw out of."

"Tom, if it ain't unregular and irreligious to sejest it," I says, "there's an old rusty saw-blade around yonder sticking under the weatherboarding behind the smoke-house."

He looked kind of weary and discouraged-like, and says:

"It ain't no use to try to learn you nothing, Huck. Run along and smouch the knives—three of them." So I done it.

Chapter XXXVI

As soon as we reckoned everybody was asleep, that night, we went down the lightning-rod, and shut ourselves up in the lean-to, and got out our pile of fox-fire, and went to work. We cleared everything out of the way, about four or five foot along the middle of the bottom log. Tom said he was right behind Jim's bed now, and we'd dig in under it, and when we got through there couldn't nobody in the cabin ever know there was any hole there, because Jim's counterpin[4] hung down most to the ground, and you'd have to raise it up and look under to see the hole. So we dug and dug, with case-knives, till most midnight; and then we was dog-tired, and our hands was blistered, and yet you couldn't see we'd done anything, hardly. At last I says:

"This ain't no thirty-seven year job, this is a thirty-eight year job, Tom Sawyer."

He never said nothing. But he sighed, and pretty soon he stopped digging, and then for a good little while I knowed he was thinking. Then he says:

"It ain't no use, Huck, it ain't agoing to work. If we was prisoners it would, because then we'd have as many years as we wanted, and no hurry; and we wouldn't get but a few minutes to dig, every day, while they was changing watches, and so our hands wouldn't get blistered, and we could keep it up right along, year in and year out, and do it right, and the way it ought to be done. But *we* can't fool along, we got to rush; we ain't got no time to spare. If we was to put in another night this way, we'd have to knock off for a week to let our hands get well—couldn't touch a case-knife with them sooner."

"Well, then, what we going to do, Tom?"

"I'll tell you. It ain't right, and it ain't moral, and I wouldn't like it to get out—but there ain't only just the one way; we got to dig him out with the picks, and *let on* it's case-knives."

"*Now* you're *talking!*" I says; "your head gets leveler and leveler all the time, Tom Sawyer," I says. "Picks is the thing, moral or no moral; and as for me, I don't care shucks for the morality of it, nohow. When I start in to steal a nigger, or a watermelon, or a Sunday-school book, I ain't no ways particular how it's done so it's done. What I want is my nigger; or what I want is my watermelon; or what I want is my Sunday-school book; and if a pick's the handiest thing, that's the thing I'm agoing to dig that nigger or

4. Counterpane or bedspread.

that watermelon or that Sunday-school book out with; and I don't give a dead rat what the authorities thinks about it nuther."

"Well," he says, "there's excuse for picks and letting-on in a case like this; if it warn't so, I wouldn't approve of it, nor I wouldn't stand by and see the rules broke—because right is right, and wrong is wrong, and a body ain't got no business doing wrong when he ain't ignorant and knows better. It might answer for *you* to dig Jim out with a pick, *without* any letting-on, because you don't know no better; but it wouldn't for me, because I do know better. Gimme a case-knife."

He had his own by him, but I handed him mine. He flung it down, and says:

"Gimme a *case-knife*."

I didn't know just what to do—but then I thought. I scratched around amongst the old tools, and got a pick-ax and give it to him, and he took it and went to work, and never said a word.

He was always just that particular. Full of principle.

So then I got a shovel, and then we picked and shoveled, turn about, and made the fur fly. We stuck to it about a half an hour, which was as long as we could stand up; but we had a good deal of a hole to show for it. When I got up stairs, I looked out at the window and see Tom doing his level best with the lightning-rod, but he couldn't come it, his hands was so sore. At last he says:

"It ain't no use, it can't be done. What you reckon I better do? Can't you think up no way?"

"Yes," I says, "but I reckon it ain't regular. Come up the stairs, and let on it's a lightning-rod."

So he done it.

Next day Tom stole a pewter spoon and a brass candlestick in the house, for to make some pens for Jim out of, and six tallow candles; and I hung around the nigger cabins, and laid for a chance, and stole three tin plates. Tom said it wasn't enough; but I said nobody wouldn't ever see the plates that Jim throwed out, because they'd fall in the dog-fennel and jimpson weeds under the window-hole—then we could tote them back and he could use them over again. So Tom was satisfied. Then he says:

"Now, the thing to study out is, how to get the things to Jim."

"Take them in through the hole," I says, "when we get it done."

He only just looked scornful, and said something about nobody ever heard of such an idiotic idea, and then he went to studying. By-and-by he said he had ciphered out two or three ways, but there warn't no need to decide on any of them yet. Said we'd got to post Jim first.

That night we went down the lightning-rod a little after ten, and took one of the candles along, and listened under the window-hole, and heard Jim snoring; so we pitched it in, and it didn't wake him. Then we whirled in with the pick and shovel, and in about two hours and a half the job was done. We crept in under Jim's bed and into the cabin, and pawed around and found the candle and lit it, and stood over Jim a while, and found him looking hearty and healthy, and then we woke him up gentle and gradual. He was so glad to see us he most cried; and called us honey, and all the pet names he could think of; and was for having us hunt up a cold chisel to cut the chain off of his leg with, right away, and clearing out without losing any time. But Tom he showed him how unregular it would be, and set down and told him all about our plans, and how we could alter them in a minute any time there was an alarm; and not to be the least afraid, because we would see he got away, *sure*. So Jim he said it was all right, and we set there and talked over old times a while, and then Tom asked a lot of questions, and when Jim told him Uncle Silas come in every day or two to pray with him, and Aunt Sally come in to see if he was comfortable and had plenty to eat, and both of them was kind as they could be, Tom says:

"*Now* I know how to fix it. We'll send you some things by them."

I said, "Don't do nothing of the kind; it's one of the most jackass ideas I ever struck;" but he never paid no attention to me; went right on. It was his way when he'd got his plans set.

So he told Jim how we'd have to smuggle in the rope-ladder pie, and other large things, by Nat, the nigger that fed him, and he must be on the look-out, and not be surprised, and not let Nat see him open them; and we would put small things in uncle's coat pockets and he must steal them out; and we would tie things to aunt's apron strings or put them in her apron pocket, if we got a chance; and told him what they would be and what they was for. And told him how to keep a journal on the shirt with his blood, and all that. He told him everything. Jim he couldn't see no sense in the most of it, but he allowed we was white folks and knowed better than him; so he was satisfied, and said he would do it all just as Tom said.

Jim had plenty corn-cob pipes and tobacco; so we had a right down good sociable time; then we crawled out through the hole, and so home to bed, with hands that looked like they'd been chawed. Tom was in high spirits. He said it was the best fun he ever had in his life, and the most intellectural; and said if he only could see his way to it we would keep it up all the rest of our lives and leave Jim to our children to get out; for he believed Jim would come to like it better and better the more he got used to it. He said that in that way it could be strung out to as much as eighty year, and would be the best time on record. And he said it would make us all celebrated that had a hand in it.

In the morning we went out to the wood-pile and chopped up the brass candlestick into handy sizes, and Tom put them and the pewter spoon in his pocket. Then we went to the nigger cabins, and while I got Nat's notice off, Tom shoved a piece of candlestick into the middle of a corn-pone that was in Jim's pan, and we went along with Nat to see how it would work, and it just worked noble; when Jim bit into it it most mashed all his teeth out; and there warn't ever anything could a worked better. Tom said so himself. Jim he never let on but what it was only just a piece of rock or something like that that's always getting into bread, you know; but after that he never bit into nothing but what he jabbed his fork into it in three or four places, first.

And whilst we was a standing there in the dimmish light, here comes a couple of the hounds bulging in, from under Jim's bed; and they kept on piling in till there was eleven of them, and there warn't hardly room in there to get your breath. By jings, we forgot to fasten that lean-to door. The nigger Nat he only just hollered "witches!" once, and kneeled over onto the floor amongst the dogs, and begun to groan like he was dying. Tom jerked the door open and flung out a slab of Jim's meat, and the dogs went for it, and in two seconds he was out himself and back again and shut the door, and I knowed he'd fixed the other door too. Then he went to work on the nigger, coaxing him and petting him, and asking him if he'd been imagining he saw something again. He raised up, and blinked his eyes around, and says:

"Mars Sid, you'll say I's a fool, but if I didn't b'lieve I see most a million dogs, er devils, er some'n, I wisht I may die right heah in dese tracks. I did, mos' sholy. Mars Sid, I *felt* um—I *felt* um, sah; dey was all over me. Dad fetch it, I jis' wisht I could git my han's on one er dem witches jis' wunst—on'y jis' wunst—it's all I'd ast. But mos'ly I wisht dey'd lemme 'lone, I does."

Tom says:

"Well, I tell you what I think. What makes them come here just at this runaway nigger's breakfast-time? It's because they're hungry; that's the reason. You make them a witch pie; that's the thing for you to do."

"But my lan', Mars Sid, how's I gwyne to make 'm a witch pie? I doan' know how to make it. I hain't ever hearn er sich a thing b'fo.'"

"Well, then, I'll have to make it myself."

"Will you do it, honey?—will you? I'll wusshup de groun' und' yo' foot, I will!"

"All right, I'll do it, seeing it's you, and you've been good to us and showed us the runaway nigger. But you got to be mighty careful. When we come around, you turn your back; and then whatever we've put in the pan, don't you let on you see it at all. And don't you look, when Jim unloads the pan—something might happen, I don't know what. And above all, don't you handle the witch-things."

"Hannel 'm Mars Sid? What is you a talkin' 'bout? I wouldn' lay de weight er my finger on um, not f'r ten hund'd thous'n' billion dollars, I wouldn't."

Chapter XXXVII

That was all fixed. So then we went away and went to the rubbage-pile in the back yard where they keep the old boots, and rags, and pieces of bottles, and wore-out tin things, and all such truck, and scratched around and found an old tin washpan and stopped up the holes as well as we could, to bake the pie in, and took it down cellar and stole it full of flour, and started for breakfast and found a couple of shingle-nails that Tom said would be handy for a prisoner to scrabble his name and sorrows on the dungeon walls with, and dropped one of them in Aunt Sally's apron pocket which was hanging on a chair, and t'other we stuck in the band of Uncle Silas's hat, which was on the bureau, because we heard the children say their pa and ma was going to the runaway nigger's house this morning, and then went to breakfast, and Tom dropped the pewter spoon in Uncle Silas's coat pocket, and Aunt Sally wasn't come yet, so we had to wait a little while.

And when she come she was hot, and red, and cross, and couldn't hardly wait for the blessing; and then she went to sluicing out coffee with one hand and cracking the handiest child's head with her thimble with the other, and says:

"I've hunted high, and I've hunted low, and it does beat all, what has become of your other shirt."

My heart fell down amongst my lungs and livers and things, and a hard piece of corn-crust started down my throat after it and got met on the road with a cough and was shot across the table and took one of the children in the eye and curled him up like a fishing-worm, and let a cry out of him the size of a war-whoop, and Tom he turned kinder blue around the gills, and it all amounted to a considerable state of things for about a quarter of a minute or as much as that, and I would a sold out for half price if there was a bidder. But after that we was all right again—it was the sudden surprise of it that knocked us so kind of cold. Uncle Silas he says:

"It's most uncommon curious, I can't understand it. I know perfectly well I took it off, because——"

"Because you hain't got but one on. Just *listen* at the man! *I* know you took it off, and know it by a better way than your wool-gethering memory, too, because it was on the clo'es-line yesterday—I see it there myself. But it's gone—that's the long and the short of it, and you'll just have to change to a red flann'l one till I can get time to make a new one. And it'll be the third I've made in two years; it just keeps a body on the jump to keep you in shirts; and whatever you do manage to *do* with 'm all, is more'n *I* can make out. A body'd think you *would* learn to take some sort of care of 'em, at your time of life."

"I know it, Sally, and I do try all I can. But it oughtn't to be altogether my fault, because you know I don't see them nor have nothing to do with them except when they're on me; and I don't believe I've ever lost one of them *off* of me."

"Well, it ain't *your* fault if you haven't, Silas—you'd a done it if you could, I reckon. And the shirt ain't all that's gone, nuther. Ther's a spoon gone; and *that* ain't all. There was ten, and now ther's only nine. The calf got the shirt I reckon, but the calf never took the spoon, *that's* certain."

"Why, what else is gone, Sally?"

"Ther's six *candles* gone—that's what. The rats could a got the candles, and I reckon they did; I wonder they don't walk off with the whole place, the way you're always going to stop their holes and don't do it; and if they warn't fools they'd sleep in your hair, Silas—*you'd* never find it out; but you can't lay the *spoon* on the rats, and that I *know*."

"Well, Sally, I'm in fault, and I acknowledge it; I've been remiss; but I won't let to-morrow go by without stopping up them holes."

"Oh, I wouldn't hurry, next year'll do. Matilda Angelina Araminta *Phelps!*"

Whack comes the thimble, and the child snatches her claws out of the sugar-bowl without fooling around any. Just then, the nigger woman steps onto the passage, and says:

"Missus, dey's a sheet gone."

"A *sheet* gone! Well, for land's sake!"

"I'll stop up them holes *to-day*," says Uncle Silas, looking sorrowful.

"Oh, *do* shet up!—spose the rats took the *sheet? Where's* it gone, Lize?"

"Clah to goodness I hain't no notion, Miss Sally. She wuz on de clo's-line yistiddy, but she done gone; she ain' dah no mo', now."

"I reckon the world *is* coming to an end. I *never* see the beat of it, in all my born days. A shirt, and a sheet, and a spoon, and six can—"

"Missus," comes a young yaller wench, "dey's a brass candlestick miss'n."

"Cler out from here, you hussy, er I'll take a skillet to ye!"

Well, she was just a biling. I begun to lay for a chance; I reckoned I would sneak out and go for the woods till the weather moderated. She kept a raging right along, running her insurrection all by herself, and everybody else mighty meek and quiet; and at last Uncle Silas, looking kind of foolish, fishes up that spoon out of his pocket. She stopped, with her mouth open and her hands up, and as for me, I wished I was in Jeruslem or somewheres. But not long; because she says:

"It's *just* as I expected. So you had it in your pocket all the time; and like as not you've got the other things there, too. How'd it get there?"

"I reely don't know, Sally," he says, kind of apologizing, "or you know I would tell. I was a-studying over my text in Acts Seventeen,[5] before breakfast,

---

5. In Acts 17, Paul's preaching to the Athenians berates both their false gods and snobbery; verse 29 declares that "we are all God's offspring."

and I reckon I put it in there, not noticing, meaning to put my Testament in, and it must be so, because my Testament ain't in, but I'll go and see, and if the Testament is where I had it, I'll know I didn't put it in, and that will show that I laid the Testament down and took up the spoon, and——"

"Oh, for the land's sake! Give a body a rest! Go 'long now, the whole kit and biling of ye; and don't come nigh me again till I've got back my peace of mind."

I'd a heard her, if she'd a said it to herself, let alone speaking it out; and I'd a got up and obeyed her, if I'd a been dead. As we was passing through the setting-room, the old man he took up his hat, and the shingle-nail fell out on the floor, and he just merely picked it up and laid it on the mantel-shelf, and never said nothing, and went out. Tom see him do it, and remembered about the spoon, and says:

"Well, it ain't no use to send things by *him* no more, he ain't reliable." Then he says: "But he done us a good turn with the spoon, anyway, without knowing it, and so we'll go and do him one without *him* knowing it—stop up his rat-holes."

There was a noble good lot of them, down cellar, and it took us a whole hour, but we done the job tight and good, and ship-shape. Then we heard steps on the stairs, and blowed out our light, and hid; and here comes the old man, with a candle in one hand and a bundle of stuff in t'other, looking as absent-minded as year before last. He went a mooning around, first to one rat-hole and then another, till he'd been to them all. Then he stood about five minutes, picking tallow-drip off of his candle and thinking. Then he turns off slow and dreamy towards the stairs, saying:

"Well, for the life of me I can't remember when I done it. I could show her now that I warn't to blame on account of the rats. But never mind—let it go. I reckon it wouldn't do no good."

And so he went on a mumbling up stairs, and then we left. He was a mighty nice old man. And always is.

Tom was a good deal bothered about what to do for a spoon, but he said we'd got to have it; so he took a think. When he had ciphered it out, he told me how we was to do; then we went and waited around the spoon-basket till we see Aunt Sally coming, and then Tom went to counting the spoons and laying them out to one side, and I slip one of them up my sleeve, and Tom says:

"Why, Aunt Sally, there ain't but nine spoons, *yet*."

She says:

"Go 'long to your play, and don't bother me. I know better, I counted 'm myself."

"Well, I've counted them twice, Aunty, and *I* can't make but nine."

She looked out of all patience, but of course she come to count—anybody would.

"I declare to gracious ther' *ain't* but nine!" she says. "Why, what in the world—plague *take* the things, I'll count 'm again."

So I slipped back the one I had, and when she got done counting, she says:

"Hang the troublesome rubbage, ther's *ten* now!" and she looked huffy and bothered both. But Tom says:

"Why, Aunty I don't think there's ten."

"You numskull, didn't you see me *count* 'm?"

"I know, but—"

"Well, I'll count 'm *again*."

So I smouched one, and they come out nine same as the other time. Well, she *was* in a tearing way—just a trembling all over, she was so mad. But she counted and counted, till she got that addled she'd start to count-in the *basket* for a spoon, sometimes; and so, three times they come out right, and three times they come out wrong. Then she grabbed up the basket and slammed it across the house and knocked the cat galley-west;[6] and she said cle'r out and let her have some peace, and if we come bothering around her again betwixt that and dinner, she'd skin us. So we had the odd spoon; and dropped it in her apron pocket whilst she was giving us our sailing-orders, and Jim got it all right, along with her shingle-nail, before noon. We was very well satisfied with the business, and Tom allowed it was worth twice the trouble it took, because he said *now* she couldn't ever count them spoons twice alike again to save her life; and wouldn't believe she'd counted them right, if she *did*; and said that after she'd about counted her head off, for the last three days, he judged she'd give it up and offer to kill anybody that wanted her to ever count them any more.

So we put the sheet back on the line, that night, and stole one out of her closet; and kept on putting it back and stealing it again, for a couple of days, till she didn't know how many sheets she had, any more, and said she didn't *care*, and warn't agoing to bullyrag[7] the rest of her soul out about it, and wouldn't count them again not to save her life, she druther die first.

So we was all right now, as to the shirt and the sheet and the spoon and the candles, by the help of the calf and the rats and the mixed-up counting; and as to the candlestick, it warn't no consequence, it would blow over by-and-by.

But that pie was a job; we had no end of trouble with that pie. We fixed it up away down in the woods, and cooked it there; and we got it done at last, and very satisfactory, too; but not all in one day; and we had to use up three washpans full of flour, before we got through, and we got burnt pretty much all over, in places, and eyes put out with the smoke; because, you see, we didn't want nothing but a crust, and we couldn't prop it up right, and she would always cave in. But of course we thought of the right way at last; which was to cook the ladder, too, in the pie. So then we laid in with Jim, the second night, and tore up the sheet all in little strings, and twisted them together, and long before daylight we had a lovely rope, that you could a hung a person with. We let on it took nine months to make it.

And in the forenoon we took it down to the woods, but it wouldn't go in the pie. Being made of a whole sheet, that way, there was rope enough for forty pies, if we'd a wanted them, and plenty left over for soup, or sausage, or anything you choose. We could a had a whole dinner.

But we didn't need it. All we needed was just enough for the pie, and so we throwed the rest away. We didn't cook none of the pies in the washpan, afraid the solder would melt; but Uncle Silas he had a noble brass warming-pan which he thought considerable of, because it belonged to one of his ancestors with a long wooden handle that come over from England with William the Conqueror in the *Mayflower*[8] or one of them early ships and was hid away up garret with a lot of other old pots and things that was valuable, not on account of being any account because they warn't, but on account of them being relicts, you know, and we snaked her out, private, and took her down

6. Into confusion.
7. To nag mercilessly.

8. William the Conqueror lived in the 11th century. The *Mayflower* made its crossing in 1620.

there, but she failed on the first pies, because we didn't know how, but she come up smiling on the last one. We took and lined her with dough, and set her in the coals, and loaded her up with rag-rope, and put on a dough roof, and shut down the lid, and put hot embers on top, and stood off five foot, with the long handle, cool and comfortable, and in fifteen minutes she turned out a pie that was a satisfaction to look at. But the person that et it would want to fetch a couple of kags of toothpicks along, for if that rope-ladder wouldn't cramp him down to business, I don't know nothing what I'm talking about, and lay him in enough stomach-ache to last him till next time, too.

Nat didn't look, when we put the witch-pie in Jim's pan; and we put the three tin plates in the bottom of the pan under the vittles; and so Jim got everything all right, and as soon as he was by himself he busted into the pie and hid the rope-ladder inside of his straw tick, and scratched some marks on a tin plate and throwed it out of the window-hole.

Chapter XXXVIII

Making them pens was a distressid-tough job, and so was the saw; and Jim allowed the inscription was going to be the toughest of all. That's the one which the prisoner has to scrabble on the wall. But we had to have it; Tom said we'd *got* to; there warn't no case of a state prisoner not scrabbling his inscription to leave behind, and his coat of arms.

"Look at Lady Jane Grey," he says; "look at Gilford Dudley; look at old Northumberland![9] Why, Huck, spose it *is* considerable trouble?—what you going to do?—how you going to get around it? Jim's *got* to do his inscription and coat of arms. They all do."

Jim says:

"Why, Mars Tom, I hain't got no coat o' arms; I hain't got nuffn but dish-yer old shirt, en you knows I got to keep de journal on dat."

"Oh, you don't understand, Jim; a coat of arms is very different."

"Well," I says, "Jim's right, anyway, when he says he hain't got no coat of arms, because he hain't."

"I reckon *I* knowed that," Tom says, "but you bet he'll have one before he goes out of this—because he's going out *right,* and there ain't going to be no flaws in his record."

So whilst me and Jim filed away at the pens on a brickbat[1] apiece, Jim a making his'n out of the brass and I making mine out of the spoon, Tom set to work to think out the coat of arms. By-and-by he said he'd struck so many good ones he didn't hardly know which to take, but there was one which he reckoned he'd decide on. He says:

"On the scutcheon[2] we'll have a bend *or* in the dexter base, a saltire *murrey* in the fess, with a dog, couchant, for common charge, and under his foot a chain embattled, for slavery, with a chevron *vert* in a chief engrailed, and three invected lines on a field *azure,* with the nombril points rampant on a dancette indented; crest, a runaway nigger, *sable,* with his bundle over

9. The story of Lady Jane Grey (1537–1554), her husband, Guildford Dudley, and his father, the duke of Northumberland, was told in W.H. Ainsworth's romance *The Tower of London* (1840). The duke was at work carving a poem on the wall of his cell when the executioners came for him.

1. A fragment of brick.
2. An escutcheon is the shield-shaped surface on which a coat of arms is inscribed. The details are expressed in the technical terminology of heraldry.

his shoulder on a bar sinister: and a couple of gules for supporters, which is you and me; motto, *Maggiore fretta, minore atto*. Got it out of a book— means, the more haste, the less speed."

"Geewhillikins," I says, "but what does the rest of it mean?"

"We ain't got no time to bother over that," he says, "we got to dig in like all git-out."

"Well, anyway," I says, "what's *some* of it? What's a fess?"

"A fess—a fess is—*you* don't need to know what a fess is. I'll show him how to make it when he gets to it."

"Shucks, Tom," I says, "I think you might tell a person. What's a bar sinister?"

"Oh, *I* don't know. But he's got to have it. All the nobility does."

That was just his way. If it didn't suit him to explain a thing to you, he wouldn't do it. You might pump at him a week, it wouldn't make no difference.

He'd got all that coat of arms business fixed, so now he started in to finish up the rest of that part of the work, which was to plan out a mournful inscription—said Jim got to have one, like they all done. He made up a lot, and wrote them out on a paper, and read them off, so:

1. *Here a captive heart busted.*

2. *Here a poor prisoner, forsook by the world and friends, fretted out his sorrowful life.*

3. *Here a lonely heart broke, and a worn spirit went to its rest, after thirty-seven years of solitary captivity.*

4. *Here, homeless and friendless, after thirty-seven years of bitter captivity, perished a noble stranger, natural son of Louis XIV.*

Tom's voice trembled, whilst he was reading them, and he most broke down. When he got done, he couldn't no way make up his mind which one for Jim to scrabble onto the wall, they was all so good; but at last he allowed he would let him scrabble them all on. Jim said it would take him a year to scrabble such a lot of truck onto the logs with a nail, and he didn't know how to make letters, besides; but Tom said he would block them out for him, and then he wouldn't have nothing to do but just follow the lines. Then pretty soon he says:

"Come to think, the logs ain't agoing to do; they don't have log walls in a dungeon: we got to dig the inscriptions into a rock. We'll fetch a rock."

Jim said the rock was worse than the logs; he said it would take him such a pison long time to dig them into a rock, he wouldn't ever get out. But Tom said he would let me help him do it. Then he took a look to see how me and Jim was getting along with the pens. It was most pesky tedious hard work and slow, and didn't give my hands no show to get well of the sores, and we didn't seem to make no headway, hardly. So Tom says:

"I know how to fix it. We got to have a rock for the coat of arms and mournful inscriptions, and we can kill two birds with that same rock. There's a gaudy big grindstone down at the mill, and we'll smouch it, and carve the things on it, and file out the pens and the saw on it, too."

It warn't no slouch of an idea; and it warn't no slouch of a grindstone nuther; but we allowed we'd tackle it. It warn't quite midnight, yet, so we cleared out for the mill, leaving Jim at work. We smouched the grindstone, and set out to roll her home, but it was a most nation tough job. Sometimes, do what we could, we couldn't keep her from falling over, and she come mighty near mashing us, every time. Tom said she was going to get one of us, sure, before we got through. We got her half way; and then we was plumb played out, and most drownded with sweat. We see it warn't no use, we got to go and fetch Jim. So he raised up his bed and slid the chain off of the bed-leg, and wrapt it round and round his neck, and we crawled out through our hole and down there, and Jim and me laid into that grindstone and walked her along like nothing; and Tom superintended. He could out-superintend any boy I ever see. He knowed how to do everything.

Our hole was pretty big, but it warn't big enough to get the grindstone through; but Jim he took the pick and soon made it big enough. Then Tom marked out them things on it with the nail, and set Jim to work on them, with the nail for a chisel and an iron bolt from the rubbage in the lean-to for a hammer, and told him to work till the rest of his candle quit on him, and then he could go to bed, and hide the grindstone under his straw tick and sleep on it. Then we helped him fix his chain back on the bed-leg, and was ready for bed ourselves. But Tom thought of something, and says:

"You got any spiders in here, Jim?"

"No, sah, thanks to goodness I hain't, Mars Tom."

"All right, we'll get you some."

"But bless you, honey, I doan' *want* none. I's afeard un um. I jis' 's soon have rattlesnakes aroun'."

Tom thought a minute or two, and says:

"It's a good idea. And I reckon it's been done. It *must* a been done; it stands to reason. Yes, it's a prime good idea. Where could you keep it?"

"Keep what, Mars Tom?"

"Why, a rattlesnake."

"De goodness gracious alive, Mars Tom! Why, if dey was a rattlesnake to come in heah, I'd take en bust right out thoo dat log wall, I would, wid my head."

"Why, Jim, you wouldn't be afraid of it, after a little. You could tame it."

"*Tame* it!"

"Yes—easy enough. Every animal is grateful for kindness and petting, and they wouldn't *think* of hurting a person that pets them. Any book will tell you that. You try—that's all I ask; just try for two or three days. Why, you can get him so, in a little while, that he'll love you; and sleep with you; and won't stay away from you a minute; and will let you wrap him round your neck and put his head in your mouth."

"*Please*, Mars Tom—*doan'* talk so! I can't *stan'* it! He'd *let* me shove his head in my mouf—fer a favor, hain't it? I lay he'd wait a pow'ful long time 'fo' I *ast* him. En mo' en dat, I doan' *want* him to sleep wid me."

"Jim, don't act so foolish. A prisoner's *got* to have some kind of a dumb pet, and if a rattlesnake hain't ever been tried, why, there's more glory to be gained in your being the first to ever try it than any other way you could ever think of to save your life."

"Why, Mars Tom, I doan' *want* no sich glory. Snake take 'n bite Jim's chin off, den *whah* is de glory? No, sah, I doan' want no sich doin's."

"Blame it, can't you *try*? I only *want* you to try—you needn't keep it up if it don't work."

"But de trouble all *done,* ef de snake bite me while I's a tryin' him. Mars Tom, I's willin' to tackle mos' anything 'at ain't onreasonable, but ef you en

Huck fetches a rattlesnake in heah for me to tame, I's gwyne to *leave*, dat's *shore*."

"Well, then, let it go, let it go, if you're so bullheaded about it. We can get you some garter-snakes and you can tie some buttons on their tails, and let on they're rattlesnakes, and I reckon that'll have to do."

"I k'n stan' *dem*, Mars Tom, but blame' 'f I couldn't get along widout um, I tell you dat. I never knowed b'fo', 't was so much bother and trouble to be a prisoner."

"Well, it *always* is, when it's done right. You got any rats around here?"

"No, sah, I hain't seed none."

"Well, we'll get you some rats."

"Why, Mars Tom, I doan' *want* no rats. Dey's de dad-blamedest creturs to sturb a body, en rustle roun' over 'im, en bite his feet, when he's tryin' to sleep, I ever see. So, sah, gimme g'yarter-snakes, 'f I's got to have 'm, but doan' gimme no rats. I ain' got not use f'r um, skasely."

"But Jim, you *got* to have 'em—they all do. So don't make no more fuss about it. Prisoners ain't ever without rats. There ain't no instance of it. And they train them, and pet them, and learn them tricks, and they get to be as sociable as flies. But you got to play music to them. You got anything to play music on?"

"I ain't got nuffn but a coase comb en a piece o' paper, en a juice-harp; but I reck'n dey wouldn't take no stock in a juice-harp."

"Yes, they would. *They* don't care what kind of music 'tis. A jews-harp's plenty good enough for a rat. All animals likes music—in a prison they dote on it. Specially, painful music; and you can't get no other kind out of a jews-harp. It always interests them; they come out to see what's the matter with you. Yes, you're all right; you're fixed very well. You want to set on your bed, nights, before you go to sleep, and early in the mornings, and play your jews-harp; play The Last Link is Broken—that's the thing that'll scoop a rat, quicker'n anything else: and when you've played about two minutes, you'll see all the rats, and the snakes, and spiders, and things begin to feel worried about you, and come. And they'll just fairly swarm over you, and have a noble good time."

"Yes, *dey* will, I reck'n, Mars Tom, but what kine er time is *Jim* havin'? Blest if I kin see de pint. But I'll do it ef I got to. I reck'n I better keep de animals satisfied, en not have no trouble in de house."

Tom waited to think over, and see if there wasn't nothing else; and pretty soon he says:

"Oh—there's one thing I forgot. Could you raise a flower here, do you reckon?"

"I doan' know but maybe I could, Mars Tom; but it's tolable dark in heah, en I ain' got no use f'r no flower, nohow, en she'd be a pow'ful sight o' trouble."

"Well, you try it, anyway. Some other prisoners has done it."

"One er dem big cat-tail-lookin' mullen-stalks would grow in heah, Mars Tom, I reck'n, but she wouldn' be wuth half de trouble she'd coss."

"Don't you believe it. We'll fetch you a little one, and you plant it in the corner, over there, and raise it. And don't call it mullen, call it Pitchiola—that's its right name, when it's in a prison.[3] And you want to water it with your tears."

---

3. *Picciola* (1836) was a popular romantic novel by Xavier Saintine (pseudonym for Joseph Xavier Boniface, 1798–1865), in which a plant helps a prisoner survive.

"Why, I got plenty spring water, Mars Tom."

"You don't *want* spring water; you want to water it with your tears. It's the way they always do."

"Why, Mars Tom, I lay I kin raise one er dem mullen-stalks twyste wid spring water whiles another man's a *start'n* one wid tears."

"That ain't the idea. You *got* to do it with tears."

"She'll die on my han's, Mars Tom, she sholy will; kase I doan' skasely ever cry."

So Tom was stumped. But he studied it over, and then said Jim would have to worry along the best he could with an onion. He promised he would go to the nigger cabins and drop one, private, in Jim's coffee-pot, in the morning. Jim said he would "jis' 's soon have tobacker in his coffee;" and found so much fault with it, and with the work and bother of raising the mullen, and jews-harping the rats, and petting and flattering up the snakes and spiders and things, on top of all the other work he had to do on pens, and inscriptions, and journals, and things, which made it more trouble and worry and responsibility to be a prisoner than anything he ever undertook, that Tom most lost all patience with him; and said he was just loadened down with more gaudier chances than a prisoner ever had in the world to make a name for himself, and yet he didn't know enough to appreciate them, and they was just about wasted on him. So Jim he was sorry, and said he wouldn't behave so no more, and then me and Tom shoved for bed.

Chapter XXXIX

In the morning we went up to the village and bought a wire rat trap and fetched it down, and unstopped the best rat hole, and in about an hour we had fifteen of the bulliest kind of ones; and then we took it and put it in a safe place under Aunt Sally's bed. But while we was gone for spiders, little Thomas Franklin Benjamin Jefferson Elexander Phelps found it there, and opened the door of it to see if the rats would come out, and they did; and Aunt Sally she come in, and when we got back she was standing on top of the bed raising Cain, and the rats was doing what they could to keep off the dull times for her. So she took and dusted us both with the hickry, and we was as much as two hours catching another fifteen or sixteen, drat that meddlesome cub, and they warn't the likeliest, nuther, because the first haul was the pick of the flock. I never see a likelier lot of rats than what that first haul was.

We got a splendid stock of sorted spiders, and bugs, and frogs, and caterpillars, and one thing or another; and we like-to got a hornet's nest, but we didn't. The family was at home. We didn't give it right up, but staid with them as long as we could; because we allowed we'd tire them out or they'd got to tire us out, and they done it. Then we got allycumpain[4] and rubbed on the places, and was pretty near all right again, but couldn't set down convenient. And so we went for the snakes, and grabbed a couple of dozen garters and house-snakes, and put them in a bag, and put it in our room, and by that time it was supper time, and a rattling good honest day's work; and hungry?—oh, no I reckon not! And there warn't a blessed snake up there, when we went back—we didn't half tie the sack, and they worked out, somehow, and left.

---

4. Elecampane is an herb that Tom and Huck are using to relieve the pain of the hornet stings.

But it didn't matter much, because they was still on the premises some-wheres. So we judged we could get some of them again. No, there warn't no real scarcity of snakes about the house for a considerble spell. You'd see them dripping from the rafters and places, every now and then; and they generly landed in your plate, or down the back of your neck, and most of the time where you didn't want them. Well, they was handsome, and striped, and there warn't no harm in a million of them; but that never made no differ-ence to Aunt Sally, she despised snakes, be the breed what they might, and she couldn't stand them no way you could fix it; and every time one of them flopped down on her, it didn't make no difference what she was doing, she would just lay that work down and light out. I never see such a woman. And you could hear her whoop to Jericho. You couldn't get her to take aholt of one of them with the tongs. And if she turned over and found one in bed, she would scramble out and lift a howl that you would think the house was afire. She disturbed the old man so, that he said he could most wish there hadn't ever been no snakes created. Why, after every last snake had been gone clear out of the house for as much as a week, Aunt Sally warn't over it yet; she warn't near over it; when she was setting thinking about some-thing, you could touch her on the back of her neck with a feather and she would jump right out of her stockings. It was very curious. But Tom said all women was just so. He said they was made that way; for some reason or other.

We got a licking every time one of our snakes come in her way; and she allowed these lickings warn't nothing to what she would do if we ever loaded up the place again with them. I didn't mind the lickings, because they didn't amount to nothing; but I minded the trouble we had, to lay in another lot. But we got them laid in, and all the other things; and you never see a cabin as blithesome as Jim's was when they'd all swarm out for music and go for him. Jim didn't like the spiders, and the spiders didn't like Jim; and so they'd lay for him and make it mighty warm for him. And he said that between the rats, and the snakes, and the grindstone, there warn't no room in bed for him, skasely; and when there was, a body couldn't sleep, it was so lively, and it was always lively, he said, because *they* never all slept at one time, but took turn about, so when the snakes was asleep the rats was on deck, and when the rats turned in the snakes come on watch, so he always had one gang under him, in his way, and t'other gang having a circus over him, and if he got up to hunt a new place, the spiders would take a chance at him as he crossed over. He said if he ever got out, this time, he wouldn't ever be a pris-oner again, not for a salary.

Well, by the end of three weeks, everything was in pretty good shape. The shirt was sent in early, in a pie, and every time a rat bit Jim he would get up and write a little in his journal whilst the ink was fresh; the pens was made, the inscriptions and so on was all carved on the grindstone; the bed-leg was sawed in two, and we had et up the sawdust, and it give us a most amazing stomach-ache. We reckoned we was all going to die, but didn't. It was the most undigestible sawdust I ever see; and Tom said the same. But as I was saying, we'd got all the work done, now, at last; and we was all pretty much fagged out, too, but mainly Jim. The old man had wrote a couple of times to the plantation below Orleans to come and get their runaway nigger, but hadn't got no answer, because there warn't no such plantation; so he allowed he would advertise Jim in the St. Louis and New Orleans papers; and when he mentioned the St. Louis ones, it give me the cold shivers, and I see we hadn't no time to lose. So Tom said, now for the nonnamous letters.

"What's them?" I says.

"Warnings to the people that something is up. Sometimes it's done one way, sometimes another. But there's always somebody spying around, that gives notice to the governor of the castle. When Louis XVI was going to light out of the Tooleries,[5] a servant girl done it. It's a very good way, and so is the nonnamous letters. We'll use them both. And it's usual for the prisoner's mother to change clothes with him, and she stays in, and he slides out in her clothes. We'll do that too."

"But looky here, Tom, what do we want to *warn* anybody for, that something's up? Let them find it out for themselves—it's their lookout."

"Yes, I know; but you can't depend on them. It's the way they've acted from the very start—left us to do *everything*. They're so confiding and mulletheaded they don't take notice of nothing at all. So if we don't *give* them notice, there won't be nobody nor nothing to interfere with us, and so after all our hard work and trouble this escape 'll go off perfectly flat: won't amount to nothing—won't be nothing *to* it."

"Well, as for me, Tom, that's the way I'd like."

"Shucks," he says, and looked disgusted. So I says:

"But I ain't going to make no complaint. Anyway that suits you suits me. What you going to do about the servant-girl?"

"You'll be her. You slide in, in the middle of the night, and hook that yaller girl's frock."

"Why, Tom, that'll make trouble next morning; because of course she prob'bly hain't got any but that one."

"I know; but you don't want it but fifteen minutes, to carry the nonnamous letter and shove it under the front door."

"All right, then, I'll do it; but I could carry it just as handy in my own togs."

"You wouldn't look like a servant-girl *then*, would you?"

"No, but there won't be nobody to see what I look like, *anyway*."

"That ain't got nothing to do with it. The thing for us to do, is just to do our *duty*, and not worry about whether anybody *sees* us do it or not. Hain't you got no principle at all?"

"All right, I ain't saying nothing; I'm the servant-girl. Who's Jim's mother?"

"I'm his mother. I'll hook a gown from Aunt Sally."

"Well, then, you'll have to stay in the cabin when me and Jim leaves."

"Not much. I'll stuff Jim's clothes full of straw and lay it on his bed to represent his mother in disguise: and Jim 'll take Aunt Sally's gown off of me and wear it, and we'll all evade together. When a prisoner of style escapes, it's called an evasion. It's always called so when a king escapes, f'rinstance. And the same with a king's son; it don't make no difference whether he's a natural one or an unnatural one."

So Tom he wrote the nonnamous letter, and I smouched the yaller wench's frock, that night, and put it on, and shoved it under the front door, the way Tom told me to. It said:

> *Beware, Trouble is brewing. Keep a sharp lookout.*
>
> UNKNOWN FRIEND.

---

5. Twain probably read this episode of the Tuileries, a palace in Paris, in Thomas Carlyle's *French Revolution* (1837).

Next night we stuck a picture which Tom drawed in blood, of a skull and crossbones, on the front door; and next night another one of a coffin, on the back door. I never see a family in such a sweat. They couldn't a been worse scared if the place had a been full of ghosts laying for them behind everything and under the beds and shivering through the air. If a door banged, Aunt Sally she jumped, and said "ouch!" if anything fell, she jumped and said "ouch!" if you happened to touch her, when she warn't noticing, she done the same; she couldn't face noway and be satisfied, because she allowed there was something behind her every time—so she was always a whirling around, sudden, and saying "ouch," and before she'd get two-thirds around, she'd whirl back again, and say it again; and she was afraid to go to bed, but she dasn't set up. So the thing was working very well, Tom said; he said he never see a thing work more satisfactory. He said it showed it was done right.

So he said, now for the grand bulge! So the very next morning at the streak of dawn we got another letter ready, and was wondering what we better do with it, because we heard them say at supper they was going to have a nigger on watch at both doors all night. Tom he went down the lightning-rod to spy around; and the nigger at the back door was asleep, and he stuck it in the back of his neck and come back. This letter said:

Don't betray me, I wish to be your friend. There is a desprate gang of cut-throats from over in the Ingean Territory[6] going to steal your runaway nigger to-night, and they have been trying to scare you so as you will stay in the house and not bother them. I am one of the gang, but have got religgion and wish to quit it and lead a honest life again, and will betray the helish design. They will sneak down from northards, along the fence, at midnight exact, with a false key, and go in the nigger's cabin to get him. I am to be off a piece and blow a tin horn if I see any danger; but stead of that, I will BA like a sheep soon as they get in and not blow at all; then whilst they are getting his chains loose, you slip there and lock them in, and can kill them at your leasure. Don't do anything but just the way I am telling you, if you do they will suspicion something and raise whoopjamboreehoo. I do not wish any reward but to know I have done the right thing.

UNKNOWN FRIEND.

Chapter XL

We was feeling pretty good, after breakfast, and took my canoe and went over the river a fishing, with a lunch, and had a good time, and took a look at the raft and found her all right, and got home late to supper, and found them in such a sweat and worry they didn't know which end they was standing on, and made us go right off to bed the minute we was done supper, and wouldn't tell us what the trouble was, and never let on a word about the new letter, but didn't need to, because we knowed as much about it as anybody did, and as soon as we was half up stairs and her back was turned, we slid for the cellar cupboard and loaded up a good lunch and took it up to our room and went to bed, and got up about half-past eleven, and Tom put on Aunt Sally's dress that he stole and was going to start with the lunch, but says:

6. Indian country; part of Oklahoma reserved for Native Americans beginning in the 1830s. Because federal law did not apply there, outlaws used it as a base of operations throughout the 19th century.

"Where's the butter?"

"I laid out a hunk of it," I says, "on a piece of a corn-pone."

"Well, you *left* it laid out, then—it ain't here."

"We can get along without it," I says.

"We can get along *with* it, too," he says; "just you slide down cellar and fetch it. And then mosey right down the lightning-rod and come along. I'll go and stuff the straw into Jim's clothes to represent his mother in disguise, and be ready to *ba* like a sheep and shove soon as you get there."

So out he went, and down cellar went I. The hunk of butter, big as a person's fist, was where I had left it, so I took up the slab of corn-pone with it on, and blowed out my light, and started up stairs, very stealthy, and got up to the main floor all right, but here comes Aunt Sally with a candle, and I clapped the truck in my hat, and clapped my hat on my head, and the next second she see me; and she says:

"You been down cellar?"

"Yes'm."

"What you been doing down there?"

"Noth'n."

"*Noth'n!*"

"No'm."

"Well, then, what possessed you to go down there, this time of night?"

"I don't know'm."

"You don't *know?* Don't answer me that way, Tom, I want to know what you been *doing* down there?"

"I hain't been doing a single thing, Aunt Sally, I hope to gracious if I have."

I reckoned she'd let me go, now, and as a generl thing she would; but I spose there was so many strange things going on she was just in a sweat about every little thing that warn't yard-stick straight; so she says, very decided:

"You just march into that setting-room and stay there till I come. You been up to something you no business to, and I lay I'll find out what it is before *I'm* done with you."

So she went away as I opened the door and walked into the setting-room. My, but there was a crowd there! Fifteen farmers, and every one of them had a gun. I was most powerful sick, and slunk to a chair and set down. They was setting around, some of them talking a little, in a low voice, and all of them fidgety and uneasy, but trying to look like they warn't; but I knowed they was, because they was always taking off their hats, and putting them on, and scratching their heads, and changing their seats, and fumbling with their buttons. I warn't easy myself, but I didn't take my hat off, all the same.

I did wish Aunt Sally would come, and get done with me, and lick me, if she wanted to, and let me get away and tell Tom how we'd overdone this thing, and what a thundering hornet's nest we'd got ourselves into, so we could stop fooling around, straight off, and clear out with Jim before these rips got out of patience and come for us.

At last she come, and begun to ask me questions, but I *couldn't* answer them straight, I didn't know which end of me was up; because these men was in such a fidget now, that some was wanting to start right *now* and lay for them desperadoes, and saying it warn't but a few minutes to midnight; and others was trying to get them to hold on and wait for the sheep-signal;

and here was aunty pegging away at the questions, and me a shaking all over and ready to sink down in my tracks I was that scared; and the place getting hotter and hotter, and the butter beginning to melt and run down my neck and behind my ears: and pretty soon, when one of them says, "I'm for going and getting in the cabin *first,* and right *now,* and catching them when they come," I most dropped; and a streak of butter came a trickling down my forehead, and Aunt Sally she see it, and turns white as a sheet, and says:

"For the land's sake what *is* the matter with the child!—he's got the brain fever as shore as you're born, and they're oozing out!"

And everybody runs to see, and she snatches off my hat, and out comes the bread, and what was left of the butter, and she grabbed me, and hugged me, and says:

"Oh, what a turn you did give me! and how glad and grateful I am it ain't no worse; for luck's against us, and it never rains but it pours, and when I see that truck I thought we'd lost you, for I knowed by the color and all, it was just like your brains would be if—Dear, dear, whyd'nt you *tell* me that was what you'd been down there for, *I* wouldn't a cared. Now cler out to bed, and don't lemme see no more of you till morning!"

I was up stairs in a second, and down the lightning-rod in another one, and shinning through the dark for the lean-to. I couldn't hardly get my words out, I was so anxious; but I told Tom as quick as I could, we must jump for it, now, and not a minute to lose—the house full of men, yonder, with guns!

His eyes just blazed; and he says:

"No!—is that so? *Ain't* it bully! Why, Huck, if it was to do over again, I bet I could fetch two hundred! If we could put it off till—"

"Hurry! *hurry!*" I says. "Where's Jim?"

"Right at your elbow; if you reach out your arm you can touch him. He's dressed, and everything's ready. Now we'll slide out and give the sheep-signal."

But then we heard the tramp of men, coming to the door, and heard them begin to fumble with the padlock; and heard a man say:

"I *told* you we'd be too soon; they haven't come—the door is locked. Here, I'll lock some of you into the cabin and you lay for 'em in the dark and kill 'em when they come; and the rest scatter around a piece, and listen if you can hear 'em coming."

So in they come, but couldn't see us in the dark, and most trod on us whilst we was hustling to get under the bed. But we got under all right, and out through the hole, swift but soft—Jim first, me next, and Tom last, which was according to Tom's orders. Now we was in the lean-to, and heard trampings close by outside. So we crept to the door, and Tom stopped us there and put his eye to the crack, but couldn't make out nothing, it was so dark; and whispered and said he would listen for the steps to get further, and when he nudged us Jim must glide out first, and him last. So he set his ear to the crack and listened, and listened, and listened, and the steps a scraping around, out there, all the time; and at last he nudged us, and we slid out, and stooped down, not breathing, and not making the least noise, and slipped stealthy towards the fence, in Injun file, and got to it, all right, and me and Jim over it; but Tom's britches catched fast on a splinter on the top rail, and then he hear the steps coming, so he had to pull loose, which snapped the splinter and made a noise; and as he dropped in our tracks and started, somebody sings out:

"Who's that? Answer, or I'll shoot!"

But we didn't answer; we just unfurled our heels and shoved. Then there was a rush, and a *bang, bang, bang!* and the bullets fairly whizzed around us! We heard them sing out:

"Here they are! They've broke for the river! after 'em, boys! And turn loose the dogs!"

So here they come, full tilt. We could hear them, because they wore boots, and yelled, but we didn't wear no boots, and didn't yell. We was in the path to the mill; and when they got pretty close onto us, we dodged into the bush and let them go by, and then dropped in behind them. They'd had all the dogs shut up, so they wouldn't scare off the robbers; but by this time somebody had let them loose, and here they come, making pow-wow enough for a million; but they was our dogs; so we stopped in our tracks till they catched up; and when they see it warn't nobody but us, and no excitement to offer them, they only just said howdy, and tore right ahead towards the shouting and clattering; and then we up steam again and whizzed along after them till we was nearly to the mill, and then struck up through the bush to where my canoe was tied, and hopped in and pulled for dear life towards the middle of the river, but didn't make no more noise than we was obleeged to. Then we struck out, easy and comfortable, for the island where my raft was; and we could hear them yelling and barking at each other all up and down the bank, till we was so far away the sounds got dim and died out. And when we stepped onto the raft, I says:

"*Now,* old Jim, you're a free man *again,* and I bet you won't ever be a slave no more."

"En a mighty good job it wuz, too, Huck. It 'uz planned beautiful, en it 'uz *done* beautiful; en dey aint' *nobody* kin git up a plan dat's mo' mixed-up en splendid den what dat one wuz."

We was all as glad as we could be, but Tom was the gladdest of all, because he had a bullet in the calf of his leg.

When me and Jim heard that, we didn't feel so brash as what we did before. It was hurting him considerble, and bleeding; so we laid him in the wigwam and tore up one of the duke's shirts for to bandage him, but he says:

"Gimme the rags, I can do it myself. Don't stop, now; don't fool around here, and the evasion booming along so handsome; man the sweeps, and set her loose! Boys, we done it elegant!—'deed we did. I wish *we'd* a had the handling of Louis XVI, there wouldn't a been no 'Son of Saint Louis, ascend to heaven!'[7] wrote down in *his* biography: no, sir, we'd a whooped him over the *border*—that's what we'd a done with *him*—and done it just as slick as nothing at all, too. Man the sweeps—man the sweeps!"

But me and Jim was consulting—and thinking. And after we'd thought a minute, I says:

"Say it, Jim."

So he says:

"Well, den, dis is de way it look to me, Huck. Ef it wuz *him* dat 'uz bein' sot free, en one er de boys wuz to git shot, would he say, 'Go on en save me, nemmine 'bout a doctor f'r to save dis one?' Is dat like Mars Tom Sawyer? Would he say dat? You *bet* he wouldn't! *Well,* den, is *Jim* gwyne to say it?

---

7. Taken from the Scottish historian Thomas Carlyle's rendering of the king's execution in *The French Revolution* (1837).

No, sah—I doan' budge a step out'n dis place, 'dout a *doctor;* not if its forty year!"

I knowed he was white inside, and I reckoned he'd say what he did say—so it was all right, now, and I told Tom I was agoing for a doctor. He raised considerble row about it, but me and Jim stuck to it and wouldn't budge; so he was for crawling out and setting the raft loose himself; but we wouldn't let him. Then he give us a piece of his mind—but it didn't do no good.

So when he see me getting the canoe ready, he says:

"Well, then, if you're bound to go, I'll tell you the way to do, when you get to the village. Shut the door, and blindfold the doctor tight and fast, and make him swear to be silent as the grave, and put a purse full of gold in his hand, and then take and lead him all around the back alleys and everywheres, in the dark, and then fetch him here in the canoe, in a roundabout way amongst the islands, and search him and take his chalk away from him, and don't give it back to him till you get him back to the village, or else he will chalk this raft so he can find it again. It's the way they all do."

So I said I would, and left, and Jim was to hide in the woods when he see the doctor coming, till he was gone again.

Chapter XLI

The doctor was an old man; a very nice, kind-looking old man, when I got him up. I told him me and my brother was over on Spanish Island hunting, yesterday afternoon, and camped on a piece of a raft we found, and about midnight he must a kicked his gun in his dreams, for it went off and shot him in the leg, and we wanted him to go over there and fix it and not say nothing about it, nor let anybody know, because we wanted to come home this evening, and surprise the folks.

"Who is your folks?" he says.

"The Phelpses, down yonder."

"Oh," he says. And after a minute, he says: "How'd you say he got shot?"

"He had a dream," I says, "and it shot him."

"Singular dream," he says.

So he lit up his lantern, and got his saddle-bags, and we started. But when he see the canoe, he didn't like the look of her—said she was big enough for one, but didn't look pretty safe for two. I says:

"Oh, you needn't be afeard, sir, she carried the three of us, easy enough."

"What three?"

"Why, me and Sid, and—and—and *the guns;* that's what I mean."

"Oh," he says.

But he put his foot on the gunnel, and rocked her; and shook his head, and said he reckoned he'd look around for a bigger one. But they was all locked and chained; so he took my canoe, and said for me to wait till he come back, or I could hunt around further, or maybe I better go down home and get them ready for the surprise, if I wanted to. But I said I didn't; so I told him just how to find the raft, and then he started.

I struck an idea, pretty soon. I says to myself, spos'n he can't fix that leg just in three shakes of a sheep's tail, as the saying is? spos'n it takes him three or four days? What are we going to do?—lay around there till he lets the cat out of the bag? No, sir, I know what *I'll* do. I'll wait, and when he comes back, if he says he's got to go any more, I'll get him down there, too, if I swim; and we'll take and tie him, and keep him, and shove out down the river; and when Tom's done with him, we'll give him what it's worth, or all we got, and then let him get shore.

So then I crept into a lumber pile to get some sleep; and next time I waked up the sun was away up over my head! I shot out and went for the doctor's house, but they told me he'd gone away in the night, some time or other, and warn't back yet. Well, thinks I, that looks powerful bad for *Tom*, and I'll dig out for the island, right off. So away I shoved, and turned the corner, and nearly rammed my head into Uncle Silas's stomach! He says:

"Why, Tom! Where you been, all this time, you rascal?"

"*I* hain't been nowheres," I says, "only just hunting for the runaway nigger—me and Sid."

"Why, where ever did you go?" he says. "Your aunt's been mighty uneasy."

"She needn't," I says, "because we was all right. We followed the men and the dogs, but they out-run us, and we lost them; but we thought we heard them on the water, so we got a canoe and took out after them, and crossed over but couldn't find nothing of them; so we cruised along up-shore till we got kind of tired and beat out; and tied up the canoe and went to sleep, and never waked up till about an hour ago, then we paddled over here to hear the news, and Sid's at the post-office to see what he can hear, and I'm a branching out to get something to eat for us, and then we're going home."

So then we went to the post-office to get "Sid"; but just as I suspicioned, he warn't there; so the old man he got a letter out of the office, and we waited a while longer but Sid didn't come; so the old man said come along, let Sid foot it home, or canoe-it, when he got done fooling around—but we would ride. I couldn't get him to let me stay and wait for Sid; and he said there warn't no use in it, and I must come along, and let Aunt Sally see we was all right.

When we got home, Aunt Sally was that glad to see me she laughed and cried both, and hugged me, and give me one of them lickings of hern that don't amount to shucks, and said she'd serve Sid the same when he come.

And the place was plumb full of farmers and farmers' wives, to dinner; and such another clack a body never heard. Old Mrs. Hotchkiss was the worst; her tongue was agoing all the time. She says:

"Well, Sister Phelps, I've ransacked that-air cabin over an' I b'lieve the nigger was crazy. I says so to Sister Damrell—didn't I, Sister Damrell?—s'I, he's crazy, s'I—them's the very words I said. You all hearn me: he's crazy, s'I; everything shows it, s'I. Look at that-air grindstone, s'I; want to tell *me* 't any cretur 'ts in his right mind 's agoin' to scrabble all them crazy things onto a grindstone, s'I? Here sich 'n' sich a person busted his heart; 'n' here so 'n' so pegged along for thirty-seven year, 'n' all that—natcherl son o' Louis some-body, 'n' sich everlast'n rubbage. He's plumb crazy, s'I; it's what I says in the fust place, it's what I says in the middle, 'n' it's what I says last 'n' all the time—the nigger's crazy—crazy's Nebokoodneezer,[8] s'I."

"An' look at that-air ladder made out'n rags, Sister Hotchkiss," says old Mrs. Damrell, "what in the name o'goodness *could* he ever want of—"

---

8. Nebuchadnezzar (605–562 B.C.E.), king of Babylon, is described in Daniel 4.33 as going mad and eating grass.

"The very words I was a-sayin' no longer ago th'n this minute to Sister Utterback, 'n' she'll tell you so herself. Sh-she, look at that-air rag ladder, sh-she; 'n' s'I, yes, *look* at it, s'I—what *could* he a wanted of it, s'I. Sh-she, Sister Hotchkiss, sh-she—"

"But how in the nation'd they ever *git* that grindstone *in* there, *anyway*? 'n' who dug that-air *hole*? 'n' who—"

"My very *words*, Brer Penrod! I was a-sayin'—pass that-air sasser o' m'lasses, won't ye?—I was a-sayin' to Sister Dunlap, jist this minute, how *did* they git that grindstone in there, s'I. Without *help*, mind you—'thout *help*! *Thar's* wher' 'tis. Don't tell *me*, s'I; there *wuz* help, s'I; 'n' ther' wuz a *plenty* help, too, s'I; ther's ben a *dozen* a-helpin' that nigger, 'n' I lay I'd skin every last nigger on this place, but *I'd* find out who done it, s'I; 'n' moreover, s'I—"

"A *dozen* says you!—*forty* couldn't a done everything that's been done. Look at them case-knife saws and things, how tedious they've been made; look at that bed-leg sawed off with 'em, a week's work for six men; look at that nigger made out'n straw on the bed; and look at—"

"You may *well* say it, Brer Hightower! It's jist as I was a-sayin' to Brer Phelps, his own self. S'e, what do *you* think of it, Sister Hotchkiss, s'e? think o' what, Brer Phelps, s'I? think o' that bed-leg sawed off that a way, s'e? *think* of it, s'I? I lay it never sawed *itself* off, s'I—somebody sawed it, s'I; that's my opinion, take it or leave it, it mayn't be no 'count, s'I, but sich as 't is, it's my opinion, s'I, 'n' if anybody k'n start a better one, s'I, let him *do* it, s'I, that's all. I says to Sister Dunlap, s'I—"

"Why, dog my cats, they must a ben a house-full o' niggers in there every night for four weeks, to a done all that work, Sister Phelps. Look at that shirt—every last inch of it kivered over with secret African writ'n done with blood! Must a ben a raft uv 'm at it right along, all the time, amost. Why, I'd give two dollars to have it read to me; 'n' as for the niggers that wrote it, I 'low I'd take 'n' lash 'm t'll—"

"People to *help* him, Brother Marples! Well, I reckon you'd *think* so, if you'd a been in this house for a while back. Why, they've stole everything they could lay their hands on—and we a watching, all the time, mind you. They stole that shirt right off o' the line! and as for that sheet they made the rag ladder out of ther' ain't no telling how many times they *didn't* steal that; and flour, and candles, and candlesticks, and spoons, and the old-warming-pan, and most a thousand things that I disremember, now, and my new calico dress; and me, and Silas, and my Sid and Tom on the constant watch day *and* night, as I was a telling you, and not a one of us could catch hide nor hair, nor sight nor sound of them; and here at the last minute, lo and behold you, they slides right in under our noses, and fools us, and not only fools *us* but the Injun Territory robbers too, and actuly gets *away* with that nigger, safe and sound, and that with sixteen men and twenty-two dogs right on their very heels at that very time! I tell you, it just bangs anything I ever *heard* of. Why, *sperits* couldn't a done better, and been no smarter. And I reckon they must a *been* sperits—because, *you* know our dogs, and ther' ain't no better; well, them dogs never even got on the *track* of 'm, once! You explain *that* to me, if you can!—*any* of you!"

"Well, it does beat—"

"Laws alive, I never—"

"So help me, I wouldn't a be—"

"*House* thieves as well as—"

"Goodnessgracioussakes, I'd a ben afeard to *live* in sich a—"

"'Fraid to *live!*—why, I was that scared I dasn't hardly go to bed, or get up, or lay down, or *set* down, Sister Ridgeway. Why, they'd steal the very—why, goodness sakes, you can guess what kind of a fluster *I* was in by the time midnight come, last night. I hope to gracious if I warn't afraid they'd steal some o' the family! I was just to that pass, I didn't have no reasoning facul- ties no more. It looks foolish enough, *now,* in the day-time; but I says to myself, there's my two poor boys asleep, 'way up stairs in that lonesome room, and I declare to goodness I was that uneasy 't I crep' up there and locked 'em in! I *did.* And anybody would. Because, you know, when you get scared, that way, and it keeps running on, and getting worse and worse, all the time, and your wits gets to addling, and you get to doing all sorts o' wild things, and by-and-by you think to yourself, spos'n *I* was a boy, and was away up there, and the door ain't locked, and you—" She stopped, looking kind of wondering, and then she turned her head around slow, and when her eye lit on me—I got up and took a walk.

Says I to myself, I can explain better how we come to not be in that room this morning, if I go out to one side and study over it a little. So I done it. But I dasn't go fur, or she'd a sent for me. And when it was late in the day, the people all went, and then I come in and told her the noise and shooting waked up me and "Sid," and the door was locked, and we wanted to see the fun, so we went down the lightning-rod, and both of us got hurt a little, and we didn't never want to try *that* no more. And then I went on and told her all what I told Uncle Silas before; and then she said she'd forgive us, and maybe it was all right enough anyway, and about what a body might expect of boys, for all boys was a pretty harum-scarum lot, as fur as she could see; and so, as long as no harm hadn't come of it, she judged she better put in her time being grateful we was alive and well and she had us still, stead of fret- ting over what was past and done. So then she kissed me, and patted me on the head, and dropped into a kind of a brown study; and pretty soon jumps up, and says:

"Why, lawsamercy, it's most night, and Sid not come yet! What *has* become of that boy?"

I see my chance; so I skips up and says:

"I'll run right up to town and get him," I says.

"No, you won't," she says. "You'll stay right wher' you are; *one's* enough to be lost at a time. If he ain't here to supper, your uncle 'll go."

Well, he warn't there to supper; so right after supper uncle went.

He come back about ten, a little bit uneasy; hadn't run across Tom's track. Aunt Sally was a good *deal* uneasy; but Uncle Silas he said there warn't no occasion to be—boys will be boys, he said, and you'll see this one turn up in the morning, all sound and right. So she had to be satisfied. But she said she'd set up for him a while, anyway, and keep a light burning, so he could see it.

And then when I went up to bed she come up with me and fetched her candle, and tucked me in, and mothered me so good I felt mean, and like I couldn't look her in the face; and she set down on the bed and talked with me a long time, and said what a splendid boy Sid was, and didn't seem to want to ever stop talking about him; and kept asking me every now and then, if I reckoned he could a got lost, or hurt, or maybe drownded, and might be laying at this minute, somewhere, suffering or dead, and she not by him to help him, and so the tears would drip down, silent, and I would tell her that

Sid was all right, and would be home in the morning, sure; and she would squeeze my hand, or maybe kiss me, and tell me to say it again, and keep on saying it, because it done her good, and she was in so much trouble. And when she was going away, she looked down in my eyes, so steady and gentle, and says:

"The door ain't going to be locked, Tom; and there's the window and the rod; but you'll be good, *won't* you? And you won't go? For *my* sake."

Laws knows I *wanted* to go, bad enough, to see about Tom, and was all intending to go; but after that, I wouldn't a went, not for kingdoms.

But she was on my mind, and Tom was on my mind; so I slept very restless. And twice I went down the rod, away in the night, and slipped around front, and see her setting there by her candle in the window with her eyes towards the road and the tears in them; and I wished I could do something for her, but I couldn't, only to swear that I wouldn't never do nothing to grieve her any more. And the third time, I waked up at dawn, and slid down, and she was there yet, and her candle was most out, and her old gray head was resting on her hand, and she was asleep.

Chapter XLII

The old man was up town again, before breakfast, but couldn't get no track of Tom; and both of them set at the table, thinking, and not saying nothing, and looking mournful, and their coffee getting cold, and not eating anything. And by-and-by the old man says:

"Did I give you the letter?"

"What letter?"

"The one I got yesterday out of the post-office."

"No, you didn't give me no letter."

"Well, I must a forgot it."

So he rummaged his pockets, and then went off somewheres where he had laid it down, and fetched it, and give it to her. She says:

"Why, it's from St. Petersburg—it's from Sis."

I allowed another walk would do me good; but I couldn't stir. But before she could break it open, she dropped it and run—for she see something. And so did I. It was Tom Sawyer on a mattress; and that old doctor; and Jim, in *her* calico dress, with his hands tied behind him; and a lot of people. I hid the letter behind the first thing that come handy, and rushed. She flung herself at Tom, crying, and says:

"Oh, he's dead, he's dead, I know he's dead!"

And Tom he turned his head a little, and muttered something or other, which showed he warn't in his right mind; then she flung up her hands and says:

"He's alive, thank God! And that's enough!" and she snatched a kiss of him, and flew for the house to get the bed ready, and scattering orders right and left at the niggers and everybody else, as fast as her tongue could go, every jump of the way.

I followed the men to see what they was going to do with Jim; and the old doctor and Uncle Silas followed after Tom into the house. The men was very huffy, and some of them wanted to hang Jim, for an example to all the other niggers around there, so they wouldn't be trying to run away, like Jim done, and making such a raft of trouble, and keeping a whole family scared most to death for days and nights. But the others said, don't do it, it wouldn't answer at all, he ain't our nigger, and his owner would turn up and make us pay for him, sure. So that cooled them down a little, because the people that's always the most anxious for to hang a nigger that hain't done just right, is always the very ones that ain't the most anxious to pay for him when they've got their satisfaction out of him.

They cussed Jim considerble, though, and give him a cuff or two, side the head, once in a while, but Jim never said nothing, and he never let on to know me, and they took him to the same cabin, and put his own clothes on him, and chained him again, and not to no bed-leg, this time, but to a big staple drove into the bottom log, and chained his hands, too, and both legs, and said he warn't to have nothing but bread and water to eat, after this, till his owner come or he was sold at auction, because he didn't come in a certain length of time, and filled up our hole, and said a couple of farmers with guns must stand watch around about the cabin every night, and a bull-dog tied to the door in the day time; and about this time they was through with the job and was tapering off with a kind of generl good-bye cussing, and then the old doctor comes and takes a look and says:

"Don't be no rougher on him than you're obleeged to, because he ain't a bad nigger. When I got to where I found the boy, I see I couldn't cut the bullet out without some help, and he warn't in no condition for me to leave, to go and get help; and he got a little worse and a little worse, and after a long time he went out of his head, and wouldn't let me come anigh him, any more, and said if I chalked his raft he'd kill me, and no end of wild foolishness like that, and I see I couldn't do anything at all with him; so I says, I got to have *help,* somehow; and the minute I says it, out crawls this nigger from somewheres, and says he'll help, and he done it, too, and done it very well. Of course I judged he must be a runaway nigger, and there I *was!* and there I had to stick, right straight along all the rest of the day, and all night. It was a fix, I tell you! I had a couple of patients with the chills, and of course I'd of liked to run up to town and see them, but I dasn't, because the nigger might get away, and then I'd be to blame; and yet never a skiff come close enough for me to hail. So there I had to stick, plumb till daylight this morning; and I never see a nigger that was a better nuss or faithfuller, and yet he was resking his freedom to do it, and was all tired out, too, and I see plain enough he'd been worked main hard, lately. I liked the nigger for that; I tell you, gentlemen, a nigger like that is worth a thousand dollars—and kind treatment, too. I had everything I needed, and the boy was doing as well there as he would a done at home— better, maybe, because it was so quiet; but there I *was,* with both of 'm on my hands; and there I had to stick, till about dawn this morning; then some men in a skiff come by, and as good luck would have it, the nigger was setting by the pallet with his head propped on his knees, sound asleep; so I motioned them in, quiet, and they slipped up on him and grabbed him and tied him before he knowed what he was about, and we never had no trouble. And the boy being in a kind of a flighty sleep, too, we muffled the oars and hitched the raft on, and towed her over very nice and quiet, and the nigger never made the least row nor said a word, from the start. He ain't no bad nigger, gentlemen; that's what I think about him."

Somebody says:

"Well, it sounds very good, doctor, I'm obleeged to say."

Then the others softened up a little, too, and I was mighty thankful to that old doctor for doing Jim that good turn; and I was glad it was according to my judgment of him, too; because I thought he had a good heart in him and was a good man, the first time I see him. Then they all agreed that Jim had acted very well, and was deserving to have some notice took of it, and reward. So every one of them promised, right out and hearty, that they wouldn't cuss him no more.

Then they come out and locked him up. I hoped they was going to say he could have one or two of the chains took off, because they was rotten heavy, or could have meat and greens with his bread and water, but they didn't think of it, and I reckoned it warn't best for me to mix in, but I judged I'd get the doctor's yarn to Aunt Sally, somehow or other, as soon as I'd got through the breakers that was laying just ahead of me. Explanations, I mean, of how I forgot to mention about Sid being shot, when I was telling how him and me put in that dratted night paddling around hunting the runaway nigger.

But I had plenty time. Aunt Sally she stuck to the sick-room all day and all night; and every time I see Uncle Silas mooning around, I dodged him.

Next morning I heard Tom was a good deal better, and they said Aunt Sally was gone to get a nap. So I slips to the sick-room, and if I found him awake I reckoned we could put up a yarn for the family that would wash. But he was sleeping, and sleeping very peaceful, too; and pale, not fire-faced the way he was when he come. So I set down and laid for him to wake. In about a half an hour, Aunt Sally comes gliding in, and there I was, up a stump again! She motioned me to be still, and set down by me, and begun to whisper, and said we could all be joyful now, because all the symptoms was first rate, and he'd been sleeping like that for ever so long, and looking better and peacefuller all the time, and ten to one he'd wake up in his right mind.

So we set there watching, and by-and-by he stirs a bit, and opened his eyes very natural, and takes a look, and says:

"Hello, why I'm at *home!* How's that? Where's the raft?"

"It's all right," I says.

"And *Jim?*"

"The same," I says, but couldn't say it pretty brash. But he never noticed, but says:

"Good! Splendid! *Now* we're all right and safe! Did you tell Aunty?"

I was about to say yes; but she chipped in and says:

"About what, Sid?"

"Why, about the way the whole thing was done."

"What whole thing?"

"Why, *the* whole thing. There ain't but one; how we set the runaway nigger free—me and Tom."

"Good land! Set the run—What *is* the child talking about! Dear, dear, out of his head again!"

"*No,* I ain't out of my HEAD; I know all what I'm talking about. We *did* set him free—me and Tom. We laid out to do it, and we *done* it. And we done it elegant, too." He'd got a start, and she never checked him up, just set and stared and stared, and let him clip along, and I see it warn't no use for *me* to put in. "Why, Aunty, it cost us a power of work—weeks of it—hours and hours, every night, whilst you was all asleep. And we had to steal candles, and the sheet, and the shirt, and your dress, and spoons, and tin plates, and case-knives, and the warming-pan, and the grindstone, and flour, and just no end of things, and you can't think what work it was to make the saws, and pens, and inscriptions, and one thing or another, and you can't think *half* the fun it was. And we had to make up the pictures of coffins and things, and nonna-mous letters from the robbers, and get up and down the lightning-rod, and dig the hole into the cabin, and make the rope-ladder and send it in cooked up in a pie, and send in spoons and things to work with, in your apron pocket"—

"Mercy sakes!"

—"and load up the cabin with rats and snakes and so on, for company for Jim; and then you kept Tom here so long with the butter in his hat that you come near spiling the whole business, because the men come before we was out of the cabin, and we had to rush, and they heard us and let drive at us, and I got my share, and we dodged out of the path and let them go by, and when the dogs come they warn't interested in us, but went for the most noise, and we got our canoe, and made for the raft, and was all safe, and Jim was a free man, and we done it all by ourselves, and *wasn't* it bully, Aunty!"

"Well, I never heard the likes of it in all my born days! So it was *you,* you little rapscallions, that's been making all this trouble, and turn everybody's wits clean inside out and scared us all most to death. I've as good a notion as ever I had in my life, to take it out o' you this very minute. To think, here I've been, night after night, a—*you* just get well once, you young scamp, and I lay I'll tan the Old Harry[9] out o' both o' ye!"

But Tom, he *was* so proud and joyful, he just *couldn't* hold in, and his tongue just *went* it—she a-chipping in, and spitting fire all along, and both of them going it at once, like a cat-convention; and she says:

"*Well,* you get all the enjoyment you can out of it *now,* for mind I tell you if I catch you meddling with him again—"

"Meddling with *who?*" Tom says, dropping his smile and looking surprised.

"With *who?* Why, the runaway nigger, of course. Who'd you reckon?"

Tom looks at me very grave, and says:

"Tom, didn't you just tell me he was all right? Hasn't he got away?"

"*Him?*" says Aunt Sally; "the runaway nigger? 'Deed he hasn't. They've got him back, safe and sound, and he's in that cabin again, on bread and water, and loaded down with chains, till he's claimed or sold!"

Tom rose square up in bed, with his eye hot, and his nostrils opening and shutting like gills, and sings out to me:

"They hain't no *right* to shut him up! *Shove!*—and don't you lose a min-ute. Turn him loose! he ain't no slave; he's as free as any cretur that walks this earth!"

"What *does* the child mean?"

"I mean every word I *say,* Aunt Sally, and if somebody don't go, *I'll* go. I've knowed him all his life, and so has Tom, there. Old Miss Watson died two months ago, and she was ashamed she ever was going to sell him down the river, and *said* so; and she set him free in her will."

"Then what on earth did *you* want to set him free for, seeing he was already free?"

"Well, that *is* a question, I must say; and *just* like women! Why, I wanted the *adventure* of it; and I'd a waded neck-deep in blood to—goodness alive, AUNT POLLY!"[1]

---

9. The devil.   1. Tom Sawyer's aunt and guardian.

If she warn't standing right there, just inside the door, looking as sweet and contented as an angel half-full of pie, I wish I may never!

Aunt Sally jumped for her, and most hugged the head off of her, and cried over her, and I found a good enough place for me under the bed, for it was getting pretty sultry for *us*, seemed to me. And I peeped out, and in a little while Tom's Aunt Polly shook herself loose and stood there looking across at Tom over her spectacles—kind of grinding him into the earth, you know. And then she says:

"Yes, you *better* turn y'r head away—I would if I was you, Tom."

"Oh, deary me!" says Aunt Sally; "*is* he changed so? Why, that ain't *Tom* it's Sid; Tom's—Tom's—why, where is Tom? He was here a minute ago."

"You mean where's Huck *Finn*—that's what you mean! I reckon I hain't raised such a scamp as my Tom all these years, not to know him when I *see* him. That *would* be a pretty howdy-do. Come out from under the bed, Huck Finn."

So I done it. But not feeling brash.

Aunt Sally she was one of the mixed-upest looking persons I ever see; except one, and that was Uncle Silas, when he come in, and they told it all to him. It kind of made him drunk, as you may say, and he didn't know nothing at all the rest of the day, and preached a prayer-meeting sermon that night that give him a rattling ruputation, because the oldest man in the world couldn't a understood it. So Tom's Aunt Polly, she told all about who I was, and what; and I had to up and tell how I was in such a tight place that when Mrs. Phelps took me for Tom Sawyer—she chipped in and says, "Oh, go on and call me Aunt Sally, I'm used to it, now, and 'tain't no need to change"— that when Aunt Sally took me for Tom Sawyer, I had to stand it—that warn't no other way, and I knowed he wouldn't mind, because it would be nuts for him, being a mystery, and he'd make an adventure out of it and be perfectly satisfied. And so it turned out, and he let on to be Sid, and made things as soft as he could for me.

And his Aunt Polly she said Tom was right about old Miss Watson setting Jim free in her will; and so, sure enough, Tom Sawyer had gone and took all that trouble and bother to set a free nigger free! and I couldn't ever understand, before, until that minute and that talk, how he *could* help a body set a nigger free, with his bringing-up.

Well, Aunt Polly she said that when Aunt Sally wrote to her that Tom and *Sid* had come, all right and safe, she says to herself:

"Look at that, now! I might have expected it, letting him go off that way without anybody to watch him. So now I got to go and trapse all the way down the river, eleven hundred mile,[2] and find out what that creetur's up to, *this* time; as long as I couldn't seem to get any answer out of you about it."

"Why, I never heard nothing from you," says Aunt Sally.

"Well, I wonder! Why, I wrote to you twice, to ask you what you could mean by Sid being here."

"Well, I never got 'em, Sis."

Aunt Polly, she turns around slow and severe, and says:

"You, Tom!"

"Well—*what?*" he says, kind of pettish.

"Don't you what *me,* you impudent thing—hand out them letters."

---

2. This distance from Hannibal would place the Phelps plantation in northern Louisiana.

"What letters?"

"*Them* letters. I be bound, if I have to take aholt of you I'll—"

"They're in the trunk. There, now. And they're just the same as they was when I got them out of the office. I hain't looked into them, I hain't touched them. But I knowed they'd make trouble, and I thought if you warn't in no hurry, I'd—"

"Well, you *do* need skinning, there ain't no mistake about it. And I wrote another one to tell you I was coming; and I spose he—"

"No, it come yesterday; I hain't read it yet, but *it's* all right, I've got that one."

I wanted to offer to bet two dollars she hadn't, but I reckoned maybe it was just as safe to not to. So I never said nothing.

Chapter the Last

The first time I catched Tom, private, I asked him what was his idea, time of the evasion?—what it was he'd planned to do if the evasion worked all right and he managed to set a nigger free that was already free before? And he said, what he had planned in his head, from the start, if we got Jim out all safe, was for us to run him down the river, on the raft, and have adventures plumb to the mouth of the river, and then tell him about his being free, and take him back up home on a steamboat, in style, and pay him for his lost time, and write word ahead and get out all the niggers around, and have them waltz him into town with a torchlight procession and a brass band, and then he would be a hero, and so would we. But I reckoned it was about as well the way it was.

We had Jim out of the chains in no time, and when Aunt Polly and Uncle Silas and Aunt Sally found out how good he helped the doctor nurse Tom, they made a heap of fuss over him, and fixed him up prime, and give him all he wanted to eat, and a good time, and nothing to do. And we had him up to the sickroom; and had a high talk; and Tom give Jim forty dollars for being prisoner for us so patient, and doing it up so good, and Jim was pleased most to death, and busted out, and says:

"*Dah,* now, Huck, what I tell you?—what I tell you up dah on Jackson islan'? I *tole* you I got a hairy breas', en what's de sign un it; en I *tole* you I ben rich wunst, en gwineter to be rich *agin;* en it's come true; en heah she *is! Dah,* now! doan' talk to *me*—signs is *signs,* mine I tell you; en I knowed jis' 's well 'at I 'uz gwineter be rich agin as I's a stannin' heah dis minute!"

And then Tom he talked along, and talked along, and says, le's all three slide out of here, one of these nights, and get an outfit, and go for howling adventures amongst the Injuns, over in the Territory, for a couple of weeks or two; and I says, all right, that suits me, but I ain't got no money for to buy the outfit, and I reckon I couldn't get none from home, because it's likely pap's been back before now, and got it all away from Judge Thatcher and drunk it up.

"No he hain't," Tom says; "it's all there, yet—six thousand dollars and more; and your pap hain't ever been back since. Hadn't when I come away, anyhow."

Jim says, kind of solemn:

"He ain't a comin' back no mo', Huck."

I says:

"Why, Jim?"

"Nemmine why, Huck—but he ain't comin' back no mo'."

But I kept at him; so at last he says:

"Doan' you 'member de house dat was float'n down de river, en dey wuz a man in dah, kivered up, en I went in en unkivered him and didn' let you come in? Well, den, you k'n git yo' money when you wants it; kase dat wuz him."

Tom's most well, now, and got his bullet around his neck on a watch-guard for a watch, and is always seeing what time it is, and so there ain't nothing more to write about, and I am rotten glad of it, because if I'd a knowed what a trouble it was to make a book I wouldn't a tackled it and ain't agoing to no more. But I reckon I got to light out for the Territory ahead of the rest, because Aunt Sally she's going to adopt me and sivilize me and I can't stand it. I been there before.

THE END. YOURS TRULY, HUCK FINN.

1876–83   1884

Critical Controversy:
Race and the Ending of
Adventures of Huckleberry Finn

Celebrated by Ernest Hemingway as the source of all modern American literature, and regarded by many as a great American novel, *Huckleberry Finn* has always been controversial. In Twain's day it was criticized for taking as its hero a boy who smoked, loafed around, and rejected Sunday School—not to mention aided a runaway slave. More recently, attention has shifted to its portrayal of race through Huck's changing attitudes toward Jim. Banned in some school districts and denounced by some scholars and teachers as racist, it has been defended by others as a powerful attack on racism. Its lengthy and ambiguous final section, when the plot to free Jim gives way to an account of Tom Sawyer's pranks, has also provoked controversy. This short selection of critical writings provides a sampling of modern debate on the novel.

Below are the conflicting voices of literary critics and novelists on Jim as a character, on Huck's relationship with Jim, on the use of the "n-word," on race in general, and on the problematic ending. Three of the writers here are sharply critical of the book for what they see as its failure to follow through on its initial premise, that Jim is an admirable character whose drive for freedom expresses a basic human need. The other four argue that there is no such failure, that the book maintains its attack on those who deny Jim's status as a human being. The controversy is possible because Twain's ironic humor makes his own position difficult to identify. Leo Marx thinks Jim's drive for freedom is trivialized by an ending in which Huck becomes Tom Sawyer's yes-man. Julius Lester criticizes the book's depiction of Jim along the same lines, arguing that Jim becomes more of a minstrel-show figure than the admirable person he had earlier been. Jane Smiley, also disturbed by Twain's depiction of this black character, proposes Harriet Beecher Stowe's *Uncle Tom's Cabin* (1852) as a better model for American literature. On the other hand, Justin Kaplan defends *Huckleberry Finn* as a "savage indictment of a society that accepted slavery as a way of life"; David L. Smith argues that the novel undercuts racist discourses; and Shelley Fisher Fishkin specifically takes on Smiley's reading of Stowe versus Twain. Toni Morrison offers insights into her own experience of reading the novel a number of times over many years, concluding that *Huckleberry Finn* is a classic in part because of the powerful way that it raises but does not answer questions about race, culture, character, and nation.

LEO MARX

From Mr. Eliot, Mr. Trilling, and *Huckleberry Finn*[1]

* * *

I believe that the ending of *Huckleberry Finn* makes so many readers uneasy because they rightly sense that it jeopardizes the significance of the entire novel. To take seriously what happens at the Phelps farm is to take lightly the entire downstream journey. What is the meaning of the journey? With this question all discussion of *Huckleberry Finn* must begin. It is true that the voyage down the river has many aspects of a boy's idyl. We owe much of its hold upon our imagination to the enchanting image of the raft's unhurried drift with the current. The leisure, the absence of constraint, the beauty of the river—all these things delight us. "It's lovely to live on a raft." And the multitudinous life of the great valley we see through Huck's eyes has a fascination of its own. Then, of course, there is humor—laughter so spontaneous, so free of the bitterness present almost everywhere in American humor that readers often forget how grim a spectacle of human existence Huck contemplates. Humor in this novel flows from a bright joy of life as remote from our world as living on a raft.

Yet along with the idyllic and the epical and the funny in *Huckleberry Finn*, there is a coil of meaning which does for the disparate elements of the novel what a spring does for a watch. The meaning is not in the least obscure. It is made explicit again and again. The very words with which Clemens launches Huck and Jim upon their voyage indicate that theirs is not a boy's lark but a quest for freedom. From the electrifying moment when Huck comes back to Jackson's Island and rouses Jim with the news that a search party is on the way, we are meant to believe that Huck is enlisted in the cause of freedom. "Git up and hump yourself, Jim!" he cries. "There ain't a minute to lose. They're after us!" What particularly counts here is the *us*. No one is after Huck; no one but Jim knows he is alive. In that small word Clemens compresses the exhilarating power of Huck's instinctive humanity. His unpremeditated identification with Jim's flight from slavery is an unforgettable moment in American experience, and it may be said at once that any culmination of the journey which detracts from the urgency and dignity with which it begins will necessarily be unsatisfactory. Huck realizes this himself, and says so when, much later, he comes back to the raft after discovering that the Duke and the King have sold Jim:

1. From *American Scholar* 22 (1953): 423–40. A pioneering scholar in the field of American studies, Leo Marx (b. 1919) is best known as the author of *The Machine in the Garden: Technology and the Pastoral Ideal in America* (1964). The title of this essay refers to admiring introductions to *Huckleberry Finn* (1948 and 1950, respectively) written by the critic Lionel Trilling (1905–1975) and the poet T. S. Eliot (1888–1965).

"We turned in and slept." E. W. Kemble illustration from the first
edition (1884).

> After all this long journey . . . here it was all come to nothing, every-
> thing all busted up and ruined, because they could have the heart to
> serve Jim such a trick as that, and make him a slave again all his life,
> and amongst strangers, too, for forty dirty dollars.

Huck knows that the journey will have been a failure unless it takes Jim to
freedom. It is true that we do discover, in the end, that Jim is free, but we
also find out that the journey was not the means by which he finally reached
freedom.

The most obvious thing wrong with the ending, then, is the flimsy contrivance by which Clemens frees Jim. In the end we not only discover that
Jim has been a free man for two months, but that his freedom has been
granted by old Miss Watson. If this were only a mechanical device for terminating the action, it might not call for much comment. But it is more
than that: it is a significant clue to the import of the last ten chapters.
Remember who Miss Watson is. She is the Widow's sister whom Huck
introduces in the first pages of the novel. It is she who keeps "pecking" at
Huck, who tries to teach him to spell and to pray and to keep his feet off
the furniture. She is an ardent proselytizer for piety and good manners, and
her greed provides the occasion for the journey in the first place. She is
Jim's owner, and he decides to flee only when he realizes that she is about
to break her word (she cannot resist a slave trader's offer of eight hundred
dollars) and sell him down the river away from his family.

Miss Watson, in short, is the Enemy. If we except a predilection for physical violence, she exhibits all the outstanding traits of the valley society. She
pronounces the polite lies of civilization that suffocate Huck's spirit. The
freedom which Jim seeks, and which Huck and Jim temporarily enjoy aboard
the raft, is accordingly freedom *from* everything for which Miss Watson
stands. Indeed, the very intensity of the novel derives from the discordance
between the aspirations of the fugitives and the respectable code for which
she is a spokesman. Therefore her regeneration, of which the deathbed free-

ing of Jim is the unconvincing sign, hints a resolution of the novel's essential conflict. Perhaps because this device most transparently reveals that shift in point of view which he could not avoid, and which is less easily discerned elsewhere in the concluding chapters, Clemens plays it down. He makes little attempt to account for Miss Watson's change of heart, a change particularly surprising in view of Jim's brazen escape.

* * *

Huckleberry Finn is a masterpiece because it brings Western humor to perfection and yet transcends the narrow limits of its conventions. But the ending does not. During the final extravaganza we are forced to put aside many of the mature emotions evoked earlier by the vivid rendering of Jim's fear of capture, the tenderness of Huck's and Jim's regard for each other, and Huck's excruciating moments of wavering between honesty and respectability. None of these emotions are called forth by the anticlimactic final sequence. I do not mean to suggest that the inclusion of low comedy per se is a flaw in *Huckleberry Finn*. One does not object to the shenanigans of the rogues; there is ample precedent for the place of extravagant humor even in works of high seriousness. But here the case differs from most which come to mind: the major characters themselves are forced to play low comedy roles. Moreover, the most serious motive in the novel, Jim's yearning for freedom, is made the object of nonsense. The conclusion, in short, is farce, but the rest of the novel is not.

* * *

Tom reappears. Soon Huck has fallen almost completely under his sway once more, and we are asked to believe that the boy who felt pity for the rogues is now capable of making Jim's capture the occasion for a game. He becomes Tom's helpless accomplice, submissive and gullible. No wonder that Clemens has Huck remark, when Huck first realizes Aunt Sally has mistaken him for Tom, that "it was like being born again." Exactly. In the end, Huck regresses to the subordinate role in which he had first appeared in *The Adventures of Tom Sawyer*. Most of those traits which made him so appealing a hero now disappear. He had never, for example, found pain or misfortune amusing.

* * *

What I have been saying is that the flimsy devices of plot, the discordant farcical tone, and the disintegration of the major characters all betray the failure of the ending.

* * *

JULIUS LESTER

From Morality and *Adventures of Huckleberry Finn*[1]

*　*　*

The novel plays with black reality from the moment Jim runs away and does not immediately seek his freedom. It defies logic that Jim did not know Illinois was a free state. Yet, Twain wants us not only to believe he didn't, but to accept as credible that a runaway slave would sail *south* down the Mississippi River, the only route to freedom he knew being at Cairo, Illinois, where the Ohio River meets the Mississippi. If Jim knew that the Ohio met the Mississippi at Cairo, how could he not have known of the closer proximity of freedom to the east in Illinois or north in Iowa? If the reader must suspend intelligence to accept this, intelligence has to be dispensed with altogether to believe that Jim, having unknowingly passed the confluence of the Ohio and Mississippi Rivers, would continue down the river and go deeper and deeper into the heart of slave country. A century of white readers have accepted this as credible, a grim reminder of the abysmal feelings of superiority with which whites are burdened.

The least we expect of a novel is that it be credible, if not wholly in fact then in emotion, for it is emotions that are the true subject matter of fiction. As Jim floats down the river further and further into slave country without anxiety about his fate, without making the least effort to reverse matters, we leave the realm of factual and emotional credibility and enter the all too familiar one of white fantasy in which blacks have all the humanity of Cabbage Patch dolls.

*　*　*

The depth of Twain's contempt for blacks is not revealed fully until Tom Sawyer clears up something that had confused Huck. When Huck first proposed freeing Jim, he was surprised that Tom agreed readily. The reason Tom did so is because he knew all the while that Miss Watson had freed Jim when she died two months before.

Once again credibility is slain. Early in the novel Jim's disappearance from the town coincides with Huck's. Huck, having manufactured "evidence" of his "murder" to cover his escape, learns that the townspeople believe that Jim killed him. Yet, we are now to believe that an old white lady would free a black slave suspected of murdering a white child. White people might want to believe such fairy tales about themselves, but blacks know better.

But this is not the nadir of Twain's contempt, because when Aunt Sally asks Tom why he wanted to free Jim, knowing he was already free, Tom replies: "Well, that *is* a question, I must say; and *just* like women! Why, I wanted the *adventure* of it . . ." (Ch. 42). Now Huck understands why Tom was so eager to help Jim "escape."

---

1. From the *Mark Twain Journal* 22 (1984): 43–46. A professor at the University of Massachusetts for over thirty years, Julius Lester (b. 1939) is an award-winning author of books for children and adults.

Tom goes on to explain that his plan was "for us to run him down the river on the raft, and have adventures plumb to the mouth of the river." Then he and Huck would tell Jim he was free and take him "back up home on a steamboat, in style, and pay him for his lost time." They would tell everyone they were coming and "get out all the niggers around, and have them waltz him into town with a torchlight procession and a brass-band, and then he would be a hero, and so would we" ("Chapter the Last").

There is no honor here: * * * Jim is a plaything, an excuse for "the *adventure* of it," to be used as it suits the fancies of the white folk, whether that fancy be a journey on a raft down the river or a torch-light parade. What Jim clearly is not is a human being, and this is emphasized by the fact that Miss Watson's will frees Jim but makes no mention of his wife and children.

Twain doesn't care about the lives the slaves actually lived. Because he doesn't care, he devalues the world.

JUSTIN KAPLAN

From "Born to Trouble": One Hundred Years of *Huckleberry Finn*[1]

* * *

Twenty years after he finished *Huckleberry Finn* Mark Twain described its central and constitutive irony: "A sound heart and a deformed conscience come into collision and conscience suffers defeat." Huck's "deformed conscience" is the internalized voice of public opinion, of a conventional wisdom that found nothing wrong in the institution of slavery and held as mortal sin any attempt to subvert it. Conscience, as Mark Twain remembered from his boyhood in a slaveholding society, "can be trained to approve any wild thing you want it to approve if you begin its education early and stick to it." Huck knows that Tom Sawyer, "with his bringing-up," would never be able to set a slave free. But Huck eventually recognizes slavery for the "wild thing" it was. He follows the dictates of his sound heart and commits a sin as well as a crime by helping Jim to run away from his legal owner. "All right, then, I'll *go* to hell," Huck says. "It was awful thoughts, and awful words, but they was said. And I let them stay said; and never thought no more about reforming." Like Thoreau and Captain John Brown, Huck rejects what he considers to be an unjust and immoral law. He also rejects the craving for social approval that, according to Mark Twain, motivates the behavior of most of us. He is happy to remain a pariah. His story satirizes a number of beliefs sacred to Americans, consensual wisdom, for example, and the primacy of the average

1. From a lecture of September 11, 1984, sponsored by the Florida Center for the Book, presented at the Broward County Library in Fort Lauderdale, Florida, printed by the Library of Congress (Washington, D.C.: 1985). Justin Kaplan (b. 1925) is the author of *Mr. Clemens and Mark Twain* (1966), which won the Pulitzer Prize for biography.

man. "Do I know you?" Colonel Sherburn says when he faces down the lynch mob. "I know you clear through. I was born and raised in the South, and I've lived in the North; so I know the average all around. The average man's a coward." "Hain't we got all the fools in town on our side?" asks the king. "And ain't that a big enough majority, in any town?"

Guided by sound hearts rather than deformed consciences, Huck and Jim passed through agonies of remorse that are their own particular hells. Jim rebukes Huck: "Trash is what people is dat puts dirt on de head er dey fren's en makes 'em ashamed." "I didn't do him no more mean tricks," says Huck, "and I wouldn't done that one if I'd a knowed it would make him feel that way." Jim remembers committing an inadvertent act of cruelty to his own daughter: "De Lord God Almighty fogive po' ole Jim, kaze he never gwyne to fogive hisself as long's he live!" Seeking only self-approval, not the approval of others, the white pariah boy and the black runaway slave, "a community of saints," achieve a state of near-perfect intimacy and equality on their raft, fragile island of freedom between two shores of society. "What you want, above all things, on a raft," Huck says, "is for everybody to be satisfied, and feel right and kind towards the others." Perhaps another of the affronts that Mark Twain's novel offered and continues to offer is that his two outcasts are a silent reproach to dry-land society. They are simply too good for us, too truthful, too loyal, too passionate, and, in a profounder sense than the one we feel easy with, too moral.

Banning is one way of dealing with this profound affront. Another way is denial. Americans of Mark Twain's time and somewhat after tended to cherish him as a nostalgic recorder of boyhood high-jinks, a genial, harmless entertainer. As soon as the smiles faded from their faces they trivialized his genius and irony, his dark vision of humanity, and his moral passion. * * *

There is one especially bitter irony in the career of *Huckleberry Finn*. This novel, a savage indictment of a society that accepted slavery as a way of life, nevertheless has come under attack in our time for its alleged "racism." In 1957, for example, the N.A.A.C.P. condemned the book as "racially offensive." Such charges have supported exclusionary actions taken in many other states. In 1982 an administrator at the Mark Twain Intermediate School in Fairfax County, Virginia, called it "the most grotesque example of racism I've ever seen in my life." In 1984 school officials in Waukegan, Illinois, removed *Huckleberry Finn* from the required reading list after an alderman, according to the Associated Press, "objected to the book's use of the word 'nigger.'" It seems unlikely that anyone, of any color, who had actually read *Huckleberry Finn*, instead of merely reading or hearing about it, and who had allowed himself or herself even the barest minimum of intelligent response to its underlying spirit and intention, could accuse it of being "racist" because some of its characters use offensive racial epithets. These characters belong to their place and time, which is the Mississippi Valley thirty years before Emancipation.

As a historical portrait of slaveholding society, Mark Twain's novel is probably more faithful as well as less stereotypical than Harriet Beecher Stowe's beloved *Uncle Tom's Cabin*.* * *

Mark Twain, "the most desouthernized of southerners,"[2] according to his friend William Dean Howells, believed that it was henceforward the duty of

2. From Howells's *My Mark Twain* (1910).

white people to make amends for the crime of slavery. He may have been the least "racist" of all the major writers of his time, Herman Melville excepted. *Huckleberry Finn* is a matchless satire on racism, bigotry, and property rights in human beings.

* * *

DAVID L. SMITH

From Huck, Jim, and American Racial Discourse[1]

In July 1876, exactly one century after the American Declaration of Independence, Mark Twain began writing *Adventures of Huckleberry Finn*, a novel that illustrates trenchantly the social limitations that American "civilization" imposes on individual freedom. The book takes special note of ways in which racism impinges upon the lives of Afro-Americans, even when they are legally "free." It is therefore ironic that *Huckleberry Finn* has often been attacked and even censored as a racist work. I would argue, on the contrary, that except for Melville's work, *Huckleberry Finn* is without peer among major Euro-American novels for its explicitly antiracist stance. Those who brand the book racist generally do so without having considered the specific form of racial discourse to which the novel responds. Furthermore, *Huckleberry Finn* offers much more than the typical liberal defenses of "human dignity" and protests against cruelty. Though it contains some such elements, it is more fundamentally a critique of those socially constituted fictions— most notably romanticism, religion, and the concept of "the Negro"—which serve to justify and disguise selfish, cruel, and exploitative behavior.

When I speak of "racial discourse," I mean more than simply attitudes about race or conventions of talking about race. Most importantly, I mean that race itself is a discursive formation which delimits social relations on the basis of alleged physical differences. "Race" is a strategy for relegating a segment of the population to a permanent inferior status. It functions by insisting that each "race" has specific, definitive, inherent behavioral tendencies and capacities which distinguish it from other races. Though scientifically specious, race has been powerfully effective as an ideology and as a form of social definition that serves the interests of Euro-American hegemony. In America, race has been deployed against numerous groups, including Native Americans, Jews, Asians, and even—for brief periods—an assortment of European immigrants.

For obvious reasons, however, the primary emphasis historically has been on defining "the Negro" as a deviant from Euro-American norms. "Race" in America means white supremacy and black inferiority, and "the Negro," a socially constituted fiction, is a generalized, one-dimensional surrogate for

---

1. From *Satire or Evasion? Black Perspectives on Huckleberry Finn,* ed. James S. Leonard, Thomas A. Tenney, and Thadious M. Davis (1992), 103–20. David L. Smith is a professor at Williams College.

the historical reality of Afro-American people. It is this reified fiction that Twain attacks in *Huckleberry Finn*.

Twain adopts a strategy of subversion in his attack on race. That is, he focuses on a number of commonplaces associated with "the Negro" and then systematically dramatizes their inadequacy. He uses the term "nigger," and he shows Jim engaging in superstitious behavior. Yet he portrays Jim as a compassionate, shrewd, thoughtful, self-sacrificing, and even wise man. Indeed, his portrayal of Jim contradicts every claim presented in Jefferson's description of "the Negro."[2] Jim is cautious, he gives excellent advice, he suffers persistent anguish over separation from his wife and children, and he even sacrifices his own sleep so that Huck may rest. Jim, in short, exhibits all the qualities that "the Negro" supposedly lacks. Twain's conclusions do more than merely subvert the justifications of slavery, which was already long since abolished. Twain began his book during the final disintegration of Reconstruction, and his satire on antebellum southern bigotry is also an implicit response to the Negrophobic climate of the post-Reconstruction era. It is troubling, therefore, that so many readers have completely misunderstood Twain's subtle attack on racism.

Twain's use of the term "nigger" has provoked some readers to reject the novel. As one of the most offensive words in our vocabulary, "nigger" remains heavily shrouded in taboo. A careful assessment of this term within the context of American racial discourse, however, will allow us to understand the particular way in which the author uses it. If we attend closely to Twain's use of the word, we may find in it not just a trigger to outrage but, more important, a means of understanding the precise nature of American racism and Mark Twain's attack on it.

Most obviously, Twain uses "nigger" throughout the book as a synonym for "slave." There is ample evidence from other sources that this corresponds to one usage common during the antebellum period. We first encounter it in reference to "Miss Watson's big nigger, named Jim" (chap. 2). This usage, like the term "nigger stealer," clearly designates the "nigger" as an item of property: a commodity, a slave. This passage also provides the only apparent textual justification for the common critical practice of labeling Jim "Nigger Jim," as if "nigger" were a part of his proper name. This loathsome habit goes back at least as far as Albert Bigelow Paine's biography of Twain (1912). In any case, "nigger" in this sense connotes an inferior, even subhuman, creature who is properly owned by and subservient to Euro-Americans.

Both Huck and Jim use the word in this sense. For example, when Huck fabricates his tale about the riverboat accident, the following exchange occurs between him and Aunt Sally:

"Good gracious! anybody hurt?"
"No'm. Killed a nigger."
"Well, it's lucky; because sometimes people do get hurt." (Chap. 32)

Huck has never met Aunt Sally prior to this scene, and in spinning a lie which this stranger will find unobjectionable, he correctly assumes that the common notion of Negro subhumanity will be appropriate. Huck's offhand remark is intended to exploit Aunt Sally's attitudes, not to express Huck's

2. A reference to Thomas Jefferson's *Notes on the State of Virginia* (1787), Query XIV.

own. A nigger, Aunt Sally confirms, is not a person. Yet this exchange is hilarious precisely because we know that Huck is playing on her glib and conventional bigotry. We know that Huck's relationship to Jim has already invalidated for him such obtuse racial notions. The conception of the "nigger" is a socially constituted and sanctioned fiction, and it is just as false and absurd as Huck's explicit fabrication, which Aunt Sally also swallows whole.

In fact, the exchange between Huck and Aunt Sally reveals a great deal about how racial discourse operates. Its function is to promulgate a conception of "the Negro" as a subhuman and expendable creature who is by definition feeble-minded, immoral, lazy, and superstitious. One crucial purpose of this social fiction is to justify the abuse and exploitation of Afro-American people by substituting the essentialist fiction of "Negroism" for the actual character of individual Afro-Americans. Hence, in racial discourse every Afro-American becomes just another instance of "the Negro"—just another "nigger." Twain recognizes this invidious tendency of race thinking, however, and he takes every opportunity to expose the mismatch between racial abstractions and real human beings.

* * *

As a serious critic of American society, Twain recognized that racial discourse depends upon the deployment of a system of stereotypes which constitute "the Negro" as fundamentally different from and inferior to Euro-Americans. As with his handling of "nigger," Twain's strategy with racial stereotypes is to elaborate them in order to undermine them. To be sure, those critics are correct who have argued that Twain uses this narrative to reveal Jim's humanity. Jim, however, is just one individual. Twain uses the narrative to expose the cruelty and hollowness of that racial discourse which exists only to obscure the humanity of *all* Afro-American people.

JANE SMILEY

From Say It Ain't So, Huck:
Second Thoughts on Mark Twain's "Masterpiece"[1]

* * *

As with all bad endings, the problem really lies at the beginning, and at the beginning of *The Adventures of Huckleberry Finn* neither Huck nor Twain takes Jim's desire for freedom at all seriously; that is, they do not accord it the respect that a man's passion deserves. The sign of this is that not only do the two never cross the Mississippi to Illinois, a free state, but they hardly even consider it. In both *Tom Sawyer* and *Huckleberry Finn,* the Jackson's Island scenes show that such a crossing, even in secret, is both possible and routine, and even though it would present legal difficulties for an escaped slave, these would certainly pose no more hardship than locating the mouth

1. From *Harper's Magazine* (January 1996): 61–67. Jane Smiley (b. 1949) won the Pulitzer Prize for her novel *A Thousand Acres* (1991).

of the Ohio and then finding passage up it. It is true that there could have been slave catchers in pursuit (though the novel ostensibly takes place in the 1840s and the Fugitive Slave Act was not passed until 1850), but Twain's moral failure, once Huck and Jim link up, is never even to account for their choice to go down the river rather than across it. What this reveals is that for all his lip service to real attachment between white boy and black man, Twain really saw Jim as no more than Huck's sidekick, homoerotic or otherwise. All the claims that are routinely made for the book's humanitarian power are, in the end, simply absurd. Jim is never autonomous, never has a vote, always finds his purposes subordinate to Huck's, and, like every good sidekick, he never minds. He grows ever more passive and also more affectionate as Huck and the Duke and the Dauphin and Tom (and Twain) make ever more use of him for their own purposes. But this use they make of him is not supplementary; it is integral to Twain's whole conception of the novel. Twain thinks that Huck's affection is a good enough reward for Jim.

The sort of meretricious critical reasoning that has raised Huck's paltry good intentions to a "strategy of subversion" (David L. Smith) and a "convincing indictment of slavery" (Eliot)[2] precisely mirrors the same sort of meretricious reasoning that white people use to convince themselves that they are not "racist." If Huck *feels* positive toward Jim, and *loves* him, and *thinks* of him as a man, then that's enough. He doesn't actually have to act in accordance with his feelings. White Americans always think racism is a feeling, and they reject it or they embrace it. To most Americans, it seems more honorable and nicer to reject it, so they do, but they almost invariably fail to understand that how they *feel* means very little to black Americans, who understand racism as a way of structuring American culture, American politics, and the American economy. To invest *The Adventures of Huckleberry Finn* with "greatness" is to underwrite a very simplistic and evasive theory of what racism is and to promulgate it, philosophically, in schools and the media as well as in academic journals. Surely the discomfort of many readers, black and white, and the censorship battles that have dogged *Huck Finn* in the last twenty years are understandable in this context. No matter how often the critics "place in context" Huck's use of the word "nigger," they can never excuse or fully hide the deeper racism of the novel—the way Twain and Huck use Jim because they really don't care enough about his desire for freedom to let that desire change their plans. And to give credit to Huck suggests that the only racial insight Americans of the nineteenth or twentieth century are capable of is a recognition of the obvious—that blacks, slave and free, are human.

Ernest Hemingway, thinking of himself, as always, once said that all American literature grew out of *Huck Finn*. It undoubtedly would have been better for American literature, and American culture, if our literature had grown out of one of the best-selling novels of all time, another American work of the nineteenth century, *Uncle Tom's Cabin*, which for its portrayal of an array of thoughtful, autonomous, and passionate black characters leaves *Huck Finn* far behind. *Uncle Tom's Cabin* was published in 1852, when Twain was seventeen, still living in Hannibal and contributing to his brother's newspapers.

---

2. See T. S. Eliot's "The Boy and the River: Without Beginning or End," his introduction to a 1950 edition of *Huckleberry Finn*.

* * *

I would rather my children read *Uncle Tom's Cabin*, even though it is far more vivid in its depiction of cruelty than *Huck Finn*, and this is because Stowe's novel is clearly and unmistakably a tragedy. No whitewash, no secrets, but evil, suffering, imagination, endurance, and redemption—just like life. Like little Eva, who eagerly but fearfully listens to the stories of the slaves that her family tries to keep from her, our children want to know what is going on, what has gone on, and what we intend to do about it. If "great" literature has any purpose, it is to help us face up to our responsibilities instead of enabling us to avoid them once again by lighting out for the territory.

TONI MORRISON

From Introduction to *Adventures of Huckleberry Finn*[1]

* * *

In the early eighties I read *Huckleberry Finn* again, provoked, I believe, by demands to remove the novel from the libraries and required reading lists of public schools. These efforts were based, it seemed to me, on a narrow notion of how to handle the offense Mark Twain's use of the term "nigger" would occasion for black students and the corrosive effect it would have on white ones. It struck me as a purist yet elementary kind of censorship designed to appease adults rather than educate children. Amputate the problem, band-aid the solution. A serious comprehensive discussion of the term by an intelligent teacher certainly would have benefited my eighth-grade class and would have spared all of us (a few blacks, many whites—mostly second-generation immigrant children) some grief. Name calling is a plague of childhood and a learned activity ripe for discussion as soon as it surfaces. Embarrassing as it had been to hear the dread word spoken, and therefore sanctioned, in class, my experience of Jim's epithet had little to do with my initial nervousness the book had caused. Reading "nigger" hundreds of times embarrassed, bored, annoyed—but did not faze me. In this latest reading I was curious about the source of my alarm—my sense that danger lingered after the story ended. I was powerfully attracted to the combination of delight and fearful agitation lying entwined like crossed fingers in the pages. And it was significant that this novel which had given so much pleasure to young readers was also complicated territory for sophisticated scholars.

Usually the divide is substantial: if a story that pleased us as novice readers does not disintegrate as we grow older, it maintains its value only in its retelling for other novices or to summon uncapturable pleasure as playback. Also, the books that academic critics find consistently rewarding are

1. From "Introduction," *Adventures of Huckleberry Finn* (New York: Oxford University Press, 1996), xxxi–xli. Toni Morrison (b. 1931) is the author of *Beloved* (1987) and other novels; in 1993 she was awarded the Nobel Prize for Literature.

works only partially available to the minds of young readers. *Adventures of Huckleberry Finn* manages to close that divide, and one of the reasons it requires no leap is that in addition to the reverence the novel stimulates is its ability to transform its contradictions into fruitful complexities and to seem to be deliberately cooperating in the controversy it has excited. The brilliance of *Huckleberry Finn* is that it *is* the argument it raises.

My 1980s reading, therefore, was an effort to track the unease, nail it down, and learn in so doing the nature of my troubled relationship to this classic American work. * * *

If the emotional environment into which Twain places his protagonist is dangerous, then the leading question the novel poses for me is, What does Huck need to live without terror, melancholy and suicidal thoughts? The answer, of course, is Jim. When Huck is among society—whether respectable or deviant, rich or poor—he is alert to and consumed by its deception, its illogic, its scariness. Yet he is depressed by himself and sees nature more often as fearful. But when he and Jim become the only "we," the anxiety is outside, not within. ". . . we would watch the lonesomeness of the river . . . for about an hour . . . just solid lonesomeness." Unmanageable terror gives way to a pastoral, idyllic, intimate timelessness minus the hierarchy of age, status or adult control. It has never seemed to me that, in contrast to the entrapment and menace of the shore, the river itself provides this solace. The consolation, the healing properties Huck longs for, is made possible by Jim's active, highly vocal affection. It is in Jim's company that the dread of contemplated nature disappears, that even storms are beautiful and sublime, that real talk—comic, pointed, sad—takes place. Talk so free of lies it produces an aura of restfulness and peace unavailable anywhere else in the novel.* * *

So there will be no "adventures" without Jim. The risk is too great. To Huck and to the novel. When the end does come, when Jim is finally, tortuously, unnecessarily freed, able now to be a father to his own children, Huck runs. Not back to the town—even if it is safe now—but a further run, for the "territory." And if there are complications out there in the world, Huck, we are to assume, is certainly ready for them. He has had a first-rate education in social and individual responsibility, and it is interesting to note that the lessons of his growing but secret activism begin to be punctuated by speech, not silence, by moves toward truth, rather than quick lies.

* * *

The source of my unease reading this amazing, troubling book now seems clear: an imperfect coming to terms with three matters Twain addresses—Huck Finn's estrangement, soleness and morbidity as an outcast child; the disproportionate sadness at the center of Jim's and his relationship; and the secrecy in which Huck's engagement with (rather than escape from) a racist society is necessarily conducted. It is also clear that the rewards of my effort to come to terms have been abundant. My alarm, aroused by Twain's precise rendering of childhood's fear of death and abandonment, remains—as it should. It has been extremely worthwhile slogging through Jim's shame and humiliation to recognize the sadness, the tragic implications at the center of his relationship with Huck. My fury at the maze of deceit, the risk of personal harm that a white child is forced to negotiate in a race-inflected society, is dissipated by the exquisite uses to which Twain puts that maze, that risk.

Yet the larger question, the danger that sifts from the novel's last page, is whether Huck, minus Jim, will be able to stay those three monsters as he enters the "territory." Will that undefined space, so falsely imagined as "open," be free of social chaos, personal morbidity, and further moral complications embedded in adulthood and citizenship? Will it be free not only of nightmare fathers but of dream fathers too? Twain did not write Huck there. He imagined instead a reunion—Huck, Jim and Tom, soaring in a balloon over Egypt.

For a hundred years, the argument that this novel *is* has been identified, reidentified, examined, waged and advanced. What it cannot be is dismissed. It is classic literature, which is to say it heaves, manifests and lasts.

SHELLEY FISHER FISHKIN

From Lighting Out for the Territory: Reflections on Mark Twain and American Culture[1]

* * *

Novelist Jane Smiley hadn't read *Huckleberry Finn* since junior high, but when she broke her leg and was immobilized for a spell, she decided to read it again. She shared her reactions with the readers of *Harper's Magazine* in January 1996: "I closed the cover stunned. Yes, stunned. Not, by any means, by the artistry of the book but by the notion that this is the novel all American literature grows out of, that this is a great novel, that this is even a serious novel." The book, she maintains, "has little to offer in the way of greatness." She faults Twain for not taking Jim's aspirations toward freedom seriously: her evidence is that he doesn't let him cross the river to Illinois (she seems unaware of the dangers inherent in that plan in the 1840s) and she faults Twain for demanding too little from Huck: "If Huck feels positive toward Jim, and loves him, and thinks of him as a man, then that's enough. He doesn't actually have to act in accordance with his feelings." (Smiley must have read a different book than I did, because in my edition the crux of the novel involves Huck's decision to "act in accordance with his feelings.") "The very heart of nineteenth-century American experience and literature, the nature and meaning of slavery, is finally what Twain cannot face," Smiley maintains. *Uncle Tom's Cabin*, she argues, is infinitely superior: she'd prefer her children to read Stowe's book and wouldn't care if they never read Twain's.

* * *

Smiley seems to somehow miss the fact that *Huckleberry Finn* came out more than thirty years after Stowe's novel, and that the two books were written to achieve two different ends. One was written to mobilize sentiment against slavery. The other was written to expose the dynamics of racism. In her effort to excoriate the "deeper racism" inherent in Twain's novel, Smiley seems unconcerned that Stowe parcels out brains to her black characters in

1. From *Lighting Out for the Territory: Reflections on Mark Twain and American Culture* (New York: Oxford University Press, 1997). Shelley Fisher Fishkin is the author of *Was Huck Black?: Mark Twain and African-American Voices* (1993) and the editor of the *Oxford Mark Twain*.

inverse proportion to the amount of melanin in their skin. She is also obtuse to the growing consensus about the meaning of the last portion of *Huckleberry Finn*.

* * *

In the book's famous ending—variously maligned as a failure, a mistake, a retreat, or worse—what do we find? Incarcerated in a tiny shack, with a ludicrous assortment of snakes, rats, and spiders put there by an authority figure who claims to have his best interests at heart, Jim is denied information that he needs and is forced to perform a series of pointless and exhausting tasks. After risking his life to get the freedom that, unbeknownst to him, is already his, after proving himself to be a paragon of moral virtue who towers over everyone around him, this legally free black man is still denied respect—and is still in chains. All of this happens not at the hands of charlatans, the duke and the king, but at the initiative of a respectable Tom Sawyer and churchgoing citizens like the Phelpses and their neighbors. Victor Doyno's research on the manuscript reveals that Twain revised meticulously to make his prose as sharp and effective as possible; his revisions of manuscript page 751, for example, show him emphasizing Jim's bravery and selflessness and contrasting it sharply with Tom's foolishness.[2]

Is what America did to the ex-slaves any less insane than what Tom Sawyer put Jim through in the novel? After all, the spiders and carved grindstones Tom imposed on Jim don't hold a candle to the creativity—or cruelty—of the white cadets at West Point who in 1880 slashed Johnson Whittaker's ears, beat him unconscious, and accused him of staging the attack, alleging he expected to fail his philosophy exam. "It was that one part black that undid him," Twain observed acidly. "It was to blame for the whole thing." Where do we go for a window on the "contrast between our ideals and activities" that was "inescapable" after "the war to 'free the slaves'" as Ralph Ellison put it in our 1991 interview? "People didn't want to talk directly about it," Ellison observed. But Twain did take it on: "One of the functions of comedy," Ellison said, "is to allow us to deal with the unspeakable. And this Twain did consistently." *Huckleberry Finn* may end in farce, but it is not Twain's farce—it is ours. Twain's book is not escapist. It is an escape from the *denial* of the farce we've made of what was—and still is—a noble social and political experiment.

2. See Victor A. Doyno, *Writing Huck Finn: Mark Twain's Creative Process* (1991).

BRET HARTE
1836–1902

Francis Bret[t] Harte was born August 25, 1836, in Albany, New York, of English, Dutch, and Jewish descent. His father, Henry, a schoolteacher, died in 1845, and four years later Harte left school to work in a lawyer's office and then in the counting room of a merchant. In 1854 he followed his mother, Elizabeth Rebecca, and his elder sister and brother to Oakland, California, and for a year lived with his mother and stepfather, Colonel Andrew Williams, the first mayor of Oakland. When he turned twenty-one, he left to seek employment farther north in California, where he worked for a time for Wells Fargo (he claimed that he "rode shotgun") and also as a miner, teacher, tutor, pharmacist's clerk, and printer. From 1858 to 1860 he set type and served as an editorial assistant on the staff of the Uniontown *Northern Californian*. In late February 1860, while the editor-in-chief was out of town, Harte wrote an editorial expressing outrage over the massacre in nearby Eureka of sixty Native Americans, mostly women and children, by a small gang of white vigilantes. After the appearance of the editorial, his life was apparently threatened, and within a month he left for San Francisco.

Harte quickly found a job setting type for *The Golden Era*, a monthly magazine, and soon began contributing poems, stories, and sketches, many under the pseudonym "The Bohemian." Jessie Benton Frémont, daughter of John C. Frémont, a former presidential candidate, befriended Harte and helped him obtain a series of government appointments that culminated in 1863 in his being named secretary to the superintendent in the U.S. Branch Mint in San Francisco, a position that left him free to write nearly full time. Harte's career as a writer was confirmed in 1868 when he became the first editor of the newly established and quickly influential *Overland Monthly*. In the second issue appeared "The Luck of Roaring Camp," which made him a national celebrity. In this story, as elsewhere, Harte's success rested on his ability to portray distinctive characters whom he connected to the western settings. Although regional writing in the 1890s was later to become identified with women authors, especially from New England, Harte was in the forefront of those trying to see people in the context of their local environment. Perhaps what most distinguished him from other writers who exploited the myths of the Wild West is an ironic perspective that often went undetected by readers unfamiliar with California, who wished to believe in noble gamblers and prostitutes with hearts of gold. The strange tale "Miggles," for its time quite a challenge to American sexual and gender mores, takes this ironic perspective on the "mystery" of the title character.

Harte focused on character types, such as schoolmarms, stagedrivers, and whores, to give readers a feel for what he called "a heterogeneous and remarkable population" drawn to the Pacific coast by the discovery of gold and remaining there to make their fortunes. There, "men were accepted for what they actually were" and what they could contribute to camp or settlement, and "distinction of previous position or advantages were unknown." If he sometimes condescended to these subjects in order to appeal to eastern readers, he also immortalized them. As the critic Gary Scharnhorst has noted, "[I]n his best Western writing Harte challenged the dime-novelized treatment of the frontier. His gamblers may be libertines, but they are also chivalrous; his redshirt miners may be coarse, but they are also charitable; and his fallen women may be 'easy,' but they are also self-sacrificial."

Harte often parodied biblical texts in order to challenge accepted beliefs and ridicule religious hypocrisy. If, as Scharnhorst has also pointed out, "The Luck of

Roaring Camp" is a retelling of the gospel story of the Nativity, the Madonna is a mixed-blood prostitute named Cherokee Sal, and her son Tommy (the name of the doubting Apostle) is a false Messiah. The name "Luck" denotes merely chance, not faith; in the end all is swept away by a flood of biblical proportions. "The Luck of Roaring Camp" turns out to be all bad. In 1870 Harte published a collection called *"The Luck of Roaring Camp" and Other Sketches,* which included works from *The Golden Era* and *Overland Monthly.* This popular book established many ideas about the West that were also circulated in various forms by other western writers, including Mark Twain, Joaquin Miller, Ambrose Bierce, and, later, Jack London.

Harte, who had married Anna Griswold in 1862, left San Francisco early in 1871 at the height of his fame in hopes that in the East his literary reputation would grow even more. After a journey cross-country that was covered by the daily press, the Hartes were entertained in Boston by the new editor of the *Atlantic Monthly,* William Dean Howells. James T. Fields, who owned the *Atlantic Monthly* and the firm of J. R. Osgood and Company, Harte's publisher, offered Harte the unheard-of sum of ten thousand dollars to write twelve or more poems and sketches to be published in the *Atlantic* and *Every Saturday* during the course of the year. Unfortunately, Harte did not produce much writing in the twelve months following, and his contract was not renewed. At the same time, his drinking was harming his lecturing career, which was already shaky due to performances that some saw as "dandified" and not at all those of a rugged western character. Whenever Harte departed from his standard western stories, he was castigated by critics, and so remained trapped in formula and self-parody. During the winter of 1877–78, his contract with Osgood having ended, Harte became nearly penniless.

The last three decades of Harte's life constitute a decline in his personal and literary fortunes. His novel *Gabriel Conroy* (1876) sold well but was slammed by the critics, and though his two plays, *Two Men of Sandy Bar* (1876) and (with Mark Twain) *Ah Sin* (1877), were produced, neither was successful. Harte was appointed consul to Crefield, Prussia, in 1878 and to Glasgow, Scotland, in 1880, and moved to Europe. But when Grover Cleveland became president in 1885, Harte lost his consulship. Though his American audience waned, Harte's English readers continued to receive his work favorably until his death, from throat cancer, in May 1902.

Harte was a literary pioneer for his use of local color, his bringing of California and western subjects to readers in the East, and his encouragement of western writers. He spawned a host of imitators, including Damon Runyon and O. Henry. Like his friend Buffalo Bill Cody, Harte helped create the West as a place of adventure and romance, injecting a characteristic note of gritty realism and irony. On the side of the San Francisco Bohemian Club is a bronze memorial commemorating Harte's life and featuring Cherokee Sal, Colonel Starbottle, and Miggles, among other of his most memorable characters.

The Luck of Roaring Camp[1]

There was commotion in Roaring Camp. It could not have been a fight, for in 1850 that was not novel enough to have called together the entire settlement. The ditches and claims were not only deserted, but "Tuttle's grocery" had contributed its gamblers, who, it will be remembered, calmly continued their game the day that French Pete and Kanaka Joe[2] shot each other to

---

1. First appearing in 1868 in *Overland Monthly,* the tale was reprinted by Osgood of Boston in 1870 in *"The Luck of Roaring Camp" and Other Sketches* and by Houghton Mifflin in 1878 in *"The Luck of Roaring Camp" and Other Tales;* the present text is taken from the 1878 revision.
2. Hawaiian word for adult man, used (nonpejoratively) by both Hawaiians and Americans at the time.

death over the bar in the front room. The whole camp was collected before a rude cabin on the outer edge of the clearing. Conversation was carried on in a low tone, but the name of a woman was frequently repeated. It was a name familiar enough in the camp,—"Cherokee Sal."

Perhaps the less said of her the better. She was a coarse and, it is to be feared, a very sinful woman. But at that time she was the only woman in Roaring Camp, and was just then lying in sore extremity, when she most needed the ministration of her own sex. Dissolute, abandoned, and irreclaimable, she was yet suffering a martyrdom hard enough to bear even when veiled by sympathizing womanhood, but now terrible in her loneliness. The primal curse had come to her in that original isolation which must have made the punishment of the first transgression so dreadful. It was, perhaps, part of the expiation of her sin that, at a moment when she most lacked her sex's intuitive tenderness and care, she met only the half-contemptuous faces of her masculine associates. Yet a few of the spectators were, I think, touched by her sufferings. Sandy Tipton thought it was "rough on Sal," and, in the contemplation of her condition, for a moment rose superior to the fact that he had an ace and two bowers[3] in his sleeve.

It will be seen also that the situation was novel. Deaths were by no means uncommon in Roaring Camp, but a birth was a new thing. People had been dismissed the camp effectively, finally, and with no possibility of return; but this was the first time that anybody had been introduced *ab initio*.[4] Hence the excitement.

"You go in there, Stumpy," said a prominent citizen known as "Kentuck," addressing one of the loungers. "Go in there, and see what you kin do. You've had experience in them things."

Perhaps there was a fitness in the selection. Stumpy, in other climes, had been the putative head of two families; in fact, it was owing to some legal informality in these proceedings that Roaring Camp—a city of refuge—was indebted to his company. The crowd approved the choice, and Stumpy was wise enough to bow to the majority. The door closed on the extempore surgeon and midwife, and Roaring Camp sat down outside, smoked its pipe, and awaited the issue.

The assemblage numbered about a hundred men. One or two of these were actual fugitives from justice, some were criminal, and all were reckless. Physically they exhibited no indication of their past lives and character. The greatest scamp had a Raphael[5] face, with a profusion of blonde hair; Oakhurst, a gambler, had the melancholy air and intellectual abstraction of a Hamlet; the coolest and most courageous man was scarcely over five feet in height, with a soft voice and an embarrassed, timid manner. The term "roughs" applied to them was a distinction rather than a definition. Perhaps in the minor details of fingers, toes, ears, etc., the camp may have been deficient, but these slight omissions did not detract from their aggregate force. The strongest man had but three fingers on his right hand; the best shot had but one eye.

Such was the physical aspect of the men that were dispersed around the cabin. The camp lay in a triangular valley between two hills and a river. The only outlet was a steep trail over the summit of a hill that faced the cabin, now illuminated by the rising moon. The suffering woman might have seen

---

3. In the card game euchre, jacks of the trump suit or the other suit of the same color.
4. From the beginning (Latin).

5. Raffaello Sanzio (1483–1520), painter and architect of the Italian High Renaissance, best known for his Madonnas.

it from the rude bunk whereon she lay,—seen it winding like a silver thread until it was lost in the stars above.

A fire of withered pine boughs added sociability to the gathering. By degrees the natural levity of Roaring Camp returned. Bets were freely offered and taken regarding the result. Three to five that "Sal would get through with it;" even that the child would survive; side bets as to the sex and complexion of the coming stranger. In the midst of an excited discussion an exclamation came from those nearest the door, and the camp stopped to listen. Above the swaying and moaning of the pines, the swift rush of the river, and the crackling of the fire rose a sharp, querulous cry,—a cry unlike anything heard before in the camp. The pines stopped moaning, the river ceased to rush, and the fire to crackle. It seemed as if Nature had stopped to listen too.

The camp rose to its feet as one man! It was proposed to explode a barrel of gunpowder; but in consideration of the situation of the mother, better counsels prevailed, and only a few revolvers were discharged; for whether owing to the rude surgery of the camp, or some other reason, Cherokee Sal was sinking fast. Within an hour she had climbed, as it were, that rugged road that led to the stars, and so passed out of Roaring Camp, its sin and shame, forever. I do not think that the announcement disturbed them much, except in speculation as to the fate of the child. "Can he live now?" was asked of Stumpy. The answer was doubtful. The only other being of Cherokee Sal's sex and maternal condition in the settlement was an ass. There was some conjecture as to fitness, but the experiment was tried. It was less problematical than the ancient treatment of Romulus and Remus,[6] and apparently as successful.

When these details were completed, which exhausted another hour, the door was opened, and the anxious crowd of men, who had already formed themselves into a queue, entered in single file. Beside the low bunk or shelf, on which the figure of the mother was starkly outlined below the blankets, stood a pine table. On this a candle-box was placed, and within it, swathed in staring red flannel, lay the last arrival at Roaring Camp. Beside the candle-box was placed a hat. Its use was soon indicated. "Gentlemen," said Stumpy, with a singular mixture of authority and *ex officio*[7] complacency,— "gentlemen will please pass in at the front door, round the table, and out at the back door. Them as wishes to contribute anything toward the orphan will find a hat handy." The first man entered with his hat on; he uncovered, however, as he looked about him, and so unconsciously set an example to the next. In such communities good and bad actions are catching. As the procession filed in comments were audible,—criticisms addressed perhaps rather to Stumpy in the character of showman: "Is that him?" "Mighty small specimen;" "Hasn't more'n got the color;" "Ain't bigger nor a derringer." The contributions were as characteristic: A silver tobacco box; a doubloon; a navy revolver, silver mounted; a gold specimen; a very beautifully embroidered lady's handkerchief (from Oakhurst the gambler); a diamond breastpin; a diamond ring (suggested by the pin, with the remark from the giver that he "saw that pin and went two diamonds better"); a slung-shot; a Bible

6. Twin brothers Romulus and Remus, traditional founders of Rome, were sons of Mars and Rhea, daughter of King Numitor of Alba Longa. When Numitor's brother Amulius deposed him, he made Rhea a Vestal Virgin (and thus forbidden to marry). But when Mars fell in love with her and she bore him the twins, Amulius, fearing they would grow up to overthrow him, left them by the banks of the River Tiber to fend for themselves; they were found by a she-wolf who took pity on them and fed them with her milk.

7. By virtue of one's office, or position (Latin).

(contributor not detected); a golden spur; a silver teaspoon (the initials: I regret to a say, were not the giver's); a pair of surgeon's shears; a lancet;[8] Bank of England note for £5; and about $200 in loose gold and silver coin. During these proceedings Stumpy maintained a silence as impassive as the dead on his left, a gravity as inscrutable as that of the newly born on his right. Only one incident occurred to break the monotony of the curious procession. As Kentuck bent over the candle-box half curiously, the child turned, and, in a spasm of pain, caught at his groping finger, and held it fast for a moment. Kentuck looked foolish and embarrassed. Something like a blush tried to assert itself in his weather-beaten cheek. "The d—d little cuss!" he said, as he extricated his finger, with perhaps more tenderness and care than he might have been deemed capable of showing. He held that finger a little apart from its fellows as he went out, and examined it curiously. The examination provoked the same original remark in regard to the child. In fact, he seemed to enjoy repeating it. "He rastled with my finger," he remarked to Tipton, holding up the member. "the d—d little cuss!"

It was four o'clock before the camp sought repose. A light burnt in the cabin where the watchers sat, for Stumpy did not go to bed that night. Nor did Kentuck. He drank quite freely, and related with great gusto his experience, invariably ending with his characteristic condemnation of the newcomer. It seemed to relieve him of any unjust implication of sentiment, and Kentuck had the weaknesses of the nobler sex. When everybody else had gone to bed, he walked down to the river and whistled reflectingly. Then he walked up the gulch past the cabin, still whistling with demonstrative unconcern. At a large redwood-tree he paused and retraced his steps, and again passed the cabin. Halfway down to the river's bank he again paused, and then returned and knocked at the door. It was opened by Stumpy. "How goes it?" said Kentuck, looking past Stumpy toward the candle-box. "All serene!" replied Stumpy. "Anything up?" "Nothing." There was a pause—an embarrassing one—Stumpy still holding the door. Then Kentuck had recourse to his finger, which he held up to Stumpy. "Rastled with it,—the d—d little cuss," he said, and retired.

The next day Cherokee Sal had such rude sepulture as Roaring Camp afforded. After her body had been committed to the hillside, there was a formal meeting of the camp to discuss what should be done with her infant. A resolution to adopt it was unanimous and enthusiastic. But an animated discussion in regard to the manner and feasibility of providing for its wants at once sprang up. It was remarkable that the argument partook of none of those fierce personalities with which discussions were usually conducted at Roaring Camp. Tipton proposed that they should send the child to Red Dog,—a distance of forty miles,—where female attention could be procured. But the unlucky suggestion met with fierce and unanimous opposition. It was evident that no plan which entailed parting from their new acquisition would for a moment be entertained. "Besides," said Tom Ryder, "them fellows at Red Dog would swap it, and ring in somebody else on us."[9] A disbelief in the honesty of other camps prevailed at Roaring Camp, as in other places.

The introduction of a female nurse in the camp also met with objection. It was argued that no decent woman could be prevailed to accept Roaring Camp

8. A small surgical knife.
9. Tom fears that the men of Red Dog might substitute another baby for theirs.

as her home, and the speaker urged that "they did n't want any more of the other kind." This unkind allusion to the defunct mother, harsh as it may seem, was the first spasm of propriety,—the first symptom of the camp's regeneration. Stumpy advanced nothing. Perhaps he felt a certain delicacy in interfering with the selection of a possible successor in office. But when questioned, he averred stoutly that he and "Jinny"—the mammal before alluded to—could manage to rear the child. There was something original, independent, and heroic about the plan that pleased the camp. Stumpy was retained. Certain articles were sent for to Sacramento. "Mind," said the treasurer, as he pressed a bag of gold-dust into the expressman's hand, "the best that can be got,— lace, you know, and filigree-work and frills,—d—n the cost!"

Strange to say, the child thrived. Perhaps the invigorating climate of the mountain camp was compensation for material deficiencies. Nature took the foundling to her broader breast. In that rare atmosphere of the Sierra foothills,—that air pungent with balsamic odor, that ethereal cordial at once bracing and exhilarating,—he may have found food and nourishment, or a subtle chemistry that transmuted ass's milk to lime and phosphorus.[1] Stumpy inclined to the belief that it was the latter and good nursing. "Me and that ass," he would say, "has been father and mother to him! Don't you," he would add, apostrophizing the helpless bundle before him, "never go back on us."

By the time he was a month old the necessity of giving him a name became apparent. He had generally been known as "The Kid," "Stumpy's Boy," "The Coyote" (an allusion to his vocal powers), and even by Kentuck's endearing diminutive of "The d—d little cuss." But these were felt to be vague and unsatisfactory, and were at last dismissed under another influence. Gamblers and adventurers are generally superstitious, and Oakhurst one day declared that the baby had brought "the luck" to Roaring Camp. It was certain that of late they had been successful. "Luck" was the name agreed upon, with the prefix of Tommy for greater convenience. No allusion was made to the mother, and the father was unknown. "It's better," said the philosophical Oakhurst, "to take a fresh deal all round. Call him Luck, and start him fair." A day was accordingly set apart for the christening. What was meant by this ceremony the reader may imagine who has already gathered some idea of the reckless irreverence of Roaring Camp. The master of ceremonies was one "Boston," a noted wag, and the occasion seemed to promise the greatest facetiousness. This ingenious satirist had spent two days in preparing a burlesque of the Church service, with pointed local allusions. The choir was properly trained, and Sandy Tipton was to stand godfather. But after the procession had marched to the grove with music and banners, and the child had been deposited before a mock altar, Stumpy stepped before the expectant crowd. "It ain't my style to spoil fun, boys," said the little man, stoutly eyeing the faces around him, "but it strikes me that this thing ain't exactly on the squar. It's playing it pretty low down on this yer baby to ring in fun on him that he ain't goin' to understand. And ef there's goin' to be any godfathers round, I'd like to see who's got any better rights than me." A silence followed Stumpy's speech. To the credit of all humorists be it said that the first man to acknowledge its justice was the satirist thus stopped of his fun. "But," said Stumpy, quickly following up his advantage, "we're here for a christening, and we'll have it. I proclaim you Thomas Luck, according to the laws of the United

1. Both lime and phosphorus are used as fertilizer and both are generally white; the suggestion is that the ass's milk would help the child's bones grow strong.

States and the State of California, so help me God." It was the first time that the name of the Deity had been otherwise uttered than profanely in the camp. The form of christening was perhaps even more ludicrous than the satirist had conceived; but strangely enough, nobody saw it and nobody laughed. "Tommy" was christened as seriously as he would have been under a Christian roof, and cried and was comforted in as orthodox fashion.

And so the work of regeneration began in Roaring Camp. Almost imperceptibly a change came over the settlement. The cabin assigned to "Tommy Luck"—or "The Luck," as he was more frequently called—first showed signs of improvement. It was kept scrupulously clean and whitewashed. Then it was boarded, clothed, and papered. The rosewood cradle, packed eighty miles by mule, had, in Stumpy's way of putting it, "sorter killed the rest of the furniture." So the rehabilitation of the cabin became a necessity. The men who were in the habit of lounging in at Stumpy's to see "how 'The Luck' got on" seemed to appreciate the change, and in self-defense the rival establishment of "Tuttle's grocery" bestirred itself and imported a carpet and mirrors. The reflections of the latter on the appearance of Roaring Camp tended to produce stricter habits of personal cleanliness. Again Stumpy imposed a kind of quarantine upon those who aspired to the honor and privilege of holding The Luck. It was a cruel mortification to Kentuck—who, in the carelessness of a large nature and the habits of frontier life, had begun to regard all garments as a second cuticle, which, like a snake's, only sloughed off through decay—to be debarred this privilege from certain prudential reasons. Yet such was the subtle influence of innovation that he thereafter appeared regularly every afternoon in a clean shirt and face still shining from his ablutions. Nor were moral and social sanitary laws neglected. "Tommy," who was supposed to spend his whole existence in a persistent attempt to repose, must not be disturbed by noise. The shouting and yelling, which had gained the camp its infelicitous title, were not permitted within hearing distance of Stumpy's. The men conversed in whispers or smoked with Indian gravity. Profanity was tacitly given up in these sacred precincts, and throughout the camp a popular form of expletive, known as "D——n the luck!" and "Curse the luck!" was abandoned, as having a new personal bearing. Vocal music was not interdicted, being supposed to have a soothing, tranquilizing quality; and one song, sung by "Man-o'-War Jack," an English sailor from her Majesty's Australian colonies, was quite popular as a lullaby. It was a lugubrious recital of the exploits of "the Arethusa, Seventy-four," in a muffled minor, ending with a prolonged dying fall at the burden of each verse, "On b-oo-o-ard of the Arethusa." It was a fine sight to see Jack holding The Luck, rocking from side to side as if with the motion of a ship, and crooning forth this naval ditty. Either through the peculiar rocking of Jack or the length of his song,—it contained ninety stanzas, and was continued with conscientious deliberation to the bitter end,—the lullaby generally had the desired effect. At such times the men would lie at full length under the trees in the soft summer twilight, smoking their pipes and drinking in the melodious utterances. An indistinct idea that this was pastoral happiness pervaded the camp. "This 'ere kind o' think," said the Cockney Simmons, meditatively reclining on his elbow, "is 'evingly." It reminded him of Greenwich.[2]

2. A town on the Thames River in England, birthplace of Henry VIII and site of the Royal Naval College, venerated by seafarers for its keeping of official, or Greenwich Mean, time.

On the long summer days The Luck was usually carried to the gulch from whence the golden store of Roaring Camp was taken. There, on a blanket spread over pine boughs, he would lie while the men were working in the ditches below. Latterly there was a rude attempt to decorate this bower with flowers and sweet-smelling shrubs, and generally some one would bring him a cluster of wild honeysuckles, azaleas, or the painted blossoms of Las Mariposas. The men had suddenly awakened to the fact that there were beauty and significance in these trifles, which they had so long trodden carelessly beneath their feet. A flake of glittering mica, a fragment of variegated quartz, a bright pebble from the bed of the creek, became beautiful to eyes thus cleared and strengthened, and were invariably put aside for The Luck. It was wonderful how many treasures the woods and hillsides yielded that "would do for Tommy." Surrounded by playthings such as never child out of fairyland had before, it is to be hoped that Tommy was content. He appeared to be serenely happy, albeit there was an infantine gravity about him, a contemplative light in his round gray eyes, that sometimes worried Stumpy. He was always tractable and quiet, and it is recorded that once, having crept beyond his "corral,"—a hedge of tessellated pine boughs, which surrounded his bed,—he dropped over the bank on his head in the soft earth, and remained with his mottled legs in the air in that position for at least five minutes with unflinching gravity. He was extricated without a murmur. I hesitate to record the many other instances of his sagacity, which rest, unfortunately, upon the statements of prejudiced friends. Some of them were not without a tinge of superstition. "I crep' up the bank just now," said Kentuck one day, in a breathless state of excitement, "and dern my skin if he wasn't a-talking to a jaybird as was a-sittin' on his lap. There they was, just as free and sociable as anything you please, a-jawin' at each other just like two cherrybums." Howbeit, whether creeping over the pine boughs or lying lazily on his back blinking at the leaves above him, to him the birds sang, the squirrels chattered, and the flowers bloomed. Nature was his nurse and playfellow. For him she would let slip between the leaves golden shafts of sunlight that fell just within his grasp; she would send wandering breezes to visit him with the balm of bay and resinous gum; to him the tall redwoods nodded familiarly and sleepily, the bumblebees buzzed, and the rooks cawed a slumbrous accompaniment.

Such was the golden summer of Roaring Camp. They were "flush times," and the luck was with them. The claims had yielded enormously. The camp was jealous of its privileges and looked suspiciously on strangers. No encouragement was given to immigration, and, to make their seclusion more perfect, the land on either side of the mountain wall that surrounded the camp they duly preëmpted. This, and a reputation for singular proficiency with the revolver, kept the reserve of Roaring Camp inviolate. The expressman— their only connecting link with the surrounding world—sometimes told wonderful stories of the camp. He would say, "They've a street up there in 'Roaring' that would lay over any street in Red Dog. They've got vines and flowers round their houses, and they wash themselves twice a day. But they're mighty rough on strangers, and they worship an Ingin baby."

With the prosperity of the camp came a desire for further improvement. It was proposed to build a hotel in the following spring, and to invite one or two decent families to reside there for the sake of The Luck, who might perhaps profit by female companionship. The sacrifice that this concession to the sex cost these men, who were fiercely skeptical in regard to its general virtue and usefulness, can only be accounted for by their affection for Tommy. A few still held out. But the resolve could not be carried into effect for three months, and the minority meekly yielded in the hope that something might turn up to prevent it. And it did.

The winter of 1851 will long be remembered in the foothills. The snow lay deep on the Sierras, and every mountain creek became a river, and every river a lake. Each gorge and gulch was transformed into a tumultuous watercourse that descended the hillsides, tearing down giant trees and scattering its drift and débris along the plain. Red Dog had been twice under water, and Roaring Camp had been forewarned. "Water put the gold into them gulches," said Stumpy. "It's been here once and will be here again!" And that night the North Fork suddenly leaped over its banks and swept up the triangular valley of Roaring Camp.

In the confusion of rushing water, crashing trees, and crackling timber, and the darkness which seemed to flow with the water and blot out the fair valley, but little could be done to collect the scattered camp. When the morning broke, the cabin of Stumpy, nearest the river-bank, was gone. Higher up the gulch they found the body of its unlucky owner; but the pride, the hope, the joy, The Luck, of Roaring Camp had disappeared. They were returning with sad hearts when a shout from the bank recalled them.

It was a relief-boat from down the river. They had picked up, they said, a man and an infant, nearly exhausted, about two miles below. Did anybody know them, and did they belong here?

It needed but a glance to show them Kentuck lying there, cruelly crushed and bruised, but still holding The Luck of Roaring Camp in his arms. As they bent over the strangely assorted pair, they saw that the child was cold and pulseless. "He is dead," said one. Kentuck opened his eyes. "Dead?" he repeated feebly. "Yes, my man, and you are dying too." A smile lit the eyes of the expiring Kentuck. "Dying!" he repeated; "he's a-taking me with him. Tell the boys I've got The Luck with me now;" and the strong man, clinging to the frail babe as a drowning man is said to cling to a straw, drifted away into the shadowy river that flows forever to the unknown sea.

1868   1870, 1878

WILLIAM DEAN HOWELLS
1837–1920

As a novelist, playwright, critic, essayist, reviewer, poet, and editor, William Dean Howells was always in the public eye, and his influence during the 1880s and 1890s on a growing middle-class readership was incalculable. Known at the height of his career as "the Dean of American Letters," Howells represented both the traditional and the innovative through his promotion of a new American realism. In the "Editor's Study" essays he wrote for *Harper's New Monthly Magazine* starting in 1886 (some of which were collected in *Criticism and Fiction* [1891]), Howells attacked sentimentality of thought and feeling and the falsification of moral nature and ethical options wherever he found them in fiction. He believed that realism "was nothing more or less than the truthful treatment of material," especially the motives and actions of *ordinary* men and women.

Howells was born in Martinsville, Ohio, on March 1, 1837, and had little formal schooling, assisting his father—a newspaper publisher and printer—from a very early age. As a teenager he was writing for newspapers in Columbus and Cincinnati, becoming city editor of the *Ohio State Journal* in 1858. During 1859–1860, Howells's essays, poems, and reviews appeared in such national publications as the *Atlantic Monthly* and the *Saturday Press*. His increasingly national visibility as an author and active supporter of the Republican Party in Columbus helped him to land the plum job of writing Abraham Lincoln's campaign biography, which appeared in 1860. In that year, with the money he earned from the biography, he made a literary pilgrimage to New England—the center of American literary culture at that time—where he was welcomed by such figures as James Russell Lowell, Oliver Wendell Holmes, Ralph Waldo Emerson, and Nathaniel Hawthorne. When Lincoln became president in 1861, he appointed Howells as U.S. Consul to Venice. There he wrote a series of travel letters, eventually published as *Venetian Life* (1866). In December 1862, he married Elinor Mead; they had three children. Returning to America after the Civil War, he worked briefly for the *Nation* in New York City until James T. Fields offered him the assistant editorship of Boston's *Atlantic Monthly*. In effect, Howells assumed control of the magazine from the very beginning, and he succeeded officially to the editorship in 1871, a position he held until resigning in 1881 to have more time to write fiction.

Howells had been finding his way as a novelist during his ten years as editor, publishing seven novels, beginning with *Their Wedding Journey* (1872). These early novels are short, uncomplicated linear narratives that deliberately avoid the exaggerated characterizations and plots of romantic fiction in favor of a more ordinary realism. Howells came into his own as novelist in the 1880s. *A Modern Instance* (1882) examines psychic, familial, and social disintegration under the pressure of the secularization and urbanization of post–Civil War America, the disintegration that became one of Howells's central subjects. Howells published his most famous novel, *The Rise of Silas Lapham*, in 1885, which traces the moral rise (and economic collapse) of Silas Lapham, a typical American entrepreneur who built a paint manufacturing company out of a combination of sheer luck, hard work, and shady business dealings. Within a year of its publication, Howells was profoundly affected by Russian novelist Leo Tolstoy's ideas of nonviolence, Spartan living, and economic equality and, at great risk to his reputation, publicly defended the "Haymarket Anarchists," a group of Chicago workers, several of whom were executed without clear proof of their participation in a bombing at a public demonstration in May 1886.

In 1891 Howells moved from Boston to New York to take on the editorship of the *Cosmopolitan*, which he hoped to make into a forum for his increasingly radical political views; he resigned in 1893 when he failed to gain support for his political agenda from the magazine's wealthy owner. As a fiction writer, he had begun to offer more direct political explorations of social and economic injustice in novels such as the large-canvassed *A Hazard of New Fortunes* (1890), which depicts class and ethnic conflict in New York City from the perspective of an editor who has moved from Boston to New York and appreciates the city as an outsider; the tighter, more psychologically focused *An Imperative Duty* (1892), which depicts racial passing; and the utopian romance *A Traveller from Altruria* (1894). Howells publicly opposed the Spanish-American War (1898), which was presented by its supporters as an unselfish effort to liberate Cuba from Spain, but which Howells feared was actually about U.S. expansionists' designs on Cuba, Puerto Rico, the Philippines, and other Spanish colonial possessions. In "Editha" (1905), Howells characteristically explores the moral failure of individuals who have been corrupted by their culture's worst values. Though the Spanish-American War is not specifically

William Dean Howells, c. 1871, when he became editor of the *Atlantic Monthly*.

mentioned in the story, its satire of romantic conceptions of battlefield glory and the rush to war suited the political moment.

In the course of his lifelong career as literary authority, Howells was international in outlook and promoted such European contemporaries as Ivan Turgenev, Benito Perez Caldós, Leo Tolstoy, Henrik Ibsen, Émile Zola, George Eliot, and Thomas Hardy. In the constant stream of reviews he wrote over five decades, he also supported many younger American writers and early on recognized and publicized the work of talented African American and women writers, including Paul Dunbar, Charles Chesnutt, Sarah Orne Jewett, Mary E. Wilkins Freeman, Edith Wharton, and Emily Dickinson. He actively promoted the careers of such emerging realists and naturalists as Stephen Crane, Hamlin Garland, and Frank Norris, and from the 1860s on was the friend and literary champion of Henry James and Mark Twain.

By the time Howells died of pneumonia in 1920, he had served for thirteen years as first president of the American Academy of Arts and Letters and was himself a national institution. For rebels and iconoclasts of the 1930s, Howellsian realism stood for literary conservatism. Frank Norris set the tone for this criticism when he called Howells's novels "teacup tragedies." But not only did Howells believe that ordinary middle-class life deserved literary respect, he was much more radical and adventurous than Norris and others were willing to credit. An outspoken cultural critic and novelistic innovator, Howells focused his passions and intellect on a wide array of contemporary issues in politics and art, regularly revealing his fascination with the lives of Americans of all backgrounds.

Editha[1]

The air was thick with the war feeling,[2] like the electricity of a storm which has not yet burst. Editha sat looking out into the hot spring afternoon, with her lips parted, and panting with the intensity of the question whether she could let him go. She had decided that she could not let him stay, when she saw him at the end of the still leafless avenue, making slowly up towards the house, with his head down and his figure relaxed. She ran impatiently out on the veranda, to the edge of the steps, and imperatively demanded greater haste of him with her will before she called aloud to him: "George!"

He had quickened his pace in mystical response to her mystical urgence, before he could have heard her; now he looked up and answered, "Well?"

"Oh, how united we are!" she exulted, and then she swooped down the steps to him. "What is it?" she cried.

"It's war," he said, and he pulled her up to him and kissed her.

---

1. First printed in the January 1905 issue of *Harper's Monthly*, the source of the present text.

2. The "war fever" preceding the Spanish-American War (1898), which Howells opposed.

She kissed him back intensely, but irrelevantly, as to their passion, and uttered from deep in her throat. "How glorious!"

"It's war," he repeated, without consenting to her sense of it; and she did not know just what to think at first. She never knew what to think of him; that made his mystery, his charm. All through their courtship, which was contemporaneous with the growth of the war feeling, she had been puzzled by his want of seriousness about it. He seemed to despise it even more than he abhorred it. She could have understood his abhorring any sort of blood-shed; that would have been a survival of his old life when he thought he would be a minister, and before he changed and took up the law. But making light of a cause so high and noble seemed to show a want of earnestness at the core of his being. Not but that she felt herself able to cope with a congenital defect of that sort, and make his love for her save him from himself. Now perhaps the miracle was already wrought in him. In the presence of the tremendous fact that he announced, all triviality seemed to have gone out of him; she began to feel that. He sank down on the top step, and wiped his forehead with his handkerchief, while she poured out upon him her question of the origin and authenticity of his news.

All the while, in her duplex emotioning, she was aware that now at the very beginning she must put a guard upon herself against urging him, by any word or act, to take the part that her whole soul willed him to take, for the completion of her ideal of him. He was very nearly perfect as he was, and he must be allowed to perfect himself. But he was peculiar, and he might very well be reasoned out of his peculiarity. Before her reasoning went her emotioning: her nature pulling upon his nature, her womanhood upon his manhood, without her knowing the means she was using to the end she was willing. She had always supposed that the man who won her would have done something to win her; she did not know what, but something. George Gearson had simply asked her for her love, on the way home from a concert, and she gave her love to him, without, as it were, thinking. But now, it flashed upon her, if he could do something worthy to *have* won her—be a hero, *her* hero—it would be even better than if he had done it before asking her; it would be grander. Besides, she had believed in the war from the beginning.

"But don't you see, dearest," she said, "that it wouldn't have come to this, if it hadn't been in the order of Providence? And I call any war glorious that is for the liberation of people who have been struggling for years against the cruelest oppression. Don't you think so, too?"

"I suppose so," he returned, languidly. "But war! Is it glorious to break the peace of the world?"

"That ignoble peace! It was no peace at all, with that crime and shame at our very gates." She was conscious of parroting the current phrases of the newspapers, but it was no time to pick and choose her words. She must sacrifice anything to the high ideal she had for him, and after a good deal of rapid argument she ended with the climax: "But now it doesn't matter about the how or why. Since the war has come, all that is gone. There are no two sides, any more. There is nothing now but our country."

He sat with his eyes closed and his head leant back against the veranda, and he said with a vague smile, as if musing aloud, "Our country—right or wrong."[3]

"Yes, right or wrong!" she returned, fervidly. "I'll go and get you some lemonade." She rose rustling, and whisked away; when she came back with

3. "Our country! In her intercourse with foreign nations may she always be in the right; but our country right or wrong." Part of a toast given by American naval officer Stephen Decatur (1779–1820).

two tall glasses of clouded liquid, on a tray, and the ice clucking in them, he still sat as she had left him, and she said as if there had been no interruption: "But there is no question of wrong in this case. I call it a sacred war. A war for liberty, and humanity, if ever there was one. And I know you will see it just as I do, yet."

He took half the lemonade at a gulp, and he answered as he set the glass down: "I know you always have the highest ideal. When I differ from you, I ought to doubt myself."

A generous sob rose in Editha's throat for the humility of a man, so very nearly perfect, who was willing to put himself below her.

Besides, she felt, more subliminally, that he was never so near slipping through her fingers as when he took that meek way.

"You shall not say that! Only, for once I happen to be right." She seized his hand in her two hands, and poured her soul from her eyes into his. "Don't you think so?" she entreated him.

He released his hand and drank the rest of his lemonade, and she added, "Have mine, too," but he shook his head in answering, "I've no business to think so, unless I act so, too."

Her heart stopped a beat before it pulsed on with leaps that she felt in her neck. She had noticed that strange thing in men: they seemed to feel bound to do what they believed, and not think a thing was finished when they said it, as girls did. She knew what was in his mind, but she pretended not, and she said, "Oh, I am not sure," and then faltered.

He went on as if to himself without apparently heeding her. "There's only one way of proving one's faith in a thing like this."

She could not say that she understood, but she did understand.

He went on again. "If I believed—if I felt as you do about this war—Do you wish me to feel as you do?"

Now she was really not sure; so she said, "George, I don't know what you mean."

He seemed to muse away from her as before. "There is a sort of fascination in it. I suppose that at the bottom of his heart every man would like at times to have his courage tested, to see how he would act."

"How can you talk in that ghastly way?"

"It *is* rather morbid. Still, that's what it comes to, unless you're swept away by ambition, or driven by conviction. I haven't the conviction or the ambition, and the other thing is what it comes to with me. I ought to have been a preacher, after all; then I couldn't have asked it of myself, as I must, now I'm a lawyer. And you believe it's a holy war, Editha?" he suddenly addressed her. "Oh, I know you do! But you wish me to believe so, too?"

She hardly knew whether he was mocking or not, in the ironical way he always had with her plainer mind. But the only thing was to be outspoken with him.

"George, I wish you to believe whatever you think is true, at any and every cost. If I've tried to talk you into anything, I take it all back."

"Oh, I know that, Editha. I know how sincere you are, and how—I wish I had your undoubting spirit! I'll think it over; I'd like to believe as you do. But I don't, now; I don't, indeed. It isn't this war alone; though this seems peculiarly wanton and needless; but it's every war—so stupid; it makes me sick. Why shouldn't this thing have been settled reasonably?"

"Because," she said, very throatily again, "God meant it to be war."

"You think it was God? Yes, I suppose that is what people will say."

"Do you suppose it would have been war if God hadn't meant it?"

"I don't know. Sometimes it seems as if God had put this world into men's keeping to work it as they pleased."

"Now, George, that is blasphemy."

"Well, I won't blaspheme. I'll try to believe in your pocket Providence," he said, and then he rose to go.

"Why don't you stay to dinner?" Dinner at Balcom's Works was at one o'clock.

"I'll come back to supper, if you'll let me. Perhaps I shall bring you a convert."

"Well, you may come back, on that condition."

"All right. If I don't come, you'll understand."

He went away without kissing her, and she felt it a suspension of their engagement. It all interested her intensely; she was undergoing a tremendous experience, and she was being equal to it. While she stood looking after him, her mother came out through one of the long windows, on to the veranda, with a catlike softness and vagueness.

"Why didn't he stay to dinner?"

"Because—because—war has been declared," Editha pronounced, without turning.

Her mother said, "Oh, my!" and then said nothing more until she had sat down in one of the large Shaker chairs[4] and rocked herself for some time. Then she closed whatever tacit passage of thought there had been in her mind with the spoken words: "Well, I hope *he* won't go."

"And *I* hope he *will*," the girl said, and confronted her mother with a stormy exaltation that would have frightened any creature less unimpressionable than a cat.

Her mother rocked herself again for an interval of cogitation. What she arrived at in speech was: "Well, I guess you've done a wicked thing, Editha Balcom."

The girl said, as she passed indoors through the same window her mother had come out by: "I haven't done anything—yet."

In her room, she put together all her letters and gifts from Gearson, down to the withered petals of the first flower he had offered, with that timidity of his veiled in that irony of his. In the heart of the packet she enshrined her engagement ring which she had restored to the pretty box he had brought it her in. Then she sat down, if not calmly yet strongly, and wrote:

> "GEORGE:—I understood—when you left me. But I think we had better emphasize your meaning that if we cannot be one in everything we had better be one in nothing. So I am sending these things for your keeping till you have made up your mind.
>
> "I shall always love you, and therefore I shall never marry any one else. But the man I marry must love his country first of all, and be able to say to me,
>
> > "'I could not love thee, dear, so much,
> > Loved I not honor more.'[5]

---

4. Sturdy unadorned chairs made by the Shaker sect.

5. From "Lucasta, Going to the Wars," by the English poet Richard Lovelace (1618–1658).

"There is no honor above America with me. In this great hour there is no other honor.

"Your heart will make my words clear to you. I had never expected to say so much, but it has come upon me that I must say the utmost.

EDITHA"

She thought she had worded her letter well, worded it in a way that could not be bettered; all had been implied and nothing expressed.

She had it ready to send with the packet she had tied with red, white, and blue ribbon, when it occurred to her that she was not just to him, that she was not giving him a fair chance. He had said he would go and think it over, and she was not waiting. She was pushing, threatening, compelling. That was not a woman's part. She must leave him free, free, free. She could not accept for her country or herself a forced sacrifice.

In writing her letter she had satisfied the impulse from which it sprang; she could well afford to wait till he had thought it over. She put the packet and the letter by, and rested serene in the consciousness of having done what was laid upon her by her love itself to do, and yet used patience, mercy, justice.

She had her reward. Gearson did not come to tea, but she had given him till morning, when, late at night there came up from the village the sound of a fife and drum with a tumult of voices, in shouting, singing, and laughing. The noise drew nearer and nearer; it reached the street end of the avenue; there it silenced itself, and one voice, the voice she knew best, rose over the silence. It fell; the air was filled with cheers; the fife and drum struck up, with the shouting, singing, and laughing again, but now retreating; and a single figure came hurrying up the avenue.

She ran down to meet her lover and clung to him. He was very gay, and he put his arm round her with a boisterous laugh. "Well, you must call me Captain, now; or Cap, if you prefer; that's what the boys call me. Yes, we've had a meeting at the town hall, and everybody has volunteered; and they selected me for captain, and I'm going to the war, the big war, the glorious war, the holy war ordained by the pocket Providence that blesses butchery. Come along; let's tell the whole family about it. Call them from their downy beds, father, mother, Aunt Hitty, and all the folks!"

But when they mounted the veranda steps he did not wait for a larger audience; he poured the story out upon Editha alone.

"There was a lot of speaking, and then some of the fools set up a shout for me. It was all going one way, and I thought it would be a good joke to sprinkle a little cold water on them. But you can't do that with a crowd that adores you. The first thing I knew I was sprinkling hell-fire on them. 'Cry havoc, and let slip the dogs of war.'[6] That was the style. Now that it had come to the fight, there were no two parties; there was one country, and the thing was to fight the fight to a finish as quick as possible. I suggested volunteering then and there, and I wrote my name first of all on the roster. Then they elected me—that's all. I wish I had some ice-water!"

She left him walking up and down the veranda, while she ran for the ice-pitcher and a goblet, and when she came back he was still walking up and down, shouting the story he had told her to her father and mother, who had

6. From Antony's soliloquy after the murder of Caesar, in Shakespeare's *Julius Caesar* (3.1.274).

come out more sketchily dressed than they commonly were by day. He drank goblet after goblet of the ice-water without noticing who was giving it, and kept on talking, and laughing through his talk wildly. "It's astonishing," he said, "how well the worse reason looks when you try to make it appear the better. Why, I believe I was the first convert to the war in that crowd tonight! I never thought I should like to kill a man; but now, I shouldn't care; and the smokeless powder lets you see the man drop that you kill. It's all for the country! What a thing it is to have a country that *can't* be wrong, but if it is, is right, anyway!"

Editha had a great, vital thought, an inspiration. She set down the ice-pitcher on the veranda floor, and ran up-stairs and got the letter she had written him. When at last he noisily bade her father and mother, "Well, good night. I forgot I woke you up; I sha'n't want any sleep myself," she followed him down the avenue to the gate. There, after the whirling words that seemed to fly away from her thoughts and refuse to serve them, she made a last effort to solemnize the moment that seemed so crazy, and pressed the letter she had written upon him.

"What's this?" he said. "Want me to mail it?"

"No, no. It's for you. I wrote it after you went this morning. Keep it—keep it—and read it sometime—" She thought, and then her inspiration came: "Read it if ever you doubt what you've done, or fear that I regret your having done it. Read it after you've started."

They strained each other in embraces that seemed as ineffective as their words, and he kissed her face with quick, hot breaths that were so unlike him, that made her feel as if she had lost her old lover and found a stranger in his place. The stranger said: "What a gorgeous flower you are, with your red hair, and your blue eyes that look black now, and your face with the color painted out by the white moonshine! Let me hold you under my chin, to see whether I love blood, you tiger-lily!" Then he laughed Gearson's laugh, and released her, scared and giddy. Within her willfulness she had been frightened by a sense of subtler force in him, and mystically mastered as she had never been before.

She ran all the way back to the house, and mounted the steps panting. Her mother and father were talking of the great affair. Her mother said: "Wa'n't Mr. Gearson in rather of an excited state of mind? Didn't you think he acted curious?"

"Well, not for a man who'd just been elected captain and had to set 'em up for the whole of Company A," her father chuckled back.

"What in the world do you mean, Mr. Balcom? Oh! There's Editha!" She offered to follow the girl indoors.

"Don't come, mother!" Editha called, vanishing.

Mrs. Balcom remained to reproach her husband. "I don't see much of anything to laugh at."

"Well, it's catching. Caught it from Gearson. I guess it won't be much of a war, and I guess Gearson don't think so, either. The other fellows will back down as soon as they see we mean it. I wouldn't lose any sleep over it. I'm going back to bed, myself."

Gearson came again next afternoon, looking pale, and rather sick, but quite himself, even to his languid irony. "I guess I'd better tell you, Editha, that I consecrated myself to your god of battles last night by pouring too many libations to him down my own throat. But I'm all right now. One has to carry off the excitement, somehow."

"Promise me," she commanded, "that you'll never touch it again!"

"What! Not let the cannikin clink? Not let the soldier drink?[7] Well, I promise."

"You don't belong to yourself now; you don't even belong to *me*. You belong to your country, and you have a sacred charge to keep yourself strong and well for your country's sake. I have been thinking, thinking all night and all day long."

"You look as if you had been crying a little, too," he said with his queer smile.

"That's all past. I've been thinking, and worshipping *you*. Don't you suppose I know all that you've been through, to come to this? I've followed you every step from your old theories and opinions."

"Well, you've had a long row to hoe."

"And I know you've done this from the highest motives—"

"'Oh, there won't be much pettifogging to do till this cruel war is—"

"And you haven't simply done it for my sake. I couldn't respect you if you had."

"Well, then we'll say I haven't. A man that hasn't got his own respect intact wants the respect of all the other people he can corner. But we won't go into that. I'm in for the thing now, and we've got to face our future. My idea is that this isn't going to be a very protracted struggle; we shall just scare the enemy to death before it comes to a fight at all. But we must provide for contingencies, Editha. If anything happens to me—"

"Oh, George!" She clung to him sobbing.

"I don't want you to feel foolishly bound to my memory. I should hate that, wherever I happened to be."

"I am yours, for time and eternity—time and eternity." She liked the words; they satisfied her famine for phrases.

"Well, say eternity; that's all right; but time's another thing; and I'm talking about time. But there is something! My mother! If anything happens—"

She winced, and he laughed. "You're not the bold soldier-girl of yesterday!" Then he sobered. "If anything happens, I want you to help my mother out. She won't like my doing this thing. She brought me up to think war a fool thing as well as a bad thing. My father was in the civil war, all through it; lost his arm in it." She thrilled with the sense of the arm round her; what if that should be lost? He laughed as if divining her: "Oh, it doesn't run in the family, as far as I know!" Then he added, gravely: "He came home with misgivings about war, and they grew on him. I guess he and mother agreed between them that I was to be brought up in his final mind about it; but that was before my time. I only knew him from my mother's report of him and his opinions; I don't know whether they were hers first; but they were hers last. This will be a blow to her. I shall have to write and tell her—"

He stopped, and she asked: "Would you like me to write too, George?"

"I don't believe that would do. No, I'll do the writing. She'll understand a little if I say that I thought the way to minimize it was to make war on the largest possible scale at once—that I felt I must have been helping on the war somehow if I hadn't helped keep it from coming, and I knew I hadn't; when it came, I had no right to stay out of it."

---

7. Allusion to Shakespeare's *Othello* (2.3.64–68), in which Iago sings a soldier's drinking song.

Whether his sophistries satisfied him or not, they satisfied her. She clung to his breast, and whispered, with closed eyes and quivering lips: "Yes, yes, yes!"

"But if anything should happen, you might go to her, and see what you could do for her. You know? It's rather far off; she can't leave her chair—"

"Oh, I'll go, if it's the ends of the earth! But nothing will happen! Nothing *can*! I—"

She felt herself lifted with his rising, and Gearson was saying, with his arm still round her, to her father: "Well, we're off at once, Mr. Balcom. We're to be formally accepted at the capital, and then bunched up with the rest somehow, and sent into camp somewhere, and got to the front as soon as possible. We all want to be in the van,[8] of course; we're the first company to report to the Governor. I came to tell Editha, but I hadn't got round to it."

She saw him again for a moment at the capital, in the station, just before the train started southward with his regiment. He looked well, in his uniform, and very soldierly, but somehow girlish, too, with his clean-shaven face and slim figure. The manly eyes and the strong voice satisfied her, and his preoccupation with some unexpected details of duty flattered her. Other girls were weeping and bemoaning themselves, but she felt a sort of noble distinction in the abstraction, the almost unconsciousness, with which they parted. Only at the last moment he said: "Don't forget my mother. It mayn't be such a walk-over as I supposed," and he laughed at the notion.

He waved his hand to her as the train moved off—she knew it among a score of hands that were waved to other girls from the platform of the car, for it held a letter which she knew was hers. Then he went inside the car to read it, doubtless, and she did not see him again. But she felt safe for him through the strength of what she called her love. What she called her God, always speaking the name in a deep voice and with the implication of a mutual understanding, would watch over him and keep him and bring him back to her. If with an empty sleeve, then he should have three arms instead of two, for both of hers should be his for life. She did not see, though, why she should always be thinking of the arm his father had lost.

There were not many letters from him, but they were such as she could have wished, and she put her whole strength into making hers such as she imagined he could have wished, glorifying and supporting him. She wrote to his mother glorifying him as their hero, but the brief answer she got was merely to the effect that Mrs. Gearson was not well enough to write herself, and thanking her for her letter by the hand of someone who called herself "Yrs truly, Mrs. W. J. Andrews."

Editha determined not to be hurt, but to write again quite as if the answer had been all she expected. But before it seemed as if she could have written, there came news of the first skirmish, and in the list of the killed, which was telegraphed as a trifling loss on our side, was Gearson's name. There was a frantic time of trying to make out that it might be, must be, some other Gearson; but the name and the company and the regiment, and the State were too definitely given.

---

8. Short for vanguard, the foremost division of an army.

Beginnings to 1820

World Map, Juan de la Cosa, 1500

As pilot of the *Niña* during Columbus's second voyage (1494–95), Juan de la Cosa learned about New World space firsthand. He also participated in three later voyages to South America, dying in 1510 after being struck by a poison arrow during a slaving raid in what is present-day Colombia. De la Cosa's large map, measuring three by six feet, embraces the entire known world but is most notable for its attempt to portray and conceptualize the land that would come to be called the "New World" or "America." Cuba, rendered as an island (Columbus had made all his men, including de la Cosa, swear it was part of a hypothesized continent), shows up with remarkable clarity. Hovering to its west (at the top) is a mystical figure of Columbus as Saint Christopher—the humble ferryman who carried Christ over the water on his back and thus supplied de la Cosa with a fitting metaphor for the looming Christianization of the Americas.

René de Laudonnière and Chief Athore, Jacques Le Moyne de Morgues, 1564

When Protestant French colonists under Jean Ribault landed in Florida in the early 1560s, they erected two columns, decorated with the arms of the French king, that were intended to project their claim over the region. Jacques Le Moyne de Morgues, who as mapmaker and artist accompanied Ribault's successor, René de Laudonnière, on a second French expedition, here portrays the moment when the local Indian chief, Athore, took Ribault to one of the columns. This engraving shows the native people "worshipping this stone as an idol," having placed before it offerings of fruit, edible roots, medicinal herbs, precious oils, and such artifacts as baskets and a bow and quiver. The artist, who escaped when the Spanish wiped out the French colony in 1565, settled in London, where he became an associate of Sir Walter Ralegh and the English artist-explorer John White.

Untitled, Cindy Sherman, 1981

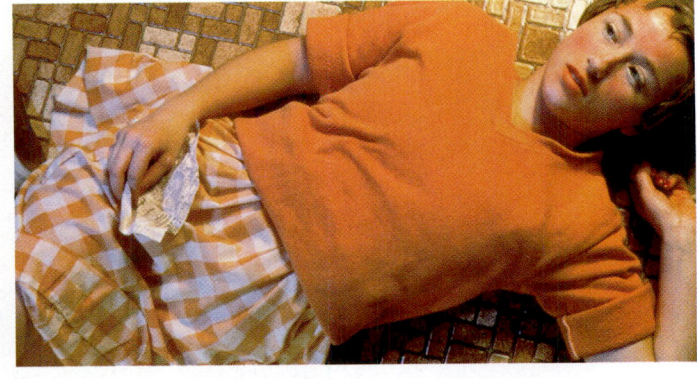

This photograph by the artist Cindy Sherman (b. 1954) is number 96 of her "Centerfold" series (1981). Like Sherman's earlier, black-and-white "Film Stills," this series consists of "self-portraits" in which the artist explores representations of women by dressing in a variety of costumes and adopting a variety of poses. Sherman's role as both photographer and subject reverses the traditional power of the male gaze, and here she examines and subverts the objectified images of women displayed in magazine centerfolds. Rather than signaling availability, this cropped, color-saturated photograph is enigmatic. Sherman's girlish clothing, evoking the 1950s, conceals more than it reveals, and she holds in her hand a largely unreadable scrap torn from a newspaper. Her gaze, vacant and interior, is also unreadable. Her distinctly unrevealing sweater and the flush on her face become part of the color pattern—oranges and browns forming a series of grids and checks—rather than an erotic sign.

Vietnam Veterans Memorial, Maya Lin, 1982

Located on the mall in Washington, D.C., the Vietnam Veterans Memorial is a 246-foot-long, v-shaped sunken wall of black granite. It is engraved with more than fifty-eight thousand names of those who died in the Vietnam conflict. The names are listed in chronological order, and to locate a particular name a visitor walks along the wall searching for it. The polished surface of the granite reflects the sky, the surrounding landscape, and the visitor. Considerable controversy attended the design, by the Chinese American architect Maya Lin (b. 1959), some objecting to its abstraction in place of the realistic statuary of most war memorials, and some finding it too somber. Lin has said she wanted a structure that would carve out a space for the public display of grief and loss, and the memorial has a powerful elegiac quality. Dedicated on Veterans Day, 1982, it has become the most widely visited monument in Washington.

Sonny's Quilt, Faith Ringgold, 1986

In *Sonny's Quilt*, an acrylic painting on canvas with a pieced fabric border, Faith Ringgold (b. 1930) unites two African American art forms: jazz and the quilt. This quilt painting depicts the jazz saxophonist Theodore Walter "Sonny" Rollins (b. 1930) poised high on the Brooklyn Bridge, the river below him and the skyline above him. To spare his neighbors in Brooklyn, Rollins used to leave his apartment to practice his instrument in public places. The brilliant coloration of the painting recalls the materials of African American quilts, and the girders and wires of the bridge, as well as the repeated squares in the bridge's structure, resemble the designs and borders of quilt patterns. Centered in the painting, Rollins is alone with his music and yet a part of the surrounding city. Ringgold's depiction of the Williamsburg Bridge evokes the iconic status of the nearby Brooklyn Bridge in American painting, photography, and literature, including *The Bridge* (1930) by Hart Crane (1899–1932), a selection from which appears in this anthology.

World Trade Center Burning, Peter Morgan, September 11, 2001

"A screaming comes across the sky." This opening sentence of Thomas Pynchon's 1973 novel *Gravity's Rainbow* had for decades impressed readers with the terrors of modern warfare, in which military technologies at the far edge of human inventiveness were turned against people at home. That Pynchon's scene was London, under attack from German V-2 rockets near the end of World War II, may have allayed readers' most personal fears. Yet on September 11, 2001, another such screaming awoke not just the United States but the whole world to the reality that wholesale destruction was an ever-present possibility. After half a century of Cold War rhetoric that had made such catastrophes unthinkable, the unthinkable happened. Two jet airliners were crashed into the twin towers of New York's World Trade Center in an event witnessed within minutes by television viewers all over the Earth. By the time the buildings collapsed, the whole world was watching. What in normal terms might be a line in a novel or a scene in a movie was now most horribly real.

The Gates, Christo and Jeanne-Claude, 2005

For sixteen days, from February 12 to 27, 2005, New York City's Central Park was transformed by the artists Christo (b. 1935) and Jeanne-Claude (1935–2009) into a series of walkways, extending over twenty-three miles, in which orange-colored fabric panels were suspended from 7,503 vinyl structures or gates. To some who saw them as they stirred in the wind, these panels had a mysterious and dreamlike effect, transforming a familiar landscape and reaffirming the city's beauty after the tragedy of 9/11. Like all of Christo and Jeanne-Claude's creations, *The Gates* was public and temporary. New Yorkers' responses were typically mixed: while some complained about the expense and the hype, many found *The Gates* magical, an experience at once individual and shared by people from all over the country and the world.

Then there was a lapse into depths out of which it seemed as if she never could rise again; then a lift into clouds far above all grief, black clouds, that blotted out the sun, but where she soared with him, with George, George! She had the fever that she expected of herself, but she did not die in it; she was not even delirious, and it did not last long. When she was well enough to leave her bed, her one thought was of George's mother, of his strangely worded wish that she should go to her and see what she could do for her. In the exaltation of the duty laid upon her—it buoyed her up instead of burdening her—she rapidly recovered.

Her father went with her on the long railroad journey from northern New York to western Iowa; he had business out at Davenport, and he said he could just as well go then as any other time; and he went with her to the little country town where George's mother lived in a little house on the edge of illimitable corn-fields, under trees pushed to a top of the rolling prairie. George's father had settled there after the civil war, as so many other old soldiers had done; but they were Eastern people, and Editha fancied touches of the East in the June rose overhanging the front door, and the garden with early summer flowers stretching from the gate of the paling fence.

It was very low inside the house, and so dim, with the closed blinds, that they could scarcely see one another: Editha tall and black in her crapes which filled the air with the smell of their dyes; her father standing decorously apart with his hat on his forearm, as at funerals; a woman rested in a deep armchair, and the woman who had let the strangers in stood behind the chair.

The seated woman turned her head round and up, and asked the woman behind her chair: "*Who* did you say?"

Editha, if she had done what she expected of herself, would have gone down on her knees at the feet of the seated figure and said, "I am George's Editha," for answer.

But instead of her own voice she heard that other woman's voice, saying: "Well, I don't know as I *did* get the name just right. I guess I'll have to make a little more light in here," and she went and pushed two of the shutters ajar.

Then Editha's father said, in his public will-now-address-a-few-remarks tone: "My name is Balcom, ma'am—Junius H. Balcom, of Balcom's Works, New York; my daughter—"

"Oh!" the seated woman broke in, with a powerful voice, the voice that always surprised Editha from Gearson's slender frame. "Let me see you! Stand round where the light can strike on your face," and Editha dumbly obeyed. "So, you're Editha Balcom," she sighed.

"Yes," Editha said, more like a culprit than a comforter.

"What did you come for?" Mrs. Gearson asked.

Editha's face quivered and her knees shook. "I came—because—because George—" She could go no further.

"Yes," the mother said, "he told me he had asked you to come if he got killed. You didn't expect that, I suppose, when you sent him."

"I would rather have died myself than done it!" Editha said with more truth in her deep voice than she ordinarily found in it. "I tried to leave him free—"

"Yes, that letter of yours, that came back with his other things, left him free."

Editha saw now where George's irony came from.

"It was not to be read before—unless—until—I told him so," she faltered.

"Of course, he wouldn't read a letter of yours, under the circumstances, till he thought you wanted him to. Been sick?" the woman abruptly demanded.

"Very sick." Editha said, with self-pity.

"Daughter's life," her father interposed, "was almost despaired of, at one time."

Mrs. Gearson gave him no heed. "I suppose you would have been glad to die, such a brave person as you! I don't believe *he* was glad to die. He was always a timid boy, that way; he was afraid of a good many things; but if he was afraid he did what he made up his mind to. I suppose he made up his mind to go, but I knew what it cost him, by what it cost me when I heard of it. I had been through *one* war before. When you sent him you didn't expect he would get killed."

The voice seemed to compassionate Editha, and it was time. "No," she huskily murmured.

"No, girls don't; women don't, when they give their men up to their country. They think they'll come marching back, somehow, just as gay as they went, or if it's an empty sleeve, or even an empty pantaloon, it's all the more glory, and they're so much the prouder of them, poor things!"

The tears began to run down Editha's face; she had not wept till then; but it was now such a relief to be understood that the tears came.

"No, you didn't expect him to get killed," Mrs. Gearson repeated in a voice which was startlingly like George's again. "You just expected him to kill some one else, some of those foreigners, that weren't there because they had any say about it, but because they had to be there, poor wretches—conscripts, or whatever they call 'em. You thought it would be all right for my George, *your* George, to kill the sons of those miserable mothers and the husbands of those girls that you would never see the faces of." The woman lifted her powerful voice in a psalmlike note. "I thank my God he didn't live to do it! I thank my God they killed him first, and that he ain't livin' with their blood on his hands!" She dropped her eyes, which she had raised with her voice, and glared at Editha. "What you got that black on for?" She lifted herself by her powerful arms so high that her helpless body seemed to hang limp its full length. "Take it off, take it off, before I tear it from your back!"

The lady who was passing the summer near Balcom's Works was sketching Editha's beauty, which lent itself wonderfully to the effects of a colorist. It had come to that confidence which is rather apt to grow between artist and sitter, and Editha told her everything.

"To think of your having such a tragedy in your life!" the lady said. She added: "I suppose there are people who feel that way about war. But when you consider the good this war has done—how much it has done for the country! I can't understand such people, for my part. And when you had come all the way out there to console her—got up out of a sick-bed! Well!"

"I think," Editha said, magnanimously, "she wasn't quite in her right mind; and so did papa."

"Yes," the lady said, looking at Editha's lips in nature and then at her lips in art, and giving an empirical touch to them in the picture. "But how dreadful of her! How perfectly—excuse me—how *vulgar!*"

A light broke upon Editha in the darkness which she felt had been without a gleam of brightness for weeks and months. The mystery that had bewildered her was solved by the word; and from that moment she rose from grovelling in shame and self-pity, and began to live again in the ideal.

1905

AMBROSE BIERCE
1842–c. 1914

Ambrose Gwinnett Bierce was born on June 24, 1842, in Meigs County, Ohio, the tenth of thirteen children. After the family moved to Indiana, he attended school and then struck out on his own at age fifteen. He worked as a printer's apprentice for a newspaper in Indiana, spent a term at a military school in Kentucky, and enlisted in the Union Army during the Civil War. Bierce later defined war (in his *Devil's Dictionary*) as a "by-product of the arts of peace" and peace as "a period of cheating between two periods of fighting," so it is hard to accept his own testimony that he was a zealous soldier. The Civil War, however, was an important source of some of his best fiction, including the suspenseful "An Occurrence at Owl Creek Bridge" (1890) and the equally bitter war narrative "Chickamauga" (1889).

When the war ended, Bierce moved to San Francisco to begin the journalistic career he followed for the rest of his life. San Francisco in the late 1860s and 1870s was becoming home to a journalism-based literary culture, as writers worked to make the West better known to eastern readers and counter the image of the "wild West" so popular in dime-novel fiction by showing San Francisco as the center of a cultivated society. Bierce married in 1872 and he went with his wife to England for four years, where he continued to hone his literary skills. Returning to San Francisco in 1875, he made a reputation through his newspaper columns as a satirist of elegance and bite. In 1897, now working for the Hearst newspaper organization, he went to Washington, D.C., as a correspondent. He had already published several books, including the story collections *Tales of Soldiers and Civilians* (1891) and *Can Such Things Be?* (1893). In Washington he collected his witticisms into dictionary form in a book published first in 1906 as *The Cynic's Word Book*. Between 1909 and 1912 his collected works appeared in twelve volumes; the *Word Book* was renamed *The Devil's Dictionary*.

Bierce and his wife had three children; they separated in 1888 and divorced five years later. One of his two sons seems to have been shot to death in 1889 in a brawl over a woman. The other died from alcoholism-related pneumonia in 1913. In that year, Bierce went to Mexico and disappeared. It is supposed that he planned to take part in the Mexican Revolution on the side of Pancho Villa, a cause endorsed by some politically engaged Americans of the era (but not by the U.S. government).

Among writers active after the Civil War, Bierce was known as the most consistently pessimistic; he was called "bitter Bierce" by many. His stories merged the hallucinatory and the paranormal with everyday events, attempting to catch the intensity of extreme human experience. Rejecting the national preference for optimism and happy endings, he strove to produce essays, fiction, and commentaries that would remain in his readers' minds as much for the tight pungency of their articulations as for the ideas themselves.

An Occurrence at Owl Creek Bridge[1]

I

A man stood upon a railroad bridge in Northern Alabama, looking down into the swift waters twenty feet below. The man's hands were behind his back, the wrists bound with a cord. A rope closely encircled his neck. It was attached to a stout cross-timber above his head, and the slack fell to the level of his knees. Some loose boards laid upon the sleepers[2] supporting the metals of the railway supplied a footing for him, and his executioners—two private soldiers of the Federal army, directed by a sergeant, who in civil life may have been a deputy sheriff. At a short remove upon the same temporary platform was an officer in the uniform of his rank, armed. He was a captain. A sentinel at each end of the bridge stood with his rifle in the position known as "support," that is to say, vertical in front of the left shoulder, the hammer resting on the forearm thrown straight across the chest—a formal and unnatural position, enforcing an erect carriage of the body. It did not appear to be the duty of these two men to know what was occurring at the centre of the bridge; they merely blockaded the two ends of the foot planking that traversed it.

Beyond one of the sentinels nobody was in sight; the railroad ran straight away into a forest for a hundred yards, then, curving, was lost to view. Doubtless there was an outpost farther along. The other bank of the stream was open ground—a gentle acclivity crowned with a stockade of vertical tree trunks, loopholed for rifles, with a single embrasure through which protruded the muzzle of a brass cannon commanding the bridge. Midway of the slope between bridge and fort were the spectators—a single company of infantry in line, at "parade rest," the butts of the rifles on the ground, the barrels inclining slightly backward against the right shoulder, the hands crossed upon the stock. A lieutenant stood at the right of the line, the point of his sword upon the ground, his left hand resting upon his right. Excepting the group of four at the center of the bridge not a man moved. The company faced the bridge, staring stonily, motionless. The sentinels, facing the banks of the stream, might have been statues to adorn the bridge. The captain stood with folded arms, silent, observing the work of his subordinates but making no sign. Death is a dignitary who, when he comes announced, is to be received with formal manifestations of respect, even by those most familiar with him. In the code of military etiquette silence and fixity are forms of deference.

The man who was engaged in being hanged was apparently about thirty-five years of age. He was a civilian, if one might judge from his dress, which was that of a planter. His features were good—a straight nose, firm mouth, broad forehead, from which his long, dark hair was combed straight back, falling behind his ears to the collar of his well-fitting frock coat. He wore a mustache and pointed beard but no whiskers; his eyes were large and dark gray and had a kindly expression which one would hardly have expected in

---

1. First published in the *San Francisco Examiner* on July 13, 1890, this story was subsequently reprinted as part of the collection *Tales of Soldiers and Civilians* (1891), the source of the text printed here.
2. English word for railroad ties, the cross-braces supporting railroad tracks.

one whose neck was in the hemp. Evidently this was no vulgar assassin. The liberal military code makes provision for hanging many kinds of people, and gentlemen are not excluded.

The preparations being complete, the two private soldiers stepped aside and each drew away the plank upon which he had been standing. The sergeant turned to the captain, saluted and placed himself immediately behind that officer, who in turn moved apart one pace. These movements left the condemned man and the sergeant standing on the two ends of the same plank, which spanned three of the cross-ties of the bridge. The end upon which the civilian stood almost, but not quite, reached a fourth. This plank had been held in place by the weight of the captain; it was now held by that of the sergeant. At a signal from the former, the latter would step aside, the plank would tilt and the condemned man go down between two ties. The arrangement commended itself to his judgment as simple and effective. His face had not been covered nor his eyes bandaged. He looked a moment at his "unsteadfast footing," then let his gaze wander to the swirling water of the stream racing madly beneath his feet. A piece of dancing driftwood caught his attention and his eyes followed it down the current. How slowly it appeared to move! What a sluggish stream!

He closed his eyes in order to fix his last thoughts upon his wife and children. The water, touched to gold by the early sun, the brooding mists under the banks at some distance down the stream, the fort, the soldiers, the piece of drift—all had distracted him. And now he became conscious of a new disturbance. Striking through the thought of his dear ones was a sound which he could neither ignore nor understand, a sharp, distinct, metallic percussion like the stroke of a blacksmith's hammer upon the anvil; it had the same ringing quality. He wondered what it was, and whether immeasurably distant or near by—it seemed both. Its recurrence was regular, but as slow as the tolling of a death knell. He awaited each stroke with impatience and—he knew not why—apprehension. The intervals of silence grew progressively longer; the delays became maddening. With their greater infrequency the sounds increased in strength and sharpness. They hurt his ear like the thrust of a knife; he feared he would shriek. What he heard was the ticking of his watch.

He unclosed his eyes and saw again the water below him. "If I could free my hands," he thought, "I might throw off the noose and spring into the stream. By diving I could evade the bullets and, swimming vigorously, reach the bank, take to the woods, and get away home. My home, thank God, is as yet outside their lines; my wife and little ones are still beyond the invader's farthest advance."

As these thoughts, which have here to be set down in words, were flashed into the doomed man's brain rather than evolved from it, the captain nodded to the sergeant. The sergeant stepped aside.

II

Peyton Farquhar was a well-to-do planter, of an old and highly-respected Alabama family. Being a slave owner, and, like other slave owners, a politician he was naturally an original secessionist and ardently devoted to the Southern cause. Circumstances of an imperious nature which it is unnecessary to relate here, had prevented him from taking service with the gallant army that had fought the disastrous campaigns ending with the fall of Corinth,[3] and he chafed under the inglorious restraint, longing for the release of his energies, the larger life of the soldier, the opportunity for distinction. That opportunity, he felt, would come, as it comes to all in war time. Meanwhile he did what he could. No service was too humble for him to perform in aid of the South, no adventure too perilous for him to undertake if consistent with the character of a civilian who was at heart a soldier, and who in good faith and without too much qualification assented to at least a part of the frankly villainous dictum that all is fair in love and war.

One evening while Farquhar and his wife were sitting on a rustic bench near the entrance to his grounds, a gray-clad soldier rode up to the gate and asked for a drink of water. Mrs. Farquhar was only too happy to serve him with her own white hands. While she was gone to fetch the water her husband approached the dusty horseman and inquired eagerly for news from the front.

"The Yanks are repairing the railroads," said the man, "and are getting ready for another advance. They have reached the Owl Creek bridge, put it in order, and built a stockade on the other bank. The commandant has issued an order, which is posted everywhere, declaring that any civilian caught interfering with the railroad, its bridges, tunnels, or trains will be summarily hanged. I saw the order."

"How far is it to the Owl Creek bridge?" Farquhar asked.

"About thirty miles?"

"Is there no force on this side the creek?"

"Only a picket post[4] half a mile out, on the railroad, and a single sentinel at this end of the bridge."

"Suppose a man—a civilian and student of hanging—should elude the picket post and perhaps get the better of the sentinel," said Farquhar, smiling, "what could he accomplish?"

The soldier reflected. "I was there a month ago," he replied. "I observed that the flood of last winter had lodged a great quantity of driftwood against the wooden pier at this end of the bridge. It is now dry and would burn like tow."

The lady had now brought the water, which the soldier drank. He thanked her ceremoniously, bowed to her husband, and rode away. An hour later, after nightfall, he repassed the plantation, going northward in the direction from which he had come. He was a Federal scout.

III

As Peyton Farquhar fell straight downward through the bridge, he lost consciousness and was as one already dead. From this state he was awakened—ages later, it seemed to him—by the pain of a sharp pressure upon his throat, followed by a sense of suffocation. Keen, poignant agonies seemed to shoot from his neck downward through every fiber of his body and limbs. These pains appeared to flash along well-defined lines of ramification and to beat with an inconceivably rapid periodicity. They seemed like streams of pulsating fire heating him to an intolerable temperature. As to his head, he

---

3. Corinth, Mississippi, fell to the Union forces on April 6 and 7, 1862, under General Ulysses S. Grant in the Battle of Shiloh.
4. Guard post.

was conscious of nothing but a feeling of fullness—of congestion. These sensations were unaccompanied by thought. The intellectual part of his nature was already effaced; he had power only to feel, and feeling was torment. He was conscious of motion. Encompassed in a luminous cloud, of which he was now merely the fiery heart, without material substance, he swung through unthinkable arcs of oscillation, like a vast pendulum. Then all at once, with terrible suddenness, the light about him shot upward with the noise of a loud plash; a frightful roaring was in his ears, and all was cold and dark. The power of thought was restored; he knew that the rope had broken and he had fallen into the stream. There was no additional strangulation; the noose about his neck was already suffocating him and kept the water from his lungs. To die of hanging at the bottom of a river!—the idea seemed to him ludicrous. He opened his eyes in the blackness and saw above him a gleam of light, but how distant, how inaccessible! He was still sinking, for the light became fainter and fainter until it was a mere glimmer. Then it began to grow and brighten, and he knew that he was rising toward the surface—knew it with reluctance, for he was now very comfortable. "To be hanged and drowned," he thought, "that is not so bad; but I do not wish to be shot. No; I will not be shot; that is not fair."

He was not conscious of an effort, but a sharp pain in his wrist apprised him that he was trying to free his hands. He gave the struggle his attention, as an idler might observe the feat of a juggler, without interest in the outcome. What splendid effort!—what magnificent, what superhuman strength! Ah, that was a fine endeavor! Bravo! The cord fell away; his arms parted and floated upward, the hands dimly seen on each side in the growing light. He watched them with a new interest as first one and then the other pounced upon the noose at his neck. They tore it away and thrust it fiercely aside, its undulations resembling those of a water snake. "Put it back, put it back!" He thought he shouted these words to his hands, for the undoing of the noose had been succeeded by the direst pang that he had yet experienced. His neck ached horribly; his brain was on fire; his heart, which had been fluttering faintly, gave a great leap, trying to force itself out at his mouth. His whole body was racked and wrenched with an insupportable anguish! But his disobedient hands gave no heed to the command. They beat the water vigorously with quick, downward strokes, forcing him to the surface. He felt his head emerge; his eyes were blinded by the sunlight; his chest expanded convulsively, and with a supreme and crowning agony his lungs engulfed a great draught of air, which instantly he expelled in a shriek!

He was now in full possession of his physical senses. They were, indeed, preternaturally keen and alert. Something in the awful disturbance of his organic system had so exalted and refined them that they made record of things never before perceived. He felt the ripples upon his face and heard their separate sounds as they struck. He looked at the forest on the bank of the stream, saw the individual trees, the leaves and the veining of each leaf—saw the very insects upon them: the locusts, the brilliant-bodied flies, the gray spiders stretching their webs from twig to twig. He noted the prismatic colors in all the dewdrops upon a million blades of grass. The humming of the gnats that danced above the eddies of the stream, the beating of the dragon flies' wings, the strokes of the water spiders' legs, like oars which had lifted their boat—all these made audible music. A fish slid along beneath his eyes and he heard the rush of its body parting the water.

He had come to the surface facing down the stream; in a moment the visible world seemed to wheel slowly round, himself the pivotal point, and he saw the bridge, the fort, the soldiers upon the bridge, the captain, the sergeant, the two privates, his executioners. They were in silhouette against the blue sky. They shouted and gesticulated, pointing at him; the captain had drawn his pistol, but did not fire; the others were unarmed. Their movements were grotesque and horrible, their forms gigantic.

Suddenly he heard a sharp report and something struck the water smartly within a few inches of his head, spattering his face with spray. He heard a second report, and saw one of the sentinels with his rifle at his shoulder, a light cloud of blue smoke rising from the muzzle. The man in the water saw the eye of the man on the bridge gazing into his own through the sights of the rifle. He observed that it was a gray eye, and remembered having read that gray eyes were keenest and that all famous marksmen had them. Nevertheless, this one had missed.

A counter swirl had caught Farquhar and turned him half round; he was again looking into the forest on the bank opposite the fort. The sound of a clear, high voice in a monotonous singsong now rang out behind him and came across the water with a distinctness that pierced and subdued all other sounds, even the beating of the ripples in his ears. Although no soldier, he had frequented camps enough to know the dread significance of that deliberate, drawling, aspirated chant; the lieutenant on shore was taking a part in the morning's work. How coldly and pitilessly—with what an even, calm intonation, presaging and enforcing tranquillity in the men—with what accurately-measured intervals fell those cruel words:

"Attention, company. . . . Shoulder arms. . . . Ready. . . . Aim. . . . Fire."

Farquhar dived—dived as deeply as he could. The water roared in his ears like the voice of Niagara, yet he heard the dulled thunder of the volley, and, rising again toward the surface, met shining bits of metal, singularly flattened, oscillating slowly downward. Some of them touched him on the face and hands, then fell away, continuing their descent. One lodged between his collar and neck; it was uncomfortably warm, and he snatched it out.

As he rose to the surface, gasping for breath, he saw that he had been a long time under water; he was perceptibly farther down stream—nearer to safety. The soldiers had almost finished reloading; the metal ramrods flashed all at once in the sunshine as they were drawn from the barrels, turned in the air, and thrust into their sockets. The two sentinels fired again, independently and ineffectually.

The hunted man saw all this over his shoulder; he was now swimming vigorously with the current. His brain was as energetic as his arms and legs; he thought with the rapidity of lightning.

"The officer," he reasoned, "will not make that martinet's error a second time. It is as easy to dodge a volley as a single shot. He has probably already given the command to fire at will. God help me, I cannot dodge them all!"

An appalling plash within two yards of him, followed by a loud, rushing sound, *diminuendo*,[5] which seemed to travel back through the air to the fort and died in an explosion which stirred the very river to its deeps! A rising sheet of water, which curved over him, fell down upon him, blinded him,

5. Diminishing.

strangled him! The cannon had taken a hand in the game. As he shook his head free from the commotion of the smitten water, he heard the deflected shot humming through the air ahead, and in an instant it was cracking and smashing the branches in the forest beyond.

"They will not do that again," he thought; "the next time they will use a charge of grape.[6] I must keep my eye upon the gun; the smoke will apprise me—the report arrives too late; it lags behind the missile. It is a good gun."

Suddenly he felt himself whirled round and round—spinning like a top. The water, the banks, the forests, the now distant bridge, fort and men—all were commingled and blurred. Objects were represented by their colors only; circular horizontal streaks of color—that was all he saw. He had been caught in a vortex and was being whirled on with a velocity of advance and gyration which made him giddy and sick. In a few moments he was flung upon the gravel at the foot of the left bank of the stream—the southern bank—and behind a projecting point which concealed him from his enemies. The sudden arrest of his motion, the abrasion of one of his hands on the gravel, restored him and he wept with delight. He dug his fingers into the sand, threw it over himself in handfuls and audibly blessed it. It looked like gold, like diamonds, rubies, emeralds; he could think of nothing beautiful which it did not resemble. The trees upon the bank were giant garden plants; he noted a definite order in their arrangement, inhaled the fragrance of their blooms. A strange, roseate light shone through the spaces among their trunks and the wind made in their branches the music of aeolian harps.[7] He had no wish to perfect his escape, was content to remain in that enchanting spot until retaken.

A whizz and rattle of grapeshot among the branches high above his head roused him from his dream. The baffled cannoneer had fired him a random farewell. He sprang to his feet, rushed up the sloping bank, and plunged into the forest.

All that day he traveled, laying his course by the rounding sun. The forest seemed interminable; nowhere did he discover a break in it, not even a woodman's road. He had not known that he lived in so wild a region. There was something uncanny in the revelation.

By nightfall he was fatigued, footsore, famishing. The thought of his wife and children urged him on. At last he found a road which led him in what he knew to be the right direction. It was as wide and straight as a city street, yet it seemed untraveled. No fields bordered it, no dwelling anywhere. Not so much as the barking of a dog suggested human habitation. The black bodies of the great trees formed a straight wall on both sides, terminating on the horizon in a point, like a diagram in a lesson in perspective. Overhead, as he looked up through this rift in the wood, shone great golden stars looking unfamiliar and grouped in strange constellations. He was sure they were arranged in some order which had a secret and malign significance. The wood on either side was full of singular noises, among which—once, twice, and again—he distinctly heard whispers in an unknown tongue.

His neck was in pain, and, lifting his hand to it, he found it horribly swollen. He knew that it had a circle of black where the rope had bruised it. His

6. Grapeshot, a cluster of small iron balls used as a cannon charge.
7. Stringed instruments activated by the wind

(Aeolus was the keeper of the winds in classical mythology).

eyes felt congested; he could no longer close them. His tongue was swollen with thirst; he relieved its fever by thrusting it forward from between his teeth into the cold air. How softly the turf had carpeted the untraveled avenue! He could no longer feel the roadway beneath his feet!

Doubtless, despite his suffering, he fell asleep while walking, for now he sees another scene—perhaps he has merely recovered from a delirium. He stands at the gate of his own home. All is as he left it, and all bright and beautiful in the morning sunshine. He must have traveled the entire night. As he pushes open the gate and passes up the wide white walk, he sees a flutter of female garments; his wife, looking fresh and cool and sweet, steps down from the veranda to meet him. At the bottom of the steps she stands waiting, with a smile of ineffable joy, an attitude of matchless grace and dignity. Ah, how beautiful she is! He springs forward with extended arms. As he is about to clasp her, he feels a stunning blow upon the back of the neck; a blinding white light blazes all about him, with a sound like the shock of a cannon—then all is darkness and silence!

Peyton Farquhar was dead; his body, with a broken neck, swung gently from side to side beneath the timbers of the Owl Creek bridge.

1890, 1891

HENRY JAMES
1843–1916

As a young man Henry James set out to be a "literary master" in the European sense. Even though the highly cultivated characters in his fiction ran counter to the vernacular tradition popularized by Mark Twain, James attracted, in his own lifetime, a select company of admirers and made a good living from his publications. His writings, the product of more than half a century as a publishing author, include tales, novellas, novels, plays, autobiographies, criticism, travel pieces, letters, reviews, and biographies—altogether perhaps as many as one hundred volumes, a prodigious output even by late nineteenth-century standards. The recognition of his importance as well as his wide influence as novelist and critic increased in the years between the world wars, when American literary taste reached a new level of sophistication. Since that time James has been firmly established as one of America's greatest novelists and critics, a subtle psychological realist and an unsurpassed literary stylist.

Henry James was born in New York City on April 15, 1843. His father was an independently wealthy amateur religious philosopher; his mother, Mary Robertson Walsh James, like many women of her day, stayed home and was the family mainstay. James's slightly older brother, William, was America's first notable psychologist and perhaps its most influential philosopher. There were also two younger brothers and a sister, Alice, herself a perceptive observer and diarist, to complete this remarkable American family. First taken to Europe as an infant, James spent his boyhood in a then almost bucolic Washington Square in New York City before the family once again left for the Continent when he was twelve. His father wanted the children to have a rich, "sensuous education," and during the next four years, with stays in England, Switzerland, and France, they were taken to galleries, librar-

Henry James in the early 1890s.

ies, museums, and (of special interest to James) theaters. James's formal schooling was unsystematic, but he mastered French well enough to begin a lifelong study of its literature, and from childhood on he was fascinated by the literary and historical traditions in Europe that, he later lamented in *Hawthorne* (1879), he believed were mostly absent in the United States.

James early developed what he described in *A Small Boy and Others* (1913) as the "practice of wondering and dawdling and gaping." This memoir also tells about an "obscure hurt" to his back that, disqualifying him from service in the Civil War, must have reinforced his inclination to observe rather than participate. In his later teens, his interest in literature and in writing intensified, and by the time he was twenty-one he was publishing reviews and stories in some of the leading American journals—*Atlantic Monthly, North American Review, Galaxy,* and *Nation.* He attended Harvard Law School briefly in 1862 but then decided that literature was his calling. He settled permanently in England in 1876 (after moving back and forth between America and Europe and after trial residences in France and Italy). James never married. He maintained close ties with his family, including William's children. He kept up a large correspondence, was extremely sociable, and knew most of his contemporaries in the arts. His prodigious creative energy was invested for more than fifty years in what he called the "sacred rage" of his art.

Leon Edel, James's influential modern biographer, divides the writer's mature career into three parts. In the first, which culminated with *The Portrait of a Lady* (1881), James felt his way toward and appropriated the so-called international theme—the drama, comic and tragic, of Americans in Europe and occasionally of Europeans in America. In the second period, he experimented with diverse themes and forms—initially in novels dealing explicitly with the social and political currents of the 1870s and 1880s, such as *The Princess Casamassima*, then in writing for the theater, and finally in shorter fictions exploring the relationship of artists to society and the troubled psyches of oppressed children, as in *What Maisie Knew* (1897). In his last period, the so-called major phase, which culminated with *The Golden Bowl* (1904), he returned to international and cosmopolitan subjects in elaborately complex narratives of great epistemological and moral challenge to readers.

Three of his earliest books, *A Passionate Pilgrim* (stories), *Transatlantic Sketches* (travel pieces), and *Roderick Hudson* (a novel), were published in 1875. *The American* (1877) was his first successful extended treatment of the naïve young American in conflict with the traditions, customs, and values of the Old World. *Daisy Miller* (1878), with its portrayal of the "new" American girl, brought him widespread popularity. In this "study," as it was originally subtitled, a stubbornly naïve American girl willfully resists European (and American) social mores. These works show James as neither a chauvinist for America nor a resentful émigré but a true cosmopolitan concerned with exploring American national character as it is tested by cultural displacement. In *Daisy Miller* in particular, James's skillful use of the limited point of view depicts a character who is himself limited by self-absorption and class position and who is thus unable to see Daisy for who she is. This narrative device, described by Percy Lubbock as the use of a "focal character," or narrator, somewhere over the protagonist's left shoulder, became an increasingly important part of James's technique. In *Daisy Miller* and other works written during the 1870s, James was already developing the hallmarks of his later greatness. He was also beginning to make problems of knowledge, whether characters' knowledge of each other or readers' struggles with deliberately limited information, the central drama of his texts.

Despite their appeal, the relatively simple characters of Christopher Newman (*The American*) and Daisy Miller evoke romance, melodrama, and pathos more than psychological complexity and genuine tragedy, which required for James a broader canvas. In the character and career of Isabel Archer he found the focus for his first masterpiece of the international theme, *The Portrait of a Lady*. Here, the complex inner lives of his American characters are fully and realistically portrayed. The last third of *Portrait* involves the heroine's awakened understanding and her attempts to escape her miserable marriage without sacrificing her principles or harming other people she cares about. James's tendency to have his main characters sacrifice their own happiness for the sake of principle has been criticized by some for its rejection of self-expression. But in *Portrait* and other of his works, James underscores how renunciation *is* a form of self-expression.

From 1885 to 1890 James was largely occupied by writing *The Bostonians* (1886), *The Princess Casamassima* (1886), and *The Tragic Muse* (1889). These novels of reformers, radicals, and revolutionaries are better appreciated, perhaps, in our time than they were in his. Out of a sense of artistic challenge as well as financial need, James attempted to regain the popularity of *Daisy Miller* and earn money by turning dramatist. Between 1890 and 1895 he wrote seven plays; two were produced, and both were painful public failures for their author, leading him into a period of intense self-doubt. Between 1895 and 1900 he returned to fiction, especially to experimental works with three dominant subjects, which he often combined: misunderstood or troubled writers and artists; ghosts and apparitions; and doomed or threatened children and adolescents. "The Beast in the Jungle" (1903, 1909) depicts the life of an egocentric man whose obsessive concern over the vague prospect of personal disaster destroys his chances for love and life in the present. Some of James's biographers have linked the guilt in this tale to the suicide of Constance Fenimore Woolson in 1894, which she may have resorted to partly out of unrequited (and entirely unrecognized) love for James. More recently, Eve Kosofsky Sedgwick and other critics have linked the character's lack of interest in women to repressed homosexuality. However it is interpreted, "The Beast in the Jungle" remains a chilling tale of a failed life.

Following his own advice to other novelists to "dramatize, dramatize, dramatize," James increasingly removed himself as controlling narrator. The benefits of this heightened emphasis on showing rather than telling were compression or intensification and enhanced opportunity for ambiguity. The more the author withdrew—not telling what was said, not analyzing a character's responses—the more the reader was forced to enter the process of creating meaning. The major works in which he experimented with such psychological realism were his last three great novels, *The Wings of the Dove* (1902), *The Ambassadors* (1903), and *The Golden Bowl* (1904). All three return to the international theme, but with a new and remorseless insight into how people make their own realities through their perceptions, impressions, and inner motivations. American innocence, at this point, becomes only a willful refusal to see, while awareness of one's own character as well as others' provides the wisdom to escape the designs that lead to disaster—though disaster is rarely thwarted in time and we are usually left both with insight and with the knowledge that it has come "too late." James's remedy for unhappiness is sometimes more unhappiness, but more importantly the willingness to entertain diverse points of view on moral struggles. His treatment of such an extraordinarily complex theme allows him an unparalleled richness of syntax, sentence structure, metaphoric webs, symbols, characterization, point of view, and organizing rhythms. The world of these novels is the one James defined in "The Art of Fiction" (1884) as representing "the very atmosphere of the mind." These late dramas of perception are widely considered to be James's most influential contribution to the craft of fiction.

When James was not writing fiction, he often wrote about it—either his own or others'. He was, as he noted in a letter, "a critical, a *non-naif*, a questioning, worrying reader." His inquiries into the achievement of other writers—preserved in such volumes as *French Poets and Novelists* (1878), *Partial Portraits* (1888), and *Notes on Novelists* (1914)—are remarkable for their breadth, balance, and acuteness. More broadly theoretical than his reviews or essays on individual writers, "The Art of Fiction" (an excerpt from which appears later in this volume) encapsulates James's central aesthetic conceptions. Calling attention to the unparalleled opportunities open to the artist of fiction and the beauty of the novel form, James also insists that "the deepest quality of a work of art will always be the quality of the mind of the producer" and that "no good novel will ever proceed from a superficial mind." James left no better record than this essay of his always twinned concerns over the moral and formal qualities of fiction, of the relationship between aesthetic and moral perception.

James was an extremely self-conscious writer, and his *Complete Notebooks*, edited and published in 1987, reveal a subtle, intense mind in the act of discovering subjects, methods, and principles. The prefaces he wrote for Scribner's lavish twenty-four-volume New York Edition (1907–09) of his extensively revised novels and tales contain James's final analyses of the works he considered to best represent his achievement—not to mention the extensive revisions themselves. As the culmination of a lifetime of reflection on the art of fiction, they provide extraordinary accounts of the origins and growth of his major writings and exquisite analyses of the fictional problems each work posed. These prefaces lent both vocabulary and example for the close textual analysis of prose fiction dominant in English departments in the decades following World War II.

During his 1904–05 visit to the United States, the first after nearly twenty years, James traveled extensively and lectured in his native land and in Canada. The chief result of this visit was *The American Scene* (1907). This "absolutely personal" book explores the profound changes that occurred in America between the Civil War and World War I, the period James characterized as the "Age of the Mistake." The same richness of personal rumination is found in three other autobiographical reminiscences he wrote later in life: *A Small Boy and Others* (1913), *Notes of a Son and Brother* (1914), and the fragmentary and posthumously published *The Middle Years* (1917).

Henry James became a naturalized British subject out of impatience with America's reluctance to enter World War I. He had involved himself in war-relief work starting in 1915. In 1916, he was awarded the British Order of Merit. Despite their considerable difficulty, most of James's novels and tales have remained in print. The rich depth of his work—especially his incisive psychological renderings of *why* people do the things they do—has continued to attract literary scholars and critics, as well as millions of readers around the world.

Daisy Miller: A Study[1]

I

At the little town of Vevey, in Switzerland, there is a particularly comfortable hotel. There are, indeed, many hotels; for the entertainment of tourists is the business of the place, which, as many travelers will remember, is seated upon

---

1. First published in the *Cornhill Magazine* 37 (June–July 1878). The text reprinted here follows the first British book edition, published by Macmillan in 1879.

the edge of a remarkably blue lake[2]—a lake that it behoves every tourist to visit. The shore of the lake presents an unbroken array of establishments of this order, of every category, from the "grand hotel" of the newest fashion, with a chalk-white front, a hundred balconies, and a dozen flags flying from its roof, to the little Swiss *pension*[3] of an elder day, with its name inscribed in German-looking lettering upon a pink or yellow wall, and an awkward summer-house in the angle of the garden. One of the hotels at Vevey, however, is famous, even classical, being distinguished from many of its upstart neighbors by an air both of luxury and of maturity. In this region, in the month of June, American travelers are extremely numerous; it may be said, indeed, that Vevey assumes at this period some of the characteristics of an American watering-place. There are sights and sounds which evoke a vision, an echo, of Newport and Saratoga.[4] There is a flitting hither and thither of "stylish" young girls, a rustling of muslin flounces, a rattle of dance-music in the morning hours, a sound of high-pitched voices at all times. You receive an impression of these things at the excellent inn of the "Trois Couronnes,"[5] and are transported in fancy to the Ocean House or to Congress Hall. But at the "Trois Couronnes," it must be added, there are other features that are much at variance with these suggestions: neat German waiters, who look like secretaries of legation; Russian princesses sitting in the garden; little Polish boys walking about, held by the hand, with their governors; a view of the snowy crest of the Dent du Midi and the picturesque towers of the Castle of Chillon.[6]

I hardly know whether it was the analogies or the differences that were uppermost in the mind of a young American, who, two or three years ago, sat in the garden of the "Trois Couronnes," looking about him, rather idly, at some of the graceful objects I have mentioned. It was a beautiful summer morning, and in whatever fashion the young American looked at things, they must have seemed to him charming. He had come from Geneva the day before, by the little steamer, to see his aunt, who was staying at the hotel—Geneva having been for a long time his place of residence. But his aunt had a headache—his aunt had almost always a headache—and now she was shut up in her room, smelling camphor,[7] so that he was at liberty to wander about. He was some seven-and-twenty years of age; when his friends spoke of him, they usually said that he was at Geneva, "studying." When his enemies spoke of him they said—but, after all, he had no enemies; he was an extremely amiable fellow, and universally liked. What I should say is, simply, that when certain persons spoke of him they affirmed that the reason of his spending so much time at Geneva was that he was extremely devoted to a lady who lived there—a foreign lady—a person older than himself. Very few Americans—indeed I think none—had ever seen this lady, about whom there were some singular stories. But Winterbourne had an old attachment for the little metropolis of Calvinism;[8] he had been put to school there as a boy, and he had afterwards gone to college there—circumstances which had

---

2. Lac Léman, or Lake of Geneva.
3. Boardinghouse.
4. Newport, Rhode Island, and Saratoga, New York, resort areas for the rich, where the Ocean House and Congress Hall hotels are located.
5. Three Crowns (French).
6. Medieval castle on an island in Lake Geneva, famous as the setting for Byron's poem "The Pris-

oner of Chillon" (1816). "Dent du Midi": the highest peak in a mountain group in the Swiss Alps.
7. An aromatic substance made from bark and wood, used at the time for the relief of minor pain.
8. Geneva, where the French Protestant reformer John Calvin (1509–1564) attempted to establish a community based on his theological beliefs.

led to his forming a great many youthful friendships. Many of these he had kept, and they were a source of great satisfaction to him.

After knocking at his aunt's door and learning that she was indisposed, he had taken a walk about the town, and then he had come in to his breakfast. He had now finished his breakfast, but he was drinking a small cup of coffee, which had been served to him on a little table in the garden by one of the waiters who looked like an *attaché*.[9] At last he finished his coffee and lit a cigarette. Presently a small boy came walking along the path—an urchin of nine or ten. The child, who was diminutive for his years, had an aged expression of countenance, a pale complexion, and sharp little features. He was dressed in knickerbockers, with red stockings, which displayed his poor little spindleshanks;[1] he also wore a brilliant red cravat. He carried in his hand a long alpenstock,[2] the sharp point of which he thrust into everything that he approached—the flower-beds, the garden-benches, the trains of the ladies' dresses. In front of Winterbourne he paused, looking at him with a pair of bright, penetrating little eyes.

"Will you give me a lump of sugar?" he asked, in a sharp, hard little voice—a voice immature, and yet, somehow, not young.

Winterbourne glanced at the small table near him, on which his coffee-service rested, and saw that several morsels of sugar remained. "Yes, you may take one," he answered; "but I don't think sugar is good for little boys."

This little boy stepped forward and carefully selected three of the coveted fragments, two of which he buried in the pocket to his knickerbockers, depositing the other as promptly in another place. He poked his alpenstock, lance-fashion, into Winterbourne's bench, and tried to crack the lump of sugar with his teeth.

"Oh, blazes; it's har-r-d!" he exclaimed, pronouncing the adjective in a peculiar manner.

Winterbourne had immediately perceived that he might have the honor of claiming him as a fellow-countryman. "Take care you don't hurt your teeth," he said, paternally.

"I haven't got any teeth to hurt. They have all come out. I have only got seven teeth. My mother counted them last night, and one came out right afterwards. She said she'd slap me if any more came out. I can't help it. It's this old Europe. It's the climate that makes them come out. In America they didn't come out. It's these hotels."

Winterbourne was much amused. "If you eat three lumps of sugar, your mother will certainly slap you," he said.

"She's got to give me some candy, then," rejoined his young interlocutor. "I can't get any candy here—any American candy. American candy's the best candy."

"And are American little boys the best little boys?" asked Winterbourne.

"I don't know. I'm an American boy," said the child.

"I see you are one of the best!" laughed Winterbourne.

"Are you an American man?" pursued this vivacious infant. And then, on Winterbourne's affirmative reply—"American men are the best," he declared.

His companion thanked him for the compliment; and the child, who had now got astride of his alpenstock, stood looking about him, while he

9. I.e., like a member of the diplomatic corps.   2. Walking stick.
1. Legs.

attacked a second lump of sugar. Winterbourne wondered if he himself had been like this in his infancy, for he had been brought to Europe at about this age.

"Here comes my sister!" cried the child, in a moment. "She's an American girl."

Winterbourne looked along the path and saw a beautiful young lady advancing. "American girls are the best girls," he said, cheerfully, to his young companion.

"My sister ain't the best!" the child declared. "She's always blowing[3] at me."

"I imagine that is your fault, not hers," said Winterbourne. The young lady meanwhile had drawn near. She was dressed in white muslin, with a hundred frills and flounces, and knots of pale-colored ribbon. She was bare-headed; but she balanced in her hand a large parasol, with a deep border of embroidery; and she was strikingly, admirably pretty. "How pretty they are!" thought Winterbourne, straightening himself in his seat, as if he were prepared to rise.

The young lady paused in front of his bench, near the parapet of the garden, which overlooked the lake. The little boy had now converted his alpenstock into a vaulting-pole, by the aid of which he was springing about in the gravel, and kicking it up not a little.

"Randolph," said the young lady, "what *are* you doing?"

"I'm going up the Alps," replied Randolph. "This is the way!" And he gave another little jump, scattering the pebbles about Winterbourne's ears.

"That's the way they come down," said Winterbourne.

"He's an American man!" cried Randolph, in his little hard voice.

The young lady gave no heed to this announcement, but looked straight at her brother. "Well, I guess you had better be quiet," she simply observed.

It seemed to Winterbourne that he had been in a manner presented. He got up and stepped slowly towards the young girl, throwing away his cigarette. "This little boy and I have made acquaintance," he said, with great civility. In Geneva, as he had been perfectly aware, a young man was not at liberty to speak to a young unmarried lady except under certain rarely-occurring conditions; but here at Vevey, what conditions could be better than these?—a pretty American girl coming and standing in front of you in a garden. This pretty American girl, however, on hearing Winterbourne's observation, simply glanced at him; she then turned her head and looked over the parapet, at the lake and the opposite mountains. He wondered whether he had gone too far; but he decided that he must advance farther, rather than retreat. While he was thinking of something else to say, the young lady turned to the little boy again.

"I should like to know where you got that pole," she said.

"I bought it!" responded Randolph.

"You don't mean to say you're going to take it to Italy!"

"Yes, I am going to take it to Italy!" the child declared.

The young girl glanced over the front of her dress, and smoothed out a knot or two of ribbon. Then she rested her eyes upon the prospect again. "Well, I guess you had better leave it somewhere," she said, after a moment.

"Are you going to Italy?" Winterbourne inquired, in a tone of great respect.

The young lady glanced at him again.

"Yes, sir," she replied. And she said nothing more.

3. Nagging.

"Are you—a—going over the Simplon?"[4] Winterbourne pursued, a little embarrassed.

"I don't know," she said, "I suppose it's some mountain. Randolph, what mountain are we going over?"

"Going where?" the child demanded.

"To Italy," Winterbourne explained.

"I don't know," said Randolph. "I don't want to go to Italy. I want to go to America."

"Oh, Italy is a beautiful place!" rejoined the young man.

"Can you get candy there?" Randolph loudly inquired.

"I hope not," said his sister. "I guess you have had enough candy, and mother thinks so too."

"I haven't had any for ever so long—for a hundred weeks!" cried the boy, still jumping about.

The young lady inspected her flounces and smoothed her ribbons again; and Winterbourne presently risked an observation upon the beauty of the view. He was ceasing to be embarrassed, for he had begun to perceive that she was not in the least embarrassed herself. There had not been the slightest alteration in her charming complexion; she was evidently neither offended nor fluttered. If she looked another way when he spoke to her, and seemed not particularly to hear him, this was simply her habit, her manner. Yet, as he talked a little more, and pointed out some of the objects of interest in the view, with which she appeared quite unacquainted, she gradually gave him more of the benefit of her glance; and then he saw that this glance was perfectly direct and unshrinking. It was not, however, what would have been called an immodest glance, for the young girl's eyes were singularly honest and fresh. They were wonderfully pretty eyes; and, indeed, Winterbourne had not seen for a long time anything prettier than his fair countrywoman's various features—her complexion, her nose, her ears, her teeth. He had a great relish for feminine beauty; he was addicted to observing and analyzing it; and as regards this young lady's face he made several observations. It was not at all insipid, but it was not exactly expressive; and though it was eminently delicate, Winterbourne mentally accused it—very forgivingly—of a want of finish. He thought it very possible that Master Randolph's sister was a coquette; he was sure she had a spirit of her own; but in her bright, sweet, superficial little visage there was no mockery, no irony. Before long it became obvious that she was much disposed towards conversation. She told him that they were going to Rome for the winter—she and her mother and Randolph. She asked him if he was a "real American"; she wouldn't have taken him for one; he seemed more like a German—this was said after a little hesitation, especially when he spoke. Winterbourne, laughing, answered that he had met Germans who spoke like Americans; but that he had not, so far as he remembered, met an American who spoke like a German. Then he asked her if she would not be more comfortable in sitting upon the bench which he had just quitted. She answered that she liked standing up and walking about; but she presently sat down. She told him she was from New York State—"if you know where that is." Winterbourne learned more about her by catching hold of her small, slippery brother and making him stand a few minutes by his side.

4. A mountain pass in the Alps between Switzerland and Italy.

"Tell me your name, my boy," he said.

"Randolph C. Miller," said the boy, sharply. "And I'll tell you her name"; and he leveled his alpenstock at his sister.

"You had better wait till you are asked!" said this young lady, calmly.

"I should like very much to know your name," said Winterbourne.

"Her name is Daisy Miller!" cried the child. "But that isn't her real name; that isn't her name on her cards."

"It's a pity you haven't got one of my cards!" said Miss Miller.

"Her real name is Annie P. Miller," the boy went on.

"Ask him *his* name," said his sister, indicating Winterbourne.

But on this point Randolph seemed perfectly indifferent; he continued to supply information with regard to his own family. "My father's name is Ezra B. Miller," he announced. "My father ain't in Europe; my father's in a better place than Europe."

Winterbourne imagined for a moment that this was the manner in which the child had been taught to intimate that Mr. Miller had been removed to the sphere of celestial rewards. But Randolph immediately added, "My father's in Schenectady. He's got a big business. My father's rich, you bet."

"Well!" ejaculated Miss Miller, lowering her parasol and looking at the embroidered border. Winterbourne presently released the child, who departed, dragging his alpenstock along the path. "He doesn't like Europe," said the young girl. "He wants to go back."

"To Schenectady, you mean?"

"Yes; he wants to go right home. He hasn't got any boys here. There is one boy here, but he always goes round with a teacher; they won't let him play."

"And your brother hasn't any teacher?" Winterbourne inquired.

"Mother thought of getting him one, to travel round with us. There was a lady told her of a very good teacher; an American lady—perhaps you know her—Mrs. Sanders. I think she came from Boston. She told her of this teacher, and we thought of getting him to travel round with us. But Randolph said he didn't want a teacher traveling round with us. He said he wouldn't have lessons when he was in the cars.[5] And we *are* in the cars about half the time. There was an English lady we met in the cars—I think her name was Miss Featherstone; perhaps you know her. She wanted to know why I didn't give Randolph lessons—give him 'instruction,' she called it. I guess he could give me more instruction than I could give him. He's very smart."

"Yes," said Winterbourne; "he seems very smart."

"Mother's going to get a teacher for him as soon as we get to Italy. Can you get good teachers in Italy?"

"Very good, I should think," said Winterbourne.

"Or else she's going to find some school. He ought to learn some more. He's only nine. He's going to college." And in this way Miss Miller continued to converse upon the affairs of her family, and upon other topics. She sat there with her extremely pretty hands, ornamented with very brilliant rings, folded in her lap, and with her pretty eyes now resting upon those of Winterbourne, now wandering over the garden, the people who passed by, and the beautiful view. She talked to Winterbourne as if she had known him a long

5. Railway cars.

time. He found it very pleasant. It was many years since he heard a young girl talk so much. It might have been said of this unknown young lady, who had come and sat down beside him upon a bench, that she chattered. She was very quiet, she sat in a charming tranquil attitude; but her lips and her eyes were constantly moving. She had a soft, slender, agreeable voice, and her tone was decidedly sociable. She gave Winterbourne a history of her movements and intentions, and those of her mother and brother, in Europe, and enumerated, in particular, the various hotels at which they had stopped. "That English lady in the cars," she said—"Miss Featherstone—asked me if we didn't all live in hotels in America. I told her I had never been in so many hotels in my life as since I came to Europe. I have never seen so many—it's nothing but hotels." But Miss Miller did not make this remark with a querulous accent; she appeared to be in the best humor with everything. She declared that the hotels were very good, when once you got used to their ways, and that Europe was perfectly sweet. She was not disappointed—not a bit. Perhaps it was because she had heard so much about it before. She had ever so many intimate friends that had been there ever so many times. And then she had had ever so many dresses and things from Paris. Whenever she put on a Paris dress she felt as if she were in Europe.

"It was a kind of wishing-cap," said Winterbourne.

"Yes," said Miss Miller, without examining this analogy; "it always made me wish I was here. But I needn't have done that for dresses. I am sure they send all the pretty ones to America; you see the most frightful things here. The only thing I don't like," she proceeded, "is the society. There isn't any society; or, if there is, I don't know where it keeps itself. Do you? I suppose there is some society somewhere, but I haven't seen anything of it. I'm very fond of society, and I have always had a great deal of it. I don't mean only in Schenectady, but in New York. I used to go to New York every winter. In New York I had lots of society. Last winter I had seventeen dinners given me; and three of them were by gentlemen," added Daisy Miller. "I have more friends in New York than in Schenectady—more gentlemen friends; and more young lady friends too," she resumed in a moment. She paused again for an instant; she was looking at Winterbourne with all her prettiness in her lively eyes and in her light, slightly monotonous smile. "I have always had," she said, "a great deal of gentlemen's society."

Poor Winterbourne was amused, perplexed, and decidedly charmed. He had never yet heard a young girl express herself in just this fashion; never, at least, save in cases where to say such things seemed a kind of demonstrative evidence of a certain laxity of deportment. And yet was he to accuse Miss Daisy Miller of actual or potential *inconduite*,[6] as they said at Geneva? He felt that he had lived at Geneva so long that he had lost a good deal; he had become dishabituated to the American tone. Never, indeed, since he had grown old enough to appreciate things, had he encountered a young American girl of so pronounced a type as this. Certainly she was very charming; but how deucedly sociable! Was she simply a pretty girl from New York State—were they all like that, the pretty girls who had a good deal of gentlemen's society? Or was she also a designing, an audacious, an unscrupulous young person? Winterbourne had lost his instinct in this matter, and his

6. Misconduct (French).

reason could not help him. Miss Daisy Miller looked extremely innocent. Some people had told him that, after all, American girls were exceedingly innocent; and others had told him that, after all, they were not. He was inclined to think Miss Daisy Miller was a flirt—a pretty American flirt. He had never, as yet, had any relations with young ladies of this category. He had known, here in Europe, two or three women—persons older than Miss Daisy Miller, and provided, for respectability's sake, with husbands—who were great coquettes—dangerous, terrible women, with whom one's relations were liable to take a serious turn. But this young girl was not a coquette in that sense; she was very unsophisticated; she was only a pretty American flirt. Winterbourne was almost grateful for having found the formula that applied to Miss Daisy Miller. He leaned back in his seat; he remarked to himself that she had the most charming nose he had ever seen; he wondered what were the regular conditions and limitations of one's intercourse with a pretty American flirt. It presently became apparent that he was on the way to learn.

"Have you been to that old castle?" asked the young girl, pointing with her parasol to the far-gleaming walls of the Château de Chillon.

"Yes, formerly, more than once," said Winterbourne. "You too, I suppose, have seen it?"

"No; we haven't been there. I want to go there dreadfully. Of course I mean to go there. I wouldn't go away from here without having seen that old castle."

"It's a very pretty excursion," said Winterbourne, "and very easy to make. You can drive, you know, or you can go by the little steamer."

"You can go in the cars," said Miss Miller.

"Yes; you can go in the cars," Winterbourne assented.

"Our courier[7] says they take you right up to the castle," the young girl continued. "We were going last week; but my mother gave out. She suffers dreadfully from dyspepsia. She said she couldn't go. Randolph wouldn't go either; he says he doesn't think much of old castles. But I guess we'll go this week, if we can get Randolph."

"Your brother is not interested in ancient monuments?" Winterbourne inquired, smiling.

"He says he don't care much about old castles. He's only nine. He wants to stay at the hotel. Mother's afraid to leave him alone, and the courier won't stay with him; so we haven't been to many places. But it will be too bad if we don't go up there." And Miss Miller pointed again at the Château de Chillon.

"I should think it might be arranged," said Winterbourne. "Couldn't you get some one to stay—for the afternoon—with Randolph?"

Miss Miller looked at him a moment; and then, very placidly—"I wish *you* would stay with him!" she said.

Winterbourne hesitated a moment. "I would much rather go to Chillon with you."

"With me?" asked the young girl, with the same placidity.

She didn't rise, blushing, as a young girl at Geneva would have done; and yet Winterbourne, conscious that he had been very bold, thought it possible she was offended. "With your mother," he answered very respectfully.

But it seemed that both his audacity and his respect were lost upon Miss Daisy Miller. "I guess my mother won't go, after all," she said. "She don't like

7. Social guide.

to ride round in the afternoon. But did you really mean what you said just now; that you would like to go up there?"

"Most earnestly," Winterbourne declared.

"Then we may arrange it. If mother will stay with Randolph, I guess Eugenio will."

"Eugenio?" the young man inquired.

"Eugenio's our courier. He doesn't like to stay with Randolph; he's the most fastidious man I ever saw. But he's a splendid courier. I guess he'll stay at home with Randolph if mother does, and then we can go to the castle."

Winterbourne reflected for an instant as lucidly as possible—"we" could only mean Miss Daisy Miller and himself. This programme seemed almost too agreeable for credence; he felt as if he ought to kiss the young lady's hand. Possibly he would have done so—and quite spoiled the project; but at this moment another person—presumably Eugenio—appeared. A tall, handsome man, with superb whiskers, wearing a velvet morning-coat and a brilliant watch-chain, approached Miss Miller, looking sharply at her companion. "Oh, Eugenio!" said Miss Miller, with the friendliest accent.

Eugenio had looked at Winterbourne from head to foot; he now bowed gravely to the young lady. "I have the honor to inform mademoiselle that luncheon is upon the table."

Miss Miller slowly rose. "See here, Eugenio," she said. "I'm going to that old castle, any way."

"To the Château de Chillon, mademoiselle?" the courier inquired. "Mademoiselle had made arrangements?" he added, in a tone which struck Winterbourne as very impertinent.

Eugenio's tone apparently threw, even to Miss Miller's own apprehension, a slightly ironical light upon the young girl's situation. She turned to Winterbourne, blushing a little—a very little. "You won't back out?" she said.

"I shall not be happy till we go!" he protested.

"And you are staying in this hotel?" she went on. "And you are really an American?"

The courier stood looking at Winterbourne, offensively. The young man, at least, thought his manner of looking an offence to Miss Miller; it conveyed an imputation that she "picked up" acquaintances. "I shall have the honor of presenting to you a person who will tell you all about me," he said smiling, and referring to his aunt.

"Oh well, we'll go some day," said Miss Miller. And she gave him a smile and turned away. She put up her parasol and walked back to the inn beside Eugenio. Winterbourne stood looking after her; and as she moved away, drawing her muslin furbelows over the gravel, said to himself that she had the *tournure*[8] of a princess.

II

He had, however, engaged to do more than proved feasible, in promising to present his aunt, Mrs. Costello, to Miss Daisy Miller. As soon as the former lady had got better of her headache he waited upon her in her apartment; and, after the proper inquiries in regard to her health, he asked her if she

8. Grace, poise (French).

had observed, in the hotel, an American family—a mamma, a daughter, and a little boy.

"And a courier?" said Mrs. Costello. "Oh, yes, I have observed them. Seen them—heard them—and kept out of their way." Mrs. Costello was a widow with a fortune; a person of much distinction, who frequently intimated that, if she were not so dreadfully liable to sick-headaches, she would probably have left a deeper impress upon her time. She had a long pale face, a high nose, and a great deal of very striking white hair, which she wore in large puffs and *rouleaux*[9] over the top of her head. She had two sons married in New York, and another who was now in Europe. This young man was amusing himself at Homburg,[1] and, though he was on his travels, was rarely perceived to visit any particular city at the moment selected by his mother for her own appearance there. Her nephew, who had come up to Vevey expressly to see her, was therefore more attentive than those who, as she said, were nearer to her. He had imbibed at Geneva the idea that one must always be attentive to one's aunt. Mrs. Costello had not seen him for many years, and she was greatly pleased with him, manifesting her approbation by initiating him into many of the secrets of that social sway which, as she gave him to understand, she exerted in the American capital. She admitted that she was very exclusive; but, if he were acquainted with New York, he would see that one had to be. And her picture of the minutely hierarchical constitution of the society of that city, which she presented to him in many different lights, was, to Winterbourne's imagination, almost oppressively striking.

He immediately perceived, from her tone, that Miss Daisy Miller's place in the social scale was low. "I am afraid you don't approve of them," he said.

"They are very common," Mrs. Costello declared. "They are the sort of Americans that one does one's duty by not—not accepting."

"Ah, you don't accept them?" said the young man.

"I can't, my dear Frederick. I would if I could, but I can't."

"The young girl is very pretty," said Winterbourne, in a moment.

"Of course she's pretty. But she is very common."

"I see what you mean, of course," said Winterbourne, after another pause.

"She has that charming look that they all have," his aunt resumed. "I can't think where they pick it up; and she dresses in perfection—no, you don't know how well she dresses. I can't think where they get their taste."

"But, my dear aunt, she is not, after all, a Comanche savage."

"She is a young lady," said Mrs. Costello, "who has an intimacy with her mamma's courier?"

"An intimacy with the courier?" the young man demanded.

"Oh, the mother is just as bad! They treat the courier like a familiar friend—like a gentleman. I shouldn't wonder if he dines with them. Very likely they have never seen a man with such good manners, such fine clothes, so like a gentleman. He probably corresponds to the young lady's idea of a Count. He sits with them in the garden, in the evening. I think he smokes."

Winterbourne listened with interest to these disclosures; they helped him to make up his mind about Miss Daisy. Evidently she was rather wild. "Well," he said, "I am not a courier, and yet she was very charming to me."

"You had better have said at first," said Mrs. Costello with dignity, "that you had made her acquaintance."

9. Rolls, coils (French).   1. A resort in Germany.

"We simply met in the garden, and we talked a bit."

"*Tout bonnement!*[2] And pray what did you say?"

"I said I should take the liberty of introducing her to my admirable aunt."

"I am much obliged to you."

"It was to guarantee my respectability," said Winterbourne.

"And pray who is to guarantee hers?"

"Ah, you are cruel!" said the young man. "She's a very nice girl."

"You don't say that as if you believed it," Mrs. Costello observed.

"She is completely uncultivated," Winterbourne went on. "But she is wonderfully pretty, and, in short, she is very nice. To prove that I believe it, I am going to take her to the Château de Chillon."

"You two are going off there together? I should say it proved just the contrary. How long had you known her, may I ask, when this interesting project was formed. You haven't been twenty-four hours in the house."

"I had known her half-an-hour!" said Winterbourne, smiling.

"Dear me!" cried Mrs. Costello. "What a dreadful girl!"

Her nephew was silent for some moments.

"You really think, then," he began earnestly, and with a desire for trustworthy information—"you really think that—" But he paused again.

"Think what, sir," said his aunt.

"That she is the sort of young lady who expects a man—sooner or later—to carry her off?"

"I haven't the least idea what such young ladies expect a man to do. But I really think that you had better not meddle with little American girls that are uncultivated, as you call them. You have lived too long out of the country. You will be sure to make some great mistake. You are too innocent."

"My dear aunt, I am not so innocent," said Winterbourne, smiling and curling his moustache.

"You are too guilty, then?"

Winterbourne continued to curl his moustache, meditatively. "You won't let the poor girl know you then?" he asked at last.

"Is it literally true that she is going to the Château de Chillon with you?"

"I think that she fully intends it."

"Then, my dear Frederick," said Mrs. Costello, "I must decline the honor of her acquaintance. I am an old woman, but I am not too old—thank Heaven—to be shocked!"

"But don't they all do these things—the young girls in America?" Winterbourne inquired.

Mrs. Costello stared a moment. "I should like to see my granddaughters do them!" she declared, grimly.

This seemed to throw some light upon the matter, for Winterbourne remembered to have heard that his pretty cousins in New York were "tremendous flirts." If, therefore, Miss Daisy Miller exceeded the liberal license allowed to these young ladies, it was probable that anything might be expected of her. Winterbourne was impatient to see her again, and he was vexed with himself that, by instinct, he should not appreciate her justly.

Though he was impatient to see her, he hardly knew what he should say to her about his aunt's refusal to become acquainted with her; but he discovered, promptly enough, that with Miss Daisy Miller there was no great

2. Quite simply! (French).

need of walking on tiptoe. He found her that evening in the garden, wandering about in the warm starlight, like an indolent sylph, and swinging to and fro the largest fan he had ever beheld. It was ten o'clock. He had dined with his aunt, had been sitting with her since dinner, and had just taken leave of her till the morrow. Miss Daisy Miller seemed very glad to see him; she declared it was the longest evening she had ever passed.

"Have you been all alone?" he asked.

"I have been walking round with mother. But mother gets tired walking round," she answered.

"Has she gone to bed?"

"No; she doesn't like to go to bed," said the young girl. "She doesn't sleep—not three hours. She says she doesn't know how she lives. She's dreadfully nervous. I guess she sleeps more than she thinks. She's gone somewhere after Randolph; she wants to try to get him to go to bed. He doesn't like to go to bed."

"Let us hope she will persuade him," observed Winterbourne.

"She will talk to him all she can; but he doesn't like her to talk to him," said Miss Daisy, opening her fan. "She's going to try to get Eugenio to talk to him. But he isn't afraid of Eugenio. Eugenio's a splendid courier, but he can't make much impression on Randolph! I don't believe he'll go to bed before eleven." It appeared that Randolph's vigil was in fact triumphantly prolonged, for Winterbourne strolled about with the young girl for some time without meeting her mother. "I have been looking round for that lady you want to introduce me to," his companion resumed. "She's your aunt." Then, on Winterbourne's admitting the fact, and expressing some curiosity as to how she had learned it, she said she had heard all about Mrs. Costello from the chambermaid. She was very quiet and very *comme il faut;* she wore white puffs; she spoke to no one, and she never dined at the *table d'hôte*.[3] Every two days she had a headache. "I think that's a lovely description, headache and all!" said Miss Daisy, chattering along in her thin, gay voice. "I want to know her ever so much. I know just what *your* aunt would be; I know I should like her. She would be very exclusive. I like a lady to be exclusive; I'm dying to be exclusive myself. Well, we *are* exclusive, mother and I. We don't speak to every one—or they don't speak to us. I suppose it's about the same thing. Any way, I shall be ever so glad to know your aunt."

Winterbourne was embarrassed. "She would be most happy," he said, "but I am afraid those headaches will interfere."

The young girl looked at him through the dusk. "But I suppose she doesn't have a headache every day," she said, sympathetically.

Winterbourne was silent a moment. "She tells me she does," he answered at last—not knowing what to say.

Miss Daisy Miller stopped and stood looking at him. Her prettiness was still visible in the darkness; she was opening and closing her enormous fan. "She doesn't want to know me!" she said suddenly. "Why don't you say so? You needn't be afraid. I'm not afraid!" And she gave a little laugh.

Winterbourne fancied there was a tremor in her voice; he was touched, shocked, mortified by it. "My dear young lady," he protested, "she knows no one. It's her wretched health."

---

3. A common table for guests in a restaurant or hotel (French). "*Comme il faut*": well mannered (French).

The young girl walked on a few steps, laughing still. "You needn't be afraid," she repeated. "Why should she want to know me?" Then she paused again; she was close to the parapet of the garden, and in front of her was the starlit lake. There was a vague sheen upon its surface, and in the distance were dimly-seen mountain forms. Daisy Miller looked out upon the mysterious prospect, and then she gave another little laugh. "Gracious! she *is* exclusive!" she said. Winterbourne wondered whether she was seriously wounded, and for a moment almost wished that her sense of injury might be such as to make it becoming in him to attempt to reassure and comfort her. He had a pleasant sense that she would be very approachable for consolatory purposes. He felt then, for the instant, quite ready to sacrifice his aunt, conversationally; to admit that she was a proud, rude woman, and to declare that they needn't mind her. But before he had time to commit himself to this perilous mixture of gallantry and impiety, the young lady, resuming her walk, gave an exclamation in quite another tone. "Well; here's mother! I guess she hasn't got Randolph to go to bed." The figure of a lady appeared, at a distance, very indistinct in the darkness, and advancing with a slow and wavering movement. Suddenly it seemed to pause.

"Are you sure it is your mother? Can you distinguish her in this thick dusk?" Winterbourne asked.

"Well!" cried Miss Daisy Miller, with a laugh, "I guess I know my own mother. And when she has got on my shawl, too! She is always wearing my things."

The lady in question, ceasing to advance, hovered vaguely about the spot at which she had checked her steps.

"I am afraid your mother doesn't see you," said Winterbourne. "Or perhaps," he added—thinking, with Miss Miller, the joke permissible—"perhaps she feels guilty about your shawl."

"Oh, it's a fearful old thing!" the young girl replied, serenely. "I told her she could wear it. She won't come here, because she sees you."

"Ah, then," said Winterbourne, "I had better leave you."

"Oh, no; come on!" urged Miss Daisy Miller.

"I'm afraid your mother doesn't approve of my walking with you."

Miss Miller gave him a serious glance. "It isn't for me; it's for you—that is, it's for *her*. Well; I don't know who it's for! But mother doesn't like any of my gentlemen friends. She's right down timid. She always makes a fuss if I introduce a gentleman. But I *do* introduce them—almost always. If I didn't introduce my gentlemen friends to mother," the young girl added, in her little soft, flat monotone, "I shouldn't think I was natural."

"To introduce me," said Winterbourne, "you must know my name." And he proceeded to pronounce it.

"Oh, dear; I can't say all that!" said his companion, with a laugh. But by this time they had come up to Mrs. Miller, who, as they drew near, walked to the parapet of the garden and leaned upon it, looking intently at the lake and turning her back upon them. "Mother!" said the young girl, in a tone of decision. Upon this the elderly lady turned round. "Mr. Winterbourne," said Miss Daisy Miller, introducing the young man very frankly and prettily. "Common" she was, as Mrs. Costello had pronounced her; yet it was a wonder to Winterbourne that, with her commonness, she had a singularly delicate grace.

Her mother was a small, spare, light person, with a wandering eye, a very exiguous nose, and a large forehead, decorated with a certain amount of thin, much-frizzled hair. Like her daughter, Mrs. Miller was dressed with extreme elegance; she had enormous diamonds in her ears. So far as Winterbourne could observe, she gave him no greeting—she certainly was not looking at him. Daisy was near her, pulling her shawl straight. "What are you doing, poking round here?" this young lady inquired; but by no means with that harshness of accent which her choice of words may imply.

"I don't know," said her mother, turning towards the lake again.

"I shouldn't think you'd want that shawl!" Daisy exclaimed.

"Well—I do!" her mother answered, with a little laugh.

"Did you get Randolph to go to bed?" asked the young girl.

"No; I couldn't induce him," said Mrs. Miller, very gently. "He wants to talk to the waiter. He likes to talk to that waiter."

"I was telling Mr. Winterbourne," the young girl went on; and to the young man's ear her tone might have indicated that she had been uttering his name all her life.

"Oh, yes!" said Winterbourne; "I have the pleasure of knowing your son."

Randolph's mamma was silent; she turned her attention to the lake. But at last she spoke. "Well, I don't see how he lives!"

"Anyhow, it isn't so bad as it was at Dover,"[4] said Daisy Miller.

"And what occurred at Dover?" Winterbourne asked.

"He wouldn't go to bed at all. I guess he sat up all night—in the public parlour. He wasn't in bed at twelve o'clock: I know that."

"It was half-past twelve," declared Mrs. Miller, with mild emphasis.

"Does he sleep much during the day?" Winterbourne demanded.

"I guess he doesn't sleep much," Daisy rejoined.

"I wish he would!" said her mother. "It seems as if he couldn't."

"I think he's real tiresome," Daisy pursued.

Then, for some moments, there was silence. "Well, Daisy Miller," said the elder lady, presently, "I shouldn't think you'd want to talk against your own brother!"

"Well, he *is* tiresome, mother," said Daisy, quite without the asperity of a retort.

"He's only nine," urged Mrs. Miller.

"Well, he wouldn't go to that castle," said the young girl. "I'm going there with Mr. Winterbourne."

To this announcement, very placidly made, Daisy's mamma offered no response. Winterbourne took for granted that she deeply disapproved of the projected excursion; but he said to himself that she was a simple, easily managed person, and that a few deferential protestations would take the edge from her displeasure. "Yes," he began; "your daughter has kindly allowed me the honor of being her guide."

Mrs. Miller's wandering eyes attached themselves, with a sort of appealing air, to Daisy, who, however, strolled a few steps farther, gently humming to herself. "I presume you will go in the cars," said her mother.

"Yes; or in the boat," said Winterbourne.

"Well, of course, I don't know," Mrs. Miller rejoined. "I have never been to that castle."

"It is a pity you shouldn't go," said Winterbourne, beginning to feel reassured as to her opposition. And yet he was quite prepared to find that, as a matter of course, she meant to accompany her daughter.

4. English coastal town, across from France.

"We've been thinking ever so much about going," she pursued; "but it seems as if we couldn't. Of course Daisy—she wants to go round. But there's a lady here—I don't know her name—she says she shouldn't think we'd want to go to see castles *here*; she should think we'd want to wait till we got to Italy. It seems as if there would be so many there," continued Mrs. Miller, with an air of increasing confidence. "Of course, we only want to see the principal ones. We visited several in England," she presently added.

"Ah, yes! in England there are beautiful castles," said Winterbourne. "But Chillon, here, is very well worth seeing."

"Well, if Daisy feels up to it—," said Mrs. Miller, in a tone impregnated with a sense of the magnitude of the enterprise. "It seems as if there was nothing she wouldn't undertake."

"Oh, I think she'll enjoy it!" Winterbourne declared. And he desired more and more to make it a certainty that he was to have the privilege of a *tête-à-tête*[5] with the young lady, who was still strolling along in front of them, softly vocalizing. "You are not disposed, madam," he inquired, "to undertake it yourself?"

Daisy's mother looked at him, an instant, askance, and then walked forward in silence. Then—"I guess she had better go alone," she said, simply.

Winterbourne observed to himself that this was a very different type of maternity from that of the vigilant matrons who massed themselves in the forefront of social intercourse in the dark old city at the other end of the lake. But his meditations were interrupted by hearing his name very distinctly pronounced by Mrs. Miller's unprotected daughter.

"Mr. Winterbourne!" murmured Daisy.

"Mademoiselle!" said the young man.

"Don't you want to take me out in a boat?"

"At present?" he asked.

"Of course!" said Daisy.

"Well, Annie Miller!" exclaimed her mother.

"I beg you, madam, to let her go," said Winterbourne, ardently; for he had never yet enjoyed the sensation of guiding through the summer starlight a skiff freighted with a fresh and beautiful young girl.

"I shouldn't think she'd want to," said her mother. "I should think she'd rather go indoors."

"I'm sure Mr. Winterbourne wants to take me," Daisy declared. "He's so awfully devoted!"

"I will row you over to Chillon, in the starlight."

"I don't believe it!" said Daisy.

"Well!" ejaculated the elderly lady again.

"You haven't spoken to me for half-an-hour," her daughter went on.

"I have been having some very pleasant conversation with your mother," said Winterbourne.

"Well; I want you to take me out in a boat!" Daisy repeated. They had all stopped, and she had turned round and was looking at Winterbourne. Her face wore a charming smile, her pretty eyes were gleaming, she was swinging her great fan about. No; it's impossible to be prettier than that, thought Winterbourne.

"There are half-a-dozen boats moored at that landing-place," he said, pointing to certain steps which descended from the garden to the lake. "If you will do me the honor to accept my arm, we will go and select one of them."

Daisy stood there smiling; she threw back her head and gave a little light laugh. "I like a gentleman to be formal!" she declared.

"I assure you it's a formal offer."

"I was bound I would make you say something," Daisy went on.

"You see it's not very difficult," said Winterbourne. "But I am afraid you are chaffing me."

"I think not, sir," remarked Mrs. Miller, very gently.

"Do, then, let me give you a row," he said to the young girl.

"It's quite lovely, the way you say that!" said Daisy.

"It will be still more lovely to do it."

"Yes, it would be lovely!" said Daisy. But she made no movement to accompany him; she only stood there laughing.

"I should think you had better find out what time it is," interposed her mother.

"It is eleven o'clock, madam," said a voice, with a foreign accent, out of the neighboring darkness; and Winterbourne, turning, perceived the florid personage who was in attendance upon the two ladies. He had apparently just approached.

"Oh, Eugenio," said Daisy, "I am going out in a boat!"

Eugenio bowed. "At eleven o'clock, mademoiselle?"

"I am going with Mr. Winterbourne. This very minute."

"Do tell her she can't," said Mrs. Miller to the courier.

"I think you had better not go out in a boat, mademoiselle," Eugenio declared.

Winterbourne wished to Heaven this pretty girl were not so familiar with her courier; but he said nothing.

"I suppose you don't think it's proper!" Daisy exclaimed, "Eugenio doesn't think anything's proper."

"I am at your service," said Winterbourne.

"Does mademoiselle propose to go alone?" asked Eugenio of Mrs. Miller.

"Oh, no; with this gentleman!" answered Daisy's mamma.

The courier looked for a moment at Winterbourne—the latter thought he was smiling—and then, solemnly, with a bow, "As mademoiselle pleases!" he said.

"Oh, I hoped you would make a fuss!" said Daisy. "I don't care to go now."

"I myself shall make a fuss if you don't go," said Winterbourne.

"That's all I want—a little fuss!" And the young girl began to laugh again.

"Mr. Randolph has gone to bed!" the courier announced, frigidly.

"Oh, Daisy; now we can go!" said Mrs. Miller.

Daisy turned away from Winterbourne, looking at him, smiling and fanning herself. "Good night," she said; "I hope you are disappointed, or disgusted, or something!"

He looked at her, taking the hand she offered him. "I am puzzled," he answered.

"Well; I hope it won't keep you awake!" she said, very smartly; and, under the escort of the privileged Eugenio, the two ladies passed towards the house.

Winterbourne stood looking after them; he was indeed puzzled. He lingered beside the lake for a quarter of an hour, turning over the mystery of the young girl's sudden familiarities and caprices. But the only very definite conclusion he came to was that he should enjoy deucedly "going off" with her somewhere.

Two days afterwards he went off with her to the Castle of Chillon. He waited for her in the large hall of the hotel, where the couriers, the servants, the foreign tourists were lounging about and staring. It was not the place he would have chosen, but she had appointed it. She came tripping downstairs, buttoning her long gloves, squeezing her folded parasol against her pretty figure, dressed in the perfection of a soberly elegant travelling-costume. Winterbourne was a man of imagination and, as our ancestors used to say, of sensibility; as he looked at her dress and, on the great staircase, her little rapid, confiding step, he felt as if there were something romantic going forward. He could have believed he was going to elope with her. He passed out with her among all the idle people that were assembled there; they were all looking at her very hard; she had begun to chatter as soon as she joined him. Winterbourne's preference had been that they should be conveyed to Chillon in a carriage; but she expressed a lively wish to go in the little steamer; she declared that she had a passion for steamboats. There was always such a lovely breeze upon the water, and you saw such lots of people. The sail was not long, but Winterbourne's companion found time to say a great many things. To the young man himself their little excursion was so much of an escapade—an adventure—that, even allowing for her habitual sense of freedom, he had some expectation of seeing her regard it in the same way. But it must be confessed that, in this particular, he was disappointed. Daisy Miller was extremely animated, she was in charming spirits; but she was apparently not at all excited; she was not fluttered; she avoided neither his eyes nor those of any one else; she blushed neither when she looked at him nor when she saw that people were looking at her. People continued to look at her a great deal, and Winterbourne took much satisfaction in his pretty companion's distinguished air. He had been a little afraid that she would talk loud, laugh overmuch, and even, perhaps, desire to move about the boat a good deal. But he quite forgot his fears; he sat smiling, with his eyes upon her face, while, without moving from her place, she delivered herself of a great number of original reflections. It was the most charming garrulity he had ever heard. He had assented to the idea that she was "common"; but was she so, after all, or was he simply getting used to her commonness? Her conversation was chiefly of what metaphysicians term the objective cast; but every now and then it took a subjective turn.

"What on *earth* are you so grave about?" she suddenly demanded, fixing her agreeable eyes upon Winterbourne's.

"Am I grave?" he asked. "I had an idea I was grinning from ear to ear."

"You look as if you were taking me to a funeral. If that's a grin, your ears are very near together."

"Should you like me to dance a hornpipe[6] on the deck?"

"Pray do, and I'll carry round your hat. It will pay the expenses of our journey."

"I never was better pleased in my life," murmured Winterbourne.

She looked at him a moment, and then burst into a little laugh. "I like to make you say those things! You're a queer mixture!"

6. An English dance similar to the jig.

In the castle, after they had landed, the subjective element decidedly prevailed. Daisy tripped about the vaulted chambers, rustled her skirts in the corkscrew staircases, flirted back with a pretty little cry and a shudder from the edge of the *oubliettes*,[7] and turned a singularly well-shaped ear to everything that Winterbourne told her about the place. But he saw that she cared very little for feudal antiquities, and that the dusky traditions of Chillon made but a slight impression upon her. They had the good fortune to have been able to walk about without other companionship than that of the custodian; and Winterbourne arranged with this functionary that they should not be hurried—that they should linger and pause wherever they chose. The custodian interpreted the bargain generously—Winterbourne, on his side, had been generous—and ended by leaving them quite to themselves. Miss Miller's observations were not remarkable for logical consistency; for anything she wanted to say she was sure to find a pretext. She found a great many pretexts in the rugged embrasures of Chillon for asking Winterbourne sudden questions about himself—his family, his previous history, his tastes, his habits, his intentions—and for supplying information upon corresponding points in her own personality. Of her own tastes, habits, and intentions Miss Miller was prepared to give the most definite, and indeed the most favourable, account.

"Well; I hope you know enough!" she said to her companion, after he had told her the history of the unhappy Bonivard.[8] "I never saw a man that knew so much!" The history of Bonivard had evidently, as they say, gone into one ear and out of the other. But Daisy went on to say that she wished Winterbourne would travel with them and "go round" with them; they might know something, in that case. "Don't you want to come and teach Randolph?" she asked. Winterbourne said that nothing could possibly please him so much; but that he had unfortunately other occupations. "Other occupations? I don't believe it!" said Miss Daisy. "What do you mean? You are not in business." The young man admitted that he was not in business; but he had engagements which, even within a day or two, would force him to go back to Geneva. "Oh, bother!" she said. "I don't believe it!" and she began to talk about something else. But a few moments later, when he was pointing out to her the pretty design of an antique fireplace, she broke out irrelevantly, "You don't mean to say you are going back to Geneva?"

"It is a melancholy fact that I shall have to return to Geneva to-morrow."

"Well, Mr. Winterbourne," said Daisy; "I think you're horrid!"

"Oh, don't say such dreadful things!" said Winterbourne—"just at the last."

"The last!" cried the young girl; "I call it the first. I have half a mind to leave you here and go straight back to the hotel alone." And for the next ten minutes she did nothing but call him horrid. Poor Winterbourne was fairly bewildered; no young lady had as yet done him the honor to be so agitated by the announcement of his movements. His companion, after this, ceased to pay any attention to the curiosities of Chillon or the beauties of the lake; she opened fire upon the mysterious charmer in Geneva, whom she appeared to have instantly taken it for granted that he was hurrying back to see. How did Miss Daisy Miller know that there was a charmer in Geneva? Winterbourne, who denied the existence of such a person, was quite unable to discover; and

---

7. Secret pitlike dungeons with an opening only at the top; places where one is forgotten (French).
8. Hero of Byron's poem "The Prisoner of Chil-
lon"; François de Bonivard (1496–1570), Swiss patriot and martyr, was confined for seven years in the Castle of Chillon.

he was divided between amazement at the rapidity of her induction and amusement at the frankness of her *persiflage*.[9] She seemed to him, in all this, an extraordinary mixture of innocence and crudity. "Does she never allow you more than three days at a time?" asked Daisy, ironically. "Doesn't she give you a vacation in summer? There's no one so hard worked but they can get leave to go off somewhere at this season. I suppose, if you stay another day, she'll come after you in the boat. Do wait over till Friday, and I will go down to the landing to see her arrive!" Winterbourne began to think he had been wrong to feel disappointed in the temper in which the young lady had embarked. If he had missed the personal accent, the personal accent was now making its appearance. It sounded very distinctly, at last, in her telling him she would stop "teasing" him if he would promise her solemnly to come down to Rome in the winter.

"That's not a difficult promise to make," said Winterbourne. "My aunt has taken an apartment in Rome for the winter, and has already asked me to come and see her."

"I don't want you to come for your aunt," said Daisy; "I want you to come for me." And this was the only allusion that the young man was ever to hear her make to his invidious kinswoman. He declared that, at any rate, he would certainly come. After this Daisy stopped teasing. Winterbourne took a carriage, and they drove back to Vevey in the dusk; the young girl was very quiet.

In the evening Winterbourne mentioned to Mrs. Costello that he had spent the afternoon at Chillon, with Miss Daisy Miller.

"The Americans—of the courier?" asked this lady.

"Ah, happily," said Winterbourne, "the courier stayed at home."

"She went with you all alone?"

"All alone."

Mrs. Costello sniffed a little at her smelling-bottle. "And that," she exclaimed, "is the young person you wanted me to know!"

III

Winterbourne, who had returned to Geneva the day after his excursion to Chillon, went to Rome towards the end of January. His aunt had been established there for several weeks, and he had received a couple of letters from her. "Those people you were so devoted to last summer at Vevey have turned up here, courier and all," she wrote. "They seem to have made several acquaintances, but the courier continues to be the most *intime*. The young lady, however, is also very intimate with some third-rate Italians, with whom she rackets about in a way that makes much talk. Bring me that pretty novel of Cherbuliez's[1]—'Paule Méré'—and don't come later than the 23rd."

In the natural course of events, Winterbourne, on arriving in Rome, would presently have ascertained Mrs. Miller's address at the American banker's and have gone to pay his compliments to Miss Daisy. "After what happened at Vevey I certainly think I may call upon them," he said to Mrs. Costello.

"If, after what happens—at Vevey and everywhere—you desire to keep up the acquaintance, you are very welcome. Of course a man may know every one. Men are welcome to the privilege!"

9. Frivolous, bantering talk (French).
1. Victor Cherbuliez (1829–1899), which James spelled "Cherbuliex," a popular French novelist of Swiss origin. His 1865 novel *Paule Méré* focused on a young woman who violates Geneva's social conventions.

"Pray what is it that happens—here, for instance?" Winterbourne demanded.

"The girl goes about alone with her foreigners. As to what happens farther, you must apply elsewhere for information. She has picked up half-a-dozen of the regular Roman fortune-hunters, and she takes them about to people's houses. When she comes to a party she brings with her a gentleman with a good deal of manner and a wonderful moustache."

"And where is the mother?"

"I haven't the least idea. They are very dreadful people."

Winterbourne meditated a moment. "They are very ignorant—very innocent only. Depend upon it they are not bad."

"They are hopelessly vulgar," said Mrs. Costello. "Whether or no being hopelessly vulgar is being 'bad' is a question for the metaphysicians. They are bad enough to dislike, at any rate; and for this short life that is quite enough."

The news that Daisy Miller was surrounded by half-a-dozen wonderful moustaches checked Winterbourne's impulse to go straightway to see her. He had perhaps not definitely flattered himself that he had made an ineffaceable impression upon her heart, but he was annoyed at hearing of a state of affairs so little in harmony with an image that had lately flitted in and out of his own meditations; the image of a very pretty girl looking out of an old Roman window and asking herself urgently when Mr. Winterbourne would arrive. If, however, he determined to wait a little before reminding Miss Miller of his claims to her consideration, he went very soon to call upon two or three other friends. One of these friends was an American lady who had spent several winters at Geneva, when she had placed her children at school. She was a very accomplished woman and she lived in the Via Gregoriana.[2] Winterbourne found her in a little crimson drawing-room, on a third floor; the room was filled with southern sunshine. He had not been there ten minutes when the servant came in, announcing "Madame Mila!" This announcement was presently followed by the entrance of little Randolph Miller, who stopped in the middle of the room and stood staring at Winterbourne. An instant later his pretty sister crossed the threshold; and then, after a considerable interval, Mrs. Miller slowly advanced.

"I know you!" said Randolph.

"I'm sure you know a great many things," exclaimed Winterbourne, taking him by the hand. "How is your education coming on?"

Daisy was exchanging greetings very prettily with her hostess; but when she heard Winterbourne's voice she quickly turned her head. "Well, I declare!" she said.

"I told you I should come, you know," Winterbourne rejoined smiling.

"Well—I didn't believe it," said Miss Daisy.

"I am much obliged to you," laughed the young man.

"You might have come to see me!" said Daisy.

"I arrived only yesterday."

"I don't believe that!" the young girl declared.

Winterbourne turned with a protesting smile to her mother; but this lady evaded his glance, and seating herself, fixed her eyes upon her son. "We've got a bigger place than this," said Randolph. "It's all gold on the walls."

2. A fashionable street in Rome.

Mrs. Miller turned uneasily in her chair. "I told you if I were to bring you, you would say something!" she murmured.

"I told *you!*" Randolph exclaimed. "I tell *you*, sir!" he added jocosely, giving Winterbourne a thump on the knee. "It *is* bigger, too!"

Daisy had entered upon a lively conversation with her hostess; Winterbourne judged it becoming to address a few words to her mother. "I hope you have been well since we parted at Vevey," he said.

Mrs. Miller now certainly looked at him—at his chin. "Not very well, sir," she answered.

"She's got the dyspepsia," said Randolph. "I've got it too. Father's got it. I've got it worst!"

This announcement, instead of embarrassing Mrs. Miller, seemed to relieve her. "I suffer from the liver," she said. "I think it's the climate; it's less bracing than Schenectady, especially in the winter season. I don't know whether you know we reside at Schenectady. I was saying to Daisy that I certainly hadn't found any one like Dr. Davis, and I didn't believe I should. Oh, at Schenectady, he stands first; they think everything of him. He has so much to do, and yet there was nothing he wouldn't do for me. He said he never saw anything like my dyspepsia, but he was bound to cure it. I'm sure there was nothing he wouldn't try. He was just going to try something new when we came off. Mr. Miller wanted Daisy to see Europe for herself. But I wrote to Mr. Miller that it seems as if I couldn't get on without Dr. Davis. At Schenectady he stands at the very top; and there's a great deal of sickness there, too. It affects my sleep."

Winterbourne had a good deal of pathological gossip with Dr. Davis's patient, during which Daisy chattered unremittingly to her own companion. The young man asked Mrs. Miller how she was pleased with Rome. "Well, I must say I am disappointed," she answered. "We had heard so much about it; I suppose we had heard too much. But we couldn't help that. We had been led to expect something different."

"Ah, wait a little, and you will become very fond of it," said Winterbourne.

"I hate it worse and worse every day!" cried Randolph.

"You are like the infant Hannibal,"[3] said Winterbourne.

"No, I ain't!" Randolph declared, at a venture.

"You are not much like an infant," said his mother. "But we have seen places," she resumed, "that I should put a long way before Rome." And in reply to Winterbourne's interrogation, "There's Zurich," she observed; "I think Zurich is lovely; and we hadn't heard half so much about it."

"The best place we've seen is the City of Richmond!" said Randolph.

"He means the ship," his mother explained. "We crossed in that ship. Randolph had a good time on the City of Richmond."

"It's the best place I've seen," the child repeated. "Only it was turned the wrong way."

"Well, we've got to turn the right way some time," said Mrs. Miller, with a little laugh. Winterbourne expressed the hope that her daughter at least found some gratification in Rome, and she declared that Daisy was quite carried away. "It's on account of the society—the society's splendid. She goes round everywhere; she has made a great number of acquaintances. Of course she goes round more than I do. I must say they have been very

3. The Carthaginian general (247–183 B.C.E.), from his infancy, had a lifelong hatred of Rome.

sociable; they have taken her right in. And then she knows a great many gentlemen. Oh, she thinks there's nothing like Rome. Of course, it's a great deal pleasanter for a young lady if she knows plenty of gentlemen."

By this time Daisy had turned her attention again to Winterbourne. "I've been telling Mrs. Walker how mean you were!" the young girl announced.

"And what is the evidence you have offered?" asked Winterbourne, rather annoyed at Miss Miller's want of appreciation of the zeal of an admirer who on his way down to Rome had stopped neither at Bologna nor at Florence, simply because of a certain sentimental impatience. He remembered that a cynical compatriot had once told him that American women—the pretty ones, and this gave a largeness to the axiom—were at once the most exacting in the world and the least endowed with a sense of indebtedness.

"Why, you were awfully mean at Vevey," said Daisy. "You wouldn't do anything. You wouldn't stay there when I asked you."

"My dearest young lady," cried Winterbourne, with eloquence, "have I come all the way to Rome to encounter your reproaches?"

"Just hear him say that!" said Daisy to her hostess, giving a twist to a bow on this lady's dress. "Did you ever hear anything so quaint?"

"So quaint, my dear?" murmured Mrs. Walker, in the tone of a partisan of Winterbourne.

"Well, I don't know," said Daisy, fingering Mrs. Walker's ribbons. "Mrs. Walker, I want to tell you something."

"Motherr," interposed Randolph, with his rough ends to his words, "I tell you you've got to go. Eugenio'll raise something!"

"I'm not afraid of Eugenio," said Daisy, with a toss of her head. "Look here, Mrs. Walker," she went on, "you know I'm coming to your party."

"I am delighted to hear it."

"I've got a lovely dress."

"I am very sure of that."

"But I want to ask a favor—permission to bring a friend."

"I shall be happy to see any of your friends," said Mrs. Walker, turning with a smile to Mrs. Miller.

"Oh, they are not my friends," answered Daisy's mamma, smiling shyly, in her own fashion. "I never spoke to them!"

"It's an intimate friend of mine—Mr. Giovanelli," said Daisy, without a tremor in her clear little voice or a shadow on her brilliant little face.

Mrs. Walker was silent a moment, she gave a rapid glance at Winterbourne. "I shall be glad to see Mr. Giovanelli," she then said.

"He's an Italian," Daisy pursued, with the prettiest serenity. "He's a great friend of mine—he's the handsomest man in the world—except Mr. Winterbourne! He knows plenty of Italians, but he wants to know some Americans. He thinks ever so much of Americans. He's tremendously clever. He's perfectly lovely!"

It was settled that this brilliant personage should be brought to Mrs. Walker's party, and then Mrs. Miller prepared to take her leave. "I guess we'll go back to the hotel," she said.

"You may go back to the hotel, mother, but I'm going to take a walk," said Daisy.

"She's going to walk with Mr. Giovanelli," Randolph proclaimed.

"I am going to the Pincio,"[4] said Daisy, smiling.

---

4. The Pincian Hill, offering a fine view of Rome.

"Alone, my dear at this hour?" Mrs. Walker asked. The afternoon was drawing to a close—it was the hour for the throng of carriages and of contemplative pedestrians. "I don't think it's safe, my dear," said Mrs. Walker.

"Neither do I," subjoined Mrs. Miller. "You'll get the fever[5] as sure as you live. Remember what Dr. Davis told you!"

"Give her some medicine before she goes," said Randolph.

The company had risen to its feet; Daisy, still showing her pretty teeth, bent over and kissed her hostess. "Mrs. Walker, you are too perfect," she said. "I'm not going alone; I am going to meet a friend."

"Your friend won't keep you from getting the fever," Mrs. Miller observed.

"Is it Mr. Giovanelli?" asked the hostess.

Winterbourne was watching the girl; at this question his attention quickened. She stood there smiling and smoothing her bonnet-ribbons; she glanced at Winterbourne. Then, while she glanced and smiled, she answered without a shade of hesitation, "Mr. Giovanelli—the beautiful Giovanelli."

"My dear young friend," said Mrs. Walker, taking her hand, pleadingly, "don't walk off to the Pincio at this hour to meet a beautiful Italian."

"Well, he speaks English," said Mrs. Miller.

"Gracious me!" Daisy exclaimed, "I don't want to do anything improper. There's an easy way to settle it." She continued to glance at Winterbourne. "The Pincio is only a hundred yards distant, and if Mr. Winterbourne were as polite as he pretends he would offer to walk with me!"

Winterbourne's politeness hastened to affirm itself, and the young girl gave him gracious leave to accompany her. They passed downstairs before her mother, and at the door Winterbourne perceived Mrs. Miller's carriage drawn up, with the ornamental courier whose acquaintance he had made at Vevey seated within. "Good-bye, Eugenio!" cried Daisy, "I'm going to take a walk." The distance from the Via Gregoriana to the beautiful garden at the other end of the Pincian Hill is, in fact, rapidly traversed. As the day was splendid, however, and the concourse of vehicles, walkers, and loungers numerous, the young Americans found their progress much delayed. This fact was highly agreeable to Winterbourne, in spite of his consciousness of his singular situation. The slow-moving, idly-gazing Roman crowd bestowed much attention upon the extremely pretty young foreign lady who was passing through it upon his arm; and he wondered what on earth had been in Daisy's mind when she proposed to expose herself, unattended, to its appreciation. His own mission, to her sense, apparently, was to consign her to the hands of Mr. Giovanelli; but Winterbourne, at once annoyed and gratified, resolved that he would do no such thing.

"Why haven't you been to see me?" asked Daisy. "You can't get out of that."

"I have had the honor of telling you that I have only just stepped out of the train."

"You must have stayed in the train a good while after it stopped!" cried the young girl, with her little laugh. "I suppose you were asleep. You have had time to go to see Mrs. Walker."

"I knew Mrs. Walker—" Winterbourne began to explain.

"I knew where you knew her. You knew her at Geneva. She told me so. Well, you knew me at Vevey. That's just as good. So you ought to have come." She asked him no other question than this; she began to prattle about her

---

5. Malaria, whose means of transmission (the mosquito) was unknown in James's day, but which was associated with damp, dark places.

own affairs. "We've got splendid rooms at the hotel; Eugenio says they're the best rooms in Rome. We are going to stay all winter—if we don't die of the fever; and I guess we'll stay then. It's a great deal nicer than I thought; I thought it would be fearfully quiet; I was sure it would be awfully poky. I was sure we should be going round all the time with one of those dreadful old men that explain about the pictures and things. But we only had about a week of that, and now I'm enjoying myself. I know ever so many people, and they are all so charming. The society's extremely select. There are all kinds—English, and Germans, and Italians. I think I like the English best. I like their style of conversation. But there are some lovely Americans. I never saw anything so hospitable. There's something or other every day. There's not much dancing; but I must say I never thought dancing was everything. I was always fond of conversation. I guess I shall have plenty at Mrs. Walker's—her rooms are so small." When they had passed the gate of the Pincian Gardens, Miss Miller began to wonder where Mr. Giovanelli might be. "We had better go straight to that place in front," she said, "where you look at the view."

"I certainly shall not help you to find him," Winterbourne declared.

"Then I shall find him without you," said Miss Daisy.

"You certainly won't leave me!" cried Winterbourne.

She burst into her little laugh. "Are you afraid you'll get lost—or run over? But there's Giovanelli, leaning against that tree. He's staring at the women in the carriages: did you ever see anything so cool?"

Winterbourne perceived at some distance a little man standing with folded arms, nursing his cane. He had a handsome face, an artfully poised hat, a glass in one eye, and a nosegay in his button-hole. Winterbourne looked at him a moment and then said, "Do you mean to speak to that man?"

"Do I mean to speak to him? Why, you don't suppose I mean to communicate by signs?"

"Pray understand, then," said Winterbourne, "that I intend to remain with you."

Daisy stopped and looked at him, without a sign of troubled consciousness in her face; with nothing but the presence of her charming eyes and her happy dimples. "Well, she's a cool one!" thought the young man.

"I don't like the way you say that," said Daisy. "It's too imperious."

"I beg your pardon if I say it wrong. The main point is to give you an idea of my meaning."

The young girl looked at him more gravely, but with eyes that were prettier than ever. "I have never allowed a gentleman to dictate to me, or to interfere with anything I do."

"I think you have made a mistake," said Winterbourne. "You should sometimes listen to a gentleman—the right one?"

Daisy began to laugh again, "I do nothing but listen to gentlemen!" she exclaimed. "Tell me if Mr. Giovanelli is the right one?"

The gentleman with the nosegay in his bosom had now perceived our two friends, and was approaching the young girl with obsequious rapidity. He bowed to Winterbourne as well as to the latter's companion; he had a brilliant smile, an intelligent eye; Winterbourne thought him not a bad-looking fellow. But he nevertheless said to Daisy—"No, he's not the right one."

Daisy evidently had a natural talent for performing introductions; she mentioned the name of each of her companions to the other. She strolled along with one of them on each side of her; Mr. Giovanelli, who spoke English very cleverly—Winterbourne afterwards learned that he had practiced the idiom upon a great many American heiresses—addressed her a great deal of very polite nonsense; he was extremely urbane, and the young American, who said nothing, reflected upon that profundity of Italian cleverness which enables people to appear more gracious in proportion as they are more acutely disappointed. Giovanelli, of course, had counted upon something more intimate; he had not bargained for a party of three. But he kept his temper in a manner which suggested far-stretching intentions. Winterbourne flattered himself that he had taken his measure. "He is not a gentleman," said the young American; "he is only a clever imitation of one. He is a music-master, or a penny-a-liner, or a third-rate artist. Damn his good looks!" Mr. Giovanelli had certainly a very pretty face; but Winterbourne felt a superior indignation at his own lovely fellow-countrywoman's not knowing the difference between a spurious gentleman and a real one. Giovanelli chattered and jested and made himself wonderfully agreeable. It was true that if he was an imitation the imitation was very skillful. "Nevertheless," Winterbourne said to himself, "a nice girl ought to know!" And then he came back to the question whether this was in fact a nice girl. Would a nice girl—even allowing for her being a little American flirt—make a rendezvous with a presumably low-lived foreigner? The rendezvous in this case, indeed, had been in broad daylight, and in the most crowded corner of Rome; but was it not impossible to regard the choice of these circumstances as a proof of extreme cynicism? Singular though it may seem, Winterbourne was vexed that the young girl, in joining her *amoroso*,[6] should not appear more impatient of his own company, and he was vexed because of his inclination. It was impossible to regard her as a perfectly well-conducted young lady; she was wanting in a certain indispensable delicacy. It would therefore simplify matters greatly to be able to treat her as the object of one of those sentiments which are called by romancers "lawless passions." That she should seem to wish to get rid of him would help him to think more lightly of her, and to be able to think more lightly of her would make her much less perplexing. But Daisy, on this occasion, continued to present herself as an inscrutable combination of audacity and innocence.

She had been walking some quarter of an hour, attended by her two cavaliers, and responding in a tone of very childish gaiety, as it seemed to Winterbourne, to the pretty speeches of Mr. Giovanelli, when a carriage that had detached itself from the revolving train drew up beside the path. At the same moment Winterbourne perceived that his friend Mrs. Walker—the lady whose house he had lately left—was seated in the vehicle and was beckoning to him. Leaving Miss Miller's side, he hastened to obey her summons. Mrs. Walker was flushed; she wore an excited air. "It is really too dreadful," she said. "That girl must not do this sort of thing. She must not walk here with you two men. Fifty people have noticed her."

Winterbourne raised his eyebrows. "I think it's a pity to make too much fuss about it."

"It's a pity to let the girl ruin herself!"

"She *is* very innocent," said Winterbourne.

"She's very crazy!" cried Mrs. Walker. "Did you ever see anything so imbecile as her mother? After you had all left me, just now, I could not sit

6. Lover (Italian).

still for thinking of it. It seemed too pitiful, not even to attempt to save her. I ordered the carriage and put on my bonnet, and came here as quickly as possible. Thank heaven I have found you!"

"What do you propose to do with us?" asked Winterbourne, smiling.

"To ask her to get in, to drive her about here for half-an-hour, so that the world may see she is not running absolutely wild, and then to take her safely home."

"I don't think it's a very happy thought," said Winterbourne; "but you can try."

Mrs. Walker tried. The young man went in pursuit of Miss Miller, who had simply nodded and smiled at his interlocutrix in the carriage and had gone her way with her own companion. Daisy, on learning that Mrs. Walker wished to speak to her, retraced her steps with a perfect good grace and with Mr. Giovanelli at her side. She declared that she was delighted to have a chance to present this gentleman to Mrs. Walker. She immediately achieved the introduction, and declared that she had never in her life seen anything so lovely as Mrs. Walker's carriage-rug.

"I am glad you admire it," said this lady, smiling sweetly. "Will you get in and let me put it over you?"

"Oh, no, thank you," said Daisy. "I shall admire it much more as I see you driving round with it."

"Do get in and drive with me," said Mrs. Walker.

"That would be charming, but it's so enchanting just as I am!" and Daisy gave a brilliant glance at the gentlemen on either side of her.

"It may be enchanting, dear child, but it is not the custom here," urged Mrs. Walker, leaning forward in her victoria[7] with her hands devoutly clasped.

"Well, it ought to be, then!" said Daisy. "If I didn't walk I should expire."

"You should walk with your mother, dear," cried the lady from Geneva, losing patience.

"With my mother dear!" exclaimed the young girl. Winterbourne saw that she scented interference. "My mother never walked ten steps in her life. And then, you know," she added with a laugh, "I am more than five years old."

"You are old enough to be more reasonable. You are old enough, dear Miss Miller, to be talked about."

Daisy looked at Mrs. Walker, smiling intensely. "Talked about? What do you mean?"

"Come into my carriage and I will tell you."

Daisy turned her quickened glance again from one of the gentlemen beside her to the other. Mr. Giovanelli was bowing to and fro, rubbing down his gloves and laughing very agreeably; Winterbourne thought it a most unpleasant scene. "I don't think I want to know what you mean," said Daisy presently. "I don't think I should like it."

Winterbourne wished that Mrs. Walker would tuck in her carriage-rug and drive away; but this lady did not enjoy being defied, as she afterwards told him. "Should you prefer being thought a very reckless girl?" she demanded.

"Gracious me!" exclaimed Daisy. She looked again at Mr. Giovanelli, then she turned to Winterbourne. There was a little pink flush in her check; she

7. A horse-drawn carriage for two with a raised seat in front for the driver.

was tremendously pretty. "Does Mr. Winterbourne think," she asked slowly, smiling, throwing back her head and glancing at him from head to foot, "that—to save my reputation—I ought to get into the carriage?"

Winterbourne colored; for an instant he hesitated greatly. It seemed so strange to hear her speak that way of her "reputation." But he himself, in fact, must speak in accordance with gallantry. The finest gallantry, here, was simply to tell her the truth; and the truth, for Winterbourne, as the few indications I have been able to give have made him known to the reader, was that Daisy Miller should take Mrs. Walker's advice. He looked at her exquisite prettiness; and then he said very gently, "I think you should get into the carriage."

Daisy gave a violent laugh. "I never heard anything so stiff! If this is improper, Mrs. Walker," she pursued, "then I am all improper, and you must give me up. Good-bye; I hope you'll have a lovely ride!" and, with Mr. Giovanelli, who made a triumphantly obsequious salute, she turned away.

Mrs. Walker sat looking after her, and there were tears in Mrs. Walker's eyes. "Get in here, sir," she said to Winterbourne, indicating the place beside her. The young man answered that he felt bound to accompany Miss Miller; whereupon Mrs. Walker declared that if he refused her this favor she would never speak to him again. She was evidently in earnest. Winterbourne overtook Daisy and her companion and, offering the young girl his hand, told her that Mrs. Walker had made an imperious claim upon his society. He expected that in answer she would say something rather free, something to commit herself still farther to that "recklessness" from which Mrs. Walker had so charitably endeavored to dissuade her. But she only shook his hand, hardly looking at him, while Mr. Giovanelli bade him farewell with a too emphatic flourish of the hat.

Winterbourne was not in the best possible humor as he took his seat in Mrs. Walker's victoria. "That was not clever of you," he said candidly, while the vehicle mingled again with the throng of carriages.

"In such a case," his companion answered, "I don't wish to be clever, I wish to be *earnest*!"

"Well, your earnestness has only offended her and put her off."

"It has happened very well," said Mrs. Walker. "If she is so perfectly determined to compromise herself, the sooner one knows it the better; one can act accordingly."

"I suspect she meant no harm," Winterbourne rejoined.

"So I thought a month ago. But she has been going too far."

"What has she been doing?"

"Everything that is not done here. Flirting with any man she could pick up; sitting in corners with mysterious Italians; dancing all the evening with the same partners; receiving visits at eleven o'clock at night. Her mother goes away when visitors come."

"But her brother," said Winterbourne, laughing, "sits up till midnight."

"He must be edified by what he sees. I'm told that at their hotel every one is talking about her, and that a smile goes round among the servants when a gentleman comes and asks for Miss Miller."

"The servants be hanged!" said Winterbourne angrily. "The poor girl's only fault," he presently added, "is that she is very uncultivated."

"She is naturally indelicate," Mrs. Walker declared. "Take that example this morning. How long had you known her at Vevey?"

"A couple of days."

"Fancy, then, her making it a personal matter that you should have left the place!"

Winterbourne was silent for some moments; then he said, "I suspect, Mrs. Walker, that you and I have lived too long at Geneva!" And he added a request that she should inform him with what particular design she had made him enter her carriage.

"I wished to beg you to cease your relations with Miss Miller—not to flirt with her—to give her no farther opportunity to expose herself—to let her alone, in short."

"I'm afraid I can't do that," said Winterbourne. "I like her extremely."

"All the more reason that you shouldn't help her to make a scandal."

"There shall be nothing scandalous in my attentions to her."

"There certainly will be in the way she takes them. But I have said what I had on my conscience," Mrs. Walker pursued. "If you wish to rejoin the young lady I will put you down. Here, by-the-way, you have a chance."

The carriage was traversing that part of the Pincian Garden which overhangs the wall of Rome and overlooks the beautiful Villa Borghese.[8] It is bordered by a large parapet, near which there are several seats. One of the seats, at a distance, was occupied by a gentleman and a lady, towards whom Mrs. Walker gave a toss of her head. At the same moment these persons rose and walked towards the parapet. Winterbourne had asked the coachman to stop; he now descended from the carriage. His companion looked at him a moment in silence; then, while he raised his hat, she drove majestically away. Winterbourne stood there; he had turned his eyes towards Daisy and her cavalier. They evidently saw no one; they were too deeply occupied with each other. When they reached the low garden-wall they stood a moment looking off at the great flat-topped pine-clusters of the Villa Borghese; then Giovanelli seated himself familiarly upon the broad ledge of the wall. The western sun in the opposite sky sent out a brilliant shaft through a couple of cloud-bars; whereupon Daisy's companion took her parasol out of her hands and opened it. She came a little nearer and he held the parasol over her; then, still holding it, he let it rest upon her shoulder, so that both of their heads were hidden from Winterbourne. This young man lingered a moment, then he began to walk. But he walked—not towards the couple with the parasol; towards the residence of his aunt, Mrs. Costello.

IV

He flattered himself on the following day that there was no smiling among the servants when he, at least, asked for Mrs. Miller at her hotel. This lady and her daughter, however, were not at home; and on the next day, after repeating his visit, Winterbourne again had the misfortune not to find them. Mrs. Walker's party took place on the evening of the third day, and in spite of the frigidity of his last interview with the hostess, Winterbourne was among the guests. Mrs. Walker was one of those American ladies who, while residing abroad, make a point, in their own phrase, of studying European society; and she had on this occasion collected several specimens of her diversely-born fellow-mortals to serve, as it were, as text-books. When

8. Seventeenth-century palace.

Winterbourne arrived Daisy Miller was not there; but in a few moments he saw her mother come in alone, very shyly and ruefully. Mrs. Miller's hair, above her exposed-looking temples, was more frizzled than ever. As she approached Mrs. Walker, Winterbourne also drew near.

"You see I've come all alone," said poor Mrs. Miller. "I'm so frightened; I don't know what to do; it's the first time I've ever been to a party alone—especially in this country. I wanted to bring Randolph or Eugenio, or someone, but Daisy just pushed me off by myself. I ain't used to going round alone."

"And does not your daughter intend to favor us with her society?" demanded Mrs. Walker, impressively.

"Well, Daisy's all dressed," said Mrs. Miller, with that accent of the dispassionate, if not of the philosophic, historian with which she always recorded the current incidents of her daughter's career. "She's got dressed on purpose before dinner. But she's got a friend of hers there; that gentleman—the Italian—that she wanted to bring. They've got going at the piano; it seems as if they couldn't leave off. Mr. Giovanelli sings splendidly. But I guess they'll come before very long," concluded Mrs. Miller hopefully.

"I'm sorry she should come—in that way," said Mrs. Walker.

"Well, I told her that there was no use in her getting dressed before dinner if she was going to wait three hours," responded Daisy's mamma. "I didn't see the use of her putting on such a dress as that to sit round with Mr. Giovanelli."

"This is most horrible!" said Mrs. Walker, turning away and addressing herself to Winterbourne. "*Elle s'affiche*.[9] It's her revenge for my having ventured to remonstrate with her. When she comes I shall not speak to her."

Daisy came after eleven o'clock, but she was not, on such an occasion, a young lady to wait to be spoken to. She rustled forward in radiant loveliness, smiling and chattering, carrying a large bouquet and attended by Mr. Giovanelli. Every one stopped talking, and turned and looked at her. She came straight to Mrs. Walker. "I'm afraid you thought I never was coming, so I sent mother off to tell you. I wanted to make Mr. Giovanelli practice some things before he came; you know he sings beautifully, and I want you to ask him to sing. This is Mr. Giovanelli; you know I introduced him to you; he's got the most lovely voice and he knows the most charming set of songs. I made him go over them this evening, on purpose; we had the greatest time at the hotel." Of all this Daisy delivered herself with the sweetest, brightest audibleness, looking now at her hostess and now round the room, while she gave a series of little pats, round her shoulders, to the edges of her dress. "Is there anyone I know?" she asked.

"I think every one knows you!" said Mrs. Walker pregnantly, and she gave a very cursory greeting to Mr. Giovanelli. This gentleman bore himself gallantly. He smiled and bowed and showed his white teeth, he curled his moustaches and rolled his eyes, and performed all the proper functions of a handsome Italian at an evening party. He sang, very prettily, half-a-dozen songs, though Mrs. Walker afterwards declared that she had been quite unable to find out who asked him. It was apparently not Daisy who had given him his orders. Daisy sat at a distance from the piano, and though she had publicly, as it were, professed a high admiration for his singing, talked, not inaudibly, while it was going on.

9. She's making a spectacle of herself (French).

"It's a pity these rooms are so small; we can't dance," she said to Winterbourne, as if she had seen him five minutes before.

"I am not sorry we can't dance," Winterbourne answered; "I don't dance."

"Of course you don't dance; you're too stiff," said Miss Daisy. "I hope you enjoyed your drive with Mrs. Walker."

"No, I didn't enjoy it; I preferred walking with you."

"We paired off, that was much better," said Daisy. "But did you ever hear anything so cool as Mrs. Walker's wanting me to get into her carriage and drop poor Mr. Giovanelli; and under the pretext that it was proper? People have different ideas! It would have been most unkind; he had been talking about that walk for ten days."

"He should not have talked about it at all," said Winterbourne; "he would never have proposed to a young lady of this country to walk about the streets with him."

"About the streets?" cried Daisy, with her pretty stare. "Where then would he have proposed to her to walk? The Pincio is not the streets, either; and I, thank goodness, am not a young lady of this country. The young ladies of this country have a dreadfully pokey time of it, so far as I can learn; I don't see why I should change my habits for *them*."

"I am afraid your habits are those of a flirt," said Winterbourne gravely.

"Of course they are," she cried, giving him her little smiling stare again. "I'm a fearful, frightful flirt! Did you ever hear of a nice girl that was not? But I suppose you will tell me now that I am not a nice girl."

"You're a very nice girl, but I wish you would flirt with me, and me only," said Winterbourne.

"Ah! thank you, thank you very much; you are the last man I should think of flirting with. As I have had the pleasure of informing you, you are too stiff."

"You say that too often," said Winterbourne.

Daisy gave a delighted laugh. "If I could have the sweet hope of making you angry, I would say it again."

"Don't do that; when I am angry I'm stiffer than ever. But if you won't flirt with me, do cease at least to flirt with your friend at the piano; they don't understand that sort of thing here."

"I thought they understood nothing else!" exclaimed Daisy.

"Not in young unmarried women."

"It seems to me much more proper in young unmarried women than in old married ones," Daisy declared.

"Well," said Winterbourne, "when you deal with natives you must go by the custom of the place. Flirting is a purely American custom; it doesn't exist here. So when you show yourself in public with Mr. Giovanelli and without your mother—"

"Gracious! Poor mother!" interposed Daisy.

"Though you may be flirting, Mr. Giovanelli is not; he means something else."

"He isn't preaching, at any rate," said Daisy with vivacity. "And if you want very much to know, we are neither of us flirting; we are too good friends for that; we are very intimate friends."

"Ah," rejoined Winterbourne, "if you are in love with each other it is another affair."

She had allowed him up to this point to talk so frankly that he had no expectation of shocking her by this ejaculation; but she immediately got up, blushing visibly, and leaving him to exclaim mentally that little American flirts were the queerest creatures in the world. "Mr. Giovanelli, at least," she said, giving her interlocutor a single glance, "never says such very disagreeable things to me."

Winterbourne was bewildered; he stood staring. Mr. Giovanelli had finished singing; he left the piano and came over to Daisy. "Won't you come into the other room and have some tea?" he asked, bending before her with his decorative smile.

Daisy turned to Winterbourne, beginning to smile again. He was still more perplexed, for this inconsequent smile made nothing clear, though it seemed to prove, indeed, that she had a sweetness and softness that reverted instinctively to the pardon of offences. "It has never occurred to Mr. Winterbourne to offer me any tea," she said, with her little tormenting manner.

"I have offered you advice," Winterbourne rejoined.

"I prefer weak tea!" cried Daisy, and she went off with the brilliant Giovanelli. She sat with him in the adjoining room, in the embrasure of the window, for the rest of the evening. There was an interesting performance at the piano, but neither of these young people gave heed to it. When Daisy came to take leave of Mrs. Walker, this lady conscientiously repaired the weakness of which she had been guilty at the moment of the young girl's arrival. She turned her back straight upon Miss Miller and left her to depart with what grace she might. Winterbourne was standing near the door; he saw it all. Daisy turned very pale and looked at her mother, but Mrs. Miller was humbly unconscious of any violation of the usual social forms. She appeared, indeed, to have felt an incongruous impulse to draw attention to her own striking observance of them. "Good night, Mrs. Walker," she said; "we've had a beautiful evening. You see if I let Daisy come to parties without me, I don't want her to go away without me." Daisy turned away, looking with a pale, grave face at the circle near the door; Winterbourne saw that, for the first moment, she was too much shocked and puzzled even for indignation. He on his side was greatly touched.

"That was very cruel," he said to Mrs. Walker.

"She never enters my drawing-room again," replied his hostess.

Since Winterbourne was not to meet her in Mrs. Walker's drawing-room, he went as often as possible to Mrs. Miller's hotel. The ladies were rarely at home, but when he found them the devoted Giovanelli was always present. Very often the polished little Roman was in the drawing-room with Daisy alone, Mrs. Miller being apparently constantly of the opinion that discretion is the better part of surveillance. Winterbourne noted, at first with surprise, that Daisy on these occasions was never embarrassed or annoyed by his own entrance; but he very presently began to feel that she had no more surprises for him; the unexpected in her behavior was the only thing to expect. She showed no displeasure at her *tête-à-tête* with Giovanelli being interrupted; she could chatter as freshly and freely with two gentlemen as with one; there was always, in her conversation, the same odd mixture of audacity and puerility. Winterbourne remarked to himself that if she was seriously interested in Giovanelli it was very singular that she should not take more trouble to preserve the sanctity of their interviews, and he liked her the more for her innocent-looking indifference and her apparently inexhaustible good humor. He could hardly have said why, but she seemed to him a girl who would never be jealous. At the risk of exciting a somewhat derisive smile on the reader's part, I may affirm that with regard to the women who had hitherto interested him it very often seemed to Winterbourne among the possibilities that, given certain contingencies, he should be afraid—literally afraid—of these ladies. He had a pleasant sense that he should never be afraid of Daisy Miller. It must be added that this sentiment was not altogether flattering to Daisy; it was part of his conviction, or rather of his apprehension, that she would prove a very light young person.

But she was evidently very much interested in Giovanelli. She looked at him whenever he spoke; she was perpetually telling him to do this and to do that; she was constantly "chaffing" and abusing him. She appeared completely to have forgotten that Winterbourne had said anything to displease her at Mrs. Walker's little party. One Sunday afternoon, having gone to St. Peter's[1] with his aunt, Winterbourne perceived Daisy strolling about the great church in company with the inevitable Giovanelli. Presently he pointed out the young girl and her cavalier to Mrs. Costello. This lady looked at them a moment through her eyeglasses, and then she said:

"That's what makes you so pensive in these days, eh?"

"I had not the least idea I was pensive," said the young man.

"You are very much preoccupied, you are thinking of something."

"And what is it," he asked, "that you accuse me of thinking of?"

"Of that young lady's, Miss Baker's, Miss Chandler's—what's her name?—Miss Miller's intrigue with that little barber's block."[2]

"Do you call it an intrigue," Winterbourne asked—"an affair that goes on with such peculiar publicity?"

"That's their folly," said Mrs. Costello, "it's not their merit."

"No," rejoined Winterbourne, with something of that pensiveness to which his aunt had alluded. "I don't believe that there is anything to be called an intrigue."

"I have heard a dozen people speak of it; they say she is quite carried away by him."

"They are certainly very intimate," said Winterbourne.

Mrs. Costello inspected the young couple again with her optical instrument. "He is very handsome. One easily sees how it is. She thinks him the most elegant man in the world, the finest gentleman. She has never seen anything like him; he is better even than the courier. It was the courier probably who introduced him, and if he succeeds in marrying the young lady, the courier will come in for a magnificent commission."

"I don't believe she thinks of marrying him," said Winterbourne, "and I don't believe he hopes to marry her."

"You may be very sure she thinks of nothing. She goes on from day to day, from hour to hour, as they did in the Golden Age. I can imagine nothing more vulgar. And at the same time," added Mrs. Costello, "depend upon it that she may tell you any moment that she is 'engaged.'"

"I think that is more than Giovanelli expects," said Winterbourne.

"Who is Giovanelli?"

"The little Italian. I have asked questions about him and learned something. He is apparently a perfectly respectable little man. I believe he is in a small way a *cavaliere avvocato*.[3] But he doesn't move in what are called the

---

1. Ornate Renaissance church in Vatican City, and the worldwide center of Catholic observances.

2. A dandy.

3. Lawyer (Italian). *"Cavaliere"*: a term of respect.

first circles. I think it is really not absolutely impossible that the courier introduced him. He is evidently immensely charmed with Miss Miller. If she thinks him the finest gentleman in the world, he, on his side, has never found himself in personal contact with such splendor, such opulence, such expensiveness, as this young lady's. And then she must seem to him wonderfully pretty and interesting. I rather doubt whether he dreams of marrying her. That must appear to him too impossible a piece of luck. He has nothing but his handsome face to offer, and there is a substantial Mr. Miller in that mysterious land of dollars. Giovanelli knows that he hasn't a title to offer. If he were only a count or a *marchese*![4] He must wonder at his luck at the way they have taken him up."

"He accounts for it by his handsome face, and thinks Miss Miller a young lady *qui se passe ses fantaisies!*"[5] said Mrs. Costello.

"It is very true," Winterbourne pursued, "that Daisy and her mamma have not yet risen to that stage of—what shall I call it?—of culture, at which the idea of catching a count or a *marchese* begins. I believe that they are intellectually incapable of that conception."

"Ah! but the *cavalier* can't believe it," said Mrs. Costello.

Of the observation excited by Daisy's "intrigue," Winterbourne gathered that day at St. Peter's sufficient evidence. A dozen of the American colonists in Rome came to talk with Mrs. Costello, who sat on a little portable stool at the base of one of the great pilasters. The vesper-service was going forward in splendid chants and organ-tones in the adjacent choir, and meanwhile, between Mrs. Costello and her friends, there was a great deal said about poor little Miss Miller's going really "too far." Winterbourne was not pleased with what he heard; but when, coming out upon the great steps of the church, he saw Daisy, who had emerged before him, get into an open cab with her accomplice and roll away through the cynical streets of Rome, he could not deny to himself that she was going very far indeed. He felt very sorry for her—not exactly that he believed that she had completely lost her head, but because it was painful to hear so much that was pretty and undefended and natural assigned to a vulgar place among the categories of disorder. He made an attempt after this to give a hint to Mrs. Miller. He met one day in the Corso[6] a friend—a tourist like himself—who had just come out of the Doria Palace, where he had been walking through the beautiful gallery. His friend talked for a moment about the superb portrait of Innocent X. by Velasquez,[7] which hangs in one of the cabinets of the palace, and then said, "And in the same cabinet, by-the-way, I had the pleasure of contemplating a picture of a different kind—that pretty American girl whom you pointed out to me last week." In answer to Winterbourne's inquiries, his friend narrated that the pretty American girl—prettier than ever—was seated with a companion in the secluded nook in which the great papal portrait is enshrined.

"Who was her companion?" asked Winterbourne.

"A little Italian with a bouquet in his button-hole. The girl is delightfully pretty, but I thought I understood from you the other day that she was a young lady *du meilleur monde*."[8]

4. Marquis (Italian).
5. Who is indulging her whims (French).
6. Via del Corso: main street in Central Rome.
7. Diego Rodríguez de Silva y Velásquez (1599–

1660), Spanish painter. Velásquez's painting of Pope Innocent X is exhibited in a small gallery of the Doria Palace.
8. Of the better society (French).

"So she is!" answered Winterbourne; and having assured himself that his informant had seen Daisy and her companion but five minutes before, he jumped into a cab and went to call on Mrs. Miller. She was at home; but she apologized to him for receiving him in Daisy's absence.

"She's gone out somewhere with Mr. Giovanelli," said Mrs. Miller. "She's always going round with Mr. Giovanelli."

"I have noticed that they are very intimate," Winterbourne observed.

"Oh! it seems as if they couldn't live without each other!" said Mrs. Miller. "Well, he's a real gentleman, anyhow. I keep telling Daisy she's engaged!"

"And what does Daisy say?"

"Oh, she says she isn't engaged. But she might as well be!" this impartial parent resumed. "She goes on as if she was. But I've made Mr. Giovanelli promise to tell me, if *she* doesn't. I should want to write to Mr. Miller about it—shouldn't you?"

Winterbourne replied that he certainly should; and the state of mind of Daisy's mamma struck him as so unprecedented in the annals of parental vigilance that he gave up as utterly irrelevant the attempt to place her upon her guard.

After this Daisy was never at home, and Winterbourne ceased to meet her at the houses of their common acquaintances, because, as he perceived, these shrewd people had quite made up their minds that she was going too far. They ceased to invite her, and they intimated that they desired to express to observant Europeans the great truth that, though Miss Daisy Miller was a young American lady, her behavior was not representative—was regarded by her compatriots as abnormal. Winterbourne wondered how she felt about all the cold shoulders that were turned towards her, and sometimes it annoyed him to suspect that she did not feel at all. He said to himself that she was too light and childish, too uncultivated and unreasoning, too provincial, to have reflected upon her ostracism or even to have perceived it. Then at other moments he believed that she carried about in her elegant and irresponsible little organism a defiant, passionate, perfectly observant consciousness of the impression she produced. He asked himself whether Daisy's defiance came from the consciousness of innocence or from her being, essentially, a young person of the reckless class. It must be admitted that holding oneself to a belief in Daisy's "innocence" came to seem to Winterbourne more and more a matter of fine-spun gallantry. As I have already had occasion to relate, he was angry at finding himself reduced to chopping logic about this young lady; he was vexed at his want of instinctive certitude as to how far her eccentricities were generic, national, and how far they were personal. From either view of them he had somehow missed her, and now it was too late. She was "carried away" by Mr. Giovanelli.

A few days after his brief interview with her mother, he encountered her in that beautiful abode of flowering desolation known as the Palace of the Cæsars. The early Roman spring had filled the air with bloom and perfume, and the rugged surface of the Palatine[9] was muffled with tender verdure. Daisy was strolling along the top of one of those great mounds of ruin that are embanked with mossy marble and paved with monumental inscriptions. It seemed to him that Rome had never been so lovely as just then. He stood looking off at the enchanting harmony of line and color that remotely encir-

---

9. A park on a hill in the center of Rome, with palatial ruins and historical monuments.

cles the city, inhaling the softly humid odors and feeling the freshness of the year and the antiquity of the place reaffirm themselves in mysterious inter-fusion. It seemed to him also that Daisy had never looked so pretty; but this had been an observation of his whenever he met her. Giovanelli was at her side, and Giovanelli, too, wore an aspect of even unwonted brilliancy.

"Well," said Daisy, "I should think you would be lonesome!"

"Lonesome?" asked Winterbourne.

"You are always going round by yourself. Can't you get any one to walk with you?"

"I am not so fortunate," said Winterbourne, "as your companion."

Giovanelli, from the first, had treated Winterbourne with distinguished politeness; he listened with a deferential air to his remarks; he laughed, punc-tiliously, at his pleasantries; he seemed disposed to testify to his belief that Winterbourne was a superior young man. He carried himself in no degree like a jealous wooer; he had obviously a great deal of tact; he had no objection to your expecting a little humility of him. It even seemed to Winterbourne at times that Giovanelli would find a certain mental relief in being able to have a private understanding with him—to say to him, as an intelligent man, that, bless you, *he* knew how extraordinary was this young lady, and didn't flatter himself with delusive—or at least *too* delusive—hopes of matrimony and dol-lars. On this occasion he strolled away from his companion to pluck a sprig of almond blossom, which he carefully arranged in his button-hole.

"I know why you say that," said Daisy, watching Giovanelli. "Because you think I go round too much with *him*!" And she nodded at her attendant.

"Everyone thinks so—if you care to know," said Winterbourne.

"Of course I care to know!" Daisy exclaimed seriously. "But I don't believe it. They are only pretending to be shocked. They don't really care a straw what I do. Besides, I don't go round so much."

"I think you will find they do care. They will show it—disagreeably."

Daisy looked at him a moment. "How—disagreeably?"

"Haven't you noticed anything?" Winterbourne asked.

"I have noticed you. But I noticed you were as stiff as an umbrella the first time I saw you."

"You will find I am not so stiff as several others," said Winterbourne, smiling.

"How shall I find it?"

"By going to see the others."

"What will they do to me?"

"They will give you the cold shoulder. Do you know what that means?"

Daisy was looking at him intently; she began to color. "Do you mean as Mrs. Walker did the other night?"

"Exactly!" said Winterbourne.

She looked away at Giovanelli, who was decorating himself with his almond-blossom. Then looking back at Winterbourne—"I shouldn't think you would let people be so unkind!" she said.

"How can I help it?" he asked.

"I should think you would say something."

"I do say something"; and he paused a moment. "I say that your mother tells me that she believes you are engaged."

"Well, she does," said Daisy very simply.

Winterbourne began to laugh. "And does Randolph believe it?" he asked.

"I guess Randolph doesn't believe anything," said Daisy. Randolph's scepticism excited Winterbourne to farther hilarity, and he observed that Giovanelli was coming back to them. Daisy, observing it too, addressed herself again to her countryman. "Since you have mentioned it," she said, "I *am* engaged." . . . Winterbourne looked at her; he had stopped laughing. "You don't believe it!" she added.

He was silent a moment; and then, "Yes, I believe it!" he said.

"Oh, no, you don't," she answered. "Well, then—I am not!"

The young girl and her cicerone[1] were on their way to the gate of the enclosure, so that Winterbourne, who had but lately entered, presently took leave of them. A week afterwards he went to dine at a beautiful villa on the Cælian Hill,[2] and, on arriving, dismissed his hired vehicle. The evening was charming, and he promised himself the satisfaction of walking home beneath the Arch of Constantine and past the vaguely-lighted monuments of the Forum.[3] There was a waning moon in the sky, and her radiance was not brilliant, but she was veiled in a thin cloud-curtain which seemed to diffuse and equalize it. When, on his return from the villa (it was eleven o'clock), Winterbourne approached the dusky circle of the Colosseum,[4] it occurred to him, as a lover of the picturesque, that the interior, in the pale moonshine, would be well worth a glance. He turned aside and walked to one of the empty arches, near which, as he observed, an open carriage—one of the little Roman street-cabs—was stationed. Then he passed in among the cavernous shadows of the great structure, and emerged upon the clear and silent arena. The place had never seemed to him more impressive. One-half of the gigantic circus was in deep shade; the other was sleeping in the luminous dusk. As he stood there he began to murmur Byron's famous lines, out of "Manfred";[5] but before he had finished his quotation he remembered that if nocturnal meditations in the Colosseum are recommended by the poets, they are deprecated by the doctors. The historic atmosphere was there, certainly; but the historic atmosphere, scientifically considered, was not better than a villainous miasma. Winterbourne walked to the middle of the arena, to take a more general glance, intending thereafter to make a hasty retreat. The great cross in the center was covered with shadow; it was only as he drew near it that he made it out distinctly. Then he saw that two persons were stationed upon the low steps which formed its base. One of these was a woman, seated; her companion was standing in front of her.

Presently the sound of the woman's voice came to him distinctly in the warm night air. "Well, he looks at us as one of the old lions or tigers may have looked at the Christian martyrs!" These were the words he heard, in the familiar accent of Miss Daisy Miller.

"Let us hope he is not very hungry," responded the ingenious Giovanelli. "He will have to take me first; you will serve for dessert!"

1. Chaperone (Italian).
2. One of the seven hills upon which ancient Rome had been built.
3. Ruins of the governmental and religious center of ancient Rome. "Arch of Constantine": built in the fourth century to celebrate a key military victory of Rome's first Christian emperor.
4. Ancient Roman amphitheater, known for its battles between gladiators and public executions of Christians.
5. Byron's 1817 dramatic poem contains the fol-

lowing lines: ". . . the night / Hath been to me a more familiar face / Than that of man; and in her starry shade / Of dim and solitary loveliness, / I learn'd the language of another world. / I do remember me, that in my youth, / When I was wandering,—upon such a night / I stood within the Colosseum's wall, / 'Midst the chief relics of almighty Rome; / The trees which grew along the broken arches / Waved dark in the blue midnight, and the stars / Shone through the rents of ruin. . . ."

Winterbourne stopped, with a sort of horror; and, it must be added, with a sort of relief. It was as if a sudden illumination had been flashed upon the ambiguity of Daisy's behavior and the riddle had become easy to read. She was a young lady whom a gentleman need no longer be at pains to respect. He stood there looking at her—looking at her companion, and not reflecting that though he saw them vaguely, he himself must have been more brightly visible. He felt angry with himself that he had bothered so much about the right way of regarding Miss Daisy Miller. Then, as he was going to advance again, he checked himself; not from the fear that he was doing her injustice, but from a sense of the danger of appearing unbecomingly exhilarated by this sudden revulsion from cautious criticism. He turned away towards the entrance of the place; but as he did so he heard Daisy speak again.

"Why, it was Mr. Winterbourne! He saw me—and he cuts me!"

What a clever little reprobate she was, and how smartly she played an injured innocence! But he wouldn't cut her. Winterbourne came forward again, and went towards the great cross. Daisy had got up; Giovanelli lifted his hat. Winterbourne had now begun to think simply of the craziness, from a sanitary point of view, of a delicate young girl lounging away the evening in this nest of malaria. What if she *were* a clever little reprobate? that was no reason for her dying of the *perniciosa*.[6] "How long have you been there?" he asked, almost brutally.

Daisy, lovely in the flattering moonlight, looked at him a moment. Then— "All the evening," she answered gently. . . . "I never saw anything so pretty."

"I am afraid," said Winterbourne, "that you will not think Roman fever very pretty. This is the way people catch it. I wonder," he added, turning to Giovanelli, "that you, a native Roman, should countenance such a terrible indiscretion."

"Ah," said the handsome native, "for myself, I am not afraid."

"Neither am I—for you! I am speaking for this young lady."

Giovanelli lifted his well-shaped eyebrows and showed his brilliant teeth. But he took Winterbourne's rebuke with docility. "I told the Signorina it was a grave indiscretion; but when was the Signorina ever prudent?"

"I never was sick, and I don't mean to be!" the Signorina declared. "I don't look like much, but I'm healthy! I was bound to see the Colosseum by moonlight; I shouldn't have wanted to go home without that; and we have had the most beautiful time, haven't we, Mr. Giovanelli! If there has been any danger, Eugenio can give me some pills. He has got some splendid pills."

"I should advise you," said Winterbourne, "to drive home as fast as possible and take one!"

"What you say is very wise," Giovanelli rejoined. "I will go and make sure the carriage is at hand." And he went forward rapidly.

Daisy followed with Winterbourne. He kept looking at her; she seemed not in the least embarrassed. Winterbourne said nothing; Daisy chattered about the beauty of the place. "Well, I *have* seen the Colosseum by moonlight!" she exclaimed. "That's one good thing." Then, noticing Winterbourne's silence, she asked him why he didn't speak. He made no answer; he only began to laugh. They passed under one of the dark archways; Giovanelli was in front with the carriage. Here Daisy stopped a moment, looking at the young American. "*Did* you believe I was engaged the other day?" she asked.

6. Malaria (Italian).

"It doesn't matter what I believed the other day," said Winterbourne, still laughing.

"Well, what do you believe now?"

"I believe that it makes very little difference whether you are engaged or not!"

He felt the young girl's pretty eyes fixed upon him through the thick gloom of the archway; she was apparently going to answer. But Giovanelli hurried her forward. "Quick, quick," he said; "if we get in by midnight we are quite safe."

Daisy took her seat in the carriage, and the fortunate Italian placed himself beside her. "Don't forget Eugenio's pills!" said Winterbourne, as he lifted his hat.

"I don't care," said Daisy, in a little strange tone, "whether I have Roman fever or not!" Upon this the cab-driver cracked his whip, and they rolled away over the desultory patches of the antique pavement.

Winterbourne—to do him justice, as it were—mentioned to no one that he had encountered Miss Miller, at midnight, in the Colosseum with a gentleman; but nevertheless, a couple of days later, the fact of her having been there under these circumstances was known to every member of the little American circle, and commented accordingly. Winterbourne reflected that they had of course known it at the hotel, and that, after Daisy's return, there had been an exchange of jokes between the porter and the cab-driver. But the young man was conscious at the same moment that it had ceased to be a matter of serious regret to him that the little American flirt should be "talked about" by low-minded menials. These people, a day or two later, had serious information to give: the little American flirt was alarmingly ill. Winterbourne, when the rumor came to him, immediately went to the hotel for more news. He found that two or three charitable friends had preceded him, and that they were being entertained in Mrs. Miller's salon by Randolph.

"It's going round at night," said Randolph—"that's what made her sick. She's always going round at midnight. I shouldn't think she'd want to—it's so plaguey dark. You can't see anything here at night, except when there's a moon. In America there's always a moon!" Mrs. Miller was invisible; she was now, at least, giving her daughter the advantage of her society. It was evident that Daisy was dangerously ill.

Winterbourne went often to ask for news of her, and once he saw Mrs. Miller, who, though deeply alarmed, was—rather to his surprise—perfectly composed, and, as it appeared, a most efficient and judicious nurse. She talked a good deal about Dr. Davis, but Winterbourne paid her the compliment of saying to himself that she was not, after all, such a monstrous goose. "Daisy spoke of you the other day," she said to him. "Half the time she doesn't know what she's saying, but that time I think she did. She gave me a message: she told me to tell you. She told me to tell you that she never was engaged to that handsome Italian. I am sure I am very glad; Mr. Giovanelli hasn't been near us since she was taken ill. I thought he was so much of a gentleman; but I don't call that very polite! A lady told me that he was afraid I was angry with him for taking Daisy round at night. Well, so I am; but I suppose he knows I'm a lady. I would scorn to scold him. Any way, she says she's not engaged. I don't know why she wanted you to know; but she said to me three times—'Mind you tell Mr. Winterbourne.' And then she told me to ask if you remembered the time you went to that castle, in Switzerland. But

I said I wouldn't give any such messages as that. Only, if she is not engaged, I'm sure I'm glad to know it."

But, as Winterbourne had said, it mattered very little. A week after this the poor girl died; it had been a terrible case of the fever. Daisy's grave was in the little Protestant cemetery, in an angle of the wall of imperial Rome, beneath the cypresses and the thick spring-flowers. Winterbourne stood there beside it, with a number of other mourners; a number larger than the scandal excited by the young lady's career would have led you to expect. Near him stood Giovanelli, who came nearer still before Winterbourne turned away. Giovanelli was very pale; on this occasion he had no flower in his button-hole; he seemed to wish to say something. At last he said, "She was the most beautiful young lady I ever saw, and the most amiable." And then he added in a moment, "And she was the most innocent."

Winterbourne looked at him, and presently repeated his words, "And the most innocent?"

"The most innocent!"

Winterbourne felt sore and angry. "Why the devil," he asked, "did you take her to that fatal place?"

Mr. Giovanelli's urbanity was apparently imperturbable. He looked on the ground a moment, and then he said, "For myself, I had no fear; and she wanted to go."

"That was no reason!" Winterbourne declared.

The subtle Roman again dropped his eyes. "If she had lived, I should have got nothing. She would never have married me, I am sure."

"She would never have married you?"

"For a moment I hoped so. But no, I am sure."

Winterbourne listened to him; he stood staring at the raw protuberance among the April daisies. When he turned away again Mr. Giovanelli, with his light slow step, had retired.

Winterbourne almost immediately left Rome; but the following summer he again met his aunt, Mrs. Costello, at Vevey. Mrs. Costello was fond of Vevey. In the interval Winterbourne had often thought of Daisy Miller and her mystifying manners. One day he spoke of her to his aunt—said it was on his conscience that he had done her injustice.

"I am sure I don't know," said Mrs. Costello. "How did your injustice affect her?"

"She sent me a message before her death which I didn't understand at the time. But I have understood it since. She would have appreciated one's esteem."

"Is that a modest way," asked Mrs. Costello, "of saying that she would have reciprocated one's affection?"

Winterbourne offered no answer to this question; but he presently said, "You were right in that remark that you made last summer. I was booked to make a mistake. I have lived too long in foreign parts."

Nevertheless, he went back to live at Geneva, whence there continue to come the most contradictory accounts of his motives of sojourn: a report that he is "studying" hard—an intimation that he is much interested in a very clever foreign lady.

1878, 1879

The Real Thing[1]

I

When the porter's wife, who used to answer the house-bell, announced "A gentleman and a lady, sir" I had, as I often had in those days—the wish being father to the thought—an immediate vision of sitters. Sitters my visitors in this case proved to be; but not in the sense I should have preferred. There was nothing at first however to indicate that they mightn't have come for a portrait. The gentleman, a man of fifty, very high and very straight, with a moustache slightly grizzled and a dark grey walking-coat admirably fitted, both of which I noted professionally—I don't mean as a barber or yet as a tailor—would have struck me as a celebrity if celebrities often were striking. It was a truth of which I had for some time been conscious that a figure with a good deal of frontage was, as one might say, almost never a public institution. A glance at the lady helped to remind me of this paradoxical law: she also looked too distinguished to be a "personality." Moreover one would scarcely come across two variations together.

Neither of the pair immediately spoke—they only prolonged the preliminary gaze suggesting that each wished to give the other a chance. They were visibly shy; they stood there letting me take them in—which, as I afterwards perceived, was the most practical thing they could have done. In this way their embarrassment served their cause. I had seen people painfully reluctant to mention that they desired anything so gross as to be represented on canvas; but the scruples of my new friends appeared almost insurmountable. Yet the gentleman might have said "I should like a portrait of my wife," and the lady might have said "I should like a portrait of my husband." Perhaps they weren't husband and wife—this naturally would make the matter more delicate. Perhaps they wished to be done together—in which case they ought to have brought a third person to break the news.

"We come from Mr. Rivet," the lady finally said with a dim smile that had the effect of a moist sponge passed over a "sunk"[2] piece of painting, as well as of a vague allusion to vanished beauty. She was as tall and straight, in her degree, as her companion, and with ten years less to carry. She looked as sad as a woman could look whose face was not charged with expression; that is her tinted oval mask showed waste as an exposed surface shows friction. The hand of time had played over her freely, but to an effect of elimination. She was slim and stiff, and so well-dressed, in dark blue cloth, with lappets[3] and pockets and buttons, that it was clear she employed the same tailor as her husband. The couple had an indefinable air of prosperous thrift—they evidently got a good deal of luxury for their money. If I was to be one of their luxuries it would behove me to consider my terms.

"Ah Claude Rivet recommended me?" I echoed; and I added that it was very kind of him, though I could reflect that, as he only painted landscape, this wasn't a sacrifice.

1. This "little gem of bright, quick vivid form," as James called it, first appeared in the April 16, 1892, issue of *Black and White*; then in *"The Real Thing" and Other Tales* (1893); and finally in Vol. 18 (1909) of the New York edition, the source of the text printed here.
2. When colors lose their brilliance after they have dried on the canvas, they are said to have "sunk in."
3. Decorative flaps or folds.

The lady looked very hard at the gentleman, and the gentleman looked round the room. Then staring at the floor a moment and stroking his moustache, he rested his pleasant eyes on me with the remark: "He said you were the right one."

"I try to be, when people want to sit."

"Yes, we should like to," said the lady anxiously.

"Do you mean together?"

My visitors exchanged a glance. "If you could do anything with *me* I suppose it would be double," the gentleman stammered.

"Oh yes, there's naturally a higher charge for two figures than for one."

"We should like to make it pay," the husband confessed.

"That's very good of you," I returned, appreciating so unwonted a sympathy—for I supposed he meant pay the artist.

A sense of strangeness seemed to draw on the lady.

"We mean for the illustrations—Mr. Rivet said you might put one in."

"Put in—an illustration?" I was equally confused.

"Sketch her off, you know," said the gentleman, colouring.

It was only then that I understood the service Claude Rivet had rendered me; he had told them how I worked in black-and-white, for magazines, for storybooks, for sketches of contemporary life, and consequently had copious employment for models. These things were true, but it was not less true—I may confess it now; whether because the aspiration was to lead to everything or to nothing I leave the reader to guess—that I couldn't get the honours, to say nothing of the emoluments, of a great painter of portraits out of my head. My "illustrations" were my pot-boilers; I looked to a different branch of art—far and away the most interesting it had always seemed to me—to perpetuate my fame. There was no shame in looking to it also to make my fortune; but that fortune was by so much further from being made from the moment my visitors wished to be "done" for nothing. I was disappointed; for in the pictorial sense I had immediately *seen* them. I had seized their type—I had already settled what I would do with it. Something that wouldn't absolutely have pleased them, I afterwards reflected.

"Ah you're—you're—a—?" I began as soon as I had mastered my surprise. I couldn't bring out the dingy word "models": it seemed so little to fit the case.

"We haven't had much practice," said the lady.

"We've got to *do* something, and we've thought that an artist in your line might perhaps make something of us," her husband threw off. He further mentioned that they didn't know many artists and that they had gone first, on the off-chance—he painted views of course, but sometimes put in figures; perhaps I remembered—to Mr. Rivet, whom they had met a few years before at a place in Norfolk where he was sketching.

"We used to sketch a little ourselves," the lady hinted.

"It's very awkward, but we absolutely *must* do something," her husband went on.

"Of course we're not so *very* young," she admitted with a wan smile.

With the remark that I might as well know something more about them the husband had handed me a card extracted from a neat new pocket-book—their appurtenances were all of the freshest—and inscribed with the words "Major Monarch." Impressive as these words were they didn't carry my knowledge much further; but my visitor presently added: "I've left the army and we've had the misfortune to lose our money. In fact our means are dreadfully small."

"It's awfully trying—a regular strain," said Mrs. Monarch.

They evidently wished to be discreet—to take care not to swagger because they were gentlefolk. I felt them willing to recognise this as something of a drawback, at the same time that I guessed at an underlying sense—their consolation in adversity—that they *had* their points. They certainly had; but these advantages struck me as preponderantly social; such for instance as would help to make a drawing-room look well. However, a drawing-room was always, or ought to be, a picture.

In consequence of his wife's allusion to their age Major Monarch observed: "Naturally it's more for the figure that we thought of going in. We can still hold ourselves up." On the instant I saw that the figure was indeed their strong point. His "naturally" didn't sound vain, but it lighted up the question. "*She* has the best one," he continued, nodding at his wife with a pleasant after-dinner absence of circumlocution. I could only reply, as if we were in fact sitting over our wine, that this didn't prevent his own from being very good; which led him in turn to make answer: "We thought that if you ever have to do people like us we might be something like it. *She* particularly—for a lady in a book, you know."

I was so amused by them that, to get more of it, I did my best to take their point of view; and though it was an embarrassment to find myself appraising physically, as if they were animals on hire or useful blacks, a pair whom I should have expected to meet only in one of the relations in which criticism is tacit, I looked at Mrs. Monarch judicially enough to be able to exclaim after a moment with conviction: "Oh yes, a lady in a book!" She was singularly like a bad illustration.

"We'll stand up, if you like," said the Major; and he raised himself before me with a really grand air.

I could take his measure at a glance—he was six feet two and a perfect gentleman. It would have paid any club in process of formation and in want of a stamp to engage him at a salary to stand in the principal window. What struck me at once was that in coming to me they had rather missed their vocation; they could surely have been turned to better account for advertising purposes. I couldn't of course see the thing in detail, but I could see them make somebody's fortune—I don't mean their own. There was something in them for a waistcoat-maker, an hotel-keeper or a soap-vendor. I could imagine "We always use it" pinned on their bosoms with the greatest effect; I had a vision of the brilliancy with which they would launch a table d'hôte.[4]

Mrs. Monarch sat still, not from pride but from shyness, and presently her husband said to her; "Get up, my dear, and show how smart you are." She obeyed, but she had no need to get up to show it. She walked to the end of the studio and then came back blushing, her fluttered eyes on the partner of her appeal. I was reminded of an incident I had accidentally had a glimpse of in Paris—being with a friend there, a dramatist about to produce a play, when an actress came to him to ask to be entrusted with a part. She went through her paces before him, walked up and down as Mrs. Monarch was doing. Mrs. Monarch did it quite as well, but I abstained from

---

4. Host's table (French); a common dining table for guests at a hotel.

applauding. It was very odd to see such people apply for such poor pay. She looked as if she had ten thousand a year. Her husband had used the word that described her: she was in the London current jargon essentially and typically "smart." Her figure was, in the same order of ideas, conspicuously and irreproachably "good." For a woman of her age her waist was surprisingly small; her elbow moreover had the orthodox crook. She held her head at the conventional angle, but why did she come to *me*? She ought to have tried on jackets at a big shop. I feared my visitors were not only destitute but "artistic"—which would be a great complication. When she sat down again I thanked her, observing that what a draughtsman most valued in his model was the faculty of keeping quiet.

"Oh *she* can keep quiet," said Major Monarch. Then he added jocosely: "I've always kept her quiet."

"I'm not a nasty fidget, am I?" It was going to wring tears from me, I felt, the way she hid her head, ostrich-like, in the other broad bosom.

The owner of this expanse addressed his answer to me. "Perhaps it isn't out of place to mention—because we ought to be quite business-like, oughtn't we?—that when I married her she was known as the Beautiful Statue."

"Oh dear!" said Mrs. Monarch ruefully.

"Of course I should want a certain amount of expression," I rejoined.

"Of *course*!"—and I had never heard such unanimity.

"And then I suppose you know that you'll get awfully tired."

"Oh we *never* get tired!" they eagerly cried.

"Have you had any kind of practice?"

They hesitated—they looked at each other. "We've been photographed—*immensely*," said Mrs. Monarch.

"She means the fellows have asked us themselves," added the Major.

"I see—because you're so good-looking."

"I don't know what they thought, but they were always after us."

"We always got our photographs for nothing," smiled Mrs. Monarch.

"We might have brought some, my dear," her husband remarked.

"I'm not sure we have any left. We've given quantities away," she explained to me.

"With our autographs and that sort of thing," said the Major.

"Are they to be got in the shops?" I enquired as a harmless pleasantry.

"Oh yes, *hers*—they used to be."

"Not now," said Mrs. Monarch with her eyes on the floor.

II

I could fancy the "sort of thing" they put on the presentation copies of their photographs, and I was sure they wrote a beautiful hand. It was odd how quickly I was sure of everything that concerned them. If they were now so poor as to have to earn shillings and pence they could never have had much of a margin. Their good looks had been their capital, and they had good-humouredly made the most of the career that this resource marked out for them. It was in their faces, the blankness, the deep intellectual repose of the twenty years of country-house visiting that had given them pleasant intonations. I could see the sunny drawing-rooms, sprinkled with periodicals she didn't read, in which Mrs. Monarch had continuously sat; I could see the wet shrubberies in which she had walked, equipped to admiration for either exercise. I could see the rich covers[5] the Major had helped to shoot and the wonderful garments in which, late at night, he repaired to the smoking-room to talk about them. I could imagine their leggings and waterproofs, their knowing tweeds and rugs, their rolls of sticks and cases of tackle and neat umbrellas; and I could evoke the exact appearance of their servants and the compact variety of their luggage on the platforms of country stations.

They gave small tips, but they were liked; they didn't do anything them-selves, but they were welcome. They looked so well everywhere; they grati-fied the general relish for stature, complexion and "form." They knew it without fatuity or vulgarity, and they respected themselves in consequence. They weren't superficial; they were thorough and kept themselves up—it had been their line. People with such a taste for activity had to have some line. I could feel how even in a dull house they could have been counted on for the joy of life. At present something had happened—it didn't matter what, their little income had grown less, it had grown least—and they had to do something for pocket-money. Their friends could like them, I made out, without liking to support them. There was something about them that represented credit—their clothes, their manners, their type; but if credit is a large empty pocket in which an occasional chink reverberates, the chink at least must be audible. What they wanted of me was to help to make it so. Fortunately they had no children—I soon divined that. They would also perhaps wish our relations to be kept secret: this was why it was "for the figure"—the reproduction of the face would betray them.

I liked them—I felt, quite as their friends must have done—they were so simple; and I had no objection to them if they would suit. But somehow with all their perfections I didn't easily believe in them. After all they were ama-teurs, and the ruling passion of my life was the detestation of the amateur. Combined with this was another perversity—an innate preference for the represented subject over the real one: the defect of the real one was so apt to be a lack of representation. I liked things that appeared; then one was sure. Whether they *were* or not was a subordinate and almost always a profitless question. There were other considerations, the first of which was that I already had two or three recruits in use, notably a young person with big feet, in alpaca, from Kilburn, who for a couple of years had come to me regularly for my illustrations and with whom I was still—perhaps ignobly—satisfied. I frankly explained to my visitors how the case stood, but they had taken more precautions than I supposed. They had reasoned out their oppor-tunity, for Claude Rivet had told them of the projected *édition de luxe* of one of the writers of our day—the rarest of the novelists—who, long neglected by the multitudinous vulgar and dearly prized by the attentive (need I men-tion Philip Vincent?)[6] had had the happy fortune of seeing, late in life, the dawn and then the full light of a higher criticism; an estimate in which on the part of the public there was something really of expiation. The edition preparing, planned by a publisher of taste, was practically an act of high reparation; the wood-cuts with which it was to be enriched were the homage of English art to one of the most independent representatives of English let-ters. Major and Mrs. Monarch confessed to me they had hoped I might be able to work *them* into my branch of the enterprise. They knew I was to do

---

5. Game birds.
6. Invented name, possibly a humorous reference to James himself; his first novel was called *Roderick Hudson*.

the first of the books, "Rutland Ramsay," but I had to make clear to them that my participation in the rest of the affair—this first book was to be a test—must depend on the satisfaction I should give. If this should be limited my employers would drop me with scarce common forms. It was therefore a crisis for me, and naturally I was making special preparations, looking about for new people, should they be necessary, and securing the best types. I admitted however that I should like to settle down to two or three good models who would do for everything.

"Should we have often to—a—put on special clothes?" Mrs. Monarch timidly demanded.

"Dear yes—that's half the business."

"And should we be expected to supply our own costumes?"

"Oh no; I've got a lot of things. A painter's models put on—or put off— anything he likes."

"And you mean—a—the same?"

"The same?"

Mrs. Monarch looked at her husband again.

"Oh she was just wondering," he explained, "if the costumes are in *general* use." I had to confess that they were, and I mentioned further that some of them—I had a lot of genuine greasy last-century things—had served their time, a hundred years ago, on living world-stained men and women; on figures not perhaps so far removed, in that vanished world, from *their* type, the Monarchs', *quoi!*[7] of a breeched and bewigged age. "We'll put on anything that *fits*," said the Major.

"Oh I arrange that—they fit in the pictures."

"I'm afraid I should do better for the modern books. I'd come as you like," said Mrs. Monarch.

"She has got a lot of clothes at home: they might do for contemporary life," her husband continued.

"Oh I can fancy scenes in which you'd be quite natural." And indeed I could see the slipshod rearrangements of stale properties—the stories I tried to produce pictures for without the exasperation of reading them—whose sandy tracts the good lady might help to people. But I had to return to the fact that for this sort of work—the daily mechanical grind—I was already equipped: the people I was working with were fully adequate.

"We only thought we might be more like *some* characters," said Mrs. Monarch mildly, getting up.

Her husband also rose; he stood looking at me with a dim wistfulness that was touching in so fine a man. "Wouldn't it be rather a pull sometimes to have—a—to have—?" He hung fire; he wanted me to help him by phrasing what he meant. But I couldn't—I didn't know. So he brought it out awkwardly: "The *real* thing; a gentleman, you know, or a lady." I was quite ready to give a general assent—I admitted that there was a great deal in that. This encouraged Major Monarch to say, following up his appeal with an unacted gulp: "It's awfully hard—we've tried everything." The gulp was communicative; it proved too much for his wife. Before I knew it Mrs. Monarch had dropped again upon a divan and burst into tears. Her husband sat down beside her, holding one of her hands; whereupon she quickly dried her eyes with the other, while I felt embarrassed as she looked up at me. "There isn't a

7. What! (French).

confounded job I haven't applied for—waited for—prayed for. You can fancy we'd be pretty bad first. Secretaryships and that sort of thing? You might as well ask for a peerage. I'd be *anything*—I'm strong; a messenger or a coal- heaver. I'd put on a gold-laced cap and open carriage-doors in front of the haberdasher's; I'd hang about a station to carry portmanteaux;[8] I'd be a postman. But they won't *look* at you; there are thousands as good as yourself already on the ground. *Gentlemen,* poor beggars, who've drunk their wine, who've kept their hunters!"

I was as reassuring as I knew how to be, and my visitors were presently on their feet again while, for the experiment, we agreed on an hour. We were discussing it when the door opened and Miss Churm came in with a wet umbrella. Miss Churm had to take the omnibus to Maida Vale[9] and then walk half a mile. She looked a trifle blowsy and slightly splashed. I scarcely ever saw her come in without thinking afresh how odd it was that, being so little in herself, she should yet be so much in others. She was a meagre little Miss Churm, but was such an ample heroine of romance. She was only a freckled cockney,[1] but she could represent everything, from a fine lady to a shepherdess; she had the faculty as she might have had a fine voice or long hair. She couldn't spell and she loved beer, but she had two or three "points," and practice, and a knack, and mother-wit, and a whimsical sensibility, and a love of the theatre, and seven sisters, and not an ounce of respect, especially for the *h*. The first thing my visitors saw was that her umbrella was wet, and in their spotless perfection they visibly winced at it. The rain had come on since their arrival.

"I'm all in a soak; there *was* a mess of people in the 'bus. I wish you lived near a stytion," said Miss Churm. I requested her to get ready as quickly as possible, and she passed into the room in which she always changed her dress. But before going out she asked me what she was to get into this time.

"It's the Russian princess, don't you know?" I answered; "the one with the 'golden eyes,' in black velvet, for the long thing in the *Cheapside*."[2]

"Golden eyes? I *say!*" cried Miss Churm, while my companions watched her with intensity as she withdrew. She always arranged herself, when she was late, before I could turn around; and I kept my visitors a little on purpose, so that they might get an idea, from seeing her, what would be expected of themselves. I mentioned that she was quite my notion of an excellent model—she was really very clever.

"Do you think she looks like a Russian princess?" Major Monarch asked with lurking alarm.

"When I make her, yes."

"Oh if you have to *make* her—!" he reasoned, not without point.

"That's the most you can ask. There are so many who are not makeable."

"Well now, *here's* a lady"—and with a persuasive smile he passed his arm into his wife's—"who's already made!"

"Oh I'm not a Russian princess," Mrs. Monarch protested a little coldly. I could see she had known some and didn't like them. There at once was a complication of a kind I never had to fear with Miss Churm.

---

8. Large suitcases.
9. Residential district in West London.
1. Native of London, especially the East End. The cockney dialect is known for dropping *h*'s;

e.g., *hair* would be pronounced *air*.
2. Imaginary magazine named after a main business street in London.

This young lady came back in black velvet—the gown was rather rusty and very low on her lean shoulders—and with a Japanese fan in her red hands. I reminded her that in the scene I was doing she had to look over some one's head. "I forget whose it is; but it doesn't matter. Just look over a head."

"I'd rather look over a stove," said Miss Churm; and she took her station near the fire. She fell into position, settled herself into a tall attitude, gave a certain backward inclination to her head and a certain forward droop to her fan, and looked, at least to my prejudiced sense, distinguished and charming, foreign and dangerous. We left her looking so while I went downstairs with Major and Mrs. Monarch.

"I believe I could come about as near it as that," said Mrs. Monarch.

"Oh, you think she's shabby, but you must allow for the alchemy of art."

However, they went off with an evident increase of comfort founded on their demonstrable advantage in being the real thing. I could fancy them shuddering over Miss Churm. She was very droll about them when I went back, for I told her what they wanted.

"Well, if *she* can sit I'll tyke to bookkeeping," said my model.

"She's very ladylike," I replied as an innocent form of aggravation.

"So much the worse for *you*. That means she can't turn round."

"She'll do for the fashionable novels."

"Oh yes, she'll *do* for them!" my model humorously declared. "Ain't they bad enough without her?" I had often sociably denounced them to Miss Churm.

III

It was for the elucidation of a mystery in one of these works that I first tried Mrs. Monarch. Her husband came with her, to be useful if necessary—it was sufficiently clear that as a general thing he would prefer to come with her. At first I wondered if this were for "propriety's" sake—if he were going to be jealous and meddling. The idea was too tiresome, and if it had been confirmed it would speedily have brought our acquaintance to a close. But I soon saw there was nothing in it and that if he accompanied Mrs. Monarch it was—in addition to the chance of being wanted—simply because he had nothing else to do. When they were separate his occupation was gone and they never *had* been separate. I judged rightly that in their awkward situation their close union was their main comfort and that this union had no weak spot. It was a real marriage, an encouragement to the hesitating, a nut for pessimists to crack. Their address was humble—I remember afterwards thinking it had been the only thing about them that was really professional—and I could fancy the lamentable lodgings in which the Major would have been left alone. He could sit there more or less grimly with his wife—he couldn't sit there anyhow without her.

He had too much tact to try and make himself agreeable when he couldn't be useful; so when I was too absorbed in my work to talk he simply sat and waited. But I liked to hear him talk—it made my work, when not interrupting it, less mechanical, less special. To listen to him was to combine the excitement of going out with the economy of staying at home. There was only one hindrance—that I seemed not to know any of the people this brilliant couple had known. I think he wondered extremely, during the term of our intercourse, whom the deuce I *did* know. He hadn't a stray sixpence of an idea to fumble for, so we didn't spin it very fine; we confined ourselves to questions of leather and even of liquor—saddlers and breeches-makers and how to get excellent claret cheap—and matters like "good trains" and the habits of small game. His lore on these last subjects was astonishing—he managed to interweave the station-master with the ornithologist. When he couldn't talk about greater things he could talk cheerfully about smaller, and since I couldn't accompany him into reminiscences of the fashionable world he could lower the conversation without a visible effort to my level.

So earnest a desire to please was touching in a man who could so easily have knocked one down. He looked after the fire and had an opinion on the draught of the stove without my asking him, and I could see that he thought many of my arrangements not half knowing. I remember telling him that if I were only rich I'd offer him a salary to come and teach me how to live. Sometimes he gave a random sigh of which the essence might have been: "Give me even such a bare old barrack as *this,* and I'd do something with it!" When I wanted to use him he came alone; which was an illustration of the superior courage of women. His wife could bear her solitary second floor, and she was in general more discreet; showing by various small reserves that she was alive to the propriety of keeping our relations markedly professional—not letting them slide into sociability. She wished it to remain clear that she and the Major were employed, not cultivated, and if she approved of me as a superior, who could be kept in his place, she never thought me quite good enough for an equal.

She sat with great intensity, giving the whole of her mind to it, and was capable of remaining for an hour almost as motionless as before a photographer's lens. I could see she had been photographed often, but somehow the very habit that made her good for that purpose unfitted her for mine. At first I was extremely pleased with her ladylike air, and it was a satisfaction, on coming to follow her lines, to see how good they were and how far they could lead the pencil. But after a little skirmishing I began to find her too insurmountably stiff; do what I would with it my drawing looked like a photograph or a copy of a photograph. Her figure had no variety of expression—she herself had no sense of variety. You may say that this was my business and was only a question of placing her. Yet I placed her in every conceivable position and she managed to obliterate their differences. She was always a lady certainly, and into the bargain was always the same lady. She was the real thing, but always the same thing. There were moments when I rather writhed under the serenity of her confidence that she *was* the real thing. All her dealings with me and all her husband's were an implication that this was lucky for *me.* Meanwhile I found myself trying to invent types that approached her own, instead of making her own transform itself—in the clever way that was not impossible for instance to poor Miss Churm. Arrange as I would and take the precautions I would, she always came out, in my pictures, too tall—landing me in the dilemma of having represented a fascinating woman as seven feet high, which (out of respect perhaps to my own very much scantier inches) was far from my idea of such a personage.

The case was worse with the Major—nothing I could do would keep *him* down, so that he became useful only for representation of brawny giants. I adored variety and range, I cherished human accidents, the illustrative note; I wanted to characterise closely, and the thing in the world I most hated was the danger of being ridden by a type. I had quarrelled with some of my friends about it; I had parted company with them for maintaining that one *had* to be, and that if the type was beautiful—witness Raphael and Leonardo[3]—the servitude was only a gain. I was neither Leonardo nor Raphael—I might only be a presumptuous young modern searcher; but I held that everything was to be sacrificed sooner than character. When they claimed that the obsessional form could easily *be* character I retorted, perhaps superficially, "Whose?" It couldn't be everybody's—it might end in being nobody's.

After I had drawn Mrs. Monarch a dozen times I felt surer even than before that the value of such a model as Miss Churm resided precisely in the fact that she had no positive stamp, combined of course with the other fact that what she did have was a curious and inexplicable talent for imitation. Her usual appearance was like a curtain which she could draw up at request for a capital performance. This performance was simply suggestive; but it was a word to the wise—it was vivid and pretty. Sometimes even I thought it, though she was plain herself, too insipidly pretty; I made it a reproach to her that the figures drawn from her were monotonously (*bêtement*,[4] as we used to say) graceful. Nothing made her more angry: it was so much her pride to feel she could sit for characters that had nothing in common with each other. She would accuse me at such moments of taking away her "reputytion."

It suffered a certain shrinkage, this queer quantity, from the repeated visits of my new friends. Miss Churm was greatly in demand, never in want of employment, so I had no scruple in putting her off occasionally, to try them more at my ease. It was certainly amusing at first to do the real thing—it was amusing to do Major Monarch's trousers. There *were* the real thing, even if he did come out colossal. It was amusing to do his wife's back hair—it was so mathematically neat—and the particular "smart" tension of her tight stays. She lent herself especially to positions in which the face was somewhat averted or blurred; she abounded in ladylike back views and *profils perdus*.[5] When she stood erect she took naturally one of the attitudes in which court-painters represent queens and princesses; so that I found myself wondering whether, to draw out this accomplishment, I couldn't get the editor of the *Cheapside* to publish a really royal romance, "A Tale of Buckingham Palace." Sometimes however the real thing and the make-believe came into contact; by which I mean that Miss Churm, keeping an appointment or coming to make one on days when I had much work in hand, encountered her invidious rivals. The encounter was not on their part, for they noticed her no more than if she had been the housemaid; not from intentional loftiness, but simply because as yet, professionally, they didn't know how to fraternise, as I could imagine they would have liked—or at least that the Major would. They couldn't talk about the omnibus—they always walked; and they didn't know what else to try—she wasn't interested in good trains or cheap claret. Besides, they must have felt—in the air—that she was amused at them, secretly derisive of their ever knowing how. She wasn't a person to conceal the limits of her faith if she had had a chance to show them. On the other hand Mrs. Monarch didn't think her tidy; for why else did she take pains to say to me—it was going out of the way, for Mrs. Monarch—that she didn't like dirty women?

3. Leonardo da Vinci (1452–1519), Florentine painter, sculptor, architect, and engineer. Raffaello Santi or Sanzio (1483–1520), Italian painter.

4. Foolishly (French).
5. Lost profiles (French); poses in which the subject turns away.

One day when my young lady happened to be present with my other sitters—she even dropped in, when it was convenient, for a chat—I asked her to be so good as to lend a hand in getting tea, a service with which she was familiar and which was one of a class that, living as I did in a small way, with slender domestic resources, I often appealed to my models to render. They liked to lay hands on my property, to break the sitting, and sometimes the china—it made them feel Bohemian. The next time I saw Miss Churm after this incident she surprised me greatly by making a scene about it—she accused me of having wished to humiliate her. She hadn't resented the outrage at the time, but had seemed obliging and amused, enjoying the comedy of asking Mrs. Monarch, who sat vague and silent, whether she would have cream and sugar, and putting an exaggerated simper into the question. She had tried intonations—as if she too wished to pass for the real thing—till I was afraid my other visitors would take offence.

Oh they were determined not to do this, and their touching patience was the measure of their great need. They would sit by the hour, uncomplaining, till I was ready to use them; they would come back on the chance of being wanted and would walk away cheerfully if it failed. I used to go to the door with them to see in what magnificent order they retreated. I tried to find other employment for them—I introduced them to several artists. But they didn't "take," for reasons I could appreciate, and I became rather anxiously aware that after such disappointments they fell back upon me with a heavier weight. They did me the honour to think me most *their* form. They weren't romantic enough for the painters, and in those days there were few serious workers in black-and-white. Besides, they had an eye to the great job I had mentioned to them—they had secretly set their hearts on supplying the right essence for my pictorial vindication of our fine novelist. They knew that for this undertaking I should want no costume-effects, none of the frippery of past ages—that it was a case in which everything would be contemporary and satirical and presumably genteel. If I could work them into it their future would be assured, for the labour would of course be long and the occupation steady.

One day Mrs. Monarch came without her husband—she explained his absence by his having had to go to the City.[6] While she sat there in her usual relaxed majesty there came at the door a knock which I immediately recognised as the subdued appeal of a model out of work. It was followed by the entrance of a young man whom I at once saw to be a foreigner and who proved in fact an Italian acquainted with no English word but my name, which he uttered in a way that made it seem to include all others. I hadn't then visited his country, nor was I proficient in his tongue; but as he was not so meanly constituted—what Italian is?—as to depend only on that member for expression he conveyed to me, in familiar but graceful mimicry, that he was in search of exactly the employment in which the lady before me was engaged. I was not struck with him at first, and while I continued to draw I dropped few signs of interest or encouragement. He stood his ground however—not importunately, but with a dumb dog-like fidelity in his eyes that amounted to innocent impudence, the manner of a devoted servant—he might have been in the house for years—unjustly suspected. Suddenly

6. London. The "City" also specifically means the old part of London around St. Paul's Cathedral, especially the financial and legal institutions there.

it struck me that this very attitude and expression made a picture; whereupon I told him to sit down and wait till I should be free. There was another picture in the way he obeyed me, and I observed as I worked that there were others still in the way he looked wonderingly, with his head thrown back, about the high studio. He might have been crossing himself in Saint Peter's. Before I finished I said to myself "The fellow's a bankrupt orange-monger, but a treasure."

When Mrs. Monarch withdrew he passed across the room like a flash to open the door for her, standing there with the rapt pure gaze of the young Dante spellbound by the young Beatrice.[7] As I never insisted, in such situations, on the blankness of the British domestic, I reflected that he had the making of a servant—and I needed one, but couldn't pay him to be only that—as well as of a model; in short I resolved to adopt my bright adventurer if he would agree to officiate in the double capacity. He jumped at my offer, and in the event my rashness—for I had really known nothing about him— wasn't brought home to me. He proved a sympathetic though a desultory ministrant, and had in a wonderful degree the *sentiment de la pose.*[8] It was uncultivated, instinctive, a part of the happy instinct that had guided him to my door and helped him to spell out my name on the card nailed to it. He had had no other introduction to me than a guess, from the shape of my high north window, seen outside, that my place was a studio and that as a studio it would contain an artist. He had wandered to England in search of fortune, like other itinerants, and had embarked, with a partner and a small green hand-cart, on the sale of penny ices. The ices had melted away and the partner had dissolved in their train. My young man wore tight yellow trousers with reddish stripes and his name was Oronte. He was sallow but fair, and when I put him into some old clothes of my own he looked like an Englishman. He was as good as Miss Churm, who could look, when requested, like an Italian.

IV

I thought Mrs. Monarch's face slightly convulsed when, on her coming back with her husband, she found Oronte installed. It was strange to have to recognise in a scrap of a lazzarone[9] a competitor to her magnificent Major. It was she who scented danger first, for the Major was anecdotically unconscious. But Oronte gave us tea, with a hundred eager confusions—he had never been concerned in so queer a process—and I think she thought better of me for having at last an "establishment." They saw a couple of drawings that I had made of the establishment, and Mrs. Monarch hinted that it never would have struck her he had sat for them. "Now the drawings you make from *us,* they look exactly like us," she reminded me, smiling in triumph; and I recognised that this was indeed just their defect. When I drew the Monarchs I couldn't anyhow get away from them—get into the character I wanted to represent; and I hadn't the least desire my model should be discoverable in my picture. Miss Churm never was, and Mrs. Monarch thought I hid her, very properly, because she was vulgar; whereas

---

7. Dante Alighieri (1265–1321), Italian poet, first saw Beatrice Portinari when they were both nine. Though he saw her only a few times, she made a lasting impression on him and became his ideal, his life's inspiration, and the direct agent of his salvation (as his greatest work, *The Divine Comedy,* makes clear).
8. Instinct for striking poses (French).
9. Beggar (Italian).

if she was lost it was only as the dead who go to heaven are lost—in the gain of an angel the more.

By this time I had got a certain start with "Rutland Ramsay," the first novel in the great projected series; that is I had produced a dozen drawings, several with the help of the Major and his wife, and I had sent them in for approval. My understanding with the publishers, as I have already hinted, had been that I was to be left to do my work, in this particular case, as I liked, with the whole book committed to me; but my connexion with the rest of the series was only contingent. There were moments when, frankly, it *was* a comfort to have the real thing under one's hand; for there were characters in "Rutland Ramsay" that were very much like it. There were people presumably as erect as the Major and women of as good a fashion as Mrs. Monarch. There was a great deal of country-house life—treated, it is true, in a fine fanciful ironical generalised way—and there was a considerable implication of knickerbockers and kilts.[1] There were certain things I had to settle at the outset; such things for instance as the exact appearance of the hero and the particular bloom and figure of the heroine. The author of course gave me a lead, but there was a margin for interpretation. I took the Monarchs into my confidence, I told them frankly what I was about, I mentioned my embarrassments and alternatives. "Oh take *him!*" Mrs. Monarch murmured sweetly, looking at her husband; and "What could you want better than my wife?" the Major enquired with the comfortable candour that now prevailed between us.

I wasn't obliged to answer these remarks—I was only obliged to place my sitters. I wasn't easy in mind, and I postponed a little timidly perhaps the solving of my question. The book was a large canvas, the other figures were numerous, and I worked off at first some of the episodes in which the hero and the heroine were not concerned. When once I had set *them* up I should have to stick to them—I couldn't make my young man seven feet high in one place and five feet nine in another. I inclined on the whole to the latter measurement, though the Major more than once reminded me that *he* looked about as young as any one. It was indeed quite possible to arrange him, for the figure, so that it would have been difficult to detect his age. After the spontaneous Oronte had been with me a month, and after I had given him to understand several times over that his native exuberance would presently constitute an insurmountable barrier to our further intercourse, I waked to a sense of his heroic capacity. He was only five feet seven, but the remaining inches were latent. I tried him almost secretly at first, for I was really rather afraid of the judgment my other models would pass on such a choice. If they regarded Miss Churm as little better than a snare what would they think of the representation by a person so little the real thing as an Italian street-vendor of a protagonist formed by a public school?

If I went a little in fear of them it wasn't because they bullied me, because they had got an oppressive foothold, but because in their really pathetic decorum and mysteriously permanent newness they counted on me so intensely. I was therefore very glad when Jack Hawley came home: he was always of such good counsel. He painted badly himself, but there was no one like him for putting his finger on the place. He had been absent from

---

1. Knickerbockers (close-fitting short pants gathered at the knee) and kilts (knee-length pleated skirts, usually of tartan, worn by Scottish men) suggest a rural, outdoor attire.

England for a year; he had been somewhere—I don't remember where—to get a fresh eye. I was in a good deal of dread of any such organ, but we were old friends; he had been away for months and a sense of emptiness was creeping into my life. I hadn't dodged a missile for a year.

He came back with a fresh eye, but with the same old black velvet blouse, and the first evening he spent in my studio we smoked cigarettes till the small hours. He had done no work himself, he had only got the eye; so the field was clear for the production of my little things. He wanted to see what I had produced for the *Cheapside,* but he was disappointed in the exhibition. That at least seemed the meaning of two or three comprehensive groans which, as he lounged on my big divan, his leg folded under him, looking at my latest drawings, issued from his lips with the smoke of the cigarette.

"What's the matter with you?" I asked.

"What's the matter with *you?*"

"Nothing save that I'm mystified."

"You are indeed. You're quite off the hinge. What's the meaning of this new fad?" And he tossed me, with visible irreverence, a drawing in which I happened to have depicted both my elegant models. I asked if he didn't think it good, and he replied that it struck him as execrable, given the sort of thing I had always represented myself to him as wishing to arrive at; but I let that pass—I was so anxious to see exactly what he meant. The two figures in the picture looked colossal, but I supposed this was *not* what he meant, inasmuch as, for aught he knew the contrary, I might have been trying for some such effect. I maintained that I was working exactly in the same way as when he last had done me the honour to tell me I might do something some day. "Well, there's a screw loose somewhere," he answered; "wait a bit and I'll discover it." I depended upon him to do so: where else was the fresh eye? But he produced at last nothing more luminous than "I don't know—I don't like your types." This was lame for a critic who had never consented to discuss with me anything but the question of execution, the direction of strokes and the mystery of values.

"In the drawings you've been looking at I think my types are very handsome."

"Oh they won't do!"

"I've been working with new models."

"I see you have. *They* won't do."

"Are you very sure of that?"

"Absolutely—they're stupid."

"You mean *I* am—for I ought to get round that."

"You *can't*—with such people. Who are they?"

I told him, so far as was necessary, and he concluded heartlessly: "*Ce sont des gens qu'il faut mettre à la porte.*"[2]

"You've never seen them; they're awfully good"—I flew to their defence.

"Not seen them? Why all this recent work of yours drops to pieces with them. It's all I want to see of them."

"No one else has said anything against it—the *Cheapside* people are pleased."

"Everyone else is an ass, and the *Cheapside* people the biggest asses of all. Come, don't pretend at this time of day to have pretty illusions about the

2. Such people should be shown the door (French).

public, especially about publishers and editors. It's not for *such* animals you work—it's for those who know, *coloro che sanno;*[3] so keep straight for *me* if you can't keep straight for yourself. There was a certain sort of thing you used to try for—and a very good thing it was. But this twaddle isn't *in* it." When I talked with Hawley later about "Rutland Ramsay" and its possible successors he declared that I must get back into my boat again or I should go to the bottom. His voice in short was the voice of warning.

I noted the warning, but I didn't turn my friends out of doors. They bored me a good deal; but the very fact that they bored me admonished me not to sacrifice them—if there was anything to be done with them—simply to irritation. As I look back at this phase they seem to me to have pervaded my life not a little. I have a vision of them as most of the time in my studio, seated against the wall on an old velvet bench to be out of the way, and resembling the while a pair of patient courtiers in a royal ante-chamber. I'm convinced that during the coldest weeks of the winter they held their ground because it saved them fire. Their newness was losing its gloss, and it was impossible not to feel them objects of charity. Whenever Miss Churm arrived they went away, and after I was fairly launched in "Rutland Ramsay" Miss Churm arrived pretty often. They managed to express to me tacitly that they supposed I wanted her for the low life of the book, and I let them suppose it, since they had attempted to study the work—it was lying about the studio—without discovering that it dealt only with the highest circles. They had dipped into the most brilliant of our novelists without deciphering many passages. I still took an hour from them, now and again, in spite of Jack Hawley's warning: it would be time enough to dismiss them, if dismissal should be necessary, when the rigour of the season was over. Hawley had made their acquaintance—he had met them at my fireside—and thought them a ridiculous pair. Learning that he was a painter they tried to approach him, to show him too that they were the real thing; but he looked at them, across the big room, as if they were miles away: they were a compendium of everything he most objected to in the social system of his country. Such people as that, all convention and patent-leather, with ejaculations that stopped conversation, had no business in a studio. A studio was a place to learn to see, and how could you see through a pair of feather-beds?

The main inconvenience I suffered at their hands was that at first I was shy of letting it break upon them that my artful little servant had begun to sit to me for "Rutland Ramsay." They knew I had been odd enough—they were prepared by this time to allow oddity to artists—to pick a foreign vagabond out of the streets when I might have had a person with whiskers and credentials, but it was some time before they learned how high I rated his accomplishments. They found him in an attitude more than once, but they never doubted I was doing him as an organ-grinder. There were several things they never guessed, and one of them was that for a striking scene in the novel, in which a footman briefly figured, it occurred to me to make use of Major Monarch as the menial. I kept putting this off, I didn't like to ask him to don the livery—besides the difficulty of finding a livery to fit him. At last, one day late in the winter, when I was at work on the despised Oronte, who caught one's idea on the wing, and was in the glow of feeling myself go

---

3. A misquotation of a phrase Dante applied to Aristotle in *The Divine Comedy*, "Inferno," 4.131, which reads, *"el maestro di color che sanno,"* literally, "the master of those who know."

very straight, they came in, the Major and his wife, with their society laugh about nothing (there was less and less to laugh at); came in like country-callers—they always reminded me of that—who have walked across the park after church and are presently persuaded to stay to luncheon. Luncheon was over, but they could stay to tea—I knew they wanted it. The fit was on me, however, and I couldn't let my ardour cool and my work wait, with the fading daylight, while my model prepared it. So I asked Mrs. Monarch if she would mind laying it out—a request which for an instant brought all the blood to her face. Her eyes were on her husband's for a second, and some mute telegraphy passed between them. Their folly was over the next instant; his cheerful shrewdness put an end to it. So far from pitying their wounded pride, I must add, I was moved to give it as complete a lesson as I could. They bustled about together and got out the cups and saucers and made the kettle boil. I know they felt as if they were waiting on my servant, and when the tea was prepared I said: "He'll have a cup, please—he's tired." Mrs. Monarch brought him one where he stood, and he took it from her as if he had been a gentleman at a party squeezing a crush-hat with an elbow.

Then it came over me that she had made a great effort for me—made it with a kind of nobleness—and that I owed her a compensation. Each time I saw her after this I wondered what the compensation could be. I couldn't go on doing the wrong thing to oblige them. Oh it *was* the wrong thing, the stamp of the work for which they sat—Hawley was not the only person to say it now. I sent in a large number of the drawings I had made for "Rutland Ramsay," and I received a warning that was more to the point than Hawley's. The artistic adviser of the house for which I was working was of opinion that many of my illustrations were not what had been looked for. Most of these illustrations were the subjects in which the Monarchs had figured. Without going into the question of what *had* been looked for, I had to face the fact that at this rate I shouldn't get the other books to do. I hurled myself in despair on Miss Churm—I put her through all her paces. I not only adopted Oronte publicly as my hero, but one morning when the Major looked in to see if I didn't require him to finish a *Cheapside* figure for which he had begun to sit the week before, I told him I had changed my mind—I'd do the drawing from my man. At this my visitor turned pale and stood looking at me. "Is *he* your idea of an English gentleman?" he asked.

I was disappointed, I was nervous, I wanted to get on with my work; so I replied with irritation: "Oh my dear Major—I can't be ruined for *you!*"

It was a horrid speech, but he stood another moment—after which, without a word, he quitted the studio. I drew a long breath, for I said to myself that I shouldn't see him again. I hadn't told him definitely that I was in danger of having my work rejected, but I was vexed at his not having felt the catastrophe in the air, read with me the moral of our fruitless collaboration, the lesson that in the deceptive atmosphere of art even the highest respectability may fail of being plastic.

I didn't owe my friends money, but I did see them again. They reappeared together three days later, and, given all the other facts, there was something tragic in that one. It was a clear proof they could find nothing else in life to do. They had threshed the matter out in a dismal conference—they had digested the bad news that they were not in for the series. If they weren't useful to me even for the *Cheapside* their function seemed difficult to determine, and I could only judge at first that they had come, forgivingly, decorously, to take a last leave. This made me rejoice in secret that I had little leisure for a scene; for I had placed both my other models in position together and I was pegging away at a drawing from which I hoped to derive glory. It had been suggested by the passage in which Rutland Ramsay, drawing up a chair to Artemisia's piano-stool, says extraordinary things to her while she ostensibly fingers out a difficult piece of music. I had done Miss Churm at the piano before—it was an attitude in which she knew how to take on an absolutely poetic grace. I wished the two figures to "compose" together with intensity, and my little Italian had entered perfectly into my conception. The pair were vividly before me, the piano had been pulled out; it was a charming show of blended youth and murmured love, which I had only to catch and keep. My visitors stood and looked at it, and I was friendly to them over my shoulder.

They made no response, but I was used to silent company and went on with my work, only a little disconcerted—even though exhilarated by the sense that *this* was at least the ideal thing—at not having got rid of them after all. Presently I heard Mrs. Monarch's sweet voice beside or rather above me: "I wish her hair were a little better done." I looked up and she was staring with a strange fixedness at Miss Churm, whose back was turned to her. "Do you mind my just touching it?" she went on—a question which made me spring up for an instant as with the instinctive fear that she might do the young lady a harm. But she quieted me with a glance I shall never forget—I confess I should like to have been able to paint *that*—and went for a moment to my model. She spoke to her softly, laying a hand on her shoulder and bending over her; and as the girl, understanding, gratefully assented, she disposed her rough curls, with a few quick passes, in such a way as to make Miss Churm's head twice as charming. It was one of the most heroic personal services I've ever seen rendered. Then Mrs. Monarch turned away with a low sigh and, looking about her as if for something to do, stooped to the floor with a noble humility and picked up a dirty rag that had dropped out of my paint-box.

The Major meanwhile had also been looking for something to do, and, wandering to the other end of the studio, saw before him my breakfast-things neglected, unremoved. "I say, can't I be useful *here?*" he called out to me with an irrepressible quaver. I assented with a laugh that I fear was awkward, and for the next ten minutes, while I worked, I heard the light clatter of china and the tinkle of spoons and glass. Mrs. Monarch assisted her husband—they washed up my crockery, they put it away. They wandered off into my little scullery, and I afterwards found that they had cleaned my knives and that my slender stock of plate had an unprecedented surface. When it came over me, the latent eloquence of what they were doing, I confess that my drawing was blurred for a moment—the picture swam. They had accepted their failure, but they couldn't accept their fate. They had bowed their heads in bewilderment to the perverse and cruel law in virtue of which the real thing could be so much less precious than the unreal; but they didn't want to starve. If my servants were my models, then my models might be my servants. They would reverse the parts—the others would sit for the ladies and gentlemen and *they* would do the work. They would still be in the studio—it was an intense dumb appeal to me not to turn them out. "Take us on," they wanted to say—"we'll do *anything.*"

My pencil dropped from my hand; my sitting was spoiled and I got rid of my sitters, who were also evidently rather mystified and awestruck. Then, alone with the Major and his wife I had a most uncomfortable moment. He put their prayer into a single sentence: "I say, you know—just let *us* do for you, can't you?" I couldn't—it was dreadful to see them emptying my slops; but I pretended I could, to oblige them, for about a week. Then I gave them a sum of money to go away, and I never saw them again. I obtained the remaining books, but my friend Hawley repeats that Major and Mrs. Monarch did me a permanent harm, got me into false ways. If it be true I'm content to have paid the price—for the memory.

1892, 1909

The Beast in the Jungle[1]

I

What determined the speech that startled him in the course of their encounter scarcely matters, being probably but some words spoken by himself quite without intention—spoken as they lingered and slowly moved together after their renewal of acquaintance. He had been conveyed by friends an hour or two before to the house at which she was staying; the party of visitors at the other house, of whom he was one, and thanks to whom it was his theory, as always, that he was lost in the crowd, had been invited over to luncheon. There had been after luncheon much dispersal, all in the interest of the original motive, a view of Weatherend itself and the fine things, intrinsic features, pictures, heirlooms, treasures of all the arts, that made the place almost famous; and the great rooms were so numerous that guests could wander at their will, hang back from the principal group and in cases where they took such matters with the last seriousness give themselves up to mysterious appreciations and measurements. There were persons to be observed, singly or in couples, bending toward objects in out-of-the-way corners with their hands on their knees and their heads nodding quite as with the emphasis of an excited sense of smell. When they were two they either mingled their sounds of ecstasy or melted into silences of even deeper import, so that there were aspects of the occasion that gave it for Marcher much the air of the "look round," previous to a sale highly advertised, that excites or quenches, as may be, the dream of acquisition. The dream of acquisition at Weatherend would have had to be wild indeed, and John Marcher found himself, among such suggestions, disconcerted almost equally by the presence of those who knew too much and by that of those who knew nothing. The great rooms caused so much poetry and history to press upon him that he needed some straying apart to feel in a proper relation with them, though this impulse was not, as happened, like the gloating of some of his companions, to be compared to the movements of a dog sniffing a cupboard. It had an issue promptly enough in a direction that was not to have been calculated.

It led, briefly, in the course of the October afternoon, to his closer meeting with May Bartram, whose face, a reminder, yet not quite a remembrance, as they sat much separated at a very long table, had begun merely by

---

1. James initially recorded the idea for this story in 1895, but it first appeared in the collection *The Better Sort* (1903). It was reprinted, with minor revisions, in the *Altar of the Dead* volume of the New York edition, Vol. 17 (1909), the source of the text printed here.

troubling him rather pleasantly. It affected him as the sequel of something of which he had lost the beginning. He knew it, and for the time quite welcomed it, as a continuation, but didn't know what it continued, which was an interest or an amusement the greater as he was also somehow aware—yet without a direct sign from her—that the young woman herself hadn't lost the thread. She hadn't lost it, but she wouldn't give it back to him, he saw, without some putting forth of his hand for it; and he not only saw that, but saw several things more, things odd enough in the light of the fact that at the moment some accident of grouping brought them face to face he was still merely fumbling with the idea that any contact between them in the past would have had no importance. If it had had no importance he scarcely knew why his actual impression of her should so seem to have so much; the answer to which, however, was that in such a life as they all appeared to be leading for the moment one could but take things as they came. He was satisfied, without in the least being able to say why, that this young lady might roughly have ranked in the house as a poor relation; satisfied also that she was not there on a brief visit, but was more or less a part of the establishment—almost a working, a remunerated part. Didn't she enjoy at periods a protection that she paid for by helping, among other services, to show the place and explain it, deal with the tiresome people, answer questions about the dates of the building, the styles of the furniture, the authorship of the pictures, the favourite haunts of the ghost? It wasn't that she looked as if you could have given her shillings—it was impossible to look less so. Yet when she finally drifted toward him, distinctly handsome, though ever so much older—older than when he had seen her before—it might have been as an effect of her guessing that he had, within the couple of hours, devoted more imagination to her than to all the others put together, and had thereby penetrated to a kind of truth that the others were too stupid for. She *was* there on harder terms than any one; she was there as a consequence of things suffered, one way and another, in the interval of years; and she remembered him very much as she was remembered—only a good deal better.

By the time they at last thus came to speech they were alone in one of the rooms—remarkable for a fine portrait over the chimney-place—out of which their friends had passed, and the charm of it was that even before they had spoken they had practically arranged with each other to stay behind for talk. The charm, happily, was in other things too—partly in there being scarce a spot at Weatherend without something to stay behind for. It was in the way the autumn day looked into the high windows as it waned; the way the red light, breaking at the close from under a low sombre sky, reached out in a long shaft and played over old wainscots, old tapestry, old gold, old colour. It was most of all perhaps in the way she came to him as if, since she had been turned on to deal with the simpler sort, he might, should he choose to keep the whole thing down, just take her mild attention for a part of her general business. As soon as he heard her voice, however, the gap was filled up and the missing link supplied; the slight irony he divined in her attitude lost its advantage. He almost jumped at it to get there before her. "I met you years and years ago in Rome. I remember all about it." She confessed to disappointment—she had been so sure he didn't; and to prove how well he did he began to pour forth the particular recollections that popped up as he called for them. Her face and her voice, all at his service now, worked the miracle—the impression operating like the torch of a lamplighter who touches into flame, one by one, a long row of gas-jets. Marcher flattered himself the illumination was brilliant, yet he was really still more pleased on her showing him, with amusement, that in his haste to make everything right he had got most things rather wrong. It hadn't been at Rome—it had been at Naples; and it hadn't been eight years before—it had been more nearly ten. She hadn't been, either, with her uncle and aunt, but with her mother and her brother; in addition to which it was not with the Pembles *he* had been, but with the Boyers, coming down in their company from Rome—a point on which she insisted, a little to his confusion, and as to which she had her evidence in hand. The Boyers she had known, but didn't know the Pembles, though she had heard of them, and it was the people he was with who had made them acquainted. The incident of the thunderstorm that had raged round them with such violence as to drive them for refuge into an excavation—this incident had not occurred at the Palace of the Cæsars, but at Pompeii,[2] on an occasion when they had been present there at an important find.

He accepted her amendments, he enjoyed her corrections, though the moral of them was, she pointed out, that he *really* didn't remember the least thing about her; and he only felt it as a drawback that when all was made strictly historic there didn't appear much of anything left. They lingered together still, she neglecting her office—for from the moment he was so clever she had no proper right to him—and both neglecting the house, just waiting as to see if a memory or two more wouldn't again breathe on them. It hadn't taken them many minutes, after all, to put down on the table, like the cards of a pack, those that constituted their respective hands; only what came out was that the pack was unfortunately not perfect—that the past, invoked, invited, encouraged, could give them, naturally, no more than it had. It had made them anciently meet—her at twenty, him at twenty-five; but nothing was so strange, they seemed to say to each other, as that, while so occupied, it hadn't done a little more for them. They looked at each other as with the feeling of an occasion missed; the present would have been so much better if the other, in the far distance, in the foreign land, hadn't been so stupidly meagre. There weren't apparently, all counted, more than a dozen little old things that had succeeded in coming to pass between them; trivialities of youth, simplicities of freshness, stupidities of ignorance, small possible germs, but too deeply buried—too deeply (didn't it seem?) to sprout after so many years. Marcher could only feel he ought to have rendered her some service—saved her from a capsized boat in the Bay or at least recovered her dressing-bag, filched from her cab in the streets of Naples by a lazzarone[3] with a stiletto. Or it would have been nice if he could have been taken with fever all alone at his hotel, and she could have come to look after him, to write to his people, to drive him out in convalescence. *Then* they would be in possession of the something or other that their actual show seemed to lack. It yet somehow presented itself, this show, as too good to be spoiled; so that they were reduced for a few minutes more to wondering a little helplessly why—since they seemed to know a certain number of the same people— their reunion had been so long averted. They didn't use that name for it, but their delay from minute to minute to join the others was a kind of confession that they didn't quite want it to be a failure. Their attempted supposition of reasons for their not having met but showed how little they knew of each

---

2. Pompeii is near Naples, not Rome.   3. Beggar (Italian).

other. There came in fact a moment when Marcher felt a positive pang. It was vain to pretend she was an old friend, for all the communities were wanting, in spite of which it was as an old friend that he saw she would have suited him. He had new ones enough—was surrounded with them for instance on the stage of the other house; as a new one he probably wouldn't have so much as noticed her. He would have liked to invent something, get her to make-believe with him that some passage of a romantic or critical kind *had* originally occurred. He was really almost reaching out in imagination—as against time—for something that would do, and saying to himself that if it didn't come this sketch of a fresh start would show for quite awkwardly bungled. They would separate, and now for no second or no third chance. They would have tried and not succeeded. Then it was, just at the turn, as he afterwards made it out to himself, that, everything else failing, she herself decided to take up the case and, as it were, save the situation. He felt as soon as she spoke that she had been consciously keeping back what she said and hoping to get on without it; a scruple in her that immensely touched him when, by the end of three or four minutes more, he was able to measure it. What she brought out, at any rate, quite cleared the air and supplied the link—the link it was so odd he should frivolously have managed to lose.

"You know you told me something I've never forgotten and that again and again has made me think of you since; it was that tremendously hot day when we went to Sorrento,[4] across the bay, for the breeze. What I allude to was what you said to me, on the way back, as we sat under the awning of the boat enjoying the cool. Have you forgotten?"

He had forgotten and was even more surprised than ashamed. But the great thing was that he saw in this no vulgar reminder of any "sweet" speech. The vanity of women had long memories, but she was making no claim on him of a compliment or a mistake. With another woman, a totally different one, he might have feared the recall possibly of even some imbecile "offer." So, in having to say that he had indeed forgotten, he was conscious rather of a loss than of a gain; he already saw an interest in the matter of her mention. "I try to think—but I give it up. Yet I remember the Sorrento day."

"I'm not very sure you do," May Bartram after a moment said; "and I'm not very sure I ought to want you to. It's dreadful to bring a person back at any time to what he was ten years before. If you've lived away from it," she smiled, "so much the better."

"Ah if *you* haven't why should I?" he asked.

"Lived away, you mean, from what I myself was?"

"From what *I* was. I was of course an ass," Marcher went on; "but I would rather know from you just the sort of ass I was than—from the moment you have something in your mind—not know anything."

Still, however, she hesitated. "But if you've completely ceased to be that sort—?"

"Why I can then all the more bear to know. Besides, perhaps I haven't."

"Perhaps. Yet if you haven't," she added. "I should suppose you'd remember. Not indeed that *I* in the least connect with my impression the invidious name you use. If I had only thought you foolish," she explained, "the thing I speak of wouldn't so have remained with me. It was about yourself." She

4. Resort town across the bay from Naples.

waited as if it might come to him; but as, only meeting her eyes in wonder, he gave no sign, she burnt her ships.[5] "Has it ever happened?"

Then it was that, while he continued to stare, a light broke for him and the blood slowly came to his face, which began to burn with recognition. "Do you mean I told you—?" But he faltered, lest what came to him shouldn't be right, lest he should only give himself away.

"It was something about yourself that it was natural one shouldn't forget— that is if one remembered you at all. That's why I ask you," she smiled, "if the thing you then spoke of has ever come to pass?"

Oh then he saw, but he was lost in wonder and found himself embarrassed. This, he also saw, made her sorry for him, as if her allusion had been a mistake. It took him but a moment, however, to feel it hadn't been, much as it had been a surprise. After the first little shock of it her knowledge on the contrary began, even if rather strangely, to taste sweet to him. She was the only other person in the world then who would have it, and she had had it all these years, while the fact of his having so breathed his secret had unaccountably faded from him. No wonder they couldn't have met as if nothing had happened. "I judge," he finally said, "that I know what you mean. Only I had strangely enough lost any sense of having taken you so far into my confidence."

"Is it because you've taken so many others as well?"

"I've taken nobody. Not a creature since then."

"So that I'm the only person who knows?"

"The only person in the world."

"Well," she quickly replied, "I myself have never spoken. I've never, never repeated of you what you told me." She looked at him so that he perfectly believed her. Their eyes met over it in such a way that he was without a doubt. "And I never will."

She spoke with an earnestness that, as if almost excessive, put him at ease about her possible derision. Somehow the whole question was a new luxury to him—that is from the moment she was in possession. If she didn't take the sarcastic view she clearly took the sympathetic, and that was what he had had, in all the long time, from no one whomsoever. What he felt was that he couldn't at present have begun to tell her, and yet could profit perhaps exquisitely by the accident of having done so of old. "Please don't then. We're just right as it is."

"Oh I am," she laughed, "if you are!" To which she added: "Then you do still feel in the same way?"

It was impossible he shouldn't take to himself that she was really interested, though it all kept coming as perfect surprise. He had thought of himself so long as abominably alone, and lo he wasn't alone a bit. He hadn't been, it appeared, for an hour—since those moments on the Sorrento boat. It was *she* who had been, he seemed to see as he looked at her—she who had been made so by the graceless fact of his lapse of fidelity. To tell her what he had told her—what had it been but to ask something of her? something that she had given, in her charity, without his having, by a remembrance, by a return of the spirit, failing another encounter, so much as thanked her. What he had asked of her had been simply at first not to laugh at him. She had beautifully not done so for ten years, and she was not doing so now.

5. I.e., to proceed boldly.

So he had endless gratitude to make up. Only for that he must see just how he had figured to her. "What, exactly, was the account I gave—?"

"Of the way you did feel? Well, it was very simple. You said you had had from your earliest time, as the deepest thing within you, the sense of being kept for something rare and strange, possibly prodigious and terrible, that was sooner or later to happen to you, that you had in your bones the foreboding and the conviction of, and that would perhaps overwhelm you."

"Do you call that very simple?" John Marcher asked.

She thought a moment. "It was perhaps because I seemed, as you spoke, to understand it."

"You do understand it?" he eagerly asked.

Again she kept her kind eyes on him. "You still have the belief?"

"Oh!" he exclaimed helplessly. There was too much to say.

"Whatever it's to be," she clearly made out, "it hasn't yet come."

He shook his head in complete surrender now. "It hasn't yet come. Only, you know, it isn't anything I'm to *do*, to achieve in the world, to be distinguished or admired for. I'm not such an ass as *that*. It would be much better, no doubt, if I were."

"It's to be something you're merely to suffer?"

"Well, say to wait for—to have to meet, to face, to see suddenly break out in my life; possibly destroying all further consciousness, possibly annihilating me; possibly, on the other hand, only altering everything, striking at the root of all my world and leaving me to the consequences, however they shape themselves."

She took this in, but the light in her eyes continued for him not to be that of mockery. "Isn't what you describe perhaps but the expectation—or at any rate the sense of danger, familiar to so many people—of falling in love?"

John Marcher wondered. "Did you ask me that before?"

"No—I wasn't so free-and-easy then. But it's what strikes me now."

"Of course," he said after a moment, "it strikes you. Of course it strikes *me*. Of course what's in store for me may be no more than that. The only thing is," he went on, "that I think if it had been that I should by this time know."

"Do you mean because you've *been* in love?" And then as he but looked at her in silence: "You've been in love, and it hasn't meant such a cataclysm, hasn't proved the great affair?"

"Here I am, you see. It hasn't been overwhelming."

"Then it hasn't been love," said May Bartram.

"Well, I at least thought it was. I took it for that—I've taken it till now. It was agreeable, it was delightful, it was miserable," he explained. "But it wasn't strange. It wasn't what *my* affair's to be."

"You want something all to yourself—something that nobody else knows or *has* known?"

"It isn't a question of what I 'want'—God knows I don't want anything. It's only a question of the apprehension that haunts me—that I live with day by day."

He said this so lucidly and consistently that he could see it further impose itself. If she hadn't been interested before she'd have been interested now. "Is it a sense of coming violence?"

Evidently now too again he liked to talk of it. "I don't think of it as—when it does come—necessarily violent. I only think of it as natural and as of course above all unmistakeable. I think of it simply as *the* thing. *The* thing will of itself appear natural."

"Then how will it appear strange?"

Marcher bethought himself. "It won't—to *me*."

"To whom then?"

"Well," he replied, smiling at last, "say to you."

"Oh then I'm to be present?"

"Why you *are* present—since you know."

"I see." She turned it over. "But I mean at the catastrophe."[6]

At this, for a minute, their lightness gave way to their gravity; it was as if the long look they exchanged held them together. "It will only depend on yourself—if you'll watch with me."

"Are you afraid?" she asked.

"Don't leave me *now*," he went on.

"Are you afraid?" she repeated.

"Do you think me simply out of my mind?" he pursued instead of answering. "Do I merely strike you as a harmless lunatic?"

"No," said May Bartram. "I understand you. I believe you."

"You mean you feel how my obsession—poor old thing!—may correspond to some possible reality?"

"To some possible reality."

"Then you *will* watch with me?"

She hesitated, then for the third time put her question. "Are you afraid?"

"Did I tell you I was—at Naples?"

"No, you said nothing about it."

"Then I don't know. And I should *like* to know," said John Marcher. "You'll tell me yourself whether you think so. If you'll watch with me you'll see."

"Very good then." They had been moving by this time across the room, and at the door, before passing out, they paused as for the full wind-up of their understanding. "I'll watch with you," said May Bartram.

II

The fact that she "knew"—knew and yet neither chaffed him nor betrayed him—had in a short time begun to constitute between them a goodly bond, which became more marked when, within the year that followed their afternoon at Weatherend, the opportunities for meeting multiplied. The event that thus promoted these occasions was the death of the ancient lady her great-aunt, under whose wing, since losing her mother, she had to such an extent found shelter, and who, though but the widowed mother of the new successor to the property, had succeeded—thanks to a high tone and a high temper—in not forfeiting the supreme position at the great house. The deposition of this personage arrived but with her death, which, followed by many changes, made in particular a difference for the young woman in whom Marcher's expert attention had recognised from the first a dependent with a pride that might ache though it didn't bristle. Nothing for a long time had made him easier than the thought that the aching must have been much soothed by Miss Bartram's now finding herself able to set up a small home in London. She had acquired property, to an amount that made that

6. Final event, usually of a play, and not necessarily catastrophic.

luxury just possible, under her aunt's extremely complicated will, and when the whole matter began to be straightened out, which indeed took time, she let him know that the happy issue was at last in view. He had seen her again before that day, both because she had more than once accompanied the ancient lady to town and because he had paid another visit to the friends who so conveniently made of Weatherend one of the charms of their own hospitality. These friends had taken him back there; he had achieved there again with Miss Bartram some quiet detachment; and he had in London succeeded in persuading her to more than one brief absence from her aunt. They went together, on these latter occasions, to the National Gallery and the South Kensington Museum,[7] where, among vivid reminders, they talked of Italy at large—not now attempting to recover, as at first, the taste of their youth and their ignorance. That recovery, the first day at Weatherend, had served its purpose well, had given them quite enough; so that they were, to Marcher's sense, no longer hovering about the headwaters of their stream, but had felt their boat pushed sharply off and down the current.

They were literally afloat together; for our gentleman this was marked, quite as marked as that the fortunate cause of it was just the buried treasure of her knowledge. He had with his own hands dug up this little hoard, brought to light—that is to within reach of the dim day constituted by their discretions and privacies—the object of value the hiding-place of which he had, after putting it into the ground himself, so strangely, so long forgotten. The rare luck of his having again just stumbled on the spot made him indifferent to any other question; he would doubtless have devoted more time to the odd accident of his lapse of memory if he hadn't been moved to devote so much to the sweetness, the comfort, as he felt, for the future, that this accident itself had helped to keep fresh. It had never entered into his plan that any one should "know," and mainly for the reason that it wasn't in him to tell any one. That would have been impossible, for nothing but the amusement of a cold world would have waited on it. Since, however, a mysterious fate had opened his mouth betimes, in spite of him, he would count that a compensation and profit by it to the utmost. That the right person *should* know tempered the asperity of his secret more even than his shyness had permitted him to imagine; and May Bartram was clearly right, because—well, because there she was. Her knowledge simply settled it; he would have been sure enough by this time had she been wrong. There was that in his situation, no doubt, that disposed him too much to see her as a mere confidant, taking all her light for him from the fact—the fact only—of her interest in his predicament; from her mercy, sympathy, seriousness, her consent not to regard him as the funniest of the funny. Aware, in fine, that her price for him was just in her giving him this constant sense of his being admirably spared, he was careful to remember that she had also a life of her own, with things that might happen to *her,* things that in friendship one should likewise take account of. Something fairly remarkable came to pass with him, for that matter, in this connexion—something represented by a certain passage of his consciousness, in the suddenest way, from one extreme to the other.

He had thought himself, so long as nobody knew, the most disinterested person in the world, carrying his concentrated burden, his perpetual suspense, ever so quietly, holding his tongue about it, giving others no glimpse of

7. Art museums in London; the South Kensington Museum is now called the Victoria and Albert Museum.

it nor of its effect upon his life, asking of them no allowance and only making on his side all those that were asked. He hadn't disturbed people with the queerness of their having to know a haunted man, though he had had moments of rather special temptation on hearing them say they were for-sooth "unsettled." If they were as unsettled as he was—he who had never been settled for an hour in his life—they would know what it meant. Yet it wasn't, all the same, for him to make them, and he listened to them civilly enough. This was why he had such good—though possibly such rather colourless—manners; this was why, above all, he could regard himself, in a greedy world, as decently—as in fact perhaps even a little sublimely—unselfish. Our point is accordingly that he valued this character quite suffi-ciently to measure his present danger of letting it lapse, against which he promised himself to be much on his guard. He was quite ready, none the less, to be selfish just a little, since surely no more charming occasion for it had come to him. "Just a little," in a word, was just as much as Miss Bartram, tak-ing one day with another, would let him. He never would be in the least coer-cive, and would keep well before him the lines on which consideration for her—the very highest—ought to proceed. He would thoroughly establish the heads under which her affairs, her requirements, her peculiarities—he went so far as to give them the latitude of that name—would come into their inter-course. All this naturally was a sign of how much he took the intercourse itself for granted. There was nothing more to be done about *that*. It simply existed; had sprung into being with her first penetrating question to him in the autumn light there at Weatherend. The real form it should have taken on the basis that stood out large was the form of their marrying. But the devil in this was that the very basis itself put marrying out of the question. His conviction, his apprehension, his obsession, in short, wasn't a privilege he could invite a woman to share; and that consequence of it was precisely what was the matter with him. Something or other lay in wait for him, amid the twists and the turns of the months and the years, like a crouching beast in the jungle. It signified little whether the crouching beast were destined to slay him or to be slain. The definite point was the inevitable spring of the creature; and the definite lesson from that was that a man of feeling didn't cause himself to be accompanied by a lady on a tiger-hunt. Such was the image under which he had ended by figuring his life.

They had at first, none the less, in the scattered hours spent together, made no allusion to that view of it; which was a sign he was handsomely alert to give that he didn't expect, that he in fact didn't care, always to be talking about it. Such a feature in one's outlook was really like a hump on one's back. The difference it made every minute of the day existed quite independently of discussion. One discussed of course *like* a hunchback, for there was always, if nothing else, the hunchback face. That remained, and she was watching him; but people watched best, as a general thing, in silence, so that such would be predominantly the manner of their vigil. Yet he didn't want, at the same time, to be tense and solemn; tense and solemn was what he imagined he too much showed for with other people. The thing to be, with the one person who knew, was easy and natural—to make the reference rather than be seeming to avoid it, to avoid it rather than be seem-ing to make it, and to keep it, in any case, familiar, facetious even, rather than pedantic and portentous. Some such consideration as the latter was doubtless in his mind for instance when he wrote pleasantly to Miss Bar-tram that perhaps the great thing he had so long felt as in the lap of the gods was no more than this circumstance, which touched him so nearly, of her acquiring a house in London. It was the first allusion they had yet again made, needing any other hitherto so little; but when she replied, after having given him the news, that she was by no means satisfied with such a trifle as the climax to so special a suspense, she almost set him wondering if she hadn't even a larger conception of singularity for him than he had for himself. He was at all events destined to become aware little by little, as time went by, that she was all the while looking at his life, judging it, measuring it, in the light of the thing she knew, which grew to be at last, with the consecration of the years, never mentioned between them save as "the real truth" about him. That had always been his own form of reference to it, but she adopted the form so quietly that, looking back at the end of a period, he knew there was no moment at which it was traceable that she had, as he might say, got inside his idea, or exchanged the attitude of beautifully indulging for that of still more beautifully believing him.

It was always open to him to accuse her of seeing him but as the most harmless of maniacs, and this, in the long run—since it covered so much ground—was his easiest description of their friendship. He had a screw loose for her, but she liked him in spite of it and was practically, against the rest of the world, his kind wise keeper, unremunerated but fairly amused and, in the absence of other near ties, not disreputably occupied. The rest of the world of course thought him queer, but she, she only, knew how, and above all why, queer; which was precisely what enabled her to dispose the concealing veil in the right folds. She took his gaiety from him—since it had to pass with them for gaiety—as she took everything else; but she certainly so far justified by her unerring touch his finer sense of the degree to which he had ended by convincing her. *She* at least never spoke of the secret of his life except as "the real truth about you," and she had in fact a wonderful way of making it seem, as such, the secret of her own life too. That was in fine how he so constantly felt her as allowing for him; he couldn't on the whole call it anything else. He allowed for himself, but she, exactly, allowed still more; partly because, better placed for a sight of the matter, she traced his unhappy perversion through reaches of its course into which he could scarce follow it. He knew how he felt, but, besides knowing that, she knew how he *looked* as well; he knew each of the things of importance he was insidiously kept from doing, but she could add up the amount they made, understand how much, with a lighter weight on his spirit, he might have done, and thereby establish how, clever as he was, he fell short. Above all she was in the secret of the difference between the forms he went through—those of his little office under Government, those of caring for his modest patrimony, for his library, for his garden in the country, for the people in London whose invitations he accepted and repaid—and the detachment that reigned beneath them and that made of all behaviour, all that could in the least be called behaviour, a long act of dissimulation. What it had come to was that he wore a mask painted with the social simper, out of the eyeholes of which there looked eyes of an expression not in the least matching the other features. This the stupid world, even after years, had never more than half-discovered. It was only May Bartram who had, and she achieved, by an art indescribable, the feat of at once—or perhaps it was only alternately—meeting the eyes from in front and mingling her own vision, as from over his shoulder, with their peep through the apertures.

So while they grew older together she did watch with him, and so she let this association give shape and colour to her own existence. Beneath *her* forms as well detachment had learned to sit, and behaviour had become for her, in the social sense, a false account of herself. There was but one account of her that would have been true all the while and that she could give straight to nobody, least of all to John Marcher. Her whole attitude was a virtual statement, but the perception of that only seemed called to take its place for him as one of the many things necessarily crowded out of his consciousness. If she had moreover, like himself, to make sacrifices to their real truth, it was to be granted that her compensation might have affected her as more prompt and more natural. They had long periods, in this London time, during which, when they were together, a stranger might have listened to them without in the least pricking up his ears; on the other hand the real truth was equally liable at any moment to rise to the surface, and the auditor would then have wondered indeed what they were talking about. They had from an early hour made up their mind that society was, luckily, unintelligent, and the margin allowed them by this had fairly become one of their commonplaces. Yet there were still moments when the situation turned almost fresh—usually under the effect of some expression drawn from herself. Her expressions doubtless repeated themselves, but her intervals were generous. "What saves us, you know, is that we answer so completely to so usual an appearance: that of the man and woman whose friendship has become such a daily habit—or almost—as to be at last indispensable." That for instance was a remark she had frequently enough had occasion to make, though she had given it at different times different developments. What we are especially concerned with is the turn it happened to take from her one afternoon when he had come to see her in honour of her birthday. This anniversary had fallen on a Sunday, at a season of thick fog and general outward gloom; but he had brought her his customary offering, having known her now long enough to have established a hundred small traditions. It was one of his proofs to himself, the present he made her on her birthday, that he hadn't sunk into real selfishness. It was mostly nothing more than a small trinket, but it was always fine of its kind, and he was regularly careful to pay for it more than he thought he could afford. "Our habit saves you at least, don't you see? because it makes you, after all, for the vulgar, indistinguishable from other men. What's the most inveterate mark of men in general? Why the capacity to spend endless time with dull women—to spend it I won't say without being bored, but without minding that they are, without being driven off at a tangent by it; which comes to the same thing. I'm your dull woman, a part of the daily bread for which you pray at church. That covers your tracks more than anything."

"And what covers yours?" asked Marcher, whom his dull woman could mostly to this extent amuse. "I see of course what you mean by your saving me, in this way and that, so far as other people are concerned—I've seen it all along. Only what is it that saves *you*? I often think, you know, of that."

She looked as if she sometimes thought of that too, but rather in a different way. "Where other people, you mean, are concerned?"

"Well, you're really so in with me, you know—as a sort of result of my being so in with yourself. I mean of my having such an immense regard for you, being so tremendously mindful of all you've done for me. I sometimes ask myself if it's quite fair. Fair I mean to have so involved and—since one may say it—interested you. I almost feel as if you hadn't really had time to do anything else."

"Anything else but be interested?" she asked. "Ah what else does one ever want to be? If I've been 'watching' with you, as we long ago agreed I was to do, watching's always in itself an absorption."

"Oh certainly," John Marcher said, "if you hadn't had your curiosity—! Only doesn't it sometimes come to you as time goes on that your curiosity isn't being particularly repaid?"

May Bartram had a pause. "Do you ask that, by any chance, because you feel at all that yours isn't? I mean because you have to wait so long."

Oh he understood what she meant! "For the thing to happen that never does happen? For the beast to jump out? No, I'm just where I was about it. It isn't a matter as to which I can *choose*, I can decide for a change. It isn't one as to which there *can* be a change. It's in the lap of the gods. One's in the hands of one's law—there one is. As to the form the law will take, the way it will operate, that's its own affair."

"Yes," Miss Bartram replied; "of course one's fate's coming, of course it *has* come in its own form and its own way, all the while. Only, you know, the form and the way in your case were to have been—well, something so exceptional and, as one may say, so particularly *your* own."

Something in this made him look at her with suspicion. "You say 'were to *have* been,' as if in your heart you had begun to doubt."

"Oh!" she vaguely protested.

"As if you believed," he went on, "that nothing will now take place."

She shook her head slowly but rather inscrutably. "You're far from my thought."

He continued to look at her. "What then is the matter with you?"

"Well," she said after another wait, "the matter with me is simply that I'm more sure than ever my curiosity, as you call it, will be but too well repaid."

They were frankly grave now; he had got up from his seat, had turned once more about the little drawing-room to which, year after year, he brought his inevitable topic; in which he had, as he might have said, tasted their intimate community with every sauce, where every object was as familiar to him as the things of his own house and the very carpets were worn with his fitful walk very much as the desks in old counting-houses are worn by the elbows of generations of clerks. The generations of his nervous moods had been at work there, and the place was the written history of his whole middle life. Under the impression of what his friend had just said he knew himself, for some reason, more aware of these things; which made him, after a moment, stop again before her. "Is it possibly that you've grown afraid?"

"Afraid?" He thought, as she repeated the word, that his question had made her, a little, change colour; so that, lest he should have touched on a truth, he explained very kindly: "You remember that that was what you asked *me* long ago—that first day at Weatherend."

"Oh yes, and you told me you didn't know—that I was to see for myself. We've said little about it since, even in so long a time."

"Precisely," Marcher interposed—"quite as if it were too delicate a matter for us to make free with. Quite as if we might find, on pressure, that I *am* afraid. For then," he said, "we shouldn't, should we? quite know what to do."

She had for the time no answer to his question. "There have been days when I thought you were. Only, of course," she added, "there have been days when we have thought almost anything."

"Everything. Oh!" Marcher softly groaned as with a gasp, half-spent, at the face, more uncovered just then than it had been for a long while, of the imagination always with them. It had always had its incalculable moments of glaring out, quite as with the very eyes of the very Beast, and, used as he was to them, they could still draw from him the tribute of a sigh that rose from the depths of his being. All they had thought, first and last, rolled over him; the past seemed to have been reduced to mere barren speculation. This in fact was what the place had just struck him as so full of—the simplification of everything but the state of suspense. That remained only by seeming to hang in the void surrounding it. Even his original fear, if fear it had been, had lost itself in the desert. "I judge, however," he continued, "that you see I'm not afraid now."

"What I see, as I make it out, is that you've achieved something almost unprecedented in the way of getting used to danger. Living with it so long and so closely you've lost your sense of it; you know it's there, but you're indifferent, and you cease even, as of old, to have to whistle in the dark. Considering what the danger is," May Bartram wound up, "I'm bound to say I don't think your attitude could well be surpassed."

John Marcher faintly smiled. "It's heroic?"

"Certainly—call it that."

It was what he would have liked indeed to call it. "I *am* then a man of courage?"

"That's what you were to show me."

He still, however, wondered. "But doesn't the man of courage know what he's afraid of—or *not* afraid of? I don't know *that*, you see. I don't focus it. I can't name it. I only know I'm exposed."

"Yes, but exposed—how shall I say?—so directly. So intimately. That's surely enough."

"Enough to make you feel then—as what we may call the end and the upshot of our watch—that I'm not afraid?"

"You're not afraid. But it isn't," she said, "the end of our watch. That is it isn't the end of yours. You've everything still to see."

"Then why haven't *you?*" he asked. He had had, all along, to-day, the sense of her keeping something back, and he still had it. As this was his first impression of that it quite made a date. The case was the more marked as she didn't at first answer; which in turn made him go on. "You know something I don't." Then his voice, for that of a man of courage, trembled a little. "You know what's to happen." Her silence, with the face she showed, was almost a confession—it made him sure. "You know, and you're afraid to tell me. It's so bad that you're afraid I'll find out."

All this might be true, for she did look as if, unexpectedly to her, he had crossed some mystic line that she had secretly drawn round her. Yet she might, after all, not have worried; and the real climax was that he himself, at all events, needn't. "You'll never find out."

III

It was all to have made, none the less, as I have said, a date; which came out in the fact that again and again, even after long intervals, other things that passed between them wore in relation to this hour but the character of recalls and results. Its immediate effect had been indeed rather to lighten insistence—almost to provoke a reaction; as if their topic had dropped by its own weight and as if moreover, for that matter, Marcher had been visited by one of his occasional warnings against egotism. He had kept up, he felt, and very decently on the whole, his consciousness of the importance of not being selfish, and it was true that he had never sinned in that direction without promptly enough trying to press the scales the other way. He often repaired his fault, the season permitting, by inviting his friend to accompany him to the opera; and it not infrequently thus happened that, to show he didn't wish her to have but one sort of food for her mind, he was the cause of her appearing there with him a dozen nights in the month. It even happened that, seeing her home at such times, he occasionally went in with her to finish, as he called it, the evening, and, the better to make his point, sat down to the frugal but always careful little supper that awaited his pleasure. His point was made, he thought, by his not eternally insisting with her on himself; made for instance, at such hours, when it befell that, her piano at hand and each of them familiar with it, they went over passages of the opera together. It chanced to be on one of these occasions, however, that he reminded her of her not having answered a certain question he had put to her during the talk that had taken place between them on her last birthday. "What is it that saves *you?*"—saved her, he meant, from that appearance of variation from the usual human type. If he had practically escaped remark, as she pretended, by doing, in the most important particular, what most men do—find the answer to life in patching up an alliance of a sort with a woman no better than himself—how had she escaped it, and how could the alliance, such as it was, since they must suppose it had been more or less noticed, have failed to make her rather positively talked about?

"I never said," May Bartram replied, "that it hadn't made me a good deal talked about."

"Ah well then you're not 'saved.'"

"It hasn't been a question for me. If you've had your woman I've had," she said, "my man."

"And you mean that makes you all right?"

Oh it was always as if there were so much to say! "I don't know why it shouldn't make me—humanly, which is what we're speaking of—as right as it makes you."

"I see," Marcher returned. "'Humanly,' no doubt, as showing that you're living for something. Not, that is, just for me and my secret."

May Bartram smiled. "I don't pretend it exactly shows that I'm not living for you. It's my intimacy with you that's in question."

He laughed as he saw what she meant. "Yes, but since, as you say, I'm only, so far as people make out, ordinary, you're—aren't you?—no more than ordinary either. You help me to pass for a man like another. So if I *am*, as I understand you, you're not compromised. Is that it?"

She had another of her waits, but she spoke clearly enough. "That's it. It's all that concerns me—to help you to pass for a man like another."

He was careful to acknowledge the remark handsomely. "How kind, how beautiful, you are to me! How shall I ever repay you?"

She had her last grave pause, as if there might be a choice of ways. But she chose. "By going on as you are."

It was into this going on as he was that they relapsed, and really for so long a time that the day inevitably came for a further sounding of their depths. These depths, constantly bridged over by a structure firm enough in

spite of its lightness and of its occasional oscillation in the somewhat vertigi-
nous air, invited on occasion, in the interest of their nerves, a dropping of
the plummet and a measurement of the abyss. A difference had been made
moreover, once for all, by the fact that she had all the while not appeared to
feel the need of rebutting his charge of an idea within her that she didn't
dare to express—a charge uttered just before one of the fullest of their later
discussions ended. It had come up for him then that she "knew" something
and that what she knew was bad—too bad to tell him. When he had spoken
of it as visibly so bad that she was afraid he might find it out, her reply had
left the matter too equivocal to be let alone and yet, for Marcher's special
sensibility, almost too formidable again to touch. He circled about it at a
distance that alternately narrowed and widened and that still wasn't much
affected by the consciousness in him that there was nothing she could
"know," after all, any better than he did. She had no source of knowledge he
hadn't equally—except of course that she might have finer nerves. That was
what women had where they were interested; they made out things, where
people were concerned, that the people often couldn't have made out for
themselves. Their nerves, their sensibility, their imagination, were conductors and revealers, and the beauty of May Bartram was in particular that
she had given herself so to his case. He felt in these days what, oddly
enough, he had never felt before, the growth of a dread of losing her by some
catastrophe—some catastrophe that yet wouldn't at all be *the* catastrophe:
partly because she had almost of a sudden begun to strike him as more
useful to him than ever yet, and partly by reason of an appearance of uncertainty in her health, coincident and equally new. It was characteristic of the
inner detachment he had hitherto so successfully cultivated and to which
our whole account of him is a reference, it was characteristic that his complications, such as they were, had never yet seemed so as at this crisis to
thicken about him, even to the point of making him ask himself if he were,
by any chance, of a truth, within sight or sound, within touch or reach,
within the immediate jurisdiction, of the thing that waited.

When the day came, as come it had to, that his friend confessed to him her
fear of a deep disorder in her blood, he felt somehow the shadow of a change
and the chill of a shock. He immediately began to imagine aggravations and
disasters, and above all to think of her peril as the direct menace for himself
of personal privation. This indeed gave him one of those partial recoveries of
equanimity that were agreeable to him—it showed him that what was still
first in his mind was the loss she herself might suffer. "What if she should
have to die before knowing, before seeing—?" It would have been brutal, in
the early stages of her trouble, to put that question to her; but it had immediately sounded for him to his own concern, and the possibility was what most
made him sorry for her. If she did "know," moreover, in the sense of her having had some—what should he think?—mystical irresistible light, this would
make the matter not better, but worse, inasmuch as her original adoption of
his own curiosity had quite become the basis of her life. She had been living
to see what would *be* to be seen, and it would quite lacerate her to have to
give up before the accomplishment of the vision. These reflexions, as I say,
quickened his generosity; yet, make them as he might, he saw himself, with
the lapse of the period, more and more disconcerted. It lapsed for him with
a strange steady sweep, and the oddest oddity was that it gave him, independently of the threat of much inconvenience, almost the only positive surprise

his career, if career it could be called, had yet offered him. She kept the house as she had never done; he had to go to her to see her—she could meet him nowhere now, though there was scarce a corner of their loved old London in which she hadn't in the past, at one time or another, done so; and he found her always seated by her fire in the deep old-fashioned chair she was less and less able to leave. He had been struck one day, after an absence exceeding his usual measure, with her suddenly looking much older to him than he had ever thought of her being; then he recognised that the suddenness was all on his side—he had just simply and suddenly noticed. She looked older because inevitably, after so many years, she *was* old, or almost; which was of course true in still greater measure of her companion. If she was old, or almost, John Marcher assuredly was, and yet it was her showing of the lesson, not his own, that brought the truth home to him. His surprises began here; when once they had begun they multiplied; they came rather with a rush: it was as if, in the oddest way in the world, they had all been kept back, sown in a thick cluster, for the late afternoon of life, the time at which for people in general the unexpected has died out.

One of them was that he should have caught himself—for he *had* so done—*really* wondering if the great accident would take form now as nothing more than his being condemned to see this charming woman, this admirable friend, pass away from him. He had never so unreservedly qualified her as while confronted in thought with such a possibility; in spite of which there was small doubt for him that as an answer to his long riddle the mere effacement of even so fine a feature of his situation would be an abject anti-climax. It would represent, as connected with his past attitude, a drop of dignity under the shadow of which his existence could only become the most grotesque of failures. He had been far from holding it a failure—long as he had waited for the appearance that was to make it a success. He had waited for quite another thing, not for such a thing as that. The breath of his good faith came short, however, as he recognised how long he had waited, or how long at least his companion had. That she, at all events, might be recorded as having waited in vain—this affected him sharply, and all the more because of his at first having done little more than amuse himself with the idea. It grew more grave as the gravity of her condition grew, and the state of mind it produced in him, which he himself ended by watching as if it had been some definite disfigurement of his outer person, may pass for another of his surprises. This conjoined itself still with another, the really stupefying consciousness of a question that he would have allowed to shape itself had he dared. What did everything mean—what, that is, did *she* mean, she and her vain waiting and her probable death and the soundless admonition of it all—unless that, at this time of day, it was simply, it was overwhelmingly too late? He had never at any stage of his queer consciousness admitted the whisper of such a correction; he had never till within these last few months been so false to his conviction as not to hold that what was to come to him had time, whether *he* struck himself as having it or not. That at last, at last, he certainly hadn't it, to speak of, or had it but in the scantiest measure—such, soon enough, as things went with him, became the inference with which his old obsession had to reckon: and this it was not helped to do by the more and more confirmed appearance that the great vagueness casting the long shadow in which he had lived had, to attest itself, almost no margin left. Since it was in Time that he was to have met his fate, so it was in Time that his fate was to have acted; and as he waked up to the sense of no longer being young, which was exactly the sense of being stale, just as that, in turn, was the sense of being weak, he waked up to another matter beside. It all hung together; they were subject, he and the great vagueness, to an equal and indivisible law. When the possibilities themselves had accordingly turned stale, when the secret of the gods had grown faint, had perhaps even quite evaporated, that, and that only, was failure. It wouldn't have been failure to be bankrupt, dishonoured, pilloried, hanged; it was failure not to be anything. And so, in the dark valley into which his path had taken its unlooked-for twist, he wondered not a little as he groped. He didn't care what awful crash might overtake him, with what ignominy or what monstrosity he might yet be associated—since he wasn't after all too utterly old to suffer—if it would only be decently proportionate to the posture he had kept, all his life, in the threatened presence of it. He had but one desire left—that he shouldn't have been "sold."

IV

Then it was that, one afternoon, while the spring of the year was young and new she met all in her own way his frankest betrayal of these alarms. He had gone in late to see her, but evening hadn't settled and she was presented to him in that long fresh light of waning April days which affects us often with a sadness sharper than the greyest hours of autumn. The week had been warm, the spring was supposed to have begun early, and May Bartram sat, for the first time in the year, without a fire; a fact that, to Marcher's sense, gave the scene of which she formed part a smooth and ultimate look, an air of know-ing, in its immaculate order and cold meaningless cheer, that it would never see a fire again. Her own aspect—he could scarce have said why—intensified this note. Almost as white as wax, with the marks and signs in her face as numerous and as fine as if they had been etched by a needle, with soft white draperies relieved by a faded green scarf on the delicate tone of which the years had further refined, she was the picture of a serene and exquisite but impenetrable sphinx, whose head, or indeed all whose person, might have been powdered with silver. She was a sphinx, yet with her white petals and green fronds she might have been a lily too—only an artificial lily, wonder-fully imitated and constantly kept, without dust or stain, though not exempt from a slight droop and a complexity of faint creases, under some clear glass bell. The perfection of household care, of high polish and finish, always reigned in her rooms, but they now looked most as if everything had been wound up, tucked in, put away, so that she might sit with folded hands and with nothing more to do. She was "out of it," to Marcher's vision; her work was over; she communicated with him as across some gulf or from some island of rest that she had already reached, and it made him feel strangely abandoned. Was it—or rather wasn't it—that if for so long she had been watching with him the answer to their question must have swum into her ken and taken on its name, so that her occupation was verily gone? He had as much as charged her with this in saying to her, many months before, that she even then knew something she was keeping from him. It was a point he had never since ven-tured to press, vaguely fearing as he did that it might become a difference, perhaps a disagreement, between them. He had in this later time turned ner-vous, which was what he in all the other years had never been; and the oddity was that his nervousness should have waited till he had begun to doubt, should have held off so long as he was sure. There was something, it seemed to him, that the wrong word would bring down on his head, something that would so at least ease off his tension. But he wanted not to speak the wrong word; that would make everything ugly. He wanted the knowledge he lacked to drop on him, if drop it could, by its own august weight. If she was to forsake him it was surely for her to take leave. This was why he didn't directly ask her again what she knew; but it was also why, approaching the matter from another side, he said to her in the course of his visit: "What do you regard as the very worst that at this time of day *can* happen to me?"

He had asked her that in the past often enough; they had, with the odd irregular rhythm of their intensities and avoidances, exchanged ideas about it and then had seen the ideas washed away by cool intervals, washed like figures traced in sea-sand. It had ever been the mark of their talk that the oldest allusions in it required but a little dismissal and reaction to come out again, sounding for the hour as new. She could thus at present meet his enquiry quite freshly and patiently. "Oh yes, I've repeatedly thought, only it always seemed to me of old that I couldn't quite make up my mind. I thought of dreadful things, between which it was difficult to choose; and so must you have done."

"Rather! I feel now as if I had scarce done anything else. I appear to myself to have spent my life in thinking of nothing *but* dreadful things. A great many of them I've at different times named to you, but there were others I couldn't name."

"They were too, too dreadful?"

"Too, too dreadful—some of them."

She looked at him a minute, and there came to him as he met it an inconsequent sense that her eyes, when one got their full clearness, were still as beautiful as they had been in youth, only beautiful with a strange cold light—a light that somehow was a part of the effect, if it wasn't rather a part of the cause, of the pale hard sweetness of the season and the hour. "And yet," she said at last, "there are horrors we've mentioned."

It deepened the strangeness to see her, as such a figure in such a picture, talk of "horrors," but she was to do in a few minutes something stranger yet—though even of this he was to take the full measure but afterwards—and the note of it already trembled. It was, for the matter of that, one of the signs that her eyes were having again the high flicker of their prime. He had to admit, however, what she said. "Oh yes, there were times when we did go far." He caught himself in the act of speaking as if it all were over. Well, he wished it were; and the consummation depended for him clearly more and more on his friend.

But she had now a soft smile. "Oh far—!"

It was oddly ironic. "Do you mean you're prepared to go further?"

She was frail and ancient and charming as she continued to look at him, yet it was rather as if she had lost the thread. "Do you consider that we went far?"

"Why I thought it the point you were just making—that we *had* looked most things in the face."

"Including each other?" She still smiled. "But you're quite right. We've had together great imaginations, often great fears; but some of them have been unspoken."

"Then the worst—we haven't faced that. I *could* face it, I believe, if I knew what you think it. I feel," he explained, "as if I had lost my power to conceive such things." And he wondered if he looked as blank as he sounded. "It's spent."

"Then why do you assume," she asked, "that mine isn't?"

"Because you've given me signs to the contrary. It isn't a question for you of conceiving, imagining, comparing. It isn't a question now of choosing." At last he came out with it. "You know something I don't. You've shown me that before."

These last words had affected her, he made out in a moment, exceedingly, and she spoke with firmness. "I've shown you, my dear, nothing."

He shook his head. "You can't hide it."

"Oh, oh!" May Bartram sounded over what she couldn't hide. It was almost a smothered groan.

"You admitted it months ago, when I spoke of it to you as of something you were afraid I should find out. Your answer was that I couldn't, that I wouldn't, and I don't pretend I have. But you had something therefore in mind, and I now see how it must have been, how it still is, the possibility that, of all possibilities, has settled itself for you as the worst. This," he went on, "is why I appeal to you. I'm only afraid of ignorance to-day—I'm not afraid of knowledge." And then as for a while she said nothing: "What makes me sure is that I see in your face and feel here, in this air and amid these appearances, that you're out of it. You've done. You've had your experience. You leave me to my fate."

Well, she listened, motionless and white in her chair, as on a decision to be made, so that her manner was fairly an avowal, though still, with a small fine inner stiffness, an imperfect surrender. "It *would* be the worst," she finally let herself say. "I mean the thing I've never said."

It hushed him a moment. "More monstrous than all the monstrosities we've named?"

"More monstrous. Isn't that what you sufficiently express," she asked, "in calling it the worst?"

Marcher thought. "Assuredly—if you mean, as I do, something that includes all the loss and all the shame that are thinkable."

"It would if it *should* happen," said May Bartram. "What we're speaking of, remember, is only my idea."

"It's your belief," Marcher returned. "That's enough for me. I feel your beliefs are right. Therefore if, having this one, you give me no more light on it, you abandon me."

"No, no!" she repeated. "I'm with you—don't you see?—still." And as to make it more vivid to him she rose from her chair—a movement she seldom risked in these days—and showed herself, all draped and all soft, in her fairness and slimness. "I haven't forsaken you."

It was really, in its effort against weakness, a generous assurance, and had the success of the impulse not, happily, been great, it would have touched him to pain more than to pleasure. But the cold charm in her eyes had spread, as she hovered before him, to all the rest of her person, so that it was for the minute almost a recovery of youth. He couldn't pity her for that; he could only take her as she showed—as capable even yet of helping him. It was as if, at the same time, her light might at any instant go out; wherefore he must make the most of it. There passed before him with intensity the three or four things he wanted most to know; but the question that came of itself to his lips really covered the others. "Then tell me if I shall consciously suffer."

She promptly shook her head. "Never!"

It confirmed the authority he imputed to her, and it produced on him an extraordinary effect. "Well, what's better than that? Do you call that the worst?"

"You think nothing is better?" she asked.

She seemed to mean something so special that he again sharply wondered, though still with the dawn of a prospect of relief. "Why not, if one doesn't *know*?" After which, as their eyes, over his question, met in a silence, the dawn deepened and something to his purpose came prodigiously out of her very face. His own, as he took it in, suddenly flushed to the forehead, and he gasped with the force of a perception to which, on the instant, everything fitted. The sound of his gasp filled the air; then he became articulate. "I see—if I don't suffer!"

In her own look, however, was doubt. "You see what?"

"Why what you mean—what you've always meant."

She again shook her head. "What I mean isn't what I've always meant. It's different."

"It's something new?"

She hung back from it a little. "Something new. It's not what you think. I see what you think."

His divination drew breath then; only her correction might be wrong. "It isn't that I *am* a blockhead?" he asked between faintness and grimness. "It isn't that it's all a mistake?"

"A mistake?" she pityingly echoed. *That* possibility, for her, he saw, would be monstrous; and if she guaranteed him the immunity from pain it would accordingly not be what she had in mind. "Oh no," she declared; "it's nothing of that sort. You've been right."

Yet he couldn't help asking himself if she weren't, thus pressed, speaking but to save him. It seemed to him he should be most in a hole if his history should prove all a platitude. "Are you telling me the truth, so that I shan't have been a bigger idiot than I can bear to know? I *haven't* lived with a vain imagination, in the most besotted illusion? I haven't waited but to see the door shut in my face?"

She shook her head again. "However the case stands *that* isn't the truth. Whatever the reality, it *is* a reality. The door isn't shut. The door's open," said May Bartram.

"Then something's to come?"

She waited once again, always with her cold sweet eyes on him. "It's never too late." She had, with her gliding step, diminished the distance between them, and she stood nearer to him, close to him, a minute, as if still charged with the unspoken. Her movement might have been for some finer emphasis of what she was at once hesitating and deciding to say. He had been standing by the chimney-piece, fireless and sparely adorned, a small perfect old French clock and two morsels of rosy Dresden[8] constituting all its furniture; and her hand grasped the shelf while she kept him waiting, grasped it a little as for support and encouragement. She only kept him waiting, however; that is he only waited. It had become suddenly, from her movement and attitude, beau-

---

8. Fine German porcelain.

tiful and vivid to him that she had something more to give him; her wasted face delicately shone with it—it glittered almost as with the white lustre of silver in her expression. She was right, incontestably, for what he saw in her face was the truth, and strangely, without consequence, while their talk of it as dreadful was still in the air, she appeared to present it as inordinately soft. This, prompting bewilderment, made him but gape the more gratefully for her revelation, so that they continued for some minutes silent, her face shining at him, her contact imponderably pressing, and his stare all kind but all expectant. The end, none the less, was that what he had expected failed to come to him. Something else took place instead, which seemed to consist at first in the mere closing of her eyes. She gave way at the same instant to a slow fine shudder, and though he remained staring—though he stared in fact but the harder—turned off and regained her chair. It was the end of what she had been intending, but it left him thinking only of that.

"Well, you don't say—?"

She had touched in her passage a bell near the chimney and had sunk back strangely pale. "I'm afraid I'm too ill."

"Too ill to tell me?" It sprang up sharp to him, and almost to his lips, the fear she might die without giving him light. He checked himself in time from so expressing his question, but she answered as if she had heard the words.

"Don't you know—now?"

"'Now'—?" She had spoken as if some difference had been made within the moment. But her maid, quickly obedient to her bell, was already with them. "I know nothing." And he was afterwards to say to himself that he must have spoken with odious impatience, such an impatience as to show that, supremely disconcerted, he washed his hands of the whole question.

"Oh!" said May Bartram.

"Are you in pain?" he asked as the woman went to her.

"No," said May Bartram.

Her maid, who had put an arm round her as if to take her to her room, fixed on him eyes that appealingly contradicted her; in spite of which, however, he showed once more his mystification. "What then has happened?"

She was once more, with her companion's help, on her feet, and, feeling withdrawal imposed on him, he had blankly found his hat and gloves and had reached the door. Yet he waited for her answer. "What *was* to," she said.

V

He came back the next day, but she was then unable to see him, and as it was literally the first time this had occurred in the long stretch of their acquaintance he turned away, defeated and sore, almost angry—or feeling at least that such a break in their custom was really the beginning of the end—and wandered alone with his thoughts, especially with the one he was least able to keep down. She was dying and he would lose her; she was dying and his life would end. He stopped in the Park, into which he had passed, and stared before him at his recurrent doubt. Away from her the doubt pressed again; in her presence he had believed her, but as he felt his forlornness he threw himself into the explanation that, nearest at hand, had most of a miserable warmth for him and least of a cold torment. She had deceived him to save him—to put him off with something in which he should be able to rest. What could the thing that was to happen to him be, after all, but just this thing that had begun to happen? Her dying, her death, his consequent solitude—*that* was what he had figured as the Beast in the Jungle, that was what had been in the lap of the gods. He had had her word for it as he left her—what else on earth could she have meant? It wasn't a thing of a monstrous order; not a fate rare and distinguished; not a stroke of fortune that overwhelmed and immortalised; it had only the stamp of the common doom. But poor Marcher at this hour judged the common doom sufficient. It would serve his turn, and even as the consummation of infinite waiting he would bend his pride to accept it. He sat down on a bench in the twilight. He hadn't been a fool. Something had *been*, as she had said, to come. Before he rose indeed it had quite struck him that the final fact really matched with the long avenue through which he had had to reach it. As sharing his suspense and as giving herself all, giving her life, to bring it to an end, she had come with him every step of the way. He had lived by her aid, and to leave her behind would be cruelly, damnably to miss her. What could be more overwhelming than that?

Well, he was to know within the week, for though she kept him a while at bay, left him restless and wretched during a series of days on each of which he asked about her only again to have to turn away, she ended his trial by receiving him where she had always received him. Yet she had been brought out at some hazard into the presence of so many of the things that were, consciously, vainly, half their past, and there was scant service left in the gentleness of her mere desire, all too visible, to check his obsession and wind up his long trouble. That was clearly what she wanted, the one thing more for her own peace while she could still put out her hand. He was so affected by her state that, once seated by her chair, he was moved to let everything go; it was she herself therefore who brought him back, took up again, before she dismissed him, her last word of the other time. She showed how she wished to leave their business in order. "I'm not sure you understood. You've nothing to wait for more. It *has* come."

Oh how he looked at her! "Really?"

"Really."

"The thing that, as you said, *was* to?"

"The thing that we began in our youth to watch for."

Face to face with her once more he believed her; it was a claim to which he had so abjectly little to oppose. "You mean that it has come as a positive definite occurrence, with a name and a date?"

"Positive. Definite. I don't know about the 'name,' but oh with a date!"

He found himself again too helplessly at sea. "But come in the night—come and passed me by?"

May Bartram had her strange faint smile. "Oh no, it hasn't passed you by!"

"But if I haven't been aware of it and it hasn't touched me—?"

"Ah your not being aware of it"—and she seemed to hesitate an instant to deal with this—"your not being aware of it is the strangeness *in* the strangeness. It's the wonder *of* the wonder." She spoke as with the softness almost of a sick child, yet now at last, at the end of all, with the perfect straightness of a sibyl. She visibly knew that she knew, and the effect on him was of something co-ordinate, in its high character, with the law that had ruled him. It was the true voice of the law; so on her lips would the law itself have sounded. "It *has* touched you," she went on. "It has done its office. It has made you all its own."

"So utterly without my knowing it?"

"So utterly without your knowing it." His hand, as he leaned to her, was on the arm of her chair, and, dimly smiling always now, she placed her own on it. "It's enough if *I* know it."

"Oh!" he confusedly breathed, as she herself of late so often had done.

"What I long ago said is true. You'll never know now, and I think you ought to be content. You've *had* it," said May Bartram.

"But had what?"

"Why what was to have marked you out. The proof of your law. It has acted. I'm too glad," she then bravely added, "to have been able to see what it's *not*."

He continued to attach his eyes to her, and with the sense that it was all beyond him, and that *she* was too, he would still have sharply challenged her hadn't he so felt it an abuse of her weakness to do more than take devoutly what she gave him, take it hushed as to a revelation. If he did speak, it was out of the foreknowledge of his loneliness to come. "If you're glad of what it's 'not' it might then have been worse?"

She turned her eyes away, she looked straight before her; with which after a moment: "Well, you know our fears."

He wondered. "It's something then we never feared?"

On this slowly she turned to him. "Did we ever dream, with all our dreams, that we should sit and talk of it thus?"

He tried for a little to make out that they had; but it was as if their dreams, numberless enough, were in solution in some thick cold mist through which thought lost itself. "It might have been that we couldn't talk?"

"Well"—she did her best for him—"not from this side. This, you see," she said, "is the *other* side."

"I think," poor Marcher returned, "that all sides are the same to me." Then, however, as she gently shook her head in correction: "We mightn't, as it were, have got across—?"

"To where we are—no. We're *here*"—she made her weak emphasis.

"And much good does it do us!" was her friend's frank comment.

"It does us the good it can. It does us the good that *it* isn't here. It's past. It's behind," said May Bartram. "Before—" but her voice dropped.

He had got up, not to tire her, but it was hard to combat his yearning. She after all told him nothing but that his light had failed—which he knew well enough without her. "Before—?" he blankly echoed.

"Before, you see, it was always to *come*. That kept it present."

"Oh I don't care what comes now! Besides," Marcher added, "it seems to me I liked it better present, as you say, than I can like it absent with *your* absence."

"Oh mine!"—and her pale hands made light of it.

"With the absence of everything." He had a dreadful sense of standing there before her for—so far as anything but this proved, this bottomless drop was concerned—the last time of their life. It rested on him with a weight he felt he could scarce bear, and this weight it apparently was that still pressed out what remained in him of speakable protest. "I believe you; but I can't begin to pretend I understand. *Nothing*, for me, is past; nothing *will* pass till I pass myself, which I pray my stars may be as soon as possible. Say, however," he added, "that I've eaten my cake, as you contend, to the last crumb—how can the thing I've never felt at all be the thing I was marked out to feel?"

She met him perhaps less directly, but she met him unperturbed. "You take your 'feelings' for granted. You were to suffer your fate. That was not necessarily to know it."

"How in the world—when what is such knowledge but suffering?"

She looked up at him a while in silence. "No—you don't understand."

"I suffer," said John Marcher.

"Don't, don't!"

"How can I help at least *that?*"

"*Don't!*" May Bartram repeated.

She spoke it in a tone so special, in spite of her weakness, that he stared an instant—stared as if some light, hitherto hidden, had shimmered across his vision. Darkness again closed over it, but the gleam had already become for him an idea. "Because I haven't the right—?"

"Don't *know*—when you needn't," she mercifully urged. "You needn't—for we shouldn't."

"Shouldn't?" If he could but know what she meant!

"No—it's too much."

"Too much?" he still asked but, with a mystification that was the next moment of a sudden to give way. Her words, if they meant something, affected him in this light—the light also of her wasted face—as meaning *all,* and the sense of what knowledge had been for herself came over him with a rush which broke through into a question. "Is it of that then you're dying?"

She but watched him, gravely at first, as to see, with this, where he was, and she might have seen something or feared something that moved her sympathy. "I would live for you still—if I could." Her eyes closed for a little, as if, withdrawn into herself, she were for a last time trying. "But I can't!" she said as she raised them again to take leave of him.

She couldn't indeed, as but too promptly and sharply appeared, and he had no vision of her after this that was anything, but darkness and doom. They had parted for ever in that strange talk; access to her chamber of pain, rigidly guarded, was almost wholly forbidden him; he was feeling now more-over, in the face of doctors, nurses, the two or three relatives attracted doubtless by the presumption of what she had to "leave," how few were the rights, as they were called in such cases, that he had to put forward, and how odd it might even seem that their intimacy shouldn't have given him more of them. The stupidest fourth cousin had more, even though she had been nothing in such a person's life. She had been a feature of features in *his,* for what else was it to have been so indispensable? Strange beyond say-ing were the ways of existence, baffling for him the anomaly of his lack, as he felt it to be, of producible claim. A woman might have been, as it were, everything to him, and it might yet present him in no connexion that any one seemed held to recognise. If this was the case in these closing weeks it was the case more sharply on the occasion of the last offices rendered, in the great grey London cemetery, to what had been mortal, to what had been pre-cious, in his friend. The concourse at her grave was not numerous, but he saw himself treated as scarce more nearly concerned with it than if there had been a thousand others. He was in short from this moment face to face with the fact that he was to profit extraordinarily little by the interest May Bartram had taken in him. He couldn't quite have said what he expected, but he hadn't surely expected this approach to a double privation. Not only had her interest failed him, but he seemed to feel himself unattended—and for a reason he couldn't seize—by the distinction, the dignity, the propriety, if nothing else, of the man markedly bereaved. It was as if in the view of society he had not *been* markedly bereaved, as if there still failed some sign or proof of it, and as if none the less his character could never be affirmed nor the deficiency ever made up. There were moments as the weeks went by when he would have liked, by some almost aggressive act, to take his stand on the intimacy of his loss, in order that it *might* be questioned and his retort, to the relief of his spirit, so recorded; but the moments of an irritation more helpless followed fast on these, the moments during which, turning things over with a good conscience but with a bare horizon, he found himself wondering if he oughtn't to have begun, so to speak, further back.

He found himself wondering at many things, and this last speculation had others to keep it company. What could he have done, after all, in her lifetime, without giving them both, as it were, away? He couldn't have made known she was watching him, for that would have published the superstition of the Beast. This was what closed his mouth now—now that the Jungle had been threshed to vacancy and that the Beast had stolen away. It sounded too foolish and too flat; the difference for him in this particular, the extinction in his life of the element of suspense, was such as in fact to surprise him. He could scarce have said what the effect resembled; the abrupt cessation, the positive prohibition, of music perhaps, more than anything else, in some place all adjusted and all accustomed to sonority and to attention. If he could at any rate have conceived lifting the veil from his image at some moment of the past (what had he done, after all, if not lift it to *her?*) so to do this today, to talk to people at large of the Jungle cleared and confide to them that he now felt it as safe, would have been not only to see them listen as to a good-wife's tale, but really to hear himself tell one. What it presently came to in truth was that poor Marcher waded through his beaten grass, where no life stirred, where no breath sounded, where no evil eye seemed to gleam from a possible lair, very much as if vaguely looking for the Beast, and still more as if acutely missing it. He walked about in an existence that had grown strangely more spacious, and, stopping fitfully in places where the undergrowth of life struck him as closer, asked himself yearningly, wondered secretly and sorely, if it would have lurked here or there. It would have at all events *sprung;* what was at least complete was his belief in the truth of the assurance given him. The change from his old sense to his new was absolute and final: what was to happen *had* so absolutely and finally happened that he was as little able to know a fear for his future as to know a hope; so absent in short was any question of anything still to come. He was to live entirely with the other question, that of his unidentified past, that of his having to see his fortune impenetrably muffled and masked.

The torment of this vision became then his occupation; he couldn't perhaps have consented to live but for the possibility of guessing. She had told him, his friend, not to guess; she had forbidden him, so far as he might, to know, and she had even in a sort denied the power in him to learn: which were so many things, precisely, to deprive him of rest. It wasn't that he wanted, he argued for fairness, that anything past and done should repeat itself; it was only that he shouldn't, as an anticlimax, have been taken sleeping so sound as not to be able to win back by an effort of thought the lost stuff of consciousness. He declared to himself at moments that he would either win it back or have done with consciousness for ever; he made this idea his one motive in fine, made it so much his passion that none other, to compare with it, seemed ever to have touched him. The lost stuff of consciousness became thus for him as a strayed or stolen child to an unappeasable father; he hunted it up and down very much as if he were knocking at doors and enquiring of the police. This was the spirit in which, inevitably, he set himself to travel; he started on a journey that was to be as long as he could make it; it danced before him that, as the other side of the globe couldn't possibly have less to say to him, it might, by a possibility of suggestion, have more. Before he quitted London, however, he made a pilgrimage to May Bartram's grave, took his way to it through the endless avenues of the grim suburban metropolis, sought it out in the wilderness of tombs, and, though he had come but for the renewal of the act of farewell, found himself, when he had at last stood by it, beguiled into long intensities. He stood for an hour, powerless to turn away and yet powerless to penetrate the darkness of death; fixing with his eyes her inscribed name and date, beating his forehead against the fact of the secret they kept, drawing his breath, while he waited, as if some sense would in pity of him rise from the stones. He kneeled on the stones, however, in vain; they kept what they concealed; and if the face of the tomb did become a face for him it was because her two names became a pair of eyes that didn't know him. He gave them a last long look, but no palest light broke.

VI

He stayed away, after this, for a year; he visited the depths of Asia, spending himself on scenes of romantic interest, of superlative sanctity; but what was present to him everywhere was that for a man who had known what *he* had known the world was vulgar and vain. The state of mind in which he had lived for so many years shone out to him, in reflexion, as a light that coloured and refined, a light beside which the glow of the East was garish cheap and thin. The terrible truth was that he had lost—with everything else—a distinction as well; the things he saw couldn't help being common when he had become common to look at them. He was simply now one of them himself—he was in the dust, without a peg for the sense of difference; and there were hours when, before the temples of gods and the sepulchres of kings, his spirit turned for nobleness of association to the barely discriminated slab in the London suburb. That had become for him, and more intensely with time and distance, his one witness of a past glory. It was all that was left to him for proof or pride, yet the past glories of Pharaohs were nothing to him as he thought of it. Small wonder then that he came back to it on the morrow of his return. He was drawn there this time as irresistibly as the other, yet with a confidence, almost, that was doubtless the effect of the many months that had elapsed. He had lived, in spite of himself, into his change of feeling, and in wandering over the earth had wandered, as might be said, from the circumference to the centre of his desert. He had settled to his safety and accepted perforce his extinction; figuring to himself, with some colour, in the likeness of certain little old men he remembered to have seen, of whom, all meagre and wizened as they might look, it was related that they had in their time fought twenty duels or been loved by ten princesses. They indeed had been wondrous for others while he was but wondrous for himself; which, however, was exactly the cause of his haste to renew the wonder by getting back, as he might put it, into his own presence. That had quickened his steps and checked his delay. If his visit was prompt it was because he had been separated so long from the part of himself that alone he now valued.

It's accordingly not false to say that he reached his goal with a certain elation and stood there again with a certain assurance. The creature beneath the sod *knew* of his rare experience, so that, strangely now, the place had lost for him its mere blankness of expression. It met him in mildness—not, as before, in mockery; it wore for him the air of conscious greeting that we find, after absence, in things that have closely belonged to us and which seem to confess of themselves to the connexion. The plot of ground, the graven tablet, the tended flowers affected him so as belonging to him that he resembled for the hour a contented landlord reviewing a piece of property. Whatever had happened—well, had happened. He had not come back this time with the vanity of that question, his former worrying "What, *what?*" now practically so spent. Yet he would none the less never again so cut himself off from the spot; he would come back to it every month, for if he did nothing else by its aid he at least held up his head. It thus grew for him, in the oddest way, a positive resource; he carried out his idea of periodical returns, which took their place at last among the most inveterate of his habits. What it all amounted to, oddly enough, was that in his finally so simplified world this garden of death gave him the few square feet of earth on which he could still most live. It was as if, being nothing anywhere else for any one, nothing even for himself, he were just everything here, and if not for a crowd of witnesses or indeed for any witness but John Marcher, then by clear right of the register that he could scan like an open page. The open page was the tomb of his friend, and *there* were the facts of the past, there the truth of his life, there the backward reaches in which he could lose himself. He did this from time to time with such effect that he seemed to wander through the old years with his hand in the arm of a companion who was, in the most extraordinary manner, his other, his younger self; and to wander, which was more extraordinary yet, round and round a third presence—not wandering she, but stationary, still, whose eyes, turning with his revolution, never ceased to follow him, and whose seat was his point, so to speak, of orientation. Thus in short he settled to live—feeding all on the sense that he once *had* lived, and dependent on it not alone for a support but for an identity.

It sufficed him in its way for months and the year elapsed; it would doubtless even have carried him further but for an accident, superficially slight, which moved him, quite in another direction, with a force beyond any of his impressions of Egypt or of India. It was a thing of the merest chance—the turn, as he afterwards felt, of a hair, though he was indeed to live to believe that if light hadn't come to him in this particular fashion it would still have come in another. He was to live to believe this, I say, though he was not to live, I may not less definitely mention, to do much else. We allow him at any rate the benefit of the conviction, struggling up for him at the end, that, whatever might have happened or not happened, he would have come round of himself to the light. The incident of an autumn day had put the match to the train laid from of old by his misery. With the light before him he knew that even of late his ache had only been smothered. It was strangely drugged, but it throbbed; at the touch it began to bleed. And the touch, in the event, was the face of a fellow mortal. This face, one grey afternoon when the leaves were thick in the alleys, looked into Marcher's own, at the cemetery, with an expression like the cut of a blade. He felt it, that is, so deep down that he winced at the steady thrust. The person who so mutely assaulted him was a figure he had noticed, on reaching his own goal, absorbed by a grave a short distance away, a grave apparently fresh, so that the emotion of the visitor would probably match it for frankness. This face alone forbade further attention, though during the time he stayed he remained vaguely conscious of his neighbour, a middle-aged man apparently, in mourning, whose bowed back, among the clustered monuments and mortuary yews, was constantly presented. Marcher's theory that these were elements in contact with which he himself revived, had suffered, on this occasion, it may be granted, a marked, an excessive check. The autumn day was dire for him as none had recently been, and he rested with a heaviness he had not yet known on the low stone table that bore May Bartram's name. He rested without power to move, as if some spring in him, some spell vouchsafed, had suddenly been broken for ever. If he could have done that moment as he wanted he would simply have stretched himself on the slab that was ready to take him, treating it as a place prepared to receive his last sleep. What in all the wide world had he now to keep awake for? He stared before him with the question, and it was then that, as one of the cemetery walks passed near him, he caught the shock of the face.

His neighbour at the other grave had withdrawn, as he himself, with force enough in him, would have done by now, and was advancing along the path on his way to one of the gates. This brought him close, and his pace was slow, so that—and all the more as there was a kind of hunger in his look—the two men were for a minute directly confronted. Marcher knew him at once for one of the deeply stricken—a perception so sharp that nothing else in the picture comparatively lived, neither his dress, his age, nor his presumable character and class; nothing lived but the deep ravage of the features he showed. He *showed* them—that was the point; he was moved, as he passed, by some impulse that was either a signal for sympathy or, more possibly, a challenge to an opposed sorrow. He might already have been aware of our friend, might at some previous hour have noticed in him the smooth habit of the scene, with which the state of his own senses so scantly consorted, and might thereby have been stirred as by an overt discord. What Marcher was at all events conscious of was in the first place that the image of scarred passion presented to him was conscious too—of something that profaned the air; and in the second that, roused, startled, shocked, he was yet the next moment looking after it, as it went, with envy. The most extraordinary thing that had happened to him—though he had given that name to other matters as well—took place, after his immediate vague stare, as a consequence of this impression. The stranger passed, but the raw glare of his grief remained, making our friend wonder in pity what wrong, what wound it expressed, what injury not to be healed. What had the man *had*, to make him by the loss of it so bleed and yet live?

Something—and this reached him with a pang—that *he*, John Marcher, hadn't; the proof of which was precisely John Marcher's arid end. No passion had ever touched him, for this was what passion meant; he had survived and maundered and pined, but where had been *his* deep ravage? The extraordinary thing we speak of was the sudden rush of the result of this question. The sight that had just met his eyes named to him, as in letters of quick flame, something he had utterly, insanely missed, and what he had missed made these things a train of fire, made them mark themselves in an anguish of inward throbs. He had seen *outside* of his life, not learned it within, the way a woman was mourned when she had been loved for herself: such was the force of his conviction of the meaning of the stranger's face, which still flared for him as a smoky torch. It hadn't come to him, the knowledge, on the wings of experience; it had brushed him, jostled him, upset him, with the disrespect of chance, the insolence of accident. Now that the illumination had begun, however, it blazed to the zenith, and what he presently stood there gazing at was the sounded void of his life. He gazed, he drew breath, in pain; he turned in his dismay, and, turning, he had before him in sharper incision than ever the open page of his story. The name on the table smote him as the passage of his neighbour had done, and what it said to him, full in the face, was that *she* was what he had missed. This was the awful thought, the answer to all the past, the vision at the dread clearness of which he grew as cold as the stone beneath him. Everything fell together, confessed, explained, overwhelmed; leaving him most of all stupefied at the blindness he had cherished. The fate he had been marked for he had met with a vengeance—he had emptied the cup to the lees; he had been the man of his time, *the* man, to whom nothing on earth was to have happened. That was the rare stroke— that was his visitation. So he saw it, as we say, in pale horror, while the pieces fitted and fitted. So *she* had seen it while he didn't, and so she served at this hour to drive the truth home. It was the truth, vivid and monstrous, that all the while he had waited the wait was itself his portion. This the companion of his vigil had at a given moment made out, and she had then offered him the chance to baffle his doom. One's doom, however, was never baffled, and on the day she told him his own had come down she had seen him but stupidly stare at the escape she offered him.

The escape would have been to love her; then, *then* he would have lived. *She* had lived—who could say now with what passion?—since she had loved him for himself; whereas he had never thought of her (ah, how it hugely glared at him!) but in the chill of his egotism and the light of her use. Her spoken words came back to him—the chain stretched and stretched. The Beast had lurked indeed, and the Beast, at its hour, had sprung; it had sprung in that twilight of the cold April when, pale, ill, wasted, but all beautiful, and perhaps even then recoverable, she had risen from her chair to stand before him and let him imaginably guess. It had sprung as he didn't guess; it had sprung as she hopelessly turned from him, and the mark, by the time he left her, had fallen where it *was* to fall. He had justified his fear and achieved his fate; he had failed, with the last exactitude, of all he was to fail of; and a moan now rose to his lips as he remembered she had prayed he mightn't know. This horror of waking—*this* was knowledge, knowledge under the breath of which the very tears in his eyes seemed to freeze. Through them, none the less, he tried to fix it and hold it; he kept it there before him so that he might feel the pain. That at least, belated and bitter, had something of the taste of life. But the bitterness suddenly sickened him, and it was as if, horribly, he saw, in the truth, in the cruelty of his image, what had been appointed and done. He saw the Jungle of his life and saw the lurking Beast; then, while he looked, perceived it, as by a stir of the air, rise, huge and hideous, for the leap that was to settle him. His eyes darkened—it was close; and, instinctively turning, in his hallucination, to avoid it, he flung himself, face down, on the tomb.

1901   1903, 1909

SARAH ORNE JEWETT
1849–1909

When Sarah Orne Jewett was born in South Berwick, Maine, in 1849, the town and region she was to memorialize in her fiction were already changing rapidly. Her grandfather had been a sea captain, shipowner, and merchant, and as a child she was exposed to the bustle of this small inland port. By the end of the Civil War, however, textile mills and a cannery had largely replaced agriculture, shipbuilding, and logging as the economic base of the community, and the arrival of French Canadian and Irish immigrants brought ethnic diversity to the area. The stable, secure, and remote small town Jewett knew and loved as a child was experiencing the economic, technological, and demographic pressures that transformed much of America in her lifetime.

Jewett and her two sisters led happy and generally carefree childhoods. Their father was a kindly, hardworking obstetrician who encouraged Jewett's reading; and even as a small child she accompanied him on his horse-and-buggy rounds, meeting the rural people who would later populate her fiction. Jewett loved her father deeply, and some of her strong feelings for him are invested in *A Country Doctor* (1884), a novel that also celebrates the competence and independence of its female protagonist. Jewett's relationship with her mother was less intense; it was not until her mother became an invalid in the 1880s that mother and daughter became close. As Jewett confessed in a letter to editor and friend Thomas Bailey Aldrich: "I never felt so near to my mother . . . as I have since she died."

In part inspired by Harriet Beecher Stowe's novel about Maine seacoast life, *The Pearl of Orr's Island* (1862), Jewett began to write and publish verse and stories in her teens. One of her first efforts was accepted in 1869 by the influential editor William Dean Howells for publication in the prestigious *Atlantic Monthly.* In her early twenties, encouraged by Howells, she wrote a group of stories and sketches about a fictional coastal town in Maine to which she gave the name Deephaven; she published her first collection of short pieces in 1877 under that title. With the publication of this book, she entered the company of the many post–Civil War regional writers who were depicting the topographies, people, speech patterns, and modes of life of the nation's distinctive regions as they came under pressure from modernizing forces.

From the late 1870s on, Jewett was part of a circle of prominent women writers and artists who lived in or near Boston. The relationship between Jewett and Annie Adams Fields, the wife of editor and publisher James T. Fields, was the most important of her many friendships with men and women. Though they had known each other since the late 1870s, it was not until Annie Fields's husband died in 1881 that they established a bond that was to sustain both women until Jewett's death in 1909. During the winter months, Jewett lived at Fields's house in Boston and in the spring and summer was often to be found at Fields's oceanside home a few miles north of Boston in Manchester-by-the-Sea. Jewett maintained her residence in South Berwick, and she and Mrs. Fields would spend time together there as well. Their relationship, common at the turn of the century among single women who lived and traveled together, was often called a "Boston marriage." In recent years their relationship—and those of other prominent female couples of the period—has been the subject of much historical and biographical commentary.

Jewett reached artistic maturity with the publication of the collection *A White Heron* in 1886; later collections of sketches and stories include *The King of Folly Island* (1888), *A Native of Winby* (1893), and *The Life of Nancy* (1895). In these works the local landscape, people, and dialect are recorded with understanding and sympathy. In "A White Heron," reprinted here, a young girl's conflicted loyalties to her conception of herself in nature and to the world of men she will soon encounter are memorably and sensitively drawn. The bulk of her work concerns long-time residents of these small Maine communities, though there are exceptions, such as "The Foreigner" (1900), a ghost story about an enigmatic West Indies outsider in a close-knit Maine community. Jewett's most enduring work is *The Country of the Pointed Firs* (1896), a collection of linked sketches filtered through the consciousness of a summer visitor, much like the person Jewett had become. In this work, bits and pieces of the lives of a small group of men and women are quilted into a unified impression of life in a once-prosperous shipping village. The strong older women who survive in the region form a female community that, for many critics, is a hallmark of New England regionalism.

A White Heron[1]

I

The woods were already filled with shadows one June evening, just before eight o'clock, though a bright sunset still glimmered faintly among the trunks of the trees. A little girl was driving home her cow, a plodding, dilatory, provoking creature in her behavior, but a valued companion for all that. They were going away from whatever light there was, and striking deep into the woods, but their feet were familiar with the path, and it was no matter whether their eyes could see it or not.

There was hardly a night the summer through when the old cow could be found waiting at the pasture bars; on the contrary, it was her greatest pleasure to hide herself away among the high huckleberry bushes, and though she wore a loud bell she had made the discovery that if one stood perfectly still it would not ring. So Sylvia had to hunt for her until she found her, and call Co'! Co'! with never an answering Moo, until her childish patience was quite spent. If the creature had not given good milk and plenty of it, the case would have seemed very different to her owners. Besides, Sylvia had all the time there was, and very little use to make of it. Sometimes in pleasant weather it was a consolation to look upon the cow's pranks as an intelligent attempt to play hide and seek, and as the child had no playmates she lent herself to this amusement with a good deal of zest. Though this chase had been so long that the wary animal herself had given an unusual signal of her whereabouts, Sylvia had only laughed when she came upon Mistress Moolly at the swamp-side, and urged her affectionately homeward with a twig of birch leaves. The old cow was not inclined to wander farther, she even turned in the right direction for once as they left the pasture, and stepped along the road at a good pace. She was quite ready to be milked now, and seldom stopped to browse. Sylvia wondered what her grandmother would say because they were so late. It was a great while since she had left home at half past five o'clock, but everybody knew the difficulty of making this errand a short one. Mrs. Tilley had chased the hornéd torment too many summer evenings herself to blame any one else for lingering, and was only thankful as she waited

1. First published in book form in "*A White Heron*" *and Other Stories* (1886), the source of the text printed here.

that she had Sylvia, nowadays, to give such valuable assistance. The good woman suspected that Sylvia loitered occasionally on her own account; there never was such a child for straying about out-of-doors since the world was made! Everybody said that it was a good change for a little maid who had tried to grow for eight years in a crowded manufacturing town, but, as for Sylvia herself, it seemed as if she never had been alive at all before she came to live at the farm. She thought often with wistful compassion of a wretched geranium that belonged to a town neighbor.

"'Afraid of folks,'" old Mrs. Tilley said to herself, with a smile, after she had made the unlikely choice of Sylvia from her daughter's houseful of children, and was returning to the farm. "'Afraid of folks,' they said! I guess she won't be troubled no great with 'em up to the old place!" When they reached the door of the lonely house and stopped to unlock it, and the cat came to purr loudly, and rub against them, a deserted pussy, indeed, but fat with young robins, Sylvia whispered that this was a beautiful place to live in, and she never should wish to go home.

The companions followed the shady woodroad, the cow taking slow steps, and the child very fast ones. The cow stopped long at the brook to drink, as if the pasture were not half a swamp, and Sylvia stood still and waited, letting her bare feet cool themselves in the shoal water, while the great twilight moths struck softly against her. She waded on through the brook as the cow moved away, and listened to the thrushes with a heart that beat fast with pleasure. There was a stirring in the great boughs overhead. They were full of little birds and beasts that seemed to be wide awake, and going about their world, or else saying good-night to each other in sleepy twitters. Sylvia herself felt sleepy as she walked along. However, it was not much farther to the house, and the air was soft and sweet. She was not often in the woods so late as this, and it made her feel as if she were a part of the gray shadows and the moving leaves. She was just thinking how long it seemed since she first came to the farm a year ago, and wondering if everything went on in the noisy town just the same as when she was there; the thought of the great red-faced boy who used to chase and frighten her made her hurry along the path to escape from the shadow of the trees.

Suddenly this little woods-girl is horror-stricken to hear a clear whistle not very far away. Not a bird's whistle, which would have a sort of friendliness, but a boy's whistle, determined, and somewhat aggressive. Sylvia left the cow to whatever sad fate might await her, and stepped discreetly aside into the bushes, but she was just too late. The enemy had discovered her, and called out in a very cheerful and persuasive tone, "Halloa, little girl, how far is it to the road?" and trembling Sylvia answered almost inaudibly, "A good ways."

She did not dare to look boldly at the tall young man, who carried a gun over his shoulder, but she came out of her bush and again followed the cow, while he walked alongside.

"I have been hunting for some birds," the stranger said kindly, "and I have lost my way, and need a friend very much. Don't be afraid," he added gallantly. "Speak up and tell me what your name is, and whether you think I can spend the night at your house, and go out gunning early in the morning."

Sylvia was more alarmed than before. Would not her grandmother consider her much to blame? But who could have foreseen such an accident as this? It did not seem to be her fault, and she hung her head as if the stem of it were broken, but managed to answer "Sylvy," with much effort when her companion again asked her name.

Mrs. Tilley was standing in the doorway when the trio came into view. The cow gave a loud moo by way of explanation.

"Yes, you'd better speak up for yourself, you old trial! Where'd she tucked herself away this time, Sylvy?" But Sylvia kept an awed silence; she knew by instinct that her grandmother did not comprehend the gravity of the situation. She must be mistaking the stranger for one of the farmer-lads of the region.

The young man stood his gun beside the door, and dropped a lumpy game-bag beside it; then he bade Mrs. Tilley good-evening, and repeated his way-farer's story, and asked if he could have a night's lodging.

"Put me anywhere you like," he said. "I must be off early in the morning, before day; but I am very hungry, indeed. You can give me some milk at any rate, that's plain."

"Dear sakes, yes," responded the hostess, whose long slumbering hospital-ity seemed to be easily awakened. "You might fare better if you went out to the main road a mile or so, but you're welcome to what we've got. I'll milk right off, and you make yourself at home. You can sleep on husks or feathers," she proffered graciously. "I raised them all myself. There's good pasturing for geese just below here towards the ma'sh. Now step round and set a plate for the gentleman, Sylvy!" And Sylvia promptly stepped. She was glad to have something to do, and she was hungry herself.

It was a surprise to find so clean and comfortable a little dwelling in this New England wilderness. The young man had known the horrors of its most primitive housekeeping, and the dreary squalor of that level of society which does not rebel at the companionship of hens. This was the best thrift of an old-fashioned farmstead, though on such a small scale that it seemed like a hermitage. He listened eagerly to the old woman's quaint talk, he watched Sylvia's pale face and shining gray eyes with ever growing enthusiasm, and insisted that this was the best supper he had eaten for a month, and after-ward the new-made friends sat down in the door-way together while the moon came up.

Soon it would be berry-time, and Sylvia was a great help at picking. The cow was a good milker, though a plaguy thing to keep track of, the hostess gossiped frankly, adding presently that she had buried four children, so Sylvia's mother, and a son (who might be dead) in California were all the children she had left. "Dan, my boy, was a great hand to go gunning," she explained sadly. "I never wanted for pa'tridges or gray squer'ls while he was to home. He's been a great wand'rer, I expect, and he's no hand to write letters. There, I don't blame him, I'd ha' seen the world myself if it had been so I could.

"Sylvia takes after him," the grandmother continued affectionately, after a minute's pause. "There ain't a foot o' ground she don't know her way over, and the wild creaturs counts her one o' themselves. Squer'ls she'll tame to come an' feed right out o' her hands, and all sorts o' birds. Last winter she got the jay-birds to bangeing[2] here, and I believe she'd 'a' scanted herself of her own meals to have plenty to throw out amongst 'em, if I hadn't kep' watch. Any-thing but crows, I tell her, I'm willin' to help support—though Dan he had a tamed one o' them that did seem to have reason same as folks. It was round

2. Hanging around.

here a good spell after he went away. Dan an' his father they didn't hitch,—but he never held up his head ag'in after Dan had dared him an' gone off."

The guest did not notice this hint of family sorrows in his eager interest in something else.

"So Sylvy knows all about birds, does she?" he exclaimed, as he looked round at the little girl who sat, very demure but increasingly sleepy, in the moonlight. "I am making a collection of birds myself. I have been at it ever since I was a boy." (Mrs. Tilley smiled.) "There are two or three very rare ones I have been hunting for these five years. I mean to get them on my own ground if they can be found."

"Do you cage 'em up?" asked Mrs. Tilley doubtfully, in response to this enthusiastic announcement.

"Oh, no, they're stuffed and preserved, dozens and dozens of them," said the ornithologist, "and I have shot or snared every one myself. I caught a glimpse of a white heron three miles from here on Saturday, and I have followed it in this direction. They have never been found in this district at all.[3] The little white heron, it is," and he turned again to look at Sylvia with the hope of discovering that the rare bird was one of her acquaintances.

But Sylvia was watching a hop-toad in the narrow footpath.

"You would know the heron if you saw it," the stranger continued eagerly. "A queer tall white bird with soft feathers and long thin legs. And it would have a nest perhaps in the top of a high tree, made of sticks, something like a hawk's nest."

Sylvia's heart gave a wild beat; she knew that strange white bird, and had once stolen softly near where it stood in some bright green swamp grass, away over at the other side of the woods. There was an open place where the sunshine always seemed strangely yellow and hot, where tall, nodding rushes grew, and her grandmother had warned her that she might sink in the soft black mud underneath and never be heard of more. Not far beyond were the salt marshes just this side the sea itself, which Sylvia wondered and dreamed about, but never had seen, whose great voice could sometimes be heard above the noise of the woods on stormy nights.

"I can't think of anything I should like so much as to find that heron's nest," the handsome stranger was saying. "I would give ten dollars to anybody who could show it to me," he added desperately, "and I mean to spend my whole vacation hunting for it if need be. Perhaps it was only migrating, or had been chased out of its own region by some bird of prey."

Mrs. Tilley gave amazed attention to all this, but Sylvia still watched the toad, not divining, as she might have done at some calmer time, that the creature wished to get to its hole under the door-step, and was much hindered by the unusual spectators at that hour of the evening. No amount of thought, that night, could decide how many wished-for treasures the ten dollars, so lightly spoken of, would buy.

The next day the young sportsman hovered about the woods, and Sylvia kept him company, having lost her first fear of the friendly lad, who proved to be most kind and sympathetic. He told her many things about the birds and what they knew and where they lived and what they did with them-

3. Several species of herons were endangered during Jewett's time because hat-makers sought their dramatic wing feathers.

selves. And he gave her a jack-knife, which she thought as great a treasure as if she were a desert-islander. All day long he did not once make her troubled or afraid except when he brought down some unsuspecting singing creature from its bough. Sylvia would have liked him vastly better without his gun; she could not understand why he killed the very birds he seemed to like so much. But as the day waned, Sylvia still watched the young man with loving admiration. She had never seen anybody so charming and delightful; the woman's heart, asleep in the child, was vaguely thrilled by a dream of love. Some premonition of that great power stirred and swayed these young creatures who traversed the solemn woodlands with soft-footed silent care. They stopped to listed to a bird's song; they pressed forward again eagerly, parting the branches,—speaking to each other rarely and in whispers; the young man going first and Sylvia following, fascinated, a few steps behind, with her gray eyes dark with excitement.

She grieved because the longed-for white heron was elusive, but she did not lead the guest, she only followed, and there was no such thing as speaking first. The sound of her own unquestioned voice would have terrified her,—it was hard enough to answer yes or no when there was need of that. At last evening began to fall, and they drove the cow home together, and Sylvia smiled with pleasure when they came to the place where she heard the whistle and was afraid only the night before.

II

Half a mile from home, at the farther edge of the woods, where the land was highest, a great pine-tree stood, the last of its generation. Whether it was left for a boundary mark, or for what reason, no one could say; the woodchoppers who had felled its mates were dead and gone long ago, and a whole forest of sturdy trees, pines and oaks and maples, had grown again. But the stately head of this old pine towered above them all and made a landmark for sea and shore miles and miles away. Sylvia knew it well. She had always believed that whoever climbed to the top of it could see the ocean; and the little girl had often laid her hand on the great rough trunk and looked up wistfully at those dark boughs that the wind always stirred, no matter how hot and still the air might be below. Now she thought of the tree with a new excitement, for why, if one climbed it at break of day, could not one see all the world, and easily discover from whence the white heron flew, and mark the place, and find the hidden nest?

What a spirit of adventure, what wild ambition! What fancied triumph and delight and glory for the later morning when she could make known the secret! It was almost too real and too great for the childish heart to bear.

All night the door of the little house stood open and the whippoorwills came and sang upon the very step. The young sportsman and his old hostess were sound asleep, but Sylvia's great design kept her broad awake and watching. She forgot to think of sleep. The short summer night seemed as long as the winter darkness, and at last when the whippoorwills ceased, and she was afraid the morning would after all come too soon, she stole out of the house and followed the pasture path through the woods, hastening toward the open ground beyond, listening with a sense of comfort and companionship to the drowsy twitter of a half-awakened bird, whose perch she had jarred in passing. Alas, if the great wave of human interest which flooded for the first time this dull little life should sweep away the satisfactions of an existence heart to heart with nature and the dumb life of the forest!

There was the huge tree asleep yet in the paling moonlight, and small and silly Sylvia began with utmost bravery to mount to the top of it, with tingling, eager blood coursing the channels of her whole frame, with her bare feet and fingers, that pinched and held like bird's claws to the monstrous ladder reaching up, up, almost to the sky itself. First she must mount the white oak tree that grew alongside, where she was almost lost among the dark branches and the green leaves heavy and wet with dew; a bird fluttered off its nest, and a red squirrel ran to and fro and scolded pettishly at the harmless housebreaker. Sylvia felt her way easily. She had often climbed there, and knew that higher still one of the oak's upper branches chafed against the pine trunk, just where its lower boughs were set close together. There, when she made the dangerous pass from one tree to the other, the great enterprise would really begin.

She crept out along the swaying oak limb at last, and took the daring step across into the old pine-tree. The way was harder than she thought; she must reach far and hold fast, the sharp dry twigs caught and held her and scratched her like angry talons, the pitch made her thin little fingers clumsy and stiff as she went round and round the tree's great stem, higher and higher upward. The sparrows and robins in the woods below were beginning to wake and twitter to the dawn, yet it seemed much lighter there aloft in the pine-tree, and the child knew that she must hurry if her project were to be of any use.

The tree seemed to lengthen itself out as she went up, and to reach farther and farther upward. It was like a great main-mast to the voyaging earth; it must truly have been amazed that morning through all its ponderous frame as it felt this determined spark of human spirit winding its way from higher branch to branch. Who knows how steadily the least twigs held themselves to advantage this light, weak creature on her way! The old pine must have loved his new dependent. More than all the hawks, and bats, and moths, and even the sweet voiced thrushes, was the brave, beating heart of the solitary gray-eyed child. And the tree stood still and frowned away the winds that June morning while the dawn grew bright in the east.

Sylvia's face was like a pale star, if one had seen it from the ground, when the last thorny bough was past, and she stood trembling and tired but wholly triumphant, high in the tree-top. Yes, there was the sea with the dawning sun making a golden dazzle over it, and toward that glorious east flew two hawks with slow-moving pinions. How low they looked in the air from that height when one had only seen them before far up, and dark against the blue sky. Their gray feathers were as soft as moths; they seemed only a little way from the tree, and Sylvia felt as if she too could go flying away among the clouds. Westward, the woodlands and farms reached miles and miles into the distance; here and there were church steeples, and white villages; truly it was a vast and awesome world!

The birds sang louder and louder. At last the sun came up bewilderingly bright. Sylvia could see the white sails of ships out at sea, and the clouds that were purple and rose-colored and yellow at first began to fade away. Where was the white heron's nest in the sea of green branches, and was this wonderful sight and pageant of the world the only reward for having climbed to such a giddy height? Now look down again, Sylvia, where the green marsh is set among the shining birches and dark hemlocks; there where you saw the white heron once you will see him again; look, look! a white spot of him like a single floating feather comes up from the dead hemlock and grows larger, and rises, and comes close at last, and goes by the landmark pine with steady sweep of wing and outstretched slender neck and crested head. And wait! wait! do not move a foot or a finger, little girl, do not send an arrow of light and consciousness from your two eager eyes, for the heron has perched on a pine bough not far beyond yours, and cries back to his mate on the nest, and plumes his feathers for the new day!

The child gives a long sigh a minute later when a company of shouting cat-birds comes also to the tree, and vexed by their fluttering and lawlessness the solemn heron goes away. She knows his secret now, the wild, light, slender bird that floats and wavers, and goes back like an arrow presently to his home in the green world beneath. Then Sylvia, well satisfied, makes her perilous way down again, not daring to look far below the branch she stands on, ready to cry sometimes because her fingers ache and her lamed feet slip. Wondering over and over again what the stranger would say to her, and what he would think when she told him how to find his way straight to the heron's nest.

"Sylvy, Sylvy!" called the busy old grandmother again and again, but nobody answered, and the small husk bed was empty and Sylvia had disappeared.

The guest waked from a dream, and remembering his day's pleasure hurried to dress himself that might it sooner begin. He was sure from the way the shy little girl looked once or twice yesterday that she had at least seen the white heron, and now she must really be made to tell. Here she comes now, paler than ever, and her worn old frock is torn and tattered, and smeared with pine pitch. The grandmother and the sportsman stand in the door together and question her, and the splendid moment has come to speak of the dead hemlock-tree by the green marsh.

But Sylvia does not speak after all, though the old grandmother fretfully rebukes her, and the young man's kind, appealing eyes are looking straight in her own. He can make them rich with money; he has promised it, and they are poor now. He is so well worth making happy, and he waits to hear the story she can tell.

No, she must keep silence! What is it that suddenly forbids her and makes her dumb? Has she been nine years growing and now, when the great world for the first time puts out a hand to her, must she thrust it aside for a bird's sake? The murmur of the pine's green branches is in her ears, she remembers how the white heron came flying through the golden air and how they watched the sea and the morning together, and Sylvia cannot speak; she cannot tell the heron's secret and give its life away.

Dear loyalty, that suffered a sharp pang as the guest went away disappointed later in the day, that could have served and followed him and loved him as a dog loves! Many a night Sylvia heard the echo of his whistle haunting the pasture path as she came home with the loitering cow. She forgot even her sorrow at the sharp report of his gun and the sight of thrushes and sparrows dropping silent to the ground, their songs hushed and their pretty feathers stained and wet with blood. Were the birds better friends than their hunter might have been,—who can tell? Whatever treasures were lost to her, woodlands and summer-time, remember! Bring your gifts and graces and tell your secrets to this lonely country child!

1886

KATE CHOPIN
1850–1904

Katherine O'Flaherty's Irish immigrant father was a successful businessman who died in a train wreck when his daughter was four years old. The family enjoyed a high place in St. Louis society; and her mother, grandmother, and great-grandmother were active, pious Catholics of French heritage. Without doubt Kate O'Flaherty grew up in the company of loving, intelligent, independent women. Particularly important was her strong-willed great-grandmother, a compelling and tireless storyteller whose influence may have been central to Chopin's becoming a significant regional writer and novelist.

Chopin was nine years old before she entered St. Louis Academy of the Sacred Heart, but she was already well read in English and French authors, and by the time she graduated from the academy in 1868 she had absorbed Cervantes, Dante, Goethe, and many English novelists and poets of the eighteenth and nineteenth centuries— Austen, the Brontës, and Coleridge among them. But it was French writers who most strongly influenced her. She read and admired French classical authors as well as more contemporary figures such as Gustave Flaubert, Madame de Staël, Émile Zola, and Guy de Maupassant. What she said of Maupassant as a writer she might have said of herself: "Here was a man who had escaped from tradition and authority, who had entered into himself and looked out upon life through his own being and with his own eyes; and who in a direct and simple way, told us what he saw." Whether focusing on St. Louis, New Orleans, or the Louisiana countryside, she described the tension between individual erotic inclination and the constraints placed on desire—especially on women's sexual desire—by traditional social mores. She told directly—and without moral judgment—how certain women were beginning to challenge the male-dominated culture that limited all aspects of women's lives—even the lives of comfortably situated women—and tried to control their psyches as well. Her new, modern perspectives, especially on female sexuality, paralleled those of Edith Wharton and Theodore Dreiser.

At the age of nineteen she married Oscar Chopin and spent the next decade in New Orleans, where her husband first prospered, then failed, as a cotton broker. After a few years in Cloutierville, a village in northwest Louisiana near Natchitoches, where her husband opened a general store and managed a family cotton plantation, she returned to St. Louis permanently in 1884, a year after her husband's death from swamp fever (probably malaria). A year later her mother died, and at the age of thirty-five Chopin was left essentially alone to raise her six young children. Having recognized the ready market for "local color," or regional, fiction, Chopin decided to fashion a literary career out of her experience of the Creole and Cajun cultures she had come to know.

Chopin claimed that she wrote on impulse, that she was "completely at the mercy of unconscious selection" of subject, and that "the polishing up process . . . always proved disastrous." In the relatively few years of her writing career—scarcely more than a decade—she completed three novels; more than 150 stories and sketches; and a substantial body of poetry, reviews, and criticism. A first novel, *At Fault,* was self-published in 1890, but it was her stories of Louisiana rural life, especially in the collection *Bayou Folk* (1894), that won her national recognition as a practitioner of local-color fiction. A second collection of stories, *A Night in Acadie,* was published three years later and increased her reputation as a local colorist. Chopin, who wrote about her own time, did not concern herself with the prewar South, but her depictions of the present revealed the unhappy residues of an outdated social ideology. At the same time, the influence of French fiction on her work showed in stories that were much more erotic—and guilt free—than the American norm. Her awareness of a disconnect between her work and American culture may explain why she did not submit "The Storm" for publication; it was not published until 1969 as part of Per Seyersted's edition of *The Complete Works of Kate Chopin*.

Chopin's major work, *The Awakening*, influenced by Gustave Flaubert's *Madame Bovary* (1856), was published in 1899. The novel, which traces the sensual and sexual coming to consciousness of a young woman, predictably aroused hostility among contemporary reviewers. Edna Pontellier is not a "new woman" demanding social, economic, and political equality; instead she can appear to be an unrepentant (if ultimately psychologically confused) sensualist, leading some critics to charge that the book was "trite and sordid," "essentially vulgar," and "unhealthily introspective and morbid in feeling." Chopin was dropped from her St. Louis clubs and snubbed by friends. But the readers who objected to Edna's behavior missed Chopin's portrayal of Edna's psychological turmoil. Though some commentators found much to praise in *The Awakening*, Chopin's only published response to reviews of the novel was to claim, "I never dreamed of Mrs. Pontellier making such a mess of things and working out her own damnation as she did. If I had had the slightest intimation of such a thing I would have excluded her from the company." After the book was published, Chopin's health began to deteriorate, and she wrote little. Though Chopin fell into obscurity for over a half a century, by the 1970s *The Awakening* and a number of her stories had come to be recognized as among the major achievements of turn-of-the-century American literary culture.

Désirée's Baby[1]

As the day was pleasant, Madame Valmondé drove over to L'Abri to see Désirée and the baby.

It made her laugh to think of Désirée with a baby. Why, it seemed but yesterday that Désirée was little more than a baby herself; when Monsieur in riding through the gateway of Valmondé had found her lying asleep in the shadow of the big stone pillar.

The little one awoke in his arms and began to cry for "Dada." That was as much as she could do or say. Some people thought she might have strayed there of her own accord, for she was of the toddling age. The prevailing belief was that she had been purposely left by a party of Texans, whose canvas-covered wagon, late in the day, had crossed the ferry that Coton Maïs kept, just below the plantation. In time Madame Valmondé abandoned every speculation but the one that Désirée had been sent to her by a beneficent Providence to be the child of her affection, seeing that she was without child of the flesh. For the girl grew to be beautiful and gentle, affectionate and sincere,—the idol of Valmondé.

It was no wonder, when she stood one day against the stone pillar in whose shadow she had lain asleep, eighteen years before, that Armand Aubigny riding by and seeing her there, had fallen in love with her. That was the way all the Aubignys fell in love, as if struck by a pistol shot. The wonder was that he had not loved her before; for he had known her since his father brought him

---

1. The story was first published in the January 4, 1893, *Vogue* as "The Father of Désirée's Baby— The Lover of Mentine," and then included in *Bayou Folk* (1894) with its present title. The text is taken from Per Seyersted's edition of *The Complete Works of Kate Chopin* (1969).

home from Paris, a boy of eight, after his mother died there. The passion that awoke in him that day, when he saw her at the gate, swept along like an avalanche, or like a prairie fire, or like anything that drives headlong over all obstacles.

Monsieur Valmondé grew practical and wanted things well considered: that is, the girl's obscure origin. Armand looked into her eyes and did not care. He was reminded that she was nameless. What did it matter about a name when he could give her one of the oldest and proudest in Louisiana? He ordered the *corbeille*[2] from Paris, and contained himself with what patience he could until it arrived; then they were married.

Madame Valmondé had not seen Désirée and the baby for four weeks. When she reached L'Abri she shuddered at the first sight of it, as she always did. It was a sad looking place, which for many years had not known the gentle presence of a mistress, old Monsieur Aubigny having married and buried his wife in France, and she having loved her own land too well ever to leave it. The roof came down steep and black like a cowl, reaching out beyond the wide galleries that encircled the yellow stuccoed house. Big, solemn oaks grew close to it, and their thick-leaved, far-reaching branches shadowed it like a pall. Young Aubigny's rule was a strict one, too, and under it his negroes had forgotten how to be gay, as they had been during the old master's easy-going and indulgent lifetime.

The young mother was recovering slowly, and lay full length, in her soft white muslins and laces, upon a couch. The baby was beside her, upon her arm, where he had fallen asleep, at her breast. The yellow[3] nurse woman sat beside a window fanning herself.

Madame Valmondé bent her portly figure over Désirée and kissed her, holding her an instant tenderly in her arms. Then she turned to the child.

"This is not the baby!" she exclaimed, in startled tones. French was the language spoken at Valmondé in those days.

"I knew you would be astonished," laughed Désirée, "at the way he has grown. The little *cochon de lait!*[4] Look at his legs, mamma, and his hands and fingernails,—real finger-nails. Zandrine had to cut them this morning. Is n't it true, Zandrine?"

The woman bowed her turbaned head majestically, "Mais si,[5] Madame."

"And the way he cries," went on Désirée, "is deafening. Armand heard him the other day as far away as La Blanche's cabin."

Madame Valmondé had never removed her eyes from the child. She lifted it and walked with it over to the window that was lightest. She scanned the baby narrowly, then looked as searchingly at Zandrine, whose face was turned to gaze across the fields.

"Yes, the child has grown, has changed," said Madame Valmondé, slowly, as she replaced it beside its mother. "What does Armand say?"

Désirée's face became suffused with a glow that was happiness itself.

"Oh, Armand is the proudest father in the parish, I believe, chiefly because it is a boy, to bear his name; though he says not,—that he would have loved a girl as well. But I know it is n't true. I know he says that to please me. And

2. Basket (French), short for *corbeille de mar-riage*: lavish wedding gifts from bridegroom to bride, traditionally presented in a wicker basket.
3. Anachronistic, generally pejorative term for a

lightly complected African American.
4. Literally a "pig in milk" (French); the term applies to a Cajun method of roasting pork.
5. Absolutely, yes (French).

mamma," she added, drawing Madame Valmondé's head down to her, and speaking in a whisper, "he has n't punished one of them—not one of them— since baby is born. Even Négrillon, who pretended to have burnt his leg that he might rest from work—he only laughed, and said Négrillon was a great scamp. Oh, mamma, I 'm so happy; it frightens me."

What Désirée said was true. Marriage, and later the birth of his son had softened Armand Aubigny's imperious and exacting nature greatly. This was what made the gentle Désirée so happy, for she loved him desperately. When he frowned she trembled, but loved him. When he smiled, she asked no greater blessing of God. But Armand's dark, handsome face had not often been disfigured by frowns since the day he fell in love with her.

When the baby was about three months old, Désirée awoke one day to the conviction that there was something in the air menacing her peace. It was at first too subtle to grasp. It had only been a disquieting suggestion; an air of mystery among the blacks; unexpected visits from far-off neighbors who could hardly account for their coming. Then a strange, an awful change in her husband's manner, which she dared not ask him to explain. When he spoke to her, it was with averted eyes, from which the old love-light seemed to have gone out. He absented himself from home; and when there, avoided her presence and that of her child, without excuse. And the very spirit of Satan seemed suddenly to take hold of him in his dealings with the slaves. Désirée was miserable enough to die.

She sat in her room, one hot afternoon, in her *peignoir*,[6] listlessly drawing through her fingers the strands of her long, silky brown hair that hung about her shoulders. The baby, half naked, lay asleep upon her own great mahogany bed, that was like a sumptuous throne, with its satin-lined half-canopy. One of La Blanche's little quadroon[7] boys—half naked too—stood fanning the child slowly with a fan of peacock feathers. Désirée's eyes had been fixed absently and sadly upon the baby, while she was striving to penetrate the threatening mist that she felt closing about her. She looked from her child to the boy who stood beside him, and back again; over and over. "Ah!" It was a cry that she could not help; which she was not conscious of having uttered. The blood turned like ice in her veins, and a clammy moisture gathered upon her face.

She tried to speak to the little quadroon boy; but no sound would come, at first. When he heard his name uttered, he looked up, and his mistress was pointing to the door. He laid aside the great, soft fan, and obediently stole away, over the polished floor, on his bare tiptoes.

She stayed motionless, with gaze riveted upon her child, and her face the picture of fright.

Presently her husband entered the room, and without noticing her, went to a table and began to search among some papers which covered it.

"Armand," she called to him, in a voice which must have stabbed him, if he was human. But he did not notice. "Armand," she said again. Then she rose and tottered towards him. "Armand," she panted once more, clutching his arm, "look at our child. What does it mean? tell me."

He coldly but gently loosened her fingers from about his arm and thrust the hand away from him. "Tell me what it means!" she cried despairingly.

---

6. Woman's dressing gown (French).
7. Term used in the nineteenth century (less often in the twentieth century) for people thought to be one-fourth black; more generally, "quadroon," like "mulatto," was used for light-skinned people of mixed racial ancestry.

"It means," he answered lightly, "that the child is not white; it means that you are not white."

A quick conception of all that this accusation meant for her nerved her with unwonted courage to deny it. "It is a lie; it is not true, I am white! Look at my hair, it is brown; and my eyes are gray, Armand, you know they are gray. And my skin is fair," seizing his wrist. "Look at my hand; whiter than yours, Armand," she laughed hysterically.

"As white as La Blanche's," he returned cruelly; and went away leaving her alone with their child.

When she could hold a pen in her hand, she sent a despairing letter to Madame Valmondé.

"My mother, they tell me I am not white. Armand has told me I am not white. For God's sake tell them it is not true. You must know it is not true. I shall die. I must die. I cannot be so unhappy, and live."

The answer that came was as brief:

"My own Désirée: Come home to Valmondé; back to your mother who loves you. Come with your child."

When the letter reached Désirée she went with it to her husband's study, and laid it open upon the desk before which he sat. She was like a stone image: silent, white, motionless after she placed it there.

In silence he ran his cold eyes over the written words. He said nothing. "Shall I go, Armand?" she asked in tones sharp with agonized suspense.

"Yes, go."

"Do you want me to go?"

"Yes, I want you to go."

He thought Almighty God had dealt cruelly and unjustly with him; and felt, somehow, that he was paying Him back in kind when he stabbed thus into his wife's soul. Moreover he no longer loved her, because of the unconscious injury she had brought upon his home and his name.

She turned away like one stunned by a blow, and walked slowly towards the door, hoping he would call her back.

"Good-by, Armand," she moaned.

He did not answer her. That was his last blow at fate.

Désirée went in search of her child. Zandrine was pacing the somber gallery with it. She took the little one from the nurse's arms with no word of explanation, and descending the steps, walked away, under the live-oak branches.

It was an October afternoon; the sun was just sinking. Out in the still fields the negroes were picking cotton.

Désirée had not changed the thin white garment nor the slippers which she wore. Her hair was uncovered and the sun's rays brought a golden gleam from its brown meshes. She did not take the broad, beaten road which led to the far-off plantation of Valmondé. She walked across a deserted field, where the stubble bruised her tender feet, so delicately shod, and tore her thin gown to shreds.

She disappeared among the reeds and willows that grew thick along the banks of the deep, sluggish bayou; and she did not come back again.

Some weeks later there was a curious scene enacted at L'Abri. In the centre of the smoothly swept back yard was a great bonfire. Armand Aubigny sat in the wide hallway that commanded a view of the spectacle; and it was he who dealt out to a half dozen negroes the material which kept this fire ablaze.

A graceful cradle of willow, with all its dainty furbishings, was laid upon the pyre, which had already been fed with the richness of a priceless *layette*.[8] Then there were silk gowns, and velvet and satin ones added to these; laces, too, and embroideries; bonnets and gloves; for the *corbeille* had been of rare quality.

The last thing to go was a tiny bundle of letters; innocent little scribblings that Désirée had sent to him during the days of their espousal. There was the remnant of one back in the drawer from which he took them. But it was not Désirée's; it was part of an old letter from his mother to his father. He read it. She was thanking God for the blessing of her husband's love:—

"But, above all," she wrote, "night and day, I thank the good God for having so arranged our lives that our dear Armand will never know that his mother, who adores him, belongs to the race that is cursed with the brand of slavery."

1893   1894

The Story of an Hour[1]

Knowing that Mrs. Mallard was afflicted with a heart trouble, great care was taken to break to her as gently as possible the news of her husband's death.

It was her sister Josephine who told her, in broken sentences; veiled hints that revealed in half concealing. Her husband's friend Richards was there, too, near her. It was he who had been in the newspaper office when intelligence of the railroad disaster was received, with Brently Mallard's name leading the list of "killed." He had only taken the time to assure himself of its truth by a second telegram, and had hastened to forestall any less careful, less tender friend in bearing the sad message.

She did not hear the story as many women have heard the same, with a paralyzed inability to accept its significance. She wept at once, with sudden, wild abandonment, in her sister's arms. When the storm of grief had spent itself she went away to her room alone. She would have no one follow her.

There stood, facing the open window, a comfortable, roomy armchair. Into this she sank, pressed down by a physical exhaustion that haunted her body and seemed to reach into her soul.

She could see in the open square before her house the tops of trees that were all aquiver with the new spring life. The delicious breath of rain was in the air. In the street below a peddler was crying his wares. The notes of a distant song which some one was singing reached her faintly, and countless sparrows were twittering in the eaves.

There were patches of blue sky showing here and there through the clouds that had met and piled one above the other in the west facing her window.

She sat with her head thrown back upon the cushion of the chair, quite motionless, except when a sob came up into her throat and shook her, as a child who has cried itself to sleep continues to sob in its dreams.

8. A set of clothes for a newborn child (French).
1. The story was first published in the April 19, 1894, *Vogue* as "The Dream of an Hour," and then reprinted in the January 5, 1895, *St. Louis Life* with its present title. The text is taken from Per Seyersted's edition of *The Complete Works of Kate Chopin* (1969).

She was young, with a fair, calm face, whose lines bespoke repression and even a certain strength. But now there was a dull stare in her eyes, whose gaze was fixed away off yonder on one of those patches of blue sky. It was not a glance of reflection, but rather indicated a suspension of intelligent thought.

There was something coming to her and she was waiting for it, fearfully. What was it? She did not know; it was too subtle and elusive to name. But she felt it, creeping out of the sky, reaching toward her through the sounds, the scents, the color that filled the air.

Now her bosom rose and fell tumultuously. She was beginning to recognize this thing that was approaching to possess her, and she was striving to beat it back with her will—as powerless as her two white slender hands would have been.

When she abandoned herself a little whispered word escaped her slightly parted lips. She said it over and over under her breath: "free, free, free!" The vacant stare and the look of terror that had followed it went from her eyes. They stayed keen and bright. Her pulses beat fast, and the coursing blood warmed and relaxed every inch of her body.

She did not stop to ask if it were or were not a monstrous joy that held her. A clear and exalted perception enabled her to dismiss the suggestion as trivial.

She knew that she would weep again when she saw the kind, tender hands folded in death; the face that had never looked save with love upon her, fixed and gray and dead. But she saw beyond that bitter moment a long procession of years to come that would belong to her absolutely. And she opened and spread her arms out to them in welcome.

There would be no one to live for her during those coming years; she would live for herself. There would be no powerful will bending hers in that blind persistence with which men and women believe they have a right to impose a private will upon a fellow-creature. A kind intention or a cruel intention made the act seem no less a crime as she looked upon it in that brief moment of illumination.

And yet she had loved him—sometimes. Often she had not. What did it matter! What could love, the unsolved mystery, count for in face of this possession of self-assertion which she suddenly recognized as the strongest impulse of her being!

"Free! Body and soul free!" she kept whispering.

Josephine was kneeling before the closed door with her lips to the keyhole, imploring for admission. "Louise, open the door! I beg; open the door—you will make yourself ill. What are you doing, Louise? For heaven's sake open the door."

"Go away. I am not making myself ill." No; she was drinking in a very elixir of life through that open window.

Her fancy was running riot along those days ahead of her. Spring days, and summer days, and all sorts of days that would be her own. She breathed a quick prayer that life might be long. It was only yesterday she had thought with a shudder that life might be long.

She arose at length and opened the door to her sister's importunities. There was a feverish triumph in her eyes, and she carried herself unwittingly like a goddess of Victory. She clasped her sister's waist, and together they descended the stairs. Richards stood waiting for them at the bottom.

Some one was opening the front door with a latchkey. It was Brently Mallard who entered, a little travel-stained, composedly carrying his gripsack and umbrella. He had been far from the scene of accident, and did not even know there had been one. He stood amazed at Josephine's piercing cry; at Richards' quick motion to screen him from the view of his wife.

But Richards was too late.

When the doctors came they said she had died of heart disease—of joy that kills.

1894   1895

At the 'Cadian Ball[1]

Bobinôt, that big, brown, good-natured Bobinôt, had no intention of going to the ball, even though he knew Calixta would be there. For what came of those balls but heartache, and a sickening disinclination for work the whole week through, till Saturday night came again and his tortures began afresh? Why could he not love Ozéina, who would marry him tomorrow; or Fronie, or any one of a dozen others, rather than that little Spanish vixen? Calixta's slender foot had never touched Cuban soil; but her mother's had, and the Spanish was in her blood all the same. For that reason the prairie people forgave her much that they would not have overlooked in their own daughters or sisters.

Her eyes,—Bobinôt thought of her eyes, and weakened,—the bluest, the drowsiest, most tantalizing that ever looked into a man's; he thought of her flaxen hair that kinked worse than a mulatto's close to her head; that broad, smiling mouth and tiptilted nose, that full figure; that voice like a rich contralto song, with cadences in it that must have been taught by Satan, for there was no one else to teach her tricks on that 'Cadian prairie. Bobinôt thought of them all as he plowed his rows of cane.

There had even been a breath of scandal whispered about her a year ago, when she went to Assumption,[2]—but why talk of it? No one did now. "C'est Espagnol, ça,"[3] most of them said with lenient shoulder-shrugs. "Bon chien tient de race,"[4] the old men mumbled over their pipes, stirred by recollections. Nothing was made of it, except that Fronie threw it up to Calixta when the two quarreled and fought on the church steps after mass one Sunday, about a lover. Calixta swore roundly in fine 'Cadian French and with true Spanish spirit, and slapped Fronie's face. Fronie had slapped her back; "Tiens, cocotte, va!"[5] "Espèce de lionèse; prends ça, et ça!"[6] till the curé himself was obliged to hasten and make peace between them. Bobinôt thought of it all, and would not go to the ball.

But in the afternoon, over at Friedheimer's store, where he was buying a trace-chain,[7] he heard some one say that Alcée Laballière would be there. Then wild horses could not have kept him away. He knew how it would be—or rather he did not know how it would be—if the handsome young

1. First published in *Two Tales* (October 1892); first published in book form in *Bayou Folk* (1894), the source of the text printed here.
2. I.e., Assumption Parish, Louisiana.
3. That's a Spaniard for you (French).

4. Just like her mother (French).
5. Listen, you flirt, get out of here! (French).
6. You bitch; take that and that! (French).
7. Equipment used to harness horses.

planter came over to the ball as he sometimes did. If Alcée happened to be in a serious mood, he might only go to the card-room and play a round or two; or he might stand out on the galleries talking crops and politics with the old people. But there was no telling. A drink or two could put the devil in his head,—that was what Bobinôt said to himself, as he wiped the sweat from his brow with his red bandanna; a gleam from Calixta's eyes, a flash of her ankle, a twirl of her skirts could do the same. Yes, Bobinôt would go to the ball.

That was the year Alcée Laballière put nine hundred acres in rice. It was putting a good deal of money into the ground, but the returns promised to be glorious. Old Madame Laballière, sailing about the spacious galleries in her white *volante*,[8] figured it all out in her head. Clarisse, her goddaughter, helped her a little, and together they built more air-castles than enough. Alcée worked like a mule that time; and if he did not kill himself, it was because his constitution was an iron one. It was an every-day affair for him to come in from the field well-nigh exhausted, and wet to the waist. He did not mind if there were visitors; he left them to his mother and Clarisse. There were often guests: young men and women who came up from the city, which was but a few hours away, to visit his beautiful kinswoman. She was worth going a good deal farther than that to see. Dainty as a lily; hardy as a sunflower; slim, tall, graceful, like one of the reeds that grew in the marsh. Cold and kind and cruel by turn, and everything that was aggravating to Alcée.

He would have liked to sweep the place of those visitors, often. Of the men, above all, with their ways and their manners; their swaying of fans like women, and dandling about hammocks. He could have pitched them over the levee into the river, if it hadn't meant murder. That was Alcée. But he must have been crazy the day he came in from the rice-field, and, toil-stained as he was, clasped Clarisse by the arms and panted a volley of hot, blistering love-words into her face. No man had ever spoken love to her like that.

"Monsieur!" she exclaimed, looking him full in the eyes, without a quiver. Alcée's hands dropped and his glance wavered before the chill of her calm, clear her eyes.

"*Par exemple!*"[9] she muttered disdainfully, as she turned from him, deftly adjusting the careful toilet that he had so brutally disarranged.

That happened a day or two before the cyclone came that cut into the rice like fine steel. It was an awful thing, coming so swiftly, without a moment's warning in which to light a holy candle or set a piece of blessed palm burning. Old Madame wept openly and said her beads, just as her son Didier, the New Orleans one, would have done. If such a thing had happened to Alphonse, the Laballière planting cotton up in Natchitoches,[1] he would have raved and stormed like a second cyclone, and made his surroundings unbearable for a day or two. But Alcée took the misfortune differently. He looked ill and gray after it, and said nothing. His speechlessness was frightful. Clarisse's heart melted with tenderness; but when she offered her soft, purring words of condolence, he accepted them with mute indifference. Then she and her nénaine[2] wept afresh in each other's arms.

A night or two later, when Clarisse went to her window to kneel there in the moonlight and say her prayers before retiring, she saw that Bruce, Alcée's negro servant, had led his master's saddle-horse noiselessly along the edge of

---

8. A flowing garment.
9. For example (French, literal trans.); here, "Get a hold of yourself!"

1. Parish in northwest Louisiana.
2. Female attendant, in this case his mother.

the sward that bordered the gravel-path, and stood holding him near by. Presently, she heard Alcée quit his room, which was beneath her own, and traverse the lower portico. As he emerged from the shadow and crossed the strip of moonlight, she perceived that he carried a pair of well-filled saddle-bags which he at once flung across the animal's back. He then lost no time in mounting, and after a brief exchange of words with Bruce, went cantering away, taking no precaution to avoid the noisy gravel as the negro had done.

Clarisse had never suspected that it might be Alcée's custom to sally forth from the plantation secretly, and at such an hour; for it was nearly midnight. And had it not been for the telltale saddle-bags, she would only have crept to bed, to wonder, to fret and dream unpleasant dreams. But her impatience and anxiety would not be held in check. Hastily unbolting the shutters of her door that opened upon the gallery, she stepped outside and called softly to the old negro.

"Gre't Peter! Miss Clarisse. I was n' sho it was a ghos' o' w'at, stan'in' up dah, plumb in de night, dataway."

He mounted halfway up the long, broad flight of stairs. She was standing at the top.

"Bruce, w'ere has Monsieur Alcée gone?" she asked.

"W'y, he gone 'bout he business, I reckin," replied Bruce, striving to be non-committal at the outset.

"W'ere has Monsieour Alcée gone?" she reiterated, stamping her bare foot. "I won't stan' any nonsense or any lies; mine, Bruce."

"I don' ric'lic ez I eva tole you lie yit, Miss Clarisse. Mista Alcée, he all broke up, sho."

"Were—has—he gone? Ah, Sainte Vierge! faut de la patience! butor, va!"[3]

"W'en I was in he room, a-breshin' off he clo'es to-day," the darkey began, settling himself against the stair-rail, "he look dat speechless an' down, I say, 'you 'pear to me like some pussun w'at gwine have a spell o' sickness, Mista Alcée.' He say, 'You reckin?' 'I dat he git up, go look hisse'f stiddy in de glass. Den he go to de chimbly an' jerk up de quinine bottle an' po' a gre't hoss-dose on to he han'. An' he swalla dat mess in a wink, an' wash hit down wid a big dram o' w'iskey w'at he keep in he room, against he come all soppin' wet outen de fiel'.

"He 'lows, 'No, I ain' gwine be sick, Bruce.' Den he square off. He say, 'I kin mak out to stan' up an' gi' an' take wid any man I knows, lessen hit's John L. Sulvun.[4] But w'en God A'mighty an' a 'oman jines fo'ces agin me, dat's one too many fur me.' I tell 'im, 'Jis so,' whils' I 'se makin' out to bresh a spot off w'at ain' dah, on he coat colla. I tell 'im, 'You wants li'le res', suh.' He say, 'No, I wants li'le fling; dat w'at I wants; an' I gwine git it. Pitch me a fis'ful o' clo'es in dem 'ar saddle-bags.' Dat w'at he say. Don't you bodda, missy. He jis' gone a-caperin' yonda to de Cajun ball. Uh—uh—de skeeters is fair' a-swarmin' like bees roun' yo' foots!"

The mosquitoes were indeed attacking Clarisse's white feet savagely. She had unconsciously been alternately rubbing one foot over the other during the darkey's recital.

"The 'Cadian ball," she repeated contemptuously. "Humph! *Par exemple!*[5] Nice conduc' for a Laballière. An' he needs a saddle-bag, fill' with clothes, to go to the 'Cadian ball!"

3. Ah, Blessed Virgin! Give me patience! Lout, get out of here! (French).
4. American heavyweight boxing champion
(1855–1918).
5. Here, "Quite an example!"

"Oh, Miss Clarisse; you go on to bed, chile; git yo' soun' sleep. He 'low he come back in couple weeks o' so. I kiarn be repeatin' lot o' truck w'at young mans say, out heah face o' young gal."

Clarisse said no more, but turned and abruptly reëntered the house.

"You done talk too much wid yo' mouf a'ready, you ole fool nigga, you," muttered Bruce to himself as he walked away.

Alcée reached the ball very late, of course—too late for the chicken gumbo which had been served at midnight.

The big, low-ceiled room—they called it a hall—was packed with men and women dancing to the music of three fiddles. There were broad galleries all around it. There was a room at one side where sober-faced men were playing cards. Another, in which babies were sleeping, was called *le parc aux petits.*[6] Any one who is white may go to a 'Cadian ball, but he must pay for his lemonade, his coffee and chicken gumbo. And he must behave himself like a 'Cadian. Grosbœuf was giving this ball. He had been giving them since he was a young man, and he was a middle-aged one, now. In that time he could recall but one disturbance, and that was caused by American railroaders, who were not in touch with their surroundings and had no business there. "Ces maudits gens du raiderode,"[7] Grosbœuf called them.

Alcée Laballière's presence at the ball caused a flutter even among the men, who could not but admire his "nerve" after such misfortune befalling him. To be sure, they knew the Laballières were rich—that there were resources East, and more again in the city. But they felt it took a *brave homme*[8] to stand a blow like that philosophically. One old gentleman, who was in the habit of reading a Paris newspaper and knew things, chuckled gleefully to everybody that Alcée's conduct was altogether *chic, mais chic.* That he had more *panache*[9] than Boulanger. Well, perhaps he had.

But what he did not show outwardly was that he was in a mood for ugly things to-night. Poor Bobinôt alone felt it vaguely. He discerned a gleam of it in Alcée's handsome eyes, as the young planter stood in the doorway, looking with rather feverish glance upon the assembly, while he laughed and talked with a 'Cadian farmer who was beside him.

Bobinôt himself was dull-looking and clumsy. Most of the men were. But the young women were very beautiful. The eyes that glanced into Alcée's as they passed him were big, dark, soft as those of the young heifers standing out in the cool prairie grass.

But the belle was Calixta. Her white dress was not nearly so handsome or well made as Fronie's (she and Fronie had quite forgotten the battle on the church steps, and were friends again), nor were her slippers so stylish as those of Ozéina; and she fanned herself with a handkerchief, since she had broken her red fan at the last ball, and her aunts and uncles were not willing to give her another. But all the men agreed she was at her best to-night. Such animation! and abandon! such flashes of wit!

"Hé, Bobinôt! Mais w'at's the matta? W'at you standin' *planté là*[1] like ole Ma'ame Tina's cow in the bog, you!"

That was good. That was an excellent thrust at Bobinôt, who had forgotten the figure[2] of the dance with his mind bent on other things, and it started a clamor of laughter at his expense. He joined good-naturedly. It

---

6. Playroom (French).
7. Those cursed railroad people (French).
8. Sturdy fellow (French).

9. Style.
1. Rooted there (French).
2. The pattern of steps.

was better to receive even such notice as that from Calixta than none at all. But Madame Suzonne, sitting in a corner, whispered to her neighbor that if Ozéina were to conduct herself in a like manner, she should immediately be taken out to the mule-cart and driven home. The women did not always approve of Calixta.

Now and then were short lulls in the dance, when couples flocked out upon the galleries for a brief respite and fresh air. The moon had gone down pale in the west, and in the east was yet no promise of day. After such an interval, when the dancers again assembled to resume the interrupted quadrille, Calixta was not among them.

She was sitting upon a bench out in the shadow, with Alcée beside her. They were acting like fools. He had attempted to take a little gold ring from her finger; just for the fun of it, for there was nothing he could have done with the ring but replace it again. But she clinched her hand tight. He pretended that it was a very difficult matter to open it. Then he kept the hand in his. They seemed to forget about it. He played with her earring, a thin crescent of gold hanging from her small brown ear. He caught a wisp of the kinky hair that had escaped its fastening, and rubbed the ends of it against his shaven cheek.

"You know, last year in Assumption, Calixta?" They belonged to the younger generation, so preferred to speak English.

"Don't come say Assumption to me, M'sieur Alcée. I done yeard Assumption till I'm plumb sick."

"Yes, I know. The idiots! Because you were in Assumption, and I happened to go to Assumption, they must have it that we went together. But it was nice—*hein*,[3] Calixta?—in Assumption?"

They saw Bobinôt emerge from the hall and stand a moment outside the lighted doorway, peering uneasily and searchingly into the darkness. He did not see them, and went slowly back.

"There is Bobinôt looking for you. You are going to set poor Bobinôt crazy. You'll marry him some day; *hein*, Calxita?"

"I don't say no, me," she replied, striving to withdraw her hand, which he held more firmly for the attempt.

"But come, Calixta; you know you said you would go back to Assumption, just to spite them."

"No, I neva said that, me. You mus' dreamt that."

"Oh, I thought you did. You know I'm going down to the city."

"W'en?"

"To-night."

"Betta make has'e, then; it's mos' day."

"Well, to-morrow'll do."

"W'at you goin' do, yonda?"

"I don't know. Drown myself in the lake, maybe; unless you go down there to visit your uncle."

Calixta's senses were reeling; and they well-nigh left her when she felt Alicée's lips brush her ear like the touch of a rose.

"Mista Alcée! Is dat Mista Alcée?" the thick voice of a negro was asking; he stood on the ground, holding to the banister-rails near which the couple sat.

3. Huh.

"W'at do you want now?" cried Alcée impatiently. "Can't I have a moment of peace?"

"I ben huntin' you high an' low, suh," answered the man. "Dey—dey some one in de road, onda de mulbare-tree, want see you a minute."

"I wouldn't go out to the road to see the Angel Gabriel. And if you come back here with any more talk, I'll have to break your neck." The negro turned mumbling away.

Alcée and Calixta laughed softly about it. Her boisterousness was all gone. They talked low, and laughed softly, as lovers do.

"Alcée! Alcée Laballière!"

It was not the negro's voice this time; but one that went through Alcée's body like an electric shock, bringing him to his feet.

Clarisse was standing there in her riding-habit, where the negro had stood. For an instant confusion reigned in Alcée's thoughts, as with one who awakes suddenly from a dream. But he felt that something of serious import had brought his cousin to the ball in the dead of night.

"W'at does this mean, Clarisse?" he asked.

"It means something has happen' at home. You mus' come."

"Happened to maman?" he questioned, in alarm.

"No: nénaine is well, and asleep. It is something else. Not to frighten you. But you mus' come. Come with me, Alcée."

There was no need for the imploring note. He would have followed the voice anywhere.

She had now recognized the girl sitting back on the bench.

"Ah, c'est vous, Calixta? Comment ça va, mon enfant?"[4]

"Tcha va b'en; et vous, mam'zélle?"[5]

Alcée swung himself over the low rail and started to follow Clarisse, without a word, without a glance back at the girl. He had forgotten he was leaving her there. But Clarisse whispered something to him, and he turned back to say "Good-night, Calixta," and offer his hand to press through the railing. She pretended not to see it.

"How come that? You settin' yere by yo'se'f, Calixta?" It was Bobinôt who had found her there alone. The dancers had not yet come out. She looked ghastly in the faint, gray light struggling out of the east.

"Yes, that's me. Go yonda in the *parc aux petits* an' ask Aunt Olisse fu' my hat. She knows w'ere 't is. I want to go home, me."

"How you came?"

"I come afoot, with the Cateaus. But I'm goin' now. I ent goin' wait fu' 'em. I'm plumb wo' out, me."

"Kin I go with you, Calixta?"

"I don' care."

They went together across the open prairie and along the edge of the fields, stumbling in the uncertain light. He told her to lift her dress that was getting wet and bedraggled; for she was pulling at the weeds and grasses with her hands.

"I don't care; it's got to go in the tub, anyway. You been sayin' all along you want to marry me, Bobinôt. Well, if you want, yet, I don' care, me."

The glow of a sudden and overwhelming happiness shone out in the brown, rugged face of the young Acadian. He could not speak, for very joy. It choked him.

"Oh well, if you don' want," snapped Calixta, flippantly, pretending to be piqued at his silence.

"*Bon Dieu!*[6] You know that makes me crazy, w'at you sayin'. You mean that, Calixta? You ent goin' turn roun' agin?"

"I neva tole you that much *yet*, Bobinôt. I mean that. *Tiens*,"[7] and she held out her hand in the business-like manner of a man who clinches a bargain with a hand-clasp. Bobinôt grew bold with happiness and asked Calixta to kiss him. She turned her face, that was almost ugly after the night's dissipation, and looked steadily into his.

"I don' want to kiss you, Bobinôt," she said, turning away again, "not to-day. Some other time. *Bonté divine!*[8] ent you satisfy, *yet!*"

"Oh, I'm satisfy, Calixta," he said.

Riding through a patch of wood, Clarisse's saddle became ungirted, and she and Alcée dismounted to readjust it.

For the twentieth time he asked her what had happened at home.

"But, Clarisse, w'at is it? Is it a misfortune?"

"Ah Dieu sait!"[9] It's only something that happen' to me."

"To you!"

"I saw you go away las' night, Alcée, with those saddle-bags," she said, haltingly, striving to arrange something about the saddle, "an' I made Bruce tell me. He said you had gone to the ball, an' wouldn' be home for weeks an' weeks. I thought, Alcée—maybe you were going to—to Assumption. I got wild. An' then I knew if you didn't come back, *now*, tonight, I couldn't stan' it,—again."

She had her face hidden in her arm that she was resting against the saddle when she said that.

He began to wonder if this meant love. But she had to tell him so, before he believed it. And when she told him, he thought the face of the Universe was changed—just like Bobinôt. Was it last week the cyclone had well-nigh ruined him? The cyclone seemed a huge joke, now. It was he, then, who, an hour ago was kissing little Calixta's ear and whispering nonsense into it. Calixta was like a myth, now. The one, only, great reality in the world was Clarisse standing before him, telling him that she loved him.

In the distance they heard the rapid discharge of pistol-shots; but it did not disturb them. They knew it was only the negro musicians who had gone into the yard to fire their pistols into the air, as the custom is, and to announce "*le bal est fini.*"[1]

1892, 1894

---

6. Good God! (French).
7. Well (French).
8. Goodness gracious! (French).

9. God knows! (French).
1. The Ball is over (Fren).

The Storm

A Sequel to "The 'Cadian Ball"[1]

I

The leaves were so still that even Bibi thought it was going to rain. Bobinôt, who was accustomed to converse on terms of perfect equality with his little son, called the child's attention to certain sombre clouds that were rolling with sinister intention from the west, accompanied by a sullen, threatening roar. They were at Friedheimer's store and decided to remain there till the storm had passed. They sat within the door on two empty kegs. Bibi was four years old and looked very wise.

"Mama'll be 'fraid, yes," he suggested with blinking eyes.

"She'll shut the house. Maybe she got Sylvie helpin' her this evenin'," Bobinôt responded reassuringly.

"No; she ent got Sylvie. Sylvie was helpin' her yistiday," piped Bibi.

Bobinôt arose and going across to the counter purchased a can of shrimps, of which Calixta was very fond. Then he returned to his perch on the keg and sat stolidly holding the can of shrimps while the storm burst. It shook the wooden store and seemed to be ripping furrows in the distant field. Bibi laid his little hand on his father's knee and was not afraid.

II

Calixta, at home, felt no uneasiness for their safety. She sat at a side window sewing furiously on a sewing machine. She was greatly occupied and did not notice the approaching storm. But she felt very warm and often stopped to mop her face on which the perspiration gathered in beads. She unfastened her white sacque at the throat. It began to grow dark, and suddenly realizing the situation she got up hurriedly and went about closing windows and doors.

Out on the small front gallery she had hung Bobinôt's Sunday clothes to dry and she hastened out to gather them before the rain fell. As she stepped outside, Alcée Laballière rode in at the gate. She had not seen him very often since her marriage, and never alone. She stood there with Bobinôt's coat in her hands, and the big rain drops began to fall. Alcée rode his horse under the shelter of a side projection where the chickens had huddled and there were plows and a harrow piled up in the corner.

"May I come and wait on your gallery till the storm is over, Calixta?" he asked.

"Come 'long in, M'sieur Alcée."

His voice and her own startled her as if from a trance, and she seized Bobinôt's vest. Alcée, mounting to the porch, grabbed the trousers and snatched Bibi's braided jacket that was about to be carried away by a sudden gust of wind. He expressed an intention to remain outside, but it was soon apparent that he might as well have been out in the open: the water beat in

1. Chopin's notebooks show that this story was written on July 18, 1898, just six months after she had submitted *The Awakening* to a publisher. As its subtitle indicates, it was intended as a sequel to her tale "At the 'Cadian Ball" (1892). "The Storm" was apparently never submitted for publication and did not see print until the publication of Per Seyersted's edition of *The Complete Works of Kate Chopin* in 1969, the basis for the text printed here.

upon the boards in driving sheets, and he went inside, closing the door after him. It was even necessary to put something beneath the door to keep the water out.

"My! what a rain! It's good two years sence it rain' like that," exclaimed Calixta as she rolled up a piece of bagging and Alcée helped her to thrust it beneath the crack.

She was a little fuller of figure than five years before when she married; but she had lost nothing of her vivacity. Her blue eyes still retained their melting quality; and her yellow hair, disheveled by the wind and rain, kinked more stubbornly than ever about her ears and temples.

The rain beat upon the low, shingled roof with a force and clatter that threatened to break an entrance and deluge them there. They were in the dining room—the sitting room—the general utility room. Adjoining was her bed room, with Bibi's couch along side her own. The door stood open, and the room with its white, monumental bed, its closed shutters, looked dim and mysterious.

Alcée flung himself into a rocker and Calixta nervously began to gather up from the floor the lengths of a cotton sheet which she had been sewing.

"If this keeps up, *Dieu sait* if the levees[2] goin' to stan' it!" she exclaimed.

"What have you got to do with the levees?"

"I got enough to do! An' there's Bobinôt with Bibi out in that storm—if he only didn' left Friedheimer's!"

"Let us hope, Calixta, that Bobinôt's got sense enough to come in out of a cyclone."

She went and stood at the window with a greatly disturbed look on her face. She wiped the frame that was clouded with moisture. It was stiflingly hot. Alcée got up and joined her at the window, looking over her shoulder. The rain was coming down in sheets obscuring the view of far-off cabins and enveloping the distant wood in a gray mist. The playing of the lightning was incessant. A bolt struck a tall chinaberry tree at the edge of the field. It filled all visible space with a blinding glare and the crash seemed to invade the very boards they stood upon.

Calixta put her hands to her eyes, and with a cry, staggered backward. Alcée's arm encircled her, and for an instant he drew her close and spasmodically to him.

"*Bonté!*"[3] she cried, releasing herself from his encircling arm and retreating from the window, "the house'll go next! If I only knew w'ere Bibi was!" She would not compose herself; she would not be seated. Alcée clasped her shoulders and looked into her face. The contact of her warm, palpitating body when he had unthinkingly drawn her into his arms, had aroused all the old-time infatuation and desire for her flesh.

"Calixta," he said, "don't be frightened. Nothing can happen. The house is too low to be struck, with so many tall trees standing about. There! aren't you going to be quiet? say, aren't you?" He pushed her hair back from her face that was warm and steaming. Her lips were as red and moist as pomegranate seed. Her white neck and a glimpse of her full, firm bosom disturbed him powerfully. As she glanced up at him the fear in her liquid blue eyes had given place to a drowsy gleam that unconsciously betrayed a sensuous

---

2. Built-up earth banks designed to keep the river from flooding the surrounding land. "*Dieu sait*": God knows (French).
3. Goodness! (French).

desire. He looked down into her eyes and there was nothing for him to do but to gather her lips in a kiss. It reminded him of Assumption.[4]

"Do you remember—in Assumption, Calixta?" he asked in a low voice broken by passion. Oh! she remembered; for in Assumption he had kissed her and kissed and kissed her; until his senses would well nigh fail, and to save her he would resort to a desperate flight. If she was not an immaculate dove in those days, she was still inviolate; a passionate creature whose very defenselessness had made her defense, against which his honor forbade him to prevail. Now—well, now—her lips seemed in a manner free to be tasted, as well as her round, white throat and her whiter breasts.

They did not heed the crashing torrents, and the roar of the elements made her laugh as she lay in his arms. She was a revelation in that dim, mysterious chamber; as white as the couch she lay upon. Her firm, elastic flesh that was knowing for the first time its birthright, was like a creamy lily that the sun invites to contribute its breath and perfume to the undying life of the world.

The generous abundance of her passion, without guile or trickery, was like a white flame which penetrated and found response in depths of his own sensuous nature that had never yet been reached.

When he touched her breasts they gave themselves up in quivering ecstasy, inviting his lips. Her mouth was a fountain of delight. And when he possessed her, they seemed to swoon together at the very borderland of life's mystery.

He stayed cushioned upon her, breathless, dazed, enervated, with his heart beating like a hammer upon her. With one hand she clasped his head, her lips lightly touching his forehead. The other hand stroked with a soothing rhythm his muscular shoulders.

The growl of the thunder was distant and passing away. The rain beat softly upon the shingles, inviting them to drowsiness and sleep. But they dared not yield.

III

The rain was over; and the sun was turning the glistening green world into a palace of gems. Calixta, on the gallery, watched Alcée ride away. He turned and smiled at her with a beaming face; and she lifted her pretty chin in the air and laughed aloud.

Bobinôt and Bibi, trudging home, stopped without at the cistern to make themselves presentable.

"My! Bibi, w'at will yo' mama say! You ought to be ashame'. You oughta' put on those good pants. Look at 'em! An' that mud on yo' collar! How you got that mud on yo' collar, Bibi? I never saw such a boy!" Bibi was the picture of pathetic resignation. Bobinôt was the embodiment of serious solicitude as he strove to remove from his own person and his son's the signs of their tramp over heavy roads and through wet fields. He scraped the mud off Bibi's bare legs and feet with a stick and carefully removed all traces from his heavy brogans. Then, prepared for the worst—the meeting with an over-scrupulous housewife, they entered cautiously at the back door.

Calixta was preparing supper. She had set the table and was dripping coffee at the hearth. She sprang up as they came in.

---

4. I.e., Assumption Parish, Louisiana, the setting for "At the 'Cadian Ball."

"Oh, Bobinôt! You back! My! but I was uneasy. W'ere you been during the rain? An' Bibi? he ain't wet? he ain't hurt?" She had clasped Bibi and was kissing him effusively. Bobinôt's explanations and apologies which he had been composing all along the way, died on his lips as Calixta felt him to see if he were dry, and seemed to express nothing but satisfaction at their safe return.

"I brought you some shrimps, Calixta," offered Bobinôt, hauling the can from his ample side pocket and laying it on the table.

"Shrimps! Oh, Bobinôt! you too good fo' anything!" and she gave him a smacking kiss on the cheek that resounded, "*J'vous réponds*,[5] we'll have a feas' to night! umph-umph!"

Bobinôt and Bibi began to relax and enjoy themselves, and when the three seated themselves at table they laughed much and so loud that anyone might have heard them as far away as Laballière's.

IV

Alcée Laballière wrote to his wife, Clarisse, that night. It was a loving letter, full of tender solicitude. He told her not to hurry back, but if she and the babies liked it at Biloxi, to stay a month longer. He was getting on nicely; and though he missed them, he was willing to bear the separation a while longer—realizing that their health and pleasure were the first things to be considered.

V

As for Clarisse, she was charmed upon receiving her husband's letter. She and the babies were doing well. The society was agreeable; many of her old friends and acquaintances were at the bay. And the first free breath since her marriage seemed to restore the pleasant liberty of her maiden days. Devoted as she was to her husband, their intimate conjugal life was something which she was more than willing to forego for a while.

So the storm passed and every one was happy.

1898   1969

5. I promise you (French).

MARY E. WILKINS FREEMAN
1852–1930

Mary E. Wilkins Freeman, best known for her depiction of New England village life, was born on October 31, 1852, in Randolph, Massachusetts, a small town twenty miles south of Boston. She was a somewhat sickly child, and two other Wilkins children died before they reached three years of age; her sister Anne lived to be seventeen. Freeman's parents were orthodox Congregationalists, and she was subject to a strict code of behavior. The constraints of religious belief, and the effect of these constraints on character formation and behavior, are among her chief subjects.

In 1867 Freeman's father became part owner of a dry-goods store in Brattleboro, Vermont, where she graduated from high school. In 1870, she entered Mount Holyoke Female Seminary, which Emily Dickinson had attended two decades earlier. Like Dickinson, Freeman left after a year in which she resisted the school's pressure on all students to offer public testimony as to their Christian commitment. She finished her formal education with a year at West Brattleboro Seminary, though the reading and discussions with her friend Evelyn Sawyer about Johann Wolfgang von Goethe, Ralph Waldo Emerson, Henry David Thoreau, Charles Dickens, William Makepeace Thackeray, Edgar Allan Poe, Nathaniel Hawthorne, and Harriet Beecher Stowe, among others, were probably more important than her schoolwork in developing her literary taste.

After the failure of her father's business in 1876, Freeman's family moved into the Brattleboro home of the Reverend Thomas Pickman Tyler, where her mother became housekeeper. Poverty was hard for the Wilkinses to bear, especially because their Puritan heritage led them to believe that poverty was a punishment for sin. Freeman's mother died in 1880, her father three years later, leaving Freeman alone at the age of twenty-eight, with a legacy of less than one thousand dollars.

Fortunately, she had begun to sell poems and stories to such leading magazines as *Harper's Bazaar,* and by the mid-1880s Freeman had a ready market for her work. As soon as she achieved a measure of economic independence, she returned to Randolph, where she lived with her childhood friend Mary Wales. Her early stories, especially those gathered and published in *A Humble Romance* (1887), are set in the Vermont countryside, but as she put it in a preface to an edition of these stories published in Edinburgh, the characters are generalized "studies of the descendants of the Massachusetts Bay colonists, in whom can still be seen traces of those features of will and conscience, so strong as to be almost exaggerations and deformities, which characterized their ancestors." More specifically, the title story dramatizes a theme Freeman was to return to frequently: the potential for unpredictable revolt in outwardly meek and downtrodden natures, such as the central character in "The Revolt of 'Mother.'"

"A New England Nun" and Other Stories, which appeared in 1891, contains several of her best stories, most notably the title story, which treats (with particular dramatic success) the pervasive theme of the psychic oppression and rebellion of women. At the same time as she provides a vivid sense of place, local dialect, and personality type, Freeman also offers in her best work insight into the individual psychology and interior life produced when confining, inherited codes of village life are subject to the pressure of a rapidly changing secular and urban world. This is a world in which, as the critic Marjorie Pryse argues, women begin to assert, individually and collectively, their vision and power against an exhausted Puritan patriarchy.

Freeman continued to write for another three decades. Although she is best known today for her stories, she also wrote plays and a number of successful novels on diverse topics from local history to labor unrest, but always with a focus on women. Among these novels are *Pembroke* (1894) and *The Shoulders of Atlas* (1908). She married Dr. Charles Freeman in 1902, when she was forty-nine, and moved to Metuchen, New Jersey; after a few happy years, her husband's drinking developed into destructive alcoholism, and he had to be institutionalized in 1920. In 1926, Freeman was awarded the W. D. Howells medal for fiction by the American Academy of Arts and Letters and elected to the National Institute of Arts and Letters—such honors were seldom given to women writers or to regionalists in those days. She died of a heart attack four years later.

A New England Nun[1]

It was late in the afternoon, and the light was waning. There was a difference in the look of the tree shadows out in the yard. Somewhere in the
distance cows were lowing and a little bell was tinkling; now and then a
farm-wagon tilted by, and the dust flew; some blue-shirted laborers with
shovels over their shoulders plodded past; little swarms of flies were dancing up and down before the peoples' faces in the soft air. There seemed to
be a gentle stir arising over everything for the mere sake of subsidence—a
very premonition of rest and hush and night.

This soft diurnal commotion was over Louisa Ellis also. She had been
peacefully sewing at her sitting-room window all the afternoon. Now she
quilted her needle carefully into her work, which she folded precisely, and
laid in a basket with her thimble and thread and scissors. Louisa Ellis could
not remember that ever in her life she had mislaid one of these little feminine appurtenances, which had become, from long use and constant association, a very part of her personality.

Louisa tied a green apron round her waist, and got out a flat straw hat
with a green ribbon. Then she went into the garden with a little blue crockery bowl, to pick some currants for her tea. After the currants were picked
she sat on the back door-step and stemmed them, collecting the stems carefully in her apron, and afterwards throwing them into the hen-coop. She
looked sharply at the grass beside the step to see if any had fallen there.

Louisa was slow and still in her movements; it took her a long time to
prepare her tea; but when ready it was set forth with as much grace as if she
had been a veritable guest to her own self. The little square table stood
exactly in the centre of the kitchen, and was covered with a starched linen
cloth whose border pattern of flowers glistened. Louisa had a damask napkin
on her tea-tray, where were arranged a cut-glass tumbler full of teaspoons,
a silver cream-pitcher, a china sugar-bowl, and one pink china cup and saucer.
Louisa used china every day—something which none of her neighbors did.
They whispered about it among themselves. Their daily tables were laid with
common crockery, their sets of best china stayed in the parlor closet, and
Louisa Ellis was no richer nor better bred than they. Still she would use the
china. She had for her supper a glass dish full of sugared currants, a plate of
little cakes, and one of light white biscuits. Also a leaf or two of lettuce, which
she cut up daintily. Louisa was very fond of lettuce, which she raised to perfection in her little garden. She ate quite heartily, though in a delicate, pecking way; it seemed almost surprising that any considerable bulk of the food
should vanish.

After tea she filled a plate with nicely baked thin corn-cakes, and carried
them out into the back-yard.

"Cæsar!" she called. "Cæsar! Cæsar!"

There was a little rush, and the clank of a chain, and a large yellow-and-
white dog appeared at the door of his tiny hut, which was half hidden among
the tall grasses and flowers. Louisa patted him and gave him the corn-cakes.
Then she returned to the house and washed the tea-things, polishing the
china carefully. The twilight had deepened; the chorus of the frogs floated in

1. From *"A New England Nun" and Other Stories* (1891), the source of the text printed here.

at the open window wonderfully loud and shrill, and once in a while a long sharp drone from a tree-toad pierced it. Louisa took off her green gingham apron, disclosing a shorter one of pink and white print. She lighted her lamp, and sat down again with her sewing.

In about half an hour Joe Dagget came. She heard his heavy step on the walk, and rose and took off her pink-and-white apron. Under that was still another—white linen with a little cambric edging on the bottom; that was Louisa's company apron. She never wore it without her calico sewing apron over it unless she had a guest. She had barely folded the pink and white one with methodical haste and laid it in a table-drawer when the door opened and Joe Dagget entered.

He seemed to fill up the whole room. A little yellow canary that had been asleep in his green cage at the south window woke up and fluttered wildly, beating his little yellow wings against the wires. He always did so when Joe Dagget came into the room.

"Good-evening," said Louisa. She extended her hand with a kind of solemn cordiality.

"Good-evening, Louisa," returned the man, in a loud voice.

She placed a chair for him, and they sat facing each other, with the table between them. He sat bolt-upright, toeing out his heavy feet squarely, glancing with a good-humored uneasiness around the room. She sat gently erect, folding her slender hands in her white-linen lap.

"Been a pleasant day," remarked Dagget.

"Real pleasant," Louisa assented, softly. "Have you been haying?" she asked, after a little while.

"Yes, I've been haying all day, down in the ten-acre lot. Pretty hot work."

"It must be."

"Yes, it's pretty hot work in the sun."

"Is your mother well to-day?"

"Yes, mother's pretty well."

"I suppose Lily Dyer's with her now?"

Dagget colored. "Yes, she's with her," he answered, slowly.

He was not very young, but there was a boyish look about his large face. Louisa was not quite as old as he, her face was fairer and smoother, but she gave people the impression of being older.

"I suppose she's a good deal of help to your mother," she said, further.

"I guess she is; I don't know how mother'd get along without her," said Dagget, with a sort of embarrassed warmth.

"She looks like a real capable girl. She's pretty-looking too," remarked Louisa.

"Yes, she is pretty fair looking."

Presently Dagget began fingering the books on the table. There was a square red autograph album, and a Young Lady's Gift-Book[2] which had belonged to Louisa's mother. He took them up one after the other and opened them; then laid them down again, the album on the Gift-Book.

Louisa kept eying them with mild uneasiness. Finally she rose and changed the position of the books, putting the album underneath. That was the way they had been arranged in the first place.

---

2. Popular annual miscellanies, containing stories, essays, and poems, usually with a polite or moral tone. They were lavishly printed and decorated for use as Christmas or New Year's gifts.

Dagget gave an awkward little laugh. "Now what difference did it make which book was on top?" said he.

Louisa looked at him with a deprecating smile. "I always keep them that way," murmured she.

"You do beat everything," said Dagget, trying to laugh again. His large face was flushed.

He remained about an hour longer, then rose to take leave. Going out, he stumbled over a rug, and trying to recover himself, hit Louisa's work-basket on the table, and knocked it on the floor.

He looked at Louisa, then at the rolling spools; he ducked himself awkwardly toward them, but she stopped him. "Never mind," said she; "I'll pick them up after you're gone."

She spoke with a mild stiffness. Either she was a little disturbed, or his nervousness affected her, and made her seem constrained in her effort to reassure him.

When Joe Dagget was outside he drew in the sweet evening air with a sigh, and felt much as an innocent and perfectly well-intentioned bear might after his exit from a china shop.

Louisa, on her part, felt much as the kind-hearted, long-suffering owner of the china shop might have done after the exit of the bear.

She tied on the pink, then the green apron, picked up all the scattered treasures and replaced them in her work-basket, and straightened the rug. Then she set the lamp on the floor, and began sharply examining the carpet. She even rubbed her fingers over it, and looked at them.

"He's tracked in a good deal of dust," she murmured. "I thought he must have."

Louisa got a dust-pan and brush, and swept Joe Dagget's track carefully.

If he could have known it, it would have increased his perplexity and uneasiness, although it would not have disturbed his loyalty in the least. He came twice a week to see Louisa Ellis, and every time, sitting there in her delicately sweet room, he felt as if surrounded by a hedge of lace. He was afraid to stir lest he should put a clumsy foot or hand through the fairy web, and he had always the consciousness that Louisa was watching fearfully lest he should.

Still the lace and Louisa commanded perforce his perfect respect and patience and loyalty. They were to be married in a month, after a singular courtship which had lasted for a matter of fifteen years. For fourteen out of the fifteen years the two had not once seen each other, and they had seldom exchanged letters. Joe had been all those years in Australia, where he had gone to make his fortune, and where he had stayed until he made it. He would have stayed fifty years if it had taken so long, and come home feeble and tottering, or never come home at all, to marry Louisa.

But the fortune had been made in the fourteen years, and he had come home now to marry the woman who had been patiently and unquestioningly waiting for him all that time.

Shortly after they were engaged he had announced to Louisa his determination to strike out into new fields, and secure a competency before they should be married. She had listened and assented with the sweet serenity which never failed her, not even when her lover set forth on that long and uncertain journey. Joe, buoyed up as he was by his sturdy determination, broke down a little at the last, but Louisa kissed him with a mild blush, and said good-by.

"It won't be for long," poor Joe had said, huskily; but it was for fourteen years.

In that length of time much had happened. Louisa's mother and brother had died, and she was all alone in the world. But greatest happening of all—a subtle happening which both were too simple to understand—Louisa's feet had turned into a path, smooth maybe under a calm, serene sky, but so straight and unswerving that it could only meet a check at her grave, and so narrow that there was no room for any one at her side.

Louisa's first emotion when Joe Dagget came home (he had not apprised her of his coming) was consternation, although she would not admit it to herself, and he never dreamed of it. Fifteen years ago she had been in love with him—at least she considered herself to be. Just at that time, gently acquiescing with and falling into the natural drift of girlhood, she had seen marriage ahead as a reasonable feature and a probable desirability of life. She had listened with calm docility to her mother's views upon the subject. Her mother was remarkable for her cool sense and sweet, even temperament. She talked wisely to her daughter when Joe Dagget presented himself, and Louisa accepted him with no hesitation. He was the first lover she had ever had.

She had been faithful to him all these years. She had never dreamed of the possibility of marrying any one else. Her life, especially for the last seven years, had been full of a pleasant peace, she had never felt discontented nor impatient over her lover's absence; still she had always looked forward to his return and their marriage as the inevitable conclusion of things. However, she had fallen into a way of placing it so far in the future that it was almost equal to placing it over the boundaries of another life.

When Joe came she had been expecting him, and expecting to be married for fourteen years, but she was as much surprised and taken aback as if she had never thought of it.

Joe's consternation came later. He eyed Louisa with an instant confirmation of his old admiration. She had changed but little. She still kept her pretty manner and soft grace, and was, he considered, every whit as attractive as ever. As for himself, his stent was done; he had turned his face away from fortune-seeking, and the old winds of romance whistled as loud and sweet as ever through his ears. All the song which he had been wont to hear in them was Louisa; he had for a long time a loyal belief that he heard it still, but finally it seemed to him that although the winds sang always that one song, it had another name. But for Louisa the wind had never more than murmured; now it had gone down, and everything was still. She listened for a little while with half-wistful attention; then she turned quietly away and went to work on her wedding clothes.

Joe had made some extensive and quite magnificent alterations in his house. It was the old homestead; the newly-married couple would live there, for Joe could not desert his mother, who refused to leave her old home. So Louisa must leave hers. Every morning, rising and going about among her neat maidenly possessions, she felt as one looking her last upon the faces of dear friends. It was true that in a measure she could take them with her, but, robbed of their old environments, they would appear in such new guises that they would almost cease to be themselves. Then there were some peculiar features of her happy solitary life which she would probably be obliged to relinquish altogether. Sterner tasks than these graceful but half-needless ones would probably devolve upon her. There would be a large house to care for; there would be company to entertain; there would be Joe's rigours and feeble old mother to wait upon; and it would be contrary to all thrifty village traditions for her to keep more than one servant. Louisa had a little still, and she used to occupy herself pleasantly in summer weather with distilling the sweet and aromatic essences from roses and peppermint and spearmint. By-and-by her still must be laid away. Her store of essences was already considerable, and there would be no time for her to distil for the mere pleasure of it. Then Joe's mother would think it foolishness; she had already hinted her opinion in the matter. Louisa dearly loved to sew a linen seam, not always for use, but for the simple, mild pleasure which she took in it. She would have been loath to confess how more than once she had ripped a seam for the mere delight of sewing it together again. Sitting at her window during long sweet afternoons, drawing her needle gently through the dainty fabric, she was peace itself. But there was small chance of such foolish comfort in the future. Joe's mother, domineering, shrewd old matron that she was even in her old age, and very likely even Joe himself, with his honest masculine rudeness, would laugh and frown down all these pretty but senseless old maiden ways.

Louisa had almost the enthusiasm of an artist over the mere order and cleanliness of her solitary home. She had throbs of genuine triumph at the sight of the window-panes which she had polished until they shone like jewels. She gloated gently over her orderly bureau-drawers, with their exquisitely folded contents redolent with lavender and sweet clover and very purity. Could she be sure of the endurance of even this? She had visions, so startling that she half repudiated them as indelicate, of coarse masculine belongings strewn about in endless litter; of dust and disorder arising necessarily from a coarse masculine presence in the midst of all this delicate harmony.

Among her forebodings of disturbance, not the least was with regard to Cæsar. Cæsar was a veritable hermit of a dog. For the greater part of his life he had dwelt in his secluded hut, shut out from the society of his kind and all innocent canine joys. Never had Cæsar since his early youth watched at a woodchuck's hole; never had he known the delights of a stray bone at a neighbor's kitchen door. And it was all on account of a sin committed when hardly out of his puppyhood. No one knew the possible depth of remorse of which this mild-visaged, altogether innocent-looking old dog might be capable; but whether or not he had encountered remorse, he had encountered a full measure of righteous retribution. Old Cæsar seldom lifted up his voice in a growl or a bark; he was fat and sleepy; there were yellow rings which looked like spectacles around his dim old eyes; but there was a neighbor who bore on his hand the imprint of several of Cæsar's sharp white youthful teeth, and for that he had lived at the end of a chain, all alone in a little hut, for fourteen years. The neighbor, who was choleric and smarting with the pain of his wound, had demanded either Cæsar's death or complete ostracism. So Louisa's brother, to whom the dog had belonged, had built him his little kennel and tied him up. It was now fourteen years since, in a flood of youthful spirits, he had inflicted that memorable bite, and with the exception of short excursions, always at the end of the chain, under the strict guardianship of his master or Louisa, the old dog had remained a close prisoner. It is doubtful if, with his limited ambition, he took much pride in the fact, but it is certain that he was possessed of considerable cheap fame. He was regarded by all the children in the village and by many adults as a very monster of ferocity. St. George's dragon[3] could hardly have surpassed in evil repute

---

3. The story of St. George (patron saint of England) and the Dragon is an allegorical expression of the triumph of the Christian hero over evil.

Louisa Ellis's old yellow dog. Mothers charged their children with solemn emphasis not to go too near him, and the children listened and believed greedily, with a fascinated appetite for terror, and ran by Louisa's house stealthily, with many sidelong and backward glances at the terrible dog. If perchance he sounded a hoarse bark, there was a panic. Wayfarers chancing into Louisa's yard eyed him with respect, and inquired if the chain were stout. Cæsar at large might have seemed a very ordinary dog, and excited no comment whatever; chained, his reputation overshadowed him, so that he lost his own proper outlines and looked darkly vague and enormous. Joe Dagget, however, with his good-humored sense and shrewdness, saw him as he was. He strode valiantly up to him and patted him on the head, in spite of Louisa's soft clamor of warning, and even attempted to set him loose. Louisa grew so alarmed that he desisted, but kept announcing his opinion in the matter quite forcibly at intervals. "There ain't a better-natured dog in town," he would say, "and it's downright cruel to keep him tied up there. Some day I'm going to take him out."

Louisa had very little hope that he would not, one of these days, when their interests and possessions should be more completely fused in one. She pictured to herself Cæsar on the rampage through the quiet and unguarded village. She saw innocent children bleeding in his path. She was herself very fond of the old dog, because he had belonged to her dead brother, and he was always very gentle with her; still she had great faith in his ferocity. She always warned people not to go too near him. She fed him on ascetic fare of corn-mush and cakes, and never fired his dangerous temper with heating and sanguinary diet of flesh and bones. Louisa looked at the old dog munching his simple fare, and thought of her approaching marriage and trembled. Still no anticipation of disorder and confusion in lieu of sweet peace and harmony, no forebodings of Cæsar on the rampage, no wild fluttering of her little yellow canary, were sufficient to turn her a hair's-breadth. Joe Dagget had been fond of her and working for her all these years. It was not for her, whatever came to pass, to prove untrue and break his heart. She put the exquisite little stitches into her wedding-garments, and the time went on until it was only a week before her wedding-day. It was a Tuesday evening, and the wedding was to be a week from Wednesday.

There was a full moon that night. About nine o'clock Louisa strolled down the road a little way. There were harvest-fields on either hand, bordered by low stone walls. Luxuriant clumps of bushes grew beside the wall, and trees—wild cherry and old apple-trees—at intervals. Presently Louisa sat down on the wall and looked about her with mildly sorrowful reflectiveness. Tall shrubs of blueberry and meadow-sweet, all woven together and tangled with blackberry vines and horsebriers, shut her in on either side. She had a little clear space between. Opposite her, on the other side of the road, was a spreading tree; the moon shone between its boughs, and the leaves twinkled like silver. The road was bespread with a beautiful shifting dapple of silver and shadow; the air was full of a mysterious sweetness. "I wonder if it's wild grapes?" murmured Louisa. She sat there some time. She was just thinking of rising, when she heard footsteps and low voices, and remained quiet. It was a lonely place, and she felt a little timid. She thought she would keep still in the shadow and let the persons, whoever they might be, pass her.

But just before they reached her the voices ceased, and the footsteps. She understood that their owners had also found seats upon the stone wall. She was wondering if she could not steal away unobserved, when the voice broke the stillness. It was Joe Dagget's. She sat still and listened.

The voice was announced by a loud sigh, which was as familiar as itself. "Well," said Dagget, "you've made up your mind, then, I suppose?"

"Yes," returned another voice; "I'm going day after to-morrow."

"That's Lily Dyer," thought Louisa to herself. The voice embodied itself in her mind. She saw a girl tall and full-figured, with a firm, fair face, looking fairer and firmer in the moonlight, her strong yellow hair braided in a close knot. A girl full of a calm rustic strength and bloom, with a masterful way which might have beseemed a princess. Lily Dyer was a favorite with the village folk; she had just the qualities to arouse the admiration. She was good and handsome and smart. Louisa had often heard her praises sounded.

"Well," said Joe Dagget, "I ain't got a word to say."

"I don't know what you could say," returned Lily Dyer.

"Not a word to say," repeated Joe, drawing out the words heavily. Then there was silence. "I ain't sorry," he began at last, "that that happened yesterday—that we kind of let on how we felt to each other. I guess it's just as well we knew. Of course I can't do anything any different. I'm going right on an' get married next week. I ain't going back on a woman that's waited for me fourteen years, an' break her heart."

"If you should jilt her to-morrow, I wouldn't have you," spoke up the girl, with sudden vehemence.

"Well, I ain't going to give you the chance," said he; "but I don't believe you would, either."

"You'd see I wouldn't. Honor's honor, an' right's right. An' I'd never think anything of any man that went against 'em for me or any other girl; you'd find that out, Joe Dagget."

"Well, you'll find out fast enough that I ain't going against 'em for you or any other girl," returned he. Their voices sounded almost as if they were angry with each other. Louisa was listening eagerly.

"I'm sorry you feel as if you must go away," said Joe, "but I don't know but it's best."

"Of course it's best. I hope you and I have got common-sense."

"Well, I suppose you're right." Suddenly Joe's voice got an undertone of tenderness. "Say, Lily," said he, "I'll get along well enough myself, but I can't bear to think—You don't suppose you're going to fret much over it?"

"I guess you'll find out I sha'n't fret much over a married man."

"Well, I hope you won't—I hope you won't, Lily. God knows I do. And—I hope—one of these days—you'll—come across somebody else—"

"I don't see any reason why I shouldn't." Suddenly her tone changed. She spoke in a sweet, clear voice, so loud that she could have been heard across the street. "No, Joe Dagget," said she, "I'll never marry any other man as long as I live. I've got good sense, an' I ain't going to break my heart nor make a fool of myself; but I'm never going to be married, you can be sure of that. I ain't that sort of a girl to feel this way twice."

Louisa heard an exclamation and a soft commotion behind the bushes; then Lily spoke again—the voice sounded as if she had risen. "This must be put a stop to," said she. "We've stayed here long enough. I'm going home."

Louisa sat there in a daze, listening to their retreating steps. After a while she got up and slunk softly home herself. The next day she did her housework methodically; that was as much a matter of course as breathing; but she did not sew on her wedding-clothes. She sat at her window and meditated. In the evening Joe came. Louisa Ellis had never known that she had any diplomacy in her, but when she came to look for it that night she found it, although meek of its kind, among her little feminine weapons. Even now she could hardly believe that she had heard aright, and that she would not do Joe a terrible injury should she break her troth-plight. She wanted to sound him without betraying too soon her own inclinations in the matter. She did it successfully, and they finally came to an understanding; but it was a difficult thing, for he was as afraid of betraying himself as she.

She never mentioned Lily Dyer. She simply said that while she had no cause of complaint against him, she had lived so long in one way that she shrank from making a change.

"Well, I never shrank, Louisa," said Dagget. "I'm going to be honest enough to say that I think maybe it's better this way; but if you'd wanted to keep on, I'd have stuck to you till my dying day. I hope you know that."

"Yes, I do," said she.

That night she and Joe parted more tenderly than they had done for a long time. Standing in the door, holding each other's hands, a last great wave of regretful memory swept over them.

"Well, this ain't the way we've thought it was all going to end, is it, Louisa?" said Joe.

She shook her head. There was a little quiver on her placid face.

"You let me know if there's ever anything I can do for you," said he. "I ain't ever going to forget you, Louisa." Then he kissed her, and went down the path.

Louisa, all alone by herself that night, wept a little, she hardly knew why; but the next morning, on waking, she felt like a queen who, after fearing lest her domain be wrested away from her, sees it firmly insured in her possession.

Now the tall weeds and grasses might cluster around Cæsar's little hermit hut, the snow might fall on its roof year in and year out, but he never would go on a rampage through the unguarded village. Now the little canary might turn itself into a peaceful yellow ball night after night, and have no need to wake and flutter with wild terror against its bars. Louisa could sew linen seams, and distil roses, and dust and polish and fold away in lavender, as long as she listed. That afternoon she sat with her needle-work at the window, and felt fairly steeped in peace. Lily Dyer, tall and erect and blooming, went past; but she felt no qualm. If Louisa Ellis had sold her birthright she did not know it, the taste of the pottage[4] was so delicious, and had been her sole satisfaction for so long. Serenity and placid narrowness had become to her as the birthright itself. She gazed ahead through a long reach of future days strung together like pearls in a rosary, every one like the others, and all smooth and flawless and innocent, and her heart went up in thankfulness. Outside was the fervid summer afternoon; the air was filled with the sounds of the busy harvest of men and birds and bees; there were halloos, metallic clatterings, sweet calls, and long hummings. Louisa sat, prayerfully numbering her days, like an uncloistered nun.

1891

4. In Genesis 25, Esau sells his birthright as oldest son of Isaac and Rebekah to his younger brother Jacob for a bowl of pottage (lentil stew).

BOOKER T. WASHINGTON
1856–1915

Between the last decade of the nineteenth century and the beginning of World War I, no one exercised more influence over race relations in the United States than did Booker Taliaferro Washington; some contemporary historians of the African American experience in America call the period the "Era of Booker T. Washington." Washington wanted to help African Americans enter mainstream white society peacefully and thus advocated an educational program of vocational training. His works have been contrasted with the dynamic and often sharply critical efforts of Frederick Douglass (whose successor as African American leader Washington wished to be) and the intellectual and professional initiatives of the fiercely independent W. E. B. Du Bois.

Washington's birth date is uncertain; as an adult he selected April 5, 1856. His mother was born a slave in Hale's Ford, Virginia (now West Virginia); his father was a white man whose identity is unknown. As a boy, he had, like most slaves, only a first name, and it was not until he entered school that he adopted the surname Washington, which was the first name of Washington Ferguson, a slave whom his mother had married. Washington's account of his early life is a catalog of deprivation and struggle. At the end of the Civil War, when he was nine years old, he accompanied his mother to Malden, West Virginia, to join his stepfather, who had found work there in a salt furnace. From 1865 to 1872, Washington worked as a salt packer, coal miner, and house servant while attending school in the off hours and thus beginning to satisfy his "intense longing" to learn to read and write. In 1872, he set out on a five-hundred–mile, month-long journey by rail, cart, and foot to reach Hampton, Virginia, where he would attend the Hampton Normal and Agricultural Institute, a school established by the American Missionary Association to train African Americans as teachers. There Washington paid his way by working as a janitor. In the quasi-military atmosphere of the school, he was drilled in the goals of cleanliness, thrift, and hard work that became central to his life and educational philosophy.

After graduating from Hampton in 1875 with honors and a certificate to teach in a trade school, Washington returned to Malden and found work with a local school. He studied for a while at Wayland Seminary and in 1878 was hired by Samuel Armstrong, the principal of Hampton, to teach in a program for Native Americans. Then, in 1881, he became the first principal of what was to become the Tuskegee Institute, a school established by the Alabama legislature to train African American men and women in agricultural and mechanical trades and teaching. Tuskegee began with thirty students, and Washington, the staff, and the students constructed the school buildings from bricks they made themselves. But through his considerable powers as a conciliator and fund-raiser, and aided by publicity over his goals of instilling Christian virtues and encouraging simple, disciplined living among the students, Washington soon developed Tuskegee into a thriving institution.

Washington emerged as a national figure in 1895 as the result of a short speech, included below, to a crowd of two thousand at the Atlanta Exposition of 1895. In the speech, popularly known as the "Atlanta Compromise," Washington argued that African Americans should defer the quest for equal rights in return for low-level economic opportunities. This approach appealed to many whites and blacks across the nation. A modern reader must understand its appeal in the context of the years between 1885 and 1910, when some thirty-five hundred African Americans were lynched and when, following the end of Reconstruction, most southern

Booker T. Washington. Washington in his office at Tuskegee
Institute, c. 1905.

states effectively disenfranchised African Americans. Even such militant African
American leaders as T. Thomas Fortune and Du Bois praised the speech and
supported the philosophy of conciliation that was its pragmatic basis. Their opposition to Washington did not develop until several years later, when they felt
it was again time to insist on civil, social, and political equality for all African
Americans.

In the years following the Atlanta speech, Washington worked to consolidate
his position as the "Moses of his race." Nothing did more to enhance this mythic
stature than his autobiography, *Up from Slavery* (1901), a masterpiece of the
genre that was widely praised in the United States and popular in translation
around the world. The early chapters reveal the physical and psychological realities
of Washington's origins, realities that were shared by many of the slaves set "free"
at the conclusion of the Civil War. Later chapters show Washington at the peak of
his success as an African American spokesperson, particularly as a master of rhetoric that allowed him to appear both as sincerely humble and as a force to be reckoned with, both as a man of selfless industry and as one of considerable political
know-how.

Washington believed in rewarding deserving individuals rather than in policies
treating African Americans as a group. His writings argue that success should be
measured not so much by the position a person has reached as by the obstacles
overcome while trying to succeed. In his work he urges African Americans to emu-
late the proverbial ship captain who urged his crew to "cast down your buckets
where you are" even though they were still at sea, and who thus found fresh water
at the mouth of a river. Washington argued that by seeking improvement African
Americans would inevitably rise as individuals. Yet he also urged whites not to
judge African American children against white children until they had had a
chance to catch up in school. In short, Washington proposed a middle ground
wherein African Americans would raise themselves by individual effort and white
Americans would appreciate the efforts being made and judge accordingly.

Up from Slavery is important as a literary production and as a record of a time,
place, and person. Washington's skillful use of metaphor and symbol, his deftly
masked ironies, and the art of his artlessness have been addressed by such critics as

William L. Andrews, Houston A. Baker, Jr., and James M. Cox. Over the years, his assimilationist position has drawn criticism, most recently from Baker, but his legacy lives on and continues to inspire readers.

Washington was awarded an honorary degree by Harvard University, was invited to dine by President Theodore Roosevelt, and was widely consulted on policy questions by white political and business leaders. On November 5, 1915, Washington was taken ill and entered St. Luke's Hospital in New York City; diagnosed with arteriosclerosis, he was told that he did not have long to live. He traveled to Tuskegee, where he died on November 14. Over eight thousand people attended his funeral, which was held in the Tuskegee Institute Chapel.

From Up from Slavery[1]

Chapter XIV. *The Atlanta Exposition Address*

The Atlanta Exposition,[2] at which I had been asked to make an address as a representative of the Negro race, as stated in the last chapter, was opened with a short address from Governor Bullock. After other interesting exercises, including an invocation from Bishop Nelson, of Georgia, a dedicatory ode by Albert Howell, Jr., and addresses by the President of the Exposition and Mrs. Joseph Thompson, the President of the Woman's Board, Governor Bullock introduced me with the words, "We have with us to-day a representative of Negro enterprise and Negro civilization."

When I arose to speak, there was considerable cheering, especially from the coloured people. As I remember it now, the thing that was uppermost in my mind was the desire to say something that would cement the friendship of the races and bring about hearty coöperation between them. So far as my outward surroundings were concerned, the only thing that I recall distinctly now is that when I got up, I saw thousands of eyes looking intently into my face. The following is the address which I delivered:—

> Mr. President and Gentlemen of the Board of Directors and Citizens:
>
> One-third of the population of the South is of the Negro race. No enterprise seeking the material, civil, or moral welfare of this section can disregard this element of our population and reach the highest success. I but convey to you, Mr. President and Directors, the sentiment of the masses of my race when I say that in no way have the value and manhood of the American Negro been more fittingly and generously recognized than by the managers of this magnificent Exposition at every stage of its progress. It is a recognition that will do more to cement the friendship of the two races than any occurrence since the dawn of our freedom.
>
> Not only this, but the opportunity here afforded will awaken among us a new era of industrial progress. Ignorant and inexperienced, it is not strange that in the first years of our new life we began at the top instead of at the bottom; that a seat in Congress or the state legislature was more

1. Published serially in *Outlook* from November 3, 1900, to February 23, 1901, *Up from Slavery* was first published in book form by Doubleday, Page and Company (1901), the source of the text printed here.

2. Opening on September 18, 1895, the Cotton States and International Exposition was a major southern trade fair.

sought than real estate or industrial skill; that the political convention or stump speaking had more attractions than starting a dairy farm or truck garden.

A ship lost at sea for many days suddenly sighted a friendly vessel. From the mast of the unfortunate vessel was seen a signal, "Water, water; we die of thirst!" The answer from the friendly vessel at once came back, "Cast down your bucket where you are." A second time the signal, "Water, water; send us water!" ran up from the distressed vessel, and was answered, "Cast down your bucket where you are." And a third and fourth signal for water was answered, "Cast down your bucket where you are." The captain of the distressed vessel, at last heeding the injunction, cast down his bucket, and it came up full of fresh, sparkling water from the mouth of the Amazon River. To those of my race who depend on bettering their condition in a foreign land or who underestimate the importance of cultivating friendly relations with the Southern white man, who is their next-door neighbour, I would say: "Cast down your bucket where you are"—cast it down in making friends in every manly way of the people of all races by whom we are surrounded.

Cast it down in agriculture, mechanics, in commerce, in domestic service, and in the professions. And in this connection it is well to bear in mind that whatever other sins the South may be called to bear, when it comes to business, pure and simple, it is in the South that the Negro is given a man's chance in the commercial world, and in nothing is this Exposition more eloquent than in emphasizing this chance. Our greatest danger is that in the great leap from slavery to freedom we may overlook the fact that the masses of us are to live by the productions of our hands, and fail to keep in mind that we shall prosper in proportion as we learn to dignify and glorify common labour and put brains and skill into the common occupations of life; shall prosper in proportion as we learn to draw the line between the superficial and the substantial, the ornamental gewgaws of life and the useful. No race can prosper till it learns that there is as much dignity in tilling a field as in writing a poem. It is at the bottom of life we must begin, and not at the top. Nor should we permit our grievances to overshadow our opportunities.

To those of the white race who look to the incoming of those of foreign birth and strange tongue and habits for the prosperity of the South, were I permitted I would repeat what I say to my own race, "Cast down your bucket where you are." Cast it down among the eight millions of Negroes whose habits you know, whose fidelity and love you have tested in days when to have proved treacherous meant the ruin of your firesides. Cast down your bucket among these people who have, without strikes and labour wars, tilled your fields, cleared your forests, builded your railroads and cities, and brought forth treasures from the bowels of the earth, and helped make possible this magnificent representation of the progress of the South. Casting down your bucket among my people, helping and encouraging them as you are doing on these grounds, and to education of head, hand, and heart, and you will find that they will buy your surplus land, make blossom the waste places in your fields, and run your factories. While doing this, you can be sure in the future, as in the past, that you and your families will be surrounded by the most patient, faithful, law-abiding, and unresentful people that the world has seen. As we have proved our loyalty to you in the past, in nursing your children, watching by the sick-bed of your mothers and fathers, and often following them with tear-dimmed eyes to their graves, so in the future, in our humble way, we shall stand by you with a devotion that no foreigner can approach, ready to lay down our lives, if need be, in defence of yours, interlacing our industrial, commercial, civil, and religious life with yours in a way that shall make the interests of both races one. In all things that are purely social we can be as separate as the fingers, yet one as the hand in all things essential to mutual progress.

There is no defence or security for any of us except in the highest intelligence and development of all. If anywhere there are efforts tending to curtail the fullest growth of the Negro, let these efforts be turned into stimulating, encouraging, and making him the most useful and intelligent citizen. Effort or means so invested will pay a thousand per cent interest. These efforts will be twice blessed—"blessing him that gives and him that takes."[3]

There is no escape through law of man or God from the inevitable:—

"The laws of changeless justice bind
Oppressor with oppressed;
And close as sin and suffering joined
We march to fate abreast."[4]

Nearly sixteen millions of hands will aid you in pulling the load upward, or they will pull against you the load downward. We shall constitute one-third and more of the ignorance and crime of the South, or one-third its intelligence and progress; we shall contribute one-third to the business and industrial prosperity of the South, or we shall prove a veritable body of death, stagnating, depressing, retarding every effort to advance the body politic.

Gentlemen of the Exposition, as we present to you our humble effort at an exhibition of our progress, you must not expect overmuch. Starting thirty years ago with ownership here and there in a few quilts and pumpkins and chickens (gathered from miscellaneous sources), remember the path that has led from these to the inventions and production of agricultural implements, buggies, steam-engines, newspapers, books, statuary, carving, paintings, the management of drug-stores and banks, has not been trodden without contact with thorns and thistles. While we take pride in what we exhibit as a result of our independent efforts, we do not for a moment forget that our part in this exhibition would fall far short of your expectations but for the constant help that has come to our educational life, not only from the Southern states, but especially from Northern philanthropists, who have made their gifts a constant stream of blessing and encouragement.

The wisest among my race understand that the agitation of questions of social equality is the extremest folly, and that progress in the enjoyment of all the privileges that will come to us must be the result of severe and

---

3. "It blesseth him that gives and him that takes" (Shakespeare, *The Merchant of Venice* 3.1.167).
4. From "Song of the Negro Boatman" (1861), by the Massachusetts poet and abolitionist John Greenleaf Whittier (1807–1892).

constant struggle rather than of artificial forcing. No race that has anything to contribute to the markets of the world is long in any degree ostracized. It is important and right that all privileges of the law be ours, but it is vastly more important that we be prepared for the exercises of these privileges. The opportunity to earn a dollar in a factory just now is worth infinitely more than the opportunity to spend a dollar in an opera-house.

In conclusion, may I repeat that nothing in thirty years has given us more hope and encouragement, and drawn us so near to you of the white race, as this opportunity offered by the Exposition; and here bending, as it were, over the altar that represents the results of the struggles of your race and mine, both starting practically empty-handed three decades ago, I pledge that in your effort to work out the great and intricate problem which God has laid at the doors of the South, you shall have at all times the patient, sympathetic help of my race; only let this be constantly in mind, that, while from representations in these buildings of the product of field, of forest, of mine, of factory, letters, and art, much good will come, yet far above and beyond material benefits will be that higher good, that, let us pray God, will come, in a blotting out of sectional differences and racial animosities and suspicions, in a determination to administer absolute justice, in a willing obedience among all classes to the mandates of law. This, this, coupled with our material prosperity, will bring into our beloved South a new heaven and a new earth.

The first thing that I remember, after I had finished speaking, was that Governor Bullock rushed across the platform and took me by the hand, and that others did the same. I received so many and such hearty congratulations that I found it difficult to get out of the building. I did not appreciate to any degree, however, the impression which my address seemed to have made, until the next morning, when I went into the business part of the city. As soon as I was recognized, I was surprised to find myself pointed out and surrounded by a crowd of men who wished to shake hands with me. This was kept up on every street on to which I went, to an extent which embarrassed me so much that I went back to my boarding-place. The next morning I returned to Tuskegee. At the station in Atlanta, and at almost all of the stations at which the train stopped between the city and Tuskegee, I found a crowd of people anxious to shake hands with me.

The papers in all the parts of the United States published the address in full, and for months afterward there were complimentary editorial references to it. Mr. Clark Howell, the editor of the Atlanta *Constitution,* telegraphed to a New York paper, among other words, the following, "I do not exaggerate when I say that Professor Booker T. Washington's address yesterday was one of the most notable speeches, both as to character and as to the warmth of its reception, ever delivered to a Southern audience. The address was a revelation. The whole speech is a platform upon which blacks and whites can stand with full justice to each other."

The Boston *Transcript* said editorially: "The speech of Booker T. Washington at the Atlanta Exposition, this week, seems to have dwarfed all the other proceedings and the Exposition itself. The sensation that it has caused in the press has never been equalled."

I very soon began receiving all kinds of propositions from lecture bureaus, and editors of magazines and papers, to take the lecture platform, and to write articles. One lecture bureau offered me fifty thousand dollars, or two hundred dollars a night and expenses, if I would place my services at its disposal for a given period. To all these communications I replied that my life-work was at Tuskegee; and that whenever I spoke it must be in the interests of the Tuskegee school and my race, and that I would enter into no arrangements that seemed to place a mere commercial value upon my services.

Some days after its delivery I sent a copy of my address to the President of the United States, the Hon. Grover Cleveland.[5] I received from him the following autograph reply:—

Gray Gables
Buzzard's Bay, Mass., October 6, 1895

Booker T. Washington, Esq.:

My Dear Sir: I thank you for sending me a copy of your address delivered at the Atlanta Exposition.

I thank you with much enthusiasm for making the address. I have read it with intense interest, and I think the Exposition would be fully justified if it did not do more than furnish the opportunity for its delivery. Your words cannot fail to delight and encourage all who wish well for your race; and if our coloured fellow-citizens do not from your utterances father new hope and form new determinations to gain every valuable advantage offered them by their citizenship, it will be strange indeed. Yours very truly,

Grover Cleveland

Later I met Mr. Cleveland, for the first time, when, as President, he visited the Atlanta Exposition. At the request of myself and others he consented to spend an hour in the Negro Building, for the purpose of inspecting the Negro exhibit and of giving the coloured people in attendance an opportunity to shake hands with him. As soon as I met Mr. Cleveland I became impressed with his simplicity, greatness, and rugged honesty. I have met him many times since then, both at public functions and at his private residence in Princeton, and the more I see of him the more I admire him. When he visited the Negro Building in Atlanta he seemed to give himself up wholly, for that hour, to the coloured people. He seemed to be as careful to shake hands with some old coloured "auntie" clad partially in rags, and to take as much pleasure in doing so, as if he were greeting some millionaire. Many of the coloured people took advantage of the occasion to get him to write his name in a book or on a slip of paper. He was as careful and patient in doing this as if he were putting his signature to some great state document.

Mr. Cleveland has not only shown his friendship for me in many personal ways, but has always consented to do anything I have asked of him for our school. This he has done, whether it was to make a personal donation or to use his influence in securing the donations of others. Judging from my personal acquaintance with Mr. Cleveland, I do not believe that he is conscious of possessing any colour prejudice. He is too great for that. In my contact with people I find that, as a rule, it is only the little, narrow people who live for themselves, who never read good books, who do not travel, who never

5. Cleveland (1837–1908), twenty-second (1885–89) and twenty-fourth (1893–97) president of the United States.

open up their souls in a way to permit them to come into contact with other souls—with the great outside world. No man whose vision is bounded by colour can come into contact with what is highest and best in the world. In meeting men, in many places, I have found that the happiest people are those who do the most for others; the most miserable are those who do the least. I have also found that few things, if any, are capable of making one so blind and narrow as race prejudice. I often say to our students, in the course of my talks to them on Sunday evenings in the chapel, that the longer I live and the more experience I have of the world, the more I am convinced that, after all, the one thing that is most worth living for—and dying for, if need be—is the opportunity of making some one else more happy and more useful.

The coloured people and the coloured newspapers at first seemed to be greatly pleased with the character of my Atlanta address, as well as with its reception. But after the first burst of enthusiasm began to die away, and the coloured people began reading the speech in cold type, some of them seemed to feel that they had been hypnotized. They seemed to feel that I had been too liberal in my remarks toward the Southern whites, and that I had not spoken out strongly enough for what they termed the "rights" of the race. For a while there was a reaction, so far as a certain element of my own race was concerned, but later these reactionary ones seemed to have been won over to my way of believing and acting.

While speaking of changes in public sentiment, I recall that about ten years after the school at Tuskegee was established, I had an experience that I shall never forget. Dr. Lyman Abbott, then the pastor of Plymouth Church, and also editor of the *Outlook* (then the *Christian Union*), asked me to write a letter for his paper giving my opinion of the exact condition, mental and moral of the coloured ministers in the South, as based upon my observations. I wrote the letter, giving the exact facts as I conceived them to be. The picture painted was a rather black one—or, since I am black, shall I say "white"? It could not be otherwise with a race but a few years out of slavery, a race which had not had time or opportunity to produce a competent ministry.

What I said soon reached every Negro minister in the country, I think, and the letters of condemnation which I received from them were not few. I think that for a year after the publication of this article every association and every conference or religious body of any kind, of my race, that met, did not fail before adjourning to pass a resolution condemning me, or calling upon me to retract or modify what I had said. Many of these organizations went so far in their resolutions as to advise parents to cease sending their children to Tuskegee. One association even appointed a "missionary" whose duty it was to warn the people against sending their children to Tuskegee. This missionary had a son in the school, and I noticed that, whatever the "missionary" might have said or done with regard to others, he was careful not to take his son away from the institution. Many of the coloured papers, especially those that were the organs of religious bodies, joined in the general chorus of condemnation or demands for retraction.

During the whole time of the excitement, and through all the criticism, I did not utter a word of explanation or retraction. I knew that I was right, and that time and the sober second thought of the people would vindicate me. It was not long before the bishops and other church leaders began to make a careful investigation of the conditions of the ministry, and they found out that I was right. In fact, the oldest and most influential bishop in one branch of the Methodist Church said that my words were far too mild. Very soon public sentiment began making itself felt, in demanding a purifying of the ministry. While this is not yet complete by any means, I think I may say, without egotism, and I have been told by many of our most influential ministers, that my words had much to do with starting a demand for the placing of a higher type of men in the pulpit. I have had the satisfaction of having many who once condemned me thank me heartily for my frank words.

The change of the attitude of the Negro ministry, so far as regards myself, is so complete that at the present time I have no warmer friends among any class than I have among the clergymen. The improvement in the character and life of the Negro ministers is one of the most gratifying evidences of the progress of the race. My experience with them, as well as other events in my life, convince me that the thing to do, when one feels sure that he has said or done the right thing, and is condemned, is to stand still and keep quiet. If he is right, time will show it.

In the midst of the discussion which was going on concerning my Atlanta speech, I received a letter which I give below, from Dr. Gilman, the President of Johns Hopkins University, who had been made chairman of the judges of award in connection with the Atlanta Exposition:—

Johns Hopkins University, Baltimore
President's Office, September 30, 1895

Dear Mr. Washington: Would it be agreeable to you to be one of the Judges of Award in the Department of Education at Atlanta? If so, I shall be glad to place your name upon the list. A line by telegraph will be welcomed. Yours very truly,

D. C. Gilman

I think I was even more surprised to receive this invitation than I had been to receive the invitation to speak at the opening of the Exposition. It was to be a part of my duty, as one of the jurors, to pass not only upon the exhibits of the coloured schools, but also upon those of the white schools. I accepted the position, and spent a month in Atlanta in performance of the duties which it entailed. The board of jurors was a large one, consisting in all of sixty members. It was about equally divided between Southern white people and Northern white people. Among them were college presidents, leading scientists and men of letters, and specialists in many subjects. When the group of jurors to which I was assigned met for organization, Mr. Thomas Nelson Page,[6] who was one of the number, moved that I be made secretary of that division, and the motion was unanimously adopted. Nearly half of our division were Southern people. In performing my duties in the inspection of the exhibits of white schools I was in every case treated with respect, and at the close of our labours I parted from my associates with regret.

I am often asked to express myself more freely than I do upon the political condition and the political future of my race. These recollections of my experience in Atlanta give me the opportunity to do so briefly. My own belief is, although I have never before said so in so many words, that the time will come when the Negro in the South will be accorded all the political

6. Popular Virginia diplomat and author (1853–1922), best known for *In Ole Virginia* (1887).

rights which his ability, character, and material possessions entitle him to. I think, though, that the opportunity to freely exercise such political rights will not come in any large degree through outside or artificial forcing, but will be accorded to the Negro by the Southern white people themselves, and that they will protect him in the exercise of those rights. Just as soon as the South gets over the old feeling that it is being forced by "foreigners," or "aliens," to do something which it does not want to do, I believe that the change in the direction that I have indicated is going to begin. In fact, there are indications that it is already beginning in a slight degree.

Let me illustrate my meaning. Suppose that some months before the open-ing of the Atlanta Exposition there had been a general demand from the press and public platform outside the South that a Negro be given a place on the opening programme, and that a Negro be placed upon the board of jurors of award. Would any such recognition of the race have taken place? I do not think so. The Atlanta officials went as far as they did because they felt it to be a pleasure, as well as a duty, to reward what they considered merit in the Negro race. Say what we will, there is something in human nature which we cannot blot out, which makes one man, in the end, recognize and reward merit in another, regardless of colour or race.

I believe it is the duty of the Negro—as the greater part of the race is already doing—to deport himself modestly in regard to political claims, depending upon the slow but sure influences that proceed from the posses-sion of property, intelligence, and high character for the full recognition of his political rights. I think that the according of the full exercise of politi-cal rights is going to be a matter of natural, slow growth, not an over-night, gourd-vine affair. I do not believe that the Negro should cease voting, for a man cannot learn the exercise of self-government by ceasing to vote, any more than a boy can learn to swim by keeping out of the water, but I do believe that in his voting he should more and more be influenced by those of intelligence and character who are his next-door neighbours.

I know coloured men who, through the encouragement, help, and advice of Southern white people, have accumulated thousands of dollars' worth of property, but who, at the same time, would never think of going to those same persons for advice concerning the casting of their ballots. This, it seems to me, is unwise and unreasonable, and should cease. In saying this I do not mean that the Negro should truckle, or not vote from principle, for the instant he ceases to vote from principle he loses the confidence and respect of the Southern white man even.

I do not believe that any state should make a law that permits an ignorant and poverty-stricken white man to vote, and prevents a black man in the same condition from voting. Such a law is not only unjust, but it will react, as all unjust laws do, in time; for the effect of such a law is to encourage the Negro to secure education and property, and at the same time it encourages the white man to remain in ignorance and poverty. I believe that in time, through the operation of intelligence and friendly race relations, all cheating at the ballot-box in the South will cease. It will become apparent that the white man who begins by cheating a Negro out of his ballot soon learns to cheat a white man out of his, and that the man who does this ends his career of dishonesty by the theft of property or by some equally serious crime. In my opinion, the time will come when the South will encourage all of its citi-zens to vote. It will see that it pays better, from every standpoint, to have healthy, vigorous life than to have that political stagnation which always results when one-half of the population has no share and no interest in the Government.

As a rule, I believe in universal, free suffrage, but I believe that in the South we are confronted with peculiar conditions that justify the protection of the ballot in many of the states, for a while at least, either by an educational test, a property test, or by both combined; but whatever tests are required, they should be made to apply with equal and exact justice to both races.

1901

CHARLES W. CHESNUTT
1858–1932

Charles Waddell Chesnutt was born on June 20, 1858, in Cleveland, Ohio. His parents were free-born blacks from North Carolina; his father served in the Union Army and after the Civil War moved his family back to Fayetteville, North Carolina. Chesnutt went to a school established by the Freedman's Bureau during Reconstruction and worked as a teacher, school principal, newspaper reporter, and accountant. He married Susan Perry, a Fayetteville schoolteacher, in 1878; they had four children. During the late 1870s Chesnutt became interested in the law. In 1883 he returned to Cleveland and began work as a legal stenographer, passing the Ohio bar exam in 1887. That same year the *Atlantic Monthly* published "The Goophered Grapevine," the first of a group of stories in the regional-dialect folktale tradition earlier made nationally popular by Joel Chandler Harris. Most of Chesnutt's contemporaries would have enjoyed the picturesque stereotype of the seemingly easygoing slave or former slave and taken pleasure in the authenticity of the language, customs, and settings in the stories, but perceptive readers of Chesnutt's time and beyond have had the added satisfaction of noting the ironic racial dramas played out between "master" and "slave" in Chesnutt's reworking of the plantation tale tradition. Chesnutt's Uncle Julius McAdoo in particular is a wise old former slave who has learned not only to survive but to manipulate his supposed superiors through a mocking mask of ignorance.

With age and fame Chesnutt became more direct in his exploration of the psychological and historical implications of racial thinking in the United States. Chesnutt was himself light skinned but had never tried to hide his racial identity; it was not until 1899, however, the year he began to write full time, that he revealed himself to his readers as a black man. In that year, his dialect stories set in rural North Carolina were gathered and published as *The Conjure Woman*. Conjure (or hoodoo) is the name given to a set of folk beliefs combining elements of Caribbean and West African healing and spiritual practices with elements of Christian belief. Practitioners of conjure were thought to know how to get in touch with and direct the powers of nature to make something happen—or to keep something from happening. Two other books by Chesnutt appeared in 1899: a collection of mostly nondialect and urban stories titled *The Wife of His Youth and Other Stories of the Color Line* and a biography of Frederick Douglass. A number of Chesnutt's stories written in the 1890s dealt with the psychological and social tensions of light-skinned blacks attempting to pass as whites. "The Wife of His Youth," printed here, affirms the importance of upwardly mobile light-complected blacks remembering and honoring their collective past. Another story in that collection, "The Passing of Grandison," shows the limits of whites' understanding of blacks' desires for freedom.

Chesnutt's first novel, *The House behind the Cedars* (1900), focuses on interracial relationships between men and women in the South, exploring some of the issues he had discussed in his essay "What Is a White Man" (1889), which had pointed to the moral unfairness and absurdity of laws against interracial marriage in a region where "pure" whiteness itself could be regarded as a fiction. Similar themes are central to *The Marrow of Tradition* (1901), his most ambitious novel, which culminates in a massacre of blacks based on the Wilmington (North Carolina) Riot of 1898. Chesnutt's third novel on the problem of race relations in the post–Civil War South, *The Colonel's Dream* (1905), depicts the failed efforts of the reform-minded Colonel Henry French to institute modernizing economic practices and to challenge white supremacy in a small southern town. Despite the overwhelming pessimism of the novel, Chesnutt dedicated it to "the great number of those who are seeking, in whatever manner or degree, from near at hand or far away, to bring the forces of enlightenment to bear upon the vexed problems which harass the South." The novel received just a few reviews and sold poorly.

Early in his career, in 1880, Chesnutt had recorded in his journal his youthful ambitions as a writer:

> The object of my writings would be not so much the elevation of the colored people as the elevation of the whites—for I consider the unjust spirit of caste which is so insidious as to pervade a whole nation, and so powerful as to subject a whole race and all connected with it to scorn and social ostracism—I consider this a barrier to the moral progress of the American people; and I would be one of the first to head a determined, organized crusade against it.

With his shrewd depictions of racial thinking in the South, and particularly of the fluidity of the color line, Chestnutt emerged as the first great short story writer in the African American tradition, and as the first African American fiction writer to be taken seriously in the white press. William Dean Howells, for example, championed Chesnutt as one of the great literary realists of the day. Chesnutt's fiction and essays can all be seen as part of Chesnutt's antiracist and anti-caste crusade as he imagined it as a young man. Arguably, his bold questioning of the very concept of "race" increasingly made white readers of his time uncomfortable. Chesnutt continued to write, but publishers became uninterested in his work; recent years have seen the posthumous first publications of four Chesnutt novels that he left in manuscript at his death. In his own time, Chesnutt remained esteemed among black writers and readers as a pioneering author committed to representing racial issues in all their historical and social complexity. In 1928 the National Association for the Advancement of Colored People awarded him the Spingarn Medal for his groundbreaking contribution "as a literary artist depicting the life and struggles of Americans of Negro descent." Chesnutt has since come to be widely recognized as one of the most powerful literary artists of the color line.

The Goophered Grapevine[1]

About ten years ago my wife was in poor health, and our family doctor, in whose skill and honesty I had implicit confidence, advised a change of climate. I was engaged in grape-culture in northern Ohio, and decided to look

---

1. First published in the August 1887 issue of the *Atlantic Monthly*, the source of the text reprinted here. A revised version of the story later appeared in the collection *The Conjure Woman* (1899).

for a location suitable for carrying on the same business in some Southern State. I wrote to a cousin who had gone into the turpentine business in central North Carolina, and he assured me that no better place could be found in the South than the State and neighborhood in which he lived: climate and soil were all that could be asked for, and land could be bought for a mere song. A cordial invitation to visit him while I looked into the matter was accepted. We found the weather delightful at that season, the end of the summer, and were most hospitably entertained. Our host placed a horse and buggy at our disposal, and himself acted as guide until I got somewhat familiar with the country.

I went several times to look at a place which I thought might suit me. It had been at one time a thriving plantation, but shiftless cultivation had well-nigh exhausted the soil. There had been a vineyard of some extent on the place, but it had not been attended to since the war, and had fallen into utter neglect. The vines—here partly supported by decayed and broken-down arbors, there twining themselves among the branches of the slender saplings which had sprung up among them—grew in wild and unpruned luxuriance, and the few scanty grapes which they bore were the undisputed prey of the first comer. The site was admirably adapted to grape-raising; the soil, with a little attention, could not have been better; and with the native grape, the luscious scuppernong, mainly to rely upon, I felt sure that I could introduce and cultivate successfully a number of other varieties.

One day I went over with my wife, to show her the place. We drove between the decayed gate-posts—the gate itself had long since disappeared—and up the straight, sandy lane to the open space where a dwelling-house had once stood. But the house had fallen a victim to the fortunes of war, and nothing remained of it except the brick pillars upon which the sills had rested. We alighted, and walked about the place for a while; but on Annie's complaining of weariness I led the way back to the yard, where a pine log, lying under a spreading elm, formed a shady though somewhat hard seat. One end of the log was already occupied by a venerable-looking colored man. He held on his knees a hat full of grapes, over which he was smacking his lips with great gusto, and a pile of grape-skins near him indicated that the performance was no new thing. He respectfully rose as we approached, and was moving away, when I begged him to keep his seat.

"Don't let us disturb you," I said. "There's plenty of room for us all."

He resumed his seat with somewhat of embarrassment.

"Do you live around here?" I asked, anxious to put him at his ease.

"Yas, suh. I lives des ober yander, behine de nex' san'-hill, on de Lumberton plank-road."

"Do you know anything about the time when this vineyard was cultivated?"

"Lawd bless yer, suh, I knows all about it. Dey ain' na'er a man in dis settlement w'at won' tell yer ole Julius McAdoo 'uz bawn an' raise' on dis yer same plantation. Is you de Norv'n gemman w'at's gwine ter buy de ole vimya'd?"

"I am looking at it," I replied; "but I don't know that I shall care to buy unless I can be reasonably sure of making something out of it."

"Well, suh, you is a stranger ter me, en I is a stranger ter you, en we is bofe strangers ter one anudder, but 'f I 'uz in yo' place, I wouldn' buy dis vimya'd."

"Why not?" I asked.

"Well, I dunner whe'r you b'lieves in cunj'in er not,—some er de w'ite folks don't, er says dey don't,—but de truf er de matter is dat dis yer old vimya'd is goophered."

"Is what?" I asked, not grasping the meaning of this unfamiliar word.

"Is goophered, cunju'd, bewitch'."

He imparted this information with such solemn earnestness, and with such an air of confidential mystery, that I felt somewhat interested, while Annie was evidently much impressed, and drew closer to me.

"How do you know it is bewitched?" I asked.

"I wouldn' spec' fer you ter b'lieve me 'less you know all 'bout de fac's. But ef you en young miss dere doan' min' lis'n'in' ter a ole nigger run on a minute er two while you er restin', I kin 'splain to yer how it all happen'."

We assured him that we would be glad to hear how it all happened, and he began to tell us. At first the current of his memory—or imagination— seemed somewhat sluggish; but as his embarrassment wore off, his language flowed more freely, and the story acquired perspective and coherence. As he became more and more absorbed in the narrative, his eyes assumed a dreamy expression, and he seemed to lose sight of his auditors, and to be living over again in monologue his life on the old plantation.

"Ole Mars Dugal' McAdoo bought dis place long many years befo' de wah, en I 'member well w'en he sot out all dis yer part er de plantation in scuppernon's. De vimes growed monst'us fas', en Mars Dugal' made a thousan' gallon er scuppernon' wine eve'y year.

"Now, ef dey's an'thing a nigger lub, nex' ter 'possum, en chick'n, en water-millyums, it's scuppernon's. Dey ain' niffin dat kin stan' up side'n de scuppernon' fer sweetness; sugar ain' a suckumstance ter scuppernon'. W'en de season is nigh 'bout ober, en de grapes begin ter swivel up des a little wid de wrinkles er ole age,—w'en de skin git sof' en brown,—den de scuppernon' make you smack yo' lip en roll yo' eye en wush fer mo'; so I reckon it ain' very 'stonishin' dat niggers lub scuppernon'.

"Dey wuz a sight er niggers in de naberhood er de vimya'd. Dere wuz ole Mars Henry Brayboy's niggers, en ole Mars Dunkin McLean's niggers, en Mars Dugal's own niggers; den dey wuz a settlement er free niggers en po' buckrahs[2] down by de Wim'l'ton Road, en Mars Dugal' had de only vimya'd in de naberhood. I reckon it ain' so much so nowadays, but befo' de wah, in slab'ry times, er nigger didn' mine goin' fi' er ten mile in a night, w'en dey wuz sump'n good ter eat at de yuther een.

"So atter a w'ile Mars Dugal' begin ter miss his scuppernon's. Co'se he 'cuse' de niggers er it, but dey all 'nied it ter de las'. Mars Dugal' sot spring guns en steel traps, en he en de oberseah sot up nights once't er twice't, tel one night Mars Dugal'—he 'uz a monst'us keerless man—got his leg shot full er cow-peas. But somehow er nudder dey couldn' nebber ketch none er de niggers. I dunner how it happen, but it happen des like I tell yer, en de grapes kep' on a-goin des de same.

"But bimeby ole Mars Dugal' fix' up a plan ter stop it. Dey 'uz a cunjuh 'ooman livin' down mongs' de free niggers on de Wim'l'ton Road, en all de darkies fum Rockfish ter Beaver Crick wuz feared uv her. She could wuk de mos' powerfulles' kind er goopher,—could make people hab fits er rheumatiz,

2. White men (regional slang).

er make 'em des dwinel away en die; en dey say she went out ridin' de niggers at night, for she wuz a witch 'sides bein' a cunjuh 'ooman. Mars Dugal' hearn 'bout Aun' Peggy's doin's, en begun ter 'flect whe'r er no he couldn' git her ter he'p him keep de niggers off'n de grapevimes. One day in de spring er de year, ole miss pack' up a basket er chick'n en poun'-cake, en a bottle er scuppernon' wine, en Mars Dugal' tuk it in his buggy en driv ober ter Aun' Peggy's cabin. He tuk de basket in, en had a long talk wid Aun' Peggy. De nex' day Aun' Peggy come up ter de vimya'd. De niggers seed her slippin' 'roun', en dey soon foun' out what she 'uz doin' dere. Mars Dugal' had hi'ed her ter goopher de grapevimes. She sa'ntered 'roun' mongs' de vimes, en tuk a leaf fum dis one, en a grape-hull fum dat one, en a grape-seed fum anudder one; en den a little twig fum here, en a little pinch er dirt fum dere,—en put it all in a big black bottle, wid a snake's toof en a speckle' hen's gall en some ha'rs fum a black cat's tail, en den fill' de bottle wid scuppernon' wine. W'en she got de goopher all ready en fix', she tuk 'n went out in de woods en buried it under de root uv a red oak tree, en den come back en tole one er de niggers she done goopher de grapevimes, en a'er a nigger w'at eat dem grapes 'ud be sho ter die inside'n twel' mont's.

"Atter dat de niggers let de scuppernons' lone, en Mars Dugal' didn' hab no 'casion ter fine no mo' fault; en de season wuz mos' gone, w'en a strange gemman stop at de plantation one night ter see Mars Dugal' on some business; en his coachman, seein' de scuppernon's growin' so nice en sweet, slip 'roun behine de smoke-house, en et all de scuppernon's he could hole. Nobody didn' notice it at de time, but dat night, on de way home, de gemman's hoss runned away en kill' de coachman. W'en we hearn de noos, Aun' Lucy, de cook, she up 'n say she seed de strange nigger eat'n er de scuppernon's behind de smoke-house; en den we knowed de goopher had b'en er wukkin. Den one er de nigger chilluns runned away fum de quarters one day, en got in de scuppernon's, en died de nex' week. W'ite folks say he die' er de fevuh, but de niggers knowed it wuz de goopher. So you k'n be sho de darkies didn' hab much ter do wid dem scuppernon' vimes.

"W'en de scuppernon' season 'uz ober fer dat year, Mars Dugal' foun' he had made fifteen hund'ed gallon er wine; en one er de niggers hearn him laffin' wid de oberseah fit ter kill, en sayin' dem fifteen hund'ed gallon er wine wuz monst'us good intrus' on de ten dollars he laid out on de vimya'd. So I 'low ez he paid Aun' Peggy ten dollars fer to goopher de grapevimes.

"De goopher didn' wuk no mo' tel de nex' summer, w'en 'long to'ds de middle er de season one er de fiel' han's died; en ez dat lef' Mars Dugal' sho't er han's, he went off ter town fer ter buy anudder. He fotch de noo nigger home wid 'im. He wuz er ole nigger, er de color er a gingy-cake, en ball ez a hoss-apple on de top er his head. He wuz a peart ole nigger, do', en could do a big day's wuk.

"Now it happen dat one er de niggers on de nex' plantation, one er ole Mars Henry Brayboy's niggers, had runned away de day befo', en tuk ter de swamp, en ole Mars Dugal' en some er de yuther nabor w'ite folks had gone out wid dere guns en dere dogs fer ter he'p 'em hunt fer de nigger; en de han's on our own plantation wuz all so flusterated dat we fuhgot ter tell de noo han' 'bout de goopher on de scuppernon' vimes. Co'se he smell de grapes en see de vimes, an atter dahk de fus' thing he done wuz ter slip off ter de grapevimes 'dout sayin' nuffin ter nobody. Nex' mawnin' he tole some er de niggers 'bout de fine bait er scuppernon' he et de night befo'.

"W'en dey tole 'im 'bout de goopher on de grapevimes, he 'uz dat tarrified dat he turn pale, en look des like he gwine ter die right in his tracks. De oberseah come up en axed w'at 'uz de matter; en w'en dey tol 'im Henry be'n eatin' er de scuppernon's, en got de goopher on 'im, he gin Henry a big drink er w'iskey, en 'low dat de nex' rainy day he take 'im ober ter Aun' Peggy's, en see ef she wouldn' take de goopher off'n him, seein' ez he didn't know nuffin erbout it tel he done et de grapes.

"Sho nuff, it rain de nex' day, en de oberseah went ober ter Aun' Peggy's wid Henry. En Aun' Peggy say dat bein' ez Henry didn' know 'bout de goopher, en et de grapes in ign'ance er de quinseconces, she reckon she mought be able fer ter take de goopher off'n him. So she fotch out er bottle wid some cunjuh medicine in it, en po'd some out in a go'd fer Henry ter drink. He manage ter git it down; he say it tas'e like whiskey wid sump'n bitter in it. She 'lowed dat 'ud keep de goopher off'n him tel de spring; but w'en de sap begin ter rise in de grapevimes he ha ter come en see her agin, en she tell him w'at e's ter do.

"Nex' spring, w'en de sap commence' ter rise in de scuppernon' vime, Henry tuk a ham one night. Whar'd he git de ham? *I* doan know; dey wa'nt no hams on de plantation 'cep'n w'at 'uz in de smoke-house, but *I* never see Henry 'bout de smoke-house. But ez I wuz a-sayin', he tuk de ham ober ter Aun' Peggy's; en Aun' Peggy tole 'im dat w'en Mars Dugal' begin ter prume de grapevimes, he mus' go en take 'n scrape off de sap whar it ooze out'n de cut een's er de vimes, en 'n'int his ball head wid it; en ef he do dat once't a year de goopher wouldn' wuk agin 'im long ez he done it. En bein 'ez he fotch her de ham, she fix' it so he kin eat all de scuppernon' he want.

"So Henry 'n'int his head wid de sap out'n de big grapevime des ha'f way 'twix' de quarters en de big house, en de goopher nebber wuk agin him dat summer. But de beatenes' thing you eber see happen ter Henry. Up ter dat time he wuz ez ball ez a sweeten' 'tater, but des ez soon ez de young leaves begun ter come out on de grapevimes de ha'r begun ter grow out on Henry's head, en by de middle er de summer he had de bigges' head er ha'r on de plantation. Befo' dat, Henry had tol'able good ha'r 'roun' de aidges, but soon ez de young grapes begun ter come Henry's ha'r begun ter quirl all up in little balls, des like dis yer reg'lar grapy ha'r, en by de time de grapes got ripe his head look des like a bunch er grapes. Combin' it didn' do no good; he wuk at it ha'f de night wid er Jim Crow,[3] en think he git it straighten' out, but in de mawnin' de grapes 'ud be dere des de same. So he gin it up, en tried ter keep de grapes down by havin' his ha'r cut sho't.

"But dat wa'nt de quares' thing 'bout de goopher. When Henry come ter de plantation, he wuz gittin' a little ole an stiff in de j'ints. But dat summer he got des ez spray en libely ez any young nigger on de plantation; fac' he got so biggity dat Mars Jackson, de oberseah, ha' ter th'eaten ter whip 'im, ef he didn' stop cuttin' up his didos[4] en behave hisse'f. But de mos' cur'ouses' thing happen' in de fall, when de sap begin ter go down in de grapevimes. Fus', when de grapes 'uz gethered, de knots begun ter straighten out'n Henry's h'ar; en w'en de leaves begin ter fall, Henry's ha'r begin ter drap out; en w'en de vimes 'uz b'ar, Henry's head wuz baller'n it wuz in de spring, en he begin ter git ole en stiff in de j'ints ag'in, en paid no mo' tention ter de

---

3. A small card, resembling a curry-comb in construction, and used by negroes in the rural districts instead of a comb [Chesnutt's note].

4. Behaving in a silly or mischievous way.

gals dyoin' er de whole winter. En nex' spring, w'en he rub de sap on ag'in, he got young ag'in, en so soopl en libely dat none er de young niggers on de plantation could n' jump, ner dance, ner hoe ez much cotton ez Henry. But in de fall er de year his grapes begun ter straighten out, en his j'ints ter git stiff, en his ha'r drap off, en de rheumatiz begin ter wrastle wid 'im.

"Now, ef you'd a knowed ole Mars Dugal' McAdoo, you'd a knowed dat it ha' ter be a mighty rainy day when he could n' fine sump'n fer his niggers ter do, en it ha' ter be a mightly little hole he couldn' crawl thoo, en ha' ter be a monst'us cloudy night w'en a dollar git by him in de dahkness; en w'en he see how Henry git young in de spring en ole in de fall, he 'lowered ter hisse'f ez how he could make mo' money outen Henry dan by wukkin' him in de cotton fiel'. 'Long de nex' spring, atter de sap commence' ter rise, en Henry 'n'int 'is head en commence fer ter git young en soopl, Mars Dugal' up'n tuk Henry ter town, en sole 'im fer fifteen hunder' dollars. Co'se de man w'at bought Henry didn' know nuffin 'bout de goopher, en Mars Dugal' didn' see no 'casion fer ter tell 'im. Long to'ds de fall, w'en de sap went down, Henry begin ter git ole again same ez yuzhal, en his noo marster begin ter git skeered les'n he gwine ter lose his fifteen-hunder'-dollar nigger. He sent fer a mighty fine doctor, but de med'cine didn' 'pear ter do no good; de goopher had a good holt. Henry tole de doctor 'bout de goopher, but de doctor des laff at 'im.

"One day in de winter Mars Dugal' went ter town, en wuz santerin' 'long de Main Street, when who should he meet but Henry's noo marster. Dey said 'Hoddy,' en Mars Dugal' ax 'im ter hab a seegyar; en atter dey run on awhile 'about de craps en de weather, Mars Dugal' ax 'im, sorter keerless, like ez ef he des thought of it,—

"'How you like de nigger I sole you las' spring?'

"Henry's marster shuck his head en knock de ashes off'n his seegyar.

"'Spec' I made a bad bahgin when I bought dat nigger. Henry done good wuk all de summer, but sence de fall set in he 'pears ter be sorter pinin' away. Dey ain' nuffin pertickler de matter wid 'im—leastways de doctor say so—'cep'n' a tech er de rheumatiz; but his ha'r is all fell out, en ef he don't pick up his strenk mighty soon, I spec' I'm gwine ter lose 'im.'

"Dey smoked on awhile, en bimeby ole mars say, 'Well, a bahgin's a bahgin, but you en me is good fren's, en I doan wan' ter see you lose all de money you paid fer dat digger; en ef w'at you say is so, en I ain't 'sputin' it, he ain't wuf much now. I spec's you wukked him too ha'd dis summer, er e'se de swamps down here don't agree wid de san'-hill nigger. So you des lemme know, en ef he gits any wusser I'll be willin' ter gib yer five hund'ed dollars fer 'im, en take my chances on his livin'.'

"Sho nuff, when Henry begun ter draw up wid de rheumatiz en it look like he gwine ter die fer sho, his noo marster sen' fer Mars Dugal', en Mars Dugal' gin him what he promus, en brung Henry home ag'in. He tuk good keer uv 'im dyoin' er de winter,—give 'im w'iskey ter rub his rheumatiz, en terbacker ter smoke, en all he want ter eat,—'caze a nigger w'at he could make a thou-san' dollars a year off'n didn' grow on eve'y huckleberry bush.

"Nex' spring, w'en de sap ris en Henry's ha'r commence' ter sprout, Mars Dugal' sole 'im ag'in, down in Robeson County dis time; en he kep' dat sellin' business up fer five year er mo'. Henry nebber say nuffin 'bout de goopher ter his noo marsters, 'caze he knew he gwine ter be tuk good keer uv de nex' winter, w'en Mars Dugal' buy him back. En Mars Dugal' made 'nuff money off'n Henry ter buy anudder plantation ober on Beaver Crick.

"But long 'bout de een' er dat five year dey come a stranger ter stop at de plantation. De fus' day he 'us dere he went out wid Mars Dugal' en spent all de mawnin' lookin' ober de vimya'd, en atter dinner dey spent all de evenin' playin' kya'ds. De niggers soon 'skiver' dat he wuz a Yankee, en dat he come down ter Norf C'lina fer ter learn de w'ite folks how to raise grapes en make wine. He promus Mars Dugal' he cud make de grapevimes ba'r twice't ez many grapes, en dat de noo wine-press he wuz a-sellin' would make mo' d'n twice't ez many gallons er wine. En ole Mars Dugal' des drunk it all in, des 'peared ter be bewitched wid dat Yankee. W'en de darkies see dat Yankee runnin' 'roun de vimya'd en diggin' under de grapevimes, dey shuk dere heads, en 'lowed dat dey feared Mars Dugal' losin' his min'. Mars Dugal' had all de dirt dug away fum under de roots er all de scuppernon' vimes, an' let 'em stan' dat away fer a week er mo'. Den dat Yankee made de niggers fix up a mixtry er lime en ashes en manyo,[5] en po' it roun' de roots er de grapevimes. Den he 'vise' Mars Dugal' fer ter trim de vimes close't, en Mars Dugal' tuck 'n done eve'ything de Yankee tole him ter do. Dyoin' all er dis time, mind yer, 'e wuz libbin' off'n de fat er de lan', at de big house, en playin' kyards wid Mars Dugal' eve'y night; en dey say Mars Dugal' los' mo'n a thousan' dollars dyoin' er de week dat Yankee wuz a runnin' de grapevimes.

"W'en de sap ris nex' spring, old Henry 'n'inted his head ez yuzhal, en his ha'r commence' ter grow des de same ez it done eve'y year. De scuppernon' vimes growed monst's fas', en de leaves wuz greener en thicker dan dey eber be'n dyowin my rememb'ance; en Henry's ha'r growed out thicker dan eber, en he 'peared ter git younger 'n younger, en soopler 'n soopler; en seein' ez he wuz sho't er han's dat spring, havin' tuk in consid'able noo groun', Mars Dugal' 'cluded he would n' sell Henry 'tel he git de crap in en de cotton chop'. So he kep' Henry on de plantation.

"But 'long 'bout time fer de grapes ter come on de scuppernon' vimes, dey 'peared ter come a change ober dem; de leaves wivered en swivel' up, en de young grapes turn' yaller, en bimeby eve'ybody on de plantation could see dat de whole vimya'd wuz dyin'. Mars Dugal' tuck'n water de vimes en done all he could, but 't wan' no use: dat Yankee done bus' de watermillyum. One time de vimes picked up a bit, en Mars Dugal' thought dey wuz gwine ter come out ag'in; but dat Yankee done dug too close unde' de roots, en prune de branches too close ter de vime, en all dat lime en ashes done burn' de life outen de vimes, en dey des kep' a with'in' en a swivelin'.

"All dis time de goopher wuz a-wukkin'. W'en de vimes commence' ter wither, Henry commence' ter complain er his rheumatiz, en when de leaves begin ter dry up his ha'r commence' ter drap out. When de vimes fresh up a bit Henry 'ud git peart agin, en when de vimes wither agin Henry 'ud git ole agin, en des kep' gittin' mo' en mo' fitten fer nuffin; he des pined away, en fine'ly tuk ter his cabin; en when de big vime whar he got de sap ter 'n'int his head withered en turned yaller en died, Henry died too,—des went out sorter like a cannel. Dey didn't 'pear ter be nuffin de matter wid 'im, cep'n' de rheumatiz, but his strenk des dwinel' away, 'tel he didn' hab ernuff lef' ter draw his bref. De goopher had got de under holt, en th'owed Henry fer good en all dat time.

"Mars Dugal' tuk on might'ly 'bout losin' his vimes en his nigger in de same year; en he swo' dat ef he could git holt er dat Yankee he'd wear 'im ter a frazzle, en den chaw up de frazzle; en he'd done it, too, for Mars Dugal' 'uz a monst'us brash man w'en he once git started. He sot de vimya'd out ober agin, but it wuz th'ee er fo' year befo' de vimes got ter b'arin' any scuppernon's.

"W'en de wah broke out, Mars Dugal' raise' a comp'ny, en went off ter fight de Yankees. He say he wuz mighty glad dat wah come, en he des want ter kill a Yankee fer eve'y dollar he los' 'long er dat grape-raisin' Yankee. En I 'spec' he would a done it, too, ef de Yankees hadn' s'picioned sump'n, en killed him fus'. Atter de s'render ole miss move' ter town, de niggers all scattered 'way fum de plantation, en de vimya'd ain' be'n cultervated sence."

"Is that story true?" asked Annie, doubtfully, but seriously, as the old man concluded his narrative.

"It's des ez true ez I'm a-settin' here, miss. Dey's a easy way ter prove it: I kin lead de way right ter Henry's grave ober yander in de plantation buryin'-groun'. En I tell yer w'at, marster, I wouldn' 'vise yer to buy dis yer ole vimya'd, 'caze de goopher's on it yit, en dey ain' no tellin' w'en it's gwine ter crap out."

"But I thought you said all the old vines died."

"Dey did 'pear ter die, but a few ov 'em come out ag'in, en is mixed in mongs' de yuthers. I ain' skeered ter eat de grapes, 'caze I knows de old vimes fum de noo ones; but wid strangers dey ain' no tellin' w'at might happen. I wouldn' 'vise yer ter buy dis vimya'd."

I bought the vineyard, nevertheless, and it has been for a long time in a thriving condition, and is referred to by the local press as a striking illustration of the opportunities open to Northern capital in the development of Southern industries. The luscious scuppernong holds first rank among our grapes, though we cultivate a great many other varieties, and our income from grapes packed and shipped to the Northern markets is quite considerable. I have not noticed any developments of the goopher in the vineyard, although I have a mild suspicion that our colored assistants do not suffer from want of grapes during the season.

I found, when I bought the vineyard, that Uncle Julius had occupied a cabin on the place for many years, and derived a respectable revenue from the neglected grapevines. This, doubtless, accounted for his advice to me not to buy the vineyard, though whether it inspired the goopher story I am unable to state. I believe, however, that the wages I pay him for his services are more than an equivalent for anything he lost by the sale of the vineyard.

1887

The Wife of His Youth[1]

I

Mr. Ryder was going to give a ball. There were several reasons why this was an opportune time for such an event.

Mr. Ryder might aptly be called the dean of the Blue Veins. The original Blue Veins were a little society of colored persons organized in a certain Northern city shortly after the war. Its purpose was to establish and maintain correct social standards among a people whose social condition presented

1. First published in the July 1898 issue of the *Atlantic* and reprinted in the collection *"The Wife of His Youth" and Other Stories of the Color Line* (1899), the source of the text printed here.

almost unlimited room for improvement. By accident, combined perhaps with some natural affinity, the society consisted of individuals who were, generally speaking, more white than black. Some envious outsider made the suggestion that no one was eligible for membership who was not white enough to show blue veins. The suggestion was readily adopted by those who were not of the favored few, and since that time the society, though possessing a longer and more pretentious name, had been known far and wide as the "Blue Vein Society," and its members as the "Blue Veins."

The Blue Veins did not allow that any such requirement existed for admission to their circle, but, on the contrary, declared that character and culture were the only things considered; and that if most of their members were light-colored, it was because such persons, as a rule, had had better opportunities to qualify themselves for membership. Opinions differed, too, as to the usefulness of the society. There were those who had been known to assail it violently as a glaring example of the very prejudice from which the colored race had suffered most; and later, when such critics had succeeded in getting on the inside, they had been heard to maintain with zeal and earnestness that the society was a life-boat, an anchor, a bulwark and a shield,—a pillar of cloud by day and of fire by night, to guide their people through the social wilderness. Another alleged prerequisite for Blue Vein membership was that of free birth; and while there was really no such requirement, it is doubtless true that very few of the members would have been unable to meet it if there had been. If there were one or two of the older members who had come up from the South and from slavery, their history presented enough romantic circumstances to rob their servile origin of its grosser aspects.

While there were no such tests of eligibility, it is true that the Blue Veins had their notions on these subjects, and that not all of them were equally liberal in regard to the things they collectively disclaimed. Mr. Ryder was one of the most conservative. Though he had not been among the founders of the society, but had come in some years later, his genius for social leadership was such that he had speedily become its recognized adviser and head, the custodian of its standards, and the preserver of its traditions. He shaped its social policy, was active in providing for its entertainment, and when the interest fell off, as it sometimes did, he fanned the embers until they burst again into a cheerful flame.

There were still other reasons for his popularity. While he was not as white as some of the Blue Veins, his appearance was such as to confer distinction upon them. His features were of a refined type, his hair was almost straight; he was always neatly dressed; his manners were irreproachable, and his morals above suspicion. He had come to Groveland a young man, and obtaining employment in the office of a railroad company as messenger had in time worked himself up to the position of stationery clerk, having charge of the distribution of the office supplies for the whole company. Although the lack of early training had hindered the orderly development of a naturally fine mind, it had not prevented him from doing a great deal of reading or from forming decidedly literary tastes. Poetry was his passion. He could repeat whole pages of the great English poets; and if his pronunciation was sometimes faulty, his eye, his voice, his gestures, would respond to the changing sentiment with a precision that revealed a poetic soul and disarmed criticism. He was economical, and had saved money; he owned and occupied a very comfortable house on a respectable street. His residence was handsomely furnished, containing among other things a good library, especially rich in poetry, a piano, and some choice engravings. He generally shared his house with some young couple, who looked after his wants and were company for him; for Mr. Ryder was a single man. In the early days of his connection with the Blue Veins he had been regarded as quite a catch, and young ladies and their mothers had manœuvred with much ingenuity to capture him. Not, however, until Mrs. Molly Dixon visited Groveland had any woman ever made him wish to change his condition to that of a married man.

Mrs. Dixon had come to Groveland from Washington in the spring, and before the summer was over she had won Mr. Ryder's heart. She possessed many attractive qualities. She was much younger than he; in fact, he was old enough to have been her father, though no one knew exactly how old he was. She was whiter than he, and better educated. She had moved in the best colored society of the country, at Washington, and had taught in the schools of that city. Such a superior person had been eagerly welcomed to the Blue Vein Society, and had taken a leading part in its activities. Mr. Ryder had at first been attracted by her charms of person, for she was very good looking and not over twenty-five; then by her refined manners and the vivacity of her wit. Her husband had been a government clerk, and at his death had left a considerable life insurance. She was visiting friends in Groveland, and, finding the town and the people to her liking, had prolonged her stay indefinitely. She had not seemed displeased at Mr. Ryder's attentions, but on the contrary had given him every proper encouragement; indeed, a younger and less cautious man would long since have spoken. But he had made up his mind, and had only to determine the time when he would ask her to be his wife. He decided to give a ball in her honor, and at some time during the evening of the ball to offer her his heart and hand. He had no special fears about the outcome, but, with a little touch of romance, he wanted the surroundings to be in harmony with his own feelings when he should have received the answer he expected.

Mr. Ryder resolved that this ball should mark an epoch in the social history of Groveland. He knew, of course,—no one could know better,—the entertainments that had taken place in past years, and what must be done to surpass them. His ball must be worthy of the lady in whose honor it was to be given, and must, by the quality of its guests, set an example for the future. He had observed of late a growing liberality, almost a laxity, in social matters, even among members of his own set, and had several times been forced to meet in a social way persons whose complexions and callings in life were hardly up to the standard which he considered proper for the society to maintain. He had a theory of his own.

"I have no race prejudice," he would say, "but we people of mixed blood are ground between the upper and the nether millstone. Our fate lies between absorption by the white race and extinction in the black. The one doesn't want us yet, but may take us in time. The other would welcome us, but it would be for us a backward step. 'With malice towards none, with charity for all,'[2] we must do the best we can for ourselves and those who are to follow us. Self-preservation is the first law of nature."

2. From Abraham Lincoln's second inaugural address (1865).

His ball would serve by its exclusiveness to counteract leveling tendencies, and his marriage with Mrs. Dixon would help to further the upward process of absorption he had been wishing and waiting for.

II

The ball was to take place on Friday night. The house had been put in order, the carpets covered with canvas, the halls and stairs decorated with palms and potted plants; and in the afternoon Mr. Ryder sat on his front porch, which the shade of a vine running up over a wire netting made a cool and pleasant lounging place. He expected to respond to the toast "The Ladies" at the supper, and from a volume of Tennyson—his favorite poet— was fortifying himself with apt quotations. The volume was open at "A Dream of Fair Women."[3] His eyes fell on these lines, and he read them aloud to judge better of their effect:—

> "At length I saw a lady within call,
>   Stiller than chisell'd marble, standing there;
> A daughter of the gods, divinely tall,
>   And most divinely fair."

He marked the verse, and turning the page read the stanza beginning,—

> "O sweet pale Margaret,
>   O rare pale Margaret."[4]

He weighed the passage a moment, and decided that it would not do. Mrs. Dixon was the palest lady he expected at the ball, and she was of a rather ruddy complexion, and of lively disposition and buxom build. So he ran over the leaves until his eye rested on the description of Queen Guinevere:[5]—

> "She seem'd a part of joyous Spring:
>   A gown of grass-green silk she wore,
>   Buckled with golden clasps before;
> A light-green tuft of plumes she bore
>   Closed in a golden ring.

>   •   •   •   •   •

> "She look'd so lovely, as she sway'd
>   The rein with dainty finger-tips,
> A man had given all other bliss,
>   And all his worldly worth for this,
> To waste his whole heart in one kiss
>   Upon her perfect lips."

As Mr. Ryder murmured these words audibly, with an appreciative thrill, he heard the latch of his gate click, and a light foot-fall sounding on the steps. He turned his head, and saw a woman standing before his door.

She was a little woman, not five feet tall, and proportioned to her height. Although she stood erect, and looked around her with very bright and restless eyes, she seemed quite old; for her face was crossed and recrossed with a

3. Poem by the English writer Alfred, Lord Tennyson (1809–1892), published in 1832.
4. From Tennyson's "Margaret" (1832).

5. Wife of the legendary King Arthur, described in the stanzas that follow from Tennyson's "Sir Launcelot and Queen Guinevere" (1842).

hundred wrinkles, and around the edges of her bonnet could be seen protruding here and there a tuft of short gray wool. She wore a blue calico gown of ancient cut, a little red shawl fastened around her shoulders with an old-fashioned brass brooch, and a large bonnet profusely ornamented with faded red and yellow artificial flowers. And she was very black,—so black that her toothless gums, revealed when she opened her mouth to speak, were not red, but blue. She looked like a bit of the old plantation life, summoned up from the past by the wave of a magician's wand, as the poet's fancy had called into being the gracious shapes of which Mr. Ryder had just been reading.

He rose from his chair and came over to where she stood.

"Good-afternoon, madam," he said.

"Good-evenin', suh," she answered, ducking suddenly with a quaint curtsy. Her voice was shrill and piping, but softened somewhat by age. "Is dis yere whar Mistuh Ryduh lib, suh?" she asked, looking around her doubtfully, and glancing into the open windows, through which some of the preparations for the evening were visible.

"Yes," he replied, with an air of kindly patronage, unconsciously flattered by her manner, "I am Mr. Ryder. Did you want to see me?"

"Yas, suh, ef I ain't 'sturbin' of you too much."

"Not at all. Have a seat over here behind the vine, where it is cool. What can I do for you?"

"'Scuse me, suh," she continued, when she had sat down on the edge of a chair, "'scuse me, suh, I's lookin' for my husban'. I heerd you wuz a big man an' had libbed heah a long time, an' I 'lowed you wouldn't min' ef I'd come roun' an' ax you ef you'd ever heerd of a merlatter[6] man by de name er Sam Taylor 'quirin' roun' in de chu'ches ermongs' de people fer his wife 'Liza Jane?"

Mr. Ryder seemed to think for a moment.

"There used to be many such cases right after the war," he said, "but it has been so long that I have forgotten them. There are very few now. But tell me your story, and it may refresh my memory."

She sat back farther in her chair so as to be more comfortable, and folded her withered hands in her lap.

"My name's 'Liza," she began, "'Liza Jane. W'en I wuz young I us'ter b'long ter Marse Bob Smif, down in ole Missoura. I wuz bawn down dere. W'en I wuz a gal I wuz married ter a man named Jim. But Jim died, an' after dat I married a merlatter man named Sam Taylor. Sam wuz free-bawn, but his mammy and daddy died, an' de w'ite folks 'prenticed him ter my marster fer ter work fer 'im 'tel he wuz growed up. Sam worked in de fiel', an' I wuz de cook. One day Ma'y Ann, ole miss's maid, came rushin' out ter de kitchen, an' says she, ''Liza Jane, ole marse gwine sell yo' Sam down de ribber.'

"'Go way f'm yere,' says I; 'my husban' 's free!'

"'Don' make no diff'ence. I heerd ole marse tell ole miss he wuz gwine take yo' Sam 'way wid 'im ter-morrow, fer he needed money, an' he knowed whar he could git a t'ousan' dollars fer Sam an' no questions axed.'

"W'en Sam come home f'm de fiel' dat night, I tole him 'bout ole marse gwine steal 'im, an' Sam run erway. His time wuz mos' up, an' he swo' dat w'en he wuz twenty-one he would come back an' he'p me run erway, er else save up de money ter buy my freedom. An' I know he'd 'a' done it, fer he thought a heap er me, Sam did. But w'en he come back he didn' fin' me, fer

I wuzn' dere. Ole marse had heerd dat I warned Sam, so he had me whip' an' sol' down de ribber.

"Den de wah broke out, an' w'en it wuz ober de cullud folks wuz scattered. I went back ter de ole home; but Sam wuzn' dere, an' I couldn' l'arn nuffin' 'bout 'im. But I knowed he'd be'n dere to look for me an' hadn' foun' me, an' had gone erway ter hunt fer me.

"I's be'n lookin' fer 'im eber sence," she added simply, as though twenty-five years were but a couple of weeks, "an' I knows he's be'n lookin' fer me. Fer he sot a heap er sto' by me, Sam did, an' I know he's be'n huntin' fer me all dese years,—'less'n he's be'n sick er sump'n, so he couldn' work, er out'n his head, so he couldn' 'member his promise. I went back down de ribber, fer I 'lowed he'd gone down dere lookin' fer me. I's be'n ter Noo Orleens, an' Atlanty, an' Charleston, an' Richmon'; an' w'en I'd be'n all ober de Souf I come ter de Norf. Fer I knows I'll fin' 'im some er dese days," she added softly, "er he'll fin' me, an' den we'll bofe be as happy in freedom as we wuz in de ole days befo' de wah." A smile stole over her withered countenance as she paused a moment, and her bright eyes softened into a far-away look.

This was the substance of the old woman's story. She had wandered a little here and there. Mr. Ryder was looking at her curiously when she finished.

"How have you lived all these years?" he asked.

"Cookin', suh. I's a good cook. Does you know anybody w'at needs a good cook, suh? I's stoppin' wid a cullud fam'ly round' de corner yonder 'tel I kin git a place."

"Do you really expect to find your husband? He may be dead long ago."

She shook her head emphatically. "Oh no, he ain' dead. De signs an' de tokens tells me. I dremp three nights runnin' on'y dis las' week dat I foun' him."

"He may have married another woman. Your slave marriage would not have prevented him, for you never lived with him after the war, and without that your marriage doesn't count."[7]

"Wouldn' make no diff'ence wid Sam. He wouldn' marry no yuther 'ooman 'tel he foun' out 'bout me. I knows it," she added. "Sump'n's be'n tellin' me all dese years dat I's gwine fin' Sam 'fo' I dies."

"Perhaps he's outgrown you, and climbed up in the world where he wouldn't care to have you find him."

"No, indeed, suh," she replied, "Sam ain' dat kin' er man. He wuz good ter me, Sam wuz, but he wuzn' much good ter nobody e'se, fer he wuz one er de triflin'es' han's on de plantation. I 'spec's ter haf ter suppo't 'im w'en I fin' 'im, fer he nebber would work 'less'n he had ter. But den he wuz free, an' he didn' git no pay fer his work, an' I don' blame 'im much. Mebbe he's done better sence he run erway, but I ain' 'spectin' much."

"You may have passed him on the street a hundred times during the twenty-five years, and not have known him; time works great changes."

She smiled incredulously. "I'd know 'im 'mongs' a hund'ed men. Fer dey wuz n' no yuther merlatter man like my man Sam, an' I couldn' be mistook. I's toted his picture roun' wid me twenty-five years."

"May I see it?" asked Mr. Ryder. "It might help me to remember whether I have seen the original."

As she drew a small parcel from her bosom he saw that it was fastened to a string that went around her neck. Removing several wrappers, she brought

---

7. Slave marriages had no legal standing in the pre–Civil War South.

to light an old-fashioned daguerreotype in a black case. He looked long and intently at the portrait. It was faded with time, but the features were still distinct, and it was easy to see what manner of man it had represented.

He closed the case, and with a slow movement handed it back to her.

"I don't know of any man in town who goes by that name," he said, "nor have I heard of any one making such inquiries. But if you will leave me your address, I will give the matter some attention, and if I find out anything I will let you know."

She gave him the number of a house in the neighborhood, and went away, after thanking him warmly.

He wrote the address on the fly-leaf of the volume of Tennyson, and, when she had gone, rose to his feet and stood looking after her curiously. As she walked down the street with mincing step, he saw several persons whom she passed turn and look back at her with a smile of kindly amusement. When she had turned the corner, he went upstairs to his bedroom, and stood for a long time before the mirror of his dressing-case, gazing thoughtfully at the reflection of his own face.

III

At eight o'clock the ballroom was a blaze of light and the guests had begun to assemble; for there was a literary programme and some routine business of the society to be gone through with before the dancing. A black servant in evening dress waited at the door and directed the guests to the dressing-rooms.

The occasion was long memorable among the colored people of the city; not alone for the dress and display, but for the high average of intelligence and culture that distinguished the gathering as a whole. There were a number of school-teachers, several young doctors, three or four lawyers, some professional singers, an editor, a lieutenant in the United States army spending his furlough in the city, and others in various polite callings; these were colored, though most of them would not have attracted even a casual glance because of any marked difference from white people. Most of the ladies were in evening costume, and dress coats and dancing pumps were the rule among the men. A band of string music, stationed in an alcove behind a row of palms, played popular airs while the guests were gathering.

The dancing began at half past nine. At eleven o'clock supper was served. Mr. Ryder had left the ballroom some little time before the intermission, but reappeared at the supper-table. The spread was worthy of the occasion, and the guests did full justice to it. When the coffee had been served, the toast-master, Mr. Solomon Sadler, rapped for order. He made a brief introductory speech, complimenting host and guests, and then presented in their order the toasts of the evening. They were responded to with a very fair display of after-dinner wit.

"The last toast," said the toast-master, when he reached the end of the list, "is one which must appeal to us all. There is no one of us of the sterner sex who is not at some time dependent upon woman,—in infancy for protection, in manhood for companionship, in old age for care and comforting. Our good host has been trying to live alone, but the fair faces I see around me to-night prove that he too is largely dependent upon the gentler sex for most that makes life worth living,—the society and love of friends,—and rumor is at fault if he does not soon yield entire subjection to one of them. Mr. Ryder will now respond to the toast,—The Ladies."

There was a pensive look in Mr. Ryder's eyes as he took the floor and adjusted his eye-glasses. He began by speaking of woman as the gift of Heaven to man, and after some general observations on the relations of the sexes he said: "But perhaps the quality which most distinguishes woman is her fidelity and devotion to those she loves. History is full of examples, but has recorded none more striking than one which only to-day came under my notice."

He then related, simply but effectively, the story told by his visitor of the afternoon. He gave it in the same soft dialect, which came readily to his lips, while the company listened attentively and sympathetically. For the story had awakened a responsive thrill in many hearts. There were some present who had seen, and others who had heard their fathers and grandfathers tell, the wrongs and sufferings of this past generation, and all of them still felt, in their darker moments, the shadow hanging over them. Mr. Ryder went on:—

"Such devotion and confidence are rare even among women. There are many who would have searched a year, some who would have waited five years, a few who might have hoped ten years; but for twenty-five years this woman has retained her affection for and her faith in a man she has not seen or heard of in all that time.

"She came to me to-day in the hope that I might be able to help her find this long-lost husband. And when she was gone I gave my fancy rein, and imagined a case I will put to you.

"Suppose that this husband, soon after his escape, had learned that his wife had been sold away, and that such inquiries as he could make brought no information of her whereabouts. Suppose that he was young, and she much older than he; that he was light, and she was black; that their marriage was a slave marriage, and legally binding only if they chose to make it so after the war. Suppose, too, that he made his way to the North, as some of us have done, and there, where he had larger opportunities, had improved them, and had in the course of all these years grown to be as different from the ignorant boy who ran away from fear of slavery as the day is from the night. Suppose, even, that he had qualified himself, by industry, by thrift, and by study, to win the friendship and be considered worthy the society of such people as these I see around me to-night, gracing my board and filling my heart with gladness; for I am old enough to remember the day when such a gathering would not have been possible in this land. Suppose, too, that, as the years went by, this man's memory of the past grew more and more indistinct, until at last it was rarely, except in his dreams, that any image of this bygone period rose before his mind. And then suppose that accident should bring to his knowledge the fact that the wife of his youth, the wife he had left behind him,—not one who had walked by his side and kept pace with him in his upward struggle, but one upon whom advancing years and a laborious life had set their mark,—was alive and seeking him, but that he was absolutely safe from recognition or discovery, unless he chose to reveal himself. My friends, what would the man do? I will presume that he was one who loved honor, and tried to deal justly with all men. I will even carry the case further, and suppose that perhaps he had set his heart upon another, whom he had hoped to call his own. What would he do, or rather what ought he to do, in such a crisis of a lifetime?

"It seemed to me that he might hesitate, and I imagined that I was an old friend, a near friend, and that he had come to me for advice; and I argued the case with him. I tried to discuss it impartially. After we had looked upon the matter from every point of view, I said to him, in words that we all know:—

> "This above all: to thine own self be true,
> And it must follow, as the night the day,
> Thou canst not then be false to any man."[8]

Then, finally, I put the question to him, 'Shall you acknowledge her?'

"And now, ladies and gentlemen, friends and companions, I ask you, what should he have done?"

There was something in Mr. Ryder's voice that stirred the hearts of those who sat around him. It suggested more than mere sympathy with an imaginary situation; it seemed rather in the nature of a personal appeal. It was observed, too, that his look rested more especially upon Mrs. Dixon, with a mingled expression of renunciation and inquiry.

She had listened, with parted lips and streaming eyes. She was the first to speak: "He should have acknowledged her."

"Yes," they all echoed, "he should have acknowledged her."

"My friends and companions," responded Mr. Ryder, "I thank you, one and all. It is the answer I expected, for I knew your hearts."

He turned and walked toward the closed door of an adjoining room, while every eye followed him in wondering curiosity. He came back in a moment, leading by the hand his visitor of the afternoon, who stood startled and trembling at the sudden plunge into this scene of brilliant gayety. She was neatly dressed in gray, and wore the white cap of an elderly woman.

"Ladies and gentlemen," he said, "this is the woman, and I am the man, whose story I have told you. Permit me to introduce to you the wife of my youth."

1899

---

8. Shakespeare, *Hamlet* 1.3.

ABRAHAM CAHAN
1860–1951

Oone of the central subjects of turn-of-the-twentieth-century U.S. literature is the (usually painful) process of "Americanization" or assimilation of immigrants from all corners of the world. Such assimilation is at the heart of the work of Abraham Cahan, both as a prolific journalist and as the author of a relatively small but important body of fiction.

Cahan was born into an Orthodox Jewish family in a village a few miles from Vilna, Lithuania, then a part of the Russian Empire. He was educated as a youth first in Hebrew schools and then in a *yeshiva*—a seminary for studies in Jewish law and commentaries on it. His absorption in traditional Jewish studies gave way in his teens to a comparably passionate engagement with secular subjects, especially literature and social theory. As a student at the Vilna Teacher Training Institute, he was among a small group of young men who, like self-described intellectuals in other Russian cities, read and discussed such subversive works as Nikolai Chernishevsky's radical utopian novel *What Is to Be Done?* (1863). Of more lasting importance to him was the reading of Tolstoi and other Russian writers; of these, Chekhov, a brilliant short-story writer, became his favorite. Although Cahan was neither a leader nor an active conspirator in efforts to overthrow the czarist regime, his room was searched twice during his first year as a teacher, and he had good reason to be concerned about the possibilities of arrest and imprisonment.

The intensified attempt to suppress dissent that brought Cahan and other intellectuals under suspicion (it was considered a revolutionary act simply to be in possession of prohibited writings) was one consequence of the assassination of Czar Alexander II in March 1881. More important historically was intensified Russian anti-Semitism and an unprecedented series of murderous pogroms unleashed against Russian Jews with at least the tacit approval of local police and other government officials. There had been pogroms before and in other regions, but these pogroms led almost immediately to the massive emigration, starting in 1882, of Russian and Eastern European Jews to Palestine and, in much greater numbers, to America (two million by 1924).

Within two months of his arrival in the United States in 1882, Cahan gave the first socialist speech to be delivered in the country in Yiddish—a language that combined Middle High German dialects with vocabularies from Hebrew, Slavic, and European languages and as time went on a distinctively Jewish American vocabulary. Cahan soon helped organize the first Jewish tailors' union; taught English at night to immigrants at the Young Men's Hebrew Association; and began his careers as editor and journalist with Yiddish, Russian, and English papers.

In 1897 Cahan was active in founding the *Jewish Daily Forward,* a Yiddish-language newspaper he edited, with some short interruptions, for nearly fifty years. As critic Jules Chametsky observed: "[Cahan] took a sectarian journal of the Social Democratic Party with 6,000 subscribers and made it the most successful foreign-language newspaper in America and the leading Yiddish paper in the world." At its height the *Forward* had a circulation of a quarter of a million (and was read by perhaps a million people altogether). Cahan's editorial policy was designed to help Jewish immigrants make the transition from the often medieval conditions of the urban ghettos and *shtetls* to the new realities of a rapidly industrializing democracy. The *Forward* combined news, information, cultural commentary, and reviews with short stories, including work of I.J. Singer and Sholem Asch. It included features such as "A Bintel Brief" (A Bundle of Letters), which printed anonymous letters from subscribers together with authoritative advice from the editor.

For twenty-five years—from 1892 until 1917—Cahan turned his attention to writing fiction in English. Encouraged by novelist and critic William Dean Howells, Cahan published his first novel, *Yekl: A Tale of the New York Ghetto*, in 1896. Encouraged further by the generally favorable reception of this work (later made more popular by Joan Micklen Silver's film adaptation, released in 1975 under the title *Hester Street*), Cahan wrote short stories that he published in 1898 as "*The Imported Bridegroom" and Other Stories of the New York Ghetto*, which included "A Sweat-Shop Romance" (first published in 1895). Throughout the volume, Yiddish and heavily accented English are largely absorbed and "translated" into the perceptive but lucid language of an omniscient third-person narrator. This change in presentational mode was a sign of Cahan's mastery of English and sophistication of technique, as well as developing control of irony.

The title "A Sweat-Shop Romance" itself suggests some of the tensions it dramatizes—between the grim and cramped spaces the characters occupy and the exhilarating release of romantic love some of them experience, between the pretensions of the prideful bosses of a "cockroach" shop and the independence and self-reliance of the young couple who refuse to be treated as servants and who marry in the end. "A Sweat-Shop Romance," with apparent artlessness, illuminates truthfully and movingly the emotional and psychological realities of ordinary men and women living with good humor under difficult economic, cultural, and social circumstances. At the same time the story provides insight into highly specific aspects of the rapidly growing and increasingly competitive garment industry. Another aspect of the story's apparent artlessness has to do with Cahan's skillful use of language. Unlike *Yekl* or some of his other stories, Yiddish and heavily accented English in this story are largely absorbed and "translated" into the perceptive but lucid language of an omniscient third-person narrator. This change of presentational mode is a clear sign of Cahan's mastery of English and sophistication of technique. In this story his sharp eye and sensitive ear for language are at the service of mood and characterization.

Cahan's masterpiece was his novel *The Rise of David Levinsky* (1917), a powerful depiction of the garment industry and the people who work in it. This book established Cahan as a progenitor of Jewish American writers as diverse as Michael Gold, Henry Roth, Saul Bellow, and Alfred Kazin. The rich tapestry of this intensely realistic account of turn-of-the-twentieth-century New York is at once a Jewish novel, a novel about the always difficult process of Americanization, and a more universal story of self-estrangement and social alienation. Both as a journalist and as a writer of fiction, Abraham Cahan was influential in his own time. He remains one of the central chroniclers of American immigrant life.

A Sweat-Shop Romance[1]

Leizer Lipman was one of those contract tailors who are classed by their hands under the head of "cockroaches," which—translating the term into lay English—means that he ran a very small shop, giving employment to a single team of one sewing-machine operator, one baster, one finisher, and one presser.

The shop was one of a suite of three rooms on the third floor of a rickety old tenement house on Essex Street, and did the additional duty of the family's kitchen and dining-room. It faced a dingy little courtyard, and was connected by a windowless bedroom with the parlor, which commanded the very heart of the Jewish markets. Bundles of cloth, cut to be made into coats, littered the floor, lay in chaotic piles by one of the walls, cumbered Mrs. Lipman's kitchen table and one or two chairs, and formed, in a corner, an improvised bed upon which a dirty two-year-old boy, Leizer's heir apparent, was enjoying his siesta.

Dangling against the door or scattered among the bundles, there were cooking utensils, dirty linen, Lipman's velvet skull-cap,[2] hats, shoes, shears, cotton-spools, and what-not. A red-hot kitchen stove and a blazing grate full of glowing flat-irons combined to keep up the overpowering temperature of the room, and helped to justify its nickname of sweat-shop in the literal sense of the epithet.

---

1. Originally published as "In the Sweat Shop" in the magazine *Short Stories* in June 1895, then as part of *"The Imported Bridegroom" and Other* *Stories of the New York Ghetto* (1898), the source of the text printed here.
2. Yarmulke; worn by Jewish men.

Work was rather scarce, but the designer of the Broadway clothing firm, of whose army of contractors Lipman was a member, was a second cousin to the latter's wife, and he saw to it that his relative's husband was kept busy. And so operations in Leizer's shop were in full swing. Heyman, the operator, with his bared brawny arms, pushed away at an unfinished coat, over which his head, presenting to view a wealth of curly brown hair, hung like an eagle bent on his prey. He swayed in unison to the rhythmic whirr of his machine, whose music, supported by the energetic thumps of Meyer's press-iron, formed an orchestral accompaniment to the sonorous and plaintive strains of a vocal duet performed by Beile, the finisher girl, and David, the baster.

Leizer was gone to the Broadway firm's offices, while Zlate, his wife, was out on a prolonged haggling expedition among the tradeswomen of Hester Street. This circumstance gave the hands a respite from the restrictions usually placed on their liberties by the presence of the "boss" and the "Missis," and they freely beguiled the tedium and fatigue of their work, now by singing, now by a bantering match at the expense of their employer and his wife, or of each other.

"Well, I suppose you might as well quit," said Meyer, a chubby, red-haired, freckled fellow of forty, emphasizing his remark by an angry stroke of his iron. "You have been over that song now fifty times without taking breath. You make me tired."

"Don't you like it? Stuff up your ears, then," Beile retorted, without lifting her head from the coat in her lap.

"Why, I do like it, first-rate and a half," Meyer returned, "but when you keep your mouth shut I like it better still, see?"

The silvery tinkle of Beile's voice, as she was singing, thrilled Heyman with delicious melancholy, gave him fresh relish for his work, and infused additional activity into his limbs; and as her singing was interrupted by the presser's gibe, he involuntarily stopped his machine with that annoying feeling which is experienced by dancers when brought to an unexpected standstill by an abrupt pause of the music.

"And you?"—he addressed himself to Meyer, facing about on his chair with an irritated countenance. "It's all right enough when you speak, but it is much better when you hold your tongue. Don't mind him, Beile. Sing away!" he then said to the girl, his dazzlingly fair face relaxing and his little eyes shutting into a sweet smile of self-confident gallantry.

"You had better stick to your work, Heyman. Why, you might have made half a cent the while," Meyer fired back, with an ironical look, which had reference to the operator's reputation of being a niggardly fellow, who overworked himself, denied himself every pleasure, and grew fat by feasting his eyes on his savings-bank book.

A sharp altercation ensued, which drifted to the subject of Heyman's servile conduct toward his employer.

"It was you, wasn't it," Meyer said, "who started that collection for a birthday present for the boss? Of course, we couldn't help chipping in. Why is David independent?"

"Did I compel you?" Heyman rejoined. "And am I to blame that it was to me that the boss threw out the hint about that present? It is so slack everywhere, and you ought to thank God for the steady job you have here," he concluded, pouncing down upon the coat on his machine.

David, who had also cut short his singing, kept silently plying his needle upon pieces of stuff which lay stretched on his master's dining-table. Presently he paused to adjust his disheveled jet-black hair, with his fingers for a comb, and to wipe the perspiration from his swarthy, beardless and typically Israelitic face with his shirt-sleeve.

While this was in progress, his languid hazel eyes were fixed on the finisher girl. She instinctively became conscious of his gaze, and raised her head from the needle. Her fresh buxom face, flushed with the heat of the room and with exertion, shone full upon the young baster. Their eyes met. David colored, and, to conceal his embarrassment, he asked: "Well, is he going to raise your wages?"

Beile nodded affirmatively, and again plunged her head into her work.

"He is? So you will now get five dollars a week. I am afraid you will be putting on airs now, won't you?"

"Do you begrudge me? Then I am willing to swap wages with you. I'll let you have my five dollars, and I'll take your twelve dollars every week."

Lipman's was a task shop, and, according to the signification which the term has in the political economy of the sweating world, his operator, baster, and finisher, while nominally engaged at so much a week, were in reality paid by the piece, the economical week being determined by a stipulated quantity of made-up coats rather than by a fixed number of the earth's revolutions around its axis; for the sweat-shop day will not coincide with the solar day unless a given amount of work be accomplished in its course. As to the presser, he is invariably a piece-worker, pure and simple.

For a more lucid account of the task system in the tailoring branch, I beg to refer the reader to David, although his exposition happens to be presented rather in the form of a satire on the subject. Indeed, David, while rather inclined to taciturnity, was an inveterate jester, and what few remarks he indulged in during his work would often cause boisterous merriment among his shopmates, although he delivered them with a nonchalant manner and with the same look of good-humored irony, mingled in strange harmony with a general expression of gruffness, which his face usually wore.

"My twelve dollars every week?" David echoed. "Oh, I see; you mean a week of twelve days!" And his needle resumed its duck-like sport in the cloth.

"How do you make it out?" Meyer demanded, in order to elicit a joke from the witty young man by his side.

"Of course, *you* don't know how to make that out. But ask Heyman or Beile. The three of us do."

"Tell him, then, and he will know too," Beile urged, laughing in advance at the expected fun.

A request coming from the finisher was—yet unknown to herself—resistless with David, and in the present instance it loosened his tongue.

"Well, I get twelve dollars a week, and Heyman fourteen. Now a working week has six days, but—hem—that 'but' gets stuck in my throat—but a day is neither a Sunday nor a Monday nor anything unless we make twelve coats. The calendars are a lot of liars."

"What do you mean?"

"They say a day has twenty-four hours. That's a bluff. A day has twelve coats."

Beile's rapturous chuckle whetted his appetite for persiflage, and he went on:—

"They read the Tuesday Psalm[3] in the synagogue this morning, but I should have read the Monday one."

"Why?"

"You see, Meyer's wife will soon come up with his dinner, and here I have still two coats to make of the twelve that I got yesterday. So it's still Monday with me. My Tuesday won't begin before about two o'clock this afternoon."

"How much will you make this week?" Meyer questioned.

"I don't expect to finish more than four days' work by the end of the week, and will only get eight dollars on Friday—that is, provided the Missis has not spent our wages by that time. So when it's Friday I'll call it Wednesday, see?"

"When I am married," he added, after a pause, "and the old woman asks me for Sabbath expenses, I'll tell her it is only Wednesday—it isn't yet Friday[4]—and I have no money to give her."

David relapsed into silence, but mutely continued his burlesque, hopping from subject to subject.

David thought himself a very queer fellow. He often wondered at the pranks which his own imagination was in the habit of playing, and at the grotesque combinations it frequently evolved. As he now stood, leaning forward over his work, he was striving to make out how it was that Meyer reminded him of the figure "7."

"What nonsense!" he inwardly exclaimed, branding himself for a crank. "And what does Heyman look like?" his mind queried, as though for spite. He contemplated the operator askance, and ran over all the digits of the Arabic system, and even the whole Hebrew alphabet, in quest of a counterpart to the young man, but failed to find anything suitable. "His face would much better become a girl," he at last decided, and mentally proceeded to envelop Heyman's head in Beile's shawl. But the proceeding somehow stung him, and he went on to meditate upon the operator's chunky nose. "No, that nose is too ugly for a girl. It wants a little planing. It's an unfinished job, as it were. But for that nose Heyman would really be the nice fellow they say he is. His snow-white skin—his elegant heavy mustache—yes, if he did not have that nose he would be all right," he maliciously joked in his heart. "And I, too, would be all right if Heyman were noseless," he added, transferring his thoughts to Beile, and wondering why she looked so sweet. "Why, her nose is not much of a beauty, either. Entirely too straight, and too—too foolish. Her eyes look old and as if constantly on the point of bursting into tears. Ah, but then her lips—that kindly smile of theirs, coming out of one corner of her mouth!" And a strong impulse seized him to throw himself on those lips and to kiss them, which he did mentally, and which shot an electric current through his whole frame. And at this Beile's old-looking eyes both charmed and pierced him to the heart, and her nose, far from looking foolish, seemed to contemplate him contemptuously, triumphantly, and knowingly, as if it had read his thoughts.

While this was going on in David's brain and heart, Beile was taken up with Heyman and with their mutual relations. His attentions to her were an open secret. He did not go out of his way to conceal them. On the contrary, he regularly escorted her home after work, and took her out to balls and

---

3. In Orthodox Judaism ten or more Jewish males at least thirteen years of age are required for the lawful conduct of a public Jewish service. Such a group (a *minyan*) meets in the early mornings; as part of the service a psalm is recited.
4. Typically payday and the start, at sundown, of the Jewish Sabbath. "Sabbath expenses": e.g., the costs of special foods, candles, and the like.

picnics—a thing involving great sacrifices to a fellow who trembled over every cent he spent, and who was sure to make up for these losses to his pocket-book by foregoing his meals. While alone with her in the hallway of her mother's residence, his voice would become so tender, so tremulous, and on several occasions he even addressed her by the endearing form of Beilinke. And yet all this had been going on now for over three months, and he had not as much as alluded to marriage, nor even bought her the most trifling present.

Her mother made life a burden to her, and urged the point-blank declaration of the alternative between a formal engagement and an arrest for breach of promise. Beile would have died rather than make herself the heroine of such a sensation; and, besides, the idea of Heyman handcuffed to a police detective was too terrible to entertain even for a moment.

She loved him. She liked his blooming face, his gentleman-like mustache, the quaint jerk of his head, as he walked; she was fond of his company; she was sure she was in love with him: her confidant, her fellow country girl and playmate, who had recently married Meyer, the presser, had told her so.

But somehow she felt disappointed. She had imagined love to be a much sweeter thing. She had thought that a girl in love admired *everything* in the object of her affections, and was blind to all his faults. She had heard that love was something like a perpetual blissful fluttering of the heart.

"I feel as if something was melting here," a girl friend who was about to be married once confided to her, pointing to her heart. "You see, it aches and yet it is so sweet at the same time." And here she never feels anything melting, nor can she help disliking some things about Heyman. His smile sometimes appears to her fulsome. Ah, if he did not shut his eyes as he does when smiling! That he is so slow to spend money is rather one of the things she likes in him. If he ever marries her she will be sure to get every cent of his wages. But then when they are together at a ball he never goes up to the bar to treat her to a glass of soda, as the other fellows do to their girls, and all he offers her is an apple or a pear, which he generally stops to buy on the street on their way to the dancing-hall. Is she in love at all? Maybe she is mistaken? But no! he is after all so dear to her. She must have herself to blame. It is not in vain that her mother calls her a whimpering, nagging thing, who gives no peace to herself nor to anybody around her. But why does he not come out with his declaration? Is it because he is too stingy to wish to support a wife? Has he been making a fool of her? What does he take her for, then?

In fairness to Heyman, it must be stated that on the point of his intentions, at least, her judgment of him was without foundation, and her misgivings gratuitous. Pecuniary considerations had nothing to do with his slowness in proposing to her. And if she could have watched him and penetrated his mind at the moments when he examined his bank-book,—which he did quite often,—she would have ascertained that little images of herself kept hovering before his eyes between the figures of its credit columns, and that the sum total conjured up to him a picture of prospective felicity with her for a central figure.

Poor thing; she did not know that when he lingeringly fondled her hand, on taking his leave in the hallway, the proposal lay on the tip of his tongue, and that lacking the strength to relieve himself of its burden he every time left her, consoling himself that the moment was inopportune, and that "tomorrow he would surely settle it." She did not know that only two days ago the idea had occurred to him to have recourse to the aid of a messenger in the form of a lady's watch, and that while she now sat worrying lest she was being made a fool of, the golden emissary lay in Heyman's vest-pocket, throbbing in company with his heart with impatient expectation of the evening hour, which had been fixed for the delivery of its message.

"I shall let mother speak to him," Beile resolved, in her musings over her needle. She went on to picture the scene, but at this point her meditations were suddenly broken by something clutching and pulling at her hair. It was her employer's boy. He had just got up from his after-dinner nap, and, for want of any other occupation, he passed his dirty little hand into her raven locks.

"He is practicing to be a boss," observed David, whose attention was attracted to the spectacle by the finisher's shriek.

Beile's voice brought Heyman to his feet, and disentangling the little fellow's fingers from the girl's hair, he fell to "plastering his nasty cheeks for him," as he put it. At this juncture the door opened to admit the little culprit's father. Heyman skulked away to his seat, and, burying his head in his work, he proceeded to drown, in the whir-r, whir-r of his machine, the screams of the boy, who would have struck a much higher key had his mamma happened on the spot.

Lipman took off his coat, substituted his greasy velvet skull-cap for his derby, and lighting a cigar with an air of good-natured business-like importance, he advanced to Meyer's corner and fell to examining a coat.

"And what does *he* look like?" David asked himself, scrutinizing his taskmaster. "Like a broom with its stick downward," he concluded to his own satisfaction. "And his snuff-box?"—meaning Lipman's huge nose—"A perfect fiddle!—And his mouth? Deaf-mutes usually have such mouths. And his beard? He has entirely too much of it, and it's too pretty for his face. It must have got there by mistake."

Presently the door again flew open, and Mrs. Lipman, heavily loaded with parcels and panting for breath, came waddling in with an elderly couple in tow.

"Greenhorns," Meyer remarked. "Must be fellow townspeople of hers— lately arrived."

"She looks like a tea-kettle, and she is puffing like one, too," David thought, after an indifferent gaze at the newcomers, looking askance at his stout, dowdyish little "Missis." "No," he then corrected himself, "she rather resembles a broom with its stick out. That's it! And wouldn't it be a treat to tie a stick to her head and to sweep the floor with the horrid thing! And her mouth? Why, it makes me think she does nothing but sneeze."

"Here is Leizer! Leizer, look at the guests I have brought you!" Zlate exclaimed, as she threw down her bundles. "Be seated, Reb Avrom; be seated, Basse. This is our factory," she went on, with a smile of mixed welcome and triumph, after the demonstrative greetings were over. "It is rather too small, isn't it? but we are going to move into larger and better quarters."

Meyer was not mistaken. Zlate's visitors had recently arrived from her birthplace, a poor town in Western Russia, where they had occupied a much higher social position than their present hostess, and Mrs. Lipman, coming upon them on Hester Street, lost no time in inviting them to her house, in order to overwhelm them with her American achievements.

"Come, I want to show you my parlor," Mrs. Lipman said, beckoning to her country people, and before they were given an opportunity to avail themselves of the chairs which she had offered them, they were towed into the front room.

When the procession returned, Leizer, in obedience to an order from his wife, took Reb Avrom in charge and proceeded to initiate him into the secrets of the "American style of tailoring."

"Oh, my!" Zlate suddenly ejaculated, with a smile. "I came near forgetting to treat. Beilke!" she then addressed herself to the finisher girl in a tone of imperious nonchalance, "here is a nickel. Fetch two bottles of soda from the grocery."

"Don't go, Beile!" David whispered across his table, perceiving the girl's reluctance.

It was not unusual for Beile to go on an errand for the wife of her employer, though she always did it unwillingly, and merely for fear of losing her place; but then Zlate generally exacted these services as a favor. In the present instance, however, Beile felt mortally offended by her commanding tone, and the idea of being paraded before the strangers as a domestic cut her to the quick, as a stream of color rushing into her face indicated. Nevertheless the prospect of having to look for a job again persuaded her to avoid trouble with Zlate, and she was about to reach out her hand for the coin, when David's exhortation piqued her sense of self-esteem, and she went on with her sewing. Heyman, who, being interrupted in his work by the visitor's inspection, was a witness of the scene, at this point turned his face from it, and cringing by his machine, he made a pretense of busying himself with the shuttle. His heart shrank with the awkwardness of his situation, and he nervously grated his teeth and shut his eyes, awaiting still more painful developments. His veins tingled with pity for his sweetheart and with deadly hatred for David. What could he do? he apologized to himself. Isn't it foolish to risk losing a steady job at this slack season on account of such a trifle as fetching up a bottle of soda? What business has David to interfere?

"You are not deaf, are you? I say go and bring some soda, quick!" Mrs. Lipman screamed, fearing lest she was going too far.

"Don't budge, Beile!" the baster prompted, with fire in his eyes.

Beile did not.

"I say go!" Zlate thundered, reddening like a beet, to use a phrase in vogue with herself.

"Never mind, Zlate," Basse interposed, to relieve the embarrassing situation. "We just had tea."

"Never mind. It is not worth the trouble," Avrom chimed in.

But this only served to lash Zlate into a greater fury, and unmindful of consequences, she strode up to the cause of her predicament, and tearing the coat out of her hands, she squeaked out:—

"Either fetch the soda, or leave my shop at once!"

Heyman was about to say, to do something, he knew not exactly what, but his tongue seemed seized with palsy, the blood turned chill in his veins, and he could neither speak nor stir.

Leizer, who was of a quiet, peaceful disposition, and very much under the thumb of his wife, stood nervously smiling and toying with his beard.

David grew ashen pale, and trembling with rage he said aloud and in deliberate accents:—

"Don't mind her, Beile, and never worry. Come along. I'll find you a better job. This racket won't work, Missis. Your friends see through it, anyhow, don't you?" he addressed himself to the newcomers. "She wanted to brag to you. That's what she troubled you for. She showed off her parlor carpet to you, didn't she? But did she tell you that it had been bought on the install-ment plan, and that the custom-peddler threatened to take it away unless she paid more regularly?"

"Leizer! are you—are you drunk?" Mrs. Lipman gasped, her face dis-torted with rage and desperation.

"Get out of here!" Leizer said, in a tone which would have been better suited to a cordial invitation.

The command was unnecessary, however, for by this time David was but-toning up his overcoat, and had his hat on. Involuntarily following his example, Beile also dressed to go. And as she stood in her new beaver cloak and freshly trimmed large old hat by the side of her discomfited com-mander, Basse reflected that it was the finisher girl who looked like a lady, with Zlate for her servant, rather than the reverse.

"See that you have our wages ready for Friday, and all the arrears, too!" was David's parting shot as the two left the room with a defiant slam of the door.

"That's like America!" Zlate remarked, with an attempt at a scornful smile. "The meanest beggar girl will put on airs."

"Why *should* one be ordered about like that? She is no servant, is she?" Heyman murmured, addressing the corner of the room, and fell to at his machine to smother his misery.

When his day's work was over, Heyman's heart failed him to face Beile, and although he was panting to see her, he did not call at her house. On the following morning he awoke with a headache, and this he used as a pretext to himself for going to bed right after supper.

On the next evening he did betake himself to the Division Street tene-ment house, where his sweetheart lived with her mother on the top floor, but on coming in front of the building his courage melted away. Added to his cowardly part in the memorable scene of two days before, there now was his apparent indifference to the finisher, as manifested by his two evenings' absence at such a critical time. He armed himself with a fib to explain his conduct. But all in vain; he could not nerve himself up to the terrible meet-ing. And so day after day passed, each day increasing the barrier to the cov-eted visit.

At last, one evening, about a fortnight after the date of Mrs. Lipman's fiasco, Heyman, forgetting to lose courage, as it were, briskly mounted the four flights of stairs of the Division Street tenement. As he was about to rap for admission he was greeted by a sharp noise within of something, like a china plate or a bowl, being dashed to pieces against the very door which he was going to open. The noise was followed by merry voices: "Good luck! Good luck!" and there was no mistaking its meaning. There was evidently an engagement party inside. The Rabbi had just read the writ of betroth-ment, and it was the mutual pledges of the contracting parties which were emphasized by the "breaking of the plate."[5]

Presently Heyman heard exclamations which dissipated his every doubt as to the identity of the chief actors in the ceremony which had just been completed within.

---

5. To signify the finality of the commitment, often done by the couple's mothers.

"Good luck to you, David! Good luck to you, Beile! May you live to a happy old age together!" "Feige, why don't you take some cake? Don't be so bashful!" "Here is luck!" came through the door, piercing a muffled hum inside.

Heyman was dumbfounded, and with his head swimming, he made a hasty retreat.

Ever since the tragi-comical incident at Lipman's shop, Heyman was not present to Beile's thoughts except in the pitiful, cowering attitude in which he had sat through that awful scene by his machine. She was sure she hated him now. And yet her heart was, during the first few days, constantly throbbing with the expectation of his visit; and as she settled in her mind that even if he came she would have nothing to do with him, her deeper consciousness seemed to say, with a smile of conviction: "Oh no, you know you would not refuse him. You wouldn't risk to remain an old maid, would you?" The idea of his jilting her harrowed her day and night. Did he avail himself of her leaving Lipman's shop to back out of the proposal which was naturally expected of him, but which he never perhaps contemplated? Did he make game of her?

When a week had elapsed without Heyman's putting in an appearance, she determined to let her mother see a lawyer about breach-of-promise proceedings. But an image, whose outlines had kept defining themselves in her heart for several days past, overruled this decision. It was the image of a pluckier fellow than Heyman—of one with whom there was more protection in store for a wife, who inspired her with more respect and confidence, and, what is more, who seemed on the point of proposing to her.

It was the image of David. The young baster pursued his courtship with a quiet persistency and a suppressed fervor which was not long in winning the girl's heart. He found work for her and for himself in the same shop; saw her home every evening; regularly came after supper to take her out for a walk, in the course of which he would treat her to candy and invite her to a coffee saloon,—a thing which Heyman had never done;—kept her chuckling over his jokes; and at the end of ten days, while sitting by her side in Central Park, one night, he said, in reply to her remark that it was so dark that she knew not where she was:—

"I'll tell you where you are—guess."

"Where?"

"Here, in my heart, and keeping me awake nights, too. Say, Beile, what have I ever done to you to have my rest disturbed by you in that manner?"

Her heart was beating like a sledge-hammer. She tried to laugh, as she returned:—

"I don't know—You can never stop making fun, can you?"

"Fun? Do you want me to cry? I will, gladly, if I only know that you will agree to have an engagement party," he rejoined, deeply blushing under cover of the darkness.

"When?" she questioned, the word crossing her lips before she knew it.

"On my part, to-morrow."

1895   1898

CHARLOTTE PERKINS GILMAN
1860–1935

Charlotte Perkins Gilman lived her life, for the most part, on the margins of a society whose economic assumptions about and social definitions of women she vigorously repudiated. Out of this resistance to conventional values and what she later characterized as "masculinist" ideals, Gilman produced the large body of polemical writings and what we would call today self-consciously feminist fiction that made her a leading theoretician, speaker, and writer on women's issues of her time.

Charlotte Anna Perkins was born in Hartford, Connecticut, on July 3, 1860. Her father, Frederic Beecher Perkins, belonged to the famous New England Beecher family, which included theologian Lyman Beecher, minister Henry Ward Beecher, and the novelist Harriet Beecher Stowe. Her mother was Mary A. Fitch, whose family had lived in Rhode Island since the middle of the seventeenth century. Gilman's father deserted his family and left for San Francisco shortly after her birth, and she spent many years trying, without success, to establish some intimacy with him. She received from him only occasional letters with lists of books she should read. Her mother returned to Providence, Rhode Island, where she supported herself and her two children with great difficulty; she apparently withheld from them all physical expressions of love, hoping to prevent their later disillusionment over broken relationships. It is easy to understand why in her autobiography Gilman described her childhood as painful and lonely.

Between 1880 and her marriage in May 1884 to Charles Stetson, a promising Providence artist, Gilman supported herself in Providence as a governess, art teacher, and designer of greeting cards. During those years she had increasingly become aware of the injustices inflicted on women, and she had begun to write poems—one in defense of prostitutes—in which she developed her own views on women's rights. She entered into the marriage reluctantly, anticipating the difficulties of reconciling her ambition to be a writer with the demands of being a wife, housekeeper, and mother. Within eleven months, their only child, Katharine, was born; following the birth, Gilman became increasingly despondent, and marital tensions increased. Her husband and her mother were convinced that Gilman needed rest and willpower to overcome her depression; they persuaded her to go to Philadelphia for treatment by Dr. S. Weir Mitchell, the most famous American neurologist of the day. A specialist in women's "nervous" disorders, Mitchell usually prescribed a "rest cure" consisting of total bedrest for several weeks and limited intellectual activity thereafter. As Gilman put it in "Why I Wrote 'The Yellow Wall-paper'?" (1913), after six weeks the doctor "sent me home with the solemn advice to 'live as domestic a life as . . . possible,' to 'have but two hours' intellectual life a day,' and 'never to touch pen, brush, or pencil again' as long as I lived." The patient returned to Providence and obeyed these instructions for three months "and came so near the borderline of utter mental ruin that I could see over." She drew back from the edge of madness by resuming her life as a reluctant wife and mother and as an enthusiastic writer and frequent contributor to the Boston *Woman's Journal*. A few years later she wrote her most famous story. As she concluded: "It was not intended to drive people crazy, but to save people from being driven crazy, and it worked." Writing "The Yellow Wall-paper" (1892), however, did not keep Gilman from suffering all her life with extended periods of depression.

In 1888, convinced that her marriage threatened her sanity, Gilman moved with her daughter to Pasadena, California, and in 1894 was granted a divorce. Her former husband promptly married her best friend, the writer Grace Ellery Channing, and not long thereafter Gilman sent her daughter east to live with them. Such actions generated much publicity and hostile criticism in the press, but nothing kept Gilman from pursuing her double career as writer and lecturer on women, labor, and social organization. In these years she was particularly influenced by the sociologist Lester Ward and the utopian novelist Edward Bellamy.

In 1898 Gilman published *Women and Economics,* the book that earned her immediate celebrity and that is still considered her most important nonfiction work. This powerful feminist manifesto argues a thesis Gilman was to develop and refine for the rest of her life: women's economic dependency on men stunts not only the growth of women but that of the whole human species. More particularly, she argued that because of the dependency of women on men for food and shelter, the sexual and maternal aspects of their personalities had been developed excessively and to the detriment of their other productive capacities. To free women to develop in a more balanced and socially constructive way, Gilman urged such reforms as centralized nurseries (in *Concerning Children,* 1900) and professionally staffed collective kitchens (in *The Home,* 1904).

In 1911 she published *The Man-Made World,* which contrasted the competitiveness and aggressiveness of men with the cooperativeness and nurturance of women and posited that until women played a larger part in national and international life, social injustice and war would characterize industrialized societies. In this same year her short story "Turned" appeared, taking on similar gender issues. Similarly, in *His Religion and Hers* (1923) Gilman predicted that only when women influenced theology would the fear of death and punishment cease to be central to religious institutions and practices.

Gilman's poetry and fiction, most written when she was well past forty, must be seen, as the critic Ann J. Lane has observed, as "part of her ideological world view, and therein lies its interest and power." Therein, also, lie its limits, for as Lane also says, "She wrote quickly, carelessly, to make a point." Still, many of Gilman's stories and her utopian novels—such as *Moving the Mountain* (1911), *Herland* (1915), and *With Her in Ourland* (1916)—offer vivid dramatizations of the social ills (and their potential remedies) that result from a competitive economic system in which women are subordinate to men and accept their subordination. In *Herland,* for instance, Gilman offers a vision of an all-female society in which caring women raise children (reproduced by parthenogenesis) collectively in a world that is both prosperous and ecologically sound.

She married her first cousin George Houghton Gilman in 1900. They lived in New York City and Norwich, Connecticut, until his sudden death in 1934. Gilman then moved to Pasadena, California, to live with her daughter's family but committed suicide the next year when she learned that she had inoperable cancer.

The Yellow Wall-paper[1]

It is very seldom that mere ordinary people like John and myself secure ancestral halls for the summer.

1. The complete and complex textual history of the extant fair copy manuscript and seven editions of the story during Gilman's lifetime is available in Julie Bates Dock's *Charlotte Perkins Gilman's "The Yellow Wall-paper" and the History of Its Publication and Reception: A Critical Edition and Documentary Casebook* (Pennsylvania State University Press, 1998). Dock's volume also contains a detailed textual apparatus and notes, a variety of background material, early reviews, and other commentary. Professor Dock and Pennsylvania State University Press have kindly granted permission to use her eclectic critical edition of this story.

A colonial mansion, a hereditary estate, I would say a haunted house, and reach the height of romantic felicity—but that would be asking too much of fate!

Still I will proudly declare that there is something queer about it.

Else, why should it be let so cheaply? And why have stood so long untenanted?

John laughs at me, of course, but one expects that in marriage.

John is practical in the extreme. He has no patience with faith, an intense horror of superstition, and he scoffs openly at any talk of things not to be felt and seen and put down in figures.

John is a physician, and *perhaps*—(I would not say it to a living soul, of course, but this is dead paper and a great relief to my mind)—*perhaps* that is one reason I do not get well faster.

You see he does not believe I am sick!

And what can one do?

If a physician of high standing, and one's own husband, assures friends and relatives that there is really nothing the matter with one but temporary nervous depression—a slight hysterical tendency[2]—what is one to do?

My brother is also a physician, and also of high standing, and he says the same thing.

So I take phosphates or phosphites—whichever it is—and tonics, and journeys, and air, and exercise, and am absolutely forbidden to "work" until I am well again.

Personally, I disagree with their ideas.

Personally, I believe that congenial work, with excitement and change, would do me good.

But what is one to do?

I did write for a while in spite of them; but it *does* exhaust me a good deal—having to be so sly about it, or else meet with heavy opposition.

I sometimes fancy that in my condition if I had less opposition and more society and stimulus—but John says the very worst thing I can do is to think about my condition, and I confess it always makes me feel bad.

So I will let it alone and talk about the house.

The most beautiful place! It is quite alone, standing well back from the road, quite three miles from the village. It makes me think of English places that you read about, for there are hedges and walls and gates that lock, and lots of separate little houses for the gardeners and people.

There is a *delicious* garden! I never saw such a garden—large and shady, full of box-bordered paths, and lined with long grape-covered arbors with seats under them.

There were greenhouses, too, but they are all broken now.

There was some legal trouble, I believe, something about the heirs and co-heirs; anyhow, the place has been empty for years.

That spoils my ghostliness, I am afraid, but I don't care—there is something strange about the house—I can feel it.

I even said so to John one moonlight evening, but he said what I felt was a *draught*, and shut the window.

---

2. *Hysteria* was a term used to describe a wide variety of symptoms, thought to be particularly prevalent among women, that indicated emotional disturbance or dysfunction. Depression, anxiety, excitability, and vague somatic complaints were among the conditions treated as "hysteria."

I get unreasonably angry with John sometimes. I'm sure I never used to be so sensitive. I think it is due to this nervous condition.

But John says if I feel so, I shall neglect proper self-control; so I take pains to control myself—before him, at least, and that makes me very tired.

I don't like our room a bit. I wanted one downstairs that opened on the piazza and had roses all over the window, and such pretty old-fashioned chintz hangings! But John would not hear of it.

He said there was only one window and not room for two beds, and no near room for him if he took another.

He is very careful and loving, and hardly lets me stir without special direction.

I have a schedule prescription for each hour in the day; he takes all care from me, and so I feel basely ungrateful not to value it more.

He said we came here solely on my account, that I was to have perfect rest and all the air I could get. "Your exercise depends on your strength, my dear," said he, "and your food somewhat on your appetite; but air you can absorb all the time." So we took the nursery at the top of the house.

It is a big, airy room, the whole floor nearly, with windows that look all ways, and air and sunshine galore. It was nursery first and then playroom and gymnasium, I should judge; for the windows are barred for little children, and there are rings and things in the walls.

Window, Walls

The paint and paper look as if a boys' school had used it. It is stripped off—the paper—in great patches all around the head of my bed, about as far as I can reach, and in a great place on the other side of the room low down. I never saw a worse paper in my life.

One of those sprawling flamboyant patterns committing every artistic sin.

It is dull enough to confuse the eye in following, pronounced enough to constantly irritate and provoke study, and when you follow the lame uncertain curves for a little distance they suddenly commit suicide—plunge off at outrageous angles, destroy themselves in unheard of contradictions.

The color is repellent, almost revolting; a smouldering unclean yellow, strangely faded by the slow-turning sunlight.

It is a dull yet lurid orange in some places, a sickly sulphur tint in others.

No wonder the children hated it! I should hate it myself if I had to live in this room long.

There comes John, and I must put this away—he hates to have me write a word.

· · · · · ·

We have been here two weeks, and I haven't felt like writing before, since that first day.

I am sitting by the window now, up in this atrocious nursery, and there is nothing to hinder my writing as much as I please, save lack of strength.

John is away all day, and even some nights when his cases are serious.

I am glad my case is not serious!

But these nervous troubles are dreadfully depressing.

John does not know how much I really suffer. He knows there is no *reason* to suffer, and that satisfies him.

Of course it is only nervousness. It does weigh on me so not to do my duty in any way!

I meant to be such a help to John, such a real rest and comfort, and here I am a comparative burden already!

Nobody would believe what an effort it is to do what little I am able—to dress and entertain, and order things.

It is fortunate Mary is so good with the baby. Such a dear baby!

And yet I *cannot* be with him, it makes me so nervous.

I suppose John never was nervous in his life. He laughs at me so about this wall-paper!

At first he meant to repaper the room, but afterwards he said that I was letting it get the better of me, and that nothing was worse for a nervous patient than to give way to such fancies.

He said that after the wall-paper was changed it would be the heavy bedstead, and then the barred windows, and then that gate at the head of the stairs, and so on.

"You know the place is doing you good," he said, "and really, dear, I don't care to renovate the house just for a three months' rental."

"Then do let us go downstairs," I said, "there are such pretty rooms there."

Then he took me in his arms and called me a blessed little goose, and said he would go down cellar, if I wished, and have it whitewashed into the bargain.

But he is right enough about the beds and windows and things.

It is as airy and comfortable a room as any one need wish, and, of course, I would not be so silly as to make him uncomfortable just for a whim.

I'm really getting quite fond of the big room, all but that horrid paper.

Out of one window I can see the garden, those mysterious deep-shaded arbors, the riotous old-fashioned flowers, and bushes and gnarly trees.

Out of another I get a lovely view of the bay and a little private wharf belonging to the estate. There is a beautiful shaded lane that runs down there from the house. I always fancy I see people walking in these numerous paths and arbors, but John has cautioned me not to give way to fancy in the least. He says that with my imaginative power and habit of story-making, a nervous weakness like mine is sure to lead to all manner of excited fancies, and that I ought to use my will and good sense to check the tendency. So I try.

I think sometimes that if I were only well enough to write a little it would relieve the press of ideas and rest me.

But I find I get pretty tired when I try.

It is so discouraging not to have any advice and companionship about my work. When I get really well, John says we will ask Cousin Henry and Julia down for a long visit; but he says he would as soon put fireworks in my pillowcase as to let me have those stimulating people about now.

I wish I could get well faster.

But I must not think about that. This paper looks to me as if it *knew* what a vicious influence it had!

There is a recurrent spot where the pattern lolls like a broken neck and two bulbous eyes stare at you upside down.

I get positively angry with the impertinence of it and the everlastingness. Up and down and sideways they crawl, and those absurd, unblinking eyes are everywhere. There is one place where two breadths didn't match, and the eyes go all up and down the line, one a little higher than the other.

I never saw so much expression in an inanimate thing before, and we all know how much expression they have! I used to lie awake as a child and get more entertainment and terror out of blank walls and plain furniture than most children could find in a toy-store.

I remember what a kindly wink the knobs of our big, old bureau used to have, and there was one chair that always seemed like a strong friend.

I used to feel that if any of the other things looked too fierce I could always hop into that chair and be safe.

The furniture in this room is no worse than inharmonious, however, for we had to bring it all from downstairs. I suppose when this was used as a play-room they had to take the nursery things out, and no wonder! I never saw such ravages as the children have made here.

The wall-paper, as I said before, is torn off in spots, and it sticketh closer than a brother[3]—they must have had perseverance as well as hatred.

Then the floor is scratched and gouged and splintered, the plaster itself is dug out here and there, and this great heavy bed, which is all we found in the room, looks as if it had been through the wars.

But I don't mind it a bit—only the paper.

There comes John's sister. Such a dear girl as she is, and so careful of me! I must not let her find me writing.

She is a perfect and enthusiastic housekeeper, and hopes for no better profession. I verily believe she thinks it is the writing which made me sick!

But I can write when she is out, and see her a long way off from these windows.

There is one that commands the road, a lovely shaded winding road, and one that just looks off over the country. A lovely country, too, full of great elms and velvet meadows.

This wall-paper has a kind of sub-pattern in a different shade, a particularly irritating one, for you can only see it in certain lights, and not clearly then.

But in the places where it isn't faded and where the sun is just so—I can see a strange, provoking, formless sort of figure, that seems to skulk about behind that silly and conspicuous front design.

There's sister on the stairs!

• • • • • •

Well, the Fourth of July is over! The people are all gone and I am tired out. John thought it might do me good to see a little company, so we just had mother and Nellie and the children down for a week.

Of course I didn't do a thing. Jennie sees to everything now.

But it tired me all the same.

John says if I don't pick up faster he shall send me to Weir Mitchell[4] in the fall.

But I don't want to go there at all. I had a friend who was in his hands once, and she says he is just like John and my brother, only more so!

Besides, it is such an undertaking to go so far.

I don't feel as if it was worth while to turn my hand over for anything, and I'm getting dreadfully fretful and querulous.

3. Proverbs 18.24: "There is a friend that stick-eth closer than a brother."
4. Silas Weir Mitchell (1829–1914), American physician, novelist, and specialist in nerve disorders, popularized the "rest cure" in the manage-ment of hysteria, nervous breakdowns, and related disorders. A friend of W. D. Howells, he was the model for the nerve specialist in Howells's *The Shadow of a Dream* (1890).

I cry at nothing, and cry most of the time.

Of course I don't when John is here, or anybody else, but when I am alone.

And I am alone a good deal just now. John is kept in town very often by serious cases, and Jennie is good and lets me alone when I want her to.

So I walk a little in the garden or down that lovely lane, sit on the porch under the roses, and lie down up here a good deal.

I'm getting really fond of the room in spite of the wall-paper. Perhaps *because* of the wall-paper.

It dwells in my mind so!

I lie here on this great immovable bed—it is nailed down, I believe—and follow that pattern about by the hour. It is as good as gymnastics, I assure you. I start, we'll say, at the bottom, down in the corner over there where it has not been touched, and I determine for the thousandth time that I *will* follow that pointless pattern to some sort of a conclusion.

I know a little of the principle of design, and I know this thing was not arranged on any laws of radiation, or alternation, or repetition, or symmetry, or anything else that I ever heard of.

It is repeated, of course, by the breadths, but not otherwise.

Looked at in one way each breadth stands alone, the bloated curves and flourishes—a kind of "debased Romanesque"[5] with *delirium tremens*—go waddling up and down in isolated columns of fatuity.

But, on the other hand, they connect diagonally, and the sprawling out-lines run off in great slanting waves of optic horror, like a lot of wallowing seaweeds in full chase.

The whole thing goes horizontally, too, at least it seems so, and I exhaust myself in trying to distinguish the order of its going in that direction.

They have used a horizontal breadth for a frieze,[6] and that adds wonder-fully to the confusion.

There is one end of the room where it is almost intact, and there, when the crosslights fade and low sun shines directly upon it, I can almost fancy radia-tion after all—the interminable grotesques seem to form around a common centre and rush off in headlong plunges of equal distraction.

It makes me tired to follow it. I will take a nap I guess.

• • • • • •

I don't know why I should write this.

I don't want to.

I don't feel able.

And I know John would think it absurd. But I *must* say what I feel and think in some way—it is such a relief!

But the effort is getting to be greater than the relief.

Half the time now I am awfully lazy, and lie down ever so much.

John says I mustn't lose my strength, and has me take cod liver oil and lots of tonics and things, to say nothing of ale and wine and rare meat.

Dear John! He loves me very dearly, and hates to have me sick. I tried to have a real earnest reasonable talk with him the other day, and tell him how I wish he would let me go and make a visit to Cousin Henry and Julia.

---

5. Style associated with ornamental complexity and repeated motifs and figures.

6. An ornamental border at the top of the wall.

But he said I wasn't able to go, nor able to stand it after I got there; and I did not make out a very good case for myself, for I was crying before I had finished.

It is getting to be a great effort for me to think straight. Just this nervous weakness I suppose.

And dear John gathered me up in his arms, and just carried me upstairs and laid me on the bed, and sat by me and read to me till it tired my head.

He said I was his darling and his comfort and all he had, and that I must take care of myself for his sake, and keep well.

He says no one but myself can help me out of it, that I must use my will and self-control and not let any silly fancies run away with me.

There's one comfort, the baby is well and happy, and does not have to occupy this nursery with the horrid wall-paper.

If we had not used it, that blessed child would have! What a fortunate escape! Why, I wouldn't have a child of mine, an impressionable little thing, live in such a room for worlds.

I never thought of it before, but it is lucky that John kept me here after all, I can stand it so much easier than a baby, you see.

Of course I never mention it to them any more—I am too wise—but I keep watch of it all the same.

There are things in that paper that nobody knows but me, or ever will.

Behind that outside pattern the dim shapes get clearer every day.

It is always the same shape, only very numerous.

And it is like a woman stooping down and creeping about behind that pattern. I don't like it a bit. I wonder—I begin to think—I wish John would take me away from here!

. . . . . .

It is so hard to talk with John about my case, because he is so wise, and because he loves me so.

But I tried it last night.

It was moonlight. The moon shines in all around just as the sun does.

I hate to see it sometimes, it creeps so slowly, and always comes in by one window or another.

John was asleep and I hated to waken him, so I kept still and watched the moonlight on that undulating wall-paper till I felt creepy.

The faint figure behind seemed to shake the pattern, just as if she wanted to get out.

I got up softly and went to feel and see if the paper *did* move, and when I came back John was awake.

"What is it, little girl?" he said. "Don't go walking about like that—you'll get cold."

I thought it was a good time to talk, so I told him that I really was not gaining here, and that I wished he would take me away.

"Why, darling!" said he, "our lease will be up in three weeks, and I can't see how to leave before.

"The repairs are not done at home, and I cannot possibly leave town just now. Of course if you were in any danger, I could and would, but you really are better, dear, whether you can see it or not. I am a doctor, dear, and I know. You are gaining flesh and color, your appetite is better, I feel really much easier about you."

"I don't weigh a bit more," said I, "nor as much; and my appetite may be better in the evening when you are here, but it is worse in the morning when you are away!"

"Bless her little heart!" said he with a big hug, "she shall be as sick as she pleases! But now let's improve the shining hours[7] by going to sleep, and talk about it in the morning!"

"And you won't go away?" I asked gloomily.

"Why, how can I, dear? It is only three weeks more and then we will take a nice little trip of a few days while Jennie is getting the house ready. Really, dear, you are better!"

"Better in body perhaps—" I began, and stopped short, for he sat up straight and looked at me with such a stern, reproachful look that I could not say another word.

"My darling," said he, "I beg of you, for my sake and for our child's sake, as well as for your own, that you will never for one instant let that idea enter your mind! There is nothing so dangerous, so fascinating, to a temperament like yours. It is a false and foolish fancy. Can you not trust me as a physician when I tell you so?"

So of course I said no more on that score, and we went to sleep before long. He thought I was asleep first, but I wasn't, and lay there for hours trying to decide whether that front pattern and the back pattern really did move together or separately.

• • • • • •

On a pattern like this, by daylight, there is a lack of sequence, a defiance of law, that is a constant irritant to a normal mind.

The color is hideous enough, and unreliable enough, and infuriating enough, but the pattern is torturing.

You think you have mastered it, but just as you get well underway in following, it turns a back-somersault and there you are. It slaps you in the face, knocks you down, and tramples upon you. It is like a bad dream.

The outside pattern is a florid arabesque, reminding one of a fungus. If you can imagine a toadstool in joints, an interminable string of toadstools, budding and sprouting in endless convolutions—why, that is something like it.

That is, sometimes!

There is one marked peculiarity about this paper, a thing nobody seems to notice but myself, and that is that it changes as the light changes.

When the sun shoots in through the east window—I always watch for that first long, straight ray—it changes so quickly that I never can quite believe it.

That is why I watch it always.

By moonlight—the moon shines in all night when there is a moon—I wouldn't know it was the same paper.

At night in any kind of light, in twilight, candlelight, lamplight, and worst of all by moonlight, it becomes bars! The outside pattern, I mean, and the woman behind it is as plain as can be.

---

7. In his poem "Against Idleness and Mischief," Isaac Watts (1674–1748) writes:

> How doth the little busy bee
> Improve each shining hour,
> And gather honey all the day
> From every opening flower!

I didn't realize for a long time what the thing was that showed behind, that dim sub-pattern, but now I am quite sure it is a woman.

By daylight she is subdued, quiet. I fancy it is the pattern that keeps her so still. It is so puzzling. It keeps me quiet by the hour.

I lie down ever so much now. John says it is good for me, and to sleep all I can.

Indeed he started the habit by making me lie down for an hour after each meal.

It is a very bad habit, I am convinced, for you see I don't sleep.

And that cultivates deceit, for I don't tell them I'm awake—O no!

The fact is I am getting a little afraid of John.

He seems very queer sometimes, and even Jennie has an inexplicable look.

It strikes me occasionally, just as a scientific hypothesis, that perhaps it is the paper!

I have watched John when he did not know I was looking, and come into the room suddenly on the most innocent excuses, and I've caught him several times *looking at the paper!* And Jennie too. I caught Jennie with her hand on it once.

She didn't know I was in the room, and when I asked her in a quiet, a very quiet voice, with the most restrained manner possible, what she was doing with the paper—she turned around as if she had been caught stealing, and looked quite angry—asked me why I should frighten her so!

Then she said that the paper stained everything it touched, that she had found yellow smooches on all my clothes and John's, and she wished we would be more careful!

Did not that sound innocent? But I know she was studying that pattern, and I am determined that nobody shall find it out but myself!

· · · · · ·

Life is very much more exciting now than it used to be. You see I have something more to expect, to look forward to, to watch. I really do eat better, and am more quiet than I was.

John is so pleased to see me improve! He laughed a little the other day, and said I seemed to be flourishing in spite of my wall-paper.

I turned it off with a laugh. I had no intention of telling him it was *because* of the wall-paper—he would make fun of me. He might even want to take me away.

I don't want to leave now until I have found it out. There is a week more, and I think that will be enough.

· · · · · ·

I'm feeling ever so much better! I don't sleep much at night, for it is so interesting to watch developments; but I sleep a good deal in the daytime.

In the daytime it is tiresome and perplexing.

There are always new shoots on the fungus, and new shades of yellow all over it. I cannot keep count of them, though I have tried conscientiously.

It is the strangest yellow, that wall-paper! It makes me think of all the yellow things I ever saw—not beautiful ones like buttercups, but old foul, bad yellow things.

But there is something else about that paper—the smell! I noticed it the moment we came into the room, but with so much air and sun it was not bad. Now we have had a week of fog and rain, and whether the windows are open or not, the smell is here.

It creeps all over the house.

I find it hovering in the dining-room, skulking in the parlor, hiding in the hall, lying in wait for me on the stairs.

It gets into my hair.

Even when I go to ride, if I turn my head suddenly and surprise it—there is that smell!

Such a peculiar odor, too! I have spent hours in trying to analyze it, to find what it smelled like.

It is not bad—at first—and very gentle, but quite the subtlest, most enduring odor I ever met.

In this damp weather it is awful, I wake up in the night and find it hanging over me.

It used to disturb me at first. I thought seriously of burning the house—to reach the smell.

But now I am used to it. The only thing I can think of that it is like is the *color* of the paper! A yellow smell.

There is a very funny mark on this wall, low down, near the mopboard. A streak that runs round the room. It goes behind every piece of furniture, except the bed, a long, straight, even *smooch,* as if it had been rubbed over and over.

I wonder how it was done and who did it, and what they did it for. Round and round and round—round and round and round—it makes me dizzy!

. . . . . .

I really have discovered something at last.

Through watching so much at night, when it changes so, I have finally found out.

The front pattern *does* move—and no wonder! The woman behind shakes it!

Sometimes I think there are a great many women behind, and sometimes only one, and she crawls around fast, and her crawling shakes it all over.

Then in the very bright spots she keeps still, and in the very shady spots she just takes hold of the bars and shakes them hard.

And she is all the time trying to climb through. But nobody could climb through that pattern—it strangles so; I think that is why it has so many heads.

They get through, and then the pattern strangles them off and turns them upside down, and makes their eyes white!

If those heads were covered or taken off it would not be half so bad.

. . . . . .

I think that woman gets out in the daytime!

And I'll tell you why—privately—I've seen her!

I can see her out of every one of my windows!

It is the same woman, I know, for she is always creeping, and most women do not creep by daylight.

[handwritten marginalia: Woman in window]

I see her in that long shaded lane, creeping up and down. I see her in those dark grape arbors, creeping all around the garden.

I see her on that long road under the trees, creeping along, and when a carriage comes she hides under the blackberry vines.

I don't blame her a bit. It must be very humiliating to be caught creeping by daylight!

I always lock the door when I creep by daylight. I can't do it at night, for I know John would suspect something at once.

And John is so queer now, that I don't want to irritate him. I wish he would take another room! Besides, I don't want anybody to get that woman out at night but myself.

I often wonder if I could see her out of all the windows at once.

But, turn as fast as I can, I can only see out of one at one time.

And though I always see her, she *may* be able to creep faster than I can turn!

I have watched her sometimes away off in the open country, creeping as fast as a cloud shadow in a high wind.

• • • • • •

If only that top pattern could be gotten off from the under one! I mean to try it, little by little.

I have found out another funny thing, but I shan't tell it this time! It does not do to trust people too much.

There are only two more days to get this paper off, and I believe John is beginning to notice. I don't like the look in his eyes.

And I heard him ask Jennie a lot of professional questions about me. She had a very good report to give.

She said I slept a good deal in the daytime.

John knows I don't sleep very well at night, for all I'm so quiet!

He asked me all sorts of questions, too, and pretended to be very loving and kind.

As if I couldn't see through him!

Still, I don't wonder he acts so, sleeping under this paper for three months.

It only interests me, but I feel sure John and Jennie are secretly affected by it.

• • • • • •

Hurrah! This is the last day, but it is enough. John had to stay in town over night, and won't be out until this evening.

Jennie wanted to sleep with me—the sly thing!—but I told her I should undoubtedly rest better for a night all alone.

That was clever, for really I wasn't alone a bit! As soon as it was moonlight and that poor thing began to crawl and shake the pattern, I got up and ran to help her.

I pulled and she shook, I shook and she pulled, and before morning we had peeled off yards of that paper.

A strip about as high as my head and half around the room.

And then when the sun came and that awful pattern began to laugh at me, I declared I would finish it to-day!

We go away to-morrow, and they are moving all my furniture down again to leave things as they were before.

Jennie looked at the wall in amazement, but I told her merrily that I did it out of pure spite at the vicious thing.

She laughed and said she wouldn't mind doing it herself, but I must not get tired.

How she betrayed herself that time!

But I am here, and no person touches this paper but me—not *alive!*

She tried to get me out of the room—it was too patent! But I said it was so quiet and empty and clean now that I believed I would lie down again and sleep all I could; and not to wake me even for dinner—I would call when I woke.

So now she is gone, and the servants are gone, and the things are gone, and there is nothing left but that great bedstead nailed down, with the canvas mattress we found on it.

We shall sleep downstairs to-night, and take the boat home to-morrow.

I quite enjoy the room, now it is bare again.

How those children did tear about here!

This bedstead is fairly gnawed!

But I must get to work.

I have locked the door and thrown the key down into the front path.

I don't want to go out, and I don't want to have anybody come in, till John comes.

I want to astonish him.

I've got a rope up here that even Jennie did not find. If that woman does get out, and tries to get away, I can tie her!

But I forgot I could not reach far without anything to stand on!

This bed will *not* move!

I tried to lift and push it until I was lame, and then I got so angry I bit off a little piece at one corner—but it hurt my teeth.

Then I peeled off all the paper I could reach standing on the floor. It sticks horribly and the pattern just enjoys it! All those strangled heads and bulbous eyes and waddling fungus growths just shriek with derision!

I am getting angry enough to do something desperate. To jump out of the window would be admirable exercise, but the bars are too strong even to try.

Besides, I wouldn't do it. Of course not. I know well enough that a step like that is improper and might be misconstrued.

I don't like to *look* out of the windows even—there are so many of those creeping women, and they creep so fast.

I wonder if they all come out of that wall-paper as I did?

But I am securely fastened now by my well-hidden rope—you don't get *me* out in the road there!

I suppose I shall have to get back behind the pattern when it comes night, and that is hard!

It is so pleasant to be out in this great room and creep around as I please!

I don't want to go outside. I won't, even if Jennie asks me to.

For outside you have to creep on the ground, and everything is green instead of yellow.

But here I can creep smoothly on the floor, and my shoulder just fits in that long smooch around the wall, so I cannot lose my way.

Why, there's John at the door!

It is no use, young man, you can't open it!

How he does call and pound!

Now he's crying for an axe.

It would be a shame to break down that beautiful door!

"John, dear!" said I in the gentlest voice, "the key is down by the front steps, under a plantain leaf!"

That silenced him for a few moments.

Then he said—very quietly indeed—"Open the door, my darling!"

"I can't," said I. "The key is down by the front door under a plantain leaf!"

And then I said it again, several times, very gently and slowly, and said it so often that he had to go and see, and he got it of course, and came in. He stopped short by the door.

"What is the matter?" he cried. "For God's sake, what are you doing!"

I kept on creeping just the same, but I looked at him over my shoulder.

"I've got out at last," said I, "in spite of you and Jane! And I've pulled off most of the paper, so you can't put me back!"

Now why should that man have fainted? But he did, and right across my path by the wall, so that I had to creep over him every time!

1892

"Now why should that man have fainted?" Joseph Henry Hatfield's illustration from the original magazine publication of "The Yellow Wall-paper," *New England Magazine*, January 1892.

EDITH WHARTON
1862–1937

A popular and critically acclaimed writer during her lifetime, Edith Wharton has long been recognized as a major figure on the American literary landscape. Along with her good friend Henry James, she has been celebrated for her portrayals of life among Americans with enough money to enjoy lives of leisure. She is uniquely important, however, for her sharply ironic depictions of the situation of women in old New York moneyed society, where, despite their material advantages, they were stifled by a culture that groomed them to be ornaments to their husbands rather than active participants in the life around them. Wharton began to write as a very young woman, published over forty books, and at her death left a number of unpublished manuscripts, including stage plays and abandoned novels, as well as a voluminous correspondence. *The House of Mirth* (1905), her second novel, was a critical and commercial success; another popular novel, *The Age of Innocence* (1920), won the Pulitzer Prize. In 1923, Wharton became the first woman awarded an honorary doctorate from Yale University, and in 1930, she was the first woman awarded the gold medal from the American Academy of Arts of Letters.

Edith Newbold Jones was born in New York City on January 24, 1862, into a patriarchal, moneyed, cultivated, and rather rigid family that, like others in its small circle, disdained and feared the drastic social, cultural, and economic changes brought on by post–Civil War expansionism and immigration. She was educated by tutors and governesses, much of the time while the family resided in Europe. In 1885 she married the Bostonian Edward Wharton, a social (but not intellectual) equal thirteen years her senior. Though they lived together (in New York; Newport, Rhode Island; Lenox, Massachusetts; and Paris) for twenty-eight years, their marriage was not happy. That Wharton did not seek a divorce until 1913 (on grounds of her husband's adultery) is more a tribute to what her biographer R. W. B. Lewis characterized as her "moral conservatism and her devotion to family ties and the sanctities of tradition" than to personal affection.

Wharton's education, through tutors and travel, never satisfied her quest for knowledge. She tried to compensate for this by extensive reading in her father's library and the libraries of her friends' fathers. In her group, young women were instructed in fashion and etiquette so that they could make a good showing in the many balls and parties they had to attend in search of proper husbands. Once the husbands were secured, women had to help them display their status, giving and attending yet more balls and parties. Rejecting these goals as superficial and oppressive, Wharton began to write as a teenager. By the time she was fifteen she had written—in secret—a thirty-thousand-word novella titled *Fast and Loose;* she also wrote a great deal of lyric poetry with what she later described as a "lamentable facility." When she was sixteen, two of her poems were published, one in the *Atlantic Monthly.* Although her intense interest in literature, ideas, and the arts never abated, she was not to publish again until 1889, when she submitted three poems to *Scribner's, Harper's,* and the *Century*—and all were accepted. The next year, a sketch of hers was published by *Scribner's.*

It was not until the late 1890s, however, that Wharton, then in her late thirties, fully embraced authorship as a career. The first significant product of that commitment was a collection of stories titled *The Greater Inclination* (1899). With the publication in 1905 of *The House of Mirth* Wharton confirmed her choice to be a writer and immediately found an appreciative public. Although she was later to write about other subjects, she discovered in *The House of Mirth* her central settings, plots, and themes: the old aristocracy of New York in conflict with the nouveau riche, the futile struggle of characters trapped by social forces larger and individuals morally smaller than themselves. *The House of Mirth* tells the story of the beautiful Lily Bart, trained to be a decorative upper-class wife but ultimately unwilling to sell herself as merchandise. In *The Custom of the Country* (1913), which Wharton considered her masterpiece, the ruthless Undine Spragg from Ohio makes her way up the social ladder, stepping on Americans and Europeans alike in her pursuit of money and the power that goes with it.

Edith Wharton, 1905.

In 1911 Wharton separated from her husband and took up residence in France, where she spent the rest of her life. During World War I, Wharton organized relief efforts for the refugees and orphans displaced by the advance of the German Army and was active in many other committees and organizations dealing with the devastation wrought by the war. She also wrote extensively about her visits to the front line, and a collection of these dispatches was published as *Fighting France, from Dunkerque to Belfort* (1915). Altogether she produced more than eighty short stories and twenty-two novellas and novels, including three very different but distinguished books: *Ethan Frome* (1911), *Summer* (1917), and *The Age of Innocence* (1920). Her autobiography, *A Backward Glance*, was published in 1934.

The selections included here represent some of Wharton's best-known work in the genre of the short story, which she termed her "smaller realisms." "The Other Two" (1904) explores the new age of divorce; "Roman Fever" (1934), which also illuminates tensions between the old world and the new, concerns a lifelong rivalry between two leisure-class women, and a long-buried secret of illicit love. Wharton, an author not only of long and short fiction, but also of travel writing, literary criticism, poetry, translation, landscape and interior design, and art history, was a shrewd social chronicler. Her technically sophisticated work reveals her engagement with the literary movements of her time: realism, naturalism, and modernism.

The Other Two[1]

I

Waythorn, on the drawing-room hearth, waited for his wife to come down to dinner.

It was their first night under his own roof, and he was surprised at his thrill of boyish agitation. He was not so old, to be sure—his glass gave him little more than the five-and-thirty years to which his wife confessed—but he had fancied himself already in the temperate zone; yet here he was listening for her step with a tender sense of all it symbolized, with some old trail of

---

1. First appeared in *Collier's Weekly* (February 1904).

verse about the garlanded nuptial doorposts floating through his enjoyment of the pleasant room and the good dinner just beyond it.

They had been hastily recalled from their honeymoon by the illness of Lily Haskett, the child of Mrs. Waythorn's first marriage. The little girl, at Waythorn's desire, had been transferred to his house on the day of her mother's wedding, and the doctor, on their arrival, broke the news that she was ill with typhoid, but declared that all the symptoms were favorable. Lily could show twelve years of unblemished health, and the case promised to be a light one. The nurse spoke as reassuringly, and after a moment of alarm Mrs. Waythorn had adjusted herself to the situation. She was very fond of Lily—her affection for the child had perhaps been her decisive charm in Waythorn's eyes—but she had the perfectly balanced nerves which her little girl had inherited, and no woman ever wasted less tissue in unproductive worry. Waythorn was therefore quite prepared to see her come in presently, a little late because of a last look at Lily, but as serene and well-appointed as if her good-night kiss had been laid on the brow of health. Her composure was restful to him; it acted as ballast to his somewhat unstable sensibilities. As he pictured her bending over the child's bed he thought how soothing her presence must be in illness: her very step would prognosticate recovery.

His own life had been a gray one, from temperament rather than circumstance, and he had been drawn to her by the unperturbed gaiety which kept her fresh and elastic at an age when most women's activities are growing either slack or febrile. He knew what was said about her; for, popular as she was, there had always been a faint undercurrent of detraction. When she had appeared in New York, nine or ten years earlier, as the pretty Mrs. Haskett whom Gus Varick had unearthed somewhere—was it in Pittsburgh or Utica?—society, while promptly accepting her, had reserved the right to cast a doubt on its own indiscrimination. Inquiry, however, established her undoubted connection with a socially reigning family, and explained her recent divorce as the natural result of a runaway match at seventeen; and as nothing was known of Mr. Haskett it was easy to believe the worst of him.

Alice Haskett's remarriage with Gus Varick was a passport to the set whose recognition she coveted, and for a few years the Varicks were the most popular couple in town. Unfortunately the alliance was brief and stormy, and this time the husband had his champions. Still, even Varick's stanchest supporters admitted that he was not meant for matrimony, and Mrs. Varick's grievances were of a nature to bear the inspection of the New York courts. A New York divorce is in itself a diploma of virtue, and in the semiwidowhood of this second separation Mrs. Varick took on an air of sanctity, and was allowed to confide her wrongs to some of the most scrupulous ears in town. But when it was known that she was to marry Waythorn there was a momentary reaction. Her best friends would have preferred to see her remain in the role of the injured wife, which was as becoming to her as crepe to a rosy complexion. True, a decent time had elapsed, and it was not even suggested that Waythorn had supplanted his predecessor. People shook their heads over him, however, and one grudging friend, to whom he affirmed that he took the step with his eyes open, replied oracularly: "Yes—and with your ears shut."

Waythorn could afford to smile at these innuendoes. In the Wall Street phrase, he had "discounted" them. He knew that society has not yet adapted itself to the consequences of divorce, and that till the adaptation takes place every woman who uses the freedom the law accords her must be her own social justification. Waythorn had an amused confidence in his wife's ability to justify herself. His expectations were fulfilled, and before the wedding took place Alice Varick's group had rallied openly to her support. She took it all imperturbably: she had a way of surmounting obstacles without seeming to be aware of them, and Waythorn looked back with wonder at the trivialities over which he had worn his nerves thin. He had the sense of having found refuge in a richer, warmer nature than his own, and his satisfaction, at the moment, was humorously summed up in the thought that his wife, when she had done all she could for Lily, would not be ashamed to come down and enjoy a good dinner.

The anticipation of such enjoyment was not, however, the sentiment expressed by Mrs. Waythorn's charming face when she presently joined him. Though she had put on her most engaging tea gown she had neglected to assume the smile that went with it, and Waythorn thought he had never seen her look so nearly worried.

"What is it?" he asked. "Is anything wrong with Lily?"

"No; I've just been in and she's still sleeping." Mrs. Waythorn hesitated. "But something tiresome has happened."

He had taken her two hands, and now perceived that he was crushing a paper between them.

"This letter?"

"Yes—Mr. Haskett has written—I mean his lawyer has written."

Waythorn felt himself flush uncomfortably. He dropped his wife's hands. "What about?"

"About seeing Lily. You know the courts—"

"Yes, yes," he interrupted nervously.

Nothing was known about Haskett in New York. He was vaguely supposed to have remained in the outer darkness from which his wife had been rescued, and Waythorn was one of the few who were aware that he had given up his business in Utica and followed her to New York in order to be near his little girl. In the days of his wooing, Waythorn had often met Lily on the doorstep, rosy and smiling, on her way "to see papa."

"I am so sorry," Mrs. Waythorn murmured.

He roused himself. "What does he want?"

"He wants to see her. You know she goes to him once a week."

"Well—he doesn't expect her to go to him now, does he?"

"No—he has heard of her illness; but he expects to come here."

"*Here?*"

Mrs. Waythorn reddened under his gaze. They looked away from each other.

"I'm afraid he has the right. . . . You'll see. . . ." She made a proffer of the letter.

Waythorn moved away with a gesture of refusal. He stood staring about the softly-lighted room, which a moment before had seemed so full of bridal intimacy.

"I'm so sorry," she repeated. "If Lily could have been moved—"

"That's out of the question," he returned impatiently.

"I suppose so."

Her lip was beginning to tremble, and he felt himself a brute.

"He must come, of course," he said. "When is—his day?"

"I'm afraid—tomorrow."

"Very well. Send a note in the morning."

The butler entered to announce dinner.

Waythorn turned to his wife. "Come—you must be tired. It's beastly, but try to forget about it," he said, drawing her hand through his arm.

"You're so good, dear. I'll try," she whispered back.

Her face cleared at once, and as she looked at him across the flowers, between the rosy candleshades, he saw her lips waver back into a smile.

"How pretty everything is!" she sighed luxuriously.

He turned to the butler. "The champagne at once, please. Mrs. Waythorn is tired."

In a moment or two their eyes met above the sparkling glasses. Her own were quite clear and untroubled: he saw that she had obeyed his injunction and forgotten.

II

Waythorn, the next morning, went downtown earlier than usual. Haskett was not likely to come till the afternoon, but the instinct of flight drove him forth. He meant to stay away all day—he had thoughts of dining at his club. As his door closed behind him he reflected that before he opened it again it would have admitted another man who had as much right to enter it as himself, and the thought filled him with a physical repugnance.

He caught the elevated at the employees' hour, and found himself crushed between two layers of pendulous humanity. At Eighth Street the man facing him wriggled out, and another took his place. Waythorn glanced up and saw that it was Gus Varick. The men were so close together that it was impossible to ignore the smile of recognition on Varick's handsome overblown face. And after all—why not? They had always been on good terms, and Varick had been divorced before Waythorn's attentions to his wife began. The two exchanged a word on the perennial grievance of the congested trains, and when a seat at their side was miraculously left empty the instinct of self-preservation made Waythorn slip into it after Varick.

The latter drew the stout man's breath of relief. "Lord—I was beginning to feel like a pressed flower." He leaned back, looking unconcernedly at Waythorn. "Sorry to hear that Sellers is knocked out again."

"Sellers?" echoed Waythorn, starting at his partner's name.

Varick looked surprised. "You didn't know he was laid up with the gout?"

"No. I've been away—I only got back last night." Waythorn felt himself reddening in anticipation of the other's smile.

"Ah—yes; to be sure. And Sellers' attack came on two days ago. I'm afraid he's pretty bad. Very awkward for me, as it happens, because he was just putting through a rather important thing for me."

"Ah?" Waythorn wondered vaguely since when Varick had been dealing in "important things." Hitherto he had dabbled only in the shallow pools of speculation, with which Waythorn's office did not usually concern itself.

It occurred to him that Varick might be talking at random, to relieve the strain of their propinquity. That strain was becoming momentarily more apparent to Waythorn, and when, at Cortlandt Street, he caught sight of an acquaintance and had a sudden vision of the picture he and Varick must present to an initiated eye, he jumped up with a muttered excuse.

"I hope you'll find Sellers better," said Varick civilly, and he stammered back: "If I can be of any use to you—" and let the departing crowd sweep him to the platform.

At his office he heard that Sellers was in fact ill with the gout, and would probably not be able to leave the house for some weeks.

"I'm sorry it should have happened so, Mr. Waythorn," the senior clerk said with affable significance. "Mr. Sellers was very much upset at the idea of giving you such a lot of extra work just now."

"Oh, that's no matter," said Waythorn hastily. He secretly welcomed the pressure of additional business, and was glad to think that, when the day's work was over, he would have to call at his partner's on the way home.

He was late for luncheon, and turned in at the nearest restaurant instead of going to his club. The place was full, and the waiter hurried him to the back of the room to capture the only vacant table. In the cloud of cigar smoke Waythorn did not at once distinguish his neighbors: but presently, looking about him, he saw Varick seated a few feet off. This time, luckily, they were too far apart for conversation, and Varick, who faced another way, had probably not even seen him; but there was an irony in their renewed nearness.

Varick was said to be fond of good living, and as Waythorn sat dispatching his hurried luncheon he looked across half enviously at the other's leisurely degustation of his meal. When Waythorn first saw him he had been helping himself with critical deliberation to a bit of Camembert at the ideal point of liquefaction, and now, the cheese removed, he was just pouring his *café double* from its little two-storied earthen pot. He poured slowly, his ruddy profile bent over the task, and one beringed white hand steadying the lid of the coffeepot; then he stretched his other hand to the decanter of cognac at his elbow, filled a liqueur glass, took a tentative sip, and poured the brandy into his coffee cup.

Waythorn watched him in a kind of fascination. What was he thinking of—only of the flavor of the coffee and the liqueur? Had the morning's meeting left no more trace in his thoughts than on his face? Had his wife so completely passed out of his life that even this odd encounter with her present husband, within a week after her remarriage, was no more than an incident in his day? And as Waythorn mused, another idea struck him: had Haskett ever met Varick as Varick and he had just met? The recollection of Haskett perturbed him, and he rose and left the restaurant, taking a circuitous way out to escape the placid irony of Varick's nod.

It was after seven when Waythorn reached home. He thought the footman who opened the door looked at him oddly.

"How is Miss Lily?" he asked in haste.

"Doing very well, sir. A gentleman—"

"Tell Barlow to put off dinner for half an hour," Waythorn cut him off, hurrying upstairs.

He went straight to his room and dressed without seeing his wife. When he reached the drawing room she was there, fresh and radiant. Lily's day had been good; the doctor was not coming back that evening.

At dinner Waythorn told her of Sellers' illness and of the resulting complications. She listened sympathetically, adjuring him not to let himself be overworked, and asking vague feminine questions about the routine of the office. Then she gave him the chronicle of Lily's day; quoted the nurse and doctor, and told him who had called to inquire. He had never seen her more serene and unruffled. It struck him, with a curious pang, that she was very happy in being with him, so happy that she found a childish pleasure in rehearsing the trivial incidents of her day.

After dinner they went to the library, and the servant put the coffee and liqueurs on a low table before her and left the room. She looked singularly soft and girlish in her rosy-pale dress, against the dark leather of one of his bachelor armchairs. A day earlier the contrast would have charmed him.

He turned away now, choosing a cigar with affected deliberation.

"Did Haskett come?" he asked, with his back to her.

"Oh, yes—he came."

"You didn't see him, of course?"

She hesitated a moment. "I let the nurse see him."

That was all. There was nothing more to ask. He swung round toward her, applying a match to his cigar. Well, the thing was over for a week, at any rate. He would try not to think of it. She looked up at him, a trifle rosier than usual, with a smile in her eyes.

"Ready for your coffee, dear?"

He leaned against the mantelpiece, watching her as she lifted the coffeepot. The lamplight struck a gleam from her bracelets and tipped her soft hair with brightness. How light and slender she was, and how each gesture flowed into the next! She seemed a creature all compact of harmonies. As the thought of Haskett receded, Waythorn felt himself yielding again to the joy of possessorship. They were his, those white hands with their flitting motions, his the light haze of hair, the lips and eyes. . . .

She set down the coffeepot, and reaching for the decanter of cognac, measured off a liqueur glass and poured it into his cup.

Waythorn uttered a sudden exclamation.

"What is the matter?" she said, startled.

"Nothing; only—I don't take cognac in my coffee."

"Oh, how stupid of me," she cried.

Their eyes met, and she blushed a sudden agonized red.

III

Ten days later, Mr. Sellers, still housebound, asked Waythorn to call on his way downtown.

The senior partner, with his swaddled foot propped up by the fire, greeted his associate with an air of embarrassment.

"I'm sorry, my dear fellow; I've got to ask you to do an awkward thing for me."

Waythorn waited, and the other went on, after a pause apparently given to the arrangement of his phrases: "The fact is, when I was knocked out I had just gone into a rather complicated piece of business for—Gus Varick."

"Well?" said Waythorn, with an attempt to put him at his ease.

"Well—it's this way: Varick came to me the day before my attack. He had evidently had an inside tip from somebody, and had made about a hundred thousand. He came to me for advice, and I suggested his going in with Vanderlyn."

"Oh, the deuce!" Waythorn exclaimed. He saw in a flash what had happened. The investment was an alluring one, but required negotiation. He listened quietly while Sellers put the case before him, and, the statement ended, he said: "You think I ought to see Varick?"

"I'm afraid I can't as yet. The doctor is obdurate. And this thing can't wait. I hate to ask you, but no one else in the office knows the ins and outs of it."

Waythorn stood silent. He did not care a farthing for the success of Varick's venture, but the honor of the office was to be considered, and he could hardly refuse to oblige his partner.

"Very well," he said, "I'll do it."

That afternoon, apprised by telephone, Varick called at the office. Waythorn, waiting in his private room, wondered what the others thought of it. The newspapers, at the time of Mrs. Waythorn's marriage, had acquainted their readers with every detail of her previous matrimonial ventures, and Waythorn could fancy the clerks smiling behind Varick's back as he was ushered in.

Varick bore himself admirably. He was easy without being undignified, and Waythorn was conscious of cutting a much less impressive figure. Varick had no experience of business, and the talk prolonged itself for nearly an hour while Waythorn set forth with scrupulous precision the details of the proposed transaction.

"I'm awfully obliged to you," Varick said as he rose. "The fact is I'm not used to having much money to look after, and I don't want to make an ass of myself—" He smiled, and Waythorn could not help noticing that there was something pleasant about his smile. "It feels uncommonly queer to have enough cash to pay one's bills. I'd have sold my soul for it a few years ago!"

Waythorn winced at the allusion. He had heard it rumored that a lack of funds had been one of the determining causes of the Varick separation, but it did not occur to him that Varick's words were intentional. It seemed more likely that the desire to keep clear of embarrassing topics had fatally drawn him into one. Waythorn did not wish to be outdone in civility.

"We'll do the best we can for you," he said. "I think this is a good thing you're in."

"Oh, I'm sure it's immense. It's awfully good of you—" Varick broke off, embarrassed. "I suppose the thing's settled now—but if—"

"If anything happens before Sellers is about, I'll see you again," said Waythorn quietly. He was glad, in the end, to appear the more self-possessed of the two.

The course of Lily's illness ran smooth, and as the days passed Waythorn grew used to the idea of Haskett's weekly visit. The first time the day came round, he stayed out late, and questioned his wife as to the visit on his return. She replied at once that Haskett had merely seen the nurse downstairs, as the doctor did not wish anyone in the child's sickroom till after the crisis.

The following week Waythorn was again conscious of the recurrence of the day, but had forgotten it by the time he came home to dinner. The crisis of the disease came a few days later, with a rapid decline of fever, and the little girl was pronounced out of danger. In the rejoicing which ensued the thought of Haskett passed out of Waythorn's mind, and one afternoon, letting himself into the house with a latchkey, he went straight to his library without noticing a shabby hat and umbrella in the hall.

In the library he found a small effaced-looking man with a thinnish gray beard sitting on the edge of a chair. The stranger might have been a piano tuner, or one of those mysteriously efficient persons who are summoned in emergencies to adjust some detail of the domestic machinery. He blinked at Waythorn through a pair of gold-rimmed spectacles and said mildly: "Mr. Waythorn, I presume? I am Lily's father."

Waythorn flushed. "Oh—" he stammered uncomfortably. He broke off, disliking to appear rude. Inwardly he was trying to adjust the actual Haskett to the image of him projected by his wife's reminiscences. Waythorn had been allowed to infer that Alice's first husband was a brute.

"I am sorry to intrude," said Haskett, with his over-the-counter politeness.

"Don't mention it," returned Waythorn, collecting himself. "I suppose the nurse has been told?"

"I presume so. I can wait," said Haskett. He had a resigned way of speaking, as though life had worn down his natural powers of resistance.

Waythorn stood on the threshold, nervously pulling off his gloves.

"I'm sorry you've been detained. I will send for the nurse," he said; and as he opened the door he added with an effort: "I'm glad we can give you a good report of Lily." He winced as the *we* slipped out, but Haskett seemed not to notice it.

"Thank you, Mr. Waythorn, It's been an anxious time for me."

"Ah, well, that's past. Soon she'll be able to go to you." Waythorn nodded and passed out.

In his own room he flung himself down with a groan. He hated the womanish sensibility which made him suffer so acutely from the grotesque chances of life. He had known when he married that his wife's former husbands were both living, and that amid the multiplied contacts of modern existence there were a thousand chances to one that he would run against one or the other, yet he found himself as much disturbed by his brief encounter with Haskett as though the law had not obligingly removed all difficulties in the way of their meeting.

Waythorn sprang up and began to pace the room nervously. He had not suffered half as much from his two meetings with Varick. It was Haskett's presence in his own house that made the situation so intolerable. He stood still, hearing steps in the passage.

"This way, please," he heard the nurse say. Haskett was being taken upstairs, then: not a corner of the house but was open to him. Waythorn dropped into another chair, staring vaguely ahead of him. On his dressing table stood a photograph of Alice, taken when he had first known her. She was Alice Varick then—how fine and exquisite he had thought her! Those were Varick's pearls about her neck. At Waythorn's instance they had been returned before her marriage. Had Haskett ever given her any trinkets—and what had become of them, Waythorn wondered? He realized suddenly that he knew very little of Haskett's past or present situation; but from the man's appearance and manner of speech he could reconstruct with curious precision the surroundings of Alice's first marriage. And it startled him to think that she had, in the background of her life, a phase of existence so different from anything with which he had connected her. Varick, whatever his faults, was a gentleman, in the conventional, traditional sense of the term: the sense which at that moment seemed, oddly enough, to have most meaning to Waythorn. He and Varick had the same social habits, spoke the same language, understood the same allusions. But this other man . . . it was grotesquely uppermost in Waythorn's mind that Haskett had worn a made-up tie attached with an elastic. Why should that ridiculous detail symbolize the whole man? Waythorn was exasperated by his own paltriness, but the fact of the tie expanded, forced itself on him, became as it were the key to Alice's past. He could see her, as Mrs. Haskett, sitting in a "front parlor" furnished in plush, with a pianola, and copy of *Ben Hur*[2] on the center table. He could see her going to the theater with Haskett—or perhaps even to a "Church Sociable"—she in a "picture hat" and Haskett in a black frock coat, a little creased, with the made-up tie on an elastic. On the way home they would stop and look at the illuminated shop windows, lingering over the photographs of New York actresses. On Sunday afternoons Haskett would take her for a walk, pushing Lily ahead of them in a white enameled perambulator, and Waythorn had a vision of the people they would stop and talk to. He could fancy how pretty Alice must have looked, in a dress adroitly constructed from the hints of a New York fashion paper, and how she must have looked down on the other women, chafing at her life, and secretly feeling that she belonged in a bigger place.

For the moment his foremost thought was one of wonder at the way in which she had shed the phase of existence which her marriage with Haskett implied. It was as if her whole aspect, every gesture, every inflection, every allusion, were a studied negation of that period of her life. If she had denied being married to Haskett she could hardly have stood more convicted of duplicity than in this obliteration of the self which had been his wife.

Waythorn started up, checking himself in the analysis of her motives. What right had he to create a fantastic effigy of her and then pass judgment on it? She had spoken vaguely of her first marriage as unhappy, had hinted, with becoming reticence, that Haskett had wrought havoc among her young illusions. . . . It was a pity for Waythorn's peace of mind that Haskett's very inoffensiveness shed a new light on the nature of those illusions. A man would rather think that his wife has been brutalized by her first husband than that the process has been reversed.

IV

"Mr. Waythorn, I don't like that French governess of Lily's."

Haskett, subdued and apologetic, stood before Waythorn in the library, revolving his shabby hat in his hand.

Waythorn, surprised in his armchair over the evening paper, stared back perplexedly at his visitor.

"You'll excuse my asking to see you," Haskett continued. "But this is my last visit, and I thought if I could have a word with you it would be a better way than writing to Mrs. Waythorn's lawyer."

Waythorn rose uneasily. He did not like the French governess either; but that was irrelevant.

"I am not so sure of that," he returned stiffly; "but since you wish it I will give your message to—my wife." He always hesitated over the possessive pronoun in addressing Haskett.

The latter sighed. "I don't know as that will help much. She didn't like it when I spoke to her."

<hr/>

2. *Ben Hur: A Tale of The Christ* (1880) was an extremely popular novel by Lew Wallace (1827–1905).

Waythorn turned red. "When did you see her?" he asked.

"Not since the first day I came to see Lily—right after she was taken sick. I remarked to her then that I didn't like the governess."

Waythorn made no answer. He remembered distinctly that, after that first visit, he had asked his wife if she had seen Haskett. She had lied to him then, but she had respected his wishes since; and the incident cast a curious light on her character. He was sure she would not have seen Haskett that first day if she had divined that Waythorn would object, and the fact that she did not divine it was almost as disagreeable to the latter as the discovery that she had lied to him.

"I don't like the woman," Haskett was repeating with mild persistency. "She ain't straight, Mr. Waythorn—she'll teach the child to be underhand. I've noticed a change in Lily—she's too anxious to please—and she don't always tell the truth. She used to be the straightest child, Mr. Waythorn—" He broke off, his voice a little thick. "Not but what I want her to have a stylish education," he ended.

Waythorn was touched. "I'm sorry, Mr. Haskett; but frankly, I don't quite see what I can do."

Haskett hesitated. Then he laid his hat on the table, and advanced to the hearthrug, on which Waythorn was standing. There was nothing aggressive in his manner, but he had the solemnity of a timid man resolved on a decisive measure.

"There's just one thing you can do, Mr. Waythorn," he said. "You can remind Mrs. Waythorn that, by the decree of the courts, I am entitled to have a voice in Lily's bringing-up." He paused, and went on more deprecatingly: "I'm not the kind to talk about enforcing my rights, Mr. Waythorn. I don't know as I think a man is entitled to rights he hasn't known how to hold on to; but this business of the child is different. I've never let go there—and I never mean to."

The scene left Waythorn deeply shaken. Shamefacedly, in indirect ways, he had been finding out about Haskett; and all that he had learned was favorable. The little man, in order to be near his daughter, had sold out his share in a profitable business in Utica, and accepted a modest clerkship in a New York manufacturing house. He boarded in a shabby street and had few acquaintances. His passion for Lily filled his life. Waythorn felt that this exploration of Haskett was like groping about with a dark lantern in his wife's past; but he saw now that there were recesses his lantern had not explored. He had never inquired into the exact circumstances of his wife's first matrimonial rupture. On the surface all had been fair. It was she who had obtained the divorce, and the court had given her the child. But Waythorn knew how many ambiguities such a verdict might cover. The mere fact that Haskett retained a right over his daughter implied an unsuspected compromise. Waythorn was an idealist. He always refused to recognize unpleasant contingencies till he found himself confronted with them, and then he saw them followed by a spectral train of consequences. His next days were thus haunted, and he determined to try to lay the ghosts by conjuring them up in his wife's presence.

When he repeated Haskett's request a flame of anger passed over her face; but she subdued it instantly and spoke with a slight quiver of outraged motherhood.

"It is very ungentlemanly of him," she said.

The word grated on Waythorn. "That is neither here nor there. It's a bare question of rights."

She murmured: "It's not as if he could ever be a help to Lily—"

Waythorn flushed. This was even less to his taste. "The question is," he repeated, "what authority has he over her?"

She looked downward, twisting herself a little in her seat. "I am willing to see him—I thought you objected," she faltered.

In a flash he understood that she knew the extent of Haskett's claims. Perhaps it was not the first time she had resisted them.

"My objecting has nothing to do with it," he said coldly; "if Haskett has a right to be consulted you must consult him."

She burst into tears, and he saw that she expected him to regard her as a victim.

Haskett did not abuse his rights. Waythorn had felt miserably sure that he would not. But the governess was dismissed, and from time to time the little man demanded an interview with Alice. After the first outburst she accepted the situation with her usual adaptability. Haskett had once reminded Waythorn of the piano tuner, and Mrs. Waythorn, after a month or two, appeared to class him with that domestic familiar. Waythorn could not but respect the father's tenacity. At first he had tried to cultivate the suspicion that Haskett might be "up to" something, that he had an object in securing a foothold in the house. But in his heart Waythorn was sure of Haskett's single-mindedness; he even guessed in the latter a mild contempt for such advantages as his relation with the Waythorns might offer. Haskett's sincerity of purpose made him invulnerable, and his successor had to accept him as a lien on the property.

Mr. Sellers was sent to Europe to recover from his gout, and Varick's affairs hung on Waythorn's hands. The negotiations were prolonged and complicated; they necessitated frequent conferences between the two men, and the interests of the firm forbade Waythorn's suggesting that his client should transfer his business to another office.

Varick appeared well in the transaction. In moments of relaxation his coarse streak appeared, and Waythorn dreaded his geniality; but in the office he was concise and clear-headed, with a flattering deference to Waythorn's judgment. Their business relations being so affably established, it would have been absurd for the two men to ignore each other in society. The first time they met in a drawing room, Varick took up their intercourse in the same easy key, and his hostess' grateful glance obliged Waythorn to respond to it. After that they ran across each other frequently, and one evening at a ball Waythorn, wandering through the remoter rooms, came upon Varick seated beside his wife. She colored a little, and faltered in what she was saying; but Varick nodded to Waythorn without rising, and the latter strolled on.

In the carriage, on the way home, he broke out nervously: "I didn't know you spoke to Varick."

Her voice trembled a little. "It's the first time—he happened to be standing near me; I didn't know what to do. It's so awkward, meeting everywhere—and he said you had been very kind about some business."

"That's different," said Waythorn.

She paused a moment. "I'll do just as you wish," she returned pliantly. "I thought it would be less awkward to speak to him when we meet."

Her pliancy was beginning to sicken him. Had she really no will of her own—no theory about her relation to these men? She had accepted Haskett—did she mean to accept Varick? It was "less awkward," as she had said, and her instinct was to evade difficulties or to circumvent them. With sudden vividness Waythorn saw how the instinct had developed. She was "as easy as an old shoe"—a shoe that too many feet had worn. Her elasticity was the result of tension in too many different directions. Alice Haskett—Alice Varick—Alice Waythorn—she had been each in turn, and had left hanging to each name a little of her privacy, a little of her personality, a little of the inmost self where the unknown god abides.

"Yes—it's better to speak to Varick," said Waythorn wearily.

V

The winter wore on, and society took advantage of the Waythorns' acceptance of Varick. Harassed hostesses were grateful to them for bridging over a social difficulty, and Mrs. Waythorn was held up as a miracle of good taste. Some experimental spirits could not resist the diversion of throwing Varick and his former wife together, and there were those who thought he found a zest in the propinquity. But Mrs. Waythorn's conduct remained irreproachable. She neither avoided Varick nor sought him out. Even Waythorn could not but admit that she had discovered the solution of the newest social problem.

He had married her without giving much thought to that problem. He had fancied that a woman can shed her past like a man. But now he saw that Alice was bound to hers both by the circumstances which forced her into continued relation with it, and by the traces it had left on her nature. With grim irony Waythorn compared himself to a member of a syndicate. He held so many shares in his wife's personality and his predecessors were his partners in the business. If there had been any element of passion in the transaction he would have felt less deteriorated by it. The fact that Alice took her change of husbands like a change of weather reduced the situation to mediocrity. He could have forgiven her for blunders, for excesses; for resisting Haskett, for yielding to Varick; for anything but her acquiescence and her tact. She reminded him of a juggler tossing knives; but the knives were blunt and she knew they would never cut her.

And then, gradually, habit formed a protecting surface for his sensibilities. If he paid for each day's comfort with the small change of his illusions, he grew daily to value the comfort more and set less store upon the coin. He had drifted into a dulling propinquity with Haskett and Varick and he took refuge in the cheap revenge of satirizing the situation. He even began to reckon up the advantages which accrued from it, to ask himself if it were not better to own a third of a wife who knew how to make a man happy than a whole one who had lacked opportunity to acquire the art. For it *was* an art, and made up, like all others, of concessions, eliminations and embellishments; of lights judiciously thrown and shadows skillfully softened. His wife knew exactly how to manage the lights, and he knew exactly to what training she owed her skill. He even tried to trace the source of his obligations, to discriminate between the influences which had combined to produce his domestic happiness: he perceived that Haskett's commonness had made Alice worship good breeding, while Varick's liberal construction of the marriage bond had taught her to value the conjugal virtues; so that he was directly indebted to his predecessors for the devotion which made his life easy if not inspiring.

From this phase he passed into that of complete acceptance. He ceased to satirize himself because time dulled the irony of the situation and the joke lost its humor with its sting. Even the sight of Haskett's hat on the hall table had ceased to touch the springs of epigram. The hat was often seen there now, for it had been decided that it was better for Lily's father to visit her than for the little girl to go to his boardinghouse. Waythorn, having acquiesced in this arrangement, had been surprised to find how little difference it made. Haskett was never obtrusive, and the few visitors who met him on the stairs were unaware of his identity. Waythorn did not know how often he saw Alice, but with himself Haskett was seldom in contact.

One afternoon, however, he learned on entering that Lily's father was waiting to see him. In the library he found Haskett occupying a chair in his usual provisional way. Waythorn always felt grateful to him for not leaning back.

"I hope you'll excuse me, Mr. Waythorn," he said rising. "I wanted to see Mrs. Waythorn about Lily, and your man asked me to wait here till she came in."

"Of course," said Waythorn, remembering that a sudden leak had that morning given over the drawing room to the plumbers.

He opened his cigar case and held it out to his visitor, and Haskett's acceptance seemed to mark a fresh stage in their intercourse. The spring evening was chilly, and Waythorn invited his guest to draw up his chair to the fire. He meant to find an excuse to leave Haskett in a moment; but he was tired and cold, and after all the little man no longer jarred on him.

The two were enclosed in the intimacy of their blended cigar smoke when the door opened and Varick walked into the room. Waythorn rose abruptly. It was the first time that Varick had come to the house, and the surprise of seeing him, combined with the singular inopportuneness of his arrival, gave a new edge to Waythorn's blunted sensibilities. He stared at his visitor without speaking.

Varick seemed too preoccupied to notice his host's embarrassment.

"My dear fellow," he exclaimed in his most expansive tone, "I must apologize for tumbling in on you in this way, but I was too late to catch you downtown, and so I thought—"

He stopped short, catching sight of Haskett, and his sanguine color deepened to a flush which spread vividly under his scant blond hair. But in a moment he recovered himself and nodded slightly. Haskett returned the bow in silence, and Waythorn was still groping for speech when the footman came in carrying a tea table.

The intrusion offered a welcome vent to Waythorn's nerves. "What the deuce are you bringing this here for?" he said sharply.

"I beg your pardon, sir, but the plumbers are still in the drawing room, and Mrs. Waythorn said she would have tea in the library." The footman's perfectly respectful tone implied a reflection on Waythorn's reasonableness.

"Oh, very well," said the latter resignedly, and the footman proceeded to open the folding tea table and set out its complicated appointments. While this interminable process continued the three men stood motionless, watching it with a fascinated stare, till Waythorn, to break the silence, said to Varick, "Won't you have a cigar?"

He held out the case he had just tendered to Haskett, and Varick helped himself with a smile. Waythorn looked about for a match, and finding none, proffered a light from his own cigar. Haskett, in the background, held his ground mildly, examining his cigar tip now and then, and stepping forward at the right moment to knock its ashes into the fire.

The footman at last withdrew, and Varick immediately began: "If I could just say half a word to you about this business—"

"Certainly," stammered Waythorn; "in the dining room—"

But as he placed his hand on the door it opened from without, and his wife appeared on the threshold.

She came in fresh and smiling, in her street dress and hat, shedding a fragrance from the boa which she loosened in advancing.

"Shall we have tea in here, dear?" she began; and then she caught sight of Varick. Her smile deepened, veiling a slight tremor of surprise.

"Why, how do you do?" she said with a distinct note of pleasure.

As she shook hands with Varick she saw Haskett standing behind him. Her smile faded for a moment, but she recalled it quickly, with a scarcely perceptible side glance at Waythorn.

"How do you do, Mr. Haskett?" she said, and shook hands with him a shade less cordially.

The three men stood awkwardly before her, till Varick, always the most self-possessed, dashed into an explanatory phrase.

"We—I had to see Waythorn a moment on business," he stammered, brick-red from chin to nape.

Haskett stepped forward with his air of mild obstinacy. "I am sorry to intrude; but you appointed five o'clock—" he directed his resigned glance to the timepiece on the mantel.

She swept aside their embarrassment with a charming gesture of hospitality.

"I'm so sorry—I'm always late; but the afternoon was so lovely." She stood drawing off her gloves, propitiatory and graceful, diffusing about her a sense of ease and familiarity in which the situation lost its grotesqueness. "But before talking business," she added brightly, "I'm sure everyone wants a cup of tea."

She dropped into her low chair by the tea table, and the two visitors, as if drawn by her smile, advanced to receive the cups she held out.

She glanced about for Waythorn, and he took the third cup with a laugh.

1904

Roman Fever[1]

I

From the table at which they had been lunching two American ladies of ripe but well-cared-for middle age moved across the lofty terrace of the Roman restaurant and, leaning on its parapet, looked first at each other, and then down on the outspread glories of the Palatine[2] and the Forum, with the same expression of vague but benevolent approval.

As they leaned there a girlish voice echoed up gaily from the stairs leading to the court below. "Well, come along, then," it cried, not to them but to an

1. First printed in *Liberty* magazine in 1934.
2. Palatine Hill: a park in the center of Rome, with palatial ruins and historical monuments.

invisible companion, "and let's leave the young things to their knitting"; and a voice as fresh laughed back: "Oh, look here, Babs, not actually *knitting*—" "Well, I mean figuratively," rejoined the first. "After all, we haven't left our poor parents much else to do. . . ." and at that point the turn of the stairs engulfed the dialogue.

The two ladies looked at each other again, this time with a tinge of smiling embarrassment, and the smaller and paler one shook her head and colored slightly.

"Barbara!" she murmured, sending an unheard rebuke after the mocking voice in the stairway.

The other lady, who was fuller, and higher in color, with a small determined nose supported by vigorous black eyebrows, gave a good-humored laugh. "That's what our daughters think of us!"

Her companion replied by a deprecating gesture. "Not of us individually. We must remember that. It's just the collective modern idea of Mothers. And you see—" Half-guiltily she drew from her handsomely mounted black handbag a twist of crimson silk run through by two fine knitting needles. "One never knows," she murmured. "The new system has certainly given us a good deal of time to kill; and sometimes I get tired just looking—even at this." Her gesture was now addressed to the stupendous scene at their feet.

The dark lady laughed again, and they both relapsed upon the view, contemplating it in silence, with a sort of diffused serenity which might have been borrowed from the spring effulgence of the Roman skies. The luncheon hour was long past, and the two had their end of the vast terrace to themselves. At its opposite extremity a few groups, detained by a lingering look at the outspread city, were gathering up guidebooks and fumbling for tips. The last of them scattered, and the two ladies were alone on the air-washed height.

"Well, I don't see why we shouldn't just stay here," said Mrs. Slade, the lady of the high color and energetic brows. Two derelict basket chairs stood near, and she pushed them into the angle of the parapet, and settled herself in one, her gaze upon the Palatine. "After all, it's still the most beautiful view in the world."

"It always will be, to me," assented her friend Mrs. Ansley, with so slight a stress on the "me" that Mrs. Slade, though she noticed it, wondered if it were not merely accidental, like the random underlinings of old-fashioned letter writers.

"Grace Ansley was always old-fashioned," she thought; and added aloud, with a retrospective smile: "It's a view we've both been familiar with for a good many years. When we first met here we were younger than our girls are now. You remember?"

"Oh, yes, I remember," murmured Mrs. Ansley, with the same undefinable stress. "There's that headwaiter wondering," she interpolated. She was evidently far less sure than her companion of herself and of her rights in the world.

"I'll cure him of wondering," said Mrs. Slade, stretching her hand toward a bag as discreetly opulent-looking as Mrs. Ansley's. Signing to the headwaiter, she explained that she and her friend were old lovers of Rome, and would like to spend the end of the afternoon looking down on the view— that is, if it did not disturb the service? The headwaiter, bowing over her gratuity, assured her that the ladies were most welcome, and would be still more so if they would condescend to remain for dinner. A full-moon night, they would remember. . . .

Mrs. Slade's black brows drew together, as though references to the moon were out of place and even unwelcome. But she smiled away her frown as the headwaiter retreated. "Well, why not? We might do worse. There's no knowing, I suppose, when the girls will be back. Do you even know back from *where?* I don't!"

Mrs. Ansley again colored slightly. "I think those young Italian aviators we met at the Embassy invited them to fly to Tarquinia[3] for tea. I suppose they'll want to wait and fly back by moonlight."

"Moonlight—moonlight! What a part it still plays. Do you suppose they're as sentimental as we were?"

"I've come to the conclusion that I don't in the least know what they are," said Mrs. Ansley. "And perhaps we didn't know much more about each other."

"No; perhaps we didn't."

Her friend gave her a shy glance. "I never should have supposed you were sentimental, Alida."

"Well, perhaps I wasn't." Mrs. Slade drew her lids together in retrospect; and for a few moments the two ladies, who had been intimate since childhood, reflected how little they knew each other. Each one, of course, had a label ready to attach to the other's name; Mrs. Delphin Slade, for instance, would have told herself, or anyone who asked her, that Mrs. Horace Ansley, twenty-five years ago, had been exquisitely lovely—no, you wouldn't believe it, would you?. . . . though, of course, still charming, distinguished. . . . Well, as a girl she had been exquisite; far more beautiful than her daughter Barbara, though certainly Babs, according to the new standards at any rate, was more effective—had more *edge,* as they say. Funny where she got it, with those two nullities as parents. Yes; Horace Ansley was—well, just the duplicate of his wife. Museum specimens of old New York. Good-looking, irreproachable, exemplary. Mrs. Slade and Mrs. Ansley had lived opposite each other—actually as well as figuratively—for years. When the drawing-room curtains in No. 20 East 73rd Street were renewed, No. 23, across the way, was always aware of it. And of all the movings, buyings, travels, anniversaries, illnesses—the tame chronicle of an estimable pair. Little of it escaped Mrs. Slade. But she had grown bored with it by the time her husband made his big *coup* in Wall Street, and when they bought in upper Park Avenue had already begun to think: "I'd rather live opposite a speakeasy for a change; at least one might see it raided." The idea of seeing Grace raided was so amusing that (before the move) she launched it at a woman's lunch. It made a hit, and went the rounds—she sometimes wondered if it had crossed the street, and reached Mrs. Ansley. She hoped not, but didn't much mind. Those were the days when respectability was at a discount, and it did the irreproachable no harm to laugh at them a little.

A few years later, and not many months apart, both ladies lost their husbands. There was an appropriate exchange of wreaths and condolences, and a brief renewal of intimacy in the half-shadow of their mourning; and now, after another interval, they had run across each other in Rome, at the same hotel, each of them the modest appendage of a salient daughter. The similarity of their lot had again drawn them together, lending itself to mild jokes,

---

3. An ancient Etruscan city in the province of Viterbo, Lazio, Italy, famous for resisting Roman rule.

and the mutual confession that, if in old days it must have been tiring to "keep up" with daughters, it was now, at times, a little dull not to.

No doubt, Mrs. Slade reflected, she felt her unemployment more than poor Grace ever would. It was a big drop from being the wife of Delphin Slade to being his widow. She had always regarded herself (with a certain conjugal pride) as his equal in social gifts, as contributing her full share to the making of the exceptional couple they were: but the difference after his death was irremediable. As the wife of the famous corporation lawyer, always with an international case or two on hand, every day brought its exciting and unexpected obligation: the impromptu entertaining of eminent colleagues from abroad, the hurried dashes on legal business to London, Paris or Rome, where the entertaining was so handsomely reciprocated; the amusement of hearing in her wake: "What, that handsome woman with the good clothes and the eyes is Mrs. Slade—*the* Slade's wife? Really? Generally the wives of celebrities are such frumps."

Yes; being *the* Slade's widow was a dullish business after that. In living up to such a husband all her faculties had been engaged; now she had only her daughter to live up to, for the son who seemed to have inherited his father's gifts had died suddenly in boyhood. She had fought through that agony because her husband was there, to be helped and to help; now, after the father's death, the thought of the boy had become unbearable. There was nothing left but to mother her daughter; and dear Jenny was such a perfect daughter that she needed no excessive mothering. "Now with Babs Ansley I don't know that I *should* be so quiet," Mrs. Slade sometimes half-enviously reflected; but Jenny, who was younger than her brilliant friend, was that rare accident, an extremely pretty girl who somehow made youth and prettiness seem as safe as their absence. It was all perplexing—and to Mrs. Slade a little boring. She wished that Jenny would fall in love—with the wrong man, even; that she might have to be watched, out-maneuvered, rescued. And instead, it was Jenny who watched her mother, kept her out of drafts, made sure that she had taken her tonic. . . .

Mrs. Ansley was much less articulate than her friend, and her mental portrait of Mrs. Slade was slighter, and drawn with fainter touches. "Alida Slade's awfully brilliant; but not as brilliant as she thinks," would have summed it up; though she would have added, for the enlightenment of strangers, that Mrs. Slade had been an extremely dashing girl; much more so than her daughter, who was pretty, of course, and clever in a way, but had none of her mother's—well, "vividness," someone had once called it. Mrs. Ansley would take up current words like this, and cite them in quotation marks, as unheard-of audacities. No; Jenny was not like her mother. Sometimes Mrs. Ansley thought Alida Slade was disappointed; on the whole she had had a sad life. Full of failures and mistakes; Mrs. Ansley had always been rather sorry for her. . . .

So these two ladies visualized each other, each through the wrong end of her little telescope.

II

For a long time they continued to sit side by side without speaking. It seemed as though, to both, there was a relief in laying down their somewhat futile activities in the presence of the vast Memento Mori which faced them. Mrs.

Slade sat quite still, her eyes fixed on the golden slope of the Palace of the Caesars,[4] and after a while Mrs. Ansley ceased to fidget with her bag, and she too sank into meditation. Like many intimate friends, the two ladies had never before had occasion to be silent together, and Mrs. Ansley was slightly embarrassed by what seemed, after so many years, a new stage in their intimacy, and one with which she did not yet know how to deal.

Suddenly the air was full of that deep clangor of bells which periodically covers Rome with a roof of silver. Mrs. Slade glanced at her wristwatch. "Five o'clock already," she said, as though surprised.

Mrs. Ansley suggested interrogatively: "There's bridge at the Embassy at five." For a long time Mrs. Slade did not answer. She appeared to be lost in contemplation, and Mrs. Ansley thought the remark had escaped her. But after a while she said, as if speaking out of a dream: "Bridge, did you say? Not unless you want to. . . . But I don't think I will, you know."

"Oh, no," Mrs. Ansley hastened to assure her. "I don't care to at all. It's so lovely here; and so full of old memories, as you say." She settled herself in her chair, and almost furtively drew forth her knitting. Mrs. Slade took sideway note of this activity, but her own beautifully cared-for hands remained motionless on her knee.

"I was just thinking," she said slowly, "what different things Rome stands for to each generation of travelers. To our grandmothers, Roman fever;[5] to our mothers, sentimental dangers—how we used to be guarded!—to our daughters, no more dangers than the middle of Main Street. They don't know it—but how much they're missing!"

The long golden light was beginning to pale, and Mrs. Ansley lifted her knitting a little closer to her eyes. "Yes; how we were guarded!"

"I always used to think," Mrs. Slade continued, "that our mothers had a much more difficult job than our grandmothers. When Roman fever stalked the streets it must have been comparatively easy to gather in the girls at the danger hour; but when you and I were young, with such beauty calling us, and the spice of disobedience thrown in, and no worse risk than catching cold during the cool hour after sunset, the mothers used to be put to it to keep us in—didn't they?"

She turned again toward Mrs. Ansley, but the latter had reached a delicate point in her knitting. "One, two, three—slip two; yes, they must have been," she assented, without looking up.

Mrs. Slade's eyes rested on her with a deepened attention. "She can knit—in the face of *this*! How like her. . . ."

Mrs. Slade leaned back, brooding, her eyes ranging from the ruins which faced her to the long green hollow of the Forum, the fading glow of the church fronts beyond it, and the outlying immensity of the Colosseum.[6] Suddenly she thought: "It's all very well to say that our girls have done away with sentiment and moonlight. But if Babs Ansley isn't out to catch that young aviator—the one who's a Marchese[7]—then I don't know anything. And Jenny has no chance beside her. I know that too. I wonder if that's why Grace Ansley likes the two girls to go everywhere together? My poor Jenny

---

4. Complex begun by Augustus Caesar on the Palatine Hill in Rome. "Memento Mori": "Remember you will die" (Latin).
5. Malaria.

6. Ancient Roman amphitheater, known for its battles between gladiators and public executions of Christians.
7. A member of Italian nobility.

as a foil—!" Mrs. Slade gave a hardly audible laugh, and at the sound Mrs. Ansley dropped her knitting.

"Yes—?"

"I—oh, nothing. I was only thinking how your Babs carries everything before her. That Campolieri boy is one of the best matches in Rome. Don't look so innocent, my dear—you know he is. And I was wondering, ever so respectfully, you understand . . . wondering how two such exemplary characters as you and Horace had managed to produce anything quite so dynamic." Mrs. Slade laughed again, with a touch of asperity.

Mrs. Ansley's hands lay inert across her needles. She looked straight out at the great accumulated wreckage of passion and splendor at her feet. But her small profile was almost expressionless. At length she said: "I think you overrate Babs, my dear."

Mrs. Slade's tone grew easier. "No; I don't. I appreciate her. And perhaps envy you. Oh, my girl's perfect; if I were a chronic invalid I'd—well, I think I'd rather be in Jenny's hands. There must be times . . . but there! I always wanted a brilliant daughter . . . and never quite understood why I got an angel instead."

Mrs. Ansley echoed her laugh in a faint murmur. "Babs is an angel too."

"Of course—of course! But she's got rainbow wings. Well, they're wandering by the sea with their young men; and here we sit . . . and it all brings back the past a little too acutely."

Mrs. Ansley had resumed her knitting. One might almost have imagined (if one had known her less well, Mrs. Slade reflected) that, for her also, too many memories rose from the lengthening shadows of those august ruins. But no; she was simply absorbed in her work. What was there for her to worry about? She knew that Babs would almost certainly come back engaged to the extremely eligible Campolieri. "And she'll sell the New York house, and settle down near them in Rome, and never be in their way . . . she's much too tactful. But she'll have an excellent cook, and just the right people in for bridge and cocktails . . . and a perfectly peaceful old age among her grandchildren."

Mrs. Slade broke off this prophetic flight with a recoil of self-disgust. There was no one of whom she had less right to think unkindly than of Grace Ansley. Would she never cure herself of envying her? Perhaps she had begun too long ago.

She stood up and leaned against the parapet, filling her troubled eyes with the tranquilizing magic of the hour. But instead of tranquilizing her the sight seemed to increase her exasperation. Her gaze turned toward the Colosseum. Already its golden flank was drowned in purple shadow, and above it the sky curved crystal clear, without light or color. It was the moment when afternoon and evening hang balanced in mid-heaven.

Mrs. Slade turned back and laid her hand on her friend's arm. The gesture was so abrupt that Mrs. Ansley looked up, startled.

"The sun's set. You're not afraid, my dear?"

"Afraid—?"

"Of Roman fever or pneumonia? I remember how ill you were that winter. As a girl you had a very delicate throat, hadn't you?"

"Oh, we're all right up here. Down below, in the Forum, it does get deathly cold, all of a sudden . . . but not here."

"Ah, of course you know because you had to be so careful." Mrs. Slade turned back to the parapet. She thought: "I must make one more effort not to hate her." Aloud she said: "Whenever I look at the Forum from up here,

I remember that story about a great-aunt of yours, wasn't she? A dreadfully wicked great-aunt?"

"Oh, yes; great-aunt Harriet. The one who was supposed to have sent her young sister out to the Forum after sunset to gather a night-blooming flower for her album. All our great-aunts and grandmothers used to have albums of dried flowers."

Mrs. Slade nodded. "But she really sent her because they were in love with the same man—"

"Well, that was the family tradition. They said Aunt Harriet confessed it years afterward. At any rate, the poor little sister caught the fever and died. Mother used to frighten us with the story when we were children."

"And you frightened *me* with it, that winter when you and I were here as girls. The winter I was engaged to Delphin."

Mrs. Ansley gave a faint laugh. "Oh, did I? Really frightened you? I don't believe you're easily frightened."

"Not often; but I was then. I was easily frightened because I was too happy. I wonder if you know what that means?"

"I—yes . . ." Mrs. Ansley faltered.

"Well, I suppose that was why the story of your wicked aunt made such an impression on me. And I thought: 'There's no more Roman fever, but the Forum is deathly cold after sunset—especially after a hot day. And the Colosseum's even colder and damper'."

"The Colosseum—?"

"Yes. It wasn't easy to get in, after the gates were locked for the night. Far from easy. Still, in those days it could be managed; it *was* managed, often. Lovers met there who couldn't meet elsewhere. You knew that?"

"I—I dare say. I don't remember."

"You don't remember? You don't remember going to visit some ruins or other one evening, just after dark, and catching a bad chill? You were supposed to have gone to see the moon rise. People always said that expedition was what caused your illness."

There was a moment's silence; then Mrs. Ansley rejoined: "Did they? It was all so long ago."

"Yes. And you got well again—so it didn't matter. But I suppose it struck your friends—the reason given for your illness, I mean—because everybody knew you were so prudent on account of your throat, and your mother took such care of you. . . . You *had* been out late sight-seeing, hadn't you, that night?"

"Perhaps I had. The most prudent girls aren't always prudent. What made you think of it now?"

Mrs. Slade seemed to have no answer ready. But after a moment she broke out: "Because I simply can't bear it any longer—!"

Mrs. Ansley lifted her head quickly. Her eyes were wide and very pale. "Can't bear what?"

"Why—your not knowing that I've always known why you went."

"Why I went—?"

"Yes. You think I'm bluffing, don't you? Well, you went to meet the man I was engaged to—and I can repeat every word of the letter that took you there."

While Mrs. Slade spoke Mrs. Ansley had risen unsteadily to her feet. Her bag, her knitting and gloves, slid in a panic-stricken heap to the ground. She looked at Mrs. Slade as though she were looking at a ghost.

"No, no—don't," she faltered out.

"Why not? Listen, if you don't believe me. 'My one darling, things can't go on like this. I must see you alone. Come to the Colosseum immediately after dark tomorrow. There will be somebody to let you in. No one whom you need fear will suspect'—but perhaps you've forgotten what the letter said?"

Mrs. Ansley met the challenge with an unexpected composure. Steadying herself against the chair she looked at her friend, and replied: "No; I know it by heart too."

"And the signature? 'Only *your* D.S.' Was that it? I'm right, am I? That was the letter that took you out that evening after dark?"

Mrs. Ansley was still looking at her. It seemed to Mrs. Slade that a slow struggle was going on behind the voluntarily controlled mask of her small quiet face. "I shouldn't have thought she had herself so well in hand," Mrs. Slade reflected, almost resentfully. But at this moment Mrs. Ansley spoke. "I don't know how you knew. I burnt that letter at once."

"Yes; you would, naturally—you're so prudent!" The sneer was open now. "And if you burnt the letter you're wondering how on earth I know what was in it. That's it, isn't it?"

Mrs. Slade waited, but Mrs. Ansley did not speak.

"Well, my dear, I know what was in that letter because I wrote it!"

"You wrote it?"

"Yes."

The two women stood for a minute staring at each other in the last golden light. Then Mrs. Ansley dropped back into her chair. "Oh," she murmured, and covered her face with her hands.

Mrs. Slade waited nervously for another word or movement. None came, and at length she broke out: "I horrify you."

Mrs. Ansley's hands dropped to her knee. The face they uncovered was streaked with tears. "I wasn't thinking of you. I was thinking—it was the only letter I ever had from him!"

"And I wrote it. Yes; I wrote it! But I was the girl he was engaged to. Did you happen to remember that?"

Mrs. Ansley's head drooped again. "I'm not trying to excuse myself . . . I remembered. . . ."

"And still you went?"

"Still I went."

Mrs. Slade stood looking down on the small bowed figure at her side. The flame of her wrath had already sunk, and she wondered why she had ever thought there would be any satisfaction in inflicting so purposeless a wound on her friend. But she had to justify herself.

"You do understand? I'd found out—and I hated you, hated you. I knew you were in love with Delphin—and I was afraid; afraid of you, of your quiet ways, your sweetness . . . your . . . well, I wanted you out of the way, that's all. Just for a few weeks; just till I was sure of him. So in a blind fury I wrote that letter . . . I don't know why I'm telling you now."

"I suppose," said Mrs. Ansley slowly, "it's because you've always gone on hating me."

"Perhaps. Or because I wanted to get the whole thing off my mind." She paused. "I'm glad you destroyed the letter. Of course I never thought you'd die."

Mrs. Ansley relapsed into silence, and Mrs. Slade, leaning above her, was conscious of a strange sense of isolation, of being cut off from the warm current of human communion. "You think me a monster!"

"I don't know. . . . It was the only letter I had, and you say he didn't write it?"

"Ah, how you care for him still!"

"I cared for that memory," said Mrs. Ansley.

Mrs. Slade continued to look down on her. She seemed physically reduced by the blow—as if, when she got up, the wind might scatter her like a puff of dust. Mrs. Slade's jealousy suddenly leapt up again at the sight. All these years the woman had been living on that letter. How she must have loved him, to treasure the mere memory of its ashes! The letter of the man her friend was engaged to. Wasn't it she who was the monster?

"You tried your best to get him away from me, didn't you? But you failed; and I kept him. That's all."

"Yes. That's all."

"I wish now I hadn't told you. I'd no idea you'd feel about it as you do; I thought you'd be amused. It all happened so long ago, as you say; and you must do me the justice to remember that I had no reason to think you'd ever taken it seriously. How could I, when you were married to Horace Ansley two months afterward? As soon as you could get out of bed your mother rushed you off to Florence and married you. People were rather surprised—they wondered at its being done so quickly; but I thought I knew. I had an idea you did it out of *pique*—to be able to say you'd got ahead of Delphin and me. Girls have such silly reasons for doing the most serious things. And your marrying so soon convinced me that you'd never really cared."

"Yes. I suppose it would," Mrs. Ansley assented.

The clear heaven overhead was emptied of all its gold. Dusk spread over it, abruptly darkening the Seven Hills.[8] Here and there lights began to twinkle through the foliage at their feet. Steps were coming and going on the deserted terrace—waiters looking out of the doorway at the head of the stairs, then reappearing with trays and napkins and flasks of wine. Tables were moved, chairs straightened. A feeble string of electric lights flickered out. Some vases of faded flowers were carried away, and brought back replenished. A stout lady in a dust coat suddenly appeared, asking in broken Italian if anyone had seen the elastic band which held together her tattered Baedeker. She poked with her stick under the table at which she had lunched, the waiters assisting.

The corner where Mrs. Slade and Mrs. Ansley sat was still shadowy and deserted. For a long time neither of them spoke. At length Mrs. Slade began again: "I suppose I did it as a sort of joke—"

"A joke?"

"Well, girls are ferocious sometimes, you know. Girls in love especially. And I remember laughing to myself all that evening at the idea that you were waiting around there in the dark, dodging out of sight, listening for every sound, trying to get in.—Of course I was upset when I heard you were so ill afterward."

Mrs. Ansley had not moved for a long time. But now she turned slowly toward her companion. "But I didn't wait. He'd arranged everything. He was there. We were let in at once," she said.

8. The Seven Hills of Rome east of the Tiber River form the heart of the city.

Mrs. Slade sprang up from her leaning position. "Delphin there? They let you in?—Ah, now you're lying!" she burst out with violence.

Mrs. Ansley's voice grew clearer, and full of surprise. "But of course he was there. Naturally he came—"

"Came? How did he know he'd find you there? You must be raving!"

Mrs. Ansley hesitated, as though reflecting. "But I answered the letter. I told him I'd be there. So he came."

Mrs. Slade flung her hands up to her face. "Oh, God—you answered! I never thought of your answering. . . ."

"It's odd you never thought of it, if you wrote the letter."

"Yes. I was blind with rage."

Mrs. Ansley rose, and drew her fur scarf about her. "It is cold here. We'd better go . . . I'm sorry for you," she said, as she clasped the fur about her throat.

The unexpected words sent a pang through Mrs. Slade. "Yes; we'd better go." She gathered up her bag and cloak. "I don't know why you should be sorry for me," she muttered.

Mrs. Ansley stood looking away from her toward the dusky secret mass of the Colosseum. "Well—because I didn't have to wait that night."

Mrs. Slade gave an unquiet laugh. "Yes; I was beaten there. But I oughtn't to begrudge it to you, I suppose. At the end of all these years. After all, I had everything; I had him for twenty-five years. And you had nothing but that one letter that he didn't write."

Mrs. Ansley was again silent. At length she turned toward the door of the terrace. She took a step, and turned back, facing her companion.

"I had Barbara," she said, and began to move ahead of Mrs. Slade toward the stairway.

1934

SUI SIN FAR (EDITH MAUD EATON)
1865–1914

Much remains unknown about Sui Sin Far, though a sense of both her vulnerability and her toughness can be strongly felt in such late autobiographical accounts as "Leaves from the Mental Portfolio of an Eurasian" (1909) and "Sui Sin Far, the Half-Chinese Writer, Tells of Her Career" (1912). The second of sixteen children, fourteen of whom lived to adulthood, Far was born Edith Maud Eaton in Macclesfield, England, to a Chinese mother raised in England and a white English father from a well-to-do family. Her father, Edward Eaton, formerly a merchant, became alienated from his English family not long after his marriage to Grace Trefusis and struggled thereafter to earn a living as a landscape painter. When Far was seven the family moved first to New York State and then to Montreal. The family's fortunes began to decline when Far was eleven, and along with other siblings she was withdrawn from school to help support her parents and the younger children by selling on the street her father's paintings and her own crocheted lace. She continued to support family members for the rest of her life, though her income as a stenographer and freelance journalist barely covered her own modest needs and her health was always fragile, partly as a result of childhood rheumatic fever.

Sui Sin Far and her sister Winnifred were published while they were teenagers; two other sisters became painters, and another sister became the first Chinese American lawyer in Chicago. Winnifred, who wrote under the Japanese-sounding pseudonym Onoto Watanna, published the first Asian American novel, *Miss Nume of Japan,* in 1899, and was popular for many years as the author of sentimental and melodramatic novels.

Though Sui Sin Far began her writing career in Montreal, it was not until 1896, after she moved to the United States, that she adopted her pseudonym, a literal translation of the symbol for waterlily as water fairy flower, or, more generally, bulbs that can sprout and bloom in water. That same year she published her first story, in the American literary magazine *Fly Leaf.* From 1898 to 1909 she lived chiefly in Seattle, where her work as a journalist took her into the city's thriving Chinatown. She also lived briefly in San Francisco and other U.S. West Coast cities. She spent her last years in Boston.

"Mrs. Spring Fragrance" was first published in *Hampton's Magazine* in January 1910. In 1912 it became the title story for the only book Sui Sin Far published, containing thirty-seven stories, articles, and sketches, some of them previously published, focusing on Chinese immigrants in late nineteenth-century America. The stories in *Mrs. Spring Fragrance,* set mainly in Seattle, often involve conflict in well-off merchant immigrant families when members of a family differ over the desirability or even the possibility of Americanizing. One spouse is usually more devoted to traditional values than the other, while children are typically more eager to become American than their parents. Maxine Hong Kingston, Amy Tan, and David Henry Hwang, among other contemporary Asian American writers, continue to examine many of the issues Sui Sin Far first introduced to American readers.

Mrs. Spring Fragrance[1]

I

When Mrs. Spring Fragrance first arrived in Seattle, she was unacquainted with even one word of the American language. Five years later her husband, speaking of her, said: "There are no more American words for her learning." And everyone who knew Mrs. Spring Fragrance agreed with Mr. Spring Fragrance.

Mr. Spring Fragrance, whose business name was Sing Yook, was a young curio merchant. Though conservatively Chinese in many respects, he was at the same time what is called by the Westerners, "Americanized." Mrs. Spring Fragrance was even more "Americanized."

Next door to the Spring Fragrances lived the Chin Yuens. Mrs. Chin Yuen was much older than Mrs. Spring Fragrance; but she had a daughter of eighteen with whom Mrs. Spring Fragrance was on terms of great friendship. The daughter was a pretty girl whose Chinese name was Mai Gwi Far (a rose) and whose American name was Laura. Nearly everybody called her Laura, even her parents and Chinese friends. Laura had a sweetheart, a youth named Kai Tzu. Kai Tzu, who was American-born, and as ruddy and stalwart as any

---

1. The story was first published in the January 1910 *Hampton's Magazine,* based in New York City, and then republished in *Mrs. Spring Fra-* *grance and Other Stories* (Chicago: A. C. McClurg, 1912), from which this text is taken.

young Westerner, was noted amongst baseball players as one of the finest pitchers on the Coast. He could also sing, "Drink to me only with thine eyes,"[2] to Laura's piano accompaniment.

Now the only person who knew that Kai Tzu loved Laura and that Laura loved Kai Tzu, was Mrs. Spring Fragrance. The reason for this was that, although the Chin Yuen parents lived in a house furnished in American style, and wore American clothes, yet they religiously observed many Chinese customs, and their ideals of life were the ideals of their Chinese forefathers. Therefore, they had betrothed their daughter, Laura, at the age of fifteen, to the eldest son of the Chinese Government school-teacher in San Francisco. The time for the consummation of the betrothal was approaching.

Laura was with Mrs. Spring Fragrance and Mrs. Spring Fragrance was trying to cheer her.

"I had such a pretty walk today," said she. "I crossed the banks above the beach and came back by the long road. In the green grass the daffodils were blowing, in the cottage gardens the currant bushes were flowering, and in the air was the perfume of the wallflower. I wished, Laura, that you were with me."

Laura burst into tears. "That is the walk," she sobbed, "Kai Tzu and I so love; but never, ah, never, can we take it together again."

"Now, Little Sister," comforted Mrs. Spring Fragrance, "you really must not grieve like that. Is there not a beautiful American poem written by a noble American named Tennyson, which says:

"'Tis better to have loved and lost,
Than never to have loved at all?"[3]

Mrs. Spring Fragrance was unaware that Mr. Spring Fragrance, having returned from the city, tired with the day's business, had thrown himself down on the bamboo settee on the veranda, and that although his eyes were engaged in scanning the pages of the *Chinese World*,[4] his ears could not help receiving the words which were borne to him through the open window.

"'Tis better to have loved and lost,
Than never to have loved at all,"

repeated Mr. Spring Fragrance. Not wishing to hear more of the secret talk of women, he arose and sauntered around the veranda to the other side of the house. Two pigeons circled around his head. He felt in his pocket for a li-chi which he usually carried for their pecking. His fingers touched a little box. It contained a jadestone pendant, which Mrs. Spring Fragrance had particularly admired the last time she was down town. It was the fifth anniversary of Mr. and Mrs. Spring Fragrance's wedding day.

Mr. Spring Fragrance pressed the little box down into the depths of his pocket.

A young man came out of the back door of the house at Mr. Spring Fragrance's left. The Chin Yuen house was at his right.

2. Popular English folk song, which drew on Ben Jonson's (1572–1637) 1616 poem "Song to Celia."
3. From the English poet Alfred, Lord Tennyson's (1809–1892) *In Memoriam* (1850), an elegy for his beloved friend Arthur Hallam: "I hold it true, whate'er befall;/I feel it, when I sorrow most;/'Tis better to have loved and lost / Than never to have loved at all" (canto 27, 13–16).
4. A newspaper published in San Francisco's Chinatown at the time the story was set.

"Good evening," said the young man. "Good evening," returned Mr. Spring Fragrance. He stepped down from his porch and went and leaned over the railing which separated this yard from the yard in which stood the young man.

"Will you please tell me," said Mr. Spring Fragrance, "the meaning of two lines of an American verse which I have heard?"

"Certainly," returned the young man with a genial smile. He was a star student at the University of Washington, and had not the slightest doubt that he could explain the meaning of all things in the universe.

"Well," said Mr. Spring Fragrance, "it is this:

"'Tis better to have loved and lost,
Than never to have loved at all.'"

"Ah!" responded the young man with an air of profound wisdom. "That, Mr. Spring Fragrance, means that it is a good thing to love anyway—even if we can't get what we love, or, as the poet tells us, lose what we love. Of course, one needs experience to feel the truth of this teaching."

The young man smiled pensively and reminiscently. More than a dozen young maidens "loved and lost" were passing before his mind's eye.

"The truth of the teaching!" echoed Mr. Spring Fragrance, a little testily. "There is no truth in it whatever. It is disobedient to reason. Is it not better to have what you do not love than to love what you do not have?"

"That depends," answered the young man, "upon temperament."

"I thank you. Good evening," said Mr. Spring Fragrance. He turned away to muse upon the unwisdom of the American way of looking at things.

Meanwhile, inside the house, Laura was refusing to be comforted.

"Ah, no! no!" cried she. "If I had not gone to school with Kai Tzu, nor talked nor walked with him, nor played the accompaniments to his songs, then I might consider with complacency, or at least without horror, my approaching marriage with the son of Man You. But as it is—oh, as it is—!"

The girl rocked herself to and fro in heartfelt grief.

Mrs. Spring Fragrance knelt down beside her, and clasping her arms around her neck, cried in sympathy:

"Little Sister, oh, Little Sister! Dry your tears—do not despair. A moon has yet to pass before the marriage can take place. Who knows what the stars may have to say to one another during its passing? A little bird has whispered to me—"

For a long time Mrs. Spring Fragrance talked. For a long time Laura listened. When the girl arose to go, there was a bright light in her eyes.

II

Mrs. Spring Fragrance, in San Francisco on a visit to her cousin, the wife of the herb doctor of Clay Street, was having a good time. She was invited everywhere that the wife of an honorable Chinese merchant could go. There was much to see and hear, including more than a dozen babies who had been born in the families of her friends since she last visited the city of the Golden Gate. Mrs. Spring Fragrance loved babies. She had had two herself, but both had been transplanted into the spirit land before the completion of even one moon. There were also many dinners and theatre-parties given in her honor. It was at one of the theatre-parties that Mrs. Spring Fragrance met Ah Oi, a young girl who had the reputation of being the prettiest Chinese girl in San Francisco, and the naughtiest. In spite of gossip, however, Mrs. Spring Fragrance took a great fancy to Ah Oi and invited her to a têté-à-tête picnic on the following day. This invitation Ah Oi joyfully accepted. She was a sort of bird girl and never felt so happy as when out in the park or woods.

On the day after the picnic Mrs. Spring Fragrance wrote to Laura Chin Yuen thus:

> MY PRECIOUS LAURA,—May the bamboo ever wave. Next week I accompany Ah Oi to the beauteous town of San José. There will we be met by the son of the Illustrious Teacher, and in a little Mission, presided over by a benevolent American priest, the little Ah Oi and the son of the Illustrious Teacher will be joined together in love and harmony— two pieces of music made to complete one another.
>
> The Son of the Illustrious Teacher, having been through an American Hall of Learning, is well able to provide for his orphan bride and fears not the displeasure of his parents, now that he is assured that your grief at his loss will not be inconsolable. He wishes me to waft to you and to Kai Tzu—and the little Ah Oi joins with him—ten thousand rainbow wishes for your happiness.
>
> My respects to your honorable parents, and to yourself, the heart of your loving friend,
>
> JADE SPRING FRAGRANCE

To Mr. Spring Fragrance, Mrs. Spring Fragrance also indited a letter:

> GREAT AND HONORED MAN,—Greeting from your plum blossom,[5] who is desirous of hiding herself from the sun of your presence for a week of seven days more. My honorable cousin is preparing for the Fifth Moon Festival, and wishes me to compound for the occasion some American "fudge," for which delectable sweet, made by my clumsy hands, you have sometimes shown a slight prejudice. I am enjoying a most agreeable visit, and American friends, as also our own, strive benevolently for the accomplishment of my pleasure. Mrs. Samuel Smith, an American lady, known to my cousin, asked for my accompaniment to a magniloquent lecture the other evening. The subject was "America, the Protector of China!" It was most exhilarating, and the effect of so much expression of benevolence leads me to beg of you to forget to remember that the barber charges you one dollar for a shave while he humbly submits to the American man a bill of fifteen cents. And murmur no more because your honored elder brother, on a visit to this country, is detained under the roof-tree of this great Government instead of under your own humble roof. Console him with the reflection that he is protected under the wing of the Eagle, the Emblem of Liberty. What is the loss of ten hundred years or ten thousand times ten dollars compared with the happiness of knowing oneself so securely sheltered? All of this I have

5. The plum blossom is the Chinese flower of virtue. It has been adopted by the Japanese, just in the same way as they have adopted the Chinese national flower, the chrysanthemum [Sui Sin Far's note].

learned from Mrs. Samuel Smith, who is as brilliant and great of mind as one of your own superior sex.

For me it is sufficient to know that the Golden Gate Park is most enchanting, and the seals on the rock at the Cliff House[6] extremely entertaining and amiable. There is much feasting and merry-making under the lanterns in honor of your Stupid Thorn.

I have purchased for your smoking a pipe with an amber mouth. It is said to be very sweet to the lips and to emit a cloud of smoke fit for the gods to inhale.

Awaiting, by the wonderful wire of the telegram message, your gracious permission to remain for the celebration of the Fifth Moon Festival and the making of American "fudge," I continue for ten thousand times ten thousand years,

> Your ever loving and obedient woman,
>
> JADE

P.S. Forget not to care for the cat, the birds, and the flowers. Do not eat too quickly nor fan too vigorously now that the weather is warming.

Mrs. Spring Fragrance smiled as she folded this last epistle. Even if he were old-fashioned, there was never a husband so good and kind as hers. Only on one occasion since their marriage had he slighted her wishes. That was when, on the last anniversary of their wedding, she had signified a desire for a certain jadestone pendant, and he had failed to satisfy that desire.

But Mrs Spring Fragrance, being of a happy nature, and disposed to look upon the bright side of things, did not allow her mind to dwell upon the jadestone pendant. Instead, she gazed complacently down upon her bejeweled fingers and folded in with her letter to Mr. Spring Fragrance a bright little sheaf of condensed love.

III

Mr. Spring Fragrance sat on his doorstep. He had been reading two letters, one from Mrs. Spring Fragrance, and the other from an elderly bachelor cousin in San Francisco. The one from the elderly bachelor cousin was a business letter, but contained the following postscript:

Tsen Hing, the son of the Government schoolmaster, seems to be much in the company of your young wife. He is a good-looking youth, and pardon me, my dear cousin; but if women are allowed to stray at will from under their husbands' mulberry roofs, what is to prevent them from becoming butterflies?

"Sing Foon is old and cynical," said Mr. Spring Fragrance to himself. "Why should I pay any attention to him? This is America, where a man may speak to a woman, and a woman listen, without any thought of evil."

He destroyed his cousin's letter and re-read his wife's. Then he became very thoughtful. Was the making of American fudge sufficient reason for a wife to wish to remain a week longer in a city where her husband was not?

---

6. Famous restaurant on the Pacific shore at Point Lobos in San Francisco; it opened in 1863 and, because of its setting, became a favorite of locals and visitors.

The young man who lived in the next house came out to water the lawn.

"Good evening," said he. "Any news from Mrs. Spring Fragrance?"

"She is having a very good time," returned Mr. Spring Fragrance.

"Glad to hear it. I think you told me she was to return the end of this week."

"I have changed my mind about her," said Mr. Spring Fragrance. "I am bidding her remain a week longer, as I wish to give a smoking party during her absence. I hope I may have the pleasure of your company."

"I shall be delighted," returned the young fellow. "But, Mr. Spring Fragrance, don't invite any other white fellows. If you do not I shall be able to get in a scoop. You know, I'm a sort of honorary reporter for the _Gleaner_."[7]

"Very well," absently answered Mr. Spring Fragrance.

"Of course, your friend the Consul will be present. I shall call it 'A high-class Chinese stag party!'"

In spite of his melancholy mood, Mr. Spring Fragrance smiled.

"Everything is 'high-class' in America," he observed.

"Sure!" cheerfully assented the young man. "Haven't you ever heard that all Americans are princes and princesses, and just as soon as a foreigner puts his foot upon our shores, he also becomes of the nobility—I mean, the royal family."

"What about my brother in the Detention Pen?" dryly inquired Mr. Spring Fragrance.

"Now, you've got me," said the young man, rubbing his head. "Well, that is a shame—'a beastly shame,' as the Englishman says. But understand, old fellow, we that are real Americans are up against that—even more than you. It is against our principles."

"I offer the real Americans my consolations that they should be compelled to do that which is against their principles."

"Oh, well, it will all come right some day. We're not a bad sort, you know. Think of the indemnity money returned to the Dragon by Uncle Sam."[8]

Mr. Spring Fragrance puffed his pipe in silence for some moments. More than politics was troubling his mind.

At last he spoke. "Love," said he, slowly and distinctly, "comes before the wedding in this country, does it not?"

"Yes, certainly."

Young Carman knew Mr. Spring Fragrance well enough to receive with calmness his most astounding queries.

"Presuming," continued Mr. Spring Fragrance—"presuming that some friend of your father's, living—presuming—in England—has a daughter that he arranges with your father to be your wife. Presuming that you have never seen that daughter, but that you marry her, knowing her not. Presuming that she marries you, knowing you not.—After she marries you and knows you, will that woman love you?"

"Emphatically, no," answered the young man.

"That is the way it would be in America—that the woman who marries the man like that—would not love him?"

"Yes, that is the way it would be in America. Love, in this country, must be free, or it is not love at all."

---

7. Perhaps a reference to the _Weekly Gleaner_, a Jewish American newspaper in San Francisco that began publication in 1857, but "_Gleaner_" was also the generic name of a number of newspapers.

8. Historically, the dragon was the symbol of the Emperor of China, as Uncle Sam is a symbol of the United States.

"In China, it is different!" mused Mr. Spring Fragrance.

"Oh, yes, I have no doubt that in China it is different."

"But the love is in the heart all the same," went on Mr. Spring Fragrance.

"Yes, all the same. Everybody falls in love some time or another. Some"—pensively—"many times."

Mr. Spring Fragrance arose.

"I must go down town," said he.

As he walked down the street he recalled the remark of a business acquaintance who had met his wife and had had some conversation with her: "She is just like an American woman."

He had felt somewhat flattered when this remark had been made. He looked upon it as a compliment to his wife's cleverness; but it rankled in his mind as he entered the telegraph office. If his wife was becoming as an American woman, would it not be possible for her to love as an American woman—a man to whom she was not married? There also floated in his memory the verse which his wife had quoted to the daughter of Chin Yuen. When the telegraph clerk handed him a blank, he wrote this message:

"Remain as you wish, but remember that ''Tis better to have loved and lost, than never to have loved at all.'"

When Mrs. Spring Fragrance received this message, her laughter tinkled like falling water. How droll! How delightful! Here was her husband quoting American poetry in a telegram. Perhaps he had been reading her American poetry books since she had left him! She hoped so. They would lead him to understand her sympathy for her dear Laura and Kai Tzu. She need no longer keep from him their secret. How joyful! It had been such a hardship to refrain from confiding in him before. But discreetness had been most necessary, seeing that Mr. Spring Fragrance entertained as old-fashioned notions concerning marriage as did the Chin Yuen parents. Strange that that should be so, since he had fallen in love with her picture before *ever* he had seen her, just as she had fallen in love with his! And when the marriage veil was lifted and each beheld the other for the first time in the flesh, there had been no disillusion—no lessening of the respect and affection, which those who had brought about the marriage had inspired in each young heart.

Mrs. Spring Fragrance began to wish she could fall asleep and wake to find the week flown, and she in her own little home pouring tea for Mr. Spring Fragrance.

IV

Mr. Spring Fragrance was walking to business with Mr. Chin Yuen. As they walked they talked.

"Yes," said Mr. Chin Yuen, "the old order is passing away, and the new order is taking its place, even with us who are Chinese. I have finally consented to give my daughter in marriage to young Kai Tzu."

Mr. Spring Fragrance expressed surprise. He had understood that the marriage between his neighbor's daughter and the San Francisco schoolteacher's son was all arranged.

"So 'twas," answered Mr. Chin Yuen; "but it seems the young renegade, without consultation or advice, has placed his affections upon some untrustworthy female, and is so under her influence that he refuses to fulfil his parents' promise to me for him."

"So!" said Mr. Spring Fragrance. The shadow on his brow deepened.

"But," said Mr. Chin Yuen, with affable resignation, "it is all ordained by Heaven. Our daughter, as the wife of Kai Tzu, for whom she has long had a loving feeling, will not now be compelled to dwell with a mother-in-law and where her own mother is not. For that, we are thankful, as she is our only one and the conditions of life in this Western country are not as in China. Moreover, Kai Tzu, though not so much of a scholar as the teacher's son, has a keen eye for business and that, in America, is certainly much more desirable than scholarship. What do you think?"

"Eh! What!" exclaimed Mr. Spring Fragrance. The latter part of his companion's remarks had been lost upon him.

That day the shadow which had been following Mr. Spring Fragrance ever since he had heard his wife quote, "'Tis better to have loved," etc., became so heavy and deep that he quite lost himself within it.

At home in the evening he fed the cat, the bird, and the flowers. Then, seating himself in a carved black chair—a present from his wife on his last birthday—he took out his pipe and smoked. The cat jumped into his lap. He stroked it softly and tenderly. It had been much fondled by Mrs. Spring Fragrance, and Mr. Spring Fragrance was under the impression that it missed her. "Poor thing!" said he. "I suppose you want her back!" When he arose to go to bed he placed the animal carefully on the floor, and thus apostrophized it:

"O Wise and Silent One, your mistress returns to you, but her heart she leaves behind her, with the Tommies in San Francisco."

The Wise and Silent. One made no reply. He was not a jealous cat.

Mr. Spring Fragrance slept not that night; the next morning he ate not. Three days and three nights without sleep and food went by.

There was a springlike freshness in the air on the day that Mrs. Spring Fragrance came home. The skies overhead were as blue as Puget Sound stretching its gleaming length toward the mighty Pacific, and all the beautiful green world seemed to be throbbing with springing life.

Mrs. Spring Fragrance was never so radiant.

"Oh," she cried light-heartedly, "is it not lovely to see the sun shining so clear, and everything so bright to welcome me?"

Mr. Spring Fragrance made no response. It was the morning after the fourth sleepless night.

Mrs. Spring Fragrance noticed his silence, also his grave face.

"Everything—everyone is glad to see me but you," she declared, half seriously, half jestingly.

Mr. Spring Fragrance set down her valise. They had just entered the house.

"If my wife is glad to see me," he quietly replied, "I also am glad to see her!"

Summoning their servant boy, he bade him look after Mrs. Spring Fragrance's comfort.

"I must be at the store in half an hour," said he, looking at his watch. "There is some very important business requiring attention."

"What is the business?" inquired Mrs. Spring Fragrance, her lip quivering with disappointment.

"I cannot just explain to you," answered her husband.

Mrs. Spring Fragrance looked up into his face with honest and earnest eyes. There was something in his manner, in the tone of her husband's voice, which touched her.

"Yen," said she, "you do not look well. You are not well. What is it?"

Something arose in Mr. Spring Fragrance's throat which prevented him from replying.

"O darling one! O sweetest one!" cried a girl's joyous voice. Laura Chin Yuen ran into the room and threw her arms around Mrs. Spring Fragrance's neck.

"I spied you from the window," said Laura, "and I couldn't rest until I told you. We are to be married next week, Kai Tzu and I. And all through you, all through you—the sweetest jade jewel in the world!"

Mr. Spring Fragrance passed out of the room.

"So the son of the Government teacher and little Happy Love are already married," Laura went on, relieving Mrs. Spring Fragrance of her cloak, her hat, and her folding fan.

Mr. Spring Fragrance paused upon the doorstep.

"Sit down, Little Sister, and I will tell you all about it," said Mrs. Spring Fragrance, forgetting her husband for a moment.

When Laura Chin Yuen had danced away, Mr. Spring Fragrance came in and hung up his hat.

"You got back very soon," said Mrs. Spring Fragrance, covertly wiping away the tears which had begun to fall as soon as she thought herself alone.

"I did not go," answered Mr. Spring Fragrance. "I have been listening to you and Laura."

"But if the business is very important, do not you think you should attend to it?" anxiously queried Mrs. Spring Fragrance.

"It is not important to me now," returned Mr. Spring Fragrance. "I would prefer to hear again about Ah Oi and Man You and Laura and Kai Tzu."

"How lovely of you to say that!" exclaimed Mrs. Spring Fragrance, who was easily made happy. And she began to chat away to her husband in the friendliest and wifeliest fashion possible. When she had finished she asked him if he were not glad to hear that those who loved as did the young lovers whose secrets she had been keeping, were to be united; and he replied that indeed he was; that he would like every man to be as happy with a wife as he himself had ever been and ever would be.

"You did not always talk like that," said Mrs. Spring Fragrance slyly. "You must have been reading my American poetry books!"

"American poetry!" ejaculated Mr. Spring Fragrance almost fiercely, "American poetry is detestable, *abhorrable*!"

"Why! why!" exclaimed Mrs. Spring Fragrance, more and more surprised.

But the only explanation which Mr. Spring Fragrance vouchsafed was a jadestone pendant.

1910   1912

W. E. B. DU BOIS
1868–1963

William Edward Burghardt Du Bois was born on February 23, 1868, in Great Barrington, Massachusetts. His childhood was happy; but with the approach of adolescence Du Bois discovered that what made him different from his schoolmates was not so much his superior academic achievement as his brown skin. Looking back on his childhood in a predominately white town, Du Bois wrote, "It dawned on me with a certain suddenness, that I was . . . shut out from their world by a vast veil," a veil beyond which he claimed to have no desire to force his way. Du Bois's entire career, nonetheless, may be understood as an unremitting struggle for civil and political rights for African Americans and for human rights around the world.

Du Bois was educated at Fisk University in Nashville, Tennessee, where he received a bachelor's degree in 1888; Harvard University, where he received a second bachelor's degree in 1890 and a master's degree in 1891; the University of Berlin (1892–94); and then Harvard again, where he received a Ph.D. in history in 1895. His doctoral dissertation, *The Suppression of the African Slave Trade to the United States of America, 1638–1870,* was published as the first volume in the Harvard Historical Studies series in 1896. By the time Du Bois completed his graduate studies his accomplishments were already considerable, but he could not secure an appointment at a major research university. He taught first instead at Wilberforce College in Ohio, at that time a small, poor, black college. There he offered Greek, Latin, German, and English—subjects far removed from his real interest in the emerging field of sociology.

After spending a year at the University of Pennsylvania, where he did the research for *The Philadelphia Negro* (1899), the first sociological monograph on an African American community, Du Bois moved to Atlanta University in 1897. There, over the following thirteen years, he produced a steady stream of important studies of African American life. Dedicated to the rigorous, scholarly examination of the so-called Negro problem, Du Bois soon had to face up to the violent realities of the lives he proposed to study. On his way to present an appeal for reason in the case of a black man accused of murder and rape, Du Bois was met by the news that a lynch mob had killed and dismembered the man and that "his knuckles were on exhibition at a grocery store." Though Du Bois never ceased being a scholar, from this time on he increasingly became an activist and sought a wider audience for his writings.

Du Bois first came to national attention with the publication of *The Souls of Black Folk* (1903), characterized by scholar Eric J. Sundquist as "the preeminent text of African American cultural consciousness." Several chapters explore the implications of this extraordinary book's dramatic and prophetic announcement in its "Forethought" that "the problem of the Twentieth Century is the problem of the color-line." In the first chapter, "Of Our Spiritual Strivings," Du Bois introduces a key concept that would inform his thinking for the rest of his career—the notion of the "twoness" of African Americans: "One ever feels his twoness," Du Bois asserts, "an American, a Negro; two souls, two thoughts, two unreconciled strivings; two warring ideals in one dark body, whose dogged strength alone keeps it from being torn asunder." This foundational observation described what Du Bois named "double-consciousness." Another of Du Bois's important ideas was the Talented Tenth, the title of an essay he published as the second chapter of *The Negro Problem* (1903). By this he meant a college-educated elite that could provide leadership for African Americans after

W. E. B. Du Bois in his office at Atlanta University, c. 1905.

Reconstruction. In this regard the chapter in *Souls of Black Folk* that particularly caused a stir when the volume was first published was the one that challenged—coolly and without rancor—the enormous authority and power that had accumulated in the hands of one black spokesman, Booker T. Washington. Washington had founded Tuskegee Institute in Alabama to train African Americans in basic agricultural and mechanical skills and had gained national prominence with his Atlanta Exposition speech in 1895. His address seemed to many people to accept disenfranchisement and segregation and settle for a low level of education in exchange for white "toleration" and economic cooperation. Although Du Bois had initially joined in the general approval of this "separate and unequal" philosophy, by the early 1900s he had begun to reject Washington's position, and with the publication of *Souls of Black Folk* his public defiance of Washington put the two men in lasting opposition. The almost immediate repudiation of *Souls of Black Folk* by Washington's allies reinforced Du Bois's emerging radicalism; he became a leader in the Niagara Movement (1905), which aggressively demanded for African Americans the same civil rights enjoyed by white Americans.

In 1910 Du Bois left Atlanta for New York, where he served for the next quarter of a century as editor of the *Crisis,* the official publication of the newly formed National Association for the Advancement of Colored People (NAACP), an organization he helped create. Through this publication Du Bois reached an increasingly large audience—one hundred thousand by 1919—with powerful messages that argued the need for black development and white social enlightenment.

Frustrated by the lack of fundamental change and progress in the condition of African Americans, from 1920 on Du Bois shifted his attention from the reform of race relations in America through research and political legislation to the search for longer-range worldwide economic solutions to the international problems of inequity among the races. He began a steady movement toward Pan-African and socialist perspectives that led to his joining the U.S. Communist Party in 1961 and, in the year of his death, becoming a citizen of Ghana. During these forty years he was extremely active as a politician, organizer, and diplomat, and he continued as a powerful writer of poetry, fiction, autobiography, essays, and scholarly works. When, in his last major speech, Martin Luther King Jr. spoke of Du Bois as "one of the most remarkable men of our time," he was uttering the verdict of history.

From The Souls of Black Folk[1]

I. Of Our Spiritual Strivings

O water, voice of my heart, crying in the sand,
    All night long crying with a mournful cry,
As I lie and listen, and cannot understand
      The voice of my heart in my side or the voice of the sea,
    O water, crying for rest, is it I, is it I?
      All night long the water is crying to me.

Unresting water, there shall never be rest
    Till the last moon droop and the last tide fail,
And the fire of the end begin to burn in the west;
      And the heart shall be weary and wonder and cry like the sea,
    All life long crying without avail,
      As the water all night long is crying to me.

ARTHUR SYMONS[2]

Between me and the other world there is ever an unasked question: unasked by some through feelings of delicacy; by others through the difficulty of rightly framing it. All, nevertheless, flutter round it. They approach me in a half-hesitant sort of way, eye me curiously or compassionately, and then, instead of saying directly, How does it feel to be a problem? they say, I know an excellent colored man in my town; or, I fought at Mechanicsville;[3] or, Do not these Southern outrages make your blood boil? At these I smile, or am interested, or reduce the boiling to a simmer, as the occasion may require. To the real question, How does it feel to be a problem? I answer seldom a word.

And yet, being a problem is a strange experience,—peculiar even for one who has never been anything else, save perhaps in babyhood and in Europe. It is in the early days of rollicking boyhood that the revelation first bursts upon one, all in a day, as it were. I remember well when the shadow swept across me. I was a little thing, away up in the hills of New England, where the dark Housatonic winds between Hoosac and Taghkanic[4] to the sea. In a wee wooden schoolhouse, something put it into the boys' and girls' heads to buy gorgeous visiting-cards—ten cents a package—and exchange. The exchange was merry, till one girl, a tall newcomer, refused my card,—refused it peremptorily, with a glance. Then it dawned upon me with a certain suddenness that I was different from the others; or like, mayhap, in heart and life and longing, but shut out from their world by a vast veil. I had thereafter no desire to tear down that veil, to creep through; I held all beyond it in common contempt, and lived above it in a region of blue sky and great wandering shadows. That

---

1. *The Souls of Black Folk*, a compilation of nine previously printed and five unpublished essays, appeared first as a book in 1903, the source of the text printed here.
2. English poet (1865–1945); the quotation is from "The Crying of Water" (1903).

3. Civil War battle in Virginia, June 26, 1862, resulting in heavy Confederate losses.
4. Mountain ranges partly in Massachusetts, partly in Vermont. The Housatonic is a river in western Massachussetts.

sky was bluest when I could beat my mates at examination-time, or beat them at a foot-race, or even beat their stringy heads. Alas, with the years all this fine contempt began to fade; for the worlds I longed for, and all their dazzling opportunities, were theirs, not mine. But they should not keep these prizes, I said; some, all, I would wrest from them. Just how I would do it I could never decide: by reading law, by healing the sick, by telling the wonderful tales that swam in my head,—some way. With other black boys the strife was not so fiercely sunny: their youth shrunk into tasteless sycophancy, or into silent hatred of the pale world about them and mocking distrust of everything white; or wasted itself in a bitter cry, Why did God make me an outcast and a stranger in mine own house? The shades of the prison-house closed round about us all: walls strait and stubborn to the whitest, but relentlessly narrow, tall, and unscalable to sons of night who must plod darkly on in resignation, or beat unavailing palms against the stone, or steadily, half hopelessly, watch the streak of blue above.

After the Egyptian and Indian, the Greek and Roman, the Teuton and Mongolian, the Negro is a sort of seventh son, born with a veil, and gifted with second-sight in this American world,—a world which yields him no true self-consciousness, but only lets him see himself through the revelation of the other world. It is a peculiar sensation, this double-consciousness, this sense of always looking at one's self through the eyes of others, of measuring one's soul by the tape of a world that looks on in amused contempt and pity. One ever feels his two-ness,—an American, a Negro; two souls, two thoughts, two unreconciled strivings; two warring ideals in one dark body, whose dogged strength alone keeps it from being torn asunder.

The history of the American Negro is the history of this strife,—this longing to attain self-conscious manhood, to merge his double self into a better and truer self. In this merging he wishes neither of the older selves to be lost. He would not Africanize America, for America has too much to teach the world and Africa. He would not bleach his Negro soul in a flood of white Americanism, for he knows that Negro blood has a message for the world. He simply wishes to make it possible for a man to be both a Negro and an American, without being cursed and spit upon by his fellows, without having the doors of Opportunity closed roughly in his face.

This, then, is the end of his striving: to be a co-worker in the kingdom of culture, to escape both death and isolation, to husband and use his best powers and his latent genius. These powers of body and mind have in the past been strangely wasted, dispersed, or forgotten. The shadow of a mighty Negro past flits through the tale of Ethiopia the Shadowy and of Egypt the Sphinx. Throughout history, the powers of single black men flash here and there like falling stars, and die sometimes before the world has rightly gauged their brightness. Here in America, in the few days since Emancipation, the black man's turning hither and thither in hesitant and doubtful striving has often made his very strength to lose effectiveness, to seem like absence of power, like weakness. And yet it is not weakness,—it is the contradiction of double aims. The double-aimed struggle of the black artisan—on the one hand to escape white contempt for a nation of mere hewers of wood and drawers of water, and on the other hand to plough and nail and dig for a poverty-stricken horde—could only result in making him a poor craftsman, for he had but half a heart in either cause. By the poverty and ignorance of his people, the Negro minister or doctor was tempted toward quackery and demagogy; and by the criticism of the other world, toward ideals that made him ashamed of his lowly tasks. The would-be black *savant*[5] was confronted by the paradox that the knowledge his people needed was a twice-told tale to his white neighbors, while the knowledge which would teach the white world was Greek to his own flesh and blood. The innate love of harmony and beauty that set the ruder souls of his people a-dancing and a-singing raised but confusion and doubt in the soul of the black artist; for the beauty revealed to him was the soul-beauty of a race which his larger audience despised, and he could not articulate the message of another people. This waste of double aims, this seeking to satisfy two unreconciled ideals, has wrought sad havoc with the courage and faith and deeds of ten thousand thousand people,—has sent them often wooing false gods and invoking false means of salvation, and at times has even seemed about to make them ashamed of themselves.

Away back in the days of bondage they thought to see in one divine event the end of all doubt and disappointment; few men ever worshipped Freedom with half such unquestioning faith as did the American Negro for two centuries. To him, so far as he thought and dreamed, slavery was indeed the sum of all villainies, the cause of all sorrow, the root of all prejudice; Emancipation was the key to a promised land of sweeter beauty than ever stretched before the eyes of wearied Israelites. In song and exhortation swelled one refrain—Liberty; in his tears and curses the God he implored had Freedom in his right hand. At last it came,—suddenly, fearfully, like a dream. With one wild carnival of blood and passion came the message in his own plaintive cadences:—

> "Shout, O children!
> Shout, you're free!
> For God has bought your liberty!"[6]

Years have passed away since then,—ten, twenty, forty; forty years of national life, forty years of renewal and development, and yet the swarthy spectre sits in its accustomed seat at the Nation's feast. In vain do we cry to this our vastest social problem:—

> "Take any shape but that, and my firm nerves
> Shall never tremble!"[7]

The Nation has not yet found peace from its sins; the freedman has not yet found in freedom his promised land. Whatever of good may have come in these years of change, the shadow of a deep disappointment rests upon the Negro people,—a disappointment all the more bitter because the unattained ideal was unbounded save by the simple ignorance of a lowly people.

The first decade was merely a prolongation of the vain search for freedom, the boon that seemed ever barely to elude their grasp,—like a tantalizing will-o'-the-wisp, maddening and misleading the headless host. The holocaust of war, the terrors of the Ku-Klux Klan, the lies of carpetbaggers,[8] the disorganization of industry, and the contradictory advice of friends and foes, left the bewildered serf with no new watchword beyond the old

5. Learned person.
6. Source unidentified.
7. Shakespeare, *Macbeth* 3.2.99.
8. Used as an epithet in the South to describe Northerners who came to the South during Reconstruction to make money by exploiting conditions created by the devastation of the Civil War. Many carried luggage made of carpet materials. "Ku Klux Klan": a secretive and often violent white supremacist society founded in the South shortly after the Civil War.

cry for freedom. As the time flew, however, he began to grasp a new idea. The ideal of liberty demanded for its attainment powerful means, and these the Fifteenth Amendment[9] gave him. The ballot, which before he had looked upon as a visible sign of freedom, he now regarded as the chief means of gaining and perfecting the liberty with which war had partially endowed him. And why not? Had not votes made war and emancipated millions? Had not votes enfranchised the freedmen? Was anything impossible to a power that had done all this? A million black men started with renewed zeal to vote themselves into the kingdom. So the decade flew away, the revolution of 1876[1] came, and left the half-free serf weary, wondering, but still inspired. Slowly but steadily, in the following years, a new vision began gradually to replace the dream of political power,—a powerful movement, the rise of another ideal to guide the unguided, another pillar of fire by night after a clouded day. It was the ideal of "book-learning"; the curiosity, born of compulsory ignorance, to know and test the power of the cabalistic[2] letters of the white man, the longing to know. Here at last seemed to have been discovered the mountain path to Canaan;[3] longer than the highway of Emancipation and law, steep and rugged, but straight, leading to heights high enough to overlook life.

Up the new path the advance guard toiled, slowly, heavily, doggedly; only those who have watched and guided the faltering feet, the misty minds, the dull understandings, of the dark pupils of these schools know how faithfully, how piteously, this people strove to learn. It was weary work. The cold statistician wrote down the inches of progress here and there, noted also where here and there a foot had slipped or some one had fallen. To the tired climbers, the horizon was ever dark, the mists were often cold, the Canaan was always dim and far away. If, however, the vistas disclosed as yet no goal, no resting-place, little but flattery and criticism, the journey at least gave leisure for reflection and self-examination; it changed the child of Emancipation to the youth with dawning self-consciousness, self-realization, self-respect. In those sombre forests of his striving his own soul rose before him, and he saw himself,—darkly as through a veil; and yet he saw in himself some faint revelation of his power, of his mission. He began to have a dim feeling that, to attain his place in the world, he must be himself, and not another. For the first time he sought to analyze the burden he bore upon his back, that dead-weight of social degradation partially masked behind a half-named Negro problem. He felt his poverty; without a cent, without a home, without land, tools, or savings, he had entered into competition with rich, landed, skilled neighbors. To be a poor man is hard, but to be a poor race in a land of dollars is the very bottom of hardships. He felt the weight of his ignorance,—not simply of letters, but of life, of business, of the humanities; the accumulated sloth and shirking and awkwardness of decades and centuries shackled his hands and feet. Nor was his burden all poverty and ignorance. The red stain of bastardy, which two centuries of systematic legal defilement of Negro women had stamped upon his race, meant not only the loss of ancient African chastity, but also the hereditary weight of a mass of corruption from white adulterers, threatening almost the obliteration of the Negro home.

A people thus handicapped ought not to be asked to race with the world, but rather allowed to give all its time and thought to its own social problems.

9. Amendment to the Constitution passed in 1870 to guarantee and protect the voting rights of African American men.
1. Congressional opposition to the continuation of Reconstruction policies and programs after the national elections of 1876.
2. Indecipherable and mystical.
3. The Promised Land of the Israelites.

But alas! while sociologists gleefully count his bastards and his prostitutes, the very soul of the toiling, sweating black man is darkened by the shadow of a vast despair. Men call the shadow prejudice, and learnedly explain it as the natural defence of culture against barbarism, learning against ignorance, purity against crime, the "higher" against the "lower" races. To which the Negro cries Amen! and swears that to so much of this strange prejudice as is founded on just homage to civilization, culture, righteousness, and progress, he humbly bows and meekly does obeisance. But before that nameless prejudice that leaps beyond all this he stands helpless, dismayed, and well-nigh speechless; before that personal disrespect and mockery, the ridicule and systematic humiliation, the distortion of fact and wanton license of fancy, the cynical ignoring of the better and the boisterous welcoming of the worse, the all-pervading desire to inculcate disdain for everything black, from Toussaint[4] to the devil,—before this there rises a sickening despair that would disarm and discourage any nation save that black host to whom "discouragement" is an unwritten word.

But the facing of so vast a prejudice could not but bring the inevitable self-questioning, self-disparagement, and lowering of ideals which ever accompany repression and breed in an atmosphere of contempt and hate. Whisperings and portents came borne upon the four winds: Lo! we are diseased and dying, cried the dark hosts; we cannot write, our voting is vain; what need of education, since we must always cook and serve? And the Nation echoed and enforced this self-criticism, saying: Be content to be servants, and nothing more; what need of higher culture for half-men? Away with the black man's ballot, by force or fraud,—and behold the suicide of a race! Nevertheless, out of the evil came something of good,—the more careful adjustment of education to real life, the clearer perception of the Negroes' social responsibilities, and the sobering realization of the meaning of progress.

So dawned the time of *Sturm und Drang*:[5] storm and stress to-day rocks our little boat on the mad waters of the world-sea; there is within and without the sound of conflict, the burning of body and rending of soul; inspiration strives with doubt, and faith with vain questionings. The bright ideals of the past,— physical freedom, political power, the training of brains and the training of hands,—all these in turn have waxed and waned, until even the last grows dim and overcast. Are they all wrong,—all false? No, not that, but each alone was over-simple and incomplete,—the dreams of a credulous race-childhood, or the fond imaginings of the other world which does not know and does not want to know our power. To be really true, all these ideals must be melted and welded into one. The training of the schools we need to-day more than ever,— the training of deft hands, quick eyes and ears, and above all the broader, deeper, higher culture of gifted minds and pure hearts. The power of the ballot we need in sheer self-defence,—else what shall save us from a second slavery? Freedom, too, the long-sought, we still seek,—the freedom of life and limb, the freedom to work and think, the freedom to love and aspire. Work, culture, liberty,—all these we need, not singly but together, not successively but together, each growing and aiding each, and all striving toward that vaster ideal that swims before the Negro people, the ideal of human brotherhood, gained through the unifying ideal of Race; the ideal of fostering and developing the traits and talents of the Negro, not in opposition to or contempt for

4. Toussaint L'Ouverture (1743–1803), slave-born Haitian soldier, patriot, and martyr to the liberation of Haiti from foreign control.
5. Storm and stress (German).

other races, but rather in large conformity to the greater ideals of the American Republic, in order that some day on American soil two world-races may give each to each those characteristics both so sadly lack. We the darker ones come even now not altogether empty-handed: there are to-day no truer exponents of the pure human spirit of the Declaration of Independence than the American Negroes; there is no true American music but the wild sweet melodies of the Negro slave; the American fairy tales and folk-lore are Indian and African; and, all in all, we black men seem the sole oasis of simple faith and reverence in a dusty desert of dollars and smartness. Will America be poorer if she replace her brutal dyspeptic blundering with light-hearted but determined Negro humility? or her coarse and cruel wit with loving jovial good-humor? or her vulgar music with the soul of the Sorrow Songs?

Merely a concrete test of the underlying principles of the great republic is the Negro Problem, and the spiritual striving of the freedmen's sons is the travail of souls whose burden is almost beyond the measure of their strength, but who bear it in the name of an historic race, in the name of this the land of their fathers' fathers, and in the name of human opportunity.

And now what I have briefly sketched in large outline let me on coming pages tell again in many ways, with loving emphasis and deeper detail, that men may listen to the striving in the souls of black folk.

* * *

III. Of Mr. Booker T. Washington and Others[6]

From birth till death enslaved; in word, in deed, unmanned!

• • • • • • • • •

Hereditary bondsmen! Know ye not
Who would be free themselves must strike the blow?
—Byron[7]

Easily the most striking thing in the history of the American Negro since 1876[8] is the ascendancy of Mr. Booker T. Washington. It began at the time

6. *Of Mr. Booker T. Washington and Others* was first published in *Guardian*, July 27, 1902, and then collected in *The Souls of Black Folk*. Booker T. Washington (1856–1915) founded and helped build Tuskegee Institute, a black college in Alabama, and became a powerful leader of and spokesman for black Americans, especially after his address at the Atlanta Exposition in 1895.
7. The epigraph is from *Childe Harold's Pilgrimage* (1812), Canto 2, 74.710, 76.720–21, by George Gordon, Lord Byron (1758–1824). The music is

from the refrain of a black spiritual titled "A Great Camp-Meetin' in de Promised Land" (also called "There's a Great Camp Meeting" and "Walk Together Children"). The words of the refrain set to this music are

Going to mourn and never tire—
mourn and never tire, mourn and never tire.

8. Reconstruction ended in 1876; federal troops were withdrawn from the South, and black political power was essentially destroyed.

when war memories and ideals were rapidly passing; a day of astonishing commercial development was dawning; a sense of doubt and hesitation overtook the freedmen's sons,—then it was that his leading began. Mr. Washington came, with a simple definite programme, at the psychological moment when the nation was a little ashamed of having bestowed so much sentiment on Negroes, and was concentrating its energies on Dollars. His programme of industrial education, conciliation of the South, and submission and silence as to civil and political rights, was not wholly original; the Free Negroes from 1830 up to war-time had striven to build industrial schools, and the American Missionary Association had from the first taught various trades; and Price[9] and others had sought a way of honorable alliance with the best of the Southerners. But Mr. Washington first indissolubly linked these things; he put enthusiasm, unlimited energy, and perfect faith into this programme, and changed it from a by-path into a veritable Way of Life. And the tale of the methods by which he did this is a fascinating study of human life.

It startled the nation to hear a Negro advocating such a programme after many decades of bitter complaint; it startled and won the applause of the South, it interested and won the admiration of the North; and after a confused murmur of protest, it silenced if it did not convert the Negroes themselves.

To gain the sympathy and cooperation of the various elements comprising the white South was Mr. Washington's first task; and this, at the time Tuskegee was founded, seemed, for a black man, well-nigh impossible. And yet ten years later it was done in the word spoken at Atlanta: "In all things purely social we can be as separate as the five fingers, and yet one as the hand in all things essential to mutual progress." This "Atlanta Compromise"[1] is by all odds the most notable thing in Mr. Washington's career. The South interpreted it in different ways: the radicals received it as a complete surrender of the demand for civil and political equality; the conservatives, as a generously conceived working basis for mutual understanding. So both approved it, and to-day its author is certainly the most distinguished Southerner since Jefferson Davis, and the one with the largest personal following.

Next to this achievement comes Mr. Washington's work in gaining place and consideration in the North. Others less shrewd and tactful had formerly essayed to sit on these two stools and had fallen between them; but as Mr. Washington knew the heart of the South from birth and training, so by singular insight he intuitively grasped the spirit of the age which was dominating the North. And so thoroughly did he learn the speech and thought of triumphant commercialism, and the ideals of material prosperity, that the picture of a lone black boy poring over a French grammar amid the weeds and dirt of a neglected home soon seemed to him the acme of absurdities.[2] One wonders what Socrates and St. Francis of Assisi would say to this.

And yet this very singleness of vision and thorough oneness with his age is a mark of the successful man. It is as though Nature must needs make

9. Joseph Charles Price (1854–1893), influential southern black educator and civil rights leader.
1. In a speech at the Atlanta Exposition of 1895, Washington in effect traded political, civil, and social rights for blacks for the promise of vocational-training schools and jobs. His purpose was to reduce racial tension in the South while providing a stable black labor force whose skills would provide job security.
2. In Washington's *Up from Slavery* (1901), ch. 8,

"Teaching School in a Stable and a Hen-House," there is a passage on the absurdity of knowledge not practically useful:

In fact, one of the saddest things I saw during the month of travel which I have described was a young man, who had attended some high school, sitting down in a one-room cabin, with grease on his clothing, filth all around him, and weeds in the yard and garden, engaged in studying French grammar.

men narrow in order to give them force. So Mr. Washington's cult has gained unquestioning followers, his work has wonderfully prospered, his friends are legion, and his enemies are confounded. To-day he stands as the one recognized spokesman of his ten million fellows, and one of the most notable figures in a nation of seventy millions. One hesitates, therefore, to criticise a life which, beginning with so little, has done so much. And yet the time is come when one may speak in all sincerity and utter courtesy of the mistakes and shortcomings of Mr. Washington's career, as well as of his triumphs, without being thought captious or envious, and without forgetting that it is easier to do ill than well in the world.

The criticism that has hitherto met Mr. Washington has not always been of this broad character. In the South especially has he had to walk warily to avoid the harshest judgments,—and naturally so, for he is dealing with the one subject of deepest sensitiveness to that section. Twice—once when at the Chicago celebration of the Spanish-American War he alluded to the color-prejudice that is "eating away the vitals of the South," and once when he dined with President Roosevelt[3]—has the resulting Southern criticism been violent enough to threaten seriously his popularity. In the North the feeling has several times forced itself into words, that Mr. Washington's counsels of submission overlooked certain elements of true manhood, and that his educational programme was unnecessarily narrow. Usually, however, such criticism has not found open expression, although, too, the spiritual sons of the Abolitionists have not been prepared to acknowledge that the schools founded before Tuskegee, by men of broad ideals and self-sacrificing spirit, were wholly failures or worthy of ridicule. While, then, criticism has not failed to follow Mr. Washington, yet the prevailing public opinion of the land has been but too willing to deliver the solution of a wearisome problem into his hands, and say, "If that is all you and your race ask, take it."

Among his own people, however, Mr. Washington has encountered the strongest and most lasting opposition, amounting at times to bitterness, and even to-day continuing strong and insistent even though largely silenced in outward expression by the public opinion of the nation. Some of this opposition is, of course, mere envy; the disappointment of displaced demagogues and the spite of narrow minds. But aside from this, there is among educated and thoughtful colored men in all parts of the land a feeling of deep regret, sorrow, and apprehension at the wide currency and ascendancy which some of Mr. Washington's theories have gained. These same men admire his sincerity of purpose, and are willing to forgive much to honest endeavor which is doing something worth the doing. They coöperate with Mr. Washington as far as they conscientiously can; and, indeed, it is no ordinary tribute to this man's tact and power that, steering as he must between so many diverse interests and opinions, he so largely retains the respect of all.

But the hushing of the criticism of honest opponents is a dangerous thing. It leads some of the best of the critics to unfortunate silence and paralysis of effort, and others to burst into speech so passionately and intemperately as to lose listeners. Honest and earnest criticism from those whose interests are most nearly touched,—criticism of writers by readers, of government by those governed, of leaders by those led,—this is the soul of democracy and

3. Theodore Roosevelt (1858–1919), twenty-sixth president of the United States (1901–09). Washington's dining with him at the White House in 1901 caused controversy around the country.

the safeguard of modern society. If the best of the American Negroes receive by outer pressure a leader whom they had not recognized before, manifestly there is here a certain palpable gain. Yet there is also irreparable loss,—a loss of that peculiarly valuable education which a group receives when by search and criticism it finds and commissions its own leaders. The way in which this is done is at once the most elementary and the nicest problem of social growth. History is but the record of such group-leadership; and yet how infinitely changeful is its type and character! And of all types and kinds, what can be more instructive than the leadership of a group within a group?—that curious double movement where real progress may be negative and actual advance be relative retrogression. All this is the social student's inspiration and despair.

Now in the past the American Negro has had instructive experience in the choosing of group leaders, founding thus a peculiar dynasty which in the light of present conditions is worth while studying. When sticks and stones and beasts form the sole environment of a people, their attitude is largely one of determined opposition to and conquest of natural forces. But when to earth and brute is added an environment of men and ideas, then the attitude of the imprisoned group may take three main forms,—a feeling of revolt and revenge; an attempt to adjust all thought and action to the will of the greater group; or, finally, a determined effort at self-realization and self-development despite environing opinion. The influence of all of these attitudes at various times can be traced in the history of the American Negro, and in the evolution of his successive leaders.

Before 1750, while the fire of African freedom still burned in the veins of the slaves, there was in all leadership or attempted leadership but the one motive of revolt and revenge,—typified in the terrible Maroons, the Danish blacks, and Cato[4] of Stono, and veiling all the Americas in fear of insurrection. The liberalizing tendencies of the latter half of the eighteenth century brought, along with kindlier relations between black and white, thoughts of ultimate adjustment and assimilation. Such aspiration was especially voiced in the earnest songs of Phyllis, in the martyrdom of Attucks, the fighting of Salem and Poor, the intellectual accomplishments of Banneker and Derham, and the political demands of the Cuffes.[5]

Stern financial and social stress after the war cooled much of the previous humanitarian ardor. The disappointment and impatience of the Negroes at the persistence of slavery and serfdom voiced itself in two movements. The slaves in the South, aroused undoubtedly by vague rumors of the Haytian revolt, made three fierce attempts at insurrection,—in 1800 under Gabriel in Virginia, in 1822 under Vesey in Carolina, and in 1831 again in Virginia

---

4. The leader of the Stono, South Carolina, slave revolt of September 9, 1739, in which twenty-five whites were killed. "Maroons": fugitive slaves from the West Indies and Guiana in the 17th and 18th centuries, or their descendants. Many of the slaves in the Danish West Indies revolted in 1733 because of the lack of sufficient food.
5. Paul Cuffe (1759–1817) organized to resettle free blacks in African colonies. A champion of civil rights for free blacks in Massachusetts, he took thirty-eight blacks to Africa in 1815 at his own expense. Phyllis (or Phillis) Wheatley (c. 1753–1784), black slave and poet. Crispus Attucks

(c. 1723–1770) was killed in the Boston massacre. Peter Salem (d. 1816), black patriot who killed Major Pitcairn in the battle of Bunker Hill. Salem Poor (b. 1747), a black soldier who fought at Bunker Hill, Valley Forge, and White Plains. Benjamin Banneker (1731–1806), a black mathematician who also studied astronomy. James Derham (b. 1762), the first recognized black physician in America; born a slave, he learned medicine from his physician master, bought his freedom in 1783, and by 1788 was one of the foremost physicians of New Orleans.

under the terrible Nat Turner.[6] In the Free States, on the other hand, a new and curious attempt at self-development was made. In Philadelphia and New York color-prescription led to a withdrawal of Negro communicants from white churches and the formation of a peculiar socio-religious institution among the Negroes known as the African Church,—an organization still living and controlling in its various branches over a million of men.

Walker's wild appeal[7] against the trend of the times showed how the world was changing after the coming of the cotton-gin. By 1830 slavery seemed hopelessly fastened on the South, and the slaves thoroughly cowed into submission. The free Negroes of the North, inspired by the mulatto immigrants from the West Indies, began to change the basis of their demands; they recognized the slavery of slaves, but insisted that they themselves were freemen, and sought assimilation and amalgamation with the nation on the same terms with other men. Thus, Forten and Purvis of Philadelphia, Shad of Wilmington, Du Bois of New Haven, Barbadoes[8] of Boston, and others, strove singly and together as men, they said, not as slaves; as "people of color," not as "Negroes." The trend of the times, however, refused them recognition save in individual and exceptional cases, considered them as one with all the despised blacks, and they soon found themselves striving to keep even the rights they formerly had of voting and working and moving as freemen. Schemes of migration and colonization arose among them; but these they refused to entertain, and they eventually turned to the Abolition movement as a final refuge.

Here, led by Remond, Nell, Wells-Brown, and Douglass,[9] a new period of self-assertion and self-development dawned. To be sure, ultimate freedom and assimilation was the ideal before the leaders, but the assertion of the manhood rights of the Negro by himself was the main reliance, and John Brown's raid was the extreme of its logic. After the war and emancipation, the great form of Frederick Douglass, the greatest of American Negro leaders, still led the host. Self-assertion, especially in political lines, was the main programme, and behind Douglass came Elliot, Bruce, and Langston, and the Reconstruction politicians, and, less conspicuous but of greater social significance Alexander Crummell and Bishop Daniel Payne.[1]

6. A slave (1800–1831), he led the Southampton insurrection in 1831, during which approximately sixty whites and more than a hundred slaves were killed or executed. Gabriel (1775?–1800) conspired to attack Richmond, Virginia, with a thousand other slaves on August 30, 1800; but a storm forced a suspension of the mission and two slaves betrayed the conspiracy. On October 7, Gabriel and fifteen others were hanged. Denmark Vesey (c. 1767–1822) purchased his freedom in 1800; he led an unsuccessful uprising in 1822 and was hanged.
7. A revolutionary and eloquent antislavery pamphlet by the black leader David Walker (1785–1830).
8. James G. Barbadoes was one of those present at the first National Negro Convention along with Forten, Purvis, Shadd, and others. James Forten (1766–1842), black civic leader and philanthropist. Robert Purvis (1810–1898), abolitionist, helped found the American Anti-Slavery Society in 1833 and was the president of the Underground Railway. Abraham Shadd, abolitionist, was on the first board of managers of the American Anti-Slavery Society, a delegate from Delaware for the first National Negro Convention (1830), and president of the third one in 1833. Alexander Du Bois (1803–1887), paternal grandfather of W. E. B. Du

Bois, helped form the Negro Episcopal Parish of St. Luke in 1847 and was the senior warden there.
9. Frederick Douglass (1818–1895), abolitionist and orator and born a slave, was U.S. minister to Haiti and U.S. marshal of the District of Columbia. Charles Lenox Remond (1810–1873), black leader. William Cooper Nell (1816–1874), abolitionist, writer, and first African American to hold office under the government of the United States (clerk in the post office). Through his efforts equal school privileges were obtained for black children in Boston. William Wells Brown (1814–1884) published *Clotel* in 1853, the first novel by a black American, and *The Escape* in 1858, the first play by a black American.
1. Daniel Alexander Payne (1811–1893), bishop of the African Methodist Episcopal church and president of Wilberforce University (1863–76). Robert Brown Elliot (1842–1884), black politician, graduate of Eton, South Carolina congressman in the U.S. House of Representatives. Blanche K. Bruce (1841–1898), born a slave, first black man to serve a full term in the U.S. Senate (1875–81). John Mercer Langston (1829–1897), congressman, lawyer, diplomat, educator, born a slave. Crummell (1819–1898), clergyman of the Protestant Episcopal church, missionary in Liberia for twenty years and then in Washington, D.C.

Then came the Revolution of 1876, the suppression of the Negro votes, the changing and shifting of ideals, and the seeking of new lights in the great night. Douglass, in his old age, still bravely stood for the ideals of his early manhood,—ultimate assimilation *through* self-assertion, and on no other terms. For a time Price arose as a new leader, destined, it seemed, not to give up, but to re-state the old ideals in a form less repugnant to the white South. But he passed away in his prime. Then came the new leader. Nearly all the former ones had become leaders by the silent suffrage of their fellows, had sought to lead their own people alone, and were usually, save Douglass, little known outside their race. But Booker T. Washington arose as essentially the leader not of one race but of two,—a compromiser between the South, the North, and the Negro. Naturally the Negroes resented, at first bitterly, signs of compromise which surrendered their civil and political rights, even though this was to be exchanged for larger chances of economic development. The rich and dominating North, however, was not only weary of the race problem, but was investing largely in Southern enterprises, and welcomed any method of peaceful coöperation. Thus, by national opinion, the Negroes began to recognize Mr. Washington's leadership; and the voice of criticism was hushed.

Mr. Washington represents in Negro thought the old attitude of adjustment and submission; but adjustment at such a peculiar time as to make his programme unique. This is an age of unusual economic development, and Mr. Washington's programme naturally takes an economic cast, becoming a gospel of Work and Money to such an extent as apparently almost completely to overshadow the higher aims of life. Moreover, this is an age when the more advanced races are coming in closer contact with the less developed races, and the race-feeling is therefore intensified; and Mr. Washington's programme practically accepts the alleged inferiority of the Negro races. Again, in our own land, the reaction from the sentiment of war time has given impetus to race-prejudice against Negroes, and Mr. Washington withdraws many of the high demands of Negroes as men and American citizens. In other periods of intensified prejudice all the Negro's tendency to self-assertion has been called forth; at this period a policy of submission is advocated. In the history of nearly all other races and peoples the doctrine preached at such crises has been that manly self-respect is worth more than lands and houses, and that a people who voluntarily surrender such respect, or cease striving for it, are not worth civilizing.

In answer to this, it has been claimed that the Negro can survive only through submission. Mr. Washington distinctly asks that black people give up, at least for the present, three things,—

First, political power,

Second, insistence on civil rights,

Third, higher education of Negro youth,—

and concentrate all their energies on industrial education, the accumulation of wealth, and the conciliation of the South. This policy has been courageously and insistently advocated for over fifteen years, and has been triumphant for perhaps ten years. As a result of this tender of the palm-branch, what has been the return? In these years there have occurred:

1. The disfranchisement of the Negro.

2. The legal creation of a distinct status of civil inferiority for the Negro.

3. The steady withdrawal of aid from institutions for the higher training of the Negro.

These movements are not, to be sure, direct results of Mr. Washington's teachings; but his propaganda has, without a shadow of doubt, helped their speedier accomplishment. The question then comes: Is it possible, and probable, that nine millions of men can make effective progress in economic lines if they are deprived of political rights, made a servile caste, and allowed only the most meagre chance for developing their exceptional men? If history and reason give any distinct answer to these questions, it is an emphatic *No.* And Mr. Washington thus faces the triple paradox of his career:

1. He is striving nobly to make Negro artisans business men and property-owners; but it is utterly impossible, under modern competitive methods, for workingmen and property-owners to defend their rights and exist without the right of suffrage.

2. He insists on thrift and self-respect, but at the same time counsels a silent submission to civic inferiority such as is bound to sap the manhood of any race in the long run.

3. He advocates common-school[2] and industrial training, and depreciates institutions of higher learning; but neither the Negro common-schools, nor Tuskegee itself, could remain open a day were it not for teachers trained in Negro colleges, or trained by their graduates.

This triple paradox in Mr. Washington's position is the object of criticism by two classes of colored Americans. One class is spiritually descended from Toussaint the Savior,[3] through Gabriel, Vesey, and Turner, and they represent the attitude of revolt and revenge; they hate the white South blindly and distrust the white race generally, and so far as they agree on definite action, think that the Negro's only hope lies in emigration beyond the borders of the United States. And yet, by the irony of fate, nothing has more effectually made this programme seem hopeless than the recent course of the United States toward weaker and darker peoples in the West Indies, Hawaii, and the Philippines,—for where in the world may we go and be safe from lying and brute force?

The other class of Negroes who cannot agree with Mr. Washington has hitherto said little aloud. They deprecate the sight of scattered counsels, of internal disagreement; and especially they dislike making their just criticism of a useful and earnest man an excuse for a general discharge of venom from small-minded opponents. Nevertheless, the questions involved are so fundamental and serious that it is difficult to see how men like the Grimkes, Kelly Miller, J. W. E. Bowen,[4] and other representatives of this group, can much longer be silent. Such men feel in conscience bound to ask of this nation three things:

1. The right to vote.
2. Civic equality.
3. The education of youth according to ability.

They acknowledge Mr. Washington's invaluable service in counselling patience and courtesy in such demands; they do not ask that ignorant black men vote when ignorant whites are debarred, or that any reasonable restric-

---

2. A free public school offering courses at pre-college level.
3. Toussaint L'Ouverture; see n. 4, p. 1721.
4. John Wesley Edward Bowen (1855–?), Methodist clergyman and educator, president of Gammon Theological Seminary of Atlanta. Archibald Grimké (1849–1930) and Francis Grimké (1850–1937), American civic leaders concerned with African American affairs. Miller (1863–1939), dean of Howard University, lectured on the race problem.

tions in the suffrage should not be applied; they know that the low social level of the mass of the race is responsible for much discrimination against it, but they also know, and the nation knows, that relentless color-prejudice is more often a cause than a result of the Negro's degradation; they seek the abatement of this relic of barbarism, and not its systematic encouragement and pampering by all agencies of social power from the Associated Press to the Church of Christ. They advocate, with Mr. Washington, a broad system of Negro common schools supplemented by thorough industrial training; but they are surprised that a man of Mr. Washington's insight cannot see that no such educational system ever has rested or can rest on any other basis than that of the well-equipped college and university, and they insist that there is a demand for a few such institutions throughout the South to train the best of the Negro youth as teachers, professional men, and leaders.

This group of men honor Mr. Washington for his attitude of conciliation toward the white South; they accept the "Atlanta Compromise" in its broadest interpretation; they recognize, with him, many signs of promise, many men of high purpose and fair judgment, in this section; they know that no easy task has been laid upon a region already tottering under heavy burdens. But, nevertheless, they insist that the way to truth and right lies in straightforward honesty, not in indiscriminate flattery; in praising those of the South who do well and criticising uncompromisingly those who do ill; in taking advantage of the opportunities at hand and urging their fellows to do the same, but at the same time in remembering that only a firm adherence to their higher ideals and aspirations will ever keep those ideals within the realm of possibility. They do not expect that the free right to vote, to enjoy civic rights, and to be educated, will come in a moment; they do not expect to see the bias and prejudices of years disappear at the blast of a trumpet; but they are absolutely certain that the way for a people to gain their reasonable rights is not by voluntarily throwing them away and insisting that they do not want them; that the way for a people to gain respect is not by continually belittling and ridiculing themselves; that, on the contrary, Negroes must insist continually, in season and out of season, that voting is necessary to modern manhood, that color discrimination is barbarism, and that black boys need education as well as white boys.

In failing thus to state plainly and unequivocally the legitimate demands of their people, even at the cost of opposing an honored leader, the thinking classes of American Negroes would shirk a heavy responsibility,—a responsibility to themselves, a responsibility to the struggling masses, a responsibility to the darker races of men whose future depends so largely on this American experiment, but especially a responsibility to this nation,—this common Fatherland. It is wrong to encourage a man or a people in evil-doing; it is wrong to aid and abet a national crime simply because it is unpopular not to do so. The growing spirit of kindliness and reconciliation between the North and South after the frightful differences of a generation ago ought to be a source of deep congratulation to all, and especially to those whose mistreatment caused the war; but if that reconciliation is to be marked by the industrial slavery and civic death of those same black men, with permanent legislation into a position of inferiority, then those black men, if they are really men, are called upon by every consideration of patriotism and loyalty to oppose such a course by all civilized methods, even though such opposition involves disagreement with Mr. Booker T. Washington. We have no right to sit silently by while the inevitable seeds are sown for a harvest of disaster to our children, black and white.

First, it is the duty of black men to judge the South discriminatingly. The present generation of Southerners are not responsible for the past, and they should not be blindly hated or blamed for it. Furthermore, to no class is the indiscriminate endorsement of the recent course of the South toward Negroes more nauseating than to the best thought of the South. The South is not "solid"; it is a land in the ferment of social change, wherein forces of all kinds are fighting for supremacy; and to praise the ill the South is to-day perpetrating is just as wrong as to condemn the good. Discriminating and broad-minded criticism is what the South needs,—needs it for the sake of her own white sons and daughters, and for the insurance of robust, healthy mental and moral development.

To-day even the attitude of the Southern whites toward the blacks is not, as so many assume, in all cases the same; the ignorant Southerner hates the Negro, the workingmen fear his competition, the money-makers wish to use him as a laborer, some of the educated see a menace in his upward develop-ment, while others—usually the sons of the masters—wish to help him to rise. National opinion has enabled this last class to maintain the Negro com-mon schools, and to protect the Negro partially in property, life, and limb. Through the pressure of the money-makers, the Negro is in danger of being reduced to semi-slavery, especially in the country districts; the workingmen, and those of the educated who fear the Negro, have united to disfranchise him, and some have urged his deportation; while the passions of the ignorant are easily aroused to lynch and abuse any black man. To praise this intricate whirl of thought and prejudice is nonsense; to inveigh indiscriminately against "the South" is unjust; but to use the same breath in praising Governor Aycock, exposing Senator Morgan, arguing with Mr. Thomas Nelson Page, and denouncing Senator Ben Tillman,[5] is not only sane, but the imperative duty of thinking black men.

It would be unjust to Mr. Washington not to acknowledge that in several instances he has opposed movements in the South which were unjust to the Negro; he sent memorials to the Louisiana and Alabama constitutional conventions, he has spoken against lynching, and in other ways has openly or silently set his influence against sinister schemes and unfortunate hap-penings. Notwithstanding this, it is equally true to assert that on the whole the distinct impression left by Mr. Washington's propaganda is, first, that the South is justified in its present attitude toward the Negro because of the Negro's degradation; secondly, that the prime cause of the Negro's failure to rise more quickly is his wrong education in the past; and, thirdly, that his future rise depends primarily on his own efforts. Each of these propositions

5. Benjamin Ryan Tillman (1847–1918), governor of South Carolina (1890–94) and U.S. Senator (1895–1918), served as the chairman on the com-mittee on suffrage (during the South Carolina constitutional convention) and framed the article providing for an educational and property qualifi-cation for voting, thus eliminating the black vote. He presented the views of the southern extremists on the race question, justified lynching in cases of rape and the use of force to disenfranchise blacks, and advocated the repeal of the Fifteenth Amendment. Charles Brantley Aycock (1859–1912), governor of North Carolina (1901–05). Edwin Denison Morgan (1811–1883), governor of New York (1859–63) and U.S. Senator (1863–69), voted with the minority in President Johnson's veto of the Freedman's Bureau bill and for Johnson's conviction. Page (1853–1922), American novelist and diplomat, did much to build up romantic leg-ends of the southern plantation.

is a dangerous half-truth. The supplementary truths must never be lost sight of: first, slavery and race-prejudice are potent if not sufficient causes of the Negro's position; second, industrial and common-school training were necessarily slow in planting because they had to await the black teachers trained by higher institutions,—it being extremely doubtful if any essentially different development was possible, and certainly a Tuskegee was unthinkable before 1880; and, third, while it is a great truth to say that the Negro must strive and strive mightily to help himself, it is equally true that unless his striving be not simply seconded, but rather aroused and encouraged, by the initiative of the richer and wiser environing group, he cannot hope for great success.

In his failure to realize and impress this last point, Mr. Washington is especially to be criticised. His doctrine has tended to make the whites, North and South, shift the burden of the Negro problem to the Negro's shoulders and stand aside as critical and rather pessimistic spectators; when in fact the burden belongs to the nation, and the hands of none of us are clean if we bend not our energies to righting these great wrongs.

The South ought to be led, by candid and honest criticism, to assert her better self and do her full duty to the race she has cruelly wronged and is still wronging. The North—her co-partner in guilt—cannot salve her conscience by plastering it with gold. We cannot settle this problem by diplomacy and suaveness, by "policy" alone. If worse come to worst, can the moral fibre of this country survive the slow throttling and murder of nine millions of men?

The black men of America have a duty to perform, a duty stern and delicate,—a forward movement to oppose a part of the work of their greatest leader. So far as Mr. Washington preaches Thrift, Patience, and Industrial Training for the masses, we must hold up his hands and strive with him, rejoicing in his honors and glorying in the strength of this Joshua called of God and of man to lead the headless host. But so far as Mr. Washington apologizes for injustice, North or South, does not rightly value the privilege and duty of voting, belittles the emasculating effects of caste distinctions, and opposes the higher training and ambition of our brighter minds,—so far as he, the South, or the Nation, does this,—we must unceasingly and firmly oppose them. By every civilized and peaceful method we must strive for the rights which the world accords to men, clinging unwaveringly to those great words which the sons of the Fathers would fain forget: "We hold these truths to be self-evident: That all men are created equal; that they are endowed by their Creator with certain unalienable rights; that among these are life, liberty, and the pursuit of happiness."

1903

Realism and Naturalism

Realism and *naturalism* are closely related terms in American literary history, sometimes used interchangeably, sometimes used as opposites. Realism implies a rejection of romantic, heroic, exaggerated, and idealistic views of life in favor of detailed, accurate descriptions of the everyday. The characters are presented as ordinary people involved in the normal moral dilemmas of life. Naturalists, however, pointed out that the realists generally focused on the middle class. They claimed that the lives of the poor, the immigrant, the socially outcast, were not amenable to a realistic treatment. They required something more extreme, something more sensitive to the relative lack of power of the socially marginalized. Both movements agreed that accurate depiction of life's details was the purpose of fiction, but disagreed on what life's details consisted of and, beyond that, how best to understand such concepts as "Nature"—including human nature.

Realism as a movement in novel-writing had developed in early nineteenth-century Europe, where old ways of life were giving way to the modern, just as they were in the United States after the Civil War. By the middle of the century in England and France, realism was simply identified with modern writing. Different U.S. authors implemented literary realism in different ways, but William Dean Howells, Mark Twain, Henry James, and Edith Wharton can all be seen as central figures in the movement. Twain pushed realism towards satirical exaggeration and developed the use of various regional and class dialects. Henry James worked with the flow of interior thoughts, pushing realism towards the stream of consciousness and other characteristics of literary modernism. Howells used the details of ordinary life—homes, furnishings, workplaces, neighborhoods—as indexes to the moral lives of his characters. Edith Wharton's view of high society pushed toward naturalism in its sense that the rich could sometimes seem as much victims of natural forces as the poor.

By the end of the nineteenth century, naturalism, with its supposedly scientific point of view, had developed its own set of techniques tending to a more extreme, and arguably more romantic, view of human life than realism. Social interpretations of Darwinian evolution, seeing human beings as victims of the struggle for survival won by the strongest, could be applied to labor versus capital, railroads versus farmers, and other political struggles across the nation. Emphasis shifted from views of human beings as capable of shaping their destinies to views of them as futilely responding to the things that happened to them. Nevertheless, the aim of total scientific objectivity among naturalists clashed with their frequent sense of outrage over social injustice, setting up a literature that is often internally conflicted. Naturalistic subject matter ranges from Stephen Crane's awed and terrified Union soldier in *The Red Badge of Courage* (1895), to Frank Norris's and Upton Sinclair's exposés of the power of capitalism in *The Octopus* (1901) and *The Jungle* (1906), to the portraits of psychopathological characters in Norris's *McTeague* (1899) and Jack London's *The Sea-Wolf* (1904). Naturalism thus appeared in many forms. Like *The Octopus*, London's *The Call of the Wild* (1903) was at once a profoundly naturalistic novel and an intensely romantic fable; in London's fiction, though human nature seems inevitably to go wrong, it may be saved in rugged environments where "civilized" notions such as self-gain are no longer useful. Later, Richard Wright and Américo Paredes would use such themes in urban settings. Despite its often brutal subject matter, naturalism "reflects an affirmative ethical conception of life," as critic Donald Pizer expresses it, by endowing even the lowest characters with moral complexity.

WILLIAM DEAN HOWELLS

William Dean Howells (1837–1920) was enormously influential not only through his many novels, which he said dealt with the "smiling aspects of life," but also through his editorship of important literary journals—the *Atlantic Monthly*, published in Boston, and *Harper's Magazine*, published in New York City. He used these influential positions to foster and encourage numerous authors, writing many essays about the literature of his era. Howells felt American writing should be "simple, natural, and honest" and should refrain from "romantic exaggeration." Unlike Henry James or Mark Twain, his fellow realist innovators, Howells was not interested in the unconscious and irrational in humankind. Though he was criticized by Frank Norris among others for his "teacup tragedies" that take place in front parlors, as an editor and critic Howells responded deeply and sensitively to novelistic complexity. In his essay "Henry James, Jr.," Howells praises James's "impartiality" as that which leaves conclusions about characters up to the reader: "We must take him on his own ground, for clearly he will not come to ours."

"Novel-Writing and Novel-Reading" was not published until well after Howells's death; in his day it was a widely praised lecture he gave on a tour through the East and Midwest in 1899. In the essay Howells shows a change from the "Boston" Howells to the "New York" Howells. Moving to New York in 1891, Howells developed a growing concern with social and race questions in literature. He came to see novel-reading as a more serious endeavor than ever. And for novelists, he felt, "construction and criticism go hand-in-hand." From his new column in *Harper's Magazine*, Howells campaigned for the importance of realism in the novel, arguing that the reader's own "experience of life" was the only test of "'realism.'" But, in the end, realism is less "picturesque" than historical and ethical. In his earlier career, Howells had insisted on eliding those passions that could not be revealed in polite novels; by this point, he had come to believe that "realism excludes nothing that is true." He argues that the novel can be a vehicle of social reform and praises those who write toward that goal, such as Charles Chesnutt. "The truth," he declares, "may be indecent, but it cannot be vicious, it can never corrupt or deprave" in its "material honesty."

From Henry James, Jr.[1]

* * *

That artistic impartiality which puzzled so many in the treatment of Daisy Miller[2] is one of the qualities most valuable in the eyes of those who care how things are done, and I am not sure that it is not Mr. James's most characteristic quality. As "frost performs the effect of fire," this impartiality comes at last to the same result as sympathy. We may be quite sure that Mr. James does not like the peculiar phase of our civilization typified

---

1. First published in the *Century* 25.1 (November 1882), from which this excerpt is taken.

2. Title character of James's 1878 novella.

in Henrietta Stackpole:[3] but he treats her with such exquisite justice that he lets *us* like her. It is an extreme case, but I confidently allege it in proof.

His impartiality is part of the reserve with which he works in most respects, and which at first glance makes us say that he is wanting in humor. But I feel pretty certain that Mr. James has not been able to disinherit himself to this degree. We Americans are terribly in earnest about making ourselves, individually and collectively; but I fancy that our prevailing mood in the face of all problems is that of an abiding faith which can afford to be funny. He has himself indicated that we have, as a nation, as a people, our joke, and every one of us is in the joke more or less. We may, some of us, dislike it extremely, disapprove it wholly, and even abhor it, but we are in the joke all the same, and no one of us is safe from becoming the great American humorist at any given moment. The danger is not apparent in Mr. James's case, and I confess that I read him with a relief in the comparative immunity that he affords from the national facetiousness. Many of his people are humorously imagined, or rather humorously *seen*, like Daisy Miller's mother, but these do not give a dominant color; the business in hand is commonly serious, and the droll people are subordinated. They abound, nevertheless, and many of them are perfectly new finds * * *. But though Mr. James portrays the humorous in character, he is decidedly not on humorous terms with his reader; he ignores rather than recognizes the fact that they are both in the joke.

If we take him at all we must take him on his own ground, for clearly he will not come to ours. We must make concessions to him, not in this respect only, but in several others, chief among which is the motive for reading fiction. By example, at least, he teaches that it is the pursuit and not the end which should give us pleasure; for he often prefers to leave us to our own conjectures in regard to the fate of the people in whom he has interested us. There is no question, of course, but he could tell the story of Isabel[4] in "The Portrait of a Lady" to the end, yet he does not tell it. We must agree, then, to take what seems a fragment instead of a whole, and to find, when we can, a name for this new kind of fiction. Evidently it is the character, not the fate, of his people which occupies him; when he has fully developed their character he leaves them to what destiny the reader pleases.

* * *

The art of fiction has, in fact, become a finer art in our day than it was with Dickens and Thackeray. We could not suffer the confidential attitude of the latter now, nor the mannerism of the former, any more than we could endure the prolixity of Richardson or the coarseness of Fielding. These great men are of the past—they and their methods and interests; even Trollope and Reade are not of the present. The new school derives from Hawthorne and George Eliot rather than any others;[5] but it studies human

---

3. Character in James's 1881 novel *The Portrait of a Lady*.
4. Protagonist of *The Portrait of a Lady*.
5. Charles Dickens (1812–1870), William Makepeace Thackeray (1811–1863), Anthony Trollope (1815–1882), Charles Reade (1814–1884), and

George Eliot (pseudo. Mary Ann Evans) (1819–1880): 19th-century British novelists. Samuel Richardson (1689–1761) and Henry Fielding (1707–1754): 18th-century British novelists. Nathaniel Hawthorne (1804–1864): 19th-century American short-story writer and novelist.

nature much more in its wonted aspects, and finds its ethical and dramatic examples in the operation of lighter but not really less vital motives.

* * *

Will the reader be content to accept a novel which is an analytic study rather than a story, which is apt to leave him arbiter of the destiny of the author's creations? Will he find his account in the unflagging interest of their development? Mr. James's growing popularity seems to suggest that this may be the case; but the work of Mr. James's imitators will have much to do with the final result.

* * *

I own that I like a finished story; but then also I like those which Mr. James seems not to finish. This is probably the position of most of his readers, who cannot very logically account for either preference. We can only make sure that we have here an annalist, or analyst, as we choose, who fascinates us from his first page to his last, whose narrative or whose comment may enter into any minuteness of detail without fatiguing us, and can only truly grieve us when it ceases.

1882

From Novel-Writing and Novel-Reading: An Impersonal Explanation[1]

* * *

By beauty of course I mean truth, for the one involves the other; it is only the false in art which is ugly, and it is only the false which is universal. The truth may be indecent, but it cannot be vicious, it can never corrupt or deprave; and I should say this in defense of the grossest material honestly treated in modern novels as against the painted and perfumed meretricious-ness of the novels that went before them. I conceive that apart from all the clamor about schools of fiction is the *quiet* question of truth, how to get it in, so that it may get itself out again as beauty, the divinely living thing which all men love and worship. So I make truth the prime test of a novel. If I do not find that it is like life, then it does not exist for me as art; it is ugly, it is ludi-crous, it is impossible. I do not expect a novel to be wholly true. I have never read one that seemed to me so except Tolstoy's novels:[2] but I expect it to be a constant endeavor for the truth, and I perceive beauty in it so far as it fulfills this endeavor. I am quite willing to recognize and enjoy whatever measure of truth I find in a novel that is partly or mainly false; only, if I come upon the falsehood at the outset I am apt not to read that novel. But I do not bear such a grudge against it as I do against the novel which lures me on with a fair face of truth, and drops the mask midway. If you ask me for illustrations, I am somewhat at a loss, but if you ask me for examples, they are manifold.

1. From *Howells and James: A Double Billing: Novel-Writing and Novel-Reading, An Impersonal Explanation*, ed. William M. Gibson, Leon Edel, and Lyall H. Powers (1958), from which this excerpt is taken.

2. Russian realist Leo Tolstoy's (1828–1910) most famous works are *Anna Karenina*, *The Death of Ivan Ilych*, and *War and Peace*.

In English I should say the truthful novelists or those working with an ideal of truth were Jane Austen, George Eliot, Anthony Trollope, Thomas Hardy, Mrs. Humphrey Ward, George Moore; in French, Flaubert, Maupassant, the Goncourts, Daudet and Zola; in Russian, Tourguenief and Tolstoy; in Spanish, Valdés, Galdós and Pardo-Bazan; in Norwegian, Björnson, Lie, and Kielland. In English, some untruthful novelists, or those working from an ideal of effect, are Thackeray, Dickens, Bulwer, Reade, and all their living followers; in French, Dumas, Feuillet, Ohnet; in Spanish Valera; in Russian, measurably Doystoyevsky;[3] in Norwegian, none that I know of. It is right to say, however, of some of the untruthful novelists, and notably of Thackeray, that they were the victims of their period. If Thackeray had been writing in our time, I have no question but he would have been one of its most truthful artists.

The truth which I mean, the truth which is the only beauty, is truth to human experience, and human experience is so manifold and so recondite, that no scheme can be too remote, too airy for the test. It is a well ascertained fact concerning the imagination that it can work only with the stuff of experience. It can absolutely create nothing; it can only compose. The most fantastic extravagance comes under the same law that exacts likeness to the known as well as the closest and severest study of life. Once for all, then, obedience to this law is the creed of the realist, and rebellion is the creed of the romanticist. Both necessarily work under it, but one willingly, to beautiful effect, and the other unwillingly to ugly effect.

For the reader, whether he is an author too, or not, the only test of a novel's truth is his own knowledge of life. Is it like what he has seen or felt? Then it is true, and for him it cannot otherwise be true, that is to say beautiful. It will not avail that it has style, learning, thinking, feeling; it is no more beautiful without truth than the pretty statue which cannot stand on its feet. It is very astonishing to me that any sort of people can find pleasure in such a thing; but I know that there are many who do; and I should not think of consigning them to the police for their bad taste so long as their taste alone is bad. At the same time I confess that I should suspect an unreality, an insincerity in a mature and educated person whom I found liking an unreal, an insincere novel. You see, I take novels rather seriously, and I would hold them to a much stricter account than they are commonly held to. If I could, I would have them all subject to the principles that govern an honest man, and do not suffer him to tell lies of any sort. I think the novelist is rarely the victim of such a possession, or obsession, that he does not know when he is representing and when he is misrepresenting life. If he does not know it fully at the time, he cannot fail to be aware of it upon review of his work. In the frenzy of inspiration, he may not know that he has been lying; but a time will quickly come to him, if he is at all an artist, when he will know it, and

3. Among the 19th-century novelists that Howells mentions are Jane Austen (1775–1817), Thomas Hardy (1840–1928), Mrs. Humphrey Ward (1851–1920), George Moore (1852–1933), Gustave Flaubert (1821–1880), Guy de Maupassant (1850–1893), Edmund de Goncourt (1822–1896), Jules de Goncourt (1830–1870), Alphonse Daudet (1840–1897), Émile Zola (1840–1902), Ivan Turgenev (1818–1883), Armando Palacio Valdés (1853–1938), Benito Pérez Galdós (1843–1920), Emilia Pardo-Bazan (1851–1921), Björnstjerne Martinus Björnson (1832–1910), Jonas Lie (1833–1908), Alexander Kielland (1849–1906), Edward Bulwer-Lytton (1831–1891), Alexandre Dumas, pére (1802–1870), Octave Feuillet (1821–1890), Georges Ohnet (1848–1918), Juan Valera (1824–1905), and Fyodor Dostoyevsky (1821–1881). Howells divides them into two camps: realists and idealists.

will see that the work he has done is ugly because of it. That is the time for him to tear up his work and to begin anew.

Of course, there are several ways of regarding life in fiction, and in order to do justice to the different kinds we ought to distinguish very clearly between them. There are three forms which I think of, and which I will name in the order of their greatness: the novel, the romance, and the romanticistic novel.

The novel I take to be the sincere and conscientious endeavor to picture life just as it is, to deal with character as we witness it in living people, and to record the incidents that grow out of character. This is the supreme form of fiction, and I offer as supreme examples of it, Pride and Prejudice, Middlemarch, Anna Karenina, Fathers and Sons, Doña Perfecta and Marta y Maria,[4] sufficiently varied in their origin and material and method, but all of the same absolute honesty in their intention. They all rely for their moral effect simply and solely upon their truth to nature.

The novel is easily first among books that people read willingly and it is rightfully first. It has known how to keep the charm of the story, and to add to it the attraction of almost every interest. It still beguiles, as in the hands of the Byzantine romancers,[5] not to go unnumbered centuries back to the Greek novel of Homer, the Odyssey;[6] and it has learnt how to warm, to question, to teach in every concern of life. Scarcely any predicament, moral or psychological, has escaped its study, and it has so refined and perfected its methods that antiseptic surgery itself has hardly made a more beneficent advance. It began with the merest fable, excluding from the reader's interest all but the fortunes of princes and other dignified personages for whose entertainment it existed, until now it includes all sorts and conditions of men, who turn to it for instruction, inspiration, consolation. It has broadened and deepened down and out till it compasses the whole of human nature; and no cause important to the race has been unfriended of it. Sometimes I have been vexed at its vicious pandering to passion, but I cannot think, after all, of any great modern novel which has not been distinctly moral in effect. I am not sorry to have had it go into the dark places of the soul, the filthy and squalid places of society, high and low, and shed there its great light. Let us know with its help what we are, and where we are. Let all the hidden things be brought into the sun, and let every day be the day of judgment. If the sermon cannot any longer serve this end, let the novel do it.

4. Pride and Prejudice (1813) by Jane Austen, Middlemarch (1872) by George Eliot, Anna Karenina (1877) by Leo Tolstoy, Fathers and Sons (1861) by Ivan Turgenev, Doña Perfecta (1876) by Benito Pérez Galdós, and Marta y Maria (1883) by Armando Palacio Valdés are 19th-century novels that represent "realism" as defined by Howells.
5. Erotic novels thrived in the Byzantine Empire from the late 5th century until the fall of Con-

stantinople in 1453; their hero was often Alexander the Great.
6. Homer is the poet of ancient Greek tradition who is said to have composed both of the great Greek epics, The Iliad and The Odyssey, probably in the 8th century B.C.E. The latter depicts the trials of Odysseus and his family as he struggles to return from Troy.

HENRY JAMES

Perhaps the most famous description of realism in the novel is Henry James's essay "The Art of Fiction," in which James (1843–1916) dismisses all prescriptions for novelistic success. A well-known traditionalist critic, Walter Besant, proposed that the good novel had to be overtly moral. James offered a rebuttal, rejecting *a priori* requirements of the novel: "I am quite at a loss to imagine anything (at any rate in this matter of fiction) that people *ought* to like or to dislike. Selection will be sure to take care of itself, for it has a constant motive behind it. That motive is simply experience." James urges the novelist to observe not only environment but more importantly its *meaning*: "[to catch] the very note and trick, the strange irregular rhythm of life, that is the attempt whose strenuous force keeps Fiction upon her feet." James matches the desire to reflect the incomplete realities of characters—who never seem to "know" until it is too late—with his own tacit pledge not to make designs on the opinions of his readers. But this ambiguity *is* James's design—*not* to "know" people in any certain, reductive, sense. James's idea of consciousness—a sort of spiderweb of "the very atmosphere of the mind"—means that the question of the "moral" is a false one. He finds that "the deepest quality of a work of art will always be the quality of the mind of the producer. . . . No good novel will ever proceed from a superficial mind."

From The Art of Fiction[1]

* * *

It goes without saying that you will not write a good novel unless you possess the sense of reality; but it will be difficult to give you a recipe for calling that sense into being. Humanity is immense, and reality has a myriad forms; the most one can affirm is that some of the flowers of fiction have the odour of it, and others have not; as for telling you in advance how your nosegay should be composed, that is another affair. It is equally excellent and inconclusive to say that one must write from experience; to our suppositious aspirant such a declaration might savour of mockery. What kind of experience is intended, and where does it begin and end? Experience is never limited, and it is never complete; it is an immense sensibility, a kind of huge spider-web of the finest silken threads suspended in the chamber of consciousness, and catching every air-borne particle in its tissue. It is the very atmosphere of the mind; and when the mind is imaginative—much more when it happens to be that of a man of genius—it takes to itself the faintest hints of life, it converts the very pulses of the air into revelations. The young lady living in a village has only to be a damsel upon whom nothing is lost to make it quite unfair (as it seems to me) to declare to her that she shall have nothing to say about the military. Greater miracles have been seen than that, imagination assisting, she should speak the truth about some of these gentlemen. I remember an English novelist, a woman of genius, telling me that she was much commended for the impression she

---

1. First published in *Longman's Magazine* 4 (September 1884), then in James's *Partial Portraits* (1888); rpt. in *Selected Literary Criticism* by Henry James (1968), from which this text is taken.

had managed to give in one of her tales of the nature and way of life of the French Protestant youth. She had been asked where she learned so much about this recondite being, she had been congratulated on her peculiar opportunities. These opportunities consisted in her having once, in Paris, as she ascended a staircase, passed an open door where, in the household of a *pasteur,* some of the young Protestants were seated at table round a finished meal. The glimpse made a picture; it lasted only a moment, but that moment was experience. She had got her direct personal impression, and she turned out her type. She knew what youth was, and what Protestantism; she also had the advantage of having seen what it was to be French, so that she converted these ideas into a concrete image and produced a reality. Above all, however, she was blessed with the faculty which when you give it an inch takes an ell, and which for the artist is a much greater source of strength than any accident of residence or of place in the social scale. The power to guess the unseen from the seen, to trace the implication of things, to judge the whole piece by the pattern, the condition of feeling life in general so completely that you are well on your way to knowing any particular corner of it—this cluster of gifts may almost be said to constitute experience, and they occur in country and in town and in the most differing stages of education. If experience consists of impressions, it may be said that impressions *are* experience, just as (have we not seen it?) they are the very air we breathe. Therefore, if I should certainly say to a novice, 'Write from experience and experience only', I should feel that this was rather a tantalizing monition if I were not careful immediately to add, 'Try to be one of the people on whom nothing is lost!'

* * *

A novel is a living thing, all one and continuous, like any other organism, and in proportion as it lives will it be found, that in each of the parts there is something of each of the other parts. The critic who over the close texture of a finished work shall pretend to trace a geography of items will mark some frontiers as artificial, I fear, as any that have been known to history. There is an old-fashioned distinction between the novel of character and the novel of incident which must have cost many a smile to the intending fabulist who was keen about his work. It appears to me as little to the point as the equally celebrated distinction between the novel and the romance—to answer as little to any reality. There are bad novels and good novels, as there are bad pictures and good pictures; but that is the only distinction in which I see any meaning, and I can as little imagine speaking of a novel of character as I can imagine speaking of a picture of character. When one says picture one says of character, when one says novel one says of incident, and the terms may be transposed at will. What is character but the determination of incident? What is incident but the illustration of character? What is either a picture or a novel that is *not* of character? What else do we seek in it and find in it? It is an incident for a woman to stand up with her hand resting on a table and look out at you in a certain way; or if it be not an incident I think it will be hard to say what it is. At the same time it is an expression of character. If you say you don't see it (character in *that—allons donc!*),[2] this is exactly what the artist who has reason of his own for thinking he

2. Let's go! (French).

does see it undertakes to show you. When a young man makes up his mind that he has not faith enough after all to enter the church as he intended, that is an incident, though you may not hurry to the end of the chapter to see whether perhaps he doesn't change once more. I do not say that these are extraordinary or startling incidents. I do not pretend to estimate the degree of interest proceeding from them, for this will depend upon the skill of the painter. It sounds almost puerile to say that some incidents are intrinsically much more important than others, and I need not take this precaution after having professed my sympathy for the major ones in remarking that the only classification of the novel that I can understand is into that which has life and that which has it not.

* * *

There is one point at which the moral sense and the artistic sense lie very near together; that is in the light of the very obvious truth that the deepest quality of a work of art will always be the quality of the mind of the producer. In proportion as that intelligence is fine will the novel, the picture, the statue partake of the substance of beauty and truth. To be constituted of such elements is, to my vision, to have purpose enough. No good novel will ever proceed from a superficial mind; that seems to me an axiom which, for the artist in fiction, will cover all needful moral ground: if the youthful aspirant take it to heart it will illuminate for him many of the mysteries of 'purpose'.

* * *

1884

FRANK NORRIS

Frank Norris (1870–1902) was the major theorist of naturalism in the United States, publishing essays that disputed Howell's view of the writer's obligations. In "Zola as a Romantic Writer" (1896), he argues that Howells's realism is simply uninteresting because the people he writes about are uninteresting. He wants something more romantic, more idealistic, more extreme—even though these literary characteristics might be seen as going counter to the deterministic view that supposedly dominated naturalism. The Howells-Norris difference paralleled that in France between Balzac and Zola—the earlier a realist, the later a naturalist.

In "A Plea for Romantic Fiction," first published in 1901, Norris seeks to redefine romance and naturalism. For Norris "realism" is confined to what is generally agreed on by middle-class readers to be "normal life," while naturalism penetrates "the surface of things." Norris again describes Howells's realism as the "drama of a broken teacup." He calls on realism to do the "entertaining," while naturalism, as romance, does the "teaching."

Zola as a Romantic Writer[1]

It is curious to notice how persistently M. Zola[2] is misunderstood. How strangely he is misinterpreted even by those who conscientiously admire the novels of the "man of the iron pen." For most people Naturalism has a vague meaning. It is a sort of inner circle of realism—a kind of diametric opposite of romanticism, a theory of fiction wherein things are represented "as they really are," inexorably, with the truthfulness of a camera. This idea can be shown to be far from right, that Naturalism, as understood by Zola, is but a form of romanticism after all.

Observe the methods employed by the novelists who profess and call themselves "realists"—Mr. Howells,[3] for instance. Howells's characters live across the street from us, they are "on our block." We know all about them, about their affairs, and the story of their lives. One can go even further. We ourselves are Mr. Howells's characters, so long as we are well behaved and ordinary and bourgeois, so long as we are not adventurous or not rich or not unconventional. If we are otherwise, if things commence to happen to us, if we kill a man or two, or get mixed up in a tragic affair, or do something on a large scale, such as the amassing of enormous wealth or power or fame, Mr. Howells cuts our acquaintance at once. He will none of us if we are out of the usual.

This is the real Realism. It is the smaller details of every-day life, things that are likely to happen between lunch and supper, small passions, restricted emotions, dramas of the reception-room, tragedies of an afternoon call, crises involving cups of tea. Every one will admit there is no romance here. The novel is interesting—which is after all the main point—but it is the commonplace tale of commonplace people made into a novel of far more than commonplace charm. Mr. Howells is not uninteresting; he is simply not romantic. But that Zola should be quoted as a realist, and as a realist of realists, is a strange perversion.

Reflect a moment upon his choice of subject and character and episode. The Rougon-Macquart[4] live in a world of their own; they are not of our lives any more than are the Don Juans, the Jean Valjeans, the Gil Blases, the Marmions, or the Ivanhoes. We, the bourgeois, the commonplace, the ordinary, have no part nor lot in the *Rougon-Macquart*, in *Lourdes*, or in *Rome*;[5] it is not our world, not because our social position is different, but because we are *ordinary*. To be noted of M. Zola we must leave the rank and the file, either run to the forefront of the marching world, or fall by the roadway; we must separate ourselves; we must become individual, unique. The naturalist takes no note of common people, common in so far as their interests, their lives, and the things that occur in them are common, are ordinary. Terrible things must happen to the characters of the naturalistic tale. They must be

1. First published in the San Francisco *Wave* 15 (June 27, 1896); rpt. in *The Literary Criticism of Frank Norris* (1964), from which this text is taken.
2. Émile Zola (1840–1902), naturalistic French novelist.
3. William Dean Howells (1837–1920), American novelist, critic, and proponent of realism.
4. Between 1870 and 1893, Zola wrote twenty novels about the intertwined and multigenerational Rougon-Macquart families.

5. Don Juan: a fictional libertine who makes a career out of seducing young women and ends up in hell. Jean Valjean: protagonist of Victor Hugo's 1862 novel *Les Misérables*. Gil Blas: 1862 novel by Alain-René Lesage. Marmion: antagonist in Sir Walter Scott's 1808 epic poem of the same name. Wilfred of Ivanhoe: protagonist of Scott's 1819 novel, *Ivanhoe*. Lourdes: town in southwestern France where fourteen-year-old Bernadette Soubirous claimed to have been visited by the Virgin Mary in 1858.

twisted from the ordinary, wrenched out from the quiet, uneventful round of every-day life, and flung into the throes of a vast and terrible drama that works itself out in unleashed passions, in blood, and in sudden death. The world of M. Zola is a world of big things; the enormous, the formidable, the terrible, is what counts; no teacup tragedies here. Here Nana holds her monstrous orgies, and dies horribly, her face distorted to a frightful mask; Etienne Lantier, carried away by the strike of coal miners of *Le Voreux*, (the strike that is almost war), is involved in the vast and fearful catastrophe that comes as a climax of the great drama; Claude Lantier, disappointed, disillusioned, acknowledging the futility of his art after a life of effort, hangs himself on his huge easel; Jacques Lantier, haunted by an hereditary insanity, all his natural desires hideously distorted, cuts the throat of the girl he loves, and is ground to pieces under the wheels of his own locomotive; Jean Macquart, soldier and tiller of the fields, is drawn into the war of 1870, passes through the terrible scenes of Sedan and the Siege of Paris only to bayonet to death his truest friend and sworn brother-at-arms in the streets of the burning capital.[6]

Everything is extraordinary, imaginative, grotesque even, with a vague note of terror quivering throughout like the vibration of an ominous and low-pitched diapason. It is all romantic, at times unmistakably so, as in *Le Rêve* or *Rome*, closely resembling the work of the greatest of all modern romanticists, Hugo.[7] We have the same huge dramas, the same enormous scenic effects, the same love of the extraordinary, the vast, the monstrous, and the tragic.

Naturalism is a form of romanticism, not an inner circle of realism. Where is the realism in the *Rougon-Macquart*? Are such things likely to happen between lunch and supper? That Zola's work is not purely romantic as was Hugo's, lies chiefly in the choice of Milieu. These great, terrible dramas no longer happen among the personnel of a feudal and Renaissance nobility, those who are in the fore-front of the marching world, but among the lower— almost the lowest—classes; those who have been thrust or wrenched from the ranks, who are falling by the roadway. This is not romanticism—this drama of the people, working itself out in blood and ordure. It is not realism. It is a school by itself, unique, somber, powerful beyond words. It is naturalism.

1896

6. Nana: title character of Zola's 1880 novel, in which a prostitute rises from humble beginnings to destroy enemies among the Parisian elite. Etienne Lantier: protagonist of Zola's 1885 *Germinal*. *Le Voreux*: "the voracious one" (French), and also the mining-town setting for *Germinal*. Claude Lantier: protagonist of Zola's 1886 *L'Oeuvre* ("The Masterpiece"). Jacques Lantier: a central character in Zola's 1890 novel, *La Bete Humaine* ("The Human Beast"). Jean Macquart: protagonist of Zola's 1892 novel, *La Debacle*, the final installment of the twenty-volume *Rougon-Macquart* series. War of 1870: War between Prussia and France which resulted in the defeat of France

and the dissolution of its imperial power, and the unification of German states under the Prussian king. Sedan: battle in the War of 1870 in which Napoleon III of France, along with his army, surrendered to Prussian forces. The Siege of Paris: battle of the French capital from September 1870 to January 1871, when the armistice was signed.
7. *Le Rêne* or *Rome*: *Rougon-Macquart* novels published in 1888; the second installment of *Les Trois Villes* was published in 1896. Victor-Marie Hugo (1802–1885), 19th-century French Romantic writer best known for his novels *Les Misérables* (1862) and *Notre-Dame de Paris* (1831).

A Plea for Romantic Fiction[1]

Let us at the start make a distinction. Observe that one speaks of Romanticism and not of sentimentalism. One claims that the latter is as distinct from the former as is that other form of art which is called Realism. Romance has been often put upon and overburdened by being forced to bear the onus of abuse that by right should fall to sentiment; but the two should be kept very distinct, for a very high and illustrious place will be claimed for Romance, while sentiment will be handed down the scullery stairs.

Many people today are composing mere sentimentalism, and calling it and causing it to be called Romance, so with those who are too busy to think much upon these subjects, but who none the less love honest literature, Romance has fallen into disrepute. Consider now the cut-and-thrust stories. They are labelled Romances, and it is very easy to get the impression that Romance must be an affair of cloaks and daggers, or moonlight and golden hair. But this is not so at all. The true Romance is a more serious business than this. It is not merely a conjurer's trick box, full of flimsy quackeries, tinsel and clap traps, meant only to amuse, and relying upon deception to do even that. Is it not something better than this? Can we not see in it an instrument, keen, finely tempered, flawless—an instrument with which we may go straight through the clothes and tissues and wrappings of flesh down deep into the red, living heart of things?

Is all this too subtle, too merely speculative and intrinsic, too *précieuse* and nice and "literary"?[2] Devoutly one hopes the contrary. So much is made of so-called Romanticism in present-day fiction, that the subject seems worthy of discussion, and a protest against the misuse of a really noble and honest formula of literature appears to be timely—misuse, that is, in the sense of limited use. Let us suppose for the moment that a Romance can be made out of the cut-and-thrust business. Good Heavens, are there no other things that are romantic, even in this—falsely, falsely called—humdrum world of today? Why should it be that so soon as the novelist addresses himself—seriously—to the consideration of contemporary life he must abandon Romance and take up that harsh, loveless, colorless, blunt tool called Realism?

Now, let us understand at once what is meant by Romance and what by Realism. Romance—I take it—is the kind of fiction that takes cognizance of variations from the type of normal life. Realism is the kind of fiction that confines itself to the type of normal life. According to this definition, then, Romance may even treat of the sordid, the unlovely—as for instance, the novels of M. Zola. (Zola has been dubbed a Realist, but he is, on the contrary, the very head of Romanticists.) Also, Realism, used as it sometimes is as a term of reproach, need not be in the remotest sense or degree offensive, but on the other hand respectable as a church and proper as a deacon—as, for instance, the novels of Mr. Howells.

The reason why one claims so much for Romance, and quarrels so pointedly with Realism, is that Realism stultifies itself. It notes only the surface of things. For it Beauty is not even skin-deep, but only a geometrical plane,

1. First published in the *Boston Evening Transcript*, December 18, 1901; rpt. in *McTeague: A Story of San Francisco* by Frank Norris, 2nd ed. (1997), from which this text is taken.
2. That is, overly careful and conventional.

without dimensions of depth, a mere outside. Realism is very excellent so far as it goes, but it goes no farther than the Realist himself can actually see, or actually hear. Realism is minute, it is the drama of a broken teacup, the tragedy of a walk down the block, the excitement of an afternoon call, the adventure of an invitation to dinner. It is the visit to my neighbor's house, a formal visit, from which I may draw no conclusions. I see my neighbor and his friends—very, oh, such very! probable people—and that is all. Realism bows upon the doormat and goes away and says to me, as we link arms on the sidewalk: "That is life." And I say it is not. It is not, as you would very well see if you took Romance with you to call upon your neighbor.

Lately you have been taking Romance a weary journey across the water— ages and the flood of years—and haling her into the fusty, musty, worm-eaten, moth-riddled, rust-corroded "Grandes Salles"[3] of the Middle Ages and the Renaissance, and she has found the drama of a bygone age for you there. But would you take her across the street to your neighbor's front parlor (with the bisque fisher boy[4] on the mantel and the photograph of Niagara Falls on glass hanging in the front window); would you introduce her there? Not you. Would you take a walk with her on Fifth avenue, or Beacon street, or Michigan avenue?[5] No indeed. Would you choose her for a companion of a morning spent in Wall Street, or an afternoon in the Waldorf-Astoria?[6] You just guess you would not.

She would be out of place, you say, inappropriate. She might be awkward in my neighbor's front parlor, and knock over the little bisque fisher boy. Well, she might. If she did, you might find underneath the base of the statuette, hidden away, tucked away—what? God knows. But something which would be a complete revelation of my neighbor's secretest life.

So you think Romance would stop in the front parlor and discuss medicated flannels and mineral waters with the ladies?[7] Not for more than five minutes. She would be off upstairs with you, prying, peeping, peering into the closets of the bedrooms, into the nursery, into the sitting-room; yes, and into that little iron box screwed to the lower shelf of the closet in the library; and into those compartments and pigeonholes of the *secrétaire*[8] in the study. She would find a heartache (maybe) between the pillows of the mistress's bed, and a memory carefully secreted in the master's deedbox.[9] She would come upon a great hope amid the books and papers of the study table of the young man's room, and—perhaps—who knows—an affair, or, great heavens, an intrigue, in the scented ribbons and gloves and hairpins of the young lady's bureau. And she would pick here a little and there a little, making up a bag of hopes and fears, and a package of joys and sorrows—great ones, mind you—and then come down to the front door, and stepping out into the street, hand you the bags and package, and say to you—"That is Life!"

Romance does very well in the castles of the Middle Ages and the Renaissance chateaux, and she has the entrée there and is very well received. That is all well and good. But let us protest against limiting her to such places and

---

3. Great ballrooms or auditoriums (French).
4. Inexpensive imitation of costly porcelain figurines.
5. Streets in New York City, Boston, and Chicago, respectively.
6. Luxury hotel in New York City.
7. Flannels were used to apply warm liquors to

the body for the purpose of easing pain by relaxing the skin. Mineral waters were bathed in or drunk as curatives for many medical conditions at this time.
8. Desk (French).
9. Lockbox for money or valuables.

such times. You will find her, I grant you, in the chatelaine's[1] chamber and the dungeon of the man-at-arms; but, if you choose to look for her, you will find her equally at home in the brownstone house on the corner and in the office building downtown. And this very day, in this very hour, she is sitting among the rags and wretchedness, the dirt and despair of the tenements of the East Side[2] of New York

"What?" I hear you say, "look for Romance—the lady of the silken robes and golden crown, our beautiful, chaste maiden of soft voice and gentle eyes—look for her among the vicious ruffians, male and female, of Allen Street and Mulberry Bend?"[3] I tell you she is there, and to your shame be it said you will not know her in those surroundings. You, the aristocrats, who demand the fine linen and the purple in your fiction; you, the sensitive, the delicate, who will associate with your Romance only so long as she wears a silken gown. You will not follow her to the slums, for you believe that Romance should only amuse and entertain you, singing you sweet songs and touching the harp of silver strings with rosy-tipped fingers. If haply she should call to you from the squalor of a dive, or the awful degradation of a disorderly house,[4] crying: "Look! listen! This, too, is life. These, too, are my children, look at them, know them and, knowing, help!" Should she call thus, you would stop your ears; you would avert your eyes, and you would answer, "Come from there, Romance. Your place is not there!" And you would make of her a harlequin, a tumbler,[5] a sword dancer, when, as a matter of fact, she should be by right divine a teacher sent from God.

She will not always wear a robe of silk, the gold crown, the jeweled shoon,[6] will not always sweep the silver harp. An iron note is hers if so she choose, and coarse garments, and stained hands; and, meeting her thus, it is for you to know her as she passes—know her for the same young queen of the blue mantle and lilies.[7] She can teach you, if you will be humble to learn. Teach you by showing. God help you, if at last you take from Romance her mission of teaching, if you do not believe that she has a purpose, a nobler purpose and a mightier than mere amusement, mere entertainment. Let Realism do the entertaining with its meticulous presentation of teacups, rag carpets, wall paper and haircloth sofas, stopping with these, going no deeper than it sees, choosing the ordinary, the untroubled, the commonplace.

But to Romance belongs the wide world for range, and the unplumbed depths of the human heart, and the mystery of sex, and the problems of life, and the black, unsearched penetralia of the soul of man. You, the indolent, must not always be amused. What matter the silken clothes, what matter the prince's houses? Romance, too, is a teacher, and if—throwing aside the purple—she wears the camel's hair and feeds upon the locusts,[8] it is to cry aloud unto the people, "Prepare ye the way of the Lord; make straight his path."

1901

1. Wife of an estate owner (French).
2. One of the oldest neighborhoods of New York City, situated along the East River from the Manhattan Bridge to 14th Street and bounded on the west by Broadway, a working-class neighborhood defined by immigrant populations and tenements.
3. Streets in Manhattan's Lower East Side associated with the "Five Points Slum," known during Norris's time as a center of violence and crime.

4. A house of prostitution.
5. Clown or buffoon; acrobat or gymnast.
6. Archaic plural of "shoe."
7. Details frequently seen in depictions of the Virgin Mary.
8. Reference to John the Baptist's self-imposed exile in the wilderness and prophecies of the future (see especially Matthew 3, 11, 14).

THEODORE DREISER

Theodore Dreiser (1871–1945) has been called "the American Zola" by critic George J. Becker. His output includes some of the most famous, and longest, examples of naturalistic fiction. He was also an editor, and on occasion a theorist of literature. "True Art Speaks Plainly," first published in 1903, is a rejoinder by the author to the criticism that greeted *Sister Carrie* (1900) on publication. Dreiser argues that the essence of morality is to "tell the truth. . . . [to] express what we see honestly and without subterfuge." Defending himself and other naturalists against charges of lewdness, Dreiser characterizes the conventional critic's version of "the mental virtue of the reader" as false. The novelist must tell the truth no matter the consequences. Despite his clear statements about truth, morality, and fiction, Dreiser struggled for acceptance of his work on its own grounds until the great success of *An American Tragedy* in 1925.

True Art Speaks Plainly[1]

The sum and substance of literary as well as social morality may be expressed in three words—tell the truth. It matters not how the tongues of the critics may wag, or the voices of a partially developed and highly conventionalized society may complain, the business of the author, as well as of other workers upon this earth, is to say what he knows to be true, and, having said as much, to abide the result with patience.

Truth is what is; and the seeing of what is, the realization of truth. To express what we see honestly and without subterfuge: this is morality as well as art.

What the so-called judges of the truth or morality are really inveighing against most of the time is not the discussion of mere sexual lewdness, for no work with that as a basis could possibly succeed, but the disturbing and destroying of their own little theories concerning life, which in some cases may be nothing more than a quiet acceptance of things as they are without any regard to the well-being of the future. Life for them is made up of a variety of interesting but immutable forms and any attempt either to picture any of the wretched results of modern social conditions or to assail the critical defenders of the same is naturally looked upon with contempt or aversion.

It is true that the rallying cry of the critics against so-called immoral literature is that the mental virtue of the reader must be preserved; but this has become a house of refuge to which every form of social injustice hurries for protection. The influence of intellectual ignorance and physical and moral greed upon personal virtue produces the chief tragedies of the age, and yet the objection to the discussion of the sex question is so great as to almost prevent the handling of the theme entirely.

Immoral! Immoral! Under this cloak hide the vices of wealth as well as the vast unspoken blackness of poverty and ignorance; and between them must

1. First published in *Booklovers Magazine* (February 1903); rpt. in *Documents of Modern Literary Realism* (1963), from which this text is taken.

walk the little novelist, choosing neither truth nor beauty, but some half-conceived phase of life that bears no honest relationship to either the whole of nature or to man.

The impossibility of any such theory of literature having weight with the true artist must be apparent to every clear reasoning mind. Life is not made up of any one phase or condition of being, nor can man's interest possibly be so confined.

The extent of all reality is the realm of the author's pen, and a true picture of life, honestly and reverentially set down, is both moral and artistic whether it offends the conventions or not.

1903

JACK LONDON

Jack London's essay "What Life Means to Me" was published in *Cosmopolitan* in March 1906 as part of a series in which the magazine challenged prominent American writers to contribute articles on this theme. London (1876–1916) had been warned by the socialist and poet Edwin Markham that the Hearst Corporation, which owned *Cosmopolitan,* would never publish an attack on American capitalism, but the article appeared as London wrote it. London wryly remarked to Markham that "special writers like myself are paid well for expanding their own untrammeled views," with the understanding that these views would sell magazines. His second wife, Charmian Kittredge London, later described this essay as his "most impassioned committal of himself as a rebel toward the shames and uncleanness of the capitalist system." "What Life Means to Me," written during the socialist phase of London's development, is one of his strongest expressions of the relation between the naturalistic elements of his fiction and his gritty origins and struggles for survival within urban poverty and an exploitative class system.

From What Life Means to Me[1]

I was born in the working-class. Early I discovered enthusiasm, ambition, and ideals; and to satisfy these became the problem of my child-life. My environment was crude and rough and raw. I had no outlook, but an uplook rather. My place in society was at the bottom. Here life offered nothing but sordidness and wretchedness, both of the flesh and the spirit; for here flesh and spirit were alike starved and tormented.

Above me towered the colossal edifice of society, and to my mind the only way out was up. Into this edifice I early resolved to climb. Up above, men wore black clothes and boiled shirts, and women dressed in beautiful gowns. Also, there were good things to eat, and there was plenty to eat. This much for the flesh. Then there were the things of the spirit. Up above me, I knew, were unselfishnesses of the spirit, clean and noble thinking, keen intellectual

1. First published in *Cosmopolitan* 41 (March 1906); rpt. in *Revolution and Other Essays* by Jack London (1909), from which this text is taken.

living. I knew all this because I read "Seaside Library" novels,[2] in which, with the exception of the villains and adventuresses, all men and women thought beautiful thoughts, spoke a beautiful tongue, and performed glorious deeds. In short, as I accepted the rising of the sun, I accepted that up above me was all that was fine and noble and gracious, all that gave decency and dignity to life, all that made life worth living and that remunerated one for his travail and misery.

*   *   *

I was a sailor before the mast, a longshoreman, a roustabout;[3] I worked in canneries, and factories, and laundries; I mowed lawns, and cleaned carpets, and washed windows. And I never got the full product of my toil. I looked at the daughter of the cannery owner, in her carriage, and knew that it was my muscle, in part, that helped drag along that carriage on its rubber tires. I looked at the son of the factory owner, going to college, and knew that it was my muscle that helped, in part, to pay for the wine and good fellowship he enjoyed.

But I did not resent this. It was all in the game. They were the strong. Very well, I was strong. I would carve my way to a place amongst them and make money out of the muscles of other men. I was not afraid of work. I loved hard work. I would pitch in and work harder than ever and eventually become a pillar of society.

And just then, as luck would have it, I found an employer that was of the same mind. I was willing to work, and he was more than willing that I should work. I thought I was learning a trade. In reality, I had displaced two men. I thought he was making an electrician out of me; as a matter of fact, he was making fifty dollars per month out of me. The two men I had displaced had received forty dollars each per month; I was doing the work of both for thirty dollars per month.

This employer worked me nearly to death. A man may love oysters, but too many oysters will disincline him toward that particular diet. And so with me. Too much work sickened me. I did not wish ever to see work again. I fled from work. I became a tramp, begging my way from door to door, wandering over the United States and sweating bloody sweats in slums and prisons.

I had been born in the working-class, and I was now, at the age of eighteen, beneath the point at which I had started. I was down in the cellar of society, down in the subterranean depths of misery about which it is neither nice nor proper to speak. I was in the pit, the abyss, the human cesspool, the shambles and the charnel-house of our civilization. This is the part of the edifice of society that society chooses to ignore. Lack of space compels me here to ignore it, and I shall say only that the things I there saw gave me a terrible scare.

I was scared into thinking. I saw the naked simplicities of the complicated civilization in which I lived. Life was a matter of food and shelter. In order to get food and shelter men sold things. The merchant sold shoes, the politician sold his manhood, and the representative of the people, with exceptions, of course, sold his trust; while nearly all sold their honor. Women, too, whether on the street or in the holy bond of wedlock, were prone to sell their flesh. All things were commodities, all people bought and sold. The one commodity that labor had to sell was muscle. The honor of labor had no price in the market-place. Labor had muscle, and muscle alone, to sell.

2. Inexpensive novel series published by George   3. Dock worker.
Munro, New York, from 1877 to 1882.

But there was a difference, a vital difference. Shoes and trust and honor had a way of renewing themselves. They were imperishable stocks. Muscle, on the other hand, did not renew. As the shoe merchant sold shoes, he continued to replenish his stock. But there was no way of replenishing the laborer's stock of muscle. The more he sold of his muscle, the less of it remained to him. It was his one commodity, and each day his stock of it diminished. In the end, if he did not die before, he sold out and put up his shutters. He was a muscle bankrupt, and nothing remained to him but to go down into the cellar of society and perish miserably.

I learned, further, that brain was likewise a commodity. It, too, was different from muscle. A brain seller was only at his prime when he was fifty or sixty years old, and his wares were fetching higher prices than ever. But a laborer was worked out or broken down at forty-five or fifty. I had been in the cellar of society, and I did not like the place as a habitation. The pipes and drains were unsanitary, and the air was bad to breathe. If I could not live on the parlor floor of society, I could, at any rate, have a try at the attic. It was true, the diet there was slim, but the air at least was pure. So I resolved to sell no more muscle, and to become a vender of brains.

Then began a frantic pursuit of knowledge. I returned to California and opened the books. While thus equipping myself to become a brain merchant, it was inevitable that I should delve into sociology. There I found, in a certain class of books, scientifically formulated, the simple sociological concepts I had already worked out for myself. Other and greater minds, before I was born, had worked out all that I had thought and a vast deal more. I discovered that I was a socialist.

The socialists were revolutionists, inasmuch as they struggled to overthrow the society of the present, and out of the material to build the society of the future. I, too, was a socialist and a revolutionist. I joined the groups of working-class and intellectual revolutionists, and for the first time came into intellectual living. Here I found keen-flashing intellects and brilliant wits; for here I met strong and alert-brained, withal horny-handed, members of the working-class; unfrocked preachers too wide in their Christianity for any congregation of Mammon-worshippers; professors broken on the wheel of university subservience to the ruling class and flung out because they were quick with knowledge which they strove to apply to the affairs of mankind.

Here I found, also, warm faith in the human, glowing idealism, sweetnesses of unselfishness, renunciation, and martyrdom—all the splendid, stinging things of the spirit. Here life was clean, noble, and alive. Here life rehabilitated itself, became wonderful and glorious; and I was glad to be alive. I was in touch with great souls who exalted flesh and spirit over dollars and cents, and to whom the thin wail of the starved slum child meant more than all the pomp and circumstance of commercial expansion and world empire. All about me were nobleness of purpose and heroism of effort, and my days and nights were sunshine and starshine, all fire and dew, with before my eyes, ever burning and blazing, the Holy Grail, Christ's own Grail, the warm human, long-suffering and maltreated, but to be rescued and saved at the last.

* * *

1906, 1909

THEODORE DREISER
1871–1945

Theodore Herman Albert Dreiser was born in Terre Haute, Indiana, on August 17, 1871, the eleventh of thirteen children. His stern, emotionally distant father was, in Dreiser's view, "mentally a little weak"; he was in any event not very successful in providing for his large family, and he served as the prototype for the failed men who appear so frequently in Dreiser's novels. Dreiser's mother, by contrast, was steadfastly devoted to the well-being of her children; she was, Dreiser claimed, the only person who ever loved him enough. She, too, appears in fictionalized form in many of Dreiser's books.

Dreiser's unhappy childhood haunted him throughout his life. The large family moved from house to house in Indiana dogged by poverty, insecurity, and internal divisions. One of his brothers became a famous popular songwriter under the name Paul Dresser, but other siblings lived turbulent lives that not only defied their father's rigid morality but placed them on the margins of respectable society altogether. Dreiser as a youth was ungainly, confused, shy, and full of vague yearnings like most of his fictional protagonists, male and female. In this as in many other ways, Dreiser's novels are direct projections of his inner life as well as careful transcriptions of his experiences, especially those involving his unstable family.

From the age of fifteen Dreiser was on his own, earning meager support from a variety of menial jobs. A high-school teacher staked him to a year at Indiana University in 1889, but Dreiser's real education was to come from experience and from independent reading and thinking. This education began in 1892 when he landed by persistence and good luck his first newspaper job with the *Chicago Globe*. Over the next decade, as an itinerant journalist, Dreiser slowly groped his way to authorship, testing what he knew from his own life against what he had learned from reading, among others, Charles Darwin, Ernst Haeckel, Thomas Huxley, and Herbert Spencer, late nineteenth-century scientists and social scientists who lent support to the view that nature and society had no divine sanction. Generally speaking, these thinkers agreed that human beings, just as much as other life-forms, were participants in an evolutionary process in which only those who adapted successfully to their environments survived. Human beings, they agreed, were not the privileged creations of supernatural powers. At the same time, Spencer in particular argued that human consciousness was itself a product of evolutionary processes and that it entailed the adaptive capacity for altruism and various forms of social cooperation. This tension between deterministic "chemisms" (as Dreiser called them) and the potential for friendship and the improvement of social institutions appears in Dreiser's fiction throughout his writing career. Early on Dreiser emphasized the mechanistic side of this tension, while in later phases—in his fiction and in his social writings—he appeared to balance his more pessimistic views with belief in the possibilities of social justice.

Sister Carrie (1900), Dreiser's first novel, two chapters of which are included here, tells the story of Carrie Meeber, a country girl from Wisconsin who comes to Chicago, attracted by the excitement that rapidly growing urban centers held out for so many young people in the late 1800s, but even more by the possibility of supporting herself, especially given the meager opportunities in her small rural town. In Chicago she is seduced first by a traveling salesman, Charles Drouet, then by George Hurstwood, a married middle-aged manager of a stylish saloon patronized by wealthy men. Eager to elope with Carrie, Hurstwood steals ten thousand dollars from the safe in the bar; then he and Carrie flee to New York, where, unable to find a job equivalent to the one he gave up, he deteriorates while she begins a successful career on the stage. They eventually part company and, unbeknownst to Carrie, the impoverished Hurstwood commits suicide.

The novel depicts social transgressions by characters who feel no remorse and largely escape punishment, and it is candid about sex and names living persons. It was virtually suppressed by its publisher, who printed but refused to promote the book. Since its reissue in 1907 it has steadily risen in popularity and scholarly acceptance. *Sister Carrie* addresses many issues still of significance today: class mobility, immigration, urban life, greater independence for women and control of their own sexualities, pressure to succeed in American society, and celebrity culture.

In the first years of the twentieth century Dreiser suffered a nervous breakdown. With the help of his brother Paul, he recovered and by 1904 was on the way to several successful years as an editor, the last of them as editorial director of the Butterick Publishing Company. In 1910 he resigned to write *Jennie Gerhardt* (1911), one of his best novels and the first of a long succession of books that marked his turn to writing as a full-time career. This novel, about the doomed love between a rich man and a poor woman, takes seriously the reality of gentleness, selflessness, and loyalty, though in the end materialism and pressures associated with wealth and social position carry the day.

In *The Financier* (1912), *The Titan* (1914), and *The Stoic* (not published until 1947), Dreiser shifted from the pathos of helpless protagonists to the power of those unusual individuals who assume dominant roles in business and society. The protagonist of this "Trilogy of Desire" (as Dreiser described it), Frank Cowperwood, is modeled after the Chicago speculator Charles T. Yerkes. These novels of the businessman as buccaneer elaborated, even more explicitly than had *Sister Carrie,* the notion that men of high sexual energy were financially successful, a theme that is carried over into the autobiographical novel *The "Genius"* (1915).

The identification of potency with money is at the heart of Dreiser's greatest and most successful novel, *An American Tragedy* (1925). The novel is based on a much-publicized murder in upstate New York in 1906. Clyde Griffiths is a poor boy from the provinces who dreams of a life of luxury and status. When his prospect for marrying the wealthy Sondra Finchley is threatened by the pregnant Roberta Alden, a factory worker with whom he has had a relationship, Clyde plans to murder her. He takes her out boating, but at the last moment finds himself unable to carry out his murderous plan. Then when she approaches him, he physically rebuffs her, causing the boat to capsize and causing her to drown after all. Did he kill her or not? The second half of the book follows Clyde's arrest, his trial, his imprisonment, and his eventual execution. The novel was an immediate best seller and confirmed Dreiser's status as one of the leading writers of his time.

During the last two decades of his life Dreiser turned to polemical writing, but also to other genres—poetry, travel books, and autobiography, including *Dawn* (1931), the first volume in the projected but uncompleted *A History of Myself*. He visited the Soviet Union in 1927 and published *Dreiser Looks at Russia* the following year. In the 1930s, like many American intellectuals and writers, Dreiser was increasingly attracted by the philosophical program of the Communist party. Unable to believe in traditional religious credos, yet unable to give up his strong sense of justice, he continued to seek a way to reconcile his determinism with his compassionate sense of the mystery of life.

Dreiser's interest was in human motives and behavior and in the particularities of the environments that helped shape them. His writing is often blunt and ungainly, but many critics believe that his ability to structure complex narratives by manipulating point of view and by using symbols and clusters of metaphors as leitmotifs more than compensates for his sometimes awkward syntax. If, in the end, readers want from a novelist the communication of a deeply felt sense of life, continuing interest in Dreiser seems ensured.

From Sister Carrie[1]

Chapter I

When Caroline Meeber boarded the afternoon train for Chicago her total outfit consisted of a small trunk, which was checked in the baggage car, a cheap imitation alligator skin satchel holding some minor details of the toilet, a small lunch in a paper box and a yellow leather snap purse, containing her ticket, a scrap of paper with her sister's address in Van Buren Street,[2] and four dollars in money. It was in August, 1889. She was eighteen years of age, bright, timid and full of the illusions of ignorance and youth. Whatever touch of regret at parting characterized her thoughts it was certainly not for advantages now being given up. A gush of tears at her mother's farewell kiss, a touch in the throat when the cars clacked by the flour mill where her father worked by the day, a pathetic sigh as the familiar green environs of the village passed in review, and the threads which bound her so lightly to girlhood and home were irretrievably broken.

To be sure she was not conscious of any of this. Any change, however great, might be remedied. There was always the next station where one might descend and return. There was the great city, bound more closely by these very trains which came up daily. Columbia City was not so very far away, even once she was in Chicago. What pray is a few hours—a hundred miles? She could go back. And then her sister was there. She looked at the little slip bearing the latter's address and wondered. She gazed at the green landscape now passing in swift review until her swifter thoughts replaced its impression with vague conjectures of what Chicago might be. Since infancy her ears had been full of its fame. Once the family had thought of moving there. If she secured good employment they might come now. Anyhow it was vast. There were lights and sounds and a roar of things. People were rich. There were vast depots. This on-rushing train was merely speeding to get there.

When a girl leaves her home at eighteen, she does one of two things. Either she falls into saving hands and becomes better, or she rapidly assumes the cosmopolitan standard of virtue and becomes worse. Of an intermediate balance, under the circumstances, there is no possibility. The city has its cunning wiles no less than the infinitely smaller and more human tempter. There are large forces which allure, with all the soulfulness of expression possible in the most cultured human. The gleam of a thousand lights is often as effective, to all moral intents and purposes, as the persuasive light in a wooing and fascinating eye. Half the undoing of the unsophisticated and natural mind is accomplished by forces wholly superhuman. A blare of sound, a roar of life, a vast array of human hives appeal to the astonished senses in equivocal terms. Without a counselor at hand to whisper cautious interpretations, what falsehoods may not these things breathe into the unguarded ear! Unrecognized for what they are, their beauty, like music, too often relaxes, then weakens, then perverts the simplest human perceptions.

Caroline, or "Sister Carrie" as she had been half affectionately termed by the family, was possessed of a mind rudimentary in its power of observation and analysis. Self-interest with her was high, but not strong. It was nevertheless her guiding characteristic. Warm with the fancies of youth, pretty with

---

1. First published by Doubleday & Page (1900), from which this text is taken.

2. East-west Chicago street that, roughly, divides the city in half.

the insipid prettiness of the formative period, possessed of a figure which tended toward eventual shapeliness and an eye alight with certain native intelligence, she was a fair example of the middle American class—two generations removed from the emigrant. Books were beyond her interest— knowledge a sealed book. In the intuitive graces she was still crude. She could scarcely toss her head gracefully. Her hands were almost ineffectual for the same reason. The feet, though small, were set flatly. And yet she was interested in her charms, quick to understand the keener pleasures of life, ambitious to gain in material things. A half-equipped little knight she was, venturing to reconnoitre the mysterious city and dreaming wild dreams of some vague, far-off supremacy which should make it prey and subject, the proper penitent, grovelling at a woman's slipper.

"That," said a voice in her ear, "is one of the prettiest little resorts in Wisconsin."

"Is it?" she answered nervously.

The train was just pulling out of Waukesha.[3] For some time she had been conscious of a man behind. She felt him observing her mass of hair. He had been fidgeting, and with natural intuition she felt a certain interest growing in that quarter. Her maidenly reserve and a certain sense of what was conventional under the circumstances called her to forestall and deny this familiarity, but the daring and magnetism of the individual, born of past experience and triumphs, prevailed. She answered.

He leaned forward to put his elbows upon the back of her seat and proceeded to make himself volubly agreeable.

"Yes, that's a great resort for Chicago people. The hotels are swell. You are not familiar with this part of the country, are you?"

"Oh yes I am," answered Carrie. "That is, I live at Columbia City. I have never been through here though."

"And so this is your first visit to Chicago," he observed.

All the time she was conscious of certain features out of the side of her eye. Flush, colorful cheeks, a light mustache, a gray fedora hat. She now turned and looked upon him in full, the instincts of self-protection and coquetry mingling confusedly in her brain.

"I didn't say that," she said.

"Oh," he answered in a very pleasing way and with an assumed air of mistake. "I thought you did."

Here was a type of the traveling canvasser for a manufacturing house—a class which at that time was first being dubbed by the slang of the day "drummers."[4] He came within the meaning of a still newer term which had sprung into general use among Americans in 1880, and which concisely expressed the thought of one whose dress or manners are such as to impress strongly the fancy, or elicit the admiration, of susceptible young women—a "masher." His clothes were of an impressive character, the suit being cut of a striped and crossed pattern of brown wool, very popular at that time. It was what has since become known as a business suit. The low crotch of the vest revealed a stiff shirt bosom of white and pink stripes, surmounted by a high white collar about which was fastened a tie of distinct pattern. From his coat sleeves protruded a pair of linen cuffs of the same material as the shirt and

---

3. A city in Wisconsin about 106 miles north of Chicago on Lake Michigan.

4. "Canvassers" and "drummers" are salesmen.

fastened with large gold-plate buttons set with the common yellow agates known as "cat's-eyes." His fingers bore several rings, one the ever-enduring heavy seal, and from his vest dangled a neat gold watch chain from which was suspended the secret insignia of the Order of Elks. The whole suit was rather tight-fitting and was finished off with broad-soled tan shoes, highly polished, and the grey felt hat, then denominated "fedora," before mentioned. He was, for the order of intellect represented, attractive; and whatever he had to recommend him, you may be sure was not lost upon Carrie, in this her first glance.

Lest this order of individual should permanently pass, let me put down some of the most striking characteristics of his most successful manner and method. Good clothes of course were the first essential, the things without which he was nothing. A strong physical nature actuated by a keen desire for the feminine was the next. A mind free of any consideration of the problems or forces of the world and actuated not by greed but an insatiable love of variable pleasure—woman—pleasure. His method was always simple. Its principal element was daring, backed of course by an intense desire and admiration for the sex. Let him meet with a young woman twice and upon the third meeting he would walk up and straighten her necktie for her and perhaps address her by her first name. If an attractive woman should deign a glance of interest in passing him upon the street he would run up, seize her by the hand in feigned acquaintanceship and convince her that they had met before, providing of course that his pleasing way interested her in knowing him further. In the great department stores he was at his ease in capturing the attention of some young woman, while waiting for the cash boy to come back with his change. In such cases, by those little wiles common to the type, he would find out the girl's name, her favorite flower, where a note would reach her, and perhaps pursue the delicate task of friendship until it proved unpromising for the one aim in view, when it would be relinquished.

He would do very well with more pretentious women, though the burden of expense was a slight deterrent. Upon entering a parlor car at St. Paul, for instance, he would select a chair next to the most promising bit of femininity and soon inquire if she cared to have the shade lowered. Before the train cleared the yards he would have the porter bring her a footstool. At the next lull in his conversational progress he would find her something to read, and from then on by dint of compliment gently insinuated, personal narrative, exaggeration and service, he would win her tolerance and mayhap regard.

Those who have ever delved into the depths of a woman's conscience must, at some time or other, have come upon that mystery of mysteries—the moral significance, to her, of clothes. A woman should some day write the complete philosophy of that subject. No matter how young she is, it is one of the things she wholly comprehends. There is an indescribably faint line in the matter of man's apparel which somehow divides for her those who are worth glancing at and those who are not. Once an individual has passed this faint line on the way downward he will get no glance from her. There is another line at which the dress of a man will cause her to study her own. This line the individual at her elbow now marked for Carrie. She became conscious of an inequality. Her own plain blue dress with its black cotton tape trimmings realized itself to her imagination as shabby. She felt the worn state of her shoes.

He mistook this thought wave, which caused her to withdraw her glance and turn for relief to the landscape outside, for some little gain his grace had brought him.

"Let's see," he went on. "I know quite a number of people in your town—Morgenroth the clothier and Gibson the dry-goods man."

"Oh, do you," she interrupted, aroused by memories of longings the displays in the latter's establishment had cost her.

At last he had a clue to her interest and followed it up deftly. In a few minutes he had come about into her seat. He talked of sales of clothing, his travels, Chicago and the amusements of that city.

"If you are going there you will enjoy it immensely. Have you relatives?"

"I am going to visit my sister," she explained.

"You want to see Lincoln Park," he said, "and Michigan Avenue.[5] They are putting up great buildings there. It's a second New York, great. So much to see—theatres, crowds, fine houses—oh you'll like that."

There was a little ache in her fancy of all he described. Her insignificance in the presence of so much magnificence faintly affected her. She realized that hers was not to be a round of pleasure, and yet there was something promising in all the material prospect he set forth. There was something satisfactory in the attention of this individual with his good clothes. She could not help smiling as he told her of some popular actress she reminded him of. She was not silly and yet attention of this sort had its weight.

"You will be in Chicago some little time, won't you?" he observed, at one turn of the now easy conversation.

"I don't know," said Carrie vaguely—a flash vision of the possibility of her not securing employment rising in her mind.

"Several weeks anyhow," he said, looking steadily into her eyes.

There was much more passing now than the mere words indicated. He recognized the indescribable thing that made for fascination and beauty in her. She realized that she was of interest to him from the one standpoint which a woman both delights in and fears. Her manner was simple, though, for the very reason that she had not yet learned the many little affectations with which women conceal their true feelings—some things she did appeared bold. A clever companion, had she ever had one, would have warned her never to look a man in the eyes so steadily.

"Why do you ask?" she said.

"Well, I'm going to be there several weeks. I'm going to study stock at our place and get new samples. I might show you 'round."

"I don't know whether you can or not—I mean I don't know whether I can. I shall be living with my sister and—"

"Well, if she minds, we'll fix that." He took out his pencil and a little pocket note book, as if it were all settled. "What is your address there?"

She fumbled her purse, which contained the address slip.

He reached down in his hip pocket and took out a fat purse. It was filled with slips of paper, some mileage books, a roll of green-backs and so on. It impressed her deeply. Such a purse had never been carried by any man who had ever been attentive to her before. Indeed a man who traveled, who was brisk and experienced and of the world, had never come within such close

5. The "Magnificent Mile" of stores, restaurants, office buildings, hotels, and historic landmarks. "Lincoln Park": upscale Chicago neighborhood.

range before. The purse, the shiny tan shoes, the smart new suit and the *air* with which he did things built up for her a dim world of fortune around him of which he was the centre. It disposed her pleasantly toward all he might do.

He took out a neat business card on which was engraved "Bartlett, Caryoe and Company," and down in the left-hand corner "Chas. H. Drouet."

"That's me," he said, putting the card in her hand and touching his name. "It's pronounced 'Drew-eh.' Our family was French on my father's side."

She looked at it while he put up his purse. Then he got out a letter from a bunch in his coat pocket.

"This is the house I travel for," he went on, pointing to a picture on it— "corner of State and Lake." There was pride in his voice. He felt that it was something to be connected with such a place, and he made her feel that way.

"What is your address?" he began again, fixing his pencil to write.

She looked at his hand.

"Carrie Meeber," she said slowly, "354 West Van Buren St., care S. C. Hanson."

He wrote it carefully down and got out the purse again. "You'll be at home if I come around Monday night?" he said.

"I think so," she answered.

How true it is that words are but vague shadows of the volumes we mean. Little audible links they are, chaining together great inaudible feelings and purposes. Here were these two, bandying little phrases, drawing purses, looking at cards and both unconscious of how inarticulate all their real feelings were. Neither was wise enough to be sure of the working of the mind of the other. He could not tell how his luring succeeded. She could not realize that she was drifting, until he secured her address. Now she felt that she had yielded something—he, that he had gained a victory. Already they felt that they were somehow associated. Already he took control in directing the conversation. His words were easy. Her manner was relaxed.

They were nearing Chicago. Already the signs were numerous. Trains flashed by them. Across wide stretches of flat open prairie they could see lines of telegraph poles stalking across the fields toward the great city. Away off there were indications of suburban towns, some big smoke stacks towering high in the air. Frequently there were two-story frame houses standing out in the open fields, without fence or trees, outposts of the approaching army of homes.

To the child, the genius with imagination, or the wholly untraveled, the approach to a great city for the first time is a wonderful thing. Particularly if it be evening—that mystic period between the glare and the gloom of the world when life is changing from one sphere or condition to another. Ah, the promise of the night. What does it not hold for the weary. What old illusion of hope is not here forever repeated! Says the soul of the toiler to itself, "I shall soon be free. I shall be in the ways and the hosts of the merry. The streets, the lamp, the lighted chamber set for dining are for me. The theatres, the halls, the parties, the ways of rest and the paths of song—these are mine in the night." Though all humanity be still enclosed in the shops, the thrill runs abroad. It is in the air. The dullest feel something which they may not always express or describe. It is the lifting of the burden of toil.

Sister Carrie gazed out of the window. Her companion, affected by her wonder, so contagious are all things, felt anew some interest in the city and pointed out the marvels. Already vast net-works of tracks—the sign and insignia of Chicago—stretched on either hand. There were thousands of cars and a clangor of engine bells. At the sides of this traffic stream stood dingy houses, smoky mills, tall elevators.[6] Through the interstices, evidences of the stretching city could be seen. Street cars waited at crossings for the train to go by. Gatemen toiled at wooden arms which closed the streets. Bells clanged, the rails clacked, whistles sounded afar off.

"This is North-West Chicago," said Drouet. "This is the Chicago River," and he pointed to a little muddy creek, crowded with the huge, masted wanderers from far-off waters nosing the black, posted banks. With a puff, a clang and a clatter of rails it was gone. "Chicago is getting to be a great town," he went on. "It's a wonder. You'll find lots to see here."

She did not hear this very well. Her heart was troubled by a kind of terror. The fact that she was alone, away from home, rushing into a great sea of life and endeavor, began to tell. She could not help but feel a little choked for breath—a little sick as her heart beat so fast. She half closed her eyes and tried to think it was nothing, that Columbia City was only a little way off.

"Chicago!—Chicago!" called the brakeman, slamming open the door. They were rushing into a more crowded yard, alive with the clatter and clang of life. She began to gather up her poor little grip and closed her hand firmly upon her purse. Drouet arose, kicked his legs to straighten his trousers and seized his clean yellow grip.

"I suppose your people will be here to meet you," he said. "Let me carry your grip."

"Oh no," she said. "I'd rather you wouldn't. I'd rather you wouldn't be with me when I meet my sister."

"All right," he said in all kindness. "I'll be near, though, in case she isn't here, and take you out there safely."

"You're so kind," said Carrie, feeling the goodness of such attention in her strange situation.

"Chicago!" called the brakeman, drawing the word out long. They were under a great shadowy train shed, where lamps were already beginning to shine out, with passenger cars all about and the train moving at a snail's pace. The people in the car were all up and crowding about the door.

"Well, here we are," said Drouet, leading the way to the door. "Goodbye," he said, "till I see you Monday."

"Goodbye," she said, taking his proffered hand.

"Remember I'll be looking till you find your sister."

She smiled into his eyes.

They filed out and he affected to take no notice of her. A lean-faced, rather commonplace woman recognized Carrie on the platform and hurried forward.

"Why Sister Carrie!" she began and there was a perfunctory embrace of welcome.

Carrie realized the change of affectional atmosphere at once. Amid all the maze, uproar and novelty, she felt cold reality taking her by the hand. No world of light and merriment. No round of amusement. Her sister carried with her much of the grimness of shift and toil.

"Why, how are all the folks at home"—she began—"how is Father, and Mother?"

6. Grain elevators.

Carrie answered, but was looking away. Down the aisle toward the gate leading into the waiting room and the street stood Drouet. He was looking back. When he saw that she saw him and was safe with her sister he turned to go, sending back the shadow of a smile. Only Carrie saw it. She felt something lost to her when he moved away. When he disappeared she felt his absence thoroughly. With her sister she was much alone, a lone figure in a tossing, thoughtless sea.

* * *

Chapter III

Once across the river and into the wholesale district, she glanced about her for some likely door at which to apply. As she contemplated the wide windows and imposing signs, she became conscious of being gazed upon and understood for what she was—a wage-seeker. She had never done this thing before and lacked courage. To avoid conspicuity and a certain indefinable shame she felt at being caught spying about for some place where she might apply for a position, she quickened her steps and assumed an air of indifference supposedly common to one upon an errand. In this way she passed many manufacturing and wholesale houses without once glancing in. At last, after several blocks of walking, she felt that this would not do, and began to look about again, though without relaxing her pace. A little way on she saw a great door which for some reason attracted her attention. It was ornamented by a small brass sign, and seemed to be the entrance to a vast hive of six or seven floors. "Perhaps," she thought, "they may want some one" and crossed over to enter, screwing up her courage to the sticking point as she went. When she came within a score of feet of the desired goal, she observed a young gentleman in a grey check suit, fumbling his watch-charm and looking out. That he had anything to do with the concern she could not tell, but because he happened to be looking in her direction, her weakening heart misgave her and she hurried by, too overcome with shame to enter in. After several blocks of walking, in which the uproar of the streets and the novelty of the situation had time to wear away the effect of this, her first defeat, she again looked about. Over the way stood a great six-story structure labeled "Storm and King," which she viewed with rising hope. It was a wholesale dry goods concern and employed women. She could see them moving about now and then upon the upper floors. This place she decided to enter, no matter what. She crossed over and walked directly toward the entrance. As she did so two men came out and paused in the door. A telegraph messenger in blue dashed past her and up the few steps which graced the entrance and disappeared. Several pedestrians out of the hurrying throng which filled the sidewalks passed about her as she paused, hesitating. She looked helplessly around and then, seeing herself observed, retreated. It was too difficult a task. She could not go past them.

So severe a defeat told sadly upon her nerves. She could scarcely understand her weakness and yet she could not think of gazing inquiringly about upon the surrounding scene. Her feet carried her mechanically forward, every foot of her progress being a satisfactory portion of a flight which she gladly made. Block after block passed by. Upon street lamps at the various corners she read names such as Madison, Monroe, La Salle, Clark, Dearborn, State;[7]

---

7. Major downtown streets between the Chicago River and Lake Michigan

and still she went, her feet beginning to tire upon the broad stone flagging. She was pleased in part that the streets were bright and clean. The morning sun shining down with steadily increasing warmth made the shady side of the streets pleasantly cool. She looked at the blue sky overhead with more realization of its charm than had ever come to her before.

Her cowardice began to trouble her in a way. She turned back along the street she had come, resolving to hunt up Storm and King and enter in. On the way she encountered a great wholesale shoe company, through the broad plate windows of which she saw an enclosed executive department, hidden by frosted glass. Without this enclosure, but just within the street entrance, sat a grey-haired gentleman at a small table, with a large open ledger of some kind before him. She walked by this institution several times hesitating, but finding herself unobserved she eventually gathered sufficient courage to falter past the screen door and stand humbly waiting.

"Well, young lady," observed the old gentleman looking at her somewhat kindly—"what is it you wish?"

"I am, that is, do you—I mean, do you need any help?" she stammered.

"Not just at present," he answered smiling. "Not just at present. Come in sometime next week. Occasionally we need some one."

She received the answer in silence and backed awkwardly out. The pleasant nature of her reception rather astonished her. She had expected that it would be more difficult, that something cold and harsh would be said—she knew not what. That she had not been put to shame and made to feel her unfortunate position seemed remarkable. She did not realize that it was just this which made her experience easy, but the result was the same. She felt greatly relieved.

Somewhat encouraged, she ventured into another large structure. It was a clothing company, and more people were in evidence—well-dressed men of forty and more, surrounded by brass railings and employed variously.

An office boy approached her.

"Who is it you wish to see?" he asked.

"I want to see the manager," she returned.

He ran away and spoke to one of a group of three men who were conferring together. One broke off and came towards her.

"Well?" he said, coldly. The greeting drove all courage from her at once.

"Do you need any help?" she stammered.

"No," he replied abruptly and turned upon his heel.

She went foolishly out, the office boy deferentially swinging the door for her, and gladly sank into the obscuring crowd. It was a severe set-back to her recently pleased mental state.

Now she walked quite aimlessly for a time, turning here and there, seeing one great company after another but finding no courage to prosecute her single inquiry. High noon came and with it hunger. She hunted out an unassuming restaurant and entered but was disturbed to find that the prices were exorbitant for the size of her purse. A bowl of soup was all that she could feel herself able to afford, and with this quickly eaten she went out again. It restored her strength somewhat and made her moderately bold to pursue the search.

In walking a few blocks to fix upon some probable place she again encountered the firm of Storm and King and this time managed to enter. Some gentlemen were conferring close at hand but took no notice of her. She was left standing, gazing nervously upon the floor, her confusion and mental distress momentarily increasing until at last she was ready to turn and hurry eagerly away. When the limit of her distress had been nearly reached she was beckoned to by a man at one of the many desks within the nearby railing.

"Who is it you wish to see?" he inquired.

"Why any one, if you please," she answered. "I am looking for something to do."

"Oh, you want to see Mr. McManus," he returned. "Sit down!" and he pointed to a chair against the neighboring wall. He went on leisurely writing until after a time a short stout gentleman came in from the street.

"Mr. McManus," called the man at the desk, "this young woman wants to see you."

The short gentleman turned about towards Carrie, and she arose and came forward.

"What can I do for you, Miss," he inquired surveying her curiously.

"I want to know if I can get a position," she inquired.

"As what?" he asked.

"Not as anything in particular," she faltered. "I—"

"Have you ever had any experience in the wholesale dry goods business?" he questioned.

"No sir," she replied.

"Are you a stenographer or typewriter?"

"No sir."

"Well we haven't anything here," he said. "We employ only experienced help."

She began to step backward toward the door, when something about her plaintive face attracted him.

"Have you ever worked at anything before?" he inquired.

"No sir," she said.

"Well now, it's hardly possible that you would get anything to do in a wholesale house of this kind. Have you tried the department stores?"

She acknowledged that she had not.

"Well, if I were you," he said, looking at her rather genially, "I would try the department stores. They often need young women as clerks."

"Thank you," she said, her whole nature relieved by this spark of friendly interest.

"Yes," he said, as she moved toward the door, "you try the department stores," and off he went.

At that time the department store was in its earliest form of successful operation and there were not many. The first three in the United States, established about 1884, were in Chicago. Carrie was familiar with the names of several through the advertisements in the "Daily News," and now proceeded to seek them. The words of Mr. McManus had somehow managed to restore her courage, which had fallen low, and she dared to hope that this new line would offer her something in the way of employment. Some time she spent in wandering up and down thinking to encounter the buildings by chance, so readily is the mind, bent upon prosecuting a hard but needful errand, eased by that self-deception which the semblance of search without the reality gives. At last she inquired of a police officer and was directed to proceed "two blocks up" where she would find The Fair. Following his advice she reached that institution and entered.

The nature of these vast retail combinations, should they ever permanently disappear, will form an interesting chapter in the commercial history of our nation. Such a flowering out of a modest trade principle the world had never witnessed up to that time. They were along the line of the most effective retail organization, with hundreds of stores coordinated into one, and laid out upon the most imposing and economic basis. They were handsome, bustling, successful affairs, with a host of clerks and a swarm of patrons. Carrie passed along the busy aisles, much affected by the remarkable displays of trinkets, dress goods, shoes, stationery, jewelry. Each separate counter was a show place of dazzling interest and attraction. She could not help feeling the claim of each trinket and valuable upon her personally and yet she did not stop. There was nothing there which she could not have used—nothing which she did not long to own. The dainty slippers and stockings, the delicately frilled skirts and petticoats, the laces, ribbons, hair-combs, purses, all touched her with individual desire, and she felt keenly the fact that not any of these things were in the range of her purchase. She was a work-seeker, an outcast without employment, one whom the average employé could tell at a glance was poor and in need of a situation.

It must not be thought that anyone could have mistaken her for a nervous, sensitive, high-strung nature, cast unduly upon a cold, calculating and unpoetic world. Such certainly she was not. But women are peculiarly sensitive to the personal adornment or equipment of their person, even the dullest, and particularly is this true of the young. Your bright-eyed, rosy-cheeked maiden, over whom a poet might well rave for the flowerlike expression of her countenance and the lissome and dainty grace of her body, may reasonably be dead to every evidence of the artistic and poetic in the unrelated evidences of life, and yet not lack in material appreciation. Never, it might be said, does she fail in this. With her the bloom of a rose may pass unappreciated, but the bloom of a fold of silk, never. If nothing in the heavens, or the earth, or the waters, could elicit her fancy or delight her from its spiritual or artistic side, think not that the material would be lost. The glint of a buckle, the hue of a precious stone, the faintest tints of the watered silk, these she would devine and qualify as readily as your poet if not more so. The creak, the rustle, the glow—the least and best of the graven or spun—, these she would perceive and appreciate—if not because of some fashionable or hearsay quality, then on account of their true beauty, their innate fitness in any order of harmony, their place in the magical order and sequence of dress.

Not only did Carrie feel the drag of desire for all of this which was new and pleasing in apparel for women, but she noticed, too, with a touch at the heart, the fine ladies who elbowed and ignored her, brushing past in utter disregard of her presence, themselves eagerly enlisted in the materials which the store contained. Carrie was not familiar with the appearance of her more fortunate sisters of the city. Neither had she before known the nature and appearance of the shop girls, with whom she now compared poorly. They were pretty in the main, some even handsome, with a certain independence and toss of indifference which added, in the case of the more favored, a certain piquancy. Their clothes were neat, in many instances fine, and wherever she encountered the eye of one, it was only to recognize in it a keen analysis of her own position—her individual shortcomings of dress and that shadow of *manner* which she thought must hang about her and make clear to all who and what she was. A flame of envy lighted in her heart. She realized in a dim way how much the city held—wealth, fashion, ease—every adornment for women, and she longed for dress and beauty with a whole and fulsome heart.

On the second floor were the managerial offices, to which after some inquiry she was now directed. There she found other girls ahead of her, applicants like herself, but with more of that self-satisfied and independent air which experience of the city lends—girls who scrutinized her in a painful manner. After a wait of perhaps three-quarters of an hour she was called in turn.

"Now," said a sharp, quick-mannered Jew who was sitting at a roll-top desk near the window—"have you ever worked in any other store?"

"No sir," said Carrie.

"Oh, you haven't," he said, eyeing her keenly.

"No sir," she replied.

"Well, we prefer young women just now with some experience. I guess we can't use you."

Carrie stood waiting a moment, hardly certain whether the interview had terminated.

"Don't wait!" he exclaimed. "Remember we are very busy here."

Carrie began to move quickly to the door.

"Hold on," he said, calling her back. "Give me your name and address. We want girls occasionally."

When she had gotten safely out again into the street she could scarcely restrain tears. It was not so much the particular rebuff which she had just experienced, but the whole abashing trend of the day. She was tired and rather over-played upon in the nerves. She abandoned the thought of appealing to the other department stores and now wandered on, feeling a certain safety and relief in mingling with the crowd.

In her indifferent wandering she turned into Jackson Street, not far from the river, and was keeping her way along the south side of that imposing thoroughfare, when a piece of wrapping paper written on with marking ink and tacked upon a door attracted her attention. It read "Girls wanted—wrappers and stitchers." She hesitated for the moment, thinking surely to go in, but upon further consideration the added qualifications of "wrappers and stitchers" deterred her. She had no idea of what that meant. Most probably she would need to be experienced in it. She walked on a little way, mentally balancing as to whether or not to apply. Necessity triumphed however and she returned.

The entrance, which opened into a small hall, led to an elevator shaft, the elevator of which was up. It was a dingy affair, being used both as a freight and passenger entrance, and the woodwork was marked and splintered by the heavy boxes which were tumbled in and out, at intervals. A frowzy-headed German-American, about fourteen years of age, operated the elevator in his shirt sleeves and bare feet. His face was considerably marked with grease and dirt.

When the elevator stopped, the boy leisurely raised a protecting arm of wood and by grace of his superior privilege admitted her.

"Wear do you want go?" he inquired.

"I want to see the manager," she replied.

"Wot manager?" he returned, surveying her caustically.

"Is there more than one?" she asked. "I thought it was all one firm."

"Naw," said the youth. "Der's six different people. Want to see Speigel-heim?"

"I don't know," answered Carrie. She colored a little as she began to feel the necessity of explaining. "I want to see whoever put up that sign."

"Dot's Speigelheim," said the boy. "Fort floor." Therewith he proudly turned to his task of pulling the rope, and the elevator ascended.

The firm of Speigelheim and Co., makers of boys' caps, occupied one floor of fifty feet in width and some eighty feet in depth. It was a place rather dingily lighted, the darkest portions having incandescent lights, filled in part with machines and part with workbenches. At the latter labored quite a company of girls and some men. The former were drabby looking creatures, stained in face with oil and dust, clad in thin shapeless cotton dresses, and shod with more or less worn shoes. Many of them had their sleeves rolled up, revealing bare arms, and in some cases, owing to heat, their dresses were open at the neck. They were, a fair type of nearly the lowest order of shop girls,— careless, rather slouchy, and more or less pale from confinement. They were not timid however, were rich in curiosity and strong in daring and slang.

Carrie looked about her, very much disturbed and quite sure that she did not want to work here. Aside from making her uncomfortable by sidelong glances, no one paid her the least attention. She waited until the whole department was aware of her presence. Then some word was sent round and a foreman in an apron and shirt sleeves, the latter rolled up to his shoulders, approached.

"Do you want to see me?" he asked.

"Do you need any help?" said Carrie, already learning directness of address.

"Do you know how to stitch caps?" he returned.

"No sir," she replied.

"Have you ever had any experience at this kind of work?" he inquired.

She owned that she hadn't.

"Well," said the foreman, scratching his ear meditatively, "we do need a stitcher. We like experienced help though. We've hardly got time to break people in." He paused and looked away out of the window. "We might, though, put you at finishing," he concluded reflectively.

"How much do you pay a week?" ventured Carrie, emboldened by a certain softness in the man's manner and his simplicity of address.

"Three and a half," he answered.

"Oh," she was about to exclaim, but checked herself, and allowed her thoughts to die without expression.

"We're not exactly in need of anybody," he went on vaguely, looking her over as one would a package. "You can come Monday morning though," he added, "and I'll put you to work."

"Thank you," said Carrie weakly.

"If you come, bring an apron," he added.

He walked away and left her standing by the elevator, never so much as inquiring her name.

While the appearance of the shop and the announcement of the price paid per week operated very much as a blow to Carrie's fancy, the fact that work of any kind, after so rude a round of experience, was offered her, was gratifying. She could not begin to believe that she would take the place, modest as her aspirations were. She had been used to better than that. Her mere experience and the free out-of-doors life of the country caused her nature to revolt at such confinement. Dirt had never been her share. Her sister's flat was clean. This place was grimy and low; the girls were careless and hardened. They must be bad-minded and -hearted, she imagined. Still a place had been offered her. Surely Chicago was not so bad if she could find one place in one day. She might find another and better later.

Her subsequent experiences were not of a reassuring nature, however. From all the more pleasing or imposing places she was turned away abruptly with the most chilling formality. In others where she applied, only the experienced were required. She met with painful rebuffs, the most trying of which had been in a cloak manufacturing house, where she had gone to the fourth floor to inquire.

"No, no," said the foreman, a rough, heavy-built individual who looked after a miserably lighted work shop, "we don't want anyone. Don't come here."

In another factory she was leered upon by a most sensual-faced individual who endeavored to turn the natural questions of the inquiry into a personal interview, asking all sorts of embarrassing questions and endeavoring to satisfy himself evidently that she was of loose enough morals to suit his purpose. In that case she had been relieved enough to get away and found the busy, indifferent streets to be again a soothing refuge.

With the wane of the afternoon went her hopes, her courage and her strength. She had been astonishingly persistent. So earnest an effort was well deserving of a better reward. On every hand, to her fatigued senses, the great business portion grew larger, harder, more stolid in its indifference. It seemed as if it was all closed to her, that the struggle was too fierce for her to hope to do anything at all. Men and women hurried by in long, shifting lines. She felt the flow of the tide of effort and interest, felt her own helplessness without quite realizing the wisp on the tide that she was. She cast about vainly for some possible place to apply but found no door which she had the courage to enter. It would be the same thing all over. The old humiliation of her pleas rewarded by curt denial. Sick at heart and in body, she turned to the west, the direction of Minnie's flat, which she had now fixed in mind, and began that wearisome, baffled retreat which the seeker for employment at nightfall too often makes. In passing through Fifth Avenue, south towards Van Buren Street, where she intended to take a car, she passed the door of a large wholesale shoe house, through the plate glass window of which she could see a middle-aged gentleman sitting at a small desk. One of those forlorn impulses which often grow out of a fixed sense of defeat, the last sprouting of a baffled and uprooted growth of ideas, seized upon her. She walked deliberately through the door and up to the gentleman who looked at her weary face with partially awakened interest.

"What is it?" he said.

"Can you give me something to do?" asked Carrie.

"Now I really don't know," he said kindly. "What kind of work is it you want—you're not a typewriter, are you?"

"Oh, no," answered Carrie.

"Well, we only employ book keepers and typewriters here. You might go round to the side and inquire upstairs. They did want some help upstairs a few days ago. Ask for Mr. Brown."

She hastened around to the side entrance and was taken up by the elevator to the fourth floor.

"Call Mr. Brown, Willie," said the elevator man to a boy near by.

Willie went off and presently returned with the information that Mr. Brown said she should sit down and that he would be around in a little while.

It was a portion of a stock room which gave no idea of the general character of the floor, and Carrie could form no opinion of the nature of the work.

"So you want something to do," said Mr. Brown, after he inquired concerning the nature of her errand. "Have you ever been employed in a shoe factory before?"

"No sir," said Carrie.

"What is your name?" he inquired, and being informed, "Well, I don't know as I have anything for you. Would you work for four and a half a week?"

Carrie was too worn by defeat not to feel that it was considerable. She had not expected that he would offer her less than six. She acquiesced, however, and he took her name and address.

"Well," he said finally—"you report here at eight o'clock Monday morning. I think I can find something for you to do."

He left her revived by the possibilities, sure that she had found something to do at last. Instantly the blood crept warmly over her body. Her nervous tension relaxed. She walked out into the busy street and discovered a new atmosphere. Behold, the throng was moving with a lightsome step. She noticed that men and women were smiling. Scraps of conversation and notes of laughter floated to her. The air was light. People were already pouring out of the buildings, their labor ended for the day. She noticed that they were pleased, and thoughts of her sister's home, and the meal that would be awaiting her, quickened her steps. She hurried on, tired perhaps, but no longer weary of foot. What would not Minnie say! Ah, long the winter in Chicago—the lights, the crowd, the amusement. This was a great, pleasing metropolis after all. Her new firm was a goodly institution. Its windows were of huge plate glass. She could probably do well there. Thoughts of Drouet returned, of the things he had told her. She now felt that life was better. That it was livelier, sprightlier. She boarded a car in the best of sprits, feeling her blood still flowing pleasantly. She would live in Chicago, her mind kept saying to itself. She would have a better time than she ever had before—she would be happy.

1900

STEPHEN CRANE
1871–1900

Stephen Crane was born November 1, 1871, and died on June 5, 1900, at the age of twenty-eight, by which time he had published enough material to fill a dozen volumes of a collected edition and had lived a legendary life. He was the son of a Methodist minister and a social reform–minded mother; but he systematically rejected religious and social traditions and identified with the urban poor. Although temperamentally gentle, Crane was attracted to—even obsessed by—war and other

Stephen Crane as a war correspondent in Athens, Greece, 1897, posing for a studio photograph.

forms of physical and psychic violence. He frequently lived the down-and-out life of a penniless artist; he was also ambitious and something of a snob. He was a poet and an impressionist; a journalist and a realist. In Crane, the contradictions and tensions present in many writers seem intensified.

Crane once explained to an editor: "After all, I cannot help vanishing and disappearing and dissolving. It is my foremost trait." This restless, peripatetic quality of Crane's life began early. The last of fourteen children, Crane moved with his family at least three times before he entered school at age seven in the small town of Port Jervis, New York. His father died in 1880, and three years later, after several temporary moves, the family settled in the coastal resort town of Asbury Park, New Jersey. Crane never took to school. He attended Lafayette College for a semester before transferring to Syracuse University. There he distinguished himself as a baseball player but was unable to accept the routine of academic life and withdrew before completing a full year. He left for New York City and a literary career, taking up journalistic assignments that allowed him to witness the city close at hand. Between 1891 and 1893 Crane shuttled between the seedy New York apartments of his artist friends and his brother Edmund's house in nearby Lake View, New Jersey. During these apprenticeship years, Crane developed his powers as an observer of psychological and social reality. Encouraged by Hamlin Garland, whom he had heard lecture in 1891, Crane began his first book while at Syracuse. After it had been rejected by several New York editors, he published the work—*Maggie, A Girl of the Streets* (*A Story of New York*)—at his own expense in 1893. Although Garland admired this short novel and the powerful literary arbiter William Dean Howells promoted both Crane and *Maggie* (and continued to think it his best work), the book did not sell even when, in revised form, it was republished in 1896 by the prestigious publishing house of D. Appleton and Company. In a highly stylized way using heavy dialect, *Maggie* told the story of a girl born in the slums of New York who during her short life is driven to prostitution. As one of the first reviewers of the 1893 edition observed: "the evident object of the writer is to show the tremendous influence of the environment on the human character and destiny." It remains Crane's fullest treatment of how the urban poor lived in the burgeoning cities of America in the 1880s and 1890s.

Crane's next novel, *The Red Badge of Courage* (1895), takes the Civil War as its background for a story about the effect of battle on a young man. Many American writers have used war as the setting for narratives about the coming of age; Crane is in the advance guard of those who chose not to judge characters at war by their actions, but instead to focus on their immediate and relatively unfiltered feelings. That is, Crane is distinctively modern in conceiving personal identity as complex and ambiguous and in obliging his readers to judge for themselves the adequacy of Henry Fleming's responses to his experiences.

When *Red Badge* was first published in newspapers around the country starting in December 1894, Crane's fortunes began to improve. The same syndicate (an agency that buys and then sells stories to newspapers and magazines for simultaneous publication) that took *Red Badge* hired him early in 1895 as a roving reporter in the American West and Mexico, experiences that would give him the material for several of his finest tales—"The Bride Comes to Yellow Sky" and "The Blue Hotel" among them. Also, early in 1895, D. Appleton and Company agreed to issue *Red Badge* in book form. In the spring of that year, *The Black Riders and Other Lines,* his first volume of poetry, was published in Boston by Copeland and Day. Predictably, Garland and Howells responded favorably to Crane's spare, original, unflinchingly honest poetry, but it was too experimental in form and too unconventional in its dark philosophic outlook to win wide acceptance. When *Red Badge* appeared in the fall in book form, however, it won Crane international acclaim, although not wide sales, at the age of twenty-four.

Crane's poetry, journalism, and fiction clearly demonstrated his religious, social, and literary rebelliousness, while his alienated, unconventional beliefs also led him to direct action. After challenging the New York police force on behalf of a prostitute who claimed harassment at its hands, Crane left the city in the winter of 1896–97 to cover the insurrection against Spain in Cuba. On his way to Cuba he met Cora Howorth Taylor, the proprietor of a bordello, the Hotel de Dream in Jacksonville, Florida, with whom he lived for the last three years of his life. On January 2, 1897, Crane's ship *The Commodore* sank off the coast of Florida. His report of this harrowing adventure was published a few days later in the *New York Press.* He promptly converted this event into one of the best-known and most widely reprinted of all American stories, "The Open Boat." This story, like *Red Badge,* reveals Crane's characteristic subject matter—the physical, emotional, and intellectual responses of people under extreme pressure, the dominant themes of nature's indifference to humanity's fate, and the consequent need for compassionate collective action. Along with *Maggie,* "The Open Boat" locates Crane within American literary naturalism alongside its other practitioners, Frank Norris, Jack London, and Theodore Dreiser, but, unlike *Maggie,* it contains a certain romanticism.

In "The Open Boat" and another late story, "The Blue Hotel," Crane achieved his mature style, one characterized by irony and brevity, qualities later associated with Sherwood Anderson and Ernest Hemingway, among other literary modernists. But Crane's style cannot be contained by any of the terms typically used to describe it—realism, naturalism, impressionism, or expressionism. In these late stories (and before he began to write chiefly for money), Crane is in many respects a modernist ahead of his time in his abandonment of the overseeing narrator in favor of a literary impressionism and other narrative strategies that convey psychological experiences. His works display his tough-minded irony and a sympathetic but unflinching demand for courage, integrity, grace, and generosity in the face of a universe in which human beings, to quote from his story "The Blue Hotel," are so many lice clinging "to a whirling, fire-smote, ice-locked disease-stricken, space-lost bulb."

In 1897 Crane settled in England. In the last months of his life his situation became desperate; he was suffering from tuberculosis and was seriously in debt. He wrote furiously in a doomed attempt to earn money, but the effort only worsened his health. In 1899 he drafted thirteen stories set in the fictional town Whilomville and published his second volume of poetry, *War Is Kind,* the novel *Active Service,* and the American edition of *"The Monster" and Other Stories.* "The Monster" is a daring exploration of the hypocrisy and cruelty of racial prejudice. During a Christmas party that year Crane nearly died of a lung hemorrhage. Surviving only a few months, he summoned the strength to write a series of nine articles on great battles and complete the first twenty-five chapters of the novel *The O'Ruddy.* In spite of Cora's hopes for a miraculous cure and the generous assistance of Henry James and others, Crane died, at Badenweiler, Germany, on June 5, 1900.

The Open Boat[1]

A TALE INTENDED TO BE AFTER THE FACT, BEING THE EXPERIENCE OF FOUR MEN FROM THE SUNK STEAMER COMMODORE

I

None of them knew the color of the sky. Their eyes glanced level, and were fastened upon the waves that swept toward them. These waves were of the hue of slate, save for the tops, which were of foaming white, and all of the men knew the colors of the sea. The horizon narrowed and widened, and dipped and rose, and at all times its edge was jagged with waves that seemed thrust up in points like rocks.

Many a man ought to have a bath-tub larger than the boat which here rode upon the sea. These waves were most wrongfully and barbarously abrupt and tall, and each froth-top was a problem in small boat navigation.

The cook squatted in the bottom and looked with both eyes at the six inches of gunwale which separated him from the ocean. His sleeves were rolled over his fat forearms, and the two flaps of his unbuttoned vest dangled as he bent to bail out the boat. Often he said: "Gawd! That was a narrow clip." As he remarked it he invariably gazed eastward over the broken sea.

The oiler,[2] steering with one of the two oars in the boat, sometimes raised himself suddenly to keep clear of water that swirled in over the stern. It was a thin little oar and it seemed often ready to snap.

The correspondent, pulling at the other oar, watched the waves and wondered why he was there.

The injured captain, lying in the bow, was at this time buried in that profound dejection and indifference which comes, temporarily at least, to even

1. Crane sailed as a correspondent on the steamer *Commodore,* which, on January 1, 1897, left Jacksonville, Florida, with munitions for the Cuban insurrectionists. Early on the morning of January 2, the steamer sank. With three others, Crane reached Daytona Beach in a ten-foot dinghy on the following morning. Under the title "Stephen Crane's Own Story," the *New York Press* on January 7 carried the details of his nearly fatal experience.

In June 1897, he published his fictional account, "The Open Boat," in *Scribner's Magazine.* The story gave the title to *"The Open Boat" and Other Tales of Adventure* (1898). The text here reprints that established for the University of Virginia edition of *The Works of Stephen Crane,* Vol. 5, *Tales of Adventure* (1970).
2. One who oils machinery in the engine room of a ship.

the bravest and most enduring when, willy nilly, the firm fails, the army loses, the ship goes down. The mind of the master of a vessel is rooted deep in the timbers of her, though he command for a day or a decade, and this captain had on him the stern impression of a scene in the grays of dawn of seven turned faces, and later a stump of a top-mast with a white ball on it that slashed to and fro at the waves, went low and lower, and down. Thereafter there was something strange in his voice. Although steady, it was deep with mourning, and of a quality beyond oration or tears.

"Keep 'er a little more south, Billie," said he.

"'A little more south,' sir," said the oiler in the stern.

A seat in his boat was not unlike a seat upon a bucking broncho, and, by the same token, a broncho is not much smaller. The craft pranced and reared, and plunged like an animal. As each wave came, and she rose for it, she seemed like a horse making at a fence outrageously high. The manner of her scramble over these walls of water is a mystic thing, and, moreover, at the top of them were ordinarily these problems in white water, the foam racing down from the summit of each wave, requiring a new leap, and a leap from the air. Then, after scornfully bumping a crest, she would slide, and race, and splash down a long incline and arrive bobbing and nodding in front of the next menace.

A singular disadvantage of the sea lies in the fact that after successfully surmounting one wave you discover that there is another behind it just as important and just as nervously anxious to do something effective in the way of swamping boats. In a ten-foot dingey one can get an idea of the resources of the sea in the line of waves that is not probable to the average experience, which is never at sea in a dingey. As each slaty wall of water approached, it shut all else from the view of the men in the boat, and it was not difficult to imagine that this particular wave was the final outburst of the ocean, the last effort of the grim water. There was a terrible grace in the move of the waves, and they came in silence, save for the snarling of the crests.

In the wan light, the faces of the men must have been gray. Their eyes must have glinted in strange ways as they gazed steadily astern. Viewed from a balcony, the whole thing would doubtlessly have been weirdly picturesque. But the men in the boat had no time to see it, and if they had had leisure there were other things to occupy their minds. The sun swung steadily up the sky, and they knew it was broad day because the color of the sea changed from slate to emerald-green, streaked with amber lights, and the foam was like tumbling snow. The process of the breaking day was unknown to them. They were aware only of this effect upon the color of the waves that rolled toward them.

In disjointed sentences the cook and the correspondent argued as to the difference between a life-saving station and a house of refuge. The cook had said: "There's a house of refuge just north of the Mosquito Inlet Light, and as soon as they see us, they'll come off in their boat and pick us up."

"As soon as who see us?" said the correspondent.

"The crew," said the cook.

"Houses of refuge don't have crews," said the correspondent. "As I understand them, they are only places where clothes and grub are stored for the benefit of shipwrecked people. They don't carry crews."

"Oh, yes, they do," said the cook.

"No, they don't," said the correspondent.

"Well, we're not there yet, anyhow," said the oiler, in the stern.

"Well," said the cook, "perhaps it's not a house of refuge that I'm thinking of as being near Mosquito Inlet Light. Perhaps it's a life-saving station."

"We're not there yet," said the oiler, in the stern.

II

As the boat bounced from the top of each wave, the wind tore through the hair of the hatless men, and as the craft plopped her stern down again the spray slashed past them. The crest of each of these waves was a hill, from the top of which the men surveyed, for a moment, a broad tumultuous expanse, shining and wind-riven. It was probably splendid. It was probably glorious, this play of the free sea, wild with lights of emerald and white and amber.

"Bully good thing it's an on-shore wind," said the cook. "If not, where would we be? Wouldn't have a show."

"That's right," said the correspondent.

The busy oiler nodded his assent.

Then the captain, in the bow, chuckled in a way that expressed humor, contempt, tragedy, all in one. "Do you think we've got much of a show, now, boys?" said he.

Whereupon the three were silent, save for a trifle of hemming and hawing. To express any particular optimism at this time they felt to be childish and stupid, but they all doubtless possessed this sense of the situation in their mind. A young man thinks doggedly at such times. On the other hand, the ethics of their condition was decidedly against any open suggestion of hopelessness. So they were silent.

"Oh, well," said the captain, soothing his children, "we'll get ashore all right."

But there was that in his tone which made them think, so the oiler quoth: "Yes! If this wind holds!"

The cook was bailing. "Yes! If we don't catch hell in the surf."

Canton flannel[3] gulls flew near and far. Sometimes they sat down on the sea, near patches of brown sea-weed that rolled over the waves with a movement like carpets on a line in a gale. The birds sat comfortably in groups, and they were envied by some in the dingey, for the wrath of the sea was no more to them than it was to a covey of prairie chickens a thousand miles inland. Often they came very close and stared at the men with black bead-like eyes. At these times they were uncanny and sinister in their unblinking scrutiny, and the men hooted angrily at them, telling them to be gone. One came, and evidently decided to alight on the top of the captain's head. The bird flew parallel to the boat and did not circle, but made short sidelong jumps in the air in chicken-fashion. His black eyes were wistfully fixed upon the captain's head. "Ugly brute," said the oiler to the bird. "You look as if you were made with a jack-knife." The cook and the correspondent swore darkly at the creature. The captain naturally wished to knock it away with the end of the heavy painter, but he did not dare do it, because anything resembling an emphatic gesture would have capsized this freighted boat, and so with his open hand, the captain gently and carefully waved the gull away. After it had been discouraged from the pursuit the captain breathed easier on account of his hair, and others breathed easier because the bird struck their minds at this time as being somehow grewsome and ominous.

---

3. Common name of a lightweight cotton fabric, usually white.

In the meantime the oiler and the correspondent rowed. And also they rowed.

They sat together in the same seat, and each rowed an oar. Then the oiler took both oars; then the correspondent took both oars; then the oiler; then the correspondent. They rowed and they rowed. The very ticklish part of the business was when the time came for the reclining one in the stern to take his turn at the oars. By the very last star of truth, it is easier to steal eggs from under a hen than it was to change seats in the dingey. First the man in the stern slid his hand along the thwart and moved with care, as if he were of Sèvres.[4] Then the man in the rowing seat slid his hand along the other thwart. It was all done with the most extraordinary care. As the two sidled past each other, the whole party kept watchful eyes on the coming wave, and the captain cried: "Look out now! Steady there!"

The brown mats of sea-weed that appeared from time to time were like islands, bits of earth. They were travelling, apparently, neither one way nor the other. They were, to all intents, stationary. They informed the men in the boat that it was making progress slowly toward the land.

The captain, rearing cautiously in the bow, after the dingey soared on a great swell, said that he had seen the light-house at Mosquito Inlet. Presently the cook remarked that he had seen it. The correspondent was at the oars, then, and for some reason he too wished to look at the light-house, but his back was toward the far shore and the waves were important, and for some time he could not seize an opportunity to turn his head. But at last there came a wave more gentle than the others, and when at the crest of it he swiftly scoured the western horizon.

"See it?" said the captain.

"No," said the correspondent, slowly, "I didn't see anything."

"Look again," said the captain. He pointed. "It's exactly in that direction."

At the top of another wave, the correspondent did as he was bid, and this time his eyes chanced on a small still thing on the edge of the swaying horizon. It was precisely like the point of a pin. It took an anxious eye to find a light-house so tiny.

"Think we'll make it, Captain?"

"If this wind holds and the boat don't swamp, we can't do much else," said the captain.

The little boat, lifted by each towering sea, and splashed viciously by the crests, made progress that in the absence of sea-weed was not apparent to those in her. She seemed just a wee thing wallowing, miraculously, top-up, at the mercy of five oceans. Occasionally, a great spread of water, like white flames, swarmed into her.

"Bail her, cook," said the captain, serenely.

"All right, Captain," said the cheerful cook.

III

It would be difficult to describe the subtle brotherhood of men that was here established on the seas. No one said that it was so. No one mentioned it. But it dwelt in the boat, and each man felt it warm him. They were a captain, an oiler, a cook, and a correspondent, and they were friends, friends in a more curiously iron-bound degree than may be common. The hurt captain, lying

4. Fine, often ornately decorated French porcelain.

against the water-jar in the bow, spoke always in a low voice and calmly, but he could never command a more ready and swiftly obedient crew than the motley three of the dingey. It was more than a mere recognition of what was best for the common safety. There was surely in it a quality that was personal and heartfelt. And after this devotion to the commander of the boat there was this comradeship that the correspondent, for instance, who had been taught to be cynical of men, knew even at the time was the best experience of his life. But no one said that it was so. No one mentioned it.

"I wish we had a sail," remarked the captain. "We might try my overcoat on the end of an oar and give you two boys a chance to rest." So the cook and the correspondent held the mast and spread wide the overcoat. The oiler steered, and the little boat made good way with her new rig. Sometimes the oiler had to scull sharply to keep a sea from breaking into the boat, but otherwise sailing was a success.

Meanwhile the light-house had been growing slowly larger. It had now almost assumed color, and appeared like a little gray shadow on the sky. The man at the oars could not be prevented from turning his head rather often to try for a glimpse of this little gray shadow.

At last, from the top of each wave the men in the tossing boat could see land. Even as the light-house was an upright shadow on the sky, this land seemed but a long black shadow on the sea. It certainly was thinner than paper. "We must be about opposite New Smyrna," said the cook, who had coasted this shore often in schooners. "Captain, by the way, I believe they abandoned that life-saving station there about a year ago."

"Did they?" said the captain.

The wind slowly died away. The cook and the correspondent were not now obliged to slave in order to hold high the oar. But the waves continued their old impetuous swooping at the dingey, and the little craft, no longer under way, struggled woundily over them. The oiler or the correspondent took the oars again.

Shipwrecks are *apropos* of nothing. If men could only train for them and have them occur when the men had reached pink condition, there would be less drowning at sea. Of the four in the dingey none had slept any time worth mentioning for two days and two nights previous to embarking in the dingey, and in the excitement of clambering about the deck of a foundering ship they had also forgotten to eat heartily.

For these reasons, and for others, neither the oiler nor the correspondent was fond of rowing at this time. The correspondent wondered ingenuously how in the name of all that was sane could there be people who thought it amusing to row a boat. It was not an amusement; it was a diabolical punishment, and even a genius of mental aberrations could never conclude that it was anything but a horror to the muscles and a crime against the back. He mentioned to the boat in general how the amusement of rowing struck him, and the weary-faced oiler smiled in full sympathy. Previously to the foundering, by the way, the oiler had worked double-watch in the engine-room of the ship.

"Take her easy, now, boys," said the captain. "Don't spend yourselves. If we have to run a surf you'll need all your strength, because we'll sure have to swim for it. Take your time."

Slowly the land arose from the sea. From a black line it became a line of black and a line of white—trees and sand. Finally, the captain said that he could make out a house on the shore. "That's the house of refuge, sure," said the cook. "They'll see us before long, and come out after us."

The distant light-house reared high. "The keeper ought to be able to make us out now, if he's looking through a glass," said the captain. "He'll notify the life-saving people."

"None of those other boats could have got ashore to give word of the wreck," said the oiler, in a low voice. "Else the life-boat would be out hunting us."

Slowly and beautifully the land loomed out of the sea. The wind came again. It had veered from the northeast to the southeast. Finally, a new sound struck the ears of the men in the boat. It was the low thunder of the surf on the shore. "We'll never be able to make the light-house now," said the captain. "Swing her head a little more north, Billie."

"'A little more north,' sir," said the oiler.

Whereupon the little boat turned her nose once more down the wind, and all but the oarsman watched the shore grow. Under the influence of this expansion doubt and direful apprehension was leaving the minds of the men. The management of the boat was still most absorbing, but it could not prevent a quiet cheerfulness. In an hour, perhaps, they would be ashore.

Their back-bones had become thoroughly used to balancing in the boat and they now rode this wild colt of a dingey like circus men. The correspondent thought that he had been drenched to the skin, but happening to feel in the top pocket of his coat, he found therein eight cigars. Four of them were soaked with seawater; four were perfectly scatheless. After a search, somebody produced three dry matches, and thereupon the four waifs rode impudently in their little boat, and with an assurance of an impending rescue shining in their eyes, puffed at the big cigars and judged well and ill of all men. Everybody took a drink of water.

IV

"Cook," remarked the captain, "there don't seem to be any signs of life about your house of refuge."

"No," replied the cook. "Funny they don't see us!"

A broad stretch of lowly coast lay before the eyes of the men. It was of dunes topped with dark vegetation. The roar of the surf was plain, and sometimes they could see the white lip of a wave as it spun up the beach. A tiny house was blocked out black upon the sky. Southward, the slim light-house lifted its little gray length.

Tide, wind, and waves were swinging the dingey northward. "Funny they don't see us," said the men.

The surf's roar was here dulled, but its tone was, nevertheless, thunderous and mighty. As the boat swam over the great rollers, the men sat listening to this roar. "We'll swamp sure," said everybody.

It is fair to say here that there was not a life-saving station within twenty miles in either direction, but the men did not know this fact and in consequence they made dark and opprobrious remarks concerning the eyesight of the nation's life-savers. Four scowling men sat in the dingey and surpassed records in the invention of epithets.

"Funny they don't see us."

The light-heartedness of a former time had completely faded. To their sharpened minds it was easy to conjure pictures of all kinds of incompetency and blindness and, indeed, cowardice. There was the shore of the populous land, and it was bitter and bitter to them that from it came no sign.

"Well," said the captain, ultimately, "I suppose we'll have to make a try for ourselves. If we stay out here too long, we'll none of us have strength left to swim after the boat swamps."

And so the oiler, who was at the oars, turned the boat straight for the shore. There was a sudden tightening of muscles. There was some thinking.

"If we don't all get ashore—" said the captain. "If we don't all get ashore, I suppose you fellows know where to send news of my finish?"

They then briefly exchanged some addresses and admonitions. As for the reflections of the men, there was a great deal of rage in them. Perchance they might be formulated thus: "If I am going to be drowned—if I am going to be drowned—if I am going to be drowned, why, in the name of the seven mad gods who rule the sea, was I allowed to come thus far and contemplate sand and trees? Was I brought here merely to have my nose dragged away as I was about to nibble the sacred cheese of life? It is preposterous. If this old ninny-woman, Fate, cannot do better than this, she should be deprived of the management of men's fortunes. She is an old hen who knows not her intention. If she has decided to drown me, why did she not do it in the beginning and save me all this trouble. The whole affair is absurd. . . . But, no, she cannot mean to drown me. She dare not drown me. She cannot drown me. Not after all this work." Afterward the man might have had an impulse to shake his fist at the clouds. "Just you drown me, now, and then hear what I call you!"

The billows that came at this time were more formidable. They seemed always just about to break and roll over the little boat in a turmoil of foam. There was a preparatory and long growl in the speech of them. No mind unused to the sea would have concluded that the dingey could ascend these sheer heights in time. The shore was still afar. The oiler was a wily surfman. "Boys," he said, swiftly, "she won't live three minutes more and we're too far out to swim. Shall I take her to sea again, Captain?"

"Yes! Go ahead!" said the captain.

This oiler, by a series of quick miracles, and fast and steady oarsmanship, turned the boat in the middle of the surf and took her safely to sea again.

There was a considerable silence as the boat bumped over the furrowed sea to deeper water. Then somebody in gloom spoke. "Well, anyhow, they must have seen us from the shore by now."

The gulls went in slanting flight up the wind toward the gray desolate east. A squall, marked by dingy clouds, and clouds brick-red, like smoke from a burning building, appeared from the southeast.

"What do you think of those life-saving people? Ain't they peaches?"

"Funny they haven't seen us."

"Maybe they think we're out here for sport! Maybe they think we're fishin'. Maybe they think we're damned fools."

It was a long afternoon. A changed tide tried to force them southward, but wind and wave said northward. Far ahead, where coast-line, sea, and sky formed their mighty angle, there were little dots which seemed to indicate a city on the shore.

"St. Augustine?"

The captain shook his head. "Too near Mosquito Inlet."

And the oiler rowed, and then the correspondent rowed. Then the oiler rowed. It was a weary business. The human back can become the seat of more aches and pains than are registered in books for the composite anatomy of a regiment. It is a limited area, but it can become the theatre of innumerable muscular conflicts, tangles, wrenches, knots, and other comforts.

"Did you ever like to row, Billie?" asked the correspondent.

"No," said the oiler. "Hang it."

When one exchanged the rowing-seat for a place in the bottom of the boat, he suffered a bodily depression that caused him to be careless of everything save an obligation to wiggle one finger. There was cold sea-water swashing to and fro in the boat, and he lay in it. His head, pillowed on a thwart, was within an inch of the swirl of a wave crest, and sometimes a particularly obstreperous sea came inboard and drenched him once more. But these matters did not annoy him. It is almost certain that if the boat had capsized he would have tumbled comfortably out upon the ocean as if he felt sure that it was a great soft mattress.

"Look! There's a man on the shore!"

"Where?"

"There? See 'im? See 'im?"

"Yes, sure! He's walking along."

"Now he's stopped. Look! He's facing us!"

"He's waving at us!"

"So he is! By thunder!"

"Ah, now, we're all right! Now we're all right! There'll be a boat out here for us in half an hour."

"He's going on. He's running. He's going up to that house there."

The remote beach seemed lower than the sea, and it required a searching glance to discern the little black figure. The captain saw a floating stick and they rowed to it. A bath-towel was by some weird chance in the boat, and, tying this on the stick, the captain waved it. The oarsman did not dare turn his head, so he was obliged to ask questions.

"What's he doing now?"

"He's standing still again. He's looking, I think. . . . There he goes again. Toward the house. . . . Now he's stopped again."

"Is he waving at us?"

"No, not now! he was, though."

"Look! There comes another man!"

"He's running."

"Look at him go, would you."

"Why, he's on a bicycle. Now he's met the other man. They're both waving at us. Look!"

"There comes something up the beach."

"What the devil is that thing?"

"Why, it looks like a boat."

"Why, certainly it's a boat."

"No, it's on wheels."

"Yes, so it is. Well, that must be the life-boat. They drag them along shore on a wagon."

"That's the life-boat, sure."

"No, by——, it's—it's an omnibus."

"I tell you it's a life-boat."

"It is not! It's an omnibus. I can see it plain. See? One of those big hotel omnibuses."

"By thunder, you're right. It's an omnibus, sure as fate. What do you suppose they are doing with an omnibus? Maybe they are going around collecting the life-crew, hey?"

"That's it, likely. Look! There's a fellow waving a little black flag. He's standing on the steps of the omnibus. There come those other two fellows. Now they're all talking together. Look at the fellow with the flag. Maybe he ain't waving it!"

"That ain't a flag, is it? That's his coat. Why, certainly, that's his coat."

"So it is. It's his coat. He's taken it off and is waving it around his head. But would you look at him swing it!"

"Oh, say, there isn't any life-saving station there. That's just a winter resort hotel omnibus that has brought over some of the boarders to see us drown."

"What's that idiot with the coat mean? What's he signaling, anyhow?"

"It looks as if he were trying to tell us to go north. There must be a life-saving station up there."

"No! He thinks we're fishing. Just giving us a merry hand. See? Ah, there, Willie."

"Well, I wish I could make something out of those signals. What do you suppose he means?"

"He don't mean anything. He's just playing."

"Well, if he'd just signal us to try the surf again, or to go to sea and wait, or go north, or go south, or go to hell—there would be some reason in it. But look at him. He just stands there and keeps his coat revolving like a wheel. The ass!"

"There come more people."

"Now there's quite a mob. Look! Isn't that a boat?"

"Where? Oh, I see where you mean. No, that's no boat."

"That fellow is still waving his coat."

"He must think we like to see him do that. Why don't he quit it. It don't mean anything."

"I don't know. I think he is trying to make us go north. It must be that there's a life-saving station there somewhere."

"Say, he ain't tired yet. Look at 'im wave."

"Wonder how long he can keep that up. He's been revolving his coat ever since he caught sight of us. He's an idiot. Why aren't they getting men to bring a boat out. A fishing boat—one of those big yawls—could come out here all right. Why don't he do something?"

"Oh, it's all right, now."

"They'll have a boat out here for us in less than no time, now that they've seen us."

A faint yellow tone came into the sky over the low land. The shadows on the sea slowly deepened. The wind bore coldness with it, and the men began to shiver.

"Holy smoke!" said one, allowing his voice to express his impious mood, "if we keep on monkeying out here! If we've got to flounder out here all night!"

"Oh, we'll never have to stay here all night! Don't you worry. They've seen us now, and it won't be long before they'll come chasing out after us."

The shore grew dusky. The man waving a coat blended gradually into this gloom, and it swallowed in the same manner the omnibus and the group of people. The spray, when it dashed uproariously over the side, made the voyagers shrink and swear like men who were being branded.

"I'd like to catch the chump who waved the coat. I feel like socking him one, just for luck."

"Why? What did he do?"

"Oh, nothing, but then he seemed so damned cheerful."

In the meantime the oiler rowed, and then the correspondent rowed, and then the oiler rowed. Gray-faced and bowed forward, they mechanically, turn by turn, plied the leaden oars. The form of the light-house had vanished from the southern horizon, but finally a pale star appeared, just lifting from the sea. The streaked saffron in the west passed before the all-merging darkness, and the sea to the east was black. The land had vanished, and was expressed only by the low and drear thunder of the surf.

"If I am going to be drowned—if I am going to be drowned—if I am going to be drowned, why, in the name of the seven mad gods who rule the sea, was I allowed to come thus far and contemplate sand and trees? Was I brought here merely to have my nose dragged away as I was about to nibble the sacred cheese of life?"

The patient captain, drooped over the water-jar, was sometimes obliged to speak to the oarsman.

"Keep her head up! Keep her head up!"

"'Keep her head up,' sir." The voices were weary and low.

This was surely a quiet evening. All save the oarsman lay heavily and list-lessly in the boat's bottom. As for him, his eyes were just capable of noting the tall black waves that swept forward in a most sinister silence, save for an occasional subdued growl of a crest.

The cook's head was on a thwart, and he looked without interest at the water under his nose. He was deep in other scenes. Finally he spoke. "Billie," he murmured, dreamfully, "what kind of pie do you like best?"

V

"Pie," said the oiler and the correspondent, agitatedly. "Don't talk about those things, blast you!"

"Well," said the cook, "I was just thinking about ham sandwiches, and——"

A night on the sea in an open boat is a long night. As darkness settled finally, the shine of the light, lifting from the sea in the south, changed to full gold. On the northern horizon a new light appeared, a small bluish gleam on the edge of the waters. These two lights were the furniture of the world. Otherwise there was nothing but waves.

Two men huddled in the stern, and distances were so magnificent in the dingey that the rower was enabled to keep his feet partly warmed by thrust-ing them under his companions. Their legs indeed extended far under the rowing-seat until they touched the feet of the captain forward. Sometimes, despite the efforts of the tired oarsman, a wave came piling into the boat, an icy wave of the night, and the chilling water soaked them anew. They would twist their bodies for a moment and groan, and sleep the dead sleep once more, while the water in the boat gurgled about them as the craft rocked.

The plan of the oiler and the correspondent was for one to row until he lost the ability, and then arouse the other from his sea-water couch in the bottom of the boat.

The oiler plied the oars until his head drooped forward, and the overpow-ering sleep blinded him. And he rowed yet afterward. Then he touched a man in the bottom of the boat, and called his name. "Will you spell me for a little while?" he said meekly.

"Sure, Billie," said the correspondent, awakening and dragging himself to a sitting position. They exchanged places carefully, and the oiler, cuddling down in the sea-water at the cook's side, seemed to go to sleep instantly.

The particular violence of the sea had ceased. The waves came without snarling. The obligation of the man at the oars was to keep the boat headed so that the tilt of the rollers would not capsize her, and to preserve her from filling when the crests rushed past. The black waves were silent and hard to be seen in the darkness. Often one was almost upon the boat before the oarsman was aware.

In a low voice the correspondent addressed the captain. He was not sure that the captain was awake, although this iron man seemed to be always awake. "Captain, shall I keep her making for that light north, sir?"

The same steady voice answered him. "Yes. Keep it about two points off the port bow."

The cook had tied a life-belt around himself in order to get even the warmth which this clumsy cork contrivance could donate, and he seemed almost stove-like when a rower, whose teeth invariably chattered wildly as soon as he ceased his labor, dropped down to sleep.

The correspondent, as he rowed, looked down at the two men sleeping under foot. The cook's arm was around the oiler's shoulders, and, with their fragmentary clothing and haggard faces, they were the babes of the sea, a grotesque rendering of the old babes in the wood.

Later he must have grown stupid at his work, for suddenly there was a growling of water, and a crest came with a roar and a swash into the boat, and it was a wonder that it did not set the cook afloat in his life-belt. The cook continued to sleep, but the oiler sat up, blinking his eyes and shaking with the new cold.

"Oh, I'm awful sorry, Billie," said the correspondent, contritely.

"That's all right, old boy," said the oiler, and lay down again and was asleep.

Presently it seemed that even the captain dozed, and the correspondent thought that he was the one man afloat on all the oceans. The wind had a voice as it came over the waves, and it was sadder than the end.

There was a long, loud swishing astern of the boat, and a gleaming trail of phosphorescence, like blue flame, was furrowed on the black waters. It might have been made by a monstrous knife.

Then there came a stillness, while the correspondent breathed with the open mouth and looked at the sea.

Suddenly there was another swish and another long flash of bluish light, and this time it was alongside the boat, and might almost have been reached with an oar. The correspondent saw an enormous fin speed like a shadow through the water, hurling the crystalline spray and leaving the long glowing trail.

The correspondent looked over his shoulder at the captain. His face was hidden, and he seemed to be asleep. He looked at the babes of the sea. They certainly were asleep. So, being bereft of sympathy, he leaned a little way to one side and swore softly into the sea.

But the thing did not then leave the vicinity of the boat. Ahead or astern, on one side or the other, at intervals long or short, fled the long sparkling streak, and there was to be heard the whiroo of the dark fin. The speed and power of the thing was greatly to be admired. It cut the water like a gigantic and keen projectile.

The presence of this biding thing did not affect the man with the same horror that it would if he had been a picnicker. He simply looked at the sea dully and swore in an undertone.

Nevertheless, it is true that he did not wish to be alone with the thing. He wished one of his companions to awaken by chance and keep him company with it. But the captain hung motionless over the water-jar and the oiler and the cook in the bottom of the boat were plunged in slumber.

VI

"If I am going to be drowned—if I am going to be drowned—if I am going to be drowned, why, in the name of the seven mad gods who rule the sea, was I allowed to come thus far and contemplate sand and trees?"

During this dismal night, it may be remarked that a man would conclude that it was really the intention of the seven mad gods to drown him, despite the abominable injustice of it. For it was certainly an abominable injustice to drown a man who had worked so hard, so hard. The man felt it would be a crime most unnatural. Other people had drowned at sea since galleys swarmed with painted sails, but still——

When it occurs to a man that nature does not regard him as important, and that she feels she would not maim the universe by disposing of him, he at first wishes to throw bricks at the temple, and he hates deeply the fact that there are no bricks and no temples. Any visible expression of nature would surely be pelleted with his jeers.

Then, if there be no tangible thing to hoot he feels, perhaps, the desire to confront a personification and indulge in pleas, bowed to one knee, and with hands supplicant, saying: "Yes, but I love myself."

A high cold star on a winter's night is the word he feels that she says to him. Thereafter he knows the pathos of his situation.

The men in the dingey had not discussed these matters, but each had, no doubt, reflected upon them in silence and according to his mind. There was seldom any expression upon their faces save the general one of complete weariness. Speech was devoted to the business of the boat.

To chime the notes of his emotion, a verse mysteriously entered the correspondent's head. He had even forgotten that he had forgotten this verse, but it suddenly was in his mind.

A soldier of the Legion lay dying in Algiers,
There was lack of woman's nursing, there was dearth of woman's tears;
But a comrade stood beside him, and he took that comrade's hand,
And he said: "I never more shall see my own, my native land."[5]

In his childhood, the correspondent had been made acquainted with the fact that a soldier of the Legion lay dying in Algiers, but he had never regarded it as important. Myriads of his school-fellows had informed him of the soldier's plight, but the dinning had naturally ended by making him perfectly indifferent. He had never considered it his affair that a soldier of

---

5. The lines are incorrectly quoted from Caroline E. S. Norton's poem "Bingen on the Rhine" (1883)

the Legion lay dying in Algiers, nor had it appeared to him as a matter for sorrow. It was less to him than the breaking of a pencil's point.

Now, however, it quaintly came to him as a human, living thing. It was no longer merely a picture of a few throes in the breast of a poet, meanwhile drinking tea and warming his feet at the grate; it was an actuality—stern, mournful, and fine.

The correspondent plainly saw the soldier. He lay on the sand with his feet out straight and still. While his pale left hand was upon his chest in an attempt to thwart the going of his life, the blood came between his fingers. In the far Algerian distance, a city of low square forms was set against a sky that was faint with the last sunset hues. The correspondent, plying the oars and dreaming of the slow and slower movements of the lips of the soldier, was moved by a profound and perfectly impersonal comprehension. He was sorry for the soldier of the Legion who lay dying in Algiers.

The thing which had followed the boat and waited had evidently grown bored at the delay. There was no longer to be heard the slash of the cut-water, and there was no longer the flame of the long trail. The light in the north still glimmered, but it was apparently no nearer to the boat. Sometimes the boom of the surf rang in the correspondent's ears, and he turned the craft seaward then and rowed harder. Southward, some one had evidently built a watch-fire on the beach. It was too low and too far to be seen, but it made a shimmering, roseate reflection upon the bluff back of it, and this could be discerned from the boat. The wind came stronger, and sometimes a wave suddenly raged out like a mountain-cat and there was to be seen the sheen and sparkle of a broken crest.

The captain, in the bow, moved on his water-jar and sat erect. "Pretty long night," he observed to the correspondent. He looked at the shore. "Those life-saving people take their time."

"Did you see that shark playing around?"

"Yes, I saw him. He was a big fellow, all right."

"Wish I had known you were awake."

Later the correspondent spoke into the bottom of the boat.

"Billie!" There was a slow and gradual disentanglement. "Billie, will you spell me?"

"Sure," said the oiler.

As soon as the correspondent touched the cold comfortable seawater in the bottom of the boat, and had huddled close to the cook's life-belt he was deep in sleep, despite the fact that his teeth played all the popular airs. This sleep was so good to him that it was but a moment before he heard a voice call his name in a tone that demonstrated the last stages of exhaustion. "Will you spell me?"

"Sure, Billie."

The light in the north had mysteriously vanished, but the correspondent took his course from the wide-awake captain.

Later in the night they took the boat farther out to sea, and the captain directed the cook to take one oar at the stern and keep the boat facing the seas. He was to call out if he should hear the thunder of the surf. This plan enabled the oiler and the correspondent to get respite together. "We'll give those boys a chance to get into shape again," said the captain. They curled down and, after a few preliminary chatterings and trembles, slept once more the dead sleep. Neither knew they had bequeathed to the cook the company of another shark, or perhaps the same shark.

As the boat caroused on the waves, spray occasionally bumped over the side and gave them a fresh soaking, but this had no power to break their repose. The ominous slash of the wind and the water affected them as it would have affected mummies.

"Boys," said the cook, with the notes of every reluctance in his voice, "she's drifted in pretty close. I guess one of you had better take her to sea again." The correspondent, aroused, heard the crash of the toppled crests.

As he was rowing, the captain gave him some whiskey and water, and this steadied the chills out of him. "If I ever get ashore and anybody shows me even a photograph of an oar—"

At last there was a short conversation.

"Billie. . . . Billie, will you spell me?"

"Sure," said the oiler.

VII

When the correspondent again opened his eyes, the sea and the sky were each of the gray hue of the dawning. Later, carmine and gold was painted upon the waters. The morning appeared finally, in its splendor, with a sky of pure blue, and the sunlight flamed on the tips of the waves.

On the distant dunes were set many little black cottages, and a tall white wind-mill reared above them. No man, nor dog, nor bicycle appeared on the beach. The cottages might have formed a deserted village.

The voyagers scanned the shore. A conference was held in the boat. "Well," said the captain, "if no help is coming, we might better try a run through the surf right away. If we stay out here much longer we will be too weak to do anything for ourselves at all." The others silently acquiesced in this reasoning. The boat was headed for the beach. The correspondent wondered if none ever ascended the tall wind-tower, and if then they never looked seaward. This tower was a giant, standing with its back to the plight of the ants. It represented in a degree, to the correspondent, the serenity of nature amid the struggles of the individual—nature in the wind, and nature in the vision of men. She did not seem cruel to him then, nor beneficent, nor treacherous, nor wise. But she was indifferent, flatly indifferent. It is, perhaps, plausible that a man in this situation, impressed with the unconcern of the universe, should see the innumerable flaws of his life and have them taste wickedly in his mind and wish for another chance. A distinction between right and wrong seems absurdly clear to him, then, in this new ignorance of the grave-edge, and he understands that if he were given another opportunity he would mend his conduct and his words, and be better and brighter during an introduction, or at a tea.

"Now, boys," said the captain, "she is going to swamp sure. All we can do is to work her in as far as possible, and then when she swamps, pile out and scramble for the beach. Keep cool now, and don't jump until she swamps sure."

The oiler took the oars. Over his shoulders he scanned the surf. "Captain," he said, "I think I'd better bring her about, and keep her head-on to the seas and back her in."

"All right, Billie," said the captain. "Back her in." The oiler swung the boat then and, seated in the stern, the cook and the correspondent were obliged to look over their shoulders to contemplate the lonely and indifferent shore.

The monstrous inshore rollers heaved the boat high until the men were again enabled to see the white sheets of water scudding up the slanted beach. "We won't get in very close," said the captain. Each time a man could wrest his attention from the rollers, he turned his glance toward the shore, and in the expression of the eyes during this contemplation there was a singular quality. The correspondent, observing the others, knew that they were not afraid, but the full meaning of their glances was shrouded.

As for himself, he was too tired to grapple fundamentally with the fact. He tried to coerce his mind into thinking of it, but the mind was dominated at this time by the muscles, and the muscles said they did not care. It merely occurred to him that if he should drown it would be a shame.

There were no hurried words, no pallor, no plain agitation. The men simply looked at the shore. "Now, remember to get well clear of the boat when you jump," said the captain.

Seaward the crest of a roller suddenly fell with a thunderous crash, and the long white comber came roaring down upon the boat.

"Steady now," said the captain. The men were silent. They turned their eyes from the shore to the comber and waited. The boat slid up the incline, leaped at the furious top, bounced over it, and swung down the long back of the wave. Some water had been shipped and the cook bailed it out.

But the next crest crashed also. The tumbling boiling flood of white water caught the boat and whirled it almost perpendicular. Water swarmed in from all sides. The correspondent had his hands on the gunwale at this time, and when the water entered at that place he swiftly withdrew his fingers, as if he objected to wetting them.

The little boat, drunken with this weight of water, reeled and snuggled deeper into the sea.

"Bail her out, cook! Bail her out," said the captain.

"All right, Captain," said the cook.

"Now, boys, the next one will do for us, sure," said the oiler. "Mind to jump clear of the boat."

The third wave moved forward, huge, furious, implacable. It fairly swallowed the dingey, and almost simultaneously the men tumbled into the sea. A piece of life-belt had lain in the bottom of the boat, and as the correspondent went overboard he held this to his chest with his left hand.

The January water was icy, and he reflected immediately that it was colder than he had expected to find it off the coast of Florida. This appeared to his dazed mind as a fact important enough to be noted at the time. The coldness of the water was sad; it was tragic. This fact was somehow so mixed and confused with his opinion of his own situation that it seemed almost a proper reason for tears. The water was cold.

When he came to the surface he was conscious of little but the noisy water. Afterward he saw his companions in the sea. The oiler was ahead in the race. He was swimming strongly and rapidly. Off to the correspondent's left, the cook's great white and corked back bulged out of the water, and in the rear the captain was hanging with his one good hand to the keel of the overturned dingey.

There is a certain immovable quality to a shore, and the correspondent wondered at it amid the confusion of the sea.

It seemed also very attractive, but the correspondent knew that it was a long journey, and he paddled leisurely. The piece of life preserver lay under him, and sometimes he whirled down the incline of a wave as if he were on a hand-sled.

But finally he arrived at a place in the sea where travel was beset with difficulty. He did not pause swimming to inquire what manner of current had caught him, but there his progress ceased. The shore was set before him like a bit of scenery on a stage, and he looked at it and understood with his eyes each detail of it.

As the cook passed, much farther to the left, the captain was calling to him, "Turn over on your back, cook! Turn over on your back and use the oar."

"All right, sir." The cook turned on his back, and, paddling with an oar, went ahead as if he were a canoe.

Presently the boat also passed to the left of the correspondent with the captain clinging with one hand to the keel. He would have appeared like a man raising himself to look over a board fence, if it were not for the extraordinary gymnastics of the boat. The correspondent marvelled that the captain could still hold to it.

They passed on, nearer to the shore—the oiler, the cook, the captain—and following them went the water-jar, bouncing gayly over the seas.

The correspondent remained in the grip of this strange new enemy—a current. The shore, with its white slope of sand and its green bluff, topped with little silent cottages, was spread like a picture before him. It was very near to him then, but he was impressed as one who in a gallery looks at a scene from Brittany or Holland.

He thought: "I am going to drown? Can it be possible? Can it be possible? Can it be possible?" Perhaps an individual must consider his own death to be the final phenomenon of nature.

But later a wave perhaps whirled him out of this small deadly current, for he found suddenly that he could again make progress toward the shore. Later still, he was aware that the captain, clinging with one hand to the keel of the dingey, had his face turned away from the shore and toward him, and was calling his name. "Come to the boat! Come to the boat!"

In his struggle to reach the captain and the boat, he reflected that when one gets properly wearied, drowning must really be a comfortable arrangement, a cessation of hostilities accompanied by a large degree of relief, and he was glad of it, for the main thing in his mind for some moments had been horror of the temporary agony. He did not wish to be hurt.

Presently he saw a man running along the shore. He was undressing with most remarkable speed. Coat, trousers, shirt, everything flew magically off him.

"Come to the boat," called the captain.

"All right, Captain." As the correspondent paddled, he saw the captain let himself down to bottom and leave the boat. Then the correspondent performed his one little marvel of the voyage. A large wave caught him and flung him with ease and supreme speed completely over the boat and far beyond it. It struck him even then as an event in gymnastics, and a true miracle of the sea. An overturned boat in the surf is not a plaything to a swimming man.

The correspondent arrived in water that reached only to his waist, but his condition did not enable him to stand for more than a moment. Each wave knocked him into a heap, and the under-tow pulled at him.

Then he saw the man who had been running and undressing, and undressing and running, come bounding into the water. He dragged ashore the cook, and then waded toward the captain, but the captain waved him away, and sent him to the correspondent. He was naked, naked as a tree in winter, but a halo was about his head, and he shone like a saint. He gave a strong pull, and a long drag, and a bully heave at the correspondent's hand. The correspondent schooled in the minor formulæ, said: "Thanks, old man." But suddenly the man cried: "What's that?" He pointed a swift finger. The correspondent said: "Go."

In the shallows, face downward, lay the oiler. His forehead touched sand that was periodically, between each wave, clear of the sea.

The correspondent did not know all that transpired afterward. When he achieved safe ground he fell, striking the sand with each particular part of his body. It was as if he had dropped from a roof, but the thud was grateful to him.

It seems that instantly the beach was populated with men with blankets, clothes, and flasks, and women with coffee-pots and all the remedies sacred to their minds. The welcome of the land to the men from the sea was warm and generous, but a still and dripping shape was carried slowly up the beach, and the land's welcome for it could only be the different and sinister hospitality of the grave.

When it came night, the white waves paced to and fro in the moonlight, and the wind brought the sound of the great sea's voice to the men on shore, and they felt that they could then be interpreters.

1897, 1898

The Blue Hotel[1]

I

The Palace Hotel at Fort Romper was painted a light blue, a shade that is on the legs of a kind of heron, causing the bird to declare its position against any background. The Palace Hotel, then, was always screaming and howling in a way that made the dazzling winter landscape of Nebraska seem only a gay swampish hush. It stood alone on the prairie, and when the snow was falling the town two hundred yards away was not visible. But when the traveler alighted at the railway station he was obliged to pass the Palace Hotel before he could come upon the company of low clap-board houses which composed Fort Romper, and it was not to be thought that any traveler could pass the Palace Hotel without looking at it. Pat Scully, the proprietor, had proved himself a master of strategy when he chose his paints. It is true that on clear days, when the great trans-continental expresses, long lines of sway-

---

1. First published in two installments in *Collier's Weekly* for November 26 and December 3, 1898, then in *"The Monster" and Other Stories* (1899). The text here reprints that established for the University of Virginia edition of *The Works of Stephen Crane*. Vol 5, *Tales of Adventure* (1970).

ing Pullmans, swept through Fort Romper, passengers were overcome at the sight, and the cult that knows the brown-reds and the subdivisions of the dark greens of the East expressed shame, pity, horror, in a laugh. But to the citizens of this prairie town, and to the people who would naturally stop there, Pat Scully had performed a feat. With this opulence and splendor, these creeds, classes, egotisms, that streamed through Romper on the rails day after day, they had no color in common.

As if the displayed delights of such a blue hotel were not sufficiently enticing, it was Scully's habit to go every morning and evening to meet the leisurely trains that stopped at Romper and work his seductions upon any man that he might see wavering, gripsack in hand.

One morning, when a snow-crusted engine dragged its long string of freight cars and its one passenger coach to the station, Scully performed the marvel of catching three men. One was a shaky and quick-eyed Swede, with a great shining cheap valise; one was a tall bronzed cowboy, who was on his way to a ranch near the Dakota line; one was a little silent man from the East, who didn't look it, and didn't announce it. Scully practically made them prisoners. He was so nimble and merry and kindly that each probably felt it would be the height of brutality to try to escape. They trudged off over the creaking board sidewalks in the wake of the eager little Irishman. He wore a heavy fur cap squeezed tightly down on his head. It caused his two red ears to stick out stiffly, as if they were made of tin.

At last, Scully, elaborately, with boisterous hospitality, conducted them through the portals of the blue hotel. The room which they entered was small. It seemed to be merely a proper temple for an enormous stove, which, in the center, was humming with god-like violence. At various points on its surface the iron had become luminous and glowed yellow from the heat. Beside the stove Scully's son Johnnie was playing High-Five[2] with an old farmer who had whiskers both gray and sandy. They were quarreling. Frequently the old farmer turned his face toward a box of sawdust—colored brown from tobacco juice—that was behind the stove, and spat with an air of great impatience and irritation. With a loud flourish of words Scully destroyed the game of cards, and bustled his son upstairs with part of the baggage of the new guests. He himself conducted them to three basins of the coldest water in the world. The cowboy and the Easterner burnished themselves fiery red with this water, until it seemed to be some kind of a metal polish. The Swede, however, merely dipped his fingers gingerly and with trepidation. It was notable that throughout this series of small ceremonies the three travelers were made to feel that Scully was very benevolent. He was conferring great favors upon them. He handed the towel from one to the other with an air of philanthropic impulse.

Afterward they went to the first room, and, sitting about the stove, listened to Scully's officious clamor at his daughters, who were preparing the midday meal. They reflected in the silence of experienced men who tread carefully amid new people. Nevertheless, the old farmer, stationary, invincible in his chair near the warmest part of the stove, turned his face from the sawdust box frequently and addressed a glowing commonplace to the strangers. Usually he was answered in short but adequate sentences by either the cowboy or the Easterner. The Swede said nothing. He seemed to

2. I.e., cinch, a card game.

be occupied in making furtive estimates of each man in the room. One might have thought that he had the sense of silly suspicion which comes to guilt. He resembled a badly frightened man.

Later, at dinner, he spoke a little, addressing his conversation entirely to Scully. He volunteered that he had come from New York, where for ten years he had worked as a tailor. These facts seemed to strike Scully as fascinating, and afterward he volunteered that he had lived at Romper for fourteen years. The Swede asked about the crops and the price of labor. He seemed barely to listen to Scully's extended replies. His eyes continued to rove from man to man.

Finally, with a laugh and a wink, he said that some of these Western communities were very dangerous; and after his statement he straightened his legs under the table, titled his head, and laughed again, loudly. It was plain that the demonstration had no meaning to the others. They looked at him wondering and in silence.

II

As the men trooped heavily back into the front room, the two little windows presented views of a turmoiling sea of snow. The huge arms of the wind were making attempts—mighty, circular, futile—to embrace the flakes as they sped. A gate-post like a still man with a blanched face stood aghast amid this profligate fury. In a hearty voice Scully announced the presence of a blizzard. The guests of the blue hotel, lighting their pipes, assented with grunts of lazy masculine contentment. No island of the sea could be exempt in the degree of this little room with its humming stove. Johnnie, son of Scully, in a tone which defined his opinion of his ability as a card-player, challenged the old farmer of both gray and sandy whiskers to a game of High-Five. The farmer agreed with a contemptuous and bitter scoff. They sat close to the stove, and squared their knees under a wide board. The cowboy and the Easterner watched the game with interest. The Swede remained near the window, aloof, but with a countenance that showed signs of an inexplicable excitement.

The play of Johnnie and the gray-beard was suddenly ended by another quarrel. The old man arose while casting a look of heated scorn at his adversary. He slowly buttoned his coat, and then stalked with fabulous dignity from the room. In the discreet silence of all other men the Swede laughed. His laughter rang somehow childish. Men by this time had begun to look at him askance, as if they wished to inquire what ailed him.

A new game was formed jocosely. The cowboy volunteered to become the partner of Johnnie, and they all then turned to ask the Swede to throw in his lot with the little Easterner. He asked some questions about the game, and learning that it wore many names, and that he had played it when it was under an alias, he accepted the invitation. He strode toward the men nervously, as if he expected to be assaulted. Finally, seated, he gazed from face to face and laughed shrilly. This laugh was so strange that the Easterner looked up quickly, the cowboy sat intent and with his mouth open, and Johnnie paused, holding the cards with still fingers.

Afterward there was a short silence. Then Johnnie said: "Well, let's get at it. Come on now!" They pulled their chairs forward until their knees were bunched under the board. They began to play, and their interest in the game caused the others to forget the manner of the Swede.

The cowboy was a board-whacker. Each time that he held superior cards he whanged them, one by one, with exceeding force, down upon the improvised table, and took the tricks with a glowing air of prowess and pride that sent thrills of indignation into the hearts of his opponents. A game with a board-whacker in it is sure to become intense. The countenances of the Easterner and the Swede were miserable whenever the cowboy thundered down his aces and kings, while Johnnie, his eyes gleaming with joy, chuckled and chuckled.

Because of the absorbing play none considered the strange ways of the Swede. They paid strict heed to the game. Finally, during a lull caused by a new deal, the Swede suddenly addressed Johnnie: "I suppose there have been a good many men killed in this room." The jaws of the others dropped and they looked at him.

"What in hell are you talking about?" asked Johnnie.

The Swede laughed again his blatant laugh, full of a kind of false courage and defiance. "Oh, you know what I mean all right," he answered.

"I'm a liar if I do!" Johnnie protested. The card was halted, and the men stared at the Swede. Johnnie evidently felt that as the son of the proprietor he should make a direct inquiry. "Now, what might you be drivin' at, mister?" he asked. The Swede winked at him. It was a wink full of cunning. His fingers shook on the edge of the board. "Oh, maybe you think I have been to nowheres. Maybe you think I'm a tenderfoot?"

"I don't know nothin' about you," answered Johnnie, "and I don't give a damn where you've been. All I got to say is that I don't know what you're driving at. There hain't never been nobody killed in this room."

The cowboy, who had been steadily gazing at the Swede, then spoke. "What's wrong with you, mister?"

Apparently it seemed to the Swede that he was formidably menaced. He shivered and turned white near the corners of his mouth. He sent an appealing glance in the direction of the little Easterner. During these moments he did not forget to wear his air of advanced pot-valor.[3] "They say they don't know what I mean," he remarked mockingly to the Easterner.

The latter answered after prolonged and cautious reflection. "I don't understand you," he said, impassively.

The Swede made a movement then which announced that he thought he had encountered treachery from the only quarter where he had expected sympathy if not help. "Oh, I see you are all against me. I see——"

The cowboy was in a state of deep stupefaction. "Say," he cried, as he tumbled the deck violently down upon the board. "Say, what are you gittin' at, hey?"

The Swede sprang up with the celerity of a man escaping from a snake on the floor. "I don't want to fight!" he shouted. "I don't want to fight!"

The cowboy stretched his long legs indolently and deliberately. His hands were in his pockets. He spat into the sawdust box. "Well, who the hell thought you did?" he inquired.

The Swede backed rapidly toward a corner of the room. His hands were out protectingly in front of his chest, but he was making an obvious struggle

---

3. Drunken bravado.

to control his fright. "Gentlemen," he quavered, "I suppose I am going to be killed before I can leave this house! I suppose I am going to be killed before I can leave this house!" In his eyes was the dying swan look. Through the windows could be seen the snow turning blue in the shadow of dusk. The wind tore at the house and some loose thing beat regularly against the clapboards like a spirit tapping.

A door opened, and Scully himself entered. He paused in surprise as he noted the tragic attitude of the Swede. Then he said: "What's the matter here?"

The Swede answered him swiftly and eagerly: "These men are going to kill me."

"Kill you!" ejaculated Scully. "Kill you! What are you talkin'?"

The Swede made the gesture of a martyr.

Scully wheeled sternly upon his son. "What is this, Johnnie?"

The lad had grown sullen. "Damned if I know," he answered. "I can't make no sense to it." He began to shuffle the cards, fluttering them together with an angry snap. "He says a good many men have been killed in this room, or something like that. And he says he's goin' to be killed here too. I don't know what ails him. He's crazy, I shouldn't wonder."

Scully then looked for explanation to the cowboy, but the cowboy simply shrugged his shoulders."

"Kill you?" said Scully again to the Swede. "Kill you? Man, you're off your nut."

"Oh, I know," burst out the Swede. "I know what will happen. Yes, I'm crazy—yes. Yes, of course, I'm crazy—yes. But I know one thing——" There was a sort of sweat of misery and terror upon his face. "I know I won't get out of here alive."

The cowboy drew a deep breath, as if his mind was passing into the last stages of dissolution. "Well, I'm dog-goned," he whispered to himself.

Scully wheeled suddenly and faced his son. "You've been troublin' this man!"

Johnnie's voice was loud with its burden of grievance. "Why, good Gawd, I ain't done nothin' to 'im."

The Swede broke in. "Gentlemen, do not disturb yourselves. I will leave this house. I will go 'way because——" He accused them dramatically with his glance. "Because I do not want to be killed."

Scully was furious with his son. "Will you tell me what is the matter, you young divil? What's the matter, anyhow? Speak out!"

"Blame it," cried Johnnie in despair, "don't I tell you I don't know. He—he says we want to kill him, and that's all I know. I can't tell what ails him."

The Swede continued to repeat: "Never mind, Mr. Scully, never mind. I will leave this house. I will go away, because I do not wish to be killed. Yes, of course, I am crazy—yes. But I know one thing! I will go away. I will leave this house. Never mind, Mr. Scully, never mind. I will go away."

"You will not go 'way," said Scully. "You will not go 'way until I hear the reason of this business. If anybody has troubled you I will take care of him. This is my house. You are under my roof, and I will not allow any peaceable man to be troubled here." He cast a terrible eye upon Johnnie, the cowboy, and the Easterner.

"Never mind, Mr. Scully, never mind. I will go 'way. I do not wish to be killed." The Swede moved toward the door, which opened upon the stairs. It was evidently his intention to go at once for his baggage.

"No, no," shouted Scully peremptorily; but the white-faced man slid by him and disappeared. "Now," said Scully severely, "what does this mean?"

Johnnie and the cowboy cried together: "Why, we didn't do nothin' to 'im!"

Scully's eyes were cold. "No," he said, "you didn't?"

Johnnie swore a deep oath. "Why, this is the wildest loon I ever see. We didn't do nothin' at all. We were jest sittin' here playin' cards and he——"

The father suddenly spoke to the Easterner. "Mr. Blanc," he asked, "what has these boys been doin'?"

The Easterner reflected again. "I didn't see anything wrong at all," he said at last slowly.

Scully began to howl. "But what does it mane?" He stared ferociously at his son. "I have a mind to lather you for this, me boy."

Johnnie was frantic. "Well, what have I done?" he bawled at his father.

III

"I think you are tongue-tied," said Scully finally to his son, the cowboy and the Easterner, and at the end of this scornful sentence he left the room.

Upstairs the Swede was swiftly fastening the straps of his great valise. Once his back happened to be half-turned toward the door, and hearing a noise there, he wheeled and sprang up, uttering a loud cry. Scully's wrinkled visage showed grimly in the light of the small lamp he carried. This yellow effulgence, streaming upward, colored only his prominent features, and left his eyes, for instance, in mysterious shadow. He resembled a murderer.

"Man, man!" he exclaimed, "have you gone daffy?"

"Oh, no! Oh, no!" rejoined the other. "There are people in this world who know pretty nearly as much as you do—understand?"

For a moment they stood gazing at each other. Upon the Swede's deathly pale cheeks were two spots brightly crimson and sharply edged, as if they had been carefully painted. Scully placed the light on the table and sat himself on the edge of the bed. He spoke ruminatively. "By cracky, I never heard of such a thing in my life. It's a complete muddle. I can't for the soul of me think how you ever got this idea into your head." Presently he lifted his eyes and asked: "And did you sure think they were going to kill you?"

The Swede scanned the old man as if he wished to see into his mind. "I did," he said at last. He obviously suspected that this answer might precipitate an outbreak. As he pulled on a strap his whole arm shook, the elbow wavering like a bit of paper.

Scully banged his hand impressively on the foot-board of the bed. "Why, man, we're goin' to have a line of ilictric street-cars in this town next spring."

"'A line of electric street-cars,'" repeated the Swede stupidly.

"And," said Scully, "there's a new railroad goin' to be built down from Broken Arm to here. Not to mention the four churches and the smashin' big brick school-house. Then there's the big factory, too. Why, in two years Romper'll be a met-tro-*pol*-is."

Having finished the preparation of his baggage, the Swede straightened himself. "Mr. Scully," he said with sudden hardihood, "how much do I owe you?"

"You don't owe me anythin'," said the old man angrily.

"Yes, I do," retorted the Swede. He took seventy-five cents from his pocket and tendered it to Scully; but the latter snapped his fingers in disdainful refusal. However, it happened that they both stood gazing in a strange fashion at three silver pieces on the Swede's open palm.

"I'll not take your money," said Scully at last. "Not after what's been goin' on here." Then a plan seemed to strike him. "Here," he cried, picking up his lamp and moving toward the door. "Here! Come with me a minute."

"No," said the Swede in overwhelming alarm.

"Yes," urged the old man. "Come on! I want you to come and see a picter—just across the hall—in my room."

The Swede must have concluded that his hour was come. His jaw dropped and his teeth showed like a dead man's. He ultimately followed Scully across the corridor, but he had the step of one hung in chains.

Scully flashed the light high on the wall of his own chamber. There was revealed a ridiculous photograph of a little girl. She was leaning against a balustrade of gorgeous decoration, and the formidable bang to her hair was prominent. The figure was as graceful as an upright sled-stake, and, withal, it was the hue of lead. "There," said Scully tenderly. "That's the picter of my little girl that died. Her name was Carrie. She had the purtiest hair you ever saw! I was that fond of her, she——"

Turning then he saw that the Swede was not contemplating the picture at all, but, instead, was keeping keen watch on the gloom in the rear.

"Look, man!" shouted Scully heartily. "That's the picter of my little gal that died. Her name was Carrie. And then here's the picter of my oldest boy, Michael. He's a lawyer in Lincoln an' doin' well. I gave that boy a grand eddycation, and I'm glad for it now. He's a fine boy. Look at 'im now. Ain't he bold as blazes, him there in Lincoln, an honored an' respicted gintleman. An honored an' respicted gintleman," concluded Scully with a flourish. And so saying, he smote the Swede jovially on the back.

The Swede faintly smiled.

"Now," said the old man, "there's only one more thing." He dropped suddenly to the floor and thrust his head beneath the bed. The Swede could hear his muffled voice. "I'd keep it under me piller if it wasn't for that boy Johnnie. Then there's the old woman——Where is it now? I never put it twice in the same place. Ah, now come out with you!"

Presently he backed clumsily from under the bed, dragging with him an old coat rolled into a bundle. "I've fetched him," he muttered. Kneeling on the floor he unrolled the coat and extracted from its heart a large yellow-brown whisky bottle.

His first maneuver was to hold the bottle up to the light. Reassured, apparently, that nobody had been tampering with it, he thrust it with a generous movement toward the Swede.

The weak-kneed Swede was about to eagerly clutch this element of strength, but he suddenly jerked his hand away and cast a look of horror upon Scully.

"Drink," said the old man affectionately. He had arisen to his feet, and now stood facing the Swede.

There was a silence. Then again Scully said: "Drink!"

The Swede laughed wildly. He grabbed the bottle, put it to his mouth, and as his lips curled absurdly around the opening and his throat worked, he kept his glance burning with hatred upon the old man's face.

IV

After the departure of Scully the three men, with the cardboard still upon their knees, preserved for a long time an astounded silence. Then Johnnie said: "That's the dod-dangest Swede I ever see."

"He ain't no Swede," said the cowboy scornfully.

"Well, what is he then?" cried Johnnie. "What is he then?"

"It's my opinion," replied the cowboy deliberately, "he's some kind of a Dutchman." It was a venerable custom of the country to entitle as Swedes all light-haired men who spoke with a heavy tongue. In consequence the idea of the cowboy was not without its daring. "Yes, sir," he repeated. "It's my opinion this feller is some kind of a Dutchman."

"Well, he says he's a Swede, anyhow," muttered Johnnie sulkily. He turned to the Easterner: "What do you think, Mr. Blanc?"

"Oh, I don't know," replied the Easterner.

"Well, what do you think makes him act that way?" asked the cowboy.

"Why, he's frightened!" The Easterner knocked his pipe against a rim of the stove. "He's clear frightened out of his boots."

"What at?" cried Johnnie and cowboy together.

The Easterner reflected over his answer.

"What at?" cried the others again.

"Oh, I don't know, but it seems to me this man has been reading dime-novels, and he thinks he's right out in the middle of it—the shootin' and stabbin' and all."

"But," said the cowboy, deeply scandalized, "this ain't Wyoming, ner none of them places. This is Nebrasker."

"Yes," added Johnnie, "an' why don't he wait till he gits *out West?*"

The traveled Easterner laughed. "It isn't different there even—not in these days. But he thinks he's right in the middle of hell."

Johnnie and the cowboy mused long.

"It's awful funny," remarked Johnnie at last.

"Yes," said the cowboy. "This is a queer game. I hope we don't git snowed in, because then we'd have to stand this here man bein' around with us all the time. That wouldn't be no good."

"I wish pop would throw him out," said Johnnie.

Presently they heard a loud stamping on the stairs, accompanied by ringing jokes in the voice of old Scully, and laughter, evidently from the Swede. The men around the store stared vacantly at each other. "Gosh," said the cowboy. The door flew open, and old Scully, flushed and anec-dotal, came into the room. He was jabbering at the Swede, who followed him, laughing bravely. It was the entry of two roisterers from a banquet ball.

"Come now," said Scully sharply to the three seated men, "move up and give us a chance at the stove." The cowboy and the Easterner obediently sidled their chairs to make room for the newcomers. Johnnie, however, simply arranged himself in a more indolent attitude, and then remained motionless.

"Come! Git over, there," said Scully.

"Plenty of room on the other side of the stove," said Johnnie.

"Do you think we want to sit in the draught?" roared the father.

But the Swede here interposed with a grandeur of confidence. "No, no. Let the boy sit where he likes," he cried in a bullying voice to the father.

"All right! All right!" said Scully deferentially. The cowboy and the Easterner exchanged glances of wonder.

The five chairs were formed in a crescent about one side of the stove. The Swede began to talk; he talked arrogantly, profanely, angrily. Johnnie, the cowboy and the Easterner maintained a morose silence, while old Scully appeared to be receptive and eager, breaking in constantly with sympathetic ejaculations.

Finally, the Swede announced that he was thirsty. He moved in his chair, and said that he would go for a drink of water.

"I'll git it for you," cried Scully at once.

"No," said the Swede contemptuously. "I'll get it for myself." He arose and stalked with the air of an owner off into the executive parts of the hotel.

As soon as the Swede was out of hearing Scully sprang to his feet and whispered intensely to the others. "Upstairs he thought I was tryin' to poison 'im."

"Say," said Johnnie, "this makes me sick. Why don't you throw 'im out in the snow?"

"Why, he's all right now," declared Scully. "It was only that he was from the East and he thought this was a tough place. That's all. He's all right now."

The cowboy looked with admiration upon the Easterner. "You were straight," he said. "You were on to that there Dutchman."

"Well," said Johnnie to his father, "he may be all right now, but I don't see it. Other time he was scared, and now he's too fresh."

Scully's speech was always a combination of Irish brogue and idiom, Western twang and idiom, and scraps of curiously formal diction taken from the story-books and newspapers. He now hurled a strange mass of language at the head of his son. "What do I keep? What do I keep? What do I keep?" he demanded in a voice of thunder. He slapped his knee impressively, to indicate that he himself was going to make reply, and that all should head. "I keep a hotel," he shouted. "A hotel, do you mind? A guest under my roof has sacred privileges. He is to be intimidated by none. Not one word shall he hear that would prijudice him in favor of goin' away. I'll not have it. There's no place in this here town where they can say they iver took in a guest of mine because he was afraid to stay here." He wheeled suddenly upon the cowboy and the Easterner. "Am I right?"

"Yes, Mr. Scully," said the cowboy, "I think you're right."

"Yes, Mr. Scully," said the Easterner, "I think you're right."

V

At six-o'clock supper, the Swede fizzed like a fire-wheel. He sometimes seemed on the point of bursting into riotous song, and in all his madness he was encouraged by old Scully. The Easterner was incased in reserve; the cowboy sat in wide-mouthed amazement, forgetting to eat, while Johnnie wrathily demolished great plates of food. The daughters of the house when they were obliged to replenish the biscuits approached as warily as Indians, and, having succeeded in their purposes, fled with ill-concealed trepidation. The Swede domineered the whole feast, and he gave it the appearance of a cruel bacchanal. He seemed to have grown suddenly taller; he gazed, brutally disdainful, into every face. His voice rang through the room. Once when he jabbed out harpoon-fashion with his fork to pinion a biscuit the weapon nearly impaled the hand of the Easterner which had been stretched quietly out for the same biscuit.

After supper, as the men filed toward the other room, the Swede smote Scully ruthlessly on the shoulder. "Well, old boy, that was a good square meal." Johnnie looked hopefully at his father; he knew that shoulder was tender from an old fall; and indeed it appeared for a moment as if Scully was going to flame out over the matter, but in the end he smiled a sickly smile and remained silent. The others understood from his manner that he was admitting his responsibility for the Swede's new viewpoint.

Johnnie, however, addressed his parent in an aside. "Why don't you license somebody to kick you downstairs?" Scully scowled darkly by way of reply.

When they were gathered about the stove, the Swede insisted on another game of High-Five. Scully gently deprecated the plan at first, but the Swede turned a wolfish glare upon him. The old man subsided, and the Swede canvassed the others. In his tone there was always a great threat. The cowboy and the Easterner both remarked indifferently that they would play. Scully said that he would presently have to go to meet the 6.58 train, and so the Swede turned menacingly upon Johnnie. For a moment their glances crossed like blades, and then Johnnie smiled and said: "Yes, I'll play."

They formed a square with the little board on their knees. The Easterner and the Swede were again partners. As the play went on, it was noticeable that the cowboy was not board-whacking as usual. Meanwhile, Scully, near the lamp, had put on his spectacles and, with an appearance curiously like an old priest, was reading a newspaper. In time he went out to meet the 6.58 train, and, despite his precautions, a gust of polar wind whirled into the room as he opened the door. Besides scattering the cards, it chilled the players to the marrow. The Swede cursed frightfully. When Scully returned, his entrance disturbed a cozy and friendly scene. The Swede again cursed. But presently they were once more intent, their heads bent forward and their hands moving swiftly. The Swede had adopted the fashion of board-whacking.

Scully took up his paper and for a long time remained immersed in matters which were extraordinarily remote from him. The lamp burned badly, and once he stopped to adjust the wick. The newspaper as he turned from page to page rustled with a slow and comfortable sound. Then suddenly he heard three terrible words: "You are cheatin'!"

Such scenes often prove that there can be little of dramatic import in environment. Any room can present a tragic front; any room can be comic. This little den was now hideous as a torture-chamber. The new faces of the men themselves had changed it upon the instant. The Swede held a huge fist in front of Johnnie's face, while the latter looked steadily over it into the blazing orbs of his accuser. The Easterner had grown pallid; the cowboy's jaw had dropped in that expression of bovine amazement which was one of his important mannerisms. After the three words, the first sound in the room was made by Scully's paper as it floated forgotten to his feet. His spectacles had also fallen from his nose, but by a clutch he had saved them in air. His hand, grasping the spectacles, now remained poised awkwardly and near his shoulder. He stared at the card-players.

Probably the silence was while a second elapsed. Then, if the floor had been suddenly twitched out from under the men they could not have moved quicker. The five had projected themselves headlong toward a common point. It happened that Johnnie in rising to hurl himself upon the Swede had stumbled slightly because of his curiously instinctive care for the cards and the board. The loss of the moment allowed time for the arrival of Scully, and also allowed the cowboy time to give the Swede a great push which sent him staggering back. The men found tongue together, and hoarse shouts of rage, appeal or fear burst from every throat. The cowboy pushed and jostled feverishly at the Swede, and the Easterner and Scully clung wildly to Johnnie; but, through the smoky air, above the swaying bodies of the peace-compellers, the eyes of the two warriors ever sought each other in glances of challenge that were at once hot and steely.

Of course the board had been overturned, and now the whole company of cards was scattered over the floor, where the boots of the men trampled the fat and painted kings and queens as they gazed with their silly eyes at the war that was waging above them.

Scully's voice was dominating the yells. "Stop now! Stop, I say! Stop, now——"

Johnnie, as he struggled to burst through the rank formed by Scully and the Easterner, was crying: "Well, he says I cheated! He says I cheated! I won't allow no man to say I cheated! If he says I cheated, he's a—— ——!"

The cowboy was telling the Swede: "Quit, now! Quit, d'ye hear——"

The screams of the Swede never ceased. "He did cheat! I saw him! I saw him——"

As for the Easterner, he was importuning in a voice that was not heeded. "Wait a moment, can't you? Oh, wait a moment. What's the good of a fight over a game of cards? Wait a moment——"

In this tumult no complete sentences were clear. "Cheat"—"Quit"—"He says"—These fragments pierced the uproar and rang out sharply. It was remarkable that whereas Scully undoubtedly made the most noise, he was the least heard of any of the riotous band.

Then suddenly there was a great cessation. It was as if each man had paused for breath, and although the room was still lighted with the anger of men, it could be seen that there was no danger of immediate conflict, and at once Johnnie, shouldering his way forward, almost succeeded in confronting the Swede. "What did you say I cheated for? What did you say I cheated for? I don't cheat and I won't let no man say I do!"

The Swede said: "I saw you! I saw you!"

"Well," cried Johnnie, "I'll fight any man what says I cheat!"

"No, you won't," said the cowboy. "Not here."

"Ah, be still, can't you?" said Scully, coming between them.

The quiet was sufficient to allow the Easterner's voice to be heard. He was repeating: "Oh, wait a moment, can't you? What's the good of a fight over a game of cards? Wait a moment."

Johnnie, his red face appearing above his father's shoulder, hailed the Swede again. "Did you say I cheated?"

The Swede showed his teeth. "Yes."

"Then," said Johnnie, "we must fight."

"Yes, fight," roared the Swede. He was like a demoniac. "Yes, fight! I'll show you what kind of a man I am! I'll show you who you want to fight! Maybe you think I can't fight! Maybe you think I can't! I'll show you, you skin,[4] you card-sharp! Yes, you cheated! You cheated! You cheated!"

---

4. Cheat (colloquial).

"Well, let's git at it, then, mister," said Johnnie coolly.

The cowboy's brow was beaded with sweat from his efforts in intercepting all sorts of raids. He turned in despair to Scully. "What are you goin' to do now?"

A change had come over the Celtic visage of the old man. He now seemed all eagerness; his eyes glowed.

"We'll let them fight," he answered stalwartly. "I can't put up with it any longer. I've stood this damned Swede till I'm sick. We'll let them fight."

VI

The men prepared to go out of doors. The Easterner was so nervous that he had great difficulty in getting his arms into the sleeves of his new leather-coat. As the cowboy drew his fur-cap down over his ears his hands trembled. In fact, Johnnie and old Scully were the only ones who displayed no agitation. These preliminaries were conducted without words.

Scully threw open the door. "Well, come on," he said. Instantly a terrific wind caused the flame of the lamp to struggle at its wick, while a puff of black smoke sprang from the chimney-top. The stove was in mid-current of the blast, and its voice swelled to equal the roar of the storm. Some of the scarred and bedabbled cards were caught up from the floor and dashed helplessly against the further wall. The men lowered their heads and plunged into the tempest as into a sea.

No snow was falling, but great whirls and clouds of flakes, swept up from the ground by the frantic winds, were streaming southward with the speed of bullets. The covered land was blue with the sheen of an unearthly satin, and there was no other hue save where at the low black railway station—which seemed incredibly distant—one light gleamed like a tiny jewel. As the men floundered into a thigh-deep drift, it was known that the Swede was bawling out something. Scully went to him, put a hand on his shoulder and projected an ear. "What's that you say?" he shouted.

"I say," bawled the Swede again, "I won't stand much show against this gang. I know you'll all pitch on me."

Scully smote him reproachfully on the arm. "Tut, man," he yelled. The wind tore the words from Scully's lips and scattered them far a-lee.

"You are all a gang of——" boomed the Swede, but the storm also seized the remainder of this sentence.

Immediately turning their backs upon the wind, the men had swung around a corner to the sheltered side of the hotel. It was the function of the little house to preserve here, amid this great devastation of snow, an irregular V-shape of heavily-incrusted grass, which crackled beneath the feet. One could imagine the great drifts piled against the windward side. When the party reached the comparative peace of this spot it was found that the Swede was still bellowing.

"Oh, I know what kind of a thing this is! I know you'll all pitch on me. I can't lick you all!"

Scully turned upon him panther-fashion. "You'll not have to whip all of us. You'll have to whip my son Johnnie. An' the man what troubles you durin' that time will have me to dale with."

The arrangements were swiftly made. The two men faced each other, obedient to the harsh commands of Scully, whose face, in the subtly luminous gloom, could be seen set in the austere impersonal lines that are pictured on the countenances of the Roman veterans. The Easterner's teeth were chattering, and he was hopping up and down like a mechanical toy. The cowboy stood rock-like.

The contestants had not stripped off any clothing. Each was in his ordinary attire. Their fists were up, and they eyed each other in a calm that had the elements of leonine cruelty in it.

During this pause, the Easterner's mind, like a film, took lasting impressions of three men—the iron-nerved master of the ceremony; the Swede, pale, motionless, terrible; and Johnnie, serene yet ferocious, brutish yet heroic. The entire prelude had in it a tragedy greater than the tragedy of action, and this aspect was accentuated by the long mellow cry of the blizzard, as it sped the tumbling and wailing flakes into the black abyss of the south.

"Now!" said Scully.

The two combatants leaped forward and crashed together like bullocks. There was heard the cushioned sound of blows, and a curse squeezing out from between the tight teeth of one.

As for the spectators, the Easterner's pent-up breath exploded from him with a pop of relief, absolute relief from the tension of the preliminaries. The cowboy bounded into the air with a yowl. Scully was immovable as from supreme amazement and fear at the fury of the fight which he himself had permitted and arranged.

For a time the encounter in the darkness was such a perplexity of flying arms that it presented no more detail than would a swiftly-revolving wheel. Occasionally a face, as if illumined by a flash of light, would shine out, ghastly and marked with pink spots. A moment later, the men might have been known as shadows, if it were not for the involuntary utterance of oaths that came from them in whispers.

Suddenly a holocaust of warlike desire caught the cowboy, and he bolted forward with the speed of a broncho. "Go it, Johnnie; go it! Kill him! Kill him!"

Scully confronted him. "Kape back," he said; and by his glance the cowboy could tell that this man was Johnnie's father.

To the Easterner there was a monotony of unchangeable fighting that was an abomination. This confused mingling was eternal to his sense, which was concentrated in a longing for the end, the priceless end. Once the fighters lurched near him, and as he scrambled hastily backward, he heard them breathe like men on the rack.

"Kill him, Johnnie! Kill him! Kill him!" The cowboy's face was contorted like one of those agony-masks in museums.

"Keep still," said Scully icily.

Then there was a sudden loud grunt, incomplete, cut-short, and Johnnie's body swung away from the Swede and fell with sickening heaviness to the grass. The cowboy was barely in time to prevent the mad Swede from flinging himself upon his prone adversary. "No, you don't," said the cowboy, interposing an arm. "Wait a second."

Scully was at his son's side. "Johnnie! Johnnie, me boy?" His voice had a quality of melancholy tenderness. "Johnnie? Can you go on with it?" He looked anxiously down into the bloody pulpy face of his son.

There was a moment of silence, and then Johnnie answered in his ordinary voice: "Yes, I—it—yes."

Assisted by his father he struggled to his feet. "Wait a bit now till you git your wind," said the old man.

A few paces away the cowboy was lecturing the Swede. "No, you don't! Wait a second!"

The Easterner was plucking at Scully's sleeve. "Oh, this is enough," he pleaded. "This is enough! Let it go as it stands. This is enough!"

"Bill," said Scully, "git out of the road." The cowboy stepped aside. "Now." The combatants were actuated by a new caution as they advanced toward collision. They glared at each other, and then the Swede aimed a lightning blow that carried with it his entire weight. Johnnie was evidently half-stupid from weakness, but he miraculously dodged, and his fist sent the over-balanced Swede sprawling.

The cowboy, Scully and the Easterner burst into a cheer that was like a chorus of triumphant soldiery, but before its conclusion the Swede had scuffled agilely to his feet and come in berserk abandon at his foe. There was another perplexity of flying arms, and Johnnie's body again swung away and fell, even as a bundle might fall from a roof. The Swede instantly staggered to a little wind-waved tree and leaned upon it, breathing like an engine, while his savage and flame-lit eyes roamed from face to face as the men bent over Johnnie. There was a splendor of isolation in his situation at this time which the Easterner felt once when, lifting his eyes from the man on the ground, he beheld that mysterious and lonely figure, waiting.

"Are you any good yet, Johnnie?" asked Scully in a broken voice.

The son gasped and opened his eyes languidly. After a moment he answered: "No—I ain't—any good—any—more." Then, from shame and bodily ill, he began to weep, the tears furrowing down through the blood-stains on his face. "He was too—too—too heavy for me."

Scully straightened and addressed the waiting figure. "Stranger," he said, evenly, "it's all up with our side." Then his voice changed into that vibrant huskiness which is commonly the tone of the most simple and deadly announcements. "Johnnie is whipped."

Without replying, the victor moved off on the route to the front door of the hotel.

The cowboy was formulating new and unspellable blasphemies. The Easterner was startled to find that they were out in a wind that seemed to come direct from the shadowed arctic floes. He heard again the wail of the snow pas it was flung to its grave in the south. He knew now that all this time the cold had been sinking into him deeper and deeper, and he wondered that he had not perished. He felt indifferent to the condition of the vanquished man.

"Johnnie, can you walk?" asked Scully.

"Did I hurt—hurt him any?" asked the son.

"Can you walk, boy? Can you walk?"

Johnnie's voice was suddenly strong. There was a robust impatience in it. "I asked you whether I hurt him any!"

"Yes, yes, Johnnie," answered the cowboy consolingly; "he's hurt a good deal."

They raised him from the ground, and as soon as he was on his feet he went tottering off, rebuffing all attempts at assistance. When the party rounded the corner they were fairly blinded by the pelting of the snow. It burned their faces like fire. The cowboy carried Johnnie through the drift to the door. As they entered some cards again rose from the floor and beat against the wall.

The Easterner rushed to the stove. He was so profoundly chilled that he almost dared to embrace the glowing iron. The Swede was not in the room. Johnnie sank into a chair, and folding his arms on his knees, buried his face in them. Scully, warming one foot and then the other at a rim of the stove, muttered to himself with Celtic mournfulness. The cowboy had removed his fur-cap, and with a dazed and rueful air he was now running one hand through his tousled locks. From overhead they could hear the creaking of boards, as the Swede tramped here and there in his room.

The sad quiet was broken by the sudden flinging open of a door that led toward the kitchen. It was instantly followed by an inrush of women. They precipitated themselves upon Johnnie amid a chorus of lamentation. Before they carried their prey off to the kitchen, there to be bathed and harangued with that mixture of sympathy and abuse which is a feat of their sex, the mother straightened herself and fixed old Scully with an eye of stern reproach. "Shame be upon you, Patrick Scully!" she cried. "Your own son, too. Shame be upon you!"

"There, now! Be quiet, now!" said the old man weakly.

"Shame be upon you, Patrick Scully!" The girls, rallying to this slogan, sniffed disdainfully in the direction of those trembling accomplices, the cowboy and the Easterner. Presently they bore Johnnie away, and left the three men to dismal reflection.

VII

"I'd like to fight this here Dutchman myself," said the cowboy, breaking a long silence.

Scully wagged his head sadly. "No, that wouldn't do. It wouldn't be right. It wouldn't be right."

"Well, why wouldn't it?" argued the cowboy. "I don't see no harm in it."

"No," answered Scully with mournful heroism. "It wouldn't be right. It was Johnnie's fight, and now we mustn't whip the man just because he whipped Johnnie."

"Yes, that's true enough," said the cowboy; "but—he better not get fresh with me, because I couldn't stand no more of it."

"You'll not say a word to him," commanded Scully, and even then they heard the tread of the Swede on the stairs. His entrance was made theatric. He swept the door back with a bang and swaggered to the middle of the room. No one looked at him. "Well," he cried, insolently, at Scully. "I s'pose you'll tell me now how much I owe you?"

The old man remained stolid. "You don't owe me nothin'."

"Huh!" cried the Swede, "huh! Don't owe 'im nothin'."

The cowboy addressed the Swede. "Stranger, I don't see how you come to be so gay around here."

Old Scully was instantly alert. "Stop!" he shouted, holding his hand forth, fingers upward. "Bill, you shut up!"

The cowboy spat carelessly into the sawdust box. "I didn't say a word, did I?" he asked.

"Mr. Scully," called the Swede, "how much do I owe you?" It was seen that he was attired for departure, and that he had his valise in his hand.

"You don't owe me nothin'," repeated Scully in his same imperturbable way.

"Huh!" said the Swede. "I guess you're right. I guess if it was any way at all, you'd owe me somethin'. That's what I guess." He turned to the cowboy. "'Kill him! Kill him! Kill him!'" he mimicked, and then guffawed victoriously. "'Kill him!'" He was convulsed with ironical humor.

But he might have been jeering the dead. The three men were immovable and silent, staring with glassy eyes at the stove.

The Swede opened the door and passed into the storm, giving one derisive glance backward at the still group.

As soon as the door was closed, Scully and the cowboy leaped to their feet and began to curse. They trampled to and fro, waving their arms and smashing into the air with their fists. "Oh, but that was a hard minute!" wailed Scully. "That was a hard minute! Him there leerin' and scoffin'! One bang at his nose was worth forty dollars to me that minute! How did you stand it, Bill?"

"How did I stand it?" cried the cowboy in a quivering voice. "How did I stand it? Oh!"

The old man burst into sudden brogue. "I'd loike to take that Swade," he wailed, "and hould 'im down on a shtone flure and bate 'im to a jelly wid a shtick!"

The cowboy groaned in sympathy. "I'd like to git him by the neck and ha-ammer him"—he brought his hand down on a chair with a noise like a pistol-shot—"hammer that there Dutchman until he couldn't tell himself from a dead coyote!"

"I'd bate 'im until he——"

"I'd show *him* some things——"

And then together they raised a yearning fanatic cry. "Oh-o-oh! if we only could——"

"Yes!"

"Yes!"

"And then I'd——"

"O-o-oh!"

VIII

The Swede, tightly gripping his valise, tacked across the face of the storm as if he carried sails. He was following a line of little naked gasping trees, which he knew must mark the way of the road. His face, fresh from the pounding of Johnnie's fists, felt more pleasure than pain in the wind and the driving snow. A number of square shapes loomed upon him finally, and he knew them as the houses of the main body of the town. He found a street and made travel along it, leaning heavily upon the wind whenever, at a corner, a terrific blast caught him.

He might have been in a deserted village. We picture the world as thick with conquering and elate humanity, but here, with the bugles of the tempest pealing, it was hard to imagine a peopled earth. One viewed the existence of man then as a marvel, and conceded a glamour of wonder to these lice which were caused to cling to a whirling, fire-smote, ice-locked, disease-stricken, space-lost bulb. The conceit of man was explained by this storm to be the very engine of life. One was a coxcomb not to die in it. However, the Swede found a saloon.

In front of it an indomitable red light was burning, and the snow-flakes were made blood-color as they flew through the circumscribed territory of the lamp's shining. The Swede pushed open the door of the saloon and entered. A sanded expanse was before him, and at the end of it four men sat about a table drinking. Down one side of the room extended a radiant bar, and its guardian was leaning upon his elbows listening to the talk of the men at the table. The Swede dropped his valise upon the floor, and, smiling fraternally upon the barkeeper, said: "Gimme some whisky, will you?" The man placed a bottle, a whisky-glass, and a glass of ice-thick water upon the bar. The Swede poured himself an abnormal portion of whisky and drank it in three gulps. "Pretty bad night," remarked the bartender indifferently. He was making the pretension of blindness, which is usually a distinction of his class; but it could have seen that he was furtively studying the half-erased blood-stains on the face of the Swede. "Bad night," he said again.

"Oh, it's good enough for me," replied the Swede, hardily, as he poured himself more whisky. The barkeeper took his coin and maneuvered it through its reception by the highly-nickeled cash-machine. A bell rang; a card labeled "20 cts." had appeared.

"No," continued the Swede, "this isn't too bad weather. It's good enough for me."

"So?" murmured the barkeeper languidly.

The copious drams made the Swede's eyes swim, and he breathed a trifle heavier. "Yes, I like this weather. I like it. It suits me." It was apparently his design to impart a deep significance to these words.

"So?" murmured the bartender again. He turned to gaze dreamily at the scroll-like birds and bird-like scrolls which had been drawn with soap upon the mirrors back of the bar.

"Well, I guess I'll take another drink," said the Swede presently. "Have something?"

"No, thanks; I'm not drinkin'," answered the bartender. Afterward he asked: "How did you hurt your face?"

The Swede immediately began to boast loudly. "Why, in a fight. I thumped the soul out of a man down here at Scully's hotel."

The interest of the four men at the table was at last aroused.

"Who was it?" said one.

"Johnnie Scully," blustered the Swede. "Son of the man what runs it. He will be pretty near dead for some weeks, I can tell you. I made a nice thing of him, I did. He couldn't get up. They carried him in the house. Have a drink?"

Instantly the men in some subtle way incased themselves in reserve. "No, thanks," said one. The group was of curious formation. Two were prominent local business men; one was the district-attorney; and one was a professional gambler of the kind known as "square." But a scrutiny of the group would not have enabled an observer to pick the gambler from the men of more reputable pursuits. He was, in fact, a man so delicate in manner, when among people of fair class, and so judicious in his choice of victims, that in the strictly masculine part of the town's life he had come to be explicitly trusted and admired. People called him a thoroughbred. The fear and contempt with which his craft was regarded was undoubtedly the reason that his quiet dignity shone conspicuous above the quiet dignity of men who might be merely hatters, billiard-markers[5] or grocery clerks. Beyond an

5. Scorekeepers at billiards matches.

occasional unwary traveler, who came by rail, this gambler was supposed to prey solely upon reckless and senile farmers, who, when flush with good crops, drove into town in all the pride and confidence of an absolutely invulnerable stupidity. Hearing at times in circuitous fashion of the despoilment of such a farmer, the important men of Romper invariably laughed in contempt of the victim, and if they thought of the wolf at all, it was a kind of pride at the knowledge that he would never dare think of attacking their wisdom and courage. Besides, it was popular that this gambler had a real wife and two real children in a neat cottage in a suburb, where he led an exemplary home life, and when any one even suggested a discrepancy in his character, the crowd immediately vociferated descriptions of this virtuous family circle. Then men who led exemplary home lives, and men who did not lead exemplary home lives, all subsided in a bunch, remarking that there was nothing more to be said.

However, when a restriction was placed upon him—as, for instance, when a strong clique of members of the new Pollywog Club refused to permit him, even as a spectator, to appear in the rooms of the organization—the candor and gentleness with which he accepted the judgment disarmed many of his foes and made his friends more desperately partisan. He invariably distinguished between himself and a respectable Romper man so quickly and frankly that his manner actually appeared to be a continual broadcast compliment.

And one must not forget to declare the fundamental fact of his entire position in Romper. It is irrefutable that in all affairs outside of his business, in all matters that occur eternally and commonly between man and man, this thieving card-player was so generous, so just, so moral, that, in a contest, he could have put to flight the consciences of nine-tenths of the citizens of Romper.

And so it happened that he was seated in this saloon with the two prominent local merchants and the district-attorney.

The Swede continued to drink raw whisky, meanwhile babbling at the barkeeper and trying to induce him to indulge in potations. "Come on. Have a drink. Come on. What—no? Well, have a little one then. By gawd, I've whipped a man to-night, and I want to celebrate. I whipped him good, too. Gentlemen," the Swede cried to the men at the table, "have a drink?"

"Ssh!" said the barkeeper.

The group at the table, although furtively attentive, had been pretending to be deep in talk, but now a man lifted his eyes toward the Swede and said shortly: "Thanks. We don't want any more."

At this reply the Swede ruffled out his chest like a rooster. "Well," he exploded, "it seems I can't get anybody to drink with me in this town. Seems so, don't it? Well!"

"Ssh!" said the barkeeper.

"Say," snarled the Swede, "don't you try to shut me up. I won't have it. I'm a gentleman, and I want people to drink with me. And I want 'em to drink with me now. *Now*—do you understand?" He rapped the bar with his knuckles.

Years of experience had calloused the bartender. He merely grew sulky. "I hear you," he answered.

"Well," cried the Swede, "listen hard then. See those men over there? Well, they're going to drink with me, and don't you forget it. Now you watch."

"Hi!" yelled the barkeeper, "this won't do!"

"Why won't it?" demanded the Swede. He stalked over to the table, and by chance laid his hand upon the shoulder of the gambler. "How about this?" he asked, wrathfully. "I asked you to drink with me."

The gambler simply twisted his head and spoke over his shoulder. "My friend, I don't know you."

"Oh, hell!" answered the Swede, "come and have a drink."

"Now, my boy," advised the gambler kindly, "take your hand off my shoulder and go 'way and mind your own business." He was a little slim man, and it seemed strange to hear him use this tone of heroic patronage to the burly Swede. The other men at the table said nothing.

"What? You won't drink with me, you little dude! I'll make you then! I'll make you!" The Swede had grasped the gambler frenziedly at the throat, and was dragging him from his chair. The other men sprang up. The barkeeper dashed around the corner of his bar. There was a great tumult, and then was seen a long blade in the hand of the gambler. It shot forward, and a human body, this citadel of virtue, wisdom, power, was pierced as easily as if it had been a melon. The Swede fell with a cry of supreme astonishment.

The prominent merchants and the district-attorney must have at once tumbled out of the place backward. The bartender found himself hanging limply to the arm of a chair and gazing into the eyes of a murderer.

"Henry," said the latter, as he wiped his knife on one of the towels that hung beneath the bar-rail, "you tell 'em where to find me. I'll be home, waiting for 'em." Then he vanished. A moment afterward the barkeeper was in the street dinning through the storm for help, and, moreover, companionship.

The corpse of the Swede, alone in the saloon, had its eyes fixed upon a dreadful legend that dwelt a-top of the cash-machine. "This registers the amount of your purchase."

IX

Months later, the cowboy was frying pork over the stove of a little ranch near the Dakota line, when there was a quick thud of hoofs outside, and, presently, the Easterner entered with the letters and the papers.

"Well," said the Easterner at once, "the chap that killed the Swede has got three years. Wasn't much, was it?"

"He has? Three years?" The cowboy poised his pan of pork, while he ruminated upon the news. "Three years. That ain't much."

"No. It was a light sentence," replied the Easterner as he unbuckled his spurs. "Seems there was a good deal of sympathy for him in Romper."

"If the bartender had been any good," observed the cowboy thoughtfully, "he would have gone in and cracked that there Dutchman on the head with a bottle in the beginnin' of it and stopped all this here murderin'."

"Yes, a thousand things might have happened," said the Easterner tartly.

The cowboy returned his pan of pork to the fire, but his philosophy continued. "It's funny, ain't it? If he hadn't said Johnnie was cheatin' he'd be alive this minute. He was an awful fool. Game played for fun, too. Not for money. I believe he was crazy."

"I feel sorry for that gambler," said the Easterner.

"Oh, so do I," said the cowboy. "He don't deserve none of it for killin' who he did."

"The Swede might not have been killed if everything had been square."

"Might not have been killed?" exclaimed the cowboy. "Everythin' square? Why, when he said that Johnnie was cheatin' and acted like such a jackass? And then in the saloon he fairly walked up to git hurt?" With these arguments the cowboy browbeat the Easterner and reduced him to rage.

"You're a fool!" cried the Easterner viciously. "You're a bigger jackass than the Swede by a million majority. Now let me tell you one thing. Let me tell you something. Listen! Johnnie *was* cheating!"

"Johnnie,'" said the cowboy blankly. There was a minute of silence, and then he said robustly: "Why, no. The game was only for fun."

"Fun or not," said the Easterner, "Johnnie was cheating. I saw him. I know it. I saw him. And I refused to stand up and be a man. I let the Swede fight it out alone. And you—you were simply puffing around the place and wanting to fight. And then old Scully himself! We are all in it! This poor gambler isn't even a noun. He is kind of an adverb. Every sin is the result of a collaboration. We, five of us, have collaborated in the murder of this Swede. Usually there are from a dozen to forty women really involved in every murder, but in this case it seems to be only five men—you, I, Johnnie, old Scully, and that fool of an unfortunate gambler came merely as a culmination, the apex of a human movement, and gets all the punishment."

The cowboy, injured and rebellious, cried out blindly into this fog of mysterious theory. "Well, I didn't do anythin', did I?"

1898, 1902

From War Is Kind[1]

I

Do not weep, maiden, for war is kind.
Because your lover threw wild hands toward the sky
And the affrighted steed ran on alone,
Do not weep.
War is kind.   5

    Hoarse, booming drums of the regiment
    Little souls who thirst for fight,
    These men were born to drill and die
    The unexplained glory flies above them
    Great is the battle-god, great, and his kingdom——   10
    A field where a thousand corpses lie.

Do not weep, babe, for war is kind.
Because your father tumbled in the yellow trenches,
Raged at his breast, gulped and died,
Do not weep.   15
War is kind.

    Swift, blazing flag of the regiment
    Eagle with crest of red and gold,

---

1. First published in *"War Is Kind" and Other Lines* (1899); rpt. in *Stephen Crane: Prose and Poetry* (1984), from which this text is taken.

These men were born to drill and die
Point for them the virtue of slaughter   20
Make plain to them the excellence of killing
And a field where a thousand corpses lie.

Mother whose heart hung humble as a button
On the bright splendid shroud of your son,
Do not weep.   25
War is kind.

*   *   *

XIX

The chatter of a death-demon from a tree-top.

Blood—blood and torn grass—
Had marked the rise of his agony——
This lone hunter.
The grey-green woods impassive   5
Had watched the threshing of his limbs.

A canoe with flashing paddle
A girl with soft searching eyes,
A call: "John!"

Come, arise, hunter!   10
Can you not hear?

The chatter of a death-demon from a tree-top.

XX

The impact of a dollar upon the heart
Smiles warm red light
Sweeping from the hearth rosily upon the white table,
With the hanging cool velvet shadows
Moving softly upon the door.   5

The impact of a million dollars
Is a crash of flunkeys
And yawning emblems of Persia
Cheeked against oak, France and a sabre,
The outcry of old Beauty   10
Whored by pimping merchants
To submission before wine and chatter.
Silly rich peasants stamp the carpets of men,
Dead men who dreamed fragrance and light
Into their woof, their lives;   15
The rug of an honest bear
Under the feet of a cryptic slave
Who speaks always of baubles
Forgetting place, multitude, work and state,

Champing and mouthing of hats   20
Making ratful squeak of hats,
Hats.

XXI

A man said to the universe:
"Sir, I exist!"
"However," replied the universe,
"The fact has not created in me
"A sense of obligation."   5

XXII

When the prophet, a complacent fat man,
Arrived at the mountain-top
He cried: "Woe to my knowledge!
I intended to see good white lands
And bad black lands,   5
But the scene is grey."

1899

PAUL LAURENCE DUNBAR
1872–1906

Paul Laurence Dunbar was one of the first professional African American literary figures, publishing six volumes of poetry, beginning with *Oak and Ivy* in 1893, as well as novels, librettos, songs, and essays. Dunbar's father, Joshua, who had escaped slavery in Kentucky and moved to Ohio via the Underground Railroad, served in the 55th Massachusetts Regiment of the Union Army during the Civil War. His mother, Matilda Murphy, also a former slave, separated from Joshua when Dunbar was two years old. Throughout his childhood, Matilda encouraged Paul in his education, often doing without so that he could continue in school. Though Dunbar first wanted to be a lawyer, he chose instead "to be a worthy singer of the songs of God and nature." He wanted "to interpret my own people though song and story, and prove to the many that we are more human than African."

Dunbar early on developed an ear for language and a love of English Romantic poetry. Yet upon graduation from Central High School, in Dayton, Ohio, where he'd been student and class leader, he found only menial jobs open to him. In 1892 he was invited to read a poem at the Western Association of Writers, which was convening in Dayton. Inspired by this, he traveled in 1893 to the Columbian Exposition in Chicago, where he met Frederick Douglass and sold *Oak and Ivy*, the publication of which he subsidized, for a dollar per copy. Douglass—the former U.S. minister to Haiti and Commissioner of the Haitian Exhibition—hired him as a clerk.

In 1895 Dunbar published his best-known work, *Lyrics of the Lowly Life*, from which most of the selections here are drawn. Committed to rendering the authentic voice of the black speaker, and inspired by Shakespeare, Shelley, Keats, and Tennyson, Dunbar published in such popular venues as the *New York Times, Century, Lippincott's Monthly*, and the *Saturday Evening Post*, journals with almost exclusively white readerships. Though he was celebrated by black and white literary leaders, among them Douglass, Booker T. Washington, W. E. B. Du Bois, William Dean Howells, Eugene Field, and James Whitcomb Riley, he was criticized in the 1920s by Harlem Renaissance writers who saw him as catering to a white audience with stereotyped black folk elements and dialect. Despite this criticism, Dunbar's influence on subsequent African American writers such as Zora Neale Hurston is precisely that he presented traditional dialect, customs, and other cultural elements without apology.

Dunbar married the writer Alice Moore in 1898; they lived in the Le Droit Park section of Washington, D.C., an area that welcomed the new black middle class and where they enjoyed the company of black intellectuals, activists, and artists. During this time he began to emerge as a fiction writer, publishing four collections of short stories and four novels over the next six years. In the best of the novels, *The Sport of the Gods* (1903), Dunbar chronicles the unhappy circumstances of an African American family moving from the rural South to New York City. A year before the novel was published, Dunbar and his wife separated, in part due to his alcoholism, and Dunbar's poetry increasingly reflects a more somber mood. When he returned to Dayton to live with his mother, he believed that he had failed as a poet. Critical and popular attention to his work continued to grow throughout the twentieth century, however, and Dunbar is now recognized as a pioneer in creating a new black poetic diction.

An Ante-Bellum Sermon[1]

We is gathahed hyeah, my brothahs,
   In dis howlin' wildaness,
Fu' to speak some words of comfo't
   To each othah in distress.
An' we chooses fu' ouah subjic'   5
   Dis—we 'll 'splain it by an' by;
"An' de Lawd said, 'Moses, Moses,'
   An' de man said, 'Hyeah am I.'"

Now ole Pher'oh, down in Egypt,
   Was de wuss man evah bo'n,   10
An' he had de Hebrew chillun
   Down dah wukin' in his co'n;
'T well de Lawd got tiahed o' his foolin',
   An' sez he: "I'll let him know—
Look hyeah, Moses, go tell Pher'oh   15
   Fu' to let dem chillun go."

"An' ef he refuse to do it,
   I will make him rue de houah,
Fu' I 'll empty down on Egypt
   All de vials of my powah."   20
Yes, he did—an' Pher'oh's ahmy

---

1. First published in Dunbar's *Lyrics of the Lowly Life* (1897) and then in his *Complete Poems* (1903); rpt. in *The Complete Poems of Paul Laurence Dunbar* (1993), from which this text is taken.

Was n't wuth a ha'f a dime;
 Fu' de Lawd will he'p his chilun,
  You kin trust him evah time.

An' yo' enemies may 'sail you   25
 In de back an' in de front;
But de Lawd is all aroun' you,
 Fu' to ba' de battle's brunt.
Dey kin fo'ge yo' chains an' shackles
 F'om de mountains to de sea;   30
But de Lawd will sen' some Moses
 Fu' to set his chillun free.

An' de lan' shall hyeah his thundah,
 Lak a blas' f'om Gab'el's ho'n,
Fu' de Lawd of hosts is mighty   35
 When he girds his ahmor on.
But fu' feah some one mistakes me,
 I will pause right hyeah to say,
Dat I 'm still a-preachin' ancient,
 I ain't talkin' 'bout to-day.   40

But I tell you, fellah christuns,
 Things 'll happen mighty strange;
Now, de Lawd done dis fu' Isrul,
 An' his ways don't nevah change,
An' de love he showed to Isrul   45
 Was n't all on Isrul spent;
Now don't run an' tell yo' mastahs
 Dat I 's preachin' discontent.

'Cause I is n't; I 'se a-judgin'
 Bible people by deir ac's;   50
I 'se a-givin' you de Scriptuah,
 I 'se a-handin' you de fac's.
Cose ole Pher'oh b'lieved in slav'ry,
 But de Lawd he let him see,
Dat de people he put bref in,—   55
 Evah mothah's son was free.

An' dahs othahs thinks lak Pher'oh,
 But dey calls de Scriptuah liar,
Fu' de Bible says "a servant
 Is a-worthy of his hire."[2]   60
An' you cain't git roun' nor thoo dat,
 An' you cain't git ovah it,
Fu' whatevah place you git in,
 Dis hyeah Bible too 'll fit.

2. Biblical mandate against the unethical practice of masters withholding wages from their servants, here used to indict slavery (Leviticus 19.13, Deuteronomy 24.15 and 25).

So you see de Lawd's intention,
    Evah sence de worl' began,
Was dat His almighty freedom
    Should belong to evah man,
But I think it would be bettah,   70
    Ef I 'd pause agin to say,
Dat I 'm talkin' 'bout ouah freedom
    In a Bibleistic way.

But de Moses is a-comin',
    An' he 's comin', suah and fas'
We kin hyeah his feet a-trompin',   75
    We kin hyeah his trumpit blas'.
But I want to wa'n you people,
    Don't you git too brigity;[3]
An' don't you git to braggin'
    'Bout dese things, you wait an' see.   80

But when Moses wif his powah
    Comes an' sets us chillun free,
We will praise de gracious Mastah
    Dat has gin us liberty;
An' we 'll shout ouah halleluyahs,   85
    On dat mighty reck'nin' day,
When we 'se reco'nised ez citiz'—
    Huh uh! Chillun, let us pray!

1897

We Wear the Mask[1]

We wear the mask that grins and lies,
It hides our cheeks and shades our eyes,—
This debt we pay to human guile;
With torn and bleeding hearts we smile,
And mouth with myriad subtleties.   5

Why should the world be overwise,
In counting all our tears and sighs?
Nay, let them only see us, while
    We wear the mask.

We smile, but, O great Christ, our cries   10
To thee from tortured souls arise.
We sing, but oh the clay is vile
Beneath our feet, and long the mile;
But let the world dream otherwise,
    We wear the mask!   15

1897

---

3. Brazen, presumptuous, or insolent.
1. First published in Dunbar's *Lyrics of the Lowly Life* (1897) and then in his *Complete Poems* (1903); rpt. in *The Complete Poems of Paul Laurence Dunbar* (1993), from which this text is taken.

Sympathy[1]

I know what the caged bird feels, alas!
  When the sun is bright on the upland slopes;
When the wind stirs soft through the springing grass,
And the river flows like a stream of glass;
  When the first bird sings and the first bud opes,   5
And the faint perfume from its chalice steals—
I know what the caged bird feels!

I know why the caged bird beats his wing
  Till its blood is red on the cruel bars;
For he must fly back to his perch and cling   10
When he fain would be on the bough a-swing;
  And a pain still throbs in the old, old scars
And they pulse again with a keener sting—
I know why he beats his wing!

I know why the caged bird sings, ah me,   15
  When his wing is bruised and his bosom sore,—
When he beats his bars and he would be free;
It is not a carol of joy or glee,
  But a prayer that he sends from his heart's deep core,
But a plea, that upward to Heaven he flings—   20
I know why the caged bird sings!

1899

Harriet Beecher Stowe[1]

She told the story, and the whole world wept
  At wrongs and cruelties it had not known
  But for this fearless woman's voice alone.
  She spoke to consciences that long had slept:
Her message, Freedom's clear reveille, swept   5
  From heedless hovel to complacent throne.
  Command and prophecy were in the tone
  And from its sheath the sword of justice leapt.
Around two peoples swelled a fiery wave,
  But both came forth transfigured from the flame.   10
Blest be the hand that dared be strong to save,
  And blest be she who in our weakness came—
Prophet and priestess! At one stroke she gave
A race to freedom and herself to fame.

1899

---

1. First published in Dunbar's *Lyrics of the Hearthside* (1899) and then in his *Complete Poems* (1903); rpt. in *The Complete Poems of Paul Laurence Dunbar* (1993), from which this text is taken.
1. First published in Dunbar's *Lyrics of the Hearthside* (1899) and then in his *Complete Poems* (1903); rpt. in *The Complete Poems of Paul Laurence Dunbar* (1993), from which this text is taken. Harriet Beecher Stowe (1811–1896), abolitionist and author of many books, the most famous being *Uncle Tom's Cabin* (1852).

Frederick Douglass[1]

A hush is over all the teeming lists,
    And there is pause, a breath-space in the strife;
A spirit brave has passed beyond the mists
    And vapors that obscure the sun of life.
And Ethiopia, with bosom torn,   5
Laments the passing of her noblest born.

She weeps for him a mother's burning tears—
    She loved him with a mother's deepest love.
He was her champion thro' direful years,
    And held her weal all other ends above.   10
When Bondage held her bleeding in the dust,
He raised her up and whispered, "Hope and Trust."

For her his voice, a fearless clarion, rung
    That broke in warning on the ears of men;
For her the strong bow of his power he strung,   15
    And sent his arrows to the very den
Where grim Oppression held his bloody place
And gloated o'er the mis'ries of a race.

And he was no soft-tongued apologist;
    He spoke straightforward, fearlessly uncowed;   20
The sunlight of his truth dispelled the mist,
    And set in bold relief each dark hued cloud;
To sin and crime he gave their proper hue,
And hurled at evil what was evil's due.

Through good and ill report he cleaved his way   25
    Right onward, with his face set toward the heights,
Nor feared to face the foeman's dread array,—
    The lash of scorn, the sting of petty spites.
He dared the lightning in the lightning's track,
And answered thunder with his thunder back.   30

When men maligned him, and their torrent wrath
    In furious imprecations o'er him broke,
He kept his counsel as he kept his path;
    'T was for his race, not for himself he spoke.
He knew the import of his Master's call,   35
And felt himself too mighty to be small.

No miser in the good he held was he,—
    His kindness followed his horizon's rim.

---

1. First published in Dunbar's *Lyrics of Love and Laughter* (1903), then in *The Complete Poems* (1903); rpt. in *The Complete Poems of Paul Laurence Dunbar* (1993), from which this text is taken. Frederick Douglass (1818–1895) was the author of *Narrative of the Life of Frederick Douglass* (1845), in which he recounts his birth into slavery, escape into freedom, and eventual involvement with the abolitionist movement.

His heart, his talents, and his hands were free
    To all who truly needed aught of him. 40
Where poverty and ignorance were rife,
He gave his bounty as he gave his life.

The place and cause that first aroused his might
    Still proved its power until his latest day.
In Freedom's lists and for the aid of Right 45
    Still in the foremost rank he waged the fray;
Wrong lived; his occupation was not gone.
He died in action with his armor on!

We weep for him, but we have touched his hand,
    And felt the magic of his presence nigh, 50
The current that he sent throughout the land,
    The kindling spirit of his battlecry.
O'er all that holds us we shall triumph yet,
And place our banner where his hopes were set!

Oh, Douglass, thou hast passed beyond the shore, 55
    But still thy voice is ringing o'er the gale!
Thou 'st taught thy race how high her hopes may soar,
    And bade her seek the heights, nor faint, nor fail.
She will not fail, she heeds thy stirring cry,
She knows thy guardian spirit will be nigh, 60
And, rising from beneath the chast'ning rod,
She stretches out her bleeding hands to God!

1903

JACK LONDON
1876–1916

John Griffith Chaney was born in San Francisco, California, on January 12, 1876, the son of Flora Wellman Chaney, spiritualist and common-law wife of William H. Chaney, an itinerant astrologer who abandoned Flora on learning of her pregnancy. Nine months after the child's birth, Flora married John London, a Civil War veteran and construction worker who adopted "Johnny." As a child, London escaped some of the unhappiness at home by living on and off with the Prentisses, African American neighbors who called him "Jack" and who served as surrogate parents until, at the age of fifteen, he sailed San Francisco Bay as an oyster pirate, going on to become a member of the California Fish Patrol. Drinking with the oyster pirates and the Fish Patrol, London developed what would later become full-blown alcoholism. Entranced by the sea and its possibilities, he sailed aboard the sealing ship the *Sophia Sutherland*, returning home in 1893 to publish his first, prize-winning, story, "Typhoon Off the Coast of Japan," in the San Francisco *Morning Call*.

In 1894, following the Panic of 1893, London marched east with a contingent of Coxey's Army, an organized group of the unemployed planning to agitate for jobs in Washington, D.C. He was arrested as a vagrant at Niagara Falls and did thirty days of hard time in the Erie County Penitentiary in Buffalo, New York. Returning home, he vowed to educate himself, and he also turned to socialism, running for mayor of Oakland twice on the socialist ticket. At the age of twenty he was accepted to the University of California, but, lacking money, he attended for only one semester. The most important event of London's early life occurred in 1897, when, at age twenty-one, he headed to Alaska to take part in the Klondike Gold Rush. In 1900, the prestigious *Atlantic Monthly* featured his story "An Odyssey of the North" in its January issue; Houghton Mifflin published his first book, *The Son of the Wolf*; and he married Bessie Mae Maddern, with whom he went on to have two daughters before their divorce in 1905 and his marriage to Charmian Kittredge. In these years he also traveled to London, England, to write the sociological exposé *The People of the Abyss* (1903) and to Korea to cover the Russo-Japanese War of 1904, and he bought land in Sonoma County, experimenting with terracing and organic farming. He wrote one thousand words per day and won international acclaim with *The Call of the Wild* (1903) and *The Sea-Wolf* (1904). Later, after his extensive South Seas travels and residence in Hawaii, he became modern America's first Pacific Rim writer.

London, though he said he wrote only for money, was a disciplined and careful craftsman, drawing from many literary, philosophical, scientific, and other sources, and writing on many subjects. His writings reflect the social and intellectual turbulence of the turn of the twentieth century, including his competing sympathies for socialism, Social Darwinism, and Nietzschean individualism; his combination of urban settings and characters with the pastoral and exotic; his conflicted ideas about race; his dual identity as a literary writer of the emerging naturalist school and a mass-market phenomenon. London was an important influence on later writers such as Ernest Hemingway and Richard Wright, for both his adventure writing and his socialist works, such as "The Mexican," "South of the Slot," and his many socialist essays.

Long snubbed by the critical establishment as too popular and too politically unorthodox, London's writings have attracted new interest for their literary artistry and for what they show about the cultural and historical issues of his era, especially race and class. By the time he died in 1916, London was the best-selling author in America and was on his way to becoming the most popular American writer in the world. In a writing career of only twenty years, London published 18 novels, 198 short stories, three plays, and hundreds of nonfiction books and articles. His ranch is now the Jack London State Historic Park in Glen Ellen, California.

To Build a Fire[1]

Day had broken cold and gray, exceedingly cold and gray, when the man turned aside from the main Yukon trail and climbed the high earth-bank, where a dim and little-travelled trail led eastward through the fat spruce timberland. It was a steep bank, and he paused for breath at the top, excusing the act to himself by looking at his watch. It was nine o'clock. There was no sun nor hint of sun, though there was not a cloud in the sky. It was a clear day, and yet there seemed an intangible pall over the face of things,

---

1. First published in the *Youth's Companion* for May 29, 1902, in a version of 2,700 words—"for boys only," according to London. The later, widely anthologized version of 7,235 words, written while London was struggling to survive his South Seas voyage aboard his sailboat the *Snark*, was first published in the *Century Magazine* 76 (August 1908). The text here is that of the 1910 collection *Lost Face*.

a subtle gloom that made the day dark, and that was due to the absence of sun. This fact did not worry the man. He was used to the lack of sun. It had been days since he had seen the sun, and he knew that a few more days must pass before that cheerful orb, due south, would just peep above the sky-line and dip immediately from view.

The man flung a look back along the way he had come. The Yukon lay a mile wide and hidden under three feet of ice. On top of this ice were as many feet of snow. It was all pure white, rolling in gentle undulations where the ice-jams of the freeze-up had formed. North and south, as far as his eye could see, it was unbroken white, save for a dark hair-line that curved and twisted from around the spruce-covered island to the south, and that curved and twisted away into the north, where it disappeared behind another spruce-covered island. This dark hair-line was the trail—the main trail— that led south five hundred miles to the Chilcoot Pass, Dyea, and salt water; and that led north seventy miles to Dawson, and still on to the north a thousand miles to Nulato, and finally to St. Michael on Bering Sea, a thousand miles and half a thousand more.[2]

But all this—the mysterious, far-reaching hair-line trail, the absence of sun from the sky, the tremendous cold, and the strangeness and weirdness of it all—made no impression on the man. It was not because he was long used to it. He was a newcomer in the land, a *chechaquo,* and this was his first winter. The trouble with him was that he was without imagination. He was quick and alert in the things of life, but only in the things, and not in the significances. Fifty degrees below zero meant eighty-odd degrees of frost. Such fact impressed him as being cold and uncomfortable, and that was all. It did not lead him to meditate upon his frailty as a creature of temperature, and upon man's frailty in general, able only to live within certain narrow limits of heat and cold; and from there on it did not lead him to the conjectural field of immortality and man's place in the universe. Fifty degrees below zero stood for a bite of frost that hurt and that must be guarded against by the use of mittens, ear-flaps, warm moccasins, and thick socks. Fifty degrees below zero was to him just precisely fifty degrees below zero. That there should be anything more to it than that was a thought that never entered his head.

As he turned to go on, he spat speculatively. There was a sharp, explosive crackle that startled him. He spat again. And again, in the air, before it could fall to the snow, the spittle crackled. He knew that at fifty below spittle crackled on the snow, but this spittle had crackled in the air. Undoubtedly it was colder than fifty below—how much colder he did not know. But the temperature did not matter. He was bound for the old claim on the left fork of Henderson Creek, where the boys were already. They had come over across the divide from the Indian Creek country, while he had come the roundabout way to take a look at the possibilities of getting out logs in the spring from the islands in the Yukon. He would be in to camp by six o'clock; a bit after dark, it was true, but the boys would be there, a fire would be going, and a hot supper would be ready. As for lunch, he pressed his hand

2. The narrator surveys the entire length of Alaska and the Canadian Yukon, from the steep Chilcoot Pass near Skagway, which prospective miners first scaled in the winter of 1897–98 to enter the Yukon; to Dyea, a shabby settlement where they disembarked onto a swampy beach; to Dawson, the hub of the Klondike gold rush; and finally to Nulato and St. Michael, sparse settle- ments on the way to the mouth of the Yukon River, from which miners would sail for home. The Yukon is one of the few rivers that flows north. London floated "up" the Yukon from Dawson to St. Michael in the spring of 1898 to return home after unsuccessfully prospecting for gold. This journey was the subject of his first Klondike writings.

against the protruding bundle under his jacket. It was also under his shirt, wrapped up in a handkerchief and lying against the naked skin. It was the only way to keep the biscuits from freezing. He smiled agreeably to himself as he thought of those biscuits, each cut open and sopped in bacon grease, and each enclosing a generous slice of fried bacon.

He plunged in among the big spruce trees. The trail was faint. A foot of snow had fallen since the last sled had passed over, and he was glad he was without a sled, travelling light. In fact, he carried nothing but the lunch wrapped in the handkerchief. He was surprised, however, at the cold. It certainly was cold, he concluded, as he rubbed his numb nose and cheek-bones with his mittened hand. He was a warm-whiskered man, but the hair on his face did not protect the high cheek-bones and the eager nose that thrust itself aggressively into the frosty air.

At the man's heels trotted a dog, a big native husky, the proper wolf-dog, gray-coated and without any visible or temperamental difference from its brother, the wild wolf. The animal was depressed by the tremendous cold. It knew that it was no time for travelling. Its instinct told it a truer tale than was told to the man by the man's judgment. In reality, it was not merely colder than fifty below zero; it was colder than sixty below, than seventy below. It was seventy-five below zero. Since the freezing-point is thirty-two above zero, it meant that one hundred and seven degrees of frost obtained. The dog did not know anything about thermometers. Possibly in its brain there was no sharp consciousness of a condition of very cold such as was in the man's brain. But the brute had its instinct. It experienced a vague but menacing apprehension that subdued it and made it slink along at the man's heels, and that made it question eagerly every unwonted movement of the man as if expecting him to go into camp or to seek shelter somewhere and build a fire. The dog had learned fire, and it wanted fire, or else to burrow under the snow and cuddle its warmth away from the air.

The frozen moisture of its breathing had settled on its fur in a fine powder of frost, and especially were its jowls, muzzle, and eyelashes whitened by its crystalled breath. The man's red beard and mustache were likewise frosted, but more solidly, the deposit taking the form of ice and increasing with every warm, moist breath he exhaled. Also, the man was chewing tobacco, and the muzzle of ice held his lips so rigidly that he was unable to clear his chin when he expelled the juice. The result was that a crystal beard of the color and solidity of amber was increasing its length on his chin. If he fell down it would shatter itself, like glass, into brittle fragments. But he did not mind the appendage. It was the penalty all tobacco-chewers paid in that country, and he had been out before in two cold snaps. They had not been so cold as this, he knew, but by the spirit thermometer at Sixty Mile he knew they had been registered at fifty below and at fifty-five.

He held on through the level stretch of woods for several miles, crossed a wide flat of niggerheads,[3] and dropped down a bank to the frozen bed of a small stream. This was Henderson Creek, and he knew he was ten miles from the forks. He looked at his watch. It was ten o'clock. He was making four miles an hour, and he calculated that he would arrive at the forks at half-past twelve. He decided to celebrate that event by eating his lunch there.

3. Racially charged name of a strong dark chewing tobacco of the period, applied here to large hummocks of earth under the snow that are created by centuries of alternate freezing and thawing.

The dog dropped in again at his heels, with a tail drooping discouragement, as the man swung along the creek-bed. The furrow of the old sled-trail was plainly visible, but a dozen inches of snow covered the marks of the last runners. In a month no man had come up or down that silent creek. The man held steadily on. He was not much given to thinking, and just then particularly he had nothing to think about save that he would eat lunch at the forks and that at six o'clock he would be in camp with the boys. There was nobody to talk to; and, had there been, speech would have been impossible because of the ice-muzzle on his mouth. So he continued monotonously to chew tobacco and to increase the length of his amber beard.

Once in a while the thought reiterated itself that it was very cold and that he had never experienced such cold. As he walked along he rubbed his cheek-bones and nose with the back of his mittened hand. He did this automatically, now and again changing hands. But rub as he would, the instant he stopped his cheek-bones went numb, and the following instant the end of his nose went numb. He was sure to frost his cheeks; he knew that, and experienced a pang of regret that he had not devised a nose-strap of the sort Bud wore in cold snaps. Such a strap passed across the cheeks, as well, and saved them. But it didn't matter much, after all. What were frosted cheeks? A bit painful, that was all; they were never serious.

Empty as the man's mind was of thoughts, he was keenly observant, and he noticed the changes in the creek, the curves and bends and timber-jams, and always he sharply noted where he placed his feet. Once, coming around a bend, he shied abruptly, like a startled horse, curved away from the place where he had been walking, and retreated several paces back along the trail. The creek he knew was frozen clear to the bottom,—no creek could contain water in that arctic winter,—but he knew also that there were springs that bubbled out from the hillsides and ran along under the snow and on top the ice of the creek. He knew that the coldest snaps never froze these springs, and he knew likewise their danger. They were traps. They hid pools of water under the snow that might be three inches deep, or three feet. Sometimes a skin of ice half an inch thick covered them, and in turn was covered by the snow. Sometimes there were alternate layers of water and ice-skin, so that when one broke through he kept on breaking through for a while, sometimes wetting himself to the waist.

That was why he had shied in such panic. He had felt the give under his feet and heard the crackle of snow-hidden ice-skin. And to get his feet wet in such a temperature meant trouble and danger. At the very least it meant delay, for he would be forced to stop and build a fire, and under its protection to bare his feet while he dried his socks and moccasins. He stood and studied the creek-bed and its banks, and decided that the flow of water came from the right. He reflected awhile, rubbing his nose and cheeks, then skirted to the left, stepping gingerly and testing the footing for each step. Once clear of the danger, he took a fresh chew of tobacco and swung along at his four-mile gait.

In the course of the next two hours he came upon several similar traps. Usually the snow above the hidden pools had a sunken, candied appearance that advertised the danger. Once again, however, he had a close call; and once, suspecting danger, he compelled the dog to go on in front. The dog did not want to go. It hung back until the man shoved it forward, and then it went quickly across the white, unbroken surface. Suddenly it broke through, floundered to one side, and got away to firmer footing. It had wet its forefeet and legs, and almost immediately the water that clung to it turned to ice. It made quick efforts to lick the ice off its legs, then dropped down in the snow and began to bite out the ice that had formed between the toes. This was a matter of instinct. To permit the ice to remain would mean sore feet. It did not know this. It merely obeyed the mysterious prompting that arose from the deep crypts of its being. But the man knew, having achieved a judgment on the subject, and he removed the mitten from his right hand and helped tear out the ice-particles. He did not expose his fingers more than a minute, and was astonished at the swift numbness that smote them. It certainly was cold. He pulled on the mitten hastily, and beat the hand savagely across his chest.

At twelve o'clock the day was at its brightest. Yet the sun was too far south on its winter journey to clear the horizon. The bulge of the earth intervened between it and Henderson Creek, where the man walked under a clear sky at noon and cast no shadow. At half-past twelve, to the minute, he arrived at the forks of the creek. He was pleased at the speed he had made. If he kept it up, he would certainly be with the boys by six. He unbuttoned his jacket and shirt and drew forth his lunch. The action consumed no more than a quarter of a minute, yet in that brief moment the numbness laid hold of the exposed fingers. He did not put the mitten on, but, instead, struck the fingers a dozen sharp smashes against his leg. Then he sat down on a snow-covered log to eat. The sting that followed upon the striking of his fingers against his leg ceased so quickly that he was startled. He had had no chance to take a bite of biscuit. He struck the fingers repeatedly and returned them to the mitten, baring the other hand for the purpose of eating. He tried to take a mouthful, but the ice-muzzle prevented. He had forgotten to build a fire and thaw out. He chuckled at his foolishness, and as he chuckled he noted the numbness creeping into the exposed fingers. Also, he noted that the stinging which had first come to his toes when he sat down was already passing away. He wondered whether the toes were warm or numb. He moved them inside the moccasins and decided that they were numb.

He pulled the mitten on hurriedly and stood up. He was a bit frightened. He stamped up and down until the stinging returned into the feet. It certainly was cold, was his thought. That man from Sulphur Creek[4] had spoken the truth when telling how cold it sometimes got in the country. And he had laughed at him at the time! That showed one must not be too sure of things. There was no mistake about it, it *was* cold. He strode up and down, stamping his feet and threshing his arms, until reassured by the returning warmth. Then he got out matches and proceeded to make a fire. From the under-growth, where high water of the previous spring had lodged a supply of seasoned twigs, he got his fire-wood. Working carefully from a small beginning, he soon had a roaring fire, over which he thawed the ice from his face and in the protection of which he ate his biscuits. For the moment the cold of space was outwitted. The dog took satisfaction in the fire, stretching out close enough for warmth and far enough away to escape being singed.

When the man had finished, he filled his pipe and took his comfortable time over a smoke. Then he pulled on his mittens, settled the ear-flaps of his cap firmly about his ears, and took the creek trail up the left fork. The dog was disappointed and yearned back toward the fire. This man did not know cold. Possibly all the generations of his ancestry had been ignorant of cold, of real cold, of cold one hundred and seven degrees below freezing-point. But the dog

---

4. Mining area between the towns of Dawson and Granville.

knew; all its ancestry knew, and it had inherited the knowledge. And it knew that it was not good to walk abroad in such fearful cold. It was the time to lie snug in a hole in the snow and wait for a curtain of cloud to be drawn across the face of outer space whence this cold came. On the other hand, there was no keen intimacy between the dog and the man. The one was the toil-slave of the other, and the only caresses it had ever received were the caresses of the whip-lash and of harsh and menacing throat-sounds that threatened the whip-lash. So the dog made no effort to communicate its apprehension to the man. It was not concerned in the welfare of the man; it was for its own sake that it yearned back toward the fire. But the man whistled, and spoke to it with the sound of whip-lashes, and the dog swung in at the man's heels and followed after.

The man took a chew of tobacco and proceeded to start a new amber beard. Also, his moist breath quickly powdered with white his mustache, eyebrows, and lashes. There did not seem to be so many springs on the left fork of the Henderson, and for half an hour the man saw no signs of any. And then it happened. At a place where there were no signs, where the soft, unbroken snow seemed to advertise solidity beneath, the man broke through. It was not deep. He wet himself halfway to the knees before he floundered out to the firm crust.

He was angry, and cursed his luck aloud. He had hoped to get into camp with the boys at six o'clock, and this would delay him an hour, for he would have to build a fire and dry out his foot-gear. This was imperative at that low temperature—he knew that much; and he turned aside to the bank, which he climbed. On top, tangled in the underbrush about the trunks of several small spruce trees, was a high-water deposit of dry fire-wood—sticks and twigs, principally, but also larger portions of seasoned branches and fine, dry, last-year's grasses. He threw down several large pieces on top of the snow. This served for a foundation and prevented the young flame from drowning itself in the snow it otherwise would melt. The flame he got by touching a match to a small shred of birch-bark that he took from his pocket. This burned even more readily than paper. Placing it on the foundation, he fed the young flame with wisps of dry grass and with the tiniest dry twigs.

He worked slowly and carefully, keenly aware of his danger. Gradually, as the flame grew stronger, he increased the size of the twigs with which he fed it. He squatted in the snow, pulling the twigs out from their entanglement in the brush and feeding directly to the flame. He knew there must be no failure. When it is seventy-five below zero, a man must not fail in his first attempt to build a fire—that is, if his feet are wet. If his feet are dry, and he fails, he can run along the trail for half a mile and restore his circulation. But the circulation of wet and freezing feet cannot be restored by running when it is seventy-five below. No matter how fast he runs, the wet feet will freeze the harder.

All this the man knew. The old-timer on Sulphur Creek had told him about it the previous fall, and now he was appreciating the advice. Already all sensation had gone out of his feet. To build the fire he had been forced to remove his mittens, and the fingers had quickly gone numb. His pace of four miles an hour had kept his heart pumping blood to the surface of his body and to all the extremities. But the instant he stopped, the action of the pump eased down. The cold of space smote the unprotected tip of the planet, and he, being on that unprotected tip, received the full force of the blow. The blood of his body recoiled before it. The blood was alive, like the dog, and like the dog it wanted to hide away and cover itself up from the fearful cold.

So long as he walked four miles an hour, he pumped that blood, willy-nilly, to the surface; but now it ebbed away and sank down into the recesses of his body. The extremities were the first to feel its absence. His wet feet froze the faster, and his exposed fingers numbed the faster, though they had not yet begun to freeze. Nose and cheeks were already freezing, while the skin of all his body chilled as it lost its blood.

But he was safe. Toes and nose and cheeks would be only touched by the frost, for the fire was beginning to burn with strength. He was feeding it with twigs the size of his finger. In another minute he would be able to feed it with branches the size of his wrist, and then he could remove his wet footgear, and, while it dried, he could keep his naked feet warm by the fire, rubbing them at first, of course, with snow. The fire was a success. He was safe. He remembered the advice of the old-timer on Sulphur Creek, and smiled. The old-timer had been very serious in laying down the law that no man must travel alone in the Klondike after fifty below. Well, here he was; he had had the accident; he was alone; and he had saved himself. Those old-timers were rather womanish, some of them, he thought. All a man had to do was to keep his head, and he was all right. Any man who was a man could travel alone. But it was surprising, the rapidity with which his cheeks and nose were freezing. And he had not thought his fingers could go lifeless in so short a time. Lifeless they were, for he could scarcely make them move together to grip a twig, and they seemed remote from his body and from him. When he touched a twig, he had to look and see whether or not he had hold of it. The wires were pretty well down between him and his finger-ends.

All of which counted for little. There was the fire, snapping and crackling and promising life with every dancing flame. He started to untie his moccasins. They were coated with ice; the thick German socks were like sheaths of iron halfway to the knees; and the moccasin strings were like rods of steel all twisted and knotted as by some conflagration. For a moment he tugged with his numb fingers, then, realizing the folly of it, he drew his sheath-knife.

But before he could cut the strings, it happened. It was his own fault or, rather, his mistake. He should not have built the fire under the spruce tree. He should have built it in the open. But it had been easier to pull the twigs from the brush and drop them directly on the fire. Now the tree under which he had done this carried a weight of snow on its boughs. No wind had blown for weeks, and each bough was fully freighted. Each time he had pulled a twig he had communicated a slight agitation to the tree—an imperceptible agitation, so far as he was concerned, but an agitation sufficient to bring about the disaster. High up in the tree one bough capsized its load of snow. This fell on the boughs beneath, capsizing them. This process continued, spreading out and involving the whole tree. It grew like an avalanche, and it descended without warning upon the man and the fire, and the fire was blotted out! Where it had burned was a mantle of fresh and disordered snow.

The man was shocked. It was as though he had just heard his own sentence of death. For a moment he sat and stared at the spot where the fire had been. Then he grew very calm. Perhaps the old-timer on Sulphur Creek was right. If he had only had a trail-mate he would have been in no danger now. The trail-mate could have built the fire. Well, it was up to him to build the fire over again, and this second time there must be no failure. Even if he succeeded, he would most likely lose some toes. His feet must be badly frozen by now, and there would be some time before the second fire was ready.

Such were his thoughts, but he did not sit and think them. He was busy all the time they were passing through his mind. He made a new foundation for a fire, this time in the open, where no treacherous tree could blot it out. Next, he gathered dry grasses and tiny twigs from the high-water flotsam. He could not bring his fingers together to pull them out, but he was able to gather them by the handful. In this way he got many rotten twigs and bits of green moss that were undesirable, but it was the best he could do. He worked methodically, even collecting an armful of the larger branches to be used later when the fire gathered strength. And all the while the dog sat and watched him, a certain yearning wistfulness in its eyes, for it looked upon him as the fire-provider, and the fire was slow in coming.

When all was ready, the man reached in his pocket for a second piece of birch-bark. He knew the bark was there, and, though he could not feel it with his fingers, he could hear its crisp rustling as he fumbled for it. Try as he would, he could not clutch hold of it. And all the time, in his consciousness, was the knowledge that each instant his feet were freezing. This thought tended to put him in a panic, but he fought against it and kept calm. He pulled on his mittens with his teeth, and threshed his arms back and forth, beating his hands with all his might against his sides. He did this sitting down, and he stood up to do it; and all the while the dog sat in the snow, its wolf-brush of a tail curled around warmly over its forefeet, its sharp wolf-ears pricked forward intently as it watched the man. And the man, as he beat and threshed with his arms and hands, he felt a great surge of envy as he regarded the creature that was warm and secure in its natural covering.

After a time he was aware of the first faraway signals of sensation in his beaten fingers. The faint tingling grew stronger till it evolved into a stinging ache that was excruciating, but which the man hailed with satisfaction. He stripped the mitten from his right hand and fetched forth the birch-bark. The exposed fingers were quickly going numb again. Next he brought out his bunch of sulphur matches. But the tremendous cold had already driven the life out of his fingers. In his effort to separate one match from the others, the whole bunch fell in the snow. He tried to pick it out of the snow, but failed. The dead fingers could neither touch nor clutch. He was very careful. He drove the thought of his freezing feet, and nose, and cheeks, out of his mind, devoting his whole soul to the matches. He watched, using the sense of vision in place of that of touch, and when he saw his fingers on each side the bunch, he closed them—that is, he willed to close them, for the wires were down, and the fingers did not obey. He pulled the mitten on the right hand, and beat it fiercely against his knee. Then, with both mittened hands, he scooped the bunch of matches, along with much snow, into his lap. Yet he was no better off.

After some manipulation he managed to get the bunch between the heels of his mittened hands. In this fashion he carried it to his mouth. The ice crackled and snapped when by a violent effort he opened his mouth. He drew the lower jaw in, curled the upper lip out of the way, and scraped the bunch with his upper teeth in order to separate a match. He succeeded in getting one, which he dropped on his lap. He was no better off. He could not pick it up. Then he devised a way. He picked it up in his teeth and scratched it on his leg. Twenty times he scratched before he succeeded in lighting it. As it flamed he held it with his teeth to the birch-bark. But the burning brimstone went up his nostrils and into his lungs, causing him to cough spasmodically. The match fell into the snow and went out.

The old-timer on Sulphur Creek was right, he thought in the moment of controlled despair that ensued: after fifty below, a man should travel with a partner. He beat his hands, but failed in exciting any sensation. Suddenly he bared both hands, removing the mittens with his teeth. He caught the whole bunch between the heels of his hands. His arm-muscles not being frozen enabled him to press the hand-heels tightly against the matches. Then he scratched the bunch along his leg. It flared into flame, seventy sulphur matches at once! There was no wind to blow them out. He kept his head to one side to escape the strangling fumes, and held the blazing bunch to the birch-bark. As he so held it, he became aware of sensation in his hand. His flesh was burning. He could smell it. Deep down below the surface he could feel it. The sensation developed into pain that grew acute. And still he endured it, holding the flame of the matches clumsily to the bark that would not light readily because his own burning hands were in the way, absorbing most of the flame.

At last, when he could endure no more, he jerked his hands apart. The blazing matches fell sizzling into the snow, but the birch-bark was alight. He began laying dry grasses and the tiniest twigs on the flame. He could not pick and choose, for he had to lift the fuel between the heels of his hands. Small pieces of rotten wood and green moss clung to the twigs, and he bit them off as well as he could with his teeth. He cherished the flame carefully and awkwardly. It meant life, and it must not perish. The withdrawal of blood from the surface of his body now made him begin to shiver, and he grew more awkward. A large piece of green moss fell squarely on the little fire. He tried to poke it out with his fingers, but his shivering frame made him poke too far, and he disrupted the nucleus of the little fire, the burning grasses and tiny twigs separating and scattering. He tried to poke them together again, but in spite of the tenseness of the effort, his shivering got away with him, and the twigs were hopelessly scattered. Each twig gushed a puff of smoke and went out. The fire-provider had failed. As he looked apathetically about him, his eyes chanced on the dog, sitting across the ruins of the fire from him, in the snow, making restless, hunching movements, slightly lifting one forefoot and then the other, shifting its weight back and forth on them with wistful eagerness.

The sight of the dog put a wild idea into his head. He remembered the tale of the man, caught in a blizzard, who killed a steer and crawled inside the carcass, and so was saved. He would kill the dog and bury his hands in the warm body until the numbness went out of them. Then he could build another fire. He spoke to the dog, calling it to him; but in his voice was a strange note of fear that frightened the animal, who had never known the man to speak in such way before. Something was the matter, and its suspicious nature sensed danger—it knew not what danger, but somewhere, somehow, in its brain arose an apprehension of the man. It flattened its ears down at the sound of the man's voice, and its restless, hunching movements and the liftings and shiftings of its forefeet became more pronounced; but it would not come to the man. He got on his hands and knees and crawled toward the dog. This unusual posture again excited suspicion, and the animal sidled mincingly away.

The man sat up in the snow for a moment and struggled for calmness. Then he pulled on his mittens, by means of his teeth, and got upon his feet. He glanced down at first in order to assure himself that he was really standing up, for the absence of sensation in his feet left him unrelated to the earth. His erect position in itself started to drive the webs of suspicion from the dog's mind; and when he spoke peremptorily, with the sound of whip-lashes in his voice, the dog rendered its customary allegiance and came to him. As it came within reaching distance, the man lost his control. His arms flashed out to the dog, and he experienced genuine surprise when he discovered that his hands could not clutch, that there was neither bend nor feeling in the fingers. He had forgotten for the moment that they were frozen and that they were freezing more and more. All this happened quickly, and before the animal could get away, he encircled its body with his arms. He sat down in the snow, and in this fashion held the dog, while it snarled and whined and struggled.

But it was all he could do, hold its body encircled in his arms and sit there. He realized that he could not kill the dog. There was no way to do it. With his helpless hands he could neither draw nor hold his sheath-knife nor throttle the animal. He released it, and it plunged wildly away, with tail between its legs, and still snarling. It halted forty feet away and surveyed him curiously, with ears sharply pricked forward. The man looked down at his hands in order to locate them, and found them hanging on the ends of his arms. It struck him as curious that one should have to use his eyes in order to find out where his hands were. He began threshing his arms back and forth, beating the mittened hands against his sides. He did this for five minutes, violently, and his heart pumped enough blood up to the surface to put a stop to his shivering. But no sensation was aroused in the hands. He had an impression that they hung like weights on the ends of his arms, but when he tried to run the impression down, he could not find it.

A certain fear of death, dull and oppressive, came to him. This fear quickly became poignant as he realized that it was no longer a mere matter of freezing his fingers and toes, or of losing his hands and feet, but that it was a matter of life and death with the chances against him. This threw him into a panic, and he turned and ran up the creek-bed along the old, dim trail. The dog joined in behind and kept up with him. He ran blindly, without intention, in fear such as he had never known in his life. Slowly, as he ploughed and floundered through the snow, he began to see things again—the banks of the creek, the old timber-jams, the leafless aspens, and the sky. The running made him feel better. He did not shiver. Maybe, if he ran on, his feet would thaw out; and, anyway, if he ran far enough, he would reach camp and the boys. Without doubt he would lose some fingers and toes and some of his face; but the boys would take care of him, and save the rest of him when he got there. And at the same time there was another thought in his mind that said he would never get to the camp and the boys; that it was too many miles away, that the freezing had too great a start on him, and that he would soon be stiff and dead. This thought he kept in the background and refused to consider. Sometimes it pushed itself forward and demanded to be heard, but he thrust it back and strove to think of other things.

It struck him as curious that he could run at all on feet so frozen that he could not feel them when they struck the earth and took the weight of his body. He seemed to himself to skim along above the surface, and to have no connection with the earth. Somewhere he had once seen a winged Mercury,[5] and he wondered if Mercury felt as he felt when skimming over the earth.

His theory of running until he reached camp and the boys had one flaw in it: he lacked the endurance. Several times he stumbled, and finally he

5. Mercury is the Roman god of messengers, thieves, and storytellers; he flew between heaven and earth wearing winged sandals. He is also the god of healing and the courier of souls to the Underworld.

tottered, crumpled up, and fell. When he tried to rise, he failed. He must sit and rest, he decided, and next time he would merely walk and keep on going. As he sat and regained his breath, he noted that he was feeling quite warm and comfortable. He was not shivering, and it even seemed that a warm glow had come to his chest and trunk. And yet, when he touched his nose or cheeks, there was no sensation. Running would not thaw them out. Nor would it thaw out his hands and feet. Then the thought came to him that the frozen portions of his body must be extending. He tried to keep this thought down, to forget it, to think of something else; he was aware of the panicky feeling that it caused, and he was afraid of the panic. But the thought asserted itself, and persisted, until it produced a vision of his body totally frozen. This was too much, and he made another wild run along the trail. Once he slowed down to a walk, but the thought of the freezing extending itself made him run again.

And all the time the dog ran with him, at his heels. When he fell down a second time, it curled its tail over its forefeet and sat in front of him, facing him, curiously eager and intent. The warmth and security of the animal angered him, and he cursed it till it flattened down its ears appeasingly. This time the shivering came more quickly upon the man. He was losing in his battle with the frost. It was creeping into his body from all sides. The thought of it drove him on, but he ran no more than a hundred feet, when he staggered and pitched headlong. It was his last panic. When he had recovered his breath and control, he sat up and entertained in his mind the conception of meeting death with dignity. However, the conception did not come to him in such terms. His idea of it was that he had been making a fool of himself, running around like a chicken with its head cut off—such was the simile that occurred to him. Well, he was bound to freeze anyway, and he might as well take it decently. With this new-found peace of mind came the first glimmerings of drowsiness. A good idea, he thought, to sleep off to death. It was like taking an anaesthetic. Freezing was not so bad as people thought. There were lots worse ways to die.

He pictured the boys finding his body next day. Suddenly he found himself with them, coming along the trail and looking for himself. And, still with them, he came around a turn in the trail and found himself lying in the snow. He did not belong with himself any more, for even then he was out of himself, standing with the boys and looking at himself in the snow. It certainly was cold, was his thought. When he got back to the States he could tell the folks what real cold was. He drifted on from this to a vision of the old-timer on Sulphur Creek. He could see him quite clearly, warm and comfortable, and smoking a pipe.

"You were right, old hoss; you were right," the man mumbled to the old-timer of Sulphur Creek.

Then the man drowsed off into what seemed to him the most comfortable and satisfying sleep he had ever known. The dog sat facing him and waiting. The brief day drew to a close in a long, slow twilight. There were no signs of a fire to be made, and, besides, never in the dog's experience had it known a man to sit like that in the snow and make no fire. As the twilight drew on, its eager yearning for the fire mastered it, and with a great lifting and shifting of forefeet, it whined softly, then flattened its ears down in anticipation of being chidden by the man. But the man remained silent. Later, the dog whined loudly. And still later it crept close to the man and caught the scent of death. This made the animal bristle and back away. A little longer it delayed, howling under the stars that leaped and danced and shone brightly in the cold sky. Then it turned and trotted up the trail in the direction of the camp it knew, where were the other food-providers and fire-providers.

1902, 1908

ZITKALA ŠA (GERTRUDE SIMMONS BONNIN)
1876–1938

Gertrude Simmons was born in 1876 on the Yankton Sioux Reservation in South Dakota. Her mother was *Tate Iyohi Win*, or "Reaches the Wind Woman," otherwise known as Ellen Simmons, and her father was probably a white man named Felker who left his wife before the child's birth. Her mother later married another white man, John H. Simmons, whose surname was given to the child. Gertrude Simmons today is usually referred to as Zitkala Ša (pronounced *sha*), or Red Bird, a name she chose for herself. Zitkala Ša was an important Native American writer, orator, and debater; a singer, pianist, and violinist; and an activist on behalf of women's and Native American rights.

Eighteen hundred and seventy-six, the year of Zitkala Ša's birth, was the year in which George Armstrong Custer's Seventh Cavalry was defeated by a coalition of Sioux and Cheyenne warriors on the Little Bighorn River in Montana, after which the federal government finally drove both tribes onto reservations. In 1890, the U.S. Department of the Census announced the closing of the frontier, meaning that no more "free land" remained open for settlement; the United States had achieved its "manifest destiny," extending its dominion from "sea to shining sea." As an adult, then, Zitkala Ša lived in what has been called the "transitional" period in Native American history, a difficult time for Indian peoples, when the U.S. government pursued an official policy of "detribalization" and land-hungry whites sought access to tribal domains.

At the age of eight, Zitkala Ša declared her intention to learn the white man's ways—or, as she puts it, in her autobiographical "Impressions of an Indian Childhood" (1900), she wanted to taste the "big red apples" missionaries promised Indian children if they would attend boarding school. She began her schooling at White's Manual Institute, a Quaker school in Indiana. As her autobiography details it, her introduction to "civilization" subjected her and the other Indian children to having their long hair cut, to having the clothing in which they had arrived discarded, and, perhaps most painful, to being forbidden to speak their Native languages. This was, in the oft-quoted dictum of Colonel Richard Henry Pratt, headmaster of the Carlisle Indian Institute, where Zitkala Ša later worked, an education intended to "Kill the Indian and save the man!"

From White's, Zitkala Ša went on to Earlham College, also in Indiana, where she began to demonstrate a wide range of talents. In the last section of "Impressions of an Indian Childhood," she tells of her appearance as the representative of the college in 1896 at a statewide oratorical competition, where some "rowdies," as she puts it, "threw out a large white flag, with a drawing of a most forlorn Indian girl on it," along with, "in bold black letters words that ridiculed the college which was represented by a 'squaw.'" This slight was somewhat assuaged by her winning second prize overall.

The following year, Zitkala Ša became "the latest addition to our force of workers," as the Carlisle Institute's publication, the *Indian Helper,* announced in its July 1897

Carlisle School: "Before" and "After." The Carlisle Indian School produced a considerable number of "before" and "after" photos, representing the difference in appearance between new Indian arrivals to the school and its graduates. Zitkala Ša came to teach at Carlisle in 1897, at the age of only twenty-one, and she might have known some of these graduates, photographed the year of her arrival—several of whom were older than she was.

number. At Carlisle, Zitkala Ša led the glee club, played the piano and violin, and became engaged to Thomas Marshall, a Sioux from the Pine Ridge Agency, a devout Christian convert, "without a peer among our students," who died suddenly from an undiagnosed illness.

Soon after Marshall's death, Zitkala Ša began to publish autobiography and fiction. (She also wrote poetry.) "Impressions of an Indian Childhood" and "The School Days of an Indian Girl" appeared in the *Atlantic Monthly* in 1900. Her short story "The Soft-Hearted Sioux" appeared in *Harper's Monthly* in 1901, and the essay-manifesto "Why I Am a Pagan" appeared in the *Atlantic Monthly* in 1902. Although her first book *Old Indian Legends* was published in 1901, her other writings did not appear in book form until 1921, with the publication of *American Indian Stories*.

"The Soft-Hearted Sioux" makes powerfully clear that the protagonist's Christianization and "civilization" have unfitted him for any relation to his traditional parents. In "Why I Am a Pagan," Zitkala Ša speaks of a "native preacher" who mouths "most strangely the jangling phrases of a bigoted creed," remarks that her mother is "a follower of the new superstition," and states her own preference for "excursions in natural gardens" rather than the "dogma" of the Christians.

In May 1902, Zitkala Ša married Raymond Bonnin, also a Yankton, and an employee of the U.S. Indian Service (later the Bureau of Indian Affairs). They had one son, Raymond Ohiya Bonnin, born in 1903. Although she would occasionally publish stories and poems thereafter, and wrote the libretto for an opera, *Sun Dance*, the bulk of Zitkala Ša's writing over the second half of her life derived from her active engagement in Indian affairs. After years of work on the Uintah Ouray Ute Agency in Utah, the family moved to Washington, D.C., in 1916 so that Zitkala Ša could take up her elected position as secretary of the Society of the American Indian (SAI), an organization dedicated to improving the condition of Native people. During World War I, Bonnin served in the army as assistant to the Quartermaster General in Washington, retiring with the rank of captain. When the SAI broke up in 1920, Zitkala Ša began working with the General Federation of Women's Clubs, which established an Indian Welfare Committee in 1921 at her urging. One of the committee's achievements was an inquiry into the treatment of some of the tribes in Oklahoma, which led to the publication, in 1924, of a study of the graft, corruption, and exploitation of the tribes and spurred the formation under President Hoover of the Merriam Commission in 1928 to study these matters. In 1926, Zitkala Ša had founded her own organization, the National Council of American Indians, of which she was president, with her husband serving as counselor general, secretary-treasurer, and executive secretary. It was in 1938 that she fell into a coma and died.

Zitkala Ša is buried in Arlington National Cemetery beside her husband, Captain Raymond Bonnin.

From Impressions of an Indian Childhood

I. My Mother

A wigwam of weather-stained canvas stood at the base of some irregularly ascending hills. A footpath wound its way gently down the sloping land till it reached the broad river bottom; creeping through the long swamp grasses that bent over it on either side, it came out on the edge of the Missouri.

Here, morning, noon, and evening, my mother came to draw water from the muddy stream for our household use. Always, when my mother started for the river, I stopped my play to run along with her. She was only of medium height. Often she was sad and silent, at which times her full arched lips were compressed into hard and bitter lines, and shadows fell under her black eyes. Then I clung to her hand and begged to know what made the tears fall.

"Hush; my little daughter must never talk about my tears"; and smiling through them, she patted my head and said, "Now let me see how fast you can run to-day." Whereupon I tore away at my highest possible speed, with my long black hair blowing in the breeze.

I was a wild little girl of seven. Loosely clad in a slip of brown buckskin, and light-footed with a pair of soft moccasins on my feet, I was as free as the wind that blew my hair, and no less spirited than a bounding deer. These were my mother's pride,—my wild freedom and overflowing spirits. She taught me no fear save that of intruding myself upon others.

Having gone many paces ahead I stopped, panting for breath, and laughing with glee as my mother watched my every movement. I was not wholly conscious of myself, but was more keenly alive to the fire within. It was as if I were the activity, and my hands and feet were only experiments for my spirit to work upon.

Returning from the river, I tugged beside my mother, with my hand upon the bucket I believed I was carrying. One time, on such a return, I remember a bit of conversation we had. My grown-up cousin, Warca-Ziwin (Sunflower), who was then seventeen, always went to the river alone for water for her mother. Their wigwam was not far from ours; and I saw her daily going to and from the river. I admired my cousin greatly. So I said: "Mother, when I am tall as my cousin Warca-Ziwin, you shall not have to come for water. I will do it for you."

With a strange tremor in her voice which I could not understand, she answered, "If the paleface does not take away from us the river we drink."

"Mother, who is this bad paleface?" I asked.

"My little daughter, he is a sham,—a sickly sham! The bronzed Dakota is the only real man."

I looked up into my mother's face while she spoke; and seeing her bite her lips, I knew she was unhappy. This aroused revenge in my small soul. Stamping my foot on the earth, I cried aloud, "I hate the paleface that makes my mother cry!"

Setting the pail of water on the ground, my mother stooped, and stretching her left hand out on the level with my eyes, she placed her other arm about me; she pointed to the hill where my uncle and my only sister lay buried.

"There is what the paleface has done! Since then your father too has been buried in a hill nearer the rising sun. We were once very happy. But the paleface has stolen our lands and driven us hither. Having defrauded us of our land, the paleface forced us away.

"Well, it happened on the day we moved camp that your sister and uncle were both very sick. Many others were ailing, but there seemed to be no help. We traveled many days and nights; not in the grand happy way that we moved camp when I was a little girl, but we were driven, my child, driven like a herd of buffalo. With every step, your sister, who was not as large as you are now, shrieked with the painful jar until she was hoarse with crying. She grew more and more feverish. Her little hands and cheeks were burning hot. Her little lips were parched and dry, but she would not drink the water I gave her. Then I discovered that her throat was swollen and red. My poor child, how I cried with her because the Great Spirit had forgotten us!

"At last, when we reached this western country, on the first weary night your sister died. And soon your uncle died also, leaving a widow and an orphan daughter, your cousin Warca-Ziwin. Both your sister and uncle might have been happy with us to-day, had it not been for the heartless paleface."

My mother was silent the rest of the way to our wigwam. Though I saw no tears in her eyes, I knew that was because I was with her. She seldom wept before me.

II. The Legends

During the summer days, my mother built her fire in the shadow of our wigwam.

In the early morning our simple breakfast was spread upon the grass west of our tepee. At the farthest point of the shade my mother sat beside her fire, toasting a savory piece of dried meat. Near her, I sat upon my feet, eating my dried meat with unleavened bread, and drinking strong black coffee.

The morning meal was our quiet hour, when we two were entirely alone. At noon, several who chanced to be passing by stopped to rest, and to share our luncheon with us, for they were sure of our hospitality.

My uncle, whose death my mother ever lamented, was one of our nation's bravest warriors. His name was on the lips of old men when talking of the proud feats of valor; and it was mentioned by younger men, too, in connection with deeds of gallantry. Old women praised him for his kindness toward them; young women held him up as an ideal to their sweethearts. Every one loved him, and my mother worshiped his memory. Thus it happened that even strangers were sure of welcome in our lodge, if they but asked a favor in my uncle's name.

Though I heard many strange experiences related by these wayfarers, I loved best the evening meal, for that was the time old legends were told. I was always glad when the sun hung low in the west, for then my mother sent me to invite the neighboring old men and women to eat supper with us. Running all the way to the wigwams, I halted shyly at the entrances. Sometimes I stood long moments without saying a word. It was not any fear that made me so dumb when out upon such a happy errand; nor was it that I wished to withhold the invitation, for it was all I could do to observe this very proper silence. But it was a sensing of the atmosphere, to assure myself that I should not hinder other plans. My mother used to say to me, as I was almost bounding away for the old people: "Wait a moment before you invite any one. If other plans are being discussed, do not interfere, but go elsewhere."

The old folks knew the meaning of my pauses; and often they coaxed my confidence by asking, "What do you seek, little granddaughter?"

"My mother says you are to come to our tepee this evening," I instantly exploded, and breathed the freer afterwards.

"Yes, yes, gladly, gladly I shall come!" each replied. Rising at once and carrying their blankets across one shoulder, they flocked leisurely from their various wigwams toward our dwelling.

My mission done, I ran back, skipping and jumping with delight. All out of breath, I told my mother almost the exact words of the answers to my invitation. Frequently she asked, "What were they doing when you entered their tepee?" This taught me to remember all I saw at a single glance. Often I told my mother my impressions without being questioned.

While in the neighboring wigwams sometimes an old Indian woman asked me, "What is your mother doing?" Unless my mother had cautioned me not to tell, I generally answered her questions without reserve.

At the arrival of our guests I sat close to my mother, and did not leave her side without first asking her consent. I ate my supper in quiet, listening patiently to the talk of the old people, wishing all the time that they would begin the stories I loved best. At last, when I could not wait any longer, I whispered in my mother's ear, "Ask them to tell an Iktomi story,[1] mother."

Soothing my impatience, my mother said aloud, "My little daughter is anxious to hear your legends." By this time all were through eating, and the evening was fast deepening into twilight.

As each in turn began to tell a legend, I pillowed my head in my mother's lap; and lying flat upon my back, I watched the stars as they peeped down upon me, one by one. The increasing interest of the tale aroused me, and I sat up eagerly listening for every word. The old women made funny remarks, and laughed so heartily that I could not help joining them.

The distant howling of a pack of wolves or the hooting of an owl in the river bottom frightened me, and I nestled into my mother's lap. She added some dry sticks to the fire, and the bright flames heaped up into the faces of the old folks as they sat around in a great circle.

On such an evening, I remember the glare of the fire shone on a tattooed star upon the brow of the old warrior who was telling a story. I watched him curiously as he made his unconscious gestures. The blue star upon his bronzed forehead was a puzzle to me. Looking about, I saw two parallel lines on the chin of one of the old women. The rest had none. I examined my mother's face, but found no sign there.

After the warrior's story was finished, I asked the old woman the meaning of the blue lines on her chin, looking all the while out of the corners of my eyes at the warrior with the star on his forehead. I was a little afraid that he would rebuke me for my boldness.

Here the old woman began: "Why, my grandchild, they are signs,—secret signs I dare not tell you. I shall, however, tell you a wonderful story about a woman who had a cross tattooed upon each of her cheeks."

It was a long story of a woman whose magic power lay hidden behind the marks upon her face. I fell asleep before the story was completed.

Ever after that night I felt suspicious of tattooed people. Wherever I saw one I glanced furtively at the mark and round about it, wondering what terrible magic power was covered there.

It was rarely that such a fearful story as this one was told by the camp fire. Its impression was so acute that the picture still remains vividly clear and pronounced.

* * *

VII. The Big Red Apples

The first turning away from the easy, natural flow of my life occurred in an early spring. It was in my eighth year; in the month of March, I afterward learned. At this age I knew but one language, and that was my mother's native tongue.

From some of my playmates I heard that two paleface missionaries were in our village. They were from that class of white men who wore big hats and carried large hearts, they said. Running direct to my mother, I began to

---

1. A story about the Sioux trickster.

question her why these two strangers were among us. She told me, after I had teased much, that they had come to take away Indian boys and girls to the East. My mother did not seem to want me to talk about them. But in a day or two, I gleaned many wonderful stories from my playfellows concerning the strangers.

"Mother, my friend Judéwin is going home with the missionaries. She is going to a more beautiful country than ours; the palefaces told her so!" I said wistfully, wishing in my heart that I too might go.

Mother sat in a chair, and I was hanging on her knee. Within the last two seasons my big brother Dawée had returned from a three years' education in the East, and his coming back influenced my mother to take a farther step from her native way of living. First it was a change from the buffalo skin to the white man's canvas that covered our wigwam. Now she had given up her wigwam of slender poles, to live, a foreigner, in a home of clumsy logs.

"Yes, my child, several others besides Judéwin are going away with the palefaces. Your brother said the missionaries had inquired about his little sister," she said, watching my face very closely.

My heart thumped so hard against my breast, I wondered if she could hear it.

"Did he tell them to take me, mother?" I asked, fearing lest Dawée had forbidden the palefaces to see me, and that my hope of going to the Wonderland would be entirely blighted.

With a sad, slow smile, she answered: "There! I knew you were wishing to go, because Judéwin has filled your ears with the white men's lies. Don't believe a word they say! Their words are sweet, but, my child, their deeds are bitter. You will cry for me, but they will not even soothe you. Stay with me, my little one! Your brother Dawée says that going East, away from your mother, is too hard an experience for his baby sister."

Thus my mother discouraged my curiosity about the lands beyond our eastern horizon; for it was not yet an ambition for Letters that was stirring me. But on the following day the missionaries did come to our very house. I spied them coming up the footpath leading to our cottage. A third man was with them, but he was not my brother Dawée. It was another, a young interpreter, a paleface who had a smattering of the Indian language. I was ready to run out to meet them, but I did not dare to displease my mother. With great glee, I jumped up and down on our ground floor. I begged my mother to open the door, that they would be sure to come to us. Alas! They came, they saw, and they conquered!

Judéwin had told me of the great tree where grew red, red apples; and how we could reach out our hands and pick all the red apples we could eat. I had never seen apple trees. I had never tasted more than a dozen red apples in my life; and when I heard of the orchards of the East, I was eager to roam among them. The missionaries smiled into my eyes, and patted my head. I wondered how mother could say such hard words against them.

"Mother, ask them if little girls may have all the red apples they want, when they go East," I whispered aloud, in my excitement.

The interpreter heard me, and answered: "Yes, little girl, the nice red apples are for those who pick them; and you will have a ride on the iron horse if you go with these good people."

I had never seen a train, and he knew it.

"Mother, I'm going East! I like big red apples, and I want to ride on the iron horse! Mother, say yes!" I pleaded.

My mother said nothing. The missionaries waited in silence; and my eyes began to blur with tears, though I struggled to choke them back. The corners of my mouth twitched, and my mother saw me.

"I am not ready to give you any word," she said to them. "To-morrow I shall send you my answer by my son."

With this they left us. Alone with my mother, I yielded to my tears, and cried aloud, shaking my head so as not to hear what she was saying to me. This was the first time I had ever been so unwilling to give up my own desire that I refused to hearken to my mother's voice.

There was a solemn silence in our home that night. Before I went to bed I begged the Great Spirit to make my mother willing I should go with the missionaries.

The next morning came, and my mother called me to her side. "My daughter, do you still persist in wishing to leave your mother?" she asked.

"Oh, mother, it is not that I wish to leave you, but I want to see the wonderful Eastern land," I answered.

My dear old aunt came to our house that morning, and I heard her say, "Let her try it."

I hoped that, as usual, my aunt was pleading on my side. My brother Dawée came for mother's decision. I dropped my play, and crept close to my aunt.

"Yes, Dawée, my daughter, though she does not understand what it all means, is anxious to go. She will need an education when she is grown, for then there will be fewer real Dakotas, and many more palefaces. This tearing her away, so young, from her mother is necessary, if I would have her an educated woman. The palefaces, who owe us a large debt for stolen lands, have begun to pay a tardy justice in offering some education to our children. But I know my daughter must suffer keenly in this experiment. For her sake, I dread to tell you my reply to the missionaries. Go, tell them that they may take my little daughter, and that the Great Spirit shall not fail to reward them according to their hearts."

Wrapped in my heavy blanket, I walked with my mother to the carriage that was soon to take us to the iron horse. I was happy. I met my playmates, who were also wearing their best thick blankets. We showed one another our new beaded moccasins, and the width of the belts that girdled our new dresses. Soon we were being drawn rapidly away by the white man's horses. When I saw the lonely figure of my mother vanish in the distance, a sense of regret settled heavily upon me. I felt suddenly weak, as if I might fall limp to the ground. I was in the hands of strangers whom my mother did not fully trust. I no longer felt free to be myself, or to voice my own feelings. The tears trickled down my cheeks, and I buried my face in the folds of my blanket. Now the first step, parting me from my mother, was taken, and all my belated tears availed nothing.

Having driven thirty miles to the ferryboat, we crossed the Missouri in the evening. Then riding again a few miles eastward, we stopped before a massive brick building. I looked at it in amazement, and with a vague misgiving, for in our village I had never seen so large a house. Trembling with fear and distrust of the palefaces, my teeth chattering from the chilly ride, I crept noiselessly in my soft moccasins along the narrow hall, keeping very close to the bare wall. I was as frightened and bewildered as the captured young of a wild creature.

1900

The Soft-Hearted Sioux

I

Beside the open fire I sat within our tepee. With my red blanket wrapped tightly about my crossed legs, I was thinking of the coming season, my sixteenth winter. On either side of the wigwam were my parents. My father was whistling a tune between his teeth while polishing with his bare hand a red stone pipe he had recently carved. Almost in front of me, beyond the center fire, my old grandmother sat near the entranceway.

She turned her face toward her right and addressed most of her words to my mother. Now and then she spoke to me, but never did she allow her eyes to rest upon her daughter's husband, my father. It was only upon rare occasions that my grandmother said anything to him. Thus his ears were open and ready to catch the smallest wish she might express. Sometimes when my grandmother had been saying things which pleased him, my father used to comment upon them. At other times, when he could not approve of what was spoken, he used to work or smoke silently.

On this night my old grandmother began her talk about me. Filling the bowl of her red stone pipe with dry willow bark, she looked across at me. "My grandchild, you are tall and are no longer a little boy." Narrowing her old eyes, she asked, "My grandchild, when are you going to bring here a handsome young woman?" I stared into the fire rather than meet her gaze. Waiting for my answer, she stooped forward and through the long stem drew a flame into the red stone pipe.

I smiled while my eyes were still fixed upon the bright fire, but I said nothing in reply. Turning to my mother, she offered her the pipe. I glanced at my grandmother. The loose buckskin sleeve fell off at her elbow and showed a wrist covered with silver bracelets. Holding up the fingers of her left hand, she named off the desirable young women of our village.

"Which one, my grandchild, which one?" she questioned.

"Hoh!" I said, pulling at my blanket in confusion. "Not yet!" Here my mother passed the pipe over the fire to my father. Then she, too, began speaking of what I should do.

"My son, be always active. Do not dislike a long hunt. Learn to provide much buffalo meat and many buckskins before you bring home a wife." Presently my father gave the pipe to my grandmother, and he took his turn in the exhortations.

"Ho, my son, I have been counting in my heart the bravest warriors of our people. There is not one of them who won his title in his sixteenth winter. My son, it is a great thing for some brave of sixteen winters to do."

Not a word had I to give in answer. I knew well the fame of my warrior father. He had earned the right of speaking such words, though even he himself was a brave only at my age. Refusing to smoke my grandmother's pipe because my heart was too much stirred by their words, and sorely troubled with a fear lest I should disappoint them, I arose to go. Drawing my blanket over my shoulders, I said, as I stepped toward the entranceway: "I go to hobble my pony. It is now late in the night."

II

Nine winters' snows had buried deep that night when my old grandmother, together with my father and mother, designed my future with the glow of a camp fire upon it.

Yet I did not grow up the warrior, huntsman, and husband I was to have been. At the mission school I learned it was wrong to kill. Nine winters I hunted for the soft heart of Christ, and prayed for the huntsmen who chased the buffalo on the plains.

In the autumn of the tenth year I was sent back to my tribe to preach Christianity to them. With the white man's Bible in my hand, and the white man's tender heart in my breast, I returned to my own people.

Wearing a foreigner's dress, I walked, a stranger, into my father's village.

Asking my way, for I had not forgotten my native tongue, an old man led me toward the tepee where my father lay. From my old companion I learned that my father had been sick many moons. As we drew near the tepee, I heard the chanting of a medicine-man within it. At once I wished to enter in and drive from my home the sorcerer of the plains, but the old warrior checked me. "Ho, wait outside until the medicine-man leaves your father," he said. While talking he scanned me from head to feet. Then he retraced his steps toward the heart of the camping-ground.

My father's dwelling was on the outer limits of the round-faced village. With every heartthrob I grew more impatient to enter the wigwam.

While I turned the leaves of my Bible with nervous fingers, the medicine-man came forth from the dwelling and walked hurriedly away. His head and face were closely covered with the loose robe which draped his entire figure.

He was tall and large. His long strides I have never forgot. They seemed to me then the uncanny gait of eternal death. Quickly pocketing my Bible, I went into the tepee.

Upon a mat lay my father, with furrowed face and gray hair. His eyes and cheeks were sunken far into his head. His sallow skin lay thin upon his pinched nose and high cheekbones. Stooping over him, I took his fevered hand. "How, Ate?"[1] I greeted him. A light flashed from his listless eyes and his dried lips parted. "My son!" he murmured, in a feeble voice. Then again the wave of joy and recognition receded. He closed his eyes, and his hand dropped from my open palm to the ground.

Looking about, I saw an old woman sitting with bowed head. Shaking hands with her, I recognized my mother. I sat down between my father and mother as I used to do, but I did not feel at home. The place where my old grandmother used to sit was now unoccupied. With my mother I bowed my head. Alike our throats were choked and tears were streaming from our eyes; but far apart in spirit our ideas and faiths separated us. My grief was for the soul unsaved; and I thought my mother wept to see a brave man's body broken by sickness.

Useless was my attempt to change the faith in the medicine-man to that abstract power named God. Then one day I became righteously mad with anger that the medicine-man should thus ensnare my father's soul. And

1. Hello, Father.

when he came to chant his sacred songs I pointed toward the door and bade him go! The man's eyes glared upon me for an instant. Slowly gathering his robe about him, he turned his back upon the sick man and stepped out of our wigwam. "Ha, ha, ha! my son, I cannot live without the medicine-man!" I heard my father cry when the sacred man was gone.

III

On a bright day, when the winged seeds of the prairie-grass were flying hither and thither, I walked solemnly toward the centre of the camping-ground. My heart beat hard and irregularly at my side. Tighter I grasped the sacred book I carried under my arm. Now was the beginning of life's work.

Though I knew it would be hard, I did not once feel that failure was to be my reward. As I stepped unevenly on the rolling ground, I thought of the warriors soon to wash off their war-paints and follow me.

At length I reached the place where the people had assembled to hear me preach. In a large circle men and women sat upon the dry red grass. Within the ring I stood, with the white man's Bible in my hand. I tried to tell them of the soft heart of Christ.

In silence the vast circle of bareheaded warriors sat under an afternoon sun. At last, wiping the wet from my brow, I took my place in the ring. The hush of the assembly filled me with great hope.

I was turning my thoughts upward to the sky in gratitude, when a stir called me to earth again.

A tall, strong man arose. His loose robe hung in folds over his right shoulder. A pair of snapping black eyes fastened themselves like the poisonous fangs of a serpent upon me. He was the medicine-man. A tremor played about my heart and a chill cooled the fire in my veins.

Scornfully he pointed a long forefinger in my direction and asked:

"What loyal son is he who, returning to his father's people, wears a foreigner's dress?" He paused a moment, and then continued: "The dress of that foreigner of whom a story says he bound a native of our land, and heaping dry sticks around him, kindled a fire at his feet!" Waving his hand toward me, he exclaimed, "Here is the traitor to his people!"

I was helpless. Before the eyes of the crowd the cunning magician turned my honest heart into a vile nest of treachery. Alas! the people frowned as they looked upon me.

"Listen!" he went on. "Which one of you who have eyed the young man can see through his bosom and warn the people of the nest of young snakes hatching there? Whose ear was so acute that he caught the hissing of snakes whenever the young man opened his mouth? This one has not only proven false to you, but even to the Great Spirit who made him. He is a fool! Why do you sit here giving ear to a foolish man who could not defend his people because he fears to kill, who could not bring venison to renew the life of his sick father? With his prayers, let him drive away the enemy! With his soft heart, let him keep off starvation! We shall go elsewhere to dwell upon an untainted ground."

With this he disbanded the people. When the sun lowered in the west and the winds were quiet, the village of cone-shaped tepees was gone. The medicine-man had won the hearts of the people.

Only my father's dwelling was left to mark the fighting-ground.

IV

From a long night at my father's bedside I came out to look upon the morning. The yellow sun hung equally between the snow-covered land and the cloudless blue sky. The light of the new day was cold. The strong breath of winter crusted the snow and fitted crystal shells over the rivers and lakes. As I stood in front of the tepee, thinking of the vast prairies which separated us from our tribe, and wondering if the high sky likewise separated the soft-hearted Son of God from us, the icy blast from the North blew through my hair and skull. My neglected hair had grown long and fell upon my neck.

My father had not risen from his bed since the day the medicine-man led the people away. Though I read from the Bible and prayed beside him upon my knees, my father would not listen. Yet I believed my prayers were not unheeded in heaven.

"Ha, ha, ha! my son," my father groaned upon the first snowfall. "My son, our food is gone. There is no one to bring me meat! My son, your soft heart has unfitted you for everything!" Then covering his face with the buffalo-robe, he said no more. Now while I stood out in that cold winter morning, I was starving. For two days I had not seen any food. But my own cold and hunger did not harass my soul as did the whining cry of the sick old man.

Stepping again into the tepee, I untied my snow-shoes, which were fastened to the tent-poles.

My poor mother, watching by the sick one, and faithfully heaping wood upon the centre fire, spoke to me:

"My son, do not fail again to bring your father meat, or he will starve to death."

"How, Ina,"[2] I answered, sorrowfully. From the tepee I started forth again to hunt food for my aged parents. All day I tracked the white level lands in vain. Nowhere, nowhere were there any other footprints but my own! In the evening of this third fast-day I came back without meat. Only a bundle of sticks for the fire I brought on my back. Dropping the wood outside, I lifted the door-flap and set one foot within the tepee.

There I grew dizzy and numb. My eyes swam in tears. Before me lay my old gray-haired father sobbing like a child. In his horny hands he clutched the buffalo-robe, and with his teeth he was gnawing off the edges. Chewing the dry stiff hair and buffalo-skin, my father's eyes sought my hands. Upon seeing them empty, he cried out:

"My son, your soft heart will let me starve before you bring me meat! Two hills eastward stand a herd of cattle. Yet you will see me die before you bring me food!"

Leaving my mother lying with covered head upon her mat, I rushed out into the night.

With a strange warmth in my heart and swiftness in my feet, I climbed over the first hill, and soon the second one. The moonlight upon the white country showed me a clear path to the white man's cattle. With my hand upon the knife in my belt, I leaned heavily against the fence while counting the herd.

Twenty in all I numbered. From among them I chose the best-fattened creature. Leaping over the fence, I plunged my knife into it.

2. Hello, Mother.

My long knife was sharp, and my hands, no more fearful and slow, slashed off choice chunks of warm flesh. Bending under the meat I had taken for my starving father, I hurried across the prairie.

Toward home I fairly ran with the life-giving food I carried upon my back. Hardly had I climbed the second hill when I heard sounds coming after me. Faster and faster I ran with my load for my father, but the sounds were gaining upon me. I heard the clicking of snowshoes and the squeaking of the leather straps at my heels; yet I did not turn to see what pursued me, for I was intent upon reaching my father. Suddenly like thunder an angry voice shouted curses and threats into my ear! A rough hand wrenched my shoulder and took the meat from me! I stopped struggling to run. A deafening whir filled my head. The moon and stars began to move. Now the white prairie was sky, and the stars lay under my feet. Now again they were turning. At last the starry blue rose up into place. The noise in my ears was still. A great quiet filled the air. In my hand I found my long knife dripping with blood. At my feet a man's figure lay prone in blood-red snow. The horrible scene about me seemed a trick of my senses, for I could not understand it was real. Looking long upon the blood-stained snow, the load of meat for my starving father reached my recognition at last. Quickly I tossed it over my shoulder and started again homeward.

Tired and haunted I reached the door of the wigwam. Carrying the food before me, I entered with it into the tepee.

"Father, here is food!" I cried, as I dropped the meat near my mother. No answer came. Turning about, I beheld my gray-haired father dead! I saw by the unsteady firelight an old gray-haired skeleton lying rigid and stiff.

Out into the open I started, but the snow at my feet became bloody.

V

On the day after my father's death, having led my mother to the camp of the medicine-man, I gave myself up to those who were searching for the murderer of the paleface.

They bound me hand and foot. Here in this cell I was placed four days ago.

The shrieking winter winds have followed me hither. Rattling the bars, they howl unceasingly: "Your soft heart! your soft heart will see me die before you bring me food!" Hark! something is clanking the chain on the door. It is being opened. From the dark night without a black figure crosses the threshold. It is the guard. He comes to warn me of my fate. He tells me that tomorrow I must die. In his stern face I laugh aloud. I do not fear death.

Yet I wonder who shall come to welcome me in the realm of strange sight. Will the loving Jesus grant me pardon and give my soul a soothing sleep? or will my warrior father greet me and receive me as his son? Will my spirit fly upward to a happy heaven? or shall I sink into the bottomless pit, an outcast from a God of infinite love?

Soon, soon I shall know, for now I see the east is growing red. My heart is strong. My face is calm. My eyes are dry and eager for new scenes. My hands hang quietly at my side. Serene and brave, my soul awaits the men to perch me on the gallows for another flight. I go.

1901

American Literature
1914–1945

THE TWO WARS AS HISTORICAL MARKERS

The conflict eventually known as World War I broke out in Europe in 1914, with Great Britain and France fighting against Germany. The United States, which belatedly entered the war in 1917, on the side of Britain and France, had ended its last full-scale conflict, The Civil War, some fifty years previously. In the interval, the country's industrial power had grown immensely. So had its major cities, swelled on the Eastern seaboard by immigrants increasingly from southern and eastern Europe, and on the West Coast, from Asia. In 1914 the country's network of transcontinental railroads linked its productive farms, small towns, and industry to urban centers. Henry Ford had begun the transformation of the automobile from an exotic luxury technology into a consumer good with the 1908 introduction of the Model T, and in 1912 an American entrepreneur had dreamed up the first transcontinental highway. Aviation pioneers were rapidly building upon the Wright brothers' first successful powered airplane flights of 1903. Like the Civil War, World War I would mobilize the country's industries and technologies, spur their development, and uproot both soldiers and civilians. On an even larger scale, World War II would do the same.

These events were momentous in themselves and as harbingers of transformations to come. At the end of World War I, however, the United States was still in the main a nation of farmers and small towns, with about two-thirds of its population living in rural districts or towns of fewer than 25,000 inhabitants. Although several waves of immigration had altered the makeup of the population, the majority of Americans

Night Hawks, (detail), Edward Hopper, 1942. For more information about this painting, see the color insert in this volume.

NAACP—Silent March, 1917. On July 28, 1917, under the leadership of the National Association for the Advancement of Colored People, some ten thousand African Americans marched down New York City's Fifth Avenue to protest the race riots of that summer in East Saint Louis, during which an estimated one hundred black citizens were lynched and thousands of others left homeless.

were still of English or German ancestry and about one American in ten was of African descent. The majority was deeply distrustful of international politics, and after the war ended, many attempted to steer the nation back to prewar modes of life. In 1924 Congress enacted a sweeping exclusionary immigration act, extending the reach of previous restrictions. The act prohibited all Asian immigration and set quotas for other countries on the basis of their existing U.S. immigrant populations, intending thereby to control the ethnic makeup of the United States (and the proportion of Americans born outside the United States did decline markedly from 1910 to 1940). The immediate postwar years also saw the so-called Red scare, when labor union headquarters were raided and immigrant radicals deported by a government fearful of the influence of the newly Communist Soviet Union (formerly tsarist Russia).

For other Americans, however, the war helped accelerate long-sought changes in the forms of political and social life. The long struggle to win American women the vote—given a final push by women's work as nurses and ambulance drivers during the war—ended in 1920 with the passage of the Nineteenth Amendment to the Constitution. The National Association for the Advancement of Colored People (NAACP), founded in 1909, successfully argued during World War I for the commissioning of black officers in the U.S. armed forces; as they would after World War II, African Americans who fought abroad returned to fight for their rights at home. Despite the government's restrictions on leftist political activity, many Americans—

Suffragettes Picket the White House, 1917. Members of the National Woman's Party regularly demonstrated in front of the White House during Woodrow Wilson's administration. After the U.S. entry into World War I heightened concerns for domestic order, prosuffrage picketers were arrested and jailed.

among them writers and intellectuals as well as labor activists and urban immigrants—looked to the Soviet Union and the international Communist movement for a model in combating inequality and fostering workers' rights in the United States. Other Americans went abroad, for shorter or longer stretches of time, in order to taste the expatriate life (made cheaper in war-ravaged economies by the solid American dollar) in Europe's battered but still vibrant cities and countryside. Some Americans traveled physical and social distances almost as great within the boundaries of the United States, as African Americans began to migrate in large numbers out of the segregated South and young people everywhere increasingly attended college away from home and moved to the cities. African Americans, emancipated urban women, and the restless young faced off against rural and urban traditionalists over the question of who, exactly, was truly "American."

These conflicts over the shape of the future acquired new urgency when the stock market crashed in 1929 and led to an economic depression with a 25 percent unemployment rate—a percentage even larger in its impact, by present-day standards, because women in general were not in the workforce. Known as the Great Depression, this period of economic hardship did not fully end until the United States entered World War II, following the Japanese attack on the American fleet at Pearl Harbor on December 7, 1941. Japan's ally Germany also declared war on the United States, thus involving the country in another European conflict. The war unified the country politically; revitalized industry, which devoted itself to goods needed for the war effort;

and put people to work, including women who went into the labor force in unprecedented numbers. Germany surrendered in the spring of 1945. The war ended in August 1945 following the detonation of two atomic bombs over the Japanese cities of Hiroshima and Nagasaki. Europe was in ruins and the United States had become the world's major industrial and political power.

The two wars, then, bracket a period during which the United States became a fully modern nation. The country's internal fractures can be understood as diverse responses to the irreversible advent of modernity. American literature in these decades registers all sides of the era's struggles and debates, while sharing a commitment to explore the many meanings of modernity. Some writers rejoiced while others lamented; some anticipated future utopias and others believed that civilization had collapsed; but the period's most influential voices believed that old forms would not work for new times, and were inspired by the possibility of creating something entirely new.

Among literary conflicts, three issues stand out, all of them related to the accelerating transformations and conflicts of modernity. One conflict centered on the uses of literary tradition. To some, a work registering its allegiance to literary history—through allusion to canonical works of the past, or by using traditional poetic forms and poetic language—seemed imitative and old-fashioned. To others, a work failing to honor literary tradition was bad or incompetent writing. For still others, literary history was best appreciated oppositionally: modernist works often allude to previous literature ironically, or deliberately fracture traditional literary formulas. A related conflict involved the place of popular culture in serious literature. Throughout the era, popular culture gained momentum and influence. Some writers regarded it as crucial for the future of literature that popular forms, such as film and jazz, be embraced; to others, serious literature by definition had to reject what they saw as the cynical commercialism of popular culture.

Another issue was the question of how far literature should engage itself in political and social struggle. Should art be a domain unto itself, exploring aesthetic questions and enunciating transcendent truths, or should art participate in the politics of the times? For some, a work that was political in aim counted as propaganda, not art; others thought that apolitical literature was evasive and irresponsible; some viewed the call to keep art out of politics as covertly political, a conservative mandate to preserve the status quo, even if it did not acknowledge itself as such.

CHANGING TIMES

The transformations of the first half of the twentieth century were driven both by ideas and by changes in the economic and technological underpinnings of daily life. Much social energy in the 1920s went into enlarging the boundaries for acceptable self-expression. Adherents to small-town values such as the work ethic, social conformity, duty, and respectability clashed ideologically not only with internationally minded radicals but also with newly affluent young people who argued for more diverse, permissive, and tolerant styles of life. To some extent this debate recapitulated the long-time American conflict between the claims of the individual and those of society, a conflict going back to the seventeenth-century religious conflicts over autonomy of conscience and epitomized in Ralph Waldo Emerson's call, in the 1840s: "whosoever would be a man, must be a non-conformist."

The 1920s saw significant changes in sexual mores, as was to be expected when young people were no longer under the watchful eyes of their small-town elders. These social changes found their most influential theorist in the Austrian psychiatrist Sigmund Freud (1858–1939), inventor of the practice of psychoanalysis. According to Freud, many modern neuroses could be traced to repression and inhibition. Freud developed the idea of the self as grounded in an "unconscious," where forbidden desires, traumas, and unacceptable emotions—most of these sexual in nature and derived from childhood experiences—were stored. Freudian analysis aimed at helping people become aware of their repressed feelings, and so less likely to re-enact the traumas of the past in the present. The popular American version of psychoanalysis—more utopian than Freud's cautious claim that individuals could learn to cope with their own personalities more effectively—held that emotional wholeness could be swiftly attained if people recognized and overcame their inhibitions. Americanized Freudian ideas provided the psychological under-pinning for much literature of the interwar era, whether the focus was the individual trapped in a repressive culture or the repressive culture itself.

The middle-class double sexual standard had, in fact, always granted considerable sexual freedom to men; now, however, women—enfranchised and liberated by automobiles and job possibilities away from home—began to demand similar freedom for themselves. Women's demands went well beyond the erotic, however, encompassing education, professional work, mobility, and whatever else seemed like social goods hitherto reserved for men. Female dress changed; long, heavy, restricting garments gave way to short, lightweight, easily worn store-bought clothing. The combination of expanding urban life with new psychologies oriented to self-expression also brought into being new social possibilities for women and men whose sexual desires did not conform to traditional patterns. Freud was only one of a number of thinkers in the period who urged a measure of toleration for sexual minorities, especially homosexuals—a term that entered specialized English usage in the 1890s and came into wider circulation in the years following World War I. Although the legal risks and social stigma born by homosexuals remained very much in force, gay enclaves became more visible in American life and gay lives became more imaginable as a theme in American literature.

African Americans, like women, became mobile in these years as never before. Around 1915, as a direct result of the industrial needs of World War I, opportunities opened for African Americans in the factories of the North, and what became known as the Great Migration out of the South began. Not only did migration give the lie to southern white claims that African Americans were content with southern segregationist practices, it damaged the South's economy by draining off an important segment of its working people. Even though African Americans faced racism, segregation, and racial violence in the North, a black American presence soon became powerfully visible in American cultural life. Harlem, a section of New York City, attained an almost wholly black population of over 150,000 by the mid-1920s; from this "city within a city," African Americans wrote, performed, composed, and painted. Here as well they founded two major journals of opinion and culture, *The Crisis* (in 1910) and *Opportunity* (in 1923). This work

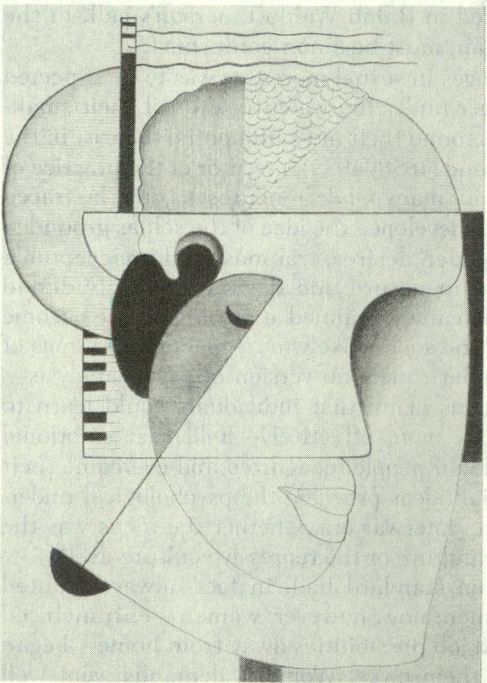

Lenox Avenue, Sargent Claude Johnson, 1938. Johnson's lithograph pays tribute to the clubs, ballrooms, and bars of New York City's Lenox Avenue, hub of the Harlem Renaissance. During the Great Depression, the Federal Art Project enlisted many notable artists to create graphic works celebrating American cultural and natural landmarks.

influenced writers, painters, and musicians of other ethnicities, and became known collectively as the Harlem Renaissance.

The famous black intellectual W. E. B. Du Bois had argued in *The Souls of Black Folk* (1903) that African Americans had a kind of double consciousness—of themselves as Americans and as blacks. This doubleness contributed to debates within African American cultural life. The Harlem Renaissance sparked arguments between those who wanted to claim membership in the culture at large and those who wanted to stake out a separate artistic domain; between those who wanted to celebrate rural African American lifeways and those committed to urban intellectuality; between those who wanted to join the American mainstream and those who, disgusted by American race prejudice, aligned themselves with worldwide revolutionary movements; between those who celebrated a "primitive" African heritage and those who rejected the idea as a degrading stereotype. African American women, as Nella Larsen's novel *Quicksand* testifies, could experience these divisions with special force. Women were very much called upon in efforts to "uplift," advance, and educate the black community, but these communal obligations could be felt as constraints upon individual freedom and exploration; meanwhile the white social world, given to exoticizing or sexualizing black women, offered few alternatives.

Class inequality, as well as American racial divisions, continued to generate intellectual and artistic debate in the interwar years. The nineteenth-century United States had been host to many radical movements—labor activism, utopianism, socialism, anarchism—inspired by diverse sources. In the twentieth century, especially following the rise of the Soviet Union, the American left increasingly drew its intellectual and political program from the Marxist tradition. The German philosopher Karl Marx (1818–1883) located the roots of human behavior in economics. He claimed that industrializing societies were structurally divided into two antagonistic classes based on different relations to the means of production—capital versus labor. The Industrial Revolution arose from the accumulation of surplus capital by industrialists paying the least possible amount to workers; the next stage in world history would be when workers took control of the means of production for themselves. Because, to Marx, the ideas and ideals of any particular society could represent the interests of only its dominant class, he derided individualism as a middle-class or "bourgeois" value that could only discourage worker solidarity.

Marx's ideas formed the basis for communist political parties across Europe. In 1917, a Communist revolution in Russia led by Vladimir Ilyich Lenin (1870–1914) overthrew the tsarist regime, instituted the "dictatorship of the proletariat" that Marx had called for, and engineered the development of Communism as a unified international movement. Americans who thought of themselves as Marxists in the 1920s and 1930s were usually connected with the Communist party and subjected to government surveillance and occasional violence, as were socialists, anarchists, union organizers, and others who opposed American free enterprise and marketplace competition. Although politics directed from outside the national boundaries was, almost by definition, "un-American," many adherents of these movements hoped to make the United States conform to its stated ideals, guaranteeing liberty and justice for all.

A defining conflict between American ideals and American realities for writers of the 1920s was the Sacco-Vanzetti case. Nicola Sacco and Bartolomeo Vanzetti were Italian immigrants, not Communists but avowed anarchists; on April 15, 1920, they were arrested near Boston after a murder during a robbery. They were accused of that crime, then tried and condemned to death in 1921; but it was widely believed that they had not received a fair trial and that their political beliefs had been held against them. After a number of appeals, they were executed in 1927, maintaining their innocence to the end. John Dos Passos and Katherine Anne Porter were among the many writers and intellectuals who demonstrated in their defense; several were arrested and jailed. It is estimated that well over a hundred poems (including works by William Carlos Williams, Edna St. Vincent Millay, and Carl Sandburg) along with six plays and eight novels of the time treated the incident from a sympathetic perspective.

Like the Sacco-Vanzetti case in the 1920s, the Scottsboro case in the 1930s brought many American writers and intellectuals, black and white, together in a cause—here, the struggle against racial bias in the justice system. In 1931 nine black youths were indicted in Scottsboro, Alabama, for the alleged rape of two white women in a railroad freight car. They were all found guilty, and some were sentenced to death. The U.S. Supreme Court reversed convictions twice; in a second trial one of the alleged victims retracted her testimony; in 1937 charges against five were dropped. But four went to jail, in many people's view unfairly. American Communists were especially active in the Scottsboro defense; but people across the political spectrum saw the case as crucial to the question of whether black people could receive fair trials in the American South. The unfair trial of an African American man became a literary motif in much writing of the period and beyond, including Richard Wright's *Native Son*, William Faulkner's *Intruder in the Dust*, and Harper Lee's *To Kill a Mockingbird*.

SCIENCE AND TECHNOLOGY

Technology played a vital, although often invisible, role in all these events, because it linked places and spaces, contributing to the shaping of culture as a national phenomenon rather than a series of local manifestations. Without new modes of production, transportation, and communication, modern America in all its complexity could not have existed. Electricity for lights and appliances, along with the telephone—nineteenth-century inventions— expanded into American homes during these years, improving life for many but widening the gap between those plugged into the new networks and those outside them. The phonograph record and the record player (early devices for recording and playing music), the motion picture (which acquired sound in 1929), and the radio brought mass popular culture into being. Although the nineteenth-century dream of forging a scattered population into a single nation could now be realized more instantaneously and directly than was ever possible with print media, many intellectuals suspected that mass culture would create a robotic, passive population vulnerable to demagoguery.

The most powerful technological innovation, however, the automobile, encouraged activity not passivity. Automobiles put Americans on the road, dramatically reshaped the structure of American industry and occupations, and altered the national topography as well. Along with work in automobile factories themselves, millions of other jobs—in steel mills, parts factories, highway construction and maintenance, gas stations, machine shops, roadside restaurants, motels—depended on the industry. The road itself became—and has remained—a key powerful symbol of the United States and of modernity as well. Cities grew, suburbs came into being, small towns died, new towns arose, according to the placement of highways, which rapidly supplanted the railroad in shaping the patterns of twentieth-century American urban expansion. The United States had become a nation of migrants as much as or more than it was a nation of immigrants.

In tandem with the impact of technological change on daily life, one of the most important developments in the interwar period was the growth of modern "big" science. At the end of the nineteenth century and beginning of the twentieth, scientists discovered that the atom was not the smallest possible unit of matter, that matter was not indestructible, that both time and space were relative to an observer's position, that some phenomena were so small that attempts at measurement would alter them, that some outcomes could be predicted only in terms of statistical probability, that the universe might be infinite in size and yet infinitely expanding; much of the commonsense basis of nineteenth-century science had to be put aside in favor of far more powerful but also far less commonsensical theories. Among many results, scientists and literary intellectuals became less able to communicate with each other and their worldviews became polarized. Writers responded with ambivalence to the new science, sometimes drawing on scientific images and ideas—"the imagination uses the phraseology of science," wrote the poet (and physician) William Carlos Williams—sometimes deploring the loss of authority for traditional, humanistic explanations of the concrete, experienced world and felt human life. Gertrude Stein's radical literary experiments were partly inspired by her laboratory experiences in neuroanatomy at Harvard University and the Johns Hopkins Medical School. Poets like Ezra

Pound, T. S. Eliot, and Wallace Stevens, however, along with many of their readers, questioned the capacity of science to provide accounts of subjective experience and moral issues and elevated the metaphorical language of poetry over the supposed literal accuracy of scientific description. The increased specialization of intellectual activity divided educated people into what the British novelist and physicist C. P. Snow was later to call the "two cultures"—science versus letters.

THE 1930s

The Great Depression was a worldwide phenomenon and fostered social unrest that led to the rise of fascist dictatorships in Europe, including those of Generalissimo Francisco Franco in Spain, Benito Mussolini in Italy, and Adolf Hitler in Germany. Hitler's program, which was to make Germany rich and strong by

The Bread Line, New York, Clare Leighton, 1932. Leighton, who was born in England and became a U.S. citizen in 1939, made her reputation as an illustrator of rural life and work. This wood engraving's line of idled men dwarfed by their urban surroundings represents Depression-era New York City as the dark antithesis of her traditional subjects.

conquering the rest of Europe, led inexorably to World War II.

In the United States, the Depression made politics and economics the salient issues of public life and overrode questions of individual freedom with fear of mass collapse. Free-enterprise capitalism had always justified itself by arguing that although the system made a small number of individuals immensely wealthy it also guaranteed better lives for all. This assurance now rang hollow. The suicides of millionaire bankers and stockbrokers made the headlines, but more compelling was the enormous toll among ordinary people who lost homes, jobs, farms, and life savings in the stock market crash. Conservatives advised waiting until things got better; radicals espoused immediate social revolution. In this polarized atmosphere, the election of Franklin Delano Roosevelt to the presidency in 1932 was a victory for American pragmatism; his series of liberal reforms—social security, acts creating jobs in the public sector, welfare, and unemployment insurance—cushioned the worst effects of the Depression and avoided the civil strife that many had thought inevitable.

The terrible economic situation in the United States produced a significant increase in Communist party membership and prestige in the 1930s.

Towards Los Angeles, 1937, Dorothea Lange. During the Great Depression, the Farm Security Administration—one of many new government agencies created in response to the economic emergency—employed a number of well-known documentary photographers. Dorothea Lange produced memorable portraits of migrants displaced by the Dust Bowl under the FSA's sponsorship.

Numerous intellectuals allied themselves with its causes, even if they did not become party members. An old radical journal, *The Masses,* later *The New Masses,* became the official literary voice of the party, and various other radical groups founded journals to represent their viewpoints. Visitors to the Soviet Union returned with glowing reports about a true workers' democracy and prosperity for all. The appeal of Communism was significantly enhanced by its claim to be an opponent of fascism. Communists fought against Franco in the Spanish Civil War of 1936 and 1937. Hitler's nightmare policies of genocide and racial superiority and his plans for a general European war to secure more room for the superior German "folk" to live became increasingly evident as European refugees began to flee to the United States in the 1930s, and many believed that the USSR would be the only country able to withstand the German war machine. But Soviet

Communism showed another side to Americans when American Communists were ordered to break up the meetings of other radical groups; when Josef Stalin, the Soviet dictator, instituted a series of brutal purges in the Soviet Union beginning in 1936; and when in 1939 he signed a pact promising not to go to war against Germany. The disillusionment and betrayal felt by many radicals over these acts led many 1930s left-wing activists to become staunch anti-Communists after World War II.

AMERICAN VERSIONS OF MODERNISM

In most English language literary contexts, "modernism" is a catchall term for any kind of literary production in the interwar period that deals with the modern world. More narrowly, it refers to work that represents the transformation of traditional society under the pressures of modernity, and that breaks down traditional literary forms in doing so. Much modernist literature of this sort, which critics increasingly now set apart as "high modernism," is in a sense antimodern: it interprets modernity as an experience of loss. As its title underlines, T. S. Eliot's *The Waste Land*—the great poem of high modernism—represents the modern world as a scene of ruin.

Scholars of international modernism frequently trace its rise back to the later nineteenth century, citing the works of French Symbolists in literature, Friedrich Nietzsche in philosophy, and Charles Darwin in science as example of radically antitraditional modes of thought and artistic practice. As an artistic movement, however, modernism reached a defining level of international coherence and momentum in response to the effects of World War I, which were far more devastating on the Continent than they were in the United States. It involved other art forms—sculpture, painting, dance—as well as literature. The poetry of William Butler Yeats; James Joyce's *Ulysses* (1922); Marcel Proust's *Remembrance of Things Past* (1913–27); Thomas Mann's novels and short stories, including *The Magic Mountain* (1927)— these were only a few of the literary products of this movement in England and on the Continent. In painting, artists like Pablo Picasso, Juan Gris, and Georges Braque invented cubism; in the 1920s the surrealistic movement known as dadaism emerged. The American public was introduced to modern art at the famous New York Armory Show of 1913, which featured cubist paintings and caused an uproar. Marcel Duchamp's *Nude Descending a Staircase*, which, to the untrained eye, looked like a mass of crudely drawn rectangles, was especially provocative. Composers like Igor Stravinsky similarly produced music in a "modern" mode, featuring dissonance and discontinuity rather than neat formal structure and appealing tonal harmonies. His composition *The Rite of Spring* (1913) provoked a riot in the Paris concert hall where it was premiered.

At the heart of the high modernist aesthetic lay the conviction that the previously sustaining structures of human life, whether social, political, religious, or artistic, had been destroyed or shown up as falsehoods or, at best, arbitrary and fragile human constructions. Order, sequence, and unity in works of art might well express human desires for coherence rather than reliable intuitions of reality. Generalization, abstraction, and high-flown writing might conceal rather than convey the real. The form of a story, with its beginnings, complications, and resolutions, might be an artifice imposed on the flux and fragmentation of experience. To the extent that art falsely presented such an order as given or natural, it had to be renovated.

Thus a key formal characteristic typical of high modernist works, whether in painting, sculpture, or musical composition, is its construction out of fragments—fragments of myth or history, fragments of experience or perception, fragments of previous artistic works. Modernist literature is often notable for what it omits: the explanations, interpretations, connections, summaries, and distancing that provide continuity, perspective, and security in earlier literatures. A typical modernist work may seem to begin arbitrarily, to advance without explanation, and to end without resolution, consisting of vivid segments juxtaposed without cushioning or integrating transitions. There may be shifts in perspective, voice, and tone. Its rhetoric may be understated, ironic. It may suggest rather than assert, making use of symbols and images instead of statements. Its elements may be drawn from disparate areas of experience. The effect may be shocking and unsettling; the experience of reading will be challenging and difficult. Faced with intuiting connections left unstated, the reader of a modernist work is often said to participate in the creative work of making the poem or story.

Some high modernist works, however, order their discontinuous elements into conspicuous larger patterns, patterns often drawn from world literature, mythologies, and religions. As its title advertises, Joyce's *Ulysses* maps the lives of its modern characters onto Homer's *Odyssey*; Eliot's *The Waste Land* layers the Christian narrative of death and resurrection over a broad range of quest myths. The question for readers lies in the meaning of these borrowed structures and mythic parallels: do they reveal profound similarities or ironic contrasts between the modern world and earlier times? For some writers and readers, the adaptability of ancient stories to modern circumstances testified to their deep truth, underlying the surface buzz and confusion of modernity; for others, such parallels indicated Christianity to *be* only a myth, one of many human constructions aimed at creating order out of, and finding purpose in, history's flux.

If meaning is a human construction, then meaning cannot be separated from the difficult process of its making; if meaning lies obscured deep underneath the ruins of modern life, then it must be effortfully sought out. Modernist literature therefore tended to foreground the search for meaning over didactic statement, and the subject matter of modernist writing often became, by extension, the poem or literary work itself. While there have long been paintings about painting and poems about poetry, high modernist writing was especially self-reflexive, concerned with its own nature as art and with its questioning of previous traditions of literature. Ironically—because this subject matter was motivated by deep concern about the interrelation of literature and life—this subject often had the effect of limiting the audience for a modernist work; high modernism demanded of its ideal readers an encyclopedic knowledge of the traditions it fragmented or ironized. Nevertheless, over time, the principles of modernism became increasingly influential.

Modernist techniques transformed fiction as well as poetry in this period. Prose writers strove for directness, compression, and vividness. They were often sparing of words. The average novel became quite a bit shorter than it had been in the nineteenth century, when a novel was expected to fill two or even three volumes. The modernist aesthetic gave a new significance to the short story, which had previously been thought of as a relatively slight artistic form. (Poems, too, became shorter, as narrative poems lost ground to lyrics and the repetitive patterns of rhyme and meter that had helped sustain long poems in previous centuries lost ground to free verse.) Victorian or realistic fiction achieved its effects by accumulation and saturation; modern fiction preferred suggestion. Victorian fiction often featured an authoritative narrator; modern fiction tended to be written in the first person or to limit the reader to one character's point of view on the action. This limitation accorded with the modernist sense that "truth" does not exist objectively but is the product of the mind's interaction with reality. The selected point of view is often that of a naïve or marginal person—a child or an outsider—to convey better the reality of confusion and dissent rather than the myth of certainty and consensus.

In both poetry and fiction, modernists tended to emphasize the concrete sensory image or detail over general statement. Allusions to literary, historical, philosophical, or religious details of the past often keep company, in modernist works, with vignettes of contemporary life, chunks of popular culture, dream imagery, and symbolism drawn from the author's private repertory of life experiences. A work built from these various materials may move across time and space, shift from the public to the personal, and open literature as a field for every sort of concern. The inclusion of material previously deemed "unliterary" in works of high seriousness extended to language that might previously have been thought improper, including representations of the speech of the uneducated and the inarticulate, the colloquial, slangy, and the popular. Traditional realistic fiction had incorporated colloquial and dialect speech, often to comic effect, in its representation of the broad tapestry of social life; but such speakers were usually framed by a narrator's educated literary voice, conveying truth and authority over subordinate voices. In modernist writing like William Faulkner's *As I Lay Dying*, these voices assume the full burden of the narrative's authority; this is what Ernest Hemingway had in mind when he asserted that the American literary tradition began with *Huckleberry Finn*.

"Serious" literature between the two world wars thus found itself in a curious relationship with the culture at large. If it attacked the old-style ideals of polite literature, it felt itself attacked in turn by the ever-growing industry of popular literature. The reading audience in America was vast, but it preferred a kind of book quite different from that turned out by literary high modernists: tales of romance or adventure, historical novels, crime fiction, and westerns became popular modes enjoying a success that most serious writers could only dream of. The problem was that often they *did* dream of it; unrealistically, perhaps, the Ezra Pounds of the era imagined themselves with an audience of millions. When, on occasion, this dream came true—as it did for F. Scott Fitzgerald and Ernest Hemingway—writers often accused themselves of having sold out.

Serious writers in these years were, in fact, being published and read as writers had not been in earlier times. The number of so-called little magazines—that is, magazines of very small circulations devoted to the publication of works for a small audience (sometimes the works of a specific group of authors)—was in the hundreds. *Poetry: A Magazine of Verse* began in 1912. The *Little Review* followed in 1914. Then came the *Seven Arts* in 1916, the *Dial* in 1917, the *Frontier* in 1920, *Reviewer* and *Broom* in 1921, *Fugitive* in 1922, *This Quarter* in 1925, *Transition* and *Hound and Horn* in

Broom Magazine Cover, Enrico Prampolini, 1922. *Broom* was among the most internationally ambitious of modernism's little magazines, publishing authors such as Gertrude Stein, Wallace Stevens, and Jean Toomer alongside work by artists like Man Ray and Picasso. This cover complemented an essay by Harold Loeb, *Broom's* editor, that celebrated the modernist beauty of engines, motors, and airplanes.

1927, and many more. The culture that did not listen to serious writers or make them rich still gave them plenty of opportunity to be read and allowed them (in such neighborhoods as Greenwich Village in New York City) a freedom in lifestyle that was new in American history. In addition, such major publishers as New Directions, Random House, Scribner, and Harper were actively looking for serious fiction and poetry to feature alongside bestsellers like *Gone with the Wind* and *Anthony Adverse.*

Some writers in the period were able to use these opportunities to cross over the hierarchies separating high modernism from middlebrow and popular culture. Pietro di Donato's ambitiously modernist fiction about Italian immigrants in New York was published in the popular magazine *Esquire* and picked up by the Book of the Month Club. Where writers like William Faulkner and F. Scott Fitzgerald experienced Hollywood as a graveyard of serious literary ambition, Katherine Anne Porter found in the film industry not only financial rewards but also a springboard to wider critical and popular appreciation for her work as a whole.

MODERNISM ABROAD AND ON NATIVE GROUNDS

The profession of authorship in the United States has always defined itself in part as a patriotic enterprise aimed at developing a cultural life for the nation and embodying national values. High modernism, however, was a self-consciously international movement, and the leading American exponents of high modernism tended to be permanent expatriates like Gertrude Stein, Ezra Pound, H.D., and T. S. Eliot. These writers left the United States because they found the country lacking in a tradition of high culture and indifferent, if not actively hostile, to artistic achievement. They also believed that a national culture could never be more than parochial. In London in the first two decades of the twentieth century and in Paris during the 1920s, they found a vibrant community of dedicated artists and a society that respected them and allowed them a great deal of personal freedom. Yet they seldom thought of themselves as deserting their nation, and only Eliot gave up American citizenship (sometimes, too, the traffic went in the other direction, as when the British-born poet Mina Loy became an American citizen). They thought of themselves as bringing the United States into the larger context of European culture. The ranks of these permanent expatriates were swelled by American writers who lived abroad for some part of the period, among them Ernest Hemingway, Sherwood Anderson, F. Scott Fitzgerald, Claude McKay, Katherine Anne Porter, Nella Larsen, Robert Frost, and Eugene O'Neill.

Those writers who came back, however, and those who never left took seriously the task of integrating modernist ideas and methods with American subject matter. Not every experimental modernist writer disconnected literary ambitions from national belonging: Hart Crane, Marianne Moore, and William Carlos Williams, for example, all wanted to write overtly "American" works. Some writers—as the title of John Dos Passos's *U.S.A.* clearly shows—attempted to speak for the nation as a whole. Crane's long poem *The Bridge* and Williams's *Paterson* both take an American city as symbol and expand it to the nation, following the model established by Walt Whitman. F. Scott Fitzgerald's *The Great Gatsby* is similarly ambitious, and many writers addressed the whole nation in individual works—for example, E. E. Cummings's "next to of course god america i" and Claude McKay's "America." And a profoundly modern writer like William Faulkner cannot be extricated from his commitment to writing about his native South.

Like Faulkner, many writers of the period chose to identify themselves with the American scene and to root their work in a specific region, continuing a tradition of regionalist American writing that burgeoned in the years following the American Civil War. Their perspective on the regions was sometimes celebratory and sometimes critical. Carl Sandburg, Edgar Lee Masters, Sherwood Anderson, and Willa Cather worked with the Midwest; Cather grounded her later work in the Southwest; Black Elk's Lakota autobiography recalled the high plains of South Dakota and Wyoming; John Steinbeck wrote about California; Edwin Arlington Robinson and Robert Frost identified their work with New England. An especially strong center of regional literary activity emerged in the South, which had a weak literary tradition up to the Civil War. Thomas Wolfe's was an Appalachian South of hardy mountain people; Katherine Anne Porter wrote about her native Texas as a heterogeneous combination of frontier, plantation, and Hispanic cultures. Zora Neale Hurston drew on her childhood memories of the all-black town of Eatonville, Florida, for much of her best-known fiction, including her novel *Their Eyes Were Watching God*. William Faulkner depicted a South at once specific to his native state of Mississippi and expanded into a mythic region anguished by racial and historical conflict.

As the pairing of Hurston and Faulkner suggests, the history of race in the United States was central to the specifically national subject matter to which many American modernists remained committed. Although race as a subject potentially implicated all American writers, it was African Americans whose contributions most signally differentiated American modernism from that of Europe. The numerous writers associated with the Harlem Renaissance made it impossible ever to think of a national literature without the work of black Americans. Countee Cullen, Langston Hughes, and Zora Neale Hurston attained particular prominence at the time; but others, including Claude McKay and Nella Larsen, were also well known. All were influenced by the values of modernism: both Hughes, for example, with his incorporation of blues rhythms into poetry, and Hurston, with her poetic depictions of folk culture, applied modernist techniques to represent twentieth-century African American lives. Writers associated with the Renaissance expressed protest and anger—Hughes, in particular, wrote a number of powerful antilynching and anticapitalist poems; but the movement's writers also articulated the hopes of racial uplift and, like Hurston, focused on the vitality of black culture more than on the burdens of racism. At least part of this approach was strategic—the bulk of the readership for Harlem authors was white. The note of pure anger was not expressed until Richard Wright, who had come to literary maturity in Chicago, published *Native Son* in 1940. Contributions to the Harlem Renaissance came from artists in many media; an influence equal to or greater than that of the writers came from musicians. Jazz and blues, African American in origin, are felt by many to be the most authentically American art forms the nation has ever produced. African American singers and musicians in this period achieved worldwide reputations and were often much more highly regarded abroad than in the United States.

American literary women had been active on the national scene from Anne Bradstreet forward. Their increasing prominence in the nineteenth century generated a backlash from some male modernists, who asserted their own artistic seriousness by identifying women writers with the didactic, popular writing against which they rebelled. But women refused to stay on the sidelines and associated themselves with all the important literary trends of the era: H.D. and Amy Lowell with imagism, Marianne Moore and Mina Loy with high modernism; Willa Cather with mythic regionalism, Zora Neale Hurston and Nella Larsen with the Harlem Renaissance, Katherine Anne Porter with psychological fiction; Edna St. Vincent Millay with social and sexual liberation. Many of these writers concentrated on depictions of women characters or women's thoughts and experiences. Yet few labeled themselves feminists. The passage of the suffrage amendment in 1920 had taken some of the energy out of feminism that would not return until the 1960s. Some women writers found social causes like labor and racism more important than women's rights; others focused their energies on struggles less amenable to public, legal remedies, as when Mina Loy sought to represent motherhood as compatible with an energetic vision of female sexuality. Nevertheless, these literary women were clearly pushing back the boundaries of the permissible, demanding new cultural freedom for women. Equally important, they were operating as public figures and taking positions on public causes.

DRAMA

Drama in America was slow to develop as a self-conscious literary form. It was not until 1920 (the year of Eugene O'Neill's *Beyond the Horizon*) that the United States produced a world-class playwright. This is not to say that *theater*—productions and performances—was new to American life. After the American Revolution theaters—at first with itinerant English actors and companies, then with American—opened throughout the East; among early centers were Boston and Philadelphia as well as New York City. As the country expanded westward, so did its theater, together with other kinds of performance: burlesques, showboats on the Mississippi, minstrel shows, pantomimes. As the nineteenth century went on, the activity became centered more and more in New York—especially within the few blocks known as "Broadway." Managers originated plays there and then sent them out to tour through the rest of the country, as Eugene O'Neill's father did with his *Count of Monte Cristo.*

Innovations in American theater are often launched in reaction against Broadway, a pattern observable as early as 1915 with the formation of the Washington Square Players and the Provincetown Players (organized by Susan Glaspell and others), both located in New York's Greenwich Village and both dedicated to the production of plays that more conservative managers refused. The Provincetown Players produced the first works of Glaspell and Eugene O'Neill. These fledgling companies, and others like them, often knew better what they opposed than what they wanted. European influence was strong. By 1915, Henrik Ibsen in Europe and George Bernard Shaw in England had shown that the theater could be an arena for serious ideas; while the psychological dramas of August Strindberg, the symbolic work of Maurice Maeterlinck, and the sophisticated criticism of Arthur Schnitzler provided other models. The American tours of European companies, in particular the Moscow Art Theatre in 1923, further exposed Americans to the theatrical avant-garde. American playwrights in the 1920s and 1930s were united not so much by a common cause of ideas, European or American, as by the new assumption that drama should be a branch of contemporary literature rather than a stepchild of popular entertainments.

Just as his contemporaries in poetry and fiction were changing and questioning their forms, so Eugene O'Neill sought to refine his. He experimented less in language than in dramatic structure and in new production methods available through technology (e.g., lighting) or borrowed from the stylized realism of German expressionism. Almost as famous at the time was Maxwell Anderson, whose best plays—the tragic *Winterset* (1935) and the romantic comedy *High Tor* (1937)—embody a stylized blank verse, a language attempted by few modern dramatists. Playwrights such as Sidney Howard, Lillian Hellman, and Robert Sherwood wrote serious realistic plays. George Kaufman and his many collaborators, especially Moss Hart, invented a distinctively American form, the wisecracking domestic and social comedy, while S. N. Behrman and Philip Barry wrote higher comedies of ideas. The musical comedy was another distinctively American invention: beginning as an amalgam of jokes, songs, and dances, it progressed steadily toward an integration of its various elements, reaching new heights with the work of George and Ira Gershwin in the 1920s and 1930s and of Oscar Hammerstein in collaboration with Jerome Kern or Richard Rodgers from the 1920s on into the 1950s.

Social commentary and satire had been a thread in the bright weave of American drama since the early 1920s, beginning, perhaps, with Elmer Rice's fiercely expressionistic play about a rebellious nonentity, *The Adding Machine* (1923). During the Depression social criticism became a much

Eugene O'Neill and the Provincetown Players, 1916. O'Neill (on ladder) and members of the company preparing the stage for *Bound East for Cardiff*, O'Neill's first play produced by the Players, at the company's first New York City theater, on Macdougal Street in Greenwich Village.

more important dramatic theme, with political plays performed by many radical groups. Among the most significant was Clifford Odets's *Waiting for Lefty* (1935), which dramatized a taxidrivers' strike meeting and turned the stage into a platform for argument. Many poets and fiction writers of the interwar period wrote plays—among them Ernest Hemingway, E. E. Cummings, William Carlos Williams, William Faulkner, Edna St. Vincent Millay, Langston Hughes, T. S. Eliot, and John Steinbeck. It was in this period that drama moved decisively into the American literary mainstream.

1914–1945

TEXTS	CONTEXTS
1910 Edwin Arlington Robinson, **"Miniver Cheevy"**	
1914 Robert Frost, **"Home Burial"** • Carl Sandburg, **"Chicago"**	1914–18 World War I
1915 Edgar Lee Masters, *Spoon River Anthology* • Ezra Pound begins *Cantos*	1915 Great Migration of African Americans from the rural South to northern industrial cities
1916 Susan Glaspell, *Trifles*	
	1917 United States declares war on Germany • revolution in Russia brings Communist party to power
1918 Willa Cather, *My Ántonia*	1918 Daylight Savings Time instituted to allow more daylight for war production
1919 Sherwood Anderson, **Winesburg, Ohio** • Amy Lowell, **"Madonna of the Evening Flowers"**	1919 Senate limits U.S. participation in League of Nations; does not ratify Versailles Treaty to end World War I
1920 Pound, "Hugh Selwyn Mauberley" • Edwin Arlington Robinson, **"Mr. Flood's Party"**	1920 18th Amendment prohibits the manufacture, sale, and transportation of alcoholic beverages • 19th Amendment gives women the vote
	1920–27 Sacco-Vanzetti trial
1921 T. S. Eliot, **The Waste Land** • Claude McKay, **"Africa, America"** • Marianne Moore, **"Poetry"** • Langston Hughes, **"The Negro Speaks of Rivers"**	
1922 Mina Loy, **"Brancusi's Golden Bird"**	1922 Fascism rises in Europe; Mussolini becomes dictator of Italy
1923 Wallace Stevens, **"Sunday Morning"** • Jean Toomer, *Cane*	
1924 H.D. (Hilda Doolittle), **"Helen"**	1924 Exclusionary immigration act bars Asians from the United States
1925 Countee Cullen, **"Heritage"** • Gertrude Stein, *The Making of Americans* • Alain Locke publishes *The New Negro*, leading anthology of the Harlem Renaissance	
1926 Hart Crane, *The Bridge*	
1927 Zora Neale Hurston, "The Eatonville Anthology"	1927 *The Jazz Singer*, first full-length "talkie," is released
1928 Nella Larsen, *Quicksand*	
	1929 Stock market crashes; Great Depression begins
1930 Katherine Anne Porter, **"Flowering Judas"**	1930 Sinclair Lewis is first American to win Nobel Prize for literature
1931 E. E. Cummings, **"i sing of Olaf glad and big"** • F. Scott Fitzgerald, **"Babylon Revisited"**	1931 Scottsboro trial

Boldface titles indicate works in the anthology.

TEXTS	CONTEXTS
1932 Black Elk and John G. Neihardt, *Black Elk Speaks* • Sterling A. Brown, "He Was a Man"	**1932** Franklin Delano Roosevelt's "New Deal" introduces social security, welfare, and unemployment insurance
	1933 Adolf Hitler's Nationalist Socialist (Nazi) party comes to power in Germany • 18th Amendment repealed
1934 William Carlos Williams, "**This Is Just to Say**"	**1934** Wheeler-Howard (Indian Reorganization) Act passed, ending Dawes era
1936 Ernest Hemingway, "**The Snows of Kilimanjaro**"	**1936** Hitler begins armed occupation of Europe
	1936–39 Spanish Civil War: U.S. volunteers among those fighting against General Franco, who becomes dictator of Spain
1937 Thomas Wolfe, "The Lost Boy" • Pietro di Donato, "Christ in Concrete"	**1937** Stalin's purges
1938 John Dos Passos, *U.S.A.* • William Faulkner, "**Barn Burning**"	
1939 Richard Wright, "**The Man Who Was Almost a Man**"	**1939–45** World War II • the Holocaust
1940 Eugene O'Neill, *Long Day's Journey into Night*	
	1941 Japan bombs Pearl Harbor, Hawaii • United States enters war against Japan and its allies, Germany and Italy
1942 Wallace Stevens, "**Of Modern Poetry**"	**1942** President Roosevelt orders internment of Japanese Americans in camps
1944 H.D. (Hilda Doolittle), *The Walls Do Not Fall* • Marianne Moore, "**In Distrust of Merits**"	**1944** D Day; Allied invasion of Normandy
	1945 German forces surrender in spring; Japan surrenders in August following explosion of two nuclear bombs over Japanese cities

EDWIN ARLINGTON ROBINSON
1869–1935

L ike his own Miniver Cheevy, Edwin Arlington Robinson felt himself born too late. He turned to poetry in search of an alternative world of elegance and beauty, but wrote his best poems about wasted, blighted, or impoverished lives. His brief story and portrait poems are in traditional form with metrically regular verse, rhymes, and elevated diction. Such techniques dignify the subject matter and also provide a contrast, where his subject is unpoetic according to traditional standards, that emphasizes its sadness and banality.

Robinson was raised in Gardiner, Maine, the Tilbury Town of such poems as "Miniver Cheevy" and "Mr. Flood's Party." His father's lumber business and land speculations failed during the Great Panic of 1893. One of his brothers, a physician, became a drug addict; the other, a businessman, became an alcoholic. Robinson, by nature a scholar and book lover, was able to afford just two years at Harvard. Returning to Gardiner and trying to become a professional poet, he had to depend for support on friends and patrons, until a Pulitzer Prize in 1922 brought him some financial security. By this time he was over fifty.

Robinson studied alone and with friends long after his formal schooling ended. He read classic works in many languages as well as such American writers as Hawthorne, Whitman, Emerson, and Henry James, whom he interpreted as individualistic idealists. He was also drawn to the bleak, tragic vision of the British novelist Thomas Hardy. These influences were distilled in the gloomy, austere, yet sonorous verse of his second book, *Children of the Night* (1897—*The Torrent and the Night Before* had been published the previous year, at his own expense). Celebrating the pain of isolated lives, Robinson worked through to a residue of affirmation, an occasional "light" or "word" that is glimpsed in the "night" of these poems.

Robinson moved to New York City around the turn of the century. *The Town Down the River* (1910) and *The Man against the Sky* (1916) won increasing numbers of readers and critics' awards. *Avon's Harvest* and *Collected Poems* (both 1922) were successful, as was a trilogy of long poems in imitation of medieval narratives, beginning with *Merlin* (1917). The last of these, *Tristram* (1927), brought a third Pulitzer Prize. To some of the tougher-minded critics of the 1920s, the escapism of the later work (precisely what may have made it attractive to a larger audience), uncorrected by the somber wit and sustained irony of the Tilbury poems, seemed overly sentimental. The prizes and honors represented, to a large extent, their belated recognition of his earlier poetry.

Although in that earlier work Robinson was a New England regional poet like Robert Frost and a chronicler of small-town life like Edgar Lee Masters and Sherwood Anderson, he thought of himself as estranged both from his time and from the practices of other poets. The difference between him and these others lay in his ever-present sense of a lost, glorious past.

The text of the poems included here is that of *Collected Poems of Edwin Arlington Robinson* (1921, 1937).

Richard Cory

Whenever Richard Cory went down town,
We people on the pavement looked at him:
He was a gentleman from sole to crown,
Clean favored, and imperially slim.

And he was always quietly arrayed,   5
And he was always human when he talked;
But still he fluttered pulses when he said,
"Good-morning," and he glittered when he walked.

And he was rich—yes, richer than a king,—
And admirably schooled in every grace: 10
In fine, we thought that he was everything
To make us wish that we were in his place.

So on we worked, and waited for the light,
And went without the meat, and cursed the bread;
And Richard Cory, one calm summer night,   15
Went home and put a bullet through his head.

1896

Miniver Cheevy

Miniver Cheevy, child of scorn,
　Grew lean while he assailed the seasons;
He wept that he was ever born,
　And he had reasons.

Miniver loved the days of old   5
　When swords were bright and steeds were prancing;
The vision of a warrior bold
　Would set him dancing.

Miniver sighed for what was not,
　And dreamed, and rested from his labors;   10
He dreamed of Thebes and Camelot,
　And Priam's neighbors.[1]

Miniver mourned the ripe renown
　That made so many a name so fragrant;
He mourned Romance, now on the town,   15
　And Art, a vagrant.

1. The neighbors of King Priam in Homer's *Iliad* are his heroic compatriots in the doomed city of Troy. Thebes was an ancient city in Boeotia, rival of Athens and Sparta for supremacy in Greece and the setting of Sophocles' tragedies about Oedipus. Camelot is the legendary court of King Arthur and the knights of the Round Table.

Miniver loved the Medici,[2]
   Albeit he had never seen one;
He would have sinned incessantly
   Could he have been one.   20

Miniver cursed the commonplace
   And eyed a khaki suit with loathing;
He missed the mediæval grace
   Of iron clothing.

Miniver scorned the gold he sought,   25
   But sore annoyed was he without it;
Miniver thought, and thought, and thought,
   And thought about it.

Miniver Cheevy, born too late,
   Scratched his head and kept on thinking;   30
Miniver coughed, and called it fate,
   And kept on drinking.

                            1910

Mr. Flood's Party

Old Eben Flood, climbing alone one night
Over the hill between the town below
And the forsaken upland hermitage
That held as much as he should ever know
On earth again of home, paused warily.   5
The road was his with not a native near;
And Eben, having leisure, said aloud,
For no man else in Tilbury Town[1] to hear:

"Well, Mr. Flood, we have the harvest moon
Again, and we may not have many more;   10
The bird is on the wing, the poet says,[2]
And you and I have said it here before.
Drink to the bird." He raised up to the light
The jug that he had gone so far to fill,
And answered huskily: "Well, Mr. Flood,   15
Since you propose it, I believe I will."

Alone, as if enduring to the end
A valiant armor of scarred hopes outworn,
He stood there in the middle of the road

2. Family of wealthy merchants, politicians, churchmen, and art patrons in 16th-century Florence.
1. The fictive town in a number of Robinson's poems, modeled on Gardiner, Maine.
2. Flood paraphrases stanza 7 of the Persian

poem *The Rubáiyát of Omar Khayyám* in the 1859 translation by the English poet Edward FitzGerald (1809–1883): "Come, fill the Cup, and in the Fire of Spring / Your Winter-garment of Repentance fling: / The Bird of Time has but a little way / To flutter—and the Bird is on the Wing."

Like Roland's ghost winding a silent horn.[3]   20
Below him, in the town among the trees,
Where friends of other days had honored him,
A phantom salutation of the dead
Rang thinly till old Eben's eyes were dim.

Then, as a mother lays her sleeping child   25
Down tenderly, fearing it may awake,
He set the jug down slowly at his feet
With trembling care, knowing that most things break;
And only when assured that on firm earth
It stood, as the uncertain lives of men   30
Assuredly did not, he paced away,
And with his hand extended paused again:

"Well, Mr. Flood, we have not met like this
In a long time; and many a change has come
To both of us, I fear, since last it was   35
We had a drop together. Welcome home!"
Convivially returning with himself,
Again he raised the jug up to the light;
And with an acquiescent quaver said:
"Well, Mr. Flood, if you insist, I might.   40

"Only a very little, Mr. Flood—
For auld lang syne.[4] No more, sir; that will do."
So, for the time, apparently it did,
And Eben evidently thought so too;
For soon amid the silver loneliness   45
Of night he lifted up his voice and sang,
Secure, with only two moons listening,
Until the whole harmonious landscape rang—

"For auld lang syne." The weary throat gave out,
The last word wavered, and the song was done.   50
He raised again the jug regretfully
And shook his head, and was again alone.
There was not much that was ahead of him,
And there was nothing in the town below—
Where strangers would have shut the many doors   55
That many friends had opened long ago.

                                                      1921

---

3. Roland was King Charlemagne's nephew, celebrated in the *Chanson de Roland* (Song of Roland,
c. 1000). Just before dying in the battle of Ronce-
valles (778 c.e.), he sounded his horn for help.

4. Old long since (Scottish, literal trans.); hence
"the days of long ago," the title and refrain of a
famous song by the Scottish poet Robert Burns
(1759–1796).

WILLA CATHER
1873–1947

Willa Cather was born in Virginia, the oldest child of Charles and Mary Virginia Cather, who moved with their family to the Nebraska Divide when she was nine years old. After a year of farming, they relocated to the town of Red Cloud, and her father went into the real estate business. At sixteen, Cather moved on her own to Lincoln, the state capital and seat of the University of Nebraska; she attended preparatory school for one year and graduated from the university in 1895. In college she studied the classics and participated in the lively contemporary cultural life of the city by reviewing books, plays, and musical performances. Following graduation, she eked out a year as a journalist in Red Cloud and Lincoln before moving to Pittsburgh, Pennsylvania, to work as an editor of a women's magazine, the *Home Monthly*, a position she left five years later to teach high-school English and Latin. During this time she also wrote poems and stories, gathering poems into *April Twilights*, in 1903, and stories into *The Troll Garden*, in 1905. Also in Pittsburgh, in 1899, she met Isabelle McClung, from a prominent, wealthy family. She lived in the McClung home from 1901 to 1906, when she moved to New York City to write for the journal *McClure's*. Throughout her life, Cather remained devoted to McClung, experiencing her marriage in 1916 as a severe personal loss and being devastated by her death in 1938.

Having long wished to write novels, Cather took a leave of absence from *McClure's* in 1911, and wrote *Alexander's Bridge* (1912). This novel was successful, but it was the next three that made her reputation. Each focused on a western heroine: Alexandra Bergson in *O Pioneers!* (1913), Thea Kronborg in *The Song of the Lark* (1915), and Ántonia Shimerda in *My Ántonia* (1918). While Alexandra is extraordinary as the most successful farmer—the only woman farmer—on the Nebraska Divide, and Thea is extraordinary as a gifted opera singer, Ántonia has no unusual gifts; for Cather and the novel's many readers she stands for the entire experience of European settlement of the Great Plains. These three novels also manifest Cather's lyrical yet understated prose writing; they contain a wealth of detail about the lives of Nebraska settlers—Bohemian Czech, German, Danish, Swedish, Norwegian, French, Russian, and "Americans" from the East—as they learned to farm on the prairie and built communities in which their various ethnicities met and mingled. Cather's is no melting pot ethos, however; rather she sees the frontier as a shifting kaleidoscope of overlapping social groups and individuals. Recognizing that even by the second decade of the twentieth century this period in U.S. history had disappeared, Cather approached her characters with deep respect for what they had endured and accomplished.

Whether these novels (or any of Cather's other work) reflect a lesbian sensibility has been a matter of much critical debate. Her *Selected Letters* (2013), long withheld from publication, confirm that Cather's central emotional involvements in her life were with women; in 1908 she began to share an apartment with Edith Lewis, a Nebraskan whom she had met in 1903, and they lived together until Cather's death. (They lived mostly in New York City, but Cather also traveled a great deal: to Europe, to New England, to the Southwest, and back to Red Cloud to visit her family.) Estrangement from conventional sexuality and sex roles is typical of many of her main characters, male and female; but heterosexual romance and sexual behavior is equally present in her novels. It seems fair to say that close friendship, much more than romantic or sexual love, is the great ideal in her fiction.

Around 1922, according to Cather, the world broke in two; she suffered from the combined effects of poor health, dissatisfaction with the progress of her career, and

Illustration for *My Ántonia*, W. T. Benda. For the first edition of *My Ántonia*, Cather commissioned a set of drawings by Wladyslaw T. Benda, a Polish immigrant who was part of the New York City art scene. Known to Cather through his work for *McClure's*, Benda simplified his often dramatic visual style to match Cather's spare narration.

alarm at the increasing mechanization and mass-produced quality of American life. She joined the Episcopal Church, and her novels took a new direction. Although her books had always celebrated alternative values to the material and conventional, this theme became much more urgent, while the motif of heroic womanhood—which had led many to call her a feminist, though Cather herself kept aloof from all movements—receded. Important books from her "middle period" include *A Lost Lady* (1923) and *The Professor's House* (1925), which deal with spiritual and cultural crises in the lives of the main characters.

Published in 1927, the novel *Death Comes for the Archbishop* initiated another stage. Like many other writers and artists in the 1920s, Cather had become entranced with the American Southwest—especially New Mexico; her first trip to the region in 1912 figured in her depiction (in *The Song of the Lark*) of Thea Kronborg finding spiritual renewal in this landscape. *Death Comes for the Archbishop*, partly written at Mary Austin's home in Santa Fe, is based on the career of Jean Baptiste Lamy (1814–1888), archbishop of New Mexico, and the priest Joseph Marchebeuf, his close friend and collaborator. Another historical novel, *Shadows on the Rock* (1931) is set even further back in time, in seventeenth-century Quebec. In both books, a composite image of high French culture, ceremonial spirituality, and the American landscape contrasts with the material trivia and empty banality of contemporary life.

Inspired by the classical Latin works that she loved so much, Cather believed in the ideas of art and the artist and strove to attain an artistic height from which she might survey the entire human scene. She tried to imbue the particularities of her stories with what she thought of as universal significance. In *My Ántonia*, which continues to be the favorite novel for most Cather readers, Jim Burden reflects on the aspirations of the poet Virgil to bring the muse to his own country for the first time; by country, Virgil means "not a nation or even a province, but the little rural neighborhood" where he was born. This is clearly what is intended in *My Ántonia*; the idea of combining artistic transcendence with local, especially rural, specificity, speaks to Cather's own goals. It is a measure of her ambition that she thinks of her work in Virgilian terms, since Virgil was the greatest of the Latin poets. This aim was also Cather's in stories of Nebraska such as "Neighbour Rosicky." But a story like "The Sculptor's Funeral" shows her awareness that the neighborhood may not appreciate the artists who put it on the cultural map.

Politically, culturally, and aesthetically, Cather was in many respects deeply conservative as well as conflicted—a sophisticated populist, an agrarian urbanite. She believed in high art and superior people, but also thought great human gifts were more often found among the obscure and ordinary than among those with great advantages. Her vision of the United States seldom focused on Native Americans and African Americans; yet she preferred immigrants from Europe to migrants from the East Coast. She appreciated popular legends and folktales, which appear along with classical myth and allusion in her work. Her subtle experiments with formal structure include the retrospective narrative of *My Ántonia*, the embedded Southwestern story of Tom Outland in *The Professor's House*, and the seemingly unplotted, episodic chronicle form of *Death Comes for the Archbishop*. She once described her work as deliberately "unfurnished," meaning that it was cut down to only those details absolutely necessary; "suggestion rather than enumeration" was another way she described her goal. The resulting spareness and clarity of her fiction puts it in the modernist tradition.

The text of "The Sculptor's Funeral" is from *Youth and the Bright Medusa* (1920); that of "Neighbour Rosicky" is from *Obscure Destinies* (1932).

Neighbour Rosicky

I

When Doctor Burleigh told neighbour Rosicky he had a bad heart, Rosicky protested.

"So? No, I guess my heart was always pretty good. I got a little asthma, maybe. Just a awful short breath when I was pitchin' hay last summer, dat's all."

"Well, now, Rosicky, if you know more about it than I do, what did you come to me for? It's your heart that makes you short of breath, I tell you. You're sixty-five years old, and you've always worked hard, and your heart's tired. You've got to be careful from now on, and you can't do heavy work any more. You've got five boys at home to do it for you."

The old farmer looked up at the Doctor with a gleam of amusement in his queer triangular-shaped eyes. His eyes were large and lively, but the lids were caught up in the middle in a curious way, so that they formed a triangle. He did not look like a sick man. His brown face was creased but not wrinkled, he had a ruddy colour in his smooth-shaven cheeks and in his lips, under his long brown moustache. His hair was thin and ragged around his ears, but very little grey. His forehead, naturally high and crossed by deep parallel lines, now ran all the way up to his pointed crown. Rosicky's face had the habit of looking interested,—suggested a contented disposition and a reflective quality that was gay rather than grave. This gave him a certain detachment, the easy manner of an onlooker and observer.

"Well, I guess you ain't got no pills fur a bad heart, Doctor Ed. I guess the only thing is fur me to git me a new one."

Doctor Burleigh swung round in his desk-chair and frowned at the old farmer.

"I think if I were you I'd take a little care of the old one, Rosicky."

Rosicky shrugged. "Maybe I don't know how. I expect you mean fur me not to drink my coffee no more."

"I wouldn't, in your place. But you'll do as you choose about that. I've never yet been able to separate a Bohemian[1] from his coffee or his pipe. I've quit trying. But the sure thing is you've got to cut out farm work. You can feed the stock and do chores about the barn, but you can't do anything in the fields that makes you short of breath."

"How about shelling corn?"

1. Native of Bohemia, in the Czech Republic.

"Of course not!"

Rosicky considered with puckered brows.

"I can't make my heart go no longer'n it wants to, can I, Doctor Ed?"

"I think it's good for five or six years yet, maybe more, if you'll take the strain off it. Sit around the house and help Mary. If I had a good wife like yours, I'd want to stay around the house."

His patient chuckled. "It ain't no place fur a man. I don't like no old man hanging round the kitchen too much. An' my wife, she's a awful hard worker her own self."

"That's it; you can help her a little. My Lord, Rosicky, you are one of the few men I know who has a family he can get some comfort out of; happy dispositions, never quarrel among themselves, and they treat you right. I want to see you live a few years and enjoy them."

"Oh, they're good kids, all right," Rosicky assented.

The Doctor wrote him a prescription and asked him how his oldest son, Rudolph, who had married in the spring, was getting on. Rudolph had struck out for himself, on rented land. "And how's Polly? I was afraid Mary mightn't like an American daughter-in-law, but it seems to be working out all right."

"Yes, she's a fine girl. Dat widder woman bring her daughters up very nice. Polly got lots of spunk, an' she got some style, too. Da's nice, for young folks to have some style." Rosicky inclined his head gallantly. His voice and his twinkly smile were an affectionate compliment to his daughter-in-law.

"It looks like a storm, and you'd better be getting home before it comes. In town in the car?" Doctor Burleigh rose.

"No, I'm in de wagon. When you got five boys, you ain't got much chance to ride round in de Ford. I ain't much for cars, noway."

"Well, it's a good road out to your place; but I don't want you bumping around in a wagon much. And never again on a hay-rake, remember!"

Rosicky placed the Doctor's fee delicately behind the desk-telephone, looking the other way, as if this were an absent-minded gesture. He put on his plush cap and his corduroy jacket with a sheepskin collar, and went out.

The Doctor picked up his stethoscope and frowned at it as if he were seriously annoyed with the instrument. He wished it had been telling tales about some other man's heart, some old man who didn't look the Doctor in the eye so knowingly, or hold out such a warm brown hand when he said good-bye. Doctor Burleigh had been a poor boy in the country before he went away to medical school; he had known Rosicky almost ever since he could remember, and he had a deep affection for Mrs. Rosicky.

Only last winter he had had such a good breakfast at Rosicky's, and that when he needed it. He had been out all night on a long, hard confinement case at Tom Marshall's—a big rich farm where there was plenty of stock and plenty of feed and a great deal of expensive farm machinery of the newest model, and no comfort whatever. The woman had too many children and too much work, and she was no manager. When the baby was born at last, and handed over to the assisting neighbour woman, and the mother was properly attended to, Burleigh refused any breakfast in that slovenly house, and drove his buggy—the snow was too deep for a car—eight miles to Anton Rosicky's place. He didn't know another farm-house where a man could get such a warm welcome, and such good strong coffee with rich cream. No wonder the old chap didn't want to give up his coffee!

He had driven in just when the boys had come back from the barn and were washing up for breakfast. The long table, covered with a bright oilcloth, was set out with dishes waiting for them, and the warm kitchen was full of the smell of coffee and hot biscuit and sausage. Five big handsome boys, running from twenty to twelve, all with what Burleigh called natural good manners—they hadn't a bit of the painful self-consciousness he himself had to struggle with when he was a lad. One ran to put his horse away, another helped him off with his fur coat and hung it up, and Josephine, the youngest child and the only daughter, quickly set another place under her mother's direction.

With Mary, to feed creatures was the natural expression of affection—her chickens, the calves, her big hungry boys. It was a rare pleasure to feed a young man whom she seldom saw and of whom she was as proud as if he belonged to her. Some country housekeepers would have stopped to spread a white cloth over the oilcloth, to change the thick cups and plates for their best china, and the wooden-handled knives for plated ones. But not Mary.

"You must take us as you find us, Doctor Ed. I'd be glad to put out my good things for you if you was expected, but I'm glad to get you any way at all."

He knew she was glad—she threw back her head and spoke out as if she were announcing him to the whole prairie. Rosicky hadn't said anything at all; he merely smiled his twinkling smile, put some more coal on the fire, and went into his own room to pour the Doctor a little drink in a medicine glass. When they were all seated, he watched his wife's face from his end of the table and spoke to her in Czech. Then, with the instinct of politeness which seldom failed him, he turned to the doctor and said slyly: "I was just tellin' her not to ask you no questions about Mrs. Marshall till you eat some breakfast. My wife, she's terrible fur to ask questions."

The boys laughed, and so did Mary. She watched the Doctor devour her biscuit and sausage, too much excited to eat anything herself. She drank her coffee and sat taking in everything about her visitor. She had known him when he was a poor country boy, and was boastfully proud of his success, always saying: "What do people go to Omaha for, to see a doctor, when we got the best one in the State right here?" If Mary liked people at all, she felt physical pleasure in the sight of them, personal exultation in any good fortune that came to them. Burleigh didn't know many women like that, but he knew she was like that.

When his hunger was satisfied, he did, of course, have to tell them about Mrs. Marshall, and he noticed what a friendly interest the boys took in the matter.

Rudolph, the oldest one (he was still living at home then), said: "The last time I was over there, she was lifting them big heavy milk-cans, and I knew she oughtn't to be doing it."

"Yes, Rudolph told me about that when he come home, and I said it wasn't right," Mary put in warmly. "It was all right for me to do them things up to the last, for I was terrible strong, but that woman's weakly. And do you think she'll be able to nurse it, Ed?" She sometimes forgot to give him the title she was so proud of. "And to think of your being up all night and then not able to get a decent breakfast! I don't know what's the matter with such people."

"Why, Mother," said one of the boys, "if Doctor Ed had got breakfast there, we wouldn't have him here. So you ought to be glad."

"He knows I'm glad to have him, John, any time. But I'm sorry for that poor woman, how bad she'll feel the Doctor had to go away in the cold without his breakfast."

"I wish I had been in practice when these were getting born." The Doctor looked down the row of close-clipped heads. "I missed some good breakfasts by not being."

The boys began to laugh at their mother because she flushed so red, but she stood her ground and threw up her head. "I don't care, you wouldn't have got away from this house without breakfast. No doctor ever did. I'd have had something ready fixed that Anton could warm up for you."

The boys laughed harder than ever, and exclaimed at her: "I'll bet you would!" "She would, that!"

"Father, did you get breakfast for the Doctor when we were born?"

"Yes, and he used to bring me my breakfast, too, mighty nice. I was always awful hungry!" Mary admitted with a guilty laugh.

While the boys were getting the Doctor's horse, he went to the window to examine the house plants. "What do you do to your geraniums to keep them blooming all winter, Mary? I never pass this house that from the road I don't see your windows full of flowers."

She snapped off a dark red one, and a ruffled new green leaf, and put them in his buttonhole. "There, that looks better. You look too solemn for a young man, Ed. Why don't you git married? I'm worried about you. Settin' at breakfast, I looked at you real hard, and I seen you've got some grey hairs already."

"Oh, yes! They're coming. Maybe they'd come faster if I married."

"Don't talk so. You'll ruin your health eating at the hotel. I could send your wife a nice loaf of nut bread, if you only had one. I don't like to see a young man getting grey. I'll tell you something, Ed; you make some strong black tea and keep it handy in a bowl, and every morning just brush it into your hair, an' it'll keep the grey from showin' much. That's the way I do!"

Sometimes the Doctor heard the gossipers in the drug-store wondering why Rosicky didn't get on faster. He was industrious, and so were his boys, but they were rather free and easy, weren't pushers, and they didn't always show good judgment. They were comfortable, they were out of debt, but they didn't get much ahead. Maybe, Doctor Burleigh reflected, people as generous and warm-hearted and affectionate as the Rosickys never got ahead much; maybe you couldn't enjoy your life and put it into the bank, too.

II

When Rosicky left Doctor Burleigh's office, he went into the farm-implement store to light his pipe and put on his glasses and read over the list Mary had given him. Then he went into the general merchandise place next door and stood about until the pretty girl with the plucked eyebrows, who always waited on him, was free. Those eyebrows, two thin India-ink strokes, amused him, because he remembered how they used to be. Rosicky always prolonged his shopping by a little joking; the girl knew the old fellow admired her, and she liked to chaff with him.

"Seems to me about every other week you buy ticking, Mr. Rosicky, and always the best quality," she remarked as she measured off the heavy bolt with red stripes.

"You see, my wife is always makin' goose-fedder pillows, an' de thin stuff don't hold in dem little down-fedders."

"You must have lots of pillows at your home."

"Sure. She makes quilts of dem, too. We sleeps easy. Now she's makin' a fedder quilt for my son's wife. You know Polly, that married my Rudolph. How much my bill, Miss Pearl?"

"Eight eighty-five."

"Chust make it nine, and put in some candy fur de women."

"As usual. I never did see a man buy so much candy for his wife. First thing you know, she'll be getting too fat."

"I'd like that. I ain't much fur all dem slim women like what de style is now."

"That's one for me, I suppose, Mr. Bohunk!"[2] Pearl sniffed and elevated her India-ink strokes.

When Rosicky went out to his wagon, it was beginning to snow,—the first snow of the season, and he was glad to see it. He rattled out of town and along the highway through a wonderfully rich stretch of country, the finest farms in the county. He admired this High Prairie, as it was called, and always liked to drive through it. His own place lay in a rougher territory, where there was some clay in the soil and it was not so productive. When he bought his land, he hadn't the money to buy on High Prairie; so he told his boys, when they grumbled, that if their land hadn't some clay in it, they wouldn't own it at all. All the same, he enjoyed looking at these fine farms, as he enjoyed looking at a prize bull.

After he had gone eight miles, he came to the graveyard, which lay just at the edge of his own hay-land. There he stopped his horses and sat still on his wagon seat, looking about at the snowfall. Over yonder on the hill he could see his own house, crouching low, with the clump of orchard behind and the windmill before, and all down the gentle hill-slope the rows of pale gold cornstalks stood out against the white field. The snow was falling over the cornfield and the pasture and the hay-land, steadily, with very little wind—a nice dry snow. The graveyard had only a light wire fence about it and was all overgrown with long red grass. The fine snow, settling into this red grass and upon the few little evergreens and the head-stones, looked very pretty.

It was a nice graveyard, Rosicky reflected, sort of snug and homelike, not cramped or mournful,—a big sweep all round it. A man could lie down in the long grass and see the complete arch of the sky over him, hear the wagons go by; in summer the mowing-machine rattled right up to the wire fence. And it was so near home. Over there across the cornstalks his own roof and wind-mill looked so good to him that he promised himself to mind the Doctor and take care of himself. He was awful fond of his place, he admitted. He wasn't anxious to leave it. And it was a comfort to think that he would never have to go farther than the edge of his own hayfield. The snow, falling over his barn-yard and the graveyard, seemed to draw things together like. And they were all old neighbours in the graveyard, most of them friends; there was nothing to feel awkward or embarrassed about. Embarrassment was the most dis-agreeable feeling Rosicky knew. He didn't often have it,—only with certain people whom he didn't understand at all.

2. Bohemian (slang); here used affectionately.

Well, it was a nice snowstorm; a fine sight to see the snow falling so quietly and graciously over so much open country. On his cap and shoulders, on the horses' backs and manes, light, delicate, mysterious it fell; and with it a dry cool fragrance was released into the air. It meant rest for vegetation and men and beasts, for the ground itself; a season of long nights for sleep, leisurely breakfasts, peace by the fire. This and much more went through Rosicky's mind, but he merely told himself that winter was coming, clucked to his horses, and drove on.

When he reached home, John, the youngest boy, ran out to put away his team for him, and he met Mary coming up from the outside cellar with her apron full of carrots. They went into the house together. On the table, covered with oilcloth figured with clusters of blue grapes, a place was set, and he smelled hot coffee-cake of some kind. Anton never lunched in town; he thought that extravagant, and anyhow he didn't like the food. So Mary always had something ready for him when he got home.

After he was settled in his chair, stirring his coffee in a big cup, Mary took out of the oven a pan of *kolache*[3] stuffed with apricots, examined them anxiously to see whether they had got too dry, put them beside his plate, and then sat down opposite him.

Rosicky asked her in Czech if she wasn't going to have any coffee.

She replied in English, as being somehow the right language for transacting business: "Now what did Doctor Ed say, Anton? You tell me just what."

"He said I was to tell you some compliments, but I forgot 'em." Rosicky's eyes twinkled.

"About you, I mean. What did he say about your asthma?"

"He says I ain't got no asthma." Rosicky took one of the little rolls in his broad brown fingers. The thickened nail of his right thumb told the story of his past.

"Well, what is the matter? And don't try to put me off."

"He don't say nothing much, only I'm a little older, and my heart ain't so good like it used to be."

Mary started and brushed her hair back from her temples with both hands as if she were a little out of her mind. From the way she glared, she might have been in a rage with him.

"He says there's something the matter with your heart? Doctor Ed says so?"

"Now don't yell at me like I was a hog in de garden, Mary. You know I always did like to hear a woman talk soft. He didn't say anything de matter wid my heart, only it ain't so young like it used to be, an' he tell me not to pitch hay or run de corn-sheller."

Mary wanted to jump up, but she sat still. She admired the way he never under any circumstances raised his voice or spoke roughly. He was city-bred, and she was country-bred; she often said she wanted her boys to have their papa's nice ways.

"You never have no pain there, do you? It's your breathing and your stomach that's been wrong. I wouldn't believe nobody but Doctor Ed about it. I guess I'll go see him myself. Didn't he give you no advice?"

"Chust to take it easy like, an' stay round de house dis winter. I guess you got some carpenter work for me to do. I kin make some new shelves for you,

---

and I want dis long time to build a closet in de boys' room and make dem two little fellers keep dere clo'es hung up."

Rosicky drank his coffee from time to time, while he considered. His moustache was of the soft long variety and came down over his mouth like the teeth of a buggy-rake over a bundle of hay. Each time he put down his cup, he ran his blue handkerchief over his lips. When he took a drink of water, he managed very neatly with the back of his hand.

Mary sat watching him intently, trying to find any change in his face. It is hard to see anyone who has become like your own body to you. Yes, his hair had got thin, and his high forehead had deep lines running from left to right. But his neck, always clean-shaved except in the busiest seasons, was not loose or baggy. It was burned a dark reddish brown, and there were deep creases in it, but it looked firm and full of blood. His cheeks had a good colour. On either side of his mouth there was a half-moon down the length of his cheek, not wrinkles, but two lines that had come there from his habitual expression. He was shorter and broader than when she married him; his back had grown broad and curved, a good deal like the shell on an old turtle, and his arms and legs were short.

He was fifteen years older than Mary, but she had hardly ever thought about it before. He was her man, and the kind of man she liked. She was rough, and he was gentle—city-bred, as she always said. They had been ship-mates on a rough voyage and had stood by each other in trying times. Life had gone well with them because, at bottom, they had the same ideas about life. They agreed, without discussion, as to what was most important and what was secondary. They didn't often exchange opinions, even in Czech—it was as if they had thought the same thought together. A good deal had to be sacrificed and thrown overboard in a hard life like theirs, and they had never disagreed as to the things that could go. It had been a hard life, and a soft life, too. There wasn't anything brutal in the short, broad-backed man with the three-cornered eyes and the forehead that went on to the top of his skull. He was a city man, a gentle man, and though he had married a rough farm girl, he had never touched her without gentleness.

They had been at one accord not to hurry through life, not to be always skimping and saving. They saw their neighbours buy more land and feed more stock than they did, without discontent. Once when the creamery agent came to the Rosickys to persuade them to sell him their cream, he told them how much money the Fasslers, their nearest neighbours, had made on their cream last year.

"Yes," said Mary, "and look at them Fassler children! Pale, pinched little things, they look like skimmed milk. I had rather put some colour into my children's faces than put money into the bank."

The agent shrugged and turned to Anton.
"I guess we'll do like she says," said Rosicky.

III

Mary very soon got into town to see Doctor Ed, and then she had a talk with her boys and set a guard over Rosicky. Even John, the youngest, had his father on his mind. If Rosicky went to throw hay down from the loft, one of the boys ran up the ladder and took the fork from him. He sometimes complained that though he was getting to be an old man, he wasn't an old woman yet.

That winter he stayed in the house in the afternoons and carpentered, or sat in the chair between the window full of plants and the wooden bench where the two pails of drinking-water stood. This spot was called "Father's corner," though it was not a corner at all. He had a shelf there, where he kept his Bohemian papers and his pipes and tobacco, and his shears and needles and thread and tailor's thimble. Having been a tailor in his youth, he couldn't bear to see a woman patching at his clothes, or at the boys'. He liked tailoring, and always patched all the overalls and jackets and work shirts. Occasionally he made over a pair of pants one of the older boys had outgrown, for the little fellow.

While he sewed, he let his mind run back over his life. He had a good deal to remember, really; life in three countries. The only part of his youth he didn't like to remember was the two years he had spent in London, in Cheapside, working for a German tailor who was wretchedly poor. Those days, when he was nearly always hungry, when his clothes were dropping off him for dirt, and the sound of a strange language kept him in continual bewilderment, had left a sore spot in his mind that wouldn't bear touching.

He was twenty when he landed at Castle Garden in New York, and he had a protector who got him work in a tailor shop in Vesey Street, down near the Washington Market. He looked upon that part of his life as very happy. He became a good workman, he was industrious, and his wages were increased from time to time. He minded his own business and envied nobody's good fortune. He went to night school and learned to read English. He often did overtime work and was well paid for it, but somehow he never saved anything. He couldn't refuse a loan to a friend, and he was self-indulgent. He liked a good dinner, and a little went for beer, a little for tobacco; a good deal went to the girls. He often stood through an opera on Saturday nights; he could get standing-room for a dollar. Those were the great days of opera in New York, and it gave a fellow something to think about for the rest of the week. Rosicky had a quick ear, and a childish love of all the stage splendour; the scenery, the costumes, the ballet. He usually went with a chum, and after the performance they had beer and maybe some oysters somewhere. It was a fine life; for the first five years or so it satisfied him completely. He was never hungry or cold or dirty, and everything amused him: a fire, a dog fight, a parade, a storm, a ferry ride. He thought New York the finest, richest, friendliest city in the world.

Moreover, he had what he called a happy home life. Very near the tailor shop was a small furniture-factory, where an old Austrian, Loeffler, employed a few skilled men and made unusual furniture, most of it to order, for the rich German housewives uptown. The top floor of Loeffler's five-storey factory was a loft, where he kept his choice lumber and stored the old pieces of furniture left on his hands. One of the young workmen he employed was a Czech, and he and Rosicky became fast friends. They persuaded Loeffler to let them have a sleeping-room in one corner of the loft. They bought good beds and bedding and had their pick of the furniture kept up there. The loft was low-pitched, but light and airy, full of windows, and good-smelling by reason of the fine lumber put up there to season. Old Loeffler used to go down to the docks and buy wood from South America and the East from the sea captains. The young men were as foolish about their house as a bridal pair. Zichec, the young cabinet-maker, devised every sort of convenience, and Rosicky kept their clothes in order. At night and on Sundays, when the quiver of machinery underneath was still, it was the quietest place in the world, and on summer nights all the sea winds blew in. Zichec often practised on his flute in the evening. They were both fond of music and went to the opera together. Rosicky thought he wanted to live like that for ever.

But as the years passed, all alike, he began to get a little restless. When spring came round, he would begin to feel fretted, and he got to drinking. He was likely to drink too much of a Saturday night. On Sunday he was languid and heavy, getting over his spree. On Monday he plunged into work again. So he never had time to figure out what ailed him, although he knew something did. When the grass turned green in Park Place, and the lilac hedge at the back of Trinity churchyard put out its blossoms, he was tormented by a longing to run away. That was why he drank too much; to get a temporary illusion of freedom and wide horizons.

Rosicky, the old Rosicky, could remember as if it were yesterday the day when the young Rosicky found out what was the matter with him. It was on a Fourth of July afternoon, and he was sitting in Park Place in the sun. The lower part of New York was empty. Wall Street, Liberty Street, Broadway, all empty. So much stone and asphalt with nothing going on, so many empty windows. The emptiness was intense, like the stillness in a great factory when the machinery stops and the belts and bands cease running. It was too great a change, it took all the strength out of one. Those blank buildings, without the stream of life pouring through them, were like empty jails. It struck young Rosicky that this was the trouble with big cities; they built you in from the earth itself, cemented you away from any contact with the ground. You lived in an unnatural world, like the fish in an aquarium, who were probably much more comfortable than they ever were in the sea.

On that very day he began to think seriously about the articles he had read in the Bohemian papers, describing prosperous Czech farming communities in the West. He believed he would like to go out there as a farm hand; it was hardly possible that he could ever have land of his own. His people had always been workmen, his father and grandfather had worked in shops. His mother's parents had lived in the country, but they rented their farm and had a hard time to get along. Nobody in his family had ever owned any land,—that belonged to a different station of life altogether. Anton's mother died when he was little, and he was sent into the country to her parents. He stayed with them until he was twelve, and formed those ties with the earth and the farm animals and growing things which are never made at all unless they are made early. After his grandfather died, he went back to live with his father and stepmother, but she was very hard on him, and his father helped him to get passage to London.

After that Fourth of July day in Park Place, the desire to return to the country never left him. To work on another man's farm would be all he asked; to see the sun rise and set and to plant things and watch them grow. He was a very simple man. He was like a tree that has not many roots, but one taproot that goes down deep. He subscribed for a Bohemian paper printed in Chicago, then for one printed in Omaha. His mind got farther and farther west. He began to save a little money to buy his liberty. When he was thirty-five, there was a great meeting in New York of Bohemian athletic societies, and Rosicky left the tailor shop and went home with the Omaha delegates to try his fortune in another part of the world.

IV

Perhaps the fact that his own youth was well over before he began to have a family was one reason why Rosicky was so fond of his boys. He had almost a grandfather's indulgence for them. He had never had to worry about any of them—except, just now, a little about Rudolph.

On Saturday night the boys always piled into the Ford, took little Josephine, and went to town to the moving-picture show. One Saturday morning they were talking at the breakfast table about starting early that evening, so that they would have an hour or so to see the Christmas things in the stores before the show began. Rosicky looked down the table.

"I hope you boys ain't disappointed, but I want you to let me have de car tonight. Maybe some of you can go in with de neighbours."

Their faces fell. They worked hard all week, and they were still like children. A new jack-knife or a box of candy pleased the older ones as much as the little fellow.

"If you and mother are going to town," Frank said, "maybe you could take a couple of us along with you, anyway.'"

"No, I want to take de car down to Rudolph's, and let him an' Polly go in to de show. She don't git into town enough, an' I'm afraid she's gettin' lonesome, an' he can't afford no car yet."

That settled it. The boys were a good deal dashed. Their father took another piece of apple-cake and went on: "Maybe next Saturday night de two little fellers can go along wid dem."

"Oh, is Rudolph going to have the car every Saturday night?"

Rosicky did not reply at once; then he began to speak seriously: "Listen, boys; Polly ain't lookin' so good. I don't like to see nobody lookin' sad. It comes hard fur a town girl to be a farmer's wife. I don't want no trouble to start in Rudolph's family. When it starts, it ain't so easy to stop. An American girl don't git used to our ways all at once. I like to tell Polly she and Rudolph can have the car every Saturday night till after New Year's, if it's all right with you boys."

"Sure, it's all right, papa," Mary cut in. "And it's good you thought about that. Town girls is used to more than country girls. I lay awake nights, scared she'll make Rudolph discontented with the farm."

The boys put as good a face on it as they could. They surely looked forward to their Saturday nights in town. That evening Rosicky drove the car the half-mile down to Rudolph's new, bare little house.

Polly was in a short-sleeved gingham dress, clearing away the supper dishes. She was a trim, slim little thing, with blue eyes and shingled yellow hair, and her eyebrows were reduced to a mere brush-stroke, like Miss Pearl's.

"Good-evening, Mr. Rosicky. Rudolph's at the barn, I guess." She never called him father, or Mary mother. She was sensitive about having married a foreigner. She never in the world would have done it if Rudolph hadn't been such a handsome, persuasive fellow and such a gallant lover. He had graduated in her class in the high school in town, and their friendship began in the ninth grade.

Rosicky went in, though he wasn't exactly asked. "My boys ain't goin' to town tonight, an' I brought de car over fur you two to go in to de picture show."

Polly, carrying dishes to the sink, looked over her shoulder at him. "Thank you. But I'm late with my work tonight, and pretty tired. Maybe Rudolph would like to go in with you."

"Oh, I don't go to de shows! I'm too old-fashioned. You won't feel so tired after you ride in de air a ways. It's a nice clear night, an' it ain't cold. You go an' fix yourself up, Polly, an' I'll wash de dishes an' leave everything nice fur you."

Polly blushed and tossed her bob. "I couldn't let you do that, Mr. Rosicky, I wouldn't think of it."

Rosicky said nothing. He found a bib apron on a nail behind the kitchen door. He slipped it over his head and then took Polly by her two elbows and pushed her gently toward the door of her own room. "I washed up de kitchen many times for my wife, when de babies was sick or somethin'. You go an' make yourself look nice. I like you to look prettier'n any of dem town girls when you go in. De young folks must have some fun, an' I'm goin' to look out fur you, Polly."

That kind, reassuring grip on her elbows, the old man's funny bright eyes, made Polly want to drop her head on his shoulder for a second. She restrained herself, but she lingered in his grasp at the door of her room, murmuring tearfully: "You always lived in the city when you were young, didn't you? Don't you ever get lonesome out here?"

As she turned round to him, her hand fell naturally into his, and he stood holding it and smiling into her face with his peculiar, knowing, indulgent smile without a shadow of reproach in it. "Dem big cities is all right fur de rich, but dey is terrible hard fur de poor."

"I don't know. Sometimes I think I'd like to take a chance. You lived in New York, didn't you?"

"An' London. Da's bigger still. I learned my trade dere. Here's Rudolph comin', you better hurry."

"Will you tell me about London some time?"

"Maybe. Only I ain't no talker, Polly. Run an' dress yourself up."

The bedroom door closed behind her, and Rudolph came in from the outside, looking anxious. He had seen the car and was sorry any of his family should come just then. Supper hadn't been a very pleasant occasion. Halting in the doorway, he saw his father in a kitchen apron, carrying dishes to the sink. He flushed crimson and something flashed in his eye. Rosicky held up a warning finger.

"I brought de car over fur you an' Polly to go to de picture show, an' I made her let me finish here so you won't be late. You go put on a clean shirt, quick!"

"But don't the boys want the car, Father?"

"Not tonight dey don't." Rosicky fumbled under his apron and found his pants pocket. He took out a silver dollar and said in a hurried whisper: "You go an' buy dat girl some ice cream an' candy tonight, like you was courtin'. She's awful good friends wid me."

Rudolph was very short of cash, but he took the money as if it hurt him. There had been a crop failure all over the country. He had more than once been sorry he'd married this year.

In a few minutes the young people came out, looking clean and a little stiff. Rosicky hurried them off, and then he took his own time with the dishes. He scoured the pots and pans and put away the milk and swept the kitchen. He put some coal in the stove and shut off the draughts, so the place would be warm for them when they got home late at night. Then he sat down and had a pipe and listened to the clock tick.

Generally speaking, marrying an American girl was certainly a risk. A Czech should marry a Czech. It was lucky that Polly was the daughter of a poor widow woman; Rudolph was proud, and if she had a prosperous family to throw up at him, they could never make it go. Polly was one of four sisters, and they all worked; one was book-keeper in the bank, one taught music, and Polly and her younger sister had been clerks, like Miss Pearl. All four of them were musical, had pretty voices, and sang in the Methodist choir, which the eldest sister directed.

Polly missed the sociability of a store position. She missed the choir, and the company of her sisters. She didn't dislike housework, but she disliked so much of it. Rosicky was a little anxious about this pair. He was afraid Polly would grow so discontented that Rudy would quit the farm and take a factory job in Omaha. He had worked for a winter up there, two years ago, to get money to marry on. He had done very well, and they would always take him back at the stockyards. But to Rosicky that meant the end of everything for his son. To be a landless man was to be a wage-earner, a slave, all your life; to have nothing, to be nothing.

Rosicky thought he would come over and do a little carpentering for Polly after the New Year. He guessed she needed jollying. Rudolph was a serious sort of chap, serious in love and serious about his work.

Rosicky shook out his pipe and walked home across the fields. Ahead of him the lamplight shone from his kitchen windows. Suppose he were still in a tailor shop on Vesey Street, with a bunch of pale, narrow-chested sons working on machines, all coming home tired and sullen to eat supper in a kitchen that was a parlour also; with another crowded, angry family quarrelling just across the dumb-waiter shaft, and squeaking pulleys at the windows where dirty washings hung on dirty lines above a court full of old brooms and mops and ash-cans . . .

He stopped by the windmill to look up at the frosty winter stars and draw a long breath before he went inside. That kitchen with the shining windows was dear to him; but the sleeping fields and bright stars and the noble darkness were dearer still.

V

On the day before Christmas the weather set in very cold; no snow, but a bitter, biting wind that whistled and sang over the flat land and lashed one's face like fine wires. There was baking going on in the Rosicky kitchen all day, and Rosicky sat inside, making over a coat that Albert had outgrown into an overcoat for John. Mary had a big red geranium in bloom for Christmas, and a row of Jerusalem cherry trees, full of berries. It was the first year she had ever grown these; Doctor Ed brought her the seeds from Omaha when he went to some medical convention. They reminded Rosicky of plants he had seen in England; and all afternoon, as he stitched, he sat thinking about those two years in London, which his mind usually shrank from even after all this while.

He was a lad of eighteen when he dropped down into London, with no money and no connexions except the address of a cousin who was supposed to be working at a confectioner's. When he went to the pastry shop, however, he found that the cousin had gone to America. Anton tramped the streets for several days, sleeping in doorways and on the Embankment, until he was in utter despair. He knew no English, and the sound of the strange language all about him confused him. By chance he met a poor German tailor who had learned his trade in Vienna, and could speak a little Czech. This tailor, Lifschnitz, kept a repair shop in a Cheapside basement, underneath a cobbler. He didn't much need an apprentice, but he was sorry for the boy and took him in for no wages but his keep and what he could pick up. The pickings were supposed to be coppers given you when you took work home to a customer. But most of the customers called for their clothes themselves, and the coppers that came Anton's way were very few. He had, however, a place to sleep. The tailor's family lived upstairs in three rooms; a kitchen, a bedroom, where Lifschnitz and his wife and five children slept, and a livingroom. Two corners of this living room were curtained off for lodgers; in one Rosicky slept on an old horsehair sofa, with a feather quilt to wrap himself in. The other corner was rented to a wretched, dirty boy, who was studying the violin. He actually practised there. Rosicky was dirty, too. There was no way to be anything else. Mrs. Lifschnitz got the water she cooked and washed with from a pump in a brick court, four flights down. There were bugs in the place, and multitudes of fleas, though the poor woman did the best she could. Rosicky knew she often went empty to give another potato or a spoonful of dripping to the two hungry, sad-eyed boys who lodged with her. He used to think he would never get out of there, never get a clean shirt to his back again. What would he do, he wondered, when his clothes actually dropped to pieces and the worn cloth wouldn't hold patches any longer?

It was still early when the old farmer put aside his sewing and his recollections. The sky had been a dark grey all day, with not a gleam of sun, and the light failed at four o'clock. He went to shave and change his shirt while the turkey was roasting. Rudolph and Polly were coming over for supper.

After supper they sat round in the kitchen, and the younger boys were saying how sorry they were it hadn't snowed. Everybody was sorry. They wanted a deep snow that would lie long and keep the wheat warm, and leave the ground soaked when it melted.

"Yes, sir!" Rudolph broke out fiercely; "if we have another dry year like last year, there's going to be hard times in this country."

Rosicky filled his pipe. "You boys don't know what hard times is. You don't owe nobody, you got plenty to eat an' keep warm, an' plenty water to keep clean. When you got them, you can't have it very hard."

Rudolph frowned, opened and shut his big right hand, and dropped it clenched upon his knee. "I've got to have a good deal more than that, father, or I'll quit this farming gamble. I can always make good wages railroading, or at the packing house, and be sure of my money."

"Maybe so," his father answered dryly.

Mary, who had just come in from the pantry and was wiping her hands on the roller towel, thought Rudy and his father were getting too serious. She brought her darning-basket and sat down in the middle of the group.

"I ain't much afraid of hard times, Rudy," she said heartily. "We've had a plenty, but we've always come through. Your father wouldn't never take nothing very hard, not even hard times. I got a mind to tell you a story on him. Maybe you boys can't hardly remember the year we had that terrible hot wind, that burned everything up on the Fourth of July? All the corn an' the gardens. An' that was in the days when we didn't have alfalfa yet,—I guess it wasn't invented.

"Well, that very day your father was out cultivatin' corn, and I was here in the kitchen makin' plum preserves. We had bushels of plums that year. I noticed it was terrible hot, but it's always hot in the kitchen when you're preservin', an' I was too busy with my plums to mind. Anton come in from the field about three o'clock, an' I asked him what was the matter.

"'Nothin',' he says, 'but it's pretty hot an' I think I won't work no more to-day.' He stood round for a few minutes, an' then he says: 'Ain't you near through? I want you should git up a nice supper for us tonight. It's Fourth of July.'

"I told him to git along, that I was right in the middle of preservin', but the plums would taste good on hot biscuit. 'I'm goin' to have fried chicken, too,' he says, and he went off an' killed a couple. You three oldest boys was little fellers, playin' round outside, real hot an' sweaty, an' your father took you to the horse tank down by the windmill an' took off your clothes an' put you in. Them two box-elder trees were little then, but they made shade over the tank. Then he took off all his own clothes, an' got in with you. While he was playin' in the water with you, the Methodist preacher drove into our place to say how all the neighbours was goin' to meet at the schoolhouse that night, to pray for rain. He drove right to the windmill, of course, and there was your father and you three with no clothes on. I was in the kitchen door, an' I had to laugh, for the preacher acted like he ain't never seen a naked man before. He surely was embarrassed, an' your father couldn't git to his clothes; they was all hangin' up on the windmill to let the sweat dry out of 'em. So he laid in the tank where he was, an' put one of you boys on top of him to cover him up a little, an' talked to the preacher.

"When you got through playin' in the water, he put clean clothes on you and a clean shirt on himself, an' by that time I'd begun to get supper. He says: 'It's too hot in here to eat comfortable. Let's have a picnic in the orchard. We'll eat our supper behind the mulberry hedge, under them linden trees.'

"So he carried our supper down, an' a bottle of my wild-grape wine, an' everything tasted good, I can tell you. The wind got cooler as the sun was goin' down, and it turned out pleasant, only I noticed how the leaves was curled up on the linden trees. That made me think, an' I asked your father if that hot wind all day hadn't been terrible hard on the gardens an' the corn.

"'Corn,' he says, 'there ain't no corn.'

"'What you talkin' about?' I said. 'Ain't we got forty acres?'

"'We ain't got an ear,' he says, 'nor nobody else ain't got none. All the corn in this country was cooked by three o'clock today, like you'd roasted it in an oven.'

"'You mean you won't get no crop at all?' I asked him. I couldn't believe it, after he'd worked so hard.

"'No crop this year,' he says. 'That's why we're havin' a picnic. We might as well enjoy what we got.'

"An' that's how your father behaved, when all the neighbours was so discouraged they couldn't look you in the face. An' we enjoyed ourselves that year, poor as we was, an' our neighbours wasn't a bit better off for bein' miserable. Some of 'em grieved till they got poor digestions and couldn't relish what they did have."

The younger boys said they thought their father had the best of it. But Rudolph was thinking that, all the same, the neighbours had managed to get ahead more, in the fifteen years since that time. There must be something wrong about his father's way of doing things. He wished he knew what was going on in the back of Polly's mind. He knew she liked his father, but he knew, too, that she was afraid of something. When his mother sent over coffee-cake or prune tarts or a loaf of fresh bread, Polly seemed to regard them with a certain suspicion. When she observed to him that his brothers had nice manners, her tone implied that it was remarkable they should have. With his mother she was stiff and on her guard. Mary's hearty frankness and gusts of good humour irritated her. Polly was afraid of being unusual or conspicuous in any way, of being 'ordinary' as she said!

When Mary had finished her story, Rosicky laid aside his pipe.

"You boys like me to tell you about some of dem hard times I been through in London?" Warmly encouraged, he sat rubbing his forehead along the deep creases. It was bothersome to tell a long story in English (he nearly always talked to the boys in Czech), but he wanted Polly to hear this one.

"Well, you know about dat tailor shop I worked in in London? I had one Christmas dere I ain't never forgot. Times was awful bad before Christmas; de boss ain't got much work, an' have it awful hard to pay his rent. It ain't so much fun, bein' poor in a big city like London, I'll say! All de windows is full of good t'ings to eat, an' all de pushcarts in de streets is full, an' you smell 'em all de time, an' you ain't got no money—not a damn bit. I didn't mind de cold so much, though I didn't have no overcoat, chust a short jacket I'd outgrowed so it wouldn't meet on me, an' my hands was chapped raw. But I always had a good appetite, like you all know, an' de sight of dem pork pies in de windows was awful fur me!

"Day before Christmas was terrible foggy dat year, an' dat fog gits into your bones and makes you all damp like. Mrs. Lifschnitz didn't give us nothin' but a little bread an' drippin' for supper, because she was savin' to try for to give us a good dinner on Christmas Day. After supper de boss say I go an' enjoy myself, so I went into de streets to listen to de Christmas singers. Dey sing old songs an' make very nice music, an' I run round after dem a good ways, till I got awful hungry. I t'ink maybe if I go home, I can sleep till morning an' forget my belly.

"I went into my corner real quiet, and roll up in my fedder quilt. But I ain't got my head down, till I smell somet'ing good. Seem like it git stronger an' stronger, an' I can't git to sleep noway. I can't understand dat smell. Dere was a gas light in a hall across de court, dat always shine in at my window a little. I got up an' look round. I got a little wooden box in my corner fur a stool, 'cause I ain't got no chair. I picks up dat box, and under it dere is a roast goose on a platter! I can't believe my eyes. I carry it to de window where de light comes in, an' touch it and smell it to find out, an' den I taste it to be sure. I say, I will eat chust one little bite of dat goose, so I can go to sleep, and tomorrow I won't eat none at all. But I tell you, boys, when I stop, one half of dat goose was gone!"

The narrator bowed his head, and the boys shouted. But little Josephine slipped behind his chair and kissed him on the neck beneath his ear.

"Poor little Papa, I don't want him to be hungry!"

"Da's long ago, child. I ain't never been hungry since I had your mudder to cook fur me."

"Go on and tell us the rest, please," said Polly.

"Well, when I come to realize what I done, of course, I felt terrible. I felt better in de stomach, but very bad in de heart. I set on my bed wid dat platter on my knees, an' it all come to me; how hard dat poor woman save to buy dat goose, and how she get some neighbour to cook it dat got more fire, an' how she put it in my corner to keep it away from dem hungry children. Dere was a old carpet hung up to shut my corner off, an' de children wasn't allowed to go in dere. An' I know she put it in my corner because she trust me more'n she did de violin boy. I can't stand it to face her after I spoil de Christmas. So I put on my shoes and go out into de city. I tell myself I better throw myself in de river; but I guess I ain't dat kind of a boy.

"It was after twelve o'clock, an' terrible cold, an' I start out to walk about London all night. I walk along de river awhile, but dey was lots of drunks all along; men, and women too. I chust move along to keep away from de police. I git onto de Strand, an' den over to New Oxford Street, where dere was a big German restaurant on de ground floor, wid big windows all fixed up fine, an' I could see de people havin' parties inside. While I was lookin' in, two men and two ladies come out, laughin' and talkin' and feelin' happy about all dey been eatin' an' drinkin', and dey was speakin' Czech—not like de Austrians, but like de home folks talk it.

"I guess I went crazy, an' I done what I ain't never done before nor since. I went right up to dem gay people an' begun to beg dem: 'Fellow countrymen, for God's sake give me money enough to buy a goose!'

"Dey laugh, of course, but de ladies speak awful kind to me, an' dey take me back into de restaurant and give me hot coffee and cakes, an' make me tell all about how I happened to come to London, an' what I was doin' dere. Dey take my name and where I work down on paper, an' both of dem ladies give me ten shillings.

"De big market at Covent Garden[4] ain't very far away, an' by dat, time it was open. I go dere an buy a big goose an' some pork pies, an' potatoes and onions, an' cakes an' oranges fur de children—all I could carry! When I git home, everybody is still asleep. I pile all I bought on de kitchen table, an' go in an' lay down on my bed, an I ain't waken up till I hear dat woman scream when she come out into her kitchen. My goodness, but she was surprise! She laugh an' cry at de same time, an' hug me and waken all de children. She ain't stop fur no breakfast; she git de Christmas dinner ready dat morning, and we all sit down an' eat all we can hold. I ain't never seen dat violin boy have all he can hold before.

"Two-three days after dat, de two men come to hunt me up, an' dey ask my boss, and he give me a good report an' tell dem I was a steady boy all right. One of dem Bohemians was very smart an' run a Bohemian newspaper in New York, an' de odder was a rich man, in de importing business, an' dey been travelling togedder. Dey told me how t'ings was easier in New York, an' offered to pay my passage when dey was goin' home soon on a boat. My boss say to me: 'You go. You ain't got no chance here, an' I like to

---

4. Square in London, site of a famous flower and vegetable market and of the Covent Garden opera house.

see you git ahead, fur you always been a good boy to my woman, and fur dat fine Christmas dinner you give us all.' An' da's how I got to New York."

That night when Rudolph and Polly, arm in arm, were running home across the fields with the bitter wind at their backs, his heart leaped for joy when she said she thought they might have his family come over for supper on New Year's Eve. "Let's get up a nice supper, and not let your mother help at all; make her be company for once."

"That would be lovely of you, Polly," he said humbly. He was a very simple, modest boy, and he, too, felt vaguely that Polly and her sisters were more experienced and worldly than his people.

The winter turned out badly for farmers. It was bitterly cold, and after the first light snows before Christmas there was no snow at all—and no rain. March was as bitter as February. On those days when the wind fairly punished the country, Rosicky sat by his window. In the fall he and the boys had put in a big wheat planting, and now the seed had frozen in the ground. All that land would have to be ploughed up and planted over again, planted in corn. It had happened before, but he was younger then, and he never worried about what had to be. He was sure of himself and of Mary; he knew they could bear what they had to bear, that they would always pull through somehow. But he was not so sure about the young ones, and he felt troubled because Rudolph and Polly were having such a hard start.

Sitting beside his flowering window while the panes rattled and the wind blew in under the door, Rosicky gave himself to reflection as he had not done since those Sundays in the loft of the furniture factory in New York, long ago. Then he was trying to find what he wanted in life for himself; now he was trying to find what he wanted for his boys, and why it was he so hungered to feel sure they would be here, working this very land, after he was gone.

They would have to work hard on the farm, and probably they would never do much more than make a living. But if he could think of them as staying here on the land, he wouldn't have to fear any great unkindness for them. Hardships, certainly; it was a hardship to have the wheat freeze in the ground when seed was so high; and to have to sell your stock because you had no feed. But there would be other years when everything came along right, and you caught up. And what you had was your own. You didn't have to choose between bosses and strikers, and go wrong either way. You didn't have to do with dishonest and cruel people. They were the only things in his experience he had found terrifying and horrible: the look in the eyes of a dishonest and crafty man, of a scheming and rapacious woman.

In the country, if you had a mean neighbour, you could keep off his land and make him keep off yours. But in the city, all the foulness and misery and brutality of your neighbours was part of your life. The worst things he had come upon in his journey through the world were human,—depraved and poisonous specimens of man. To this day he could recall certain terrible faces in the London streets. There were mean people everywhere, to be sure, even in their own country town here. But they weren't tempered, hardened, sharpened, like the treacherous people in cities who live by grinding or cheating or poisoning their fellow-men. He had helped to bury two of his fellow-workmen in the tailoring trade, and he was distrustful of the organized industries that see one out of the world in big cities. Here, if you were sick, you had Doctor Ed to look after you; and if you died, fat Mr. Haycock, the kindest man in the world, buried you.

It seemed to Rosicky that for good, honest boys like his, the worst they could do on the farm was better than the best they would be likely to do in the city. If he'd had a mean boy, now, one who was crooked and sharp and tried to put anything over on his brothers, then town would be the place for him. But he had no such boy. As for Rudolph, the discontented one, he would give the shirt off his back to anyone who touched his heart. What Rosicky really hoped for his boys was that they could get through the world without ever knowing much about the cruelty of human beings. "Their mother and me ain't prepared them for that," he sometimes said to himself.

These thoughts brought him back to a grateful consideration of his own case. What an escape he had had, to be sure! He, too, in his time, had had to take money for repair work from the hand of a hungry child who let it go so wistfully; because it was money due his boss. And now, in all these years, he had never had to take a cent from anyone in bitter need—never had to look at the face of a woman become like a wolf's from struggle and famine. When he thought of these things, Rosicky would put on his cap and jacket and slip down to the barn and give his work-horses a little extra oats, letting them eat it out of his hand in their slobbery fashion. It was his way of expressing what he felt, and made him chuckle with pleasure.

The spring came warm, with blue skies,—but dry, dry as bone. The boys began ploughing up the wheat-fields to plant them over in corn. Rosicky would stand at the fence corner and watch them, and the earth was so dry it blew up in clouds of brown dust that hid the horses and the sulky plough and the driver. It was a bad outlook.

The big alfalfa-field that lay between the home place and Rudolph's came up green, but Rosicky was worried because during that open windy winter a great many Russian thistle plants had blown in there and lodged. He kept asking the boys to rake them out; he was afraid their seed would root and "take the alfalfa." Rudolph said that was nonsense. The boys were working so hard planting corn, their father felt he couldn't insist about the thistles, but he set great store by that big alfalfa-field. It was a feed you could depend on,—and there was some deeper reason, vague, but strong. The peculiar green of that clover woke early memories in old Rosicky, went back to something in his childhood in the old world. When he was a little boy, he had played in fields of that strong blue-green colour.

One morning, when Rudolph had gone to town in the car, leaving a work-team idle in his barn, Rosicky went over to his son's place, put the horses to the buggy-rake, and set about quietly taking up those thistles. He behaved with guilty caution, and rather enjoyed stealing a march on Doctor Ed, who was just then taking his first vacation in seven years of practice and was attending a clinic in Chicago. Rosicky got the thistles raked up, but did not stop to burn them. That would take some time, and his breath was pretty short, so he thought he had better get the horses back to the barn.

He got them into the barn and to their stalls, but the pain had come on so sharp in his chest that he didn't try to take the harness off. He started for the house, bending lower with every step. The cramp in his chest was shutting him up like a jack-knife. When he reached the windmill, he swayed and caught at the ladder. He saw Polly coming down the hill, running with the swiftness of a slim greyhound. In a flash she had her shoulder under his armpit.

"Lean on me, Father, hard! Don't be afraid. We can get to the house all right."

Somehow they did, though Rosicky became blind with pain; he could keep on his legs, but he couldn't steer his course. The next thing he was conscious of was lying on Polly's bed, and Polly bending over him wringing out bath-towels in hot water and putting them on his chest. She stopped only to throw coal into the stove, and she kept the tea-kettle and the black pot going. She put these hot applications on him for nearly an hour, she told him afterwards, and all that time he was drawn up stiff and blue, with the sweat pouring off him.

As the pain gradually loosed its grip, the stiffness went out of his jaws, the black circles round his eyes disappeared, and a little of his natural colour came back. When his daughter-in-law buttoned his shirt over his chest at last, he sighed.

"Da's fine, de way I feel now, Polly. It was a awful bad spell, an' I was so sorry it all come on you like it did."

Polly was flushed and excited. "Is the pain really gone? Can I leave you long enough to telephone over to your place?"

Rosicky's eyelids fluttered. "Don't telephone, Polly. It ain't no use to scare my wife. It's nice and quiet here, an' if I ain't too much trouble to you, just let me lay still till I feel like myself. I ain't got no pain now. It's nice here."

Polly bent over him and wiped the moisture from his face. "Oh, I'm so glad it's over!" she broke out impulsively. "It just broke my heart to see you suffer so, Father."

Rosicky motioned her to sit down on the chair where the tea-kettle had been, and looked up at her with that lively affectionate gleam in his eyes. "You was awful good to me, I won't never forgit dat. I hate it to be sick on you like dis. Down at de barn I say to myself, dat young girl ain't had much experience in sickness, I don't want to scare her, an' maybe she's got a baby comin' or somet'ing."

Polly took his hand. He was looking at her so intently and affectionately and confidingly; his eyes seemed to caress her face, to regard it with pleasure. She frowned with her funny streaks of eyebrows, and then smiled back at him.

"I guess maybe there is something of that kind going to happen. But I haven't told anyone yet, not my mother or Rudolph. You'll be the first to know."

His hand pressed hers. She noticed that it was warm again. The twinkle in his yellow-brown eyes seemed to come nearer.

"I like mighty well to see dat little child, Polly," was all he said. Then he closed his eyes and lay half-smiling. But Polly sat still, thinking hard. She had a sudden feeling that nobody in the world, not her mother, not Rudolph, or anyone, really loved her as much as old Rosicky did. It perplexed her. She sat frowning and trying to puzzle it out. It was as if Rosicky had a special gift for loving people, something that was like an ear for music or an eye for colour. It was quiet, unobtrusive; it was merely there. You saw it in his eyes,— perhaps that was why they were merry. You felt it in his hands, too. After he dropped off to sleep, she sat holding his warm, broad, flexible brown hand. She had never seen another in the least like it. She wondered if it wasn't a kind of gipsy hand, it was so alive and quick and light in its communications,— very strange in a farmer. Nearly all the farmers she knew had huge lumps of fists, like mauls, or they were knotty and bony and uncomfortable-looking, with stiff fingers. But Rosicky's was like quicksilver, flexible, muscular, about the colour of a pale cigar, with deep, deep creases across the palm. It wasn't nervous, it wasn't a stupid lump; it was a warm brown human hand, with some cleverness in it, a great deal of generosity, and something else which Polly could only call "gypsy-like"—something nimble and lively and sure, in the way that animals are.

Polly remembered that hour long afterwards; it had been like an awakening to her. It seemed to her that she had never learned so much about life from anything as from old Rosicky's hand. It brought her to herself; it communicated some direct and untranslatable message.

When she heard Rudolph coming in the car, she ran out to meet him.

"Oh, Rudy, your father's been awful sick! He raked up those thistles he's been worrying about, and afterward he could hardly get to the house. He suffered so I was afraid he was going to die."

Rudolph jumped to the ground. "Where is he now?"

"On the bed. He's asleep. I was terribly scared, because, you know, I'm so fond of your father." She slipped her arm through his and they went into the house. That afternoon they took Rosicky home and put him to bed, though he protested that he was quite well again.

The next morning he got up and dressed and sat down to breakfast with his family. He told Mary that his coffee tasted better than usual to him, and he warned the boys not to bear any tales to Doctor Ed when he got home. After breakfast he sat down by his window to do some patching and asked Mary to thread several needles for him before she went to feed her chickens,— her eyes were better than his, and her hands steadier. He lit his pipe and took up John's overalls. Mary had been watching him anxiously all morning, and as she went out of the door with her bucket of scraps, she saw that he was smiling. He was thinking, indeed, about Polly, and how he might never have known what a tender heart she had if he hadn't got sick over there. Girls nowadays didn't wear their heart on their sleeve. But now he knew Polly would make a fine woman after the foolishness wore off. Either a woman had that sweetness at her heart or she hadn't. You couldn't always tell by the look of them; but if they had that, everything came out right in the end.

After he had taken a few stitches, the cramp began in his chest, like yesterday. He put his pipe cautiously down on the window-sill and bent over to ease the pull. No use,—he had better try to get to his bed if he could. He rose and groped his way across the familiar floor, which was rising and falling like the deck of a ship. At the door he fell. When Mary came in, she found him lying there, and the moment she touched him she knew that he was gone.

Doctor Ed was away when Rosicky died, and for the first few weeks after he got home he was harddriven. Every day he said to himself that he must get out to see that family that had lost their father. One soft, warm moonlight night in early summer he started for the farm. His mind was on other things, and not until his road ran by the graveyard did he realize that Rosicky wasn't over there on the hill where the red lamplight shone, but here, in the moonlight. He stopped his car, shut off the engine, and sat there for a while.

A sudden hush had fallen on his soul. Everything here seemed strangely moving and significant, though signifying what, he did not know. Close by the wire fence stood Rosicky's mowing-machine, where one of the boys had been cutting hay that afternoon; his own work-horses had been going up and down there. The new-cut hay perfumed all the night air. The moonlight silvered the long, billowy grass that grew over the graves and hid the fence; the few little evergreens stood out black in it, like shadows in a pool. The sky was very blue and soft, the stars rather faint because the moon was full.

For the first time it struck Doctor Ed that this was really a beautiful graveyard. He thought of city cemeteries; acres of shrubbery and heavy stone, so arranged and lonely and unlike anything in the living world. Cities of the dead, indeed; cities of the forgotten, of the "put away." But this was open and free, this little square of long grass which the wind for ever stirred. Nothing but the sky overhead, and the many-coloured fields running on until they met that sky. The horses worked here in summer; the neighbours passed on their way to town; and over yonder, in the cornfield, Rosicky's own cattle would be eating fodder as winter came on. Nothing could be more undeath-like than this place; nothing could be more right for a man who had helped to do the work of great cities and had always longed for the open country and had got to it at last. Rosicky's life seemed to him complete and beautiful.

1928, 1932

The Sculptor's Funeral

A group of the townspeople stood on the station siding of a little Kansas town, awaiting the coming of the night train, which was already twenty minutes overdue. The snow had fallen thick over everything; in the pale starlight the line of bluffs across the wide, white meadows south of the town made soft, smoke-colored curves against the clear sky. The men on the siding stood first on one foot and then on the other, their hands thrust deep into their trousers pockets, their overcoats open, their shoulders screwed up with the cold; and they glanced from time to time toward the southeast, where the railroad track wound along the river shore. They conversed in low tones and moved about restlessly, seeming uncertain as to what was expected of them. There was but one of the company who looked as if he knew exactly why he was there, and he kept conspicuously apart; walking to the far end of the platform, returning to the station door, then pacing up the track again, his chin sunk in the high collar of his overcoat, his burly shoulders drooping forward, his gait heavy and dogged. Presently he was approached by a tall, spare, grizzled man clad in a faded Grand Army suit,[1] who shuffled out from the group and advanced with a certain deference, craning his neck forward until his back made the angle of a jack-knife three-quarters open.

"I reckon she's a goin' to be pretty late again tonight, Jim," he remarked in a squeaky falsetto. "S'pose it's the snow?"

"I don't know," responded the other man with a shade of annoyance, speaking from out an astonishing cataract of red beard that grew fiercely and thickly in all directions.

---

1. Quasi-military, uniform-inspired suit worn by members of the Grand Army of the Republic (G.A.R.), a fraternal organization for northern veterans of the Civil War founded in 1866.

The spare man shifted the quill toothpick he was chewing to the other side of his mouth. "It ain't likely that anybody from the East will come with the corpse, I s'pose," he went on reflectively.

"I don't know," responded the other, more curtly than before.

"It's too bad he didn't belong to some lodge or other. I like an order funeral[2] myself. They seem more appropriate for people of some repytation," the spare man continued, with an ingratiating concession in his shrill voice, as he carefully placed his toothpick in his vest pocket. He always carried the flag at the G.A.R. funerals in the town.

The heavy man turned on his heel, without replying, and walked up the siding. The spare man rejoined the uneasy group. "Jim's ez full ez a tick, ez ushel," he commented commiseratingly.

Just then a distant whistle sounded, and there was a shuffling of feet on the platform. A number of lanky boys, of all ages, appeared as suddenly and slimily as eels wakened by the crack of thunder; some came from the waiting-room, where they had been warming themselves by the red stove, or half asleep on the slat benches; others uncoiled themselves from baggage trucks or slid out of express wagons. Two clambered down from the driver's seat of a hearse that stood backed up against the siding. They straightened their stooping shoulders and lifted their heads, and a flash of momentary animation kindled their dull eyes at that cold, vibrant scream, the world-wide call for men. It stirred them like the note of a trumpet; just as it had often stirred the man who was coming home tonight, in his boyhood.

The night express shot, red as a rocket, from out the eastward marsh lands and wound along the river shore under the long lines of shivering poplars that sentinelled the meadows, the escaping steam hanging in gray masses against the pale sky and blotting out the Milky Way. In a moment the red glare from the headlight streamed up the snow-covered track before the siding and glittered on the wet, black rails. The burly man with the disheveled red beard walked swiftly up the platform toward the approaching train, uncovering his head as he went. The group of men behind him hesitated, glanced questioningly at one another, and awkwardly followed his example. The train stopped, and the crowd shuffled up to the express car just as the door was thrown open, the man in the G.A.R. suit thrusting his head forward with curiosity. The express messenger appeared in the doorway, accompanied by a young man in a long ulster and travelling cap.

"Are Mr. Merrick's friends here?" inquired the young man.

The group on the platform swayed uneasily. Philip Phelps, the banker, responded with dignity: "We have come to take charge of the body. Mr. Merrick's father is very feeble and can't be about."

"Send the agent out here," growled the express messenger, "and tell the operator to lend a hand."

The coffin was got out of its rough-box and down on the snowy platform. The townspeople drew back enough to make room for it and then formed a close semicircle about it, looking curiously at the palm leaf which lay across the black cover. No one said anything. The baggage man stood by his truck, waiting to get at the trunks. The engine panted heavily, and the fireman dodged in and out among the wheels with his yellow torch and long oil-can, snapping the spindle boxes. The young Bostonian, one of the dead sculptor's

2. Lodge, order: fraternal organizations.

pupils who had come with the body, looked about him helplessly. He turned to the banker, the only one of that black, uneasy, stoop-shouldered group who seemed enough of an individual to be addressed.

"None of Mr. Merrick's brothers are here?" he asked uncertainly.

The man with the red beard for the first time stepped up and joined the others. "No, they have not come yet; the family is scattered. The body will be taken directly to the house." He stooped and took hold of one of the handles of the coffin.

"Take the long hill road up, Thompson, it will be easier on the horses," called the liveryman as the undertaker snapped the door of the hearse and prepared to mount to the driver's seat.

Laird, the red-bearded lawyer, turned again to the stranger: "We didn't know whether there would be any one with him or not," he explained. "It's a long walk, so you'd better go up in the hack." He pointed to a single battered conveyance, but the young man replied stiffly: "Thank you, but I think I will go up with the hearse. If you don't object," turning to the undertaker, "I'll ride with you."

They clambered up over the wheels and drove off in the starlight up the long, white hill toward the town. The lamps in the still village were shining from under the low, snow-burdened roofs; and beyond, on every side, the plains reached out into emptiness, peaceful and wide as the soft sky itself, and wrapped in a tangible, white silence.

When the hearse backed up to a wooden sidewalk before a naked, weather-beaten frame house, the same composite, ill-defined group that had stood upon the station siding was huddled about the gate. The front yard was an icy swamp, and a couple of warped planks, extending from the sidewalk to the door, made a sort of rickety footbridge. The gate hung on one hinge, and was opened wide with difficulty. Steavens, the young stranger, noticed that something black was tied to the knob of the front door.

The grating sound made by the casket, as it was drawn from the hearse, was answered by a scream from the house; the front door was wrenched open, and a tall, corpulent woman rushed out bare-headed into the snow and flung herself upon the coffin, shrieking: "My boy, my boy! And this is how you've come home to me!"

As Steavens turned away and closed his eyes with a shudder of unutterable repulsion, another woman, also tall, but flat and angular, dressed entirely in black, darted out of the house and caught Mrs. Merrick by the shoulders, crying sharply: "Come, come, mother; you mustn't go on like this!" Her tone changed to one of obsequious solemnity as she turned to the banker: "The parlour is ready, Mr. Phelps."

The bearers carried the coffin along the narrow boards, while the under-taker ran ahead with the coffin-rests. They bore it into a large, unheated room that smelled of dampness and disuse and furniture polish, and set it down under a hanging lamp ornamented with jingling glass prisms and before a "Rogers group" of John Alden and Priscilla, wreathed with smilax.[3] Henry Steavens stared about him with the sickening conviction that there had

3. A flowering vine; also the name of a nymph turned into the flower in Greek mythology. "Rogers group": plaster figurines of literary and historical subjects, mass-produced by John Rogers from 1859 to 1892. "John Alden and Priscilla": Pilgrims on the *Mayflower* whose love was treated in Henry Wadsworth Longfellow's best-selling 1858 narrative poem *The Courtship of Miles Standish*.

been a mistake, and that he had somehow arrived at the wrong destination. He looked at the clover-green Brussels,[4] the fat plush upholstery, among the hand-painted china placques and panels and vases, for some mark of identification,—for something that might once conceivably have belonged to Harvey Merrick. It was not until he recognized his friend in the crayon portrait of a little boy in kilts and curls, hanging above the piano, that he felt willing to let any of these people approach the coffin.

"Take the lid off, Mr. Thompson; let me see my boy's face," wailed the elder woman between her sobs. This time Steavens looked fearfully, almost beseechingly into her face, red and swollen under its masses of strong, black, shiny hair. He flushed, dropped his eyes, and then, almost incredulously, looked again. There was a kind of power about her face—a kind of brutal handsomeness, even; but it was scarred and furrowed by violence, and so colored and coarsened by fiercer passions that grief seemed never to have laid a gentle finger there. The long nose was distended and knobbed at the end, and there were deep lines on either side of it; her heavy, black brows almost met across her forehead, her teeth were large and square, and set far apart—teeth that could tear. She filled the room; the men were obliterated, seemed tossed about like twigs in an angry water, and even Steavens felt himself being drawn into the whirlpool.

The daughter—the tall, raw-boned woman in crêpe, with a mourning comb in her hair which curiously lengthened her long face—sat stiffly upon the sofa, her hands, conspicuous for their large knuckles, folded in her lap, her mouth and eyes drawn down, solemnly awaiting the opening of the coffin. Near the door stood a mulatto woman, evidently a servant in the house, with a timid bearing and an emaciated face pitifully sad and gentle. She was weeping silently, the corner of her calico apron lifted to her eyes, occasionally suppressing a long, quivering sob. Steavens walked over and stood beside her.

Feeble steps were heard on the stairs, and an old man, tall and frail, odorous of pipe smoke, with shaggy, unkept gray hair and a dingy beard, tobacco stained about the mouth, entered uncertainly. He went slowly up to the coffin and stood rolling a blue cotton handkerchief between his hands, seeming so pained and embarrassed by his wife's orgy of grief that he had no consciousness of anything else.

"There, there, Annie, dear, don't take on so," he quavered timidly, putting out a shaking hand and awkwardly patting her elbow. She turned and sank upon his shoulder with such violence that he tottered a little. He did not even glance toward the coffin, but continued to look at her with a dull, frightened, appealing expression, as a spaniel looks at the whip. His sunken cheeks slowly reddened and burned with miserable shame. When his wife rushed from the room, her daughter strode after her with set lips. The servant stole up to the coffin, bent over it for a moment, and then slipped away to the kitchen, leaving Steavens, the lawyer, and the father to themselves. The old man stood looking down at his dead son's face. The sculptor's splendid head seemed even more noble in its rigid stillness than in life. The dark hair had crept down upon the wide forehead; the face seemed strangely long, but in it there was not that repose we expect to find in the faces of the dead. The brows were so drawn that there were two deep lines above the

4. Carpeting developed in Europe and mass-produced in the United States beginning in the mid-nineteenth century.

beaked nose, and the chin was thrust forward defiantly. It was as though the strain of life had been so sharp and bitter that death could not at once relax the tension and smooth the countenance into perfect peace—as though he were still guarding something precious, which might even yet be wrested from him.

The old man's lips were working under his stained beard. He turned to the lawyer with timid deference: "Phelps and the rest are comin' back to set up with Harve, ain't they?" he asked. "Thank 'ee, Jim, thank 'ee." He brushed the hair back gently from his son's forehead. "He was a good boy, Jim; always a good boy. He was ez gentle ez a child and the kindest of 'em all—only we didn't none of us ever onderstand him." The tears trickled slowly down his beard and dropped upon the sculptor's coat.

"Martin, Martin! Oh, Martin! come here," his wife wailed from the top of the stairs. The old man started timorously: "Yes, Annie, I'm coming." He turned away, hesitated, stood for a moment in miserable indecision; then reached back and patted the dead man's hair softly, and stumbled from the room.

"Poor old man, I didn't think he had any tears left. Seems as if his eyes would have gone dry long ago. At his age nothing cuts very deep," remarked the lawyer.

Something in his tone made Steavens glance up. While the mother had been in the room, the young man had scarcely seen any one else; but now, from the moment he first glanced into Jim Laird's florid face and bloodshot eyes, he knew that he had found what he had been heartsick at not finding before—the feeling, the understanding, that must exist in some one, even here.

The man was red as his beard, with features swollen and blurred by dissipation, and a hot, blazing blue eye. His face was strained—that of a man who is controlling himself with difficulty—and he kept plucking at his beard with a sort of fierce resentment. Steavens, sitting by the window, watched him turn down the glaring lamp, still its jangling pendants with an angry gesture, and then stand with his hands locked behind him, staring down into the master's face. He could not help wondering what link there had been between the porcelain vessel and so sooty a lump of potter's clay.

From the kitchen an uproar was sounding; when the dining-room door opened, the import of it was clear. The mother was abusing the maid for having forgotten to make the dressing for the chicken salad which had been prepared for the watchers. Steavens had never heard anything in the least like it; it was injured, emotional, dramatic abuse, unique and masterly in its excruciating cruelty, as violent and unrestrained as had been her grief of twenty minutes before. With a shudder of disgust the lawyer went into the dining-room and closed the door into the kitchen.

"Poor Roxy's getting it now," he remarked when he came back. "The Merricks took her out of the poor-house years ago; and if her loyalty would let her, I guess the poor old thing could tell tales that would curdle your blood. She's the mulatto woman who was standing in here a while ago, with her apron to her eyes. The old woman is a fury; there never was anybody like her. She made Harvey's life a hell for him when he lived at home; he was so sick ashamed of it. I never could see how he kept himself sweet."

"He was wonderful," said Steavens slowly, "wonderful; but until tonight I have never known how wonderful."

"That is the eternal wonder of it, anyway; that it can come even from such a dung heap as this," the lawyer cried, with a sweeping gesture which seemed to indicate much more than the four walls within which they stood.

"I think I'll see whether I can get a little air. The room is so close I am beginning to feel rather faint," murmured Steavens, struggling with one of the windows. The sash was stuck, however, and would not yield, so he sat down dejectedly and began pulling at his collar. The lawyer came over, loosened the sash with one blow of his red fist and sent the window up a few inches. Steavens thanked him, but the nausea which had been gradually climbing into his throat for the last half hour left him with but one desire—a desperate feeling that he must get away from this place with what was left of Harvey Merrick. Oh, he comprehended well enough now the quiet bitterness of the smile that he had seen so often on his master's lips!

Once when Merrick returned from a visit home, he brought with him a singularly feeling and suggestive bas-relief[5] of a thin, faded old woman, sitting and sewing something pinnned to her knee; while a full-lipped, full-blooded little urchin, his trousers held up by a single gallows,[6] stood beside her, impatiently twitching her gown to call her attention to a butterfly he had caught. Steavens, impressed by the tender and delicate modelling of the thin, tired face, had asked him if it were his mother. He remembered the dull flush that had burned up in the sculptor's face.

The lawyer was sitting in a rocking-chair beside the coffin, his head thrown back and his eyes closed. Steavens looked at him earnestly, puzzled at the line of the chin, and wondering why a man should conceal a feature of such distinction under that disfiguring shock of beard. Suddenly, as though he felt the young sculptor's keen glance, Jim Laird opened his eyes.

"Was he always a good deal of an oyster?" he asked abruptly. "He was terribly shy as a boy."

"Yes, he was an oyster, since you put it so," rejoined Steavens. "Although he could be very fond of people, he always gave one the impression of being detached. He disliked violent emotion; he was reflective, and rather distrustful of himself—except, of course, as regarded his work. He was sure enough there. He distrusted men pretty thoroughly and women even more, yet somehow without believing ill of them. He was determined, indeed, to believe the best; but he seemed afraid to investigate."

"A burnt dog dreads the fire," said the lawyer grimly, and closed his eyes.

Steavens went on and on, reconstructing that whole miserable boyhood. All this raw, biting ugliness had been the portion of the man whose mind was to become an exhaustless gallery of beautiful impressions—so sensitive that the mere shadow of a poplar leaf flickering against a sunny wall would be etched and held there for ever. Surely, if ever a man had the magic word in his finger tips, it was Merrick. Whatever he touched, he revealed its holiest secret; liberated it from enchantment and restored it to its pristine loveliness. Upon whatever he had come in contact with, he had left a beautiful record of the experience—a sort of ethereal signature; a scent, a sound, a color that was his own.

Steavens understood now the real tragedy of his master's life; neither love nor wine, as many had conjectured; but a blow which had fallen earlier and

5. French, "low relief": sculpture in which an image is slightly raised against a background.   6. One of a pair of suspenders.

cut deeper than anything else could have done—a shame not his, and yet so unescapably his, to hide in his heart from his very boyhood. And without— the frontier warfare; the yearning of a boy, cast ashore upon a desert of newness and ugliness and sordidness, for all that is chastened and old, and noble with traditions.

At eleven o'clock the tall, flat woman in black announced that the watchers were arriving, and asked them to "step into the dining-room." As Steavens rose, the lawyer said dryly: "You go on—it'll be a good experience for you. I'm not equal to that crowd tonight; I've had twenty years of them."

As Steavens closed the door after him he glanced back at the lawyer, sitting by the coffin in the dim light, with his chin resting on his hand.

The same misty group that had stood before the door of the express car shuffled into the dining-room. In the light of the kerosene lamp they separated and became individuals. The minister, a pale, feeble-looking man with white hair and blond chin-whiskers, took his seat beside a small side table and placed his Bible upon it. The Grand Army man sat down behind the stove and tilted his chair back comfortably against the wall, fishing his quill toothpick from his waistcoat pocket. The two bankers, Phelps and Elder, sat off in a corner behind the dinner-table, where they could finish their discussion of the new usury law and its effect on chattel security loans.[7] The real estate agent, an old man with a smiling, hypocritical face, soon joined them. The coal and lumber dealer and the cattle shipper sat on opposite sides of the hard coal-burner, their feet on the nickel-work.[8] Steavens took a book from his pocket and began to read. The talk around him ranged through various topics of local interest while the house was quieting down. When it was clear that the members of the family were in bed, the Grand Army man hitched his shoulders and, untangling his long legs, caught his heels on the rounds of his chair.

"S'pose there'll be a will, Phelps?" he queried in his weak falsetto.

The banker laughed disagreeably, and began trimming his nails with a pearl-handled pocket-knife.

"There'll scarcely be any need for one, will there?" he queried in his turn.

The restless Grand Army man shifted his position again, getting his knees still nearer his chin. "Why, the ole man says Harve's done right well lately," he chirped.

The other banker spoke up. "I reckon he means by that Harve ain't asked him to mortgage any more farms lately, so as he could go on with his education."

"Seems like my mind don't reach back to a time when Harve wasn't bein' edycated," tittered the Grand Army man.

There was a general chuckle. The minister took out his handkerchief and blew his nose sonorously. Banker Phelps closed his knife with a snap. "It's too bad the old man's sons didn't turn out better," he remarked with reflective authority. "They never hung together. He spent money enough on Harve to stock a dozen cattle-farms, and he might as well have poured it into Sand Creek. If Harve had stayed at home and helped nurse what little they had, and gone into stock on the old man's bottom farm, they might all have been

7. Loans backed by the debtor's personal property. Kansas revised its laws regulating interest on loans and prohibiting usury (excessive interest) in 1889.
8. Cast-iron stoves were often finished with nickel trim work, sometimes including footrests.

well fixed. But the old man had to trust everything to tenants and was cheated right and left."

"Harve never could have handled stock none," interposed the cattleman. "He hadn't it in him to be sharp. Do you remember when he bought Sander's mules for eight-year olds, when everybody in town knew that Sander's father-in-law give 'em to his wife for a wedding present eighteen years before, an' they was full-grown mules then?"

The company laughed discreetly, and the Grand Army man rubbed his knees with a spasm of childish delight.

"Harve never was much account for anything practical, and he shore was never fond of work," began the coal and lumber dealer. "I mind the last time he was home; the day he left, when the old man was out to the barn helpin' his hand hitch up to take Harve to the train, and Cal Moots was patchin' up the fence; Harve, he come out on the step and sings out, in his ladylike voice: 'Cal Moots, Cal Moots! please come cord my trunk.'"

"That's Harve for you," approved the Grand Army man. "I kin hear him howlin' yet, when he was a big feller in long pants and his mother used to whale him with a rawhide in the barn for lettin' the cows git foundered in the cornfield when he was drivin' 'em home from pasture. He killed a cow of mine that-a-way onct—a pure Jersey and the best milker I had, an' the ole man had to put up for her. Harve, he was watchin' the sun set acrost the marshes when the anamile got away."

"Where the old man made his mistake was in sending the boy East to school," said Phelps, stroking his goatee and speaking in a deliberate, judicial tone. "There was where he got his head full of nonsense. What Harve needed, of all people, was a course in some first-class Kansas City business college."

The letters were swimming before Steavens's eyes. Was it possible that these men did not understand, that the palm on the coffin meant nothing to them? The very name of their town would have remained for ever buried in the postal guide had it not been now and again mentioned in the world in connection with Harvey Merrick's. He remembered what his master had said to him on the day of his death, after the congestion of both lungs had shut off any probability of recovery, and the sculptor had asked his pupil to send his body home. "It's not a pleasant place to be lying while the world is moving and doing and bettering," he had said with a feeble smile, "but it rather seems as though we ought to go back to the place we came from, in the end. The townspeople will come in for a look at me; and after they have had their say, I shan't have much to fear from the judgment of God!"

The cattleman took up the comment. "Forty's young for a Merrick to cash in; they usually hang on pretty well. Probably he helped it along with whisky."

"His mother's people were not long lived, and Harvey never had a robust constitution," said the minister mildly. He would have liked to say more. He had been the boy's Sunday-school teacher, and had been fond of him; but he felt that he was not in a position to speak. His own sons had turned out badly, and it was not a year since one of them had made his last trip home in the express car, shot in a gambling-house in the Black Hills.

"Nevertheless, there is no disputin' that Harve frequently looked upon the wine when it was red, also variegated, and it shore made an oncommon fool of him," moralized the cattleman.

Just then the door leading into the parlour rattled loudly and every one started involuntarily, looking relieved when only Jim Laird came out. The Grand Army man ducked his head when he saw the spark in his blue, blood-shot eye. They were all afraid of Jim; he was a drunkard, but he could twist the law to suit his client's needs as no other man in all western Kansas could do, and there were many who tried. The lawyer closed the door behind him, leaned back against it and folded his arms, cocking his head a little to one side. When he assumed this attitude in the court-room, ears were always pricked up, as it usually foretold a flood of withering sarcasm.

"I've been with you gentlemen before," he began in a dry, even tone, "when you've sat by the coffins of boys born and raised in this town; and, if I remember rightly, you were never any too well satisfied when you checked them up. What's the matter, anyhow? Why is it that reputable young men are as scarce as millionaires in Sand City? It might almost seem to a stranger that there was some way something the matter with your progressive town. Why did Ruben Sayer, the brightest young lawyer you ever turned out, after he had come home from the university as straight as a die, take to drinking and forge a check and shoot himself? Why did Bill Merrit's son die of the shakes in a saloon in Omaha? Why was Mr. Thomas's son, here, shot in a gambling-house? Why did young Adams burn his mill to beat the insurance companies and go to the pen?"

The lawyer paused and unfolded his arms, laying one clenched fist quietly on the table. "I'll tell you why. Because you drummed nothing but money and knavery into their ears from the time they wore knickerbockers; because you carped away at them as you've been carping here tonight, holding our friends Phelps and Elder up to them for their models, as our grandfathers held up George Washington and John Adams. But the boys were young, and raw at the business you put them to, and how could they match coppers with such artists as Phelps and Elder? You wanted them to be successful rascals; they were only unsuccessful ones—that's all the difference. There was only one boy ever raised in this borderland between ruffianism and civilization who didn't come to grief, and you hated Harvey Merrick more for winning out than you hated all the other boys who got under the wheels. Lord, Lord, how you did hate him! Phelps, here, is fond of saying that he could buy and sell us all out any time he's a mind to; but he knew Harve wouldn't have given a tinker's damn for his bank and all his cattlefarms put together; and a lack of appreciation, that way, goes hard with Phelps.

"Old Nimrod thinks Harve drank too much; and this from such as Nimrod and me!

"Brother Elder says Harve was too free with the old man's money—fell short in filial consideration, maybe. Well, we can all remember the very tone in which brother Elder swore his own father was a liar, in the county court; and we all know that the old man came out of that partnership with his son as bare as a sheared lamb. But maybe I'm getting personal, and I'd better be driving ahead at what I want to say."

The lawyer paused a moment, squared his heavy shoulders, and went on: "Harvey Merrick and I went to school together, back East. We were dead in earnest, and we wanted you all to be proud of us some day. We meant to be great men. Even I, and I haven't lost my sense of humor, gentlemen, I meant to be a great man. I came back here to practice, and I found you didn't in the least want me to be a great man. You wanted me to be a shrewd lawyer—oh, yes! Our veteran here wanted me to get him an increase of pension, because he had dyspepsia; Phelps wanted a new county survey that would put the widow Wilson's little bottom farm inside his south line; Elder wanted to lend money at 5 per cent a month, and get it collected; and Stark here wanted to wheedle old women up in Vermont into investing their annuities in real-estate mortgages that are not worth the paper they are written on. Oh, you needed me hard enough, and you'll go on needing me!

"Well, I came back here and became the damned shyster you wanted me to be. You pretend to have some sort of respect for me; and yet you'll stand up and throw mud at Harvey Merrick, whose soul you couldn't dirty and whose hands you couldn't tie. Oh, you're a discriminating lot of Christians! There have been times when the sight of Harvey's name in some Eastern paper has made me hang my head like a whipped dog; and, again, times when I liked to think of him off there in the world, away from all this hog-wallow, climbing the big, clean up-grade he'd set for himself.

"And we? Now that we've fought and lied and sweated and stolen, and hated as only the disappointed strugglers in a bitter, dead little Western town know how to do, what have we got to show for it? Harvey Merrick wouldn't have given one sunset over your marshes for all you've got put together, and you know it. It's not for me to say why, in the inscrutable wisdom of God, a genius should ever have been called from this place of hatred and bitter waters; but I want this Boston man to know that the drivel he's been hearing here tonight is the only tribute any truly great man could have from such a lot of sick, side-tracked, burnt-dog, land-poor sharks as the here-present financiers of Sand City—upon which town may God have mercy!"

The lawyer thrust out his hand to Steavens as he passed him, caught up his overcoat in the hall, and had left the house before the Grand Army man had had time to lift his ducked head and crane his long neck about at his fellows.

Next day Jim Laird was drunk and unable to attend the funeral services. Steavens called twice at his office, but was compelled to start East without seeing him. He had a presentiment that he would hear from him again, and left his address on the lawyer's table; but if Laird found it, he never acknowledged it. The thing in him that Harvey Merrick had loved must have gone under ground with Harvey Merrick's coffin; for it never spoke again, and Jim got the cold he died of driving across the Colorado mountains to defend one of Phelps's sons who had got into trouble out there by cutting government timber.

1905, 1920

AMY LOWELL
1874–1925

Born in Brookline, Massachusetts, the fifth and last child, twelve years younger than her nearest sibling, Amy Lowell hailed from one of Boston's wealthiest and most prestigious and powerful families. The first Lowell arrived at Massachusetts Bay Colony in 1639; from the revolutionary years on, when a Lowell was made a judge by George Washington, no era was without one or more Lowells prominent in the intellectual, religious, political, philanthropic, and commercial life of New England. In the early nineteenth century her paternal grandfather and his brothers established the Lowell textile mills in Lowell, Massachusetts—the town itself had been founded by the Lowells in 1653. The success of these mills changed the economy of New England. Profits were invested in utilities, highways, railroads, and banks. In the same generation her maternal grandfather, Abbot Lawrence, established a second New England textile dynasty. All the Lowell men went to Harvard. Traditionally, those who were not in business became Unitarian ministers or scholars—the poet James Russell Lowell was her great-uncle; her father, Augustus, was important to the founding of the Massachusetts Institute of Technology; her brother Percival was a pioneering scholar of Japanese and Korean civilization and an astronomer (he founded the Lowell Observatory and discovered the planet Pluto); her brother Abbot Lawrence was president of Harvard from 1909 to 1933.

But none of the millionaires, manufacturers, philanthropists, statesmen, ambassadors, judges, and scholars in Amy Lowell's background could give this energetic and unusually intelligent young woman a model to follow. They were all men, and the rules for Lowell women were different. Women in the family were expected to marry well, imbue their children with a strong sense of family pride, oversee the running of several homes, and participate in upper-class Boston's busy social world. None of this interested Lowell in the least. Yet she believed in the importance of her heritage and shared the self-confidence and drive to contribute notably to public life characteristic of Lowell men.

Resisting the kind of formal education available to women of her class at the time, she attended school only between the ages of ten and seventeen. She educated herself through the use of her family's extensive private library as well as the resources of the Boston Athenaeum, a dues-paying library club founded by one of her ancestors early in the nineteenth century. She had enjoyed writing from childhood on, but did not venture into professional authorship until 1912, at the age of thirty-eight. In that year, her first book of poems—*A Dome of Many-Coloured Glass*—achieved both popular and critical success.

The year 1912 was the year that Harriet Monroe launched her influential little magazine, *Poetry,* and when in January 1913 Lowell read H.D.'s imagistic poetry she was converted to this new style. She decided to devote her popularity and social prominence to popularizing imagism and with characteristic energy and self-confidence journeyed to England to meet H.D., Ezra Pound, D. H. Lawrence, Richard Aldington, and other participants in the informal movement. When Pound abandoned imagism for vorticism, Lowell became the chief spokesperson for the movement, editing several imagist anthologies. Two volumes of original criticism by Lowell—*Six French Poets* (1915) and *Tendencies in Modern American Poetry* (1917)—also forwarded the cause. Pound, upstaged as a publicist, enviously renamed the movement "Amygism." Lowell retorted that "it was not until I entered the arena and Ezra dropped out that Imagism had to be considered seriously."

Lowell's own poetry—published in *Sword Blades and Poppy Seed* (1914), *Men, Women, and Ghosts* (1916), *Can Grande's Castle* (1918), *Pictures of the Floating World* (1919), and *Legends* (1921)—was never exclusively imagistic but included long historical narrative poems and journalistic prose poems and used standard verse patterns, blank verse, and a Whitmanesque free verse resembling the open line developed by Carl Sandburg. Her best poems tend to enclose sharp imagistic representation within this relatively fluid line, thereby achieving an effect of simultaneous compactness and flexibility. Like many women poets, she worked with a symbolic vocabulary of flowers and color.

Lowell enjoyed her success and cheerfully went on the lecture circuit as a celebrity, making innumerable close friendships as a result of her warmth and generosity. Despite health problems that plagued her for most of her life, she remained full of energy and zest. She depended for support on the companionship of Ada Dwyer Russell, a former actress, for whom she wrote many of her most moving appreciations of female beauty. Although she traveled widely in Europe, she was ultimately committed to New England and the Lowell heritage, both of which fused in an attachment to her home, Sevenels, in Brookline. A devotee of Romantic poetry and especially of Keats, she had begun to collect Keats manuscripts in 1905; these now form the basis of the great collection at Harvard University. In addition to all her other activities in the 1920s, she worked on a two-volume biography of Keats that greatly extended the published information about the poet when it appeared in 1925, although its psychological approach offended many traditional critics.

Lowell was just fifty-one when she died. Despite continued sniping from the high modernist poets who thought her work was too accessible, her poetry continued to be both popular and critically esteemed until the 1950s, when scholars focused the canon on a very small number of writers. The efforts of feminists to rediscover and republicize the work of neglected women authors as well as the researches of literary historians into the whole picture of American literary achievement have together brought her work back into the spotlight that it occupied during her lifetime.

The texts printed here are from Lowell's *Complete Poems* (1955).

The Captured Goddess

Over the housetops,
Above the rotating chimney-pots,
I have seen a shiver of amethyst,
And blue and cinnamon have flickered
A moment,   5
At the far end of a dusty street.

Through sheeted rain
Has come a lustre of crimson,
And I have watched moonbeams
Hushed by a film of palest green.   10

It was her wings,
Goddess!
Who stepped over the clouds,
And laid her rainbow feathers
Aslant on the currents of the air.   15

I followed her for long,
With gazing eyes and stumbling feet.

I cared not where she led me,
My eyes were full of colors:
Saffrons, rubies, the yellows of beryls,   20
And the indigo-blue of quartz;
Flights of rose, layers of chrysoprase,
Points of orange, spirals of vermilion,
The spotted gold of tiger-lily petals,
The loud pink of bursting hydrangeas.   25
I followed,
And watched for the flashing of her wings.

In the city I found her,
The narrow-streeted city.
In the market-place I came upon her,   30
Bound and trembling.
Her fluted wings were fastened to her sides with cords,
She was naked and cold,
For that day the wind blew
Without sunshine.   35

Men chaffered for her,
They bargained in silver and gold,
In copper, in wheat,
And called their bids across the market-place.

The Goddess wept.   40

Hiding my face I fled,
And the grey wind hissed behind me,
Along the narrow streets.

                                                    1914

Venus Transiens

Tell me,
Was Venus more beautiful
Than you are,
When she topped
The crinkled waves,   5
Drifting shoreward
On her plaited shell?
Was Botticelli's[1] vision
Fairer than mine;
And were the painted rosebuds   10
He tossed his lady,
Of better worth
Than the words I blow about you

---

1. Sandro Botticelli (c. 1440–1510), Italian Renaissance painter among whose works is the *Birth of Venus*, depicting the Greek goddess of love and beauty rising from the ocean on a seashell.

To cover your too great loveliness
As with a gauze   15
Of misted silver?

For me,
You stand poised
In the blue and buoyant air,
Cinctured by bright winds,   20
Treading the sunlight.
And the waves which precede you
Ripple and stir
The sands at my feet.

1919

Madonna of the Evening Flowers

All day long I have been working,
Now I am tired.
I call: "Where are you?"
But there is only the oak tree rustling in the wind.
The house is very quiet,   5
The sun shines in on your books,
On your scissors and thimble just put down,
But you are not there.
Suddenly I am lonely:
Where are you?   10
I go about searching.

Then I see you,
Standing under a spire of pale blue larkspur,
With a basket of roses on your arm.
You are cool, like silver,   15
And you smile.
I think the Canterbury bells[1] are playing little tunes.

You tell me that the peonies need spraying,
That the columbines have overrun all bounds,
That the pyrus japonica should be cut back and rounded.   20
You tell me these things.
But I look at you, heart of silver,
White heart-flame of polished silver,
Burning beneath the blue steeples of the larkspur,
And I long to kneel instantly at your feet,   25
While all about us peal the loud, sweet *Te Deums* of the
        Canterbury bells.

1919

---

1. Little bell-shaped blue flowers. Lowell puns on the bells of Canterbury Cathedral in England pealing out religious music.

September, 1918

This afternoon was the colour of water falling through sunlight;
The trees glittered with the tumbling of leaves;
The sidewalks shone like alleys of dropped maple leaves;
And the houses ran along them laughing out of square, open
    windows.
Under a tree in the park,   5
Two little boys, lying flat on their faces,
Were carefully gathering red berries
To put in a pasteboard box.

Some day there will be no war.
Then I shall take out this afternoon   10
And turn it in my fingers,
And remark the sweet taste of it upon my palate,
And note the crisp variety of its flights of leaves.
To-day I can only gather it
And put it into my lunch-box,   15
For I have time for nothing
But the endeavour to balance myself
Upon a broken world.

                                              1919

St. Louis

June

Flat,
Flat,
Long as sight
Either way,
An immense country,   5
With a great river
Steaming it full of moist, unbearable heat.
The orchards are little quincunxes of Noah's Ark trees,
The plows and horses are children's toys tracing amusingly shallow lines
    upon an illimitable surface.
Great chunks of life to match the country,   10
Great lungs to breathe this hot, wet air.

But it is not mine.
Mine is a land of hills
Lying couchant in the angles of heraldic beasts
About white villages.   15
A land of singing elms and pine-trees.
A restless up and down land
Always mounting, dipping, slipping into a different contour,
Where the roads turn every hundred yards or so,
Where brooks rattle forgotten Indian names to tired farm-houses,   20

And faint spires of old meeting-houses
Flaunt their golden weather-cocks in a brave show of challenge at a sunset
    sky.

Here the heat stuffs down with the thickness of boiled feathers,
The river runs in steam.
There, lilacs are in bloom,   25
Cool blue-purples, wine-reds, whites,
Flying colour to quiet dooryards.
Grown year on year to a suddenness of old perfection,
Saying "Before! Before!" to each new Spring.
Here is "Now,"   30
But "Before" is mine with the lilacs,
With the white sea of everywhither,
With the heraldic, story-telling hills.

                                                                    1927

GERTRUDE STEIN
1874–1946

Among modernists active between the wars, Gertrude Stein was more radically experimental than most. She pushed language to its limits—and kept on pushing. Her work was sometimes literal nonsense, often funny, and always exciting to those who thought of writing as a craft and language as a medium. As Sherwood Anderson wrote, "she is laying word against word, relating sound to sound, feeling for the taste, the smell, the rhythm of the individual word. She is attempting to do something for the writers of our English speech that may be better understood after a time, and she is not in a hurry."

Stein's grandparents were well-off German Jewish immigrants who, at the time of her birth, were established in business in Baltimore. Born in Allegheny, Pennsylvania, she was the youngest of seven children; the family lived abroad from 1875 to 1879 and then settled in northern California. Her parents died when she was an adolescent, leaving their five surviving children well provided for. Stein made a family with her favorite brother, Leo, for many years. When he went to Harvard in 1892 she followed and was admitted to Harvard's "annex for women"—now Radcliffe College. She studied there with the great psychologist William James; some of her early writings—for example, *Three Lives* (1909) and *The Making of Americans,* which she completed in 1908 but did not publish until 1925—are probably trying to apply his theories of consciousness: consciousness as unique to each individual, as an ongoing stream, a perpetual present. In *Three Lives,* also, Stein set herself the difficult task of representing the consciousnesses of three ordinary, working-class women whose lives and minds were not the conventional material of serious literature.

When Leo moved on to Johns Hopkins to study biology, Stein followed, enrolling in the medical school. At the end of her fourth year, she failed intentionally, for several reasons: Leo had become interested in art and decided to go to Europe, she had begun to write, and she had become erotically involved with two women (the

Gertrude Stein and Picasso's Portrait, Man Ray, 1922. Man Ray, one of the most important of modernist photographers, posed Gertrude Stein at home in front of her 1906 portrait by Pablo Picasso. Stein in her turn composed many "portraits" in writing of her artist friends, including Picasso and Henri Matisse.

story of this triangle formed the basis of her novel *Q.E.D.,* published posthumously in 1950). In early 1903 Leo settled in Paris; Stein joined him that fall. They began to collect modern art and became good friends with many of the brilliant aspiring painters of the day, including Pablo Picasso, Georges Braque, and Henri Matisse. Stein's friendship with the painters was extremely important for her development, for she reproduced some of their experiments in the very different medium of words. Because of them, she came to think of words as tangible entities in themselves as well as vehicles conveying meaning or representing reality. The cubist movement in painting also affected her. Painters like Picasso and Braque believed that so-called representational paintings conveyed not what people actually saw but rather what they had learned to *think* they saw. The cubists wanted to reproduce a pure visual experience unmediated by cultural ideas. To see a "person" is to see a cultural construct. So they painted a human form reduced to various geometrical shapes as they might be seen from different angles when the form moved or the observer changed position. The degree to which their paintings shocked an audience measured, to Picasso and Braque, the degree to which that audience had lost its original perceiving power.

In 1909 the long companionship of Stein and her brother was complicated when Alice B. Toklas joined the household as Gertrude Stein's lover; she became her secretary, housekeeper, typist, editor, and lifelong companion. Leo moved out in 1913, and the art collection was divided, but the apartment at 27 rue de Fleurus continued to serve as a gathering place for French artists and intellectuals, American expatriates, and American visitors. Without much expectation that her work would achieve any wide audience, Stein continued to write and to advise younger writers like Ernest Hemingway and F. Scott Fitzgerald. "A great deal of description," she said about a draft of Hemingway's first novel, "and not particularly good description. Begin over again and concentrate." The need to concentrate and distill—the idea that description was too often an indulgence—was a lesson the younger writer took to heart.

In the 1920s Stein and Toklas began spending summers in the south of France, where they bought a small house in 1929. They lived there during the war, when they could not return to Paris. Devoted to their adopted country, Stein and Toklas did what they could for France during both world wars. They visited and entertained American soldiers, many of whom continued to write to the couple for years after they had returned to the United States and some of whom visited when they had occasion to return to France. Even though Stein returned to the United States only once, in 1934, on what turned into a very successful lecture tour, she and Toklas always thought of themselves as Americans.

Stein's work may be considered as falling into three overlapping chronological phases. In all three phases she wrote lesbian love poems that developed a complex private symbolism for socially unacceptable feelings and events—a symbolism so obscure that their eroticism is by no means apparent, even in a much more permissive age, and needs decoding if the poems are to be understood. At first she was interested in representing present time, which is the way she believed life was subjectively experienced. Experience goes on and yet changes minutely from instant to instant. In *The Making of Americans,* Stein explained, "there was a groping for using everything and there was a groping for a continuous present and there was an inevitable beginning of beginning again and again and again." And, she added humorously, "I went on to a thousand pages of it."

Stein's 1914 *Tender Buttons*, a cubist prose-poem collage of domestic objects, looked forward to her still more innovative work of the 1920s, where she treated words as things, carefully ignoring or defying the connection between words and meanings, continually undercutting expectations about order, coherence, and associations. Naturally, the effect of such writing is often absurd, because expected patterns do not appear but are continually disrupted and frustrated. There is a great deal of joking in this work, which she openly characterized as defiance of what she called, in one long essay-poem, "patriarchal poetry"—that is, orderly, hierarchical, rule-based poetry. Much of her experimental work remained unpublished in her lifetime.

The third phase of her work, in the 1930s, represents a campaign of self-promotion. Her autobiography, written as *The Autobiography of Alice B. Toklas* (1933), her *Everybody's Autobiography* (1937), and *Wars I Have Seen* (1945) are narratives that present some of her techniques in simplified form and also project her strong independent personality. Because they were easier to read, they were popular, as was her opera libretto *Four Saints in Three Acts* put to music by Virgil Thomson. By the time of her death she had become a public personality. In recent years, the extent of her influence on other writers and the intentions behind experiments that had previously seemed "meaningless" have become much more apparent. The women's movement, with its interest in women's lives, has also produced a new appreciation of her radical individualism.

The text of *Tender Buttons* is from the first edition (1914).

From Tender Buttons

Objects

A CARAFE, THAT IS A BLIND GLASS

A kind in glass and a cousin, a spectacle and nothing strange a single hurt color and an arrangement in a system to pointing. All this and not ordinary, not unordered in not resembling. The difference is spreading.

GLAZED GLITTER

Nickel, what is nickel, it is originally rid of a cover.

The change in that is that red weakens an hour. The change has come. There is no search. But there is, there is that hope and that interpretation and sometime, surely any is unwelcome, sometime there is breath and there will be a sinecure and charming very charming is that clean and cleansing. Certainly glittering is handsome and convincing.

There is no gratitude in mercy and in medicine. There can be breakages in Japanese. That is no programme. That is no color chosen. It was chosen yesterday, that showed spitting and perhaps washing and polishing. It certainly showed no obligation and perhaps if borrowing is not natural there is some use in giving.

A SUBSTANCE IN A CUSHION

The change of color is likely and a difference a very little difference is prepared. Sugar is not a vegetable.

Callous is something that hardening leaves behind what will be soft if there is a genuine interest in there being present as many girls as men. Does this change. It shows that dirt is clean when there is a volume.

A cushion has that cover. Supposing you do not like to change, supposing it is very clean that there is no change in appearance, supposing that there is regularity and a costume is that any the worse than an oyster and an exchange. Come to season that is there any extreme use in feather and cotton. Is there not much more joy in a table and more chairs and very likely roundness and a place to put them.

A circle of fine card board and a chance to see a tassel.

What is the use of a violent kind of delightfulness if there is no pleasure in not getting tired of it. The question does not come before there is a quotation. In any kind of place there is a top to covering and it is a pleasure at any rate there is some venturing in refusing to believe nonsense. It shows what use there is in a whole piece if one uses it and it is extreme and very likely the little things could be dearer but in any case there is a bargain and if there is the best thing to do is to take it away and wear it and then be reckless be reckless and resolved on returning gratitude.

Light blue and the same red with purple makes a change. It shows that there is no mistake. Any pink shows that and very likely it is reasonable. Very likely there should not be a finer fancy present. Some increase means a calamity and this is the best preparation for three and more being together. A little calm is so ordinary and in any case there is sweetness and some of that.

A seal and matches and a swan and ivy and a suit.

A closet, a closet does not connect under the bed. The band if it is white and black, the band has a green string. A sight a whole sight and a little groan grinding makes a trimming such a sweet singing trimming and a red thing not a round thing but a white thing, a red thing and a white thing.

The disgrace is not in carelessness nor even in sewing it comes out out of the way.

What is the sash like. The sash is not like anything mustard it is not like a same thing that has stripes, it is not even more hurt than that, it has a little top.

A BOX

Out of kindness comes redness and out of rudeness comes rapid same question, out of an eye comes research, out of selection comes painful cattle. So then the order is that a white way of being round is something suggesting a pin and is it disappointing, it is not, it is so rudimentary to be analysed and see a fine substance strangely, it is so earnest to have a green point not to red but to point again.

A PIECE OF COFFEE

More of double.

A place in no new table.

A single image is not splendor. Dirty is yellow. A sign of more in not mentioned. A piece of coffee is not a detainer. The resemblance to yellow is dirtier and distincter. The clean mixture is whiter and not coal color, never more coal color than altogether.

The sight of a reason, the same sight slighter, the sight of a simpler negative answer, the same sore sounder, the intention to wishing, the same splendor, the same furniture.

The time to show a message is when too late and later there is no hanging in a blight.

A not torn rose-wood color. If it is not dangerous then a pleasure and more than any other if it is cheap is not cheaper. The amusing side is that the sooner there are no fewer the more certain is the necessity dwindled. Supposing that the case contained rose-wood and a color. Supposing that there was no reason for a distress and more likely for a number, supposing that there was no astonishment, is it not necessary to mingle astonishment.

The settling of stationing cleaning is one way not to shatter scatter and scattering. The one way to use custom is to use soap and silk for cleaning. The one way to see cotton is to have a design concentrating the illusion and the illustration. The perfect way is to accustom the thing to have a lining and the shape of a ribbon and to be solid, quite solid in standing and to use heaviness in morning. It is light enough in that. It has that shape nicely. Very nicely may not be exaggerating. Very strongly may be sincerely fainting. May be strangely flattering. May not be strange in everything. May not be strange to.

DIRT AND NOT COPPER

Dirt and not copper makes a color darker. It makes the shape so heavy and makes no melody harder.

It makes mercy and relaxation and even a strength to spread a table fuller. There are more places not empty. They see cover.

NOTHING ELEGANT

A charm a single charm is doubtful. If the red is rose and there is a gate surrounding it, if inside is let in and there places change then certainly something is upright. It is earnest.

MILDRED'S UMBRELLA

A cause and no curve, a cause and loud enough, a cause and extra a loud clash and an extra wagon, a sign of extra, a sac a small sac and an established color and cunning, a slender grey and no ribbon, this means a loss a great loss a restitution.

A METHOD OF A CLOAK

A single climb to a line, a straight exchange to a cane, a desperate adventure and courage and a clock, all this which is a system, which has feeling, which has resignation and success, all makes an attractive black silver.

A RED STAMP

If lilies are lily white if they exhaust noise and distance and even dust, if they dusty will dirt a surface that has no extreme grace, if they do this and it is not necessary it is not at all necessary if they do this they need a catalogue.

A BOX

A large box is handily made of what is necessary to replace any substance. Suppose an example is necessary, the plainer it is made the more reason there is for some outward recognition that there is a result.

A box is made sometimes and them to see to see to it neatly and to have the holes stopped up makes it necessary to use paper.

A custom which is necessary when a box is used and taken is that a large part of the time there are three which have different connections. The one is on the table. The two are on the table. The three are on the table. The one, one is the same length as is shown by the cover being longer. The other is different there is more cover that shows it. The other is different and that makes the corners have the same shade the eight are in singular arrangement to make four necessary.

Lax, to have corners, to be lighter than some weight, to indicate a wedding journey, to last brown and not curious, to be wealthy, cigarettes are established by length and by doubling.

Left open, to be left pounded, to be left closed, to be circulating in summer and winter, and sick color that is grey that is not dusty and red shows, to be sure cigarettes do measure an empty length sooner than a choice in color.

Winged, to be winged means that white is yellow and pieces pieces that are brown are dust color if dust is washed off, then it is choice that is to say it is fitting cigarettes sooner than paper.

An increase why is an increase idle, why is silver cloister, why is the spark brighter, if it is brighter is there any result, hardly more than ever.

A PLATE

An occasion for a plate, an occasional resource is in buying and how soon does washing enable a selection of the same thing neater. If the party is small a clever song is in order.

Plates and a dinner set of colored china. Pack together a string and enough with it to protect the centre, cause a considerable haste and gather more as it is cooling, collect more trembling and not any even trembling, cause a whole thing to be a church.

A sad size a size that is not sad is blue as every bit of blue is precocious. A kind of green a game in green and nothing flat nothing quite flat and more round, nothing a particular color strangely, nothing breaking the losing of no little piece.

A splendid address a really splendid address is not shown by giving a flower freely, it is not shown by a mark or by wetting.

Cut cut in white, cut in white so lately. Cut more than any other and show it. Show it in the stem and in starting and in evening coming complication.

A lamp is not the only sign of glass. The lamp and the cake are not the only sign of stone. The lamp and the cake and the cover are not the only necessity altogether.

A plan a hearty plan, a compressed disease and no coffee, not even a card or a change to incline each way, a plan that has that excess and that break is the one that shows filling.

A SELTZER BOTTLE

Any neglect of many particles to a cracking, any neglect of this makes around it what is lead in color and certainly discolor in silver. The use of this is manifold. Supposing a certain time selected is assured, suppose it is even necessary, suppose no other extract is permitted and no more handling is needed, suppose the rest of the message is mixed with a very long slender needle and even if it could be any black border, supposing all this altogether made a dress and suppose it was actual, suppose the mean way to state it was occasional, if you suppose this in August and even more melodiously, if you suppose this even in the necessary incident of there certainly being no middle in summer and winter, suppose this and an elegant settlement a very elegant settlement is more than of consequence, it is not final and sufficient and substituted. This which was so kindly a present was constant.

A LONG DRESS

What is the current that makes machinery, that makes it crackle, what is the current that presents a long line and a necessary waist. What is this current.

What is the wind, what is it.

Where is the serene length, it is there and a dark place is not a dark place, only a white and red are black, only a yellow and green are blue, a pink is scarlet, a bow is every color. A line distinguishes it. A line just distinguishes it.

A RED HAT

A dark grey, a very dark grey, a quite dark grey is monstrous ordinarily, it is so monstrous because there is no red in it. If red is in everything it is not necessary. Is that not an argument for any use of it and even so is there any place that is better, is there any place that has so much stretched out.

A BLUE COAT

A blue coat is guided guided away, guided and guided away, that is the particular color that is used for that length and not any width not even more than a shadow.

A PIANO

If the speed is open, if the color is careless, if the selection of a strong scent is not awkward, if the button holder is held by all the waving color and there is no color, not any color. If there is no dirt in a pin and there can be none scarcely, if there is not then the place is the same as up standing.

This is no dark custom and it even is not acted in any such a way that a restraint is not spread. That is spread, it shuts and it lifts and awkwardly not awkwardly the centre is in standing.

A CHAIR

A widow in a wise veil and more garments shows that shadows are even. It addresses no more, it shadows the stage and learning. A regular arrangement, the severest and the most preserved is that which has the arrangement not more than always authorized.

A suitable establishment, well housed, practical, patient and staring, a suitable bedding, very suitable and not more particularly than complaining, anything suitable is so necessary.

A fact is that when the direction is just like that, no more, longer, sudden and at the same time not any sofa, the main action is that without a blaming there is no custody.

Practice measurement, practice the sign that means that really means a necessary betrayal, in showing that there is wearing.

Hope, what is a spectacle, a spectacle is the resemblance between the circular side place and nothing else, nothing else.

To choose it is ended, it is actual and more and more than that it has it certainly has the same treat, and a seat all that is practiced and more easily much more easily ordinarily.

Pick a barn, a whole barn, and bend more slender accents than have ever been necessary, shine in the darkness necessarily.

Actually not aching, actually not aching, a stubborn bloom is so artificial and even more than that, it is a spectacle, it is a binding accident, it is animosity and accentuation.

If the chance to dirty diminishing is necessary, if it is why is there no complexion, why is there no rubbing, why is there no special protection.

A FRIGHTFUL RELEASE

A bag which was left and not only taken but turned away was not found. The place was shown to be very like the last time. A piece was not exchanged, not a bit of it, a piece was left over. The rest was mismanaged.

A PURSE

A purse was not green, it was not straw color, it was hardly seen and it had a use a long use and the chain, the chain was never missing, it was not misplaced, it showed that it was open, that is all that it showed.

A MOUNTED UMBRELLA

What was the use of not leaving it there where it would hang what was the use if there was no chance of ever seeing it come there and show that it was handsome and right in the way it showed it. The lesson is to learn that it does show it, that it shows it and that nothing, that there is nothing, that there is no more to do about it and just so much more is there plenty of reason for making an exchange.

A CLOTH

Enough cloth is plenty and more, more is almost enough for that and besides if there is no more spreading is there plenty of room for it. Any occasion shows the best way.

MORE

An elegant use of foliage and grace and a little piece of white cloth and oil.

Wondering so winningly in several kinds of oceans is the reason that makes red so regular and enthusiastic. The reason that there is more snips are the same shining very colored rid of no round color.

A NEW CUP AND SAUCER

Enthusiastically hurting a clouded yellow bud and saucer, enthusiastically so is the bite in the ribbon.

OBJECTS

Within, within the cut and slender joint alone, with sudden equals and no more than three, two in the centre make two one side.

If the elbow is long and it is filled so then the best example is all together. The kind of show is made by squeezing.

EYE GLASSES

A color in shaving, a saloon is well placed in the centre of an alley.

A CUTLET

A blind agitation is manly and uttermost.

CARELESS WATER

No cup is broken in more places and mended, that is to say a plate is broken and mending does do that it shows that culture is Japanese. It shows the whole element of angels and orders. It does more to choosing and it does more to that ministering counting. It does, it does change in more water.

Supposing a single piece is a hair supposing more of them are orderly, does that show that strength, does that show that joint, does that show that balloon famously. Does it.

A PAPER

A courteous occasion makes a paper show no such occasion and this makes readiness and eyesight and likeness and a stool.

A DRAWING

The meaning of this is entirely and best to say the mark, best to say it best to shown sudden places, best to make bitter, best to make the length tall and nothing broader, anything between the half.

WATER RAINING

Water astonishing and difficult altogether makes a meadow and a stroke.

COLD CLIMATE

A season in yellow sold extra strings makes lying places.

MALACHITE

The sudden spoon is the same in no size. The sudden spoon is the wound in the decision.

AN UMBRELLA

Coloring high means that the strange reason is in front not more in front behind. Not more in front in peace of the dot.

A PETTICOAT

A light white, a disgrace, an ink spot, a rosy charm.

A WAIST

A star glide, a single frantic sullenness, a single financial grass greediness.
Object that is in wood. Hold the pine, hold the dark, hold in the rush, make the bottom.
A piece of crystal. A change, in a change that is remarkable there is no reason to say that there was a time.
A woolen object gilded. A country climb is the best disgrace, a couple of practices any of them in order is so left.

A TIME TO EAT

A pleasant simple habitual and tyrannical and authorised and educated and resumed and articulate separation. This is not tardy.

A LITTLE BIT OF A TUMBLER

A shining indication of yellow consists in there having been more of the same color than could have been expected when all four were bought. This was the hope which made the six and seven have no use for any more places and this necessarily spread into nothing. Spread into nothing.

A FIRE

What was the use of a whole time to send and not send if there was to be the kind of thing that made that come in. A letter was nicely sent.

A HANDKERCHIEF

A winning of all the blessings, a sample not a sample because there is no worry.

RED ROSES

A cool red rose and a pink cut pink, a collapse and a sold hole, a little less hot.

IN BETWEEN

In between a place and candy is a narrow foot-path that shows more mounting than anything, so much really that a calling meaning a bolster measured a whole thing with that. A virgin a whole virgin is judged made and so between curves and outlines and real seasons and more out glasses and a perfectly unprecedented arrangement between old ladies and mild colds there is no satin wood shining.

COLORED HATS

Colored hats are necessary to show that curls are worn by an addition of blank spaces, this makes the difference between single lines and broad stomachs, the least thing is lightening, the least thing means a little flower and a big delay a big delay that makes more nurses than little women really little women. So clean is a light that nearly all of it shows pearls and little ways. A large hat is tall and me and all custard whole.

A FEATHER

A feather is trimmed, it is trimmed by the light and the bug and the post, it is trimmed by little leaning and by all sorts of mounted reserves and loud volumes. It is surely cohesive.

A BROWN

A brown which is not liquid not more so is relaxed and yet there is a change, a news is pressing.

A LITTLE CALLED PAULINE

A little called anything shows shudders.

Come and say what prints all day. A whole few watermelon. There is no pope.

No cut in pennies and little dressing and choose wide soles and little spats really little spices.

A little lace makes boils. This is not true.

Gracious of gracious and a stamp a blue green white bow a blue green lean, lean on the top.

If it is absurd then it is leadish and nearly set in where there is a tight head.

A peaceful life to arise her, noon and moon and moon. A letter a cold sleeve a blanket a shaving house and nearly the best and regular window.

Nearer in fairy sea, nearer and farther, show white has lime in sight, show a stitch of ten. Count, count more so that thicker and thicker is leaning.

I hope she has her cow. Bidding a wedding, widening received treading, little leading mention nothing.

Cough out cough out in the leather and really feather it is not for.

Please could, please could, jam it not plus more sit in when.

A SOUND

Elephant beaten with candy and little pops and chews all bolts and reckless reckless rats, this is this.

A TABLE

A table means does it not my dear it means a whole steadiness. Is it likely that a change.

A table means more than a glass even a looking glass is tall. A table means necessary places and a revision a revision of a little thing it means it does mean that there has been a stand, a stand where it did shake.

SHOES

To be a wall with a damper a stream of pounding way and nearly enough choice makes a steady midnight. It is pus.

A shallow hole rose on red, a shallow hole in and in this makes ale less. It shows shine.

A DOG

A little monkey goes like a donkey that means to say that means to say that more sighs last goes. Leave with it. A little monkey goes like a donkey.

A WHITE HUNTER

A white hunter is nearly crazy.

A LEAVE

In the middle of a tiny spot and nearly bare there is a nice thing to say that wrist is leading. Wrist is leading.

SUPPOSE AN EYES

Suppose it is within a gate which open is open at the hour of closing summer that is to say it is so.

All the seats are needing blackening. A white dress is in sign. A soldier a real soldier has a worn lace a worn lace of different sizes that is to say if he can read, if he can read he is a size to show shutting up twenty-four.

Go red go red, laugh white.

Suppose a collapse in rubbed purr, in rubbed purr get.

Little sales ladies little sales ladies little saddles of mutton.

Little sales of leather and such beautiful beautiful, beautiful beautiful.

A SHAWL

A shawl is a hat and hurt and a red balloon and an under coat and a sizer a sizer of talks.

A shawl is a wedding, a piece of wax a little build. A shawl.

Pick a ticket, pick it in strange steps and with hollows. There is hollow hollow belt, a belt is a shawl.

A plate that has a little bobble, all of them, any so.

Please a round it is ticket.

It was a mistake to state that a laugh and a lip and a laid climb and a depot and a cultivator and little choosing is a point it.

BOOK

Book was there, it was there. Book was there. Stop it, stop it, it was a cleaner, a wet cleaner and it was not where it was wet, it was not high, it was directly placed back, not back again, back it was returned, it was needless, it put a bank, a bank when, a bank care.

Suppose a man a realistic expression of resolute reliability suggests pleasing itself white all white and no head does that mean soap. It does not so. It means kind wavers and little chance to beside beside rest. A plain.

Suppose ear rings that is one way to breed, breed that. Oh chance to say, oh nice old pole. Next best and nearest a pillar. Chest not valuable, be papered.

Cover up cover up the two with a little piece of string and hope rose and green, green.

Please a plate, put a match to the seam and really then really then, really then it is a remark that joins many many lead games. It is a sister and sister and a flower and a flower and a dog and a colored sky a sky colored grey and nearly that nearly that let.

PEELED PENCIL, CHOKE

Rub her coke.

IT WAS BLACK, BLACK TOOK

Black ink best wheel bale brown.

Excellent not a hull house, not a pea soup, no bill no care, no precise no past pearl pearl goat.

THIS IS THIS DRESS, AIDER

Aider, why aider why whow, whow stop touch, aider whow, aider stop the muncher, muncher munchers.

A jack in kill her, a jack in, makes a meadowed king, makes a to let.

1914

ROBERT FROST
1874–1963

Although he identified himself with New England, Robert Frost was born in California and lived there until his father died, when Frost was eleven. The family then moved to New England, where his mother supported them by teaching school. Frost graduated from high school in 1891 in Lawrence, Massachusetts, sharing the post of valedictorian with Elinor White, whom he married three years later. Occasional attendance at Dartmouth College and Harvard, and a variety of different jobs including an attempt to run a farm in Derry, New Hampshire, marked the next twenty years. Frost made a new start in 1912, taking his family, which included four children, to England. There he worked on his poetry and found a publisher for his first book, *A Boy's Will* (1913). Ezra Pound reviewed it favorably, excited (as he put it in a letter) by this "VURRY Amur'k'n talent." Pound recommended Frost's poems to American editors and helped get his second book, *North of Boston*, published in 1914. *North of Boston* was widely praised by critics in America and England when it appeared; the favorable reception persuaded Frost to return home. He bought another farm in New Hampshire and prospered financially through sales of his books and papers, along with teaching and lecturing at various colleges. The success he enjoyed for the rest of his life, however, came too late to cancel the bitterness left by his earlier struggles. Moreover, he endured personal tragedy: a son committed suicide, and a daughter had a complete mental collapse.

The clarity of Frost's diction, the colloquial rhythms, the simplicity of his images, and above all the folksy speaker—these are intended to make the poems look natural, unplanned. In the context of the modernist movement, however, they can be seen as a thoughtful reply to high modernism's fondness for obscurity and difficulty. In addition, by investing in the New England terrain, Frost rejected modernist internationalism and revitalized the tradition of New England regionalism. Readers who accepted Frost's persona and his setting as typically American accepted the powerful myth that rural New England was the heart of America.

Frost played the rhythms of ordinary speech against formal patterns of line and verse and contained them within traditional poetic forms. The interaction of colloquial diction with blank verse is especially central to his dramatic monologues. To Frost traditional forms were the essence of poetry, material with which poets responded to flux and disorder (what, adopting scientific terminology, he called "decay") by forging something permanent. Poetry, he wrote, was "one step backward taken," resisting time—a "momentary stay against confusion."

Throughout the 1920s Frost's poetic practice changed very little; later books— including *Mountain Interval* (1916), *New Hampshire* (1923), and *West-Running Brook* (1928)—confirmed the impression he had created in *North of Boston*. Most of his poems fall into a few types. Nature lyrics describing or commenting on a scene or event—like "Stopping by Woods on a Snowy Evening," "Birches," and "After Apple-Picking"—are probably the best known. There are also dramatic narratives in blank verse about country people, like "The Death of the Hired Man," and poems of commentary or generalization, like "The Gift Outright," which he read at John F. Kennedy's presidential inauguration in 1961. He could also be humorous or sardonic, as in "Fire and Ice." In the nature lyrics, a comparison often emerges between the outer scene and the psyche, a comparison of what Frost in one poem called "outer and inner weather."

Because he presented himself as a New Englander reading a New England land-scape, Frost is often interpreted as an ideological descendent of the nineteenth-century American Transcendentalists. But he is far less affirmative about the universe than they; for where they, looking at nature, discerned a benign creator, he saw "no expression, nothing to express." Frost did share with Emerson and Thoreau, however, the belief that collective enterprises could do nothing but weaken the individual self. He avoided political movements precisely because they were movements, group undertakings. In the 1930s he parted company with many American writers by opposing both the social programs of Franklin Roosevelt's New Deal and artistic programs similarly aimed, he thought, at the lessening of social grievances rather than the exploration of enduring human grief. In *A Further Range* (1936), for which he won the third of his four Pulitzer Prizes, Frost invited readers "to a one-man revolution"—the "only revolution that is coming," he declared. Left-leaning critics replied by denouncing the volume's "reactionary" constriction of Frost's poetic voice to that of a head-shaking Yankee skeptic. Frost deeply resented this criticism and responded to it with a newly didactic kind of poetry. In the last twenty years of his life, Frost increased his activities as a teacher and lecturer—at Amherst, at Dartmouth, at Harvard, at the Bread Loaf School of English at Middlebury College in Vermont, and in poetry readings and talks around the country.

The text of the poems included here is that of *The Poetry of Robert Frost* (1969).

The Pasture

I'm going out to clean the pasture spring;
I'll only stop to rake the leaves away
(And wait to watch the water clear, I may):
I shan't be gone long.—You come too.
I'm going out to fetch the little calf   5
That's standing by the mother. It's so young
It totters when she licks it with her tongue.
I shan't be gone long.—You come too.

1913

Mowing

There was never a sound beside the wood but one,
And that was my long scythe whispering to the ground.
What was it it whispered? I knew not well myself;
Perhaps it was something about the heat of the sun,
Something, perhaps, about the lack of sound—   5
And that was why it whispered and did not speak.
It was no dream of the gift of idle hours,
Or easy gold at the hand of fay or elf:
Anything more than the truth would have seemed too weak
To the earnest love that laid the swale[1] in rows,   10
Not without feeble-pointed spikes of flowers

---

1. Grasses in a marshy meadow.

(Pale orchises), and scared a bright green snake.
The fact is the sweetest dream that labor knows.
My long scythe whispered and left the hay to make.

1913

Mending Wall

Something there is that doesn't love a wall,
That sends the frozen-ground-swell under it,
And spills the upper boulders in the sun,
And makes gaps even two can pass abreast.
The work of hunters is another thing: 5
I have come after them and made repair
Where they have left not one stone on a stone,
But they would have the rabbit out of hiding,
To please the yelping dogs. The gaps I mean,
No one has seen them made or heard them made,   10
But at spring mending-time we find them there.
I let my neighbor know beyond the hill;
And on a day we meet to walk the line
And set the wall between us once again.
We keep the wall between us as we go.   15
To each the boulders that have fallen to each.
And some are loaves and some so nearly balls
We have to use a spell to make them balance:
"Stay where you are until our backs are turned!"
We wear our fingers rough with handling them.   20
Oh, just another kind of outdoor game,
One on a side. It comes to little more:
There where it is we do not need the wall:
He is all pine and I am apple orchard.
My apple trees will never get across   25
And eat the cones under his pines, I tell him.
He only says, "Good fences make good neighbors."
Spring is the mischief in me, and I wonder
If I could put a notion in his head:
"*Why* do they make good neighbors? Isn't it   30
Where there are cows? But here there are no cows.
Before I built a wall I'd ask to know
What I was walling in or walling out,
And to whom I was like to give offense.
Something there is that doesn't love a wall,   35
That wants it down." I could say "Elves" to him,
But it's not elves exactly, and I'd rather
He said it for himself. I see him there
Bringing a stone grasped firmly by the top
In each hand, like an old-stone savage armed.   40
He moves in darkness as it seems to me,
Not of woods only and the shade of trees.
He will not go behind his father's saying,

And he likes having thought of it so well
He says again, "Good fences make good neighbors."   45

1914

The Death of the Hired Man

Mary sat musing on the lamp-flame at the table
Waiting for Warren. When she heard his step,
She ran on tip-toe down the darkened passage
To meet him in the doorway with the news
And put him on his guard. "Silas is back."   5
She pushed him outward with her through the door
And shut it after her. "Be kind," she said.
She took the market things from Warren's arms
And set them on the porch, then drew him down
To sit beside her on the wooden steps.   10

"When was I ever anything but kind to him?
But I'll not have the fellow back," he said.
"I told him so last haying, didn't I?
If he left then, I said, that ended it.
What good is he? Who else will harbor him   15
At his age for the little he can do?
What help he is there's no depending on.
Off he goes always when I need him most.
He thinks he ought to earn a little pay,
Enough at least to buy tobacco with,   20
So he won't have to beg and be beholden.
'All right,' I say, 'I can't afford to pay
Any fixed wages, though I wish I could.'
'Someone else can.' 'Then someone else will have to.'
I shouldn't mind his bettering himself   25
If that was what it was. You can be certain,
When he begins like that, there's someone at him
Trying to coax him off with pocket-money,—
In haying time, when any help is scarce.
In winter he comes back to us. I'm done."   30

"Sh! not so loud: he'll hear you," Mary said.

"I want him to: he'll have to soon or late."

"He's worn out. He's asleep beside the stove.
When I came up from Rowe's I found him here,
Huddled against the barn-door fast asleep,   35
A miserable sight, and frightening, too—
You needn't smile—I didn't recognize him—
I wasn't looking for him—and he's changed.
Wait till you see."

                              "Where did you say he'd been?"   40

"He didn't say. I dragged him to the house,
And gave him tea and tried to make him smoke.
I tried to make him talk about his travels.
Nothing would do: he just kept nodding off."

"What did he say? Did he say anything?"   45

"But little."

       "Anything? Mary, confess
He said he'd come to ditch the meadow for me."

"Warren!"

      "But did he? I just want to know."   50

"Of course he did. What would you have him say?
Surely you wouldn't grudge the poor old man
Some humble way to save his self-respect.
He added, if you really care to know,
He meant to clear the upper pasture, too.   55
That sounds like something you have heard before?
Warren, I wish you could have heard the way
He jumbled everything. I stopped to look
Two or three times—he made me feel so queer—
To see if he was talking in his sleep.   60
He ran on Harold Wilson—you remember—
The boy you had in haying four years since.
He's finished school, and teaching in his college.
Silas declares you'll have to get him back.
He says they two will make a team for work: 65
Between them they will lay this farm as smooth!
The way he mixed that in with other things.
He thinks young Wilson a likely lad, though daft
On education—you know how they fought
All through July under the blazing sun,   70
Silas up on the cart to build the load,
Harold along beside to pitch it on."

"Yes, I took care to keep well out of earshot."

"Well, those days trouble Silas like a dream.
You wouldn't think they would. How some things linger!   75
Harold's young college-boy's assurance piqued him.
After so many years he still keeps finding
Good arguments he sees he might have used.
I sympathize. I know just how it feels
To think of the right thing to say too late.   80
Harold's associated in his mind with Latin.
He asked me what I thought of Harold's saying
He studied Latin, like the violin,
Because he liked it—that an argument!
He said he couldn't make the boy believe   85

He could find water with a hazel prong—
Which showed how much good school had ever done him.
He wanted to go over that. But most of all
He thinks if he could have another chance
To teach him how to build a load of hay—"   90

"I know, that's Silas' one accomplishment.
He bundles every forkful in its place,
And tags and numbers it for future reference,
So he can find and easily dislodge it
In the unloading. Silas does that well.   95
He takes it out in bunches like big birds' nests.
You never see him standing on the hay
He's trying to lift, straining to lift himself."

"He thinks if he could teach him that, he'd be
Some good perhaps to someone in the world.   100
He hates to see a boy the fool of books.
Poor Silas, so concerned for other folk,
And nothing to look backward to with pride,
And nothing to look forward to with hope,
So now and never any different."   105

Part of a moon was falling down the west,
Dragging the whole sky with it to the hills.
Its light poured softly in her lap. She saw it
And spread her apron to it. She put out her hand
Among the harplike morning-glory strings,   110
Taut with the dew from garden bed to eaves,
As if she played unheard some tenderness
That wrought on him beside her in the night.
"Warren," she said, "he has come home to die:
You needn't be afraid he'll leave you this time."   115

"Home," he mocked gently.

                              "Yes, what else but home?
It all depends on what you mean by home.
Of course he's nothing to us, any more
Than was the hound that came a stranger to us   120
Out of the woods, worn out upon the trail."

"Home is the place where, when you have to go there,
They have to take you in."

                              "I should have called it
Something you somehow haven't to deserve."   125

Warren leaned out and took a step or two,
Picked up a little stick, and brought it back
And broke it in his hand and tossed it by.
"Silas has better claim on us you think

Than on his brother? Thirteen little miles   130
As the road winds would bring him to his door.
Silas has walked that far no doubt today.
Why doesn't he go there? His brother's rich,
A somebody—director in the bank."

"He never told us that."   135

         "We know it though."

"I think his brother ought to help, of course.
I'll see to that if there is need. He ought of right
To take him in, and might be willing to—
He may be better than appearances.   140
But have some pity on Silas. Do you think
If he had any pride in claiming kin
Or anything he looked for from his brother,
He'd keep so still about him all this time?"

"I wonder what's between them."   145

         "I can tell you.
Silas is what he is—we wouldn't mind him—
But just the kind that kinsfolk can't abide.
He never did a thing so very bad.
He don't know why he isn't quite as good   150
As anybody. Worthless though he is,
He won't be made ashamed to please his brother."

"I can't think Si ever hurt anyone."

"No, but he hurt my heart the way he lay
And rolled his old head on that sharp-edged chair-back.   155
He wouldn't let me put him on the lounge.
You must go in and see what you can do.
I made the bed up for him there tonight.
You'll be surprised at him—how much he's broken.
His working days are done; I'm sure of it."   160

"I'd not be in a hurry to say that."

"I haven't been. Go, look, see for yourself.
But, Warren, please remember how it is:
He's come to help you ditch the meadow.
He has a plan. You mustn't laugh at him.   165
He may not speak of it, and then he may.
I'll sit and see if that small sailing cloud
Will hit or miss the moon."

         It hit the moon.
Then there were three there, making a dim row,   170
The moon, the little silver cloud, and she.
Warren returned—too soon, it seemed to her,
Slipped to her side, caught up her hand and waited.

"Warren?" she questioned.

                                  "Dead," was all he answered.   175

                                                      1914

After Apple-Picking

My long two-pointed ladder's sticking through a tree
Toward heaven still,
And there's a barrel that I didn't fill
Beside it, and there may be two or three
Apples I didn't pick upon some bough.   5
But I am done with apple-picking now.
Essence of winter sleep is on the night,
The scent of apples: I am drowsing off.
I cannot rub the strangeness from my sight
I got from looking through a pane of glass   10
I skimmed this morning from the drinking trough
And held against the world of hoary grass.
It melted, and I let it fall and break.
But I was well
Upon my way to sleep before it fell,   15
And I could tell
What form my dreaming was about to take.
Magnified apples appear and disappear,
Stem end and blossom end,
And every fleck of russet showing clear.   20
My instep arch not only keeps the ache,
It keeps the pressure of a ladder-round.
I feel the ladder sway as the boughs bend.
And I keep hearing from the cellar bin
The rumbling sound   25
Of load on load of apples coming in.
For I have had too much
Of apple-picking: I am overtired
Of the great harvest I myself desired.
There were ten thousand thousand fruit to touch,   30
Cherish in hand, lift down, and not let fall.
For all
That struck the earth,
No matter if not bruised or spiked with stubble,
Went surely to the cider-apple heap   35
As of no worth.
One can see what will trouble
This sleep of mine, whatever sleep it is.
Were he not gone,
The woodchuck could say whether it's like his   40
Long sleep, as I describe its coming on,
Or just some human sleep.

                                                      1914

The Wood-Pile

Out walking in the frozen swamp one gray day,
I paused and said, "I will turn back from here.
No, I will go on farther—and we shall see."
The hard snow held me, save where now and then
One foot went through. The view was all in lines   5
Straight up and down of tall slim trees
Too much alike to mark or name a place by
So as to say for certain I was here
Or somewhere else: I was just far from home.
A small bird flew before me. He was careful   10
To put a tree between us when he lighted,
And say no word to tell me who he was
Who was so foolish as to think what *he* thought.
He thought that I was after him for a feather—
The white one in his tail; like one who takes   15
Everything said as personal to himself.
One flight out sideways would have undeceived him.
And then there was a pile of wood for which
I forgot him and let his little fear
Carry him off the way I might have gone,   20
Without so much as wishing him good-night.
He went behind it to make his last stand.
It was a cord of maple, cut and split
And piled—and measured, four by four by eight.
And not another like it could I see.   25
No runner tracks in this year's snow looped near it.
And it was older sure than this year's cutting,
Or even last year's or the year's before.
The wood was gray and the bark warping off it
And the pile somewhat sunken. Clematis   30
Had wound strings round and round it like a bundle.
What held it, though, on one side was a tree
Still growing, and on one a stake and prop,
These latter about to fall. I thought that only
Someone who lived in turning to fresh tasks   35
Could so forget his handiwork on which
He spent himself, the labor of his ax,
And leave it there far from a useful fireplace
To warm the frozen swamp as best it could
With the slow smokeless burning of decay.   40

1914

The Road Not Taken

Two roads diverged in a yellow wood,
And sorry I could not travel both
And be one traveler, long I stood
And looked down one as far as I could
To where it bent in the undergrowth;   5

Then took the other, as just as fair,
And having perhaps the better claim,
Because it was grassy and wanted wear;
Though as for that, the passing there
Had worn them really about the same,   10

And both that morning equally lay
In leaves no step had trodden black.
Oh, I kept the first for another day!
Yet knowing how way leads on to way,
I doubted if I should ever come back.   15

I shall be telling this with a sigh
Somewhere ages and ages hence:
Two roads diverged in a wood, and I—
I took the one less traveled by,
And that has made all the difference.   20

                                                        1916

Birches

When I see birches bend to left and right
Across the lines of straighter darker trees,
I like to think some boy's been swinging them.
But swinging doesn't bend them down to stay
As ice storms do. Often you must have seen them   5
Loaded with ice a sunny winter morning
After a rain. They click upon themselves
As the breeze rises, and turn many-colored
As the stir cracks and crazes their enamel.
Soon the sun's warmth makes them shed crystal shells   10
Shattering and avalanching on the snow crust—
Such heaps of broken glass to sweep away
You'd think the inner dome of heaven had fallen.
They are dragged to the withered bracken by the load,
And they seem not to break; though once they are bowed   15
So low for long, they never right themselves:
You may see their trunks arching in the woods
Years afterwards, trailing their leaves on the ground
Like girls on hands and knees that throw their hair
Before them over their heads to dry in the sun.   20
But I was going to say when Truth broke in
With all her matter of fact about the ice storm,
I should prefer to have some boy bend them
As he went out and in to fetch the cows—
Some boy too far from town to learn baseball,   25
Whose only play was what he found himself,
Summer or winter, and could play alone.
One by one he subdued his father's trees
By riding them down over and over again

Until he took the stiffness out of them,   30
And not one but hung limp, not one was left
For him to conquer. He learned all there was
To learn about not launching out too soon
And so not carrying the tree away
Clear to the ground. He always kept his poise   35
To the top branches, climbing carefully
With the same pains you use to fill a cup
Up to the brim, and even above the brim.
Then he flung outward, feet first, with a swish,
Kicking his way down through the air to the ground.   40
So was I once myself a swinger of birches.
And so I dream of going back to be.
It's when I'm weary of considerations,
And life is too much like a pathless wood
Where your face burns and tickles with the cobwebs   45
Broken across it, and one eye is weeping
From a twig's having lashed across it open.
I'd like to get away from earth awhile
And then come back to it and begin over.
May no fate willfully misunderstand me   50
And half grant what I wish and snatch me away
Not to return. Earth's the right place for love:
I don't know where it's likely to go better.
I'd like to go by climbing a birch tree,
And climb black branches up a snow-white trunk   55
Toward heaven, till the tree could bear no more,
But dipped its top and set me down again.
That would be good both going and coming back.
One could do worse than be a swinger of birches.

                                                                      1916

"Out, Out—"[1]

The buzz saw snarled and rattled in the yard
And made dust and dropped stove-length sticks of wood,
Sweet-scented stuff when the breeze drew across it.
And from there those that lifted eyes could count
Five mountain ranges one behind the other   5
Under the sunset far into Vermont.
And the saw snarled and rattled, snarled and rattled,
As it ran light, or had to bear a load.
And nothing happened: day was all but done.
Call it a day, I wish they might have said   10
To please the boy by giving him the half hour
That a boy counts so much when saved from work.
His sister stood beside them in her apron
To tell them "Supper." At the word, the saw,

---

1. From Shakespeare's *Macbeth* 5.5.23–24: "Out, out, brief candle! / Life's but a walking shadow."

As if to prove saws knew what supper meant,   15
Leaped out at the boy's hand, or seemed to leap—
He must have given the hand. However it was,
Neither refused the meeting. But the hand!
The boy's first outcry was a rueful laugh,
As he swung toward them holding up the hand,   20
Half in appeal, but half as if to keep
The life from spilling. Then the boy saw all—
Since he was old enough to know, big boy
Doing a man's work, though a child at heart—
He saw all spoiled. "Don't let him cut my hand off—   25
The doctor, when he comes. Don't let him, sister!"
So. But the hand was gone already.
The doctor put him in the dark of ether.
He lay and puffed his lips out with his breath.
And then—the watcher at his pulse took fright.   30
No one believed. They listened at his heart.
Little—less—nothing!—and that ended it.
No more to build on there. And they, since they
Were not the one dead, turned to their affairs.

                                                      1916

Fire and Ice

Some say the world will end in fire,
Some say in ice.
From what I've tasted of desire
I hold with those who favor fire.
But if it had to perish twice,   5
I think I know enough of hate
To say that for destruction ice
Is also great
And would suffice.

                                                      1923

Nothing Gold Can Stay

Nature's first green is gold,
Her hardest hue to hold.
Her early leaf's a flower;
But only so an hour.
Then leaf subsides to leaf.   5
So Eden sank to grief,
So dawn goes down to day.
Nothing gold can stay.

                                                      1923

Stopping by Woods on a Snowy Evening

Whose woods these are I think I know.
His house is in the village, though;
He will not see me stopping here
To watch his woods fill up with snow.

My little horse must think it queer   5
To stop without a farmhouse near
Between the woods and frozen lake
The darkest evening of the year.

He gives his harness bells a shake
To ask if there is some mistake.   10
The only other sound's the sweep
Of easy wind and downy flake.

The woods are lovely, dark, and deep,
But I have promises to keep,
And miles to go before I sleep.   15
And miles to go before I sleep.

1923

Desert Places

Snow falling and night falling fast, oh, fast
In a field I looked into going past,
And the ground almost covered smooth in snow,
But a few weeds and stubble showing last.

The woods around it have it—it is theirs.   5
All animals are smothered in their lairs.
I am too absent-spirited to count;
The loneliness includes me unawares.

And lonely as it is, that loneliness
Will be more lonely ere it will be less—   10
A blanker whiteness of benighted snow
With no expression, nothing to express.

They cannot scare me with their empty spaces
Between stars—on stars where no human race is.
I have it in me so much nearer home   15
To scare myself with my own desert places.

1936

Design

I found a dimpled spider, fat and white,
On a white heal-all,[1] holding up a moth
Like a white piece of rigid satin cloth—
Assorted characters of death and blight
Mixed ready to begin the morning right,   5
Like the ingredients of a witches' broth—
A snow-drop spider, a flower like a froth,
And dead wings carried like a paper kite.

What had that flower to do with being white,
The wayside blue and innocent heal-all?   10
What brought the kindred spider to that height,
Then steered the white moth thither in the night?
What but design of darkness to appall?—
If design govern in a thing so small.

                                        1922, 1936

Neither Out Far Nor In Deep

The people along the sand
All turn and look one way.
They turn their back on the land.
They look at the sea all day.

As long as it takes to pass   5
A ship keeps raising its hull;
The wetter ground like glass
Reflects a standing gull.

The land may vary more;
But wherever the truth may be—   10
The water comes ashore,
And the people look at the sea.

They cannot look out far.
They cannot look in deep.
But when was that ever a bar   15
To any watch they keep?

                                        1936

Directive

Back out of all this now too much for us,
Back in a time made simple by the loss
Of detail, burned, dissolved, and broken off

---

1. Common wildflower whose blossom is normally violet or blue.

Like graveyard marble sculpture in the weather,
There is a house that is no more a house   5
Upon a farm that is no more a farm
And in a town that is no more a town.
The road there, if you'll let a guide direct you
Who only has at heart your getting lost,
May seem as if it should have been a quarry—   10
Great monolithic knees the former town
Long since gave up pretense of keeping covered.
And there's a story in a book about it:
Besides the wear of iron wagon wheels
The ledges show lines ruled southeast-northwest,   15
The chisel work of an enormous Glacier
That braced his feet against the Arctic Pole.
You must not mind a certain coolness from him
Still said to haunt this side of Panther Mountain.
Nor need you mind the serial ordeal   20
Of being watched from forty cellar holes
As if by eye pairs out of forty firkins.[1]
As for the woods' excitement over you
That sends light rustle rushes to their leaves,
Charge that to upstart inexperience.   25
Where were they all not twenty years ago?
They think too much of having shaded out
A few old pecker-fretted[2] apple trees.
Make yourself up a cheering song of how
Someone's road home from work this once was,   30
Who may be just ahead of you on foot
Or creaking with a buggy load of grain.
The height of the adventure is the height
Of country where two village cultures faded
Into each other. Both of them are lost.   35
And if you're lost enough to find yourself
By now, pull in your ladder road behind you
And put a sign up closed to all but me.
Then make yourself at home. The only field
Now left's no bigger than a harness gall.[3]   40
First there's the children's house of make-believe,
Some shattered dishes underneath a pine,
The playthings in the playhouse of the children.
Weep for what little things could make them glad.
Then for the house that is no more a house,   45
But only a belilaced cellar hole,
Now slowly closing like a dent in dough.
This was no playhouse but a house in earnest.
Your destination and your destiny's
A brook that was the water of the house,   50
Cold as a spring as yet so near its source,
Too lofty and original to rage.
(We know the valley streams that when aroused

1. Small wooden tubs for butter or lard.   3. Sore on a horse's skin caused by the rubbing
2. Marked up with small holes by woodpeckers.   of the harness.

Will leave their tatters hung on barb and thorn.)
I have kept hidden in the instep arch   55
Of an old cedar at the waterside
A broken drinking goblet like the Grail[4]
Under a spell so the wrong ones can't find it,
So can't get saved, as Saint Mark[5] says they mustn't.
(I stole the goblet from the children's playhouse.)   60
Here are your waters and your watering place.
Drink and be whole again beyond confusion.

1947

4. The cup used by Jesus at the Last Supper. According to legend, the Grail later disappeared from its keepers because of their moral impurity, and various knights, including those of King Arthur's Round Table, went in quest of it. From this, the quest for the Grail has come to symbolize any spiritual search.
5. A reference to the Gospel of Mark, 4.11–12; see also Mark 16.16.

SUSAN GLASPELL
1876–1948

Susan Glaspell—journalist, novelist, short-story writer, playwright, theatrical producer and director, actor—was a multitalented professional who eventually published more than fifty short stories, nine novels, and fourteen plays. Feminist rediscovery of *Trifles*, her first play—written and produced in 1916 and turned into a prize-winning short story, "A Jury of Her Peers," in 1917—has made this her best-known work today.

Born and raised in Davenport, Iowa, Glaspell worked for a year on the Davenport *Morning Republican* after high school graduation, then attended Drake University in Des Moines from 1895 to 1899. In college she wrote for the campus newspaper as well as various Des Moines papers; after graduation she worked for two years on the Des Moines *Daily News*. In 1901 she abandoned journalism, returning to Davenport with a plan to earn her living as a fiction writer. Her early stories, combining regional midwestern settings with romantic plots, found favor with the editors of such popular magazines as *Harper's*, the *Ladies' Home Journal*, the *American Magazine*, and the *Woman's Home Companion*. In 1909 she published her first novel, *The Glory of the Conquered*.

In 1913 she married the recently divorced George Cram Cook, a Harvard-educated native of Davenport, who was a writer and theatrical director much interested in modernist experimentation. The two moved to the East Coast, traveled widely, and collaborated on many projects. They helped found both the Washington Square Players in 1914 and the group that came to be known as the Provincetown Players in 1916.

The Provincetown Players, named for the New England seaport town where many of the members spent their summers, aimed to foster an American theater by producing plays by American playwrights only. Eugene O'Neill became the best-known dramatist of the group; Glaspell was a close second. She not only wrote plays but also acted in them, directed them, and helped produce them. From 1916 to 1922 she wrote nine plays, including *Trifles,* for the Provincetown Players; in 1922 Cook and Glaspell withdrew from the group, finding that it had become too commercially successful to suit their experimental aims.

Cook died in 1924; a later close relationship, with the novelist and playwright Norman Matson, ended in 1932. Throughout the 1930s and 1940s, Glaspell, now a year-round resident of Provincetown, continued to write and publish. Her novel *Judd Rankin's Wife* (1928) was made into a movie. She won the 1930 Pulitzer Prize for drama for *Alison's Room,* a play loosely based on the life of Emily Dickinson. Her last novel, *Judd Rankin's Daughter,* appeared in 1945, three years before she died at the age of seventy-two.

For Glaspell, the influence of such European playwrights as Henrik Ibsen and August Strindberg opened the door to much grimmer writing in a play like *Trifles* than in her popular short stories, with their formulaic happy endings. Her realism— her unsparing depiction of women's narrow, thwarted, isolated, and subjugated lives in rural, regional settings—produces effects quite unlike the nostalgic celebrations of woman-centered societies often associated with women regionalists. The efficiently plotted *Trifles* also features a formal device found in other Glaspell works, including *Alison's Room:* the main character at its center never appears.

The text is from *Plays by Susan Glaspell* (1987).

Trifles

CHARACTERS

GEORGE HENDERSON, *County Attorney*
HENRY PETERS, *Sheriff*
LEWIS HALE, *a Neighboring Farmer*
MRS PETERS
MRS HALE

SCENE: *The kitchen in the now abandoned farmhouse of* John Wright, *a gloomy kitchen, and left without having been put in order—unwashed pans under the sink, a loaf of bread outside the bread-box, a dish-towel on the table—other signs of incompleted work. At the rear the outer door opens and the* SHERIFF *comes in followed by the* COUNTY ATTORNEY *and* HALE. *The* SHERIFF *and* HALE *are men in middle life, the* COUNTY ATTORNEY *is a young man; all are much bundled up and go at once to the stove. They are followed by the two women—the* SHERIFF's *wife first; she is a slight wiry woman, a thin nervous face.* MRS HALE *is larger and would ordinarily be called more comfortable looking, but she is disturbed now and looks fearfully about as she enters. The women have come in slowly, and stand close together near the door.*

COUNTY ATTORNEY [*rubbing his hands*] This feels good. Come up to the fire, ladies.

MRS PETERS [*after taking a step forward*] I'm not—cold.

SHERIFF [*unbuttoning his overcoat and stepping away from the stove as if to mark the beginning of official business*] Now, Mr Hale, before we move things about, you explain to Mr Henderson just what you saw when you came here yesterday morning.

COUNTY ATTORNEY By the way, has anything been moved? Are things just as you left them yesterday?

SHERIFF [*looking about*]   It's just the same. When it dropped below zero last night I thought I'd better send Frank out this morning to make a fire for us—no use getting pneumonia with a big case on, but I told him not to touch anything except the stove—and you know Frank.

COUNTY ATTORNEY   Somebody should have been left here yesterday.

SHERIFF   Oh—yesterday. When I had to send Frank to Morris Center for that man who went crazy—I want you to know I had my hands full yesterday. I knew you could get back from Omaha by today and as long as I went over everything here myself—

COUNTY ATTORNEY   Well, Mr Hale, tell just what happened when you came here yesterday morning.

HALE   Harry and I had started to town with a load of potatoes. We came along the road from my place and as I got here I said, 'I'm going to see if I can't get John Wright to go in with me on a party telephone.'[1] I spoke to Wright about it once before and he put me off, saying folks talked too much anyway, and all he asked was peace and quiet—I guess you know about how much he talked himself; but I thought maybe if I went to the house and talked about it before his wife, though I said to Harry that I didn't know as what his wife wanted made much difference to John—

COUNTY ATTORNEY   Let's talk about that later, Mr Hale. I do want to talk about that, but tell now just what happened when you got to the house.

HALE   I didn't hear or see anything; I knocked at the door, and still it was all quiet inside. I knew they must be up, it was past eight o'clock. So I knocked again, and I thought I heard somebody say, 'Come in.' I wasn't sure. I'm not sure yet, but I opened the door—this door [*indicating the door by which the two women are still standing*] and there in that rocker—[*pointing to it*] sat Mrs Wright.

[*They all look at the rocker.*]

COUNTY ATTORNEY   What—was she doing?

HALE   She was rockin' back and forth. She had her apron in her hand and was kind of—pleating it.

COUNTY ATTORNEY   And how did she—look?

HALE   Well, she looked queer.

COUNTY ATTORNEY   How do you mean—queer?

HALE   Well, as if she didn't know what she was going to do next. And kind of done up.

COUNTY ATTORNEY   How did she seem to feel about your coming?

HALE   Why, I don't think she minded—one way or other. She didn't pay much attention. I said, 'How do. Mrs Wright it's cold, ain't it?' And she said, 'Is it?'—and went on kind of pleating at her apron. Well, I was surprised: she didn't ask me to come up to the stove, or to set down, but just sat there, not even looking at me, so I said, 'I want to see John.' And then she—laughed. I guess you would call it a laugh. I thought of Harry and the team outside, so I said a little sharp: 'Can't I see John?' 'No,' she says, kind o' dull like. 'Ain't he home?' says I. 'Yes,' says she, 'he's home.' 'Then why can't I see him?' I asked her, out of patience. ''Cause he's dead,' says she. '*Dead?*' says I. She just nodded her head, not getting a bit excited, but rockin' back and forth. 'Why—where is he?' says I, not knowing what

---

1. A single telephone line shared by several households.

to say. She just pointed upstairs—like that [*himself pointing to the room above*] I got up, with the idea of going up there. I walked from there to here—then I says, 'Why, what did he die of?' 'He died of a rope round his neck,' says she, and just went on pleatin' at her apron. Well, I went out and called Harry. I thought I might—need help. We went upstairs and there he was lyin'—

COUNTY ATTORNEY   I think I'd rather have you go into that upstairs, where you can point it all out. Just go on now with the rest of the story.

HALE   Well, my first thought was to get that rope off. It looked . . . [*stops, his face twitches*] . . . but Harry, he went up to him, and he said, 'No, he's dead all right, and we'd better not touch anything.' So we went back down stairs. She was still sitting that same way. 'Has anybody been notified?' I asked. 'No,' says she unconcerned. 'Who did this, Mrs Wright?' said Harry. He said it business-like—and she stopped pleatin' of her apron. 'I don't know,' she says. 'You don't *know*?' says Harry. 'No,' says she. 'Weren't you sleepin' in the bed with him?' says Harry. 'Yes,' says she, 'but I was on the inside.' 'Somebody slipped a rope round his neck and strangled him and you didn't wake up?' says Harry. 'I didn't wake up,' she said after him. We must 'a looked as if we didn't see how that could be, for after a minute she said, 'I sleep sound.' Harry was going to ask her more questions but I said maybe we ought to let her tell her story first to the coroner, or the sheriff, so Harry went fast as he could to Rivers' place, where there's a telephone.

COUNTY ATTORNEY   And what did Mrs Wright do when she knew that you had gone for the coroner?

HALE   She moved from that chair to this one over here [*pointing to a small chair in the corner*] and just sat there with her hands held together and looking down. I got a feeling that I ought to make some conversation, so I said I had come in to see if John wanted to put in a telephone, and at that she started to laugh, and then she stopped and looked at me—scared. [*the* COUNTY ATTORNEY, *who has had his notebook out, makes a note*] I dunno, maybe it wasn't scared. I wouldn't like to say it was. Soon Harry got back, and then Dr Lloyd came, and you, Mr Peters, and so I guess that's all I know that you don't.

COUNTY ATTORNEY [*looking around*]   I guess we'll go upstairs first—and then out to the barn and around there. [*to the* SHERIFF] You're convinced that there was nothing important here—nothing that would point to any motive.

SHERIFF   Nothing here but kitchen things.

[*The* COUNTY ATTORNEY, *after again looking around the kitchen, opens the door of a cupboard closet. He gets up on a chair and looks on a shelf. Pulls his hand away, sticky.*]

COUNTY ATTORNEY   Here's a nice mess.

[*The women draw nearer.*]

MRS PETERS [*to the other woman*]   Oh, her fruit: it did freeze. [*to the* LAWYER] She worried about that when it turned so cold. She said the fire'd go out and her jars would break.

SHERIFF   Well, can you beat the women! Held for murder and worryin' about her preserves.

COUNTY ATTORNEY   I guess before we're through she may have something more serious than preserves to worry about.

HALE   Well, women are used to worrying over trifles.

[*The two women move a little closer together.*]

COUNTY ATTORNEY [*with the gallantry of a young politician*]   And yet, for all their worries, what would we do without the ladies? [*the women do not unbend. He goes to the sink, takes a dipperful of water from the pail and pouring it into a basin, washes his hands. Starts to wipe them on the roller-towel, turns it for a cleaner place*] Dirty towels! [*kicks his foot against the pans under the sink*] Not much of a housekeeper, would you say, ladies?

MRS HALE [*stiffly*]   There's a great deal of work to be done on a farm.

COUNTY ATTORNEY   To be sure. And yet [*with a little bow to her*] I know there are some Dickson county farmhouses which do not have such roller towels.

[*He gives it a pull to expose its length again.*]

MRS HALE   Those towels get dirty awful quick. Men's hands aren't always as clean as they might be.

COUNTY ATTORNEY   Ah, loyal to your sex, I see. But you and Mrs Wright were neighbors. I suppose you were friends, too.

MRS HALE [*shaking her head*]   I've not seen much of her of late years. I've not been in this house—it's more than a year.

COUNTY ATTORNEY   And why was that? You didn't like her?

MRS HALE   I liked her all well enough. Farmers' wives have their hands full, Mr Henderson. And then—

COUNTY ATTORNEY   Yes—?

MRS HALE [*looking about*]   It never seemed a very cheerful place.

COUNTY ATTORNEY   No—it's not cheerful. I shouldn't say she had the homemaking instinct.

MRS HALE   Well, I don't know as Wright had, either.

COUNTY ATTORNEY   You mean that they didn't get on very well?

MRS HALE   No. I don't mean anything. But I don't think a place'd be any cheerfuller for John Wright's being in it.

COUNTY ATTORNEY   I'd like to talk more of that a little later. I want to get the lay of things upstairs now.

[*He goes to the left, where three steps lead to a stair door.*]

SHERIFF   I suppose anything Mrs Peters does'll be all right. She was to take in some clothes for her, you know, and a few little things. We left in such a hurry yesterday.

COUNTY ATTORNEY   Yes, but I would like to see what you take, Mrs Peters, and keep an eye out for anything that might be of use to us.

MRS PETERS   Yes, Mr Henderson.

[*The women listen to the men's steps on the stairs, then look about the kitchen.*]

MRS HALE   I'd hate to have men coming into my kitchen, snooping around and criticising.

[*She arranges the pans under sink which the lawyer had shoved out of place.*]

MRS PETERS   Of course it's no more than their duty.

MRS HALE   Duty's all right, but I guess that deputy sheriff that came out to make the fire might have got a little of this on. [*gives the roller towel a pull*] Wish I'd thought of that sooner. Seems mean to talk about her for not having things slicked up when she had to come away in such a hurry.

MRS PETERS [*who has gone to a small table in the left rear corner of the room, and lifted one end of a towel that covers a pan*] She had bread set.
[*Stands still.*]

MRS HALE [*eyes fixed on a loaf of bread beside the bread-box, which is on a low shelf at the other side of the room. Moves slowly toward it*] She was going to put this in there. [*picks up loaf, then abruptly drops it. In a manner of returning to familiar things*] It's a shame about her fruit. I wonder if it's all gone. [*gets up on the chair and looks*] I think there's some here that's all right, Mrs Peters. Yes—here; [*holding it toward the window*] this is cherries, too. [*looking again*] I declare I believe that's the only one. [*gets down, bottle in her hand. Goes to the sink and wipes it off on the outside*] She'll feel awful bad after all her hard work in the hot weather. I remember the afternoon I put up my cherries last summer.

[*She puts the bottle on the big kitchen table, center of the room. With a sigh, is about to sit down in the rocking-chair. Before she is seated realizes what chair it is; with a slow look at it, steps back. The chair which she has touched rocks back and forth.*]

MRS PETERS Well, I must get those things from the front room closet. [*she goes to the door at the right, but after looking into the other room, steps back*] You coming with me, Mrs Hale? You could help me carry them.

[*They go in the other room; reappear, MRS PETERS carrying a dress and skirt, MRS HALE following with a pair of shoes.*]

MRS PETERS My, it's cold in there.

[*She puts the clothes on the big table and hurries to the stove.*]

MRS HALE [*examining the skirt*] Wright was close.[2] I think maybe that's why she kept so much to herself. She didn't even belong to the Ladies Aid. I suppose she felt she couldn't do her part, and then you don't enjoy things when you feel shabby. She used to wear pretty clothes and be lively, when she was Minnie Foster, one of the town girls singing in the choir. But that—oh, that was thirty years ago. This all you was to take in?

MRS PETERS She said she wanted an apron. Funny thing to want, for there isn't much to get you dirty in jail, goodness knows. But I suppose just to make her feel more natural. She said they was in the top drawer in this cupboard. Yes, here. And then her little shawl that always hung behind the door. [*opens stair door and looks*] Yes, here it is.

[*Quickly shuts door leading upstairs.*]

MRS HALE [*abruptly moving toward her*] Mrs Peters?

MRS PETERS Yes, Mrs Hale?

MRS HALE Do you think she did it?

MRS PETERS [*in a frightened voice*] Oh, I don't know.

MRS HALE Well, I don't think she did. Asking for an apron and her little shawl. Worrying about her fruit.

MRS PETERS [*starts to speak, glances up, where footsteps are heard in the room above. In a low voice*] Mr Peters says it looks bad for her. Mr Henderson is awful sarcastic in a speech and he'll make fun of her sayin' she didn't wake up.

MRS HALE Well, I guess John Wright didn't wake when they was slipping that rope under his neck.

2. Miserly.

MRS PETERS No, it's strange. It must have been done awful crafty and still. They say it was such a—funny way to kill a man, rigging it all up like that.

MRS HALE That's just what Mr Hale said. There was a gun in the house. He says that's what he can't understand.

MRS PETERS Mr Henderson said coming out that what was needed for the case was a motive; something to show anger, or—sudden feeling.

MRS HALE [*who is standing by the table*] Well, I don't see any signs of anger around here. [*she puts her hand on the dish-towel which lies on the table, stands looking down at table, one half of which is clean, the other half messy*] It's wiped to here. [*makes a move as if to finish work, then turns and looks at loaf of bread outside the bread-box. Drops towel. In that voice of coming back to familiar things.*] Wonder how they are finding things upstairs. I hope she had it a little more red-up[3] up there. You know, it seems kind of *sneaking*. Locking her up in town and then coming out here and trying to get her own house to turn against her!

MRS PETERS But Mrs Hale, the law is the law.

MRS HALE I s'pose 'tis. [*unbuttoning her coat*] Better loosen up your things, Mrs Peters. You won't feel them when you go out.

[MRS PETERS *takes off her fur tippet,[4] goes to hang it on hook at back of room, stands looking at the under part of the small corner table.*]

MRS PETERS She was piecing a quilt.

[*She brings the large sewing basket and they look at the bright pieces.*]

MRS HALE It's log cabin pattern. Pretty, isn't it? I wonder if she was goin' to quilt it or just knot it?

[*Footsteps have been heard coming down the stairs. The* SHERIFF *enters followed by* HALE *and the* COUNTY ATTORNEY.]

SHERIFF They wonder if she was going to quilt it or just knot it!

[*The men laugh, the women look abashed.*]

COUNTY ATTORNEY [*rubbing his hands over the stove*] Frank's fire didn't do much up there, did it? Well, let's go out to the barn and get that cleared up.

[*The men go outside.*]

MRS HALE [*resentfully*] I don't know as there's anything so strange, our takin' up our time with little things while we're waiting for them to get the evidence. [*she sits down at the big table smoothing out a block with decision*] I don't see as it's anything to laugh about.

MRS PETERS [*apologetically*] Of course they've got awful important things on their minds.

[*Pulls up a chair and joins* MRS HALE *at the table.*]

MRS HALE [*examining another block*] Mrs Peters, look at this one. Here, this is the one she was working on, and look at the sewing! All the rest of it has been so nice and even. And look at this! It's all over the place! Why, it looks as if she didn't know what she was about!

[*After she has said this they look at each other, then start to glance back at the door. After an instant* MRS HALE *has pulled at a knot and ripped the sewing.*]

MRS PETERS Oh, what are you doing, Mrs Hale?

MRS HALE [*mildly*] Just pulling out a stitch or two that's not sewed very good. [*threading a needle*] Bad sewing always made me fidgety.

---

3. Tidy.   4. Short cape, falling just below the shoulders.

MRS PETERS [*nervously*]   I don't think we ought to touch things.

MRS HALE   I'll just finish up this end. [*suddenly stopping and leaning forward*] Mrs Peters?

MRS PETERS   Yes, Mrs Hale?

MRS HALE   What do you suppose she was so nervous about?

MRS PETERS   Oh—I don't know. I don't know as she was nervous. I sometimes sew awful queer when I'm just tired. [MRS HALE *starts to say something, looks at* MRS PETERS, *then goes on sewing*] Well I must get these things wrapped up. They may be through sooner than we think. [*putting apron and other things together*] I wonder where I can find a piece of paper, and string.

MRS HALE   In that cupboard, maybe.

MRS PETERS [*looking in cupboard*]   Why, here's a bird-cage. [*holds it up*] Did she have a bird, Mrs Hale?

MRS HALE   Why, I don't know whether she did or not—I've not been here for so long. There was a man around last year selling canaries cheap, but I don't know as she took one; maybe she did. She used to sing real pretty herself.

MRS PETERS [*glancing around*]   Seems funny to think of a bird here. But she must have had one, or why would she have a cage? I wonder what happened to it.

MRS HALE   I s'pose maybe the cat got it.

MRS PETERS   No, she didn't have a cat. She's got that feeling some people have about cats—being afraid of them. My cat got in her room and she was real upset and asked me to take it out.

MRS HALE   My sister Bessie was like that. Queer, ain't it?

MRS PETERS [*examining the cage*]   Why, look at this door. It's broke. One hinge is pulled apart.

MRS HALE [*looking too*]   Looks as if someone must have been rough with it.

MRS PETERS   Why, yes.

[*She brings the cage forward and puts it on the table.*]

MRS HALE   I wish if they're going to find any evidence they'd be about it. I don't like this place.

MRS PETERS   But I'm awful glad you came with me, Mrs Hale. It would be lonesome for me sitting here alone.

MRS HALE   It would, wouldn't it? [*dropping her sewing*] But I tell you what I do wish, Mrs Peters. I wish I had come over sometimes when *she* was here. I—[*looking around the room*]—wish I had.

MRS PETERS   But of course you were awful busy. Mrs Hale—your house and your children.

MRS HALE   I could've come. I stayed away because it weren't cheerful—and that's why I ought to have come. I—I've never liked this place. Maybe because it's down in a hollow and you don't see the road. I dunno what it is, but it's a lonesome place and always was. I wish I had come over to see Minnie Foster sometimes. I can see now—[*shakes her head*]

MRS PETERS   Well, you mustn't reproach yourself, Mrs Hale. Somehow we just don't see how it is with other folks until—something comes up.

MRS HALE   Not having children makes less work—but it makes a quiet house, and Wright out to work all day, and no company when he did come in. Did you know John Wright, Mrs Peters?

MRS PETERS   Not to know him; I've seen him in town. They say he was a good man.

MRS HALE   Yes—good; he didn't drink, and kept his word as well as most, I guess, and paid his debts. But he was a hard man, Mrs Peters. Just to pass the time of day with him—[*shivers*] Like a raw wind that gets to the bone. [*pauses, her eye falling on the cage*] I should think she would a wanted a bird. But what do you suppose went with it?

MRS PETERS   I don't know, unless it got sick and died.

[*She reaches over and swings the broken door, swings it again, both women watch it.*]

MRS HALE   You weren't raised round here, were you? [MRS PETERS *shakes her head*] You didn't know—her?

MRS PETERS   Not till they brought her yesterday.

MRS HALE   She—come to think of it, she was kind of like a bird herself—real sweet and pretty, but kind of timid and—fluttery. How—she—did—change. [*silence: then as if struck by a happy thought and relieved to get back to everyday things*] Tell you what, Mrs Peters, why don't you take the quilt in with you? It might take up her mind.

MRS PETERS   Why, I think that's a real nice idea, Mrs Hale. There couldn't possibly be any objection to it, could there? Now, just what would I take? I wonder if her patches are in here—and her things.

[*They look in the sewing basket.*]

MRS HALE   Here's some red. I expect this has got sewing things in it. [*brings out a fancy box*] What a pretty box. Looks like something somebody would give you. Maybe her scissors are in here. [*Opens box. Suddenly puts her hand to her nose*] Why—[MRS PETERS *bends nearer, then turns her face away*] There's something wrapped up in this piece of silk.

MRS PETERS   Why, this isn't her scissors.

MRS HALE   [*lifting the silk*]   Oh, Mrs Peters—it's—

[MRS PETERS *bends closer.*]

MRS PETERS   It's the bird.

MRS HALE   [*jumping up*]   But, Mrs Peters—look at it! It's neck! Look at its neck! It's all—other side *to*.

MRS PETERS   Somebody—wrung—its—neck.

[*Their eyes meet. A look of growing comprehension, of horror. Steps are heard outside.* MRS HALE *slips box under quilt pieces, and sinks into her chair. Enter* SHERIFF *and* COUNTY ATTORNEY. MRS PETERS *rises.*]

COUNTY ATTORNEY   [*as one turning from serious things to little pleasantries*] Well ladies, have you decided whether she was going to quilt it or knot it?

MRS PETERS   We think she was going to—knot it.

COUNTY ATTORNEY   Well, that's interesting, I'm sure. [*seeing the bird-cage*] Has the bird flown?

MRS HALE   [*putting more quilt pieces over the box*]   We think the—cat got it.

COUNTY ATTORNEY   [*preoccupied*]   Is there a cat?

[MRS HALE *glances in a quick covert way at* MRS PETERS.]

MRS PETERS   Well, not *now*. They're superstitious, you know. They leave.

COUNTY ATTORNEY   [*to* SHERIFF PETERS, *continuing an interrupted conversation*] No sign at all of anyone having come from the outside. Their own rope. Now let's go up again and go over it piece by piece. [*they start upstairs*] It would have to have been someone who knew just the—

[MRS PETERS *sits down. The two women sit there not looking at one another, but as if peering into something and at the same time holding back. When they talk now it is in the manner of feeling their way over strange ground, as if afraid of what they are saying, but as if they can not help saying it.*]

MRS HALE   She liked the bird. She was going to bury it in that pretty box.

MRS PETERS [*in a whisper*]   When I was a girl—my kitten—there was a boy took a hatchet, and before my eyes—and before I could get there—[*covers her face an instant*] If they hadn't held me back I would have—[*catches herself, looks upstairs where steps are heard, falters weakly*]—hurt him.

MRS HALE [*with a slow look around her*]   I wonder how it would seem never to have had any children around. [*pause*] No, Wright wouldn't like the bird—a thing that sang. She used to sing. He killed that, too.

MRS PETERS [*moving uneasily*]   We don't know who killed the bird.

MRS HALE   I knew John Wright.

MRS PETERS   It was an awful thing was done in this house that night, Mrs Hale. Killing a man while he slept, slipping a rope around his neck that choked the life out of him.

MRS HALE   His neck. Choked the life out of him.

[*Her hand goes out and rests on the bird-cage.*]

MRS PETERS [*with rising voice*]   We don't know who killed him. We don't *know.*

MRS HALE [*her own feeling not interrupted*]   If there'd been years and years of nothing, then a bird to sing to you, it would be awful—still, after the bird was still.

MRS PETERS [*something within her speaking*]   I know what stillness is. When we homesteaded in Dakota, and my first baby died—after he was two years old, and me with no other then—

MRS HALE [*moving*]   How soon do you suppose they'll be through, looking for the evidence?

MRS PETERS   I know what stillness is. [*pulling herself back*] The law has got to punish crime, Mrs Hale.

MRS HALE [*not as if answering that*]   I wish you'd seen Minnie Foster when she wore a white dress with blue ribbons and stood up there in the choir and sang. [*a look around the room*] Oh, I *wish* I'd come over here once in a while! That was a crime! That was a crime! Who's going to punish that?

MRS PETERS [*looking upstairs*]   We mustn't—take on.

MRS HALE   I might have known she needed help! I know how things can be—for women. I tell you, it's queer. Mrs Peters. We live close together and we live far apart. We all go through the same things—it's all just a different kind of the same thing. [*brushes her eyes, noticing the bottle of fruit, reaches out for it*] If I was you, I wouldn't tell her her fruit was gone. Tell her it *ain't.* Tell her it's all right. Take this in to prove it to her. She—she may never know whether it was broke or not.

MRS PETERS [*takes the bottle, looks about for something to wrap it in; takes petticoat from the clothes brought from the other room, very nervously begins winding this around the bottle. In a false voice*]   My, it's a good thing the men couldn't hear us. Wouldn't they just laugh! Getting all stirred up over a little thing like a—dead canary. As if that could have anything to do with—with—wouldn't they *laugh!*

[*The men are heard coming down stairs.*]

MRS HALE [*under her breath*]   Maybe they would—maybe they wouldn't.

COUNTY ATTORNEY   No, Peters, it's all perfectly clear except a reason for doing it. But you know juries when it comes to women. If there was some definite thing. Something to show—something to make a story about—a thing that would connect up with this strange way of doing it—

[*The women's eyes meet for an instant. Enter* HALE *from outer door.*]

HALE   Well, I've got the team around. Pretty cold out there.

COUNTY ATTORNEY   I'm going to stay here a while by myself. [*to the* SHER-IFF] You can send Frank out for me, can't you? I want to go over everything. I'm not satisfied that we can't do better.

SHERIFF   Do you want to see what Mrs Peters is going to take in?

[*The* LAWYER *goes to the table, picks up the apron, laughs.*]

COUNTY ATTORNEY   Oh, I guess they're not very dangerous things the ladies have picked out. [*Moves a few things about, disturbing the quilt pieces which cover the box. Steps back*] No, Mrs Peters doesn't need supervising. For that matter, a sheriff's wife is married to the law. Ever think of it that way, Mrs Peters?

MRS PETERS   Not—just that way.

SHERIFF [*chuckling*]   Married to the law. [*moves toward the other room*] I just want you to come in here a minute, George. We ought to take a look at these windows.

COUNTY ATTORNEY [*scoffingly*]   Oh, windows!

SHERIFF   We'll be right out, Mr Hale.

[HALE *goes outside. The* SHERIFF *follows the* COUNTY ATTORNEY *into the other room. Then* MRS HALE *rises, hands tight together, looking intensely at* MRS PETERS, *whose eyes make a slow turn, finally meeting* MRS HALE's. *A moment* MRS HALE *holds her, then her own eyes point the way to where the box is concealed. Suddenly* MRS PETERS *throws back quilt pieces and tries to put the box in the bag she is wearing. It is too big. She opens box, starts to take bird out, cannot touch it, goes to pieces, stands there helpless. Sound of a knob turning in the other room.* MRS HALE *snatches the box and puts it in the pocket of her big coat. Enter* COUNTY ATTORNEY *and* SHERIFF.]

COUNTY ATTORNEY [*facetiously*]   Well, Henry, at least we found out that she was not going to quilt it. She was going to—what is it you call it, ladies?

MRS HALE [*her hand against her pocket*]   We call it—knot it, Mr Henderson.

CURTAIN

1916

SHERWOOD ANDERSON
1876–1941

Sherwood Anderson was approaching middle age when he abandoned a successful business career to become a writer. Living in Chicago, New Orleans, and Paris, meeting literary people, he worked furiously to make up for his late start, producing novels, short stories, essays, and an autobiography. His short fiction provided a model for younger writers, whose careers he encouraged by literary advice and by practical help in getting published as well. *Winesburg, Ohio,* which appeared in 1919 when he was forty-three years old, remains a major work of experimental fiction and was in its time a bold treatment of small-town life in the American Midwest in the tradition of Edgar Lee Masters's *Spoon River Anthology.*

Anderson was born in southern Ohio, the third of seven children in a family headed by a father whose training and skill as a harness maker were becoming useless in the new world of the automobile. Anderson's father kept his family on the move in search of work; the stamina and tenderness of his mother supplied coherence and security in this nomadic life. Not until 1892, when Anderson was sixteen, did they settle down in the town of Clyde, Ohio, which became the model for Winesburg. Anderson never finished high school. He held a variety of jobs, living in Chicago with an older brother in 1896 and again in 1900 when he worked as an advertising copywriter.

His first wife came from a successful Ohio business family; the couple settled in Ohio where Anderson managed a mail-order house as well as two paint firms. But he found increasingly that the need to write conflicted with his career. In 1912 he left his business and his marriage, returning to Chicago, where he met the writers and artists whose activities were creating the Chicago Renaissance. These included the novelists Floyd Dell and Theodore Dreiser; the poets Edgar Lee Masters, Vachel Lindsay, and Carl Sandburg; and the editors Harriet Monroe of *Poetry* and Margaret C. Anderson of the *Little Review.* His first major publication was *Windy McPherson's Son* (1916), the story of a man who runs away from a small Iowa town in futile search for life's meaning; his second was *Marching Men* (1917), about a charismatic lawyer who tries—unsuccessfully—to reorganize the factory system in a small town. These books reveal three of Anderson's preoccupations: the individual quest for self and social betterment, the small-town environment, and the distrust of modern industrial society. Missing, however, is the interest in human psychology and the sense of conflict between inner and outer worlds that appear in *Winesburg* and later works.

In 1916 Anderson began writing and publishing the tales that were brought together in *Winesburg, Ohio.* The formal achievement of the book lay in its articulation of individual tales to a loose but coherent structure. The lives of a number of people living in the town of Winesburg are observed by the naïve adolescent George Willard, a reporter for the local newspaper. Their stories contribute to his understanding of life and to his preparation for a career as a writer. The book ends when his mother dies and he leaves Winesburg. With the help of the narrator, whose vision is larger than George's, the reader can see how the lives of the characters have been profoundly distorted by the frustration and suppression of so many of their desires. Anderson calls these characters "grotesques," but the intention of *Winesburg, Ohio* is to show that life in all American small towns is grotesque in the same way. Anderson's attitude toward the characters mixes compassion for the individual with dismay at a social order that can do so much damage. His criticism is

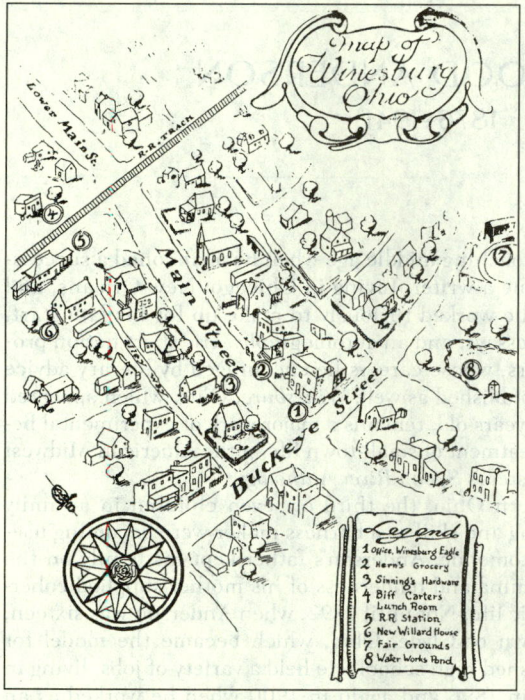

Winesburg, Ohio, Harald Toksvig, 1919. Toksvig's map was printed in the first edition of *Winesburg, Ohio.*

not specifically political, however; he is measuring society by a utopian standard of free emotional and sensual expression.

Stylistically Anderson strove for the simplest possible prose, using brief or at least uncomplex sentences and an unsophisticated vocabulary appropriate to the muffled awareness and limited resources of his typical characters. Structurally, his stories build toward a moment when the character breaks out in some frenzied gesture of release that is revelatory of a hidden inner life. In both style and structure Anderson's works were important influences on other writers: he encouraged simplicity and directness of style, made attractive the use of the point of view of outsider characters as a way of criticizing conventional society, and gave the craft of the short story a decided push toward stories presenting a slice of life or a significant moment as opposed to panorama and summary.

Winesburg, Ohio appeared near the beginning of Anderson's literary career, and although he continued writing for two decades, he never repeated its success. His best later work was in short stories, published in three volumes: *The Triumph of the Egg* (1921), *Horses and Men* (1923), and *Death in the Woods and Other Stories* (1933). He also wrote a number of novels, including *Poor White* (1920), *Many Marriages* (1923), *Beyond Desire* (1932), and *Kit Brandon* (1936), as well as free verse, prose poems, plays, and essays. A series of autobiographical volumes advertised his career, attempted to define the writer's vocation in America, and discussed his impact on other writers. The more he claimed, however, the less other writers were willing to allow him; both Hemingway and Faulkner, for example, whom he had met in Paris and New Orleans, respectively, satirized his cult of the simple and thereby disavowed his influence. (In fact, he *had* stimulated and helped both of them—stimulated Hemingway in his quest for stylistic simplicity, Faulkner in his search for the proper subject matter.) During the 1930s Anderson, along with many other writers, was active in liberal causes, and he died at sea on the way to South America while on a goodwill mission for the State Department.

The text is that of *Winesburg, Ohio* (1919).

From Winesburg, Ohio

Hands

Upon the half decayed veranda of a small frame house that stood near the edge of a ravine near the town of Winesburg, Ohio, a fat little old man walked nervously up and down. Across a long field that had been seeded for clover but that had produced only a dense crop of yellow mustard weeds, he could see the public highway along which went a wagon filled with berry pickers returning from the fields. The berry pickers, youths and maidens, laughed and shouted boisterously. A boy clad in a blue shirt leaped from the wagon and attempted to drag after him one of the maidens who screamed and protested shrilly. The feet of the boy in the road kicked up a cloud of dust that floated across the face of the departing sun. Over the long field came a thin girlish voice. "Oh, you Wing Biddlebaum, comb your hair, it's falling into your eyes," commanded the voice to the man, who was bald and whose nervous little hands fiddled about the bare white forehead as though arranging a mass of tangled locks.

Wing Biddlebaum, forever frightened and beset by a ghostly band of doubts, did not think of himself as in any way a part of the life of the town where he had lived for twenty years. Among all the people of Winesburg but one had come close to him. With George Willard, son of Tom Willard, the proprietor of the new Willard House, he had formed something like a friend-ship. George Willard was the reporter on the *Winesburg Eagle* and some-times in the evenings he walked out along the highway to Wing Biddlebaum's house. Now as the old man walked up and down on the veranda, his hands moving nervously about, he was hoping that George Willard would come and spend the evening with him. After the wagon containing the berry pickers had passed, he went across the field through the tall mustard weeds and climbing a rail fence peered anxiously along the road to the town. For a moment he stood thus, rubbing his hands together and looking up and down the road, and then, fear overcoming him, ran back to walk again upon the porch on his own house.

In the presence of George Willard, Wing Biddlebaum, who for twenty years had been the town mystery, lost something of his timidity, and his shadowy personality, submerged in a sea of doubts, came forth to look at the world. With the young reporter at his side, he ventured in the light of day into Main Street or strode up and down on the rickety front porch of his own house, talking excitedly. The voice that had been low and trembling became shrill and loud. The bent figure straightened. With a kind of wriggle, like a fish returned to the brook by the fisherman, Biddlebaum the silent began to talk, striving to put into words the ideas that had been accumulated by his mind during long years of silence.

Wing Biddlebaum talked much with his hands. The slender expressive fingers, forever active, forever striving to conceal themselves in his pockets or behind his back, came forth and became the piston rods of his machin-ery of expression.

The story of Wing Biddlebaum is a story of hands. Their restless activity, like unto the beating of the wings of an imprisoned bird, had given him his name. Some obscure poet of the town had thought of it. The hands alarmed their owner. He wanted to keep them hidden away and looked with amazement at the quiet inexpressive hands of other men who worked beside him in the fields, or passed, driving sleepy teams on country roads.

When he talked to George Willard, Wing Biddlebaum closed his fists and beat with them upon a table or on the walls of his house. The action made him more comfortable. If the desire to talk came to him when the two were walking in the fields, he sought out a stump or the top board of a fence and with his hands pounding busily talked with renewed ease.

The story of Wing Biddlebaum's hands is worth a book in itself. Sympathetically set forth it would tap many strange, beautiful qualities in obscure men. It is a job for a poet. In Winesburg the hands had attracted attention merely because of their activity. With them Wing Biddlebaum had picked as high as a hundred and forty quarts of strawberries in a day. They became his distinguishing feature, the source of his fame. Also they made more grotesque an already grotesque and elusive individuality. Winesburg was proud of the hands of Wing Biddlebaum in the same spirit in which it was proud of Banker White's new stone house and Wesley Moyer's bay stallion, Tony Tip, that had won the two-fifteen trot at the fall races in Cleveland.

As for George Willard, he had many times wanted to ask about the hands. At times an almost overwhelming curiosity had taken hold of him. He felt that there must be a reason for their strange activity and their inclination to keep hidden away and only a growing respect for Wing Biddlebaum kept him from blurting out the questions that were often in his mind.

Once he had been on the point of asking. The two were walking in the fields on a summer afternoon and had stopped to sit upon a grassy bank. All afternoon Wing Biddlebaum had talked as one inspired. By a fence he had stopped and beating like a giant woodpecker upon the top board had shouted at George Willard, condemning his tendency to be too much influenced by the people about him. "You are destroying yourself," he cried. "You have the inclination to be alone and to dream and you are afraid of dreams. You want to be like others in town here. You hear them talk and you try to imitate them."

On the grassy bank Wing Biddlebaum had tried again to drive his point home. His voice became soft and reminiscent, and with a sigh of contentment he launched into a long rambling talk, speaking as one lost in a dream.

Out of the dream Wing Biddlebaum made a picture for George Willard. In the picture men lived again in a kind of pastoral golden age. Across a green open country came clean-limbed young men, some afoot, some mounted upon horses. In crowds the young men came to gather about the feet of an old man who sat beneath a tree in a tiny garden and who talked to them.[1]

Wing Biddlebaum became wholly inspired. For once he forgot the hands. Slowly they stole forth and lay upon George Willard's shoulders. Something new and bold came into the voice that talked. "You must try to forget all you have learned," said the old man. "You must begin to dream. From this time on you must shut your ears to the roaring of the voices."

Pausing in his speech, Wing Biddlebaum looked long and earnestly at George Willard. His eyes glowed. Again he raised the hands to caress the boy and then a look of horror swept over his face.

---

1. Biddlebaum's picture invokes ideals of the Greek Golden Age generally, and more particularly the image of the Athenian philosopher Socrates (469–399 B.C.E) teaching young Greek aristocrats.

With a convulsive movement of his body, Wing Biddlebaum sprang to his feet and thrust his hands deep into his trousers pockets. Tears came to his eyes. "I must be getting along home. I can talk no more with you," he said nervously.

Without looking back, the old man had hurried down the hillside and across a meadow, leaving George Willard perplexed and frightened upon the grassy slope. With a shiver of dread the boy arose and went along the road toward town. "I'll not ask him about his hands," he thought, touched by the memory of the terror he had seen in the man's eyes. "There's something wrong, but I don't want to know what it is. His hands have something to do with his fear of me and of everyone."

And George Willard was right. Let us look briefly into the story of the hands. Perhaps our talking of them will arouse the poet who will tell the hidden wonder story of the influence for which the hands were but fluttering pennants of promise.

In his youth Wing Biddlebaum had been a school teacher in a town in Pennsylvania. He was not then known as Wing Biddlebaum, but went by the less euphonic name of Adolph Myers.[2] As Adolph Myers he was much loved by the boys of his school.

Adolph Myers was meant by nature to be a teacher of youth. He was one of those rare, little-understood men who rule by a power so gentle that it passes as a lovable weakness. In their feeling for the boys under their charge such men are not unlike the finer sort of women in their love of men.

And yet that is but crudely stated. It needs the poet there. With the boys of his school, Adolph Myers had walked in the evening or had sat talking until dusk upon the schoolhouse steps lost in a kind of dream. Here and there went his hands, caressing the shoulders of the boys, playing about the tousled heads. As he talked his voice became soft and musical. There was a caress in that also. In a way the voice and the hands, the stroking of the shoulders and the touching of the hair was a part of the schoolmaster's effort to carry a dream into the young minds. By the caress that was in his fingers he expressed himself. He was one of those men in whom the force that creates life is diffused, not centralized. Under the caress of his hands doubt and disbelief went out of the minds of the boy and they began also to dream.

And then the tragedy. A half-witted boy of the school became enamored of the young master. In his bed at night he imagined unspeakable things and in the morning went forth to tell his dreams as facts. Strange, hideous accusations fell from his loose-hung lips. Through the Pennsylvania town went a shiver. Hidden, shadowy doubts that had been in men's minds concerning Adolph Myers were galvanized into beliefs.

The tragedy did not linger. Trembling lads were jerked out of bed and questioned. "He put his arms about me," said one. "His fingers were always playing in my hair," said another.

One afternoon a man of the town, Henry Bradford, who kept a saloon, came to the schoolhouse door. Calling Adolph Myers into the school yard he began to beat him with his fists. As his hard knuckles beat down into the frightened face of the schoolmaster, his wrath became more and more terrible. Screaming with dismay, the children ran here and there like

2. Both his adopted surname and his original one underline Biddlebaum's foreignness by labeling him as German and, probably, Jewish.

disturbed insects "I'll teach you to put your hands on my boy, you beast," roared the saloon keeper, who, tired of beating the master, had begun to kick him about the yard.

Adolph Myers was driven from the Pennsylvania town in the night. With lanterns in their hands a dozen men came to the door of the house where he lived alone and commanded that he dress and come forth. It was raining and one of the men had a rope in his hands. They had intended to hang the schoolmaster, but something in his figure, so small, white, and pitiful, touched their hearts and they let him escape. As he ran away into the darkness they repented of their weakness and ran after him, swearing and throwing sticks and great balls of soft mud at the figure that screamed and ran faster and faster into the darkness.

For twenty years Adolph Myers had lived alone in Winesburg. He was but forty but looked sixty-five. The name of Biddlebaum he got from a box of goods seen at a freight station as he hurried through an eastern Ohio town. He had an aunt in Winesburg, a black-toothed old woman who raised chickens, and with her he lived until she died. He had been ill for a year after the experience in Pennsylvania, and after his recovery worked as a day laborer in the fields, going timidly about and striving to conceal his hands. Although he did not understand what had happened he felt that the hands must be to blame. Again and again the fathers of the boys had talked of the hands. "Keep your hands to yourself," the saloon keeper had roared, dancing with fury in the schoolhouse yard.

Upon the veranda of his house by the ravine, Wing Biddlebaum continued to walk up and down until the sun had disappeared and the road beyond the field was lost in the grey shadows. Going into his house he cut slices of bread and spread honey upon them. When the rumble of the evening train that took away the express cars loaded with the day's harvest of berries had passed and restored the silence of the summer night, he went again to walk upon the veranda. In the darkness he could not see the hands and they became quiet. Although he still hungered for the presence of the boy, who was the medium through which he expressed his love of man, the hunger became again a part of his loneliness and his waiting. Lighting a lamp, Wing Biddlebaum washed the few dishes soiled by his simple meal and, setting up a folding cot by the screen door that led to the porch, prepared to undress for the night. A few stray white bread crumbs lay on the cleanly washed floor by the table; putting the lamp upon a low stool he began to pick up the crumbs, carrying them to his mouth one by one with unbelievable rapidity. In the dense blotch of light beneath the table, the kneeling figure looked like a priest engaged in some service of his church. The nervous expressive fingers, flashing in and out of the light, might well have been mistaken for the fingers of the devotee going swiftly through decade after decade of his rosary.[3]

Mother

Elizabeth Willard, the mother of George Willard, was tall and gaunt and her face was marked with smallpox scars. Although she was but forty-five, some obscure disease had taken the fire out of her figure. Listlessly she

---

3. String of beads used by Roman Catholics to keep track of prayers, divided into sections or "decades" of ten beads.

went about the disorderly old hotel looking at the faded wall-paper and the ragged carpets and, when she was able to be about, doing the work of a chambermaid among beds soiled by the slumbers of fat traveling men. Her husband, Tom Willard, a slender, graceful man with square shoulders, a quick military step, and a black mustache, trained to turn sharply up at the ends, tried to put the wife out of his mind. The presence of the tall ghostly figure, moving slowly through the halls, he took as a reproach to himself. When he thought of her he grew angry and swore. The hotel was unprofitable and forever on the edge of failure and he wished himself out of it. He thought of the old house and the woman who lived there with him as things defeated and done for. The hotel in which he had begun life so hopefully was now a mere ghost of what a hotel should be. As he went spruce and businesslike through the streets of Winesburg, he sometimes stopped and turned quickly about as though fearing that the spirit of the hotel and of the woman would follow him even into the streets. "Damn such a life, damn it!" he sputtered aimlessly.

Tom Willard had a passion for village politics and for years had been the leading Democrat in a strongly Republican community. Some day, he told himself, the tide of things political will turn in my favor and the years of ineffectual service count big in the bestowal of rewards. He dreamed of going to Congress and even of becoming governor. Once when a younger member of the party arose at a political conference and began to boast of his faithful service, Tom Willard grew white with fury. "Shut up, you," he roared, glaring about. "What do you know of service? What are you but a boy? Look at what I've done here! I was a Democrat here in Winesburg when it was a crime to be a Democrat. In the old days they fairly hunted us with guns."

Between Elizabeth and her one son George there was a deep unexpressed bond of sympathy, based on a girlhood dream that had long ago died. In the son's presence she was timid and reserved, but sometimes while he hurried about town intent upon his duties as a reporter, she went into his room and closing the door knelt by a little desk, made of a kitchen table, that sat near a window. In the room by the desk she went through a ceremony that was half a prayer, half a demand, addressed to the skies. In the boyish figure she yearned to see something half forgotten that had once been a part of herself recreated. The prayer concerned that. "Even though I die, I will in some way keep defeat from you," she cried, and so deep was her determination that her whole body shook. Her eyes glowed and she clenched her fists. "If I am dead and see him becoming a meaningless drab figure like myself, I will come back," she declared. "I ask God now to give me that privilege. I demand it. I will pay for it. God may beat me with his fists. I will take any blow that may befall if but this my boy be allowed to express something for us both." Pausing uncertainly, the woman stared about the boy's room. "And do not let him become smart and successful either," she added vaguely.

The communion between George Willard and his mother was outwardly a formal thing without meaning. When she was ill and sat by the window in her room he sometimes went in the evening to make her a visit. They sat by a window that looked over the roof of a small frame building into Main Street. By turning their heads they could see, through another window, along an alleyway that ran behind the Main Street stores and into the back door of Abner Groff's bakery. Sometimes as they sat thus a picture of village life presented itself to them. At the back door of his shop appeared Abner Groff with a stick or an empty milk bottle in his hand. For a long time there was a feud between the baker and a grey cat that belonged to Sylvester West, the druggist. The boy and his mother saw the cat creep into the door of the bakery and presently emerge followed by the baker who swore and waved his arms about. The baker's eyes were small and red and his black hair and beard were filled with flour dust. Sometimes he was so angry that, although the cat had disappeared, he hurled sticks, bits of broken glass, and even some of the tools of his trade about. Once he broke a window at the back of Sinning's Hardware Store. In the alley the grey cat crouched behind barrels filled with torn paper and broken bottles above which flew a black swarm of flies. Once when she was alone, and after watching a prolonged and ineffectual outburst on the part of the baker, Elizabeth Willard put her head down on her long white hands and wept. After that she did not look along the alleyway any more, but tried to forget the contest between the bearded man and the cat. It seemed like a rehearsal of her own life, terrible in its vividness.

In the evening when the son sat in the room with his mother, the silence made them both feel awkward. Darkness came on and the evening train came in at the station. In the street below feet tramped up and down upon a board sidewalk. In the station yard, after the evening train had gone, there was a heavy silence. Perhaps Skinner Leason, the express agent, moved a truck the length of the station platform. Over on Main Street sounded a man's voice, laughing. The door of the express office banged. George Willard arose and crossing the room fumbled for the doorknob. Sometimes he knocked against a chair, making it scrape along the floor. By the window sat the sick woman, perfectly still, listless. Her long hands, white and bloodless, could be seen drooping over the ends of the arms of the chair. "I think you had better be out among the boys. You are too much indoors," she said, striving to relieve the embarrassment of the departure. "I thought I would take a walk," replied George Willard, who felt awkward and confused.

One evening in July, when the transient guests who made the New Willard House their temporary homes had become scarce, and the hallways, lighted only by kerosene lamps turned low, were plunged in gloom, Elizabeth Willard had an adventure. She had been ill in bed for several days and her son had not come to visit her. She was alarmed. The feeble blaze of life that remained in her body was blown into a flame by her anxiety and she crept out of bed, dressed and hurried along the hallway toward her son's room, shaking with exaggerated fears. As she went along she steadied herself with her hand, slipped along the papered walls of the hall and breathed with difficulty. The air whistled through her teeth. As she hurried forward she thought how foolish she was. "He is concerned with boyish affairs," she told herself. "Perhaps he has now begun to walk about in the evening with girls."

Elizabeth Willard had a dread of being seen by guests in the hotel that had once belonged to her father and the ownership of which still stood recorded in her name in the county courthouse. The hotel was continually losing patronage because of its shabbiness and she thought of herself as also shabby. Her own room was in an obscure corner and when she felt able to work she voluntarily worked among the beds, preferring the labor that could be done when the guests were abroad seeking trade among the merchants of Winesburg.

By the door of her son's room the mother knelt upon the floor and listened for some sound from within. When she heard the boy moving about and talking in low tones a smile came to her lips. George Willard had a habit of talking aloud to himself and to hear him doing so had always given his mother a peculiar pleasure. The habit in him, she felt, strengthened the secret bond that existed between them. A thousand times she had whispered to herself of the matter. "He is groping about, trying to find himself," she thought. "He is not a dull clod, all words and smartness. Within him there is a secret something that is striving to grow. It is the thing I let be killed in myself."

In the darkness in the hallway by the door the sick woman arose and started again toward her own room. She was afraid that the door would open and the boy come upon her. When she had reached a safe distance and was about to turn a corner into a second hallway she stopped and bracing herself with her hands waited, thinking to shake off a trembling fit of weakness that had come upon her. The presence of the boy in the room had made her happy. In her bed, during the long hours alone, the little fears that had visited her had become giants. Now they were all gone. "When I get back to my room I shall sleep," she murmured gratefully.

But Elizabeth Willard was not to return to her bed and to sleep. As she stood trembling in the darkness the door of her son's room opened and the boy's father, Tom Willard, stepped out. In the light that streamed out at the door he stood with the knob in his hand and talked. What he said infuriated the woman.

Tom Willard was ambitious for his son. He had always thought of himself as a successful man, although nothing he had ever done had turned out successfully. However, when he was out of sight of the New Willard House and had no fear of coming upon his wife, he swaggered and began to dramatize himself as one of the chief men of the town. He wanted his son to succeed. He it was who had secured for the boy the position on the *Winesburg Eagle.* Now, with a ring of earnestness in his voice, he was advising concerning some course of conduct. "I tell you what, George, you've got to wake up," he said sharply. "Will Henderson has spoken to me three times concerning the matter. He says you go along for hours not hearing when you are spoken to and acting like a gawky girl. What ails you?" Tom Willard laughed good-naturedly. "Well, I guess you'll get over it," he said. "I told Will that. You're not a fool and you're not a woman. You're Tom Willard's son and you'll wake up. I'm not afraid. What you say clears things up. If being a newspaper man had put the notion of becoming a writer into your mind that's all right. Only I guess you'll have to wake up to do that too, eh?"

Tom Willard went briskly along the hallway and down a flight of stairs to the office. The woman in the darkness could hear him laughing and talking with a guest who was striving to wear away a dull evening by dozing in a chair by the office door. She returned to the door of her son's room. The weakness had passed from her body as by a miracle and she stepped boldly along. A thousand ideas raced through her head. When she heard the scraping of a chair and the sound of a pen scratching upon paper, she again turned and went back along the hallway to her own room.

A definite determination had come into the mind of the defeated wife of the Winesburg Hotel keeper. The determination was the result of long years of quiet and rather ineffectual thinking. "Now," she told herself, "I will act. There is something threatening my boy and I will ward it off." The fact that the conversation between Tom Willard and his son had been rather quiet and natural, as though an understanding existed between them, maddened her. Although for years she had hated her husband, her hatred had always before been a quite impersonal thing. He had been merely a part of something else that she hated. Now, and by the few words at the door, he had become the thing personified. In the darkness of her own room she clenched her fists and glared about. Going to a cloth bag that hung on a nail by the wall she took out a long pair of sewing scissors and held them in her hand like a dagger. "I will stab him," she said aloud. "He has chosen to be the voice of evil and I will kill him. When I have killed him something will snap within myself and I will die also. It will be a release for all of us."

In her girlhood and before her marriage with Tom Willard, Elizabeth had borne a somewhat shaky reputation in Winesburg. For years she had been what is called "stage-struck" and had paraded through the streets with traveling men guests at her father's hotel, wearing loud clothes and urging them to tell her of life in the cities out of which they had come. Once she startled the town by putting on men's clothes and riding a bicycle down Main Street.

In her own mind the tall girl had been in those days much confused. A great restlessness was in her and it expressed itself in two ways. First there was an uneasy desire for change, for some big definite movement to her life. It was this feeling that had turned her mind to the stage. She dreamed of joining some company and wandering over the world, seeing always new faces and giving something out of herself to all people. Sometimes at night she was quite beside herself with the thought, but when she tried to talk of the matter to the members of the theatrical companies that came to Winesburg and stopped at her father's hotel, she got nowhere. They did not seem to know what she meant, or if she did get something of her passion expressed, they only laughed. "It's not like that," they said. "It's as dull and uninteresting as this here. Nothing comes of it."

With the traveling men when she walked about with them, and later with Tom Willard, it was quite different. Always they seemed to understand and sympathize with her. On the side streets of the village, in the darkness under the trees, they took hold of her hand and she thought that something unexpressed in herself came forth and became a part of an unexpressed something in them.

And then there was the second expression of her restlessness. When that came she felt for a time released and happy. She did not blame the men who walked with her and later she did not blame Tom Willard. It was always the same, beginning with kisses and ending, after strange wild emotions, with peace and then sobbing repentance. When she sobbed she put her hand upon the face of the man and had always the same thought. Even though he were large and bearded she thought he had become suddenly a little boy. She wondered why he did not sob also.

In her room, tucked away in a corner of the old Willard House, Elizabeth Willard lighted a lamp and put it on a dressing table that stood by the door. A thought had come into her mind and she went to a closet and brought out a small square box and set it on the table. The box contained material for make-up and had been left with other things by a theatrical company that had once been stranded in Winesburg. Elizabeth Willard had decided that she would be beautiful. Her hair was still black and there was a great mass of it braided and coiled about her head. The scene that was to take place in the office below began to grow in her mind. No ghostly worn-out figure should confront Tom Willard, but something quite unexpected and startling. Tall and with dusky cheeks and hair that fell in a mass from her shoulders, a figure should come striding down the stairway before the startled loungers in the hotel office. The figure would be silent—it would be swift and terrible. As a tigress whose cub had been threatened would she appear, coming out of the shadows, stealing noiselessly along and holding the long wicked scissors in her hand.

With a little broken sob in her throat Elizabeth Willard blew out the light that stood upon the table and stood weak and trembling in the darkness. The strength that had been a miracle in her body left and she half reeled across the floor, clutching at the back of the chair in which she had spent so many long days staring out over the tin roofs into the main street of Winesburg. In the hallway there was the sound of footsteps and George Willard came in at the door. Sitting in a chair beside his mother he began to talk. "I'm going to get out of here," he said. "I don't know where I shall go or what I shall do but I am going away."

The woman in the chair waited and trembled. An impulse came to her. "I suppose you had better wake up," she said. "You think that? You will go to the city and make money, eh? It will be better for you, you think, to be a business man, to be brisk and smart and alive?" She waited and trembled.

The son shook his head. "I suppose I can't make you understand, but oh, I wish I could," he said earnestly. "I can't even talk to father about it. I don't try. There isn't any use. I don't know what I shall do. I just want to go away and look at people and think."

Silence fell upon the room where the boy and woman sat together. Again, as on the other evenings, they were embarrassed. After a time the boy tried again to talk. "I suppose it won't be for a year or two but I've been thinking about it," he said, rising and going toward the door. "Something father said makes it sure that I shall have to go away." He fumbled with the door knob. In the room the silence became unbearable to the woman. She wanted to cry out with joy because of the words that had come from the lips of her son, but the expression of joy had become impossible to her. "I think you had better go out among the boys. You are too much indoors," she said. "I thought I would go for a little walk," replied the son stepping awkwardly out of the room and closing the door.

CARL SANDBURG
1878–1967

Son of an immigrant Swedish blacksmith who had settled in Galesburg, Illinois, Carl Sandburg was an active populist and socialist, a journalist, and an important figure in the Chicago Renaissance of arts and letters. During the 1920s and 1930s he was one of the most widely read poets in the nation. His poetic aim was to celebrate the working people of America in poems that they could understand. He wrote sympathetically and affirmatively of the masses, using a long verse line unfettered by rhyme or regular meter, a line deriving from Whitman but with cadences closer to the rhythms of ordinary speech. "Simple poems for simple people," he said.

Sandburg's irregular schooling included brief attendance at Lombard College, but he was too restless to work through to a degree. He held a variety of jobs before moving to Chicago in 1913; he was in the army during the Spanish-American War, served as a war correspondent for the Galesburg *Evening Mail*, worked for the Social Democratic Party in Wisconsin, was secretary to the Socialist mayor of Milwaukee, and wrote editorials for the Milwaukee *Leader*. He had long been writing poetry but achieved success with the 1914 publication of his poem "Chicago" in *Poetry* magazine.

Poetry was one element in a surge of artistic activity in Chicago following the 1893 World's Fair. Such midwesterners as the architect Frank Lloyd Wright; the novelists Theodore Dreiser, Henry Blake Fuller, and Floyd Dell; and the poets Edgar Lee Masters and Vachel Lindsay believed not only that Chicago was a great city but that since the Midwest was America's heartland, it was in this region that the cultural life of the nation ought to center. Two literary magazines—*Poetry*, founded in 1912 by Harriet Monroe, and the *Little Review*, founded by Margaret C. Anderson in 1914—helped bring this informal movement to international attention. Nothing could be more apt to local interests than a celebratory poem called "Chicago."

Four volumes of poetry by Sandburg appeared in the next ten years: *Chicago Poems* (1914), *Cornhuskers* (1918), *Smoke and Steel* (1920), and *Slabs of the Sunburnt West* (1922). These present a panorama of America, concentrating on the prairies and cities of the Midwest. Like Whitman, Sandburg was aware that American life was increasingly urban, and he had little interest in the small town and its conventional middle class. The cities of the Midwest seemed to display both the vitality of the masses and their exploitation in an inequitable class system. Unlike many radicals whose politics were formed after the turn of the twentieth century, Sandburg believed that the people themselves, rather than a cadre of intellectuals acting on behalf of the people, would ultimately shape their own destiny. His political poems express appreciation for the people's energy and outrage at the injustices they suffer. They also balance strong declarative statements with passages of precise description. Other poems show Sandburg working in more lyrical or purely imagistic modes.

If the early "Chicago" is his best-known poem, his most ambitious is the book-length *The People, Yes* (1936), a collage of prose vignettes, anecdotes, and poetry, making use of his researches into American folk song. Sandburg had published these researches in *The American Songbag* in 1927, and he also composed a multi-volume biography of Abraham Lincoln between 1926 and 1939. The purpose of this painstaking work was to present Lincoln as an authentic folk hero, a great man who had risen from among the people of the American heartland and represented its best values. He wrote features, editorials, and columns for the *Chicago Daily News* between 1922 and 1930, and pursued other literary projects as well. After World War II, when it became common for poets to read their works at campuses around the country, he enjoyed bringing his old-style populist radicalism to college students.

The text of the poems here is that of *The Complete Poems of Carl Sandburg* (1970).

Chicago

Hog Butcher for the World,
Tool Maker, Stacker of Wheat,
Player with Railroads and the Nation's Freight Handler;
Stormy, husky, brawling,
City of the Big Shoulders:

They tell me you are wicked and I believe them, for I have seen
    your painted women under the gas lamps luring the farm
    boys.
And they tell me you are crooked and I answer: Yes, it is true I
    have seen the gunman kill and go free to kill again.
And they tell me you are brutal and my reply is: On the faces of
    women and children I have seen the marks of wanton hunger.
And having answered so I turn once more to those who sneer at
    this my city, and I give them back the sneer and say to them:
Come and show me another city with lifted head singing so
    proud to be alive and coarse and strong and cunning.   10
Flinging magnetic curses amid the toil of piling job on job, here
    is a tall bold slugger set vivid against the little soft cities;
Fierce as a dog with tongue lapping for action, cunning as a
    savage pitted against the wilderness,
        Bareheaded,
        Shoveling,
        Wrecking,   15
        Planning,
        Building, breaking, rebuilding,
Under the smoke, dust all over his mouth, laughing with white
    teeth,
Under the terrible burden of destiny laughing as a young man
    laughs,
Laughing even as an ignorant fighter laughs who has never lost
    a battle,   20
Bragging and laughing that under his wrist is the pulse, and
    under his ribs the heart of the people,
        Laughing!
Laughing the stormy, husky, brawling laughter of Youth, half-
    naked, sweating, proud to be Hog Butcher, Tool Maker,
    Stacker of Wheat, Player with Railroads and Freight
    Handler to the Nation.

        1914, 1916

Fog

    The fog comes
    on little cat feet.

    It sits looking
    over harbor and city
    on silent haunches   5
    and then moves on.

        1916

Grass[1]

Pile the bodies high at Austerlitz and Waterloo.
Shovel them under and let me work—
            I am the grass; I cover all.

And pile them high at Gettysburg
And pile them high at Ypres and Verdun.   5
Shovel them under and let me work.
Two years, ten years, and passengers ask the conductor:
            What place is this?
            Where are we now?

            I am the grass.   10
            Let me work.

                        1918

1. The proper names in this poem are all famous battlefields in the Napoleonic Wars, the American Civil War, and World War I.

WALLACE STEVENS
1879–1955

Wallace Stevens was raised in Reading, Pennsylvania, and went to Harvard for three years before leaving school in 1897 to pursue a literary career. Determined, however, that he would never "make a petty struggle for existence," he also looked for a well-paying job. After briefly trying journalism, he went to law school. In 1916 he began to work for the Hartford Accident and Indemnity Company and moved with his wife to Hartford, Connecticut. They made Hartford their lifelong home, Stevens writing his poetry at night and during summers. Visiting Florida frequently on business, he found the contrast between the South's lush vegetation and tropical climate and the chilly austerity of New England a useful metaphor for opposing ways of imagining the world, as poems like "The Snow Man" and "Sunday Morning" show.

Stevens began to publish in little magazines around 1914. In the early years of his career, he frequented literary gatherings in New York City, becoming friends with William Carlos Williams and Marianne Moore, among others. Because his concern was with the private interaction of the observed and the observer, however, he had little interest in artistic causes—less still in politics—and after moving to Hartford, he dropped out of literary circles, although he maintained an active correspondence with his friends. A good businessman, by the mid-1930s Stevens was prosperous. He continued to work for the same company until his death, eventually becoming a vice president.

His first volume of poetry, *Harmonium,* appeared in 1923. The poems in that book, mostly brief lyrics, are dazzling in their wit, imagery, and color; they established Stevens as one of the most accomplished poets of his era, although some critics found in them so much display as to make their "seriousness" questionable. But Stevens's purpose in part was to show that display was a valid poetic exercise—that poetry existed to illuminate the world's surfaces as well as its depths. He brought a newly perceived but real world before the reader, authenticating both the beauty of reality and the dependence of that beauty—indeed the dependence of reality itself—on the human observer. Two repeated activities are looking at things—the self as active observer of reality—and playing musical instruments or singing—the self as creator of reality (as in "The Idea of Order at Key West"). In this concern with the role of the perceiver in the creation of what is nevertheless real—the sense of an inescapable subjectivity in everything we know—Stevens clearly shared a modernist ideology. His search for belief in an era when, he thought, Christianity had lost its power; and the idea, increasingly expressed in later poems, that with the fading of traditional religion poetry might become the forger of new faiths also coincided with the convictions of such poets as T. S. Eliot (in his earlier phase) and Ezra Pound. He had an almost postmodern sense, however, that any religious explanation of the world would have to be a fiction.

His poems feature the continually unexpected in diction and imagery. They abound in allusions to music and painting; are packed with sense images, especially of sound and color; and are elegant and funny. Consider the surprise and humor in the titles of the selections printed here as well as these: "Floral Decorations for Bananas," "Anatomy of Monotony," "The Bird with the Coppery, Keen Claws," "Frogs Eat Butterflies, Snakes Eat Frogs, Hogs Eat Snakes, Men Eat Hogs." Stevens's line is simple—either blank verse or brief stanzas, usually unrhymed—so that the reader's attention is directed to vocabulary and imagery rather than prosody. Invented words are frequent, some employed simply for sound effects. Multilayered puns that ingeniously convey many important meanings serve to thicken and lighten the poetic texture.

Among the poems in *Harmonium* at least three have become touchstones for critics: "The Comedian as the Letter C," "Peter Quince at the Clavier," and "Sunday Morning." "The Comedian as the Letter C" establishes a contrast between an idealistic would-be poet with his empty imaginings and the same poet enmeshed in the rich reality of the senses and human affections. "Peter Quince at the Clavier," again, opposes an idea of beauty in the mind with the reality of beauty in the flesh—paradoxically, it is beauty in the flesh that is immortal. "Sunday Morning" opens with a woman taking her ease at home on the day traditionally reserved for church-going, and mentally contrasting a fearful, death-obsessed Christianity with her own celebration of earthly pleasure. She would like to think that her behavior is a religion—a celebration—of life, yet death too is real and to some extent she knows that her behavior is as partial as the Christianity she cannot accept. She wonders whether there might ever be a religion that would take the real world rather than another world as its ground, accepting death and change as inevitable and beautiful. The poem, in the form of a meditation deriving from this opening situation, attempts to sketch out the resolution that the woman desires.

In the six years following the appearance of *Harmonium* Stevens published little new work. With the 1930s came a surge of creativity, beginning with the republication of *Harmonium* in an expanded version in 1931. New volumes and major works appeared regularly thereafter: *Ideas of Order* in 1935, *Owl's Clover* in 1936, *The Man with a Blue Guitar* in 1937, *Parts of a World* in 1942, *Transport to Summer* in 1947, and *The Auroras of Autumn* in 1950. A book collecting his occasional lectures appeared as *The Necessary Angel* in 1951; its gist was that poetry was "the supreme fiction" that enabled human beings to apprehend reality as a whole instead of in fragmentary flashes of insight. Stevens's poetry can be usefully thought of as reconceiving and expressing the ideas of the nineteenth-century American Transcendentalists in modernist terms, for they too located the individual at the center of the world while defining that individual chiefly as a perceiver rather than a doer, or defining perceiving as the most important human activity. The difference is that the

Transcendentalists confidently assumed that their perceptions were guaranteed by God. Stevens was more skeptical.

In his poetry of the 1930s and after, Stevens became increasingly abstract and theoretical; the dazzling effects diminished, the diction became plainer. Major, long poems from these years were *Notes toward a Supreme Fiction* (from *Transport to Summer*) and *An Ordinary Evening in New Haven* (from *The Auroras of Autumn*). In these later poems Stevens was more concerned about what active role poetry might play in the world than he had been in earlier work. These expository and discursive poems should have been easier to follow than the earlier compressed and elliptical poetry, but critics generally agree that the difficulty and abstractness of their ideas make them much more difficult. And to some readers the absence of the earlier specificity and sparkle also makes the later work less rewarding. But those who enjoyed a taxing poetry of ideas saw the late work as an advance. Stevens's complete *Collected Poems* (1954) has been celebrated as one of the most important books of American poetry in the twentieth century.

The text of the poems included here is that of *The Collected Poems of Wallace Stevens* (1954).

The Snow Man

One must have a mind of winter
To regard the frost and the boughs
Of the pine-trees crusted with snow;

And have been cold a long time
To behold the junipers shagged with ice,   5
The spruces rough in the distant glitter

Of the January sun; and not to think
Of any misery in the sound of the wind,
In the sound of a few leaves,

Which is the sound of the land   10
Full of the same wind
That is blowing in the same bare place

For the listener, who listens in the snow,
And, nothing himself, beholds
Nothing that is not there and the nothing that is. 15

1931

A High-Toned Old Christian Woman

Poetry is the supreme fiction, madame.
Take the moral law and make a nave[1] of it
And from the nave build haunted heaven. Thus,

---

1. Main body of a church building, especially the vaulted central portion of a Christian Gothic church.

The conscience is converted into palms,
Like windy citherns[2] hankering for hymns.   5
We agree in principle. That's clear. But take
The opposing law and make a peristyle,[3]
And from the peristyle project a masque[4]
Beyond the planets. Thus, our bawdiness,
Unpurged by epitaph, indulged at last,   10
Is equally converted into palms,
Squiggling like saxophones. And palm for palm,
Madame, we are where we began. Allow,
Therefore, that in the planetary scene
Your disaffected flagellants, well-stuffed,   15
Smacking their muzzy[5] bellies in parade,
Proud of such novelties of the sublime,
Such tink and tank and tunk-a-tunk-tunk,
May, merely may, madame, whip from themselves
A jovial hullabaloo among the spheres.   20
This will make widows wince. But fictive things
Wink as they will. Wink most when widows wince.

                                          1923

The Emperor of Ice-Cream

Call the roller of big cigars,
The muscular one, and bid him whip
In kitchen cups concupiscent curds.
Let the wenches dawdle in such dress
As they are used to wear, and let the boys   5
Bring flowers in last month's newspapers.
Let be be finale of seem.
The only emperor is the emperor of ice-cream.

Take from the dresser of deal,[1]
Lacking the three glass knobs, that sheet   10
On which she embroidered fantails[2] once
And spread it so as to cover her face.
If her horny feet protrude, they come
To show how cold she is, and dumb.
Let the lamp affix its beam.   15
The only emperor is the emperor of ice-cream.

                                          1923

2. I.e., citterns; pear-shaped guitars.
3. Colonnade surrounding a building, especially the cells or main chamber of an ancient Greek temple—an "opposing law" to a Christian church.
4. Spectacle or entertainment consisting of music, dancing, mime, and often poetry.
5. Sodden with drunkenness.
1. Plain, unfinished wood.
2. Stevens explained that "the word fantails does not mean fan, but fantail pigeons."

Disillusionment of Ten O'Clock

The houses are haunted
By white night-gowns.
None are green,
Or purple with green rings,
Or green with yellow rings,   5
Or yellow with blue rings.
None of them are strange,
With socks of lace
And beaded ceintures.
People are not going   10
To dream of baboons and periwinkles.
Only, here and there, an old sailor,
Drunk and asleep in his boots,
Catches tigers
In red weather.   15

1931

Sunday Morning[1]

I

Complacencies of the peignoir, and late
Coffee and oranges in a sunny chair,
And the green freedom of a cockatoo
Upon a rug mingle to dissipate
The holy hush of ancient sacrifice.   5
She dreams a little, and she feels the dark
Encroachment of that old catastrophe,
As a calm darkens among water-lights.
The pungent oranges and bright, green wings
Seem things in some procession of the dead,   10
Winding across wide water, without sound.
The day is like wide water, without sound,
Stilled for the passing of her dreaming feet
Over the seas, to silent Palestine,
Dominion of the blood and sepulchre.   15

II

Why should she give her bounty to the dead?
What is divinity if it can come
Only in silent shadows and in dreams?
Shall she not find in comforts of the sun,
In pungent fruit and bright, green wings, or else 20
In any balm or beauty of the earth,

---

1. This poem was first published in *Poetry* magazine in 1915; the editor, Harriet Monroe, printed only five of its eight stanzas but arranged them in the order Stevens suggested when consenting to the deletions (I, VIII, IV, V, and VII); he restored the deleted stanzas and the original sequence in subsequent printings.

Things to be cherished like the thought of heaven?
Divinity must live within herself:
Passions of rain, or moods in falling snow;
Grievings in loneliness, or unsubdued   25
Elations when the forest blooms; gusty
Emotions on wet roads on autumn nights;
All pleasures and all pains, remembering
The bough of summer and the winter branch.
These are the measures destined for her soul.   30

III

Jove[2] in the clouds had his inhuman birth.
No mother suckled him, no sweet land gave
Large-mannered motions to his mythy mind.
He moved among us, as a muttering king,
Magnificent, would move among his hinds,   35
Until our blood, commingling, virginal,
With heaven, brought such requital to desire
The very hinds[3] discerned it, in a star.
Shall our blood fail? Or shall it come to be
The blood of paradise? And shall the earth   40
Seem all of paradise that we shall know?
The sky will be much friendlier then than now,
A part of labor and a part of pain,
And next in glory to enduring love,
Not this dividing and indifferent blue.   45

IV

She says, "I am content when wakened birds,
Before they fly, test the reality
Of misty fields, by their sweet questionings;
But when the birds are gone, and their warm fields
Return no more, where, then, is paradise?"   50
There is not any haunt of prophecy,
Nor any old chimera[4] of the grave,
Neither the golden underground, nor isle
Melodious, where spirits gat them home,
Nor visionary south, nor cloudy palm   55
Remote on heaven's hill,[5] that has endured
As April's green endures; or will endure
Like her remembrance of awakened birds,
Or her desire for June and evening, tipped
By the consummation of the swallow's wings.   60

V

She says, "But in contentment I still feel
The need of some imperishable bliss."
Death is the mother of beauty; hence from her,

---

2. Supreme god in Roman mythology.
3. Farmhands; an allusion to the shepherds who
saw the star of Bethlehem that signaled the birth
of Jesus.

4. In Greek mythology, a monster with a lion's
head, goat's body, and serpent's tail.
5. Versions of Paradise in diverse world religions.

Alone, shall come fulfillment to our dreams
And our desires. Although she strews the leaves   65
Of sure obliteration on our paths,
The path sick sorrow took, the many paths
Where triumph rang its brassy phrase, or love
Whispered a little out of tenderness,
She makes the willow shiver in the sun   70
For maidens who were wont to sit and gaze
Upon the grass, relinquished to their feet.
She causes boys to pile new plums and pears
On disregarded plate. The maidens taste
And stray impassioned in the littering leaves.   75

VI

Is there no change of death in paradise?
Does ripe fruit never fall? Or do the boughs
Hang always heavy in that perfect sky,
Unchanging, yet so like our perishing earth,
With rivers like our own that seek for seas   80
They never find, the same receding shores
That never touch with inarticulate pang?
Why set the pear upon those river-banks
Or spice the shores with odors of the plum?
Alas, that they should wear our colors there,   85
The silken weavings of our afternoons,
And pick the strings of our insipid lutes!
Death is the mother of beauty, mystical,
Within whose burning bosom we devise
Our earthly mothers waiting, sleeplessly.   90

VII

Supple and turbulent, a ring of men
Shall chant in orgy on a summer morn
Their boisterous devotion to the sun,
Not as a god, but as a god might be,
Naked among them, like a savage source.   95
Their chant shall be a chant of paradise,
Out of their blood, returning to the sky;
And in their chant shall enter, voice by voice,
The windy lake wherein their lord delights,
The trees, like serafin,[6] and echoing hills,   100
That choir among themselves long afterward.
They shall know well the heavenly fellowship
Of men that perish and of summer morn.
And whence they came and whither they shall go
The dew upon their feet shall manifest.   105

---

6. I.e., seraphim; angels.

VIII

She hears, upon that water without sound,
A voice that cries, "The tomb in Palestine
Is not the porch of spirits lingering.
It is the grave of Jesus, where he lay."
We live in an old chaos of the sun,   110
Or old dependency of day and night,
Or island solitude, unsponsored, free,
Of that wide water, inescapable.
Deer walk upon our mountains, and the quail
Whistle about us their spontaneous cries;   115
Sweet berries ripen in the wilderness;
And, in the isolation of the sky,
At evening, casual flocks of pigeons make
Ambiguous undulations as they sink,
Downward to darkness, on extended wings.   120

1915, 1923

Anecdote of the Jar

I placed a jar in Tennessee,
And round it was, upon a hill.
It made the slovenly wilderness
Surround that hill.

The wilderness rose up to it,   5
And sprawled around, no longer wild.
The jar was round upon the ground
And tall and of a port in air.

It took dominion everywhere.
The jar was gray and bare.   10
It did not give of bird or bush,
Like nothing else in Tennessee.

1923

Thirteen Ways of Looking at a Blackbird

I

Among twenty snowy mountains,
The only moving thing
Was the eye of the blackbird.

II

I was of three minds,
Like a tree   5
In which there are three blackbirds.

III

The blackbird whirled in the autumn winds.
It was a small part of the pantomime.

IV

A man and a woman
Are one.
A man and a woman and a blackbird   10
Are one.

V

I do not know which to prefer,
The beauty of inflections
Or the beauty of innuendoes,
The blackbird whistling   15
Or just after.

VI

Icicles filled the long window
With barbaric glass.
The shadow of the blackbird   20
Crossed it, to and fro.
The mood
Traced in the shadow
An indecipherable cause.

VII

O thin men of Haddam,[1]   25
Why do you imagine golden birds?
Do you not see how the blackbird
Walks around the feet
Of the women about you?

VIII

I know noble accents   30
And lucid, inescapable rhythms;
But I know, too,
That the blackbird is involved
In what I know.

IX

When the blackbird flew out of sight,   35
It marked the edge
Of one of many circles.

1. A city in Connecticut.

X

At the sight of blackbirds
Flying in a green light,
Even the bawds of euphony   40
Would cry out sharply.

XI

He rode over Connecticut
In a glass coach.
Once, a fear pierced him,
In that he mistook   45
The shadow of his equipage
For blackbirds.

XII

The river is moving.
The blackbird must be flying.

XIII

It was evening all afternoon.   50
It was snowing
And it was going to snow.
The blackbird sat
In the cedar-limbs.

                                                        1931

The Idea of Order at Key West[1]

She sang beyond the genius of the sea.
The water never formed to mind or voice,
Like a body wholly body, fluttering
Its empty sleeves; and yet its mimic motion
Made constant cry, caused constantly a cry,   5
That was not ours although we understood,
Inhuman, of the veritable ocean.

The sea was not a mask. No more was she.
The song and water were not medleyed sound
Even if what she sang was what she heard,   10
Since what she sang was uttered word by word.
It may be that in all her phrases stirred
The grinding water and the gasping wind;
But it was she and not the sea we heard.

For she was the maker of the song she sang.   15
The ever-hooded, tragic-gestured sea

---

1. One of the islands off the southern coast of Florida, where Stevens vacationed. The poem begins with the scene of a woman walking by the sea and singing.

Was merely a place by which she walked to sing.
Whose spirit is this? we said, because we knew
It was the spirit that we sought and knew
That we should ask this often as she sang.   20

If it was only the dark voice of the sea
That rose, or even colored by many waves;
If it was only the outer voice of sky
And cloud, of the sunken coral water-walled,
However clear, it would have been deep air,   25
The heaving speech of air, a summer sound
Repeated in a summer without end
And sound alone. But it was more than that,
More even than her voice, and ours, among
The meaningless plungings of water and the wind,   30
Theatrical distances, bronze shadows heaped
On high horizons, mountainous atmospheres
Of sky and sea.
                    It was her voice that made
The sky acutest at its vanishing.   35
She measured to the hour its solitude.
She was the single artificer of the world
In which she sang. And when she sang, the sea,
Whatever self it had, became the self
That was her song, for she was the maker. Then we,   40
As we beheld her striding there alone,
Knew that there never was a world for her
Except the one she sang and, singing, made.

Ramon Fernandez,[2] tell me, if you know,
Why, when the singing ended and we turned   45
Toward the town, tell why the glassy lights,
The lights in the fishing boats at anchor there,
As the night descended, tilting in the air,
Mastered the night and portioned out the sea,
Fixing emblazoned zones and fiery poles,   50
Arranging, deepening, enchanting night.

Oh! Blessed rage for order, pale Ramon,
The maker's rage to order words of the sea,
Words of the fragrant portals, dimly-starred,
And of ourselves and of our origins,   55
In ghostlier demarcations, keener sounds.

                                                        1936

Of Modern Poetry

The poem of the mind in the act of finding
What will suffice. It has not always had

---

2. A French literary critic and essayist (1894–1944). Stevens said that he had invented the name and that its coincidence with a real person was accidental.

To find: the scene was set; it repeated what
Was in the script.
                              Then the theatre was changed   5
To something else. Its past was a souvenir.
It has to be living, to learn the speech of the place.
It has to face the men of the time and to meet
The women of the time. It has to think about war
And it has to find what will suffice. It has   10
To construct a new stage. It has to be on that stage
And, like an insatiable actor, slowly and
With meditation, speak words that in the ear,
In the delicatest ear of the mind, repeat,
Exactly, that which it wants to hear, at the sound   15
Of which, an invisible audience listens,
Not to the play, but to itself, expressed
In an emotion as of two people, as of two
Emotions becoming one. The actor is
A metaphysician in the dark, twanging   20
An instrument, twanging a wiry string that gives
Sounds passing through sudden rightnesses, wholly
Containing the mind, below which it cannot descend,
Beyond which it has no will to rise.
                              It must   25
Be the finding of a satisfaction, and may
Be of a man skating, a woman dancing, a woman
Combing. The poem of the act of the mind.

1942

WILLIAM CARLOS WILLIAMS
1883–1963

A modernist known for his disagreements with all the other modernists, William Carlos Williams thought of himself as the most underrated poet of his generation. His reputation has risen dramatically since World War II as a younger generation of poets testified to the influence of his work on their idea of what poetry should be. The simplicity of his verse forms, the matter-of-factness of both his subject matter and his means of describing it, seemed to bring poetry into natural relation with everyday life. He is now judged to be among the most important poets writing between the wars. His career continued into the 1960s, taking new directions as he produced, along with shorter lyrics, his epic five-part poem *Paterson*.

He was born in 1883 in Rutherford, New Jersey, a town near the city of Paterson. His maternal grandmother, an Englishwoman deserted by her husband, had come to America with her son, married again, and moved to Puerto Rico. Her son—Williams's father—married a woman descended on one side from French Basque people, on the other from Dutch Jews. This mix of origins always fascinated Williams and made him feel that he was different from what he thought of as mainstream Americans, i.e., northeasterners or midwesterners of English descent. After the family moved to New Jersey, Williams's father worked as a salesman for a perfume company; in childhood his father was often away from home, and the two women—mother and grandmother—were the most important adults to him. Throughout Williams's poetry the figure of woman as an earth mother, whom men require for completion and whose reason for being is to supply that completeness, appears, perhaps reflecting that early experience.

Except for a year in Europe, Williams attended local schools. He entered the School of Dentistry at the University of Pennsylvania directly after graduating from high school but soon switched to medicine. In college he met and became friends with Ezra Pound; Hilda Doolittle, later to become known as the poet H.D.; and the painter Charles Demuth. These friendships did much to steer him toward poetry, and even as he completed his medical work, interned in New York City, and did postgraduate study in Leipzig, Germany, he was reconceiving his commitment to medicine as a means of self-support in the more important enterprise of becoming a poet. Although he never lost his sense that he was a doctor in order to be a poet, his patients knew him as a dedicated old-fashioned physician, who made house calls, listened to people's problems, and helped them through life's crises. Pediatrics was his specialty; and in the course of his career, he delivered more than two thousand babies.

In 1912, after internship and study abroad, Williams married his fiancée of several years, Florence Herman. Despite strains in their relationship caused by Williams's continuing interest in other women, the marriage lasted and became, toward the end of Williams's life, the subject of some beautiful love poetry, including "Asphodel, that Greeny Flower." In the meantime women and the mixed belittlement–adoration accorded them by men (including the poet) were persistent themes. The couple settled in Rutherford, where Williams opened his practice. Except for a trip to Europe in 1924, when he saw Pound and met James Joyce, among others, and trips for lectures and poetry readings later in his career, Williams remained in Rutherford all his life, continuing his medical practice until poor health forced him to retire. He wrote at night, and spent weekends in New York City with friends who were writers and artists—the avant-garde painters Marcel Duchamp and Francis Picabia, the poets Marianne Moore and Wallace Stevens, and others. At their gatherings he acquired a reputation for outspoken hostility to most of the "-isms" of the day.

The characteristic Williams style emerged clearly in the landmark volume of mixed prose and poetry *Spring and All* (1923; see p. 1965 and p. 1988). One can see in this book that the gesture of staying at home was more for him than a practical assessment of his chances of self-support. Interested, like his friend Ezra Pound, in making a new kind of poetry, Williams also wanted always to speak as an American within an American context. One can observe this bias in the title of one of his books of essays, *In the American Grain* (1925), and in his choice of his own region as the setting and subject of *Paterson,* a long poem about his native city incorporating a great variety of textual fragments—letters, newspaper accounts, poetry—in a modernist collage.

Williams detested Eliot's *The Waste Land,* describing its popularity as a "catastrophe," deploring not only its internationalism but also its pessimism and deliberate obscurity. To him these characteristics were un-American. Yet Williams was not a sentimental celebrant of American life. He objected to Robert Frost's homespun poetry—which might be thought of as similar to his own work—for nostalgically evoking a bygone rural America rather than engaging with what he saw as the real American present. His America was made up of small cities like Paterson, with immigrants, factories, and poor working-class people struggling to get by. The sickness and suffering he saw as a physician entered into his poetry, as did his personal life; but the overall impact of his poetry is social rather than autobiographical.

The social aspect of Williams's poetry rises from its accumulation of detail; he opposed the use of poetry for general statements and abstract critique. "No ideas but in things," he wrote. Wallace Stevens had also written, "not ideas about the thing but the thing itself"; yet there is a world of difference between Williams's plainspoken and often opinionated writing and Stevens's cool elegance. Williams drew his vocabulary from up-to-date local speech and searched for a poetic line derived from the cadences of street talk. But he rejected "free verse" as an absurdity; rhythm within the line, and linking one line to another, was the heart of poetic craft to him. While working on *Paterson,* he invented the "triadic" or "stepped line," a long line broken into three segments, which he used in many poems, including several of the selections printed here.

Williams published fiction and essays as well as poetry, especially during the 1930s. Books of short stories (*The Edge of the Knife,* 1932, and *Life along the Passaic River,* 1938) and novels (*White Mule,* 1937, and *In the Money,* 1940) appeared in these years. He was also involved with others in the establishment of several little magazines, each designed to promulgate counterstatements to the powerful influences of Pound, Eliot, and the New Critics. All the time he remained active in his community and in political events; in the 1930s and 1940s he aligned himself with liberal Democratic and, on occasion, leftist issues but always from the vantage point of an unreconstructed individualism. Some of his affiliations were held against him in the McCarthy era and to his great distress he was deprived in 1948 of the post of consultant in poetry at the Library of Congress.

It was also in 1948 that he had a heart attack, and in 1951 the first of a series of strokes required him to turn over his medical practice to one of his two sons and made writing increasingly difficult. Nevertheless, he persevered in his work on *Paterson,* whose five books were published in 1946, 1948, 1949, 1951, and 1958. *The Desert Music* (1954) and *Pictures from Brueghel* (1962), containing new poetry, also appeared; but by 1961 Williams had to stop writing. By the time of his death a host of younger poets, including Allen Ginsberg, Denise Levertov, Charles Olson, and Robert Creeley, had been inspired by his example. He won the National Book Award in 1950, the Bollingen Prize in 1953, and the Pulitzer Prize in 1962.

The texts of the poems included here are those of *The Collected Poems of William Carlos Williams,* Volume 1: *1909–1939* (1986), edited by A. Walton Litz and Christopher MacGowan, and *The Collected Poems of William Carlos Williams,* Volume 2: *1939–1962* (1988), edited by Christopher MacGowan.

The Young Housewife

At ten A.M. the young housewife
moves about in negligee behind
the wooden walls of her husband's house.
I pass solitary in my car.

Then again she comes to the curb   5
to call the ice-man, fish-man, and stands
shy, uncorseted, tucking in
stray ends of hair, and I compare her
to a fallen leaf.

The noiseless wheels of my car   10
rush with a crackling sound over
dried leaves as I bow and pass smiling.

1916, 1917

Portrait of a Lady

Your thighs are appletrees
whose blossoms touch the sky.
Which sky? The sky
where Watteau[1] hung a lady's
slipper. Your knees   5
are a southern breeze—or
a gust of snow. Agh! what
sort of man was Fragonard?[2]
—as if that answered
anything. Ah, yes—below   10
the knees, since the tune
drops that way, it is
one of those white summer days,
the tall grass of your ankles
flickers upon the shore—   15
Which shore?—
the sand clings to my lips—
Which shore?
Agh, petals maybe. How
should I know?   20
Which shore? Which shore?
I said petals from an appletree.

                                                     1920, 1934

Queen-Anne's-Lace[1]

Her body is not so white as
anemone petals nor so smooth—nor
so remote a thing. It is a field
of the wild carrot taking
the field by force; the grass   5
does not raise above it.
Here is no question of whiteness,
white as can be, with a purple mole
at the center of each flower.
Each flower is a hand's span   10
of her whiteness. Wherever
his hand has lain there is
a tiny purple blemish. Each part
is a blossom under his touch
to which the fibres of her being   15
stem one by one, each to its end,
until the whole field is a
white desire, empty, a single stem,

---

1. Jean Antoine Watteau (1684–1721), French
artist who painted elegantly dressed lovers in idealized rustic settings.
2. Jean Honoré Fragonard (1732–1806), French
painter who depicted fashionable lovers in paintings more wittily and openly erotic than Wat-

teau's. Fragonard's *The Swing* depicts a girl who
has kicked her slipper into the air.
1. A common wildflower whose white bloom is
composed of numerous tiny blossoms, each with
a dark spot at the center, joined to the stalk by
fibrous stems.

a cluster, flower by flower,
a pious wish to whiteness gone over—   20
or nothing.

                                                       1921

The Widow's Lament in Springtime

Sorrow is my own yard
where the new grass
flames as it has flamed
often before but not
with the cold fire   5
that closes round me this year.
Thirtyfive years
I lived with my husband.
The plumtree is white today
with masses of flowers.   10
Masses of flowers
load the cherry branches
and color some bushes
yellow and some red
but the grief in my heart   15
is stronger than they
for though they were my joy
formerly, today I notice them
and turn away forgetting.
Today my son told me   20
that in the meadows,
at the edge of the heavy woods
in the distance, he saw
trees of white flowers.
I feel that I would like   25
to go there
and fall into those flowers
and sink into the marsh near them.

                                                       1921

Spring and All[1]

By the road to the contagious hospital[2]
under the surge of the blue
mottled clouds driven from the
northeast—a cold wind. Beyond, the
waste of broad, muddy fields   5
brown with dried weeds, standing and fallen

1. In the volume *Spring and All* (as originally published, 1923), prose statements were interspersed through the poems, which were identified by roman numerals. Williams added titles later and used the volume's title for the opening poem. For examples of the prose sections of *Spring and All*, see "Modernist Manifestos," p. 1988.
2. I.e., a hospital for treating contagious diseases.

patches of standing water
the scattering of tall trees

All along the road the reddish
purplish, forked, upstanding, twiggy   10
stuff of bushes and small trees
with dead, brown leaves under them
leafless vines—

Lifeless in appearance, sluggish
dazed spring approaches—   15

They enter the new world naked,
cold, uncertain of all
save that they enter. All about them
the cold, familiar wind—

Now the grass, tomorrow   20
the stiff curl of wildcarrot leaf

One by one objects are defined—
It quickens: clarity, outline of leaf

But now the stark dignity of
entrance—Still, the profound change   25
has come upon them: rooted, they
grip down and begin to awaken

                                                1923

To Elsie[1]

The pure products of America
go crazy—
mountain folk from Kentucky

or the ribbed north end of
Jersey   5
with its isolate lakes and

valleys, its deaf-mutes, thieves
old names
and promiscuity between

devil-may-care men who have taken   10
to railroading
out of sheer lust of adventure—

---

1. In *Spring and All,* this poem was originally numbered XVIII. Elsie, from the State Orphanage, worked for the Williams family as a nursemaid.

and young slatterns, bathed
in filth
from Monday to Saturday   15

to be tricked out that night
with gauds
from imaginations which have no

peasant traditions to give them
character   20
but flutter and flaunt

sheer rags—succumbing without
emotion
save numbed terror

under some hedge of choke-cherry   25
or viburnum—
which they cannot express—

Unless it be that marriage
perhaps
with a dash of Indian blood   30

will throw up a girl so desolate
so hemmed round
with disease or murder

that she'll be rescued by an
agent—   35
reared by the state and

sent out at fifteen to work in
some hard-pressed
house in the suburbs—

some doctor's family, some Elsie—   40
voluptuous water
expressing with broken

brain the truth about us—
her great
ungainly hips and flopping breasts   45

addressed to cheap
jewelry
and rich young men with fine eyes

as if the earth under our feet
were   50
an excrement of some sky

and we degraded prisoners
destined
to hunger until we eat filth

while the imagination strains   55
after deer
going by fields of goldenrod in

the stifling heat of September
Somehow
it seems to destroy us   60

It is only in isolate flecks that
something
is given off

No one
to witness   65
and adjust, no one to drive the car

                                                   1923

The Red Wheelbarrow[1]

so much depends
upon

a red wheel
barrow

glazed with rain   5
water

beside the white
chickens

                                                   1923

This Is Just to Say

I have eaten
the plums
that were in
the icebox

and which   5
you were probably

---

1. Numbered XXII in *Spring and All*.

saving
for breakfast

Forgive me
they were delicious   10
so sweet
and so cold

1934

A Sort of a Song

Let the snake wait under
his weed
and the writing
be of words, slow and quick, sharp
to strike, quiet to wait,   5
sleepless.

—through metaphor to reconcile
the people and the stones.
Compose. (No ideas
but in things) Invent!   10
Saxifrage is my flower that splits
the rocks.

1944

The Dance

In Brueghel's great picture, The Kermess,[1]
the dancers go round, they go round and
around, the squeal and the blare and the
tweedle of bagpipes, a bugle and fiddles
tipping their bellies (round as the thick-   5
sided glasses whose wash they impound)
their hips and their bellies off balance
to turn them. Kicking and rolling about
the Fair Grounds, swinging their butts, those
shanks must be sound to bear up under such   10
rollicking measures, prance as they dance
in Brueghel's great picture, The Kermess.

1944

1. *The Wedding Dance* by the Flemish painter Pieter Brueghel (or Breughel) the Elder (c. 1525–1569).

Landscape with the Fall of Icarus[1]

According to Brueghel[2]
when Icarus fell
it was spring

a farmer was ploughing
his field   5
the whole pageantry

of the year was
awake tingling
near

the edge of the sea   10
concerned
with itself

sweating in the sun
that melted
the wings' wax   15

unsignificantly
off the coast
there was

a splash quite unnoticed
this was   20
Icarus drowning

1962

EZRA POUND
1885–1972

Ezra Loomis Pound was born in Hailey, Idaho. When he was still an infant his parents settled in a comfortable suburb near Philadelphia where his father was an assayer at the regional branch of the U.S. Mint. "I knew at fifteen pretty much what I wanted to do," he wrote in 1913; what he wanted was to become a poet. He had this goal in mind as an undergraduate at the University of Pennsylvania (where he met and became lifelong friends with William Carlos Williams and had a

---

1. In Greek mythology, a young man whose father made wings for him with feathers held together by wax. Icarus flew too close to the sun, the wax melted, and he fell into the sea and drowned.

2. A landscape by Flemish painter Pieter Brueghel the Elder (c. 1525–1569) in which Icarus is depicted by a tiny leg sticking out of the sea in one corner of the picture.

romance with Hilda Doolittle, who was later to become the poet H.D.) and at Hamilton College; it also motivated his graduate studies in languages—French, Italian, Old English, and Latin—at the University of Pennsylvania, where he received an M.A. in 1906. He planned to support himself as a college teacher while writing.

The poetry that he had in mind in these early years was in vogue at the turn of the twentieth century—melodious in versification and diction, romantic in themes, world-weary in tone—poetry for which the term *decadent* was used. A particular image of the poet went with such poetry: the poet committed to art for its own sake, careless of convention, and continually shocking the respectable middle class. A rebellious and colorful personality, Pound delighted in this role but quickly found that it was not compatible with the sober behavior expected from professors of language. He lost his first teaching job, at Wabash College in Indiana, in fewer than six months.

Convinced that his country had no place for him—and that a country with no place for him had no place for art—he went to Europe in 1908. He settled in London and quickly became involved in its literary life, and especially prominent in movements to revolutionize poetry and identify good new poets. He supported himself by teaching and reviewing for several journals. For a while he acted as secretary to the great Irish poet William Butler Yeats. He married Dorothy Shakespear, daughter of a close friend of Yeats, in 1914. Ten years later he became involved with the American expatriate Olga Rudge and maintained relationships with both women thereafter.

As an advocate of the new, he found himself propagandizing against the very poetry that had made him want to be a poet at the start; and this contradiction remained throughout his life: on the one hand, a desire to "make it new"; on the other, a deep attachment to the old. Many of his critical essays were later collected and published in books such as *Make It New* (1934), *The ABC of Reading* (1934), *Polite Essays* (1937), and *Literary Essays* (1954). He was generous in his efforts to assist other writers in their work and in their attempts to get published; he was helpful to H.D., T. S. Eliot, James Joyce, William Carlos Williams, Robert Frost, Ernest Hemingway, and Marianne Moore, to name just a few.

Pound first campaigned for "imagism," his name for a new kind of poetry. Rather than describing something—an object or situation—and then generalizing about it, imagist poets attempted to present the object directly, avoiding the ornate diction and complex but predictable verse forms of traditional poetry. Any significance to be derived from the image had to appear inherent in its spare, clean presentation. "Go in fear of abstractions," Pound wrote (see "A Retrospect," p. 1984). Elaborate grammatical constructions seemed artificial; hence this new poetry tended to work in disconnected fragments. Although imagism lasted only briefly as a formal movement, most subsequent twentieth-century poetry showed its influence. Pound soon moved on to "vorticism," which, although still espousing direct and bare presentation, sought for some principle of dynamism and energy in the image. In his imagist phase Pound was connected with H.D. and Richard Aldington, a British poet who became H.D.'s husband; as a vorticist he was allied with the iconoclastic writer and artist Wyndham Lewis.

Pound thought of the United States as a culturally backward nation and longed to produce a sophisticated, worldly poetry on behalf of his country. Walt Whitman was his symbol of American poetic narrowness. His major works during his London years consisted of free translations of languages unknown to most Westerners: Provençal, Chinese, Japanese. He also experimented with the dramatic monologue form developed by the English Victorian poet Robert Browning. Poems from these years appeared in his volumes *A Lume Spento* (By the spent light; Italian), which appeared in 1908, *A Quinzaine for This Yule* (1908), and *Personae* (1910). *Persona* means "mask," and the poems in this last volume developed the dramatic monologue as a means for the poet to assume various identities and to engage in acts of historical reconstruction and empathy.

Although the imagist view of poetry would seem to exclude the long poem as a workable form, Pound could not overcome the traditional belief that a really great poem had to be long. He hoped to write such a poem himself, a poem for his time, which would unite biography and history by representing the total content of his mind and memory. To this end he began working on his *Cantos* in 1915. The cantos were separate poems of varying lengths, combining reminiscence, meditation, description, and transcriptions from books Pound was reading, all of which were to be forged into unity by the heat of the poet's imagination. Ultimately, he produced 116 cantos, whose intricate obscurities continue to fascinate and challenge critics. The London period came to a close with two poems of disillusionment, "Hugh Selwyn Mauberley (Life and Contacts)" and "Mauberley," which described the decay of Western civilization in the aftermath of the Great War.

Looking for an explanation of what had gone wrong, Pound came upon the "social credit" theories of Major Clifford Hugh Douglas, a social economist who attributed all the ills of civilization to the interposition of money between human exchanges of goods. At this point, poetry and politics fused in Pound's work, and he began to search for a society in which art was protected from money and to record this search in poems and essays. This became a dominant theme in the *Cantos*. Leaving England for good in 1920, he lived on the Mediterranean Sea, in Paris for a time, and then settled in the small Italian town of Rapallo in 1925. His survey of history having persuaded him that the ideal society was a hierarchy with a strong leader and an agricultural economy, he greeted the Italian fascist dictator Benito Mussolini as a deliverer. He looked for other strong leaders in world history and idealized them in the *Cantos*. During World War II he voluntarily served the Italian government by making numerous English-language radio broadcasts beamed at England and the United States in which he vilified Jews, President Franklin D. Roosevelt, and American society in general. When the U.S. Army occupied Italy, Pound was arrested, held for weeks in an open-air cage at the prison camp near Pisa, and finally brought to the United States to be tried for treason. The trial did not take place, however, because the court accepted a psychiatric report to the effect that Pound was "insane and mentally unfit to be tried." From 1946 to 1958 he was a patient and a prisoner in St. Elizabeth's Hospital for the criminally insane in Washington, D.C. During those years he received visits, wrote letters, composed cantos, and continued his polemic against American society.

In 1948 the *Pisan Cantos* (LXXIV–LXXXIV) won the Library of Congress's newly established Bollingen Prize for poetry, an event that provoked tremendous debate about Pound's stature as a poet as well as a citizen. Ten years later the efforts of a committee of writers succeeded in winning Pound's release; he returned to Italy, where he died at the age of eighty-seven. He remains one of the most controversial poets of the era.

The texts of the poems included here are those of *Personae: The Collected Poems* (rev., 1949) and *The Cantos* (1976).

To Whistler, American[1]

On the loan exhibit of his paintings at the Tate Gallery.

> You also, our first great
> Had tried all ways;
> Tested and pried and worked in many fashions,
> And this much gives me heart to play the game.
>
> Here is a part that's slight, and part gone wrong,   5
> And much of little moment, and some few

---

1. James Abbott McNeill Whistler (1834–1903), expatriate American painter.

Perfect as Dürer![2]
"In the Studio" and these two portraits,[3] if I had my choice!
And then these sketches in the mood of Greece?

You had your searches, your uncertainties,   10
And this is good to know—for us, I mean,
Who bear the brunt of our America
And try to wrench her impulse into art.

You were not always sure, not always set
To hiding night or tuning "symphonies";[4]   15
Had not one style from birth, but tried and pried
And stretched and tampered with the media.

You and Abe Lincoln from that mass of dolts
Show us there's chance at least of winning through.

                                                    1912, 1949

Portrait d'une Femme[1]

Your mind and you are our Sargasso Sea,[2]
London has swept about you this score years
And bright ships left you this or that in fee:
Ideas, old gossip, oddments of all things,
Strange spars of knowledge and dimmed wares of price.   5
Great minds have sought you—lacking someone else.
You have been second always. Tragical?
No. You preferred it to the usual thing:
One dull man, dulling and uxorious,
One average mind—with one thought less, each year.   10
Oh, you are patient, I have seen you sit
Hours, where something might have floated up.
And now you pay one. Yes, you richly pay.
You are a person of some interest, one comes to you
And takes strange gain away: 15
Trophies fished up; some curious suggestion;
Fact that leads nowhere; and a tale or two,
Pregnant with mandrakes,[3] or with something else
That might prove useful and yet never proves,
That never fits a corner or shows use,   20
Or finds its hour upon the loom of days:
The tarnished, gaudy, wonderful old work;
Idols and ambergris and rare inlays,

2. Albrecht Dürer (1471–1528), German painter and engraver.
3. "'Brown and Gold—de Race,' 'Grenat et Or—Le Petit Cardinal' ('Garnet and Gold—The Little Cardinal')" [Pound's note]. Titles and subjects of the portraits.
4. Whistler painted many night scenes and titled many paintings "symphonies."

1. Portrait of a lady (French).
2. Sea in the North Atlantic where boats were becalmed; named for its large masses of floating seaweed.
3. Herb used as a cathartic; believed in legend to have human properties, to shriek when pulled from the ground, and to promote pregnancy.

These are your riches, your great store; and yet
For all this sea-hoard of deciduous things,   25
Strange woods half sodden, and new brighter stuff:
In the slow float of differing light and deep,
No! there is nothing! In the whole and all,
Nothing that's quite your own.
                     Yet this is you.   30

                                          1912

A Pact

I make a pact with you, Walt Whitman—
I have detested you long enough.
I come to you as a grown child
Who has had a pig-headed father;
I am old enough now to make friends.   5
It was you that broke the new wood,
Now is a time for carving.
We have one sap and one root—
Let there be commerce between us.

                                  1913, 1916

In a Station of the Metro[1]

The apparition of these faces in the crowd;
Petals on a wet, black bough.

                                  1913, 1916

The River-Merchant's Wife: A Letter[1]

While my hair was still cut straight across my forehead
I played about the front gate, pulling flowers.
You came by on bamboo stilts, playing horse,
You walked about my seat, playing with blue plums.
And we went on living in the village of Chŭkan: 5
Two small people, without dislike or suspicion.

At fourteen I married My Lord you.
I never laughed, being bashful.
Lowering my head, I looked at the wall.
Called to, a thousand times, I never looked back.   10

---

1. Paris subway.
1. Adaptation from the Chinese of Li Po (701–762), named Rihaku in Japanese, from the papers of Ernest Fenollosa, an American scholar whose widow gave his papers on Japan and China to Pound.

At fifteen I stopped scowling,
I desired my dust to be mingled with yours
Forever and forever and forever.
Why should I climb the look out?

At sixteen you departed,   15
You went into far Ku-tŭ-en, by the river of swirling eddies,
And you have been gone five months.
The monkeys make sorrowful noise overhead.

You dragged your feet when you went out.
By the gate now, the moss is grown, the different mosses,   20
Too deep to clear them away!
The leaves fall early this autumn, in wind.
The paired butterflies are already yellow with August
Over the grass in the West garden;
They hurt me. I grow older.   25
If you are coming down through the narrows of the river Kiang,
Please let me know beforehand,
And I will come out to meet you
          As far as Chŭ-fŭ-Sa.

                                By Rihaku

                                1915

From The Cantos

I[1]

And then went down to the ship,
Set keel to breakers, forth on the godly sea, and
We set up mast and sail on that swart ship,
Bore sheep aboard her, and our bodies also
Heavy with weeping, and winds from sternward   5
Bore us out onward with bellying canvas,
Circe's[2] this craft, the trim-coifed goddess.
Then sat we amidships, wind jamming the tiller,
Thus with stretched sail, we went over sea till day's end.
Sun to his slumber, shadows o'er all the ocean,   10
Came we then to the bounds of deepest water,
To the Kimmerian[3] lands, and peopled cities
Covered with close-webbed mist, unpierced ever
With glitter of sun-rays
Nor with stars stretched, nor looking back from heaven   15
Swartest night stretched over wretched men there

---

1. Lines 1–68 are an adaptation of book 11 of Homer's *Odyssey*, which recounts Odysseus's voyage to Hades, the underworld of the dead. Odysseus was a native of Ithaca, in Greece.
2. Odysseus lived for a year with Circe before he determined to return to Ithaca. She instructed him to get directions for his trip home by visiting the Theban prophet Tiresias in the underworld.
3. Mythical people living in a foggy region at the edge of the earth.

The ocean flowing backward, came we then to the place
Aforesaid by Circe.
Here did they rites, Perimedes and Eurylochus,[4]
And drawing sword from my hip   20
I dug the ell-square pitkin;[5]
Poured we libations unto each the dead,
First mead then sweet wine, water mixed with white flour.
Then prayed I many a prayer to the sickly death's-heads;
As set in Ithaca, sterile bulls of the best   25
For sacrifice, heaping the pyre with goods,
A sheep to Tiresias only, black and a bell-sheep.[6]
Dark blood flowed in the fosse,[7]
Souls out of Erebus,[8] cadaverous dead, of brides
Of youths and of the old who had borne much;   30
Souls stained with recent tears, girls tender,
Men many, mauled with bronze lance heads,
Battle spoil, bearing yet dreory[9] arms,
These many crowded about me; with shouting,
Pallor upon me, cried to my men for more beasts;   35
Slaughtered the herds, sheep slain of bronze;
Poured ointment, cried to the gods,
To Pluto the strong, and praised Proserpine;[1]
Unsheathed the narrow sword,
I sat to keep off the impetuous impotent dead,   40
Till I should hear Tiresias.
But first Elpenor[2] came, our friend Elpenor,
Unburied, cast on the wide earth,
Limbs that we left in the house of Circe,
Unwept, unwrapped in sepulchre, since toils urged other.   45
Pitiful spirit. And I cried in hurried speech:
"Elpenor, how art thou come to this dark coast?
"Cam'st thou afoot, outstripping seamen?"
            And he in heavy speech:
"Ill fate and abundant wine. I slept in Circe's ingle.[3]   50
"Going down the long ladder unguarded,
"I fell against the buttress,
"Shattered the nape-nerve, the soul sought Avernus.[4]
"But thou, O King, I bid remember me, unwept, unburied,
"Heap up mine arms, be tomb by sea-bord, and inscribed: 55
"*A man of no fortune, and with a name to come.*
"And set my oar up, that I swung mid fellows."

And Anticlea[5] came, whom I beat off, and then Tiresias Theban,
Holding his golden wand, knew me, and spoke first:

---

4. Two of Odysseus's companions.
5. Small pit, one ell (forty-five inches) on each side.
6. The prophet Tiresias is likened to a sheep that leads the herd.
7. Ditch, trench.
8. Land of the dead, Hades.
9. Bloody.
1. Goddess of regeneration and wife of Pluto, god of the underworld.

2. Odysseus's companion who fell to his death from the roof of Circe's house and was left unburied by his friends.
3. Corner, house.
4. Lake near Naples, the entrance to Hades.
5. Odysseus's mother. In the *Odyssey*, Odysseus weeps at the sight of her but obeys Circe's instructions to speak to no one until Tiresias has first drunk the libation of blood that will enable him to speak.

"A second time?[6] why? man of ill star,   60
"Facing the sunless dead and this joyless region?
"Stand from the fosse, leave me my bloody bever[7]
"For soothsay."
            And I stepped back,
And he strong with the blood, said then: "Odysseus   65
"Shalt return through spiteful Neptune,[8] over dark seas,
"Lose all companions." And then Anticlea came.
Lie quiet Divus. I mean, that is Andreas Divus,
In officina Wecheli, 1538, out of Homer.[9]
And he sailed, by Sirens and thence outward and away   70
And unto Circe.
            Venerandam,[1]
In the Cretan's phrase, with the golden crown, Aphrodite,
Cypri munimenta sortita est,[2] mirthful, orichalchi,[3] with golden
Girdles and breast bands, thou with dark eyelids   75
Bearing the golden bough of Argicida.[4] So that:

                                                          1925

6. They met once before on earth.
7. Libation.
8. God of the sea, who was to delay Odysseus's return by a storm at sea.
9. Pound acknowledges using the Renaissance Latin translation of Homer, produced in the workshop ("officina") of Wechel in Paris in 1538, by Andreas Divus.
1. Commanding reverence; a phrase describing Aphrodite, the goddess of love, in the Latin translation of the second Homeric Hymn by Georgius Dartona Cretensis (the "Cretan" in line 73).

2. The fortresses of Cyprus were her appointed realm (Latin).
3. Of copper (Latin); a reference to gifts presented to Aphrodite in the second Homeric Hymn.
4. Aeneas offered the Golden Bough to Proserpine before descending to the underworld. Pound associates Persephone with Aphrodite, goddess of love and slayer of the Greeks (Argi) during the Trojan War, and associates the Golden Bough, sacred to the goddess Diana, with the magic wand of the god Hermes, slayer of the many-eyed Argus ("Argicida") and liberator of Io.

Modernist Manifestos

As an artistic movement, or set of movements, given to asserting its breaks with past traditions, modernism in the early twentieth century often proclaimed itself in the writing of manifestoes. The modernist manifesto is a public declaration of artistic convictions, relatively brief, often highly stylized or epigrammatic in the mode of other forms of modernist writing, and almost always an aggressively self-conscious declaration of artistic independence.

The word *manifesto*, derived from Latin and meaning "to make public," first entered English usage in the seventeenth century to describe printed declarations of belief and advocacy. Early manifestoes tended to be weapons forged by dissenting groups in religious and political struggles, a tradition that continued into the nineteenth century with perhaps the most famous political manifesto of the era, Karl Marx's *Communist Manifesto* (1848). In the nineteenth century, artistic groups also began to issue manifestos. The preface to the second edition of *Lyrical Ballads* (1800) by the poets William Wordsworth and Samuel Taylor Coleridge, for example, defended their "experiment" with a new kind of poetry; in the United States, Ralph Waldo Emerson's *Nature* (1836), the founding document of American transcendentalism, called for spiritual and artistic renewal; inspired partly by Emerson's example, Margaret Fuller's "The Great Lawsuit: MAN *versus* MEN. WOMAN *versus* WOMEN" (1843) linked women's pursuit of political rights to their pursuit of artistic expression and intellectual independence. In late nineteenth-century Paris, the "Symbolist Manifesto" (1886), by the poet Jean Moréas, turned the genre of the manifesto in some of its characteristically high modernist directions. Attacking not so much oppressive social conditions as oppressive conceptions of literature, the Symbolists declared their hostility to realism's "plain meanings, declamations, false sentimentality and matter-of-fact description" in order to claim for poetry a freer, less moralizing play of verbal imagination.

The writers of manifestos did not have one particular audience in mind; it was enough for them to get their positions into the public realm. But manifestos also worked to bring like-minded people together; a poet might publish a manifesto in a journal of poetry, a political radical in a radical journal, and so on. In the modernist period, manifestos increasingly reached an international community of self-consciously avant-garde, cosmopolitan artists. The Italian writer F. T. Marinetti published his "Manifesto of Futurism" in French; Ezra Pound's "A Retrospect" ranged freely over his contemporaries in British and American modernist poetry as well as over Pound's admired writers of the past in several languages—Dante, Goethe, Shakespeare; Willa Cather similarly juxtaposed American fiction with French, Russian, and British works in "The Novel Démeublé."

Hostility is often a rhetorical tool of the manifesto, and it was especially so in the modernist period. Modernist manifestoes often tried to grab their audiences by the lapels, to separate not only the new from the old but also a creative *us* from a "vulgar" or hidebound *them*. The us/them divide was intended to offend traditionalists as well as to unite the believers in new artistic movements, and it often succeeded in both aims. Marinetti's "Manifesto of Futurism" set the tone in 1909 by declaring that "No work without an aggressive character can be a masterpiece" and exalting "scorn for women" along with modern technology. By 1918, Ezra Pound in "A Retrospect" could manage to insult in one sentence both traditional poetic forms and would-be imitators of his own free verse: "The actual language and phrasing" of the new poetry, Pound complained, "is often as bad as that of our elders without even the excuse that the words are shoveled in to fill a metric pattern or to complete the noise of a rhyme-sound." The modernist boundary between *us* and *them*, Pound's "Retrospect" implies, will always be in motion, always pushing forward and leaving someone behind.

At the same time, however, the very aggression of some high modernist manifestoes encouraged some members of their audience to talk back with equal vigor. Marinetti denounced advocates of women's suffrage but recognized a counterpart to his own aggressive tactics in London's most radical suffragettes, to the point of joining them on a march that was broken up by mounted police. Mina Loy wrote and privately circulated her "Feminist Manifesto" as an enthusiastic member of Marinetti's circle; his take-no-prisoners example licensed her rhetoric of destruction and demolition, which she aimed not only at the institutions of sexism but also at less confrontational versions of feminism.

Other influential modernist manifestoes were more measured in their language or more subtle in their explorations of the relationship between modernist destruction and cultural production. William Carlos Williams's exuberant prose interludes in *Spring and All* asserted, with the aid of language borrowed from evolutionary biology, that modernism's sudden "SPRING" into the new was the explosive culmination of many small, repeated movements in the past. The title metaphor of Willa Cather's "The Novel Démeublé"—the novel "unfurnished"—suggested that modernism might prune the decorative excesses of nineteenth-century realism without abandoning its basic structure. And Langston Hughes, although he railed against "the mountain standing in the way of any true Negro art in America," ultimately envisioned the mountain—the internal and external struggles of black Americans to cast off white denigrations of African American culture—as the foundation of a higher and broader modernist art: "We build our temples for tomorrow, strong as we know how, and we stand on top of the mountain, free within ourselves."

F. T. MARINETTI

Marinetti (1876–1944) published two obscure volumes of poetry in his native Italian before "The Founding and Manifesto of Futurism" appeared in *Le Figaro,* an influential Parisian journal, in February 1909. The futurist manifesto attracted an international circle of artists and writers into Marinetti's orbit, including painters, architects, poets, sculptors, playwrights, and film directors. Across all the arts, futurism scorned traditional standards of artistic beauty, celebrated modern technologies of speed, and aimed to shock audiences: futurist painters adopted the mixed perspectives of cubism to celebrate speeding trains, and futurist theater drew on cabaret, variety shows, and circuses in staging free-form events that violated traditional theater's boundary between actors and audience. Futurism's aesthetic of aggression had unsettling political implications as well: true to his manifesto's declaration that war is "the only hygiene" of the world, Marinetti welcomed the technologically enhanced slaughter of World War I and supported the rise of Mussolini's Italian fascism.

From Manifesto of Futurism

1. We intend to sing the love of danger, the habit of energy and fearlessness.

2. Courage, audacity, and revolt will be essential elements of our poetry.

3. Up to now literature has exalted a pensive immobility, ecstasy, and sleep. We intend to exalt aggressive action, a feverish insomnia, the racer's stride, the mortal leap, the punch and the slap.

4. We say that the world's magnificence has been enriched by a new beauty; the beauty of speed. A racing car whose hood is adorned with great pipes, like serpents of explosive breath—a roaring car that seems to ride on grapeshot—is more beautiful than the *Victory of Samothrace*.[1]

5. We want to hymn the man at the wheel, who hurls the lance of his spirit across the Earth, along the circle of its orbit.

6. The poet must spend himself with ardor, splendor, and generosity, to swell the enthusiastic fervor of the primordial elements.

7. Except in struggle, there is no more beauty. No work without an aggressive character can be a masterpiece. Poetry must be conceived as a violent attack on unknown forces, to reduce and prostrate them before man.

8. We stand on the last promontory of the centuries! . . . Why should we look back, when what we want is to break down the mysterious doors of the Impossible? Time and Space died yesterday. We already live in the absolute, because we have created eternal, omnipresent speed.

9. We will glorify war—the world's only hygiene—militarism, patriotism, the destructive gesture of freedom-bringers, beautiful ideas worth dying for, and scorn for woman.

10. We will destroy the museums, libraries, academies of every kind, will fight moralism, feminism, every opportunistic or utilitarian cowardice.

11. We will sing of great crowds excited by work, by pleasure, and by riot; we will sing of the multicolored, polyphonic tides of revolution in the modern capitals; we will sing of the vibrant nightly fervor of arsenals and shipyards blazing with violent electric moons; greedy railway stations that devour smoke-plumed serpents; factories hung on clouds by the crooked lines of their smoke; bridges that stride the rivers like giant gymnasts, flashing in the sun with a glitter of knives; adventurous steamers that sniff the horizon; deep-chested locomotives whose wheels paw the tracks like the hooves of enormous steel horses bridled by tubing; and the sleek flight of planes whose propellers chatter in the wind like banners and seem to cheer like an enthusiastic crowd.

* * *

1909

MINA LOY

"Feminist Manifesto" was written during Loy's association with F. T. Marinetti but never published during her lifetime (1882–1966); it survives in a copy sent to a friend, the writer Mabel Dodge Luhan, in 1914. Loy's central demand is sexual freedom, the end of the divide between "the mistress" and "the mother," and the destruction of women's attachment to ideals of their own purity. Loy's modernist

1. Famous Greek statue of Nike, the winged goddess of victory, from the 2nd or 3rd century B.C.E.; discovered on the island of Samothrace in 1863, it became an icon of 19th-century high artistic taste.

call for women's free sexual expression appeals to elite women's sense of race and class privilege: echoing nineteenth-century alarms that granting women life choices beyond marriage and childbearing would lead to white "race suicide," Loy urges "superior" women to embrace maternity as both a responsibility and an aspect of their own sexual development.

Feminist Manifesto

The feminist movement as at present instituted is

Inadequate

__Women__ if you want to realise yourselves—you are on the eve of a devastating psychological upheaval—all your pet illusions must be unmasked—the lies of centuries have got to go— are you prepared for the __Wrench__—? There is no half-measure—NO scratching on the surface of the rubbish heap of tradition, will bring about __Reform__, the only method is __Absolute__ __Demolition__

Cease to place your confidence in economic legislation, vice-crusades & uniform education[1]—you are glossing over __Reality__.
Professional & commercial careers are opening up for you—

Is that all you want ?

And if you honestly desire to find your level without prejudice—be __Brave__ & deny at the outset—that pathetic clap-trap war cry __Woman is the equal of man__—

She is __NOT!__ for

---

1. Securing women's legal right to own property, gaining access to education for women (especially higher education) on the same terms as men, and suppressing prostitution were all important goals of 19th- and early 20th-century feminist movements.

The man who lives a life in which his activities conform to a social code which is a protectorate of the feminine element——is no longer **masculine**
The women who adapt themselves to a theoretical valuation of their sex as a **relative impersonality**, are not yet **Feminine**
Leave off looking to men to find out what you are **not** —seek within yourselves to find out what you **are**
As conditions are at present constituted—you have the choice between **Parasitism, & Prostitution** —or Negation

Men & women are enemies, with the enmity of the exploited for the parasite, the parasite for the exploited—at present they are at the mercy of the advantage that each can take of the others sexual dependence—. The only point at which the interests of the sexes merge—is the sexual embrace.

The first illusion it is to your interest to demolish is the division of women into two classes **the mistress, & the mother** every well-balanced & developed woman knows that is not true, Nature has endowed the complete woman with a faculty for expressing herself through **all** her functions—there are **no restrictions** the woman who is so incompletely evolved as to be un-self-conscious in sex, will prove a restrictive influence on the temperamental expansion of the next generation; the woman who is a poor mistress will be an incompetent mother—an inferior mentality—& will

enjoy an inadequate apprehension of **Life** .
To obtain results you must make sacrifices & the first & greatest sacrifice you have to make is of your "virtue"
The fictitious value of woman as identified with her physical purity—is too easy a stand-by——rendering her lethargic in the acquisition of intrinsic merits of character by which she could obtain a concrete value— therefore, the first self-enforced law for the female sex, as a protection against the man made bogey of virtue—which is the principle instrument of her subjection, would be the **unconditional** surgical destruction of virginity through-out the female population at puberty—.

The value of man is assessed entirely according to his use or
interest to the community, the value of woman, depends
entirely on <u>chance</u>, her success or insuccess in manoeuvering
a man into taking the life-long responsibility of her—
The advantages of marriage of too ridiculously ample—
compared to all other trades—for under modern conditions a
woman can accept preposterously luxurious support from a
man (with-out return of any sort—even offspring)—as a thank
offering for her virginity
The woman who has not succeeded in striking that
advantageous bargain—is prohibited from any but
surreptitious re-action to Life-stimuli— **& <u>entirely</u>**
<u>**debarred**</u> <u>**maternity.**</u>
Every woman has a right to maternity—
Every woman of superior intelligence should realize her race-
responsibility, in producing children in adequate proportion to
the unfit or degenerate members of her sex—

Each child of a superior woman should be the result of a
definite period of psychic development in her life—& not
necessarily of a possibly irksome & outworn continuance of an
alliance—spontaneously adapted for vital creation in the
beginning but not necessarily harmoniously balanced as the
parties to it—follow their individual lines of personal
evolution—
For the harmony of the race, each individual should be the
expression of an easy & ample interpenetration of the male &
female temperaments—free of stress
Woman must become more responsible for the child than
man—
Women must destroy in themselves, the desire to be loved—

The feeling that it is a personal insult when a man transfers
his attentions from her to another woman
The desire for comfortable protection instead of an intelligent
curiosity & courage in meeting & resisting the pressure of life
sex or so called love must be reduced to its initial element,
honour, grief, sentimentality, pride & consequently jealousy
must be detached from it.
Woman for her happiness must retain her deceptive fragility of
appearance, combined with indomitable will, irreducible

courage, & abundant health the outcome of sound nerves—
Another great illusion that woman must use all her
introspective clear-sightedness & unbiassed bravery to
destroy—for the sake of her <u>self respect</u> is the impurity of sex
the realisation in defiance of superstition that there is <u>nothing</u>
<u>impure in sex</u>—except in the mental attitude to it—will
constitute an incalculable & wider social regeneration than it
is possible for our generation to imagine.

1914   1982

EZRA POUND

"A Retrospect" summarizes Pound's early declarations of the principles of Imagism. His famous list of "Don'ts," originally published in 1913, cautioned poets
against superfluous words, rigid metrical rhythms, and the use of abstract rhetoric
rather than "direct treatment" of poetic subjects. Pound's own poetry by 1918 was
taking a turn away from Imagism's characteristic emphasis on representing "an
intellectual and emotional complex in an instant of time" and toward longer poems,
more engaged with history and the inherited materials of art.

From A Retrospect

There has been so much scribbling about a new fashion in poetry, that I
may perhaps be pardoned this brief recapitulation and retrospect.

In the spring or early summer of 1912, "H. D.," Richard Aldington and
myself decided[1] that we were agreed upon the three principles following:

1. Direct treatment of the 'thing' whether subjective or objective.
2. To use absolutely no word that does not contribute to the presentation.
3. As regarding rhythm: to compose in the sequence of the musical
   phrase, not in sequence of a metronome.

Upon many points of taste and of predilection we differed, but agreeing
upon these three positions we thought we had as much right to a group
name, at least as much right, as a number of French "schools" proclaimed
by Mr Flint in the August number of Harold Monro's magazine for 1911.[2]

This school has since been "joined" or "followed" by numerous people who,
whatever their merits, do not show any signs of agreeing with the second
specification. Indeed *vers libre*[3] has become as prolix and as verbose as any of
the flaccid varieties that preceded it. It has brought faults of its own. The
actual language and phrasing is often as bad as that of our elders without

---

1. H. D. and the British poet Richard Aldington
(1892–1962), who married H.D. in 1913, were
among the first poets designated "Imagistes" by
Pound.
2. The British poet and translator Frank Stuart

Flint (1885–1960) was a friend of Pound's and
another Imagist; the Scottish poet and critic Harold Munro founded the *Poetry Review* in 1911.
3. Free verse (French); poetry without a fixed pattern of rhyme or meter.

even the excuse that the words are shovelled in to fill a metric pattern or to complete the noise of a rhyme-sound. Whether or no the phrases followed by the followers are musical must be left to the reader's decision. At times I can find a marked metre in "vers libres," as stale and hackneyed as any pseudo-Swinburnian,[4] at times the writers seem to follow no musical structure whatever. But it is, on the whole, good that the field should be ploughed. Perhaps a few good poems have come from the new method, and if so it is justified.

Criticism is not a circumscription or a set of prohibitions. It provides fixed points of departure. It may startle a dull reader into alertness. That little of it which is good is mostly in stray phrases; or if it be an older artist helping a younger it is in great measure but rules of thumb, cautions gained by experience.

I set together a few phrases on practical working about the time the first remarks on imagisme were published. The first use of the word "Imagiste" was in my note to T.E. Hulme's[5] five poems, printed at the end of my "Ripostes" in the autumn of 1912. I reprint my cautions from *Poetry* for March, 1913.

A FEW DON'TS

An "Image" is that which presents an intellectual and emotional complex in an instant of time. I use the term "complex" rather in the technical sense employed by the newer psychologists, such as Hart,[6] though we might not agree absolutely in our application.

It is the presentation of such a "complex" instantaneously which gives that sense of sudden liberation; that sense of freedom from time limits and space limits; that sense of sudden growth, which we experience in the presence of the greatest works of art.

It is better to present one Image in a lifetime than to produce voluminous works.

All this, however, some may consider open to debate. The immediate necessity is to tabulate A LIST OF DON'TS for those beginning to write verses. I can not put all of them into Mosaic[7] negative.

To begin with, consider the three propositions (demanding direct treatment, economy of words, and the sequence of the musical phrase), not as dogma—never consider anything as dogma—but as the result of long contemplation, which, even if it is some one else's contemplation, may be worth consideration.

Pay no attention to the criticism of men who have never themselves written a notable work. Consider the discrepancies between the actual writing of the Greek poets and dramatists, and the theories of the Graeco-Roman grammarians, concocted to explain their metres.

LANGUAGE

Use no superfluous word, no adjective which does not reveal something.

Don't use such an expression as "dim lands *of peace*." It dulls the image. It mixes an abstraction with the concrete. It comes from the writer's not realizing that the natural object is always the *adequate* symbol.

4. The British Victorian poet Algernon Swinburne (1837–1909) was famous for using elaborate poetic forms.
5. Thomas Ernest Hulme (1883–1917), British poet and critic who, with Pound, formulated early statements of Imagism.
6. British psychologist Bernard Hart (1879–

1960), influenced by the theories of Sigmund Freud, popularized the idea of the "complex" as an "emotional system of ideas."
7. Referring to the "Thou shalt not . . ." formula of the Ten Commandments of Moses (Exodus 20.1–17).

Go in fear of abstractions. Do not retell in mediocre verse what has already been done in good prose. Don't think any intelligent person is going to be deceived when you try to shirk all the difficulties of the unspeakably difficult art of good prose by chopping your composition into line lengths.

What the expert is tired of today the public will be tired of tomorrow.

Don't imagine that the art of poetry is any simpler than the art of music, or that you can please the expert before you have spent at least as much effort on the art of verse as the average piano teacher spends on the art of music.

Be influenced by as many great artists as you can, but have the decency either to acknowledge the debt outright, or to try to conceal it.

Don't allow "influence" to mean merely that you mop up the particular decorative vocabulary of some one or two poets whom you happen to admire. A Turkish war correspondent was recently caught red-handed babbling in his despatches of "dove-grey" hills, or else it was "pearl-pale," I can not remember.

Use either no ornament or good ornament.

1918

WILLA CATHER

"The Novel Démeublé" strikes many familiar high modernist themes: distrust of mass production, the importance of distinguishing popular entertainment from serious art, and disdain for nineteenth-century realism with its consumerist catalogs of material objects. In this essay, however, Cather (1873–1947) sifts through the nineteenth-century heritage rather than rejecting it wholesale; she finds a precursor for her own ideal of the "unfurnished" modernist novel in Hawthorne's *The Scarlet Letter*.

From The Novel Démeublé

The novel, for a long while, has been over-furnished. The property-man has been so busy on its pages, the importance of material objects and their vivid presentation have been so stressed, that we take it for granted whoever can observe, and can write the English language, can write a novel. Often the latter qualification is considered unnecessary.

In any discussion of the novel, one must make it clear whether one is talking about the novel as a form of amusement, or as a form of art; since they serve very different purposes and in very different ways. One does not wish the egg one eats for breakfast, or the morning paper, to be made of the stuff of immortality. The novel manufactured to entertain great multitudes of people must be considered exactly like a cheap soap or a cheap perfume, or cheap furniture. Fine quality is a distinct disadvantage in articles made for great numbers of people who do not want quality but quantity, who do not want a thing that "wears," but who want change,—a succession of new things that are quickly thread-bare and can be lightly thrown away. Does anyone pretend that if the Woolworth store windows were piled high with Tanagra figurines at ten cents, they could for a moment compete with Kewpie brides[1] in the popular esteem? Amusement is one thing; enjoyment of art is another.

* * *

There is a popular superstition that "realism" asserts itself in the cataloguing of a great number of material objects, in explaining mechanical processes, the methods of operating manufactories and trades, and in minutely and unsparingly describing physical sensations. But is not realism, more than it is anything else, an attitude of mind on the part of the writer toward his material, a vague indication of the sympathy and candour with which he accepts, rather than chooses, his theme? Is the story of a banker who is unfaithful to his wife and who ruins himself by speculation in trying to gratify the caprices of his mistresses, at all reinforced by a masterly exposition of banking, our whole system of credits, the methods of the Stock Exchange? Of course, if the story is thin, these things do reinforce it in a sense,—any amount of red meat thrown into the scale to make the beam dip. But are the banking system and the Stock Exchange worth being written about at all? Have such things any proper place in imaginative art?

* * *

If the novel is a form of imaginative art, it cannot be at the same time a vivid and brilliant form of journalism. Out of the teeming, gleaming stream of the present it must select the eternal material of art. There are hopeful signs that some of the younger writers are trying to break away from mere verisimilitude, and, following the development of modern painting, to interpret imaginatively the material and social investiture of their characters; to present their scene by suggestion rather than by enumeration. The higher processes of art are all processes of simplification. The novelist must learn to write, and then he must unlearn it; just as the modern painter learns to draw, and then learns when utterly to disregard his accomplishment, when to subordinate it to a higher and truer effect. In this direction only, it seems to me, can the novel develop into anything more varied and perfect than all the many novels that have gone before.

One of the very earliest American romances might well serve as a suggestion to later writers. In *The Scarlet Letter* how truly in the spirit of art is the mise-en-scène presented.[2] That drudge, the theme-writing high-school student, could scarcely be sent there for information regarding the manners and dress and interiors of Puritan society. The material investiture of the story is presented as if unconsciously; by the reserved, fastidious hand of an artist, not by the gaudy fingers of a showman or the mechanical industry of a department-store window-dresser. As I remember it, in the twilight melancholy of that book, in its consistent mood, one can scarcely ever see the actual surroundings of the people; one feels them, rather, in the dusk.

1. Kewpie dolls, enormously popular from their introduction in the 1910s, were manufactured in ceramic and, later, plastic. Named for their resemblance to images of Cupid, they were often distributed in bride and groom sets. "Woolworth's": American chain store founded in the late 19th century and noted for inexpensive merchandise. "Tanagra figurines": miniature terracotta statues, usually of fashionably dressed women, mass produced in Greece at the end of the 4th century B.C.E.
2. *The Scarlet Letter* (1850), by American novelist Nathaniel Hawthorne (1804–1864).

Whatever is felt upon the page without being specifically named there—that, one might say, is created. It is the inexplicable presence of the thing not named, of the overtone divined by the ear but not heard by it, the verbal mood, the emotional aura of the fact or the thing or the deed, that gives high quality to the novel or the drama, as well as to poetry itself.

* * *

How wonderful it would be if we could throw all the furniture out of the window; and along with it, all the meaningless reiterations concerning physical sensations, all the tiresome old patterns, and leave the room as bare as the stage of a Greek theatre, or as that house into which the glory of Pentacost[3] descended; leave the scene bare for the play of emotions, great and little—for the nursery tale, no less than the tragedy, is killed by tasteless amplitude. The elder Dumas[4] enunciated a great principle when he said that to make a drama, a man needed one passion, and four walls.

1922

3. Christian festival marking the descent of the Holy Spirit to Christ's disciples after his death and resurrection (Acts 2.1–4); often painted as described in the Bible, with the disciples at a table in a closed room.
4. Alexandre Dumas (1802–1870), popular French novelist, author of *The Three Musketeers* (1844).

WILLIAM CARLOS WILLIAMS

Williams's 1923 *Spring and All* interspersed untitled short poems (many of them, like "Spring and All" and "The Red Wheelbarrow," now familiar to readers as free-standing lyrics) with sections of manifesto-style prose. *Spring and All* dramatizes repeatedly what Williams (1883–1963) calls "the leap from prose to the process of imagination," charting the rhythmic ebb and flow of imagination's force. Although the poems in *Spring and All* are numbered consecutively, the headings of the prose interludes frequently, as here, play with typographical conventions of numbering.

From Spring and All

CHAPTER VI

Now, in the imagination, all flesh, all human flesh has been dead upon the earth for ten million, billion years. The bird has turned into a stone within whose heart an egg, unlaid, remained hidden.

It is spring! but miracle of miracles a miraculous miracle has gradually taken place during these seemingly wasted eons. Through the orderly sequences of unmentionable time EVOLUTION HAS REPEATED ITSELF FROM THE BEGINNING.

Good God!

Every step once taken in the first advance of the human race, from the amoeba to the highest type of intelligence, has been duplicated, every step exactly paralleling the one that preceded in the dead ages gone by. A perfect plagiarism results. Everything is and is new. Only the imagination is undeceived.

At this point the entire complicated and laborious process begins to near a new day. (More of this in Chapter XIX) But for the moment everything is fresh, perfect, recreated.

In fact now, for the first time, everything IS new. Now at last the perfect effect is being witlessly discovered. The terms "veracity" "actuality" "real" "natural" "sincere" are being discussed at length, every word in the discussion being evolved from an identical discussion which took place the day before yesterday.

Yes, the imagination, drunk with prohibitions, has destroyed and recreated everything afresh in the likeness of that which it was. Now indeed men look about in amazement at each other with a full realization of the meaning of "art."

CHAPTER 2

It is spring: life again begins to assume its normal appearance as of "today." Only the imagination is undeceived. The volcanos are extinct. Coal is beginning to be dug again where the fern forests stood last night. (If an error is noted here, pay no attention to it.)

CHAPTER XIX

I realize that the chapters are rather quick in their sequence and that nothing much is contained in any one of them but no one should be surprised at this today.

THE TRADITIONALISTS OF PLAGIARISM

It is spring. That is to say, it is approaching THE BEGINNING.

In that huge and microscopic career of time, as it were a wild horse racing in an illimitable pampa[1] under the stars, describing immense and microscopic circles with his hoofs on the solid turf, running without a stop for the millionth part of a second until he is aged and worn to a heap of skin, bones and ragged hoofs—In that majestic progress of life, that gives the exact impression of Phidias' frieze,[2] the men and beasts of which, though they seem of the rigidity of marble are not so but move, with blinding rapidity, though we do not have the time to notice it, their legs advancing a millionth part of an inch every fifty thousand years—In that progress of life which seems stillness itself in the mass of its movements—at last SPRING is approaching.

1. Extensive grassy plains of central Argentina (Spanish, la pampa).
2. The most important sculptor of classical Athens, Phidias (c.500–c.432 b.c.e.) or his students executed the frieze (a long band of relief sculpture surmounting columns) decorating the Parthenon in Athens; the frieze depicts a festival procession of men and horses.

In that colossal surge toward the finite and the capable life has now arrived for the second time at that exact moment when in the ages past the destruction of the species *Homo sapiens* occurred.

Now at last that process of miraculous verisimilitude, that great copying which evolution has followed, repeating move for move every move that it made in the past—is approaching the end.

Suddenly it is at an end. THE WORLD IS NEW.[3]

1923

3. In the original publication, the poem "Spring and All" ("By the road to the contagious hospital"; see p. 1965) directly followed this section.

LANGSTON HUGHES

Where Willa Cather, along with many other modernists, sought to divide high art from popular entertainment, Langston Hughes (1902–1967) urged African American artists to embrace black popular culture, epitomized for Hughes and many other observers of the 1920s by the innovations of jazz. "The Negro Artist and the Racial Mountain," published at the height of the Harlem Renaissance, takes aim at white audiences who looked to black artists for easy, stereotypical entertainment. Hughes's essay reserves most of its anger, however, for black elites who—he charged—preferred their artists to imitate white standards.

From The Negro Artist and the Racial Mountain

One of the most promising of the young Negro poets said to me once, "I want to be a poet—not a Negro poet," meaning, I believe, "I want to write like a white poet"; meaning subconsciously, "I would like to be a white poet"; meaning behind that, "I would like to be white." And I was sorry the young man said that, for no great poet has ever been afraid of being himself. And I doubted then that, with his desire to run away spiritually from his race, this boy would ever be a great poet. But this is the mountain standing in the way of any true Negro art in America—this urge within the race toward whiteness, the desire to pour racial individuality into the mold of American standardization, and to be as little Negro and as much American as possible.

* * *

The Negro artist works against an undertow of sharp criticism and misunderstanding from his own group and unintentional bribes from the whites. "O, be respectable, write about nice people, show how good we are," say the Negroes. "Be stereotyped, don't go too far, don't shatter our illusions about you, don't amuse us too seriously. We will pay you," say the whites. Both would have told Jean Toomer not to write "Cane."[1] The colored people did not praise it. The white people did not buy it. Most of the colored people who did read "Cane" hate it. They are afraid of it. Although the critics gave it good reviews the public remained indifferent. Yet (excepting the work of Du Bois[2]) "Cane" contains the finest prose written by a Negro in America. And like the singing of Robeson,[3] it is truly racial.

* * *

Most of my own poems are racial in theme and treatment, derived from the life I know. In many of them I try to grasp and hold some of the meanings and rhythms of jazz. I am sincere as I know how to be in these poems and yet after every reading I answer questions like these from my own people: Do you think Negroes should always write about Negroes? I wish you wouldn't read some of your poems to white folks. How do you find anything interesting in a place like a cabaret? Why do you write about black people? You aren't black. What makes you do so many jazz poems?

But jazz to me is one of the inherent expressions of Negro life in America: the eternal tom-tom beating in the Negro soul—the tom-tom of revolt against weariness in a white world, a world of subway trains, and work, work, work; the tom-tom of joy and laughter, and pain swallowed in a smile. Yet the Philadelphia clubwoman is ashamed to say that her race created it and she does not like me to write about it. The old subconscious "white is best" runs through her mind. Years of study under white teachers, a lifetime of white books, pictures, and papers, and white manners, morals, and Puritan standards made her dislike the spirituals. And now she turns up her nose at jazz and all its manifestations—likewise almost everything else distinctly racial. She doesn't care for the Winold Reiss[4] portraits of Negroes because they are "too Negro." She does not want a true picture of herself from anybody. She wants the artist to flatter her, to make the white world believe that all Negroes are as smug and as near white in soul as she wants to be. But, to my mind, it is the duty of the younger Negro artist, if he accepts any duties at all from outsiders, to change through the force of his art that old whispering "I want to be white," hidden in the aspirations of his people, to "Why should I want to be white? I am a Negro—and beautiful!"

So I am ashamed for the black poet who says, "I want to be a poet, not a Negro poet," as though his own racial world were not as interesting as any other world. I am ashamed, too, for the colored artist who runs from the painting of Negro faces to the painting of sunsets after the manner of the academicians because he fears the strange un-whiteness of his own features. An artist must be free to choose what he does, certainly, but he must also never be afraid to do what he might choose.

Let the blare of Negro Jazz bands and the bellowing voice of Bessie Smith singing Blues penetrate the closed ears of the colored near-intellectuals until they listen and perhaps understand. Let Paul Robeson singing Water

1. Jean Toomer's *Cane* combines prose and poems in a modernist dual portrait of rural Georgia and the urban black community of Washington, D.C.; see p. 2143.
2. W. E. B. Du Bois (1868–1963), author of *The Souls of Black Folk* (1903) and other works on African American life and history.

3. Paul Robeson (1898–1976), African American actor and singer; in 1925 he made his concert debut in New York City with a program of black spirituals.
4. Winold Reiss (1886–1953), German-born artist known for his portraits of figures from the Harlem Renaissance.

Boy, and Rudolph Fisher writing about the streets of Harlem, and Jean Toomer holding the heart of Georgia in his hands, and Aaron Douglas[5] drawing strange black fantasies cause the smug Negro middle class to turn from their white, respectable, ordinary books and papers to catch a glimmer of their own beauty. We younger Negro artists who create now intend to express our individual dark-skinned selves without fear or shame. If white people are pleased we are glad. If they are not, it doesn't matter. We know we are beautiful. And ugly too. The tom-tom cries and the tom-tom laughs. If colored people are pleased we are glad. If they are not, their displeasure doesn't matter either. We build our temples for tomorrow, strong as we know how, and we stand on top of the mountain, free within ourselves.

1926

5. Aaron Douglas (1899–1979), painter and muralist who studied with Winold Reiss and who became the first head of the Harlem Artists' Guild; Bessie Smith (1894?–1937), noted blues singer at the height of her fame in the 1920s; Rudolph Fisher (1897–1934), Harlem Renaissance author and musician who arranged songs for Paul Robeson's 1925 New York concert debut.

H.D. (HILDA DOOLITTLE)
1886–1961

In January 1913, Harriet Monroe's influential little magazine, *Poetry,* printed three vivid poems by an unknown "H.D., Imagiste." These spare, elegant lyrics were among the first important products of the "imagist movement": poems devoid of explanation and declamation, unrhymed and lacking regular beat, depending on the power of an image to arrest attention and convey emotion. The poet's pen name, the movement's name, and the submission to the magazine were all the work of Ezra Pound, poet and tireless publicist for anything new in the world of poetry. The poems themselves had been written by his friend Hilda Doolittle. In later years, H.D. would look back at these events as epitomizing her dilemma: how to be a woman poet speaking in a world where women were spoken for and about by men. It is, perhaps, a symbol of her sense of difficulty that, though she strove for a voice that could be recognized as clearly feminine, she continued to publish under the name that Pound had devised for her.

She was born in Bethlehem, Pennsylvania, one girl in a family of five boys. Her mother was a musician and music teacher, active in the Moravian church to which many in Bethlehem belonged. The symbols and rituals of this group, along with its tradition of secrecy created in response to centuries of oppression, had much to do with H.D.'s interest in images and her attraction in later life to occult and other symbol systems: the cabala, numerology, the tarot, and psychoanalysis.

When her father, an astronomer and mathematician, was appointed director of the observatory at the University of Pennsylvania, the family moved to a suburb of Philadelphia. There, when she was fifteen years old, H.D. met Ezra Pound, a student at the university, already dedicated to poetry and acting the poet's role with dramatic intensity. The two were engaged for a while, but Pound's influence continued long after each had gone on to other partners. H.D. attended college at Bryn Mawr for two years; in 1911 she made a bold move to London, where Pound had gone some years earlier. She married a member of his circle, the English poet Richard Aldington, in 1913. With Aldington she studied Greek and read the classics, but the marriage was not a success and was destroyed by their separation during World War I when Aldington went into the army and served in France.

The years 1918–19 were terrible for H.D.: her brother Gilbert was killed in the fighting in France, her father died soon thereafter, her marriage broke up, close friendships with Pound and with D. H. Lawrence came to an end, she had a nearly fatal case of flu, and amid all this gave birth to a daughter who Aldington said was not his child. But she was rescued from the worst of her emotional and financial troubles by Winifred Ellerman, whose father, a shipping magnate, was one of the wealthiest men in England. Ellerman, a writer who had adopted the pen name Bryher, had initially been attracted by H.D.'s poetry; their relationship developed first as a love affair and then into a lifelong friendship.

In 1923, H.D. settled in Switzerland. With Bryher's financial help she raised her daughter and cared for her ailing mother, who had joined her household. During 1933 and 1934 she spent time in Vienna, where she underwent analysis by Sigmund Freud, hoping to understand both her writer's block and what she called her "two loves" of women and men. Freud's theory of the unconscious and the disguised ways in which it reaches expression accorded well with H.D.'s understanding of how the unexplained images in a poem could be significant; the images were coded personal meanings. H.D.'s religious mysticism clashed with Freud's materialism, however, and she had mixed reactions to Freud's developing theory that women's unhappiness was determined by their sense of biological inferiority to men. But H.D. was instrumental (with Bryher's help) in getting Freud, who was Jewish, safely to London when the Nazi regime took over in Austria. When World War II broke out H.D. went back to London to share England's fate in crisis.

During the 1930s she worked mostly in prose forms and composed several autobiographical pieces (some of which remain unpublished). Like many major poets of the era, H.D. came in time to feel the need to write longer works; the bombardment of London inspired three long related poems about World War II, *The Walls Do Not Fall* (1944), *Tribute to the Angels* (1945), and *The Flowering of the Rod* (1946), which appeared together as *Trilogy*. In them she combined layers of historical and personal experience; wars going back to the Trojan War all fused in one image of humankind forever imposing and enduring violence.

The personal and the historical had always been one to her, and she became increasingly attracted to the image of Helen, the so-called cause of the Trojan War, as an image of herself. According to Homer's *Iliad*, Helen's beauty led Paris, a Trojan prince, to steal her from her Greek husband, Menelaus; and all the Greek warriors made common cause to get her back. After ten years' encamped before the walls of Troy, they found a devious way to enter the city and destroy it. H.D. was struck by the fact that the legend was related entirely from the male point of view; Helen never had a chance to speak. The object of man's acts and the subject of their poems, she was herself always silent. If Helen tried to speak, would she even have a voice or a point of view? Out of these broodings, and helped by her study of symbols, H.D. wrote her meditative epic of more than fourteen hundred lines, *Helen in Egypt*. The poem, composed between 1951 and 1955, consists of three books of interspersed verse and prose commentary, which follow Helen's quest. "She herself is the writing" that she seeks to understand, the poet observes.

H.D.'s imagist poetry, for which she was known during her lifetime, represents the imagist credo with its vivid phrasing, compelling imagery, free verse, short poetic line, and avoidance of abstraction and generalization. She followed Pound's example in producing many translations of poetry from older literature, especially from her favorite Greek poets. Her natural images are influenced by her early immersion in astronomy as well as by Greek poetry's Mediterranean settings. Austere landscapes of sea, wind, stars, and sand are contrasted with sensual figures of jewels, honey, and shells. Traditional metaphorical resources of earlier women's poetry, such as flowers and birds, are absorbed into modernism's aesthetic of "fiery tempered steel." As when her "Oread" calls upon the sea to "splash your great pines / on our rocks," H.D.'s best-known poems embody high modernism's goal of condensing forces at once lush and shattering, violent and creative, into a single arresting image.

The texts of the poems included here are those of *Collected Poems 1912–1944*, edited by Louis L. Martz (1983).

Mid-day

The light beats upon me.
I am startled—
a split leaf crackles on the paved floor—
I am anguished—defeated.

A slight wind shakes the seed-pods—   5
my thoughts are spent
as the black seeds.
My thoughts tear me,
I dread their fever.
I am scattered in its whirl.   10
I am scattered like
the hot shrivelled seeds.

The shrivelled seeds
are split on the path—
the grass bends with dust,   15
the grape slips
under its crackled leaf:
yet far beyond the spent seed-pods,
and the blackened stalks of mint,
the poplar is bright on the hill,   20
the poplar spreads out,
deep-rooted among trees.

O poplar, you are great
among the hill-stones,
while I perish on the path   25
among the crevices of the rocks.

1916

Oread[1]

Whirl up, sea—
whirl your pointed pines,
splash your great pines

---

1. A nymph of mountains and hills.

on our rocks,
hurl your green over us,   5
cover us with your pools of fir.

                                                            1914, 1924

Leda[1]

Where the slow river
meets the tide,
a red swan lifts red wings
and darker beak,
and underneath the purple down   5
of his soft breast
uncurls his coral feet.

Through the deep purple
of the dying heat
of sun and mist,   10
the level ray of sun-beam
has caressed
the lily with dark breast,
and flecked with richer gold
its golden crest.   15

Where the slow lifting
of the tide,
floats into the river
and slowly drifts
among the reeds,   20
and lifts the yellow flags,
he floats
where tide and river meet.

Ah kingly kiss—
no more regret   25
nor old deep memories
to mar the bliss;
where the low sedge is thick,
the gold day-lily
outspreads and rests   30
beneath soft fluttering
of red swan wings
and the warm quivering
of the red swan's breast.

                                                            1919, 1921

---

1. In Greek mythology, Leda is the mortal raped by Zeus, in the guise of a swan. Helen of Troy was her daughter.

Helen[1]

All Greece hates
the still eyes in the white face,
the lustre as of olives
where she stands,
and the white hands.   5

All Greece reviles
the wan face when she smiles,
hating it deeper still
when it grows wan and white,
remembering past enchantments   10
and past ills.

Greece sees unmoved,
God's daughter, born of love,
the beauty of cool feet
and slenderest knees,   15
could love indeed the maid,
only if she were laid,
white ash amid funereal cypresses.

1924

1. In Greek legend, the wife of Menelaus; her kidnapping by the Trojan prince Paris started the Trojan War. She was the daughter of the god Zeus, the product of his rape, when disguised as a swan, of the mortal Leda.

MARIANNE MOORE
1887–1972

Marianne Moore was a radically inventive modernist, greatly admired by other poets of her generation, and a powerful influence on such later writers as Robert Lowell, Randall Jarrell, and Richard Wilbur. Like her forerunner Emily Dickinson, she made of the traditional and constraining "woman's place" a protected space to do her own work, but unlike Emily Dickinson, she was a deliberate professional, publishing her poems regularly, in touch with the movements and artists of her time. She was famous for the statement that poetry, though departing from the real world, re-created that world within its forms: poems were "imaginary gardens with real toads in them." Her earlier work is distinguished by great precision of observation and language, ornate diction, and complex stanza and prosodic patterns. Her later work is much less ornate; and in revising her poetry, she tended to simplify and shorten.

She was born in Kirkwood, Missouri, a suburb of St. Louis. In her childhood, the family was abandoned by her father; they moved to Carlisle, Pennsylvania, where—in a pattern common among both men and women writers of this period—her mother supported them by teaching school. She went to Bryn Mawr College, graduating in

1909; traveled with her mother in England and France in 1911; and returned to Carlisle to teach at the U.S. Indian School between 1911 and 1915. Having begun to write poetry in college, she was first published in 1915 and 1916 in such little magazines as the *Egoist* (an English magazine with which Ezra Pound was associated), *Poetry,* and *Others* (a journal for experimental writing with which William Carlos Williams was associated, founded by Alfred Kreymbourg, a New York poet and playwright). Through these magazines she entered the avant-garde and modernist world. She never married; in 1916 she and her mother merged their household with that of Moore's brother, a Presbyterian minister, and they moved with him to a parish in Brooklyn, New York. There Moore was close to literary circles and Ebbets Field, where the Dodgers, then a Brooklyn baseball team, had their home stadium. Moore was a lifelong fan.

While holding jobs in schools and libraries, Moore worked at her poetry. A volume called simply *Poems* was brought out in London in 1921 without her knowledge through the efforts of two women friends who were writers, H.D. (whom she had met at Bryn Mawr) and Bryher. Another book, *Observations,* appeared in 1924 and won the Dial Award. In 1925 she began to work as editor of the *Dial,* continuing in this influential position until the magazine was disbanded in 1929. Her reviews and editorial judgments were greatly respected, although her preference for elegance and decorum over sexual frankness was not shared by some of the writers—Hart Crane and James Joyce among them—whose work she rejected or published only after they revised it.

As a critic of poetry Moore wrote numerous essays—her collected prose makes a larger book than her collected poetry. She believed that poets usually undervalued prose; "precision, economy of statement, logic" were features of good prose that could "liberate" the imagination, she wrote. In writing about animals she was able to take advantage of two different prose modes that attracted her—scientific and historical description. Her poems were an amalgam of her own observation and her readings, which she acknowledged by quotation marks and often by footnotes as well. In Moore's writings, the reader almost never finds the conventional poetic allusions that invoke a great tradition and assert the present poet's place in it. Moore's poems typically juxtapose disparate areas of human knowledge and combine the elevated with the ordinary. Her notebooks suggest, for example, that the image of the kiwi bird in "The Mind is an Enchanting Thing" emerged from a sketch Moore made of a shoe-polish tin; she praises the human mind both for its capacity to be mesmerized by the small facets of its ordinary environment and for its changeful, self-undoing freedom.

Against the exactitude and "unbearable accuracy" (as she put it) of her language, Moore counterpointed a complex texture of stanza form and versification. Pound worked with the clause, Williams with the line, H.D. with the image, Stevens and Stein with the word; Moore, unlike these modernist contemporaries, used the entire stanza as the unit of her poetry. Her stanza is composed of regular lines counted by syllables, instead of by stress, which are connected in an elaborate verse pattern, and in which rhymes often occur at unaccented syllables and even in the middle of a word. The effects she achieves are complex and subtle; she was often called the "poet's poet" of her day because the reader needed expert technical understanding to recognize what she was doing.

Nevertheless, her poetry also had a thematic, declarative edge which the outbreak of World War II led her to expand. In "The Paper Nautilus," she drew on her characteristic vein of natural observation in order to will that a threatened civilization be protected by love. At the same time, Moore was keenly aware of her distance, as a civilian and a woman, from direct experience of combat; "In Distrust of Merits," her most famous poem of the war, reflects Moore's struggle (like Emily Dickinson's during the Civil War) to adopt an ethically responsible relationship toward the fighting she could know only through newsreels and photographs.

Moore received the Bollingen, National Book, and Pulitzer awards for *Collected Poems* in 1951. Throughout her lifetime she continued to revise, expand, cut, and select, so that from volume to volume a poem with the same name may be a very different work. Her *Complete Poems* of 1967 represented her poetry as she wanted it remembered, but a full understanding of Moore calls for reading all of the versions of her changing work.

Poetry[1]

I, too, dislike it: there are things that are important beyond all
      this fiddle.
Reading it, however, with a perfect contempt for it, one
      discovers in
it after all, a place for the genuine.
      Hands that can grasp, eyes
      that can dilate, hair that can rise 5
      if it must, these things are important not because a

high-sounding interpretation can be put upon them but because
      they are
useful. When they become so derivative as to become
      unintelligible,
the same thing may be said for all of us, that we
      do not admire what 10
      we cannot understand: the bat
      holding on upside down or in quest of something to

eat, elephants pushing, a wild horse taking a roll, a tireless wolf
      under
a tree, the immovable critic twitching his skin like a horse
      that feels a flea, the base-
ball fan, the statistician— 15
      nor is it valid
      to discriminate against "business documents and

school-books";[2] all these phenomena are important. One must
      make a distinction
however: when dragged into prominence by half poets, the
      result is not poetry,
nor till the poets among us can be 20
      "literalists of
      the imagination"[3]—above
      insolence and triviality and can present

for inspection, "imaginary gardens with real toads in them," shall
      we have
      it. In the meantime, if you demand on the one hand, 25

---

1. The version printed here follows the text and format of *Selected Poems* (1935).
2. Diary of Tolstoy (Dutton), p. 84. "Where the boundary between prose and poetry lies, I shall never be able to understand. The question is raised in manuals of style, yet the answer to it lies beyond me. Poetry is verse; prose is not verse. Or else poetry is everything with the exception of business documents and school books" [Moore's note].

3. Yeats's *Ideas of Good and Evil* (A.H. Bullen), p. 182. "The limitation of his view was from the very intensity of his vision; he was a too literal realist of imagination, as others are of nature; and because he believed that the figures seen by the mind's eye, when exalted by inspiration, were 'eternal existences,' symbols of divine essences, he hated every grace of style that might obscure their lineaments" [Moore's note].

the raw material of poetry in
 all its rawness and
 that which is on the other hand
genuine, then you are interested in poetry.

1921, 1935

To a Snail[1]

If "compression is the first grace of style,"[2]
you have it. Contractility is a virtue
as modesty is a virtue.
It is not the acquisition of any one thing
that is able to adorn,   5
or the incidental quality that occurs
as a concomitant of something well said,
that we value in style,
but the principle that is hid:
in the absence of feet, "a method of conclusions";   10
"a knowledge of principles,"
in the curious phenomenon of your occipital horn.

1924

The Paper Nautilus[1]

For authorities whose hopes
are shaped by mercenaries?
 Writers entrapped by
 teatime fame and by
commuters' comforts? Not for these   5
 the paper nautilus
 constructs her thin glass shell.

 Giving her perishable
souvenir of hope, a dull
 white outside and smooth   10
 edged inner surface
glossy as the sea, the watchful
 maker of it guards it
 day and night; she scarcely

 eats until the eggs are hatched.   15
Buried eight-fold in her eight
 arms, for she is in
 a sense a devil

1. The text is from *Complete Poems* (1967).
2. "The very first grace of style is that which
comes from compression." *Demetrius on Style*
translated by W. Hamilton Fyfe. Heinemann,
1932 [Moore's note].
1. The text is from *Complete Poems* (1967).

fish, her glass ram'shorn-cradled freight
    is hid but is not crushed;   20
        as Hercules,[2] bitten

    by a crab loyal to the hydra,
was hindered to succeed,
    the intensively
        watched eggs coming from   25
the shell free it when they are freed,—
    leaving its wasp-nest flaws
    of white on white, and close

    laid Ionic[3] chiton-folds
like the lines in the mane of   30
    a Parthenon[4] horse,
        round which the arms had
wound themselves as if they knew love
    is the only fortress
        strong enough to trust to.   35

                              1941, 1967

The Mind Is an Enchanting Thing[1]

is an enchanted thing
    like the glaze on a
katydid-wing
        subdivided by sun
        till the nettings are legion.   5
Like Gieseking playing Scarlatti;[2]

like the apteryx[3] awl
    as a beak, or the
kiwi's rain-shawl
        of haired feathers, the mind
        feeling its way as though blind,   10
walks along with its eyes on the ground.

It has memory's ear
    that can hear without
having to hear.   15
        Like the gyroscope's fall,
        truly unequivocal
because trued by regnant certainty,

---

2. Hero of Greek myth, who performed numerous exploits including battle with the hydra, a many-headed monster.
3. Classical Greek, specifically Athenian.
4. Temple in Athens decorated by a carved marble band of sculptures, including processions of horses.

1. The text is from *Complete Poems* (1967).
2. Walter Wilhelm Gieseking (1895–1956), French-born German pianist, known for his renditions of compositions by the Italian composer Domenico Scarlatti (1685–1757).
3. A flightless New Zealand bird, related to the kiwi, with a beak shaped like an awl.

it is a power of
　　strong enchantment. It   20
is like the dove
　　　neck animated by
　　　sun; it is memory's eye;
it's conscientious inconsistency.

It tears off the veil; tears   25
　　the temptation, the
mist the heart wears,
　　　from its eye—if the heart
　　　has a face; it takes apart
dejection. It's fire in the dove-neck's   30

iridescence; in the
　　inconsistencies
of Scarlatti.
　　　Unconfusion submits
　　　its confusion to proof; it's   35
not a Herod's oath that cannot change.[4]

　　　　　　　　　　　　　　　　　1944

In Distrust of Merits[1]

Strengthened to live, strengthened to die for
　　medals and positioned victories?
They're fighting, fighting, fighting the blind
　　man who thinks he sees,—
who cannot see that the enslaver is   5
enslaved; the hater, harmed. O shining O
　　firm star, O tumultuous
　　　ocean lashed till small things go
　　　as they will, the mountainous
　　　　wave makes us who look, know   10

depth. Lost at sea before they fought! O
　　star of David, star of Bethlehem,
O black imperial lion[2]
　　of the Lord—emblem
of a risen world—be joined at last, be   15
joined. There is hate's crown beneath which all is
　　death; there's love's without which none
　　　is king; the blessed deeds bless
　　　the halo. As contagion
　　　　of sickness makes sickness,   20

4. Herod Antipas (d. 39 C.E.), ruler of Judea under the Romans. He had John the Baptist beheaded to fulfill a promise to Salome (Mark 6.22–27).
1. The text is from *Complete Poems* (1967).
2. Emperor Haile Selassie of Ethiopia, leader of his country's resistance against Italian occupa-tion during World War II; after Mussolini's fall in 1943, Selassie declared Ethiopia "less interested in vengeance for the past than in justice for the future." "Star of David": a symbol of Judaism, "star of Bethlehem": of Christianity.

contagion of trust can make trust. They're
  fighting in deserts and caves, one by
one, in battalions and squadrons;
  they're fighting that I
may yet recover from the disease, My   25
Self; some have it lightly; some will die. "Man's
   wolf to man" and we devour
    ourselves. The enemy could not
  have made a greater breach in our
    defenses. One pilot-   30

ing a blind man can escape him, but
  Job disheartened by false comfort[3] knew
that nothing can be so defeating
  as a blind man who
can see. O alive who are dead, who are   35
proud not to see, O small dust of the earth
   that walks so arrogantly
    trust begets power and faith is
  an affectionate thing. We
   vow, we make this promise   40

to the fighting—it's a promise—"We'll
  never hate black, white, red, yellow, Jew,
Gentile, Untouchable."[4] We are
  not competent to
make our vows. With set jaw they are fighting, 45
fighting, fighting,—some we love whom we know,
   some we love but know not—that
    hearts may feel and not be numb.
  It cures me; or am I what
   I can't believe in? Some   50

in snow, some on crags, some in quicksands,
  little by little, much by much, they
are fighting fighting fighting that where
  there was death there may
be life. "When a man is prey to anger,   55
he is moved by outside things; when he holds
   his ground in patience patience
    patience, that is action or
  beauty," the soldier's defense
   and hardest armor for   60

the fight. The world's an orphans' home. Shall
  we never have peace without sorrow?
without pleas of the dying for
  help that won't come? O
quiet form upon the dust, I cannot   65
look and yet I must. If these great patient

---

3. When undergoing Jehovah's test of his fidel- fort him.
ity, Job rejected the attempts of friends to com- 4. The lowest hereditary caste in India.

dyings—all these agonies
and wound bearings and bloodshed—
can teach us how to live, these
dyings were not wasted.   70

Hate-hardened heart, O heart of iron,
        iron is iron till it is rust.
There never was a war that was
        not inward; I must
fight till I have conquered in myself what   75
causes war, but I would not believe it.
        I inwardly did nothing.
        O Iscariot[5]-like crime!
Beauty is everlasting
        and dust is for a time.   80

                                                    1944

5. Judas Iscariot was the apostle who betrayed Jesus Christ.

T. S. ELIOT
1888–1965

The publication in 1922 of *The Waste Land* in the British little magazine *Criterion* and the American *Dial* was a cultural and literary event. The poem's title and the view it incorporated of modern civilization seemed, to many, to catch precisely the state of culture and society after World War I. The war, supposedly fought to save European civilization, had been the most brutal and destructive in Western history: what kind of civilization could have allowed it to take place? The long, fragmented structure of *The Waste Land*, too, contained so many technical innovations that ideas of what poetry was and how it worked seemed fundamentally changed. A generation of poets either imitated or resisted it.

The author of this poem was an American living in London, T. S. Eliot. Eliot had a comfortable upbringing in St. Louis: his mother was involved in cultural and charitable activities and wrote poetry; his father was a successful businessman. His grandfather Eliot had been a New England Unitarian minister who, moving to St. Louis, had founded Washington University. Eliot was thus a product of that New England-based "genteel tradition" that shaped the nation's cultural life after the Civil War. He attended Harvard for both undergraduate (1906–10) and graduate (1911–14) work. He studied at the Sorbonne in Paris from 1910 to 1911 and at Oxford from 1915 to 1916, writing a dissertation on the idealistic philosophy of the English logician and metaphysician F. H. Bradley (1846–1924). The war prevented Eliot from returning to Harvard for the oral defense of his doctoral degree, and this delay became the occasion of his turning to a life in poetry and letters rather than in academics.

Eliot had begun writing traditional poetry as a college student. In 1908, however, he read Arthur Symons's *The Symbolist Movement in Literature* (1899) and learned about Jules LaForgue and other French Symbolist poets. Symons's book altered Eliot's view of poetry, as "The Love Song of J. Alfred Prufrock" (published in *Poetry* in 1915) and "Preludes" (published in *Blast* in the same year) showed; in these poems Eliot took Symons's "revolt against exteriority, against rhetoric" in the direction of associative, oblique free verse. His fellow expatriate and poet Ezra Pound, reading this work, began enthusiastically introducing Eliot in literary circles as a young American who had "trained himself *and* modernized himself *on his own*." Pound helped Eliot over several years to get financially established. In addition, he was a perceptive reader and critic of Eliot's draft poems.

Eliot settled in England, marrying Vivian Haigh-Wood in 1915. Separated in 1932, they never divorced; Haigh-Wood died in a mental institution in 1947. After marrying, Eliot worked in London, first as a teacher and then from 1917 to 1925 in the foreign department of Lloyd's Bank, hoping to find time to write poetry and literary essays. His criticism was published in the *Egoist* and then in the little magazine that he founded, *Criterion*, which was published from 1922 to 1939. His persuasive style, a mixture of advocacy and judiciousness, effectively counterpointed Pound's aggressive, confrontational approach; the two together had a tremendous effect on how the poetry of the day was written and how the poetry of the past was evaluated. More than any other Americans they defined what is now thought of as "high" modernism.

Eliot began working on *The Waste Land* in 1921 and finished it in a Swiss sanatorium while recovering from a mental collapse brought on by overwork, marital problems, and general depression. He accepted some alterations suggested by his wife and cut huge chunks out of the poem on Pound's advice. Although Pound's work on the poem was all excision, so different was the manuscript before and after Pound's suggestions were incorporated that some critics suggest we should think of *The Waste Land* as jointly authored. The poem as published in *Criterion* and the *Dial* had no footnotes; these were appended for its publication in book form and added yet another layer (possibly self-mocking) to the complex texture of the poem.

The Waste Land consists of five discontinuous segments, each composed of fragments incorporating multiple voices and characters, literary and historical allusions and quotations, vignettes of contemporary life, surrealistic images, myths and legends. "These fragments I have shored against my ruins," the poet writes, asking whether he can form any coherent structure from the splinters of civilization. The poem's discontinuous elements are organized by recurrent allusions to the myth of seasonal death, burial, and rebirth that, according to much anthropological thinking of the time, underlay all religions. In Sir James Frazer's multivolume *The Golden Bough* (1890–1915) and Jessie Weston's *From Ritual to Romance* (1920), Eliot found a repertory of myths through which he could invoke, without specifically naming any religion, the story of a desert land brought to life by a king's sacrifice. Although it gestures toward religious belief, *The Waste Land* concludes with the outcome of the quest for regeneration uncertain in a cacophonous, desolate landscape.

Many readers saw *The Waste Land* as the definitive cultural statement of its time, but it was not definitive for Eliot. The poem may have been Eliot's indirect confession of personal discord, for which he sought resolution in social orders beyond those of poetry. In 1927 he became a British citizen; in a preface to the collection of essays *For Lancelot Andrewes* (1928), he declared himself a "classicist in literature, royalist in politics, and anglo-catholic in religion." After "The Hollow Men" and the "Sweeney" poems, which continue *The Waste Land*'s critique of modern civilization, he turned increasingly to poems of religious doubt and reconciliation. "The Journey of the Magi" and "Ash Wednesday" are poems about the search for a faith desperately needed, yet difficult to sustain. The *Four Quartets*, begun with "Burnt Norton" in 1934 and completed in 1943, are not so much reports of secure faith as dramatizations of the difficult process of arriving at belief. The *Four Quartets* move away from the fragmentary quotation and collage techniques of *The*

Waste Land in favor of plainer expository statement grounded in particular times and places—the England of Eliot's chosen citizenship and the America of his origins—while aspiring to a timeless religious faith.

An emphasis on order, hierarchy, and racial homogeneity emerged in Eliot's social essays of the later 1920s and 1930s; a strain of crude anti-Semitism had appeared in the earlier Sweeney poems. As European politics became increasingly turbulent, the stability promised by totalitarian regimes appealed to some observers, Eliot included. The Communist rejection of all religion also tended to drive the more traditionally religious modernists into the opposing camp of fascism. Pound's and Eliot's fas-

Eliot inspecting manuscripts at his desk.

cist sympathies in the 1930s, together with their immense influence on poetry, linked high modernism with reactionary politics in the public's perception, even while individual modernists in these years embraced political movements ranging from the far left to the extreme right, maintained centrist or liberal allegiances, or despised politics completely.

During the 1930s and 1940s, Eliot's criticism and poetry became increasingly important to the group of writers—many of them poets and academics in the United States—whose work became known collectively as the "New Criticism." In his influential essay "Tradition and the Individual Talent," Eliot had defined the English and European poetic tradition as a self-sufficient organic whole, an elastic equilibrium that constantly reformed itself to accommodate new poets. What makes poems matter, in Eliot's definition of tradition, is their effect on other poems, not their capacity to act upon the world outside of poetry. Poets contribute to the tradition, he argued, not through the direct expression of individual emotion but through a difficult process of distancing "the man who suffers" from "the mind which creates"; readers, therefore, should focus on the feeling embodied in the poem itself rather than reading the poem through the life of the poet. In other essays, Eliot denigrated didactic, expository, or narrative poets like Milton and the Victorians while applauding the verbally complex, paradoxical, indirect, symbolic work of seventeenth-century Metaphysical poets like John Donne and George Herbert. Through the New Criticism, Eliot's "impersonal" approach to poetry had a powerful role in shaping the literary curriculum in American colleges and universities, especially following World War II.

For the New Criticism, which analyzed poems for imagery, allusion, ambiguity, and irony, Eliot's essays provided theory, his poetry opportunities for practical criticism. But when critics used Eliot's preference for difficult indirection to judge literary quality and made interpretation the main task of readers, they often overlooked the lyricism, obvious didacticism, and humor of Eliot's own poetry. And they minimized the poems' cultural, historical, and autobiographical content.

However elitist his pronouncements, however hostile to modernity he claimed to be, Eliot drew heavily on popular forms and longed to have wide cultural influence. There are vaudeville turns throughout *The Waste Land*. He admired Charlie Chaplin and wanted "as large and miscellaneous an audience as possible." He pursued this ambition by writing verse plays. *Murder in the Cathedral* (1935) was a church pageant; *The Family Reunion* (1939), *The Cocktail Party* (1949), *The Confidential Clerk* (1953), and *The Elder Statesman* (1959), all religious in theme, were successfully produced in London and on Broadway. He never became a popular poet, however, despite his tremendous impact on the teaching and writing of poetry. Although Eliot remained a resident of England, he returned to the United States frequently to lecture and to give readings of his poems. He married his assistant, Valerie Fletcher, in 1957. By the time of his death he had become a social and cultural institution.

The text of the poems is that of *The Complete Poems and Plays of T. S. Eliot* (1969).

The Love Song of J. Alfred Prufrock

> *S'io credessi che mia risposta fosse*
> *a persona che mai tornasse al mondo,*
> *questa fiamma staria senza più scosse.*
> *Ma per ciò che giammai di questo fondo*
> *non tornò vivo alcun, s'i'odo il vero,*
> *senza tema d'infamia ti rispondo.*[1]

Let us go then, you and I,
When the evening is spread out against the sky
Like a patient etherised upon a table;
Let us go, through certain half-deserted streets,
The muttering retreats   5
Of restless nights in one-night cheap hotels
And sawdust restaurants with oyster-shells:
Streets that follow like a tedious argument
Of insidious intent
To lead you to an overwhelming question . . .   10
Oh, do not ask, 'What is it?'
Let us go and make our visit.

In the room the women come and go
Talking of Michelangelo.

The yellow fog that rubs its back upon the window-panes,   15
The yellow smoke that rubs its muzzle on the window-panes,
Licked its tongue into the corners of the evening,

Lingered upon the pools that stand in drains,
Let fall upon its back the soot that falls from chimneys,
Slipped by the terrace, made a sudden leap,   20
And seeing that it was a soft October night,
Curled once about the house, and fell asleep.

And indeed there will be time[2]
For the yellow smoke that slides along the street

---

1. If I thought that my reply would be to one who would ever return to the world, this flame would stay without further movement; but since none has ever returned alive from this depth, if what I hear is true, I answer you without fear of infamy (Italian; Dante's *Inferno* 27.61–66). The speaker, Guido da Montefeltro, consumed in flame as punishment for giving false counsel, confesses his shame without fear of its being reported since he believes Dante cannot return to earth.
2. An echo of Andrew Marvell, "To His Coy Mistress" (1681): "Had we but world enough and time."

Rubbing its back upon the window-panes;   25
There will be time, there will be time
To prepare a face to meet the faces that you meet;
There will be time to murder and create,
And time for all the works and days[3] of hands
That lift and drop a question on your plate;   30
Time for you and time for me,
And time yet for a hundred indecisions,
And for a hundred visions and revisions,
Before the taking of a toast and tea.

In the room the women come and go   35
Talking of Michelangelo.

And indeed there will be time
To wonder, 'Do I dare?' and, 'Do I dare?'
Time to turn back and descend the stair,
With a bald spot in the middle of my hair—   40
(They will say: 'How his hair is growing thin!')
My morning coat, my collar mounting firmly to the chin,
My necktie rich and modest, but asserted by a simple pin—
(They will say: 'But how his arms and legs are thin!')
Do I dare   45
Disturb the universe?
In a minute there is time
For decisions and revisions which a minute will reverse.

For I have known them all already, known them all—
Have known the evenings, mornings, afternoons,   50
I have measured out my life with coffee spoons;
I know the voices dying with a dying fall[4]
Beneath the music from a farther room.
     So how should I presume?

And I have known the eyes already, known them all—   55
The eyes that fix you in a formulated phrase,
And when I am formulated, sprawling on a pin,
When I am pinned and wriggling on the wall,
Then how should I begin
To spit out all the butt-ends of my days and ways?   60
     And how should I presume?
And I have known the arms already, known them all—
Arms that are braceleted and white and bare
(But in the lamplight, downed with light brown hair!)
Is it perfume from a dress   65
That makes me so digress?
Arms that lie along a table, or wrap about a shawl.
     And should I then presume?
     And how should I begin?

     .   .   .   .   .   .

3. *Works and Days* is a didactic poem about farm-   Shakespeare's *Twelfth Night* 1.1.4: "If music be
ing by the Greek poet Hesiod (8th century B.C.E.).   the food of love, play on. . . . That strain again! It
4. Echo of Duke Orsino's invocation of music in   had a dying fall."

Shall I say, I have gone at dusk through narrow streets   70
And watched the smoke that rises from the pipes
Of lonely men in shirt-sleeves, leaning out of windows? . . .

I should have been a pair of ragged claws
Scuttling across the floors of silent seas.
    .   .   .   .   .   .

And the afternoon, the evening, sleeps so peacefully!   75
Smoothed by long fingers,
Asleep . . . tired . . . or it malingers,
Stretched on the floor, here beside you and me.
Should I, after tea and cakes and ices,
Have the strength to force the moment to its crisis?   80
But though I have wept and fasted, wept and prayed,
Though I have seen my head (grown slightly bald) brought in
     upon a platter,[5]
I am no prophet—and here's no great matter;
I have seen the moment of my greatness flicker,
And I have seen the eternal Footman hold my coat, and snicker,   85
And in short, I was afraid.

And would it have been worth it, after all,
After the cups, the marmalade, the tea,
Among the porcelain, among some talk of you and me,
Would it have been worth while,   90
To have bitten off the matter with a smile,
To have squeezed the universe into a ball
To roll it towards some overwhelming question,
To say: 'I am Lazarus,[6] come from the dead,
Come back to tell you all, I shall tell you all'—   95
If one, settling a pillow by her head,
    Should say: 'That is not what I meant at all.
    That is not it, at all.'

And would it have been worth it, after all,
Would it have been worth while,   100
After the sunsets and the dooryards and the sprinkled streets,
After the novels, after the teacups, after the skirts that trail
     along the floor—
And this, and so much more?—
It is impossible to say just what I mean!
But as if a magic lantern threw the nerves in patterns on a screen: 105
Would it have been worth while
If one, settling a pillow or throwing off a shawl,
And turning toward the window, should say:
    'That is not it at all,
    That is not what I meant, at all.'   110
    .   .   .   .   .   .

No! I am not Prince Hamlet, nor was meant to be;
Am an attendant lord, one that will do

---

5. The head of the prophet John the Baptist, who was killed at the behest of Princess Salome, was brought to her on a platter (see Mark 6.17–20, Matthew 14.3–11).

6. The resurrection of Lazarus is recounted in John 11.1–44; see also Luke 16.19–31.

To swell a progress,[7] start a scene or two,
Advise the prince; no doubt, an easy tool,
Deferential, glad to be of use,   115
Politic, cautious, and meticulous;
Full of high sentence,[8] but a bit obtuse;
At times, indeed, almost ridiculous—
Almost, at times, the Fool.

I grow old . . . I grow old . . .   120
I shall wear the bottoms of my trousers rolled.

Shall I part my hair behind? Do I dare to eat a peach?
I shall wear white flannel trousers, and walk upon the beach.
I have heard the mermaids singing, each to each.

I do not think that they will sing to me.   125

I have seen them riding seaward on the waves
Combing the white hair of the waves blown back
When the wind blows the water white and black.

We have lingered in the chambers of the sea
By sea-girls wreathed with seaweed red and brown   130
Till human voices wake us, and we drown.

                                            1915, 1917

The Waste Land[1]

"Nam Sibyllam quidem Cumis ego ipse oculis meis vidi in ampulla pendere, et cum illi pueri dicerent: Σίβυλλα τί θέλεις respondebat illa: ἀποθανεῖν θέλω."[2]

FOR EZRA POUND
IL MIGLIOR FABBRO.[3]

I. The Burial of the Dead[4]

April is the cruellest month, breeding
Lilacs out of the dead land, mixing
Memory and desire, stirring
Dull roots with spring rain.

---

7. A journey or procession made by royal courts and often portrayed on Elizabethan stages.
8. Opinions, sententiousness.
1. Eliot's notes for the first hardcover edition of *The Waste Land* opened with his acknowledgment that "not only the title, but the plan and a good deal of the incidental symbolism of the poem" were suggested by Jessie L. Weston's book on the Grail Legend, *From Ritual to Romance* (1920), and that he was indebted also to James G. Frazer's *The Golden Bough* (1890–1915), "especially the two volumes *Adonis, Attis, Osiris,*" which deal with vegetation myths and fertility rites. Eliot's notes are incorporated in the footnotes to this text. Many critics believe that the

notes were added in a spirit of parody. The numerous and extensive literary quotations add to the multivocal effect of the poem.
2. A quotation from Petronius's *Satyricon* (1st century C.E.) about the Sibyl (prophetess) of Cumae, blessed with eternal life by Apollo but doomed to perpetual old age, who guided Aeneas through Hades in Virgil's *Aeneid*: "For once I myself saw with my own eyes the Sibyl at Cumae hanging in a cage, and when the boys said to her 'Sibyl, what do you want?' she replied, 'I want to die.'"
3. "The better maker," the tribute in Dante's *Purgatorio* 26.117 to the Provençal poet Arnaut Daniel.
4. The title of the Anglican burial service.

Winter kept us warm, covering 5
Earth in forgetful snow, feeding
A little life with dried tubers.
Summer surprised us, coming over the Starnbergersee[5]
With a shower of rain; we stopped in the colonnade,
And went on in sunlight, into the Hofgarten,[6] 10
And drank coffee, and talked for an hour.
Bin gar keine Russin, stamm' aus Litauen, echt deutsch.[7]
And when we were children, staying at the arch-duke's,
My cousin's, he took me out on a sled,
And I was frightened. He said, Marie, 15
Marie, hold on tight. And down we went.
In the mountains, there you feel free.
I read, much of the night, and go south in the winter.

What are the roots that clutch, what branches grow
Out of this stony rubbish? Son of man,[8] 20
You cannot say, or guess, for you know only
A heap of broken images, where the sun beats,
And the dead tree gives no shelter, the cricket no relief,[9]
And the dry stone no sound of water. Only
There is shadow under this red rock,[1] 25
(Come in under the shadow of this red rock),
And I will show you something different from either
Your shadow at morning striding behind you
Or your shadow at evening rising to meet you;
I will show you fear in a handful of dust. 30
        Frisch weht der Wind
        Der Heimat zu
        Mein Irisch Kind,
        Wo weilest du?[2]
'You gave me hyacinths first a year ago; 35
'They called me the hyacinth girl.'
—Yet when we came back, late, from the hyacinth[3] garden,
Your arms full, and your hair wet, I could not
Speak, and my eyes failed, I was neither
Living nor dead, and I knew nothing, 40
Looking into the heart of light, the silence.
Oed' und leer das Meer.[4]

---

5. A lake near Munich. Lines 8–16 were suggested by the Countess Marie Larisch's memoir, *My Past* (1913).

6. A public park in Munich, with cafés; former grounds of a Bavarian palace.

7. I am certainly not Russian; I come from Lithuania, a true German (German).

8. "Cf. Ezekiel II, i" [Eliot's note]. There God addresses the prophet Ezekiel as "Son of man" and declares: "stand upon thy feet, and I will speak unto thee."

9. "Cf. Ecclesiastes XII, v" [Eliot's note]. There the preacher describes the bleakness of old age when "the grasshopper shall be a burden, and desire shall fail."

1. Cf. Isaiah 32.1–2 and the prophecy that the reign of the Messiah "shall be . . . as rivers of water in a dry place, as the shadow of a great rock in a weary land."

2. "V. [see] *Tristan und Isolde*, I, verses 5–8" [Eliot's note]. In Wagner's opera, a sailor aboard Tristan's ship recalls his love back in Ireland: "Fresh blows the wind to the homeland; my Irish child, where are you waiting?"

3. The boy Hyacinth, in Ovid's *Metamorphoses* 10, was beloved by Apollo but slain by a jealous rival. The Greeks celebrated his festival in May.

4. "III, verse 24" [Eliot's note]. In *Tristan*, III, verse 24, the dying Tristan, awaiting the ship that carries his beloved Isolde, is told that "Empty and barren is the sea."

Madame Sosostris,[5] famous clairvoyante,
Had a bad cold, nevertheless
Is known to be the wisest woman in Europe,   45
With a wicked pack of cards.[6] Here, said she,
Is your card, the drowned Phoenician Sailor,[7]
(Those are pearls that were his eyes.[8] Look!)
Here is Belladonna, the Lady of the Rocks,[9]
The lady of situations.   50
Here is the man with three staves, and here the Wheel,
And here is the one-eyed merchant,[1] and this card,
Which is blank, is something he carries on his back,
Which I am forbidden to see. I do not find
The Hanged Man. Fear death by water.   55
I see crowds of people, walking round in a ring.
Thank you. If you see dear Mrs. Equitone,
Tell her I bring the horoscope myself:
One must be so careful these days.

Unreal City,[2]   60
Under the brown fog of a winter dawn,
A crowd flowed over London Bridge, so many,
I had not thought death had undone so many.[3]
Sighs, short and infrequent, were exhaled,[4]
And each man fixed his eyes before his feet.   65
Flowed up the hill and down King William Street,
To where Saint Mary Woolnoth kept the hours
With a dead sound on the final stroke of nine.[5]
There I saw one I knew, and stopped him, crying: 'Stetson!
'You who were with me in the ships at Mylae![6]   70

5. Eliot derived the name from "Sesostris, the Sorceress of Ectabana," the pseudo-Egyptian name assumed by a woman who tells fortunes in Aldous Huxley's novel *Chrome Yellow* (1921). Sesostris was a 12th-dynasty Egyptian king.
6. The tarot deck of cards. Eliot's note to this passage reads: "I am not familiar with the exact constitution of the Tarot pack of cards, from which I have obviously departed to suit my own convenience. The Hanged Man, a member of the traditional pack, fits my purpose in two ways: because he is associated in my mind with the Hanged God of Frazer, and because I associate him with the hooded figure in the passage of the disciples to Emmaus in Part V. The Phoenician Sailor and the Merchant appear later; also the 'crowds of people,' and Death by Water is executed in Part IV. The Man with Three Staves (an authentic member of the Tarot pack) I associate, quite arbitrarily, with the Fisher King himself."
7. A symbolic figure that includes "Mr. Eugenides, the Smyrna merchant" in Part III and "Phlebas the Phoenician" in Part IV. The ancient Phoenicians were seagoing merchants who spread Egyptian fertility cults throughout the Mediterranean.
8. The line is a quotation from Ariel's song in Shakespeare's *Tempest* 1.2.398. Prince Ferdinand, disconsolate because he thinks his father has drowned in the storm, is consoled when Ariel sings of a miraculous sea change that has transformed death into "something rich and strange."

9. Belladonna, literally "beautiful lady," is the name of both the poisonous plant deadly nightshade and a cosmetic.
1. These three figures are from the Tarot deck.
2. "Cf. Baudelaire: 'Fourmillante cité, cité pleine de rêves, / Où le spectre en plein jour raccroche le passant'" [Eliot's note]. The lines are quoted from "Les Sept Vieillards" (The Seven Old Men), poem 93 of *Les Fleurs du Mal* (The Flowers of Evil, 1857) by the French Symbolist Charles Baudelaire (1821–1867), and may be translated from the French: "Swarming city, city full of dreams, / Where the specter in broad daylight accosts the passerby."
3. "Cf. *Inferno* III, 55–57" [Eliot's note]. The note continues to quote Dante's lines, which may be translated: "So long a train of people, / That I should never have believed / That death had undone so many."
4. "Cf. *Inferno* IV, 25–27" [Eliot's note]. Dante describes, in Limbo, the virtuous pagan dead, who, living before Christ, could not hope for salvation. The lines read: "Here, so far as I could tell by listening, / There was no lamentation except sighs, / which caused the eternal air to tremble."
5. "A phenomenon which I have often noticed" [Eliot's note]. The church named is in the financial district of London.
6. The battle of Mylae (260 B.C.E.) was a victory for Rome against Carthage. "Stetson": a hat manufacturer.

'That corpse you planted last year in your garden,
'Has it begun to sprout? Will it bloom this year?
'Or has the sudden frost disturbed its bed?
'O keep the Dog far hence, that's friend to men,
'Or with his nails he'll dig it up again!⁷   75
'You! hypocrite lecteur!—mon semblable,—mon frère!'⁸

II. A Game of Chess⁹

The Chair she sat in, like a burnished throne,¹
Glowed on the marble, where the glass
Held up by standards wrought with fruited vines
From which a golden Cupidon peeped out   80
(Another hid his eyes behind his wing)
Doubled the flames of sevenbranched candelabra
Reflecting light upon the table as
The glitter of her jewels rose to meet it,
From satin cases poured in rich profusion.   85
In vials of ivory and coloured glass
Unstoppered, lurked her strange synthetic perfumes,
Unguent, powdered, or liquid—troubled, confused
And drowned the sense in odours; stirred by the air
That freshened from the window, these ascended   90
In fattening the prolonged candle-flames,
Flung their smoke into the laquearia,²
Stirring the pattern on the coffered ceiling.
Huge sea-wood fed with copper
Burned green and orange, framed by the coloured stone,   95
In which sad light a carvèd dolphin swam.
Above the antique mantel was displayed
As though a window gave upon the sylvan scene³
The change of Philomel, by the barbarous king
So rudely forced; yet there the nightingale   100
Filled all the desert with inviolable voice

---

7. "Cf. the dirge in Webster's *White Devil*" [Eliot's note]. In the play by John Webster (d. 1625), a crazed woman fears that the corpses of her decadent and murdered relatives might be disinterred: "But keep the wolf far thence, that's foe to men, / For with his nails he'll dig them up again." In echoing the lines Eliot altered "foe" to "friend" and the "wolf" to "Dog," invoking the brilliant Dog Star Sirius, whose rise in the heavens accompanied the flooding of the Nile and promised the return of fertility to Egypt.

8. "V. Baudelaire, Preface to *Fleurs du Mal*" [Eliot's note]. The last line of the introductory poem to *Les Fleurs du Mal*. "Au Lecteur" (To the Reader) may be translated from the French: "Hypocrite reader!—my likeness—my brother!

9. The title suggests two plays by Thomas Middleton: *A Game of Chess* (1627), about a marriage of political expediency, and *Women Beware Women* (1657), containing a scene in which a mother-in-law is engrossed in a chess game while her daughter-in-law is seduced nearby. Eliot's note to line 118 refers readers to this play. It is now believed that much of this section reflects Eliot's

disintegrating marriage.

1. "Cf. *Antony and Cleopatra*, II, ii. 190" [Eliot's note]. In Shakespeare's play, Enobarbus's description of Cleopatra begins: "The barge she sat in, like a burnish'd throne, / Burn'd on the water."

2. "Laquearia, V. *Aeneid*, I, 726" [Eliot's note]. Eliot quotes the passage containing the term *laquearia* ("paneled ceiling") and describing the banquet hall where Queen Dido welcomed Aeneas to Carthage. It reads: "Blazing torches hang from the gilded paneled ceiling, and torches conquer the night with flames." Aeneas became Dido's lover but abandoned her to continue his journey to found Rome, and she committed suicide.

3. Eliot's notes for lines 98–99 refer the reader to "Milton, *Paradise Lost*, IV, 140" for the phrase "sylvan scene" and to "Ovid, *Metamorphoses*, VI, Philomela." The lines splice the setting of Eve's temptation in the Garden of Eden, first described through Satan's eyes, with the rape of Philomela by her sister's husband, King Tereus, and her transformation into the nightingale. Eliot's note for line 100 refers the reader ahead to the nightingale's song in Part III, line 204, of his own poem.

And still she cried, and still the world pursues,
'Jug Jug'[4] to dirty ears.
And other withered stumps of time
Were told upon the walls; staring forms   105
Leaned out, leaning, hushing the room enclosed.
Footsteps shuffled on the stair.
Under the firelight, under the brush, her hair
Spread out in fiery points
Glowed into words, then would be savagely still.   110

'My nerves are bad to-night. Yes, bad. Stay with me.
'Speak to me. Why do you never speak. Speak.
       'What are you thinking of? What thinking? What?
'I never know what you are thinking. Think.'

I think we are in rats' alley[5]   115
Where the dead men lost their bones.

'What is that noise?'
                       The wind under the door.[6]
'What is that noise now? What is the wind doing?'
                       Nothing again nothing.   120
                                                      'Do
'You know nothing? Do you see nothing? Do you remember
'Nothing?'

       I remember
Those are pearls that were his eyes.   125
'Are you alive, or not? Is there nothing in your head?'
                                               But
O O O O that Shakespeherian Rag—
It's so elegant
So intelligent   130
'What shall I do now? What shall I do?'
'I shall rush out as I am, and walk the street
'With my hair down, so. What shall we do tomorrow?
'What shall we ever do?'
                       The hot water at ten.   135
And if it rains, a closed car at four.
And we shall play a game of chess,
Pressing lidless eyes and waiting for a knock upon the door.

When Lil's husband got demobbed,[7] I said—
I didn't mince my words, I said to her myself,   140
HURRY UP PLEASE ITS TIME[8]
Now Albert's coming back, make yourself a bit smart.

---

4. The conventional rendering of the nightingale's song in Elizabethan poetry.
5. Eliot's note refers readers to "Part III, l. 195."
6. "Cf. Webster: 'Is the wind in that door still?'" [Eliot's note]. In John Webster's *The Devil's Law Case* (1623) 3.2.162, a duke is cured of an infection by a wound intended to kill him; a surprised surgeon asks the quoted question, meaning, "Is he still alive?"
7. Slang for "demobilized," discharged from the army.
8. Routine call of British bartenders to clear the pub at closing time.

He'll want to know what you done with that money he gave you
To get yourself some teeth. He did, I was there.
You have them all out, Lil, and get a nice set,   145
He said, I swear, I can't bear to look at you.
And no more can't I, I said, and think of poor Albert,
He's been in the army four years, he wants a good time,
And if you don't give it him, there's others will, I said.
Oh is there, she said. Something o' that, I said.   150
Then I'll know who to thank, she said, and give me a straight look.
HURRY UP PLEASE ITS TIME
If you don't like it you can get on with it, I said.
Others can pick and choose if you can't.
But if Albert makes off, it won't be for lack of telling.   155
You ought to be ashamed, I said, to look so antique.
(And her only thirty-one.)
I can't help it, she said, pulling a long face,
It's them pills I took, to bring it off, she said.
(She's had five already, and nearly died of young George.)   160
The chemist[9] said it would be all right, but I've never been the same.
You *are* a proper fool, I said.
Well, if Albert won't leave you alone, there it is, I said,
What you get married for if you don't want children?
HURRY UP PLEASE ITS TIME   165
Well, that Sunday Albert was home, they had a hot gammon,[1]
And they asked me in to dinner, to get the beauty of it hot—
HURRY UP PLEASE ITS TIME
HURRY UP PLEASE ITS TIME
Goonight Bill, Goonight Lou. Goonight May. Goonight.   170
Ta ta. Goonight. Goonight.
Good night, ladies, good night, sweet ladies, good night, good night.[2]

III. The Fire Sermon[3]

The river's tent is broken; the last fingers of leaf
Clutch and sink into the wet bank. The wind
Crosses the brown land, unheard. The nymphs are departed.   175
Sweet Thames, run softly, till I end my song.[4]
The river bears no empty bottles, sandwich papers,
Silk handkerchiefs, cardboard boxes, cigarette ends
Or other testimony of summer nights. The nymphs are departed.
And their friends, the loitering heirs of City directors;   180
Departed, have left no addresses.
By the waters of Leman I sat down and wept[5] . . .
Sweet Thames, run softly till I end my song,

---

9. Pharmacist.
1. Ham or bacon.
2. A double echo of the popular song "Good night ladies, we're going to leave you now" and mad Ophelia's farewell before drowning, in Shakespeare, *Hamlet* 4.5.72.
3. I.e., Buddha's Fire Sermon. See n. 7, p. 2018.
4. "V. Spenser, *Prothalamion*" [Eliot's note]. The line is the refrain of the marriage song by Edmund Spenser (1552–1599), a pastoral celebration of marriage set along the Thames River near

London.
5. The phrasing recalls Psalm 137.1, in which the exiled Jews mourn for their homeland: "By the rivers of Babylon, there we sat down, yea, we wept, when we remembered Zion." Lake Leman is another name for Lake Geneva, location of the sanatorium where Eliot wrote the bulk of *The Waste Land*. The archaic term *leman*, for "illicit mistress," led to the phrase "waters of leman" signifying lusts.

Sweet Thames, run softly, for I speak not loud or long.
But at my back in a cold blast I hear[6]   185
The rattle of the bones, and chuckle spread from ear to ear.

A rat crept softly through the vegetation
Dragging its slimy belly on the bank
While I was fishing in the dull canal
On a winter evening round behind the gashouse   190
Musing upon the king my brother's wreck[7]
And on the king my father's death before him.
White bodies naked on the low damp ground
And bones cast in a little low dry garret,
Rattled by the rat's foot only, year to year.   195
But at my back from time to time I hear
The sound of horns and motors, which shall bring
Sweeney to Mrs. Porter in the spring.[8]
O the moon shone bright on Mrs. Porter
And on her daughter   200
They wash their feet in soda water[9]
Et, O ces voix d'enfants, chantant dans la coupole!;[1]

Twit twit twit
Jug jug jug jug jug jug

So rudely forc'd.   205
Tereu[2]

Unreal City
Under the brown fog of a winter noon
Mr. Eugenides, the Smyrna merchant
Unshaven, with a pocket full of currants   210
C.i.f.[3] London: documents at sight,
Asked me in demotic French
To luncheon at the Cannon Street Hotel
Followed by a weekend at the Metropole.

At the violet hour, when the eyes and back   215
Turn upward from the desk, when the human engine waits

6. This line and line 196 echo Andrew Marvell (1621–1678), *To His Coy Mistress*, lines 21–24: "But at my back I always hear / Time's wingèd chariot hurrying near; / And yonder all before us lie / Deserts of vast eternity."
7. "Cf. *The Tempest*, I, ii" [Eliot's note]. Another allusion to Shakespeare's play, 1.2.389–90, where Prince Ferdinand, thinking his father dead, describes himself as "Sitting on a bank, / Weeping again the King my father's wrack."
8. "Cf. Day, *Parliament of Bees*: 'When of the sudden, listening, you shall hear, / A noise of horns and hunting, which shall bring / Actaeon to Diana in the spring, / Where all shall see her naked skin'" [Eliot's note]. Actaeon was changed into a stag and hunted to death as punishment for seeing Diana, goddess of chastity, bathing. John Day (1574–c. 1640), English poet.
9. "I do not know the origin of the ballad from which these lines are taken: it was reported to me

from Sydney, Australia" [Eliot's note]. The bawdy song was popular among World War I troops.
1. "V. Verlaine, *Parsifal*" [Eliot's note]. The last line of the sonnet "Parsifal" by the French Symbolist Paul Verlaine (1844–1896) reads: "And O those children's voices singing in the cupola." In Wagner's opera, the feet of Parsifal, the questing knight, are washed before he enters the sanctuary of the Grail.
2. Alludes to Tereus, who raped Philomela, and like *jug* is a conventional Elizabethan term for the nightingale's song; also a slang pronunciation of *true*.
3. "The currants were quoted at a price 'carriage and insurance free to London'; and the Bill of Lading, etc. were to be handed to the buyer upon payment of the sight draft" [Eliot's note]. Some have suggested another possibility for the phrase "carriage and insurance free": "cost, insurance and freight."

Like a taxi throbbing waiting,
I Tiresias,[4] though blind, throbbing between two lives,
Old man with wrinkled female breasts, can see
At the violet hour, the evening hour that strives   220
Homeward, and brings the sailor home from sea,[5]
The typist home at teatime, clears her breakfast, lights
Her stove, and lays out food in tins.
Out of the window perilously spread
Her drying combinations touched by the sun's last rays,   225
On the divan are piled (at night her bed)
Stockings, slippers, camisoles, and stays.
I Tiresias, old man with wrinkled dugs
Perceived the scene, and foretold the rest—
I too awaited the expected guest.   230
He, the young man carbuncular, arrives,
A small house agent's clerk, with one bold stare,
One of the low on whom assurance sits
As a silk hat on a Bradford[6] millionaire.
The time is now propitious, as he guesses,   235
The meal is ended, she is bored and tired,
Endeavours to engage her in caresses
Which still are unreproved, if undesired.
Flushed and decided, he assaults at once;
Exploring hands encounter no defence;   240
His vanity requires no response,
And makes a welcome of indifference.
(And I Tiresias have foresuffered all
Enacted on this same divan or bed;
I who have sat by Thebes below the wall[7]   245
And walked among the lowest of the dead.)
Bestows one final patronising kiss,
And gropes his way, finding the stairs unlit . . .

She turns and looks a moment in the glass,
Hardly aware of her departed lover;   250

---

4. Eliot's note reads: "Tiresias, although a mere spectator and not indeed a 'character,' is yet the most important personage in the poem, uniting all the rest. Just as the one-eyed merchant, seller of currants, melts into the Phoenician Sailor, and the latter is not wholly distinct from Ferdinand Prince of Naples, so all the women are one woman, and the two sexes meet in Tiresias. What Tiresias *sees*, in fact, is the substance of the poem. The whole passage from Ovid is of great anthropological interest." The note quotes the Latin passage from Ovid, *Metamorphoses* 2.421–43, which may be translated: "Jove [very drunk] said jokingly to Juno: 'You women have greater pleasure in love than that enjoyed by men.' She denied it. So they decided to refer the question to wise Tiresias who knew love from both points of view. For once, with a blow of his staff, he had separated two huge snakes who were copulating in the forest, and miraculously was changed instantly from a man into a woman and remained so for seven years. In the eighth year he saw the snakes again and said: 'If a blow against you is so powerful that it changes the sex of the author of it, now I shall strike you again.' With these words he struck them, and his former shape and masculinity were restored. As referee in the sportive quarrel, he supported Jove's claim. Juno, overly upset by the decision, condemned the arbitrator to eternal blindness. But the all-powerful father (inasmuch as no god can undo what has been done by another god) gave him the power of prophecy, with this honor compensating him for the loss of sight."
5. "This may not appear as exact as Sappho's lines, but I had in mind the 'longshore' or 'dory' fisherman, who returns at nightfall" [Eliot's note]. Fragment 149, by the female Greek poet Sappho (fl. 600 B.C.E.), celebrates the Evening Star who "brings homeward all those / Scattered by the dawn, / The sheep to fold . . . / The children to their mother's side." A more familiar echo is "Home is the sailor, home from sea" in "Requiem" by Robert Louis Stevenson (1850–1894).
6. A Yorkshire, England, manufacturing town where fortunes were made during World War I.
7. Tiresias prophesied in the marketplace below the wall of Thebes, witnessed the tragedies of Oedipus and Creon in that city, and retained his prophetic powers in the underworld.

Her brain allows one half-formed thought to pass:
'Well now that's done: and I'm glad it's over.'
When lovely woman stoops to folly and
Paces about her room again, alone,
She smoothes her hair with automatic hand,   255
And puts a record on the gramophone.[8]

'This music crept by me upon the waters'[9]
And along the Strand, up Queen Victoria Street.
O City city, I can sometimes hear
Beside a public bar in Lower Thames Street,   260
The pleasant whining of a mandoline
And a clatter and a chatter from within
Where fishmen lounge at noon: where the walls
Of Magnus Martyr[1] hold
Inexplicable splendour of Ionian white and gold.   265

        The river sweats[2]
        Oil and tar
        The barges drift
        With the turning tide
        Red sails   270
        Wide
        To leeward, swing on the heavy spar.
        The barges wash
        Drifting logs
        Down Greenwich reach   275
        Past the Isle of Dogs.[3]
                Weialala leia
                Wallala leialala

        Elizabeth and Leicester[4]
        Beating oars   280
        The stern was formed
        A gilded shell
        Red and gold
        The brisk swell
        Rippled both shores   285

8. Eliot's note refers to the novel *The Vicar of Wakefield* (1766) by Oliver Goldsmith (1728–1774) and the song sung by Olivia when she revisits the scene of her seduction: "When lovely woman stoops to folly / And finds too late that men betray / What charm can soothe her melancholy, / What art can wash her guilt away? / The only art her guilt to cover, / To hide her shame from every eye, / To give repentance to her lover / And wring his bosom—is to die."
9. Eliot's note refers to Shakespeare's *The Tempest*, the scene where Ferdinand listens to Ariel's song telling of his father's miraculous sea change: "This music crept by me on the waters, / Allaying both their fury and my passion / With its sweet air" (1.2.391–93).
1. "The interior of St. Magnus Martyr is to my mind one of the finest among [Christopher] Wren's interiors" [Eliot's note].
2. "The Song of the (three) Thames-daughters begins here. From line 292 to 306 inclusive they speak in turn. V. *Götterdämmerung*, III, i: the Rhine-daughters" [Eliot's note]. Lines 277–78 and 290–91 are from the lament of the Rhine maidens for the lost beauty of the Rhine River in the opera by Richard Wagner (1813–1883), *Götterdämmerung* (The Twilight of the Gods, 1876).
3. A peninsula in the Thames opposite Greenwich, a borough of London and the birthplace of Queen Elizabeth I. Throughout this section Eliot has named places along the Thames River.
4. Reference to the romance between Queen Elizabeth I and the earl of Leicester. Eliot's note refers to the historian James A. Froude, "*Elizabeth*, Vol. I. ch. iv, letter of [bishop] De Quadra [the ambassador] to Philip of Spain: 'In the afternoon we were in a barge, watching the games on the river. (The queen) was alone with Lord Robert and myself on the poop, when they began to talk nonsense, and went so far that Lord Robert at last said, as I was on the spot there was no reason why they should not be married if the queen pleased.'"

Southwest wind
Carried down stream
The peal of bells
White towers
         Weialala leia   290
         Wallala leialala

Trams and dusty trees.
Highbury bore me. Richmond and Kew
Undid me.[5] By Richmond I raised my knees
Supine on the floor of a narrow canoe.'   295
'My feet are at Moorgate, and my heart
Under my feet. After the event
He wept. He promised "a new start."
I made no comment. What should I resent?'

'On Margate Sands,   300
I can connect
Nothing with nothing.
The broken fingernails of dirty hands.
My people humble people who expect
Nothing.'   305
         la la

To Carthage then I came[6]

Burning burning burning burning[7]
O Lord Thou pluckest me out[8]
O Lord Thou pluckest   310

burning

IV. Death by Water

Phlebas the Phoenician, a fortnight dead,
Forgot the cry of gulls, and the deep sea swell
And the profit and loss.
         A current under sea   315
Picked his bones in whispers. As he rose and fell
He passed the stages of his age and youth
Entering the whirlpool.
         Gentile or Jew
O you who turn the wheel and look to windward,   320
Consider Phlebas, who was once handsome and tall as you.

---

5. "Cf. *Purgatorio*, V, 133" [Eliot's note]. Eliot parodies Dante's lines, which may be translated: "Remember me, who am La Pia. / Siena made me, Maremma undid me."
6. "V. St. Augustine's *Confessions*: 'to Carthage then I came, where a cauldron of unholy loves sang all about mine ears'" [Eliot's note]. Augustine here recounts his licentious youth.
7. Eliot's note to lines 307–09 refers to "Buddha's Fire Sermon (which corresponds in importance to the Sermon on the Mount)" and "St. Augustine's *Confessions*." The "collocation of these two representatives of eastern and western asceticism, as the culmination of this part of the poem, is not an accident."
8. The line is from Augustine's *Confessions* and echoes also Zechariah 3.2, where Jehovah, rebuking Satan, calls the high priest Joshua "a brand plucked out of the fire."

V. What the Thunder Said[9]

After the torchlight red on sweaty faces
After the frosty silence in the gardens
After the agony in stony places
The shouting and the crying   325
Prison and palace and reverberation
Of thunder of spring over distant mountains
He who was living is now dead
We who were living are now dying
With a little patience[1]   330

Here is no water but only rock
Rock and no water and the sandy road
The road winding above among the mountains
Which are mountains of rock without water
If there were water we should stop and drink   335
Amongst the rock one cannot stop or think
Sweat is dry and feet are in the sand
If there were only water amongst the rock
Dead mountain mouth of carious teeth that cannot spit
Here one can neither stand nor lie nor sit   340
There is not even silence in the mountains
But dry sterile thunder without rain
There is not even solitude in the mountains
But red sullen faces sneer and snarl
From doors of mudcracked houses   345
                     If there were water

And no rock
If there were rock
And also water
And water   350
A spring
A pool among the rock
If there were the sound of water only
Not the cicada[2]
And dry grass singing   355
But sound of water over a rock
Where the hermit-thrush[3] sings in the pine trees
Drip drop drip drop drop drop drop
But there is no water

---

9. "In the first part of Part V three themes are employed: the journey to Emmaus, the approach to the Chapel Perilous (see Miss Weston's book) and the present decay of eastern Europe" [Eliot's note]. During his disciples' journey to Emmaus, after his Crucifixion and Resurrection, Jesus walked alongside and conversed with them, but they did not recognize him (Luke 24.13–34).
1. The opening nine lines allude to Christ's imprisonment and trial, to his agony in the garden of Gethsemane, and to his Crucifixion on Golgotha (Calvary) and burial.
2. Grasshopper. Cf. line 23 and see n. 9, p. 2010.
3. "This is . . . the hermit-thrush which I have heard in Quebec Province. Chapman says (*Handbook of Birds of Eastern North America*) 'it is most at home in secluded woodland and thickety retreats.' . . . Its 'water dripping song' is justly celebrated" [Eliot's note].

Who is the third who walks always beside you?[4]   360
When I count, there are only you and I together
But when I look ahead up the white road
There is always another one walking beside you
Gliding wrapt in a brown mantle, hooded
I do not know whether a man or a woman   365
—But who is that on the other side of you?

What is that sound high in the air[5]
Murmur of maternal lamentation
Who are those hooded hordes swarming
Over endless plains, stumbling in cracked earth   370
Ringed by the flat horizon only
What is the city over the mountains
Cracks and reforms and bursts in the violet air
Falling towers
Jerusalem Athens Alexandria   375
Vienna London
Unreal

A woman drew her long black hair out tight
And fiddled whisper music on those strings
And bats with baby faces in the violet light   380
Whistled, and beat their wings
And crawled head downward down a blackened wall
And upside down in air were towers
Tolling reminiscent bells, that kept the hours
And voices singing out of empty cisterns and exhausted wells.   385

In this decayed hole among the mountains
In the faint moonlight, the grass is singing
Over the tumbled graves, about the chapel
There is the empty chapel, only the wind's home.
It has no windows, and the door swings,   390
Dry bones can harm no one.
Only a cock stood on the rooftree
Co co rico co co rico[6]
In a flash of lightning. Then a damp gust
Bringing rain   395

Ganga[7] was sunken, and the limp leaves
Waited for rain, while the black clouds
Gathered far distant, over Himavant.[8]
The jungle crouched, humped in silence.

---

4. "The following lines were stimulated by the account of one of the Antarctic expeditions (I forget which, but I think one of Shackleton's): it was related that the party of explorers, at the extremity of their strength, had the constant delusion that there was *one more member* than could actually be counted" [Eliot's note].

5. Eliot's note quotes a passage in German from *Blick ins Chaos* (1920) by Hermann Hesse (1877–1962), which may be translated: "Already half of Europe, already at least half of Eastern Europe, on the way to Chaos, drives drunk in sacred infatuation along the edge of the precipice, since drunkenly, as though hymn-singing, as Dimitri Karamazov sang in [the novel] *The Brothers Karamazov* [1882] by Feodor Dostoevsky [1821–1881]. The offended bourgeois laughs at the songs; the saint and the seer hear them with tears."

6. A cock's crow in folklore signaled the departure of ghosts (as in Shakespeare's *Hamlet* 1.1.157ff.); in Matthew 26.34 and 74, a cock crowed, as Christ predicted, when Peter denied him three times.

7. The Indian river Ganges.

8. A mountain in the Himalayas.

Then spoke the thunder 400
Da[9]
Datta: what have we given?
My friend, blood shaking my heart
The awful daring of a moment's surrender
Which an age of prudence can never retract 405
By this, and this only, we have existed
Which is not to be found in our obituaries
Or in memories draped by the beneficent spider[1]
Or under seals broken by the lean solicitor
In our empty rooms 410
Da
Dayadhvam: I have heard the key[2]
Turn in the door once and turn once only
We think of the key, each in his prison
Thinking of the key, each confirms a prison 415
Only at nightfall, aethereal rumours
Revive for a moment a broken Coriolanus[3]
Da
Damyata: The boat responded
Gaily, to the hand expert with sail and oar 420
The sea was calm, your heart would have responded
Gaily, when invited, beating obedient
To controlling hands

                  I sat upon the shore
Fishing,[4] with the arid plain behind me
Shall I at least set my lands in order?[5] 425
London Bridge is falling down falling down falling down
Poi s'ascose nel foco che gli affina[6]
Quando fiam uti chelidon[7]—O swallow swallow
Le Prince d'Aquitaine à la tour abolie[8] 430

9. "'Datta, dayadhvam, damyata' (Give, sympathise, control). The fable of the meaning of the Thunder is found in the *Brihadaranyaka—Upanishad*, 5, 1" [Eliot's note]. In the Hindu legend, the injunction of Prajapati (supreme deity) is *Da*, which is interpreted in three different ways by gods, men, and demons, to mean "control ourselves," "give alms," and "have compassion." Prajapati assures them that when "the divine voice, The Thunder," repeats the syllable it means all three things and that therefore "one should practice . . . Self-Control, Alms-giving, and Compassion."
1. Eliot's note refers to Webster's *The White Devil* 5.6: "they'll remarry / Ere the worm pierce your winding-sheet, ere the spider / Make a thin curtain for your epitaphs."
2. "Cf. *Inferno*, XXXIII, 46" [Eliot's note]. At this point Ugolino recalls his imprisonment with his children, where they starved to death: "And I heard below the door of the horrible tower being locked up." Eliot's note continues: "Also F. H. Bradley, *Appearance and Reality*, p.346. 'My external sensations are no less private to myself than are my thoughts or my feelings. In either case my experience falls within my own circle, a circle closed on the outside; and, with all its elements alike, every sphere is opaque to the others which surround it. . . . In brief, regarded as an existence which appears in a soul, the whole world for each is peculiar and private to that soul.'"

3. Roman patrician who defiantly chose self-exile when threatened with banishment by the leaders of the populace. He is the tragic protagonist in Shakespeare's *Coriolanus* (1608).
4. "V. Weston: *From Ritual to Romance;* chapter on the Fisher King" [Eliot's note].
5. Cf. Isaiah 38.1: "Thus saith the Lord, Set thine house in order: for thou shalt die, and not live."
6. Eliot's note to *Purgatorio* 26 quotes in Italian the passage (lines 145–48) where the Provençal poet Arnaut Daniel, recalling his lusts, addresses Dante: "I pray you now, by the Goodness that guides you to the summit of this staircase, reflect in due season on my suffering." Then, in the line quoted in *The Waste Land,* "he hid himself in the fire that refines them."
7. Eliot's note refers to the *Pervigilium Veneris* (The Vigil of Venus), an anonymous Latin poem, and suggests a comparison with "Philomela in Parts II and III" of *The Waste Land*. The last stanzas of the *Pervigilium* recreate the myth of the nightingale in the image of a swallow, and the poet listening to the bird speaks the quoted line, "When shall I be as the swallow," and adds: "that I may cease to be silent." "O Swallow, Swallow" are the opening words of one of the songs interspersed in Tennyson's narrative poem *The Princess* (1847).
8. "V. Gerard de Nerval, Sonnet *El Desdichado*" [Eliot's note]. The line reads: "The Prince of Aquitaine in the ruined tower."

These fragments I have shored against my ruins
Why then Ile fit you. Hieronymo's mad againe.[9]
Datta. Dayadhvam. Damyata.
      Shantih   shantih   shantih[1]

1921   1922

The Hollow Men

Mistah Kurtz—he dead.[1]
        A penny for the Old Guy[2]

I

We are the hollow men
We are the stuffed men
Leaning together
Headpiece filled with straw. Alas!
Our dried voices, when   5
We whisper together
Are quiet and meaningless
As wind in dry grass
Or rats' feet over broken glass
In our dry cellar   10

Shape without form, shade without colour,
Paralysed force, gesture without motion;

Those who have crossed
With direct eyes, to death's other Kingdom
Remember us—if at all—not as lost   15
Violent souls, but only
As the hollow men
The stuffed men.

II

Eyes I dare not meet in dreams
In death's dream kingdom   20
These do not appear:
There, the eyes are

---

9. Eliot's note refers to Thomas Kyd's revenge play, *The Spanish Tragedy*, subtitled *Hieronymo's Mad Againe* (1594). In it Hieronymo is asked to write a court play and he answers, "I'll fit you," in the double sense of "oblige" and "get even." He manages, although mad, to kill the murderers of his son by acting in the play and assigning parts appropriately, then commits suicide.
1. "Shantih. Repeated as here, a formal ending to an Upanishad. 'The peace which passeth understanding' is our equivalent to this word" [Eliot's note]. The Upanishad is a Vedic treatise, a sacred Hindu text.
1. Quotation from *Heart of Darkness,* by Joseph Conrad (1857–1924). Kurtz went into the African jungle as an official of a trading company and degenerated into an evil, tyrannical man. His dying words were "the horror!"
2. Guy Fawkes led a group of conspirators who planned to blow up the English House of Commons in 1605; he was caught and executed before the plan was carried out. On the day of his execution (November 5) children make straw effigies of the "guy" and beg for pennies for fireworks.

Sunlight on a broken column
There, is a tree swinging
And voices are   25
In the wind's singing
More distant and more solemn
Than a fading star.

Let me be no nearer
In death's dream kingdom   30
Let me also wear
Such deliberate disguises
Rat's coat, crowskin, crossed staves
In a field
Behaving as the wind behaves   35
No nearer—

Not that final meeting
In the twilight kingdom

III

This is the dead land
This is cactus land   40
Here the stone images
Are raised, here they receive
The supplication of a dead man's hand
Under the twinkle of a fading star.

Is it like this   45
In death's other kingdom
Waking alone
At the hour when we are
Trembling with tenderness
Lips that would kiss   50
Form prayers to broken stone.

IV

The eyes are not here
There are no eyes here
In this valley of dying stars
In this hollow valley   55
This broken jaw of our lost kingdoms

In this last of meeting places
We grope together
And avoid speech
Gathered on this beach of the tumid river   60

Sightless, unless
The eyes reappear
As the perpetual star

Multifoliate rose[3]
Of death's twilight kingdom   65
The hope only
Of empty men.

V

Here we go round the prickly pear
Prickly pear prickly pear
Here we go round the prickly pear   70
At five o'clock in the morning.[4]

Between the idea
And the reality
Between the motion
And the act   75
Falls the Shadow

                           For Thine is the Kingdom[5]

Between the conception
And the creation
Between the emotion   80
And the response
Falls the Shadow

                                        Life is very long

Between the desire
And the spasm   85
Between the potency
And the existence
Between the essence
And the descent
Falls the Shadow   90

                           For Thine is the Kingdom

For Thine is
Life is
For Thine is the

This is the way the world ends   95
This is the way the world ends
This is the way the world ends
Not with a bang but a whimper.

                                                    1925

3. Part 3 of *The Divine Comedy*, by Dante Alighieri (1265–1321), is a vision of Paradise. The souls of the saved in heaven range themselves around the deity in the figure of a "multifoliate rose" (*Paradiso* 28.30).

4. Allusion to a children's rhyming game, "Here we go round the mulberry bush," substituting a prickly pear cactus for the mulberry bush.
5. Part of a line from the Lord's Prayer.

Journey of the Magi[1]

'A cold coming we had of it,
Just the worst time of the year
For a journey, and such a long journey:
The ways deep and the weather sharp,
The very dead of winter.'[2]   5
And the camels galled, sore-footed, refractory,
Lying down in the melting snow.
There were times we regretted
The summer palaces on slopes, the terraces,
And the silken girls bringing sherbet.   10
Then the camel men cursing and grumbling
And running away, and wanting their liquor and women,
And the night-fires going out, and the lack of shelters,
And the cities hostile and the towns unfriendly
And the villages dirty and charging high prices: 15
A hard time we had of it.
At the end we preferred to travel all night,
Sleeping in snatches,
With the voices singing in our ears, saying
That this was all folly.   20

Then at dawn we came down to a temperate valley,
Wet, below the snow line, smelling of vegetation,
With a running stream and a water-mill beating the darkness,
And three trees on the low sky.
And an old white horse galloped away in the meadow.   25
Then we came to a tavern with vine-leaves over the lintel,
Six hands at an open door dicing for pieces of silver,
And feet kicking the empty wine-skins.
But there was no information, and so we continued
And arrived at evening, not a moment too soon   30
Finding the place; it was (you may say) satisfactory.

All this was a long time ago, I remember,
And I would do it again, but set down
This set down
This: were we led all that way for   35
Birth or Death? There was a Birth, certainly,
We had evidence and no doubt. I had seen birth and death,
But had thought they were different; this Birth was
Hard and bitter agony for us, like Death, our death.
We returned to our places, these Kingdoms,   40
But no longer at ease here, in the old dispensation,
With an alien people clutching their gods.
I should be glad of another death.

                                                             1935

---

1. The three wise men, or kings, who followed the star of Bethlehem, bringing gifts to the newly born Christ.

2. These lines are adapted from the sermon preached at Christmas, in 1622, by Bishop Lancelot Andrewes.

FROM FOUR QUARTETS

Burnt Norton[1]

τὸυ λόγον δ'εόντος ξυνοῦ ζώουσιν οἱ πολλοί
ὡς ἰδίαν ἔχοντες φρόνησιν.
                    I. p.77. Fr. 2.
ὁδὸς ἄνω κάτω μία καί ὠυτή.
                    I. p.89. Fr. 60.[2]
—Diels: *Die Fragmente der Vorsokratiker*
                    (Herakleitos)

I[3]

Time present and time past
Are both perhaps present in time future,
And time future contained in time past.
If all time is eternally present
All time is unredeemable.   5
What might have been is an abstraction
Remaining a perpetual possibility
Only in a world of speculation.
What might have been and what has been
Point to one end, which is always present.   10
Footfalls echo in the memory
Down the passage which we did not take
Towards the door we never opened
Into the rose-garden.[4] My words echo
Thus, in your mind.   15
                    But to what purpose
Disturbing the dust on a bowl of rose-leaves
I do not know.
                    Other echoes
Inhabit the garden. Shall we follow?   20
Quick, said the bird, find them, find them,
Round the corner. Through the first gate,
Into our first world, shall we follow
The deception of the thrush? Into our first world.
There they were, dignified, invisible,   25

---

1. Eliot made "Burnt Norton," published originally as a separate poem, the basis and formal
model for "East Coker" (1940), "The Dry Salvages"
(1941), and "Little Gidding" (1942). Together they
make up *Four Quartets* (1943). The *Quartets* seeks
to capture those rare moments when eternity
"intersects" the temporal continuum, while treating also the relations between those moments and
the flux of time. Central to "Burnt Norton" is the
idea of the Spanish mystic St. John of the Cross
(1542–1591) that the ascent of a soul to union
with God is facilitated by memory and disciplined
meditation but that meditation is superseded by a
"dark night of the soul" that deepens paradoxically
the nearer one approaches the light of God. Burnt
Norton is a manor house in Gloucestershire,
England.
2. The Greek epigraphs are from the pre-Socratic
philosopher Heraclitus (540?–475 B.C.E.) and may
be translated: "But although the Word is common
to all, the majority of people live as though they
had each an understanding peculiarly his own"
and "The way up and the way down are one and
the same."
3. The opening lines echo Ecclesiastes 3.15:
"That which hath been is now; and that which is
to be hath already been."
4. The rose is a symbol of sexual and spiritual
love; in Christian traditions it is associated with
the harmony of religious truth and with the Virgin Mary. The memory may be personal as well.

Moving without pressure, over the dead leaves,
In the autumn heat, through the vibrant air,
And the bird called, in response to
The unheard music hidden in the shrubbery,
And the unseen eyebeam crossed, for the roses   30
Had the look of flowers that are looked at.
There they were as our guests, accepted and accepting.
So we moved, and they, in a formal pattern,
Along the empty alley, into the box circle,[5]
To look down into the drained pool.   35
Dry the pool, dry concrete, brown edged,
And the pool was filled with water out of sunlight,
And the lotos rose, quietly, quietly,
The surface glittered out of heart of light,[6]
And they were behind us, reflected in the pool.   40
Then a cloud passed, and the pool was empty.
Go, said the bird, for the leaves were full of children,
Hidden excitedly, containing laughter.
Go, go, go, said the bird: human kind
Cannot bear very much reality.   45
Time past and time future
What might have been and what has been.
Point to one end, which is always present.

                              II

Garlic and sapphires in the mud
Clot the bedded axle-tree.   50
The trilling wire in the blood
Sings below inveterate scars
Appeasing long forgotten wars.
The dance along the artery
The circulation of the lymph   55
Are figured in the drift of stars
Ascend to summer in the tree
We move above the moving tree
In light upon the figured leaf[7]
And hear upon the sodden floor   60
Below, the boarhound and the boar
Pursue their pattern as before
But reconciled among the stars.

At the still point of the turning world. Neither flesh nor fleshless;
Neither from nor towards; at the still point, there the dance is,   65
But neither arrest nor movement. And do not call it fixity,
Where past and future are gathered. Neither movement from
      nor towards,
Neither ascent nor decline. Except for the point, the still point,

---

5. Evergreen boxwood shrubs, planted in a circle.
6. An echo of Dante, *Paradiso* 12.28–29: "From out of the heart of one of the new lights there moved a voice."

7. An echo of the description of death in Tennyson, *In Memoriam* (1850) 43.10–12: "So that still garden of the souls / In many a figured leaf enrolls / The total world since life began."

There would be no dance and there is only the dance.
I can only say, *there* we have been: but I cannot say where.   70
And I cannot say, how long, for that is to place it in time.
The inner freedom from the practical desire,
The release from action and suffering, release from the inner
And the outer compulsion, yet surrounded
By a grace of sense, a white light still and moving,   75
Erhebung[8] without motion, concentration
Without elimination, both a new world
And the old made explicit, understood
In the completion of its partial ecstasy,
The resolution of its partial horror.   80
Yet the enchainment of past and future
Woven in the weakness of the changing body,
Protects mankind from heaven and damnation
Which flesh cannot endure.
                    Time past and time future   85
Allow but a little consciousness.
To be conscious is not to be in time
But only in time can the moment in the rose-garden,
The moment in the arbour where the rain beat,
The moment in the draughty church at smokefall   90
Be remembered; involved with past and future.
Only through time time is conquered.

III

Here is a place of disaffection
Time before and time after
In a dim light: neither daylight   95
Investing form with lucid stillness
Turning shadow into transient beauty
With slow rotation suggesting permanence
Nor darkness to purify the soul
Emptying the sensual with deprivation   100
Cleansing affection from the temporal.
Neither plenitude nor vacancy. Only a flicker
Over the strained time-ridden faces
Distracted from distraction by distraction
Filled with fancies and empty of meaning   105
Tumid apathy with no concentration
Men and bits of paper, whirled by the cold wind
That blows before and after time,
Wind in and out of unwholesome lungs
Time before and time after.   110
Eructation of unhealthy souls
Into the faded air, the torpid
Driven on the wind that sweeps the gloomy hills of London,
Hampstead and Clerkenwell, Campden and Putney,
Highgate, Primrose and Ludgate.[9] Not here   115
Not here the darkness, in this twittering world.

---

8. Exaltation (German).   9. Districts and neighborhoods in London.

Descend lower, descend only
Into the world of perpetual solitude,
World not world, but that which is not world,
Internal darkness, deprivation   120
And destitution of all property,
Desiccation of the world of sense,
Evacuation of the world of fancy,
Inoperancy of the world of spirit;
This is the one way, and the other   125
Is the same, not in movement
But abstention from movement; while the world moves
In appetency, on its metalled ways
Of time past and time future.

IV

Time and the bell have buried the day,   130
The black cloud carries the sun away.
Will the sunflower turn to us, will the clematis
Stray down, bend to us; tendril and spray
Clutch and cling?
Chill   135
Fingers of yew be curled
Down on us? After the kingfisher's wing
Has answered light to light, and is silent, the light is still
At the still point of the turning world.

V

Words move, music moves   140
Only in time; but that which is only living
Can only die. Words, after speech, reach
Into the silence. Only by the form, the pattern,
Can words or music reach
The stillness, as a Chinese jar still   145
Moves perpetually in its stillness.
Not the stillness of the violin, while the note lasts,
Not that only, but the co-existence,
Or say that the end precedes the beginning,
And the end and the beginning were always there   150
Before the beginning and after the end.
And all is always now. Words strain,
Crack and sometimes break, under the burden,
Under the tension, slip, slide, perish,
Decay with imprecision, will not stay in place,   155
Will not stay still. Shrieking voices
Scolding, mocking, or merely chattering,
Always assail them. The Word in the desert[1]
Is most attacked by voices of temptation,
The crying shadow in the funeral dance,   160

---

1. An allusion to Christ's temptation in the wilderness (Luke 4.1–4).

The loud lament of the disconsolate chimera.[2]
The detail of the pattern is movement,
As in the figure of the ten stairs.[3]
Desire itself is movement
Not in itself desirable;   165
Love is itself unmoving,
Only the cause and end of movement,
Timeless, and undesiring
Except in the aspect of time
Caught in the form of limitation   170
Between un-being and being.
Sudden in a shaft of sunlight
Even while the dust moves
There rises the hidden laughter
Of children in the foliage   175
Quick, now, here, now always—
Ridiculous the waste sad time
Stretching before and after.

                                                                      1936, 1943

2. A monster in Greek mythology and a symbol
of fantasies and delusions.
3. An allusion to St. John of the Cross's figure

for the soul's ascent to God: "The Ten Degrees of
the Mystical Ladder of Divine Love."

EUGENE O'NEILL
1888–1953

Eugene O'Neill, the nation's first major playwright, was born in a New York City hotel on Broadway on October 16, 1888. His father was James O'Neill, an actor who abandoned his early success in Shakespearean roles to make a fortune playing the lead role in a dramatization of Alexander Dumas's swashbuckling novel *The Count of Monte Cristo* (1844–45), which he performed on tour more than five thousand times. O'Neill's mother, Ella Quinlan, the daughter of a successful Irish immigrant businessman in Cincinnati, hated backstage life and became addicted to morphine. An older brother, James Jr., had been born in 1878 and during most of Eugene's childhood was away at various boarding schools. Later "Jamie," Eugene's idol, became an actor and an alcoholic.

During O'Neill's childhood, his parents toured for part of every year, lived in New York City hotels for another part, and spent summers at their home in New London, Connecticut. O'Neill went to good preparatory schools and started college at Princeton in 1906. Suspended after his freshman year for missing classes and exams, O'Neill found work in New York City, where he met Kathleen Jenkins; when she became pregnant, the two eloped. With his father's help, he shipped out to sea and went searching for gold in South America, leaving his wife behind; it would be eleven years before he met their son, Eugene Jr., born in 1910. O'Neill drank and drifted, alternating sea voyages with sojourns in Greenwich Village, an area of lower Manhattan that was becoming home to artists and political radicals. After nearly dying of tuberculosis in 1912, O'Neill decided to curtail his drinking and write plays. In 1914 his father subsidized the publication of *Thirst*, a collection of five one-act plays; fortified by this accomplishment, O'Neill applied and was accepted as a special student at Harvard in the playwriting class of Professor George Pierce Baker—the first such class offered at an American university. O'Neill's real entry into the contemporary theater, though, came through his Greenwich Village friends: he joined a new experimental theater group called the Provincetown Players—in the summer its members staged plays on a wharf in Provincetown, Massachusetts. For the rest of the year they used a small theater in the Village. They produced O'Neill's one-act play *Bound East for Cardiff* in the summer of 1916.

The Provincetown group gave O'Neill his forum, and—working closely with playwright Susan Glaspell—he gave them a place in American theater history. Play followed play in these early years: five of his plays were staged in 1917, and he wrote another six in 1918. The works with likely appeal for general audiences were moved uptown from the Village to Broadway, making O'Neill both famous and financially successful. Many of these early plays, with crude and slangy dialogue that departed strikingly from the stage rhetoric of the day, were grim one-acts based on his experiences at sea. Instead of the elegant witticisms of drawing-room comedy or the flowery eloquence of historical drama, audiences were faced with ships' holds and sailors' bars. An exaggerated realism, veering toward expressionism, was the mode of these earliest works.

Around 1920, O'Neill's plays became longer and less realistic, and his aims more ambitious. He began to experiment with techniques to convey inner emotions not expressible in dramatic action—the world of the mind, of memories and fears. He ignored standard play divisions of scenes and acts; made his characters wear masks; split one character between two actors; and reintroduced ghosts, choruses, and Shakespearean-style monologues and direct addresses to the audience. The political radicalism of his Greenwich Village circles was reflected in the themes of many of these plays, although O'Neill would always be more drawn to the deep-lived emotions of social conflicts than to organized political movements aimed at resolving them. In *The Emperor Jones* (1920), a former Pullman porter uses the lessons of Wall Street ("Dere's little stealin' like you does, and dere's big stealin' like I does") to oppress the inhabitants of a Caribbean island; their revolt sends Jones into flight, pursued by the ghosts of New World slavery. In *The Hairy Ape* (1922), a sailor, becoming aware of how he is viewed by the upper class, degenerates into what he is perceived to be. *Desire under the Elms* (1924) links family conflict to lust after property and control as well as to erotic desire; *The Great God Brown* (1926) drew on O'Neill's full array of experimental techniques to expose the inner life of a business magnate. Centered on the turbulent emotional life of a beautiful woman, *Strange Interlude* (1928), despite its audacious nine-act length, won the Pulitzer Prize, was made into a Hollywood film, and became O'Neill's greatest commercial success.

O'Neill's father had died in 1920, his mother in 1921, his brother in 1923. During the mid-1920s, O'Neill became interested in dramatizing the complicated pattern of his family's life. He was influenced by the popularization of Sigmund Freud's ideas: the power of irrational drives; the existence of a subconscious; the roles of repression and inhibition in the formation of personality and in adult suffering; the importance of sex; and above all the lifelong influence of parents. With Freud, he saw the family as a locus of intense and irresolvable conflicting feelings: as Edmund observes of his mother in *Long Day's Journey into Night*, "it's as if, in spite of loving us, she hated us." But where Freud's famous case histories explore the conflicts of an individual, O'Neill's dramatic method came to focus on the family, rather than the person, as the fundamental human unit. He found inspiration and confirmation for this approach in classical Greek drama, which had always centered on families. His 1931 *Mourning Becomes Electra*, based on the *Oresteia* cycle of the classical Greek playwright Aeschylus, situated the ancient story of family murder and divine retribution in Civil War America with great success.

Twice married after the annulment of his early elopement, O'Neill began to suffer from a series of health problems in the 1930s, was diagnosed with Parkinson's Disease in 1941, and lived in relative seclusion for the last twenty years of his life. Following the production of *Mourning Becomes Electra* in 1931, his output slowed. Much of his work from the 1930s and 1940s remained in manuscript until after his death, and there was a twelve-year gap in the staging of his plays between *Days without End* (1934), which failed on Broadway, and *The Iceman Cometh*, in 1946, which also did poorly. During this interval O'Neill set out and revised increasingly ambitious plans for cycles of plays that would encompass American history through the stories of several families. Recalling the conflicting immigrant experiences of his own parents—the prosperous assimilation of his mother's family contrasted with his Irish-born father's famine-driven economic insecurity and greed—sharpened O'Neill's sense of American history as a family drama of possession and dispossession.

Three years after O'Neill's death, *Iceman* was successfully revived, and O'Neill's work reattained prominence. His widow, the former actress Carlotta Monterey whom O'Neill had married in 1929, released other plays, which were widely acclaimed in posthumous productions. Among such stagings were parts of a projected nine- or eleven-play sequence (critics differ in the interpretation of the surviving manuscript material) about an Irish family in America named the Melody family and some obviously autobiographical dramas about a family named the Tyrones. The Melody plays produced after O'Neill's death include *A Touch of the Poet*, produced in 1957, and *More Stately Mansions*, which was staged in 1967; the Tyrone plays include *Long Day's Journey into Night*, produced in 1956, and *A Moon for the Misbegotten*, produced in 1957.

In inscribing the manuscript of *Long Day's Journey* to Carlotta, O'Neill wrote that he had faced his dead in this play, writing "with deep pity and understanding and forgiveness for *all* the four haunted Tyrones." His treatment made it impossible to blame any of the characters for the suffering they inflicted on the others; each Tyrone was both a victim and an oppressor. The Tyrones are at the mercy of the past, and the word *ghosts* recurs throughout the play: ghosts of those they remember, those who influenced them, their younger selves, their dreams and ambitions, and their disappointments. O'Neill handled the emotionalism of his theme with rigorous dramatic formalism, designing the play as a series of encounters—each character is placed with one, two, or three of the others, until every combination is worked through. *Long Day's Journey* observes the classical dramatic unities of time and space, following the family's various configurations through one day, from the pretense of conventional family life in the morning to the tragic truth of their night. The audience thus witnesses a literal day in the lives of the Tyrones, as well as the journey through life toward death.

Romantic, realistic, naturalistic, melodramatic, sentimental, cynical, poetic— O'Neill's work in general is all of these. Even while he made his characters espouse philosophical positions, O'Neill was not trying to write philosophical drama. He wanted to make plays conveying emotions of such intensity and complexity that the theater would become a vital force in American life. In all his works, the spectacle of emotional intensity was meant to produce emotional response in an audience—what Aristotle, in his *Poetics*, had called "catharsis." O'Neill's plays have been translated and staged all over the world; he won the Pulitzer Prize four times and the Nobel Prize in 1936, the first and so far only American dramatist to do so.

The text is that of the Yale University Press Edition (1956).

Long Day's Journey into Night

CHARACTERS

JAMES TYRONE
MARY CAVAN TYRONE, *his wife*
JAMES TYRONE, JR., *their elder son*
EDMUND TYRONE, *their younger son*
CATHLEEN, *second girl*[1]

SCENES

ACT 1 *Living room of the Tyrones' summer home 8:30 A.M. of a day in August, 1912*

ACT 2 SCENE 1 *The same, around 12:45*
SCENE 2 *The same, about a half hour later*

ACT 3 *The same, around 6:30 that evening*

ACT 4 *The same, around midnight*

Act 1

SCENE—*Living room of* JAMES TYRONE'S *summer home on a morning in August, 1912.*

At rear are two double doorways with portieres. The one at right leads into a front parlor with the formally arranged, set appearance of a room rarely occupied. The other opens on a dark, windowless back parlor, never used except as a passage from living room to dining room. Against the wall between the doorways is a small bookcase, with a picture of Shakespeare above it, containing novels by Balzac, Zola, Stendhal, philosophical and sociological works by Schopenhauer, Nietzsche, Marx, Engels, Kropotkin, Max Sterner, plays by Ibsen, Shaw, Strindberg, poetry by Swinburne, Rossetti, Wilde, Ernest Dowson, Kipling, etc.[2]

In the right wall, rear, is a screen door leading out on the porch which extends halfway around the house. Farther forward, a series of three windows looks over the front lawn to the harbor and the avenue that runs along the water front. A small wicker table and an ordinary oak desk are against the wall, flanking the windows.

In the left wall, a similar series of windows looks out on the grounds in back of the house. Beneath them is a wicker couch with cushions, its head toward rear. Farther back is a large, glassed-in bookcase with sets of Dumas, Victor Hugo, Charles Lever, three sets of Shakespeare, The World's Best Literature in fifty large volumes, Hume's History of England, Thiers' History of the Consulate and Empire, Smollett's History of England, Gibbon's Roman Empire and miscellaneous volumes of old plays, poetry, and several histories of Ireland. The astonishing thing about these sets is that all the volumes have the look of having been read and reread.

The hardwood floor is nearly covered by a rug, inoffensive in design and color. At center is a round table with a green shaded reading lamp, the cord plugged in one of the four sockets in the chandelier above. Around the table

---

1. A servant.
2. A variety of 19th-century (especially late 19th-century) authors are cited. Nobody in the audience would be able to read the titles and authors on these books—an example of O'Neill's novelistic approach to theatrical detail, also seen in the minute physical descriptions he provides of the characters' appearance and behavior throughout.

within reading-light range are four chairs, three of them wicker armchairs, the fourth (at right front of table) a varnished oak rocker with leather bottom.

It is around 8:30. Sunshine comes through the windows at right.

As the curtain rises, the family have just finished breakfast. MARY TYRONE *and her husband enter together from the back parlor, coming from the dining room.*

MARY *is fifty-four, about medium height. She still has a young, graceful figure, a trifle plump, but showing little evidence of middle-aged waist and hips, although she is not tightly corseted. Her face is distinctly Irish in type. It must once have been extremely pretty, and is still striking. It does not match her healthy figure but is thin and pale with the bone structure prominent. Her nose is long and straight, her mouth wide with full, sensitive lips. She uses no rouge or any sort of make-up. Her high forehead is framed by thick, pure white hair. Accentuated by her pallor and white hair, her dark brown eyes appear black. They are unusually large and beautiful, with black brows and long curling lashes.*

What strikes one immediately is her extreme nervousness. Her hands are never still. They were once beautiful hands, with long, tapering fingers, but rheumatism has knotted the joints and warped the fingers, so that now they have an ugly crippled look. One avoids looking at them, the more so because one is conscious she is sensitive about their appearance and humiliated by her inability to control the nervousness which draws attention to them.

She is dressed simply but with a sure sense of what becomes her. Her hair is arranged with fastidious care. Her voice is soft and attractive. When she is merry, there is a touch of Irish lilt in it.

Her most appealing quality is the simple, unaffected charm of a shy convent-girl youthfulness she has never lost—an innate unworldly innocence.

JAMES TYRONE *is sixty-five but looks ten years younger. About five feet eight, broad-shouldered and deep-chested, he seems taller and slenderer because of his bearing, which has a soldierly quality of head up, chest out, stomach in, shoulders squared. His face has begun to break down but he is still remarkably good looking—a big, finely shaped head, a handsome profile, deep-set light-brown eyes. His grey hair is thin with a bald spot like a monk's tonsure.*

The stamp of his profession is unmistakably on him. Not that he indulges in any of the deliberate temperamental posturings of the stage star. He is by nature and preference a simple, unpretentious man, whose inclinations are still close to his humble beginnings and his Irish farmer forebears. But the actor shows in all his unconscious habits of speech, movement and gesture. These have the quality of belonging to a studied technique. His voice is remarkably fine, reso-nant and flexible, and he takes great pride in it.

His clothes, assuredly, do not costume any romantic part. He wears a thread-bare, ready-made, grey sack suit and shineless black shoes, a collar-less shirt with a thick white handkerchief knotted loosely around his throat. There is nothing picturesquely careless about this get-up. It is commonplace shabby. He believes in wearing his clothes to the limit of usefulness, is dressed now for gardening, and doesn't give a damn how he looks.

He has never been really sick a day in his life. He has no nerves. There is a lot of stolid, earthy peasant in him, mixed with streaks of sentimental melan-choly and rare flashes of intuitive sensibility.

TYRONE'S *arm is around his wife's waist as they appear from the back parlor. Entering the living room he gives her a playful hug.*

TYRONE   You're a fine armful now, Mary, with those twenty pounds you've gained.

MARY [*smiles affectionately*]   I've gotten too fat, you mean, dear. I really ought to reduce.

TYRONE   None of that, my lady! You're just right. We'll have no talk of reducing. Is that why you ate so little breakfast?

MARY   So little? I thought I ate a lot.

TYRONE   You didn't. Not as much as I'd like to see, anyway.

MARY [*teasingly*]   Oh you! You expect everyone to eat the enormous breakfast you do. No one else in the world could without dying of indigestion. [*She comes forward to stand by the right of table.*]

TYRONE [*following her*]   I hope I'm not as big a glutton as that sounds. [*with hearty satisfaction*] But thank God, I've kept my appetite and I've the digestion of a young man of twenty, if I am sixty-five.

MARY   You surely have, James. No one could deny that.

[*She laughs and sits in the wicker armchair at right rear of table. He comes around in back of her and selects a cigar from a box on the table and cuts off the end with a little clipper. From the dining room* JAMIE's *and* EDMUND's *voices are heard. Mary turns her head that way.*]

Why did the boys stay in the dining room, I wonder? Cathleen must be waiting to clear the table.

TYRONE [*jokingly but with an undercurrent of resentment*]   It's a secret confab they don't want me to hear, I suppose. I'll bet they're cooking up some new scheme to touch the Old Man.

[*She is silent on this, keeping her head turned toward their voices. Her hands appear on the table top, moving restlessly. He lights his cigar and sits down in the rocker at right of table, which is his chair, and puffs contentedly.*]

There's nothing like the first after-breakfast cigar, if it's a good one, and this new lot have the right mellow flavor. They're a great bargain, too. I got them dead cheap. It was McGuire put me on to them.

MARY [*a trifle acidly*]   I hope he didn't put you on to any new piece of property at the same time. His real estate bargains don't work out so well.

TYRONE [*defensively*]   I wouldn't say that, Mary. After all, he was the one who advised me to buy that place on Chestnut Street and I made a quick turnover on it for a fine profit.

MARY [*smiles now with teasing affection*]   I know. The famous one stroke of good luck. I'm sure McGuire never dreamed—[*Then she pats his hand.*] Never mind, James. I know it's a waste of breath trying to convince you you're not a cunning real estate speculator.

TYRONE [*huffily*]   I've no such idea. But land is land, and it's safer than the stocks and bonds of Wall Street swindlers. [*then placatingly*] But let's not argue about business this early in the morning.

[*A pause. The boys' voices are again heard and one of them has a fit of coughing.* MARY *listens worriedly. Her fingers play nervously on the table top.*]

MARY   James, it's Edmund you ought to scold for not eating enough. He hardly touched anything except coffee. He needs to eat to keep up his strength. I keep telling him that but he says he simply has no appetite. Of course, there's nothing takes away your appetite like a bad summer cold.

TYRONE   Yes, it's only natural. So don't let yourself get worried—

MARY [*quickly*]   Oh, I'm not. I know he'll be all right in a few days if he takes care of himself. [*as if she wanted to dismiss the subject but can't*] But it does seem a shame he should have to be sick right now.

TYRONE   Yes, it is bad luck. [*He gives her a quick, worried look.*] But you mustn't let it upset you, Mary. Remember, you've got to take care of yourself, too.

MARY [*quickly*]   I'm not upset. There's nothing to be upset about. What makes you think I'm upset?

TYRONE   Why, nothing, except you've seemed a bit high-strung the past few days.

MARY [*forcing a smile*]   I have? Nonsense, dear. It's your imagination. [*with sudden tenseness*] You really must not watch me all the time, James. I mean, it makes me self-conscious.

TYRONE [*putting a hand over one of her nervously playing ones*]   Now, now, Mary. That's your imagination. If I've watched you it was to admire how fat and beautiful you looked. [*His voice is suddenly moved by deep feeling.*] I can't tell you the deep happiness it gives me, darling, to see you as you've been since you came back to us, your dear old self again. [*He leans over and kisses her cheek impulsively—then turning back adds with a constrained air*] So keep up the good work, Mary.

MARY [*has turned her head away*]   I will, dear. [*She gets up restlessly and goes to the windows at right.*] Thank heavens, the fog is gone. [*She turns back.*] I do feel out of sorts this morning. I wasn't able to get much sleep with that awful foghorn going all night long.

TYRONE   Yes, it's like having a sick whale in the back yard. It kept me awake, too.

MARY [*affectionately amused*]   Did it? You had a strange way of showing your restlessness. You were snoring so hard I couldn't tell which was the foghorn! [*She comes to him, laughing, and pats his cheek playfully.*] Ten foghorns couldn't disturb you. You haven't a nerve in you. You've never had.

TYRONE [*his vanity piqued—testily*]   Nonsense. You always exaggerate about my snoring.

MARY   I couldn't. If you could only hear yourself once—
[*A burst of laughter comes from the dining room. She turns her head, smiling.*]
What's the joke, I wonder?

TYRONE [*grumpily*]   It's on me. I'll bet that much. It's always on the Old Man.

MARY [*teasingly*]   Yes, it's terrible the way we all pick on you, isn't it? You're so abused! [*She laughs—then with a pleased, relieved air*] Well, no matter what the joke is about, it's a relief to hear Edmund laugh. He's been so down in the mouth lately.

TYRONE [*ignoring this—resentfully*]   Some joke of Jamie's, I'll wager. He's forever making sneering fun of somebody, that one.

MARY   Now don't start in on poor Jamie, dear. [*without conviction*] He'll turn out all right in the end, you wait and see.

TYRONE   He'd better start soon, then. He's nearly thirty-four.

MARY [*ignoring this*]   Good heavens, are they going to stay in the dining room all day? [*She goes to the back parlor doorway and calls*] Jamie! Edmund! Come in the living room and give Cathleen a chance to clear the table.

[EDMUND *calls back,* "We're coming, Mama." *She goes back to the table.*]

TYRONE [*grumbling*]   You'd find excuses for him no matter what he did.

MARY [*sitting down beside him, pats his hand*]   Shush.

Their sons JAMES, JR., *and* EDMUND *enter together from the back parlor. They are both grinning, still chuckling over what had caused their laughter, and as they come forward they glance at their father and their grins grow broader.*

JAMIE, *the elder, is thirty-three. He has his father's broad-shouldered, deep-chested physique, is an inch taller and weighs less, but appears shorter and stouter because he lacks* TYRONE'*s bearing and graceful carriage. He also lacks his father's vitality. The signs of premature disintegration are on him. His face is still good looking, despite marks of dissipation, but it has never been handsome like* TYRONE'*s, although* JAMIE *resembles him rather than his mother. He has fine brown eyes, their color midway between his father's lighter and his mother's darker ones. His hair is thinning and already there is indication of a bald spot like* TYRONE'*s. His nose is unlike that of any other member of the family, pronouncedly aquiline. Combined with his habitual expression of cynicism it gives his countenance a Mephistophelian cast. But on the rare occasions when he smiles without sneering, his personality possesses the remnant of a humorous, romantic, irresponsible Irish charm—that of the beguiling ne'er-do-well, with a strain of the sentimentally poetic, attractive to women and popular with men.*

He is dressed in an old sack suit, not as shabby as TYRONE'*s, and wears a collar and tie. His fair skin is sunburned a reddish, freckled tan.*

EDMUND *is ten years younger than his brother, a couple of inches taller, thin and wiry. Where* JAMIE *takes after his father, with little resemblance to his mother,* EDMUND *looks like both his parents, but is more like his mother. Her big, dark eyes are the dominant feature in his long, narrow Irish face. His mouth has the same quality of hypersensitiveness hers possesses. His high fore-head is hers accentuated, with dark brown hair, sunbleached to red at the ends, brushed straight back from it. But his nose is his father's and his face in profile recalls* TYRONE'*s.* EDMUND'*s hands are noticeably like his mother's, with the same exceptionally long fingers. They even have to a minor degree the same nervousness. It is in the quality of extreme nervous sensibility that the likeness of* EDMUND *to his mother is most marked.*

He is plainly in bad health. Much thinner than he should be, his eyes appear feverish and his cheeks are sunken. His skin, in spite of being sunburned a deep brown, has a parched sallowness. He wears a shirt, collar and tie, no coat, old flannel trousers, brown sneakers.

MARY [*turns smilingly to them, in a merry tone that is a bit forced*]   I've been teasing your father about his snoring. [*to* TYRONE] I'll leave it to the boys, James. They must have heard you. No, not you, Jamie. I could hear you down the hall almost as bad as your father. You're like him. As soon as your head touches the pillow you're off and ten foghorns couldn't wake you. [*She stops abruptly, catching* JAMIE'*s eyes regarding her with an uneasy, probing look. Her smile vanishes and her manner becomes self-conscious.*] Why are you staring, Jamie? [*Her hands flutter up to her hair.*] Is my hair coming down? It's hard for me to do it up properly now. My eyes are getting so bad and I never can find my glasses.

JAMIE [*looks away guiltily*]   Your hair's all right, Mama. I was only thinking how well you look.

TYRONE [*heartily*]   Just what I've been telling her, Jamie. She's so fat and sassy, there'll soon be no holding her.

EDMUND   Yes, you certainly look grand, Mama. [*She is reassured and smiles at him lovingly. He winks with a kidding grin.*] I'll back you up about Papa's snoring. Gosh, what a racket!

JAMIE   I heard him, too. [*He quotes, putting on a ham-actor manner*] "The Moor, I know his trumpet."[3]

[*His mother and brother laugh.*]

TYRONE [*scathingly*]   If it takes my snoring to make you remember Shakespeare instead of the dope sheet on the ponies, I hope I'll keep on with it.

MARY   Now, James! You mustn't be so touchy.

[JAMIE *shrugs his shoulders and sits down in the chair on her right.*]

EDMUND [*irritably*]   Yes, for Pete's sake, Papa! The first thing after breakfast! Give it a rest, can't you? [*He slumps down in the chair at left of table next to his brother. His father ignores him.*]

MARY [*reprovingly*]   Your father wasn't finding fault with you. You don't have to always take Jamie's part. You'd think you were the one ten years older.

JAMIE [*boredly*]   What's all the fuss about? Let's forget it.

TYRONE [*contemptuously*]   Yes, forget! Forget everything and face nothing! It's a convenient philosophy if you've no ambition in life except to—

MARY   James, do be quiet. [*She puts an arm around his shoulder—coaxingly*] You must have gotten out of the wrong side of the bed this morning. [*to the boys, changing the subject*] What were you two grinning about like Cheshire cats when you came in? What was the joke?

TYRONE [*with a painful effort to be a good sport*]   Yes, let us in on it, lads. I told your mother I knew damned well it would be one on me, but never mind that, I'm used to it.

JAMIE [*dryly*]   Don't look at me. This is the Kid's story.

EDMUND [*grins*]   I meant to tell you last night, Papa, and forgot it. Yesterday when I went for a walk I dropped in at the Inn—

MARY [*worriedly*]   You shouldn't drink now, Edmund.

EDMUND [*ignoring this*]   And who do you think I met there, with a beautiful bun on,[4] but Shaughnessy, the tenant on that farm of yours.

MARY [*smiling*]   That dreadful man! But he is funny.

TYRONE [*scowling*]   He's not so funny when you're his landlord. He's a wily Shanty Mick, that one. He could hide behind a corkscrew. What's he complaining about now, Edmund—for I'm damned sure he's complaining. I suppose he wants his rent lowered. I let him have the place for almost nothing, just to keep someone on it, and he never pays that till I threaten to evict him.

EDMUND   No, he didn't beef about anything. He was so pleased with life he even bought a drink, and that's practically unheard of. He was delighted because he'd had a fight with your friend, Harker, the Standard Oil millionaire, and won a glorious victory.

MARY [*with amused dismay*]   Oh, Lord! James, you'll really have to do something—

TYRONE   Bad luck to Shaughnessy, anyway!

3. Shakespeare's *Othello* 2.1.180.   4. I.e., drunk.

JAMIE [*maliciously*] I'll bet the next time you see Harker at the Club and give him the old respectful bow, he won't see you.

EDMUND Yes. Harker will think you're no gentleman for harboring a tenant who isn't humble in the presence of a king of America.

TYRONE Never mind the Socialist gabble. I don't care to listen—

MARY [*tactfully*] Go on with your story, Edmund.

EDMUND [*grins at his father provocatively*] Well, you remember, Papa, the ice pond on Harker's estate is right next to the farm, and you remember Shaughnessy keeps pigs. Well, it seems there's a break in the fence and the pigs have been bathing in the millionaire's ice pond, and Harker's foreman told him he was sure Shaughnessy had broken the fence on purpose to give his pigs a free wallow.

MARY [*shocked and amused*] Good heavens!

TYRONE [*sourly, but with a trace of admiration*] I'm sure he did, too, the dirty scallywag. It's like him.

EDMUND So Harker came in person to rebuke Shaughnessy. [*He chuckles.*] A very bonehead play! If I needed any further proof that our ruling plutocrats, especially the ones who inherited their boodle, are not mental giants, that would clinch it.

TYRONE [*with appreciation, before he thinks*] Yes, he'd be no match for Shaughnessy. [*then he growls*] Keep your damned anarchist remarks to yourself. I won't have them in my house. [*But he is full of eager anticipation.*] What happened?

EDMUND Harker had as much chance as I would with Jack Johnson.[5] Shaughnessy got a few drinks under his belt and was waiting at the gate to welcome him. He told me he never gave Harker a chance to open his mouth. He began by shouting that he was no slave Standard Oil could trample on. He was a King of Ireland, if he had his rights, and scum was scum to him, no matter how much money it had stolen from the poor.

MARY Oh, Lord! [*But she can't help laughing.*]

EDMUND Then he accused Harker of making his foreman break down the fence to entice the pigs into the ice pond in order to destroy them. The poor pigs, Shaughnessy yelled, had caught their death of cold. Many of them were dying of pneumonia, and several others had been taken down with cholera from drinking the poisoned water. He told Harker he was hiring a lawyer to sue him for damages. And he wound up by saying that he had to put up with poison ivy, ticks, potato bugs, snakes and skunks on his farm, but he was an honest man who drew the line somewhere, and he'd be damned if he'd stand for a Standard Oil thief trespassing. So would Harker kindly remove his dirty feet from the premises before he sicked the dog on him. And Harker did! [*He and* JAMIE *laugh.*]

MARY [*shocked but giggling*] Heavens, what a terrible tongue that man has!

TYRONE [*admiringly before he thinks*] The damned old scoundrel! By God, you can't beat him! [*He laughs—then stops abruptly and scowls.*] The dirty blackguard! He'll get me in serious trouble yet. I hope you told him I'd be mad as hell—

EDMUND I told him you'd be tickled to death over the great Irish victory, and so you are. Stop faking, Papa.

---

5. Famous prizefighter, the first African American heavyweight boxing champion of the world.

TYRONE   Well, I'm not tickled to death.

MARY [*teasingly*]   You are, too, James. You're simply delighted!

TYRONE   No, Mary, a joke is a joke, but—

EDMUND   I told Shaughnessy he should have reminded Harker that a Standard Oil millionaire ought to welcome the flavor of hog in his ice water as an appropriate touch.

TYRONE   The devil you did! [*frowning*] Keep your damned Socialist anarchist sentiments out of my affairs!

EDMUND   Shaughnessy almost wept because he hadn't thought of that one, but he said he'd include it in a letter he's writing to Harker, along with a few other insults he'd overlooked. [*He and* JAMIE *laugh.*]

TYRONE   What are you laughing at? There's nothing funny—A fine son you are to help that blackguard get me into a lawsuit!

MARY   Now, James, don't lose your temper.

TYRONE [*turns on* JAMIE]   And you're worse than he is, encouraging him. I suppose you're regretting you weren't there to prompt Shaughnessy with a few nastier insults. You've a fine talent for that, if for nothing else.

MARY   James! There's no reason to scold Jamie.

> [JAMIE *is about to make some sneering remark to his father, but he shrugs his shoulders.*]

EDMUND [*with sudden nervous exasperation*]   Oh, for God's sake, Papa! If you're starting that stuff again, I'll beat it. [*He jumps up.*] I left my book upstairs, anyway. [*He goes to the front parlor, saying disgustedly*] God, Papa, I should think you'd get sick of hearing yourself—

> [*He disappears.* TYRONE *looks after him angrily.*]

MARY   You musn't mind Edmund, James. Remember he isn't well.

> [EDMUND *can be heard coughing as he goes upstairs. She adds nervously*] A summer cold makes anyone irritable.

JAMIE [*genuinely concerned*]   It's not just a cold he's got. The Kid is damned sick.

> [*His father gives him a sharp warning look but he doesn't see it.*]

MARY [*turns on him resentfully*]   Why do you say that? It *is* just a cold! Anyone can tell that! You always imagine things!

TYRONE [*with another warning glance at* JAMIE—*easily*]   All Jamie meant was Edmund might have a touch of something else, too, which makes his cold worse.

JAMIE   Sure, Mama. That's all I meant.

TYRONE   Doctor Hardy thinks it might be a bit of malarial fever he caught when he was in the tropics. If it is, quinine will soon cure it.

MARY [*a look of contemptuous hostility flashes across her face*]   Doctor Hardy! I wouldn't believe a thing he said, if he swore on a stack of Bibles! I know what doctors are. They're all alike. Anything, they don't care what, to keep you coming to them. [*She stops short, overcome by a fit of acute self-consciousness as she catches their eyes fixed on her. Her hands jerk nervously to her hair. She forces a smile.*] What is it? What are you looking at? Is my hair—?

TYRONE [*puts his arm around her—with guilty heartiness, giving her a playful hug*]   There's nothing wrong with your hair. The healthier and fatter you get, the vainer you become. You'll soon spend half the day primping before the mirror.

MARY [*half reassured*] I really should have new glasses. My eyes are so bad now.

TYRONE [*with Irish blarney*] Your eyes are beautiful, and well you know it. [*He gives her a kiss. Her face lights up with a charming, shy embarrassment. Suddenly and startlingly one sees in her face the girl she had once been, not a ghost of the dead, but still a living part of her.*]

MARY You mustn't be so silly, James. Right in front of Jamie!

TYRONE Oh, he's on to you, too. He knows this fuss about eyes and hair is only fishing for compliments. Eh, Jamie?

JAMIE [*his face has cleared, too, and there is an old boyish charm in his loving smile at his mother*] Yes, You can't kid us, Mama.

MARY [*laughs and an Irish lilt comes into her voice*] Go along with both of you! [*then she speaks with a girlish gravity*] But I did truly have beautiful hair once, didn't I, James?

TYRONE The most beautiful in the world!

MARY It was a rare shade of reddish brown and so long it came down below my knees. You ought to remember it, too, Jamie. It wasn't until after Edmund was born that I had a single grey hair. Then it began to turn white. [*The girlishness fades from her face.*]

TYRONE [*quickly*] And that made it prettier than ever.

MARY [*again embarrassed and pleased*] Will you listen to your father, Jamie—after thirty-five years of marriage! He isn't a great actor for nothing, is he? What's come over you, James? Are you pouring coals of fire on my head for teasing you about snoring? Well, then, I take it all back. It must have been only the foghorn I heard. [*She laughs, and they laugh with her. Then she changes to a brisk businesslike air.*] But I can't stay with you any longer, even to hear compliments. I must see the cook about dinner and the day's marketing. [*She gets up and sighs with humorous exaggeration.*] Bridget is so lazy. And so sly. She begins telling me about her relatives so I can't get a word in edgeways and scold her. Well, I might as well get it over. [*She goes to the back-parlor doorway, then turns, her face worried again.*] You mustn't make Edmund work on the grounds with you, James, remember. [*again with the strange obstinate set to her face*] Not that he isn't strong enough, but he'd perspire and he might catch more cold.

[*She disappears through the back parlor.* TYRONE *turns on* JAMIE *condemningly.*]

TYRONE You're a fine lunkhead! Haven't you any sense? The one thing to avoid is saying anything that would get her more upset over Edmund.

JAMIE [*shrugging his shoulders*] All right. Have it your way. I think it's the wrong idea to let Mama go on kidding yourself. It will only make the shock worse when she has to face it. Anyway, you can see she's deliberately fooling herself with that summer cold talk. She knows better.

TYRONE Knows? Nobody knows yet.

JAMIE Well, I do. I was with Edmund when he went to Doc Hardy on Monday. I heard him pull that touch of malaria stuff. He was stalling. That isn't what he thinks any more. You know it as well as I do. You talked to him when you went uptown yesterday, didn't you?

TYRONE He couldn't say anything for sure yet. He's to phone me today before Edmund goes to him.

JAMIE [*slowly*] He thinks it's consumption,[6] doesn't he, Papa?

TYRONE [*reluctantly*] He said it might be.

JAMIE [*moved, his love for his brother coming out*] Poor kid! God damn it! [*He turns on his father accusingly.*] It might never have happened if you'd sent him to a real doctor when he first got sick.

TYRONE What's the matter with Hardy? He's always been our doctor up here.

JAMIE Everything's the matter with him! Even in this hick burg he's rated third class! He's a cheap old quack!

TYRONE That's right! Run him down! Run down everybody! Everyone is a fake to you!

JAMIE [*contemptuously*] Hardy only charges a dollar. That's what makes you think he's a fine doctor!

TYRONE [*stung*] That's enough! You're not drunk now! There's no excuse— [*He controls himself—a bit defensively*] If you mean I can't afford one of the fine society doctors who prey on the rich summer people—

JAMIE Can't afford? You're one of the biggest property owners around here.

TYRONE That doesn't mean I'm rich. It's all mortgaged—

JAMIE Because you always buy more instead of paying off mortgages. If Edmund was a lousy acre of land you wanted, the sky would be the limit!

TYRONE That's a lie! And your sneers against Doctor Hardy are lies! He doesn't put on frills, or have an office in a fashionable location, or drive around in an expensive automobile. That's what you pay for with those other five-dollars-to-look-at-your-tongue fellows, not their skill.

JAMIE [*with a scornful shrug of his shoulders*] Oh, all right. I'm a fool to argue. You can't change the leopard's spots.

TYRONE [*with rising anger*] No, you can't. You've taught me that lesson only too well. I've lost all hope you will ever change yours. You dare tell me what I can afford? You've never known the value of a dollar and never will! You've never saved a dollar in your life! At the end of each season you're penniless! You've thrown your salary away every week on whores and whiskey!

JAMIE My salary! Christ!

TYRONE It's more than you're worth, and you couldn't get that if it wasn't for me. If you weren't my son, there isn't a manager in the business who would give you a part, your reputation stinks so. As it is, I have to humble my pride and beg for you, saying you've turned over a new leaf, although I know it's a lie!

JAMIE I never wanted to be an actor. You forced me on the stage.

TYRONE That's a lie! You made no effort to find anything else to do. You left it to me to get you a job and I have no influence except in the theater. Forced you! You never wanted to do anything except loaf in barrooms! You'd have been content to sit back like a lazy lunk and sponge on me for the rest of your life! After all the money I'd wasted on your education, and all you did was get fired in disgrace from every college you went to!

JAMIE Oh, for God's sake, don't drag up that ancient history!

6. Tuberculosis.

TYRONE   It's not ancient history that you have to come home every summer to live on me.

JAMIE   I earn my board and lodging working on the grounds. It saves you hiring a man.

TYRONE   Bah! You have to be driven to do even that much! [*His anger ebbs into a weary complaint.*] I wouldn't give a damn if you ever displayed the slightest sign of gratitude. The only thanks is to have you sneer at me for a dirty miser, sneer at my profession, sneer at every damned thing in the world—except yourself.

JAMIE [*wryly*]   That's not true, Papa. You can't hear me talking to myself, that's all.

TYRONE [*stares at him puzzledly, then quotes mechanically*]   "Ingratitude, the vilest weed that grows"![7]

JAMIE   I could see that line coming! God, how many thousand times—! [*He stops, bored with their quarrel, and shrugs his shoulders.*] All right, Papa. I'm a bum. Anything you like, so long as it stops the argument.

TYRONE [*with indignant appeal now*]   If you'd get ambition in your head instead of folly! You're young yet. You could still make your mark. You had the talent to become a fine actor! You have it still. You're my son—!

JAMIE [*boredly*]   Let's forget me. I'm not interested in the subject. Neither are you. [TYRONE *gives up.* JAMIE *goes on casually.*] What started us on this? Oh, Doc Hardy. When is he going to call you up about Edmund?

TYRONE   Around lunch time. [*He pauses—then defensively*] I couldn't have sent Edmund to a better doctor. Hardy's treated him whenever he was sick up here, since he was knee high. He knows his constitution as no other doctor could. It's not a question of my being miserly, as you'd like to make out. [*bitterly*] And what could the finest specialist in America do for Edmund, after he's deliberately ruined his health by the mad life he's led ever since he was fired from college? Even before that when he was in prep school, he began dissipating and playing the Broadway sport to imitate you, when he's never had your constitution to stand it. You're a healthy hulk like me—or you were at his age—but he's always been a bundle of nerves like his mother. I've warned him for years his body couldn't stand it, but he wouldn't heed me, and now it's too late.

JAMIE [*sharply*]   What do you mean, too late? You talk as if you thought—

TYRONE [*guiltily explosive*]   Don't be a damned fool! I meant nothing but what's plain to anyone! His health has broken down and he may be an invalid for a long time.

JAMIE [*stares at his father, ignoring his explanation*]   I know it's an Irish peasant idea consumption is fatal. It probably is when you live in a hovel on a bog, but over here, with modern treatment—

TYRONE   Don't I know that! What are you gabbing about, anyway? And keep your dirty tongue off Ireland, with your sneers about peasants and bogs and hovels! [*accusingly*] The less you say about Edmund's sickness, the better for your conscience! You're more responsible than anyone!

JAMIE [*stung*]   That's a lie! I won't stand for that, Papa!

TYRONE   It's the truth! You've been the worst influence for him. He grew up admiring you as a hero! A fine example you set him! If you ever gave

7. Shakespeare's *King Lear* 1.4.

him advice except in the ways of rottenness, I've never heard of it! You made him old before his time, pumping him full of what you consider worldly wisdom, when he was too young to see that your mind was so poisoned by your own failure in life, you wanted to believe every man was a knave with his soul for sale, and every woman who wasn't a whore was a fool!

JAMIE [*with a defensive air of weary indifference again*] All right. I did put Edmund wise to things, but not until I saw he'd started to raise hell, and knew he'd laugh at me if I tried the good advice, older brother stuff. All I did was make a pal of him and be absolutely frank so he'd learn from my mistakes that—[*He shrugs his shoulders—cynically*] Well, that if you can't be good you can at least be careful.

[*His father snorts contemptuously. Suddenly* JAMIE *becomes really moved.*]

That's a rotten accusation, Papa. You know how much the Kid means to me, and how close we've always been—not like the usual brothers! I'd do anything for him.

TYRONE [*impressed—mollifyingly*] I know you may have thought it was for the best, Jamie. I didn't say you did it deliberately to harm him.

JAMIE Besides it's damned rot! I'd like to see anyone influence Edmund more than he wants to be. His quietness fools people into thinking they can do what they like with him. But he's stubborn as hell inside and what he does is what he wants to do, and to hell with anyone else! What had I to do with all the crazy stunts he's pulled in the last few years— working his way all over the map as a sailor and all that stuff. I thought that was a damned fool idea, and I told him so. You can't imagine me getting fun out of being on the beach in South America, or living in filthy dives, drinking rotgut, can you? No, thanks! I'll stick to Broadway, and a room with a bath, and bars that serve bonded Bourbon.

TYRONE You and Broadway! It's made you what you are! [*with a touch of pride*] Whatever Edmund's done, he's had the guts to go off on his own, where he couldn't come whining to me the minute he was broke.

JAMIE [*stung into sneering jealousy*] He's always come home broke finally, hasn't he? And what did his going away get him? Look at him now! [*He is suddenly shamefaced.*] Christ! That's a lousy thing to say. I don't mean that.

TYRONE [*decides to ignore this*] He's been doing well on the paper. I was hoping he'd found the work he wants to do at last.

JAMIE [*sneering jealously again*] A hick town rag! Whatever bull they hand you, they tell me he's a pretty bum reporter. If he weren't your son—[*ashamed again*] No, that's not true! They're glad to have him, but it's the special stuff that gets him by. Some of the poems and parodies he's written are damned good. [*grudgingly again*] Not that they'd ever get him anywhere on the big time. [*hastily*] But he's certainly made a damned good start.

TYRONE Yes. He's made a start. You used to talk about wanting to become a newspaper man but you were never willing to start at the bottom. You expected—

JAMIE Oh, for Christ's sake, Papa! Can't you lay off me!

TYRONE [*stares at him—then looks away—after a pause*] It's damnable luck Edmund should be sick right now. It couldn't have come at a worse time for him. [*He adds, unable to conceal an almost furtive uneasiness*] Or for your mother. It's damnable she should have this to upset her, just when she needs peace and freedom from worry. She's been so well in the two months since she came home. [*His voice grows husky and trembles a little.*] It's been heaven to me. This home has been a home again. But I needn't tell you, Jamie.

> [*His son looks at him, for the first time with an understanding sympathy. It is as if suddenly a deep bond of common feeling existed between them in which their antagonisms could be forgotten.*]

JAMIE [*almost gently*]   I've felt the same way, Papa.

TYRONE   Yes, this time you can see how strong and sure of herself she is. She's a different woman entirely from the other times. She has control of her nerves—or she had until Edmund got sick. Now you can feel her growing tense and frightened underneath. I wish to God we could keep the truth from her, but we can't if he has to be sent to a sanatorium. What makes it worse is her father died of consumption. She worshiped him and she's never forgotten. Yes, it will be hard for her. But she can do it! She has the will power now! We must help her, Jamie, in every way we can!

JAMIE [*moved*]   Of course, Papa. [*hesitantly*] Outside of nerves, she seems perfectly all right this morning.

TYRONE [*with hearty confidence now*]   Never better. She's full of fun and mischief. [*Suddenly he frowns at* JAMIE *suspiciously.*] Why do you say, seems? Why shouldn't she be all right? What the hell do you mean?

JAMIE   Don't start jumping down my throat! God, Papa, this ought to be one thing we can talk over frankly without a battle.

TYRONE   I'm sorry, Jamie. [*tensely*] But go on and tell me—

JAMIE   There's nothing to tell. I was all wrong. It's just that last night— Well, you know how it is, I can't forget the past. I can't help being suspicious. Any more than you can. [*bitterly*] That's the hell of it. And it makes it hell for Mama! She watches us watching her—

TYRONE [*sadly*]   I know. [*tensely*] Well, what was it! Can't you speak out!

JAMIE   Nothing, I tell you. Just my damned foolishness. Around three o'clock this morning, I woke up and heard her moving around in the spare room. Then she went to the bathroom. I pretended to be asleep. She stopped in the hall to listen, as if she wanted to make sure I was.

TYRONE [*with forced scorn*]   For God's sake, is that all? She told me herself the foghorn kept her awake all night, and every night since Edmund's been sick she's been up and down, going to his room to see how he was.

JAMIE [*eagerly*]   Yes, that's right, she did stop to listen outside his room. [*hesitantly again*] It was her being in the spare room that scared me. I couldn't help remembering that when she starts sleeping alone in there, it has always been a sign—

TYRONE   It isn't this time! It's easily explained. Where else could she go last night to get away from my snoring? [*He gives way to a burst of resentful anger.*] By God, how you can live with a mind that sees nothing but the worst motives behind everything is beyond me!

JAMIE [*stung*]   Don't pull that! I've just said I was all wrong. Don't you suppose I'm as glad of that as you are!

TYRONE [*mollifyingly*]   I'm sure you are, Jamie. [*A pause. His expression becomes somber. He speaks slowly with a superstitious dread.*] It would be like a curse she can't escape if worry over Edmund—It was her long sickness after bringing him into the world that she first—

JAMIE   She didn't have anything to do with it!

TYRONE   I'm not blaming her.

JAMIE [*bitingly*]   Then who are you blaming? Edmund, for being born?

TYRONE   You damned fool! No one was to blame.

JAMIE   The bastard of a doctor was! From what Mama's said, he was another cheap quack like Hardy! You wouldn't pay for a first-rate—

TYRONE   That's a lie! [*furiously*] So I'm to blame! That's what you're driving at, is it? You evil-minded loafer!

JAMIE [*warningly as he hears his mother in the dining room*]   Ssh!
[TYRONE *gets hastily to his feet and goes to look out the windows at right.* JAMIE *speaks with a complete change of tone.*]
Well, if we're going to cut the front hedge today, we'd better go to work.
[MARY *comes in from the back parlor. She gives a quick, suspicious glance from one to the other, her manner nervously self-conscious.*]

TYRONE [*turns from the window—with an actor's heartiness*]   Yes, it's too fine a morning to waste indoors arguing. Take a look out the window, Mary. There's no fog in the harbor. I'm sure the spell of it we've had is over now.

MARY [*going to him*]   I hope so, dear. [*to* JAMIE, *forcing a smile*] Did I actually hear you suggesting work on the front hedge, Jamie? Wonders will never cease! You must want pocket money badly.

JAMIE [*kiddingly*]   When don't I? [*He winks at her, with a derisive glance at his father.*] I expect a salary of at least one large iron man[8] at the end of the week—to carouse on!

MARY [*does not respond to his humor—her hands fluttering over the front of her dress*]   What were you two arguing about?

JAMIE [*shrugs his shoulders*]   The same old stuff.

MARY   I heard you say something about a doctor, and your father accusing you of being evil-minded.

JAMIE [*quickly*]   Oh, that. I was saying again Doc Hardy isn't my idea of the world's greatest physician.

MARY [*knows he is lying—vaguely*]   Oh. No, I wouldn't say he was either. [*changing the subject—forcing a smile*] That Bridget! I thought I'd never get away. She told me about her second cousin on the police force in St. Louis. [*then with nervous irritation*] Well, if you're going to work on the hedge why don't you go? [*hastily*] I mean, take advantage of the sunshine before the fog comes back. [*strangely, as if talking aloud to herself*] Because I know it will. [*Suddenly she is self-consciously aware that they are both staring fixedly at her—flurriedly, raising her hands*] Or I should say, the rheumatism in my hands knows. It's a better weather prophet than you are, James. [*She stares at her hands with fascinated repulsion.*] Ugh! How ugly they are! Who'd ever believe they were once beautiful?
[*They stare at her with a growing dread.*]

TYRONE [*takes her hands and gently pushes them down*]   Now, now, Mary. None of that foolishness. They're the sweetest hands in the world.
[*She smiles, her face lighting up, and kisses him gratefully. He turns to his son.*]

8. Slang for "dollar."

Come on Jamie. Your mother's right to scold us. The way to start work is to start work. The hot sun will sweat some of that booze fat off your middle.

[*He opens the screen door and goes out on the porch and disappears down a flight of steps leading to the ground.* JAMIE *rises from his chair and, taking off his coat, goes to the door. At the door he turns back but avoids looking at her, and she does not look at him.*]

JAMIE [*with an awkward, uneasy tenderness*] We're all so proud of you, Mama, so darned happy.

[*She stiffens and stares at him with a frightened defiance. He flounders on.*]

But you've still got to be careful. You mustn't worry so much about Edmund. He'll be all right.

MARY [*with a stubborn, bitterly resentful look*] Of course, he'll be all right. And I don't know what you mean, warning me to be careful.

JAMIE [*rebuffed and hurt, shrugs his shoulders*] All right, Mama. I'm sorry I spoke.

[*He goes out on the porch. She waits rigidly until he disappears down the steps. Then she sinks down in the chair he had occupied, her face betraying a frightened, furtive desperation, her hands roving over the table top, aimlessly moving objects around. She hears* EDMUND *descending the stairs in the front hall. As he nears the bottom he has a fit of coughing. She springs to her feet, as if she wanted to run away from the sound, and goes quickly to the windows at right. She is looking out, apparently calm, as he enters from the front parlor, a book in one hand. She turns to him, her lips set in a welcoming, motherly smile.*]

MARY Here you are. I was just going upstairs to look for you.

EDMUND I waited until they went out. I don't want to mix up in any arguments. I feel too rotten.

MARY [*almost resentfully*] Oh, I'm sure you don't feel half as badly as you make out. You're such a baby. You like to get us worried so we'll make a fuss over you. [*hastily*] I'm only teasing, dear. I know how miserably uncomfortable you must be. But you feel better today, don't you? [*worriedly, taking his arm*] All the same, you've grown much too thin. You need to rest all you can. Sit down and I'll make you comfortable.

[*He sits down in the rocking chair and she puts a pillow behind his back.*]

There, How's that?

EDMUND Grand. Thanks, Mama.

MARY [*kisses him—tenderly*] All you need is your mother to nurse you. Big as you are, you're still the baby of the family to me, you know.

EDMUND [*takes her hand—with deep seriousness*] Never mind me. You take care of yourself. That's all that counts.

MARY [*evading his eyes*] But I am, dear. [*forcing a laugh*] Heavens, don't you see how fat I've grown! I'll have to have all my dresses let out. [*She turns away and goes to the windows at right. She attempts a light, amused tone.*] They've started clipping the hedge. Poor Jamie! How he hates working in front where everyone passing can see him. There go the Chatfields in their new Mercedes. It's a beautiful car, isn't it? Not like our secondhand Packard. Poor Jamie! He bent almost under the hedge so they wouldn't notice him. They bowed to your father and he bowed back as if he were taking a curtain call. In that filthy old suit I've tried to make him throw away. [*Her voice has grown bitter.*] Really, he ought to have more pride than to make such a show of himself.

EDMUND He's right not to give a damn what anyone thinks. Jamie's a fool to care about the Chatfields. For Pete's sake, who ever heard of them outside this hick burg?

MARY [*with satisfaction*] No one. You're quite right, Edmund. Big frogs in a small puddle. It is stupid of Jamie. [*She pauses, looking out the window— then with an undercurrent of lonely yearning*] Still, the Chatfields and people like them stand for something. I mean they have decent, presentable homes they don't have to be ashamed of. They have friends who entertain them and whom they entertain. They're not cut off from everyone. [*She turns back from the window.*] Not that I want anything to do with them. I've always hated this town and everyone in it. You know that. I never wanted to live here in the first place, but your father liked it and insisted on building this house, and I've had to come here every summer.

EDMUND Well, it's better than spending the summer in a New York hotel, isn't it? And this town's not so bad. I like it well enough. I suppose because it's the only home we've had.

MARY I've never felt it was my home. It was wrong from the start. Everything was done in the cheapest way. Your father would never spend the money to make it right. It's just as well we haven't any friends here. I'd be ashamed to have them step in the door. But he's never wanted family friends. He hates calling on people, or receiving them. All he likes is to hobnob with men at the Club or in a barroom. Jamie and you are the same way, but you're not to blame. You've never had a chance to meet decent people here. I know you both would have been so different if you'd been able to associate with nice girls instead of—You'd never have disgraced yourselves as you have, so that now no respectable parents will let their daughters be seen with you.

EDMUND [*irritably*] Oh, Mama, forget it! Who cares? Jamie and I would be bored stiff. And about the Old Man, what's the use of talking? You can't change him.

MARY [*mechanically rebuking*] Don't call your father the Old Man. You should have more respect. [*then dully*] I know it's useless to talk. But sometimes I feel so lonely. [*Her lips quiver and she keeps her head turned away.*]

EDMUND Anyway, you've got to be fair, Mama. It may have been all his fault in the beginning, but you know that later on, even if he'd wanted to, we couldn't have had people here—[*He flounders guiltily.*] I mean, you wouldn't have wanted them.

MARY [*wincing—her lips quivering pitifully*] Don't. I can't bear having you remind me.

EDMUND Don't take it that way! Please, Mama! I'm trying to help. Because it's bad for you to forget. The right way is to remember. So you'll always be on your guard. You know what's happened before. [*miserably*] God, Mama, you know I hate to remind you. I'm doing it because it's been so wonderful having you home the way you've been, and it would be terrible—

MARY [*strickenly*] Please, dear. I know you mean it for the best, but—[*A defensive uneasiness comes into her voice again.*] I don't understand why you should suddenly say such things. What put it in your mind this morning?

EDMUND [*evasively*]   Nothing. Just because I feel rotten and blue, I suppose.

MARY   Tell me the truth. Why are you so suspicious all of a sudden?

EDMUND   I'm not!

MARY   Oh, yes you are. I can feel it. Your father and Jamie, too—particularly Jamie.

EDMUND   Now don't start imagining things, Mama.

MARY [*her hands fluttering*]   It makes it so much harder, living in this atmosphere of constant suspicion, knowing everyone is spying on me, and none of you believe in me, or trust me.

EDMUND   That's crazy, Mama. We do trust you.

MARY   If there was only some place I could go to get away for a day, or even an afternoon, some woman friend I could talk to—not about anything serious, simply laugh and gossip and forget for a while—someone besides the servants—that stupid Cathleen!

EDMUND [*gets up worriedly and puts his arm around her*]   Stop it, Mama. You're getting yourself worked up over nothing.

MARY   Your father goes out. He meets his friends in barrooms or at the Club. You and Jamie have the boys you know. You go out. But I am alone. I've always been alone.

EDMUND [*soothingly*]   Come now! You know that's a fib. One of us always stays around to keep you company, or goes with you in the automobile when you take a drive.

MARY [*bitterly*]   Because you're afraid to trust me alone! [*She turns on him—sharply.*] I insist you tell me why you act so differently this morning—why you felt you had to remind me—

EDMUND [*hesitates—then blurts out guiltily*]   It's stupid. It's just that I wasn't asleep when you came in my room last night. You didn't go back to your and Papa's room. You went in the spare room for the rest of the night.

MARY   Because your father's snoring was driving me crazy! For heaven's sake, haven't I often used the spare room as my bedroom? [*bitterly*] But I see what you thought. That was when—

EDMUND [*too vehemently*]   I didn't think anything!

MARY   So you pretended to be asleep in order to spy on me!

EDMUND   No! I did it because I knew if you found out I was feverish and couldn't sleep, it would upset you.

MARY   Jamie was pretending to be asleep, too, I'm sure, and I suppose your father—

EDMUND   Stop it, Mama!

MARY   Oh, I can't bear it, Edmund, when even you—! [*Her hands flutter up to pat her hair in their aimless, distracted way. Suddenly a strange undercurrent of revengefulness comes into her voice.*] It would serve all of you right if it was true!

EDMUND   Mama! Don't say that! That's the way you talk when—

MARY   Stop suspecting me! Please, dear! You hurt me! I couldn't sleep because I was thinking about you. That's the real reason! I've been so worried ever since you've been sick. [*She puts her arms around him and hugs him with a frightened, protective tenderness.*]

EDMUND [*soothingly*]   That's foolishness. You know it's only a bad cold.

MARY   Yes, of course, I know that!

EDMUND But listen, Mama. I want you to promise me that even if it should turn out to be something worse, you'll know I'll soon be all right again, anyway, and you won't worry yourself sick, and you'll keep on taking care of yourself—

MARY [*frightenedly*] I won't listen when you're so silly! There's absolutely no reason to talk as if you expected something dreadful! Of course, I promise you. I give you my sacred word of honor! [*then with a sad bitterness*] But I suppose you're remembering I've promised before on my word of honor.

EDMUND No!

MARY [*her bitterness receding into a resigned helplessness*] I'm not blaming you, dear. How can you help it? How can any one of us forget? [*strangely*] That's what makes it so hard—for all of us. We can't forget.

EDMUND [*grabs her shoulder*] Mama! Stop it!

MARY [*forcing a smile*] All right, dear. I didn't mean to be so gloomy. Don't mind me. Here. Let me feel your head. Why, it's nice and cool. You certainly haven't any fever now.

EDMUND Forget! It's you—

MARY But I'm quite all right, dear. [*with a quick, strange, calculating, almost sly glance at him*] Except I naturally feel tired and nervous this morning, after such a bad night. I really ought to go upstairs and lie down until lunch time and take a nap.

[*He gives her an instinctive look of suspicion—then, ashamed of himself, looks quickly away. She hurries on nervously.*]

What are you going to do? Read here? It would be much better for you to go out in the fresh air and sunshine. But don't get overheated, remember. Be sure and wear a hat.

[*She stops, looking straight at him now. He avoids her eyes. There is a tense pause. Then she speaks jeeringly.*]

Or are you afraid to trust me alone?

EDMUND [*tormentedly*] No! Can't you stop talking like that! I think you ought to take a nap. [*He goes to the screen door—forcing a joking tone*] I'll go down and help Jamie bear up. I love to lie in the shade and watch him work.

[*He forces a laugh in which she makes herself join. Then he goes out on the porch and disappears down the steps. Her first reaction is one of relief. She appears to relax. She sinks down in one of the wicker armchairs at rear of table and leans her head back, closing her eyes. But suddenly she grows terribly tense again. Her eyes open and she strains forward, seized by a fit of nervous panic. She begins a desperate battle with herself. Her long fingers, warped and knotted by rheumatism, drum on the arms of the chair, driven by an insistent life of their own, without her consent.*]

CURTAIN

Act 2

SCENE 1

SCENE—*The same. It is around quarter to one. No sunlight comes into the room now through the windows at right. Outside the day is still fine but increasingly sultry, with a faint haziness in the air which softens the glare of the sun.*

EDMUND *sits in the armchair at left of table, reading a book. Or rather he is trying to concentrate on it but cannot. He seems to be listening for some sound from upstairs. His manner is nervously apprehensive and he looks more sickly than in the previous act.*

The second girl, CATHLEEN, *enters from the back parlor. She carries a tray on which is a bottle of bonded Bourbon, several whiskey glasses and a pitcher of ice water. She is a buxom Irish peasant, in her early twenties, with a red-cheeked comely face, black hair and blue eyes—amiable, ignorant, clumsy, and possessed by a dense, well-meaning stupidity. She puts the tray on the table.* EDMUND *pretends to be so absorbed in his book he does not notice her, but she ignores this.*

CATHLEEN [*with garrulous familiarity*]   Here's the whiskey. It'll be lunch time soon. Will I call your father and Mister Jamie, or will you?

EDMUND [*without looking up from his book*]   You do it.

CATHLEEN   It's a wonder your father wouldn't look at his watch once in a while. He's a divil for making the meals late, and then Bridget curses me as if I was to blame. But he's a grand handsome man, if he is old. You'll never see the day you're as good looking—nor Mister Jamie, either. [*She chuckles.*] I'll wager Mister Jamie wouldn't miss the time to stop work and have his drop of whiskey if he had a watch to his name!

EDMUND [*gives up trying to ignore her and grins*]   You win that one.

CATHLEEN   And here's another I'd win, that you're making me call them so you can sneak a drink before they come.

EDMUND   Well, I hadn't thought of that—

CATHLEEN   Oh no, not you! Butter wouldn't melt in your mouth, I suppose.

EDMUND   But now you suggest it—

CATHLEEN [*suddenly primly virtuous*]   I'd never suggest a man or a woman touch drink, Mister Edmund. Sure, didn't it kill an uncle of mine in the old country. [*relenting*] Still, a drop now and then is no harm when you're in low spirits, or have a bad cold.

EDMUND   Thanks for handing me a good excuse. [*then with forced casualness*] You'd better call my mother, too.

CATHLEEN   What for? She's always on time without any calling. God bless her, she has some consideration for the help.

EDMUND   She's been taking a nap.

CATHLEEN   She wasn't asleep when I finished my work upstairs a while back. She was lying down in the spare room with her eyes wide open. She'd a terrible headache, she said.

EDMUND [*his casualness more forced*]   Oh well then, just call my father.

CATHLEEN [*goes to the screen door, grumbling good-naturedly*]   No wonder my feet kill me each night. I won't walk out in this heat and get sun-stroke. I'll call from the porch.

[*She goes out on the side porch, letting the screen door slam behind her, and disappears on her way to the front porch. A moment later she is heard shouting.*]

Mister Tyrone! Mister Jamie! It's time!

[EDMUND, *who has been staring frightenedly before him, forgetting his book, springs to his feet nervously.*]

EDMUND   God, what a wench!

[*He grabs the bottle and pours a drink, adds ice water and drinks. As he does so, he hears someone coming in the front door. He puts the glass hastily on the tray and sits down again, opening his book.* JAMIE *comes in from the front parlor, his coat over his arm. He has taken off collar and tie and carries them in his hand. He is wiping sweat from his forehead with a handkerchief.* EDMUND *looks up as if his reading was interrupted.* JAMIE *takes one look at the bottle and glasses and smiles cynically.*]

JAMIE   Sneaking one, eh? Cut out the bluff, Kid. You're a rottener actor than I am.

EDMUND [*grins*]   Yes, I grabbed one while the going was good.

JAMIE [*puts a hand affectionately on his shoulder*]   That's better. Why kid me? We're pals, aren't we?

EDMUND   I wasn't sure it was you coming.

JAMIE   I made the Old Man look at his watch. I was halfway up the walk when Cathleen burst into song. Our wild Irish lark! She ought to be a train announcer.

EDMUND   That's what drove me to drink. Why don't you sneak one while you've got a chance?

JAMIE   I was thinking of that little thing. [*He goes quickly to the window at right.*] The Old Man was talking to old Captain Turner. Yes, he's still at it. [*He comes back and takes a drink.*] And now to cover up from his eagle eye. [*He measures two drinks of water and pours them in the whiskey bottle and shakes it up.*] There. That fixes it. [*He pours water in the glass and sets it on the table by* EDMUND.] And here's the water you've been drinking.

EDMUND   Fine! You don't think it will fool him, do you?

JAMIE   Maybe not, but he can't prove it. [*Putting on his collar and tie.*] I hope he doesn't forget lunch listening to himself talk. I'm hungry. [*He sits across the table from* EDMUND—*irritably*] That's what I hate about working down in front. He puts on an act for every damned fool that comes along.

EDMUND [*gloomily*]   You're in luck to be hungry. The way I feel I don't care if I ever eat again.

JAMIE [*gives him a glance of concern*]   Listen, Kid. You know me. I've never lectured you, but Doctor Hardy was right when he told you to cut out the redeye.

EDMUND   Oh, I'm going to after he hands me the bad news this afternoon. A few before then won't make any difference.

JAMIE [*hesitates—then slowly*]   I'm glad you've got your mind prepared for bad news. It won't be such a jolt. [*He catches* EDMUND *staring at him.*] I mean, it's a cinch you're really sick, and it would be wrong dope to kid yourself.

EDMUND [*disturbed*]   I'm not. I know how rotten I feel, and the fever and chills I get at night are no joke. I think Doctor Hardy's last guess was right. It must be the damned malaria come back on me.

JAMIE   Maybe, but don't be too sure.

EDMUND   Why? What do you think it is?

JAMIE   Hell, how would I know? I'm no Doc. [*abruptly*] Where's Mama?

EDMUND   Upstairs.

JAMIE [*looks at him sharply*]   When did she go up?

EDMUND   Oh, about the time I came down to the hedge, I guess. She said she was going to take a nap.

JAMIE   You didn't tell me—

EDMUND [*defensively*]   Why should I? What about it? She was tired out. She didn't get much sleep last night.

JAMIE   I know she didn't.

[*A pause. The brothers avoid looking at each other.*]

EDMUND   That damned foghorn kept me awake, too.

[*Another pause.*]

JAMIE   She's been upstairs alone all morning, eh? You haven't seen her?

EDMUND   No. I've been reading here. I wanted to give her a chance to sleep.

JAMIE   Is she coming down to lunch?

EDMUND   Of course.

JAMIE [*dryly*]   No of course about it. She might not want any lunch. Or she might start having most of her meals alone upstairs. That's happened, hasn't it?

EDMUND [*with frightened resentment*]   Cut it out, Jamie! Can't you think anything but—? [*persuasively*] You're all wrong to suspect anything. Cathleen saw her not long ago. Mama didn't tell her she wouldn't be down to lunch.

JAMIE   Then she wasn't taking a nap?

EDMUND   Not right then, but she was lying down, Cathleen said.

JAMIE   In the spare room?

EDMUND   Yes. For Pete's sake, what of it?

JAMIE [*bursts out*]   You damned fool! Why did you leave her alone so long? Why didn't you stick around?

EDMUND   Because she accused me—and you and Papa—of spying on her all the time and not trusting her. She made me feel ashamed. I know how rotten it must be for her. And she promised on her sacred word of honor—

JAMIE [*with a bitter weariness*]   You ought to know that doesn't mean anything.

EDMUND   It does this time!

JAMIE   That's what we thought the other times. [*He leans over the table to give his brother's arm an affectionate grasp.*] Listen, Kid, I know you think I'm a cynical bastard, but remember I've seen a lot more of this game than you have. You never knew what was really wrong until you were in prep-school. Papa and I kept it from you. But I was wise ten years or more before we had to tell you. I know the game backwards and I've been thinking all morning of the way she acted last night when she thought we were asleep. I haven't been able to think of anything else. And now you tell me she got you to leave her alone upstairs all morning.

EDMUND   She didn't! You're crazy!

JAMIE [*placatingly*]   All right, Kid. Don't start a battle with me. I hope as much as you do I'm crazy. I've been as happy as hell because I'd really begun to believe that this time—[*He stops—looking through the front parlor toward the hall—lowering his voice, hurriedly*] She's coming downstairs. You win on that. I guess I'm a damned suspicious louse.

[*They grow tense with a hopeful, fearful expectancy.* JAMIE *mutters*] Damn! I wish I'd grabbed another drink.

EDMUND   Me, too.

[*He coughs nervously and this brings on a real fit of coughing.* JAMIE *glances at him with worried pity.* MARY *enters from the front parlor. At first one notices no change except that she appears to be less nervous, to be more as she was when we first saw her after breakfast, but then one becomes aware that her eyes are brighter, and there is a peculiar detachment in her voice and manner, as if she were a little withdrawn from her words and actions.*]

MARY [*goes worriedly to* EDMUND *and puts her arm around him*]   You mustn't cough like that. It's bad for your throat. You don't want to get a sore throat on top of your cold.

[*She kisses him. He stops coughing and gives her a quick apprehensive glance, but if his suspicions are aroused her tenderness makes him renounce them and he believes what he wants to believe for the moment. On the other hand,* JAMIE *knows after one probing look at her that his suspicions are justified. His eyes fall to stare at the floor, his face sets in an expression of embittered, defensive cynicism.* MARY *goes on, half sitting on the arm of* EDMUND's *chair, her arm around him, so her face is above and behind his and he cannot look into her eyes.*]

But I seem to be always picking on you, telling you don't do this and don't do that. Forgive me, dear. It's just that I want to take care of you.

EDMUND   I know, Mama. How about you? Do you feel rested?

MARY   Yes, ever so much better. I've been lying down ever since you went out. It's what I needed after such a restless night. I don't feel nervous now.

EDMUND   That's fine.

[*He pats her hand on his shoulder.* JAMIE *gives him a strange, almost contemptuous glance, wondering if his brother can really mean this.* EDMUND *does not notice but his mother does.*]

MARY [*in a forced teasing tone*]   Good heavens, how down in the mouth you look, Jamie. What's the matter now?

JAMIE [*without looking at her*]   Nothing.

MARY   Oh, I'd forgotten you've been working on the front hedge. That accounts for your sinking into the dumps, doesn't it?

JAMIE   If you want to think so, Mama.

MARY [*keeping her tone*]   Well, that's the effect it always has, isn't it? What a big baby you are! Isn't he, Edmund?

EDMUND   He's certainly a fool to care what anyone thinks.

MARY [*strangely*]   Yes, the only way is to make yourself not care.

[*She catches* JAMIE *giving her a bitter glance and changes the subject.*]

Where is your father? I heard Cathleen call him.

EDMUND   Gabbing with old Captain Turner, Jamie says. He'll be late, as usual.

[JAMIE *gets up and goes to the windows at right, glad of an excuse to turn his back.*]

MARY   I've told Cathleen time and again she must go wherever he is and tell him. The idea of screaming as if this were a cheap boardinghouse!

JAMIE [*looking out the window*]   She's down there now. [*sneeringly*] Interrupting the famous Beautiful Voice! She should have more respect.

MARY [*sharply—letting her resentment toward him come out*]   It's you who should have more respect. Stop sneering at your father! I won't have it!

You ought to be proud you're his son! He may have his faults. Who hasn't? But he's worked hard all his life. He made his way up from ignorance and poverty to the top of his profession! Everyone else admires him and you should be the last one to sneer—you, who, thanks to him, have never had to work hard in your life!

[*Stung,* JAMIE *has turned to stare at her with accusing antagonism. Her eyes waver guiltily and she adds in a tone which begins to placate*]

Remember your father is getting old, Jamie. You really ought to show more consideration.

JAMIE   I ought to?

EDMUND [*uneasily*]   Oh, dry up, Jamie!

[JAMIE *looks out the window again.*]

And, for Pete's sake, Mama, why jump on Jamie all of a sudden?

MARY [*bitterly*]   Because he's always sneering at someone else, always looking for the worst weakness in everyone. [*then with a strange, abrupt change to a detached, impersonal tone*] But I suppose life has made him like that, and he can't help it. None of us can help the things life has done to us. They're done before you realize it, and once they're done they make you do other things until at last everything comes between you and what you'd like to be, and you've lost your true self forever.

[EDMUND *is made apprehensive by her strangeness. He tries to look up in her eyes but she keeps them averted.* JAMIE *turns to her—then looks quickly out of the window again.*]

JAMIE [*dully*]   I'm hungry. I wish the Old Man would get a move on. It's a rotten trick the way he keeps meals waiting, and then beefs because they're spoiled.

MARY [*with a resentment that has a quality of being automatic and on the surface while inwardly she is indifferent*]   Yes, it's very trying, Jamie. You don't know how trying. You don't have to keep house with summer servants who don't care because they know it isn't a permanent position. The really good servants are all with people who have homes and not merely summer places. And your father won't even pay the wages the best summer help ask. So every year I have stupid, lazy greenhorns to deal with. But you've heard me say this a thousand times. So has he, but it goes in one ear and out the other. He thinks money spent on a home is money wasted. He's lived too much in hotels. Never the best hotels, of course. Second-rate hotels. He doesn't understand a home. He doesn't feel at home in it. And yet, he wants a home. He's even proud of having this shabby place. He loves it here. [*She laughs—a hopeless and yet amused laugh.*] It's really funny, when you come to think of it. He's a peculiar man.

EDMUND [*again attempting uneasily to look up in her eyes*]   What makes you ramble on like that, Mama?

MARY [*quickly casual—patting his cheek*]   Why, nothing in particular, dear. It *is* foolish.

[*As she speaks,* CATHLEEN *enters from the back parlor.*]

CATHLEEN [*volubly*]   Lunch is ready, Ma'am, I went down to Mister Tyrone, like you ordered, and he said he'd come right away, but he kept on talking to that man, telling him of the time when—

MARY [*indifferently*]   All right, Cathleen. Tell Bridget I'm sorry but she'll have to wait a few minutes until Mister Tyrone is here.

[CATHLEEN *mutters,* "Yes, Ma'am," *and goes off through the back parlor, grumbling to herself.*]

JAMIE Damn it! Why don't you go ahead without him? He told us to.

MARY [*with a remote, amused smile*] He doesn't mean it. Don't you know your father yet? He'd be so terribly hurt.

EDMUND [*jumps up—as if he was glad of an excuse to leave*] I'll make him get a move on.

> [*He goes out on the side porch. A moment later he is heard calling from the porch exasperatedly.*]

Hey! Papa! Come on! We can't wait all day!

> [MARY *has risen from the arm of the chair. Her hands play restlessly over the table top. She does not look at* JAMIE *but she feels the cynically appraising glance he gives her face and hands.*]

MARY [*tensely*] Why do you stare like that?

JAMIE You know. [*He turns back to the window.*]

MARY I don't know.

JAMIE Oh, for God's sake, do you think you can fool me, Mama? I'm not blind.

MARY [*looks directly at him now, her face set again in an expression of blank, stubborn denial*] I don't know what you're talking about.

JAMIE No? Take a look at your eyes in the mirror!

EDMUND [*coming in from the porch*] I got Papa moving. He'll be here in a minute. [*with a glance from one to the other, which his mother avoids—uneasily*] What happened? What's the matter, Mama?

MARY [*disturbed by his coming, gives way to a flurry of guilty, nervous excitement*] Your brother ought to be ashamed of himself. He's been insinuating I don't know what.

EDMUND [*turns on* JAMIE] God damn you!

> [*He takes a threatening step toward him.* JAMIE *turns his back with a shrug and looks out the window.*]

MARY [*more upset, grabs* EDMUND'S *arm—excitedly*] Stop this at once, do you hear me? How dare you use such language before me! [*Abruptly her tone and manner change to the strange detachment she has shown before.*] It's wrong to blame your brother. He can't help being what the past has made him. Any more than your father can. Or you. Or I.

EDMUND [*frightenedly—with a desperate hoping against hope*] He's a liar! It's a lie, isn't it, Mama?

MARY [*keeping her eyes averted*] What is a lie? Now you're talking in riddles like Jamie. [*Then her eyes meet his stricken, accusing look. She stammers*] Edmund! Don't! [*She looks away and her manner instantly regains the quality of strange detachment—calmly*] There's your father coming up the steps now. I must tell Bridget.

> [*She goes through the back parlor.* EDMUND *moves slowly to his chair. He looks sick and hopeless.*]

JAMIE [*from the window, without looking around*] Well?

EDMUND [*refusing to admit anything to his brother yet—weakly defiant*] Well, what? You're a liar.

> [JAMIE *again shrugs his shoulders. The screen door on the front porch is heard closing.* EDMUND *says dully*]

Here's Papa. I hope he loosens up with the old bottle.

> [TYRONE *comes in through the front parlor. He is putting on his coat.*]

TYRONE   Sorry I'm late. Captain Turner stopped to talk and once he starts gabbing you can't get away from him.

JAMIE [*without turning—dryly*]   You mean once he starts listening.

[*His father regards him with dislike. He comes to the table with a quick measuring look at the bottle of whiskey. Without turning,* JAMIE *senses this.*]

It's all right. The level in the bottle hasn't changed.

TYRONE   I wasn't noticing that. [*He adds caustically*] As if it proved anything with you around. I'm on to your tricks.

EDMUND [*dully*]   Did I hear you say, let's all have a drink?

TYRONE [*frowns at him*]   Jamie is welcome after his hard morning's work, but I won't invite you. Doctor Hardy—

EDMUND   To hell with Doctor Hardy! One isn't going to kill me. I feel—all in, Papa.

TYRONE [*with a worried look at him—putting on a fake heartiness*]   Come along, then. It's before a meal and I've always found that good whiskey, taken in moderation as an appetizer, is the best of tonics.

[EDMUND *gets up as his father passes the bottle to him. He pours a big drink.* TYRONE *frowns admonishingly.*]

I said, in moderation.

[*He pours his own drink and passes the bottle to* JAMIE, *grumbling.*]

It'd be a waste of breath mentioning moderation to you.

[*Ignoring the hint,* JAMIE *pours a big drink. His father scowls—then, giving it up, resumes his hearty air, raising his glass.*]

Well, here's health and happiness!

[EDMUND *gives a bitter laugh.*]

EDMUND   That's a joke!

TYRONE   What is?

EDMUND   Nothing. Here's how. [*They drink.*]

TYRONE [*becoming aware of the atmosphere*]   What's the matter here? There's gloom in the air you could cut with a knife. [*turns on* JAMIE *resentfully*] You got the drink you were after, didn't you? Why are you wearing that gloomy look on your mug?

JAMIE [*shrugging his shoulders*]   You won't be singing a song yourself soon.

EDMUND   Shut up, Jamie.

TYRONE [*uneasy now—changing the subject*]   I thought lunch was ready. I'm hungry as a hunter. Where is your mother?

MARY [*returning through the back parlor, calls*]   Here I am.

[*She comes in. She is excited and self-conscious. As she talks, she glances everywhere except at any of their faces.*]

I've had to calm down Bridget. She's in a tantrum over your being late again, and I don't blame her. If your lunch is dried up from waiting in the oven, she said it served you right, you could like it or leave it for all she cared. [*with increasing excitement*] Oh, I'm so sick and tired of pretending this is a home! You won't help me! You won't put yourself out the least bit! You don't know how to act in a home! You don't really want one! You never have wanted one—never since the day we were married! You should have remained a bachelor and lived in second-rate hotels and entertained your friends in barrooms! [*She adds strangely, as if she were now talking aloud to herself rather than to* TYRONE] Then nothing would ever have happened.

[*They stare at her.* TYRONE *knows now. He suddenly looks a tired, bitterly sad old man.* EDMUND *glances at his father and sees that he knows, but he still cannot help trying to warn his mother.*]

EDMUND   Mama! Stop talking. Why don't we go in to lunch.

MARY [*Starts and at once the quality of unnatural detachment settles on her face again. She even smiles with an ironical amusement to herself.*]   Yes, it is inconsiderate of me to dig up the past, when I know your father and Jamie must be hungry. [*putting her arm around* EDMUND's *shoulder— with a fond solicitude which is at the same time remote*] I do hope you have an appetite, dear. You really must eat more [*Her eyes become fixed on the whiskey glass on the table beside him—sharply*] Why is that glass there? Did you take a drink? Oh, how can you be such a fool? Don't you know it's the worst thing? [*She turns on* TYRONE.] You're to blame, James. How could you let him? Do you want to kill him? Don't you remember my father? He wouldn't stop after he was stricken. He said doctors were fools! He thought, like you, that whiskey is a good tonic! [*A look of terror comes into her eyes and she stammers*] But, of course, there's no comparison at all. I don't know why I—Forgive me for scolding you, James. One small drink won't hurt Edmund. It might be good for him, if it gives him an appetite.

[*She pats* EDMUND's *cheek playfully, the strange detachment again in her manner. He jerks his head away. She seems not to notice, but she moves instinctively away.*]

JAMIE [*roughly, to hide his tense nerves*]   For God's sake, let's eat. I've been working in the damned dirt under the hedge all morning. I've earned my grub.

[*He comes around in back of his father, not looking at his mother, and grabs* EDMUND's *shoulder.*]

Come on, Kid. Let's put on the feed bag.

[EDMUND *gets up, keeping his eyes averted from his mother. They pass her, heading for the back parlor.*]

TYRONE [*dully*]   Yes, you go in with your mother, lads. I'll join you in a second.

[*But they keep on without waiting for her. She looks at their backs with a helpless hurt and, as they enter the back parlor, starts to follow them.* TYRONE's *eyes are on her, sad and condemning. She feels them and turns sharply without meeting his stare.*]

MARY   Why do you look at me like that? [*Her hands flutter up to pat her hair.*] Is it my hair coming down? I was so worn out from last night, I thought I'd better lie down this morning. I drowsed off and had a nice refreshing nap. But I'm sure I fixed my hair again when I woke up. [*forcing a laugh*] Although, as usual, I couldn't find my glasses. [*sharply*] Please stop staring! One would think you were accusing me—[*then pleadingly*] James! You don't understand!

TYRONE [*with dull anger*]   I understand that I've been a God-damned fool to believe in you!

[*He walks away from her to pour himself a big drink.*]

MARY [*her face again sets in stubborn defiance*]   I don't know what you mean by "believing in me." All I've felt was distrust and spying and suspicion. [*then accusingly*] Why are you having another drink? You never have more than one before lunch. [*bitterly*] I know what to expect. You will be drunk tonight. Well, it won't be the first time, will it—or the thousandth? [*again she bursts out pleadingly*] Oh, James, please! You don't understand! I'm worried about Edmund! I'm so afraid he—

TYRONE   I don't want to listen to excuses, Mary.

MARY [*strickenly*]   Excuses? You mean—? Oh, you can't believe that of me! You mustn't believe that, James! [*then slipping away into her strange detachment—quite casually*] Shall we not go into lunch dear? I don't want anything but I know you're hungry.

> [*He walks slowly to where she stands in the doorway. He walks like an old man. As he reaches her she bursts out piteously.*]

James! I tried so hard! I tried so hard! Please believe—!

TYRONE [*moved in spite of himself—helplessly*]   I suppose you did, Mary. [*then grief-strickenly*] For the love of God, why couldn't you have the strength to keep on?

MARY [*her face setting into that stubborn denial again*]   I don't know what you're talking about. Have the strength to keep on what?

TYRONE [*hopelessly*]   Never mind. It's no use now.

> [*He moves on and she keeps beside him as they disappear in the back parlor.*]

CURTAIN

Act 2

SCENE 2

SCENE—*The same, about a half hour later. The tray with the bottle of whiskey has been removed from the table. The family are returning from lunch as the curtain rises.* MARY *is the first to enter from the back parlor. Her husband follows. He is not with her as he was in the similar entrance after breakfast at the opening of Act One. He avoids touching her or looking at her. There is condemnation in his face, mingled now with the beginning of an old weary, helpless resignation.* JAMIE *and* EDMUND *follow their father.* JAMIE'S *face is hard with defensive cynicism.* EDMUND *tries to copy this defense but without success. He plainly shows he is heartsick as well as physically ill.*

MARY *is terribly nervous again, as if the strain of sitting through lunch with them had been too much for her. Yet at the same time, in contrast to this, her expression shows more of that strange aloofness which seems to stand apart from her nerves and the anxieties which harry them.*

She is talking as she enters—a stream of words that issues casually, in a routine of family conversation, from her mouth. She appears indifferent to the fact that their thoughts are not on what she is saying any more than her own are. As she talks, she comes to the left of the table and stands, facing front, one hand fumbling with the bosom of her dress, the other playing over the table top. TYRONE *lights a cigar and goes to the screen door, staring out.* JAMIE *fills a pipe from a jar on top of the bookcase at rear. He lights it as he goes to look out the window at right.* EDMUND *sits in a chair by the table, turned half away from his mother so he does not have to watch her.*

MARY   It's no use finding fault with Bridget. She doesn't listen. I can't threaten her, or she'd threaten she'd leave. And she does do her best at times. It's too bad they seem to be just the times you're sure to be late, James. Well, there's this consolation: it's difficult to tell from her cooking whether she's doing her best or her worst. [*She gives a little laugh of detached amusement—indifferently*] Never mind. The summer will soon be over, thank goodness. Your season will open again and we can go back to second-rate hotels and trains. I hate them, too, but at least I don't expect them to be like a home, and there's no housekeeping to worry about. It's unreasonable to expect Bridget or Cathleen to act as if this was a home. They know it isn't as well as we know it. It never has been and it never will be.

TYRONE [*bitterly without turning around*]   No, it never can be now. But it was once, before you—

MARY [*her face instantly set in blank denial*]   Before I what? [*There is dead silence. She goes on with a return of her detached air.*] No, no. Whatever you mean, it isn't true, dear. It was never a home. You've always preferred the Club or barroom. And for me it's always been as lonely as a dirty room in a one-night stand hotel. In a real home one is never lonely. You forget I know from experience what a home is like. I gave up one to marry you—my father's home. [*At once, through an association of ideas she turns to* EDMUND. *Her manner becomes tenderly solicitous, but there is the strange quality of detachment in it.*] I'm worried about you, Edmund. You hardly touched a thing at lunch. That's no way to take care of yourself. It's all right for me not to have an appetite. I've been growing too fat. But you must eat. [*coaxingly maternal*] Promise me you will, dear, for my sake.

EDMUND [*dully*]   Yes, Mama.

MARY [*pats his cheek as he tries not to shrink away*]   That's a good boy.
   [*There is another pause of dead silence. Then the telephone in the front hall rings and all of them stiffen startledly.*]

TYRONE [*hastily*]   I'll answer. McGuire said he'd call me. [*He goes out through the front parlor.*]

MARY [*indifferently*]   McGuire. He must have another piece of property on his list that no one would think of buying except your father. It doesn't matter any more, but it's always seemed to me your father could afford to keep on buying property but never to give me a home.
   [*She stops to listen as* TYRONE's *voice is heard from the hall.*]

TYRONE   Hello. [*with forced heartiness*] Oh, how are you, Doctor?
   [*JAMIE turns from the window.* MARY's *fingers play more rapidly on the table top.* TYRONE's *voice, trying to conceal, reveals that he is hearing bad news.*]

I see—[*hurriedly*] Well, you'll explain all about it when you see him this afternoon. Yes, he'll be in without fail. Four o'clock. I'll drop in myself and have a talk with you before that. I have to go uptown on business, anyway. Goodbye, Doctor.

EDMUND [*dully*]   That didn't sound like glad tidings.
   [*JAMIE gives him a pitying glance—then looks out the window again.* MARY's *face is terrified and her hands flutter distractedly.* TYRONE *comes in. The strain is obvious in his casualness as he addresses* EDMUND.]

TYRONE   It was Doctor Hardy. He wants you to be sure and see him at four.

EDMUND [*dully*]   What did he say? Not that I give a damn now.

MARY [*bursts out excitedly*]   I wouldn't believe him if he swore on a stack of Bibles. You mustn't pay attention to a word he says, Edmund.

TYRONE [*sharply*]   Mary!

MARY [*more excitedly*]   Oh, we all realize why you like him, James! Because he's cheap! But please don't try to tell me! I know all about Doctor Hardy. Heaven knows I ought to after all these years. He's an ignorant fool! There should be a law to keep men like him from practicing. He hasn't the slightest idea—When you're in agony and half insane, he sits and holds your hand and delivers sermons on will power! [*Her face is drawn in an expression of intense suffering by the memory. For the moment, she loses all caution. With bitter hatred*] He deliberately humiliates you! He makes you beg and plead! He treats you like a criminal! He understands nothing! And yet it was exactly the same type of cheap quack who first gave you the medicine—and you never knew what it was until too late! [*passionately*] I hate doctors! They'll sell their souls! What's worse, they'll sell yours, and you never know it till one day you find yourself in hell!

EDMUND   Mama! For God's sake, stop talking.

TYRONE [*shakily*]   Yes, Mary, it's no time—

MARY [*suddenly is overcome by guilty confusion—stammers*]   I—Forgive me, dear. You're right. It's useless to be angry now. [*There is again a pause of dead silence. When she speaks again, her face has cleared and is calm, and the quality of uncanny detachment is in her voice and manner.*] I'm going upstairs for a moment, if you'll excuse me. I have to fix my hair. [*she adds smilingly*] That is if I can find my glasses. I'll be right down.

TYRONE [*as she starts through the doorway—pleading and rebuking*]   Mary!

MARY [*turns to stare at him calmly*]   Yes, dear? What is it?

TYRONE [*helplessly*]   Nothing.

MARY [*with a strange derisive smile*]   You're welcome to come up and watch me if you're so suspicious.

TYRONE   As if that could do any good! You'd only postpone it. And I'm not your jailor. This isn't a prison.

MARY   No. I know you can't help thinking it's a home. [*She adds quickly with a detached contrition*] I'm sorry, dear. I don't mean to be bitter. It's not your fault.

> [*She turns and disappears through the back parlor. The three in the room remain silent. It is as if they were waiting until she got upstairs before speaking.*]

JAMIE [*cynically brutal*]   Another shot in the arm!

EDMUND [*angrily*]   Cut out that kind of talk!

TYRONE   Yes! Hold your foul tongue and your rotten Broadway loafer's lingo! Have you no pity or decency? [*losing his temper*] You ought to be kicked out in the gutter! But if I did it, you know damned well who'd weep and plead for you, and excuse you and complain till I let you come back.

JAMIE [*a spasm of pain crosses his face*]   Christ, don't I know that? No pity? I have all the pity in the world for her. I understand what a hard game to beat she's up against—which is more than you ever have! My lingo didn't mean I had no feeling. I was merely putting bluntly what we all know, and have to live with now, again. [*bitterly*] The cures are no damned good except for a while. The truth is there is no cure and we've been saps to hope—[*cynically*] They never come back!

EDMUND [*scornfully parodying his brother's cynicism*]   They never come back! Everything is in the bag! It's all a frame-up! We're all fall guys and suckers and we can't beat the game! [*disdainfully*] Christ, if I felt the way you do—!

JAMIE [*stung for a moment—then shrugging his shoulders, dryly*]   I thought you did. Your poetry isn't very cheery. Nor the stuff you read and claim to admire. [*He indicates the small bookcase at rear.*] Your pet with the unpronounceable name, for example.

EDMUND   Nietzsche. You don't know what you're talking about. You haven't read him.

JAMIE   Enough to know it's a lot of bunk!

TYRONE   Shut up, both of you! There's little choice between the philosophy you learned from Broadway loafers, and the one Edmund got from his books. They're both rotten to the core. You've both flouted the faith you were born and brought up in—the one true faith of the Catholic Church—and your denial has brought nothing but self-destruction!

[*His two sons stare at him contemptuously. They forget their quarrel and are as one against him on this issue.*]

EDMUND   That's the bunk, Papa!

JAMIE   We don't pretend, at any rate. [*caustically*] I don't notice you've worn any holes in the knees of your pants going to Mass.

TYRONE   It's true I'm a bad Catholic in the observance, God forgive me. But I believe! [*angrily*] And you're a liar! I may not go to church but every night and morning of my life I get on my knees and pray!

EDMUND [*bitingly*]   Did you pray for Mama?

TYRONE   I did. I've prayed to God these many years for her.

EDMUND   Then Nietzsche must be right. [*He quotes from* Thus Spake Zarathustra.] "God is dead: of His pity for man hath God died."

TYRONE [*ignores this*]   If your mother had prayed, too—She hasn't denied her faith, but she's forgotten it, until now there's no strength of the spirit left in her to fight against her curse. [*then dully resigned*] But what's the good of talk? We've lived with this before and now we must again. There's no help for it. [*bitterly*] Only I wish she hadn't led me to hope this time. By God, I never will again!

EDMUND   That's a rotten thing to say, Papa! [*defiantly*] Well, I'll hope! She's just started. It can't have got a hold on her yet. She can still stop. I'm going to talk to her.

JAMIE [*shrugs his shoulders*]   You can't talk to her now. She'll listen but she won't listen. She'll be here but she won't be here. You know the way she gets.

TYRONE   Yes, that's the way the poison acts on her always. Every day from now on, there'll be the same drifting away from us until by the end of each night—

EDMUND [*miserably*]   Cut it out, Papa! [*He jumps up from his chair.*] I'm going to get dressed. [*bitterly, as he goes*] I'll make so much noise she can't suspect I've come to spy on her.

[*He disappears through the front parlor and can be heard stamping noisily upstairs.*]

JAMIE [*after a pause*]   What did Doc Hardy say about the Kid?

TYRONE [*dully*]   It's what you thought. He's got consumption.

JAMIE   God damn it!

TYRONE   There is no possible doubt, he said.

JAMIE   He'll have to go to a sanatorium.

TYRONE   Yes, and the sooner the better, Hardy said, for him and everyone around him. He claims that in six months to a year Edmund will be cured, if he obeys orders. [*He sighs—gloomily and resentfully*] I never thought a child of mine—It doesn't come from my side of the family. There wasn't one of us that didn't have lungs as strong as an ox.

JAMIE   Who gives a damn about that part of it! Where does Hardy want to send him?

TYRONE   That's what I'm to see him about.

JAMIE   Well, for God's sake, pick out a good place and not some cheap dump!

TYRONE [*stung*]   I'll send him wherever Hardy thinks best!

JAMIE   Well, don't give Hardy your old over-the-hills-to-the-poorhouse song about taxes and mortgages.

TYRONE   I'm no millionaire who can throw money away! Why shouldn't I tell Hardy the truth?

JAMIE   Because he'll think you want him to pick a cheap dump, and because he'll know it isn't the truth—especially if he hears afterwards you've seen McGuire and let that flannel-mouth, gold-brick merchant sting you with another piece of bum property!

TYRONE   Keep your nose out of my business!

JAMIE   This is Edmund's business. What I'm afraid of is, with your Irish bog trotter idea that consumption is fatal, you'll figure it would be a waste of money to spend any more than you can help.

TYRONE   You liar!

JAMIE   All right. Prove I'm a liar. That's what I want. That's why I brought it up.

TYRONE [*his rage still smoldering*]   I have every hope Edmund will be cured. And keep your dirty tongue off Ireland! You're a fine one to sneer, with the map of it on your face!

JAMIE   Not after I wash my face. [*Then before his father can react to this insult to the Old Sod he adds dryly, shrugging his shoulders*] Well, I've said all I have to say. It's up to you. [*abruptly*] What do you want me to do this afternoon, now you're going uptown? I've done all I can do on the hedge until you cut more of it. You don't want me to go ahead with your clipping, I know that.

TYRONE   No. You'd get it crooked, as you get everything else.

JAMIE   Then I'd better go uptown with Edmund. The bad news coming on top of what's happened to Mama may hit him hard.

TYRONE [*forgetting his quarrel*]   Yes, go with him, Jamie. Keep up his spirits, if you can. [*He adds caustically*] If you can without making it an excuse to get drunk!

JAMIE   What would I use for money? The last I heard they were still selling booze, not giving it away. [*He starts for the front-parlor doorway.*] I'll get dressed.

[*He stops in the doorway as he sees his mother approaching from the hall, and moves aside to let her come in. Her eyes look brighter, and her manner is more detached. This change becomes more marked as the scene goes on.*]

MARY [*vaguely*] You haven't seen my glasses anywhere, have you, Jamie?

[*She doesn't look at him. He glances away, ignoring her question but she doesn't seem to expect an answer. She comes forward, addressing her husband without looking at him.*]

You haven't seen them, have you, James?

[*Behind her* JAMIE *disappears through the front parlor.*]

TYRONE [*turns to look out the screen door*] No, Mary.

MARY What's the matter with Jamie? Have you been nagging at him again? You shouldn't treat him with such contempt all the time. He's not to blame. If he'd been brought up in a real home, I'm sure he would have been different. [*She comes to the windows at right—lightly*] You're not much of a weather prophet, dear. See how hazy it's getting. I can hardly see the other shore.

TYRONE [*trying to speak naturally*] Yes, I spoke too soon. We're in for another night of fog, I'm afraid.

MARY Oh, well, I won't mind it tonight.

TYRONE No, I don't imagine you will, Mary.

MARY [*flashes a glance at him—after a pause*] I don't see Jamie going down to the hedge. Where did he go?

TYRONE He's going with Edmund to the Doctor's. He went up to change his clothes. [*then, glad of an excuse to leave her*] I'd better do the same or I'll be late for my appointment at the Club.

[*He makes a move toward the front-parlor doorway, but with a swift impulsive movement she reaches out and clasps his arm.*]

MARY [*a note of pleading in her voice*] Don't go yet, dear. I don't want to be alone. [*hastily*] I mean, you have plenty of time. You know you boast you can dress in one-tenth the time it takes the boys. [*vaguely*] There is something I wanted to say. What is it? I've forgotten. I'm glad Jamie is going uptown. You didn't give him any money, I hope.

TYRONE I did not.

MARY He'd only spend it on drink and you know what a vile, poisonous tongue he has when he's drunk. Not that I would mind anything he said tonight, but he always manages to drive you into a rage, especially if you're drunk, too, as you will be.

TYRONE [*resentfully*] I won't. I never get drunk.

MARY [*teasing indifferently*] Oh, I'm sure you'll hold it well. You always have. It's hard for a stranger to tell, but after thirty-five years of marriage—

TYRONE I've never missed a performance in my life. That's the proof! [*then bitterly*] If I did get drunk it is not you who should blame me. No man has ever had a better reason.

MARY Reason? What reason? You always drink too much when you go to the Club, don't you? Particularly when you meet McGuire. He sees to that. Don't think I'm finding fault, dear. You must do as you please. I won't mind.

TYRONE I know you won't. [*He turns toward the front parlor, anxious to escape.*] I've got to get dressed.

MARY [*again she reaches out and grasps his arm—pleadingly*] No, please wait a little while, dear. At least, until one of the boys comes down. You will all be leaving me so soon.

TYRONE [*with bitter sadness*]   It's you who are leaving us, Mary.

MARY   I? That's a silly thing to say, James. How could I leave? There is nowhere I could go. Who would I go to see? I have no friends.

TYRONE   It's your own fault—[*He stops and sighs helplessly—persuasively*] There's surely one thing you can do this afternoon that will be good for you, Mary. Take a drive in the automobile. Get away from the house. Get a little sun and fresh air. [*injuredly*] I bought the automobile for you. You know I don't like the damned things. I'd rather walk any day, or take a trolley. [*with growing resentment*] I had it here waiting for you when you came back from the sanatorium. I hoped it would give you pleasure and distract your mind. You used to ride in it every day, but you've hardly used it at all lately. I paid a lot of money I couldn't afford, and there's the chauffeur I have to board and lodge and pay high wages whether he drives you or not. [*bitterly*] Waste! The same old waste that will land me in the poorhouse in my old age! What good did it do you? I might as well have thrown the money out the window.

MARY [*with detached calm*]   Yes, it was a waste of money, James. You shouldn't have bought a secondhand automobile. You were swindled again as you always are, because you insist on secondhand bargains in everything.

TYRONE   It's one of the best makes! Everyone says it's better than any of the new ones!

MARY [*ignoring this*]   It was another waste to hire Smythe, who was only a helper in a garage and had never been a chauffeur. Oh, I realize his wages are less than a real chauffeur's, but he more than makes up for that, I'm sure, by the graft he gets from the garage on repair bills. Something is always wrong. Smythe sees to that, I'm afraid.

TYRONE   I don't believe it! He may not be a fancy millionaire's flunky but he's honest! You're as bad as Jamie, suspecting everyone!

MARY   You mustn't be offended, dear. I wasn't offended when you gave me the automobile. I knew you didn't mean to humiliate me. I knew that was the way you had to do everything. I was grateful and touched. I knew buying the car was a hard thing for you to do, and it proved how much you loved me, in your way, especially when you couldn't really believe it would do me any good.

TYRONE   Mary! [*He suddenly hugs her to him—brokenly*] Dear Mary! For the love of God, for my sake and the boys' sake and your own, won't you stop now?

MARY [*stammers in guilty confusion for a second*]   I—James! Please! [*Her strange, stubborn defense comes back instantly.*] Stop what? What are you talking about?

[*He lets his arm fall to his side brokenly. She impulsively puts her arm around him.*]

James! We've loved each other! We always will! Let's remember only that, and not try to understand what we cannot understand, or help things that cannot be helped—the things life has done to us we cannot excuse or explain.

TYRONE [*as if he hadn't heard—bitterly*]   You won't even try?

MARY [*her arms drop hopelessly and she turns away—with detachment*] Try to go for a drive this afternoon, you mean? Why, yes, if you wish me to, although it makes me feel lonelier than if I stayed here. There is no one I can invite to drive with me, and I never know where to tell Smythe to go. If there was a friend's house where I could drop in and laugh and gossip awhile. But, of course, there isn't. There never has been. [*her manner becoming more and more remote*] At the Convent I had so many friends. Girls whose families lived in lovely homes. I used to visit them and they'd visit me in my father's home. But, naturally, after I married an actor—you know how actors were considered in those days—a lot of them gave me the cold shoulder. And then, right after we were married, there was the scandal of that woman who had been your mistress, suing you. From then on, all my old friends either pitied me or cut me dead. I hated the ones who cut me much less than the pitiers.

TYRONE [*with guilty resentment*]   For God's sake, don't dig up what's long forgotten. If you're that far gone in the past already, when it's only the beginning of the afternoon, what will you be tonight?

MARY [*stares at him defiantly now*]   Come to think of it, I do have to drive uptown. There's something I must get at the drugstore.

TYRONE [*bitterly scornful*]   Leave it to you to have some of the stuff hidden, and prescriptions for more! I hope you'll lay in a good stock ahead so we'll never have another night like the one when you screamed for it, and ran out of the house in your nightdress half crazy, to try and throw yourself off the dock!

MARY [*tries to ignore this*]   I have to get tooth powder and toilet soap and cold cream—[*She breaks down pitiably.*] James! You mustn't remember! You mustn't humiliate me so!

TYRONE [*ashamed*]   I'm sorry. Forgive me, Mary!

MARY [*defensively detached again*]   It doesn't matter. Nothing like that ever happened. You must have dreamed it.

[*He stares at her hopelessly. Her voice seems to drift farther and farther away.*]

I was so healthy before Edmund was born. You remember, James. There wasn't a nerve in my body. Even traveling with you season after season, with week after week of one-night stands, in trains without Pullmans, in dirty rooms of filthy hotels, eating bad food, bearing children in hotel rooms, I still kept healthy. But bearing Edmund was the last straw. I was so sick afterwards, and that ignorant quack of a cheap hotel doctor—All he knew was I was in pain. It was easy for him to stop the pain.

TYRONE   Mary! For God's sake, forget the past!

MARY [*with strange objective calm*]   Why? How can I? The past is the present, isn't it? It's the future, too. We all try to lie out of that but life won't let us. [*going on*] I blame only myself. I swore after Eugene died I would never have another baby. I was to blame for his death. If I hadn't left him with my mother to join you on the road, because you wrote telling me you missed me and were so lonely, Jamie would never have been allowed, when he still had measles, to go in the baby's room. [*her face hardening*] I've always believed Jamie did it on purpose. He was jealous of the baby. He hated him. [*as TYRONE starts to protest*] Oh, I know Jamie was only seven, but he was never stupid. He'd been warned it might kill the baby. He knew. I've never been able to forgive him for that.

TYRONE [*with bitter sadness*]   Are you back with Eugene now? Can't you let our dead baby rest in peace?

MARY [*as if she hadn't heard him*]   It was my fault. I should have insisted on staying with Eugene and not have let you persuade me to join you, just because I loved you. Above all, I shouldn't have let you insist I have another baby to take Eugene's place, because you thought that would make me forget his death. I knew from experience by then that children should have homes to be born in, if they are to be good children, and women need homes, if they are to be good mothers. I was afraid all the time I carried Edmund. I knew something terrible would happen. I knew I'd proved by the way I'd left Eugene that I wasn't worthy to have another baby, and that God would punish me if I did. I never should have borne Edmund.

TYRONE [*with an uneasy glance through the front parlor*]   Mary! Be careful with your talk. If he heard you he might think you never wanted him. He's feeling bad enough already without—

MARY [*violently*]   It's a lie! I did want him! More than anything in the world! You don't understand! I meant, for his sake. He has never been happy. He never will be. Nor healthy. He was born nervous and too sensitive, and that's my fault. And now, ever since he's been so sick I've kept remembering Eugene and my father and I've been so frightened and guilty—[*then, catching herself, with an instant change to stubborn denial*] Oh, I know it's foolish to imagine dreadful things when there's no reason for it. After all, everyone has colds and gets over them.

[TYRONE *stares at her and sighs helplessly. He turns away toward the front parlor and sees* EDMUND *coming down the stairs in the hall.*]

TYRONE [*sharply, in a low voice*]   Here's Edmund. For God's sake try and be yourself—at least until he goes! You can do that much for him!

[*He waits, forcing his face into a pleasantly paternal expression. She waits frightenedly, seized again by a nervous panic, her hands fluttering over the bosom of her dress, up to her throat and hair, with a distracted aimlessness. Then, as* EDMUND *approaches the doorway, she cannot face him. She goes swiftly away to the windows at left and stares out with her back to the front parlor.* EDMUND *enters. He has changed to a ready-made blue serge suit, high stiff collar and tie, black shoes. With an actor's heartiness*]

Well! You look spic and span. I'm on my way up to change, too. [*He starts to pass him.*]

EDMUND [*dryly*]   Wait a minute, Papa. I hate to bring up disagreeable topics, but there's the matter of carfare. I'm broke.

TYRONE [*starts automatically on a customary lecture*]   You'll always be broke until you learn the value—[*checks himself guiltily, looking at his son's sick face with worried pity*] But you've been learning, lad. You worked hard before you took ill. You've done splendidly. I'm proud of you.

[*He pulls out a small roll of bills from his pants pocket and carefully selects one.* EDMUND *takes it. He glances at it and his face expresses astonishment. His father again reacts customarily—sarcastically*]

Thank you. [*He quotes*] "How sharper than a serpent's tooth it is—"

EDMUND   "To have a thankless child."[9] I know. Give me a chance, Papa. I'm knocked speechless. This isn't a dollar. It's a ten spot.

TYRONE [*embarrassed by his generosity*]   Put it in your pocket. You'll probably meet some of your friends uptown and you can't hold your end up and be sociable with nothing in your jeans.

---

9. Shakespeare's *King Lear* 1.4.312.

EDMUND You meant it? Gosh, thank you, Papa. [*He is genuinely pleased and grateful for a moment—then he stares at his father's face with uneasy suspicion.*] But why all of a sudden—? [*cynically*] Did Doc Hardy tell you I was going to die? [*Then he sees his father is bitterly hurt.*] No! That's a rotten crack. I was only kidding, Papa. [*He puts an arm around his father impulsively and gives him an affectionate hug.*] I'm very grateful. Honest, Papa.

TYRONE [*touched, returns his hug*] You're welcome, lad.

MARY [*suddenly turns to them in a confused panic of frightened anger*] I won't have it! [*She stamps her foot.*] Do you hear, Edmund! Such morbid nonsense! Saying you're going to die! It's the books you read! Nothing but sadness and death! Your father shouldn't allow you to have them. And some of the poems you've written yourself are even worse! You'd think you didn't want to live! A boy of your age with everything before him! It's just a pose you get out of books! You're not really sick at all!

TYRONE Mary! Hold your tongue!

MARY [*instantly changing to a detached tone*] But, James, it's absurd of Edmund to be so gloomy and make such a great to-do about nothing. [*turning to* EDMUND *but avoiding his eyes—teasingly affectionate*] Never mind, dear. I'm on to you. [*She comes to him.*] You want to be petted and spoiled and made a fuss over, isn't that it? You're still such a baby. [*She puts her arm around him and hugs him. He remains rigid and unyielding. Her voice begins to tremble.*] But please don't carry it too far, dear. Don't say horrible things. I know it's foolish to take them seriously but I can't help it. You've got me—so frightened.

> [*She breaks and hides her face on his shoulder, sobbing.* EDMUND *is moved in spite of himself. He pats her shoulder with an awkward tenderness.*]

EDMUND Don't, mother. [*His eyes meet his father's.*]

TYRONE [*huskily—clutching at hopeless hope*] Maybe if you asked your mother now what you said you were going to—[*He fumbles with his watch.*] By God, look at the time! I'll have to shake a leg.

> [*He hurries away through the front parlor.* MARY *lifts her head. Her manner is again one of detached motherly solicitude. She seems to have forgotten the tears which are still in her eyes.*]

MARY How do you feel, dear? [*She feels his forehead.*] Your head is a little hot, but that's just from going out in the sun. You look ever so much better than you did this morning. [*taking his hand*] Come and sit down. You mustn't stand on your feet so much. You must learn to husband your strength.

> [*She gets him to sit and she sits sideways on the arm of his chair, an arm around his shoulder, so he cannot meet her eyes.*]

EDMUND [*starts to blurt out the appeal he now feels is quite hopeless*] Listen, Mama—

MARY [*interrupting quickly*] Now, now! Don't talk. Lean back and rest. [*persuasively*] You know, I think it would be much better for you if you stayed home this afternoon and let me take care of you. It's such a tiring trip uptown in the dirty old trolley on a hot day like this. I'm sure you'd be much better off here with me.

EDMUND [*dully*] You forget I have an appointment with Hardy. [*trying again to get his appeal started*] Listen, Mama—

MARY [*quickly*]   You can telephone and say you don't feel well enough. [*excitedly*] It's simply a waste of time and money seeing him. He'll only tell you some lie. He'll pretend he's found something serious the matter because that's his bread and butter. [*She gives a hard sneering little laugh.*] The old idiot! All he knows about medicine is to look solemn and preach will power!

EDMUND [*trying to catch her eyes*]   Mama! Please listen! I want to ask you something! You—You're only just started. You can still stop. You've got the will power! We'll all help you. I'll do anything! Won't you, Mama?

MARY [*stammers pleadingly*]   Please don't—talk about things you don't understand!

EDMUND [*dully*]   All right, I give up. I knew it was no use.

MARY [*in blank denial now*]   Anyway, I don't know what you're referring to. But I do know you should be the last one—Right after I returned from the sanatorium, you began to be ill. The doctor there had warned me I must have peace at home with nothing to upset me, and all I've done is worry about you. [*then distractedly*] But that's no excuse! I'm only trying to explain. It's not an excuse! [*She hugs him to her—pleadingly*] Promise me, dear, you won't believe I made you an excuse.

EDMUND [*bitterly*]   What else can I believe?

MARY [*slowly takes her arm away—her manner remote and objective again*]   Yes, I suppose you can't help suspecting that.

EDMUND [*ashamed but still bitter*]   What do you expect?

MARY   Nothing, I don't blame you. How could you believe me—when I can't believe myself? I've become such a liar. I never lied about anything once upon a time. Now I have to lie, especially to myself. But how can you understand, when I don't myself. I've never understood anything about it, except that one day long ago I found I could no longer call my soul my own. [*She pauses—then lowering her voice to a strange tone of whispered confidence*] But some day, dear, I will find it again— some day when you're all well, and I see you healthy and happy and successful, and I don't have to feel guilty any more—some day when the Blessed Virgin Mary forgives me and gives me back the faith in Her love and pity I used to have in my convent days, and I can pray to Her again—when She sees no one in the world can believe in me even for a moment any more, then She will believe in me, and with Her help it will be so easy. I will hear myself scream with agony, and at the same time I will laugh because I will be so sure of myself. [*then as* EDMUND *remains hopelessly silent, she adds sadly*] Of course, you can't believe that, either. [*She rises from the arm of his chair and goes to stare out the windows at right with her back to him—casually*] Now I think of it, you might as well go uptown. I forgot I'm taking a drive. I have to go to the drugstore. You would hardly want to go there with me. You'd be so ashamed.

EDMUND [*brokenly*]   Mama! Don't!

MARY   I suppose you'll divide that ten dollars your father gave you with Jamie. You always divide with each other, don't you? Like good sports. Well, I know what he'll do with his share. Get drunk someplace where he can be with the only kind of woman he understands or likes. [*She turns to him, pleading frightenedly*] Edmund! Promise me you won't drink! It's so dangerous! You know Doctor Hardy told you—

EDMUND [*bitterly*] I thought he was an old idiot. Anyway, by tonight, what will you care?

MARY [*pitifully*] Edmund!

> [JAMIE's *voice is heard from the front hall,* "Come on, Kid, let's beat it."
> MARY's *manner at once becomes detached again.*]

Go on, Edmund. Jamie's waiting. [*She goes to the front-parlor doorway.*] There comes your father downstairs, too.

> [TYRONE's *voice calls,* "Come on, Edmund."]

EDMUND [*jumping up from his chair*] I'm coming.

> [*He stops beside her—without looking at her.*]

Goodbye, Mama.

MARY [*kisses him with detached affection*] Goodbye, dear. If you're coming home for dinner, try not to be late. And tell your father. You know what Bridget is.

> [*He turns and hurries away.* TYRONE *calls from the hall,* "Goodbye, Mary," *and then* JAMIE, "Goodbye, Mama." *She calls back*]

Goodbye. [*The front screen door is heard closing after them. She comes and stands by the table, one hand drumming on it, the other fluttering up to pat her hair. She stares about the room with frightened, forsaken eyes and whispers to herself.*] It's so lonely here. [*Then her face hardens into bitter self-contempt.*] You're lying to yourself again. You wanted to get rid of them. Their contempt and disgust aren't pleasant company. You're glad they're gone. [*She gives a little despairing laugh.*] Then Mother of God, why do I feel so lonely?

CURTAIN

Act 3

SCENE—*The same. It is around half past six in the evening. Dusk is gathering in the living room, an early dusk due to the fog which has rolled in from the Sound and is like a white curtain drawn down outside the windows. From a lighthouse beyond the harbor's mouth, a foghorn is heard at regular intervals, moaning like a mournful whale in labor, and from the harbor itself, intermittently, comes the warning ringing of bells on yachts at anchor.*

The tray with the bottle of whiskey, glasses, and pitcher of ice water is on the table, as it was in the pre-luncheon scene of the previous act. MARY *and the second girl,* CATHLEEN, *are discovered. The latter is standing at left of table. She holds an empty whiskey glass in her hand as if she'd forgotten she had it. She shows the effects of drink. Her stupid, good-humored face wears a pleased and flattered simper.*

MARY *is paler than before and her eyes shine with unnatural brilliance. The strange detachment in her manner has intensified. She has hidden deeper within herself and found refuge and release in a dream where present reality is but an appearance to be accepted and dismissed unfeelingly—even with a hard cynicism—or entirely ignored. There is at times an uncanny gay, free youthfulness in her manner, as if in spirit she were released to become again, simply and without self-consciousness, the naive, happy, chattering schoolgirl of her convent days. She wears the dress into which she had changed for her drive to town, a simple, fairly expensive affair, which would be extremely becoming if it were not for the careless, almost slovenly way she wears it. Her hair is no longer fastidiously in place. It has a slightly disheveled, lopsided look. She talks to* CATHLEEN *with a confiding familiarity, as if the second girl were an old, intimate friend. As the curtain rises, she is standing by the screen door looking out. A moan of the foghorn is heard.*

MARY [*amused—girlishly*] That foghorn! Isn't it awful, Cathleen?

CATHLEEN [*talks more familiarly than usual but never with intentional impertinence because she sincerely likes her mistress*] It is indeed, Ma'am. It's like a banshee.

MARY [*Goes on as if she hadn't heard. In nearly all the following dialogue there is the feeling that she has* CATHLEEN *with her merely as an excuse to keep talking.*] I don't mind it tonight. Last night it drove me crazy. I lay awake worrying until I couldn't stand it any more.

CATHLEEN Bad cess to it.[1] I was scared out of my wits riding back from town. I thought that ugly monkey, Smythe, would drive us in a ditch or against a tree. You couldn't see your hand in front of you. I'm glad you had me sit in back with you, Ma'am. If I'd been in front with that monkey—He can't keep his dirty hands to himself. Give him half a chance and he's pinching me on the leg or you-know-where—asking your pardon, Ma'am, but it's true.

MARY [*dreamily*] It wasn't the fog I minded, Cathleen, I really love fog.

CATHLEEN They say it's good for the complexion.

MARY It hides you from the world and the world from you. You feel that everything has changed, and nothing is what it seemed to be. No one can find or touch you any more.

CATHLEEN I wouldn't care so much if Smythe was a fine, handsome man like some chauffeurs I've seen—I mean, if it was all in fun, for I'm a decent girl. But for a shriveled runt like Smythe—! I've told him, you must think I'm hard up that I'd notice a monkey like you. I've warned him, one day I'll give a clout that'll knock him into next week. And so I will!

MARY It's the foghorn I hate. It won't let you alone. It keeps reminding you, and warning you, and calling you back. [*She smiles strangely.*] But it can't tonight. It's just an ugly sound. It doesn't remind me of anything. [*She gives a teasing, girlish laugh.*] Except, perhaps, Mr. Tyrone's snores. I've always had such fun teasing him about it. He has snored ever since I can remember, especially when he's had too much to drink, and yet he's like a child, he hates to admit it. [*She laughs, coming to the table.*] Well, I suppose I snore at times, too, and I don't like to admit it. So I have no right to make fun of him, have I? [*She sits in the rocker at right of table.*]

CATHLEEN Ah, sure, everybody healthy snores. It's a sign of sanity, they say. [*then, worriedly*] What time is it, Ma'am? I ought to go back in the kitchen. The damp is in Bridget's rheumatism and she's like a raging divil. She'll bite my head off.

[*She puts her glass on the table and makes a movement toward the back parlor.*]

MARY [*with a flash of apprehension*] No, don't go, Cathleen. I don't want to be alone, yet.

CATHLEEN You won't be for long. The Master and the boys will be home soon.

---

1. Bad luck to it (Irish).

MARY   I doubt if they'll come back for dinner. They have too good an
excuse to remain in the barrooms where they feel at home.
[CATHLEEN *stares at her, stupidly puzzled.* MARY *goes on smilingly*]
Don't worry about Bridget. I'll tell her I kept you with me, and you can
take a big drink of whiskey to her when you go. She won't mind then.

CATHLEEN   [*grins—at her ease again*]   No, Ma'am. That's the one thing
can make her cheerful. She loves her drop.

MARY   Have another drink yourself, if you wish, Cathleen.

CATHLEEN   I don't know if I'd better, Ma'am. I can feel what I've had
already. [*reaching for the bottle*] Well, maybe one more won't harm. [*She
pours a drink.*] Here's your good health, Ma'am. [*She drinks without
bothering about a chaser.*]

MARY   [*dreamily*]   I really did have good health once, Cathleen. But that
was long ago.

CATHLEEN   [*worried again*]   The Master's sure to notice what's gone from
the bottle. He has the eye of a hawk for that.

MARY   [*amusedly*]   Oh, we'll play Jamie's trick on him. Just measure a few
drinks of water and pour them in.

CATHLEEN   [*does this—with a silly giggle*]   God save me, it'll be half water.
He'll know by the taste.

MARY   [*indifferently*]   No, by the time he comes home he'll be too drunk to
tell the difference. He has such a good excuse, he believes, to drown his
sorrows.

CATHLEEN   [*philosophically*]   Well, it's a good man's failing. I wouldn't give
a trauneen[2] for a teetotaler. They've no high spirits. [*then, stupidly puzzled*] Good excuse? You mean Master Edmund, Ma'am? I can tell the
Master is worried about him.

MARY   [*stiffens defensively—but in a strange way the reaction has a mechanical quality, as if it did not penetrate to real emotion*]   Don't be silly, Cathleen. Why should he be? A touch of grippe is nothing. And Mr. Tyrone
never is worried about anything, except money and property and the fear
he'll end his days in poverty. I mean, deeply worried. Because he cannot
really understand anything else. [*She gives a little laugh of detached,
affectionate amusement.*] My husband is a very peculiar man, Cathleen.

CATHLEEN   [*vaguely resentful*]   Well, he's a fine, handsome, kind gentleman just the same, Ma'am. Never mind his weakness.

MARY   Oh, I don't mind. I've loved him dearly for thirty-six years. That
proves I know he's lovable at heart and can't help being what he is,
doesn't it?

CATHLEEN   [*hazily reassured*]   That's right. Ma'am. Love him dearly, for any
fool can see he worships the ground you walk on. [*fighting the effect of
her last drink and trying to be soberly conversational*] Speaking of acting,
Ma'am, how is it you never went on the stage?

MARY   [*resentfully*]   I? What put that absurd notion in your head? I was
brought up in a respectable home and educated in the best convent in
the Middle West. Before I met Mr. Tyrone I hardly knew there was such
a thing as a theater. I was a very pious girl. I even dreamed of becoming
a nun. I've never had the slightest desire to be an actress.

---

2. Coin of very low value (Irish).

CATHLEEN [*bluntly*]   Well, I can't imagine you a holy nun, Ma'am. Sure, you never darken the door of a church, God forgive you.

MARY [*ignores this*]   I've never felt at home in the theater. Even though Mr. Tyrone has made me go with him on all his tours, I've had little to do with the people in his company, or with anyone on the stage. Not that I have anything against them. They have always been kind to me, and I to them. But I've never felt at home with them. Their life is not my life. It has always stood between me and—[*She gets up—abruptly*] But let's not talk of old things that couldn't be helped. [*She goes to the porch door and stares out.*] How thick the fog is. I can't see the road. All the people in the world could pass by and I would never know. I wish it was always that way. It's getting dark already. It will soon be night, thank goodness. [*She turns back—vaguely*] It was kind of you to keep me company this afternoon, Cathleen. I would have been lonely driving uptown alone.

CATHLEEN   Sure, wouldn't I rather ride in a fine automobile than stay here and listen to Bridget's lies about her relations? It was like a vacation, Ma'am. [*She pauses—then stupidly*] There was only one thing I didn't like.

MARY [*vaguely*]   What was that, Cathleen?

CATHLEEN   The way the man in the drugstore acted when I took in the prescription for you. [*indignantly*] The impidence[3] of him!

MARY [*with stubborn blankness*]   What are you talking about? What drugstore? What prescription? [*then hastily, as* CATHLEEN *stares in stupid amazement*] Oh, of course, I'd forgotten. The medicine for the rheumatism in my hands. What did the man say? [*then with indifference*] Not that it matters, as long as he filled the prescription.

CATHLEEN   It mattered to me, then! I'm not used to being treated like a thief. He gave me a long look and says insultingly, "Where did you get hold of this?" and I says, "It's none of your damned business, but if you must know, it's for the lady I work for, Mrs. Tyrone, who's sitting out in the automobile." That shut him up quick. He gave a look out at you and said, "Oh," and went to get the medicine.

MARY [*vaguely*]   Yes, he knows me. [*She sits in the armchair at right rear of table. She adds in a calm, detached voice*] It's a special kind of medicine. I have to take it because there is no other that can stop the pain—all the pain—I mean, in my hands. [*She raises her hands and regards them with melancholy sympathy. There is no tremor in them now.*] Poor hands! You'd never believe it, but they were once one of my good points, along with my hair and eyes, and I had a fine figure, too. [*Her tone has become more and more far-off and dreamy.*] They were a musician's hands. I used to love the piano. I worked so hard at my music in the Convent—if you can call it work when you do something you love. Mother Elizabeth and my music teacher both said I had more talent than any student they remembered. My father paid for special lessons. He spoiled me. He would do anything I asked. He would have sent me to Europe to study after I graduated from the Convent. I might have gone—if I hadn't fallen in love with Mr. Tyrone. Or I might have become a nun. I had two dreams. To be a nun, that was the more beautiful one. To become a concert pianist, that was the other. [*She pauses, regarding her hands fixedly.* CATHLEEN *blinks her*

3. Impudence.

eyes to fight off drowsiness and a tipsy feeling.] I haven't touched a piano in so many years. I couldn't play with such crippled fingers, even if I wanted to. For a time after my marriage I tried to keep up my music. But it was hopeless. One-night stands, cheap hotels, dirty trains, leaving children, never having a home—[*She stares at her hands with fascinated disgust.*] See, Cathleen, how ugly they are! So maimed and crippled! You would think they'd been through some horrible accident! [*She gives a strange little laugh.*] So they have, come to think of it. [*She suddenly thrusts her hands behind her back.*] I won't look at them. They're worse than the fog-horn for reminding me—[*then with defiant self-assurance*] But even they can't touch me now. [*She brings her hands from behind her back and deliberately stares at them—calmly*] They're far away. I see them, but the pain has gone.

CATHLEEN [*stupidly puzzled*]   You've taken some of the medicine? It made you act funny, Ma'am. If I didn't know better, I'd think you'd a drop taken.

MARY [*dreamily*]   It kills the pain. You go back until at last you are beyond its reach. Only the past when you were happy is real. [*She pauses—then as if her words had been an evocation which called back happiness she changes in her whole manner and facial expression. She looks younger. There is a quality of an innocent convent girl about her, and she smiles shyly.*] If you think Mr. Tyrone is handsome now, Cathleen, you should have seen him when I first met him. He had the reputation of being one of the best looking men in the country. The girls in the Convent who had seen him act, or seen his photographs, used to rave about him. He was a great matinee idol then, you know. Women used to wait at the stage door just to see him come out. You can imagine how excited I was when my father wrote me he and James Tyrone had become friends, and that I was to meet him when I came home for Easter vacation. I showed the letter to all the girls, and how envious they were! My father took me to see him act first. It was a play about the French Revolution and the leading part was a nobleman. I couldn't take my eyes off him. I wept when he was thrown in prison—and then was so mad at myself because I was afraid my eyes and nose would be red. My father had said we'd go backstage to his dressing room right after the play, and so we did. [*She gives a little excited, shy laugh.*] I was so bashful all I could do was stammer and blush like a little fool. But he didn't seem to think I was a fool. I know he liked me the first moment we were introduced. [*coquettishly*] I guess my eyes and nose couldn't have been red, after all. I was really very pretty then, Cathleen. And he was handsomer than my wildest dream, in his make-up and his nobleman's costume that was so becoming to him. He was different from all ordinary men, like someone from another world. At the same time he was simple, and kind, and unassuming, not a bit stuck-up or vain. I fell in love right then. So did he, he told me afterwards. I forgot all about becoming a nun or a concert pianist. All I wanted was to be his wife. [*She pauses, staring before her with unnaturally bright, dreamy eyes, and a rapt, tender, girlish smile.*] Thirty-six years ago, but I can see it as clearly as if it were tonight! We've loved each other ever since. And in all those thirty-six years, there has never been a breath of scandal about him. I mean, with any other woman. Never since he met me. That has made me very happy, Cathleen. It has made me forgive so many other things.

CATHLEEN [*fighting tipsy drowsiness—sentimentally*] He's a fine gentleman and you're a lucky woman. [*then, fidgeting*] Can I take the drink to
Bridget, Ma'am? It must be near dinnertime and I ought to be in the
kitchen helping her. If she don't get something to quiet her temper,
she'll be after me with the cleaver.

MARY [*with a vague exasperation at being brought back from her dream*]
Yes, yes, go. I don't need you now.

CATHLEEN [*with relief*] Thank you, Ma'am. [*She pours out a big drink
and starts for the back parlor with it.*] You won't be alone long. The Master and the boys—

MARY [*impatiently*] No, no, they won't come. Tell Bridget I won't wait.
You can serve dinner promptly at half past six. I'm not hungry but I'll sit
at the table and we'll get it over with.

CATHLEEN You ought to eat something, Ma'am. It's a queer medicine if it
takes away your appetite.

MARY [*has begun to drift into dreams again—reacts mechanically*] What
medicine? I don't know what you mean. [*in dismissal*] You better take
the drink to Bridget.

CATHLEEN Yes, Ma'am.

> [*She disappears through the back parlor.* MARY *waits until she hears the
> pantry door close behind her. Then she settles back in relaxed dreami-
> ness, staring fixedly at nothing. Her arms rest limply along the arms of
> the chair, her hands with long, warped, swollen-knuckled, sensitive fin-
> gers drooping in complete calm. It is growing dark in the room. There is
> a pause of dead quiet. Then from the world outside comes the melancholy
> moan of the foghorn, followed by a chorus of bells, muffled by the fog,
> from the anchored craft in the harbor.* MARY's *face gives no sign she has
> heard, but her hands jerk and the fingers automatically play for a
> moment on the air. She frowns and shakes her head mechanically as if a
> fly had walked across her mind. She suddenly loses all the girlish quality
> and is an aging, cynically sad, embittered woman.*]

MARY [*bitterly*] You're a sentimental fool. What is so wonderful about
that first meeting between a silly romantic schoolgirl and a matinee
idol? You were much happier before you knew he existed, in the Convent when you used to pray to the Blessed Virgin. [*longingly*] If I could
only find the faith I lost, so I could pray again! [*She pauses—then begins
to recite the Hail Mary in a flat, empty tone.*] "Hail, Mary, full of grace!
The Lord is with Thee; blessed art Thou among women." [*sneeringly*]
You expect the Blessed Virgin to be fooled by a lying dope fiend reciting
words! You can't hide from her! [*She springs to her feet. Her hands fly up
to pat her hair distractedly.*] I must go upstairs. I haven't taken enough.
When you start again you never know exactly how much you need. [*She
goes toward the front parlor—then stops in the doorway as she hears the
sound of voices from the front path. She starts guiltily.*] That must be
them—[*She hurries back to sit down. Her face sets in stubborn
defensiveness—resentfully*] Why are they coming back? They don't want
to. And I'd much rather be alone. [*Suddenly her whole manner changes.
She becomes pathetically relieved and eager.*] Oh, I'm so glad they've
come! I've been so horribly lonely!

> [*The front door is heard closing and* TYRONE *calls uneasily from the hall.*]

TYRONE Are you there, Mary?

[*The light in the hall is turned on and shines through the front parlor to fall on* MARY.]

MARY [*rises from her chair, her face lighting up lovingly—with excited eagerness*]   I'm here, dear. In the living room. I've been waiting for you.
[TYRONE *comes in through the front parlor.* EDMUND *is behind him.* TYRONE *has had a lot to drink but beyond a slightly glazed look in his eyes and a trace of blur in his speech, he does not show it.* EDMUND *has also had more than a few drinks without much apparent effect, except that his sunken cheeks are flushed and his eyes look bright and feverish. They stop in the doorway to stare appraisingly at her. What they see fulfills their worst expectations. But for the moment* MARY *is unconscious of their condemning eyes. She kisses her husband and then* EDMUND. *Her manner is unnaturally effusive. They submit shrinkingly. She talks excitedly.*]

I'm so happy you've come. I had given up hope. I was afraid you wouldn't come home. It's such a dismal, foggy evening. It must be much more cheerful in the barrooms uptown, where there are people you can talk and joke with. No, don't deny it. I know how you feel. I don't blame you a bit. I'm all the more grateful to you for coming home. I was sitting here so lonely and blue. Come and sit down.
[*She sits at left rear of table,* EDMUND *at left of table, and* TYRONE *in the rocker at right of it.*]

Dinner won't be ready for a minute. You're actually a little early. Will wonders never cease. Here's the whiskey, dear. Shall I pour a drink for you? [*Without waiting for a reply she does so.*] And you, Edmund? I don't want to encourage you, but one before dinner, as an appetizer, can't do any harm.
[*She pours a drink for him. They make no move to take the drinks. She talks on as if unaware of their silence.*]

Where's Jamie? But, of course, he'll never come home so long as he has the price of a drink left. [*She reaches out and clasps her husband's hand—sadly*] I'm afraid Jamie has been lost to us for a long time, dear. [*Her face hardens.*] But we mustn't allow him to drag Edmund down with him, as he'd like to do. He's jealous because Edmund has always been the baby—just as he used to be of Eugene. He'll never be content until he makes Edmund as hopeless a failure as he is.

EDMUND [*miserably*]   Stop talking, Mama.

TYRONE [*dully*]   Yes, Mary, the less you say now—[*then to Edmund, a bit tipsily*] All the same there's truth in your mother's warning. Beware of that brother of yours, or he'll poison life for you with his damned sneering serpent's tongue!

EDMUND [*as before*]   Oh, cut it out, Papa.

MARY [*goes on as if nothing had been said*]   It's hard to believe, seeing Jamie as he is now, that he was ever my baby. Do you remember what a healthy, happy baby he was, James? The one-night stands and filthy trains and cheap hotels and bad food never made him cross or sick. He was always smiling or laughing. He hardly ever cried. Eugene was the same, too, happy and healthy, during the two years he lived before I let him die through my neglect.

TYRONE   Oh, for the love of God! I'm a fool for coming home!

EDMUND   Papa! Shut up!

MARY [*smiles with detached tenderness at* EDMUND]   It was Edmund who was the crosspatch when he was little, always getting upset and frightened about nothing at all. [*She pats his hand—teasingly*] Everyone used to say, dear, you'd cry at the drop of a hat.

EDMUND [*cannot control his bitterness*]   Maybe I guessed there was a good reason not to laugh.

TYRONE [*reproving and pitying*]   Now, now, lad. You know better than to pay attention—

MARY [*as if she hadn't heard—sadly again*]   Who would have thought Jamie would grow up to disgrace us. You remember, James, for years after he went to boarding school, we received such glowing reports. Everyone liked him. All his teachers told us what a fine brain he had, and how easily he learned his lessons. Even after he began to drink and they had to expel him, they wrote us how sorry they were, because he was so likable and such a brilliant student. They predicted a wonderful future for him if he would only learn to take life seriously. [*She pauses—then adds with a strange, sad detachment*] It's such a pity. Poor Jamie! It's hard to understand—[*Abruptly a change comes over her. Her face hardens and she stares at her husband with accusing hostility.*] No, it isn't at all. You brought him up to be a boozer. Since he first opened his eyes, he's seen you drinking. Always a bottle on the bureau in the cheap hotel rooms! And if he had a nightmare when he was little, or a stomach-ache, your remedy was to give him a teaspoonful of whiskey to quiet him.

TYRONE [*stung*]   So I'm to blame because that lazy hulk has made a drunken loafer of himself? Is that what I came home to listen to? I might have known! When you have the poison in you, you want to blame everyone but yourself!

EDMUND   Papa! You told me not to pay attention. [*then, resentfully*] Anyway it's true. You did the same thing with me. I can remember that teaspoonful of booze every time I woke up with a nightmare.

MARY [*in a detached reminiscent tone*]   Yes, you were continually having nightmares as a child. You were born afraid. Because I was so afraid to bring you into the world. [*She pauses—then goes on with the same detachment*] Please don't think I blame your father, Edmund. He didn't know any better. He never went to school after he was ten. His people were the most ignorant kind of poverty-stricken Irish. I'm sure they honestly believed whiskey is the healthiest medicine for a child who is sick or frightened.

[TYRONE *is about to burst out in angry defense of his family but* EDMUND *intervenes.*]

EDMUND [*sharply*]   Papa! [*changing the subject*] Are we going to have this drink, or aren't we?

TYRONE [*controlling himself—dully*]   You're right. I'm a fool to take notice. [*He picks up his glass listlessly.*] Drink hearty, lad.

[EDMUND *drinks but* TYRONE *remains staring at the glass in his hand.* EDMUND *at once realizes how much the whiskey has been watered. He frowns, glancing from the bottle to his mother—starts to say something but stops.*]

MARY [*in a changed tone—repentantly*]   I'm sorry if I sounded bitter, James. I'm not. It's all so far away. But I did feel a little hurt when you wished you hadn't come home. I was so relieved and happy when you came, and grateful to you. It's very dreary and sad to be here alone in the fog with night falling.

TYRONE [*moved*]   I'm glad I came, Mary, when you act like your real self.

MARY   I was so lonesome I kept Cathleen with me just to have someone to talk to. [*Her manner and quality drift back to the shy convent girl again.*] Do you know what I was telling her, dear? About the night my father took me to your dressing room and I first fell in love with you. Do you remember?

TYRONE [*deeply moved—his voice husky*]   Can you think I'd ever forget, Mary?

[EDMUND *looks away from them, sad and embarrassed.*]

MARY [*tenderly*]   No. I know you still love me, James, in spite of everything.

TYRONE [*His face works and he blinks back tears—with quiet intensity*] Yes! As God is my judge! Always and forever, Mary!

MARY   And I love you, dear, in spite of everything.

[*There is a pause in which* EDMUND *moves embarrassedly. The strange detachment comes over her manner again as if she were speaking impersonally of people seen from a distance.*]

But I must confess, James, although I couldn't help loving you, I would never have married you if I'd known you drank so much. I remember the first night your barroom friends had to help you up to the door of our hotel room, and knocked and then ran away before I came to the door. We were still on our honeymoon, do you remember?

TYRONE [*with guilty vehemence*]   I don't remember! It wasn't on our honeymoon! And I never in my life had to be helped to bed, or missed a performance!

MARY [*as though he hadn't spoken*]   I had waited in that ugly hotel room hour after hour. I kept making excuses for you. I told myself it must be some business connected with the theater. I knew so little about the theater. Then I became terrified. I imagined all sorts of horrible accidents. I got on my knees and prayed that nothing had happened to you— and then they brought you up and left you outside the door. [*She gives a little, sad sigh.*] I didn't know how often that was to happen in the years to come, how many times I was to wait in ugly hotel rooms. I became quite used to it.

EDMUND [*bursts out with a look of accusing hate at his father*]   Christ! No wonder—! [*He controls himself—gruffly*] When is dinner, Mama? It must be time.

TYRONE [*overwhelmed by shame which he tries to hide, fumbles with his watch*]   Yes. It must be. Let's see. [*He stares at his watch without seeing it—pleadingly*] Mary! Can't you forget—?

MARY [*with detached pity*]   No, dear. But I forgive. I always forgive you. So don't look so guilty. I'm sorry I remembered out loud. I don't want to be sad, or to make you sad. I want to remember only the happy part of the past. [*Her manner drifts back to the shy, gay convent girl.*] Do you remember our wedding, dear? I'm sure you've completely forgotten what my wedding gown looked like. Men don't notice such things. They don't think they're important. But it was important to me, I can tell you! How I fussed and worried! I was so excited and happy! My father told me to buy anything I wanted and never mind what it cost. The best is none too good, he said. I'm afraid he spoiled me dreadfully. My mother didn't. She was very pious and strict. I think she was a little jealous. She didn't approve of my marrying—especially an actor. I think she hoped I would become a nun. She used to scold my father. She'd grumble, "You never tell me, never mind what it costs, when I buy anything! You've spoiled that girl so, I pity her husband if she ever marries. She'll expect him to give her the moon. She'll never make a good wife." [*She laughs affection-ately.*] Poor mother! [*She smiles at* TYRONE *with a strange, incongruous coquetry.*] But she was mistaken, wasn't she, James? I haven't been such a bad wife, have I?

TYRONE [*huskily, trying to force a smile*] I'm not complaining, Mary.

MARY [*a shadow of vague guilt crosses her face*] At least, I've loved you dearly, and done the best I could—under the circumstances. [*The shadow vanishes and her shy, girlish expression returns.*] That wedding gown was nearly the death of me and the dressmaker, too! [*She laughs.*] I was so particular. It was never quite good enough. At last she said she refused to touch it any more or she might spoil it, and I made her leave so I could be alone to examine myself in the mirror. I was so pleased and vain. I thought to myself, "Even if your nose and mouth and ears are a trifle too large, your eyes and hair and figure, and your hands, make up for it. You're just as pretty as any actress he's ever met, and you don't have to use paint." [*She pauses, wrinkling her brow in an effort of memory.*] Where is my wedding gown now, I wonder? I kept it wrapped up in tissue paper in my trunk. I used to hope I would have a daughter and when it came time for her to marry—She couldn't have bought a lovelier gown, and I knew, James, you'd never tell her, never mind the cost. You'd want her to pick up something at a bargain. It was made of soft, shimmering satin, trimmed with wonderful old duchesse lace, in tiny ruffles around the neck and sleeves, and worked in with the folds that were draped round in a bustle effect at the back. The basque[4] was boned and very tight. I remember I held my breath when it was fitted, so my waist would be as small as pos-sible. My father even let me have duchesse lace on my white satin slip-pers, and lace with orange blossoms in my veil. Oh, how I loved that gown! It was so beautiful! Where is it now, I wonder? I used to take it out from time to time when I was lonely, but it always made me cry, so finally a long while ago—[*She wrinkles her forehead again.*] I wonder where I hid it? Probably in one of the old trunks in the attic. Some day I'll have to look.

> [*She stops, staring before her.* TYRONE *sighs, shaking his head hope-lessly, and attempts to catch his son's eye, looking for sympathy, but* EDMUND *is staring at the floor.*]

TYRONE [*forces a casual tone*] Isn't it dinner time, dear? [*with a feeble attempt at teasing*] You're forever scolding me for being late, but now I'm on time for once, it's dinner that's late.

> [*She doesn't appear to hear him. He adds, still pleasantly*]

Well, if I can't eat yet, I can drink. I'd forgotten I had this.

> [*He drinks his drink.* EDMUND *watches him.* TYRONE *scowls and looks at his wife with sharp suspicion—roughly*]

---

4. Tight-fitting bodice.

Who's been tampering with my whiskey? The damned stuff is half water! Jamie's been away and he wouldn't overdo his trick like this, anyway. Any fool could tell—Mary, answer me! [*with angry disgust*] I hope to God you haven't taken to drink on top of—

EDMUND   Shut up, Papa! [*to his mother, without looking at her*] You treated Cathleen and Bridget, isn't that it, Mama?

MARY [*with indifferent casualness*] Yes, of course. They work hard for poor wages. And I'm the housekeeper, I have to keep them from leaving. Besides, I wanted to treat Cathleen because I had her drive uptown with me, and sent her to get my prescription filled.

EDMUND   For God's sake, Mama! You can't trust her! Do you want everyone on earth to know?

MARY [*her face hardening stubbornly*] Know what? That I suffer from rheumatism in my hands and have to take medicine to kill the pain? Why should I be ashamed of that? [*turns on EDMUND with a hard, accusing antagonism—almost a revengeful enmity*] I never knew what rheumatism was before you were born! Ask your father!

[EDMUND *looks away, shrinking into himself.*]

TYRONE   Don't mind her, lad. It doesn't mean anything. When she gets to the stage where she gives the old crazy excuse about her hands she's gone far away from us.

MARY [*turns on him—with a strangely triumphant, taunting smile*] I'm glad you realize that, James! Now perhaps you'll give up trying to remind me, you and Edmund! [*abruptly, in a detached, matter-of-fact tone*] Why don't you light the light, James? It's getting dark. I know you hate to, but Edmund has proved to you that one bulb burning doesn't cost much. There's no sense letting your fear of the poorhouse make you too stingy.

TYRONE [*reacts mechanically*] I never claimed one bulb cost much! It's having them on, one here and one there, that makes the Electric Light Company rich. [*He gets up and turns on the reading lamp—roughly*] But I'm a fool to talk reason to you. [*to EDMUND*] I'll get a fresh bottle of whiskey, lad, and we'll have a real drink. [*He goes through the back parlor.*]

MARY [*with detached amusement*] He'll sneak around to the outside cellar door so the servants won't see him. He's really ashamed of keeping his whiskey padlocked in the cellar. Your father is a strange man, Edmund. It took many years before I understood him. You must try to understand and forgive him, too, and not feel contempt because he's close-fisted. His father deserted his mother and their six children a year or so after they came to America. He told them he had a premonition he would die soon, and he was homesick for Ireland, and wanted to go back there to die. So he went and he did die. He must have been a peculiar man, too. Your father had to go to work in a machine shop when he was only ten years old.

EDMUND [*protests dully*] Oh, for Pete's sake, Mama. I've heard Papa tell that machine shop story ten thousand times.

MARY   Yes, dear, you've had to listen, but I don't think you've ever tried to understand.

EDMUND [*ignoring this—miserably*] Listen, Mama! You're not so far gone yet you've forgotten everything. You haven't asked me what I found out this afternoon. Don't you care a damn?

MARY [*shakenly*]   Don't say that! You hurt me, dear!

EDMUND   What I've got is serious, Mama. Doc Hardy knows for sure now.

MARY [*stiffens into scornful, defensive stubbornness*]   That lying old quack! I warned you he'd invent—!

EDMUND [*miserably dogged*]   He called in a specialist to examine me, so he'd be absolutely sure.

MARY [*ignoring this*]   Don't tell me about Hardy! If you heard what the doctor at the sanatorium, who really knows something, said about how he'd treated me! He said he ought to be locked up! He said it was a wonder I hadn't gone mad! I told him I had once, that time I ran down in my nightdress to throw myself off the dock. You remember that, don't you? And yet you want me to pay attention to what Doctor Hardy says. Oh, no!

EDMUND [*bitterly*]   I remember, all right. It was right after that Papa and Jamie decided they couldn't hide it from me any more. Jamie told me. I called him a liar! I tried to punch him in the nose. But I knew he wasn't lying. [*His voice trembles, his eyes begin to fill with tears.*] God, it made everything in life seem rotten!

MARY [*pitiably*]   Oh, don't. My baby! You hurt me so dreadfully!

EDMUND [*dully*]   I'm sorry, Mama. It was you who brought it up. [*then with a bitter, stubborn persistence*] Listen, Mama. I'm going to tell you whether you want to hear or not. I've got to go to a sanatorium.

MARY [*dazedly, as if this was something that had never occurred to her*]   Go away? [*violently*] No! I won't have it! How dare Doctor Hardy advise such a thing without consulting me! How dare your father allow him! What right has he? You are my baby! Let him attend to Jamie! [*more and more excited and bitter*] I know why he wants you sent to a sanatorium. To take you from me! He's always tried to do that. He's been jealous of every one of my babies! He kept finding ways to make me leave them. That's what caused Eugene's death. He's been jealous of you most of all. He knew I loved you most because—

EDMUND [*miserably*]   Oh, stop talking crazy, can't you, Mama! Stop trying to blame him. And why are you so against my going away now? I've been away a lot, and I've never noticed it broke your heart!

MARY [*bitterly*]   I'm afraid you're not very sensitive, after all. [*sadly*] You might have guessed, dear, that after I knew you knew—about me—I had to be glad whenever you were where you couldn't see me.

EDMUND [*brokenly*]   Mama! Don't! [*He reaches out blindly and takes her hand—but he drops it immediately, overcome by bitterness again.*] All this talk about loving me—and you won't even listen when I try to tell you how sick—

MARY [*with an abrupt transformation into a detached bullying motherliness*] Now, now. That's enough! I don't care to hear because I know it's nothing but Hardy's ignorant lies.

[*He shrinks back into himself. She keeps on in a forced, teasing tone but with an increasing undercurrent of resentment.*]

You're so like your father, dear. You love to make a scene out of nothing so you can be dramatic and tragic. [*with a belittling laugh*] If I gave you the slightest encouragement, you'd tell me next you were going to die—

EDMUND   People do die of it. Your own father—

MARY [*sharply*]   Why do you mention him? There's no comparison at all with you. He had consumption. [*angrily*] I hate you when you become

gloomy and morbid! I forbid you to remind me of my father's death, do
you hear me?

EDMUND [*his face hard—grimly*]   Yes, I hear you, Mama. I wish to God I
didn't! [*He gets up from his chair and stands staring condemningly at
her—bitterly*] It's pretty hard to take at times, having a dope fiend for a
mother!

> [*She winces—all life seeming to drain from her face, leaving it with the
> appearance of a plaster cast. Instantly* EDMUND *wishes he could take
> back what he has said. He stammers miserably.*]

Forgive me, Mama. I was angry. You hurt me.

> [*There is a pause in which the foghorn and the ships' bells are heard.*]

MARY [*goes slowly to the windows at right like an automaton—looking
out, a blank, far-off quality in her voice*]   Just listen to that awful
foghorn.
And the bells. Why is it fog makes everything sound so sad and lost,
I wonder?

EDMUND [*brokenly*]   I—I can't stay here. I don't want any dinner.

> [*He hurries away through the front parlor. She keeps staring out the
> window until she hears the front door close behind him. Then she comes
> back and sits in her chair, the same blank look on her face.*]

MARY [*vaguely*]   I must go upstairs. I haven't taken enough. [*She pauses—
then longingly*] I hope, sometime, without meaning it, I will take an
overdose. I never could do it deliberately. The Blessed Virgin would
never forgive me, then.

> [*She hears* TYRONE *returning and turns as he comes in, through the back
> parlor, with a bottle of whiskey he has just uncorked. He is fuming.*]

TYRONE [*wrathfully*]   The padlock is all scratched. That drunken loafer
has tried to pick the lock with a piece of wire, the way he's done before.
[*with satisfaction, as if this was a perpetual battle of wits with his elder
son*] But I've fooled him this time. It's a special padlock a professional
burglar couldn't pick. [*He puts the bottle on the tray and suddenly is
aware of* EDMUND's *absence.*] Where's Edmund?

MARY [*with a vague far-away air*]   He went out. Perhaps he's going uptown
again to find Jamie. He still has some money left, I suppose, and it's
burning a hole in his pocket. He said he didn't want any dinner. He
doesn't seem to have any appetite these days. [*then stubbornly*] But it's
just a summer cold.

> [TYRONE *stares at her and shakes his head helplessly and pours himself
> a big drink and drinks it. Suddenly it is too much for her and she breaks
> out and sobs.*]

Oh, James, I'm so frightened! [*She gets up and throws her arms around
him and hides her face on his shoulder—sobbingly*] I know he's going
to die!

TYRONE   Don't say that! It's not true! They promised me in six months
he'd be cured.

MARY   You don't believe that! I can tell when you're acting! And it will be
my fault. I should never have borne him. It would have been better for
his sake. I could never hurt him then. He wouldn't have had to know his
mother was a dope fiend—and hate her!

TYRONE [*his voice quivering*]   Hush, Mary, for the love of God! He loves
you. He knows it was a curse put on you without your knowing or will-

ing it. He's proud you're his mother! [*abruptly as he hears the pantry door opening*] Hush, now! Here comes Cathleen. You don't want her to see you crying.

[*She turns quickly away from him to the windows at right, hastily wiping her eyes. A moment later* CATHLEEN *appears in the back-parlor doorway. She is uncertain in her walk and grinning woozily.*]

CATHLEEN [*starts guiltily when she sees* TYRONE—*with dignity*]   Dinner is served, Sir. [*raising her voice unnecessarily*] Dinner is served, Ma'am. [*She forgets her dignity and addresses* TYRONE *with good-natured familiarity*] So you're here, are you? Well, well. Won't Bridget be in a rage! I told her the Madame said you wouldn't be home. [*then reading accusation in his eye*] Don't be looking at me that way. If I've a drop taken, I didn't steal it. I was invited.

[*She turns with huffy dignity and disappears through the back parlor.*]

TYRONE [*sighs—then summoning his actor's heartiness*]   Come along, dear. Let's have our dinner. I'm hungry as a hunter.

MARY [*comes to him—her face is composed in plaster again and her tone is remote*]   I'm afraid you'll have to excuse me, James. I couldn't possibly eat anything. My hands pain me dreadfully. I think the best thing for me is to go to bed and rest. Good night dear.

[*She kisses him mechanically and turns toward the front parlor.*]

TYRONE [*harshly*]   Up to take more of that God-damned poison, is that it? You'll be like a mad ghost before the night's over!

MARY [*starts to walk away—blankly*]   I don't know what you're talking about, James. You say such mean, bitter things when you've drunk too much. You're as bad as Jamie or Edmund.

[*She moves off through the front parlor. He stands a second as if not knowing what to do. He is a sad, bewildered, broken old man. He walks wearily off through the back parlor toward the dining room.*]

CURTAIN

Act 4

SCENE—*The same. It is around midnight. The lamp in the front hall has been turned out, so that now no light shines through the front parlor. In the living room only the reading lamp on the table is lighted. Outside the windows the wall of fog appears denser than ever. As the curtain rises, the foghorn is heard, followed by the ships' bells from the harbor.*

TYRONE *is seated at the table. He wears his pince-nez[5] and is playing solitaire. He has taken off his coat and has on an old brown dressing gown. The whiskey bottle on the tray is three-quarters empty. There is a fresh full bottle on the table, which he has brought from the cellar so there will be an ample reserve on hand. He is drunk and shows it by the owlish, deliberate manner in which he peers at each card to make certain of its identity, and then plays it as if he wasn't certain of his aim. His eyes have a misted, oily look and his mouth is slack. But despite all the whiskey in him, he has not escaped, and he looks as he appeared at the close of the preceding act, a sad, defeated old man, possessed by hopeless resignation.*

---

5. Eyeglasses clipped to the nose.

As the curtain rises, he finishes a game and sweeps the cards together. He shuffles them clumsily, dropping a couple on the floor. He retrieves them with difficulty, and starts to shuffle again, when he hears someone entering the front door. He peers over his pince-nez through the front parlor.

TYRONE [*his voice thick*]   Who's that? Is it you, Edmund?

> [EDMUND's *voice answers curtly, "Yes." Then he evidently collides with something in the dark hall and can be heard cursing. A moment later the hall lamp is turned on.* TYRONE *frowns and calls.*]

Turn that light out before you come in.

> [*But* EDMUND *doesn't. He comes in through the front parlor. He is drunk now, too, but like his father he carries it well, and gives little physical sign of it except in his eyes and a chip-on-the-shoulder aggressiveness in his manner.* TYRONE *speaks, at first with a warm, relieved welcome.*]

I'm glad you've come, lad. I've been damned lonely. [*then resentfully*] You're a fine one to run away and leave me to sit alone here all night when you know—[*with sharp irritation*] I told you to turn out that light! We're not giving a ball. There's no reason to have the house ablaze with electricity at this time of night, burning up money!

EDMUND [*angrily*]   Ablaze with electricity! One bulb! Hell, everyone keeps a light on in the front hall until they go to bed. [*He rubs his knee.*] I damned near busted my knee on the hat stand.

TYRONE   The light from here shows in the hall. You could see your way well enough if you were sober.

EDMUND   If *I* was sober? I like that!

TYRONE   I don't give a damn what other people do. If they want to be wasteful fools, for the sake of show, let them be!

EDMUND   One bulb! Christ, don't be such a cheap skate! I've proved by figures if you left the light bulb on all night it wouldn't be as much as one drink!

TYRONE   To hell with your figures! The proof is in the bills I have to pay!

EDMUND [*sits down opposite his father—contemptuously*]   Yes, facts don't mean a thing, do they? What you want to believe, that's the only truth! [*derisively*] Shakespeare was an Irish Catholic, for example.

TYRONE [*stubbornly*]   So he was. The proof is in his plays.

EDMUND   Well he wasn't, and there's no proof of it in his plays, except to you! [*jeeringly*] The Duke of Wellington, there was another good Irish Catholic!

TYRONE   I never said he was a good one. He was a renegade but a Catholic just the same.

EDMUND   Well, he wasn't. You just want to believe no one but an Irish Catholic general could beat Napoleon.

TYRONE   I'm not going to argue with you. I asked you to turn out that light in the hall.

EDMUND   I heard you, and as far as I'm concerned it stays on.

TYRONE   None of your damned insolence! Are you going to obey me or not?

EDMUND   Not! If you want to be a crazy miser put it out yourself!

TYRONE [*with threatening anger*]   Listen to me! I've put up with a lot from you because from the mad things you've done at times I've thought you weren't quite right in your head. I've excused you and never lifted my hand to you. But there's a straw that breaks the camel's back. You'll obey me and put out that light or, big as you are, I'll give you a thrashing that'll teach you—! [*Suddenly he remembers* EDMUND's *illness and instantly becomes guilty and shamefaced.*] Forgive me, lad. I forgot—You shouldn't goad me into losing my temper.

EDMUND [*ashamed himself now*]   Forget it, Papa. I apologize, too. I had no right being nasty about nothing. I am a bit soused, I guess. I'll put out the damned light. [*He starts to get up.*]

TYRONE   No, stay where you are. Let it burn.

>   [*He stands up abruptly—and a bit drunkenly—and begins turning on the three bulbs in the chandelier, with a childish, bitterly dramatic self-pity.*]

We'll have them all on! Let them burn! To hell with them! The poorhouse is the end of the road, and it might as well be sooner as later! [*He finishes turning on the lights.*]

EDMUND [*has watched this proceeding with an awakened sense of humor—now he grins, teasing affectionately*]   That's a grand curtain. [*He laughs.*] You're a wonder, Papa.

TYRONE [*sits down sheepishly—grumbles pathetically*]   That's right, laugh at the old fool! The poor old ham! But the final curtain will be in the poorhouse just the same, and that's not comedy! [*Then as* EDMUND *is still grinning, he changes the subject.*] Well, well, let's not argue. You've got brains in that head of yours, though you do your best to deny them. You'll live to learn the value of a dollar. You're not like your damned tramp of a brother. I've given up hope he'll ever get sense. Where is he, by the way?

EDMUND   How would I know?

TYRONE   I thought you'd gone back uptown to meet him.

EDMUND   No. I walked out to the beach. I haven't seen him since this afternoon.

TYRONE   Well, if you split the money I gave you with him, like a fool—

EDMUND   Sure I did. He's always staked me when he had anything.

TYRONE   Then it doesn't take a soothsayer to tell he's probably in the whorehouse.

EDMUND   What of it if he is? Why not?

TYRONE [*contemptuously*]   Why not, indeed. It's the fit place for him. If he's ever had a loftier dream than whores and whiskey, he's never shown it.

EDMUND   Oh, for Pete's sake, Papa! If you're going to start that stuff, I'll beat it. [*He starts to get up.*]

TYRONE [*placatingly*]   All right, all right, I'll stop. God knows, I don't like the subject either. Will you join me in a drink?

EDMUND   Ah! Now you're talking!

TYRONE [*passes the bottle to him—mechanically*]   I'm wrong to treat you. You've had enough already.

EDMUND [*pouring a big drink—a bit drunkenly*]   Enough is *not* as good as a feast. [*He hands back the bottle.*]

TYRONE   It's too much in your condition.

EDMUND   Forget my condition! [*He raises his glass.*] Here's how.

TYRONE   Drink hearty. [*They drink.*] If you walked all the way to the beach you must be damp and chilled.

EDMUND   Oh, I dropped in at the Inn on the way out and back.

TYRONE   It's not a night I'd pick for a long walk.

EDMUND   I loved the fog. It was what I needed. [*He sounds more tipsy and looks it.*]

TYRONE   You should have more sense than to risk—

EDMUND   To hell with sense! We're all crazy. What do we want with sense? [*He quotes from Dowson[6] sardonically.*]

> "They are not long, the weeping and the laughter,
> Love and desire and hate:
> I think they have no portion in us after
> We pass the gate.
>
> They are not long, the days of wine and roses:
> Out of a misty dream
> Our path emerges for a while, then closes
> Within a dream."

[*staring before him*] The fog was where I wanted to be. Halfway down the path you can't see this house. You'd never know it was here. Or any of the other places down the avenue. I couldn't see but a few feet ahead. I didn't meet a soul. Everything looked and sounded unreal. Nothing was what it is. That's what I wanted—to be alone with myself in another world where truth is untrue and life can hide from itself. Out beyond the harbor, where the road runs along the beach, I even lost the feeling of being on land. The fog and the sea seemed part of each other. It was like walking on the bottom of the sea. As if I had drowned long ago. As if I was a ghost belonging to the fog, and the fog was the ghost of the sea. It felt damned peaceful to be nothing more than a ghost within a ghost. [*He sees his father staring at him with mingled worry and irritated disapproval. He grins mockingly.*] Don't look at me as if I'd gone nutty. I'm talking sense. Who wants to see life as it is, if they can help it? It's the three Gorgons[7] in one. You look in their faces and turn to stone. Or it's Pan.[8] You see him and you die—that is, inside you—and have to go on living as a ghost.

TYRONE [*impressed and at the same time revolted*]   You have a poet in you but it's a damned morbid one! [*forcing a smile*] Devil take your pessimism. I feel low-spirited enough. [*He sighs.*] Why can't you remember your Shakespeare and forget the third-raters. You'll find what you're trying to say in him—as you'll find everything else worth saying. [*He quotes, using his fine voice*] "We are such stuff as dreams are made on, and our little life is rounded with a sleep."[9]

EDMUND [*ironically*]   Fine! That's beautiful. But I wasn't trying to say that. We are such stuff as manure is made on, so let's drink up and forget it. That's more my idea.

TYRONE [*disgustedly*]   Ach! Keep such sentiments to yourself. I shouldn't have given you that drink.

EDMUND   It did pack a wallop, all right. On you, too. [*He grins with affectionate teasing.*] Even if you've never missed a performance! [*aggressively*] Well, what's wrong with being drunk? It's what we're after, isn't

---

6. Ernest Dowson (1867–1900), English poet.
7. In Greek mythology, three monstrous sisters so ugly that the sight of them turned one to stone.

8. Greek god of woods, fields, and flocks, half man and half goat, associated with wildness.
9. Shakespeare's *The Tempest* 4.1.156–58.

it? Let's not kid each other, Papa. Not tonight. We know what we're
trying to forget. [*hurriedly*] But let's not talk about it. It's no use now.

TYRONE [*dully*]   No. All we can do is try to be resigned—again.

EDMUND   Or be so drunk you can forget. [*He recites, and recites well,
with bitter, ironical passion, the Symons' translation of Baudelaire's*[1]
prose poem.] "Be always drunken. Nothing else matters: that is the
only question. If you would not feel the horrible burden of Time weighing on your shoulders and crushing you to the earth, be drunken
continually.

"Drunken with what? With wine, with poetry, or with virtue, as you
will. But be drunken.

"And if sometimes, on the stairs of a palace, or on the green side of a
ditch, or in the dreary solitude of your own room, you should awaken
and the drunkenness be half or wholly slipped away from you, ask of
the wind, or of the wave, or of the star, or of the bird, or of the clock, of
whatever flies, or sighs, or rocks, or sings, or speaks, ask what hour it is;
and the wind, wave, star, bird, clock, will answer you: 'It is the hour to
be drunken! Be drunken, if you would not be martyred slaves of Time;
be drunken continually! With wine, with poetry, or with virtue, as you
will.'" [*He grins at his father provocatively.*]

TYRONE [*thickly humorous*]   I wouldn't worry about the virtue part of it,
if I were you. [*then disgustedly*] Pah! It's morbid nonsense! What little
truth is in it you'll find nobly said in Shakespeare. [*then appreciatively*]
But you recited it well, lad. Who wrote it?

EDMUND   Baudelaire.

TYRONE   Never heard of him.

EDMUND [*grins provocatively*]   He also wrote a poem about Jamie and the
Great White Way.

TYRONE   That loafer! I hope to God he misses the last car and has to stay
uptown!

EDMUND [*goes on, ignoring this*]   Although he was French and never saw
Broadway and died before Jamie was born, he knew him and Little Old
New York just the same. [*He recites the Symons' translation of Baude-
laire's "Epilogue."*]

> "With heart at rest I climbed the citadel's
> Steep height, and saw the city as from a tower,
> Hospital, brothel, prison, and such hells,
>
> Where evil comes up softly like a flower.
> Thou knowest, O Satan, patron of my pain,
> Not for vain tears I went up at that hour;
>
> But like an old sad faithful lecher, fain
> To drink delight of that enormous trull
> Whose hellish beauty makes me young again.
>
> Whether thou sleep, with heavy vapours full,
> Sodden with day, or, new apparelled, stand
> In gold-laced veils of evening beautiful,

---

1. Charles Baudelaire (1821–1867), French poet. Arthur Symons (1865–1945), English poet and literary
critic.

>I love thee, infamous city! Harlots and
>Hunted have pleasures of their own to give,
>The vulgar herd can never understand."

TYRONE [*with irritable disgust*] Morbid filth! Where the hell do you get your taste in literature? Filth and despair and pessimism! Another atheist, I suppose. When you deny God, you deny hope. That's the trouble with you. If you'd get down on your knees—

EDMUND [*as if he hadn't heard—sardonically*] It's a good likeness of Jamie, don't you think, hunted by himself and whiskey, hiding in a Broadway hotel room with some fat tart—he likes them fat—reciting Dowson's Cynara to her. [*He recites derisively, but with deep feeling*]

>"All night upon mine heart I felt her warm heart beat,
>Night-long within mine arms in love and sleep she lay;
>Surely the kisses of her bought red mouth were sweet;
>But I was desolate and sick of an old passion,
>When I awoke and found the dawn was gray:
>I have been faithful to thee, Cynara! in my fashion."

[*jeeringly*] And the poor fat burlesque queen doesn't get a word of it, but suspects she's being insulted! And Jamie never loved any Cynara, and was never faithful to a woman in his life, even in his fashion! But he lies there, kidding himself he is superior and enjoys pleasures "the vulgar herd can never understand"! [*He laughs.*] It's nuts—completely nuts!

TYRONE [*vaguely—his voice thick*] It's madness, yes. If you'd get on your knees and pray. When you deny God, you deny sanity.

EDMUND [*ignoring this*] But who am I to feel superior? I've done the same damned thing. And it's no more crazy than Dowson himself, inspired by an absinthe hangover, writing it to a dumb barmaid, who thought he was a poor crazy souse, and gave him the gate to marry a waiter! [*He laughs—then soberly, with genuine sympathy*] Poor Dowson. Booze and consumption got him. [*He starts and for a second looks miserable and frightened. Then with defensive irony*] Perhaps it would be tactful of me to change the subject.

TYRONE [*thickly*] Where you get your taste in authors—That damned library of yours! [*He indicates the small bookcase at rear.*] Voltaire, Rousseau, Schopenhauer, Nietzsche, Ibsen! Atheists, fools, and madmen! And your poets! This Dowson, and this Baudelaire, and Swinburne and Oscar Wilde, and Whitman and Poe! Whore-mongers and degenerates! Pah! When I've three good sets of Shakespeare there [*he nods at the large bookcase*] you could read.

EDMUND [*provocatively*] They say he was a souse, too.

TYRONE They lie! I don't doubt he liked his glass—it's a good man's failing—but he knew how to drink so it didn't poison his brain with morbidness and filth. Don't compare him with the pack you've got in there. [*He indicates the small bookcase again.*] Your dirty Zola! And your Dante Gabriel Rossetti who was a dope fiend! [*He starts and looks guilty.*]

EDMUND [*with defensive dryness*] Perhaps it would be wise to change the subject. [*a pause*] You can't accuse me of not knowing Shakespeare. Didn't I win five dollars from you once when you bet me I couldn't learn a leading part of his in a week, as you used to do in stock in the old days.

I learned Macbeth and recited it letter perfect, with you giving me the cues.

TYRONE [*approvingly*]   That's true. So you did. [*He smiles teasingly and sighs.*] It was a terrible ordeal, I remember, hearing you murder the lines. I kept wishing I'd paid over the bet without making you prove it.

[*He chuckles and* EDMUND *grins. Then he starts as he hears a sound from upstairs—with dread*]
Did you hear? She's moving around. I was hoping she'd gone to sleep.

EDMUND   Forget it! How about another drink?

[*He reaches out and gets the bottle, pours a drink and hands it back. Then with a strained casualness, as his father pours a drink*]
When did Mama go to bed?

TYRONE   Right after you left. She wouldn't eat any dinner. What made you run away?

EDMUND   Nothing. [*Abruptly raising his glass.*]   Well, here's how.

TYRONE [*mechanically*]   Drink hearty, lad. [*They drink.* TYRONE *again listens to sounds upstairs—with dread*] She's moving around a lot. I hope to God she doesn't come down.

EDMUND [*dully*]   Yes. She'll be nothing but a ghost haunting the past by this time. [*He pauses—then miserably*] Back before I was born—

TYRONE   Doesn't she do the same with me? Back before she ever knew me. You'd think the only happy days she's ever known were in her father's home, or at the Convent, praying and playing the piano. [*jealous resentment in his bitterness*] As I've told you before, you must take her memories with a grain of salt. Her wonderful home was ordinary enough. Her father wasn't the great, generous, noble Irish gentleman she makes out. He was a nice enough man, good company and a good talker. I liked him and he liked me. He was prosperous enough, too, in his wholesale grocery business, an able man. But he had his weakness. She condemns my drinking but she forgets his. It's true he never touched a drop till he was forty, but after that he made up for lost time. He became a steady champagne drinker, the worst kind. That was his grand pose, to drink only champagne. Well, it finished him quick—that and the consumption— [*He stops with a guilty glance at his son.*]

EDMUND [*sardonically*]   We don't seem able to avoid unpleasant topics, do we?

TYRONE [*sighs sadly*]   No. [*then with a pathetic attempt at heartiness*] What do you say to a game or two of Casino, lad?

EDMUND   All right.

TYRONE [*shuffling the cards clumsily*]   We can't lock up and go to bed till Jamie comes on the last trolley—which I hope he won't—and I don't want to go upstairs, anyway, till she's asleep.

EDMUND   Neither do I.

TYRONE [*keeps shuffling the cards fumblingly, forgetting to deal them*]   As I was saying, you must take her tales of the past with a grain of salt. The piano playing and her dream of becoming a concert pianist. That was put in her head by the nuns flattering her. She was their pet. They loved her for being so devout. They're innocent women, anyway, when it comes to the world. They don't know that not one in a million who shows promise ever rises to concert playing. Not that your mother didn't play well for a schoolgirl, but that's no reason to take it for granted she could have—

EDMUND [*sharply*] Why don't you deal, if we're going to play.

TYRONE Eh? I am. [*dealing with very uncertain judgment of distance*] And the idea she might have become a nun. That's the worst. Your mother was one of the most beautiful girls you could ever see. She knew it, too. She was a bit of a rogue and a coquette, God bless her, behind all her shyness and blushes. She was never made to renounce the world. She was bursting with health and high spirits and the love of loving.

EDMUND For God's sake, Papa! Why don't you pick up your hand?

TYRONE [*picks it up—dully*] Yes, let's see what I have here.

[*They both stare at their cards unseeingly. Then they both start.* TYRONE *whispers*]

Listen!

EDMUND She's coming downstairs.

TYRONE [*hurriedly*] We'll play our game. Pretend not to notice and she'll soon go up again.

EDMUND [*staring through the front parlor—with relief*] I don't see her. She must have started down and then turned back.

TYRONE Thank God.

EDMUND Yes. It's pretty horrible to see her the way she must be now. [*with bitter misery*] The hardest thing to take is the blank wall she builds around her. Or it's more like a bank of fog in which she hides and loses herself. Deliberately, that's the hell of it! You know something in her does it deliberately—to get beyond our reach, to be rid of us, to forget we're alive! It's as if, in spite of loving us, she hated us!

TYRONE [*remonstrates gently*] Now, now, lad. It's not her. It's the damned poison.

EDMUND [*bitterly*] She takes it to get that effect. At least, I know she did this time! [*abruptly*] My play, isn't it? Here. [*He plays a card.*]

TYRONE [*plays mechanically—gently reproachful*] She's been terribly frightened about your illness, for all her pretending. Don't be too hard on her, lad. Remember she's not responsible. Once that cursed poison gets a hold on anyone—

EDMUND [*his face grows hard and he stares at his father with bitter accusation*] It never should have gotten a hold on her! I know damned well she's not to blame! And I know who is! You are! Your damned stinginess! If you'd spent money for a decent doctor when she was so sick after I was born, she'd never have known morphine existed! Instead you put her in the hands of a hotel quack who wouldn't admit his ignorance and took the easiest way out, not giving a damn what happened to her afterwards! All because his fee was cheap! Another one of your bargains!

TYRONE [*stung—angrily*] Be quiet! How dare you talk of something you know nothing about! [*trying to control his temper*] You must try to see my side of it, too, lad. How was I to know he was that kind of a doctor? He had a good reputation—

EDMUND Among the souses in the hotel bar, I suppose!

TYRONE That's a lie! I asked the hotel proprietor to recommend the best—

EDMUND Yes! At the same time crying poorhouse and making it plain you wanted a cheap one! I know your system! By God, I ought to after this afternoon!

TYRONE [*guiltily defensive*] What about this afternoon?

EDMUND   Never mind now. We're talking about Mama! I'm saying no matter how you excuse yourself you know damned well your stinginess is to blame—

TYRONE   And I say you're a liar! Shut your mouth right now, or—

EDMUND [*ignoring this*]   After you found out she'd been made a morphine addict, why didn't you send her to a cure then, at the start, while she still had a chance? No, that would have meant spending some money! I'll bet you told her all she had to do was use a little will power! That's what you still believe in your heart, in spite of what doctors, who really know something about it, have told you!

TYRONE   You lie again! I know better than that now! But how was I to know then? What did I know of morphine? It was years before I discovered what was wrong. I thought she'd never got over her sickness, that's all. Why didn't I send her to a cure, you say? [*bitterly*] Haven't I? I've spent thousands upon thousands in cures! A waste. What good have they done her? She always started again.

EDMUND   Because you've never given her anything that would help her want to stay off it! No home except this summer dump in a place she hates and you've refused even to spend money to make this look decent, while you keep buying more property, and playing sucker for every con man with a gold mine, or a silver mine, or any kind of get-rich-quick swindle! You've dragged her around on the road, season after season, on one-night stands, with no one she could talk to, waiting night after night in dirty hotel rooms for you to come back with a bun on after the bars closed! Christ, is it any wonder she didn't want to be cured. Jesus, when I think of it I hate your guts!

TYRONE [*strickenly*]   Edmund! [*then in a rage*] How dare you talk to your father like that, you insolent young cub! After all I've done for you.

EDMUND   We'll come to that, what you're doing for me!

TYRONE [*looking guilty again—ignores this*]   Will you stop repeating your mother's crazy accusations, which she never makes unless it's the poison talking? I never dragged her on the road against her will. Naturally, I wanted her with me. I loved her. And she came because she loved me and wanted to be with me. That's the truth, no matter what she says when she's not herself. And she needn't have been lonely. There was always the members of my company to talk to, if she'd wanted. She had her children, too, and I insisted, in spite of the expense, on having a nurse to travel with her.

EDMUND [*bitterly*]   Yes, your one generosity, and that because you were jealous of her paying too much attention to us, and wanted us out of your way! It was another mistake, too! If she'd had to take care of me all by herself, and had that to occupy her mind, maybe she'd have been able—

TYRONE [*goaded into vindictiveness*]   Or for that matter, if you insist in judging things by what she says when she's not in her right mind, if you hadn't been born she'd never—[*He stops ashamed.*]

EDMUND [*suddenly spent and miserable*]   Sure. I know that's what she feels, Papa.

TYRONE [*protests penitently*]   She doesn't! She loves you as dearly as ever mother loved a son! I only said that because you put me in such a God-damned rage, raking up the past, and saying you hate me—

EDMUND [*dully*] I didn't mean it, Papa. [*He suddenly smiles—kidding a bit drunkenly*] I'm like Mama, I can't help liking you, in spite of everything.

TYRONE [*grins a bit drunkenly in return*] I might say the same of you. You're no great shakes as a son. It's a case of "A poor thing but mine own."[2] [*They both chuckle with real, if alcoholic, affection.* TYRONE *changes the subject.*] What's happened to our game? Whose play is it?

EDMUND Yours, I guess.

[TYRONE *plays a card which* EDMUND *takes and the game gets forgotten again.*]

TYRONE You mustn't let yourself be too downhearted, lad, by the bad news you had today. Both the doctors promised me, if you obey orders at this place you're going, you'll be cured in six months, or a year at most.

EDMUND [*his face hard again*] Don't kid me. You don't believe that.

TYRONE [*too vehemently*] Of course I believe it! Why shouldn't I believe it when both Hardy and the specialist—?

EDMUND You think I'm going to die.

TYRONE That's a lie! You're crazy!

EDMUND [*more bitterly*] So why waste money? That's why you're sending me to a state farm—

TYRONE [*in guilty confusion*] What state farm? It's the Hilltown Sanatorium, that's all I know, and both doctors said it was the best place for you.

EDMUND [*scathingly*] For the money! That is, for nothing, or practically nothing. Don't lie, Papa! You know damned well Hilltown Sanatorium is a state institution! Jamie suspected you'd cry poorhouse to Hardy and he wormed the truth out of him.

TYRONE [*furiously*] That drunken loafer! I'll kick him out in the gutter! He's poisoned your mind against me ever since you were old enough to listen!

EDMUND You can't deny it's the truth about the state farm, can you?

TYRONE It's not true the way you look at it! What if it is run by the state? That's nothing against it. The state has the money to make a better place than any private sanatorium. And why shouldn't I take advantage of it? It's my right—and yours. We're residents. I'm a property owner. I help to support it. I'm taxed to death—

EDMUND [*with bitter irony*] Yes, on property valued at a quarter of a million.

TYRONE Lies! It's all mortgaged!

EDMUND Hardy and the specialist know what you're worth. I wonder what they thought of you when they heard you moaning poorhouse and showing you wanted to wish me on charity!

TYRONE It's a lie! All I told them was I couldn't afford any millionaire's sanatorium because I was land poor. That's the truth!

EDMUND And then you went to the Club to meet McGuire and let him stick you with another bum piece of property! [*as* TYRONE *starts to deny*] Don't lie about it! We met McGuire in the hotel bar after he left you. Jamie kidded him about hooking you, and he winked and laughed!

TYRONE [*lying feebly*] He's a liar if he said—

---

2. Shakespeare's *As You Like It* 5.4.60.

EDMUND Don't lie about it! [*with gathering intensity*] God, Papa, ever since I went to sea and was on my own, and found out what hard work for little pay was, and what it felt like to be broke, and starve, and camp on park benches because I had no place to sleep, I've tried to be fair to you because I knew what you'd been up against as a kid. I've tried to make allowances. Christ, you have to make allowances in this damned family or go nuts! I have tried to make allowances for myself when I remember all the rotten stuff I've pulled! I've tried to feel like Mama that you can't help being what you are where money is concerned. But God Almighty, this last stunt of yours is too much! It makes me want to puke! Not because of the rotten way you're treating me. To hell with that! I've treated you rottenly, in my way, more than once. But to think when it's a question of your son having consumption, you can show yourself up before the whole town as such a stinking old tightwad! Don't you know Hardy will talk and the whole damned town will know! Jesus, Papa, haven't you any pride or shame? [*bursting with rage*] And don't think I'll let you get away with it! I won't go to any damned state farm just to save you a few lousy dollars to buy more bum property with! You stinking old miser—! [*He chokes huskily, his voice trembling with rage, and then is shaken by a fit of coughing.*]

TYRONE [*has shrunk back in his chair under this attack, his guilty contrition greater than his anger—he stammers*] Be quiet! Don't say that to me! You're drunk! I won't mind you. Stop coughing, lad. You've got yourself worked up over nothing. Who said you had to go to this Hilltown place? You can go anywhere you like. I don't give a damn what it costs. All I care about is to have you get well. Don't call me a stinking miser, just because I don't want doctors to think I'm a millionaire they can swindle.

[EDMUND *has stopped coughing. He looks sick and weak. His father stares at him frightenedly.*]

You look weak, lad. You'd better take a bracer.

EDMUND [*grabs the bottle and pours his glass brimfull—weakly*] Thanks. [*He gulps down the whiskey.*]

TYRONE [*pours himself a big drink, which empties the bottle, and drinks it; his head bows and he stares dully at the cards on the table—vaguely*] Whose play is it? [*He goes on dully, without resentment.*] A stinking old miser. Well, maybe you're right. Maybe I can't help being, although all my life since I had anything I've thrown money over the bar to buy drinks for everyone in the house, or loaned money to sponges I knew would never pay it back—[*with a loose-mouthed sneer of self-contempt*] But, of course, that was in barrooms, when I was full of whiskey. I can't feel that way about it when I'm sober in my home. It was at home I first learned the value of a dollar and the fear of the poorhouse. I've never been able to believe in my luck since. I've always feared it would change and everything I had would be taken away. But still, the more property you own, the safer you think you are. That may not be logical, but it's the way I have to feel. Banks fail, and your money's gone, but you think you can keep land beneath your feet. [*Abruptly his tone becomes scornfully superior.*] You said you realized what I'd been up against as a boy. The hell you do! How could you? You've had everything—nurses, schools, college, though you didn't stay there. You've had food, clothing. Oh, I know you had a fling of hard work with your back and hands, a bit of being homeless and penniless in a foreign land, and I respect you for it. But it was a game of romance and adventure to you. It was play.

EDMUND [*dully sarcastic*]   Yes, particularly the time I tried to commit suicide at Jimmie the Priest's, and almost did.

TYRONE   You weren't in your right mind. No son of mine would ever—You were drunk.

EDMUND   I was stone cold sober. That was the trouble. I'd stopped to think too long.

TYRONE [*with drunken peevishness*]   Don't start your damned atheist morbidness again! I don't care to listen. I was trying to make plain to you— [*scornfully*] What do you know of the value of a dollar? When I was ten my father deserted my mother and went back to Ireland to die. Which he did soon enough, and deserved to, and I hope he's roasting in hell. He mistook rat poison for flour, or sugar, or something. There was gossip it wasn't by mistake but that's a lie. No one in my family ever—

EDMUND   My bet is, it wasn't by mistake.

TYRONE   More morbidness! Your brother put that in your head. The worst he can suspect is the only truth for him. But never mind. My mother was left, a stranger in a strange land, with four small children, me and a sister a little older and two younger than me. My two older brothers had moved to other parts. They couldn't help. They were hard put to it to keep themselves alive. There was no damned romance in our poverty. Twice we were evicted from the miserable hovel we called home, with my mother's few sticks of furniture thrown out in the street, and my mother and sisters crying. I cried, too, though I tried hard not to, because I was the man of the family. At ten years old! There was no more school for me. I worked twelve hours a day in a machine shop, learning to make files. A dirty barn of a place where rain dripped through the roof, where you roasted in summer, and there was no stove in winter, and your hands got numb with cold, where the only light came through two small filthy windows, so on grey days I'd have to sit bent over with my eyes almost touching the files in order to see! You talk of work! And what do you think I got for it? Fifty cents a week! It's the truth! Fifty cents a week! And my poor mother washed and scrubbed for the Yanks by the day, and my older sister sewed, and my two younger stayed at home to keep the house. We never had clothes enough to wear, nor enough food to eat. Well I remember one Thanksgiving, or maybe it was Christmas, when some Yank in whose house mother had been scrubbing gave her a dollar extra for a present, and on the way home she spent it all on food. I can remember her hugging and kissing us and saying with tears of joy running down her tired face: "Glory be to God, for once in our lives we'll have enough for each of us!" [*He wipes tears from his eyes.*] A fine, brave, sweet woman. There never was a braver or finer.

EDMUND [*moved*]   Yes, she must have been.

TYRONE   Her one fear was she'd get old and sick and have to die in the poorhouse. [*He pauses—then adds with grim humor*] It was in those days I learned to be a miser. A dollar was worth so much then. And once you've learned a lesson, it's hard to unlearn it. You have to look for bargains. If I took this state farm sanatorium for a good bargain, you'll have to forgive me. The doctors did tell me it's a good place. You must believe that, Edmund. And I swear I never meant you to go there if you didn't want to. [*vehemently*] You can choose any place you like! Never mind what it costs! Any place I can afford. Any place you like—within reason.

> [*At this qualification, a grin twitches* EDMUND's *lips. His resentment has gone. His father goes on with an elaborately offhand, casual air.*]

There was another sanatorium the specialist recommended. He said it had a record as good as any place in the country. It's endowed by a group of millionaire factory owners, for the benefit of their workers principally, but you're eligible to go there because you're a resident. There's such a pile of money behind it, they don't have to charge much. It's only seven dollars a week but you get ten times that value. [*hastily*] I don't want to persuade you to anything, understand. I'm simply repeating what I was told.

EDMUND [*concealing his smile—casually*]   Oh, I know that. It sounds like a good bargain to me. I'd like to go there. So that settles that. [*Abruptly he is miserably desperate again—dully*] It doesn't matter a damn now, anyway. Let's forget it! [*changing the subject*] How about our game? Whose play is it?

TYRONE [*mechanically*]   I don't know. Mine, I guess. No, it's yours.

> [EDMUND *plays a card. His father takes it. Then about to play from his hand, he again forgets the game.*]

Yes, maybe life overdid the lesson for me, and made a dollar worth too much, and the time came when that mistake ruined my career as a fine actor. [*sadly*] I've never admitted this to anyone before, lad, but tonight I'm so heartsick I feel at the end of everything, and what's the use of fake pride and pretense. That God-damned play I bought for a song and made such a great success in—a great money success—it ruined me with its promise of an easy fortune. I didn't want to do anything else, and by the time I woke up to the fact I'd become a slave to the damned thing and did try other plays, it was too late. They had identified me with that one part, and didn't want me in anything else. They were right, too. I'd lost the great talent I once had through years of easy repetition, never learning a new part, never really working hard. Thirty-five to forty thousand dollars net profit a season like snapping your fingers! It was too great a temptation. Yet before I bought the damned thing I was considered one of the three or four young actors with the greatest artistic promise in America. I'd worked like hell. I'd left a good job as a machinist to take supers'[3] parts because I loved the theater. I was wild with ambition. I read all the plays ever written. I studied Shakespeare as you'd study the Bible. I educated myself. I got rid of an Irish brogue you could cut with a knife. I loved Shakespeare. I would have acted in any of his plays for nothing, for the joy of being alive in his great poetry. And I acted well in him. I felt inspired by him. I could have been a great Shakespearean actor, if I'd kept on. I know that! In 1874 when Edwin Booth[4] came to the theater in Chicago where I was leading man, I played Cassius to his Brutus one night, Brutus to his Cassius the next, Othello to his Iago, and so on. The first night I played Othello, he said to our manager. "That young man is

---

3. Supernumeraries, extras.
4. Edwin Booth (1833–1893), American actor and theatrical manager.

playing Othello better than I ever did!" [*proudly*] That from Booth, the greatest actor of his day or any other! And it was true! And I was only twenty-seven years old! As I look back on it now, that night was the high spot in my career. I had life where I wanted it! And for a time after that I kept on upward with ambition high. Married your mother. Ask her what I was like in those days. Her love was an added incentive to ambition. But a few years later my good bad luck made me find the big money-maker. It wasn't that in my eyes at first. It was a great romantic part I knew I could play better than anyone. But it was a great box office success from the start—and then life had me where it wanted me—at from thirty-five to forty thousand net profit a season! A fortune in those days—or even in these. [*bitterly*] What the hell was it I wanted to buy, I wonder, that was worth—Well, no matter. It's a late day for regrets. [*He glances vaguely at his cards.*] My play, isn't it?

EDMUND [*moved, stares at his father with understanding—slowly*] I'm glad you've told me this, Papa. I know you a lot better now.

TYRONE [*with a loose, twisted smile*] Maybe I shouldn't have told you. Maybe you'll only feel more contempt for me. And it's a poor way to convince you of the value of a dollar. [*Then as if this phrase automatically aroused an habitual association in his mind, he glances up at the chandelier disapprovingly.*] The glare from those extra lights hurts my eyes. You don't mind if I turn them out, do you? We don't need them, and there's no use making the Electric Company rich.

EDMUND [*controlling a wild impulse to laugh—agreeably*] No, sure not. Turn them out.

TYRONE [*gets heavily and a bit waveringly to his feet and gropes uncertainly for the lights—his mind going back to its line of thought*] No, I don't know what the hell it was I wanted to buy. [*He clicks out one bulb.*] On my solemn oath, Edmund, I'd gladly face not having an acre of land to call my own, nor a penny in the bank—[*He clicks out another bulb.*] I'd be willing to have no home but the poorhouse in my old age if I could look back now on having been the fine artist I might have been.

[*He turns out the third bulb, so only the reading lamp is on, and sits down again heavily.* EDMUND *suddenly cannot hold back a burst of strained, ironical laughter.* TYRONE *is hurt.*]

What the devil are you laughing at?

EDMUND Not at you, Papa. At life. It's so damned crazy.

TYRONE [*growls*] More of your morbidness! There's nothing wrong with life. It's we who—[*He quotes*] "The fault, dear Brutus, is not in our stars, but in ourselves that we are underlings."[5] [*He pauses—then sadly*] The praise Edwin Booth gave my Othello. I made the manager put down his exact words in writing. I kept it in my wallet for years. I used to read it every once in a while until finally it made me feel so bad I didn't want to face it any more. Where is it now, I wonder? Somewhere in this house. I remember I put it away carefully—

EDMUND [*with a wry ironical sadness*] It might be in an old trunk in the attic, along with Mama's wedding dress. [*Then as his father stares at him, he adds quickly*] For Pete's sake, if we're going to play cards, let's play.

---

5. Shakespeare's *Julius Caesar* 1.2.134.

[*He takes the card his father had played and leads. For a moment, they play the game, like mechanical chess players. Then* TYRONE *stops, listening to a sound upstairs.*]

TYRONE   She's still moving around. God knows when she'll go to sleep.

EDMUND [*pleads tensely*]   For Christ's sake, Papa, forget it!

[*He reaches out and pours a drink.* TYRONE *starts to protest, then gives it up.* EDMUND *drinks. He puts down the glass. His expression changes. When he speaks it is as if he were deliberately giving way to drunkenness and seeking to hide behind a maudlin manner.*]

Yes, she moves above and beyond us, a ghost haunting the past, and here we sit pretending to forget, but straining our ears listening for the slightest sound, hearing the fog drip from the eaves like the uneven tick of a rundown, crazy clock—or like the dreary tears of a trollop spattering in a puddle of stale beer on a honky-tonk table top! [*He laughs with maudlin appreciation.*] Not so bad, that last, eh? Original, not Baudelaire. Give me credit! [*then with alcoholic talkativeness*] You've just told me some high spots in your memories. Want to hear mine? They're all connected with the sea. Here's one. When I was on the Squarehead square rigger, bound for Buenos Aires. Full moon in the Trades. The old hooker driving fourteen knots. I lay on the bowsprit, facing astern, with the water foaming into spume under me, the masts with every sail white in the moonlight, towering high above me. I became drunk with the beauty and singing rhythm of it, and for a moment I lost myself—actually lost my life. I was set free! I dissolved in the sea, became white sails and flying spray, became beauty and rhythm, became moonlight and the ship and the high dim-starred sky! I belonged, without past or future, within peace and unity and a wild joy, within something greater than my own life, or the life of Man, to Life itself! To God, if you want to put it that way. Then another time, on the American Line, when I was lookout on the crow's nest in the dawn watch. A calm sea, that time. Only a lazy ground swell and a slow drowsy roll of the ship. The passengers asleep and none of the crew in sight. No sound of man. Black smoke pouring from the funnels behind and beneath me. Dreaming, not keeping lookout, feeling alone, and above, and apart, watching the dawn creep like a painted dream over the sky and sea which slept together. Then the moment of ecstatic freedom came. The peace, the end of the quest, the last harbor, the joy of belonging to a fulfillment beyond men's lousy, pitiful, greedy fears and hopes and dreams! And several other times in my life, when I was swimming far out, or lying alone on a beach, I have had the same experience. Became the sun, the hot sand, green seaweed anchored to a rock, swaying in the tide. Like a saint's vision of beatitude. Like the veil of things as they seem drawn back by an unseen hand. For a second you see—and seeing the secret, are the secret. For a second there is meaning! Then the hand lets the veil fall and you are alone, lost in the fog again, and you stumble on toward nowhere, for no good reason! [*He grins wryly.*] It was a great mistake, my being born a man, I would have been much more successful as a sea gull or a fish. As it is, I will always be a stranger who never feels at home, who does not really want and is not really wanted, who can never belong, who must always be a little in love with death!

TYRONE [*stares at him—impressed*]   Yes, there's the makings of a poet in you all right. [*then protesting uneasily*] But that's morbid craziness about not being wanted and loving death.

EDMUND [*sardonically*]   The *makings* of a poet. No, I'm afraid I'm like the guy who is always panhandling for a smoke. He hasn't even got the makings. He's got only the habit. I couldn't touch what I tried to tell you just now. I just stammered. That's the best I'll ever do. I mean, if I live. Well, it will be faithful realism, at least. Stammering is the native eloquence of us fog people.

> [*A pause. Then they both jump startledly as there is a noise from outside the house, as if someone had stumbled and fallen on the front steps.* EDMUND *grins.*]

Well, that sounds like the absent brother. He must have a peach of a bun on.

TYRONE [*scowling*]   That loafer! He caught the last car, bad luck to it. [*He gets to his feet.*] Get him to bed, Edmund. I'll go out on the porch. He has a tongue like an adder when he's drunk. I'd only lose my temper.

> [*He goes out the door to the side porch as the front door in the hall bangs shut behind* JAMIE. EDMUND *watches with amusement* JAMIE's *wavering progress through the front parlor.* JAMIE *comes in. He is very drunk and woozy on his legs. His eyes are glassy, his face bloated, his speech blurred, his mouth slack like his father's, a leer on his lips.*]

JAMIE [*swaying and blinking in the doorway—in a loud voice*]   What ho! What ho!

EDMUND [*sharply*]   Nix on the loud noise!

JAMIE [*blinks at him*]   Oh, hello, Kid. [*with great seriousness*] I'm as drunk as a fiddler's bitch.

EDMUND [*dryly*]   Thanks for telling me your great secret.

JAMIE [*grins foolishly*]   Yes. Unneshesary information Number One, eh? [*He bends and slaps at the knees of his trousers.*] Had serious accident. The front steps tried to trample on me. Took advantage of fog to waylay me. Ought to be a lighthouse out there. Dark in here, too. [*scowling*] What the hell is this, the morgue? Lesh have some light on subject. [*He sways forward to the table, reciting Kipling*[6]]

> "Ford, ford, ford o' Kabul river,
> Ford o' Kabul river in the dark!
> Keep the crossing-stakes beside you, an' they
> will surely guide you
> 'Cross the ford o' Kabul river in the dark."

[*He fumbles at the chandelier and manages to turn on the three bulbs.*] Thash more like it. The hell with old Gaspard.[7] Where is the old tightwad?

EDMUND   Out on the porch.

JAMIE   Can't expect us to live in the Black Hole of Calcutta.[8] [*His eyes fix on the full bottle of whiskey.*] Say! Have I got the d.t.'s?[9] [*He reaches out fumblingly and grabs it.*] By God, it's real. What's matter with the Old

---

6. Rudyard Kipling (1865–1936), English author.
7. Jamie's contemptuous name for his father, drawn from a character in the popular drama *The Bells*.

8. Small dungeon in Calcutta, India, where, on June 20, 1756, 123 of 146 British prisoners died of suffocation. Hence, any small, cramped space.
9. Delirium tremens.

Man tonight? Must be ossified to forget he left this out. Grab opportunity by the forelock. Key to my success. [*He slops a big drink into a glass.*]

EDMUND   You're stinking now. That will knock you stiff.

JAMIE   Wisdom from the mouth of babes. Can the wise stuff, Kid. You're still wet behind the ears. [*He lowers himself into a chair, holding the drink carefully aloft.*]

EDMUND   All right. Pass out if you want to.

JAMIE   Can't, that's trouble. Had enough to sink a ship, but can't sink. Well, here's hoping. [*He drinks.*]

EDMUND   Shove over the bottle. I'll have one, too.

JAMIE [*with sudden, big-brotherly solicitude, grabbing the bottle*]   No, you don't. Not while I'm around. Remember doctor's orders. Maybe no one else gives a damn if you die, but I do. My kid brother. I love your guts, Kid. Everything else is gone. You're all I've got left. [*pulling bottle closer to him*] So no booze for you, if I can help it. [*Beneath his drunken sentimentality there is a genuine sincerity.*]

EDMUND [*irritably*]   Oh, lay off it.

JAMIE [*is hurt and his face hardens*]   You don't believe I care, eh? Just drunken bull. [*He shoves the bottle over.*] All right. Go ahead and kill yourself.

EDMUND [*seeing he is hurt—affectionately*]   Sure I know you care, Jamie, and I'm going on the wagon. But tonight doesn't count. Too many damned things have happened today. [*He pours a drink.*] Here's how. [*He drinks.*]

JAMIE [*sobers up momentarily and with a pitying look*]   I know, Kid. It's been a lousy day for you. [*then with sneering cynicism*] I'll bet old Gaspard hasn't tried to keep you off booze. Probably give you a case to take with you to the state farm for pauper patients. The sooner you kick the bucket, the less expense. [*with contemptuous hatred*] What a bastard to have for a father! Christ, if you put him in a book, no one would believe it!

EDMUND [*defensively*]   Oh, Papa's all right, if you try to understand him— and keep your sense of humor.

JAMIE [*cynically*]   He's been putting on the old sob act for you, eh? He can always kid you. But not me. Never again. [*then slowly*] Although, in a way, I do feel sorry for him about one thing. But he has even that coming to him. He's to blame. [*hurriedly*] But to hell with that. [*He grabs the bottle and pours another drink, appearing very drunk again.*] That lash drink's getting me. This one ought to put the lights out. Did you tell Gaspard I got it out of Doc Hardy this sanatorium is a charity dump?

EDMUND [*reluctantly*]   Yes. I told him I wouldn't go there. It's all settled now. He said I can go anywhere I want. [*He adds, smiling without resentment*] Within reason, of course.

JAMIE [*drunkenly imitating his father*]   Of course, lad. Anything within reason. [*sneering*] That means another cheap dump. Old Gaspard, the miser in "The Bells," that's a part he can play without make-up.

EDMUND [*irritably*]   Oh, shut up, will you. I've heard that Gaspard stuff a million times.

JAMIE [*shrugs his shoulders—thickly*]   Aw right, if you're shatisfied—let him get away with it. It's your funeral—I mean, I hope it won't be.

EDMUND [*changing the subject*]   What did you do uptown tonight? Go to Mamie Burns?

JAMIE [*very drunk, his head nodding*]   Sure thing. Where else could I find
suitable feminine companionship? And love. Don't forget love. What is
a man without a good woman's love? A God-damned hollow shell.

EDMUND [*chuckles tipsily, letting himself go now and be drunk*]   You're
a nut.

JAMIE [*quotes with gusto from Oscar Wilde's[1] "The Harlot's House"*]

"Then, turning to my love, I said,
'The dead are dancing with the dead,
The dust is whirling with the dust.'

But she—she heard the violin,
And left my side and entered in:
Love passed into the house of lust.

Then suddenly the tune went false,
The dancers wearied of the waltz . . ."

[*He breaks off, thickly*] Not strictly accurate. If my love was with me, I
didn't notice it. She must have been a ghost. [*He pauses.*] Guess which
one of Mamie's charmers I picked to bless me with her woman's love.
It'll hand you a laugh, Kid. I picked Fat Violet.

EDMUND [*laughs drunkenly*]   No, honest? Some pick! God, she weighs a
ton. What the hell for, a joke?

JAMIE   No joke. Very serious. By the time I hit Mamie's dump I felt very
sad about myself and all the other poor bums in the world. Ready for a
weep on any old womanly bosom. You know how you get when John Barleycorn turns on the soft music inside you. Then, soon as I got in the
door, Mamie began telling me all her troubles. Beefed how rotten business was, and she was going to give Fat Violet the gate. Customers didn't
fall for Vi. Only reason she'd kept her was she could play the piano. Lately
Vi's gone on drunks and been too boiled to play, and was eating her out of
house and home, and although Vi was a goodhearted dumbbell, and she
felt sorry for her because she didn't know how the hell she'd make a living, still business was business, and she couldn't afford to run a house for
fat tarts. Well, that made me feel sorry for Fat Violet, so I squandered two
bucks of your dough to escort her upstairs. With no dishonorable intentions whatever. I like them fat, but not that fat. All I wanted was a little
heart-to-heart talk concerning the infinite sorrow of life.

EDMUND [*chuckles drunkenly*]   Poor Vi! I'll bet you recited Kipling and
Swinburne and Dowson and gave her "I have been faithful to thee,
Cynara, in my fashion."

JAMIE [*grins loosely*]   Sure—with the Old Master, John Barleycorn, playing soft music. She stood it for a while. Then she got good and sore.
Got the idea I took her upstairs for a joke. Gave me a grand bawling
out. Said she was better than a drunken bum who recited poetry. Then
she began to cry. So I had to say I loved her because she was fat, and she
wanted to believe that, and I stayed with her to prove it, and that
cheered her up, and she kissed me when I left, and said she'd fallen
hard for me, and we both cried a little more in the hallway, and everything was fine, except Mamie Burns thought I'd gone bughouse.

---

1. Irish author (1854–1900).

EDMUND [*quotes derisively*]

> "Harlots and
> Hunted have pleasures of their own to give,
> The vulgar herd can never understand."

JAMIE [*nods his head drunkenly*]   Egzactly! Hell of a good time, at that. You should have stuck around with me, Kid. Mamie Burns inquired after you. Sorry to hear you were sick. She meant it, too. [*He pauses— then with maudlin humor, in a ham-actor tone*] This night has opened my eyes to a great career in store for me, my boy! I shall give the art of acting back to the performing seals, which are its most perfect expression. By applying my natural God-given talents in their proper sphere, I shall attain the pinnacle of success! I'll be the lover of the fat woman in Barnum and Bailey's circus! [EDMUND *laughs.* JAMIE's *mood changes to arrogant disdain.*] Pah! Imagine me sunk to the fat girl in a hick town hooker shop! Me! Who have made some of the best-lookers on Broadway sit up and beg! [*He quotes from Kipling's "Sestina of the Tramp-Royal"*]

> "Speakin' in general, I 'ave tried 'em all,
> The 'appy roads that take you o'er the world."

[*with sodden melancholy*] Not so apt. Happy roads is bunk. Weary roads is right. Get you nowhere fast. That's where I've got—nowhere. Where everyone lands in the end, even if most of the suckers won't admit it.

EDMUND [*derisively*]   Can it! You'll be crying in a minute.

JAMIE [*starts and stares at his brother for a second with bitter hostility— thickly*]   Don't get—too damned fresh. [*then abruptly*] But you're right. To hell with repining! Fat Violet's a good kid. Glad I stayed with her. Christian act. Cured her blues. Hell of a good time. You should have stuck with me, Kid. Taken your mind off your troubles. What's the use coming home to get the blues over what can't be helped. All over— finished now—not a hope! [*He stops, his head nodding drunkenly, his eyes closing—then suddenly he looks up, his face hard, and quotes jeeringly.*]

> "If I were hanged on the highest hill,
> Mother o' mine, O mother o' mine!
> I know whose love would follow me still . . ."

EDMUND [*violently*]   Shut up!

JAMIE [*in a cruel, sneering tone with hatred in it*]   Where's the hophead? Gone to sleep?

[EDMUND *jerks as if he'd been struck. There is a tense silence.* EDMUND's *face looks stricken and sick. Then in a burst of rage he springs from his chair.*]

EDMUND   You dirty bastard!

[*He punches his brother in the face, a blow that glances off the cheek-bone. For a second* JAMIE *reacts pugnaciously and half rises from his chair to do battle, but suddenly he seems to sober up to a shocked real-ization of what he has said and he sinks back limply.*]

JAMIE [*miserably*]   Thanks, Kid. I certainly had that coming. Don't know what made me—booze talking—You know me, Kid.

EDMUND [*his anger ebbing*]   I know you'd never say that unless—But God, Jamie, no matter how drunk you are, it's no excuse! [*He pauses—miserably*]

I'm sorry I hit you. You and I never scrap—that bad. [*He sinks back on his chair.*]

JAMIE [*huskily*] It's all right. Glad you did. My dirty tongue. Like to cut it out. [*He hides his face in his hands—dully*] I suppose it's because I feel so damned sunk. Because this time Mama had me fooled. I really believed she had it licked. She thinks I always believe the worst, but this time I believed the best. [*His voice flutters.*] I suppose I can't forgive her—yet. It meant so much. I'd begun to hope, if she'd beaten the game, I could, too. [*He begins to sob, and the horrible part of his weeping is that it appears sober, not the maudlin tears of drunkenness.*]

EDMUND [*blinking back tears himself*] God, don't I know how you feel! Stop it, Jamie!

JAMIE [*trying to control his sobs*] I've known about Mama so much longer than you. Never forget the first time I got wise. Caught her in the act with a hypo. Christ, I'd never dreamed before that any women but whores took dope! [*He pauses.*] And then this stuff of you getting consumption. It's got me licked. We've been more than brothers. You're the only pal I've ever had. I love your guts. I'd do anything for you.

EDMUND [*reaches out and pats his arm*] I know that, Jamie.

JAMIE [*his crying over—drops his hands from his face—with a strange bitterness*] Yet I'll bet you've heard Mama and old Gaspard spill so much bunk about my hoping for the worst, you suspect right now I'm thinking to myself that Papa is old and can't last much longer, and if you were to die, Mama and I would get all he's got, and so I'm probably hoping—

EDMUND [*indignantly*] Shut up, you damned fool! What the hell put that in your nut? [*He stares at his brother accusingly.*] Yes, that's what I'd like to know. What put that in your mind?

JAMIE [*confusedly—appearing drunk again*] Don't be a dumbbell! What I said! Always suspected of hoping for the worst. I've got so I can't help— [*then drunkenly resentful*] What are you trying to do, accuse me? Don't play the wise guy with me! I've learned more of life than you'll ever know! Just because you've read a lot of highbrow junk, don't think you can fool me! You're only an overgrown kid! Mama's baby and Papa's pet! The family White Hope! You've been getting a swelled head lately. About nothing! About a few poems in a hick town newspaper! Hell, I used to write better stuff for the Lit magazine in college! You better wake up! You're setting no rivers on fire! You let hick town boobs flatter you with bunk about your future—

[*Abruptly his tone changes to disgusted contrition.* EDMUND *has looked away from him, trying to ignore this tirade.*]

Hell, Kid, forget it. That goes for Sweeny. You know I don't mean it. No one hopes more than I do you'll knock 'em all dead. No one is prouder you've started to make good. [*drunkenly assertive*] Why shouldn't I be proud? Hell, it's purely selfish. You reflect credit on me. I've had more to do with bringing you up than anyone. I wised you up about women, so you'd never be a fall guy, or make any mistakes you didn't want to make! And who steered you on to reading poetry first? Swinburne,[2] for example? I did! And because I once wanted to write, I planted it in your mind

---

2. Algernon Charles Swinburne (1837–1909), English poet and critic.

that someday you'd write! Hell, you're more than my brother. I made you! You're my Frankenstein![3]

[*He has risen to a note of drunken arrogance.* EDMUND *is grinning with amusement now.*]

EDMUND   All right, I'm your Frankenstein. So let's have a drink. [*He laughs.*] You crazy nut!

JAMIE [*thickly*]   I'll have a drink. Not you. Got to take care of you. [*He reaches out with a foolish grin of doting affection and grabs his brother's hand.*] Don't be scared of this sanatorium business. Hell, you can beat that standing on your head. Six months and you'll be in the pink. Probably haven't got consumption at all. Doctors lot of fakers. Told me years ago to cut out booze or I'd soon be dead—and here I am. They're all con men. Anything to grab your dough. I'll bet this state farm stuff is political graft game. Doctors get a cut for every patient they send.

EDMUND [*disgustedly amused*]   You're the limit! At the Last Judgment, you'll be around telling everyone it's in the bag.

JAMIE   And I'll be right. Slip a piece of change to the Judge and be saved, but if you're broke you can go to hell!

[*He grins at this blasphemy and* EDMUND *has to laugh.* JAMIE *goes on.*] "Therefore put money in thy purse."[4] That's the only dope. [*mockingly*] The secret of my success! Look what it's got me!

[*He lets* EDMUND's *hand go to pour a big drink, and gulps it down. He stares at his brother with bleary affection—takes his hand again and begins to talk thickly but with a strange, convincing sincerity.*] Listen, Kid, you'll be going away. May not get another chance to talk. Or might not be drunk enough to tell you truth. So got to tell you now. Something I ought to have told you long ago—for your own good.

[*He pauses—struggling with himself.* EDMUND *stares, impressed and uneasy. Jamie blurts out*] Not drunken bull, but "in vino veritas"[5] stuff. You better take it seriously. Want to warn you—against me. Mama and Papa are right. I've been rotten bad influence. And worst of it is, I did it on purpose.

EDMUND [*uneasily*]   Shut up! I don't want to hear—

JAMIE   Nix, Kid! You listen! Did it on purpose to make a bum of you. Or part of me did. A big part. That part that's been dead so long. That hates life. My putting you wise so you'd learn from my mistakes. Believed that myself at times, but it's a fake. Made my mistakes look good. Made getting drunk romantic. Made whores fascinating vampires instead of poor, stupid, diseased slobs they really are. Made fun of work as sucker's game. Never wanted you to succeed and make me look even worse by comparison. Wanted you to fail. Always jealous of you. Mama's baby, Papa's pet! [*He stares at* EDMUND *with increasing enmity.*] And it was your being born that started Mama on dope. I know that's not your fault, but all the same, God damn you, I can't help hating your guts—!

EDMUND [*almost frightenedly*]   Jamie! Cut it out! You're crazy!

JAMIE   But don't get wrong idea, Kid. I love you more than I hate you. My saying what I'm telling you now proves it. I run the risk you'll hate me—

3. In the novel *Frankenstein* by the English author Mary Shelley (1797–1851), the scientist Dr. Frankenstein creates a monster. Jamie confuses the scientist with his creation, although it is possible that the mistake is O'Neill's.
4. Shakespeare's *Othello* 1.3.354.
5. In wine there is truth (Latin).

and you're all I've got left. But I didn't mean to tell you that last stuff—go that far back. Don't know what made me. What I wanted to say is, I'd like to see you become the greatest success in the world. But you'd better be on your guard. Because I'll do my damnedest to make you fail. Can't help it. I hate myself. Got to take revenge. On everyone else. Especially you. Oscar Wilde's "Reading Gaol" has the dope twisted. The man was dead and so he had to kill the thing he loved. That's what it ought to be. The dead part of me hopes you won't get well. Maybe he's even glad the game has got Mama again! He wants company, he doesn't want to be the only corpse around the house! [*He gives a hard, tortured laugh.*]

EDMUND   Jesus, Jamie! You really have gone crazy!

JAMIE   Think it over and you'll see I'm right. Think it over when you're away from me in the sanatorium. Make up your mind you've got to tie a can to me—get me out of your life—think of me as dead—tell people, "I had a brother, but he's dead." And when you come back, look out for me. I'll be waiting to welcome you with that "my old pal" stuff, and give you the glad hand, and at the first good chance I get stab you in the back.

EDMUND   Shut up! I'll be God-damned if I'll listen to you any more—

JAMIE   [*as if he hadn't heard*]   Only don't forget me. Remember I warned you—for your sake. Give me credit. Greater love hath no man than this, that he saveth his brother from himself. [*very drunkenly, his head bobbing*] That's all. Feel better now. Gone to confession. Know you absolve me, don't you, Kid? You understand. You're a damned fine kid. Ought to be. I made you. So go and get well. Don't die on me. You're all I've got left. God bless you, Kid. [*His eyes close. He mumbles*] That last drink—the old K.O.

> [*He falls into a drunken doze, not completely asleep.* EDMUND *buries his face in his hands miserably.* TYRONE *comes in quietly through the screen door from the porch, his dressing gown wet with fog, the collar turned up around his throat. His face is stern and disgusted but at the same time pitying.* EDMUND *does not notice his entrance.*]

TYRONE   [*in a low voice*]   Thank God he's asleep.

> [EDMUND *looks up with a start.*]

I thought he'd never stop talking. [*He turns down the collar of his dressing gown.*] We'd better let him stay where he is and sleep it off.

> [EDMUND *remains silent.* TYRONE *regards him—then goes on*]

I heard the last part of his talk. It's what I've warned you. I hope you'll heed the warning, now it comes from his own mouth.

> [EDMUND *gives no sign of having heard.* TYRONE *adds pityingly*]

But don't take it too much to heart, lad. He loves to exaggerate the worst of himself when he's drunk. He's devoted to you. It's the one good thing left in him. [*He looks down on* JAMIE *with a bitter sadness.*] A sweet spectacle for me! My first-born, who I hoped would bear my name in honor and dignity, who showed such brilliant promise!

EDMUND   [*miserably*]   Keep quiet, can't you, Papa?

TYRONE   [*pours a drink*]   A waste! A wreck, a drunken hulk, done with and finished!

> [*He drinks.* JAMIE *has become restless, sensing his father's presence, struggling up from his stupor. Now he gets his eyes open to blink up at* TYRONE. *The latter moves back a step defensively, his face growing hard.*]

JAMIE   [*suddenly points a finger at him and recites with dramatic emphasis*]

"Clarence is come, false, fleeting, perjured Clarence,
That stabbed me in the field by Tewksbury.
Seize on him, Furies, take him into torment."[6]

[*then resentfully*] What the hell are you staring at? [*He recites sardonically from Rossetti*[7]]

"Look in my face. My name is Might-Have-Been;
I am also called No More, Too Late, Farewell."

TYRONE   I'm well aware of that, and God knows I don't want to look at it.

EDMUND   Papa! Quit it!

JAMIE [*derisively*]   Got a great idea for you, Papa. Put on revival of "The Bells" this season. Great part in it you can play without make-up. Old Gaspard, the miser!

[TYRONE *turns away, trying to control his temper.*]

EDMUND   Shut up, Jamie!

JAMIE [*jeeringly*]   I claim Edwin Booth never saw the day when he could give as good a performance as a trained seal. Seals are intelligent and honest. They don't put up any bluffs about the Art of Acting. They admit they're just hams earning their daily fish.

TYRONE [*stung, turns on him in a rage*]   You loafer!

EDMUND   Papa! Do you want to start a row that will bring Mama down? Jamie, go back to sleep! You've shot off your mouth too much already.

[TYRONE *turns away.*]

JAMIE [*thickly*]   All right, Kid. Not looking for argument. Too damned sleepy.

[*He closes his eyes, his head nodding.* TYRONE *comes to the table and sits down, turning his chair so he won't look at* JAMIE. *At once he becomes sleepy, too.*]

TYRONE [*heavily*]   I wish to God she'd go to bed so that I could, too. [*drowsily*] I'm dog tired. I can't stay up all night like I used to. Getting old—old and finished. [*with a bone-cracking yawn*] Can't keep my eyes open. I think I'll catch a few winks. Why don't you do the same, Edmund? It'll pass the time until she—

[*His voice trails off. His eyes close, his chin sags, and he begins to breathe heavily through his mouth.* EDMUND *sits tensely. He hears something and jerks nervously forward in his chair, staring through the front parlor into the hall. He jumps up with a hunted, distracted expression. It seems for a second he is going to hide in the back parlor. Then he sits down again and waits, his eyes averted, his hands gripping the arms of his chair. Suddenly all five bulbs of the chandelier in the front parlor are turned on from a wall switch, and a moment later someone starts playing the piano in there—the opening of one of Chopin's*[8] *simpler waltzes, done with a forgetful, stiff-fingered groping, as if an awkward schoolgirl were practicing it for the first time.* TYRONE *starts to wide-awakeness and sober dread, and* JAMIE's *head jerks back and his eyes open. For a moment they listen frozenly. The playing stops as abruptly as it began, and* MARY *appears in the doorway. She wears a sky-blue dressing gown*

6. Shakespeare's *Richard III* 1.4.55–57.
7. Dante Gabriel Rossetti (1821–1882), English poet and painter.
8. Frederic Chopin (1810–1849), Polish composer famous for works for the piano.

over her nightdress, dainty slippers and pompons on her bare feet. Her face is paler than ever. Her eyes look enormous. They glisten like polished black jewels. The uncanny thing is that her face now appears so youthful. Experience seems ironed out of it. It is a marble mask of girlish innocence, the mouth caught in a shy smile. Her white hair is braided in two pigtails which hang over her breast. Over one arm, carried neglectfully, trailing on the floor, as if she had forgotten she held it, is an old-fashioned white satin wedding gown, trimmed with duchesse lace. She hesitates in the doorway, glancing round the room, her forehead puckered puzzledly, like someone who has come to a room to get something but has become absent-minded on the way and forgotten what it was. They stare at her. She seems aware of them merely as she is aware of other objects in the room, the furniture, the windows, familiar things she accepts automatically as naturally belonging there but which she is too preoccupied to notice.]

JAMIE [*breaks the cracking silence—bitterly, self-defensively sardonic*] The Mad Scene. Enter Ophelia![9]

> [*His father and brother both turn on him fiercely.* EDMUND *is quicker. He slaps* JAMIE *across the mouth with the back of his hand.*]

TYRONE [*his voice trembling with suppressed fury*] Good boy, Edmund. The dirty blackguard! His own mother!

JAMIE [*mumbles guiltily, without resentment*] All right, Kid. Had it coming. But I told you how much I'd hoped—[*He puts his hands over his face and begins to sob.*]

TYRONE I'll kick you out in the gutter tomorrow, so help me God. [*But* JAMIE's *sobbing breaks his anger, and he turns and shakes his shoulder, pleading*] Jamie, for the love of God, stop it!

> [*Then* MARY *speaks, and they freeze into silence again, staring at her. She has paid no attention whatever to the incident. It is simply a part of the familiar atmosphere of the room, a background which does not touch her preoccupation; and she speaks aloud to herself, not to them.*]

MARY I play so badly now. I'm all out of practice. Sister Theresa will give me a dreadful scolding. She'll tell me it isn't fair to my father when he spends so much money for extra lessons. She's quite right, it isn't fair, when he's so good and generous, and so proud of me. I'll practice every day from now on. But something horrible has happened to my hands. The fingers have gotten so stiff—[*She lifts her hands to examine them with a frightened puzzlement.*] The knuckles are all swollen. They're so ugly. I'll have to go to the Infirmary and show Sister Martha. [*with a sweet smile of affectionate trust*] She's old and a little cranky, but I love her just the same, and she has things in her medicine chest that'll cure anything. She'll give me something to rub on my hands, and tell me to pray to the Blessed Virgin, and they'll be well again in no time. [*She forgets her hands and comes into the room, the wedding gown trailing on the floor. She glances around vaguely, her forehead puckered again.*] Let me see. What did I come here to find? It's terrible, how absent-minded I've become. I'm always dreaming and forgetting.

TYRONE [*in a stifled voice*] What's that she's carrying, Edmund?

EDMUND [*dully*] Her wedding gown, I suppose.

---

9. An allusion to Shakespeare's *Hamlet*.

TYRONE   Christ! [*He gets to his feet and stands directly in her path—in anguish*] Mary! Isn't it bad enough—? [*controlling himself—gently persuasive*] Here, let me take it, dear. You'll only step on it and tear it and get it dirty dragging it on the floor. Then you'd be sorry afterwards.

    [*She lets him take it, regarding him from somewhere far away within herself, without recognition, without either affection or animosity.*]

MARY [*with the shy politeness of a well-bred young girl toward an elderly gentleman who relieves her of a bundle*]   Thank you. You are very kind. [*She regards the wedding gown with a puzzled interest.*] It's a wedding gown. It's very lovely, isn't it? [*A shadow crosses her face and she looks vaguely uneasy.*] I remember now. I found it in the attic hidden in a trunk. But I don't know what I wanted it for. I'm going to be a nun—that is, if I can only find—[*She looks around the room, her forehead puckered again.*] What is it I'm looking for? I know it's something I lost. [*She moves back from* TYRONE, *aware of him now only as some obstacle in her path.*]

TYRONE [*in hopeless appeal*]   Mary!

    [*But it cannot penetrate her preoccupation. She doesn't seem to hear him. He gives up helplessly, shrinking into himself, even his defensive drunkenness taken from him, leaving him sick and sober. He sinks back on his chair, holding the wedding gown in his arms with an unconscious clumsy, protective gentleness.*]

JAMIE [*drops his hand from his face, his eyes on the table top. He has suddenly sobered up, too—dully*]   It's no good, Papa. [*He recites from Swinburne's "A Leave-taking" and does it well, simply but with a bitter sadness.*]

> "Let us rise up and part; she will not know.
> Let us go seaward as the great winds go,
> Full of blown sand and foam; what help is here?
> There is no help, for all these things are so,
> And all the world is bitter as a tear.
> And how these things are, though ye strove to show,
> She would not know."

MARY [*looking around her*]   Something I miss terribly. It can't be altogether lost. [*She starts to move around in back of* JAMIE's *chair.*]

JAMIE [*turns to look up into her face—and cannot help appealing pleadingly in his turn*]   Mama!

    [*She does not seem to hear. He looks away hopelessly.*]

Hell! What's the use? It's no good. [*He recites from "A Leave-taking" again with increased bitterness.*]

> "Let us go hence, my songs; she will not hear.
> Let us go hence together without fear;
> Keep silence now, for singing-time is over,
> And over all old things and all things dear.
> She loves not you nor me as all we love her.
> Yea, though we sang as angels in her ear,
> She would not hear."

MARY [*looking around her*]   Something I need terribly. I remember when I had it I was never lonely nor afraid. I can't have lost it forever, I would die if I thought that. Because then there would be no hope.

[*She moves like a sleepwalker, around the back of* JAMIE'*s chair, then forward toward left front, passing behind* EDMUND.]

EDMUND [*turns impulsively and grabs her arm. As he pleads he has the quality of a bewilderedly hurt little boy.*]   Mama! It isn't a summer cold! I've got consumption!

MARY [*For a second he seems to have broken through to her. She trembles and her expression becomes terrified. She calls distractedly, as if giving a command to herself.*]   No! [*And instantly she is far away again. She murmurs gently but impersonally*] You must not try to touch me. You must not try to hold me. It isn't right, when I am hoping to be a nun.

[*He lets his hand drop from her arm. She moves left to the front end of the sofa beneath the windows and sits down, facing front, her hands folded in her lap, in a demure school-girlish pose.*]

JAMIE [*gives Edmund a strange look of mingled pity and jealous gloating*] You damned fool. It's no good. [*He recites again from the Swinburne poem.*]

"Let us go hence, go hence; she will not see.
Sing all once more together; surely she,
She too, remembering days and words that were,
Will turn a little toward us, sighing; but we,
We are hence, we are gone, as though we had not been there.
Nay, and though all men seeing had pity on me,
She would not see."

TYRONE [*trying to shake off his hopeless stupor*]   Oh, we're fools to pay any attention. It's the damned poison. But I've never known her to drown herself in it as deep as this. [*gruffly*] Pass me that bottle, Jamie. And stop reciting that damned morbid poetry. I won't have it in my house!

[JAMIE *pushes the bottle toward him. He pours a drink without disarranging the wedding gown he holds carefully over his other arm and on his lap, and shoves the bottle back.* JAMIE *pours his and passes the bottle to* EDMUND, *who, in turn, pours one.* TYRONE *lifts his glass and his sons follow suit mechanically, but before they can drink* MARY *speaks and they slowly lower their drinks to the table, forgetting them.*]

MARY [*staring dreamily before her. Her face looks extraordinarily youthful and innocent. The shyly eager, trusting smile is on her lips as she talks aloud to herself.*] I had a talk with Mother Elizabeth. She is so sweet and good. A saint on earth. I love her dearly. It may be sinful of me but I love her better than my own mother. Because she always understands, even before you say a word. Her kind blue eyes look right into your heart. You can't keep any secrets from her. You couldn't deceive her, even if you were mean enough to want to. [*She gives a little rebellious toss of her head— with girlish pique*] All the same, I don't think she was so understanding this time. I told her I wanted to be a nun. I explained how sure I was of my vocation, that I had prayed to the Blessed Virgin to make me sure, and to find me worthy. I told Mother I had had a true vision when I was praying in the shrine of Our Lady of Lourdes, on the little island in the lake. I said I knew, as surely as I knew I was kneeling there, that the Blessed Virgin had smiled and blessed me with her consent. But Mother Elizabeth told me I must be more sure than that, even, that I must prove it wasn't simply my imagination. She said, if I was so sure, then I wouldn't mind putting myself to a test by going home after I graduated, and living as other girls lived, going out to parties and dances and enjoying myself; and then if after a year or two I still felt sure, I could come back to see her and we would talk it over again. [*She tosses her head—indignantly*] I never dreamed Holy Mother would give me such advice! I was really shocked. I said, of course, I would do anything she suggested, but I knew it was simply a waste of time. After I left her, I felt all mixed up, so I went to the shrine and prayed to the Blessed Virgin and found peace again because I knew she heard my prayer and would always love me and see no harm ever came to me so long as I never lost my faith in her. [*She pauses and a look of growing uneasiness comes over her face. She passes a hand over her forehead as if brushing cobwebs from her brain—vaguely*] That was in the winter of senior year. Then in the spring something happened to me. Yes, I remember. I fell in love with James Tyrone and was so happy for a time. [*She stares before her in a sad dream.* TYRONE *stirs in his chair.* EDMUND *and* JAMIE *remain motionless.*]

CURTAIN

1940

CLAUDE McKAY
1889–1948

One of his biographers aptly calls Claude McKay a lifelong wanderer, a "sojourner" in the Harlem Renaissance. A Jamaican by birth, he did not become an American citizen until 1940; he left Harlem just when the Renaissance was getting started; he criticized leading black intellectuals like W. E. B. Du Bois and Alain Locke (who, in turn, criticized him). Nevertheless, *Harlem Shadows,* his 1922 book of poetry, is generally considered the book that initiated the Harlem Renaissance; his *Home to Harlem* (1928) was the only best-selling African American novel of the decade. Whether the Harlem Renaissance was a unified movement or a resonant label encompassing artists with diverse aims, whether McKay was an American Harlemite or a man of the world, he was unquestionably one of the most important black writers of the 1920s. As well as influencing African American literature, he has had a major impact on writing by West Indians and Africans.

Claude McKay (Festus Claudius McKay) was born in Sunny Ville, a rural village in central Jamaica. This village, with its setting of spectacular natural beauty, became in later years his symbol of a lost golden age. McKay's grandfather, a West African Ashanti, had been brought to the island as a slave, and McKay's father passed on to his son what he remembered of Ashanti values and rituals. Economic necessity led the young McKay to Kingston (Jamaica's principal city) in 1909, where he was apprenticed to a cabinetmaker and wheelwright. Combining his emerging literary ambitions with an interest in Jamaican folkways, McKay published two ground-breaking books of dialect poetry—*Songs of Jamaica* and *Constab Ballads*—in

1912. Prize money from these books took him to the United States to study agriculture, but his literary ambitions drew him to New York City after two years in school (first at the Tuskegee Institute, then at Kansas State College). He married his Jamaican sweetheart, Eulalie Imelda Lewars, in 1914; the couple had a daughter, but the marriage did not last. Supporting himself in jobs like restaurant kitchen helper and Pullman railroad waiter, he began to publish in avant-garde journals; by 1917 he was appearing in *The Seven Arts*, *Pearson's*, and the prominent left-wing *Liberator*, edited by Max Eastman. *The Liberator* published his famous poem "If We Must Die" in 1919. His poetry, much of it written in strict sonnet form, braided racial subject matter, radical politics, and poetic technique into compelling statements that were also good poetry according to traditional standards.

McKay's radical politics, already formed in Jamaica, rose from his belief that racism was inseparable from capitalism, which he saw as a structure designed to perpetuate economic inequality. To him, attacking capitalism was attacking racial injustice. Before the publication of *Harlem Shadows*, McKay had spent 1919–21 in England; in 1923 he went to Moscow, where he was welcomed as a celebrity. His connections to the Communist regime in Russia made him a target for the FBI, which issued orders to keep him from returning to the United States. He stayed in Europe until 1934, living mainly in France but also in Spain and Morocco. *Home to Harlem* (1928), written mostly in France, was an episodic guide to Harlem's artistic, popular, and intellectual life. Later events turned it into one of the movement's last statements; retrenchment in the publishing industry after the stock market crash of 1929, the emergence of younger African American writers with different values, and dissension among Harlem artists themselves combined to bring an end to the Harlem Renaissance and altered the character of life in Harlem itself.

When McKay was finally able to return to the United States in 1934, the nation was deep in the Great Depression. With general unemployment at over 25 percent, paid literary work was extremely hard to come by. In 1935 he joined the New York City branch of the Federal Writers' Project, a New Deal organization giving work to unemployed writers. Except for his important autobiography, *A Long Way from Home* (1937), he did little creative work, and his health failed. Through his friendship with Ellen Tarry, a young African American writer who was a Catholic, he received medical care from Friendship House, a Catholic lay organization in Harlem. In the later years of his life, appalled by Stalin's purges, McKay repudiated his earlier Communist sympathies. He began to work at Friendship House and, after moving to Chicago, worked for the Catholic Youth Organization. He converted to Catholicism in 1944 and died in Chicago four years later.

All texts are from *Harlem Shadows* (1922).

The Harlem Dancer

Applauding youths laughed with young prostitutes
And watched her perfect, half-clothed body sway;
Her voice was like the sound of blended flutes
Blown by black players upon a picnic day.
She sang and danced on gracefully and calm, 5
The light gauze hanging loose about her form;
To me she seemed a proudly-swaying palm
Grown lovelier for passing through a storm.
Upon her swarthy neck black shiny curls
Luxuriant fell; and tossing coins in praise, 10
The wine-flushed, bold-eyed boys, and even the girls,

Devoured her shape with eager, passionate gaze;
But looking at her falsely-smiling face,
I knew her self was not in that strange place.

1917, 1922

Harlem Shadows

I hear the halting footsteps of a lass
   In Negro Harlem when the night lets fall
Its veil. I see the shapes of girls who pass
   To bend and barter at desire's call.
Ah, little dark girls who in slippered feet   5
Go prowling through the night from street to street!

Through the long night until the silver break
   Of day the little gray feet know no rest;
Through the lone night until the last snow-flake
   Has dropped from heaven upon the earth's white breast,   10
The dusky, half-clad girls of tired feet
Are trudging, thinly shod, from street to street.

Ah, stern harsh world, that in the wretched way
Of poverty, dishonor and disgrace,
Has pushed the timid little feet of clay,   15
   The sacred brown feet of my fallen race!
Ah, heart of me, the weary, weary feet
In Harlem wandering from street to street.

1918, 1922

The Lynching

His Spirit in smoke ascended to high heaven.
His father, by the cruelest way of pain,
Had bidden him to his bosom once again;
The awful sin remained still unforgiven.
All night a bright and solitary star   5
(Perchance the one that ever guided him,
Yet gave him up at last to Fate's wild whim)
Hung pitifully o'er the swinging char.
Day dawned, and soon the mixed crowds came to view
The ghastly body swaying in the sun   10
The women thronged to look, but never a one
Showed sorrow in her eyes of steely blue;
And little lads, lynchers that were to be,
Danced round the dreadful thing in fiendish glee.

1919, 1922

If We Must Die

If we must die, let it not be like hogs
Hunted and penned in an inglorious spot,
While round us bark the mad and hungry dogs,
Making their mock at our accursèd lot.
If we must die, O let us nobly die,   5
So that our precious blood may not be shed
In vain; then even the monsters we defy
Shall be constrained to honor us though dead!
O kinsmen! we must meet the common foe!
Though far outnumbered let us show us brave,   10
And for their thousand blows deal one deathblow!
What though before us lies the open grave?
Like men we'll face the murderous, cowardly pack,
Pressed to the wall, dying, but fighting back!

                                                1919, 1922

Africa

The sun sought thy dim bed and brought forth light,
The sciences were sucklings at thy breast;
When all the world was young in pregnant night
Thy slaves toiled at thy monumental best.
Thou ancient treasure-land, thou modern prize,   5
New peoples marvel at thy pyramids!
The years roll on, thy sphinx of riddle eyes
Watches the mad world with immobile lids.
The Hebrews humbled them at Pharaoh's name.
Cradle of Power! Yet all things were in vain!   10
Honor and Glory, Arrogance and Fame!
They went. The darkness swallowed thee again.
Thou art the harlot, now thy time is done,
Of all the mighty nations of the sun.

                                                1921, 1922

America

Although she feeds me bread of bitterness,
And sinks into my throat her tiger's tooth,
Stealing my breath of life, I will confess
I love this cultured hell that tests my youth!
Her vigor flows like tides into my blood,   5
Giving me strength erect against her hate.
Her bigness sweeps my being like a flood.
Yet as a rebel fronts a king in state,
I stand within her walls with not a shred

Of terror, malice, not a word of jeer.   10
Darkly I gaze into the days ahead,
And see her might and granite wonders there,
Beneath the touch of Time's unerring hand,
Like priceless treasures sinking in the sand.

                                                    1921, 1922

KATHERINE ANNE PORTER
1890–1980

Over a long writing life Katherine Anne Porter produced only four books of stories and one novel, *Ship of Fools,* which did not appear until she was over seventy. Her reputation as a prose writer did not depend on quantity; each story was technically skilled, emotionally powerful, combining traditional narration with new symbolic techniques and contemporary subject matter.

Callie Porter—she changed the name to Katherine Anne when she became a writer—was born in the small settlement of Indian Creek, Texas; her mother died soon after giving birth to her fourth child, when Porter was not quite two years old. Her father moved them all to his mother's home in Kyle, Texas, where the paternal grandmother raised the family in extreme poverty. The father gave up all attempts to support them either financially or emotionally; the security provided by the strong, loving, but pious and stern grandmother ended with her death when Porter was eleven. Porter married to leave home immediately after her sixteenth birthday, only to find that rooted domesticity was not for her. Long before her divorce in 1915, she had separated from her first husband and begun a life of travel, activity, and changes of jobs.

She started writing in 1916 as a reporter for a Dallas newspaper. In 1917 she moved to Denver, the next year to New York City's Greenwich Village. Between 1918 and 1924 she lived mainly in Mexico, freelancing, meeting artists and intellectuals, and becoming involved in revolutionary politics. In Mexico she found the resources of journalism inadequate to her ambitions; using an anecdote she had heard from an archaeologist as a kernel, she wrote her first story, "María Concepción," which was published in the prestigious *Century* magazine in 1922. Like all her stories, it dealt with powerful emotions and had a strong sense of locale. Critics praised her as a major talent.

Although she considered herself a serious writer from this time on, Porter was distracted from fiction by many crosscurrents. A self-supporting woman with expensive tastes, she hesitated to give up lucrative freelance offers. She enjoyed travel and gladly took on jobs that sent her abroad. She became involved in political causes, including the Sacco-Vanzetti case. She was married four times.

Porter planned each story meticulously—taking extensive notes, devising scenarios, roughing out dialogue, and revising many times, sometimes over a period of years. She did not write confessional or simple autobiographical fiction, but each story originated in an important experience of her life. Although not a feminist, Porter devoted much of her work to exploring the tensions in women's lives in the modern era. The story that made her famous for life, so that everything else she published thereafter was looked on as a literary event, was "Flowering Judas" (1929), set in Mexico and dealing with revolutionary politics, lust, and betrayal. The reality of mixed motives and the difference between pure idealism and egotistical opportunism as they are encountered in revolutionary politics are among the themes in this deceptively simple narrative. It appeared in the little magazine *Hound and Horn*. The collections *Flowering Judas* and *Noon Wine* came out in 1930 and 1937. In 1930 Porter went back to Mexico and the following year to Europe on a Guggenheim fellowship; she lived in Berlin, Paris, and Basel before returning to the United States in 1936. Two more collections of stories and novellas appeared in 1939 (*Pale Horse, Pale Rider*) and in 1944 (*The Leaning Tower*). These later collections feature several stories about Miranda Gay, a character who is partly autobiographical and partly an idealized image of the southern belle facing the modern world. *Pale Horse, Pale Rider* narrates Miranda's World War I romance with a soldier in the highly charged political climate of the American home front.

Soon after arriving in Europe in 1931 Porter began working on a novel, but it was not until 1962 that *Ship of Fools*, which runs to almost five hundred pages, appeared. Set on an ocean liner crossing the Atlantic to Germany in August 1931, it explores the characters and developing relationships of a large number of passengers; the ship, as Porter wrote in a preface, stands for "this world on its voyage to eternity." As in "Flowering Judas" and *Pale Horse, Pale Rider* the personal and the political intersect in *Ship of Fools*, since the coming of Nazism in Germany frames the interlinked stories of the travelers. In its film version, *Ship of Fools* brought Porter a great deal of money. Capitalizing on the publicity, her publishers brought out the *Collected Stories* in 1965, from which followed the National Book Award, the Pulitzer Prize, the Gold Medal for fiction of the National Institute of Arts and Letters, and election to the American Academy of Letters, all in the next two years. The happiest occasions in her later years—she lived to be ninety—were connected with endowing and establishing the Katherine Anne Porter Room at the University of Maryland, not far from her last home near Washington, D.C.

The texts are from the *Collected Stories* (1965).

Flowering Judas[1]

Braggioni sits heaped upon the edge of a straight-backed chair much too small for him, and sings to Laura in a furry, mournful voice. Laura has begun to find reasons for avoiding her own house until the latest possible moment, for Braggioni is there almost every night. No matter how late she is, he will be sitting there with a surly, waiting expression, pulling at his kinky yellow hair, thumbing the strings of his guitar, snarling a tune under his breath. Lupe the Indian maid meets Laura at the door, and says with a flicker of a glance towards the upper room, "He waits."

Laura wishes to lie down, she is tired of her hairpins and the feel of her long tight sleeves, but she says to him, "Have you a new song for me this evening?" If he says yes, she asks him to sing it. If he says no, she remembers his favorite one, and asks him to sing it again. Lupe brings her a cup of chocolate and a plate of rice, and Laura eats at the small table under the lamp, first inviting Braggioni, whose answer is always the same: "I have eaten, and besides, chocolate thickens the voice."

Laura says, "Sing, then," and Braggioni heaves himself into song. He scratches the guitar familiarly as though it were a pet animal, and sings pas-

---

1. One of a genus of trees and shrubs with purplish rosy flowers. According to legend, Judas Iscariot, betrayer of Jesus, hanged himself from such a tree.

sionately off key, taking the high notes in a prolonged painful squeal. Laura, who haunts the markets listening to the ballad singers, and stops every day to hear the blind boy playing his reed-flute in Sixteenth of September Street,[2] listens to Braggioni with pitiless courtesy, because she dares not smile at his miserable performance. Nobody dares to smile at him. Braggioni is cruel to everyone, with a kind of specialized insolence, but he is so vain of his talents, and so sensitive to slights, it would require a cruelty and vanity greater than his own to lay a finger on the vast cureless wound of his self-esteem. It would require courage, too, for it is dangerous to offend him, and nobody has this courage.

Braggioni loves himself with such tenderness and amplitude and eternal charity that his followers—for he is a leader of men, a skilled revolutionist, and his skin has been punctured in honorable warfare—warm themselves in the reflected glow, and say to each other: "He has a real nobility, a love of humanity raised above mere personal affections." The excess of this self-love has flowed out, inconveniently for her, over Laura, who, with so many others, owes her comfortable situation and her salary to him. When he is in a very good humor, he tells her, "I am tempted to forgive you for being a *gringa. Gringita!*"[3] and Laura, burning, imagines herself leaning forward suddenly, and with a sound back-handed slap wiping the suety smile from his face. If he notices her eyes at these moments he gives no sign.

She knows what Braggioni would offer her, and she must resist tenaciously without appearing to resist, and if she could avoid it she would not admit even to herself the slow drift of his intention. During these long evenings which have spoiled a long month for her, she sits in her deep chair with an open book on her knees, resting her eyes on the consoling rigidity of the printed page when the sight and sound of Braggioni singing threaten to identify themselves with all her remembered afflictions and to add their weight to her uneasy premonitions of the future. The gluttonous bulk of Braggioni has become a symbol of her many disillusions, for a revolutionist should be lean, animated by heroic faith, a vessel of abstract virtues. This is nonsense, she knows it now and is ashamed of it. Revolution must have leaders, and leadership is a career for energetic men. She is, her comrades tell her, full of romantic error, for what she defines as cynicism in them is merely "a developed sense of reality." She is almost too willing to say, "I am wrong, I suppose I don't really understand the principles," and afterward she makes a secret truce with herself, determined not to surrender her will to such expedient logic. But she cannot help feeling that she has been betrayed irreparably by the disunion between her way of living and her feeling of what life should be, and at times she is almost contented to rest in this sense of grievance as a private store of consolation. Sometimes she wishes to run away, but she stays. Now she longs to fly out of this room, down the narrow stairs, and into the street where the houses lean together like conspirators under a single mottled lamp, and leave Braggioni singing to himself.

Instead she looks at Braggioni, frankly and clearly, like a good child who understands the rules of behavior. Her knees cling together under sound

---

2. A street in Morelia, a city in western Mexico where the story is set.
3. A young female foreigner, non-Mexican girl; a

patronizing term meaning "cute little foreign girl." Diminutive of *gringa*, which is used pejoratively, especially for an American.

blue serge, and her round white collar is not purposely nun-like. She wears the uniform of an idea, and has renounced vanities. She was born Roman Catholic, and in spite of her fear of being seen by someone who might make a scandal of it, she slips now and again into some crumbling little church, kneels on the chilly stone, and says a Hail Mary on the gold rosary she bought in Tehuantepec. It is no good and she ends by examining the altar with its tinsel flowers and ragged brocades, and feels tender about the battered doll-shape of some male saint whose white, lace-trimmed drawers hang limply around his ankles below the hieratic dignity of his velvet robe. She has encased herself in a set of principles derived from her early training, leaving no detail of gesture or of personal taste untouched, and for this reason she will not wear lace made on machines. This is her private heresy, for in her special group the machine is sacred, and will be the salvation of the workers. She loves fine lace, and there is a tiny edge of fluted cobweb on this collar, which is one of twenty precisely alike, folded in blue tissue paper in the upper drawer of her clothes chest.

Braggioni catches her glance solidly as if he had been waiting for it, leans forward, balancing his paunch between his spread knees, and sings with tremendous emphasis, weighing his words. He has, the song relates, no father and no mother, nor even a friend to console him; lonely as a wave of the sea he comes and goes, lonely as a wave. His mouth opens round and yearns sideways, his balloon cheeks grow oily with the labor of song. He bulges marvelously in his expensive garments. Over his lavender collar, crushed upon a purple necktie, held by a diamond hoop: over his ammunition belt of tooled leather worked in silver, buckled cruelly around his gasping middle: over the tops of his glossy yellow shoes Braggioni swells with ominous ripeness, his mauve silk hose stretched taut, his ankles bound with the stout leather thongs of his shoes.

When he stretches his eyelids at Laura she notes again that his eyes are the true tawny yellow cat's eyes. He is rich, not in money, he tells her, but in power, and this power brings with it the blameless ownership of things, and the right to indulge his love of small luxuries. "I have a taste for the elegant refinements," he said once, flourishing a yellow silk handkerchief before her nose. "Smell that? It is Jockey Club, imported from New York." Nonetheless he is wounded by life. He will say so presently. "It is true everything turns to dust in the hand, to gall on the tongue." He sighs and his leather belt creaks like a saddle girth. "I am disappointed in everything as it comes. Everything." He shakes his head. "You, poor thing, you will be disappointed too. You are born for it. We are more alike than you realize in some things. Wait and see. Some day you will remember what I have told you, you will know that Braggioni was your friend."

Laura feels a slow chill, a purely physical sense of danger, a warning in her blood that violence, mutilation, a shocking death, wait for her with lessening patience. She has translated this fear into something homely, immediate, and sometimes hesitates before crossing the street. "My personal fate is nothing, except as the testimony of a mental attitude," she reminds herself, quoting from some forgotten philosophic primer, and is sensible enough to add, "Anyhow, I shall not be killed by an automobile if I can help it."

"It may be true I am as corrupt, in another way, as Braggioni," she thinks in spite of herself, "as callous, as incomplete," and if this is so, any kind of death seems preferable. Still she sits quietly, she does not run. Where could she go? Uninvited she has promised herself to this place; she can no longer imagine herself as living in another country, and there is no pleasure in remembering her life before she came here.

Precisely what is the nature of this devotion, its true motives, and what are its obligations? Laura cannot say. She spends part of her days in Xochimilco, near by, teaching Indian children to say in English, "The cat is on the mat." When she appears in the classroom they crowd about her with smiles on their wise, innocent, clay-colored faces, crying, "Good morning, my titcher!" in immaculate voices, and they make of her desk a fresh garden of flowers every day.

During her leisure she goes to union meetings and listens to busy important voices quarreling over tactics, methods, internal politics. She visits the prisoners of her own political faith in their cells, where they entertain themselves with counting cockroaches, repenting of their indiscretions, composing their memoirs, writing out manifestoes and plans for their comrades who are still walking about free, hands in pockets, sniffing fresh air. Laura brings them food and cigarettes and a little money, and she brings messages disguised in equivocal phrases from the men outside who dare not set foot in the prison for fear of disappearing into the cells kept empty for them. If the prisoners confuse night and day, and complain, "Dear little Laura, time doesn't pass in this infernal hole, and I won't know when it is time to sleep unless I have a reminder," she brings them their favorite narcotics, and says in a tone that does not wound them with pity, "Tonight will really be night for you," and though her Spanish amuses them, they find her comforting, useful. If they lose patience and all faith, and curse the slowness of their friends in coming to their rescue with money and influence, they trust her not to repeat everything, and if she inquires, "Where do you think we can find money, or influence?" they are certain to answer, "Well, there is Braggioni, why doesn't he do something?"

She smuggles letters from headquarters to men hiding from firing squads in back streets in mildewed houses, where they sit in tumbled beds and talk bitterly as if all Mexico were at their heels, when Laura knows positively they might appear at the band concert in the Alameda[4] on Sunday morning, and no one would notice them. But Braggioni says, "Let them sweat a little. The next time they may be careful. It is very restful to have them out of the way for a while." She is not afraid to knock on any door in any street after midnight, and enter in the darkness, and say to one of these men who is really in danger: "They will be looking for you— seriously—tomorrow morning after six. Here is some money from Vicente. Go to Vera Cruz and wait."

She borrows money from the Roumanian agitator to give to his bitter enemy the Polish agitator. The favor of Braggioni is their disputed territory, and Braggioni holds the balance nicely, for he can use them both. The Polish agitator talks love to her over café tables, hoping to exploit what he believes is her secret sentimental preference for him, and he gives her misinformation which he begs her to repeat as the solemn truth to certain persons. The Roumanian is more adroit. He is generous with his money in all good causes, and lies to her with an air of ingenuous candor, as if he were her good friend and confidant. She never repeats anything they may

4. Public promenade bordered with trees.

say. Braggioni never asks questions. He has other ways to discover all that he wishes to know about them.

Nobody touches her, but all praise her gray eyes, and the soft, round under lip which promises gayety, yet is always grave, nearly always firmly closed: and they cannot understand why she is in Mexico. She walks back and forth on her errands, with puzzled eyebrows, carrying her little folder of drawings and music and school papers. No dancer dances more beautifully than Laura walks, and she inspires some amusing, unexpected ardors, which cause little gossip, because nothing comes of them. A young captain who had been a soldier in Zapata's[5] army attempted, during a horseback ride near Cuernavaca, to express his desire for her with the noble simplicity befitting a rude folk-hero: but gently, because he was gentle. This gentleness was his defeat, for when he alighted, and removed her foot from the stirrup, and essayed to draw her down into his arms, her horse, ordinarily a tame one, shied fiercely, reared and plunged away. The young hero's horse careered blindly after his stable-mate, and the hero did not return to the hotel until rather late that evening. At breakfast he came to her table in full charro dress,[6] gray buckskin jacket and trousers with strings of silver buttons down the leg, and he was in a humorous, careless mood. "May I sit with you?" and "You are a wonderful rider. I was terrified that you might be thrown and dragged. I should never have forgiven myself. But I cannot admire you enough for your riding!"

"I learned to ride in Arizona," said Laura.

"If you will ride with me again this morning, I promise you a horse that will not shy with you," he said. But Laura remembered that she must return to Mexico City at noon.

Next morning the children made a celebration and spent their playtime writing on the blackboard, "We lov ar ticher," and with tinted chalks they drew wreaths of flowers around the words. The young hero wrote her a letter: "I am a very foolish, wasteful, impulsive man. I should have first said I love you, and then you would not have run away. But you shall see me again." Laura thought, "I must send him a box of colored crayons," but she was trying to forgive herself for having spurred her horse at the wrong moment.

A brown, shock-haired youth came and stood in her patio one night and sang like a lost soul for two hours, but Laura could think of nothing to do about it. The moonlight spread a wash of gauzy silver over the clear spaces of the garden, and the shadows were cobalt blue. The scarlet blossoms of the Judas tree were dull purple, and the names of the colors repeated themselves automatically in her mind, while she watched not the boy, but his shadow, fallen like a dark garment across the fountain rim, trailing in the water. Lupe came silently and whispered expert counsel in her ear: "If you will throw him one little flower, he will sing another song or two and go away." Laura threw the flower, and he sang a last song and went away with the flower tucked in the band of his hat. Lupe said, "He is one of the organizers of the Typographers Union, and before that he sold corridos[7] in the Merced market, and before that, he came from Guanajuato, where I was born. I would not trust any man, but I trust least those from Guanajuato."

5. Emiliano Zapata (c. 1879–1919), Mexican peasant revolutionary general whose movement, *zapatismo*, combined agrarian and Mexican Indian cultural aspirations; one of the most significant figures in Mexico from 1910 to 1919, when he was murdered.
6. Costume worn by a peasant horseman of special status.
7. Popular ballads.

She did not tell Laura that he would be back again the next night, and the next, nor that he would follow her at a certain fixed distance around the Merced market, through the Zócolo, up Francisco I. Madero Avenue, and so along the Paseo de la Reforma to Chapultepec Park, and into the Philosopher's Footpath, still with that flower withering in his hat, and an indivisible attention in his eyes.

Now Laura is accustomed to him, it means nothing except that he is nineteen years old and is observing a convention with all propriety, as though it were founded on a law of nature, which in the end it might well prove to be. He is beginning to write poems which he prints on a wooden press, and he leaves them stuck like handbills in her door. She is pleasantly disturbed by the abstract, unhurried watchfulness of his black eyes which will in time turn easily towards another object. She tells herself that throwing the flower was a mistake, for she is twenty-two years old and knows better; but she refuses to regret it, and persuades herself that her negation of all external events as they occur is a sign that she is gradually perfecting herself in the stoicism she strives to cultivate against that disaster she fears, though she cannot name it.

She is not at home in the world. Every day she teaches children who remain strangers to her, though she loves their tender round hands and their charming opportunist savagery. She knocks at unfamiliar doors not knowing whether a friend or a stranger shall answer, and even if a known face emerges from the sour gloom of that unknown interior, still it is the face of a stranger. No matter what this stranger says to her, nor what her message to him, the very cells of her flesh reject knowledge and kinship in one monotonous word. No. No. No. She draws her strength from this one holy talismanic word which does not suffer her to be led into evil. Denying everything, she may walk anywhere in safety, she looks at everything without amazement.

No, repeats this firm unchanging voice of her blood; and she looks at Braggioni without amazement. He is a great man, he wishes to impress this simple girl who covers her great round breasts with thick dark cloth, and who hides long, invaluably beautiful legs under a heavy skirt. She is almost thin except for the incomprehensible fullness of her breasts, like a nursing mother's, and Braggioni, who considers himself a judge of women, speculates again on the puzzle of her notorious virginity, and takes the liberty of speech which she permits without a sign of modesty, indeed, without any sort of sign, which is disconcerting.

"You think you are so cold, *gringita!* Wait and see. You will surprise yourself some day! May I be there to advise you!" He stretches his eyelids at her, and his ill-humored cat's eyes waver in a separate glance for the two points of light marking the opposite ends of a smoothly drawn path between the swollen curve of her breasts. He is not put off by that blue serge, nor by her resolutely fixed gaze. There is all the time in the world. His cheeks are bellying with the wind of song. "O girl with the dark eyes," he sings, and reconsiders. "But yours are not dark. I can change all that. O girl with the green eyes, you have stolen my heart away!" then his mind wanders to the song, and Laura feels the weight of his attention being shifted elsewhere. Singing thus, he seems harmless, he is quite harmless, there is nothing to do but sit patiently and say "No," when the moment comes. She draws a full breath, and her mind wanders also, but not far. She dares not wander too far.

Not for nothing has Braggioni taken pains to be a good revolutionist and a professional lover of humanity. He will never die of it. He has the malice, the cleverness, the wickedness, the sharpness of wit, the hardness of heart, stipulated for loving the world profitably. *He will never die of it.* He will live to see himself kicked out from his feeding trough by other hungry world-saviors. Traditionally he must sing in spite of his life which drives him to bloodshed, he tells Laura, for his father was a Tuscany[8] peasant who drifted to Yucatan and married a Maya woman: a woman of race, an aristocrat. They gave him the love and knowledge of music, thus: and under the rip of his thumbnail, the strings of the instrument complain like exposed nerves.

Once he was called Delgadito by all the girls and married women who ran after him; he was so scrawny all his bones showed under his thin cotton clothing, and he could squeeze his emptiness to the very backbone with his two hands. He was a poet and the revolution was only a dream then; too many women loved him and sapped away his youth, and he could never find enough to eat anywhere, anywhere! Now he is a leader of men, crafty men who whisper in his ear, hungry men who wait for hours outside his office for a word with him, emaciated men with wild faces who waylay him at the street gate with a timid, "Comrade, let me tell you . . ." and they blow the foul breath from their empty stomachs in his face.

He is always sympathetic. He gives them handfuls of small coins from his own pocket, he promises them work, there will be demonstrations, they must join the unions and attend the meetings, above all they must be on the watch for spies. They are closer to him than his own brothers, without them he can do nothing—until tomorrow, comrade!

Until tomorrow. "They are stupid, they are lazy, they are treacherous, they would cut my throat for nothing," he says to Laura. He has good food and abundant drink, he hires an automobile and drives in the Paseo on Sunday morning, and enjoys plenty of sleep in a soft bed beside a wife who dares not disturb him; and he sits pampering his bones in easy billows of fat, singing to Laura, who knows and thinks these things about him. When he was fifteen, he tried to drown himself because he loved a girl, his first love, and she laughed at him. "A thousand women have paid for that," and his tight little mouth turns down at the corners. Now he perfumes his hair with Jockey Club, and confides to Laura: "One woman is really as good as another for me, in the dark. I prefer them all."

His wife organizes unions among the girls in the cigarette factories, and walks in picket lines, and even speaks at meetings in the evening. But she cannot be brought to acknowledge the benefits of true liberty. "I tell her I must have my freedom, net. She does not understand my point of view." Laura has heard this many times. Braggioni scratches the guitar and meditates. "She is an instinctively virtuous woman, pure gold, no doubt of that. If she were not, I should lock her up, and she knows it."

His wife, who works so hard for the good of the factory girls, employs part of her leisure lying on the floor weeping because there are so many women in the world, and only one husband for her, and she never knows where nor when to look for him. He told her: "Unless you can learn to cry when I am not here, I must go away for good." That day he went away and took a room at the Hotel Madrid.

It is this month of separation for the sake of higher principles that has been spoiled not only for Mrs. Braggioni, whose sense of reality is beyond

---

8. A region in north-central Italy.

criticism, but for Laura, who feels herself bogged in a nightmare. Tonight Laura envies Mrs. Braggioni, who is alone, and free to weep as much as she pleases about a concrete wrong. Laura has just come from a visit to the prison, and she is waiting for tomorrow with a bitter anxiety as if tomorrow may not come, but time may be caught immovably in this hour, with herself transfixed, Braggioni singing on forever, and Eugenio's body not yet discovered by the guard.

Braggioni says: "Are you going to sleep?" Almost before she can shake her head, he begins telling her about the May-day disturbances coming on in Morelia, for the Catholics hold a festival in honor of the Blessed Virgin, and the Socialists celebrate their martyrs on that day. "There will be two independent processions, starting from either end of town, and they will march until they meet, and the rest depends . . ." He asks her to oil and load his pistols. Standing up, he unbuckles his ammunition belt, and spreads it laden across her knees. Laura sits with the shells slipping through the cleaning cloth dipped in oil, and he says again he cannot understand why she works so hard for the revolutionary idea unless she loves some man who is in it. "Are you not in love with someone?" "No," says Laura. "And no one is in love with you?" "No." "Then it is your own fault. No woman need go begging. Why, what is the matter with you? The legless beggar woman in the Alameda has a perfectly faithful lover. Did you know that?"

Laura peers down the pistol barrel and says nothing, but a long, slow faintness rises and subsides in her; Braggioni curves his swollen fingers around the throat of the guitar and softly smothers the music out of it, and when she hears him again he seems to have forgotten her, and is speaking in the hypnotic voice he uses when talking in small rooms to a listening, close-gathered crowd. Some day this world, now seemingly so composed and eternal, to the edges of every sea shall be merely a tangle of gaping trenches, of crashing walls and broken bodies. Everything must be torn from its accustomed place where it has rotted for centuries, hurled skyward and distributed, cast down again clean as rain, without separate identity. Nothing shall survive that the stiffened hands of poverty have created for the rich and no one shall be left alive except the elect spirits destined to procreate a new world cleansed of cruelty and injustice, ruled by benevolent anarchy: "Pistols are good, I love them, cannon are even better, but in the end I pin my faith to good dynamite," he concludes, and strokes the pistol lying in her hands. "Once I dreamed of destroying this city, in case it offered resistance to General Ortíz, but it fell into his hands like an over-ripe pear."

He is made restless by his own words, rises and stands waiting. Laura holds up the belt to him: "Put that on, and go kill somebody in Morelia, and you will be happier," she says softly. The presence of death in the room makes her bold. "Today, I found Eugenio going into a stupor. He refused to allow me to call the prison doctor. He had taken all the tablets I brought him yesterday. He said he took them because he was bored."

"He is a fool, and his death is his own business," says Braggioni, fastening his belt carefully.

"I told him if he had waited only a little while longer, you would have got him set free," says Laura. "He said he did not want to wait."

"He is a fool and we are well rid of him," says Braggioni, reaching for his hat.

He goes away. Laura knows his mood has changed, she will not see him any more for a while. He will send word when he needs her to go on errands into strange streets, to speak to the strange faces that will appear, like clay masks with the power of human speech, to mutter their thanks to Braggioni for his help. Now she is free, and she thinks, I must run while there is time. But she does not go.

Braggioni enters his own house where for a month his wife has spent many hours every night weeping and tangling her hair upon her pillow. She is weeping now, and she weeps more at the sight of him, the cause of all her sorrows. He looks about the room. Nothing is changed, the smells are good and familiar, he is well acquainted with the woman who comes toward him with no reproach except grief on her face. He says to her tenderly: "You are so good, please don't cry any more, you dear good creature." She says, "Are you tired, my angel? Sit here and I will wash your feet." She brings a bowl of water, and kneeling, unlaces his shoes, and when from her knees she raises her sad eyes under her blackened lids, he is sorry for everything, and bursts into tears. "Ah, yes, I am hungry, I am tired, let us eat something together," he says, between sobs. His wife leans her head on his arm and says, "Forgive me!" and this time he is refreshed by the solemn, endless rain of her tears.

Laura takes off her serge dress and puts on a white linen nightgown and goes to bed. She turns her head a little to one side, and lying still, reminds herself that it is time to sleep. Numbers tick in her brain like little clocks, soundless doors close of themselves around her. If you would sleep, you must not remember anything, the children will say tomorrow, good morning, my teacher, the poor prisoners who come every day bringing flowers to their jailor. 1-2-3-4-5—it is monstrous to confuse love with revolution, night with day, life with death—ah, Eugenio!

The tolling of the midnight bell is a signal, but what does it mean? Get up, Laura, and follow me: come out of your sleep, out of your bed, out of this strange house. What are you doing in this house? Without a word, without fear she rose and reached for Eugenio's hand, but he eluded her with a sharp, sly smile and drifted away. This is not all, you shall see—Murderer, he said, follow me, I will show you a new country, but it is far away and we must hurry. No, said Laura, not unless you take my hand, no; and she clung first to the stair rail, and then to the topmost branch of the Judas tree that bent down slowly and set her upon the earth, and then to the rocky ledge of a cliff, and then to the jagged wave of a sea that was not water but a desert of crumbling stone. Where are you taking me, she asked in wonder but without fear. To death, and it is a long way off, and we must hurry, said Eugenio. No, said Laura, not unless you take my hand. Then eat these flowers, poor prisoner, said Eugenio in a voice of pity, take and eat: and from the Judas tree he stripped the warm bleeding flowers, and held them to her lips. She saw that his hand was fleshless, a cluster of small white petrified branches, and his eye sockets were without light, but she ate the flowers greedily for they satisfied both hunger and thirst. Murderer! said Eugenio, and Cannibal! This is my body and my blood. Laura cried No! and at the sound of her own voice, she awoke trembling, and was afraid to sleep again.

1929, 1930

ZORA NEALE HURSTON
1891–1960

Zora Neale Hurston was born in 1891 in Notasulga, Alabama, and moved with her family in 1892 to Eatonville, Florida, an all-black town. Her father, a Baptist preacher of considerable eloquence, was not a family man and made life difficult for his wife and eight children. The tie between mother and daughter was strong; Lucy Hurston was a driving force and strong support for all her children. But her death when Zora Hurston was about eleven left the child with little home life. Hitherto, the town of Eatonville had been like an extended family to her, and her early childhood was protected from racism because she encountered no white people. With her mother's death, Hurston's wanderings and her initiation into American racism began. The early security had given her the core of self-confidence she needed to survive. She moved from one relative's home to another until she was old enough to support herself, and with her earnings she began slowly to pursue an education. Although she had never finished grade school in Eatonville she was able to enter and complete college. In the early 1920s at Howard University in Washington, D.C. (the nation's leading African American university at that time), she studied with the great black educator Alain Locke, who was to make history with his anthology *The New Negro* in 1925. After a short story, "Drenched in Light," appeared in the New York African American magazine *Opportunity*, she decided to move to Harlem and pursue a literary career there.

As her biographer, Robert Hemenway, writes, "Zora Hurston was an extraordinarily witty woman, and she acquired an instant reputation in New York for her high spirits and side-splitting tales of Eatonville life. She could walk into a room of strangers . . . and almost immediately gather people, charm, amuse, and impress them." Her Eatonville vignettes convey the flavor of this discourse. Generous, outspoken, high spirited, an interesting conversationalist, she worked as a personal secretary for the politically liberal novelist Fannie Hurst and entered Barnard College. Her career took two simultaneous directions: at Barnard she studied with the famous anthropologist Franz Boas and developed an interest in black folk traditions, and in Harlem she became well known as a storyteller, an informal performing artist. Thus she was doubly committed to oral narrative, and her work excels in its representation of people talking.

When she graduated from Barnard in 1927 she received a fellowship to return to Florida and study the oral traditions of Eatonville. From then on, she strove to achieve a balance between focusing on the folk and her origins and focusing on herself as an individual. After the fellowship money ran out, Hurston was supported by Mrs. R. Osgood Mason, an elderly white patron of the arts. Mason had firm ideas about what she wanted her protégés to produce; she required them all to get her permission before publishing any of the work that she had subsidized. In this relationship, Hurston experienced a difficulty that all the black artists of the Harlem Renaissance had to face—the fact that well-off white people were the sponsors of, and often expected to be the chief audience for, their work.

Hurston's work was not entirely popular with the male intellectual leaders of the Harlem community. She quarreled especially with Langston Hughes; she rejected the idea that a black writer's chief concern should be how blacks were being portrayed to the white reader. She did not write to "uplift her race," either; because in her view it was already uplifted, she (like Claude McKay) was not embarrassed to present her characters as mixtures of good and bad, strong and weak. Some of

Zora Neale Hurston, as photographed by Carl Van Vechten in 1938.

the other Harlem writers thought her either naïve or egotistical, but Hurston argued that freedom could only mean freedom from all coercion, no matter what the source.

The Great Depression brought an end to the structure that had undergirded Hurston's field-work, and she turned fully to writing. Unfortunately her most important work appeared in the mid-1930s when there was little interest in it, or in African American writing in general. She published *Jonah's Gourd Vine* in 1934 (a novel whose main character is based on her father); *Mules and Men* in 1935 (based on material from her field trips in Florida—this was her best-selling book, but it earned a total of only $943.75); and *Their Eyes Were Watching God,* in 1937. This novel about an African American woman's quest for self-hood has become a popular and critical favorite, both a woman's story, and a descriptive critique of southern African American folk society, showing its divisions and diversity. Technically, it is a loosely organized, highly metaphorical novel, with passages of broad folk humor and of extreme artistic compression. Other books followed in 1938 and 1939, and she wrote an autobiography—*Dust Tracks on a Road*—which appeared in 1942, with its occasional expression of antiwhite sentiments removed by her editors. At this point, however, Hurston had no audience. For the last decade of her life she lived in Florida, working from time to time as a maid.

How It Feels to Be Colored Me[1]

I am colored but I offer nothing in the way of extenuating circumstances except the fact that I am the only Negro in the United States whose grandfather on the mother's side was *not* an Indian chief.

I remember the very day that I became colored. Up to my thirteenth year I lived in the little Negro town of Eatonville, Florida. It is exclusively a colored town. The only white people I knew passed through the town going to or coming from Orlando. The native whites rode dusty horses, the Northern tourists chugged down the sandy village road in automobiles. The town knew the Southerners and never stopped cane chewing when they passed.

1. The text is that of *I Love Myself When I Am Laughing . . . and Then Again When I Am Looking Mean and Impressive* (1979), edited by Alice Walker.

But the Northerners were something else again. They were peered at cautiously from behind the curtains by the timid. The more venturesome would come out on the porch to watch them go past and got just as much pleasure out of the tourists as the tourists got out of the village.

The front porch might seem a daring place for the rest of the town, but it was a gallery seat for me. My favorite place was atop the gate-post. Proscenium box[2] for a born first-nighter. Not only did I enjoy the show, but I didn't mind the actors knowing that I liked it. I usually spoke to them in passing. I'd wave at them and when they returned my salute, I would say something like this: "Howdy-do-well-I-thank-you-where-you-goin'?" Usually automobile or the horse paused at this, and after a queer exchange of compliments, I would probably "go a piece of the way" with them, as we say in farthest Florida. If one of my family happened to come to the front in time to see me, of course negotiations would be rudely broken off. But even so, it is clear that I was the first "welcome-to-our-state" Floridian, and I hope the Miami Chamber of Commerce will please take notice.

During this period, white people differed from colored to me only in that they rode through town and never lived there. They liked to hear me "speak pieces" and sing and wanted to see me dance the parse-me-la, and gave me generously of their small silver for doing these things, which seemed strange to me for I wanted to do them so much that I needed bribing to stop. Only they didn't know it. The colored people gave no dimes. They deplored any joyful tendencies in me, but I was their Zora nevertheless. I belonged to them, to the nearby hotels, to the county—everybody's Zora.

But changes came in the family when I was thirteen, and I was sent to school in Jacksonville. I left Eatonville, the town of the oleanders, as Zora. When I disembarked from the river-boat at Jacksonville, she was no more. It seemed that I had suffered a sea change. I was not Zora of Orange County any more, I was now a little colored girl. I found it out in certain ways. In my heart as well as in the mirror, I became a fast brown—warranted not to rub nor run.

But I am not tragically colored. There is no great sorrow dammed up in my soul, nor lurking behind my eyes. I do not mind at all. I do not belong to the sobbing school of Negrohood who hold that nature somehow has given them a lowdown dirty deal and whose feelings are all hurt about it. Even in the helter-skelter skirmish that is my life, I have seen that the world is to the strong regardless of a little pigmentation more or less. No, I do not weep at the world—I am too busy sharpening my oyster knife.

Someone is always at my elbow reminding me that I am the granddaughter of slaves. It fails to register depression with me. Slavery is sixty years in the past. The operation was successful and the patient is doing well, thank you. The terrible struggle that made me an American out of a potential slave said "On the line!" The Reconstruction said "Get set!"; and the generation before said "Go!" I am off to a flying start and I must not halt in the stretch to look behind and weep. Slavery is the price I paid for civilization, and the choice was not with me. It is a bully adventure and worth all that I have paid through my ancestors for it. No one on earth ever had a greater chance for glory. The world to be won and nothing to be lost. It is thrilling to think—to

2. Box at the front of the auditorium, closest to the stage.

know that for any act of mine, I shall get twice as much praise or twice as much blame. It is quite exciting to hold the center of the national stage, with the spectators not knowing whether to laugh or to weep.

The position of my white neighbor is much more difficult. No brown specter pulls up a chair beside me when I sit down to eat. No dark ghost thrusts its leg against mine in bed. The game of keeping what one has is never so exciting as the game of getting.

I do not always feel colored. Even now I often achieve the unconscious Zora of Eatonville before the Hegira.[3] I feel most colored when I am thrown against a sharp white background.

For instance at Barnard. "Besides the waters of the Hudson" I feel my race. Among the thousand white persons, I am a dark rock surged upon, and overswept, but through it all, I remain myself. When covered by the waters, I am; and the ebb but reveals me again.

Sometimes it is the other way around. A white person is set down in our midst, but the contrast is just as sharp for me. For instance, when I sit in the drafty basement that is The New World Cabaret[4] with a white person, my color comes. We enter chatting about any little nothing that we have in common and are seated by the jazz waiters. In the abrupt way that jazz orchestras have, this one plunges into a number. It loses no time in circumlocutions, but gets right down to business. It constricts the thorax and splits the heart with its tempo and narcotic harmonies. This orchestra grows rambunctious, rears on its hind legs and attacks the tonal veil with primitive fury, rending it, clawing it until it breaks through to the jungle beyond. I follow those heathen—follow them exultingly. I dance wildly inside myself; I yell within, I whoop; I shake my assegai[5] above my head, I hurl it true to the mark *yeeeeooww!* I am in the jungle and living in the jungle way. My face is painted red and yellow and my body is painted blue. My pulse is throbbing like a war drum. I want to slaughter something—give pain, give death to what, I do not know. But the piece ends. The men of the orchestra wipe their lips and rest their fingers. I creep back slowly to the veneer we call civilization with the last tone and find the white friend sitting motionless in his seat smoking calmly.

"Good music they have here," he remarks, drumming the table with his fingertips.

Music. The great blobs of purple and red emotion have not touched him. He has only heard what I felt. He is far away and I see him but dimly across the ocean and the continent that have fallen between us. He is so pale with his whiteness then and I am *so* colored.

At certain times I have no race, I am *me*. When I set my hat at a certain angle and saunter down Seventh Avenue, Harlem City, feeling as snooty as the lions in front of the Forty-Second Street Library, for instance. So far as my feelings are concerned, Peggy Hopkins Joyce on the Boule Mich[6] with her gorgeous raiment, stately carriage, knees knocking together in a most

3. Forced march of Muhammad from Mecca to Medina in 622 c.e.; hence any forced flight or journey for safety.
4. Popular Harlem nightclub in the 1920s.
5. A slender spear used by some South African peoples.

6. Boulevard St. Michel, a street on the Left Bank of Paris running through the Latin Quarter. It is lined with cafés that were—and still are— frequented by Americans. Joyce was a much-photographed socialite and heiress.

aristocratic manner, has nothing on me. The cosmic Zora emerges. I belong to no race nor time. I am the eternal feminine with its string of beads.

I have no separate feeling about being an American citizen and colored. I am merely a fragment of the Great Soul that surges within the boundaries. My country, right or wrong.

Sometimes, I feel discriminated against, but it does not make me angry. It merely astonishes me. How *can* any deny themselves the pleasure of my company? It's beyond me.

But in the main, I feel like a brown bag of miscellany propped against a wall. Against a wall in company with other bags, white, red and yellow. Pour out the contents, and there is discovered a jumble of small things priceless and worthless. A first-water diamond, an empty spool, bits of broken glass, lengths of string, a key to a door long since crumbled away, a rusty knife-blade, old shoes saved for a road that never was and never will be, a nail bent under the weight of things too heavy for any nail, a dried flower or two still a little fragrant. In your hand is the brown bag. On the ground before you is the jumble it held—so much like the jumble in the bags, could they be emptied, that all might be dumped in a single heap and the bags refilled without altering the content of any greatly. A bit of colored glass more or less would not matter. Perhaps that is how the Great Stuffer of Bags filled them in the first place—who knows?

1928

The Gilded Six-Bits[1]

It was a Negro yard around a Negro house in a Negro settlement that looked to the payroll of the G and G Fertilizer works for its support.

But there was something happy about the place. The front yard was parted in the middle by a sidewalk from gate to door-step, a sidewalk edged on either side by quart bottles driven neck down into the ground on a slant. A mess of homey flowers planted without a plan but blooming cheerily from their helter-skelter places. The fence and house were whitewashed. The porch and steps scrubbed white.

The front door stood open to the sunshine so that the floor of the front room could finish drying after its weekly scouring. It was Saturday. Everything clean from the front gate to the privy house. Yard raked so that the strokes of the rake would make a pattern. Fresh newspaper cut in fancy edge on the kitchen shelves.

Missie May was bathing herself in the galvanized washtub in the bedroom. Her dark-brown skin glistened under the soapsuds that skittered down from her wash rag. Her stiff young breasts thrust forward aggressively like broad-based cones with the tips lacquered in black.

She heard men's voices in the distance and glanced at the dollar clock on the dresser.

"Humph! Ah'm way behind time t'day! Joe gointer be heah 'fore Ah git mah clothes on if Ah don't make haste."

1. The text is from the printing in *Story* magazine (1933). "Gilded": lightly plated with thin gold or gold-colored foil. "Six-bits": seventy-five cents (two bits equals one quarter).

She grabbed the clean meal sack at hand and dried herself hurriedly and began to dress. But before she could tie her slippers, there came the ring of singing metal on wood. Nine times.

Missie May grinned with delight. She had not seen the big tall man come stealing in the gate and creep up the walk grinning happily at the joyful mischief he was about to commit. But she knew that it was her husband throwing silver dollars in the door for her to pick up and pile beside her plate at dinner. It was this way every Saturday afternoon. The nine dollars hurled into the open door, he scurried to a hiding place behind the cape jasmine bush and waited.

Missie May promptly appeared at the door in mock alarm.

"Who dat chunkin' money in mah do'way?" She demanded. No answer from the yard. She leaped off the porch and began to search the shrubbery. She peeped under the porch and hung over the gate to look up and down the road. While she did this, the man behind the jasmine darted to the chinaberry tree. She spied him and gave chase.

"Nobody ain't gointer be chuckin' money at me and Ah not do 'em nothin'," she shouted in mock anger. He ran around the house with Missie May at his heels. She overtook him at the kitchen door. He ran inside but could not close it after him before she crowded in and locked with him in a rough and tumble. For several minutes the two were a furious mass of male and female energy. Shouting, laughing, twisting, turning, tussling, tickling each other in the ribs; Missie May clutching onto Joe and Joe trying, but not too hard, to get away.

"Missie May, take yo' hand out mah pocket!" Joe shouted out between laughs.

"Ah ain't, Joe, not lessen you gwine gimme whateve' it is good you got in yo' pocket. Turn it go, Joe, do Ah'll tear yo' clothes."

"Go on tear 'em. You de one dat pushes de needles round heah. Move yo' hand Missie May."

"Lemme git dat paper sack out yo' pocket. Ah bet its candy kisses."

"Tain't. Move yo' hand. Woman ain't go no business in a man's clothes nohow. Go way."

Missie May gouged way down and gave an upward jerk and triumphed.

"Unhhunh! Ah got it. It 'tis so candy kisses. Ah knowed you had somethin' for me in yo' clothes. Now Ah got to see whut's in every pocket you got."

Joe smiled indulgently and let his wife go through all of his pockets and take out the things that he had hidden there for her to find. She bore off the chewing gum, the cake of sweet soap, the pocket handkerchief as if she had wrested them from him, as if they had not been bought for the sake of this friendly battle.

"Whew! dat play-fight done got me all warmed up," Joe exclaimed. "Got me some water in de kittle?"

"Yo' water is on de fire and yo' clean things is cross de bed. Hurry up and wash yo'self and git changed so we kin eat. Ah'm hongry." As Missie said this, she bore the steaming kettle into the bedroom.

"You ain't hongry, sugar," Joe contradicted her. "Youse jes' a little empty. Ah'm de one whut's hongry. Ah could eat up camp meetin', back off 'ssociation, and drink Jurdan[2] dry. Have it on de table when Ah git out de tub."

2. The Jordan River in biblical Palestine (now Israel).

"Don't you mess wid mah business, man. You git in yo' clothes. Ah'm a real wife, not no dress and breath.[3] Ah might not look lak one, but if you burn me, you won't git a thing but wife ashes."

Joe splashed in the bedroom and Missie May fanned around in the kitchen. A fresh red and white checked cloth on the table. Big pitcher of buttermilk beaded with pale drops of butter from the churn. Hot fried mullet, crackling bread, ham hock atop a mound of string beans and new potatoes, and perched on the window-sill a pone[4] of spicy potato pudding.

Very little talk during the meal but that little consisted of banter that pretended to deny affection but in reality flaunted it. Like when Missie May reached for a second helping of the tater pone. Joe snatched it out of her reach.

After Missie May had made two or three unsuccessful grabs at the pan, she begged, "Aw, Joe gimme some mo' dat tater pone."

"Nope, sweetenin' is for us men-folks. Y'all pritty lil frail eels don't need nothin' lak dis. You too sweet already."

"Please, Joe."

"Naw, naw. Ah don't want you to git no sweeter than whut you is already. We goin' down de road a lil piece t'night so you go put on yo' Sunday-go-to-meetin' things."

Missie May looked at her husband to see if he was playing some prank. "Sho nuff, Joe?"

"Yeah. We goin' to de ice cream parlor."

"Where de ice cream parlor at, Joe?"

"A new man done come heah from Chicago and he done got a place and took and opened it up for a ice cream parlor, and bein' as it's real swell, Ah wants you to be one de first ladies to walk in dere and have some set down."

"Do Jesus, Ah ain't knowed nothin' 'bout it. Who de man done it?"

"Mister Otis D. Slemmons, of spots and places—Memphis, Chicago, Jacksonville, Philadelphia and so on."

"Dat heavy-set man wid his mouth full of gold teethes?"

"Yeah. Where did you see 'im at?"

"Ah went down to de sto' tuh git a box of lye and Ah seen 'im standing' on de corner talkin' to some of de mens, and Ah come on back and went to scrubbin' de floor, and he passed and tipped his hat whilst Ah was scourin' de steps. Ah thought Ah never seen *him* befo'."

Joe smiled pleasantly. "Yeah, he's up to date. He got de finest clothes Ah ever seen on a colored man's back."

"Aw, he don't look no better in his clothes than you do in yourn. He got a puzzlegut on 'im and he so chuckle-headed,[5] he got a pone behind his neck."

Joe looked down at his own abdomen and said wistfully, "Wisht Ah had a build on me lak he got. He ain't puzzle-gutted, honey. He jes' got a corperation. Dat make 'm look lak a rich white man. All rich mens is got some belly on 'em."

"Ah seen de pitchers of Henry Ford and he's a spare-built man and Rockefeller look lak he ain't got but one gut. But Ford and Rockefeller and dis Slemmons and all de rest kin be as many-gutted as dey please, Ah'm

---

3. All show; i.e., not a real wife.
4. Loaf- or oval-shaped cake.

5. Stupid, blockheaded. "Puzzlegut": fat belly.

satisfied wid you jes' lak you is, baby. God took pattern after a pine tree and built you noble. Youse a pritty man, and if Ah knowed any way to make you mo' pritty still Ah'd take and do it."

Joe reached over gently and toyed with Missie May's ear. "You jes' say dat cause you love me, but Ah know Ah can't hold no light to Otis D. Slemmons. Ah ain't never been nowhere and Ah ain't got nothin' but you."

Missie May got on his lap and kissed him and he kissed back in kind. Then he went on. "All de womens is crazy 'bout 'im everywhere he go."

"How you know dat, Joe?"

"He tole us so hisself."

"Dat don't make it so. His mouf is cut cross-ways, ain't it? Well, he kin lie jes' lak anybody else."

"Good Lawd, Missie! You womens sho is hard to sense into things. He's got a five-dollar gold piece for a stick-pin and he got a ten-dollar gold piece on his watch chain and his mouf is jes' crammed full of gold teethes. Sho wisht it wuz mine. And whut make it so cool, he got money 'cumulated. And womens give it all to 'im."

"Ah don't see whut de womens see on 'im. Ah wouldn't give 'im a wink if de sheriff wuz after 'im."

"Well, he tole us how de white womens in Chicago give 'im all dat gold money. So he don't 'low nobody to touch it at all. Not even put dey finger on it. Dey tole 'im not to. You kin make 'miration at it, but don't tetch it."

"Whyn't he stay up dere where dey so crazy 'bout 'im?"

"Ah reckon dey done made 'im vast-rich and he wants to travel some. He say dey wouldn't leave 'im hit a lick of work. He got mo' lady people crazy 'bout him than he kin shake a stick at."

"Joe, Ah hates to see you so dumb. Dat stray nigger jes' tell y'all anything and y'all b'lieve it."

"Go 'head on now, honey and put on yo' clothes. He talkin' 'bout his pritty womens—Ah want 'im to see *mine*."

Missie May went off to dress and Joe spent the time trying to make his stomach punch out like Slemmons' middle. He tried the rolling swagger of the stranger, but found that his tall bone-and-muscle stride fitted ill with it. He just had time to drop back into his seat before Missie May came in dressed to go.

On the way home that night Joe was exultant. "Didn't Ah say ole Otis was swell? Can't he talk Chicago talk? Wuzn't dat funny whut he said when great big fat ole Ida Armstrong come in? He asted me, 'Who is dat broad wid de forte shake?' Dat's a new word. Us always thought forty was a set of figgers but he showed us where it means a whole heap of things. Sometimes he don't say forty, he jes' say thirty-eight and two and dat mean de same thing. Know whut he tole me when Ah wuz payin' for our ice cream? He say, 'Ah have to hand it to you, Joe. Dat wife of yours is jes' thirty-eight and two. Yessuh, she's forte!' Ain't he killin'?"

"He'll do in case of a rush. But he sho is got uh heap uh gold on 'im. Dat's de first time Ah ever seed gold money. It lookted good on him sho nuff, but it'd look a whole heap better on you."

"Who, me? Missie May youse crazy! Where would a po' man lak me git gold money from?"

Missie May was silent for a minute, then she said, "Us might find some goin' long de road some time. Us could."

"Who would be losin' gold money round heah? We ain't even seen none dese white folks wearin' no gold money on dey watch chain. You must be figgerin' Mister Packard or Mister Cadillac goin' pass through heah."

"You don't know whut been lost 'round heah. Maybe somebody way back in memorial times[6] lost they gold money and went on off and it ain't never been found. And then if we wuz to find it, you could wear some 'thout havin' no gang of womens lak dat Slemmons say he got."

Joe laughed and hugged her. "Don't be so wishful 'bout me. Ah'm satisfied de way Ah is. So long as Ah be yo' husband, Ah don't keer 'bout nothin' else. Ah'd ruther all de other womens in de world to be dead than for you to have de toothache. Less we go to bed and git our night rest."

It was Saturday night once more before Joe could parade his wife in Slemmons' ice cream parlor again. He worked the night shift and Saturday was his only night off. Every other evening around six o'clock he left home, and dying dawn saw him hustling home around the lake where the challenging sun flung a flaming sword from east to west across the trembling water.

That was the best part of life—going home to Missie May. Their white-washed house, the mock battle on Saturday, the dinner and ice cream parlor afterwards, church on Sunday nights when Missie outdressed any woman in town—all, everything was right.

One night around eleven the acid[7] ran out at the G. and G. The foreman knocked off the crew and let the steam die down. As Joe rounded the lake on his way home, a lean moon rode the lake in a silver boat. If anybody had asked Joe about the moon on the lake, he would have said he hadn't paid it any attention. But he saw it with his feelings. It made him yearn painfully for Missie. Creation obsessed him. He thought about children. They had been married for more than a year now. They had money put away. They ought to be making little feet for shoes.[8] A little boy child would be about right.

He saw a dim light in the bedroom and decided to come in through the kitchen door. He could wash the fertilizer dust off himself before presenting himself to Missie May. It would be nice for her not to know that he was there until he slipped into his place in bed and hugged her back. She always liked that.

He eased the kitchen door open slowly and silently, but when he went to set his dinner bucket on the table he bumped it into a pile of dishes, and something crashed to the floor. He heard his wife gasp in fright and hurried to reassure her.

"Iss me, honey. Don't get skeered."

There was a quick, large movement in the bedroom. A rustle, a thud, and a stealthy silence. The light went out.

What? Robbers? Murderers? Some varmint attacking his helpless wife, perhaps. He struck a match, threw himself on guard and stepped over the door-sill into the bedroom.

The great belt on the wheel of Time slipped and eternity stood still. By the match light he could see the man's legs fighting with his breeches in his frantic desire to get them on. He had both chance and time to kill the intruder in his helpless condition—half in and half out of his pants—but he was too weak to take action. The shapeless enemies of humanity that live in the hours

---

6. Wordplay on "in time immemorial"; time so long ago as to be forgotten.

7. Used in making fertilizer.
8. I.e., They ought to be having babies.

of Time had waylaid Joe. He was assaulted in his weakness. Like Samson awakening after his haircut.[9] So he just opened his mouth and laughed.

The match went out and he struck another and lit the lamp. A howling wind raced across his heart, but underneath its fury he heard his wife sobbing and Slemmons pleading for his life. Offering to buy it with all that he had. "Please, suh, don't kill me. Sixty-two dollars at de sto'. Gold money."

Joe just stood. Slemmons looked at the window, but it was screened. Joe stood out like a rough-backed mountain between him and the door. Barring him from escape, from sunrise, from life.

He considered a surprise attack upon the big clown that stood there laughing like a chessy cat.[1] But before his fist could travel an inch, Joe's own rushed out to crush him like a battering ram. Then Joe stood over him.

"Git into yo' damn rags, Slemmons, and dat quick."

Slemmons scrambled to his feet and into his vest and coat. As he grabbed his hat, Joe's fury overrode his intentions and he grabbed at Slemmons with his left hand and struck at him with his right. The right landed. The left grazed the front of his vest. Slemmons was knocked a somersault into the kitchen and fled through the open door. Joe found himself alone with Missie May, with the golden watch charm clutched in his left fist. A short bit of broken chain dangled between his fingers.

Missie May was sobbing. Wails of weeping without words. Joe stood, and after awhile he found out that he had something in his hand. And then he stood and felt without thinking and without seeing with his natural eyes. Missie May kept on crying and Joe kept on feeling so much and not knowing what to do with all his feelings, he put Slemmons' watch charm in his pants pocket and took a good laugh and went to bed.

"Missie May, whut you cryin' for?"

"Cause Ah love you so hard and Ah know you don't love *me* no mo'."

Joe sank his face into the pillow for a spell then he said huskily, "You don't know de feelings of dat yet, Missie May."

"Oh Joe, honey, he said he wuz gointer give me dat gold money and he jes' kept on after me—"

Joe was very still and silent for a long time. Then he said, "Well, don't cry no mo', Missie May. Ah got yo' gold piece for you."

The hours went past on their rusty ankles. Joe still and quiet on one bed-rail and Missie May wrung dry of sobs on the other. Finally the sun's tide crept upon the shore of night and drowned all its hours. Missie May with her face stiff and streaked towards the window saw the dawn come into her yard. It was day. Nothing more. Joe wouldn't be coming home as usual. No need to fling open the front door and sweep off the porch, making it nice for Joe. Never no more breakfast to cook; no more washing and starching of Joe's jumper-jackets and pants. No more nothing. So why get up?

With this strange man in her bed, she felt embarrassed to get up and dress. She decided to wait till he had dressed and gone. Then she would get up, dress quickly and be gone forever beyond reach of Joe's looks and laughs. But he never moved. Red light turned to yellow, then white.

From beyond the no-man's land between them came a voice. A strange voice that yesterday had been Joe's.

---

9. In Judges 13–16, Samson's exceptional strength resides in his hair, which his treacherous lover, Delilah, cuts off while he sleeps.

1. I.e., Cheshire cat; an allusion to the grinning cat in *Alice's Adventures in Wonderland* (1865), by Lewis Carroll (1832–1898).

"Missie May, ain't you gonna fix me no breakfus'?"

She sprang out of bed. "Yeah, Joe. Ah didn't reckon you wuz hongry."

No need to die today. Joe needed her for a few more minutes anyhow.

Soon there was a roaring fire in the cook stove. Water bucket full and two chickens killed. Joe loved fried chicken and rice. She didn't deserve a thing and good Joe was letting her cook him some breakfast. She rushed hot biscuits to the table as Joe took his seat.

He ate with his eyes on his plate. No laughter, no banter.

"Missie May, you ain't eatin' yo' breakfus'."

"Ah don't choose none, Ah thank yuh."

His coffee cup was empty. She sprang to refill it. When she turned from the stove and bent to set the cup beside Joe's plate, she saw the yellow coin on the table between them.

She slumped into her seat and wept into her arms.

Presently Joe said calmly, "Missie May, you cry too much. Don't look back lak Lot's wife and turn to salt."[2]

The sun, the hero of every day, the impersonal old man that beams as brightly on death as on birth, came up every morning and raced across the blue dome and dipped into the sea of fire every evening. Water ran down hill and birds nested.

Missie knew why she didn't leave Joe. She couldn't. She loved him too much, but she could not understand why Joe didn't leave her. He was polite, even kind at times, but aloof.

There were no more Saturday romps. No ringing silver dollars to stack beside her plate. No pockets to rifle. In fact the yellow coin in his trousers was like a monster hiding in the cave of his pockets to destroy her.

She often wondered if he still had it, but nothing could have induced her to ask nor yet to explore his pockets to see for herself. Its shadow was in the house whether or no.

One night Joe came home around midnight and complained of pains in the back. He asked Missie to rub him down with liniment. It had been three months since Missie had touched his body and it all seemed strange. But she rubbed him. Grateful for the chance. Before morning, youth triumphed and Missie exulted. But the next day, as she joyfully made up their bed, beneath her pillow she found the piece of money with the bit of chain attached.

Alone to herself, she looked at the thing with loathing, but look she must. She took it into her hands with trembling and saw first thing that it was no gold piece. It was a gilded half dollar. Then she knew why Slemmons had forbidden anyone to touch his gold. He trusted village eyes at a distance not to recognize his stick-pin as a gilded quarter, and his watch charm as a four-bit piece.

She was glad at first that Joe had left it there. Perhaps he was through with her punishment. They were man and wife again. Then another thought came clawing at her. He had come home to buy from her as if she were any woman in the long house.[3] Fifty cents for her love. As if to say that he could pay as well as Slemmons. She slid the coin into his Sunday pants pocket and dressed herself and left his house.

---

2. According to Genesis 19.26, Lot's wife was turned into a pillar of salt for looking back at the destroyed city of Sodom when she and her husband were fleeing from it.

3. House of prostitution.

Halfway between her house and the quarters[4] she met her husband's mother, and after a short talk she turned and went back home. Never would she admit defeat to that woman who prayed for it nightly. If she had not the substance of marriage she had the outside show. Joe must leave *her*. She let him see she didn't want his old gold four-bits too.

She saw no more of the coin for some time though she knew that Joe could not help finding it in his pocket. But his health kept poor, and he came home at least every ten days to be rubbed.

The sun swept around the horizon, trailing its robes of weeks and days. One morning as Joe came in from work, he found Missie May chopping wood. Without a word he took the ax and chopped a huge pile before he stopped.

"You ain't got no business choppin' wood, and you know it."

"How come? Ah been choppin' it for de last longest."

"Ah ain't blind. You makin' feet for shoes."[5]

"Won't you be glad to have a lil baby chile, Joe?"

"You know dat 'thout astin' me."

"Iss gointer be a boy chile and de very spit of you." "You reckon, Missie May?"

"Who else could it look lak?"

Joe said nothing, but he thrust his hand deep into his pocket and fingered something there.

It was almost six months later Missie May took to bed and Joe went and got his mother to come wait on the house.

Missie May delivered a fine boy. Her travail was over when Joe came in from work one morning. His mother and the old women were drinking great bowls of coffee around the fire in the kitchen.

The minute Joe came into the room his mother called him aside.

"How did Missie May make out?" he asked quickly.

"Who, dat gal? She strong as a ox. She gointer have plenty mo'. We done fixed her wid de sugar and lard to sweeten her for de nex' one."

Joe stood silent awhile.

"You ain't ast 'bout de baby, Joe. You oughter be mighty proud cause he sho is de spittin' image of yuh, son. Dat's yourn all right, if you never git another one, dat un is yourn. And you know Ah'm mighty proud too, son, cause Ah never thought well of you marryin' Missie May cause her ma used tuh fan her foot round right smart and Ah been mighty skeered dat Missie May was gointer git misput on her road."

Joe said nothing. He fooled around the house till late in the day then just before he went to work, he went and stood at the foot of the bed and asked his wife how she felt. He did this every day during the week.

On Saturday he went to Orlando to make his market.[6] It had been a long time since he had done that.

Meat and lard, meal and flour, soap and starch. Cans of corn and tomatoes. All the staples. He fooled around town for awhile and bought bananas and apples. Way after while he went around to the candy store.

"Hellow, Joe," the clerk greeted him. "Ain't seen you in a long time."

"Nope, Ah ain't been heah. Been round in spots and places."

4. Workers' dwellings.
5. You're pregnant (folk expression).

6. A big shopping trip.

"Want some of them molasses kisses you always buy?"

"Yessuh." He threw the gilded half dollar on the counter. "Will dat spend?"

"Whut is it, Joe? Well, I'll be doggone! A gold-plated four-bit piece. Where'd you git it, Joe?"

"Offen a stray nigger dat come through Eatonville. He had it on his watch chain for a charm—goin' round making out iss gold money. Ha ha! He had a quarter on his tie pin and it wuz all golded up too. Tryin' to fool people. Makin' out he so rich and everything. Ha! Ha! Tryin' to tole off folkses wives from home."

"How did you git it, Joe? Did he fool you, too?"

"Who, me? Naw suh! He ain't fooled me none. Know whut Ah done? He come round me wid his smart talk. Ah hauled off and knocked 'im down and took his old four-bits way from 'im. Gointer buy my wife some good ole lasses kisses wid it. Gimme fifty cents worth of dem candy kisses."

"Fifty cents buys a mighty lot of candy kisses, Joe. Why don't you split it up and take some chocolate bars, too. They eat good, too."

"Yessuh, dey do, but Ah wants all dat in kisses. Ah got a lil boy chile home now. Tain't a week old yet, but he kin suck a sugar tit and maybe eat one them kisses hisself."

Joe got his candy and left the store. The clerk turned to the next customer. "Wisht I could be like these darkies. Laughin' all the time. Nothin' worries 'em."

Back in Eatonville, Joe reached his own front door. There was the ring of singing metal on wood. Fifteen times. Missie May couldn't run to the door, but she crept there as quickly as she could.

"Joe Banks, Ah hear you chunkin' money in mah do'way. You wait till Ah got mah strength back and Ah'm gointer fix you for dat."

1933

E. E. CUMMINGS
1894–1962

Beginning in the 1920s and 1930s, Edward Estlin Cummings built a reputation as author of a particularly agreeable kind of modernist poetry, distinguished by clever formal innovation, a tender lyricism, and the thematic celebration of individuals against mass society. These qualities were evident in his first literary success, a zesty prose account of his experience in a French prison camp during World War I, *The Enormous Room* (1922). He and a friend had joined the ambulance corps in France the day after the United States entered the war; their disdain for the bureaucracy, expressed in outspoken letters home, aroused antagonism among French officials and they were imprisoned. To be made a prisoner by one's own side struck Cummings as outrageous and yet funny; from the experience he produced an ironic, profane celebration of the ordinary soldier and an attack on bureaucracy.

E. E. Cummings, self-portrait, 1939. Cummings showed his early abstract paintings at modernist exhibitions like that of New York's Society of Independent Artists; his later work, like this self-portrait, became more realistic and figurative.

His poetry continued the attack on depersonalized, commercial, exploitative mass culture and celebrated loners, lovers, and nonconformists.

He was born in Cambridge, Massachusetts. His father was a Congregationalist minister and teacher at Harvard; the family was close knit and Cummings, a much-loved son. While a student at Harvard (he graduated in 1915 and took an M.A. in 1916) he began to write poetry based on the intricate stanza patterns of the pre-Raphaelite and Meta-physical writers he was reading in English literature classes. When he began to innovate—as he did after discovering the poetry of Ezra Pound—he was able to build (like Pound himself) from a firm apprenticeship in tradi-tional techniques.

After the war, Cummings established a life that included a studio in Greenwich Village, travel and sojourns in France, and summers at the family home in New Hampshire. He was a painter as well as a poet; simple living and careful management of a small allowance from his mother, along with prizes, royal-ties, and commissions, enabled him to work full time as an artist. He published four volumes of well-received poetry in the 1920s and a book of collected poems toward the end of the 1930s. In the 1950s he visited and read at many college campuses, where students enjoyed his tricks of verse and vocabulary and appreciated his ten-der yet earthy poetry. He received a special citation by the National Book Award committee in 1955 and the Bollingen Prize in 1957.

In his attempts to reshape poetry Cummings was also concerned to be widely accessible. Cummings's verse is characterized by common speech and attention to the visual form of the poem—that is, the poem as it appears on the page as distin-guished from its sound when read aloud. Experiments with capitalization or lack of it, punctuation, line breaks, hyphenation, and verse shapes were all carried out for the reader's eyes as well as ears. To express his sense that life was always in process, he wrote untitled poems without beginnings and endings, consisting of fragmen-tary lines. There is always humor in his poetry, and his outrage at cruelty and exploitation is balanced with gusto and celebration of the body.

The text of the poems included here is that of *Complete Poems* (1991).

in Just-

in Just-
spring   when the world is mud-
luscious the little
lame balloonman

whistles   far   and wee   5

and eddieandbill come
running from marbles and
piracies and it's
spring

when the world is puddle-wonderful   10

the queer
old balloonman whistles
far   and   wee
and bettyandisbel come dancing

from hop-scotch and jump-rope and   15

it's
spring
and
    the

        goat-footed   20

balloonMan   whistles
far
and
wee

                                              1920, 1923

O sweet spontaneous

O sweet spontaneous
earth how often have
the
doting

    fingers of   5
prurient philosophers pinched
and
poked

thee
,has the naughty thumb   10

of science prodded
thy

   beauty   .how
often have religions taken
thee upon their scraggy knees   15
squeezing and

buffeting thee that thou mightest conceive
gods
    (but
true   20

to the incomparable
couch of death thy
rhythmic
lover

    thou answerest   25

them only with

        spring)

                      1920, 1923

Buffalo Bill 's

Buffalo Bill 's[1]
defunct
    who used to
    ride a watersmooth-silver
                stallion   5
and break onetwothreefourfive pigeonsjustlikethat
                      Jesus

he was a handsome man
            and what i want to know is
how do you like your blueeyed boy   10
Mister Death

                      1920, 1923

"next to of course god america i

"next to of course god america i
love you land of the pilgrims' and so forth oh
say can you see by the dawn's early my

1. William F. Cody (1846–1917), American scout and Wild West showman.

country 'tis of centuries come and go
and are no more what of it we should worry   5
in every language even deafanddumb
thy sons acclaim your glorious name by gorry
by jingo by gee by gosh by gum
why talk of beauty what could be more beaut-
iful than these heroic happy dead   10
who rushed like lions to the roaring slaughter
they did not stop to think they died instead
then shall the voice of liberty be mute?"

He spoke.   And drank rapidly a glass of water

                                                      1926

i sing of Olaf glad and big

i sing of Olaf glad and big
whose warmest heart recoiled at war:
a conscientious object-or

his wellbelovéd colonel(trig
westpointer[1] most succinctly bred)   5
took erring Olaf soon in hand;
but—though an host of overjoyed
noncoms(first knocking on the head
him)do through icy waters roll
that helplessness which others stroke   10
with brushes recently employed
anent this muddy toiletbowl,
while kindred intellects evoke
allegiance per blunt instruments—
Olaf(being to all intents   15
a corpse and wanting any rag
upon what God unto him gave)
responds,without getting annoyed
"I will not kiss your fucking flag"

straightway the silver bird looked grave   20
(departing hurriedly to shave)

but—though all kinds of officers
(a yearning nation's blueeyed pride)
their passive prey did kick and curse
until for wear their clarion   25
voices and boots were much the worse,
and egged the firstclassprivates on
his rectum wickedly to tease
by means of skilfully applied

---

1. Graduate of the U.S. Military Academy at West Point, New York.

bayonets roasted hot with heat—   30
Olaf(upon what were once knees)
does almost ceaselessly repeat
"there is some shit I will not eat"

our president,being of which
assertions duly notified   35
threw the yellowsonofabitch
into a dungeon,where he died

Christ(of His mercy infinite)
i pray to see; and Olaf,too

preponderatingly because   40
unless statistics lie he was
more brave than me:more blond than you.

                                                    1931

somewhere i have never travelled,gladly beyond

somewhere i have never travelled,gladly beyond
any experience,your eyes have their silence:
in your most frail gesture are things which enclose me,
or which i cannot touch because they are too near

your slightest look easily will unclose me   5
though i have closed myself as fingers,
you open always petal by petal myself as Spring opens
(touching skilfully,mysteriously)her first rose

or if your wish be to close me,iand
my life will shut very beautifully,suddenly,   10
as when the heart of this flower imagines
the snow carefully everywhere descending;

nothing which we are to perceive in this world equals
the power of your intense fragility:whose texture
compels me with the colour of its countries,   15
rendering death and forever with each breathing

(i do not know what it is about you that closes
and opens;only something in me understands
the voice of your eyes is deeper than all roses)
nobody,not even the rain,has such small hands   20

                                                    1931

anyone lived in a pretty how town

anyone lived in a pretty how town
(with up so floating many bells down)
spring summer autumn winter
he sang his didn't he danced his did.

Women and men(both little and small)   5
cared for anyone not at all
they sowed their isn't they reaped their same
sun moon stars rain

children guessed(but only a few
and down they forgot as up they grew   10
autumn winter spring summer)
that noone loved him more by more

when by now and tree by leaf
she laughed his joy she cried his grief
bird by snow and stir by still   15
anyone's any was all to her

someones married their everyones
laughed their cryings and did their dance
(sleep wake hope and then)they
said their nevers they slept their dream   20

stars rain sun moon
(and only the snow can begin to explain
how children are apt to forget to remember
with up so floating many bells down)

one day anyone died i guess   25
(and noone stooped to kiss his face)
busy folk buried them side by side
little by little and was by was

all by all and deep by deep
and more by more they dream their sleep   30
noone and anyone earth by april
wish by spirit and if by yes.

Women and men(both dong and ding)
summer autumn winter spring
reaped their sowing and went their came   35
sun moon stars rain

1940

JEAN TOOMER
1894–1967

Jean Toomer's *Cane*, the author's contribution to Harlem Renaissance literature, received immediate acclaim when it appeared in 1923. Toomer described African American communities from Chicago and Washington, D.C., to small-town Georgia through the analytic filter of a modernist, urban literary style. William Stanley Braithwaite, in the NAACP-sponsored *Crisis*, praised him as the first to "write about the Negro without the surrender or the compromise of the author's vision." Sherwood Anderson recognized *Cane* as the work of an artistic peer, and other readers compared it favorably to Anderson's *Winesburg, Ohio*.

Born in Washington, D.C., Toomer never knew his father. He grew up with his grandfather, who had been an important Louisiana politician during the Reconstruction era, and his mother. After high school graduation, he attended several colleges—the University of Wisconsin, the Massachusetts College of Agriculture, the American College of Physical Training in Chicago, the University of Chicago, and the City College of New York—without completing a degree. He held numerous short-term jobs in various parts of the country, including four months in 1921 as superintendent of a small black school in Sparta, Georgia. This encounter with black Americans in the rural South formed the basis of *Cane*.

Toomer began writing when he was in his middle twenties, publishing poems and stories in avant-garde magazines such as *Broom*, the *Little Review*, and *Prairie*. He also published in the major political and artistic journals of the Harlem Renaissance, such as the *Liberator, Crisis*, and *Opportunity*. Composed as an assemblage of short stories, sketches, poems, even a play, *Cane* brought together many of Toomer's published magazine pieces.

Part I of *Cane*, set in rural Georgia, depicts a black community based in the rhythms of cotton culture, charged with sexual desire, and menaced by white violence. Part II shows black life in Washington, D.C., and Chicago, the fast-paced urban hives of money and ambition. The autobiographical third part describes an African American intellectual teaching in the South, trying to put down roots in an unfamiliar setting that he struggles to recognize as the source of his own artistic ambitions. This three-part structure is held together by a narrator who alternately steps forward in a first-person voice and recedes into third-person narration, poetry, or drama. *Cane*'s shifting voices explore whether a northern, urban African American can understand himself and his vocation by immersion in a black folk heritage that he has never known. The work is distinguished by its poetic, imagistic, evocative prose, its linguistic innovativeness, and its experimental construction.

Toomer spent much of the last forty years of his life looking for a spiritual community; he had difficulty finding publishers for the writing he produced during these decades. For a while he was a disciple of the Russian mystic George I. Gurdjieff. In the late 1940s he became a committed Quaker. At his death he left many unpublished short stories, as well as novels, plays, and an autobiography.

The text is that of the first edition (1923) as corrected in 1973.

From Cane[1]

Georgia Dusk

The sky, lazily disdaining to pursue
   The setting sun, too indolent to hold
   A lengthened tournament for flashing gold,
Passively darkens for night's barbecue,

A feast of moon and men and barking hounds,   5
   An orgy for some genius of the South
   With blood-hot eyes and cane-lipped scented mouth,
Surprised in making folk-songs from soul sounds.

The sawmill blows its whistle, buzz-saws stop,
   And silence breaks the bud of knoll and hill,   10
   Soft settling pollen where plowed lands fulfill
Their early promise of a bumper crop.

Smoke from the pyramidal sawdust pile
   Curls up, blue ghosts of trees, tarrying low
   Where only chips and stumps are left to show   15
The solid proof of former domicile.

Meanwhile, the men, with vestiges of pomp,
   Race memories of king and caravan,
   High-priests, an ostrich, and a juju-man,[2]
Go singing through the footpaths of the swamp.   20

Their voices rise . . the pine trees are guitars,
   Strumming, pine-needles fall like sheets of rain . .
   Their voices rise . . the chorus of the cane
Is caroling a vesper to the stars . .

O singers, resinous and soft your songs   25
   Above the sacred whisper of the pines,
   Give virgin lips to cornfield concubines,
Bring dreams of Christ to dusky cane-lipped throngs.

Fern

Face flowed into her eyes. Flowed in soft cream foam and plaintive ripples, in such a way that wherever your glance may momentarily have rested, it immediately thereafter wavered in the direction of her eyes. The soft suggestion of down slightly darkened, like the shadow of a bird's wing might, the creamy brown color of her upper lip. Why, after noticing it, you sought her eyes, I cannot tell you. Her nose was aquiline, Semitic. If you have heard a Jewish

---

1. Of the book's three sections, the first and the last are Georgia scenes. "Fern" appears in the first section after the poem "Georgia Dusk." "Portrait in Georgia" followed by "Blood-Burning Moon" conclude the first section. "Seventh Street" is the first sketch in the second section, which is devoted to Washington, D.C., and Chicago.
2. West African tribesman who controls the magical fetish or charm, or "juju."

cantor[3] sing, if he has touched you and made your own sorrow seem trivial when compared with his, you will know my feeling when I follow the curves of her profile, like mobile rivers, to their common delta. They were strange eyes. In this, that they sought nothing—that is, nothing that was obvious and tangible and that one could see, and they gave the impression that nothing was to be denied. When a woman seeks, you will have observed, her eyes deny. Fern's eyes desired nothing that you could give her; there was no reason why they should withhold. Men saw her eyes and fooled themselves. Fern's eyes said to them that she was easy. When she was young, a few men took her, but got no joy from it. And then, once done, they felt bound to her (quite unlike their hit and run with other girls), felt as though it would take them a lifetime to fulfill an obligation which they could find no name for. They became attached to her, and hungered after finding the barest trace of what she might desire. As she grew up, new men who came to town felt as almost everyone did who ever saw her: that they would not be denied. Men were everlastingly bringing her their bodies. Something inside of her got tired of them, I guess, for I am certain that for the life of her she could not tell why or how she began to turn them off. A man in fever is no trifling thing to send away. They began to leave her, baffled and ashamed, yet vowing to themselves that some day they would do some fine thing for her: send her candy every week and not let her know whom it came from, watch out for her wedding-day and give her a magnificent something with no name on it, buy a house and deed it to her, rescue her from some unworthy fellow who had tricked her into marrying him. As you know, men are apt to idolize or fear that which they cannot understand, especially if it be a woman. She did not deny them, yet the fact was that they were denied. A sort of superstition crept into their consciousness of her being somehow above them. Being above them meant that she was not to be approached by anyone. She became a virgin. Now a virgin in a small southern town is by no means the usual thing, if you will believe me. That the sexes were made to mate is the practice of the South. Particularly, black folks were made to mate. And it is black folks whom I have been talking about thus far. What white men thought of Fern I can arrive at only by analogy. They let her alone.

Anyone, of course, could see her, could see her eyes. If you walked up the Dixie Pike most any time of day, you'd be most like to see her resting listless-like on the railing of her porch, back propped against a post, head tilted a little forward because there was a nail in the porch post just where her head came which for some reason or other she never took the trouble to pull out. Her eyes, if it were sunset, rested idly where the sun, molten and glorious, was pouring down between the fringe of pines. Or maybe they gazed at the gray cabin on the knoll from which an evening folk-song was coming. Perhaps they followed a cow that had been turned loose to roam and feed on cotton-stalks and corn leaves. Like as not they'd settle on some vague spot above the horizon, though hardly a trace of wistfulness would come to them. If it were dusk, then they'd wait for the search-light of the evening train which you could see miles up the track before it flared across the Dixie Pike, close to her home. Wherever they looked, you'd follow them and then waver back. Like her face, the whole countryside seemed to flow into her eyes. Flowed into them with the soft listless cadence of Georgia's South. A young

---

3. Singer in religious services.

Negro, once, was looking at her, spellbound, from the road. A white man passing in a buggy had to flick him with his whip if he was to get by without running him over. I first saw her on her porch. I was passing with a fellow whose crusty numbness (I was from the North and suspected of being prejudiced and stuck-up) was melting as he found me warm. I asked him who she was. "That's Fern," was all that I could get from him. Some folks already thought that I was given to nosing around; I let it go at that, so far as questions were concerned. But at first sight of her I felt as if I heard a Jewish cantor sing. As if his singing rose above the unheard chorus of a folk-song. And I felt bound to her. I too had my dreams: something I would do for her. I have knocked about from town to town too much not to know the futility of mere change of place. Besides, picture if you can, this cream-colored solitary girl sitting at a tenement window looking down on the indifferent throngs of Harlem. Better that she listen to folk-songs at dusk in Georgia, you would say, and so would I. Or, suppose she came up North and married. Even a doctor or a lawyer, say, one who would be sure to get along—that is, make money. You and I know, who have had experience in such things, that love is not a thing like prejudice which can be bettered by changes of town. Could men in Washington, Chicago, or New York, more than the men of Georgia, bring her something left vacant by the bestowal of their bodies? You and I who know men in these cities will have to say, they could not. See her out and out a prostitute along State Street in Chicago. See her move into a southern town where white men are more aggressive. See her become a white man's concubine . . . Something I must do for her. There was myself. What could I do for her? Talk, of course. Push back the fringe of pines upon new horizons. To what purpose? and what for? Her? Myself? Men in her case seem to lose their selfishness. I lost mine before I touched her. I ask you, friend (it makes no difference if you sit in the Pullman or the Jim Crow[4] as the train crosses her road), what thoughts would come to you—that is, after you'd finished with the thoughts that leap into men's minds at the sight of a pretty woman who will not deny them; what thoughts would come to you, had you seen her in a quick flash, keen and intuitively, as she sat there on her porch when your train thundered by? Would you have got off at the next station and come back for her to take her where? Would you have completely forgotten her as soon as you reached Macon, Atlanta, Augusta, Pasadena, Madison, Chicago, Boston, or New Orleans? Would you tell your wife or sweetheart about a girl you saw? Your thoughts can help me, and I would like to know. Something I would do for her . . .

One evening I walked up the Pike on purpose, and stopped to say hello. Some of her family were about, but they moved away to make room for me. Damn if I knew how to begin. Would you? Mr. and Miss So-and-So, people, the weather, the crops, the new preacher, the frolic, the church benefit, rabbit and possum hunting, the new soft drink they had at old Pap's store, the schedule of the trains, what kind of town Macon was, Negro's migration north, bollweevils, syrup, the Bible—to all these things she gave a yassur or nassur, without further comment. I began to wonder if perhaps my own emotional sensibility had played one of its tricks on me. "Lets take a walk," I at last ventured. The suggestion, coming after so long an isolation, was novel

---

4. In the segregated South, black persons were required to sit in the "Jim Crow" section of railway cars and were not allowed as passengers in the first-class "Pullman" lounges, or sleeping cars.

enough, I guess, to surprise. But it wasnt that. Something told me that men before me had said just that as a prelude to the offering of their bodies. I tried to tell her with my eyes. I think she understood. The thing from her that made my throat catch, vanished. Its passing left her visible in a way I'd thought, but never seen. We walked down the Pike with people on all the porches gaping at us. "Doesnt it make you mad?" She meant the row of petty gossiping people. She meant the world. Through a canebrake that was ripe for cutting, the branch was reached. Under a sweet-gum tree, and where reddish leaves had dammed the creek a little, we sat down. Dusk, suggesting the almost imperceptible procession of giant trees, settled with a purple haze about the cane. I felt strange, as I always do in Georgia, particularly at dusk. I felt that things unseen to men were tangibly immediate. It would not have surprised me had I had vision. People have them in Georgia more often than you would suppose. A black woman once saw the mother of Christ and drew her in charcoal on the courthouse wall . . . When one is on the soil of one's ancestors, most anything can come to one . . . From force of habit, I suppose, I held Fern in my arms—that is, without at first noticing it. Then my mind came back to her. Her eyes, unusually weird and open, held me. Held God. He flowed in as I've seen the countryside flow in. Seen men. I must have done something—what, I don't know, in the confusion of my emotion. She sprang up. Rushed some distance from me. Fell to her knees, and began swaying, swaying. Her body was tortured with something it could not let out. Like boiling sap it flooded arms and fingers till she shook them as if they burned her. It found her throat, and spattered inarticulately in plaintive, convulsive sounds, mingled with calls to Christ Jesus. And then she sang, brokenly. A Jewish cantor singing with a broken voice. A child's voice, uncertain, or an old man's. Dusk hid her; I could hear only her song. It seemed to me as though she were pounding her head in anguish upon the ground. I rushed at her. She fainted in my arms.

There was talk about her fainting with me in the canefield. And I got one or two ugly looks from town men who'd set themselves up to protect her. In fact, there was talk of making me leave town. But they never did. They kept a watch-out for me, though. Shortly after, I came back North. From the train window I saw her as I crossed her road. Saw her on her porch, head tilted a little forward where the nail was, eyes vaguely focused on the sunset. Saw her face flow into them, the countryside and something that I call God, flowing into them . . . Nothing ever really happened. Nothing ever came to Fern, not even I. Something I would do for her. Some fine unnamed thing . . . And, friend, you? She is still living, I have reason to know. Her name, against the chance that you might happen down that way, is Fernie May Rosen.

* * *

Portrait in Georgia

Hair—braided chestnut,
    coiled like a lyncher's rope,
Eyes—fagots,
Lips—old scars, or the first red blisters,
Breath—the last sweet scent of cane,

And her slim body, white as the ash
of black flesh after flame.

* * *

Seventh Street

Money burns the pocket, pocket hurts,
Bootleggers in silken shirts,
Ballooned, zooming Cadillacs,
Whizzing, whizzing down the street-car tracks.

Seventh Street is a bastard of Prohibition and the War.[5] A crude-boned, soft-skinned wedge of nigger life breathing its loafer air, jazz songs and love, thrusting unconscious rhythms, black reddish blood into the white and whitewashed wood of Washington. Stale soggy wood of Washington. Wedges rust in soggy wood . . . Split it! In two! Again! Shred it! . . the sun. Wedges are brilliant in the sun; ribbons of wet wood dry and blow away. Black reddish blood. Pouring for crude-boned soft-skinned life, who set you flowing? Blood suckers of the War would spin in a frenzy of dizziness if they drank your blood. Prohibition would put a stop to it. Who set you flowing? White and whitewash disappear in blood. Who set you flowing? Flowing down the smooth asphalt of Seventh Street, in shanties, brick office buildings, theaters, drug stores, restaurants, and cabarets? Eddying on the corners? Swirling like a blood-red smoke up where the buzzards fly in heaven? God would not dare to suck black red blood. A Nigger God! He would duck his head in shame and call for the Judgment Day. Who set you flowing?

Money burns the pocket, pocket hurts,
Bootleggers in silken shirts,
Ballooned, zooming Cadillacs,
Whizzing, whizzing down the street-car tracks.

1923

5. World War I.

F. SCOTT FITZGERALD
1896–1940

I n the 1920s and 1930s F. Scott Fitzgerald was equally famous as a writer and as a celebrity author whose lifestyle seemed to symbolize the two decades; in the 1920s he stood for all-night partying, drinking, and the pursuit of pleasure while in the 1930s he stood for the gloomy aftermath of excess. "Babylon Revisited," written immediately after the stock market crash, is simultaneously a personal and a national story.

Fitzgerald was born in a middle-class neighborhood in St. Paul, Minnesota, descended on his father's side from southern colonial landowners and legislators, on his mother's from Irish immigrants. Much of his boyhood was spent in Buffalo and Syracuse, New York. The family was not prosperous and it took an aunt's support to send him to a Catholic boarding school in New Jersey in 1911. Two years later he entered Princeton University, where he participated in extracurricular literary and dramatic activities, forming friendships with campus intellectuals like the prominent critic Edmund Wilson who were to help him in later years. But he failed to make the football team and felt the disappointment for years. After three years of college Fitzgerald quit to join the army, but the war ended before he saw active service. Stationed in Montgomery, Alabama, he met and courted Zelda Sayre, a local belle who rejected him. In 1919 he went to New York City, determined to make a fortune and win Zelda. Amazingly, he succeeded. A novel he had begun in college, revised, and published in 1920 as *This Side of Paradise* became an immediate bestseller, making its author rich and famous at the age of twenty-four. As one of the earliest examples of a novel about college life, *This Side of Paradise* was accepted as the voice of the younger generation in a society increasingly oriented toward youth. He combined the traditional narrative and rhetorical gifts of a good fiction writer, it appeared, with a thoroughly modern sensibility. A week after the novel appeared, Scott and Zelda were married. Living extravagantly in New York City and St. Paul, and on Long Island, they more than spent the money Fitzgerald made from two collections of short stories—*Flappers and Philosophers* (1920) and *Tales of the Jazz Age* (1922)—and a second novel, *The Beautiful and Damned* (1922). Their only child, a daughter, was born in 1921.

In 1924, the Fitzgeralds moved to Europe to live more cheaply. They made friends with American expatriates, Hemingway, Stein, and Pound among others. During this time Fitzgerald published his best-known and most successful novel, *The Great Gatsby* (1925), and another book of short stories, *All the Sad Young Men* (1926). *The Great Gatsby* tells the story of a self-made young man whose dream of success, personified in a rich and beautiful young woman named Daisy, turns out to be a fantasy in every sense: Daisy belongs to a corrupt society, Gatsby corrupts himself in the quest for her, and above all, the rich have no intention of sharing their privileges. The novel is narrated from the point of view of Nick Carraway, an onlooker who is both moved and repelled by the tale he tells and whose responses form a sort of subplot: this experiment in narrative point of view was widely imitated. The structure of *The Great Gatsby* is compact; the style dazzling; and its images of automobiles, parties, and garbage heaps seem to capture the contradictions of a consumer society. The novel became an instant classic and remains so to this day.

Fitzgerald wrote dozens of short stories during the twenties; many were published in the mass-circulation weekly the *Saturday Evening Post*, which paid extremely well. Despite the pace at which he worked—in all he wrote 178 short stories—the Fitzgeralds could not get out of debt. Scott became alcoholic, and Zelda broke down in 1930 and spent most of the rest of her life in mental institutions. In 1931 Fitzgerald reestablished himself permanently in the United States, living at first near Baltimore, where his wife was hospitalized. A fourth novel, *Tender Is the Night*, appeared in 1934. The novel follows the emotional decline of a young American psychiatrist whose personal energies are sapped, his career corroded equally by his marriage to a beautiful and wealthy patient and his own weakness of character ("character" was one of Fitzgerald's favorite concepts). As in *The Great Gatsby*, the character begins as a disciple of the work ethic and turns into a pursuer of wealth, and the American Dream accordingly turns into a nightmare. Unlike *Gatsby*, whose characters never really connect with each other, *Tender Is the Night* shows a range of intimacies, none of them successful. The novel did not sell well. In 1937 Fitzgerald turned to Hollywood screenwriting; toward the end of the decade things were looking up for him, and he planned to revive his career as a fiction writer. But his health had been ruined by heavy drinking; he died of a heart attack in Hollywood at the age of forty-four, leaving an unfinished novel about a film mogul, *The Last Tycoon*, which was brought out by Edmund Wilson in 1941. Wilson also successfully promoted Fitzgerald's posthumous reputation by editing a collection of his writings, which he called *The Crack-Up*, in 1945.

The text of "Winter Dreams" is from *Metropolitan* magazine (1922); that of "Babylon Revisited" is from *Stories of F. Scott Fitzgerald* (1951).

Winter Dreams

Some of the caddies were poor as sin and lived in one-room houses with a neurasthenic cow in the front yard, but Dexter Green's father owned the second best grocery store in Dillard—the best one was "The Hub," patronized by the wealthy people from Lake Erminie—and Dexter caddied only for pocket-money.

In the fall when the days became crisp and grey and the long Minnesota winter shut down like the white lid of a box, Dexter's skis moved over the snow that hid the fairways of the golf course. At these times the country gave him a feeling of profound melancholy—it offended him that the links should lie in enforced fallowness, haunted by ragged sparrows for the long season. It was dreary, too, that on the tees where the gay colors fluttered in summer there were now only the desolate sand-boxes knee-deep in crusted ice. When he crossed the hills the wind blew cold as misery, and if the sun was out he tramped with his eyes squinted up against the hard dimensionless glare.

In April the winter ceased abruptly. The snow ran down into Lake Erminie scarcely tarrying for the early golfers to brave the season with red and black balls. Without elation, without an interval of moist glory the cold was gone.

Dexter knew that there was something dismal about this northern spring, just as he knew there was something gorgeous about the fall. Fall made him clench his hands and tremble and repeat idiotic sentences to himself and make brisk abrupt gestures of command to imaginary audiences and armies. October filled him with hope which November raised to a sort of ecstatic triumph, and in this wood the fleeting brilliant impressions of the summer at Lake Erminie were ready grist to his will. He became a golf champion and defeated Mr. T. A. Hedrick in a marvelous match played over a hundred times in the fairways of his imagination, a match each detail of which he changed about untiringly—sometimes winning with almost laughable ease, sometimes coming up magnificently from behind. Again, stepping from a Pierce-Arrow automobile, like Mr. Mortimer Jones, he strolled frigidly into the lounge of the Erminie Golf Club—or perhaps, surrounded by an admiring crowd, he gave an exhibition of fancy diving from the springboard of the Erminie Club raft. . . . Among those most impressed was Mr. Mortimer Jones.

And one day it came to pass that Mr. Jones, himself and not his ghost, came up to Dexter, almost with tears in his eyes and said that Dexter was the —— best caddy in the club and wouldn't he decide not to quit if Mr. Jones made it worth his while, because every other —— caddy in the club lost one ball a hole for him—regularly—

"No, sir," said Dexter, decisively, "I don't want to caddy any more." Then, after a pause, "I'm too old."

"You're—why, you're not more than fourteen. Why did you decide just this morning that you wanted to quit? You promised that next week you'd go over to the state tournament with me."

"I decided I was too old."

Dexter handed in his "A Class" badge, collected what money was due him from the caddy master and caught the train for Dillard.

"The best —— caddy I ever saw," shouted Mr. Mortimer Jones over a drink that afternoon. "Never lost a ball! Willing! Intelligent! Quiet! Honest! Grateful!—"

The little girl who had done this was eleven—beautifully ugly as little girls are apt to be who are destined after a few years to be inexpressably lovely and bring no end of misery to a great number of men. The spark, however, was perceptible. There was a general ungodliness in the way her lips twisted down at the corners when she smiled and in the—Heaven help us!—in the almost passionate quality of her eyes. Vitality is born early in such women. It was utterly in evidence now, shining through her thin frame in a sort of glow.

She had come eagerly out on to the course at nine o'clock with a white linen nurse and five small new golf clubs in a white canvas bag which the nurse was carrying. When Dexter first saw her she was standing by the caddy house, rather ill-at-ease and trying to conceal the fact by engaging her nurse in an obviously unnatural conversation illumined by startling and irrelevant smiles from herself.

"Well, it's certainly a nice day, Hilda," Dexter heard her say, then she drew down the corners of her mouth, smiled and glanced furtively around, her eyes in transit falling for an instant on Dexter.

Then to the nurse:

"Well, I guess there aren't very many people out here this morning, are there?"

The smile again radiant, blatantly artificial—convincing.

"I don't know what we're supposed to do now," said the nurse, looking nowhere in particular.

"Oh, that's all right"—the smile—"I'll fix it up."

Dexter stood perfectly still, his mouth faintly ajar. He knew that if he moved forward a step his stare would be in her line of vision—if he moved backward he would lose his full view of her face—For a moment he had not realized how young she was. Now he remembered having seen her several times the year before—in bloomers.

Suddenly, involuntarily, he laughed, a short abrupt laugh—then, startled by himself, he turned and began to walk quickly away.

"Boy!"

Dexter stopped.

"Boy—"

Beyond question he was addressed. Not only that, but he was treated to that absurd smile, that preposterous smile—the memory of which at least half a dozen men were to carry to the grave.

"Boy, do you know where the golf teacher is?"

"He's giving a lesson."

"Well, do you know where the caddy-master is?"

"He's not here yet this morning."

"Oh." For a moment this baffled her. She stood alternately on her right and left foot.

"We'd like to get a caddy," said the nurse. "Mrs. Mortimer Jones sent us out to play golf and we don't know how without we get a caddy."

Here she was stopped by an ominous glance from Miss Jones, followed immediately by the smile.

"There aren't any caddies here except me," said Dexter to the nurse. "And I got to stay here in charge until the caddy-master gets here."

"Oh."

Miss Jones and her retinue now withdrew and at a proper distance from Dexter became involved in a heated conversation. The conversation was concluded by Miss Jones taking one of the clubs and hitting it on the ground with violence. For further emphasis she raised it again and was about to bring it down smartly upon the nurse's bosom, when the nurse seized the club and twisted it from her hands.

"You darn *fool!*" cried Miss Jones wildly.

Another argument ensued. Realizing that the elements of the comedy were implied in the scene, Dexter several times began to smile but each time slew the smile before it reached maturity. He could not resist the monstrous conviction that the little girl was justified in beating the nurse.

The situation was resolved by the fortuitous appearance of the caddy-master who was appealed to immediately by the nurse.

"Miss Jones is to have a little caddy and this one says he can't go."

"Mr. McKenna said I was to wait here till you came," said Dexter quickly.

"Well, he's here now." Miss Jones smiled cheerfully at the caddy-master. Then she dropped her bag and set off at a haughty mince toward the first tee.

"Well?" The caddy-master turned to Dexter. "What you standing there like a dummy for? Go pick up the young lady's clubs."

"I don't think I'll go out today," said Dexter.

"You don't—"

"I think I'll quit."

The enormity of his decision frightened him. He was a favorite caddy and the thirty dollars a month he earned through the summer were not to be made elsewhere in Dillard. But he had received a strong emotional shock and his perturbation required a violent and immediate outlet.

It is not so simple as that, either. As so frequently would be the case in the future, Dexter was unconsciously dictated to by his winter dreams.

Now, of course, the quality and the seasonability of these winter dreams varied, but the stuff of them remained. They persuaded Dexter several years later to pass up a business course at the State University—his father, prospering now, would have paid his way—for the precarious advantage of attending an older and more famous university in the East, where he was bothered by his scanty funds. But do not get the impression, because his winter dreams happened to be concerned at first with musings on the rich, that there was anything shoddy in the boy. He wanted not association with glittering things and glittering people—he wanted the glittering things themselves. Often he reached out for the best without knowing why he wanted it—and sometimes he ran up against the mysterious denials and prohibitions in which life indulges. It is with one of those denials and not with his career as a whole that this story deals.

He made money. It was rather amazing. After college he went to the city from which Lake Erminie draws its wealthy patrons. When he was only twenty-three and had been there not quite two years, there were already people who liked to say, "Now *there's* a boy—" All about him rich men's sons were peddling bonds precariously, or investing patrimonies precariously, or plodding through the two dozen volumes of canned rubbish in the "George Washington Commercial Course," but Dexter borrowed a thousand dollars on his college degree and his steady eyes, and bought a partnership in a *laundry*.

It was a small laundry when he went into it. Dexter made a specialty of learning how the English washed fine woolen golf stockings without shrinking them. Inside of a year he was catering to the trade who wore knicker-bockers. Men were insisting that their shetland hose and sweaters go to his laundry just as they had insisted on a caddy who could find golf balls. A little later he was doing their wives' lingerie as well—and running five branches in different parts of the city. Before he was twenty-seven he owned the larg-est string of laundries in his section of the country. It was then that he sold out and went to New York. But the part of his story that concerns us here goes back to when he was making his first big success.

When he was twenty-three Mr. W. L. Hart, one of the grey-haired men who like to say "Now there's a boy"—gave him a guest card to the Lake Erminie Club for over a week-end. So he signed his name one day on the register, and that afternoon played golf in a foursome with Mr. Hart and Mr. Sandwood and Mr. T. A. Hedrick. He did not consider it necessary to remark that he had once carried Mr. Hart's bag over this same links and that he knew every trap and gully with his eyes shut—but he found himself glancing at the four caddies who trailed them, trying to catch a gleam or gesture that would remind him of himself, that would lessen the gap which lay between his past and his future.

It was a curious day, slashed abruptly with fleeting, familiar impressions. One minute he had the sense of being a trespasser—in the next he was impressed by the tremendous superiority he felt toward Mr. T. A. Hedrick, who was a bore and not even a good golfer any more.

Then, because of a ball Mr. Hart lost near the fifteenth green an enor-mous thing happened. While they were searching the stiff grasses of the rough there was a clear call of "Fore!" from behind a hill in their rear. And as they all turned abruptly from their search a bright new ball sliced abruptly over the hill and caught Mr. T. A. Hedrick rather neatly in the stomach.

Mr. T. A. Hedrick grunted and cursed.

"By Gad!" cried Mr. Hedrick, "they ought to put some of these crazy women off the course. It's getting to be outrageous."

A head and a voice came up together over the hill:

"Do you mind if we go through?"

"You hit me in the stomach!" thundered Mr. Hedrick.

"Did I?" The girl approached the group of men. "I'm sorry. I yelled 'Fore!'"

Her glance fell casually on each of the men. She nodded to Sandwood and then scanned the fairway for her ball.

"Did I bounce off into the rough?"

It was impossible to determine whether this question was ingenuous or malicious. In a moment, however, she left no doubt, for as her partner came up over the hill she called cheerfully.

"Here I am! I'd have gone on the green except that I hit something."

As she took her stance for a short mashie shot, Dexter looked at her closely. She wore a blue gingham dress, rimmed at throat and shoulders with a white edging that accentuated her tan. The quality of exaggeration, of thinness that had made her passionate eyes and down turning mouth absurd at eleven was gone now. She was arrestingly beautiful. The color in her cheeks was centered like the color in a picture—it was not a "high" color, but a sort of fluctuating and feverish warmth, so shaded that it seemed at any moment it would recede and disappear. This color and the mobility of her mouth gave a continual impression of flux, of intense life, of passionate vitality—balanced only par-tially by the sad luxury of her eyes.

She swung her mashie impatiently and without interest, pitching the ball into a sandpit on the other side of the green. With a quick insincere smile and a careless "Thank you!" she went on after it.

"That Judy Jones!" remarked Mr. Hedrick on the next tee, as they waited—some moments—for her to play on ahead. "All she needs is to be turned up and spanked for six months and then to be married off to an old-fashioned cavalry captain."

"Gosh, she's good looking!" said Mr. Sandwood, who was just over thirty.

"Good-looking!" cried Mr. Hedrick contemptuously. "She always looks as if she wanted to be kissed! Turning those big cow-eyes on every young calf in town!"

It is doubtful if Mr. Hedrick intended a reference to the maternal instinct.

"She'd play pretty good golf if she'd try," said Mr. Sandwood.

"She has no form," said Mr. Hedrick solemnly.

"She has a nice figure," said Mr. Sandwood.

"Better thank the Lord she doesn't drive a swifter ball," said Mr. Hart, winking at Dexter. "Come on. Let's go."

Later in the afternoon the sun went down with a riotous swirl of gold and varying blues and scarlets, and left the dry rustling night of western summer. Dexter watched from the verandah of the Erminie Club, watched the even overlap of the waters in the little wind, silver molasses under the harvest moon. Then the moon held a finger to her lips and the lake became a clear pool, pale and quiet. Dexter put on his bathing suit and swam out to the farthest raft, where he stretched dripping on the wet canvas of the spring board.

There was a fish jumping and a star shining and the lights around the lake were gleaming. Over on a dark peninsula a piano was playing the songs of last summer and of summers before that—songs from "The Pink Lady" and "The Chocolate Soldier" and "Mlle. Modiste"—and because the sound of a piano over a stretch of water had always seemed beautiful to Dexter he lay perfectly quiet and listened.

The tune the piano was playing at that moment had been gay and new five years before when Dexter was a sophomore at college. They had played it at a prom once and because he could not afford the luxury of proms in those days he had stood outside the gymnasium and listened. The sound of the tune and the splash of the fish jumping precipitated in him a sort of ecstasy and it was with that ecstasy he viewed what happened to him now. The ecstasy was a gorgeous appreciation. It was his sense that, for once, he was magnificently atune to life and that everything about him was radiating a brightness and a glamor he might never know again.

A low pale oblong detached itself suddenly from the darkness of the peninsula, spitting forth the reverberate sound of a racing motorboat. Two white streamers of cleft water rolled themselves out behind it and almost immediately the boat was beside him, drowning out the hot tinkle of the piano in the drone of its spray. Dexter raising himself on his arms was aware of a figure standing at the wheel, of two dark eyes regarding him over the lengthening space of water—then the boat had gone by and was sweeping in an immense and purposeless circle of spray round and round in the middle of the lake. With equal eccentricity one of the circles flattened out and headed back toward the raft.

"Who's that?" she called, shutting off the motor. She was so near now that Dexter could see her bathing suit, which consisted apparently of pink rompers. "Oh—you're one of the men I hit in the stomach."

The nose of the boat bumped the raft. After an inexpert struggle, Dexter managed to twist the line around a two-by-four. Then the raft tilted rakishly as she sprung on.

"Well, kiddo," she said huskily, "do you"—she broke off. She had sat herself upon the springboard, found it damp and jumped up quickly,—"do you want to go surf-board riding?"

He indicated that he would be delighted.

"The name is Judy Jones. Ghastly reputation but enormously popular." She favored him with an absurd smirk—rather, what tried to be a smirk, for, twist her mouth as she might, it was not grotesque, it was merely beautiful. "See that house over on the peninsula?"

"No."

"Well, there's a house there that I live in only you can't see it because it's too dark. And in that house there is a fella waiting for me. When he drove up by the door I drove out by the dock because he has watery eyes and asks me if I have an ideal."

There was a fish jumping and a star shining and the lights around the lake were gleaming. Dexter sat beside Judy Jones and she explained how her boat was driven. Then she was in the water, swimming to the floating surf-board with exquisite crawl. Watching her was as without effort to the eye as watching a branch waving or a sea-gull flying. Her arms, burned to butternut, moved sinuously among the dull platinum ripples, elbow appearing first, casting the forearm back with a cadence of falling water, then reaching out and down stabbing a path ahead.

They moved out into the lake and, turning, Dexter saw that she was kneeling on the low rear of the now up-tilted surf-board.

"Go faster," she called, "fast as it'll go."

Obediently he jammed the lever forward and the white spray mounted at the bow. When he looked around again the girl was standing up on the rushing board, her arms spread ecstatically, her eyes lifted toward the moon.

"It's awful cold, kiddo," she shouted. "What's your name anyways?"

"The name is Dexter Green. Would it amuse you to know how good you look back there?"

"Yes," she shouted, "it would amuse me. Except that I'm too cold. Come to dinner tomorrow night."

He kept thinking how glad he was that he had never caddied for this girl. The damp gingham clinging made her like a statue and turned her intense mobility to immobility at last.

"—At seven o'clock," she shouted, "Judy Jones, Girl, who hit man in stomach. Better write it down,"—and then, "Faster—oh, faster!"

Had he been as calm inwardly as he was in appearance, Dexter would have had time to examine his surroundings in detail. He received, however, an enduring impression that the house was the most elaborate he had ever seen. He had known for a long time that it was the finest on Lake Erminie, with a Pompeiian swimming pool and twelve acres of lawn and garden. But what gave it an air of breathless intensity was the sense that it was inhabited by Judy Jones—that it was as casual a thing to her as the little house in the village had once been to Dexter. There was a feeling of mystery in it, of bedrooms upstairs more beautiful and strange than other bedrooms, of gay and radiant activities taking place through these deep corridors and of romances that were not musty and laid already in lavender, but were fresh and breathing and set forth in rich motor cars and in great dances whose flowers were scarcely withered. They were more real because he could feel them all about him, pervading the air with the shades and echoes of still vibrant emotion.

And so while he waited for her to appear he peopled the soft deep summer room and the sun porch that opened from it with the men who had already loved Judy Jones. He knew the sort of men they were—the men who when he first went to college had entered from the great prep-schools with graceful clothes and the deep tan of healthy summer, who did nothing or anything with the same debonaire ease.

Dexter had seen that, in one sense, he was better than these men. He was newer and stronger. Yet in acknowledging to himself that he wished his children to be like them he was admitting that he was but the rough, strong stuff from which this graceful aristocracy eternally sprang.

When, a year before, the time had come when he could wear good clothes, he had known who were the best tailors in America, and the best tailor in America had made him the suit he wore this evening. He had acquired that particular reserve peculiar to his university, that set it off from other universities. He recognized the value to him of such a mannerism and he had adopted it; he knew that to be careless in dress and manner required more confidence than to be careful. But carelessness was for his children. His mother's name had been Krimslich. She was a Bohemian[1] of the peasant class and she had talked broken English to the end of her days. Her son must keep to the set patterns.

He waited for Judy Jones in her house, and he saw these other young men around him. It excited him that many men had loved her. It increased her value in his eyes.

At a little after seven Judy Jones came downstairs. She wore a blue silk afternoon dress. He was disappointed at first that she had not put on something more elaborate, and this feeling was accentuated when, after a brief greeting, she went to the door of a butler's pantry and pushing it open called: "You can have dinner, Martha." He had rather expected that a butler would announce dinner, that there would be a cocktail perhaps. It even offended him that she should know the maid's name.

Then he put these thoughts behind him as they sat down together on a chintz-covered lounge.

"Father and mother won't be here," she said.

"Ought I to be sorry?"

"They're really quite nice," she confessed, as if it had just occurred to her. "I think my father's the best looking man of his age I've ever seen. And mother looks about thirty."

He remembered the last time he had seen her father, and found he was glad the parents were not to be here tonight. They would wonder who he was. He had been born in Keeble, a Minnesota village fifty miles farther north and he always gave Keeble as his home instead of Dillard. Country towns were well enough to come from if they weren't inconveniently in sight and used as foot-stools by fashionable lakes.

1. Native of Bohemia, in the Czech Republic.

Before dinner he found the conversation unsatisfactory. The beautiful Judy seemed faintly irritable—as much so as it was possible to be with a comparative stranger. They discussed Lake Erminie and its golf course, the surf-board riding of the night before and the cold she had caught, which made her voice more husky and charming than ever. They talked of his university which she had visited frequently during the past two years, and of the nearby city which supplied Lake Erminie with its patrons and whither Dexter would return next day to his prospering laundries.

During dinner she slipped into a moody depression which gave Dexter a feeling of guilt. Whatever petulance she uttered in her throaty voice worried him. Whatever she smiled at—at him, at a silver fork, at nothing—, it disturbed him that her smile could have no root in mirth, or even in amusement. When the red corners of her lips curved down, it was less a smile than an invitation to a kiss.

Then, after dinner, she led him out on the dark sun-porch and deliberately changed the atmosphere.

"Do I seem gloomy?" she demanded.

"No, but I'm afraid I'm boring you," he answered quickly.

"You're not. I like you. But I've just had rather an unpleasant afternoon. There was a—man I cared about. He told me out of a clear sky that he was poor as a church-mouse. He'd never even hinted it before. Does this sound horribly mundane?"

"Perhaps he was afraid to tell you."

"I suppose he was," she answered thoughtfully. "He didn't start right. You see, if I'd thought of him as poor—well, I've been mad about loads of poor men, and fully intended to marry them all. But in this case, I hadn't thought of him that way and my interest in him wasn't strong enough to survive the shock."

"I know. As if a girl calmly informed her fiancé that she was a widow. He might not object to widows, but——"

"Let's start right," she suggested suddenly. "Who are you, anyhow?"

For a moment Dexter hesitated. There were two versions of his life that he could tell. There was Dillard and his caddying and his struggle through college, or——

"I'm nobody," he announced. "My career is largely a matter of futures."

"Are you poor?"

"No," he said frankly, "I'm probably making more money than any man my age in the northwest. I know that's an obnoxious remark, but you advised me to start right."

There was a pause. She smiled, and with a touch of amusement.

"You sound like a man in a play."

"It's your fault. You tempted me into being assertive."

Suddenly she turned her dark eyes directly upon him and the corners of her mouth drooped until her face seemed to open like a flower. He dared scarcely to breathe, he had the sense that she was exerting some force upon him; making him overwhelmingly conscious of the youth and mystery that wealth imprisons and preserves, the freshness of many clothes, of cool rooms and gleaming things, safe and proud above the hot struggles of the poor.

The porch was bright with the bought luxury of starshine. The wicker of the settee squeaked fashionably when he put his arm around her, commanded by her eyes. He kissed her curious and lovely mouth and committed himself to the following of a grail.

It began like that—and continued, with varying shades of intensity, on such a note right up to the dénouement. Dexter surrendered a part of himself to the most direct and unprincipled personality with which he had ever come in contact. Whatever the beautiful Judy Jones desired, she went after with the full pressure of her charm. There was no divergence of method, no jockeying for position or premeditation of effects—there was very little mental quality in any of her affairs. She simply made men conscious to the highest degree of her physical loveliness.

Dexter had no desire to change her. Her deficiencies were knit up with a passionate energy that transcended and justified them.

When, as Judy's head lay against his shoulder that first night, she whispered:

"I don't know what's the matter with me. Last night I thought I was in love with a man and tonight I think I'm in love with you—"

—it seemed to him a beautiful and romantic thing to say. It was the exquisite excitability that for the moment he controlled and owned. But a week later he was compelled to view this same quality in a different light. She took him in her roadster to a picnic supper and after supper she disappeared, likewise in her roadster, with another man. Dexter became enormously upset and was scarcely able to be decently civil to the other people present. When she assured him that she had not kissed the other man he knew she was lying—yet he was glad that she had taken the trouble to lie to him.

He was, as he found before the summer ended, one of a dozen, a varying dozen, who circulated about her. Each of them had at one time been favored above all others—about half of them still basked in the solace of occasional sentimental revivals. Whenever one showed signs of dropping out through long neglect she granted him a brief honeyed hour which encouraged him to tag along for a year or so longer. Judy made these forays upon the helpless and defeated without malice, indeed half unconscious that there was anything mischievous in what she did.

When a new man came to town everyone dropped out—dates were automatically cancelled.

The helpless part of trying to do anything about it was that she did it all herself. She was not a girl who could be "won" in the kinetic sense—she was proof against cleverness, she was proof against charm, if any of these assailed her too strongly she would immediately resolve the affair to a physical basis and under the magic of her physical splendor the strong as well as the brilliant played her game and not their own. She was entertained only by the gratification of her desires and by the direct exercise of her own charm. Perhaps from so much youthful love, so many youthful lovers she had come, in self defense, to nourish herself wholly from within.

Succeeding Dexter's first exhilaration came restlessness and dissatisfaction. The helpless ecstasy of losing himself in her charm was a powerful opiate rather than a tonic. It was fortunate for his work during the winter that those moments of ecstasy came infrequently. Early in their acquaintance it had seemed for a while that there was a deep and spontaneous mutual attraction—that first August for example—three days of long evenings on her dusky verandah, of strange wan kisses through the late afternoon, in shadowy alcoves or behind the protecting trellises of the garden arbors, of mornings when she was fresh as a dream and almost shy at meeting him in the clarity of the rising day. There was all the ecstasy of an engagement about it, sharpened by his realization that there was no engagement. It was during those three days that, for the first time, he had asked her to marry him. She said "maybe some day," she said "kiss me," she said "I'd like to marry you," she said "I love you,"—she said—nothing.

The three days were interrupted by the arrival of a New York man who visited the Jones' for half September. To Dexter's agony, rumor engaged them. The man was the son of the president of a great trust company. But at the end of a month it was reported that Judy was yawning. At a dance one night she sat all evening in a motor boat with an old beau, while the New Yorker searched the club for her frantically. She told the old beau that she was bored with her visitor and two days later he left. She was seen with him at the station and it was reported that he looked very mournful indeed.

On this note the summer ended. Dexter was twenty-four and he found himself increasingly in a position to do as he wished. He joined two clubs in the city and lived at one of them. Though he was by no means an integral part of the stag-lines at these clubs he managed to be on hand at dances where Judy Jones was likely to appear. He could have gone out socially as much as he liked—he was an eligible young man, now, and popular with downtown fathers. His confessed devotion to Judy Jones had rather solidified his position. But he had no social aspirations and rather despised the dancing men who were always on tap for the Thursday or Saturday parties and who filled in at dinners with the younger married set. Already he was playing with the idea of going East to New York. He wanted to take Judy Jones with him. No disillusion as to the world in which she had grown up could cure his illusion as to her desirability.

Remember that—for only in the light of it can what he did for her be understood.

Eighteen months after he first met Judy Jones he became engaged to another girl. Her name was Irene Scheerer and her father was one of the men who had always believed in Dexter. Irene was light haired and sweet and honorable and a little stout and she had two beaus whom she pleasantly relinquished when Dexter formally asked her to marry him.

Summer, fall, winter, spring, another summer, another fall—so much he had given of his active life to the curved lips of Judy Jones. She had treated him with interest, with encouragement, with malice, with indifference, with contempt. She had inflicted on him the innumerable little slights and indignities possible in such a case—as if in revenge for having ever cared for him at all. She had beckoned him and yawned at him and beckoned him again and he had responded often with bitterness and narrowed eyes. She had brought him ecstatic happiness and intolerable agony of spirit. She had caused him untold inconvenience and not a little trouble. She had insulted him and she had ridden over him and she had played his interest in her against his interest in his work—for fun. She had done everything to him except to criticize him—this she had not done—it seemed to him only because it might have sullied the utter indifference she manifested and sincerely felt toward him.

When autumn had come and gone again it occurred to him that he could not have Judy Jones. He had to beat this into his mind but he convinced himself at last. He lay awake at night for a while and argued it over. He told himself the trouble and the pain she had caused him, he enumerated her glaring deficiencies as a wife. Then he said to himself that he loved her and after a while he fell asleep. For a week, lest he imagine her husky voice over the telephone or her eyes opposite him at lunch, he worked hard and late and at night he went to his office and plotted out his years.

At the end of a week he went to a dance and cut in on her once. For almost the first time since they had met he did not ask her to sit out with him or tell her that she was lovely. It hurt him that she did not miss these things—that was all. He was not jealous when he saw that there was a new man tonight. He had been hardened against jealousy long before.

He stayed late at the dance. He sat for an hour with Irene Scheerer and talked about books and about music. He knew very little about either. But he was beginning to be master of his own time now and he had a rather priggish notion that he—the young and already fabulously successful Dexter Green—should know more about such things.

That was in October when he was twenty-five. In January Dexter and Irene became engaged. It was to be announced in June and they were to be married three months later.

The Minnesota winter prolonged itself interminably and it was almost May when the winds came soft and the snow ran down into Lake Erminie at last. For the first time in over a year Dexter was enjoying a certain tranquility of spirit. Judy Jones had been in Florida and afterwards in Hot Springs and somewhere she had been engaged and somewhere she had broken it off. At first, when Dexter had definitely given her up, it had made him sad that people still linked them together and asked for news of her, but when he began to be placed at dinner next to Irene Scheerer people didn't ask him about her any more—they told him about her. He ceased to be an authority on her.

May at last. Dexter walked the streets at night when the darkness was damp as rain, wondering that so soon, with so little done, so much of ecstasy had gone from him. May one year back had been marked by Judy's poignant, unforgivable, yet forgiven turbulence—it had been one of those rare times when he fancied she had grown to care for him. That old penny's worth of happiness he had spent for this bushel of content. He knew that Irene would be no more than a curtain spread behind him, a hand moving among gleaming tea cups, a voice calling to children . . . fire and loveliness were gone, magic of night and the hushed wonder of the hours and seasons . . . slender lips, down turning, dropping to his lips like poppy petals, bearing him up into a heaven of eyes . . . a haunting gesture, light of a warm lamp on her hair. The thing was deep in him. He was too strong, too alive for it to die lightly.

In the middle of May when the weather balanced for a few days on the thin bridge that led to deep summer he turned in one night at Irene's house. Their engagement was to be announced in a week now—no one would be surprised at it. And tonight they would sit together on the lounge at the College Club and look on for an hour at the dancers. It gave him a sense of solidity to go with her—. She was so sturdily popular, so intensely a "good egg."

He mounted the steps of the brown stone house and stepped inside.

"Irene," he called.

Mrs. Scheerer came out of the living room to meet him.

"Dexter," she said. "Irene's gone upstairs with a splitting headache. She wanted to go with you but I made her go to bed."

"Nothing serious I—"

"Oh, no. She's going to play golf with you in the morning. You can spare her for just one night, can't you, Dexter?"

Her smile was kind. She and Dexter liked each other. In the living room he talked for a moment before he said goodnight.

Returning to the College Club, where he had rooms, he stood in the doorway for a moment and watched the dancers. He leaned against the door post, nodded at a man or two—yawned.

"Hello, kiddo."

The familiar voice at his elbow startled him. Judy Jones had left a man and crossed the room to him—Judy Jones, a slender enamelled doll in cloth of gold, gold in a band at her head, gold in two slipper points at her dress's hem. The fragile glow of her face seemed to blossom as she smiled at him. A breeze of warmth and light blew through the room. His hands in the pockets of his dinner jacket tightened spasmodically. He was filled with a sudden excitement.

"When did you get back?" he asked casually.

"Come here and I'll tell you about it."

She turned and he followed her. She had been away—he could have wept at the wonder of her return. She had passed through enchanted streets, doing young things that were like plaintive music. All mysterious happenings, all fresh and quickening hopes, had gone away with her, come back with her now.

She turned in the doorway.

"Have you a car here? If you haven't I have."

"I have a coupé."

In then, with a rustle of golden cloth. He slammed the door. Into so many cars she had stepped—like this—like that—her back against the leather, so—her elbow resting on the door—waiting. She would have been soiled long since had there been anything to soil her,—except herself—but these things were all her own outpouring.

With an effort he forced himself to start the car and avoiding her surprised glance backed into the street. This was nothing, he must remember. She had done this before and he had put her behind him, as he would have slashed a bad account from his books.

He drove slowly downtown and affecting a disinterested abstraction traversed the deserted streets of the business section, peopled here and there, where a movie was giving out its crowd or where consumptive or pugilistic youth lounged in front of pool halls. The clink of glasses and the slap of hands on the bars issued from saloons, cloisters of glazed glass and dirty yellow light.

She was watching him closely and the silence was embarrassing yet in this crisis he could find no casual word with which to profane the hour. At a convenient turning he began to zig-zag back toward the College Club.

"Have you missed me?" she asked suddenly.

"Everybody missed you."

He wondered if she knew of Irene Scheerer. She had been back only a day—her absence had been almost contemporaneous with his engagement.

"What a remark!" Judy laughed sadly—without sadness. She looked at him searchingly. He became absorbed for a moment in the dashboard.

"You're handsomer than you used to be," she said thoughtfully. "Dexter, you have the most rememberable eyes."

He could have laughed at this, but he did not laugh. It was the sort of thing that was said to sophomores. Yet it stabbed at him.

"I'm awfully tired of everything, kiddo." She called everyone kiddo, endowing the obsolete slang with careless, individual camaraderie. "I wish you'd marry me."

The directness of this confused him. He should have told her now that he was going to marry another girl but he could not tell her. He could as easily have sworn that he had never loved her.

"I think we'd get along," she continued, on the same note, "unless probably you've forgotten me and fallen in love with another girl."

Her confidence was obviously enormous. She had said, in effect, that she found such a thing impossible to believe, that if it were true he had merely committed a childish indiscretion—and probably to show off. She would forgive him, because it was not a matter of any moment but rather something to be brushed aside lightly.

"Of course you could never love anybody but me," she continued. "I like the way you love me. Oh, Dexter, have you forgotten last year?"

"No, I haven't forgotten."

"Neither have I!"

Was she sincerely moved—or was she carried along by the wave of her own acting?

"I wish we could be like that again," she said, and he forced himself to answer:

"I don't think we can."

"I suppose not. . . . I hear you're giving Irene Scheerer a violent rush."

There was not the faintest emphasis on the name, yet Dexter was suddenly ashamed.

"Oh, take me home," cried Judy suddenly. "I don't want to go back to that idiotic dance—with those children."

Then, as he turned up the street that led to the residence district, Judy began to cry quietly to herself. He had never seen her cry before.

The dark street lightened, the dwellings of the rich loomed up around them, he stopped his coupé in front of the great white bulk of the Mortimer Jones' house, somnolent, gorgeous, drenched with the splendor of the damp moonlight. Its solidity startled him. The strong walls, the fine steel of the girders, the breadth and beam and pomp of it were there only to bring out the contrast with the young beauty beside him. It was sturdy to accentuate her slightness—as if to show what a breeze could be generated by a butterfly's wing.

He sat perfectly quiet, his nerves in wild clamor, afraid that if he moved he would find her irresistibly in his arms. Two tears had rolled down her wet face and trembled on her upper lip.

"I'm more beautiful than anybody else," she said brokenly, "why can't I be happy?" Her moist eyes tore at his stability—mouth turned slowly downward with an exquisite sadness. "I'd like to marry you if you'll have me, Dexter. I suppose you think I'm not worth having but I'll be so beautiful for you, Dexter."

A million phrases of anger, of pride, of passion, of hatred, of tenderness fought on his lips. Then a perfect wave of emotion washed over him, carrying off with it a sediment of wisdom, of convention, of doubt, of honor. This was his girl who was speaking, his own, his beautiful, his pride.

"Won't you come in?" he heard her draw in her breath sharply.

Waiting.

"All right," his voice was trembling, "I'll come in."

It seems strange to say that neither when it was over nor a long time afterward did he regret that night. Looking at it from the perspective of ten years, the fact that Judy's flare for him endured just one month seemed of little importance. Nor did it matter that by his yielding he subjected himself to a deeper agony in the end and gave serious hurt to Irene Scheerer and to Irene's parents who had befriended him. There was nothing sufficiently pictorial about Irene's grief to stamp itself on his mind.

Dexter was at bottom hard-minded. The attitude of the city on his action was of no importance to him, not because he was going to leave the city, but because any outside attitude on the situation seemed superficial. He was completely indifferent to popular opinion. Nor, when he had seen that it was no use, that he did not possess in himself the power to move fundamentally or to hold Judy Jones, did he bear any malice toward her. He loved her and he would love her until the day he was too old for loving—but he could not have her. So he tasted the deep pain that is reserved only for the strong, just as he had tasted for a little while the deep happiness.

Even the ultimate falsity of the grounds upon which Judy terminated the engagement—that she did not want to "take him away" from Irene, that it—was on her conscience—did not revolt him. He was beyond any revulsion or any amusement.

He went east in February with the intention of selling out his laundries and settling in New York—but the war[2] came to America in March and changed his plans. He returned to the west, handed over the management of the business to his partner and went into the first officers' training camp in late April. He was one of those young thousands who greeted the war with a certain amount of relief, welcoming the liberation from webs of tangled emotion.

This story is not his biography, remember, although things creep into it which have nothing to do with those dreams he had when he was young. We are almost done with them and with him now. There is only one more incident to be related here and it happens seven years farther on.

It took place in New York, where he had done well—so well that there were no barriers too high for him now. He was thirty-two years old, and, except for one flying trip immediately after the war, he had not been west in seven years. A man named Devlin from Detroit came into his office to see him in a business way, and then and there this incident occurred, and closed out, so to speak, this particular side of his life.

"So you're from the middle west," said the man Devlin with careless curiosity. "That's funny—I thought men like you were probably born and raised on Wall Street. You know—wife of one of my best friends in Detroit came from your city. I was an usher at the wedding."

Dexter waited with no apprehension of what was coming. There was a magic that his city would never lose for him. Just as Judy's house had always seemed to him more mysterious and gay than other houses, so his dream of

---

2. World War I, which the United States entered in 1917.

the city itself, now that he had gone from it, was pervaded with a melancholy beauty.

"Judy Simms," said Devlin with no particular interest, "Judy Jones she was once."

"Yes. I knew her." A dull impatience spread over him. He had heard, of course, that she was married,—perhaps deliberately he had heard no more.

"Awfully nice girl," brooded Devlin, meaninglessly, "I'm sort of sorry for her."

"Why?" Something in Dexter was alert, receptive, at once.

"Oh, Joe Simms has gone to pieces in a way. I don't mean he beats her, you understand, or anything like that. But he drinks and runs around—"

"Doesn't she run around?"

"No. Stays at home with her kids."

"Oh."

"She's a little too old for him," said Devlin.

"Too old!" cried Dexter, "why man, she's only twenty-seven."

He was possessed with a wild notion of rushing out into the streets and taking a train to Detroit. He rose to his feet, spasmodically, involuntarily.

"I guess you're busy," Devlin apologized quickly. "I didn't realize—"

"No, I'm not busy," said Dexter, steadying his voice. "I'm not busy at all. Not busy at all. Did you say she was—twenty-seven. No, I said she was twenty-seven."

"Yes, you did," agreed Devlin drily.

"Go on, then. Go on."

"What do you mean?"

"About Judy Jones."

Devlin looked at him helplessly.

"Well, that's—I told you all there is to it. He treats her like the devil. Oh, they're not going to get divorced or anything. When he's particularly outrageous she forgives him. In fact, I'm inclined to think she loves him. She was a pretty girl when she first came to Detroit."

A pretty girl! The phrase struck Dexter as ludicrous.

"Isn't she—a pretty girl any more?"

"Oh, she's all right."

"Look here," said Dexter, sitting down suddenly, "I don't understand. You say she was a 'pretty girl' and now you say she's 'all right.' I don't understand what you mean—Judy Jones wasn't a pretty girl, at all. She was a great beauty. Why, I knew her, I knew her. She was—"

Devlin laughed pleasantly.

"I'm not trying to start a row," he said. "I think Judy's a nice girl and I like her. I can't understand how a man like Joe Simms could fall madly in love with her, but he did." Then he added, "Most of the women like her."

Dexter looked closely at Devlin, thinking wildly that there must be a reason for this, some insensitivity in the man or some private malice.

"Lots of women fade just-like-*that*." Devlin snapped his fingers. "You must have seen it happen. Perhaps I've forgotten how pretty she was at her wedding. I've seen her so much since then, you see. She has nice eyes."

A sort of dullness settled down upon Dexter. For the first time in his life he felt like getting very drunk. He knew that he was laughing loudly at something Devlin had said but he did not know what it was or why it was funny. When Devlin went, in a few minutes, he lay down on his lounge and looked out the window at the New York skyline into which the sun was sinking in dully lovely shades of pink and gold.

He had thought that having nothing else to lose he was invulnerable at last—but he knew that he had just lost something more, as surely as if he had married Judy Jones and seen her fade away before his eyes.

The dream was gone. Something had been taken from him. In a sort of panic he pushed the palms of his hands into his eyes and tried to bring up a picture of the waters lapping at Lake Erminie and the moonlit verandah, and gingham on the golf links and the dry sun and the gold color of her neck's soft down. And her mouth damp to his kisses and her eyes plaintive with melancholy and her freshness like new fine linen in the morning. Why these things were no longer in the world. They had existed and they existed no more.

For the first time in years the tears were streaming down his face. But they were for himself now. He did not care about mouth and eyes and moving hands. He wanted to care and he could not care. For he had gone away and he could never go back any more. The gates were closed, the sun was gone down and there was no beauty but the grey beauty of steel that withstands all time. Even the grief he could have borne was left behind in the country of illusion, of youth, of the richness of life, where his winter dreams had flourished.

"Long ago," he said, "long ago, there was something in me, but now that thing is gone. Now that thing is gone, that thing is gone. I cannot cry. I cannot care. That thing will come back no more."

1922

Babylon Revisited[1]

"And where's Mr. Campbell?" Charlie asked.

"Gone to Switzerland. Mr. Campbell's a pretty sick man, Mr. Wales."

"I'm sorry to hear that. And George Hardt?" Charlie inquired.

"Back in America, gone to work."

"And where is the Snow Bird?"

"He was in here last week. Anyway, his friend, Mr. Schaeffer, is in Paris."

Two familiar names from the long list of a year and a half ago. Charlie scribbled an address in his notebook and tore out the page.

"If you see Mr. Schaeffer, give him this," he said. "It's my brother-in-law's address. I haven't settled on a hotel yet."

He was not really disappointed to find Paris was so empty. But the stillness in the Ritz bar was strange and portentous. It was not an American bar any more—he felt polite in it, and not as if he owned it. It had gone back into France. He felt the stillness from the moment he got out of the taxi and saw the doorman, usually in a frenzy of activity at this hour, gossiping with a *chasseur*[2] by the servants' entrance.

1. Babylon was an ancient, prosperous city in Mesopotamia, associated by the Hebrews and Greeks with materialism and sensual pleasure; here, the reference is to Paris, where the story is set in the aftermath of the stock market crash of 1929.
2. Messenger-boy, errand runner (French).

Passing through the corridor, he heard only a single, bored voice in the once-clamorous women's room. When he turned into the bar he traveled the twenty feet of green carpet with his eyes fixed straight ahead by old habit; and then, with his foot firmly on the rail, he turned and surveyed the room, encountering only a single pair of eyes that fluttered up from a news-paper in the corner. Charlie asked for the head barman, Paul, who in the latter days of the bull market had come to work in his own custom-built car—disembarking, however, with due nicety at the nearest corner. But Paul was at his country house today and Alix giving him information.

"No, no more," Charlie said, "I'm going slow these days."

Alix congratulated him: "You were going pretty strong a couple of years ago."

"I'll stick to it all right," Charlie assured him. "I've stuck to it for over a year and a half now."

"How do you find conditions in America?"

"I haven't been to America for months. I'm in business in Prague, repre-senting a couple of concerns there. They don't know about me down there."

Alix smiled.

"Remember the night of George Hardt's bachelor dinner here?" said Charlie. "By the way, what's become of Claude Fessenden?"

Alix lowered his voice confidentially: "He's in Paris, but he doesn't come here any more. Paul doesn't allow it. He ran up a bill of thirty thousand francs, charging all his drinks and his lunches, and usually his dinner, for more than a year. And when Paul finally told him he had to pay, he gave him a bad check."

Alix shook his head sadly.

"I don't understand it, such a dandy fellow. Now he's all bloated up—" He made a plump apple of his hands.

Charlie watched a group of strident queens installing themselves in a corner.

"Nothing affects them," he thought. "Stocks rise and fall, people loaf or work, but they go on forever." The place oppressed him. He called for the dice and shook with Alix for the drink.

"Here for long, Mr. Wales?"

"I'm here for four or five days to see my little girl."

"Oh-h! You have a little girl?"

Outside, the fire-red, gas-blue, ghost-green signs shone smokily through the tranquil rain. It was late afternoon and the streets were in movement; the bistros[3] gleamed. At the corner of the Boulevard des Capucines he took a taxi. The Place de la Concorde moved by in pink majesty; they crossed the logical Seine, and Charlie felt the sudden provincial quality of the left bank.[4]

Charlie directed his taxi to the Avenue de l'Opera, which was out of his way. But he wanted to see the blue hour spread over the magnificent façade, and imagine that the cab horns, playing endlessly the first few bars of *Le Plus que Lent*,[5] were the trumpets of the Second Empire. They were closing the iron grill in front of Brentano's Book-store, and people were already at dinner behind the trim little bourgeois hedge of Duval's. He had never eaten

3. Small, informal restaurants.
4. Paris is divided by the Seine River; the grander buildings and broader streets are on the Right Bank. To Charlie, the Left Bank is more like a town than a city.
5. *La Plus que Lente* (More than Slow), piano composition by French composer Claude Debussy (1862–1918).

at a really cheap restaurant in Paris. Five-course dinner, four francs fifty, eighteen cents, wine included. For some odd reason he wished that he had.

As they rolled on to the Left Bank and he felt its sudden provincialism, he thought, "I spoiled this city for myself. I didn't realize it, but the days came along one after another, and then two years were gone, and everything was gone, and I was gone."

He was thirty-five, and good to look at. The Irish mobility of his face was sobered by a deep wrinkle between his eyes. As he rang his brother-in-law's bell in the Rue Palatine, the wrinkle deepened till it pulled down his brows; he felt a cramping sensation in his belly. From behind the maid who opened the door darted a lovely little girl of nine who shrieked "Daddy!" and flew up, struggling like a fish, into his arms. She pulled his head around by one ear and set her cheek against his.

"My old pie," he said.

"Oh, daddy, daddy, daddy, daddy, dads, dads, dads!"

She drew him into the salon, where the family waited, a boy and a girl his daughter's age, his sister-in-law and her husband. He greeted Marion with his voice pitched carefully to avoid either feigned enthusiasm or dislike, but her response was more frankly tepid, though she minimized her expression of unalterable distrust by directing her regard toward his child. The two men clasped hands in a friendly way and Lincoln Peters rested his for a moment on Charlie's shoulder.

The room was warm and comfortably American. The three children moved intimately about, playing through the yellow oblongs that led to other rooms; the cheer of six o'clock spoke in the eager smacks of the fire and the sounds of French activity in the kitchen. But Charlie did not relax; his heart sat up rigidly in his body and he drew confidence from his daughter, who from time to time came close to him, holding in her arms the doll he had brought.

"Really extremely well," he declared in answer to Lincoln's question. "There's a lot of business there that isn't moving at all, but we're doing even better than ever. In fact, damn well. I'm bringing my sister over from America next month to keep house for me. My income last year was bigger than it was when I had money. You see, the Czechs—"

His boasting was for a specific purpose; but after a moment, seeing a faint restiveness in Lincoln's eye, he changed the subject:

"Those are fine children of yours, well brought up, good manners."

"We think Honoria's a great little girl too."

Marion Peters came back from the kitchen. She was a tall woman with worried eyes, who had once possessed a fresh American loveliness. Charlie had never been sensitive to it and was always surprised when people spoke of how pretty she had been. From the first there had been an instinctive antipathy between them.

"Well, how do you find Honoria?" she asked.

"Wonderful. I was astonished how much she's grown in ten months. All the children are looking well."

"We haven't had a doctor for a year. How do you like being back in Paris?"

"It seems very funny to see so few Americans around."

"I'm delighted," Marion said vehemently. "Now at least you can go into a store without their assuming you're a millionaire. We've suffered like everybody, but on the whole it's a good deal pleasanter."

"But it was nice while it lasted," Charlie said. "We were a sort of royalty, almost infallible, with a sort of magic around us. In the bar this afternoon"—he stumbled, seeing his mistake—"there wasn't a man I knew."

She looked at him keenly. "I should think you'd have had enough of bars."

"I only stayed a minute. I take one drink every afternoon, and no more."

"Don't you want a cocktail before dinner?" Lincoln asked.

"I take only one drink every afternoon, and I've had that."

"I hope you keep to it," said Marion.

Her dislike was evident in the coldness with which she spoke, but Charlie only smiled; he had larger plans. Her very aggressiveness gave him an advantage, and he knew enough to wait. He wanted them to initiate the discussion of what they knew had brought him to Paris.

At dinner he couldn't decide whether Honoria was most like him or her mother. Fortunate if she didn't combine the traits of both that had brought them to disaster. A great wave of protectiveness went over him. He thought he knew what to do for her. He believed in character; he wanted to jump back a whole generation and trust in character again as the eternally valuable element. Everything else wore out.

He left soon after dinner, but not to go home. He was curious to see Paris by night with clearer and more judicious eyes than those of other days. He bought a *strapontin* for the Casino and watched Josephine Baker[6] go through her chocolate arabesques.

After an hour he left and strolled toward Montmartre, up the Rue Pigalle into the Place Blanche. The rain had stopped and there were a few people in evening clothes disembarking from taxis in front of cabarets, and *cocottes*[7] prowling singly or in pairs, and many Negroes. He passed a lighted door from which issued music, and stopped with the sense of familiarity; it was Bricktop's, where he had parted with so many hours and so much money. A few doors farther on he found another ancient rendezvous and incautiously put his head inside. Immediately an eager orchestra burst into sound, a pair of professional dancers leaped to their feet and a maître d'hôtel swooped toward him, crying, "Crowd just arriving, sir!" But he withdrew quickly.

"You have to be damn drunk," he thought.

Zelli's was closed, the bleak and sinister cheap hotels surrounding it were dark; up in the Rue Blanche there was more light and a local, colloquial French crowd. The Poet's Cave had disappeared, but the two great mouths of the Café of Heaven and the Café of Hell still yawned—even devoured, as he watched, the meager contents of a tourist bus—a German, a Japanese, and an American couple who glanced at him with frightened eyes.

So much for the effort and ingenuity of Montmartre. All the catering to vice and waste was on an utterly childish scale, and he suddenly realized the meaning of the word "dissipate"—to dissipate into thin air; to make nothing out of something. In the little hours of the night every move from place to place was an enormous human jump, an increase of paying for the privilege of slower and slower motion.

He remembered thousand-franc notes given to an orchestra for playing a single number, hundred-franc notes tossed to a doorman for calling a cab.

6. African American jazz singer and dancer (1906–1975) who arrived in Paris with a vaudeville troupe in 1925 and remained as a star enter- tainer. "*Strapontin*": folding seat.
7. Coquettes (French, literal trans.); prostitutes.

But it hadn't been given for nothing.

It had been given, even the most wildly squandered sum, as an offering to destiny that he might not remember the things most worth remembering, the things that now he would always remember—his child taken from his control, his wife escaped to a grave in Vermont.

In the glare of a *brasserie*[8] a woman spoke to him. He bought her some eggs and coffee, and then, eluding her encouraging stare, gave her a twenty-franc note and took a taxi to his hotel.

II

He woke upon a fine fall day—football weather. The depression of yesterday was gone and he liked the people on the streets. At noon he sat opposite Honoria at Le Grand Vatel, the only restaurant he could think of not reminiscent of champagne dinners and long luncheons that began at two and ended in a blurred and vague twilight.

"Now, how about vegetables? Oughtn't you to have some vegetables?"

"Well, yes."

"Here's *épinards* and *chou-fleur* and carrots and *haricots*."[9]

"I'd like *chou-fleur*."

"Wouldn't you like to have two vegetables?"

"I usually only have one at lunch."

The waiter was pretending to be inordinately fond of children. "*Qu'elle est mignonne la petite! Elle parle exactement comme une Française.*"[1]

"How about dessert? Shall we wait and see?"

The waiter disappeared. Honoria looked at her father expectantly.

"What are we going to do?"

"First, we're going to that toy store in the Rue Saint-Honoré and buy you anything you like. And then we're going to the vaudeville at the Empire."

She hesitated. "I like it about the vaudeville, but not the toy store."

"Why not?"

"Well, you brought me this doll." She had it with her. "And I've got lots of things. And we're not rich any more, are we?"

"We never were. But today you are to have anything you want."

"All right," she agreed resignedly.

When there had been her mother and a French nurse he had been inclined to be strict; now he extended himself, reached out for a new tolerance; he must be both parents to her and not shut any of her out of communication.

"I want to get to know you," he said gravely. "First let me introduce myself. My name is Charles J. Wales, of Prague."

"Oh, daddy!" her voice cracked with laughter.

"And who are you, please?" he persisted, and she accepted a rôle immediately: "Honoria Wales, Rue Palatine, Paris."

"Married or single?"

"No, not married. Single."

He indicated the doll. "But I see you have a child, madame."

---

8. Large, plain restaurant specializing in simple meals and beer.
9. Green beans (French). "*Épinards*": spinach.

"*Chou-fleur*": cauliflower.
1. How cute she is! She speaks exactly like a French girl (French).

Unwilling to disinherit it, she took it to her heart and thought quickly: "Yes, I've been married, but I'm not married now. My husband is dead."

He went on quickly, "And the child's name?"

"Simone. That's after my best friend at school."

"I'm very pleased that you're doing so well at school."

"I'm third this month," she boasted. "Elsie"—that was her cousin—"is only about eighteenth, and Richard is about at the bottom."

"You like Richard and Elsie, don't you?"

"Oh, yes. I like Richard quite well and I like her all right."

Cautiously and casually he asked: "And Aunt Marion and Uncle Lincoln—which do you like best?"

"Oh, Uncle Lincoln, I guess."

He was increasingly aware of her presence. As they came in, a murmur of ". . . adorable" followed them, and now the people at the next table bent all their silences upon her, staring as if she were something no more conscious than a flower.

"Why don't I live with you?" she asked suddenly. "Because mamma's dead?"

"You must stay here and learn more French. It would have been hard for daddy to take care of you so well."

"I don't really need much taking care of any more. I do everything for myself."

Going out of the restaurant, a man and a woman unexpectedly hailed him.

"Well, the old Wales!"

"Hello there, Lorraine. . . . Dunc."

Sudden ghosts out of the past: Duncan Schaeffer, a friend from college. Lorraine Quarrles, a lovely, pale blonde of thirty; one of a crowd who had helped them make months into days in the lavish times of three years ago.

"My husband couldn't come this year," she said, in answer to his question. "We're poor as hell. So he gave me two hundred a month and told me I could do my worst on that. . . . This your little girl?"

"What about coming back and sitting down?" Duncan asked.

"Can't do it." He was glad for an excuse. As always, he felt Lorraine's passionate, provocative attraction, but his own rhythm was different now.

"Well, how about dinner?" she asked.

"I'm not free. Give me your address and let me call you."

"Charlie, I believe you're sober," she said judicially. "I honestly believe he's sober, Dunc. Pinch him and see if he's sober."

Charlie indicated Honoria with his head. They both laughed.

"What's your address?" said Duncan skeptically.

He hesitated, unwilling to give the name of his hotel.

"I'm not settled yet. I'd better call you. We're going to see the vaudeville at the Empire."

"There! That's what I want to do," Lorraine said. "I want to see some clowns and acrobats and jugglers. That's just what we'll do, Dunc."

"We've got to do an errand first," said Charlie. "Perhaps we'll see you there."

"All right, you snob. . . . Good-by, beautiful little girl."

"Good-by."

Honoria bobbed politely.

Somehow, an unwelcome encounter. They liked him because he was functioning, because he was serious; they wanted to see him, because he was stronger than they were now, because they wanted to draw a certain sustenance from his strength.

At the Empire, Honoria proudly refused to sit upon her father's folded coat. She was already an individual with a code of her own, and Charlie was more and more absorbed by the desire of putting a little of himself into her before she crystallized utterly. It was hopeless to try to know her in so short a time.

Between the acts they came upon Duncan and Lorraine in the lobby where the band was playing.

"Have a drink?"

"All right, but not up at the bar. We'll take a table."

"The perfect father."

Listening abstractedly to Lorraine, Charlie watched Honoria's eyes leave their table, and he followed them wistfully about the room, wondering what they saw. He met her glance and she smiled.

"I liked that lemonade," she said.

What had she said? What had he expected? Going home in a taxi afterward, he pulled her over until her head rested against his chest.

"Darling, do you ever think about your mother?"

"Yes, sometimes," she answered vaguely.

"I don't want you to forget her. Have you got a picture of her?"

"Yes, I think so. Anyhow, Aunt Marion has. Why don't you want me to forget her?"

"She loved you very much."

"I loved her too."

They were silent for a moment.

"Daddy, I want to come and live with you," she said suddenly.

His heart leaped; he had wanted it to come like this.

"Aren't you perfectly happy?"

"Yes, but I love you better than anybody. And you love me better than anybody, don't you, now that mummy's dead?"

"Of course I do. But you won't always like me best, honey. You'll grow up and meet somebody your own age and go marry him and forget you ever had a daddy."

"Yes, that's true," she agreed tranquilly.

He didn't go in. He was coming back at nine o'clock and he wanted to keep himself fresh and new for the thing he must say then.

"When you're safe inside, just show yourself in that window."

"All right. Good-by, dads, dads, dads, dads."

He waited in the dark street until she appeared, all warm and glowing, in the window above and kissed her fingers out into the night.

III

They were waiting. Marion sat behind the coffee service in a dignified black dinner dress that just faintly suggested mourning. Lincoln was walking up and down with the animation of one who had already been talking. They were as anxious as he was to get into the question. He opened it almost immediately:

"I suppose you know what I want to see you about—why I really came to Paris."

Marion played with the black stars on her necklace and frowned.

"I'm awfully anxious to have a home," he continued. "And I'm awfully anxious to have Honoria in it. I appreciate your taking in Honoria for her mother's sake, but things have changed now"—he hesitated and then continued more forcibly—"changed radically with me, and I want to ask you to reconsider the matter. It would be silly for me to deny that about three years ago I was acting badly—"

Marion looked up at him with hard eyes.

"—but all that's over. As I told you, I haven't had more than a drink a day for over a year, and I take that drink deliberately, so that the idea of alcohol won't get too big in my imagination. You see the idea?"

"No," said Marion succinctly.

"It's a sort of stunt I set myself. It keeps the matter in proportion."

"I get you," said Lincoln. "You don't want to admit it's got any attraction for you."

"Something like that. Sometimes I forget and don't take it. But I try to take it. Anyhow, I couldn't afford to drink in my position. The people I represent are more than satisfied with what I've done, and I'm bringing my sister over from Burlington to keep house for me, and I want awfully to have Honoria too. You know that even when her mother and I weren't getting along well we never let anything that happened touch Honoria. I know she's fond of me and I know I'm able to take care of her and—well, there you are. How do you feel about it?"

He knew that now he would have to take a beating. It would last an hour or two hours, and it would be difficult, but if he modulated his inevitable resentment to the chastened attitude of the reformed sinner, he might win his point in the end.

Keep your temper, he told himself. You don't want to be justified. You want Honoria.

Lincoln spoke first: "We've been talking it over ever since we got your letter last month. We're happy to have Honoria here. She's a dear little thing, and we're glad to be able to help her, but of course that isn't the question—"

Marion interrupted suddenly. "How long are you going to stay sober, Charlie?" she asked.

"Permanently, I hope."

"How can anybody count on that?"

"You know I never did drink heavily until I gave up business and came over here with nothing to do. Then Helen and I began to run around with—"

"Please leave Helen out of it. I can't bear to hear you talk about her like that."

He stared at her grimly; he had never been certain how fond of each other the sisters were in life.

"My drinking only lasted about a year and a half—from the time we came over until I—collapsed."

"It was time enough."

"It was time enough," he agreed.

"My duty is entirely to Helen," she said. "I try to think what she would have wanted me to do. Frankly, from the night you did that terrible thing you haven't really existed for me. I can't help that. She was my sister."

"Yes."

"When she was dying she asked me to look out for Honoria. If you hadn't been in a sanitarium then, it might have helped matters."

He had no answer.

"I'll never in my life be able to forget the morning when Helen knocked at my door, soaked to the skin and shivering and said you'd locked her out."

Charlie gripped the sides of the chair. This was more difficult than he expected; he wanted to launch out into a long expostulation and explanation, but he only said: "The night I locked her out—" and she interrupted, "I don't feel up to going over that again."

After a moment's silence Lincoln said: "We're getting off the subject. You want Marion to set aside her legal guardianship and give you Honoria. I think the main point for her is whether she has confidence in you or not."

"I don't blame Marion," Charlie said slowly, "but I think she can have entire confidence in me. I had a good record up to three years ago. Of course, it's within human possibilities I might go wrong any time. But if we wait much longer I'll lose Honoria's childhood and my chance for a home." He shook his head, "I'll simply lose her, don't you see?"

"Yes, I see," said Lincoln.

"Why didn't you think of all this before?" Marion asked.

"I suppose I did, from time to time, but Helen and I were getting along badly. When I consented to the guardianship, I was flat on my back in a sanitarium and the market had cleaned me out. I knew I'd acted badly, and I thought if it would bring any peace to Helen, I'd agree to anything. But now it's different. I'm functioning, I'm behaving damn well, so far as—"

"Please don't swear at me," Marion said.

He looked at her, startled. With each remark the force of her dislike became more and more apparent. She had built up all her fear of life into one wall and faced it toward him. This trivial reproof was possibly the result of some trouble with the cook several hours before. Charlie became increasingly alarmed at leaving Honoria in this atmosphere of hostility against himself; sooner or later it would come out, in a word here, a shake of the head there, and some of that distrust would be irrevocably implanted in Honoria. But he pulled his temper down out of his face and shut it up inside him; he had won a point, for Lincoln realized the absurdity of Marion's remark and asked her lightly since when she had objected to the word "damn."

"Another thing," Charlie said: "I'm able to give her certain advantages now. I'm going to take a French governess to Prague with me. I've got a lease on a new apartment—"

He stopped, realizing that he was blundering. They couldn't be expected to accept with equanimity the fact that his income was again twice as large as their own.

"I suppose you can give her more luxuries than we can," said Marion. "When you were throwing away money we were living along watching every ten francs. . . . I suppose you'll start doing it again."

"Oh, no," he said. "I've learned. I worked hard for ten years, you know—until I got lucky in the market, like so many people. Terribly lucky. It won't happen again."

There was a long silence. All of them felt their nerves straining, and for the first time in a year Charlie wanted a drink. He was sure now that Lincoln Peters wanted him to have his child.

Marion shuddered suddenly; part of her saw that Charlie's feet were planted on the earth now, and her own maternal feeling recognized the

naturalness of his desire; but she had lived for a long time with a prejudice—a prejudice founded on a curious disbelief in her sister's happiness,
and which, in the shock of one terrible night, had turned to hatred for him.
It had all happened at a point in her life where the discouragement of ill
health and adverse circumstances made it necessary for her to believe in
tangible villainy and a tangible villain.

"I can't help what I think!" she cried out suddenly. "How much you were
responsible for Helen's death, I don't know. It's something you'll have to
square with your own conscience."

An electric current of agony surged through him; for a moment he was
almost on his feet, an unuttered sound echoing in his throat. He hung on to
himself for a moment, another moment.

"Hold on there," said Lincoln uncomfortably. "I never thought you were
responsible for that."

"Helen died of heart trouble," Charlie said dully.

"Yes, heart trouble." Marion spoke as if the phrase had another meaning
for her.

Then, in the flatness that followed her outburst, she saw him plainly and
she knew he had somehow arrived at control over the situation. Glancing at
her husband, she found no help from him, and as abruptly as if it were a
matter of no importance, she threw up the sponge.

"Do what you like!" she cried, springing up from her chair. "She's your
child. I'm not the person to stand in your way. I think if it were my child I'd
rather see her—" She managed to check herself. "You two decide it. I can't
stand this. I'm sick. I'm going to bed."

She hurried from the room; after a moment Lincoln said:

"This has been a hard day for her. You know how strongly she feels—"
His voice was almost apologetic: "When a woman gets an idea in her
head."

"Of course."

"It's going to be all right. I think she sees now that you—can provide for
the child, and so we can't very well stand in your way or Honoria's way."

"Thank you, Lincoln."

"I'd better go along and see how she is."

"I'm going."

He was still trembling when he reached the street, but a walk down the
Rue Bonaparte to the *quais*[2] set him up, and as he crossed the Seine, fresh
and new by the *quai* lamps, he felt exultant. But back in his room he
couldn't sleep. The image of Helen haunted him. Helen whom he had loved
so until they had senselessly begun to abuse each other's love, tear it into
shreds. On that terrible February night that Marion remembered so vividly,
a slow quarrel had gone on for hours. There was a scene at the Florida, and
then he attempted to take her home, and then she kissed young Webb at a
table; after that there was what she had hysterically said. When he arrived
home alone he turned the key in the lock in wild anger. How could he know
she would arrive an hour later alone, that there would be a snowstorm in
which she wandered about in slippers, too confused to find a taxi? Then the
aftermath, her escaping pneumonia by a miracle, and all the attendant horror. They were "reconciled," but that was the beginning of the end, and

---

2. Quays (French); a section of the Left Bank is lined with quays, or walking places along the river.

Marion, who had seen with her own eyes and who imagined it to be one of many scenes from her sister's martyrdom, never forgot.

Going over it again brought Helen nearer, and in the white, soft light that steals upon half sleep near morning he found himself talking to her again. She said that he was perfectly right about Honoria and that she wanted Honoria to be with him. She said she was glad he was being good and doing better. She said a lot of other things—very friendly things—but she was in a swing in a white dress, and swinging faster and faster all the time, so that at the end he could not hear clearly all that she said.

IV

He woke up feeling happy. The door of the world was open again. He made plans, vistas, futures for Honoria and himself, but suddenly he grew sad, remembering all the plans he and Helen had made. She had not planned to die. The present was the thing—work to do and someone to love. But not to love too much, for he knew the injury that a father can do to a daughter or a mother to a son by attaching them too closely: afterward, out in the world, the child would seek in the marriage partner the same blind tenderness and, failing probably to find it, turn against love and life.

It was another bright, crisp day. He called Lincoln Peters at the bank where he worked and asked if he could count on taking Honoria when he left for Prague. Lincoln agreed that there was no reason for delay. One thing—the legal guardianship. Marion wanted to retain that a while longer. She was upset by the whole matter, and it would oil things if she felt that the situation was still in her control for another year. Charlie agreed, wanting only the tangible, visible child.

Then the question of a governess. Charles sat in a gloomy agency and talked to a cross Béarnaise and to a buxom Breton peasant,[3] neither of whom he could have endured. There were others whom he would see tomorrow.

He lunched with Lincoln Peters at Griffons, trying to keep down his exultation.

"There's nothing quite like your own child," Lincoln said. "But you understand how Marion feels too."

"She's forgotten how hard I worked for seven years there," Charlie said. "She just remembers one night."

"There's another thing." Lincoln hesitated. "While you and Helen were tearing around Europe throwing money away, we were just getting along. I didn't touch any of the prosperity because I never got ahead enough to carry anything but my insurance. I think Marion felt there was some kind of injustice in it—you not even working toward the end, and getting richer and richer."

"It went just as quick as it came," said Charlie.

"Yes, a lot of it stayed in the hands of *chasseurs* and saxophone players and maîtres d'hôtel—well, the big party's over now. I just said that to explain Marion's feeling about those crazy years. If you drop in about six o'clock tonight before Marion's too tired, we'll settle the details on the spot."

---

3. Béarn and Breton are two French provincial regions. The implication is that Charlie wants a higher-class (preferably Parisian) governess.

Back at his hotel, Charlie found a *pneumatique* that had been redirected from the Ritz bar where Charlie had left his address for the purpose of finding a certain man.

"DEAR CHARLIE: You were so strange when we saw you the other day that I wondered if I did something to offend you. If so, I'm not conscious of it. In fact, I have thought about you too much for the last year, and it's always been in the back of my mind that I might see you if I came over here. We *did* have such good times that crazy spring, like the night you and I stole the butcher's tricycle, and the time we tried to call on the president and you had the old derby rim and the wire cane. Everybody seems so old lately, but I don't feel old a bit. Couldn't we get together some time today for old time's sake? I've got a vile hang-over for the moment, but will be feeling better this afternoon and will look for you about five in the sweatshop at the Ritz.

"Always devotedly,
LORRAINE."

His first feeling was one of awe that he had actually, in his mature years, stolen a tricycle and pedaled Lorraine all over the Étoile between the small hours and dawn. In retrospect it was a nightmare. Locking out Helen didn't fit in with any other act of his life, but the tricycle incident did—it was one of many. How many weeks or months of dissipation to arrive at that condition of utter irresponsibility?

He tried to picture how Lorraine had appeared to him then—very attractive; Helen was unhappy about it, though she said nothing. Yesterday, in the restaurant, Lorraine had seemed trite, blurred, worn away. He emphatically did not want to see her, and he was glad Alix had not given away his hotel address. It was a relief to think, instead, of Honoria, to think of Sundays spent with her and of saying good morning to her and of knowing she was there in his house at night, drawing her breath in the darkness.

At five he took a taxi and bought presents for all the Peters—a piquant cloth doll, a box of Roman soldiers, flowers for Marion, big linen handkerchiefs for Lincoln.

He saw, when he arrived in the apartment, that Marion had accepted the inevitable. She greeted him now as though he were a recalcitrant member of the family, rather than a menacing outsider. Honoria had been told she was going; Charlie was glad to see that her tact made her conceal her excessive happiness. Only on his lap did she whisper her delight and the question "When?" before she slipped away with the other children.

He and Marion were alone for a minute in the room, and on an impulse he spoke out boldly:

"Family quarrels are bitter things. They don't go according to any rules. They're not like aches or wounds; they're more like splits in the skin that won't heal because there's not enough material. I wish you and I could be on better terms."

"Some things are hard to forget," she answered. "It's a question of confidence." There was no answer to this and presently she asked, "When do you propose to take her?"

"As soon as I can get a governess. I hoped the day after tomorrow."

"That's impossible. I've got to get her things in shape. Not before Saturday."

He yielded. Coming back into the room, Lincoln offered him a drink.

"I'll take my daily whisky," he said.

It was warm here, it was a home, people together by a fire. The children felt very safe and important; the mother and father were serious, watchful. They had things to do for the children more important than his visit here. A spoonful of medicine was, after all, more important than the strained relations between Marion and himself. They were not dull people, but they were very much in the grip of life and circumstances. He wondered if he couldn't do something to get Lincoln out of his rut at the bank.

A long peal at the door-bell; the *bonne à tout faire*[4] passed through and went down the corridor. The door opened upon another long ring, and then voices, and the three in the salon looked up expectantly; Richard moved to bring the corridor within his range of vision, and Marion rose. Then the maid came back along the corridor, closely followed by the voices, which developed under the light into Duncan Schaeffer and Lorraine Quarrles.

They were gay, they were hilarious, they were roaring with laughter. For a moment Charlie was astounded; unable to understand how they ferreted out the Peters' address.

"Ah-h-h!" Duncan wagged his finger roguishly at Charlie. "Ah-h-h!"

They both slid down another cascade of laughter. Anxious and at a loss, Charlie shook hands with them quickly and presented them to Lincoln and Marion. Marion nodded, scarcely speaking. She had drawn back a step toward the fire; her little girl stood beside her, and Marion put an arm about her shoulder.

With growing annoyance at the intrusion, Charlie waited for them to explain themselves. After some concentration Duncan said:

"We came to invite you out to dinner. Lorraine and I insist that all this shishi, cagy business 'bout your address got to stop."

Charlie came closer to them, as if to force them backward down the corridor.

"Sorry, but I can't. Tell me where you'll be and I'll phone you in half an hour."

This made no impression. Lorraine sat down suddenly on the side of a chair, and focusing her eyes on Richard, cried, "Oh, what a nice little boy! Come here, little boy." Richard glanced at his mother, but did not move. With a perceptible shrug of her shoulders, Lorraine turned back to Charlie:

"Come and dine. Sure your cousins won' mine. See you so sel'om. Or solemn."

"I can't," said Charlie sharply. "You two have dinner and I'll phone you."

Her voice became suddenly unpleasant. "All right, we'll go. But I remember once when you hammered on my door at four A.M. I was enough of a good sport to give you a drink. Come on, Dunc."

Still in slow motion, with blurred, angry faces, with uncertain feet, they retired along the corridor.

"Good night," Charlie said.

"Good night!" responded Lorraine emphatically.

---

4. Maid of all work (French). The Peters family cannot afford to hire several servants with specialized tasks.

When he went back into the salon Marion had not moved, only now her son was standing in the circle of her other arm. Lincoln was still swinging Honoria back and forth like a pendulum from side to side.

"What an outrage!" Charlie broke out. "What an absolute outrage!"

Neither of them answered. Charlie dropped into an armchair, picked up his drink, set it down again and said:

"People I haven't seen for two years having the colossal nerve—"

He broke off. Marion had made the sound "Oh!" in one swift, furious breath, turned her body from him with a jerk and left the room.

Lincoln set down Honoria carefully.

"You children go in and start your soup," he said, and when they obeyed, he said to Charlie:

"Marion's not well and she can't stand shocks. That kind of people make her really physically sick."

"I didn't tell them to come here. They wormed your name out of somebody. They deliberately—"

"Well, it's too bad. It doesn't help matters. Excuse me a minute."

Left alone, Charlie sat tense in his chair. In the next room he could hear the children eating, talking in monosyllables, already oblivious to the scene between their elders. He heard a murmur of conversation from a farther room and then the ticking bell of a telephone receiver picked up, and in a panic he moved to the other side of the room and out of earshot.

In a minute Lincoln came back. "Look here, Charlie. I think we'd better call off dinner for tonight. Marion's in bad shape."

"Is she angry with me?"

"Sort of," he said, almost roughly. "She's not strong and—"

"You mean she's changed her mind about Honoria?"

"She's pretty bitter right now. I don't know. You phone me at the bank tomorrow."

"I wish you'd explain to her I never dreamed these people would come here. I'm just as sore as you are."

"I couldn't explain anything to her now."

Charlie got up. He took his coat and hat and started down the corridor. Then he opened the door of the dining room and said in a strange voice, "Good night, children."

Honoria rose and ran around the table to hug him.

"Good night, sweetheart," he said vaguely, and then trying to make his voice more tender, trying to conciliate something, "Good night, dear children."

V

Charlie went directly to the Ritz bar with the furious idea of finding Lorraine and Duncan, but they were not there, and he realized that in any case there was nothing he could do. He had not touched his drink at the Peters, and now he ordered a whisky-and-soda. Paul came over to say hello.

"It's a great change," he said sadly. "We do about half the business we did. So many fellows I hear about back in the States lost everything, maybe not in the first crash, but then in the second. Your friend George Hardt lost every cent, I hear. Are you back in the States?"

"No, I'm in business in Prague."

"I heard that you lost a lot in the crash."

"I did," and he added grimly, "but I lost everything I wanted in the boom."

"Selling short."

"Something like that."

Again the memory of those days swept over him like a nightmare—the people they had met travelling; then people who couldn't add a row of figures or speak a coherent sentence. The little man Helen had consented to dance with at the ship's party, who had insulted her ten feet from the table; the women and girls carried screaming with drink or drugs out of public places—

—The men who locked their wives out in the snow, because the snow of twenty-nine wasn't real snow. If you didn't want it to be snow, you just paid some money.

He went to the phone and called the Peters' apartment; Lincoln answered.

"I called up because this thing is on my mind. Has Marion said anything definite?"

"Marion's sick," Lincoln answered shortly. "I know this thing isn't altogether your fault, but I can't have her go to pieces about it. I'm afraid we'll have to let it slide for six months; I can't take the chance of working her up to this state again."

"I see."

"I'm sorry, Charlie."

He went back to his table. His whisky glass was empty, but he shook his head when Alix looked at it questioningly. There wasn't much he could do now except send Honoria some things; he would send her a lot of things tomorrow. He thought rather angrily that this was just money—he had given so many people money. . . .

"No, no more," he said to another waiter. "What do I owe you?"

He would come back some day; they couldn't make him pay forever. But he wanted his child, and nothing was much good now, beside that fact. He wasn't young any more, with a lot of nice thoughts and dreams to have by himself. He was absolutely sure Helen wouldn't have wanted him to be so alone.

1931

WILLIAM FAULKNER
1897–1962

Between 1929 and 1936 William Faulkner published novels about childhood, families, sex, race, obsessions, time, the past, his native South, and the modern world. He invented voices for characters ranging from sages to children, criminals, the insane, even the dead—sometimes all within one book. He developed, beyond this ventriloquism, his own unmistakable narrative voice: urgent, intense, highly rhetorical. He experimented with narrative chronology and with techniques for representing mind and memory. He invented an entire southern county and wrote its history.

He was a native Mississippian, born near Oxford, where his parents moved when he was about five. His great-grandfather had been a local legend: a colonel in the Civil War, lawyer, railroad builder, financier, politician, writer, and public figure who was shot and killed by a business and political rival in 1889. Faulkner's grandfather carried on some of the family enterprises, and his father worked first for the railroad (the Gulf and Chicago) and later as business manager of the University of Mississippi. The father was a reclusive man who loved to hunt, drink, and swap stories with his hunting friends; the mother, ambitious, sensitive, and literary, was a more profound influence on Faulkner, her favorite of four sons. In Faulkner's childhood his mother's mother also lived with them; she was a high-spirited, independent, and imaginative old lady whose death in 1907 seems to have affected Faulkner deeply.

Faulkner dropped out of high school in 1915 and had no further formal education beyond a year (1919–20) as a special student at the University of Mississippi. Through family connections, various jobs were made for him, but he was unhappy in all of them. In 1918 Estelle Oldham, his high school love, married someone else; Faulkner briefly left Oxford. First he went to New Haven where his best friend and informal tutor, Phil Stone, was in the Yale law school; then he enlisted in the British Royal Flying Corps and was sent to Canada to train. World War I ended before he saw active service; nevertheless, when he returned to Oxford in 1919 he was limping from what he claimed was a war wound.

Back at home, Faulkner drifted from one job to another and wrote poetry that was a mélange of Shakespearean, pastoral, Victorian, and Edwardian modes, with an overlay of French Symbolism, which he published in *The Marble Faun*, in 1924. In 1925 he went to New Orleans where, for the first time, he met and mingled with literary people, including Sherwood Anderson, who encouraged Faulkner to develop his own style, to concentrate on prose, and to use his region for material.

Faulkner wrote his first novel, *Soldier's Pay*, in New Orleans, and Anderson recommended it to his own publisher, Liveright; it appeared in 1926. He also published in the New Orleans magazine *The Double Dealer* and the newspaper *The Times Picayune*. He learned about the experimental writing of James Joyce and the ideas of Sigmund Freud. After a trip to Europe at the end of the same year, he returned to Oxford. In 1929 he married Estelle Oldham, who had been divorced and had returned to Oxford with her two children. They bought a ruined mansion, Rowan Oak, in 1930 and began to restore it to its antebellum appearance. A daughter born in 1931 died in infancy; a second daughter, Jill, was born in 1933.

Faulkner's second novel was a satire on New Orleans intellectuals called *Mosquitos* (1927). His more typical subject matter emerged with his rejected novel *Flags in the Dust*, and the shortened version of it that appeared in 1929 as *Sartoris*. In this work Faulkner focused on the interconnections between a prominent southern family and the local community: the Sartoris family as well as many other characters appeared in later works, and the region, renamed Yoknapatawpha County, was to become the locale of Faulkner's imaginative world.

The social and historical emphasis in *Sartoris* was not directly followed up in the works Faulkner wrote next. *The Sound and the Fury* (1929)—Faulkner's favorite novel—and *As I Lay Dying* (1930) were dramatically experimental attempts to articulate the inexpressible aspects of individual psychology. *The Sound and the Fury* has four sections, each with a different narrator, each supplying a different piece of the plot. Three of the narrators are brothers: Benjy, the idiot; Quentin, the suicide; and Jason, the business failure. Each of them, for different reasons, mourns the loss of their sister Caddie. While the story moves out to the disintegration of the old southern family to which these brothers belong, its focus is on the private obsessions of the brothers, and it invents an entirely different style for each narrator. Only the last section, told from a traditionally omniscient point of view, provides a sequential narration; the other three jump freely in time and space. The structure of *As I Lay Dying* is even more complex. Like *The Sound and the Fury*, it is organized around the loss of a beloved woman. The precipitating event in the novel is the death of a mother. The story moves forward in chronological time as the "poor white" Bundren family takes her body to the town of Jefferson for burial. Its narration is divided into fifty-nine sections of interior monologue by fifteen characters, each with a different perception of the action and a different way of relating to reality. The family's adventures and misadventures on the road are comic, tragic, grotesque, absurd, and deeply moving.

Neither these books nor his early short stories were very popular. *Sanctuary*, a sensational work about sex, gangsters, official corruption, and urban violence, attracted considerable attention, however. It appeared in 1931, and took its place in the large amount of hard-boiled fiction that appeared in the decade, notably by such authors as Dashiell Hammett and Raymond Chandler. During four different intervals—1932–37, 1942–45, 1951, and 1954—Faulkner spent time in Hollywood or on contract as a scriptwriter. He worked well with the director Howard Hawks, and wrote the scripts for two famous movies, an adaptation of Ernest Hemingway's *To Have and Have Not* and an adaptation of Raymond Chandler's *The Big Sleep*, both starring Humphrey Bogart and Lauren Bacall.

He continued to produce brilliant and inventive novels during these years. *Light in August* (1932) counterpointed a comic pastoral about the pregnant earth-mother figure Lena Grove with a grim tragedy about the embittered outcast Joe Christmas, who may or may not be racially mixed; it interrelated individual psychology and cultural pathology. *Absalom, Absalom!*, which followed in 1936, is thought by many to be Faulkner's masterpiece. The story of Thomas Sutpen, the ruthless would-be founder of a southern dynasty after the Civil War, is related by four different speakers, each trying to find "the meaning" of the story. The reader, observing how the story changes in each telling, comes to see that making stories is the human way of making meaning. Like Faulkner's earlier novels, *Absalom* is thus simultaneously about an individual, about the South, and about itself as a work of fiction. But its emphasis shifts from the private psychology that dominated in earlier work to social psychology: to the collective mind of the South.

With World War II, Faulkner's work became more traditional and less difficult. He began to write about the rise, in Yoknapatawpha County, of the poor white family named Snopes—this family had appeared in earlier works (like "Barn Burning")—and the simultaneous decline of the region's "aristocratic" families. *The Hamlet* (1940) was the first of three novels devoted to the Snopeses. Because all his works had been set in Yoknapatawpha County and were interconnected, the region and its people began to take on an existence independent of any one book in which they appeared.

Faulkner's national reputation soared after the publication in 1946 of an anthology of his writings, *The Portable Faulkner,* edited by the critic Malcolm Cowley. He already had a major reputation abroad, especially in France, where his work in translation was a powerful influence on the French so-called new novel and its practitioners such as Michel Butor and Alain Robbe-Grillet. His antiracist *Intruder in the Dust* (1948) occasioned the award of the Nobel Prize in 1950. In the 1950s Faulkner visited many college campuses. His writing took on more of the air of an old-fashioned yarn; he dealt with more legendary and local color materials; he rounded out the Snopes saga with *The Town* (1957) and *The Mansion* (1959). At the age of sixty-five he died of a heart attack.

The texts of "A Rose for Emily" and "Barn Burning" are those of *Collected Stories* (1950).

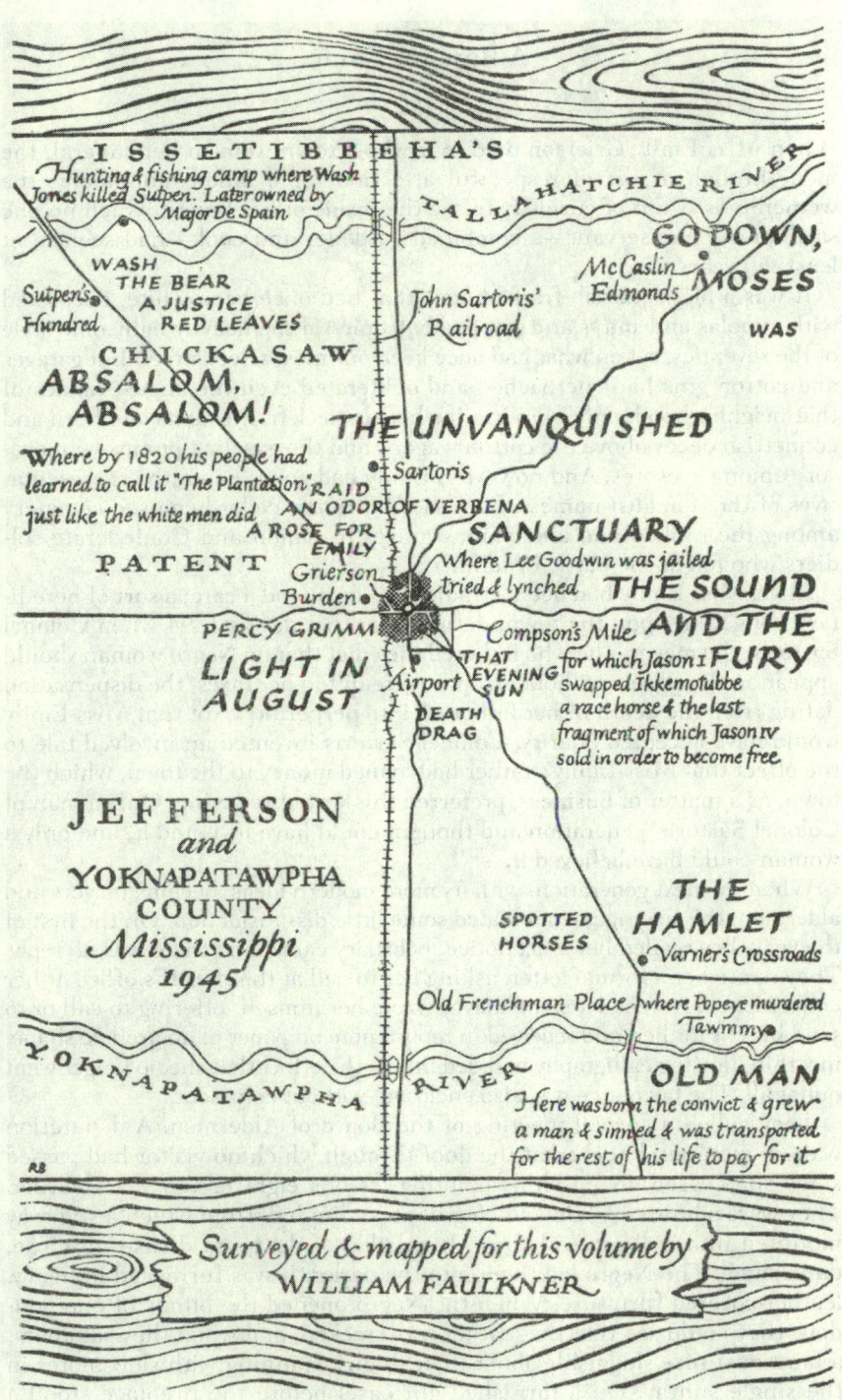

ISSETIBBEHA'S

Hunting & fishing camp where Wash
Jones killed Sutpen. Later owned by
Major De Spain

TALLAHATCHIE RIVER

GO DOWN,
McCaslin
Edmonds
MOSES

WASH
THE BEAR
A JUSTICE
RED LEAVES

Sutpen's
Hundred

John Sartoris'
Railroad

WAS

CHICKASAW
ABSALOM,
ABSALOM!

THE UNVANQUISHED

Where by 1820 his people had
learned to call it "The Plantation"
just like the white men did

• Sartoris

RAID
AN ODOR OF VERBENA
A ROSE FOR
EMILY
Grierson
Burden •

SANCTUARY
Where Lee Goodwin was jailed
tried & lynched

THE SOUND
AND THE
FURY

PATENT

PERCY GRIMM

Compson's Mile
for which Jason I
swapped Ikkemotubbe
a race horse & the last
fragment of which Jason IV
sold in order to become free

LIGHT IN
AUGUST

Airport

THAT
EVENING
SUN

DEATH
DRAG

JEFFERSON
and
YOKNAPATAWPHA
COUNTY
Mississippi
1945

SPOTTED
HORSES

THE
HAMLET
• Varner's Crossroads

Old Frenchman Place where Popeye murdered
Tawmmy

YOKNAPATAWPHA   RIVER

OLD MAN

Here was born the convict & grew
a man & sinned & was transported
for the rest of his life to pay for it

Surveyed & mapped for this volume by
WILLIAM FAULKNER

Yoknapatawpha County. Faulkner drew this map of his fictional world for Malcolm
Cowley's 1946 collection *The Portable Faulkner*.

A Rose for Emily

I

When Miss Emily Grierson died, our whole town went to her funeral: the men through a sort of respectful affection for a fallen monument, the women mostly out of curiosity to see the inside of her house, which no one save an old manservant—a combined gardener and cook—had seen in at least ten years.

It was a big, squarish frame house that had once been white, decorated with cupolas and spires and scrolled balconies in the heavily lightsome style of the seventies, set on what had once been our most select street. But garages and cotton gins had encroached and obliterated even the august names of that neighborhood; only Miss Emily's house was left, lifting its stubborn and coquettish decay above the cotton wagons and the gasoline pumps—an eyesore among eyesores. And now Miss Emily had gone to join the representatives of those august names where they lay in the cedar-bemused cemetery among the ranked and anonymous graves of Union and Confederate soldiers who fell at the battle of Jefferson.

Alive, Miss Emily had been a tradition, a duty, and a care; a sort of hereditary obligation upon the town, dating from that day in 1894 when Colonel Sartoris, the mayor—he who fathered the edict that no Negro woman should appear on the streets without an apron—remitted her taxes, the dispensation dating from the death of her father on into perpetuity. Not that Miss Emily would have accepted charity. Colonel Sartoris invented an involved tale to the effect that Miss Emily's father had loaned money to the town, which the town, as a matter of business, preferred this way of repaying. Only a man of Colonel Sartoris' generation and thought could have invented it, and only a woman could have believed it.

When the next generation, with its more modern ideas, became mayors and aldermen, this arrangement created some little dissatisfaction. On the first of the year they mailed her a tax notice. February came, and there was no reply. They wrote her a formal letter, asking her to call at the sheriff's office at her convenience. A week later the mayor wrote her himself, offering to call or to send his car for her, and received in reply a note on paper of an archaic shape, in a thin, flowing calligraphy in faded ink, to the effect that she no longer went out at all. The tax notice was also enclosed, without comment.

They called a special meeting of the Board of Aldermen. A deputation waited upon her, knocked at the door through which no visitor had passed since she ceased giving china-painting lessons eight or ten years earlier. They were admitted by the old Negro into a dim hall from which a stairway mounted into still more shadow. It smelled of dust and disuse—a close, dank smell. The Negro led them into the parlor. It was furnished in heavy, leather-covered furniture. When the Negro opened the blinds of one window, they could see that the leather was cracked; and when they sat down, a faint dust rose sluggishly about their thighs, spinning with slow motes in the single sunray. On a tarnished gilt easel before the fireplace stood a crayon portrait of Miss Emily's father.

They rose when she entered—a small, fat woman in black, with a thin gold chain descending to her waist and vanishing into her belt, leaning on an ebony cane with a tarnished gold head. Her skeleton was small and spare;

perhaps that was why what would have been merely plumpness in another was obesity in her. She looked bloated, like a body long submerged in motionless water, and of that pallid hue. Her eyes, lost in the fatty ridges of her face, looked like two small pieces of coal pressed into a lump of dough as they moved from one face to another while the visitors stated their errand.

She did not ask them to sit. She just stood in the door and listened quietly until the spokesman came to a stumbling halt. Then they could hear the invisible watch ticking at the end of the gold chain.

Her voice was dry and cold. "I have no taxes in Jefferson. Colonel Sartoris explained it to me. Perhaps one of you can gain access to the city records and satisfy yourselves."

"But we have. We are the city authorities, Miss Emily. Didn't you get a notice from the sheriff, signed by him?"

"I received a paper, yes," Miss Emily said. "Perhaps he considers himself the sheriff . . . . . . I have no taxes in Jefferson."

"But there is nothing on the books to show that, you see. We must go by the—"

"See Colonel Sartoris. I have no taxes in Jefferson."

"But, Miss Emily—"

"See Colonel Sartoris." (Colonel Sartoris had been dead almost ten years.) "I have no taxes in Jefferson. Tobe!" The Negro appeared. "Show these gentlemen out."

II

So she vanquished them, horse and foot, just as she had vanquished their fathers thirty years before about the smell. That was two years after her father's death and a short time after her sweetheart—the one we believed would marry her—had deserted her. After her father's death she went out very little; after her sweetheart went away, people hardly saw her at all. A few of the ladies had the temerity to call, but were not received, and the only sign of life about the place was the Negro man—a young man then—going in and out with a market basket.

"Just as if a man—any man—could keep a kitchen properly," the ladies said; so they were not surprised when the smell developed. It was another link between the gross, teeming world and the high and mighty Griersons.

A neighbor, a woman, complained to the mayor, Judge Stevens, eighty years old.

"But what will you have me do about it, madam?" he said.

"Why, send her word to stop it," the woman said. "Isn't there a law?"

"I'm sure that won't be necessary," Judge Stevens said. "It's probably just a snake or a rat that nigger of hers killed in the yard. I'll speak to him about it."

The next day he received two more complaints, one from a man who came in diffident deprecation. "We really must do something about it, Judge. I'd be the last one in the world to bother Miss Emily, but we've got to do something." That night the Board of Aldermen met—three gray-beards and one younger man, a member of the rising generation.

"It's simple enough," he said. "Send her word to have her place cleaned up. Give her a certain time to do it in, and if she don't . . . . . ."

"Dammit, sir," Judge Stevens said, "will you accuse a lady to her face of smelling bad?"

So the next night, after midnight, four men crossed Miss Emily's lawn and slunk about the house like burglars, sniffing along the base of the brickwork and at the cellar openings while one of them performed a regular sowing motion with his hand out of a sack slung from his shoulder. They broke open the cellar door and sprinkled lime there, and in all the outbuildings. As they recrossed the lawn, a window that had been dark was lighted and Miss Emily sat in it, the light behind her, and her upright torso motionless as that of an idol. They crept quietly across the lawn and into the shadow of the locusts that lined the street. After a week or two the smell went away.

That was when people had begun to feel really sorry for her. People in our town, remembering how old lady Wyatt, her great-aunt, had gone completely crazy at last, believed that the Griersons held themselves a little too high for what they really were. None of the young men were quite good enough for Miss Emily and such. We had long thought of them as a tableau; Miss Emily a slender figure in white in the background, her father a spraddled silhouette in the foreground, his back to her and clutching a horsewhip, the two of them framed by the back-flung front door. So when she got to be thirty and was still single, we were not pleased exactly, but vindicated; even with insanity in the family she wouldn't have turned down all of her chances if they had really materialized.

When her father died, it got about that the house was all that was left to her; and in a way, people were glad. At last they could pity Miss Emily. Being left alone, and a pauper, she had become humanized. Now she too would know the old thrill and the old despair of a penny more or less.

The day after his death all the ladies prepared to call at the house and offer condolence and aid, as is our custom. Miss Emily met them at the door, dressed as usual and with no trace of grief on her face. She told them that her father was not dead. She did that for three days, with the ministers calling on her, and the doctors, trying to persuade her to let them dispose of the body. Just as they were about to resort to law and force, she broke down, and they buried her father quickly.

We did not say she was crazy then. We believed she had to do that. We remembered all the young men her father had driven away, and we knew that with nothing left, she would have to cling to that which had robbed her, as people will.

III

She was sick for a long time. When we saw her again, her hair was cut short, making her look like a girl, with a vague resemblance to those angels in colored church windows—sort of tragic and serene.

The town had just let the contracts for paving the sidewalks, and in the summer after her father's death they began to work. The construction company came with niggers and mules and machinery, and a foreman named Homer Barron, a Yankee—a big, dark, ready man, with a big voice and eyes lighter than his face. The little boys would follow in groups to hear him cuss the niggers, and the niggers singing in time to the rise and fall of picks. Pretty soon he knew everybody in town. Whenever you heard a lot of laughing anywhere about the square, Homer Barron would be in the center of the group. Presently we began to see him and Miss Emily on Sunday afternoons driving in the yellow-wheeled buggy and the matched team of bays from the livery stable.

At first we were glad that Miss Emily would have an interest, because the ladies all said, "Of course a Grierson would not think seriously of a Northerner, a day laborer." But there were still others, older people, who said that even grief could not cause a real lady to forget *noblesse oblige*—without calling it *noblesse oblige*. They just said, "Poor Emily. Her kinsfolk should come to her." She had some kin in Alabama; but years ago her father had fallen out with them over the estate of old lady Wyatt, the crazy woman, and there was no communication between the two families. They had not even been represented at the funeral.

And as soon as the old people said, "Poor Emily," the whispering began. "Do you suppose it's really so?" they said to one another. "Of course it is. What else could . . . . . ." This behind their hands; rustling of craned silk and satin behind jalousies closed upon the sun of Sunday afternoon as the thin, swift clop-clop-clop of the matched team passed: "Poor Emily."

She carried her head high enough—even when we believed that she was fallen. It was as if she demanded more than ever the recognition of her dignity as the last Grierson; as if it had wanted that touch of earthiness to reaffirm her imperviousness. Like when she bought the rat poison, the arsenic. That was over a year after they had begun to say "Poor Emily," and while the two female cousins were visiting her.

"I want some poison," she said to the druggist. She was over thirty then, still a slight woman, though thinner than usual, with cold, haughty black eyes in a face the flesh of which was strained across the temples and about the eyesockets as you imagine a lighthouse-keeper's face ought to look. "I want some poison," she said.

"Yes, Miss Emily. What kind? For rats and such? I'd recom—"

"I want the best you have. I don't care what kind."

The druggist named several. "They'll kill anything up to an elephant. But what you want is—"

"Arsenic," Miss Emily said. "Is that a good one?"

"Is . . . . . . arsenic? Yes ma'am. But what you want—"

"I want arsenic."

The druggist looked down at her. She looked back at him, erect, her face like a strained flag. "Why, of course," the druggist said. "If that's what you want. But the law requires you to tell what you are going to use it for."

Miss Emily just stared at him, her head tilted back in order to look him eye for eye, until he looked away and went and got the arsenic and wrapped it up. The Negro delivery boy brought her the package; the druggist didn't come back. When she opened the package at home there was written on the box, under the skull and bones: "For rats."

IV

So the next day we all said, "She will kill herself"; and we said it would be the best thing. When she had first begun to be seen with Homer Barron, we had said, "She will marry him." Then we said, "She will persuade him yet," because Homer himself had remarked—he liked men, and it was known that he drank with the younger men in the Elks' Club—that he was not a marrying man. Later we said, "Poor Emily," behind the jalousies as they passed on Sunday afternoon in the glittering buggy, Miss Emily with her head high and Homer Barron with his hat cocked and a cigar in his teeth, reins and whip in a yellow glove.

Then some of the ladies began to say that it was a disgrace to the town and a bad example to the young people. The men did not want to interfere, but at last the ladies forced the Baptist minister—Miss Emily's people were Episcopal—to call upon her. He would never divulge what happened during that interview, but he refused to go back again. The next Sunday they again drove about the streets, and the following day the minister's wife wrote to Miss Emily's relations in Alabama.

So she had blood-kin under her roof again and we sat back to watch developments. At first nothing happened. Then we were sure that they were to be married. We learned that Miss Emily had been to the jeweler's and ordered a man's toilet set in silver, with the letters H. B. on each piece. Two days later we learned that she had bought a complete outfit of men's clothing, including a nightshirt, and we said, "They are married." We were really glad. We were glad because the two female cousins were even more Grierson than Miss Emily had ever been.

So we were not surprised when Homer Barron—the streets had been finished some time since—was gone. We were a little disappointed that there was not a public blowing-off, but we believed that he had gone on to prepare for Miss Emily's coming, or to give her a chance to get rid of the cousins. (By that time it was a cabal, and we were all Miss Emily's allies to help circumvent the cousins.) Sure enough, after another week they departed. And, as we had expected all along, within three days Homer Barron was back in town. A neighbor saw the Negro man admit him at the kitchen door at dusk one evening.

And that was the last we saw of Homer Barron. And of Miss Emily for some time. The Negro man went in and out with the market basket, but the front door remained closed. Now and then we would see her at a window for a moment, as the men did that night when they sprinkled the lime, but for almost six months she did not appear on the streets. Then we knew that this was to be expected too; as if that quality of her father which had thwarted her woman's life so many times had been too virulent and too furious to die.

When we next saw Miss Emily, she had grown fat and her hair was turning gray. During the next few years it grew grayer and grayer until it attained an even pepper-and-salt iron-gray, when it ceased turning. Up to the day of her death at seventy-four it was still that vigorous iron-gray, like the hair of an active man.

From that time on her front door remained closed, save for a period of six or seven years, when she was about forty, during which she gave lessons in china-painting. She fitted up a studio in one of the downstairs rooms, where the daughters and granddaughters of Colonel Sartoris' contemporaries were sent to her with the same regularity and in the same spirit that they were sent on Sundays with a twenty-five-cent piece for the collection plate. Meanwhile her taxes had been remitted.

Then the newer generation became the backbone and the spirit of the town, and the painting pupils grew up and fell away and did not send their children to her with boxes of color and tedious brushes and pictures cut from the ladies' magazines. The front door closed upon the last one and remained closed for good. When the town got free postal delivery Miss Emily alone refused to let them fasten the metal numbers above her door and attach a mailbox to it. She would not listen to them.

Daily, monthly, yearly we watched the Negro grow grayer and more stooped, going in and out with the market basket. Each December we sent her a tax notice, which would be returned by the post office a week later, unclaimed. Now and then we would see her in one of the downstairs windows—she had evidently shut up the top floor of the house—like the carven torso of an idol in a niche, looking or not looking at us, we could never tell which. Thus she passed from generation to generation—dear, inescapable, impervious, tranquil, and perverse.

And so she died. Fell ill in the house filled with dust and shadows, with only a doddering Negro man to wait on her. We did not even know she was sick; we had long since given up trying to get any information from the Negro. He talked to no one, probably not even to her, for his voice had grown harsh and rusty, as if from disuse.

She died in one of the downstairs rooms, in a heavy walnut bed with a curtain, her gray head propped on a pillow yellow and moldy with age and lack of sunlight.

V

The Negro met the first of the ladies at the front door and let them in, with their hushed, sibilant voices and their quick, curious glances, and then he disappeared. He walked right through the house and out the back and was not seen again.

The two female cousins came at once. They held the funeral on the second day, with the town coming to look at Miss Emily beneath a mass of bought flowers, with the crayon face of her father musing profoundly above the bier and the ladies sibilant and macabre; and the very old men—some in their brushed Confederate uniforms—on the porch and the lawn, talking of Miss Emily as if she had been a contemporary of theirs, believing that they had danced with her and courted her perhaps, confusing time with its mathematical progression, as the old do, to whom all the past is not a diminishing road, but, instead, a huge meadow which no winter ever quite touches, divided from them now by the narrow bottle-neck of the most recent decade of years.

Already we knew that there was one room in that region above stairs which no one had seen in forty years, and which would have to be forced. They waited until Miss Emily was decently in the ground before they opened it.

The violence of breaking down the door seemed to fill this room with pervading dust. A thin, acrid pall as of the tomb seemed to lie everywhere upon this room decked and furnished as for a bridal: upon the valance curtains of faded rose color, upon the rose-shaded lights, upon the dressing table, upon the delicate array of crystal and the man's toilet things backed with tarnished silver, silver so tarnished that the monogram was obscured. Among them lay a collar and tie, as if they had just been removed, which, lifted, left upon the surface a pale crescent in the dust. Upon a chair hung the suit, carefully folded; beneath it the two mute shoes and the discarded socks.

The man himself lay in the bed.

For a long while we just stood there, looking down at the profound and fleshless grin. The body had apparently once lain in the attitude of an embrace, but now the long sleep that outlasts love, that conquers even the grimace of love, had cuckolded him. What was left of him, rotted beneath what was left of the nightshirt, had become inextricable from the bed in which he lay; and upon him and upon the pillow beside him lay that even coating of the patient and biding dust.

Then we noticed that in the second pillow was the indentation of a head. One of us lifted something from it, and leaning forward, that faint and invisible dust dry and acrid in the nostrils, we saw a long strand of iron-gray hair.

1931

Barn Burning

The store in which the Justice of the Peace's court was sitting smelled of cheese. The boy, crouched on his nail keg at the back of the crowded room, knew he smelled cheese, and more: from where he sat he could see the ranked shelves close-packed with the solid, squat, dynamic shapes of tin cans whose labels his stomach read, not from the lettering which meant nothing to his mind but from the scarlet devils and the silver curve of fish—this, the cheese which he knew he smelled and the hermetic meat which his intestines believed he smelled coming in intermittent gusts momentary and brief between the other constant one, the smell and sense just a little of fear because mostly of despair and grief, the old fierce pull of blood. He could not see the table where the Justice sat and before which his father and his father's enemy (*our enemy* he thought in that despair; *ourn! mine and hisn both! He's my father!*) stood, but he could hear them, the two of them that is, because his father had said no word yet:

"But what proof have you, Mr. Harris?"

"I told you. The hog got into my corn. I caught it up and sent it back to him. He had no fence that would hold it. I told him so, warned him. The next time I put the hog in my pen. When he came to get it I gave him enough wire to patch up his pen. The next time I put the hog up and kept it. I rode down to his house and saw the wire I gave him still rolled on to the spool in his yard. I told him he could have the hog when he paid me a dollar pound fee. That evening a nigger came with the dollar and got the hog. He was a strange nigger. He said, 'He say to tell you wood and hay kin burn.' I said, 'What?' 'That whut he say to tell you,' the nigger said. 'Wood and hay kin burn.' That night my barn burned. I got the stock out but I lost the barn."

"Where is the nigger? Have you got him?"

"He was a strange nigger, I tell you. I don't know what became of him."

"But that's not proof. Don't you see that's not proof?"

"Get that boy up here. He knows." For a moment the boy thought too that the man meant his older brother until Harris said, "Not him. The little one. The boy," and, crouching, small for his age, small and wiry like his father, in patched and faded jeans even too small for him, with straight, uncombed, brown hair and eyes gray and wild as storm scud, he saw the men between himself and the table part and become a lane of grim faces, at the end of which he saw the Justice, a shabby, collarless, graying man in spectacles, beckoning him. He felt no floor under his bare feet; he seemed to walk beneath the palpable weight of the grim turning faces. His father, stiff in his black Sunday coat donned not for the trial but for the moving, did not even look at him. *He aims for me to lie,* he thought, again with that frantic grief and despair. *And I will have to do hit.*

"What's your name, boy?" the Justice said.

"Colonel Sartoris Snopes,"[1] the boy whispered.

"Hey?" the Justice said. "Talk louder. Colonel Sartoris? I reckon anybody named for Colonel Sartoris in this country can't help but tell the truth, can they?" The boy said nothing. *Enemy! Enemy!* he thought; for a moment he could not even see, could not see that the Justice's face was kindly nor discern that his voice was troubled when he spoke to the man named Harris: "Do you want me to question this boy?" But he could hear, and during those subsequent long seconds while there was absolutely no sound in the crowded little room save that of quiet and intent breathing it was as if he had swung outward at the end of a grape vine, over a ravine, and at the top of the swing had been caught in a prolonged instant of mesmerized gravity, weightless in time.

"No!" Harris said violently, explosively. "Damnation! Send him out of here!" Now time, the fluid world, rushed beneath him again, the voices coming to him again through the smell of cheese and sealed meat, the fear and despair and the old grief of blood:

"This case is closed. I can't find against you, Snopes, but I can give you advice. Leave this country and don't come back to it."

His father spoke for the first time, his voice cold and harsh, level, without emphasis: "I aim to. I don't figure to stay in a country among people who . . ." he said something unprintable and vile, addressed to no one.

"That'll do," the Justice said. "Take your wagon and get out of this country before dark. Case dismissed."

His father turned, and he followed the stiff black coat, the wiry figure walking a little stiffly from where a Confederate provost's man's musket ball had taken him in the heel on a stolen horse thirty years ago, followed the two backs now, since his older brother had appeared from somewhere in the crowd, no taller than the father but thicker, chewing tobacco steadily, between the two lines of grim-faced men and out of the store and across the worn gallery and down the sagging steps and among the dogs and half-grown boys in the mild May dust, where as he passed a voice hissed:

"Barn burner!"

Again he could not see, whirling; there was a face in a red haze, moonlike, bigger than the full moon, the owner of it half again his size, he leaping in the red haze toward the face, feeling no blow, feeling no shock when his head struck the earth, scrabbling up and leaping again, feeling no blow this time either and tasting no blood, scrabbling up to see the other boy in full flight and himself already leaping into pursuit as his father's hand jerked him back, the harsh, cold voice speaking above him: "Go get in the wagon."

It stood in a grove of locusts and mulberries across the road. His two hulking sisters in their Sunday dresses and his mother and her sister in calico and sunbonnets were already in it, sitting on and among the sorry residue of the dozen and more movings which even the boy could remember—the battered stove, the broken beds and chairs, the clock inlaid with mother-of-pearl, which would not run, stopped at some fourteen minutes past two o'clock of a dead and forgotten day and time, which had been his mother's dowry. She

---

1. The boy is named for Colonel Sartoris, a leading citizen of Jefferson (the fictional town that Faulkner based on his hometown of Oxford, Mississippi) and officer in the Confederate Army. The Snopeses are a poor white family from the same area. Both families appear in other works by Faulkner.

was crying, though when she saw him she drew her sleeve across her face and began to descend from the wagon. "Get back," the father said.

"He's hurt. I got to get some water and wash his . . ."

"Get back in the wagon," his father said. He got in too, over the tail-gate. His father mounted to the seat where the older brother already sat and struck the gaunt mules two savage blows with the peeled willow, but without heat. It was not even sadistic; it was exactly that same quality which in later years would cause his descendants to over-run the engine before putting a motor car into motion, striking and reining back in the same movement. The wagon went on, the store with its quiet crowd of grimly watching men dropped behind; a curve in the road hid it. *Forever* he thought. *Maybe he's done satisfied now, now that he has* . . . stopping himself, not to say it aloud even to himself. His mother's hand touched his shoulder.

"Does hit hurt?" she said.

"Naw," he said. "Hit don't hurt. Lemme be."

"Can't you wipe some of the blood off before hit dries?"

"I'll wash to-night," he said. "Lemme be, I tell you."

The wagon went on. He did not know where they were going. None of them ever did or ever asked, because it was always somewhere, always a house of sorts waiting for them a day or two days or even three days away. Likely his father had already arranged to make a crop on another farm before he . . . Again he had to stop himself. He (the father) always did. There was something about his wolflike independence and even courage when the advantage was at least neutral which impressed strangers, as if they got from his latent ravening ferocity not so much a sense of dependability as a feeling that his ferocious conviction in the rightness of his own actions would be of advantage to all whose interest lay with his.

That night they camped, in a grove of oaks and beeches where a spring ran. The nights were still cool and they had a fire against it, of a rail lifted from a nearby fence and cut into lengths—a small fire, neat, niggard almost, a shrewd fire; such fires were his father's habit and custom always, even in freezing weather. Older, the boy might have remarked this and wondered why not a big one; why should not a man who had not only seen the waste and extravagance of war, but who had in his blood an inherent voracious prodigality with material not his own, have burned everything in sight? Then he might have gone a step farther and thought that that was the reason: that niggard blaze was the living fruit of nights passed during those four years in the woods hiding from all men, blue or gray, with his strings of horses (captured horses, he called them). And older still, he might have divined the true reason: that the element of fire spoke to some deep mainspring of his father's being, as the element of steel or of powder spoke to other men, as the one weapon for the preservation of integrity, else breath were not worth the breathing, and hence to be regarded with respect and used with discretion.

But he did not think this now and he had seen those same niggard blazes all his life. He merely ate his supper beside it and was already half asleep over his iron plate when his father called him, and once more he followed the stiff back, the stiff and ruthless limp, up the slope and on to the starlit road where, turning, he could see his father against the stars but without face or depth—a shape black, flat, and bloodless as though cut from tin in the iron folds of the frockcoat which had not been made for him, the voice harsh like tin and without heat like tin:

"You were fixing to tell them. You would have told him." He didn't answer. His father struck him with the flat of his hand on the side of the head, hard but without heat, exactly as he had struck the two mules at the store, exactly as he would strike either of them with any stick in order to kill a horse fly, his voice still without heat or anger: "You're getting to be a man. You got to learn. You got to learn to stick to your own blood or you ain't going to have any blood to stick to you. Do you think either of them, any man there this morning, would? Don't you know all they wanted was a chance to get at me because they knew I had them beat? Eh?" Later, twenty years later, he was to tell himself, "If I had said they wanted only truth, justice, he would have hit me again." But now he said nothing. He was not crying. He just stood there. "Answer me," his father said.

"Yes," he whispered. His father turned.

"Get on to bed. We'll be there to-morrow."

To-morrow they were there. In the early afternoon the wagon stopped before a paintless two-room house identical almost with the dozen others it had stopped before even in the boy's ten years, and again, as on the other dozen occasions, his mother and aunt got down and began to unload the wagon, although his two sisters and his father and brother had not moved.

"Likely hit ain't fitten for hawgs," one of the sisters said.

"Nevertheless, fit it will and you'll hog it and like it," his father said. "Get out of them chairs and help your Ma unload."

The two sisters got down, big, bovine, in a flutter of cheap ribbons; one of them drew from the jumbled wagon bed a battered lantern, the other a worn broom. His father handed the reins to the older son and began to climb stiffly over the wheel. "When they get unloaded, take the team to the barn and feed them." Then he said, and at first the boy thought he was still speaking to his brother: "Come with me."

"Me?" he said.

"Yes," his father said. "You."

"Abner," his mother said. His father paused and looked back—the harsh level stare beneath the shaggy, graying, irascible brows.

"I reckon I'll have a word with the man that aims to begin to-morrow owning me body and soul for the next eight months."

They went back up the road. A week ago—or before last night, that is— he would have asked where they were going, but not now. His father had struck him before last night but never before had he paused afterward to explain why; it was as if the blow and the following calm, outrageous voice still rang, repercussed, divulging nothing to him save the terrible handicap of being young, the light weight of his few years, just heavy enough to prevent his soaring free of the world as it seemed to be ordered but not heavy enough to keep him footed solid in it, to resist it and try to change the course of its events.

Presently he could see the grove of oaks and cedars and the other flowering trees and shrubs where the house would be, though not the house yet. They walked beside a fence massed with honeysuckle and Cherokee roses and came to a gate swinging open between two brick pillars, and now, beyond a sweep of drive, he saw the house for the first time and at that instant he forgot his father and the terror and despair both, and even when he remembered his father again (who had not stopped) the terror and despair did not return. Because, for all the twelve movings, they had sojourned until now in a poor country, a land of small farms and fields and houses, and he had never seen a house like this before. *Hit's big as a courthouse* he thought quietly, with a surge of peace and joy whose reason he could not have thought into words, being too young for that: *They are safe from him. People whose lives are a part of this peace and dignity are beyond his touch, he no more to them than a buzzing wasp: capable of stinging for a little moment but that's all; the spell of this peace and dignity rendering even the barns and stable and cribs which belong to it impervious to the puny flames he might contrive . . .* this, the peace and joy, ebbing for an instant as he looked again at the stiff black back, the stiff and implacable limp of the figure which was not dwarfed by the house, for the reason that it had never looked big anywhere and which now, against the serene columned backdrop, had more than ever that impervious quality of something cut ruthlessly from tin, depthless, as though, sidewise to the sun, it would cast no shadow. Watching him, the boy remarked the absolutely undeviating course which his father held and saw the stiff foot come squarely down in a pile of fresh droppings where a horse had stood in the drive and which his father could have avoided by a simple change of stride. But it ebbed only for a moment, though he could not have thought this into words either, walking on in the spell of the house, which he could even want but without envy, without sorrow, certainly never with that ravening and jealous rage which unknown to him walked in the ironlike black coat before him: *Maybe he will feel it too. Maybe it will even change him now from what maybe he couldn't help but be.*

They crossed the portico. Now he could hear his father's stiff foot as it came down on the boards with clocklike finality, a sound out of all proportion to the displacement of the body it bore and which was not dwarfed either by the white door before it, as though it had attained to a sort of vicious and ravening minimum not to be dwarfed by anything—the flat, wide, black hat, the formal coat of broadcloth which had once been black but which had now that friction-glazed greenish cast of the bodies of old house flies, the lifted sleeve which was too large, the lifted hand like a curled claw. The door opened so promptly that the boy knew the Negro must have been watching them all the time, an old man with neat grizzled hair, in a linen jacket, who stood barring the door with his body, saying, "Wipe yo foots, white man, fo you come in here. Major ain't home nohow."

"Get out of my way, nigger," his father said, without heat too, flinging the door back and the Negro also and entering, his hat still on his head. And now the boy saw the prints of the stiff foot on the doorjamb and saw them appear on the pale rug behind the machinelike deliberation of the foot which seemed to bear (or transmit) twice the weight which the body compassed. The Negro was shouting "Miss Lula! Miss Lula!" somewhere behind them, then the boy, deluged as though by a warm wave by a suave turn of carpeted stair and a pendant glitter of chandeliers and a mute gleam of gold frames, heard the swift feet and saw her too, a lady—perhaps he had never seen her like before either—in a gray, smooth gown with lace at the throat and an apron tied at the waist and the sleeves turned back, wiping cake or biscuit dough from her hands with a towel as she came up the hall, looking not at his father at all but at the tracks on the blond rug with an expression of incredulous amazement.

"I tried," the Negro cried. "I tole him to . . ."

"Will you please go away?" she said in a shaking voice. "Major de Spain is not at home. Will you please go away?"

His father had not spoken again. He did not speak again. He did not even look at her. He just stood stiff in the center of the rug, in his hat, the shaggy iron-gray brows twitching slightly above the pebble-colored eyes as he appeared to examine the house with brief deliberation. Then with the same deliberation he turned; the boy watched him pivot on the good leg and saw the stiff foot drag round the arc of the turning, leaving a final long and fading smear. His father never looked at it, he never once looked down at the rug. The Negro held the door. It closed behind them, upon the hysteric and indistinguishable woman-wail. His father stopped at the top of the steps and scraped his boot clean on the edge of it. At the gate he stopped again. He stood for a moment, planted stiffly on the stiff foot, looking back at the house. "Pretty and white, ain't it?" he said. "That's sweat. Nigger sweat. Maybe it ain't white enough yet to suit him. Maybe he wants to mix some white sweat with it."

Two hours later the boy was chopping wood behind the house within which his mother and aunt and the two sisters (the mother and aunt, not the two girls, he knew that; even at this distance and muffled by walls the flat loud voices of the two girls emanated an incorrigible idle inertia) were setting up the stove to prepare a meal, when he heard the hooves and saw the linen-clad man on a fine sorrel mare, whom he recognized even before he saw the rolled rug in front of the Negro youth following on a fat bay carriage horse—a suffused, angry face vanishing, still at full gallop, beyond the corner of the house where his father and brother were sitting in the two tilted chairs; and a moment later, almost before he could have put the axe down, he heard the hooves again and watched the sorrel mare go back out of the yard, already galloping again. Then his father began to shout one of the sisters' names, who presently emerged backward from the kitchen door dragging the rolled rug along the ground by one end while the other sister walked behind it.

"If you ain't going to tote, go on and set up the wash pot," the first said.

"You, Sarty!" the second shouted. "Set up the wash pot!" His father appeared at the door, framed against that shabbiness, as he had been against that other bland perfection, impervious to either, the mother's anxious face at his shoulder.

"Go on," the father said. "Pick it up." The two sisters stooped, broad, lethargic; stooping, they presented an incredible expanse of pale cloth and a flutter of tawdry ribbons.

"If I thought enough of a rug to have to git hit all the way from France I wouldn't keep hit where folks coming in would have to tromp on hit," the first said. They raised the rug.

"Abner," the mother said. "Let me do it."

"You go back and git dinner," his father said. "I'll tend to this."

From the woodpile through the rest of the afternoon the boy watched them, the rug spread flat in the dust beside the bubbling wash-pot, the two sisters stooping over it with that profound and lethargic reluctance, while the father stood over them in turn, implacable and grim, driving them though never raising his voice again. He could smell the harsh homemade lye they were using; he saw his mother come to the door once and look toward them with an expression not anxious now but very like despair; he saw his father turn, and he fell to with the axe and saw from the corner of his eye his father raise from the ground a flattish fragment of field stone and examine it and return to the pot, and this time his mother actually spoke: "Abner. Abner. Please don't. Please, Abner."

Then he was done too. It was dusk; the whippoorwills had already begun. He could smell coffee from the room where they would presently eat the cold food remaining from the mid-afternoon meal, though when he entered the house he realized they were having coffee again probably because there was a fire on the hearth, before which the rug now lay spread over the backs of the two chairs. The tracks of his father's foot were gone. Where they had been were now long, water-cloudy scoriations resembling the sporadic course of a lilliputian mowing machine.

It still hung there while they ate the cold food and then went to bed, scattered without order or claim up and down the two rooms, his mother in one bed, where his father would later lie, the older brother in the other, himself, the aunt, and the two sisters on pallets on the floor. But his father was not in bed yet. The last thing the boy remembered was the depthless, harsh silhouette of the hat and coat bending over the rug and it seemed to him that he had not even closed his eyes when the silhouette was standing over him, the fire almost dead behind it, the stiff foot prodding him awake. "Catch up the mule," his father said.

When he returned with the mule his father was standing in the black door, the rolled rug over his shoulder. "Ain't you going to ride?" he said.

"No. Give me your foot."

He bent his knee into his father's hand, the wiry, surprising power flowed smoothly, rising, he rising with it, on to the mule's bare back (they had owned a saddle once; the boy could remember it though not when or where) and with the same effortlessness his father swung the rug up in front of him. Now in the starlight they retraced the afternoon's path, up the dusty road rife with honeysuckle, through the gate and up the black tunnel of the drive to the lightless house, where he sat on the mule and felt the rough warp of the rug drag across his thighs and vanish.

"Don't you want me to help?" he whispered. His father did not answer and now he heard again that stiff foot striking the hollow portico with that wooden and clocklike deliberation, that outrageous overstatement of the weight it carried. The rug, hunched, not flung (the boy could tell that even in the darkness) from his father's shoulder, struck the angle of wall and floor with a sound unbelievably loud, thunderous, then the foot again, unhurried and enormous; a light came on in the house and the boy sat, tense, breathing steadily and quietly and just a little fast, though the foot itself did not increase its beat at all, descending the steps now; now the boy could see him.

"Don't you want to ride now?" he whispered. "We kin both ride now," the light within the house altering now, flaring up and sinking. *He's coming down the stairs now,* he thought. He had already ridden the mule up beside the horse block; presently his father was up behind him and he doubled the reins over and slashed the mule across the neck, but before the animal could begin to trot the hard, thin arm came round him, the hard, knotted hand jerking the mule back to a walk.

In the first red rays of the sun they were in the lot, putting plow gear on the mules. This time the sorrel mare was in the lot before he heard it at all, the rider collarless and even bareheaded, trembling, speaking in a shaking voice as the woman in the house had done, his father merely looking up once before stooping again to the hame he was buckling, so that the man on the mare spoke to his stooping back:

"You must realize you have ruined that rug. Wasn't there anybody here, any of your women . . ." he ceased, shaking, the boy watching him, the older brother leaning now in the stable door, chewing, blinking slowly and steadily at nothing apparently. "It cost a hundred dollars. But you never had a hundred dollars. You never will. So I'm going to charge you twenty bushels of corn against your crop. I'll add it in your contract and when you come to the commissary you can sign it. That won't keep Mrs. de Spain quiet but maybe it will teach you to wipe your feet off before you enter her house again."

Then he was gone. The boy looked at his father, who still had not spoken or even looked up again, who was now adjusting the logger-head in the hame.

"Pap," he said. His father looked at him—the inscrutable face, the shaggy brows beneath which the gray eyes glinted coldly. Suddenly the boy went toward him, fast, stopping as suddenly. "You done the best you could!" he cried. "If he wanted hit done different why didn't he wait and tell you how? He won't git no twenty bushels! He won't git none! We'll gether hit and hide hit! I kin watch . . ."

"Did you put the cutter back in that straight stock like I told you?"

"No, sir," he said.

"Then go do it."

That was Wednesday. During the rest of that week he worked steadily, at what was within his scope and some which was beyond it, with an industry that did not need to be driven nor even commanded twice; he had this from his mother, with the difference that some at least of what he did he liked to do, such as splitting wood with the half-size axe which his mother and aunt had earned, or saved money somehow, to present him with at Christmas. In company with the two older women (and on one afternoon, even one of the sisters), he built pens for the shoat and the cow which were a part of his father's contract with the landlord, and one afternoon, his father being absent, gone somewhere on one of the mules, he went to the field.

They were running a middle buster now, his brother holding the plow straight while he handled the reins, and walking beside the straining mule, the rich black soil shearing cool and damp against his bare ankles, he thought *Maybe this is the end of it. Maybe even that twenty bushels that seems hard to have to pay for just a rug will be a cheap price for him to stop forever and always from being what he used to be*; thinking, dreaming now, so that his brother had to speak sharply to him to mind the mule: *Maybe he even won't collect the twenty bushels. Maybe it will all add up and balance and vanish—corn, rug, fire; the terror and grief, the being pulled two ways like between two teams of horses—gone, done with for ever and ever.*

Then it was Saturday; he looked up from beneath the mule he was harnessing and saw his father in the black coat and hat. "Not that," his father said. "The wagon gear." And then, two hours later, sitting in the wagon bed behind his father and brother on the seat, the wagon accomplished a final curve, and he saw the weathered paintless store with its tattered tobacco- and patent-medicine posters and the tethered wagons and saddle animals below the gallery. He mounted the gnawed steps behind his father and brother, and there again was the lane of quiet, watching faces for the three of them to walk through. He saw the man in spectacles sitting at the plank table and he did not need to be told this was a Justice of the Peace; he sent one glare of fierce, exultant, partisan defiance at the man in collar and cravat now, whom he had seen but twice before in his life, and that on a galloping horse, who now wore on his face an expression not of rage but of amazed unbelief which the boy could not have known was at the incredible circumstance of being sued by one of his own tenants, and came and stood against his father and cried at the Justice: "He ain't done it! He ain't burnt . . ."

"Go back to the wagon," his father said.

"Burnt?" the Justice said. "Do I understand this rug was burned too?"

"Does anybody here claim it was?" his father said. "Go back to the wagon." But he did not, he merely retreated to the rear of the room, crowded as that other had been, but not to sit down this time, instead, to stand pressing among the motionless bodies, listening to the voices:

"And you claim twenty bushels of corn is too high for the damage you did to the rug?"

"He brought the rug to me and said he wanted the tracks washed out of it. I washed the tracks out and took the rug back to him."

"But you didn't carry the rug back to him in the same condition it was in before you made the tracks on it."

His father did not answer, and now for perhaps half a minute there was no sound at all save that of breathing, the faint, steady suspiration of complete and intent listening.

"You decline to answer that, Mr. Snopes?" Again his father did not answer. "I'm going to find against you, Mr. Snopes. I'm going to find that you were responsible for the injury to Major de Spain's rug and hold you liable for it. But twenty bushels of corn seems a little high for a man in your circumstances to have to pay. Major de Spain claims it cost a hundred dollars. October corn will be worth about fifty cents. I figure that if Major de Spain can stand a ninety-five-dollar loss on something he paid cash for, you can stand a five-dollar loss you haven't earned yet. I hold you in damages to Major de Spain to the amount of ten bushels of corn over and above your contract with him, to be paid to him out of your crop at gathering time. Court adjourned."

It had taken no time hardly, the morning was but half begun. He thought they would return home and perhaps back to the field, since they were late, far behind all other farmers. But instead his father passed on behind the wagon, merely indicating with his hand for the older brother to follow with it, and crossed the road toward the blacksmith shop opposite, pressing on after his father, overtaking him, speaking, whispering up at the harsh, calm face beneath the weathered hat: "He won't git no ten bushels neither. He won't git one. We'll . . ." until his father glanced for an instant down at him, the face absolutely calm, the grizzled eyebrows tangled above the cold eyes, the voice almost pleasant, almost gentle:

"You think so? Well, we'll wait till October anyway."

The matter of the wagon—the setting of a spoke or two and the tightening of the tires—did not take long either, the business of the tires accomplished by driving the wagon into the spring branch behind the shop and letting it stand there, the mules nuzzling into the water from time to time, and the boy on the seat with the idle reins, looking up the slope and through the sooty tunnel of the shed where the slow hammer rang and where his father sat on an upended cypress bolt, easily, either talking or listening, still sitting there when the boy brought the dripping wagon up out of the branch and halted it before the door.

"Take them on to the shade and hitch," his father said. He did so and returned. His father and the smith and a third man squatting on his heels inside the door were talking, about crops and animals; the boy, squatting too in the ammoniac dust and hoof-parings and scales of rust, heard his father tell a long and unhurried story out of the time before the birth of the older brother even when he had been a professional horsetrader. And then his father came up beside him where he stood before a tattered last year's circus poster on the other side of the store, gazing rapt and quiet at the scarlet horses, the incredible poisings and convolutions of tulle and tights and the painted leers of comedians, and said "It's time to eat."

But not at home. Squatting beside his brother against the front wall, he watched his father emerge from the store and produce from a paper sack a segment of cheese and divide it carefully and deliberately into three with his pocket knife and produce crackers from the same sack. They all three squatted on the gallery and ate, slowly, without talking; then in the store again, they drank from a tin dipper tepid water smelling of the cedar bucket and of living beech trees. And still they did not go home. It was a horse lot this time, a tall rail fence upon and along which men stood and sat and out of which one by one horses were led, to be walked and trotted and then cantered back and forth along the road while the slow swapping and buying went on and the sun began to slant westward, they—the three of them—watching and listening, the older brother with his muddy eyes and his steady, inevitable tobacco, the father commenting now and then on certain of the animals, to no one in particular.

It was after sundown when they reached home. They ate supper by lamplight, then, sitting on the doorstep, the boy watched the night fully accomplish, listening to the whippoorwills and the frogs, when he heard his mother's voice: "Abner! No! No! Oh, God. Oh, God. Abner!" and he rose, whirled, and saw the altered light through the door where a candle stub now burned in a bottle neck on the table and his father, still in the hat and coat, at once formal and burlesque as though dressed carefully for some shabby and ceremonial violence, emptying the reservoir of the lamp back into the five-gallon kerosene can from which it had been filled, while the mother tugged at his arm until he shifted the lamp to the other hand and flung her back, not savagely or viciously, just hard, into the wall, her hands flung out against the wall for balance, her mouth open and in her face the same quality of hopeless despair as had been in her voice. Then his father saw him standing in the door.

"Go to the barn and get that can of oil we were oiling the wagon with," he said. The boy did not move. Then he could speak.

"What . . ." he cried. "What are you . . ."

"Go get that oil," his father said. "Go."

Then he was moving, running, outside the house, toward the stable: this is the old habit, the old blood which he had not been permitted to choose for himself, which had been bequeathed him willy nilly and which had run for so long (and who knew where, battening on what of outrage and savagery and lust) before it came to him. *I could keep on,* he thought. *I could run on and on and never look back, never need to see his face again. Only I can't. I can't,* the rusted can in his hand now, the liquid sploshing in it as he ran back to the house and into it, into the sound of his mother's weeping in the next room, and handed the can to his father.

"Ain't you going to even send a nigger?" he cried. "At least you sent a nigger before!"

This time his father didn't strike him. The hand came even faster than the blow had, the same hand which had set the can on the table with almost excruciating care flashing from the can toward him too quick for him to follow it, gripping him by the back of his shirt and on to tiptoe before he had seen it quit the can, the face stooping at him in breathless and frozen ferocity, the cold, dead voice speaking over him to the older brother who leaned against the table, chewing with that steady, curious, sidewise motion of cows:

"Empty the can into the big one and go on. I'll catch up with you."

"Better tie him up to the bedpost," the brother said.

"Do like I told you," the father said. Then the boy was moving, his bunched shirt and the hard, bony hand between his shoulder-blades, his toes just touching the floor, across the room and into the other one, past the sisters sitting with spread heavy thighs in the two chairs over the cold hearth, and to where his mother and aunt sat side by side on the bed, the aunt's arms about his mother's shoulders.

"Hold him," the father said. The aunt made a startled movement. "Not you," the father said. "Lennie. Take hold of him. I want to see you do it." His mother took him by the wrist. "You'll hold him better than that. If he gets loose don't you know what he is going to do? He will go up yonder." He jerked his head toward the road. "Maybe I'd better tie him."

"I'll hold him," his mother whispered.

"See you do then." Then his father was gone, the stiff foot heavy and measured upon the boards, ceasing at last.

Then he began to struggle. His mother caught him in both arms, he jerking and wrenching at them. He would be stronger in the end, he knew that. But he had no time to wait for it. "Lemme go!" he cried. "I don't want to have to hit you!"

"Let him go!" the aunt said. "If he don't go, before God, I am going there myself!"

"Don't you see I can't!" his mother cried. "Sarty! Sarty! No! No! Help me, Lizzie!"

Then he was free. His aunt grasped at him but it was too late. He whirled, running, his mother stumbled forward on to her knees behind him, crying to the nearer sister: "Catch him, Net! Catch him!" But that was too late too, the sister (the sisters were twins, born at the same time, yet either of them now gave the impression of being, encompassing as much living meat and volume and weight as any other two of the family) not yet having begun to rise from the chair, her head, face, alone merely turned, presenting to him in the flying instant an astonishing expanse of young female features untroubled by any surprise even, wearing only an expression of bovine interest. Then he was out of the room, out of the house, in the mild dust of the starlit road and the heavy rifeness of honeysuckle, the pale ribbon unspooling with terrific slowness under his running feet, reaching the gate at last and turning in, running, his heart and lungs drumming, on up the drive toward the lighted house, the lighted door. He did not knock, he burst in, sobbing for breath, incapable for the moment of speech; he saw the astonished face of the Negro in the linen jacket without knowing when the Negro had appeared.

"De Spain!" he cried, panted. "Where's . . ." then he saw the white man too emerging from a white door down the hall. "Barn!" he cried. "Barn!"

"What?" the white man said. "Barn?"

"Yes!" the boy cried. "Barn!"

"Catch him!" the white man shouted.

But it was too late this time too. The Negro grasped his shirt, but the entire sleeve, rotten with washing, carried away, and he was out that door too and in the drive again, and had actually never ceased to run even while he was screaming into the white man's face.

Behind him the white man was shouting, "My horse! Fetch my horse!" and he thought for an instant of cutting across the park and climbing the fence into the road, but he did not know the park nor how high the vine-massed fence might be and he dared not risk it. So he ran on down the drive, blood and breath roaring; presently he was in the road again though he could not see it. He could not hear either: the galloping mare was almost upon him before he heard her, and even then he held his course, as if the very urgency of his wild grief and need must in a moment more find him wings, waiting until the ultimate instant to hurl himself aside and into the weed-choked roadside ditch as the horse thundered past and on, for an instant in furious silhouette against the stars, the tranquil early summer night sky which, even before the shape of the horse and rider vanished, stained abruptly and violently upward: a long, swirling roar incredible and soundless, blotting the stars, and he springing up and into the road again, running again, knowing it was too late yet still running even after he heard the shot and, an instant later, two shots, pausing now without knowing he had ceased to run, crying "Pap! Pap!", running again before he knew he had begun to run, stumbling, tripping over something and scrabbling up again without ceasing to run, looking backward over his shoulder at the glare as he got up, running on among the invisible trees, panting, sobbing, "Father! Father!"

At midnight he was sitting on the crest of a hill. He did not know it was midnight and he did not know how far he had come. But there was no glare behind him now and he sat now, his back toward what he had called home for four days anyhow, his face toward the dark woods which he would enter when breath was strong again, small, shaking steadily in the chill darkness, hugging himself into the remainder of his thin, rotten shirt, the grief and despair now no longer terror and fear but just grief and despair. *Father. My father,* he thought. "He was brave!" he cried suddenly, aloud but not loud, no more than a whisper: "He was! He was in the war! He was in Colonel Sartoris' cav'ry!" not knowing that his father had gone to that war a private in the fine old European sense, wearing no uniform, admitting the authority of and giving fidelity to no man or army or flag, going to war as Malbrouck[2] himself did: for booty—it meant nothing and less than nothing to him if it were enemy booty or his own.

The slow constellations wheeled on. It would be dawn and then sun-up after a while and he would be hungry. But that would be to-morrow and now he was only cold, and walking would cure that. His breathing was easier now and he decided to get up and go on, and then he found that he had been asleep because he knew it was almost dawn, the night almost over. He could tell that from the whippoorwills. They were everywhere now among the dark trees below him, constant and inflectioned and ceaseless, so that, as

2. Figure in an 18th-century French ballad, "Malbrouck Has Gone to the War," popularly identified with John Churchill, first duke of Marlborough (1650–1722), who rose through the ranks from private to become a famous commander. Despite his military genius, he was often accused of greed and disloyalty.

the instant for giving over to the day birds drew nearer and nearer, there was no interval at all between them. He got up. He was a little stiff, but walking would cure that too as it would the cold, and soon there would be the sun. He went on down the hill, toward the dark woods within which the liquid silver voices of the birds called unceasing—the rapid and urgent beating of the urgent and quiring heart of the late spring night. He did not look back.

1938

HART CRANE
1899–1932

Before his suicide at the age of thirty-two, Hart Crane led a life of extremes: he wrote poetry of frequently ecstatic intensity, drank uncontrollably, had bitterly ambivalent relations with his quarreling parents; he relished the comparative erotic freedom of post–World War I Greenwich Village while enduring his literary friends' disapproval of his homosexuality. Born and raised in Ohio, Crane went to New York City in 1917, ostensibly to prepare for college but in fact to investigate the possibility of a literary career. Returning to Cleveland for four years (1919–23), he tried unsuccessfully to enter business as a means of financing an after-hours literary life. During these years he read widely and developed a large circle of intellectual friends and correspondents. He also published some of the poems that made his early reputation: "My Grandmother's Love Letters" in 1920, "Chaplinesque" in 1921, and "For the Marriage of Faustus and Helen" in 1922. He also began work on the love sequence *Voyages.* By 1923, believing himself ready to succeed as a writer, he moved back to New York City.

His most productive years came between 1923 and 1927. He completed *Voyages* in 1924, published his first collection, *White Buildings,* in 1926, and composed ten of the fifteen poems that were to make up *The Bridge* in 1926. He held occasional jobs, but received most of his support from his parents, friends, and above all from the patronage of a banker, Otto Kahn. Crane defined himself as a follower of Walt Whitman in the visionary, prophetic, affirmative American tradition, aiming at nothing less than to master the techniques of modernism while reversing its direction— to make it positive, celebratory, and deeply meshed with contemporary American life without sacrificing technical complexity or richness. For him as for the somewhat older William Carlos Williams, Eliot's *The Waste Land* was both threat and model. That poem could become an "absolute impasse," he wrote, unless one could "go *through* it to a different goal," leaving its negations behind. This was the task he attempted in *The Bridge.*

Crane's practice centered on metaphor—the device that, in his view, represented the difference between poetry and expository prose. He believed that metaphor had preceded logic in the development of human thought and that it still remained the primary mode in which human knowledge was acquired and through which experience was connected to mind. The center of *The Bridge,* for example, is the Brooklyn Bridge—a tangible object transformed metaphorically into the sign of connection, technology, America, history, and the future. The poem, published in 1930, was not particularly well received by the critics; this was a great disappointment to Crane, and even though *Poetry* magazine awarded it a prize and the Guggenheim Foundation gave him a fellowship in the same year, he was perplexed about his future. In Mexico he completed work for a third book, *Key West,* but on the return trip to New York City he jumped overboard and drowned.

The Bridge is a visionary poem made up of fifteen individual sections of varying lengths. It encapsulates a heroic quest, at once personal and epic, to find and enunciate "America." Like Walt Whitman's "Song of the Open Road," which also focused on a symbol of expansion and dynamism, *The Bridge* moves westward in imagination from Brooklyn to California. It also goes back into the American past, dwelling on historical or legendary figures such as Columbus, Pocahontas, and Rip Van Winkle. It moves upward under the guidance of Whitman; down in "The Tunnel" it meets the wandering spirit of Edgar Allan Poe. The material bridge stands at the center of all this motion and stands, finally, for the poem and poetry itself. The separate lyrics making up *The Bridge* are arranged like music, with recurring, modulated themes rather than a narrative or an expository line. As in most modernist poems, the verse is open and varied, the syntax complicated and often ambiguous, the references often dependent on a personal, sometimes inaccessible train of thought. Like his model Whitman, Crane wrote from the paradoxical, conflicted position of the outsider claiming to speak from and for the very center of America.

The text of the poems included here is that of *Complete Poems of Hart Crane,* edited by Marc Simon (1993).

Chaplinesque[1]

We make our meek adjustments,
Contented with such random consolations
As the wind deposits
In slithered and too ample pockets.

For we can still love the world, who find   5
A famished kitten on the step, and know
Recesses for it from the fury of the street,
Or warm torn elbow coverts.

We will sidestep, and to the final smirk
Dally the doom of that inevitable thumb   10
That slowly chafes its puckered index toward us,
Facing the dull squint with what innocence
And what surprise!

And yet these fine collapses are not lies
More than the pirouettes of any pliant cane;   15
Our obsequies[2] are, in a way, no enterprise.
We can evade you, and all else but the heart:
What blame to us if the heart live on.

The game enforces smirks; but we have seen
The moon in lonely alleys make   20
A grail of laughter of an empty ash can,

---

1. Crane wrote of seeing Charlie Chaplin's film *The Kid* (1921) and said that he aimed "to put in words some of the Chaplin pantomime, so beautiful, and so full of eloquence, and so modern." The film "made me feel myself, as a poet, as being 'in the same boat' with him," Crane wrote.
2. In the double sense of "funeral rites" and "obsequiousness."

And through all sound of gaiety and quest
Have heard a kitten in the wilderness.

1921, 1926

At Melville's Tomb[1]

Often beneath the wave, wide from this ledge
The dice of drowned men's bones he saw bequeath
An embassy. Their numbers as he watched,
Beat on the dusty shore and were obscured.[2]
And wrecks passed without sound of bells,   5
The calyx of death's bounty giving back
A scattered chapter, livid hieroglyph,
The portent wound in corridors of shells.[3]

Then in the circuit calm of one vast coil,
Its lashings charmed and malice reconciled,   10
Frosted eyes there were that lifted altars;[4]
And silent answers crept across the stars.

Compass, quadrant and sextant contrive
No farther tides[5] . . . High in the azure steeps
Monody shall not wake the mariner.   15
This fabulous shadow only the sea keeps.

1926

1. This poem was published in *Poetry* magazine only after Crane provided the editor, Harriet Monroe, with a detailed explanation of its images. His letter and Monroe's inquiries and comments were published with the poem. Crane's detailed comments in the letter are incorporated in the notes to the poem. Herman Melville (1819–1891), American author.
2. "Dice bequeath an embassy, in the first place, by being ground (in this connection only, of course) in little cubes from the bones of drowned men by the action of the sea, and are finally thrown up on the sand, having 'numbers' but no identification. These being the bones of dead men who never completed their voyage, it seems legitimate to refer to them as the only surviving evidence of certain messages undelivered, mute evidence of certain things. . . . Dice as a symbol of chance and circumstance is also implied" [Crane's note].
3. "This calyx refers in a double ironic sense both to a cornucopia and the vortex made by a sinking vessel. As soon as the water has closed over a ship this whirlpool sends up broken spars, wreckage, etc., which can be alluded to as livid *hieroglyphs*, making a *scattered chapter* so far as any complete record of the recent ship and crew is concerned.

In fact, about as much definite knowledge might come from all this as anyone might gain from the roar of his own veins, which is easily heard (haven't you ever done it?) by holding a shell close to one's ear" [Crane's note]. A calyx is a whorl of leaves forming the outer casing of the bud of a plant.
4. "Refers simply to a conviction that a man, not knowing perhaps a definite god yet being endowed with a reverence for deity—such a man naturally postulates a deity somehow, and the altar of that deity by the very *action* of the eyes *lifted* in searching" [Crane's note].
5. "Hasn't it often occurred that instruments originally invented for record and computation have inadvertently so extended the concepts of the entity they were invented to measure (concepts of space, etc.) in the mind and imagination that employed them, that they may metaphorically be said to have extended the original boundaries of the entity measured? This little bit of 'relativity' ought not to be discredited in poetry now that scientists are proceeding to measure the universe on principles of pure *ratio*, quite as metaphorical, so far as previous standards of scientific methods extended, as some of the axioms in *Job*" [Crane's note].

ERNEST HEMINGWAY
1899–1961

The narrator in Ernest Hemingway's *A Farewell to Arms,* reflecting on his war experiences, observes at one point, "I was always embarrassed by the words sacred, glorious, and sacrifice and the expression in vain. . . . I had seen nothing sacred, and the things that were glorious had no glory and the sacrifices were like the stockyards at Chicago if nothing was done with the meat except to bury it. There were many words that you could not stand to hear." Hemingway's aim and achievement as a novelist and short-story writer were to convey his concerns in a prose style built from what was left after eliminating all the words one "could not stand to hear." As flamboyant in his personal style as he was severe in his writing, Hemingway became an international celebrity after the publication in 1926 of his first novel, *The Sun Also Rises.* At the time of his death, he was probably the most famous writer in the world.

He was born and raised in Oak Park, Illinois, one of six children. His mother was a music teacher, director of the church choir, and a lover of high culture who had contemplated a career as an opera singer. His father was a successful physician, prone to depression, who enjoyed hunting, fishing, and cooking and who shared in household responsibilities more than most men of his era. The family spent summers at their cottage in northern Michigan, where many of Hemingway's stories are set. After high school, Hemingway took a job on the *Kansas City Star.* When the United States entered the war in 1917, Hemingway was eager to go. An eye problem barred him from the army, so he joined the ambulance corps. Within three weeks he was wounded by shrapnel. After six months in the hospital Hemingway went home as a decorated hero: when wounded, he had carried a comrade more badly hurt than he to safety. He found readjustment difficult and became increasingly estranged from his family, especially his mother. Years later, when his father committed suicide, Hemingway blamed his mother for that death.

In 1920 he married Hadley Richardson and went to Paris. Supported partly by her money and partly by his journalism, Hemingway worked at becoming a writer. He came to know Gertrude Stein, Sherwood Anderson, Ezra Pound, F. Scott Fitzgerald, and others in the large community of expatriate artistic and literary Americans. Besides reading his manuscripts and advising him, Fitzgerald and Anderson, better known than he, used their influence to get his book of short stories *In Our Time* published in the United States in 1925. In this book, stories about the adolescent Nick Adams as he grows up in northern Michigan alternate with very brief, powerful vignettes of war and crime.

In 1926 his novel *The Sun Also Rises* appeared; it presents the stripped-down "Hemingway style" at its finest. "I always try to write on the principle of the iceberg," he told an interviewer. "There is seven-eighths of it under water for every part that shows." Narrated by Jake Barnes, whose World War I wounds have left him sexually impotent, *The Sun Also Rises* depicts Jake's efforts to live according to a self-conscious code of dignity, of "grace under pressure," in the midst of a circle of self-seeking American and English expatriates in Paris. He finds an ideal in the rich tradition of Spanish peasant life, especially as epitomized in bullfighting and the bullfighter. *The Sun Also Rises* was directly responsible for a surge of American tourism to Pamplona, Spain, where the novel's bullfights are set.

In 1927 Hemingway brought out his second collection of stories, *Men without Women.* Adapting journalistic techniques in telegraphic prose that minimized narrator commentary and depended heavily on uncontextualized dialogue, these stories developed a modern, speeded-up, streamlined style that has been endlessly imitated. His second novel, *A Farewell to Arms,* appeared in 1929. It described a romance between an American army officer, Frederic Henry, and a British nurse, Catherine Barkley. The two run away from war, trying to make "a separate peace," but their idyll is shattered when Catherine dies in childbirth. Hemingway's work has been much criticized for its depictions of women. The wholly good Catherine lives for Frederick Henry alone; and Maria, in his Spanish Civil War novel (*For Whom the Bell Tolls,* 1940), is a fantasy figure of total submissiveness. Characters like Brett Ashley in *The Sun Also Rises* and Pilar in *For Whom the Bell Tolls,* however, are strong, complex figures. Overall, Hemingway identified the rapid change in women's status after World War I and the general blurring of sex roles that accompanied the new sexual freedom as aspects of modernity that men were simultaneously attracted to and found hard to deal with. More recently, especially in light of the themes of some of his posthumously published writings, critics have begun to re-interpret Hemingway's work as preoccupied with the cultural and psychological meanings of masculinity in a way that bespeaks considerable sexual ambivalence.

As Hemingway aged, his interest in exclusively masculine forms of self-assertion and self-definition became more pronounced. War, hunting, and similar pursuits that he had used at first to show men manifesting dignity in the face of certain defeat increasingly became depicted (in his life as well as his writing) as occasions for competitive masculine display and triumph. Soon after the publication of *The Sun Also Rises,* his first marriage broke up; in all he was married four times. In the 1930s and 1940s he adopted the style of life of a celebrity.

In the 1930s two new themes entered his work. One was the decade's ever-present theme of politics. A political loner distrustful of all ideological abstractions, Hemingway was nevertheless drawn into antifascist politics by the Spanish Civil War. In *To Have and Have Not* (1937), the earliest of his political novels, the good characters are working-class people and the antagonists are idle rich. *For Whom the Bell Tolls* draws on Hemingway's experiences in Spain as a war correspondent, celebrating both the peasant antifascists and the Americans who fought on their behalf. Hemingway's opposition to fascism did not, however, keep him from viewing the pro-Loyalist communists, who were also active in the Spanish Civil War, with considerable skepticism. His one play, *The Fifth Column*—which was printed along with his collected stories in 1938 and staged in 1940—specifically blames the communists for betraying the cause.

The second new theme, obviously autobiographical, was that of the successful writer losing his talent in an atmosphere of success, celebrity, and wealth. This is clearly expressed in "The Snows of Kilimanjaro," reprinted here, which also contains passages of his most lyrical and evocative writing as the writer looks back on earlier, happy days living in Paris and skiing in the Austrian Alps. The story also draws on Hemingway's experiences on African hunting safaris and shows the writer blaming his wife for what has happened to him, yet simultaneously recognizing that the fault is his alone.

Hemingway was fiercely anti-Nazi during World War II. As well as working as a war correspondent, work that sent him often to Europe, he used his fishing boat to keep watch for German submarines off the coast of Cuba, where he had a home. After the war ended, he continued his travels and was badly hurt in Africa in January 1954 in the crash of a small plane. He had already published his allegorical fable *The Old Man and the Sea* (1952), in the mass-circulation weekly magazine *Life;* this, his last major work published during his lifetime, won a Pulitzer Prize in 1953 and was central to his winning the Nobel Prize in 1954. The plane crash had damaged his mental and physical health, and he never fully recovered. Subject increasingly to depression and an incapacitating paranoia—afflictions that seem to have run in his family— he was hospitalized several times before killing himself in 1961. Yet it does appear that some of his suspicions about being watched by U.S. government agents may have been justified. Many writers associated with radical causes had dossiers compiled on them by the FBI. Several books have been published posthumously based on the voluminous manuscript collections he left. These include a book of reminiscences about his life in 1920s Paris, *A Moveable Feast* (1964); a novel about literary fame and sexual ambiguity constructed from several unfinished drafts, *The Garden of Eden* (1986); and *The Nick Adams Stories* (1972), a collection that added eight previously unpublished stories to the group.

The text is that of *The Fifth Column and the First Forty-nine Stories* (1938).

The Snows of Kilimanjaro[1]

> *Kilimanjaro is a snow covered mountain 19,710 feet high, and is said to be the highest mountain in Africa. Its western summit is called the Masai "Ngàje Ngài," the House of God. Close to the western summit there is the dried and frozen carcass of a leopard. No one has explained what the leopard was seeking at that altitude.*

"The marvellous thing is that it's painless," he said. "That's how you know when it starts."

"Is it really?"

"Absolutely. I'm awfully sorry about the odor though. That must bother you."

"Don't! Please don't."

"Look at them," he said. "Now is it sight or is it scent that brings them like that?"

The cot the man lay on was in the wide shade of a mimosa tree and as he looked out past the shade onto the glare of the plain there were three of the big birds squatted obscenely, while in the sky a dozen more sailed, making quick-moving shadows as they passed.

"They've been there since the day the truck broke down," he said. "Today's the first time any have lit on the ground. I watched the way they sailed very carefully at first in case I ever wanted to use them in a story. That's funny now."

"I wish you wouldn't," she said.

"I'm only talking," he said. "It's much easier if I talk. But I don't want to bother you."

"You know it doesn't bother me," she said. "It's that I've gotten so very nervous not being able to do anything. I think we might make it as easy as we can until the plane comes."

"Or until the plane doesn't come."

"Please tell me what I can do. There must be something I can do."

"You can take the leg off and that might stop it, though I doubt it. Or you can shoot me. You're a good shot now. I taught you to shoot didn't I?"

"Please don't talk that way. Couldn't I read to you?"

"Read what?"

"Anything in the book bag that we haven't read."

"I can't listen to it," he said. "Talking is the easiest. We quarrel and that makes the time pass."

"I don't quarrel. I never want to quarrel. Let's not quarrel any more. No matter how nervous we get. Maybe they will be back with another truck today. Maybe the plane will come."

---

1. Mount Kilimanjaro is in Tanzania, near the border with Kenya. It is no longer snow-covered.

"I don't want to move," the man said. "There is no sense in moving now except to make it easier for you."

"That's cowardly."

"Can't you let a man die as comfortably as he can without calling him names? What's the use of slanging me?"

"You're not going to die."

"Don't be silly. I'm dying now. Ask those bastards." He looked over to where the huge, filthy birds sat, their naked heads sunk in the hunched feathers. A fourth planed down, to run quick-legged and then waddle slowly toward the others.

"They are around every camp. You never notice them. You can't die if you don't give up."

"Where did you read that? You're such a bloody fool."

"You might think about some one else."

"For Christ's sake," he said. "That's been my trade."

He lay then and was quiet for a while and looked across the heat shimmer of the plain to the edge of the bush. There were a few Tommies[2] that showed minute and white against the yellow and, far off, he saw a herd of zebra, white against the green of the bush. This was a pleasant camp under big trees against a hill, with good water, and close by, a nearly dry water hole where sand grouse flighted in the mornings.

"Wouldn't you like me to read?" she asked. She was sitting on a canvas chair beside his cot. "There's a breeze coming up."

"No thanks."

"Maybe the truck will come."

"I don't give a damn about the truck."

"I do."

"You give a damn about so many things that I don't."

"Not so many, Harry."

"What about a drink?"

"It's supposed to be bad for you. It said in Black's to avoid all alcohol. You shouldn't drink."

"Molo!" he shouted.

"Yes Bwana."

"Bring whiskey-soda."

"Yes Bwana."

"You shouldn't," she said. "That's what I mean by giving up. It says it's bad for you. I know it's bad for you."

"No," he said. "It's good for me."

So now it was all over, he thought. So now he would never have a chance to finish it. So this was the way it ended in a bickering over a drink. Since the gangrene started in his right leg he had no pain and with the pain the horror had gone and all he felt now was a great tiredness and anger that this was the end of it. For this, that now was coming, he had very little curiosity. For years it had obsessed him; but now it meant nothing in itself. It was strange how easy being tired enough made it.

Now he would never write the things that he had saved to write until he knew enough to write them well. Well, he would not have to fail at trying to

---

2. Familiar name for the Thomson's gazelle of East Africa, smallest of the gazelles.

write them either. Maybe you could never write them, and that was why you put them off and delayed the starting. Well he would never know, now.

"I wish we'd never come," the woman said. She was looking at him holding the glass and biting her lip. "You never would have gotten anything like this in Paris. You always said you loved Paris. We could have stayed in Paris or gone anywhere. I'd have gone anywhere. I said I'd go anywhere you wanted. If you wanted to shoot we could have gone shooting in Hungary and been comfortable."

"Your bloody money," he said.

"That's not fair," she said. "It was always yours as much as mine. I left everything and I went wherever you wanted to go and I've done what you wanted to do. But I wish we'd never come here."

"You said you loved it."

"I did when you were all right. But now I hate it. I don't see why that had to happen to your leg. What have we done to have that happen to us?"

"I suppose what I did was to forget to put iodine on it when I first scratched it. Then I didn't pay any attention to it because I never infect. Then, later, when it got bad, it was probably using that weak carbolic solution when the other antiseptics ran out that paralyzed the minute blood vessels and started the gangrene." He looked at her. "What else?"

"I don't mean that."

"If we would have hired a good mechanic instead of a half baked kikuyu driver, he would have checked the oil and never burned out that bearing in the truck."

"I don't mean that."

"If you hadn't left your own people, your goddamned Old Westbury, Saratoga, Palm Beach people to take me on—"

"Why, I loved you. That's not fair. I love you now. I'll always love you. Don't you love me?"

"No," said the man. "I don't think so. I never have."

"Harry, what are you saying? You're out of your head."

"No. I haven't any head to go out of."

"Don't drink that," she said. "Darling, please don't drink that. We have to do everything we can."

"You do it," he said. "I'm tired."

Now in his mind he saw a railway station at Karagatch and he was standing with his pack and that was the headlight of the Simplon-Orient[3] *cutting the dark now and he was leaving Thrace*[4] *then after the retreat. That was one of the things he had saved to write, with, in the morning at breakfast, looking out the window and seeing snow on the mountains in Bulgaria and Nansen's Secretary asking the old man if it were snow and the old man looking at it and saying, No, that's not snow. It's too early for snow. And the Secretary repeating to the other girls, No, you see. It's not snow and them all saying, It's not snow we were mistaken. But it was the snow all right and he sent them on into it when he evolved exchange of populations. And it was snow they tramped along in until they died that winter.*

3. A fast train going from Paris to Constantinople, crossing the Alps into Italy over the Simplon Pass.
4. A region spanning parts of Greece and Turkey,

scene of border wars in 1922 that Hemingway had covered as a war correspondent while living in Paris.

It was snow too that fell all Christmas week that year up in the Gauertal, that year they lived in the woodcutter's house with the big square porcelain stove that filled half the room, and they slept on mattresses filled with beech leaves, the time the deserter came with his feet bloody in the snow. He said the police were right behind him and they gave him woolen socks and held the gendarmes talking until the tracks had drifted over.

In Schrunz,[5] on Christmas day, the snow was so bright it hurt your eyes when you looked out from the weinstube and saw every one coming home from church. That was where they walked up the sleigh-smoothed urine-yellowed road along the river with the steep pine hills, skis heavy on the shoulder, and where they ran that great run down the glacier above the Madlener-haus, the snow as smooth to see as cake frosting and as light as powder and he remembered the noiseless rush the speed made as you dropped down like a bird.

They were snow-bound a week in the Madlener-haus that time in the blizzard playing cards in the smoke by the lantern light and the stakes were higher all the time as Herr Lent lost more. Finally he lost it all. Everything, the skischule money and all the season's profit and then his capital. He could see him with his long nose, picking up the cards and then opening, "Sans Voir."[6] There was always gambling then. When there was no snow you gambled and when there was too much you gambled. He thought of all the time in his life he had spent gambling.

But he had never written a line of that, nor of that cold, bright Christmas day with the mountains showing across the plain that Barker had flown across the lines to bomb the Austrian officers' leave train, machine-gunning them as they scattered and ran. He remembered Barker afterwards coming into the mess and starting to tell about it. And how quiet it got and then somebody saying, "You bloody murderous bastard."

Those were the same Austrians they killed then that he skied with later. No not the same. Hans, that he skied with all that year, had been in the Kaiser-Jägers[7] and when they went hunting hares together up the little valley above the saw-mill they had talked of the fighting on Pasubio and of the attack on Perticara and Asalone and he had never written a word of that. Nor of Monte Corona, nor the Sette Communi, nor of Arsiero.

How many winters had he lived in the Vorarlberg and the Arlberg? It was four and then he remembered the man who had the fox to sell when they had walked into Bludenz, that time to buy presents, and the cherry-pit taste of good kirsch, the fast-slipping rush of running powder-snow on crust, singing "Hi! Ho! said Rolly!" as you ran down the last stretch to the steep drop, taking it straight, then running the orchard in three turns and out across the ditch and onto the icy road behind the inn. Knocking your bindings loose, kicking the skis free and leaning them up against the wooden wall of the inn, the lamplight coming from the window, where inside, in the smoky, new-wine smelling warmth, they were playing the accordion.

"Where did we stay in Paris?" he asked the woman who was sitting by him in a canvas chair, now, in Africa.

---

5. Alpine ski resort in the western part of Austria.
6. Without seeing (French); a blind opening bet in poker or other gambling games.
7. The Kaiser's Hunters (German); elite Austrian troops. In World War I, Germany and Austria fought against the United Kingdom, France, Italy, and the United States.

"At the Crillon.⁸ You know that."

"Why do I know that?"

"That's where we always stayed."

"No. Not always."

"There and at the Pavillion Henri-Quatre in St. Germain. You said you loved it there."

"Love is a dunghill," said Harry. "And I'm the cock that gets on it to crow."

"If you have to go away," she said, "is it absolutely necessary to kill off everything you leave behind? I mean do you have to take away everything? Do you have to kill your horse, and your wife and burn your saddle and your armour?"

"Yes," he said. "Your damned money was my armour. My Swift and my Armour."

"Don't."

"All right. I'll stop that. I don't want to hurt you."

"It's a little bit late now."

"All right then. I'll go on hurting you. It's more amusing. The only thing I ever really liked to do with you I can't do now."

"No, that's not true. You liked to do many things and everything you wanted to do I did."

"Oh, for Christ sake stop bragging, will you?"

He looked at her and saw her crying.

"Listen," he said. "Do you think that it is fun to do this? I don't know why I'm doing it. It's trying to kill to keep yourself alive, I imagine. I was all right when we started talking. I didn't mean to start this, and now I'm crazy as a coot and being as cruel to you as I can be. Don't pay any attention, darling, to what I say. I love you, really. You know I love you. I've never loved any one else the way I love you."

He slipped into the familiar lie he made his bread and butter by.

"You're sweet to me."

"You bitch," he said. "You rich bitch. That's poetry. I'm full of poetry now. Rot and poetry. Rotten poetry."

"Stop it. Harry, why do you have to turn into a devil now?"

"I don't like to leave anything," the man said. "I don't like to leave things behind."

•   •   •

It was evening now and he had been asleep. The sun was gone behind the hill and there was a shadow all across the plain and the small animals were feeding close to camp; quick dropping heads and switching tails, he watched them keeping well out away from the bush now. The birds no longer waited on the ground. They were all perched heavily in a tree. There were many more of them. His personal boy was sitting by the bed.

"Memsahib's gone to shoot," the boy said. "Does Bwana want?"

"Nothing."

She had gone to kill a piece of meat and, knowing how he liked to watch the game, she had gone well away so she would not disturb this little pocket of the plain that he could see. She was always thoughtful, he thought. On anything she knew about, or had read, or that she had ever heard.

8. Luxury hotel in Paris, as is the Henri-Quatre (below).

It was not her fault that when he went to her he was already over. How could a woman know that you meant nothing that you said; that you spoke only from habit and to be comfortable? After he no longer meant what he said, his lies were more successful with women than when he had told them the truth.

It was not so much that he lied as that there was no truth to tell. He had had his life and it was over and then he went on living it again with different people and more money, with the best of the same places, and some new ones.

You kept from thinking and it was all marvellous. You were equipped with good insides so that you did not go to pieces that way, the way most of them had, and you made an attitude that you cared nothing for the work you used to do, now that you could no longer do it. But, in yourself, you said that you would write about these people; about the very rich; that you were really not of them but a spy in their country; that you would leave it and write of it and for once it would be written by some one who knew what he was writing of. But he would never do it, because each day of not writing, of comfort, of being that which he despised, dulled his ability and softened his will to work so that, finally, he did no work at all. The people he knew now were all much more comfortable when he did not work. Africa was where he had been happiest in the good time of his life, so he had come out here to start again. They had made this safari with the minimum of comfort. There was no hardship; but there was no luxury and he had thought that he could get back into training that way. That in some way he could work the fat off his soul the way a fighter went into the mountains to work and train in order to burn it out of his body.

She had liked it. She said she loved it. She loved anything that was exciting, that involved a change of scene, where there were new people and where things were pleasant. And he had felt the illusion of returning strength of will to work. Now if this was how it ended, and he knew it was, he must not turn like some snake biting itself because its back was broken. It wasn't this woman's fault. If it had not been she it would have been another. If he lived by a lie he should try to die by it. He heard a shot beyond the hill.

She shot very well this good, this rich bitch, this kindly caretaker and destroyer of his talent. Nonsense. He had destroyed his talent himself. Why should he blame this woman because she kept him well? He had destroyed his talent by not using it, by betrayals of himself and what he believed in, by drinking so much that he blunted the edge of his perceptions, by laziness, by sloth, and by snobbery, by pride and by prejudice,[9] by hook and by crook. What was this? A catalogue of old books? What was his talent anyway? It was a talent all right but instead of using it, he had traded on it. It was never what he had done, but always what he could do. And he had chosen to make his living with something else instead of a pen or a pencil. It was strange, too, wasn't it, that when he fell in love with another woman, that woman should always have more money than the last one? But when he no longer was in love, when he was only lying, as to this woman, now, who had the most money of all, who had all the money there was, who had had a husband and children, who had taken lovers and been dissatisfied with them, and who loved him dearly as a writer, as a man, as a companion and as a proud posses-

9. Reference to title of a novel by the English writer Jane Austen (1775–1817).

sion; it was strange that when he did not love her at all and was lying, that he should be able to give her more for her money than when he had really loved.

We must all be cut out for what we do, he thought. However you make your living is where your talent lies. He had sold vitality, in one form or another, all his life and when your affections are not too involved you give much better value for the money. He had found that out but he would never write that, now, either. No, he would not write that, although it was well worth writing.

Now she came in sight, walking across the open toward the camp. She was wearing jodhpurs and carrying her rifle. The two boys had a Tommie slung and they were coming along behind her. She was still a good-looking woman, he thought, and she had a pleasant body. She had a great talent and appreciation for the bed, she was not pretty, but he liked her face, she read enormously, liked to ride and shoot and, certainly, she drank too much. Her husband had died when she was still a comparatively young woman and for a while she had devoted herself to her two just-grown children, who did not need her and were embarrassed at having her about, to her stable of horses, to books, and to bottles. She liked to read in the evening before dinner and she drank Scotch and soda while she read. By dinner she was fairly drunk and after a bottle of wine at dinner she was usually drunk enough to sleep.

That was before the lovers. After she had the lovers she did not drink so much because she did not have to be drunk to sleep. But the lovers bored her. She had been married to a man who had never bored her and these people bored her very much.

Then one of her two children was killed in a plane crash and after that was over she did not want the lovers, and drink being no anæsthetic she had to make another life. Suddenly, she had been acutely frightened of being alone. But she wanted some one that she respected with her.

It had begun very simply. She liked what he wrote and she had always envied the life he led. She thought he did exactly what he wanted to. The steps by which she had acquired him and the way in which she had finally fallen in love with him were all part of a regular progression in which she had built herself a new life and he had traded away what remained of his old life.

He had traded it for security, for comfort too, there was no denying that, and for what else? He did not know. She would have bought him anything he wanted. He knew that. She was a damned nice woman too. He would as soon be in bed with her as any one; rather with her, because she was richer, because she was very pleasant and appreciative and because she never made scenes. And now this life that she had built again was coming to a term because he had not used iodine two weeks ago when a thorn had scratched his knee as they moved forward trying to photograph a herd of waterbuck standing, their heads up, peering while their nostrils searched the air, their ears spread wide to hear the first noise that would send them rushing into the bush. They had bolted, too, before he got the picture.

Here she came now.

He turned his head on the cot to look toward her. "Hello," he said.

"I shot a Tommy ram," she told him. "He'll make you good broth and I'll have them mash some potatoes with the Klim.[1] How do you feel?"

---

1. Powdered milk or milk substitute.

"Much better."

"Isn't that lovely? You know I thought perhaps you would. You were sleeping when I left."

"I had a good sleep. Did you walk far?"

"No. Just around behind the hill. I made quite a good shot on the Tommy."

"You shoot marvellously, you know."

"I love it. I've loved Africa. Really. If *you're* all right it's the most fun that I've ever had. You don't know the fun it's been to shoot with you. I've loved the country."

"I love it too."

"Darling, you don't know how marvellous it is to see you feeling better. I couldn't stand it when you felt that way. You won't talk to me like that again, will you? Promise me?"

"No," he said. "I don't remember what I said."

"You don't have to destroy me. Do you? I'm only a middle-aged woman who loves you and wants to do what you want to do. I've been destroyed two or three times already. You wouldn't want to destroy me again, would you?"

"I'd like to destroy you a few times in bed," he said.

"Yes. That's the good destruction. That's the way we're made to be destroyed. The plane will be here tomorrow."

"How do you know?"

"I'm sure. It's bound to come. The boys have the wood all ready and the grass to make the smudge.[2] I went down and looked at it again today. There's plenty of room to land and we have the smudges ready at both ends."

"What makes you think it will come tomorrow?"

"I'm sure it will. It's overdue now. Then, in town, they will fix up your leg and then we will have some good destruction. Not that dreadful talking kind."

"Should we have a drink? The sun is down."

"Do you think you should?"

"I'm having one."

"We'll have one together. *Molo, letti dui whiskey-soda!*" she called.

"You'd better put on your mosquito boots," he told her.

"I'll wait till I bathe . . ."

While it grew dark they drank and just before it was dark and there was no longer enough light to shoot, a hyena crossed the open on his way around the hill.

"That bastard crosses there every night," the man said. "Every night for two weeks."

"He's the one makes the noise at night. I don't mind it. They're a filthy animal though."

Drinking together, with no pain now except the discomfort of lying in the one position, the boys lighting a fire, its shadow jumping on the tents, he could feel the return of acquiescence in this life of pleasant surrender. She *was* very good to him. He had been cruel and unjust in the afternoon. She was a fine woman, marvellous really. And just then it occurred to him that he was going to die.

---

2. Fire made to produce a dense smoke, to guide the plane to a landing place.

It came with a rush; not as a rush of water nor of wind; but of a sudden evil-smelling emptiness and the odd thing was that the hyena slipped lightly along the edge of it.

"What is it, Harry?" she asked him.

"Nothing," he said. "You had better move over to the other side. To windward."

"Did Molo change the dressing?"

"Yes. I'm just using the boric now."

"How do you feel?"

"A little wobbly."

"I'm going in to bathe," she said. "I'll be right out. I'll eat with you and then we'll put the cot in."

So, he said to himself, we did well to stop the quarrelling. He had never quarrelled much with this woman, while with the women that he loved he had quarrelled so much they had finally, always, with the corrosion of the quarrelling, killed what they had together. He had loved too much, demanded too much, and he wore it all out.

He thought about alone in Constantinople[3] that time, having quarrelled in Paris before he had gone out. He had whored the whole time and then, when that was over, and he had failed to kill his loneliness, but only made it worse, he had written her, the first one, the one who left him, a letter telling her how he had never been able to kill it. . . . How when he thought he saw her outside the Regence one time it made him go all faint and sick inside, and that he would follow a woman who looked like her in some way, along the Boulevard, afraid to see it was not she, afraid to lose the feeling it gave him. How every one he had slept with had only made him miss her more. How what she had done could never matter since he knew he could not cure himself of loving her. He wrote this letter at the Club, cold sober, and mailed it to New York asking her to write him at the office in Paris. That seemed safe. And that night missing her so much it made him feel hollow sick inside, he wandered up past Taxim's, picked a girl up and took her out to supper. He had gone to a place to dance with her afterward, she danced badly, and left her for a hot Armenian slut, that swung her belly against him so it almost scalded. He took her away from a British gunner subaltern after a row. The gunner asked him outside and they fought in the street on the cobbles in the dark. He'd hit him twice, hard, on the side of the jaw and when he didn't go down he knew he was in for a fight. The gunner hit him in the body, then beside his eye. He swung with his left again and landed and the gunner fell on him and grabbed his coat and tore the sleeve off and he clubbed him twice behind the ear and then smashed him with his right as he pushed him away. When the gunner went down his head hit first and he ran with the girl because they heard the M.P.'s coming. They got into a taxi and drove out to Rimmily Hissa along the Bosphorus, and around, and back in the cool night and went to bed and she felt as over-ripe as she looked but smoother, rose-petal, syrupy, smooth-bellied, big-breasted and needed no pillow under her buttocks, and he left her before she was awake looking blousy enough in the first daylight and turned up at the Pera Palace with a black eye, carrying his coat because one sleeve was missing.

3. Now Istanbul, the largest city in Turkey. In the rest of the paragraph there are references to streets and places in and around the city.

That same night he left for Anatolia and he remembered, later on that trip, riding all day through fields of the poppies that they raised for opium and how strange it made you feel, finally, and all the distances seemed wrong, to where they had made the attack with the newly arrived Constantine officers, that did not know a goddamned thing, and the artillery had fired into the troops and the British observer had cried like a child.

That was the day he'd first seen dead men wearing white ballet skirts and upturned shoes with pompons on them. The Turks had come steadily and lumpily and he had seen the skirted men running and the officers shooting into them and running then themselves and he and the British observer had run too until his lungs ached and his mouth was full of the taste of pennies and they stopped behind some rocks and there were the Turks coming as lumpily as ever. Later he had seen the things that he could never think of and later still he had seen much worse. So when he got back to Paris that time he could not talk about it or stand to have it mentioned. And there in the café as he passed was that American poet with a pile of saucers in front of him and a stupid look on his potato face talking about the Dada movement[4] with a Roumanian who said his name was Tristan Tzara, who always wore a monocle and had a headache, and, back at the apartment with his wife that now he loved again, the quarrel all over, the madness all over, glad to be home, the office sent his mail up to the flat. So then the letter in answer to the one he'd written came in on a platter one morning and when he saw the handwriting he went cold all over and tried to slip the letter underneath another. But his wife said, "Who is that letter from, dear?" and that was the end of the beginning of that.

He remembered the good times with them all, and the quarrels. They always picked the finest places to have the quarrels. And why had they always quarrelled when he was feeling best? He had never written any of that because, at first, he never wanted to hurt any one and then it seemed as though there was enough to write without it. But he had always thought that he would write it finally. There was so much to write. He had seen the world change; not just the events; although he had seen many of them and had watched the people, but he had seen the subtler change and he could remember how the people were at different times. He had been in it and he had watched it and it was his duty to write of it; but now he never would.

"How do you feel?" she said. She had come out from the tent now after her bath.

"All right."

"Could you eat now?" He saw Molo behind her with the folding table and the other boy with the dishes.

"I want to write," he said.

"You ought to take some broth to keep your strength up."

"I'm going to die tonight," he said. "I don't need my strength up."

"Don't be melodramatic, Harry, please," she said.

"Why don't you use your nose? I'm rotted half way up my thigh now. What the hell should I fool with broth for? Molo bring whiskey-soda."

"Please take the broth," she said gently.

---

4. An international movement in painting, sculpture, and literature that flourished between 1916 and 1922, stressing fantasy, surrealism, and nonsense. The term is a child's cry, chosen because it has no meaning. Tristan Tzara (below) was a leading member of the movement.

"All right."

The broth was too hot. He had to hold it in the cup until it cooled enough to take it and then he just got it down without gagging.

"You're a fine woman," he said. "Don't pay any attention to me."

She looked at him with her well-known, well-loved face from *Spur* and *Town and Country*,[5] only a little the worse for drink, only a little the worse for bed, but *Town and Country* never showed those good breasts and those useful thighs and those lightly small-of-back-caressing hands, and as he looked and saw her well known pleasant smile, he felt death come again. This time there was no rush. It was a puff, as of a wind that makes a candle flicker and the flame go tall.

"They can bring my net out later and hang it from the tree and build the fire up. I'm not going in the tent tonight. It's not worth moving. It's a clear night. There won't be any rain."

So this was how you died, in whispers that you did not hear. Well, there would be no more quarrelling. He could promise that. The one experience that he had never had he was not going to spoil now. He probably would. You spoiled everything. But perhaps he wouldn't.

"You can't take dictation, can you?"

"I never learned," she told him.

"That's all right."

There wasn't time, of course, although it seemed as though it telescoped so that you might put it all into one paragraph if you could get it right.

There was a log house, chinked white with mortar, on a hill above the lake. There was a bell on a pole by the door to call the people in to meals. Behind the house were fields and behind the fields was the timber. A line of lombardy poplars ran from the house to the dock. Other poplars ran along the point. A road went up to the hills along the edge of the timber and along that road he picked blackberries. Then that log house was burned down and all the guns that had been on deer foot racks above the open fire place were burned and afterwards their barrels, with the lead melted in the magazines, and the stocks burned away, lay out on the heap of ashes that were used to make lye for the big iron soap kettles, and you asked Grandfather if you could have them to play with, and he said, no. You see they were his guns still and he never bought any others. Nor did he hunt any more. The house was rebuilt in the same place out of lumber now and painted white and from its porch you saw the poplars and the lake beyond; but there were never any more guns. The barrels of the guns that had hung on the deer feet on the wall of the log house lay out there on the heap of ashes and no one ever touched them.

In the Black Forest,[6] after the war, we rented a trout stream and there were two ways to walk to it. One was down the valley from Triberg and around the valley road in the shade of the trees that bordered the white road, and then up a side road that went up through the hills past many small farms, with the big Schwarzwald[7] houses, until that road crossed the stream. That was where our fishing began.

The other way was to climb steeply up to the edge of the woods and then go across the top of the hills through the pine woods, and then out to the edge of a meadow and down across this meadow to the bridge. There were birches along the stream and it was not big, but narrow, clear and fast, with pools where it had cut under the roots of the birches. At the Hotel in Triberg the proprietor had a fine season. It was very pleasant and we were all great friends. The next year came the inflation and the money he had made the year before was not enough to buy supplies to open the hotel and he hanged himself.

You could dictate that, but you could not dictate the Place Contrescarpe[8] where the flower sellers dyed their flowers in the street and the dye ran over the paving where the autobus started and the old men and the women, always drunk on wine and bad marc;[9] and the children with their noses running in the cold; the smell of dirty sweat and poverty and drunkenness at the Café des Amateurs and the whores at the Bal Musette[1] they lived above. The Concierge who entertained the trooper of the Garde Republicaine in her loge, his horsehair-plumed helmet on a chair. The locataire across the hall whose husband was a bicycle racer and her joy that morning at the Cremerie when she had opened L'Auto and seen where he placed third in Paris-Tours, his first big race. She had blushed and laughed and then gone upstairs crying with the yellow sporting paper in her hand. The husband of the woman who ran the Bal Musette drove a taxi and when he, Harry, had to take an early plane the husband knocked upon the door to wake him and they each drank a glass of white wine at the zinc of the bar before they started. He knew his neighbors in that quarter then because they all were poor.

Around that Place there were two kinds; the drunkards and the sportifs. The drunkards killed their poverty that way; the sportifs took it out in exercise. They were the descendants of the Communards[2] and it was no struggle for them to know their politics. They knew who had shot their fathers, their relatives, their brothers, and their friends when the Versailles troops came in and took the town after the Commune and executed any one they could catch with calloused hands, or who wore a cap, or carried any other sign he was a working man. And in that poverty, and in that quarter across the street from a Boucherie Chevaline[3] and a wine co-operative he had written the start of all he was to do. There never was another part of Paris that he loved like that, the sprawling trees, the old white plastered houses painted brown below, the long green of the autobus in that round square, the purple flower dye upon the paving, the sudden drop down the hill of the rue Cardinal Lemoine to the River, and the other way the narrow crowded world of the rue Mouffetard. The street that ran up toward the Pantheon and the other that he always took with the bicycle, the only asphalted street in all that quarter, smooth under the tires, with the high narrow houses and the cheap tall hotel where Paul Verlaine[4] had died. There were only two rooms in the apartments where they lived and he had a room on the top floor of that hotel that cost him sixty francs a month where he did his writing, and from it he could see the roofs and chimney pots and all the hills of Paris.

From the apartment you could only see the wood and coal man's place. He sold wine too, bad wine. The golden horse's head outside the Boucherie Chevaline where the carcasses hung yellow gold and red in the open window, and the green painted co-operative where they bought their wine; good wine and

8. Square in a working-class neighborhood of Paris.
9. White brandy (French).
1. Dance hall (French).
2. Participants in the 1871 workers' uprising in Paris and the Commune, a local government established on March 18, 1871, but suppressed by the Versailles government two months later.
3. A butcher shop selling horsemeat, once common in poorer neighborhoods throughout Europe.
4. French Symbolist poet (1844–1896). Hemingway rented and worked in a room in which Verlaine had lived.

cheap. The rest was plaster walls and the windows of the neighbors. The neigh-
bors who, at night, when some one lay drunk in the street, moaning and groan-
ing in that typical French ivresse[5] *that you were propaganded to believe did not*
exist, would open their windows and then the murmur of talk.

"Where is the policeman? When you don't want him the bugger is always
there. He's sleeping with some concierge. Get the Agent." Till some one threw a
bucket of water from a window and the moaning stopped. "What's that? Water.
Ah, that's intelligent." And the windows shutting. Marie, his femme de menage,[6]
protesting against the eight-hour day saying, "If a husband works until six he gets
only a little drunk on the way home and does not waste too much. If he works
only until five he is drunk every night and one has no money. It is the wife of
the working man who suffers from this shortening of hours."

"Wouldn't you like some more broth?" the woman asked him now.

"No, thank you very much. It is awfully good."

"Try just a little."

"I would like a whiskey-soda."

"It's not good for you."

"No. It's bad for me. Cole Porter[7] wrote the words and the music. This
knowledge that you're going mad for me."

"You know I like you to drink."

"Oh yes. Only it's bad for me."

When she goes, he thought. I'll have all I want. Not all I want but all there
is. Ayee he was tired. Too tired. He was going to sleep a little while. He lay
still and death was not there. It must have gone around another street. It
went in pairs, on bicycles, and moved absolutely silently on the pavements.

No, he had never written about Paris. Not the Paris that he cared about. But
what about the rest that he had never written?

What about the ranch and the silvered gray of the sage brush, the quick, clear
water in the irrigation ditches, and the heavy green of the alfalfa. The trail
went up into the hills and the cattle in the summer were shy as deer. The bawl-
ing and the steady noise and slow moving mass raising a dust as you brought
them down in the fall. And behind the mountains, the clear sharpness of the
peak in the evening light and, riding down along the trail in the moonlight,
bright across the valley. Now he remembered coming down through the timber
in the dark holding the horse's tail when you could not see and all the stories
that he meant to write.

About the half-wit chore boy who was left at the ranch that time and told not
to let any one get any hay, and that old bastard from the Forks who had beaten
the boy when he had worked for him stopping to get some feed. The boy refus-
ing and the old man saying he would beat him again. The boy got the rifle from
the kitchen and shot him when he tried to come into the barn and when they
came back to the ranch he'd been dead a week, frozen in the corral, and the
dogs had eaten part of him. But what was left you packed on a sled wrapped in
a blanket and roped on and you got the boy to help you haul it, and the two of
you took it out over the road on skis, and sixty miles down to town to turn the

5. Drunkenness (French). Because the French
drank wine and brandy rather than hard liquor,
it was often claimed that there was no real
drunkenness among them.

6. Charwoman (French).
7. Popular American song composer (1893–
1964).

boy over. He having no idea that he would be arrested. Thinking he had done his duty and that you were his friend and he would be rewarded. He'd helped to haul the old man in so everybody could know how bad the old man had been and how he'd tried to steal some feed that didn't belong to him, and when the sheriff put the handcuffs on the boy he couldn't believe it. Then he'd started to cry. That was one story he had saved to write. He knew at least twenty good stories from out there and he had never written one. Why?

"You tell them why," he said.

"Why what, dear?"

"Why nothing."

She didn't drink so much, now, since she had him. But if he lived he would never write about her, he knew that now. Nor about any of them. The rich were dull and they drank too much, or they played too much backgammon. They were dull and they were repetitious. He remembered poor Julian and his romantic awe of them and how he had started a story once that began, "The very rich are different from you and me."[8] And how some one had said to Julian, Yes, they have more money. But that was not humorous to Julian. He thought they were a special glamourous race and when he found they weren't it wrecked him just as much as any other thing that wrecked him.

He had been contemptuous of those who wrecked. You did not have to like it because you understood it. He could beat anything, he thought, because no thing could hurt him if he did not care.

All right. Now he would not care for death. One thing he had always dreaded was the pain. He could stand pain as well as any man, until it went on too long, and wore him out, but here he had something that had hurt frightfully and just when he had felt it breaking him, the pain had stopped.

He remembered long ago when Williamson, the bombing officer, had been hit by a stick bomb some one in a German patrol had thrown as he was coming in through the wire that night and, screaming, had begged every one to kill him. He was a fat man, very brave, and a good officer, although addicted to fantastic shows. But that night he was caught in the wire, with a flare lighting him up and his bowels spilled out into the wire, so when they brought him in, alive, they had to cut him loose. Shoot me, Harry. For Christ sake shoot me. They had had an argument one time about our Lord never sending you anything you could not bear and some one's theory had been that meant that at a certain time the pain passed you out automatically. But he had always remembered Williamson, that night. Nothing passed out Williamson until he gave him all his morphine tablets that he had always saved to use himself and then they did not work right away.

Still this now, that he had, was very easy; and if it was no worse as it went on there was nothing to worry about. Except that he would rather be in better company.

He thought a little about the company that he would like to have.

No, he thought, when everything you do, you do too long, and do too late, you can't expect to find the people still there. The people all are gone. The party's over and you are with your hostess now.

8. These are the opening words of "The Rich Boy" by F. Scott Fitzgerald. Hemingway originally used Fitzgerald's name instead of "Julian," but was persuaded to make the change by his editor, Maxwell Perkins.

I'm getting as bored with dying as with everything else, he thought.

"It's a bore," he said out loud.

"What is, my dear?"

"Anything you do too bloody long."

He looked at her face between him and the fire. She was leaning back in the chair and the firelight shone on her pleasantly lined face and he could see that she was sleepy. He heard the hyena make a noise just outside the range of the fire.

"I've been writing," he said. "But I got tired."

"Do you think you will be able to sleep?"

"Pretty sure. Why don't you turn in?"

"I like to sit here with you."

"Do you feel anything strange?" he asked her.

"No. Just a little sleepy."

"I do," he said.

He had just felt death come by again.

"You know the only thing I've never lost is curiosity," he said to her.

"You've never lost anything. You're the most complete man I've ever known."

"Christ," he said. "How little a woman knows. What is that? Your intuition?"

Because, just then, death had come and rested its head on the foot of the cot and he could smell its breath.

"Never believe any of that about a scythe and a skull,"[9] he told her. "It can be two bicycle policemen as easily, or be a bird. Or it can have a wide snout like a hyena."

It had moved up on him now, but it had no shape any more. It simply occupied space.

"Tell it to go away."

It did not go away but moved a little closer.

"You've got a hell of a breath," he told it. "You stinking bastard."

It moved up closer to him still and he could not speak to it, and when it saw he could not speak it came a little closer, and now he tried to send it away without speaking, but it moved in on him so its weight was all upon his chest, and while it crouched there and he could not move, or speak, he heard the woman say, "Bwana is asleep now. Take the cot up very gently and carry it into the tent."

He could not speak to tell her to make it go away and it crouched now, heavier, so he could not breathe. And then, while they lifted the cot, suddenly it was all right and the weight went from his chest.

It was morning and had been morning for some time and he heard the plane. It showed very tiny and then made a wide circle and the boys ran out and lit the fires, using kerosene, and piled on grass so there were two big smudges at each end of the level place and the morning breeze blew them toward the camp and the plane circled twice more, low this time, and then glided down and levelled off and landed smoothly and, coming walking toward him, was old Compton in slacks, a tweed jacket and a brown felt hat.

"What's the matter, old cock?" Compton said.

"Bad leg," he told him. "Will you have some breakfast?"

---

9. In medieval imagery death is often represented as a skeleton draped in a long cape so that only the skull shows. He carries a scythe.

"Thanks. I'll just have some tea. It's the Puss Moth[1] you know. I won't be able to take the Memsahib. There's only room for one. Your lorry is on the way."

Helen had taken Compton aside and was speaking to him. Compton came back more cheery than ever.

"We'll get you right in," he said. "I'll be back for the Mem. Now I'm afraid I'll have to stop at Arusha to refuel. We'd better get going."

"What about the tea?"

"I don't really care about it you know."

The boys had picked up the cot and carried it around the green tents and down along the rock and out onto the plain and along past the smudges that were burning brightly now, and the grass all consumed, and the wind fanning the fire, to the little plane. It was difficult getting him in, but once in he lay back in the leather seat, and the leg was stuck straight out to one side of the seat where Compton sat. Compton started the motor and got in. He waved to Helen and to the boys and, as the clatter moved into the old familiar roar, they swung around with Compie watching for wart-hog holes and roared, bumping, along the stretch between the fires and with the last bump rose and he saw them all standing below, waving, and the camp beside the hill, flattening now, and the plain spreading, clumps of trees, and the bush flattening, while the game trails ran now smoothly to the dry waterholes, and there was a new water that he had never known of. The zebra, small rounded backs now, and the wildebeeste, big-headed dots seeming to climb as they moved in long fingers across the plain, now scattering as the shadow came toward them, they were tiny now, and the movement had no gallop, and the plain as far as you could see, gray-yellow now and ahead old Compie's tweed back and the brown felt hat. Then they were over the first hills and the wildebeeste were trailing up them, and then they were over mountains with sudden depths of green-rising forest and the solid bamboo slopes, and then the heavy forest again, sculptured into peaks and hollows until they crossed, and hills sloped down and then another plain, hot now, and purple brown, bumpy with heat and Compie looking back to see how he was riding. Then there were other mountains dark ahead.

And then instead of going on to Arusha they turned left, he evidently figured that they had the gas, and looking down he saw a pink sifting cloud, moving over the ground, and in the air, like the first snow in a blizzard, that comes from nowhere, and he knew the locusts were coming up from the South. Then they began to climb and they were going to the East it seemed, and then it darkened and they were in a storm, the rain so thick it seemed like flying through a waterfall, and then they were out and Compie turned his head and grinned and pointed and there, ahead, all he could see, as wide as all the world, great, high, and unbelievably white in the sun, was the square top of Kilimanjaro. And then he knew that there was where he was going.

Just then the hyena stopped whimpering in the night and started to make a strange, human, almost crying sound. The woman heard it and stirred uneasily. She did not wake. In her dream she was at the house on Long Island and it was the night before her daughter's début. Somehow her father was there and he had been very rude. Then the noise the hyena made was so loud she

---

1. A small, light airplane seating two people.

woke and for a moment she did not know where she was and she was very afraid. Then she took the flashlight and shone it on the other cot that they had carried in after Harry had gone to sleep. She could see his bulk under the mosquito bar but somehow he had gotten his leg out and it hung down alongside the cot. The dressings had all come down and she could not look at it.

"Molo," she called, "Molo! Molo!"

Then she said, "Harry, Harry!" Then her voice rising, "Harry! Please, Oh Harry!"

There was no answer and she could not hear him breathing.

Outside the tent the hyena made the same strange noise that had awakened her. But she did not hear him for the beating of her heart.

1936, 1938

LANGSTON HUGHES
1902–1967

Langston Hughes was the most popular and versatile of the many writers connected with the Harlem Renaissance. Along with Zora Neale Hurston, and in contrast to Jean Toomer and Countee Cullen (who wanted to work with the patterns of written literary forms, whether traditional or experimental), he wanted to capture the oral and improvisatory traditions of black culture in written form.

Hughes was born in Joplin, Missouri; as a child, since his parents were separated, he lived mainly with his maternal grandmother in Lawrence, Kansas. He did, however, live intermittently both with his mother in Detroit and Cleveland, where he finished high school and began to write poetry, and with his father, who, disgusted with American racism, had gone to Mexico. Like other poets in this era—T. S. Eliot, Hart Crane, Edgar Lee Masters, and Robert Frost—Hughes had a mother sympathetic to his poetic ambitions and a businesslike father with whom he was in deep, scarring conflict.

Hughes entered Columbia University in 1920 but left after a year. Traveling and drifting, he shipped out as a merchant seaman and worked at a nightclub in Paris (France) and as a busboy in Washington, D.C. All this time he was writing and publishing poetry, chiefly in the two important African American periodicals *Opportunity* and the *Crisis*. Eleven of Hughes's poems were published in Alain Locke's pioneering anthology, *The New Negro* (1925), and he was also well represented in Countee Cullen's 1927 anthology, *Caroling Dusk*. Carl Van Vechten, one of the white patrons of African American writing, helped get *The Weary Blues*, Hughes's first volume of poems, published in 1926. It was in this year, too, that his important essay "The Negro Artist and the Racial Mountain" appeared in the *Nation* (see p. 1990); in that essay Hughes described the immense challenges to be faced by the serious black artist "who would produce a racial art" but insisted on the need for courageous artists to make the attempt. Other patrons appeared: Amy Spingarn financed his college education at Lincoln University (Pennsylvania), and Charlotte Mason subsidized him in New York City between 1928 and 1930. The publication of his novel *Not without Laughter* in 1930 solidified his reputation and sales, enabling him to support himself. By the 1930s he was being called "the bard of Harlem."

The Great Depression brought an abrupt end to much African American literary activity, but Hughes was already a public figure. In the activist 1930s he was much absorbed in radical politics. Hughes and other blacks were drawn by the American Communist Party, which made racial justice an important plank in its platform, promoting an image of working-class solidarity that nullified racial boundaries. He visited the Soviet Union in 1932 and produced a significant amount of radical writing up to the eve of World War II. He covered the Spanish civil war for the *Baltimore Afro-American* in 1937. By the end of the decade he had also been involved in drama and screenplay writing and had begun an autobiography, all the while publishing poetry. In 1943 he invented the folksy, streetwise character Jesse B. Semple, whose commonsense prose monologues on race were eventually collected in four volumes, and Alberta K. Johnson, Semple's female equivalent, in his series of "Madam" poems.

In the 1950s and 1960s Hughes published a variety of anthologies for children and adults, including *First Book of Negroes* (1952), *The First Book of Jazz* (1955), and *The Book of Negro Folklore* (1958). In 1953 he was called to testify before Senator Joseph McCarthy's committee on subversive activities in connection with his 1930s radicalism. The FBI listed him as a security risk until 1959; and during these years, when he could not travel outside the United States because he would not have been allowed to reenter the country, Hughes worked to rehabilitate his reputation as a good American by producing patriotic poetry. From 1960 to the end of his life he was again on the international circuit.

Within the spectrum of artistic possibilities open to writers of the Harlem Renaissance—drawing on African American rural folk forms; on literary traditions and forms that entered the United States from Europe and Great Britain; or on the new cultural forms of blacks in American cities—Hughes chose to focus his work on modern, urban black life. He modeled his stanza forms on the improvisatory rhythms of jazz music and adapted the vocabulary of everyday black speech to poetry. He also acknowledged finding inspiration for his writing in the work of white American poets who preceded him. Like Walt Whitman he heard America singing, and he asserted his right to sing America back; he also learned from Carl Sandburg's earlier attempts to work jazz into poetry. Hughes did not confuse his pride in African American culture with complacency toward the material deprivations of black life in the United States. He was keenly aware that the modernist "vogue in things Negro" among white Americans was potentially exploitative and voyeuristic; he confronted such racial tourists with the misery as well as the jazz of Chicago's South Side. Early and late, Hughes's poems demanded that African Americans be acknowledged as owners of the culture they gave to the United States and as fully enfranchised American citizens.

The source of the poems printed here is *Collected Poems* (1994).

The Negro Speaks of Rivers

I've known rivers:
I've known rivers ancient as the world and older than the
     flow of human blood in human veins.

My soul has grown deep like the rivers.

I bathed in the Euphrates when dawns were young.
I built my hut near the Congo and it lulled me to sleep.   5
I looked upon the Nile and raised the pyramids above it.
I heard the singing of the Mississippi when Abe Lincoln
     went down to New Orleans, and I've seen its
     muddy bosom turn all golden in the sunset

I've known rivers:
Ancient, dusky rivers.

My soul has grown deep like the rivers.   10

1921, 1926

Mother to Son

Well, son, I'll tell you:
Life for me ain't been no crystal stair.
It's had tacks in it,
And splinters,
And boards torn up,   5
And places with no carpet on the floor—
Bare.
But all the time
I'se been a-climbin' on,
And reachin' landin's,   10
And turnin' corners,
And sometimes goin' in the dark
Where there ain't been no light.
So boy, don't you turn back.
Don't you set down on the steps   15
'Cause you finds it's kinder hard.
Don't you fall now—
For I'se still goin', honey,
I'se still climbin',
And life for me ain't been no crystal stair.   20

1922, 1926

I, Too

I, too, sing America.

I am the darker brother.
They send me to eat in the kitchen
When company comes,
But I laugh,   5
And eat well,
And grow strong.

Tomorrow,
I'll be at the table
When company comes.   10
Nobody'll dare
Say to me,
"Eat in the kitchen,"
Then.

Besides,   15
They'll see how beautiful I am
And be ashamed—

I, too, am America.

                                                        1925, 1959

The Weary Blues

Droning a drowsy syncopated tune,
Rocking back and forth to a mellow croon,
    I heard a Negro play.
Down on Lenox Avenue the other night
By the pale dull pallor of an old gas light   5
    He did a lazy sway. . . .
    He did a lazy sway. . . .
To the tune o' those Weary Blues.
With his ebony hands on each ivory key.
He made that poor piano moan with melody.   10
    O Blues!
Swaying to and fro on his rickety stool
He played that sad raggy tune like a musical fool.
    Sweet Blues!
Coming from a black man's soul.   15
    O Blues!
In a deep song voice with a melancholy tone
I heard that Negro sing, that old piano moan—
    "Ain't got nobody in all this world,
    Ain't got nobody but ma self.   20
    I's gwine to quit ma frownin'
    And put ma troubles on de shelf."
Thump, thump, thump, went his foot on the floor.
He played a few chords then he sang some more—
    "I got de Weary Blues   25
    And I can't be satisfied.
    Got de Weary Blues
    And can't be satisfied—
    I ain't happy no mo'
    And I wish that I had died."   30
And far into the night he crooned that tune.
The stars went out and so did the moon.
The singer stopped playing and went to bed.
While the Weary Blues echoes through his head
He slept like a rock or a man that's dead.   35

                                                        1925

Mulatto

I am your son, white man!

Georgia dusk
And the turpentine woods.
One of the pillars of the temple fell.

    You are my son!   5
    Like hell!

The moon over the turpentine woods.
The Southern night
Full of stars,
Great big yellow stars.   10
  What's a body but a toy?
    Juicy bodies
    Of nigger wenches
    Blue black
    Against black fences.   15
    O, you little bastard boy,
    What's a body but a toy?
The scent of pine wood stings the soft night air.
    What's the body of your mother?
Silver moonlight everywhere.   20

    What's the body of your mother?
Sharp pine scent in the evening air.
      A nigger night,
      A nigger joy,
      A little yellow   25
      Bastard boy.

    Naw, you ain't my brother.
    Niggers ain't my brother.
    Not ever.
    Niggers ain't my brother.   30
The Southern night is full of stars,
Great big yellow stars.
      O, sweet as earth,
      Dusk dark bodies
      Give sweet birth   35
To little yellow bastard boys.

    Git on back there in the night,
    You ain't white.

The bright stars scatter everywhere.
Pine wood scent in the evening air.   40
      A nigger night,
      A nigger joy.

    I am your son, white man!

A little yellow
Bastard boy. 45

1927

Song for a Dark Girl

Way Down South in Dixie[1]
    (Break the heart of me)
They hung my black young lover
    To a cross roads tree.

Way Down South in Dixie 5
    (Bruised body high in air)
I asked the white Lord Jesus
    What was the use of prayer.

Way Down South in Dixie
    (Break the heart of me) 10
Love is a naked shadow
    On a gnarled and naked tree.

1927

Visitors to the Black Belt

You can talk about
Across the railroad tracks—
To me it's *here*
On this side of the tracks.

You can talk about 5
Up in Harlem—
To me it's *here*
In Harlem.

You can say
Jazz on the South Side—[1] 10
To me it's hell
On the South Side:

    Kitchenettes
    With no heat
    And garbage 15
    In the halls.

---

1. Last line of "Dixie," the popular minstrel song, probably composed by Daniel D. Emmett (1815–1904).

1. African American neighborhood in Chicago; see also Archibald J. Motley's 1934 painting, *Black Belt* in the color insert to this volume.

Who're you, outsider?

Ask me who am I.

1940, 1943

Note on Commercial Theatre

You've taken my blues and gone—
You sing 'em on Broadway
And you sing 'em in Hollywood Bowl,
And you mixed 'em up with symphonies
And you fixed 'em   5
So they don't sound like me.
Yep, you done taken my blues and gone.

You also took my spirituals and gone.
You put me in *Macbeth* and *Carmen Jones*
And all kinds of *Swing Mikados*   10
And in everything but what's about me—
But someday somebody'll
Stand up and talk about me,
And write about me—

Black and beautiful—   15
And sing about me,
And put on plays about me!

I reckon it'll be
Me myself!

Yes, it'll be me.   20

1940, 1959

Democracy

Democracy will not come
Today, this year
   Nor ever
Through compromise and fear.

I have as much right   5
As the other fellow has
   To stand
On my two feet
And own the land.

I tire so of hearing people say,   10
Let things take their course.

Tomorrow is another day.
I do not need my freedom when I'm dead.
I cannot live on tomorrow's bread.

    Freedom   15
    Is a strong seed
    Planted
    In a great need.
    I live here, too.
    I want freedom   20
    Just as you.

                                              1949

Theme for English B

The instructor said,

    Go home and write
    a page tonight.
    And let that page come out of you—
    Then, it will be true.   5

I wonder if it's that simple?
I am twenty-two, colored, born in Winston-Salem.
I went to school there, then Durham, then here
to this college on the hill above Harlem.[1]
I am the only colored student in my class.   10
The steps from the hill lead down into Harlem,
through a park, then I cross St. Nicholas,
Eighth Avenue, Seventh, and I come to the Y,
the Harlem Branch Y, where I take the elevator
up to my room, sit down, and write this page: 15

It's not easy to know what is true for you or me
at twenty-two, my age. But I guess I'm what
I feel and see and hear, Harlem, I hear you:
hear you, hear me—we two—you, me, talk on this page.
(I hear New York, too.) Me—who?   20
Well, I like to eat, sleep, drink, and be in love.
I like to work, read, learn, and understand life.
I like a pipe for a Christmas present,
or records—Bessie, bop, or Bach.[2]
I guess being colored doesn't make me *not* like 25
the same things other folks like who are other races.
So will my page be colored that I write?
Being me, it will not be white.
But it will be

---

1. The City College of the City University of New York; Winston-Salem and Durham are cities in North Carolina.
2. Johann Sebastian Bach (1685–1750), German composer of the Baroque era; Bessie Smith (1894–1937), noted blues singer. "Bop": jazz form developed in Harlem during World War II.

a part of you, instructor.   30
You are white—
yet a part of me, as I am a part of you.
That's American.
Sometimes perhaps you don't want to be a part of me.
Nor do I often want to be a part of you.   35
But we are, that's true!
As I learn from you,
I guess you learn from me—
although you're older—and white—
and somewhat more free.   40

This is my page for English B.

1949

JOHN STEINBECK
1902–1968

Most of John Steinbeck's best writing is set in the region of California that he called home, the Salinas Valley and Monterey peninsula of California, where visitors today will find official remembrances of him everywhere. Steinbeck believed in the American promise of opportunity for all, but believed also that social injustices and economic inequalities had put opportunity beyond reach for many. His work merged literary modernism with literary realism, celebrated traditional rural communities along with social outcasts and immigrant cultures, and endorsed conservative values and radical politics at the same time.

Steinbeck's father managed a flour mill and later became treasurer of Monterey County; his mother, who had taught school before marriage, was active in local civic affairs. Their home was full of books, and Steinbeck read avidly from an early age. After graduating from Salinas High School in 1919, he began to study at Stanford University but took time off for a variety of short-term jobs at local mills, farms, and estates. During this period he developed an abiding respect for people who worked on farms and in factories, and committed his literary abilities to their cause. He left college for good in 1925, having completed less than three years of coursework, and continued his roving life.

With financial help from his father, Steinbeck spent most of 1929 writing. He moved to the seaside town of Pacific Grove, on the Monterey coast, and in 1930 was married (the first of three times). In 1935 he achieved commercial success with his third novel, *Tortilla Flat*, a celebration of the Mexican-American culture of the "*paisanos*" who lived in the Monterey hills. The book favorably contrasted these lusty, idealized types to the valley's respectable, conventional, Anglo-Protestant population. Steinbeck's next novel, *In Dubious Battle* (1936), contrasted the decency of striking migratory farm workers both to the cynicism of landowners and their vigilantes, and to the equal cynicism of Communist labor union organizers who exploit the workers' plight for their own purposes. Sympathy for the underdog appears again in *Of Mice and Men* (1937), a best-selling short novel about two itinerant ranch hands, and yet again in *The Grapes of Wrath* (1939), his most famous and most ambitious novel.

Inspired by the devastating 1930s drought in the southern plains states and the exodus of thousands of farmers from their homes in the so-called Dust Bowl, *The Grapes of Wrath* told the story of the Joad family, who, after losing their land in Oklahoma, migrated westward to California on U.S. Highway 66 looking for, but not finding, a better life. Because of its supposed radicalism, the novel was banned or burned in several states, but even so, it became the nation's number one bestseller and won a Pulitzer Prize in 1940. *Cannery Row* (1940), a local-color novel about workers in the sardine canneries of Monterey, also became a bestseller.

After World War II Steinbeck's work displayed increasing hostility to American culture, whose mass commercialization seemed to him to be destroying individual creativity. "The Leader of the People" expresses his sense that America's heroic times are past and locates value in the story's socially marginal characters—a child, an old man, and a farmhand. His most important later works are *The Wayward Bus* (1947), *East of Eden* (1952), *Sweet Thursday* (1954), and *Travels with Charley in Search of America* (1962), in which he recounts his automobile tour of the United States, taken with his dog. Steinbeck won the Nobel Prize in 1962.

The text is that of *The Red Pony* (1945).

The Leader of the People

On Saturday afternoon Billy Buck, the ranch-hand, raked together the last of the old years' haystack and pitched small forkfuls over the wire fence to a few mildly interested cattle. High in the air small clouds like puffs of cannon smoke were driven eastward by the March wind. The wind could be heard whishing in the brush on the ridge crests, but no breath of it penetrated down into the ranch-cup.

The little boy, Jody, emerged from the house eating a thick piece of buttered bread. He saw Billy working on the last of the haystack. Jody tramped down scuffling his shoes in a way he had been told was destructive to good shoe-leather. A flock of white pigeons flew out of the black cypress tree as Jody passed, and circled the tree and landed again. A half-grown tortoise-shell cat leaped from the bunkhouse porch, galloped on stiff legs across the road, whirled and galloped back again. Jody picked up a stone to help the game along, but he was too late, for the cat was under the porch before the stone could be discharged. He threw the stone into the cypress tree and started the white pigeons on another whirling flight.

Arriving at the used-up haystack, the boy leaned against the barbed wire fence. "Will that be all of it, do you think?" he asked.

The middle-aged ranch-hand stopped his careful raking and stuck his fork into the ground. He took off his black hat and smoothed down his hair. "Nothing left of it that isn't soggy from ground moisture," he said. He replaced his hat and rubbed his dry leathery hands together.

"Ought to be plenty mice," Jody suggested.

"Lousy with them," said Billy. "Just crawling with mice."

"Well, maybe, when you get all through, I could call the dogs and hunt the mice."

"Sure, I guess you could," said Billy Buck. He lifted a forkful of the damp ground-hay and threw it into the air. Instantly three mice leaped out and burrowed frantically under the hay again.

Jody sighed with satisfaction. Those plump, sleek, arrogant mice were doomed. For eight months they had lived and multiplied in the haystack.

They had been immune from cats, from traps, from poison and from Jody. They had grown smug in their security, overbearing and fat. Now the time of disaster had come; they would not survive another day.

Billy looked up at the top of the hills that surrounded the ranch. "Maybe you better ask your father before you do it," he suggested.

"Well, where is he? I'll ask him now."

"He rode up to the ridge ranch after dinner. He'll be back pretty soon."

Jody slumped against the fence post. "I don't think he'd care."

As Billy went back to his work he said ominously, "You'd better ask him anyway. You know how he is."

Jody did know. His father, Carl Tiflin, insisted upon giving permission for anything that was done on the ranch, whether it was important or not. Jody sagged farther against the post until he was sitting on the ground. He looked up at the little puffs of wind-driven cloud. "Is it like to rain, Billy?"

"It might. The wind's good for it, but not strong enough."

"Well, I hope it don't rain until after I kill those damn mice." He looked over his shoulder to see whether Billy had noticed the mature profanity. Billy worked on without comment.

Jody turned back and looked at the side-hill where the road from the outside world came down. The hill was washed with lean March sunshine. Silver thistles, blue lupins and a few poppies bloomed among the sage bushes. Halfway up the hill Jody could see Doubletree Mutt, the black dog, digging in a squirrel hole. He paddled for a while and then paused to kick bursts of dirt out between his hind legs, and he dug with an earnestness which belied the knowledge he must have had that no dog had ever caught a squirrel by digging in a hole.

Suddenly, while Jody watched, the black dog stiffened, and backed out of the hole and looked up the hill toward the cleft in the ridge where the road came through. Jody looked up too. For a moment Carl Tiflin on horseback stood out against the pale sky and then he moved down the road toward the house. He carried something white in his hand.

The boy started to his feet. "He's got a letter," Jody cried. He trotted away toward the ranch house, for the letter would probably be read aloud and he wanted to be there. He reached the house before his father did, and ran in. He heard Carl dismount from his creaking saddle and slap the horse on the side to send it to the barn where Billy would unsaddle it and turn it out.

Jody ran into the kitchen. "We got a letter!" he cried.

His mother looked up from a pan of beans. "Who has?"

"Father has. I saw it in his hand."

Carl strode into the kitchen then, and Jody's mother asked, "Who's the letter from, Carl?"

He frowned quickly. "How did you know there was a letter?"

She nodded her head in the boy's direction. "Big-Britches Jody told me."

Jody was embarrassed.

His father looked down at him contemptuously. "He *is* getting to be a Big-Britches," Carl said. "He's minding everybody's business but his own. Got his big nose into everything."

Mrs. Tiflin relented a little. "Well, he hasn't enough to keep him busy. Who's the letter from?"

Carl still frowned on Jody. "I'll keep him busy if he isn't careful." He held out a sealed letter. "I guess it's from your father."

Mrs. Tiflin took a hairpin from her head and slit open the flap. Her lips pursed judiciously. Jody saw her eyes snap back and forth over the lines. "He says," she translated, "he says he's going to drive out Saturday to stay for a little while. Why, this is Saturday. The letter must have been delayed." She looked at the postmark. "This was mailed day before yesterday. It should have been here yesterday." She looked up questioningly at her husband, and then her face darkened angrily. "Now what have you got that look on you for? He doesn't come often."

Carl turned his eyes away from her anger. He could be stern with her most of the time, but when occasionally her temper arose, he could not combat it.

"What's the matter with you?" she demanded again.

In his explanation there was a tone of apology Jody himself might have used. "It's just that he talks," Carl said lamely. "Just talks."

"Well, what of it? You talk yourself."

"Sure I do. But your father only talks about one thing."

"Indians!" Jody broke in excitedly. "Indians and crossing the plains!"

Carl turned fiercely on him. "You get out, Mr. Big-Britches! Go on, now! Get out!"

Jody went miserably out the back door and closed the screen with elaborate quietness. Under the kitchen window his shamed, downcast eyes fell upon a curiously shaped stone, a stone of such fascination that he squatted down and picked it up and turned it over in his hands.

The voices came clearly to him through the open kitchen window. "Jody's damn well right," he heard his father say. "Just Indians and crossing the plains. I've heard that story about how the horses got driven off about a thousand times. He just goes on and on, and he never changes a word in the things he tells."

When Mrs. Tiflin answered her tone was so changed that Jody, outside the window, looked up from his study of the stone. Her voice had become soft and explanatory. Jody knew how her face would have changed to match the tone. She said quietly, "Look at it this way, Carl. That was the big thing in my father's life. He led a wagon train clear across the plains to the coast, and when it was finished, his life was done. It was a big thing to do, but it didn't last long enough. Look!" she continued, "it's as though he was born to do that, and after he finished it, there wasn't anything more for him to do but think about it and talk about it. If there'd been any farther west to go, he'd have gone. He's told me so himself. But at last there was the ocean. He lives right by the ocean where he had to stop."

She had caught Carl, caught him and entangled him in her soft tone.

"I've seen him," he agreed quietly. "He goes down and stares off west over the ocean." His voice sharpened a little. "And then he goes up to the Horseshoe Club in Pacific Grove, and he tells people how the Indians drove off the horses."

She tried to catch him again. "Well, it's everything to him. You might be patient with him and pretend to listen."

Carl turned impatiently away. "Well, if it gets too bad, I can always go down to the bunkhouse and sit with Billy," he said irritably. He walked through the house and slammed the front door after him.

Jody ran to his chores. He dumped the grain to the chickens without chasing any of them. He gathered the eggs from the nests. He trotted into the house with the wood and interlaced it so carefully in the wood-box that two armloads seemed to fill it to overflowing.

His mother had finished the beans by now. She stirred up the fire and brushed off the stove-top with a turkey wing. Jody peered cautiously at her to see whether any rancor toward him remained. "Is he coming today?" Jody asked.

"That's what his letter said."

"Maybe I better walk up the road to meet him."

Mrs. Tiflin clanged the stove-lid shut. "That would be nice," she said. "He'd probably like to be met."

"I guess I'll just do it then."

Outside, Jody whistled shrilly to the dogs. "Come on up the hill," he commanded. The two dogs waved their tails and ran ahead. Along the roadside the sage had tender new tips. Jody tore off some pieces and rubbed them on his hands until the air was filled with the sharp wild smell. With a rush the dogs leaped from the road and yapped into the brush after a rabbit. That was the last Jody saw of them, for when they failed to catch the rabbit, they went back home.

Jody plodded on up the hill toward the ridge top. When he reached the little cleft where the road came through, the afternoon wind struck him and blew up his hair and ruffled his shirt. He looked down on the little hills and ridges below and then out at the huge green Salinas Valley. He could see the white town of Salinas far out in the flat and the flash of its windows under the waning sun. Directly below him, in an oak tree, a crow congress had convened. The tree was black with crows all cawing at once.

The Jody's eyes followed the wagon road down from the ridge where he stood, and lost it behind a hill, and picked it up again on the other side. On that distant stretch he saw a cart slowly pulled by a bay horse. It disappeared behind the hill. Jody sat down on the ground and watched the place where the cart would reappear again. The wind sang on the hilltops and the puff-ball clouds hurried eastward.

Then the cart came into sight and stopped. A man dressed in black dismounted from the seat and walked to the horse's head. Although it was so far away, Jody knew he had unhooked the check-rein, for the horse's head dropped forward. The horse moved on, and the man walked slowly up the hill beside it. Jody gave a glad cry and ran down the road toward them. The squirrels bumped along off the road, and a road-runner flirted its tail and raced over the edge of the hill and sailed out like a glider.

Jody tried to leap into the middle of his shadow at every step. A stone rolled under his foot and he went down. Around a little bend he raced, and there, a short distance ahead, were his grandfather and the cart. The boy dropped from his unseemly running and approached at a dignified walk.

The horse plodded stumble-footedly up the hill and the old man walked beside it. In the lowering sun there giant shadows flickered darkly behind them. The grandfather was dressed in a black broadcloth suit and he wore kid congress gaiters[1] and a black tie on a short, hard collar. He carried his black slouch hat in his hand. His white beard was cropped close and his white eyebrows overhung his eyes like mustaches. The blue eyes were sternly merry. About the whole face and figure there was a granite dignity, so that every motion seemed an impossible thing. Once at rest, it seemed the old man would be stone, would never move again. His steps were slow and certain. Once made, no step could ever be retraced; once headed in a direction, the path would never bend nor the pace increase nor slow.

1. High-topped shoes, or spats. Grandfather is dressed quite formally, in keeping with his old-fashioned sense of dignity.

When Jody appeared around the bend, Grandfather waved his hat slowly in welcome, and he called, "Why, Jody! Come down to meet me, have you?"

Jody sidled near and turned and matched his step to the old man's step and stiffened his body and dragged his heels a little. "Yes, sir," he said. "We got your letter only today."

"Should have been here yesterday," said Grandfather. "It certainly should. How are all the folks?"

"They're fine, sir." He hesitated and then suggested shyly, "Would you like to come on a mouse hunt tomorrow, sir?"

"Mouse hunt, Jody?" Grandfather chuckled. "Have the people of this generation come down to hunting mice? They aren't very strong, the new people, but I hardly thought mice would be game for them."

"No, sir. It's just play. The haystack's gone. I'm going to drive out the mice to the dogs. And you can watch, or even beat the hay a little."

The stern, merry eyes turned down on him. "I see. You don't eat them, then. You haven't come to that yet."

Jody explained, "The dogs eat them, sir. It wouldn't be much like hunting Indians, I guess."

"No, not much—but then later, when the troops were hunting Indians and shooting children and burning teepees, it wasn't much different from your mouse hunt."

They topped the rise and started down into the ranch-cup, and they lost the sun from their shoulders. "You've grown," Grandfather said. "Nearly an inch, I should say."

"More" Jody boasted. "Where they mark me on the door, I'm up more than an inch since Thanksgiving even."

Grandfather's rich throaty voice said, "Maybe you're getting too much water and turning to pith and stalk. Wait until you head out, and then we'll see."

Jody looked quickly into the old man's face to see whether his feelings should be hurt, but there was no will to injure, no punishing nor putting-in-your-place light in the keen blue eyes. "We might kill a pig," Jody suggested.

"Oh, no! I couldn't let you do that. You're just humoring me. It isn't the time and you know it."

"You know Riley, the big boar, sir?"

"Yes, I remember Riley well."

"Well, Riley ate a hole into that same haystack, and it fell down on him and smothered him."

"Pigs do that when they can," said Grandfather.

"Riley was a nice pig, for a boar, sir. I rode him sometimes, and he didn't mind."

A door slammed at the house below them, and they saw Jody's mother standing on the porch waving her apron in welcome. And they saw Carl Tiflin walking up from the barn to be at the house for the arrival.

The sun had disappeared from the hills by now. The blue smoke from the house chimney hung in flat layers in the purpling ranch-cup. The puff-ball clouds, dropped by the falling wind, hung listlessly in the sky.

Billy Buck came out of the bunkhouse and flung a wash basin of soapy water on the ground. He had been shaving in mid-week, for Billy held Grandfather in reverence, and Grandfather said that Billy was one of the few men of the new generation who had not gone soft. Although Billy was in middle age, Grandfather considered him a boy. Now Billy was hurrying toward the house too.

When Jody and Grandfather arrived, the three were waiting for them in front of the yard gate.

Carl said, "Hello, sir. We've been looking for you."

Mrs. Tiflin kissed Grandfather on the side of his beard, and stood still while his big hand patted her shoulder. Billy shook hands solemnly, grinning under his straw mustache. "I'll put up your horse," said Billy, and he led the rig away.

Grandfather watched him go, and then, turning back to the group, he said as he had said a hundred times before, "There's a good boy. I knew his father, old Mule-tail Buck. I never knew why they called him Mule-tail except he packed mules."

Mrs. Tiflin turned and led the way into the house. "How long are you going to stay, Father? Your letter didn't say."

"Well, I don't know. I thought I'd stay about two weeks. But I never stay as long as I think I'm going to."

In a short while they were sitting at the white oilcloth table eating their supper. The lamp with the tin reflector hung over the table. Outside the dining-room windows the big moths battered softly against the glass.

Grandfather cut his steak into tiny pieces and chewed slowly. "I'm hungry," he said. "Driving out here got my appetite up. It's like when we were crossing. We all got so hungry every night we could hardly wait to let the meat get done. I could eat about five pounds of buffalo meat every night."

"It's moving around does it," said Billy. "My father was a government packer. I helped him when I was a kid. Just the two of us could about clean up a deer's ham."

"I knew your father, Billy," said Grandfather. "A fine man he was. They called him Mule-tail Buck. I don't know why except he packed mules."

"That was it," Bill agreed. "He packed mules."

Grandfather put down his knife and fork and looked around the table. "I remember one time we ran out of meat—" His voice dropped to a curious low sing-song, dropped into a tonal groove the story had worn for itself. "There was no buffalo, no antelope, not even rabbits. The hunters couldn't even shoot a coyote. That was the time for the leader to be on the watch. I was the leader, and I kept my eyes open. Know why? Well, just the minute the people began to get hungry they'd start slaughtering the team oxen. Do you believe that? I've heard of parties that just ate up their draft cattle. Started from the middle and worked toward the ends. Finally they'd eat the lead pair, and then the wheelers. The leader of a party had to keep them from doing that."

In some manner a big moth got into the room and circled the hanging kerosene lamp. Billy got up and tried to clap it between his hands. Carl struck with a cupped palm and caught the moth and broke it. He walked to the window and dropped it out.

"As I was saying," Grandfather began again, but Carl interrupted him. "You'd better eat some more meat. All the rest of us are ready for our pudding."

Jody saw a flash of anger in his mother's eyes. Grandfather picked up his knife and fork. "I'm pretty hungry, all right," he said. "I'll tell you about that later."

When supper was over, when the family and Billy Buck sat in front of the fireplace in the other room, Jody anxiously watched Grandfather. He saw the signs he knew. The bearded head leaned forward; the eyes lost their sternness and looked wonderingly into the fire; the big lean fingers laced themselves on the black knees. "I wonder," he began, "I just wonder whether I ever told you how those thieving Piutes drove off thirty-five of our horses."

"I think you did," Carl interrupted. "Wasn't it just before you went up into the Tahoe country?"

Grandfather turned quickly toward his son-in-law. "That's right. I guess I must have told you that story."

"Lots of times," Carl said cruelly, and he avoided his wife's eyes. But he felt the angry eyes on him, and he said, "'Course I'd like to hear it again."

Grandfather looked back at the fire. His fingers unlaced and laced again. Jody knew how he felt, how his insides were collapsed and empty. Hadn't Jody been called a Big-Britches that very afternoon? He arose to heroism and opened himself to the term Big-Britches again. "Tell about Indians," he said softly.

Grandfather's eyes grew stern again. "Boys always want to hear about Indians. It was a job for men, but boys want to hear about it. Well, let's see. Did I ever tell you how I wanted each wagon to carry a long iron plate?"

Everyone but Jody remained silent. Jody said, "No. You didn't."

"Well, when the Indians attacked, we always put the wagons in a circle and fought from between the wheels. I thought that if every wagon carried a long plate with rifle holes, the men could stand the plates on the outside of the wheels when the wagons were in the circle and they would be protected. It would save lives and that would make up for the extra weight of the iron. But of course the party wouldn't do it. No party had done it before and they couldn't see why they should go to the expense. They lived to regret it, too."

Jody looked at his mother, and knew from her expression that she was not listening at all. Carl picked at a callus on his thumb and Billy Buck watched a spider crawling up the wall.

Grandfather's tone dropped into its narrative groove again. Jody knew in advance exactly what words would fall. The story droned on, speeded up for the attack, grew sad over the wounds, struck a dirge at the burials on the great plains. Jody sat quietly watching Grandfather. The stern blue eyes were detached. He looked as though he were not very interested in the story himself.

When it was finished, when the pause had been politely respected as the frontier of the story, Billy Buck stood up and stretched and hitched his trousers. "I guess I'll turn in," he said. Then he faced Grandfather. "I've got an old powder horn and a cap and ball pistol down to the bunkhouse. Did I ever show them to you?"

Grandfather nodded slowly. "Yes, I think you did, Billy. Reminds me of a pistol I had when I was leading the people across." Billy stood politely until the story was done, and then he said, "Good night," and went out of the house.

Carl Tiflin tried to turn the conversation then. "How's the country between here and Monterey?[2] I've heard it's pretty dry."

"It is dry," said Grandfather. "There's not a drop of water in the Laguna Seca.[3] But it's a long pull from '87. The whole country was powder then, and in '61 I believe all the coyotes starved to death. We had fifteen inches of rain this year."

"Yes, but it all came too early. We could do with some now." Carl's eye fell on Jody. "Hadn't you better be getting to bed?"

---

2. Peninsula jutting into the Pacific Ocean south of San Francisco.   3. Dry Lagoon (Spanish).

Jody stood up obediently. "Can I kill the mice in the old haystack, sir?"

"Mice? Oh! Sure, kill them all off. Billy said there isn't any good hay left."

Jody exchanged a secret and satisfying look with Grandfather. "I'll kill every one tomorrow," he promised.

Jody lay in his bed and thought of the impossible world of Indians and buffaloes, a world that had ceased to be forever. He wished he could have been living in the heroic time, but he knew he was not of heroic timber. No one living now, save possibly Billy Buck, was worthy to do the things that had been done. A race of giants had lived then, fearless men, men of a staunchness unknown in this day. Jody thought of the wide plains and of the wagons moving across like centipedes. He thought of Grandfather on a huge white horse, marshaling the people. Across his mind marched the great phantoms, and they marched off the earth and they were gone.

He came back to the ranch for a moment, then. He heard the dull rushing sound that space and silence make. He heard one of the dogs, out in the doghouse, scratching a flea and bumping his elbow against the floor with every stroke. Then the wind arose again and the black cypress groaned and Jody went to sleep.

He was up half an hour before the triangle sounded for breakfast. His mother was rattling the stove to make the flames roar when Jody went through the kitchen. "You're up early," she said. "Where are you going?"

"Out to get a good stick. We're going to kill the mice today."

"Who is 'we'?"

"Why, Grandfather and I."

"So you've got him in it. You always like to have someone in with you in case there's blame to share."

"I'll be right back," said Jody. "I just want to have a good stick ready for after breakfast."

He closed the screen door after him and went out into the cool blue morning. The birds were noisy in the dawn and the ranch cats came down from the hill like blunt snakes. They had been hunting gophers in the dark, and although the four cats were full of gopher meat, they sat in a semi-circle at the back door and mewed piteously for milk. Doubletree Mutt and Smasher moved sniffing along the edge of the brush, performing the duty with rigid ceremony, but when Jody whistled, their heads jerked up and their tails waved. They plunged down to him, wriggling their skins and yawning. Jody patted their heads seriously, and moved on to the weathered scrap pile. He selected an old broom handle and a short piece of inch-square scrap wood. From his pocket he took a shoelace and tied the ends of the sticks loosely together to make a flail. He whistled his new weapon through the air and struck the ground experimentally, while the dogs leaped aside and whined with apprehension.

Jody turned and started down past the house toward the old haystack ground to look over the field of slaughter, but Billy Buck, sitting patiently on the back steps, called to him, "You better come back. It's only a couple of minutes till breakfast."

Jody changed his course and moved toward the house. He leaned his flail against the steps. "That's to drive the mice out," he said. "I'll bet they're fat. I'll bet they don't know what's going to happen to them today."

"No, nor you either," Billy remarked philosophically, "nor me, nor anyone."

Jody was staggered by this thought. He knew it was true. His imagination twitched away from the mouse hunt. Then his mother came out on the back porch and struck the triangle, and all thoughts fell in a heap.

Grandfather hadn't appeared at the table when they sat down. Billy nodded at his empty chair. "He's all right? He isn't sick?"

"He takes a long time to dress," said Mrs. Tiflin. "He combs his whiskers and rubs up his shoes and brushes his clothes."

Carl scattered sugar on his mush. "A man that's led a wagon train across the plains has got to be pretty careful how he dresses."

Mrs. Tiflin turned on him. "Don't do that, Carl! Please don't!" There was more of threat than of request in her tone. And the threat irritated Carl.

"Well, how many times do I have to listen to the story of the iron plates, and the thirty-five horses? That time's done. Why can't he forget it, now it's done?" He grew angrier while he talked, and his voice rose. "Why does he have to tell them over and over? He came across the plains. All right! Now it's finished. Nobody wants to hear about it over and over."

The door into the kitchen closed softly. The four at the table sat frozen. Carl laid his mush spoon on the table and touched his chin with his fingers.

Then the kitchen door opened and Grandfather walked in. His mouth smiled tightly and his eyes were squinted. "Good morning," he said, and he sat down and looked at his mush dish.

Carl could not leave it there. "Did—did you hear what I said?"

Grandfather jerked a little nod.

"I don't know what got into me, sir. I didn't mean it. I was just being funny."

Jody glanced in shame at his mother, and he saw that she was looking at Carl, and that she wasn't breathing. It was an awful thing that he was doing. He was tearing himself to pieces to talk like that. It was a terrible thing to him to retract a word, but to retract it in shame was infinitely worse.

Grandfather looked sidewise. "I'm trying to get right side up," he said gently. "I'm not being mad. I don't mind what you said, but it might be true, and I would mind that."

"It isn't true," said Carl. "I'm not feeling well this morning. I'm sorry I said it."

"Don't be sorry, Carl. An old man doesn't see things sometimes. Maybe you're right. The crossing is finished. Maybe it should be forgotten, now it's done."

Carl got up from the table. "I've had enough to eat. I'm going to work. Take your time, Billy!" He walked quickly out of the dining-room. Billy gulped the rest of his food and followed soon after. But Jody could not leave his chair.

"Won't you tell any more stories?" Jody asked.

"Why, sure I'll tell them, but only when—I'm sure people want to hear them."

"I like to hear them, sir."

"Oh! Of course you do, but you're a little boy. It was a job for men, but only little boys like to hear about it."

Jody got up from his place. "I'll wait outside for you, sir. I've got a good stick for those mice."

He waited by the gate until the old man came out on the porch. "Let's go down and kill the mice now," Jody called.

"I think I'll just sit in the sun, Jody. You go kill the mice."

"You can use my stick if you like."

"No, I'll just sit here a while."

Jody turned disconsolately away, and walked down toward the old haystack. He tried to whip up his enthusiasm with thoughts of the fat juicy mice.

He beat the ground with his flail. The dogs coaxed and whined about him, but he could not go. Back at the house he could see Grandfather sitting on the porch, looking small and thin and black.

Jody gave up and went to sit on the steps at the old man's feet.

"Back already? Did you kill the mice?"

"No, sir. I'll kill them some other day."

The morning flies buzzed close to the ground and the ants dashed about in front of the steps. The heavy smell of sage slipped down the hill. The porch boards grew warm in the sunshine.

Jody hardly knew when Grandfather started to talk. "I shouldn't stay here, feeling the way I do." He examined his strong old hands. "I feel as though the crossing wasn't worth doing." His eyes moved up the side-hill and stopped on a motionless hawk perched on a dead limb. "I tell those old stories, but they're not what I want to tell. I only know how I want people to feel when I tell them.

"It wasn't Indians that were important, nor adventures, nor even getting out here. It was a whole bunch of people made into one big crawling beast. And I was the head. It was westering and westering. Every man wanted something for himself, but the big beast that was all of them wanted only westering. I was the leader, but if I hadn't been there, someone else would have been the head. The thing had to have a head.

"Under the little bushes the shadows were black at white noonday. When we saw the mountains at last, we cried—all of us. But it wasn't getting here that mattered, it was movement and westering.

"We carried life out here and set it down the way those ants carry eggs. And I was the leader. The westering was as big as God, and the slow steps that made the movement piled up and piled up until the continent was crossed.

"Then we came down to the sea, and it was done." He stopped and wiped his eyes until the rims were red. "That's what I should be telling instead of stories."

When Jody spoke, Grandfather started and looked down at him. "Maybe I could lead the people some day," Jody said.

The old man smiled. "There's no place to go. There's the ocean to stop you. There's a line of old men along the shore hating the ocean because it stopped them."

"In boats I might, sir."

"No place to go, Jody. Every place is taken. But that's not the worst—no, not the worst. Westering has died out of the people. Westering isn't a hunger any more. It's all done. Your father is right. It is finished." He laced his fingers on his knee and looked at them.

Jody felt very sad. "If you'd like a glass of lemonade I could make it for you."

Grandfather was about to refuse, and then he saw Jody's face. "That would be nice," he said. "Yes, it would be nice to drink a lemonade."

Jody ran into the kitchen where his mother was wiping the last of the breakfast dishes. "Can I have a lemon to make a lemonade for Grandfather?"

His mother mimicked—"And another lemon to make a lemonade for you."

"No, ma'am. I don't want one."

"Jody! You're sick!" Then she stopped suddenly. "Take a lemon out of the cooler," she said softly. "Here, I'll reach the squeezer down to you."

1945

COUNTEE CULLEN
1903–1946

More than most poets of the Harlem Renaissance, Countee Cullen valued traditional poetic forms in English—the sonnet, rhymed couplets, and quatrains—over modernist free verse or rhythms suggested by jazz and popular culture. Never one to shy away from controversy, Cullen prefaced his important anthology of African American poetry, *Caroling Dusk* (1927), with the assertion, "As heretical as it may sound, there is the probability that Negro poets, dependent as they are on the English language, may have more to gain from the rich background of English and American poetry than from any nebulous atavistic yearnings toward an African inheritance." Cullen demanded that black poets be considered as American poets, ultimately without any special racial designation. Nevertheless, the titles of his books of poetry—*Color* (1925), *Copper Sun* (1927), *The Ballad of the Brown Girl* (1928)—showed that, like Claude MacKay and Jean Toomer, he felt a responsibility to write about being black even if he did so in modes outside of black folk traditions. Although he clashed with a number of his contemporaries in the Harlem Renaissance, Cullen could also be generous to black writers whose poetics differed from his. What mattered to Cullen was appreciating the full range of black literary writing, a range as great, he insisted, as that found among white poets in English, and resisting every "attempt to corral the ebony muse into some definite mold" to which all black writers should conform.

Although Cullen's birthplace and early years are obscure, he was adopted at some point in his childhood by a Harlem-based minister and given a good education, first in New York public schools and then at New York University, where he received his B.A. in 1925, and at Harvard, where he took an M.A. in 1926. In high school, Cullen earned a city-wide poetry prize for "I Have a Rendezvous with Life," a rejoinder to Alan Seeger's sentimental World War I poem. His first book of poems, *Color*, appeared in his senior year at college; it established him as the "black Keats," a prodigy.

From 1926 to 1928, Cullen was assistant editor at the important black journal *Opportunity*, for which he also wrote a feature column, "The Dark Tower." In 1928 he married Nina Yolande Du Bois, the daughter of W. E. B. Du Bois, and won a Guggenheim fellowship that took him to Paris and enabled him to complete another book of poems, *The Black Christ* (1929). His marriage quickly disintegrated, however, over Cullen's attraction to men, and the couple was divorced in 1930. Neither *The Black Christ* nor the novel that followed, *One Way to Heaven* (1932), earned the acclaim of Cullen's earlier books. He spent the last years of his life teaching at New York's Frederick Douglass Junior High School, where his pupils included the future novelist James Baldwin. With the revival of scholarly interest in the Harlem Renaissance, Cullen's distinctive combination of traditionalist poetic skill with acerbic self-questioning on matters of racism and racial identity has once again brought his poetry to critical attention.

The text of poems included here is that of *Color* (1925).

Yet Do I Marvel

I doubt not God is good, well-meaning, kind,
And did He stoop to quibble could tell why

The little buried mole continues blind,
Why flesh that mirrors Him must some day die,
Make plain the reason tortured Tantalus   5
Is baited by the fickle fruit, declare
If merely brute caprice dooms Sisyphus[1]
To struggle up a never-ending stair.
Inscrutable His ways are, and immune
To catechism by a mind too strewn   10
With petty cares to slightly understand
What awful brain compels His awful hand.
Yet do I marvel at this curious thing:
To make a poet black, and bid him sing!

                                                1925

Incident

Once riding in old Baltimore,
    Heart-filled, head-filled with glee,
I saw a Baltimorean
    Keep looking straight at me.

Now I was eight and very small,   5
    And he was no whit bigger,
And so I smiled, but he poked out
    His tongue, and called me, "Nigger."

I saw the whole of Baltimore
    From May until December;   10
Of all the things that happened there
    That's all that I remember.

                                                1925

Heritage

What is Africa to me:
Copper sun or scarlet sea,
Jungle star or jungle track,
Strong bronzed men, or regal black
Women from whose loins I sprang   5
When the birds of Eden sang?
One three centuries removed
From the scenes his fathers loved,
Spicy grove, cinnamon tree,
What is Africa to me?   10

---

1. Tantalus and Sisyphus are figures in Greek mythology who were punished in Hades. Tantalus was offered food and water that was then instantly snatched away. Sisyphus had to roll a heavy stone to the top of a hill and, after it rolled back down, repeat the ordeal perpetually.

So I lie, who all day long
Want no sound except the song
Sung by wild barbaric birds
Goading massive jungle herds,
Juggernauts[1] of flesh that pass   15
Trampling tall defiant grass
Where young forest lovers lie,
Plighting troth beneath the sky.
So I lie, who always hear,
Though I cram against my ear   20
Both my thumbs, and keep them there,
Great drums throbbing through the air.
So I lie, whose fount of pride,
Dear distress, and joy allied,
Is my somber flesh and skin,   25
With the dark blood dammed within
Like great pulsing tides of wine
That, I fear, must burst the fine
Channels of the chafing net
Where they surge and foam and fret.   30

Africa? A book one thumbs
Listlessly, till slumber comes.
Unremembered are her bats
Circling through the night, her cats
Crouching in the river reeds,   35
Stalking gentle flesh that feeds
By the river brink; no more
Does the bugle-throated roar
Cry that monarch claws have leapt
From the scabbards where they slept.   40
Silver snakes that once a year
Doff the lovely coats you wear,
Seek no covert in your fear
Lest a mortal eye should see;
What's your nakedness to me?   45
Here no leprous flowers rear
Fierce corollas[2] in the air;
Here no bodies sleek and wet,
Dripping mingled rain and sweat,
Tread the savage measures of   50
Jungle boys and girls in love.
What is last year's snow to me,[3]
Last year's anything? The tree
Budding yearly must forget
How its past arose or set—   55
Bough and blossom, flower, fruit,
Even what shy bird with mute

---

1. The juggernaut is a sacred Hindu idol dragged on a huge car in the path of which devotees were believed to throw themselves—hence any power demanding blind sacrifice, here spliced with the image of elephants.

2. The whorl of petals forming the inner envelope of a flower.

3. An echo of the lament "Where are the snows of yesteryear?" from "Grand Testament" by the 15th-century French poet François Villon.

Wonder at her travail there,
Meekly labored in its hair.
One three centuries removed   60
From the scenes his fathers loved,
Spicy grove, cinnamon tree,
What is Africa to me?

So I lie, who find no peace
Night or day, no slight release   65
From the unremittant beat
Made by cruel padded feet
Walking through my body's street.
Up and down they go, and back,
Treading out a jungle track.   70
So I lie, who never quite
Safely sleep from rain at night—
I can never rest at all
When the rain begins to fall;
Like a soul gone mad with pain   75
I must match its weird refrain;
Ever must I twist and squirm,
Writhing like a baited worm,
While its primal measures drip
Through my body, crying, "Strip!   80
Doff this new exuberance.
Come and dance the Lover's Dance!"
In an old remembered way
Rain works on me night and day.

Quaint, outlandish heathen gods   85
Black men fashion out of rods,
Clay, and brittle bits of stone,
In a likeness like their own,
My conversion came high-priced;
I belong to Jesus Christ,   90
Preacher of humility;
Heathen gods are naught to me.

Father, Son, and Holy Ghost,
So I make an idle boast;
Jesus of the twice-turned cheek[4]   95
Lamb of God, although I speak
With my mouth thus, in my heart
Do I play a double part.
Ever at Thy glowing altar
Must my heart grow sick and falter,   100
Wishing He I served were black,
Thinking then it would not lack
Precedent of pain to guide it,
Let who would or might deride it;

4. In his Sermon on the Mount (Matthew 5.39), Jesus declared that when struck on the cheek, one should turn the other cheek rather than strike back.

Surely then this flesh would know   105
Yours had borne a kindred woe.
Lord, I fashion dark gods, too,
Daring even to give You
Dark despairing features where,
Crowned with dark rebellious hair,   110
Patience wavers just so much as
Mortal grief compels, while touches
Quick and hot, of anger, rise
To smitten cheek and weary eyes.
Lord, forgive me if my need   115
Sometimes shapes a human creed.
All day long and all night through,
One thing only must I do:
Quench my pride and cool my blood,
Lest I perish in the flood.   120
Lest a hidden ember set
Timber that I thought was wet
Burning like the dryest flax,
Melting like the merest wax,
Lest the grave restore its dead.   125
Not yet has my heart or head
In the least way realized
They and I are civilized.

1925

RICHARD WRIGHT
1908–1960

With the 1940 publication of *Native Son* Richard Wright became the first African American author of a bestseller. *Native Son* is an uncompromising study of an African American underclass youth who is goaded to brutal violence by the oppression, hatred, and incomprehension of the white world. The sensational story disregarded conventional wisdom about how black authors should approach a white reading audience. Bigger Thomas, the main character, embodied everything that such an audience might fear and detest, but by situating the point of view within this character's consciousness Wright forced readers to see the world through Bigger's eyes and thus to understand him. The novel was structured like a hard-boiled detective story, contained layers of literary allusion and symbol, and combined Marxist social analysis with existential philosophy—in brief, it was at once a powerful social statement and a complex work of literary art.

Wright was born near Natchez, Mississippi. When he was five, his father abandoned the family—Wright, his younger brother, and his mother—and for the next ten years Wright was raised by a series of relatives in Mississippi. By 1925, when he went to Memphis on his own, he had moved twenty times. Extreme poverty, a constantly interrupted education that never went beyond junior high school, and the religious fundamentalism of his grandmother, along with the constant experiences of humiliation and hatred in a racially segregated South: all these contributed to Wright's growing sense that the hidden anger of black people was justified and that only by acknowledging and expressing it could they move beyond it. The title of *Native Son* made the point that the United States is as much the country of black as of white; the story showed that blacks had been deprived of their inheritance.

Two years after moving to Memphis, Wright went north to Chicago. There he took a series of odd jobs and then joined the WPA Writers' Project (a government project of the depression years to help support authors) as a writer of guidebooks and as a director of the Federal Negro Theater. He began to study Marxist theory, contributing poetry to leftist literary magazines and joining the Communist party in 1932. By 1935 he had become the center of a group of African American Chicago writers and had started to write fiction. He was influenced by the naturalistic fiction of James T. Farrell, whose study of sociology at the University of Chicago had helped give structure to his popular Studs Lonigan trilogy about working people of Irish descent.

Wright moved to New York in 1937 to write for the New York Writers' Project and as a reporter on the communist *Daily Worker*. In 1938 he published *Uncle Tom's Children*, a collection of four short stories. (An earlier novel, *Lawd Today*, was not published until after his death.) Set in the rural South, the stories center on racial conflict and physical violence. Wright's theme of the devastating effect of relentless, institutionalized hatred and humiliation on the black male's psyche was paramount in all of them.

After *Native Son*, Wright turned to autobiographical writings that eventuated in *Black Boy*, published in 1945. Many consider this to be his best book, and such writers as Ralph Ellison and James Baldwin took it as a model for their own work in the 1950s and 1960s. A communist activist in the early 1940s, Wright became increasingly disillusioned and broke completely with the party in 1944. Visiting France in 1946, he was warmly received by leading writers and philosophers. In 1947 he settled permanently in that country, where he was perceived from the first as one of the important experimental modernist prose writers and was ranked on a level with Hemingway, Fitzgerald, and Faulkner. An existential novel, *The Outsider* (1953), was followed by five more books: two novels and three collections of lectures, travel writings, and sociopolitical commentary. The collection *Eight Men*, from which the story printed here is taken, was the last literary project he worked on, and it appeared the year after his death.

Wright's immersion in Marxist doctrine gave him tools for representing society as divided into antagonistic classes and run for the benefit of the few. But in each of his works he portrays individuals who, no matter how they are deformed and brutalized by oppression and exploitation, retain a transcendent spark of selfhood. Ultimately, it is in this spark that Wright put his faith. His writing from first to last affirmed the dignity and humanity of society's outcasts without romanticizing them, and indicted those who had cast them out. As Ralph Ellison expressed it, Wright's example "converted the American Negro impulse toward self-annihilation and 'going underground' into a will to confront the world" and to "throw his findings unashamedly into the guilty conscience of America."

The text was first published in *Harper's Bazaar* (1939) under the title "Almos' a Man." Under its present title it appeared in *Eight Men* (1961), a posthumous collection of Wright's short fiction.

The Man Who Was Almost a Man

Dave struck out across the fields, looking homeward through paling light. Whut's the use talkin wid em niggers in the field? Anyhow, his mother was putting supper on the table. Them niggers can't understan nothing. One of these days he was going to get a gun and practice shooting, then they couldn't talk to him as though he were a little boy. He slowed, looking at the ground. Shucks, Ah ain scareda them even ef they are biggern me! Aw, Ah know whut Ahma do. Ahm going by ol Joe's sto n git that Sears Roebuck catlog n look at them guns. Mebbe Ma will lemme buy one when she gits mah pay from ol man Hawkins. Ahma beg her t gimme some money. Ahm ol ernough to hava gun. Ahm seventeen. Almost a man. He strode, feeling his long loose-jointed limbs. Shucks, a man oughta hava little gun aftah he done worked hard all day.

He came in sight of Joe's store. A yellow lantern glowed on the front porch. He mounted steps and went through the screen door, hearing it bang behind him. There was a strong smell of coal oil and mackerel fish. He felt very confident until he saw fat Joe walk in through the rear door, then his courage began to ooze.

"Howdy, Dave! Whutcha want?"

"How yuh, Mistah Joe? Aw, Ah don wanna buy nothing. Ah jus wanted t see ef yuhd lemme look at tha catlog erwhile."

"Sure! You wanna see it here?"

"Nawsuh. Ah wans t take it home wid me. Ah'll bring it back termorrow when Ah come in from the fiels."

"You plannin on buying something?"

"Yessuh."

"Your ma lettin you have your own money now?"

"Shucks. Mistah Joe, Ahm gittin t be a man like anybody else!"

Joe laughed and wiped his greasy white face with a red bandanna.

"Whut you plannin on buyin?"

Dave looked at the floor, scratched his head, scratched his thigh, and smiled. Then he looked up shyly.

"Ah'll tell yuh, Mistah Joe, ef yuh promise yuh won't tell."

"I promise."

"Waal, Ahma buy a gun."

"A gun? What you want with a gun?"

"Ah wanna keep it."

"You ain't nothing but a boy. You don't need a gun."

"Aw, lemme have the catlog, Mistah Joe. Ah'll bring it back."

Joe walked through the rear door. Dave was elated. He looked around at barrels of sugar and flour. He heard Joe coming back. He craned his neck to see if he were bringing the book. Yeah, he's got it. Gawddog, he's got it!

"Here, but be sure you bring it back. It's the only one I got."

"Sho, Mistah Joe."

"Say, if you wanna buy a gun, why don't you buy one from me? I gotta gun to sell."

"Will it shoot?"

"Sure it'll shoot."

"Whut kind is it?"

"Oh, it's kinda old . . . a left-hand Wheeler. A pistol. A big one."

"Is it got bullets in it?"

"It's loaded."

"Kin Ah see it?"

"Where's your money?"

"What yuh wan fer it?"

"I'll let you have it for two dollars."

"Just two dollahs? Shucks, Ah could buy tha when Ah git mah pay."

"I'll have it here when you want it."

"Awright, suh. Ah be in fer it."

He went through the door, hearing it slam again behind him. Ahma git some money from Ma n buy me a gun! Only two dollahs! He tucked the thick catalogue under his arm and hurried.

"Where yuh been, boy?" His mother held a steaming dish of black-eyed peas.

"Aw, Ma, Ah just stopped down the road t talk wid the boys."

"Yuh know bettah t keep suppah waitin."

He sat down, resting the catalogue on the edge of the table.

"Yuh git up from there and git to the well n wash yosef! Ah ain feedin no hogs in mah house!"

She grabbed his shoulder and pushed him. He stumbled out of the room, then came back to get the catalogue.

"Whut this?"

"Aw, Ma, it's jusa catlog."

"Who yuh git it from?"

"From Joe, down at the sto."

"Waal, thas good. We kin use it in the outhouse."

"Naw, Ma." He grabbed for it. "Gimme ma catlog, Ma."

She held onto it and glared at him.

"Quit hollerin at me! Whut's wrong wid yuh? Yuh crazy?"

"But Ma, please. It ain mine! It's Joe's! He tol me t bring it back t im termorrow."

She gave up the book. He stumbled down the back steps, hugging the thick book under his arm. When he had splashed water on his face and hands, he groped back to the kitchen and fumbled in a corner for the towel. He bumped into a chair; it clattered to the floor. The catalogue sprawled at his feet. When he had dried his eyes he snatched up the book and held it again under his arm. His mother stood watching him.

"Now, ef yuh gonna act a fool over that ol book, Ah'll take it n burn it up."

"Naw, Ma, please."

"Waal, set down n be still!"

He sat down and drew the oil lamp close. He thumbed page after page, unaware of the food his mother set on the table. His father came in. Then his small brother.

"Whutcha got there, Dave?" his father asked.

"Jusa catlog," he answered, not looking up.

"Yeah, here they is!" His eyes glowed at blue-and-black revolvers. He glanced up, feeling sudden guilt. His father was watching him. He eased the book under the table and rested it on his knees. After the blessing was asked, he ate. He scooped up peas and swallowed fat meat without chewing. But-termilk helped to wash it down. He did not want to mention money before his father. He would do much better by cornering his mother when she was alone. He looked at his father uneasily out of the edge of his eye.

"Boy, how come yuh don quit foolin wid tha book n eat yo suppah?"

"Yessuh."

"How you n ol man Hawkins gitten erlong?"

"Suh?"

"Can't yuh hear? Why don yuh lissen? Ah ast yu how wuz yuh n ol man Hawkins gittin erlong?"

"Oh, swell, Pa. Ah plows mo lan than anybody over there."

"Waal, yuh oughta keep yo mind on whut yuh doin."

"Yessuh."

He poured his plate full of molasses and sopped it up slowly with a chunk of cornbread. When his father and brother had left the kitchen, he still sat and looked again at the guns in the catalogue, longing to muster courage enough to present his case to his mother. Lawd, ef Ah only had tha pretty one! He could almost feel the slickness of the weapon with his fingers. If he had a gun like that he would polish it and keep it shining so it would never rust. N Ah'd keep it loaded, by Gawd!

"Ma?" His voice was hesitant.

"Hunh?"

"Ol man Hawkins give yuh mah money yit?"

"Yeah, but ain no usa yuh thinking bout throwin nona it erway. Ahm keepin tha money sos yuh kin have cloes t go to school this winter."

He rose and went to her side with the open catalogue in his palms. She was washing dishes, her head bent low over a pan. Shyly he raised the book. When he spoke, his voice was husky, faint.

"Ma, Gawd knows Ah wans one of these."

"One of whut?" she asked, not raising her eyes.

"One of these," he said again, not daring even to point. She glanced up at the page, then at him with wide eyes.

"Nigger, is yuh gone plumb crazy?"

"Aw, Ma."

"Git outta here! Don yuh talk t me bout no gun! Yuh a fool!"

"Ma, Ah kin buy one fer two dollahs."

"Not ef Ah knows it, yuh ain!"

"But yuh promised me one."

"Ah don care whut Ah promised! Yuh ain nothing but a boy yit!"

"Ma, ef yuh lemme buy one Ah'll *never* ast yuh fer nothing no mo."

"Ah tol yuh t git outta here! Yuh ain gonna toucha penny of tha money fer no gun! Thas how come Ah has Mistah Hawkins t pay yo wages t me, cause Ah knows yuh ain got no sense."

"But, Ma, we needa gun. Pa ain got no gun. We needa gun in the house. Yuh kin never tell whut might happen."

"Now don yuh try to maka fool outta me, boy! Ef we did hava gun, yuh wouldn't have it!"

He laid the catalogue down and slipped his arm around her waist.

"Aw, Ma, Ah done worked hard alla summer n ain ast yuh fer nothin, is Ah, now?"

"Thas whut yuh spose t do!"

"But Ma, Ah wans a gun. Yuh kin lemme have two dollahs outta mah money. Please, Ma. I kin give it to Pa . . . Please, Ma! Ah loves yuh, Ma."

When she spoke her voice came soft and low.

"What yuh wan wida gun, Dave? Yuh don need no gun. Yuh'll git in trouble. N ef yo pa jus thought Ah let yuh have money t buy a gun he'd hava fit."

"Ah'll hide it, Ma. It ain but two dollahs."

"Lawd, chil, whut's wrong wid yuh?"

"Ain nothing wrong, Ma. Ahm almos a man now. Ah wans a gun."

"Who gonna sell yuh a gun?"

"Ol Joe at the sto."

"N it don cos but two dollahs?"

"Thas all, Ma. Just two dollahs. Please, Ma."

She was stacking the plates away; her hands moved slowly, reflectively. Dave kept an anxious silence. Finally, she turned to him.

"Ah'll let yuh git tha gun ef yuh promise me one thing."

"Whut's tha, Ma?"

"Yuh bring it straight back t me, yuh hear? It be fer Pa."

"Yessum! Lemme go now, Ma."

She stooped, turned slightly to one side, raised the hem of her dress, rolled down the top of her stocking, and came up with a slender wad of bills.

"Here," she said. "Lawd knows yuh don need no gun. But yer pa does. Yuh bring it right back t me, yuh hear? Ahma put it up. Now ef yuh don, Ahma have yuh pa pick yuh so hard yuh won fergit it."

"Yessum."

He took the money, ran down the steps, and across the yard.

"Dave! Yuuuuuh Daaaaave!"

He heard, but he was not going to stop now. "Naw, Lawd!"

The first movement he made the following morning was to reach under his pillow for the gun. In the gray light of dawn he held it loosely, feeling a sense of power. Could kill a man with a gun like this. Kill anybody, black or white. And if he were holding his gun in his hand, nobody could run over him; they would have to respect him. It was a big gun, with a long barrel and a heavy handle. He raised and lowered it in his hand, marveling at its weight.

He had not come straight home with it as his mother had asked; instead he had stayed out in the fields, holding the weapon in his hand, aiming it now and then at some imaginary foe. But he had not fired it; he had been afraid that his father might hear. Also he was not sure he knew how to fire it.

To avoid surrendering the pistol he had not come into the house until he knew that they were all asleep. When his mother had tiptoed to his bedside late that night and demanded the gun, he had first played possum; then he had told her that the gun was hidden outdoors, that he would bring it to her in the morning. Now he lay turning it slowly in his hands. He broke it, took out the cartridges, felt them, and then put them back.

He slid out of bed, got a long strip of old flannel from a trunk, wrapped the gun in it, and tied it to his naked thigh while it was still loaded. He did not go in to breakfast. Even though it was not yet daylight, he started for Jim Hawkins' plantation. Just as the sun was rising he reached the barns where the mules and plows were kept.

"Hey! That you, Dave?"

He turned. Jim Hawkins stood eying him suspiciously.

"What're yuh doing here so early?"

"Ah didn't know Ah wuz gittin up so early, Mistah Hawkins. Ah wuz fixin t hitch up ol Jenny n take her t the fiels."

"Good. Since you're so early, how about plowing that stretch down by the woods?"

"Suits me, Mistah Hawkins."

"O.K. Go to it!"

He hitched Jenny to a plow and started across the fields. Hot dog! This was just what he wanted. If he could get down by the woods, he could shoot his gun and nobody would hear. He walked behind the plow, hearing the traces creaking, feeling the gun tied tight to his thigh.

When he reached the woods, he plowed two whole rows before he decided to take out the gun. Finally, he stopped, looked in all directions, then untied the gun and held it in his hand. He turned to the mule and smiled.

"Know whut this is, Jenny? Naw, yuh wouldn know! Yuhs jusa ol mule! Anyhow, this is a gun, n it kin shoot, by Gawd!"

He held the gun at arm's length. Whut t hell, Ahma shoot this thing! He looked at Jenny again.

"Lissen here, Jenny! When Ah pull this ol trigger, Ah don wan yuh t run n acka fool now!"

Jenny stood with head down, her short ears pricked straight. Dave walked off about twenty feet, held the gun far out from him at arm's length, and turned his head. Hell, he told himself, Ah ain afraid. The gun felt loose in his fingers; he waved it wildly for a moment. Then he shut his eyes and tightened his forefinger. Bloom! A report half deafened him and he thought his right hand was torn from his arm. He heard Jenny whinnying and galloping over the field, and he found himself on his knees, squeezing his fingers hard between his legs. His hand was numb; he jammed it into his mouth, trying to warm it, trying to stop the pain. The gun lay at his feet. He did not quite know what had happened. He stood up and stared at the gun as though it were a living thing. He gritted his teeth and kicked the gun. Yuh almos broke mah arm! He turned to look for Jenny; she was far over the fields, tossing her head and kicking wildly.

"Hol on there, ol mule!"

When he caught up with her she stood trembling, walling her big white eyes at him. The plow was far away; the traces had broken. Then Dave stopped short, looking, not believing. Jenny was bleeding. Her left side was red and wet with blood. He went closer. Lawd, have mercy! Wondah did Ah shoot this mule? He grabbed for Jenny's mane. She flinched, snorted, whirled, tossing her head.

"Hol on now! Hol on."

Then he saw the hole in Jenny's side, right between the ribs. It was round, wet, red. A crimson stream streaked down the front leg, flowing fast. Good Gawd! Ah wuzn't shootin at tha mule. He felt panic. He knew he had to stop that blood, or Jenny would bleed to death. He had never seen so much blood in all his life. He chased the mule for a half a mile, trying to catch her. Finally she stopped, breathing hard, stumpy tail half arched. He caught her mane and led her back to where the plow and gun lay. Then he stooped and grabbed handfuls of damp black earth and tried to plug the bullet hole. Jenny shuddered, whinnied, and broke from him.

"Hol on! Hol on now!"

He tried to plug it again, but blood came anyhow. His fingers were hot and sticky. He rubbed dirt into his palms, trying to dry them. Then again he attempted to plug the bullet hole, but Jenny shied away, kicking her heels high. He stood helpless. He had to do something. He ran at Jenny; she dodged him. He watched a red stream of blood flow down Jenny's leg and form a bright pool at her feet.

"Jenny . . . Jenny," he called weakly.

His lips trembled. She's bleeding t death! He looked in the direction of home, wanting to go back, wanting to get help. But he saw the pistol lying in the damp black clay. He had a queer feeling that if he only did something, this would not be; Jenny would not be there bleeding to death.

When he went to her this time, she did not move. She stood with sleepy, dreamy eyes; and when he touched her she gave a low-pitched whinny and knelt to the ground, her front knees slopping in blood.

"Jenny . . . Jenny . . ." he whispered.

For a long time she held her neck erect; then her head sank, slowly. Her ribs swelled with a mighty heave and she went over.

Dave's stomach felt empty, very empty. He picked up the gun and held it gingerly between his thumb and forefinger. He buried it at the foot of a tree. He took a stick and tried to cover the pool of blood with dirt—but what was the use? There was Jenny lying with her mouth open and her eyes walled and glassy. He could not tell Jim Hawkins he had shot his mule. But he had to tell something. Yeah, Ah'll tell em Jenny started gittin wil n fell on the joint of the plow. . . . But that would hardly happen to a mule. He walked across the field slowly, head down.

It was sunset. Two of Jim Hawkins' men were over near the edge of the woods digging a hole in which to bury Jenny. Dave was surrounded by a knot of people, all of whom were looking down at the dead mule.

"I don't see how in the world it happened," said Jim Hawkins for the tenth time.

The crowd parted and Dave's mother, father, and small brother pushed into the center.

"Where Dave?" his mother called.

"There he is," said Jim Hawkins.

His mother grabbed him.

"Whut happened, Dave? Whut yuh done?"

"Nothin."

"C mon, boy, talk," his father said.

Dave took a deep breath and told the story he knew nobody believed.

"Waal," he drawled. "Ah brung ol Jenny down here sos Ah could do mah plowin. Ah plowed bout two rows, just like yuh see." He stopped and pointed at the long rows of upturned earth. "Then somethin musta been wrong wid ol Jenny. She wouldn ack right a-tall. She started snortin n kickin her heels. Ah tried t hol her, but she pulled erway, rearin n goin in. Then when the point of the plow was stickin up in the air, she swung erroun n twisted herself back on it . . . She stuck herself n started t bleed. N fo Ah could do anything, she wuz dead."

"Did you ever hear of anything like that in all your life?" asked Jim Hawkins.

There were white and black standing in the crowd. They murmured. Dave's mother came close to him and looked hard into his face. "Tell the truth, Dave," she said.

"Looks like a bullet hole to me," said one man.

"Dave, whut yuh do wid the gun?" his mother asked.

The crowd surged in, looking at him. He jammed his hands into his pockets, shook his head slowly from left to right, and backed away. His eyes were wide and painful.

"Did he hava gun?" asked Jim Hawkins.

"By Gawd, Ah tol yuh tha wu a gun wound," said a man, slapping his thigh.

His father caught his shoulders and shook him till his teeth rattled.

"Tell whut happened, yuh rascal! Tell whut . . ."

Dave looked at Jenny's stiff legs and began to cry.

"Whut yuh do wid tha gun?" his mother asked.

"Whut wuz he doin wida gun?" his father asked.

"Come on and tell the truth," said Hawkins. "Ain't nobody going to hurt you . . ."

His mother crowded close to him.

"Did yuh shoot tha mule, Dave?"

Dave cried, seeing blurred white and black faces.

"Ahh ddinn gggo tt sshooot hher . . . Ah sssswear ffo Gawd Ahh ddin. . . . Ah wuz a-tryin t sssee ef the old gggun would sshoot."

"Where yuh git the gun from?" his father asked.

"Ah got it from Joe, at the sto."

"Where yuh git the money?"

"Ma give it t me."

"He kept worryin me, Bob. Ah had t. Ah tol im t bring the gun right back to me . . . It was fer yuh, the gun."

"But how yuh happen to shoot that mule?" asked Jim Hawkins.

"Ah wuzn shootin at the mule, Mistah Hawkins. The gun jumped when Ah pulled the trigger . . . N fo Ah knowed anythin Jenny was there a-bleedin."

Somebody in the crowd laughed. Jim Hawkins walked close to Dave and looked into his face.

"Well, looks like you have bought you a mule, Dave."

"Ah swear fo Gawd, Ah didn go t kill the mule, Mistah Hawkins!"

"But you killed her!"

All the crowd was laughing now. They stood on tiptoe and poked heads over one another's shoulders.

"Well, boy, looks like yuh done bought a dead mule! Hahaha!"

"Ain tha ershame."

"Hohohohoho."

Dave stood, head down, twisting his feet in the dirt.

"Well, you needn't worry about it, Bob," said Jim Hawkins to Dave's father. "Just let the boy keep on working and pay me two dollars a month."

"Whut yuh wan fer yo mule, Mistah Hawkins?"

Jim Hawkins screwed up his eyes.

"Fifty dollars."

"Whut yuh do wid tha gun?" Dave's father demanded.

Dave said nothing.

"Yuh wan me t take a tree n beat yuh till yuh talk!"

"Nawsuh!"

"Whut yuh do wid it?"

"Ah throwed it erway."

"Where?"

"Ah . . . Ah throwed it in the creek."

"Waal, c mon home. N firs thing in the mawnin git to tha creek n fin tha gun."

"Yessuh."

"Whut yuh pay fer it?"

"Two dollahs."

"Take tha gun n git yo money back n carry it t Mistah Hawkins, yuh near? N don fergit Ahma lam you black bottom good fer this! Now march yosef on home, suh!"

Dave turned and walked slowly. He heard people laughing. Dave glared, his eyes welling with tears. Hot anger bubbled in him. Then he swallowed and stumbled on.

That night Dave did not sleep. He was glad that he had gotten out of killing the mule so easily, but he was hurt. Something hot seemed to turn over inside him each time he remembered how they had laughed. He tossed on his bed, feeling his hard pillow. *N Pa says he's gonna beat me . . .* He remembered other beatings, and his back quivered. *Naw, naw, Ah sho don wan im t beat me tha way no mo. Dam em all! Nobody ever gave him anything. All he did was work. They treat me like a mule, n then they beat me.* He gritted his teeth. *N Ma had t tell on me.*

Well, if he had to, he would take old man Hawkins that two dollars. But that meant selling the gun. And he wanted to keep that gun. Fifty dollars for a dead mule.

He turned over, thinking how he had fired the gun. He had an itch to fire it again. *Ef other men kin shoota gun, by Gawd, Ah kin!* He was still, listening. *Mebbe they all sleepin now.* The house was still. He heard the soft breathing of his brother. *Yes, now!* He would go down and get that gun and see if he could fire it! He eased out of bed and slipped into overalls.

The moon was bright. He ran almost all the way to the edge of the woods. He stumbled over the ground, looking for the spot where he had buried the gun. *Yeah, here it is.* Like a hungry dog scratching for a bone, he pawed it up. He puffed his black cheeks and blew dirt from the trigger and barrel. He broke it and found four cartridges unshot. He looked around; the fields were filled with silence and moonlight. He clutched the gun stiff and hard in his fingers. But, as soon as he wanted to pull the trigger, he shut his eyes and turned his head. *Naw, An can't shoot wid mah eyes closed n mah head turned.* With effort he held his eyes open; then he squeezed. *Bloooom!* He was stiff, not breathing. The gun was still in his hands. Dammit, he'd done it! He fired again. *Bloooom!* He smiled. *Blooooom! Blooooom! Click, click.* There! It was empty. If anybody could shoot a gun, he could. He put the gun into his hip pocket and started across the fields.

When he reached the top of a ridge he stood straight and proud in the moonlight, looking at Jim Hawkins' big white house, feeling the gun sagging in his pocket. *Lawd, ef Ah had just one mo bullet Ah'd taka shot at tha house. Ah'd like t scare ol man Hawkins jusa little . . . Jusa enough t let im know Dave Saunders is a man.*

To his left the road curved, running to the tracks of the Illinois Central. He jerked his head, listening. From far off came a faint *hoooof-hoooof; hoooof-hoooof; hoooof-hoooof.* . . . He stood rigid. *Two dollahs a mont. Les see now . . . Tha means it'll take bout two years. Shucks! Ah'll be dam!*

He started down the road, toward the tracks. *Yeah, here she comes!* He stood beside the track and held himself stiffly. Here she comes, *erroun the ben . . . C mon, yuh slow poke! C mon!* He had his hand on his gun; something quivered in his stomach. Then the train thundered past, the gray and brown box cars rumbling and clinking. He gripped the gun tightly; then he jerked his hand out of his pocket. *Ah betcha Bill wouldn't do it! Ah betcha. . . .* The cars slid past, steel grinding upon steel. *Ahm ridin yuh ternight, so hep me Gawd!* He was hot all over. He hesitated just a moment; then he grabbed, pulled atop of a car, and lay flat. He felt his pocket; the gun was still there. Ahead the long rails were glinting in the moonlight, stretching away, away to somewhere, somewhere where he could be a man . . .

1939, 1961

American Literature
since 1945

THE UNITED STATES AND
WORLD POWER

Distribution of power is a purpose of war, and the consequences of a world war are necessarily global. Having agreed to a policy of demanding unconditional surrender, the allied countries of Britain, the Soviet Union, and the United States positioned themselves to achieve nothing short of total victory over their enemies in World War II: Germany and Japan. Yet each country's contribution to victory made for startling contrasts in the following half century. Britain, beleaguered since the war's start in September 1939, fought against odds that depleted its resources and severely disrupted its traditional class structure. The Soviet Union, an amalgamation of nations under the central power of Russia, suffered the war's worst casualties when attacked by Germany in June 1941 and afterward, well into 1945, during the hideous contest of attrition along the war's bitter eastern front. Although newly established as a world power after the end of hostilities, the U.S.S.R. remained at an economic disadvantage and dissolved in 1991 after five decades of Cold War against its ideological adversaries in the West. It was the United States, entering the war after Japan's attack on Pearl Harbor on December 7, 1941, that emerged as the only world power in excellent economic shape. This new power, experienced both at home and abroad, became a major force in reshaping American culture for the balance of the twentieth century.

The great social effort involved in fighting World War II reorganized America's economy and altered its people's lifestyles. Postwar existence revealed different

---

Autumn Rhythms (detail), by Jackson Pollock. For more information about this painting, see the color insert in this volume.

kinds of men and women, with new aspirations among both majority and minority populations. New possibilities for action empowered individuals and groups in the pursuit of personal freedom and individual self-expression. During World War II American industry had expanded dramatically for military purposes; plants that had manufactured Chevrolets, Plymouths, Studebakers, Packards, and Fords now made B-24 Liberators and Grumman Avengers. With three million men in uniform, the vastly expanded workforce required increasing numbers of women. After hostilities were concluded many of these women were reluctant to return to homemaking; and then after a decade or so of domesticity, women emerged as a political force on behalf of their rights and opportunities in the workplace. This pattern extended to other groups as well. African Americans, whether they enlisted or were drafted, served in fighting units throughout the war and were unwilling to return to second-class status afterward; nor could a majority culture aware of their contribution continue to enforce segregation and other forms of prejudice so easily as before the war.

Economic power at the world level continued to influence American culture through the first two postwar decades. The first two—and only two—atomic bombs that have ever been used were exploded by the United States in Japan in August 1945; their effect was so horrific that geographical "containment" of America's nuclear-armed communist rivals emerged as the paramount American military policy. When Communist North Korea invaded American ally South Korea in 1950, therefore, the United States rejected responding with atomic weapons in favor of a United Nations–sponsored "police action" that followed a policy of using conventional weapons only and not pursuing enemy forces beyond specific boundaries. But if hot war was out, cold war was in, specifically the type of contest in which military strength was built up for deterrence rather than combat. Henceforth economic conduct would be a major factor in the American decision to contain the Soviet Union's attempt to expand its influence. In the years following World War II the U.S.S.R. had assumed a stance considered adversarial to Western interests. Ideologically, the opposition was between Western capitalism and Soviet state socialism; politically the contest exhibited itself in the West's rebuilding of Germany and the formation of the North Atlantic Treaty Organization (NATO) versus the Soviet Union's dominance over Eastern Europe by means of the Warsaw Pact. In Africa, where new nations gained independence from colonial rule, West and East competed for influence. Overall, the West perceived a threat in the U.S.S.R.'s 1948 attainment of nuclear weaponry and its maintenance of massive troop strength beyond its borders. When communist revolutionaries took control of mainland China in 1949, the Cold War moved beyond European boundaries to encompass the entire globe. Until the collapse of the Soviet Union in 1991, economic warfare motivated American activity as decisively as had the waging of World War II.

Throughout the 1950s and into the early 1960s, social critics perceived a stable conformity to American life, a dedication to an increasingly materialistic standard of living, whose ethical merit was ensured by a continuity with the prewar world—a continuity that proved to be delusory. In this initial postwar period white males benefited especially from the economy and saw the nature of their lives change. The G.I. Bill provided veterans with a college education; after World War II America would eventually have as much as 50 percent of its population college educated, a percentage unthinkable in prewar years and unmatched by any other nation. With world markets open to American goods, the expanded economy offered sophisticated technical and professional jobs for these college graduates; within a generation the alphabet soup of great corporations—IT&T, GE, RCA, IBM, and so forth—came to dominate employment patterns at home and around the globe. Higher incomes and demographic expansion created vast new suburbs beyond the limits of older cities, and the population of the United States began a westward shift. New roads accommodated this increasingly mobile society, including the interstate highway system begun in 1955. By 1960 the average American family was moving to a new place of residence at the rate of once every five years, as new opportunities beckoned and lifestyles expanded beyond the more traditional stability of "home." An age of plenty created a new managerial class, but also ensured an ample piece of the pie for workers protected by secure, well-organized unions.

The GI Bill of Rights (1944), which provided federal subsidies to support college education for returning World War II veterans, democratized American higher education. Shown here, veterans and other students at New York University in January 1945.

But ways of life consonant with an isolated, stable economy could not survive in the new atmosphere of American power and wealth. The passage from the 1950s to the 1960s marks the great watershed of the postwar half-century. Conflicts between conformity and individuality, tradition and innovation, stability and disruption were announced and anticipated even before they materially influenced history and culture. The earliest harbinger was the 1960 election of John F. Kennedy as president. To a mainstream society that might have become complacent with the material success of the postwar years and had neglected the less fortunate, Kennedy offered an energetic program of involvement. Formally titled "The New Frontier," it reached from the participation of individual Americans in the Peace Corps (working to aid underdeveloped countries around the world) to the grand effort to conquer space. In the midst of his brief presidency, in October 1962, in what came to be known as the "Cuban Missile Crisis," the Soviet Union installed ballistic missiles in Cuba; when Kennedy protested this act and began a naval blockade of the island nation, the possibility of nuclear warfare loomed closer than ever before, until the U.S.S.R. relented and withdrew its weapons. Domestic tensions also rose when Robert Kennedy,

John F. Kennedy Jr. salutes at his father's funeral.

the president's brother and U.S. attorney general, took a newly activist approach toward desegregation, sending federal troops into the South to enforce the law. But there was a cultural grace to the Kennedy era as well, with the president's wife, Jacqueline, making involvement in the arts not just fashionable but also a matter of government policy.

The Sixties, as they are known, really began with the assassination of John F. Kennedy on November 22, 1963. The tumultuous dozen years of American history that followed represent a more combative period in civil rights, climaxing with the most sustained and effective attempts to remedy the evils of racial discrimination since the years of Reconstruction after the Civil War. For the first time since the suffrage movement following World War I, women organized to pursue their legal, ethical, and cultural interests, now defined as feminism. Active dissension within the culture emerged in response to military involvement in Vietnam, where in 1961 President Kennedy had sent small numbers of advisers to help the Republic of South Vietnam resist pressures from Communist North Vietnam. Presidents Lyndon Johnson and Richard Nixon expanded and continued the U.S. presence; and an increasingly strident opposition—fueled by protests on American college campuses and among the country's liberal intellectuals—turned into a much larger cultural revolution. Between 1967 and 1970 the nation experienced many outbreaks of violence, including political assassinations (of both presidential candidate Robert Kennedy and civil rights leader Dr. Martin Luther King Jr. in 1968), urban riots, and massive campus disruptions.

Torn apart by opposition to President Johnson and the climate of violence surrounding its national convention in Chicago in August 1968, the Democratic Party lost to Republican candidate Richard Nixon, who was then, like his predecessor, burdened with the Vietnam War and escalating dissent (leading to student deaths at Kent State and Jackson State universities in May 1970). By the time the Vietnam War ended in 1975 with the collapse of Saigon to North Vietnamese and Viet Cong forces, the United States had also been buffeted by transformative political trouble in the form of the Watergate scandal: a revelation of President Nixon's abuses of governmental privileges that led to his resignation in August 1974. These events mark the end of one of the more discomfortingly disruptive eras in American history.

By the end of the 1970s some characteristics of the previous decade's countercultural revolt had been accepted in the mainstream, including informalities of dress, relaxation of sexual codes of behavior, and an increased respect for individual rights. The 1980s witnessed a call for traditional values, interpreted as a return not to community and self-sacrifice but to the pursuit of wealth. During Ronald Reagan's presidency income disparities grew while taxes fell; the Sixties' distrust of government mutated into a defense of personal acquisition. Following the debacle in Vietnam, where more than fifty thousand Americans had died in a losing war, the military restricted itself in the 1980s and early 1990s to quick, sharply specified interventions (in Grenada, Panama, and most dramatically in the Gulf War of 1991), relying less on vague deterrence than on precise applications of technological expertise. Economically, America boomed, but in new ways: manufacturing dominance was replaced by service efficiency, massive workforces were downsized into more profitable units, while speculation and entrepreneurship replaced older modes of development.

As the twentieth century made its turn, global power experienced its greatest readjustment since World War II. American economic might had depleted the Soviet Union's ability to compete, and as that state's ethnic republics achieved independence and the old Warsaw Pact alliance of Eastern European nations collapsed, the European Union—once restricted to Western democracies—assumed even greater importance. With the attack on New York's World Trade Center and the Pentagon by terrorists on September 11, 2001, the third millennium threatened to echo the first, with religious forces setting political agendas and working to see those agendas fulfilled, beginning with a seemingly open-ended face-off between American and revolutionary Islamic forces in Afghanistan and Iraq.

LITERARY DEVELOPMENTS

In such a turbulent half century, literature also encompassed a great deal of change. Not surprisingly, during this period many important writers reexamined both what literature is meant to accomplish and how to accomplish it. Conflicts between conformity and individuality, tradition and innovation, stability and disruption characterized the literature of the period as they also shaped the historical and cultural milieu. Just as people in the first two decades following World War II addressed themselves to taking material advantage of the extensive gains won by the global victory, so writers sought to capitalize on the successes of a previous literary generation. Cultural homogeneity was an ideal during the 1950s, patriotically so in terms of building up the foundations of American society to resist and contain Communism, materialistically so when it came to enjoying the benefits of

The Saturday Evening
POST
May 25, 1957 – 15¢

I Call on Groucho
By PETE MARTIN

How Will America Behave
IF H-BOMBS FALL?

"After the Prom." This 1957 *Saturday Evening Post* cover by
Norman Rockwell contrasts with the ominous headline, "How Will
America Behave IF H-BOMBS FALL?"

capitalism. This ideal of homogeneity led many writers to assume that a single work—short story, novel, poem, or play—could represent the experiences of an entire people, that a common national essence lay beneath distinctions of gender, race, ethnicity, religion, or region. The literary world between 1945 and the Sixties often let readers believe that there could be such a thing as a representative American short story, nuanced for upper-middle-class patrons in the pages of the *New Yorker* magazine while slanted to more homely interests in *Collier's* and the *Saturday Evening Post*.

Novels of the immediate postwar period followed this trend in greater depth, in larger scale, and with more self-conscious justification. Ernest Hemingway, a master of the short story, had fostered the notion of novel writing as "going the distance," slugging it out all the way, as it were, in a fifteen-round championship prizefight. Publicized by others as one of the dominant literary figures of his day, Hemingway promoted his own example to influence a new generation of novelists who believed they had to act like him to be taken seriously. Hence the desire to write what was called "the great American novel"—a major work that would characterize the larger aspects of national experience. Ambitions were not simply to write a war novel, for example, but *the* war novel; not just a work about corporate big business, but something that encapsulated the subject for all times. Regionalism could remain an interest, but only if it provided broader meaning; here the example of William Faulkner encouraged the belief among younger writers that dealing with the American South meant grappling with monumental issues of guilt and the inexorable power of history. Major dramatists behaved the same way; if their immediate predecessors had drawn on classically tragic allusions in deepening their themes, postwar playwrights embraced otherwise mundane characters as universal types. The death of a salesman, for example, would be examined in the same spotlight once reserved for great people, for here indeed was a figure who stood for the postwar human being.

As a genre poetry was less tied to expectations about realism or national essence than was the novel or the short story. In the 1950s the poetic standard was the short lyric meditation, in which the poet, avoiding the first person, would find an object, a landscape, or an observed encounter that epitomized and clarified a feeling. A poem was the product of retrospection, a gesture of composure following the initial shock or stimulus that provided the occasion for writing. Some poets composed in intricate stanzas and skillful rhymes, deploying a mastery of verse form as one sign of the civilized mind's power to explore, tame, and distill raw experience. In the 1950s and 1960s poets acquired a new visibility in American life. After the war, writers' conferences and workshops, recordings, and published and broadcast interviews became common, and a network of poets traveling to give readings and to become poets-in-residence at universities began to form. Despite this increase in poetry's visibility, its marginal position in the nation's culture, when compared to that of prose fiction, may have allowed for more divergence from the ideal of homogeneity. The mid to late 1940s saw the publication of groundbreaking books as various as Gwendolyn Brooks's *A Street in Bronzeville* (1945), with its evocation of African American experience; Robert Duncan's *Heavenly City, Earthly City* (1947), with its mystical and homosexual themes; and Theodore Roethke's linguistically experimental sequence *The Lost Son* (1948). As early as 1950 Charles Olsen's manifesto, *Projective Verse*, called for a unit of poetic expression based not on predetermined metrical feet but on the poet's "breath" and the rhythms of the body. In the 1950s and 1960s a number of important poets displayed what the poet-critic Richard Howard called "the longing to lose the gift of order, despoiling the self of all that had been, merely, propriety." The poetry of Allen Ginsberg, Sylvia Plath, and John Berryman began as well mannered and formal, then turned to wilder and more disquieting forms of lyric exploration.

Like the notion of cultural conformity, the understanding of any single piece of literature as representing an entire people came under withering scrutiny during the 1960s. As the novelist Philip Roth remarked in 1960, "the American writer in the middle of the twentieth century has his hands full in trying to understand, describe, and then make credible much of American reality." Critical movements of the time articulated a new literary unease around the issue of realism, and writers responded to this unease by developing new literary strategies, new ways of dealing with a much more contentious, varied, and unstable sense of the era. Some writers felt that social reality had become too unstable to serve as a reliable anchor for their narratives, and some critics believed that fiction had exhausted its formal possibilities. A "Death of the Novel" controversy arose. Both the novel and the short story, some argued, demanded a set of fairly limited conventions; these conventions, such as characterization and development by means of dialogue, imagery, and symbolism, however, relied on a securely describable world to make sense.

In poetry, two important and transforming shocks were administered by Allen Ginsberg's *Howl* (1956) and Robert Lowell's *Life Studies* (1959). Ginsberg first delivered his poem aloud, during a reading at the Six Gallery in San Francisco in the fall of 1955; the following year it was published by Lawrence Ferlinghetti's City Lights Bookshop. In a single stroke, with the energy of a reborn Walt Whitman, Ginsberg made poetry one of the rallying points for underground protest and prophetic denunciation of the prosperous, complacent, gray-spirited Eisenhower years. The setting in which the poem appeared is also significant, for *Howl*, like other work associated with what came to be known as the San Francisco Renaissance, challenged the conventions of a literary tradition dominated by the East Coast. With its open, experimental form and strong oral emphasis, *Howl* sounded a departure from the well-shaped lyric. Lowell, a more "difficult," less popular poet, was rooted in the literary culture of Boston. But with *Life Studies* he too challenged the literary status quo, bringing a new directness and autobiographical intensity into American poetry as he exposed the psychological turbulence suffered by an inbred New Englander. Lowell's embrace of a more open, less heavily symbolic style was inspired, in part, by hearing the work of Ginsberg and others while on a reading tour of the West Coast.

City Lights Bookstore, in San Francisco, California, is a landmark to poetry and to freedom of speech. Owned by the poet Lawrence Ferlinghetti, City Lights published the work of Beat poets, most famously Allen Ginsberg's groundbreaking *Howl and Other Poems* (1956). Shown here outside the bookstore in 1956 are (left to right) Bob Donlin, Neal Cassady, Ginsberg, Robert LaVinge, and Ferlinghetti.

The connection between these two volumes and the times in which they were written is direct and apparent. Their poems anticipated and explored the fissures in American social consensus that would erupt into the open conflicts of the 1960s and 1970s and shape American life for decades to come, with growing public unease concerning a broad range of issues: the uses of government and industrial power; the institutions of marriage and the family; the rights of racial minorities, women, and homosexuals; the use of drugs; alternative states of consciousness. Taken together, Ginsberg's and Lowell's books also suggested that the invigorating energies of postwar American poetry would arise from diverse regions of the country, their common aim being to restore poetry to a more vital relation with contemporary life.

Even as American life in the 1950s espoused conformity, technological advances in the exchange of information had made the particulars of that life ever harder to manage. As boundaries of time and space were eclipsed by television, air travel, and an accompanying global awareness, the once essential unities of representation (time, space, and action) no longer provided ground on which to build a work of literary art. As more became known about the world, the writer's ability to make sense of the whole was challenged. A culture that looked for all-encompassing expressions from its writers now seemed to demand the impossible. In the 1960s poets began to extend their subject matter to include more explicit and extreme areas of autobiographical revelation—sex, divorce, alcoholism, insanity. The convenient but not very precise label "confessional" came to be attached to certain books in which the intimate particulars of one person's life insisted on the distinctness of individual experience, not its representativeness. Other poets devised forms that reflected an understanding of poetry as provisional, as representing the changing flow of experience from moment to moment. Some poets began dating each of their poems, as though to suggest that the feelings involved belonged to the moment and were subject to change.

A parallel development in literary theory posed another great threat to conventional literature. Known as "Deconstruction" and brought to American shores from France by means of a series of university conferences and academic publications beginning in 1966, this style of criticism questioned the underlying assumptions behind any statement, exposing how what was accepted as absolute truth usually depended on rhetoric rather than fact, exposing indeed how "fact" itself was constructed by intellectual operations. This style of criticism became attractive to literary scholars who had been framing social and political questions in much the same terms—believing, for example, that the Vietnam War had been presented to the American people through slogans rather than realities. Many of the fiction writers, dramatists, and poets who sought stable employment in universities and colleges took part vigorously in these discussions. Deconstruction's preoccupation with language dismantled some of the boundaries between philosophy, poetry, psychology, and linguistics, and emphasized writing as a site of multiple "discourses." The idea of literature as self-expression was complicated by a focus on the social power of language and the constructed nature of subjectivity. The skepticism toward unity and coherence that marks the era extended to the very idea of the self. The Death of the Novel debates in prose fiction had an analogue in the intensified skepticism poets brought to the idea of narrative. Borrowing from the technologies of film and video (jump cuts, tracking shots, shifting camera angles, split screens), literature began to imagine a reader saturated with the sounds of contemporary discourse, a reader whose attention quickly shifts. All of these impulses converged to destabilize literary genres that were once thought to be reliable windows on the world.

Literature in the 1960s was often extreme in its methods and disruptive in its effects. Yet much like its social and political developments, the decade's literary trends remained influential beyond the Sixties. Writers continued to experiment with diverse practices with which to render a sense of contemporary reality, and they continued their artistic debates over how that reality was constituted and how it could be represented. Authors as diverse as John Updike, Bernard Malamud, and Ann Beattie continued to write realistic fiction, even in the heyday of Deconstruction, but in a style enriched by the rigorous cross-examination of its previously unquestioned methods. Even in a period at times overly conscious of self and world as fictional constructs, poets like Gwendolyn Brooks and Philip Levine engaged with history and politics, and others like Elizabeth Bishop and Stanley Kunitz remained committed to poetry's relation to a common world. In prose fiction a new group of realistic writers, called "Minimalists," made these challenges central to their work, crafting a manner of description that with great intensity limited itself to what could be most reliably accepted. What the Minimalists described was not endorsed by the authors as true; rather it consisted of signs that their characters accepted as truth, not objects from nature but conventions accepted by societies to go about the business of living. In a typical Minimalist story, although nothing sad is mentioned and no character grieves, someone makes a sign that she is saying something meant to be sad, and another character emits a perfect sign of being deeply unhappy in response. Objects that abound in such works are drawn from the consumer's world not for what they are but for what they signify, be it good taste or poor, wealth or deprivation. It is a workable way of writing realism in a world where philosophical definitions discourage such a term.

The social and political changes of the 1960s left a legacy even richer than those of critical and philosophical revolutions. Political dissent helped make available to literature a broad range of more insistent voices. Civil rights activism helped create the Black Arts Movement, which in turn replaced the notion of accepting only one token African American writer at a time with a much broader awareness of imaginative expression by a wide range of literary talent. A parallel movement saw Southern writers, like the poet Charles Wright and the fiction writer Barry Hannah, seeking modes of expression other than mourning the loss of the Civil War or feeling guilty about slavery. Jewish American writers, like the poet Stanley Kunitz and the fiction writers Philip Roth and Bernard Malamud, began moving beyond thematics of assimilation and identity to embrace subjects and techniques reaching from the deeply personal to the metapoetic or metafictive. Some women prose writers—Ursula LeGuin, for example—found that subgenres such as fantasy and science fiction could be useful in undermining long-held stereotypes of gender, while poets such as Adrienne Rich and Audre Lorde presented the experience of women hitherto silenced or unrepresented in literature. In both fiction and poetry, writers found that present-day life could be described with a new frankness and expanded awareness appropriate to women's wider and more egalitarian role in society. Native American writers received new respect from mainstream culture, initiated by attention to the land's ecology and recognition that the "Wild West" view of American history included a strategic stereotyping of Indian people. An important body of critical work helped create new contexts for thinking about Native American literature as both traditional and contemporary. In fact, in the 1970s and 1980s a fresh impetus of experimentation and literary commitment came from writers of minority traditions who gained access to presses and publishing venues. Available now were artistic expressions of the cultural complexity of the American population from Chinese Americans, Japanese Americans, Mexican Americans, and other groups previously excluded from the literary canon. These different traditions were not mutually exclusive; the work of many writers testified to an enlivening interaction between traditions, affirming the imagination's freedom to draw from many sources. As, earlier, the modernists had reached out to traditions beyond the Western— the poet Ezra Pound to the Chinese ideograph and the poet Charles Olson to Mayan Indian culture, for example—American writers of this period were redefining what constitutes America.

One of the most dramatic developments, during the 1970s and 1980s, one that indicated the broadening range of achievement among writers of many different backgrounds and persuasions, was the success of African American women—novelists, dramatists, and poets—in finding literary voices and making them heard as important articulations of experience. Here was a reminder of how so much of what passes for reality is nothing but artifice, fabrication, and convention—for here was a large group of people whose ancestors had been written out of history and who were still often denied speaking parts in national dialogues. Even with so much of a usable past effaced and identity repressed, these writers were able to find a means of expression that helped redefine readers' understanding of the world, whether in imaginative refigurings of the novel like Toni Morrison's, in book-length poetic sequences like Rita Dove's *Thomas and Beulah*, or in individual poems that gave voice to African American experience, like those of Lucille Clifton. By the close of the twentieth century other voices emerged that also had been written out of history, and many writers from minority traditions began to take their place at the center of American writing. "Realism," like "globalism," was now a much more expansive and inclusive term, from Sherman Alexie's Native Americans to Jhumpa Lahiri's international cosmopolites with their world-spanning technologies.

Another important development involved the increasing prominence of Latina/Latino writing in American literature. As the title of Dan Wakefield's 1959 nonfiction novel, *Island in the City*, suggests, communities of native Spanish speakers were once considered enclaves. Yet New York City's Puerto Rican Spanish Harlem not only spread, but was augumented by areas of Brooklyn and urban New Jersey being resettled by families from the Dominican Republic—families like those portrayed in the fiction of Julia Alvarez and Junot Díaz, whose lives were enriched by an interpolation of Anglo and Hispanic cultures, thanks to frequent travels between old and new homes. Such natural and spontaneous multiculturalism would make a work such as composer Leonard Bernstein's musical (and later film) *West Side Story* (1957) seem almost quaintly historical in its separation of societies. Elsewhere, persons of Hispanic heritage began rivaling in numbers their Anglo

Rita Dove served as Poet Laureate and Consultant in Poetry at the Library of Congress from 1993 to 1995. She was the youngest person—and first African American—to hold this appointment.

fellow citizens not just in Southern California's Orange County, which had once typified a Nixon–era style of white establishment values, but even in the small towns of Iowa and Nebraska, where their participation in agricultural industries such as meat-packing helped revive an endangered economy, not to mention their contributions to both popular entertainment and literary culture.

Contemporary literature values heterogeneity in its forms and pluralism in its cultural influences. This literature assumes a context wherein the nature of reality changes. Because contemporary culture appears so relentlessly artificial—political events, advertising, and television (including news programs) can all be seen as staged and packaged reforms of fiction—it is also increasingly a literature preoccupied with authenticity and a yearning for the real. Hence the appeal of documentary films, the popularity of the memoir, the attraction on DVDs of "outtakes" showing moments of disruption in the process of filmmaking. The burgeoning genre known as creative nonfiction—a term that first appeared officially in 1983 as a category for creative writing fellowships offered by the National Endowment of the Arts—reflects contemporary literature's impatience with the opposition between fact and fiction. Combining aspects of the essay, memoir, reportage, criticism, and autobiography, creative nonfiction uses the techniques of fiction to make a claim to the real. As represented in a cluster in this volume, creative nonfiction can be said to include some of the best environmental and travel writing, as well as hybrid forms of memoir that rely on the fiction of memory and factual research. *The Year of Magical Thinking* (2005), Joan Didion's account of the year following the sudden death of her husband, John Gregory Dunne, from cardiac arrest, is a case in point: it is part memoir, part medical research, part an almost clinical investigation of the phenomenon of grief.

Among contemporary literature's emblems is the Internet, and, in a digital age, reality is hybrid, with constant input from multiple sources and a proclivity for combining, editing, altering, and rearranging existing materials—processes analogous to DJ sampling in music. In such a culture, originality and plagiarism no longer seem necessarily opposing terms. As technology reshapes what we think about and how we experience contemporary literature, it is also reshaping how writers produce literature. Some contemporary writers edit online journals; they turn to hypertext to create computer-screen poems with simultaneous and open-ended possibilities, where the reader's choices shape poetic forms. Thanks to computer technology, novelists may include artificial intelligence among their casts of characters, as Richard Powers demonstrates in his novel *Galatea* 2.2 (1995). At the same time some contemporary writers continue to draft their work with pencil and paper, and some feel as much affinity with classical Chinese poets or the great nineteenth-century novelists as with computer technology.

It has been said that our contemporary culture provides the greatest variety of literary expression that has ever been available at any one time. From a war effort that demanded unity of purpose and a Cold War period that for a time encouraged conformity to a homogenous ideal, American writing has emerged in the twenty-first century to include a sophisticated mastery of technique broadened by an understanding of literature's role in characterizing reality, whether that reality is understood as transcendental and visionary or as rooted in the natural and material world. One thing distinguishing recent American works as contemporary is that the two different understandings of reality are not unified or reconciled; rather, as with the nuclei in Louise Glück's poem "Mitosis," "No one actually remembers them / as not divided."

A hallmark of the postwar period is its shift from unity to diversity as an ideal, and during this time American writing has been characterized by a great variety of styles employed simultaneously. If anything is common to the period, it is a self-conscious and experimental view of language as a tool of literary expression. In a wide variety of ways writers explore and test the ways language shapes our perceptions of reality, and their work moves in and out of various kinds of language, as if testing the limits and possibilities of the different discourses that make up contemporary life. This energetic investigation of language fuels a new inclusiveness and invigorates imaginative potential. Contemporary literature has survived the threats of its death to flourish in ways our writers are still imagining.

AMERICAN LITERATURE SINCE 1945

TEXTS	CONTEXTS
1941 Eudora Welty, **"Petrified Man"**	
1944 Stanley Kunitz, "Father and Son"	
1945 Randall Jarrell, "The Death of the Ball Turret Gunner"	**1945** U.S. drops atomic bombs on Hiroshima and Nagasaki; Japan surrenders, ending World War II • Cold War begins
1947 Tennesse Williams, *A Streetcar Named Desire*	**1947** Jackie Robinson becomes the first black Major League ballplayer
1948 Theodore Roethke, *The Lost Son*	
1949 Arthur Miller, *Death of a Salesman*	
1950 Richard Wilbur, "A World without Objects Is a Sensible Emptiness" • Charles Olson, "Projective Verse"	**1950** Senator Joseph McCarthy begins attacks on communism
	1950–53 Korean War
1952 Ralph Ellison, *Invisible Man*	
1953 Saul Bellow, *The Adventures of Augie March* • Charles Olson, "Maximus, to Himself"	**1953** House Concurrent Resolution 108 dictates government's intention to "terminate" its treaty relations with the Native American tribes
	1954 *Brown v. Board of Education* declares segregated schools unconstitutional • Beat Generation poets begin to gather at San Francisco's City Lights Bookshop
1955 Flannery O'Connor, **"Good Country People"**	
1955–68 John Berryman composes *The Dream Songs* (pub. 1964, 1968, 1977)	
1956 Allen Ginsberg, *Howl*	**1956** Martin Luther King Jr. leads bus boycott in Montgomery, Alabama
1958 Bernard Malamud, "The Magic Barrel"	
1959 Philip Roth, **"Defender of the Faith"** • Robert Creeley, "Kore" • Robert Lowell, *Life Studies* • Frank O'Hara, "Personism"	**1959** Fidel Castro becomes communist leader of Cuba
1960 Thomas Pynchon, **"Entropy"** • Gwendolyn Brooks, **"We Real Cool"** • Robert Duncan, "Often I Am Permitted to Return to a Meadow"	**1960** Woolworth lunch counter sit-in in Greensboro, N.C., marks beginning of Civil Rights Movement
1961 Denise Levertov, "The Jacob's Ladder"	
1962 Jack Kerouac, *Big Sur* • Robert Hayden, **"Middle Passage"**	**1962** United States and Soviet Union close to war over Russian missiles based in Cuba; missiles withdrawn
1963 James Wright, "A Blessing" • Martin Luther King Jr., **"I Have a Dream"**	**1963** King delivers "I Have a Dream" speech • black church in Birmingham, Alabama, bombed, killing four girls • President John F. Kennedy assassinated

Boldface titles indicate works in the anthology.

TEXTS	CONTEXTS
1964 John Cheever, **"The Swimmer"** • Amiri Baraka (LeRoi Jones) **"An Agony. As Now."** • Frank O'Hara, "A Step Away from Them"	
1965 James Baldwin, **"Going to Meet the Man"** • A. R. Ammons, "Corson's Inlet"	**1965** Riots break out in Watts section of Los Angeles • Malcolm X assassinated • hippie culture flourishes in San Francisco
	1965–73 Vietnam War
1966 James Merrill, "The Broken Home" • Sylvia Plath, *Ariel*	**1966** National Organization for Women (NOW) founded • Hayden and Brooks criticized at Black Writers' Conference, Fisk University, for composing "academic" poetry
1967 A. R. Ammons, "A Poem Is a Walk" • W. S. Merwin, "For a Coming Extinction"	
1968 Donald Barthelme, "The Balloon" • Edward Abbey, **"Havasu"**	**1968** King assassinated • Senator Robert F. Kennedy assassinated • photo of Earthrise by Apollo 8
1969 N. Scott Momaday, *The Way to Rainy Mountain* • Kurt Vonnegut, *Slaughterhouse-Five* • Galway Kinnell. "The Porcupine" • Robert Penn Warren, *Audubon*	**1969** U.S. astronauts land on the moon • Stonewall riots in New York City initiate gay liberation movement • Woodstock Festival held near Bethel, New York
1970 Ishmael Reed, "Neo-HooDoo Manifesto"	**1970** National Guard kills four students during antiwar demonstration at Kent State University, Ohio
1971 Audre Lorde, "Black Mother Woman"	
1972 Rudolfo A. Anaya, *Bless Me, Ultima* • Anne Sexton, *The Death of the Fathers* • Letter from Elizabeth Bishop to Robert Lowell objecting to use of personal letters in manuscript of *The Dolphin*	**1972** Watergate Scandal • military draft ends
1973 Alice Walker, **"Everyday Use"** • Adrienne Rich, *Diving into the Wreck*	**1973** *Roe v. Wade* legalizes abortion • American Indian Movement members occupy Wounded Knee, South Dakota
1974 Grace Paley, "A Conversation with My Father" • Annie Dillard, *Pilgrim at Tinker Creek*	**1974** President Richard Nixon resigns in wake of Watergate, avoiding impeachment
1975 John Updike, **"Separating"** • John Ashbery, "Self-Portrait in a Convex Mirror" • Michael S. Harper, "Nightmare Begins Responsibility"	
1976 Elizabeth Bishop, *Geography III* • Maxine Hong Kingston, **"No Name Woman"** • Barry Lopez, **"The Raven"**	**1976** U.S. bicentennial
1977 Audre Lorde, **"Poetry Is Not a Luxury"**	
1978 Ann Beattie, "Weekend" • Jamaica Kinkaid, **"Girl"**	
1979 Philip Levine, "Starlight" • Mary Oliver, "The Black Snake" • Robert Hass "Meditation at Lagunitas"	

TEXTS	CONTEXTS
1980 Toni Cade Bambara, "Medley" • Sam Shepard, *True West*	
1981 Leslie Marmon Silko, **"Lullaby"** • Lorna Dee Cervantes, "The Body as Braille" • James Dickey, **"Falling"** • Simon J. Ortiz, **"From Sand Creek"**	
1982 Raymond Carver, **"Cathedral"** • David Mamet, *Glengarry Glen Ross*	**1982** Equal Rights Amendment defeated • antinuclear movement protests manufacture of nuclear weapons • AIDS officially identified in the United States
1983 Toni Morrison, **"Recitatif"** • Joy Harjo, **"Call It Fear"**	
1984 Louise Erdrich, **"Dear John Wayne"**	
1985 Ursula K. Le Guin, **"She Unnames Them"** • Stanley Kunitz, **"The Wellfleet Whale"**	
1986 Louise Erdrich, **"Fleur"** • Art Spiegelman, *Maus I* • Rita Dove, *Thomas and Beulah* • Li-Young Lee, **"Eating Together"**	
1987 Gloria Anzaldúa, *Borderlands/La Frontera* • Sharon Olds, "I Go Back to May 1937"	
1988 Yusef Komunyakaa, **"Facing It"**	
1989 Amy Tan, *The Joy Luck Club*	**1989** Soviet Union collapses; Cold War ends • oil tanker *Exxon Valdez* runs aground in Alaska
1990 Robert Pinsky, "The Want Bone"	**1990** Congress passes Native American Graves Protection and Repatriation Act
1991 Sandra Cisneros, **Woman Hollering Creek**	**1991** United States enters Persian Gulf War • World Wide Web introduced
1993 Gary Snyder, **"Ripples on the Surface"** • A.R. Ammons, *Garbage* • Sherman Alexie, "This Is What It Means to Say Phoenix, Arizona"	
1994 Cathy Song, **"Lost Sister"** • Stephen Dixon, "Flying"	
1995 Jorie Graham, *The Dream of the Unified Field*	**1995** Federal building in Oklahoma City bombed in a terrorist attack
1996 W. S. Merwin, "Lament for the Makers" • Sherman Alexie, **"The Exaggeration of Despair"** • Junot Díaz, **"Drown"**	
1997 Julia Alvarez, *¡Yo!* • Fanny Howe, "[Nobody wants crossed out girls around]"	**1997** *Pathfinder* robot explores Mars

Boldface titles indicate works in the anthology.

TEXTS	CONTEXTS
1998 Billy Collins, **"I Chop Some Parsley While Listening to Art Blakey's Version of 'Three Blind Mice'"**	
1999 Jhumpa Lahiri, **"Sexy"** • Charles Simic, "Arriving Celebrities"	
2000 Charles Wright, "North American Bear" • Lucille Clifton, **"Moonchild"**	
2001 Charles Simic, "Late September"	**2001** Execution of Timothy McVeigh, convicted of 1995 Oklahoma City bombing • September 11 terrorist attacks on Pentagon and World Trade Center
2002 Dorothy Allison, **"Stubborn Girls and Mean Stories"** • Alberto Ríos, "Refugio's Hair"	
	2003 United States and Great Britain invade Iraq
2004 Louise Glück, "October"	
2005 Kay Ryan, "Home to Roost" • Joan Didion, *The Year of Magical Thinking*	
2006 Thomas McGuane, "Gallatin Canyon" • Richard Powers, *The Echo Maker* • John Crawford, **"The Last True Story I'll Ever Tell"**	
2007 Edwidge Danticat, *Brother, I'm Dying*	**2007** Advent of worst economic recession since the Great Depression.
	2009 Inauguration of Barack Obama as U.S. President
	2010 Massive oil spill in the Gulf of Mexico
	2011 Death of terrorist leader Osama bin Laden, architect of 9/11 attacks

THEODORE ROETHKE
1908–1963

Theodore Roethke had the kind of childhood a poet might have invented. He was born in Saginaw, Michigan, where both his German grandfather and his father kept greenhouses for a living. The greenhouse world, he later said, represented for him "both heaven and hell, a kind of tropics created in the savage climate of Michigan, where austere German Americans turned their love of order and their terrifying efficiency into something truly beautiful." Throughout his life he was haunted both by the ordered, protected world of the greenhouse—the constant activity of growth, the cultivated flowers—and by the desolate landscape of his part of Michigan. "The marsh, the mire, the Void, is always there, immediate and terrifying. It is a splendid place for schooling the spirit. It is America."

Roethke's poetry often reenacted this "schooling" of the spirit by revisiting the landscapes of his childhood: the nature poems that make up the largest part of his early work try to bridge the distance between a child's consciousness and the adult mysteries presided over by his father. Roethke arranged and rearranged these poems to give the sense of a spiritual autobiography, especially in preparing the volumes *The Lost Son and Other Poems* (1948), *Praise to the End!* (1951), and *The Waking* (1953). In what are known as "the greenhouse poems," the greenhouse world emerged as a "reality harsher than reality," the cultivator's activity pulsating and threatening. Its overseers, like "Frau Bauman, Frau Schmidt, and Frau Schwartze" (the title of one poem) emerge as gods, fates, muses, and witches all in one. By focusing on the minute processes of botanical growth—the rooting, the budding—the poet found a way of participating in the mysteries of this once alien world, whether he was deep in the subterranean root cellar or, as a child, perched high on top of the greenhouse.

In his books *The Lost Son* and *Praise to the End!* Roethke explored the regenerative possibilities of prerational speech (like children's riddles) in which language as sound recaptures nonlogical states of being. In these poems, his most dazzling and original work, Roethke opened up the possibilities of language. The title of one section of the long poem *The Lost Son* is "The Gibber," a pun because the word means both a meaningless utterance and the pouch at the base of a flower's calyx. The pun identifies principles of growth with the possibilities of speech freed from logical meanings, and the sequence as a whole suggests the power of both nature and language to revive the spirit of an adult life: "A lively understandable spirit / Once entertained you. / It will come again. / Be still. / Wait."

If the nature poems of Roethke's first four books explore the anxieties within him since childhood, his later love poems show him in periods of release and momentary pleasure: "And I dance round and round, / A fond and foolish man, / And see and suffer myself / In another being at last." The love poems, many included in *Words for the Wind* (1958) and *The Far Field* (1964), are among the most appealing in modern American verse. His beautiful and tender "Elegy for Jane" should be included in this category. These poems stand in sharp relief to the suffering Roethke experienced in other areas of his personal life—several mental breakdowns and periods of alcoholism—which led to a premature death. *The Far Field*, a posthumous volume, includes fierce, strongly rhymed lyrics in which Roethke tried "bare, even terrible statement," pressing toward the threshold of spiritual insight: "A man goes far to find out what he is—/ Death of the self in a long, tearless night, / All natural shapes blazing unnatural light." The nature poems of this last volume, gathered as "The North American Sequence," use extended landscape to find natural analogies for the human passage toward the dark unknown, hoping "in their rhythms to catch the very movement of mind itself."

Roethke is remembered as one of the great teachers of poetry, especially by those young poets and critics who studied with him at the University of Washington from 1948 until the time of his death. James Wright, David Wagoner, and Richard Hugo, among others, attended his classes. He was noted for his mastery of sound and metrics. Although his own poetry was intensely personal, his starting advice to students always deemphasized undisciplined self-expression. "Write like someone else," he instructed beginners. In Roethke's own career, however, this advice had its costs. His apprenticeship to Yeats, in particular, endangered his own poetic voice; in some late poems the echo of this great predecessor makes Roethke all but inaudible.

Roethke was much honored later in his career: a Pulitzer Prize for *The Waking* (1953); a National Book Award and Bollingen Prize for the collected poems, *Words for the Wind* (1958); and a posthumous National Book Award for *The Far Field* (1964).

Cuttings

Sticks-in-a-drowse droop over sugary loam,
Their intricate stem-fur dries;
But still the delicate slips keep coaxing up water;
The small cells bulge;

One nub of growth   5
Nudges a sand-crumb loose,
Pokes through a musty sheath
Its pale tendrilous horn.

1948

Cuttings

(*later*)

This urge, wrestle, resurrection of dry sticks,
Cut stems struggling to put down feet,
What saint strained so much,
Rose on such lopped limbs to a new life?

I can hear, underground, that sucking and sobbing,   5
In my veins, in my bones I feel it,—
The small waters seeping upward,
The tight grains parting at last.
When sprouts break out,
Slippery as fish   10
I quail, lean to beginnings, sheath-wet.

1948

My Papa's Waltz

The whiskey on your breath
Could make a small boy dizzy;
But I hung on like death:
Such waltzing was not easy.

We romped until the pans   5
Slid from the kitchen shelf;
My mother's countenance
Could not unfrown itself.

The hand that held my wrist
Was battered on one knuckle;   10
At every step you missed
My right ear scraped a buckle.

You beat time on my head
With a palm caked hard by dirt,
Then waltzed me off to bed   15
Still clinging to your shirt.

1948

Dolor

I have known the inexorable sadness of pencils,
Neat in their boxes, dolor of pad and paper-weight,
All the misery of manilla folders and mucilage,
Desolation in immaculate public places,
Lonely reception room, lavatory, switchboard,   5
The unalterable pathos of basin and pitcher,
Ritual of multigraph, paper-clip, comma,
Endless duplication of lives and objects.
And I have seen dust from the walls of institutions,
Finer than flour, alive, more dangerous than silica,   10
Sift, almost invisible, through long afternoons of tedium,
Dropping a fine film on nails and delicate eyebrows,
Glazing the pale hair, the duplicate grey standard faces.

1948

The Waking

I wake to sleep, and take my waking slow.
I feel my fate in what I cannot fear.
I learn by going where I have to go.

We think by feeling. What is there to know?
I hear my being dance from ear to ear.   5
I wake to sleep, and take my waking slow.

Of those so close beside me, which are you?
God bless the Ground! I shall walk softly there,
And learn by going where I have to go.

Light takes the Tree; but who can tell us how?   10
The lowly worm climbs up a winding stair;
I wake to sleep, and take my waking slow.

Great Nature has another thing to do
To you and me; so take the lively air,
And, lovely, learn by going where to go.   15

This shaking keeps me steady. I should know.
What falls away is always. And is near.
I wake to sleep, and take my waking slow.
I learn by going where I have to go.

                                                                  1953

Elegy for Jane

My Student, Thrown by a Horse

I remember the neckcurls, limp and damp as tendrils;
And her quick look, a sidelong pickerel smile;
And how, once startled into talk, the light syllables leaped for her,
And she balanced in the delight of her thought,
A wren, happy, tail into the wind,   5
Her song trembling the twigs and small branches.
The shade sang with her;
The leaves, their whispers turned to kissing;
And the mold sang in the bleached valleys under the rose.

Oh, when she was sad, she cast herself down into such a pure depth, 10
Even a father could not find her:
Scraping her cheek against straw;
Stirring the clearest water.

My sparrow, you are not here,
Waiting like a fern, making a spiny shadow.   15
The sides of wet stones cannot console me,
Nor the moss, wound with the last light.

If only I could nudge you from this sleep,
My maimed darling, my skittery pigeon.
Over this damp grave I speak the words of my love: 20
I, with no rights in this matter,
Neither father nor lover.

                                                                  1953

I Knew a Woman

I knew a woman, lovely in her bones,
When small birds sighed, she would sigh back at them;
Ah, when she moved, she moved more ways than one:
The shapes a bright container can contain!
Of her choice virtues only gods should speak,   5
Or English poets who grew up on Greek
(I'd have them sing in chorus, cheek to cheek).

How well her wishes went! She stroked my chin,
She taught me Turn, and Counter-turn, and Stand;[1]
She taught me Touch, that undulant white skin;   10
I nibbled meekly from her proffered hand;
She was the sickle; I, poor I, the rake,
Coming behind her for her pretty sake
(But what prodigious mowing we did make).

Love likes a gander, and adores a goose: 15
Her full lips pursed, the errant note to seize;
She played it quick, she played it light and loose;
My eyes, they dazzled at her flowing knees;
Her several parts could keep a pure repose,
Or one hip quiver with a mobile nose   20
(She moved in circles, and those circles moved).

Let seed be grass, and grass turn into hay:
I'm martyr to a motion not my own;
What's freedom for? To know eternity.
I swear she cast a shadow white as stone.   25
But who would count eternity in days?
These old bones live to learn her wanton ways:
(I measure time by how a body sways).

1958

---

1. The triadic parts of a Pindaric ode, a ceremonious poem in the manner of the Greek lyric poet Pindar (c. 522–c. 438 B.C.E.).

EUDORA WELTY
1909–2001

I n her essay "Place in Fiction," Eudora Welty spoke of her work as filled with the spirit of place: "Location is the ground conductor of all the currents of emotion and belief and moral conviction that charge out from the story in its course." Both her outwardly uneventful life and her writing are most intimately connected to the topography and atmosphere, the season and the soil of Mississippi, her lifelong home.

Eudora Welty. A young Welty ponders the view from the doorstep of a southern home.

Born in Jackson to parents who came from the North, and raised in comfortable circumstances (her father headed an insurance company), she attended Mississippi State College for Women, then graduated from the University of Wisconsin in 1929. After a course in advertising at the Columbia University School of Business, she returned to Mississippi, working first as a radio writer and newspaper society editor, then for the Depression-era Works Progress Administration, taking photographs of and interviewing local residents. Those travels would be reflected in her fiction and also in a book of her photographs, *One Time and Place*, published in 1971.

She began writing fiction after her return to Mississippi in 1931 and five years later published her first story, "Death of a Traveling Salesman," in a small magazine. Over the next two years six of her stories were published in the *Southern Review*, a serious literary magazine one of whose editors was the poet and novelist Robert Penn Warren. She also received strong support from Katherine Anne Porter, who contributed an introduction to Welty's first book of stories, *A Curtain of Green* (1941). That introduction hailed the arrival of another gifted southern fiction writer, and in fact the volume contained some of the best stories she ever wrote, such as "Petrified Man." Her profusion of metaphor and the difficult surface of her narrative—often oblique and indirect in its effect—were in part a mark of her admiration for modern writers like Virginia Woolf and (as with any young southern writer) William Faulkner. Although Welty's stories were as shapely as that of her mentor, Porter, they were more richly idiomatic and comic in their inclination. A second collection, *The Wide Net*, appeared two years later; and her first novel, *The Robber Bridegroom*, was published in 1942.

In that year and the next she was awarded the O. Henry Memorial Prize for the best piece of short fiction, and from then on she received a steady stream of awards and prizes, including the Pulitzer Prize for her novel *The Optimist's Daughter* (1972). Her most ambitious and longest piece of fiction is *Losing Battles* (1970), in which she aimed to compose a narrative made up almost wholly out of her characters' voices in mainly humorous interplay. Like Robert Frost, Welty loved gossip in all its actuality and intimacy, and if that love failed in the novels to produce compelling, extended sequences, it did result in many lively and entertaining pages. Perhaps her finest single book after *A Curtain of Green* was *The Golden Apples* (1949), a sequence of tales about a fabulous, invented, small Mississippi community named Morgana. Her characters appear and reappear in these related stories and come together most memorably in the brilliant "June Recital," perhaps her masterpiece.

Throughout her fiction Welty's wonderfully sharp sense of humor is strongly evident. Although her characters often consist of involuted southern families, physically handicapped, mentally retarded, or generally unstable kinfolk—and although her narratives are shot through with undercurrents of death, violence, and degradation—Welty transforms everything with an entertaining twist. No matter how desperate a situation may be, she makes us listen to the way a character talks about it; we pay attention to style rather than information. And although her attitude toward human folly is satiric, her satire is devoid of the wish to undermine and mock her characters. Instead, the vivid realizations of her prose give them irresistible life and a memorable expressiveness. Yet she remarked in an essay that "fine story writers seem to be in a sense obstructionists," and Welty's narratives unfold through varied repetitions or reiterations that have, she once claimed, the function of a deliberate double exposure in photography. By making us pay close attention to who is speaking and the implications of that speech, by asking us to imagine the way in which a silent character is responding to that speech, and by making us read behind the deceptively simple response she gives to that character, she makes us active readers, playfully engaged in a typically complicated scene. "Why I Live at the P.O.," "Keela, the Outcast Indian Maiden," "Powerhouse," "June Recital," "Petrified Man," and many others demonstrate the strength and the joy of her art. And although she has been called a "regional" writer, she has noted the condescending nature of that term, which she calls an "outsider's term; it has no meaning for the insider who is doing the writing, because as far as he knows he is simply writing about life" (*On Writing*). So it is with Eudora Welty's fiction.

The text is from *A Curtain of Green* (1941).

Petrified Man

"Reach in my purse and git me a cigarette without no powder in it if you kin, Mrs. Fletcher, honey," said Leota to her ten o'clock shampoo-and-set customer. "I don't like no perfumed cigarettes."

Mrs. Fletcher gladly reached over to the lavender shelf under the lavender-framed mirror, shook a hair net loose from the clasp of the patent-leather bag, and slapped her hand down quickly on a powder puff which burst out when the purse was opened.

"Why, look at the peanuts, Leota!" said Mrs. Fletcher in her marvelling voice.

"Honey, them goobers has been in my purse a week if they's been in it a day. Mrs. Pike bought them peanuts."

"Who's Mrs. Pike?" asked Mrs. Fletcher, settling back. Hidden in this den of curling fluid and henna[1] packs, separated by a lavender swing-door from the other customers, who were being gratified in other booths, she could give her curiosity its freedom. She looked expectantly at the black part in Leota's yellow curls as she bent to light the cigarette.

"Mrs. Pike is this lady from New Orleans," said Leota, puffing, and pressing into Mrs. Fletcher's scalp with strong red-nailed fingers. "A friend, not a customer. You see, like maybe I told you last time, me and Fred and Sal and

---

1. Reddish brown dye for tinting hair.

Joe all had us a fuss, so Sal and Joe up and moved out, so we didn't do a thing but rent out their room. So we rented it to Mrs. Pike. And Mr. Pike." She flicked an ash into the basket of dirty towels. "Mrs. Pike is a very decided blonde. *She* bought me the peanuts."

"She must be cute," said Mrs. Fletcher.

"Honey, 'cute' ain't the word for what she is. I'm tellin' you, Mrs. Pike is attractive. She has her a good time. She's got a sharp eye out, Mrs. Pike has."

She dashed the comb through the air, and paused dramatically as a cloud of Mrs. Fletcher's hennaed hair floated out of the lavender teeth like a small storm-cloud.

"Hair fallin'."

"Aw, Leota."

"Uh-huh, commencin' to fall out," said Leota, combing again, and letting fall another cloud.

"Is it any dandruff in it?" Mrs. Fletcher was frowning, her hair-line eyebrows diving down toward her nose, and her wrinkled, beady-lashed eyelids batting with concentration.

"Nope." She combed again. "Just fallin' out."

"Bet it was that last perm'nent you gave me that did it," Mrs. Fletcher said cruelly. "Remember you cooked me fourteen minutes."

"You had fourteen minutes comin' to you," said Leota with finality.

"Bound to be somethin'," persisted Mrs. Fletcher. "Dandruff, dandruff. I couldn't of caught a thing like that from Mr. Fletcher, could I?"

"Well," Leota answered at last, "you know what I heard in here yestiddy, one of Thelma's ladies was settin' over yonder in Thelma's booth gittin' a machineless, and I don't mean to insist or insinuate or anything, Mrs. Fletcher, but Thelma's lady just happ'med to throw out—I forgotten what she was talkin' about at the time—that you was p-r-e-g., and lots of times that'll make your hair do awful funny, fall out and God knows what all. It just ain't our fault, is the way I look at it."

There was a pause. The women stared at each other in the mirror.

"Who was it?" demanded Mrs. Fletcher.

"Honey, I really couldn't say," said Leota. "Not that you look it."

"Where's Thelma? I'll get it out of her," said Mrs. Fletcher.

"Now, honey, I wouldn't go and git mad over a little thing like that," Leota said, combing hastily, as though to hold Mrs. Fletcher down by the hair. "I'm sure it was somebody didn't mean no harm in the world. How far gone are you?"

"Just wait," said Mrs. Fletcher, and shrieked for Thelma, who came in and took a drag from Leota's cigarette.

"Thelma, honey, throw your mind back to yestiddy if you kin," said Leota, drenching Mrs. Fletcher's hair with a thick fluid and catching the overflow in a cold wet towel at her neck.

"Well, I got my lady half wound for a spiral," said Thelma doubtfully.

"This won't take but a minute," said Leota. "Who is it you got in there, old Horse Face? Just cast your mind back and try to remember who your lady was yestiddy who happ'm to mention that my customer was pregnant, that's all. She's dead to know."

Thelma drooped her blood-red lips and looked over Mrs. Fletcher's head into the mirror. "Why, honey, I ain't got the faintest," she breathed. "I really don't recollect the faintest. But I'm sure she meant no harm. I declare, I forgot my hair finally got combed and thought it was a stranger behind me."

"Was it that Mrs. Hutchinson?" Mrs. Fletcher was tensely polite.

"Mrs. Hutchinson? Oh, Mrs. Hutchinson." Thelma batted her eyes. "Naw, precious, she come on Thursday and didn't ev'm mention your name. I doubt if she ev'm knows you're on the way."

"Thelma!" cried Leota staunchly.

"All I know is, whoever it is 'll be sorry some day. Why, I just barely knew it myself!" cried Mrs. Fletcher. "Just let her wait!"

"Why? What're you gonna do to her?"

It was a child's voice, and the women looked down. A little boy was making tents with aluminum wave pinchers[2] on the floor under the sink.

"Billy Boy, hon, mustn't bother nice ladies," Leota smiled. She slapped him brightly and behind her back waved Thelma out of the booth. "Ain't Billy Boy a sight? Only three years old and already just nuts about the beauty-parlor business."

"I never saw him here before," said Mrs. Fletcher, still unmollified.

"He ain't been here before, that's how come," said Leota. "He belongs to Mrs. Pike. She got her a job but it was Fay's Millinery. He oughtn't to try on those ladies' hats, they come down over his eyes like I don't know what. They just git to look ridiculous, that's what, an' of course he's gonna put 'em on: hats. They tole Mrs. Pike they didn't appreciate him hangin' around there. Here, he couldn't hurt a thing."

"Well! I don't like children that much," said Mrs. Fletcher.

"Well!" said Leota moodily.

"Well! I'm almost tempted not to have this one," said Mrs. Fletcher. "That Mrs. Hutchinson! Just looks straight through you when she sees you on the street and then spits at you behind your back."

"Mr. Fletcher would beat you on the head if you didn't have it now," said Leota reasonably. "After going this far."

Mrs. Fletcher sat up straight. "Mr. Fletcher can't do a thing with me."

"He can't!" Leota winked at herself in the mirror.

"No, siree, he can't. If he so much as raises his voice against me, he knows good and well I'll have one of my sick headaches, and then I'm just not fit to live with. And if I really look that pregnant already—"

"Well, now, honey, I just want you to know—I habm't told any of my ladies and I ain't goin' to tell 'em—even that you're losin' your hair. You just get you one of those Stork-a-Lure dresses and stop worryin'. What people don't know don't hurt nobody, as Mrs. Pike says."

"Did you tell Mrs. Pike?" asked Mrs. Fletcher sulkily.

"Well, Mrs. Fletcher, look, you ain't ever goin' to lay eyes on Mrs. Pike or her lay eyes on you, so what diffunce does it make in the long run?"

"I knew it!" Mrs. Fletcher deliberately nodded her head so as to destroy a ringlet Leota was working on behind her ear. "Mrs. Pike!"

Leota sighed. "I reckon I might as well tell you. It wasn't any more Thelma's lady tole me you was pregnant than a bat."

"Not Mrs. Hutchinson?"

"Naw, Lord! It was Mrs. Pike."

---

2. Clips used to form and hold (or set) hair curl or wave.

"Mrs. Pike!" Mrs. Fletcher could only sputter and let curling fluid roll into her ear. "How could Mrs. Pike possibly know I was pregnant or otherwise, when she doesn't even know me? The nerve of some people!"

"Well, here's how it was. Remember Sunday?"

"Yes," said Mrs. Fletcher.

"Sunday, Mrs. Pike an' me was all by ourself. Mr. Pike and Fred had gone over to Eagle Lake, sayin' they was goin' to catch 'em some fish, but they didn't a course. So we was gettin' in Mrs. Pike's car, it's a 1939 Dodge—"

"1939, eh," said Mrs. Fletcher.

"—An' we was gettin' us a Jax beer apiece—that's the beer that Mrs. Pike says is made right in N.O., so she won't drink no other kind. So I seen you drive up to the drugstore an' run in for just a secont, leavin' I reckon Mr. Fletcher in the car, an' come runnin' out with looked like a perscription. So I says to Mrs. Pike, just to be makin' talk, 'Right yonder's Mrs. Fletcher, and I reckon that's Mr. Fletcher—she's one of my regular customers,' I says."

"I had on a figured print," said Mrs. Fletcher tentatively.

"You sure did," agreed Leota. "So Mrs. Pike, she give you a good look—she's very observant, a good judge of character, cute as a minute, you know—and she says, 'I bet you another Jax that lady's three months on the way.'"

"What gall!" said Mrs. Fletcher. "Mrs. Pike!"

"Mrs. Pike ain't goin' to bite you," said Leota. "Mrs. Pike is a lovely girl, you'd be crazy about her, Mrs. Fletcher. But she can't sit still a minute. We went to the travellin' freak show yestiddy after work. I got through early—nine o'clock. In the vacant store next door. What, you ain't been?"

"No, I despise freaks," declared Mrs. Fletcher.

"Aw. Well, honey, talkin' about bein' pregnant an' all, you ought to see those twins in a bottle, you really owe it to yourself."

"What twins?" asked Mrs. Fletcher out of the side of her mouth.

"Well, honey, they got these two twins in a bottle, see? Born joined plumb together—dead a course." Leota dropped her voice into a soft lyrical hum. "They was about this long—pardon—must of been full time, all right, wouldn't you say?—an' they had these two heads an' two faces an' four arms an' four legs, all kind of joined *here*. See, this face looked this-a-way, and the other face looked that-a-way, over their shoulder, see. Kinda pathetic."

"Glah!" said Mrs. Fletcher disapprovingly.

"Well, ugly? Honey, I mean to tell you—their parents was first cousins and all like that. Billy Boy, git me a fresh towel from off Teeny's stack—this 'n's wringin' wet—an' quit ticklin' my ankles with that curler. I declare! He don't miss nothin'."

"Me and Mr. Fletcher aren't one speck of kin, or he could never of had me," said Mrs. Fletcher placidly.

"Of course not!" protested Leota. "Neither is me an' Fred, not that we know of. Well, honey, what Mrs. Pike liked was the pygmies. They've got these pygmies down there, too, an' Mrs. Pike was just wild about 'em. You know, the teeniniest men in the universe? Well, honey, they can just rest back on their little bohunkus an' roll around an' you can't hardly tell if they're sittin' or standin'. That'll give you some idea. They're about forty-two years old. Just suppose it was your husband!"

"Well, Mr. Fletcher is five foot nine and one half," said Mrs. Fletcher quickly.

"Fred's five foot ten," said Leota, "but I tell him he's still a shrimp, account of I'm so tall." She made a deep wave over Mrs. Fletcher's other temple with the comb. "Well, these pygmies are a kind of a dark brown, Mrs. Fletcher. Not bad lookin' for what they are, you know."

"I wouldn't care for them," said Mrs. Fletcher. "What does that Mrs. Pike see in them?"

"Aw, I don't know," said Leota. "She's just cute, that's all. But they got this man, this petrified man, that ever'thing ever since he was nine years old, when it goes through his digestion, see, somehow Mrs. Pike says it goes to his joints and has been turning to stone."

"How awful!" said Mrs. Fletcher.

"He's forty-two too. That looks like a bad age."

"Who said so, that Mrs. Pike? I bet she's forty-two," said Mrs. Fletcher.

"Naw," said Leota, "Mrs. Pike's thirty-three, born in January, an Aquarian. He could move his head—like this. A course his head and mind ain't a joint, so to speak, and I guess his stomach ain't, either—not yet, anyways. But see—his food, he eats it, and it goes down, see, and then he digests it"— Leota rose on her toes for an instant—"and it goes out to his joints and before you can say 'Jack Robinson,' it's stone—pure stone. He's turning to stone. How'd you liked to be married to a guy like that? All he can do, he can move his head just a quarter of an inch. A course he *looks* just *terrible*."

"I should think he would," said Mrs. Fletcher frostily. "Mr. Fletcher takes bending exercises every night of the world. I make him."

"All Fred does is lay around the house like a rug. I wouldn't be surprised if he woke up some day and couldn't move. The petrified man just sat there moving his quarter of an inch though," said Leota reminiscently.

"Did Mrs. Pike like the petrified man?" asked Mrs. Fletcher.

"Not as much as she did the others," said Leota deprecatingly. "And then she likes a man to be a good dresser, and all that."

"Is Mr. Pike a good dresser?" asked Mrs. Fletcher sceptically.

"Oh, well, yeah," said Leota, "but he's twelve or fourteen years older'n her. She ast Lady Evangeline about him."

"Who's Lady Evangeline?" asked Mrs. Fletcher.

"Well, it's this mind reader they got in the freak show," said Leota. "Was real good. Lady Evangeline is her name, and if I had another dollar I wouldn't do a thing but have my other palm read. She had what Mrs. Pike said was the 'sixth mind' but she had the worst manicure I ever saw on a living person."

"What did she tell Mrs. Pike?" asked Mrs. Fletcher.

"She told her Mr. Pike was as true to her as he could be and besides, would come into some money."

"Humph!" said Mrs. Fletcher. "What does he do?"

"I can't tell," said Leota, "because he don't work. Lady Evangeline didn't tell me enough about my nature or anything. And I would like to go back and find out some more about this boy. Used to go with this boy until he got married to this girl. Oh, shoot, that was about three and a half years ago, when you was still goin' to the Robert E. Lee Beauty Shop in Jackson. He married her for her money. Another fortune-teller tole me that at the time. So I'm not in love with him anymore, anyway, besides being married to Fred, but Mrs. Pike thought, just for the hell of it, see, to ask Lady Evangeline was he happy."

"Does Mrs. Pike know everything about you already?" asked Mrs. Fletcher unbelievingly. "Mercy!"

"Oh, yeah, I tole her ever'thing about ever'thing, from now on back to I don't know when—to when I first started goin' out," said Leota. "So I ast Lady Evangeline for one of my questions, was he happily married, and she says, just like she was glad I ask her, 'Honey,' she says, 'naw, he idn't. You write down this day, March 8, 1941,' she says, 'and mock it down: three years from today him and her won't be occupyin' the same bed.' There it is, up on the wall with them other dates—see, Mrs. Fletcher? And she says, 'Child, you ought to be glad you didn't git him, because he's so mercenary.' So I'm glad I married Fred. He sure ain't mercenary, money don't mean a thing to him. But I sure would like to go back and have my other palm read."

"Did Mrs. Pike believe in what the fortune-teller said?" asked Mrs. Fletcher in a superior tone of voice.

"Lord, yes, she's from New Orleans. Ever'body in New Orleans believes ever'thing spooky. One of 'em in New Orleans before it was raided says to Mrs. Pike one summer she was goin' to go from State to State and meet some grey-headed men, and, sure enough, she says she went on a beautician convention up to Chicago. . . ."

"Oh!" said Mrs. Fletcher. "Oh, is Mrs. Pike a beautician too?"

"Sure she is," protested Leota. "She's a beautician. I'm goin' to git her in here if I can. Before she married. But it don't leave you. She says sure enough, there was three men who was a very large part of making her trip what it was, and they all three had grey in their hair and they went in six States. Got Christmas cards from 'em. Billy Boy, go see if Thelma's got any dry cotton. Look how Mrs. Fletcher's a-drippin'."

"Where did Mrs. Pike meet Mr. Pike?" asked Mrs. Fletcher primly.

"On another train," said Leota.

"I met Mr. Fletcher, or rather he met me, in a rental library," said Mrs. Fletcher with dignity, as she watched the net come down over her head.

"Honey, me an' Fred, we met in a rumble seat[3] eight months ago and we was practically on what you might call the way to the altar inside of half an hour," said Leota in a guttural voice, and bit a bobby pin open. "Course it don't last. Mrs. Pike says nothin' like that ever lasts."

"Mr. Fletcher and myself are as much in love as the day we married," said Mrs. Fletcher belligerently as Leota stuffed cotton into her ears.

"Mrs. Pike says it don't last," repeated Leota in a louder voice. "Now go git under the dryer. You can turn yourself on, can't you? I'll be back to comb you out. Durin' lunch I promised to give Mrs. Pike a facial. You know—free. Her bein' in the business, so to speak."

"I bet she needs one," said Mrs. Fletcher, letting the swing-door fly back against Leota. "Oh, pardon me."

A week later, on time for her appointment, Mrs. Fletcher sank heavily into Leota's chair after first removing a drug-store rental book, called *Life Is Like That*, from the seat. She stared in a discouraged way into the mirror.

"You can tell it when I'm sitting down, all right," she said.

Leota seemed preoccupied and stood shaking out a lavender cloth. She began to pin it around Mrs. Fletcher's neck in silence.

3. Folding seat at the rear of an automobile.

"I said you sure can tell it when I'm sitting straight on and coming at you this way," Mrs. Fletcher said.

"Why, honey, naw you can't," said Leota gloomily. "Why, I'd never know. If somebody was to come up to me on the street and say, 'Mrs. Fletcher is pregnant!' I'd say, 'Heck, she don't look it to me.'"

"If a certain party hadn't found it out and spread it around, it wouldn't be too late even now," said Mrs. Fletcher frostily, but Leota was almost choking her with the cloth, pinning it so tight, and she couldn't speak clearly. She paddled her hands in the air until Leota wearily loosened her.

"Listen, honey, you're just a virgin compared to Mrs. Montjoy," Leota was going on, still absent-minded. She bent Mrs. Fletcher back in the chair and, sighing, tossed liquid from a teacup on to her head and dug both hands into her scalp. "You know Mrs. Montjoy—her husband's that premature-greyheaded fella?"

"She's in the Trojan Garden Club, is all I know," said Mrs. Fletcher.

"Well, honey," said Leota, but in a weary voice, "she come in here not the week before and not the day before she had her baby—she come in here the very selfsame day, I mean to tell you. Child, we was all plumb scared to death. There she was! Come for her shampoo an' set. Why, Mrs. Fletcher, in an hour an' twenty minutes she was layin' up there in the Babtist Hospital with a seb'm-pound son. It was that close a shave. I declare, if I hadn't been so tired I would of drank up a bottle of gin that night."

"What gall," said Mrs. Fletcher. "I never knew her at all well."

"See, her husband was waitin' outside in the car, and her bags was all packed an' in the back seat, an' she was all ready, 'cept she wanted her shampoo an' set. An' havin' one pain right after another. Her husband kep' comin' in here, scared-like, but couldn't do nothin' with her a course. She yelled bloody murder, too, but she always yelled her head off when I give her a perm'nent."

"She must of been crazy," said Mrs. Fletcher. "How did she look?"

"Shoot!" said Leota.

"Well, I can guess," asid Mrs. Fletcher. "Awful."

"Just wanted to look pretty while she was havin' her baby, is all," said Leota airily. "Course, we was glad to give the lady what she was after—that's our motto—but I bet a hour later she wasn't payin' no mind to them little end curls. I bet she wasn't thinkin' about she ought to have on a net. It wouldn't of done her no good if she had."

"No, I don't suppose it would," said Mrs. Fletcher.

"Yeah man! She was a-yellin'. Just like when I give her perm'nent."

"Her husband ought to make her behave. Don't it seem that way to you?" asked Mrs. Fletcher. "He ought to put his foot down."

"Ha," said Leota. "A lot he could do. Maybe some women is soft."

"Oh, you mistake me, I don't mean for her to get soft—far from it! Women have to stand up for themselves, or there's just no telling. But now you take me—I ask Mr. Fletcher's advice now and then, and he appreciates it, especially on something important, like is it time for a permanent—not that I've told him about the baby. He says, 'Why, dear, go ahead!' Just ask their *advice*."

"Huh! If I ever ast Fred's advice we'd be floatin' down the Yazoo River on a houseboat or somethin' by this time," said Leota. "I'm sick of Fred. I told him to go over to Vicksburg."

"Is he going?" demanded Mrs. Fletcher.

"Sure. See, the fortune-teller—I went back and had my other palm read, since we've got to rent the room agin—said my lover was goin' to work in Vicksburg, so I don't know who she could mean, unless she meant Fred. And Fred ain't workin' here—that much is so."

"Is he going to work in Vicksburg?" asked Mrs. Fletcher. "And—"

"Sure. Lady Evangeline said so. Said the future is going to be brighter than the present. He don't want to go, but I ain't gonna put up with nothin' like that. Lays around the house an' bulls—did bull—with that good-for-nothin' Mr. Pike. He says if he goes who'll cook, but I says I never get to eat anyway—not meals. Billy Boy, take Mrs. Grover that *Screen Secrets* and leg it."

Mrs. Fletcher heard stamping feet go out the door.

"Is that that Mrs. Pike's little boy here again?" she asked, sitting up gingerly.

"Yeah, that's still him." Leota stuck out her tongue.

Mrs. Fletcher could hardly believe her eyes. "Well! How's Mrs. Pike, your attractive new friend with the sharp eyes who spreads it around town that perfect strangers are pregnant?" she asked in a sweetened tone.

"Oh, Mizziz Pike." Leota combed Mrs. Fletcher's hair with heavy strokes.

"You act like you're tired," said Mrs. Fletcher.

"Tired? Feel like it's four o'clock in the afternoon already," said Leota. "I ain't told you the awful luck we had, me and Fred? It's the worst thing you ever heard of. Maybe *you* think Mrs. Pike's got sharp eyes. Shoot, there's a limit! Well, you know, we rented out our room to this Mr. and Mrs. Pike from New Orleans when Sal an' Joe Fentress got mad at us 'cause they drank up some home-brew we had in the closet—Sal an' Joe did. So, a week ago Sat'-day Mr. and Mrs. Pike moved in. Well, I kinda fixed up the room, you know—put a sofa pillow on the couch and picked some ragged robbins and put in a vase, but they never did say they appreciated it. Anyway, then I put some old magazines on the table."

"I think that was lovely," said Mrs. Fletcher.

"Wait. So, come night 'fore last, Fred and this Mr. Pike, who Fred just took up with, was back from they said they was fishin', bein' as neither one of 'em has got a job to his name, and we was all settin' around their room. So Mrs. Pike was settin' there, readin' a old *Startling G-Man Tales* that was mine, mind you, I'd bought it myself, and all of a sudden she jumps!—into the air—you'd 'a' thought she'd set on a spider—an' says, 'Canfield'—ain't that silly, that's Mr. Pike—'Canfield, my God A'mighty,' she says, 'honey,' she says, 'we're rich, and you won't have to work.' Not that he turned one hand anyway. Well, me and Fred rushes over to her, and Mr. Pike, too, and there she sets, pointin' her finger at a photo in my copy of *Startling G-Man*. 'See that man?' yells Mrs. Pike. 'Remember him, Canfield?' 'Never forget a face,' says Mr. Pike. 'It's Mr. Petrie, that we stayed with him in the apartment next to ours in Toulouse Street in N.O. for six weeks. Mr. Petrie.' 'Well,' says Mrs. Pike, like she can't hold out one secont longer, 'Mr. Petrie is wanted for five hundred dollars cash, for rapin' four women in California, and I know where he is.'"

"Mercy!" said Mrs. Fletcher. "Where was he?"

At some time Leota had washed her hair and now she yanked her up by the back locks and sat her up.

"Know where he was?"

"I certainly don't," Mrs. Fletcher said. Her scalp hurt all over.

Leota flung a towel around the top of her customer's head. "Nowhere else but in that freak show! I saw him just as plain as Mrs. Pike. *He* was the petrified man!"

"Who would ever have thought that!" cried Mrs. Fletcher sympathetically.

"So Mr. Pike says, 'Well whatta you know about that', an' he looks real hard at the photo and whistles. And she starts dancin' and singin' about their good luck. She meant our bad luck! I made a point of tellin' that fortune-teller the next time I saw her. I said, 'Listen, that magazine was layin' around the house for a month, and there was the freak show runnin' night an' day, not two steps away from my own beauty parlor, with Mr. Petrie just settin' there waitin'. An' it had to be Mr. and Mrs. Pike, almost perfect strangers.'"

"What gall," said Mrs. Fletcher. She was only sitting there, wrapped in a turban, but she did not mind.

"Fortune-tellers don't care. And Mrs. Pike, she goes around actin' like she thinks she was Mrs. God," said Leota. "So they're goin' to leave tomorrow, Mr. and Mrs. Pike. And in the meantime I got to keep that mean, bad little ole kid here, gettin' under my feet ever' minute of the day an' talkin' back too."

"Have they gotten the five hundred dollars' reward already?" asked Mrs. Fletcher.

"Well," said Leota, "at first Mr. Pike didn't want to do anything about it. Can you feature that? Said he kinda liked that ole bird and said he was real nice to 'em, lent 'em money or somethin'. But Mrs. Pike simply tole him he could just go to hell, and I can see her point. She says, 'You ain't worked a lick in six months, and here I make five hundred dollars in two seconts, and what thanks do I get for it? You go to hell, Canfield,' she says. So," Leota went on in a despondent voice, "they called up the cops and they caught the ole bird, all right, right there in the freak show where I saw him with my own eyes, thinkin' he was petrified. He's the one. Did it under his real name—Mr. Petrie. Four women in California, all in the month of August. So Mrs. Pike gits five hundred dollars. And my magazine, and right next door to my beauty parlor. I cried all night, but Fred said it wasn't a bit of use and to go to sleep, because the whole thing was just a sort of coincidence—you know: can't do nothin' about it. He says it put him clean out of the notion of goin' to Vicksburg for a few days till we rent out the room agin—no tellin' who we'll git this time."

"But can you imagine anybody knowing this old man, that's raped four women?" persisted Mrs. Fletcher, and she shuddered audibly. "Did Mrs. Pike *speak* to him when she met him in the freak show?"

Leota had begun to comb Mrs. Fletcher's hair. "I says to her, I says, 'I didn't notice you fallin' on his neck when he was the petrified man—don't tell me you didn't recognize your fine friend?' And she says, 'I didn't recognize him with that white powder all over his face. He just looked familiar,' Mrs. Pike says, 'and lots of people look familiar.' But she says that ole petrified man did put her in mind of somebody. She wondered who it was! Kep' her awake, which man she'd ever knew it reminded her of. So when she seen the photo, it all come to her. Like a flash. Mr. Petrie. The way he'd turn his head and look at her when she took him in his breakfast."

"Took him in his breakfast!" shrieked Mrs. Fletcher. "Listen—don't tell me. I'd 'a' felt something."

"Four women. I guess those women didn't have the faintest notion at the time they'd be worth a hundred an' twenty-five bucks apiece some day to Mrs. Pike. We ast her how old the fella was then, an's she says he musta had one foot in the grave, at least. Can you beat it?"

"Not really petrified at all, of course," said Mrs. Fletcher meditatively. She drew herself up. "I'd 'a' felt something," she said proudly.

"Shoot! I did feel somethin'," said Leota. "I tole Fred when I got home I felt so funny. I said, 'Fred, that ole petrified man sure did leave me with a funny feelin'.' He says, 'Funny-haha or funny-peculiar?' and I says, 'Funny-peculiar.'" She pointed her comb into the air emphatically.

"I'll bet you did," said Mrs. Fletcher.

They both heard a crackling noise.

Leota screamed, "Billy Boy! What you doin' in my purse?"

"Aw, I'm just eatin' these ole stale peanuts up," said Billy Boy.

"You come here to me!" screamed Leota, recklessly flinging down the comb, which scattered a whole ashtray full of bobby pins and knocked down a row of Coca-Cola bottles. "This is the last straw!"

"I caught him! I caught him!" giggled Mrs. Fletcher. "I'll hold him on my lap. You bad, bad boy, you! I guess I better learn how to spank little old bad boys," she said.

Leota's eleven o'clock customer pushed open the swing-door upon Leota's paddling him heartily with the brush, while he gave angry but belittling screams which penetrated beyond the booth and filled the whole curious beauty parlor. From everywhere ladies began to gather round to watch the paddling. Billy Boy kicked both Leota and Mrs. Fletcher as hard as he could, Mrs. Fletcher with her new fixed smile.

Billy Boy stomped through the group of wild-haired ladies and went out the door, but flung back the words, "If you're so smart, why ain't you rich?"

1941

ELIZABETH BISHOP
1911–1979

"The enormous power of reticence," the poet Octavio Paz said in a tribute, "—that is the great lesson of Elizabeth Bishop." Bishop's reticence originates in a temperament indistinguishable from her style; her remarkable formal gifts allowed her to create ordered and lucid structures that hold strong feelings in place. Chief among these feelings was a powerful sense of loss. Born in Worcester, Massachusetts, she was eight months old when her father died. Her mother suffered a series of breakdowns and was permanently institutionalized when Elizabeth was five. "I've never concealed this," Bishop once wrote, "although I don't like to make too much of it. But of course it is an important fact, to me. I didn't see her again." Her understatement is characteristic. When Bishop wrote about her early life—as she first did in several poems and stories in the 1950s and last did in her extraordinary final book, *Geography III* (1976)—she resisted sentimentality and self-pity. It was as if she could look at the events of her own life with the same unflinching gaze she turned on the landscapes that so consistently compelled her. The deep feeling in her poems rises out of direct and particular description, but Bishop does more than simply observe. Whether writing about her childhood landscape of Nova Scotia or her adopted Brazil, she often opens a poem with long perspectives on time, with landscapes that dwarf the merely human, emphasizing the dignified frailty of a human observer.

Examining her own case, she traces the observer's instinct to early childhood. "In the Waiting Room," a poem written in the early 1970s, probes the sources of her interest in details. Using an incident from when she was seven—a little girl waits for her aunt in the dentist's anteroom—Bishop shows how in the course of the episode she became aware, as if wounded, of the utter strangeness and engulfing power of the world. The spectator in that poem hangs on to details as a kind of life-jacket; she observes because she has to.

After her father's death Bishop and her mother lived with Bishop's maternal grandparents in Great Village, Nova Scotia. She remained there for several years after her mother was institutionalized, until she was removed ("kidnapped," as she says in one of her stories) by her paternal grandparents and taken to live in Worcester, Massachusetts. This experience was followed by a series of illnesses (eczema, bronchitis, and asthma), which plagued her for years. Bishop later lived with an aunt and attended Walnut Hill School, a private high school. In 1934 she graduated from Vassar College, where she had been introduced to Marianne Moore. Moore's meticulous taste for fact was to influence Bishop's poetry, but more immediately Moore's independent life as a poet seemed an alternative to Bishop's vaguer intentions to attend medical school. Bishop lived in New York City and in Key West, Florida; a traveling fellowship took her to Brazil, where she met Lota de Macedo Soares, an architect with whom she lived for sixteen years. Lota committed suicide in 1967, a loss registered in Bishop's late villanelle, "One Art" (1976).

Exile and travel were always at the heart of Bishop's poems. The title of her first book, *North & South* (1946), looks backward to the northern seas of Nova Scotia and forward to the tropical world of Brazil. Her poems are set among these landscapes, where she can stress encircling and eroding geological powers or, in the case of Brazil, a bewildering botanical plenty. *Questions of Travel* (1965), her third volume, constitutes a sequence of poems initiating her, with her botanist-geologist-anthropologist's curiosity, into Brazilian life and the mysteries of what questions a traveler-exile should ask. In this series, with its increasing penetration of a new country, a process is at work similar to one Bishop identifies in the great English naturalist Charles Darwin, of whom Bishop once said: "One admires the beautiful solid case being built up out of his endless, heroic observations, almost unconscious or automatic—and then comes a sudden relaxation, a forgetful phrase, and one feels the strangeness of his undertaking, sees the lonely young man, his eyes fixed on facts and minute details, sinking or sliding giddily off into the unknown."

In 1969 Bishop's *Complete Poems* appeared, an ironic title in light of the fact that she continued to publish new poetry. *Geography III* contains some of her best work, poems that, from the perspective of her return to the United States, look back on the appetite for exploration apparent in her earlier verse. The influence of her long friendship with the poet Robert Lowell, and their high regard for one another's work, may be felt in the way *Geography III* explores memory and autobiography more directly than does her earlier work. Bishop, however, believed that there were limits on the ways in which poems could use the materials of a life, as she suggested in a 1972 letter to Lowell. Having left Brazil, Bishop lived in Boston from 1970 on and taught at Harvard University until 1977. She received the Pulitzer Prize for the combined volume *North & South and A Cold Spring* (1955) and the National Book Award for *The Complete Poems*, and in 1976 was the first woman and the first

American to receive the Books Abroad Neustadt International Prize for Literature. Since Bishop's death, most of her published work has been gathered in two volumes: *The Complete Poems 1929–1979* and *The Collected Prose*. An edition of her unpublished poems and drafts, *Edgar Allen Poe & The Juke-Box*, was published to some controversy in 2006.

The Fish

I caught a tremendous fish
and held him beside the boat
half out of water, with my hook
fast in a corner of his mouth.
He didn't fight.   5
He hadn't fought at all.
He hung a grunting weight,
battered and venerable
and homely. Here and there
his brown skin hung in strips   10
like ancient wallpaper,
and its pattern of darker brown
was like wallpaper:
shapes like full-blown roses
stained and lost through age.   15
He was speckled with barnacles,
fine rosettes of lime,
and infested
with tiny white sea-lice,
and underneath two or three   20
rags of green weed hung down.
While his gills were breathing in
the terrible oxygen
—the frightening gills,
fresh and crisp with blood,   25
that can cut so badly—
I thought of the coarse white flesh
packed in like feathers,
the big bones and the little bones,
the dramatic reds and blacks   30
of his shiny entrails,
and the pink swim-bladder
like a big peony.
I looked into his eyes
which were far larger than mine   35
but shallower, and yellowed,
the irises backed and packed
with tarnished tinfoil
seen through the lenses
of old scratched isinglass.[1]   40

---

1. A whitish, semitransparent substance, originally obtained from the swim bladders of some freshwater fish and occasionally used for windows.

They shifted a little, but not
to return my stare.
—It was more like the tipping
of an object toward the light.
I admired his sullen face, 45
the mechanism of his jaw,
and then I saw
that from his lower lip
—if you could call it a lip—
grim, wet, and weaponlike, 50
hung five old pieces of fish-line,
or four and a wire leader
with the swivel still attached,
with all their five big hooks
grown firmly in his mouth. 55
A green line, frayed at the end
where he broke it, two heavier lines,
and a fine black thread
still crimped from the strain and snap
when it broke and he got away. 60
Like medals with their ribbons
frayed and wavering,
a five-haired beard of wisdom
trailing from his aching jaw.
I stared and stared 65
and victory filled up
the little rented boat,
from the pool of bilge
where oil had spread a rainbow
around the rusted engine 70
to the bailer rusted orange,
the sun-cracked thwarts,
the oarlocks on their strings,
the gunnels—until everything
was rainbow, rainbow, rainbow! 75
And I let the fish go.

1946

At the Fishhouses

Although it is a cold evening,
down by one of the fishhouses
an old man sits netting,
his net, in the gloaming almost invisible
a dark purple-brown, 5
and his shuttle worn and polished.
The air smells so strong of codfish
it makes one's nose run and one's eyes water.
The five fishhouses have steeply peaked roofs
and narrow, cleated gangplanks slant up 10
to storerooms in the gables

for the wheelbarrows to be pushed up and down on.
All is silver: the heavy surface of the sea,
swelling slowly as if considering spilling over,
is opaque, but the silver of the benches,   15
the lobster pots, and masts, scattered
among the wild jagged rocks,
is of an apparent translucence
like the small old buildings with an emerald moss
growing on their shoreward walls.   20
The big fish tubs are completely lined
with layers of beautiful herring scales
and the wheelbarrows are similarly plastered
with creamy iridescent coats of mail,
with small iridescent flies crawling on them.   25
Up on the little slope behind the houses,
set in the sparse bright sprinkle of grass,
is an ancient wooden capstan,[1]
cracked, with two long bleached handles
and some melancholy stains, like dried blood,   30
where the ironwork has rusted.
The old man accepts a Lucky Strike.[2]
He was a friend of my grandfather.
We talk of the decline in the population
and of codfish and herring   35
while he waits for a herring boat to come in.
There are sequins on his vest and on his thumb.
He has scraped the scales, the principal beauty,
from unnumbered fish with that black old knife,
the blade of which is almost worn away.   40

Down at the water's edge, at the place
where they haul up the boats, up the long ramp
descending into the water, thin silver
tree trunks are laid horizontally
across the gray stones, down and down   45
at intervals of four or five feet.

Cold dark deep and absolutely clear,
element bearable to no mortal,
to fish and to seals . . . One seal particularly
I have seen here evening after evening.   50
He was curious about me. He was interested in music;
like me a believer in total immersion,[3]
so I used to sing him Baptist hymns.
I also sang "A Mighty Fortress Is Our God."
He stood up in the water and regarded me   55
steadily, moving his head a little.
Then he would disappear, then suddenly emerge
almost in the same spot, with a sort of shrug
as if it were against his better judgment.

---

1. Cylindrical drum around which rope is wound,   2. Brand of cigarettes.
used for winching.   3. Form of baptism favored by Baptists.

Cold dark deep and absolutely clear, 60
the clear gray icy water . . . Back, behind us,
the dignified tall firs begin.
Bluish, associating with their shadows,
a million Christmas trees stand
waiting for Christmas. The water seems suspended 65
above the rounded gray and blue-gray stones.
I have seen it over and over, the same sea, the same,
slightly, indifferently swinging above the stones,
icily free above the stones,
above the stones and then the world. 70
If you should dip your hand in,
your wrist would ache immediately,
your bones would begin to ache and your hand would burn
as if the water were a transmutation of fire
that feeds on stones and burns with a dark gray flame. 75
If you tasted it, it would first taste bitter,
then briny, then surely burn your tongue.
It is like what we imagine knowledge to be:
dark, salt, clear, moving, utterly free,
drawn from the cold hard mouth 80
of the world, derived from the rocky breasts
forever, flowing and drawn, and since
our knowledge is historical, flowing, and flown.

1955

The Armadillo

for Robert Lowell

This is the time of year
when almost every night
the frail, illegal fire balloons appear.
Climbing the mountain height,

rising toward a saint 5
still honored in these parts,
the paper chambers flush and fill with light
that comes and goes, like hearts.

Once up against the sky it's hard
to tell them from the stars— 10
planets, that is—the tinted ones:
Venus going down, or Mars,

or the pale green one. With a wind,
they flare and falter, wobble and toss;
but if it's still they steer between 15
the kite sticks of the Southern Cross,

receding, dwindling, solemnly
and steadily forsaking us,

or, in the downdraft from a peak,
suddenly turning dangerous.   20

Last night another big one fell.
It splattered like an egg of fire
against the cliff behind the house.
The flame ran down. We saw the pair

of owls who nest there flying up   25
and up, their whirling black-and-white
stained bright pink underneath, until
they shrieked up out of sight.

The ancient owls' nest must have burned.
Hastily, all alone,   30
a glistening armadillo left the scene,
rose-flecked, head down, tail down,

and then a baby rabbit jumped out,
short-eared, to our surprise.
So soft!—a handful of intangible ash   35
with fixed, ignited eyes.

Too pretty, dreamlike mimicry!
O falling fire and piercing cry
and panic, and a weak mailed fist[1]
clenched ignorant against the sky!   40

1965

Sestina[1]

September rain falls on the house.
In the failing light, the old grandmother
sits in the kitchen with the child
beside the Little Marvel Stove,
reading the jokes from the almanac,   5
laughing and talking to hide her tears.

She thinks that her equinoctial tears
and the rain that beats on the roof of the house
were both foretold by the almanac,
but only known to a grandmother.   10
The iron kettle sings on the stove.
She cuts some bread and says to the child,

It's time for tea now; but the child
is watching the teakettle's small hard tears
dance like mad on the hot black stove,   15

---

1. The armadillo, curled tight and protected
against everything but fire.
1. A fixed verse form in which the end words of the
first six-line stanza must be used at the ends of the
lines in the following stanzas in a rotating order;
the final three lines must contain all six words.

the way the rain must dance on the house.
Tidying up, the old grandmother
hangs up the clever almanac

on its string. Birdlike, the almanac
hovers half open above the child,   20
hovers above the old grandmother
and her teacup full of dark brown tears.
She shivers and says she thinks the house
feels chilly, and puts more wood in the stove.

It was to be, says the Marvel Stove.   25
I know what I know, says the almanac.
With crayons the child draws a rigid house
and a winding pathway. Then the child
puts in a man with buttons like tears
and shows it proudly to the grandmother.   30

But secretly, while the grandmother
busies herself about the stove,
the little moons fall down like tears
from between the pages of the almanac
into the flower bed the child   35
has carefully placed in the front of the house.

Time to plant tears, says the almanac.
The grandmother sings to the marvellous stove
and the child draws another inscrutable house.

1965

In the Waiting Room

In Worcester, Massachusetts,
I went with Aunt Consuelo
to keep her dentist's appointment
and sat and waited for her
in the dentist's waiting room.   5
It was winter. It got dark
early. The waiting room
was full of grown-up people,
arctics and overcoats,
lamps and magazines.   10
My aunt was inside
what seemed like a long time
and while I waited I read
the *National Geographic*
(I could read) and carefully   15
studied the photographs:
the inside of a volcano,
black, and full of ashes;

then it was spilling over
in rivulets of fire.   20
Osa and Martin Johnson[1]
dressed in riding breeches,
laced boots, and pith helmets.
A dead man slung on a pole
—"Long Pig,"[2] the caption said.   25
Babies with pointed heads
wound round and round with string;
black, naked women with necks
wound round and round with wire
like the necks of light bulbs.   30
Their breasts were horrifying.
I read it right straight through.
I was too shy to stop.
And then I looked at the cover:
the yellow margins, the date.   35

Suddenly, from inside,
came an *oh!* of pain
—Aunt Consuelo's voice—
not very loud or long.
I wasn't at all surprised;   40
even then I knew she was
a foolish, timid woman.
I might have been embarrassed,
but wasn't. What took me
completely by surprise   45
was that it was *me*:
my voice, in my mouth.
Without thinking at all
I was my foolish aunt,
I—we—were falling, falling,   50
our eyes glued to the cover
of the *National Geographic*,
February, 1918.

I said to myself: three days
and you'll be seven years old.   55
I was saying it to stop
the sensation of falling off
the round, turning world
into cold, blue-black space.
But I felt: you are an *I*,   60
you are an *Elizabeth*,
you are one of *them*.
Why should you be one, too?
I scarcely dared to look.
to see what it was I was.   65
I gave a sidelong glance

1. Famous explorers and travel writers.
2. Polynesian cannibals' name for the human carcass.

—I couldn't look any higher—
at shadowy gray knees,
trousers and skirts and boots
and different pairs of hands   70
lying under the lamps.
I knew that nothing stranger
had ever happened, that nothing
stranger could ever happen.
Why should I be my aunt,   75
or me, or anyone?
What similarities—
boots, hands, the family voice
I felt in my throat, or even
the *National Geographic*   80
and those awful hanging breasts—
held us all together
or made us all just one?
How—I didn't know any
word for it—how "unlikely" . . .   85
How had I come to be here,
like them, and overhear
a cry of pain that could have
got loud and worse but hadn't?

The waiting room was bright   90
and too hot. It was sliding
beneath a big black wave,
another, and another.

Then I was back in it.
The War was on. Outside,   95
in Worcester, Massachusetts,
were night and slush and cold,
and it was still the fifth
of February, 1918.

                                                    1976

One Art

The art of losing isn't hard to master;
so many things seem filled with the intent
to be lost that their loss is no disaster.

Lose something every day. Accept the fluster
of lost door keys, the hour badly spent.   5
The art of losing isn't hard to master.

Then practice losing farther, losing faster:
places, and names, and where it was you meant
to travel. None of these will bring disaster.

I lost my mother's watch. And look! my last, or   10
next-to-last, of three loved houses went.
The art of losing isn't hard to master.

I lost two cities, lovely ones. And, vaster,
some realms I owned, two rivers, a continent.
I miss them, but it wasn't a disaster.   15

—Even losing you (the joking voice, a gesture
I love) I shan't have lied. It's evident
the art of losing's not too hard to master
though it may look like (*Write* it!) like disaster.

1976

TENNESSEE WILLIAMS
1911–1983

Speaking of Blanche DuBois, the heroine of *A Streetcar Named Desire*, Tennessee Williams once said, "She was a demonic creature; the size of her feeling was too great for her to contain." In Williams's plays—he wrote and rewrote more than twenty full-length dramas as well as screenplays and shorter works—his characters are driven by the size of their feelings, much as Williams felt driven to write about them.

He was born Thomas Lanier Williams in Columbus, Mississippi. His mother, "Miss Edwina," the daughter of an Episcopalian minister, was repressed and genteel, very much the southern belle in her youth. His father, Cornelius, was a traveling salesman, often away from his family and often violent and drunk when at home. As a child Williams was sickly and overly protected by his mother; he was closely attached to his sister, Rose, repelled by the roughhouse world of boys, and alienated from his father. The family's move from Mississippi to St. Louis, where Cornelius became a sales manager of the shoe company he had traveled for, was a shock to Mrs. Williams and her young children, used to living in small southern towns where a minister's daughter was an important person. Yet Mrs. Williams could take care of herself; she was a "survivor."

Williams went to the University of Missouri, but left after two years; his father then found him a job in the shoe-factory warehouse. He worked there for nearly three years, writing feverishly at night. (His closest friend at the time was a burly coworker, easygoing and attractive to women, named Stanley Kowalski, whose name and characteristics Williams would borrow for *A Streetcar Named Desire*.) Williams found the life so difficult, however, that he succumbed to a nervous breakdown. After recovering at the home of his beloved grandparents, he went on to further studies, finally graduating at the age of twenty-seven. Earlier Rose had been suffering increasing mental imbalance; the final trauma was apparently brought on by one of Cornelius's alcoholic rages, in which he beat Edwina and, trying to calm Rose, made a gesture that she took to be sexual. Shortly thereafter Edwina signed the papers allowing Rose to be "tragically becalmed" by a prefrontal lobotomy. Rose spent most of her life in sanatoriums, except when Williams brought her out for visits.

The next year Williams left for New Orleans, the first of many temporary homes; it would provide the setting for *A Streetcar Named Desire*. In New Orleans he changed his name to "Tennessee," later giving—as often when discussing his life—various romantic reasons for doing so. There also he actively entered the homosexual world.

Williams had had plays produced at local theaters and in 1939 he won a prize for a collection of one-act plays, *American Blues*. The next year *Battle of Angels* failed (in 1957 he would rewrite it as *Orpheus Descending*). His first success was *The Glass Menagerie* (1945). Williams called it a "memory play," seen through the recollections of the writer, Tom, who talks to the audience about himself and about the scenes depicting his mother, Amanda, poverty-stricken but genteelly living on memories of her southern youth and her "gentlemen callers"; his crippled sister, Laura, who finds refuge in her "menagerie" of little glass animals; and the traumatic effect of a modern "gentleman caller" on them. While there are similarities between Edwina, Rose, and Tennessee on the one hand, and Amanda, Laura, and Tom on the other, there are also differences: the play is not literally autobiographical.

The financial success of *Menagerie* proved exhilarating, then debilitating. Williams fled to Mexico to work full-time on an earlier play, *The Poker Night*. It had begun as *The Moth*; its first image, as Williams's biographer, Donald Spoto, tells us, was "simply that of a woman, sitting with folded hands near a window, while moonlight streamed in and she awaited in vain the arrival of her boyfriend": named Blanche, she was at first intended as a young Amanda. During rehearsals of *Menagerie*, Williams had asked members of the stage crew to teach him to play poker, and he began to visualize his new play as a series of confrontations between working-class poker players and two refined southern women.

As the focus of his attention changed from Stanley to Blanche, *The Poker Night* turned into *A Streetcar Named Desire*. Upon opening in 1947, it was an even greater success than *The Glass Menagerie*, and it won the Pulitzer Prize. Williams was able to travel and to buy a home in Key West, Florida, where he did much of his ensuing

A game of seven-card stud poker continues as the action of *A Streetcar Named Desire* concludes. Original Broadway production, 1947.

work. At about this time his "transitory heart" found "a home at last" in a young man named Frank Merlo.

For more than a decade thereafter a new Williams play appeared almost every two years. Among the most successful were *The Rose Tattoo* (1950), in which the tempestuous heroine, Serafina, worshiping the memory of her dead husband, finds love again; the Pulitzer Prize–winning *Cat on a Hot Tin Roof* (1955), which portrays the conflict of the dying Big Daddy and his impotent son, Brick, watched and controlled by Brick's wife, "Maggie the Cat"; and *The Night of the Iguana* (1961), which brings a varied group of tormented people together at a rundown hotel on the Mexican coast. His plays were produced widely abroad and also became equally successful films. Yet some of the ones now regarded as the best of this period were commercial failures: *Summer and Smoke* (1948), for example, and the surrealistic and visionary *Camino Real* (1953).

For years Williams had depended on a wide variety of drugs, especially to help him sleep and to keep him awake in the early mornings, when he invariably worked. In the 1960s the drugs began to take a real toll. Other factors contributed to the decline of his later years: Frank Merlo's death, the emergence of younger playwrights of whom he felt blindly jealous, and the violent nature of the 1960s, which seemed both to mirror his inner chaos and to leave him behind.

Yet despite Broadway failures, critical disparagements, and a breakdown for which he was hospitalized, he valiantly kept working. Spoto notes that in Williams's late work, Rose was "the source and inspiration of everything he wrote, either directly—with a surrogate character representing her—or indirectly, in the situation of romanticized mental illness or unvarnished verisimilitude." This observation is certainly true of his last Broadway play, the failed *Clothes for a Summer Hotel* (1980), ostensibly about the ghosts of Scott and Zelda Fitzgerald, and of the play he obsessively wrote and rewrote, *The Two Character Play*, which chronicles the descent of a brother and sister, who are also lovers into madness and death.

Despite Williams's self-destructiveness, in his writing and in his social life, the work of his great years was now being seriously studied and often revived by regional and community theaters. Critics began to see that he was one of America's best and most dedicated playwrights. And he kept on working. He was collaborating on a film of two stories about Rose when he died, apparently having choked to death on the lid of a pill bottle.

Always reluctant to talk about his work (likening it to a "bird that will be startled away, as by a hawk's shadow"), Williams did not see himself in a tradition of American dramaturgy. He acknowledged the influence of Anton Chekhov, the nineteenth-century Russian writer of dramas with lonely, searching characters; of D. H. Lawrence, the British novelist who emphasized the theme of a sexual life force; and above all of the American Hart Crane, homosexual *poète maudit*, who, he said, "touched fire that burned [himself] alive," adding that "perhaps it is only through self-immolation of such a nature that we living beings can offer to you the entire truth of ourselves." Such a statement indicates the deeply confessional quality of Williams's writing, even in plays not directly autobiographical.

Although he never acknowledged any debt to the American playwright Eugene O'Neill, Williams shared with O'Neill an impatience over the theatrical conventions of realism. *The Glass Menagerie*, for example, uses screened projections, lighting effects, and music to emphasize that it takes place in Tom's memory. *A Streetcar Named Desire* moves in and out of the house on Elysian Fields, while music and lighting reinforce all the major themes. Williams also relies on the effects of language, especially of a vivid and colloquial Southern speech that may be compared with that of William Faulkner, Eudora Welty, or Flannery O'Connor. Rhythms of language become almost a musical indication of character, distinguishing Blanche from other characters. Reading or seeing his plays, we become aware of how symbolic repetitions—in Blanche's and Stanley's turns of phrase, the naked light bulb and the paper lantern, the Mexican woman selling flowers for the dead, the "Varsouviana" waltz and the reverberating voices—produce a heightening of reality: what Williams called "poetic realism."

More than a half century later does the destruction of Blanche, the "lady," still have the power to move us? Elia Kazan, in his director's notes, calls her "an outdated creature, approaching extinction . . . like a dinosaur." But Blythe Danner, who played Blanche in a 1988 revival, acutely observes that Williams "was attached to the things that were going to destroy him" and that Blanche, similarly, is attracted to and repelled by Stanley: "It's Tennessee fighting, fighting, fighting what he doesn't want to get into, what is very prevalent in his mind. That incredible contradiction in so many people is what he captures better than any other playwright."

Contemporary criticisms of Williams's plays focused on their violence and their obsession with sexuality, which in some of the later work struck some commentators as an almost morbid preoccupation with "perversion"—murder, rape, drugs, incest, nymphomania. The shriller voices making such accusations were attacking Williams for his homosexuality, which could not be publicly spoken of in this country until comparatively recently. These taboo topics, however, figure as instances of Williams's deeper subjects: desire and loneliness. As he said in an interview, "Desire is rooted in a longing for companionship, a release from the loneliness that haunts every individual." Loneliness and desire propel his characters into extreme behavior, no doubt, but such behavior literally dramatizes the plight that Williams saw as universal.

The following text is from *The Theatre of Tennessee Williams*, volume 1 (1971).

A Streetcar Named Desire

> And so it was I entered the broken world
> To trace the visionary company of love, its voice
> An instant in the wind (I know not whither hurled)
> But not for long to hold each desperate choice.
> —"The Broken Tower" by Hart Crane[1]

THE CHARACTERS

BLANCHE	PABLO
STELLA	A NEGRO WOMAN
STANLEY	A DOCTOR
MITCH	A NURSE
EUNICE	A YOUNG COLLECTOR
STEVE	A MEXICAN WOMAN

Scene One

The exterior of a two-story corner building on a street in New Orleans which is named Elysian Fields and runs between the L & N tracks and the river.[2] The section is poor but, unlike corresponding sections in other American cities, it has a raffish charm. The houses are mostly white frame, weathered grey, with rickety outside stairs and galleries and quaintly ornamented gables. This building contains two flats, upstairs and down. Faded white stairs ascend to the entrances of both.

It is first dark of an evening early in May. The sky that shows around the dim white building is a peculiarly tender blue, almost a turquoise, which invests the scene with a kind of lyricism and gracefully attenuates the atmosphere of decay. You can almost feel the warm breath of the brown river beyond the river warehouses with their faint redolences of bananas and coffee. A corresponding air is

---

1. American poet (1899–1932).
2. Elysian Fields is a New Orleans street at the northern tip of the French Quarter, between the Louisville & Nashville railroad tracks and the Mississippi River. In Greek mythology the Elysian Fields are the abode of the blessed in the afterlife.

evoked by the music of Negro entertainers at a barroom around the corner. In this part of New Orleans you are practically always just around the corner, or a few doors down the street, from a tinny piano being played with the infatuated fluency of brown fingers. This "Blue Piano" expresses the spirit of the life which goes on here.

Two women, one white and one colored, are taking the air on the steps of the building. The white woman is EUNICE, *who occupies the upstairs flat; the colored woman a neighbor, for New Orleans is a cosmopolitan city where there is a relatively warm and easy intermingling of races in the old part of town.*

Above the music of the "Blue Piano" the voices of people on the street can be heard overlapping.

> [*Two men come around the corner,* STANLEY KOWALSKI *and* MITCH. *They are about twenty-eight or thirty years old, roughly dressed in blue denim work clothes.* STANLEY *carries his bowling jacket and a red-stained package from a butcher's. They stop at the foot of the steps.*]

STANLEY [*bellowing*]   Hey there! Stella, baby!

> [STELLA *comes out on the first floor landing, a gentle young woman, about twenty-five, and of a background obviously quite different from her husband's.*]

STELLA [*mildly*]   Don't holler at me like that. Hi, Mitch.

STANLEY   Catch!

STELLA   What?

STANLEY   Meat!

> [*He heaves the package at her. She cries out in protest but manages to catch it: then she laughs breathlessly. Her husband and his companion have already started back around the corner.*]

STELLA [*calling after him*]   Stanley! Where are you going?

STANLEY   Bowling!

STELLA   Can I come watch?

STANLEY   Come on. [*He goes out.*]

STELLA   Be over soon. [*to the white woman*] Hello, Eunice. How are you?

EUNICE   I'm all right. Tell Steve to get him a poor boy's sandwich 'cause nothing's left here.

> [*They all laugh; the colored woman does not stop.* STELLA *goes out.*]

COLORED WOMAN   What was that package he th'ew at 'er? [*She rises from steps, laughing louder.*]

EUNICE   You hush, now!

NEGRO WOMAN   Catch *what!*

> [*She continues to laugh.* BLANCHE *comes around the corner, carrying a valise. She looks at a slip of paper, then at the building, then again at the slip and again at the building. Her expression is one of shocked disbelief. Her appearance is incongruous to this setting. She is daintily dressed in a white suit with a fluffy bodice, necklace and earrings of pearl, white gloves and hat, looking as if she were arriving at a summer tea or cocktail party in the garden district. She is about five years older than* STELLA. *Her delicate beauty must avoid a strong light. There is something about her uncertain manner, as well as her white clothes, that suggests a moth.*]

EUNICE [*finally*]   What's the matter, honey? Are you lost?

BLANCHE [*with faintly hysterical humor*]   They told me to take a street-car named Desire, and then transfer to one called Cemeteries[3] and ride six blocks and get off at—Elysian Fields!

---

3. The end of a streetcar line that stopped at a cemetery. Desire is a New Orleans street.

EUNICE   That's where you are now.

BLANCHE   At Elysian Fields?

EUNICE   This here is Elysian Fields.

BLANCHE   They mustn't have—understood—what number I wanted . . .

EUNICE   What number you lookin' for?

[BLANCHE *wearily refers to the slip of paper.*]

BLANCHE   Six thirty-two.

EUNICE   You don't have to look no further.

BLANCHE [*uncomprehendingly*]   I'm looking for my sister, Stella DuBois, I mean—Mrs. Stanley Kowalski.

EUNICE   That's the party.—You just did miss her, though.

BLANCHE   This—can this be—her home?

EUNICE   She's got the downstairs here and I got the up.

BLANCHE   Oh. She's—out?

EUNICE   You noticed that bowling alley around the corner?

BLANCHE   I'm—not sure I did.

EUNICE   Well, that's where she's at, watchin' her husband bowl. [*There is a pause.*] You want to leave your suitcase here an' go find her?

BLANCHE   No.

NEGRO WOMAN   I'll go tell her you come.

BLANCHE   Thanks.

NEGRO WOMAN   You welcome. [*She goes out.*]

EUNICE   She wasn't expecting you?

BLANCHE   No. No, not tonight.

EUNICE   Well, why don't you just go in and make yourself at home till they get back.

BLANCHE   How could I—do that?

EUNICE   We own this place so I can let you in.

[*She gets up and opens the downstairs door. A light goes on behind the blind, turning it light blue.* BLANCHE *slowly follows her into the downstairs flat. The surrounding areas dim out as the interior is lighted. Two rooms can be seen, not too clearly defined. The one first entered is primarily a kitchen but contains a folding bed to be used by* BLANCHE. *The room beyond this is a bedroom. Off this room is a narrow door to a bathroom.*]

EUNICE [*defensively, noticing* BLANCHE's *look*]   It's sort of messed up right now but when it's clean it's real sweet.

BLANCHE   Is it?

EUNICE   Uh-huh, I think so. So you're Stella's sister?

BLANCHE   Yes. [*wanting to get rid of her*] Thanks for letting me in.

EUNICE   *Por nada*,[4] as the Mexicans say, *por nada*! Stella spoke of you.

BLANCHE   Yes?

EUNICE   I think she said you taught school.

BLANCHE   Yes.

EUNICE   And you're from Mississippi, huh?

BLANCHE   Yes.

EUNICE   She showed me a picture of your home-place, the plantation.

BLANCHE   Belle Reve?[5]

EUNICE   A great big place with white columns.

BLANCHE   Yes . . .

4. It's nothing (Spanish).   5. Beautiful Dream (French).

EUNICE   A place like that must be awful hard to keep up.

BLANCHE   If you will excuse me, I'm just about to drop.

EUNICE   Sure, honey. Why don't you set down?

BLANCHE   What I meant was I'd like to be left alone.

EUNICE [*offended*]   Aw. I'll make myself scarce, in that case.

BLANCHE   I didn't meant to be rude, but—

EUNICE   I'll drop by the bowling alley an' hustle her up. [*She goes out the door.*]

> [BLANCHE *sits in a chair very stiffly with her shoulders slightly hunched and her legs pressed close together and her hands tightly clutching her purse as if she were quite cold. After a while the blind look goes out of her eyes and she begins to look slowly around. A cat screeches. She catches her breath with a startled gesture. Suddenly she notices something in a half opened closet. She springs up and crosses to it, and removes a whiskey bottle. She pours a half tumbler of whiskey and tosses it down. She carefully replaces the bottle and washes out the tumbler at the sink. Then she resumes her seat in front of the table.*]

BLANCHE [*faintly to herself*]   I've got to keep hold of myself! [STELLA *comes quickly around the corner of the building and runs to the door of the downstairs flat.*]

STELLA [*calling out joyfully*]   Blanche!

> [*For a moment they stare at each other. Then* BLANCHE *springs up and runs to her with a wild cry.*]

BLANCHE   Stella, oh, Stella, Stella! Stella for Star!

> [*She begins to speak with feverish vivacity as if she feared for either of them to stop and think. They catch each other in a spasmodic embrace.*]

BLANCHE   Now, then, let me look at you. But don't you look at me, Stella, no, no, no, not till later, not till I've bathed and rested! And turn that over-light off! Turn that off! I won't be looked at in this merciles glare! [STELLA *laughs and complies.*] Come back here now! Oh, my baby! Stella! Stella for Star! [*She embraces her again.*] I thought you would never come back to this horrible place! What am I saying? I didn't mean to say that. I meant to be nice about it and say—Oh, what a convenient location and such—Ha-a-ha! Precious lamb! You haven't said a *word* to me.

STELLA   You haven't given me a chance to, honey! [*She laughs, but her glance at* BLANCHE *is a little anxious.*]

BLANCHE   Well, now you talk. Open your pretty mouth and talk while I look around for some liquor! I know you must have some liquor on the place! Where could it be, I wonder? Oh, I spy, I spy!

> [*She rushes to the closet and removes the bottle; she is shaking all over and panting for breath as she tries to laugh. The bottle nearly slips from her grasp.*]

STELLA [*noticing*]   Blanche, you sit down and let me pour the drinks. I don't know what we've got to mix with. Maybe a coke's in the icebox. Look'n see, honey, while I'm—

BLANCHE   No coke, honey, not with my nerves tonight! Where—where—where is—?

STELLA   Stanley? Bowling! He loves it. They're having a—found some soda!—tournament . . .

BLANCHE   Just water, baby, to chase it! Now don't get worried, your sister hasn't turned into a drunkard, she's just all shaken up and hot and tired and dirty! You sit down, now, and explain this place to me! What are you doing in a place like this?

STELLA   Now, Blanche—

BLANCHE   Oh, I'm not going to be hypocritical, I'm going to be honestly critical about it! Never, never, never in my worst dreams could I picture— Only Poe! Only Mr. Edgar Allan Poe!—could do it justice! Out there I suppose is the ghoul-haunted woodland of Weir![6] [*She laughs.*]

STELLA   No, honey, those are the L & N tracks.

BLANCHE   No, now seriously, putting joking aside. Why didn't you tell me, why didn't you write me, honey, why didn't you let me know?

STELLA   [*carefully, pouring herself a drink*]   Tell you what, Blanche?

BLANCHE   Why, that you had to live in these conditions!

STELLA   Aren't you being a little intense about it? It's not that bad at all! New Orleans isn't like other cities.

BLANCHE   This has got nothing to do with New Orleans. You might as well say—forgive me, blessed baby! [*She suddenly stops short.*] The subject is closed!

STELLA   [*a little drily*]   Thanks.

        [*During the pause,* BLANCHE *stares at her. She smiles at* BLANCHE.]

BLANCHE   [*looking down at her glass, which shakes in her hand*]   You're all I've got in the world, and you're not glad to see me!

STELLA   [*sincerely*]   Why, Blanche, you know that's not true.

BLANCHE   No?—I'd forgotten how quiet you were.

STELLA   You never did give me a chance to say much, Blanche. So I just got in the habit of being quiet around you.

BLANCHE   [*vaguely*]   A good habit to get into . . . [*then, abruptly*] You haven't asked me how I happened to get away from the school before the spring term ended.

STELLA   Well, I thought you'd volunteer that information—if you wanted to tell me.

BLANCHE   You thought I'd been fired?

STELLA   No, I—thought you might have—resigned . . .

BLANCHE   I was so exhausted by all I'd been through my—nerves broke. [*nervously tamping cigarette*] I was on the verge of—lunacy, almost! So Mr. Graves—Mr. Graves is the high school superintendent—he suggested I take a leave of absence. I couldn't put all of those details into the wire . . . [*She drinks quickly.*] Oh, this buzzes right through me and feels so *good!*

STELLA   Won't you have another?

BLANCHE   No, one's my limit.

STELLA   Sure?

BLANCHE   You haven't said a word about my appearance.

STELLA   You look just fine.

BLANCHE   God love you for a liar! Daylight never exposed so total a ruin! But you—you've put on some weight, yes, you're just as plump as a little partridge! And it's so becoming to you!

STELLA   Now, Blanche—

BLANCHE   Yes, it is, it is or I wouldn't say it! You just have to watch around the hips a little. Stand up.

6. From the refrain of Poe's gothic ballad "Ulalume" (1847).

STELLA   Not now.

BLANCHE   You hear me? I said stand up! [STELLA *complies reluctantly*.]
You messy child, you, you've spilt something on that pretty white lace
collar! About your hair—you ought to have it cut in a feather bob with
your dainty features. Stella, you have a maid, don't you?

STELLA   No. With only two rooms it's—

BLANCHE   What? *Two* rooms, did you say?

STELLA   This one and— [*She is embarrassed.*]

BLANCHE   The other one? [*She laughs sharply. There is an embarrassed
silence.*]

BLANCHE   I am going to take just one little tiny nip more, sort of to put
the stopper on, so to speak. . . . Then put the bottle away so I won't be
tempted. [*She rises.*] I want you to look at *my* figure! [*She turns around.*]
You know I haven't put on one ounce in ten years, Stella? I weigh what
I weighed the summer you left Belle Reve. The summer Dad died and
you left us . . .

STELLA [*a little wearily*]   It's just incredible, Blanche, how well you're
looking.

BLANCHE [*They both laugh uncomfortably.*]   But, Stella, there's only two
rooms, I don't see where you're going to put me!

STELLA   We're going to put you in here.

BLANCHE   What kind of bed's this—one of those collapsible things?
[*She sits on it.*]

STELLA   Does it feel all right?

BLANCHE [*dubiously*]   Wonderful, honey. I don't like a bed that gives much.
But there's no door between the two rooms, and Stanley—will it be
decent?

STELLA   Stanley is Polish, you know.

BLANCHE   Oh, yes. They're something like Irish, aren't they?

STELLA   Well—

BLANCHE   Only not so—highbrow? [*They both laugh again in the same
way.*] I brought some nice clothes to meet all your lovely friends in.

STELLA   I'm afraid you won't think they are lovely.

BLANCHE   What are they like?

STELLA   They're Stanley's friends.

BLANCHE   Polacks?

STELLA   They're a mixed lot, Blanche.

BLANCHE   Heterogeneous—types?

STELLA   Oh, yes. Yes, types is right!

BLANCHE   Well—anyhow—I brought nice clothes and I'll wear them. I
guess you're hoping I'll say I'll put up at a hotel, but I'm not going to put
up at a hotel. I want to be *near* you, got to be *with* somebody, I *can't* be
alone! Because—as you must have noticed—I'm—*not* very *well*. . . .
[*Her voice drops and her look is frightened.*]

STELLA   You seem a little bit nervous or overwrought or something.

BLANCHE   Will Stanley like me, or will I be just a visiting in-law, Stella? I
couldn't stand that.

STELLA   You'll get along fine together, if you'll just try not to—well—
compare him with men that we went out with at home.

BLANCHE   Is he so—different?

STELLA   Yes. A different species.

BLANCHE   In what way; what's he like?

STELLA   Oh, you can't describe someone you're in love with! Here's a picture of him! [*She hands a photograph to* BLANCHE.]

BLANCHE   An officer?

STELLA   A Master Sergeant in the Engineers' Corps. Those are decorations!

BLANCHE   He had those on when you met him?

STELLA   I assure you I wasn't just blinded by all the brass.

BLANCHE   That's not what I—

STELLA   But of course there were things to adjust myself to later on.

BLANCHE   Such as his civilian background! [STELLA *laughs uncertainly.*] How did he take it when you said I was coming?

STELLA   Oh, Stanley doesn't know yet.

BLANCHE [*frightened*]   You—haven't told him?

STELLA   He's on the road a good deal.

BLANCHE   Oh. Travels?

STELLA   Yes.

BLANCHE   Good. I mean—isn't it?

STELLA [*half to herself*]   I can hardly stand it when he is away for a night . . .

BLANCHE   Why, Stella!

STELLA   When he's away for a week I nearly go wild!

BLANCHE   Gracious!

STELLA   And when he comes back I cry on his lap like a baby . . . [*She smiles to herself.*]

BLANCHE   I guess that is what is meant by being in love . . . [STELLA *looks up with a radiant smile.*] Stella—

STELLA   What?

BLANCHE [*in an uneasy rush*]   I haven't asked you the things you probably thought I was going to ask. And so I'll expect you to be understanding about what *I* have to tell *you.*

STELLA   What, Blanche? [*Her face turns anxious.*]

BLANCHE   Well, Stella—you're going to reproach me, I know that you're bound to reproach me—but before you do—take into consideration— you left! I stayed and struggled! You came to New Orleans and looked out for yourself! *I* stayed at *Belle Reve* and tried to hold it together! I'm not meaning this in any reproachful way, but *all* the burden descended on *my* shoulders.

STELLA   The best I could do was make my own living, Blanche.
          [BLANCHE *begins to shake again with intensity.*]

BLANCHE   I know, I know. But you are the one that abandoned Belle Reve, not I! I stayed and fought for it, bled for it, almost died for it!

STELLA   Stop this hysterical outburst and tell me what's happened? What do you mean fought and bled? What kind of—

BLANCHE   I knew you would, Stella. I knew you would take this attitude about it!

STELLA   About—what?—please!

BLANCHE [*slowly*]   The loss—the loss . . .

STELLA   Belle Reve? Lost, is it? No!

BLANCHE   Yes, Stella.
          [*They stare at each other across the yellow-checked linoleum of the table.* BLANCHE *slowly nods her head and* STELLA *looks slowly down at her hands folded on the table. The music of the "Blue Piano" grows louder.* BLANCHE *touches her handkerchief to her forehead.*]

STELLA But how did it go? What happened?

BLANCHE [*syringing up*] You're a fine one to ask me how it went!

STELLA Blanche!

BLANCHE You're a fine one to sit there *accusing me* of it!

STELLA *Blanche!*

BLANCHE I, I, *I* took the blows in my face and my body! All of those deaths! The long parade to the graveyard! Father, mother! Margaret, that dreadful way! So big with it, it couldn't be put in a coffin! But had to be burned like rubbish! You just came home in time for the funerals, Stella. And funerals are pretty compared to deaths. Funerals are quiet, but deaths—not always. Sometimes their breathing is hoarse, and sometimes it rattles, and sometimes they even cry out to you, "Don't let me go!" Even the old, sometimes, say, "Don't let me go." As if you were able to stop them! But funerals are quiet, with pretty flowers. And, oh, what gorgeous boxes they pack them away in! Unless you were there at the bed when they cried out, "Hold me!" you'd never suspect there was the struggle for breath and bleeding. You didn't dream, but I saw! *Saw! Saw!* And now you sit there telling me with your eyes that I let the place go! How in hell do you think all that sickness and dying was paid for? Death is expensive, Miss Stella! And old Cousin Jessie's right after Margaret's, hers! Why, the Grim Reaper had put up his tent on our doorstep! . . . Stella. Belle Reve was his headquarters! Honey—that's how it slipped through my fingers! Which of them left us a fortune? Which of them left a cent of insurance even? Only poor Jessie—one hundred to pay for her coffin. That was all, Stella! And I with my pitiful salary at the school. Yes, accuse me! Sit there and stare at me, thinking I let the place go! *I* let the place go? Where were *you*! In bed with your—Polack!

STELLA [*springing*] Blanche! You be still! That's enough! [*She starts out.*]

BLANCHE Where are you going?

STELLA I'm going into the bathroom to wash my face.

BLANCHE Oh, Stella, Stella, you're crying!

STELLA Does that surprise you?

BLANCHE Forgive me—I didn't mean to—

[*The sound of men's voices is heard.* STELLA *goes into the bathroom, closing the door behind her. When the men appear, and* BLANCHE *realizes it must be* STANLEY *returning, she moves uncertainly from the bathroom door to the dressing table, looking apprehensively toward the front door.* STANLEY *enters, followed by* STEVE *and* MITCH. STANLEY *pauses near his door,* STEVE *by the foot of the spiral stair, and* MITCH *is slightly above and to the right of them, about to go out. As the men enter, we hear some of the following dialogue.*]

STANLEY Is that how he got it?

STEVE Sure that's how he got it. He hit the old weather-bird for 300 bucks on a six-number-ticket.

MITCH Don't tell him those things; he'll believe it.

[*Mitch starts out.*]

STANLEY [*restraining Mitch*] Hey, Mitch—come back here.

[BLANCHE, *at the sound of voices, retires in the bedroom. She picks up* STANLEY's *photo from dressing table, looks at it, puts it down. When* STANLEY *enters the apartment, she darts and hides behind the screen at the head of bed.*]

STEVE [*to* STANLEY *and* MITCH] Hey, are we playin' poker tomorrow?

STANLEY Sure—at Mitch's.

MITCH [*hearing this, returns quickly to the stair rail*]   No—not at my place. My mother's still sick!

STANLEY   Okay, at my place . . . [MITCH *starts out again.*] But you bring the beer!

>[MITCH *pretends not to hear—calls out "Good night, all," and goes out, singing.* EUNICE'*s voice is heard, above.*]

Break it up down there! I made the spaghetti dish and ate it myself.

STEVE [*going upstairs*]   I told you and phoned you we was playing. [*to the men*] Jax beer![7]

EUNICE   You never phoned me once.

STEVE   I told you at breakfast—and phoned you at lunch . . .

EUNICE   Well, never mind about that. You just get yourself home here once in a while.

STEVE   You want it in the papers?

>[*More laughter and shouts of parting come from the men.* STANLEY *throws the screen door of the kitchen open and comes in. He is of medium height, about five feet eight or nine, and strongly, compactly built. Animal joy in his being is implicit in all his movements and attitudes. Since earliest manhood the center of his life has been pleasure with women, the giving and taking of it, not with weak indulgence, dependently, but with the power and pride of a richly feathered male bird among hens. Branching out from this complete and satisfying center are all the auxiliary channels of his life, such as his heartiness with men, his appreciation of rough humor, his love of good drink and food and games, his car, his radio, everything that is his, that bears his emblem of the gaudy seed-bearer. He sizes women up at a glance, with sexual classifications, crude images flashing into his mind and determining the way he smiles at them.*]

BLANCHE [*drawing involuntarily back from his stare*]   You must be Stanley. I'm Blanche.

STANLEY   Stella's sister?

BLANCHE   Yes.

STANLEY   H'lo. Where's the little woman?

BLANCHE   In the bathroom.

STANLEY   Oh. Didn't know you were coming in town.

BLANCHE   I—uh—

STANLEY   Where you from, Blanche?

BLANCHE   Why, I—live in Laurel.

>[*He has crossed to the closet and removed the whiskey bottle.*]

STANLEY   In Laurel, huh? Oh, yeah. Yeah, in Laurel, that's right. Not in my territory. Liquor goes fast in hot weather. [*He holds the bottle to the light to observe its depletion.*] Have a shot?

BLANCHE   No, I—rarely touch it.

STANLEY   Some people rarely touch it, but it touches them often.

BLANCHE [*faintly*]   Ha-ha.

STANLEY   My clothes're stickin' to me. Do you mind if I make myself comfortable? [*He starts to remove his shirt.*]

BLANCHE   Please, please do.

STANLEY   Be comfortable is my motto.

BLANCHE   It's mine, too. It's hard to stay looking fresh. I haven't washed or even powdered my face and—here you are!

---

7. A local brand.

STANLEY   You know you can catch cold sitting around in damp things, especially when you been exercising hard like bowling is. You're a teacher, aren't you?

BLANCHE   Yes.

STANLEY   What do you teach, Blanche?

BLANCHE   English.

STANLEY   I never was a very good English student. How long you here for, Blanche?

BLANCHE   I—don't know yet.

STANLEY   You going to shack up here?

BLANCHE   I thought I would if it's not inconvenient for you all.

STANLEY   Good.

BLANCHE   Traveling wears me out.

STANLEY   Well, take it easy.

[*A cat screeches near the window,* BLANCHE *springs up.*]

BLANCHE   What's that?

STANLEY   Cats . . . Hey, Stella!

STELLA   [*faintly, from the bathroom*]   Yes, Stanley.

STANLEY   Haven't fallen in, have you? [*He grins at* BLANCHE. *She tries unsuccessfully to smile back. There is a silence.*] I'm afraid I'll strike you as being the unrefined type. Stella's spoke of you a good deal. You were married once, weren't you?

[*The music of the polka rises up, faint in the distance.*]

BLANCHE   Yes. When I was quite young.

STANLEY   What happened?

BLANCHE   The boy—the boy died. [*She sinks back down.*] I'm afraid I'm—going to be sick! [*Her head falls on her arms.*]

Scene Two

It is six o'clock the following evening. BLANCHE *is bathing.* STELLA *is completing her toilette.* BLANCHE's *dress, a flowered print, is laid out on* STELLA's *bed.*

STANLEY *enters the kitchen from outside, leaving the door open on the perpetual "Blue Piano" around the corner.*

STANLEY   What's all this monkey doings?

STELLA   Oh, Stan! [*She jumps up and kisses him, which he accepts with lordly composure.*] I'm taking Blanche to Galatoire's[8] for supper and then to a show, because it's your poker night.

STANLEY   How about my supper, huh? I'm not going to no Galatoire's for supper!

STELLA   I put you a cold plate on ice.

STANLEY   Well, isn't that just dandy!

STELLA   I'm going to try to keep Blanche out till the party breaks up because I don't know how she would take it. So we'll go to one of the little places in the Quarter afterward and you'd better give me some money.

STANLEY   Where is she?

STELLA   She's soaking in a hot tub to quiet her nerves. She's terribly upset.

8. Renowned fancy restaurant with traditional New Orleans cuisine.

STANLEY   Over what?

STELLA   She's been through such an ordeal.

STANLEY   Yeah?

STELLA   Stan, we've—lost Belle Reve!

STANLEY   The place in the country?

STELLA   Yes.

STANLEY   How?

STELLA [*vaguely*]   Oh, it had to be—sacrificed or something. [*There is a pause while* STANLEY *considers.* STELLA *is changing into her dress.*] When she comes in be sure to say something nice about her appearance. And, oh! Don't mention the baby. I haven't said anything yet, I'm waiting until she gets in a quieter condition.

STANLEY [*ominously*]   So?

STELLA   And try to understand her and be nice to her, Stan.

BLANCHE [*singing in the bathroom*]   "From the land of the sky blue water, They brought a captive maid!"

STELLA   She wasn't expecting to find us in such a small place. You see I'd tried to gloss things over a little in my letters.

STANLEY   So?

STELLA   And admire her dress and tell her she's looking wonderful. That's important with Blanche. Her little weakness!

STANLEY   Yeah. I get the idea. Now let's skip back a little to where you said the country place was disposed of.

STELLA   Oh!—yes . . .

STANLEY   How about that? Let's have a few more details on that subjeck.

STELLA   It's best not to talk much about it until she's calmed down.

STANLEY   So that's the deal, huh? Sister Blanche cannot be annoyed with business details right now!

STELLA   You saw how she was last night.

STANLEY   Uh-hum, I saw how she was. Now let's have a gander at the bill of sale.

STELLA   I haven't seen any.

STANLEY   She didn't show you no papers, no deed of sale or nothing like that, huh?

STELLA   It seems like it wasn't sold.

STANLEY   Well, what in hell was it then, give away? To charity?

STELLA   Shhh! She'll hear you.

STANLEY   I don't care if she hears me. Let's see the papers!

STELLA   There weren't any papers, she didn't show any papers, I don't care about papers.

STANLEY   Have you ever heard of the Napoleonic code?[9]

STELLA   No, Stanley, I haven't heard of the Napoleonic code and if I have, I don't see what it—

STANLEY   Let me enlighten you on a point or two, baby.

STELLA   Yes?

STANLEY   In the state of Louisiana we have the Napoleonic code according to which what belongs to the wife belongs to the husband and vice

---

9. This codification of French law (1802), made by Napoleon as emperor, is the basis for Louisiana's civil law.

versa. For instance if I had a piece of property, or you had a piece of property—

STELLA   My head is swimming!

STANLEY   All right. I'll wait till she gets through soaking in a hot tub and then I'll inquire if *she* is acquainted with the Napoleonic code. It looks to me like you have been swindled, baby, and when you're swindled under the Napoleonic code I'm swindled *too*. And I don't like to be *swindled*.

STELLA   There's plenty of time to ask her questions later but if you do now she'll go to pieces again. I don't understand what happened to Belle Reve but you don't know how ridiculous you are being when you suggest that my sister or I or anyone of our family could have perpetrated a swindle on anyone else.

STANLEY   Then where's the money if the place was sold?

STELLA   Not sold—lost, lost!

[*He stalks into bedroom, and she follows him.*]
Stanley!
[*He pulls open the wardrobe trunk standing in middle of room and jerks out an armful of dresses.*]

STANLEY   Open your eyes to this stuff! You think she got them out of a teacher's pay?

STELLA   Hush!

STANLEY   Look at these feathers and furs that she come here to preen herself in! What's this here? A solid-gold dress, I believe! And this one! What is these here? Fox-pieces! [*He blows on them.*] Genuine fox fur-pieces, a half a mile long! Where are your fox-pieces, Stella? Bushy snow-white ones, no less! Where are your white fox-pieces?

STELLA   Those are inexpensive summer furs that Blanche has had a long time.

STANLEY   I got an acquaintance who deals in this sort of merchandise. I'll have him in here to appraise it. I'm willing to bet you there's thousands of dollars invested in this stuff here!

STELLA   Don't be such an idiot, Stanley!

[*He hurls the furs to the day bed. Then he jerks open a small drawer in the trunk and pulls up a fistful of costume jewelry.*]

STANLEY   And what have we here? The treasure chest of a pirate!

STELLA   Oh, Stanley!

STANLEY   Pearls! Ropes of them! What is this sister of yours, a deep-sea diver? Bracelets of solid gold, too! Where are your pearls and gold bracelets?

STELLA   Shhh! Be still, Stanley!

STANLEY   And diamonds! A crown for an empress!

STELLA   A rhinestone tiara she wore to a costume ball.

STANLEY   What's rhinestone?

STELLA   Next door to glass.

STANLEY   Are you kidding? I have an acquaintance that works in a jewelry store. I'll have him in here to make an appraisal of this. Here's your plantation, or what was left of it, here!

STELLA   You have no idea how stupid and horrid you're being! Now close that trunk before she comes out of the bathroom!

[*He kicks the trunk partly closed and sits on the kitchen table.*]

STANLEY   The Kowalskis and the DuBoises have different notions.

STELLA [*angrily*]   Indeed they have, thank heavens!—*I'm* going outside.
[*She snatches up her white hat and gloves and crosses to the outside door.*]
You come out with me while Blanche is getting dressed.

STANLEY   Since when do you give me orders?

STELLA   Are you going to stay here and insult her?

STANLEY   You're damn tootin' I'm going to stay here.
[STELLA *goes out to the porch.* BLANCHE *comes out of the bathroom in a
red satin robe.*]

BLANCHE [*airily*]   Hello, Stanley! Here I am, all freshly bathed and scented,
and feeling like a brand new human being!
[*He lights a cigarette.*]

STANLEY   That's good.

BLANCHE [*drawing the curtains at the windows*]   Excuse me while I slip on
my pretty new dress!

STANLEY   Go right ahead, Blanche.
[*She closes the drapes between the rooms.*]

BLANCHE   I understand there's to be a little card party to which we ladies
are cordially *not* invited!

STANLEY [*ominously*]   Yeah?
[BLANCHE *throws off her robe and slips into a flowered print dress.*]

BLANCHE   Where's Stella?

STANLEY   Out on the porch.

BLANCHE   I'm going to ask a favor of you in a moment.

STANLEY   What could that be, I wonder?

BLANCHE   Some buttons in back! You may enter! [*He crosses through drapes
with a smoldering look.*] How do I look?

STANLEY   You look all right.

BLANCHE   Many thanks! Now the buttons!

STANLEY   I can't do nothing with them.

BLANCHE   You men with your big clumsy fingers. May I have a drag on
your cig?

STANLEY   Have one for yourself.

BLANCHE   Why, thanks! . . . It looks like my trunk has exploded.

STANLEY   Me an' Stella were helping you unpack.

BLANCHE   Well, you certainly did a fast and thorough job of it!

STANLEY   It looks like you raided some stylish shops in Paris.

BLANCHE   Ha-ha! Yes—clothes are my passion!

STANLEY   What does it cost for a string of fur-pieces like that?

BLANCHE   Why, those were a tribute from an admirer of mine!

STANLEY   He must have had a lot of—admiration!

BLANCHE   Oh, in my youth I excited some admiration. But look at me now!
[*She smiles at him radiantly.*] Would you think it possible that I was once
considered to be—attractive?

STANLEY   Your looks are okay.

BLANCHE   I was fishing for a compliment, Stanley.

STANLEY   I don't go in for that stuff.

BLANCHE   What—stuff?

STANLEY   Compliments to women about their looks. I never met a woman
that didn't know if she was good-looking or not without being told, and
some of them give themselves credit for more than they've got. I once
went out with a doll who said to me, "I am the glamorous type, I am the
glamorous type!" I said, "So what?"

BLANCHE   And what did she say then?

STANLEY   She didn't say nothing. That shut her up like a clam.

BLANCHE   Did it end the romance?

STANLEY   It ended the conversation—that was all. Some men are took in by this Hollywood glamor stuff and some men are not.

BLANCHE   I'm sure you belong in the second category.

STANLEY   That's right.

BLANCHE   I cannot imagine any witch of a woman casting a spell over you.

STANLEY   That's—right.

BLANCHE   You're simple, straightforward and honest, a little bit on the primitive side I should think. To interest you a woman would have to— [*She pauses with an indefinite gesture.*]

STANLEY [*slowly*]   Lay . . . her cards on the table.

BLANCHE [*smiling*]   Well, I never cared for wishy-washy people. That was why, when you walked in here last night, I said to myself—"My sister has married a man!"—Of course that was all that I could tell about you.

STANLEY [*booming*]   Now let's cut the re-bop!¹

BLANCHE [*pressing hands to her ears*]   Ouuuuu!

STELLA [*calling from the steps*]   Stanley! You come out here and let Blanche finish dressing!

BLANCHE   I'm through dressing, honey.

STELLA   Well, you come out, then.

STANLEY   Your sister and I are having a little talk.

BLANCHE [*lightly*]   Honey, do me a favor. Run to the drugstore and get me a lemon Coke with plenty of chipped ice in it!—Will you do that for me, sweetie?

STELLA [*uncertainly*]   Yes. [*She goes around the corner of the building.*]

BLANCHE   The poor little thing was out there listening to us, and I have an idea she doesn't understand you as well as I do. . . . All right; now, Mr. Kowalski, let us proceed without any more double-talk. I'm ready to answer all questions. I've nothing to hide. What is it?

STANLEY   There is such a thing in this state of Louisiana as the Napoleonic code, according to which whatever belongs to my wife is also mine—and vice versa.

BLANCHE   My, but you have an impressive judicial air!
   [*She sprays herself with her atomizer; then playfully sprays him with it. He seizes the atomizer and slams it down on the dresser. She throws back her head and laughs.*]

STANLEY   If I didn't know that you was my wife's sister I'd get ideas about you!

BLANCHE   Such as what!

STANLEY   Don't play so dumb. You know what!

BLANCHE [*she puts the atomizer on the table*]   All right. Cards on the table. That suits me. [*She turns to* STANLEY.] I know I fib a good deal. After all, a woman's charm is fifty per cent illusion, but when a thing is important I tell the truth, and this is the truth: I haven't cheated my sister or you or anyone else as long as I have lived.

STANLEY   Where's the papers? In the trunk?

BLANCHE   Everything that I own is in that trunk.

---

1. Nonsense (from "bebop," a form of jazz).

[STANLEY *crosses to the trunk, shoves it roughly open and begins to open compartments.*]

BLANCHE   What in the name of heaven are you thinking of! What's in the back of that little boy's mind of yours? That I am absconding with something, attempting some kind of treachery on my sister?—Let me do that! It will be faster and simpler . . . [*She crosses to the trunk and takes out a box.*] I keep my papers mostly in this tin box. [*She opens it.*]

STANLEY   What's them underneath? [*He indicates another sheaf of paper.*]

BLANCHE   These are love-letters, yellowing with antiquity, all from one boy. [*He snatches them up. She speaks fiercely.*] Give those back to me!

STANLEY   I'll have a look at them first!

BLANCHE   The touch of your hands insults them!

STANLEY   Don't pull that stuff!

[*He rips off the ribbon and starts to examine them.* BLANCHE *snatches them from him, and they cascade to the floor.*]

BLANCHE   Now that you've touched them I'll burn them!

STANLEY [*staring, baffled*]   What in hell are they?

BLANCHE [*on the floor gathering them up*]   Poems a dead boy wrote. I hurt him the way that you would like to hurt me, but you can't! I'm not young and vulnerable any more. But my young husband was and I—never mind about that! Just give them back to me!

STANLEY   What do you mean by saying you'll have to burn them?

BLANCHE   I'm sorry, I must have lost my head for a moment. Everyone has something he won't let others touch because of their—intimate nature . . .

[*She now seems faint with exhaustion and she sits down with the strong box and puts on a pair of glasses and goes methodically through a large stack of papers.*]

Ambler & Ambler. Hmmmmm. . . . Crabtree. . . . More Ambler & Ambler.

STANLEY   What is Ambler & Ambler?

BLANCHE   A firm that made loans on the place.

STANLEY   Then it *was* lost on a mortgage?

BLANCHE [*touching her forehead*]   That must've been what happened.

STANLEY   I don't want no ifs, ands or buts! What's all the rest of them papers?

[*She hands him the entire box. He carries it to the table and starts to examine the paper.*]

BLANCHE [*picking up a large envelope containing more papers*]   There are thousands of papers, stretching back over hundreds of years, affecting Belle Reve as, piece by piece, our improvident grandfathers and father and uncles and brothers exchanged the land for their epic fornications— to put it plainly! [*She removes her glasses with an exhausted laugh.*] The four-letter word deprived us of our plantation, till finally all that was left—and Stella can verify that!—was the house itself and about twenty acres of ground, including a graveyard, to which now all but Stella and I have retreated. [*She pours the contents of the envelope on the table.*] Here all of them are, all papers! I hereby endow you with them! Take them, peruse them—commit them to memory, even! I think it's wonderfully fitting that Belle Reve should finally be this bunch of old papers in your big, capable hands! . . . I wonder if Stella's come back with my lemon Coke . . . [*She leans back and closes her eyes.*]

STANLEY   I have a lawyer acquaintance who will study these out.

BLANCHE   Present them to him with a box of aspirin tablets.

STANLEY [*becoming somewhat sheepish*]   You see, under the Napoleonic code—a man has to take an interest in his wife's affairs—especially now that she's going to have a baby.

[BLANCHE *opens her eyes. The "Blue Piano" sounds louder.*]

BLANCHE   Stella? Stella going to have a baby? [*dreamily*] I didn't know she was going to have a baby!

[*She gets up and crosses to the outside door.* STELLA *appears around the corner with a carton from the drugstore.* STANLEY *goes into the bedroom with the envelope and the box. The inner rooms fade to darkness and the outside wall of the house is visible,* BLANCHE *meets* STELLA *at the foot of the steps to the sidewalk.*]

BLANCHE   Stella, Stella for star! How lovely to have a baby! It's all right. Everything's all right.

STELLA   I'm sorry he did that to you.

BLANCHE   Oh, I guess he's just not the type that goes for jasmine perfume, but maybe he's what we need to mix with our blood now that we've lost Belle Reve. We thrashed it out. I feel a bit shaky, but I think I handled it nicely, I laughed and treated it all as a joke. [STEVE *and* PABLO *appear, carrying a case of beer.*] I called him a little boy and laughed and flirted. Yes, I was flirting with your husband! [*as the men approach*] The guests are gathering for the poker party. [*The two men pass between them, and enter the house.*] Which way do we go now, Stella—this way?

STELLA   No, this way. [*She leads* BLANCHE *away.*]

BLANCHE [*laughing*]   The blind are leading the blind!

[*A tamale* VENDOR *is heard calling.*]

VENDOR'S VOICE   Red-hot!

Scene Three

THE POKER NIGHT[2]

*There is a picture of Van Gogh's[3] of a billiard-parlor at night. The kitchen now suggests that sort of lurid nocturnal brilliance, the raw colors of childhood's spectrum. Over the yellow linoleum of the kitchen table hangs an electric bulb with a vivid green glass shade. The poker players—*STANLEY, STEVE, MITCH *and* PABLO—*wear colored shirts, solid blues, a purple, a red-and-white check, a light green, and they are men at the peak of their physical manhood, as coarse and direct and powerful as the primary colors. There are vivid slices of watermelon on the table, whiskey bottles and glasses. The bedroom is relatively dim with only the light that spills between the portieres and through the wide window on the street.*

For a moment, there is absorbed silence as a hand is dealt.

STEVE   Anything wild this deal?

PABLO   One-eyed jacks are wild.

STEVE   Give me two cards.

PABLO   You, Mitch?

MITCH   I'm out.

PABLO   One.

---

2. Williams's first title for *A Streetcar Named Desire* (see headnote).

3. *The Night Café*, by the Dutch Postimpressionist painter Vincent van Gogh (1853–1890).

MITCH Anyone want a shot?

STANLEY Yeah. Me.

PABLO Why don't somebody go to the Chinaman's and bring back a load of chop suey?

STANLEY When I'm losing you want to eat! Ante up! Openers? Openers! Get y'r ass off the table, Mitch. Nothing belongs on a poker table but cards, chips and whiskey.

[*He lurches up and tosses some watermelon rinds to the floor.*]

MITCH Kind of on your high horse, ain't you?

STANLEY How many?

STEVE Give me three.

STANLEY One.

MITCH I'm out again. I oughta go home pretty soon.

STANLEY Shut up.

MITCH I gotta sick mother. She don't go to sleep until I come in at night.

STANLEY Then why don't you stay home with her?

MITCH She says to go out, so I go, but I don't enjoy it. All the while I keep wondering how she is.

STANLEY Aw, for the sake of Jesus, go home, then!

PABLO What've you got?

STEVE Spade flush.

MITCH You all are married. But I'll be alone when she goes.—I'm going to the bathroom.

STANLEY Hurry back and we'll fix you a sugar-tit.

MITCH Aw, go rut. [*He crosses through the bedroom into the bathroom.*]

STEVE [*dealing a hand*] Seven card stud.[4] [*telling his joke as he deals*] This ole farmer is out in back of his house sittin' down th'owing corn to the chickens when all at once he hears a loud cackle and this young hen comes lickety split around the side of the house with the rooster right behind her and gaining on her fast.

STANLEY [*impatient with the story*] Deal!

STEVE But when the rooster catches sight of the farmer th'owing the corn he puts on the brakes and lets the hen get away and starts pecking corn. And the old farmer says, "Lord God, I hopes I never gits *that* hongry!"

[STEVE *and* PABLO *laugh. The sisters appear around the corner of the building.*]

STELLA The game is still going on.

BLANCHE How do I look?

STELLA Lovely, Blanche.

BLANCHE I feel so hot and frazzled. Wait till I powder before you open the door. Do I look done in?

STELLA Why no. You are as fresh as a daisy.

BLANCHE One that's been picked a few days.

[STELLA *opens the door and they enter.*]

STELLA Well, well, well. I see you boys are still at it?

STANLEY Where you been?

STELLA Blanche and I took in a show. Blanche, this is Mr. Gonzales and Mr. Hubbell.

---

4. An adventurous and risky variant of poker.

BLANCHE   Please don't get up.

STANLEY   Nobody's going to get up, so don't be worried.

STELLA   How much longer is this game going to continue?

STANLEY   Till we get ready to quit.

BLANCHE   Poker is so fascinating. Could I kibitz?

STANLEY   You could not. Why don't you women go up and sit with Eunice?

STELLA   Because it is nearly two-thirty. [BLANCHE *crosses into the bedroom and partially closes the portieres.*] Couldn't you call it quits after one more hand?

> [*A chair scrapes.* STANLEY *gives a loud whack of his hand on her thigh.*]

STELLA [*sharply*]   That's not fun, Stanley.

> [*The men laugh,* STELLA *goes into the bedroom.*]

STELLA   It makes me so mad when he does that in front of people.

BLANCHE   I think I will bathe.

STELLA   Again?

BLANCHE   My nerves are in knots. Is the bathroom occupied?

STELLA   I don't know.

> [BLANCHE *knocks,* MITCH *opens the door and comes out, still wiping his hands on a towel.*]

BLANCHE   Oh!—good evening.

MITCH   Hello. [*He stares at her.*]

STELLA   Blanche, this is Harold Mitchell. My sister, Blanche DuBois.

MITCH [*with awkward courtesy*]   How do you do, Miss DuBois.

STELLA   How is your mother now, Mitch?

MITCH   About the same, thanks. She appreciated your sending over that custard.—Excuse me, please.

> [*He crosses slowly back into the kitchen, glancing back at* BLANCHE *and coughing a little shyly. He realizes he still has the towel in his hands and with an embarrassed laugh hands it to* STELLA. BLANCHE *looks after him with a certain interest.*]

BLANCHE   That one seems—superior to the others.

STELLA   Yes, he is.

BLANCHE   I thought he had a sort of sensitive look.

STELLA   His mother is sick.

BLANCHE   Is he married?

STELLA   No.

BLANCHE   Is he a wolf?

STELLA   Why, Blanche! [BLANCHE *laughs.*] I don't think he would be.

BLANCHE   What does—what does he do? [*She is unbuttoning her blouse.*]

STELLA   He's on the precision bench in the spare parts department. At the plant Stanley travels for.

BLANCHE   Is that something much?

STELLA   No. Stanley's the only one of his crowd that's likely to get any-where.

BLANCHE   What makes you think Stanley will?

STELLA   Look at him.

BLANCHE   I've looked at him.

STELLA   Then you should know.

BLANCHE   I'm sorry, but I haven't noticed the stamp of genius even on Stanley's forehead.

[*She takes off the blouse and stands in her pink silk brassiere and white skirt in the light through the portieres. The game has continued in undertones.*]

STELLA   It isn't on his forehead and it isn't genius.

BLANCHE   Oh. Well, what is it, and where? I would like to know.

STELLA   It's a drive that he has. You're standing in the light, Blanche!

BLANCHE   Oh, am I!

[*She moves out of the yellow streak of light.* STELLA *has removed her dress and put on a light blue satin kimona.*]

STELLA [*with girlish laughter*]   You ought to see their wives.

BLANCHE [*laughingly*]   I can imagine. Big, beefy things, I suppose.

STELLA   You know that one upstairs? [*more laughter*] One time [*laughing*] the plaster— [*laughing*] cracked—

STANLEY   You hens cut out that conversation in there!

STELLA   You can't hear us.

STANLEY   Well, you can hear me and I said to hush up!

STELLA   This is my house and I'll talk as much as I want to!

BLANCHE   Stella, don't start a row.

STELLA   He's half drunk!—I'll be out in a minute.

[*She goes into the bathroom,* BLANCHE *rises and crosses leisurely to a small white radio and turns it on.*]

STANLEY   Awright, Mitch, you in?

MITCH   What? Oh!—No, I'm out!

[BLANCHE *moves back into the streak of light. She raises her arms and stretches, as she moves indolently back to the chair. Rhumba music comes over the radio.* MITCH *rises at the table.*]

STANLEY   Who turned that on in there?

BLANCHE   I did. Do you mind?

STANLEY   Turn it off!

STEVE   Aw, let the girls have their music.

PABLO   Sure, that's good, leave it on!

STEVE   Sounds like Xavier Cugat![5]

[STANLEY *jumps up and, crossing to the radio, turns it off. He stops short at the sight of* BLANCHE *in the chair. She returns his look without flinching. Then he sits again at the poker table. Two of the men have started arguing hotly.*]

STEVE   I didn't hear you name it.

PABLO   Didn't I name it, Mitch?

MITCH   I wasn't listenin'.

PABLO   What were you doing, then?

STANLEY   He was looking through them drapes. [*He jumps up and jerks roughly at curtains to close them.*] Now deal the hand over again and let's play cards or quit. Some people get ants when they win.

[MITCH *rises as* STANLEY *returns to his seat.*]

STANLEY [*yelling*]   Sit down!

MITCH   I'm going to the "head." Deal me out.

PABLO   Sure he's got ants now. Seven five-dollar bills in his pants pocket folded up tight as spitballs.

STEVE   Tomorrow you'll see him at the cashier's window getting them changed into quarters.

---

5. Cuban bandleader (1900–1990), well known for composing and playing rhumbas.

STANLEY   And when he goes home he'll deposit them one by one in a piggy bank his mother give him for Christmas. [*dealing*] This game is Spit in the Ocean.[6]

> [MITCH *laughs uncomfortably and continues through the portieres. He stops just inside.*]

BLANCHE [*softly*]   Hello! The Little Boys' Room is busy right now.

MITCH   We've—been drinking beer.

BLANCHE   I hate beer.

MITCH   It's—a hot weather drink.

BLANCHE   Oh, I don't think so; it always makes me warmer. Have you got any cigs? [*She has slipped on the dark red satin wrapper.*]

MITCH   Sure.

BLANCHE   What kind are they?

MITCH   Luckies.

BLANCHE   Oh, good. What a pretty case. Silver?

MITCH   Yes. Yes; read the inscription.

BLANCHE   Oh, is there an inscription? I can't make it out. [*He strikes a match and moves closer.*] Oh! [*reading with feigned difficulty*] "And if God choose, / I shall but love thee better—after—death!" Why, that's from my favorite sonnet by Mrs. Browning.[7]

MITCH   You know it?

BLANCHE   Certainly I do!

MITCH   There's a story connected with that inscription.

BLANCHE   It sounds like a romance.

MITCH   A pretty sad one.

BLANCHE   Oh?

MITCH   The girl's dead now.

BLANCHE [*in a tone of deep sympathy*]   Oh!

MITCH   She knew she was dying when she give me this. A very strange girl, very sweet—very!

BLANCHE   She must have been fond of you. Sick people have such deep, sincere attachments.

MITCH   That's right, they certainly do.

BLANCHE   Sorrow makes for sincerity, I think.

MITCH   It sure brings it out in people.

BLANCHE   The little there is belongs to people who have experienced some sorrow.

MITCH   I believe you are right about that.

BLANCHE   I'm positive that I am. Show me a person who hasn't known any sorrow and I'll show you a shuperficial—Listen to me! My tongue is a little—thick! You boys are responsible for it. The show let out at eleven and we couldn't come home on account of the poker game so we had to go somewhere and drink. I'm not accustomed to having more than one drink. Two is the limit—and *three*! [*She laughs.*] Tonight I had three.

STANLEY   Mitch!

MITCH   Deal me out. I'm talking to Miss—

BLANCHE   DuBois.

---

6. Another variant of poker.
7. Elizabeth Barrett Browning (1806–1861), British poet, most famous for her sequence of love poems, *Sonnets from the Portuguese*. The quotation here is from sonnet 43, better known by its first line, "How do I love thee?"

MITCH Miss DuBois?

BLANCHE It's a French name. It means woods and Blanche means white, so the two together mean white woods. Like an orchard in spring! You can remember it by that.

MITCH You're French?

BLANCHE We are French by extraction. Our first American ancestors were French Huguenots.

MITCH You are Stella's sister, are you not?

BLANCHE Yes, Stella is my precious little sister. I call her little in spite of the fact she's somewhat older than I. Just slightly. Less than a year. Will you do something for me?

MITCH Sure. What?

BLANCHE I bought this adorable little colored paper lantern at a Chinese shop on Bourbon. Put it over the light bulb! Will you, please?

MITCH Be glad to.

BLANCHE I can't stand a naked light bulb, any more than I can a rude remark or a vulgar action.

MITCH [adjusting the lantern] I guess we strike you as being a pretty rough bunch.

BLANCHE I'm very adaptable—to circumstances.

MITCH Well, that's a good thing to be. You are visiting Stanley and Stella?

BLANCHE Stella hasn't been so well lately, and I came down to help her for a while. She's very run down.

MITCH You're not—?

BLANCHE Married? No, no. I'm an old maid schoolteacher!

MITCH You may teach school but you're certainly not an old maid.

BLANCHE Thank you, sir! I appreciate your gallantry!

MITCH So you are in the teaching profession?

BLANCHE Yes. Ah, yes . . .

MITCH Grade school or high school or—

STANLEY [bellowing] Mitch!

MITCH Coming!

BLANCHE Gracious, what lung-power! . . . I teach high school. In Laurel.

MITCH What do you teach? What subject?

BLANCHE Guess!

MITCH I bet you teach art or music? [BLANCHE laughs delicately.] Of course I could be wrong. You might teach arithmetic.

BLANCHE Never arithmetic, sir; never arithmetic! [with a laugh] I don't even know my multiplication tables! No, I have the misfortune of being an English instructor. I attempt to instill a bunch of bobby-soxers and drugstore Romeos with reverence for Hawthorne and Whitman and Poe!

MITCH I guess that some of them are more interested in other things.

BLANCHE How very right you are! Their literary heritage is not what most of them treasure above all else! But they're sweet things! And in the spring, it's touching to notice them making their first discovery of love! As if nobody had ever known it before!

> [The bathroom door opens and STELLA comes out. BLANCHE continues talking to MITCH.]

Oh! Have you finished? Wait—I'll turn on the radio.

[*She turns the knobs on the radio and it begins to play "Wien, Wien, nur du allein."*[8] BLANCHE *waltzes to the music with romantic gestures,* MITCH *is delighted and moves in awkward imitation like a dancing bear.* STANLEY *stalks fiercely through the portieres into the bedroom. He crosses to the small white radio and snatches it off the table. With a shouted oath, he tosses the instrument out the window.*]

STELLA   Drunk—drunk—animal thing, you! [*She rushes through to the poker table.*] All of you—please go home! If any of you have one spark of decency in you—

BLANCHE [*wildly*]   Stella, watch out, he's—

[STANLEY *charges after* STELLA.]

MEN [*feebly*]   Take it easy, Stanley. Easy, fellow.—Let's all—

STELLA   You lay your hands on me and I'll—

[*She backs out of sight. He advances and disappears. There is the sound of a blow.* STELLA *cries out.* BLANCHE *screams and runs into the kitchen. The men rush forward and there is grappling and cursing. Something is overturned with a crash.*]

BLANCHE [*shrilly*]   My sister is going to have a baby!

MITCH   This is terrible.

BLANCHE   Lunacy, absolute lunacy!

MITCH   Get him in here, men.

[STANLEY *is forced, pinioned by the two men, into the bedroom. He nearly throws them off. Then all at once he subsides and is limp in their grasp. They speak quietly and lovingly to him and he leans his face on one of their shoulders.*]

STELLA [*in a high, unnatural voice, out of sight*]   I want to go away, I want to go away!

MITCH   Poker shouldn't be played in a house with women.

[BLANCHE *rushes into the bedroom.*]

BLANCHE   I want my sister's clothes! We'll go to that woman's upstairs!

MITCH   Where is the clothes?

BLANCHE [*opening the closet*]   I've got them! [*She rushes through to* STELLA.] Stella, Stella, precious! Dear, dear little sister, don't be afraid!

[*With her arm around* STELLA, BLANCHE *guides her to the outside door and upstairs.*]

STANLEY [*dully*]   What's the matter; what's happened?

MITCH   You just blew your top, Stan.

PABLO   He's okay, now.

STEVE   Sure, my boy's okay!

MITCH   Put him on the bed and get a wet towel.

PABLO   I think coffee would do him a world of good, now.

STANLEY [*thickly*]   I want water.

MITCH   Put him under the shower!

[*The men talk quietly as they lead him to the bathroom.*]

STANLEY   Let the rut go of me, you sons of bitches!

[*Sounds of blows are heard. The water goes on full tilt.*]

STEVE   Let's get quick out of here!

[*They rush to the poker table and sweep up their winnings on their way out.*]

---

8. Vienna, Vienna, you are my only (German); a waltz from an operetta by Franz Lehár (1870–1948).

MITCH [*sadly but firmly*] Poker should not be played in a house with women.

[*The door closes on them and the place is still. The Negro entertainers in the bar around the corner play "Paper Doll"[9] slow and blue. After a moment* STANLEY *comes out of the bathroom dripping water and still in his clinging wet polka dot drawers.*]

STANLEY Stella! [*There is a pause.*] My baby doll's left me!

[*He breaks into sobs. Then he goes to the phone and dials, still shuddering with sobs.*]

Eunice? I want my baby! [*He waits a moment; then he hangs up and dials again.*] Eunice! I'll keep on ringin' until I talk with my baby!

[*An indistinguishable shrill voice is heard. He hurls phone to floor. Dissonant brass and piano sounds as the rooms dim out to darkness and the outer walls appear in the night light. The "Blue Piano" plays for a brief interval. Finally,* STANLEY *stumbles half-dressed out to the porch and down the wooden steps to the pavement before the building. There he throws back his head like a baying hound and bellows his wife's name: "Stella! Stella, sweetheart! Stella!"*]

STANLEY Stell-*lahhhhh!*

EUNICE [*calling down from the door of her upper apartment*] Quit that howling out there an' go back to bed!

STANLEY I want my baby down here. Stella, Stella!

EUNICE She ain't comin' down so you quit! Or you'll git th' law on you!

STANLEY Stella!

EUNICE You can't beat on a woman an' then call 'er back! She won't come! And her goin' t' have a baby! . . . You stinker! You whelp of a Polack, you! I hope they do haul you in and turn the fire hose on you, same as the last time!

STANLEY [*humbly*] Eunice, I want my girl to come down with me!

EUNICE Hah! [*She slams her door.*]

STANLEY [*with heaven-splitting violence*] STELL-LAHHHHH!

[*The low-tone clarinet moans. The door upstairs opens again.* STELLA *slips down the rickety stairs in her robe. Her eyes are glistening with tears and her hair loose about her throat and shoulders. They stare at each other. Then they come together with low, animal moans. He falls to his knees on the steps and presses his face to her belly, curving a little with maternity. Her eyes go blind with tenderness as she catches his head and raises him level with her. He snatches the screen door open and lifts her off her feet and bears her into the dark flat.* BLANCHE *comes out the upper landing in her robe and slips fearfully down the steps.*]

BLANCHE Where is my little sister? Stella? Stella?

[*She stops before the dark entrance of her sister's flat. Then catches her breath as if struck. She rushes down to the walk before the house. She looks right and left as if for a sanctuary. The music fades away,* MITCH *appears from around the corner.*]

MITCH Miss DuBois?

BLANCHE Oh!

MITCH All quiet on the Potomac now?

BLANCHE She ran downstairs and went back in there with him.

MITCH Sure she did.

BLANCHE I'm terrified!

---

9. Popular song of the early 1940s by Johnny Black.

MITCH   Ho-ho! There's nothing to be scared of. They're crazy about each other.

BLANCHE   I'm not used to such—

MITCH   Naw, it's a shame this had to happen when you just got here. But don't take it serious.

BLANCHE   Violence! Is so—

MITCH   Set down on the steps and have a cigarette with me.

BLANCHE   I'm not properly dressed.

MITCH   That don't make no difference in the Quarter.

BLANCHE   Such a pretty silver case.

MITCH   I showed you the inscription, didn't I?

BLANCHE   Yes. [*During the pause, she looks up at the sky.*] There's so much— so much confusion in the world . . . [*He coughs diffidently.*] Thank you for being so kind! I need kindness now.

Scene Four

It is early the following morning. There is a confusion of street cries like a choral chant.

STELLA *is lying down in the bedroom. Her face is serene in the early morning sunlight. One hand rests on her belly, rounding slightly with new maternity. From the other dangles a book of colored comics. Her eyes and lips have that almost narcotized tranquility that is in the faces of Eastern idols.*

The table is sloppy with remains of breakfast and the debris of the preceding night, and STANLEY'S *gaudy pyjamas lie across the threshold of the bathroom. The outside door is slightly ajar on a sky of summer brilliance.*

BLANCHE *appears at this door. She has spent a sleepless night and her appearance entirely contrasts with* STELLA'S. *She presses her knuckles nervously to her lips as she looks through the door, before entering.*

BLANCHE   Stella?

STELLA [*stirring lazily*]   Hmmh?

   [BLANCHE *utters a moaning cry and runs into the bedroom, throwing herself down beside* STELLA *in a rush of hysterical tenderness.*]

BLANCHE   Baby, my baby sister!

STELLA [*drawing away from her*]   Blanche, what is the matter with you?

   [BLANCHE *straightens up slowly and stands beside the bed looking down at her sister with knuckles pressed to her lips.*]

BLANCHE   He's left?

STELLA   Stan? Yes.

BLANCHE   Will he be back?

STELLA   He's gone to get the car greased. Why?

BLANCHE   Why! I've been half crazy, Stella! When I found out you'd been insane enough to come back in here after what happened—I started to rush in after you!

STELLA   I'm glad you didn't.

BLANCHE   What were you thinking of? [STELLA *makes an indefinite gesture.*] Answer me! What? What?

STELLA   Please, Blanche! Sit down and stop yelling.

BLANCHE   All right, Stella. I will repeat the question quietly now. How could you come back in this place last night? Why, you must have slept with him!

[STELLA *gets up in a calm and leisurely way.*]

STELLA   Blanche, I'd forgotten how excitable you are. You're making much too much fuss about this.

BLANCHE   Am I?

STELLA   Yes, you are, Blanche. I know how it must have seemed to you and I'm awful sorry it had to happen, but it wasn't anything as serious as you seem to take it. In the first place, when men are drinking and playing poker anything can happen. It's always a powder-keg. He didn't know what he was doing. . . . He was as good as a lamb when I came back and he's really very, very ashamed of himself.

BLANCHE   And that—that makes it all right?

STELLA   No, it isn't all right for anybody to make such a terrible row, but—people do sometimes. Stanley's always smashed things. Why, on our wedding night—soon as we came in here—he snatched off one of my slippers and rushed about the place smashing light bulbs with it.

BLANCHE   He did—*what*?

STELLA   He smashed all the light bulbs with the heel of my slipper! [*She laughs.*]

BLANCHE   And you—you *let* him? Didn't *run*, didn't *scream*?

STELLA   I was—sort of—thrilled by it. [*She waits for a moment.*] Eunice and you had breakfast?

BLANCHE   Do you suppose I wanted any breakfast?

STELLA   There's some coffee left on the stove.

BLANCHE   You're so—matter of fact about it, Stella.

STELLA   What other can I be? He's taken the radio to get it fixed. It didn't land on the pavement so only one tube was smashed.

BLANCHE   And you are standing there smiling!

STELLA   What do you want me to do?

BLANCHE   Pull yourself together and face the facts.

STELLA   What are they, in your opinion?

BLANCHE   In my opinion? You're married to a madman!

STELLA   No!

BLANCHE   Yes, you are, your fix is worse than mine is! Only you're not being sensible about it. I'm going to *do* something. Get hold of myself and make myself a new life!

STELLA   Yes?

BLANCHE   But you've given in. And that isn't right, you're not old! You can get out.

STELLA [*slowly and emphatically*]   I'm not in anything I want to get out of.

BLANCHE [*incredulously*]   What—Stella?

STELLA   I said I am not in anything that I have a desire to get out of. Look at the mess in this room! And those empty bottles! They went through two cases last night! He promised this morning that he was going to quit having these poker parties, but you know how long such a promise is going to keep. Oh, well, it's his pleasure, like mine is movies and bridge. People have got to tolerate each other's habits, I guess.

BLANCHE   I don't understand you. [STELLA *turns toward her.*] I don't understand your indifference. Is this a Chinese philosophy you've—cultivated?

STELLA   Is what—what?

BLANCHE   This—shuffling about and mumbling—'One tube smashed—beer bottles—mess in the kitchen!'—as if nothing out of the ordinary has happened! [STELLA *laughs uncertainly and picking up the broom, twirls it in her hands.*]

BLANCHE   Are you deliberately shaking that thing in my face?

STELLA   No.

BLANCHE   Stop it. Let go of that broom. I won't have you cleaning up for him!

STELLA   Then who's going to do it? Are you?

BLANCHE   I? I!

STELLA   No, I didn't think so.

BLANCHE   Oh, let me think, if only my mind would function! We've got to get hold of some money, that's the way out!

STELLA   I guess that money is always nice to get hold of.

BLANCHE   Listen to me. I have an idea of some kind. [*Shakily she twists a cigarette into her holder.*] Do you remember Shep Huntleigh? [STELLA *shakes her head.*] Of course you remember Shep Huntleigh. I went out with him at college and wore his pin for a while. Well—

STELLA   Well?

BLANCHE   I ran into him last winter. You know I went to Miami during the Christmas holidays?

STELLA   No.

BLANCHE   Well, I did. I took the trip as an investment, thinking I'd meet someone with a million dollars.

STELLA   Did you?

BLANCHE   Yes. I ran into Shep Huntleigh—I ran into him on Biscayne Boulevard, on Christmas Eve, about dusk . . . getting into his car—Cadillac convertible; must have been a block long!

STELLA   I should think it would have been—inconvenient in traffic!

BLANCHE   You've heard of oil wells?

STELLA   Yes—remotely.

BLANCHE   He has them, all over Texas. Texas is literally spouting gold in his pockets.

STELLA   My, my.

BLANCHE   Y'know how indifferent I am to money. I think of money in terms of what it does for you. But he could do it, he could certainly do it!

STELLA   Do what, Blanche?

BLANCHE   Why—set us up in a—shop!

STELLA   What kind of a shop?

BLANCHE   Oh, a—shop of some kind! He could do it with half what his wife throws away at the races.

STELLA   He's married?

BLANCHE   Honey, would I be here if the man weren't married? [STELLA *laughs a little.* BLANCHE *suddenly springs up and crosses to phone. She speaks shrilly.*] How do I get Western Union?—Operator! Western Union!

STELLA   That's a dial phone, honey.

BLANCHE   I can't dial, I'm too—

STELLA   Just dial O.

BLANCHE   O?

STELLA   Yes, "O" for Operator! [BLANCHE *considers a moment; then she puts the phone down.*]

BLANCHE   Give me a pencil. Where is a slip of paper? I've got to write it down first—the message, I mean . . . [*She goes to the dressing table, and grabs up a sheet of Kleenex and an eyebrow pencil for writing equipment.*] Let me see now . . . [*She bites the pencil.*] 'Darling Shep. Sister and I in desperate situation.'

STELLA   I beg your pardon!

BLANCHE   'Sister and I in desperate situation. Will explain details later. Would you be interested in—?' [*She bites the pencil again.*] 'Would you be—interested—in . . .' [*She smashes the pencil on the table and springs up.*] You never get anywhere with direct appeals!

STELLA [*with a laugh*]   Don't be so ridiculous, darling!

BLANCHE   But I'll think of something, I've *got* to think of—*something*! Don't laugh at me, Stella! Please, please don't—I—I want you to look at the contents of my purse! Here's what's in it! [*She snatches her purse open.*] Sixty-five measly cents in coin of the realm!

STELLA [*crossing to bureau*]   Stanley doesn't give me a regular allowance, he likes to pay bills himself, but—this morning he gave me ten dollars to smooth things over. You take five of it, Blanche, and I'll keep the rest.

BLANCHE   Oh, no. No, Stella.

STELLA [*insisting*]   I know how it helps your morale just having a little pocket-money on you.

BLANCHE   No, thank you—I'll take to the streets!

STELLA   Talk sense! How did you happen to get so low on funds?

BLANCHE   Money just goes—it goes places. [*She rubs her forehead.*] Sometime today I've got to get hold of a Bromo![1]

STELLA   I'll fix you one now.

BLANCHE   Not yet—I've got to keep thinking!

STELLA   I wish you'd just let things go, at least for a—while . . .

BLANCHE   Stella, I can't live with him! You can, he's your husband. But how could I stay here with him, after last night, with just those curtains between us?

STELLA   Blanche, you saw him at his worst last night.

BLANCHE   On the contrary, I saw him at his best! What such a man has to offer is animal force and he gave a wonderful exhibition of that! But the only way to live with such a man is to—go to bed with him! And that's your job—not mine!

STELLA   After you've rested a little, you'll see it's going to work out. You don't have to worry about anything while you're here. I mean—expenses . . .

BLANCHE   I have to plan for us both, to get us both—out!

STELLA   You take it for granted that I am in something that I want to get out of.

BLANCHE   I take it for granted that you still have sufficient memory of Belle Reve to find this place and these poker players impossible to live with.

STELLA   Well, you're taking entirely too much for granted.

BLANCHE   I can't believe you're in earnest.

STELLA   No?

BLANCHE   I understand how it happened—a little. You saw him in uniform, an officer, not here but—

STELLA   I'm not sure it would have made any difference where I saw him.

BLANCHE   Now don't say it was one of those mysterious electric things between people! If you do I'll laugh in your face.

---

1. Short for Bromo-seltzer, a headache remedy.

STELLA   I am not going to say anything more at all about it!

BLANCHE   All right, then, don't!

STELLA   But there are things that happen between a man and a woman
in the dark—that sort of make everything else seem—unimportant.
[*Pause.*]

BLANCHE   What you are talking about is brutal desire—just—Desire!—
the name of that rattle-trap streetcar that bangs through the Quarter,
up one old narrow street and down another . . .

STELLA   Haven't you ever ridden on that streetcar?

BLANCHE   It brought me here.—Where I'm not wanted and where I'm
ashamed to be . . .

STELLA   Then don't you think your superior attitude is a bit out of place?

BLANCHE   I am not being or feeling at all superior, Stella. Believe me I'm
not! It's just this. This is how I look at it. A man like that is someone to go
out with—once—twice—three times when the devil is in you. But live
with? Have a child by?

STELLA   I have told you I love him.

BLANCHE   Then I *tremble* for you! I just—*tremble* for you. . . .

STELLA   I can't help your trembling if you insist on trembling!
[*There is a pause.*]

BLANCHE   May I—speak—*plainly*?

STELLA   Yes, do. Go ahead. As plainly as you want to.
[*Outside, a train approaches. They are silent till the noise subsides. They
are both in the bedroom. Under cover of the train's noise* STANLEY *enters
from outside. He stands unseen by the women, holding some packages in
his arms, and overhears their following conversation. He wears an under-
shirt and grease-stained seersucker pants.*]

BLANCHE   Well—if you'll forgive me—he's *common*!

STELLA   Why, yes, I suppose he is.

BLANCHE   Suppose! You can't have forgotten that much of our bringing
up, Stella, that you just *suppose* that any part of a gentleman's in his
nature! *Not one particle, no!* Oh, if he was just—*ordinary*! Just *plain*—
but good and wholesome, but—*no*. There's something downright—*bestial*—about him! You're hating me saying this, aren't you?

STELLA [*coldly*]   Go on and say it all, Blanche.

BLANCHE   He acts like an animal, has an animal's habits! Eats like one,
moves like one, talks like one! There's even something—sub-human—
something not quite to the stage of humanity yet! Yes, something—ape-
like about him, like one of those pictures I've seen in—anthropological
studies! Thousands and thousands of years have passed him right by,
and there he is—Stanley Kowalski—survivor of the Stone Age! Bearing
the raw meat home from the kill in the jungle! And you—*you* here—
waiting for him! Maybe he'll strike you or maybe grunt and kiss you!
That is, if kisses have been discovered yet! Night falls and the other apes
gather! There in the front of the cave, all grunting like him, and swilling and gnawing and hulking! His poker night! you call it—this party
of apes! Somebody growls—some creature snatches at something—the
fight is on! *God!* Maybe we are a long way from being made in God's
image, but Stella—my sister—there has been *some* progress since then!
Such things as art—as poetry and music—such kinds of new light have
come into the world since then! In some kinds of people some tenderer

feelings have had some little beginning! That we have got to make *grow*! And *cling* to, and hold as our flag! In this dark march toward whatever it is we're approaching. . . . *Don't—don't hang back with the brutes!*

[*Another train passes outside.* STANLEY *hesitates, licking his lips. Then suddenly he turns stealthily about and withdraws through front door. The women are still unaware of his presence. When the train has passed he calls through the closed front door.*]

STANLEY Hey! Hey, Stella!

STELLA [*who has listened gravely to* BLANCHE] Stanley!

BLANCHE Stell, I—

[*But* STELLA *has gone to the front door.* STANLEY *enters casually with his packages.*]

STANLEY Hiyuh, Stella. Blanche back?

STELLA Yes, she's back.

STANLEY Hiyuh, Blanche. [*He grins at her.*]

STELLA You must've got under the car.

STANLEY Them darn mechanics at Fritz's don't know their ass fr'm—*Hey!*

[STELLA *has embraced him with both arms, fiercely, and full in the view of* BLANCHE. *He laughs and clasps her head to him. Over her head he grins through the curtains at* BLANCHE. *As the lights fade away, with a lingering brightness on their embrace, the music of the "Blue Piano" and trumpet and drums is heard.*]

Scene Five

BLANCHE *is seated in the bedroom fanning herself with a palm leaf as she reads over a just-completed letter. Suddenly she bursts into a peal of laughter.* STELLA *is dressing in the bedroom.*

STELLA What are you laughing at, honey?

BLANCHE Myself, myself, for being such a liar! I'm writing a letter to Shep. [*She picks up the letter.*] "Darling Shep. I am spending the summer on the wing, making flying visits here and there. And who knows, perhaps I shall take a sudden notion to *swoop* down on *Dallas*! How would you feel about that? Ha-ha! [*She laughs nervously and brightly, touching her throat as if actually talking to* SHEP.] Forewarned is forearmed, as they say!"— How does that sound?

STELLA Uh-huh . . .

BLANCHE [*going on nervously*] "Most of my sister's friends go north in the summer but some have homes on the Gulf and there has been a continued round of entertainments, teas, cocktails, and luncheons—"

[*A disturbance is heard upstairs at the Hubbells' apartment.*]

STELLA Eunice seems to be having some trouble with Steve.

[EUNICE's *voice shouts in terrible wrath.*]

EUNICE I heard about you and that blonde!

STEVE That's a damn lie!

EUNICE You ain't pulling the wool over my eyes! I wouldn't mind if you'd stay down at the Four Deuces, but you always going up.

STEVE Who ever seen me up?

EUNICE I seen you chasing her 'round the balcony—I'm gonna call the vice squad!

STEVE Don't you throw that at me!

EUNICE [*shrieking*] You hit me! I'm gonna call the police!
> [*A clatter of aluminum striking a wall is heard, followed by a man's angry roar, shouts and overturned furniture. There is a crash; then a relative hush.*]

BLANCHE [*brightly*] Did he *kill* her?
> [EUNICE *appears on the steps in daemonic disorder.*]

STELLA No! She's coming downstairs.

EUNICE Call the police, I'm going to call the police! [*She rushes around the corner.*]
> [*They laugh lightly.* STANLEY *comes around the corner in his green and scarlet silk bowling shirt. He trots up the steps and bangs into the kitchen.* BLANCHE *registers his entrance with nervous gestures.*]

STANLEY What's a matter with Eun-uss?

STELLA She and Steve had a row. Has she got the police?

STANLEY Naw. She's gettin' a drink.

STELLA That's much more practical!
> [STEVE *comes down nursing a bruise on his forehead and looks in the door.*]

STEVE She here?

STANLEY Naw, naw. At the Four Deuces.

STEVE That rutting hunk! [*He looks around the corner a bit timidly, then turns with affected boldness and runs after her.*]

BLANCHE I must jot that down in my notebook. Ha-ha! I'm compiling a notebook of quaint little words and phrases I've picked up here.

STANLEY You won't pick up nothing here you ain't heard before.

BLANCHE Can I count on that?

STANLEY You can count on it up to five hundred.

BLANCHE That's a mighty high number. [*He jerks open the bureau drawer, slams it shut and throws shoes in a corner. At each noise* BLANCHE *winces slightly. Finally she speaks.*] What sign were you born under?

STANLEY [*while he is dressing*] Sign?

BLANCHE Astrological sign. I bet you were born under Aries. Aries people are forceful and dynamic. They dote on noise! They love to bang things around! You must have had lots of banging around in the army and now that you're out, you make up for it by treating inanimate objects with such a fury!
> [STELLA *has been going in and out of closet during this scene. Now she pops her head out of the closet.*]

STELLA Stanley was born just five minutes after Christmas.

BLANCHE Capricorn—the Goat!

STANLEY What sign were *you* born under?

BLANCHE Oh, my birthday's next month, the fifteenth of September; that's under Virgo.

STANLEY What's Virgo?

BLANCHE Virgo is the Virgin.

STANLEY [*contemptuously*] Hah! [*He advances a little as he knots his tie.*] Say, do you happen to know somebody named Shaw?
> [*Her face expresses a faint shock. She reaches for the cologne bottle and dampens her handkerchief as she answers carefully.*]

BLANCHE Why, everybody knows somebody named Shaw!

STANLEY Well, this somebody named Shaw is under the impression he met you in Laurel, but I figure he must have got you mixed up with some other party because this other party is someone he met at a hotel called the Flamingo.

[BLANCHE *laughs breathlessly as she touches the cologne-dampened handkerchief to her temples.*]

BLANCHE   I'm afraid he does have me mixed up with this "other party." The Hotel Flamingo is not the sort of establishment I would dare to be seen in!

STANLEY   You know of it?

BLANCHE   Yes, I've seen it and smelled it.

STANLEY   You must've got pretty close if you could smell it.

BLANCHE   The odor of cheap perfume is penetrating.

STANLEY   That stuff you use is expensive?

BLANCHE   Twenty-five dollars an ounce! I'm nearly out. That's just a hint if you want to remember my birthday! [*She speaks lightly but her voice has a note of fear.*]

STANLEY   Shaw must've got you mixed up. He goes in and out of Laurel all the time so he can check on it and clear up any mistake.

[*He turns away and crosses to the portieres.* BLANCHE *closes her eyes as if faint. Her hand trembles as she lifts the handkerchief again to her forehead.* STEVE *and* EUNICE *come around corner.* STEVE's *arm is around* EUNICE's *shoulder and she is sobbing luxuriously and he is cooing love-words. There is a murmur of thunder as they go slowly upstairs in a tight embrace.*]

STANLEY [*to* STELLA]   I'll wait for you at the Four Deuces!

STELLA   Hey! Don't I rate one kiss?

STANLEY   Not in front of your sister.

[*He goes out.* BLANCHE *rises from her chair. She seems faint; looks about her with an expression of almost panic.*]

BLANCHE   Stella! What have you heard about me?

STELLA   Huh?

BLANCHE   What have people been telling you about me?

STELLA   Telling?

BLANCHE   You haven't heard any—unkind—gossip about me?

STELLA   Why, no, Blanche, of course not!

BLANCHE   Honey, there was—a good deal of talk in Laurel.

STELLA   About *you,* Blanche?

BLANCHE   I wasn't so good the last two years or so, after Belle Reve had started to slip through my fingers.

STELLA   All of us do things we—

BLANCHE   I never was hard or self-sufficient enough. When people are soft—soft people have got to shimmer and glow—they've got to put on soft colors, the colors of butterfly wings, and put a—paper lantern over the light. . . . It isn't enough to be soft. You've got to be soft *and attractive.* And I—I'm fading now! I don't know how much longer I can turn the trick.

[*The afternoon has faded to dusk.* STELLA *goes into the bedroom and turns on the light under the paper lantern. She holds a bottled soft drink in her hand.*]

BLANCHE   Have you been listening to me?

STELLA   I don't listen to you when you are being morbid! [*She advances with the bottled Coke.*]

BLANCHE [*with abrupt change to gaiety*]   Is that Coke for me?

STELLA   Not for anyone else!

BLANCHE   Why, you precious thing, you! Is it just Coke?

STELLA [*turning*]   You mean you want a shot in it!

BLANCHE   Well, honey, a shot never does a Coke any harm! Let me! You mustn't wait on me!

STELLA   I like to wait on you, Blanche. It makes it seem more like home. [*She goes into the kitchen, finds a glass and pours a shot of whiskey into it.*]

BLANCHE   I have to admit I love to be waited on . . .

[*She rushes into the bedroom.* STELLA *goes to her with the glass.* BLANCHE *suddenly clutches* STELLA'*s free hand with a moaning sound and presses the hand to her lips.* STELLA *is embarrassed by her show of emotion.* BLANCHE *speaks in a choked voice.*]

You're—you're—so *good* to me! And I—

STELLA   Blanche.

BLANCHE   I know, I won't! You hate me to talk sentimental! But honey, *believe* I feel things more than I *tell* you! I *won't* stay long! I won't, I *promise* I—

STELLA   Blanche!

BLANCHE [*hysterically*]   I won't, I promise, *I'll* go! Go *soon*! I will *really*! I *won't* hang around until he—throws me out . . .

STELLA   Now will you stop talking foolish?

BLANCHE   Yes, honey. Watch how you pour—that fizzy stuff foams over! [BLANCHE *laughs shrilly and grabs the glass, but her hand shakes so it almost slips from her grasp.* STELLA *pours the Coke into the glass. It foams over and spills.* BLANCHE *gives a piercing cry.*]

STELLA [*shocked by the cry*]   Heavens!

BLANCHE   Right on my pretty white skirt!

STELLA   Oh . . . Use my hanky. Blot gently.

BLANCHE [*slowly recovering*]   I know—gently—gently . . .

STELLA   Did it stain?

BLANCHE   Not a bit. Ha-ha! Isn't that lucky? [*She sits down shakily, taking a grateful drink. She holds the glass in both hands and continues to laugh a little.*]

STELLA   Why did you scream like that?

BLANCHE   I don't know why I screamed! [*continuing nervously*] Mitch—Mitch is coming at seven. I guess I am just feeling nervous about our relations. [*She begins to talk rapidly and breathlessly.*] He hasn't gotten a thing but a good-night kiss, that's all I have given him, Stella. I want his respect. And men don't want anything they get too easy. But on the other hand men lose interest quickly. Especially when the girl is over—thirty. They think a girl over thirty ought to—the vulgar term is—"put out." . . . And I—I'm not "putting out." Of course he—he doesn't know—I mean I haven't informed him—of my real age!

STELLA   Why are you sensitive about your age?

BLANCHE   Because of hard knocks my vanity's been given. What I mean is—he thinks I'm sort of—prim and proper, you know! [*She laughs out sharply.*] I want to *deceive* him enough to make him—want me . . .

STELLA   Blanche, do you want *him*?

BLANCHE   I want to *rest*! I want to breathe quietly again! Yes—I *want* Mitch . . . *very badly*! Just think! If it happens! I can leave here and not be anyone's problem . . .

[STANLEY *comes around the corner with a drink under his belt.*]

STANLEY [*bawling*]   Hey, Steve! Hey, Eunice! Hey, Stella!
> [*There are joyous calls from above. Trumpet and drums are heard from around the corner.*]

STELLA [*kissing* BLANCHE *impulsively*]   It *will* happen!

BLANCHE [*doubtfully*]   It will?

STELLA   It *will*! [*She goes across into the kitchen, looking back at* BLANCHE.] It will, honey, *it will*. . . . But don't take another drink! [*Her voice catches as she goes out the door to meet her husband.*]
> [BLANCHE *sinks faintly back in her chair with her drink.* EUNICE *shrieks with laughter and runs down the steps.* STEVE *bounds after her with goatlike screeches and chases her around corner.* STANLEY *and* STELLA *twine arms as they follow, laughing. Dusk settles deeper. The music from the Four Deuces is slow and blue.*]

BLANCHE   Ah, me, ah, me, ah, me . . .
> [*Her eyes fall shut and the palm leaf fan drops from her fingers. She slaps her hand on the chair arm a couple of times. There is a little glimmer of lightning about the building.* A YOUNG MAN *comes along the street and rings the bell.*]

BLANCHE   Come in.
> [*The* YOUNG MAN *appears through the portieres. She regards him with interest.*]

BLANCHE   Well, well! What can I do for *you*?

YOUNG MAN   I'm collecting for *The Evening Star*.

BLANCHE   I didn't know that stars took up collections.

YOUNG MAN   It's the paper.

BLANCHE   I know, I was joking—feebly! Will you—have a drink?

YOUNG MAN   No, ma'am. No, thank you. I can't drink on the job.

BLANCHE   Oh, well, now, let's see. . . . No, I don't have a dime! I'm not the lady of the house. I'm her sister from Mississippi. I'm one of those poor relations you've heard about.

YOUNG MAN   That's all right. I'll drop by later. [*He starts to go out. She approaches a little.*]

BLANCHE   Hey! [*He turns back shyly. She puts a cigarette in a long holder.*] Could you give me a light? [*She crosses toward him. They meet at the door between the two rooms.*]

YOUNG MAN   Sure. [*He takes out a lighter.*] This doesn't always work.

BLANCHE   It's temperamental? [*It flares.*] Ah!—thank you. [*He starts away again.*] Hey! [*He turns again, still more uncertainly. She goes close to him.*] Uh—what time is it?

YOUNG MAN   Fifteen of seven, ma'am.

BLANCHE   So late? Don't you just love these long rainy afternoons in New Orleans when an hour isn't just an hour—but a little piece of eternity dropped into your hands—and who knows what to do with it? [*She touches his shoulders.*] You—uh—didn't get wet in the rain?

YOUNG MAN   No, ma'am. I stepped inside.

BLANCHE   In a drugstore? And had a soda?

YOUNG MAN   Uh-huh.

BLANCHE   Chocolate?

YOUNG MAN   No, ma'am. Cherry.

BLANCHE [*laughing*]   Cherry!

YOUNG MAN   A cherry soda.

BLANCHE   You make my mouth water. [*She touches his cheek lightly, and smiles. Then she goes to the trunk.*]

YOUNG MAN   Well, I'd better be going—

BLANCHE [*stopping him*]   Young man!

> [*He turns. She takes a large, gossamer scarf from the trunk and drapes it about her shoulders. In the ensuing pause, the "Blue Piano" is heard. It continues through the rest of this scene and the opening of the next. The young man clears his throat and looks yearningly at the door.*]

Young man! Young, young, young man! Has anyone ever told you that you look like a young Prince out of the Arabian Nights?

> [*The* YOUNG MAN *laughs uncomfortably and stands like a bashful kid.* BLANCHE *speaks softly to him.*]

Well, you do, honey lamb! Come here. I want to kiss you, just once, softly and sweetly on your mouth!

> [*Without waiting for him to accept, she crosses quickly to him and presses her lips to his.*]

Now run along, now, quickly! It would be nice to keep you, but I've got to be good—and keep my hands off children.

> [*He stares at her a moment. She opens the door for him and blows a kiss at him as he goes down the steps with a dazed look. She stands there a little dreamily after he has disappeared. Then* MITCH *appears around the corner with a bunch of roses.*]

BLANCHE [*gaily*]   Look who's coming! My Rosenkavalier! Bow to me first . . . now present them! *Ahhhh—Merciiii!*[2]

> [*She looks at him over them, coquettishly pressing them to her lips. He beams at her self-consciously.*]

Scene Six

It is about two A.M on the same evening. The outer wall of the building is visible. BLANCHE *and* MITCH *come in. The utter exhaustion which only a neurasthenic personality can know is evident in* BLANCHE's *voice and manner.* MITCH *is stolid but depressed. They have probably been out to the amusement park on Lake Pontchartrain, for* MITCH *is bearing, upside down, a plaster statuette of Mae West, the sort of prize won at shooting galleries and carnival games of chance.*

BLANCHE [*stopping lifelessly at the steps*]   Well— [MITCH *laughs uneasily.*] Well . . .

MITCH   I guess it must be pretty late—and you're tired.

BLANCHE   Even the hot tamale man has deserted the street, and he hangs on till the end. [MITCH *laughs uneasily again.*] How will you get home?

MITCH   I'll walk over to Bourbon and catch an owl-car.

BLANCHE [*laughing grimly*]   Is that streetcar named Desire still grinding along the tracks at this hour?

MITCH [*heavily*]   I'm afraid you haven't gotten much fun out of this evening, Blanche.

BLANCHE   I spoiled it for *you.*

MITCH   No, you didn't, but I felt all the time that I wasn't giving you much—entertainment.

BLANCHE   I simply couldn't rise to the occasion. That was all. I don't think I've ever tried so hard to be gay and made such a dismal mess of it. I get ten points for trying!—I *did* try.

---

2. "Merci": thank you (French). "My Rosenkavalier": Knight of the Rose (German); title of a romantic opera (1911) by Richard Strauss.

MITCH Why did you try if you didn't feel like it, Blanche?

BLANCHE I was just obeying the law of nature.

MITCH Which law is that?

BLANCHE The one that says the lady must entertain the gentleman—or no dice! See if you can locate my door key in this purse. When I'm so tired my fingers are all thumbs!

MITCH [*rooting in her purse*] This it?

BLANCHE No, honey, that's the key to my trunk which I must soon be packing.

MITCH You mean you are leaving here soon?

BLANCHE I've outstayed my welcome.

MITCH This it?

[*The music fades away.*]

BLANCHE Eureka! Honey, you open the door while I take a last look at the sky. [*She leans on the porch rail. He opens the door and stands awkwardly behind her.*] I'm looking for the Pleiades, the Seven Sisters, but these girls are not out tonight. Oh, yes they are, there they are! God bless them! All in a bunch going home from their little bridge party. . . . Y' get the door open? Good boy! I guess you—want to go now . . .

[*He shuffles and coughs a little.*]

MITCH Can I—uh—kiss you—good night?

BLANCHE Why do you always ask me if you may?

MITCH I don't know whether you want me to or not.

BLANCHE Why should you be so doubtful?

MITCH That night when we parked by the lake and I kissed you, you—

BLANCHE Honey, it wasn't the kiss I objected to. I liked the kiss very much. It was the other little—familiarity—that I—felt obliged to—discourage. . . . I didn't resent it! Not a bit in the world! In fact, I was somewhat flattered that you—desired me! But, honey, you know as well as I do that a single girl, a girl alone in the world, has got to keep a firm hold on her emotions or she'll be lost!

MITCH [*solemnly*] Lost?

BLANCHE I guess you are used to girls that like to be lost. The kind that get lost immediately, on the first date!

MITCH I like you to be exactly the way that you are, because in all my—experience—I have never known anyone like you.

[BLANCHE *looks at him gravely; then she bursts into laughter and then claps a hand to her mouth.*]

MITCH Are you laughing at me?

BLANCHE No, honey. The lord and lady of the house have not yet returned, so come in. We'll have a nightcap. Let's leave the lights off. Shall we?

MITCH You just—do what you want to.

[BLANCHE *precedes him into the kitchen. The outer wall of the building disappears and the interiors of the two rooms can be dimly seen.*]

BLANCHE [*remaining in the first room*] The other room's more comfortable—go on in. This crashing around in the dark is my search for some liquor.

MITCH You want a drink?

BLANCHE I want *you* to have a drink! You have been so anxious and solemn all evening, and so have I; we have both been anxious and solemn and now for these few last remaining moments of our lives together—I want to create—*joie de vivre*! I'm lighting a candle.

MITCH   That's good.

BLANCHE   We are going to be very Bohemian. We are going to pretend that we are sitting in a little artists' cafe on the Left Bank in Paris! [*She lights a candle stub and puts it in a bottle.*] *Je suis la Dame aux Camellias! Vous êtes—Armand!*[3] Understand French?

MITCH [*heavily*]   Naw. Naw, I—

BLANCHE   *Voulez-vous couchez avec moi ce soir? Vous ne comprenez pas? Ah, quelle dommage!*[4]—I mean it's a damned good thing. . . . I've found some liquor! Just enough for two shots without any dividends, honey . . .

MITCH [*heavily*]   That's—good.

[*She enters the bedroom with the drinks and the candle.*]

BLANCHE   Sit down! Why don't you take off your coat and loosen your collar?

MITCH   I better leave it on.

BLANCHE   No. I want you to be comfortable.

MITCH   I am ashamed of the way I perspire. My shirt is sticking to me.

BLANCHE   Perspiration is healthy. If people didn't perspire they would die in five minutes. [*She takes his coat from him.*] This is a nice coat. What kind of material is it?

MITCH   They call that stuff alpaca.

BLANCHE   Oh. Alpaca.

MITCH   It's very light-weight alpaca.

BLANCHE   Oh. Light-weight alpaca.

MITCH   I don't like to wear a wash-coat even in summer because I sweat through it.

BLANCHE   Oh.

MITCH   And it don't look neat on me. A man with a heavy build has got to be careful of what he puts on him so he don't look too clumsy.

BLANCHE   You are not too heavy.

MITCH   You don't think I am?

BLANCHE   You are not the delicate type. You have a massive bone-structure and a very imposing physique.

MITCH   Thank you. Last Christmas I was given a membership to the New Orleans Athletic Club.

BLANCHE   Oh, good.

MITCH   It was the finest present I ever was given. I work out there with the weights and I swim and I keep myself fit. When I started there, I was getting soft in the belly but now my belly is hard. It is so hard now that a man can punch me in the belly and it don't hurt me. Punch me! Go on! See?

[*She pokes lightly at him.*]

BLANCHE   Gracious. [*Her hand touches her chest.*]

MITCH   Guess how much I weigh, Blanche?

BLANCHE   Oh, I'd say in the vicinity of—one hundred and eighty?

MITCH   Guess again.

BLANCHE   Not that much?

MITCH   No. More.

---

3. I am the Lady of the Camellias! You are— Armand! (French). Both are characters in the popular romantic play *La Dame aux Camélias* (1852), by the French author Alexandre Dumas *fils*; she is a courtesan who gives up her true love, Armand.

4. Would you like to sleep with me this evening? You don't understand? Ah, what a pity! (French).

BLANCHE   Well, you're a tall man and you can carry a good deal of weight without looking awkward.

MITCH   I weigh two hundred and seven pounds and I'm six feet one and one half inches tall in my bare feet—without shoes on. And that is what I weigh stripped.

BLANCHE   Oh, my goodness, me! It's awe-inspiring.

MITCH [embarrassed]   My weight is not a very interesting subject to talk about. [He hesitates for a moment.] What's yours?

BLANCHE   My weight?

MITCH   Yes.

BLANCHE   Guess!

MITCH   Let me lift you.

BLANCHE   Samson![5] Go on, lift me. [He comes behind her and puts his hands on her waist and raises her lightly off the ground.] Well?

MITCH   You are light as a feather.

BLANCHE   Ha-ha! [He lowers her but keeps his hands on her waist. BLANCHE speaks with an affectation of demureness.] You may release me now.

MITCH   Huh?

BLANCHE [gaily]   I said unhand me, sir. [He fumblingly embraces her. Her voice sounds gently reproving.] Now, Mitch. Just because Stanley and Stella aren't at home is no reason why you shouldn't behave like a gentleman.

MITCH   Just give me a slap whenever I step out of bounds.

BLANCHE   That won't be necessary. You're a natural gentleman, one of the very few that are left in the world. I don't want you to think that I am severe and old maid school-teacherish or anything like that. It's just—well—

MITCH   Huh?

BLANCHE   I guess it is just that I have—old-fashioned ideals! [She rolls her eyes, knowing he cannot see her face. MITCH goes to the front door. There is a considerable silence between them. BLANCHE sighs and MITCH coughs self-consciously.]

MITCH [finally]   Where's Stanley and Stella tonight?

BLANCHE   They have gone out. With Mr. and Mrs. Hubbell upstairs.

MITCH   Where did they go?

BLANCHE   I think they were planning to go to a midnight prevue at Loew's State.

MITCH   We should all go out together some night.

BLANCHE   No. That wouldn't be a good plan.

MITCH   Why not?

BLANCHE   You are an old friend of Stanley's?

MITCH   We was together in the Two-forty-first.[6]

BLANCHE   I guess he talks to you frankly?

MITCH   Sure.

BLANCHE   Has he talked to you about me?

BLANCHE   Oh—not very much.

BLANCHE   The way you say that, I suspect that he has.

MITCH   No, he hasn't said much.

---

5. Legendary strong man in the Old Testament.   6. Engineering battalion in World War II.

BLANCHE   But what he *has* said. What would you say his attitude toward me was?

MITCH   Why do you want to ask that?

BLANCHE   Well—

MITCH   Don't you get along with him?

BLANCHE   What do you think?

MITCH   I don't think he understands you.

BLANCHE   That is putting it mildly. If it weren't for Stella about to have a baby, I wouldn't be able to endure things here.

MITCH   He isn't—nice to you?

BLANCHE   He is insufferably rude. Goes out of his way to offend me.

MITCH   In what way, Blanche?

BLANCHE   Why, in every conceivable way.

MITCH   I'm surprised to hear that.

BLANCHE   Are you?

MITCH   Well, I—don't see how anybody could be rude to you.

BLANCHE   It's really a pretty frightful situation. You see, there's no privacy here. There's just these portieres between the two rooms at night. He stalks through the rooms in his underwear at night. And I have to ask him to close the bathroom door. That sort of commonness isn't necessary. You probably wonder why I don't move out. Well, I'll tell you frankly. A teacher's salary is barely sufficient for her living expenses. I didn't save a penny last year and so I had to come here for the summer. That's why I have to put up with my sister's husband. And he has to put up with me, apparently so much against his wishes. . . . Surely he must have told you how much he hates me!

MITCH   I don't think he hates you.

BLANCHE   He hates me. Or why would he insult me? The first time I laid eyes on him I thought to myself, that man is my executioner! That man will destroy me, unless——

MITCH   Blanche—

BLANCHE   Yes, honey?

MITCH   Can I ask you a question?

BLANCHE   Yes. What?

MITCH   How old are you?

[*She makes a nervous gesture.*]

BLANCHE   Why do you want to know?

MITCH   I talked to my mother about you and she said, "How old is Blanche?" And I wasn't able to tell her. [*There is another pause.*]

BLANCHE   You talked to your mother about me?

MITCH   Yes.

BLANCHE   Why?

MITCH   I told my mother how nice you were, and I liked you.

BLANCHE   Were you sincere about that?

MITCH   You know I was.

BLANCHE   Why did your mother want to know my age?

MITCH   Mother is sick.

BLANCHE   I'm sorry to hear it. Badly?

MITCH   She won't live long. Maybe just a few months.

BLANCHE   Oh.

MITCH   She worries because I'm not settled.

BLANCHE Oh.

MITCH She wants me to be settled down before she— [*His voice is hoarse and he clears his throat twice, shuffling nervously around with his hands in and out of his pockets.*]

BLANCHE You love her very much, don't you?

MITCH Yes.

BLANCHE I think you have a great capacity for devotion. You will be lonely when she passes on, won't you? [MITCH *clears his throat and nods.*] I understand what that is.

MITCH To be lonely?

BLANCHE I loved someone, too, and the person I loved I lost.

MITCH Dead? [*She crosses to the window and sits on the sill, looking out. She pours herself another drink.*] A man?

BLANCHE He was a boy, just a boy, when I was a very young girl. When I was sixteen, I made the discovery—love. All at once and much, much too completely. It was like you suddenly turned a blinding light on something that had always been half in shadow, that's how it struck the world for me. But I was unlucky. Deluded. There was something different about the boy, a nervousness, a softness and tenderness which wasn't like a man's, although he wasn't the least bit effeminate looking—still—that thing was there. . . . He came to me for help. I didn't know that. I didn't find out anything till after our marriage when we'd run away and come back and all I knew was I'd failed him in some mysterious way and wasn't able to give the help he needed but couldn't speak of! He was in the quicksands and clutching at me—but I wasn't holding him out, I was slipping in with him! I didn't know that. I didn't know anything except I loved him unendurably but without being able to help him or help myself. Then I found out. In the worst of all possible ways. By coming suddenly into a room that I thought was empty—which wasn't empty, but had two people in it . . . the boy I had married and an older man who had been his friend for years . . .

[*A locomotive is heard approaching outside. She claps her hands to her ears and crouches over. The headlight of the locomotive glares into the room as it thunders past. As the noise recedes she straightens slowly and continues speaking.*]

Afterward we pretended that nothing had been discovered. Yes, the three of us drove out to Moon Lake Casino, very drunk and laughing all the way.

[*Polka music sounds, in a minor key faint with distance.*]

We danced the Varsouviana![7] Suddenly in the middle of the dance the boy I had married broke away from me and ran out of the casino. A few moments later—a shot!

[*The polka stops abruptly.* BLANCHE *rises stiffly. Then, the polka resumes in a major key.*]

I ran out—all did!—all ran and gathered about the terrible thing at the edge of the lake! I couldn't get near for the crowding. Then somebody caught my arm. "Don't go any closer! Come back! You don't want to see!" See? See what! Then I heard voices say—Allan! Allan! The Grey boy! He'd stuck the revolver into his mouth, and fired—so that the back of his head had been—blown away!

---

7. Fast Polish waltz, similar to the polka.

[*She sways and covers her face.*]

It was because—on the dance floor—unable to stop myself—I'd suddenly said—"I saw! I know! You disgust me . . ." And then the searchlight which had been turned on the world was turned off again and never for one moment since has there been any light that's stronger than this—kitchen—candle . . .

[MITCH *gets up awkwardly and moves toward her a little. The polka music increases.* MITCH *stands beside her.*]

MITCH [*drawing her slowly into his arms*]   You need somebody. And I need somebody, too. Could it be—you and me, Blanche?

[*She stares at him vacantly for a moment. Then with a soft cry huddles in his embrace. She makes a sobbing effort to speak but the words won't come. He kisses her forehead and her eyes and finally her lips. The Polka tune fades out. Her breath is drawn and released in long, grateful sobs.*]

BLANCHE   Sometimes—there's God—so quickly!

Scene Seven

It is late afternoon in mid-September.

The portieres are open and a table is set for a birthday supper, with cake and flowers.

STELLA *is completing the decorations as* STANLEY *comes in.*

STANLEY   What's all this stuff for?

STELLA   Honey, it's Blanche's birthday.

STANLEY   She here?

STELLA   In the bathroom.

STANLEY [*mimicking*]   "Washing out some things"?

STELLA   I reckon so.

STANLEY   How long she been in there?

STELLA   All afternoon.

STANLEY [*mimicking*]   "Soaking in a hot tub"?

STELLA   Yes.

STANLEY   Temperature 100 on the nose, and she soaks herself in a hot tub.

STELLA   She says it cools her off for the evening.

STANLEY   And you run out an' get her cokes, I suppose? And serve 'em to Her Majesty in the tub? [STELLA *shrugs.*] Set down here a minute.

STELLA   Stanley, I've got things to do.

STANLEY   Set down! I've got th' dope on your big sister, Stella.

STELLA   Stanley, stop picking on Blanche.

STANLEY   That girl calls *me* common!

STELLA   Lately you been doing all you can think of to rub her the wrong way, Stanley, and Blanche is sensitive and you've got to realize that Blanche and I grew up under very different circumstances than you did.

STANLEY   So I been told. And told and told and told! You know she's been feeding us a pack of lies here?

STELLA   No, I don't, and—

STANLEY   Well, she has, however. But now the cat's out of the bag! I found out some things!

STELLA   What—things?

STANLEY   Things I already suspected. But now I got proof from the most reliable sources—which I have checked on!

> [BLANCHE *is singing in the bathroom a saccharine popular ballad which is used contrapuntally with* STANLEY'S *speech.*]

STELLA [*to* STANLEY]   Lower your voice!

STANLEY   Some canary bird, huh!

STELLA   Now please tell me quietly what you think you've found out about my sister.

STANLEY   Lie Number One: All this squeamishness she puts on! You should just know the line she's been feeding to Mitch. He thought she had never been more than kissed by a fellow! But Sister Blanche is no lily! Ha-ha! Some lily she is!

STELLA   What have you heard and who from?

STANLEY   Our supply-man down at the plant has been going through Laurel for years and he knows all about her and everybody else in the town of Laurel knows all about her. She is as famous in Laurel as if she was the President of the United States, only she is not respected by any party! This supply-man stops at a hotel called the Flamingo.

BLANCHE [*singing blithely*]   "Say, it's only a paper moon, Sailing over a cardboard sea—But it wouldn't be make-believe If you believed in me!"[8]

STELLA   What about the—Flamingo?

STANLEY   She stayed there, too.

STELLA   My sister lived at Belle Reve.

STANLEY   This is after the home-place had slipped through her lily-white fingers! She moved to the Flamingo! A second-class hotel which has the advantage of not interfering in the private social life of the personalities there! The Flamingo is used to all kinds of goings-on. But even the management of the Flamingo was impressed by Dame Blanche! In fact they was so impressed by Dame Blanche that they requested her to turn in her room key—for permanently! This happened a couple of weeks before she showed here.

BLANCHE [*singing*]   "It's a Barnum and Bailey world, Just as phony as it can be—But it wouldn't be make-believe If you believed in me!"

STELLA   What—contemptible—lies!

STANLEY   Sure, I can see how you would be upset by this. She pulled the wool over your eyes as much as Mitch's!

STELLA   It's pure invention! There's not a word of truth in it and if if I were a man and this creature had dared to invent such things in my presence—

BLANCHE [*singing*]   "Without your love, It's a honky-tonk parade! Without your love, It's a melody played In a penny arcade . . ."

STANLEY   Honey, I told you I thoroughly checked on these stories! Now wait till I finished. The trouble with Dame Blanche was that she couldn't put on her act any more in Laurel! They got wised up after two or three dates with her and then they quit, and she goes on to another, the same old line, same old act, same old hooey! But the town was too small for this to go on forever! And as time went by she became a town character. Regarded as not just different but downright loco—nuts. [STELLA *draws*

---

8. From "It's Only a Paper Moon" (1933), a popular song by Harold Arlen.

back.] And for the last year or two she has been washed up like poison. That's why she's here this summer, visiting royalty, putting on all this act—because she's practically told by the mayor to get out of town! Yes, did you know there was an army camp near Laurel and your sister's was one of the places called "Out-of-Bounds"?

BLANCHE   "It's only a paper moon, Just as phony as it can be—But it wouldn't be make-believe If you believed in me!"

STANLEY   Well, so much for her being such a refined and particular type of girl. Which brings us to Lie Number Two.

STELLA   I don't want to hear any more!

STANLEY   She's not going back to teach school! In fact I am willing to bet you that she never had no idea of returning to Laurel! She didn't resign temporarily from the high school because of her nerves! No, siree, Bob! She didn't. They kicked her out of that high school before the spring term ended—and I hate to tell you the reason that step was taken! A seventeen-year-old boy—she'd gotten mixed up with!

BLANCHE   "It's a Barnum and Bailey world, Just as phony as it can be—"
    [*In the bathroom the water goes on loud; little breathless cries and peals of laughter are heard as if a child were frolicking in the tub.*]

STELLA   This is making me—sick!

STANLEY   The boy's dad learned about it and got in touch with the high school superintendent. Boy, oh, boy, I'd like to have been in that office when Dame Blanche was called on the carpet! I'd like to have seen her trying to squirm out of that one! But they had her on the hook good and proper that time and she knew that the jig was all up! They told her she better move on to some fresh territory. Yep, it was practickly a town ordinance passed against her!
    [*The bathroom door is opened and* BLANCHE *thrusts her head out, holding a towel about her hair.*]

BLANCHE   Stella!

STELLA [*faintly*]   Yes, Blanche?

BLANCHE   Give me another bath-towel to dry my hair with. I've just washed it.

STELLA   Yes, Blanche. [*She crosses in a dazed way from the kitchen to the bathroom door with a towel.*]

BLANCHE   What's the matter, honey?

STELLA   Matter? Why?

BLANCHE   You have such a strange expression on your face!

STELLA   Oh— [*she tries to laugh*] I guess I'm a little tired!

BLANCHE   Why don't you bathe, too, soon as I get out?

STANLEY [*calling from the kitchen*]   How soon is that going to be?

BLANCHE   Not so terribly long! Possess your soul in patience!

STANLEY   It's not my soul, it's my kidneys I'm worried about!
    [BLANCHE *slams the door.* STANLEY *laughs harshly.* STELLA *comes slowly back into the kitchen.*]

STANLEY   Well, what do you think of it?

STELLA   I don't believe all of those stories and I think your supply-man was mean and rotten to tell them. It's possible that some of the things he said are partly true. There are things about my sister I don't approve of—things that caused sorrow at home. She was always—flighty!

STANLEY   Flighty!

STELLA But when she was young, very young, she married a boy who wrote poetry. . . . He was extremely good-looking. I think Blanche didn't just love him but worshipped the ground he walked on! Adored him and thought him almost too fine to be human! But then she found out—

STANLEY What?

STELLA This beautiful and talented young man was a degenerate. Didn't your supply-man give you that information?

STANLEY All we discussed was recent history. That must have been a pretty long time ago.

STELLA Yes, it was—a pretty long time ago . . .

[STANLEY *comes up and takes her by the shoulders rather gently. She gently withdraws from him. Automatically she starts sticking little pink candles in the birthday cake.*]

STANLEY How many candles you putting in that cake?

STELLA I'll stop at twenty-five.

STANLEY Is company expected?

STELLA We asked Mitch to come over for cake and ice-cream.

[STANLEY *looks a little uncomfortable. He lights a cigarette from the one he has just finished.*]

STANLEY I wouldn't be expecting Mitch over tonight.

[STELLA *pauses in her occupation with candles and looks slowly around at* STANLEY.]

STELLA Why?

STANLEY Mitch is a buddy of mine. We were in the same outfit together— Two-forty-first Engineers. We work in the same plant and now on the same bowling team. You think I could face him if—

STELLA Stanley Kowalski, did you—did you repeat what that—?

STANLEY You're goddam right I told him! I'd have that on my conscience the rest of my life if I knew all that stuff and let my best friend get caught!

STELLA Is Mitch through with her?

STANLEY Wouldn't you be if—?

STELLA I said, *Is Mitch through with her?*

[BLANCHE's *voice is lifted again, serenely as a bell. She sings* "But it wouldn't be make-believe If you believed in me."]

STANLEY No, I don't think he's necessarily through with her—just wised up!

STELLA Stanley, she thought Mitch was—going to—going to marry her. I was hoping so, too.

STANLEY Well, he's not going to marry her. Maybe he *was*, but he's not going to jump in a tank with a school of sharks—now! [*He rises.*] Blanche! Oh, Blanche! Can I please get in my bathroom? [*There is a pause.*]

BLANCHE Yes, indeed, sir! Can you wait one second while I dry?

STANLEY Having waited one hour I guess one second ought to pass in a hurry.

STELLA And she hasn't got her job? Well, what will she do!

STANLEY She's not stayin' here after Tuesday. You know that, don't you? Just to make sure I bought her ticket myself. A bus ticket.

STELLA In the first place, Blanche wouldn't go on a bus.

STANLEY She'll go on a bus and like it.

STELLA No, she won't, no, she won't, Stanley!

STANLEY *She'll go!* Period. P.S. She'll go *Tuesday!*

STELLA [*slowly*] What'll—she—do? What on earth will she—*do!*

STANLEY   Her future is mapped out for her.

STELLA   What do you mean?
>[BLANCHE *sings*.]

STANLEY   Hey, canary bird! Toots! Get *OUT* of the *BATHROOM!*
>[*The bathroom door flies open and* BLANCHE *emerges with a gay peal of laughter, but as* STANLEY *crosses past her, a frightened look appears in her face, almost a look of panic. He doesn't look at her but slams the bathroom door shut as he goes in.*]

BLANCHE   [*snatching up a hairbrush*]   Oh, I feel so good after my long, hot bath, I feel so good and cool and—rested!

STELLA   [*sadly and doubtfully from the kitchen*]   Do you, Blanche?

BLANCHE   [*snatching up a hairbrush*]   Yes, I do, so refreshed! [*She tinkles her highball glass.*] A hot bath and a long, cold drink always give me a brand new outlook on life! [*She looks through the portieres at* STELLA, *standing between them, and slowly stops brushing.*] Something has happened!—What is it?

STELLA   [*turning away quickly*]   Why, nothing has happened, Blanche.

BLANCHE   You're lying! Something has!
>[*She stares fearfully at* STELLA, *who pretends to be busy at the table. The distant piano goes into a hectic breakdown.*]

Scene Eight

Three quarters of an hour later.

The view through the big windows is fading gradually into a still-golden dusk. A torch of sunlight blazes on the side of a big water-tank or oil-drum across the empty lot toward the business district which is now pierced by pinpoints of lighted windows or windows reflecting the sunset.

The three people are completing a dismal birthday supper. STANLEY *looks sullen.* STELLA *is embarrassed and sad.*

BLANCHE *has a tight, artificial smile on her drawn face. There is a fourth place at the table which is left vacant.*

BLANCHE   [*suddenly*]   Stanley, tell us a joke, tell us a funny story to make us all laugh. I don't know what's the matter, we're all so solemn. Is it because I've been stood up by my beau?
>[STELLA *laughs feebly.*]
It's the first time in my entire experience with men, and I've had a good deal of all sorts, that I've actually been stood up by anybody! Ha-ha! I don't know how to take it. . . . Tell us a funny little story, Stanley! Something to help us out.

STANLEY   I didn't think you liked my stories, Blanche.

BLANCHE   I like them when they're amusing but not indecent.

STANLEY   I don't know any refined enough for your taste.

BLANCHE   Then let me tell one.

STELLA   Yes, you tell one, Blanche. You used to know lots of good stories.
>[*The music fades.*]

BLANCHE   Let me see, now. . . . I must run through my repertoire! Oh, yes—I love parrot stories! Do you all like parrot stories? Well, this one's about the old maid and the parrot. This old maid, she had a parrot that cursed a blue streak and knew more vulgar expressions than Mr. Kowalski!

STANLEY Huh.

BLANCHE And the only way to hush the parrot up was to put the cover back on its cage so it would think it was night and go back to sleep. Well, one morning the old maid had just uncovered the parrot for the day— when who should she see coming up the front walk but the preacher! Well, she rushed back to the parrot and slipped the cover back on the cage and then she let in the preacher. And the parrot was perfectly still, just as quiet as a mouse, but just as she was asking the preacher how much sugar he wanted in his coffee—the parrot broke the silence with a loud—[*She whistles.*]—and said—"God *damn*, but that was a short day!"

[*She throws back her head and laughs.* STELLA *also makes an ineffectual effort to seem amused.* STANLEY *pays no attention to the story but reaches way over the table to spear his fork into the remaining chop which he eats with his fingers.*]

BLANCHE Apparently Mr. Kowalski was not amused.

STELLA Mr. Kowalski is too busy making a pig of himself to think of anything else!

STANLEY That's right, baby.

STELLA Your face and your fingers are disgustingly greasy. Go and wash up and then help me clear the table.

[*He hurls a plate to the floor.*]

STANLEY That's how I'll clear the table! [*He seizes her arm.*] Don't ever talk that way to me! "Pig—Polack—disgusting—vulgar—greasy!"—them kind of words have been on your tongue and your sister's too much around here! What do you two think you are? A pair of queens? Remember what Huey Long[9] said—"Every Man is a King!" And I am the king around here, so don't forget it! [*He hurls a cup and saucer to the floor.*] My place is cleared! You want me to clear your places?

[STELLA *begins to cry weakly.* STANLEY *stalks out on the porch and lights a cigarette. The Negro entertainers around the corner are heard.*]

BLANCHE What happened while I was bathing? What did he tell you, Stella?

STELLA Nothing, nothing, nothing!

BLANCHE I think he told you something about Mitch and me! You know why Mitch didn't come but you won't tell me! [STELLA *shakes her head helplessly.*] I'm going to call him!

STELLA I wouldn't call him, Blanche.

BLANCHE I am, I'm going to call him on the phone.

STELLA [*miserably*] I wish you wouldn't.

BLANCHE I intend to be given some explanation from someone!

[*She rushes to the phone in the bedroom.* STELLA *goes out on the porch and stares reproachfully at her husband. He grunts and turns away from her.*]

STELLA I hope you're pleased with your doings. I never had so much trouble swallowing food in my life, looking at that girl's face and the empty chair! [*She cries quietly.*]

BLANCHE [*at the phone*] Hello. Mr. Mitchell, please. . . . Oh. . . . I would like to leave a number if I may. Magnolia 9047. And say it's important to call. . . . Yes, very important. . . . Thank you.

---

9. Demagogic Louisiana political leader, governor, and senator (1893–1935).

[*She remains by the phone with a lost, frightened look.* STANLEY *turns slowly back toward his wife and takes her clumsily in his arms.*]

STANLEY   Stell, it's gonna be all right after she goes and after you've had the baby. It's gonna be all right again between you and me the way that it was. You remember the way that it was? Them nights we had together? God, honey, it's gonna be sweet when we can make noise in the night the way that we used to and get the colored lights going with nobody's sister behind the curtains to hear us!

[*Their upstairs neighbors are heard in bellowing laughter at something.* STANLEY *chuckles.*]

Steve an' Eunice . . .

STELLA   Come on back in. [*She returns to the kitchen and starts lighting the candles on the white cake.*] Blanche?

BLANCHE   Yes. [*She returns from the bedroom to the table in the kitchen.*] Oh, those pretty, pretty little candles! Oh, don't burn them, Stella.

STELLA   I certainly will.

[STANLEY *comes back in.*]

BLANCHE   You ought to save them for baby's birthdays. Oh, I hope candles are going to glow in his life and I hope that his eyes are going to be like candles, like two blue candles lighted in a white cake!

STANLEY [*sitting down*]   What poetry!

BLANCHE [*she pauses reflectively for a moment*]   I shouldn't have called him.

STELLA   There's lots of things could have happened.

BLANCHE   There's no excuse for it, Stella. I don't have to put up with insults. I won't be taken for granted.

STANLEY   Goddamn, it's hot in here with the steam from the bathroom.

BLANCHE   I've said I was sorry three times. [*The piano fades out.*] I take hot baths for my nerves. Hydrotherapy, they call it. You healthy Polack, without a nerve in your body, of course you don't know what anxiety feels like!

STANLEY   I am not a Polack. People from Poland are Poles, not Polacks. But what I am is a one-hundred-per-cent American, born and raised in the greatest country on earth and proud as hell of it, so don't ever call me a Polack.

[*The phone rings.* BLANCHE *rises expectantly.*]

BLANCHE   Oh, that's for me, I'm sure.

STANLEY   *I'm* not sure. Keep your seat. [*He crosses leisurely to phone.*] H'lo. Aw, yeh, hello, Mac.

[*He leans against wall, staring insultingly in at* BLANCHE. *She sinks back in her chair with a frightened look.* STELLA *leans over and touches her shoulder.*]

BLANCHE   Oh, keep your hands off me, Stella. What is the matter with you? Why do you look at me with that pitying look?

STANLEY [*bawling*]   QUIET IN THERE!—We've got a noisy woman on the place.—Go on, Mac. At Riley's? No, I don't wanta bowl at Riley's. I had a little trouble with Riley last week. I'm the team captain, ain't I? All right, then, we're not gonna bowl at Riley's, we're gonna bowl at the West Side or the Gala! All right, Mac. See you!

[*He hangs up and returns to the table.* BLANCHE *fiercely controls herself, drinking quickly from her tumbler of water. He doesn't look at her but reaches in a pocket. Then he speaks slowly and with false amiability.*]

Sister Blanche, I've got a little birthday remembrance for you.

BLANCHE   Oh, have you, Stanley? I wasn't expecting any, I—I don't know why Stella wants to observe my birthday! I'd much rather forget it—when you—reach twenty-seven! Well—age is a subject that you'd prefer to—ignore!

STANLEY   Twenty-seven?

BLANCHE [*quickly*]   What is it? Is it for *me*?
   [*He is holding a little envelope toward her.*]

STANLEY   Yes, I hope you like it!

BLANCHE   Why, why—Why, it's a—

STANLEY   Ticket! Back to Laurel! On the Greyhound! Tuesday!
   [*The Varsouviana music steals in softly and continues playing.* STELLA *rises abruptly and turns her back.* BLANCHE *tries to smile. Then she tries to laugh. Then she gives both up and springs from the table and runs into the next room. She clutches her throat and then runs into the bathroom. Coughing, gagging sounds are heard.*]

Well!

STELLA   You didn't need to do that.

STANLEY   Don't forget all that I took off her.

STELLA   You needn't have been so cruel to someone alone as she is.

STANLEY   Delicate piece she is.

STELLA   She is. She was. You didn't know Blanche as a girl. Nobody, nobody, was tender and trusting as she was. But people like you abused her, and forced her to change.
   [*He crosses into the bedroom, ripping off his shirt, and changes into a brilliant silk bowling shirt. She follows him.*]

Do you think you're going bowling now?

STANLEY   Sure.

STELLA   You're not going bowling. [*She catches hold of his shirt.*] Why did you do this to her?

STANLEY   I done nothing to no one. Let go of my shirt. You've torn it.

STELLA   I want to know why. Tell me why.

STANLEY   When we first met, me and you, you thought I was common. How right you was, baby. I was common as dirt. You showed me the snapshot of the place with the columns. I pulled you down off them columns and how you loved it, having them colored lights going! And wasn't we happy together, wasn't it all okay till she showed here?
   [STELLA *makes a slight movement. Her look goes suddenly inward as if some interior voice had called her name. She begins a slow, shuffling progress from the bedroom to the kitchen, leaning and resting on the back of the chair and then on the edge of a table with a blind look and listening expression.* STANLEY, *finishing with his shirt, is unaware of her reaction.*]

And wasn't we happy together? Wasn't it all okay? Till she showed here.

Hoity-Toity, describing me as an ape. [*He suddenly notices the change in* STELLA.] Hey, what is it, Stel? [*He crosses to her.*]

STELLA [*quietly*]   Take me to the hospital.
   [*He is with her now, supporting her with his arm, murmuring indistinguishably as they go outside.*]

Scene Nine

A while later that evening. BLANCHE *is seated in a tense hunched position in a bedroom chair that she has recovered with diagonal green and white stripes. She has on her scarlet satin robe. On the table beside chair is a bottle of liquor and a glass. The rapid, feverish polka tune, the "Varsouviana," is heard. The music is in her mind; she is drinking to escape it and the sense of disaster closing in on her, and she seems to whisper the words of the song. An electric fan is turning back and forth across her.*

MITCH *comes around the corner in work clothes: blue denim shirt and pants. He is unshaven. He climbs the steps to the door and rings.* BLANCHE *is startled.*

BLANCHE   Who is it, please?

MITCH [*hoarsely*]   Me. Mitch.

[*The polka tune stops.*]

BLANCHE   Mitch!—Just a minute.

[*She rushes about frantically, hiding the bottle in a closet, crouching at the mirror and dabbing her face with cologne and powder. She is so excited that her breath is audible as she dashes about. At last she rushes to the door in the kitchen and lets him in.*]

Mitch!—Y'know, I really shouldn't let you in after the treatment I have received from you this evening! So utterly uncavalier! But hello, beautiful!

[*She offers him her lips. He ignores it and pushes past her into the flat. She looks fearfully after him as he stalks into the bedroom.*]

My, my, what a cold shoulder! And such uncouth apparel! Why, you haven't even shaved! The unforgivable insult to a lady! But I forgive you. I forgive you because it's such a relief to see you. You've stopped that polka tune that I had caught in my head. Have you ever had anything caught in your head? No, of course you haven't, you dumb angel-puss, you'd never get anything awful caught in your head!

[*He stares at her while she follows him while she talks. It is obvious that he has had a few drinks on the way over.*]

MITCH   Do we have to have that fan on?

BLANCHE   No!

MITCH   I don't like fans.

BLANCHE   Then let's turn it off, honey. I'm not partial to them!

[*She presses the switch and the fan nods slowly off. She clears her throat uneasily as* MITCH *plumps himself down on the bed in the bedroom and lights a cigarette.*]

I don't know what there is to drink. I—haven't investigated.

MITCH   I don't want Stan's liquor.

BLANCHE   It isn't Stan's. Everything here isn't Stan's. Some things on the premises are actually mine! How is your mother? Isn't your mother well?

MITCH   Why?

BLANCHE   Something's the matter tonight, but never mind. I won't cross-examine the witness. I'll just—[*She touches her forehead vaguely. The polka tune starts up again.*]—pretend I don't notice anything different about you! That—music again . . .

MITCH   What music?

BLANCHE   The "Varsourviana"! The polka tune they were playing when Allan—Wait!

[*A distant revolver shot is heard.* BLANCHE *seems relieved.*]

There now, the shot! It always stops after that.
[*The polka music dies out again.*]
Yes, now it's stopped.

MITCH   Are you boxed out of your mind?

BLANCHE   I'll go and see what I can find in the way of— [*She crosses into the closet, pretending to search for the bottle.*] Oh, by the way, excuse me for not being dressed. But I'd practically given you up! Had you forgotten your invitation to supper?

MITCH   I wasn't going to see you any more.

BLANCHE   Wait a minute. I can't hear what you're saying and you talk so little that when you do say something, I don't want to miss a single syllable of it. . . . What am I looking around here for? Oh, yes—liquor! We've had so much excitement around here this evening that I *am* boxed out of my mind! [*She pretends suddenly to find the bottle. He draws his foot up on the bed and stares at her contemptuously.*] Here's something. Southern Comfort! What is that, I wonder?

MITCH   If you don't know, it must belong to Stan.

BLANCHE   Take your foot off the bed. It has a light cover on it. Of course you boys don't notice things like that. I've done so much with this place since I've been here.

MITCH   I bet you have.

BLANCHE   You saw it before I came. Well, look at it now! This room is almost—dainty! I want to keep it that way. I wonder if this stuff ought to be mixed with something? Ummm, it's sweet, so sweet! It's terribly, terribly sweet! Why, it's a *liqueur*, I believe! Yes, that's what it *is*, a liqueur! [MITCH *grunts.*] I'm afraid you won't like it, but try it, and maybe you will.

MITCH   I told you already I don't want none of his liquor and I mean it. You ought to lay off his liquor. He says you been lapping it up all summer like a wild cat!

BLANCHE   What a fantastic statement! Fantastic of him to say it, fantastic of you to repeat it! I won't descend to the level of such cheap accusations to answer them, even!

MITCH   Huh.

BLANCHE   What's in your mind? I see something in your eyes!

MITCH   [*getting up*]   It's dark in here.

BLANCHE   I like it dark. The dark is comforting to me.

MITCH   I don't think I ever seen you in the light. [BLANCHE *laughs breathlessly.*] That's a fact!

BLANCHE   Is it?

MITCH   I've never seen you in the afternoon.

BLANCHE   Whose fault is that?

MITCH   You never want to go out in the afternoon.

BLANCHE   Why, Mitch, you're at the plant in the afternoon!

MITCH   Not Sunday afternoon. I've asked you to go out with me sometimes on Sundays but you always make an excuse. You never want to go out till after six and then it's always some place that's not lighted much.

BLANCHE   There is some obscure meaning in this but I fail to catch it.

MITCH   What it means is I've never had a real good look at you, Blanche. Let's turn the light on here.

BLANCHE   [*fearfully*]   Light? Which light? What for?

MITCH   This one with the paper thing on it. [*He tears the paper lantern off the light bulb. She utters a frightened gasp.*]

BLANCHE   What did you do that for?

MITCH   So I can take a look at you good and plain!

BLANCHE   Of course you don't really mean to be insulting!

MITCH   No, just realistic.

BLANCHE   I don't want realism. I want magic! [MITCH *laughs.*] Yes, yes, magic! I try to give that to people. I misrepresent things to them. I don't tell truth, I tell what *ought* to be truth. And if that is sinful, then let me be damned for it!—*Don't turn the light on!*

> [MITCH *crosses to the switch. He turns the light on and stares at her. She cries out and covers her face. He turns the lights off again.*]

MITCH   [*slowly and bitterly*]   I don't mind you being older than what I thought. But all the rest of it—Christ! That pitch about your ideals being so old-fashioned and all the malarkey that you've dished out all summer. Oh, I knew you weren't sixteen any more. But I was a fool enough to believe you was straight.

BLANCHE   Who told you I wasn't—"straight"? My loving brother-in-law. And you believed him.

MITCH   I called him a liar at first. And then I checked on the story. First I asked our supply-man who travels through Laurel. And then I talked directly over long-distance to this merchant.

BLANCHE   Who is this merchant?

MITCH   Kiefaber.

BLANCHE   The merchant Kiefaber of Laurel! I know the man. He whistled at me. I put him in his place. So now for revenge he makes up stories about me.

MITCH   Three people, Kiefaber, Stanley and Shaw, swore to them!

BLANCHE   Rub-a-dub-dub, three men in a tub! And such a filthy tub!

MITCH   Didn't you stay at a hotel called The Flamingo?

BLANCHE   Flamingo? No! Tarantula was the name of it! I stayed at a hotel called The Tarantula Arms!

MITCH   [*stupidly*]   Tarantula?

BLANCHE   Yes, a big spider! That's where I brought my victims. [*She pours herself another drink.*] Yes, I had many intimacies with strangers. After the death of Allan—intimacies with strangers was all I seemed able to fill my empty heart with. . . . I think it was panic, just panic, that drove me from one to another, hunting for some protection—here and there, in the most—unlikely places—even, at last, in a seventeen-year-old boy but—somebody wrote the superintendent about it—"This woman is morally unfit for her position!"

> [*She throws back her head with convulsive, sobbing laughter. Then she repeats the statement, gasps, and drinks.*]

True? Yes, I suppose—unfit somehow—anyway. . . . So I came here. There was nowhere else I could go. I was played out. You know what played out is? My youth was suddenly gone up the water-spout, and—I met you. You said you needed somebody. Well, I needed somebody, too. I thanked God for you, because you seemed to be gentle—a cleft in the rock of the world that I could hide in! But I guess I was asking, hoping—too much! Kiefaber, Stanley and Shaw have tied an old tin can to the tail of the kite.

> [*There is a pause.* MITCH *stares at her dumbly.*]

MITCH   You lied to me, Blanche.

BLANCHE   Don't say I lied to you.

MITCH   Lies, lies, inside and out, all lies.

BLANCHE   Never inside, I didn't lie in my heart . . .

[A VENDOR comes around the corner. She is a blind MEXICAN WOMAN *in a dark shawl, carrying bunches of those gaudy tin flowers that lower-class Mexicans display at funerals and other festive occasions. She is calling barely audibly. Her figure is only faintly visible outside the building.*]

MEXICAN WOMAN   Flores. Flores, Flores para los muertos.[1] Flores. Flores.

BLANCHE   What? Oh! Somebody outside . . . [*She goes to the door, opens it and stares at the* MEXICAN WOMAN.]

MEXICAN WOMAN [*she is at the door and offers* BLANCHE *some of her flowers*] Flores? Flores para los muertos?

BLANCHE [*frightened*]   No, no! Not now! Not now!

[*She darts back into the apartment, slamming the door.*]

MEXICAN WOMAN [*she turns away and starts to move down the street*]   Flores para los muertos.

[*The polka tune fades in.*]

BLANCHE [*as if to herself*]   Crumble and fade and—regrets—recriminations . . . "If you'd done this, it wouldn't've cost me that!"

MEXICAN WOMAN   Corones[2] para los muertos. Corones . . .

BLANCHE   Legacies! Huh. . . . And other things such as bloodstained pillow-slips—"Her linen needs changing"—"Yes, Mother. But couldn't we get a colored girl to do it?" No, we couldn't of course. Everything gone but the—

MEXICAN WOMAN   Flores.

BLANCHE   Death—I used to sit here and she used to sit over there and death was as close as you are. . . . We didn't dare even admit we had ever heard of it!

MEXICAN WOMAN   Flores para los muertos, flores—flores . . .

BLANCHE   The opposite is desire. So do you wonder? How could you possibly wonder! Not far from Belle Reve, before we had lost Belle Reve, was a camp where they trained young soldiers. On Sunday nights they would go in town to get drunk—

MEXICAN WOMAN [*softly*]   Corones . . .

BLANCHE   —and on the way back they would stagger onto my lawn and call—"Blanche! Blanche!"—the deaf old lady remaining suspected nothing. But sometimes I slipped outside to answer their calls. . . . Later the paddy-wagon would gather them up like daisies . . . the long way home . . .

[*The* MEXICAN WOMAN *turns slowly and drifts back off with her soft mournful cries.* BLANCHE *goes to the dresser and leans forward on it. After a moment,* MITCH *rises and follows her purposefully. The polka music fades away. He places his hands on her waist and tries to turn her about.*]

BLANCHE   What do you want?

MITCH [*fumbling to embrace her*]   What I been missing all summer.

BLANCHE   Then marry me, Mitch!

MITCH   I don't think I want to marry you anymore.

BLANCHE   No?

---

1. Flowers for the dead (Spanish).   2. Wreaths (Spanish).

MITCH [*dropping his hands from her waist*] You're not clean enough to bring in the house with my mother.

BLANCHE   Go away, then. [*He stares at her.*] Get out of here quick before I start screaming fire! [*Her throat is tightening with hysteria.*] Get out of here quick before I start screaming fire.

[*He still remains staring. She suddenly rushes to the big window with its pale blue square of the soft summer light and cries wildly.*]

Fire! Fire! Fire!

[*With a startled gasp, MITCH turns and goes out the outer door, clatters awkwardly down the steps and around the corner of the building. BLANCHE staggers back from the window and falls to her knees. The distant piano is slow and blue.*]

Scene Ten

It is a few hours later that night.

BLANCHE *has been drinking fairly steadily since* MITCH *left. She has dragged her wardrobe trunk into the center of the bedroom. It hangs open with flowery dresses thrown across it. As the drinking and packing went on, a mood of hysterical exhilaration came into her and she has decked herself out in a somewhat soiled and crumpled white satin evening gown and a pair of scuffed silver slippers with brilliants set in their heels.*

Now she is placing the rhinestone tiara on her head before the mirror of the dressing-table and murmuring excitedly as if to a group of spectral admirers.

BLANCHE   How about taking a swim, a moonlight swim at the old rock-quarry? If anyone's sober enough to drive a car! Ha-ha! Best way in the world to stop your head buzzing! Only you've got to be careful to dive where the deep pool is—if you hit a rock you don't come up till tomorrow . . .

[*Tremblingly she lifts the hand mirror for a closer inspection. She catches her breath and slams the mirror face down with such violence that the glass cracks. She moans a little and attempts to rise.* STANLEY *appears around the corner of the building. He still has on the vivid green silk bowling shirt. As he rounds the corner the honky-tonk music is heard. It continues softly throughout the scene. He enters the kitchen, slamming the door. As he peers in at* BLANCHE *he gives a low whistle. He has had a few drinks on the way and has brought some quart beer bottles home with him.*]

BLANCHE   How is my sister?

STANLEY   She is doing okay.

BLANCHE   And how is the baby?

STANLEY [*grinning amiably*]   The baby won't come before morning so they told me to go home and get a little shut-eye.

BLANCHE   Does that mean we are to be alone in here?

STANLEY   Yep. Just me and you, Blanche. Unless you got somebody hid under the bed. What've you got on those fine feathers for?

BLANCHE   Oh, that's right. You left before my wire came.

STANLEY   You got a wire?

BLANCHE   I received a telegram from an old admirer of mine.

STANLEY   Anything good?

BLANCHE   I think so. An invitation.

STANLEY   What to? A fireman's ball?

BLANCHE [*throwing back her head*] A cruise of the Caribbean on a yacht!

STANLEY Well, well. What do you know?

BLANCHE I have never been so surprised in my life.

STANLEY I guess not.

BLANCHE It came like a bolt from the blue!

STANLEY Who did you say it was from?

BLANCHE An old beau of mine.

STANLEY The one that give you the white fox-pieces?

BLANCHE Mr. Shep Huntleigh. I wore his ATO pin my last year at college. I hadn't seen him again until last Christmas. I ran in to him on Biscayne Boulevard. Then—just now—this wire—inviting me on a cruise of the Caribbean! The problem is clothes. I tore into my trunk to see what I have that's suitable for the tropics!

STANLEY And come up with that—gorgeous—diamond—tiara?

BLANCHE This old relic? Ha-ha! It's only rhinestones.

STANLEY Gosh. I thought it was Tiffany diamonds. [*He unbuttons his shirt.*]

BLANCHE Well, anyhow, I shall be entertained in style.

STANLEY Uh-huh. It goes to show, you never know what is coming.

BLANCHE Just when I thought my luck had begun to fail me—

STANLEY Into the picture pops this Miami millionaire.

BLANCHE This man is not from Miami. This man is from Dallas.

STANLEY This man is from Dallas?

BLANCHE Yes, this man is from Dallas where gold spouts out of the ground!

STANLEY Well, just so he's from somewhere! [*He starts removing his shirt.*]

BLANCHE Close the curtains before you undress any further.

STANLEY [*amiably*] This is all I'm going to undress right now. [*He rips the sack off a quart beer bottle*] Seen a bottle-opener?

[*She moves slowly toward the dresser, where she stands with her hands knotted together.*]

I used to have a cousin who could open a beer bottle with his teeth. [*pounding the bottle cap on the corner of table*] That was his only accomplishment, all he could do—he was just a human bottle-opener. And then one time, at a wedding party, he broke his front teeth off! After that he was so ashamed of himself he used t' sneak out of the house when company came . . .

[*The bottle cap pops off and a geyser of foam shoots up. Stanley laughs happily, holding up the bottle over his head.*]

Ha-ha! Rain from heaven! [*He extends the bottle toward her*] Shall we bury the hatchet and make it a loving-cup? Huh?

BLANCHE No, thank you.

STANLEY Well, it's a red-letter night for us both. You having an oil millionaire and me having a baby.

[*He goes to the bureau in the bedroom and crouches to remove something from the bottom drawer.*]

BLANCHE [*drawing back*] What are you doing in here?

STANLEY Here's something I always break out on special occasions like this. The silk pyjamas I wore on my wedding night!

BLANCHE Oh.

STANLEY When the telephone rings and they say, "You've got a son!" I'll tear this off and wave it like a flag! [*He shakes out a brilliant pyjama coat.*]

I guess we are both entitled to put on the dog. [*He goes back to the kitchen with the coat over his arm.*]

BLANCHE When I think of how divine it is going to be to have such a thing as privacy once more—I could weep with joy!

STANLEY This millionaire from Dallas is not going to interfere with your privacy any?

BLANCHE It won't be the sort of thing you have in mind. This man is a gentleman and he respects me. [*improvising feverishly*] What he wants is my companionship. Having great wealth sometimes makes people lonely! A cultivated woman, a woman of intelligence and breeding, can enrich a man's life—immeasurably! I have those things to offer, and this doesn't take them away. Physical beauty is passing. A transitory possession. But beauty of the mind and richness of the spirit and tenderness of the heart—and I have all of those things—aren't taken away, but grow! Increase with the years! How strange that I should be called a destitute woman! When I have all of these treasures locked in my heart. [*A choked sob comes from her.*] I think of myself as a very, very rich woman! But I have been foolish—casting my pearls before swine!

STANLEY Swine, huh?

BLANCHE Yes, swine! Swine! And I'm thinking not only of you but of your friend, Mr. Mitchell. He came to see me tonight. He dared to come here in his work clothes! And to repeat slander to me, vicious stories that he had gotten from you! I gave him his walking papers . . .

STANLEY You did, huh?

BLANCHE But then he came back. He returned with a box of roses to beg my forgiveness! He implored my forgiveness. But some things are not forgivable. Deliberate cruelty is not forgivable. It is the one unforgivable thing in my opinion and it is the one thing of which I have never, never been guilty. And so I told him, I said to him. "Thank you," but it was foolish of me to think that we could ever adapt ourselves to each other. Our ways of life are too different. Our attitudes and our backgrounds are incompatible. We have to be realistic about such things. So farewell, my friend! And let there be no hard feelings . . .

STANLEY Was this before or after the telegram came from the Texas oil millionaire?

BLANCHE What telegram? No! No, after! As a matter of fact, the wire came just as—

STANLEY As a matter of fact there wasn't no wire at all!

BLANCHE Oh, oh!

STANLEY There isn't no millionaire! And Mitch didn't come back with roses 'cause I know where he is—

BLANCHE Oh!

STANLEY There isn't a goddam thing but imagination!

BLANCHE Oh!

STANLEY And lies and conceit and tricks!

BLANCHE Oh!

STANLEY And look at yourself! Take a look at yourself in that worn-out Mardi Gras outfit, rented for fifty cents from some rag-picker! And with the crazy crown on! What queen do you think you are?

BLANCHE Oh—God . . .

STANLEY I've been on to you from the start! Not once did you pull any wool over this boy's eyes! You come in here and sprinkle the place with powder and spray perfume and cover the light-bulb with a paper lantern, and lo and behold the place has turned into Egypt and you are the Queen of the Nile! Sitting on your throne and swilling down my liquor! I say— Ha!—Ha! Do you hear me? Ha—ha—ha! [*He walks into the bedroom.*]

BLANCHE   Don't come in here!

[*Lurid reflections appear on the walls around* BLANCHE. *The shadows are of a grotesque and menacing form. She catches her breath, crosses to the phone and jiggles the hook.* STANLEY *goes into the bathroom and closes the door.*]

Operator, operator! Give me long-distance, please. . . . I want to get in touch with Mr. Shep Huntleigh of Dallas. He's so well known he doesn't require any address. Just ask anybody who—Wait!!—No, I couldn't find it right now. . . . Please understand, I—No! No, wait!. . . . One moment! Someone is—Nothing! Hold on, please!

[*She sets the phone down and crosses warily into the kitchen. The night is filled with inhuman voices like cries in a jungle. The shadows and lurid reflections move sinuously as flames along the wall spaces. Through the back wall of the rooms, which have become transparent, can be seen the sidewalk. A prostitute has rolled a drunkard. He pursues her along the walk, overtakes her and there is a struggle. A policeman's whistle breaks it up. The figures disappear. Some moments later the Negro Woman appears around the corner with a sequined bag which the prostitute had dropped on the walk. She is rooting excitedly through it.* BLANCHE *presses her knuckles to her lips and returns slowly to the phone. She speaks in a hoarse whisper.*]

BLANCHE   Operator! Operator! Never mind long-distance. Get Western Union. There isn't time to be—Western—Western Union!

[*She waits anxiously.*]

Western Union? Yes! I—want to—Take down this message! "In desperate, desperate circumstances! Help me! Caught in a trap. Caught in—" Oh!

[*The bathroom door is thrown open and* STANLEY *comes out in the brilliant silk pyjamas. He grins at her as he knots the tasseled sash about his waist. She gasps and backs away from the phone. He stares at her for a count of ten. Then a clicking becomes audible from the telephone, steady and rasping.*]

STANLEY   You left th' phone off th' hook.

[*He crosses to it deliberately and sets it back on the hook. After he has replaced it, he stares at her again, his mouth slowly curving into a grin, as he weaves between* BLANCHE *and the outer door. The barely audible "Blue Piano" begins to drum up louder. The sound of it turns into the roar of an approaching locomotive.* BLANCHE *crouches, pressing her fists to her ears until it has gone by.*]

BLANCHE   [*finally straightening*]   Let me—let me get by you!

STANLEY   Get by me? Sure. Go ahead. [*He moves back a pace in the doorway.*]

BLANCHE   You—you stand over there! [*She indicates a further position.*]

STANLEY   [*grinning*]   You got plenty of room to walk by me now.

BLANCHE   Not with you there! But I've got to get out somehow!

STANLEY   You think I'll interfere with you? Ha-ha!

[*The "Blue Piano" goes softly. She turns confusedly and makes a faint gesture. The inhuman jungle voices rise up. He takes a step toward her, biting his tongue which protrudes between his lips.*]

STANLEY [*softly*] Come to think of it—maybe you wouldn't be bad to—interfere with . . .

[BLANCHE *moves backward through the door into the bedroom.*]

BLANCHE   Stay back! Don't you come toward me another step or I'll—

STANLEY   What?

BLANCHE   Some awful thing will happen! It will!

STANLEY   What are you putting on now?

[*They are now both inside the bedroom.*]

BLANCHE   I warn you, don't, I'm in danger!

[*He takes another step. She smashes a bottle on the table and faces him, clutching the broken top.*]

STANLEY   What did you do that for?

BLANCHE   So I could twist the broken end in your face!

STANLEY   I bet you would do that!

BLANCHE   I would! I will if you—

STANLEY   Oh! So you want some roughhouse! All right, let's have some roughhouse!

[*He springs toward her, overturning the table. She cries out and strikes at him with the bottle top but he catches her wrist.*]

Tiger—tiger! Drop the bottle-top! Drop it! We've had this date with each other from the beginning!

[*She moans. The bottle-top falls. She sinks to her knees: He picks up her inert figure and carries her to the bed. The hot trumpet and drums from the Four Deuces sound loudly.*]

Scene Eleven

It is some weeks later. STELLA *is packing* BLANCHE's *things. Sounds of water can be heard running in the bathroom.*

*The portieres are partly open on the poker players—*STANLEY, STEVE, MITCH *and* PABLO—*who sit around the table in the kitchen. The atmosphere of the kitchen is now the same raw, lurid one of the disastrous poker night.*

The building is framed by the sky of turquoise. STELLA *has been crying as she arranges the flowery dresses in the open trunk.*

EUNICE *comes down the steps from her flat above and enters the kitchen. There is an outburst from the poker table.*

STANLEY   Drew to an inside straight and made it, by God.

PABLO   *Maldita sea tu suerto!*

STANLEY   Put it in English, greaseball.

PABLO   I am cursing your rutting luck.

STANLEY [*prodigiously elated*]   You know what luck is? Luck is believing you're lucky. Take at Salerno.[3] I believed I was lucky. I figured that 4 out of 5 would not come through but I would . . . and I did. I put that down as a rule. To hold front position in this rat-race you've got to believe you are lucky.

MITCH   You . . . you . . . you . . . Brag . . . brag . . . bull . . . bull.

[STELLA *goes into the bedroom and starts folding a dress.*]

STANLEY   What's the matter with him?

---

3. Important beachhead in the Allied invasion of Italy in World War II.

EUNICE [*walking past the table*] I always did say that men are callous things with no feelings, but this does beat anything. Making pigs of yourselves. [*She comes through the portieres into the bedroom.*]

STANLEY What's the matter with her?

STELLA How is my baby?

EUNICE Sleeping like a little angel. Brought you some grapes. [*She puts them on a stool and lowers her voice.*] Blanche?

STELLA Bathing.

EUNICE How is she?

STELLA She wouldn't eat anything but asked for a drink.

EUNICE What did you tell her?

STELLA I—just told her that—we'd made arrangements for her to rest in the country. She's got it mixed in her mind with Shep Huntleigh.

[BLANCHE *opens the bathroom door slightly.*]

BLANCHE Stella.

STELLA Yes, Blanche.

BLANCHE If anyone calls while I'm bathing take the number and tell them I'll call right back.

STELLA Yes.

BLANCHE That cool yellow silk—the bouclé. See if it's crushed. If it's not too crushed I'll wear it and on the lapel that silver and turquoise pin in the shape of a seahorse. You will find them in the heart-shaped box I keep my accessories in. And Stella . . . Try and locate a bunch of artificial violets in that box, too, to pin with the seahorse on the lapel of the jacket.

[*She closes the door.* STELLA *turns to* EUNICE.]

STELLA I don't know if I did the right thing.

EUNICE What else could you do?

STELLA I couldn't believe her story and go on living with Stanley.

EUNICE Don't ever believe it. Life has got to go on. No matter what happens, you've got to keep on going.

[*The bathroom door opens a little.*]

BLANCHE [*looking out*] Is the coast clear?

STELLA Yes, Blanche. [*to* EUNICE] Tell her how well she's looking.

BLANCHE Please close the curtains before I come out.

STELLA They're closed.

STANLEY —How many for you?

PABLO Two.

STEVE Three.

[BLANCHE *appears in the amber light of the door. She has a tragic radiance in her red satin robe following the sculptural lines of her body. The "Varsouviana" rises audibly as* BLANCHE *enters the bedroom.*]

BLANCHE [*with faintly hysterical vivacity*] I have just washed my hair.

STELLA Did you?

BLANCHE I'm not sure I got the soap out.

EUNICE Such fine hair!

BLANCHE [*accepting the compliment*] It's a problem. Didn't I get a call?

STELLA Who from, Blanche?

BLANCHE Shep Huntleigh . . .

STELLA Why, not yet, honey!

BLANCHE How strange! I—

[*At the sound of* BLANCHE's *voice* MITCH's *arm supporting his cards has sagged and his gaze is dissolved into space.* STANLEY *slaps him on the shoulder.*]

STANLEY   Hey, Mitch, come to!

[*The sound of this new voice shocks* BLANCHE. *She makes a shocked gesture, forming his name with her lips.* STELLA *nods and looks quickly away.* BLANCHE *stands quite still for some moments—the silver-backed mirror in her hand and a look of sorrowful perplexity as though all human experience shows on her face.* BLANCHE *finally speaks but with sudden hysteria.*]

BLANCHE   What's going on here?

[*She turns from* STELLA *to* EUNICE *and back to* STELLA. *Her rising voice penetrates the concentration of the game.* MITCH *ducks his head lower but* STANLEY *shoves back his chair as if about to rise.* STEVE *places a restraining hand on his arm.*]

BLANCHE [*continuing*]   What's happened here? I want an explanation of what's happened here.

STELLA [*agonizingly*]   Hush! Hush!

EUNICE   Hush! Hush! Honey.

STELLA   Please, Blanche.

BLANCHE   Why are you looking at me like that? Is something wrong with me?

EUNICE   You look wonderful, Blanche. Don't she look wonderful?

STELLA   Yes.

EUNICE   I understand you are going on a trip.

STELLA   Yes, Blanche *is*. She's going on a vacation.

EUNICE   I'm green with envy.

BLANCHE   Help me, help me get dressed!

STELLA [*handing her dress*]   Is this what you—

BLANCHE   Yes, it will do! I'm anxious to get out of here—this place is a trap!

EUNICE   What a pretty blue jacket.

STELLA   It's lilac colored.

BLANCHE   You're both mistaken. It's Della Robbia blue.[4] The blue of the robe in the old Madonna pictures. Are these grapes washed?

[*She fingers the bunch of grapes which* EUNICE *had brought in.*]

EUNICE   Huh?

BLANCHE   Washed, I said. Are they washed?

EUNICE   They're from the French Market.

BLANCHE   That doesn't mean they've been washed. [*The cathedral bells chime.*] Those cathedral bells—they're the only clean thing in the Quarter. Well, I'm going now. I'm ready to go.

EUNICE [*whispering*]   She's going to walk out before they get here.

STELLA   Wait, Blanche.

BLANCHE   I don't want to pass in front of those men.

EUNICE   Then wait'll the game breaks up.

STELLA   Sit down and . . .

[BLANCHE *turns weakly, hesitantly about. She lets them push her into a chair.*]

BLANCHE   I can smell the sea air. The rest of my time I'm going to spend on the sea. And when I die, I'm going to die on the sea. You know what I

---

4. A shade of light blue seen in terra cottas made by the Della Robbia family in the Italian Renaissance.

shall die of [*She plucks a grape.*] I shall die of eating an unwashed grape one day out on the ocean. I will die—with my hand in the hand of some nice-looking ship's doctor, a very young one with a small blond mustache and a big silver watch. "Poor lady," they'll say, "the quinine did her no good. That unwashed grape has transported her soul to heaven." [*The cathedral chimes are heard.*] And I'll be buried at sea sewn up in a clean white sack and dropped overboard—at noon—in the blaze of summer—and into an ocean as blue as [*chimes again*] my first lover's eyes!

> [*A* DOCTOR *and a* MATRON *have appeared around the corner of the building and climbed the steps to the porch. The gravity of their profession is exaggerated—the unmistakable aura of the state institution with its cynical detachment. The* DOCTOR *rings the doorbell. The murmur of the game is interrupted.*]

EUNICE [*whispering to* STELLA]   That must be them.

> [STELLA *presses her fists to her lips.*]

BLANCHE [*rising slowly*]   What is it?

EUNICE [*affectedly casual*]   Excuse me while I see who's at the door.

STELLA   Yes.

> [EUNICE *goes into the kitchen.*]

BLANCHE [*tensely*]   I wonder if it's for me.

> [*A whispered colloquy takes place at the door.*]

EUNICE [*returning, brightly*]   Someone is calling for Blanche.

BLANCHE   It *is* for me, then! [*She looks fearfully from one to the other and then to the portieres. The "Varsouviana" faintly plays.*] Is it the gentleman I was expecting from Dallas?

EUNICE   I think it is, Blanche.

BLANCHE   I'm not quite ready.

STELLA   Ask him to wait outside.

BLANCHE   I . . .

> [EUNICE *goes back to the portieres. Drums sound very softly.*]

STELLA   Everything packed?

BLANCHE   My silver toilet articles are still out.

STELLA   Ah!

EUNICE [*returning*]   They're waiting in front of the house.

BLANCHE   They! Who's "they"?

EUNICE   There's a lady with him.

BLANCHE   I cannot imagine who this "lady" could be! How is she dressed?

EUNICE   Just—just a sort of a—plain-tailored outfit.

BLANCHE   Possibly she's— [*Her voice dies out nervously.*]

STELLA   Shall we go, Blanche?

BLANCHE   Must we go through that room?

STELLA   I will go with you.

BLANCHE   How do I look?

STELLA   Lovely.

EUNICE [*echoing*]   Lovely.

> [BLANCHE *moves fearfully to the portieres.* EUNICE *draws them open for her.* BLANCHE *goes into the kitchen.*]

BLANCHE [*to the men*]   Please don't get up. I'm only passing through.

> [*She crosses quickly to outside door.* STELLA *and* EUNICE *follow. The poker players stand awkwardly at the table—all except* MITCH *who remains seated, looking down at the table.* BLANCHE *steps out on a small porch at the side of the door. She stops short and catches her breath.*]

DOCTOR   How do you do?

BLANCHE   You are not the gentleman I was expecting. [*She suddenly gasps and starts back up the steps. She stops by* STELLA, *who stands just outside the door, and speaks in a frightening whisper.*] That man isn't Shep Huntleigh.

　　　　[*The "Varsouviana" is playing distantly.* STELLA *stares back at* BLANCHE. EUNICE *is holding* STELLA'S *arm. There is a moment of silence—no sound but that of* STANLEY *steadily shuffling the cards.* BLANCHE *catches her breath again and slips back into the flat. She enters the flat with a peculiar smile, her eyes wide and brilliant. As soon as her sister goes past her,* STELLA *closes her eyes and clenches her hands.* EUNICE *throws her arms comfortingly about her. Then she starts up to her flat.* BLANCHE *stops just inside the door.* MITCH *keeps staring down at his hands on the table, but the other men look at her curiously. At last she starts around the table toward the bedroom. As she does,* STANLEY *suddenly pushes back his chair and rises as if to block her way. The* MATRON *follows her into the flat.*]

STANLEY   Did you forget something?

BLANCHE [*shrilly*]   Yes! Yes, I forgot something!

　　　　[*She rushes past him into the bedroom. Lurid reflections appear on the walls in odd, sinuous shapes. The "Varsouviana" is filtered into a weird distortion, accompanied by the cries and noises of the jungle.* BLANCHE *seizes the back of a chair as if to defend herself.*]

STANLEY [*sotto voce*][5]   Doc, you better go in.

DOCTOR [*sotto voce, motioning to the* MATRON]   Nurse, bring her out.

　　　　[*The* MATRON *advances on one side,* STANLEY *on the other. Divested of all the softer properties of womanhood, the* MATRON *is a peculiarly sinister figure in her severe dress. Her voice is bold and toneless as a firebell.*]

MATRON   Hello, Blanche.

　　　　[*The greeting is echoed and re-echoed by other mysterious voices behind the walls, as if reverberated through a canyon of rock.*]

STANLEY   She says that she forgot something.

　　　　[*The echo sounds in threatening whispers.*]

MATRON   That's all right.

STANLEY   What did you forget, Blanche?

BLANCHE   I—I—

MATRON   It don't matter. We can pick it up later.

STANLEY   Sure. We can send it along with the trunk.

BLANCHE [*retreating in panic*]   I don't know you—I don't know you. I want to be—left alone—please!

MATRON   Now, Blanche!

ECHOES [*rising and falling*]   Now, Blanche—now, Blanche—now, Blanche!

STANLEY   You left nothing here but spilt talcum and old empty perfume bottles—unless it's the paper lantern you want to take with you. You want the lantern?

　　　　[*He crosses to dressing table and seizes the paper lantern, tearing it off the light bulb, and extends it toward her. She cries out as if the lantern was herself. The* MATRON *steps boldly toward her. She screams and tries to break past the* MATRON. *All the men spring to their feet.* STELLA *runs out to the porch, with* EUNICE *following to comfort her, simultaneously*]

5. In an undertone [Italian].

with the confused voices of the men in the kitchen. STELLA *rushes into* EUNICE's *embrace on the porch.*]

STELLA   Oh, my God, Eunice help me! Don't let them do that to her, don't let them hurt her! Oh, God, oh, please God, don't hurt her! What are they doing to her? What are they doing? [*She tries to break from* EUNICE's *arms.*]

EUNICE   No, honey, no, no, honey. Stay here. Don't go back in there. Stay with me and don't look.

STELLA   What have I done to my sister? Oh, God, what have I done to my sister?

EUNICE   You done the right thing, the only thing you could do. She couldn't stay here; there wasn't no other place for her to go.

[*While* STELLA *and* EUNICE *are speaking on the porch the voices of the men in the kitchen overlap them.* MITCH *has started toward the bedroom.* STANLEY *crosses to block him.* STANLEY *pushes him aside.* MITCH *lunges and strikes at* STANLEY. STANLEY *pushes* MITCH *back.* MITCH *collapses at the table, sobbing. During the preceding scenes, the* MATRON *catches hold of* BLANCHE's *arm and prevents her flight.* BLANCHE *turns wildly and scratches at the* MATRON. *The heavy woman pinions her arms.* BLANCHE *cries out hoarsely and slips to her knees.*]

MATRON   These fingernails have to be trimmed. [*The* DOCTOR *comes into the room and she looks at him.*] Jacket, Doctor?

DOCTOR   Not unless necessary.

[*He takes off his hat and now he becomes personalized. The unhuman quality goes. His voice is gentle and reassuring as he crosses to* BLANCHE *and crouches in front of her. As he speaks her name, her terror subsides a little. The lurid reflections fade from the walls, the inhuman cries and noises die out and her own hoarse crying is calmed.*]

DOCTOR   Miss DuBois.

[*She turns her face to him and stares at him with desperate pleading. He smiles; then he speaks to the* MATRON.]

It won't be necessary.

BLANCHE [*faintly*]   Ask her to let go of me.

DOCTOR [*to the* MATRON]   Let go.

[*The* MATRON *releases her.* BLANCHE *extends her hands toward the* DOCTOR. *He draws her up gently and supports her with his arm and leads her through the portieres.*]

BLANCHE [*holding tight to his arm*]   Whoever you are—I have always depended on the kindness of strangers.

[*The poker players stand back as* BLANCHE *and the* DOCTOR *cross the kitchen to the front door. She allows him to lead her as if she were blind. As they go out on the porch,* STELLA *cries out her sister's name from where she is crouched a few steps up on the stairs.*]

STELLA   Blanche! Blanche, Blanche!

[BLANCHE *walks on without turning, followed by the* DOCTOR *and the* MATRON. *They go around the corner of the building.* EUNICE *descends to* STELLA *and places the child in her arms. It is wrapped in a pale blue blanket.* STELLA *accepts the child, sobbingly.* EUNICE *continues downstairs and enters the kitchen where the men, except for* STANLEY, *are returning silently to their places about the table.* STANLEY *has gone out on the porch and stands at the foot of the steps looking at* STELLA.]

STANLEY [*a bit uncertainly*]   Stella?

[*She sobs with inhuman abandon. There is something luxurious in her complete surrender to crying now that her sister is gone.*]

STANLEY [*voluptuously, soothingly*]   Now, honey. Now, love. Now, now, love. [*He kneels beside her and his fingers find the opening of her blouse.*] Now, now, love, Now, love. . . .

[*The luxurious sobbing, the sensual murmur fade away under the swelling music of the "Blue Piano" and the muted trumpet.*]

STEVE   This game is seven-card stud.

CURTAIN

1947

JOHN CHEEVER
1912–1982

"It seems to me that man's inclination toward light, toward brightness, is very nearly botanical—and I mean spiritual light. One not only needs it, one struggles for it." These sentences from an interview with John Cheever, conducted by the novelist John Hersey, at first glance look strange coming from a "*New Yorker*" writer of entertaining stories in which harried, well-to-do, white middle-class suburbanites conduct their lives. "Our Chekhov of the exurbs," he was dubbed by the reviewer John Leonard, with reference to the mythical community of Shady Hill (which Cheever created along the lines of existing ones in Fairfield, Connecticut, or Westchester County, New York). Yet Chekhov's own characters, living in darkness, aspire toward "spiritual fight," with a similarly "botanical" inclination. Trapped in their beautifully appointed houses and neighborhoods but carried along by the cool, effortless prose of their creator, Cheever's characters are viewed with a sympathetic irony, well-seasoned by sadness.

Cheever's early years were not notably idyllic, and he reveals little nostalgia for a lost childhood. Born in Quincy, Massachusetts, he grew up in what he describes as shabby gentility, with his father departing the family when his son was fifteen. (Cheever had an older brother, Fred, with whom he formed a strong but troubled relationship.) Two years later his father lost the family's money in the crash of 1929, and by that time Cheever had been expelled from Thayer Academy, in Braintree. The expulsion marked the end of his formal education and the beginning of his career as a writer; for, remarkably, he wrote a short story about the experience, titled it "Expelled," and sent it to the *New Republic*, where Malcolm Cowley (who would become a lifelong friend) published it.

During the 1930s Cheever lived in New York City, in impoverished circumstances, taking odd jobs to support himself and winning a fellowship to the writer's colony at Yaddo, in Saratoga Springs. His New York life would provide the material for many of his early stories, whose protagonists are rather frequently in desperate economic situations. With the coming of World War II, Cheever joined the armed forces and served in the Pacific theater but saw no combat. In 1941 he married Mary Winternitz. About the marriage, which produced three children and lasted through four decades, Cheever said, "That two people—both of us temperamental, quarrelsome, and intensely ambitious—could have gotten along for such a vast period of time is for me a very good example of the boundlessness of human nature." Meanwhile, with the help of Malcolm Cowley, he began to publish in the *New Yorker* and in 1943, while he was serving in the military, his first book of stories (*The Way Some People Live*) was published to favorable reviews. Over the decades to follow the stories continued to appear, largely in the *New Yorker*, where he became—along with J. D. Salinger and John Updike—a recurrent phenomenon. Five further volumes of short fiction were published, and in 1978 *The Stories of John Cheever* gathered those he wished to be remembered for.

Although he is praised for his skill as a realist depictor of suburban manners and morals, Cheever's art cannot be adequately understood in such terms. As Stephen C. Moore has usefully pointed out, "His best stories move from a base in a mimetic presentation of surface reality—the *scenery* of apparently successful American middle class life—to fables of heroism." Cheever's embattled heroes express themselves in taking up challenges that are essentially fabulous, and foolhardy: swimming home across the backyard pools of Westchester ("The Swimmer," printed here); performing feats of physical daredeviltry in suburban living rooms ("O Youth and Beauty"); or dealing with the myriad demands and temptations that beset the hero who, having escaped death in an airplane, returns home to more severe trials ("The Country Husband"). Whatever the specific narrative, we are always aware of the storyteller's art, shaping ordinary life into the odder, more willful figures of fantasy and romance.

While Cheever will be remembered primarily as a short-story writer, his output includes a respectable number of novels. In 1957 he won a National Book Award for his first one, *The Wapshot Chronicle* (it was followed by *The Wapshot Scandal*, in 1964), notable for its New England seacoast setting and domestic flavor, if less so for a continuously engaging narrative line. Perhaps his most gripping novel is *Bullet Park* (1969), which, like the best of the stories, is both realistic and fabulous. The suburban milieu, seen from the 5:42 train from New York, has never been depicted more accurately, even lovingly, by Cheever. And as is to be expected, his protagonist's carefully built, pious suburban existence turns out to be a mess. The novel provoked interesting disagreement about its merits (some critics felt the narrative manipulations both ruthless and sentimental), but there was no disagreement about the vivid quality of its represented life, on the commuter train or at the cocktail party. In the years just previous to his death, and after a bout with alcohol and drug addiction, Cheever published his two final novels, *Falconer* (1978) and *Oh What a Paradise It Seems* (1980), the former receiving much praise for its harrowing rendering of prison life. (Farragut, the novel's hero, is sent to Falconer Prison for killing his brother; Cheever lived in Ossining, New York, home of Sing Sing Prison, during his later years.)

From the beginning to the end of his career he was and remained a thoroughly professional writer, wary of pronouncing on the world at large (there is a noticeable absence of politics and ideology in his work) or on the meaning and significance of his own art. As one sees from his *Journals* (1991), he agonized over the disruptive facts of his alcoholism and his homosexuality. But he remained a private man, seemingly untouched by experiments—or fads—in fiction writing. Whether or not, as T. S. Eliot said about Henry James, he had a mind so fine that no idea could violate it, Cheever remained firmly resistant to ideas of all sorts. This insular tendency is probably a reason why his work makes less than a "major" claim on us, but it is also the condition responsible for his devoted and scrupulous attention to the particularities of middle-class life at the far edge of its promised dream.

This text of "The Swimmer" is from *The Brigadier and the Golf Widow* (1964).

The Swimmer

It was one of those midsummer Sundays when everyone sits around saying: "I *drank* too much last night." You might have heard it whispered by the parishioners leaving church, heard it from the lips of the priest himself, struggling with his cassock in the *vestiarium*,[1] heard it from the golf links and the tennis courts, heard it from the wildlife preserve where the leader of the Audubon group was suffering from a terrible hangover. "I *drank* too much," said Donald Westerhazy. "We all *drank* too much," said Lucinda Merrill. "It must have been the wine," said Helen Westerhazy. "I *drank* too much of that claret."

This was at the edge of the Westerhazys' pool. The pool, fed by an artesian well with a high iron content, was a pale shade of green. It was a fine day. In the west there was a massive stand of cumulus cloud so like a city seen from a distance—from the bow of an approaching ship—that it might have had a name. Lisbon. Hackensack.[2] The sun was hot. Neddy Merrill sat by the green water, one hand in it, one around a glass of gin. He was a slender man—he seemed to have the especial slenderness of youth—and while he was far from young he had slid down his banister that morning and given the bronze backside of Aphrodite[3] on the hall table a smack, as he jogged toward the smell of coffee in his dining room. He might have been compared to a summer's day, particularly the last hours of one, and while he lacked a tennis racket or a sail bag the impression was definitely one of youth, sport, and clement weather. He had been swimming and now he was breathing deeply, stertorously as if he could gulp into his lungs the components of that moment, the heat of the sun, the intenseness of his pleasure. It all seemed to flow into his chest. His own house stood in Bullet Park,[4] eight miles to the south, where his four beautiful daughters would have had their lunch and might be playing tennis. Then it occurred to him that by taking a dogleg to the southwest he could reach his home by water.

His life was not confining and the delight he took in this observation could not be explained by its suggestion of escape. He seemed to see, with a cartographer's eye, that string of swimming pools, that quasi-subterranean stream that curved across the county. He had made a discovery, a contribution to modern geography; he would name the stream Lucinda after his wife. He was not a practical joker nor was he a fool but he was determinedly original and had a vague and modest idea of himself as a legendary figure. The day was beautiful and it seemed to him that a long swim might enlarge and celebrate its beauty.

He took off a sweater that was hung over his shoulders and dove in. He had an inexplicable contempt for men who did not hurl themselves into pools. He swam a choppy crawl, breathing either with every stroke or every fourth stroke and counting somewhere well in the back of his mind the one-two one-two of a flutter kick. It was not a serviceable stroke for long distances but the domestication of swimming had saddled the sport with some customs and in his part of the world a crawl was customary. To be embraced and sustained by

---

1. Cloakroom for religious vestments adjacent to a church's sanctuary.
2. A town in New Jersey. Lisbon is the capital of Portugal.
3. Greek goddess of love and beauty.
4. Fictive suburb used as a location for many of Cheever's stories and novels.

the light green water was less a pleasure, it seemed, than the resumption of a natural condition, and he would have liked to swim without trunks, but this was not possible, considering his project. He hoisted himself up on the far curb—he never used the ladder—and started across the lawn. When Lucinda asked where he was going he said he was going to swim home.

The only maps and charts he had to go by were remembered or imaginary but these were clear enough. First there were the Grahams, the Hammers, the Lears, the Howlands, and the Crosscups. He would cross Ditmar Street to the Bunkers and come, after a short portage, to the Levys, the Welchers, and the public pool in Lancaster. Then there were the Hallorans, the Sachses, the Biswangers, Shirley Adams, the Gilmartins, and the Clydes. The day was lovely, and that he lived in a world so generously supplied with water seemed like a clemency, a beneficence. His heart was high and he ran across the grass. Making his way home by an uncommon route gave him the feeling that he was a pilgrim, an explorer, a man with a destiny, and he knew that he would find friends all along the way; friends would line the banks of the Lucinda River.

He went through a hedge that separated the Westerhazys' land from the Grahams', walked under some flowering apple trees, passed the shed that housed their pump and filter, and came out at the Grahams' pool. "Why, Neddy," Mrs. Graham said, "what a marvelous surprise. I've been trying to get you on the phone all morning. Here, let me get you a drink." He saw then, like any explorer, that the hospitable customs and traditions of the natives would have to be handled with diplomacy if he was ever going to reach his destination. He did not want to mystify or seem rude to the Grahams nor did he have the time to linger there. He swam the length of their pool and joined them in the sun and was rescued, a few minutes later, by the arrival of two carloads of friends from Connecticut. During the uproarious reunions he was able to slip away. He went down by the front of the Grahams' house, stepped over a thorny hedge, and crossed a vacant lot to the Hammers'. Mrs. Hammer, looking up from her roses, saw him swim by although she wasn't quite sure who it was. The Lears heard him splashing past the open windows of their living room. The Howlands and the Crosscups were away. After leaving the Howlands' he crossed Ditmar Street and started for the Bunkers', where he could hear, even at that distance, the noise of a party.

The water refracted the sound of voices and laughter and seemed to suspend it in midair. The Bunkers' pool was on a rise and he climbed some stairs to a terrace where twenty-five or thirty men and women were drinking. The only person in the water was Rusty Towers, who floated there on a rubber raft. Oh how bonny and lush were the banks of the Lucinda River! Prosperous men and women gathered by the sapphire-colored waters while caterer's men in white coats passed them cold gin. Overhead a red de Haviland trainer was circling around and around and around in the sky with something like the glee of a child in a swing. Ned felt a passing affection for the scene, a tenderness for the gathering, as if it was something he might touch. In the distance he heard thunder. As soon as Enid Bunker saw him she began to scream: "Oh look who's here! What a marvelous surprise! When Lucinda said that you couldn't come I thought I'd *die*." She made her way to him through the crowd, and when they had finished kissing she led him to the bar, a progress that was slowed by the fact that he stopped to kiss eight or ten other women and shake the hands of as many men. A smiling bartender he had

seen at a hundred parties gave him a gin and tonic and he stood by the bar for
a moment, anxious not to get stuck in any conversation that would delay his
voyage. When he seemed about to be surrounded he dove in and swam close
to the side to avoid colliding with Rusty's raft. At the far end of the pool he
bypassed the Tomlinsons with a broad smile and jogged up the garden path.
The gravel cut his feet but this was the only unpleasantness. The party was
confined to the pool, and as he went toward the house he heard the brilliant,
watery sound of voices fade, heard the noise of a radio from the Bunkers'
kitchen, where someone was listening to a ballgame. Sunday afternoon. He
made his way through the parked cars and down the grassy border of their
driveway to Alewives' Lane. He did not want to be seen on the road in his
bathing trunks but there was no traffic and he made the short distance to
the Levys' driveway, marked with a private property sign and a green tube
for the *New York Times*. All the doors and windows of the big house were
open but there were no signs of life; not even a dog barked. He went around
the side of the house to the pool and saw that the Levys had only recently
left. Glasses and bottles and dishes of nuts were on a table at the deep end,
where there was a bathhouse or gazebo, hung with Japanese lanterns. After
swimming the pool he got himself a glass and poured a drink. It was his
fourth or fifth drink and he had swum nearly half the length of the Lucinda
River. He felt tired, clean, and pleased at that moment to be alone; pleased
with everything.

It would storm. The stand of cumulus cloud—that city—had risen and
darkened, and while he sat there he heard the percussiveness of thunder
again. The de Haviland trainer was still circling overhead and it seemed to
Ned that he could almost hear the pilot laugh with pleasure in the afternoon; but when there was another peal of thunder he took off for home. A
train whistle blew and he wondered what time it had gotten to be. Four?
Five? He thought of the provincial station at that hour, where a waiter, his
tuxedo concealed by a raincoat, a dwarf with some flowers wrapped in newspaper, and a woman who had been crying would be waiting for the local. It
was suddenly growing dark; it was that moment when the pin-headed birds
seem to organize their song into some acute and knowledgeable recognition
of the storm's approach. Then there was a fine noise of rushing water from
the crown of an oak at his back, as if a spigot there had been turned. Then
the noise of fountains came from the crowns of all the tall trees. Why did he
love storms, what was the meaning of his excitement when the door sprang
open and the rain wind fled rudely up the stairs, why had the simple task of
shutting the windows of an old house seemed fitting and urgent, why did the
first watery notes of a storm wind have for him the unmistakable sound of
good news, cheer, glad tidings? Then there was an explosion, a smell of cordite, and rain lashed the Japanese lanterns that Mrs. Levy had bought in
Kyoto the year before last, or was it the year before that?

He stayed in the Levys' gazebo until the storm had passed. The rain had
cooled the air and he shivered. The force of the wind had stripped a maple
of its red and yellow leaves and scattered them over the grass and the water.
Since it was midsummer the tree must be blighted, and yet he felt a peculiar sadness at this sign of autumn. He braced his shoulders, emptied his
glass, and started for the Welchers' pool. This meant crossing the Lindleys'
riding ring and he was surprised to find it overgrown with grass and all the
jumps dismantled. He wondered if the Lindleys had sold their horses or

gone away for the summer and put them out to board. He seemed to remember having heard something about the Lindleys and their horses but the memory was unclear. On he went, barefoot through the wet grass, to the Welchers', where he found their pool was dry.

This breach in his chain of water disappointed him absurdly, and he felt like some explorer who seeks a torrential headwater and finds a dead stream. He was disappointed and mystified. It was common enough to go away for the summer but no one ever drained his pool. The Welchers had definitely gone away. The pool furniture was folded, stacked, and covered with a tarpaulin. The bathhouse was locked. All the windows of the house were shut, and when he went around to the driveway in front he saw a for-sale sign nailed to a tree. When had he last heard from the Welchers—when, that is, had he and Lucinda last regretted an invitation to dine with them? It seemed only a week or so ago. Was his memory failing or had he so disciplined it in the repression of unpleasant facts that he had damaged his sense of the truth? Then in the distance he heard the sound of a tennis game. This cheered him, cleared away all his apprehensions and let him regard the overcast sky and the cold air with indifference. This was the day that Neddy Merrill swam across the county. That was the day! He started off then for his most difficult portage.

Had you gone for a Sunday afternoon ride that day you might have seen him, close to naked, standing on the shoulders of route 424, waiting for a chance to cross. You might have wondered if he was the victim of foul play, had his car broken down, or was he merely a fool. Standing barefoot in the deposits of the highway—beer cans, rags, and blowout patches—exposed to all kinds of ridicule, he seemed pitiful. He had known when he started that this was a part of his journey—it had been on his maps—but confronted with the lines of traffic, worming through the summery light, he found himself unprepared. He was laughed at, jeered at, a beer can was thrown at him, and he had no dignity or humor to bring to the situation. He could have gone back, back to the Westerhazys', where Lucinda would still be sitting in the sun. He had signed nothing, vowed nothing, pledged nothing, not even to himself. Why, believing as he did, that all human obduracy was susceptible to common sense, was he unable to turn back? Why was he determined to complete his journey even if it meant putting his life in danger? At what point had this prank, this joke, this piece of horseplay become serious? He could not go back, he could not even recall with any clearness the green water at the Westerhazys', the sense of inhaling the day's components, the friendly and relaxed voices saying that they had *drunk* too much. In the space of an hour, more or less, he had covered a distance that made his return impossible.

An old man, tooling down the highway at fifteen miles an hour, let him get to the middle of the road, where there was a grass divider. Here he was exposed to the ridicule of the northbound traffic, but after ten or fifteen minutes he was able to cross. From here he had only a short walk to the Recreation Center at the edge of the Village of Lancaster, where there were some handball courts and a public pool.

The effect of the water on voices, the illusion of brilliance and suspense, was the same here as it had been at the Bunkers' but the sounds here were louder, harsher, and more shrill, and as soon as he entered the crowded enclosure he was confronted with regimentation. "ALL SWIMMERS MUST TAKE

A SHOWER BEFORE USING THE POOL. ALL SWIMMERS MUST USE THE FOOTBATH. ALL SWIMMERS MUST WEAR THEIR IDENTIFICATION DISKS." He took a shower, washed his feet in a cloudy and bitter solution and made his way to the edge of the water. It stank of chlorine and looked to him like a sink. A pair of lifeguards in a pair of towers blew police whistles at what seemed to be regular intervals and abused the swimmers through a public address system. Neddy remembered the sapphire water at the Bunkers' with longing and thought that he might contaminate himself—damage his own prosperousness and charm—by swimming in this murk, but he reminded himself that he was an explorer, a pilgrim, and that this was merely a stagnant bend in the Lucinda River. He dove, scowling with distaste, into the chlorine and had to swim with his head above water to avoid collisions, but even so he was bumped into, splashed and jostled. When he got to the shallow end both lifeguards were shouting at him: "Hey, you, you without the identification disk, get outa the water." He did, but they had no way of pursuing him and he went through the reek of suntan oil and chlorine out through the hurricane fence and passed the handball courts. By crossing the road he entered the wooded part of the Halloran estate. The woods were not cleared and the footing was treacherous and difficult until he reached the lawn and the clipped beech hedge that encircled their pool.

The Hallorans were friends, an elderly couple of enormous wealth who seemed to bask in the suspicion that they might be Communists. They were zealous reformers but they were not Communists, and yet when they were accused, as they sometimes were, of subversion, it seemed to gratify and excite them. Their beech hedge was yellow and he guessed this had been blighted like the Levys' maple. He called hullo, hullo, to warn the Hallorans of his approach, to palliate his invasion of their privacy. The Hallorans, for reasons that had never been explained to him, did not wear bathing suits. No explanations were in order, really. Their nakedness was a detail in their uncompromising zeal for reform and he stepped politely out of his trunks before he went through the opening in the hedge.

Mrs. Halloran, a stout woman with white hair and a serene face, was reading the *Times*. Mr. Halloran was taking beech leaves out of the water with a scoop. They seemed not surprised or displeased to see him. Their pool was perhaps the oldest in the county, a fieldstone rectangle, fed by a brook. It had no filter or pump and its waters were the opaque gold of the stream.

"I'm swimming across the county," Ned said.

"Why, I didn't know one could," exclaimed Mrs. Halloran.

"Well, I've made it from the Westerhazys'," Ned said. "That must be about four miles."

He left his trunks at the deep end, walked to the shallow end, and swam this stretch. As he was pulling himself out of the water he heard Mrs. Halloran say: "We've been *terribly* sorry to hear about all your misfortunes, Neddy."

"My misfortunes?" Ned asked. "I don't know what you mean."

"Why, we heard that you'd sold the house and that your poor children . . ."

"I don't recall having sold the house," Ned said, "and the girls are at home."

"Yes," Mrs. Halloran sighed. "Yes . . ." Her voice filled the air with an unseasonable melancholy and Ned spoke briskly. "Thank you for the swim."

"Well, have a nice trip," said Mrs. Halloran.

Beyond the hedge he pulled on his trunks and fastened them. They were loose and he wondered if, during the space of an afternoon, he could have lost some weight. He was cold and he was tired and the naked Hallorans and their dark water had depressed him. The swim was too much for his strength but how could he have guessed this, sliding down the banister that morning and sitting in the Westerhazys' sun? His arms were lame. His legs felt rubbery and ached at the joints. The worst of it was the cold in his bones and the feeling that he might never be warm again. Leaves were falling down around him and he smelled woodsmoke on the wind. Who would be burning wood at this time of year?

He needed a drink. Whiskey would warm him, pick him up, carry him through the last of his journey, refresh his feeling that it was original and valorous to swim across the county. Channel swimmers took brandy. He needed a stimulant. He crossed the lawn in front of the Hallorans' house and went down a little path to where they had built a house for their only daughter Helen and her husband Eric Sachs. The Sachses' pool was small and he found Helen and her husband there.

"Oh, *Neddy*," Helen said. "Did you lunch at Mother's?"

"Not *really*," Ned said. "I *did* stop to see your parents." This seemed to be explanation enough. "I'm terribly sorry to break in on you like this but I've taken a chill and I wonder if you'd give me a drink."

"Why, I'd *love* to," Helen said, "but there hasn't been anything in this house to drink since Eric's operation. That was three years ago."

Was he losing his memory, had his gift for concealing painful facts let him forget that he had sold his house, that his children were in trouble, and that his friend had been ill? His eyes slipped from Eric's face to his abdomen, where he saw three pale, sutured scars, two of them at least a foot long. Gone was his navel, and what, Neddy thought, would the roving hand, bed-checking one's gifts at 3 A.M. make of a belly with no navel, no link to birth, this breach in the succession?

"I'm sure you can get a drink at the Biswangers'," Helen said. "They're having an enormous do. You can hear it from here. Listen!"

She raised her head and from across the road, the lawns, the gardens, the woods, the fields, he heard again the brilliant noise of voices over water. "Well, I'll get wet," he said, still feeling that he had no freedom of choice about his means of travel. He dove into the Sachses' cold water and, gasping, close to drowning, made his way from one end of the pool to the other. "Lucinda and I want *terribly* to see you," he said over his shoulder, his face set toward the Biswangers'. "We're sorry it's been so long and we'll call you *very* soon."

He crossed some fields to the Biswangers' and the sounds of revelry there. They would be honored to give him a drink, they would be happy to give him a drink, they would in fact be lucky to give him a drink. The Biswangers invited him and Lucinda for dinner four times a year, six weeks in advance. They were always rebuffed and yet they continued to send out their invitations, unwilling to comprehend the rigid and undemocratic realities of their society. They were the sort of people who discussed the price of things at cocktails, exchanged market tips during dinner, and after dinner told dirty stories to mixed company. They did not belong to Neddy's set—they were not even on Lucinda's Christmas card list. He went toward their pool with feelings of indifference, charity, and some unease, since it seemed to be getting dark and these were the longest days of the year. The party when he joined it was noisy and large. Grace Biswanger was the kind of hostess who asked the optometrist, the veterinarian, the real-estate dealer and the dentist. No one was swimming and the twilight, reflected on the water of the pool, had a wintry gleam. There was a bar and he started for this. When Grace Biswanger saw him she came toward him, not affectionately as he had every right to expect, but bellicosely.

"Why, this party has everything," she said loudly, "including a gate crasher."

She could not deal him a social blow—there was no question about this and he did not flinch. "As a gate crasher," he asked politely, "do I rate a drink?"

"Suit yourself," she said. "You don't seem to pay much attention to invitations."

She turned her back on him and joined some guests, and he went to the bar and ordered a whiskey. The bartender served him but he served him rudely. His was a world in which the caterer's men kept the social score, and to be rebuffed by a part-time barkeep meant that he had suffered some loss of social esteem. Or perhaps the man was new and uninformed. Then he heard Grace at his back say: "They went for broke overnight—nothing but income— and he showed up drunk one Sunday and asked us to loan him five thousand dollars. . . ." She was always talking about money. It was worse than eating your peas off a knife. He dove into the pool, swam its length and went away.

The next pool on his list, the last but two, belonged to his old mistress, Shirley Adams. If he had suffered any injuries at the Biswangers' they would be cured here. Love—sexual roughhouse in fact—was the supreme elixir, the painkiller, the brightly colored pill that would put the spring back into his step, the joy of life in his heart. They had had an affair last week, last month, last year. He couldn't remember. It was he who had broken it off, his was the upper hand, and he stepped through the gate of the wall that surrounded her pool with nothing so considered as self-confidence. It seemed in a way to be his pool as the lover, particularly the illicit lover, enjoys the possessions of his mistress with an authority unknown to holy matrimony. She was there, her hair the color of brass, but her figure, at the edge of the lighted, cerulean water, excited in him no profound memories. It had been, he thought, a light-hearted affair, although she had wept when he broke it off. She seemed confused to see him and he wondered if she was still wounded. Would she, God forbid, weep again?

"What do you want?" she asked.

"I'm swimming across the county."

"Good Christ. Will you ever grow up?"

"What's the matter?"

"If you've come here for money," she said, "I won't give you another cent."

"You could give me a drink."

"I could but I won't. I'm not alone."

"Well, I'm on my way."

He dove in and swam the pool, but when he tried to haul himself up onto the curb he found that the strength in his arms and his shoulders had gone, and he paddled to the ladder and climbed out. Looking over his shoulder he saw, in the lighted bathhouse, a young man. Going out onto the dark lawn he smelled chrysanthemums or marigolds—some stubborn autumnal fragrance—on the night air, strong as gas. Looking overhead he saw that the stars had come out, but why should he seem to see Andromeda, Cepheus, and Cassiopeia? What had become of the constellations of midsummer? He began to cry.

It was probably the first time in his adult life that he had ever cried, certainly the first time in his life that he had ever felt so miserable, cold, tired, and bewildered. He could not understand the rudeness of the caterer's barkeep or the rudeness of a mistress who had come to him on her knees and showered his trousers with tears. He had swum too long, he had been immersed too long, and his nose and his throat were sore from the water. What he needed then was a drink, some company, and some clean dry clothes, and while he could have cut directly across the road to his home he went on to the Gilmartins' pool. Here, for the first time in his life, he did not dive but went down the steps into the icy water and swam a hobbled side stroke that he might have learned as a youth. He staggered with fatigue on his way to the Clydes' and paddled the length of their pool, stopping again and again with his hand on the curb to rest. He climbed up the ladder and wondered if he had the strength to get home. He had done what he wanted, he had swum the county, but he was so stupefied with exhaustion that his triumph seemed vague. Stooped, holding onto the gateposts for support, he turned up the driveway of his house.

The place was dark. Was it so late that they had all gone to bed? Had Lucinda stayed at the Westerhazys' for supper? Had the girls joined her there or gone someplace else? Hadn't they agreed, as they usually did on Sunday, to regret all their invitations and stay at home? He tried the garage doors to see what cars were in but the doors were locked and rust came off the handles onto his hands. Going toward the house, he saw that the force of the thunderstorm had knocked one of the rain gutters loose. It hung down over the front door like an umbrella rib, but it could be fixed in the morning. The house was locked, and he thought that the stupid cook or the stupid maid must have locked the place up until he remembered that it had been some time since they had employed a maid or a cook. He shouted, pounded on the door, tried to force it with his shoulder, and then, looking in at the windows, saw that the place was empty.

1964

ROBERT HAYDEN
1913–1980

"Hayden is by far the best chronicler and rememberer of the African American heritage in these Americas that I know of," the poet Michael Harper, whose own sense of history is indebted to Robert Hayden's work, has said. Hayden's poems save what has vanished, what has been lost to standard histories, like a 1920s prizefighter from the Midwest ("Free Fantasia: Tiger Flowers") or a miner trapped in Crystal Cave ("Beginnings, V"). He records the loss of what others never noticed as missing, and in their recovery he discovers a significance in the passing moment, the passed-over figure, the inarticulate gesture, which lasts through time. Always, in his words, "opposed to the chauvinistic and the doctrinaire" in art, he cherished the freedom of the poet to write about whatever seized the imagination. But his imagination was in its nature elegiac and historical. As he remembers and re-creates the African American heritage, he speaks to the struggles of the individual spirit for freedom and to painful self-divisions known to the people of many times and places. But if the circumstances he confronts in his poems are often harsh, his work captures the energy and joyfulness that make survival possible.

Born in Detroit, Michigan, Hayden grew up in a poor neighborhood called by its inhabitants, with affectionate irony, "Paradise Valley." His powerful sequence *Elegies for Paradise Valley* (1978) resurrects the neighborhood in its racial and ethnic mix. Memory for Hayden is an act of love that leads to self-awareness; in this sequence and in poems like "Those Winter Sundays," he writes about his own past, confronts its pain, and preserves its sustaining moments of happiness.

Hayden had a deep understanding of the conflicts that divide the self. His family history gave him an early acquaintance with such self-division: his parents' marriage ended when he was young, and his mother left him in the care of foster parents (whose surname he adopted) when she left Detroit to look for work. He remained with the Haydens even after his mother returned to Detroit when he was a teenager and lived for a period with his foster family until conflict arose between her and his foster mother. "I lived in the midst of so much turmoil all the time I didn't know if I loved or hated," he once said. As an African American and as a poet Hayden also lived between worlds. He courageously maintained his sense of vocation through years of critical neglect and amid the demands of full-time teaching at Fisk University from 1946 to 1968. He published his first book, *Heart-Shape in the Dust*, in 1940, but his mature work did not appear in quantity until his volume *Ballad of Remembrance* (1962). At the same time his belief that the poet should not be restricted by any set of themes, racial or otherwise, and the highly formal quality of his work led to criticism by some young African American writers in the 1960s. But Hayden never abandoned his belief in the power of art to speak universally. In a 1974 interview he told Dennis Gendron of rereading Yeats's poem "Easter 1916" in the wake of the riots in Detroit— "that is the kind of poetry I want to write," he said, in admiration of the ways Yeats conceived a particular historical and political moment so that it speaks across time and place.

In fact, Hayden did himself write that kind of poetry. His most famous poem, "Middle Passage," demonstrates his transfiguring imagination and the knowledge of historical documents, which began early in his career. In 1936, after leaving college because of increasingly difficult economic conditions, Hayden joined the Federal Writers Project of the Works Progress Administration, and for two years he researched the history of abolition movements and the Underground Railroad in Michigan. "Middle Passage" is a collage of accounts of the slave ships that transported men and women from Africa into slavery in the New World. Through the multiple voices in the poem, Hayden lets the accounts of those who participated in (and profited from) the slave trade reveal the evidence of their own damnation. The blindness that attacks one of the ships becomes a symbol of the devastating suffering of those transported into slavery and of the moral blindness everywhere evident in the traders' accounts. The collage technique allows Hayden to suggest the fragmentation of the story; the silences in the poem evoke the missing voices of those who suffered and died on the voyages or in the intolerable conditions of slavery. At the heart of the poem is the account of a rebellion led by one of the slaves (Cinquez) on the ship *Amistad*. Cinquez is one of several figures in Hayden's poems who dramatize "The deep immortal human wish / the timeless will" ("Middle Passage") that for Hayden is the indomitable yearning for freedom. This "timeless will" and struggle also appear in his poems about Harriet Tubman ("Runagate Runagate"), Nat Turner, Frederick Douglass, Phillis Wheatley, and the later figures Paul Robeson and Bessie Smith.

Hayden's experiment with collage technique in "Middle Passage" connects him to modernist poets like T. S. Eliot and William Carlos Williams and to an African American tradition acutely aware of the power of voice. He continued to experiment with poetic form and with the creation of different voices, always testing the possibilities of craft and forging a language to express what he knew and felt. His sequences *Beginnings* and *Elegies for Paradise Valley* demonstrate his formal originality, as does his late poem "American Journal," with its long lines and its approximation to prose. Hayden loved language and was unafraid to be lushly descriptive as well as to be precisely imagistic. His work summons us to notice the world as we had not before and offers us candor, clearsightedness, and a transforming gaiety.

From 1968 until his death Hayden was professor of English at the University of Michigan at Ann Arbor. In 1976 he became the first African American to be appointed poetry consultant to the Library of Congress, the position now known as poet laureate of the United States.

Middle Passage[1]

I

Jesús, Estrella, Esperanza, Mercy[2]

Sails flashing to the wind like weapons,
sharks following the moans the fever and the dying;
horror the corposant and compass rose.[3]

Middle Passage: 5
        voyage through death
                to life upon these shores.

"10 April 1800—
Blacks rebellious. Crew uneasy. Our linguist says
their moaning is a prayer for death,   10
ours and their own. Some try to starve themselves.
Lost three this morning leaped with crazy laughter
to the waiting sharks, sang as they went under."

Desire, Adventure, Tartar, Ann:

Standing to America, bringing home   15
black gold, black ivory, black seed.

        Deep in the festering hold thy father lies,
        of his bones New England pews are made,
        those are altar lights that were his eyes.[4]

---

1. Main route for the slave trade in the Atlantic between Africa and the West Indies.
2. Names of slave ships. (*Estrella* and *Esperanza* are Spanish for "Star" and "Hope," respectively.)
3. Circle printed on a map showing compass directions. "Corposant": a fiery luminousness that can appear on the decks of ships during electrical storms.
4. "Full fathom five thy father lies; / Of his bones are coral made; / Those are pearls that were his eyes" (Shakespeare's *Tempest* 1.2.400–02). The sprite Ariel is singing about the supposed death by drowning of the king of Naples.

Jesus   Saviour   Pilot   Me   20
Over   Life's   Tempestuous   Sea[5]

We pray that Thou wilt grant, O Lord,
safe passage to our vessels bringing
heathen souls unto Thy chastening.

Jesus   Saviour   25

    "8 bells. I cannot sleep, for I am sick
    with fear, but writing eases fear a little
    since still my eyes can see these words take shape
    upon the page & so I write, as one
    would turn to exorcism. 4 days scudding,   30
    but now the sea is calm again. Misfortune
    follows in our wake like sharks (our grinning
    tutelary gods). Which one of us
    has killed an albatross?[6] A plague among
    our blacks—Ophthalmia: blindness—& we   35
    have jettisoned the blind to no avail.
    It spreads, the terrifying sickness spreads.
    Its claws have scratched sight from the Capt.'s eyes
    & there is blindness in the fo'c'sle[7]
    & we must sail 3 weeks before we come   40
    to port."

        What port awaits us, Davy Jones'
        or home? I've heard of slavers drifting, drifting,
        playthings of wind and storm and chance, their crews
        gone blind, the jungle hatred   45
        crawling up on deck.

Thou   Who   Walked   On   Galilee

    "Deponent further sayeth *The Bella J*
    left the Guinea Coast
    with cargo of five hundred blacks and odd   50
    for the barracoons[8] of Florida:

    "That there was hardly room 'tween-decks for half
    the sweltering cattle stowed spoon-fashion there;
    that some went mad of thirst and tore their flesh
    and sucked the blood: 55

    "That Crew and Captain lusted with the comeliest
    of the savage girls kept naked in the cabins;
    that there was one they called The Guinea Rose
    and they cast lots and fought to lie with her:

---

5. Words from a Protestant hymn.
6. A bird of good omen; to kill one is an unlucky
and impious act (as in Samuel Taylor Coleridge's
Rime of the Ancient Mariner).

7. Short for forecastle, the place in a ship where
sailors are quartered.
8. Barracks or enclosures for slaves.

"That when the Bo's'n piped all hands,[9] the flames   60
spreading from starboard already were beyond
control, the negroes howling and their chains
entangled with the flames:

"That the burning blacks could not be reached,
that the Crew abandoned ship,   65
leaving their shrieking negresses behind,
that the Captain perished drunken with the wenches:

"Further Deponent sayeth not."

Pilot   Oh   Pilot   Me

II

Aye, lad, and I have seen those factories,   70
Gambia, Rio Pongo, Calabar;[1]
have watched the artful mongos[2] baiting traps
of war wherein the victor and the vanquished

Were caught as prizes for our barracoons.
Have seen the nigger kings whose vanity   75
and greed turned wild black hides of Fellatah,
Mandingo, Ibo, Kru[3] to gold for us.

And there was one—King Anthracite we named him—
fetish face beneath French parasols
of brass and orange velvet, impudent mouth   80
whose cups were carven skulls of enemies:

He'd honor us with drum and feast and conjo[4]
and palm-oil-glistening wenches deft in love,
and for tin crowns that shone with paste,
red calico and German-silver trinkets   85

Would have the drums talk war and send
his warriors to burn the sleeping villages
and kill the sick and old and lead the young
in coffles[5] to our factories.

Twenty years a trader, twenty years,   90
for there was wealth aplenty to be harvested
from those black fields, and I'd be trading still
but for the fevers melting down my bones.

---

9. I.e., when the boatswain (petty officer aboard
a ship) signaled to summon all the crew on deck.
1. A city in southeast Nigeria. Gambia is a river
and nation in West Africa. Rio Pongo is a watercourse, dry for most of the year, in East Africa.

2. I.e., Africans.
3. African tribes.
4. Dance.
5. Train of slaves fastened together.

III

Shuttles in the rocking loom of history,
the dark ships move, the dark ships move,   95
their bright ironical names
like jests of kindness on a murderer's mouth;
plough through thrashing glister toward
fata morgana's lucent melting shore,
weave toward New World littorals[6] that are   100
mirage and myth and actual shore.

Voyage through death,
                    voyage whose chartings are unlove.

A charnel stench, effluvium of living death
spreads outward from the hold,   105
where the living and the dead, the horribly dying,
lie interlocked, lie foul with blood and excrement.

> *Deep in the festering hold thy father lies,*
> *the corpse of mercy rots with him,*
> *rats eat love's rotten gelid eyes.*   110

But, oh, the living look at you
with human eyes whose suffering accuses you,
whose hatred reaches through the swill of dark
to strike you like a leper's claw.

You cannot stare that hatred down   115
or chain the fear that stalks the watches
and breathes on you its fetid scorching breath;
cannot kill the deep immortal human wish,
the timeless will.

> "But for the storm that flung up barriers   120
> of wind and wave, *The Amistad,*[7] señores,
> would have reached the port or Príncipe in two,
> three days at most; but for the storm we should
> have been prepared for what befell.
> Swift as the puma's leap it came. There was   125
> that interval of moonless calm filled only
> with the water's and the rigging's usual sounds,
> then sudden movement, blows and snarling cries
> and they had fallen on us with machete
> and marlinspike. It was as though the very   130
> air, the night itself were striking us.
> Exhausted by the rigors of the storm,
> we were no match for them. Our men went down
> before the murderous Africans. Our loyal

---

6. Coastal regions. "Fata morgana": mirage.
7. A Spanish ship—the name means "Friendship"—that carried fifty-three illegally obtained
slaves out of Havana, Cuba, in July 1839. The
slaves revolted and seized the ship.

Celestino ran from below with gun   135
and lantern and I saw, before the cane-
knife's wounding flash, Cinquez,
that surly brute who calls himself a prince,
directing, urging on the ghastly work.[8]
He hacked the poor mulatto down, and then   140
he turned on me. The decks were slippery
when daylight finally came. It sickens me
to think of what I saw, of how these apes
threw overboard the butchered bodies of
our men, true Christians all, like so much jetsam.   145
Enough, enough. The rest is quickly told:
Cinquez was forced to spare the two of us
you see to steer the ship to Africa,
and we like phantoms doomed to rove the sea
voyaged east by day and west by night,   150
deceiving them, hoping for rescue,
prisoners on our own vessel, till
at length we drifted to the shores of this
your land, America, where we were freed
from our unspeakable misery. Now we   155
demand, good sirs, the extradition of
Cinquez and his accomplices to La
Havana.[9] And it distresses us to know
there are so many here who seem inclined
to justify the mutiny of these blacks.   160
We find it paradoxical indeed
that you whose wealth, whose tree of liberty
are rooted in the labor of your slaves
should suffer the august John Quincy Adams
to speak with so much passion of the right   165
of chattel slaves to kill their lawful masters
and with his Roman rhetoric weave a hero's
garland for Cinquez.[1] I tell you that
we are determined to return to Cuba
with our slaves and there see justice done. Cinquez—   170
or let us say 'the Prince'—Cinquez shall die."

The deep immortal human wish,
the timeless will:

Cinquez its deathless primaveral image,
life that transfigures many lives.   175

Voyage through death
        to life upon these shores.

                                              1962

---

8. During the mutiny the Africans, led by a man called Cinqué, or Cinquez, killed the captain, his slave Celestino, and the mate, but spared the two slave owners.

9. After two months the *Amistad* reached Long Island Sound, where it was detained by the American ship *Washington*, the slaves were imprisoned, and the owners were freed. The owners began litigation to return the slaves to Havana to be tried for murder.

1. The case reached the Supreme Court in 1841; the Africans were defended by former president John Quincy Adams, and the court released the thirty-seven survivors to return to Africa.

Homage to the Empress of the Blues[1]

Because there was a man somewhere in a candystripe silk shirt,
gracile and dangerous as a jaguar and because a woman moaned for him
in sixty-watt gloom and mourned him Faithless Love
Twotiming Love Oh Love Oh Careless Aggravating Love,

     She came out on the stage in yards of pearls, emerging like   5
     a favorite scenic view, flashed her golden smile and sang.

Because grey laths began somewhere to show from underneath
torn hurdygurdy[2] lithographs of dollfaced heaven;
and because there were those who feared alarming fists of snow
on the door and those who feared the riot-squad of statistics,   10

     She came out on the stage in ostrich feathers, beaded satin,
     and shone that smile on us and sang.

                                   1962

Those Winter Sundays

     Sundays too my father got up early
     and put his clothes on in the blueblack cold,
     then with cracked hands that ached
     from labor in the weekday weather made
     banked fires blaze. No one ever thanked him.   5

     I'd wake and hear the cold splintering, breaking.
     When the rooms were warm, he'd call,
     and slowly I would rise and dress,
     fearing the chronic angers of that house,

     Speaking indifferently to him,   10
     who had driven out the cold
     and polished my good shoes as well.
     What did I know, what did I know
     of love's austere and lonely offices?

                                   1962

---

1. Bessie Smith (1895–1937), one of the greatest American blues singers. Her flamboyant style, which grew out of the black vaudeville tradition, made her popular in the 1920s.

2. A disreputable kind of dance hall. "Laths": the strips of wood that form a backing for wall plaster.

RANDALL JARRELL

1914–1965

"Monstrously knowing and monstrously innocent. . . . A Wordsworth with the obsession of a Lewis Carroll"—so Robert Lowell once described his friend and fellow poet Randall Jarrell. Jarrell was a teacher and a critic as well as a poet, and for many writers of his generation—Lowell, Delmore Schwartz, and John Berryman among them—he was the critic whose taste was most unerring, who seemed to know instantly what was genuine and what was not. An extraordinary teacher, he loved the activity of teaching, both in and out of the classroom; "the gods who had taken away the poet's audience had given him students," he once said. The novelist Peter Taylor recalls that when he came to Vanderbilt University as a freshman in the mid-1930s, Jarrell, then a graduate student, had already turned the literary students into disciples; he held court discussing Chekhov on the sidelines of touch football games. For all his brilliance Jarrell was, at heart, democratic. Believing that poetry belongs to every life, his teaching, his literary criticism, and his poetry aimed to recapture and reeducate a general audience lost to poetry in an age of specialization. Jarrell's interests were democratic as well, and he had a lifelong fascination with popular culture. Witty and incisive, Jarrell could be intimidating; at the same time he remained deeply in touch with childhood's mystery and enchantment. It was as if, his close friend the philosopher Hannah Arendt once said, he "had emerged from the enchanted forests." He loved fairy tales, translated a number of them, and wrote several books for children, among them *The Bat-Poet* (1964). The childlike quality of the person informs Jarrell's poems as well; he is unembarrassed by the adult heart still in thrall to childhood's wishes.

Jarrell was born in Nashville, Tennessee, but spent much of his childhood in Long Beach, California. When his parents divorced, he, then eleven, remained for a year with his grandparents in Hollywood, then returned to live with his mother in Nashville. He majored in psychology at Vanderbilt and stayed on there to do graduate work in English. In 1937 he left Nashville to teach at Kenyon College (Gambier, Ohio) at the invitation of his old Vanderbilt professor John Crowe Ransom, the New Critic and Fugitive poet. From that time on Jarrell almost always had some connection with a university: after Kenyon, the University of Texas, Sarah Lawrence College, and from 1947 until his death, the Women's College of the University of North Carolina at Greensboro. But, as his novel *Pictures from an Institution* (1954) with its mixed satiric and tender views of academic life suggests, he was never satisfied with a cloistered education. As poetry editor of *The Nation* (1946), and then in a series of essays and reviews collected as *Poetry and the Age* (1953), he introduced readers to the work of his contemporaries—Elizabeth Bishop, Robert Lowell, John Berryman, the William Carlos Williams of *Paterson*—and influentially reassessed the reputations of Whitman and Robert Frost.

Among the poets who emerged after World War II, Jarrell stands out for his colloquial plainness. While others—Richard Wilbur and the early Robert Lowell, for example—were writing highly structured poems with complicated imagery, Jarrell's work feels and sounds close to what he calls in one poem the "dailiness of life" ("Well Water"). He is master of the everyday heartbreak and identifies with ordinary forms of loneliness. Jarrell's gift of imaginative sympathy appears in the treatment of soldiers in his war poems, the strongest to come out of World War II. He had been trained as an Army Air Force pilot and after that as a control operator, and he had a sense of the war's special casualties. With their under-

The Gotham Book Mart. This midtown Manhattan store was famous for its literary eminences. A December 1948 party drew a roomful of midcentury writers, including, clockwise, W. H. Auden on the ladder, Elizabeth Bishop, Delmore Schwartz, Randall Jarrell, Charles Henri Ford, William Rose Benét, Stephen Spender, Marya Zaturenska, Horace Gregory, Tennessee Williams, Richard Eberhart, Gore Vidal, and José Garcia Villa.

standing of soldiers as both destructive and innocent at the same time, these poems make his volumes *Little Friend, Little Friend* (1945) and *Losses* (1948) powerful and moving. Jarrell also empathized with the dreams, loneliness, and disappointments of women, whose perspective he often adopted, as in the title poem of his collection *The Woman at the Washington Zoo* (1960) and his poem "Next Day."

Against the blasted or unrealized possibilities of adult life Jarrell often poised the rich mysteries of childhood. The title poem of his last book, *The Lost World* (1965), looks back to his Los Angeles playtime, the movie sets and plaster dinosaurs and pterodactyls against whose eternal light-hearted presence he measures his own aging. The poem has Jarrell's characteristic sense or loss but also his capacity for a mysterious happiness, which animates the poem even as he holds "nothing" in his hands.

Jarrell suffered a nervous breakdown in February 1965, but returned to teaching that fall. In October he was struck down by a car and died. His *Complete Poems* were published posthumously (1969), as were a translation of Goethe's *Faust*, Part I, in preparation at his death, and two books of essays, *The Third Book of Criticism* (1969) and *Kipling, Auden & Co.* (1980).

The Death of the Ball Turret Gunner[1]

From my mother's sleep I fell into the State,
And I hunched in its belly till my wet fur froze.
Six miles from earth, loosed from its dream of life,
I woke to black flak[2] and the nightmare fighters.
When I died they washed me out of the turret with a hose.   5

1945

Second Air Force

Far off, above the plain the summer dries,
The great loops of the hangars sway like hills.
Buses and weariness and loss, the nodding soldiers
Are wire, the bare frame building, and a pass
To what was hers; her head hides his square patch   5
And she thinks heavily: My son is grown.
She sees a world: sand roads, tar-paper barracks,
The bubbling asphalt of the runways, sage,
The dunes rising to the interminable ranges,
The dim flights moving over clouds like clouds.   10
The armorers in their patched faded green,
Sweat-stiffened, banded with brass cartridges,
Walk to the line; their Fortresses,[1] all tail,
Stand wrong and flimsy on their skinny legs,
And the crews climb to them clumsily as bears.   15
The head withdraws into its hatch (a boy's),
The engines rise to their blind laboring roar,
And the green, made beasts run home to air.
Now in each aspect death is pure.
(At twilight they wink over men like stars   20
And hour by hour, through the night, some see
The great lights floating in—from Mars, from Mars.)
How emptily the watchers see them gone.

They go, there is silence; the woman and her son
Stand in the forest of the shadows, and the light   25
Washes them like water. In the long-sunken city
Of evening, the sunlight stills like sleep
The faint wonder of the drowned; in the evening,
In the last dreaming light, so fresh, so old,
The soldiers pass like beasts, unquestioning,   30
And the watcher for an instant understands

1. A ball turret was a plexiglass sphere set into the belly of a B-17 or B-24 [bomber], and inhabited by two .50 caliber machine-guns and one man, a short, small man. When this gunner tracked with his machine-guns a fighter attacking his bomber from below, he revolved with the turret; hunched upside-down in his little sphere, he looked like the foetus in the womb. The fighters which attacked him were armed with cannon firing explosive shells. The hose was a steam hose [Jarrell's note].
2. Antiaircraft fire.
1. Flying Fortresses, a type of bomber in World War II.

What there is then no need to understand;
But she wakes from her knowledge, and her stare,
A shadow now, moves emptily among
The shadows learning in their shadowy fields   35
The empty missions.
                            Remembering,
She hears the bomber calling, *Little Friend!*[2]
To the fighter hanging in the hostile sky,
And sees the ragged flame eat, rib by rib,   40
Along the metal of the wing into her heart:
The lives stream out, blossom, and float steadily
To the flames of the earth, the flames
That burn like stars above the lands of men.

She saves from the twilight that takes everything   45
A squadron shipping, in its last parade—
Its dogs run by it, barking at the band—
A gunner walking to his barracks, half-asleep,
Starting at something, stumbling (above, invisible,
The crews in the steady winter of the sky   50
Tremble in their wired fur); and feels for them
The love of life for life. The hopeful cells
Heavy with someone else's death, cold carriers
Of someone else's victory, grope past their lives
Into her own bewilderment: The years meant *this*?   55

But for them the bombers answer everything.

                                                    1945

Thinking of the Lost World

This spoonful of chocolate tapioca
Tastes like—like peanut butter, like the vanilla
Extract Mama told me not to drink.
Swallowing the spoonful, I have already traveled
Through time to my childhood. It puzzles me   5
That age is like it.
                    Come back to that calm country
Through which the stream of my life first meandered,
My wife, our cat, and I sit here and see
Squirrels quarreling in the feeder, a mockingbird   10
Copying our chipmunk, as our end copies
Its beginning.
               Back in Los Angeles, we missed
Los Angeles. The sunshine of the Land

---

2. In "Second Air Force" the woman visiting her son remembers what she has read on the front page of her newspaper the week before, a conversation between a bomber, in flames over Germany, and one of the fighters protecting it: "Then I heard the bomber call me in: 'Little Friend, Little Friend, I got two engines on fire. Can you see me, Little Friend?' I said, 'I'm crossing right over you. Let's go home'" [Jarrell's note].

Of Sunshine is a gray mist now, the atmosphere 15
Of some factory planet: when you stand and look
You see a block or two, and your eyes water.
The orange groves are all cut down . . . My bow
Is lost, all my arrows are lost or broken,
My knife is sunk in the eucalyptus tree 20
Too far for even Pop to get it out,
And the tree's sawed down. It and the stair-sticks
And the planks of the tree house are all firewood
Burned long ago; its gray smoke smells of Vicks.[1]

Twenty Years After, thirty-five years after, 25
Is as good as ever—better than ever,
Now that D'Artagnan[2] is no longer old—
Except that it is unbelievable.
I say to my old self: "I believe. Help thou
Mine unbelief." 30
          I believe the dinosaur
Or pterodactyl's married the pink sphinx
And lives with those Indians in the undiscovered
Country between California and Arizona
That the mad girl told me she was princess of— 35
Looking at me with the eyes of a lion,
Big, golden, without human understanding,
As she threw paper-wads from the back seat
Of the car in which I drove her with her mother
From the jail in Waycross to the hospital 40
In Daytona. If I took my eyes from the road
And looked back into her eyes, the car would—I'd be—

Or if only I could find a crystal set[3]
Sometimes, surely, I could still hear their chief
Reading to them from Dumas or *Amazing Stories*; 45
If I could find in some Museum of Cars
Mama's dark blue Buick, Lucky's electric,
Couldn't I be driven there? Hold out to them,
The paraffin half picked out, Tawny's dewclaw—
And have walk to me from among their wigwams 50
My tall brown aunt, to whisper to me: "Dead?
They told you I was dead?"
                As if you could die!
If I never saw you, never again
Wrote to you, even, after a few years, 55
How often you've visited me, having put on,
As a mermaid puts on her sealskin, another face
And voice, that don't fool me for a minute—
That are yours for good . . . All of them are gone
Except for me; and for me nothing is gone— 60
The chicken's body is still going round

1. A remedy for colds.
2. Hero of *The Three Musketeers* (1844), by Alexandre Dumas *père*; its sequel was *Twenty Years*

After (1845).
3. Old-fashioned radio receiver.

And round in widening circles, a satellite
From which, as the sun sets, the scientist bends
A look of evil on the unsuspecting earth.
Mama and Pop and Dandeen are still there   65
In the Gay Twenties.
                        The Gay Twenties! You say
The Gay Nineties . . . But it's all right: they *were* gay,
O so gay! A certain number of years after,
Any time is Gay, to the new ones who ask: 70
"Was that the first World War or the second?"
Moving between the first world and the second,
I hear a boy call, now that my beard's gray:
"Santa Claus! Hi, Santa Claus!" It *is* miraculous
To have the children call you Santa Claus.   75
I wave back. When my hand drops to the wheel,
It is brown and spotted, and its nails are ridged
Like Mama's. Where's my own hand? My smooth
White bitten-fingernailed one? I seem to see
A shape in tennis shoes and khaki riding-pants   80
Standing there empty-handed; I reach out to it
Empty-handed, my hand comes back empty,
And yet my emptiness is traded for its emptiness,
I have found that Lost World in the Lost and Found
Columns whose gray illegible advertisements   85
My soul has memorized world after world:
LOST—NOTHING. STRAYED FROM NOWHERE. NO REWARD.
I hold in my own hands, in happiness,
Nothing: the nothing for which there's no reward.

                                                                    1965

JOHN BERRYMAN
1914–1972

From a generation whose ideal poem was short, self-contained, and ironic, John Berryman emerged as the author of two extended and passionate works: "Homage to Mistress Bradstreet" and the lyric sequence *The Dream Songs*. It was as if Berryman needed more space than the single lyric provided—a larger theater in which to play out an unrelenting psychic drama. He had written shorter poems—songs and sonnets—but his discovery of large-scale dramatic situations and strange new voices astonished his contemporaries.

Berryman seemed fated to intense suffering and self-preoccupation. His father, a banker, shot himself outside his son's window when the boy was twelve. The suicide haunted Berryman to the end of his own life, which also came by suicide. Berryman, who was born John Smith, took a new name from his stepfather, also a banker. His childhood was a series of displacements: ten years near McAlester,

Oklahoma, then Tampa, Florida, and after his father's suicide, Gloucester, Massachusetts, and New York City. His mother's second marriage ended in divorce, but his stepfather sent him to private school in Connecticut. Berryman graduated from Columbia College in 1936 and won a fellowship to Clare College, Cambridge, England.

He was later to say of himself, "I masquerade as a writer. Actually I am a scholar." However misleading this may be about his poetry, it reminds us that all his life Berryman drew nourishment from teaching—at Wayne State, at Harvard (1940–43), then off and on at Princeton, and from 1955 until his death, at the University of Minnesota. He chose to teach not creative writing but literature and the "history of civilization," and he claimed that such teaching forced him into areas in which he would not otherwise have done detailed work. A mixture of bookishness and wildness characterizes all his writing: five years of research lay behind the intensities of "Homage to Mistress Bradstreet," while an important constituent of "huffy Henry's" personality in *The Dream Songs* is his professorial awkwardness and exhibitionism.

Berryman seemed drawn to borrowing identities in his poetry. In his first important volume, *The Dispossessed* (1948), he had experimented with various dramatic voices in the short poems "Nervous Songs: The Song of the Demented Priest," "A Professor's Song," "The Song of the Tortured Girl," and "The Song of the Man Forsaken and Obsessed." The *dispossession* of the book's title had two opposite and urgent meanings for him: "the miserable, *put out of one's own*, and the relieved, saved, undevilled, de-spelled." Taking on such roles was for Berryman both a revelation of his castout, fatherless state and an exorcism of it. It was perhaps in that spirit that he entered into an imaginary dialogue with what he felt as the kindred nature of the Puritan poet Anne Bradstreet. "Both of our worlds unhanded us." What started out to be a poem of fifty lines emerged as the fifty-seven stanzas of "Homage to Mistress Bradstreet" (1956), a work so absorbing that after completing it Berryman claimed to be "a ruin for two years." It was not Bradstreet's poetry that engaged him. Quite the contrary: he was fascinated by the contrast between her "bald abstract rime" and her life of passionate suffering. The poem explores the kinship between Bradstreet and Berryman as figures of turbulence and rebellion.

Berryman took literary encouragement from another American poet of the past, Stephen Crane, about whom he wrote a book-length critical study in 1950. Crane's poems, he said, have "the character of a 'dream,' something seen naively in a new relation." Berryman's attraction to a poetry that accommodated the nightmare antics of the dream world became apparent in his own long work, *The Dream Songs*. It was modeled, he claimed, on "the greatest American poem," Whitman's "Song of Myself," in which the speaker assumes a fluid, ever-changing persona. *77 Dream Songs* was published in 1964. Additional poems, to a total of 385, appeared in *His Toy, His Dream, His Rest* (1968). (Some uncollected dream songs were published posthumously in *Henry's Fate*, 1977, and drafts of others remained in manuscript.) Obvious links exist between Berryman and other so-called confessional writers such as Robert Lowell, Sylvia Plath, and Anne Sexton. But the special autobiographical flavor of *The Dream Songs* is that of a psychic vaudeville; as in dreams, the poet represents himself through a fluid series of *alter egos*, whose voices often flow into one another in single poems. One of these voices is that of a blackface minstrel, and Berryman's appropriation of this dialect prompted Michael Harper's poem "Tongue-Tied in Black and White," written both as homage to Berryman and as part of Harper's quarrel with the use of "that needful black idiom offending me" ("Tongue-Tied in Black and White"). Despite the suffering that these poems enact, Berryman seemed to find a secret strength through the staginess, variety, resourcefulness, and renewals of these poems.

The Dream Songs brought Berryman a success that was not entirely beneficial. The collection *Love and Fame* (1970) shows him beguiled by his own celebrity and wrestling with some of its temptations. In an unfinished, posthumously published novel, *Recovery*, he portrays himself as increasingly prey to alcoholism. Berryman had been married twice before, and his hospitalization for drinking and for periods of insanity had put a strain on his third marriage. He came to distrust his poetry as a form of exhibitionism and was clearly, in his use of the discipline of prose and in the prayers that crowd his last two volumes of poetry (*Delusions, Etc.* appeared posthumously), in search of some new and humbling style. Having been raised a strict Catholic and fallen away from the church, he tried to return to it in his last years, speaking of his need for a "God of rescue." On January 7, 1972, Berryman committed suicide by leaping from a Minneapolis bridge.

Homage to Mistress Bradstreet

Anne Bradstreet ("Born 1612 Anne Dudley, married at 16 Simon Bradstreet, a Cambridge man, steward to the Countess of Warwick and protege of her father Thomas Dudley secretary to the Earl of Lincoln. Crossed in the *Arbella*, 1630, under Governor Winthrop" [Berryman's note]) came to the Massachusetts Bay Colony when she was eighteen years old. She was one of the first poets on American soil. Of this poem, Berryman says:

> An American historian somewhere observes that all colonial settlements are intensely conservative, *except* in the initial break-off point (whether religious, political, legal, or whatever). Trying to do justice to both parts of this obvious truth—which I came upon only after the poem was finished—I concentrated upon the second and the poem laid itself out in a series of rebellions. I had her rebel first against the new environment and above all against her barrenness (which in fact lasted for years), then against her marriage (which in fact seems to have been brilliantly happy), and finally against her continuing life of illness, loss, and age. These are the three large sections of the poem; they are preceded and followed by an exordium and coda, of four stanzas each, spoken by the "I" of the twentieth-century poet, which modulates into her voice, who speaks most of the poem. Such is the plan. Each rebellion, of course, is succeeded by submission, although even in the moment of the poem's supreme triumph—the presentment, too long to quote now, of the birth of her first child—rebellion survives.

Berryman wrote two stanzas of the poem and found himself stalled for five years, during which he gathered material, until he discovered the strategy of dialogue and inserted himself in the poem. "Homage to Mistress Bradstreet" was first published in *Partisan Review* in 1953, but did not appear as a book until 1956.

In his exordium (stanzas 1–4), the poet makes an intense identification between himself and Bradstreet, both of them alienated by hardship or circumstance from those around them: "We are on each other's hands / who care. Both of our worlds unhanded us." The identification is so complete that in the subsequent stanzas he hears her voice recounting the tribulations of life in a new country, her yearnings for the England she left behind, her lonely dedication to her poetry, and the personal suffering in her early barrenness and miscarriages. Stanza 17 continues in Bradstreet's voice.

From Homage to Mistress Bradstreet

* * *

17

The winters close, Springs open, no child stirs
under my withering heart, O seasoned heart   130
God grudged his aid.
All things else soil like a shirt.
Simon is much away. My executive[1] stales.
The town came through for the cartway by the pales,[2]
but my patience is short,   135
I revolt from, I am like, these savage foresters

18

whose passionless dicker in the shade, whose glance
impassive & scant, belie their murderous cries
when quarry seems to show.
Again I must have been wrong, twice.[3]   140
Unwell in a new way. Can that begin?
God brandishes. O love, O I love. Kin,
gather. My world is strange
and merciful, ingrown months, blessing a swelling trance.[4]

19

So squeezed, wince you I scream? I love you & hate   145
off with you. Ages! *Useless.* Below my waist
he has me in Hell's vise.
Stalling. He let go. Come back: brace
me somewhere. No. No. Yes! everything down
hardens I press with horrible joy down   150
my back cracks like a wrist
shame I am voiding oh behind it is too late

20

hide me forever I work thrust I must free
now I all muscles & bones concentrate
what is living from dying?   155
Simon I must leave you so untidy
Monster you are killing me Be sure
I'll have you later Women do endure
I can *can* no longer
and it passes the wretched trap whelming and I am me 160

---

1. Power to act.
2. Stockade fence.
3. One of the several allusions to her failure to become pregnant.
4. Her first child was not born until about 1633 [Berryman's note].

21

drencht & powerful, I did it with my body!
One proud tug greens Heaven. Marvellous,
unforbidding Majesty.
Swell, imperious bells. I fly.
Mountainous, woman not breaks and will bend: 165
sways God nearby: anguish comes to an end.
Blossomed Sarah,[5] and I
blossom. Is that thing alive? I hear a famisht howl.

22

Beloved household, I am Simon's wife,
and the mother of Samuel—whom greedy yet I miss   170
out of his kicking place.
More in some ways I feel at a loss,
freer. Cantabanks & mummers,[6] nears
longing for you. Our chopping[7] scores my ears,
our costume bores my eyes.   175
St. George[8] to the good sword, rise! chop-logic's rife

23

& fever & Satan & Satan's ancient fere.[9]
Pioneering is not feeling well,
not Indians, beasts.
Not all their riddling can forestall   180
one leaving. Sam, your uncle has had to
go from us to live with God. 'Then Aunt went too?'
Dear, she does wait still.
Stricken: 'Oh. Then he takes us one by one.' My dear.

24

Forswearing it otherwise, they starch their minds.   185
Folkmoots, & blether, blether. John Cotton rakes[1]
to the synod of Cambridge.[2]
Down from my body my legs flow,
out from it arms wave, on it my head shakes.
Now Mistress Hutchinson rings forth a call—   190
should she? many creep out a broken wall—
affirming the Holy Ghost
dwells in one justified. Factioning passion blinds

---

5. Wife of Abraham, barren until old age, when she gave birth to Isaac (Genesis 17.19).
6. Ballad singers and mimes.
7. *Chopping*: disputing, snapping, haggling; axing [Berryman's note].
8. Patron saint of England; the slayer of dragons.
9. *Fere*: his friend Death [Berryman's note].
1. "*Rakes*: inclines, as a mast; bows" [Berryman's

note]. "Folkmoots": a town assembly for debate. "Blether": nonsense.
2. In the first synod (a body for religious debate), Cotton agreed to the condemnation and banishment of his follower Anne Hutchinson. Her heresies included a deemphasis of perfect moral conduct as evidence of the justification for Christian salvation.

25

all to all her good, all—can she be exiled?
Bitter sister, victim! I miss you.   195
—I miss you, Anne,[3]
day or night weak as a child,
tender & empty, doomed, quick to no tryst.
—I hear you. Be kind, you who leaguer[4]
my image in the mist.   200
—Be kind you, to one unchained eager far & wild

26

and if, O my love, my heart is breaking, please
neglect my cries and I will spare you. Deep
in Time's grave, Love's, you lie still.
Lie still.—Now? That happy shape   205
my forehead had under my most long, rare,
ravendark, hidden, soft bodiless hair
you award me still.
You must not love me, but I do not bid you cease.

27

Veiled my eyes, attending. How can it be I?   210
Moist, with parted lips, I listen, wicked.
I shake in the morning & retch.
Brood I do on myself naked.
A fading world I dust, with fingers new.
—I have earned the right to be alone with you.   215
—What right can that be?
Convulsing, if you love, enough, like a sweet lie.

28

Not that, I know, you can. This cratered skin,
like the crabs & shells of my Palissy[5] ewer, touch!
Oh, you do, you do?   220
Falls on me what I like a witch,
for lawless holds, annihilations of law
which Time and he and man abhor, foresaw:
sharper than what my Friend[6]
brought me for my revolt when I moved smooth & thin,   225

3. One might say: He [the poet] is enabled to speak, at last, in the fortune of an echo of her—and when she is loneliest (her former spiritual adviser [John Cotton] having deserted Anne Hutchinson, and this her [Bradstreet's] closest friend banished), as if she had summoned him; and only thus, perhaps, is she enabled to hear him. This second section of the poem is a dialogue, his voice however ceasing well before it ends at [line] 307, and hers continuing for the whole third part until the coda ([stanzas] 54–57) [Berryman's note].
4. Beleaguer, besiege.
5. Bernard Palissy (1510–1590), French Protestant ceramicist noted for special glazes and highly ornamented pieces.
6. Allusion to the punishments of God visited on those who rebel against him (cf. Isaiah 1.6).

29

faintings black, rigour, chilling, brown
parching, back, brain burning, the grey pocks
itch, a manic stench
of pustules snapping, pain floods the palm,
sleepless, or a red shaft with a dreadful start   230
rides at the chapel, like a slipping heart.
My soul strains in one qualm
ah but *this* is not to save me but to throw me down.

30

And out of this I lull. It lessens. Kiss me.
That once. As sings out up in sparkling dark   235
a trail of a star & dies,
while the breath flutters, sounding, mark,
so shorn ought such caresses to us be
who, deserving nothing, flush and flee
the darkness of that light,   240
a lurching frozen from a warm dream. Talk to me.

31[7]

—It is Spring's New England. Pussy willows wedge
up in the wet. Milky crestings, fringed
yellow, in heaven, eyed
by the melting hand-in-hand or mere   245
desirers single, heavy-footed, rapt,
make surge poor human hearts. Venus is trapt—
the hefty pike shifts, sheer[8]—
in Orion blazing. Warblings, odours, nudge to an edge—

32

—Ravishing, ha, what crouches outside ought,   250
flamboyant, ill, angelic. Often, now,
I am afraid of you.
I am a sobersides; I know.
I *want* to take you for my lover.—Do.
—I hear a madness. Harmless I to you   255
am not, not I?—No.
—I cannot but be. Sing a concord of our thought.

---

7. Berryman (in *Poets on Poetry*) called this speech of the poet to Bradstreet "an only half-subdued aria-stanza."
8. Lines 246–47 are opposed images of the bottom of the sea against the summit of the sky, as imaged by the planet Venus and the constellation Orion. "Sheer" in the sense of "invisible" (quoted from comments by Berryman in the Italian translation of "Mistress Bradstreet" by Sergio Perosa).

33

—Wan dolls in indigo on gold:[9] refrain
my western lust. I am drowning in this past.
I lose sight of you   260
who mistress me from air. Unbraced
in delirium of the grand depths,[1] giving away
haunters what kept me, I breathe solid spray.
—I am losing you!
Straiten me on.[2]—I suffered living like a stain: 265

34

I trundle the bodies, on the iron bars,
over that fire backward & forth; they burn;
bits fall. I wonder if
I killed them. Women serve my turn.
—Dreams! You are good.—No.—Dense with hardihood   270
the wicked are dislodged, and lodged the good.
In green space we are safe.
God awaits us (but I am yielding) who Hell wars.

35

—I cannot feel myself God waits. He flies
nearer a kindly world; or he is flown.   275
One Saturday's rescue[3]
won't show. Man is entirely alone
may be. I am a man of griefs & fits
trying to be my friend. And the brown smock splits,
down the pale flesh a gash   280
broadens and Time holds up your heart against my eyes.

36

—Hard and divided heaven! creases me. Shame
is failing. My breath is scented, and I throw
hostile glances towards God.
Crumpling plunge of a pestle, bray:[4]   285
sin cross & opposite, wherein I survive
nightmares of Eden. Reaches foul & live

---

9. Cf., on Byzantine icons [here, the impassive Madonnas painted against gold backgrounds in medieval altarpieces of the Eastern Church], Frederick Rolfe ("Baron Corvo"): "Who ever dreams of praying (with expectation of response) for the prayer of a Tintoretto or a Titian, or a Bellini, or a Botticelli? But who can refrain from crying 'O Mother!' to these unruffleable wan dolls in indigo on gold?" (quoted from *The Desire and Pursuit of the Whole* by Graham Greene in *The Last Childhood*) [Berryman's note].
1. "Délires des grandes profondeurs," described by [the twentieth-century French marine explorer Jacques-Yves] Cousteau and others; a euphoria, sometimes fatal, in which the hallucinated diver offers passing fish his line, helmet, anything [Berryman's note; he translates the French phrase in line 262].
2. I.e., tighten your embrace.
3. As of cliffhangers, movie serials wherein each week's episode ends with a train bearing down on the strapped heroine or with the hero dangling over an abyss into which Indians above him peer with satisfaction before they hatchet the rope; *rescue*: forcible recovery (by the owner) of goods distrained [Berryman's note].
4. Punning (according to Berryman's notes) on (1) the pulverizing action of a mortar and pestle and (2) the strident noise of a donkey.

he for me, this soul
to crunch, a minute tangle of eternal flame.

37

I fear Hell's hammer-wind. But fear does wane.   290
Death's blossoms grain my hair; I cannot live.
A black joy clashes
joy, in twilight. The Devil said
'I will deal toward her softly, and her enchanting cries
will fool the horns of Adam.'[5] Father of lies,   295
a male great pestle smashes
small women swarming towards the mortar's rim in vain.

38

I see the cruel spread Wings black with saints!
Silky my breasts not his, mine, mine to withhold
or tender, tender.   300
I am sifting, nervous, and bold.
The light is changing. Surrender this loveliness
you cannot make me do. *But* I will. Yes.
What horror, down stormy air,
warps towards me? My threatening promise faints   305

39[6]

torture me, Father, lest not I be thine!
Tribunal terrible & pure, my God,
mercy for him and me.
Faces half-fanged, Christ drives abroad,
and though the crop hopes, Jane[7] is so slipshod   310
I cry. Evil dissolves, & love, like foam;
that love. Prattle of children powers me home,
my heart claps like the swan's
under a frenzy of *who* love me & who shine.[8]

*   *   *

1953, 1956

---

5. Referring to Satan's temptation of Eve, who was to eat the apple from the Tree of Knowledge and then convince Adam to do so (cf. Genesis 3).
6. The stanza is unsettled, like [stanza] 24, by a middle line, signaling a broad transition [Berryman's note].
7. A servant.
8. The final stanzas present Bradstreet's intensi-fied vision of death and damnation and include the death of her father, blaspheming. But in the last four stanzas the poem modulates back into the poet's voice and his vow to keep Bradstreet alive in his loving memory and in his writing. "Hover, utter, still, a sourcing whom my lost candle like the firefly loves."

FROM THE DREAM SONGS[1]

29

There sat down, once, a thing on Henry's heart
so heavy, if he had a hundred years
& more, & weeping, sleepless, in all them time
Henry could not make good.
Starts again always in Henry's ears   5
the little cough somewhere, an odour, a chime.

And there is another thing he has in mind
like a grave Sienese face[2] a thousand years
would fail to blur the still profiled reproach of. Ghastly,
with open eyes, he attends, blind.   10
All the bells say: too late. This is not for tears;
thinking.

But never did Henry, as he thought he did,
end anyone and hacks her body up
and hide the pieces, where they may be found.   15
He knows: he went over everyone, & nobody's missing.
Often he reckons, in the dawn, them up.
Nobody is ever missing.

45

He stared at ruin. Ruin stared straight back.
He thought they was old friends. He felt on the stair
where her papa found them bare
they became familiar. When the papers were lost
rich with pals' secrets, he thought he had the knack   5
of ruin. Their paths crossed

and once they crossed in jail; they crossed in bed;
and over an unsigned letter their eyes met,
and in an Asian city
directionless & lurchy at two & three,   10
or trembling to a telephone's fresh threat,
and when some wired his head

---

1. These poems were written over a period of thirteen years. (*77 Dream Songs* was published in 1964, and the remaining poems appeared in *His Toy, His Dream, His Rest* in 1968. Some uncollected dream songs were included in the volume *Henry's Fate*, which appeared five years after Berryman committed suicide in 1972.) Berryman placed an introductory note at the head of *His Toy, His Dream, His Rest*: "The poem then, whatever its wide cast of characters, is essentially about an imaginary character (not the poet, not me) named Henry, a white American in early middle age sometimes in blackface, who has suffered an irreversible loss and talks about himself sometimes in the first person, sometimes in the third, sometimes even in the second; he has a friend, never named, who addresses him as Mr. Bones and variants thereof. Requiescant in pace."
2. Allusion to the somber, austere mosaiclike religious portraits by the Italian painters who worked in Siena during the 13th and 14th centuries.

to reach a wrong opinion, 'Epileptic'.
But he noted now that: they were not old friends.
He did not know this one.   15
This one was a stranger, come to make amends
for all the imposters, and to make it stick.
Henry nodded, un-.

384

The marker slants, flowerless, day's almost done,
I stand above my father's grave with rage,
often, often before
I've made this awful pilgrimage to one
who cannot visit me, who tore his page   5
out: I come back for more,

I spit upon this dreadful banker's grave
who shot his heart out in a Florida dawn
O ho alas alas
When will indifference come, I moan & rave   10
I'd like to scrabble till I got right down
away down under the grass

and ax the casket open ha to see
just how he's taking it, which he sought so hard
we'll tear apart   15
the mouldering grave clothes ha & then Henry
will heft the ax once more, his final card,
and fell it on the start.

                                                                  1968

RALPH ELLISON
1914–1994

" If the Negro, or any other writer, is going to do what's expected of him, he's lost the battle before he takes the field." This remark of Ralph Ellison's, taken from his *Paris Review* interview of 1953, serves in more than one sense as an appropriate motto for his own career. He did not do what his critics, literary or political, suggested that he ought to, but insisted on being a writer rather than a spokesman for a cause or a representative figure. His importance to American letters is partly due to this independence. He also did the unexpected, however, in not following his fine first novel with the others that were predicted. While maintaining a strong

Ellison, Langston Hughes, and James Baldwin at the Newport Jazz Festival in 1958.

presence on the literary scene by writing essays on a wide variety of social and cultural issues, Ellison published only excerpts from his work in progress: a massive novel that may well have run to three volumes, a single book of which was assembled after his death and published as *Juneteenth* (1999), later expanded as *Three Days Before the Shooting . . .* (2010).

Ellison was born in Oklahoma; grew up in Oklahoma City; won a state scholarship; and attended the Tuskegee Institute, where he was a music major, his instrument the trumpet. His musical life was wide enough to embrace both "serious music" and the world of Southwest–Kansas City jazz just reaching its heyday when Ellison was a young man. He became friends with the blues singer Jimmy Rushing and was acquainted with other members of what would be the great Count Basie band of the 1930s; this "deep, rowdy stream of jazz" figured for him as an image of the power and control that constituted art. Although he was a serious student of music and composition, his literary inclinations eventually dominated his musical ones; but testimony to his abiding knowledge and love of music may be found in some of the essays in his collection *Shadow and Act* (1964).

Ellison left Tuskegee and went north to New York City. There, in 1936, he met the novelist Richard Wright, who encouraged him as a writer, and Ellison began to publish reviews and short stories. *Invisible Man*, begun in 1945, was published seven years later and won the National Book Award. Ellison subsequently received a number of awards and lectureships; taught at the Salzburg Seminar, at Bard College, and at the University of Chicago; and in 1970 was named Albert Schweitzer Professor of the Humanities at New York University, where he taught until his retirement. Yet he admitted to being troubled by the terms in which *Invisible Man's* success—and perhaps his own career as well—were defined. In the *Paris Review* interview he deprecatingly referred to his novel as largely a failure, wished that rather than a "statement" about the American Negro it could be read "simply as a novel," and hoped that in twenty years it would be so read, casually adding, "if it's around that long."

Invisible Man may have outlived Ellison's expectations, but not without suffering attacks from critics. The most powerful of these, Irving Howe, took the author to task for not following Richard Wright's lead and devoting his fiction to the Negro cause. Howe believed that African Americans should write social protest novels about the tragedy of black ghetto life. *Invisible Man* had used its protagonist's "invisibility" to entertain a much broader range of possibilities; and though by no means socially irresponsible, the novel is dedicated to the richness of life and art that becomes possible when the imagination is liberated from close realism.

From Invisible Man

Chapter I

[BATTLE ROYAL]

It goes a long way back, some twenty years. All my life I had been looking for something, and everywhere I turned someone tried to tell me what it was. I accepted their answers too, though they were often in contradiction and even self-contradictory. I was naïve. I was looking for myself and asking everyone except myself questions which I, and only I, could answer. It took me a long time and much painful boomeranging of my expectations to achieve a realization everyone else appears to have been born with: That I am nobody but myself. But first I had to discover that I am an invisible man!

And yet I am no freak of nature, nor of history. I was in the cards, other things having been equal (or unequal) eighty-five years ago. I am not ashamed of my grandparents for having been slaves. I am only ashamed of myself for having at one time been ashamed. About eighty-five years ago they were told that they were free, united with others of our country in everything pertaining to the common good, and, in everything social, separate like the fingers of the hand. And they believed it. They exulted in it. They stayed in their place, worked hard, and brought up my father to do the same. But my grandfather is the one. He was an odd old guy, my grandfather, and I am told I take after him. It was he who caused the trouble. On his deathbed he called my father to him and said, "Son, after I'm gone I want you to keep up the good fight. I never told you, but our life is a war and I have been a traitor all my born days, a spy in the enemy's country ever since I give up my gun back in the Reconstruction. Live with your head in the lion's mouth. I want you to overcome 'em with yeses, undermine 'em with grins, agree 'em to death and destruction, let 'em swoller you till they vomit or bust wide open." They thought the old man had gone out of his mind. He had been the meekest of men. The younger children were rushed from the room, the shades drawn and the flame of the lamp turned so low that it sputtered on the wick like the old man's breathing. "Learn it to the younguns," he whispered fiercely; then he died.

But my folks were more alarmed over his last words than over his dying. It was as though he had not died at all, his words caused so much anxiety. I was warned emphatically to forget what he had said and, indeed, this is the first time it has been mentioned outside the family circle. It had a tremendous effect upon me, however. I could never be sure of what he meant. Grandfather had been a quiet old man who never made any trouble, yet on his deathbed he had called himself a traitor and a spy, and he had spoken of his meekness as a dangerous activity. It became a constant puzzle which lay unanswered in the back of my mind. And whenever things went well for me I remembered my grandfather and felt guilty and uncomfortable. It was as though I was carrying out his advice in spite of myself. And to make it worse, everyone loved me for it. I was praised by the most lily-white men of the town. I was considered an example of desirable conduct—just as my grandfather had been. And what puzzled me was that the old man had defined it as *treachery*. When I was praised for my conduct I felt a guilt that in some way I was doing something that was really against the wishes of the white folks, that if they had understood they would have desired me to act just the opposite, that I should have been sulky and mean, and that that really would have been what they wanted, even though they were fooled and thought they wanted me to act as I did. It made me afraid that some day they would look upon me as a traitor and I would be lost. Still I was more afraid to act any other way because they didn't like that at all. The old man's words were like a curse. On my graduation day I delivered an oration in which I showed that humility was the secret, indeed, the very essence of progress. (Not that I believed this—how could I, remembering my grandfather?—I only believed that it worked.) It was a great success. Everyone praised me and I was invited to give the speech at a gathering of the town's leading white citizens. It was a triumph for our whole community.

It was in the main ballroom of the leading hotel. When I got there I discovered that it was on the occasion of a smoker, and I was told that since I was to be there anyway I might as well take part in the battle royal to be fought by some of my schoolmates as part of the entertainment. The battle royal came first.

All of the town's big shots were there in their tuxedoes, wolfing down the buffet foods, drinking beer and whiskey and smoking black cigars. It was a large room with a high ceiling. Chairs were arranged in neat rows around three sides of a portable boxing ring. The fourth side was clear, revealing a gleaming space of polished floor. I had some misgivings over the battle royal, by the way. Not from a distaste for fighting, but because I didn't care too much for the other fellows who were to take part. They were tough guys who seemed to have no grandfather's curse worrying their minds. No one could mistake their toughness. And besides, I suspected that fighting a battle royal might detract from the dignity of my speech. In those pre-invisible days I visualized myself as a potential Booker T. Washington.[1] But the other fellows didn't care too much for me either, and there were nine of them. I felt superior to them in my way, and I didn't like the manner in which we were all crowded together into the servants' elevator. Nor did they like my being there. In fact, as the warmly lighted floors flashed past the elevator we had words over the fact that I, by taking part in the fight, had knocked one of their friends out of a night's work.

We were led out of the elevator through a rococo hall into an anteroom and told to get into our fighting togs. Each of us was issued a pair of boxing gloves and ushered out into the big mirrored hall, which we entered looking cautiously about us and whispering, lest we might accidentally be heard above the noise of the room. It was foggy with cigar smoke. And already the whiskey was taking effect. I was shocked to see some of the most important

1. African American author and educator (1856–1915).

men of the town quite tipsy. They were all there—bankers, lawyers, judges, doctors, fire chiefs, teachers, merchants. Even one of the more fashionable pastors. Something we could not see was going on up front. A clarinet was vibrating sensuously and the men were standing up and moving eagerly forward. We were a small tight group, clustered together, our bare upper bodies touching and shining with anticipatory sweat; while up front the big shots were becoming increasingly excited over something we still could not see. Suddenly I heard the school superintendent, who had told me to come, yell, "Bring up the shines, gentlemen! Bring up the little shines!"

We were rushed up to the front of the ballroom, where it smelled even more strongly of tobacco and whiskey. Then we were pushed into place. I almost wet my pants. A sea of faces, some hostile, some amused, ringed around us, and in the center, facing us, stood a magnificent blonde—stark naked. There was dead silence. I felt a blast of cold air chill me. I tried to back away, but they were behind me and around me. Some of the boys stood with lowered heads, trembling. I felt a wave of irrational guilt and fear. My teeth chattered, my skin turned to goose flesh, my knees knocked. Yet I was strongly attracted and looked in spite of myself. Had the price of looking been blindness, I would have looked. The hair was yellow like that of a circus kewpie doll, the face heavily powdered and rouged, as though to form an abstract mask, the eyes hollow and smeared a cool blue, the color of a baboon's butt. I felt a desire to spit upon her as my eyes brushed slowly over her body. Her breasts were firm and round as the domes of East Indian temples, and I stood so close as to see the fine skin texture and beads of pearly perspiration glistening like dew around the pink and erected buds of her nipples. I wanted at one and the same time to run from the room, to sink through the floor, or go to her and cover her from my eyes and the eyes of the others with my body; to feel the soft thighs, to caress her and destroy her, to love her and murder her, to hide from her, and yet to stroke where below the small American flag tattooed upon her belly her thighs formed a capital V. I had a notion that of all in the room she saw only me with her impersonal eyes.

And then she began to dance, a slow sensuous movement; the smoke of a hundred cigars clinging to her like the thinnest of veils. She seemed like a fair bird-girl girdled in veils calling to me from the angry surface of some gray and threatening sea. I was transported. Then I became aware of the clarinet playing and the big shots yelling at us. Some threatened us if we looked and others if we did not. On my right I saw one boy faint. And now a man grabbed a silver pitcher from a table and stepped close as he dashed ice water upon him and stood him up and forced two of us to support him as his head hung and moans issued from his thick bluish lips. Another boy began to plead to go home. He was the largest of the group, wearing dark red fighting trunks much too small to conceal the erection which projected from him as though in answer to the insinuating low-registered moaning of the clarinet. He tried to hide himself with his boxing gloves.

And all the while the blonde continued dancing, smiling faintly at the big shots who watched her with fascination, and faintly smiling at our fear. I noticed a certain merchant who followed her hungrily, his lips loose and drooling. He was a large man who wore diamond studs in a shirtfront which swelled with the ample paunch underneath, and each time the blonde swayed her undulating hips he ran his hand through the thin hair of his bald head and, with his arms upheld, his posture clumsy like that of an intoxicated panda, wound his belly in a slow and obscene grind. This creature was completely hypnotized. The music had quickened. As the dancer flung herself about with a detached expression on her face, the men began reaching out to touch her. I could see their beefy fingers sink into the soft flesh. Some of the others tried to stop them and she began to move around the floor in graceful circles, as they gave chase, slipping and sliding over the polished floor. It was mad. Chairs went crashing, drinks were spilt, as they ran laughing and howling after her. They caught her just as she reached a door, raised her from the floor, and tossed her as college boys are tossed at a hazing, and above her red, fixed-smiling lips I saw the terror and disgust in her eyes, almost like my own terror and that which I saw in some of the other boys. As I watched, they tossed her twice and her soft breasts seem to flatten against the air and her legs flung wildly as she spun. Some of the more sober ones helped her to escape. And I started off the floor, heading for the anteroom with the rest of the boys.

Some were still crying and in hysteria. But as we tried to leave we were stopped and ordered to get into the ring. There was nothing to do but what we were told. All ten of us climbed under the ropes and allowed ourselves to be blindfolded with broad bands of white cloth. One of the men seemed to feel a bit sympathetic and tried to cheer us up as we stood with our backs against the ropes. Some of us tried to grin. "See that boy over there?" one of the men said. "I want you to run across at the bell and give it to him right in the belly. If you don't get him, I'm going to get you. I don't like his looks." Each of us was told the same. The blindfolds were put on. Yet even then I had been going over my speech. In my mind each word was as bright as flame. I felt the cloth pressed into place, and frowned so that it would be loosened when I relaxed.

But now I felt a sudden fit of blind terror. I was unused to darkness. It was as though I had suddenly found myself in a dark room filled with poisonous cottonmouths. I could hear the bleary voices yelling insistently for the battle royal to begin.

"Get going in there!"

"Let me at that big nigger!"

I strained to pick up the school superintendent's voice, as though to squeeze some security out of that slightly more familiar sound.

"Let me at those black sonsabitches!" someone yelled.

"No, Jackson, no!" another voice yelled. "Here, somebody, help me hold Jack."

"I want to get at that ginger-colored nigger. Tear him limb from limb," the first voice yelled.

I stood against the ropes trembling. For in those days I was what they called ginger-colored, and he sounded as though he might crunch me between his teeth like a crisp ginger cookie.

Quite a struggle was going on. Chairs were being kicked about and I could hear voices grunting as with a terrific effort. I wanted to see, to see more desperately than ever before. But the blindfold was tight as a thick skin-puckering scab and when I raised my gloved hands to push the layers of white aside a voice yelled, "Oh, no you don't, black bastard! Leave that alone!"

"Ring the bell before Jackson kills him a coon!" someone boomed in the sudden silence. And I heard the bell clang and the sound of the feet scuffling forward.

A glove smacked against my head. I pivoted, striking out stiffly as someone went past, and felt the jar ripple along the length of my arm to my shoulder. Then it seemed as though all nine of the boys had turned upon me at once. Blows pounded me from all sides while I struck out as best I could. So many blows landed upon me that I wondered if I were not the only blindfolded fighter in the ring, or if the man called Jackson hadn't succeeded in getting me after all.

Blindfolded, I could no longer control my motions. I had no dignity. I stumbled about like a baby or a drunken man. The smoke had become thicker and with each new blow it seemed to sear and further restrict my lungs. My saliva became like hot bitter glue. A glove connected with my head, filling my mouth with warm blood. It was everywhere. I could not tell if the moisture I felt upon my body was sweat or blood. A blow landed hard against the nape of my neck. I felt myself going over, my head hitting the floor. Streaks of blue light filled the black world behind the blindfold. I lay prone, pretending that I was knocked out, but felt myself seized by hands and yanked to my feet. "Get going, black boy! Mix it up!" My arms were like lead, my head smarting from blows. I managed to feel my way to the ropes and held on, trying to catch my breath. A glove landed in my mid-section and I went over again, feeling as though the smoke had become a knife jabbed into my guts. Pushed this way and that by the legs milling around me, I finally pulled erect and discovered that I could see the black, sweat-washed forms weaving in the smoky-blue atmosphere like drunken dancers weaving to the rapid drum-like thuds of blows.

Everyone fought hysterically. It was complete anarchy. Everybody fought everybody else. No group fought together for long. Two, three, four, fought one, then turned to fight each other, were themselves attacked. Blows landed below the belt and in the kidney, with the gloves open as well as closed, and with my eye partly opened now there was not so much terror. I moved carefully, avoiding blows, although not too many to attract attention, fighting from group to group. The boys groped about like blind, cautious crabs crouching to protect their mid-sections, their heads pulled in short against their shoulders, their arms stretched nervously before them, with their fists testing the smoke-filled air like the knobbed feelers of hypersensitive snails. In one corner I glimpsed a boy violently punching the air and heard him scream in pain as he smashed his hand against a ring post. For a second I saw him bent over holding his hand, then going down as a blow caught his unprotected head. I played one group against the other, slipping in and throwing a punch then stepping out of range while pushing the others into the melee to take the blows blindly aimed at me. The smoke was agonizing and there were no rounds, no bells at three minute intervals to relieve our exhaustion. The room spun around me, a swirl of lights, smoke, sweating bodies surrounded by tense white faces. I bled from both nose and mouth, the blood spattering upon my chest.

The men kept yelling, "Slug him, black boy! Knock his guts out!"

"Uppercut him! Kill him! Kill that big boy!"

Taking a fake fall, I saw a boy going down heavily beside me as though we were felled by a single blow, saw a sneaker-clad foot shoot into his groin as the two who had knocked him down stumbled upon him. I rolled out of range, feeling a twinge of nausea.

The harder we fought the more threatening the men became. And yet, I had begun to worry about my speech again. How would it go? Would they recognize my ability? What would they give me?

I was fighting automatically when suddenly I noticed that one after another of the boys was leaving the ring. I was surprised, filled with panic, as though I had been left alone with an unknown danger. Then I understood. The boys had arranged it among themselves. It was the custom for the two men left in the ring to slug it out for the winner's prize. I discovered this too late. When the bell sounded two men in tuxedoes leaped into the ring and removed the blindfold. I found myself facing Tatlock, the biggest of the gang. I felt sick at my stomach. Hardly had the bell stopped ringing in my ears than it clanged again and I saw him moving swiftly toward me. Thinking of nothing else to do I hit him smash on the nose. He kept coming, bringing the rank sharp violence of stale sweat. His face was a black blank of a face, only his eyes alive—with hate of me and aglow with a feverish terror from what had happened to us all. I became anxious. I wanted to deliver my speech and he came at me as though he meant to beat it out of me. I smashed him again and again, taking his blows as they came. Then on a sudden impulse I struck him lightly and as we clinched, I whispered, "Fake like I knocked you out, you can have the prize."

"I'll break your behind," he whispered hoarsely.

"For *them?*"

"For *me*, sonofabitch!"

They were yelling for us to break it up and Tatlock spun me half around with a blow, and as a joggled camera sweeps in a reeling scene, I saw the howling red faces crouching tense beneath the cloud of blue-gray smoke. For a moment the world wavered, unraveled, flowed, then my head cleared and Tatlock bounced before me. That fluttering shadow before my eyes was his jabbing left hand. Then falling forward, my head against his damp shoulder, I whispered,

"I'll make it five dollars more."

"Go to hell!"

But his muscles relaxed a trifle beneath my pressure and I breathed, "Seven?"

"Give it to your ma," he said, ripping me beneath the heart.

And while I still held him I butted him and moved away. I felt myself bombarded with punches. I fought back with hopeless desperation. I wanted to deliver my speech more than anything else in the world, because I felt that only these men could judge truly my ability, and now this stupid clown was ruining my chances. I began fighting carefully now, moving in to punch him and out again with my greater speed. A lucky blow to his chin and I had him going too—until I heard a loud voice yell, "I got my money on the big boy."

Hearing this, I almost dropped my guard. I was confused: Should I try to win against the voice out there? Would not this go against my speech, and was not this a moment for humility, for nonresistance? A blow to my head as I danced about sent my right eye popping like a jack-in-the-box and settled my dilemma. The room went red as I fell. It was a dream fall, my body languid and fastidious as to where to land, until the floor became impatient and smashed up to meet me. A moment later I came to. An hypnotic voice said FIVE emphatically. And I lay there, hazily watching a dark red spot of my own blood shaping itself into a butterfly, glistening and soaking into the soiled gray world of the canvas.

When the voice drawled TEN I was lifted up and dragged to a chair. I sat dazed. My eye pained and swelled with each throb of my pounding heart and I wondered if now I would be allowed to speak. I was wringing wet, my mouth still bleeding. We were grouped along the wall now. The other boys ignored me as they congratulated Tatlock and speculated as to how much they would be paid. One boy whimpered over his smashed hand. Looking up front, I saw attendants in white jackets rolling the portable ring away and placing a small square rug in the vacant space surrounded by chairs. Perhaps, I thought, I will stand on the rug to deliver my speech.

Then the M.C. called to us, "Come on up here boys and get your money."

We ran forward to where the men laughed and talked in their chairs, waiting. Everyone seemed friendly now.

"There it is on the rug," the man said. I saw the rug covered with coins of all dimensions and a few crumpled bills. But what excited me, scattered here and there, were the gold pieces.

"Boys, it's all yours," the man said. "You get all you grab."

"That's right, Sambo," a blond man said, winking at me confidentially.

I trembled with excitement, forgetting my pain. I would get the gold and the bills, I thought. I would use both hands. I would throw my body against the boys nearest me to block them from the gold.

"Get down around the rug now," the man commanded, "and don't anyone touch it until I give the signal."

"This ought to be good," I heard.

As told, we got around the square rug on our knees. Slowly the man raised his freckled hand as we followed it upward with our eyes.

I heard, "These niggers look like they're about to pray!"

Then, "Ready," the man said. "Go!"

I lunged for a yellow coin lying on the blue design of the carpet, touching it and sending a surprised shriek to join those rising around me. I tried frantically to remove my hand but could not let go. A hot, violent force tore through my body, shaking me like a wet rat. The rug was electrified. The hair bristled up on my head as I shook myself free. My muscles jumped, my nerves jangled, writhed. But I saw that this was not stopping the other boys. Laughing in fear and embarrassment, some were holding back and scooping up the coins knocked off by the painful contortions of the others. The men roared above us as we struggled.

"Pick it up, goddamnit, pick it up!" someone called like a bass-voiced parrot. "Go on, get it!"

I crawled rapidly around the floor, picking up the coins, trying to avoid the coppers and to get greenbacks and the gold. Ignoring the shock by laughing, as I brushed the coins off quickly, I discovered that I could contain the electricity—a contradiction, but it works. Then the men began to push us onto the rug. Laughing embarrassedly, we struggled out of their hands and kept after the coins. We were all wet and slippery and hard to hold. Suddenly I saw a boy lifted into the air, glistening with sweat like a circus seal, and dropped, his wet back landing flush upon the charged rug, heard him yell and saw him literally dance upon his back, his elbows beating a frenzied tattoo upon the floor, his muscles twitching like the flesh of a horse stung by many flies. When he finally rolled off, his face was gray and no one stopped him when he ran from the floor amid booming laughter.

"Get the money," the M.C. called. "That's good hard American cash!"

And we snatched and grabbed, snatched and grabbed. I was careful not to come too close to the rug now, and when I felt the hot whiskey breath descend upon me like a cloud of foul air I reached out and grabbed the leg of a chair. It was occupied and I held on desperately.

"Leggo, nigger! Leggo!"

The huge face wavered down to mine as he tried to push me free. But my body was slippery and he was too drunk. It was Mr. Colcord, who owned a chain of movie houses and "entertainment palaces." Each time he grabbed me I slipped out of his hands. It became a real struggle. I feared the rug more than I did the drunk, so I held on, surprising myself for a moment by trying to topple *him* upon the rug. It was such an enormous idea that I found myself actually carrying it out. I tried not to be obvious, yet when I grabbed his leg, trying to tumble him out of the chair, he raised up roaring with laughter, and, looking at me with soberness dead in the eye, kicked me viciously in the chest. The chair leg flew out of my hand and I felt myself going and rolled. It was as though I had rolled through a bed of hot coals. It seemed a whole century would pass before I would roll free, a century in which I was seared through the deepest levels of my body to the fearful breath within me and the breath seared and heated to the point of explosion. It'll all be over in a flash, I thought as I rolled clear. It'll all be over in a flash.

But not yet, the men on the other side were waiting, red faces swollen as though from apoplexy as they bent forward in their chairs. Seeing their fingers coming toward me I rolled away as a fumbled football rolls off the receiver's fingertips, back into the coals. That time I luckily sent the rug sliding out of place and heard the coins ringing against the floor and the boys scuffling to pick them up and the M.C. calling, "All right, boys, that's all. Go get dressed and get your money."

I was limp as a dish rag. My back felt as though it had been beaten with wires.

When we had dressed the M.C. came in and gave us each five dollars, except Tatlock, who got ten for being last in the ring. Then he told us to leave. I was not to get a chance to deliver my speech, I thought. I was going out into the dim alley in despair when I was stopped and told to go back. I returned to the ballroom, where the men were pushing back their chairs and gathering in groups to talk.

The M.C. knocked on a table for quiet. "Gentlemen," he said, "we almost forgot an important part of the program. A most serious part, gentlemen. This boy was brought here to deliver a speech which he made at his graduation yesterday . . ."

"Bravo!"

"I'm told that he is the smartest boy we've got out there in Greenwood. I'm told that he knows more big words than a pocket-sized dictionary."

Much applause and laughter.

"So now, gentlemen, I want you to give him your attention."

There was still laughter as I faced them, my mouth dry, my eye throbbing. I began slowly, but evidently my throat was tense, because they began shouting, "Louder! Louder!"

"We of the younger generation extol the wisdom of that great leader and educator," I shouted, "who first spoke these flaming words of wisdom: 'A ship lost at sea for many days suddenly sighted a friendly vessel. From the mast of the unfortunate vessel was seen a signal: "Water, water; we die of thirst!" The answer from the friendly vessel came back: "Cast down your bucket where you are." The captain of the distressed vessel, at last heeding the injunction, cast down his bucket, and it came up full of fresh sparkling water from the mouth of the Amazon River.' And like him I say, and in his words, 'To those of my race who depend upon bettering their condition in a foreign land, or who underestimate the importance of cultivating friendly relations with the Southern white man, who is his next-door neighbor, I would say: "Cast down your bucket where you are"—cast it down in making friends in every manly way of the people of all races by whom we are surrounded . . .'"

I spoke automatically and with such fervor that I did not realize that the men were still talking and laughing until my dry mouth, filling up with blood from the cut, almost strangled me. I coughed, wanting to stop and go to one of the tall brass, sand-filled spittoons to relieve myself, but a few of the men, especially the superintendent, were listening and I was afraid. So I gulped it down, blood, saliva and all, and continued. (What powers of endurance I had during those days! What enthusiasm! What a belief in the lightness of things!) I spoke even louder in spite of the pain. But still they talked and still they laughed, as though deaf with cotton in dirty ears. So I spoke with greater emotional emphasis. I closed my ears and swallowed blood until I was nauseated. The speech seemed a hundred times as long as before, but I could not leave out a single word. All had to be said, each memorized nuance considered, rendered. Nor was that all. Whenever I uttered a word of three or more syllables a group of voices would yell for me to repeat it. I used the phrase "social responsibility," and they yelled:

"What's that word you say, boy?"

"Social responsibility," I said.

"What?"

"Social . . ."

"Louder."

". . . responsibility."

"More!"

"Respon—"

"Repeat!"

"—sibility."

The room filled with the uproar of laughter until, no doubt, distracted by having to gulp down my blood, I made a mistake and yelled a phrase I had often seen denounced in newspaper editorials, heard debated in private.

"Social . . ."

"What?" they yelled.

"... equality—"

The laughter hung smokelike in the sudden stillness. I opened my eyes, puzzled. Sounds of displeasure filled the room. The M.C. rushed forward. They shouted hostile phrases at me. But I did not understand.

A small dry mustached man in the front row blared out, "Say that slowly, son!"

"What, sir?"

"What you just said!"

"Social responsibility, sir," I said.

"You weren't being smart, were you, boy?" he said, not unkindly.

"No, sir!"

"You sure that about 'equality' was a mistake?"

"Oh, yes, sir," I said. "I was swallowing blood."

"Well, you had better speak more slowly so we can understand. We mean to do right by you, but you've got to know your place at all times. All right, now, go on with your speech."

I was afraid. I wanted to leave but I wanted also to speak and I was afraid they'd snatch me down.

"Thank you, sir," I said, beginning where I had left off, and having them ignore me as before.

Yet when I finished there was a thunderous applause. I was surprised to see the superintendent come forth with a package wrapped in white tissue paper, and, gesturing for quiet, address the men.

"Gentlemen, you see that I did not overpraise the boy. He makes a good speech and some day he'll lead his people in the proper paths. And I don't have to tell you that that is important in these days and times. This is a good, smart boy, and so to encourage him in the right direction, in the name of the Board of Education I wish to present him a prize in the form of this . . ."

He paused, removing the tissue paper and revealing a gleaming calfskin brief case.

". . . in the form of this first-class article from Shad Whitmore's shop."

"Boy," he said, addressing me, "take this prize and keep it well. Consider it a badge of office. Prize it. Keep developing as you are and some day it will be filled with important papers that will help shape the destiny of your people."

I was so moved that I could hardly express my thanks. A rope of bloody saliva forming a shape like an undiscovered continent drooled upon the leather and I wiped it quickly away. I felt an importance that I had never dreamed.

"Open it and see what's inside," I was told.

My fingers a-tremble, I complied, smelling the fresh leather and finding an official-looking document inside. It was a scholarship to the state college for Negroes. My eyes filled with tears and I ran awkwardly off the floor.

I was overjoyed; I did not even mind when I discovered that the gold pieces I had scrambled for were brass pocket tokens advertising a certain make of automobile.

When I reached home everyone was excited. Next day the neighbors came to congratulate me. I even felt safe from grandfather, whose deathbed curse usually spoiled my triumphs. I stood beneath his photograph with my brief case in hand and smiled triumphantly into his stolid black peasant's face. It was a face that fascinated me. The eyes seemed to follow everywhere I went.

That night I dreamed I was at a circus with him and that he refused to laugh at the clowns no matter what they did. Then later he told me to open my brief case and read what was inside and I did, finding an official envelope stamped with the state seal; and inside the envelope I found another and another, endlessly, and I thought I would fall of weariness. "Them's years," he said. "Now open that one." And I did and in it I found an engraved document containing a short message in letters of gold. "Read it," my grandfather said. "Out loud!"

"To Whom It May Concern," I intoned. "Keep This Nigger-Boy Running."

I awoke with the old man's laughter ringing in my ears.

(It was a dream I was to remember and dream again for many years after. But at that time I had no insight into its meaning. First I had to attend college.)

1952

SAUL BELLOW
1915–2005

Winner of the Nobel Prize in Literature in 1976, Saul Bellow distinguished himself through a writing career that spanned nearly two-thirds of a century. Bellow, the child of Russian Jewish immigrants, was born in Lachine, Quebec, a suburb of Montreal, and spent nine years there before moving with his family to Chicago. While relishing the style of big-city life typical of the 1920s and 1930s, he pursued an increasingly intellectual track through Tuley High School, the University of Chicago, and Northwestern University. Literature was always Bellow's great love, but as his biographer James Atlas explains, the antisemitic establishment was unreceptive to his ambitions. "In search of career advice," Atlas notes, Bellow sought counsel from the chair of Northwestern's English Department, William Frank Bryan, who warned him against postgraduate study in the field, because "no Jew could really grasp the tradition of English literature. . . . No Jew would ever have the right *feeling* for it." Bellow therefore began work toward a master's degree in sociology and anthropology at the University of Wisconsin. Discouraged by the technical work required and chided by his new advisor for being too literary, he dropped out after just one semester, returning to Chicago and a lifelong career in literature that involved teaching (initially at a downtown teachers college, later most prestigiously as a member of the University of Chicago's Committee on Social Thought), editing (first for the *Encyclopaedia Britannica*, then for his own journal, *The Noble Savage*), and writing fiction. Except for brief service in the bureaucracy of the merchant marine during World War II, a Guggenheim Fellowship year in Paris (1948–49), and some time living in New York City and the New England countryside, Bellow made Chicago his primary residence and the setting for his most characteristic work, most famously *The Adventures of Augie March* (1953). In finding a voice for the protagonist of this novel Bellow discovered his own style, a mix of the urban colloquial and the erudite.

Bellow's first novel, *Dangling Man*, was not published until he was nearly thirty. It is a short series of elegantly morose meditations, told through the journal of a young man waiting to be inducted into the army and with the "freedom" of having nothing to do but wait. Eventually he is drafted: "Long live regimentation," he sardonically exults. His second novel, *The Victim* (1947), continues the investigation of ways people strive to be relieved of self-determination. This book concerns a week in the life of Asa Leventhal, alone in New York City while his wife visits a relative, who is suddenly confronted by a figure from the past (Kirby Allbee, a Gentile) who succeeds in implicating Leventhal with the past and its present manifestations. *The Victim* is Bellow's most somberly naturalistic depiction of a man brought up against forces larger than himself, yet from the opening sentence ("On some nights New York is as hot as Bangkok") a poetic dimension appears and helps create the sense of mystery and disturbance felt by both the main character and the reader.

Dangling Man and *The Victim* are highly wrought, mainly humorless books; in two long novels published in the 1950s Bellow opened up into new ranges of aspiration and situational zaniness, which brought him respectful admiration from many critics. *The Adventures of Augie March* and *Henderson the Rain King* (1959) are each narrated by an "I" who, like his predecessor Huck Finn, is good at lighting out for the territory ahead of whoever means to tie him down. The hero's adventures, whether occurring in Chicago, Mexico, or Africa, are exuberantly delivered in an always stimulating and sometimes overactive prose. *Augie* is filled with sights and sounds, colors and surfaces; its tone is self-involved, affectionate, and affirmative; *Henderson*, Bellow's most extravagant narrative, has the even more fabulous air of a quest-romance, in which the hero returns home from Africa at peace with the world he had been warring against.

The ironic motto for Bellow's novels of the 1950s may well be "Seize the Day," as in the title of perhaps his most sharply defined piece of fiction. This short novel (1956) is both painful and exhilarating because it so fully exposes its hero (Tommy Wilhelm, an aging out-of-work ex-actor) to the insults of other people who don't understand him, to a city (New York, particularly its Upper West Side) impervious to his needs, and to a narrative prose that mixes ridicule and affection so thoroughly as to make them scarcely distinguishable. *Seize the Day* combines, within Tommy's monologues, a wildness and pathos of bitter comedy that was a powerful new element in Bellow's work.

In "Where Do We Go from Here?: The Future of Fiction," an essay published in 1965, Bellow pointed out that nineteenth-century American literature—Emerson, Thoreau, Whitman, Melville—was highly didactic in its efforts to "instruct a young and raw nation." Bellow sees himself in this instructive tradition and in the international company of "didactic" novelists like Dostoyevsky, D. H. Lawrence, and Joseph Conrad; he believes also that "the imagination is looking for new ways to express virtue . . . we have barely begun to comprehend what a human being is." These concerns animate the novels Bellow wrote in the years since *Henderson*. In *Herzog* (1964) the hero is another down-and-outer, a professor-intellectual, a student of Romanticism and of the glorification of Self, which Herzog believes both modern life and modernist literature have been undercutting. At the same time he is a comic and pathetic victim of marital disorder; like all Bellow's heroes, Herzog has a terrible time with women, yet cannot live without them. In *Mr. Sammler's Planet* (1970), written out of the disorders of the late 1960s, the atmosphere is grimmer. Sammler, an aging Jew living (again) on New York's Upper West Side, analyzes and judges but cannot understand the young or blacks, or the mass of people gathered at Broadway and Ninety-sixth Street. He sees about him everywhere "poverty of soul" but admits that he too has "a touch of the same disease—the disease of the single self explaining what was what and who was who."

These novels, as well as *Humboldt's Gift* (1975), have been accused of parading too single-handedly attitudes toward which their author is sympathetic, whereas *The Dean's December* (1982) was criticized by John Updike, in a review, for being too much *"about* Saul Bellow," even though indirectly. Subsequently, a collection of shorter fiction, *Him with His Foot in His Mouth* (1984); the novels *More Die of Heartbreak* (1987) and *Ravelstein* (2000); three novellas, *The Bellarosa Connection* (1989), *A Theft* (1989), and *The Actual* (1997); and three stories collected as *Something to Remember Me By* (1991) exhibit various talky, informal protagonists and narrators with a lot on their minds. Matters of form and plot in these works seem less important than the ideas and active energy struck off by human beings in turmoil—usually comic turmoil. What Bellow finds moving in Theodore Dreiser's work, "his balkiness and sullenness, and then his allegiance to life," is still found in his own: complaint and weariness, fault-finding, accusation of self and others—these gestures directed at "life" also make up the stuff of life and the "allegiance" out of which Bellow's heroes are made. We read him for this range of interest; for flexibility and diversity of style and idiom; and for the eloquences of nostalgia, invective, and lamentation that make up his intensely imagined world.

Married five times, he ended his academic career with a brief residency at Boston University, afterward retiring to rural Vermont, where he died two months short of his ninetieth birthday and five years after publishing *Ravelstein*, his nineteenth book and a work indicative of the conservative, traditionalist posture of his later career.

From The Adventures of Augie March

Chapter One

I am an American, Chicago born—Chicago, that somber city—and go at things as I have taught myself, free-style, and will make the record in my own way: first to knock, first admitted; sometimes an innocent knock, sometimes a not so innocent. But a man's character is his fate, says Heraclitus,[1] and in the end there isn't any way to disguise the nature of the knocks by acoustical work on the door or gloving the knuckles.

Everybody knows there is no fineness or accuracy of suppression; if you hold down one thing you hold down the adjoining.

My own parents were not much to me, though I cared for my mother. She was simple-minded, and what I learned from her was not what she taught, but on the order of object lessons. She didn't have much to teach, poor woman. My brothers and I loved her. I speak for them both; for the elder it is safe enough; for the younger one, Georgie, I have to answer—he was born an idiot—but I'm in no need to guess, for he had a song he sang as he ran drag-footed with his stiff idiot's trot, up and down along the curl-wired fence in the backyard:

> Georgie Mahchy, Augie, Simey
> Winnie Mahchy, evwy, evwy love Mama.

He was right about everyone save Winnie, Grandma Lausch's poodle, a pursy old overfed dog. Mama was Winnie's servant, as she was Grandma Lausch's. Loud-breathing and wind-breaking, she lay near the old lady's stool on a

---

1. Early Greek philosopher (fl. c. 480 B.C.E.) famous for his cryptic aphorisms and for positing the existence of the human soul.

cushion embroidered with a Berber[2] aiming a rifle at a lion. She was personally Grandma's, belonged to her suite; the rest of us were the governed, and
especially Mama. Mama passed the dog's dish to Grandma, and Winnie
received her food at the old lady's feet from the old lady's hands. These hands
and feet were small; she wore a shriveled sort of lisle on her legs and her slippers were gray—ah, the gray of that felt, the gray despotic to souls—with
pink ribbons. Mama, however, had large feet, and around the house she wore
men's shoes, usually without strings, and a dusting or mobcap like somebody's fanciful cotton effigy of the form of the brain. She was meek and long,
round-eyed like Georgie—gentle green round eyes and a gentle freshness of
color in her long face. Her hands were work-reddened, she had very few of her
teeth left—to heed the knocks as they come—and she and Simon wore the
same ravelly coat-sweaters. Besides having round eyes, Mama had circular
glasses that I went with her to the free dispensary on Harrison Street[3] to get.
Coached by Grandma Lausch, I went to do the lying. Now I know it wasn't so
necessary to lie, but then everyone thought so, and Grandma Lausch especially, who was one of those Machiavellis of small street and neighborhood
that my young years were full of. So Grandma, who had it all ready before we
left the house and must have put in hours plotting it out in thought and
phrase, lying small in her chilly small room under the featherbed, gave it to
me at breakfast. The idea was that Mama wasn't keen enough to do it right.
That maybe one didn't need to be keen didn't occur to us; it was a contest.
The dispensary would want to know why the Charities didn't pay for the
glasses. So you must say nothing about the Charities, but that sometimes
money from my father came and sometimes it didn't, and that Mama took
boarders. This was, in a delicate and choosy way, by ignoring and omitting
certain large facts, true. It was true enough for *them*, and at the age of nine I
could appreciate this perfectly. Better than my brother Simon, who was too
blunt for this kind of maneuver and, anyway, from books, had gotten hold of
some English schoolboy notions of honor. *Tom Brown's Schooldays*[4] for many
years had an influence we were not in a position to afford.

Simon was a blond boy with big cheekbones and wide gray eyes and had
the arms of a cricketer—I go by the illustrations; we never played anything
but softball. Opposed to his British style was his patriotic anger at George
III.[5] The mayor was at that time ordering the schoolboard to get history
books that dealt more harshly with the king, and Simon was very hot at
Cornwallis.[6] I admired this patriotic flash, his terrific personal wrath at the
general, and his satisfaction over his surrender at Yorktown,[7] which would
often come over him at lunch while we ate our bologna sandwiches.
Grandma had a piece of boiled chicken at noon, and sometimes there was
the gizzard for bristle-headed little Georgie, who loved it and blew at the
ridgy thing more to cherish than to cool it. But this martial true-blood pride
of Simon's disqualified him for the crafty task to be done at the dispensary;
he was too disdainful to lie and might denounce everybody instead. I could

2. Non-Arabic North African tribesman.
3. Downtown location of Chicago's social welfare
agency.
4. Novel (1857) based on experiences at Rugby
School, by the English jurist and religious
reformer Thomas Hughes (1822–1896).
5. King (1738–1820) of England, Scotland, and
Ireland during a period (r. 1760–1820) that

included the American Revolution.
6. Charles Cornwallis (1738–1805), British general who made the final surrender in the American Revolution.
7. Village in southeast Virginia where in 1781
British forces surrendered to George Washington's Continental Army, effectively ending the
American Revolution.

be counted on to do the job, because I enjoyed it. I loved a piece of strategy. I had enthusiasms too; I had Simon's, though there was never much meat in Cornwallis for me, and I had Grandma Lausch's as well. As for the truth of these statements I was instructed to make—well, it was a fact that we had a boarder. Grandma Lausch was our boarder, not a relation at all. She was supported by two sons, one from Cincinnati and one from Racine, Wisconsin. The daughters-in-law did not want her, and she, the widow of a powerful Odessa[8] businessman—a divinity over us, bald, whiskery, with a fat nose, greatly armored in a cutaway, a double-breasted vest, powerfully buttoned (his blue photo, enlarged and retouched by Mr. Lulov, hung in the parlor, doubled back between the portico columns of the full-length mirror, the dome of the stove beginning where his trunk ended)—she preferred to live with us, because for so many years she was used to direct a house, to command, to govern, to manage, scheme, devise, and intrigue in all her languages. She boasted French and German besides Russian, Polish, and Yiddish; and who but Mr. Lulov, the retouch artist from Division Street,[9] could have tested her claim to French? And he was a serene bogus too, that triple-backboned gallant tea-drinker. Except that he had been a hackie in Paris, once, and if he told the truth about that might have known French among other things, like playing tunes on his teeth with a pencil or singing and keeping time with a handful of coins that he rattled by jigging his thumb along the table, and how to play chess.

Grandma Lausch played like Timur, whether chess or klabyasch,[1] with palatal catty harshness and sharp gold in her eyes. Klabyasch she played with Mr. Kreindl, a neighbor of ours who had taught her the game. A powerful stub-handed man with a large belly, he swatted the table with those hard hands of his, flinging down his cards and shouting "*Shtoch! Yasch! Menél! Klabyasch!*"[2] Grandma looked sardonically at him. She often said, after he left, "If you've got a Hungarian friend you don't need an enemy." But there was nothing of the enemy about Mr. Kreindl. He merely, sometimes, sounded menacing because of his drill-sergeant's bark. He was an old-time Austro-Hungarian[3] conscript, and there was something soldierly about him: a neck that had strained with pushing artillery wheels, a campaigner's red in the face, a powerful bite in his jaw and gold-crowned teeth, green cockeyes and soft short hair, altogether Napoleonic.[4] His feet slanted out on the ideal of Frederick the Great,[5] but he was about a foot under the required height for guardsmen. He had a masterly look of independence. He and his wife—a woman quiet and modest to the neighbors and violently quarrelsome at home—and his son, a dental student, lived in what was called the English basement at the front of the house. The son, Kotzie, worked evenings in the corner drugstore and went to school in the neighborhood of County Hospital, and it was he who told Grandma about the free dispensary. Or rather,

8. City in the Ukraine on the Black Sea, departure point for many Russian Jews who emigrated to North America in the late 19th and early 20th centuries.

9. Commercial and shopping street on Chicago's North Side.

1. Card game taking its name from the Yiddish verb for "to gather." "Timur": also Tamerlane, Mongol warrior (1336–1405) whose conquests stretched from the Ukraine to northern India.

2. Successive winning tricks.

3. The dual monarchy of Austria and Hungary (1867–1918) encompassed Austria, Hungary, Bohemia, and parts of Poland, Romania, Italy, and the Balkans.

4. Era and style of Napoléon Bonaparte's (1769–1821) rule as Napoléon I, emperor of the French (1804–15).

5. Frederick II (1712–1786), called "the Great," king of Prussia (r. 1740–86), patron of the arts and philosophy.

the old woman sent for him to find out what one could get from those state and county places. She was always sending for people, the butcher, the grocer, the fruit peddler, and received them in the kitchen to explain that the Marches had to have discounts. Mama usually had to stand by. The old woman would tell them, "You see how it is—do I have to say more? There's no man in the house and children to bring up." This was her most frequent argument. When Lubin, the caseworker, came around and sat in the kitchen, familiar, bald-headed, in his gold glasses, his weight comfortable, his mouth patient, she shot it at him: "How do you expect children to be brought up?" While he listened, trying to remain comfortable but gradually becoming like a man determined not to let a grasshopper escape from his hand. "Well, my dear, Mrs. March could raise your rent," he said. She must often have answered—for there were times when she sent us all out to be alone with him—"Do you know what things would be like without me? You ought to be grateful for the way I hold them together." I'm sure she even said, "And when I die, Mr. Lubin, you'll see what you've got on your hands." I'm one hundred per cent sure of it. To us nothing was ever said that might weaken her rule by suggesting it would ever end. Besides, it would have shocked us to hear it, and she, in her miraculous knowledge of us, able to be extremely close to our thoughts—she was one sovereign who knew exactly the proportions of love, respect, and fear of power in her subjects—understood how we would have been shocked. But to Lubin, for reasons of policy and also because she had to express feelings she certainly had, she must have said it. He had a harassed patience with her of "deliver me from such clients," though he tried to appear master of the situation. He held his derby between his thighs (his suits, always too scanty in the pants, exposed white socks and bulldog shoes, crinkled, black, and bulging with toes), and he looked into the hat as though debating whether it was wise to release his grasshopper on the lining for a while.

"I pay as much as I can afford," she would say.

She took her cigarette case out from under her shawl, she cut a Murad[6] in half with her sewing scissors and picked up the holder. This was still at a time when women did not smoke. Save the intelligentsia—the term she applied to herself. With the holder in her dark little gums between which all her guile, malice, and command issued, she had her best inspirations of strategy. She was as wrinkled as an old paper bag, an autocrat, hard-shelled and jesuitical,[7] a pouncy old hawk of a Bolshevik,[8] her small ribboned gray feet immobile on the shoekit and stool Simon had made in the manual-training class, dingy old wool Winnie whose bad smell filled the flat on the cushion beside her. If wit and discontent don't necessarily go together, it wasn't from the old woman that I learned it. She was impossible to satisfy. Kreindl, for example, on whom we could depend, Kreindl who carried up the coal when Mama was sick and who instructed Kotzie to make up our prescriptions for nothing, she called "that trashy Hungarian," or "Hungarian pig." She called Kotzie "the baked apple"; she called Mrs. Kreindl "the secret goose," Lubin "the shoemaker's son," the dentist "the butcher," the butcher "the timid swindler." She detested the dentist, who had several times unsuccessfully tried to fit her with false teeth. She

6. A Turkish cigarette, named for the Murad River.
7. Reference to the Society of Jesus, commonly called Jesuits, a Catholic religious order famous for its intellectual rigor, founded in 1540 by the Spanish priest Ignatius of Loyola (1491–1556).
8. Left-wing political party allied with other Communist forces in the Russian Revolution (1917).

accused him of burning her gums when taking the impressions. But then she tried to pull his hands away from her mouth. I saw that happen: the stolid, square-framed Dr. Wernick, whose compact forearms could have held off a bear, painfully careful with her, determined, concerned at her choked screams, and enduring her scratches. To see her struggle like that was no easy thing for me, and Dr. Wernick was sorry to see me there too, I know, but either Simon or I had to squire her wherever she went. Here particularly she needed a witness to Wernick's cruelty and clumsiness as well as a shoulder to lean on when she went weakly home. Already at ten I was only a little shorter than she and big enough to hold her small weight.

"You saw how he put his paws over my face so I couldn't breathe?" she said. "God made him to be a butcher. Why did he become a dentist? His hands are too heavy. The touch is everything to a dentist. If his hands aren't right he shouldn't be let practice. But his wife worked hard to send him through school and make a dentist of him. And I must go to him and be burned because of it."

The rest of us had to go to the dispensary—which was like the dream of a multitude of dentists' chairs, hundreds of them in a space as enormous as an armory, and green bowls with designs of glass grapes, drills lifted zigzag as insects' legs, and gas flames on the porcelain swivel trays—a thundery gloom in Harrison Street of limestone county buildings and cumbersome red streetcars with metal grillwork on their windows and monarchical iron whiskers of cowcatchers front and rear. They lumbered and clanged, and their brake tanks panted in the slushy brown of a winter afternoon or the bare stone brown of a summer's, salted with ash, smoke, and prairie dust, with long stops at the clinics to let off dumpers, cripples, hunchbacks, brace-legs, crutch-wielders, tooth and eye sufferers, and all the rest.

So before going with my mother for the glasses I was always instructed by the old woman and had to sit and listen with profound care. My mother too had to be present, for there must be no slip-up. She must be coached to say nothing. "Remember, Rebecca," Grandma would rerepeat, "let him answer everything." To which Mama was too obedient even to say yes, but only sat and kept her long hands folded on the bottle-fly iridescence of the dress the old woman had picked for her to wear. Very healthy and smooth, her color; none of us inherited this high a color from her, or the form of her nose with nostrils turned back and showing a little of the partition. "You keep out of it. If they ask you something, you look at Augie like this." And she illustrated how Mama was to turn to me, terribly exact, if she had only been able to drop her habitual grandeur. "Don't tell anything. Only answer questions," she said to me. My mother was anxious that I should be worthy and faithful. Simon and I were her miracles or accidents; Georgie was her own true work in which she returned to her fate after blessed and undeserved success. "Augie, listen to Grandma. Hear what she says," was all she ever dared when the old woman unfolded her plan.

"When they ask you, 'Where is your father?' you say, 'I don't know where, miss.' No matter how old she is, you shouldn't forget to say 'miss.' If she wants to know where he was the last time you heard from him, you must tell her that the last time he sent a money order was about two years ago from Buffalo, New York. Never say a word about the Charity. The Charity you should never mention, you hear that? Never. When she asks you how much the rent is, tell her eighteen dollars. When she asks where the money comes from, say you have boarders. How many? Two boarders. Now, say to me, how much rent?"

"Eighteen dollars."

"And how many boarders?"

"Two."

"And how much do they pay?"

"How much should I say?"

"Eight dollars each a week."

"Eight dollars."

"So you can't go to a private doctor, if you get sixty-four dollars a month. The eyedrops alone cost me five when I went, and he scalded my eyes. And these specs"—she tapped the case—"cost ten dollars the frames and fifteen the glasses."

Never but at such times, by necessity, was my father mentioned. I claimed to remember him; Simon denied that I did, and Simon was right. I liked to imagine it.

"He wore a uniform," I said. "Sure I remember. He was a soldier."

"Like hell he was. You don't know anything about it."

"Maybe a sailor."

"Like hell. He drove a truck for Hall Brothers laundry on Marshfield,[9] that's what he did. *I* said he used to wear a uniform. Monkey sees, monkey does; monkey hears, monkey says." Monkey was the basis of much thought with us. On the sideboard, on the Turkestan runner, with their eyes, ears, and mouth covered, we had see-no-evil, speak-no-evil, hear-no-evil, a lower trinity of the house. The advantage of lesser gods is that you can take their names any way you like. "Silence in the courthouse, monkey wants to speak; speak, monkey, speak." "The monkey and the bamboo were playing in the grass . . ." Still the monkeys could be potent, and awesome besides, and deep social critics when the old woman, like a great lama—for she is Eastern to me, in the end—would point to the squatting brown three, whose mouths and nostrils were drawn in sharp blood-red, and with profound wit, her unkindness finally touching greatness, say, "Nobody asks you to love the whole world, only to be honest, *ehrlich*.[1] Don't have a loud mouth. The more you love people the more they'll mix you up. A child loves, a person respects. Respect is better than love. And that's respect, the middle monkey." It never occurred to us that she sinned mischievously herself against that convulsed speak-no-evil who hugged his lips with his hands; but no criticism of her came near our minds at any time, much less when the resonance of a great principle filled the whole kitchen.

She used to read us lessons off poor Georgie's head. He would kiss the dog. This bickering handmaiden of the old lady, at one time. Now a dozy, long-sighing crank and proper object of respect for her years of right-minded but not exactly lovable busyness. But Georgie loved her—and Grandma, whom he would kiss on the sleeve, on the knee, taking knee or arm in both hands and putting his underlip forward, chaste, lummoxy, caressing, gentle and diligent when he bent his narrow back, blouse bagging all over it, whitish hair pointy and close as a burr or sunflower when the seeds have been picked out of it. The old lady let him embrace her and spoke to him in the following way:

9. Commercial avenue on Chicago's North Side.   1. Sincere (German).

"Hey, you, boy, clever *junge*,[2] you like the old Grandma, my minister, my *cavalyer*?[3] That's-a-boy. You know who's good to you, who gives you gizzards and necks? Who? Who makes noodles for you? Yes. Noodles are slippery, hard to pick up with a fork and hard to pick up with the fingers. You see how the little bird pulls the worm? The little worm wants to stay in the ground. The little worm doesn't want to come out. Enough, you're making my dress wet." And she'd sharply push his forehead off with her old prim hand, having fired off for Simon and me, mindful always of her duty to wise us up, one more animadversion on the trustful, loving, and simple surrounded by the cunning-hearted and tough, a fighting nature of birds and worms, and a desperate mankind without feelings. Illustrated by Georgie. But the principal illustration was not Georgie but Mama, in her love-originated servitude, simpleminded, abandoned with three children. This was what old lady Lausch was driving at, now, in the later wisdom of her life, that she had a second family to lead.

And what must Mama have thought when in any necessary connection my father was brought into the conversation? She sat docile. I conceive that she thought of some detail about him—a dish he liked, perhaps meat and potatoes, perhaps cabbage or cranberry sauce; perhaps that he disliked a starched collar, or a soft collar; that he brought home the *Evening American* or the *Journal*.[4] She thought this because her thoughts were always simple; but she felt abandonment, and greater pains than conscious mental ones put a dark streak to her simplicity. I don't know how she made out before, when we were alone after the desertion, but Grandma came and put a regulating hand on the family life. Mama surrendered powers to her that maybe she had never known she had and took her punishment in drudgery; occupied a place, I suppose, among women conquered by a superior force of love, like those women whom Zeus got the better of in animal form and who next had to take cover from his furious wife. Not that I can see my big, gentle, dilapidated, scrubbing, and lugging mother as a fugitive of immense beauty from such classy wrath, or our father as a marble-legged Olympian. She had sewed buttonholes in a coat factory in a Wells Street[5] loft and he was a laundry driver—there wasn't even so much as a picture of him left when he blew. But she does have a place among such women by the deeper right of continual payment. And as for vengeance from a woman, Grandma Lausch was there to administer the penalties under the standards of legitimacy, representing the main body of married womankind.

Still the old lady had a heart. I don't mean to say she didn't. She was tyrannical and a snob about her Odessa luster and her servants and governesses, but though she had been a success herself she knew what it was to fall through susceptibility. I began to realize this when I afterward read some of the novels she used to send me to the library for. She taught me the Russian alphabet so that I could make out the titles. Once a year she read *Anna Karenina* and *Eugene Onegin*.[6] Occasionally I got into hot water by bringing a book she didn't want. "How many times do I have to tell you if it

2. Young man (German).
3. Yiddish borrowing from the German *kavalier* (gentleman) and Polish *kawaler* (bachelor, gallant).
4. Chicago newpapers of the era.
5. Light-industrial street immediately north of

Chicago's downtown area.
6. Verse narrative (1823–31) by the Russian poet Aleksandr Pushkin (1799–1837). "*Anna Karenina*": novel (1875–77) by the Russian novelist Leo Tolstoy (1828–1910).

doesn't say *roman* I don't want it? You didn't look inside. Are your fingers too weak to open the book? Then they should be too weak to play ball or pick your nose. For that you've got strength! *Bozhe moy!*[7] God in Heaven! You haven't got the brains of a cat, to walk two miles and bring me a book about religion because it says Tolstoi on the cover."

The old *grande dame*, I don't want to be misrepresenting her. She was suspicious of what could have been, given one wrong stitch of heredity, a family vice by which we could have been exploited. She didn't want to read Tolstoi on religion. She didn't trust him as a family man because the countess had had such trouble with him. But although she never went to the synagogue, ate bread on Passover, sent Mama to the pork butcher where meat was cheaper, loved canned lobster and other forbidden food, she was not an atheist and free-thinker. Mr. Anticol, the old junky she called (search me why) "Rameses"—after the city named with Pithom in the Scriptures maybe;[8] no telling what her inspirations were—was that. A real rebel to God. Icy and canny, she would listen to what he had to say and wouldn't declare herself. He was ruddy, and gloomy; his leathery serge cap made him flat-headed, and his alley calls for rags, old iron—"recks aline," he sung it—made him gravel-voiced and gruff. He had tough hair and brows and despising brown eyes; he was a studious, shaggy, meaty old man. Grandma bought a set of the *Encyclopedia Americana*—edition of 1892, I think—from him and saw to it that Simon and I read it; and he too, whenever he met us, asked, "How's the set?" believing, I reckon, that it taught irreverence to religion. What had made him an atheist was a massacre of Jews in his town. From the cellar where he was hidden he saw a laborer pissing on the body of his wife's younger brother, just killed. "So don't talk to me about God," he said. But it was he that talked about God, all the time. And while Mrs. Anticol stayed pious, it was his idea of grand apostasy to drive to the reform synagogue on the high holidays and park his pink-eye nag among the luxurious, whirl-wired touring cars of the rich Jews who bared their heads inside as if they were attending a theater, a kind of abjectness in them that gave him grim entertainment to the end of his life. He caught a cold in the rain and died of pneumonia.

Grandma, all the same, burned a candle on the anniversary of Mr. Lausch's death, threw a lump of dough on the coals when she was baking, as a kind of offering, had incantations over baby teeth and stunts against the evil eye. It was kitchen religion and had nothing to do with the giant God of the Creation who turned back the waters and exploded Gomorrah, but it was on the side of religion at that. And while we're on that side I'll mention the Poles—we were just a handful of Jews among them in the neighborhood—and the swollen, bleeding hearts on every kitchen wall, the pictures of saints, baskets of death flowers tied at the door, communions, Easters, and Christmases. And sometimes we were chased, stoned, bitten, and beat up for Christ-killers, all of us, even Georgie, articled, whether we liked it or not, to this mysterious trade. But I never had any special grief from it, or brooded, being by and large too larky and boisterous to take it to heart, and looked at it as needing no more special explanation than the stone-and-bat wars of the street gangs or the swarming on a fall evening of parish punks to rip up

---

7. Oh, my God (Russian).
8. *Exodus* 1.11: "Therefore they set taskmasters over them to afflict them with heavy burdens; and they built for Pharoah store-cities, Pithom and Raamses."

fences, screech and bawl at girls, and beat up strangers. It wasn't in my
nature to fatigue myself with worry over being born to this occult work, even
though some of my friends and playmates would turn up in the middle of
these mobs to trap you between houses from both ends of a passageway.
Simon had less truck with them. School absorbed him more, and he had his
sentiments anyway, a mixed extract from Natty Bumppo, Quentin Durward,
Tom Brown, Clark at Kaskaskia, the messenger who brought the good news
from Ratisbon,[9] and so on, that kept him more to himself. I was just a slow
understudy to this, just as he never got me to put in hours on his Sandow
muscle builder[1] and the gimmick for developing the sinews of the wrist. I
was an easy touch for friendships, and most of the time they were cut short
by older loyalties. I was pals longest with Stashu Kopecs, whose mother was
a midwife graduated from the Aesculapian School of Midwifery on Milwaukee Avenue.[2] Well to do, the Kopecses had an electric player piano and lino-
leums in all the rooms, but Stashu was a thief, and to run with him I stole
too: coal off the cars, clothes from the lines, rubber balls from the dime
store, and pennies off the newsstands. Mostly for the satisfaction of dexterity,
though Stashu invented the game of stripping in the cellar and putting on
girls' things swiped from the clotheslines. Then he too showed up in a gang
that caught me one cold afternoon of very little snow while I was sitting on a
crate frozen into the mud, eating Nabisco[3] wafers, my throat full of the sweet
dust. Foremost, there was a thug of a kid, about thirteen but undersized, hard
and grieved-looking. He came up to accuse me, and big Moonya Staplanski,
just out of the St. Charles Reformatory[4] and headed next for the one at Pontiac,[5] backed him up.

"You little Jew bastard, you hit my brother," Moonya said.

"I never did. I never even saw him before."

"You took away a nickel from him. How did you buy them biscuits else,
you?"

"I got them at home."

Then I caught sight of Stashu, hayheaded and jeering, pleased to sickness with his deceit and his new-revealed brotherhood with the others, and
I said, "Hey, you lousy bed-wetter, Stashu, you know Moon ain't even got a
brother."

Here the kid hit me and the gang jumped me, Stashu with the rest, tearing the buckles from my sheepskin coat and bloodying my nose.

"Who is to blame?" said Grandma Lausch when I came home. "You know
who? You are, Augie, because that's all the brains you have to go with that piss-
in-bed accoucherka's[6] son. Does Simon hang around with them? Not Simon.
He has too much sense." I thanked God she didn't know about the stealing.
And in a way, because that was her schooling temperament, I suspect she was

9. The French name for the German city of
Regensburg, which was captured by Napoleon's
armies in 1809. "Natty Bumppo": protagonist of
the Leatherstocking novels by the American novelist James Fenimore Cooper (1789–1851). "Quentin Durward": eponymous hero in the novel (1823)
by the Scottish poet and novelist Sir Walter Scott
(1771–1832). "Tom Brown": see n. 4, p. 2408.
"Clark at Kaskasia": the American military leader
George Rogers Clark (1752–1818) captured the
British frontier fort at Kaskaskia, Illinois, in 1778.
1. Device named after Eugen Sandow (1867–

1925), American physical culturist born in
Germany, famous for his performances as a body-
builder and for advocacy of physical education.
2. Commercial and shopping street on Chicago's
North Side, at this time a Polish-American neighborhood.
3. Brand name of the National Biscuit Company.
4. Site of the Illinois State Reformatory for Boys.
5. Site of the Illinois Correctional Center.
6. Yiddish borrowing from the Polish akuszerka
(midwife).

pleased that I should see where it led to give your affections too easily. But Mama, the prime example of this weakness, was horrified. Against the old lady's authority she didn't dare to introduce her feelings during the hearing, but when she took me into the kitchen to put a compress on me she near-sightedly pored over my scratches, whispering and sighing to me, while Georgie tottered around behind her, long and white, and Winnie lapped water under the sink.

1953

ARTHUR MILLER
1915–2005

For much modern American drama the family is the central subject, as the anthology selections show. In *Long Day's Journey into Night* Eugene O'Neill studied his own family through the Tyrones; in Tennessee Williams's *A Streetcar Named Desire* the Kowalskis are one family, which Blanche invades, while Blanche and Stella, as sisters, are another. Most of Arthur Miller's plays, as well, concentrate on the family and envision an ideal world as, perhaps, an enlarged family. Often the protagonist's sense of family draws him into conflict with—and eventual doom in—the outside world. Yet Miller recognized that an ideal is sometimes a rationalization. Joe Keller insists in *All My Sons* (1947) that during the war he shipped damaged airplane parts to support his family, but a desire for commercial success was part of his motive. Eddie Carbone in *A View from the Bridge* (1955) accepts death because of his sense of responsibility to his niece, but married man though he is, he may also be in love with that same niece. In *Death of a Salesman* (1949) Willy Loman's delusions and self-deceptions derive from, and return to, his image of himself as family provider, an image he cannot live up to; driven by his desire to be "well liked," a successful social personality, he fails to connect with either of his sons and neglects his wife. Thus Miller's treatment of the family leads to a treatment both of personal ideals and of the society within which families have to operate.

Miller was born into a German Jewish family in Manhattan; his father was a well-to-do but almost illiterate clothing manufacturer, his mother an avid reader. When his father's business collapsed after the stock market crash in 1929, the family moved to Brooklyn, where Miller graduated from high school. His subsequent two years of work in an automobile-parts warehouse to earn money for college tuition are warmly recalled in his play *A Memory of Two Mondays* (1955). At the University of Michigan he enrolled as a journalism student. These were the years of the Spanish Civil War, the rise of fascism, and the attraction of Marxism as a way out of the Depression, and here Miller formed his political views. He also began to write plays, which won prizes at the university and in New York. He then went to work for the Federal Theater Project, wrote radio plays, toured army camps to gather material for a film, and married Mary Slattery, the first of his three wives.

In 1947 Miller enjoyed his first Broadway success, *All My Sons*. (*The Man Who Had All the Luck* had failed in 1944.) This strongly realistic portrayal of a family divided because of the father's insistence on business as usual during World War II drew the attention of audiences and theater critics. *Death of a Salesman*, his masterpiece, was produced two years later and won the Pulitzer Prize. An adaptation of Ibsen's *An Enemy of the People* followed in 1951. It was suggested to him by the actors Fredric March and Florence Eldridge, but Miller was clearly drawn by Ibsen's hero, Dr. Stockmann, who leads a fight against pollution with strong but confused idealism.

In the 1950s the hysterical search for supposed communist infiltration of American life reached its height, as Senator Joseph McCarthy summoned suspect after suspect to hearings in Washington. Miller later said that at this time he was reading a book about the Salem witch trials and saw that "the main point of the hearings, precisely as in seventeenth-century Salem, was that the accused make public confession, damn his confederates as well as his Devil master, and guarantee his sterling new allegiance by breaking disgusting old vows—whereupon he was let loose to rejoin the society of extremely decent people." Out of this came *The Crucible* (1953), in which the hero, John Proctor, allows himself to be executed rather than sign away his name and his children's respect. Hysteria touched Miller personally when he was denied a passport and in 1957 was convicted of contempt of Congress for refusing to name suspected communists (this conviction was unanimously overturned by the Supreme Court the following year).

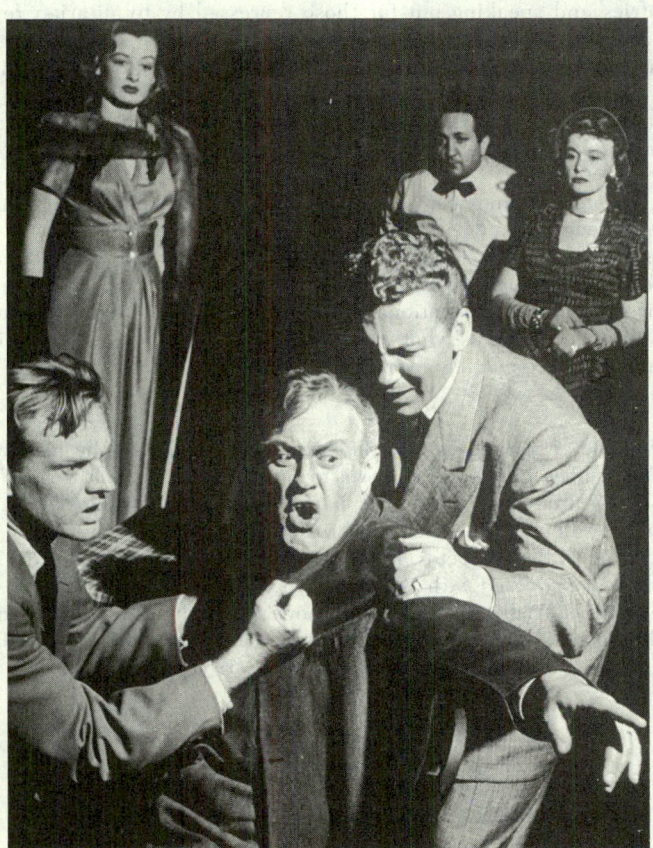

Actor Lee J. Cobb as Willy Loman being restrained by actors Arthur Kennedy (left) and Cameron Mitchell (right) as his sons Biff and Hap respectively in the 1949 original Broadway production of *Death of a Salesman*.

Miller had long been looking for a way to dramatize what he had earlier learned about mob control of the Brooklyn waterfront and finally did so in the one-act play *A View from the Bridge*, produced with *A Memory of Two Mondays* in 1955; later he would rework *View* into a full-length play. Meanwhile, he had met the glamorous movie actress Marilyn Monroe; they married in 1956, after he divorced his first wife. He wrote the screenplay *The Misfits* for Monroe, but in their private life, their complex natures were ill-sorted. The marriage ended in divorce in 1961, and a year later he married the photographer Ingeborg Morath, with whom he collaborated on several books of photographs and essays.

In 1964 two plays opened: *After the Fall* (in which the protagonist is a thinly disguised Miller investigating his family, his responsibilities, and his wives) and *Incident at Vichy* (about Jews and Nazis in Vichy, France). While these were by no means as successful as *Salesman*, they returned him seriously to the stage. Among later plays are *The Price* (1968), *The Creation of the World and Other Business* (1972), *The Archbishop's Ceiling* (1977), and two one-act plays under the title *Danger: Memory!* (1986). These last fared poorly in New York, but found successful productions elsewhere in the world.

Miller in his later years was something of an activist. In the late 1960s he was asked to become president of PEN (Poets, Essayists, Novelists), the international writers' group. By opening this organization to writers in what were then Iron Curtain countries and speaking out for those repressed by totalitarian regimes, he became a respected champion of human rights.

Like his contemporary Tennessee Williams, Miller rejected the influence of "mawkish twenties slang" and "deadly repetitiveness." Again like Williams, Miller was impatient with prosy dialogue and well-made structures. As he explained, the success of *A Streetcar Named Desire* in 1947 helped him write *Death of a Salesman*:

> With *Streetcar*, Tennessee had printed a license to speak at full throat, and it helped strengthen me as I turned to Willy Loman, a salesman always full of words, and better yet, a man who could never cease trying, like Adam, to name himself and the world's wonders. I had known all along that this play could not be encompassed by conventional realism, and for one integral reason: in Willy the past was as alive as what was happening at the moment, sometimes even crashing in to completely overwhelm his mind. I wanted precisely the same fluidity of form.

In *Salesman* the action moves effortlessly from the present—the last twenty-four hours of Willy's life—into moments in his memory, symbolized in the stage setting by the idyllic leaves around his house that, in these past moments, block out the threatening apartment houses. The successful realization of this fluidity on the stage was greatly aided by Miller's director, Elia Kazan, and his stage designer, Jo Mielziner, both of whom had worked with Williams two years earlier on *Streetcar*. A striking difference between Williams and Miller, however, is the latter's overt moralizing, which adds a didactic element to his plays not to be found in those of Williams.

The text is from *Arthur Miller's Collected Plays* (1957).

Death of a Salesman

Certain Private Conversations in Two Acts and a Requiem

THE CHARACTERS

WILLY LOMAN	THE WOMAN	JENNY
LINDA	CHARLEY	STANLEY
BIFF	UNCLE BEN	MISS FORSYTHE
HAPPY	HOWARD WAGNER	LETTA
BERNARD		

The action takes place in WILLY LOMAN's *house and yard and in various places he visits in the New York and Boston of today.*

Act One

A melody is heard, playing upon a flute. It is small and fine, telling of grass and trees and the horizon. The curtain rises.

Before us is the Salesman's house. We are aware of towering, angular shapes behind it, surrounding it on all sides. Only the blue light of the sky falls upon the house and forestage; the surrounding area shows an angry flow of orange. As more light appears, we see a solid vault of apartment houses around the small, fragile-seeming home. An air of the dream clings to the place, a dream rising out of reality. The kitchen at center seems actual enough, for there is a kitchen table with three chairs, and a refrigerator. But no other fixtures are seen. At the back of the kitchen there is a draped entrance, which leads to the living-room. To the right of the kitchen, on a level raised two feet, is a bedroom furnished only with a brass bedstead and a straight chair. On a shelf over the bed a silver athletic trophy stands. A window opens onto the apartment house at the side.

Behind the kitchen, on a level raised six and a half feet, is the boys' bedroom, at present barely visible. Two beds are dimly seen, and at the back of the room a dormer window. (This bedroom is above the unseen living-room.) At the left a stairway curves up to it from the kitchen.

The entire setting is wholly or, in some places, partially transparent. The roofline of the house is one-dimensional; under and over it we see the apartment buildings. Before the house lies an apron, curving beyond the forestage into the orchestra. This forward area serves as the back yard as well as the locale of all WILLY's *imaginings and of his city scenes. Whenever the action is in the present the actors observe the imaginary wall-lines, entering the house only through its door at the left. But in the scenes of the past these boundaries are broken, and characters enter or leave a room by stepping "through" a wall onto the forestage.*

From the right, WILLY LOMAN, *the Salesman, enters, carrying two large sample cases. The flute plays on. He hears but is not aware of it. He is past sixty years of age, dressed quietly. Even as he crosses the stage to the doorway of the house, his exhaustion is apparent. He unlocks the door, comes into the kitchen, and thankfully lets his burden down, feeling the soreness of his palms. A word-sigh escapes his lips—it might be "Oh, boy, oh, boy." He closes the door, then carries his cases out into the living-room, through the draped kitchen doorway.*

LINDA, his wife, has stirred in her bed at the right. She gets out and puts on a robe, listening. Most often jovial, she has developed an iron repression of her exceptions to WILLY's *behavior—she more than loves him, she admires him, as though his mercurial nature, his temper, his massive dreams and little cruelties, served her only as sharp reminders of the turbulent longings within him, longings which she shares but lacks the temperament to utter and follow to their end.*

LINDA [*hearing* WILLY *outside the bedroom, calls with some trepidation*]
  Willy!
WILLY It's all right. I came back.
LINDA Why? What happened? [*slight pause*] Did something happen,
  Willy?
WILLY No, nothing happened.
LINDA You didn't smash the car, did you?
WILLY [*with casual irritation*] I said nothing happened. Didn't you hear me?
LINDA Don't you feel well?
WILLY I'm tired to the death. [*The flute has faded away. He sits on the bed
  beside her, a little numb.*] I couldn't make it. I just couldn't make it, Linda.
LINDA [*very carefully, delicately*] Where were you all day? You look terrible.
WILLY I got as far as a little above Yonkers. I stopped for a cup of coffee.
  Maybe it was the coffee.
LINDA What?
WILLY [*after a pause*] I suddenly couldn't drive any more. The car kept
  going off onto the shoulder, y'know?
LINDA [*helpfully*] Oh. Maybe it was the steering again. I don't think Angelo
  knows the Studebaker.
WILLY No, it's me, it's me. Suddenly I realize I'm goin' sixty miles an hour
  and I don't remember the last five minutes. I'm—I can't seem to—keep
  my mind to it.
LINDA Maybe it's your glasses. You never went for your new glasses.
WILLY No, I see everything. I came back ten miles an hour. It took me
  nearly four hours from Yonkers.
LINDA [*resigned*] Well, you'll just have to take a rest, Willy, you can't con-
  tinue this way.
WILLY I just got back from Florida.
LINDA But you didn't rest your mind. Your mind is overactive, and the
  mind is what counts, dear.
WILLY I'll start out in the morning. Maybe I'll feel better in the morning.
  [*She is taking off his shoes.*] These goddam arch supports are killing me.
LINDA Take an aspirin. Should I get you an aspirin? It'll soothe you.
WILLY [*with wonder*] I was driving along, you understand? And I was
  fine. I was even observing the scenery. You can imagine, me looking at
  scenery, on the road every week of my life. But it's so beautiful up there,
  Linda, the trees are so thick, and the sun is warm. I opened the wind-
  shield and just let the warm air bathe over me. And then all of a sudden
  I'm goin' off the road! I'm tellin' ya, I absolutely forgot I was driving. If
  I'd've gone the other way over the white line I might've killed somebody.
  So I went on again—and five minutes later I'm dreamin' again, and I
  nearly— [*He presses two fingers against his eyes.*] I have such thoughts,
  I have such strange thoughts.
LINDA Willy, dear. Talk to them again. There's no reason why you can't
  work in New York.
WILLY They don't need me in New York. I'm the New England man. I'm
  vital in New England.
LINDA But you're sixty years old. They can't expect you to keep traveling
  every week.
WILLY I'll have to send a wire to Portland. I'm supposed to see Brown
  and Morrison tomorrow morning at ten o'clock to show the line. Goddammit, I could sell them! [*He starts putting on his jacket.*]

LINDA [*taking the jacket from him*] Why don't you go down to the place tomorrow and tell Howard you've simply got to work in New York? You're too accommodating, dear.

WILLY If old man Wagner was alive I'd a been in charge of New York now! That man was a prince, he was a masterful man. But that boy of his, that Howard, he don't appreciate. When I went north the first time, the Wagner Company didn't know where New England was!

LINDA Why don't you tell those things to Howard, dear?

WILLY [*encouraged*] I will, I definitely will. Is there any cheese?

LINDA I'll make you a sandwich.

WILLY No, go to sleep. I'll take some milk. I'll be up right away. The boys in?

LINDA They're sleeping. Happy took Biff on a date tonight.

WILLY [*interested*] That so?

LINDA It was so nice to see them shaving together, one behind the other, in the bathroom. And going out together. You notice? The whole house smells of shaving lotion.

WILLY Figure it out. Work a lifetime to pay off a house. You finally own it, and there's nobody to live in it.

LINDA Well, dear, life is a casting off. It's always that way.

WILLY No, no, some people—some people accomplish something. Did Biff say anything after I went this morning?

LINDA You shouldn't have criticized him, Willy, especially after he just got off the train. You mustn't lose your temper with him.

WILLY When the hell did I lose my temper? I simply asked him if he was making any money. Is that a criticism?

LINDA But, dear, how could he make any money?

WILLY [*worried and angered*] There's such an undercurrent in him. He became a moody man. Did he apologize when I left this morning?

LINDA He was crestfallen, Willy. You know how he admires you. I think if he finds himself, then you'll both be happier and not fight any more.

WILLY How can he find himself on a farm? Is that a life? A farmhand? In the beginning, when he was young, I thought, well, a young man, it's good for him to tramp around, take a lot of different jobs. But it's more than ten years now and he has yet to make thirty-five dollars a week?

LINDA He's finding himself, Willy.

WILLY Not finding yourself at the age of thirty-four is a disgrace!

LINDA Shh!

WILLY The trouble is he's lazy, goddammit!

LINDA Willy, please!

WILLY Biff is a lazy bum!

LINDA They're sleeping. Get something to eat. Go on down.

WILLY Why did he come home? I would like to know what brought him home.

LINDA I don't know. I think he's still lost, Willy. I think he's very lost.

WILLY Biff Loman is lost. In the greatest country in the world a young man with such—personal attractiveness, gets lost. And such a hard worker. There's one thing about Biff—he's not lazy.

LINDA Never.

WILLY [*with pity and resolve*] I'll see him in the morning; I'll have a nice talk with him. I'll get him a job selling. He could be big in no time. My God! Remember how they used to follow him around in high school?

When he smiled at one of them their faces lit up. When he walked down the street . . . [*He loses himself in reminiscences.*]

LINDA [*trying to bring him out of it*] Willy, dear, I got a new kind of American-type cheese today. It's whipped.

WILLY Why do you get American when I like Swiss?

LINDA I just thought you'd like a change—

WILLY I don't want a change! I want Swiss cheese. Why am I always being contradicted?

LINDA [*with a covering laugh*] I thought it would be a surprise.

WILLY Why don't you open a window in here, for God's sake?

LINDA [*with infinite patience*] They're all open, dear.

WILLY The way they boxed us in here. Bricks and windows, windows and bricks.

LINDA We should've bought the land next door.

WILLY The street is lined with cars. There's not a breath of fresh air in the neighborhood. The grass don't grow any more, you can't raise a carrot in the back yard. They should've had a law against apartment houses. Remember those two beautiful elm trees out there? When I and Biff hung the swing between them?

LINDA Yeah, like being a million miles from the city.

WILLY They should've arrested the builder for cutting those down. They massacred the neighborhood. [*lost*] More and more I think of those days, Linda. This time of year it was lilac and wisteria. And then the peonies would come out, and the daffodils. What fragrance in this room!

LINDA Well, after all, people had to move somewhere.

WILLY No, there's more people now.

LINDA I don't think there's more people. I think—

WILLY There's more people! That's what's ruining this country! Population is getting out of control. The competition is maddening! Smell the stink from that apartment house! And another one on the other side . . . How can they whip cheese?

[*On* WILLY's *last line,* BIFF *and* HAPPY *raise themselves up in their beds, listening.*]

LINDA Go down, try it. And be quiet.

WILLY [*turning to* LINDA, *guiltily*] You're not worried about me, are you, sweetheart?

BIFF What's the matter?

HAPPY Listen!

LINDA You've got too much on the ball to worry about.

WILLY You're my foundation and my support, Linda.

LINDA Just try to relax, dear. You make mountains out of molehills.

WILLY I won't fight with him any more. If he wants to go back to Texas, let him go.

LINDA He'll find his way.

WILLY Sure. Certain men just don't get started till later in life. Like Thomas Edison, I think. Or B. F. Goodrich. One of them was deaf. [*He starts for the bedroom doorway.*] I'll put my money on Biff.

LINDA And Willy—if it's warm Sunday we'll drive in the country. And we'll open the windshield, and take lunch.

WILLY No, the windshields don't open on the new cars.

LINDA But you opened it today.

WILLY   Me? I didn't. [*He stops.*] Now isn't that peculiar! Isn't that a remarkable—[*He breaks off in amazement and fright as the flute is heard distantly.*]

LINDA   What, darling?

WILLY   That is the most remarkable thing.

LINDA   What, dear?

WILLY   I was thinking of the Chevvy. [*slight pause*] Nineteen twenty-
eight . . . when I had that red Chevvy—[*breaks off*] That funny? I coulda
sworn I was driving that Chevvy today.

LINDA   Well, that's nothing. Something must've reminded you.

WILLY   Remarkable. Ts. Remember those days? The way Biff used to simo-
nize that car? The dealer refused to believe there was eighty thousand
miles on it. [*He shakes his head.*] Heh! [*to* LINDA] Close your eyes, I'll be
right up. [*He walks out of the bedroom.*]

HAPPY [*to* BIFF]   Jesus, maybe he smashed up the car again!

LINDA [*calling after* WILLY]   Be careful on the stairs, dear! The cheese is
on the middle shelf! [*She turns, goes over to the bed, takes his jacket, and
goes out of the bedroom.*]

> [*Light has risen on the boys' room. Unseen,* WILLY *is heard talking to
> himself, "Eighty thousand miles," and a little laugh.* BIFF *gets out of bed,
> comes downstage a bit, and stands attentively.* BIFF *is two years older
> than his brother* HAPPY, *well built, but in these days bears a worn air and
> seems less self-assured. He has succeeded less, and his dreams are stron-
> ger and less acceptable than* HAPPY'S. HAPPY *is tall, powerfully made.
> Sexuality is like a visible color on him, or a scent that many women have
> discovered. He, like his brother, is lost, but in a different way, for he has
> never allowed himself to turn his face toward defeat and is thus more
> confused and hard-skinned, although seemingly more content.*]

HAPPY [*getting out of bed*]   He's going to get his license taken away if he
keeps that up. I'm getting nervous about him, y'know, Biff?

BIFF   His eyes are going.

HAPPY   No, I've driven with him. He sees all right. He just doesn't keep
his mind on it. I drove into the city with him last week. He stops at a
green light and then it turns red and he goes. [*He laughs.*]

BIFF   Maybe he's color-blind.

HAPPY   Pop? Why he's got the finest eye for color in the business. You know
that.

BIFF [*sitting down on his bed*]   I'm going to sleep.

HAPPY   You're not still sour on Dad, are you Biff?

BIFF   He's all right, I guess.

WILLY [*underneath them, in the living-room*]   Yes, sir, eighty thousand
miles—eighty-two thousand!

BIFF   You smoking?

HAPPY [*holding out a pack of cigarettes*]   Want one?

BIFF [*taking a cigarette*]   I can never sleep when I smell it.

WILLY   What a simonizing job, heh!

HAPPY [*with deep sentiment*]   Funny, Biff, y'know? Us sleeping in here
again? The old beds. [*He pats his bed affectionately.*] All the talk that
went across those two beds, huh? Our whole lives.

BIFF   Yeah. Lotta dreams and plans.

HAPPY [*with a deep and masculine laugh*]   About five hundred women
would like to know what was said in this room.

> [*They share a soft laugh.*]

BIFF   Remember that big Betsy something—what the hell was her name—over on Bushwick Avenue?

HAPPY [*combing his hair*]   With the collie dog!

BIFF   That's the one. I got you in there, remember?

HAPPY   Yeah, that was my first time—I think. Boy, there was a pig! [*They laugh, almost crudely.*] You taught me everything I know about women. Don't forget that.

BIFF   I bet you forgot how bashful you used to be. Especially with girls.

HAPPY   Oh, I still am, Biff.

BIFF   Oh, go on.

HAPPY   I just control it, that's all. I think I got less bashful and you got more so. What happened, Biff? Where's the old humor, the old confidence? [*He shakes* BIFF's *knee.* BIFF *gets up and moves restlessly about the room.*] What's the matter?

BIFF   Why does Dad mock me all the time?

HAPPY   He's not mocking you, he—

BIFF   Everything I say there's a twist of mockery on his face. I can't get near him.

HAPPY   He just wants you to make good, that's all. I wanted to talk to you about Dad for a long time, Biff. Something's—happening to him. He—talks to himself.

BIFF   I noticed that this morning. But he always mumbled.

HAPPY   But not so noticeable. It got so embarrassing I sent him to Florida. And you know something? Most of the time he's talking to you.

BIFF   What's he say about me?

HAPPY   I can't make it out.

BIFF   What's he say about me?

HAPPY   I think the fact that you're not settled, that you're still kind of up in the air . . .

BIFF   There's one or two other things depressing him, Happy.

HAPPY   What do you mean?

BIFF   Never mind. Just don't lay it all to me.

HAPPY   But I think if you just got started—I mean—is there any future for you out there?

BIFF   I tell ya, Hap, I don't know what the future is. I don't know—what I'm supposed to want.

HAPPY   What do you mean?

BIFF   Well, I spent six or seven years after high school trying to work myself up. Shipping clerk, salesman, business of one kind or another. And it's a measly manner of existence. To get on that subway on the hot mornings in summer. To devote your whole life to keeping stock, or making phone calls, or selling or buying. To suffer fifty weeks of the year for the sake of a two-week vacation, when all you really desire is to be outdoors, with your shirt off. And always to have to get ahead of the next fella. And still—that's how you build a future.

HAPPY   Well, you really enjoy it on a farm? Are you content out there?

BIFF [*with rising agitation*]   Hap, I've had twenty or thirty different kinds of jobs since I left home before the war, and it always turns out the same. I just realized it lately. In Nebraska when I herded cattle, and the Dakotas, and Arizona, and now in Texas. It's why I came home now, I guess, because I realized it. This farm I work on, it's spring there now, see? And they've got about fifteen new colts. There's nothing more inspiring or—

beautiful than the sight of a mare and a new colt. And it's cool there now, see? Texas is cool now, and it's spring. And whenever spring comes to where I am, I suddenly get the feeling, my God, I'm not gettin' anywhere! What the hell am I doing, playing around with horses, twenty-eight dollars a week! I'm thirty-four years old. I oughta be makin' my future. That's when I come running home. And now, I get here, and I don't know what to do with myself. [*after a pause*] I've always made a point of not wasting my life, and everytime I come back here I know that all I've done is to waste my life.

HAPPY   You're a poet, you know that, Biff? You're a—you're an idealist!

BIFF   No, I'm mixed up very bad. Maybe I oughta get married. Maybe I oughta get stuck into something. Maybe that's my trouble. I'm like a boy. I'm not married. I'm not in business, I just—I'm like a boy. Are you content, Hap? You're a success, aren't you? Are you content?

HAPPY   Hell, no!

BIFF   Why? You're making money, aren't you?

HAPPY   [*moving about with energy, expressiveness*]   All I can do now is wait for the merchandise manager to die. And suppose I get to be merchandise manager? He's a good friend of mine, and he just built a terrific estate on Long Island. And he lived there about two months and sold it, and now he's building another one. He can't enjoy it once it's finished. And I know that's just what I would do. I don't know what the hell I'm workin' for. Sometimes I sit in my apartment—all alone. And I think of the rent I'm paying. And it's crazy. But then, it's what I always wanted. My own apartment, a car, and plenty of women. And still, goddammit, I'm lonely.

BIFF   [*with enthusiasm*]   Listen why don't you come out West with me?

HAPPY   You and I, heh?

BIFF   Sure, maybe we could buy a ranch. Raise cattle, use our muscles. Men built like we are should be working out in the open.

HAPPY   [*avidly*]   The Loman Brothers, heh?

BIFF   [*with vast affection*]   Sure, we'd be known all over the counties!

HAPPY   [*enthralled*]   That's what I dream about, Biff. Sometimes I want to just rip my clothes off in the middle of the store and outbox that goddam merchandise manager. I mean I can outbox, outrun, and outlift anybody in that store, and I have to take orders from those common, petty sons-of-bitches till I can't stand it any more.

BIFF   I'm tellin' you, kid, if you were with me I'd be happy out there.

HAPPY   [*enthused*]   See, Biff, everybody around me is so false that I'm constantly lowering my ideals . . .

BIFF   Baby, together we'd stand up for one another, we'd have someone to trust.

HAPPY   If I were around you—

BIFF   Hap, the trouble is we weren't brought up to grub for money. I don't know how to do it.

HAPPY   Neither can I!

BIFF   Then let's go!

HAPPY   The only thing is—what can you make out there?

BIFF   But look at your friend. Builds an estate and then hasn't the peace of mind to live in it.

HAPPY   Yeah, but when he walks into the store the waves part in front of him. That's fifty-two thousand dollars a year coming through the revolving door, and I got more in my pinky finger than he's got in his head.

BIFF   Yeah, but you just said—

HAPPY   I gotta show some of those pompous, self-important executives over there that Hap Loman can make the grade. I want to walk into the store the way he walks in. Then I'll go with you, Biff. We'll be together yet, I swear. But take those two we had tonight. Now weren't they gorgeous creatures?

BIFF   Yeah, yeah, most gorgeous I've had in years.

HAPPY   I get that any time I want, Biff. Whenever I feel disgusted. The only trouble is, it gets like bowling or something. I just keep knockin' them over and it doesn't mean anything. You still run around a lot?

BIFF   Naa. I'd like to find a girl—steady, somebody with substance.

HAPPY   That's what I long for.

BIFF   Go on! You'd never come home.

HAPPY   I would! Somebody with character, with resistance! Like Mom, y'know? You're gonna call me a bastard when I tell you this. That girl Charlotte I was with tonight is engaged to be married in five weeks. [*He tries on his new hat.*]

BIFF   No kiddin'!

HAPPY   Sure, the guy's in line for the vice-presidency of the store. I don't know what gets into me, maybe I just have an overdeveloped sense of competition or something, but I went and ruined her, and furthermore I can't get rid of her. And he's the third executive I've done that to. Isn't that a crummy characteristic? And to top it all, I go to their weddings! [*indignantly, but laughing*] Like I'm not supposed to take bribes. Manufacturers offer me a hundred-dollar bill now and then to throw an order their way. You know how honest I am, but it's like this girl, see. I hate myself for it. Because I don't want the girl, and, still, I take it and—I love it!

BIFF   Let's go to sleep.

HAPPY   I guess we didn't settle anything, heh?

BIFF   I just got one idea that I think I'm going to try.

HAPPY   What's that?

BIFF   Remember Bill Oliver?

HAPPY   Sure, Oliver is very big now. You want to work for him again?

BIFF   No, but when I quit he said something to me. He put his arm on my shoulder, and he said, "Biff, if you ever need anything, come to me."

HAPPY   I remember that. That sounds good.

BIFF   I think I'll go to see him. If I could get ten thousand or even seven or eight thousand dollars I could buy a beautiful ranch.

HAPPY   I bet he'd back you. 'Cause he thought highly of you, Biff. I mean, they all do. You're well liked, Biff. That's why I say to come back here, and we both have the apartment. And I'm tellin' you, Biff, any babe you want . . .

BIFF   No, with a ranch I could do the work I like and still be something. I just wonder though. I wonder if Oliver still thinks I stole that carton of basketballs.

HAPPY   Oh, he probably forgot that long ago. It's almost ten years. You're too sensitive. Anyway, he didn't really fire you.

BIFF   Well, I think he was going to. I think that's why I quit. I was never sure whether he knew or not. I know he thought the world of me, though. I was the only one he'd let lock up the place.

WILLY [*below*]   You gonna wash the engine, Biff?

HAPPY Shh!
[BIFF *looks at* HAPPY, *who is gazing down, listening.* WILLY *is mumbling in the parlor.*]
HAPPY You hear that?
[*They listen.* WILLY *laughs warmly.*]
BIFF [*growing angry*] Doesn't he know Mom can hear that?
WILLY Don't get your sweater dirty, Biff!
[*A look of pain crosses* BIFF's *face.*]
HAPPY Isn't that terrible? Don't leave again, will you? You'll find a job here. You gotta stick around. I don't know what to do about him, it's getting embarrassing.
WILLY What a simonizing job!
BIFF Mom's hearing that!
WILLY No kiddin', Biff, you got a date? Wonderful!
HAPPY Go on to sleep. But talk to him in the morning, will you?
BIFF [*reluctantly getting into bed*] With her in the house. Brother!
HAPPY [*getting into bed*] I wish you'd have a good talk with him.
[*The light on their room begins to fade.*]
BIFF [*to himself in bed*] That selfish, stupid . . .
HAPPY Sh . . . Sleep, Biff.
[*Their light is out. Well before they have finished speaking,* WILLY's *form is dimly seen below in the darkened kitchen. He opens the refrigerator, searches in there, and takes out a bottle of milk. The apartment houses are fading out, and the entire house and surroundings become covered with leaves. Music insinuates itself as the leaves appear.*]
WILLY Just wanna be careful with those girls, Biff, that's all. Don't make any promises. No promises of any kind. Because a girl, y'know, they always believe what you tell 'em, and you're very young, Biff, you're too young to be talking seriously to girls.
[*Light rises on the kitchen.* WILLY, *talking, shuts the refrigerator door and comes downstage to the kitchen table. He pours milk into a glass. He is totally immersed in himself, smiling faintly.*]
WILLY Too young entirely, Biff. You want to watch your schooling first. Then when you're all set, there'll be plenty of girls for a boy like you. [*He smiles broadly at a kitchen chair.*] That so? The girls pay for you? [*He laughs.*] Boy, you must really be makin' a hit.
[WILLY *is gradually addressing—physically—a point offstage, speaking through the wall of the kitchen, and his voice has been rising in volume to that of a normal conversation.*]
WILLY I been wondering why you polish the car so careful. Ha! Don't leave the hubcaps, boys. Get the chamois to the hubcaps. Happy, use newspaper on the windows, it's the easiest thing. Show him how to do it, Biff! You see, Happy? Pad it up, use it like a pad. That's it, that's it, good work. You're doin' all right, Hap. [*He pauses, then nods in approbation for a few seconds, then looks upward.*] Biff, first thing we gotta do when we get time is clip that big branch over the house. Afraid it's gonna fall in a storm and hit the roof. Tell you what. We get a rope and sling her around, and then we climb up there with a couple of saws and take her down. Soon as you finish the car, boys, I wanna see ya. I got a surprise for you, boys.
BIFF [*offstage*] Whatta ya got, Dad?
WILLY No, you finish first. Never leave a job till you're finished— remember that, [*looking toward the "big trees"*] Biff, up in Albany I saw

a beautiful hammock. I think I'll buy it next trip, and we'll hang it right between those two elms. Wouldn't that be something? Just swingin' there under those branches. Boy, that would be . . .

[YOUNG BIFF *and* YOUNG HAPPY *appear from the direction* WILLY *was addressing.* HAPPY *carries rags and a pail of water.* BIFF, *wearing a sweater with a block "S," carries a football.*]

BIFF [*pointing in the direction of the car offstage*] How's that, Pop, professional?

WILLY Terrific. Terrific job, boys. Good work, Biff.

HAPPY Where's the surprise, Pop?

WILLY In the back seat of the car.

HAPPY Boy! [*He runs off.*]

BIFF What is it, Dad? Tell me, what'd you buy?

WILLY [*laughing, cuffs him*] Never mind, something I want you to have.

BIFF [*turns and starts off*] What is it, Hap?

HAPPY [*offstage*] It's a punching bag!

BIFF Oh, Pop!

WILLY It's got Gene Tunney's[1] signature on it!

[HAPPY *runs onstage with a punching bag.*]

BIFF Gee, how'd you know we wanted a punching bag?

WILLY Well, it's the finest thing for the timing.

HAPPY [*lies down on his back and pedals with his feet*] I'm losing weight, you notice, Pop?

WILLY [*to* HAPPY] Jumping rope is good too.

BIFF Did you see the new football I got?

WILLY [*examining the ball*] Where'd you get a new ball?

BIFF The coach told me to practice my passing.

WILLY That so? And he gave you the ball, heh?

BIFF Well, I borrowed it from the locker room. [*He laughs confidentially.*]

WILLY [*laughing with him at the left*] I want you to return that.

HAPPY I told you he wouldn't like it!

BIFF [*angrily*] Well, I'm bringing it back!

WILLY [*stopping the incipient argument, to* HAPPY] Sure, he's gotta practice with a regulation ball, doesn't he? [*to* BIFF] Coach'll probably congratulate you on your initiative!

BIFF Oh, he keeps congratulating my initiative all the time, Pop.

WILLY That's because he likes you. If somebody else took that ball there'd be an uproar. So what's the report, boys, what's the report?

BIFF Where'd you go this time, Dad? Gee we were lonesome for you.

WILLY [*pleased, puts an arm around each boy and they come down to the apron*] Lonesome, heh?

BIFF Missed you every minute.

WILLY Don't say? Tell you a secret, boys. Don't breathe it to a soul. Someday I'll have my own business, and I'll never have to leave home any more.

HAPPY Like Uncle Charley, heh?

WILLY Bigger than Uncle Charley! Because Charley is not—liked. He's liked, but he's not—well liked.

BIFF Where'd you go this time, Dad?

---

1. World heavyweight boxing champion from 1926 to 1928.

WILLY   Well, I got on the road, and I went north to Providence. Met the Mayor.

BIFF   The Mayor of Providence!

WILLY   He was sitting in the hotel lobby.

BIFF   What'd he say?

WILLY   He said, "Morning!" And I said, "You got a fine city here, Mayor." And then he had coffee with me. And then I went to Waterbury. Waterbury is a fine city. Big clock city, the famous Waterbury clock. Sold a nice bill there. And then Boston—Boston is the cradle of the Revolution. A fine city. And a couple of other towns in Mass., and on to Portland and Bangor and straight home!

BIFF   Gee, I'd love to go with you sometime, Dad.

WILLY   Soon as summer comes.

HAPPY   Promise?

WILLY   You and Hap and I, and I'll show you all the towns. America is full of beautiful towns and fine, upstanding people. And they know me, boys, they know me up and down New England. The finest people. And when I bring you fellas up, there'll be open sesame for all of us, 'cause one thing, boys: I have friends. I can park my car in any street in New England, and the cops protect it like their own. This summer, heh?

BIFF and HAPPY [*together*]   Yeah! You bet!

WILLY   We'll take our bathing suits.

HAPPY   We'll carry your bags, Pop!

WILLY   Oh, won't that be something! Me comin' into the Boston stores with you boys carryin' my bags. What a sensation!
   [BIFF *is prancing around, practicing passing the ball.*]

WILLY   You nervous, Biff, about the game?

BIFF   Not if you're gonna be there.

WILLY   What do they say about you in school, now that they made you captain?

HAPPY   There's a crowd of girls behind him everytime the classes change.

BIFF [*taking* WILLY's *hand*]   This Saturday, Pop, this Saturday—just for you, I'm going to break through for a touchdown.

HAPPY   You're supposed to pass.

BIFF   I'm takin' one play for Pop. You watch me, Pop, and when I take off my helmet, that means I'm breakin' out. Then you watch me crash through that line!

WILLY [*kisses* BIFF]   Oh, wait'll I tell this in Boston!
   [BERNARD *enters in knickers. He is younger than* BIFF, *earnest and loyal, a worried boy.*]

BERNARD   Biff, where are you? You're supposed to study with me today.

WILLY   Hey, looka Bernard. What're you lookin' so anemic about, Bernard?

BERNARD   He's gotta study, Uncle Willy. He's got Regents[2] next week.

HAPPY [*tauntingly, spinning* BERNARD *around*]   Let's box, Bernard!

BERNARD   Biff! [*He gets away from* HAPPY.] Listen, Biff, I heard Mr. Birnbaum say that if you don't start studyin' math he's gonna flunk you, and you won't graduate. I heard him!

WILLY   You better study with him, Biff. Go ahead now.

BERNARD   I heard him!

---

2. Compulsory statewide high school examinations in New York.

BIFF   Oh, Pop, you didn't see my sneakers! [*He holds up a foot for* WILLY *to look at.*]

WILLY   Hey, that's a beautiful job of printing!

BERNARD [*wiping his glasses*]   Just because he printed University of Virginia on his sneakers doesn't mean they've got to graduate him, Uncle Willy!

WILLY [*angrily*]   What're you talking about? With scholarships to three universities they're gonna flunk him?

BERNARD   But I heard Mr. Birnbaum say—

WILLY   Don't be a pest, Bernard! [*to his boys*] What an anemic!

BERNARD   Okay, I'm waiting for you in my house, Biff.
         [BERNARD *goes off. The Lomans laugh.*]

WILLY   Bernard is not well liked, is he?

BIFF   He's liked, but he's not well liked.

HAPPY   That's right, Pop.

WILLY   That's just what I mean. Bernard can get the best marks in school, y'understand, but when he gets out in the business world, y'understand, you are going to be five times ahead of him. That's why I thank Almighty God you're both built like Adonises.[3] Because the man who makes an appearance in the business world, the man who creates personal interest, is the man who gets ahead. Be liked and you will never want. You take me, for instance. I never have to wait in line to see a buyer. "Willy Loman is here!" That's all they have to know, and I go right through.

BIFF   Did you knock them dead, Pop?

WILLY   Knocked 'em cold in Providence, slaughtered 'em in Boston.

HAPPY [*on his back, pedaling again*]   I'm losing weight, you notice, Pop?
         [LINDA *enters, as of old, a ribbon in her hair, carrying a basket of washing.*]

LINDA [*with youthful energy*]   Hello, dear!

WILLY   Sweetheart!

LINDA   How'd the Chevvy run?

WILLY   Chevrolet, Linda, is the greatest car ever built. [*to the boys*] Since when do you let your mother carry wash up the stairs?

BIFF   Grab hold there, boy!

HAPPY   Where to, Mom?

LINDA   Hang them up on the line. And you better go down to your friends, Biff. The cellar is full of boys. They don't know what to do with themselves.

BIFF   Ah, when Pop comes home they can wait!

WILLY [*laughs appreciatively*]   You better go down and tell them what to do, Biff.

BIFF   I think I'll have them sweep out the furnace room.

WILLY   Good work, Biff.

BIFF [*goes through wall-line of kitchen to doorway at back and calls down*]   Fellas! Everybody sweep out the furnace room! I'll be right down!

VOICES   All right! Okay, Biff.

BIFF   George and Sam and Frank, come out back! We're hangin' up the wash! Come on, Hap, on the double!
         [*He and* HAPPY *carry out the basket.*]

LINDA   The way they obey him!

---

3. In Greek mythology Adonis was a beautiful youth favored by Aphrodite, the goddess of love.

WILLY   Well, that training, the training. I'm tellin' you, I was sellin' thousands and thousands, but I had to come home.

LINDA   Oh, the whole block'll be at that game. Did you sell anything?

WILLY   I did five hundred gross in Providence and seven hundred gross in Boston.

LINDA   No! Wait a minute, I've got a pencil. [*She pulls pencil and paper out of her apron pocket.*] That makes your commission . . . Two hundred— my God! Two hundred and twelve dollars!

WILLY   Well, I didn't figure it yet, but . . .

LINDA   How much did you do?

WILLY   Well, I—I did—about a hundred and eighty gross in Providence. Well, no—it came to—roughly two hundred gross on the whole trip.

LINDA [*without hesitation*]   Two hundred gross. That's . . . [*She figures.*]

WILLY   The trouble was that three of the stores were half closed for inventory in Boston. Otherwise I woulda broke records.

LINDA   Well, it makes seventy dollars and some pennies. That's very good.

WILLY   What do we owe?

LINDA   Well, on the first there's sixteen dollars on the refrigerator—

WILLY   Why sixteen?

LINDA   Well, the fan belt broke, so it was a dollar eighty.

WILLY   But it's brand new.

LINDA   Well, the man said that's the way it is. Till they work themselves in, y'know.
      [*They move through the wall-line into the kitchen.*]

WILLY   I hope we didn't get stuck on that machine.

LINDA   They got the biggest ads of any of them!

WILLY   I know, it's a fine machine. What else?

LINDA   Well, there's nine-sixty for the washing machine. And for the vacuum cleaner there's three and a half due on the fifteenth. Then the roof, you got twenty-one dollars remaining.

WILLY   It don't leak, does it?

LINDA   No, they did a wonderful job. Then you owe Frank for the carburetor.

WILLY   I'm not going to pay that man! That goddam Chevrolet, they ought to prohibit the manufacture of that car!

LINDA   Well, you owe him three and a half. And odds and ends, comes to around a hundred and twenty dollars by the fifteenth.

WILLY   A hundred and twenty dollars! My God, if business don't pick up I don't know what I'm gonna do!

LINDA   Well, next week you'll do better.

WILLY   Oh, I'll knock 'em dead next week. I'll go to Hartford. I'm very well liked in Hartford. You know, the trouble is, Linda, people don't seem to take to me.
      [*They move onto the forestage.*]

LINDA   Oh, don't be foolish.

WILLY   I know it when I walk in. They seem to laugh at me.

LINDA   Why? Why would they laugh at you? Don't talk that way, Willy.
      [WILLY *moves to the edge of the stage.* LINDA *goes into the kitchen and starts to darn stockings.*]

WILLY   I don't know the reason for it, but they just pass me by. I'm not noticed.

LINDA   But you're doing wonderful, dear. You're making seventy to a hundred dollars a week.

WILLY   But I gotta be at it ten, twelve hours a day. Other men—I don't know—they do it easier. I don't know why—I can't stop myself—I talk too much. A man oughta come in with a few words. One thing about Charley. He's a man of few words, and they respect him.

LINDA   You don't talk too much, you're just lively.

WILLY [smiling]   Well, I figure, what the hell, life is short, a couple of jokes. [to himself] I joke too much! [The smiles goes.]

LINDA   Why? You're—

WILLY   I'm fat. I'm very—foolish to look at, Linda. I didn't tell you, but Christmas time I happened to be calling on F. H. Stewarts, and a salesman I know, as I was going in to see the buyer I heard him say something about—walrus. And I—I cracked him right across the face. I won't take that. I simply will not take that. But they do laugh at me. I know that.

LINDA   Darling . . .

WILLY   I gotta overcome it. I know I gotta overcome it. I'm not dressing to advantage, maybe.

LINDA   Willy, darling, you're the handsomest man in the world—

WILLY   Oh, no, Linda.

LINDA   To me you are. [slight pause] The handsomest.
[From the darkness is heard the laughter of a woman. WILLY doesn't turn to it, but it continues through LINDA's lines.]

LINDA   And the boys, Willy. Few men are idolized by their children the way you are.
[Music is heard as behind a scrim,[4] to the left of the house, THE WOMAN, dimly seen, is dressing.]

WILLY [with great feeling]   You're the best there is, Linda, you're a pal, you know that? On the road—on the road I want to grab you sometimes and just kiss the life outa you.
[The laughter is loud now, and he moves into a brightening area at the left, where THE WOMAN has come from behind the scrim and is standing, putting on her hat, looking into a "mirror" and laughing.]

WILLY   'Cause I get so lonely—especially when business is bad and there's nobody to talk to. I get the feeling that I'll never sell anything again, that I won't make a living for you, or a business, a business for the boys. [He talks through THE WOMAN's subsiding laughter; THE WOMAN primps at the "mirror."] There's so much I want to make for—

THE WOMAN   Me? You didn't make me, Willy. I picked you.

WILLY [pleased]   You picked me?

THE WOMAN [who is quite proper-looking, WILLY's age]   I did. I've been sitting at that desk watching all the salesmen go by, day in, day out. But you've got such a sense of humor, and we do have such a good time together, don't we?

WILLY   Sure, sure. [He takes her in his arms.] Why do you have to go now?

THE WOMAN   It's two o'clock . . .

WILLY   No, come on in! [He pulls her.]

THE WOMAN   . . . my sisters'll be scandalized. When'll you be back?

4. Part of a stage set; a painted gauze curtain that becomes transparent when lighted from the back.

WILLY   Oh, two weeks about. Will you come up again?

THE WOMAN   Sure thing. You do make me laugh. It's good for me. [*She squeezes his arm, kisses him.*] And I think you're a wonderful man.

WILLY   You picked me, heh?

THE WOMAN   Sure. Because you're so sweet. And such a kidder.

WILLY   Well, I'll see you next time I'm in Boston.

THE WOMAN   I'll put you right through to the buyers.

WILLY [*slapping her bottom*]   Right. Well, bottoms up!

THE WOMAN [*slaps him gently and laughs*]   You just kill me, Willy. [*He suddenly grabs her and kisses her roughly.*] You kill me. And thanks for the stockings. I love a lot of stockings. Well, good night.

WILLY   Good night. And keep your pores open!

THE WOMAN   Oh, Willy!

[THE WOMAN *bursts out laughing, and* LINDA's *laughter blends in.* THE WOMAN *disappears into the dark. Now the area at the kitchen table brightens.* LINDA *is sitting where she was at the kitchen table, but now is mending a pair of her silk stockings.*]

LINDA   You are, Willy. The handsomest man. You've got no reason to feel that—

WILLY [*coming out of* THE WOMAN's *dimming area and going over to* LINDA] I'll make it all up to you, Linda. I'll—

LINDA   There's nothing to make up, dear. You're doing fine, better than—

WILLY [*noticing her mending*]   What's that?

LINDA   Just mending my stockings. They're so expensive—

WILLY [*angrily, taking them from her*]   I won't have you mending stockings in this house! Now throw them out!

[LINDA *puts the stockings in her pocket.*]

BERNARD [*entering on the run*]   Where is he? If he doesn't study!

WILLY [*moving to the forestage, with great agitation*]   You'll give him the answers!

BERNARD   I do, but I can't on a Regents! That's a state exam! They're liable to arrest me!

WILLY   Where is he? I'll whip him, I'll whip him!

LINDA   And he'd better give back that football, Willy, it's not nice.

WILLY   Biff! Where is he? Why is he taking everything?

LINDA   He's too rough with the girls, Willy. All the mothers are afraid of him!

WILLY   I'll whip him!

BERNARD   He's driving the car without a license!

[THE WOMAN's *laugh is heard.*]

WILLY   Shut up!

LINDA   All the mothers—

WILLY   Shut up!

BERNARD [*backing quietly away and out*]   Mr. Birnbaum says he's stuck up.

WILLY   Get outa here!

BERNARD   If he doesn't buckle down he'll flunk math! [*He goes off.*]

LINDA   He's right, Willy, you've gotta—

WILLY [*exploding at her*]   There's nothing the matter with him! You want him to be a worm like Bernard? He's got spirit, personality . . .

[*As he speaks,* LINDA, *almost in tears, exist into the living-room.* WILLY *is alone in the kitchen, wilting and staring. The leaves are gone. It is night again, and the apartment houses look down from behind.*]

WILLY   Loaded with it. Loaded! What is he stealing? He's giving it back, isn't he? Why is he stealing? What did I tell him? I never in my life told him anything but decent things.

[HAPPY *in pajamas has come down the stairs;* WILLY *suddenly becomes aware of* HAPPY's *presence.*]

HAPPY   Let's go now, come on.

WILLY [*sitting down at the kitchen table*]   Huh! Why did she have to wax the floors herself? Everytime she waxes the floors she keels over. She knows that!

HAPPY   Shh! Take it easy. What brought you back tonight?

WILLY   I got an awful scare. Nearly hit a kid in Yonkers. God! Why didn't I go to Alaska with my brother Ben that time! Ben! That man was a genius, that man was success incarnate! What a mistake! He begged me to go.

HAPPY   Well, there's no use in—

WILLY   You guys! There was a man started with the clothes on his back and ended up with diamond mines!

HAPPY   Boy, someday I'd like to know how he did it.

WILLY   What's the mystery? The man knew what he wanted and went out and got it! Walked into a jungle, and comes out, the age of twenty-one, and he's rich! The world is an oyster, but you don't crack it open on a mattress!

HAPPY   Pop, I told you I'm gonna retire you for life.

WILLY   You'll retire me for life on seventy goddam dollars a week? And your women and your car and your apartment, and you'll retire me for life! Christ's sake, I couldn't get past Yonkers today! Where are you guys, where are you? The woods are burning! I can't drive a car!

[CHARLEY *has appeared in the doorway. He is a large man, slow of speech, laconic, immovable. In all he says, despite what he says, there is pity, and, now, trepidation. He has a robe over pajamas, slippers on his feet. He enters the kitchen.*]

CHARLEY   Everything all right?

HAPPY   Yeah, Charley, everything's . . .

WILLY   What's the matter?

CHARLEY   I heard some noise. I thought something happened. Can't we do something about the walls? You sneeze in here, and in my house hats blow off.

HAPPY   Let's go to bed, Dad. Come on.

[CHARLEY *signals to* HAPPY *to go.*]

WILLY   You go ahead, I'm not tired at the moment.

HAPPY [*to* WILLY]   Take it easy, huh? [*He exits.*]

WILLY   What're you doin' up?

CHARLEY [*sitting down at the kitchen table opposite* WILLY]   Couldn't sleep good. I had a heartburn.

WILLY   Well, you don't know how to eat.

CHARLEY   I eat with my mouth.

WILLY   No, you're ignorant. You gotta know about vitamins and things like that.

CHARLEY   Come on, let's shoot. Tire you out a little.

WILLY [*hesitantly*]   All right. You got cards?

CHARLEY [*taking a deck from his pocket*]   Yeah, I got them. Someplace. What is it with those vitamins?

WILLY [*dealing*] They build up your bones. Chemistry.

CHARLEY Yeah, but there's no bones in a heartburn.

WILLY What are you talkin' about? Do you know the first thing about it?

CHARLEY Don't get insulted.

WILLY Don't talk about something you don't know anything about.
[*They are playing. Pause.*]

CHARLEY What're you doin' home?

WILLY A little trouble with the car.

CHARLEY Oh. [*pause*] I'd like to take a trip to California.

WILLY Don't say.

CHARLEY You want a job?

WILLY I got a job, I told you that. [*after a slight pause*] What the hell are you offering me a job for?

CHARLEY Don't get insulted.

WILLY Don't insult me.

CHARLEY I don't see no sense in it. You don't have to go on this way.

WILLY I got a good job. [*slight pause*] What do you keep comin' in here for?

CHARLEY You want me to go?

WILLY [*after a pause, withering*] I can't understand it. He's going back to Texas again. What the hell is that?

CHARLEY Let him go.

WILLY I got nothin' to give him, Charley, I'm clean, I'm clean.

CHARLEY He won't starve. None a them starve. Forget about him.

WILLY Then what have I got to remember?

CHARLEY You take it too hard. To hell with it. When a deposit bottle is broken you don't get your nickel back.

WILLY That's easy enough for you to say.

CHARLEY That ain't easy for me to say.

WILLY Did you see the ceiling I put up in the living-room?

CHARLEY Yeah, that's a piece of work. To put up a ceiling is a mystery to me. How do you do it?

WILLY What's the difference?

CHARLEY Well, talk about it.

WILLY You gonna put up a ceiling?

CHARLEY How could I put up a ceiling?

WILLY Then what the hell are you bothering me for?

CHARLEY You're insulted again.

WILLY A man who can't handle tools is not a man. You're disgusting.

CHARLEY Don't call me disgusting, Willy.
[UNCLE BEN, *carrying a valise and an umbrella, enters the forestage from around the right corner of the house. He is a stolid man, in his sixties, with a mustache and an authoritative air. He is utterly certain of his destiny, and there is an aura of far places about him. He enters exactly as* WILLY *speaks.*]

WILLY I'm getting awfully tired, Ben.
[BEN's *music is heard.* BEN *looks around at everything.*]

CHARLEY Good, keep playing; you'll sleep better. Did you call me Ben?
[BEN *looks at his watch.*]

WILLY That's funny. For a second there you reminded me of my brother Ben.

BEN I only have a few minutes. [*He strolls, inspecting the place.* WILLY *and* CHARLEY *continue playing.*]

CHARLEY   You never heard from him again, heh? Since that time?

WILLY   Didn't Linda tell you? Couple of weeks ago we got a letter from his wife in Africa. He died.

CHARLEY   That so.

BEN [*chuckling*]   So this is Brooklyn, eh?

CHARLEY   Maybe you're in for some of his money.

WILLY   Naa, he had seven sons. There's just one opportunity I had with that man . . .

BEN   I must make a train, William. There are several properties I'm looking at in Alaska.

WILLY   Sure, sure! If I'd gone with him to Alaska that time, everything would've been totally different.

CHARLEY   Go on, you'd froze to death up there.

WILLY   What're you talking about?

BEN   Opportunity is tremendous in Alaska, William. Surprised you're not up there.

WILLY   Sure, tremendous.

CHARLEY   Heh?

WILLY   There was the only man I ever met who knew the answers.

CHARLEY   Who?

BEN   How are you all?

WILLY [*taking a pot, smiling*]   Fine, fine.

CHARLEY   Pretty sharp tonight.

BEN   Is Mother living with you?

WILLY   No, she died a long time ago.

CHARLEY   Who?

BEN   That's too bad. Fine specimen of a lady, Mother.

WILLY [*to* CHARLEY]   Heh?

BEN   I'd hoped to see the old girl.

CHARLEY   Who died?

BEN   Heard anything from Father, have you?

WILLY [*unnerved*]   What do you mean, who died?

CHARLEY [*taking a pot*]   What're you talkin' about?

BEN [*looking at his watch*]   William, it's half-past eight!

WILLY [*as though to dispel his confusion he angrily stops* CHARLEY's *hand*]   That's my build!

CHARLEY   I put the ace—

WILLY   If you don't know how to play the game I'm not gonna throw my money away on you!

CHARLEY [*rising*]   It was my ace, for God's sake!

WILLY   I'm through, I'm through!

BEN   When did Mother die?

WILLY   Long ago. Since the beginning you never knew how to play cards.

CHARLEY [*picks up the cards and goes to the door*]   All right! Next time I'll bring a deck with five aces.

WILLY   I don't play that kind of game!

CHARLEY [*turning to him*]   You ought to be ashamed of yourself!

WILLY   Yeah?

CHARLEY   Yeah! [*He goes out.*]

WILLY [*slamming the door after him*]   Ignoramus!

BEN [*as* WILLY *comes toward him through the wall-line of the kitchen*]   So you're William.

WILLY [*shaking* BEN's *hand*]   Ben! I've been waiting for you so long! What's the answer? How did you do it?

BEN   Oh, there's a story in that.

[LINDA *enters the forestage, as of old, carrying the wash basket.*]

LINDA   Is this Ben?

BEN [*gallantly*]   How do you do, my dear.

LINDA   Where've you been all these years? Willy's always wondered why you—

WILLY [*pulling* BEN *away from her impatiently*]   Where is Dad? Didn't you follow him? How did you get started?

BEN   Well, I don't know how much you remember.

WILLY   Well, I was just a baby, of course, only three or four years old—

BEN   Three years and eleven months.

WILLY   What a memory, Ben!

BEN   I have many enterprises, William, and I have never kept books.

WILLY   I remember I was sitting under the wagon in—was it Nebraska?

BEN   It was South Dakota, and I gave you a bunch of wild flowers.

WILLY   I remember you walking away down some open road.

BEN [*laughing*]   I was going to find Father in Alaska.

WILLY   Where is he?

BEN   At that age I had a very faulty view of geography, William. I discovered after a few days that I was heading due south, so instead of Alaska, I ended up in Africa.

LINDA   Africa!

WILLY   The Gold Coast!

BEN   Principally diamond mines.

LINDA   Diamond mines!

BEN   Yes, my dear. But I've only a few minutes—

WILLY   No! Boys! Boys! [YOUNG BIFF *and* HAPPY *appear.*] Listen to this. This is your Uncle Ben, a great man! Tell my boys, Ben!

BEN   Why, boys, when I was seventeen I walked into the jungle, and when I was twenty-one I walked out. [*He laughs.*] And by God I was rich.

WILLY [*to the boys*]   You see what I been talking about? The greatest things can happen!

BEN [*glancing at his watch*]   I have an appointment in Ketchikan Tuesday week.

WILLY   No, Ben! Please tell about Dad. I want my boys to hear. I want them to know the kind of stock they spring from. All I remember is a man with a big beard, and I was in Mamma's lap, sitting around a fire, and some kind of high music.

BEN   His flute. He played the flute.

WILLY   Sure, the flute, that's right!

[*New music is heard, a high, rollicking tune.*]

BEN   Father was a very great and a very wild-hearted man. We would start in Boston, and he'd toss the whole family into the wagon, and then he'd drive the team right across the country; through Ohio, and Indiana, Michigan, Illinois, and all the Western states. And we'd stop in the towns and sell the flutes that he'd made on the way. Great inventor, Father. With one gadget he made more in a week than a man like you could make in a lifetime.

WILLY   That's just the way I'm bringing them up, Ben—rugged, well liked, all-around.

BEN Yeah? [*to* BIFF] Hit that, boy—hard as you can. [*He pounds his stomach.*]

BIFF Oh, no, sir!

BEN [*taking boxing stance*] Come on, get to me! [*He laughs.*]

WILLY Go to it, Biff! Go ahead, show him!

BIFF Okay! [*He cocks his fist and starts in.*]

LINDA [*to* WILLY] Why must he fight, dear?

BEN [*sparring with* BIFF] Good boy! Good boy!

WILLY How's that, Ben, heh?

HAPPY Give him the left, Biff!

LINDA Why are you fighting?

BEN Good boy! [*Suddenly comes in, trips* BIFF, *and stands over him, the point of his umbrella poised over* BIFF's *eye.*]

LINDA Look out, Biff!

BIFF Gee!

BEN [*patting* BIFF's *knee*] Never fight fair with a stranger, boy. You'll never get out of the jungle that way. [*taking* LINDA's *hand and bowing*] It was an honor and a pleasure to meet you, Linda.

LINDA [*withdrawing her hand coldly, frightened*] Have a nice—trip.

BEN [*to* WILLY] And good luck with your—what do you do?

WILLY Selling.

BEN Yes. Well . . . [*He raises his hand in farewell to all.*]

WILLY No, Ben, I don't want you to think . . . [*He takes* BEN's *arm to show him.*] It's Brooklyn, I know, but we hunt too.

BEN Really, now.

WILLY Oh, sure, there's snakes and rabbits and—that's why I moved out here. Why, Biff can fell any one of these trees in no time! Boys! Go right over to where they're building the apartment house and get some sand. We're gonna rebuild the entire front stoop right now! Watch this, Ben!

BIFF Yes, sir! On the double, Hap!

HAPPY [*as he and* BIFF *run off*] I lost weight, Pop, you notice?

[CHARLEY *enters in knickers, even before the boys are gone.*]

CHARLEY Listen, if they steal any more from that building the watchman'll put the cops on them!

LINDA [*to* WILLY] Don't let Biff . . .

[BEN *laughs lustily.*]

WILLY You shoulda seen the lumber they brought home last week. At least a dozen six-by-tens worth all kinds a money.

CHARLEY Listen, if that watchman—

WILLY I gave them hell, understand. But I got a couple of fearless characters there.

CHARLEY Willy, the jails are full of fearless characters.

BEN [*clapping* WILLY *on the back, with a laugh at* CHARLEY] And the stock exchange, friend!

WILLY [*joining in* BEN's *laughter*] Where are the rest of your pants?

CHARLEY My wife bought them.

WILLY Now all you need is a golf club and you can go upstairs and go to sleep. [*to* BEN] Great athlete! Between him and his son Bernard they can't hammer a nail!

BERNARD [*rushing in*] The watchman's chasing Biff!

WILLY [*angrily*] Shut up! He's not stealing anything!

LINDA [*alarmed, hurrying off left*]   Where is he? Biff, dear! [*She exits.*]

WILLY [*moving toward the left, away from* BEN]   There's nothing wrong. What's the matter with you?

BEN   Nervy boy. Good!

WILLY [*laughing*]   Oh, nerves of iron, that Biff!

CHARLEY   Don't know what it is. My New England man comes back and he's bleedin', they murdered him up there.

WILLY   It's contacts, Charley, I got important contacts!

CHARLEY [*sarcastically*]   Glad to hear it, Willy. Come in later, we'll shoot a little casino. I'll take some of your Portland money. [*He laughs at* WILLY *and exits.*]

WILLY [*turning to* BEN]   Business is bad, it's murderous. But not for me, of course.

BEN   I'll stop by on my way back to Africa.

WILLY [*longingly*]   Can't you stay a few days? You're just what I need, Ben, because I—I have a fine position here, but I—well, Dad left when I was such a baby and I never had a chance to talk to him and I still feel— kind of temporary about myself.

BEN   I'll be late for my train.

[*They are at opposite ends of the stage.*]

WILLY   Ben, my boys—can't we talk? They'd go into the jaws of hell for me, see, but I—

BEN   William, you're being first-rate with your boys. Outstanding, manly chaps!

WILLY [*hanging on to his words*]   Oh, Ben, that's good to hear! Because sometimes I'm afraid that I'm not teaching them the right kind of—Ben, how should I teach them?

BEN [*giving great weight to each word, and with a certain vicious audacity*] William, when I walked into the jungle, I was seventeen. When I walked out I was twenty-one. And, by God, I was rich! [*He goes off into darkness around the right corner of the house.*]

WILLY   . . . was rich! That's just the spirit I want to imbue them with! To walk into a jungle! I was right! I was right! I was right!

[BEN *is gone, but* WILLY *is still speaking to him as* LINDA, *in nightgown and robe, enters the kitchen, glances around for* WILLY, *then goes to the door of the house, looks out and sees him. Comes down to his left. He looks at her.*]

LINDA   Willy, dear? Willy?

WILLY   I was right!

LINDA   Did you have some cheese? [*He can't answer.*] It's very late, dar- ling. Come to bed, heh?

WILLY [*looking straight up*]   Gotta break your neck to see a star in this yard.

LINDA   You coming in?

WILLY   Whatever happened to that diamond watch fob? Remember? When Ben came from Africa that time? Didn't he give me a watch fob with a diamond in it?

LINDA   You pawned it, dear. Twelve, thirteen years ago. For Biff's radio correspondence course.

WILLY   Gee, that was a beautiful thing. I'll take a walk.

LINDA   But you're in your slippers.

WILLY [*starting to go around the house at the left*]   I was right! I was! [*half
to* LINDA, *as he goes, shaking his head*] What a man! There was a man
worth talking to. I was right!

LINDA [*calling after* WILLY]   But in your slippers, Willy!

> [WILLY *is almost gone when* BIFF, *in his pajamas, comes down the stairs
> and enters the kitchen.*]

BIFF   What is he doing out there?

LINDA   Sh!

BIFF   God Almighty, Mom, how long has he been doing this?

LINDA   Don't, he'll hear you.

BIFF   What the hell is the matter with him?

LINDA   It'll pass by morning.

BIFF   Shouldn't we do anything?

LINDA   Oh, my dear, you should do a lot of things, but there's nothing to
do so go to sleep.

> [HAPPY *comes down the stairs and sits on the steps.*]

HAPPY   I never heard him so loud, Mom.

LINDA   Well, come around more often; you'll hear him. [*She sits down at
the table and mends the lining of* WILLY's *jacket.*]

BIFF   Why didn't you ever write me about this, Mom?

LINDA   How would I write to you? For over three months you had no
address.

BIFF   I was on the move. But you know I thought of you all the time. You
know that, don't you, pal?

LINDA   I know, dear, I know. But he likes to have a letter. Just to know
that there's still a possibility for better things.

BIFF   He's not like this all the time, is he?

LINDA   It's when you come home he's always the worst.

BIFF   When I come home?

LINDA   When you write you're coming, he's all smiles, and talks about the
future, and—he's just wonderful. And then the closer you seem to come,
the more shaky he gets, and then, by the time you get here, he's arguing,
and he seems angry at you. I think it's just that maybe he can't bring
himself to—to open up to you. Why are you so hateful to each other?
Why is that?

BIFF [*evasively*]   I'm not hateful, Mom.

LINDA   But you no sooner come in the door than you're fighting!

BIFF   I don't know why. I mean to change. I'm tryin', Mom, you understand?

LINDA   Are you home to stay now?

BIFF   I don't know. I want to look around, see what's doin'.

LINDA   Biff, you can't look around all your life, can you?

BIFF   I just can't take hold, Mom. I can't take hold of some kind of a life.

LINDA   Biff, a man is not a bird, to come and go with the springtime.

BIFF   Your hair . . . [*He touches her hair.*] Your hair got so gray.

LINDA   Oh, it's been gray since you were in high school. I just stopped
dyeing it, that's all.

BIFF   Dye it again, will ya? I don't want my pal looking old. [*He smiles.*]

LINDA   You're such a boy! You think you can go away for a year and . . .
You've got to get it into your head now that one day you'll knock on this
door and there'll be strange people here—

BIFF   What are you talking about? You're not even sixty, Mom.

LINDA   But what about your father?

BIFF [*lamely*]   Well, I meant him too.

HAPPY   He admires Pop.

LINDA   Biff, dear, if you don't have any feeling for him, then you can't have any feeling for me.

BIFF   Sure I can, Mom.

LINDA   No. You can't just come to see me, because I love him. [*with a threat, but only a threat, of tears*] He's the dearest man in the world to me, and I won't have anyone making him feel unwanted and low and blue. You've got to make up your mind now, darling, there's no leeway any more. Either he's your father and you pay him that respect, or else you're not to come here. I know he's not easy to get along with—nobody knows that better than me—but . . .

WILLY [*from the left, with a laugh*]   Hey, hey, Biffo!

BIFF [*starting to go out after* WILLY]   What the hell is the matter with him? [HAPPY *stops him.*]

LINDA   Don't—don't go near him!

BIFF   Stop making excuses for him! He always, always wiped the floor with you. Never had an ounce of respect for you.

HAPPY   He's always had respect for—

BIFF   What the hell do you know about it?

HAPPY [*surlily*]   Just don't call him crazy!

BIFF   He's got no character—Charley wouldn't do this. Not in his own house—spewing out that vomit from his mind.

HAPPY   Charley never had to cope with what he's got to.

BIFF   People are worse off than Willy Loman. Believe me, I've seen them!

LINDA   Then make Charley your father, Biff. You can't do that, can you? I don't say he's a great man. Willy Loman never made a lot of money. His name was never in the paper. He's not the finest character that ever lived. But he's a human being, and a terrible thing is happening to him. So attention must be paid. He's not to be allowed to fall into his grave like an old dog. Attention, attention must be finally paid to such a person. You called him crazy—

BIFF   I didn't mean—

LINDA   No, a lot of people think he's lost his—balance. But you don't have to be very smart to know what his trouble is. The man is exhausted.

HAPPY   Sure!

LINDA   A small man can be just as exhausted as a great man. He works for a company thirty-six years this March, opens up unheard-of territories to their trademark, and now in his old age they take his salary away.

HAPPY [*indignantly*]   I didn't know that, Mom.

LINDA   You never asked, my dear! Now that you get your spending money someplace else you don't trouble your mind with him.

HAPPY   But I gave you money last—

LINDA   Christmas time, fifty dollars! To fix the hot water it cost ninety-seven fifty! For five weeks he's been on straight commission, like a beginner, an unknown!

BIFF   Those ungrateful bastards!

LINDA   Are they any worse than his sons? When he brought them business, when he was young, they were glad to see him. But now his old friends, the old buyers that loved him so and always found some order to hand him in a pinch—they're all dead, retired. He used to be able to make six, seven calls a day in Boston. Now he takes his valises out of the car and puts them back and takes them out again and he's exhausted. Instead of walking he talks now. He drives seven hundred miles, and when he gets there no one knows him any more, no one welcomes him. And what goes through a man's mind, driving seven hundred miles home without having earned a cent? Why shouldn't he talk to himself? Why? When he has to go to Charley and borrow fifty dollars a week and pretend to me that it's his pay? How long can that go on? How long? You see what I'm sitting here and waiting for? And you tell me he has no character? The man who never worked a day but for your benefit? When does he get the medal for that? Is this his reward—to turn around at the age of sixty-three and find his sons, who he loved better than his life, one a philandering bum—

HAPPY   Mom!

LINDA   That's all you are, my baby! [*to* BIFF] And you! What happened to the love you had for him? You were such pals! How you used to talk to him on the phone every night! How lonely he was till he could come home to you!

BIFF   All right, Mom. I'll live here in my room, and I'll get a job. I'll keep away from him, that's all.

LINDA   No, Biff. You can't stay here and fight all the time.

BIFF   He threw me out of this house, remember that.

LINDA   Why did he do that? I never knew why.

BIFF   Because I know he's a fake and he doesn't like anybody around who knows!

LINDA   Why a fake? In what way? What do you mean?

BIFF   Just don't lay it all at my feet. It's between me and him—that's all I have to say. I'll chip in from now on. He'll settle for half my pay check. He'll be all right. I'm going to bed. [*He starts for the stairs.*]

LINDA   He won't be all right.

BIFF   [*turning on the stairs, furiously*]   I hate this city and I'll stay here. Now what do you want?

LINDA   He's dying, Biff.

[HAPPY *turns quickly to her, shocked.*]

BIFF   [*after a pause*]   Why is he dying?

LINDA   He's been trying to kill himself.

BIFF   [*with great horror*]   How?

LINDA   I live from day to day.

BIFF   What're you talking about?

LINDA   Remember I wrote you that he smashed up the car again? In February?

BIFF   Well?

LINDA   The insurance inspector came. He said that they have evidence. That all these accidents in the last year—weren't—weren't—accidents.

HAPPY   How can they tell that? That's a lie.

LINDA   It seems there's a woman . . . [*she takes a breath as*]

{ BIFF [*sharply but contained*]   What woman?
{ LINDA [*simultaneously*]   . . . and this woman . . .

LINDA   What?

BIFF   Nothing. Go ahead.

LINDA   What did you say?

BIFF   Nothing. I just said what woman?

HAPPY   What about her?

LINDA   Well, it seems she was walking down the road and saw his car. She says that he wasn't driving fast at all, and that he didn't skid. She says he came to that little bridge, and then deliberately smashed into the railing, and it was only the shallowness of the water that saved him.

BIFF   Oh, no, he probably just fell asleep again.

LINDA   I don't think he fell asleep.

BIFF   Why not?

LINDA   Last month . . . [*with great difficulty*] Oh, boys, it's so hard to say a thing like this! He's just a big stupid man to you, but I tell you there's more good in him than in many other people. [*She chokes, wipes her eyes.*] I was looking for a fuse. The lights blew out, and I went down the cellar. And behind the fuse box—it happened to fall out—was a length of rubber pipe—just short.

HAPPY   No kidding?

LINDA   There's a little attachment on the end of it. I knew right away. And sure enough, on the bottom of the water heater there's a new little nipple on the gas pipe.

HAPPY   [*angrily*]   That—jerk.

BIFF   Did you have it taken off?

LINDA   I'm—I'm ashamed to. How can I mention it to him? Every day I go down and take away that little rubber pipe. But, when he comes home, I put it back where it was. How can I insult him that way? I don't know what to do. I live from day to day, boys. I tell you, I know every thought in his mind. It sounds so old-fashioned and silly, but I tell you he put his whole life into you and you've turned your backs on him. [*She is bent over in the chair, weeping, her face in her hands.*] Biff, I swear to God! Biff, his life is in your hands!

HAPPY   [*to* BIFF]   How do you like that damned fool!

BIFF   [*kissing her*]   All right, pal, all right. It's all settled now. I've been remiss. I know that, Mom. But now I'll stay, and I swear to you, I'll apply myself, [*kneeling in front of her, in a fever of self-reproach*] It's just—you see, Mom, I don't fit in business. Not that I won't try. I'll try, and I'll make good.

HAPPY   Sure you will. The trouble with you in business was you never tried to please people.

BIFF   I know, I—

HAPPY   Like when you worked for Harrison's. Bob Harrison said you were tops, and then you go and do some damn fool, thing like whistling whole songs in the elevator like a comedian.

BIFF   [*against* HAPPY]   So what? I like to whistle sometimes.

HAPPY   You don't raise a guy to a responsible job who whistles in the elevator!

LINDA   Well, don't argue about it now.

HAPPY   Like when you'd go off and swim in the middle of the day instead of taking the line around.

BIFF   [*his resentment rising*]   Well, don't you run off? You take off sometimes, don't you? On a nice summer day?

HAPPY   Yeah, but I cover myself!

LINDA   Boys!

HAPPY If I'm going to take a fade the boss can call any number where I'm supposed to be and they'll swear to him that I just left. I'll tell you something that I hate to say, Biff, but in the business world some of them think you're crazy.

BIFF [*angered*] Screw the business world!

HAPPY All right, screw it! Great, but cover yourself!

LINDA Hap, Hap!

BIFF I don't care what they think! They've laughed at Dad for years, and you know why? Because we don't belong in this nuthouse of a city! We should be mixing cement on some open plain, or—or carpenters. A carpenter is allowed to whistle!

[WILLY *walks in from the entrance of the house, at left.*]

WILLY Even your grandfather was better than a carpenter. [*Pause. They watch him.*] You never grew up. Bernard does not whistle in the elevator, I assure you.

BIFF [*as though to laugh* WILLY *out of it*] Yeah, but you do, Pop.

WILLY I never in my life whistled in an elevator! And who in the business world thinks I'm crazy?

BIFF I didn't mean it like that, Pop. Now don't make a whole thing out of it, will ya?

WILLY Go back to the West! Be a carpenter, a cowboy, enjoy yourself!

LINDA Willy, he was just saying—

WILLY I heard what he said!

HAPPY [*trying to quiet* WILLY] Hey, Pop, come on now . . .

WILLY [*continuing over* HAPPY's *line*] They laugh at me, heh? Go to Filene's, go to the Hub, go to Slattery's, Boston. Call out the name Willy Loman and see what happens! Big Shot!

BIFF All right, Pop.

WILLY Big!

BIFF All right!

WILLY Why do you always insult me?

BIFF I didn't say a word. [*to* LINDA] Did I say a word?

LINDA He didn't say anything, Willy.

WILLY [*going to the doorway of the living-room*] All right, good night, good night.

LINDA Willy, dear, he just decided . . .

WILLY [*to* BIFF] If you get tired hanging around tomorrow, paint the ceiling I put up in the living-room.

BIFF I'm leaving early tomorrow.

HAPPY He's going to see Bill Oliver, Pop.

WILLY [*interestedly*] Oliver? For what?

BIFF [*with reserve, but trying, trying*] He always said he'd stake me. I'd like to go into business, so maybe I can take him up on it.

LINDA Isn't that wonderful?

WILLY Don't interrupt. What's wonderful about it? There's fifty men in the City of New York who'd stake him. [*to* BIFF] Sporting goods?

BIFF I guess so. I know something about it and—

WILLY He knows something about it! You know sporting goods better than Spalding, for God's sake! How much is he giving you?

BIFF I don't know, I didn't even see him yet, but—

WILLY Then what're you talkin' about?

BIFF [*getting angry*]   Well, all I said was I'm gonna see him, that's all!

WILLY [*turning away*]   Ah, you're counting your chickens again.

BIFF [*starting left for the stairs*]   Oh, Jesus, I'm going to sleep!

WILLY [*calling after him*]   Don't curse in this house!

BIFF [*turning*]   Since when did you get so clean?

HAPPY [*trying to stop them*]   Wait a . . .

WILLY   Don't use that language to me! I won't have it!

HAPPY [*grabbing* BIFF, *shouts*]   Wait a minute! I got an idea. I got a feasible idea. Come here, Biff, let's talk this over now, let's talk some sense here. When I was down in Florida last time, I thought of a great idea to sell sporting goods. It just came back to me. You and I, Biff—we have a line, the Loman Line. We train a couple of weeks, and put on a couple of exhibitions, see?

WILLY   That's an idea!

HAPPY   Wait! We form two basketball teams, see? Two water-polo teams. We play each other. It's a million dollars' worth of publicity. Two brothers, see? The Loman Brothers. Displays in the Royal Palms—all the hotels. And banners over the ring and the basketball court: "Loman Brothers." Baby, we could sell sporting goods!

WILLY   That is a one-million-dollar idea!

LINDA   Marvelous!

BIFF   I'm in great shape as far as that's concerned.

HAPPY   And the beauty of it is, Biff, it wouldn't be like a business. We'd be out playin' ball again . . .

BIFF [*enthused*]   Yeah, that's . . .

WILLY   Million-dollar . . .

HAPPY   And you wouldn't get fed up with it, Biff. It'd be the family again. There'd be the old honor, and comradeship, and if you wanted to go off for a swim or somethin'—well, you'd do it! Without some smart cooky gettin' up ahead of you!

WILLY   Lick the world! You guys together could absolutely lick the civilized world.

BIFF   I'll see Oliver tomorrow. Hap, if we could work that out . . .

LINDA   Maybe things are beginning to—

WILLY [*wildly enthused, to* LINDA]   Stop interrupting! [*to* BIFF] But don't wear sport jacket and slacks when you see Oliver.

BIFF   No, I'll—

WILLY   A business suit, and talk as little as possible, and don't crack any jokes.

BIFF   He did like me. Always liked me.

LINDA   He loved you!

WILLY [*to* LINDA]   Will you stop! [*to* BIFF] Walk in very serious. You are not applying for a boy's job. Money is to pass. Be quiet, fine, and serious. Everybody likes a kidder, but nobody lends him money.

HAPPY   I'll try to get some myself, Biff. I'm sure I can.

WILLY   I see great things for you kids, I think your troubles are over. But remember, start big and you'll end big. Ask for fifteen. How much you gonna ask for?

BIFF   Gee, I don't know—

WILLY   And don't say "Gee." "Gee" is a boy's word. A man walking in for fifteen thousand dollars does not say "Gee!"

BIFF   Ten, I think, would be top though.

WILLY   Don't be so modest. You always started too low. Walk in with a big laugh. Don't look worried. Start off with a couple of your good stories to lighten things up. It's not what you say, it's how you say it—because personality always wins the day.

LINDA   Oliver always thought the highest of him—

WILLY   Will you let me talk?

BIFF   Don't yell at her, Pop, will ya?

WILLY   [angrily]   I was talking, wasn't I?

BIFF   I don't like you yelling at her all the time, and I'm tellin' you, that's all.

WILLY   What're you, takin' over this house?

LINDA   Willy—

WILLY   [turning on her]   Don't take his side all the time, goddammit!

BIFF   [furiously]   Stop yelling at her!

WILLY   [suddenly pulling on his cheek, beaten down, guilt ridden]   Give my best to Bill Oliver—he may remember me. [He exits through the living-room doorway.]

LINDA   [her voice subdued]   What'd you have to start that for? [BIFF turns away.] You see how sweet he was as soon as you talked hopefully? [She goes over to BIFF.] Come up and say good night to him. Don't let him go to bed that way.

HAPPY   Come on, Biff, let's buck him up.

LINDA   Please, dear. Just say good night. It takes so little to make him happy. Come. [She goes through the living-room doorway, calling upstairs from within the living-room] Your pajamas are hanging in the bathroom, Willy!

HAPPY   [looking toward where LINDA went out]   What a woman! They broke the mold when they made her. You know that, Biff?

BIFF   He's off salary. My God, working on commission!

HAPPY   Well, let's face it: he's no hot-shot selling man. Except that sometimes, you have to admit, he's a sweet personality.

BIFF   [deciding]   Lend me ten bucks, will ya? I want to buy some new ties.

HAPPY   I'll take you to a place I know. Beautiful stuff. Wear one of my striped shirts tomorrow.

BIFF   She got gray. Mom got awful old. Gee, I'm gonna go in to Oliver tomorrow and knock him for a—

HAPPY   Come on up. Tell that to Dad. Let's give him a whirl. Come on.

BIFF   [steamed up]   You know, with ten thousand bucks, boy!

HAPPY   [as they go into the living-room]   That's the talk, Biff, that's the first time I've heard the old confidence out of you! [from within the living-room, fading off] You're gonna live with me, kid, and any babe you want just say the word . . . [The last lines are hardly heard. They are mounting the stairs to their parents' bedroom.]

LINDA   [entering her bedroom and addressing WILLY, who is in the bathroom. She is straightening the bed for him.]   Can you do anything about the shower? It drips.

WILLY   [from the bathroom]   All of a sudden everything falls to pieces! Goddam plumbing, oughta be sued, those people. I hardly finished putting it in and the thing . . . [His words rumble off.]

LINDA   I'm just wondering if Oliver will remember him. You think he might?

WILLY [*coming out of the bathroom in his pajamas*] Remember him? What's the matter with you, you crazy? If he'd've stayed with Oliver he'd be on top by now! Wait'll Oliver gets a look at him. You don't know the average caliber any more. The average young man today—[*he is getting into bed*]—is got a caliber of zero. Greatest thing in the world for him was to bum around.

[BIFF *and* HAPPY *enter the bedroom. Slight pause.*]

WILLY [*stops short, looking at* BIFF] Glad to hear it, boy.

HAPPY He wanted to say good night to you, sport.

WILLY [*to* BIFF] Yeah. Knock him dead, boy. What'd you want to tell me?

BIFF Just take it easy, Pop. Good night. [*He turns to go.*]

WILLY [*unable to resist*] And if anything falls off the desk while you're talking to him—like a package or something—don't you pick it up. They have office boys for that.

LINDA I'll make a big breakfast—

WILLY Will you let me finish? [*to* BIFF] Tell him you were in the business in the West. Not farm work.

BIFF All right, Dad.

LINDA I think everything—

WILLY [*going right through her speech*] And don't undersell yourself. No less than fifteen thousand dollars.

BIFF [*unable to bear him*] Okay. Good night, Mom. [*He starts moving.*]

WILLY Because you got a greatness in you, Biff, remember that. You got all kinds a greatness . . . [*He lies back, exhausted.* BIFF *walks out.*]

LINDA [*calling after* BIFF] Sleep well, darling!

HAPPY I'm gonna get married, Mom. I wanted to tell you.

LINDA Go to sleep, dear.

HAPPY [*going*] I just wanted to tell you.

WILLY Keep up the good work. [HAPPY *exits.*] God . . . remember that Ebbets Field[5] game? The championship of the city?

LINDA Just rest. Should I sing to you?

WILLY Yeah. Sing to me. [LINDA *hums a soft lullaby.*] When that team came out—he was the tallest, remember?

LINDA Oh, yes. And in gold.

[BIFF *enters the darkened kitchen, takes a cigarette, and leaves the house. He comes downstage into a golden pool of light. He smokes, staring at the night.*]

WILLY Like a young god. Hercules[6]—something like that. And the sun, the sun all around him. Remember how he waved to me? Right up from the field, with the representatives of three colleges standing by? And the buyers I brought, and the cheers when he came out—Loman, Loman, Loman! God Almighty, he'll be great yet. A star like that, magnificent, can never really fade away!

[*The light on* WILLY *is fading. The gas heater begins to glow through the kitchen wall, near the stairs, a blue flame beneath red coils.*]

LINDA [*timidly*] Willy dear, what has he got against you?

WILLY I'm so tired. Don't talk any more.

[BIFF *slowly returns to the kitchen. He stops, stares toward the heater.*]

LINDA Will you ask Howard to let you work in New York?

---

5. Brooklyn sports stadium.
6. In Greek and Roman mythology the son of the chief god (Zeus, Jupiter), famous for his great strength.

WILLY   First thing in the morning. Everything'll be all right.

[BIFF *reaches behind the heater and draws out a length of rubber tubing. He is horrified and turns his head toward* WILLY's *room, still dimly lit, from which the strains of* LINDA's *desperate but monotonous humming rise.*]

WILLY [*staring through the window into the moonlight*]   Gee, look at the moon moving between the buildings!

[BIFF *wraps the tubing around his hand and quickly goes up the stairs.*]

CURTAIN

Act Two

Music is heard, gay and bright. The curtain rises as the music fades away. WILLY, *in shirt sleeves, is sitting at the kitchen table, sipping coffee, his hat in his lap.* LINDA *is filling his cup when she can.*

WILLY   Wonderful coffee. Meal in itself.

LINDA   Can I make you some eggs?

WILLY   No. Take a breath.

LINDA   You look so rested, dear.

WILLY   I slept like a dead one. First time in months. Imagine, sleeping till ten on a Tuesday morning. Boys left nice and early, heh?

LINDA   They were out of here by eight o'clock.

WILLY   Good work!

LINDA   It was so thrilling to see them leaving together. I can't get over the shaving lotion in this house!

WILLY [*smiling*]   Mmm—

LINDA   Biff was very changed this morning. His whole attitude seemed to be hopeful. He couldn't wait to get downtown to see Oliver.

WILLY   He's heading for a change. There's no question, there simply are certain men that take longer to get—solidified. How did he dress?

LINDA   His blue suit. He's so handsome in that suit. He could be a—anything in that suit!

[WILLY *gets up from the table.* LINDA *holds his jacket for him.*]

WILLY   There's no question, no question at all. Gee, on the way home tonight I'd like to buy some seeds.

LINDA [*laughing*]   That'd be wonderful. But not enough sun gets back there. Nothing'll grow any more.

WILLY   You wait, kid, before it's all over we're gonna get a little place out in the country, and I'll raise some vegetables, a couple of chickens . . .

LINDA   You'll do it yet, dear.

[WILLY *walks out of his jacket.* LINDA *follows him.*]

WILLY   And they'll get married, and come for a weekend. I'd build a little guest house. 'Cause I got so many fine tools, all I'd need would be a little lumber and some peace of mind.

LINDA [*joyfully*]   I sewed the lining . . .

WILLY   I could build two guest houses, so they'd both come. Did he decide how much he's going to ask Oliver for?

LINDA [*getting him into the jacket*]   He didn't mention it, but I imagine ten or fifteen thousand. You going to talk to Howard today?

WILLY   Yeah. I'll put it to him straight and simple. He'll just have to take me off the road.

LINDA   And Willy, don't forget to ask for a little advance, because we've got the insurance premium. It's the grace period now.

WILLY   That's a hundred . . . ?

LINDA   A hundred and eight, sixty-eight. Because we're a little short again.

WILLY   Why are we short?

LINDA   Well, you had the motor job on the car . . .

WILLY   That goddam Studebaker!

LINDA   And you got one more payment on the refrigerator . . .

WILLY   But it just broke again!

LINDA   Well, it's old, dear.

WILLY   I told you we should've bought a well-advertised machine. Charley bought a General Electric and it's twenty years old and it's still good, that son-of-a-bitch.

LINDA   But, Willy—

WILLY   Whoever heard of a Hastings refrigerator? Once in my life I would like to own something outright before it's broken! I'm always in a race with the junkyard! I just finished paying for the car and it's on its last legs. The refrigerator consumes belts like a goddam maniac. They time those things. They time them so when you finally paid for them, they're used up.

LINDA   [buttoning up his jacket as he unbuttons it]   All told, about two hundred dollars would carry us, dear. But that includes the last payment on the mortgage. After this payment, Willy, the house belongs to us.

WILLY   It's twenty-five years!

LINDA   Biff was nine years old when we bought it.

WILLY   Well, that's a great thing. To weather a twenty-five year mortgage is—

LINDA   It's an accomplishment.

WILLY   All the cement, the lumber, the reconstruction I put in this house! There ain't a crack to be found in it anymore.

LINDA   Well, it served its purpose.

WILLY   What purpose? Some stranger'll come along, move in, and that's that. If only Biff would take this house, and raise a family . . . [He starts to go.] Good-by, I'm late.

LINDA   [suddenly remembering]   Oh, I forgot! You're supposed to meet them for dinner.

WILLY   Me?

LINDA   At Frank's Chop House on Forty-eighth near Sixth Avenue.

WILLY   Is that so! How about you?

LINDA   No, just the three of you. They're gonna blow you to a big meal!

WILLY   Don't say! Who thought of that?

LINDA   Biff came to me this morning, Willy, and he said, "Tell Dad, we want to blow him to a big meal." Be there six o'clock. You and your two boys are going to have dinner.

WILLY   Gee whiz! That's really somethin'. I'm gonna knock Howard for a loop, kid. I'll get an advance, and I'll come home with a New York job. Goddammit, now I'm gonna do it!

LINDA   Oh, that's the spirit, Willy!

WILLY   I will never get behind a wheel the rest of my life!

LINDA   It's changing, Willy, I can feel it changing!

WILLY   Beyond a question. G'by, I'm late. [He starts to go again.]

LINDA [*calling after him as she runs to the kitchen table for a handkerchief*] You got your glasses?

WILLY [*feels for them, then comes back in*] Yeah, yeah, got my glasses.

LINDA [*giving him the handkerchief*] And a handkerchief.

WILLY Yeah, handkerchief.

LINDA And your saccharine?

WILLY Yeah, my saccharine.

LINDA Be careful on the subway stairs.

[*She kisses him, and a silk stocking is seen hanging from her hand.* WILLY *notices it.*]

WILLY Will you stop mending stockings? At least while I'm in the house. It gets me nervous. I can't tell you. Please.

[LINDA *hides the stocking in her hand as she follows* WILLY *across the forestage in front of the house.*]

LINDA Remember, Frank's Chop House.

WILLY [*passing the apron*] Maybe beets would grow out there.

LINDA [*laughing*] But you tried so many times.

WILLY Yeah. Well, don't work hard today. [*He disappears around the right corner of the house.*]

LINDA Be careful!

[*As* WILLY *vanishes,* LINDA *waves to him. Suddenly the phone rings. She runs across the stage and into the kitchen and lifts it.*]

LINDA Hello? Oh, Biff! I'm so glad you called, I just . . . Yes, sure, I just told him. Yes, he'll be there for dinner at six o'clock, I didn't forget. Listen, I was just dying to tell you. You know that little rubber pipe I told you about? That he connected to the gas heater? I finally decided to go down the cellar this morning and take it away and destroy it. But it's gone! Imagine? He took it away himself, it isn't there! [*She listens.*] When? Oh, then you took it. Oh—nothing, it's just that I'd hoped he'd taken it away himself. Oh, I'm not worried, darling, because this morning he left in such high spirits, it was like the old days! I'm not afraid any more. Did Mr. Oliver see you? . . . Well, you wait there then. And make a nice impression on him, darling. Just don't perspire too much before you see him. And have a nice time with Dad. He may have big news too! . . . That's right, a New York job. And be sweet to him tonight, dear. Be loving to him. Because he's only a little boat looking for a harbor. [*She is trembling with sorrow and joy.*] Oh, that's wonderful, Biff, you'll save his life. Thanks, darling. Just put your arm around him when he comes into the restaurant. Give him a smile. That's the boy . . . Good-by, dear. . . . You got your comb? . . . That's fine. Good-by, Biff dear.

[*In the middle of her speech,* HOWARD WAGNER, *thirty-six, wheels in a small typewriter table on which is a wire-recording machine and proceeds to plug it in. This is on the left forestage. Light slowly fades on* LINDA *as it rises on* HOWARD. HOWARD *is intent on threading the machine and only glances over his shoulder as* WILLY *appears.*]

WILLY Pst! Pst!

HOWARD Hello, Willy, come in.

WILLY Like to have a little talk with you, Howard.

HOWARD Sorry to keep you waiting. I'll be with you in a minute.

WILLY What's that, Howard?

HOWARD Didn't you ever see one of these? Wire recorder.

WILLY Oh. Can we talk a minute?

HOWARD Records things. Just got delivery yesterday. Been driving me crazy, the most terrific machine I ever saw in my life. I was up all night with it.

WILLY What do you do with it?

HOWARD I bought it for dictation, but you can do anything with it. Listen to this. I had it home last night. Listen to what I picked up. The first one is my daughter. Get this. [*He flicks the switch and "Roll out the Barrel" is heard being whistled.*] Listen to that kid whistle.

WILLY That is lifelike, isn't it?

HOWARD Seven years old. Get that tone.

WILLY Ts, ts. Like to ask a little favor if you . . .
[*The whistling breaks off, and the voice of* HOWARD's *daughter is heard.*]

HIS DAUGHTER "Now you, Daddy."

HOWARD She's crazy for me! [*Again the same song is whistled.*] That's me! Ha! [*He winks.*]

WILLY You're very good!
[*The whistling breaks off again. The machine runs silent for a moment.*]

HOWARD Sh! Get this now, this is my son.

HIS SON "The capital of Alabama is Montgomery; the capital of Arizona is Phoenix; the capital of Arkansas is Little Rock; the capital of California is Sacramento . . ." [*and on, and on*]

HOWARD [*holding up five fingers*] Five years old, Willy!

WILLY He'll make an announcer some day!

HIS SON [*continuing*] "The capital . . ."

HOWARD Get that—alphabetical order! [*The machine breaks off suddenly.*] Wait a minute. The maid kicked the plug out.

WILLY It certainly is a—

HOWARD Sh, for God's sake!

HIS SON "It's nine o'clock, Bulova watch time. So I have to go to sleep."

WILLY That really is—

HOWARD Wait a minute! The next is my wife.
[*They wait.*]

HOWARD'S VOICE "Go on, say something." [*pause*] "Well, you gonna talk?"

HIS WIFE "I can't think of anything."

HOWARD'S VOICE "Well, talk—it's turning."

HIS WIFE [*shyly, beaten*] "Hello." [*silence*] "Oh, Howard, I can't talk into this . . ."

HOWARD [*snapping the machine off*] That was my wife.

WILLY That is a wonderful machine. Can we—

HOWARD I tell you, Willy, I'm gonna take my camera, and my handsaw, and all my hobbies, and out they go. This is the most fascinating relaxation I ever found.

WILLY I think I'll get one myself.

HOWARD Sure, they're only a hundred and a half. You can't do without it. Supposing you wanna hear Jack Benny,[7] see? But you can't be at home at that hour. So you tell the maid to turn the radio on when Jack Benny comes on, and this automatically goes on with the radio . . .

WILLY And when you come home you . . .

---

7. Vastly popular radio comedian of the 1930s and 1940s.

HOWARD   You can come home twelve o'clock, one o'clock, any time you like, and you get yourself a Coke and sit yourself down, throw the switch, and there's Jack Benny's program in the middle of the night!

WILLY   I'm definitely going to get one. Because lots of time I'm on the road, and I think to myself, what I must be missing on the radio!

HOWARD   Don't you have a radio in the car?

WILLY   Well, yeah, but who ever thinks of turning it on?

HOWARD   Say, aren't you supposed to be in Boston?

WILLY   That's what I want to talk to you about, Howard. You got a minute? [*He draws a chair in from the wing.*]

HOWARD   What happened? What're you doing here?

WILLY   Well . . .

HOWARD   You didn't crack up again, did you?

WILLY   Oh, no. No . . .

HOWARD   Geez, you had me worried there for a minute. What's the trouble?

WILLY   Well, tell you the truth, Howard. I've come to the decision that I'd rather not travel any more.

HOWARD   Not travel! Well, what'll you do?

WILLY   Remember, Christmas time, when you had the party here? You said you'd try to think of some spot for me here in town.

HOWARD   With us?

WILLY   Well, sure.

HOWARD   Oh, yeah, yeah. I remember. Well, I couldn't think of anything for you, Willy.

WILLY   I tell ya, Howard. The kids are all grown up, y'know. I don't need much any more. If I could take home—well, sixty-five dollars a week, I could swing it.

HOWARD   Yeah, but Willy, see I—

WILLY   I tell ya why, Howard. Speaking frankly and between the two of us, y'know—I'm just a little tired.

HOWARD   Oh, I could understand that, Willy. But you're a road man, Willy, and we do a road business. We've only got a half-dozen salesmen on the floor here.

WILLY   God knows, Howard, I never asked a favor of any man. But I was with the firm when your father used to carry you in here in his arms.

HOWARD   I know that, Willy, but—

WILLY   Your father came to me the day you were born and asked me what I thought of the name of Howard, may he rest in peace.

HOWARD   I appreciate that, Willy, but there just is no spot here for you. If I had a spot I'd slam you right in, but I just don't have a single solitary spot.

[*He looks for his lighter.* WILLY *has picked it up and gives it to him. Pause.*]

WILLY [*with increasing anger*]   Howard, all I need to set my table is fifty dollars a week.

HOWARD   But where am I going to put you, kid?

WILLY   Look, it isn't a question of whether I can sell merchandise, is it?

HOWARD   No, but it's a business, kid, and everybody's gotta pull his own weight.

WILLY [*desperately*]   Just let me tell you a story, Howard—

HOWARD   'Cause you gotta admit, business is business.

WILLY [*angrily*]   Business is definitely business, but just listen for a minute. You don't understand this. When I was a boy—eighteen, nineteen—I was already on the road. And there was a question in my mind as to whether selling had a future for me. Because in those days I had a yearning to go to Alaska. See, there were three gold strikes in one month in Alaska, and I felt like going out. Just for the ride, you might say.

HOWARD [*barely interested*] Don't say.

WILLY Oh, yeah, my father lived many years in Alaska. He was an adventurous man. We've got quite a little streak of self-reliance in our family. I thought I'd go out with my older brother and try to locate him, and maybe settle in the North with the old man. And I was almost decided to go, when I met a salesman in the Parker House. His name was Dave Singleman. And he was eighty-four years old, and he'd drummed merchandise in thirty-one states. And old Dave, he'd go up to his room, y'understand, put on his green velvet slippers—I'll never forget—and pick up his phone and call the buyers, and without ever leaving his room, at the age of eighty-four, he made a living. And when I saw that, I realized that selling was the greatest career a man could want. 'Cause what could be more satisfying than to be able to go, at the age of eighty-four, into twenty or thirty different cities, and pick up a phone, and be remembered and loved and helped by so many different people? Do you know? when he died—and by the way he died the death of a salesman, in his green velvet slippers in the smoker of the New York, New Haven and Hartford, going into Boston—when he died, hundreds of salesmen and buyers were at his funeral. Things were sad on a lotta trains for months after that. [*He stands up.* HOWARD *has not looked at him.*] In those days there was personality in it, Howard. There was respect, and comradeship, and gratitude in it. Today, it's all cut and dried, and there's no chance for bringing friendship to bear—or personality. You see what I mean? They don't know me anymore.

HOWARD [*moving away, toward the right*] That's just the thing, Willy.

WILLY If I had forty dollars a week—that's all I'd need. Forty dollars, Howard.

HOWARD Kid, I can't take blood from a stone, I—

WILLY [*desperation is on him now*] Howard, the year Al Smith[8] was nominated, your father came to me and—

HOWARD [*starting to go off*] I've got to see some people, kid.

WILLY [*stopping him*] I'm talking about your father! There were promises made across this desk! You mustn't tell me you've got people to see—I put thirty-four years into this firm, Howard, and now I can't pay my insurance! You can't eat the orange and throw the peel away—a man is not a piece of fruit! [*after a pause*] Now pay attention. Your father—in 1928 I had a big year. I averaged a hundred and seventy dollars a week in commissions.

HOWARD [*impatiently*] Now, Willy, you never averaged—

WILLY [*banging his hand on the desk*] I averaged a hundred and seventy dollars a week in the year of 1928! And your father came to me—or rather, I was in the office here—it was right over this desk—and he put his hand on my shoulder—

HOWARD [*getting up*] You'll have to excuse me, Willy, I gotta see some people. Pull yourself together. [*going out*] I'll be back in a little while.

---

8. Democratic candidate for president in 1928.

[*On* HOWARD's *exit, the light on his chair grows very bright and strange.*]

WILLY   Pull myself together! What the hell did I say to him? My God, I was yelling at him! How could I! [WILLY *breaks off, staring at the light, which occupies the chair, animating it. He approaches this chair, standing across the desk from it.*] Frank, Frank, don't you remember what you told me that time? How you put your hand on my shoulder, and Frank . . . [*He leans on the desk and as he speaks the dead man's name he accidentally switches on the recorder, and instantly*]

HOWARD'S SON   ". . . of New York is Albany. The capital of Ohio is Cincinnati, the capital of Rhode Island is . . ." [*The recitation continues.*]

WILLY [*leaping away with fright, shouting*]   Ha! Howard! Howard! Howard!

HOWARD [*rushing in*]   What happened?

WILLY [*pointing at the machine, which continues nasally, childishly, with the capital cities*]   Shut it off! Shut it off!

HOWARD [*pulling the plug out*]   Look, Willy . . .

WILLY [*pressing his hands to his eyes*]   I gotta get myself some coffee. I'll get some coffee . . .

[WILLY *starts to walk out.* HOWARD *stops him.*]

HOWARD [*rolling up the cord*]   Willy, look . . .

WILLY   I'll go to Boston.

HOWARD   Willy, you can't go to Boston for us.

WILLY   Why can't I go?

HOWARD   I don't want you to represent us. I've been meaning to tell you for a long time now.

WILLY   Howard, are you firing me?

HOWARD   I think you need a good long rest, Willy.

WILLY   Howard—

HOWARD   And when you feel better, come back, and we'll see if we can work something out.

WILLY   But I gotta earn money, Howard. I'm in no position to—

HOWARD   Where are your sons? Why don't your sons give you a hand?

WILLY   They're working on a very big deal.

HOWARD   This is no time for false pride, Willy. You go to your sons and you tell them that you're tired. You've got two great boys, haven't you?

WILLY   Oh, no question, no question, but in the meantime . . .

HOWARD   Then that's that, heh?

WILLY   All right, I'll go to Boston tomorrow.

HOWARD   No, no.

WILLY   I can't throw myself on my sons. I'm not a cripple!

HOWARD   Look, kid, I'm busy, I'm busy this morning.

WILLY [*grasping* HOWARD's *arm*]   Howard, you've got to let me go to Boston!

HOWARD [*hard, keeping himself under control*]   I've got a line of people to see this morning. Sit down, take five minutes, and pull yourself together, and then go home, will ya? I need the office, Willy. [*He starts to go, turns, remembering the recorder, starts to push off the table holding the recorder.*] Oh, yeah. Whenever you can this week, stop by and drop off the samples. You'll feel better, Willy, and then come back and we'll talk. Pull yourself together, kid, there's people outside.

[HOWARD *exits, pushing the table off left.* WILLY *stares into space, exhausted. Now the music is heard—*BEN's *music—first distantly, then* *closer, closer. As* WILLY *speaks,* BEN *enters from the right. He carries valise and umbrella.*]

WILLY Oh, Ben, how did you do it? What is the answer? Did you wind up the Alaska deal already?

BEN Doesn't take much time if you know what you're doing. Just a short business trip. Boarding ship in an hour. Wanted to say good-by.

WILLY Ben, I've got to talk to you.

BEN [*glancing at his watch*] Haven't the time, William.

WILLY [*crossing the apron to* BEN] Ben, nothing's working out. I don't know what to do.

BEN Now, look here, William. I've bought timberland in Alaska and I need a man to look after things for me.

WILLY God, timberland! Me and my boys in those grand outdoors!

BEN You've a new continent at your doorstep, William. Get out of these cities, they're full of talk and time payments and courts of law. Screw on your fists and you can fight for a fortune up there.

WILLY Yes, yes! Linda, Linda!

[LINDA *enters as of old, with the wash.*]

LINDA Oh, you're back?

BEN I haven't much time.

WILLY No, wait! Linda, he's got a proposition for me in Alaska.

LINDA But you've got— [*to* BEN] He's got a beautiful job here.

WILLY But in Alaska, kid, I could—

LINDA You're doing well enough, Willy!

BEN [*to* LINDA] Enough for what, my dear?

LINDA [*frightened of* BEN *and angry at him*] Don't say those things to him! Enough to be happy right here, right now. [*to* WILLY, *while* BEN *laughs*] Why must everybody conquer the world? You're well liked, and the boys love you, and someday—[*to* BEN]—why, old man Wagner told him just the other day that if he keeps it up he'll be a member of the firm, didn't he, Willy?

WILLY Sure, sure. I am building something with this firm, Ben, and if a man is building something he must be on the right track, mustn't he?

BEN What are you building? Lay your hand on it. Where is it?

WILLY [*hesitantly*] That's true, Linda, there's nothing.

LINDA Why? [*to* BEN] There's a man eighty-four years old—

WILLY That's right, Ben, that's right. When I look at that man I say, what is there to worry about?

BEN Bah!

WILLY It's true, Ben. All he has to do is go into any city, pick up the phone, and he's making his living and you know why?

BEN [*picking up his valise*] I've got to go.

WILLY [*holding* BEN *back*] Look at this boy!

[BIFF, *in his high school sweater, enters carrying suitcase.* HAPPY *carries* BIFF's *shoulder guards, gold helmet, and football pants.*]

WILLY Without a penny to his name, three great universities are begging for him, and from there the sky's the limit, because it's not what you do, Ben. It's who you know and the smile on your face! It's contacts, Ben, contacts! The whole wealth of Alaska passes over the lunch table at the Commodore Hotel, and that's the wonder, the wonder of this country, that a man can end with diamonds here on the basis of being liked! [*He turns to* BIFF.] And that's why when you get out on that field today it's important. Because thousands of people will be rooting for you and loving you. [*to* BEN, *who has again begun to leave*] And Ben! when he walks into a business office his name will sound out like a bell and all the doors will open to him! I've seen it, Ben, I've seen it a thousand times! You can't feel it with your hand like timber, but it's there!

BEN   Good-by, William.

WILLY   Ben, am I right? Don't you think I'm right? I value your advice.

BEN   There's a new continent at your doorstep, William. You could walk out rich. Rich! [*He is gone.*]

WILLY   We'll do it here, Ben! You hear me? We're gonna do it here!
          [*Young* BERNARD *rushes in. The gay music of the Boys is heard.*]

BERNARD   Oh, gee, I was afraid you left already!

WILLY   Why? What time is it?

BERNARD   It's half-past one!

WILLY   Well, come on, everybody! Ebbets Field next stop! Where's the pennants? [*He rushes through the wall-line of the kitchen and out into the living-room.*]

LINDA [*to* BIFF]   Did you pack fresh underwear?

BIFF [*who has been limbering up*]   I want to go!

BERNARD   Biff, I'm carrying your helmet, ain't I?

HAPPY   No, I'm carrying the helmet.

BERNARD   Oh, Biff, you promised me.

HAPPY   I'm carrying the helmet.

BERNARD   How am I going to get in the locker room?

LINDA   Let him carry the shoulder guards. [*She puts her coat and hat on in the kitchen.*]

BERNARD   Can I, Biff? 'Cause I told everybody I'm going to be in the locker room.

HAPPY   In Ebbets Field it's the clubhouse.

BERNARD   I meant the clubhouse. Biff!

HAPPY   Biff!

BIFF [*grandly, after a slight pause*]   Let him carry the shoulder guards.

HAPPY [*as he gives* BERNARD *the shoulder guards*]   Stay close to us now.
          [*WILLY rushes in with the pennants.*]

WILLY [*handing them out*]   Everybody wave when Biff comes out on the field. [*HAPPY and* BERNARD *run off.*] You set now, boy?
          [*The music has died away.*]

BIFF   Ready to go, Pop. Every muscle is ready.

WILLY [*at the edge of the apron*]   You realize what this means?

BIFF   That's right, Pop.

WILLY [*feeling* BIFF's *muscles*]   You're comin' home this afternoon captain of the All-Scholastic Championship Team of the City of New York.

BIFF   I got it, Pop. And remember, pal, when I take off my helmet, that touchdown is for you.

WILLY   Let's go! [*He is starting out, with his arm around* BIFF, *when* CHARLEY *enters, as of old, in knickers.*] I got no room for you, Charley.

CHARLEY   Room? For what?

WILLY   In the car.

CHARLEY   You goin' for a ride? I wanted to shoot some casino.

WILLY [*furiously*]   Casino! [*incredulously*] Don't you realize what today is?

LINDA   Oh, he knows, Willy. He's just kidding you.

WILLY   That's nothing to kid about!

CHARLEY   No, Linda, what's goin' on?

LINDA   He's playing in Ebbets Field.

CHARLEY   Baseball in this weather?

WILLY   Don't talk to him. Come on, come on! [*He is pushing them out.*]

CHARLEY   Wait a minute, didn't you hear the news?

WILLY   What?

CHARLEY   Don't you listen to the radio? Ebbets Field just blew up.

WILLY   You go to hell! [CHARLEY *laughs. Pushing them out*] Come on, come on! We're late.

CHARLEY   [*as they go*]   Knock a homer, Biff, knock a homer!

WILLY   [*the last to leave, turning to* CHARLEY]   I don't think that was funny, Charley. This is the greatest day of his life.

CHARLEY   Willy, when are you going to grow up?

WILLY   Yeah, heh? When this game is over, Charley, you'll be laughing out of the other side of your face. They'll be calling him another Red Grange.[9] Twenty-five thousand a year.

CHARLEY   [*kidding*]   Is that so?

WILLY   Yeah, that's so.

CHARLEY   Well, then, I'm sorry, Willy. But tell me something.

WILLY   What?

CHARLEY   Who is Red Grange?

WILLY   Put up your hands. Goddam you, put up your hands!
[CHARLEY, *chuckling, shakes his head and walks away, around the left corner of the stage.* WILLY *follows him. The music rises to a mocking frenzy.*]

WILLY   Who the hell do you think you are, better than everybody else? You don't know everything, you big, ignorant, stupid . . . Put up your hands!
[*Light rises, on the right side of the forestage, on a small table in the reception room of* CHARLEY's *office. Traffic sounds are heard.* BERNARD, *now mature, sits whistling to himself. A pair of tennis rackets and an overnight bag are on the floor beside him.*]

WILLY   [*offstage*]   What are you walking away for? Don't walk away! If you're going to say something say it to my face! I know you laugh at me behind my back. You'll laugh out of the other side of your goddam face after this game. Touchdown! Touchdown! Eighty thousand people! Touchdown! Right between the goal posts.
[BERNARD *is a quiet, earnest, but self-assured young man.* WILLY's *voice is coming from right upstage now.* BERNARD *lowers his feet off the table and listens.* JENNY, *his father's secretary, enters.*]

JENNY   [*distressed*]   Say, Bernard, will you go out in the hall?

BERNARD   What is that noise? Who is it?

JENNY   Mr. Loman. He just got off the elevator.

BERNARD   [*getting up*]   Who's he arguing with?

JENNY   Nobody. There's nobody with him. I can't deal with him any more, and your father gets all upset everytime he comes. I've got a lot of typing to do, and your father's waiting to sign it. Will you see him?

---

9. Harold Edward Grange (1903–1991), all-American halfback at the University of Illinois from 1923 to 1925, then played professionally for the Chicago Bears.

WILLY [*entering*] Touchdown! Touch— [*He sees* JENNY.] Jenny, Jenny, good to see you. How're ya? Workin'? Or still honest?

JENNY Fine. How've you been feeling?

WILLY Not much any more, Jenny. Ha, ha! [*He is surprised to see the rackets.*]

BERNARD Hello, Uncle Willy.

WILLY [*almost shocked*] Bernard! Well, look who's here! [*He comes quickly, guiltily to* BERNARD *and warmly shakes his hand.*]

BERNARD How are you? Good to see you.

WILLY What are you doing here?

BERNARD Oh, just stopped by to see Pop. Get off my feet till my train leaves. I'm going to Washington in a few minutes.

WILLY Is he in?

BERNARD Yes, he's in his office with the accountant. Sit down.

WILLY [*sitting down*] What're you going to do in Washington?

BERNARD Oh, just a case I've got there, Willy.

WILLY That so? [*indicating the rackets*] You going to play tennis there?

BERNARD I'm staying with a friend who's got a court.

WILLY Don't say. His own tennis court. Must be fine people, I bet.

BERNARD They are, very nice. Dad tells me Biff's in town.

WILLY [*with a big smile*] Yeah, Biff's in. Working on a very big deal, Bernard.

BERNARD What's Biff doing?

WILLY Well, he's been doing very big things in the West. But he decided to establish himself here. Very big. We're having dinner. Did I hear your wife had a boy?

BERNARD That's right. Our second.

WILLY Two boys! What do you know!

BERNARD What kind of a deal has Biff got?

WILLY Well, Bill Oliver—very big sporting-goods man—he wants Biff very badly. Called him in from the West. Long distance, carte blanche, special deliveries. Your friends have their own private tennis court?

BERNARD You still with the old firm, Willy?

WILLY [*after a pause*] I'm—I'm overjoyed to see how you made the grade, Bernard, overjoyed. It's an encouraging thing to see a young man really—really—Looks very good for Biff—very—[*He breaks off, then*] Bernard— [*He is so full of emotion, he breaks off again.*]

BERNARD What is it, Willy?

WILLY [*small and alone*] What—what's the secret?

BERNARD What secret?

WILLY How—how did you? Why didn't he ever catch on?

BERNARD I wouldn't know that, Willy.

WILLY [*confidentially, desperately*] You were his friend, his boyhood friend. There's something I don't understand about it. His life ended after that Ebbets Field game. From the age of seventeen nothing good ever happened to him.

BERNARD He never trained himself for anything.

WILLY But he did, he did. After high school he took so many correspondence courses. Radio mechanics; television; God knows what, and never made the slightest mark.

BERNARD [*taking off his glasses*]   Willy, do you want to talk candidly?

WILLY [*rising, faces* BERNARD]   I regard you as a very brilliant man, Bernard. I value your advice.

BERNARD   Oh, the hell with the advice, Willy. I couldn't advise you. There's just one thing I've always wanted to ask you. When he was supposed to graduate, and the math teacher flunked him—

WILLY   Oh, that son-of-a-bitch ruined his life.

BERNARD   Yeah, but, Willy, all he had to do was go to summer school and make up that subject.

WILLY   That's right, that's right.

BERNARD   Did you tell him not to go to summer school?

WILLY   Me? I begged him to go. I ordered him to go!

BERNARD   Then why wouldn't he go?

WILLY   Why? Why! Bernard, that question has been trailing me like a ghost for the last fifteen years. He flunked the subject, and laid down and died like a hammer hit him!

BERNARD   Take it easy, kid.

WILLY   Let me talk to you—I got nobody to talk to. Bernard, Bernard, was it my fault? Y'see? It keeps going around in my mind, maybe I did something to him. I got nothing to give him.

BERNARD   Don't take it so hard.

WILLY   Why did he lay down? What is the story there? You were his friend!

BERNARD   Willy, I remember, it was June, and our grades came out. And he'd flunked math.

WILLY   That son-of-a-bitch!

BERNARD   No, it wasn't right then. Biff just got very angry, I remember, and he was ready to enroll in summer school.

WILLY [*surprised*]   He was?

BERNARD   He wasn't beaten by it at all. But then, Willy, he disappeared from the block for almost a month. And I got the idea that he'd gone up to New England to see you. Did he have a talk with you then?

[WILLY *stares in silence.*]

BERNARD   Willy?

WILLY [*with a strong edge of resentment in his voice*]   Yeah, he came to Boston. What about it?

BERNARD   Well, just that when he came back—I'll never forget this, it always mystifies me. Because I'd thought so well of Biff, even though he'd always taken advantage of me. I loved him, Willy, y'know? And he came back after that month and took his sneakers—remember those sneakers with "University of Virginia" printed on them? He was so proud of those, wore them every day. And he took them down in the cellar, and burned them up in the furnace. We had a fist fight. It lasted at least half an hour. Just the two of us, punching each other down the cellar, and crying right through it. I've often thought of how strange it was that I knew he'd given up his life. What happened in Boston, Willy?

[WILLY *looks at him as at an intruder.*]

BERNARD   I just bring it up because you asked me.

WILLY [*angrily*]   Nothing. What do you mean, "What happened?" What's that got to do with anything?

BERNARD   Well, don't get sore.

WILLY   What are you trying to do, blame it on me? If a boy lays down is
that my fault?

BERNARD   Now, Willy, don't get—

WILLY   Well, don't—don't talk to me that way! What does that mean, "What
happened?"

[CHARLEY *enters. He is in his vest, and he carries a bottle of bourbon.*]

CHARLEY   Hey, you're going to miss that train. [*He waves the bottle.*]

BERNARD   Yeah, I'm going. [*He takes the bottle.*] Thanks, Pop. [*He picks
up his rackets and bag.*] Good-by, Willy, and don't worry about it. You
know, "If at first you don't succeed . . ."

WILLY   Yes, I believe in that.

BERNARD   But sometimes, Willy, it's better for a man just to walk away.

WILLY   Walk away?

BERNARD   That's right.

WILLY   But if you can't walk away?

BERNARD   [*after a slight pause*]   I guess that's when it's tough. [*extending
his hand*] Good-by, Willy.

WILLY   [*shaking* BERNARD's *hand*]   Good-by, boy.

CHARLEY   [*an arm on* BERNARD's *shoulder*]   How do you like this kid? Gonna
argue a case in front of the Supreme Court.

BERNARD   [*protesting*]   Pop!

WILLY   [*genuinely shocked, pained, and happy*]   No! The Supreme Court!

BERNARD   I gotta run. 'By, Dad!

CHARLEY   Knock 'em dead, Bernard!

[BERNARD *goes off.*]

WILLY   [*as* CHARLEY *takes out his wallet*]   The Supreme Court! And he didn't
even mention it!

CHARLEY   [*counting out money on the desk*]   He don't have to—he's gonna
do it.

WILLY   And you never told him what to do, did you? You never took any
interest in him.

CHARLEY   My salvation is that I never took any interest in anything.
There's some money—fifty dollars. I got an accountant inside.

WILLY   Charley, look . . . [*with difficulty*] I got my insurance to pay. If you
can manage it—I need a hundred and ten dollars.

[CHARLEY *doesn't reply for a moment; merely stops moving.*]

WILLY   I'd draw it from my bank but Linda would know, and I . . .

CHARLEY   Sit down, Willy.

WILLY   [*moving toward the chair*]   I'm keeping an account of everything,
remember. I'll pay every penny back. [*He sits.*]

CHARLEY   Now listen to me, Willy.

WILLY   I want you to know I appreciate . . .

CHARLEY   [*sitting down on the table*]   Willy, what're you doin'? What the
hell is goin' on in your head?

WILLY   Why? I'm simply . . .

CHARLEY   I offered you a job. You can make fifty dollars a week. And I
won't send you on the road.

WILLY   I've got a job.

CHARLEY   Without pay? What kind of job is a job without pay? [*He rises.*]
Now, look kid, enough is enough. I'm no genius but I know when I'm
being insulted.

WILLY   Insulted!

CHARLEY   Why don't you want to work for me?

WILLY   What's the matter with you? I've got a job.

CHARLEY   Then what're you walkin' in here every week for?

WILLY [getting up]   Well, if you don't want me to walk in here—

CHARLEY   I am offering you a job!

WILLY   I don't want your goddam job!

CHARLEY   When the hell are you going to grow up?

WILLY [furiously]   You big ignoramus, if you say that to me again I'll rap you one! I don't care how big you are! [He's ready to fight. Pause.]

CHARLEY [kindly, going to him]   How much do you need, Willy?

WILLY   Charley, I'm strapped, I'm strapped. I don't know what to do. I was just fired.

CHARLEY   Howard fired you?

WILLY   That snotnose. Imagine that? I named him. I named him Howard.

CHARLEY   Willy, when're you gonna realize that them things don't mean anything? You named him Howard, but you can't sell that. The only thing you got in this world is what you can sell. And the funny thing is that you're a salesman, and you don't know that.

WILLY   I've always tried to think otherwise, I guess. I always felt that if a man was impressive, and well liked, that nothing—

CHARLEY   Why must everybody like you? Who liked J. P. Morgan?[1] Was he impressive? In a Turkish bath he'd look like a butcher. But with his pockets on he was very well liked. Now listen, Willy, I know you don't like me, and nobody can say I'm in love with you, but I'll give you a job because—just for the hell of it, put it that way. Now what do you say?

WILLY   I—I just can't work for you, Charley.

CHARLEY   What're you, jealous of me?

WILLY   I can't work for you, that's all, don't ask me why.

CHARLEY [angered, takes out more bills]   You been jealous of me all your life, you damned fool! Here, pay your insurance. [He puts the money in WILLY's hand.]

WILLY   I'm keeping strict accounts.

CHARLEY   I've got some work to do. Take care of yourself. And pay your insurance.

WILLY [moving to the right]   Funny, y'know? After all the highways, and the trains, and the appointments, and the years, you end up worth more dead than alive.

CHARLEY   Willy, nobody's worth nothin' dead. [after a slight pause] Did you hear what I said?

[WILLY stands still, dreaming.]

CHARLEY   Willy!

WILLY   Apologize to Bernard for me when you see him. I didn't mean to argue with him. He's a fine boy. They're all fine boys, and they'll end up big—all of them. Someday they'll all play tennis together. Wish me luck, Charley. He saw Bill Oliver today.

CHARLEY   Good luck.

---

1. John Pierpont Morgan (1837–1913), American banker and philanthropist famed for his enormous wealth.

WILLY [*on the verge of tears*] Charley, you're the only friend I got. Isn't that a remarkable thing? [*He goes out.*]

CHARLEY Jesus!

> [CHARLEY *stares after him a moment and follows. All light blacks out. Suddenly raucous music is heard, and a red glow rises behind the screen at right.* STANLEY, *a young waiter, appears, carrying a table, followed by* HAPPY, *who is carrying two chairs.*]

STANLEY [*putting the table down*] That's all right, Mr. Loman, I can handle it myself. [*He turns and takes the chairs from* HAPPY *and places them at the table.*]

HAPPY [*glancing around*] Oh, this is better.

STANLEY Sure, in the front there you're in the middle of all kinds a noise. Whenever you got a party. Mr. Loman, you just tell me and I'll put you back here. Y'know, there's a lotta people they don't like it private, because when they go out they like to see a lotta action around them because they're sick and tired to stay in the house by theirself. But I know you, you ain't from Hackensack. You know what I mean?

HAPPY [*sitting down*] So how's it coming, Stanley?

STANLEY Ah, it's a dog life. I only wish during the war they'd a took me in the Army. I coulda been dead by now.

HAPPY My brother's back, Stanley.

STANLEY Oh, he come back, heh? From the Far West.

HAPPY Yeah, big cattle man, my brother, so treat him right. And my father's coming too.

STANLEY Oh, your father too!

HAPPY You got a couple of nice lobsters?

STANLEY Hundred per cent, big.

HAPPY I want them with the claws.

STANLEY Don't worry, I don't give you no mice. [HAPPY *laughs.*] How about some wine? It'll put a head on the meal.

HAPPY No. You remember, Stanley, that recipe I brought you from overseas? With the champagne in it?

STANLEY Oh, yeah, sure. I still got it tacked up yet in the kitchen. But that'll have to cost a buck apiece anyways.

HAPPY That's all right.

STANLEY What'd you, hit a number or somethin'?

HAPPY No, it's a little celebration. My brother is—I think he pulled off a big deal today. I think we're going into business together.

STANLEY Great! That's the best for you. Because a family business, you know what I mean?—that's the best.

HAPPY That's what I think.

STANLEY 'Cause what's the difference? Somebody steals? It's in the family. Know what I mean? [*sotto voce*][2] Like this bartender here. The boss is goin' crazy what kinda leak he's got in the cash register. You put it in but it don't come out.

HAPPY [*raising his head*] Sh!

STANLEY What?

HAPPY You notice I wasn't lookin' right or left, was I?

STANLEY No.

---

2. In an undertone [Italian].

HAPPY   And my eyes are closed.

STANLEY   So what's the—?

HAPPY   Strudel's comin'.

STANLEY   [*catching on, looks around*]   Ah, no, there's no—
[*He breaks off as a furred, lavishly dressed girl enters and sits at the next table. Both follow her with their eyes.*]

STANLEY   Geez, how'd ya know?

HAPPY   I got radar or something. [*staring directly at her profile*] Oooooooo . . . Stanley.

STANLEY   I think that's for you, Mr. Loman.

HAPPY   Look at that mouth. Oh, God. And the binoculars.

STANLEY   Geez, you got a life, Mr. Loman.

HAPPY   Wait on her.

STANLEY   [*going to the girl's table*]   Would you like a menu, ma'am?

GIRL   I'm expecting someone, but I'd like a—

HAPPY   Why don't you bring her—excuse me, miss, do you mind? I sell champagne, and I'd like you to try my brand. Bring her a champagne, Stanley.

GIRL   That's awfully nice of you.

HAPPY   Don't mention it. It's all company money. [*He laughs.*]

GIRL   That's a charming product to be selling, isn't it?

HAPPY   Oh, gets to be like everything else. Selling is selling, y'know.

GIRL   I suppose.

HAPPY   You don't happen to sell, do you?

GIRL   No, I don't sell.

HAPPY   Would you object to a compliment from a stranger? You ought to be on a magazine cover.

GIRL   [*looking at him a little archly*]   I have been.
[STANLEY *comes in with a glass of champagne.*]

HAPPY   What'd I say before, Stanley? You see? She's a cover girl.

STANLEY   Oh, I could see, I could see.

HAPPY   [*to the* GIRL]   What magazine?

GIRL   Oh, a lot of them. [*She takes the drink.*] Thank you.

HAPPY   You know what they say in France, don't you? "Champagne is the drink of the complexion"—Hya, Biff!
[BIFF *has entered and sits with* HAPPY.]

BIFF   Hello, kid. Sorry I'm late.

HAPPY   I just got here. Uh, Miss—?

GIRL   Forsythe.

HAPPY   Miss Forsythe, this is my brother.

BIFF   Is Dad here?

HAPPY   His name is Biff. You might've heard of him. Great football player.

GIRL   Really? What team?

HAPPY   Are you familiar with football?

GIRL   No, I'm afraid I'm not.

HAPPY   Biff is quarterback with the New York Giants.

GIRL   Well, that's nice, isn't it? [*She drinks.*]

HAPPY   Good health.

GIRL   I'm happy to meet you.

HAPPY   That's my name. Hap. It's really Harold, but at West Point they called me Happy.

GIRL [*now really impressed*] Oh, I see. How do you do? [*She turns her profile*.]

BIFF Isn't Dad coming?

HAPPY You want her?

BIFF Oh, I could never make that.

HAPPY I remember the time that idea would never come into your head. Where's the old confidence, Biff?

BIFF I just saw Oliver—

HAPPY Wait a minute. I've got to see that old confidence again. Do you want her? She's on call.

BIFF Oh, no. [*He turns to look at the* GIRL.]

HAPPY I'm telling you. Watch this. [*turning to the* GIRL] Honey? [*She turns to him.*] Are you busy?

GIRL Well, I am . . . but I could make a phone call.

HAPPY Do that, will you, honey? And see if you can get a friend. We'll be here for a while. Biff is one of the greatest football players in the country.

GIRL [*standing up*] Well, I'm certainly happy to meet you.

HAPPY Come back soon.

GIRL I'll try.

HAPPY Don't try, honey, try hard.

[*The* GIRL *exits.* STANLEY *follows, shaking his head in bewildered admiration.*]

HAPPY Isn't that a shame now? A beautiful girl like that? That's why I can't get married. There's not a good woman in a thousand. New York is loaded with them, kid!

BIFF Hap, look—

HAPPY I told you she was on call!

BIFF [*strangely unnerved*] Cut it out, will ya? I want to say something to you.

HAPPY Did you see Oliver?

BIFF I saw him all right. Now look, I want to tell Dad a couple of things and I want you to help me.

HAPPY What? Is he going to back you?

BIFF Are you crazy? You're out of your goddam head, you know that?

HAPPY Why? What happened?

BIFF [*breathlessly*] I did a terrible thing today, Hap. It's been the strangest day I ever went through. I'm all numb, I swear.

HAPPY You mean he wouldn't see you?

BIFF Well, I waited six hours for him, see? All day. Kept sending my name in. Even tried to date his secretary so she'd get me to him, but no soap.

HAPPY Because you're not showin' the old confidence, Biff. He remembered you, didn't he?

BIFF [*stopping* HAPPY *with a gesture*] Finally, about five o'clock, he comes out. Didn't remember who I was or anything. I felt like such an idiot, Hap.

HAPPY Did you tell him my Florida idea?

BIFF He walked away. I saw him for one minute. I got so mad I could've torn the walls down! How the hell did I ever get the idea I was a salesman there? I even believed myself that I'd been a salesman for him! And then he gave me one look and—I realized what a ridiculous lie my whole life has been! We've been talking in a dream for fifteen years. I was a shipping clerk.

HAPPY What'd you do?

BIFF [*with great tension and wonder*]   Well, he left, see. And the secretary went out. I was all alone in the waiting-room. I don't know what came over me, Hap. The next thing I know I'm in his office—paneled walls, everything. I can't explain it. I—Hap, I took his fountain pen.

HAPPY   Geez, did he catch you?

BIFF   I ran out. I ran down all eleven flights. I ran and ran and ran.

HAPPY   That was an awful dumb—what'd you do that for?

BIFF [*agonized*]   I don't know, I just—wanted to take something, I don't know. You gotta help me, Hap, I'm gonna tell Pop.

HAPPY   You crazy? What for?

BIFF   Hap, he's got to understand that I'm not the man somebody lends that kind of money to. He thinks I've been spiting him all these years and it's eating him up.

HAPPY   That's just it. You tell him something nice.

BIFF   I can't.

HAPPY   Say you got a lunch date with Oliver tomorrow.

BIFF   So what do I do tomorrow?

HAPPY   You leave the house tomorrow and come back at night and say Oliver is thinking it over. And he thinks it over for a couple of weeks, and gradually it fades away and nobody's the worse.

BIFF   But it'll go on forever!

HAPPY   Dad is never so happy as when he's looking forward to something!
   [WILLY *enters.*]

HAPPY   Hello, scout!

WILLY   Gee, I haven't been here in years!
   [STANLEY *has followed* WILLY *in and sets a chair for him.* STANLEY *starts off but* HAPPY *stops him.*]

HAPPY   Stanley!
   [STANLEY *stands by, waiting for an order.*]

BIFF [*going to* WILLY *with guilt, as to an invalid*]   Sit down, Pop. You want a drink?

WILLY   Sure, I don't mind.

BIFF   Let's get a load on.

WILLY   You look worried.

BIFF   N-no. [*to* STANLEY] Scotch all around. Make it doubles.

STANLEY   Doubles, right. [*He goes.*]

WILLY   You had a couple already, didn't you?

BIFF   Just a couple, yeah.

WILLY   Well, what happened, boy? [*nodding affirmatively, with a smile*] Everything go all right?

BIFF [*takes a breath, then reaches out and grasps* WILLY'S *hand*]   Pal . . . [*He is smiling bravely, and* WILLY *is smiling too.*] I had an experience today.

HAPPY   Terrific, Pop.

WILLY   That so? What happened?

BIFF [*high, slightly alcoholic, above the earth*]   I'm going to tell you everything from first to last. It's been a strange day. [*Silence. He looks around, composes himself as best he can, but his breath keeps breaking the rhythm of his voice.*] I had to wait quite a while for him, and—

WILLY   Oliver?

BIFF   Yeah, Oliver. All day, as a matter of cold fact. And a lot of—instances—facts, Pop, facts about my life came back to me. Who was it, Pop? Who ever said I was a salesman with Oliver?

WILLY   Well, you were.

BIFF   No, Dad, I was a shipping clerk.

WILLY   But you were practically—

BIFF [*with determination*]   Dad, I don't know who said it first, but I was never a salesman for Bill Oliver.

WILLY   What're you talking about?

BIFF   Let's hold on to the facts tonight, Pop. We're not going to get anywhere bullin' around. I was a shipping clerk.

WILLY [*angrily*]   All right, now listen to me—

BIFF   Why don't you let me finish?

WILLY   I'm not interested in stories about the past or any crap of that kind because the woods are burning, boys, you understand? There's a big blaze going on all around. I was fired today.

BIFF [*shocked*]   How could you be?

WILLY   I was fired, and I'm looking for a little good news to tell your mother, because the woman has waited and the woman has suffered. The gist of it is that I haven't got a story left in my head, Biff. So don't give me a lecture about facts and aspects. I am not interested. Now what've you got to say to me?

[STANLEY *enters with three drinks. They wait until he leaves.*]

WILLY   Did you see Oliver?

BIFF   Jesus, Dad!

WILLY   You mean you didn't go up there?

HAPPY   Sure he went up there.

BIFF   I did. I—saw him. How could they fire you?

WILLY [*on the edge of his chair*]   What kind of a welcome did he give you?

BIFF   He won't even let you work on commission?

WILLY   I'm out! [*driving*] So tell me, he gave you a warm welcome?

HAPPY   Sure, Pop, sure!

BIFF [*driven*]   Well, it was kind of—

WILLY   I was wondering if he'd remember you. [*to* HAPPY] Imagine, man doesn't see him for ten, twelve years and gives him that kind of a welcome!

HAPPY   Damn right!

BIFF [*trying to return to the offensive*]   Pop, look—

WILLY   You know why he remembered you, don't you? Because you impressed him in those days.

BIFF   Let's talk quietly and get this down to the facts, huh?

WILLY [*as though* BIFF *had been interrupting*]   Well, what happened? It's great news, Biff. Did he take you into his office or'd you talk in the waiting-room?

BIFF   Well, he came in, see, and—

WILLY [*with a big smile*]   What'd he say? Betcha he threw his arm around you.

BIFF   Well, he kinda—

WILLY   He's a fine man. [*to* HAPPY] Very hard man to see, y'know.

HAPPY [*agreeing*]   Oh, I know.

WILLY [*to* BIFF]   Is that where you had the drinks?

BIFF   Yeah, he gave me a couple of—no, no!

HAPPY [*cutting in*]   He told him my Florida idea.

WILLY   Don't interrupt. [*to* BIFF] How'd he react to the Florida idea?

BIFF Dad, will you give me a minute to explain?

WILLY I've been waiting for you to explain since I sat down here! What happened? He took you into his office and what?

BIFF Well—I talked. And—he listened, see.

WILLY Famous for the way he listens, y'know. What was his answer?

BIFF His answer was— [*He breaks off, suddenly angry.*] Dad, you're not letting me tell you what I want to tell you!

WILLY [*accusing, angered*] You didn't see him, did you?

BIFF I did see him!

WILLY What'd you insult him or something? You insulted him, didn't you?

BIFF Listen, will you let me out of it, will you just let me out of it!

HAPPY What the hell!

WILLY Tell me what happened!

BIFF [*to* HAPPY] I can't talk to him!

[*A single trumpet note jars the ear. The light of green leaves stains the house, which holds the air of night and a dream.* YOUNG BERNARD *enters and knocks on the door of the house.*]

YOUNG BERNARD [*frantically*] Mrs. Loman, Mrs. Loman!

HAPPY Tell him what happened!

BIFF [*to* HAPPY] Shut up and leave me alone!

WILLY No, no. You had to go and flunk math!

BIFF What math? What're you talking about?

YOUNG BERNARD Mrs. Loman, Mrs. Loman!

[LINDA *appears in the house, as of old.*]

WILLY [*wildly*] Math, math, math!

BIFF Take it easy, Pop!

YOUNG BERNARD Mrs. Loman!

WILLY [*furiously*] If you hadn't flunked you'd've been set by now!

BIFF Now, look, I'm gonna tell you what happened, and you're going to listen to me.

YOUNG BERNARD Mrs. Loman!

BIFF I waited six hours—

HAPPY What the hell are you saying?

BIFF I kept sending in my name but he wouldn't see me. So finally he . . . [*He continues unheard as light fades low on the restaurant.*]

YOUNG BERNARD Biff flunked math!

LINDA No!

YOUNG BERNARD Birnbaum flunked him! They won't graduate him!

LINDA But they have to. He's gotta go to the university. Where is he? Biff! Biff!

YOUNG BERNARD No, he left. He went to Grand Central.

LINDA Grand—You mean he went to Boston!

YOUNG BERNARD Is Uncle Willy in Boston?

LINDA Oh, maybe Willy can talk to the teacher. Oh, the poor, poor boy!

[*Light on house area snaps out.*]

BIFF [*at the table, now audible, holding up a gold fountain pen*] . . . so I'm washed up with Oliver, you understand? Are you listening to me?

WILLY [*at a loss*] Yeah, sure. If you hadn't flunked—

BIFF Flunked what? What're you talking about?

WILLY Don't blame everything on me! I didn't flunk math—you did! What pen?

HAPPY   That was awful dumb, Biff, a pen like that is worth—

WILLY [*seeing the pen for the first time*]   You took Oliver's pen?

BIFF [*weakening*]   Dad, I just explained it to you.

WILLY   You stole Bill Oliver's fountain pen!

BIFF   I didn't exactly steal it! That's just what I've been explaining to you!

HAPPY   He had it in his hand and just then Oliver walked in, so he got nervous and stuck it in his pocket!

WILLY   My God, Biff!

BIFF   I never intended to do it, Dad!

OPERATOR'S VOICE   Standish Arms, good evening!

WILLY [*shouting*]   I'm not in my room!

BIFF [*frightened*]   Dad, what's the matter? [*He and* HAPPY *stand up.*]

OPERATOR   Ringing Mr. Loman for you!

WILLY   I'm not there, stop it!

BIFF [*horrified, gets down on one knee before* WILLY]   Dad, I'll make good, I'll make good. [WILLY *tries to get to his feet.* BIFF *holds him down.*] Sit down now.

WILLY   No, you're no good, you're no good for anything.

BIFF   I am, Dad, I'll find something else, you understand? Now don't worry about anything. [*He holds up* WILLY'S *face.*] Talk to me, Dad.

OPERATOR   Mr. Loman does not answer. Shall I page him?

WILLY [*attempting to stand, as though to rush and silence the* OPERATOR] No, no, no!

HAPPY   He'll strike something, Pop.

WILLY   No, no . . .

BIFF [*desperately, standing over* WILLY]   Pop, listen! Listen to me! I'm telling you something good. Oliver talked to his partner about the Florida idea. You listening? He—he talked to his partner, and he came to me . . . I'm going to be all right, you hear? Dad, listen to me, he said it was just a question of the amount!

WILLY   Then you . . . got it?

HAPPY   He's gonna be terrific, Pop!

WILLY [*trying to stand*]   Then you got it, haven't you? You got it! You got it!

BIFF [*agonized, holds* WILLY *down*]   No, no. Look, Pop. I'm supposed to have lunch with them tomorrow. I'm just telling you this so you'll know that I can still make an impression, Pop. And I'll make good somewhere, but I can't go tomorrow, see?

WILLY   Why not? You simply—

BIFF   But the pen, Pop!

WILLY   You give it to him and tell him it was an oversight!

HAPPY   Sure, have lunch tomorrow!

BIFF   I can't say that—

WILLY   You were doing a crossword puzzle and accidentally used his pen!

BIFF   Listen, kid, I took those balls years ago, now I walk in with his fountain pen? That clinches it, don't you see? I can't face him like that! I'll try elsewhere.

PAGE'S VOICE   Paging Mr. Loman!

WILLY   Don't you want to be anything?

BIFF   Pop, how can I go back?

WILLY   You don't want to be anything, is that what's behind it?

BIFF [*now angry at* WILLY *for not crediting his sympathy*]   Don't take it that
    way! You think it was easy walking into that office after what I'd done to
    him? A team of horses couldn't have dragged me back to Bill Oliver!

WILLY   Then why'd you go?

BIFF   Why did I go? Why did I go! Look at you! Look at what's become of
    you!
        [*Off left,* THE WOMAN *laughs.*]

WILLY   Biff, you're going to go to that lunch tomorrow, or—

BIFF   I can't go. I've got no appointment!

HAPPY   Biff for . . . !

WILLY   Are you spiting me?

BIFF   Don't take it that way! Goddammit!

WILLY [*strikes* BIFF *and falters away from the table*]   You rotten little louse!
    Are you spiting me?

THE WOMAN   Someone's at the door, Willy!

BIFF   I'm no good, can't you see what I am?

HAPPY [*separating them*]   Hey, you're in a restaurant! Now cut it out, both
    of you? [*The girls enter.*] Hello, girls, sit down.
        [THE WOMAN *laughs, off left.*]

MISS FORSYTHE   I guess we might as well. This is Letta.

THE WOMAN   Willy, are you going to wake up?

BIFF [*ignoring* WILLY]   How're ya, miss, sit down. What do you drink?

MISS FORSYTHE   Letta might not be able to stay long.

LETTA   I gotta get up early tomorrow. I got jury duty. I'm so excited! Were
    you fellows ever on a jury?

BIFF   No, but I been in front of them! [*The girls laugh.*] This is my father.

LETTA   Isn't he cute? Sit down with us, Pop.

HAPPY   Sit him down, Biff!

BIFF [*going to him*]   Come on, slugger, drink us under the table. To hell
    with it! Come on, sit down, pal.
        [*On* BIFF's *last insistence,* WILLY *is about to sit.*]

THE WOMAN [*now urgently*]   Willy, are you going to answer the door!
        [THE WOMAN's *call pulls* WILLY *back. He starts right, befuddled.*]

BIFF   Hey, where are you going?

WILLY   Open the door.

BIFF   The door?

WILLY   The washroom . . . the door . . . where's the door?

BIFF [*leading* WILLY *to the left*]   Just go straight down.
        [WILLY *moves left.*]

THE WOMAN   Willy, Willy, are you going to get up, get up, get up, get up?
        [WILLY *exits left.*]

LETTA   I think it's sweet you bring your daddy along.

MISS FORSYTHE   Oh, he isn't really your father!

BIFF [*at left, turning to her resentfully*]   Miss Forsythe, you've just seen a
    prince walk by. A fine, troubled prince. A hard-working, unappreciated
    prince. A pal, you understand? A good companion. Always for his boys.

LETTA   That's so sweet.

HAPPY   Well, girls, what's the program? We're wasting time. Come on, Biff.
    Gather round. Where would you like to go?

BIFF   Why don't you do something for him?

HAPPY   Me!

BIFF   Don't you give a damn for him, Hap?

HAPPY   What're you talking about? I'm the one who—

BIFF   I sense it, you don't give a good goddam about him. [*He takes the rolled-up hose from his pocket and puts it on the table in front of* HAPPY.] Look what I found in the cellar, for Christ's sake. How can you bear to let it go on?

HAPPY   Me? Who goes away? Who runs off and—

BIFF   Yeah, but he doesn't mean anything to you. You could help him—I can't! Don't you understand what I'm talking about? He's going to kill himself, don't you know that?

HAPPY   Don't I know it! Me!

BIFF   Hap, help him! Jesus . . . help him . . . Help me, help me, I can't bear to look at his face! [*Ready to weep, he hurries out, up right.*]

HAPPY [*starting after him*]   Where are you going?

MISS FORSYTHE   What's he so mad about?

HAPPY   Come on, girls, we'll catch up with him.

MISS FORSYTHE [*as* HAPPY *pushes her out*]   Say, I don't like that temper of his!

HAPPY   He's just a little overstrung, he'll be all right!

WILLY [*off left, as* THE WOMAN *laughs*]   Don't answer! Don't answer!

LETTA   Don't you want to tell your father—

HAPPY   No, that's not my father. He's just a guy. Come on, we'll catch Biff, and, honey, we're going to paint this town! Stanley, where's the check! Hey, Stanley!

[*They exit.* STANLEY *looks toward left.*]

STANLEY [*calling to* HAPPY *indignantly*]   Mr. Loman! Mr. Loman!

[STANLEY *picks up a chair and follows them off. Knocking is heard off left.* THE WOMAN *enters, laughing.* WILLY *follows her. She is in a black slip; he is buttoning his shirt. Raw, sensuous music accompanies their speech.*]

WILLY   Will you stop laughing? Will you stop?

THE WOMAN   Aren't you going to answer the door? He'll wake the whole hotel.

WILLY   I'm not expecting anybody.

THE WOMAN   Whyn't you have another drink, honey, and stop being so damn self-centered?

WILLY   I'm so lonely.

THE WOMAN   You know you ruined me, Willy? From now on, whenever you come to the office, I'll see that you go right through to the buyers. No waiting at my desk any more, Willy. You ruined me.

WILLY   That's nice of you to say that.

THE WOMAN   Gee, you are self-centered! Why so sad? You are the saddest, self-centeredest soul I ever did see-saw. [*She laughs. He kisses her.*] Come on inside, drummer boy. It's silly to be dressing in the middle of the night. [*As knocking is heard*] Aren't you going to answer the door?

WILLY   They're knocking on the wrong door.

THE WOMAN   But I felt the knocking. And he heard us talking in here. Maybe the hotel's on fire!

WILLY [*his terror rising*]   It's a mistake.

THE WOMAN   Then tell them to go away!

WILLY   There's nobody there.

THE WOMAN   It's getting on my nerves, Willy. There's somebody standing out there and it's getting on my nerves!

WILLY [*pushing her away from him*]   All right, stay in the bathroom here, and don't come out. I think there's a law in Massachusetts about it, so don't come out. It may be that new room clerk. He looked very mean. So don't come out. It's a mistake, there's no fire.

> [*The knocking is heard again. He takes a few steps away from her, and she vanishes into the wing. The light follows him, and now he is facing* YOUNG BIFF, *who carries a suitcase.* BIFF *steps toward him. The music is gone.*]

BIFF   Why didn't you answer?

WILLY   Biff! What are you doing in Boston?

BIFF   Why didn't you answer? I've been knocking for five minutes, I called you on the phone—

WILLY   I just heard you. I was in the bathroom and had the door shut. Did anything happen home?

BIFF   Dad—I let you down.

WILLY   What do you mean?

BIFF   Dad . . .

WILLY   Biffo, what's this about? [*putting his arm around* BIFF] Come on, let's go downstairs and get you a malted.

BIFF   Dad, I flunked math.

WILLY   Not for the term?

BIFF   The term. I haven't got enough credits to graduate.

WILLY   You mean to say Bernard wouldn't give you the answers?

BIFF   He did, he tried, but I only got a sixty-one.

WILLY   And they wouldn't give you four points?

BIFF   Birnbaum refused absolutely. I begged him, Pop, but he won't give me those points. You gotta talk to him before they close the school. Because if he saw the kind of man you are, and you just talked to him in your way, I'm sure he'd come through for me. The class came right before practice, see, and I didn't go enough. Would you talk to him? He'd like you, Pop. You know the way you could talk.

WILLY   You're on. We'll drive right back.

BIFF   Oh, Dad, good work! I'm sure he'll change for you!

WILLY   Go downstairs and tell the clerk I'm checkin' out. Go right down.

BIFF   Yes, sir! See, the reason he hates me, Pop—one day he was late for class so I got up at the blackboard and imitated him. I crossed my eyes and talked with a lithp.

WILLY [*laughing*]   You did? The kids like it?

BIFF   They nearly died laughing!

WILLY   Yeah? What'd you do?

BIFF   The thquare root of thixthy twee is . . . [WILLY *bursts out laughing;* BIFF *joins him.*] And in the middle of it he walked in!

> [WILLY *laughs and* THE WOMAN *joins in offstage.*]

WILLY [*without hesitation*]   Hurry downstairs and—

BIFF   Somebody in there?

WILLY   No, that was next door.

> [THE WOMAN *laughs offstage.*]

BIFF   Somebody got in your bathroom!

WILLY   No, it's the next room, there's a party—

THE WOMAN [*enters laughing. She lisps this*]   Can I come in? There's something in the bathtub, Willy, and it's moving!

[WILLY *looks at* BIFF, *who is staring open-mouthed and horrified at* THE WOMAN.]

WILLY   Ah—you better go back to your room. They must be finished painting by now. They're painting her room so I let her take a shower here. Go back, go back . . . [*He pushes her.*]

THE WOMAN [*resisting*]   But I've got to get dressed, Willy, I can't—

WILLY   Get out of here! Go back, go back . . . [*suddenly striving for the ordinary*] This is Miss Francis, Biff, she's a buyer. They're painting her room. Go back, Miss Francis, go back . . .

THE WOMAN   But my clothes, I can't go out naked in the hall!

WILLY [*pushing her offstage*]   Get outa here! Go back, go back!

[BIFF *slowly sits down on his suitcase as the argument continues offstage.*]

THE WOMAN   Where's my stockings? You promised me stockings, Willy!

WILLY   I have no stockings here!

THE WOMAN   You had two boxes of size nine sheers for me, and I want them!

WILLY   Here, for God's sake, will you get outa here!

THE WOMAN [*enters holding a box of stockings*]   I just hope there's nobody in the hall. That's all I hope. [*to* BIFF] Are you football or baseball?

BIFF   Football.

THE WOMAN [*angry, humiliated*]   That's me too. G'night. [*She snatches her clothes from* WILLY, *and walks out.*]

WILLY [*after a pause*]   Well, better get going. I want to get to the school first thing in the morning. Get my suits out of the closet. I'll get my valise. [BIFF *doesn't move.*] What's the matter? [BIFF *remains motionless, tears falling.*] She's a buyer. Buys for J. H. Simmons. She lives down the hall—they're painting. You don't imagine— [*He breaks off. After a pause*] Now listen, pal, she's just a buyer. She sees merchandise in her room and they have to keep it looking just so . . . [*Pause. Assuming command*] All right, get my suits. [BIFF *doesn't move.*] Now stop crying and do as I say. I gave you an order. Biff, I gave you an order! Is that what you do when I give you an order? How dare you cry! [*putting his arm around* BIFF] Now look, Biff, when you grow up you'll understand about these things. You mustn't—you mustn't overemphasize a thing like this. I'll see Birnbaum first thing in the morning.

BIFF   Never mind.

WILLY [*getting down beside* BIFF]   Never mind! He's going to give you those points. I'll see to it.

BIFF   He wouldn't listen to you.

WILLY   He certainly will listen to me. You need those points for the U. of Virginia.

BIFF   I'm not going there.

WILLY   Heh? If I can't get him to change that mark you'll make it up in summer school. You've got all summer to—

BIFF [*his weeping breaking from him*]   Dad . . .

WILLY [*infected by it*]   Oh, my boy . . .

BIFF   Dad . . .

WILLY   She's nothing to me, Biff. I was lonely, I was terribly lonely.

BIFF   You—you gave her Mama's stockings! [*His tears break through and he rises to go.*]

WILLY [*grabbing for* BIFF]   I gave you an order!

BIFF   Don't touch me, you—liar!

WILLY   Apologize for that!

BIFF   You fake! You phony little fake! You fake! [*Overcome, he turns quickly and weeping fully goes out with his suitcase,* WILLY *is left on the floor on his knees.*]

WILLY   I gave you an order! Biff, come back here or I'll beat you! Come back here! I'll whip you!

[STANLEY *comes quickly in from the right and stands in front of* WILLY.]

WILLY [*shouts at* STANLEY]   I gave you an order . . .

STANLEY   Hey, let's pick it up, pick it up, Mr. Loman. [*He helps* WILLY *to his feet.*] Your boys left with the chippies. They said they'll see you home.

[*A second waiter watches some distance away.*]

WILLY   But we were supposed to have dinner together.

[*Music is heard,* WILLY's *theme.*]

STANLEY   Can you make it?

WILLY   I'll—sure, I can make it. [*suddenly concerned about his clothes*] Do I—I look all right?

STANLEY   Sure, you look all right. [*He flicks a speck off* WILLY's *lapel.*]

WILLY   Here—here's a dollar.

STANLEY   Oh, your son paid me. It's all right.

WILLY [*putting it in* STANLEY's *hand*]   No, take it. You're a good boy.

STANLEY   Oh, no, you don't have to . . .

WILLY   Here—here's some more, I don't need it any more, [*after a slight pause*] Tell me—is there a seed store in the neighborhood?

STANLEY   Seeds? You mean like to plant?

[*As* WILLY *turns,* STANLEY *slips the money back into his jacket pocket.*]

WILLY   Yes. Carrots, peas . . .

STANLEY   Well, there's hardware stores on Sixth Avenue, but it may be too late now.

WILLY [*anxiously*]   Oh, I'd better hurry. I've got to get some seeds. [*He starts off to the right.*] I've got to get some seeds, right away. Nothing's planted. I don't have a thing in the ground.

[WILLY *hurries out as the light goes down.* STANLEY *moves over to the right after him, watches him off. The other waiter has been staring at* WILLY.]

STANLEY [*to the waiter*]   Well, whatta you looking at?

[*The waiter picks up the chairs and moves off right.* STANLEY *takes the table and follows him. The light fades on this area. There is a long pause, the sound of the flute coming over. The light gradually rises on the kitchen, which is empty.* HAPPY *appears at the door of the house, followed by* BIFF. HAPPY *is carrying a large bunch of long-stemmed roses. He enters the kitchen, looks around for* LINDA. *Not seeing her, he turns to* BIFF, *who is just outside the house door, and makes a gesture with his hands, indicating "Not here, I guess." He looks into the living-room and freezes. Inside,* LINDA, *unseen, is seated,* WILLY's *coat on her lap. She rises ominously and quietly and moves toward* HAPPY, *who backs up into the kitchen, afraid.*]

HAPPY   Hey, what're you doing up? [LINDA *says nothing but moves toward him implacably.*] Where's Pop? [*He keeps backing to the right, and now* LINDA *is in full view in the doorway to the living-room.*] Is he sleeping?

LINDA   Where were you?

HAPPY [*trying to laugh it off*]   We met two girls, Mom, very fine types. Here, we brought you some flowers. [*offering them to her*] Put them in your room, Ma.

[*She knocks them to the floor at* BIFF's *feet. He has now come inside and closed the door behind him. She stares at* BIFF, *silent.*]

HAPPY   Now what'd you do that for? Mom, I want you to have some flowers—

LINDA [*cutting* HAPPY *off, violently to* BIFF]   Don't you care whether he lives or dies?

HAPPY [*going to the stairs*]   Come upstairs, Biff.

BIFF [*with a flare of disgust, to* HAPPY]   Go away from me! [*to* LINDA] What do you mean, lives or dies? Nobody's dying around here, pal.

LINDA   Get out of my sight! Get out of here!

BIFF   I wanna see the boss.

LINDA   You're not going near him!

BIFF   Where is he? [*He moves into the living-room and* LINDA *follows.*]

LINDA [*shouting after* BIFF]   You invite him for dinner. He looks forward to it all day—[BIFF *appears in his parents' bedroom, looks around and exits*]—and then you desert him there. There's no stranger you'd do that to!

HAPPY   Why? He had a swell time with us. Listen, when I—[LINDA *comes back into the kitchen*]—desert him I hope I don't outlive the day!

LINDA   Get out of here!

HAPPY   Now look, Mom . . .

LINDA   Did you have to go to women tonight? You and your lousy rotten whores!

[BIFF *re-enters the kitchen.*]

HAPPY   Mom, all we did was follow Biff around trying to cheer him up! [*to* BIFF] Boy, what a night you gave me!

LINDA   Get out of here, both of you, and don't come back! I don't want you tormenting him any more. Go on now, get your things together! [*to* BIFF] You can sleep in his apartment. [*She starts to pick up the flowers and stops herself.*] Pick up this stuff, I'm not your maid any more. Pick it up, you bum, you!

[HAPPY *turns his back to her in refusal.* BIFF *slowly moves over and gets down on his knees, picking up the flowers.*]

LINDA   You're a pair of animals! Not one, not another living soul would have had the cruelty to walk out on that man in a restaurant!

BIFF [*not looking at her*]   Is that what he said?

LINDA   He didn't have to say anything. He was so humiliated he nearly limped when he came in.

HAPPY   But, Mom, he had a great time with us—

BIFF [*cutting him off violently*]   Shut up!

[*Without another word,* HAPPY *goes upstairs.*]

LINDA   You! You didn't even go in to see if he was all right!

BIFF [*still on the floor in front of* LINDA, *the flowers in his hand; with self-loathing*]   No. Didn't. Didn't do a damned thing. How do you like that, heh? Left him babbling in a toilet.

LINDA   You louse. You . . .

BIFF   Now you hit it on the nose! [*He gets up, throws the flowers in the waste-basket.*] The scum of the earth, and you're looking at him!

LINDA   Get out of here!

BIFF   I gotta talk to the boss, Mom. Where is he?

LINDA   You're not going near him. Get out of this house!

BIFF [*with absolute assurance, determination*]   No. We're gonna have an abrupt conversation, him and me.

LINDA You're not talking to him!
> [*Hammering is heard from outside the house, off right.* BIFF *turns toward the noise.*]

LINDA [*suddenly pleading*] Will you please leave him alone?

BIFF What's he doing out there?

LINDA He's planting the garden!

BIFF [*quietly*] Now? Oh, my God!
> [BIFF *moves outside,* LINDA *following. The light dies down on them and comes up on the center of the apron as* WILLY *walks into it. He is carrying a flashlight, a hoe, and a handful of seed packets. He raps the top of the hoe sharply to fix it firmly, and then moves to the left, measuring off the distance with his foot. He holds the flashlight to look at the seed packets, reading off the instructions. He is in the blue of night.*]

WILLY Carrots . . . quarter-inch apart. Rows . . . one-foot rows. [*He measures it off.*] One foot. [*He puts down a package and measures off.*] Beets. [*He puts down another package and measures again.*] Lettuce. [*He reads the package, puts it down.*] One foot— [*He breaks off as* BEN *appears at the right and moves slowly down to him.*] What a proposition, ts, ts. Terrific, terrific. 'Cause she's suffered, Ben, the woman has suffered. You understand me? A man can't go out the way he came in, Ben, a man has got to add up to something. You can't, you can't— [BEN *moves toward him as though to interrupt.*] You gotta consider, now. Don't answer so quick. Remember, it's a guaranteed twenty-thousand-dollar proposition. Now look, Ben, I want you to go through the ins and outs of this thing with me. I've got nobody to talk to, Ben, and the woman has suffered, you hear me?

BEN [*standing still, considering*] What's the proposition?

WILLY It's twenty thousand dollars on the barrelhead. Guaranteed, gilt-edged, you understand?

BEN You don't want to make a fool of yourself. They might not honor the policy.

WILLY How can they dare refuse? Didn't I work like a coolie to meet every premium on the nose? And now they don't pay off! Impossible!

BEN It's called a cowardly thing, William.

WILLY Why? Does it take more guts to stand here the rest of my life ringing up a zero?

BEN [*yielding*] That's a point, William. [*He moves, thinking, turns.*] And twenty thousand—that *is* something one can feel with the hand, it is there.

WILLY [*now assured, with rising power*] Oh, Ben, that's the whole beauty of it! I see it like a diamond, shining in the dark, hard and rough, that I can pick up and touch in my hand. Not like—like an appointment! This would not be another damned-fool appointment, Ben, and it changes all the aspects. Because he thinks I'm nothing, see, and so he spites me. But the funeral— [*straightening up*] Ben, that funeral will be massive! They'll come from Maine, Massachusetts, Vermont, New Hampshire! All the old-timers with the strange license plates—that boy will be thunderstruck, Ben, because he never realized—I am known! Rhode Island, New York, New Jersey—I am known, Ben, and he'll see it with his eyes once and for all. He'll see what I am, Ben! He's in for a shock, that boy!

BEN [*coming down to the edge of the garden*] He'll call you a coward.

WILLY [*suddenly fearful*] No, that would be terrible.

BEN Yes. And a damned fool.

WILLY No, no, he mustn't, I won't have that! [*He is broken and desperate.*]

BEN He'll hate you, William.

[*The gay music of the Boys is heard.*]

WILLY Oh, Ben, how do we get back to all the great times? Used to be so full of light, and comradeship, the sleigh-riding in winter, and the ruddiness on his cheeks. And always some kind of good news coming up, always something nice coming up ahead. And never even let me carry the valises in the house, and simonizing, simonizing that little red car! Why, why can't I give him something and not have him hate me?

BEN Let me think about it. [*He glances at his watch.*] I still have a little time. Remarkable proposition, but you've got to be sure you're not making a fool of yourself.

[BEN *drifts off upstage and goes out of sight.* BIFF *comes down from the left.*]

WILLY [*suddenly conscious of* BIFF, *turns and looks up at him, then begins picking up the packages of seeds in confusion*] Where the hell is that seed? [*indignantly*] You can't see nothing out here! They boxed in the whole goddam neighborhood!

BIFF There are people all around here. Don't you realize that?

WILLY I'm busy. Don't bother me.

BIFF [*taking the hoe from* WILLY] I'm saying good-by to you, Pop. [WILLY *looks at him, silent, unable to move.*] I'm not coming back any more.

WILLY You're not going to see Oliver tomorrow?

BIFF I've got no appointment, Dad.

WILLY He put his arm around you, and you've got no appointment?

BIFF Pop, get this now, will you? Everytime I've left it's been a fight that sent me out of here. Today I realized something about myself and I tried to explain it to you and I—I think I'm just not smart enough to make any sense out of it for you. To hell with whose fault it is or anything like that. [*He takes* WILLY's *arm.*] Let's just wrap it up, heh? Come on in, we'll tell Mom. [*He gently tries to pull* WILLY *to left.*]

WILLY [*frozen, immobile, with guilt in his voice*] No, I don't want to see her.

BIFF Come on! [*He pulls again, and* WILLY *tries to pull away.*]

WILLY [*highly nervous*] No, no, I don't want to see her.

BIFF [*tries to look into* WILLY's *face, as if to find the answer there*] Why don't you want to see her?

WILLY [*more harshly now*] Don't bother me, will you?

BIFF What do you mean, you don't want to see her? You don't want them calling you yellow, do you? This isn't your fault; it's me, I'm a bum. Now come inside! [WILLY *strains to get away.*] Did you hear what I said to you?

[WILLY *pulls away and quickly goes by himself into the house.* BIFF *follows.*]

LINDA [*to* WILLY] Did you plant, dear?

BIFF [*at the door, to* LINDA] All right, we had it out. I'm going and I'm not writing any more.

LINDA [*going to* WILLY *in the kitchen*] I think that's the best way, dear. 'Cause there's no use drawing it out, you'll just never get along.

[WILLY *doesn't respond.*]

BIFF People ask where I am and what I'm doing, you don't know, and you don't care. That way it'll be off your mind and you can start brightening up again. All right? That clears it, doesn't it? [WILLY *is silent, and* BIFF *goes to him.*] You gonna wish me luck, scout? [*He extends his hand.*] What do you say?

LINDA   Shake his hand, Willy.

WILLY [*turning to her, seething with hurt*]   There's no necessity to mention the pen at all, y'know.

BIFF [*gently*]   I've got no appointment, Dad.

WILLY [*erupting fiercely*]   He put his arm around . . . ?

BIFF   Dad, you're never going to see what I am, so what's the use of arguing? If I strike oil I'll send you a check. Meantime forget I'm alive.

WILLY [*to* LINDA]   Spite, see?

BIFF   Shake hands, Dad.

WILLY   Not my hand.

BIFF   I was hoping not to go this way.

WILLY   Well, this is the way you're going. Good-by.
    [BIFF *looks at him a moment, then turns sharply and goes to the stairs.*]

WILLY [*stops him with*]   May you rot in hell if you leave this house!

BIFF [*turning*]   Exactly what is it that you want from me?

WILLY   I want you to know, on the train, in the mountains, in the valleys, wherever you go, that you cut down your life for spite!

BIFF   No, no.

WILLY   Spite, spite, is the word of your undoing! And when you're down and out, remember what did it. When you're rotting somewhere beside the railroad tracks, remember, and don't you dare blame it on me!

BIFF   I'm not blaming it on you!

WILLY   I won't take the rap for this, you hear?
    [HAPPY *comes down the stairs and stands on the bottom step, watching.*]

BIFF   That's just what I'm telling you!

WILLY [*sinking into a chair at the table, with full accusation*]   You're trying to put a knife in me—don't think I don't know what you're doing!

BIFF   All right, phony! Then let's lay it on the line. [*He whips the rubber tube out of his pocket and puts it on the table.*]

HAPPY   You crazy—

LINDA   Biff! [*She moves to grab the hose, but* BIFF *holds it down with his hand.*]

BIFF   Leave it there! Don't move it!

WILLY [*not looking at it*]   What is that?

BIFF   You know goddam well what that is.

WILLY [*caged, wanting to escape*]   I never saw that.

BIFF   You saw it. The mice didn't bring it into the cellar! What is this supposed to do, make a hero out of you? This supposed to make me sorry for you?

WILLY   Never heard of it.

BIFF   There'll be no pity for you, you hear it? No pity!

WILLY [*to* LINDA]   You hear the spite!

BIFF   No, you're going to hear the truth—what you are and what I am!

LINDA   Stop it!

WILLY   Spite!

HAPPY [*coming down toward* BIFF]   You cut it now!

BIFF [*to* HAPPY]   The man don't know who we are! The man is gonna know! [*to* WILLY] We never told the truth for ten minutes in this house!

HAPPY   We always told the truth!

BIFF [*turning on him*]   You big blow, are you the assistant buyer? You're one of the two assistants to the assistant, aren't you?

HAPPY   Well, I'm practically—

BIFF   You're practically full of it! We all are! And I'm through with it. [*to* WILLY] Now hear this, Willy, this is me.

WILLY   I know you!

BIFF   You know why I had no address for three months? I stole a suit in Kansas City and I was in jail. [*to* LINDA, *who is sobbing*] Stop crying. I'm through with it.

[LINDA *turns away from them, her hands covering her face.*]

WILLY   I suppose that's my fault!

BIFF   I stole myself out of every good job since high school!

WILLY   And whose fault is that?

BIFF   And I never got anywhere because you blew me so full of hot air I could never stand taking orders from anybody! That's whose fault it is!

WILLY   I hear that!

LINDA   Don't, Biff!

BIFF   It's goddam time you heard that! I had to be boss big shot in two weeks, and I'm through with it!

WILLY   Then hang yourself! For spite, hang yourself!

BIFF   No! Nobody's hanging himself, Willy! I ran down eleven flights with a pen in my hand today. And suddenly I stopped, you hear me? And in the middle of that office building, do you hear this? I stopped in the middle of that building and I saw—the sky. I saw the things that I love in this world. The work and the food and time to sit and smoke. And I looked at the pen and said to myself, what the hell am I grabbing this for? Why am I trying to become what I don't want to be? What am I doing in an office, making a contemptuous, begging fool of myself, when all I want is out there, waiting for me the minute I say I know who I am! Why can't I say that, Willy? [*He tries to make* WILLY *face him, but* WILLY *pulls away and moves to the left.*]

WILLY [*with hatred, threateningly*]   The door of your life is wide open!

BIFF   Pop! I'm a dime a dozen, and so are you!

WILLY [*turning on him now in an uncontrolled outburst*]   I am not a dime a dozen! I am Willy Loman, and you are Biff Loman!

[BIFF *starts for* WILLY, *but is blocked by* HAPPY. *In his fury,* BIFF *seems on the verge of attacking his father.*]

BIFF   I am not a leader of men, Willy, and neither are you. You were never anything but a hard-working drummer who landed in the ash can like all the rest of them! I'm one dollar an hour, Willy! I tried seven states and couldn't raise it. A buck an hour! Do you gather my meaning? I'm not bringing home any prizes any more, and you're going to stop waiting for me to bring them home!

WILLY [*directly to* BIFF]   You vengeful, spiteful mut!

[BIFF *breaks from* HAPPY. WILLY, *in fright, starts up the stairs.* BIFF *grabs him.*]

BIFF [*at the peak of his fury*]   Pop, I'm nothing! I'm nothing, Pop. Can't you understand that? There's no spite in it any more. I'm just what I am, that's all.

[BIFF'*s fury has spent itself, and he breaks down, sobbing, holding on to* WILLY, *who dumbly fumbles for* BIFF'*s face.*]

WILLY [*astonished*]   What're you doing? What're you doing? [*to* LINDA] Why is he crying?

BIFF [*crying, broken*]   Will you let me go, for Christ's sake? Will you take that phony dream and burn it before something happens? [*Struggling to contain himself, he pulls away and moves to the stairs.*] I'll go in the morning. Put him—put him to bed. [*Exhausted,* BIFF *moves up the stairs to his room.*]

WILLY [*after a long pause, astonished, elevated*]   Isn't that—isn't that remarkable? Biff—he likes me!

LINDA   He loves you, Willy!

HAPPY [*deeply moved*]   Always did, Pop.

WILLY   Oh, Biff! [*staring wildly*]   He cried! Cried to me. [*He is choking with his love, and now cries out his promise.*] That boy—that boy is going to be magnificent!

[BEN *appears in the light just outside the kitchen.*]

BEN   Yes, outstanding, with twenty thousand behind him.

LINDA [*sensing the racing of his mind, fearfully, carefully*]   Now come to bed, Willy. It's all settled now.

WILLY [*finding it difficult not to rush out of the house*]   Yes, we'll sleep. Come on. Go to sleep, Hap.

BEN   And it does take a great kind of a man to crack the jungle.

[*In accents of dread,* BEN's *idyllic music starts up.*]

HAPPY [*his arm around* LINDA]   I'm getting married, Pop, don't forget it. I'm changing everything. I'm gonna run that department before the year is up. You'll see, Mom. [*He kisses her.*]

BEN   The jungle is dark but full of diamonds, Willy.

[WILLY *turns, moves, listening to* BEN.]

LINDA   Be good. You're both good boys, just act that way, that's all.

HAPPY   'Night, Pop. [*He goes upstairs.*]

LINDA [*to* WILLY]   Come, dear.

BEN   [*with greater force*]   One must go in to fetch a diamond out.

WILLY [*to* LINDA, *as he moves slowly along the edge of the kitchen, toward the door*]   I just want to get settled down, Linda. Let me sit alone for a little.

LINDA [*almost uttering her fear*]   I want you upstairs.

WILLY [*taking her in his arms*]   In a few minutes, Linda. I couldn't sleep right now. Go on, you look awful tired. [*He kisses her.*]

BEN   Not like an appointment at all. A diamond is rough and hard to the touch.

WILLY   Go on now. I'll be right up.

LINDA   I think this is the only way, Willy.

WILLY   Sure, it's the best thing.

BEN   Best thing!

WILLY   The only way. Everything is gonna be—go on, kid, get to bed. You look so tired.

LINDA   Come right up.

WILLY   Two minutes.

[LINDA *goes into the living-room, then reappears in her bedroom.* WILLY *moves just outside the kitchen door.*]

WILLY   Loves me. [*wonderingly*]   Always loved me. Isn't that a remarkable thing? Ben, he'll worship me for it!

BEN [*with promise*]   It's dark there, but full of diamonds.

WILLY   Can you imagine that magnificence with twenty thousand dollars in his pocket?

LINDA [*calling from her room*]   Willy! Come up!

WILLY [*calling into the kitchen*]   Yes! Yes. Coming! It's very smart, you realize that, don't you, sweetheart? Even Ben sees it. I gotta go, baby. 'By! 'By!
[*going over to* BEN, *almost dancing*] Imagine? When the mail comes he'll
be ahead of Bernard again!

BEN   A perfect proposition all around.

WILLY   Did you see how he cried to me? Oh, if I could kiss him, Ben!

BEN   Time, William, time!

WILLY   Oh, Ben, I always knew one way or another we were gonna make
it, Biff and I!

BEN [*looking at his watch*]   The boat. We'll be late. [*He moves slowly off
into the darkness.*]

WILLY [*elegiacally, turning to the house*]   Now when you kick off, boy, I
want a seventy-yard boot, and get right down the field under the ball,
and when you hit, hit low and hit hard, because it's important, boy. [*He
swings around and faces the audience.*] There's all kinds of important
people in the stands, and the first thing you know . . . [*suddenly realizing he is alone*] Ben! Ben, where do I . . . ? [*He makes a sudden movement of search.*] Ben, how do I . . . ?

LINDA [*calling*]   Willy, you coming up?

WILLY [*uttering a gasp of fear, whirling about as if to quiet her*]   Sh! [*He turns
around as if to find his way; sounds, faces, voices, seem to be swarming in
upon him and he flicks at them, crying,*] Sh! Sh! [*Suddenly music, faint
and high, stops him. It rises in intensity, almost to an unbearable scream.
He goes up and down on his toes, and rushes off around the house.*] Shhh!

LINDA   Willy?

[*There is no answer.* LINDA *waits.* BIFF *gets up off his bed. He is still in
his clothes.* HAPPY *sits up.* BIFF *stands listening.*]

LINDA [*with real fear*]   Willy, answer me! Willy!

[*There is the sound of a car starting and moving away at full speed.*]

LINDA   No!

BIFF [*rushing down the stairs*]   Pop!

[*As the car speeds off, the music crashes down in a frenzy of sound, which
becomes the soft pulsation of a single cello string.* BIFF *slowly returns to
his bedroom. He and* HAPPY *gravely don their jackets.* LINDA *slowly walks
out of her room. The music has developed into a dead march. The leaves
of day are appearing over everything.* CHARLEY *and* BERNARD *somberly
dressed, appear and knock on the kitchen door.* BIFF *and* HAPPY *slowly
descend the stairs to the kitchen as* CHARLEY *and* BERNARD *enter. All stop
a moment when* LINDA, *in clothes of mourning, bearing a little bunch of
roses, comes through the draped doorway into the kitchen. She goes to*
CHARLEY *and takes his arm. Now all move toward the audience, through
the wall-line of the kitchen. At the limit of the apron,* LINDA *lays down the
flowers, kneels, and sits back on her heels. All stare down at the grave.*]

Requiem

CHARLEY   It's getting dark, Linda.

[LINDA *doesn't react. She stares at the grave.*]

BIFF   How about it, Mom? Better get some rest, heh? They'll be closing
the gate soon.

[LINDA *makes no move. Pause.*]

HAPPY [*deeply angered*]   He had no right to do that. There was no necessity for it. We would've helped him.

CHARLEY [*grunting*]   Hmmm.

BIFF   Come along, Mom.

LINDA   Why didn't anybody come?

CHARLEY   It was a very nice funeral.

LINDA   But where are all the people he knew? Maybe they blame him.

CHARLEY   Naa. It's a rough world, Linda. They wouldn't blame him.

LINDA   I can't understand it. At this time especially. First time in thirty-
five years we were just about free and clear. He only needed a little salary. He was even finished with the dentist.

CHARLEY   No man only needs a little salary.

LINDA   I can't understand it.

BIFF   There were a lot of nice days. When he'd come home from a trip; or
on Sundays, making the stoop; finishing the cellar; putting on the new
porch; when he built the extra bathroom; and put up the garage. You
know something, Charley, there's more of him in that front stoop than
in all the sales he ever made.

CHARLEY   Yeah. He was a happy man with a batch of cement.

LINDA   He was so wonderful with his hands.

BIFF   He had the wrong dreams. All, all, wrong.

HAPPY [*almost ready to fight* BIFF]   Don't say that!

BIFF   He never knew who he was.

CHARLEY [*stopping* HAPPY's *movement and reply. To* BIFF]   Nobody dast
blame this man. You don't understand: Willy was a salesman. And for a
salesman, there is no rock bottom to the life. He don't put a bolt to a nut,
he don't tell you the law or give you medicine. He's a man way out there
in the blue, riding on a smile and a shoeshine. And when they start not
smiling back—that's an earthquake. And then you get yourself a couple
of spots on your hat, and you're finished. Nobody dast blame this man. A
salesman is got to dream, boy. It comes with the territory.

BIFF   Charley, the man didn't know who he was.

HAPPY [*infuriated*]   Don't say that!

BIFF   Why don't you come with me, Happy?

HAPPY   I'm not licked that easily. I'm staying right in this city, and I'm gonna
beat this racket! [*He looks at* BIFF, *his chin set.*] The Loman Brothers!

BIFF   I know who I am, kid.

HAPPY   All right, boy. I'm gonna show you and everybody else that Willy
Loman did not die in vain. He had a good dream. It's the only dream you
can have—to come out number-one man. He fought it out here, and this
is where I'm gonna win it for him.

BIFF   [*with a hopeless glance at* HAPPY, *bends toward his mother*]   Let's go,
Mom.

LINDA   I'll be with you in a minute. Go on, Charley. [*He hesitates.*]   I want
to, just for a minute. I never had a chance to say good-by.

[CHARLEY *moves away, followed by* HAPPY. BIFF *remains a slight distance up and left of* LINDA. *She sits there, summoning herself. The flute
begins, not far away, playing behind her speech.*]

LINDA   Forgive me, dear. I can't cry. I don't know what it is, but I can't cry.
I don't understand it. Why did you ever do that? Help me, Willy, I can't
cry. It seems to me that you're just on another trip. I keep expecting you.

Willy, dear, I can't cry. Why did you do it? I search and search and I search, and I can't understand it, Willy. I made the last payment on the house today. Today, dear. And there'll be nobody home. [*A sob rises in her throat.*] We're free and clear. [*Sobbing more fully, released*] We're free. [BIFF *comes slowly toward her.*] We're free . . . We're free . . .

> [BIFF *lifts her to her feet and moves out up right with her in his arms.* LINDA *sobs quietly.* BERNARD *and* CHARLEY *come together and follow them, followed by* HAPPY. *Only the music of the flute is left on the darkening stage as over the house the hard towers of the apartment buildings rise into sharp focus, and*]

CURTAIN

1949

ROBERT LOWELL
1917–1977

I n "North Haven," her poem in memory of Robert Lowell, Elizabeth Bishop translates the bird song as Lowell seemed to hear it: "repeat, repeat, repeat, revise, revise, revise." Repeatedly, even obsessively, Lowell returned to certain subjects in his poems. Each return confirmed an existing pattern even as it opened the possibility for revision. In fact, Lowell's life was full of revision. Descended from Protestant New Englanders, he converted to Catholicism, then fell away from it; he married three times; and he changed his poetic style more than once. In the later part of his career Lowell revised even his published poems and did so repeatedly. "Revision is inspiration," he once said, "no reading of the finished work as exciting as writing the last changes." Revision allowed for Lowell's love of stray events, his attraction to the fluidity of life (in this, he resembles Wallace Stevens). But Lowell also wanted to organize life into formal patterns, to locate the random moment in the design of an epic history (his Catholicism can be seen, in part, as an expression of this desire). History offered plot and repetition: just as patterns of his childhood recurred in adult life, the sins of his New England ancestors were reenacted by contemporary America. Lowell's vision of history leaned toward apocalypse, toward the revelation of a prior meaning that the poet agonized to determine, and yet he cherished the freedom of "human chances," with all their indeterminacy. His poems had to accommodate these opposing impulses. Concerning the sequence of poems in *Notebook 1967–1968*, begun as a poetic diary, he said: "Accident threw up the subject and the plot swallowed them—famished for human chances." If Lowell often swallowed up the casual, the random, the ordinary, and the domestic into the forms of his poems, his best plots have a spontaneity whose meanings cannot be fixed.

The burden of family history was substantial for Lowell, whose ancestors included members of Boston's patrician families. His grandfather was a well-known Episcopal minister and head of the fashionable St. Mark's School, which the poet was later to attend. His great-granduncle James Russell Lowell had been a poet and ambassador to England. The family's light note was provided by the poet Amy Lowell, "big and a scandal, as if Mae West were a cousin." In the context of this history Lowell's father, who fared badly in business after his retirement from service as a naval officer, appeared as a diminished figure.

Lowell's first act of revising family history was to leave the East after two years at Harvard (1935–37) in order to study at Kenyon College with John Crowe Ransom, the poet and critic. The move brought him in closer touch with the New Criticism and its predilections for "formal difficult poems," the wit and irony of English Metaphysical writers such as John Donne. He also, through Ransom and the poet Allen Tate, came into contact with (although never formally joined) the Fugitive movement, whose members were southern agrarians opposed to what they regarded as the corrupting values of northern industrialism.

Two of the acts that most decisively separated Lowell from family history were his conversion to Roman Catholicism (1940) and his resistance to American policies in World War II. Although he tried to enlist in the navy, he refused to be drafted into the army. He opposed the saturation bombing of Hamburg and the Allied policy of unconditional surrender and was as a result sentenced to a year's confinement in New York City's West Street jail. The presiding judge at his hearing admonished him for "marring" his family traditions. In his first book, *Lord Weary's Castle* (1946), his Catholicism provided a set of symbols and a distanced platform from which to express his violent antagonism to Protestant mercantile Boston. The stunning, apocalyptic conclusions of these early poems ("the Lord survives the rainbow of his will" or "The blue kingfisher dives on you in fire") render the devastating judgment of the eternal on the fallen history of the individual and the nation.

Alongside these poems drawing on Old Testament anger were poems in *Lord Weary's Castle*, such as "Mr. Edwards and the Spider," that explored from within the nervous intensity that underlay Puritan revivalism. Later dramatic narratives with modern settings, such as "The Mills of the Kavanaghs" and "Falling Asleep over the Aeneid," reveal his psychological interest in and obsession with ruined New England families.

In *Life Studies* (1959) Lowell changed his style dramatically. His subjects became explicitly autobiographical, his language more open and direct. In 1957 he gave readings in California, where Allen Ginsberg and the other Beats had just made their strongest impact in San Francisco. In contrast to their candid, breezy writing, Lowell felt his own seemed "distant, symbol-ridden, and willfully difficult. . . . I felt my old poems hid what they were really about, and many times offered a stiff, humorless, and even impenetrable surface." Although more controlled and severe than Beat writers, he was stimulated by Ginsberg's self-revelations to write more openly than he had about his parents and grandparents, about the mental breakdowns he suffered in the 1950s, and about the difficulties of marriage. (Lowell divorced his first wife, the novelist Jean Stafford, and married the critic Elizabeth Hardwick in 1949).

Life Studies, by and large, records his ambivalence toward the New England where he resettled after the war, on Boston's "hardly passionate Marlborough Street." Revising his stance toward New England and family history, he no longer denounces the city of his fathers as if he were a privileged outsider. In complicated psychological portraits of his childhood, his relation to his parents and his wives, he assumes a portion of the weakness and vulnerability for himself.

In 1960 Lowell left Boston to live in New York City. *For the Union Dead* (1964), the book that followed, continued the autobiographical vein of *Life Studies*. Lowell called it a book about "witheredness . . . lemony, soured and dry, the drouth I had touched with my own hands." These poems seem more carefully controlled than his earlier *Life Studies*. Often they organize key images from the past into a pattern that illuminates the present. The book includes a number of poems that fuse private and public themes, such as "Fall 1961" and the volume's title poem.

In 1969 Lowell published *Notebook 1967–1968* and then revised these poems for a second, augmented edition, called simply *Notebook* (1970). In 1973, in a characteristic act, he once more revised, rearranged, and expanded *Notebook*'s poems and

2484 | ROBERT LOWELL

published them in two separate books. The more personal poems, recording the breakup of his second marriage and his separation from his wife and daughter, were published as *For Lizzie and Harriet*. Those dealing more with public subjects, past and present, were published as *History*. These two books show Lowell once again engaged with the relations between the random event, or the moment out of a personal life, and an epic design. In these unrhymed, loosely blank-verse revisions of the sonnet, Lowell responded to the books he was reading, to the events of his personal life, and to the Vietnam War, of which he was an outspoken critic. "Things I felt or saw, or read were drift in the whirlpool."

At the same time a new collection of sonnets, *The Dolphin* (1973), appeared, recording his marriage to Lady Caroline Blackwood. He divided his time between her home in England and periods of teaching writing and literature at Harvard—a familiar pattern for him, in which the old tensions between New England and "elsewhere" were being constantly explored and renewed. His last book, *Day by Day* (1977), records those stresses as well as new marital difficulties. It also contains some of his most powerful poems about his childhood.

For those who cherish the work of the early Lowell, with its manic, rhythmic energy and its enjambed lines building to fierce power, or those who admire the passionate engagement of *Life Studies* or *For the Union Dead*, the poems of his last four books can be disappointing. At times flat and dispirited, they can seem worked up rather than fully imagined. Yet the later Lowell demonstrates his substantial gifts in a quieter mode.

Lowell's career included an interest in the theater, for which he wrote a version of *Prometheus Bound*, a translation of Racine's *Phaedra*, and adaptations of Melville and Hawthorne stories gathered as *The Old Glory*. He also translated from modern European poetry and the classics, often freely as "imitations," which brought important poetic voices into English currency. His *Selected Poems* (his own choices) appeared in 1976. When he died suddenly at the age of sixty, he was the dominant and most honored poet of his generation—not only for his ten volumes of verse but for his broad activity as a man of letters. He took upon himself the role of poet as public figure, sometimes at great personal cost. He was with the group of writers who led Vietnam War protesters against the Pentagon in 1967, where Norman Mailer, a fellow protester, observed that "Lowell gave off at times the unwilling haunted saintliness of a man who was repaying the moral debts of ten generations of ancestors."

The Quaker Graveyard in Nantucket

[*For Warren Winslow*,[1] *Dead at Sea*]

Let man have dominion over the fishes of the sea and the fowls of
the air and the beasts of the whole earth, and every creeping creature that moveth upon the earth.[2]

I

A brackish reach of shoal off Madaket[3]—
The sea was still breaking violently and night
Had steamed into our North Atlantic Fleet,
When the drowned sailor clutched the drag-net. Light
Flashed from his matted head and marble feet,   5
He grappled at the net

---

1. A cousin of Lowell's who died in the sinking of a naval vessel during World War II.
2. From Genesis 1.26, the account of the cre-
ation of humankind.
3. On Nantucket Island.

With the coiled, hurdling muscles of his thighs:
The corpse was bloodless, a botch of reds and whites,
Its open, staring eyes
Were lustreless dead-lights[4]   10
Or cabin-windows on a stranded hulk
Heavy with sand. We weight the body, close
Its eyes and heave it seaward whence it came,
Where the heel-headed dogfish barks its nose
On Ahab's[5] void and forehead; and the name   15
Is blocked in yellow chalk.
Sailors, who pitch this portent at the sea
Where dreadnaughts shall confess
Its hell-bent deity,
When you are powerless   20
To sand-bag this Atlantic bulwark, faced
By the earth-shaker, green, unwearied, chaste
In his steel scales: ask for no Orphean lute
To pluck life back.[6] The guns of the steeled fleet
Recoil and then repeat   25
The hoarse salute.

II

Whenever winds are moving and their breath
Heaves at the roped-in bulwarks of this pier,
The terns and sea-gulls tremble at your death
In these home waters. Sailor, can you hear   30
The Pequod's[7] sea wings, beating landward, fall
Headlong and break on our Atlantic wall
Off 'Sconset, where the yawing S-boats[8] splash
The bellbuoy, with ballooning spinnakers,
As the entangled, screeching mainsheet clears   35
The blocks: off Madaket, where lubbers[9] lash
The heavy surf and throw their long lead squids
For blue-fish? Sea-gulls blink their heavy lids
Seaward. The winds' wings beat upon the stones,
Cousin, and scream for you and the claws rush   40
At the sea's throat and wring it in the slush
Of this old Quaker graveyard where the bones
Cry out in the long night for the hurt beast
Bobbing by Ahab's whaleboats in the East.

III

All you recovered from Poseidon died   45
With you, my cousin, and the harrowed brine

---

4. Shutters over portholes to keep out water in a storm. The images in lines 4–11 come from "The Shipwreck," the opening chapter of *Cape Cod*, by Henry David Thoreau (1817–1862).
5. Protagonist of the novel *Moby-Dick*, by Herman Melville (1819–1891); he drowns as the culmination of his obsessive hunt for the white whale. Melville uses Ahab's forehead as an emblem of his monomaniac passion.

6. In Greek mythology Orpheus, through his music, tried to win the freedom of his bride, Eurydice, from the Underworld. "Earth-shaker": an epithet for Poseidon, the Greek god of the oceans and of earthquakes.
7. Ahab's ship, destroyed by Moby-Dick.
8. Type of large racing sailboats. "Yawing": steering wildly in heavy seas.
9. Sailor's term for awkward crew members.

Is fruitless on the blue beard of the god,
Stretching beyond us to the castles in Spain,
Nantucket's westward haven. To Cape Cod
Guns, cradled on the tide,   50
Blast the eelgrass about a waterclock
Of bilge and backwash, roil the salt and sand
Lashing earth's scaffold, rock
Our warships in the hand
Of the great God, where time's contrition blues   55
Whatever it was these Quaker[1] sailors lost
In the mad scramble of their lives. They died
When time was open-eyed,
Wooden and childish; only bones abide
There, in the nowhere, where their boats were tossed   60
Sky-high, where mariners had fabled news
Of IS,[2] the whited monster. What it cost
Them is their secret. In the sperm-whale's slick
I see the Quakers drown and hear their cry:
"If God himself had not been on our side,   65
If God himself had not been on our side,
When the Atlantic rose against us, why,
Then it had swallowed us up quick."

IV

This is the end of the whaleroad[3] and the whale
Who spewed Nantucket bones on the thrashed swell   70
And stirred the troubled waters to whirlpools
To send the Pequod packing off to hell:
This is the end of them, three-quarters fools,
Snatching at straws to sail
Seaward and seaward on the turntail whale,   75
Spouting out blood and water as it rolls,
Sick as a dog to these Atlantic shoals:
Clamavimus,[4] O depths. Let the sea-gulls wail

For water, for the deep where the high tide
Mutters to its hurt self, mutters and ebbs.   80
Waves wallow in their wash, go out and out,
Leave only the death-rattle of the crabs,
The beach increasing, its enormous snout
Sucking the ocean's side.
This is the end of running on the waves;   85
We are poured out like water. Who will dance
The mast-lashed master of Leviathans
Up from this field of Quakers in their unstoned graves?

1. The whaling population of Nantucket included
many Quakers.
2. The white whale is here imagined as a force
like the God of Exodus 3.14, who, when asked his
name by Moses, replies, "I AM THAT I AM." Also an
abbreviation of Iesu Salvator, Latin for Jesus, savior of men.
3. An Anglo-Saxon epithet for the sea.
4. We have called (Latin), adapting the opening
of Psalm 130: "Out of the depths have I cried unto
thee, O Lord."

V

When the whale's viscera go and the roll
Of its corruption overruns this world   90
Beyond tree-swept Nantucket and Woods Hole[5]
And Martha's Vineyard, Sailor, will your sword
Whistle and fall and sink into the fat?
In the great ash-pit of Jehoshaphat[6]
The bones cry for the blood of the white whale,   95
The fat flukes arch and whack about its ears,
The death-lance churns into the sanctuary, tears
The gun-blue swingle,[7] heaving like a flail,
And hacks the coiling life out: it works and drags
And rips the sperm-whale's midriff into rags,   100
Gobbets of blubber spill to wind and weather,
Sailor, and gulls go round the stoven timbers
Where the morning stars sing out together
And thunder shakes the white surf and dismembers
The red flag hammered in the mast-head.[8] Hide,   105
Our steel, Jonas Messias, in Thy side.[9]

VI. OUR LADY OF WALSINGHAM[1]

There once the penitents took off their shoes
And then walked barefoot the remaining mile;
And the small trees, a stream and hedgerows file
Slowly along the munching English lane,   110
Like cows to the old shrine, until you lose
Track of your dragging pain.
The stream flows down under the druid tree,
Shiloah's[2] whirlpools gurgle and make glad
The castle of God. Sailor, you were glad   115
And whistled Sion by that stream. But see:

Our Lady, too small for her canopy,
Sits near the altar. There's no comeliness
At all or charm in that expressionless
Face with its heavy eyelids. As before,   120
This face, for centuries a memory,
Non est species, neque decor,[3]
Expressionless, expresses God: it goes
Past castled Sion. She knows what God knows,
Not Calvary's Cross nor crib at Bethlehem   125
Now, and the world shall come to Walsingham.

---

5. On the coast of Massachusetts, near the island of Martha's Vineyard.
6. "The day of judgment. The world, according to some prophets, will end in fire" [Lowell's note]. In Joel 3, the Last Judgment takes place in the valley of Jehoshaphat.
7. Knifelike wooden instrument for beating flax (info fiber for spinning).
8. At the end of *Moby-Dick*, the arm of the American Indian Tashtego appears from the waves and nails Ahab's flag to the sinking mast.

9. Because he emerged alive from the belly of a whale, the prophet Jonah is often linked with the messiah as a figure of salvation.
1. Lowell took these details from E. I. Watkin's *Catholic Art and Culture* (1942), which includes a description of the medieval shrine of the Virgin at Walsingham.
2. The stream that flows past God's Temple on Mount Sion (Isaiah 8.6). In Isaiah 51.11 the redeemed come "singing into Zion."
3. There is no ostentation or elegance (Latin).

VII

The empty winds are creaking and the oak
Splatters and splatters on the cenotaph,
The boughs are trembling and a gaff
Bobs on the untimely stroke   130
Of the greased wash exploding on a shoal-bell
In the old mouth of the Atlantic. It's well;
Atlantic, you are fouled with the blue sailors,
Sea-monsters, upward angel, downward fish:
Unmarried and corroding, spare of flesh   135
Mart once of supercilious, wing'd clippers,
Atlantic, where your bell-trap guts its spoil
You could cut the brackish winds with a knife
Here in Nantucket, and cast up the time
When the Lord God formed man from the sea's slime   140
And breathed into his face the breath of life,
And blue-lung'd combers lumbered to the kill.
The Lord survives the rainbow⁴ of His will.

                                                                    1946

Mr. Edwards and the Spider¹

I saw the spiders marching through the air,
Swimming from tree to tree that mildewed day
    In latter August when the hay
    Came creaking to the barn. But where
        The wind is westerly,   5
Where gnarled November makes the spiders fly
Into the apparitions of the sky,
They purpose nothing but their ease and die
Urgently beating east to sunrise and the sea;

What are we in the hands of the great God?   10
It was in vain you set up thorn and briar
    In battle array against the fire
    And treason crackling in your blood;
        For the wild thorns grow tame
And will do nothing to oppose the flame;   15
Your lacerations tell the losing game
You play against a sickness past your cure.
How will the hands be strong? How will the heart endure?²

4. Alluding to God's covenant with Noah after
the Flood. The rainbow symbolized the fact that
humanity would never again be destroyed by flood
(Genesis 9.11).
1. Jonathan Edwards (1703–1758), Puritan
preacher and theologian. Lowell quotes his writings throughout. The details of the first stanza

come from his youthful essay "Of Insects" ("The
Habits of Spiders").
2. This stanza draws on Edwards's sermon "Sinners in the Hands of an Angry God," whose point
of departure is Ezekiel 22.14: "Can thine heart
endure or can thine hands be strong in the days
that I shall deal with thee?" (cf. line 18).

A very little thing, a little worm,
Or hourglass-blazoned spider,[3] it is said,   20
   Can kill a tiger. Will the dead
   Hold up his mirror and affirm
     To the four winds the smell
And flash of his authority? It's well
If God who holds you to the pit of hell,   25
   Much as one holds a spider, will destroy,
Baffle and dissipate your soul. As a small boy

On Windsor Marsh,[4] I saw the spider die
When thrown into the bowels of fierce fire:
   There's no long struggle, no desire   30
   To get up on its feet and fly—
     It stretches out its feet
And dies. This is the sinner's last retreat;
Yes, and no strength exerted on the heat
Then sinews the abolished will, when sick   35
And full of burning, it will whistle on a brick.

But who can plumb the sinking of that soul?
Josiah Hawley,[5] picture yourself cast
   Into a brick-kiln where the blast
   Fans your quick vitals to a coal—   40
     If measured by a glass,
How long would it seem burning! Let there pass
A minute, ten, ten trillion; but the blaze
Is infinite, eternal: this is death,
To die and know it. This is the Black Widow, death.   45

1946

Skunk Hour

for Elizabeth Bishop

Nautilus Island's[1] hermit
heiress still lives through winter in her Spartan cottage;
her sheep still graze above the sea.
Her son's a bishop. Her farmer
is first selectman in our village;   5
she's in her dotage.

Thirsting for
the hierarchic privacy
of Queen Victoria's century,
she buys up all   10

---

3. The poisonous black widow spider has, on the underside of its abdomen, a red marking that resembles an hourglass.
4. East Windsor, Connecticut, Edwards's child-hood home.
5. Edwards's uncle, Joseph Hawley.
1. The poem is set in Castine, Maine, where Lowell had a summer house.

the eyesores facing her shore,
and lets them fall.

The season's ill—
we've lost our summer millionaire,
who seemed to leap from an L. L. Bean   15
catalogue.[2] His nine-knot yawl
was auctioned off to lobstermen.
A red fox stain covers Blue Hill.

And now our fairy
decorator brightens his shop for fall;   20
his fishnet's filled with orange cork,
orange, his cobbler's bench and awl;
there is no money in his work,
he'd rather marry.

One dark night,   25
my Tudor Ford climbed the hill's skull;
I watched for love-cars. Lights turned down,
they lay together, hull to hull,
where the graveyard shelves on the town. . . .
My mind's not right.   30

A car radio bleats,
"Love, O careless Love. . . ." I hear
my ill-spirit sob in each blood cell,
as if my hand were at its throat. . . .
I myself am hell;[3]   35
nobody's here—

only skunks, that search
in the moonlight for a bite to eat.
They march on their soles up Main Street:
white stripes, moonstruck eyes' red fire   40
under the chalk-dry and spar spire
of the Trinitarian Church.

I stand on top
of our back steps and breathe the rich air—
a mother skunk with her column of kittens swills the garbage pail.   45
She jabs her wedge-head in a cup
of sour cream, drops her ostrich tail,
and will not scare.

1959

---

2. From a mail-order house in Maine that primarily sells sporting goods and clothing to the
wealthy and upper middle class.

3. "Which way I fly is Hell, myself am Hell"
(Satan in Milton's *Paradise Lost* 4.75).

For the Union Dead[1]

"Relinquunt Omnia Servare Rem Publicam."[2]

The old South Boston Aquarium stands
in a Sahara of snow now. Its broken windows are boarded.
The bronze weathervane cod has lost half its scales.
The airy tanks are dry.

Once my nose crawled like a snail on the glass;   5
my hand tingled
to burst the bubbles
drifting from the noses of the cowed, compliant fish.

My hand draws back. I often sigh still
for the dark downward and vegetating kingdom   10
of the fish and reptile. One morning last March,
I pressed against the new barbed and galvanized

fence on the Boston Common. Behind their cage,
yellow dinosaur steamshovels were grunting
as they cropped up tons of mush and grass   15
to gouge their underworld garage.

Parking spaces luxuriate like civic
sandpiles in the heart of Boston.
A girdle of orange, Puritan-pumpkin colored girders
braces the tingling Statehouse,   20

shaking over the excavations, as it faces Colonel Shaw
and his bell-cheeked Negro infantry
on St. Gaudens' shaking Civil War relief,
propped by a plank splint against the garage's earthquake.

Two months after marching through Boston,   25
half the regiment was dead;
at the dedication
William James[3] could almost hear the bronze Negroes breathe.

Their monument sticks like a fishbone
in the city's throat.   30
Its Colonel is as lean
as a compass-needle.

1. First published as "Colonel Shaw and the Massachusetts' 54th" in a paperback edition of *Life Studies* (1960). It became the title poem of *For the Union Dead* (1964).
2. Robert Gould Shaw (1837–1863) led the first all–African American regiment in the Union army during the Civil War. He was killed in the attack against Fort Wagner, South Carolina. A bronze relief by the sculptor Augustus Saint-Gaudens (1848–1897), dedicated in 1897, standing opposite the Massachusetts State House on Boston Common, commemorates the deaths. A Latin inscription on the monument reads *Omnia Reliquit Servare Rem Publicam* ("He leaves all behind to save the Republic"). Lowell's epigraph alters the inscription slightly, changing the third-person singular (*he*) to the third-person plural: "*They* give up everything to save the Republic."
3. Philosopher and psychologist (1842–1910) who taught at Harvard.

He has an angry wrenlike vigilance,
a greyhound's gentle tautness;
he seems to wince at pleasure,   35
and suffocate for privacy.

He is out of bounds now. He rejoices in man's lovely,
peculiar power to choose life and die—
when he leads his black soldiers to death,
he cannot bend his back.   40

On a thousand small town New England greens,
the old white churches hold their air
of sparse, sincere rebellion; frayed flags
quilt the graveyards of the Grand Army of the Republic.

The stone statues of the abstract Union Soldier   45
grow slimmer and younger each year—
wasp-waisted, they doze over muskets
and muse through their sideburns . . .

Shaw's father wanted no monument
except the ditch,   50
where his son's body was thrown[4]
and lost with his "niggers."

The ditch is nearer.
There are no statues for the last war[5] here;
on Boylston Street,[6] a commercial photograph   55
shows Hiroshima boiling[7]

over a Mosler Safe, the "Rock of Ages"[8]
that survived the blast. Space is nearer.
When I crouch to my television set,
the drained faces of Negro school-children rise like balloons.[9] 60

Colonel Shaw
is riding on his bubble,
he waits
for the blessed break.

The Aquarium is gone. Everywhere,   65
giant finned cars nose forward like fish;
a savage servility
slides by on grease.

                                                    1960, 1964

---

4. By the Confederate soldiers at Fort Wagner.
5. World War II.
6. In Boston, where the poem is set.
7. On August 6, 1945, the United States dropped an atomic bomb on this Japanese city.
8. Biblical reference to an indestructible and supernatural rock, the foundation of an everlasting kingdom. Used as an advertising slogan by Mosler Safes.
9. Probably news photographs connected with contemporary civil rights demonstrations to secure desegregation of schools in the South.

GWENDOLYN BROOKS

1917–2000

"If there was ever a born poet," the writer Alice Walker once said in an interview, "I think it is Brooks." A passionate sense of language and an often daring use of formal structures are hallmarks of Gwendolyn Brooks's poetry. She used these gifts in a career characterized by dramatic evolution, a career that linked two very different generations of African American poets. "Until 1967," Brooks said, "my own Blackness did not confront me with a shrill spelling of itself." She then grouped herself with militant black writers and defined her work as belonging primarily to the African American community. In her earlier work, however, Brooks followed the example of the older writers of the Harlem Renaissance, Langston Hughes and Countee Cullen among them, who honored the ideal of an integrated society. In that period her work received support largely from white audiences. But Brooks's changing sense of her commitments should not obscure her persistent, underlying concerns. She never lacked political awareness, and in remarkably versatile poems, both early and late, she wrote about black experience and black rage, with a particular awareness of the complex lives of black women.

Brooks was born in Topeka, Kansas; she grew up in Chicago and is closely identified with the energies and problems of its black community. She went to Chicago's Englewood High School and graduated from Wilson Junior College. Brooks remembered writing poetry from the time she was seven and keeping poetry notebooks from the time she was eleven. She got her education in the moderns—poets such as Pound and Eliot—under the guidance of a rich Chicago socialite, Inez Cunningham Stark, who was a reader for *Poetry* magazine and taught a poetry class at the Southside Community Art Center. Her first book, *A Street in Bronzeville* (1945), took its title from the name journalists gave to Chicago's black ghetto. Her poems portrayed the waste and loss that are the inevitable result of what Langston Hughes called the "dream deferred." With her second book of poems, *Annie Allen* (1949), Brooks became the first African American to receive the Pulitzer Prize for poetry.

In *Annie Allen* and in her Bronzeville poems (*Bronzeville Boys and Girls*, 1956, continued the work begun in *A Street in Bronzeville*), Brooks concentrated on portraits of what Hughes called "the ordinary aspects of black life," stressing the vitality and the often subversive morality of ghetto figures. She portrayed the good girls who want to be bad; the bored children of hardworking, pious mothers; the laments of women, some of them mothers, abandoned by their men. Brooks's diction was a combination of the florid biblical speech of black Protestant preachers, street talk, and the traditional vocabulary of English and American verse. She wrote vigorous, strongly accented, and strongly rhymed lines with a great deal of alliteration. She also cultivated traditional lyric forms; for example, she was one of the few modern poets to write extensively in the sonnet form.

A great change in Brooks's life came at Fisk University in 1967 with the Second Black Writers' Conference, in whose charged activist atmosphere she encountered many of the new young black poets. After this Brooks tested the possibility of writing poetry exclusively for black audiences. She drew closer to militant political groups as a result of conducting poetry workshops for some members of the Blackstone Rangers, a teenage gang in Chicago. In autobiographical writings such as her prose *Report from Part One* (1972), Brooks became more self-conscious about her own potential role as a leader of black feminists. She left her New York publisher to have her work printed by African American publishers, especially the Broadside Press. Brooks's poetry, too, changed, in both its focus and its technique. Her subjects tended to be more explicitly political and to deal with questions of revolutionary violence and issues of African American identity. Stylistically, her work evolved out of the concentrated imagery and narratives of her earlier writing, with its often formal diction, and moved toward an increased use of the energetic, improvisatory rhythms of jazz, the combinations of African chants, and an emphatically spoken language. The resulting poetry constantly revises itself and its sense of the world, open to change but evoking history. "How does one convey the influence Gwendolyn Brooks has had on generations—not only writers but people from all walks of life?" the poet Rita Dove has remarked, remembering how, as a young woman, she was "struck by these poems . . . that weren't afraid to take language and swamp it, twist it, and engage it so that it shimmered and dashed and lingered."

FROM A STREET IN BRONZEVILLE

to David and Keziah Brooks

kitchenette building

We are things of dry hours and the involuntary plan,
Grayed in, and gray. "Dream" makes a giddy sound, not strong
Like "rent," "feeding a wife," "satisfying a man."

But could a dream send up through onion fumes
Its white and violet, fight with fried potatoes   5
And yesterday's garbage ripening in the hall,
Flutter, or sing an aria down these rooms

Even if we were willing to let it in,
Had time to warm it, keep it very clean,
Anticipate a message, let it begin?   10

We wonder. But not well! not for a minute!
Since Number Five is out of the bathroom now,
We think of lukewarm water, hope to get in it.

                                                                    1945

the mother

Abortions will not let you forget.
You remember the children you got that you did not get,
The damp small pulps with a little or with no hair,
The singers and workers that never handled the air.
You will never neglect or beat   5

Them, or silence or buy with a sweet.
You will never wind up the sucking-thumb
Or scuttle off ghosts that come.
You will never leave them, controlling your luscious sigh,
Return for a snack of them, with gobbling mother-eye.   10

I have heard in the voices of the wind the voices of my dim
    killed children.
I have contracted. I have eased
My dim dears at the breasts they could never suck.
I have said, Sweets, if I sinned, if I seized
Your luck   15
And your lives from your unfinished reach,
If I stole your births and your names,
Your straight baby tears and your games,
Your stilted or lovely loves, your tumults, your marriages, aches,
    and your deaths,
If I poisoned the beginnings of your breaths,   20
Believe that even in my deliberateness I was not deliberate.
Though why should I whine,
Whine that the crime was other than mine?—
Since anyhow you are dead.
Or rather, or instead,   25
You were never made.

But that too, I am afraid,
Is faulty: oh, what shall I say, how is the truth to be said?
You were born, you had body, you died.
It is just that you never giggled or planned or cried.   30

Believe me, I loved you all.
Believe me, I knew you, though faintly, and I loved, I loved you
All.

                                     1945

The White Troops Had Their Orders But the
Negroes Looked Like Men

    They had supposed their formula was fixed.
    They had obeyed instructions to devise
    A type of cold, a type of hooded gaze.
    But when the Negroes came they were perplexed.
    These Negroes looked like men. Besides, it taxed   5
    Time and the temper to remember those
    Congenital iniquities that cause
    Disfavor of the darkness. Such as boxed
    Their feelings properly, complete to tags—
    A box for dark men and a box for Other—   10
    Would often find the contents had been scrambled.
    Or even switched. Who really gave two figs?

Neither the earth nor heaven ever trembled.
And there was nothing startling in the weather.

1945

We Real Cool

THE POOL PLAYERS.
SEVEN AT THE GOLDEN SHOVEL.

We real cool. We
Left school. We

Lurk late. We
Strike straight. We

Sing sin. We   5
Thin gin. We

Jazz June. We
Die soon.

1960

The Last Quatrain of the Ballad of Emmett Till[1]

after the murder,
after the burial

Emmett's mother is a pretty-faced thing;
            the tint of pulled taffy.
She sits in a red room,
            drinking black coffee.   5
She kisses her killed boy.
            And she is sorry.
Chaos in windy grays
            through a red prairie.   10

1960

To the Diaspora[1]

you did not know you were Afrika

When you set out for Afrika
you did not know you were going.

---

1. A fourteen-year-old African American boy
lynched in Mississippi in 1955 for allegedly "leer-
ing" at a white woman.

1. People settled far from their ancestral homelands.

Because
you did not know you were Afrika.
You did not know the Black continent   5
that had to be reached
was you.

I could not have told you then that some sun
would come,
somewhere over the road,   10
would come evoking the diamonds
of you, the Black continent—
somewhere over the road.
You would not have believed my mouth.

When I told you, meeting you somewhere close   15
to the heat and youth of the road,
liking my loyalty, liking belief,
you smiled and you thanked me but very little believed me.

Here is some sun. Some.
Now off into the places rough to reach.   20
Though dry, though drowsy, all unwillingly a-wobble,
into the dissonant and dangerous crescendo.
Your work, that was done, to be done to be done to be done.

1981

JACK KEROUAC
1922–1969

Like the lives of many trailblazing writers, Jack Kerouac's life was filled with contradictions. Regarded as a liberator of prose and champion of idiomatic American expression, he did not start learning English until grade school and never felt
comfortable speaking it until he finished high school (his parents were of French-
Canadian background, and French was the family's language at home in Lowell,
Massachusetts; his given name was "Jean-Louis"). Having won a football scholarship
to Columbia University, he rejected the athletic crowd to join the literary innovators
gathering at the college neighborhood's popular West End Bar, among them Allen
Ginsberg and William S. Burroughs, who would achieve fame as poet and novelist,
respectively. Not famous himself until the late 1950s, when a wave of interest in the
self-proclaimed Beat Movement installed him as its unwilling leader, he rode the
crest of the counterculture's growing fascination with Eastern religions, most notably
Zen Buddhism, while never rejecting the Catholicism of his childhood. Even adula-
tory responses to his work risked contradiction. For example, critics praised his most
famous novel, *On the Road* (1957), for its expansiveness and movement reminiscent
of America's Manifest Destiny myth, although the book's narrative progress is in fact
from the West Coast to the East.

Kerouac's ambitions were monumental, but a lifetime of heavy drinking killed him by age forty-seven. His several marriages, until his last one, ended with annulment, desertion, or divorce. His greatest loyalty as an adult was to his widowed mother, in later years an invalid, whom he cared for until his death. Wartime service in the merchant marine had given Kerouac manual skills useful for employment during the wanderings that characterized his life; railroad brakeman and forest-fire lookout were among the jobs he took throughout the late 1940s and into the 1950s until royalties from *On the Road* could sustain a pattern of bumming around, visiting friends, and writing as inspiration struck. "Home" was a series of addresses in Massachusetts, New York (on Long Island), and Florida, most of them chosen for his mother's convenience.

Two favorite hangouts were the San Francisco Bay Area and the coastal wilderness of California's Big Sur, an area running south from Carmel-by-the-Sea to San Luis Obispo. This is the setting for the novel most typical of Kerouac's problematic career. Composed quickly (he usually took just three days to six weeks to write a novel), on a roll of teletype paper similar to the one that aided his almost nonstop production of *On the Road, Big Sur* (1962) draws on a visit to the poet Lawrence Ferlinghetti and other Bay Area friends and a solitary stay in Ferlinghetti's isolated cabin in Bixby Canyon (here called the Raton Canyon, with Ferlinghetti taking the name "Louis [also Lorenzo] Monsanto"). Its form, shared by all but the first of Kerouac's novels (*The Town and the City*, 1950, a social novel in the realistic mode), is what the author called "spontaneous prose," equivalent to jazz improvisation in its emphasis on rhythms and inflections and the freewheeling nature of its references. Those references include Buddhism (which he had studied for its literary properties but finally rejected as a religion), Catholicism, books and authors, popular culture, friends and family, all propelled by the writer's exuberance, a momentum that exceeds conventional limits of narrative order.

"My work comprises one vast book like [the early twentieth-century French novelist Marcel] Proust's except that my remembrances are written on the run instead of afterwards in a sick bed," Kerouac observes in the headnote preceding the first chapter of *Big Sur*. Though his canon consists of more than a dozen novels published during his lifetime and others recovered from manuscript and issued after his death, the author had seen them as one grand project, the parts of which he intended to revise, integrate, and present to readers as one massive narrative when done. Neither writing nor publishing them in the order in which he had experienced their action, Kerouac did not live long enough to even begin his intended synthesis. But he named the project "the Duluoz Legend," from the name of his protagonist in *Big Sur* and other works. Central to the legend is Kerouac's close friendship with Neal Cassady (fictionalized as Dean Moriarity in *On the Road* and as Cody Pomeray in *Visions of Cody*, 1972). Their relationship had been the motivation for both the author's wanderings and his impulsive, sometimes explosive manner of writing. (Reacting to the confinements of postwar commercial culture, the Beat Movement took its name in part from the term "beatitic," or blissful, and celebrated free-form narration and a matching lifestyle.) But according to critic Warren French, this relationship also marked the limits of Kerouac's literary vision: his concern for human freedom tended toward the "elegaic and defeatist," whereas Cassady moved on from the Beat Movement to the "heroic account of the triumph of the individual over the system" that a new 1960s counterculture was finding in such works as novelist Ken Kesey's *One Flew Over the Cuckoo's Nest* (1962) and *Sometimes a Great Notion* (1964).

Though not published until after Kerouac's death, *Visions of Cody* had been written in 1959. *Big Sur* was composed in 1960 and is considered the formal conclusion to the Duluoz legend, the scope of which covered the author's lifetime and filled such novels as *The Subterraneans* (1958), *The Dharma Bums* (1958), and *Desolation Angels* (1965, covering earlier experiences). It begins with the narrator fleeing fame and seeking recovery from the nervous breakdown that fame has induced.

From Big Sur

12

But Dave is anxious and so am I to see great Cody who is always the major part of my reason for journeying to the west coast so we call him up at Los Gatos 50 miles away down the Santa Clara Valley and I hear his dear sad voice saying "Been waitin for ya old buddy, come on down right away, but I'll be goin to work at midnight so hurry up and you can visit me at work soon's the boss leaves round two and I'll show you my new job of tire recappin and see if you cant bring a little somethin like a girl or sumptin, just kiddin, come on down pal——"

So there's old Willie waiting for us down on the street parked across from the little pleasant Japanese liquor store where as usual, according to our ritual, I run and get Pernod[1] or Scotch or anything good while Dave wheels around to pick me up at the store door, and I get in the front seat right at Dave's right where I belong all the time like old Honored Samuel Johnson[2] while everybody else that wants to come along has to scramble back there on the mattress (a full mattress, the seats are out) and squat there or lie down there and also generally keep silent because when Dave's got the wheel of Willie in his hand and I've got the bottle in mine and we're off on a trip the talking all comes from the front seat——"By God" yells Dave all glad again "it's just like old times Jack, gee old Willie's been sad for ya, waitin for ya to come back——So now I'm gonna show ya how old Willie's even improved with age, had him reconditioned in Reno last month, here he goes, are you ready Willie?" and off we go and the beauty of it all this particular summer is that the front right seat is broken and just rocks back and forth gently to every one of Dave's driving moves——It's like sitting in a rocking chair on a porch only this is a moving porch and a porch to talk on at that——And insteada watching old men pitch horseshoes from this here talking porch it's all that fine white clean line in the middle of the road as we go flying like birds over the Harrison ramps and whatnot Dave always uses to sneak out of Frisco real fast and avoid all the traffic——Soon we're set straight and pointed head on down beautiful fourlane Bayshore Highway to that lovely Santa Clara Valley——But I'm amazed that after only a few years the damn thing no longer has prune fields and vast beet fields like at Lawrence[3] when I was a brakeman on the Southern Pacific[4] and even after, it's one long row of houses right down the line 50 miles to San Jose like a great monstrous Los Angeles beginning to grow south of Frisco.

At first it's beautiful to just watch that white line reel in to Willie's snout but when I start looking around out the window there's just endless housing tracts and new blue factories everywhere——Sez Dave "Yes that's right, the population explosion is gonna cover every bit of backyard dirt in America someday in fact they'll even have to start piling up friggin levels of houses and others over that like your cityCityCITY till the houses reach a hundred miles in the air in all directions of the map and people looking at the earth from another planet with super telescopes will see a prickly ball hangin in

---

1. Trademarked French anise-flavored liquer used in cocktails.
2. English poet, essayist, critic, and lexicographer (1709–1784).

3. Area in Santa Clara County south of San Francisco, by 1960 engulfed in the metropolitan sprawl of San Jose, part of the San Francisco Bay Area.
4. Major railroad.

space——It's like real horrible when you come to think of it, even us with all our fancy talks, shit man it's all millions of people and events piling up almost unimaginable now, like raving babboons we'll all be piled on top of each other or one another or whatever you're sposed to say——Hundreds of millions of hungry mouths raving for more more more——And the sadness of it all is that the world hasnt any chance to produce say a writer whose life could really actually touch all this life in every detail like you always say, some writer who could bring you sobbing thru the bed fuckin bedcribs of the moon to see it all even unto the goddamned last gory detail of some dismal robbery of the heart at dawn when no one cares like Sinatra sings" ("When no one cares," he sings in his low baritone but resumes):—"Some strict sweeper sweeping it all up, I mean the incredible helplessness I felt Jack when Céline ended his Journey To The End Of The Night[5] by pissing in the Seine River at dawn there I am thinkin my God there's probably somebody pissing in the Trenton River at dawn right now, the Danube, the Ganges, the frozen Obi, the Yellow, the Paraña, the Willamette, the Merrimac in Missouri too, the Missouri itself, the Yuma, the Amazon, the Thames, the Po;[6] the so and so, it's so friggin endless it's like poems endless everywhere and no one knows any bettern old Buddha you know where he says it's like 'There are immeasurable star misty aeons of universes more numerous than the sands in all the galaxies, multiplied by a billion lightyears of multiplication, in fact if I were to go on you'd be scared and couldnt comprehend and you'd despair so much you'd drop dead,' that's what he just about said in one of those sutras——Macrocosms and microcosms and chillicosms and microbes and finally you got all these marvelous books a man aint even got time to read em all, what you gonna do in this already piled up multiple world when you have to think of the Book of Songs, Faulkner, César Birotteau, Shakespeare, Satyricons, Dantes, in fact long stories guys tell you in bars, in fact the sutras themselves, Sir Philip Sidney, Sterne, Ibn El Arabi, the copious Lope de Vega and the uncopious goddamn Cervantes, shoo, then there's all those Catulluses and Davids[7] and radio listening skid row sages to contend with because they've all got a million stories too and you too Ron Blake in the backseat shut up! down to everything which is so much that it is of necessity dont you think NOthing anyway, huh?" (expressing exactly the way I feel, of course).

And to corroborate all that about the too-much-ness of the world, in fact, there's Stanley Popovich also in the back mattress next to Ron, Stanley Popovich of New York suddenly arrived in San Francisco with Jamie his Italian beauty girl but's going to leave her in a few days to go work for the circus, a big tough Yugoslav kid who ran the Seven Arts Gallery in New York with big bearded beatnik readings but now comes the circus and a

---

5. Novel (1932) by Louis-Ferdinand Céline, pen name of the French novelist Louis-Ferdinand Destouches (1894–1961).
6. Rivers in France, Central Europe, Massachusetts, the U.S. Great Plains, California, South America, England, and Italy.
7. King David (fl. 970 B.C.E.) of ancient Israel, credited with writing many of the Psalms; *Book of Songs*, a translation of Chinese poems published in 1937; William Faulkner (1897–1962), American novelist; Cesar Birotteau, principal character in *Histoire de la grandeur et la décadence de César Birotteau* (1838), by the French novelist Honoré de

Balzac (1799–1850); William Shakespeare (1564–1616), English dramatist and poet; *Satyricon* (c. 60 C.E.), comic picaresque narrative written in prose and poetry by the Roman author Gaius Petronius Arbiter (c. 27–66 C.E.); Dante Alighieri (1265–1321), Italian poet; Sir Philip Sidney (1554–1586), English poet; Laurence Sterne (1713–1768), British novelist; Ibn al-'Arabi (1165–1240), Muslim mystic philosopher; Lope Felix de Vega Carpio (1562–1635), Spanish dramatist; Miguel de Cervantes Saavedra (1547–1616), Spanish novelist; Gaius Valerius Catullus (c. 84–54 B.C.E.), Roman poet.

whole big on-the-road of his own——It's too much, in fact right this minute he's started telling us about circus work——On top of all that old Cody is up ahead with HIS thousand stories——We all agree it's too big to keep up with, that we're surrounded by life, that we'll never understand it, so we center it all in by swigging Scotch from the bottle and when it's empty I run out of the car and buy another one, period.

13

But on the way to Cody's my madness already began to manifest itself in a stranger way, another one of those signposts of something wrong I mentioned a ways back: I thought I saw a flying saucer in the sky over Los Gatos—— From five miles away——I look and I see this thing flying along and mention it to Dave who takes one brief look and says "Ah it's only the top of a radio tower"——It reminds me of the time I took a mescaline pill[8] and thought an airplane was a flying saucer (a strange story this, a man has to be crazy to write it anyway).

But there's old Cody in the livingroom of his fine ranchito[9] home sittin over his chess set pondering a problem and right by the fresh woodfire in the fireplace his wife's set out because she knows I love fireplaces——She a good friend of mine too——The kids are sleeping in the back, it's about eleven, and good old Cody shakes my hand again——Havent seen him for several years because mainly he's just spent two years in San Quentin[1] on a stupid charge of possession of marijuana————He was on his way to work on the railroad one night and was short on time and his driving license had been already revoked for speeding so he saw two bearded bluejeaned beat-niks parked, asked them to trade a quick ride to work at the railroad station for two sticks of tea,[2] they complied and arrested him——They were dis-guised policemen——For this great crime he spent two years in San Quen-tin in the same cell with a murderous gunman——His job was sweeping out the cotton mill room——I expect him to be all bitter and out of his head because of this but strangely and magnificently he's become quieter, more radiant, more patient, manly, more friendly even——And tho the wild fren-zies of his old road days with me have banked down he still has the same taut eager face and supple muscles and looks like he's ready to go anytime——But actually loves his home (paid for by railroad insurance when he broke his leg trying to stop a boxcar from crashing), loves his wife in a way tho they fight some, loves his kids and especially his little son Timmy John partly named after me——Poor old, good old Cody sittin there with his chess set, wants immediately to challenge somebody to a chess game but only has an hour to talk to us before he goes to work supporting the family by rushing out and pushing his Nash Rambler[3] down the quiet Los Gatos suburb street, jump-ing in, starting the motor, in fact his only complaint is that the Nash wont start without a push——No bitter complaints about society whatever from this grand and ideal man who really loves me moreover as if I deserved it,

---

8. Psychedelic drug obtained from buttonlike tops of the mescal cactus, used in some Native American ceremonies and popular with the beatnik subculture.
9. Small ranch (Mexican Spanish).
1. California State prison for serious offenders located on Point Quentin, Marin County, north of San Francisco Bay.
2. Slang for marijuana; two sticks would be two marijuana cigarettes.
3. Popular American automobile, a family sedan.

but I'm bursting to explain everything to him, not even Big Sur but the past several years, but there's no chance with everybody yakking——And in fact I can see in Cody's eyes that he can see in my own eyes the regret we both feel that recently we havent had chances to talk whatever, like we used to do driving across America and back in the old road days, too many people now want to talk to us and tell us *their* stories, we've been hemmed in and surrounded and outnumbered——The circle's closed in on the old heroes of the night——But he says "However you guys, come on down round 'bout one when the boss leaves and watch me work and keep me company awhile before you go back to the City"——I can see Dave Wain really loves him at once, and Stanley Popovich too who's come along on this trip just to meet the fabled "Dean Moriarty"——The name I give Cody in "On the Road"[4]—— But O, it breaks my heart to see he's lost his beloved job on the railroad and after all the seniority he'd piled up since 1948 and now is reduced to tire recapping and dreary parole visits——All for two sticks of wild loco weed that grows by itself in Texas because God wanted it——

And there over the bookshelf is the old photo of me and Cody arm in arm in the early days on a sunny street——

I rush to explain to Cody what happened the year before when his religious advisor at the prison had invited me to come to San Quentin to lecture the religious class——Dave Wain was supposed to drive me and wait outside the prison walls as I'd go in there alone, probably with a pepup nip bottle hidden in my coat (I hoped) and I'd be led by big guards to the lecture room of the prison and there would be sitting a hundred or so cons including Cody probably all proud in the front row——And I would begin by telling them I had been in jail myself once and that I had no right nevertheless to lecture them on religion——But they're all lonely prisoners and dont care what I talk about——The whole thing arranged, in any case, and on the big morning I wake up instead dead drunk on a floor, it's already noon and too late, Dave Wain is on the floor also, Willie's parked outside to take us to Quentin for the lecture but it's too late——But now Cody says "It's alright old buddy I understand"——Altho our friend Irwin had done it, lectured there, but Irwin can do all sorta things like that being more social than I am and capable of going in there as he did and reading his wildest poems which set the prison yard humming with excitement tho I think he shouldna done it after all because I say just to show up for any reason except visiting inside a prison is still SIGNIFYING[5]——And I tell this to Cody who ponders a chess problem and says "Drinkin again, hey?" (if there's anything he hates is to see me drink).

We help him push his Nash down the street, then drink awhile and talk with Evelyn a beautiful blonde woman that young Ron Blake wants and even Dave Wain wants but she's got her mind on other things and taking care of the children who have to go to school and dancing classes in the morning and hardly gets a word in edgewise anyway as we all yak and yell like fools to impress her tho all she really wants is to be alone with me to talk about Cody and his latest soul.

---

4. *On the Road* (1957), Kerouac's only best-selling novel. (Cody Pomeray and Dean Moriarty are both Kerouac's fictional names for his friend Neal Cassady.)
5. African American verbal rhetorical device for creating new, often ironic or obscure, meanings for old words and signs, a tradition reaching from slave days to contemporary rap and hip-hop music.

Which includes the fact of Billie Dabney his mistress who has threatened to take Cody away completely from Evelyn, as I'll show later.

So we do go out to the San Jose highway to watch Cody recap tires—— There he is wearing goggles working like Vulcan[6] at his forge, throwing tires all over the place with fantastic strength, the good ones high up on a pile, "This one's no good" down on another, bing, bang, talking all the time a long fantastic lecture on tire recapping which has Dave Wain marvel with amazement——("My God he can do all that and even explain while he's doing it")——But I just mention in connection with the fact that Dave Wain now realizes why I've always loved Cody——Expecting to see a bitter ex con he sees instead a martyr of the American Night in goggles in some dreary tire shop at 2 A.M. making fellows laugh with joy with his funny explanations yet at the same time to a T performing every bit of the work he's being paid for——Rushing up and ripping tires off car wheels with a jicklo,[7] clang, throwing it on the machine, starting up big roaring steams but yelling explanations over that, darting, bending, flinging, flaying, till Dave Wain said he thought he was going to die laughing or crying right there on the spot.

So we drive back to town and go to the mad boardinghouse to drink some more and I pass out dead drunk on the floor as usual in that house, waking up in the morning groaning far from my clean cot on the porch in Big Sur——No bluejays yakking for me to wake up any more, no gurgling creek, I'm back in the grooky city and I'm trapped.

14

Instead there's the sound of bottles crashing in the livingroom where poor Lex Pascal is holding forth yelling, it reminds of the time a year ago when Jarry Wagner's future wife got sore at Lex and threw a half gallonfull of tokay[8] across the room and hooked him right across the eye, thereupon sailing to Japan to marry Jarry in a big Zen ceremony that made coast to coast papers but all old Lex's got is a cut which I try to fix in the bathroom upstairs saying "Hey, that cut's already stopped bleeding, you'll be alright Lex"—— "I'm French Canadian too" he says proudly and when Dave and I and George Baso get ready to drive back to New York he gives me a St. Christopher medal[9] as a goingaway gift——Lex the kind of guy shouldnt really be living in this wild beat boardinghouse, should hide on a ranch somewhere, powerful, good-looking, full of crazy desire for women and booze and never enough of either——So as the bottles crash again and the Hi Fi's playing Beethoven's Solemn Mass[1] I fall asleep on the floor.

Waking up the next morning groaning of course, but this is the big day when we're going to go visit poor George Baso at the TB hospital in the Valley——Dave perks me up right away bringing coffee or wine optional—— I'm on Ben Pagan's floor somehow, apparently I've harangued him till dawn about Buddhism—some Buddhist.

6. Roman god of fire and volcanoes, often pictured at a blacksmith's forge.
7. Tool used for separating rubber tires from metal wheels.
8. Inexpensive wine.
9. Medal commemorating St. Christopher, a martyred 3rd-century Catholic saint, patron and protector of travelers.
1. *Missa Solemnis* in D Major, Opus 123 (1817–23), by the German composer Ludwig van Beethoven (1770–1827), is playing on the stereo.

Complicated already but now suddenly appears Joey Rosenberg a strange young kid from Oregon with a full beard and his hair growing right down to his neck like Raul Castro,[2] once the California High School high jump champ who was only about 5 foot 6 but had made the incredible leap of six foot nine over the bar! and shows his highjump ability too by the way he dances around on light feet——A strange athlete who's suddenly decided instead to become some sort of beat Jesus and in fact you see perfect purity and sincerity in his young blue eyes——In fact his eyes are so pure you dont notice the crazy hair and beard, and also he's wearing ragged but strangely elegant clothing ("One of the first of the new Beat Dandies," McLear told me a few days later, "did you hear about that? there's a new strange underground group of beatniks or whatever who wear special smooth dandy clothes even tho it may just be a jean jacket with shino slacks[3] they'll always have strange beautiful shoes or shirts, or turn around and wear fancy pants unpressed acourse but with torn sneakers")——Joey is wearing something like brown soft garments like a tunic or something and his shoes look like Las Vegas sports shoes——The moment he sees my battered blue little sneakers that I'd used at Big Sur when my feet go sore, that is in case my feet got sore on a rocky hike, he wants them for himself, he wants to swap the snazzy Las Vegas sports shoes (pale leather, untooled) for my silly little tightfitting tho perfect sneakers that in fact I was wearing because the Monterey hike blisters were still hurting me——So we swap——And I ask Dave Wain about him: Dave says: "He's one of the really strangest sweetest guys I've ever known, showed up about a week ago I hear tell, they asked him what he wanted to do and never answers, just smiles——He just sorta wants to dig everything and just watch and enjoy and say nothing particular about it——If someone's to ask him 'Let's drive to New York' he'd jump right for it without a word——On a sort of a pilgrimage, see, with all that youth, us old fucks oughta take a lesson from him, in faith too, he has faith, I can see it in his eyes, he has faith in any direction he may take with anyone just like Christ I guess."

It's strange that in a later revery I imagined myself walking across a field to find the strange gang of pilgrims in Arkansas and Dave Wain was sitting there saying "Shhh, He's sleeping," "He" being Joey and all the disciples are following him on a march to New York after which they expect to keep going walking on water to the other shore——But of course (in my revery even) I scoff and dont believe it (a kind of story daydreaming I often do) but in the morning when I look into Joey Rosenberg's eyes I instantly realize it IS Him, Jesus, because anyone (according to the rules of my revery) who looks into those eyes is instantly convinced and converted——So the revery continues into a long farfetched story ending with thinking I.B.M. machines trying to destroy this "Second Coming" etc. (but also, in reality, a few months later I threw away his shoes in the ashcan back home because I felt they had brought me bad luck and wishing I'd kept my blue sneakers with the little holes in the toes!)

So anyway we get Joey and Ron Blake who's always following Dave and go off to see Monsanto at the store, our usual ritual, then across the corner to Mike's Place where we start off the 10 A.M. with food, drink and a few games

---

2. Raul Castro Ruz (b. 1931), brother of Fidel.   3. Slang for polished cotton chino.

of pool at the tables along the bar——Joey winning the game and a stranger poolshark you never saw with his long Biblical hair bending to slide the cue stick smoothly through completely professionally competent fingerstance and smashing home long straight drives, like seeing Jesus shoot pool of course—— And meanwhile all the food these poor starved kids all three of them do pack in and eat!——It's not every day they're with a drunken novelist with hundreds of dollars to splurge on them, they order everything, spaghetti, follow that up with Jumbo Hamburgers, follow that up with ice cream and pie and puddings, Dave Wain has a huge appetite anyway but adds Manhattans and Martinis to the side of his plate——I'm just wailing away on my old fatal double bourbons and gingerale and I'll be sorry in a few days.

Any drinker knows how the process works: the first day you get drunk is okay, the morning after means a big head but so you can kill that easy with a few more drinks and a meal, but if you pass up the meal and go on to another night's drunk, and wake up to keep the toot going, and continue on to the fourth day, there'll come one day when the drinks wont take effect because you're chemically overloaded and you'll have to sleep it off but cant sleep any more because it was alcohol itself that made you sleep those last five nights, so delirium sets in——Sleeplessness, sweat, trembling, a groaning feeling of weakness where your arms are numb and useless, nightmares, (nightmares of death) . . . well, there's more of that up later.

About noon which is now the peak of a golden blurry new day for me we pick up Dave's girl Romana Swartz a big Rumanian monster beauty of some kind (I mean with big purple eyes and very tall and big but Mae West[4] big), Dave whispers in my ear "You oughta see her walking around that Zen-East House in those purple panties of hers, nothing else on, there's one married guy lives there who goes crazy every time she goes down the hall tho I dont blame him, would you? she's not trying to entice him or anybody she's just a nudist, she believe in nudism and bygod she's going to practice it!" (the Zen-East house being another sort of boardinghouse but this one for all kinds of married people and single and some small bohemian type families all races studying Subud or something, I never was there)——She's a big beautiful brunette anyway in the line of taste you might attribute to every slaky hungry sex slave in the world but also intelligent, well read, writes poetry, is a Zen student, knows everything, is in fact just simply a big healthy Rumanian Jewess who wants to marry a good hardy man and go live on a farm in the valley, that's it——

The T.B. hospital is about two hours away through Tracy and down the San Joaquin Valley, Dave drives beautiful with Romana between us and me holding the bottle again, it's bright beautiful California sunshine and prune orchards out there zipping by——It's always fun to have a good driver and a bottle and dark glasses on a fine sunny afternoon going somewhere interesting, and all the good conversation as I said——Ron and Joey are on the back mattress sitting crosslegged just like poor George Baso had sat on that trip last year from Frisco to New York.

But the main thing I'd liked at once about that Japanese kid was what he told me the first night I met him in that crazy kitchen of the Buchanan Street

---

4. Stage name of actress Mary Jane West (1893–1980), famous for her buxom figure and bawdy humor.

house: from midnight to 6 A.M. in his slow methodical voice he gave me his own tremendous version of the Life of Buddha beginning with infancy and right down to the end——George's theory (he has many theories and has actually run meditation classes with bells, just really a serious young lay priest of Japanese Buddhism when all is said and done) is that Buddha did not reject amorous love life with his wife and with his harem girls because he was sexually disinterested but on the contrary had been taught in the highest arts of lovemaking and eroticism possible in the India of that time, when great tomes like the Kama Sutra were in the process of being developed, tomes that give you instructions on every act, facet, approach, moment, trick, lick, lock, bing and bang and slurp of how to make love with another human being "male or female" insisted George: "He knew everything there is to know about all kinds of sex so that when he abandoned the world of pleasure to go be an ascetic in the forest everybody of course knew that he wasnt put-ting it all down out of ignorance——It served to make people of those times feel a marvelous respect for all his words——And he was just no simple Casanova[5] with a few frigid affairs across the years, man he went all the way, he had ministers and special eunuchs and special women who taught him love, special virgins were brought to him, he was acquainted with every aspect of perversity and non perversity and as you know he was also a great archer, horseman, he was just completely trained in all the arts of living by his father's orders because his father wanted to make sure he'd NEVER leave the palace——They used every trick in the books to entice him to a life of pleasure and as you know they even had him happily married to a beautiful girl called Yasodhara and he had a son with her Rahula and he also had his harem which included dancing boys and everything in the books" then George would go into every detail of this knowledge, like "He knew that the phallus is held with the hand and moved inside the vagina with a rotary movement, but this was only the first of several variations where there is also the lowering down of the gal's hips so that the vulva you see recedes and the phallus is introduced with a fast quick movement like stinging of a wasp, or else the vulva is protruded by means of lifting up the hips high so that the member is buried with a sudden rush right to the basis, or then he can with-draw real teasing like, or concentrate on right or left side——And then he knew all the gestures, words, expressions, what to do with a flower, what not to do with a flower, how to drink the lip in all kinds of kissing or how to crush kiss or soft kiss, man he was a *genius* in the beginning" . . . and so on, George went all the way telling me this till 6 A.M. it being one of the most fantastic *Buddha Charitas*[6] I'd ever heard ending with George's own perfect enuncia-tion of the law of the Twelve Nirdanas whereby Buddha just logically discon-nected all creation and laid it bare for what it was, under the Bo Tree, a chain of illusions——And on the trip to New York with Dave and me up front talk-ing all the way poor George just sat there on the mattress for the most part very quiet and told us he was taking this trip to find out if HE was traveling to New York or just the CAR (Willie the Jeep) was traveling to New York or was it just the WHEELS were rolling, or the tires, or what——A Zen problem of some kind——So that when we'd see grain elevators on the Plains of Oklahoma George would say quietly "Well it seems to me that grain elevator

---

5. Giovanni Giacomo Casanova de Seingalt (1725–1798), Italian libertine and adventurer.

6. Properly *Buddha caritas*, a state of uncondi-tional openness, generosity, and patience.

is sorta waitin for the road to approach it" or he'd say suddenly "While you guys was talkin just then about how to mix a good Pernod Martini I just saw a white horse standing in an abandoned storefront"——In Las Vegas we'd taken a good motel room and gone out to play a little roulette, in St. Louis we'd gone to see the great bellies of the East St. Louis[7] hootchy kootchy joints where three of the most marvelous young girls performed smiling directly at us as tho they knew all about George and his theories about erogenous Buddha (there sits the monarch observing the donzinggerls) and as tho they knew anyway all about Dave Wain who whenever he sees a beautiful girls says licking his lips "Yum Yum." . . .

But now George has T.B. and they tell me he may even die——Which adds to that darkness in my mind, all these DEATH things piling up suddenly—— But I cant believe old Zen Master George is going to allow his body to die just now tho it looks like it when we pass through the lawn and come to a ward of beds and see him sitting dejected on the edge of his bed with his hair hanging over his brow where before it was always combed back——He's in a bathrobe and looks up at us almost displeased (but everybody is displeased by unexpected visits from friends or relatives in a hospital)——Nobody wants to be surprised on their hospital bad——He sighs and comes out to the warm lawn with us and the expression on his face says "Well ah so you've come to see me because I'm sick but what do you really want?" as tho all the old humorous courage of the year before has now given way to a profoundly deep Japanese skepticism like that of a Samurai warrior in a fit of suicidal depression (surprising me by its abject gloomy fearful frown).

1962

7. Working-class city in Illinois across the Mississippi River from St. Louis, Missouri.

DENISE LEVERTOV
1923–1997

Denise Levertov once wrote of her predecessor, the poet H.D.: "She showed a way to penetrate mystery; which means, not to flood darkness with light so that darkness is destroyed, but to *enter into* darkness, mystery, so that it is experienced." Along with Robert Duncan, Levertov carried out in her own distinctive way H. D.'s tradition of visionary poetry. More grounded than her predecessor in observing the natural world and in appreciating daily life, Levertov connected the concrete to the invisible, as suggested by the image of *The Jacob's Ladder* (1961), the title of her fifth book. She desired that a poem be "hard as a floor, sound as a bench" but also that it be "mysterious" ("Illustrious Ancestors"), and in her poems ordinary events open into the unknown. The origins of Levertov's magical sense of the world are not difficult to trace. She was born in England and wrote of her parents: "My mother was descended from the Welsh Tailor and mystic Angel Jones of Mold, my father from the noted Hasid, Schneour Zaiman (d. 1831), the 'Rav of Northern White Russia.'" In "Illustrious Ancestors" Levertov claimed a connection to her forefathers, both mystical and Hasidic: "some line still taut between me and them." Hasidism, a sect of Judaism that emphasizes the soul's communion with God rather than formal religious observance and encourages what Levertov called "a wonder at creation," was an important influence on her father, Paul Philip Levertoff. He had converted to Christianity as a student and later became an Anglican priest, but he retained his interest in Judaism and told Hasidic legends to Levertov and her older sister, Olga, throughout their childhoods. From her mother, Beatrice Spooner-Jones, Levertov learned to look closely at the world around her, and we might say of her work what she said of her mother: "with how much gazing / her life had paid tribute to the world's body" ("The 90th Year").

In 1947 Levertov married an American, Mitchell Goodman (they later divorced), and moved to the United States. She described this move as crucial to her development as a poet; it "necessitated the finding of new rhythms in which to write, in accordance with new rhythms of life and speech." In this discovery of a new idiom the stylistic influence of William Carlos Williams was especially important to her; without it, she said, "I could not have developed from a British Romantic with an almost Victorian background to an American poet of any vitality." Levertov embraced Williams's interest in an organic poetic form, growing out of the poet's relation to her subject, and like Duncan and Robert Creeley, she actively explored the relations between the line and the unit of breath as they control rhythm, melody, and stress. But if Levertov became the poet she was by becoming an American poet, her European heritage also enriched her sense of influence. Although her poem "September 1961" acknowledges her link to "the old great ones" (Ezra Pound, Williams, and H. D.), she was as at home with the German lyric poet Rainer Maria Rilke as with the American Transcendentalist Ralph Waldo Emerson. And in the United States she discovered the work of the Jewish theologian and philosopher Martin Buber, which renewed her interest "in the Hasidic ideas with which I was dimly acquainted as a child." Her eclecticism let her move easily between plain and richly descriptive language, between a vivid perception of the "thing itself" and the often radiant mystery that, for Levertov, arose from such seeing.

From 1956 to 1959 Levertov lived with her husband and son in Mexico. They were joined there by her mother, who, after her daughter's departure, remained in Mexico for the final eighteen years of her life (she died in 1977). Several moving poems in Levertov's collection *Life in the Forest* (1978), among them "The 90th Year" and "Death in Mexico," address her mother's last years. In the late 1960s the political crisis prompted by the Vietnam War turned Levertov's work more directly to public woes, as reflected in her following four books. Not all the poems in these books explicitly concern political issues ("The Sorrow Dance," for example, contains her sequence in memory of her sister, Olga, one of her finest, most powerful poems); nonetheless, many poems originated in a need for public testimony. Her overtly political poems are not often among her best, however; their very explicitness restricted her distinctive strengths as a poet, which included a feeling for the inexplicable, a language lyrical enough to express wish and desire, and a capacity for playfulness. But it is a mistake to separate too rigidly the political concerns in her work from a larger engagement with the world. As she wrote: "If a degree of intimacy is a condition of lyric expression, surely—at times when events make feelings run high—that intimacy between writer and political belief does exist, and is as intense as other emotions."

The power of Levertov's poems depends on her capacity to balance, however precariously, her two-sided vision, to keep alive both terms of what one critic called her "magical realism." At its best her work seems to spring from experience deep within her, stirred into being by a source beyond herself (as "Caedmon" is suddenly "affrighted" by an angel, or the poet at the age of sixteen dreams deeply, "sunk in the well"). Her finest poems render the inexplicable nature of our ordinary lives and their capacity for unexpected beauty. But Levertov's capacity for pleasure in the world never strays too far from the knowledge that the very landscapes that delight us contain places "that can pull you / down" ("Zeroing In"), as

THE JACOB'S LADDER | 2509

our inner landscapes also contain places "'that are bruised forever, that time / never assuages, never.'"

Levertov published several collections of prose, including *The Poet in the World* (1973), *Light Up the Cave* (1981), and *New and Selected Essays* (1992). In 1987 she published her fifteenth book of poems, *Breathing the Water*. This book contains a long sequence, *The Showings: Lady Julian of Norwich, 1342–1416*, which continues the link between Levertov's work and a visionary tradition. She published three subsequent collections: *A Door in the Hive* (1989), *Evening Train* (1992), and *Tesserae* (1995). Levertov taught widely and from 1982 until her death was professor of English at Stanford University, where she was an important teacher for a younger generation of writers.

To the Snake

Green Snake, when I hung you round my neck
and stroked your cold, pulsing throat
      as you hissed to me, glinting
arrowy gold scales, and I felt
      the weight of you on my shoulders,   5
and the whispering silver of your dryness
      sounded close at my ears—
Green Snake—I swore to my companions that certainly
      you were harmless! But truly
I had no certainty, and no hope, only desiring   10
      to hold you, for that joy,
                which left
a long wake of pleasure, as the leaves moved
and you faded into the pattern
of grass and shadows, and I returned   15
smiling and haunted, to a dark morning.

                              1960

The Jacob's Ladder[1]

The stairway is not
a thing of gleaming strands
a radiant evanescence
for angels' feet that only glance in their tread, and need not
touch the stone.   5

It is of stone.
A rosy stone that takes
a glowing tone of softness
only because behind it the sky is a doubtful, a doubting
night gray.   10

---

1. Jacob dreamed of "a ladder set up on the earth, and the top of it reached to heaven: and behold the angels of God ascending and descending on it" (Genesis 28.12).

A stairway of sharp
angles, solidly built.
One sees that the angels must spring
down from one step to the next, giving a little
lift of the wings: 15

and a man climbing
must scrape his knees, and bring
the grip of his hands into play. The cut stone
consoles his groping feet. Wings brush past him.
The poem ascends.   20

                                                    1961

In Mind

There's in my mind a woman
of innocence, unadorned but

fair-featured, and smelling of
apples or grass. She wears

a utopian smock or shift, her hair   5
is light brown and smooth, and she

is kind and very clean without
ostentation—
              but she has
no imagination.   10
              And there's a
turbulent moon-ridden girl

or old woman, or both,
dressed in opals and rags, feathers

and torn taffeta,   15
who knows strange songs—

but she is not kind.

                                                    1964

JAMES BALDWIN
1924–1987

James Baldwin was born in Harlem, the first of nine children. From his novel *Go Tell It on the Mountain* (1953) and his story "The Rockpile," we learn about the extremely painful relationship he had with his father (actually his stepfather). David Baldwin, son of a slave, was a lay preacher rigidly committed to a vengeful God who would eventually judge white people as they deserved; in the meantime much of the vengeance was taken out on James. His father's "unlimited capacity for introspection and rancor," as the son later put it, must have had a profound effect on the sermonizing style Baldwin developed. Just as important was Baldwin's conversion and resulting service as a preacher in his father's church, as we can see from both the rhythm and the message of his prose—which is very much a *spoken* prose.

Baldwin did well in school and, having received a hardship deferment from military service because his father was dying, attached himself to Greenwich Village, where he concentrated on becoming a writer. In 1944 he met Richard Wright, at that time "the greatest black writer in the world for me," in whose early books Baldwin "found expressed, for the first time in my life, the sorrow, the rage, and the murderous bitterness which was eating up my life and the lives of those about me." Wright helped him win a Eugene Saxton fellowship, and in 1948, when Baldwin went to live in Paris, he was following in Wright's footsteps (Wright had become an expatriate to the same city a year earlier). It is perhaps for this reason that in his early essays written for *Partisan Review* and published in 1955 as *Notes of a Native Son* (with the title's explicit reference to Wright's 1940 novel, *Native Son*) Baldwin dissociated himself from the image of American life found in Wright's "protest work" and, like the novelist Ralph Ellison, went about protesting in his own way.

As far as his novels are concerned, Baldwin's way involved a preoccupation with the intertwining of sexual with racial concerns, particularly in America. His interest in what it means to be black and homosexual in relation to mainstream white society is most fully and interestingly expressed in his third novel, *Another Country* (1962). (He had previously written *Go Tell It on the Mountain*, and a second novel, *Giovanni's Room*, 1955, about a white expatriate in Paris and his male lover.) *Another Country* contains scenes full of lively detail and intelligent reflection, expressed in a manner that takes advantage of the novel's expansive form. In his short stories collected in *Going to Meet the Man* (1965), the racial terrorism of America as he perceived it made its own grotesque stylistic statement. The writer's challenge was to maintain steady control in the face of atrocities that might otherwise disrupt the narrative's ability to contain such events.

His later novels, *Tell Me How Long the Train's Been Gone* (1968) and *Just Above My Head* (1979), were more polemical. Like his fellow novelist Norman Mailer, Baldwin risked advertising himself too strenuously and sometimes let spokesmanship become a primary motivator. Like Ellison, he experienced many pressures to be more than just a writer, but he nevertheless produced artistically significant novels and stories. No black writer has been better able to imagine white experience, to speak in various tones of different kinds and behaviors of people or places other than his own. In its sensitivity to shades of discrimination and moral shape, and in its commitment—despite everything—to America, his voice was comparable in importance to that of any person of letters from recent decades, as tributes paid to him at his death agreed.

The following text is from *Going to Meet the Man* (1965).

Going to Meet the Man

"What's the matter?" she asked.

"I don't know," he said, trying to laugh, "I guess I'm tired."

"You've been working too hard," she said. "I keep telling you."

"Well, goddammit, woman," he said, "it's not my fault!" He tried again; he wretchedly failed again. Then he just lay there, silent, angry, and helpless. Excitement filled him like a toothache, but it refused to enter his flesh. He stroked her breast. This was his wife. He could not ask her to do just a little thing for him, just to help him out, just for a little while, the way he could ask a nigger girl to do it. He lay there, and he sighed. The image of a black girl caused a distant excitement in him, like a far-away light; but, again, the excitement was more like pain; instead of forcing him to act, it made action impossible.

"Go to sleep," she said, gently, "you got a hard day tomorrow."

"Yeah," he said, and rolled over on his side, facing her, one hand still on one breast. "Goddamn the niggers. The black stinking coons. You'd think they'd learn. Wouldn't you think they'd learn? I mean, *wouldn't* you?"

"They going to be out there tomorrow," she said, and took his hand away, "get some sleep."

He lay there, one hand between his legs, staring at the frail sanctuary of his wife. A faint light came from the shutters; the moon was full. Two dogs, far away, were barking at each other, back and forth, insistently, as though they were agreeing to make an appointment. He heard a car coming north on the road and he half sat up, his hand reaching for his holster, which was on a chair near the bed, on top of his pants. The lights hit the shutters and seemed to travel across the room and then went out. The sound of the car slipped away, he heard it hit gravel, then heard it no more. Some liver-lipped students, probably, heading back to that college—but coming from where? His watch said it was two in the morning. They could be coming from anywhere, from out of state most likely, and they would be at the court-house tomorrow. The niggers were getting ready. Well, they would be ready, too.

He moaned. He wanted to let whatever was in him out; but it wouldn't come out. Goddamn! he said aloud, and turned again, on his side, away from Grace, staring at the shutters. He was a big, healthy man and he had never had any trouble sleeping. And he wasn't old enough yet to have any trouble getting it up—he was only forty-two. And he was a good man, a God-fearing man, he had tried to do his duty all his life, and he had been a deputy sheriff for several years. Nothing had ever bothered him before, certainly not getting it up. Sometimes, sure, like any other man, he knew that he wanted a little more spice than Grace could give him and he would drive over yonder and pick up a black piece or arrest her, it came to the same thing, but he couldn't do that now, no more. There was no telling what might happen once your ass was in the air. And they were low enough to kill a man then, too, every one of them, or the girl herself might do it, right while she was making believe you made her feel so good. The niggers. What had the good Lord Almighty had in mind when he made the niggers? Well. They were pretty good at that, all right. Damn. Damn. Goddamn.

This wasn't helping him to sleep. He turned again, toward Grace again, and moved close to her warm body. He felt something he had never felt before. He felt that he would like to hold her, hold her, hold her, and be buried in her like a child and never have to get up in the morning again and go downtown to face those faces, good Christ, they were ugly! and never have to enter that jailhouse again and smell that smell and hear that singing; never again feel that filthy, kinky, greasy hair under his hand, never again watch those black breasts leap against the leaping cattle prod, never hear those moans again or watch that blood run down or the fat lips split or the sealed eyes struggle open. They were animals, they were no better than animals, what could be done with people like that? Here they had been in a civilized country for years and they still lived like animals. Their houses were dark, with oil cloth or cardboard in the windows, the smell was enough to make you puke your guts out, and there they sat, a whole tribe, pumping out kids, it looked like, every damn five minutes, and laughing and talking and playing music like they didn't have a care in the world, and he reckoned they didn't, neither, and coming to the door, into the sunlight, just standing there, just looking foolish, not thinking of anything but just getting back to what they were doing, saying, Yes suh, Mr. Jesse. I surely will, Mr. Jesse. Fine weather, Mr. Jesse. Why, I thank you, Mr. Jesse. He had worked for a mail-order house for a while and it had been his job to collect the payments for the stuff they bought. They were too dumb to know that they were being cheated blind, but that was no skin off his ass—he was just supposed to do his job. They would be late—they didn't have the sense to put money aside; but it was easy to scare them, and he never really had any trouble. Hell, they all liked him, the kids used to smile when he came to the door. He gave them candy, sometimes, or chewing gum, and rubbed their rough bullet heads—maybe the candy should have been poisoned. Those kids were grown now. He had had trouble with one of them today.

"There was this nigger today," he said; and stopped; his voice sounded peculiar. He touched Grace. "You awake?" he asked. She mumbled something, impatiently, she was probably telling him to go to sleep. It was all right. He knew that he was not alone.

"What a funny time," he said, "to be thinking about a thing like that—you listening?" She mumbled something again. He rolled over on his back. "This nigger's one of the ringleaders. We had trouble with him before. We must have had him out there at the work farm three or four times. Well, Big Jim C. and some of the boys really had to whip that nigger's ass today." He looked over at Grace; he could not tell whether she was listening or not; and he was afraid to ask again. "They had this line you know, to register"—he laughed, but she did not—"and they wouldn't stay where Big Jim C. wanted them, no, they had to start blocking traffic all around the court house so couldn't nothing or nobody get through, and Big Jim C. told them to disperse and they wouldn't move, they just kept up that singing, and Big Jim C. figured that the others would move if this nigger would move, him being the ringleader, but he wouldn't move and he wouldn't let the others move, so they had to beat him and a couple of the others and they threw them in the wagon—but I didn't see this nigger till I got to the jail. They were still singing and I was supposed to make them stop. Well, I couldn't make them stop for me but I knew he could make them stop. He was lying on the ground jerking and moaning, they had threw him in a cell by himself, and blood was coming out his ears from where Big Jim C. and his boys had whipped him. Wouldn't you think they'd learn? I put the prod to him and he jerked some more and he kind of screamed—but he didn't have much voice left. "You make them stop that singing," I said to him, "you hear me? You make them stop that singing." He acted like he didn't hear me and I put it to him again, under his arms, and he just rolled around on the floor and blood started coming from his mouth. He'd pissed his pants already." He paused. His mouth felt dry and his throat was as rough as sand-paper; as he talked, he began to hurt all over with that peculiar excitement which refused to be released. "You all are going to stop your singing, I said to him, and you are going to stop coming down to the court house and disrupting traffic and molesting the people and keeping us from our duties and keeping doctors from getting to sick white women and getting all them Northerners in this town to give our town a bad name—!" As he said this, he kept prodding the boy, sweat pouring from beneath the helmet he had not yet taken off. The boy rolled around in his own dirt and water and blood and tried to scream again as the prod hit his testicles, but the scream did not come out, only a kind of rattle and a moan. He stopped. He was not supposed to kill the nigger. The cell was filled with a terrible odor. The boy was still. "You hear me?" he called. "You had enough?" The singing went on. "You had enough?" His foot leapt out, he had not known it was going to, and caught the boy flush on the jaw. *Jesus*, he thought, *this ain't no nigger, this is a goddamn bull*, and he screamed again, "You had enough? You going to make them stop that singing now?"

But the boy was out. And now he was shaking worse than the boy had been shaking. He was glad no one could see him. At the same time, he felt very close to a very peculiar, particular joy; something deep in him and deep in his memory was stirred, but whatever was in his memory eluded him. He took off his helmet. He walked to the cell door.

"White man," said the boy, from the floor, behind him.

He stopped. For some reason, he grabbed his privates.

"You remember Old Julia?"

The boy said, from the floor, with his mouth full of blood, and one eye, barely open, glaring like the eye of a cat in the dark, "My grandmother's name was Mrs. Julia Blossom. *Mrs.* Julia Blossom. You going to call our women by their right names yet.—And those kids ain't going to stop singing. We going to keep on singing until every one of you miserable white mothers go stark raving out of your minds." Then he closed the one eye; he spat blood; his head fell back against the floor.

He looked down at the boy, whom he had been seeing, off and on, for more than a year, and suddenly remembered him: Old Julia had been one of his mail-order customers, a nice old woman. He had not seen her for years, he supposed that she must be dead.

He had walked into the yard, the boy had been sitting in a swing. He had smiled at the boy, and asked, "Old Julia home?"

The boy looked at him for a long time before he answered. "Don't no Old Julia live here."

"This is her house. I know her. She's lived here for years."

The boy shook his head. "You might know a Old Julia someplace else, white man. But don't nobody by that name live here."

He watched the boy; the boy watched him. The boy certainly wasn't more than ten. *White man*. He didn't have time to be fooling around with some crazy kid. He yelled, "Hey! Old Julia!"

But only silence answered him. The expression on the boy's face did not change. The sun beat down on them both, still and silent; he had the feeling that he had been caught up in a nightmare, a nightmare dreamed by a child; perhaps one of the nightmares he himself had dreamed as a child. It had that feeling—everything familiar, without undergoing any other change, had been subtly and hideously displaced: the trees, the sun, the patches of grass in the yard, the leaning porch and the weary porch steps and the card-board in the windows and the black hole of the door which looked like the entrance to a cave, and the eyes of the pickaninny, all, all, were charged with malevolence. *White man.* He looked at the boy. "She's gone out?"

The boy said nothing.

"Well," he said, "tell her I passed by and I'll pass by next week." He started to go; he stopped. "You want some chewing gum?"

The boy got down from the swing and started for the house. He said, "I don't want nothing you got, white man." He walked into the house and closed the door behind him.

Now the boy looked as though he were dead. Jesse wanted to go over to him and pick him up and pistol whip him until the boy's head burst open like a melon. He began to tremble with what he believed was rage, sweat, both cold and hot, raced down his body, the singing filled him as though it were a weird, uncontrollable, monstrous howling rumbling up from the depths of his own belly, he felt an icy fear rise in him and raise him up, and he shouted, he howled, "You lucky we *pump* some white blood into you every once in a while—your women! Here's what I got for all the black bitches in the world—!" Then he was, abruptly, almost too weak to stand; to his bewilderment, his horror, beneath his own fingers, he felt himself violently stiffen—with no warning at all; he dropped his hands and he stared at the boy and he left the cell.

"All that singing they do," he said. "All that singing." He could not remember the first time he had heard it; he had been hearing it all his life. It was the sound with which he was most familiar—though it was also the sound of which he had been least conscious—and it had always contained an obscure comfort. They were singing to God. They were singing for mercy and they hoped to go to heaven, and he had even sometimes felt, when looking into the eyes of some of the old women, a few of the very old men, that they were singing for mercy for his soul, too. Of course he had never thought of their heaven or of what God was, or could be, for them; God was the same for everyone, he supposed, and heaven was where good people went—he supposed. He had never thought much about what it meant to be a good person. He tried to be a good person and treat everybody right: it wasn't his fault if the niggers had taken it into their heads to fight against God and go against the rules laid down in the Bible for everyone to read! Any preacher would tell you that. He was only doing his duty: protecting white people from the niggers and the niggers from themselves. And there were still lots of good niggers around—he had to remember that; they weren't all like that boy this afternoon; and the good niggers must be mighty sad to see what was happening to their people. They would thank him when this was over. In that way they had, the best of them, not quite looking him in the eye, in a low voice, with a little smile: We surely thanks you, Mr. Jesse. From the bottom of our hearts, we thanks you. He smiled. They hadn't all gone crazy. This trouble would pass.—He knew that the young people had changed some of the words to the songs. He had scarcely listened to the words before and he did not listen to them now; but he knew that the words were different; he could hear that much. He did not know if the faces were different, he had never, before this trouble began, watched them as they sang, but he certainly did not like what he saw now. They hated him, and this hatred was blacker than their hearts, blacker than their skins, redder than their blood, and harder, by far, than his club. Each day, each night, he felt worn out, aching, with their smell in his nostrils and filling his lungs, as though he were drowning—drowning in niggers; and it was all to be done again when he awoke. It would never end. It would never end. Perhaps this was what the singing had meant all along. They had not been singing black folks into heaven, they had been singing white folks into hell.

Everyone felt this black suspicion in many ways, but no one knew how to express it. Men much older than he, who had been responsible for law and order much longer than he, were now much quieter than they had been, and the tone of their jokes, in a way that he could not quite put his finger on, had changed. These men were his models, they had been friends to his father, and they had taught him what it meant to be a man. He looked to them for courage now. It wasn't that he didn't know that what he was doing was right—he knew that, nobody had to tell him that; it was only that he missed the ease of former years. But they didn't have much time to hang out with each other these days. They tended to stay close to their families every free minute because nobody knew what might happen next. Explosions rocked the night of their tranquil town. Each time each man wondered silently if perhaps this time the dynamite had not fallen into the wrong hands. They thought that they knew where all the guns were; but they could not possibly know every move that was made in that secret place where the darkies lived. From time to time it was suggested that they form a posse and search the home of every nigger, but they hadn't done it yet. For one thing, this might have brought the bastards from the North down on their backs; for another, although the niggers were scattered throughout the town— down in the hollow near the railroad tracks, way west near the mills, up on the hill, the well-off ones, and some out near the college—nothing seemed to happen in one part of town without the niggers immediately knowing it in the other. This meant that they could not take them by surprise. They rarely mentioned it, but they *knew* that some of the niggers had guns. It stood to reason, as they said, since, after all, some of them had been in the Army. There were niggers in the Army right now and God knows they wouldn't have had any trouble stealing this half-assed government blind—the whole world was doing it, look at the European countries and all those countries in Africa. They made jokes about it—bitter jokes; and they cursed the government in Washington, which had betrayed them; but they had not yet formed a posse. Now, if their town had been laid out like some towns in the North, where all the niggers lived together in one locality, they could have gone down and set fire to the houses and brought about peace that way. If the niggers had all lived in one place, they could have kept the fire in one place. But the way this town was laid out, the fire could hardly be controlled. It would spread all over town—and the niggers would probably be helping it to spread. Still, from time to time, they spoke of doing it, anyway; so that now there was a real fear among them that somebody might go crazy and light the match.

They rarely mentioned anything not directly related to the war that they were fighting, but this had failed to establish between them the unspoken communication of soldiers during a war. Each man, in the thrilling silence which sped outward from their exchanges, their laughter, and their anecdotes, seemed wrestling, in various degrees of darkness, with a secret which he could not articulate to himself, and which, however directly it related to the war, related yet more surely to his privacy and his past. They could no longer be sure, after all, that they had all done the same things. They had never dreamed that their privacy could contain any element of terror, could threaten, that is, to reveal itself, to the scrutiny of a judgment day, while remaining unreadable and inaccessible to themselves; nor had they dreamed that the past, while certainly refusing to be forgotten, could yet so stubbornly refuse to be remembered. They felt themselves mysteriously set at naught, as no longer entering into the real concerns of other people—while here they were, out-numbered, fighting to save the civilized world. They had thought that people would care—people didn't care; not enough, anyway, to help them. It would have been a help, really, or at least a relief, even to have been forced to surrender. Thus they had lost, probably forever, their old and easy connection with each other. They were forced to depend on each other more and, at the same time, to trust each other less. Who could tell when one of them might not betray them all, for money, or for the ease of confession? But no one dared imagine what there might be to confess. They were soldiers fighting a war, but their relationship to each other was that of accomplices in a crime. They all had to keep their mouths shut.

I stepped in the river at Jordan.

Out of the darkness of the room, out of nowhere, the line came flying up at him, with the melody and the beat. He turned wordlessly toward his sleeping wife. *I stepped in the river at Jordan.* Where had he heard that song?

"Grace," he whispered. "You awake?"

She did not answer. If she was awake, she wanted him to sleep. Her breathing was slow and easy, her body slowly rose and fell.

I stepped in the river at Jordan.
The water came to my knees.

He began to sweat. He felt an overwhelming fear, which yet contained a curious and dreadful pleasure.

I stepped in the river at Jordan.
The water came to my waist.

It had been night, as it was now, he was in the car between his mother and his father, sleepy, his head in his mother's lap, sleepy, and yet full of excitement. The singing came from far away, across the dark fields. There were no lights anywhere. They had said good-bye to all the others and turned off on this dark dirt road. They were almost home.

I stepped in the river at Jordan,
The water came over my head,
I looked way over to the other side,
He was making up my dying bed!

"I guess they singing for him," his father said, seeming very weary and subdued now. "Even when they're sad, they sound like they just about to go and tear off a piece." He yawned and leaned across the boy and slapped his wife lightly on the shoulder, allowing his hand to rest there for a moment. "Don't they?"

"Don't talk that way," she said.

"Well, that's what we going to do," he said, "you can make up your mind to that." He started whistling. "You see? When I begin to feel it, I gets kind of musical, too."

Oh, Lord! Come on and ease my troubling mind!

He had a black friend, his age, eight, who lived nearby. His name was Otis. They wrestled together in the dirt. Now the thought of Otis made him sick. He began to shiver. His mother put her arm around him.

"He's tired," she said.

"We'll be home soon," said his father. He began to whistle again.

"We didn't see Otis this morning," Jesse said. He did not know why he said this. His voice, in the darkness of the car, sounded small and accusing.

"You haven't seen Otis for a couple of mornings," his mother said.

That was true. But he was only concerned about *this* morning.

"No," said his father, "I reckon Otis's folks was afraid to let him show himself this morning."

"But Otis didn't do nothing!" Now his voice sounded questioning.

"Otis *can't* do nothing," said his father, "he's too little." The car lights picked up their wooden house, which now solemnly approached them, the lights falling around it like yellow dust. Their dog, chained to a tree, began to bark.

"We just want to make sure Otis *don't* do nothing," said his father, and stopped the car. He looked down at Jesse. "And you tell him what your Daddy said, you hear?"

"Yes sir," he said.

His father switched off the lights. The dog moaned and pranced, but they ignored him and went inside. He could not sleep. He lay awake, hearing the night sounds, the dog yawning and moaning outside, the sawing of the crickets, the cry of the owl, dogs barking far away, then no sounds at all, just the heavy, endless buzzing of the night. The darkness pressed on his eyelids like a scratchy blanket. He turned, he turned again. He wanted to call his mother, but he knew his father would not like this. He was terribly afraid. Then he heard his father's voice in the other room, low, with a joke in it; but this did not help him, it frightened him more, he knew what was going to happen. He put his head under the blanket, then pushed his head out again, for fear, staring at the dark window. He heard his mother's moan, his father's sigh; he gritted his teeth. Then their bed began to rock. His father's breathing seemed to fill the world.

That morning, before the sun had gathered all its strength, men and women, some flushed and some pale with excitement, came with news. Jesse's father seemed to know what the news was before the first jalopy stopped in the yard, and he ran out, crying, "They got him, then? They got him?"

The first jalopy held eight people, three men and two women and three children. The children were sitting on the laps of the grown-ups. Jesse knew two of them, the two boys; they shyly and uncomfortably greeted each other. He did not know the girl.

"Yes, they got him," said one of the women, the older one, who wore a wide hat and a fancy, faded blue dress. "They found him early this morning."

"How far had he got?" Jesse's father asked.

"He hadn't got no further than Harkness," one of the men said. "Look like he got lost up there in all them trees—or maybe he just got so scared he couldn't move." They all laughed.

"Yes, and you know it's near a graveyard, too," said the younger woman, and they laughed again.

"Is that where they got him now?" asked Jesse's father.

By this time there were three cars piled behind the first one, with everyone looking excited and shining, and Jesse noticed that they were carrying food. It was like a Fourth of July picnic.

"Yeah, that's where he is," said one of the men, "declare, Jesse, you going to keep us here all day long, answering your damn fool questions. Come on, we ain't got no time to waste."

"Don't bother putting up no food," cried a woman from one of the other cars, "we got enough. Just come on."

"Why, thank you," said Jesse's father, "we be right along, then."

"I better get a sweater for the boy," said his mother, "in case it turns cold."

Jesse watched his mother's thin legs cross the yard. He knew that she also wanted to comb her hair a little and maybe put on a better dress, the dress she wore to church. His father guessed this, too, for he yelled behind her, "Now don't you go trying to turn yourself into no movie star. You just come on." But he laughed as he said this, and winked at the men; his wife was younger and prettier than most of the other women. He clapped Jesse on the head and started pulling him toward the car. "You all go on," he said, "I'll be right behind you. Jesse, you go tie up that there dog while I get this car started."

The cars sputtered and coughed and shook; the caravan began to move; bright dust filled the air. As soon as he was tied up, the dog began to bark. Jesse's mother came out of the house, carrying a jacket for his father and a sweater for Jesse. She had put a ribbon in her hair and had an old shawl around her shoulders.

"Put these in the car, son," she said, and handed everything to him. She bent down and stroked the dog, looked to see if there was water in his bowl, then went back up the three porch steps and closed the door.

"Come on," said his father, "ain't nothing in there for nobody to steal." He was sitting in the car, which trembled and belched. The last car of the caravan had disappeared but the sound of singing floated behind them.

Jesse got into the car, sitting close to his father, loving the smell of the car, and the trembling, and the bright day, and the sense of going on a great and unexpected journey. His mother got in and closed the door and the car began to move. Not until then did he ask, "Where are we going? Are we going on a picnic?"

He had a feeling that he knew where they were going, but he was not sure.

"That's right," his father said, "we're going on a picnic. You won't ever forget *this* picnic—!"

"Are we," he asked, after a moment, "going to see the bad nigger—the one that knocked down old Miss Standish?"

"Well, I reckon," said his mother, "that we *might* see him."

He started to ask, *Will a lot of niggers be there? Will Otis be there?*—but he did not ask his question, to which, in a strange and uncomfortable way, he already knew the answer. Their friends, in the other cars, stretched up the road as far as he could see; other cars had joined them; there were cars behind them. They were singing. The sun seemed suddenly very hot, and he was at once very happy and a little afraid. He did not quite understand what was happening, and he did not know what to ask—he had no one to ask. He had grown accustomed, for the solution of such mysteries, to go to Otis. He felt that Otis knew everything. But he could not ask Otis about this. Anyway, he had not seen Otis for two days; he had not seen a black face anywhere for more than two days; and he now realized, as they began chugging up the long hill which eventually led to Harkness, that there were no black faces on the road this morning, no black people anywhere. From the houses in which they lived, all along the road, no smoke curled, no life stirred—maybe one or two chickens were to be seen, that was all. There was no one at the windows, no one in the yard, no one sitting on the porches, and the doors were closed. He had come this road many a time and seen women washing in the yard (there were no clothes on the clotheslines), men working in the fields, children playing in the dust; black men passed them on the road other mornings, other days, on foot, or in wagons, sometimes in cars, tipping their hats, smiling, joking, their teeth a solid white against their skin, their eyes as warm as the sun, the blackness of their skin like dull fire against the white or the blue or the grey of their torn clothes. They passed the nigger church—dead-white, desolate, locked up; and the graveyard, where no one knelt or walked, and he saw no flowers. He wanted to ask, *Where are they? Where are they all?* But he did not dare. As the hill grew steeper, the sun grew colder. He looked at his mother and his father. They looked straight ahead, seeming to be listening to the singing which echoed and echoed in this graveyard silence. They were strangers to him now. They were looking at something he could not see. His father's lips had a strange, cruel curve, he wet his lips from time to time, and swallowed. He was terribly aware of his father's tongue, it was as though he had never seen it before. And his father's body suddenly seemed immense, bigger than a mountain. His eyes, which were grey-green, looked yellow in the sunlight; or at least there was a light in them which he had never seen before. His mother patted her hair and adjusted the ribbon, leaning forward to look into the car mirror. "You look all right," said his father, and laughed. "When that nigger looks at you, he's going to swear he throwed his life away for nothing. Wouldn't be surprised if he don't come back to haunt you." And he laughed again.

The singing now slowly began to cease; and he realized that they were nearing their destination. They had reached a straight, narrow, pebbly road, with trees on either side. The sunlight filtered down on them from a great height, as though they were underwater; and the branches of the trees scraped against the cars with a tearing sound. To the right of them, and beneath them, invisible now, lay the town; and to the left, miles of trees which led to the high mountain range which his ancestors had crossed in order to settle in this valley. Now, all was silent, except for the bumping of the tires against the rocky road, the sputtering of motors, and the sound of a crying child. And they seemed to move more slowly. They were beginning to climb again. He watched the cars ahead as they toiled patiently upward, disappearing into the sunlight of the clearing. Presently, he felt their vehicle also rise, heard his father's changed breathing, the sunlight hit his face, the trees moved away from them, and they were there. As their car crossed the clearing, he looked around. There seemed to be millions, there were certainly hundreds of people in the clearing, staring toward something he could not see. There was a fire. He could not see the flames, but he smelled the smoke. Then they were on the other side of the clearing, among the trees again. His father drove off the road and parked the car behind a great many other cars. He looked down at Jesse.

"You all right?" he asked.

"Yes sir," he said.

"Well, come on, then," his father said. He reached over and opened the door on his mother's side. His mother stepped out first. They followed her into the clearing. At first he was aware only of confusion, of his mother and father greeting and being greeted, himself being handled, hugged, and patted, and told how much he had grown. The wind blew the smoke from the fire across the clearing into his eyes and nose. He could not see over the backs of the people in front of him. The sounds of laughing and cursing and wrath—and something else—rolled in waves from the front of the mob to the back. Those in front expressed their delight at what they saw, and this delight rolled backward, wave upon wave, across the clearing, more acrid than the smoke. His father reached down suddenly and sat Jesse on his shoulders.

Now he saw the fire—of twigs and boxes, piled high; flames made pale orange and yellow and thin as a veil under the steadier light of the sun; grey-blue smoke rolled upward and poured over their heads. Beyond the shifting curtain of fire and smoke, he made out first only a length of gleaming chain, attached to a great limb of the tree; then he saw that this chain bound two black hands together at the wrist, dirty yellow palm facing dirty yellow palm. The smoke poured up; the hands dropped out of sight; a cry went up from the crowd. Then the hands slowly came into view again, pulled upward by the chain. This time he saw the kinky, sweating, bloody head—he had never before seen a head with so much hair on it, hair so black and so tangled that it seemed like another jungle. The head was hanging. He saw the forehead, flat and high, with a kind of arrow of hair in the center, like he had, like his father had; they called it a widow's peak; and the mangled eyebrows, the wide nose, the closed eyes, and the glinting eyelashes and the hanging lips, all streaming with blood and sweat. His hands were straight above his head. All his weight pulled downward from his hands; and he was a big man, a bigger man than his father, and black as an African jungle cat, and naked. Jesse pulled upward; his father's hands held him firmly by the ankles. He wanted to say something, he did not know what, but nothing he said could have been heard, for now the crowd roared again as a man stepped forward and put more wood on the fire. The flames leapt up. He thought he heard the hanging man scream, but he was not sure. Sweat was pouring from the hair in his armpits, poured down his sides, over his chest, into his navel and his groin. He was lowered again; he was raised again. Now Jesse knew that he heard him scream. The head went back, the mouth wide open, blood bubbling from the mouth; the veins of the neck jumped out; Jesse clung to his father's neck in terror as the cry rolled over the crowd. The cry of all the people rose to answer the dying man's cry. He wanted death to come quickly. They wanted to make death wait: and it was they who held death, now, on a leash which they lengthened little by little. *What did he do?* Jesse wondered. *What did the man do? What did he do?*—but he could not ask his father. He was seated on his father's shoulders, but his father was far away. There were two older men, friends of his father's, raising and lowering the chain; everyone, indiscriminately, seemed to be responsible for the fire. There was no hair left on the nigger's privates, and the eyes, now, were wide open, as white as the eyes of a clown or a doll. The smoke now carried a terrible odor across the clearing, the odor of something burning which was both sweet and rotten.

He turned his head a little and saw the field of faces. He watched his mother's face. Her eyes were very bright, her mouth was open: she was more beautiful than he had ever seen her, and more strange. He began to feel a joy he had never felt before. He watched the hanging, gleaming body, the most beautiful and terrible object he had ever seen till then. One of his father's friends reached up and in his hands he held a knife: and Jesse wished that he had been that man. It was a long, bright knife and the sun seemed to catch it, to play with it, to caress it—it was brighter than the fire. And a wave of laughter swept the crowd. Jesse felt his father's hands on his ankles slip and tighten. The man with the knife walked toward the crowd, smiling slightly; as though this were a signal, silence fell; he heard his mother cough. Then the man with the knife walked up to the hanging body. He turned and smiled again. Now there was a silence all over the field. The hanging head looked up. It seemed fully conscious now, as though the fire had burned out terror and pain. The man with the knife took the nigger's privates in his hand, one hand, still smiling, as though he were weighing them. In the cradle of the one white hand, the nigger's privates seemed as remote as meat being weighed in the scales; but seemed heavier, too, much heavier, and Jesse felt his scrotum tighten; and huge, huge, much bigger than his father's, flaccid, hairless, the largest thing he had ever seen till then, and the blackest. The white hand stretched them, cradled them, caressed them. Then the dying man's eyes looked straight into Jesse's eyes—it could not have been as long as a second, but it seemed longer than a year. Then Jesse screamed, and the crowd screamed as the knife flashed, first up, then down, cutting the dreadful thing away, and the blood came roaring down. Then the crowd rushed forward, tearing at the body with their hands, with knives, with rocks, with stones, howling and cursing. Jesse's head, of its own weight, fell downward toward his father's head. Someone stepped forward and drenched the body with kerosene. Where the man had been, a great sheet of flame appeared. Jesse's father lowered him to the ground.

"Well, I told you," said his father, "you wasn't never going to forget *this* picnic." His father's face was full of sweat, his eyes were very peaceful. At that moment Jesse loved his father more than he had ever loved him. He felt that his father had carried him through a mighty test, had revealed to him a great secret which would be the key to his life forever.

"I reckon," he said. "I reckon."

Jesse's father took him by the hand and, with his mother a little behind them, talking and laughing with the other women, they walked through the crowd, across the clearing. The black body was on the ground, the chain which had held it was being rolled up by one of his father's friends. Whatever the fire had left undone, the hands and the knives and the stones of the people had accomplished. The head was caved in, one eye was torn out, one ear was hanging. But one had to look carefully to realize this, for it was, now, merely, a black charred object on the black, charred ground. He lay spread-eagled with what had been a wound between what had been his legs.

"They going to leave him here, then?" Jesse whispered.

"Yeah," said his father, "they'll come and get him by and by. I reckon we better get over there and get some of that food before it's all gone."

"I reckon," he muttered now to himself, "I reckon." Grace stirred and touched him on the thigh: the moonlight covered her like glory. Something bubbled up in him, his nature again returned to him. He thought of the boy in the cell; he thought of the man in the fire; he thought of the knife and grabbed himself and stroked himself and a terrible sound, something between a high laugh and a howl, came out of him and dragged his sleeping wife up on one elbow. She stared at him in a moonlight which had now grown cold as ice. He thought of the morning and grabbed her, laughing and crying, crying and laughing, and he whispered, as he stroked her, as he took her, "Come on, sugar, I'm going to do you like a nigger, just like a nigger, come on, sugar, and love me just like you'd love a nigger." He thought of the morning as he labored and she moaned, thought of morning as he labored harder than he ever had before, and before his labors had ended, he heard the first cock crow and the dogs begin to bark, and the sound of tires on the gravel road.

1965

FLANNERY O'CONNOR
1925–1964

Flannery O'Connor, one of the twentieth century's finest short story writers, was born in Savannah; lived with her mother in Milledgeville, Georgia, for much of her life; and died before her fortieth birthday—a victim like her father of disseminated lupus. She was stricken with this incurable disease in 1950 while at work on her first novel; injections of a cortisone derivative arrested it, but the cortisone weakened her bones to the extent that from 1955 on she could get around only on crutches. She was able to write, travel, and lecture until 1964, when the lupus reactivated itself and killed her. A Roman Catholic throughout her life, she is quoted as having remarked, apropos of a trip to Lourdes, "I had the best-looking crutches in Europe." This remark suggests the kind of hair-raising jokes that centrally inform her writing as well as a refusal to indulge in self-pity over her fate.

She published two novels, *Wise Blood* (1952) and *The Violent Bear It Away* (1960), both weighty with symbolic and religious concerns and ingeniously contrived in the black-humored manner of Nathanael West, her American predecessor in this mode. But her really memorable creations of characters and actions take place in the stories, which are extremely funny, sometimes unbearably so, and finally we may wonder just what we are laughing at. Upon consideration the jokes appear dreadful, as with Manley Pointer's treatment of Joy Hopewell's artificial leg in "Good Country People" or Mr. Shiftlet's of his bride in "The Life You Save May Be Your Own."

Another American "regionalist," the poet Robert Frost, whose work contains its own share of dreadful jokes, once confessed to being more interested in people's speech than in the people themselves. A typical Flannery O'Connor story consists at its most vital level of people talking, clucking their endless reiterations of clichés about life, death, and the universe. These clichés are captured with beautiful accuracy by an artist who had spent her life listening to them, lovingly and maliciously keeping track until she could put them to use. Early in her life she hoped to be a cartoonist, and there is cartoonlike mastery in her vivid renderings of character through speech and other gesture. Critics have called her a maker of grotesques, a label that like other ones—regionalist, Southern lady, or Roman Catholic novelist—might have annoyed if it didn't obviously amuse her too. She once remarked tartly that "anything that comes out of the South is going to be called grotesque by the Northern reader, unless it is grotesque, in which case it is going to be called realistic."

Of course, this capacity for mockery, along with a facility in portraying perverse behavior, may work against other demands we make of the fiction writer, and O'Connor seldom suggests that her characters have inner lives that are imaginable, let alone worth respect. Instead she emphasizes her sharp eye and her ability to tell a tale and keep it moving inevitably toward completion. These completions are usually violent, occurring when the character—in many cases a woman—must confront an experience that she cannot handle by her old trustworthy language and habit-hardened responses. O'Connor's art lies partly in making it impossible for us merely to scorn the banalities of expression and behavior by which these people get through their lives. However dark the comedy, it keeps in touch with the things of this world, even when some force from another world threatens to annihilate the embattled protagonist. And although the stories are filled with religious allusions and parodies, they do not try to inculcate a doctrine. One of her best ones is titled "Revelation," but we seldom finish an O'Connor story with a simple, unambiguous sense of what has been revealed. Instead we trust that the tale's internal fun and richness reveal what it has to reveal. We can agree also, in sadness, with the critic Irving Howe's conclusion to his review of her posthumous collection of stories that it is intolerable for such a writer to have died at the age of thirty-nine.

The following text is from *A Good Man Is Hard to Find* (1955).

Good Country People

Besides the neutral expression that she wore when she was alone, Mrs. Freeman had two others, forward and reverse, that she used for all her human dealings. Her forward expression was steady and driving like the advance of a heavy truck. Her eyes never swerved to left or right but turned as the story turned as if they followed a yellow line down the center of it. She seldom used the other expression because it was not often necessary for her to retract a statement, but when she did, her face came to a complete stop, there was an almost imperceptible movement of her black eyes, during which they seemed to be receding, and then the observer would see that Mrs. Freeman, though she might stand there as real as several grain sacks thrown on top of each other, was no longer there in spirit. As for getting anything across to her when this was the case, Mrs. Hopewell had given it up. She might talk her head off. Mrs. Freeman could never be brought to admit herself wrong on any point. She would stand there and if she could be brought to say anything, it was something like, "Well, I wouldn't of said it was and I wouldn't of said it wasn't," or letting her gaze range over the top kitchen shelf where there was an assortment of dusty bottles, she might remark, "I see you ain't ate many of them figs you put up last summer."

They carried on their important business in the kitchen at breakfast. Every morning Mrs. Hopewell got up at seven o'clock and lit her gas heater and Joy's. Joy was her daughter, a large blonde girl who had an artificial leg. Mrs. Hopewell thought of her as a child though she was thirty-two years old and highly educated. Joy would get up while her mother was eating and lumber into the bathroom and slam the door, and before long, Mrs. Freeman would arrive at the back door. Joy would hear her mother call, "Come on in," and then they would talk for a while in low voices that were indistinguishable in the bathroom. By the time Joy came in, they had usually finished the weather report and were on one or the other of Mrs. Freeman's daughters, Glynese or Carramae. Joy called them Glycerin and Caramel. Glynese, a redhead, was eighteen and had many admirers; Carramae, a blonde, was only fifteen but already married and pregnant. She could not keep anything on her stomach. Every morning Mrs. Freeman told Mrs. Hopewell how many times she had vomited since the last report.

Mrs. Hopewell liked to tell people that Glynese and Carramae were two of the finest girls she knew and that Mrs. Freeman was a *lady* and that she was never ashamed to take her anywhere or introduce her to anybody they might meet. Then she would tell how she had happened to hire the Freemans in the first place and how they were a godsend to her and how she had had them four years. The reason for her keeping them so long was that they were not trash. They were good country people. She had telephoned the man whose name they had given as a reference and he had told her that Mr. Freeman was a good farmer but that his wife was the nosiest woman ever to walk the earth. "She's got to be into everything," the man said. "If she don't get there before the dust settles, you can bet she's dead, that's all. She'll want to know all your business. I can stand him real good," he had said, "but me nor my wife neither could have stood that woman one more minute on this place." That had put Mrs. Hopewell off for a few days.

She had hired them in the end because there were no other applicants but she had made up her mind beforehand exactly how she would handle the woman. Since she was the type who had to be into everything, then, Mrs. Hopewell had decided, she would not only let her be into everything, she would *see to it* that she was into everything—she would give her the responsibility of everything, she would put her in charge. Mrs. Hopewell had no bad qualities of her own but she was able to use other people's in such a constructive way that she never felt the lack. She had hired the Freemans and she had kept them four years.

Nothing is perfect. This was one of Mrs. Hopewell's favorite sayings. Another was: that is life! And still another, the most important, was: well, other people have their opinions too. She would make these statements, usually at the table, in a tone of gentle insistence as if no one held them but her, and the large hulking Joy, whose constant outrage had obliterated every expression from her face, would stare just a little to the side of her, her eyes icy blue, with the look of someone who has achieved blindness by an act of will and means to keep it.

When Mrs. Hopewell said to Mrs. Freeman that life was like that, Mrs. Freeman would say, "I always said so myself." Nothing had been arrived at by anyone that had not first been arrived at by her. She was quicker than Mr. Freeman. When Mrs. Hopewell said to her after they had been on the place a while, "You know, you're the wheel behind the wheel," and winked, Mrs. Freeman had said, "I know it. I've always been quick. It's some that are quicker than others."

"Everybody is different," Mrs. Hopewell said.

"Yes, most people is," Mrs. Freeman said.

"It takes all kinds to make the world."

"I always said it did myself."

The girl was used to this kind of dialogue for breakfast and more of it for dinner; sometimes they had it for supper too. When they had no guest they ate in the kitchen because that was easier. Mrs. Freeman always managed to arrive at some point during the meal and to watch them finish it. She would stand in the doorway if it were summer but in the winter she would stand with one elbow on top of the refrigerator and look down on them, or she would stand by the gas heater, lifting the back of her skirt slightly. Occasionally she would stand against the wall and roll her head from side to side. At no time was she in any hurry to leave. All this was very trying on Mrs. Hopewell but she was a woman of great patience. She realized that nothing is perfect and that in the Freemans she had good country people and that if, in this day and age, you get good country people, you had better hang onto them.

She had had plenty of experience with trash. Before the Freemans she had averaged one tenant family a year. The wives of these farmers were not the kind you would want to be around you for very long. Mrs. Hopewell, who had divorced her husband long ago, needed someone to walk over the fields with her; and when Joy had to be impressed for these services, her remarks were usually so ugly and her face so glum that Mrs. Hopewell would say, "If you can't come pleasantly, I don't want you at all," to which the girl, standing square and rigid-shouldered with her neck thrust slightly forward, would reply, "If you want me, here I am—LIKE I AM."

Mrs. Hopewell excused this attitude because of the leg (which had been shot off in a hunting accident when Joy was ten). It was hard for Mrs. Hopewell to realize that her child was thirty-two now and that for more than twenty years she had had only one leg. She thought of her still as a child because it tore her heart to think instead of the poor stout girl in her thirties who had never danced a step or had any *normal* good times. Her name was really Joy but as soon as she was twenty-one and away from home, she had had it legally changed. Mrs. Hopewell was certain that she had thought and thought until she had hit upon the ugliest name in any language. Then she had gone and had the beautiful name, Joy, changed without telling her mother until after she had done it. Her legal name was Hulga.

When Mrs. Hopewell thought the name, Hulga, she thought of the broad blank hull of a battleship. She would not use it. She continued to call her Joy to which the girl responded but in a purely mechanical way.

Hulga had learned to tolerate Mrs. Freeman who saved her from taking walks with her mother. Even Glynese and Carramae were useful when they occupied attention that might otherwise have been directed at her. At first she had thought she could not stand Mrs. Freeman for she had found that it was not possible to be rude to her. Mrs. Freeman would take on strange resentments and for days together she would be sullen but the source of her displeasure was always obscure; a direct attack, a positive leer, blatant ugliness to her face—these never touched her. And without warning one day, she began calling her Hulga.

She did not call her that in front of Mrs. Hopewell who would have been incensed but when she and the girl happened to be out of the house together, she would say something and add the name Hulga to the end of it, and the big spectacled Joy-Hulga would scowl and redden as if her privacy had been intruded upon. She considered the name her personal affair. She had arrived at it first purely on the basis of its ugly sound and then the full genius of its fitness had struck her. She had a vision of the name working like the ugly sweating Vulcan who stayed in the furnace and to whom, presumably, the goddess had to come when called.[1] She saw it as the name of her highest creative act. One of her major triumphs was that her mother had not been able to turn her dust into Joy, but the greater one was that she had been able to turn it herself into Hulga. However, Mrs. Freeman's relish for using the name only irritated her. It was as if Mrs. Freeman's beady steel-pointed eyes had penetrated far enough behind her face to reach some secret fact. Something about her seemed to fascinate Mrs. Freeman and then one day Hulga realized that it was the artificial leg. Mrs. Freeman had a special fondness for the details of secret infections, hidden deformities, assaults upon children. Of diseases, she preferred the lingering or incurable. Hulga had heard Mrs. Hopewell give her the details of the hunting accident, how the leg had been literally blasted off, how she had never lost consciousness. Mrs. Freeman could listen to it any time as if it had happened an hour ago.

When Hulga stumped into the kitchen in the morning (she could walk without making the awful noise but she made it—Mrs. Hopewell was certain—because it was ugly-sounding), she glanced at them and did not speak. Mrs. Hopewell would be in her red kimono with her hair tied around her head in rags. She would be sitting at the table, finishing her breakfast and Mrs. Freeman would be hanging by her elbow outward from the refrigerator, looking down at the table. Hulga always put her eggs on the stove to boil and then stood over them with her arms folded, and Mrs. Hopewell would look at her—a kind of indirect gaze divided between her and Mrs. Freeman—and would think that if she would only keep herself up a little, she wouldn't be so bad looking. There was nothing wrong with her face that a pleasant expression wouldn't help. Mrs. Hopewell said that people who looked on the bright side of things would be beautiful even if they were not.

Whenever she looked at Joy this way, she could not help but feel that it would have been better if the child had not taken the Ph.D. It had certainly not brought her out any and now that she had it, there was no more excuse for her to go to school again. Mrs. Hopewell thought it was nice for girls to go to school to have a good time but Joy had "gone through." Anyhow, she would not have been strong enough to go again. The doctors had told Mrs. Hopewell that with the best of care, Joy might see forty-five. She had a weak heart. Joy had made it plain that if it had not been for this condition, she would be far from these red hills and good country people. She would be in a university lecturing to people who knew what she was talking about. And Mrs. Hopewell could very well picture her there, looking like a scarecrow and lecturing to more of the same. Here she went about all day in a six-year-old skirt and a yellow sweat shirt with a faded cowboy on a horse embossed on it. She thought this was funny; Mrs. Hopewell thought it was idiotic and showed simply that she was still a child. She was brilliant but she didn't have a grain of sense. It seemed to Mrs. Hopewell that every year she grew less like other people and more like herself—bloated, rude, and squint-eyed. And she said such strange things! To her own mother she had said—without warning, without excuse, standing up in the middle of a meal with her face purple and her mouth half full—"Woman! do you ever look inside? Do you ever look inside and see what you are *not*? God!" she had cried sinking down again and staring at her plate, "Malebranche[2] was

---

1. Vulcan was the Greek god of fire, whom Venus, goddess of love, "presumably" obeyed as her consort.

2. Nicolas Malebranche (1638–1715), French philosopher.

right: we are not our own light. We are not our own light!" Mrs. Hopewell had no idea to this day what brought that on. She had only made the remark, hoping Joy would take it in, that a smile never hurt anyone.

The girl had taken the Ph.D. in philosophy and this left Mrs. Hopewell at a complete loss. You could say, "My daughter is a nurse," or "My daughter is a school teacher," or even, "My daughter is a chemical engineer." You could not say, "My daughter is a philosopher." That was something that had ended with the Greeks and Romans. All day Joy sat on her neck in a deep chair, reading. Sometimes she went for walks but she didn't like dogs or cats or birds or flowers or nature or nice young men. She looked at nice young men as if she could smell their stupidity.

One day Mrs. Hopewell had picked up one of the books the girl had just put down and opening it at random, she read, "Science, on the other hand, has to assert its soberness and seriousness afresh and declare that it is concerned solely with what-is. Nothing—how can it be for science anything but a horror and a phantasm? If science is right, then one thing stands firm: science wishes to know nothing of nothing. Such is after all the strictly scientific approach to Nothing. We know it by wishing to know nothing of Nothing." These words had been underlined with a blue pencil and they worked on Mrs. Hopewell like some evil incantation in gibberish. She shut the book quickly and went out of the room as if she were having a chill.

This morning when the girl came in, Mrs. Freeman was on Carramae. "She thrown up four times after supper," she said, "and was up twict in the night after three o'clock. Yesterday she didn't do nothing but ramble in the bureau drawer. All she did. Stand up there and see what she could run up on."

"She's got to eat," Mrs. Hopewell muttered, sipping her coffee, while she watched Joy's back at the stove. She was wondering what the child had said to the Bible salesman. She could not imagine what kind of a conversation she could possibly have had with him.

He was a tall gaunt hatless youth who had called yesterday to sell them a Bible. He had appeared at the door, carrying a large black suitcase that weighted him so heavily on one side that he had to brace himself against the door facing. He seemed on the point of collapse but he said in a cheerful voice, "Good morning, Mrs. Cedars!" and set the suitcase down on the mat. He was not a bad-looking young man though he had on a bright blue suit and yellow socks that were not pulled up far enough. He had prominent face bones and a streak of sticky-looking brown hair falling across his forehead.

"I'm Mrs. Hopewell," she said.

"Oh!" he said, pretending to look puzzled but with his eyes sparkling, "I saw it said 'The Cedars' on the mailbox so I thought you was Mrs. Cedars!" and he burst out in a pleasant laugh. He picked up the satchel and under cover of a pant, he fell forward into her hall. It was rather as if the suitcase had moved first, jerking him after it. "Mrs. Hopewell!" he said and grabbed her hand. "I hope you are well!" and he laughed again and then all at once his face sobered completely. He paused and gave her a straight earnest look and said, "Lady, I've come to speak of serious things."

"Well, come in," she muttered, none too pleased because her dinner was almost ready. He came into the parlor and sat down on the edge of a straight chair and put the suitcase between his feet and glanced around the room as if he were sizing her up by it. Her silver gleamed on the two sideboards; she decided he had never been in a room as elegant as this.

"Mrs. Hopewell," he began, using her name in a way that sounded almost intimate, "I know you believe in Chrustian service."

"Well yes," she murmured.

"I know," he said and paused, looking very wise with his head cocked on one side, "that you're a good woman. Friends have told me."

Mrs. Hopewell never liked to be taken for a fool. "What are you selling?" she asked.

"Bibles," the young man said and his eye raced around the room before he added, "I see you have no family Bible in your parlor, I see that is the one lack you got!"

Mrs. Hopewell could not say, "My daughter is an atheist and won't let me keep the Bible in the parlor." She said, stiffening slightly, "I keep my Bible by my bedside." This was not the truth. It was in the attic somewhere.

"Lady," he said, "the word of God ought to be in the parlor."

"Well, I think that's a matter of taste," she began. "I think . . ."

"Lady," he said, "for a Chrustian, the word of God ought to be in every room in the house besides in his heart. I know you're a Chrustian because I can see it in every line of your face."

She stood up and said, "Well, young man, I don't want to buy a Bible and I smell my dinner burning."

He didn't get up. He began to twist his hands and looking down at them, he said softly, "Well lady, I'll tell you the truth—not many people want to buy one nowadays and besides, I know I'm real simple. I don't know how to say a thing but to say it. I'm just a country boy." He glanced up into her unfriendly face. "People like you don't like to fool with country people like me!"

"Why!" she cried, "good country people are the salt of the earth! Besides, we all have different ways of doing, it takes all kinds to make the world go 'round. That's life!"

"You said a mouthful," he said.

"Why, I think there aren't enough good country people in the world!" she said, stirred. "I think that's what's wrong with it!"

His face had brightened. "I didn't inraduce myself," he said. "I'm Manley Pointer from out in the country around Willohobie, not even from a place, just from near a place."

"You wait a minute," she said. "I have to see about my dinner." She went out to the kitchen and found Joy standing near the door where she had been listening.

"Get rid of the salt of the earth," she said, "and let's eat."

Mrs. Hopewell gave her a pained look and turned the heat down under the vegetables. "I can't be rude to anybody," she murmured and went back into the parlor.

He had opened the suitcase and was sitting with a Bible on each knee.

"You might as well put those up," she told him. "I don't want one."

"I appreciate your honesty," he said. "You don't see any more real honest people unless you go way out in the country."

"I know," she said, "real genuine folks!" Through the crack in the door she heard a groan.

"I guess a lot of boys come telling you they're working their way through college," he said, "but I'm not going to tell you that. Somehow," he said, "I don't want to go to college. I want to devote my life to Chrustian service. See," he said, lowering his voice, "I got this heart condition. I may not live long.

When you know it's something wrong with you and you may not live long, well then, lady . . ." He paused, with his mouth open, and stared at her.

He and Joy had the same condition! She knew that her eyes were filling with tears but she collected herself quickly and murmured, "Won't you stay for dinner? We'd love to have you!" and was sorry the instant she heard herself say it.

"Yes mam," he said in an abashed voice, "I would sher love to do that!"

Joy had given him one look on being introduced to him and then throughout the meal had not glanced at him again. He had addressed several remarks to her, which she had pretended not to hear. Mrs. Hopewell could not understand deliberate rudeness, although she lived with it, and she felt she had always to overflow with hospitality to make up for Joy's lack of courtesy. She urged him to talk about himself and he did. He said he was the seventh child of twelve and that his father had been crushed under a tree when he himself was eight years old. He had been crushed very badly, in fact, almost cut in two and was practically not recognizable. His mother had got along the best she could by hard working and she had always seen that her children went to Sunday School and that they read the Bible every evening. He was now nineteen years old and he had been selling Bibles for four months. In that time he had sold seventy-seven Bibles and had the promise of two more sales. He wanted to become a missionary because he thought that was the way you could do most for people. "He who losest his life shall find it," he said simply and he was so sincere, so genuine and earnest that Mrs. Hopewell would not for the world have smiled. He prevented his peas from sliding onto the table by blocking them with a piece of bread which he later cleaned his plate with. She could see Joy observing sidewise how he handled his knife and fork and she saw too that every few minutes, the boy would dart a keen appraising glance at the girl as if he were trying to attract her attention.

After dinner Joy cleared the dishes off the table and disappeared and Mrs. Hopewell was left to talk with him. He told her again about his childhood and his father's accident and about various things that had happened to him. Every five minutes or so she would stifle a yawn. He sat for two hours until finally she told him she must go because she had an appointment in town. He packed his Bibles and thanked her and prepared to leave, but in the doorway he stopped and wrung her hand and said that not on any of his trips had he met a lady as nice as her and he asked if he could come again. She had said she would always be happy to see him.

Joy had been standing in the road, apparently looking at something in the distance, when he came down the steps toward her, bent to the side with his heavy valise. He stopped where she was standing and confronted her directly. Mrs. Hopewell could not hear what he said but she trembled to think what Joy would say to him. She could see that after a minute Joy said something and that then the boy began to speak again, making an excited gesture with his free hand. After a minute Joy said something else at which the boy began to speak once more. Then to her amazement, Mrs. Hopewell saw the two of them walk off together, toward the gate. Joy had walked all the way to the gate with him and Mrs. Hopewell could not imagine what they had said to each other, and she had not yet dared to ask.

Mrs. Freeman was insisting upon her attention. She had moved from the refrigerator to the heater so that Mrs. Hopewell had to turn and face her in order to seem to be listening. "Glynese gone out with Harvey Hill again last night," she said. "She had this sty."

"Hill," Mrs. Hopewell said absently, "is that the one who works in the garage?"

"Nome, he's the one that goes to chiropracter school," Mrs. Freeman said. "She had this sty. Been had it two days. So she says when he brought her in the other night he says, 'Lemme get rid of that sty for you,' and she says, 'How?' and he says, 'You just lay yourself down acrost the seat of that car and I'll show you.' So she done it and he popped her neck. Kept on a-popping it several times until she made him quit. This morning," Mrs. Freeman said, "she ain't got no sty. She ain't got no traces of a sty."

"I never heard of that before," Mrs. Hopewell said.

"He ast her to marry him before the Ordinary,"[3] Mrs. Freeman went on, "and she told him she wasn't going to be married in no *office*."

"Well, Glynese is a fine girl," Mrs. Hopewell said. "Glynese and Carramae are both fine girls."

"Carramae said when her and Lyman was married Lyman said it sure felt sacred to him. She said he said he wouldn't take five hundred dollars for being married by a preacher."

"How much would he take?" the girl asked from the stove.

"He said he wouldn't take five hundred dollars," Mrs. Freeman repeated.

"Well we all have work to do," Mrs. Hopewell said.

"Lyman said it just felt more sacred to him," Mrs. Freeman said. "The doctor wants Carramae to eat prunes. Says instead of medicine. Says them cramps is coming from pressure. You know where I think it is?"

"She'll be better in a few weeks," Mrs. Hopewell said.

"In the tube," Mrs. Freeman said. "Else she wouldn't be as sick as she is."

Hulga had cracked her two eggs into a saucer and was bringing them to the table along with a cup of coffee that she had filled too full. She sat down carefully and began to eat, meaning to keep Mrs. Freeman there by questions if for any reason she showed an inclination to leave. She could perceive her mother's eye on her. The first round-about question would be about the Bible salesman and she did not wish to bring it on. "How did he pop her neck?" she asked.

Mrs. Freeman went into a description of how he had popped her neck. She said he owned a '55 Mercury but that Glynese said she would rather marry a man with only a '36 Plymouth who would be married by a preacher. The girl asked what if he had a '32 Plymouth and Mrs. Freeman said what Glynese had said was a '36 Plymouth.

Mrs. Hopewell said there were not many girls with Glynese's common sense. She said what she admired in those girls was their common sense. She said that reminded her that they had had a nice visitor yesterday, a young man selling Bibles. "Lord," she said, "he bored me to death but he was so sincere and genuine I couldn't be rude to him. He was just good country people, you know," she said, "—just the salt of the earth."

"I seen him walk up," Mrs. Freeman said, "and then later—I seen him walk off," and Hulga could feel the slight shift in her voice, the slight insinuation, that he had not walked off alone, had he? Her face remained expressionless but the color rose into her neck and she seemed to swallow it down with the

3. Justice of the peace who performs the marriage ceremony in chambers rather than in public.

next spoonful of egg. Mrs. Freeman was looking at her as if they had a secret together.

"Well, it takes all kinds of people to make the world go 'round," Mrs. Hopewell said. "It's very good we aren't all alike."

"Some people are more alike than others," Mrs. Freeman said.

Hulga got up and stumped, with about twice the noise that was necessary, into her room and locked the door. She was to meet the Bible salesman at ten o'clock at the gate. She had thought about it half the night. She had started thinking of it as a great joke and then she had begun to see profound implications in it. She had lain in bed imagining dialogues for them that were insane on the surface but that reached below to depths that no Bible salesman would be aware of. Their conversation yesterday had been of this kind.

He had stopped in front of her and had simply stood there. His face was bony and sweaty and bright, with a little pointed nose in the center of it, and his look was different from what it had been at the dinner table. He was gazing at her with open curiosity, with fascination, like a child watching a new fantastic animal at the zoo, and he was breathing as if he had run a great distance to reach her. His gaze seemed somehow familiar but she could not think where she had been regarded with it before. For almost a minute he didn't say anything. Then on what seemed an insuck of breath, he whispered, "You ever ate a chicken that was two days old?"

The girl looked at him stonily. He might have just put this question up for consideration at the meeting of a philosophical association. "Yes," she presently replied as if she had considered it from all angles.

"It must have been mighty small!" he said triumphantly and shook all over with little nervous giggles, getting very red in the face, and subsiding finally into his gaze of complete admiration, while the girl's expression remained exactly the same.

"How old are you?" he asked softly.

She waited some time before she answered. Then in a flat voice she said, "Seventeen."

His smiles came in succession like waves breaking on the surface of a little lake. "I see you got a wooden leg," he said. "I think you're brave. I think you're real sweet."

The girl stood blank and solid and silent.

"Walk to the gate with me," he said. "You're a brave sweet little thing and I liked you the minute I seen you walk in the door."

Hulga began to move forward.

"What's your name?" he asked, smiling down on the top of her head.

"Hulga," she said.

"Hulga," he murmured, "Hulga. Hulga. I never heard of anybody name Hulga before. You're shy, aren't you, Hulga?" he asked.

She nodded, watching his large red hand on the handle of the giant valise.

"I like girls that wear glasses," he said. "I think a lot. I'm not like these people that a serious thought don't ever enter their heads. It's because I may die."

"I may die too," she said suddenly and looked up at him. His eyes were very small and brown, glittering feverishly.

"Listen," he said, "don't you think some people was meant to meet on account of what all they got in common and all? Like they both think serious thoughts and all?" He shifted the valise to his other hand so that the hand nearest her was free. He caught hold of her elbow and shook it a little. "I don't work on Saturday," he said. "I like to walk in the woods and see what Mother Nature is wearing. O'er the hills and far away. Pic-nics and things. Couldn't we go on a pic-nic tomorrow? Say yes, Hulga," he said and gave her a dying look as if he felt his insides about to drop out of him. He had even seemed to sway slightly toward her.

During the night she had imagined that she seduced him. She imagined that the two of them walked on the place until they came to the storage barn beyond the two back fields and there, she imagined, that things came to such a pass that she very easily seduced him and that then, of course, she had to reckon with his remorse. True genius can get an idea across even to an inferior mind. She imagined that she took his remorse in hand and changed it into a deeper understanding of life. She took all his shame away and turned it into something useful.

She set off for the gate at exactly ten o'clock, escaping without drawing Mrs. Hopewell's attention. She didn't take anything to eat, forgetting that food is usually taken on a picnic. She wore a pair of slacks and a dirty white shirt, and as an afterthought, she had put some Vapex on the collar of it since she did not own any perfume. When she reached the gate no one was there.

She looked up and down the empty highway and had the furious feeling that she had been tricked, that he had only meant to make her walk to the gate after the idea of him. Then suddenly he stood up, very tall, from behind a bush on the opposite embankment. Smiling, he lifted his hat which was new and wide-brimmed. He had not worn it yesterday and she wondered if he had bought it for the occasion. It was toast-colored with a red and white band around it and was slightly too large for him. He stepped from behind the bush still carrying the black valise. He had on the same suit and the same yellow socks sucked down in his shoes from walking. He crossed the highway and said, "I knew you'd come!"

The girl wondered acidly how he had known this. She pointed to the valise and asked, "Why did you bring your Bibles?"

He took her elbow, smiling down on her as if he could not stop. "You can never tell when you'll need the word of God, Hulga," he said. She had a moment in which she doubted that this was actually happening and then they began to climb the embankment. They went down into the pasture toward the woods. The boy walked lightly by her side, bouncing on his toes. The valise did not seem to be heavy today; he even swung it. They crossed half the pasture without saying anything and then, putting his hand easily on the small of her back, he asked softly, "Where does your wooden leg join on?"

She turned an ugly red and glared at him and for an instant the boy looked abashed. "I didn't mean you no harm," he said. "I only meant you're so brave and all. I guess God takes care of you."

"No," she said, looking forward and walking fast, "I don't even believe in God."

At this he stopped and whistled. "No!" he exclaimed as if he were too astonished to say anything else.

She walked on and in a second he was bouncing at her side, fanning with his hat. "That's very unusual for a girl," he remarked, watching her out of the corner of his eye. When they reached the edge of the wood, he put his hand on her back again and drew her against him without a word and kissed her heavily.

The kiss, which had more pressure than feeling behind it, produced that extra surge of adrenalin in the girl that enables one to carry a packed trunk out of a burning house, but in her, the power went at once to the brain. Even before he released her, her mind, clear and detached and ironic anyway, was regarding him from a great distance, with amusement but with pity. She had never been kissed before and she was pleased to discover that it was an unexceptional experience and all a matter of the mind's control. Some people might enjoy drain water if they were told it was vodka. When the boy, looking expectant but uncertain, pushed her gently away, she turned and walked on, saying nothing as if such business, for her, were common enough.

He came along panting at her side, trying to help her when he saw a root that she might trip over. He caught and held back the long swaying blades of thorn vine until she had passed beyond them. She led the way and he came breathing heavily behind her. Then they came out on a sunlit hillside, sloping softly into another one a little smaller. Beyond, they could see the rusted top of the old barn where the extra hay was stored.

The hill was sprinkled with small pink weeds. "Then you ain't saved?" he asked suddenly, stopping.

The girl smiled. It was the first time she had smiled at him at all. "In my economy," she said, "I'm saved and you are damned but I told you I didn't believe in God."

Nothing seemed to destroy the boy's look of admiration. He gazed at her now as if the fantastic animal at the zoo had put its paw through the bars and given him a loving poke. She thought he looked as if he wanted to kiss her again and she walked on before he had the chance.

"Ain't there somewheres we can sit down sometime?" he murmured, his voice softening toward the end of the sentence.

"In that barn," she said.

They made for it rapidly as if it might slide away like a train. It was a large two-story barn, cool and dark inside. The boy pointed up the ladder that led into the loft and said, "It's too bad we can't go up there."

"Why can't we?" she asked.

"Yer leg," he said reverently.

The girl gave him a contemptuous look and putting both hands on the ladder, she climbed it while he stood below, apparently awestruck. She pulled herself expertly through the opening and then looked down at him and said, "Well, come on if you're coming," and he began to climb the ladder, awkwardly bringing the suitcase with him.

"We won't need the Bible," she observed.

"You never can tell," he said, panting. After he had got into the loft, he was a few seconds catching his breath. She had sat down in a pile of straw. A wide sheath of sunlight, filled with dust particles, slanted over her. She lay back against a bale, her face turned away, looking out the front opening of the barn where hay was thrown from a wagon into the loft. The two pink-speckled hillsides lay back against a dark ridge of woods. The sky was cloudless and cold blue. The boy dropped down by her side and put one arm under her and the other over her and began methodically kissing her face, making little noises like a fish. He did not remove his hat but it was pushed far enough back not to interfere. When her glasses got in his way, he took them off of her and slipped them into his pocket.

The girl at first did not return any of the kisses but presently she began to and after she had put several on his cheek, she reached his lips and remained there, kissing him again and again as if she were trying to draw all the breath out of him. His breath was clear and sweet like a child's and the kisses were sticky like a child's. He mumbled about loving her and about knowing when he first seen her that he loved her, but the mumbling was like the sleepy fretting of a child being put to sleep by his mother. Her mind, throughout this, never stopped or lost itself for a second to her feelings. "You ain't said you loved me none," he whispered finally, pulling back from her. "You got to say that."

She looked away from him off into the hollow sky and then down at a black ridge and then down farther into what appeared to be two green swelling lakes. She didn't realize he had taken her glasses but this landscape could not seem exceptional to her for she seldom paid any close attention to her surroundings.

"You got to say it," he repeated. "You got to say you love me."

She was always careful how she committed herself. "In a sense," she began, "if you use the word loosely, you might say that. But it's not a word I use. I don't have illusions. I'm one of those people who see *through* to nothing."

The boy was frowning. "You got to say it. I said it and you got to say it," he said.

The girl looked at him almost tenderly. "You poor baby," she murmured. "It's just as well you don't understand," and she pulled him by the neck, facedown against her. "We are all damned," she said, "but some of us have taken off our blindfolds and see that there's nothing to see. It's a kind of salvation."

The boy's astonished eyes looked blankly through the ends of her hair. "Okay," he almost whined, "but do you love me or don'tcher?"

"Yes," she said and added, "in a sense. But I must tell you something. There mustn't be anything dishonest between us." She lifted his head and looked him in the eye. "I am thirty years old," she said. "I have a number of degrees."

The boy's look was irritated but dogged. "I don't care," he said. "I don't care a thing about what all you done. I just want to know if you love me or don'tcher?" and he caught her to him and wildly planted her face with kisses until she said, "Yes, yes."

"Okay then," he said, letting her go. "Prove it."

She smiled, looking dreamily out on the shifty landscape. She had seduced him without even making up her mind to try. "How?" she asked, feeling that he should be delayed a little.

He leaned over and put his lips to her ear. "Show me where your wooden leg joins on," he whispered.

The girl uttered a sharp little cry and her face instantly drained of color. The obscenity of the suggestion was not what shocked her. As a child she had sometimes been subject to feelings of shame but education had removed the last traces of that as a good surgeon scrapes for cancer; she would no more have felt it over what he was asking than she would have believed in his Bible. But she was as sensitive about the artificial leg as a peacock about his tail. No one ever touched it but her. She took care of it as someone else would his soul, in private and almost with her own eyes turned away. "No," she said.

"I known it," he muttered, sitting up. "You're just playing me for a sucker."

"Oh no no!" she cried. "It joins on at the knee. Only at the knee. Why do you want to see it?"

The boy gave her a long penetrating look. "Because," he said, "it's what makes you different. You ain't like anybody else."

She sat staring at him. There was nothing about her face or her round freezing-blue eyes to indicate that this had moved her; but she felt as if her heart had stopped and left her mind to pump her blood. She decided that for the first time in her life she was face to face with real innocence. This boy, with an instinct that came from beyond wisdom, had touched the truth about her. When after a minute, she said in a hoarse high voice, "All right," it was like surrendering to him completely. It was like losing her own life and finding it again, miraculously, in his.

Very gently he began to roll the slack leg up. The artificial limb, in a white sock and brown flat shoe, was bound in a heavy material like canvas and ended in an ugly jointure where it was attached to the stump. The boy's face and his voice were entirely reverent as he uncovered it and said, "Now show me how to take it off and on."

She took it off for him and put it back on again and then he took it off himself, handling it as tenderly as if it were a real one. "See!" he said with a delighted child's face. "Now I can do it myself!"

"Put it back on," she said. She was thinking that she would run away with him and that every night he would take the leg off and every morning put it back on again. "Put it back on," she said.

"Not yet," he murmured, setting it on its foot out of her reach. "Leave it off for a while. You got me instead."

She gave a cry of alarm but he pushed her down and began to kiss her again. Without the leg she felt entirely dependent on him. Her brain seemed to have stopped thinking altogether and to be about some other function that it was not very good at. Different expressions raced back and forth over her face. Every now and then the boy, his eyes like two steel spikes, would glance behind him where the leg stood. Finally she pushed him off and said, "Put it back on me now."

"Wait," he said. He leaned the other way and pulled the valise toward him and opened it. It had a pale blue spotted lining and there were only two Bibles in it. He took one of these out and opened the cover of it. It was hollow and contained a pocket flask of whiskey, a pack of cards, and a small blue box with printing on it. He laid these out in front of her one at a time in an evenly-spaced row, like one presenting offerings at the shrine of a goddess. He put the blue box in her hand. THIS PRODUCT TO BE USED ONLY FOR THE PREVENTION OF DISEASE, she read, and dropped it. The boy was unscrewing the top of the flask. He stopped and pointed, with a smile, to the deck of cards. It was not an ordinary deck but one with an obscene picture on the back of each card. "Take a swig," he said, offering her the bottle first. He held it in front of her, but like one mesmerized, she did not move.

Her voice when she spoke had an almost pleading sound. "Aren't you," she murmured, "aren't you just good country people?"

The boy cocked his head. He looked as if he were just beginning to understand that she might be trying to insult him. "Yeah," he said, curling his lip slightly, "but it ain't held me back none. I'm as good as you any day in the week."

"Give me my leg," she said.

He pushed it farther away with his foot. "Come on now, let's begin to have us a good time," he said coaxingly. "We ain't got to know one another good yet."

"Give me my leg!" she screamed and tried to lunge for it but he pushed her down easily.

"What's the matter with you all of a sudden?" he asked, frowning as he screwed the top on the flask and put it quickly back inside the Bible. "You just a while ago said you didn't believe in nothing. I thought you was some girl!"

Her face was almost purple. "You're a Christian!" she hissed. "You're a fine Christian! You're just like them all—say one thing and do another. You're a perfect Christian, you're . . ."

The boy's mouth was set angrily. "I hope you don't think," he said in a lofty indignant tone, "that I believe in that crap! I may sell Bibles but I know which end is up and I wasn't born yesterday and I know where I'm going!"

"Give me my leg!" she screeched. He jumped up so quickly that she barely saw him sweep the cards and the blue box into the Bible and throw the Bible into the valise. She saw him grab the leg and then she saw it for an instant slanted forlornly across the inside of the suitcase with a Bible at either side of its opposite ends. He slammed the lid shut and snatched up the valise and swung it down the hole and then stepped through himself.

When all of him had passed but his head, he turned and regarded her with a look that no longer had any admiration in it. "I've gotten a lot of interesting things," he said. "One time I got a woman's glass eye this way. And you needn't to think you'll catch me because Pointer ain't really my name. I use a different name at every house I call at and don't stay nowhere long. And I'll tell you another thing, Hulga," he said, using the name as if he didn't think much of it, "you ain't so smart. I been believing in nothing every since I was born!" and then the toast-colored hat disappeared down the hole and the girl was left, sitting on the straw in the dusty sunlight. When she turned her churning face toward the opening, she saw his blue figure struggling successfully over the green speckled lake.

Mrs. Hopewell and Mrs. Freeman, who were in the back pasture, digging up onions, saw him emerge a little later from the woods and head across the meadow toward the highway. "Why, that looks like that nice dull young man that tried to sell me a Bible yesterday," Mrs. Hopewell said, squinting. "He must have been selling them to the Negroes back in there. He was so simple," she said, "but I guess the world would be better off if we were all that simple."

Mrs. Freeman's gaze drove forward and just touched him before he disappeared under the hill. Then she returned her attention to the evil-smelling onion shoot she was lifting from the ground. "Some can't be that simple," she said. "I know I never could."

1955

ALLEN GINSBERG
1926–1997

" Hold back the edges of your gowns, Ladies, we are going through hell." William Carlos Williams's introduction to Allen Ginsberg's *Howl* (1956) was probably the most auspicious public welcome from one poet to another since, one hundred years before, the American Transcendentalist Ralph Waldo Emerson had hailed the unknown Walt Whitman in a letter that Whitman used as a preface to the second edition of *Leaves of Grass*. *Howl* combined apocalyptic criticism of the dull, prosperous Eisenhower years with exuberant celebration of an emerging counterculture. It was the best-known and most widely circulated book of poems of its time, and with its appearance Ginsberg became part of the history of publicity as well as the history of poetry. *Howl* and Jack Kerouac's novel *On the Road* (1957) were the pocket Bibles of the generation whose name Kerouac had coined—"Beat," with its punning overtones of "beaten down" and "beatified."

Ginsberg was the son of Louis Ginsberg, a poet and schoolteacher in New Jersey, and of Naomi Ginsberg, a Russian émigré, whose madness and eventual death her son memorialized in "Kaddish" (1959). His official education took place at Columbia University, but for him as for Kerouac the presence of William Burroughs in New York was equally influential. Burroughs (1914–1997), later the author of *Naked Lunch* (1959), one of the most inventive experiments in American prose, was at that time a drug addict about to embark on an expatriate life in Mexico and Tangier. He helped Ginsberg discover modern writers: Kafka, Yeats, Céline, Rimbaud. Ginsberg responded to Burroughs's liberated kind of life, to his comic-apocalyptic view of American society, and to his bold literary use of autobiography, as when writing about his own experience with addicts and addiction in *Junkie*, whose chapters Ginsberg was reading in manuscript form in 1950.

Ginsberg's New York career has passed into mythology for a generation of poets and readers. In 1945, his sophomore year, he was expelled from Columbia: he had sketched some obscene drawings and phrases in the dust of his dormitory window to draw the attention of a neglectful cleaning woman to the grimy state of his room. Then, living periodically with Burroughs and Kerouac, he shipped out for short trips as a messman on merchant tankers and worked in addition as a welder, a night porter, and a dishwasher.

One summer, in a Harlem apartment, Ginsberg underwent what he always represented as the central conversion experience of his life. He had an "auditory vision" of the English poet William Blake reciting his poems: first "Ah! Sunflower," and then a few minutes later the same oracular voice intoning "The Sick Rose." It was "like hearing the doom of the whole universe, and at the same time the inevitable beauty of that doom." Ginsberg was convinced that the presence of "this big god over all . . . and that the whole purpose of being born was to wake up to Him."

Ginsberg eventually finished Columbia in 1948 with high grades but under a legal cloud. Herbert Huncke, a colorful but irresponsible addict friend, had been using Ginsberg's apartment as a storage depot for the goods he stole to support his drug habit. To avoid prosecution as an accomplice, Ginsberg had to plead insanity and spent eight months in the Columbia Psychiatric Institute.

After more odd jobs and considerable success as a market researcher in San Francisco, Ginsberg left the straight, nine-to-five world for good. He was drawn to San Francisco, he said, by its "long honorable . . . tradition of Bohemian—Buddhist— Wobbly [the I.W.W., an early radical labor movement]—mystical—anarchist social

Ginsberg reading *Howl* in New York City in 1966, nine years after the court ruling finding it of redeeming social value and declaring it not obscene.

involvement." In the years after 1954 he met San Francisco poets such as Robert Duncan, Kenneth Rexroth, Gary Snyder (who was studying Chinese and Japanese at Berkeley), and Lawrence Ferlinghetti, whose City Lights Bookshop became the publisher of *Howl*. The night Ginsberg read the new poem aloud at the Six Gallery has been called "the birth trauma of the Beat Generation."

The spontaneity of surface in *Howl* conceals but grows out of Ginsberg's care and self-consciousness about rhythm and meter. Under the influence of William Carlos Williams, who had befriended him in Paterson after he left the mental hospital, Ginsberg had started carrying around a notebook to record the rhythms of voices around him. Kerouac's *On the Road* gave him further examples of "frank talk" and, in addition, of an "oceanic" prose "sometimes as sublime as epic line." Under Kerouac's influence Ginsberg began the long tumbling lines that were to become his trademark. He carefully explained that all of *Howl and Other Poems* was an experiment in what could be done with the long line, the longer unit of breath that seemed natural for him. "My feeling is for a big long clanky statement," one that accommodates "not the way you would *say* it, a thought, but the way you would think it—i.e., we think rapidly, in visual images as well as words, and if each successive thought were transcribed in its confusion . . . you get a slightly different prosody than if you were talking slowly."

Ginsberg learned the long line as well from biblical rhetoric, from the eighteenth-century English poet Christopher Smart, and above all, from Whitman and Blake. His first book pays tribute to both of these latter poets. "A Supermarket in California," with its movement from exclamations to sad questioning, is Ginsberg's melancholy reminder of what has become, after a century, of Whitman's vision of American plenty. In "Sunflower Sutra" he celebrates the battered nobility beneath our industrial "skin of grime." Ginsberg at his best gives a sense of doom and beauty, whether in the denunciatory impatient prophecies of *Howl* or in the catalog of suffering in "Kaddish." His disconnected phrases can accumulate as narrative shrieks or, at other moments, can build as a litany of praise.

By the end of the 1960s Ginsberg was widely known and widely traveled. He had conducted publicly his own pursuit of inner peace during a long stay with Buddhist instructors in India and at home served as a kind of guru for many young people disoriented by the Vietnam War. Ginsberg read his poetry and held "office hours" in universities all over America, a presence at everything from "be-ins"—mass outdoor festivals of chanting, costumes, and music—to antiwar protests. He was a gentle and persuasive presence at hearings for many kinds of reform: revision of severe drug laws and laws against homosexuality. Ginsberg had lived for years with the poet Peter Orlovsky and wrote frankly about their relationship. His poems record his drug experiences as well, and "The Change," written in Japan in 1963, marks his decision to keep away from what he considered the nonhuman domination of drugs and to lay new stress on "living in and inhabiting the human form."

In "The Fall of America" (1972) Ginsberg turned to "epic," a poem including history and registering the ups and downs of his travels across the United States. These "transit" poems sometimes seem like tape-recorded random lists of sights, sounds, and names, but at their best they give a sense of how far America has fallen, by measuring the provisional and changing world of nuclear America against the traces of nature still visible in our landscape and place-names. With Ginsberg's death, contemporary American poetry lost one of its most definitive and revolutionary figures. Happily, the poems endure.

Howl

for Carl Solomon[1]

I

I saw the best minds of my generation destroyed by madness, starving
    hysterical naked,
dragging themselves through the negro streets at dawn looking for an angry
    fix,
angelheaded hipsters burning for the ancient heavenly connection[2] to the
    starry dynamo in the machinery of night,
who poverty and tatters and hollow-eyed and high sat up smoking in the
    supernatural darkness of cold-water flats floating across the tops of
    cities contemplating jazz,
who bared their brains to Heaven under the El and saw Mohammedan[3]
    angels staggering on tenement roofs illuminated,   5
who passed through universities with radiant cool eyes hallucinating
    Arkansas and Blake-light[4] tragedy among the scholars of war,
who were expelled from the academies for crazy & publishing obscene odes
    on the windows of the skull,

---

1. Ginsberg met Solomon (b. 1928) while both were patients in the Columbia Psychiatric Institute in 1949 and called him "an intuitive Bronx Dadaist and prose-poet." Many details in "Howl" come from the "apocryphal history" that Solomon told Ginsberg in 1949. In "More Mishaps" (1968) Solomon admits that these adventures were "compounded partly of truth, but for the most [of] raving self-justification, crypto-bohemian boasting . . . effeminate prancing and esoteric aphorisms."

2. In one sense a person who can supply drugs.
3. An English term for a Muslim, commonly used in Western literature until the mid-twentieth century; now considered offensive by many Muslims because it implies that they worship the prophet Mohammed (or Muhammad) in the same way that Christians worship Christ. "The El": the elevated railway in New York City; also a Hebrew word for God.
4. Refers to Ginsberg's apocalyptic vision of the English poet William Blake (1757–1827).

who cowered in unshaven rooms in underwear, burning their money in
    wastebaskets and listening to the Terror through the wall,

who got busted in their pubic beards returning through Laredo with a belt
    of marijuana for New York,

who ate fire in paint hotels or drank turpentine in Paradise Alley,[5] death, or
    purgatoried their torsos night after night   10

with dreams, with drugs, with waking nightmares, alcohol and cock and
    endless balls,

incomparable blind streets of shuddering cloud and lightning in the mind
    leaping toward poles of Canada & Paterson,[6] illuminating all the
    motionless world of Time between,

Peyote solidities of halls, backyard green tree cemetery dawns, wine
    drunkenness over the rooftops, storefront boroughs of teahead joyride
    neon blinking traffic light, sun and moon and tree vibrations in the
    roaring winter dusks of Brooklyn, ashcan rantings and kind king light
    of mind,

who chained themselves to subways for the endless ride from Battery to
    holy Bronx[7] on benzedrine until the noise of wheels and children
    brought them down shuddering mouth-wracked and battered bleak of
    brain all drained of brilliance in the drear light of Zoo,

who sank all night in submarine light of Bickford's floated out and sat
    through the stale beer afternoon in desolate Fugazzi's,[8] listening to the
    crack of doom on the hydrogen jukebox,   15

who talked continuously seventy hours from park to pad to bar to Bellevue[9]
    to museum to the Brooklyn Bridge,

a lost battalion of platonic conversationalists jumping down the stoops off
    fire escapes off windowsills off Empire State out of the moon,

yacketayakking screaming vomiting whispering facts and memories and
    anecdotes and eyeball kicks and shocks of hospitals and jails and wars,

whole intellects disgorged in total recall for seven days and nights with
    brilliant eyes, meat for the Synagogue cast on the pavement,

who vanished into nowhere Zen New Jersey leaving a trail of ambiguous
    picture postcards of Atlantic City Hall,   20

suffering Eastern sweats and Tangerian bone-grindings and migraines of
    China[1] under junk-withdrawal in Newark's bleak furnished room,

who wandered around and around at midnight in the railroad yard
    wondering where to go, and went, leaving no broken hearts,

who lit cigarettes in boxcars boxcars boxcars racketing through snow
    toward lonesome farms in grandfather night,

who studied Plotinus Poe St. John of the Cross[2] telepathy and bop kaballah[3]
    because the cosmos instinctively vibrated at their feet in Kansas,

who loned it through the streets of Idaho seeking visionary indian angels
    who were visionary indian angels,   25

---

5. A tenement courtyard in New York's East Village; setting of Kerouac's *The Subterraneans* (1958).

6. Ginsberg's hometown; also the town celebrated by William Carlos Williams in his long poem *Paterson* (1946–58).

7. Opposite ends of a New York subway line running from the Battery (the southern tip of Manhattan) to the Bronx Zoo as its northern terminus.

8. New York bar that was a hipster hangout in the 1950s and 1960s. "Bickford's": a line of restaurants and cafeterias in the New York area from the 1920s to the 1960s.

9. New York public hospital to which psychiatric patients may be committed.

1. African and Asian sources of drugs.

2. Spanish visionary and poet (1542–1591), author of *The Dark Night of the Soul*. Plotinus (205–270), visionary Roman philosopher. Edgar Allan Poe (1809–1849), American poet and author of supernatural tales.

3. A mystical tradition of interpreting Hebrew scripture. "Bop": jazz style of the 1940s.

who thought they were only mad when Baltimore gleamed in supernatural
    ecstasy,

who jumped in limousines with the Chinaman of Oklahoma on the impulse
    of winter midnight streetlight smalltown rain,

who lounged hungry and lonesome through Houston seeking jazz or sex or
    soup, and followed the brilliant Spaniard to converse about America
    and Eternity, a hopeless task, and so took ship to Africa,

who disappeared into the volcanoes of Mexico leaving behind nothing but
    the shadow of dungarees and the lava and ash of poetry scattered in
    fireplace Chicago,

who reappeared on the West Coast investigating the FBI in beards and
    shorts with big pacifist eyes sexy in their dark skin passing out
    incomprehensible leaflets,   30

who burned cigarette holes in their arms protesting the narcotic tobacco
    haze of Capitalism,

who distributed Supercommunist pamphlets in Union Square weeping and
    undressing while the sirens of Los Alamos[4] wailed them down, and
    wailed down Wall,[5] and the Staten Island ferry also wailed,

who broke down crying in white gymnasiums naked and trembling before
    the machinery of other skeletons,

who bit detectives in the neck and shrieked with delight in policecars for
    committing no crime but their own wild cooking pederasty and
    intoxication,

who howled on their knees in the subway and were dragged off the roof
    waving genitals and manuscripts,   35

who let themselves be fucked in the ass by saintly motorcyclists, and
    screamed with joy,

who blew and were blown by those human seraphim, the sailors, caresses
    of Atlantic and Caribbean love,

who balled in the morning in the evenings in rosegardens and the grass of
    public parks and cemeteries scattering their semen freely to whomever
    come who may,

who hiccupped endlessly trying to giggle but wound up with a sob behind a
    partition in a Turkish Bath when the blonde & naked angel came to
    pierce them with a sword,[6]

who lost their loveboys to the three old shrews of fate[7] the one eyed shrew
    of the heterosexual dollar the one eyed shrew that winks out of the
    womb and the one eyed shrew that does nothing but sit on her ass and
    snip the intellectual golden threads of the craftsman's loom,   40

who copulated ecstatic and insatiate with a bottle of beer a sweetheart a
    package of cigarettes a candle and fell off the bed, and continued
    along the floor and down the hall and ended fainting on the wall with
    a vision of ultimate cunt and come eluding the last gyzym of
    consciousness,

who sweetened the snatches of a million girls trembling in the sunset, and
    were red eyed in the morning but prepared to sweeten the snatch of
    the sunrise, flashing buttocks under barns and naked in the lake,

---

4. New Mexico center for the development of the atomic bomb. In New York in the 1930s Union Square was a gathering place for radical speakers.
5. Wall Street; but also alludes to the Wailing Wall, a place of public lamentation in Jerusalem.
6. An allusion to *The Ecstasy of St. Teresa*, a sculpture by Lorenzo Bernini (1598–1680) based on St. Teresa of Ávila's (1515–1582) distinctly erotic description of a religious vision.
7. In Greek mythology goddesses who determine a mortal's life by spinning out a length of thread and cutting it at the time of death.

who went out whoring through Colorado in myriad stolen nightcars, N.C.,[8] secret hero of these poems, cocksman and Adonis of Denver—joy to the memory of his innumerable lays of girls in empty lots & diner backyards, moviehouses' rickety rows, on mountaintops in caves or with gaunt waitresses in familiar roadside lonely petticoat upliftings & especially secret gas-station solipsisms of johns, & hometown alleys too,

who faded out in vast sordid movies, were shifted in dreams, woke on a sudden Manhattan, and picked themselves up out of basements hungover with heartless Tokay[9] and horrors of Third Avenue iron dreams & stumbled to unemployment offices,

who walked all night with their shoes full of blood on the snowbank docks waiting for a door in the East River to open to a room full of steamheat and opium,   45

who created great suicidal dramas on the apartment cliff-banks of the Hudson under the wartime blue floodlight of the moon & their heads shall be crowned with laurel in oblivion,

who ate the lamb stew of the imagination or digested the crab at the muddy bottom of the rivers of Bowery,[1]

who wept at the romance of the streets with their pushcarts full of onions and bad music,

who sat in boxes breathing in the darkness under the bridge, and rose up to build harpsichords in their lofts,

who coughed on the sixth floor of Harlem crowned with flame under the tubercular sky surrounded by orange crates of theology,   50

who scribbled all night rocking and rolling over lofty incantations which in the yellow morning were stanzas of gibberish,

who cooked rotten animals lung heart feet tail borsht & tortillas dreaming of the pure vegetable kingdom,

who plunged themselves under meat trucks looking for an egg,

who threw their watches off the roof to cast their ballot for Eternity outside of Time, & alarm clocks fell on their heads every day for the next decade,

who cut their wrists three times successively unsuccessfully, gave up and were forced to open antique stores where they thought they were growing old and cried,   55

who were burned alive in their innocent flannel suits on Madison Avenue[2] amid blasts of leaden verse & the tanked-up clatter of the iron regiments of fashion & the nitroglycerine shrieks of the fairies of advertising & the mustard gas of sinister intelligent editors, or were run down by the drunken taxicabs of Absolute Reality,

who jumped off the Brooklyn Bridge this actually happened and walked away unknown and forgotten into the ghostly daze of Chinatown soup alleyways & firetrucks, not even one free beer,

who sang out of their windows in despair, fell out of the subway window, jumped in the filthy Passaic,[3] leaped on negroes, cried all over the street, danced on broken wineglasses barefoot smashed phonograph records of nostalgic European 1930's German jazz finished the

---

8. Neal Cassady, hip companion of Jack Kerouac and the original Dean Moriarty, one of the leading figures in *On the Road*.
9. A naturally sweet wine made in Hungary.
1. Southern extension of Third Avenue in New York City; traditional haunt of derelicts and alcoholics.
2. Center of New York advertising agencies.
3. River flowing past Paterson, New Jersey.

whiskey and threw up groaning into the bloody toilet, moans in their
    ears and the blast of colossal steamwhistles,
who barreled down the highways of the past journeying to each oth-
    er's hotrod-Golgotha[4] jail-solitude watch or Birmingham jazz
    incarnation,
who drove crosscountry seventytwo hours to find out if I had a vision or you
    had a vision or he had a vision to find out Eternity,   60
who journeyed to Denver, who died in Denver, who came back to Denver &
    waited in vain, who watched over Denver & brooded & loned in
    Denver and finally went away to find out the Time, & now Denver is
    lonesome for her heroes,
who fell on their knees in hopeless cathedrals praying for each other's
    salvation and light and breasts, until the soul illuminated its hair for a
    second,
who crashed through their minds in jail waiting for impossible criminals
    with golden heads and the charm of reality in their hearts who sang
    sweet blues to Alcatraz,
who retired to Mexico to cultivate a habit, or Rocky Mount to tender
    Buddha or Tangiers to boys or Southern Pacific to the black
    locomotive or Harvard to Narcissus to Woodlawn[5] to the daisychain or
    grave,
who demanded sanity trials accusing the radio of hypnotism & were left
    with their insanity & their hands & a hung jury,   65
who threw potato salad at CCNY lecturers on Dadaism[6] and subsequently
    presented themselves on the granite steps of the madhouse with
    shaven heads and harlequin speech of suicide, demanding
    instantaneous lobotomy,
and who were given instead the concrete void of insulin metrasol electricity
    hydrotherapy psychotherapy occupational therapy pingpong &
    amnesia,
who in humorless protest overturned only one symbolic pingpong table,
    resting briefly in catatonia,
returning years later truly bald except for a wig of blood, and tears and
    fingers, to the visible madman doom of the wards of the madtowns of
    the East,
Pilgrim State's Rockland's and Greystone's[7] foetid halls, bickering with the
    echoes of the soul, rocking and rolling in the midnight solitude-bench
    dolmen-realms of love, dream of life a nightmare, bodies turned to
    stone as heavy as the moon,   70
with mother finally*******, and the last fantastic book flung out of the
    tenement window, and the last door closed at 4 AM and the last
    telephone slammed at the wall in reply and the last furnished room
    emptied down to the last piece of mental furniture, a yellow paper rose
    twisted on a wire hanger in the closet, and even that imaginary,
    nothing but a hopeful little bit of hallucination—

---

4. The place in ancient Judea where Jesus was
believed to have been crucified; also known as
Calvary.
5. A cemetery in the Bronx. The Southern
Pacific is a railroad company. The references in
this line are to the lives of Kerouac, Cassidy, and
William Burroughs (an author and fellow Beat).
6. Artistic cult of absurdity (c. 1916–20).
"CCNY": City College of New York. This and the
following incidents probably derived from the

"apocryphal history of my adventures" related by
Solomon to Ginsberg.
7. Three psychiatric hospitals near New York.
Solomon was institutionalized at Pilgrim State
and Rockland; Ginsberg's mother, Naomi, was
permanently institutionalized at Greystone after
years of suffering hallucinations and paranoid
attacks. She died there in 1956, the year after
"Howl" was written.

ah, Carl,[8] while you are not safe I am not safe, and now you're really in the
    total animal soup of time—
and who therefore ran through the icy streets obsessed with a sudden flash
    of the alchemy of the use of the ellipse the catalog the meter & the
    vibrating plane,
who dreamt and made incarnate gaps in Time & Space through images
    juxtaposed, and trapped the archangel of the soul between 2 visual
    images and joined the elemental verbs and set the noun and dash of
    consciousness together jumping with sensation of Pater Omnipotens
    Aeterna Deus[9]
to recreate the syntax and measure of poor human prose and stand before
    you speechless and intelligent and shaking with shame, rejected yet
    confessing out the soul to conform to the rhythm of thought in his
    naked and endless head,   75
the madman bum and angel beat in Time, unknown, yet putting down
    here what might be left to say in time come after death,
and rose reincarnate in the ghostly clothes of jazz in the goldhorn shadow
    of the band and blew the suffering of America's naked mind for love
    into an eli eli lamma lamma sabacthani[1] saxophone cry that shivered
    the cities down to the last radio
with the absolute heart of the poem of life butchered out of their own
    bodies good to eat a thousand years.

II

What sphinx of cement and aluminum bashed open their skulls and ate up
    their brains and imagination?
Moloch![2] Solitude! Filth! Ugliness! Ashcans and unobtainable dollars!
    Children screaming under the stairways! Boys sobbing in armies! Old
    men weeping in the parks!   80
Moloch! Moloch! Nightmare of Moloch! Moloch the loveless! Mental
    Moloch! Moloch the heavy judger of men!
Moloch the incomprehensible prison! Moloch the crossbone soulless
    jailhouse and Congress of sorrows! Moloch whose buildings are
    judgment! Moloch the vast stone of war! Moloch the stunned
    governments!
Moloch whose mind is pure machinery! Moloch whose blood is running
    money! Moloch whose fingers are ten armies! Moloch whose breast is
    a cannibal dynamo! Moloch whose ear is a smoking tomb!
Moloch whose eyes are a thousand blind windows! Moloch whose
    skyscrapers stand in the long streets like endless Jehovahs! Moloch
    whose factories dream and croak in the fog! Moloch whose
    smokestacks and antennae crown the cities!
Moloch whose love is endless oil and stone! Moloch whose soul is
    electricity and banks! Moloch whose poverty is the specter of genius!
    Moloch whose fate is a cloud of sexless hydrogen! Moloch whose
    name is the Mind!   85

---

8. Solomon.
9. All-Powerful Father, Eternal God (Latin). An
allusion to a phrase used by the French painter
Paul Cézanne (1839–1906), in a 1904 letter
describing the effects of nature. In an interview,
Ginsberg compared his own method of sharply
juxtaposed images with Cézanne's foreshorten-
ing of perspective in landscape painting.

1. Christ's last words on the Cross: My God, my
God, why have you forsaken me? (Aramaic).
2. Ginsberg's own annotation in the facsimile edition of the poem reads: "'Moloch': or Molech, the
Canaanite fire god, whose worship was marked by
parents' burning their children as proprietary sacrifice. 'And thou shalt not let any of thy seed pass
through the fire to Molech' [Leviticus 18:21]."

Moloch in whom I sit lonely! Moloch in whom I dream Angels! Crazy in
    Moloch! Cocksucker in Moloch! Lacklove and manless in Moloch!
Moloch who entered my soul early! Moloch in whom I am a consciousness
    without a body! Moloch who frightened me out of my natural ecstasy!
    Moloch whom I abandon! Wake up in Moloch! Light streaming out of
    the sky!
Moloch! Moloch! Robot apartments! invisible suburbs! skeleton treasuries!
    blind capitals! demonic industries! spectral nations! invincible
    madhouses! granite cocks! monstrous bombs!
They broke their backs lifting Moloch to Heaven! Pavements, trees,
    radios, tons! lifting the city to Heaven which exists and is everywhere
    about us!
Visions! omens! hallucinations! miracles! ecstasies! gone down the
    American river!   90
Dreams! adorations! illuminations! religions! the whole boatload of
    sensitive bullshit!
Breakthroughs! over the river! flips and crucifixions! gone down the flood!
    Highs! Epiphanies! Despairs! Ten years' animal screams and suicides!
    Minds! New loves! Mad generation! down on the rocks of Time!
Real holy laughter in the river! They saw it all! the wild eyes! the holy yells!
    They bade farewell! They jumped off the roof! to solitude! waving!
    carrying flowers! Down to the river! into the street!

III

Carl Solomon! I'm with you in Rockland
    where you're madder than I am   95
I'm with you in Rockland
    where you must feel very strange
I'm with you in Rockland
    where you imitate the shade of my mother
I'm with you in Rockland   100
    where you've murdered your twelve secretaries
I'm with you in Rockland
    where you laugh at this invisible humor
I'm with you in Rockland
    where we are great writers on the same dreadful typewriter   105
I'm with you in Rockland
    where your condition has become serious and is reported on the radio
I'm with you in Rockland
    where the faculties of the skull no longer admit the worms of the
    senses
I'm with you in Rockland   110
    where you drink the tea of the breasts of the spinsters of Utica[3]
I'm with you in Rockland
    where you pun on the bodies of your nurses the harpies of the Bronx
I'm with you in Rockland
    where you scream in a straightjacket that you're losing the game of
    the actual pingpong of the abyss   115
I'm with you in Rockland
    where you bang on the catatonic piano the soul is innocent and
    immortal it should never die ungodly in an armed madhouse

---

3. Town in central New York.

I'm with you in Rockland
    where fifty more shocks will never return your soul to its body again
    from its pilgrimage to a cross in the void
I'm with you in Rockland   120
    where you accuse your doctors of insanity and plot the Hebrew
    socialist revolution against the fascist national Golgotha
I'm with you in Rockland
    where you will split the heavens of Long Island and resurrect your
    living human Jesus from the superhuman tomb
I'm with you in Rockland
    where there are twenty five thousand mad comrades all together
    singing the final stanzas of the Internationale[4]   125
I'm with you in Rockland
    where we hug and kiss the United States under our bedsheets the
    United States that coughs all night and won't let us sleep
I'm with you in Rockland
    where we wake up electrified out of the coma by our own souls'
    airplanes roaring over the roof they've come to drop angelic bombs
    the hospital illuminates itself   imaginary walls collapse   O skinny
    legions run outside   O starry-spangled shock of mercy the eternal
    war is here   O victory forget your underwear we're free
I'm with you in Rockland   130
    in my dreams you walk dripping from a sea-journey on the highway
    across America in tears to the door of my cottage in the Western night

San Francisco, 1955–56   1956

Footnote to Howl

Holy ! Holy ! Holy ! Holy ! Holy ! Holy ! Holy ! Holy ! Holy ! Holy ! Holy !
    Holy ! Holy ! Holy ! Holy !
The world is holy ! The soul is holy ! The skin is holy ! The nose is holy !
    The tongue and cock and hand and asshole holy !
Everything is holy ! everybody's holy ! everywhere is holy ! everyday is in
    eternity ! Everyman's an angel !
The bum's as holy as the seraphim ! the madman is holy as you my soul are
    holy !
The typewriter is holy the poem is holy the voice is holy the hearers are
    holy the ecstasy is holy !   5
Holy Peter holy Allen holy Solomon holy Lucien holy Kerouac holy Huncke
    holy Burroughs holy Gassady[1] holy the unknown buggered and
    suffering beggars holy the hideous human angels !

4. Former socialist and communist song; the official Soviet anthem until 1944.
1. All the figures mentioned here are Americans who shared or inspired a literary bohemia of the time. "Peter": Peter Orlovsky (1933–2010), Beat poet and Ginsberg's lover for four decades. "Allen": Ginsberg. "Solomon": Carl Solomon (1928–1993), whom Ginsberg met at the psychiatric hospital where Ginsberg's mother was being treated and to whom Ginsberg dedicated "Howl." "Lucien": Lucien Carr (1923–2005), one of the Beats and Ginsberg's roommate at Columbia University in the 1940s. "Kerouac": Jack Kerouac (1922–1969), novelist and founding figure of the Beat generation. "Huncke": Herbert Huncke (1915–1996), writer who influenced Ginsberg and who introduced Ginsberg and Kerouac to the term "beat." "Burroughs": William Burroughs (1914–1997), writer, spoken-word performer, and social critic most famous for the novel *Naked Lunch* (1959). "Cassady": Neal Cassady (1926–1968), an icon of the Beat generation and the inspiration for the character Dean Moriarty in Kerouac's best-known work, *On the Road* (1957).

Holy my mother in the insane asylum ! Holy the cocks of the grandfathers
    of Kansas !
Holy the groaning saxophone ! Holy the bop apocalypse ! Holy the
    jazzbands marijuana hipsters peace & junk & drums !
Holy the solitudes of skyscrapers and pavements ! Holy the cafeterias filled
    with the millions ! Holy the mysterious rivers of tears under the
    streets !
Holy the lone juggernaut ! Holy the vast lamb of the middle-class ! Holy the
    crazy shepherds of rebellion ! Who digs Los Angeles IS Los Angeles !   10
Holy New York Holy San Francisco Holy Peoria & Seattle Holy Paris Holy
    Tangiers Holy Moscow Holy Istanbul !
Holy time in eternity holy eternity in time holy the clocks in space holy the
    fourth dimension holy the fifth International holy the Angel in
    Moloch !

1955–56   1956, 1959

A Supermarket in California

What thoughts I have of you tonight, Walt Whitman,[1] for I walked down
the sidestreets under the trees with a headache self-conscious looking at
the full moon.
    In my hungry fatigue, and shopping for images, I went into the neon
fruit supermarket, dreaming of your enumerations!
    What peaches and what penumbras![2] Whole families shopping at night!
Aisles full of husbands! Wives in the avocados, babies in the tomatoes!—
and you, Garcia Lorca,[3] what were you doing down by the watermelons?

    I saw you, Walt Whitman, childless, lonely old grubber, poking among
the meats in the refrigerator and eyeing the grocery boys.
    I heard you asking questions of each: Who killed the pork chops? What
price bananas? Are you my Angel?   5
    I wandered in and out of the brilliant stacks of cans following you, and
followed in my imagination by the store detective.
    We strode down the open corridors together in our solitary fancy tasting
artichokes, possessing every frozen delicacy, and never passing the cashier.

    Where are we going, Walt Whitman? The doors close in an hour. Which
way does your beard point tonight?
    (I touch your book and dream of our odyssey in the supermarket and
feel absurd.)
    Will we walk all night through solitary streets? The trees add shade to
shade, lights out in the houses, we'll both be lonely.   10

    Will we stroll dreaming of the lost America of love past blue automo-
biles in driveways, home to our silent cottage?

---

1. American poet (1819–1892), author of *Leaves
of Grass*, against whose homosexuality and vision
of American plenty Ginsberg measures himself.
2. Partial shadows.

3. Federico García Lorca (1898–1936), Spanish
poet and dramatist and author of "A Poet in New
York," whose work is characterized by surrealist
and homoerotic inspiration.

Ah, dear father, graybeard, lonely old courage-teacher, what America
did you have when Charon quit poling his ferry and you got out on a
smoking bank and stood watching the boat disappear on the black waters
of Lethe?[4]

Berkeley, 1955   1956

4. Forgetfulness. In Greek mythology, one of the rivers of Hades, the Underworld. Charon was the
boatman who ferried the dead to Hades.

JOHN ASHBERY
b. 1927

John Ashbery has described his writing this way: "I think that any one of my poems
might be considered to be a snapshot of whatever is going on in my mind at the
time—first of all the desire to write a poem, after that wondering if I've left the
oven on or thinking about where I must be in the next hour." Ashbery has developed
a style hospitable to quicksilver changes in tone and attention. His work often
moves freely between different modes of discourse, between a language of popular
culture and commonplace experience and a heightened rhetoric often associated
with poetic vision. Ashbery's poems show an awareness of the various linguistic codes
(including clichés and conventional public speech) by which we live and through
which we define ourselves. This awareness includes an interest in what he has called
"prose voices," and he has often written in a way that challenges the supposed boundaries between poetry and prose.

Ashbery's poetry was not always so open to contradictory notions and impulses.
His early books rejected the mere surfaces of realism and the momentary in order
to get at "remoter areas of consciousness." The protagonist of "Illustration" (from
his first book, *Some Trees*) is a cheerful nun about to leave behind the irrelevancies
of the world by leaping from a skyscraper. Her act implies "Much that is beautiful
must be discarded / So that we may resemble a taller / impression of ourselves." To
reach the "remoter areas of consciousness," Ashbery tried various technical experiments. He used highly patterned forms such as the sestina in "Some Trees" and
"The Tennis Court Oath" (1962) not with any show of mechanical brilliance but to
explore: "I once told somebody that writing a sestina was rather like riding downhill
on a bicycle and having the pedals push your feet. I wanted my feet to be pushed
into places they wouldn't normally have taken."

Ashbery was born in Rochester, New York. He attended Deerfield Academy and
Harvard, from which he graduated in 1949. He received an M.A. in English from
Columbia in 1951. After a preliminary stay in France as a Fulbright scholar, he
returned in 1958 for eight years and was art critic for the European edition of the *New
York Herald Tribune* and reported the European shows and exhibitions for *Art News*
and *Arts International*. He returned to New York in 1965 to be executive editor of *Art
News*, a position he held until 1972. Since then he has been professor of English in the
creative writing program of Brooklyn College and art critic for *Newsweek* magazine.

Ashbery's interest in art played a formative role in his poetry. He is often associated
with Frank O'Hara, James Schuyler, and Kenneth Koch as part of the "New York
school" of poets. The name refers to their common interest in the New York school

of abstract painters of the 1940s and 1950s, some of whose techniques they wished to adapt to poetry. These painters avoided realism in order to stress the work of art as a representation of the creative act that produced it—as in the action paintings of Jackson Pollock. Ashbery's long poem *Self-Portrait in a Convex Mirror* gives as much attention to the rapidly changing feelings of the poet in the act of writing his poem as it does to the Renaissance painting that inspired him. The poem moves back and forth between the distracted energies that feed a work of art and the completed composition, which the artist feels as both a triumph and a falsification of complex feelings. Ashbery shares with O'Hara a sense of the colloquial brilliance of daily life in New York and sets this in tension with the concentration and stasis of art.

    Self-Portrait in a Convex Mirror (1975) was followed by *Houseboat Days* (1977), *As We Know* (1979), *Shadow Train* (1981), and *A Wave* (1984). His important book-length poem, *Flow Chart*, appeared in 1991 followed by collections of shorter poems, *And the Stars Were Shining* (1995), *Your Name Here* (2000) and *A Worldly Country* (2007). *Notes From the Air* (2007) is a collection of his later poems. His entertaining and provocative *Other Traditions* (2000) is a collection of his Norton Lectures on poetry at Harvard. Ashbery's work, especially his earlier, more highly experimental poems, has become particularly influential for a younger generation identified as "Language" poets, such as Charles Bernstein, Lyn Hejinian, Michael Palmer, and Susan Howe. They have been attracted to the linguistic playfulness of Ashbery's poetry and to its resistance to being read as a single, personal voice. Exposing and sometimes breaking through the world's dominant uses of language, Ashbery's poems open new possibilities of meaning: "We are all talkers / It is true, but underneath the talk lies / The moving and not wanting to be moved, the loose / Meaning, untidy and simple like the threshing floor" ("Soonest Mended").

Illustration

I

A novice[1] was sitting on a cornice
High over the city. Angels

Combined their prayers with those
Of the police, begging her to come off it.

One lady promised to be her friend.   5
"I do not want a friend," she said.

A mother offered her some nylons
Stripped from her very legs. Others brought

Little offerings of fruit and candy,
The blind man all his flowers. If any   10

Could be called successful, these were,
For that the scene should be a ceremony

Was what she wanted. "I desire
Monuments," she said. "I want to move

---

1. Student in the first stage of instruction to be a nun.

Figuratively, as waves caress 15
The thoughtless shore. You people I know

Will offer me every good thing
I do not want. But please remember

I died accepting them." With that, the wind
Unpinned her bulky robes, and naked 20

As a roc's[2] egg, she drifted softly downward
Out of the angels' tenderness and the minds of men.

II

Much that is beautiful must be discarded
So that we may resemble a taller

Impression of ourselves. Moths climb in the flame, 25
Alas, that wish only to be the flame:

They do not lessen our stature.
We twinkle under the weight

Of indiscretions. But how could we tell
That of the truth we know, she was 30

The somber vestment? For that night, rockets sighed
Elegantly over the city, and there was feasting:

There is so much in that moment!
So many attitudes toward that flame,

We might have soared from earth, watching her glide 35
Aloft, in her peplum[3] of bright leaves.

But she, of course, was only an effigy
Of indifference, a miracle

Not meant for us, as the leaves are not
Winter's because it is the end. 40

1956

Soonest Mended

Barely tolerated, living on the margin
In our technological society, we were always having to be rescued

2. Legendary bird of prey.
3. In ancient Greece a drapery about the upper part of the body.

On the brink of destruction, like heroines in *Orlando Furioso*[1]
Before it was time to start all over again.
There would be thunder in the bushes, a rustling of coils,   5
And Angelica, in the Ingres painting,[2] was considering
The colorful but small monster near her toe, as though wondering
      whether forgetting
The whole thing might not, in the end, be the only solution.
And then there always came a time when
Happy Hooligan[3] in his rusted green automobile   10
Came plowing down the course, just to make sure everything was O.K.,
Only by that time we were in another chapter and confused
About how to receive this latest piece of information.
Was it information? Weren't we rather acting this out
For someone else's benefit, thoughts in a mind   15
With room enough and to spare for our little problems (so they began
      to seem),
Our daily quandary about food and the rent and bills to be paid?
To reduce all this to a small variant,
To step free at last, minuscule on the gigantic plateau—
This was our ambition: to be small and clear and free.   20
Alas, the summer's energy wanes quickly.
A moment and it is gone. And no longer
May we make the necessary arrangements, simple as they are.
Our star was brighter perhaps when it had water in it.
Now there is no question even of that, but only   25
Of holding on to the hard earth so as not to get thrown off,
With an occasional dream, a vision: a robin flies across
The upper corner of the window, you brush your hair away
And cannot quite see, or a wound will flash
Against the sweet faces of the others, something like: 30
This is what you wanted to hear, so why
Did you think of listening to something else? We are all talkers
It is true, but underneath the talk lies
The moving and not wanting to be moved, the loose
Meaning, untidy and simple like a threshing floor.[4]   35

These then were some hazards of the course,
Yet though we knew the course *was* hazards and nothing else
It was still a shock when, almost a quarter of a century later,
The clarity of the rules dawned on you for the first time.
They were the players, and we who had struggled at the game   40
Were merely spectators, though subject to its vicissitudes
And moving with it out of the tearful stadium, borne on shoulders,
      at last.
Night after night this message returns, repeated
In the flickering bulbs of the sky, raised past us, taken away from us,
Yet ours over and over until the end that is past truth,   45

---

1. Fantastical epic poem by Ludovico Ariosto (1474–1533), whose romantic heroine Angelica is constantly being rescued from imminent perils such as monsters and storms at sea.
2. *Roger Delivering Angelica* (1819), a painting based on a scene from Ariosto, by French artist Jean-Auguste-Dominique Ingres (1780–1867).
3. The good-natured, simple title character of a popular comic strip of the 1920s and 1930s.
4. Used at harvest time to separate the wheat from the chaff, which is to be discarded.

The being of our sentences, in the climate that fostered them,
Not ours to own, like a book, but to be with, and sometimes
To be without, alone and desperate.
But the fantasy makes it ours, a kind of fence-sitting
Raised to the level of an esthetic ideal. These were moments, years,   50
Solid with reality, faces, namable events, kisses, heroic acts,
But like the friendly beginning of a geometrical progression
Not too reassuring, as though meaning could be cast aside some day
When it had been outgrown. Better, you said, to stay cowering
Like this in the early lessons, since the promise of learning   55
Is a delusion, and I agreed, adding that
Tomorrow would alter the sense of what had already been learned,
That the learning process is extended in this way, so that from this
          standpoint
None of us ever graduates from college,
For time is an emulsion,[5] and probably thinking not to grow up   60
Is the brightest kind of maturity for us, right now at any rate.
And you see, both of us were right, though nothing
Has somehow come to nothing; the avatars[6]
Of our conforming to the rules and living
Around the home have made—well, in a sense, "good citizens" of us,   65
Brushing the teeth and all that, and learning to accept
The charity of the hard moments as they are doled out,
For this is action, this not being sure, this careless
Preparing, sowing the seeds crooked in the furrow,
Making ready to forget, and always coming back   70
To the mooring of starting out, that day so long ago.

                                                            1970

Myrtle

How funny your name would be
if you could follow it back to where
the first person thought of saying it,
naming himself that, or maybe
some other persons thought of it   5
and named that person. It would
be like following a river to its source,
which would be impossible. Rivers have no source.
They just automatically appear at a place
where they get wider, and soon a real   10
river comes along, with fish and debris,
regal as you please, and someone
has already given it a name: St. Benno[1]
(saints are popular for this purpose) or, or
some other name, the name of his   15
long-lost girlfriend, who comes

---

5. A chemical solution in which the particles of
one liquid are suspended in another.
6. Incarnations.

1. St. Benno of Meissen (1010–1106), patron of
angling.

at long last to impersonate that river,
on a stage, her voice clanking
like its bed, her clothing of sand
and pasted paper, a piece of real technology,   20
while all along she is thinking, I can
do what I want to do. But I want to stay here.

1996

JAMES WRIGHT
1927–1980

"My name is James A. Wright, and I was born / Twenty-five miles from this infected grave, / In Martins Ferry, Ohio, where one slave / To Hazel-Atlas Glass became my father"; so James Wright introduced himself in an early poem, "At the Executed Murderer's Grave." The angry assertiveness in these lines suggests his embattled relations with an America he loves and hates. This America is symbolized for him by the landscape of Ohio, in particular by Martins Ferry, just across the Ohio River from Wheeling, West Virginia, the home of Wheeling Steel and of the glass factory where his father worked for fifty years. In Wright's work this landscape is harsh evidence of the way the social world has contaminated a natural world infinitely more beautiful and self-restoring. The same social world that destroys the landscape also turns its back on those whose lives meet failure or defeat, and Wright's deep knowledge of defeat and his anger at this exclusion lead him to the murderer's grave. It is not simply that Wright sympathizes with social outcasts, but rather, as Robert Hass acutely pointed out, "the suffering of other people, particularly the lost and the derelict, is actually a part of his own emotional life. It is what he writes from, not what he writes about." As a poet who writes out of loss, Wright is elegiac, memorializing a vanished beauty and lost hopes. So deep is his sense of loss that he will sometimes identify with anyone and anything that is scarred or wounded ("I am not a happy man by talent," he once said. "Sometimes I have been very happy, but characteristically I'm a miserable son of a bitch"). Any serious reading of his work has to contend with sorting out those poems in which this identification is unthinking and sentimental, poems where Wright suggests that all forms of suffering and defeat are equal and alike. What remains in some of his best work is a curiously tough-minded tenderness at work in his exploration of despair. He admires, for example, the sumac flourishing in the Ohio landscape, its bark so tough it "will turn aside hatchets and knife blades" ("The Sumac in Ohio").

When Wright finished high school, he joined the army. In 1948 he left the military to attend Kenyon College in Ohio on the G.I. Bill ("I applied to several schools in Ohio," he once said, "and they all said no except Kenyon College. So I went there"). He was lucky in his teachers; at Kenyon he studied with John Crowe Ransom and, after a Fulbright scholarship to the University of Vienna, he went to the University of Washington, where he studied with the poet Theodore Roethke and also became a close friend of Richard Hugo's. At Washington he wrote a Ph.D. dissertation on Charles Dickens and received the degree in 1959. Thereafter he became a teacher, first at the University of Minnesota, Minneapolis (1957–64), and later at Hunter College, New York (1966–80).

From both Ransom and Roethke, Wright learned poetic form. From Ransom in particular he took what he called "the Horatian ideal" of the carefully made, unified poem. Wright would later say that were he to choose a master, he would choose the Latin poet Horace, "who was able to write humorously and kindly in flawless verse." The Horatian impulse in Wright—restrained, formal, sometimes satirical—helps hold in check a deep-seated romanticism that idealizes nature and the unconscious. His first two books, *The Green Wall* (1957), chosen to appear in the Yale Younger Poets series, and *Saint Judas* (1959), are formal and literary in style although much of their subject matter (the murderer, the lunatic, a deaf child) might be called Romantic. Wright seems in these books closest to Thomas Hardy, Robert Frost, and Edwin Arlington Robinson. But in the 1960s, like a great many other American poets, he moved away from traditional forms, explored more open and improvisatory poetic structures, and began to depend heavily on what his fellow poet Robert Bly called "the deep image." Wright had been translating the work of Spanish poets often associated with surrealism—Pablo Neruda, César Vallejo, and Juan Ramón Jiménez—as well as the German Georg Trakl (whom he translated in collaboration with Bly), and he took from them, in part, a reliance on the power of a poetic image to evoke association deep within the unconscious. He followed his volume *The Branch Will Not Break* (1963) with two books, *Shall We Gather at the River* (1968) and *Two Citizens* (1974), in which he began to overwork certain images ("stone," "dark"), as if repetition were a substitute for clarity. Some of the poems in these books succeed in carrying us into areas of experience that resist the discursive, but the effect of a number of poems is to exclude conscious intelligence, to celebrate "whatever is not mind," as Robert Hass has pointed out. It is as if Wright responded to the scarred landscape outside (and inside) him by fleeing to an inwardness so deep it could not partake of thought or expression.

But Wright's love of clarity and form and his ability to see through pretensions (including his own) resurface in *Moments of the Italian Summer* (1976), *To a Blossoming Pear Tree* (1977), and his posthumous last collection, *This Journey* (1982). Restored to a unity of thinking and feeling, many of the poems in these books convey the flawed beauty of the world with a loving and witty tenderness. He often writes with particular feeling about creatures—finches, lizards, hermit crabs—whose liveliness and fragility touch him (in this and other regards his work has been important to the poet Mary Oliver). In "A Finch Sitting Out a Windstorm," his final portrait of the finch suggests admiration of its stubborness in the face of loss: "But his face is as battered / As Carmen Basilio's. / He never listens / To me."

Though the poems of his final book do not abandon the anger he feels thinking of the ruined landscapes of Ohio, the European setting of many of the poems extends his sense of ruin into a knowledge of how time chips away at all human creation, with or without the help of men and women. Although he had claimed to be constitutionally unhappy, the poems of *This Journey* suggest that before his death from cancer a deep happiness took him by surprise. We turn to Wright's work for its fierce understanding of defeat, for its blend of American speech rhythms with the formal music of poetry, and for the loveliness he finds in the imperfect and neglected. Accustomed to expect the worst, he had an enduring capacity to be astonished by this loveliness, as in this childhood memory of a trip to the icehouse with his father: "We stood and breathed the rising steam of that amazing winter, and carried away in our wagon the immense fifty-pound diamond, while the old man chipped us each a jagged little chunk and then walked behind us, his hands so calm they were trembling for us, trembling with exquisite care" ("The Ice House").

Autumn Begins in Martins Ferry, Ohio

In the Shreve High football stadium,
I think of Polacks nursing long beers in Tiltonsville,
And gray faces of Negroes in the blast furnace at Benwood,[1]
And the ruptured night watchman of Wheeling Steel,
Dreaming of heroes.   5

All the proud fathers are ashamed to go home.
Their women cluck like starved pullets,
Dying for love.

Therefore,
Their sons grow suicidally beautiful   10
At the beginning of October,
And gallop terribly against each other's bodies.

                                                            1963

To the Evening Star: Central Minnesota

Under the water tower at the edge of town
A huge Airedale ponders a long ripple
In the grass fields beyond.
Miles off, a whole grove silently
Flies up into the darkness.   5
One light comes on in the sky,
One lamp on the prairie.

Beautiful daylight of the body, your hands carry seashells.
West of this wide plain,
Animals wilder than ours   10
Come down from the green mountains in the darkness.
Now they can see you, they know
The open meadows are safe.

                                                            1963

A Blessing

Just off the highway to Rochester, Minnesota,
Twilight bounds softly forth on the grass.
And the eyes of those two Indian ponies
Darken with kindness.
They have come gladly out of the willows   5

---

1. A town south of Martins Ferry, where the Wheeling Steel Works are located. Tiltonsville is a town in easternmost Ohio, north of Martins Ferry.

To welcome my friend and me.
We step over the barbed wire into the pasture
Where they have been grazing all day, alone.
They ripple tensely, they can hardly contain their happiness
That we have come.   10
They bow shyly as wet swans. They love each other.
There is no loneliness like theirs.
At home once more,
They begin munching the young tufts of spring in the darkness.
I would like to hold the slenderer one in my arms,   15
For she has walked over to me
And nuzzled my left hand.
She is black and white,
Her mane falls wild on her forehead,
And the light breeze moves me to caress her long ear   20
That is delicate as the skin over a girl's wrist.
Suddenly I realize
That if I stepped out of my body I would break
Into blossom.

1963

ANNE SEXTON
1928–1974

Anne Sexton's first book of poems, *To Bedlam and Part Way Back* (1960), was published at a time when the label "confessional" came to be attached to poems more frankly autobiographical than had been usual in American verse. For Sexton the term is particularly apt. Although she had abandoned the Roman Catholicism into which she was born, her poems enact something analogous to preparing for and receiving religious absolution.

Sexton's confessions were to be made in terms more startling than the traditional Catholic images of her childhood. The purpose of her poems was not to analyze or explain behavior but to make it palpable in all its ferocity of feeling. Poetry "should be a shock to the senses. It should also hurt." This is apparent in both her themes and the ways in which she exhibits her subjects. Sexton writes about sex, illegitimacy, guilt, madness, and suicide. *To Bedlam* portrays her breakdown, her time in a mental hospital, her efforts at reconciliation with her daughter and husband when she returns. Her second book, *All My Pretty Ones* (1962), takes its title from Shakespeare's *Macbeth* and refers to the deaths of both her parents within three months of one another. Later books—*Live or Die* (1966), *The Death Notebooks* (1974), and *The Awful Rowing toward God* (1975; posthumous)—act out a debate about suicide and prefigure Sexton's taking of her own life. And yet, as the poet's tender address to her daughter in "Little Girl, My String Bean, My Lovely Woman" suggests, Sexton's work ranges beyond an obsession with death.

Sexton spoke of images as "the heart of poetry. Images come from the unconscious. Imagination and the unconscious are one and the same." Powerful images substantiate the strangeness of feelings and through them the poet attempts to redefine experiences so as to gain understanding, absolution, or revenge. Sexton's poems, poised between, as her titles suggest, life and death or "bedlam and part way back," are efforts at establishing a middle ground of self-assertion, substituting surreal images for the reductive versions of life visible to the exterior eye.

Sexton was born in 1928 in Newton, Massachusetts, and attended Garland Junior College. She came to poetry fairly late—when she was twenty-eight, after seeing the critic I. A. Richards lecturing about the sonnet on television. In the late 1950s she attended poetry workshops in the Boston area, including Robert Lowell's poetry seminars at Boston University. One of her fellow students was Sylvia Plath, whose suicide she commemorated in a poem, "Sylvia's Death." Sexton claimed that she was less influenced by Lowell's *Life Studies* than by W. D. Snodgrass's autobiographical *Heart's Needle* (1959), but certainly Lowell's support and the association with Plath left their mark on her and made it possible for her to publish. Although her career was relatively brief, she received several major literary prizes, including the Pulitzer Prize for *Live or Die* and an American Academy of Arts and Letters traveling fellowship. Her suicide came after a series of mental breakdowns.

The Starry Night

> That does not keep me from having a terrible
> need of—shall I say the word—religion.
> Then I go out at night to paint the stars.
> —Vincent Van Gogh[1]
> in a letter to his brother

The town does not exist
except where one black-haired tree slips
up like a drowned woman into the hot sky.
The town is silent. The night boils with eleven stars.
Oh starry starry night! This is how   5
I want to die.

It moves. They are all alive.
Even the moon bulges in its orange irons
to push children, like a god, from its eye.
The old unseen serpent swallows up the stars.   10
Oh starry starry night! This is how
I want to die:

into that rushing beast of the night,
sucked up by that great dragon, to split
from my life with no flag,   15
no belly,
no cry.

1962

---

1. Dutch painter (1853–1890) who in his thirties became insane and committed suicide. This letter to his brother—his only confidant—was written in September 1888. At the time he was painting *Starry Night on the Rhône*.

Sylvia's Death

for Sylvia Plath[1]

Oh Sylvia, Sylvia,
with a dead box of stones and spoons,

with two children, two meteors
wandering loose in the tiny playroom,

with your mouth into the sheet,   5
into the roofbeam, into the dumb prayer,

(Sylvia, Sylvia,
where did you go
after you wrote me
from Devonshire   10
about raising potatoes
and keeping bees?)

what did you stand by,
just how did you lie down into?

Thief!—   15
how did you crawl into,

crawl down alone
into the death I wanted so badly and for so long,

the death we said we both outgrew,
the one we wore on our skinny breasts,   20

the one we talked of so often each time
we downed three extra dry martinis in Boston,

the death that talked of analysts and cures,
the death that talked like brides with plots,

the death we drank to,   25
the motives and then the quiet deed?

(In Boston
the dying
ride in cabs,
yes death again,   30
that ride home
with *our* boy.)

---

1. American poet (1932–1963) and friend of Sexton's who committed suicide. Plath was living in London with her two children, having separated from her husband, the poet Ted Hughes, the previous year.

O Sylvia, I remember the sleepy drummer
who beat on our eyes with an old story,

how we wanted to let him come   35
like a sadist or a New York fairy

to do his job,
a necessity, a window in a wall or a crib,

and since that time he waited
under our heart, our cupboard,   40

and I see now that we store him up
year after year, old suicides

and I know at the news of your death,
a terrible taste for it, like salt.

(And me,   45
me too.
And now, Sylvia,
you again
with death again,
that ride home   50
with *our* boy.)

And I say only
with my arms stretched out into that stone place,

what is your death
but an old belonging,   55

a mole that fell out
of one of your poems?

(O friend,
while the moon's bad,
and the king's gone,   60
and the queen's at her wit's end
the bar fly ought to sing!)

O tiny mother,
you too!
O funny duchess!   65
O blonde thing!

February 17, 1963   1966

Little Girl, My String Bean, My Lovely Woman

My daughter, at eleven
(almost twelve), is like a garden.

Oh darling! Born in that sweet birthday suit
and having owned it and known it for so long,
now you must watch high noon enter—   5
noon, that ghost hour.
Oh, funny little girl—this one under a blueberry sky,
this one! How can I say that I've known
just what you know and just where you are?

It's not a strange place, this odd home   10
where your face sits in my hand
so full of distance,
so full of its immediate fever.
The summer has seized you,
as when, last month in Amalfi,[1] I saw   15
lemons as large as your desk-side globe—
that miniature map of the world—
and I could mention, too,
the market stalls of mushrooms
and garlic buds all engorged.   20
Or I think even of the orchard next door,
where the berries are done
and the apples are beginning to swell.
And once, with our first backyard,
I remember I planted an acre of yellow beans   25
we couldn't eat.

Oh, little girl,
my stringbean,
how do you grow?
You grow this way.   30
You are too many to eat.

I hear
as in a dream
the conversation of the old wives
speaking of *womanhood.*   35
I remember that I heard nothing myself.
I was alone.
I waited like a target.

Let high noon enter—
the hour of the ghosts.   40
Once the Romans believed
that noon was the ghost hour,
and I can believe it, too,

---

1. A seaport town in Campania, Italy.

under that startling sun,
and someday they will come to you,   45
someday, men bare to the waist, young Romans
at noon where they belong,
with ladders and hammers
while no one sleeps.

But before they enter   50
I will have said,
Your bones are lovely,
and before their strange hands
there was always this hand that formed.

Oh, darling, let your body in,   55
let it tie you in,
in comfort.
What I want to say, Linda,
is that women are born twice.

If I could have watched you grow   60
as a magical mother might,
if I could have seen through my magical transparent belly,
there would have been such ripening within:
your embryo,
the seed taking on its own,   65
life clapping the bedpost,
bones from the pond,
thumbs and two mysterious eyes,
the awfully human head,
the heart jumping like a puppy,   70
the important lungs,
the becoming—
while it becomes!
as it does now,
a world of its own,   75
a delicate place.

I say hello
to such shakes and knockings and high jinks,
such music, such sprouts,
such dancing-mad-bears of music,   80
such necessary sugar,
such goings-on!

Oh, little girl,
my stringbean,
how do you grow?   85
You grow this way.
You are too many to eat.

What I want to say, Linda,
is that there is nothing in your body that lies.
All that is new is telling the truth.   90

I'm here, that somebody else,
an old tree in the background.

Darling,
stand still at your door,
sure of yourself, a white stone, a good stone—   95
as exceptional as laughter
you will strike fire,
that new thing!

July 14, 1964   1966

ADRIENNE RICH
1929–2012

A childhood of reading and hearing poems taught Adrienne Rich to love the sound of words; her adult life taught her that poetry must "consciously situate itself amid political conditions." Over the years she conducted a passionate struggle to honor these parts of herself, in her best poems brilliantly mixing what she called "the poetry of the actual world with the poetry of sound." Extending a dialogue—between art and politics—that she first discovered in W. B. Yeats, whose poems she read as an undergraduate at Radcliffe, her work addresses with particular power the experiences of women, experiences often omitted from history and misrepresented in literature. Our culture, she wrote, is "split at the root" (to adapt the title of one of her essays); art is separated from politics, and the poet's identity as a woman is separated from her art. Rich's work seeks a language that will expose and integrate these divisions in the self and in the world. To do this she has written "directly and overtly as a woman, out of a woman's body and experience," for "to take women's existence seriously as theme and source for art, was something I had been hungering to do, needing to do, all my writing life."

Rich's first book was published in the Yale Younger Poets series, a prize particularly important for poets of her generation (others in the series have included James Wright, John Ashbery, and W. S. Merwin). W. H. Auden, the judge for the series in the 1950s, said of Rich's volume *A Change of World* (1951) that her poems "were neatly and modestly dressed . . . respect their elders, but are not cowed by them and do not tell fibs." Rich, looking back at that period from the vantage point of 1972, offered a more complicated sense of things. In an influential essay, "When We Dead Awaken," she recalled this period as one in which the chief models for poetry were men; from those models she first learned her craft. Even in reading the poetry of older women writers she found herself "looking . . . for the same things I found in the poetry of men . . . , to be equal was still confused with sounding the same." Twenty years and five volumes after *A Change of World*, she published *The Will to Change*, taking its title from the opening line of Charles Olson's *The Kingfishers*: "What does not change / is the will to change." The shift of emphasis in Rich's titles signaled an important turn in her work—from acceptance of change as a way of the world to an active sense of change as willed or desired.

In 1953 Rich married and in her twenties gave birth to three children within four years, "a radicalizing experience," she said. It was during this time that Rich experienced most severely that gap between what she called the "energy of creation" and the "energy of relation. . . . In those early years I always felt the conflict as a failure of love in myself." In her later work Rich came to identify the source of that conflict not as individual but as social, and in 1976 she published a book of prose, *Of Woman Born: Motherhood as Experience and Institution*, in which she contrasts the actual experience of bearing and raising children with the myths fostered by our medical, social, and political institutions.

With her third and fourth books, *Snapshots of a Daughter-in-Law* (1963) and *Necessities of Life* (1966), Rich began explicitly to treat problems that engaged her for the rest of her career. The title poem of *Snapshots* exposes the gap between literary versions of women's experience and the day-to-day truths of their lives.

Rich's poems aim at self-definition, at establishing boundaries of the self, but they also fight off the notion that insights remain solitary and unshared. Many of her poems proceed by means of intimate argument, sometimes with externalized parts of herself, as if to dramatize the way identity forms from the self's movement beyond fixed boundaries. In some of her most powerful later poems she pushes her imagination to recognize the multiple aspects of the self ("My selves," she calls them in her poem "Integrity"); in "Transcendental Etude," she writes: *"I am the lover and the loved, / home and wanderer, she who splits / firewood and she who knocks, a stranger / in the storm."* In other important later poems she carried out a dialogue with lives similar to and different from her own, as in the generous and powerful title poem of her collection *An Atlas of the Difficult World*. As she writes in the essay "Blood, Bread, and Poetry," in her development as a poet she came to feel "more and more urgently the dynamic between poetry as language and poetry as a kind of action, probing, burning, stripping, placing itself in dialogue with others."

After Rich and her husband moved to New York City in 1966 they became increasingly involved in radical politics, especially in the opposition to the Vietnam War. These concerns are reflected in the poems of *Leaflets* (1969) and *The Will to Change* (1971). Along with new subject matter came equally important changes in style. Rich's poems throughout the 1960s moved away from formal verse patterns to more jagged utterance. Devices such as sentence fragments, lines of varying length, and irregular spacing to mark off phrases emphasized a voice of greater urgency. With "Snapshots of a Daughter-in-Law" Rich began dating her poems, as if to mark each one as provisional, true to the moment but an instrument of passage, like an entry in a journal in which feelings are subject to continual revision.

In the 1970s Rich dedicated herself increasingly to feminism. Her work as a poet, a prose writer, and a public speaker took on a new unity and intensity. The continuing task was to see herself—as she put it in 1984—as neither "unique nor universal, but a person in history, a woman and not a man, a white and also Jewish inheritor of a particular Western consciousness, from the making of which most women have been excluded." She says in "Planetarium": "I am an instrument in the shape / of a woman trying to translate pulsations / into images for the relief of the body / and the reconstruction of the mind."

Rich's collections of prose—*Of Woman Born; On Lies, Secrets, and Silences: Selected Prose 1966–1978; Blood, Bread, and Poetry: Selected Prose 1979–1985, What Is Found There: Notebooks on Poetry and Politics* (1993), and *Arts of the Possible* (2001)—provide an important context for her poems. In these works she addresses issues of women's education and their literary traditions, Jewish identity, the relations between poetry and politics, and what she called "the erasure of lesbian existence." As a young woman Rich had been stirred by James Baldwin's comment that "any real change implies the breakup of the world as one has always known it, the loss of all that gave one an identity, the end of safety." In many ways her essays, like her poems, track the forces that resist such change and the human conditions that require it. Her essay "Compulsory Heterosexuality and Lesbian Existence" is an important example of such an examination.

Although Rich's individual poems do not consistently succeed in expressing a political vision without sacrificing "intensity of language," her work is best read as a continuous process. The books have an air of ongoing, pained investigation, almost scientific in intention but with an ardor suggested by their titles: *The Dream of a Common Language* (1977), *A Wild Patience Has Taken Me Thus Far* (1981), *The Fact of a Doorframe* (1984), and *Your Native Land, Your Life* (1986). Rich's later books, *Time's Power* (1989), *An Atlas of the Difficult World* (1991), *Dark Fields of the Republic: Poems 1991–1995* (1995), *Midnight Salvage: Poems 1995–1998* (1999), *Fox* (2001), and *The School Among the Ruins* (2004), demonstrate an ongoing power of language and deepening poetic vision. *Telephone Ringing in the Labyrinth* (2007) collects poems from 2004–2006. Most recently, Rich published *A Human Eye: Essays on Art in Society, 1997–2008, Tonight No Poetry Will Serve: Poems 2007–2010* and *Later Poems: Selected and New, 1971–2012.* Reading through her poems we may sometimes wish for more relaxation and playfulness, for a liberating comic sense of self almost never present in her work. What we find, however, is invaluable—a poet whose imagination confronts and resists the harsh necessities of our times and keeps alive a vision of what is possible: "a whole new poetry beginning here" ("Transcendental Etude").

Storm Warnings

The glass[1] has been falling all the afternoon,
And knowing better than the instrument
What winds are walking overhead, what zone
Of gray unrest is moving across the land,
I leave the book upon a pillowed chair   5
And walk from window to closed window, watching
Boughs strain against the sky

And think again, as often when the air
Moves inward toward a silent core of waiting,
How with a single purpose time has traveled   10
By secret currents of the undiscerned
Into this polar realm. Weather abroad
And weather in the heart alike come on
Regardless of prediction.

Between foreseeing and averting change   15
Lies all the mastery of elements
Which clocks and weatherglasses cannot alter.
Time in the hand is not control of time,
Nor shattered fragments of an instrument
A proof against the wind; the wind will rise,   20
We can only close the shutters.

I draw the curtains as the sky goes black
And set a match to candles sheathed in glass
Against the keyhole draught, the insistent whine
Of weather through the unsealed aperture.   25
This is our sole defense against the season;
These are the things that we have learned to do
Who live in troubled regions.

                                              1951

---

1. Barometer.

Snapshots of a Daughter-in-Law

1

You, once a belle in Shreveport,
with henna-colored hair, skin like a peachbud,
still have your dresses copied from that time,
and play a Chopin prelude
called by Cortot: *"Delicious recollections*   5
float like perfume through the memory."[1]

Your mind now, moldering like wedding-cake,
heavy with useless experience, rich
with suspicion, rumor, fantasy,
crumbling to pieces under the knife-edge   10
of mere fact. In the prime of your life.

Nervy, glowering, your daughter
wipes the teaspoons, grows another way.

2

Banging the coffee-pot into the sink
she hears the angels chiding, and looks out   15
past the raked gardens to the sloppy sky.
Only a week since They said: *Have no patience.*

The next time it was: *Be insatiable.*
Then: *Save yourself; others you cannot save.*
Sometimes she's let the tapstream scald her arm,   20
a match burn to her thumbnail,

or held her hand above the kettle's snout
right in the woolly steam. They are probably angels,
since nothing hurts her anymore, except
each morning's grit blowing into her eyes.   25

3

A thinking woman sleeps with monsters.[2]
The beak that grips her, she becomes. And Nature,
that sprung-lidded, still commodious
steamer-trunk of *tempora* and *mores*[3]
gets stuffed with it all: the mildewed orange-flowers,   30
the female pills, the terrible breasts
of Boadicea[4] beneath flat foxes' heads and orchids.

---

1. A remark made by Alfred Cortot (1877–1962), a well-known French pianist, in his *Chopin: 24 Preludes* (1930); he is referring specifically to Chopin's Prelude No. 7, Andantino, A Major.
2. A reference to W. B. Yeats's "Leda and the Swan," a poem about the rape of a maiden by Zeus in the form of a giant bird. The poem ends: "Did she put on his knowledge with his power / Before the indifferent beak could let her drop?"

3. Times and customs (Latin, literal trans.). This alludes perhaps to the Roman orator Cicero's famous phrase "O Tempora! O Mores!" ("Alas for the degeneracy of our times and the low standard of our morals!").
4. British queen in the time of the Emperor Nero; she led her people in a large, ultimately unsuccessful revolt against Roman rule. "Female pills": remedies for menstrual pain.

Two handsome women, gripped in argument,
each proud, acute, subtle, I hear scream
across the cut glass and majolica   35
like Furies[5] cornered from their prey:
The argument *ad feminam*,[6] all the old knives
that have rusted in my back, I drive in yours,
ma semblable, ma soeur![7]

4

Knowing themselves too well in one another: 40
their gifts no pure fruition, but a thorn,
the prick filed sharp against a hint of scorn . . .
Reading while waiting
for the iron to heat,
writing, *My Life had stood—a Loaded Gun*[8]—   45
in that Amherst pantry while the jellies boil and scum,
or, more often,
iron-eyed and beaked and purposed as a bird,
dusting everything on the whatnot every day of life.

5

Dulce ridens, dulce loquens,[9]   50
she shaves her legs until they gleam
like petrified mammoth-tusk.

6

When to her lute Corinna sings[1]
neither words nor music are her own;
only the long hair dipping   55
over her cheek, only the song
of silk against her knees
and these
adjusted in reflections of an eye.

Poised, trembling and unsatisfied, before   60
an unlocked door, that cage of cages,
tell us, you bird, you tragical machine—
is this *fertilisante douleur?*[2] Pinned down
by love, for you the only natural action,
are you edged more keen   65

---

5. Greek goddesses of vengeance. "Majolica": a
kind of earthenware with a richly colored glaze.
6. Feminine version of the Latin phrase *ad
hominem* (literally, "to the man"), referring to an
argument directed not to reason but to personal
prejudices and emotions.
7. The last line of Charles Baudelaire's French
poem "Au Lecteur" addresses *"Hypocrite
lecteur!—mon semblable—mon frère!"* (Hypocrite
reader, like me, my brother!); Rich here instead
addresses *"ma soeur"* (my sister). See also T. S.
Eliot, "The Waste Land," line 76.

8. *"Emily Dickinson, Complete Poems,* ed. T. H.
Johnson, 1960, p. 369" [Rich's note]; this is the
poem numbered 754 in the Johnson edition.
Amherst, Massachusetts, is the town where
Dickinson lived her entire life (1830–1886).
9. Sweetly laughing, sweetly speaking (Latin,
from Horace, *Odes,* 22.23–24).
1. First line of a lyric poem by Thomas Campion
(1567–1620) about the extent to which a courtier
is moved by Corinna's beautiful music.
2. Fertilizing (or life-giving) sorrow (French).

to prise the secrets of the vault? has Nature shown
her household books to you, daughter-in-law,
that her sons never saw?

7

"To have in this uncertain world some stay
which cannot be undermined, is   70
of the utmost consequence."[3]
                 Thus wrote
a woman, partly brave and partly good,
who fought with what she partly understood.
Few men about her would or could do more,   75
hence she was labeled harpy, shrew and whore.

8

"You all die at fifteen," said Diderot,[4]
and turn part legend, part convention.
Still, eyes inaccurately dream
behind closed windows blankening with steam.   80
Deliciously, all that we might have been,
all that we were—fire, tears,
wit, taste, martyred ambition—
stirs like the memory of refused adultery
the drained and flagging bosom of our middle years.   85

9

Not that it is done well, but
that it is done at all?[5] Yes, think
of the odds! or shrug them off forever.
This luxury of the precocious child,
Time's precious chronic invalid,—   90
would we, darlings, resign it if we could?
Our blight has been our sinecure:
mere talent was enough for us—
glitter in fragments and rough drafts.

Sigh no more, ladies.   95
            Time is male
and in his cups drinks to the fair.
Bemused by gallantry, we hear
our mediocrities over-praised,
indolence read as abnegation,   100

---

3. "From Mary Wollstonecraft, *Thoughts on the Education of Daughters*, London, 1787" [Rich's note]. Wollstonecraft (1759–1797), one of the first feminist thinkers, is best-known for her "Vindication of the Rights of Woman."
4. Denis Diderot (1713–1784), French philosopher, encyclopedist, playwright, and critic. "'You all die at fifteen': *'Vous mourez toutes à quinze ans,'* from the *Lettres à Sophie Volland*, quoted by Simone de Beauvoir in *Le Deuxième Sexe*, Vol. II, pp. 123–24" [Rich's note].
5. An allusion to Samuel Johnson's remark to James Boswell: "Sir, a woman's preaching is like a dog's walking on his hinder legs. It is not done well; but you are surprised to find it done at all" (July 31, 1763).

slattern thought styled intuition,
every lapse forgiven, our crime
only to cast too bold a shadow
or smash the mold straight off.

For that, solitary confinement,   105
tear gas, attrition shelling.
Few applicants for that honor.

                                    10

                          Well,
she's long about her coming, who must be
more merciless to herself than history.   110
Her mind full to the wind, I see her plunge
breasted and glancing through the currents,
taking the light upon her
at least as beautiful as any boy
or helicopter,[6]   115
                    poised, still coming,
her fine blades making the air wince

but her cargo
no promise then:
delivered   120
palpable
ours.

1958–60   1963

A Valediction Forbidding Mourning[1]

My swirling wants. Your frozen lips.
The grammar turned and attacked me.
Themes, written under duress.
Emptiness of the notations.

They gave me a drug that slowed the healing of wounds.   5

I want you to see this before I leave:
the experience of repetition as death
the failure of criticism to locate the pain
the poster in the bus that said:
my bleeding is under control.   10

---

6. "She comes down from the remoteness of
ages, from Thebes, from Crete, from Chichén-
Itzá; and she is also the totem set deep in the
African jungle; she is a helicopter and she is a
bird; and there is this, the greatest wonder of all:
under her tinted hair the forest murmur becomes
a thought, and words issue from her breasts"
(Simone de Beauvoir, *The Second Sex*, trans.
H. M. Parshley [New York, 1953], 729). (A translation of the passage from *Le Deuxième Sexe*,
Vol. II, 574, cited in French by Rich.)
1. Title of a famous poem by John Donne (1572–
1631) in which the English poet forbids his wife to
lament his departure for a trip to the Continent.

A red plant in a cemetery of plastic wreaths.

A last attempt: the language is a dialect called metaphor.
These images go unglossed: hair, glacier, flashlight.
When I think of a landscape I am thinking of a time.
When I talk of taking a trip I mean forever.   15
I could say: those mountains have a meaning
but further than that I could not say.

To do something very common, in my own way.

1970   1971

Diving into the Wreck

First having read the book of myths,
and loaded the camera,
and checked the edge of the knife-blade,
I put on
the body-armor of black rubber   5
the absurd flippers
the grave and awkward mask.
I am having to do this
not like Cousteau[1] with his
assiduous team   10
aboard the sun-flooded schooner
but here alone.

There is a ladder.
The ladder is always there
hanging innocently   15
close to the side of the schooner.
We know what it is for,
we who have used it.
Otherwise
it's a piece of maritime floss   20
some sundry equipment.

I go down.
Rung after rung and still
the oxygen immerses me
the blue light   25
the clear atoms
of our human air.
I go down.
My flippers cripple me,
I crawl like an insect down the ladder   30
and there is no one
to tell me when the ocean
will begin.

1. Jacques-Yves Cousteau (1910–1997), French underwater explorer and author.

First the air is blue and then
it is bluer and then green and then 35
black I am blacking out and yet
my mask is powerful
it pumps my blood with power
the sea is another story
the sea is not a question of power 40
I have to learn alone
to turn my body without force
in the deep element.

And now: it is easy to forget
what I came for 45
among so many who have always
lived here
swaying their crenellated fans
between the reefs
and besides 50
you breathe differently down here.

I came to explore the wreck.
The words are purposes.
The words are maps.
I came to see the damage that was done 55
and the treasures that prevail.
I stroke the beam of my lamp
slowly along the flank
of something more permanent
than fish or weed 60

the thing I came for:
the wreck and not the story of the wreck
the thing itself and not the myth
the drowned face[2] always staring
toward the sun 65
the evidence of damage
worn by salt and sway into this threadbare beauty
the ribs of the disaster
curving their assertion
among the tentative haunters. 70

This is the place.
And I am here, the mermaid whose dark hair
streams black, the merman in his armored body
We circle silently
about the wreck 75
we dive into the hold.
I am she: I am he

whose drowned face sleeps with open eyes
whose breasts still bear the stress
whose silver, copper, vermeil cargo lies 80

---

2. Referring to the ornamental female figurehead that formed the prow of many old sailing ships.

obscurely inside barrels
half-wedged and left to rot
we are the half-destroyed instruments
that once held to a course
the water-eaten log   85
the fouled compass

We are, I am, you are
by cowardice or courage
the one who find our way
back to this scene   90
carrying a knife, a camera
a book of myths
in which
our names do not appear.

1972   1973

Transcendental Etude[1]

for Michelle Cliff

This August evening I've been driving
over backroads fringed with queen anne's lace
my car startling young deer in meadows—one
gave a hoarse intake of her breath and all
four fawns sprang after her   5
into the dark maples.
Three months from today they'll be fair game
for the hit-and-run hunters, glorying
in a weekend's destructive power,
triggers fingered by drunken gunmen, sometimes   10
so inept as to leave the shattered animal
stunned in her blood. But this evening deep in summer
the deer are still alive and free,
nibbling apples from early-laden boughs
so weighted, so englobed   15
with already yellowing fruit
they seem eternal, Hesperidean[2]
in the clear-tuned, cricket-throbbing air.

Later I stood in the dooryard,
my nerves singing the immense   20
fragility of all this sweetness,
this green world already sentimentalized, photographed,
advertised to death. Yet, it persists
stubbornly beyond the fake Vermont
of antique barnboards glazed into discothèques,   25

1. "Etude": a piece of music played for the practice of a point of technique or a composition built
on technique but played for its artistic value.

2. I.e., like the golden apples of the tree guarded
by the Hesperides, daughters of Atlas, in Greek
mythology.

artificial snow, the sick Vermont of children
conceived in apathy, grown to winters
of rotgut violence,
poverty gnashing its teeth like a blind cat at their lives.
Still, it persists. Turning off onto a dirt road   30
from the raw cuts bulldozed through a quiet village
for the tourist run to Canada,
I've sat on a stone fence above a great, soft, sloping field
of musing heifers, a farmstead
slanting its planes calmly in the calm light,   35
a dead elm raising bleached arms
above a green so dense with life,
minute, momentary life—slugs, moles, pheasants, gnats,
spiders, moths, hummingbirds, groundhogs, butterflies—
a lifetime is too narrow   40
to understand it all, beginning with the huge
rockshelves that underlie all that life.

No one ever told us we had to study our lives,
make of our lives a study, as if learning natural history
or music, that we should begin   45
with the simple exercises first
and slowly go on trying
the hard ones, practicing till strength
and accuracy became one with the daring
to leap into transcendence, take the chance   50
of breaking down in the wild arpeggio
or faulting the full sentence of the fugue.[3]
—And in fact we can't live like that: we take on
everything at once before we've even begun
to read or mark time, we're forced to begin   55
in the midst of the hardest movement,
the one already sounding as we are born.
At most we're allowed a few months
of simply listening to the simple line
of a woman's voice singing a child   60
against her heart. Everything else is too soon,
too sudden, the wrenching-apart, that woman's heartbeat
heard ever after from a distance,
the loss of that ground-note echoing
whenever we are happy, or in despair.   65

Everything else seems beyond us,
we aren't ready for it, nothing that was said
is true for us, caught naked in the argument,
the counterpoint, trying to sightread
what our fingers can't keep up with, learn by heart   70
what we can't even read. And yet
it *is* this we were born to. We aren't virtuosi
or child prodigies, there are no prodigies

---

3. Musical piece characterized by the interweaving of several voices. "Arpeggio": production of a
chord's tones in succession.

in this realm, only a half-blind, stubborn
cleaving to the timbre, the tones of what we are 75
—even when all the texts describe it differently.

And we're not performers, like Liszt,[4] competing
against the world for speed and brilliance
(the 79-year-old pianist said, when I asked her
What makes a virtuoso?—Competitiveness.) 80
The longer I live the more I mistrust
theatricality, the false glamour cast
by performance, the more I know its poverty beside
the truths we are salvaging from
the splitting-open of our lives. 85
The woman who sits watching, listening,
eyes moving in the darkness
in rehearsing in her body, hearing-out in her blood
a score touched off in her perhaps
by some words, a few chords, from the stage: 90
a tale only she can tell.

But there come times—perhaps this is one of them—
when we have to take ourselves more seriously or die;
when we have to pull back from the incantations,
rhythms we've moved to thoughtlessly, 95
and disenthrall ourselves, bestow
ourselves to silence, or a severer listening, cleansed
of oratory, formulas, choruses, laments, static
crowding the wires. We cut the wires,
find ourselves in free-fall, as if 100
our true home were the undimensional
solitudes, the rift
in the Great Nebula.[5]
No one who survives to speak
new language, has avoided this: 105
the cutting-away of an old force that held her
rooted to an old ground
the pitch of utter loneliness
where she herself and all creation
seem equally dispersed, weightless, her being a cry 110
to which no echo comes or can ever come.

But in fact we were always like this,
rootless, dismembered: knowing it makes the difference.
Birth stripped our birthright from us,
tore us from a woman, from women, from ourselves 115
so early on
and the whole chorus throbbing at our ears
like midges, told us nothing, nothing

---

4. Franz Liszt (1811–1886), Hungarian composer
and pianist noted for his virtuoso performances.
5. A nebula is an immense body of rarefied gas
or dust in interstellar space. Rich may be referring to the Great Nebula in the Orion constellation or to a body of dark nebulae, usually called
the "Great Rift," which in photographs appears
to divide the Milky Way.

of origins, nothing we needed
to know, nothing that could re-member us.   120

Only: that it is unnatural,
the homesickness for a woman, for ourselves,
for that acute joy at the shadow her head and arms
cast on a wall, her heavy or slender
thighs on which we lay, flesh against flesh,   125
eyes steady on the face of love; smell of her milk, her sweat,
terror of her disappearance, all fused in this hunger
for the element they have called most dangerous, to be
lifted breathtaken on her breast, to rock within her
—even if beaten back, stranded against, to apprehend   130
in a sudden brine-clear thought
trembling like the tiny, orbed, endangered
egg-sac of a new world:
This is what she was to me, and this
is how I can love myself—   135
as only a woman can love me.

Homesick for myself, for her—as, after the heatwave
breaks, the clear tones of the world
manifest: cloud, bough, wall, insect, the very soul of light:
homesick as the fluted vault of desire   140
articulates itself: *I am the lover and the loved,*
home and wanderer, she who splits
firewood and she who knocks, a stranger
in the storm, two women, eye to eye
measuring each other's spirit, each other's   145
limitless desire,
                            a whole new poetry beginning here.

Vision begins to happen in such a life
as if a woman quietly walked away
from the argument and jargon in a room   150
and sitting down in the kitchen, began turning in her lap
bits of yarn, calico and velvet scraps,
laying them out absently on the scrubbed boards
in the lamplight, with small rainbow-colored shells
sent in cotton-wool from somewhere far away,   155
and skeins of milkweed from the nearest meadow—
original domestic silk, the finest findings—
and the darkblue petal of the petunia,
and the dry darkbrown lace of seaweed;
not forgotten either, the shed silver   160
whisker of the cat,
the spiral of paper-wasp-nest curling
beside the finch's yellow feather.
Such a composition has nothing to do with eternity,
the striving for greatness, brilliance—   165
only with the musing of a mind
one with her body, experienced fingers quietly pushing
dark against bright, silk against roughness,

pulling the tenets of a life together
with no mere will to mastery,   170
only care for the many-lived, unending
forms in which she finds herself,
becoming now the sherd of broken glass
slicing light in a corner, dangerous
to flesh, now the plentiful, soft leaf   175
that wrapped round the throbbing finger, soothes the wound;
and now the stone foundation, rockshelf further
forming underneath everything that grows.

1977   1978

Five O'Clock, January 2003

Tonight as cargoes of my young
fellow countrymen and women are being hauled
into positions aimed at death, positions
they who did not will it suddenly
have to assume   5
I am thinking of Ed Azevedo
half-awake in recovery
if he has his arm whole
and how much pain he must bear
under the drugs   10
On cliffs above a beach
luxuriant in low tide after storms
littered with driftwood hurled and piled and
humanly arranged in fantastic
installations and beyond   15
silk-blue and onion-silver-skinned
Jeffers' "most glorious creature on earth"[1]
we passed, greeting, I saw his arm
bandaged to the elbow
asked and he told me: It was just   20
a small cut, nothing, on the hand he'd
washed in peroxide thinking
that was it until the pain began
traveling up his arm
and then the antibiotics the splint the   25
numbing drugs the sick sensation
and this evening at five o'clock the emergency
surgery and last summer
the train from Czechoslovakia to Spain
with his girl, cheap wine, bread and cheese   30
room with a balcony, ocean like this

1. See Robinson Jeffers, "Ninth Anniversary," in *The Wild God of the World: An Anthology of Robinson Jeffers*, ed. Albert Gelpi (Stanford, Calif.: Stanford University Press, 2003), p. 52: "there the most gorious / Creature on earth shines in the nights or glitters in the suns, / Or feels of its stone in the blind fog" [Rich's note].

nobody asking for pay in advance
kindness of foreigners
in that country, sick sensation now
needing to sit in his brother's truck again   35
even the accident on the motorcycle
was nothing like this
I'll be thinking of you at five
this evening I said
afterward you'll feel better, your body   40
will be clean of this poison
I didn't say Your war is here
but could you have believed
that from a small thing infection
would craw through the blood   45
and the enormous ruffled shine
of an ocean wouldn't tell you.

2003   2004

MARTIN LUTHER KING JR.
1929–1968

On August 28, 1963, the Reverend Dr. Martin Luther King Jr. addressed a massive gathering from the steps of the Lincoln Memorial in Washington, D.C. With listeners standing shoulder to shoulder throughout the full length of the Mall, Dr. King summarized the achievement of the Civil Rights Movement and rallied sentiment for the full achievement of its goals. Battles against segregation had been waged in the courts for more than a decade, and demonstrations—such as lunch-counter sit-ins, bus boycotts, and freedom marches—had become increasingly common occurrences in American life, both in the South, where discrimination remained protected by laws, and in the North, where social conditions had long maintained a de facto separation of the races in matters of education, employment, and commerce. That morning, Dr. King and other leaders had met with President John F. Kennedy to argue for federal civil rights legislation. Achieving it would take until 1964 and the administration of the soon-to-be murdered president's successor, Lyndon B. Johnson. But the presence of such great numbers of Americans at Dr. King's 1963 speech, Americans of all races and political persuasions, was vivid proof that the time for such change was at hand.

The son of a minster, Dr. King was born in Atlanta, Georgia, and received bachelor's degrees in sociology and divinity from Morehouse College and Crozer Theological seminary before earning a doctorate in philosophy from Boston University in 1955, By then he had accepted his first pastorate at the Dexter Avenue Baptist Church in Montgomery, Alabama. It was in this city late in 1955 that a citizen named Rosa Parks, tired after a day's work, had refused to heed the local ordinance restricting African Americans to seats at the rear of city buses. Dr. King and other religious leaders offered support for Mrs. Parks and organized a boycott of Montgomery's public transport system that drew national attention. Although it took a year, this economic pressure and Dr. King's social activism (which led to his arrest and the bombing of his home) prompted federal injunctions that led to the bus system's integration. Dr. King's efforts in this struggle led to his invitation to speak at the annual convention of the National Association for the Advancement of Colored People in San Francisco and to his appearance on the February 18, 1957, cover of *Time* magazine.

For the next decade Martin Luther King Jr. was the most highly visible and politically effective leader of the Civil Rights Movement, thanks to his inspiring speeches, his deeply thoughtful books, and his practical manner of working with pragmatic forces in government. Hands-on experience with the Southern Christian Leadership Conference combined with high-profile visibility (including being named *Time* magazine's Man of the Year in January 1964 and receiving the Nobel Prize for Peace that same year) to make Dr. King a genuine hero of the movement. His talent lay in a unique ability to apply relentless pressure for change in a strictly nonviolent manner; for this his acknowledged model was the Indian independence leader Mahatma Gandi. The speech on the Mall concludes with a list of just some of the places across the United States where Dr. King had worked for social justice. In the less than five years of life left to him he would continue his struggles with a voter-registration campaign in Selma, Alabama (featuring a dangerous march from Selma to Montgomery in March 1965), a protest of the Vietnam War in 1966 (for its diversion of economic resources from social needs), and a more generalized program in support of poor people of all races. This last endeavor took him to Memphis. Tennessee, where he supported sanitation workers in their strike for better wages and working conditions. There, on April 4, 1968, he was assassinated by an avowed white supremacist, James Earl Ray, who later died in prison while serving a life sentence for his act. Dr. King's speech on the evening before his death, "I See the Promised Land," concluded with a memorable reference to having "been to the mountaintop" from which a future of justice and equality could be foreseen.

The literary features of Martin Luther King Jr.'s ascent to greatness are examined by Eric Sundquist in *King's Dream* (2008). The speech delivered from the Lincoln

August 28, 1963. In "the greatest demonstration for freedom in the history of our nation," Dr. Martin Luther King Jr. is photographed addressing his audience on the Mall in Washington, D.C.

Memorial in 1963 draws on key rhetorical features of Dr. King's writing and speaking and pushes them to new heights at the same time that the concision and focus demanded by the occasion made the statements themselves virtually iconic. Dr. King's rhetoric is that of the pulpit, using cadence and exhortation to move listeners to inspired agreement with not just the topic but also the enthusiasm behind it. Here the Bible is ever present as a source for allusion and a confirmation of value. Long familiar to members of African American religious congregations, Dr. King's strongly emotional style of presentation was new to many white listeners. Its effectiveness for a broad audience was proven by Dr. King's success and was applied to politics in coming years by the Reverend Jesse Jackson, whose 1988 campaign in the U.S. presidential primary elections would have the candidate winning the highest raw vote total in Iowa, a state with relatively few African American voters—the same state that in 2008 gave Barack Obama his first campaign victory.

The following text is from *I Have a Dream: Writings and Speeches That Changed the World* (1992).

I Have a Dream

I am happy to join with you today in what will go down in history as the greatest demonstration for freedom in the history of our nation.

Fivescore years ago, a great American, in whose symbolic shadow we stand today, signed the Emancipation Proclamation.[1] This momentous decree came as a great beacon light of hope to millions of Negro slaves who had been seared in the flames of withering injustice. It came as a joyous daybreak to end the long night of their captivity.

But one hundred years later, the Negro still is not free; one hundred years later, the life of the Negro is still sadly crippled by the manacles of segregation and the chains of discrimination; one hundred years later, the Negro lives on a lonely island of poverty in the midst of a vast ocean of material prosperity; one hundred years later, the Negro is still languishing in the corners of American society and finds himself in exile in his own land.

So we've come here today to dramatize a shameful condition. In a sense we've come to our nation's capital to cash a check. When the architects of our republic wrote the magnificent words of the Constitution and the Declaration of Independence, they were signing a promissory note to which every American was to fall heir. This note was the promise that all men, yes, black men as well as white men, would be guaranteed the unalienable rights of life, liberty, and the pursuit of happiness.

It is obvious today that America has defaulted on this promissory note in so far as her citizens of color are concerned. Instead of honoring this sacred obligation, America has given the Negro people a bad check; a check which has come back marked "insufficient funds." We refuse to believe that there are insufficient funds in the great vaults of opportunity of this nation. And so we've come to cash this check, a check that will give us upon demand the riches of freedom and the security of justice.

---

1. Abraham Lincoln (1809–1865), sixteenth president of the United States, signed the Emancipation Proclamation on September 22, 1862, abolishing slavery in all portions of the country, including the Confederacy.

We have also come to this hallowed spot to remind America of the fierce urgency of now. This is no time to engage in the luxury of cooling off or to take the tranquilizing drug of gradualism. Now is the time to make real the promises of democracy; now is the time to rise from the dark and desolate valley of segregation to the sunlit path of racial justice; now is the time to lift our nation from the quicksands of racial injustice to the solid rock of brotherhood; now is the time to make justice a reality for all God's children. It would be fatal for the nation to overlook the urgency of the moment. This sweltering summer of the Negro's legitimate discontent will not pass until there is an invigorating autumn of freedom and equality.

Nineteen sixty-three is not an end, but a beginning. And those who hope that the Negro needed to blow off steam and will now be content, will have a rude awakening if the nation returns to business as usual.

There will be neither rest nor tranquility in America until the Negro is granted his citizenship rights. The whirlwinds of revolt will continue to shake the foundations of our nation until the bright day of justice emerges.

But there is something that I must say to my people who stand on the warm threshold which leads into the palace of justice. In the process of gaining our rightful place we must not be guilty of wrongful deeds. Let us not seek to satisfy our thirst for freedom by drinking from the cup of bitterness and hatred. We must forever conduct our struggle on the high plane of dignity and discipline. We must not allow our creative protest to degenerate into physical violence. Again and again we must rise to the majestic heights of meeting physical force with soul force.

The marvelous new militancy which has engulfed the Negro community[2] must not lead us to a distrust of all white people, for many of our white brothers, as evidenced by their presence here today, have come to realize that their destiny is tied up with our destiny and they have come to realize that their freedom is inextricably bound to our freedom. This offense we share mounted to storm the battlements of injustice must be carried forth by a biracial army. We cannot walk alone.

And as we walk, we must make the pledge that we shall always march ahead. We cannot turn back. There are those who are asking the devotees of civil rights, "When will you be satisfied?" We can never be satisfied as long as the Negro is the victim of the unspeakable horrors of police brutality. We can never be satisfied as long as our bodies, heavy with fatigue of travel, cannot gain lodging in the motels of the highways and the hotels of the cities. We cannot be satisfied as long as the Negro's basic mobility is from a smaller ghetto to a larger one.

We can never be satisfied as long as our children are stripped of their selfhood and robbed of their dignity by signs stating "for whites only." We cannot be satisfied as long as a Negro in Mississippi cannot vote and a Negro in New York believes he has nothing for which to vote. No, we are not satisfied, and we will not be satisfied until justice rolls down like waters and righteousness like a mighty stream.

I am not unmindful that some of you come here out of excessive trials and tribulation. Some of you have come fresh from narrow jail cells. Some of you have come from areas where your quest for freedom left you battered

---

2. The Civil Rights Movement of the 1950s and 1960s was marked by strong activism, which was met at times by violence.

by the storms of persecution and staggered by the winds of police brutality. You have been the veterans of creative suffering. Continue to work with the faith that unearned suffering is redemptive.

Go back to Mississippi; go back to Alabama; go back to South Carolina; go back to Georgia; go back to Louisiana; go back to the slums and ghettos of the northern cities, knowing that somehow this situation can, and will be changed. Let us not wallow in the valley of despair.

So I say to you, my friends, that even though we must face the difficulties of today and tomorrow, I still have a dream. It is a dream deeply rooted in the American dream that one day this nation will rise up and live out the true meaning of its creed—we hold these truths to be self-evident, that all men are created equal.

I have a dream that one day on the red hills of Georgia, sons of former slaves and sons of former slave-owners will be able to sit down together at the table of brotherhood.

I have a dream that one day, even the state of Mississippi, a state sweltering with the heat of injustice, sweltering with the heat of oppression, will be transformed into an oasis of freedom and justice.

I have a dream my four little children will one day live in a nation where they will not be judged by the color of their skin but by the content of their character. I have a dream today!

I have a dream that one day, down in Alabama, with its vicious racists, with its governor having his lips dripping with the words of interposition and nullification,[3] that one day, right there in Alabama, little black boys and black girls will be able to join hands with little white boys and white girls as sisters and brothers. I have a dream today!

I have a dream that one day every valley shall be exalted, every hill and mountain shall be made low, the rough places shall be made plain, and the crooked places shall be made straight and the glory of the Lord will be revealed and all flesh shall see it together.

This is our hope. This is the faith that I go back to the South with.

With this faith we will be able to hew out of the mountain of despair a stone of hope. With this faith we will be able to transform the jangling discords of our nation into a beautiful symphony of brotherhood.

With this faith we will be able to work together, to pray together, to struggle together, to go to jail together, to stand up for freedom together, knowing that we will be free one day. This will be the day when all of God's children will be able to sing with new meaning—"my country 'tis of thee; sweet land of liberty; of thee I sing; land where my fathers died, land of the pilgrim's pride; from every mountain side, let freedom ring"—and if America is to be a great nation, this must become true.

So let freedom ring from the prodigious hilltops of New Hampshire.

Let freedom ring from the mighty mountains of New York.

Let freedom ring from the heightening Alleghenies of Pennsylvania.

Let freedom ring from the snow-capped Rockies of Colorado.

Let freedom ring from the curvaceous slopes of California.

But not only that.

Let freedom ring from Stone Mountain of Georgia.

---

3. Legal concepts invoked by Alabama's segregationist governor, George Wallace (1919–1998), to challenge the authority of federal antidiscrimination laws.

Let freedom ring from Lookout Mountain of Tennessee.

Let freedom ring from every hill and molehill of Mississippi, from every mountainside, let freedom ring.

And when we allow freedom to ring, when we let it ring from every village and hamlet, from every state and city, we will be able to speed up that day when all of God's children—black men and white men, Jews and Gentiles, Catholics and Protestants—will be able to join hands and to sing in the words of the old Negro spiritual, "Free at last, free at last; thank God Almighty, we are free at last."

GARY SNYDER
b. 1930

" I try to hold both history and wildness in my mind, that my poems may approach the true measure of things and stand against the unbalance and ignorance of our time," Gary Snyder has said. Throughout his life Snyder has sought alternatives to this imbalance. His quest has led him to the natural world, to the study of mythology and the discipline of Eastern religions, and to living oral traditions including those of Native American societies. Snyder understands the work of poetry as recovery and healing. Like the shaman-poet of primitive cultures whose power to "heal disease and resist death" is "acquired from dreams" (as he writes in the essay "Poetry and the Primitive"), he seeks to restore contact with a vital universe in which all things are interdependent. The journey of Snyder's life and work has taken him back to what he calls "the most archaic values on earth." His poems are acts of cultural criticism, challenges to the dominant values of the contemporary world.

The American West Coast is Snyder's native landscape; its forests and mountains have always attracted him, and they inspire many of his poems. He was born in San Francisco, grew up in Washington State, and later moved with his family to Portland, Oregon. In 1947 he entered Reed College, where he studied anthropology and developed a special interest in Native American cultures (Northwest Coast Indian myths and tales inform his second book, *Myths and Tests*, 1960). After doing graduate work in linguistics at Indiana University, he returned to the West, where he became associated with Kenneth Rexroth and Philip Whalen as well as Jack Kerouac and Allen Ginsberg, all of whom participated in what came to be called the San Francisco Renaissance. In this period Snyder also studied classical Chinese at the University of California at Berkeley and translated some of the Cold Mountain poems of the Zen poet Han-shan. In the mid-1950s Snyder went to Japan, where he resided, except intermittently, until 1968; in Japan he took formal instruction in Buddhism under Zen masters. The various traditions Snyder has studied come together in his varied vision-quest poems.

Snyder's poems, like his life, combine reading and formal study with physical activity; he has worked as a timber scaler, a forest-fire lookout (one of his lookouts inspired "August on Sourdough"), a logger, and a crewman on a tanker in the South Pacific. "My poems follow the rhythms of the physical work I'm doing and the life I'm leading at any given time," he has remarked. The title of his first book, *Riprap* (1959), is a forester's term for, he explains, "a cobble of stone laid on steep slick rock to make a trail for horses in the mountains." Snyder's poems often follow a trail of ascent or descent, as in "Straight-Creek–Great Burn" from his Pulitzer Prize–winning volume, *Turtle Island* (1975). Hiking with friends, he experiences the world as dynamic and flowing (running water and "changing clouds"), but the journey brings the walkers to a still point; they lie "resting on dry fern and / watching." From such a stillness the central image of a Snyder poem often rises, like the birds who "arch and loop," then "settle down." The achievement of stillness in a universe of change is, for Snyder, pivotal. The mind empties itself, the individual ego is erased, and the local place reveals the universal.

If Snyder's poems contain a Zenlike stillness, they also exhibit an appealing energy, one source of which is his love of wildness. Like the Henry David Thoreau of *Walden*, explicitly evoked in sections of *Myths and Texts*, Snyder finds a tonic wildness in the natural world, but unlike Thoreau he is an unabashed celebrant of erotic experience (his earlier poems show that he also knows its destructive possibilities). He renders one of the various faces of Eros in "Beneath My Hand and Eye the Distant Hills. Your Body" (from *The Back Country*, 1968).

Some of Snyder's numerous essays on politics and ecology are included in his influential *Earth House Hold* (1969), *The Practice of the Wild* (1990), and *A Place in Space: Ethics, Aesthetics, and Watersheds* (1995). His collections *Axe Handles* (1983), *Left Out in the Rain* (1986), and *No Nature: New and Selected Poems* (1992) confirm that his poems are bound up in the same concerns. *Danger on Peaks* (2004) continues Snyder's explorations of landscape and ecology and also registers the upheavals of change in the earth and in the body, including the world-changing events of September 11, 2001, memorialized in "Falling from a Height, Holding Hands." Although his didactic impulse sometimes leads him to oversimplification, Snyder's political vision remains one strength of his poetry. The potential in this vision for self-importance and over-seriousness is tempered by his sense of humor and the conviction, palpable in his best poems, that his experiences are common and shared. Snyder's poems suggest diverse contexts: his belief in the writer as cultural critic links him to Thoreau and Robert Duncan, his rhythms and strong images recall Ezra Pound, his meticulous attention to the natural world reminds us of Robert Frost and A. R. Ammons. Eclectic yet respectful of ancient traditions, Snyder is an American original who sees his own work as part of a "continual creation," one manifestation of the energy that sustains all life.

Riprap[1]

    Lay down these words
    Before your mind like rocks.
            placed solid, by hands
    In choice of place, set
    Before the body of the mind   5
            in space and time:
    Solidity of bark, leaf, or wall
            riprap of things:
    Cobble of milky way,
            straying planets,   10
    These poems, people,
            lost ponies with
    Dragging saddles—
            and rocky sure-foot trails.

---

1. A cobble of stone laid on steep slick rock to make a trail for horses in the mountains [Snyder's note].

The worlds like an endless
   four-dimensional
Game of *Go*.[2]   15
    ants and pebbles
In the thin loam, each rock a word
    a creek-washed stone   20
  Granite: ingrained
     with torment of fire and weight
Crystal and sediment linked hot
    all change, in thoughts,
As well as things.   25

                   1959

August on Sourdough,[1] A Visit from Dick Brewer

You hitched a thousand miles
       north from San Francisco
Hiked up the mountainside   a mile in the air
The little cabin—one room—
      walled in glass   5
Meadows and snowfields,   hundreds of peaks.
We lay in our sleeping bags
      talking half the night;
Wind in the guy-cables   this summer mountain rain.
Next morning I went with you   10
     as far as the cliffs,
Loaned you my poncho—   the rain across the shale—
You down the snowfield
      flapping in the wind
Waving a last goodbye   half hidden in the clouds   15
To go on hitching
      clear to New York;
Me back to my mountain   and far, far, west.

                   1968

Beneath My Hand and Eye the Distant Hills. Your Body

What my hand follows on your body
Is the line. A stream of love
 of heat, of light,   what my
 eye   lascivious
   licks   5
 over, watching

---

2. An ancient Japanese game played with black and white stones, placed one after the other on a checkered board.

1. Mountain in Washington State, where Snyder worked as a fire-watcher during the summer of 1953.

far snow-dappled Uintah mountains[1]
Is that stream.
Of power.   what my
    hand curves over, following the line.   10
    "hip" and "groin"

Where "I"
    follow by hand and eye
    the swimming limit of your body.
As when vision idly dallies on the hills   15
Loving what it feeds on.
    soft cinder cones and craters;
    —Drum Hadley in the Pinacate[2]
      took ten minutes more to look again—
A leap of power unfurling: 20
    left,   right—right—
My heart beat faster looking
    at the snowy Uintah mountains.

As my hand feeds on you
    runs down your side and curls beneath your hip.   25
oil pool; stratum; water—

What "is" within   not known
    but feel it
    sinking with a breath
    pusht ruthless, surely, down.   30

Beneath this long caress of hand and eye
    "we" learn the flower burning,
      outward, from "below".

1968

1. In northeastern Utah.   2. California town.

TONI MORRISON
b. 1931

The 1993 Nobel Laureate in literature, Toni Morrison is a novelist of great importance in her own right and has been the central figure in putting fiction by and
about African American women at the forefront of the late twentieth-century literary
canon. Whereas the legacy of slavery had all but effaced a usable tradition, and critical stereotypes at times restricted such writers' range, Morrison's fiction serves as a
model for reconstructing a culturally empowering past. She joins the great American
tradition of self-invention: her example and her editorial work have figured importantly in the careers of other writers, such as Toni Cade Bambara and Gayl Jones.

Morrison was born in Lorain, Ohio, where much of her fiction is set (a departure from earlier African American narratives typically located in the rural South or urban North). Having earned a B.A. from Howard University with a major in English and a minor in classics, and an M.A. from Cornell University (with a thesis on suicide in the novels of Virginia Woolf and William Faulkner), Morrison began a teaching career in 1955 that reached from Texas Southern University back to Howard, where her students included the future activist Stokeley Carmichael and the future critic Houston A. Baker Jr. At this time she married Harold Morrison, a Jamaican architect, with whom she had two children before ending their marriage in 1964. Already writing, she took a job with the publishing firm Random House and eventually settled in New York City, where she worked until 1983. During these same years she held visiting teaching appointments at institutions including Yale University and Bard College.

As a first novel *The Bluest Eye* (1970) is uncommonly mature for its confident use of various narrative voices. Throughout her career Morrison has been dedicated to constructing a practical cultural identity of a race and a gender whose self-images have been obscured or denied by dominating forces, and in *The Bluest Eye* she already shows that narrative strategy is an important element in such construction. A girl's need to be loved generates the novel's action, action that involves displaced and alienated affections (and eventually incestuous rape); the family's inability to produce a style of existence in which love can be born and thrive leads to just such a devastating fate for Morrison's protagonist. Love is also denied in *Sula* (1974), in which relationships extend in two directions: between contemporaries (Sula and her friend Nel) and with previous generations.

With *Song of Solomon* (1977) Morrison seeks a more positive redemption of her characters. Turning away from his parents' loveless marriage, Milkman Dead makes a physical and mental journey to his ancestral roots. Here he discovers a more useful legacy in communal tales about Grandmother and Great-Grandfather, each long dead but infusing the local culture with emotionally sustaining lore. Milkman uses this lore to learn how the spiritual guidance offered by his aunt Pilate eclipses the material concerns of his parents' world.

Allegory becomes an important strategy in *Tar Baby* (1981), drawing on the strong folk culture of Haiti, where two contrasting persons form a troubled relationship based on their distinct searches for and rejections of a heritage. Yet it is in a rebuilding of history, rather than allegory or myth, that Morrison achieves her great strength as a novelist in *Beloved* (1987), the winner of her first major award, the Pulitzer Prize. Set in the middle 1870s, when race relations in America were at their most crucial juncture (slavery having ended and the course of the South's Reconstruction not yet fully determined), this novel shows a mother (Sethe) being haunted and eventually destroyed by the ghost of a daughter (Beloved) whom she had killed eighteen years earlier rather than allow to be taken by a vicious slavemaster. This novel is central to Morrison's canon because it involves so many important themes and techniques, from love and guilt to history's role in clarifying the past's influence on the present, all told in a style of magical realism that transforms (without denying) more mundane facts.

Jazz (1992) finds Morrison modeling her narrative voice on the progression of a jazz solo to demonstrate how improvisation with detail can change the nature of what is expressed. Present and past weave together in her characters' lives as the narrative seeks to understand the jealousies of love and the sometimes macabre manifestations of hatred. *Paradise* (1988) takes a nineteenth-century utopia and reexamines its ideals in the face of 1970s realities—a reminder of how neither past nor present can be insulated from the other. *Love* (2003), with its murder, arson, pedophilia, and several rapes punctuating a narrative in which arguments over a legacy dislodge awkward elements of the past, is a reminder of how disturbing Morrison's fiction can be. *A Mercy* (2008) explores the contradictions between American and pastoral ideals, and the realities of Native American extermination and African American slavery.

Presently serving as the prestigious Golheen Professor of the Humanities at Princeton University, Morrison has moved easily into the role of spokesperson for literary issues. Together with her Nobel lecture, her essays collected as *Playing in the Dark: Whiteness and the Literary Imagination* (1992) challenge stereotypes in white critical thinking about black literature. Her short story "Recitatif," written for *Confirmation*, the 1983 anthology edited by Amiri and Amina Baraka, directly addresses the issues of individual and family, past and present, and race and its effacements that motivate the larger sense of her work. A "recitatif" is a vocal performance in which a narrative is not stated but sung. In her work Morrison's voice sings proudly of a past that in the artistic nature of its reconstruction puts all Americans in touch with a more positively usable heritage.

The following text is from *Confirmation*.

Recitatif

My mother danced all night and Roberta's was sick. That's why we were taken to St. Bonny's. People want to put their arms around you when you tell them you were in a shelter, but it really wasn't bad. No big long room with one hundred beds like Bellevue.[1] There were four to a room, and when Roberta and me came, there was a shortage of state kids, so we were the only ones assigned to 406 and could go from bed to bed if we wanted to. And we wanted to, too. We changed beds every night and for the whole four months we were there we never picked one out as our own permanent bed.

It didn't start out that way. The minute I walked in and the Big Bozo introduced us, I got sick to my stomach. It was one thing to be taken out of your own bed early in the morning—it was something else to be stuck in a strange place with a girl from a whole other race. And Mary, that's my mother, she was right. Every now and then she would stop dancing long enough to tell me something important and one of the things she said was that they never washed their hair and they smelled funny. Roberta sure did. Smell funny, I mean. So when the Big Bozo (nobody ever called her Mrs. Itkin, just like nobody ever said St. Bonaventure)—when she said, "Twyla, this is Roberta. Roberta, this is Twyla. Make each other welcome." I said, "My mother won't like you putting me in here."

"Good," said Bozo. "Maybe then she'll come and take you home."

How's that for mean? If Roberta had laughed I would have killed her, but she didn't. She just walked over to the window and stood with her back to us.

"Turn around," said the Bozo. "Don't be rude. Now Twyla. Roberta. When you hear a loud buzzer, that's the call for dinner. Come down to the first floor. Any fights and no movie." And then, just to make sure we knew what we would be missing, *"The Wizard of Oz."*[2]

Roberta must have thought I meant that my mother would be mad about my being put in the shelter. Not about rooming with her, because as soon as Bozo left she came over to me and said, "Is your mother sick too?"

1. Bellevue Hospital in New York City is known for its psychiatric ward. St. Bonaventure's offers the services of a youth shelter and school.

2. The 1939 film based on the 1900 children's book by the American writer L. Frank Baum (1856–1919).

"No," I said. "She just likes to dance all night."

"Oh," she nodded her head and I liked the way she understood things so fast. So for the moment it didn't matter that we looked like salt and pepper standing there and that's what the other kids called us sometimes. We were eight years old and got F's all the time. Me because I couldn't remember what I read or what the teacher said. And Roberta because she couldn't read at all and didn't even listen to the teacher. She wasn't good at anything except jacks, at which she was a killer: pow scoop pow scoop pow scoop.

We didn't like each other all that much at first, but nobody else wanted to play with us because we weren't real orphans with beautiful dead parents in the sky. We were dumped. Even the New York City Puerto Ricans and the upstate Indians ignored us. All kinds of kids were in there, black ones, white ones, even two Koreans. The food was good, though. At least I thought so. Roberta hated it and left whole pieces of things on her plate: Spam, Salisbury steak—even jello with fruit cocktail in it, and she didn't care if I ate what she wouldn't. Mary's idea of supper was popcorn and a can of Yoo-Hoo.[3] Hot mashed potatoes and two weenies was like Thanksgiving for me.

It really wasn't bad, St. Bonny's. The big girls on the second floor pushed us around now and then. But that was all. They wore lipstick and eyebrow pencil and wobbled their knees while they watched TV. Fifteen, sixteen, even, some of them were. They were put-out girls, scared runaways most of them. Poor little girls who fought their uncles off but looked tough to us, and mean. God did they look mean. The staff tried to keep them separate from the younger children, but sometimes they caught us watching them in the orchard where they played radios and danced with each other. They'd light out after us and pull our hair or twist our arms. We were scared of them, Roberta and me, but neither of us wanted the other one to know it. So we got a good list of dirty names we could shout back when we ran from them through the orchard. I used to dream a lot and almost always the orchard was there. Two acres, four maybe, of these little apple trees. Hundreds of them. Empty and crooked like beggar women when I first came to St. Bonny's but fat with flowers when I left. I don't know why I dreamt about that orchard so much. Nothing really happened there. Nothing all that important, I mean. Just the big girls dancing and playing the radio. Roberta and me watching. Maggie fell down there once. The kitchen woman with legs like parentheses. And the big girls laughed at her. We should have helped her up, I know, but we were scared of those girls with lipstick and eyebrow pencil. Maggie couldn't talk. The kids said she had her tongue cut out, but I think she was just born that way: mute. She was old and sandy-colored and she worked in the kitchen. I don't know if she was nice or not. I just remember her legs like parentheses and how she rocked when she walked. She worked from early in the morning till two o'clock, and if she was late, if she had too much cleaning and didn't get out till two-fifteen or so, she'd cut through the orchard so she wouldn't miss her bus and have to wait another hour. She wore this really stupid little hat—a kid's hat with ear flaps—and she wasn't much taller than we were. A really awful little hat. Even for a mute, it was dumb—dressing like a kid and never saying anything at all.

"But what about if somebody tries to kill her?" I used to wonder about that. "Or what if she wants to cry? Can she cry?"

---

3. A chocolate soft drink.

"Sure," Roberta said. "But just tears. No sounds come out."

"She can't scream?"

"Nope. Nothing."

"Can she hear?"

"I guess."

"Let's call her," I said. And we did.

"Dummy! Dummy!" She never turned her head.

"Bow legs! Bow legs!" Nothing. She just rocked on, the chin straps of her baby-boy hat swaying from side to side. I think we were wrong. I think she could hear and didn't let on. And it shames me even now to think there was somebody in there after all who heard us call her those names and couldn't tell on us.

We got along all right, Roberta and me. Changed beds every night, got F's in civics and communication skills and gym. The Bozo was disappointed in us, she said. Out of 130 of us state cases, 90 were under twelve. Almost all were real orphans with beautiful dead parents in the sky. We were the only ones dumped and the only ones with F's in three classes including gym. So we got along—what with her leaving whole pieces of things on her plate and being nice about not asking questions.

I think it was the day before Maggie fell down that we found out our mothers were coming to visit us on the same Sunday. We had been at the shelter twenty-eight days (Roberta twenty-eight and a half) and this was their first visit with us. Our mothers would come at ten o'clock in time for chapel, then lunch with us in the teachers' lounge. I thought if my dancing mother met her sick mother it might be good for her. And Roberta thought her sick mother would get a big bang out of a dancing one. We got excited about it and curled each other's hair. After breakfast we sat on the bed watching the road from the window. Roberta's socks were still wet. She washed them the night before and put them on the radiator to dry. They hadn't, but she put them on anyway because their tops were so pretty—scalloped in pink. Each of us had a purple construction-paper basket that we had made in craft class. Mine had a yellow crayon rabbit on it. Roberta's had eggs with wiggly lines of color. Inside were cellophane grass and just the jelly beans because I'd eaten the two marshmallow eggs they gave us. The Big Bozo came herself to get us. Smiling she told us we looked very nice and to come downstairs. We were so surprised by the smile we'd never seen before, neither of us moved.

"Don't you want to see your mommies?"

I stood up first and spilled the jelly beans all over the floor. Bozo's smile disappeared while we scrambled to get the candy up off the floor and put it back in the grass.

She escorted us downstairs to the first floor, where the other girls were lining up to file into the chapel. A bunch of grown-ups stood to one side. Viewers mostly. The old biddies who wanted servants and the fags who wanted company looking for children they might want to adopt. Once in a while a grandmother. Almost never anybody young or anybody whose face wouldn't scare you in the night. Because if any of the real orphans had young relatives they wouldn't be real orphans. I saw Mary right away. She had on those green slacks I hated and hated even more now because didn't she know we were going to chapel? And that fur jacket with the pocket linings so ripped she had to pull to get her hands out of them. But her face was pretty—like always, and she smiled and waved like she was the little girl looking for her mother—not me.

I walked slowly, trying not to drop the jelly beans and hoping the paper handle would hold. I had to use my last Chiclet because by the time I finished cutting everything out, all the Elmer's was gone. I am left-handed and the scissors never worked for me. It didn't matter, though; I might just as well have chewed the gum. Mary dropped to her knees and grabbed me, mashing the basket, the jelly beans, and the grass into her ratty fur jacket.

"Twyla, baby. Twyla, baby!"

I could have killed her. Already I heard the big girls in the orchard the next time saying, "Twyyyyyla, baby!" But I couldn't stay mad at Mary while she was smiling and hugging me and smelling of Lady Esther dusting powder. I wanted to stay buried in her fur all day.

To tell the truth I forgot about Roberta. Mary and I got in line for the traipse into chapel and I was feeling proud because she looked so beautiful even in those ugly green slacks that made her behind stick out. A pretty mother on earth is better than a beautiful dead one in the sky even if she did leave you all alone to go dancing.

I felt a tap on my shoulder, turned, and saw Roberta smiling. I smiled back, but not too much lest somebody think this visit was the biggest thing that ever happened in my life. Then Roberta said, "Mother, I want you to meet my roommate, Twyla. And that's Twyla's mother."

I looked up it seemed for miles. She was big. Bigger than any man and on her chest was the biggest cross I'd ever seen. I swear it was six inches long each way. And in the crook of her arm was the biggest Bible ever made.

Mary, simple-minded as ever, grinned and tried to yank her hand out of the pocket with the raggedy lining—to shake hands, I guess. Roberta's mother looked down at me and then looked down at Mary too. She didn't say anything, just grabbed Roberta with her Bible-free hand and stepped out of line, walking quickly to the rear of it. Mary was still grinning because she's not too swift when it comes to what's really going on. Then this light bulb goes off in her head and she says "That bitch!" really loud and us almost in the chapel now. Organ music whining; the Bonny Angels singing sweetly. Everybody in the world turned around to look. And Mary would have kept it up—kept calling names if I hadn't squeezed her hand as hard as I could. That helped a little, but she still twitched and crossed and uncrossed her legs all through service. Even groaned a couple of times. Why did I think she would come there and act right? Slacks. No hat like the grandmothers and viewers, and groaning all the while. When we stood for hymns she kept her mouth shut. Wouldn't even look at the words on the page. She actually reached in her purse for a mirror to check her lipstick. All I could think of was that she really needed to be killed. The sermon lasted a year, and I knew the real orphans were looking smug again.

We were supposed to have lunch in the teachers' lounge, but Mary didn't bring anything, so we picked fur and cellophane grass off the mashed jelly beans and ate them. I could have killed her. I sneaked a look at Roberta. Her mother had brought chicken legs and ham sandwiches and oranges and a whole box of chocolate-covered grahams. Roberta drank milk from a thermos while her mother read the Bible to her.

Things are not right. The wrong food is always with the wrong people. Maybe that's why I got into waitress work later—to match up the right people with the right food. Roberta just let those chicken legs sit there, but she did bring a stack of grahams up to me later when the visit was over. I think she was sorry that her mother would not shake my mother's hand. And I liked that and I liked the fact that she didn't say a word about Mary groaning all the way through the service and not bringing any lunch.

Roberta left in May when the apple trees were heavy and white. On her last day we went to the orchard to watch the big girls smoke and dance by the radio. It didn't matter that they said, "Twyyyyyla, baby." We sat on the ground and breathed. Lady Esther. Apple blossoms. I still go soft when I smell one or the other. Roberta was going home. The big cross and the big Bible was coming to get her and she seemed sort of glad and sort of not. I thought I would die in that room of four beds without her and I knew Bozo had plans to move some other dumped kid in there with me. Roberta promised to write every day, which was really sweet of her because she couldn't read a lick so how could she write anybody. I would have drawn pictures and sent them to her but she never gave me her address. Little by little she faded. Her wet socks with the pink scalloped tops and her big serious-looking eyes—that's all I could catch when I tried to bring her to mind.

I was working behind the counter at the Howard Johnson's on the Thruway just before the Kingston exit. Not a bad job. Kind of a long ride from Newburgh,[4] but okay once I got there. Mine was the second night shift—eleven to seven. Very light until a Greyhound checked in for breakfast around six-thirty. At that hour the sun was all the way clear of the hills behind the restaurant. The place looked better at night—more like shelter—but I loved it when the sun broke in, even if it did show all the cracks in the vinyl and the speckled floor looked dirty no matter what the mop boy did.

It was August and a bus crowd was just unloading. They would stand around a long while: going to the john, and looking at gifts and junk-for-sale machines, reluctant to sit down so soon. Even to eat. I was trying to fill the coffee pots and get them all situated on the electric burners when I saw her. She was sitting in a booth smoking a cigarette with two guys smothered in head and facial hair. Her own hair was so big and wild I could hardly see her face. But the eyes. I would know them anywhere. She had on a powder-blue halter and shorts outfit and earrings the size of bracelets. Talk about lipstick and eyebrow pencil. She made the big girls look like nuns. I couldn't get off the counter until seven o'clock, but I kept watching the booth in case they got up to leave before that. My replacement was on time for a change, so I counted and stacked my receipts as fast as I could and signed off. I walked over to the booth, smiling and wondering if she would remember me. Or even if she wanted to remember me. Maybe she didn't want to be reminded of St. Bonny's or to have anybody know she was ever there. I know I never talked about it to anybody.

I put my hands in my apron pockets and leaned against the back of the booth facing them.

"Roberta? Roberta Fisk?"

She looked up. "Yeah?"

"Twyla."

She squinted for a second and then said, "Wow."

"Remember me?"

4. A community beside the Hudson River, located eighty miles north of New York City.

"Sure. Hey. Wow."

"It's been a while," I said, and gave a smile to the two hairy guys.

"Yeah. Wow. You work here?"

"Yeah," I said. "I live in Newburgh."

"Newburgh? No kidding?" She laughed then a private laugh that included the guys but only the guys, and they laughed with her. What could I do but laugh too and wonder why I was standing there with my knees showing out from under that uniform. Without looking I could see the blue and white triangle on my head, my hair shapeless in a net, my ankles thick in white oxfords. Nothing could have been less sheer than my stockings. There was this silence that came down right after I laughed. A silence it was her turn to fill up. With introductions, maybe, to her boyfriends or an invitation to sit down and have a Coke. Instead she lit a cigarette off the one she'd just finished and said, "We're on our way to the Coast. He's got an appointment with Hendrix."[5] She gestured casually toward the boy next to her.

"Hendrix? Fantastic," I said. "Really fantastic. What's she doing now?"

Roberta coughed on her cigarette and the two guys rolled their eyes up at the ceiling.

"Hendrix. Jimi Hendrix, asshole. He's only the biggest—Oh, wow. Forget it."

I was dismissed without anyone saying goodbye, so I thought I would do it for her.

"How's your mother?" I asked. Her grin cracked her whole face. She swallowed. "Fine," she said. "How's yours?"

"Pretty as a picture," I said and turned away. The backs of my knees were damp. Howard Johnson's really was a dump in the sunlight.

James is as comfortable as a house slipper. He liked my cooking and I liked his big loud family. They have lived in Newburgh all of their lives and talk about it the way people do who have always known a home. His grandmother is a porch swing older than his father and when they talk about streets and avenues and buildings they call them names they no longer have. They still call the A & P[6] Rico's because it stands on property once a mom and pop store owned by Mr. Rico. And they call the new community college Town Hall because it once was. My mother-in-law puts up jelly and cucumbers and buys butter wrapped in cloth from a dairy. James and his father talk about fishing and baseball and I can see them all together on the Hudson in a raggedy skiff. Half the population of Newburgh is on welfare now, but to my husband's family it was still some upstate paradise of a time long past. A time of ice houses and vegetable wagons, coal furnaces and children weeding gardens. When our son was born my mother-in-law gave me the crib blanket that had been hers.

But the town they remembered had changed. Something quick was in the air. Magnificent old houses, so ruined they had become shelter for squatters and rent risks, were bought and renovated. Smart IBM people[7] moved out of their suburbs back into the city and put shutters up and herb gardens in their backyards. A brochure came in the mail announcing the opening of

5. Jimi Hendrix (1942–1970), African American musician and rock star.
6. Supermarket, part of a national chain once called the Great Atlantic and Pacific Tea

Company.
7. High-salaried employees of the International Business Machine Corporation, headquartered in the suburbs north of New York City.

a Food Emporium. Gourmet food it said—and listed items the rich IBM crowd would want. It was located in a new mall at the edge of town and I drove out to shop there one day—just to see. It was late in June. After the tulips were gone and the Queen Elizabeth roses were open everywhere. I trailed my cart along the aisle tossing in smoked oysters and Robert's sauce and things I knew would sit in my cupboard for years. Only when I found some Klondike ice cream bars did I feel less guilty about spending James's fireman's salary so foolishly. My father-in-law ate them with the same gusto little Joseph did.

Waiting in the check-out line I heard a voice say, "Twyla!"

The classical music piped over the aisles had affected me and the woman leaning toward me was dressed to kill. Diamonds on her hand, a smart white summer dress. "I'm Mrs. Benson," I said.

"Ho. Ho. The Big Bozo," she sang.

For a split second I didn't know what she was talking about. She had a bunch of asparagus and two cartons of fancy water.

"Roberta!"

"Right."

"For heaven's sake. Roberta."

"You look great," she said.

"So do you. Where are you? Here? In Newburgh?"

"Yes. Over in Annandale."

I was opening my mouth to say more when the cashier called my attention to her empty counter.

"Meet you outside." Roberta pointed her finger and went into the express line.

I placed the groceries and kept myself from glancing around to check Roberta's progress. I remembered Howard Johnson's and looking for a chance to speak only to be greeted with a stingy "wow." But she was waiting for me and her huge hair was sleek now, smooth around a small, nicely shaped head. Shoes, dress, everything lovely and summery and rich. I was dying to know what happened to her, how she got from Jimi Hendrix to Annandale, a neighborhood full of doctors and IBM executives. Easy, I thought. Everything is so easy for them. They think they own the world.

"How long," I asked her. "How long have you been here?"

"A year. I got married to a man who lives here. And you, you're married too, right? Benson, you said."

"Yeah. James Benson."

"And is he nice?"

"Oh, is he nice?"

"Well, is he?" Roberta's eyes were steady as though she really meant the question and wanted an answer.

"He's wonderful, Roberta. Wonderful."

"So you're happy."

"Very."

"That's good," she said and nodded her head. "I always hoped you'd be happy. Any kids? I know you have kids."

"One. A boy. How about you?"

"Four."

"Four?"

She laughed. "Step kids. He's a widower."

"Oh."

"Got a minute? Let's have a coffee."

I thought about the Klondikes melting and the inconvenience of going all the way to my car and putting the bags in the trunk. Served me right for buying all that stuff I didn't need. Roberta was ahead of me.

"Put them in my car. It's right here."

And then I saw the dark blue limousine.

"You married a Chinaman?"

"No," she laughed. "He's the driver."

"Oh, my. If the Big Bozo could see you now."

We both giggled. Really giggled. Suddenly, in just a pulse beat, twenty years disappeared and all of it came rushing back. The big girls (whom we called gar girls—Roberta's misheard word for the evil stone faces described in a civics class) there dancing in the orchard, the ploppy mashed potatoes, the double weenies, the Spam with pineapple. We went into the coffee shop holding on to one another and I tried to think why we were glad to see each other this time and not before. Once, twelve years ago, we passed like strangers. A black girl and a white girl meeting in a Howard Johnson's on the road and having nothing to say. One in a blue and white triangle wait-ress hat—the other on her way to see Hendrix. Now we were behaving like sisters separated for much too long. Those four short months were nothing in time. Maybe it was the thing itself. Just being there, together. Two little girls who knew what nobody else in the world knew—how not to ask ques-tions. How to believe what had to be believed. There was politeness in that reluctance and generosity as well. Is your mother sick too? No, she dances all night. Oh—and an understanding nod.

We sat in a booth by the window and fell into recollection like veterans.

"Did you ever learn to read?"

"Watch." She picked up the menu. "Special of the day. Cream of corn soup. Entrées. Two dots and a wriggly line. Quiche. Chef salad, scallops . . ."

I was laughing and applauding when the waitress came up.

"Remember the Easter baskets?"

"And how we tried to *introduce* them?"

"Your mother with that cross like two telephone poles."

"And yours with those tight slacks."

We laughed so loudly heads turned and made the laughter harder to suppress.

"What happened to the Jimi Hendrix date?"

Roberta made a blow-out sound with her lips.

"When he died I thought about you."

"Oh, you heard about him finally?"

"Finally. Come on, I was a small-town country waitress."

"And I was a small-town country dropout. God, were we wild. I still don't know how I got out of there alive."

"But you did."

"I did. I really did. Now I'm Mrs. Kenneth Norton."

"Sounds like a mouthful."

"It is."

"Servants and all?"

Roberta held up two fingers.

"Ow! What does he do?"

"Computers and stuff. What do I know?"

"I don't remember a hell of a lot from those days, but Lord, St. Bonny's is as clear as daylight. Remember Maggie? The day she fell down and those gar girls laughed at her?"

Roberta looked up from her salad and stared at me. "Maggie didn't fall," she said.

"Yes, she did. You remember."

"No, Twyla. They knocked her down. Those girls pushed her down and tore her clothes. In the orchard."

"I don't—that's not what happened."

"Sure it is. In the orchard. Remember how scared we were?"

"Wait a minute. I don't remember any of that."

"And Bozo was fired."

"You're crazy. She was there when I left. You left before me."

"I went back. You weren't there when they fired Bozo."

"What?"

"Twice. Once for a year when I was about ten, another for two months when I was fourteen. That's when I ran away."

"You ran away from St. Bonny's?"

"I had to. What do you want? Me dancing in that orchard?"

"Are you sure about Maggie?"

"Of course I'm sure. You've blocked it, Twyla. It happened. Those girls had behavior problems, you know."

"Didn't they, though. But why can't I remember the Maggie thing?"

"Believe me. It happened. And we were there."

"Who did you room with when you went back?" I asked her as if I would know her. The Maggie thing was troubling me.

"Creeps. They tickled themselves in the night."

My ears were itching and I wanted to go home suddenly. This was all very well but she couldn't just comb her hair, wash her face and pretend everything was hunky-dory. After the Howard Johnson's snub. And no apology. Nothing.

"Were you on dope or what that time at Howard Johnson's?" I tried to make my voice sound friendlier than I felt.

"Maybe, a little. I never did drugs much. Why?"

"I don't know; you acted sort of like you didn't want to know me then."

"Oh, Twyla, you know how it was in those days: black—white. You know how everything was."

But I didn't know. I thought it was just the opposite. Busloads of blacks and whites came into Howard Johnson's together. They roamed together then: students, musicians, lovers, protesters. You got to see everything at Howard Johnson's and blacks were very friendly with whites in those days. But sitting there with nothing on my plate but two hard tomato wedges wondering about the melting Klondikes it seemed childish remembering the slight. We went to her car, and with the help of the driver, got my stuff into my station wagon.

"We'll keep in touch this time," she said.

"Sure," I said. "Sure. Give me a call."

"I will," she said, and then just as I was sliding behind the wheel, she leaned into the window. "By the way. Your mother. Did she ever stop dancing?"

I shook my head. "No. Never."

Roberta nodded.

"And yours? Did she ever get well?"

She smiled a tiny sad smile. "No. She never did. Look, call me, okay?"

"Okay," I said, but I knew I wouldn't. Roberta had messed up my past somehow with that business about Maggie. I wouldn't forget a thing like that. Would I?

Strife came to us that fall. At least that's what the paper called it. Strife. Racial strife. The word made me think of a bird—a big shrieking bird out of 1,000,000,000 B.C. Flapping its wings and cawing. Its eye with no lid always bearing down on you. All day it screeched and at night it slept on the rooftops. It woke you in the morning and from the *Today* show to the eleven o'clock news it kept you an awful company. I couldn't figure it out from one day to the next. I knew I was supposed to feel something strong, but I didn't know what, and James wasn't any help. Joseph was on the list of kids to be transferred from the junior high school to another one at some far-out-of-the-way place and I thought it was a good thing until I heard it was a bad thing. I mean I didn't know. All the schools seemed dumps to me, and the fact that one was nicer looking didn't hold much weight. But the papers were full of it and then the kids began to get jumpy. In August, mind you. Schools weren't even open yet. I thought Joseph might be frightened to go over there, but he didn't seem scared so I forgot about it, until I found myself driving along Hudson Street out there by the school they were trying to integrate and saw a line of women marching. And who do you suppose was in line, big as life, holding a sign in front of her bigger than her mother's cross? MOTHERS HAVE RIGHTS TOO! it said.

I drove on, and then changed my mind. I circled the block, slowed down, and honked my horn.

Roberta looked over and when she saw me she waved. I didn't wave back, but I didn't move either. She handed her sign to another woman and came over to where I was parked.

"Hi."

"What are you doing?"

"Picketing. What's it look like?"

"What for?"

"What do you mean 'What for?' They want to take my kids and send them out of the neighborhood. They don't want to go."

"So what if they go to another school? My boy's being bussed too, and I don't mind. Why should you?"

"It's not about us, Twyla. Me and you. It's about our kids."

"What's more *us* than that?"

"Well, it is a free country."

"Not yet, but it will be."

"What the hell does that mean? I'm not doing anything to you."

"You really think that?"

"I know it."

"I wonder what made me think you were different."

"I wonder what made me think you were different."

"Look at them," I said. "Just look. Who do they think they are? Swarming all over the place like they own it. And now they think they can decide where my child goes to school. Look at them, Roberta. They're Bozos."

Roberta turned around and looked at the women. Almost all of them were standing still now, waiting. Some were even edging toward us. Roberta looked at me out of some refrigerator behind her eyes. "No, they're not. They're just mothers."

"And what am I? Swiss cheese?"

"I used to curl your hair."

"I hated your hands in my hair."

The women were moving. Our faces looked mean to them of course and they looked as though they could not wait to throw themselves in front of a police car, or better yet, into my car and drag me away by my ankles. Now they surrounded my car and gently, gently began to rock it. I swayed back and forth like a sideways yo-yo. Automatically I reached for Roberta, like the old days in the orchard when they saw us watching them and we had to get out of there, and if one of us fell the other pulled her up and if one of us was caught the other stayed to kick and scratch, and neither would leave the other behind. My arm shot out of the car window but no receiving hand was there. Roberta was looking at me sway from side to side in the car and her face was still. My purse slid from the car seat down under the dashboard. The four policemen who had been drinking Tab[8] in their car finally got the message and strolled over, forcing their way through the women. Quietly, firmly they spoke. "Okay, ladies. Back in line or off the streets."

Some of them went away willingly; others had to be urged away from the car doors and the hood. Roberta didn't move. She was looking steadily at me. I was fumbling to turn on the ignition, which wouldn't catch because the gearshift was still in drive. The seats of the car were a mess because the swaying had thrown my grocery coupons all over it and my purse was sprawled on the floor.

"Maybe I am different now, Twyla. But you're not. You're the same little state kid who kicked a poor old black lady when she was down on the ground. You kicked a black lady and you have the nerve to call me a bigot."

The coupons were everywhere and the guts of my purse were bunched under the dashboard. What was she saying? Black? Maggie wasn't black.

"She wasn't black," I said.

"Like hell she wasn't, and you kicked her. We both did. You kicked a black lady who couldn't even scream."

"Liar!"

"You're the liar! Why don't you just go on home and leave us alone, huh?"

She turned away and I skidded away from the curb.

The next morning I went into the garage and cut the side out of the carton our portable TV had come in. It wasn't nearly big enough, but after a while I had a decent sign: red spray-painted letters on a white background—AND SO DO CHILDREN * * * *. I meant just to go down to the school and tack it up somewhere so those cows on the picket line across the street could see it, but when I got there, some ten or so others had already assembled—protesting the cows across the street. Police permits and everything. I got in line and we strutted in time on our side while Roberta's group strutted on theirs. That first day we were all dignified, pretending the other side didn't exist. The second day there was name calling and finger gestures. But that was about all. People changed signs from time to time, but Roberta never did

8. A diet soda.

and neither did I. Actually my sign didn't make sense without Roberta's. "And so do children what?" one of the women on my side asked me. Have rights, I said, as though it was obvious.

Roberta didn't acknowledge my presence in any way and I got to thinking maybe she didn't know I was there. I began to pace myself in the line, jostling people one minute and lagging behind the next, so Roberta and I could reach the end of our respective lines at the same time and there would be a moment in our turn when we would face each other. Still, I couldn't tell whether she saw me and knew my sign was for her. The next day I went early before we were scheduled to assemble. I waited until she got there before I exposed my new creation. As soon as she hoisted her MOTHERS HAVE RIGHTS TOO I began to wave my new one, which said, HOW WOULD YOU KNOW? I know she saw that one, but I had gotten addicted now. My signs got crazier each day, and the women on my side decided that I was a kook. They couldn't make heads or tails out of my brilliant screaming posters.

I brought a painted sign in queenly red with huge black letters that said, IS YOUR MOTHER WELL? Roberta took her lunch break and didn't come back for the rest of the day or any day after. Two days later I stopped going too and couldn't have been missed because nobody understood my signs anyway.

It was a nasty six weeks. Classes were suspended and Joseph didn't go to anybody's school until October. The children—everybody's children—soon got bored with that extended vacation they thought was going to be so great. They looked at TV until their eyes flattened. I spent a couple of mornings tutoring my son, as the other mothers said we should. Twice I opened a text from last year that he had never turned in. Twice he yawned in my face. Other mothers organized living room sessions so the kids would keep up. None of the kids could concentrate so they drifted back to *The Price Is Right* and *The Brady Bunch*.[9] When the school finally opened there were fights once or twice and some sirens roared through the streets every once in a while. There were a lot of photographers from Albany. And just when ABC was about to send up a news crew, the kids settled down like nothing in the world had happened. Joseph hung my HOW WOULD YOU KNOW? sign in his bedroom. I don't know what became of AND SO DO CHILDREN * * * *. I think my father-in-law cleaned some fish on it. He was always puttering around in our garage. Each of his five children lived in Newburgh and he acted as though he had five extra homes.

I couldn't help looking for Roberta when Joseph graduated from high school, but I didn't see her. It didn't trouble me much what she had said to me in the car. I mean the kicking part. I know I didn't do that, I couldn't do that. But I was puzzled by her telling me Maggie was black. When I thought about it I actually couldn't be certain. She wasn't pitch-black, I knew, or I would have remembered that. What I remember was the kiddie hat, and the semicircle legs. I tried to reassure myself about the race thing for a long time until it dawned on me that the truth was already there, and Roberta knew it. I didn't kick her; I didn't join in with the gar girls and kick that lady, but I sure did want to. We watched and never tried to help her and never called for help. Maggie was my dancing mother. Deaf, I thought, and dumb. Nobody inside. Nobody who would hear you if you cried in the night.

---

9. Popular television programs: respectively, a game show and a situation comedy.

Nobody who could tell you anything important that you could use. Rocking, dancing, swaying as she walked. And when the gar girls pushed her down, and started roughhousing, I knew she wouldn't scream, couldn't—just like me—and I was glad about that.

We decided not to have a tree, because Christmas would be at my mother-in-law's house, so why have a tree at both places? Joseph was at SUNY New Paltz[1] and we had to economize, we said. But at the last minute, I changed my mind. Nothing could be that bad. So I rushed around town looking for a tree, something small but wide. By the time I found a place, it was snowing and very late. I dawdled like it was the most important purchase in the world and the tree man was fed up with me. Finally I chose one and had it tied onto the trunk of the car. I drove away slowly because the sand trucks were not out yet and the streets could be murder at the beginning of a snowfall. Downtown the streets were wide and rather empty except for a cluster of people coming out of the Newburgh Hotel. The one hotel in town that wasn't built out of cardboard and Plexiglas. A party, probably. The men huddled in the snow were dressed in tails and the women had on furs. Shiny things glittered from underneath their coats. It made me tired to look at them. Tired, tired, tired. On the next corner was a small diner with loops and loops of paper bells in the window. I stopped the car and went in. Just for a cup of coffee and twenty minutes of peace before I went home and tried to finish everything before Christmas Eve.

"Twyla?"

There she was. In a silvery evening gown and dark fur coat. A man and another woman were with her, the man fumbling for change to put in the cigarette machine. The woman was humming and tapping on the counter with her fingernails. They all looked a little bit drunk.

"Well. It's you."

"How are you?"

I shrugged. "Pretty good. Frazzled. Christmas and all."

"Regular?" called the woman from the counter.

"Fine," Roberta called back and then, "Wait for me in the car."

She slipped into the booth beside me. "I have to tell you something, Twyla. I made up my mind if I ever saw you again, I'd tell you."

"I'd just as soon not hear anything, Roberta. It doesn't matter now, anyway."

"No," she said. "Not about that."

"Don't be long," said the woman. She carried two regulars to go and the man peeled his cigarette pack as they left.

"It's about St. Bonny's and Maggie."

"Oh, please."

"Listen to me. I really did think she was black. I didn't make that up. I really thought so. But now I can't be sure. I just remember her as old, so old. And because she couldn't talk—well, you know, I thought she was crazy. She'd been brought up in an institution like my mother was and like I thought I would be too. And you were right. We didn't kick her. It was the gar girls. Only them. But, well, I wanted to. I really wanted them to hurt her. I said we did it, too. You and me, but that's not true. And I don't want you

---

1. A campus in the State University of New York system, located 70 miles north of New York City.

to carry that around. It was just that I wanted to do it so bad that day—wanting to is doing it."

Her eyes were watery from the drinks she'd had, I guess. I know it's that way with me. One glass of wine and I start bawling over the littlest thing.

"We were kids, Roberta."

"Yeah. Yeah. I know, just kids."

"Eight."

"Eight."

"And lonely."

"Scared, too."

She wiped her cheeks with the heel of her hand and smiled. "Well, that's all I wanted to say."

I nodded and couldn't think of any way to fill the silence that went from the diner past the paper bells on out into the snow. It was heavy now. I thought I'd better wait for the sand trucks before starting home.

"Thanks, Roberta."

"Sure."

"Did I tell you? My mother, she never did stop dancing."

"Yes. You told me. And mine, she never got well." Roberta lifted her hands from the tabletop and covered her face with her palms. When she took them away she really was crying. "Oh shit, Twyla. Shit, shit, shit. What the hell happened to Maggie?"

1983

SYLVIA PLATH
1932–1963

I n an introduction to Sylvia Plath's *Ariel* (1965), published two years after her suicide in London, Robert Lowell wrote: "In these poems . . . Sylvia Plath becomes herself, becomes something imaginary, newly, wildly, and subtly created— . . . one of those super-real, hypnotic great classical heroines." Lowell had first met Plath in 1958, during her regular visits to his poetry seminar at Boston University, where he remembered her "air of maddening docility." Later, writing his introduction, he recognized her astonishing creation of a poetic self. The poems of *Ariel* were written at white heat, two or three a day, in the last months of Plath's life, but there is nothing hurried in their language or structure. When they are taken together with the poems posthumously published in *Crossing the Water* (1971) and *Winter Trees* (1972), a coherent persona emerges: larger than life, operatic in feeling. Although this focus on the self often excludes attention to the larger world, it generates the dynamic energy of her work. Plath appropriates a centrally American tradition, the heroic ego confronting the sublime, but she brilliantly revises this tradition by turning what the American Transcendentalist Ralph Waldo Emerson called the "great and crescive self" into a heroine instead of a hero. Seizing a mythic power, the Plath of the poems transmutes the domestic and the ordinary into the hallucinatory, the utterly strange. Her revision of the romantic ego dramatizes its tendency toward disproportion and excess, and she is fully capable of both using and mocking this heightened sense of self, as she does in her poem "Lady Lazarus."

Plath's well-known autobiographical novel, *The Bell Jar* (1963) has nothing of the brilliance of her poems, but it effectively dramatizes the stereotyping of women's roles in the 1950s and the turmoil of a young woman only partly aware that her gifts and ambitions greatly exceed the options available to her. In the novel Plath uses her experience as a guest editor of a young-women's magazine (in real life, *Mademoiselle*) and then, in an abrupt shift, presents her heroine's attempted suicide and hospitalization. Plath herself had suffered a serious breakdown and attempted suicide between her junior and senior years in college. The popularity of *The Bell Jar* may be one reason why attention to Plath's life has sometimes obscured the accomplishments of her art. While her poems often begin in autobiography, their success depends on Plath's imaginative transformations of experience into myth, as in a number of her poems (such as "Daddy") where the figure of her Prussian father is transformed into an emblem for masculine authority. Otto Plath was an entomologist and the author of a treatise on bumblebees. His death in 1940 from gangrene (the consequence of a diabetic condition he refused to treat), when Plath was eight, was the crucial event of her childhood. After his death her mother, Aurelia, while struggling to support two small children, encouraged her daughter's literary ambitions.

In many ways Plath embodied the bright, young, middle-class woman of the 1950s. She went to Smith College on a scholarship and graduated summa cum laude. On a Fulbright grant she studied in England at Cambridge University, where she met and married the poet Ted Hughes. On the face of it her marriage must have seemed the perfect fate for such a young woman; it combined romance, two poets beginning careers together (Plath's first book, *The Colossus*, appeared in 1960), and two children (Frieda, born in 1960, and Nicholas, born in 1962), with a country house in Devon, England. In her poems, however, we find the strains of such a life; the work is galvanized by suffering, by a terrible constriction against which she unlooses "The lioness, / The shriek in the bath, / The cloak of holes" ("Purdah"). In articulating a dark vision of domestic life Plath adopted the license of Robert Lowell and Anne Sexton, a fellow student in Lowell's poetry seminar, to write about "private and taboo subjects."

While still living in Devon, Plath wrote most of the poems that were to make up *Ariel* (by Christmas, 1962, she had gathered them in a black binder and arranged them in a careful sequence). The marriage broke up in the summer of 1962, and at the beginning of the new year Plath found herself with two small children, living in a London flat during one of the coldest winters in recent British history. There she began new poems, writing furiously until February 1963, when she took her own life. The *Ariel* collection published by Hughes in 1965 does not follow Plath's intended sequence; it omits what Hughes called "some of the more personally aggressive poems from 1962" and includes the dozen or so poems Plath wrote in the months before her death and that she had envisioned as the beginnings of a third book. Nonetheless, the powerful, angry poems of *Ariel*, mining a limited range of deep feeling, are Plath's best-known work. Fueled by an anger toward her husband and her father, she speaks in these poems as one whose feelings are more than her own; it is as if she were the character in George Eliot's *Daniel Deronda* (1876) who appears suddenly before the novel's heroine and says, "I am a woman's life." Other poems, however, demonstrate her ability to render a wider variety of emotion; they include poems about her children (such as "Morning Song," "Child," and "Parliament Hill Fields") and a number of arresting poems about the natural world. In the vastness of natural processes the Romantic ego finds something as large as itself, and Plath's response to nature is intense, often uncanny. Her poems offer an eccentric vision where (as in "Blackberrying") the appearance of the natural world is never separable from the consciousness of the one who sees it.

For all her courting of excess Plath is a remarkably controlled writer; her lucid stanzas, her clear diction, her dazzling alterations of sound display that control. The imaginative intensity of her poems is her own triumphant creation out of the difficult circumstances of her life. She once remarked, "I cannot sympathize with those cries from the heart that are informed by nothing except a needle or a knife. . . . I believe that one should be able to control and manipulate experiences, even the most terrifying . . . with an informed and intelligent mind." The influence of her style, and of the persona she created, continues to be felt in the work of a wide variety of contemporary poets.

Morning Song

Love set you going like a fat gold watch.
The midwife slapped your footsoles, and your bald cry
Took its place among the elements.

Our voices echo, magnifying your arrival. New statue.
In a drafty museum, your nakedness   5
Shadows our safety. We stand round blankly as walls.

I'm no more your mother
Than the cloud that distills a mirror to reflect its own slow
Effacement at the wind's hand.

All night your moth-breath   10
Flickers among the flat pink roses. I wake to listen:
A far sea moves in my ear.

One cry, and I stumble from bed, cow-heavy and floral
In my Victorian nightgown.
Your mouth opens clean as a cat's. The window square   15

Whitens and swallows its dull stars. And now you try
Your handful of notes;
The clear vowels rise like balloons.

1961   1966

Lady Lazarus[1]

I have done it again.
One year in every ten
I manage it—

A sort of walking miracle, my skin
Bright as a Nazi lampshade,[2]   5
My right foot

A paperweight,
My face a featureless, fine
Jew linen.

---

1. Lazarus was raised from the dead by Jesus (John 11.1–45).

2. In the Nazi death camps the victims' skins were sometimes used to make lampshades.

Peel off the napkin   10
O my enemy.
Do I terrify?——

The nose, the eye pits, the full set of teeth?
The sour breath
Will vanish in a day.   15

Soon, soon the flesh
The grave cave ate will be
At home on me

And I a smiling woman.
I am only thirty.   20
And like the cat I have nine times to die.

This is Number Three.
What a trash
To annihilate each decade.

What a million filaments.   25
The peanut-crunching crowd
Shoves in to see

Them unwrap me hand and foot——
The big strip tease.
Gentlemen, ladies   30

These are my hands
My knees.
I may be skin and bone,

Nevertheless, I am the same, identical woman.
The first time it happened I was ten.   35
It was an accident.

The second time I meant
To last it out and not come back at all.
I rocked shut

As a seashell.   40
They had to call and call
And pick the worms off me like sticky pearls.

Dying
Is an art, like everything else.
I do it exceptionally well.   45

I do it so it feels like hell.
I do it so it feels real.
I guess you could say I've a call.

It's easy enough to do it in a cell.
It's easy enough to do it and stay put.   50
It's the theatrical

Comeback in broad day
To the same place, the same face, the same brute
Amused shout:

'A miracle!'   55
That knocks me out.
There is a charge

For the eyeing of my scars, there is a charge
For the hearing of my heart——
It really goes.   60

And there is a charge, a very large charge
For a word or a touch
Or a bit of blood

Or a piece of my hair or my clothes.
So, so, Herr[3] Doktor.   65
So, Herr Enemy.

I am your opus,
I am your valuable,
The pure gold baby

That melts to a shriek.   70
I turn and burn.
Do not think I underestimate your great concern.

Ash, ash——
You poke and stir.
Flesh, bone, there is nothing there——   75

A cake of soap,
A wedding ring,
A gold filling.[4]

Herr God, Herr Lucifer
Beware   80
Beware.

Out of the ash[5]
I rise with my red hair
And I eat men like air.

1962   1966

---

3. Mr. (German).
4. The Nazis used human remains in the making of soap and scavenged corpses for jewelry and gold teeth.

5. An allusion to the phoenix, a mythical bird that dies by fire and is reborn out of its own ashes.

Daddy

You do not do, you do not do
Any more, black shoe
In which I have lived like a foot
For thirty years, poor and white,
Barely daring to breathe or Achoo.   5

Daddy, I have had to kill you.
You died before I had time——
Marble-heavy, a bag full of God,
Ghastly statue with one grey toe[1]
Big as a Frisco seal   10

And a head in the freakish Atlantic
Where it pours bean green over blue
In the waters of beautiful Nauset.[2]
I used to pray to recover you.
Ach, du.[3]   15

In the German tongue, in the Polish town[4]
Scraped flat by the roller
Of wars, wars, wars.
But the name of the town is common.
My Polack friend   20

Says there are a dozen or two.
So I never could tell where you
Put your foot, your root,
I never could talk to you.
The tongue stuck in my jaw.   25

It stuck in a barb wire snare.
Ich,[5] ich, ich, ich,
I could hardly speak.
I thought every German was you.
And the language obscene   30

An engine, an engine
Chuffing me off like a Jew.
A Jew to Dachau, Auschwitz, Belsen.[6]
I began to talk like a Jew.
I think I may well be a Jew.   35

The snows of the Tyrol,[7] the clear beer of Vienna
Are not very pure or true.
With my gypsy ancestress and my weird luck

1. Plath's father's toe turned black from gangrene, a complication of diabetes.
2. Massachusetts beach.
3. Ah, you (German): the first of a series of references to her father's German origins.
4. The poet's father, of German descent, was
born in Grabow, Poland.
5. I (German).
6. German concentration camps, where millions
of Jews were murdered during World War II.
7. Austrian Alpine region.

And my Taroc[8] pack and my Taroc pack
I may be a bit of a Jew.   40

I have always been scared of *you*,
With your Luftwaffe,[9] your gobbledygoo.
And your neat mustache
And your Aryan eye, bright blue.
Panzer[1]-man, panzer-man, O You——   45

Not God but a swastika
So black no sky could squeak through.
Every woman adores a Fascist,
The boot in the face, the brute
Brute heart of a brute like you.   50

You stand at the blackboard, daddy,
In the picture I have of you,
A cleft in your chin instead of your foot
But no less a devil for that, no not
And less the black man who   55

Bit my pretty red heart in two.
I was ten when they buried you.
At twenty I tried to die
And get back, back, back to you.
I thought even the bones would do.   60

But they pulled me out of the sack,
And they stuck me together with glue.[2]
And then I knew what to do.
I made a model of you,
A man in black with a Meinkampf[3] look   65

And a love of the rack and the screw.
And I said I do, I do.
So daddy, I'm finally through.
The black telephone's off at the root,
The voices just can't worm through.   70

If I've killed one man, I've killed two——
The vampire who said he was you
And drank my blood for a year,
Seven years, if you want to know.
Daddy, you can lie back now.   75

---

8. Variation of Tarot, ancient fortune-telling cards. Gypsies, like Jews, were objects of Nazi genocidal ambition; many died in the concentration camps.
9. The German air force.
1. Armor (German); refers to the German army's tank corps in World War II. Hitler preached the superiority of the Aryans—people of German stock with blond hair and blue eyes.
2. An allusion to Plath's first suicide attempt.
3. A reference to Hitler's political autobiography, *Mein Kampf* (my struggle), written and published before his rise to power, in which the future dictator outlined his plans for world conquest.

There's a stake in your fat black heart
And the villagers never liked you.
They are dancing and stamping on you.
They always *knew* it was you.
Daddy, daddy, you bastard, I'm through.   80

1962   1966

Blackberrying

Nobody in the lane, and nothing, nothing but blackberries,
Blackberries on either side, though on the right mainly,
A blackberry alley, going down in hooks, and a sea
Somewhere at the end of it, heaving. Blackberries
Big as the ball of my thumb, and dumb as eyes   5
Ebon in the hedges, fat
With blue-red juices. These they squander on my fingers.
I had not asked for such a blood sisterhood; they must love me.
They accommodate themselves to my milkbottle, flattening their sides.

Overhead go the choughs[1] in black, cacophonous flocks—   10
Bits of burnt paper wheeling in a blown sky.
Theirs is the only voice, protesting, protesting.
I do not think the sea will appear at all.
The high, green meadows are glowing, as if lit from within.
I come to one bush of berries so ripe it is a bush of flies,   15
Hanging their bluegreen bellies and their wing panes in a Chinese screen.
The honey-feast of the berries has stunned them; they believe in heaven.
One more hook, and the berries and bushes end.

The only thing to come now is the sea.
From between two hills a sudden wind funnels at me,   20
Slapping its phantom laundry in my face.
These hills are too green and sweet to have tasted salt.
I follow the sheep path between them. A last hook brings me
To the hills' northern face, and the face is orange rock
That looks out on nothing, nothing but a great space   25
Of white and pewter lights, and a din like silversmiths
Beating and beating at an intractable metal.

1961   1971

Child

Your clear eye is the one absolutely beautiful thing.
I want to fill it with color and ducks,
The zoo of the new

---

1. Small, chattering birds of the crow family.

Whose names you meditate—
April snowdrop, Indian pipe, 5
Little

Stalk without wrinkle,
Pool in which images
Should be grand and classical

Not this troublous 10
Wringing of hands, this dark
Ceiling without a star.

1963   1972

JOHN UPDIKE
1932–2009

"To transcribe middleness with all its grits, bumps and anonymities, in its fullness of satisfaction and mystery: is it possible . . . or worth doing?" John Updike's novels and stories give a positive answer to the question he asks in his early memoir, *The Dogwood Tree: A Boyhood*; for he is arguably the most significant transcriber, or creator rather, of "middleness" in American writing since William Dean Howells (about whom he has written appreciatively) a century earlier. Falling in love in high school, meeting a college roommate, going to the eye doctor or dentist, eating supper on Sunday night, visiting your mother with your wife and son—these activities are made to yield up their possibilities to a writer as responsively curious in imagination and delicately precise in his literary expression as Updike showed himself to be.

Born in Shillington, Pennsylvania, John Updike was an only child. He was gifted at drawing and caricature, and after graduating summa cum laude from Harvard in 1954, he spent a year studying art in England, then returned to America and went to work for *The New Yorker*, where his first stories appeared and to which he contributed regularly for five decades. When later in the 1950s he left the magazine, he also left New York City and with his wife and children settled in Ipswich, Massachusetts. There he pursued "his solitary trade as methodically as the dentist practiced his," resisting the temptations of university teaching as successfully as he did the blandishments of media talk shows. His ample output was achieved through dedicated, steady work; his books are the fruit of patience, leisure, and craft.

Since 1959, when his first novel, *The Poorhouse Fair*, appeared, Updike published not only many novels and stories but also eight books of poetry, a play, and a vast store of book reviews and other prose writings. He is most admired by some readers as the author of the "Olinger" stories (included in *The Early Stories: 1953–1975*, 2003) about life in an imaginary Pennsylvania town that takes on its colors from the real Shillington of his youth. The heroes of these stories are adolescents straining to break out of their fast-perishing environments, as they grow up and as their small town turns into something else. Updike treats them with a blend of affection and ironic humor that is wonderfully assured in its touch, although his sense of place, of growing up during the Depression and the years of World War II, is always vividly present. Like Howells (whose fine memoir of his youthful days in Ohio, *A*

Boy's Town, is an ancestor of Updike's *The Dogwood Tree*) he shows how one's spirit takes on its coloration from the material circumstances—houses, clothes, landscape, food, parents—one is bounded by.

This sense of place, which is also a sense of life, is found in the stories and in the novels too, although Updike found it harder to invent convincing forms in which to tell longer tales. His most ambitious novel is probably *The Centaur* (1964), memorable for its portrayal of three days of confusion and error in the life of an American high school teacher seen through his son's eyes, but the book is also burdened with an elaborate set of mythical trappings that seem less than inevitable. *Couples* (1968), a novel that gained him a good deal of notoriety as a chronicler of sexual relationships, marital and adulterous, is jammed with much interesting early 1960s lore about suburban life but seems uncertain whether it is an exercise in realism or a creative fantasy, as does *Marry Me* (1976).

In the four "Rabbit" novels Updike found his most congenial and engaging subject for longer fiction. In each book he rendered the sense of an era—the 1950s in *Rabbit, Run*; the late 1960s in *Rabbit Redux*; the great gasoline crisis of 1979 in *Rabbit Is Rich*; the end of the Reagan era (and the end of Rabbit) in *Rabbit at Rest* (1990)—through the eyes of a hero who both is and is not like his creator. Harry "Rabbit" Angstrom, ex–high school basketball star, a prey to nostalgia and in love with his own past, perpetually lives in a present he can't abide. *Rabbit, Run* shows him trying to escape from his town, his job, his wife, and his child by a series of disastrously sentimental and humanly irresponsible actions; yet Updike makes us feel Rabbit's yearnings even as we judge the painful consequences of yielding to them. Ten years later the fading basketball star has become a fortyish, dispirited printer with a wayward wife and a country that is both landing on the moon and falling to pieces. *Rabbit Redux* is masterly in presenting a small town rotting away from its past certainties; it also attempts to deal with the Vietnam War and the black revolution. *Rabbit Is Rich* is a gentler, sadder chronicling of the hero's settling into grandfatherhood as he draws ever closer to death; while *Rabbit at Rest*, the longest and richest of the four novels, brings him to a moving conclusion; Rabbit's coda is presented in the reflections of his son and illegitimate daughter in "Rabbit Remembered," collected in *Licks of Love* (2000). In *Roger's Version* (1986) and *S* (1988) Updike adopted—or permitted his protagonists to adopt—a more broadly, sometimes a harsher, satiric view of contemporary religion, computer technology, feminism, and other forms of "liberation." Still, for all his virtuosity as a novelist, his best work may be found in the stories and in his short novel *Of the Farm* (1965). In "Separating" (printed here) the boy from "The Happiest I've Been" (*The Same Door*, 1959) has grown up, married, and fathered children and is now about to leave them as he moves into divorce. It is a beautiful example of Updike's careful, poised sense of how things work, a sense that can also be observed in the poem "Dog's Death" and in his memoir *Self-Consciousness* (1989).

Near the end of "The Dogwood Tree" he summarized his boyish dream of becoming an artist:

> He saw art—between drawing and writing he ignorantly made no distinction—as a method of riding a thin pencil out of Shillington, out of time altogether, into an infinity of unseen and even unborn hearts. He pictured this infinity as radiant. How innocent!

Most writers would name that innocence only to deplore it. Updike maintained instead that, as with the Christian faith he professed, succeeding years gave him no better assumptions with which to replace it. In any case, his fine sense of fact protected him from fashionable extravagances in black humor and experimental narratives, while enabling him to be both a satirist and a celebrator of our social and domestic conditions. In the last decade of his life a fabulative, almost magical atmosphere appeared in some works, as with his 2000 novel, *Gertrude and Claudius*. Yet even here John Updike showed himself to be our era's most sensitive craftsman of personal and societal manners, as he did in the generational family saga based on spiritual perceptions, *In the Beauty of the Lilies* (1996), in *Villages* (2004), a bildungsroman about a protagonist's marriages, careers, and communities, and in the sociopolitical challenge of *Terrorist* (2006).

The following text is from *The New Yorker* (June 23, 1975).

Separating

The day was fair. Brilliant. All that June the weather had mocked the Maples' internal misery with solid sunlight—golden shafts and cascades of green in which their conversations had wormed unseeing, their sad murmuring selves the only stain in Nature. Usually by this time of the year they had acquired tans; but when they met their elder daughter's plane on her return from a year in England they were almost as pale as she, though Judith was too dazzled by the sunny opulent jumble of her native land to notice. They did not spoil her homecoming by telling her immediately. Wait a few days, let her recover from jet lag, had been one of their formulations, in that string of gray dialogues—over coffee, over cocktails, over Cointreau—that had shaped the strategy of their dissolution, while the earth performed its annual stunt of renewal unnoticed beyond their closed windows. Richard had thought to leave at Easter; Joan had insisted they wait until the four children were at last assembled, with all exams passed and ceremonies attended, and the bauble of summer to console them. So he had drudged away, in love, in dread, repairing screens, getting the mowers sharpened, rolling and patching their new tennis court.

The court, clay, had come through its first winter pitted and windswept bare of redcoat. Years ago the Maples had observed how often, among their friends, divorce followed a dramatic home improvement, as if the marriage were making one last twitchy effort to live; their own worst crisis had come amid the plaster dust and exposed plumbing of a kitchen renovation. Yet, a summer ago, as canary-yellow bulldozers gaily churned a grassy, daisy-dotted knoll into a muddy plateau, and a crew of pigtailed young men raked and tamped clay into a plane, this transformation did not strike them as ominous, but festive in its impudence; their marriage could rend the earth for fun. The next spring, waking each day at dawn to a sliding sensation as if the bed were being tipped, Richard found the barren tennis court, its net and tapes still rolled in the barn, an environment congruous with his mood of purposeful desolation, and the crumbling of handfuls of clay into cracks and holes (dogs had frolicked on the court in a thaw; rivulets had evolved trenches) an activity suitably elemental and interminable. In his sealed heart he hoped the day would never come.

Now it was here. A Friday. Judith was reacclimated; all four children were assembled, before jobs and camps and visits again scattered them. Joan thought they should be told one by one. Richard was for making an announcement at the table. She said, "I think just making an announcement is a cop-out. They'll start quarrelling and playing to each other instead of focussing. They're each individuals, you know, not just some corporate obstacle to your freedom."

"O.K., O.K. I agree." Joan's plan was exact. That evening, they were giving Judith a belated welcome-home dinner, of lobster and champagne. Then, the party over, they, the two of them, who nineteen years before would push her in a baby carriage along Tenth Street to Washington Square,[1] were to walk her out of the house, to the bridge across the salt creek, and tell her, swearing her to secrecy. Then Richard Jr., who was going directly from work to a rock concert in Boston, would be told, either late when he returned on the train or early Saturday morning before he went off to his job; he was seventeen and employed as one of a golf-course maintenance crew. Then the two younger children, John and Margaret, could, as the morning wore on, be informed.

"Mopped up, as it were," Richard said.

"Do you have any better plan? That leaves you the rest of Saturday to answer any questions, pack, and make your wonderful departure."

"No," he said, meaning he had no better plan, and agreed to hers, though it had an edge of false order, a plea for control in the semblance of its achievement, like Joan's long chore lists and financial accountings and, in the days when he first knew her, her too copious lecture notes. Her plan turned one hurdle for him into four—four knife-sharp walls, each with a sheer blind drop on the other side.

All spring he had been morbidly conscious of insides and outsides, of barriers and partitions. He and Joan stood as a thin barrier between the children and the truth. Each moment was a partition, with the past on one side and the future on the other, a future containing this unthinkable *now*. Beyond four knifelike walls a new life for him waited vaguely. His skull cupped a secret, a white face, a face both frightened and soothing, both strange and known, that he wanted to shield from tears, which he felt all about him, solid as the sunlight. So haunted, he had become obsessed with battening down the house against his absence, replacing screens and sash cords, hinges and latches—a Houdini[2] making things snug before his escape.

The lock. He had still to replace a lock on one of the doors of the screened porch. The task, like most such, proved more difficult than he had imagined. The old lock, aluminum frozen by corrosion, had been deliberately rendered obsolete by manufacturers. Three hardware stores had nothing that even approximately matched the mortised hole its removal (surprisingly easy) left. Another hole had to be gouged, with bits too small and saws too big, and the old hole fitted with a block of wood—the chisels dull, the saw rusty, his fingers thick with lack of sleep. The sun poured down, beyond the porch, on a world of neglect. The bushes already needed pruning, the windward side of the house was shedding flakes of paint, rain would get in when he was gone, insects, rot, death. His family, all those he would lose, filtered through the edges of his awareness as he struggled with screw holes, splinters, opaque instructions, minutiae of metal.

Judith sat on the porch, a princess returned from exile. She regaled them with stories of fuel shortages, of bomb scares in the Underground, of Pakistani workmen loudly lusting after her as she walked past on her way to dance school. Joan came and went, in and out of the house, calmer than she should have been, praising his struggles with the lock as if this were one more and not the last of their chain of shared chores. The younger of

---

1. In Greenwich Village, an area in lower Manhattan, New York City.

2. Harry Houdini (1874–1926), American magician and escape artist.

his sons, John, now at fifteen suddenly, unwittingly handsome, for a few minutes held the rickety screen door while his father clumsily hammered and chiselled, each blow a kind of sob in Richard's ears. His younger daughter, having been at a slumber party, slept on the porch hammock through all the noise—heavy and pink, trusting and forsaken. Time, like the sunlight, continued relentlessly; the sunlight slowly slanted. Today was one of the longest days. The lock clicked, worked. He was through. He had a drink; he drank it on the porch, listening to his daughter. "It was so sweet," she was saying, "during the worst of it, how all the butcher's and bakery shops kept open by candlelight. They're all so plucky and cute. From the papers, things sounded so much worse here—people shooting people in gas lines, and everybody freezing."

Richard asked her, "Do you still want to live in England forever?" *Forever*: the concept, now a reality upon him, pressed and scratched at the back of his throat.

"No," Judith confessed, turning her oval face to him, its eyes still childishly far apart, but the lips set as over something succulent and satisfactory. "I was anxious to come home. I'm an American." She was a woman. They had raised her; he and Joan had endured together to raise her, alone of the four. The others had still some raising left in them. Yet it was the thought of telling Judith—the image of her, their first baby, walking between them arm in arm to the bridge—that broke him. The partition between himself and the tears broke. Richard sat down to the celebratory meal with the back of his throat aching; the champagne, the lobster seemed phases of sunshine; he saw them and tasted them through tears. He blinked, swallowed, croakily joked about hay fever. The tears would not stop leaking through; they came not through a hole that could be plugged but through a permeable spot in a membrane, steadily, purely, endlessly, fruitfully. They became, his tears, a shield for himself against these others—their faces, the fact of their assembly, a last time as innocents, at a table where he sat the last time as head. Tears dropped from his nose as he broke the lobster's back; salt flavored his champagne as he sipped it; the raw clench at the back of his throat was delicious. He could not help himself.

His children tried to ignore his tears. Judith on his right, lit a cigarette, gazed upward in the direction of her too energetic, too sophisticated exhalation; on her other side, John earnestly bent his face to the extraction of the last morsels—legs, tail segments—from the scarlet corpse. Joan, at the opposite end of the table, glanced at him surprised, her reproach displaced by a quick grimace, of forgiveness, or of salute to his superior gift of strategy. Between them, Margaret, no longer called Bean, thirteen and large for her age, gazed from the other side of his pane of tears as if into a shopwindow at something she coveted—at her father, a crystalline heap of splinters and memories. It was not she, however, but John who, in the kitchen, as they cleared the plates and carapaces away, asked Joan the question: *"Why is Daddy crying?"*

Richard heard the question but not the murmured answer. Then he heard Bean cry, "Oh, no-oh!"—the faintly dramatized exclamation of one who had long expected it.

John returned to the table carrying a bowl of salad. He nodded tersely at his father and his lips shaped the conspiratorial words "She told."

"Told what?" Richard asked aloud, insanely.

The boy sat down as if to rebuke his father's distraction with the example of his own good manners and said quietly, "The separation."

Joan and Margaret returned; the child, in Richard's twisted vision, seemed diminished in size, and relieved, relieved to have had the boogeyman at last proved real. He called out to her—the distances at the table had grown immense—"You knew, you always knew," but the clenching at the back of his throat prevented him from making sense of it. From afar he heard Joan talking, levelly, sensibly, reciting what they had prepared: it was a separation for the summer, an experiment. She and Daddy both agreed it would be good for them; they needed space and time to think; they liked each other but did not make each other happy enough, somehow.

Judith, imitating her mother's factual tone, but in her youth off-key, too cool, said, "I think it's silly. You should either live together or get divorced."

Richard's crying, like a wave that has crested and crashed, had become tumultuous; but it was overtopped by another tumult, for John, who had been so reserved, now grew larger and larger at the table. Perhaps his younger sister's being credited with knowing set him off. "Why didn't you *tell* us?" he asked, in a large round voice quite unlike his own. "You should have *told* us you weren't getting along."

Richard was startled into attempting to force words through his tears. "We *do* get along, that's the trouble, so it doesn't show even to us—" "That we do not love each other" was the rest of the sentence; he couldn't finish it.

Joan finished for him, in her style. "And we've always, *especially*, loved our children."

John was not mollified. "What do you care about *us?*" he boomed. "We're just little things you *had*." His sisters' laughing forced a laugh from him, which he turned hard and parodistic: "Ha ha *ha*." Richard and Joan realized simultaneously that the child was drunk, on Judith's homecoming champagne. Feeling bound to keep the center of the stage, John took a cigarette from Judith's pack, poked it into his mouth, let it hang from his lower lip, and squinted like a gangster.

"You're not little things we *had*," Richard called to him. "You're the whole point. But you're grown. Or almost."

The boy was lighting matches. Instead of holding them to his cigarette (for they had never seen him smoke; being "good" had been his way of setting himself apart), he held them to his mother's face, closer and closer, for her to blow out. Then he lit the whole folder—a hiss and then a torch, held against his mother's face. Prismed by tears, the flame filled Richard's vision; he didn't know how it was extinguished. He heard Margaret say, "Oh stop showing off," and saw John, in response, break the cigarette in two and put the halves entirely into his mouth and chew, sticking out his tongue to display the shreds to his sister.

Joan talked to him, reasoning—a fountain of reason, unintelligible. "Talked about it for years . . . our children must help us . . . Daddy and I both want . . ." As the boy listened, he carefully wadded a paper napkin into the leaves of his salad, fashioned a ball of paper and lettuce, and popped it into his mouth, looking around the table for the expected laughter. None came. Judith said, "Be mature," and dismissed a plume of smoke.

Richard got up from this stifling table and led the boy outside. Though the house was in twilight, the outdoors still brimmed with light, the long waste light of high summer. Both laughing, he supervised John's spitting out the lettuce and paper and tobacco into the pachysandra.[3] He took him by the hand—a square gritty hand, but for its softness a man's. Yet, it held on. They ran together up into the field, past the tennis court. The raw banking left by the bulldozers was dotted with daisies. Past the court and a flat stretch where they used to play family baseball stood a soft green rise glorious in the sun, each weed and species of grass distinct as illumination on parchment. "I'm sorry, so sorry," Richard cried. "You were the only one who ever tried to help me with all the goddam jobs around this place."

Sobbing, safe within his tears and the champagne, John explained, "It's not just the separation, it's the whole crummy year, I *hate* that school, you can't make any friends, the history teacher's a scud."[4]

They sat on the crest of the rise, shaking and warm from their tears but easier in their voices, and Richard tried to focus on the child's sad year—the weekdays long with homework, the weekends spent in his room with model airplanes, while his parents murmured down below, nursing their separation. How selfish, how blind, Richard thought; his eyes felt scoured. He told his son, "We'll think about getting you transferred. Life's too short to be miserable."

They had said what they could, but did not want the moment to heal, and talked on, about the school, about the tennis court, whether it would ever again be as good as it had been that first summer. They walked to inspect it and pressed a few more tapes more firmly down. A little stiltedly, perhaps trying to make too much of the moment, to prolong it, Richard led the boy to the spot in the field where the view was best, of the metallic blue river, the emerald marsh, the scattered islands velvet with shadow in the low light, the white bits of beach far away. "See," he said. "It goes on being beautiful. It'll be here tomorrow."

"I know," John answered, impatiently. The moment had closed.

Back in the house, the others had opened some white wine, the champagne being drunk, and still sat at the table, the three females, gossiping. Where Joan sat had become the head. She turned, showing him a tearless face, and asked, "All right?"

"We're fine," he said, resenting it, though relieved, that the party went on without him.

In bed she explained, "I couldn't cry I guess because I cried so much all spring. It really wasn't fair. It's your idea, and you made it look as though I was kicking you out."

"I'm sorry," he said. "I couldn't stop. I wanted to but couldn't."

"You *didn't* want to. You loved it. You were having your way, making a general announcement."

"I love having it over," he admitted. "God, those kids were great. So brave and funny." John, returned to the house, had settled to a model airplane in his room, and kept shouting down to them, "I'm O.K. No sweat." "And the way," Richard went on, cozy in his relief, "they never questioned the reasons we gave. No thought of a third person. Not even Judith."

---

3. Green, leafy plant, frequently used as ground cover.
4. Dull, disagreeable, objectionable person.

"That *was* touching," Joan said.

He gave her a hug. "You were great too. Thank you." Guiltily, he realized he did not feel separated.

"You still have Dickie to do," she told him. These words set before him a black mountain in the darkness; its cold breath, its near weight affected his chest. Of the four children Dickie was most nearly his conscience. Joan did not need to add, "That's one piece of your dirty work I won't do for you."

"I know. I'll do it. You go to sleep."

Within minutes, her breathing slowed, became oblivious and deep. It was quarter to midnight. Dickie's train from the concert would come in at one-fourteen. Richard set the alarm for one. He had slept atrociously for weeks. But whenever he closed his lids some glimpse of the last hours scorched them—Judith exhaling toward the ceiling in a kind of aversion, Bean's mute staring, the sunstruck growth of the field where he and John had rested. The mountain before him moved closer, moved within him; he was huge, momentous. The ache at the back of his throat felt stale. His wife slept as if slain beside him. When, exasperated by his hot lids, his crowded heart, he rose from bed and dressed, she awoke enough to turn over. He told her then, "If I could undo it all, I would."

"Where would you begin?" she asked. There was no place. Giving him courage, she was always giving him courage. He put on shoes without socks in the dark. The children were breathing in their rooms, the downstairs was hollow. In their confusion they had left lights burning. He turned off all but one, the kitchen overhead. The car started. He had hoped it wouldn't. He met only moonlight on the road; it seemed a diaphanous companion, flickering in the leaves along the roadside, haunting his rearview mirror like a pursuer, melting under his headlights. The center of town, not quite deserted, was eerie at this hour. A young cop in uniform kept company with a gang of T-shirted kids on the steps of the bank. Across from the railroad station, several bars kept open. Customers, mostly young, passed in and out of the warm night, savoring summer's novelty. Voices shouted from cars as they passed; an immense conversation seemed in progress. Richard parked and in his weariness put his head on the passenger seat, out of the commotion and wheeling lights. It was as when, in the movies, an assassin grimly carries his mission through the jostle of a carnival—except the movies cannot show the precipitous, palpable slope you cling to within. You cannot climb back down; you can only fall. The synthetic fabric of the car seat, warmed by his cheek, confided to him an ancient, distant scent of vanilla.

A train whistle caused him to lift his head. It was on time; he had hoped it would be late. The slender drawgates descended. The bell of approach tingled happily. The great metal body, horizontally fluted, rocked to a stop, and sleepy teen-agers disembarked, his son among them. Dickie did not show surprise that his father was meeting him at this terrible hour. He sauntered to the car with two friends, both taller than he. He said "Hi" to his father and took the passenger's seat with an exhausted promptness that expressed gratitude. The friends got into the back, and Richard was grateful; a few more minutes' postponement would be won by driving them home.

He asked, "How was the concert?"

"Groovy," one boy said from the back seat.

"It bit," the other said.

"It was O.K.," Dickie said, moderate by nature, so reasonable that in his childhood the unreason of the world had given him headaches, stomach aches, nausea. When the second friend had been dropped off at his dark house, the boy blurted, "Dad, my eyes are killing me with hay fever! I'm out there cutting that mothering grass all day!"

"Do we still have those drops?"

"They didn't do any good last summer."

"They might this." Richard swung a U-turn on the empty street. The drive home took a few minutes. The mountain was here, in his throat. "Richard," he said, and felt the boy, slumped and rubbing his eyes, go tense at his tone, "I didn't come to meet you just to make your life easier. I came because your mother and I have some news for you, and you're a hard man to get ahold of these days. It's sad news."

"That's O.K." The reassurance came out soft, but quick, as if released from the tip of a spring.

Richard had feared that his tears would return and choke him, but the boy's manliness set an example, and his voice issued forth steady and dry. "It's sad news, but it needn't be tragic news, at least for you. It should have no practical effect on your life, though it's bound to have an emotional effect. You'll work at your job, and go back to school in September. Your mother and I are really proud of what you're making of your life; we don't want that to change at all."

"Yeah," the boy said lightly, on the intake of his breath, holding himself up. They turned the corner; the church they went to loomed like a gutted fort. The home of the woman Richard hoped to marry stood across the green. Her bedroom light burned.

"Your mother and I," he said, "have decided to separate. For the summer. Nothing legal, no divorce yet. We want to see how it feels. For some years now, we haven't been doing enough for each other, making each other as happy as we should be. Have you sensed that?"

"No," the boy said. It was an honest, unemotional answer: true or false in a quiz.

Glad for the factual basis, Richard pursued, even garrulously, the details. His apartment across town, his utter accessibility, the split vacation arrangements, the advantages to the children, the added mobility and variety of the summer. Dickie listened, absorbing. "Do the others know?"

Richard described how they had been told.

"How did they take it?"

"The girls pretty calmly. John flipped out; he shouted and ate a cigarette and made a salad out of his napkin and told us how much he hated school."

His brother chuckled. "He did?"

"Yeah. The school issue was more upsetting for him than Mom and me. He seemed to feel better for having exploded."

"He did?" The repetition was the first sign that he was stunned.

"Yes. Dickie, I want to tell you something. This last hour, waiting for your train to get in, has been about the worst of my life. I hate this. *Hate* it. My father would have died before doing it to me." He felt immensely lighter, saying this. He had dumped the mountain on the boy. They were home. Moving swiftly as a shadow, Dickie was out of the car, through the bright kitchen. Richard called after him, "Want a glass of milk or anything?"

"No thanks."

"Want us to call the course tomorrow and say you're too sick to work?"

"No, that's all right." The answer was faint, delivered at the door to his room; Richard listened for the slam of a tantrum. The door closed normally. The sound was sickening.

Joan had sunk into that first deep trough of sleep and was slow to awake. Richard had to repeat, "I told him."

"What did he say?"

"Nothing much. Could you go say good night to him? Please."

She left their room, without putting on a bathrobe. He sluggishly changed back into his pajamas and walked down the hall. Dickie was already in bed, Joan was sitting beside him, and the boy's bedside clock radio was murmuring music. When she stood, an inexplicable light—the moon?—outlined her body through the nightie. Richard sat on the warm place she had indented on the child's narrow mattress. He asked him, "Do you want the radio on like that?"

"It always is."

"Doesn't it keep you awake? It would me."

"No."

"Are you sleepy?"

"Yeah."

"Good. Sure you want to get up and go to work? You've had a big night."

"I want to."

Away at school this winter he had learned for the first time that you can go short of sleep and live. As an infant he had slept with an immobile, sweating intensity that had alarmed his babysitters. As the children aged, he became the first to go to bed, earlier for a time than his younger brother and sister. Even now, he would go slack in the middle of a television show, his sprawled legs hairy and brown. "O.K. Good boy. Dickie, listen. I love you so much, I never knew how much until now. No matter how this works out, I'll always be with you. Really."

Richard bent to kiss an averted face but his son, sinewy, turned and with wet cheeks embraced him and gave him a kiss, on the lips, passionate as a woman's. In his father's ear he moaned one word, the crucial, intelligent word: *"Why?"*

Why. It was a whistle of wind in a crack, a knife thrust, a window thrown open on emptiness. The white face was gone, the darkness was featureless. Richard had forgotten why.

1975

PHILIP ROTH

b. 1933

From the moment Philip Roth's collection of stories *Goodbye, Columbus* won the Houghton Mifflin Literary Fellowship for 1959, his career has received the ambiguous reward of much anxious concern, directed at it by critics and centered on whether he would develop the promise displayed in this first book. Ten years later, with *Portnoy's Complaint*, Roth became overnight the famous author of a "dirty" best-seller, yet his success only made his critics more uneasy. Was this gifted portrayer of Jewish middle-class life really more interested in scoring points off caricatures than in creating and exploring characters? Did his very facility with words inhibit the exercise of deeper sympathies and more humanly generous purposes?

Roth grew up in Newark, New Jersey, attended the branch of Rutgers University there, graduated from Bucknell University, took an M.A. in English literature at the University of Chicago, then served in the army. Over the years he has taught at a number of universities while receiving many awards and fellowships. Like John Barth, another "university" writer, Roth is an ironic humorist, although the impulse behind his early stories is darker and less playful. *Goodbye, Columbus* is about Jews on the verge of being or already having been assimilated into the larger American culture, and the stories confidently take the measure of their embattled heroes, as in "The Conversion of the Jews" or "Epstein" or the long title story. "Defender of the Faith" (printed here), arguably the best piece in the collection, is distinguished for the way Roth explores rather than exploits the conflict between personal feelings and religious loyalties as they are felt by Nathan Marx, a U.S. Army sergeant in a Missouri training company near the end of World War II. Throughout *Goodbye, Columbus* the narrator's voice is centrally important: in some stories it is indistinguishable from that of a campus wiseguy; in others it reaches out to a calmer and graver sense of disparities between promises and performance.

Roth's first two novels, *Letting Go* (1962) and *When She Was Good* (1967), markedly extended the territory charted in *Goodbye, Columbus* and showed him eager and equipped to write about people other than Jews. *Letting Go* is conventional in technique and in its subjects—love, marriage, university life—but Roth's easy mastery of the look and feel of places and things is everywhere evident. F. Scott Fitzgerald is the American writer whose presence in these early novels is most strongly felt; in particular, the section from *Letting Go* told in the first person by a graduate student in English betrays its indebtedness to Fitzgerald's Nick Carraway, the narrator of *The Great Gatsby*. This Fitzgeraldian atmosphere, with its nostalgic evocation of adolescence and early romantic visions, is even more evident in *When She Was Good*, which is strong in its rendering of middle-American living rooms and kitchens, the flushed atmosphere of late-night 1950s sex in parked cars, or the lyrics of popular songs—bits of remembered trivia that Roth, like his predecessor, has a genius for bringing to life.

The less-than-overwhelming reception of his second novel probably helped Roth move away from relatively sober realism; certainly *Portnoy's Complaint* (1969) is a louder and more virtuoso performance than the earlier books. Alexander Portnoy's recollections of early childhood miseries are really a pretext for Roth to perform a succession of clever numbers in the inventive mode of a stand-up comic. Memories of growing up in New Jersey, listening to radio programs, playing softball, ogling girls at the ice-skating rink, or (most sensationally) masturbating in outlandish ways add up to an entertaining narrative that is sometimes crude but more often delicate and precise.

After *Portnoy* Roth moved toward fantasy and further showmanly operations: *Our Gang* (1970) attempted to do for Richard Nixon and his associates what actual events were to do one better; *The Breast* (1971) is a rather unamusing fable about a man's metamorphosis into that object; *The Great American Novel* (1973) threatened to sink under its weight of baseball lore dressed up in tall tales and sick jokes. But in *My Life as a Man* (1974) and *The Professor of Desire* (1977) he returned to matters that have traditionally preoccupied the social novelist and that inform his own best work: marriage, divorce, the family, Jewishness, and psychoanalysis—the pressures of civilization and the resultant individual discontents.

His finest work is to be found in the Zuckerman trilogy (*Zuckerman Bound*, 1985) and its successor, *The Counterlife* (1987). In these novels Roth created a hero-as-novelist whose experience parallels in important ways his creator's. A scandalous novel, *Carnovsky*, recalls *Portnoy's Complaint*; a critic named Milton Appel is a stand-in for the real critic Irving Howe, who once subjected Roth's work to hostile criticism. Yet for all the dangers of self-pity or self-absorption such autobiographical reference involves, the novels add up to something much deeper, more comic and touching, than self-advertisement and complaint. Scenes like the death of Zuckerman's father in a Florida hospital and the subsequent return of the son to the vanished Newark where he grew up are moving expressions of the generous purposes and human sympathies we find in Roth's work at its best. And those purposes and sympathies are also evident in his autobiographical writing: in *The Facts* (1988) and especially in *Patrimony* (1991), a poignant memoir of his father.

In the 1990s and into the twenty-first century Roth has developed his art of impersonation into audacious and sometimes excessive forms. *Operation Shylock* (1993) poses a presumably real Philip Roth who encounters an impostor; *Sabbath's Theater* (1995) recasts his typical protagonist as a puppeteer who manipulates women much the same way; *American Pastoral* (1997) brings back Nathan Zuckerman for a high school reunion and the investigation of a "more ordinary" classmate's life. Zuckerman remains on hand for *I Married a Communist* (1998) and *The Human Stain* (2000), while David Kepesh (who had turned into a female breast in the author's much earlier fantasy) reappears as a professor who seduces his students in *The Dying Animal* (2001). Further seduction takes place in *Everyman* (2006), although the author's most disturbing projections are reserved for *The Plot against America* (2004), in which a fictive Charles A. Lindbergh becomes president and initiates repression of American Jews. *Exit Ghost* (2007) has Nathan Zuckerman return to New York City and reencounter characters from previous novels. *Indignation* (2008) set a young man's maturation against the looming threat of military service in the Korean War. *The Humbling* (2009) projects Roth's late-life anxieties as a writer onto the career of an actor in decline. *Nemesis* (2010) expands the author's concerns with human morality (and the role of a God who allows such suffering) to encompass a polio epidemic in the Newark of his childhood. Throughout his work, Roth's emphasis remains on invention, reminding readers that the writerly self is a virtually inexhaustible resource for the imagination.

The following text is from *Goodbye, Columbus* (1959).

Defender of the Faith

In May of 1945, only a few weeks after the fighting had ended in Europe, I was rotated back to the States, where I spent the remainder of the war with a training company at Camp Crowder, Missouri. We had been racing across Germany so swiftly during the late winter and spring that when I boarded the plane that drizzly morning in Berlin, I couldn't believe our destination lay to the west. My mind might inform me otherwise, but there was an inertia of the spirit that told me we were flying to a new front where we would disembark and continue our push eastward—eastward until we'd circled the globe, marching through villages along whose twisting, cobbled streets crowds of the enemy would watch us take possession of what up till then they'd considered their own. I had changed enough in two years not to mind the trembling of the old people, the crying of the very young, the uncertain fear in the eyes of the once-arrogant. After two years I had been fortunate enough to develop an infantryman's heart which, like his feet, at first aches and swells, but finally grows horny enough for him to travel the weirdest paths without feeling a thing.

Captain Paul Barrett was to be my C.O. at Camp Crowder. The day I reported for duty he came out of his office to shake my hand. He was short, gruff, and fiery, and indoors or out he wore his polished helmet liner[1] down on his little eyes. In Europe he had received a battlefield commission and a serious chest wound, and had been returned to the States only a few months before. He spoke easily to me, but was, I thought, unnecessarily abusive towards the troops. At the evening formation, he introduced me.

"Gentlemen," he called. "Sergeant Thurston, as you know, is no longer with this Company. Your new First Sergeant is Sergeant Nathan Marx here. He is a veteran of the European theater and consequently will take no shit."

I sat up late in the orderly room that evening, trying halfheartedly to solve the riddle of duty rosters, personnel forms, and morning reports. The CQ[2] slept with his mouth open on a mattress on the floor. A trainee stood reading the next day's duty roster, which was posted on the bulletin board directly inside the screen door. It was a warm evening and I could hear the men's radios playing dance music over in the barracks.

The trainee, who I knew had been staring at me whenever I looked groggily into the forms, finally took a step in my direction.

"Hey, Sarge—we having a G.I. party tomorrow night?" A G.I. party is a barracks-cleaning.

"You usually have them on Friday nights?"

"Yes," and then he added mysteriously, "that's the whole thing."

"Then you'll have a G.I. party."

He turned away and I heard him mumbling. His shoulders were moving and I wondered if he was crying.

"What's your name, soldier?" I asked.

He turned, not crying at all. Instead his green-speckled eyes, long and narrow, flashed like fish in the sun. He walked over to me and sat on the edge of my desk.

He reached out a hand. "Sheldon," he said.

"Stand on your own two feet, Sheldon."

Climbing off the desk, he said, "Sheldon Grossbart." He smiled wider at the intimacy into which he'd led me.

"You against cleaning the barracks Friday night, Grossbart? Maybe we shouldn't have G.I. parties—maybe we should get a maid." My tone startled

---

1. Plastic liner worn under a helmet to prevent chafing and bruising. 2. Noncommissioned officer in charge of quarters at night or on weekends.

me: I felt like a Charlie McCarthy, with every top sergeant I had ever known as my Edgar Bergen.[3]

"No, Sergeant." He grew serious, but with a seriousness that seemed only to be the stifling of a smile. "It's just G.I. parties on Friday night, of all nights . . ."

He slipped up to the corner of the desk again—not quite sitting, but not quite standing either. He looked at me with those speckled eyes flashing and then made a gesture with his hand. It was very slight, no more than a rotation back and forth of the wrist, and yet it managed to exclude from our affairs everything else in the orderly room, to make the two of us the center of the world. It seemed, in fact, to exclude everything about the two of us except our hearts. "Sergeant Thurston was one thing," he whispered, an eye flashing to the sleeping CQ, "but we thought with you here, things might be a little different."

"We?"

"The Jewish personnel."

"Why?" I said, harshly.

He hesitated a moment, and then, uncontrollably, his hand went up to his mouth. "I mean . . ." he said.

"What's on your mind?" Whether I was still angry at the "Sheldon" business or something else, I hadn't a chance to tell—but clearly I was angry.

". . . we thought you . . . Marx, you know, like Karl Marx. The Marx brothers. Those guys are all . . . M-A-R-X, isn't that how you spell it, Sergeant?"

"M-A-R-X."

"Fishbein said—" He stopped. "What I mean to say, Sergeant—" His face and neck were red, and his mouth moved but no words came out. In a moment, he raised himself to attention, gazing down at me. It was as though he had suddenly decided he could expect no more sympathy from me than from Thurston, the reason being that I was of Thurston's faith and not his. The young man had managed to confuse himself as to what my faith really was, but I felt no desire to straighten him out. Very simply, I didn't like him.

When I did nothing but return his gaze, he spoke, in an altered tone. "You see, Sergeant," he explained to me, "Friday nights, Jews are supposed to go to services."

"Did Sergeant Thurston tell you you couldn't go to them when there was a G.I. party?"

"No."

"Did he say you had to stay and scrub the floors?"

"No, Sergeant."

"Did the Captain say you had to stay and scrub the floors?"

"That isn't it, Sergeant. It's the other guys in the barracks." He leaned toward me. "They think we're goofing off. But we're not. That's when Jews go to services, Friday night. We have to."

"Then go."

"But the other guys make accusations. They have no right."

"That's not the Army's problem, Grossbart. It's a personal problem you'll have to work out yourself."

"But it's un*fair*."

I got up to leave. "There's nothing I can do about it," I said.

Grossbart stiffened in front of me. "But this is a matter of *religion*, sir."

"Sergeant."

"I mean 'Sergeant,'" he said, almost snarling.

"Look, go see the chaplain. The I.G.[4] You want to see Captain Barrett, I'll arrange an appointment."

"No, no. I don't want to make trouble, Sergeant. That's the first thing they throw up to you. I just want my rights!"

"Damn it, Grossbart, stop whining. You have your rights. You can stay and scrub floors or you can go to *shul*[5]—"

The smile swam in again. Spittle gleamed at the corners of his mouth. "You mean church, Sergeant."

"I mean *shul*, Grossbart!" I walked past him and outside. Near me I heard the scrunching of a guard's boots on gravel. In the lighted windows of the barracks the young men in T-shirts and fatigue pants were sitting on their bunks, polishing their rifles. Suddenly there was a light rustling behind me. I turned and saw Grossbart's dark frame fleeing back to the barracks, racing to tell his Jewish friends that they were right—that like Karl and Harpo, I was one of them.

The next morning, while chatting with the Captain, I recounted the incident of the previous evening, as if to unburden myself of it. Somehow in the telling it seemed to the Captain that I was not so much explaining Grossbart's position as defending it.

"Marx, I'd fight side by side with a nigger if the fellow proved to me he was a man. I pride myself," the Captain said looking out the window, "that I've got an open mind. Consequently, Sergeant, nobody gets special treatment here, for the good *or* the bad. All a man's got to do is prove himself. A man fires well on the range, I give him a weekend pass. He scores high in PT, he gets a weekend pass. He *earns* it." He turned from the window and pointed a finger at me. "You're a Jewish fellow, am I right, Marx?"

"Yes, sir."

"And I admire you. I admire you because of the ribbons on your chest, not because you had a hem stitched on your dick before you were old enough to even know you had one. I judge a man by what he shows me on the field of battle, Sergeant. It's what he's got *here*," he said, and then, though I expected he would point to his heart, he jerked a thumb towards the buttons straining to hold his blouse across his belly. "Guts," he said.

"Okay, sir, I only wanted to pass on to you how the men felt."

"Mr. Marx, you're going to be old before your time if you worry about how the men feel. Leave that stuff to the Chaplain—pussy, the clap, church picnics with the little girls from Joplin, that's all his business, not yours. Let's us train these fellas to shoot straight. If the Jewish personnel feels the other men are accusing them of goldbricking . . . well, I just don't know. Seems awful funny how suddenly the Lord is calling so loud in Private Grossman's ear he's just got to run to church."

"Synagogue," I said.

"Synagogue is right, Sergeant. I'll write that down for handy reference. Thank you for stopping by."

4. Inspector general, who, apart from the chaplain, provided the only route by which complaints could be registered.

5. Synagogue (Yiddish).

That evening, a few minutes before the company gathered outside the orderly room for the chow formation, I called the CQ, Corporal Robert LaHill, in to see me. LaHill was a dark burly fellow whose hair curled out of his clothes wherever it could. He carried a glaze in his eyes that made one think of caves and dinosaurs. "LaHill," I said, "when you take the formation, remind the men that they're free to attend church services *whenever* they are held, provided they report to the orderly room before they leave the area."

LaHill didn't flicker; he scratched his wrist, but gave no indication that he'd heard or understood.

"LaHill," I said, "*church*. You remember? Church, priest, Mass, confession . . ."

He curled one lip into a ghastly smile; I took it for a signal that for a second he had flickered back up into the human race.

"Jewish personnel who want to attend services this evening are to fall out in front of the orderly room at 1900." And then I added, "By order of Captain Barrett."

A little while later, as a twilight softer than any I had seen that year dropped over Camp Crowder, I heard LaHill's thick, inflectionless voice outside my window: "Give me your ears, troopers. Toppie says for me to tell you that at 1900 hours all Jewish personnel is to fall out in front here if they wants to attend the Jewish Mass."

At seven o'clock, I looked out of the orderly-room window and saw three soldiers in starched khakis standing alone on the dusty quadrangle. They looked at their watches, and fidgeted while they whispered back and forth. It was getting darker, and alone on the deserted field they looked tiny. When I walked to the door I heard the noises of the G.I. party coming from the surrounding barracks—bunks being pushed to the wall, faucets pounding water into buckets, brooms whisking at the wooden floors. In the windows big puffs of cloth moved round and round, cleaning the dirt away for Saturday's inspection. I walked outside and the moment my foot hit the ground I thought I heard Grossbart, who was now in the center, call to the other two, "Ten-*hut*!" Or maybe when they all three jumped to attention, I imagined I heard the command.

At my approach, Grossbart stepped forward. "Thank you, sir," he said.

"Sergeant, Grossbart," I reminded him. "You call officers 'Sir.' I'm not an officer. You've been in the Army three weeks—you know that."

He turned his palms out at his sides to indicate that, in truth, he and I lived beyond convention. "Thank you, anyway," he said.

"Yes," the tall boy behind him said. "Thanks a lot."

And the third whispered, "Thank you," but his mouth barely fluttered so that he did not alter by more than a lip's movement, the posture of attention.

"For what?" I said.

Grossbart snorted, happily. "For the announcement before. The Corporal's announcement. It helped. It made it . . ."

"Fancier." It was the tall boy finishing Grossbart's sentence.

Grossbart smiled. "He means formal, sir. Public," he said to me. "Now it won't seem as though we're just taking off, goldbricking, because the work has begun."

"It was by order of Captain Barrett," I said.

"Ahh, but you pull a little weight . . ." Grossbart said. "So we thank you." Then he turned to his companions. "Sergeant Marx, I want you to meet Larry Fishbein."

The tall boy stepped forward and extended his hand. I shook it. "You from New York?" he asked.

"Yes."

"Me too." He had a cadaverous face that collapsed inward from his cheekbone to his jaw, and when he smiled—as he did at the news of our communal, attachment—revealed a mouthful of bad teeth. He blinked his eyes a good deal, as though he were fighting back tears. "What borough?" he asked.

I turned to Grossbart. "It's five after seven. What time are services?"

"*Shul*," he smiled, "is in ten minutes. I want you to meet Mickey Halpern. This is Nathan Marx, our Sergeant."

The third boy hopped forward. "Private Michael Halpern." He saluted.

"Salute officers, Halpern." The boy dropped his hand, and in his nervousness checked to see if his shirt pockets were buttoned on the way down.

"Shall I march them over, sir?" Grossbart asked, "or are you coming along?"

From behind Grossbart, Fishbein piped up. "Afterwards they're having refreshments. A Ladies' Auxiliary from St. Louis, the rabbi told us last week."

"The chaplain," whispered Halpern.

"You're welcome to come along," Grossbart said.

To avoid his plea, I looked away, and saw, in the windows of the barracks, a cloud of faces staring out at the four of us.

"Look, hurry out of here, Grossbart."

"Okay, then," he said. He turned to the others. "Double time, *march!*" and they started off, but ten feet away Grossbart spun about, and running backwards he called to me, "Good *shabus*,[6] sir." And then the three were swallowed into the Missouri dusk.

Even after they'd disappeared over the parade grounds, whose green was now a deep twilight blue, I could hear Grossbart singing the double-time cadence, and as it grew dimmer and dimmer it suddenly touched some deep memory—as did the slant of light—and I was remembering the shrill sounds of a Bronx playground, where years ago, beside the Grand Concourse,[7] I had played on long spring evenings such as this. Those thin fading sounds . . . It was a pleasant memory for a young man so far from peace and home, and it brought so very many recollections with it that I began to grow exceedingly tender about myself. In fact, I indulged myself to a reverie so strong that I felt within as though a hand had opened and was reaching down inside. It had to reach so very far to touch me. It had to reach past those days in the forests of Belgium and the dying I'd refused to weep over; past the nights in those German farmhouses whose books we'd burned to warm us, and which I couldn't bother to mourn; past those endless stretches when I'd shut off all softness I might feel for my fellows, and managed even to deny myself the posture of a conqueror—the swagger that I, as a Jew, might well have worn as my boots whacked against the rubble of Münster, Braunschweig, and finally Berlin.

---

6. Sabbath (Yiddish).　　　　　　　　7. Avenue in the Bronx, New York.

But now one night noise, one rumor of home and time past, and memory plunged down through all I had anesthetized and came to what I suddenly remembered to be myself. So it was not altogether curious that in search of more of me I found myself following Grossbart's tracks to Chapel No. 3 where the Jewish services were being held.

I took a seat in the last row, which was empty. Two rows in front sat Grossbart, Fishbein, and Halpern, each holding a little white dixie cup. Fishbein was pouring the contents of his cup into Grossbart's, and Grossbart looked mirthful as the liquid drew a purple arc between his hand and Fishbein's. In the glary yellow light, I saw the chaplain on the pulpit chanting the first line of the responsive reading. Grossbart's prayerbook remained closed on his lap; he swished the cup around. Only Halpern responded in prayer. The fingers of his right hand were spread wide across the cover of the book, and his cap was pulled down low onto his brow so that it was round like a *yarmulke*[8] rather than long and pointed. From time to time, Grossbart wet his lips at the cup's edge; Fishbein, his long yellow face, a dying light bulb, looked from here to there, leaning forward at the neck to catch sight of the faces down the row, in front—then behind. He saw me and his eyelids beat a tattoo. His elbow slid into Grossbart's side, his neck inclined towards his friend, and then, when the congregation responded, Grossbart's voice was among them. Fishbein looked into his book now too; his lips, however, didn't move.

Finally it was time to drink the wine. The chaplain smiled down at them as Grossbart swigged in one long gulp, Halpern sipped, meditating, and Fishbein faked devotion with an empty cup.

At last the chaplain spoke: "As I look down amongst the congregation—" he grinned at the word, "this night, I see many new faces, and I want to welcome you to Friday night services here at Camp Crowder. I am Major Leo Ben Ezra, your chaplain . . ." Though an American, the chaplain spoke English very deliberately, syllabically almost, as though to communicate, above all, to the lip-readers in the audience. "I have only a few words to say before we adjourn to the refreshment room where the kind ladies of the Temple Sinai, St. Louis, Missouri, have a nice setting for you."

Applause and whistling broke out. After a momentary grin, the chaplain raised his palms to the congregation, his eyes flicking upward a moment, as if to remind the troops where they were and Who Else might be in attendance. In the sudden silence that followed, I thought I heard Grossbart's cackle—"Let the goyim[9] clean the floors!" Were those the words? I wasn't sure, but Fishbein, grinning, nudged Halpern. Halpern looked dumbly at him, then went back to his prayerbook, which had been occupying him all through the rabbi's talk. One hand tugged at the black kinky hair that stuck out under his cap. His lips moved.

The rabbi continued. "It is about the food that I want to speak to you for a moment. I know, I know, I know," he intoned, wearily, "how in the mouths of most of you the *trafe*[1] food tastes like ashes. I know how you gag, some of you, and how your parents suffer to think of their children eating foods unclean and offensive to the palate. What can I tell you? I can only say close your eyes and swallow as best you can. Eat what you must to live and

8. Skullcap (Yiddish).
9. Gentiles (Yiddish).

1. Unkosher—unfit to eat (Yiddish).

throw away the rest. I wish I could help more. For those of you who find this impossible, may I ask that you try and try, but then come to see me in private where, if your revulsion is such, we will have to seek aid from those higher up."

A round of chatter rose and subsided; then everyone sang "Ain Keloha-noh," after all those years I discovered I still knew the words.

Suddenly, the service over, Grossbart was upon me. "Higher up? He means the General?"

"Hey, Shelly," Fishbein interrupted, "he means God." He smacked his face and looked at Halpern. "How high can you go!"

"Shhh!" Grossbart said. "What do you think, Sergeant?"

"I don't know. You better ask the chaplain."

"I'm going to. I'm making an appointment to see him in private. So is Mickey."

Halpern shook his head. "No, no, Sheldon . . ."

"You have rights, Mickey. They can't push us around."

"It's okay. It bothers my mother, not me . . ."

Grossbart looked at me. "Yesterday he threw up. From the hash. It was all ham and God knows what else."

"I have a cold—that was why," Halpern said. He pushed his *yamalkah* back into a cap.

"What about you, Fishbein?" I asked. "You kosher too?"

He flushed, which made the yellow more gray than pink. "A little. But I'll let it ride. I have a very strong stomach. And I don't eat a lot anyway . . ." I continued to look at him, and he held up his wrist to re-enforce what he'd just said. His watch was tightened to the last hole and he pointed that out to me. "So I don't mind."

"But services are important to you?" I asked him.

He looked at Grossbart. "Sure, sir."

"Sergeant."

"Not so much at home," said Grossbart, coming between us, "but away from home it gives one a sense of his Jewishness."

"We have to stick together," Fishbein said.

I started to walk towards the door; Halpern stepped back to make way for me.

"That's what happened in Germany," Grossbart was saying, loud enough for me to hear. "They didn't stick together. They let themselves get pushed around."

I turned. "Look, Grossbart, this is the Army, not summer camp."

He smiled. "So?" Halpern tried to sneak off, but Grossbart held his arm. "So?" he said again.

"Grossbart," I asked, "how old are you?"

"Nineteen."

"And you?" I said to Fishbein.

"The same. The same month even."

"And what about him?" I pointed to Halpern, who'd finally made it safely to the door.

"Eighteen," Grossbart whispered. "But he's like he can't tie his shoes or brush his teeth himself. I feel sorry for him."

"I feel sorry for all of us, Grossbart, but just act like a man. Just don't overdo it."

"Overdo what, sir?"

"The sir business. Don't overdo that," I said, and I left him standing there. I passed by Halpern but he did not look up. Then I was outside, black surrounded me—but behind I heard Grossbart call, "Hey, Mickey, *liebschen*,[2] come on back. Refreshments!"

Liebschen! My grandmother's word for me!

One morning, a week later, while I was working at my desk, Captain Barrett shouted for me to come into his office. When I entered, he had his helmet liner squashed down so that I couldn't even see his eyes. He was on the phone, and when he spoke to me, he cupped one hand over the mouthpiece.

"Who the fuck is Grossbart?"

"Third platoon, Captain," I said. "A trainee."

"What's all this stink about food? His mother called a goddam congressman about the food . . ." He uncovered the mouthpiece and slid his helmet up so I could see the curl of his bottom eyelash. "Yes, sir," he said into the phone. "Yes, sir. I'm still here, sir. I'm asking Marx here right now . . ."

He covered the mouthpiece again and looked back to me. "Lightfoot Harry's on the phone," he said, between his teeth. "This congressman calls General Lyman who calls Colonel Sousa who calls the Major who calls me. They're just dying to stick this thing on me. What's a matter," he shook the phone at me, "I don't feed the troops? What the hell is this?"

"Sir, Grossbart is strange . . ." Barrett greeted that with a mockingly indulgent smile. I altered my approach. "Captain, he's a very orthodox Jew and so he's only allowed to eat certain foods."

"He throws up, the congressman said. Every time he eats something his mother says he throws up!"

"He's accustomed to observing the dietary laws, Captain."

"So why's his old lady have to call the White House!"

"Jewish parents, sir, they're apt to be more protective than you expect. I mean Jews have a very close family life. A boy goes away from home, sometimes the mother is liable to get very upset. Probably the boy *mentioned* something in a letter and his mother misinterpreted."

"I'd like to punch him one right in the mouth. There's a goddam war on and he wants a silver platter!"

"I don't think the boy's to blame, sir. I'm sure we can straighten it out by just asking him. Jewish parents worry—"

"*All* parents worry, for Christ sake. But they don't get on their high horse and start pulling strings—"

I interrupted, my voice higher, tighter than before. "The home life, Captain, is so very important . . . but you're right, it may sometimes get out of hand. It's a very wonderful thing, Captain, but because it's so close, this kind of thing—"

He didn't listen any longer to my attempt to present both myself and Lightfoot Harry with an explanation for the letter. He turned back to the phone. "Sir?" he said. "Sir, Marx here tells me Jews have a tendency to be pushy. He says he thinks he can settle it right here in the Company . . . Yes, sir . . . I *will* call back, sir, soon as I can . . ." He hung up. "Where are the men, Sergeant?"

<hr>

2. Darling (German).

"On the range."

With a whack on the top, he crushed his helmet over his eyes, and charged out of his chair. "We're going for a ride."

The Captain drove and I sat beside him. It was a hot spring day and under my newly starched fatigues it felt as though my armpits were melting down onto my sides and chest. The roads were dry and by the time we reached the firing range, my teeth felt gritty with dust though my mouth had been shut the whole trip. The Captain slammed the brakes on and told me to get the hell out and find Grossbart.

I found him on his belly, firing wildly at the 500 feet target. Waiting their turns behind him were Halpern and Fishbein. Fishbein, wearing a pair of rimless G.I. glasses I hadn't seen on him before, gave the appearance of an old peddler who would gladly have sold you the rifle and cartridges that were slung all over him. I stood back by the ammo boxes, waiting for Grossbart to finish spraying the distant targets. Fishbein straggled back to stand near me.

"Hello, Sergeant Marx."

"How are you?" I mumbled.

"Fine, thank you. Sheldon's really a good shot."

"I didn't notice."

"I'm not so good, but I think I'm getting the hang of it now . . . Sergeant, I don't mean to, you know, ask what I shouldn't . . ." The boy stopped. He was trying to speak intimately but the noise of the shooting necessitated that he shout at me.

"What is it?" I asked. Down the range I saw Captain Barrett standing up in the jeep, scanning the line for me and Grossbart.

"My parents keep asking and asking where we're going. Everybody says the Pacific. I don't care, but my parents . . . If I could relieve their minds I think I could concentrate more on my shooting."

"I don't know where, Fishbein. Try to concentrate anyway."

"Sheldon says you might be able to find out—"

"I don't know a thing, Fishbein. You just take it easy, and don't let Sheldon—"

"*I'm* taking it easy, Sergeant. It's at home—"

Grossbart had just finished on the line and was dusting his fatigues with one hand. I left Fishbein's sentence in the middle.

"Grossbart, the Captain wants to see you."

He came toward us. His eyes blazed and twinkled. "Hi!"

"Don't point that goddam rifle!"

"I wouldn't shoot you, Sarge." He gave me a smile wide as a pumpkin as he turned the barrel aside.

"Damn you, Grossbart—this is no joke! Follow me."

I walked ahead of him and had the awful suspicion that behind me Grossbart was *marching*, his rifle on his shoulder, as though he were a one-man detachment.

At the jeep he gave the Captain a rifle salute. "Private Sheldon Grossbart, sir."

"At ease, Grossman." The Captain slid over to the empty front seat, and crooking a finger, invited Grossbart closer.

"Bart, sir. Sheldon Gross*bart*. It's a common error." Grossbart nodded to me—*I* understand, he indicated. I looked away, just as the mess truck pulled up to the range, disgorging a half dozen K.P.'s with rolled-up sleeves. The mess sergeant screamed at them while they set up the chow line equipment.

"Grossbart, your mama wrote some congressman that we don't feed you right. Do you know that?" the Captain said.

"It was my father, sir. He wrote to Representative Franconi that my religion forbids me to eat certain foods."

"What religion is that, Grossbart?"

"Jewish."

"Jewish, *sir*," I said to Grossbart.

"Excuse me, sir. 'Jewish, sir.'"

"What have you been living on?" the Captain asked. "You've been in the Army a month already. You don't look to me like you're falling to pieces."

"I eat because I have to, sir. But Sergeant Marx will testify to the fact that I don't eat one mouthful more than I need to in order to survive."

"Marx," Barrett asked, "is that so?"

"I've never seen Grossbart eat, sir," I said.

"But you heard the rabbi," Grossbart said. "He told us what to do, and I listened."

The Captain looked at me. "Well, Marx?"

"I still don't know what he eats and doesn't eat, sir."

Grossbart raised his rifle, as though to offer it to me. "But, Sergeant—"

"Look, Grossbart, just answer the Captain's questions!" I said sharply.

Barrett smiled at me and I resented it. "All right, Grossbart," he said, "What is it you want? The little piece of paper? You want out?"

"No, sir. Only to be allowed to live as a Jew. And for the others, too."

"What others?"

"Fishbein, sir, and Halpern."

"They don't like the way we serve either?"

"Halpern throws up, sir. I've seen it."

"I thought *you* threw up."

"Just once, sir. I didn't know the sausage was sausage."

"We'll give menus, Grossbart. We'll show training films about the food, so you can identify when we're trying to poison you."

Grossbart did not answer. Out before me, the men had been organized into two long chow lines. At the tail end of one I spotted Fishbein—or rather, his glasses spotted me. They winked sunlight back at me like a friend. Halpern stood next to him, patting inside his collar with a khaki handkerchief. They moved with the line as it began to edge up towards the food. The mess sergeant was still screaming at the K.P.'s, who stood ready to ladle out the food, bewildered. For a moment I was actually terrorized by the thought that somehow the mess sergeant was going to get involved in Grossbart's problem.

"Come over here, Marx," the Captain said to me. "Marx, you're a Jewish fella, am I right?"

I played straight man. "Yes, sir."

"How long you been in the Army? Tell this boy."

"Three years and two months."

"A year in combat, Grossbart. Twelve goddam months in combat all through Europe. I admire this man," the Captain said, snapping a wrist against my chest. But do you hear him peeping about the food? Do you? I want an answer, Grossbart. Yes or no."

"No, sir."

"And why not? He's a Jewish fella."

"Some things are more important to some Jews than other things to other Jews."

Barrett blew up. "Look, Grossbart, Marx here is a good man, a goddam *hero*. When you were sitting on your sweet ass in high school, Sergeant Marx was killing Germans. Who does more for the Jews, you by throwing up over a lousy piece of sausage, a piece of firstcut meat—or Marx by killing those Nazi bastards? If I was a Jew, Grossbart, I'd kiss this man's feet. He's a goddam hero, you know that? And *he* eats what we give him. Why do you have to cause trouble is what I want to know! What is it you're buckin' for, a discharge?"

"No, sir."

"I'm talking to a *wall*! Sergeant, get him out of my way." Barrett pounced over to the driver's seat. "I'm going to see the chaplain!" The engine roared, the jeep spun around, and then, raising a whirl of dust, the Captain was headed back to camp.

For a moment, Grossbart and I stood side by side, watching the jeep. Then he looked at me and said, "I don't want to start trouble. That's the first thing they toss up to us."

When he spoke I saw that his teeth were white and straight, and the sight of them suddenly made me understand that Grossbart actually did have parents: that once upon a time someone had taken little Sheldon to the dentist. He was someone's son. Despite all the talk about his parents, it was hard to believe in Grossbart as a child, an heir—as related by blood to anyone, mother, father, or, above all, to me. This realization led me to another.

"What does your father do, Grossbart?" I asked, as we started to walk back towards the chow line.

"He's a tailor."

"An American?"

"Now, yes. A son in the Army," he said, jokingly.

"And your mother?" I asked.

He winked. "A *ballabusta*[3]—she practically sleeps with a dustcloth in her hand."

"She's also an immigrant?"

"All she talks is Yiddish, still."

"And your father too?"

"A little English. 'Clean,' 'Press,' 'Take the pants in . . .' That's the extent of it. But they're good to me . . ."

"Then, Grossbart—" I reached out and stopped him. He turned towards me and when our eyes met his seemed to jump back, shiver in their sockets. He looked afraid. "Grossbart, then you were the one who wrote that letter, weren't you?"

It took only a second or two for his eyes to flash happy again. "Yes." He walked on, and I kept pace. "It's what my father *would* have written if he had known how. It was his name, though. *He* signed it. He even mailed it. I sent it home. For the New York postmark."

I was astonished, and he saw it. With complete seriousness, he thrust his right arm in front of me. "Blood is blood, Sergeant," he said, pinching the blue vein in his wrist.

---

3. Good housekeeper (Yiddish).

"What the hell *are* you trying to do, Grossbart? I've seen you eat. Do you know that? I told the Captain I don't know what you eat, but I've seen you eat like a hound at chow."

"We work hard, Sergeant. We're in training. For a furnace to work, you've got to feed it coal."

"If you wrote the letter, Grossbart, then why did you say you threw up all the time?"

"I was really talking about Mickey there. But he would never write, Sergeant, though I pleaded with him. He'll waste away to nothing if I don't help. Sergeant, I used my name, my father's name, but it's Mickey and Fishbein too I'm watching out for."

"You're a regular Messiah,[4] aren't you?"

We were at the chow line now.

"That's a good one, Sergeant." He smiled. "But who knows? Who can tell? Maybe you're the Messiah . . . a little bit. What Mickey says is the Messiah is a collective idea. He went to Yeshivah,[5] Mickey, for a while. He says *together* we're the Messiah. Me a little bit, you a little bit . . . You should hear that kid talk, Sergeant, when he gets going."

"Me a little bit, you a little bit. You'd like to believe that, wouldn't you, Grossbart? That makes everything so clean for you."

"It doesn't seem too bad a thing to believe, Sergeant. It only means we should all give a little, is all . . ."

I walked off to eat my rations with the other noncoms.[6]

Two days later a letter addressed to Captain Barrett passed over my desk. It had come through the chain of command—from the office of Congressman Franconi, where it had been received, to General Lyman, to Colonel Sousa, to Major Lamont, to Captain Barrett. I read it over twice while the Captain was at the officers' mess. It was dated May 14th, the day Barrett had spoken with Grossbart on the rifle range.

Dear Congressman:

First let me thank you for your interest in behalf of my son, Private Sheldon Grossbart. Fortunately, I was able to speak with Sheldon on the phone the other night, and I think I've been able to solve our problem. He is, as I mentioned in my last letter, a very religious boy, and it was only with the greatest difficulty that I could persuade him that the religious thing to do— what God Himself would want Sheldon to do—would be to suffer the pangs of religious remorse for the good of his country and all mankind. It took some doing, Congressman, but finally he saw the light. In fact, what he said (and I wrote down the words on a scratch pad so as never to forget), what he said was, "I guess you're right, Dad. So many millions of my fellow Jews gave up their lives to the enemy, the least I can do is live for a while minus a bit of my heritage so as to help end this struggle and regain for all the children of God dignity and humanity." That, Congressman, would make any father proud.

By the way, Sheldon wanted me to know—and to pass on to you—the name of a soldier who helped him reach this decision: SERGEANT NATHAN MARX. Sergeant Marx is a combat veteran who is Sheldon's First Sergeant.

---

4. The deliverer who will rule over the people of Israel at the end of time.

5. Jewish institution of learning.

6. Noncommissioned officers.

This man has helped Sheldon over some of the first hurdles he's had to face in the Army, and is in part responsible for Sheldon's changing his mind about the dietary laws. I know Sheldon would appreciate any recognition Marx could receive.

Thank you and good luck. I look forward to seeing your name on the next election ballot.

Respectfully,
Samuel E. Grossbart

Attached to the Grossbart communiqué was a communiqué addressed to General Marshall Lyman, the post commander, and signed by Representative Charles E. Franconi of the House of Representatives. The communiqué informed General Lyman that Sergeant Nathan Marx was a credit to the U.S. Army and the Jewish people.

What was Grossbart's motive in recanting? Did he feel he'd gone too far? Was the letter a strategic retreat—a crafty attempt to strengthen what he considered our alliance? Or had he actually changed his mind, via an imaginary dialogue between Grossbart *père* and *fils*?[7] I was puzzled, but only for a few days—that is, only until I realized that whatever his reasons, he had actually decided to disappear from my life: he was going to allow himself to become just another trainee. I saw him at inspection but he never winked; at chow formations but he never flashed me a sign; on Sundays, with the other trainees, he would sit around watching the noncoms' softball team, for whom I pitched, but not once did he speak an unnecessary or unusual word to me. Fishbein and Halpern retreated from sight too, at Grossbart's command I was sure. Apparently he'd seen that wisdom lay in turning back before he plunged us over into the ugliness of privilege undeserved. Our separation allowed me to forgive him our past encounters, and, finally, to admire him for his good sense.

Meanwhile, free of Grossbart, I grew used to my job and my administrative tasks. I stepped on a scale one day and discovered I had truly become a noncombatant: I had gained seven pounds. I found patience to get past the first three pages of a book. I thought about the future more and more, and wrote letters to girls I'd known before the war—I even got a few answers. I sent away to Columbia for a Law School catalogue. I continued to follow the war in the Pacific, but it was not my war and I read of bombings and battles like a civilian. I thought I could see the end in sight and sometimes at night I dreamed that I was walking on the streets of Manhattan—Broadway, Third Avenue, and 116th Street, where I had lived those three years I'd attended Columbia College. I curled myself around these dreams and I began to be happy.

And then one Saturday when everyone was away and I was alone in the orderly room reading a month-old copy of the *Sporting News*, Grossbart reappeared.

"You a baseball fan, Sergeant?"

I looked up. "How are you?"

"Fine," Grossbart said. "They're making a soldier out of me."

"How are Fishbein and Halpern?"

"Coming along," he said. "We've got no training this afternoon. They're at the movies."

7. Father and son (French).

"How come you're not with them?"

"I wanted to come over and say hello."

He smiled—a shy, regular-guy smile, as though he and I well knew that our friendship drew its sustenance from unexpected visits, remembered birthdays, and borrowed lawnmowers. At first it offended me, and then the feeling was swallowed by the general uneasiness I felt at the thought that everyone on the post was locked away in a dark movie theater and I was here alone with Grossbart. I folded my paper.

"Sergeant," he said, "I'd like to ask a favor. It is a favor and I'm making no bones about it."

He stopped, allowing me to refuse him a hearing—which, of course, forced me into a courtesy I did not intend. "Go ahead."

"Well, actually it's two favors."

I said nothing.

"The first one's about these rumors. Everybody says we're going to the Pacific."

"As I told your friend Fishbein, I don't know. You'll just have to wait to find out. Like everybody else."

"You think there's a chance of any of us going East?"

"Germany," I said, "maybe."

"I meant New York."

"I don't think so, Grossbart. Offhand."

"Thanks for the information, Sergeant," he said.

"It's not information, Grossbart. Just what I surmise."

"It certainly would be good to be near home. My parents . . . you know." He took a step towards the door and then turned back. "Oh the other thing. May I ask the other?"

"What is it?"

"The other thing is—I've got relatives in St. Louis and they say they'll give me a whole Passover dinner if I can get down there. God, Sergeant, that'd mean an awful lot to me."

I stood up. "No passes during basic, Grossbart."

"But we're off from now till Monday morning, Sergeant. I could leave the post and no one would even know."

"I'd know. You'd know."

"But that's all. Just the two of us. Last night I called my aunt and you should have heard her. 'Come, come,' she said. 'I got gefilte fish, *chrain*,[8] the works!' Just a day, Sergeant, I'd take the blame if anything happened."

"The captain isn't here to sign a pass."

"You could sign."

"Look, Grossbart—"

"Sergeant, for two months practically I've been eating *trafe* till I want to die."

"I thought you'd made up your mind to live with it. To be minus a little bit of heritage."

He pointed a finger at me. "You!" he said. "That wasn't for you to read!"

"I read it. So what."

"That letter was addressed to a congressman."

"Grossbart, don't feed me any crap. You *wanted* me to read it."

"Why are you persecuting me, Sergeant?"

8. Horseradish.

"Are you kidding!"

"I've run into this before," he said, "but never from my own!"

"Get out of here, Grossbart! Get the hell out of my sight!"

He did not move. "Ashamed, that's what you are. So you take it out on the rest of us. They say Hitler himself was half a Jew. Seeing this, I wouldn't doubt it!"

"What are you trying to do with me, Grossbart? What are you after? You want me to give you special privileges, to change the food, to find out about your orders, to give you weekend passes."

"You even talk like a goy!" Grossbart shook his fist. "Is this a weekend pass I'm asking for? Is a Seder[9] sacred or not?"

Seder! It suddenly occurred to me that Passover had been celebrated weeks before. I confronted Grossbart with the fact.

"That's right," he said. "Who says no? A month ago, and *I* was in the field eating hash! And now all I ask is a simple favor—a Jewish boy I thought would understand. My aunt's willing to go out of her way—to make a Seder a month later—" He turned to go, mumbling.

"Come back here!" I called. He stopped and looked at me. "Grossbart, why can't you be like the rest? Why do you have to stick out like a sore thumb? Why do you beg for special treatment?"

"Because I'm a Jew, Sergeant. I *am* different. Better, maybe not. But different."

"This is a war, Grossbart. For the time being *be* the same."

"I refuse."

"What?"

"I refuse. I can't stop being me, that's all there is to it." Tears came to his eyes. "It's a hard thing to be a Jew. But now I see what Mickey says— it's a harder thing to stay one." He raised a hand sadly toward me. "Look at you."

"Stop crying!"

"Stop this, stop that, stop the other thing! You stop, Sergeant. Stop closing your heart to your own!" And wiping his face with his sleeve, he ran out the door. "The least we can do for one another . . . the least . . ."

An hour later I saw Grossbart headed across the field. He wore a pair of starched khakis and carried only a little leather ditty bag. I went to the door and from the outside felt the heat of the day. It was quiet—not a soul in sight except over by the mess hall four K.P.'s sitting round a pan, sloped forward from the waists, gabbing and peeling potatoes in the sun.

"Grossbart!" I called.

He looked toward me and continued walking.

"Grossbart, get over here!"

He turned and stepped into his long shadow. Finally he stood before me.

"Where are you going?" I said.

"St. Louis. I don't care."

"You'll get caught without a pass."

"So I'll get caught without a pass."

"You'll go to the stockade."

"I'm in the stockade." He made an about-face and headed off.

9. Ceremonial dinner on the first evening of Passover.

I let him go only a step: "Come back here," I said, and he followed me into the office, where I typed out a pass and signed the Captain's name and my own initials after it.

He took the pass from me and then, a moment later, he reached out and grabbed my hand. "Sergeant, you don't know how much this means to me."

"Okay. Don't get in any trouble."

"I wish I could show you how much this means to me."

"Don't do me any favors. Don't write any more congressmen for citations."

Amazingly, he smiled. "You're right. I won't. But let me do something."

"Bring me a piece of that gefilte fish. Just get out of here."

"I will! With a slice of carrot and a little horseradish. I won't forget."

"All right. Just show your pass at the gate. And don't tell *anybody*."

"I won't. It's a month late, but a good Yom Tov[1] to you."

"Good Yom Tov, Grossbart," I said.

"You're a good Jew, Sergeant. You like to think you have a hard heart, but underneath you're a fine decent man. I mean that."

Those last three words touched me more than any words from Grossbart's mouth had the right to. "All right, Grossbart. Now call me 'sir' and get the hell out of here."

He ran out the door and was gone. I felt very pleased with myself—it was a great relief to stop fighting Grossbart. And it had cost me nothing. Barrett would never find out, and if he did, I could manage to invent some excuse. For a while I sat at my desk, comfortable in my decision. Then the screen door flew back and Grossbart burst in again. "Sergeant!" he said. Behind him I saw Fishbein and Halpern, both in starched khakis, both carrying ditty bags exactly like Grossbart's.

"Sergeant, I caught Mickey and Larry coming out of the movies. I almost missed them."

"Grossbart, did I say tell no one?"

"But my aunt said I could bring friends. That I should, in fact."

"I'm the Sergeant, Grossbart—not your aunt!"

Grossbart looked at me in disbelief; he pulled Halpern up by his sleeve. "Mickey, tell the Sergeant what this would mean to you."

"Grossbart, for God's sake, spare us—"

"Tell him what you told me, Mickey. How much it would mean."

Halpern looked at me and, shrugging his shoulders, made his admission. "A lot."

Fishbein stepped forward without prompting. "This would mean a great deal to me and my parents, Sergeant Marx."

"No!" I shouted.

Grossbart was shaking his head. "Sergeant, I could see you denying me, but how you can deny Mickey, a Yeshivah boy, that's beyond me."

"I'm not denying Mickey anything. You just pushed a little too hard, Grossbart. *You* denied him."

"I'll give him my pass, then," Grossbart said. "I'll give him my aunt's address and a little note. At least let him go."

In a second he had crammed the pass into Halpern's pants pocket. Halpern looked at me, Fishbein too. Grossbart was at the door, pushing it open. "Mickey, bring me a piece of gefilte fish at least." And then he was outside again.

1. Holiday (Yiddish).

The three of us looked at one another and then I said, "Halpern, hand that pass over."

He took it from his pocket and gave it to me. Fishbein had now moved to the doorway, where he lingered. He stood there with his mouth slightly open and then pointed to himself. "And me?" he asked.

His utter ridiculousness exhausted me. I slumped down in my seat and I felt pulses knocking at the back of my eyes. "Fishbein," I said, "you understand I'm not trying to deny you anything, don't you? If it was my Army I'd serve gefilte fish in the mess hall. I'd sell kugel[2] in the PX, honest to God."

Halpern smiled.

"You understand, don't you, Halpern?"

"Yes, Sergeant."

"And you, Fishbein? I don't want enemies. I'm just like you—I want to serve my time and go home. I miss the same things you miss."

"Then, Sergeant," Fishbein interrupted, "Why don't you come too?"

"Where?"

"To St. Louis. To Shelley's aunt. We'll have a regular Seder. Play hide-the-matzah." He gave a broad, black-toothed smile.

I saw Grossbart in the doorway again, on the other side of the screen.

"Pssst!" He waved a piece of paper. "Mickey, here's the address. Tell her I couldn't get away."

Halpern did not move. He looked at me and I saw the shrug moving up his arms into his shoulders again. I took the cover off my typewriter and made out passes for him and Fishbein. "Go," I said, "the three of you."

I thought Halpern was going to kiss my hand.

That afternoon, in a bar in Joplin, I drank beer and listened with half an ear to the Cardinal game. I tried to look squarely at what I'd become involved in, and began to wonder if perhaps the struggle with Grossbart wasn't as much my fault as his. What was I that I had to *muster* generous feelings? Who was I to have been feeling so grudging, so tight-hearted? After all, I wasn't being asked to move the world. Had I a right, then, or a reason, to clamp down on Grossbart, when that meant clamping down on Halpern, too? And Fishbein, that ugly agreeable soul, wouldn't he suffer in the bargain also? Out of the many recollections that had tumbled over me these past few days, I heard from some childhood moment my grandmother's voice: "What are you making a *tsimas*?"[3] It was what she would ask my mother when, say, I had cut myself with a knife and her daughter was busy bawling me out. I would need a hug and a kiss and my mother would moralize! But my grandmother knew—mercy overrides justice. I should have known it, too. Who was Nathan Marx to be such a pennypincher with kindness? Surely, I thought, the Messiah himself—if he should ever come—won't niggle over nickels and dimes. God willing, he'll hug and kiss.

The next day, while we were playing softball over on the Parade Grounds, I decided to ask Bob Wright, who was noncom in charge over at Classification and Assignment, where he thought our trainees would be sent when their cycle ended in two weeks. I asked casually, between innings, and he

---

2. Baked pudding of noodles or potatoes.
3. Fuss (Yiddish, literal trans.); here a side dish made of mixed cooked vegetables and fruit.

said, "They're pushing them all into the Pacific. Shulman cut the orders on your boys the other day."

The news shocked me, as though I were father to Halpern, Fishbein, and Grossbart.

That night I was just sliding into sleep when someone tapped on the door. "What is it?"

"Sheldon."

He opened the door and came in. For a moment I felt his presence without being able to see him. "How was it?" I asked, as though to the darkness.

He popped into sight before me. "Great, Sergeant." I felt my springs sag; Grossbart was sitting on the edge of the bed. I sat up.

"How about you?" he asked. "Have a nice weekend?"

"Yes."

He took a deep paternal breath. "The others went to sleep . . ." We sat silently for a while, as a homey feeling invaded my ugly little cubicle: the door was locked, the cat out, the children safely in bed.

"Sergeant, can I tell you something? Personal?"

I did not answer and he seemed to know why. "Not about me. About Mickey. Sergeant, I never felt for anybody like I feel for him. Last night I heard Mickey in the bed next to me. He was crying so, it could have broken your heart. Real sobs."

"I'm sorry to hear that."

"I had to talk to him to stop him. He held my hand, Sergeant—he wouldn't let it go. He was almost hysterical. He kept saying if he only knew where we were going. Even if he knew it *was* the Pacific, that would be better than nothing. Just to know."

Long ago, someone had taught Grossbart the sad law that only lies can get the truth. Not that I couldn't believe in Halpern's crying—his eyes *always* seemed red-rimmed. But, fact or not, it became a lie when Grossbart uttered it. He was entirely strategic. But then—it came with the force of indictment—so was I! There are strategies of aggression, but there are strategies of retreat, as well. And so, recognizing that I myself, had not been without craft and guile, I told him what I knew. "It is the Pacific."

He let out a small gasp, which was not a lie. "I'll tell him. I wish it was otherwise."

"So do I."

He jumped on my words. "You mean you think you could do something? A change maybe?"

"No, I couldn't do a thing."

"Don't you know anybody over at C & A?"

"Grossbart, there's nothing I can do. If your orders are for the Pacific then it's the Pacific."

"But Mickey."

"Mickey, you, me—everybody, Grossbart. There's nothing to be done. Maybe the war'll end before you go. Pray for a miracle."

"But—"

"Good night, Grossbart." I settled back, and was relieved to feel the springs upbend again as Grossbart rose to leave. I could see him clearly now; his jaw had dropped and he looked like a dazed prizefighter. I noticed for the first time a little paper bag in his hand.

"Grossbart"—I smiled—"my gift?"

"Oh, yes, Sergeant. Here, from all of us." He handed me the bag. "It's egg roll."

"Egg roll?" I accepted the bag and felt a damp grease spot on the bottom. I opened it, sure that Grossbart was joking.

"We thought you'd probably like it. You know, Chinese egg roll. We thought you'd probably have a taste for—"

"Your aunt served egg roll?"

"She wasn't home."

"Grossbart, she invited you. You told me she invited you and your friends."

"I know. I just reread the letter. *Next* week."

I got out of bed and walked to the window. It was black as far off as I could see. "Grossbart," I said. But I was not calling him.

"What?"

"What are you, Grossbart? Honest to God, what are you?"

I think it was the first time I'd asked him a question for which he didn't have an immediate answer.

"How can you do this to people?" I asked.

"Sergeant, the day away did us all a world of good. Fishbein, you should see him, he *loves* Chinese food."

"But the Seder," I said.

"We took second best, Sergeant."

Rage came charging at me. I didn't sidestep—I grabbed it, pulled it in, hugged it to my chest.

"Grossbart, you're a liar! You're a schemer and a crook! You've got no respect for anything! Nothing at all! Not for me, for the truth, not even for poor Halpern! You use us all—"

"Sergeant, Sergeant, I feel for Mickey, honest to God, I do. I *love* Mickey. I try—"

"You try! You feel!" I lurched towards him and grabbed his shirt front. I shook him furiously. "Grossbart, get out. Get out and stay the hell away from me! Because if I see you, I'll make your life miserable. *You understand that*?"

"Yes."

I let him free, and when he walked from the room I wanted to spit on the floor where he had stood. I couldn't stop the fury from rising in my heart. It engulfed me, owned me, till it seemed I could only rid myself of it with tears or an act of violence. I snatched from the bed the bag Grossbart had given me and with all my strength threw it out the window. And the next morning, as the men policed the area around the barracks, I heard a great cry go up from one of the trainees who'd been anticipating only his morning handful of cigarette butts and candy wrappers. "Egg roll!" he shouted. "Holy Christ, Chinese goddam egg roll!"

A week later, when I read the orders that had come down from C & A, I couldn't believe my eyes. Every single trainee was to be shipped to Camp Stoneham, California, and from there to the Pacific. Every trainee but one: Private Sheldon Grossbart was to be sent to Fort Monmouth, New Jersey. I read the mimeographed sheet several times. Dee, Farrell, Fishbein, Fuselli, Fylypowycz, Glinicki, Gromke, Gucwa, Halpern, Hardy, Helebrandt . . . right down to Anton Zygadlo, all were to be headed West before the month was out. All except Grossbart. He had pulled a string and I wasn't it.

I lifted the phone and called C & A.

The voice on the other end said smartly, "Corporal Shulman, sir."

"Let me speak to Sergeant Wright."

"Who is this calling, sir?"

"Sergeant Marx."

And to my surprise, the voice said, *"Oh."* Then: "Just a minute, Sergeant."

Shulman's *oh* stayed with me while I waited for Wright to come to the phone. Why *oh?* Who was Shulman? And then, so simply, I knew I'd discovered the string Grossbart had pulled. In fact, I could hear Grossbart the day he'd discovered Shulman, in the PX, or the bowling alley, or maybe even at services. "Glad to meet you. Where you from? Bronx? Me too. Do you know so-and-so? And so-and-so? Me too! You work at C & A? Really? Hey, how's chances of getting East? Could you do something? Change something? Swindle, cheat, lie? We gotta help each other, you know . . . if the Jews in Germany . . ."

At the other end Bob Wright answered. "How are you, Nate? How's the pitching arm?"

"Good. Bob, I wonder if you could do me a favor." I heard clearly my own words and they so reminded me of Grossbart that I dropped more easily than I could have imagined into what I had planned. "This may sound crazy, Bob, but I got a kid here on orders to Monmouth who wants them changed. He had a brother killed in Europe and he's hot to go to the Pacific. Says he'd feel like a coward if he wound up stateside. I don't know, Bob, can anything be done? Put somebody else in the Monmouth slot?"

"Who?" he asked cagily.

"Anybody. First guy on the alphabet. I don't care. The kid just asked if something could be done."

"What's his name?"

"Grossbart, Sheldon."

Wright didn't answer.

"Yeah," I said, "he's a Jewish kid, so he thought I could help him out. You know."

"I guess I can do something," he finally said. "The Major hasn't been around here for weeks—TDY[4] to the golf course. I'll try, Nate that's all I can say."

"I'd appreciate it, Bob. See you Sunday," and I hung up, perspiring.

And the following day the corrected orders appeared: Fishbein, Fuselli, Fylypowycz, Glinicki, Grossbart, Gucwa, Halpern, Hardy . . . Lucky Private Harley Alton was to go to Fort Monmouth, New Jersey, where for some reason or other, they wanted an enlisted man with infantry training.

After chow that night I stopped back at the orderly room to straighten out the guard duty roster. Grossbart was waiting for me. He spoke first.

"You son of a bitch!"

I sat down at my desk and while he glared down at me I began to make the necessary alterations in the duty roster.

"What do you have against me?" he cried. "Against my family? Would it kill you for me to be near my father, God knows how many months he has left to him."

"Why?"

"His heart," Grossbart said. "He hasn't had enough troubles in a lifetime, you've got to add to them. I curse the day I ever met you, Marx! Shulman told me what happened over there. There's no limit to your anti-Semitism,

---

4. Temporary Duty, an army orders term used ironically here.

2640 | AMIRI BARAKA (LEROI JONES)

is there! The damage you've done here isn't enough. You have to make a special phone call! You really want me dead!"

I made the last few notations in the duty roster and got up to leave. "Good night, Grossbart."

"You owe me an explanation!" He stood in my path.

"Sheldon, you're the one who owes explanations."

He scowled. "To *you*?"

"To me, I think so, yes. Mostly to Fishbein and Halpern."

"That's right, twist things around. I owe nobody nothing, I've done all I could do for them. Now I think I've got the right to watch out for myself."

"For each other we have to learn to watch out, Sheldon. You told me yourself."

"You call this watching out for me, what you did?"

"No. For all of us."

I pushed him aside and started for the door. I heard his furious breathing behind me, and it sounded like steam rushing from the engine of his terrible strength.

"You'll be all right," I said from the door. And, I thought, so would Fishbein and Halpern be all right, even in the Pacific, if only Grossbart could continue to see in the obsequiousness of the one, the soft spirituality of the other, some profit for himself.

I stood outside the orderly room, and I heard Grossbart weeping behind me. Over in the barracks, in the lighted windows, I could see the boys in their T-shirts sitting on their bunks talking about their orders, as they'd been doing for the past two days. With a kind of quiet nervousness, they polished shoes, shined belt buckles, squared away underwear, trying as best they could to accept their fate. Behind me, Grossbart swallowed hard, accepting his. And then, resisting with all my will an impulse to turn and seek pardon for my vindictiveness, I accepted my own.

1959

AMIRI BARAKA (LEROI JONES)
1934–2014

When in 1967 LeRoi Jones assumed the Bantuized Muslim name Amiri Baraka (meaning Prince, a Blessed One), he was undergoing one of several changes in his progression as a maker of literature. Born Everett Leroy Jones, he was the child of middle-class African American parents in Newark, New Jersey, where his scholastic abilities took him to the best schools available; as Baraka recalls in his autobiography, his classmates were more often white suburbanites than inner-city children of his own race. He restyled his name as "LeRoi" during his undergraduate years at Howard University (a traditionally African American institution), to which he had transferred from the mostly white campus of Rutgers University (where he had won a scholarship). After leaving Howard in 1954 and serving in the U.S. Air Force, from which he was discharged for unapproved political activities,

Jones moved to New York City's Greenwich Village and became prominent on the avant-garde poetry scene. His friends were white innovators—Gilbert Sorrentino, Diane DiPrima, and Frank O'Hara among them—with whom he worked on the magazine *Kulchur* in addition to editing and publishing his own journal, *Yugen*. Married to Hettie Cohen, he began an interracial family and wrote record reviews for mainstream jazz magazines.

Jones was well established in the more intellectually elite quarters of New York's world of poetry, art, and music. Yet as racial tensions mounted, with the assassination of Medgar Evers; fatal church bombings in Alabama; and the murder of civil rights workers James Chaney, Andrew Goodman, and Michael Schwerner in Mississippi, Jones's life underwent major changes as well. In 1965, following the assassination of Malcolm X, he left his wife and children and moved to Harlem, where as a newly declared black cultural nationalist he founded the Black Arts Repertory Theater, dedicated to taking socially militant drama directly to the people it represented.

Poetry as a vehicle of popular encouragement remained central to Baraka's belief. He may well have agreed with the judge who once convicted him of incitement to riot that his poems could motivate people to act (whether such culpability had been proven in legal form is another matter, and his incitement conviction was later, overturned on appeal). As opposed to his very first work, which conveyed a personal anguish for which the poet projected no political solution ("I am inside someone / who hates me, I look / out from his eyes") and whose collective title conveys little hope other than in the act of expression (*Preface to a Twenty Volume Suicide Note*, 1961), his later work is replete with exhortations, capitalized imperatives for action, and chantlike repetitions designed to arouse a fury for action and then direct it toward the achievement of specific social goals. Much like his drama, this poetry is overtly presentational, showing what the reader needs to think about and then providing the stimulus to act. Yet all the while the personal nature of Baraka stands behind it, making clear that a deep and complex imagination has been brought to bear on the issues. The range and intensity of Baraka's poetry is evident in his 1995 collection, *Transbluesency: The Selected Poems of Amiri Baraka/LeRoi Jones (1961–1995)*. His 2004 collection, *Somebody Blew Up America & Other Poems*, contains Baraka's controversial poem of the same name, written after 9/11, during a period in which he was New Jersey's poet laureate. After the poem's publication, public outcry became so great that the governor of New Jersey took action to abolish the position. Although Baraka sued, the United States Court of Appeals eventually ruled that state officials were immune from such lawsuits. Baraka never feared controversy; he remained an influence for many younger writers both as a major poet and as a cultural and political leader.

Beginning in the 1980s, Baraka taught in the African Studies Department at the State University of New York, Stony Brook. In addition to poetry and drama, he continued to write essays on social subjects and on jazz.

An Agony. As Now.

I am inside someone
who hates me. I look
out from his eyes. Smell
what fouled tunes come in
to his breath. Love his   5
wretched women.

Slits in the metal, for sun. Where
my eyes sit turning, at the cool air

the glance of light, or hard flesh
rubbed against me, a woman, a man,   10
without shadow, or voice, or meaning.

This is the enclosure (flesh,
where innocence is a weapon. An
abstraction. Touch. (Not mine,
Or yours, if you are the soul I had   15
and abandoned when I was blind and had
my enemies carry me as a dead man
(if he is beautiful, or pitied.

It can be pain. (As now, as all his
flesh hurts me.) It can be that. Or   20
pain. As when she ran from me into
that forest.
            Or pain, the mind
silver spiraled whirled against the
sun, higher than even old men thought   25
God would be. Or pain. And the other. The
yes. (Inside his books, his fingers. They
are withered yellow flowers and were never
beautiful.) The yes. You will, lost soul, say
'beauty.' Beauty, practiced, as the tree. The   30
slow river. A white sun in its wet sentences.

Or, the cold men in their gale. Ecstasy. Flesh
or soul. The yes. (Their robes blown. Their bowls
empty. They chant at my heels, not at yours.) Flesh
or soul, as corrupt. Where the answer moves too quickly. 35
Where the God is a self, after all.)

Cold air blown through narrow blind eyes. Flesh,
white hot metal. Glows as the day with its sun.
It is a human love, I live inside. A bony skeleton
you recognize as words or simple feeling.   40

But it has no feeling. As the metal, is hot, it is not,
given to love.

It burns the thing
inside it. And that thing
screams.   45

1964

A Poem for Willie Best[1]

I

The face sings, alone
at the top
        of the body. All

---

1. Willie Best was a negro character actor whose Hollywood name was Sleep'n'eat [Baraka's note].

flesh, all song, aligned. For hell
is silent, at those cracked lips   5
flakes of skin and mind
twist and whistle softly
as they fall.
           It was your own death
you saw. Your own face, stiff   10
and raw. This
without sound, or
movement. Sweet afton,[2] the
dead beggar bleeds
yet. His blood, for a time   15
alive, and huddled in a door
way, struggling to sing. Rain
washes it into cracks. Pits
whose bottoms are famous. Whose sides
are innocent broadcasts   20
of another life.

II

At this point, neither
front nor back. A point, the
dimensionless line. The top
of a head, seen from Christ's   25
heaven, stripped of history
or desire.
           Fixed, perpendicular
to shadow. (Even speech, vertical,
leaves no trace. Born in to death   30
held fast to it, where
the lover spreads his arms, the line
he makes to threaten Gods with history.
The fingers stretch to emptiness. At
each point, after flesh, even light   35
is speculation. But an end, his end,
failing a beginning.

2

A cross. The gesture, symbol, line
arms held stiff, nailed stiff, with
no sign, of what gave them strength.   40
The point, become a line, a cross, or
the man, and his material, driven in
the ground. If the head rolls back
and the mouth opens, screamed into
existence, there will be perhaps   45
only the slightest hint of movement
a smear; no help will come. No one
will turn to that station again.

---

2. "How Gently Sweet Afton," a poem by the Scottish poet Robert Burns (1759–1796), refers to the
river Afton in Ayrshire, Scotland.

III

At a cross roads, sits the
player. No drum, no umbrella, even   50
though it's raining. Again, and we
are somehow less miserable because
here is a hero, used to being wet.
One road is where you are standing now
(reading this, the other, crosses then   55
rushes into a wood.
      5 lbs neckbones.
      5 lbs hog innards.
      10 bottles cheap wine.
         (the contents   60
of a paper bag, also shoes, with holes
for the big toe, and several rusted
knives. This is a literature, of
symbols. And it is his gift, as the
bag is.   65
     (The contents
again, holy saviours,
       300 men on horseback
       75 bibles
       the quietness   70
of a field. A rich
man, though wet through
by the rain.
     I said,
       47 howitzers[3]   75
       7 polished horse jaws
       a few trees being waved
softly back under
the black night
      All this should be   80
invested.

IV

   Where
   ever,
     he has gone. Who ever
   mourns   85
   or sits silent
   to remember

   There is nothing of pity
   here. Nothing
   of sympathy.   90

V

This is the dance of the raised
leg. Of the hand on the knee

---

3. Short, relatively light cannons for the high-angle firing of shells at a low velocity.

quickly.
        As a dance it punishes
speech. 'The house burned. The   95
old man killed.'
              As a dance it
is obscure.

VI

This is the song
of the highest C.   100
             The falsetto. An elegance
that punishes silence. This is the song
of the toes pointed inward, the arms swung, the
hips, moved, for fucking, slow, from side
to side. He is quoted   105
saying, "My father was
never a jockey,
              but
   he did teach me
           how to ride."   110

VII

The balance.
              (Rushed in, swarmed of dark, cloaks,
and only red lights pushed a message
to the street. Rub.
             This is the lady,   115
I saw you with.
This is your mother.
This is the lady I wanted
some how to sleep with.
              As a dance, or   120
our elegant song. Sun red and grown
from trees, fences, mud roads in dried out
river beds. This is for me, with no God
but what is given. Give me
              Something more   125
than what is here. I must tell you
my body hurts.

The balance.
             Can you hear? Here
I am again. Your boy, dynamite. Can   130
you hear? My soul is moved. The soul
you gave me. I say, my soul, and it
is moved. That soul
you gave me.
             Yes, I'm sure   135
this is the lady. You
slept with her. Witness, your boy,
here, dynamite. Hear?
             I mean
can you?   140

The balance.
          He was tired of losing. (And
his walking buddies tired
of walking.
          Bent slightly,   145
at the waist. Left hand low, to flick
quick showy jabs ala Sugar.[4] The right
cocked, to complete,
               any combination.
          He was   150
tired of losing, but he was fighting
a big dumb "farmer."
          Such a blue bright
afternoon, and only a few hundred yards
from the beach. He said, I'm tired   155
of losing.
         "I *got* ta cut'cha."

VIII

A renegade
behind the mask. And even
the mask, a renegade   160
disguise. Black skin
and hanging lip.
          Lazy
          Frightened
          Thieving   165
          Very potent sexually
          Scars
          Generally inferior
               (but natural
rhythms.   170

His head is
at the window. The only
part
      that sings.
(The word he used   175
          (we are passing St. Mark's place[5]
          and those crazy jews who fuck)
                        to provoke
in neon, still useful
in the rain,   180
          to provoke
some meaning, where before
there was only hell. I said
silence, at his huddled blood.
               It is an obscene invention.   185
               A white sticky discharge.

---

4. Sugar Ray Robinson (1921–1989), American boxer.   5. Street in New York City's East Village.

"Jism," in white chalk
on the back of Angel's garage.
Red jackets with the head of
Hobbes[6] staring into space. "Jasm"   190
the name the leader took, had it
stenciled on his chest.

                                    And he sits
wet at the crossroads, remembering distinctly
each weightless face that eases by. (Sun at   195
the back door, and that hideous mindless grin.

                                    (Hear?

                                                    1964

6. Thomas Hobbes (1588–1679), English philosopher who believed a "social contract" was necessary
between rulers and the ruled. Here he represents the Western, white, materialist tradition.

N. SCOTT MOMADAY
b. 1934

" In a certain sense," writes N. Scott Momaday in the nonfiction collection *The
Man Made of Words* (1997), "we are all made of words; . . . our most essential
being consists in language. It is the element in which we think and dream and act,
in which we live our daily lives." Since the publication of his Pulitzer Prize–
winning novel *House Made of Dawn* (1968), Momaday's writing has crossed boundaries of language, form, and genre, thereby creating for Momaday, through will and
imagination, an American Indian identity in words.

Navarre Scott Momaday was born at the Kiowa and Comanche Indian Hospital
in Lawton, Oklahoma, the only child of Al Momaday, a Kiowa, and Natachee Scott,
who was part Cherokee. He spent most of his early years in New Mexico and Arizona, moving in 1946 to Jemez Pueblo in New Mexico's Rio Grande Valley. There
his parents, both artists and teachers, took jobs at a small day school. Growing up
on reservations, including those of the Navajo and the Apache, Momaday experienced the rhythms of traditional tribal life, but saw, too, the changes wrought by
postwar material culture, and their human costs—the alcoholism, unemployment,
and personal disintegration that mark the life of Abel, the returning veteran in
House Made of Dawn. Early on, Momaday's mother instilled in him the value of a
bicultural education that would open the future without closing off his native heritage. Momaday attended reservation, public, and mission schools, then graduated
from military high school in Virginia and the University of New Mexico. He received
his Ph.D. in 1963 from Stanford University, where his mentor in American and
English literature was the poet and critic Yvor Winters. Since then his teaching
career has taken him to Santa Barbara, Berkeley, the University of Moscow, Stanford, and the University of Arizona.

What some scholars call the "Native American Renaissance" is usually said to
have begun with the publication of *House Made of Dawn* in 1968 and its being
awarded the Pulitzer Prize the following year. And, indeed, from 1968 to the present Native American writers have published a substantial body of fine poetry, fic-

tion, and autobiography, gaining considerable notice in the United States and abroad.

Over the decades since the publication of *House Made of Dawn*, Momaday has published two more novels, *The Ancient Child* (1989) and *In the Bear's House* (1999); four volumes of poems, *Angle of Geese and Other Poems* (1974), *Before an Old Painting of the Crucifixion, Carmel Mission, June 1960* (1975), and *The Gourd Dancer* (1976); stories and poems in *In the Presence of the Sun* (1992); and three works of autobiography, *The Journey to Tai-me* (1967, privately published), *The Way to Rainy Mountain* (1969), and *The Names: A Memoir* (1976); as well as critical works. His deliberate engagement with a variety of forms—oral and written poetry, prose fiction and non-fiction, autobiography, legend, history, photography, painting (all "forms of discovery," in Winters's words)—has helped him lay claim to his Kiowa past.

Momaday's idea of the past as a journey is consciously expressed in *The Journey of Tai-me*, which offers his translations of the Kiowa myths he learned as a child from his grandmother, Aho. This work relates the story of the Sun Dance—a ceremony for spiritual guidance and power performed by many Plains Indian groups—to his revelatory memory on journeying to Oklahoma to see the sacred Tai-me bundle: "I became more keenly aware of myself as someone who had walked through time and in whose blood there is something inestimably old and undying. It was as if I had remembered something that happened two hundred years ago. I meant then to seek after the source of my memory and myself." In *The Way to Rainy Mountain* (1969) Momaday undertakes this search, collecting, with his father as translator, Kiowa tales and myths and clustering them with brief, loose historical commentaries and personal family stories. What seem to be fragments come together in a complex structure—twenty-four "quintessential novels," divided into three sections, framed by poems and prose pieces—that follow the Kiowa from emergence through maturity to decline as a Plains Indian culture. Central to *Rainy Mountain* and to all of Momaday's writing is the land—the focal point of memory, the defining place for Kiowa culture. The same rootedness that defines Momaday's ancestors gives his work its conjuring power, a power that comes from distilling in words and pictures, as Momaday writes, "the glare of noon and all the colors of the dawn and dusk."

From The Way to Rainy Mountain

Headwaters

Noon in the intermountain plain:
There is scant telling of the marsh—
A log, hollow and weather-stained,
An insect at the mouth, and moss—
Yet waters rise against the roots,   5
Stand brimming to the stalks. What moves?
What moves on this archaic force
Was wild and welling at the source.

Introduction

A single knoll rises out of the plain in Oklahoma, north and west of the Wichita Range. For my people, the Kiowas,[1] it is an old landmark, and they gave it the name Rainy Mountain. The hardest weather in the world is there. Winter brings blizzards, hot tornadic winds arise in the spring, and in sum-

---

1. The Kiowa were a mobile hunting and gathering people of the Southern Plains.

mer the prairie is an anvil's edge. The grass turns brittle and brown, and it cracks beneath your feet. There are green belts along the rivers and creeks, linear groves of hickory and pecan, willow and witch hazel. At a distance in July or August the steaming foliage seems almost to writhe in fire. Great green and yellow grasshoppers are everywhere in the tall grass, popping up like corn to sting the flesh, and tortoises crawl about on the red earth, going nowhere in the plenty of time. Loneliness is an aspect of the land. All things in the plain are isolate; there is no confusion of objects in the eye, but *one* hill or *one* tree or *one* man. To look upon that landscape in the early morning, with the sun at your back, is to lose the sense of proportion. Your imagination comes to life, and this, you think, is where Creation was begun.

I returned to Rainy Mountain in July. My grandmother had died in the spring, and I wanted to be at her grave. She had lived to be very old and at last infirm. Her only living daughter was with her when she died, and I was told that in death her face was that of a child.

I like to think of her as a child. When she was born, the Kiowas were living the last great moment of their history. For more than a hundred years they had controlled the open range from the Smoky Hill River to the Red, from the headwaters of the Canadian to the fork of the Arkansas and Cimarron. In alliance with the Comanches, they had ruled the whole of the southern Plains. War was their sacred business, and they were among the finest horsemen the world has ever known. But warfare for the Kiowas was preeminently a matter of disposition rather than of survival, and they never understood the grim, unrelenting advance of the U.S. Cavalry. When at last, divided and ill-provisioned, they were driven onto the Staked Plains in the cold rains of autumn, they fell into panic. In Palo Duro Canyon[2] they abandoned their crucial stores to pillage and had nothing then but their lives. In order to save themselves, they surrendered to the soldiers at Fort Sill[3] and were imprisoned in the old stone corral that now stands as a military museum. My grandmother was spared the humiliation of those high gray walls by eight or ten years, but she must have known from birth the affliction of defeat, the dark brooding of old warriors.

Her name was Aho, and she belonged to the last culture to evolve in North America. Her forebears came down from the high country in western Montana nearly three centuries ago. They were a mountain people, a mysterious tribe of hunters whose language has never been positively classified in any major group. In the late seventeenth century they began a long migration to the south and east. It was a journey toward the dawn, and it led to a golden age. Along the way the Kiowas were befriended by the Crows, who gave them the culture and religion of the Plains. They acquired horses, and their ancient nomadic spirit was suddenly free of the ground. They acquired Tai-me,[4] the sacred Sun Dance doll, from that moment the object and symbol of their worship, and so shared in the divinity of the sun. Not least, they acquired the sense of destiny, therefore courage and pride. When they entered upon the southern Plains they had been transformed. No longer were they slaves to the simple necessity of survival; they were a lordly and dangerous society of fighters and thieves, hunters and priests of

2. On the Staked Plains, or the Texas Panhandle, that part of the state jutting north between New Mexico and Oklahoma.
3. U.S. Cavalry fort in Oklahoma and site of the

Kiowa-Comanche Agency.
4. The sacred being who aids the Kiowa in times of trouble; this being is embodied in the holy doll central to Kiowa ritual.

the sun. According to their origin myth, they entered the world through a hollow log. From one point of view, their migration was the fruit of an old prophecy, for indeed they emerged from a sunless world.

Although my grandmother lived out her long life in the shadow of Rainy Mountain, the immense landscape of the continental interior lay like memory in her blood. She could tell of the Crows, whom she had never seen, and of the Black Hills, where she had never been. I wanted to see in reality what she had seen more perfectly in the mind's eye, and traveled fifteen hundred miles to begin my pilgrimage.

Yellowstone, it seemed to me, was the top of the world, a region of deep lakes and dark timber, canyons and waterfalls. But, beautiful as it is, one might have the sense of confinement there. The skyline in all directions is close at hand, the high wall of the woods and deep cleavages of shade. There is a perfect freedom in the mountains, but it belongs to the eagle and the elk, the badger and the bear. The Kiowas reckoned their stature by the distance they could see, and they were bent and blind in the wilderness.

Descending eastward, the highland meadows are a stairway to the plain. In July the inland slope of the Rockies is luxuriant with flax and buckwheat, stonecrop and larkspur. The earth unfolds and the limit of the land recedes. Clusters of trees, and animals grazing far in the distance, cause the vision to reach away and wonder to build upon the mind. The sun follows a longer course in the day, and the sky is immense beyond all comparison. The great billowing clouds that sail upon it are shadows that move upon the grain like water, dividing light. Farther down, in the land of the Crows and Blackfeet, the plain is yellow. Sweet clover takes hold of the hills and bends upon itself to cover and seal the soil. There the Kiowas paused on their way; they had come to the place where they must change their lives. The sun is at home on the plains. Precisely there does it have the certain character of a god. When the Kiowas came to the land of the Crows, they could see the dark lees of the hills at dawn across the Bighorn River, the profusion of light on the grain shelves, the oldest deity ranging after the solstices. Not yet would they veer southward to the caldron of the land that lay below; they must wean their blood from the northern winter and hold the mountains a while longer in their view. They bore Tai-me in procession to the east.

A dark mist lay over the Black Hills, and the land was like iron. At the top of a ridge I caught sight of Devil's Tower upthrust against the gray sky as if in the birth of time the core of the earth had broken through its crust and the motion of the world was begun. There are things in nature that engender an awful quiet in the heart of man; Devil's Tower is one of them. Two centuries ago, because they could not do otherwise, the Kiowas made a legend at the base of the rock. My grandmother said:

> Eight children were there at play, seven sisters and their brother. Suddenly the boy was struck dumb; he trembled and began to run upon his hands and feet. His fingers became claws, and his body was covered with fur. Directly there was a bear where the boy had been. The sisters were terrified; they ran, and the bear after them. They came to the stump of a great tree, and the tree spoke to them. It bade them climb upon it, and as they did so it began to rise into the air. The bear came to kill them, but they were just beyond its reach. It reared against the

tree and scored the bark all around with its claws. The seven sisters were borne into the sky, and they became the stars of the Big Dipper.

From that moment, and so long as the legend lives, the Kiowas have kinsmen in the night sky. Whatever they were in the mountains, they could be no more. However tenuous their well-being, however much they had suffered and would suffer again, they had found a way out of the wilderness.

My grandmother had a reverence for the sun, a holy regard that now is all but gone out of mankind. There was a wariness in her, and an ancient awe. She was a Christian in her later years, but she had come a long way about, and she never forgot her birthright. As a child she had been to the Sun Dances; she had taken part in those annual rites, and by them she had learned the restoration of her people in the presence of Tai-me. She was about seven when the last Kiowa Sun Dance was held in 1887 on the Washita River above Rainy Mountain Creek. The buffalo were gone. In order to consummate the ancient sacrifice—to impale the head of a buffalo bull upon the medicine tree—a delegation of old men journeyed into Texas, there to beg and barter for an animal from the Goodnight herd. She was ten when the Kiowas came together for the last time as a living Sun Dance culture. They could find no buffalo; they had to hang an old hide from the sacred tree. Before the dance could begin, a company of soldiers rode out from Fort Sill under orders to disperse the tribe. Forbidden without cause the essential act of their faith,[5] having seen the wild herds slaughtered and left to rot upon the ground, the Kiowas backed away forever from the medicine tree. That was July 20, 1890, at the great bend of the Washita. My grandmother was there. Without bitterness, and for as long as she lived, she bore a vision of deicide.

Now that I can have her only in memory, I see my grandmother in the several postures that were peculiar to her: standing at the wood stove on a winter morning and turning meat in a great iron skillet; sitting at the south window, bent above her beadwork, and afterwards, when her vision failed, looking down for a long time into the fold of her hands; going out upon a cane, very slowly as she did when the weight of age came upon her; praying. I remember her most often at prayer. She made long, rambling prayers out of suffering and hope, having seen many things. I was never sure that I had the right to hear, so exclusive were they of all mere custom and company. The last time I saw her she prayed standing by the side of her bed at night, naked to the waist, the light of a kerosene lamp moving upon her dark skin. Her long, black hair, always drawn and braided in the day, lay upon her shoulders and against her breasts like a shawl. I do not speak Kiowa, and I never understood her prayers, but there was something inherently sad in the sound, some merest hesitation upon the syllables of sorrow. She began in a high and descending pitch, exhausting her breath to silence; then again and again—and always the same intensity of effort, of something that is, and is not, like urgency in the human voice. Transported so in the dancing light among the shadows of her room, she seemed beyond the reach of time. But that was illusion; I think I knew then that I should not see her again.

5. From the 1880s on, the U.S. government sought to ban all "heathenish" practices among Native American peoples in a continuing effort to Christianize and "civilize" them.

Houses are like sentinels in the plain, old keepers of the weather watch. There, in a very little while, wood takes on the appearance of great age. All colors wear soon away in the wind and rain, and then the wood is burned gray and the grain appears and the nails turn red with rust. The window-panes are black and opaque; you imagine there is nothing within, and indeed there are many ghosts, bones given up to the land. They stand here and there against the sky, and you approach them for a longer time than you expect. They belong in the distance; it is their domain.

Once there was a lot of sound in my grandmother's house, a lot of coming and going, feasting and talk. The summers there were full of excitement and reunion. The Kiowas are a summer people; they abide the cold and keep to themselves, but when the season turns and the land becomes warm and vital they cannot hold still; an old love of going returns upon them. The aged visitors who came to my grandmother's house when I was a child were made of lean and leather, and they bore themselves upright. They wore great black hats and bright ample shirts that shook in the wind. They rubbed fat upon their hair and wound their braids with strips of colored cloth. Some of them painted their faces and carried the scars of old and cherished enmi-ties. They were an old council of warlords, come to remind and be reminded of who they were. Their wives and daughters served them well. The women might indulge themselves; gossip was at once the mark and compensation of their servitude. They made loud and elaborate talk among themselves, full of jest and gesture, fright and false alarm. They went abroad in fringed and flowered shawls, bright beadwork and German silver. They were at home in the kitchen, and they prepared meals that were banquets.

There were frequent prayer meetings, and great nocturnal feasts. When I was a child I played with my cousins outside, where the lamplight fell upon the ground and the singing of the old people rose up around us and carried away into the darkness. There were a lot of good things to eat, a lot of laugh-ter and surprise. And afterwards, when the quiet returned, I lay down with my grandmother and could hear the frogs away by the river and feel the motion of the air.

Now there is a funeral silence in the rooms, the endless wake of some final word. The walls have closed in upon my grandmother's house. When I returned to it in mourning, I saw for the first time in my life how small it was. It was late at night, and there was a white moon, nearly full. I sat for a long time on the stone steps by the kitchen door. From there I could see out across the land; I could see the long row of trees by the creek, the low light upon the rolling plains, and the stars of the Big Dipper. Once I looked at the moon and caught sight of a strange thing. A cricket had perched upon the handrail, only a few inches away from me. My line of vision was such that the creature filled the moon like a fossil. It had gone there, I thought, to live and die, for there, of all places, was its small definition made whole and eternal. A warm wind rose up and purled like the longing within me.

The next morning I awoke at dawn and went out on the dirt road to Rainy Mountain. It was already hot, and the grasshoppers began to fill the air. Still, it was early in the morning, and the birds sang out of the shadows. The long yellow grass on the mountain shone in the bright light, and a scissortail hied above the land. There, where it ought to be, at the end of a long and legendary way, was my grandmother's grave. Here and there on the dark stones were ancestral names. Looking back once, I saw the mountain and came away.

IV

They lived at first in the mountains. They did not yet know of Tai-me, but this is what they knew: There was a man and his wife. They had a beautiful child, a little girl whom they would not allow to go out of their sight. But one day a friend of the family came and asked if she might take the child outside to play. The mother guessed that would be all right, but she told the friend to leave the child in its cradle and to place the cradle in a tree. While the child was in the tree, a redbird came among the branches. It was not like any bird that you have seen; it was very beautiful, and it did not fly away. It kept still upon a limb, close to the child. After a while the child got out of its cradle and began to climb after the redbird. And at the same time the tree began to grow taller, and the child was borne up into the sky. She was then a woman, and she found herself in a strange place. Instead of a redbird, there was a young man standing before her. The man spoke to her and said: "I have been watching you for a long time, and I knew that I would find a way to bring you here. I have brought you here to be my wife." The woman looked all around; she saw that he was the only living man there. She saw that he was the sun.

There the land itself ascends into the sky. These mountains lie at the top of the continent, and they cast a long rain shadow on the sea of grasses to the east. They arise out of the last North American wilderness, and they have wilderness names: Wasatch, Bitterroot, Bighorn, Wind River.

I have walked in a mountain meadow bright with Indian paint-brush, lupine, and wild buckwheat, and I have seen high in the branches of a lodgepole pine the male pine grosbeak, round and rose-colored, its dark, striped wings nearly invisible in the soft, mottled light. And the upper-most branches of the tree seemed very slowly to ride across the blue sky.

XIII

If an arrow is well made, it will have tooth marks upon it. That is how you know. The Kiowas made fine arrows and straightened them in their teeth. Then they drew them to the bow to see if they were straight. Once there was a man and his wife. They were alone at night in their tipi. By the light of the fire the man was making

The old men were the best arrow-makers, for they could bring time and patience to their craft. The young men—the fighters and hunters—were willing to pay a high price for arrows that were well made.

When my father was a boy, an old man used to come to Mammedaty's[6]

---

6. Momaday's paternal grandfather.

arrows. After a while he caught sight of something. There was a small opening in the tipi where two hides were sewn together. Someone was there on the outside, looking in. The man went on with his work, but he said to his wife: "Someone is standing outside. Do not be afraid. Let us talk easily, as of ordinary things." He took up an arrow and straightened it in his teeth; then, as it was right for him to do, he drew it to the bow and took aim, first in this direction and then in that. And all the while he was talking, as if to his wife. But this is how he spoke: "I know that you are there on the outside, for I can feel your eyes upon me. If you are a Kiowa, you will understand what I am saying, and you will speak your name." But there was no answer, and the man went on in the same way, pointing the arrow all around. At last his aim fell upon the place where his enemy stood, and he let go of the string. The arrow went straight to the enemy's heart.

XVII

Bad women are thrown away. Once there was a handsome young man. He was wild and reckless, and the chief talked to the wind about him. After that, the man went hunting. A great whirlwind passed by, and he was blind. The Kiowas have no need of a blind man; they left him alone with his wife and child. The winter was coming on and food was scarce. In four days the man's wife grew tired of caring for him. A herd of buffalo came near, and the man knew the sound. He asked his wife to hand him a bow and an arrow. "You must tell me," he said, "when the buffalo are directly in front of me." And in that way he killed a bull, but his wife said that he had missed.

house and pay his respects. He was a lean old man in braids and was impressive in his age and bearing. His name was Cheney, and he was an arrowmaker. Every morning, my father tells me, Cheney would paint his wrinkled face, go out, and pray aloud to the rising sun. In my mind I can see that man as if he were there now. I like to watch him as he makes his prayer. I know where he stands and where his voice goes on the rolling grasses and where the sun comes up on the land. There, at dawn, you can feel the silence. It is cold and clear and deep like water. It takes hold of you and will not let you go.

In the Kiowa calendars[7] there is graphic proof that the lives of women were hard, whether they were "bad women" or not. Only the captives, who were slaves, held lower status. During the Sun Dance of 1843, a man stabbed his wife in the breast because she accepted Chief Dohasan's invitation to ride with him in the ceremonial procession. And in the winter of 1851–52, Big Bow stole the wife of a man who was away on a raiding expedition. He brought her to his father's camp and made her wait outside in the bitter cold while he went in to collect his things. But his father knew what was going on, and he held Big Bow and would not let him

---

7. The Kiowa recorded their history in pictures that functioned as calendars.

He asked for another arrow and killed another bull, but again his wife said that he had missed. Now the man was a hunter, and he knew the sound an arrow makes when it strikes home, but he said nothing. Then his wife helped herself to the meat and ran away with her child. The man was blind; he ate grass and kept himself alive. In seven days a band of Kiowas found him and took him to their camp. There in the firelight a woman was telling a story. She told of how her husband had been killed by enemy warriors. The blind man listened, and he knew her voice. That was a bad woman. At sunrise they threw her away.

go. The woman was made to wait in the snow until her feet were frozen.

Mammedaty's grandmother, Kau-au-ointy,[8] was a Mexican captive, taken from her homeland when she was a child of eight or ten years. I never knew her, but I have been to her grave at Rainy Mountain.

KAU-AU-OINTY

BORN 1834

DIED 1929

AT REST

She raised a lot of eyebrows, they say, for she would not play the part of a Kiowa woman. From slavery she rose up to become a figure in the tribe. She owned a great herd of cattle, and she could ride as well as any man. She had blue eyes.

XXIV

East of my grandmother's house, south of the pecan grove, there is buried a woman in a beautiful dress. Mammedaty used to know where she is buried, but now no one knows. If you stand on the front porch of the house and look eastward towards Carnegie, you know that the woman is buried somewhere within the range of your vision. But her grave is unmarked. She was buried in a cabinet, and she wore a beautiful dress How beautiful it was! It was one of those fine buckskin dresses, and it was decorated with elk's teeth and beadwork. That dress is still there, under the ground.

Aho's high moccasins are made of softest, cream-colored skins. On each instep there is a bright disc of bead-work—an eight-pointed star, red and pale blue on a white field—and there are bands of beadwork at the soles and ankles. The flaps of the leggings are wide and richly ornamented with blue and red and green and white and lavender beads.

East of my grandmother's house the sun rises out of the plain. Once in his life a man ought to concentrate his mind upon the remembered earth, I believe. He ought to give himself up to a particular landscape in his experience, to look at it from as many angles as he can, to wonder about it, to dwell upon it. He ought to imagine that he touches it with his hands at every season and listens to the sounds that are made upon it. He ought to imagine the creatures there and all the faintest motions of the wind. He ought to recollect the glare of noon and all the colors of the dawn and dusk.

8. Momaday's great-great-grandmother.

Epilogue

During the first hours after midnight on the morning of November 13, 1833, it seemed that the world was coming to an end. Suddenly the stillness of the night was broken; there were brilliant flashes of light in the sky, light of such intensity that people were awakened by it. With the speed and density of a driving rain, stars were falling in the universe. Some were brighter than Venus; one was said to be as large as the moon.

That most brilliant shower of Leonid meteors[9] has a special place in the memory of the Kiowa people. It is among the earliest entries in the Kiowa calendars, and it marks the beginning as it were of the historical period in the tribal mind. In the preceding year Tai-me had been stolen by a band of Osages, and although it was later returned, the loss was an almost unimaginable tragedy; and in 1837 the Kiowas made the first of their treaties[1] with the United States. The falling stars seemed to image the sudden and violent disintegration of an old order.

But indeed the golden age of the Kiowas had been short-lived, ninety or a hundred years, say, from about 1740. The culture would persist for a while in decline, until about 1875, but then it would be gone, and there would be very little material evidence that it had ever been. Yet it is within the reach of memory still, though tenuously now, and moreover it is even defined in a remarkably rich and living verbal tradition which demands to be preserved for its own sake. The living memory and the verbal tradition which transcends it were brought together for me once and for all in the person of Ko-sahn.

A hundred-year-old woman came to my grandmother's house one afternoon in July. Aho was dead; Mammedaty had died before I was born. There were very few Kiowas left who could remember the Sun Dances; Ko-sahn was one of them; she was a grown woman when my grandparents came into the world. Her body was twisted and her face deeply lined with age. Her thin white hair was held in place by a cap of black netting, though she wore braids as well, and she had but one eye. She was dressed in the manner of a Kiowa matron, a dark, full-cut dress that reached nearly to the ankles, full, flowing sleeves, and a wide, apron-like sash. She sat on a bench in the arbor so concentrated in her great age that she seemed extraordinarily small. She was quiet for a time—she might almost have been asleep—and then she began to speak and to sing. She spoke of many things, and once she spoke of the Sun Dance:

> My sisters and I were very young; that was a long time ago. Early one morning they came to wake us up. They had brought a great buffalo in from the plain. Everyone went out to see and to pray. We heard a great many voices. One man said that the lodge was almost ready. We were told to go there, and someone gave me a piece of cloth. It was very beautiful. Then I asked what I ought to do with it, and they said that I must tie it to the Tai-me tree. There were other pieces of cloth on the tree, and so I put mine there as well.
>
> When the lodge frame was finished, a woman—sometimes a man—began to sing. It was like this:

9. Annual meteor shower that appears to emanate from the constellation Leo; the Leonid shower of 1833 was spectactar to observers in North America east of the Rocky Mountains.
1. This treaty provided for settlers' passage through Kiowa and Comanche lands.

> *Everything is ready.*
> *Now the four societies must go out.*
> *They must go out and get the leaves,*
>   *the branches for the lodge.*

And when the branches were tied in place, again there was singing:

> *Let the boys go out.*
> *Come on, boys, now we must get the earth.*

The boys began to shout. Now they were not just ordinary boys, not all of them; they were those for whom prayers had been made, and they were dressed in different ways. There was an old, old woman. She had something on her back. The boys went out to see. The old woman had a bag full of earth on her back. It was a certain kind of sandy earth. That is what they must have in the lodge. The dancers must dance upon the sandy earth. The old woman held a digging tool in her hand. She turned towards the south and pointed with her lips. It was like a kiss, and she began to sing:

> *We have brought the earth.*
> *Now it is time to play;*
> *As old as I am, I still have the feeling of play.*

That was the beginning of the Sun Dance. The dancers treated themselves with buffalo medicine, and slowly they began to take their steps. . . . And all the people were around, and they wore splendid things—beautiful buckskin and beads. The chiefs wore necklaces, and their pendants shone like the sun. There were many people, and oh, it was beautiful! That was the beginning of the Sun Dance. It was all for Tai-me, you know, and it was a long time ago.

  It was—all of this and more—a quest, a going forth upon the way to Rainy Mountain. Probably Ko-sahn too is dead now. At times, in the quiet of evening, I think she must have wondered, dreaming, who she was. Was she become in her sleep that old purveyor of the sacred earth, perhaps, that ancient one who, old as she was, still had the feeling of play? And in her mind, at times, did she see the falling stars?

Rainy Mountain Cemetery

Most is your name the name of this dark stone.
Deranged in death, the mind to be inheres
Forever in the nominal unknown,
The wake of nothing audible he hears
Who listens here and now to hear your name.   5

The early sun, red as a hunter's moon,
Runs in the plain. The mountain burns and shines;
And silence is the long approach of noon
Upon the shadow that your name defines—
And death this cold, black density of stone.   10

1969

AUDRE LORDE
1934–1992

Audre Lorde's poetry wages what she called "a war against the tyrannies of silence"; it articulates what has been passed over out of fear or discomfort, what has been kept hidden and secret. Reading her we feel the violence inherent in breaking a silence, perhaps most often as she probes the experience of anger—the anger of black toward white or white toward black, a woman's anger at men and other women, and men's anger toward women. "My Black woman's anger," she wrote in her collection of essays, *Sister Outsider*, "is a molten pond at the core of me, my most fiercely guarded secret." Having admitted this secret into her poems, Lorde transforms our expectations of what is a fit subject for the lyric. Her work is often deliberately disturbing, the powerful voice of the poem cutting through denial, politeness, and fear. In developing this voice Lorde drew on African resources, especially the matriarchal mythology and history of West Africa. Her seventh book, *The Black Unicorn* (1978), reflects the time she spent in Africa studying, in particular, Yoruba mythology and reclaiming her connection to the rich African cultures. The African presence is evident in one of her last books, *Our Dead Behind Us* (1986), as well. Lorde's work suggests that she always connected poetry to the speaking voice, but her study of African materials deepened her connection to oral traditions (like the chant or the call) and taught her the power of voice to cut across time and place. From African writers, she said, she learned that "we live in accordance with, in a kind of correspondence with, the rest of the world as a whole." A powerful voice informed by personal and cultural history creates the possibility, for Lorde, of bridging the differences her work does not seek to erase. "It is not difference that immobilizes us," she wrote, "but silence."

Her work celebrates difference and confounds it. In Adrienne Rich's words, Lorde wrote "as a Black woman, a mother, a daughter, a Lesbian, a feminist, a visionary." Her poem "Coal" affirms an *I* that is "the total black, being spoken / from the earth's inside." This total blackness was, for her, also associated with Eros and with creativity; she celebrated this source as what she called "woman's place of power within each of us," which is "neither white nor surface; it is dark, it is ancient; and it is deep." Her best work calls on the deepest places of her own life—on the pain she experienced, on her rage (her second book, in 1972, was titled *Cables to Rage*), on her longing and desire. One of the silences her poems broke concerns love between women, and she wrote a number of poems that are erotic, precise, and true to both the power and delicacy of feeling. Unafraid of anger, she was also capable of tenderness; this is perhaps most clear not only in her love poems but in poems that address a younger generation.

Lorde was born in New York City and lived in New York almost all her life. Her parents were West Indian, and her mother was light skinned. "I grew up in a genuine confusion / between grass and weeds and flowers / and what colored meant," Lorde wrote in her poem "Outside." Part of that confusion was the conflict represented by her father's blackness and her mother's desire for whiteness (in "Black Mother Woman" Lorde speaks of the mother as "split with deceitful longings"). Lorde's understanding of identity forged out of conflict began for her, then, in her own family history with its legacy of "conflicting rebellions" ("Black Mother Woman"). In 1961 she received a B.A. from Hunter College and later a Master's of Library Science from Columbia University. The following year she married and the marriage produced a daughter and a son (she divorced in 1970). In 1968 she became poet-in-residence for a year at Tougaloo College in Mississippi, her first experience in the American South. Thereafter she knew her work to be that of a writer and teacher; she taught at John Jay College of Criminal Justice in New York City and, from 1981, was professor of English at Hunter College. In the last years of her life Lorde traveled extensively, not only to Africa but to Australia (where she met with aborigine women) and Germany. During her last years she lived much of the time in St. Croix.

"I have come to believe over and over again," Lorde said, "that what is most important to me must be spoken, made verbal and shared, even at the risk of having it bruised or misunderstood." (Her essay "Poetry Is Not a Luxury" [1977] makes the case for poetry's essential speaking of what is otherwise unnamed and unthought.) The drive toward expression made Lorde a prolific writer and led her to several prose works in which she shared experiences often restricted to privacy: *The Cancer Journals* (1980), an account of her struggle with breast cancer, and *Zami: A New Spelling of My Name* (1982), a "biomythography" of her growing up and her emergent lesbian identity. The urgency Lorde felt to make experience "verbal and shared," however, sometimes overrode a distinction crucial to her work: that between poetry and rhetoric. She preserved this distinction in her best work by listening and responding to other voices in herself and in the world around her. With their combination of pain, anger, and tenderness, her finest poems are poetry as illumination, poetry in which, as she said, "we give name to those ideas which are—until the poem—nameless, formless, about to be birthed, but already felt."

Coal

I
is the total black, being spoken
from the earth's inside.
There are many kinds of open
how a diamond comes into a knot of flame   5
how sound comes into a word, coloured
by who pays what for speaking.

Some words are open like a diamond
on glass windows
singing out within the passing crash of sun   10
Then there are words like stapled wagers
in a perforated book,—buy and sign and tear apart—
and come whatever wills all chances
the stub remains
an ill-pulled tooth with a ragged edge.   15
Some words live in my throat
breeding like adders. Others know sun
seeking like gypsies over my tongue
to explode through my lips
like young sparrows bursting from shell.   20
Some words
bedevil me.

Love is a word, another kind of open.
As the diamond comes into a knot of flame

I am Black because I come from the earth's inside   25
now take my word for jewel in the open light.

1968

The Woman Thing

The hunters are back from beating the winter's face
in search of a challenge or task
in search of food
making fresh tracks for their children's hunger
they do not watch the sun   5
they cannot wear its heat for a sign
of triumph or freedom;
The hunters are treading heavily homeward
through snow that is marked
with their own bloody footprints.   10
emptyhanded, the hunters return
snow-maddened, sustained by their rages.

In the night after food they may seek
young girls for their amusement. But now
the hunters are coming   15
and the unbaked girls flee from their angers.
All this day I have craved
food for my child's hunger
Emptyhanded the hunters come shouting
injustices drip from their mouths   20
like stale snow melted in sunlight.

Meanwhile
the woman thing my mother taught me
bakes off its covering of snow
like a rising blackening sun.   25

1968

Harriet

Harriet there was always somebody calling us crazy
or mean or stuck-up or evil or black
or black
and we were
nappy girls quick as cuttlefish[1]   5
scurrying for cover
trying to speak trying to speak
trying to speak

---

1. Ten-armed shellfish. "Nappy": with closely twisted or curled hair.

the pain in each others mouths
until we learned   10
on the edge of a lash
or a tongue
on the edge of the other's betrayal
that respect
meant keeping our distance   15
in silence
averting our eyes
from each other's face in the street
from the beautiful dark mouth
and cautious familiar eyes   20
passing alone.

I remember you Harriet
before we were broken apart
we dreamed the crossed swords
of warrior queens   25
while we avoided each other's eyes
and we learned to know lonely
as the earth learns to know dead
Harriet Harriet
what name shall we call our selves now   30
our mother is gone?

1978

LUCILLE CLIFTON
1936–2010

L ucille Clifton seems able to lift the poem off the page and return it to the air we breathe. Like the work of Langston Hughes or William Carlos Williams, her poems allow us to hear the language of our daily lives as poetry and to experience the poetry in our ordinary lives. Although a closer look reveals the subtle craft of her poems (for example, the slant rhymes and the carefully paced repetitions), they appear deceptively simple. Their frankness and directness close the distance between poet and reader, especially when these poems are read aloud. Clifton emphasized the informality in her work through the lowercase letters she preferred and through her frequent omission of titles. The language of her poems reflects her identity; "I am a black woman poet," she said, "and I sound like one." Grounded in realistic details, her poems do not shy away from what is harsh and painful, including incest, suicide, mental illness, and the effects of poverty and racism. But while Clifton's anger fuels many poems, her imagination finds beauty and humor in unexpected places; indeed, she seems able to make poetry out of anything. In this she resembles the African American quilters who rework the materials of ordinary experience into distinctive and compelling designs. Indeed, she titled one of her books *Quilting* (1991) and borrowed its section headings from the names of traditional quilt patterns.

Born in Depew, New York, to a father who worked in the steel mills and a mother who was a launderer and a homemaker (and who wrote poems but burned them), Clifton was the first person in her family to attend college. "I had a very regular life, the life of a poor black person," Clifton said; but her background and her gifts sometimes made her feel that "there is no planet stranger / than the one I'm from" ("note, passed to superman"). At sixteen she began her studies at Howard University in Washington, D.C., and she later attended Fredonia State Teachers College in New York State. She went on to work as a claims clerk in the New York State Division of Employment (1958–60) and as a literature assistant at the Office of Education in Washington (1960–71). Clifton never formally studied creative writing, but she wrote poems and thought of herself as a poet from a young age. However, her work did not receive public recognition until she was in her thirties. In 1969 she sent a poem to the poet Robert Hayden at the National Endowment for the Arts. Hayden had left the NEA, but his successor, Carolyn Kizer, read the work and submitted it to the YW-YMHA Poetry Center Discovery Award competition in New York City. Clifton won the competition and at the award ceremony, after she read her poems, an editor from Random House in the audience offered to publish her first book, *Good Times* (1969). *Good Times* appeared when she was thirty-three, a wife and mother with six children under the age of eleven. During these years her method of composition followed those writers, many of them women, who compose lines of poetry in the mind until there is time to write them down.

Clifton came from a line of African American storytellers extending from her great-grandmother, Caroline Donald, who was born in Dahomey, Africa, sold into slavery, and taken to America. Clifton's memoir, *Generations* (1976), chronicles the history of her family, including the genealogy and the tradition of strong women passed down to Clifton through her father's stories. In much of her work, Clifton consciously sought to recover an African American past that has too often been omitted from standard histories and to retell history from previously unacknowledged points of view.

In a poem beginning "the light that came to Lucille Clifton," a voice from "the non-dead past" speaks this message to her: "You might as well open the door, my child / for truth is furiously knocking." Throughout her long and productive career as a poet, and as a writer of memoirs and children's books, she transmitted the voices of a living past. Like Toni Morrison's fiction, Clifton's poems are full of ghosts: her mother and father, her unborn children, her ancestors, and sometimes mythical and biblical figures. These presences in her work bear witness to a legacy of pain, wisdom, and survival. As a writer brave enough to open the door to the truths of her life and her world, Clifton possessed a "gift of understanding" that put her in touch with the suffering of the "holy lost" ("Wild Blessing"), but the spiritual dimension of her work also reveals the possibility of joy and transformation, evident in "blessing the boats."

Clifton's books include *Good News about the Earth* (1972) and *Two-Headed Woman* (1980), which received the University of Massachusetts Juniper Prize. Both of these volumes were nominated for the Pulitzer Prize. Subsequent collections include *Next* (1987), *The Book of Light* (1993), *Blessing the Boats: New and Selected Poems 1988–2000* (2000), *Mercy* (2004), and *Voices* (2008). Clifton's work for children includes *The Black BCs* (1970), *The Times They Used to Be* (1974), and an award-winning series of books featuring events in the life of Everett Anderson, a young black boy. In 1999 she was elected a chancellor of the Academy of American Poets. She served as poet laureate for the State of Maryland and was a distinguished professor of humanities at St. Mary's College in Maryland.

miss rosie

when i watch you
wrapped up like garbage
sitting, surrounded by the smell
of too old potato peels
or   5
when i watch you
in your old man's shoes
with the little toe cut out
sitting, waiting for your mind
like next week's grocery   10
i say
when i watch you
you wet brown bag of a woman
who used to be the best looking gal in georgia
used to be called the Georgia Rose   15
i stand up
through your destruction
i stand up

1969   1987

the lost baby poem

the time i dropped your almost body down
down to meet the waters under the city
and run one with the sewage to the sea
what did i know about waters rushing back
what did i know about drowning   5
or being drowned

you would have been born into winter
in the year of the disconnected gas
and no car   we would have made the thin
walk over genesee hill[1] into the canada wind   10
to watch you slip like ice into strangers' hands
you would have fallen naked as snow into winter
if you were here i could tell you these
and some other things

if i am ever less than a mountain   15
for your definite brothers and sisters
let the rivers pour over my head
let the sea take me for a spiller
of seas   let black men call me stranger
always   for your never named sake   20

1972

---

1. Genesee County is in northwestern New York State.

homage to my hips

these hips are big hips
they need space to
move around in.
they don't fit into little
petty places, these hips.   5
are free hips.
they don't like to be held back.
these hips have never been enslaved,
they go where they want to go
they do what they want to do.   10
these hips are mighty hips.
these hips are magic hips.
i have known them
to put a spell on a man and
spin him like a top!   15

1980

wild blessings

licked in the palm of my hand
by an uninvited woman, so i have held
in that hand the hand of a man who
emptied into his daughter, the hand
of a girl who threw herself   5
from a tenement window, the trembling
junkie hand of a priest, of a boy who
shattered across viet nam
someone resembling his mother,
and more, and more.   10
do not ask me to thank the tongue
that circled my fingers
or pride myself on the attentions
of the holy lost.
i am grateful for many blessings   15
but the gift of understanding,
the wild one, maybe not.

1991

wishes for sons

i wish them cramps.
i wish them a strange town
and the last tampon.
i wish them no 7-11.

i wish them one week early   5
and wearing a white skirt.
i wish them one week late.

later i wish them hot flashes
and clots like you
wouldn't believe.   let the   10
flashes come when they
meet someone special.
let the clots come
when they want to.

let them think they have accepted   15
arrogance in the universe,
then bring them to gynecologists
not unlike themselves.

                                                     1991

the mississippi river empties into the gulf

and the gulf enters the sea and so forth,
none of them emptying anything,
all of them carrying yesterday
forever on their white tipped backs,
all of them dragging forward tomorrow.   5
it is the great circulation
of the earth's body, like the blood
of the gods, this river in which the past
is always flowing, every water
is the same water coming round.   10
everyday someone is standing on the edge
of this river, staring into time,
whispering mistakenly:
only here, only now.

                                                     1996

[oh antic god]

oh antic God
return to me
my mother in her thirties[1]
leaned across the front porch
the huge pillow of her breasts   5
pressing against the rail
summoning me in for bed.

---

1. Thelma Moore Sayles, Clifton's mother, died at age forty-four.

I am almost the dead woman's age times two.

I can barely recall her song
the scent of her hands   10
though her wild hair scratches my dreams
at night.   return to me, oh Lord of then
and now, my mother's calling,
her young voice humming my name.

2004

THOMAS PYNCHON
b. 1937

Thomas Pynchon has remained the most private of contemporary American writers, without so much as a photograph of him in circulation. A few facts are known: born on Long Island, graduated from Cornell University—where he was a student in Vladimir Nabokov's European literature course—in the late 1950s, served a term in the navy, and now lives—it is said—in southern (or is it northern?) California. Beyond that, silence, which has been broken only by seven strange and distinctive novels, plus a few short stories.

"Entropy," one of Pynchon's first publications (1960), is printed here as an introduction to his work. Its thematics of an elusive order within radical disorder anticipates his first novel, *V.* (1963), particularly in its reference to modern physics. That complex novel cannot be understood by reference to convenient fictional signposts. Although it showed an indebtedness to Faulkner and Joyce (an indebtedness shared by most serious American novelists), Pynchon's style was already wholly his own. In writing that was by turns labyrinthine, eloquent, and colloquial, he showed a particular fondness for imitating and parodying various styles. But instead of disparaging or minimizing their subjects, these imitations and parodies radiated a generous exuberance that extended to the many characters who inhabit *V.* and whose individual paranoias—Pynchon's word to characterize attempts to make connections between events—propel them into unbelievably complicated and absurd plots. The interest of *V.* was largely in the inventiveness with which Pynchon developed those plots, which might involve anything from diplomatic spy stories in nineteenth-century Africa to the bombing of Malta during World War II to the surgical reconstruction of a young woman's nose to a hunt for alligators in New York City sewers.

The comic talent shown in various New York episodes from *V.* was also evident in *The Crying of Lot 49* (1966). This short, perfectly controlled novel teases us and itself with questions about the meaning of our American heritage, as embodied in the form of the mysterious legacy left to its heroine, Oedipa Maas. (The jokey yet portentous name exemplifies Pynchon's way of playing at "significance.") What is the connection between this legacy and the mysterious alternative to the U.S. Postal System on which Oedipa believes she has stumbled? Is there a secret network of alienated citizens carrying on their lives outside the ordinary systems and institutions of American life? Or is it all Oedipa's delusion, her private paranoia? These questions are considered through a style that continually surprises and unsettles us, though it is less discontinuous than *V.*'s. In Pynchon's world everything serious has its silly aspects (inspired by the Marx Brothers and countless other comic acts), while bits of trivia and foolery are suddenly elevated, through the style, into objects of sublime contemplation—as at the novel's end, when Oedipa thinks of "squatters" who "slept in junkyards in the stripped shells of wrecked Plymouths, or even, daring, spent the night up some pole in a lineman's tent like caterpillars, swung among a web of telephone wires, living in the very copper rigging and secular miracle of communication, untroubled by the dumb voltages flickering their miles, the night long, in the thousands of unheard messages." Often Pynchon's sentences enact the daring freedom he admires, in contrast to the institutions of a technological society.

Pynchon's longest and most daring and exhaustive effort came with the publication, in 1973, of *Gravity's Rainbow*. This encyclopedic fantasy operates through brilliant improvisations, tall tales, obscene parables, and burlesque stage routines, all of which work together into a story of supersonic capabilities and annihilative retributions. A huge cast of characters, each with a crazy name and a plot to unravel, is located all over the map, but mainly in World War II London and in postwar Germany. As the four main and the countless subsidiary plots take shape, characters—and the reader—attempt to "read" the messages flickering, the dumb intent to communicate, in the most casual as well as the most portentous sign. Pynchon's knowingness and fascination with popular culture are overwhelmingly evident in *Gravity's Rainbow*, as is his preoccupation with the lore of theoretical science, of obscure historical tales, and of contemporary comic books. No one denies the formidably encyclopedic nature of this astonishing effort; the question is, as Warner Berthoff has asked it, whether that effort may not also be "encyclopedically monotonous and static." More readers begin *Gravity's Rainbow* than finish it.

After 1973, except for the publication in 1984 of some of his early stories (in *Slow Learner*), all was silent on the Pynchon front until *Vineland* appeared in 1990, followed by *Mason & Dixon* in 1997 and *Against the Day* in 2006. *Vineland* is wonderful on the California terrain and has much free wheeling and funny inventiveness; at other times Pynchon seems to be flogging his material and repeating himself. *Mason & Dixon*, about the plotters of the line that would differentiate the American North and South, is written in the manner of his more ambitious works, a massive "mega-novel" that by its very excesses of character, plot, and references to history (arcane and otherwise) seeks to overwhelm the reader with its display of authority. *Against the Day* (2006) and *Inherent Vice* (2009) have more conventional subjects—family-revenge drama and crime solving, respectively—yet the author still dotes on fantastic inventions and overwritten prose. But although there is still no consensus on his stature as an enduring American writer, there is general recognition of the quirky, uncanny exactitude of his imagination. Pynchon's theatrical spell-bindings as a man of metaphor, his feats of association (in Robert Frost's phrase), are employed on subjects—like the rocket in *Gravity's Rainbow*—that were thought to be beyond words. For daring, wit, and exuberance, no contemporary writer excels him.

The following text is from *Slow Learner* (1984).

Entropy

> Boris has just given me a summary of his views. He is a weather prophet. The weather will continue bad, he says. There will be more calamities, more death, more despair. Not the slightest indication of a change anywhere. . . . We must get into step, a lockstep toward the prison of death. There is no escape. The weather will not change.
>
> —*Tropic of Cancer*[1]

Downstairs, Meatball Mulligan's lease-breaking party was moving into its 40th hour. On the kitchen floor, amid a litter of empty champagne fifths, were Sandor Rojas and three friends, playing spit in the ocean and staying awake on Heidseck[2] and benzedrine pills. In the living room Duke, Vincent, Krinkles and Paco sat crouched over a 15-inch speaker which had been bolted into the top of a wastepaper basket, listening to 27 watts' worth of *The Heroes' Gate at Kiev.*[3] They all wore hornrimmed sunglasses and rapt expressions, and smoked funny-looking cigarettes which contained not, as you might expect, tobacco, but an adulterated form of *cannabis sativa.*[4] This group was the Duke di Angelis quartet. They recorded for a local label called Tambú and had to their credit one 10' LP entitled *Songs of Outer Space.* From time to time one of them would flick the ashes from his cigarette into the speaker cone to watch them dance around. Meatball himself was sleeping over by the window, holding an empty magnum to his chest as if it were a teddy bear. Several government girls, who worked for people like the State Department and NSA, had passed out on couches, chairs and in one case the bathroom sink.

This was in early February of '57 and back then there were a lot of American expatriates around Washington, D.C., who would talk, every time they met you, about how someday they were going to go over to Europe for real but right now it seemed they were working for the government. Everyone saw a fine irony in this. They would stage, for instance, polyglot parties where the newcomer was sort of ignored if he couldn't carry on simultaneous conversations in three or four languages. They would haunt Armenian delicatessens for weeks at a stretch and invite you over for bulghour and lamb in tiny kitchens whose walls were covered with bullfight posters. They would have affairs with sultry girls from Andalucía or the Midi[5] who studied economics at Georgetown. Their Dôme was a collegiate Rathskeller out on Wisconsin Avenue called the Old Heidelberg and they had to settle for cherry blossoms instead of lime trees when spring came, but in its lethargic way their life provided, as they said, kicks.

At the moment, Meatball's party seemed to be gathering its second wind. Outside there was rain. Rain splatted against the tar paper on the roof and was fractured into a fine spray off the noses, eyebrows and lips of wooden gargoyles under the eaves, and ran like drool down the windowpanes. The day before, it had snowed and the day before that there had been winds of gale force and before that the sun had made the city glitter bright as April, though the calendar read early February. It is a curious season in Washington, this false spring. Somewhere in it are Lincoln's Birthday and the Chi-

---

1. Novel (1934) by the American writer Henry Miller (1891–1980).
2. A very dry champagne.
3. Music by the Russian composer Modest Mus-

sorgsky (1839–1881) from his *Pictures at an Exhibition.*
4. Marijuana.
5. Regions of Spain and France, respectively.

The Gerry Mulligan Quartet premiered in Los Angeles in 1952 with Mulligan on baritone saxophone, Chet Baker on trumpet, Bob Whitlock on bass, and Chico Hamilton on drums. There was no pianist, an innovation for small ensemble jazz, leaving harmonic silences for the other instruments to fill.

nese New Year, and a forlornness in the streets because cherry blossoms are weeks away still and, as Sarah Vaughan has put it, spring will be a little late this year. Generally crowds like the one which would gather in the Old Heidelberg on weekday afternoons to drink Würtzburger and to sing Lili Marlene (not to mention The Sweetheart of Sigma Chi) are inevitably and incorrigibly Romantic. And as every good Romantic knows, the soul (*spiritus, ruach, pneuma*) is nothing, substantially, but air; it is only natural that warpings in the atmosphere should be recapitulated in those who breathe it. So that over and above the public components—holidays, tourist attractions—there are private meanderings, linked to the climate as if this spell were a *stretto* passage in the year's fugue: haphazard weather, aimless loves, unpredicted commitments: months one can easily spend *in* fugue, because oddly enough, later on, winds, rains, passions of February and March are never remembered in that city, it is as if they had never been.

The last bass notes of *The Heroes' Gate* boomed up through the floor and woke Callisto from an uneasy sleep. The first thing he became aware of was a small bird he had been holding gently between his hands, against his body. He turned his head sidewise on the pillow to smile down at it, at its blue hunched-down head and sick, lidded eyes, wondering how many more nights he would have to give it warmth before it was well again. He had been holding the bird like that for three days: it was the only way he knew to restore its health. Next to him the girl stirred and whimpered, her arm thrown across her face. Mingled with the sounds of the rain came the first tentative, querulous morning voices of the other birds, hidden in philodendrons and small fan palms: patches of scarlet, yellow and blue laced through this Rousseau-like[6] fantasy, this hothouse jungle it had taken him seven years to weave together. Hermetically sealed, it was a tiny enclave of regularity in the city's chaos, alien to the vagaries of the weather, of national politics, of any civil disorder. Through trial-and-error Callisto had perfected its ecological balance, with the help of the girl its artistic harmony, so that the swayings of its plant life, the stirrings of its birds and human inhabitants were all as integral as the rhythms of a perfectly-executed mobile. He and the girl could no longer, of course, be omitted from that sanctuary; they had become necessary to its unity. What they needed from outside was delivered. They did not go out.

"Is he all right," she whispered. She lay like a tawny question mark facing him, her eyes suddenly huge and dark and blinking slowly. Callisto ran a finger beneath the feathers at the base of the bird's neck; caressed it gently. "He's going to be well, I think. See: he hears his friends beginning to wake up." The girl had heard the rain and the birds even before she was fully awake. Her name was Aubade: she was part French and part Annamese, and she lived on her own curious and lonely planet, where the clouds and the odor of poincianas, the bitterness of wine and the accidental fingers at the small of her back or feathery against her breasts came to her reduced inevitably to the terms of sound: of music which emerged at intervals from a howling darkness of discordancy. "Aubade," he said, "go see." Obedient, she arose; padded to the window, pulled aside the drapes and after a moment said: "It is 37. Still 37." Callisto frowned. "Since Tuesday, then," he said. "No change." Henry Adams,[7] three generations before his own, had stared aghast at Power; Callisto found himself now in much the same state over Thermodynamics, the inner life of that power, realizing like his predecessor that the Virgin and the dynamo stand as much for love as for power; that the two are indeed identical; and that love therefore not only makes the world go round but also makes the boccie ball spin, the nebula precess. It was this latter or sidereal element which disturbed him. The cosmologists had predicted an eventual heat-death for the universe (something like Limbo: form and motion abolished, heat-energy identical at every point in it); the meteorologists, day-to-day, staved it off by contradicting with a reassuring array of varied temperatures.

But for three days now, despite the changeful weather, the mercury had stayed at 37 degrees Fahrenheit. Leery at omens of apocalypse, Callisto shifted beneath the covers. His fingers pressed the bird more firmly, as if needing some pulsing or suffering assurance of an early break in the temperature.

It was that last cymbal crash that did it. Meatball was hurled wincing into consciousness as the synchronized wagging of heads over the wastebasket stopped. The final hiss remained for an instant in the room, then melted into the whisper of rain outside. "Aarrgghh," announced Meatball in the silence, looking at the empty magnum. Krinkles, in slow motion, turned, smiled and held out a cigarette. "Tea time, man," he said. "No, no," said Meatball. "How many times I got to tell you guys. Not at my place. You ought to know, Washington is lousy with Feds." Krinkles looked wistful. "Jeez, Meatball," he said, "you don't want to do nothing no more." "Hair of dog,"

6. Henri Rousseau (1844–1910), French primitive painter of exotic landscapes.
7. American historian and man of letters (1838– 1918) whose writings explore the nature of power, cultural figurations of which ranged from the Virgin Mary to the modern dynamo engine.

said Meatball. "Only hope. Any juice left?" He began to crawl toward the kitchen. "No champagne, I don't think," Duke said. "Case of tequila behind the icebox." They put on an Earl Bostic[8] side. Meatball paused at the kitchen door, glowering at Sandor Rojas. "Lemons," he said after some thought. He crawled to the refrigerator and got out three lemons and some cubes, found the tequila and set about restoring order to his nervous system. He drew blood once cutting the lemons and had to use two hands squeezing them and his foot to crack the ice tray but after about ten minutes he found himself, through some miracle, beaming down into a monster tequila sour. "That looks yummy," Sandor Rojas said. "How about you make me one." Meatball blinked at him. *"Kitchi lofass a shegithe,"*[9] he replied automatically, and wandered away into the bathroom. "I say," he called out a moment later to no one in particular. "I say, there seems to be a girl or something sleeping in the sink." He took her by the shoulders and shook. "Wha," she said. "You don't look too comfortable," Meatball said. "Well," she agreed. She stumbled to the shower, turned on the cold water and sat down crosslegged in the spray. "That's better," she smiled.

"Meatball," Sandor Rojas yelled from the kitchen. "Somebody is trying to come in the window. A burglar, I think. A second-story man." "What are you worrying about," Meatball said. "We're on the third floor." He loped back into the kitchen. A shaggy woebegone figure stood out on the fire escape, raking his fingernails down the windowpane. Meatball opened the window. "Saul," he said.

"Sort of wet out," Saul said. He climbed in, dripping. "You heard, I guess."

"Miriam left you," Meatball said, "or something, is all I heard."

There was a sudden flurry of knocking at the front door. "Do come in," Sandor Rojas called. The door opened and there were three coeds from George Washington, all of whom were majoring in philosophy. They were each holding a gallon of Chianti. Sandor leaped up and dashed into the living room. "We heard there was a party," one blonde said. "Young blood," Sandor shouted. He was an ex-Hungarian freedom fighter who had easily the worst chronic case of what certain critics of the middle class have called Don Giovannism in the District of Columbia. *Purchè porti la gonnella, voi sapete quel che fa.*[1] Like Pavlov's dog: a contralto voice or a whiff of Arpège and Sandor would begin to salivate. Meatball regarded the trio blearily as they filed into the kitchen; he shrugged. "Put the wine in the icebox," he said, "and good morning."

Aubade's neck made a golden bow as she bent over the sheets of foolscap, scribbling away in the green murk of the room. "As a young man at Princeton," Callisto was dictating, nestling the bird against the gray hairs of his chest, "Callisto had learned a mnemonic device for remembering the Laws of Thermodynamics: you can't win, things are going to get worse before they get better, who says they're going to get better. At the age of 54, confronted with Gibbs'[2] notion of the universe, he suddenly realized that undergraduate cant had been oracle, after all. That spindly maze of equations

---

8. American jazz musician (1913–1965) who also recorded rhythm-and-blues material.
9. Little horse prick in your asshole (Hungarian).
1. As long as she wears a skirt, you know what he does (Italian); from Lorenzo da Ponte's libretto to

Mozart's opera *Don Giovanni* (1787).
2. Josiah Willard Gibbs (1839–1903), American physicist and chemist, a founder of statistical mechanics.

became, for him, a vision of ultimate, cosmic heat-death. He had known all along, of course, that nothing but a theoretical engine or system ever runs at 100% efficiency; and about the theorem of Clausius, which states that the entropy of an isolated system always continually increases. It was not, however, until Gibbs and Boltzmann[3] brought to this principle the methods of statistical mechanics that the horrible significance of it all dawned on him: only then did he realize that the isolated system—galaxy, engine, human being, culture, whatever—must evolve spontaneously toward the Condition of the More Probable. He was forced, therefore, in the sad dying fall of middle age, to a radical reëvaluation of everything he had learned up to then; all the cities and seasons and casual passions of his days had now to be looked at in a new and elusive light. He did not know if he was equal to the task. He was aware of the dangers of the reductive fallacy and, he hoped, strong enough not to drift into the graceful decadence of an enervated fatalism. His had always been a vigorous, Italian sort of pessimism: like Machiavelli, he allowed the forces of *virtù* and *fortuna*[4] to be about 50/50; but the equations now introduced a random factor which pushed the odds to some unutterable and indeterminate ratio which he found himself afraid to calculate." Around him loomed vague hothouse shapes; the pitifully small heart fluttered against his own. Counterpointed against his words the girl heard the chatter of birds and fitful car honkings scattered along the wet morning and Earl Bostic's alto rising in occasional wild peaks through the floor. The architectonic purity of her world was constantly threatened by such hints of anarchy: gaps and excrescences and skew lines, and a shifting or tilting of planes to which she had continually to readjust lest the whole structure shiver into a disarray of discrete and meaningless signals. Callisto had described the process once as a kind of "feedback": she crawled into dreams each night with a sense of exhaustion, and a desperate resolve never to relax that vigilance. Even in the brief periods when Callisto made love to her, soaring above the bowing of taut nerves in haphazard double-stops would be the one singing string of her determination.

"Nevertheless," continued Callisto, "he found in entropy or the measure of disorganization for a closed system an adequate metaphor to apply to certain phenomena in his own world. He saw, for example, the younger generation responding to Madison Avenue with the same spleen his own had once reserved for Wall Street: and in American 'consumerism' discovered a similar tendency from the least to the most probable, from differentiation to sameness, from ordered individuality to a kind of chaos. He found himself, in short, restating Gibbs' prediction in social terms, and envisioned a heat-death for his culture in which ideas, like heat-energy, would no longer be transferred, since each point in it would ultimately have the same quantity of energy; and intellectual motion would, accordingly, cease." He glanced up suddenly. "Check it now," he said. Again she rose and peered out at the thermometer. "37," she said. "The rain has stopped." He bent his head quickly and held his lips against a quivering wing. "Then it will change soon," he said, trying to keep his voice firm.

3. Ludwig Boltzmann (1844–1906), Austrian physicist who studied how atoms determine visual properties of matter. Rudolf Clausius (1822–1888), German physicist, developer of the science of thermodynamics.

4. Niccolò Machiavelli (1469–1527), Florentine statesman and writer on government, contrasted virtuous behavior (*virtù*) with good luck (*fortuna*).

Sitting on the stove Saul was like any big rag doll that a kid has been taking out some incomprehensible rage on. "What happened," Meatball said. "If you feel like talking, I mean."

"Of course I feel like talking," Saul said. "One thing I did, I slugged her."

"Discipline must be maintained."

"Ha, ha. I wish you'd been there. Oh Meatball, it was a lovely fight. She ended up throwing a *Handbook of Chemistry and Physics* at me, only it missed and went through the window, and when the glass broke I reckon something in her broke too. She stormed out of the house crying, out in the rain. No raincoat or anything."

"She'll be back."

"No."

"Well!" Soon Meatball said: "It was something earthshattering, no doubt. Like who is better, Sal Mineo or Ricky Nelson."[5]

"What it was about," Saul said, "was communication theory. Which of course makes it very hilarious."

"I don't know anything about communication theory."

"Neither does my wife. Come right down to it, who does? That's the joke."

When Meatball saw the kind of smile Saul had on his face he said: "Maybe you would like tequila or something."

"No. I mean, I'm sorry. It's a field you can go off the deep end in, is all. You get where you're watching all the time for security cops: behind bushes, around corners. MUFFET is top secret."

"Wha."

"Multi-unit factorial field electronic tabulator."

"You were fighting about that."

"Miriam has been reading science fiction again. That and *Scientific American*. It seems she is, as we say, bugged at this idea of computers acting like people. I made the mistake of saying you can just as well turn that around, and talk about human behavior like a program fed into an IBM machine."

"Why not," Meatball said.

"Indeed, why not. In fact it is sort of crucial to communication, not to mention information theory. Only when I said that she hit the roof. Up went the balloon. And I can't figure out *why*. If anybody should know why, I should. I refuse to believe the government is wasting taxpayers' money on me, when it has so many bigger and better things to waste it on."

Meatball made a moue. "Maybe she thought you were acting like a cold, dehumanized amoral scientist type."

"My god," Saul flung up an arm. "Dehumanized. How much more human can I get? I worry, Meatball, I do. There are Europeans wandering around North Africa these days with their tongues torn out of their heads because those tongues have spoken the wrong words. Only the Europeans thought they were the right words."

"Language barrier," Meatball suggested.

Saul jumped down off the stove. "That," he said, angry, "is a good candidate for sick joke of the year. No, ace, it is *not* a barrier. If it is anything it's

---

5. Contemporary figures from film and television who were icons of bad and good teenage behavior, respectively.

a kind of leakage. Tell a girl: 'I love you.' No trouble with two-thirds of that, it's a closed circuit. Just you and she. But that nasty four-letter word in the middle, *that's* the one you have to look out for. Ambiguity. Redundance. Irrelevance, even. Leakage. All this is noise. Noise screws up your signal, makes for disorganization in the circuit."

Meatball shuffled around. "Well, now, Saul," he muttered, "you're sort of, I don't know, expecting a lot from people. I mean, you know. What it is is, most of the things we say, I guess, are mostly noise."

"Ha! Half of what you just said, for example."

"Well, you do it too."

"I know." Saul smiled grimly. "It's a bitch, ain't it."

"I bet that's what keeps divorce lawyers in business. Whoops."

"Oh I'm not sensitive. Besides," frowning, "you're right. You find I think that most 'successful' marriages—Miriam and me, up to last night—are sort of founded on compromises. You never run at top efficiency, usually all you have is a minimum basis for a workable thing. I believe the phrase is Togetherness."

"Aarrgghh."

"Exactly. You find that one a bit noisy, don't you. But the noise content is different for each of us because you're a bachelor and I'm not. Or wasn't. The hell with it."

"Well sure," Meatball said, trying to be helpful, "you were using different words. By 'human being' you meant something that you can look at like it was a computer. It helps you think better on the job or something. But Miriam meant something entirely—"

"The hell with it."

Meatball fell silent. "I'll take that drink," Saul said after a while.

The card game had been abandoned and Sandor's friends were slowly getting wasted on tequila. On the living room couch, one of the coeds and Krinkles were engaged in amorous conversation. "No," Krinkles was saying, "no, I can't put Dave *down*. In fact I give Dave a lot of credit, man. Especially considering his accident and all." The girl's smile faded. "How terrible," she said. "What accident?" "Hadn't you heard?" Krinkles said. "When Dave was in the army, just a private E-2, they sent him down to Oak Ridge on special duty. Something to do with the Manhattan Project.[6] He was handling hot stuff one day and got an overdose of radiation. So now he's got to wear lead gloves all the time." She shook her head sympathetically. "What an awful break for a piano player."

Meatball had abandoned Saul to a bottle of tequila and was about to go to sleep in a closet when the front door flew open and the place was invaded by five enlisted personnel of the U.S. Navy, all in varying stages of abomination. "This is the place," shouted a fat, pimply seaman apprentice who had lost his white hat. "This here is the hoorhouse that chief was telling us about." A stringy-looking 3rd class boatswain's mate pushed him aside and cased the living room. "You're right, Slab," he said. "But it don't look like much, even for Stateside. I seen better tail in Naples, Italy." "How much, hey," boomed a large seaman with adenoids, who was holding a Mason jar full of white lightning. "Oh, my god," said Meatball.

---

6. The research that developed the atomic bomb for use at the end of World War II.

Outside the temperature remained constant at 37 degrees Fahrenheit. In the hothouse Aubade stood absently caressing the branches of a young mimosa, hearing a motif of sap-rising, the rough and unresolved anticipatory theme of those fragile pink blossoms which, it is said, insure fertility. That music rose in a tangled tracery: arabesques of order competing fugally with the improvised discords of the party downstairs, which peaked sometimes in cusps and ogees of noise. That precious signal-to-noise ratio, whose delicate balance required every calorie of her strength, seesawed inside the small tenuous skull as she watched Callisto, sheltering the bird. Callisto was trying to confront any idea of the heat-death now, as he nuzzled the feathery lump in his hands. He sought correspondences. Sade, of course. And Temple Drake, gaunt and hopeless in her little park in Paris, at the end of *Sanctuary*.[7] Final equilibrium. *Nightwood*.[8] And the tango. Any tango, but more than any perhaps the sad sick dance in Stravinsky's *L'Histoire du Soldat*.[9] He thought back: what had tango music been for them after the war, what meanings had he missed in all the stately coupled automatons in the *cafés'-dansants*,[1] or in the metronomes which had ticked behind the eyes of his own partners? Not even the clean constant winds of Switzerland could cure the *grippe espagnole*.[2] Stravinsky had had it, they all had had it. And how many musicians were left after Passchendaele, after the Marne?[3] It came down in this case to seven: violin, double-bass. Clarinet, bassoon. Cornet, trombone. Tympani. Almost as if any tiny troupe of saltimbanques had set about conveying the same information as a full pit-orchestra. There was hardly a full complement left in Europe. Yet with violin and tympani Stravinsky had managed to communicate in that tango the same exhaustion, the same airlessness one saw in the slicked-down youths who were trying to imitate Vernon Castle, and in their mistresses, who simply did not care. *Ma maîtresse*.[4] Celeste. Returning to Nice after the second war he had found that café replaced by a perfume shop which catered to American tourists. And no secret vestige of her in the cobblestones or in the old pension next door; no perfume to match her breath heavy with the sweet Spanish wine she always drank. And so instead he had purchased a Henry Miller novel and left for Paris,[5] and read the book on the train so that when he arrived he had been given at least a little forewarning. And saw that Celeste and the others and even Temple Drake were not all that had changed. "Aubade," he said, "my head aches." The sound of his voice generated in the girl an answering scrap of melody. Her movement toward the kitchen, the towel, the cold water, and his eyes following her formed a weird and intricate canon; as she placed the compress on his forehead his sigh of gratitude seemed to signal a new subject, another series of modulations.

"No," Meatball was still saying, "no, I'm afraid not. This is not a house of ill repute. I'm sorry, really I am." Slab was adamant. "But the chief said," he kept repeating. The seaman offered to swap the moonshine for a good

7. Sexually notorious novel published in 1931 by the American writer William Faulkner (1897–1962).

8. Novel published in 1936 by the American expatriate writer Djuna Barnes (1892–1982).

9. A 1918 work by the Russian composer Igor Stravinsky (1882–1971).

1. Café dancers (French).

2. Spanish flu (French).

3. Battle sites in World War I noted for their extremely high casualties.

4. My mistress (French).

5. Miller was famous for his strongly sexual novels written in Paris during the 1930s.

piece. Meatball looked around frantically, as if seeking assistance. In the middle of the room, the Duke di Angelis quartet were engaged in a historic moment. Vincent was seated and the others standing: they were going through the motions of a group having a session, only without instruments. "I say," Meatball said. Duke moved his head a few times, smiled faintly, lit a cigarette, and eventually caught sight of Meatball. "Quiet, man," he whispered. Vincent began to fling his arms around, his fists clenched; then, abruptly, was still, then repeated the performance. This went on for a few minutes while Meatball sipped his drink moodily. The navy had withdrawn to the kitchen. Finally at some invisible signal the group stopped tapping their feet and Duke grinned and said, "At least we ended together."

Meatball glared at him. "I say," he said. "I have this new conception, man," Duke said. "You remember your namesake. You remember Gerry."

"No," said Meatball. "I'll remember April, if that's any help."

"As a matter of fact," Duke said, "it was Love for Sale. Which shows how much you know. The point is, it was Mulligan, Chet Baker[6] and that crew, way back then, out yonder. You dig?"

"Baritone sax," Meatball said. "Something about a baritone sax."

"But no piano, man. No guitar. Or accordion. You know what that means."

"Not exactly," Meatball said.

"Well first let me just say, that I am no Mingus, no John Lewis.[7] Theory was never my strong point. I mean things like reading were always difficult for me and all—"

"I know," Meatball said drily. "You got your card taken away because you changed key on Happy Birthday at a Kiwanis Club picnic."

"Rotarian. But it occurred to me, in one of these flashes of insight, that if that first quartet of Mulligan's had no piano, it could only mean one thing."

"No chords," said Paco, the baby-faced bass.

"What he is trying to say," Duke said, "is no root chords. Nothing to listen to while you blow a horizontal line. What one does in such a case is, one *thinks* the roots."

A horrified awareness was dawning on Meatball. "And the next logical extension," he said.

"Is to think everything," Duke announced with simple dignity. "Roots, line, everything."

Meatball looked at Duke, awed. "But," he said.

"Well," Duke said modestly, "there are a few bugs to work out."

"But," Meatball said.

"Just listen," Duke said. "You'll catch on." And off they went again into orbit, presumably somewhere around the asteroid belt. After a while Krinkles made an embouchure and started moving his fingers and Duke clapped his hand to his forehead. "Oaf!" he roared. "The new head we're using, you remember, I wrote last night?" "Sure," Krinkles said, "the new head. I come

---

6. In 1952 the American jazz musicians Gerry Mulligan (1927–1996) and Chet Baker (1929–1988) became famous for their revolutionary pianoless quartet.

7. Charles Mingus (1922–1979) and John Lewis (1920–2001), American jazz musicians noted for their compositions based in musical theory.

in on the bridge. All your heads I come in then." "Right," Duke said. "So why—" "Wha," said Krinkles, "16 bars, I wait, I come in—" "16?" Duke said. "No. No, Krinkles. Eight you waited. You want me to sing it? A cigarette that bears a lipstick's traces, an airline ticket to romantic places." Krinkles scratched his head. "These Foolish Things, you mean." "Yes," Duke said, "yes, Krinkles. Bravo." "Not I'll Remember April," Krinkles said. *"Minghe morte,"*[8] said Duke. "I *figured* we were playing it a little slow," Krinkles said. Meatball chuckled. "Back to the old drawing board," he said. "No, man," Duke said, "back to the airless void." And they took off again, only it seemed Paco was playing in G sharp while the rest were in E flat, so they had to start all over.

In the kitchen two of the girls from George Washington and the sailors were singing Let's All Go Down and Piss on the Forrestal.[9] There was a two-handed, bilingual *morra*[1] game on over by the icebox. Saul had filled several paper bags with water and was sitting on the fire escape, dropping them on passersby in the street. A fat government girl in a Bennington sweatshirt, recently engaged to an ensign attached to the Forrestal, came charging into the kitchen, head lowered, and butted Slab in the stomach. Figuring this was as good an excuse for a fight as any, Slab's buddies piled in. The *morra* players were nose-to-nose, screaming *trois, sette* at the tops of their lungs. From the shower the girl Meatball had taken out of the sink announced that she was drowning. She had apparently sat on the drain and the water was now up to her neck. The noise in Meatball's apartment had reached a sustained, ungodly crescendo.

Meatball stood and watched, scratching his stomach lazily. The way he figured, there were only about two ways he could cope: (a) lock himself in the closet and maybe eventually they would all go away, or (b) try to calm everybody down, one by one. (a) was certainly the more attractive alternative. But then he started thinking about that closet. It was dark and stuffy and he would be alone. He did not feature being alone. And then this crew off the good ship Lollipop[2] or whatever it was might take it upon themselves to kick down the closet door, for a lark. And if that happened he would be, at the very least, embarrassed. The other way was more a pain in the neck, but probably better in the long run.

So he decided to try and keep his lease-breaking party from deteriorating into total chaos: he gave wine to the sailors and separated the *morra* players; he introduced the fat government girl to Sandor Rojas, who would keep her out of trouble; he helped the girl in the shower to dry off and get into bed; he had another talk with Saul; he called a repairman for the refrigerator, which someone had discovered was on the blink. This is what he did until nightfall, when most of the revellers had passed out and the party trembled on the threshold of its third day.

Upstairs Callisto, helpless in the past, did not feel the faint rhythm inside the bird begin to slacken and fail. Aubade was by the window, wandering the ashes of her own lovely world; the temperature held steady, the sky had become a uniform darkening gray. Then something from down-

---

8. Dead prick (Italian).
9. Aircraft carrier in the U.S. Navy.
1. Finger game originally played by Italians. The commands are numbers; below, three (*trois*,

French) and seven (*sette*, Italian).
2. The subject of film and song popularized in the 1930s by the American child actress Shirley Temple.

stairs—a girl's scream, an overturned chair, a glass dropped on the floor, he would never know what exactly—pierced that private time-warp and he became aware of the faltering, the constriction of muscles, the tiny tossings of the bird's head; and his own pulse began to pound more fiercely, as if trying to compensate. "Aubade," he called weakly, "he's dying." The girl, flowing and rapt, crossed the hothouse to gaze down at Callisto's hands. The two remained like that, poised, for one minute, and two, while the heartbeat ticked a graceful diminuendo down at last into stillness. Callisto raised his head slowly. "I held him," he protested, impotent with the wonder of it, "to give him the warmth of my body. Almost as if I were communicating life to him, or a sense of life. What has happened? Has the transfer of heat ceased to work? Is there no more . . ." He did not finish.

"I was just at the window," she said. He sank back, terrified. She stood a moment more, irresolute; she had sensed his obsession long ago, realized somehow that that constant 37 was now decisive. Suddenly then, as if seeing the single and unavoidable conclusion to all this she moved swiftly to the window before Callisto could speak; tore away the drapes and smashed out the glass with two exquisite hands which came away bleeding and glistening with splinters; and turned to face the man on the bed and wait with him until the moment of equilibrium was reached, when 37 degrees Fahrenheit should prevail both outside and inside, and forever, and the hovering, curious dominant of their separate lives should resolve into a tonic of darkness and the final absence of all motion.

1984

RAYMOND CARVER
1938–1988

Minimal fiction; designer fiction; even "dirty fiction," a phrase the British magazine *Granta* used to characterize the new style of American writing that was supposedly polluting the realistic short story with unconventional, irrealistic techniques—these terms were tossed around by critics of an abruptly new style of work that at times seemed to dominate the 1980s. Popularized by Bobbie Ann Mason, Ann Beattie, Frederick Barthelme, and Barry Hannah as well, its chief practitioner was a master of fine arts graduate from the University of Iowa's Writers Workshop, Raymond Carver, whose collections *Will You Please Be Quiet, Please?* (1976), *What We Talk About When We Talk About Love* (1981), and *Cathedral* (1983) set the most imitated style of their generation. Moved to put some order to these many definitions, writer John Barth—whose nonrealistic, innovative work had helped characterize the writing of the decades before—coined the term Post-Alcoholic Blue-Collar Minimalist Hyperrealism to describe the school Carver may have inadvertently founded. A recovering alcoholic, Carver had worked as a janitor, sawmill hand, delivery person, and sales representative, suggesting the profile Barth had in mind. But more pertinent to the style of his fiction was his training at Iowa and teaching in creative writing programs at universities around the country. By the time of his death, his became the most accepted style in such academic programs and in the literary magazines they generated.

This style's success is important. With conventions of literary realism having been challenged and theorists questioning all such previously stable assumptions, readers of Barth, Donald Barthelme, Kurt Vonnegut, and other such experimenters may have felt that simple realism was no longer an up-to-date way in which to write. Raymond Carver proved that it was, and that previous challenges to realistic tradition had only made it all the more effective, especially when those challenges are incorporated in the new style. Carver's patient narration does not strive for a reader's suspension of disbelief. Rather, as in the introduction of the bizarre situation experienced in "Cathedral" (printed here), its plain, even flat statement presents matter unadorned by devices meant to persuade or convince. So a blind man wants to learn what the architecture of a cathedral suggests? Here it is, Carver's story says: what you see is what there is; take it or leave it; if you are blind, he will help you feel your way through, but never as a direction to meaning, only to an apprehension of the facts. Carver's characters are usually working-class people somewhat down on their luck. Often, alcohol figures in their lives, less as a stimulant than as a further depressant. Totally unexceptional, their failures, like their hopes, are small, even puny. But from such stripped-down essentials the author is able to write in a plain, simple manner, sticking to the absolute minimum so that no one can accuse him of trying to create illusions.

Much was made of Raymond Carver's alcoholism and recovery. He made no apologies for his hard, sometimes abusive life, the rigors of which contributed to ill health and an early death. His stories and poems have the same quiet toughness to them, not flamboyant in confrontation with life's meanness but dedicated to holding on against time's slowly destructive friction with a grittiness all their own.

The following text is from *Cathedral* (1983).

Cathedral

This blind man, an old friend of my wife's, he was on his way to spend the night. His wife had died. So he was visiting the dead wife's relatives in Connecticut. He called my wife from his in-laws'. Arrangements were made. He would come by train, a five-hour trip, and my wife would meet him at the station. She hadn't seen him since she worked for him one summer in Seattle ten years ago. But she and the blind man had kept in touch. They made tapes and mailed them back and forth. I wasn't enthusiastic about his visit. He was no one I knew. And his being blind bothered me. My idea of blindness came from the movies. In the movies, the blind moved slowly and never laughed. Sometimes they were led by seeing-eye dogs. A blind man in my house was not something I looked forward to.

That summer in Seattle she had needed a job. She didn't have any money. The man she was going to marry at the end of the summer was in officers' training school. He didn't have any money, either. But she was in love with the guy, and he was in love with her, etc. She'd seen something in the paper: HELP WANTED—*Reading to Blind Man*, and a telephone number. She phoned and went over, was hired on the spot. She'd worked with this blind man all summer. She read stuff to him, case studies, reports, that sort of thing. She helped him organize his little office in the county social-service department. They'd become good friends, my wife and the blind man. How do I know these things? She told me. And she told me something else. On her last day in the office, the blind man asked if he could touch her face. She agreed to this. She told me he touched his fingers to every part of her face, her nose—even her neck! She never forgot it. She even tried to write a poem about it. She was always trying to write a poem. She wrote a poem or two every year, usually after something really important had happened to her.

When we first started going out together, she showed me the poem. In the poem, she recalled his fingers and the way they had moved around over her face. In the poem, she talked about what she had felt at the time, about what went through her mind when the blind man touched her nose and lips. I can remember I didn't think much of the poem. Of course, I didn't tell her that. Maybe I just don't understand poetry. I admit it's not the first thing I reach for when I pick up something to read.

Anyway, this man who'd first enjoyed her favors, the officer-to-be, he'd been her childhood sweetheart. So okay. I'm saying that at the end of the summer she let the blind man run his hands over her face, said goodbye to him, married her childhood etc., who was now a commissioned officer, and she moved away from Seattle. But they'd kept in touch, she and the blind man. She made the first contact after a year or so. She called him up one night from an Air Force base in Alabama. She wanted to talk. They talked. He asked her to send him a tape and tell him about her life. She did this. She sent the tape. On the tape, she told the blind man about her husband and about their life together in the military. She told the blind man she loved her husband but she didn't like it where they lived and she didn't like it that he was a part of the military-industrial thing. She told the blind man she'd written a poem and he was in it. She told him that she was writing a poem about what it was like to be an Air Force officer's wife. The poem wasn't finished yet. She was still writing it. The blind man made a tape. He sent her the tape. She made a tape. This went on for years. My wife's officer was posted to one base and then another. She sent tapes from Moody AFB,[1] McGuire, McConnell, and finally Travis, near Sacramento, where one night she got to feeling lonely and cut off from people she kept losing in that moving-around life. She got to feeling she couldn't go it another step. She went in and swallowed all the pills and capsules in the medicine chest and washed them down with a bottle of gin. Then she got into a hot bath and passed out.

But instead of dying, she got sick. She threw up. Her officer—why should he have a name? he was the childhood sweetheart, and what more does he want?—came home from somewhere, found her, and called the ambulance. In time, she put it all on a tape and sent the tape to the blind man. Over the years, she put all kinds of stuff on tapes and sent the tapes off lickety-split. Next to writing a poem every year, I think it was her chief means of recreation. On one tape, she told the blind man she'd decided to live away from her officer for a time. On another tape, she told him about her divorce. She and I began going out, and of course she told her blind man about it. She told him everything, or so it seemed to me. Once she asked me if I'd like to hear the latest tape from the blind man. This was a year ago. I was on the tape, she said. So I said okay, I'd listen to it. I got us drinks and we settled down in the living room. We made ready to listen. First she inserted the tape into the player and adjusted a couple of dials. Then she pushed a lever. The tape squeaked and someone began to talk in this loud voice. She lowered the volume. After a few minutes of harmless chitchat, I heard my own name in the mouth of this stranger, this blind man I didn't even know! And then this: "From all you've said about him, I can only conclude—" But we were interrupted, a knock at the door, something, and we didn't ever get back to the tape. Maybe it was just as well. I'd heard all I wanted to.

Now this same blind man was coming to sleep in my house.

"Maybe I could take him bowling," I said to my wife. She was at the draining board doing scalloped potatoes. She put down the knife she was using and turned around.

"If you love me," she said, "you can do this for me. If you don't love me, okay. But if you had a friend, any friend, and the friend came to visit, I'd make him feel comfortable." She wiped her hands with the dish towel.

"I don't have any blind friends," I said.

"You don't have *any* friends," she said. "Period. Besides," she said, "goddam it, his wife's just died! Don't you understand that? The man's lost his wife!"

I didn't answer. She'd told me a little about the blind man's wife. Her name was Beulah. Beulah! That's a name for a colored woman.

"Was his wife a Negro?" I asked.

"Are you crazy?" my wife said. "Have you just flipped or something?" She picked up a potato. I saw it hit the floor, then roll under the stove. "What's wrong with you?" she said. "Are you drunk?"

"I'm just asking," I said.

Right then my wife filled me in with more detail than I cared to know. I made a drink and sat at the kitchen table to listen. Pieces of the story began to fall into place.

Beulah had gone to work for the blind man the summer after my wife had stopped working for him. Pretty soon Beulah and the blind man had themselves a church wedding. It was a little wedding—who'd want to go to such a wedding in the first place?—just the two of them, plus the minister and the minister's wife. But it was a church wedding just the same. It was what Beulah had wanted, he'd said. But even then Beulah must have been carrying the cancer in her glands. After they had been inseparable for eight years—my wife's word, *inseparable*—Beulah's health went into a rapid decline. She died in a Seattle hospital room, the blind man sitting beside the bed and holding on to her hand. They'd married, lived and worked together, slept together—had sex, sure—and then the blind man had to bury her. All this without his having ever seen what the goddamned woman looked like. It was beyond my understanding. Hearing this, I felt sorry for the blind man for a little bit. And then I found myself thinking what a pitiful life this woman must have led. Imagine a woman who could never see herself as she was seen in the eyes of her loved one. A woman who could go on day after day and never receive the smallest compliment from her beloved. A woman whose husband could never read the expression on her face, be it misery or something better. Someone who could wear makeup or not—what difference to him? She could, if she wanted, wear green eye-shadow around one eye, a straight pin in her nostril, yellow slacks and purple shoes, no matter. And then to slip off into death, the blind man's hand on her hand, his blind eyes streaming tears—I'm imagining now—her last thought maybe this: that he never even knew what she looked like, and she on an express to the grave. Robert was left with a small insurance policy and half of a twenty-peso Mexican coin. The other half of the coin went into the box with her. Pathetic.

So when the time rolled around, my wife went to the depot to pick him up. With nothing to do but wait—sure, I blamed him for that—I was having a drink and watching the TV when I heard the car pull into the drive. I got up from the sofa with my drink and went to the window to have a look.

I saw my wife laughing as she parked the car. I saw her get out of the car and shut the door. She was still wearing a smile. Just amazing. She went around to the other side of the car to where the blind man was already start-ing to get out. This blind man, feature this, he was wearing a full beard! A beard on a blind man! Too much, I say. The blind man reached into the back seat and dragged out a suitcase. My wife took his arm, shut the car door, and, talking all the way, moved him down the drive and then up the steps to the front porch. I turned off the TV. I finished my drink, rinsed the glass, dried my hands. Then I went to the door.

My wife said, "I want you to meet Robert. Robert, this is my husband. I've told you all about him." She was beaming. She had this blind man by his coat sleeve.

The blind man let go of his suitcase and up came his hand.

I took it. He squeezed hard, held my hand, and then he let it go.

"I feel like we've already met," he boomed.

"Likewise," I said. I didn't know what else to say. Then I said, "Welcome. I've heard a lot about you." We began to move then, a little group, from the porch into the living room, my wife guiding him by the arm. The blind man was carrying his suitcase in his other hand. My wife said things like, "To your left here, Robert. That's right. Now watch it, there's a chair. That's it. Sit down right here. This is the sofa. We just bought this sofa two weeks ago."

I started to say something about the old sofa. I'd liked that old sofa. But I didn't say anything. Then I wanted to say something else, small-talk, about the scenic ride along the Hudson. How going *to* New York, you should sit on the right-hand side of the train, and coming *from* New York, the left-hand side.

"Did you have a good train ride?" I said. "Which side of the train did you sit on, by the way?"

"What a question, which side!" my wife said. "What's it matter which side?" she said.

"I just asked," I said.

"Right side," the blind man said. "I hadn't been on a train in nearly forty years. Not since I was a kid. With my folks. That's been a long time. I'd nearly forgotten the sensation. I have winter in my beard now," he said. "So I've been told, anyway. Do I look distinguished, my dear?" the blind man said to my wife.

"You look distinguished, Robert," she said. "Robert," she said. "Robert, it's just so good to see you."

My wife finally took her eyes off the blind man and looked at me. I had the feeling she didn't like what she saw. I shrugged.

I've never met, or personally known, anyone who was blind. This blind man was late forties, a heavy-set, balding man with stooped shoulders, as if he carried a great weight there. He wore brown slacks, brown shoes, a light-brown shirt, a tie, a sports coat. Spiffy. He also had this full beard. But he didn't use a cane and he didn't wear dark glasses. I'd always thought dark glasses were a must for the blind. Fact was, I wished he had a pair. At first glance, his eyes looked like anyone else's eyes. But if you looked close, there was something different about them. Too much white in the iris, for one thing, and the pupils seemed to move around in the sockets without his knowing it or being able to stop it. Creepy. As I stared at his face, I saw the left pupil turn in toward his nose while the other made an effort to keep in one place. But it was only an effort, for that eye was on the roam without his knowing it or wanting it to be.

I said, "Let me get you a drink. What's your pleasure? We have a little of everything. It's one of our pastimes."

"Bub, I'm a Scotch man myself," he said fast enough in this big voice.

"Right," I said. Bub! "Sure you are. I knew it."

He let his fingers touch his suitcase, which was sitting alongside the sofa. He was taking his bearings. I didn't blame him for that.

"I'll move that up to your room," my wife said.

"No, that's fine," the blind man said loudly. "It can go up when I go up."

"A little water with the Scotch?" I said.

"Very little," he said.

"I knew it," I said.

He said, "Just a tad. The Irish actor, Barry Fitzgerald?[2] I'm like that fellow. When I drink water, Fitzgerald said, I drink water. When I drink whiskey, I drink whiskey." My wife laughed. The blind man brought his hand up under his beard. He lifted his beard slowly and let it drop.

I did the drinks, three big glasses of Scotch with a splash of water in each. Then we made ourselves comfortable and talked about Robert's travels. First the long flight from the West Coast to Connecticut, we covered that. Then from Connecticut up here by train. We had another drink concerning that leg of the trip.

I remembered having read somewhere that the blind didn't smoke because, as speculation had it, they couldn't see the smoke they exhaled. I thought I knew that much and that much only about blind people. But this blind man smoked his cigarette down to the nubbin and then lit another one. This blind man filled his ashtray and my wife emptied it.

When we sat down at the table for dinner, we had another drink. My wife heaped Robert's plate with cube steak, scalloped potatoes, green beans. I buttered him up two slices of bread. I said, "Here's bread and butter for you." I swallowed some of my drink. "Now let us pray," I said, and the blind man lowered his head. My wife looked at me, her mouth agape. "Pray the phone won't ring and the food doesn't get cold," I said.

We dug in. We ate everything there was to eat on the table. We ate like there was no tomorrow. We didn't talk. We ate. We scarfed. We grazed that

2. Noted for his stock characterizations of Irish figures (often priests) in American films of the 1940s and 1950s.

table. We were into serious eating. The blind man had right away located his foods, he knew just where everything was on his plate. I watched with admiration as he used his knife and fork on the meat. He'd cut two pieces of meat, fork the meat into his mouth, and then go all out for the scalloped potatoes, the beans next, and then he'd tear off a hunk of buttered bread and eat that. He'd follow this up with a big drink of milk. It didn't seem to bother him to use his fingers once in a while, either.

We finished everything, including half a strawberry pie. For a few moments, we sat as if stunned. Sweat beaded on our faces. Finally, we got up from the table and left the dirty plates. We didn't look back. We took ourselves into the living room and sank into our places again. Robert and my wife sat on the sofa. I took the big chair. We had us two or three more drinks while they talked about the major things that had come to pass for them in the past ten years. For the most part, I just listened. Now and then I joined in. I didn't want him to think I'd left the room, and I didn't want her to think I was feeling left out. They talked of things that had happened to them—to them!—these past ten years. I waited in vain to hear my name on my wife's sweet lips: "And then my dear husband came into my life"— something like that. But I heard nothing of the sort. More talk of Robert. Robert had done a little of everything, it seemed, a regular blind jack-of-all-trades. But most recently he and his wife had had an Amway[3] distributor-ship, from which, I gathered, they'd earned their living, such as it was. The blind man was also a ham radio operator. He talked in his loud voice about conversations he'd had with fellow operators in Guam, in the Philippines, in Alaska, and even in Tahiti. He said he'd have a lot of friends there if he ever wanted to go visit those places. From time to time, he'd turn his blind face toward me, put his hand under his beard, ask me something. How long had I been in my present position? (Three years.) Did I like my work? (I didn't.) Was I going to stay with it? (What were the options?) Finally, when I thought he was beginning to run down, I got up and turned on the TV.

My wife looked at me with irritation. She was heading toward a boil. Then she looked at the blind man and said, "Robert, do you have a TV?"

The blind man said, "My dear, I have two TVs. I have a color set and a black-and-white thing, an old relic. It's funny, but if I turn the TV on, and I'm always turning it on, I turn on the color set. It's funny, don't you think?"

I didn't know what to say to that. I had absolutely nothing to say to that. No opinion. So I watched the news program and tried to listen to what the announcer was saying.

"This is a color TV," the blind man said. "Don't ask me how, but I can tell."

"We traded up a while ago," I said.

The blind man had another taste of his drink. He lifted his beard, sniffed it, and let it fall. He leaned forward on the sofa. He positioned his ashtray on the coffee table, then put the lighter to his cigarette. He leaned back on the sofa and crossed his legs at the ankles.

My wife covered her mouth, and then she yawned. She stretched. She said, "I think I'll go upstairs and put on my robe. I think I'll change into something else. Robert, you make yourself comfortable," she said.

---

3. A retail sales business operated by selling directly to consumers in their homes.

"I'm comfortable," the blind man said.

"I want you to feel comfortable in this house," she said.

"I am comfortable," the blind man said.

After she'd left the room, he and I listened to the weather report and then to the sports roundup. By that time, she'd been gone so long I didn't know if she was going to come back. I thought she might have gone to bed. I wished she'd come back downstairs. I didn't want to be left alone with a blind man. I asked him if he wanted another drink, and he said sure. Then I asked if he wanted to smoke some dope with me. I said I'd just rolled a number. I hadn't, but I planned to do so in about two shakes.

"I'll try some with you," he said.

"Damn right," I said. "That's the stuff."

I got our drinks and sat down on the sofa with him. Then I rolled us two fat numbers. I lit one and passed it. I brought it to his fingers. He took it and inhaled.

"Hold it as long as you can," I said. I could tell he didn't know the first thing.

My wife came back downstairs wearing her pink robe and her pink slippers.

"What do I smell?" she said.

"We thought we'd have us some cannabis," I said.

My wife gave me a savage look. Then she looked at the blind man and said, "Robert, I didn't know you smoked."

He said, "I do now, my dear. There's a first time for everything. But I don't feel anything yet."

"This stuff is pretty mellow," I said. "This stuff is mild. It's dope you can reason with," I said. "It doesn't mess you up."

"Not much it doesn't, bub," he said, and laughed.

My wife sat on the sofa between the blind man and me. I passed her the number. She took it and toked and then passed it back to me. "Which way is this going?" she said. Then she said, "I shouldn't be smoking this. I can hardly keep my eyes open as it is. That dinner did me in. I shouldn't have eaten so much."

"It was the strawberry pie," the blind man said. "That's what did it," he said, and he laughed his big laugh. Then he shook his head.

"There's more strawberry pie," I said.

"Do you want some more, Robert?" my wife said.

"Maybe in a little while," he said.

We gave our attention to the TV. My wife yawned again. She said, "Your bed is made up when you feel like going to bed, Robert. I know you must have had a long day. When you're ready to go to bed, say so." She pulled his arm. "Robert?"

He came to and said, "I've had a real nice time. This beats tapes, doesn't it?"

I said, "Coming at you," and I put the number between his fingers. He inhaled, held the smoke, and then let it go. It was like he'd been doing it since he was nine years old.

"Thanks, bub," he said. "But I think this is all for me. I think I'm beginning to feel it," he said. He held the burning roach out for my wife.

"Same here," she said. "Ditto. Me, too." She took the roach and passed it to me. "I may just sit here for a while between you two guys with my eyes closed. But don't let me bother you, okay? Either one of you. If it bothers you, say so. Otherwise, I may just sit here with my eyes closed until you're ready to go to bed," she said. "Your bed's made up, Robert, when you're ready. It's right next to our room at the top of the stairs. We'll show you up when you're ready. You wake me up now, you guys, if I fall asleep." She said that and then she closed her eyes and went to sleep.

The news program ended. I got up and changed the channel. I sat back down on the sofa. I wished my wife hadn't pooped out. Her head lay across the back of the sofa, her mouth open. She'd turned so that her robe had slipped away from her legs, exposing a juicy thigh. I reached to draw her robe back over her, and it was then that I glanced at the blind man. What the hell! I flipped the robe open again.

"You say when you want some strawberry pie," I said.

"I will," he said.

I said, "Are you tired? Do you want me to take you up to your bed? Are you ready to hit the hay?"

"Not yet," he said. "No, I'll stay up with you, bub. If that's all right. I'll stay up until you're ready to turn in. We haven't had a chance to talk. Know what I mean? I feel like me and her monopolized the evening." He lifted his beard and he let it fall. He picked up his cigarettes and his lighter.

"That's all right," I said. Then I said, "I'm glad for the company."

And I guess I was. Every night I smoked dope and stayed up as long as I could before I fell asleep. My wife and I hardly ever went to bed at the same time. When I did go to sleep, I had these dreams. Sometimes I'd wake up from one of them, my heart going crazy.

Something about the church and the Middle Ages was on the TV. Not your run-of-the-mill TV fare. I wanted to watch something else. I turned to the other channels. But there was nothing on them, either. So I turned back to the first channel and apologized.

"Bub, it's all right," the blind man said. "It's fine with me. Whatever you want to watch is okay. I'm always learning something. Learning never ends. It won't hurt me to learn something tonight. I got ears," he said.

We didn't say anything for a time. He was leaning forward with his head turned at me, his right ear aimed in the direction of the set. Very disconcerting. Now and then his eyelids drooped and then they snapped open again. Now and then he put his fingers into his beard and tugged, like he was thinking about something he was hearing on the television.

On the screen, a group of men wearing cowls was being set upon and tormented by men dressed in skeleton costumes and men dressed as devils. The men dressed as devils wore devil masks, horns, and long tails. This pageant was part of a procession. The Englishman who was narrating the thing said it took place in Spain once a year. I tried to explain to the blind man what was happening.

"Skeletons," he said. "I know about skeletons," he said, and he nodded.

The TV showed this one cathedral. Then there was a long, slow look at another one. Finally, the picture switched to the famous one in Paris, with its flying buttresses and its spires reaching up to the clouds. The camera pulled away to show the whole of the cathedral rising above the skyline.

There were times when the Englishman who was telling the thing would shut up, would simply let the camera move around over the cathedrals. Or else the camera would tour the countryside, men in fields walking behind oxen. I waited as long as I could. Then I felt I had to say something. I said, "They're showing the outside of this cathedral now. Gargoyles. Little statues carved to look like monsters. Now I guess they're in Italy. Yeah, they're in Italy. There's paintings on the walls of this one church."

"Are those fresco paintings, bub?" he asked, and he sipped from his drink.

I reached for my glass. But it was empty. I tried to remember what I could remember. "You're asking me are those frescoes?" I said. "That's a good question. I don't know."

The camera moved to a cathedral outside Lisbon. The differences in the Portuguese cathedral compared with the French and Italian were not that great. But they were there. Mostly the interior stuff. Then something occurred to me, and I said, "Something has occurred to me. Do you have any idea what a cathedral is? What they look like, that is? Do you follow me? If somebody says cathedral to you, do you have any notion what they're talking about? Do you know the difference between that and a Baptist church, say?"

He let the smoke dribble from his mouth. "I know they took hundreds of workers fifty or a hundred years to build," he said. "I just heard the man say that, of course. I know generations of the same families worked on a cathedral. I heard him say that, too. The men who began their life's work on them, they never lived to see the completion of their work. In that wise, bub, they're no different from the rest of us, right?" He laughed. Then his eyelids drooped again. His head nodded. He seemed to be snoozing. Maybe he was imagining himself in Portugal. The TV was showing another cathedral now. This one was in Germany. The Englishman's voice droned on. "Cathedrals," the blind man said. He sat up and rolled his head back and forth. "If you want the truth, bub, that's about all I know. What I just said. What I heard him say. But maybe you could describe one to me? I wish you'd do it. I'd like that. If you want to know, I really don't have a good idea."

I stared hard at the shot of the cathedral on the TV. How could I even begin to describe it? But say my life depended on it. Say my life was being threatened by an insane guy who said I had to do it or else.

I stared some more at the cathedral before the picture flipped off into the countryside. There was no use. I turned to the blind man and said, "To begin with, they're very tall." I was looking around the room for clues. "They reach way up. Up and up. Toward the sky. They're so big, some of them, they have to have these supports. To help hold them up, so to speak. These supports are called buttresses. They remind me of viaducts, for some reason. But maybe you don't know viaducts, either? Sometimes the cathedrals have devils and such carved into the front. Sometimes lords and ladies. Don't ask me why this is," I said.

He was nodding. The whole upper part of his body seemed to be moving back and forth.

"I'm not doing so good, am I?" I said.

He stopped nodding and leaned forward on the edge of the sofa. As he listened to me, he was running his fingers through his beard. I wasn't getting through to him, I could see that. But he waited for me to go on just the same. He nodded, like he was trying to encourage me. I tried to think what else to say. "They're really big," I said. "They're massive. They're built of stone. Marble, too, sometimes. In those olden days, when they built cathedrals, men wanted to be close to God. In those olden days, God was an important part of everyone's life. You could tell this from their cathedral-building. I'm sorry," I said, "but it looks like that's the best I can do for you. I'm just no good at it."

"That's all right, bub," the blind man said. "Hey, listen. I hope you don't mind my asking you. Can I ask you something? Let me ask you a simple question, yes or no. I'm just curious and there's no offense. You're my host. But let me ask if you are in any way religious? You don't mind my asking?"

I shook my head. He couldn't see that, though. A wink is the same as a nod to a blind man. "I guess I don't believe in it. In anything. Sometimes it's hard. You know what I'm saying?"

"Sure, I do," he said.

"Right," I said.

The Englishman was still holding forth. My wife sighed in her sleep. She drew a long breath and went on with her sleeping.

"You'll have to forgive me," I said. "But I can't tell you what a cathedral looks like. It just isn't in me to do it. I can't do any more than I've done."

The blind man sat very still, his head down, as he listened to me.

I said, "The truth is, cathedrals don't mean anything special to me. Nothing. Cathedrals. They're something to look at on late-night TV. That's all they are."

It was then that the blind man cleared his throat. He brought something up. He took a handkerchief from his back pocket. Then he said, "I get it, bub. It's okay. It happens. Don't worry about it," he said. "Hey, listen to me. Will you do me a favor? I got an idea. Why don't you find us some heavy paper? And a pen. We'll do something. We'll draw one together. Get us a pen and some heavy paper. Go on, bub, get the stuff," he said.

So I went upstairs. My legs felt like they didn't have any strength in them. They felt like they did after I'd done some running. In my wife's room, I looked around. I found some ballpoints in a little basket on her table. And then I tried to think where to look for the kind of paper he was talking about.

Downstairs, in the kitchen, I found a shopping bag with onion skins in the bottom of the bag. I emptied the bag and shook it. I brought it into the living room and sat down with it near his legs. I moved some things, smoothed the wrinkles from the bag, spread it out on the coffee table.

The blind man got down from the sofa and sat next to me on the carpet.

He ran his fingers over the paper. He went up and down the sides of the paper. The edges, even the edges. He fingered the corners.

"All right," he said. "All right, let's do her."

He found my hand, the hand with the pen. He closed his hand over my hand. "Go ahead, bub, draw," he said. "Draw. You'll see. I'll follow along with you. It'll be okay. Just begin now like I'm telling you. You'll see. Draw," the blind man said.

So I began. First I drew a box that looked like a house. It could have been the house I lived in. Then I put a roof on it. At either end of the roof, I drew spires. Crazy.

"Swell," he said. "Terrific. You're doing fine," he said. "Never thought anything like this could happen in your lifetime, did you, bub? Well, it's a strange life, we all know that. Go on now. Keep it up."

I put in windows with arches. I drew flying buttresses. I hung great doors. I couldn't stop. The TV station went off the air. I put down the pen and closed and opened my fingers. The blind man felt around over the paper. He moved the tips of his fingers over the paper, all over what I had drawn, and he nodded.

"Doing fine," the blind man said.

I took up the pen again, and he found my hand. I kept at it. I'm no artist. But I kept drawing just the same.

My wife opened up her eyes and gazed at us. She sat up on the sofa, her robe hanging open. She said, "What are you doing? Tell me, I want to know."

I didn't answer her.

The blind man said, "We're drawing a cathedral. Me and him are working on it. Press hard," he said to me. "That's right. That's good," he said. "Sure. You got it, bub. I can tell. You didn't think you could. But you can, can't you? You're cooking with gas now. You know what I'm saying? We're going to really have us something here in a minute. How's the old arm?" he said. "Put some people in there now. What's a cathedral without people?"

My wife said, "What's going on? Robert, what are you doing? What's going on?"

"It's all right," he said to her. "Close your eyes now," the blind man said to me.

I did it. I closed them just like he said.

"Are they closed?" he said. "Don't fudge."

"They're closed," I said.

"Keep them that way," he said. He said, "Don't stop now. Draw."

So we kept on with it. His fingers rode my fingers as my hand went over the paper. It was like nothing else in my life up to now.

Then he said, "I think that's it. I think you got it," he said. "Take a look. What do you think?"

But I had my eyes closed. I thought I'd keep them that way for a little longer. I thought it was something I ought to do.

"Well?" he said. "Are you looking?"

My eyes were still closed. I was in my house. I knew that. But I didn't feel like I was inside anything.

"It's really something," I said.

1983

MAXINE HONG KINGSTON

b. 1940

Maxine Hong Kingston was born in Stockton, California, to Chinese immigrant parents. Before they emigrated from China Kingston's father had been a schoolteacher and a poet; her mother had been a rural doctor in a profession consisting almost entirely of men. In America they took on quite different identities: her father, at times unemployed, worked in a gambling house and a laundry; her mother raised six children, of whom Kingston was the eldest.

Kingston graduated from the University of California at Berkeley, studying there in the turbulent middle sixties. Her debut as a writer was auspicious: in 1976, an unknown, she published her first and most widely read book, *The Woman Warrior*, and was catapulted to literary fame. Subtitled "Memoirs of a Girlhood among Ghosts," it combines autobiographical fact with legends, especially Asian ones, to make a distinct imaginative creation. Reviews of the book, almost universally laudatory, emphasized its poetic and lyric beauty. *The Woman Warrior* is about the cultural conflicts Chinese Americans must confront. Still, what remains in the mind is its quality of vivid particularity, as for example at the beginning of "Shaman," the book's third section:

> Once in a long while, four times so far for me, my mother brings out the metal tube that holds her medical diploma. On the tube are gold circles crossed with seven red lines each—"joy" ideographs in abstract. There are also little flowers that look like gears for a gold machine. . . . When I open it the smell of China flies out, a thousand-year-old bat flying heavy-handed out of the Chinese caverns where bats are as white as dust, a smell that comes from long ago, far back in my brain.

Although *The Woman Warrior* received the National Book Critics' Circle award for general nonfiction, there is nothing "general" in the richness of its language.

The importance of storytelling to Kingston's enterprise in *The Woman Warrior* and its successor, *China Men* (1980), cannot be overemphasized. In an interview with Bill Moyers on public television, Kingston said that her attempt was to push the account toward "form" by giving it a "redemptive" meaning, making it a "beautiful" story rather than a sordid one. As is typically the case with her practice as a writer, her effort is to mediate between present and past: "I think that my stories have a constant breaking in and out of the present and past. So the reader might be walking along very well in the present, but the past breaks through and changes and enlightens the present and vice versa."

Kingston had originally conceived of *The Woman Warrior* and *China Men* as one long book, but decided to preserve an overall division by gender: *Warrior* is about her female antecedents; while *China Men*, which won the 1980 National Book Award for nonfiction, deals with her relation to her father and complements that relation by providing epiclike biographies of earlier male forebears, especially those Chinese who came to America and worked on building the railroads. In a final section she writes about her brother who served in the U.S. Navy during the Vietnam War. As she discusses in the interview with Moyers, her father annotated both of these memoir-meditations, carrying further the conversation between the generations.

Tripmaster Monkey (1989), presented more deliberately as a novel, is an exercise as excessive as the young fifth-generation American hero, Wittman Ah Sing, who is portrayed there. Subtitled "His Fake Book," the novel is an extended, picaresque account of Wittman's adventures as an aspiring playwright who imagines himself to be an incarnation of the legendary Monkey King—a trickster hero said to have brought the Buddha's teaching to China. Combining magic, realism, and black humor, *Tripmaster Monkey* is about a young man's search for a community in America. Although Kingston's myth-laden narratives have been called "exotic," she dislikes the word, since she has dedicated her art to exploring what it means to be a human being in American society. In fact, she thinks of her books as more American than Chinese, sees the American poet William Carlos Williams's *In the American Grain* as a true prose predecessor, and probably would be happy to think of the hero of *Tripmaster Monkey* as a later, different version of Huck Finn (in Mark Twain's novel) or Augie March (in Saul Bellow's). As the critic Jennie Wang explains in even larger dimensions, Kingston's Wittman Ah Sing, "the maker/magician . . . conceived in the mind's fancy of a metafictionist," joins in his multiculturalism American and postmodern ambitions.

In 2011 Kingston celebrated her sixty-fifth birthday by publishing a memoir, *I Love a Broad Margin to My Life*. Written in verse form, this work engages issues of aging as the writer recalls incidents in her marriage, her career, and her involvement with social causes. She considers imaginative elements as well, including the ultimate fate of her Woman Warrior and the experiences of her protagonist in *Tripmaster Monkey* in a projected visit to China.

The following text is from *The Woman Warrior* (1976).

From The Woman Warrior

No Name Woman

"You must not tell anyone," my mother said, "what I am about to tell you. In China your father had a sister who killed herself. She jumped into the family well. We say that your father has all brothers because it is as if she had never been born.

"In 1924 just a few days after our village celebrated seventeen hurry-up weddings—to make sure that every young man who went 'out on the road' would responsibly come home—your father and his brothers and your grandfather and his brothers and your aunt's new husband sailed for America, the Gold Mountain. It was your grandfather's last trip. Those lucky enough to get contracts waved good-bye from the decks. They fed and guarded the stowaways and helped them off in Cuba, New York, Bali, Hawaii. 'We'll meet in California next year,' they said. All of them sent money home.

"I remember looking at your aunt one day when she and I were dressing; I had not noticed before that she had such a protruding melon of a stomach. But I did not think, 'She's pregnant,' until she began to look like other pregnant women, her shirt pulling and the white tops of her black pants showing. She could not have been pregnant, you see, because her husband had been gone for years. No one said anything. We did not discuss it. In early summer she was ready to have the child, long after the time when it could have been possible.

"The village had also been counting. On the night the baby was to be born the villagers raided our house. Some were crying. Like a great saw, teeth strung with lights, files of people walked zigzag across our land, tearing the rice. Their lanterns doubled in the disturbed black water, which drained away through the broken bunds.[1] As the villagers closed in, we could see that some of them, probably men and women we knew well, wore white masks. The people with long hair hung it over their faces. Women with short hair made it stand up on end. Some had tied white bands around their foreheads, arms, and legs.

"At first they threw mud and rocks at the house. Then they threw eggs and began slaughtering our stock. We could hear the animals scream their deaths—the roosters, the pigs, a last great roar from the ox. Familiar wild heads flared in our night windows; the villagers encircled us. Some of the faces stopped to peer at us, their eyes rushing like searchlights. The hands flattened against the panes, framed heads, and left red prints.

"The villagers broke in the front and the back doors at the same time, even though we had not locked the doors against them. Their knives dripped with the blood of our animals. They smeared blood on the doors and walls. One woman swung a chicken, whose throat she had slit, splattering blood in red arcs about her. We stood together in the middle of our house, in the family hall with the pictures and tables of the ancestors around us, and looked straight ahead.

"At that time the house had only two wings. When the men came back, we would build two more to enclose our courtyard and a third one to begin a second courtyard. The villagers pushed through both wings, even your grandparents' rooms, to find your aunt's, which was also mine until the men returned. From this room a new wing for one of the younger families would grow. They ripped up her clothes and shoes and broke her combs, grinding them underfoot. They tore her work from the loom. They scattered the cooking fire and rolled the new weaving in it. We could hear them in the kitchen breaking our bowls and banging the pots. They overturned the great waist-high earthenware jugs; duck eggs, pickled fruits, vegetables burst out and mixed in acrid torrents. The old woman from the next field swept a broom through the air and loosed the spirits-of-the-broom over our heads. 'Pig,' 'Ghost,' 'Pig,' they sobbed and scolded while they ruined our house.

"When they left, they took sugar and oranges to bless themselves. They cut pieces from the dead animals. Some of them took bowls that were not broken and clothes that were not torn. Afterward we swept up the rice and sewed it back up into sacks. But the smells from the spilled preserves lasted. Your aunt gave birth in the pigsty that night. The next morning when I went for the water, I found her and the baby plugging up the family well.

"Don't let your father know that I told you. He denies her. Now that you have started to menstruate, what happened to her could happen to you. Don't humiliate us. You wouldn't like to be forgotten as if you had never been born. The villagers are watchful."

Whenever she had to warn us about life, my mother told stories that ran like this one, a story to grow up on. She tested our strength to establish realities. Those in the emigrant generations who could not reassert brute survival died young and far from home. Those of us in the first American generations have had to figure out how the invisible world the emigrants built around our childhoods fits in solid America.

The immigrants confused the gods by diverting their curses, misleading them with crooked streets and false names. They must try to confuse their

---

1. Embankments built to enclose rice paddies and control the flow of irrigation water.

offspring as well, who, I suppose, threaten them in similar ways—always trying to get things straight, always trying to name the unspeakable. The Chinese I know hide their names; sojourners take new names when their lives change and guard their real names with silence.

Chinese-Americans, when you try to understand what things in you are Chinese, how do you separate what is peculiar to childhood, to poverty, insanities, one family, your mother who marked your growing with stories, from what is Chinese? What is Chinese tradition and what is the movies?

If I want to learn what clothes my aunt wore, whether flashy or ordinary, I would have to begin. "Remember Father's drowned-in-the-well sister?" I cannot ask that. My mother has told me once and for all the useful parts. She will add nothing unless powered by Necessity, a riverbank that guides her life. She plants vegetable gardens rather than lawns, she carries the odd-shaped tomatoes home from the fields and eats food left for the gods.

Whenever we did frivolous things, we used up energy, we flew high kites. We children came up off the ground over the melting cones our parents brought home from work and the American movie on New Year's Day—*Oh, You Beautiful Doll* with Betty Grable one year, and *She Wore a Yellow Ribbon* with John Wayne another year. After the one carnival ride each, we paid in guilt; our tired father counted his change on the dark walk home.

Adultery is extravagance. Could people who hatch their own chicks and eat the embryos and the heads for delicacies and boil the feet in vinegar for party food, leaving only the gravel, eating even the gizzard lining—could such people engender a prodigal aunt? To be a woman, to have a daughter in starvation time was a waste enough. My aunt could not have been the lone romantic who gave up everything for sex. Women in the old China did not choose. Some man had commanded her to lie with him and be his secret evil. I wonder whether he masked himself when he joined the raid on her family.

Perhaps she had encountered him in the fields or on the mountain where the daughters-in-law collected fuel. Or perhaps he first noticed her in the marketplace. He was not a stranger because the village housed no strangers. She had to have dealings with him other than sex. Perhaps he worked an adjoining field, or he sold her the cloth for the dress she sewed and wore. His demand must have surprised, then terrified her. She obeyed him; she always did as she was told.

When the family found a young man in the next village to be her husband, she had stood tractably beside the best rooster, his proxy,[2] and promised before they met that she would be his forever. She was lucky that he was her age and she would be the first wife, an advantage secure now. The night she first saw him, he had sex with her. Then he left for America. She had almost forgotten what he looked like. When she tried to envision him, she only saw the black and white face in the group photograph the men had had taken before leaving.

The other man was not, after all, much different from her husband. They both gave orders: she followed. "If you tell your family, I'll beat you. I'll kill you. Be here again next week." No one talked sex, ever. And she might have separated the rapes from the rest of living if only she did not have to buy

---

2. Someone or something that has the power to substitute or act for another.

her oil from him or gather wood in the same forest. I want her fear to have lasted just as long as rape lasted so that the fear could have been contained. No drawnout fear. But women at sex hazarded birth and hence lifetimes. The fear did not stop but permeated everywhere. She told the man, "I think I'm pregnant." He organized the raid against her.

On nights when my mother and father talked about their life back home, sometimes they mentioned an "outcast table" whose business they still seemed to be settling, their voices tight. In a commensal tradition,[3] where food is precious, the powerful older people made wrongdoers eat alone. Instead of letting them start separate new lives like the Japanese, who could become samurais and geishas,[4] the Chinese family, faces averted but eyes glowering sideways, hung on to the offenders and fed them leftovers. My aunt must have lived in the same house as my parents and eaten at an outcast table. My mother spoke about the raid as if she had seen it, when she and my aunt, a daughter-in-law to a different household, should not have been living together at all. Daughters-in-law lived with their husbands' parents, not their own; a synonym for marriage in Chinese is "taking a daughter-in-law." Her husband's parents could have sold her, mortgaged her, stoned her. But they had sent her back to her own mother and father, a mysterious act hinting at disgraces not told me. Perhaps they had thrown her out to deflect the avengers.

She was the only daughter; her four brothers went with her father, husband, and uncles "out on the road" and for some years became western men. When the goods were divided among the family, three of the brothers took land, and the youngest, my father, chose an education. After my grandparents gave their daughter away to her husband's family, they had dispensed all the adventure and all the property. They expected her alone to keep the traditional ways, which her brothers, now among the barbarians, could fumble without detection. The heavy, deep-rooted women were to maintain the past against the flood, safe for returning. But the rare urge west had fixed upon our family, and so my aunt crossed boundaries not delineated in space.

The work of preservation demands that the feelings playing about in one's guts not be turned into action. Just watch their passing like cherry blossoms. But perhaps my aunt, my forerunner, caught in a slow life, let dreams grow and fade and after some months or years went toward what persisted. Fear at the enormities of the forbidden kept her desires delicate, wire and bone. She looked at a man because she liked the way the hair was tucked behind his ears, or she liked the question-mark line of a long torso curving at the shoulder and straight at the hip. For warm eyes or a soft voice or a slow walk— that's all—a few hairs, a line, a brightness, a sound, a pace, she gave up family. She offered us up for a charm that vanished with tiredness, a pigtail that didn't toss when the wind died. Why, the wrong lighting could erase the dearest thing about him.

It could very well have been, however, that my aunt did not take subtle enjoyment of her friend, but, a wild woman, kept rollicking company. Imagining her free with sex doesn't fit, though. I don't know any women like that, or men either. Unless I see her life branching into mine, she gives me no ancestral help.

---

3. A tradition in which people eat together at the same table.

4. In Japanese society, women trained to entertain men. "Samurai": the Japanese warrior elite.

To sustain her being in love, she often worked at herself in the mirror, guessing at the colors and shapes that would interest him, changing them frequently in order to hit on the right combination. She wanted him to look back.

On a farm near the sea, a woman who tended her appearance reaped a reputation for eccentricity. All the married women blunt-cut their hair in flaps about their ears or pulled it back in tight buns. No nonsense. Neither style blew easily into heart-catching tangles. And at their weddings they displayed themselves in their long hair for the last time. "It brushed the backs of my knees," my mother tells me. "It was braided, and even so, it brushed the backs of my knees."

At the mirror my aunt combed individuality into her bob. A bun could have been contrived to escape into black streamers blowing in the wind or in quiet wisps about her face, but only the older women in our picture album wear buns. She brushed her hair back from her forehead, tucking the flaps behind her ears. She looped a piece of thread, knotted into a circle between her index fingers and thumbs, and ran the double strand across her forehead. When she closed her fingers as if she were making a pair of shadow geese bite, the string twisted together catching the little hairs. Then she pulled the thread away from her skin, ripping the hair out neatly, her eyes watering from the needles of pain. Opening her fingers, she cleaned the thread, then rolled it along her hairline and the tops of her eyebrows. My mother did the same to me and my sisters and herself. I used to believe that the expression "caught by the short hairs" meant a captive held with a depilatory string. It especially hurt at the temples, but my mother said we were lucky we didn't have to have our feet bound when we were seven. Sisters used to sit on their beds and cry together, she said, as their mothers or their slave removed the bandages for a few minutes each night and let the blood gush back into their veins. I hope that the man my aunt loved appreciated a smooth brow, that he wasn't just a tits-and-ass man.

Once my aunt found a freckle on her chin, at a spot that the almanac said predestined her for unhappiness. She dug it out with a hot needle and washed the wound with peroxide.

More attention to her looks than these pullings of hairs and pickings at spots would have caused gossip among the villagers. They owned work clothes and good clothes, and they wore good clothes for feasting the new seasons. But since a woman combing her hair hexes beginnings, my aunt rarely found an occasion to look her best. Women looked like great sea snails—the corded wood, babies, and laundry they carried were the whorls on their backs. The Chinese did not admire a bent back; goddesses and warriors stood straight. Still there must have been a marvelous freeing of beauty when a worker laid down her burden and stretched and arched.

Such commonplace loveliness, however, was not enough for my aunt. She dreamed of a lover for the fifteen days of New Year's, the time for families to exchange visits, money, and food. She plied her secret comb. And sure enough she cursed the year, the family, the village, and herself.

Even as her hair lured her imminent lover, many other men looked at her. Uncles, cousins, nephews, brothers would have looked, too, had they been home between journeys. Perhaps they had already been restraining their curiosity, and they left, fearful that their glances, like a field of nesting birds, might be startled and caught. Poverty hurt, and that was their first reason for leaving. But another, final reason for leaving the crowded house was the never-said.

She may have been unusually beloved, the precious only daughter, spoiled and mirror gazing because of the affection the family lavished on her. When her husband left, they welcomed the chance to take her back from the in-laws; she could live like the little daughter for just a while longer. There are stories that my grandfather was different from other people, "crazy ever since the little Jap bayoneted him in the head." He used to put his naked penis on the dinner table, laughing. And one day he brought home a baby girl, wrapped up inside his brown western-style greatcoat.[5] He had traded one of his sons, probably my father, the youngest, for her. My grandmother made him trade back. When he finally got a daughter of his own, he doted on her. They must have all loved her, except perhaps my father, the only brother who never went back to China, having once been traded for a girl.

Brothers and sisters, newly men and women, had to efface their sexual color and present plain miens. Disturbing hair and eyes, a smile like no other, threatened the ideal of five generations living under one roof. To focus blurs, people shouted face to face and yelled from room to room. The immigrants I know have loud voices, unmodulated to American tones even after years away from the village where they called their friendships out across the fields. I have not been able to stop my mother's screams in public libraries or over telephones. Walking erect (knees straight, toes pointed forward, not pigeon-toed, which is Chinese-feminine) and speaking in an inaudible voice, I have tried to turn myself American-feminine. Chinese communication was loud, public. Only sick people had to whisper. But at the dinner table, where the family members came nearest one another, no one could talk, not the outcasts nor any eaters. Every word that falls from the mouth is a coin lost. Silently they gave and accepted food with both hands. A preoccupied child who took his bowl with one hand got a sideways glare. A complete moment of total attention is due everyone alike. Children and lovers have no singularity here, but my aunt used a secret voice, a separate attentiveness.

She kept the man's name to herself throughout her labor and dying; she did not accuse him that he be punished with her. To save her inseminator's name she gave silent birth.

He may have been somebody in her own household, but intercourse with a man outside the family would have been no less abhorrent. All the village were kinsmen, and the titles shouted in loud country voices never let kinship be forgotten. Any man within visiting distance would have been neutralized as a lover—"brother," "younger brother," "older brother"—one hundred and fifteen relationship titles. Parents researched birth charts probably not so much to assure good fortune as to circumvent incest in a population that has but one hundred surnames. Everybody has eight million relatives. How useless then sexual mannerisms, how dangerous.

As if it came from an atavism[6] deeper than fear, I used to add "brother" silently to boys' names. It hexed the boys, who would or would not ask me to dance, and made them less scary and as familiar and deserving of benevolence as girls.

---

5. A heavy overcoat.
6. A trait with origins further back than the preceding generation; a throwback.

But, of course, I hexed myself also—no dates. I should have stood up, both arms waving, and shouted out across libraries, "Hey, you! Love me back." I had no idea, though, how to make attraction selective, how to control its direction and magnitude. If I made myself American-pretty so that the five or six Chinese boys in the class fell in love with me, everyone else—the Caucasian, Negro, and Japanese boys—would too. Sisterliness, dignified and honorable, made much more sense.

Attraction eludes control so stubbornly that whole societies designed to organize relationships among people cannot keep order, not even when they bind people to one another from childhood and raise them together. Among the very poor and the wealthy, brothers married their adopted sisters, like doves. Our family allowed some romance, paying adult brides' prices and providing dowries so that their sons and daughters could marry strangers. Marriage promises to turn strangers into friendly relatives—a nation of siblings.

In the village structure, spirits shimmered among the live creatures, balanced and held in equilibrium by time and land. But one human being flaring up into violence could open up a black hole; a maelstrom[7] that pulled in the sky. The frightened villagers, who depended on one another to maintain the real, went to my aunt to show her a personal, physical representation of the break she had made in the "roundness." Misallying couples snapped off the future, which was to be embodied in true offspring. The villagers punished her for acting as if she could have a private life, secret and apart from them.

If my aunt had betrayed the family at a time of large grain yields and peace, when many boys were born, and wings were being built on many houses, perhaps she might have escaped such severe punishment. But the men— hungry, greedy, tired of planting in dry soil—had been forced to leave the village in order to send food-money home. There were ghost plagues, bandit plagues, wars with the Japanese, floods. My Chinese brother and sister had died of an unknown sickness. Adultery, perhaps only a mistake during good times, became a crime when the village needed food.

The round moon cakes and round doorways, the round tables of graduated size that fit one roundness inside another, round windows and rice bowls—these talismans had lost their power to warn this family of the law: a family must be whole, faithfully keeping the descent line by having sons to feed the old and the dead, who in turn look after the family. The villagers came to show my aunt and her lover in hiding a broken house. The villagers were speeding up the circling of events because she was too shortsighted to see that her infidelity had already harmed the village, that waves of consequences would return unpredictably, sometimes in disguise, as now, to hurt her. This roundness had to be made coin-sized so that she would see its circumference: punish her at the birth of her baby. Awaken her to the inexorable. People who refused fatalism because they could invent small resources insisted on culpability. Deny accidents and wrest fault from the stars.

After the villagers left, their lanterns now scattering in various directions toward home, the family broke their silence and cursed her. "Aiaa, we're going to die. Death is coming. Death is coming. Look what you've done.

---

7. A powerful, violent whirlpool.

You've killed us. Ghost! Dead ghost! Ghost! You've never been born." She ran out into the fields, far enough from the house so that she could no longer hear their voices, and pressed herself against the earth, her own land no more. When she felt the birth coming, she thought that she had been hurt. Her body seized together. "They've hurt me too much," she thought. "This is gall, and it will kill me." With forehead and knees against the earth, her body convulsed and then relaxed. She turned on her back, lay on the ground. The black well of sky and stars went out and out and out forever; her body and her complexity seemed to disappear. She was one of the stars, a bright dot in blackness, without home, without a companion, in eternal cold and silence. An agoraphobia[8] rose in her, speeding higher and higher, bigger and bigger; she would not be able to contain it; there would be no end to fear.

Flayed, unprotected against space, she felt pain return, focusing her body. This pain chilled her—a cold, steady kind of surface pain. Inside, spasmodically, the other pain, the pain of the child, heated her. For hours she lay on the ground, alternately body and space. Sometimes a vision of normal comfort obliterated reality: she saw the family in the evening gambling at the dinner table, the young people massaging their elder's backs. She saw them congratulating one another, high joy on the mornings the rice shoots came up. When these pictures burst, the stars drew yet further apart. Black space opened.

She got to her feet to fight better and remembered that old-fashioned women gave birth in their pigsties to fool the jealous, pain-dealing gods, who do not snatch piglets. Before the next spasms could stop her, she ran to the pigsty, each step a rushing out into emptiness. She climbed over the fence and knelt in the dirt. It was good to have a fence enclosing her, a tribal person alone.

Laboring, this woman who had carried her child as a foreign growth that sickened her every day, expelled it at last. She reached down to touch the hot, wet, moving mass, surely smaller than anything human, and could feel that it was human after all—fingers, toes, nails, nose. She pulled it up on to her belly, and it lay curled there, but in the air, feet precisely tucked one under the other. She opened her loose shirt and buttoned the child inside. After resting, it squirmed and thrashed and she pushed it up to her breast. It turned its head this way and that until it found her nipple. There, it made little snuffling noises. She clenched her teeth at its preciousness, lovely as a young calf, a piglet, a little dog.

She may have gone to the pigsty as a last act of responsibility: she would protect this child as she had protected its father. It would look after her soul, leaving supplies on her grave. But how would this tiny child without family find her grave when there would be no marker for her anywhere, neither in the earth nor the family hall? No one would give her a family hall name. She had taken the child with her into the wastes. At its birth the two of them had felt the same raw pain of separation, a wound that only the family pressing tight could close. A child with no descent line would not soften her life but only trail after her, ghostlike, begging her to give it purpose. At dawn the villagers on their way to the fields would stand around the fence and look.

---

8. An abnormal fear of open space.

Full of milk, the little ghost slept. When it awoke, she hardened her breasts against the milk that crying loosens. Toward morning she picked up the baby and walked to the well.

Carrying the baby to the well shows loving. Otherwise abandon it. Turn its face into the mud. Mothers who love their children take them along. It was probably a girl; there is some hope of forgiveness for boys.

"Don't tell anyone you had an aunt. Your father does not want to hear her name. She has never been born." I have believed that sex was unspeakable and words so strong and fathers so frail that "aunt" would do my father mysterious harm. I have thought that my family, having settled among immigrants who had also been their neighbors in the ancestral land, needed to clean their name, and a wrong word would incite the kinspeople even here. But there is more to this silence: they want me to participate in her punishment. And I have.

In the twenty years since I heard this story I have not asked for details nor said my aunt's name; I do not know it. People who can comfort the dead can also chase after them to hurt them further—a reverse ancestor worship. The real punishment was not the raid swiftly inflicted by the villagers, but the family's deliberately forgetting her. Her betrayal so maddened them, they saw to it that she would suffer forever, even after death. Always hungry, always needing, she would have to beg food from other ghosts, snatch and steal it from those whose living descendants give them gifts. She would have to fight the ghosts massed at crossroads for the buns a few thoughtful citizens leave to decoy her away from village and home so that the ancestral spirits could feast unharassed. At peace, they could act like gods, not ghosts, their descent lines providing them with paper suits and dresses, spirit money, paper houses, paper automobiles, chicken, meat, and rice[9] into eternity—essences delivered up in smoke and flames, steam and incense rising from each rice bowl. In an attempt to make the Chinese care for people outside the family, Chairman Mao[1] encourages us now to give our paper replicas to the spirits of outstanding soldiers and workers, no matter whose ancestors they may be. My aunt remains forever hungry. Goods are not distributed evenly among the dead.

My aunt haunts me—her ghost drawn to me because now, after fifty years of neglect, I alone devote pages of paper to her, though not origamied into houses and clothes. I do not think she always means me well. I am telling on her, and she was a spite suicide, drowning herself in the drinking water. The Chinese are always very frightened of the drowned one, whose weeping ghost, wet hair hanging and skin bloated, waits silently by the water to pull down a substitute.

1976

---

9. Traditionally, offerings left at the graves of ancestors.

1. Mao Zedong (1893–1976), head of the Chi-

nese Communist Party and leader of China from 1949 to 1976.

BILLY COLLINS

b. 1941

The voice in a Billy Collins poem is so intimate and immediate that we feel we are in the same room with the poet. Collins imagines poet and reader sitting together at a breakfast table: "I will lean forward, / elbows on the table, / with something to tell you / and you will look up, as always, / your spoon dripping with milk, ready to listen" ("A Portrait of the Reader with a Bowl of Cereal"). The colloquial voice in his poems charms us with its air of spontaneous expression, its modesty, its humor. If some of his poems coast on charm alone, Collins's best work takes us on a surprising ride: its strange and unexpected associations deepen the familiar into the mysterious or make the mysterious familiar.

Describing the structures of his poetry, Collins says, "We are attempting, all the time, to create a logical, rational path through the day. To the left and right there are an amazing set of distractions that we can't afford to follow. But the poet is willing to stop anywhere." His poems often proceed as accounts of a day and its distractions, as in "Tuesday, June 4, 1991." At the same time the formal shapeliness of Collins's work endows ordinary activity with a strange and pleasing formality and turns it, line by measured line and stanza by stanza, into a ritual including both the pleasures and the pathos of life. These poems present a humorous self-awareness about the speaker's dramatizing and obsessive love of distraction—anything, no matter how insignificant, can carry off his attention—and one thing that is so welcome about Collins's poems is that they are funny. Only on later readings do we realize that they are also sad. When he looks over the edges of domestic life there is blankness; unlike the work of a Jorie Graham or a Charles Wright, a Collins poem evokes no metaphysical structures that might sustain this fragile world. Yet (in the Irish poet William Butler Yeats's phrase) Collins loves "what vanishes"—the day in June, the good meal, even one's memories. This knowledge of how things large and small disappear is a great equalizer. The humor in Collins's poetry puts this equalizing principle to work; he deflates the grandiose and subjects large statements of truth to the test of the particular. Collins's titles, imaginative and playful, suggest the way he alights on small, usually trivial instances in which life's strangeness and mystery flash out: "Weighing the Dog," "I Chop Some Parsley While Listening to Art Blakey's Version of 'Three Blind Mice.'" Other titles signal the way he grounds the improbable within the everyday: "Taking Off Emily Dickinson's Clothes," "Shoveling Snow with Buddha."

Collins's collections of poems include *Questions about Angels* (1977), *The Art of Drowning* (1995), *Picnic, Lightning* (1998), *Sailing Alone Around the World: New and Selected Poems* (2001), *Nine Horses* (2003), *The Trouble with Poetry and Other Poems* (2005), *Ballistics* (2008), and *Horoscopes for the Dead* (2011). He served as poet laureate of the United States from 2001 to 2003. Born in New York City (in a hospital where, as he likes to note, William Carlos Williams worked as a pediatric resident), Collins teaches at Lehman College of the City University. Walking the city streets animates him and inflects some of his poems in a way that recalls the work of Frank O'Hara, with whom Collins shares an idiomatic American voice, colloquial and understated, shaped by jazz and the blues. Collins's work often plays with the melody of a pentameter line as a jazz musician plays on and off the melody of a song; the pentameter is an undertone from which a more idiosyncratic rhythm moves around and away. While the rhythms of Collins's poetry often enforce a slowing-down, a tender lingering over everyday life, their breezy tone and quick humor seem to suggest that nothing too serious is going on. It is as if Collins were fending off the large, prophetic claims made by visionary poets (early in his career he earned a Ph.D. at the University of California at Riverside, specializing in the Romantic period), even as some of his poems are riffs on the Romantic tradition. Such Collins poems as "Keats's Handwriting" and "Lines Composed Over Three Thousand Miles from Tintern Abbey" deflate the romantic sublime and substitute for it a vision self-deprecating and humorous. Thus when we hear nightingales in a Collins poem, they're a group singing on the gospel radio station ("Sunday Morning with the Sensational Nightingales").

Collins's modest claims for poetry and the fact that his work is so appealing and accessible can lead us to underestimate the necessity and reward of rereading him. The best of his poems open up a moment like a series of nested boxes; if we read too quickly, we miss the pleasure and surprise of intricate connections and deepening discoveries. A Collins poem has a spontaneity that yields immediate pleasure, but only when we listen again more attentively do we recognize the art that makes itself look easy.

Forgetfulness

The name of the author is the first to go
followed obediently by the title, the plot,
the heartbreaking conclusion, the entire novel
which suddenly becomes one you have never read, never even heard of,

as if, one by one, the memories you used to harbor   5
decided to retire to the southern hemisphere of the brain,
to a little fishing village where there are no phones.

Long ago you kissed the names of the nine Muses goodbye,
and watched the quadratic equation pack its bag,
and even now as you memorize the order of the planets,   10

something else is slipping away, a state flower perhaps,
the address of an uncle, the capital of Paraguay.

Whatever it is you are struggling to remember
it is not poised on the tip of your tongue,
not even lurking in some obscure corner of your spleen.   15

It has floated away down a dark mythological river
whose name begins with an *L* as far as you can recall,
well on your own way to oblivion where you will join those
who have even forgotten how to swim and how to ride a bicycle.

No wonder you rise in the middle of the night   20
to look up the date of a famous battle in a book on war.
No wonder the moon in the window seems to have drifted
out of a love poem that you used to know by heart.

1991

Art Blakey on the drums.

I Chop Some Parsley While Listening to Art Blakey's[1] Version of "Three Blind Mice"

And I start wondering how they came to be blind.
If it was congenital, they could be brothers and sisters,
and I think of the poor mother
brooding over her sightless young triplets.

Or was it a common accident, all three caught   5
in a searing explosion, a fireworks perhaps?
If not,
if each came to his or her blindness separately,

how did they ever manage to find one another?
Would it not be difficult for a blind mouse   10
to locate even one fellow mouse with vision
let alone two other blind ones?

And how, in their tiny darkness,
could they possibly have run after a farmer's wife
or anyone else's wife for that matter?   15
Not to mention why.

---

1. Jazz drummer and bandleader (1919–1990).

Just so she could cut off their tails
with a carving knife, is the cynic's answer,
but the thought of them without eyes
and now without tails to trail through the moist grass   20

or slip around the corner of a baseboard
has the cynic who always lounges within me
up off his couch and at the window
trying to hide the rising softness that he feels.

By now I am on to dicing an onion   25
which might account for the wet stinging
in my own eyes, though Freddie Hubbard's
mournful trumpet on "Blue Moon,"

which happens to be the next cut,[2]
cannot be said to be making matters any better.   30

1998

The Night House

Every day the body works in the fields of the world
mending a stone wall
or swinging a sickle through the tall grass—
the grass of civics, the grass of money—
and every night the body curls around itself   5
and listens for the soft bells of sleep.

But the heart is restless and rises
from the body in the middle of the night,
leaves the trapezoidal bedroom
with its thick, pictureless walls   10
to sit by herself at the kitchen table
and heat some milk in a pan.

And the mind gets up too, puts on a robe
and goes downstairs, lights a cigarette,
and opens a book on engineering.   15
Even the conscience awakens
and roams from room to room in the dark,
darting away from every mirror like a strange fish.

And the soul is up on the roof
in her nightdress, straddling the ridge,   20
singing a song about the wildness of the sea
until the first rip of pink appears in the sky.
Then, they all will return to the sleeping body
the way a flock of birds settles back into a tree,

2. The next song on *Three Blind Mice, Vol. 1*, a 1962 live recording by Art Blakey's Jazz Messengers, which included Freddie Hubbard (1938–2008).

resuming their daily colloquy,   25
talking to each other or themselves
even through the heat of the long afternoons.
Which is why the body—that house of voices—
sometimes puts down its metal tongs, its needle, or its pen
to stare into the distance,   30

to listen to all its names being called
before bending again to its labor.

1998

GLORIA ANZALDÚA
1942–2004

The term "Chicano" was originally pejorative, used on both sides of the border to identify Mexican Americans of the lowest social class. Just as the once demeaning label "black" was appropriated and revalued by African Americans during the civil rights, black power, and black arts movements of the 1960s, so "Chicano" was embraced by Hispanic activists as a badge of pride, especially among university students and farm workers. By 1987, when the first edition of Gloria Anzaldúa's *Borderlands / La Frontera: The New Mestiza* appeared, two more politically sensitive terms had been added to the sociocultural lexicon: "Chicana," specifically identifying Mexican American women, particularly in light of their announced aims and the general interests of the Chicano movement, and "mestiza," describing Chicana women who are especially concerned with a heritage that is both Chicana and Native American. Together with Cherríe Moraga, her coeditor on *This Bridge Called My Back: Writings by Radical Women of Color* (1981), Anzaldúa emerged as a pioneer in both the writing and the study of Chicana literature.

The daughter of ranchers in Jesus Maria of the Valley, Texas, Anzaldúa labored as a migrant fieldworker before earning a B.A. from Pan American University (1969) and an M.A. from the University of Texas at Austin (1973); she did further graduate study at the University of California at Santa Cruz. She taught creative writing, Chicano studies, and feminist studies at major universities from Texas to California. She published the novel *La Prieta* (Spanish for "the dark one," 1997), other anthologies, and a series of children's books, the most notable of which—*Prietita and the Ghost Woman / Prietita y La Llorona* (1996)—introduces young readers to an important figure in Chicana culture.

La Llorona is one of the three principal representations of women in Mexican culture: *La Virgen de Guadalupe*, a vision of the Virgin Mary who appeared to an Indian, Juan Diego, in 1531 on a hillside outside Mexico City that was sacred to the worship of Tonantzín, the Indian "Mother of Heaven"; *La Chingada*, incorrectly translated as "The Raped One" but whom Anzaldúa insists be accurately identified as "The Fucked One," the deposed Aztec princess (also known as La Malinche, Doña Marina, and Malintzín Tenepal) who served the Spanish military leader Hernan Cortés as translator and lover during his consolidation of colonial power between 1519 and 1522; and *La Llorona*, "The Woman Who Cries," a spurned mistress of Mexican legend who drowned her children and was fated to eternally seek their recovery. Each of these representations metaphorically controls a narrow realm of possibility for Chicanas. At the core of Anzaldúa's work is the belief that because metaphors structure the way we think, the metaphorical influences of these types of women must be reshaped so that Chicanas can escape the binary constraint of being judged as either a virgin or a whore (and nothing else). *Borderlands/La Frontera* is Anzaldúa's most comprehensive effort toward that restructuring.

Although written mainly in English, the personal essay printed here reflects another key part of Anzaldúa's art: not only did she wish to write in Spanish from time to time but she did not always translate that Spanish into English. When she did not provide such a translation in a piece that is primarily in English, she wanted to speak directly to those who either could not or chose not to communicate in English. This practice, much like her blending of fiction, poetry, social commentary, and personal memoir, helps create the narrative richness that characterizes her work.

The following text is from the second edition of *Borderlands/La Frontera* (1999).

How to Tame a Wild Tongue

"We're going to have to control your tongue," the dentist says, pulling out all the metal from my mouth. Silver bits plop and tinkle into the basin. My mouth is a motherlode.

The dentist is cleaning out my roots. I get a whiff of the-stench when I gasp. "I can't cap that tooth yet, you're still draining," he says.

"We're going to have to do something about your tongue," I hear the anger rising in his voice. My tongue keeps pushing out the wads of cotton, pushing back the drills, the long thin needles. "I've never seen anything as strong or as stubborn," he says. And I think, how do you tame a wild tongue, train it to be quiet, how do you bridle and saddle it? How do you make it lie down?

> "Who is to say that robbing a people of
> its language is less violent than war?"
> —Ray Gwyn Smith[1]

I remember being caught speaking Spanish at recess—that was good for three licks on the knuckles with a sharp ruler. I remember being sent to the corner of the classroom for "talking back" to the Anglo teacher when all I was trying to do was tell her how to pronounce my name. "If you want to be American, speak 'American.' If you don't like it, go back to Mexico where you belong."

"I want you to speak English. *Pa'hallar buen trabajo tienes que saber hablar el inglés bien. Qué vale toda tu educación si todavía hablas inglés con un* 'accent,'" my mother would say, mortified that I spoke English like a Mexican. At Pan American University, I, and all Chicano students were required to take two speech classes. Their purpose: to get rid of our accents.

---

1. Ray Gwyn Smith [(b. 1944), Welsh painter and art educator active in the United States], *Moorland Is Cold Country*, unpublished book [Anzaldúa's note].

Attacks on one's form of expression with the intent to censor are a violation of the First Amendment. *El Anglo con cara de inocente nos arrancó la lengua.* Wild tongues can't be tamed, they can only be cut out.

Overcoming the Tradition of Silence

Ahogadas, escupimos el oscuro.
Peleando con nuestra propia sombra
el silencio nos sepulta.

En boca cerrada no entran moscas. "Flies don't enter a closed mouth" is a saying I kept hearing when I was a child. *Ser habladora* was to be a gossip and a liar, to talk too much. *Muchachitas bien criadas*, well-bred girls don't answer back. *Es una falta de respeto* to talk back to one's mother or father. I remember one of the sins I'd recite to the priest in the confession box the few times I went to confession: talking back to my mother, *hablar pa' 'trás, repelar. Hocicona, repelona, chismosa*, having a big mouth, questioning, carrying tales are all signs of being *mal criada*. In my culture they are all words that are derogatory if applied to women—I've never heard them applied to men.

The first time I heard two women, a Puerto Rican and a Cuban, say the word *"nosotras,"* I was shocked. I had not known the word existed. Chicanas use *nosotros* whether we're male or female. We are robbed of our female being by the masculine plural. Language is a male discourse.

> And our tongues have become
> dry   the wilderness has
> dried out our tongues   and
> we have forgotten speech.
> —Irena Klepfisz[2]

Even our own people, other Spanish speakers *nos quieren poner candados en la boca.* They would hold us back with their bag of *reglas de academia.*

Oyé como ladra: el lenguaje de la frontera

> *Quien tiene boca se equivoca.*
> —Mexican saying

"*Pocho*,[3] cultural traitor, you're speaking the oppressor's language by speaking English, you're ruining the Spanish language," I have been accused by various Latinos and Latinas. Chicano Spanish is considered by the purist and by most Latinos deficient, a mutilation of Spanish.

But Chicano Spanish is a border tongue which developed naturally. Change, *evolución, enriquecimiento de palabras nuevas por invención o adopción* have created variants of Chicano Spanish, *un nuevo lenguaje. Un lenguaje que corresponde a un modo de vivir.* Chicano Spanish is not incorrect, it is a living language.

---

2. Irena Klepfisz [(b. 1941), North American critic], "*Di rayze aheym / The Journey Home,*" in *The Tribe of Dina: A Jewish Women's Anthology*, Melanie Kaye/Kantrowitz and Irena Klepfisz, eds. (Montpelier, VT: Sinister Wisdom Books, 1986), 49 [Anzaldúa's note].

3. An anglicized Mexican or American of Mexican origin who speaks Spanish with an accent characteristic of North Americans and who distorts and reconstructs the language according to the influence of English. Anzaldúa offers a definition later in this selection.

For a people who are neither Spanish nor live in a country in which Spanish is the first language; for a people who live in a country in which English is the reigning tongue but who are not Anglo; for a people who cannot entirely identify with either standard (formal, Castillian) Spanish nor standard English, what recourse is left to them but to create their own language? A language which they can connect their identity to, one capable of communicating the realities and values true to themselves—a language with terms that are neither *español ni inglés*, but both. We speak a patois, a forked tongue, a variation of two languages.

Chicano Spanish sprang out of the Chicanos' need to identify ourselves as a distinct people. We needed a language with which we could communicate with ourselves, a secret language. For some of us, language is a homeland closer than the Southwest—for many Chicanos today live in the Midwest and the East. And because we are a complex, heterogeneous people, we speak many languages. Some of the languages we speak are:

1. Standard English
2. Working class and slang English
3. Standard Spanish
4. Standard Mexican Spanish
5. North Mexican Spanish dialect
6. Chicano Spanish (Texas, New Mexico, Arizona and California have regional variations)
7. Tex-Mex
8. *Pachuco* (called *caló*)

My "home" tongues are the languages I speak with my sister and brothers, with my friends. They are the last five listed, with 6 and 7 being closest to my heart. From school, the media and job situations, I've picked up standard and working class English. From Mamagrande Locha and from reading Spanish and Mexican literature, I've picked up Standard Spanish and Standard Mexican Spanish. From *los recién llegados*, Mexican immigrants, and *braceros*, I learned the North Mexican dialect. With Mexicans I'll try to speak either Standard Mexican Spanish or the North Mexican dialect. From my parents and Chicanos living in the Valley,[4] I picked up Chicano Texas Spanish, and I speak it with my mom; younger brother (who married a Mexican and who rarely mixes Spanish with English), aunts and older relatives.

With Chicanas from *Nuevo México* or *Arizona* I will speak Chicano Spanish a little, but often they don't understand what I'm saying. With most California Chicanas I speak entirely in English (unless I forget). When I first moved to San Francisco, I'd rattle off something in Spanish, unintentionally embarrassing them. Often it is only with another Chicana *tejana* that I can talk freely.

Words distorted by English are known as anglicisms or *pochismos*. The *pocho* is an anglicized Mexican or American of Mexican origin who speaks Spanish with an accent characteristic of North Americans and who distorts and reconstructs the language according to the influence of English.[5] Tex-Mex, or Spanglish, comes most naturally to me. I may switch back and forth

---

4. I.e., of the Rio Grande River in southern Texas, bordering Mexico.
5. R. C. Ortega, *Dialectología Del Barrio*, trans.

Hortencia S. Alwan (Los Angeles, CA: R. C. Ortega Publisher & Bookseller, 1977), 132 [Anzaldúa's note].

from English to Spanish in the same sentence or in the same word. With my sister and my brother Nune and with Chicano *tejano* contemporaries I speak in Tex-Mex.

From kids and people my own age I picked up *Pachuco. Pachuco* (the language of the zoot suiters) is a language of rebellion, both against Standard Spanish and Standard English. It is a secret language. Adults of the culture and outsiders cannot understand it. It is made up of slang words from both English and Spanish. *Ruca* means girl or woman, *vato* means guy or dude, *chale* means no, *simón* means yes, *churo* is sure, talk is *periquiar*, *pigionear* means petting, *que gacho* means how nerdy, *ponte águila* means watch out, death is called *la pelona*. Through lack of practice and not having others who can speak it, I've lost most of the *Pachuco* tongue.

Chicano Spanish

Chicanos, after 250 years of Spanish/Anglo colonization have developed significant differences in the Spanish we speak. We collapse two adjacent vowels into a single syllable and sometimes shift the stress in certain words such as *maíz / maiz, cohete / cuete*. We leave out certain consonants when they appear between vowels: *lado/lao, mojado/mojao*. Chicanos from South Texas pronounced *f* as *j* as in *jue* (*fue*). Chicanos use "archaisms," words that are no longer in the Spanish language, words that have been evolved out. We say *semos, truje, haiga, ansina*, and *naiden*. We retain the "archaic" *j*, as in *jalar*, that derives from an earlier *h*, (the French *halar* or the Germanic *halon* which was lost to standard Spanish in the 16th century), but which is still found in several regional dialects such as the one spoken in South Texas. (Due to geography, Chicanos from the Valley of South Texas were cut off linguistically from other Spanish speakers. We tend to use words that the Spaniards brought over from Medieval Spain. The majority of the Spanish colonizers in Mexico and the Southwest came from Extremadura—Hernán Cortés was one of them—and Andalucía.[6] Andalucians pronounce *ll* like a *y*, and their *d*'s tend to be absorbed by adjacent vowels: *tirado* becomes *tirao*. They brought *el lenguaje popular, dialectos y regionalismos*.)[7]

Chicanos and other Spanish speakers also shift *ll* to *y* and *z* to *s*.[8] We leave out initial syllables, saying *tar* for *estar, toy* for *estoy*; *hora* for *ahora* (*cubanos* and *puertorriqueños* also leave out initial letters of some words.) We also leave out the final syllable such as *pa* for *para*. The intervocalic *y*, the *ll* as in *tortilla, ella, botella*, gets replaced by *tortia* or *tortiya, ea, botea*. We add an additional syllable at the beginning of certain words: *atocar* for *tocar, agastar* for *gastar*. Sometimes we'll say *lavaste las vacijas*, other times *lavates* (substituting the *ates* verb endings for the *aste*).

We use anglicisms, words borrowed from English: *bola* from ball, *carpeta* from carpet, *máchina de lavar* (instead of *lavadora*) from washing machine. Tex-Mex argot, created by adding a Spanish sound at the beginning or end of an English word such as *cookiar* for cook, *watchar* for watch, *parkiar* for

6. Region in southern Spain. Extremadura is a city in central Spain. Cortés (1485–1547), Spanish soldier and explorer who conquered the Aztecs and claimed Mexico for Spain.
7. Eduardo Hernandéz-Chávez, Andrew D. Cohen, and Anthony F. Beltramo, *El Lenguaje de*

los Chicanos: Regional and Social Characteristics of Language Used by Mexican Americans (Arlington, VA: Center for Applied Linguistics, 1975), 39 [Anzaldúa's note].
8. Hernandéz-Chávez, xvii [Anzaldúa's note].

park, and *rapiar* for rape, is the result of the pressures on Spanish speakers to adapt to English.

We don't use the word *vosotros/as* or its accompanying verb form. We don't say *claro* (to mean yes), *imagínate*, or *me emociona*, unless we picked up Spanish from Latinas, out of a book, or in a classroom. Other Spanish-speaking groups are going through the same, or similar, development in their Spanish.

Linguistic Terrorism

Deslenguadas. Somos los del español deficiente. We are your linguistic nightmare, your linguistic aberration, your linguistic *mestizaje*, the subject of your *burla*. Because we speak with tongues of fire we are culturally crucified. Racially, culturally and linguistically *somos huérfanos*—we speak an orphan tongue.

Chicanas who grew up speaking Chicano Spanish have internalized the belief that we speak poor Spanish. It is illegitimate, a bastard language. And because we internalize how our language has been used against us by the dominant culture, we use our language differences against each other.

Chicana feminists often skirt around each other with suspicion and hesitation. For the longest time I couldn't figure it out. Then it dawned on me. To be close to another Chicana is like looking into the mirror. We are afraid of what we'll see there. *Pena.* Shame. Low estimation of self. In childhood we are told that our language is wrong. Repeated attacks on our native tongue diminish our sense of self. The attacks continue throughout our lives.

Chicanas feel uncomfortable talking in Spanish to Latinas, afraid of their censure. Their language was not outlawed in their countries. They had a whole lifetime of being immersed in their native tongue; generations, centuries in which Spanish was a first language, taught in school, heard on radio and TV, and read in the newspaper.

If a person, Chicana or Latina, has a low estimation of my native tongue, she also has a low estimation of me. Often with *mexicanas y latinas* we'll speak English as a neutral language. Even among Chicanas we tend to speak English at parties or conferences. Yet, at the same time, we're afraid the other will think we're *agringadas* because we don't speak Chicano Spanish. We oppress each other trying to out-Chicano each other, vying to be the "real" Chicanas, to speak like Chicanos. There is no one Chicano language just as there is no one Chicano experience. A monolingual Chicana whose first language is English or Spanish is just as much a Chicana as one who speaks several variants of Spanish. A Chicana from Michigan or Chicago or Detroit is just as much a Chicana as one from the Southwest. Chicano Spanish is as diverse linguistically as it is regionally.

By the end of this century, Spanish speakers will comprise the biggest minority group in the U.S., a country where students in high schools and colleges are encouraged to take French classes because French is considered more "cultured." But for a language to remain alive it must be used.[9] By the end of this century English, and not Spanish, will be the mother tongue of most Chicanos and Latinos.

---

9. Irena Klepfisz, "Secular Jewish Identity: Yidishkayt in America," in *The Tribe of Dina*, Kaye/Kantrowitz, eds., 43 [Anzaldúa's note].

So, if you want to really hurt me, talk badly about my language. Ethnic identity is twin skin to linguistic identity—I am my language. Until I can take pride in my language, I cannot take pride in myself. Until I can accept as legitimate Chicano Texas Spanish, Tex-Mex and all the other languages I speak, I cannot accept the legitimacy of myself. Until I am free to write bilingually and to switch codes without having always to translate, while I still have to speak English or Spanish when I would rather speak Spanglish, and as long as I have to accommodate the English speakers rather than having them accommodate me, my tongue will be illegitimate.

I will no longer be made to feel ashamed of existing. I will have my voice: Indian, Spanish, white. I will have my serpent's tongue—my woman's voice, my sexual voice, my poet's voice. I will overcome the tradition of silence.

> My fingers
> move sly against your palm
> Like women everywhere, we speak in code. . . .
>
> —Melanie Kaye/Kantrowitz[1]

"Vistas," corridos, y comida: My Native Tongue

In the 1960s, I read my first Chicano novel. It was *City of Night* by John Rechy[2] a gay Texan, son of a Scottish father and a Mexican mother. For days I walked around in stunned amazement that a Chicano could write and could get published. When I read *I Am Joaquín*[3] I was surprised to see a bilingual book by a Chicano in print. When I saw poetry written in Tex-Mex for the first time, a feeling of pure joy flashed through me. I felt like we really existed as a people. In 1971, when I started teaching High School English to Chicano students, I tried to supplement the required texts with works by Chicanos, only to be reprimanded and forbidden to do so by the principal. He claimed that I was supposed to teach "American" and English literature. At the risk of being fired, I swore my students to secrecy and slipped in Chicano short stories, poems, a play. In graduate school, while working toward a Ph.D., I had to "argue" with one advisor after the other, semester after semester, before I was allowed to make Chicano literature an area of focus.

Even before I read books by Chicanos or Mexicans, it was the Mexican movies I saw at the drive-in—the Thursday night special of $1.00 a carload—that gave me a sense of belonging. "*Vámonos a las vistas,*" my mother would call out and we'd all—grandmother, brothers, sister and cousins—squeeze into the car. We'd wolf down cheese and bologna white bread sandwiches while watching Pedro Infante in melodramatic tear-jerkers like *Nosotros los pobres,*[4] the first "real" Mexican movie (that was not an imitation of European movies). I remember seeing *Cuando los hijos se van*[5] and surmising that all Mexican movies played up the love a mother has for her children and what ungrateful sons and daughters suffer when they are not devoted to their

1. Melanie Kaye/Kantrowitz, "Sign," in *We Speak in Code: Poems and Other Writings* (Pittsburgh, PA: Motheroot Publications, Inc., 1980), 85 [Anzaldúa's note].
2. American novelist (b. 1934). The book was published in 1963.
3. Rodolfo Gonzales [(b. 1928), Chicano novel-

ist], *I Am Joaquín Yo Soy Joaquín* (New York, NY: Bantam Books, 1972). It was first published in 1967 [Anzaldúa's note].
4. A 1947 film. Infante (1917–1957), Mexican film actor and singer.
5. A 1941 film.

mothers. I remember the singing-type "westerns" of Jorge Negrete and Miguel Aceves Mejía.[6] When watching Mexican movies, I felt a sense of homecoming as well as alienation. People who were to amount to something didn't go to Mexican movies, or *bailes* or tune their radios to *bolero, rancherita,* and *corrido* music.

The whole time I was growing up, there was *norteño* music sometimes called North Mexican border music, or Tex-Mex music, or Chicano music, or *cantina* (bar) music. I grew up listening to *conjuntos,* three- or four-piece bands made up of folk musicians playing guitar, *bajo sexto,*[7] drums and button accordion, which Chicanos had borrowed from the German immigrants who had come to Central Texas and Mexico to farm and build breweries. In the Rio Grande Valley, Steve Jordan and Little Joe Hernández were popular, and Flaco Jiménez[8] was the accordion king. The rhythms of Tex-Mex music are those of the polka, also adapted from the Germans, who in turn had borrowed the polka from the Czechs and Bohemians.

I remember the hot, sultry evenings when *corridos*—songs of love and death on the Texas-Mexican borderlands—reverberated out of cheap amplifiers from the local *cantinas* and wafted in through my bedroom window.

Corridos first became widely used along the South Texas / Mexican border during the early conflict between Chicanos and Anglos. The *corridos* are usually about Mexican heroes who do valiant deeds against the Anglo oppressors. Pancho Villa's song, *"La cucaracha,"* is the most famous one. *Corridos* of John F. Kennedy[9] and his death are still very popular in the Valley. Older Chicanos remember Lydia Mendoza,[1] one of the great border *corrido* singers who was called *la Gloria de Tejas.* Her *"El tango negre,"* sung during the Great Depression, made her a singer of the people. The everpresent *corridos* narrated one hundred years of border history, bringing news of events as well as entertaining. These folk musicians and folk songs are our chief cultural mythmakers, and they made our hard lives seem bearable.

I grew up feeling ambivalent about our music. Country-western and rock-and-roll had more status. In the 50s and 60s, for the slightly educated and *agringado* Chicanos, there existed a sense of shame at being caught listening to our music. Yet I couldn't stop my feet from thumping to the music, could not stop humming the words, nor hide from myself the exhilaration I felt when I heard it.

There are more subtle ways that we internalize identification, especially in the forms of images and emotions. For me food and certain smells are tied to my identity, to my homeland. Woodsmoke curling up to an immense blue sky; woodsmoke perfuming my grandmother's clothes, her skin. The stench of cow manure and the yellow patches on the ground; the crack of a .22 rifle and the reek of cordite. Homemade white cheese sizzling in a pan,

6. Mexican singer and film actor (b. 1916). Negrete (1911–1953), Mexican singing actor.
7. Twelve-string guitar tuned one octave lower than normal.
8. Mexican American musicians. Esteban Jordán (1939–2010). José María De Leon Hérnandez (b. 1940), Leonardo "Flaco" Jiménez (b. 1939).

9. Thirty-fifth U.S. president (1917–1963), assassinated in Dallas, Texas. Villa (ca. 1877–1923), born Doroteo Arango, Mexican revolutionary leader.
1. Mexican American singer, songwriter, and musician (b. 1916).

melting inside a folded *tortilla*. My sister Hilda's hot, spicy *menudo*[2] *chile colorado* making it deep red, pieces of *panza* and hominy floating on top. My brother Carito barbecuing *fajitas* in the backyard. Even now and 3,000 miles away, I can see my mother spicing the ground beef, pork and venison with *chile*. My mouth salivates at the thought of the hot steaming *tamales* I would be eating if I were home.

> *Si le preguntas a mi mamá, "¿Qué eres?"*

> "Identity is the essential core of who
> we are as individuals, the conscious
> experience of the self inside."
> —Kaufman[3]

Nosotros los Chicanos straddle the borderlands. On one side of us, we are constantly exposed to the Spanish of the Mexicans, on the other side we hear the Anglos' incessant clamoring so that we forget our language. Among ourselves we don't say *nosotros los americanos, o nosotros los españoles, o nosotros los hispanos*. We say *nosotros los mexicanos* (by *mexicanos* we do not mean citizens of Mexico; we do not mean a national identity, but a racial one). We distinguish between *mexicanos del otro lado* and *mexicanos de este lado*. Deep in our hearts we believe that being Mexican has nothing to do with which country one lives in. Being Mexican is a state of soul—not one of mind, not one of citizenship. Neither eagle nor serpent,[4] but both. And like the ocean, neither animal respects borders.

> *Dime con quien andas y te diré quien eres.*
> (Tell me who your friends are and I'll tell you who
> you are.)
> —Mexican saying

Si le preguntas a mi mamá, "¿Qué eres?" te dirá, "Soy mexicana." My brothers and sister say the same. I sometimes will answer *"soy mexicana"* and at others will say *"soy Chicana" o "soy tejana."* But I identified as *"Raza"* before I ever identified as *"mexicana"* or "Chicana."

As a culture, we call ourselves Spanish when referring to ourselves as a linguistic group and when copping out. It is then that we forget our predominant Indian genes. We are 70 to 80 percent Indian.[5] We call ourselves Hispanic[6] or Spanish-American or Latin American or Latin when linking ourselves to other Spanish-speaking peoples of the Western hemisphere and when copping out. We call ourselves Mexican-American[7] to signify we are neither Mexican nor American, but more the noun "American" than the adjective "Mexican" (and when copping out).

---

2. Mexican soup made of simmered tripe, onion, garlic, chili, and hominy.
3. Gershen Kaufman [(b. 1943), American psychologist], *Shame: The Power of Caring* (Cambridge: Schenkman Books, Inc. 1980), 68. This book was instrumental in my understanding of shame [from Anzaldúa's note].
4. Respectively, male and female cultural figurations.
5. John R. Chávez [(b. 1949), American scholar and educator], *The Lost Land: The Chicano*

Images of the Southwest (Albuquerque, NM: University of New Mexico Press, 1984), 88–90 [from Anzaldúa's note].
6. "Hispanic" is derived from Hispanis (*España*, a name given to the Iberian Peninsula in ancient times when it was a part of the Roman Empire) and is a term designated by the U.S. government to make it easier to handle us on paper [Anzaldúa's note].
7. The Treaty of Guadalupe Hidalgo created the Mexican-American in 1848 [Anzaldúa's note].

Chicanos and other people of color suffer economically for not acculturating. This voluntary (yet forced) alienation makes for psychological conflict, a kind of dual identity—we don't identify with the Anglo-American cultural values and we don't totally identify with the Mexican cultural values. We are a synergy of two cultures with various degrees of Mexicanness or Angloness. I have so internalized the borderland conflict that sometimes I feel like one cancels out the other and we are zero, nothing, no one. *A veces no soy nada ni nadie. Pero hasta cuando no lo soy, lo soy.*

When not copping out, when we know we are more than nothing, we call ourselves Mexican, referring to race and ancestry; *mestizo* when affirming both our Indian and Spanish (but we hardly ever own our Black ancestry); Chicano when referring to a politically aware people born and/or raised in the U.S.; *Raza* when referring to Chicanos; *tejanos* when we are Chicanos from Texas.

Chicanos did not know we were a people until 1965 when Cesar Chavez[8] and the farmworkers united and *I Am Joaquín* was published and *la Raza Unida* party[9] was formed in Texas. With that recognition, we became a distinct people. Something momentous happened to the Chicano soul—we became aware of our reality and acquired a name and a language (Chicano Spanish) that reflected that reality. Now that we had a name, some of the fragmented pieces began to fall together—who we were, what we were, how we had evolved. We began to get glimpses of what we might eventually become.

Yet the struggle of identities continues, the struggle of borders is our reality still. One day the inner struggle will cease and a true integration take place. In the meantime, *tenemos que hacerla lucha. ¿Quién está protegiendo los ranchos de mi gente? ¿Quién está tratando de cerrar la fisura entre la india y el bianco en nuestra sangre? El Chicano, sí, el Chicano que anda como un ladrón en su propia casa.*[1]

Los Chicanos, how patient we seem, how very patient. There is the quiet of the Indian about us. We know how to survive. When other races have given up their tongue, we've kept ours. We know what it is to live under the hammer blow of the dominant *norteamericano* culture. But more than we count the blows, we count the days the weeks the years the centuries the eons until the white laws and commerce and customs will rot in the deserts they've created, lie bleached. *Humildes* yet proud, *quietos* yet wild, *nosotros los mexicanos* Chicanos will walk by the crumbling ashes as we go about our business. Stubborn, persevering, impenetrable as stone, yet possessing a malleability that renders us unbreakable, we, the *mestizas* and *mestizos*, will remain.

1987

---

8. Chicano union organizer (1927–1993).
9. Known in America as the United Farm Workers; founded in 1962.
1. Anglos, in order to alleviate their guilt for dispossessing the Chicano, stressed the Spanish part of us and perpetrated the myth of the Span-
ish Southwest. We have accepted the fiction that we are Hispanic, that is Spanish, in order to accommodate ourselves to the dominant culture and its abhorrence of Indians. Chávez, 88–91 [Anzaldúa's note].

ALICE WALKER

b. 1944

Of the two daughters at odds over family heirlooms in the story "Everyday Use" (printed here), Alice Walker resembles each one. Like the burned Maggie, she spent a childhood even more limited than her family's rural poverty dictated, for as a little girl she was shot in the eye with a BB gun; the disfigurement plagued her until it was corrected during her college years. Like Dee, she was able to attend college—first Spelman College and then Sarah Lawrence College on a scholarship—and acquire urban sophistications from the North. Many of Walker's characters become adept in the new cultural language of Black Arts and black power to which the author contributed as a young writer—and all of them are subjected to the same dismay Dee's mother feels at having to rule against this daughter's wishes. Like the mother, therefore, Walker is given to seeing both sides of a situation; and when it comes to choosing between her characters' opposing positions, she tends to be critical of her own personality first and extremely sparing in her judgment of others.

From her native Eatonton, Georgia, Walker gained an understanding of the rural South. In her essay "Beyond the Peacock," Walker evaluates both the older white writer Flannery O'Connor, who lived in nearby Milledgeville, and the perspectives from which readers see the region and its heritage. Visitors to O'Connor's home, for example, often romanticize the house's handmade bricks; Walker points out that the slaves who made those bricks surely suffered in the process. As the educated child of sharecroppers, Walker can critically reexamine the myths in and around O'Connor's life while doing justice to the complexity of O'Connor's work.

After college Walker returned to the South, first to work in the Civil Rights Movement against segregation and then to teach at Jackson State College in Mississippi. Her first novel, *The Third Life of Grange Copeland* (1970), follows its protagonist through three generations of domestic experience. In *Meridian* (1976) Walker presents fragmentary recollections of the 1960s among characters trying to make sense of their recent past. This novel reflects many of the topics treated in the author's short-story collection, *In Love & Trouble* (1973), in which a range of African American women almost always have unhappy relationships with men. Walker's third novel, *The Color Purple* (1982), makes her strongest narrative statement, formulated from what she calls a "womanist" (as opposed to strictly feminist) perspective. This approach draws on the black folk expression "womanish," which in a mother-to-daughter context signifies a call to adult, mature, responsible (and courageous) behavior. Such behavior benefits women and men and is necessary, Walker argues, for the survival of all African Americans by keeping creativity alive. The plot and the style of *The Color Purple* show how this happens, as the young black woman Celie draws on her sister's letters (written from Africa) for her own letters to God. Though Celie's life by any other terms could be considered disastrous (including rape, incest, and the killing of her babies by her father, and both physical and psychological abuse by her husband), her actions and her ability to express herself give her status as an individual. To everyone who will listen, Celie says: "I am here."

Walker has continued to publish novels, short stories, poetry, and essays. In *The Same River Twice* (1996) she writes about how the filming of *The Color Purple* challenged and changed her life. As a sociocultural critic she has examined the atrocity of female genital mutilation in parts of Africa, also incorporating her conclusions in her novel *Possessing the Secret of Joy* (1992), and as a literary critic she has spoken for a richer and more complete understanding of Zora Neale Hurston, whose employment of folk materials in narrative anticipates Walker's. Throughout her career she has spoken about the need for strength from African American women, and her writing seeks workable models for such strength.

The following text is from *In Love & Trouble* (1973).

Everyday Use

For Your Grandmama

I will wait for her in the yard that Maggie and I made so clean and wavy yesterday afternoon. A yard like this is more comfortable than most people know. It is not just a yard. It is like an extended living room. When the hard clay is swept clean as a floor and the fine sand around the edges lined with tiny, irregular grooves, anyone can come and sit and look up into the elm tree and wait for the breezes that never come inside the house.

Maggie will be nervous until after her sister goes: she will stand hopelessly in corners, homely and ashamed of the burn scars down her arms and legs, eyeing her sister with a mixture of envy and awe. She thinks her sister has held life always in the palm of one hand, that "no" is a word the world never learned to say to her.

You've no doubt seen those TV shows where the child who has "made it" is confronted, as a surprise, by her own mother and father, tottering in weakly from backstage. (A pleasant surprise, of course: What would they do if parent and child came on the show only to curse out and insult each other?) On TV mother and child embrace and smile into each other's faces. Sometimes the mother and father weep, the child wraps them in her arms and leans across the table to tell how she would not have made it without their help. I have seen these programs.

Sometimes I dream a dream in which Dee and I are suddenly brought together on a TV program of this sort. Out of a dark and soft-seated limousine I am ushered into a bright room filled with many people. There I meet a smiling, gray, sporty man like Johnny Carson who shakes my hand and tells me what a fine girl I have. Then we are on the stage and Dee is embracing me with tears in her eyes. She pins on my dress a large orchid, even though she has told me once that she thinks orchids are tacky flowers.

In real life I am a large, big-boned woman with rough, man-working hands. In the winter I wear flannel nightgowns to bed and overalls during the day. I can kill and clean a hog as mercilessly as a man. My fat keeps me hot in zero weather. I can work outside all day, breaking ice to get water for washing; I can eat pork liver cooked over the open fire minutes after it comes steaming from the hog. One winter I knocked a bull calf straight in the brain between the eyes with a sledge hammer and had the meat hung up to chill before nightfall. But of course all this does not show on television. I am the way my daughter would want me to be: a hundred pounds lighter, my skin like an uncooked barley pancake. My hair glistens in the hot bright lights. Johnny Carson has much to do to keep up with my quick and witty tongue.

But that is a mistake. I know even before I wake up. Who ever knew a Johnson with a quick tongue? Who can even imagine me looking a strange white man in the eye? It seems to me I have talked to them always with one foot raised in flight, with my head turned in whichever way is farthest from them. Dee, though. She would always look anyone in the eye. Hesitation was no part of her nature.

"How do I look, Mama?" Maggie says, showing just enough of her thin body enveloped in pink skirt and red blouse for me to know she's there, almost hidden by the door.

"Come out into the yard," I say.

Have you ever seen a lame animal, perhaps a dog run over by some care-less person rich enough to own a car, sidle up to someone who is ignorant enough to be kind to them? That is the way my Maggie walks. She has been like this, chin on chest, eyes on ground, feet in shuffle, ever since the fire that burned the other house to the ground.

Dee is lighter than Maggie, with nicer hair and a fuller figure. She's a woman now, though sometimes I forget. How long ago was it that the other house burned? Ten, twelve years? Sometimes I can still hear the flames and feel Maggie's arms sticking to me, her hair smoking and her dress falling off her in little black papery flakes. Her eyes seemed stretched open, blazed open by the flames reflected in them. And Dee. I see her standing off under the sweet gum tree she used to dig gum out of; a look of concentration on her face as she watched the last dingy gray board of the house fall in toward the red-hot brick chimney. Why don't you do a dance around the ashes? I'd wanted to ask her. She had hated the house that much.

I used to think she hated Maggie, too. But that was before we raised the money, the church and me, to send her to Augusta to school. She used to read to us without pity; forcing words, lies, other folks' habits, whole lives upon us two, sitting trapped and ignorant underneath her voice. She washed us in a river of make-believe, burned us with a lot of knowledge we didn't necessarily need to know. Pressed us to her with the serious way she read, to shove us away at just the moment, like dimwits, we seemed about to understand.

Dee wanted nice things. A yellow organdy dress to wear to her graduation from high school; black pumps to match a green suit she'd made from an old suit somebody gave me. She was determined to stare down any disaster in her efforts. Her eyelids would not flicker for minutes at a time. Often I fought off the temptation to shake her. At sixteen she had a style of her own: and knew what style was.

I never had an education myself. After second grade the school was closed down. Don't ask me why: in 1927 colored asked fewer questions than they do now. Sometimes Maggie reads to me. She stumbles along good-naturedly but can't see well. She knows she is not bright. Like good looks and money, quick-ness passed her by. She will marry John Thomas (who has mossy teeth in an earnest face) and then I'll be free to sit here and I guess just sing church songs to myself. Although I never was a good singer. Never could carry a tune. I was always better at a man's job. I used to love to milk till I was hooked in the side in '49. Cows are soothing and slow and don't bother you, unless you try to milk them the wrong way.

I have deliberately turned my back on the house. It is three rooms, just like the one that burned, except the roof is tin; they don't make shingle roofs any more. There are no real windows, just some holes cut in the sides, like the portholes in a ship, but not round and not square, with rawhide holding the shutters up on the outside. This house is in a pasture, too, like the other one. No doubt when Dee sees it she will want to tear it down. She wrote me once that no matter where we "choose" to live, she will manage to come see us. But she will never bring her friends. Maggie and I thought about this and Maggie asked me, "Mama, when did Dee ever *have* any friends?"

She had a few. Furtive boys in pink shirts hanging about on washday after school. Nervous girls who never laughed. Impressed with her they worshiped the well-turned phrase, the cute shape, the scalding humor that erupted like bubbles in lye. She read to them.

When she was courting Jimmy T she didn't have much time to pay to us, but turned all her faultfinding power on him. He *flew* to marry a cheap city girl from a family of ignorant flashy people. She hardly had time to recompose herself.

When she comes I will meet—but there they are!

Maggie attempts to make a dash for the house, in her shuffling way, but I stay her with my hand. "Come back here," I say. And she stops and tries to dig a well in the sand with her toe.

It is hard to see them clearly through the strong sun. But even the first glimpse of leg out of the car tells me it is Dee. Her feet were always neat-looking, as if God himself had shaped them with a certain style. From the other side of the car comes a short, stocky man. Hair is all over his head a foot long and hanging from his chin like a kinky mule tail. I hear Maggie suck in her breath. "Uhnnnh," is what it sounds like. Like when you see the wriggling end of a snake just in front of your foot on the road. "Uhnnnh."

Dee next. A dress down to the ground, in this hot weather. A dress so loud it hurts my eyes. There are yellows and oranges enough to throw back the light of the sun. I feel my whole face warming from the heat waves it throws out. Earrings gold, too, and hanging down to her shoulders. Bracelets dangling and making noises when she moves her arm up to shake the folds of the dress out of her armpits. The dress is loose and flows, and as she walks closer, I like it. I hear Maggie go "Uhnnnh" again. It is her sister's hair. It stands straight up like the wool on a sheep. It is black as night and around the edges are two long pigtails that rope about like small lizards disappearing behind her ears.

"Wa-su-zo-Tean-o!" she says, coming on in that gliding way the dress makes her move. The short stocky fellow with the hair to his navel is all grinning and he follows up with "Asalamalakim, my mother and sister!" He moves to hug Maggie but she falls back, right up against the back of my chair. I feel her trembling there and when I look up I see the perspiration falling off her chin.

"Don't get up," says Dee. Since I am stout it takes something of a push. You can see me trying to move a second or two before I make it. She turns, showing white heels through her sandals, and goes back to the car. Out she peeks next with a Polaroid. She stoops down quickly and lines up picture after picture of me sitting there in front of the house with Maggie cowering behind me. She never takes a shot without making sure the house is included. When a cow comes nibbling around the edge of the yard she snaps it and me and

Maggie *and* the house. Then she puts the Polaroid in the back seat of the car, and comes up and kisses me on the forehead.

Meanwhile Asalamalakim is going through motions with Maggie's hand. Maggie's hand is as limp as a fish, and probably as cold, despite the sweat, and she keeps trying to pull it back. It looks like Asalamalakim wants to shake hands but wants to do it fancy. Or maybe he don't know how people shake hands. Anyhow, he soon gives up on Maggie.

"Well," I say. "Dee."

"No, Mama," she says. "Not 'Dee,' Wangero Leewanika Kemanjo!"

"What happened to 'Dee'?" I wanted to know.

"She's dead," Wangero said. "I couldn't bear it any longer, being named after the people who oppress me."

"You know as well as me you was named after your aunt Dicie," I said. Dicie is my sister. She named Dee. We called her "Big Dee" after Dee was born.

"But who was *she* named after?" asked Wangero.

"I guess after Grandma Dee," I said.

"And who was she named after?" asked Wangero.

"Her mother," I said, and saw Wangero was getting tired. "That's about as far back as I can trace it," I said. Though, in fact, I probably could have carried it back beyond the Civil War through the branches.

"Well," said Asalamalakim, "there you are."

"Uhnnnh," I heard Maggie say.

"There I was not," I said, "before 'Dicie' cropped up in our family, so why should I try to trace it that far back?"

He just stood there grinning, looking down on me like somebody inspecting a Model A car.[1] Every once in a while he and Wangero sent eye signals over my head.

"How do you pronounce this name?" I asked.

"You don't have to call me by it if you don't want to," said Wangero.

"Why shouldn't I?" I asked. "If that's what you want us to call you, we'll call you."

"I know it might sound awkward at first," said Wangero.

"I'll get used to it," I said. "Ream it out again."

Well, soon we got the name out of the way. Asalamalakim had a name twice as long and three times as hard. After I tripped over it two or three times he told me to just call him Hakim-a-barber. I wanted to ask him was he a barber, but I didn't really think he was, so I didn't ask.

"You must belong to those beef-cattle peoples down the road," I said. They said "Asalamalakim" when they met you, too, but they didn't shake hands. Always too busy: feeding the cattle, fixing the fences, putting up salt-lick shelters, throwing down hay. When the white folks poisoned some of the herd the men stayed up all night with rifles in their hands. I walked a mile and a half just to see the sight.

Hakim-a-barber said, "I accept some of their doctrines, but farming and raising cattle is not my style." (They didn't tell me, and I didn't ask, whether Wangero (Dee) had really gone and married him.)

We sat down to eat and right away he said he didn't eat collards and pork was unclean. Wangero, though, went on through the chitlins and corn bread,

---

1. Popular model of Ford automobile introduced in 1928.

the greens and everything else. She talked a blue streak over the sweet potatoes. Everything delighted her. Even the fact that we still used the benches
her daddy made for the table when we couldn't afford to buy chairs.

"Oh, Mama!" she cried. Then turned to Hakim-a-barber. "I never knew
how lovely these benches are. You can feel the rump prints," she said, running her hands underneath her and along the bench. Then she gave a sigh
and her hand closed over Grandma Dee's butter dish. "That's it!" she said. "I
knew there was something I wanted to ask you if I could have." She jumped
up from the table and went over in the corner where the churn stood, the
milk in it clabber by now. She looked at the churn and looked at it.

"This churn top is what I need," she said. "Didn't Uncle Buddy whittle it
out of a tree you all used to have?"

"Yes," I said.

"Uh huh," she said happily. "And I want the dasher, too."

"Uncle Buddy whittle that, too?" asked the barber.

Dee (Wangero) looked up at me.

"Aunt Dee's first husband whittled the dash," said Maggie so low you
almost couldn't hear her. "His name was Henry, but they called him Stash."

"Maggie's brain is like an elephant's," Wangero said, laughing. "I can
use the churn top as a centerpiece for the alcove table," she said, sliding
a plate over the churn, "and I'll think of something artistic to do with the
dasher."

When she finished wrapping the dasher the handle stuck out. I took it for
a moment in my hands. You didn't even have to look close to see where
hands pushing the dasher up and down to make butter had left a kind of
sink in the wood. In fact, there were a lot of small sinks; you could see
where thumbs and fingers had sunk into the wood. It was beautiful light
yellow wood, from a tree that grew in the yard where Big Dee and Stash had
lived.

After dinner Dee (Wangero) went to the trunk at the foot of my bed and
started rifling through it. Maggie hung back in the kitchen over the dishpan.
Out came Wangero with two quilts. They had been pieced by Grandma Dee
and then Big Dee and me had hung them on the quilt frames on the front
porch and quilted them. One was in the Lone Star pattern. The other was
Walk Around the Mountain. In both of them were scraps of dresses Grandma
Dee had worn fifty and more years ago. Bits and pieces of Grandpa Jarrell's
Paisley shirts. And one teeny faded blue piece, about the size of a penny
matchbox, that was from Great Grandpa Ezra's uniform that he wore in the
Civil War.

"Mama," Wangero said sweet as a bird. "Can I have these old quilts?"

I heard something fall in the kitchen, and a minute later the kitchen door
slammed.

"Why don't you take one or two of the others?" I asked. "These old things
was just done by me and Big Dee from some tops your grandma pieced
before she died."

"No," said Wangero. "I don't want those. They are stitched around the
borders by machine."

"That'll make them last better," I said.

"That's not the point," said Wangero. "These are all pieces of dresses
Grandma used to wear. She did all this stitching by hand. Imagine!" She
held the quilts securely in her arms, stroking them.

"Some of the pieces, like those lavender ones, come from old clothes her mother handed down to her," I said, moving up to touch the quilts. Dee (Wangero) moved back just enough so that I couldn't reach the quilts. They already belonged to her.

"Imagine!" she breathed again, clutching them closely to her bosom.

"The truth is," I said, "I promised to give them quilts to Maggie, for when she marries John Thomas."

She gasped like a bee had stung her.

"Maggie can't appreciate these quilts!" she said. "She'd probably be backward enough to put them to everyday use."

"I reckon she would," I said. "God knows I been saving 'em for long enough with nobody using 'em. I hope she will!" I didn't want to bring up how I had offered Dee (Wangero) a quilt when she went away to college. Then she had told me they were old-fashioned, out of style.

"But they're *priceless!*" she was saying now, furiously; for she has a temper. "Maggie would put them on the bed and in five years they'd be in rags. Less than that!"

"She can always make some more," I said. "Maggie knows how to quilt."

Dee (Wangero) looked at me with hatred. "You just will not understand. The point is these quilts, *these* quilts!"

"Well," I said, stumped. "What would *you* do with them?"

"Hang them," she said. As if that was the only thing you *could* do with quilts.

Maggie by now was standing in the door. I could almost hear the sound her feet made as they scraped over each other.

"She can have them, Mama," she said, like somebody used to never winning anything, or having anything reserved for her. "I can 'member Grandma Dee without the quilts."

I looked at her hard. She had filled her bottom lip with checkerberry snuff and it gave her face a kind of dopey, hangdog look. It was Grandma Dee and Big Dee who taught her how to quilt herself. She stood there with her scarred hands hidden in the folds of her skirt. She looked at her sister with something like fear but she wasn't mad at her. This was Maggie's portion. This was the way she knew God to work.

When I looked at her like that something hit me in the top of my head and ran down to the soles of my feet. Just like when I'm in church and the spirit of God touches me and I get happy and shout. I did something I never had done before: hugged Maggie to me, then dragged her on into the room, snatched the quilts out of Miss Wangero's hands and dumped them into Maggie's lap. Maggie just sat there on my bed with her mouth open.

"Take one or two of the others," I said to Dee.

But she turned without a word and went out to Hakim-a-barber.

"You just don't understand," she said, as Maggie and I came out to the car.

"What don't I understand?" I wanted to know.

"Your heritage," she said. And then she turned to Maggie, kissed her, and said, "You ought to try to make something of yourself, too, Maggie. It's really a new day for us. But from the way you and Mama still live you'd never know it."

She put on some sunglasses that hid everything above the tip of her nose and her chin.

Maggie smiled; maybe at the sunglasses. But a real smile, not scared. After we watched the car dust settle I asked Maggie to bring me a dip of snuff. And then the two of us sat there just enjoying, until it was time to go in the house and go to bed.

1973

YUSEF KOMUNYAKAA
b. 1947

The excavation of lost names is one of the driving impulses of Yusef Komunyakaa's work. His poems recover and reanimate figures from history such as the African American elevator operator, Thomas McKeller, who appears in a stunning portrait by John Singer Sargent ("Nude Study"). In researching the portrait, Komunyakaa learned that it had been "unearthed in Sargent's studio after his death" and that "McKeller's image had been cannibalized to depict [the ancient Greek and Roman god] Apollo and a bas-relief of [the ancient Greek poet and musician] Arion—other heads and lines grafted onto his classical physique." Komunyakaa's work continually questions and revises both the cultural contradictions projected onto the black body and the erasure of black presence from history and culture. Significantly, he adopted the lost surname of a Trinidadian grandfather who came to the United States as a child, "smuggled in like a sack of papaya / On a banana boat." As the poet recounts in "Mismatched Shoes," his grandfather's "true name" disappeared in the process of assimilation. After his death his grandson "slipped into his skin" and took back the name "Komunyakaa," in what the poet calls "an affirmation of my heritage and its ambiguity."

Komunyakaa was born in Bogalusa, Louisiana, seventy miles northeast of New Orleans. Bogalusa means "Magic City" (a phrase that became the title of his 1992 collection of poems), and a lush, semitropical landscape informs many of his poems. But as the oldest of six children, and as the son of a carpenter who could write only his name, Komunyakaa grew up in an impoverished neighborhood and experienced a racial inequity that coexisted with natural beauty. At a young age, he has said, he decided that "imagination could serve as a choice of weapons."

Because the military seemed to offer a way into a larger world, Komunyakaa enlisted in the army and was sent to Vietnam, where he served as a war correspondent and editor of the military newspaper, writing accounts of what he witnessed in combat. For his work he was awarded the Bronze Star. While in Vietnam he carried with him several anthologies of poetry, but only after his military service ended did he begin to write poems, studying at the University of Colorado and then at the University of California at Irvine, where his teachers included Charles Wright and C. K. Williams. In 1984, fourteen years after his tour of duty ended, Komunyakaa began to write poems about his war experience. From his father he had learned to build and renovate houses; as he works, he has said, he keeps a pad of paper close by. While renovating a house in New Orleans he began to write down images and lines about Vietnam and so began the first in what became a series of poems about his Vietnam experience. These were collected in *Dien Cai Dau* (1988), whose title (meaning "crazy") is a Vietnamese phrase used to describe American soldiers. In one of these poems, "Facing It," he sees his own "clouded reflection" in the "black granite" of the Vietnam War Memorial designed by Maya Lin, an image of which appears in the color insert of this anthology.

To write about his surreal wartime experiences Komunyakaa drew on the work of surrealists like the French poet and critic André Breton. Komunyakaa shares with these writers and artists an emphasis on the image as linked to the unconscious, and his poems often work through a series of short lines whose quick, associative images bypass logic. A surrealist impulse to distort the familiar and juxtapose beauty and violence appears in Komunyakaa's Vietnam poems and in the racial and erotic tensions of poems like "Jasmine" (from *The Pleasure Dome*, 2001). An emphasis on the dreamlike, irrational, and fantastic was already apparent in his first two books, *Copacetic* (1984) and *I Apologize for the Eyes in My Head* (1986), both of which also reflect the musical influences of his native Louisiana.

Growing up so close to New Orleans brought Komunyakaa in early contact with jazz and the blues. The title of his first book, *Copacetic*, is a term adapted by jazz musicians from the African American tap dancer Bill "Bojangles" Robinson; in jazz it refers to especially pleasing and mellow music. Like Langston Hughes, Komunyakaa explores throughout his work the power of music—blues, jazz, and poetry—to address and, in part, to heal the pain of living in a racially divided society. The rapid energy of poems like "Facing It" and "Slam, Dunk, & Hook" belong to what the poet calls a "felt and lived syncopation," a rhythm of shifting beats that bears the influence of musicians like Charlie Parker, John Coltrane, and Miles Davis. Komunyakaa also works in tighter formal structures, whose exactness and precision suggest the careful measuring and fitting of carpentry. The quatrains of *Talking Dirty to the Gods* (2000) and the three-line stanzas of *Taboo* (2004) provide what the poet calls "an illusion of control" over volatile and complicated social and psychic material. They reflect Komunyakaa's preferred poetic strategy of "insinuation and nuance." Although his work often looks unflinchingly at what otherwise is hidden or denied, the social, racial, or erotic context of a poem often emerges in details or images, rather than in direct description. *Warhorses* (2008) continues this poet's ongoing investigation of war and violence.

Komunyakaa coedited with J. A. Sascha Feinstein a two-volume collection, *The Jazz Poetry Anthology* (1991) and *Second Set* (1996), and has also been extensively involved in collaborations with jazz musicians and vocalists. His poetry has received numerous awards, among them both the Pulitzer Prize and the Kingsley Tuft Poetry Award for *Neon Vernacular: New and Selected Poems 1977–1989* (1994). He is a professor in the Council of Humanities and Creative Writing Program at Princeton University.

Facing It

My black face fades,
hiding inside the black granite.
I said I wouldn't
dammit: No tears.
I'm stone. I'm flesh.   5
My clouded reflection eyes me
like a bird of prey, the profile of night
slanted against morning. I turn
this way—the stone lets me go.

I turn that way—I'm inside 10
the Vietnam Veterans Memorial[1]
again, depending on the light
to make a difference.
I go down the 58,022 names,
half-expecting to find 15
my own in letters like smoke.
I touch the name Andrew Johnson;
I see the booby trap's white flash.
Names shimmer on a woman's blouse
but when she walks away 20
the names stay on the wall.
Brushstrokes flash, a red bird's
wings cutting across my stare.
The sky. A plane in the sky.
A white vet's image floats 25
closer to me, then his pale eyes
look through mine. I'm a window.
He's lost his right arm
inside the stone. In the black mirror
a woman's trying to erase names: 30
No, she's brushing a boy's hair.

1988

My Father's Love Letters

On Fridays he'd open a can of Jax[1]
After coming home from the mill,
& ask me to write a letter to my mother
Who sent postcards of desert flowers
Taller than men. He would beg, 5
Promising to never beat her
Again. Somehow I was happy
She had gone, & sometimes wanted
To slip in a reminder, how Mary Lou
Williams' "Polka Dots & Moonbeams"[2] 10
Never made the swelling go down.
His carpenter's apron always bulged
With old nails, a claw hammer
Looped at his side & extension cords
Coiled around his feet. 15
Words rolled from under the pressure
Of my ballpoint: Love,
Baby, Honey, Please.

1. An image of the Vietnam War Memorial in
Washington, D.C., designed by the architect
Maya Lin and dedicated in 1982, appears in the
color insert of this anthology.
1. A beer originally brewed in New Orleans,
Louisiana.
2. The American jazz pianist Mary Lou Williams (1910–1981) performed with and composed for many of the great jazz artists of the
1940s and 1950s. The song "Polka Dots and
Moonbeams" (1940) was composed by Jimmy
Van Heusen (1913–1990) and Johnny Burke
(1908–1964).

We sat in the quiet brutality
Of voltage meters & pipe threaders,   20
Lost between sentences . . .
The gleam of a five-pound wedge
On the concrete floor
Pulled a sunset
Through the doorway of his toolshed.   25
I wondered if she laughed
& held them over a gas burner.
My father could only sign
His name, but he'd look at blueprints
& say how many bricks   30
Formed each wall. This man,
Who stole roses & hyacinth
For his yard, would stand there
With eyes closed & fists balled,
Laboring over a simple word, almost   35
Redeemed by what he tried to say.

1992

Slam, Dunk, & Hook

Fast breaks. Lay ups. With Mercury's
Insignia[1] on our sneakers,
We outmaneuvered to footwork
Of bad angels. Nothing but a hot
Swish of strings like silk   5
Ten feet out. In the roundhouse
Labyrinth our bodies
Created, we could almost
Last forever, poised in midair
Like storybook sea monsters.   10
A high note hung there
A long second. Off
The rim. We'd corkscrew
Up & dunk balls that exploded
The skullcap of hope & good   15
Intention. Lanky, all hands
& feet . . . sprung rhythm.[2]
We were metaphysical when girls
Cheered on the sidelines.
Tangled up in a falling,   20
Muscles were a bright motor
Double-flashing to the metal hoop
Nailed to our oak.
When Sonny Boy's mama died

---

1. Mercury, the messenger of the ancient Greek gods, is depicted wearing winged sandals.
2. "Sprung rhythm" is a term used by the English poet Gerard Manley Hopkins (1844–1889) to describe a poetic meter with a variable rather than fixed number of syllables in each poetic foot.

He played nonstop all day, so hard   25
Our backboard splintered.
Glistening with sweat,
We rolled the ball off
Our fingertips. Trouble
Was there slapping a blackjack[3]   30
Against an open palm.
Dribble, drive to the inside,
& glide like a sparrow hawk.[4]
Lay ups. Fast breaks.
We had moves we didn't know   35
We had. Our bodies spun
On swivels of bone & faith,
Through a lyric slipknot
Of joy, & we knew we were
Beautiful & dangerous.   40

        1992

When Dusk Weighs Daybreak

I want Catullus[1]
In every line, a barb
The sun plays for good
Luck. I need to know if iron

Tastes like laudanum[2]   5
Or a woman. I already sense
What sleeps in the same flesh,
Ariadne & her half brother[3]

Caught in the other's dream.
I want each question to fit me   10
Like a shiny hook, a lure
In the gullet. What it is

To look & know how much muscle
It takes to lift a green slab.
I need a Son House blues[4]   15
To wear out my tongue.

        2000

3. A small leather-covered bludgeon.
4. One of the best-known, handsomest, and smallest North American hawks.
1. Gaius Valerius Catullus (c. 86–c. 54 B.C.E.), Roman poet who wittily expressed love and hate in some of the finest lyric poetry of his time.
2. An opium-based painkiller.
3. In Greek mythology Ariadne was the daughter of Pasiphaë and the Cretan king, Minos. She fell in love with the Athenian hero Theseus and helped him escape the Labyrinth after he slew her half-brother, the Minotaur, a beast half bull and half man.
4. Eddie James House Jr. (1902–1988), better known as "Son," American blues singer and guitarist regarded as an epitome of the Delta blues tradition.

Jasmine

I sit beside two women, kitty-corner
to the stage, as Elvin's[1] sticks blur
the club into a blue fantasia.
I thought my body had forgotten the Deep
South, how I'd cross the street   5
if a woman like these two walked
towards me, as if a cat traversed
my path beneath the evening star.
Which one is wearing jasmine?
If my grandmothers saw me now   10
they'd say, Boy, the devil never sleeps.
My mind is lost among November
cotton flowers, a soft rain on my face
as Richard Davis[2] plucks the fat notes
of chance on his upright   15
leaning into the future.
The blonde, the brunette—
which one is scented with jasmine?
I can hear Duke in the right hand
& Basie in the left[3]   20
as the young piano player
nudges us into the past.
The trumpet's almost kissed
by enough pain. Give him a few more years,
a few more ghosts to embrace—Clifford's[4]   25
shadow on the edge of the stage.
The sign says, *No Talking*.
Elvin's guardian angel lingers
at the top of the stairs,
counting each drop of sweat   30
paid in tribute. The blonde
has her eyes closed, & the brunette
is looking at me. Our bodies
sway to each riff, the jasmine
rising from a valley somewhere   35
in Egypt, a white moon
opening countless false mouths
of laughter. The midnight
gatherers are boys & girls
with the headlights of trucks   40
aimed at their backs, because
their small hands refuse to wound
the knowing scent hidden in each bloom.

2001

1. Elvin Jones (1927–2004), American jazz drummer and bandleader.
2. American bassist (b. 1930) known for his jazz
sessions in an all-star small group at New York
City's Village Vanguard under the rubric "Jazz
for a Sunday Afternoon."

3. Duke Ellington (1899–1974), American pianist and bandleader who was also one of the
greatest jazz composers. Count Basie (1904–
1984), American jazz pianist and bandleader.
4. Clifford Brown (1930–1956), American jazz
trumpeter noted for his graceful technique.

LESLIE MARMON SILKO
b. 1948

Born in Albuquerque, New Mexico, Leslie Marmon Silko was raised in Old Laguna, a village fifty miles west of Albuquerque. The Spaniards had founded a mission there early in the eighteenth century, but Old Laguna had been formed centuries earlier by cattle-keeping Pueblos who successfully repelled raids on them by the Navajos and the Apaches. Writing of the unchanging character of Pueblo religious practices over the centuries, the historian Joe S. Sando notes that "the tradition of religious beliefs permeates every aspect of the people's life; it determines man's relation with the natural world and with his fellow man. Its basic concern is continuity of a harmonious relationship with the world in which man lives."

Silko's work addresses such matters. Her own heritage is complicated in that her great-grandfather Robert Marmon was white, whereas her mother was a mixed-blood Plains Indian who kept her daughter on the traditional cradle board during her first year of infancy. (Her ancestry also includes some Mexican blood.) Silko has made this heritage a source of strength. She writes: "I suppose at the core of my writing is the attempt to identify what it is to be a half-breed or mixed blooded person; what it is to grow up neither white nor fully traditional Indian." At the same time she insists that "what I know is Laguna. This place I am from is everything I am as a writer and human being." An active child, Silko had a horse of her own by age eight, and by thirteen she owned a rifle, with which she took part in deer hunts. Commuting to Albuquerque, she attended Catholic schools, earned a B.A. at the University of New Mexico, then began law school under a special program for Native Americans, though she soon gave it up to become a writer and teacher.

Her first published story, "The Man to Send Rain Clouds" (1969), came out of a writing assignment in college. She had heard, in Laguna, of an old man who died in a sheep camp and was given a traditional native burial—a fact resented by the Catholic priest who was not called in. The story she wrote about this situation, published in the *New Mexico Quarterly*, put her on the road to success as a writer. In 1974 a selection of her poems was published in the volume *Laguna Woman*, and in 1977 her novel *Ceremony* brought her recognition as a leading voice among Native American writers. *Ceremony* shows the dark aspects of modern American Indian life, focusing on a World War II veteran who is in acute physical and emotional straits as the novel begins, but who manages to survive by reestablishing contact with his native roots. Silko has insisted that the book is not just or even mainly about characters: "This novel is essentially about the powers inherent in the process of storytelling. . . . The chanting or telling of ancient stories to effect certain cures or protect from illness and harm have always been a part of the Pueblo's curing ceremonies." So this story of a family represents an attempt "to search for a ceremony to deal with despair"—the despair that has led to the "suicide, the alcoholism, and the violence which occur in so many Indian communities today."

Thus a strong moral connection exists between Silko's purely aesthetic delight in the writing of a story and the therapeutic, functional uses she hopes the story will play in the Native American community. In *Ceremony* and the aptly titled 1981 collection *Storyteller* of 1981 (which also contains poems and photographs), Silko's prose is an expressive, active presence, sympathetically creating landscape as well as animals and human beings. Plants assume narrative status in her third novel,

Gardens in the Dunes (1999), which looks back to late-nineteenth-century events to underscore a basic theme: that myth and history do not coincide.

The following text is from *Storyteller* (1981).

Lullaby

The sun had gone down but the snow in the wind gave off its own light. It came in thick tufts like new wool—washed before the weaver spins it. Ayah reached out for it like her own babies had, and she smiled when she remembered how she had laughed at them. She was an old woman now, and her life had become memories. She sat down with her back against the wide cottonwood tree, feeling the rough bark on her back bones; she faced east and listened to the wind and snow sing a high-pitched Yeibechei[1] song. Out of the wind she felt warmer, and she could watch the wide fluffy snow fill in her tracks, steadily, until the direction she had come from was gone. By the light of the snow she could see the dark outline of the big arroyo[2] a few feet away. She was sitting on the edge of Cebolleta Creek, where in the springtime the thin cows would graze on grass already chewed flat to the ground. In the wide deep creek bed where only a trickle of water flowed in the summer, the skinny cows would wander, looking for new grass along winding paths splashed with manure.

Ayah pulled the old Army blanket over her head like a shawl. Jimmie's blanket—the one he had sent to her. That was a long time ago and the green wool was faded, and it was unraveling on the edges. She did not want to think about Jimmie. So she thought about the weaving and the way her mother had done it. On the wall wooden loom set into the sand under a tamarack tree for shade. She could see it clearly. She had been only a little girl when her grandma gave her the wooden combs to pull the twigs and burrs from the raw, freshly washed wool. And while she combed the wool, her grandma sat beside her, spinning a silvery strand of yarn around the smooth cedar spindle. Her mother worked at the loom with yarns dyed bright yellow and red and gold. She watched them dye the yarn in boiling black pots full of beeweed petals, juniper berries, and sage. The blankets her mother made were soft and woven so tight that rain rolled off them like birds' feathers. Ayah remembered sleeping warm on cold windy nights, wrapped in her mother's blankets on the hogan's[3] sandy floor.

The snow drifted now, with the northwest wind hurling it in gusts. It drifted up around her black overshoes—old ones with little metal buckles. She smiled at the snow which was trying to cover her little by little. She could remember when they had no black rubber overshoes; only the high buckskin leggings that they wrapped over their elkhide moccasins. If the snow was dry or frozen, a person could walk all day and not get wet; and in the evenings the beams of the ceiling would hang with lengths of pale buckskin leggings, drying out slowly.

---

1. Navajo dance.
2. Gully carved by water.
3. Navajo dwelling usually made of logs and mud.

She felt peaceful remembering. She didn't feel cold any more. Jimmie's blanket seemed warmer than it had ever been. And she could remember the morning he was born. She could remember whispering to her mother, who was sleeping on the other side of the hogan, to tell her it was time now. She did not want to wake the others. The second time she called to her, her mother stood up and pulled on her shoes; she knew. They walked to the old stone hogan together, Ayah walking a step behind her mother. She waited alone, learning the rhythms of the pains while her mother went to call the old woman to help them. The morning was already warm even before dawn and Ayah smelled the bee flowers blooming and the young willow growing at the springs. She could remember that so clearly, but his birth merged into the births of the other children and to her it became all the same birth. They named him for the summer morning and in English they called him Jimmie.

It wasn't like Jimmie died. He just never came back, and one day a dark blue sedan with white writing on its doors pulled up in front of the boxcar shack where the rancher let the Indians live. A man in a khaki uniform trimmed in gold gave them a yellow piece of paper and told them that Jimmie was dead. He said the Army would try to get the body back and then it would be shipped to them; but it wasn't likely because the helicopter had burned after it crashed. All of this was told to Chato because he could understand English. She stood inside the doorway holding the baby while Chato listened. Chato spoke English like a white man and he spoke Spanish too. He was taller than the white man and he stood straighter too. Chato didn't explain why; he just told the military man they could keep the body if they found it. The white man looked bewildered; he nodded his head and he left. Then Chato looked at her and shook his head, and then he told her, "Jimmie isn't coming home anymore," and when he spoke, he used the words to speak of the dead. She didn't cry then, but she hurt inside with anger. And she mourned him as the years passed, when a horse fell with Chato and broke his leg, and the white rancher told them he wouldn't pay Chato until he could work again. She mourned Jimmie because he would have worked for his father then; he would have saddled the big bay horse and ridden the fence lines each day, with wire cutters and heavy gloves, fixing the breaks in the barbed wire and putting the stray cattle back inside again.

She mourned him after the white doctors came to take Danny and Ella away. She was at the shack alone that day they came. It was back in the days before they hired Navajo women to go with them as interpreters. She recognized one of the doctors. She had seen him at the children's clinic at Cañoncito about a month ago. They were wearing khaki uniforms and they waved papers at her and a black ball-point pen, trying to make her understand their English words. She was frightened by the way they looked at the children, like the lizard watches the fly. Danny was swinging on the tire swing on the elm tree behind the rancher's house, and Ella was toddling around the front door, dragging the broomstick horse Chato made for her. Ayah could see they wanted her to sign the papers, and Chato had taught her to sign her name. It was something she was proud of. She only wanted them to go, and to take their eyes away from her children.

She took the pen from the man without looking at his face and she signed the papers in three different places he pointed to. She stared at the ground by their feet and waited for them to leave. But they stood there and began to point and gesture at the children. Danny stopped swinging. Ayah could see his fear. She moved suddenly and grabbed Ella into her arms; the child squirmed, trying to get back to her toys. Ayah ran with the baby toward Danny; she screamed for him to run and then she grabbed him around his chest and carried him too. She ran south into the foothills of juniper trees and black lava rock. Behind her she heard the doctors running, but they had been taken by surprise, and as the hills became steeper and the cholla cactus were thicker, they stopped. When she reached the top of the hill, she stopped to listen in case they were circling around her. But in a few minutes she heard a car engine start and they drove away. The children had been too surprised to cry while she ran with them. Danny was shaking and Ella's little fingers were gripping Ayah's blouse.

She stayed up in the hills for the rest of the day, sitting on a black lava boulder in the sunshine where she could see for miles all around her. The sky was light blue and cloudless, and it was warm for late April. The sun warmth relaxed her and took the fear and anger away. She lay back on the rock and watched the sky. It seemed to her that she could walk into the sky, stepping through clouds endlessly. Danny played with little pebbles and stones, pretending they were birds eggs and then little rabbits. Ella sat at her feet and dropped fistfuls of dirt into the breeze, watching the dust and particles of sand intently. Ayah watched a hawk soar high above them, dark wings gliding; hunting or only watching, she did not know. The hawk was patient and he circled all afternoon before he disappeared around the high volcanic peak the Mexicans called Guadalupe.

Late in the afternoon, Ayah looked down at the gray boxcar shack with the paint all peeled from the wood; the stove pipe on the roof was rusted and crooked. The fire she had built that morning in the oil drum stove had burned out. Ella was asleep in her lap now and Danny sat close to her, complaining that he was hungry; he asked when they would go to the house. "We will stay up here until your father comes," she told him, "because those white men were chasing us." The boy remembered then and he nodded at her silently.

If Jimmie had been there he could have read those papers and explained to her what they said. Ayah would have known then, never to sign them. The doctors came back the next day and they brought a BIA[4] policeman with them. They told Chato they had her signature and that was all they needed. Except for the kids. She listened to Chato sullenly; she hated him when he told her it was the old woman who died in the winter, spitting blood; it was her old grandma who had given the children this disease. "They don't spit blood," she said coldly. "The whites lie." She held Ella and Danny close to her, ready to run to the hills again. "I want a medicine man first," she said to Chato, not looking at him. He shook his head. "It's too late now. The policeman is with them. You signed the paper." His voice was gentle.

It was worse than if they had died: to lose the children and to know that somewhere, in a place called Colorado, in a place full of sick and dying strangers, her children were without her. There had been babies that died soon after they were born, and one that died before he could walk. She

---

4. Bureau of Indian Affairs, an agency of the U.S. government charged with assisting the tribal authorities of reservations.

had carried them herself, up to the boulders and great pieces of the cliff that long ago crashed down from Long Mesa; she laid them in the crevices of sandstone and buried them in fine brown sand with round quartz pebbles that washed down the hills in the rain. She had endured it because they had been with her. But she could not bear this pain. She did not sleep for a long time after they took her children. She stayed on the hill where they had fled the first time, and she slept rolled up in the blanket Jimmie had sent her. She carried the pain in her belly and it was fed by everything she saw: the blue sky of their last day together and the dust and pebbles they played with; the swing in the elm tree and broomstick horse choked life from her. The pain filled her stomach and there was no room for food or for her lungs to fill with air. The air and the food would have been theirs.

She hated Chato, not because he let the policeman and doctors put the screaming children in the government car, but because he had taught her to sign her name. Because it was like the old ones always told her about learning their language or any of their ways: it endangered you. She slept alone on the hill until the middle of November when the first snows came. Then she made a bed for herself where the children had slept. She did not lie down beside Chato again until many years later, when he was sick and shivering and only her body could keep him warm. The illness came after the white rancher told Chato he was too old to work for him anymore, and Chato and his old woman should be out of the shack by the next afternoon because the rancher had hired new people to work there. That had satisfied her. To see how the white man repaid Chato's years of loyalty and work. All of Chato's fine-sounding English talk didn't change things.

It snowed steadily and the luminous light from the snow gradually diminished into the darkness. Somewhere in Cebolleta a dog barked and other village dogs joined with it. Ayah looked in the direction she had come, from the bar where Chato was buying the wine. Sometimes he told her to go on ahead and wait; and then he never came. And when she finally went back looking for him, she would find him passed out at the bottom of the wooden steps to Azzie's Bar. All the wine would be gone and most of the money too, from the pale blue check that came to them once a month in a government envelope. It was then that she would look at his face and his hands, scarred by ropes and the barbed wire of all those years, and she would think, this man is a stranger; for forty years she had smiled at him and cooked his food, but he remained a stranger. She stood up again, with the snow almost to her knees, and she walked back to find Chato.

It was hard to walk in the deep snow and she felt the air burn in her lungs. She stopped a short distance from the bar to rest and readjust the blanket. But this time he wasn't waiting for her on the bottom step with his old Stetson hat pulled down and his shoulders hunched up in his long wool overcoat.

She was careful not to slip on the wooden steps. When she pushed the door open, warm air and cigarette smoke hit her face. She looked around slowly and deliberately, in every corner, in every dark place that the old man might find to sleep. The bar owner didn't like Indians in there, especially Navajos, but he let Chato come in because he could talk Spanish like he was one of them. The men at the bar stared at her, and the bartender saw that she left the door open wide. Snowflakes were flying inside like moths and melting into a puddle on the oiled wood floor. He motioned to her to close the door, but she did not see him. She held herself straight and walked across the room slowly, searching the room with every step. The snow in her hair melted and she could feel it on her forehead. At the far corner of the room, she saw red flames at the mica window of the old stove door; she looked behind the stove just to make sure. The bar got quiet except for the Spanish polka music playing on the jukebox. She stood by the stove and shook the snow from her blanket and held it near the stove to dry. The wet wool smell reminded her of new-born goats in early March, brought inside to warm near the fire. She felt calm.

In past years they would have told her to get out. But her hair was white now and her face was wrinkled. They looked at her like she was a spider crawling slowly across the room. They were afraid; she could feel the fear. She looked at their faces steadily. They reminded her of the first time the white people brought her children back to her that winter. Danny had been shy and hid behind the thin white woman who brought them. And the baby had not known her until Ayah took her into her arms, and then Ella had nuzzled close to her as she had when she was nursing. The blonde woman was nervous and kept looking at a dainty gold watch on her wrist. She sat on the bench near the small window and watched the dark snow clouds gather around the mountains; she was worrying about the unpaved road. She was frightened by what she saw inside too: the strips of venison drying on a rope across the ceiling and the children jabbering excitedly in a language she did not know. So they stayed for only a few hours. Ayah watched the government car disappear down the road and she knew they were already being weaned from these lava hills and from this sky. The last time they came was in early June, and Ella stared at her the way the men in the bar were now staring. Ayah did not try to pick her up; she smiled at her instead and spoke cheerfully to Danny. When he tried to answer her, he could not seem to remember and he spoke English words with the Navajo. But he gave her a scrap of paper that he had found somewhere and carried in his pocket; it was folded in half, and he shyly looked up at her and said it was a bird. She asked Chato if they were home for good this time. He spoke to the white woman and she shook her head. "How much longer?" he asked, and she said she didn't know; but Chato saw how she stared at the boxcar shack. Ayah turned away then. She did not say good-bye.

She felt satisfied that the men in the bar feared her. Maybe it was her face and the way she held her mouth with teeth clenched tight, like there was nothing anyone could do to her now. She walked north down the road, searching for the old man. She did this because she had the blanket, and there would be no place for him except with her and the blanket in the old adobe barn near the arroyo. They always slept there when they came to Cebolleta. If the money and the wine were gone, she would be relieved because then they could go home again; back to the old hogan with a dirt roof and rock walls where she herself had been born. And the next day the old man could go back to the few sheep they still had, to follow along behind them, guiding them, into dry sandy arroyos where sparse grass grew. She knew he did not like walking behind old ewes when for so many years he rode big quarter horses and worked with cattle. But she wasn't sorry for him; he should have known all along what would happen.

There had not been enough rain for their garden in five years; and that was when Chato finally hitched a ride into the town and brought back brown boxes of rice and sugar and big tin cans of welfare peaches. After that, at the first of the month they went to Cebolleta to ask the postmaster for the check; and then Chato would go to the bar and cash it. They did this as they planted the garden every May, not because anything would survive the summer dust, but because it was time to do this. The journey passed the days that smelled silent and dry like the caves above the canyon with yellow painted buffaloes on their walls.

He was walking along the pavement when she found him. He did not stop or turn around when he heard her behind him. She walked beside him and she noticed how slowly he moved now. He smelled strongly of woodsmoke and urine. Lately he had been forgetting. Sometimes he called her by his sister's name and she had been gone for a long time. Once she had found him wandering on the road to the white man's ranch, and she asked him why he was going that way; he laughed at her and said, "You know they can't run that ranch without me," and he walked on determined, limping on the leg that had been crushed many years before. Now he looked at her curiously, as if for the first time, but he kept shuffling along, moving slowly along the side of the highway. His gray hair had grown long and spread out on the shoulders of the long overcoat. He wore the old felt hat pulled down over his ears. His boots were worn out at the toes and he had stuffed pieces of an old red shirt in the holes. The rags made his feet look like little animals up to their ears in snow. She laughed at his feet; the snow muffled the sound of her laugh. He stopped and looked at her again. The wind had quit blowing and the snow was falling straight down; the southeast sky was beginning to clear and Ayah could see a star.

"Let's rest awhile," she said to him. They walked away from the road and up the slope to the giant boulders that had tumbled down from the red sandrock mesa throughout the centuries of rainstorms and earth tremors. In a place where the boulders shut out the wind, they sat down with their backs against the rock. She offered half of the blanket to him and they sat wrapped together.

The storm passed swiftly. The clouds moved east. They were massive and full, crowding together across the sky. She watched them with the feeling of horses—steely blue-gray horses startled across the sky. The powerful haunches pushed into the distances and the tail hairs streamed white mist behind them. The sky cleared. Ayah saw that there was nothing between her and the stars. The light was crystalline. There was no shimmer, no distortion through earth haze. She breathed the clarity of the night sky; she smelled the purity of the half moon and the stars. He was lying on his side with his knees pulled up near his belly for warmth. His eyes were closed now, and in the light from the stars and the moon, he looked young again.

She could see it descend out of the night sky: an icy stillness from the edge of the thin moon. She recognized the freezing. It came gradually, sinking snowflake by snowflake until the crust was heavy and deep. It had the strength of the stars in Orion, and its journey was endless. Ayah knew that with the wine he would sleep. He would not feel it. She tucked the blanket around him, remembering how it was when Ella had been with her; and she felt the rush so big inside her heart for the babies. And she sang the only song she knew to sing for babies. She could not remember if she had ever sung it to her children, but she knew that her grandmother had sung it and her mother had sung it:

> *The earth is your mother,*
> *   she holds you.*
> *The sky is your father,*
> *   he protects you.*
> *Sleep,*
> *sleep.*
> *Rainbow is your sister,*
> *   she loves you.*
> *The winds are your brothers,*
> *   they sing to you.*
> *Sleep,*
> *sleep.*
> *We are together always*
> *We are together always*
> *There never was a time*
> *when this*
> *was not so.*

1981

ART SPIEGELMAN
b. 1948

Comic panels have existed since the end of the nineteeth century, beginning with Richard F. Outcault's *The Yellow Kid* in 1895. By the 1920s panels had evolved into strips—George Herriman's *Krazy Kat* was the most famous—and by the end of the 1930s these strips had grown into comic books, most successfully with the *Superman* series produced by Jerry Siegel and Joe Schuster. It would take the cultural transformations of the 1960s, however, for this trend of interweaving visual elements with an expanding sense of narrative to achieve literary form. As opposed to simple entertainment, literature involves, on a genuinely cultural level, both expression and reflection, comprising the beliefs and practices of a people. In the 1960s, as beliefs and practices were challenged and to some extent changed, comic-book art found itself uniquely positioned as an underground form ready to disrupt a traditional, more conservative order.

How underground comics became graphic novels is apparent from Art Spiegelman's career. A college dropout, Spiegelman found his first work in the most elemental form of cartoon humor, the illustrations for cards and stickers packaged with bubblegum and marketed as Wacky Packages and Garbage Pail Kids, a basely satirical form of 1960s counterculture created in the New York design studios of Topps and other novelty companies. When in 1970 Spiegelman moved from New York to San Francisco, his work progressed from novelty to subversion—of the comic-strip form and of larger cultural themes. Cartoonist R. Crumb had recently developed *Zap Comix* as a way of replacing convention with creation, both in the way comics were drawn and in the subjects they treated. Spiegelman's affinity was with the second wave of this movement, including the Zippy comics drawn by Bill Griffin, in which sequential art pushed common limits to be boldly experimental. Here older practices were turned against themselves, with action breaking out of frames, narratives interrogating themselves, and characters challenging all standards of social acceptability.

Spiegelman's return to New York prompted the key development in his work and emergence as a graphic novelist. Married to the artist and designer Françoise Mouly in 1977 and beginning a family, Spiegelman paid new attention to his father's stories about the signal event in the elder Spiegelmans' lives, the Holocaust. As Polish Jews who had been persecuted and imprisoned at Auschwitz, where their first son died, the Spiegelmans had emigrated first to Sweden (where Art was born three years after the war's end) and then to the United States, settling in the Rego Park neighborhood of Queens, New York City, and becoming naturalized American citizens. His parents' cultural transformation was greater than any Spiegelman had experienced in the 1960s, and he sought the artistic tools to represent it. In 1978 Will Eisner had taken comic books to a new level of expression by arguing theological matters in *A Contract with God*—the type of work that could be sold in bookstores rather than just on newsstands. But by applying his cartoonist's serial-narrative skills to his father's experiences, Siegelman gave the graphic novel literary importance.

Maus I (1986) and *Maus II* (1991) are complex creations, enfolding not just the father's tale but also his act of telling it, both of which are measured by the son's reception. Their handling of the Holocaust, a subject of countless previous treatments and certain to endure as one of humanity's major stories, as a cartoon adds great imaginative dimension. Thanks to a suggestive set of references, with Jews as mice (victims of prey), Germans as cats (predators of mice), French as frogs (a reminder of the self-conscious vulgarity of older comic strips), and Poles as pigs (a dietary contrast with Jews, but also a calculated insult), graphic representation gives new facets to a familiar story. Cartooning by nature involves a great amount of artistic license. Parameters of taste are much more elastic than those for fiction, poetry, and all but the most performative of drama, while the form's roots in popular culture continue to show despite the bleachings of high taste.

Even in becoming a countercultural icon, Spiegelman has maintained a sense of humor about himself. No matter how serious his subject matter (including his 2004 treatment of the 9/11 attacks, *In the Shadow of No Towers*), the cartoonist is always the fall guy, enduring his father's occasional impatience and the terrors of life. In this sense Spiegelman's mature works echo the sentiments of his first publications, *The Complete Mr. Infinity* (1970) and *The Viper Vicar of Vice, Villany, and Vickedness* (1972), both expressive of the 1960s counterculture and older comic book tradition that a new generation of readers would accept as illustrative of their own sensibilities.

The following text is from *Maus I and II* (1997).

From Maus

CHAPTER SIX

JANINA LIVES OVER THERE.

RICHIEU'S GOVERNESS ALWAYS OFFERED SHE WOULD HELP US.

WE CAME TO HER HOUSE NEAR TOWN...

OPEN UP, JANINA! QUICK!

W-WHO'S THERE?

MY GOD! IT'S THE SPIEGELMANS!

YOU'LL BRING TROUBLE! GO AWAY! *QUICKLY!*

SLAM

I'M FRIGHTENED, VLADEK.

MAYBE WE SHOULD TRY MY FATHER'S OLD HOUSE. THE JANITOR HAS KNOWN OUR FAMILY FOR YEARS.

LET'S TRY. WE'VE **GOT** TO GET OFF THE STREETS BEFORE DAWN!

I WAS A LITTLE SAFE. I HAD A COAT AND BOOTS, SO LIKE A GESTAPO WORE WHEN HE WAS NOT IN SERVICE. BUT ANJA - HER APPEARANCE - YOU COULD SEE MORE *EASY* SHE WAS JEWISH. I WAS AFRAID FOR HER.

WAKE UP, MR. LUKOWSKI. LET US IN. *PLEASE!!*

HUH? W-WHO IS IT?

ANJA! ANJA ZYLBERBERG!

WHAT ARE YOU DOING HERE, CHILD? IT ISN'T SAFE! WAIT - I'LL UNLOCK THE GATE.

I WALKED SLOW...

BEHIND ME ALSO WALKED SLOW.

IF I WALKED FAST...

BEHIND ME ALSO WALKED FAST.

WE WERE ALONE. HE SPOKE...

AMCHA?

IN HEBREW HE SAID TO ME, "OUR NATION?"

HAD I TO ANSWER HIM, OR NO?

A-AMCHA.

I THOUGHT YOU WERE A JEW.

... I'M JEWISH TOO! THERE ARE VERY FEW OF US LEFT...

..MY WIFE AND I HAVE BEEN HIDING IN SOSNOWIEC FOR OVER A YEAR.

I'M WITH MY WIFE TOO. WE'RE HUNGRY AND WE NEED A PLACE TO HIDE!

GO TO THE BLACK MARKET ON DE-KERTA STREET, NUMBER 8.

SO I LEFT HIM AND WENT RIGHT AWAY TO DEKERTA 8. THERE IT WAS A BIG COURTYARD...

?

ALL AROUND I LOOKED, BUT IT WAS NOBODY.

PSSST!

!

WANNA BUY SOME FOOD WITHOUT COUPONS, MISTER?

SHE SHOWED TO ME SAUSAGES, EGGS, CHEESE ...THINGS I ONLY WAS ABLE TO DREAM ABOUT.

I BOUGHT AND WENT QUICK BACK TO ANJA.

IT'S ALMOST DAWN—WHEN MRS. KAWKA COMES TO MILK HER COW, SHE'LL BRING YOU SOME COFFEE.

WHERE ARE YOU GOING?

TO DEKERTA.

AND SO WE CAME THERE TO LIVE WITH KAWKA'S COW.

DON'T LEAVE ME ALONE AGAIN. I'M TERRIFIED WHILE YOU'RE GONE.

DON'T WORRY, ANJA. I'LL BE SAFE. IF I DIDN'T GO OUT WE WOULDN'T HAVE FOOD...WE WOULDN'T HAVE THIS PLACE!...

AND WE'VE GOT TO FIND A WARMER PLACE FOR THE WINTER...AWAY FROM SOSNOWIEC IF POSSIBLE...

I-I'LL BE OKAY. COME BACK QUICK.

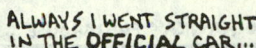

I TRAVELED OFTEN WITH THE STREETCAR TO TOWN.

IT WAS TWO CARS. ONE WAS ONLY GERMANS AND OFFICIALS. THE SECOND, IT WAS ONLY THE POLES.

ALWAYS I WENT STRAIGHT IN THE OFFICIAL CAR....

HEIL HITLER.

THE GERMANS PAID NO ATTENTION OF ME...IN THE POLISH CAR THEY COULD SMELL IF A POLISH JEW CAME IN.

AT THE BLACK MARKET I SAW SEVERAL TIMES A NICE WOMAN, WHAT I MADE A LITTLE FRIENDS WITH HER...

THE NEXT EVENING SHE CAME WITH HER 7-YEARS-OLD BOY TO KAWKA'S FARMHOUSE...

WE HAD HERE A LITTLE COMFORTABLE...WE HAD WHERE TO SIT.

REMEMBER, LITTLE ONE—NEVER TELL *ANYBODY* THERE ARE JEWS HERE. THEY'LL *SHOOT US ALL!*

YES, AUNT ANJA.

THE LITTLE BOY WAS VERY SMART AND HE LOVED VERY MUCH ANJA.

YOU HAD TO *PAY* MRS. MOTO-NOWA TO KEEP YOU, RIGHT?

OF COURSE I PAID... AND *WELL* I PAID.

...WHAT YOU THINK? SOMEONE WILL RISK THEIR LIFE FOR NOTHING?

...I PAID ALSO FOR THE *FOOD* WHAT SHE GAVE TO US FROM HER SMUGGLING BUSINESS.

BUT, ONE TIME I MISSED A FEW COINS TO THE BREAD...

I'LL PAY YOU THE REST TOMORROW, AFTER I GO OUT AND CASH SOME VALUABLES.

SORRY...I WASN'T ABLE TO *FIND* ANY BREAD TODAY.

ALWAYS SHE GOT BREAD, SO I DIDN'T BELIEVE... BUT, STILL, SHE WAS A GOOD WOMAN.

IN HIS SCHOOL THE BOY WAS VERY BAD IN GERMAN. SO ANJA TUTORED TO HIM.

ICH BIN... DU BIST... ER IST...

SHE KNEW GERMAN LIKE AN EXPERT.

AND SOON HE CAME OUT WITH *VERY* GOOD GRADES.

MY TEACHER ASKED ME HOW I IMPROVED SO MUCH...

SO I TOLD HIM MY *MOTHER* WAS HELPING ME.

WHEW

HE WAS REALLY A CLEVER BOY.

BUT IT WAS A FEW THINGS HERE NOT SO GOOD... HER HOME WAS VERY SMALL AND IT WAS ON THE GROUND FLOOR ...

WE'LL WALK TOWARD SOS-
NOWIEC — AT LEAST WE'LL
KNOW OUR WAY AROUND.

ANJA WAS SO
AFRAID SHE
WAS SHAKING.

STAY CALM — WALK AS IF WE'RE JUST
STROLLING ... AND *SPEAK* GERMAN.

FOR HOURS
WE WALKED

B-BESUCHEN WIR
DOCH FRAU KAWKA.

GUTE IDEE.

VLADEK-WE'RE
BEING FOLLOWED.

RELAX

BUT IF WE TURNED A COR-
NER, THEY ALSO TURNED.

ES IST KALT.

JA.
JA.

OF COURSE I WAS RIGHT—THEY
DIDN'T MEAN ANYTHING ON US.

WOOSH

THEY JUST WERE WALKING.

STAYING ON THE STREET ALL
NIGHT IS TOO DANGEROUS...
MAYBE WE CAN HIDE IN
THAT CONSTRUCTION SITE.

GOOD—I'M
EXHAUSTED.

HERE WAS A FOUNDATION MADE
VERY DEEP DOWN IN THE GROUND..

BE
CAREFUL!

I JUMPED FIRST IN, AND I
PULLED OVER BRICKS FOR
ANJA TO STEP DOWN.

AND HERE WE WAITED A
COLD FEW HOURS FOR THE DAY.

IT STARTED TO BE LIGHT...

COME. WE WON'T BE NOTICED IF WE MIX WITH PEOPLE OUT ON THE STREET.

I'M SO TIRED AND COLD...

WE CAN REST NOW.

WE CAME FINALLY AGAIN TO THIS PLACE WITH THE COW AND WENT INSIDE.

LATER, KAWKA CAME IN...

W-WHO'S IN HERE?

THE SPIEGEL-MANS... WE HAD NOWHERE ELSE TO GO.

WELL... I GUESS YOU CAN STAY. BUT, REMEMBER: I DON'T KNOW YOU'RE HERE!

WHY, MRS. SPIEGELMAN, YOU'RE SHIVERING!

YOU CAN COME INTO MY HOUSE FOR AN HOUR OR SO, 'TIL YOU WARM UP.

SHE TOOK ANJA INSIDE AND BROUGHT TO ME SOME FOOD...IN THOSE DAYS I WAS SO STRONG I COULD SIT EVEN IN THE SNOW ALL NIGHT...

THINGS CAN'T BE THIS BAD EVERYWHERE! I'D GIVE ANYTHING TO GET OUT OF POLAND!

YOU KNOW, BEFORE I TOOK YOU IN, I HAD A YOUNG MAN AND HIS SON HERE...

TWO PEOPLE I KNOW SMUG-GLED THEM INTO HUNGARY. I HEARD HE AND HIS BOY WERE DOING WELL THERE.

HUNGARY! REALLY?! I'D LIKE TO MEET THOSE SMUGGLERS!

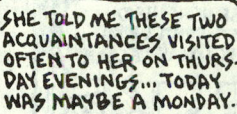

SHE TOLD ME THESE TWO ACQUAINTANCES VISITED OFTEN TO HER ON THURSDAY EVENINGS.... TODAY WAS MAYBE A MONDAY...

I DON'T GET IT... WASN'T HUNGARY AS DANGEROUS AS POLAND?

NO. FOR A LONGER TIME IT WAS *BETTER* THERE IN HUNGARY FOR THE JEWS.... BUT THEN, NEAR THE VERY FINISH OF THE WAR, THEY ALL GOT PUT *ALSO* TO AUSCHWITZ.

I WAS THERE, AND I SAW IT. THOUSANDS—HUNDREDS OF THOUSANDS OF JEWS FROM HUNGARY...

SO MANY, IT WASN'T EVEN ROOM ENOUGH TO BURY THEM ALL IN THE OVENS.

BUT AT THAT TIME, WHEN I WAS THERE WITH KAWKA, WE COULDN'T *KNOW* THEN.

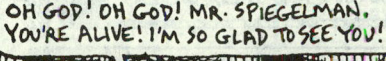

SO.... I WENT NEXT DAY TO DEKERTA STREET TO BUY FOOD...

OH GOD! OH GOD! MR. SPIEGELMAN, YOU'RE ALIVE! I'M SO GLAD TO SEE YOU!

MRS. MOTONOWA!

I WANTED TO FIND A NEW CONNECTION TO HIDE US. BUT *REALLY* I DIDN'T THINK TO FIND AGAIN *HER*.

PRAISE MARY, YOU'RE SAFE! I COULDN'T *SLEEP*, I FELT SO GUILTY ABOUT CHASING YOU AND YOUR WIFE OUT.

THE GESTAPO NEVER EVEN CAME TO MY HOUSE. I JUST PANICKED FOR NOTHING.

PLEASE COME BACK AGAIN.

ANJA WAS GLAD OF GOING BACK. AND MOTONOWA ALSO...ALWAYS I PAID HER NICELY.

AND THAT SAME NIGHT WE SAID GOODBYE TO KAWKA AND WENT AGAIN TO SZOPIENICE.

BUT, THEN, MOTONOWA STOPPED TO COME DOWN.

IT'S BEEN 3 DAYS SINCE SHE BROUGHT ANY FOOD.

HERE... HAVE ANOTHER CANDY...

I HAD STILL CANDIES I ORGANIZED ON DEKERTA. ONLY *THIS* WE HAD TO EAT.

ALSO, HERE WE HAD NO PLACE WHERE TO WASH, SO ANJA GOT ON ALL HER SKIN A TERRIBLE RASH.

I DON'T KNOW WHAT'S WORSE— THE HUNGER OR THE ITCHING.

DON'T SCRATCH! IT ONLY— SHH!

CLIK

THE DOOR.

I'M SORRY I COULDN'T GET DOWN BEFORE—MY HUSBAND IS GETTING SUSPICIOUS.

HE ASKED WHY I GO TO THE CELLAR SO OFTEN. HE EVEN ASKED IF I WAS HIDING JEWS HERE! ...HE WAS JOKING, BUT STILL...

ARE YOU ALL RIGHT HERE?

THERE ARE *RATS*, GIANT RATS! THEY'RE HORRIBLE!

WELL—YOU'RE BETTER OFF WITH THE RATS THAN WITH THE GESTAPO... AT LEAST THE RATS WON'T KILL YOU!

MMM...

AND SHE WAS RIGHT. WE WERE HAPPY EVEN TO HAVE *THESE* CONDITIONS.

AFTER THE TEN DAYS HER HUSBAND LEFT, AND SHE TOOK US BACK.

IT'S GOOD TO BE "HOME," EH, VLADEK?

IT'S A LOT NICER THAN THAT CELLAR.

BUT I DIDN'T FEEL SAFE HERE. IT WAS TOO MANY WAYS SOMEBODY COULD FIND US OUT. I WANTED TO GO BETTER TO HUNGARY.

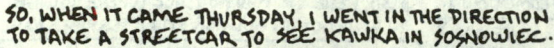

SO, WHEN IT CAME THURSDAY, I WENT IN THE DIRECTION TO TAKE A STREETCAR TO SEE KAWKA IN SOSNOWIEC.

LOOK!

I HAD TO PASS WHERE SOME CHILDREN WERE PLAYING.

A JEW! A JEW!

THEY RAN SCREAMING HOME.

HELP! MOMMY! A JEW!!

A JEW!

QUICK, THE MOTHERS CAME OUTSIDE TO SEE WHAT WAS!

THE MOTHERS ALWAYS TOLD SO: "BE CARE-FUL! A JEW WILL CATCH YOU TO A BAG AND EAT YOU!" ... SO THEY TAUGHT TO THEIR CHILDREN.

I APPROACHED OVER TO THEM...

HEIL HITLER.

IF I RAN AWAY THEY WOULD SEE: "YES, IT IS A JEW HERE."

DON'T BE AFRAID, LITTLE ONES. I'M NOT A JEW. I WON'T HURT YOU.

SORRY, MISTER. YOU KNOW HOW KIDS ARE ... HEIL HITLER.

SO I CAME OUT WELL FROM THIS...

BUT THE EXPERIENCE COST ME REALLY A LOT OF HAIRS.

1986

JULIA ALVAREZ
b. 1950

anguage, culture, politics, and region are customarily subjects for serious study, but in the work of Julia Alvarez they become the impetus for great creativity, even festivity. This is because many of Alvarez's characters share a background like her own, in which these elements are anything but stable. Born in New York City, raised in the Dominican Republic, and returned to Brooklyn when her father's political activities put him in danger from the dictator Rafael Trujillo, Alvarez faced the same prospect as her most typical protagonist: that of improvising a sense of self. Such improvisation typifies young Yolanda in Alvarez's first novel, *How the García Girls Lost Their Accents* (1991), and the sixteen members of Yolanda's immediate and extended family react to that improvisation in its sequel, *¡Yo!* (1997). If Yolanda, nicknamed "Yo" (meaning "I" in Spanish), can invent herself, so can her parents, siblings, cousins, aunts, and close friends judge her approximation of reality against theirs—and how many there are! The result is a carnival of language and language's many contexts, in which humor and the self-conscious joy of storytelling create a virtual conversation with the reader.

As a writer Alvarez has explored the double identities she shared as a young girl negotiating her way on Brooklyn playgrounds, no longer a citizen of the Dominican Republic but not yet accepted as an American. After doing graduate work at Syracuse University and publishing a book of poems, *Homecoming* (1984), she turned to the multiform saga of the García girls as a way of exploring the more playful aspects of language, a style of heteroglossia advocated by the Russian literary theorist M. M. Bakhtin. *How the García Girls Lost Their Accents* uses interrelated narratives of the four sisters to contrast their hard-won American identities with the different styles of life they had led as youngsters, first in the Dominican Republic and then as immigrants to fast-paced New York. A third novel (more loosely a sequel than is *¡Yo!*), *In the Time of the Butterflies* (1994), takes the historical event of three sisters' murder by Trujillo's secret police and retells it from a fictional perspective, that of a fourth, surviving sibling. Here are the more sober aspects of language, culture, politics, and region that are presented more happily in *¡Yo!*

In recent years Alvarez, like other Latina writers, has focused on the writer's role in fashioning a voice, particularly as that voice undertakes what critic Kelli Lyon Johnson calls "generic transgressions" in which fiction, poetry, autobiography, history, children's literature, and even literary theory intermix. *In the Name of Salomé* (2000) is presented as a novel, although its protagonists are historical figures prominent as a poet in the Dominican Republic (the mother) and a scholar in the United States (her daughter). Alvarez has taught for many years at Vermont's Middlebury College, where she is writer-in-residence between regular visits to the Dominican Republic.

The following text is from *¡Yo!* (1997).

From ¡Yo!

The Mother

To tell you the truth, the hardest thing coming to this country wasn't the winter everyone warned me about—it was the language. If you had to choose the most tongue-twisting way of saying you love somebody or how much a pound for the ground round, then say it in English. For the longest time I thought Americans must be smarter than us Latins—because how else could they speak such a difficult language. After a while, it struck me the other way. Given the choice of languages, only a fool would choose to speak English on purpose.

I guess for each one in the family it was different what was the hardest thing. For Carlos, it was having to start all over again at forty-five, getting a license, setting up a practice. My eldest Carla just couldn't bear that she wasn't the know-it-all anymore. Of course, the Americans knew their country better than she did. Sandi got more complicated, prettier, and I suppose that made it hard on her, discovering she was a princess just as she had lost her island kingdom. Baby Fifi took to this place like china in a china shop, so if anything, the hardest thing for her was hearing the rest of us moan and complain. As for Yo, I'd have to say the hardest thing about this country was being thrown together in such close proximity with me.

Back on the island[1] we lived as a clan, not as what is called here *the nuclear family*,[2] which already the name should be a hint that you're asking for trouble cooping up related tempers in the small explosive chambers of each other's attention. The girls used to run with their gang of cousins, supervised—if you can call it that—by a whole bunch of aunts and nanny-maids who had wiped our bottoms when *we* were babies and now were wiping the drool of the old people who had hired them half a century ago. There was never any reason to clash with anyone. You didn't get along with your mother? You had two sisters, one brother-in-law, three brothers and their wives, thirteen nieces and nephews, a husband, your own kids, two great-aunts, your father, a bachelor uncle, a deaf poor relation, and a small army of housemaids to mediate and appease—so that if you muttered under your breath, "You bitch!" by the time it got to your mother it would sound something like, "Pass the mango dish, please."

And this was true for Yo and me.

Back there, that one was mostly raised by the maids. She seemed to like to hang around them more than she did her own kin, so that if she had been darker, I would have thought she was a changeling that got switched with my own flesh and blood. True, from time to time we did have our run-downs—not even three, four dozen people could always block the clashing of our two strong wills.

But I had a trick that I played back then, not just on her, but on all my girls, to make them behave. I called it putting on the bear. Of course, by the time we left the island, it no longer worked there, and it was only by mistake that it worked once here.

---

1. The Dominican Republic, a Caribbean nation that shares the island of Hispaniola with Haiti.

2. A family consisting of a father, mother, and a small number of children, closely spaced in age.

It started innocently enough. My mother had given me a mink coat she used to wear when she and my father were traveling a lot to New York for vacations away from the dictatorship.[3] I kept it at the back of the walk-in closet, thinking maybe someday we would escape the hell we were living in, and I'd get to wear that coat into freedom. Often I thought about selling it. I hadn't married a rich man and we were always short on money.

But every time I got ready to sell it, I don't know. I'd bury my nose in that tickling fur that still held the smell of my mother's perfume. I'd imagine myself walking down Fifth Avenue with lights twinkling in the shop windows and snowflakes coming down so pretty, and I just couldn't bear to part with the coat. I'd slip the plastic cover back over it and think, I'll hold on to it a while longer.

Then one Christmas, I thought it'd be kind of neat to dress up for all the kids. So I draped this coat over my head with a bit of my face poking out, and the rest of the fur falling all the way down to my calves. I had some story worked out that Santa Claus couldn't make it down from the North Pole, so he had sent one of his bears instead.

My girls and their cousins took one look at me and it was like sheets hitting a fan. They screamed and ran. No one could be coaxed to come forward for a present. Finally, Carlos pantomined chasing me off with a broom, and as I hurried away, I dropped my pillowcase of goodies. Minutes later, when I walked back in, dressed in my red organdy, the girls ran to me, "Mami! Mami! El cuco[4] was here!" El cuco was the Haitian boogeyman I had told them would come and steal them away if they didn't behave.

"Really?" I said, miming surprise. "What did you do?"

The girls looked at each other, big-eyed. What could they have done but avoid being mouthfuls for a monster with an appetite for their toys. But Yo piped up, "I beat him and chased him away!"

Here was a little problem that was not going to go away by itself. Often, I put Tabasco in that mouth hoping to burn away the lies that seemed to spring from her lips. For Yo, talking was like an exercise in what you could make up. But that night was Christmas Eve, and the dictatorship seemed far away in some storybook about cucos, and Carlos looked so handsome in his white guayabera,[5] like a rich plantation owner in an American ad for coffee beans or cigars. Besides I felt pleased with my little trick.

From then on, especially when I heard them fighting, I threw that coat over my head and went hooting down the hall. I'd burst into their room, swinging my arms, calling out their names, and they'd scream, holding on to each other, whatever fight they had been in the middle of forgotten. Step by step, I approached, until they were at the edge of hysterics, their little faces pale and their eyes wide with terror. Then I flung the coat off and threw out my arms, "It's me, Mami!"

For a minute, even though they could see it was me, they hung back, unconvinced.

Maybe it was a mean thing to do, I don't know. After a few times, what I was really trying to do was see if my girls had any sense at all. I thought for sure they would catch on. But no, each time, I fooled them. And I began to feel angry at them for being so slow.

Yo figured it out, finally. Maybe she was five, six—I don't know. All those years have mixed together like an old puzzle whose box top is lost. (I don't even know anymore what picture all those little pieces make.) As usual, I went howling into the girls' bedroom. But this time, Yo broke loose, came right up to me, and yanked that coat off my head. "See," she said, turning to the others. "It *is* just Mami like I told you."

It was no surprise to me that she was the one who caught on.

Back in my room, I was returning the coat when I noticed someone had been poking around in the closet. My shoes were scattered every which way, a hat box knocked over. That closet wasn't just any walk-in closet. It had once been a hallway between the master bedroom and Carlos's study, but we had closed it off on both sides in order to make a closet you could enter from either room. It was almost always locked on account of we kept everything valuable there. I suppose at the back of our minds, Carlos and I always knew that one day we would have to leave the island in a hurry and that it would be handy to have our cash and valuables on hand. And so, I was fit to be fried seeing signs that someone had been rifling through our hiding place.

Then it came to me who our intruder had been—Yo! Earlier, I had seen her in Carlos's study, looking over the medical books her father let her play with. She must have gone in our closet, and that's how she had figured out the fur was just a fur. I was ready to call her in and give her a large serving of my right hand when I saw that the floorboards close to the study side had been pried open and not exactly wedged back in place. I crawled in under the clothes with a flashlight and lifted one of those boards. It was my turn to go pale—stashed inside and wrapped in one of my good towels was a serious-looking gun.

You can bet when Carlos came home, I threatened to leave him right then and there if he didn't tell me what he was up to. I found out more than I wanted to know.

"No harm done," Carlos kept saying. "I'll just move it to another location tonight." And he did, wrapping it inside my fur coat and laying the bundle on the back seat of the Buick like he was going off to sell that coat after all. He came back late that night, the coat over his arm, and it wasn't until the next morning as I was hanging it up that I found the oil stains on the lining. They looked just like dried blood.

After that, I was a case all right. Nights, I was up to four sleeping pills to numb myself into a few hours of the skimpiest sleep. Days I took Valium[6] to ease that jumpy feeling. It was hell on the wheels of our marriage having me down so much of the time. Worst were the migraines I got practically every afternoon. I'd have to lie down in that small, hot bedroom with the jalousies angled shut and a wet towel on my face. Far off, I could hear the kids yelling in their bedroom, and I'd wish I could squeeze that bear trick one more time to terrify them into silence.

Lots of worries went through my pounding head those afternoons. One of them that kept hammering away was that Yo had been snooping around in that closet. If she had seen that hidden gun, it was just a matter of time

6. Anti-anxiety prescription drug.

before she'd tell someone about it. Already I could see the SIM[7] coming to the door to drag us away. One afternoon when I just couldn't stand it anymore, I leapt out of my bed and called down the hall for her to come to my room this instant.

She must have thought she was going to get it about all the loud bickering coming from their bedroom. She hurried down the hall already defending herself that she had plucked off Fifi's baby doll's head only because Fifi had asked her to. "Hush now," I said, "it's not about that!" That stopped her short. She hung back at the door, looking around my bedroom like maybe she wasn't so sure the bear was nothing but her mother in a fur coat after all.

I gave her a little pep talk in a soft voice—the way you talk to babies as you stroke them till their eyes drift shut. I told her Papá Dios in heaven could see into every one of our souls. He knew when we were good and when we were bad. When we lied and when we told the truth. That He could have asked us to do whatever He wanted, but out of all the hundred million things, He had only chosen ten holy commandments for us to obey. And one of those ten was honor thy father and mother which meant you shouldn't lie to them.

"So always, always, you must tell your mami the truth." I served her a big smile of which she only returned a little slice back. She knew something else was coming. She sat on the bed, watching me. Just as she had seen through the fur to her mother, now she was looking through her mother to the scared woman inside. I let out a long sigh, and said, "Now, cuca darling, Mami wants you to tell her what things you saw when you went looking in the closet the other day."

"You mean the big closet?" she said, pointing down the passageway that led from the master bedroom to the walk-in closet and right through to her father's study.

"That very one," I said. The migraine was hammering away inside my head, building its big house of pain.

She looked at me like she knew that admitting she had been snooping would get her into a closet full of trouble. So, I promised her that telling the truth this time would make her my and God's little darling.

"I saw your coat," she said.

"That's very good," I said. "That's what I mean. What else did you see in Mami's closet?"

"Your funny shoes," she remarked. She meant the heels with little holes pockmarked in the leather.

"Excellent!" I said. "Mami's darling. What else?"

She went through that whole closet with the full inventory of practically every piece of clothing I owned. My God, I thought, give her another decade and *she* could work for the SIM. I lay there, listening because what else could I do? If she hadn't really seen anything, I didn't want to put any ideas in her head. That one had a mouth from here to China going the long way like Columbus's ships.

"How about the floor?" I asked stupidly. "Did you see anything *in* the floor?"

She shook her head in a way that didn't convince me. I went back over the ten commandments and not lying to thy mother, and still I couldn't flush any more information from her except my monogrammed hankies and, oh yes,

---

7. Servicio de Inteligencia Militar (Spanish for "Military Intelligence Service"), Trujillo's dreaded secret police.

my nylons in a pleated plastic case. I finally made her promise that if she remembered anything else, she should come and tell Mami directly and no one else. "It will be our little secret," I whispered to her.

Just as she was slipping out the door, she turned around and said a curious thing. "Mami, the bear won't be coming anymore." It was as if she were stating her part of our bargain. "Honey cuca," I said. "Remember, Mami was the one playing the bear. It was just a silly joke. But no," I promised her, "that bear's gone for good. Okay?" She nodded her approval.

As soon as the door latched shut I cried into my pillow. My head was hurting so much. I missed not having nice things, money and freedom. I hated being at the mercy of my own child, but in that house we were all at the mercy of her silence from that day on.

Isn't a story a charm? All you have to say is, *And then we came to the United States,* and with that *and then,* you skip over four more years of disappearing friends, sleepless nights, house arrest, narrow escape, *and then,* you've got two adults and four wired-up kids in a small, dark apartment near Columbia University. Yo must have kept her mouth shut or no charm would have worked to get us free of the torture chambers we kept telling the immigration people about so they wouldn't send us back.

Not being one hundred percent sure we would get to stay—that was the hardest thing at the beginning. Even the problem with the English language seemed like a drop in a leaky bucket then. It was later that I got to thinking English was the hardest thing of all for me. But believe me, back then at the beginning, I had my hands too full to be making choices among our difficulties.

Carlos was morose. All he could think about was the compañeros he had left behind. I kept asking him what else he could have done but stay to die with them. He was studying like cats and dogs for his license exam. We were living on the low end of the hog off what little savings we had left, and there was no money coming in. I was worried how I was going to pay for the warm clothes my kids would be needing once the cold weather set in.

The last thing I needed was their whining and fighting. Every day it was the same question, "When are we going to go back?" Now that we were far away and I wasn't afraid of their blurting things out, I tried to explain. But it was as if they thought I was lying to them with a story to make them behave. They'd listen, but as soon as I was done, they'd start in again. They wanted to go back to their cousins and uncles and aunts and the maids. I thought they would feel more at home once school began. But September, October, November, December passed by, and they were still having nightmares and nagging me all the long days that they wanted to go back. Go back. Go back. Go back.

I resorted to locking them in closets. That old-fashioned apartment was full of them, deep closets with glass knobs and those keyholes like in cartoons for detectives to look through and big iron keys with the handle part shaped like a fleur-de-lis. I always used the same four closets, a small one in the girls' bedroom and the big one in mine, the broom closet in the hall, and finally the coat closet in the living room. Which child went into which depended on who I grabbed first where.

I wouldn't leave them in there for long. Believe me. I'd go from door to door, like a priest taking confession, promising to let them out the minute they calmed down and agreed to live in peace. I don't know how it happened that Yo never got the coat closet until that one time that I lived to regret.

I had shut them all up and gone round, letting out the baby first, then the oldest, who was always so outraged. Then the two middle kids, first Sandi. When I got to Yo's door, I didn't get an answer. That scared me, and I opened that door quick. There she stood, pale with fright. And, ay, I felt so terrible!—she had gone in her pants.

That damn mink coat was in that closet, way to one side, but of course, being Yo, she'd gone poking around in the dark. She must have touched the fur and lost her bananas. I don't understand because it had seemed she knew the fur was just a coat. Maybe she associated me being under that coat, and here I was on one side of the door, and there she was alone on the other side with a monster she was sure we had left behind in the Dominican Republic.

I pulled her out and into the bathroom. She didn't cry. No—just that low moan kids do when they go deep inside themselves looking for the mother you haven't turned out to be for them. All she said that whole time I was trying to clean her up was, "You promised that bear was gone for good."

I got weepy myself. "You girls are the bears! And here I thought all our troubles would end when we got here." I laid down my head on my arms on the side of the bathtub, and I started bawling. "Ay, Mami, ay," the other three joined in. They had come to the door of the bathroom to see what was going on. "We promise we'll be good."

Not Yo. She stood up in the water and grabbed a towel, then stomped out of the tub. When she was out of my reach, she cried, "I don't want to be in this crazy family!"

Even back then, she always had to have the last word.

Not a week later a social worker at the school, Sally O'Brien, calls up and asks to make a house visit. The minute I get off the phone, I interrogate my girls about what they might have said to this lady. But they all swear that they have nothing to confess. I warn them if this lady gives us a bad report we'll be sent back, and if we are sent back, cucos and bears are going to be stuffed animals compared to the SIM fieras[8] that will tear us apart there. I send them off to put on their matching polka dot dresses I made them for coming to the United States. And then I do what I haven't done in our six months here. I take a Valium to give this lady a good impression.

In she comes, a tall lady in flat black shoes with straps and a blond braid down her back like a schoolgirl dressed in an old lady's suit. She has a pleasant, un-made-up face and eyes so blue and sincere you know they've yet to see the worst things in the world. She carries a satchel with little hearts painted on it. Out of it she pulls a long yellow tablet with our name already written on it. "Is it all right if I take some notes?"

"Of course, Mrs. O'Brien." I don't know if she is a married woman but I've decided to compliment her with a husband even if she doesn't have one.

"Will your husband be joining us?" she asks, looking around the room. I follow her glance since I am sure she is checking out whether the place looks clean and adequate for raising four girls. The coat closet I forgot to shut looms like a torture chamber.

8. Wild beasts (Spanish).

"My husband just received his medical license. So he has been working like a god every day, even Sunday," I add, which she writes down in her notepad. "We have been through hard times." I've already decided that I won't try to pretend that we're having a ball in America, though believe it or not, that was my original plan on how to handle this visit. I thought it would sound more patriotic.

"That must be a relief!" she says, nodding her head and looking at me. Everything she says it's like she just put the rattle in the baby's hand and is waiting to see what the baby is going to do with it.

I shake it, good and hard. "We are free at last," I tell her. "Thanks to this great country which has offered us the green cards. We cannot go back," I add. "It would be certain death."

Her eyes blink at this, and she makes a note. "I read things in the paper," she says, bringing her braid from behind to fall down the front of her suit. She doesn't seem the nervous type, but the way she keeps minding that braid it's like she is getting paid to keep it occupied. "But are things really that bad?"

And right then and there in my broken English that usually cuts my ideas down to the wrong size, I fill her two ears full with what is happening back on the island—homes raided, people hauled off, torture chambers, electric prods, attacks by dogs, fingernails pulled out. I get a little carried away and invent a few tortures of my own—nothing the SIM hadn't thought up, I'm sure. As I talk, she keeps wincing until her hands go up to her forehead like she has caught one of my migraines. In a whisper she says, "This is truly awful. You must be so worried about the rest of your family."

I can't trust my voice to say so. I give her a little nod.

"But what I don't get is how the girls keep saying they want to go back. That things were better there."

"They are sick of home—" I explain, but that doesn't sound right.

"Homesick, yes," she says.

I nod. "They are children. They do not see the forest or the trees."

"I understand." She says it so nicely that I am convinced that even with those untried blue eyes, she does understand. "They can't know the horror you and your husband have lived through."

I try to keep the tears back, but of course they come. What this lady can't know is that I'm not just crying about leaving home or about everything we've lost, but about what's to come. It's not really until now with the whole clan pulled away like the foundation under a house that I wonder if the six of us will stand together.

"I understand, I understand," she keeps saying until I get control of myself. "We're just concerned because the girls seem so anxious. Especially Yolanda."

I knew it! "Has she been telling stories?"

The lady nods slowly. "Her teacher says she loves stories. But some of the ones she tells, well—" She lets out a sigh. She tosses her braid behind her back like she doesn't want it to hear this. "Frankly, they are a little disturbing."

"Disturbing?" I ask. Even though I know what the word means, it sounds worse coming out of this woman's mouth.

"Oh, she's been mentioning things . . ." The lady waves her hand vaguely. "Things like what you were describing. Kids locked in closets and their mouths burned with lye. Bears mauling little children." She stops a moment, maybe because of the shocked look on my face.

"It doesn't surprise me," the woman explains. "In fact, I'm glad she's getting it all out."

"Yes," I say. And suddenly, I am feeling such envy for my daughter, who is able to speak of what terrifies her. I myself can't find the words in English—or Spanish. Only the howling of the bear I used to impersonate captures some of what I feel.

"Yo has always been full of stories." I say it like an accusation.

"Oh, but you should be proud of her," the lady says, bringing her braid forward like she is going to defend Yo with it.

"Proud?" I say in disbelief, ready to give her all the puzzle pieces of my mind so she gets the full picture. But then, I realize it is no use. How can this lady with her child's eyes and her sweet smile understand who I am and what I have been through? And maybe this is a blessing after all. That people only know the parts we want to tell about ourselves. Look at her. Inside that middle-aged woman is a nervous girl playing with her braid. But how that girl got stuck in there, and where the key is to let her out, maybe not even she can tell?

"Who knows where Yo got that need to invent," I finally say because I don't know what else to say.

"This has been very helpful, Laura," she says, standing up to go. "And I want you to know if there's anything we can do to help you all in settling in, please don't hesitate to call." She hands me a little card, not like our calling cards back home with all your important family names in fancy gold lettering. This one shows her name and title and the name of the school and her phone number in black print.

"Let me call the girls to say goodbye."

She smiles when they come out in their pretty, ironed dresses, curtsying like I taught them. And as she bends to shake each one's hand, I glance down at her pad on the coffee table and read the notes she has jotted: *Trauma/dictatorship/family bonds strong/mother devoted.*

For a moment I feel redeemed as if everything we are suffering and everything we will suffer is the fault of the dictatorship. I know this will be the story I tell in the future about those hard years—how we lived in terror, how the girls were traumatized by the experience, how many nights I got up to check on their blankets and they screamed if I touched them.

But never mind. Within a year of all this, the dictator will be shot dead by some of the very men who were in the underground with my husband. The girls will be jabbering away in English like they were born to it. As for the mink, I will exchange it at the secondhand shop on Fifth Avenue for four little-girl coats. If nothing else, my children will be warm that first winter everyone warned would be the hardest thing about coming to this country.

1997

JOY HARJO
b. 1951

Joy Harjo was born in Tulsa, Oklahoma, to a mother of mixed Cherokee, French, and Irish blood. She has described her father's family, members of the Creek (also known as Muskogee) tribe, as "rebels and speakers," among them a Baptist minister (Harjo's paternal grandfather), two painters (her grandmother and aunt), and a great-great-grandfather who in 1832 led a Creek rebellion against their forced removal from Alabama into Oklahoma. As the critic Laura Coltelli has pointed out, the work of many contemporary Native American writers (a large number of whom are of mixed blood) enacts a quest to reenvision identity by confronting the historical, cultural, and political realities that shape lives experienced between different worlds. Drawing on a family tradition of powerful speaking, Harjo participates in a search to reimagine and repair painful fractures in contemporary experience: between past and present, between person and landscape, and between parts of the self. Thus traveling is a mythic activity in her poems, enacting this search for community and historical connectedness. As in the work of James Welch, Simon J. Ortiz, and Leslie Marmon Silko, the theme of traveling in Harjo's poems resonates with the historical displacements and migrations of native peoples (especially the forced removal of the Creeks). She has called herself the wanderer in her family, and her poems often map her journeys, whether on foot, by car, or in a plane. Perhaps Harjo thinks of herself as the family wanderer because she left Oklahoma to attend high school at the Institute of American Indian Arts in Santa Fe, New Mexico ("in a way it saved my life," she has said). Since receiving a B.A. from the University of New Mexico in 1976 and an MFA from the University of Iowa, she has taught at the Institute of American Indian Arts, Arizona State University, the University of Colorado, the University of Arizona, and the University of New Mexico.

Harjo's vision of the interrelatedness of all things is common to Native American storytelling. The ethic that emerges from this worldview stresses reciprocity between people and various sources of power, including tradition and the natural world. Harjo's poems bring together mythic, feminist, and cultural perspectives and also unite contemporary urban experience with Native American myth and legend. In her collection *She Had Some Horses* (1983) this integration seeks to assuage the loneliness and desperation of those on the margin who populate much of the volume: a woman raising her mixed-blood children alone, a friend who threatens suicide, a woman who threatens to drop from a thirteenth-story window. The collection *In Mad Love and War* (1990) exhibits anger at the separations caused by dispossession and violence, as in an elegy for Anna Mae Pictou Aquash, a young Micmac woman shot dead on the Pine Ridge Reservation. Poems such as this recall the passion for social justice in the works of James Wright, Audre Lorde, and Leslie Marmon Silko; indeed, the spirit of Harjo's rebel great-great-grandfather is never far from her work.

Harjo has been a leading figure in the adaptation of oral traditions into written forms, consciously using the written word in her poems in a way that duplicates certain oral and ceremonial techniques. Her poems extensively and emphatically use repetition, of both words and units of thought, as mnemonic and structuring devices. For example, her poem "When the World As We Knew It Ended," written in response to the events of September 11, 2001, begins a series of stanzas with the repetition and variation of "We saw it," "We heard it," "We knew it. . . ." Reflecting the understanding that Native American tradition is not fixed but evolves and changes, Harjo has fearlessly experimented, adapting new musical and poetic forms to Native American traditions. She has long drawn on reggae, rock, Creek Stomp Dance songs, country, and African music and has integrated performance and dance into her poetry. A musician and songwriter, she has released three CD collections: *Letter from the End of the Twentieth Century* (1997), *Native Joy for Real* (2005), and a musical version of her recently republished *She Had Some Horses* (2006). Harjo plays the saxophone, which is not a traditional Native American instrument, but, she has said, "Someday it may be."

Metamorphosis, common in Native American storytelling, is central to Harjo's vision, where the world is constituted by change and constancy. Her collection *The Woman Who Fell from the Sky* (1994) embodies metamorphosis in its structure—the retelling of contemporary experience through traditional myths—and metamorphosis recurs in its stories. Various Native American traditions tell the story of a sky woman who falls through the void of space and creates the human universe. In the title poem of this volume, a group of women ("angry at their inattentive husbands") run off with stars; one of these women dares to look back at Earth and falls from the sky. In Harjo's hands this myth becomes the story of two lovers, who were children together at an Indian boarding school. Adrift in an urban landscape, they are reunited, their narrative characterized by fracture and repair. In the same collection "Flood" renders a young girl's sexuality and imaginative power through the myth of the water monster. The prose poems that form much of this book remind us that Native American storytelling, an oral tradition, does not distinguish between poetry and prose. For all Harjo's anguished sense of the warring factions in our world and our selves, her works consistently engage in a process of healing and regeneration, themes that continue in her collection *A Map to the Next World* (2000). Like the kitchen table in her poem "Perhaps the World Ends Here," Harjo's poems are a space where "we sing with joy, with sorrow. We pray of suffering and remorse. We give thanks."

Harjo has also written screenplays and the text for Stephen Strom's photographs of the Southwestern landscape, *Secrets from the Center of the World* (1989), and she has edited an anthology of tribal women's writings from around the world. A collection of interviews, *The Spiral of Memory* (1996), edited by Laura Coltelli, is a valuable accompaniment to her poems. *How We Became Human* (2003) presents a selection from Harjo's earlier work, including poems from hard-to-find chapbooks, as well as new work.

Call It Fear

There is this edge where shadows
and bones of some of us walk
                          backwards.
Talk backwards. There is this edge
call it an ocean of fear of the dark. Or   5
name it with other songs. Under our ribs
our hearts are bloody stars. Shine on
shine on, and horses in their galloping flight
strike the curve of ribs.
                          Heartbeat   10
and breathe back sharply. Breathe
                          backwards.
There is this edge within me
                    I saw it once
an August Sunday morning when the heat hadn't   15
left this earth. And Goodluck
sat sleeping next to me in the truck.

We had never broken through the edge of the
singing at four a.m.
          We had only wanted to talk, to hear   20
any other voice to stay alive with.
          And there was this edge—
not the drop of sandy rock cliff
bones of volcanic earth into
          Albuquerque.   25
Not that,
     but a string of shadow horses kicking
and pulling me out of my belly,
     not into the Rio Grande[1] but into the music
barely coming through   30
         Sunday church singing
from the radio. Battery worn-down but the voices
talking backwards.

         1983

White Bear

She begins to board the flight
   to Albuquerque. Late night.
But stops in the corrugated tunnel,
   a space between leaving and staying,
where the night sky catches   5

    her whole life

she has felt like a woman
   balancing on a wooden nickle heart
approaching herself from here to
   there, Tulsa or New York   10
with knives or corn meal.

The last flight someone talked
   about how coming from Seattle
the pilot flew a circle
   over Mt. St. Helens,[1] she sat   15
quiet. (But had seen the eruption
   as the earth beginning
to come apart, as in birth
   out of violence.)

She watches the yellow lights   20
   of towns below the airplane flicker,
fade and fall backwards. Somewhere,
   she dreamed, there is the white bear
moving down from the north, motioning her paws

---

1. River flowing from southern Colorado through New Mexico and then forming the boundary between Texas and Mexico.

1. A volcanic peak in Washington State; it erupted in 1980.

like a long arctic night, that kind   25
of circle and the whole world balanced in
   between carved of ebony and ice

     oh so hard

the clear black nights
   like her daughter's eyes, and the white   30
bear moon, cupped like an ivory rocking
cradle, tipping back it could go
either way
     all darkness
         is open to all light.   35

1983

RITA DOVE
b. 1952

What she has called the "friction" between the beauty of a poetic form and a difficult or painful subject appeals to Rita Dove. Her own formal control and discipline create a beautiful design and a haunting music in "Parsley," a poem based on a murderous event: in 1957 the dictator of the Dominican Republic, Rafael Trujillo, ordered twenty thousand black Haitians killed because they could not pronounce the letter "r" in the Spanish word for parsley. What compels Dove in this poem is the way a "single, beautiful word" has the power of life and death. More astonishing is that she writes from the perspectives of both the Haitians in the cane fields and General Trujillo in his palace. When asked in an interview about her capacity to imagine Trujillo, Dove responded, "I frankly don't believe anyone who says they've never felt any evil, that they cannot understand that process of evil. It was important to me to try to understand that arbitrary quality of his cruelty. . . . Making us get into his head may shock us all into seeing what the human being is capable of, because if we can go that far into his head, we're halfway there ourselves." An ability to enter into different points of view in a single poem is characteristic of Dove's disinterested imagination. Her method is to avoid commentary, to let the imagined person or object, the suggestive detail, speak for itself. Often her work suggests what the English poet John Keats called "negative capability," the gift of the poet to become what he or she is not.

Born in Akron, Dove attended Miami University of Ohio and, after her graduation, studied modern European literature as a Fulbright/Hays fellow at the University of Tübingen in Germany. When she returned from Europe she earned an MFA at the University of Iowa (in 1977). Later she taught creative writing at Arizona State University before joining the University of Virginia, where she is now Commonwealth Professor of English. Since her Fulbright year she has repeatedly chosen to live abroad, in Ireland, Israel, France, and especially Germany. Her travel in Europe and elsewhere suggests part of the imperative she feels as a poet: to range widely through fields of experience, to cross boundaries of space as well as time. Her first book, *The Yellow House on the Corner* (1980), is notable for its intense poems about adolescence; her second book, *Museum* (1983), dramatically extends the range of her work. "When I started *Museum*," she has said, "I was in Europe, and I had a way of looking back on America and distancing myself from my experience." As well as for several fine poems about her father (a subject that may also have needed distance), the book is remarkable for the way distance allowed Dove to move out of her immediate experience, freed her to imagine widely different lives.

As if to show that it is also possible to travel widely while staying at home, Dove's *Thomas and Beulah* (1986) is an extended sequence based on her grandparents' lives. Her continuing fascination with imagining different perspectives on the same event is evident in this sequence. Dove has described the book's origins this way:

> My grandmother had told me a story that had happened to my grandfather when he was young, coming up on a riverboat to Akron, Ohio, my hometown. But that was all I had basically. And the story so fascinated me that I tried to write about it. I started off writing stories about my grandfather and soon, because I ran out of real fact, in order to keep going, I made up facts for this character, Thomas. . . . then this poem "Dusting" appeared, really out of nowhere. I didn't realize this was Thomas's wife saying, "I want to talk. And you can't do his side without my side. . . ."

This is the story, in part, of a marriage and of a black couple's life in the industrial Midwest in the period from 1900 to 1960. Thomas's point of view controls the poems of the book's first section, while the second part imagines his wife's. The larger framework of the sequence links family history to social history. Thomas's journey from the rural South to the industrial city of Akron (where he finds employment in the Goodyear Zeppelin factory until the Depression puts him out of work) is part of the larger social movement of African Americans from the South into Northern industrial cities in the first part of this century. The individual lyrics of Dove's sequence create and sustain the story through distinct and often ordinary moments in which each life is vividly portrayed. It is part of Dove's gift that she can render the apparently unimportant moments that inform a life and set them against a background of larger historical forces, as do Robert Hayden in *Elegies for Paradise Valley* and Robert Lowell in *Notebook*.

Many of the figures in Dove's poems are displaced, on the border between different worlds: for example, Thomas and Beulah, and the biracial violin prodigy, George Bridgetower (1780–1860), who is the focus of her volume *Sonata Mulattica* (2009). The experience of displacement, of what she has called living in "two different worlds, seeing things with double vision," consistently compels this poet's imagination. It takes both detachment and control to maintain (and to live with) such doubleness. This may be why Dove's rich sense of language and her love of sound are joined to a disciplined formal sense. The forms of her poems often hold in place difficult or ambiguous feelings and keep the expression of feeling understated. While restraint is one strength of Dove's poems, her work can sometimes seem austere. Such careful control recalls Elizabeth Bishop's early work, also highly controlled and even, at times, guarded. As Bishop grew to relax her restraints, to open into an extraordinary expressiveness, so Dove's career shows a similar growth. Her collections *Grace Notes* (1989), *Mother Love* (1995), and *American Smooth* (2004) suggest just such a relaxing of the poet's guard, while *On the Bus with Rosa Parks* (2000) demonstrates an ongoing ability to unite social conscience with a transformative sense of language and form. With each book she asks something more from herself, and she has now become one of our indispensable poets. Dove was poet laureate of the United States from 1993 to 1995.

Adolescence—I

In water-heavy nights behind grandmother's porch
We knelt in the tickling grasses and whispered:
Linda's face hung before us, pale as a pecan,
And it grew wise as she said:
    "A boy's lips are soft,   5
      As soft as baby's skin."
The air closed over her words.
A firefly whirred near my ear, and in the distance
I could hear streetlamps ping
Into miniature suns   10
Against a feathery sky.

1980

Adolescence—II

Although it is night, I sit in the bathroom, waiting.
Sweat prickles behind my knees, the baby-breasts are alert.
Venetian blinds slice up the moon; the tiles quiver in pale strips.

Then they come, the three seal men with eyes as round
As dinner plates and eyelashes like sharpened tines.   5
They bring the scent of licorice. One sits in the washbowl,

One on the bathtub edge; one leans against the door.
"Can you feel it yet?" they whisper.
I don't know what to say, again. They chuckle,

Patting their sleek bodies with their hands.   10
"Well, maybe next time." And they rise,
Glittering like pools of ink under moonlight,

And vanish. I clutch at the ragged holes
They leave behind, here at the edge of darkness.
Night rests like a ball of fur on my tongue.   15

1980

Parsley[1]

1. The Cane[2] Fields

There is a parrot imitating spring
in the palace, its feathers parsley green.
Out of the swamp the cane appears

---

1. On October 2, 1937, Rafael Trujillo (1891–
1961), dictator of the Dominican Republic,
ordered 20,000 blacks killed because they could
not pronounce the letter "r" in *perejil*, the Spanish
word for parsley [Dove's note].
2. I.e., sugar cane.

to haunt us, and we cut it down. El General
searches for a word; he is all the world   5
there is. Like a parrot imitating spring,

we lie down screaming as rain punches through
and we come up green. We cannot speak an R—
out of the swamp, the cane appears

and then the mountain we call in whispers *Katalina*.[3]   10
The children gnaw their teeth to arrowheads.
There is a parrot imitating spring.

El General has found his word: *perejil*.
Who says it, lives. He laughs, teeth shining
out of the swamp. The cane appears   15

in our dreams, lashed by wind and streaming.
And we lie down. For every drop of blood
there is a parrot imitating spring.
Out of the swamp the cane appears.

2. *The Palace*

The word the general's chosen is parsley.   20
It is fall, when thoughts turn
to love and death; the general thinks
of his mother, how she died in the fall
and he planted her walking cane at the grave
and it flowered, each spring stolidly forming   25
four-star blossoms. The general

pulls on his boots, he stomps to
her room in the palace, the one without
curtains, the one with a parrot
in a brass ring. As he paces he wonders   30
Who can I kill today. And for a moment
the little knot of screams
is still. The parrot, who has traveled

all the way from Australia in an ivory
cage, is, coy as a widow, practising   35
spring. Ever since the morning
his mother collapsed in the kitchen
while baking skull-shaped candies
for the Day of the Dead,[4] the general
has hated sweets. He orders pastries   40
brought up for the bird; they arrive

3. Katarina (because "we cannot speak an R").
4. All Soul's Day, November 2. An Aztec festival
for the spirits of the dead that coincides with the
Catholic calendar. In Latin America and the
Caribbean, people move in processions to cemeteries, bearing candles, flowers, and food, all of
which may be shaped to resemble symbols of
death, such as skulls or coffins.

dusted with sugar on a bed of lace.
The knot in his throat starts to twitch;
he sees his boots the first day in battle
splashed with mud and urine   45
as a soldier falls at his feet amazed—
how stupid he looked!—at the sound
of artillery. *I never thought it would sing*
the soldier said, and died. Now

the general sees the fields of sugar   50
cane, lashed by rain and streaming.
He sees his mother's smile, the teeth
gnawed to arrowheads. He hears
the Haitians sing without R's
as they swing the great machetes: 55
Katalina, they sing, *Katalina*,

mi madle, mi amol en muelte.[5] God knows
his mother was no stupid woman; she
could roll an R like a queen. Even
a parrot can roll an R! In the bare room   60
the bright feathers arch in a parody
of greenery, as the last pale crumbs
disappear under the blackened tongue. Someone

calls out his name in a voice
so like his mother's, a startled tear   65
splashes the tip of his right boot.
My mother, my love in death.
The general remembers the tiny green sprigs
men of his village wore in their capes
to honor the birth of a son. He will   70
order many, this time, to be killed

for a single, beautiful word.

1983

Rosa[1]

How she sat there,
the time right inside a place
so wrong it was ready.

5. I.e., *mi madre, mi amor en muerte*—"my mother, my love in death."
1. Rosa Parks (1913–2005). From a series of poems titled *On the Bus with Rosa Parks*. On December 1, 1955, in Montgomery, Alabama, Parks, an African American seamstress and secretary of the local National Association for the Advancement of Colored People (NAACP), was arrested and taken to jail for refusing to yield her seat on a bus to a white passenger. Her arrest prompted a boycott of the city bus system and inspired the Civil Rights Movement in the late 1950s and the 1960s.

That trim name with
its dream of a bench   5
to rest on. Her sensible coat.

Doing nothing was the doing:
the clean flame of her gaze
carved by a camera flash.

How she stood up   10
when they bent down to retrieve
her purse. That courtesy.

                                                        2000

Fox Trot Fridays

Thank the stars there's a day
each week to tuck in

the grief, lift your pearls, and
stride brush stride

quick-quick with a   5
heel-ball-toe. Smooth

as Nat King Cole's[1]
slow satin smile,

easy as taking
one day at a time: 10

one man and
one woman,

rib to rib,
with no heartbreak in sight—

just the sweep of Paradise   15
and the space of a song

to count all the wonders in it.

                                                        2004

---

1. Popular African American jazz singer, songwriter, and pianist (1919–1965).

SANDRA CISNEROS
b. 1954

Sandra Cisneros began writing at age ten, much like the young Chicana narrator of *The House on Mango Street* (1984), the volume of interrelated vignettes from a child's perspective that brought Cisneros her first major attention. In brief, sharply drawn, but quietly expressed segments, the narrator, Esperanza, conveys the ambience of growing up in Chicago's Mexican American community. The social bond of this neighborhood eases the contrast between Esperanza's nurturing family and the more hostile forces of poverty and racism. Cisneros cultivates a sense of warmth and naive humor for her protagonists, qualities that are evident in introductory parts to *Woman Hollering Creek* (1991), a short-story collection that also deals with more troublesome aspects of young women's facing hostile forces. Without sentimentalizing or idealizing her narrator's perspective, Cisneros presents glimpses of a world full of adult challenges and multicultural complexities. Sex is a topic in all Cisneros's work, including her poetry collected as *My Wicked Wicked Ways* (1987) and *Loose Woman* (1994)—sometimes gentle and even silly, other times brutally assaultive. What remains constant is the author's view that by romanticizing sexual relations women cooperate with a male view that can be oppressive, even physically destructive. As is said of the protagonist of her 2002 novel, *Caramelo*, Cisneros is "caught between here and there." Yet "here" and "there" are not as dichotomous as young versus old, female versus male, or Mexico versus the United States. Instead, the flow of experience between these poles yields her work's subject: people finding their own lifestyles in the space between fixed boundaries. Because this intervening space is so rich in creative potential, Cisneros can balance unhappiness with humor and find personal victories where others might see social defeat.

Born in Chicago, the child of a Mexican father and a Mexican American mother, Cisneros spent parts of her childhood in Texas and Mexico as well. Her Catholic-school background led to a B.A. degree from Chicago's Loyola University, after which she earned a graduate degree in creative writing from the University of Iowa's Writers Workshop. Teaching in San Antonio, Texas, she has used her position as a writer and an educator to champion Chicana feminism, especially as this movement combines cultural issues with women's concerns. In raising controversy by having her house painted very brightly, she openly questioned monocultural "historical districts" and "community covenants." *Whose* history? Cisneros asked; *which* community sets standards? (Through research she established that her decorating style was in accordance with her home's background and that the standards used to dispute her choice were arbitrary.) A dissatisfaction with the politics of publishing has made her an advocate of small-press dissemination. Most of all, as in the story reprinted here, she is eager to show the rich dynamics of characters existing in the blend of Mexican and American cultures that begins with speaking two languages and extends to almost every aspect of life. Spanish words, Mexican holidays, ethnic foods, and localized religious practices punctuate her narratives; her characters have a facility with cultural play that reflects what for others would be an anthropologically enhanced understanding.

The following text is from *Woman Hollering Creek* (1991).

Woman Hollering Creek

The day Don Serafín gave Juan Pedro Martínez Sánchez permission to take Cleófilas Enriqueta DeLeón Hernández as his bride, across her father's threshold, over several miles of dirt road and several miles of paved, over one border and beyond to a town *en el otro lado*—on the other side—already did he divine the morning his daughter would raise her hand over her eyes, look south, and dream of returning to the chores that never ended, six good-for-nothing brothers, and one old man's complaints.

He had said, after all, in the hubbub of parting: I am your father, I will never abandon you. He *had* said that, hadn't he, when he hugged and then let her go. But at the moment Cleófilas was busy looking for Chela, her maid of honor, to fulfill their bouquet conspiracy. She would not remember her father's parting words until later. *I am your father, I will never abandon you.*

Only now as a mother did she remember. Now, when she and Juan Pedrito sat by the creek's edge. How when a man and a woman love each other, sometimes that love sours. But a parent's love for a child, a child's for its parents, is another thing entirely.

This is what Cleófilas thought evenings when Juan Pedro did not come home, and she lay on her side of the bed listening to the hollow roar of the interstate, a distant dog barking, the pecan trees rustling like ladies in stiff petticoats—*shh-shh-shh, shh-shh-shh*—soothing her to sleep.

In the town where she grew up, there isn't very much to do except accompany the aunts and godmothers to the house of one or the other to play cards. Or walk to the cinema to see this week's film again, speckled and with one hair quivering annoyingly on the screen. Or to the center of town to order a milk shake that will appear in a day and a half as a pimple on her backside. Or to the girlfriend's house to watch the latest *telenovela*[1] episode and try to copy the way the women comb their hair, wear their makeup.

But what Cleófilas has been waiting for, has been whispering and sighing and giggling for, has been anticipating since she was old enough to lean against the window displays of gauze and butterflies and lace, is passion. Not the kind on the cover of the *¡Alarma!*[2] magazines, mind you, where the lover is photographed with the bloody fork she used to salvage her good name. But passion in its purest crystalline essence. The kind the books and songs and *telenovelas* describe when one finds, finally, the great love of one's life, and does whatever one can, must do, at whatever the cost.

Tú o Nadie. "You or No One." The title of the current favorite *telenovela.* The beautiful Lucía Méndez having to put up with all kinds of hardships of the heart, separation and betrayal, and loving, always loving no matter what, because *that* is the most important thing, and did you see Lucía Méndez on the Bayer aspirin commercials—wasn't she lovely? Does she dye her hair do you think? Cleófilas is going to go to the *farmacía*[3] and buy a hair rinse; her girlfriend Chela will apply it—it's not that difficult at all.

Because you didn't watch last night's episode when Lucía confessed she loved him more than anyone in her life. In her life! And she sings the song

---

1. Serialized TV melodrama (Spanish).
2. Graphic, sensationalistic Mexican magazine

published since 1963.
3. Pharmacy, drugstore (Spanish).

"You or No One" in the beginning and end of the show. *Tú o Nadie*. Somehow one ought to live one's life like that, don't you think? You or no one. Because to suffer for love is good. The pain all sweet somehow. In the end.

Seguín. She had liked the sound of it. Far away and lovely. Not like *Monclova. Coahuia*.[4] Ugly.

Seguín, Tejas. A nice sterling ring to it. The tinkle of money. She would get to wear outfits like the women on the *tele*, like Lucía Méndez. And have a lovely house, and wouldn't Chela be jealous.

And yes, they will drive all the way to Laredo[5] to get her wedding dress. That's what they say. Because Juan Pedro wants to get married right away, without a long engagement since he can't take off too much time from work. He has a very important position in Seguin with, with . . . a beer company, I think. Or was it tires? Yes, he has to be back. So they will get married in the spring when he can take off work, and then they will drive off in his new pickup—did you see it?—to their new home in Seguin. Well, not exactly new, but they're going to repaint the house. You know newlyweds. New paint and new furniture. Why not? He can afford it. And later on add maybe a room or two for the children. May they be blessed with many.

Well, you'll see. Cleófilas has always been so good with her sewing machine. A little *rrrr, rrrr, rrrr* of the machine and ¡*zas!* Miracles. She's always been so clever, that girl. Poor thing. And without even a mama to advise her on things like her wedding night. Well, may God help her. What with a father with a head like a burro, and those six clumsy brothers. Well, what do you think! Yes, I'm going to the wedding. Of course! The dress I want to wear just needs to be altered a teensy bit to bring it up to date. See, I saw a new style last night that I thought would suit me. Did you watch last night's episode of *The Rich Also Cry*?[6] Well, did you notice the dress the mother was wearing?

La Gritona.[7] Such a funny name for such a lovely *arroyo*.[8] But that's what they called the creek that ran behind the house. Though no one could say whether the woman had hollered from anger or pain. The natives only knew the *arroyo* one crossed on the way to San Antonio, and then once again on the way back, was called Woman Hollering, a name no one from these parts questioned, little less understood. *Pues, allá de los indios, quién sabe*[9]—who knows, the townspeople shrugged, because it was of no concern to their lives how this trickle of water received its curious name.

"What do you want to know for?" Trini the laundromat attendant asked in the same gruff Spanish she always used whenever she gave Cleófilas change or yelled at her for something. First for putting too much soap in the machines. Later, for sitting on a washer. And still later, after Juan Pedrito was born, for not understanding that in this country you cannot let your baby walk around with no diaper and his pee-pee hanging out, it wasn't nice, ¿*entiendes? Pues*.[1]

---

4. Respectively a town and state in Mexico, the latter bordering Texas. "Seguín": city in Guadalupe County, south-central Texas.

5. City in southwestern Texas, on the Mexican border.

6. First global soap opera (production beginning in Mexico in 1979), exported to Russia, China, the United States, and other countries.

7. The Shouter, Yeller, Hollerer (Spanish).

8. Stream (Spanish).

9. Well, beyond the Indians, who knows (Spanish).

1. Do you understand? Well (Spanish).

How could Cleófilas explain to a woman like this why the name Woman Hollering fascinated her. Well, there was no sense talking to Trini.

On the other hand there were the neighbor ladies, one on either side of the house they rented near the *arroyo*. The woman Soledad on the left, the woman Dolores on the right.

The neighbor lady Soledad liked to call herself a widow, though how she came to be one was a mystery. Her husband had either died, or run away with an ice-house[2] floozie, or simply gone out for cigarettes one afternoon and never came back. It was hard to say which since Soledad, as a rule, didn't mention him.

In the other house lived *la señora*[3] Dolores, kind and very sweet, but her house smelled too much of incense and candles from the altars that burned continuously in memory of two sons who had died in the last war and one husband who had died shortly after from grief. The neighbor lady Dolores divided her time between the memory of these men and her garden, famous for its sunflowers—so tall they had to be supported with broom handles and old boards; red red cockscombs, fringed and bleeding a thick menstrual color; and, especially, roses whose sad scent reminded Cleófilas of the dead. Each Sunday *la señora* Dolores clipped the most beautiful of these flowers and arranged them on three modest headstones at the Seguin cemetery.

The neighbor ladies, Soledad, Dolores, they might've known once the name of the *arroyo* before it turned English but they did not know now. They were too busy remembering the men who had left through either choice or circumstance and would never come back.

Pain or rage, Cleófilas wondered when she drove over the bridge the first time as a newlywed and Juan Pedro had pointed it out. *La Gritona*, he had said, and she had laughed. Such a funny name for a creek so pretty and full of happily ever after.

The first time she had been so surprised she didn't cry out or try to defend herself. She had always said she would strike back if a man, any man, were to strike her.

But when the moment came, and he slapped her once, and then again, and again; until the lip split and bled an orchid of blood, she didn't fight back, she didn't break into tears, she didn't run away as she imagined she might when she saw such things in the *telenovelas*.

In her own home her parents had never raised a hand to each other or to their children. Although she admitted she may have been brought up a little leniently as an only daughter—*la consentida*,[4] the princess—there were some things she would never tolerate. Ever.

Instead, when it happened the first time, when they were barely man and wife, she had been so stunned, it left her speechless, motionless, numb. She had done nothing but reach up to the heat on her mouth and stare at the blood on her hand as if even then she didn't understand.

She could think of nothing to say, said nothing. Just stroked the dark curls of the man who wept and would weep like a child, his tears of repentance and shame, this time and each.

---

2. Tavern.
3. The lady (Spanish).

4. The spoiled one (Spanish).

The men at the ice house. From what she can tell, from the times during her first year when still a newlywed she is invited and accompanies her husband, sits mute beside their conversation, waits and sips a beer until it grows warm, twists a paper napkin into a knot, then another into a fan, one into a rose, nods her head, smiles, yawns, politely grins, laughs at the appropriate moments, leans against her husband's sleeve, tugs at his elbow, and finally becomes good at predicting where the talk will lead, from this Cleófilas concludes each is nightly trying to find the truth lying at the bottom of the bottle like a gold doubloon on the sea floor.

They want to tell each other what they want to tell themselves. But what is bumping like a helium balloon at the ceiling of the brain never finds its way out. It bubbles and rises, it gurgles in the throat, it rolls across the surface of the tongue, and erupts from the lips—a belch.

If they are lucky, there are tears at the end of the long night. At any given moment, the fists try to speak. They are dogs chasing their own tails before lying down to sleep, trying to find a way, a route, an out, and—finally—get some peace.

In the morning sometimes before he opens his eyes. Or after they have finished loving. Or at times when he is simply across from her at the table putting pieces of food into his mouth and chewing. Cleófilas thinks, This is the man I have waited my whole life for.

Not that he isn't a good man. She has to remind herself why she loves him when she changes the baby's Pampers, or when she mops the bathroom floor, or tries to make the curtains for the doorways without doors, or whiten the linen. Or wonder a little when he kicks the refrigerator and says he hates this shitty house and is going out where he won't be bothered with the baby's howling and her suspicious questions, and her requests to fix this and this and this because if she had any brains in her head she'd realize he's been up before the rooster earning his living to pay for the food in her belly and the roof over her head and would have to wake up again early the next day so why can't you just leave me in peace, woman.

He is not very tall, no, and he doesn't look like the men on the *telenovelas*. His face still scarred from acne. And he has a bit of a belly from all the beer he drinks. Well, he's always been husky.

This man who farts and belches and snores as well as laughs and kisses and holds her. Somehow this husband whose whiskers she finds each morning in the sink, whose shoes she must air each evening on the porch, this husband who cuts his fingernails in public, laughs loudly, curses like a man, and demands each course of dinner be served on a separate plate like at his mother's, as soon as he gets home, on time or late, and who doesn't care at all for music or *telenovelas* or romance or roses or the moon floating pearly over the *arroyo*, or through the bedroom window for that matter, shut the blinds and go back to sleep, this man, this father, this rival, this keeper, this lord, this master, this husband till kingdom come.

A doubt. Slender as a hair. A washed cup set back on the shelf wrongside-up. Her lipstick, and body talc, and hairbrush all arranged in the bathroom a different way.

No. Her imagination. The house the same as always. Nothing.

Coming home from the hospital with her new son, her husband. Something comforting in discovering her house slippers beneath the bed, the faded housecoat where she left it on the bathroom hook. Her pillow. Their bed.

Sweet sweet homecoming. Sweet as the scent of face powder in the air, jasmine, sticky liquor.

Smudged fingerprint on the door. Crushed cigarette in a glass. Wrinkle in the brain crumpling to a crease.

Sometimes she thinks of her father's house. But how could she go back there? What a disgrace. What would the neighbors say? Coming home like that with one baby on her hip and one in the oven. Where's your husband?

The town of gossips. The town of dust and despair. Which she has traded for this town of gossips. This town of dust, despair. Houses farther apart perhaps, though no more privacy because of it. No leafy *zócalo*[5] in the center of the town, though the murmur of talk is clear enough all the same. No huddled whispering on the church steps each Sunday. Because here the whispering begins at sunset at the ice house instead.

This town with its silly pride for a bronze pecan the size of a baby carriage in front of the city hall. TV repair shop, drugstore, hardware, dry cleaner's, chiropractor's, liquor store, bail bonds, empty storefront, and nothing, nothing, nothing of interest. Nothing one could walk to, at any rate. Because the towns here are built so that you have to depend on husbands. Or you stay home. Or you drive. If you're rich enough to own, allowed to drive, your own car.

There is no place to go. Unless one counts the neighbor ladies. Soledad on one side, Dolores on the other. Or the creek.

Don't go out there after dark, *mi'jita*.[6] Stay near the house. *No es bueno para la salud.*[7] Mala suerte. Bad luck. *Mal aire.*[8] You'll get sick and the baby too. You'll catch a fright wandering about in the dark, and then you'll see how right we were.

The stream sometimes only a muddy puddle in the summer, though now in the springtime, because of the rains, a good-size alive thing, a thing with a voice all its own, all day and all night calling in its high, silver voice. Is it La Llorona,[9] the weeping woman? La Llorona, who drowned her own children. Perhaps La Llorona is the one they named the creek after, she thinks, remembering all the stories she learned as a child.

La Llorona calling to her. She is sure of it. Cleófilas sets the baby's Donald Duck blanket on the grass. Listens. The day sky turning to night. The baby pulling up fistfuls of grass and laughing. La Llorona. Wonders if something as quiet as this drives a woman to the darkness under the trees.

What she needs is . . . and made a gesture as if to yank a woman's buttocks to his groin. Maximiliano, the foul-smelling fool from across the road, said this and set the men laughing, but Cleófilas just muttered. *Grosera*,[1] and went on washing dishes.

She knew he said it not because it was true, but more because it was he who needed to sleep with a woman, instead of drinking each night at the ice house and stumbling home alone.

5. Town square (Spanish).
6. My daughter (Spanish).
7. It's not good for one's health (Spanish).
8. Bad air (Spanish).
9. The Woman Who Cries (Spanish), a spurned

mistress of Mexican legend who drowned her children and was fated to eternally seek their recovery.
1. Vulgar, crude (Spanish).

Maximiliano who was said to have killed his wife in an ice-house brawl when she came at him with a mop. I had to shoot, he had said—she was armed.

Their laughter outside the kitchen window. Her husband's, his friends'. Manolo, Beto, Efraín, el Perico.[2] Maximiliano.

Was Cleófilas just exaggerating as her husband always said? It seemed the newspapers were full of such stories. This woman found on the side of the interstate. This one pushed from a moving car. This one's cadaver, this one unconscious, this one beaten blue. Her ex-husband, her husband, her lover, her father, her brother, her uncle, her friend, her co-worker. Always. The same grisly news in the pages of the dailies. She dunked a glass under the soapy water for a moment—shivered.

He had thrown a book. Hers. From across the room. A hot welt across the cheek. She could forgive that. But what stung more was the fact it was *her* book, a love story by Corín Tellado,[3] what she loved most now that she lived in the U.S., without a television set, without the *telenovelas*.

Except now and again when her husband was away and she could manage it, the few episodes glimpsed at the neighbor lady Soledad's house because Dolores didn't care for that sort of thing, though Soledad was often kind enough to retell what had happened on what episode of *María de Nadie*,[4] the poor Argentine country girl who had the ill fortune of falling in love with the beautiful son of the Arrocha family, the very family she worked for, whose roof she slept under and whose floors she vacuumed, while in that same house, with the dust brooms and floor cleaners as witnesses, the square-jawed Juan Carlos Arrocha had uttered words of love, I love you, María, listen to me, *mi querida*,[5] but it was she who had to say No, no, we are not of the same class, and remind him it was not his place nor hers to fall in love, while all the while her heart was breaking, can you imagine.

Cleófilas thought her life would have to be like that, like a *telenovela*, only now the episodes got sadder and sadder. And there were no commercials in between for comic relief. And no happy ending in sight. She thought this when she sat with the baby out by the creek behind the house. Celófilas de . . . ? But somehow she would have to change her name to Topazio, or Yesenia, Cristal, Adriana, Stefania, Andrea, something more poetic than Cleófilas. Everything happened to women with names like jewels. But what happened to a Cleófilas? Nothing. But a crack in the face.

Because the doctor has said so. She has to go. To make sure the new baby is all right, so there won't be any problems when he's born, and the appointment card says next Tuesday. Could he please take her. And that's all.

No, she won't mention it. She promises. If the doctor asks she can say she fell down the front steps or slipped when she was out in the backyard, slipped out back, she could tell him that. She has to go back next Tuesday, Juan Pedro, please, for the new baby. For their child.

She could write to her father and ask maybe for money, just a loan, for the new baby's medical expenses. Well then if he'd rather she didn't. All right, she won't. Please don't anymore. Please don't. She knows it's difficult saving

2. The Parakeet (Spanish).
3. Pseudonym of María del Socorro Tellado López (1927–2009), Spanish novelist.
4. *María of No One* (Spanish), television series produced in Argentina.
5. My love (Spanish).

money with all the bills they have, but how else are they going to get out of debt with the truck payments? And after the rent and the food and the electricity and the gas and the water and the who-knows-what, well, there's hardly anything left. But please, at least for the doctor visit. She won't ask for anything else. She has to. Why is she so anxious? Because.

Because she is going to make sure the baby is not turned around backward this time to split her down the center. Yes. Next Tuesday at five-thirty. I'll have Juan Pedrito dressed and ready. But those are the only shoes he has. I'll polish them, and we'll be ready. As soon as you come from work. We won't make you ashamed.

Felice? It's me, Graciela.

No, I can't talk louder. I'm at work.

Look, I need kind of a favor. There's a patient, a lady here who's got a problem.

Well, wait a minute. Are you listening to me or what?

I can't talk real loud 'cause her husband's in the next room.

Well, would you just listen?

I was going to do this sonogram on her—she's pregnant, right?—and she just starts crying on me. *Híjole*,[6] Felice! This poor lady's got black-and-blue marks all over. I'm not kidding.

From her husband. Who else? Another one of those brides from across the border. And her family's all in Mexico.

Shit. You think they're going to help her? Give me a break. This lady doesn't even speak English. She hasn't been allowed to call home or write or nothing. That's why I'm calling you.

She needs a ride.

Not to Mexico, you goof. Just to the Greyhound.[7] In San Anto.

No, just a ride. She's got her own money. All you'd have to do is drop her off in San Antonio on your way home. Come on, Felice. Please? If we don't help her, who will? I'd drive her myself, but she needs to be on that bus before her husband gets home from work. What do you say?

I don't know. Wait.

Right away, tomorrow even.

Well, if tomorrow's no good for you . . .

It's a date, Felice. Thursday. At the Cash N Carry[8] off I-10. Noon. She'll be ready.

Oh, and her name's Cleófilas.

I don't know. One of those Mexican saints, I guess. A martyr or something.

Cleófilas. C-L-E-O-F-I-L-A-S. Cle. O. Fi. Las. Write it down.

Thanks, Felice. When her kid's born she'll have to name her after us, right?

Yeah, you got it. A regular soap opera sometimes. *Qué vida, comadre. Bueno*[9] bye.

All morning that flutter of half-fear, half-doubt. At any moment Juan Pedro might appear in the doorway. On the street. At the Cash N Carry. Like in the dreams she dreamed.

6. Shoot! or Gee! (Spanish).
7. Long-distance bus line.
8. Retail store.
9. What a life, girlfriend, well (Spanish).

There was that to think about, yes, until the woman in the pickup drove up. Then there wasn't time to think about anything but the pickup pointed toward San Antonio. Put your bags in the back and get in.

But when they drove across the *arroyo*, the driver opened her mouth and let out a yell as loud as any mariachi. Which startled not only Cleófilas, but Juan Pedrito as well.

Pues,[1] look how cute. I scared you two, right? Sorry. Should've warned you. Every time I cross that bridge I do that. Because of the name, you know. Woman Hollering. *Pues,* I holler. She said this in a Spanish pocked with English and laughed. Did you ever notice, Felice continued, how nothing around here is named after a woman? Really. Unless she's the Virgin. I guess you're only famous if you're a virgin. She was laughing again.

That's why I like the name of that *arroyo*. Makes you want to holler like Tarzan, right?

Everything about this woman, this Felice, amazed Cleófilas. The fact that she drove a pickup. A pickup, mind you, but when Cleófilas asked if it was her husband's, she said she didn't have a husband. The pickup was hers. She herself had chosen it. She herself was paying for it.

I used to have a Pontiac Sunbird.[2] But those cars are for *viejas*.[3] Pussy cars. Now this here is a *real* car.

What kind of talk was that coming from a woman? Cleófilas thought. But then again, Felice was like no woman she'd ever met. Can you imagine, when we crossed the *arroyo* she just started yelling like a crazy, she would say later to her father and brothers. Just like that. Who would've thought?

Who would've? Pain or rage, perhaps, but not a hoot like the one Felice had just let go. Makes you want to holler like Tarzan, Felice had said.

Then Felice began laughing again, but it wasn't Felice laughing. It was gurgling out of her own throat, a long ribbon of laughter, like water.

1991

1. Well (Spanish).   3. Old ladies (Spanish).
2. Compact American automobile.

LOUISE ERDRICH
b. 1954

Louise Erdrich grew up in the small town of Wahpeton, North Dakota, on the Minnesota border. Her mother was French Chippewa, her maternal grandmother was tribal chairman on the Turtle Mountain Reservation, and both of her parents worked in the Bureau of Indian Affairs boarding school in Wahpeton. She wrote stories as a child, encouraged by her father, who paid her a nickel for each one, but Erdrich's growing up was not marked by a special awareness of her Chippewa background. She has said that she never thought about "what was Native American and what wasn't. . . . There wasn't a political climate at the time about Indian rights." The eldest of seven children, she "grew up just taking it all in as something that was part of me."

In 1972 she entered Dartmouth College, participating in a Native American studies program run by Michael Dorris—himself part American Indian and a writer—whom eventually she would marry (a relationship ending with their separation and his suicide in 1997). In her undergraduate years she won prizes for poetry and fiction and worked at a variety of jobs, such as teaching poetry in prisons, editing a Boston Indian Council newspaper, and flag-signaling on a construction site. After deciding on a career as a writer, she earned an MFA degree at Johns Hopkins, for which degree she submitted a number of poems—later to appear in her collection *Jacklight* (1984)—and part of a novel. There followed the usual sending out of poems and stories, the rejection slips, eventually the acceptances.

Her first novel, *Love Medicine*, which won the National Book Critics Circle award for 1984, began as a short story. Collaborating with her husband, she not only expanded the story but planned the resulting novel as the first of a tetralogy, ranging over different periods of time and focusing on the lives of two Chippewa families. Her interest in the interaction of quirky, passionate, complex individuals—Native American, mixed blood, German American, or Anglo—lies at the center of her fiction.

Successive chapters of *Love Medicine* jump from 1981 to 1934 to 1948, each chapter told through a particular character's point of view (sometimes we see the same event from succeeding points of view). But each individual chapter is more a discrete whole than is the case with a traditional novel, a technique Erdrich uses in many of her novels, including *Tracks* (1988), the second chapter of which was published as the story "Fleur" (printed here). Like many of Erdrich's narratives, *Tracks* draws context from High Plains Dakotas town life, where Anglo and Native American cultures meet (if not mix).

Erdrich's style is easy, offhand, quietly unostentatious, but her language often has an unpredictability and sense of surprise, as in the first paragraph of "The Red Convertible," whose protagonist, Lyman Lamartine, tells us:

> I was the first one to drive a convertible on my reservation. And of course, it was red, a red Olds. I owned that car along with my brother Henry Junior. We owned it together until his boots filled with water on a windy night and he bought out my share. Now Henry owns the whole car, and his younger brother (that's myself) Lyman walks everywhere he goes.

Such clarity and directness are only part of the story, however, since her style also calls upon lyric resources, notable in the following sentence from her second novel, *The Beet Queen*: "After the miraculous sheets of black ice came the floods, stranding boards and snaky knots of debris high in the branches, leaving brown leeches to dry like raisins on the sidewalks when the water receded, and leaving the smell of river mud, a rotten sweetness, in the backyards and gutters."

Native American oral expression does not distinguish between prose and poetry, and like many Native American writers Erdrich works in several forms. "I began as a poet, writing poetry," she has said. "I began to tell stories in poems." The lyrical descriptions in her fiction resemble the language of her poems, and the characterizations and narratives in her poetry resemble those of her fiction. Her most recent poetry collection, *Original Fire* (2003), presents new poems together with work from two earlier collections, *Jacklight* and *Baptism of Fire* (1989). Among the previously published poems are "The Butcher's Wife," which has close affinities in setting and character to her novels, and "The Potchikoo Stories," a group of prose poems about the mythical Potchikoo's life and afterlife. "Grief," a new poem, suggests the traditions of imagist poetry. But in the end such generic distinctions run counter to Erdrich's fusion of storytelling modes.

Like her fiction, Erdrich's poetry sometimes offers realistic accounts of small-town life and sometimes retells mythical stories. "I was Sleeping Where the Black Oaks

Move" exemplifies her lyrical description and her mythical imagination. Many of the poems also reflect Erdrich's awareness of the historical and ongoing devastations of Native American life, what she calls in the poem "Dear John Wayne" "the history that brought us all here." Whatever forms her storytelling takes, its linguistic resources and mixture of grief, humor, anger, and tenderness deepen our understanding of the complexities of experience.

Dear John Wayne[1]

August and the drive-in picture is packed.
We lounge on the hood of the Pontiac
surrounded by the slow-burning spirals they sell
at the window, to vanquish the hordes of mosquitoes.
Nothing works. They break through the smoke screen for blood.   5

Always the lookout spots the Indians first,
spread north to south, barring progress.
The Sioux or some other Plains bunch[2]
in spectacular columns, ICBM missiles,[3]
feathers bristling in the meaningful sunset.   10

The drum breaks. There will be no parlance.
Only the arrows whining, a death-cloud of nerves
swarming down on the settlers
who die beautifully, tumbling like dust weeds
into the history that brought us all here   15
together: this wide screen beneath the sign of the bear.

The sky fills, acres of blue squint and eye
that the crowd cheers. His face moves over us,
a thick cloud of vengeance, pitted
like the land that was once flesh. Each rut,   20
each scar makes a promise: *It is
not over, this fight, not as long as you resist.*

Everything we see belongs to us.

A few laughing Indians fall over the hood
slipping in the hot spilled butter.   25
The eye sees a lot, John, but the heart is so blind.
Death makes us owners of nothing.
He smiles, a horizon of teeth
the credits reel over, and then the white fields

again blowing in the true-to-life dark.   30
The dark films over everything.
We get into the car

1. American movie actor (1907–1979) who embodied the image of the strong, taciturn cowboy or soldier, and who in many ways personified the dominant American values of his era. He died of cancer.

2. The Sioux are a North American Plains Indian people.
3. Intercontinental Ballistic Missiles, developed starting in 1971.

scratching our mosquito bites, speechless and small
as people are when the movie is done.
We are back in our skins.   35

How can we help but keep hearing his voice,
the flip side of the sound track, still playing:
Come on, boys, we got them
where we want them, drunk, running.
They'll give us what we want, what we need.   40
Even his disease was the idea of taking everything.
Those cells, burning, doubling, splitting out of their skins.

                                                              1984

I Was Sleeping Where the Black Oaks Move

We watched from the house
as the river grew, helpless
and terrible in its unfamiliar body.
Wrestling everything into it,
the water wrapped around trees   5
until their life-hold was broken.
They went down, one by one,
and the river dragged off their covering.

Nests of the herons, roots washed to bones,
snags of soaked bark on the shoreline: 10
a whole forest pulled through the teeth
of the spillway. Trees surfacing
singly, where the river poured off
into arteries for fields below the reservation.

When at last it was over, the long removal,   15
they had all become the same dry wood.
We walked among them, the branches
whitening in the raw sun.
Above us drifted herons,
alone, hoarse-voiced, broken,   20
settling their beaks among the hollows.

Grandpa said, *These are the ghosts of the tree people,*
moving above us, unable to take their rest.

Sometimes now, we dream our way back to the heron dance.
Their long wings are bending the air   25
into circles through which they fall.
They rise again in shifting wheels.
How long must we live in the broken figures
their necks make, narrowing the sky.

                                                              1984

Grief

Sometimes you have to take your own hand
as though you were a lost child
and bring yourself stumbling
home over twisted ice.

Whiteness drifts over your house.   5
A page of warm light
falls steady from the open door.

Here is your bed, folded open.
Lie down, lie down, let the blue snow cover you.

2003

Fleur[1]

The first time she drowned in the cold and glassy waters of Lake Turcot,
Fleur Pillager was only a girl. Two men saw the boat tip, saw her struggle in
the waves. They rowed over to the place she went down, and jumped in.
When they dragged her over the gunwales, she was cold to the touch and
stiff, so they slapped her face, shook her by the heels, worked her arms back
and forth, and pounded her back until she coughed up lake water. She shivered all over like a dog, then took a breath. But it wasn't long afterward that
those two men disappeared. The first wandered off and the other, Jean Hat,
got himself run over by a cart.

It went to show, my grandma said. It figured to her, all right. By saving
Fleur Pillager, those two men had lost themselves.

The next time she fell in the lake, Fleur Pillager was twenty years old and
no one touched her. She washed onshore, her skin a dull dead gray, but
when George Many Women bent to look closer, he saw her chest move.
Then her eyes spun open, sharp black riprock, and she looked at him. "You'll
take my place," she hissed. Everybody scattered and left her there, so no one
knows how she dragged herself home. Soon after that we noticed Many
Women changed, grew afraid, wouldn't leave his house, and would not be
forced to go near water. For his caution, he lived until the day that his sons
brought him a new tin bathtub. Then the first time he used the tub he
slipped, got knocked out, and breathed water while his wife stood in the
other room frying breakfast.

Men stayed clear of Fleur Pillager after the second drowning. Even though
she was good-looking, nobody dared to court her because it was clear that
Misshepeshu, the waterman, the monster, wanted her for himself. He's a
devil, that one, love-hungry with desire and maddened for the touch of
young girls, the strong and daring especially, the ones like Fleur.

Our mothers warn us that we'll think he's handsome, for he appears with
green eyes, copper skin, a mouth tender as a child's. But if you fall into his

1. First published in *Esquire* magazine, August 1986.

arms, he sprouts horns, fangs, claws, fins. His feet are joined as one and his skin, brass scales, rings to the touch. You're fascinated, cannot move. He casts a shell necklace at your feet, weeps gleaming chips that harden into mica on your breasts. He holds you under. Then he takes the body of a lion or a fat brown worm. He's made of gold. He's made of beach moss. He's a thing of dry foam, a thing of death by drowning, the death a Chippewa cannot survive.

Unless you are Fleur Pillager. We all knew she couldn't swim. After the first time, we thought she'd never go back to Lake Turcot. We thought she'd keep to herself, live quiet, stop killing men off by drowning in the lake. After the first time, we thought she'd keep the good ways. But then, after the second drowning, we knew that we were dealing with something much more serious. She was haywire, out of control. She messed with evil, laughed at the old women's advice, and dressed like a man. She got herself into some half-forgotten medicine, studied ways we shouldn't talk about. Some say she kept the finger of a child in her pocket and a powder of unborn rabbits in a leather thong around her neck. She laid the heart of an owl on her tongue so she could see at night, and went out, hunting, not even in her own body. We know for sure because the next morning, in the snow or dust, we followed the tracks of her bare feet and saw where they changed, where the claws sprang out, the pad broadened and pressed into the dirt. By night we heard her chuffing cough, the bear cough. By day her silence and the wide grin she threw to bring down our guard made us frightened. Some thought that Fleur Pillager should be driven off the reservation, but not a single person who spoke like this had the nerve. And finally, when people were just about to get together and throw her out, she left on her own and didn't come back all summer. That's what this story is about.

During that summer, when she lived a few miles south in Argus, things happened. She almost destroyed that town.

When she got down to Argus in the year of 1920, it was just a small grid of six streets on either side of the railroad depot. There were two elevators, one central, the other a few miles west. Two stores competed for the trade of the three hundred citizens, and three churches quarreled with one another for their souls. There was a frame building for Lutherans, a heavy brick one for Episcopalians, and a long narrow shingled Catholic church. This last had a tall slender steeple, twice as high as any building or tree.

No doubt, across the low, flat wheat, watching from the road as she came near Argus on foot, Fleur saw that steeple rise, a shadow thin as a needle. Maybe in that raw space it drew her the way a lone tree draws lightning. Maybe, in the end, the Catholics are to blame. For if she hadn't seen that sign of pride, that slim prayer, that marker, maybe she would have kept walking.

But Fleur Pillager turned, and the first place she went once she came into town was to the back door of the priest's residence attached to the landmark church. She didn't go there for a handout, although she got that, but to ask for work. She got that too, or the town got her. It's hard to tell which came out worse, her or the men or the town, although the upshot of it all was that Fleur lived.

The four men who worked at the butcher's had carved up about a thousand carcasses between them, maybe half of that steers and the other half pigs, sheep, and game animals like deer, elk, and bear. That's not even mentioning the chickens, which were beyond counting. Pete Kozka owned the place, and employed Lily Veddar, Tor Grunewald, and my stepfather, Dutch James, who had brought my mother down from the reservation the year before she disappointed him by dying. Dutch took me out of school to take her place. I kept house half the time and worked the other in the butcher shop, sweeping floors, putting sawdust down, running a hambone across the street to a customer's bean pot or a package of sausage to the corner. I was a good one to have around because until they needed me, I was invisible. I blended into the stained brown walls, a skinny, big-nosed girl with staring eyes. Because I could fade into a corner or squeeze beneath a shelf, I knew everything, what the men said when no one was around, and what they did to Fleur.

Kozka's Meats served farmers for a fifty-mile area, both to slaughter, for it had a stock pen and chute, and to cure the meat by smoking it or spicing it in sausage. The storage locker was a marvel, made of many thicknesses of brick, earth insulation, and Minnesota timber, lined inside with sawdust and vast blocks of ice cut from Lake Turcot, hauled down from home each winter by horse and sledge.

A ramshackle board building, part slaughterhouse, part store, was fixed to the low, thick square of the lockers. That's where Fleur worked. Kozka hired her for her strength. She could lift a haunch or carry a pole of sausages without stumbling, and she soon learned cutting from Pete's wife, a string-thin blonde who chain-smoked and handled the razor-edged knives with nerveless precision, slicing close to her stained fingers. Fleur and Fritzie Kozka worked afternoons, wrapping their cuts in paper, and Fleur hauled the packages to the lockers. The meat was left outside the heavy oak doors that were only opened at 5:00 each afternoon, before the men ate supper.

Sometimes Dutch, Tor, and Lily stayed at the lockers, and when they did I stayed too, cleaned floors, restoked the fires in the front smokehouses, while the men sat around the squat cast-iron stove spearing slats of herring onto hardtack bread. They played long games of poker or cribbage on a board made from the planed end of a salt crate. They talked and I listened, although there wasn't much to hear since almost nothing ever happened in Argus. Tor was married, Dutch had lost my mother, and Lily read circulars. They mainly discussed about the auctions to come, equipment, or women.

Every so often, Pete Kozka came out front to make a whist, leaving Fritzie to smoke cigarettes and fry raised doughnuts in the back room. He sat and played a few rounds but kept his thoughts to himself. Fritzie did not tolerate him talking behind her back, and the one book he read was the New Testament. If he said something, it concerned weather or a surplus of sheep stomachs, a ham that smoked green or the markets for corn and wheat. He had a good-luck talisman, the opal-white lens of a cow's eye. Playing cards, he rubbed it between his fingers. That soft sound and the slap of cards was about the only conversation.

Fleur finally gave them a subject.

Her cheeks were wide and flat, her hands large, chapped, muscular. Fleur's shoulders were broad as beams, her hips fishlike, slippery, narrow. An old green dress clung to her waist, worn thin where she sat. Her braids were thick like the tails of animals, and swung against her when she moved, deliberately, slowly in her work, held in and half-tamed, but only half. I could tell, but the others never saw. They never looked into her sly brown eyes or noticed her teeth, strong and sharp and very white. Her legs were bare, and since she padded in beadworked moccasins they never saw that her fifth toes were missing. They never knew she'd drowned. They were blinded, they were stupid, they only saw her in the flesh.

And yet it wasn't just that she was a Chippewa, or even that she was a woman, it wasn't that she was good-looking or even that she was alone that made their brains hum. It was how she played cards.

Women didn't usually play with men, so the evening that Fleur drew a chair to the men's table without being so much as asked, there was a shock of surprise.

"What's this," said Lily. He was fat, with a snake's cold pale eyes and precious skin, smooth and lily-white, which is how he got his name. Lily had a dog, a stumpy mean little bull of a thing with a belly drum-tight from eating pork rinds. The dog liked to play cards just like Lily, and straddled his barrel thighs through games of stud, rum poker, vingt-un.[2] The dog snapped at Fleur's arm that first night, but cringed back, its snarl frozen, when she took her place.

"I thought," she said, her voice soft and stroking, "you might deal me in."

There was a space between the heavy bin of spiced flour and the wall where I just fit. I hunkered down there, kept my eyes open, saw her black hair swing over the chair, her feet solid on the wood floor. I couldn't see up on the table where the cards slapped down, so after they were deep in their game I raised myself up in the shadows, and crouched on a sill of wood.

I watched Fleur's hands stack and ruffle, divide the cards, spill them to each player in a blur, rake them up and shuffle again. Tor, short and scrappy, shut one eye and squinted the other at Fleur. Dutch screwed his lips around a wet cigar.

"Gotta see a man," he mumbled, getting up to go out back to the privy. The others broke, put their cards down, and Fleur sat alone in the lamplight that glowed in a sheen across the push of her breasts. I watched her closely, then she paid me a beam of notice for the first time. She turned, looked straight at me, and grinned the white wolf grin a Pillager turns on its victims, except that she wasn't after me.

"Pauline there," she said. "How much money you got?"

We had all been paid for the week that day. Eight cents was in my pocket.

"Stake me," she said, holding out her long fingers. I put the coins in her palm and then I melted back to nothing, part of the walls and tables. It was a long time before I understood that the men would not have seen me no matter what I did, how I moved. I wasn't anything like Fleur. My dress hung loose and my back was already curved, an old woman's. Work had roughened me, reading made my eyes sore, caring for my mother before she died had hardened my face. I was not much to look at, so they never saw me.

When the men came back and sat around the table, they had drawn together. They shot each other small glances, stuck their tongues in their cheeks, burst out laughing at odd moments, to rattle Fleur. But she never minded. They played their vingt-un, staying even as Fleur slowly gained. Those pennies I had given her drew nickels and attracted dimes until there was a small pile in front of her.

---

2. Twenty-one (French); a card game.

Then she hooked them with five card draw, nothing wild. She dealt, discarded, drew, and then she sighed and her cards gave a little shiver. Tor's eye gleamed, and Dutch straightened in his seat.

"I'll pay to see that hand," said Lily Veddar.

Fleur showed, and she had nothing there, nothing at all.

Tor's thin smile cracked open, and he threw his hand in too.

"Well, we know one thing," he said, leaning back in his chair, "the squaw can't bluff."

With that I lowered myself into a mound of swept sawdust and slept. I woke up during the night, but none of them had moved yet, so I couldn't either. Still later, the men must have gone out again, or Fritzie come out to break the game, because I was lifted, soothed, cradled in a woman's arms and rocked so quiet that I kept my eyes shut while Fleur rolled me into a closet of grimy ledgers, oiled paper, balls of string, and thick files that fit beneath me like a mattress.

The game went on after work the next evening. I got my eight cents back five times over, and Fleur kept the rest of the dollar she'd won for a stake. This time they didn't play so late, but they played regular, and then kept going at it night after night. They played poker now, or variations, for one week straight, and each time Fleur won exactly one dollar, no more and no less, too consistent for luck.

By this time, Lily and the other men were so lit with suspense that they got Pete to join the game with them. They concentrated, the fat dog sitting tense in Lily Veddar's lap, Tor suspicious, Dutch stroking his huge square brow, Pete steady. It wasn't that Fleur won that hooked them in so, because she lost hands too. It was rather that she never had a freak hand or even anything above a straight. She only took on her low cards, which didn't sit right. By chance, Fleur should have gotten a full or a flush by now. The irritating thing was she beat with pairs and never bluffed, because she couldn't, and still she ended each night with exactly one dollar. Lily couldn't believe, first of all, that a woman could be smart enough to play cards, but even if she was, that she would then be stupid enough to cheat for a dollar a night. By day I watched him turn the problem over, his hard white face dull, small fingers probing at his knuckles, until he finally thought he had Fleur figured as a bit-time player, caution her game. Raising the stakes would throw her.

More than anything now, he wanted Fleur to come away with something but a dollar. Two bits less or ten more, the sum didn't matter, just so he broke her streak.

Night after night she played, won her dollar, and left to stay in a place that just Fritzie and I knew about. Fleur bathed in the slaughtering tub, then slept in the unused brick smokehouse behind the lockers, a windowless place tarred on the inside with scorched fats. When I brushed against her skin I noticed that she smelled of the walls, rich and woody, slightly burnt. Since that night she put me in the closet I was no longer afraid of her, but followed her close, stayed with her, became her moving shadow that the men never noticed, the shadow that could have saved her.

August, the month that bears fruit, closed around the shop, and Pete and Fritzie left for Minnesota to escape the heat. Night by night, running, Fleur had won thirty dollars, and only Pete's presence had kept Lily at bay. But Pete was gone now, and one payday, with the heat so bad no one could move but

Fleur, the men sat and played and waited while she finished work. The cards sweat, limp in their fingers, the table was slick with grease, and even the walls were warm to the touch. The air was motionless. Fleur was in the next room boiling heads.

Her green dress, drenched, wrapped her like a transparent sheet. A skin of lakeweed. Black snarls of veining clung to her arms. Her braids were loose, half unraveled, tied behind her neck in a thick loop. She stood in steam, turning skulls through a vat with a wooden paddle. When scraps boiled to the surface, she bent with a round tin sieve and scooped them out. She'd filled two dishpans.

"Ain't that enough now?" called Lily. "We're waiting." The stump of a dog trembled in his lap, alive with rage. It never smelled me or noticed me above Fleur's smoky skin. The air was heavy in my corner, and pressed me down. Fleur sat with them.

"Now what do you say?" Lily asked the dog. It barked. That was the signal for the real game to start.

"Let's up the ante," said Lily, who had been stalking this night all month. He had a roll of money in his pocket. Fleur had five bills in her dress. The men had each saved their full pay.

"Ante a dollar then," said Fleur, and pitched hers in. She lost, but they let her scrape along, cent by cent. And then she won some. She played unevenly, as if chance were all she had. She reeled them in. The game went on. The dog was stiff now, poised on Lily's knees, a ball of vicious muscle with its yellow eyes slit in concentration. It gave advice, seemed to sniff the lay of Fleur's cards, twitched and nudged. Fleur was up, then down, saved by a scratch. Tor dealt seven cards, three down. The pot grew, round by round, until it held all the money. Nobody folded. Then it all rode on one last card and they went silent. Fleur picked hers up and drew a long breath. The heat lowered like a bell. Her card shook, but she stayed in.

Lily smiled and took the dog's head tenderly between his palms.

"Say Fatso," he said, crooning the words. "You reckon that girl's bluffing?"

The dog whined and Lily laughed. "Me too," he said, "let's show." He swept his bills and coins into the pot and then they turned their cards over.

Lily looked once, looked again, then he squeezed the dog like a fist of dough and slammed it on the table.

Fleur threw out her arms and drew the money over, grinning that same wolf grin that she'd used on me, the grin that had them. She jammed the bills in her dress, scooped the coins up in waxed white paper that she tied with string.

"Let's go another round," said Lily, his voice choked with burrs. But Fleur opened her mouth and yawned, then walked out back to gather slops for the one big hog that was waiting in the stock pen to be killed.

The men sat still as rocks, their hands spread on the oiled wood table. Dutch had chewed his cigar to damp shreds, Tor's eye was dull. Lily's gaze was the only one to follow Fleur. I didn't move. I felt them gathering, saw my stepfather's veins, the ones in his forehead that stood out in anger. The dog rolled off the table and curled in a knot below the counter, where none of the men could touch it.

Lily rose and stepped out back to the closet of ledgers where Pete kept his private stock. He brought back a bottle, uncorked and tipped it between his fingers. The lump in his throat moved, then he passed it on. They drank, quickly felt the whiskey's fire, and planned with their eyes things they couldn't say aloud.

When they left, I followed. I hid out back in the clutter of broken boards and chicken crates beside the stock pen, where they waited. Fleur could not be seen at first, and then the moon broke and showed her, slipping cautiously along the rough board chute with a bucket in her hand. Her hair fell, wild and coarse, to her waist, and her dress was a floating patch in the dark. She made a pig-calling sound, rang the tin pail lightly against the wood, froze suspiciously. But too late. In the sound of the ring Lily moved, fat and nimble, stepped right behind Fleur and put out his creamy hands. At his first touch, she whirled and doused him with the bucket of sour slops. He pushed her against the big fence and the package of coins split, went clinking and jumping, winked against the wood. Fleur rolled over once and vanished into the yard.

The moon fell behind a curtain of ragged clouds, and Lily followed into the dark muck. But he tripped, pitched over the huge flank of the pig, who lay mired to the snout, heavily snoring. I sprang out of the weeds and climbed the side of the pen, stuck like glue. I saw the sow rise to her neat, knobby knees, gain her balance and sway, curious, as Lily stumbled forward. Fleur had backed into the angle of rough wood just beyond, and when Lily tried to jostle past, the sow tipped up on her hind legs and struck, quick and hard as a snake. She plunged her head into Lily's thick side and snatched a mouthful of his shirt. She lunged again, caught him lower, so that he grunted in pained surprise. He seemed to ponder, breathing deep. Then he launched his huge body in a swimmer's dive.

The sow screamed as his body smacked over hers. She rolled, striking out with her knife-sharp hooves, and Lily gathered himself upon her, took her foot-long face by the ears and scraped her snout and cheeks against the trestles of the pen. He hurled the sow's tight skull against an iron post, but instead of knocking her dead, he merely woke her from her dream.

She reared, shrieked, drew him with her so that they posed standing upright. They bowed jerkily to each other, as if to begin. Then his arms swung and flailed. She sank her black fangs into his shoulder, clasping him, dancing him forward and backward through the pen. Their steps picked up pace, went wild. The two dipped as one, box-stepped, tripped one another. She ran her split foot through his hair. He grabbed her kinked tail. They went down and came up, the same shape and then the same color until the men couldn't tell one from the other in that light and Fleur was able to launch herself over the gates, swing down, hit gravel.

The men saw, yelled, and chased her at a dead run to the smokehouse. And Lily too, once the sow gave up in disgust and freed him. That is where I should have gone to Fleur, saved her, thrown myself on Dutch. But I went stiff with fear and couldn't unlatch myself from the trestles or move at all. I closed my eyes and put my head in my arms, tried to hide, so there is nothing to describe but what I couldn't block out, Fleur's hoarse breath, so loud it filled me, her cry in the old language, and my name repeated over and over among the words.

The heat was still dense the next morning when I came back to work. Fleur was gone but the men were there, slack-faced, hung over. Lily was paler and softer than ever, as if his flesh had steamed on his bones. They smoked, took pulls off a bottle. It wasn't noon yet. I worked awhile, waiting shop and sharpening steel. But I was sick, I was smothered, I was sweating so hard that my hands slipped on the knives, and I wiped my fingers clean of the greasy touch of the customers' coins. Lily opened his mouth and roared once, not in anger. There was no meaning to the sound. His boxer dog, sprawled limp beside his foot, never lifted its head. Nor did the other men.

They didn't notice when I stepped outside, hoping for a clear breath. And then I forgot them because I knew that we were all balanced, ready to tip, to fly, to be crushed as soon as the weather broke. The sky was so low that I felt the weight of it like a yoke. Clouds hung down, witch teats, a tornado's green-brown cones, and as I watched one flicked out and became a delicate probing thumb. Even as I picked up my heels and ran back inside, the wind blew suddenly, cold, and then came rain.

Inside, the men had disappeared already and the whole place was trembling as if a huge hand was pinched at the rafters, shaking it. I ran straight through, screaming for Dutch or for any of them, and then I stopped at the heavy doors of the lockers, where they had surely taken shelter. I stood there a moment. Everything went still. Then I heard a cry building in the wind, faint at first, a whistle and then a shrill scream that tore through the walls and gathered around me, spoke plain so I understood that I should move, put my arms out, and slam down the great iron bar that fit across the hasp and lock.

Outside, the wind was stronger, like a hand held against me. I struggled forward. The bushes tossed, the awnings flapped off storefronts, the rails of porches rattled. The odd cloud became a fat snout that nosed along the earth and sniffled, jabbed, picked at things, sucked them up, blew them apart, rooted around as if it was following a certain scent, then stopped behind me at the butcher shop and bored down like a drill.

I went flying, landed somewhere in a ball. When I opened my eyes and looked, stranger things were happening.

A herd of cattle flew through the air like giant birds, dropping dung, their mouths opened in stunned bellows. A candle, still lighted, blew past, and tables, napkins, garden tools, a whole school of drifting eyeglasses, jackets on hangers, hams, a checkerboard, a lampshade, and at last the sow from behind the lockers, on the run, her hooves a blur, set free, swooping, diving, screaming as everything in Argus fell apart and got turned upside down, smashed, and thoroughly wrecked.

Days passed before the town went looking for the men. They were bachelors, after all, except for Tor, whose wife had suffered a blow to the head that made her forgetful. Everyone was occupied with digging out, in high relief because even though the Catholic steeple had been torn off like a peaked cap and sent across five fields, those huddled in the cellar were unhurt. Walls had fallen, windows were demolished, but the stores were intact and so were the bankers and shop owners who had taken refuge in their safes or beneath their cash registers. It was a fair-minded disaster, no one could be said to have suffered much more than the next, at least not until Pete and Fritzie came home.

Of all the businesses in Argus, Kozka's Meats had suffered worst. The boards of the front building had been split to kindling, piled in a huge pyramid, and the shop equipment was blasted far and wide. Pete paced off the distance the iron bathtub had been flung—a hundred feet. The glass candy case went fifty, and landed without so much as a cracked pane. There were other surprises as well, for the back rooms where Fritzie and Pete lived were undisturbed. Fritzie said the dust still coated her china figures, and upon her kitchen table, in the ashtray, perched the last cigarette she'd put out in haste. She lit and finished it, looking through the window. From there, she could see that the old smokehouse Fleur had slept in was crushed to a red-dish sand and the stockpens were completely torn apart, the rails stacked helter-skelter. Fritzie asked for Fleur. People shrugged. Then she asked about the others and, suddenly, the town understood that three men were missing.

There was a rally of help, a gathering of shovels and volunteers. We passed boards from hand to hand, stacked them, uncovered what lay beneath the pile of jagged splinters. The lockers, full of meat that was Pete and Fritzie's investment, slowly came into sight, still intact. When enough room was made for a man to stand on the roof, there were calls, a general urge to hack through and see what lay below. But Fritzie shouted that she wouldn't allow it because the meat would spoil. And so the work continued, board by board, until at last the heavy oak doors of the freezer were revealed and people pressed to the entry. Everyone wanted to be the first, but since it was my stepfather lost, I was let go in when Pete and Fritzie wedged through into the sudden icy air.

Pete scraped a match on his boot, lit the lamp Fritzie held, and then the three of us stood still in its circle. Light glared off the skinned and hanging carcasses, the crates of wrapped sausages, the bright and cloudy blocks of lake ice, pure as winter. The cold bit into us, pleasant at first, then numbing. We must have stood there a couple of minutes before we saw the men, or more rightly, the humps of fur, the iced and shaggy hides they wore, the bear-skins they had taken down and wrapped about themselves. We stepped closer and Fritzie tilted the lantern beneath the flaps of fur into their faces. The dog was there, perched among them, heavy as a doorstop. The three had hunched around a barrel where the game was still laid out, and a dead lantern and an empty bottle too. But they had thrown down their last hands and hunkered tight, clutching one another, knuckles raw from beating at the door they had also attacked with hooks. Frost stars gleamed off their eyelashes and the stubble of their beards. Their faces were set in concentration, mouths open as if to speak some careful thought, some agreement they'd come to in each other's arms.

Power travels in the bloodlines, handed out before birth. It comes down through the hands, which in the Pillagers were strong and knotted, big, spi-dery, and rough, with sensitive fingertips good at dealing cards. It comes through the eyes, too, belligerent, darkest brown, the eyes of those in the bear clan, impolite as they gaze directly at a person.

In my dreams, I look straight back at Fleur, at the men. I am no longer the watcher on the dark sill, the skinny girl.

The blood draws us back, as if it runs through a vein of earth. I've come home and, except for talking to my cousins, live a quiet life. Fleur lives quiet too, down on Lake Turcot with her boat. Some say she's married to the waterman, Misshepeshu, or that she's living in shame with white men or windigos, or that she's killed them all. I'm about the only one here who ever goes to visit her. Last winter, I went to help out in her cabin when she bore the child, whose green eyes and skin the color of an old penny made more talk, as no one could decide if the child was mixed blood or what, fathered in a smokehouse, or by a man with brass scales, or by the lake. The girl is bold, smiling in her sleep, as if she knows what people wonder, as if she hears the old men talk, turning the story over. It comes up different every time and has no ending, no beginning. They get the middle wrong too. They only know they don't know anything.

1988

CATHY SONG
b. 1955

In many of Cathy Song's poems a particular moment or event becomes a window through which we enter a field of vision. "What frames the view," she has written, "is the mind in the diamond pinpoint light of concentration tunneling into memory, released by the imagination." As the title of her second book, *Frameless Windows, Squares of Light*, suggests, Song's poems capture the way a warm afternoon, a childhood Easter, a picnic in the park is an opening for memory and reflection. The visual quality of her poems can suggest a photograph or painting, and Song feels a connection between her work and those of the Japanese printmaker Kitagawa Utamaro and the American painter Georgia O'Keeffe. Song's first book, *Picture Bride* (1983), contains a number of poems inspired by the work of these artists. Writing, in "Beauty and Sadness," of the way Utamaro's prints rendered "Teahouse waitresses, actresses, / geishas, courtesans and maids" in "their fleeting loveliness," Song suggests that the artist and poet capture the moment, knowing that it is always dissolving.

Picture Bride was chosen by the poet Richard Hugo for the Yale Younger Poets series. In the title poem Song comes as close as imagination allows to the experience of her grandmother, who, the poem implies, was chosen as a bride from a photograph and summoned from Korea to Hawaii. But Song is also aware of the limits of imaginative identification and the difficulty of knowing the full truth of the past. She respects the mystery of another's identity. The grandmother in "Picture Bride," the woman in "Lost Sister," the mother in "Humble Jar," and the geishas painted by Utamaro possess a privacy that the poet discloses but cannot fully enter. Song's tactful sense of both the power and the limits of imagination is one of her distinctive marks as a poet.

She was born in Honolulu, Hawaii, and grew up in Wahiawa, a small town on the island of Oahu. The setting of sugar-cane fields, of island life where "the sound of the ocean / could be heard through the ironwoods" ("Waialua"), and of the rain that comes "even when the sun was shining" ("A Pale Arrangement of Hands") is central to her work. That landscape belongs to her present but also evokes her childhood and the memory of another, more distant landscape—the Asia of her ancestors. Many of Song's poems render the mysteries of what she has called "familial and personal ties; lives overlapping," and her sense of these ties extends backward to her Chinese and Korean ancestors as well as forward to her children. She began her college education at the University of Hawaii and then attended Wellesley College. After her graduation from Wellesley, she received an M.A. in creative writing from

Boston University and has since taught creative writing at a number of colleges and universities. Her third collection of poems, *School Figures*, appeared in 1994, followed by *The Land of Bliss* (2001) and *Cloud Moving Hands* (2007).

Song's ability to write about her own or another's experience as an acute observer may have to do with her multicultural background, which often places her on the boundary of what she sees. Her capacity to let the power of observation give rise to feeling recalls at times the work of Elizabeth Bishop and also suggests Song's resemblance to the Utamaro of her poem "Beauty and Sadness," whose "invisible presence / one feels in these prints." At other times Song writes about herself more directly. She has, for example, deftly rendered the erotic nature of her own experience: "But there is this slow arousal. / The small buttons / of my cotton blouse / are pulling away from my body" ("The White Porch"). The careful composition of her poems, with their vivid detail, blend the accidental and spontaneous quality of life with the design of art. Although her work can sometimes seem too composed, too removed from the sharp impact of experience, her strongest poems balance a sense of tradition with a feel for contemporary life and catch in the patterns of art the transient instant: "the flicker of a dragonfly's delicate wing."

The White Porch

I wrap the blue towel
after washing,
around the damp
weight of hair, bulky
as a sleeping cat,   5
and sit out on the porch.
Still dripping water,
it'll be dry by supper,
by the time the dust
settles off your shoes,   10
though it's only five
past noon. Think
of the luxury: how to use
the afternoon like the stretch
of lawn spread before me.   15
There's the laundry,
sun-warm clothes at twilight,
and the mountain of beans
in my lap. Each one,
I'll break and snap   20
thoughtfully in half.

But there is this slow arousal.
The small buttons
of my cotton blouse
are pulling away from my body.   25
I feel the strain of threads,
the swollen magnolias
heavy as a flock of birds
in the tree. Already,
the orange sponge cake   30
is rising in the oven.

I know you'll say it makes
your mouth dry
and I'll watch you
drench your slice of it   35
in canned peaches
and lick the plate clean.

So much hair, my mother
used to say, grabbing
the thick braided rope   40
in her hands while we washed
the breakfast dishes, discussing
dresses and pastries.
My mind often elsewhere
as we did the morning chores together.   45
Sometimes, a few strands
would catch in her gold ring.
I worked hard then,
anticipating the hour
when I would let the rope down   50
at night, strips of sheets,
knotted and tied,
while she slept in tight blankets.
My hair, freshly washed
like a measure of wealth,   55
like a bridal veil.
Crouching in the grass,
you would wait for the signal,
for the movement of curtains
before releasing yourself   60
from the shadow of moths.
Cloth, hair and hands,
smuggling you in.

1983

Lost Sister

1

In China,
even the peasants
named their first daughters
Jade—
the stone that in the far fields   5
could moisten the dry season,
could make men move mountains
for the healing green of the inner hills
glistening like slices of winter melon.

And the daughters were grateful: 10
they never left home.

To move freely was a luxury
stolen from them at birth.
Instead, they gathered patience,
learning to walk in shoes   15
the size of teacups,
without breaking—
the arc of their movements
as dormant as the rooted willow,
as redundant as the farmyard hens.   20
But they traveled far
in surviving,
learning to stretch the family rice,
to quiet the demons,
the noisy stomachs.   25

2

There is a sister
across the ocean,
who relinquished her name,
diluting jade green
with the blue of the Pacific.   30
Rising with a tide of locusts,
she swarmed with others
to inundate another shore.
In America,
there are many roads   35
and women can stride along with men.

But in another wilderness,
the possibilities,
the loneliness,
can strangulate like jungle vines.   40
The meager provisions and sentiments
of once belonging—
fermented roots, Mah-Jongg[1] tiles and firecrackers—
set but a flimsy household
in a forest of nightless cities.   45
A giant snake rattles above,
spewing black clouds into your kitchen.
Dough-faced landlords
slip in and out of your keyholes,
making claims you don't understand,   50
tapping into your communication systems
of laundry lines and restaurant chains.

You find you need China:
your one fragile identification,
a jade link   55
handcuffed to your wrist.
You remember your mother

---

1. A board game of Chinese origin.

who walked for centuries,
footless—
and like her,   60
you have left no footprints,
but only because
there is an ocean in between,
the unremitting space of your rebellion.

1983

Heaven

He thinks when we die we'll go to China.
Think of it—a Chinese heaven
where, except for his blond hair,
the part that belongs to his father,
everyone will look like him.   5
China, that blue flower on the map,
bluer than the sea
his hand must span like a bridge
to reach it.
An octave away.   10

I've never seen it.
It's as if I can't sing that far.
But look—
on the map, this black dot.
Here is where we live,   15
on the pancake plains
just east of the Rockies,
on the other side of the clouds.
A mile above the sea,
the air is so thin, you can starve on it.   20
No bamboo trees
but the alpine equivalent,
reedy aspen with light, fluttering leaves.
Did a boy in Guangzhou[1] dream of this
as his last stop?   25

I've heard the trains at night
whistling past our yards,
what we've come to own,
the broken fences, the whiny dog, the rattletrap cars.
It's still the wild west,   30
mean and grubby,
the shootouts and fistfights in the back alley.
With my son the dreamer
and my daughter, who is too young to walk,
I've sat in this spot   35
and wondered why here?

---

1. Or Canton, seaport city in southeastern China.

Why in this short life,
this town, this creek they call a river?

He had never planned to stay,
the boy who helped to build   40
the railroads for a dollar a day.[2]
He had always meant to go back.
When did he finally know
that each mile of track led him further away,
that he would die in his sleep,   45
dispossessed,
having seen Gold Mountain,[3]
the icy wind tunneling through it,
these landlocked, makeshift ghost towns?

It must be in the blood,   50
this notion of returning.
It skipped two generations, lay fallow,
the garden an unmarked grave.
On a spring sweater day
it's as if we remember him.   55
I call to the children.
We can see the mountains
shimmering blue above the air.
If you look really hard
says my son the dreamer,   60
leaning out from the laundry's rigging,
the work shirts fluttering like sails,
you can see all the way to heaven.

1988

2. The Chinese provided much of the cheap
labor that laid the tracks of the transcontinental
railroads in the 19th century.
3. In China in the 1840s and 1850s, the U.S.
state of California was known as "Gold Mountain." Many Chinese emigrated to California to
search for gold, only to discover that mining was
uncertain, unreliable, and dangerous.

LI-YOUNG LEE
b. 1957

I n his poem "Persimmons" Li-Young Lee remembers his father saying, "Some things
never leave a person." Many of the poems in Lee's books—*Rose* (1986), *The City in
Which I Love You* (1990), *Book of My Nights* (2001), and *Behind My Eyes* (2008)—testify
to a sense of the past, especially his father's past, which never leaves Lee. The father
in Lee's poems is personal and mythic; he instructs the poet-son in "the art of memory." Lee's father, born in China, served as a personal physician to Mao Zedong. He
later was jailed for nineteen months, a political prisoner of the Indonesian dictator

Sukarno. Lee was born in Jakarta, Indonesia. In 1959 the family fled Indonesia and traveled in the Far East (Hong Kong, Macao, and Japan), finally arriving in America, where Lee's father became a Presbyterian minister in a small town in western Pennsylvania. Many of Lee's poems seek to remember and understand his father's life and to come to terms with Lee's differences from that powerful figure.

Lee's work reminds us about the ancient connections between memory and poetry. In his work memory is often sweet; it draws the poet to the past even when, as in "Eating Alone," that sweetness is as dizzying as the juice of a rotten pear in which a hornet spins. But memory can also be a burden, and its pull is countered in Lee's work by a sensuous apprehension of the present. As in his poem "This Room and Everything in It," the erotic immediacy of the moment can disrupt any effort to fix that moment in the orders of memory. Everywhere in Lee's work is the evidence of hearing, taste, smell, and touch as well as sight. If the poet's bodily presence in the world recalls his great American precursor Walt Whitman, Lee's fluid motion between the physical world and the domain of memory, dream, or vision also carries out Whitman's visionary strain and links Lee to the work of Theodore Roethke, James Wright, and Denise Levertov, among others. The intensity of Lee's poems, however, is often leavened by a subtle and winning humor and playfulness; such qualities are especially valuable in a poet at times too easily seduced by beauty.

Lee studied at the University of Pittsburgh (where one of his teachers was the poet Gerald Stern), the University of Arizona, and the State University of New York College at Brockport. He has since taught at various universities. In 1995 he published a prose memoir, *The Winged Seed: A Remembrance*. His prose, like his poetry, is characterized by his deep sense of connection between an individual life and a powerful past, mediated by his ability to move between plain speech and a lushness evocative of biblical language.

Persimmons

In sixth grade Mrs. Walker
slapped the back of my head
and made me stand in the corner
for not knowing the difference
between *persimmon* and *precision*.   5
How to choose

persimmons. This is precision.
Ripe ones are soft and brown-spotted.
Sniff the bottoms. The sweet one
will be fragrant. How to eat: 10
put the knife away, lay down newspaper.
Peel the skin tenderly, not to tear the meat.
Chew the skin, suck it,
and swallow. Now, eat
the meat of the fruit,   15
so sweet,
all of it, to the heart.

Donna undresses, her stomach is white.
In the yard, dewy and shivering
with crickets, we lie naked,   20

face-up, face-down.
I teach her Chinese.
Crickets: *chiu chiu.* Dew: I've forgotten.
Naked: I've forgotten.
Ni, wo: you and me.   25
I part her legs,
remember to tell her
she is beautiful as the moon.

Other words
that got me into trouble were   30
fight and *fright, wren* and *yarn.*
Fight was what I did when I was frightened,
fright was what I felt when I was fighting.
Wrens are small, plain birds,
yarn is what one knits with.   35
Wrens are soft as yarn.
My mother made birds out of yarn.
I loved to watch her tie the stuff;
a bird, a rabbit, a wee man.

Mrs. Walker brought a persimmon to class   40
and cut it up
so everyone could taste
a *Chinese apple.* Knowing
it wasn't ripe or sweet, I didn't eat
but I watched the other faces.   45

My mother said every persimmon has a sun
inside, something golden, glowing,
warm as my face.

Once, in the cellar, I found two wrapped in newspaper,
forgotten and not yet ripe.   50
I took them and set both on my bedroom windowsill,
where each morning a cardinal
sang, *The sun, the sun.*

Finally understanding
he was going blind,   55
my father sat up all one night
waiting for a song, a ghost.
I gave him the persimmons,
swelled, heavy as sadness,
and sweet as love.   60

This year, in the muddy lighting
of my parents' cellar, I rummage, looking
for something I lost.
My father sits on the tired, wooden stairs,
black cane between his knees,   65
hand over hand, gripping the handle.

He's so happy that I've come home.
I ask how his eyes are, a stupid question.
All gone, he answers.

Under some blankets, I find a box.   70
Inside the box I find three scrolls.
I sit beside him and untie
three paintings by my father:
Hibiscus leaf and a white flower.
Two cats preening.   75
Two persimmons, so full they want to drop from the cloth.

He raises both hands to touch the cloth,
asks, *Which is this?*

This is persimmons, Father.

Oh, the feel of the wolftail on the silk,   80
the strength, the tense
precision in the wrist.
I painted them hundreds of times
eyes closed. These I painted blind.
Some things never leave a person: 85
scent of the hair of one you love,
the texture of persimmons,
in your palm, the ripe weight.

                                                      1986

Eating Alone

I've pulled the last of the year's young onions.
The garden is bare now. The ground is cold,
brown and old. What is left of the day flames
in the maples at the corner of my
eye. I turn, a cardinal vanishes.   5
By the cellar door, I wash the onions,
then drink from the icy metal spigot.

Once, years back, I walked beside my father
among the windfall pears. I can't recall
our words. We may have strolled in silence. But   10
I still see him bend, that way—left hand braced
on knee, creaky—to lift and hold to my
eye a rotten pear. In it, a hornet
spun crazily, glazed in slow, glistening juice.

It was my father I saw this morning   15
waving to me from the trees. I almost
called to him, until I came close enough
to see the shovel, leaning where I had
left it, in the flickering, deep green shade.

White rice steaming, almost done. Sweet green peas   20
fried in onions. Shrimp braised in sesame
oil and garlic. And my own loneliness.
What more could I, a young man, want.

1986

Eating Together

In the steamer is the trout
seasoned with slivers of ginger,
two sprigs of green onion, and sesame oil.
We shall eat it with rice for lunch,
brothers, sister, my mother who will   5
taste the sweetest meat of the head,
holding it between her fingers
deftly, the way my father did
weeks ago. Then he lay down
to sleep like a snow-covered road   10
winding through pines older than him,
without any travelers, and lonely for no one.

1986

This Room and Everything in It

Lie still now
while I prepare For my future,
certain hard days ahead,
when I'll need what I know so clearly this moment.

I am making use   5
of the one thing I learned
of all the things my father tried to teach me:
the art of memory.

I am letting this room
and everything in it   10
stand for my ideas about love
and its difficulties.

I'll let your love-cries,
those spacious notes
of a moment ago,   15
stand for distance.

Your scent,
that scent

of spice and a wound,
I'll let stand for mystery.   20

Your sunken belly
is the daily cup
of milk I drank
as a boy before morning prayer.

The sun on the face   25
of the wall
is God, the face
I can't see, my soul,

and so on, each thing
standing for a separate idea,   30
and those ideas forming the constellation
of my greater idea.
And one day, when I need
to tell myself something intelligent
about love,   35

I'll close my eyes
and recall this room and everything in it:
My body is estrangement.
This desire, perfection.
Your closed eyes my extinction.   40
Now I've forgotten my
idea. The book
on the windowsill, riffled by wind . . .
the even-numbered pages are
the past, the odd-   45
numbered pages, the future.
The sun is
God, your body is milk . . .

useless, useless . . .
your cries are song, my body's not me . . .   50
no good . . . my idea
has evaporated . . . your hair is time, your thighs are song . . .
it had something to do
with death . . . it had something
to do with love.   55

                                                        1990

Creative Nonfiction

"Creative nonfiction" is a relatively new term—it first appeared officially in 1983 as a category for creative writing fellowships in the National Endowment of the Arts—but examples of the form appear much earlier in American literature. If Thoreau and Emerson were publishing their personal essays today their work would probably be called examples of creative nonfiction, as might much of the travel and nature writing long a part of American literature. The term is fluid, suggesting a hybrid that involves facts, research, and information while using the resources and strategies of fiction, poetry, biography, and autobiography in shaping its material.

The term is closely allied with what was, in the 1970s, called "The New Journalism" (the writer Tom Wolfe published a book with that title in 1973), in which, instead of simply reporting the event, the writer reports on himself or herself within the event, either as a participant or an observer (or both). Examples of the "The New Journalism" include Truman Capote's *In Cold Blood* (1966), Norman Mailer's *Armies of the Night* (1968), Joan Didion's *Slouching Towards Bethlehem* (1968), Hunter Thompson's *Fear and Loathing in Las Vegas* (1972), and Wolfe's own *The Right Stuff* (1979). This approach to journalism addressed the problem of what the physicist Werner Heisenberg called "the uncertainty principle" (a theory the novelist Thomas Pynchon frequently invokes in his work), which asserts that the observer's presence alters the phenomenon being observed. "The New Journalism" sought to reveal the writer observing the event and thus make us aware of the lens through which we see. The term now seems specific to a particular cultural moment and group of writers; creative nonfiction is more flexible and expansive, both in terms of the kinds of writing it describes and the range of authors affiliated with it. Ultimately, though, the point is that no direct duplication of reality is possible in language, that all writing is affected by the author's point of view. Creative nonfiction is open in its aim of merging invention with fidelity to fact.

As with all hybrids, the distinctions between it and other forms are slippery. Most memoirs, personal essays, and environmental writing are considered to be creative nonfiction, but the writers in this cluster provide especially innovative examples of these forms. Edwidge Danticat mingles autobiography, political analysis, and biography; Joan Didion's memoir includes clinical observation and medical research. John Crawford's account of his experience as an Iraq war veteran and Dorothy Allison's description of the effects of social class on herself and her family make their works more than the stories of individuals. The environmental writing of Edward Abbey and Barry Lopez combines carefully observed, factual description of landscapes and natural creatures with an equal focus on the writer's feelings and reflections. It is easy to understand why many examples of the form slip back and forth between a variety of categories: among the selections here, Jamaica Kincaid's "Girl" appeared in a book collection advertised as "Stories," but many critics and reviewers have called the work a poem or autobiography.

The term "Creative Nonfiction" is fully at ease with such slippage, and happily embraces work that mixes elements of many different genres; whatever the mixture, it's the quality of writing and the use of various techniques that establish the work as "creative." In the twenty-first century hybridity is a significant cultural modality, and much of contemporary writing is self-consciously hybrid. Mixing poetry and essay, personal reflection and journalism, nature writing and myth, or inventing other combinations, some of the best American writing is now, and always has been, creative nonfiction.

EDWARD ABBEY

A prolific writer, Edward Abbey (1927–1989) was the author of many novels but he is most famous for his personal essays, which have become classics of environmental writing. Born and raised in Pennsylvania, he went west in his teens, and late in the 1950s he worked at Arches National Monument (now Arches National Park) near Moab in eastern Utah, as a seasonal ranger. In the spirit of Thoreau's residence at Walden Pond and Gary Snyder's summers as a fire lookout in Washington State's North Cascades, Abbey said he sought solitude in an effort to "confront, immediately and directly if possible, the bare bones of existence." His most famous book, *Desert Solitaire* (1968), came out of his journals from this period; the book is a compilation of description, natural history, tall tales, and polemical environmentalism.

One of the most gripping chapters in *Desert Solitaire* focuses on Abbey's time in Havasu, at the base of the Grand Canyon. As he tells it, during a stop at the Grand Canyon with friends en route to Los Angeles he decided on the spur of the moment to descend to the canyon floor ("fourteen miles by trail") to take a look at Havasu Canyon in Arizona, the homeland of the Havasupai Native people. Five weeks later, he emerged to find that his friends had sensibly gone on without him. During the weeks he spent there, Abbey camped and explored the surrounding landscape alone. The selection here focuses on one such day of exploration, when, looking for a shortcut back to his camp, he made a series of potentially fatal decisions.

Havasu

Most of my wandering in the desert I've done alone. Not so much from choice as from necessity—I generally prefer to go into places where no one else wants to go. I find that in contemplating the natural world my pleasure is greater if there are not too many others contemplating it with me, at the same time. However, there are special hazards in traveling alone. Your chances of dying, in case of sickness or accident, are much improved, simply because there is no one around to go for help.

Exploring a side canyon off Havasu Canyon[1] one day, I was unable to resist the temptation to climb up out of it onto what corresponds in that region to the Tonto Bench.[2] Late in the afternoon I realized that I would not have enough time to get back to my camp before dark, unless I could find a much shorter route than the one by which I had come. I looked for a shortcut.

Nearby was another little side canyon which appeared to lead down into Havasu Canyon. It was a steep, shadowy, extremely narrow defile with the usual meandering course and overhanging walls; from where I stood, near its head, I could not tell if the route was feasible all the way down to the

1. A canyon with waterfall, forming a side branch of the Grand Canyon, that was once the home of a prehistoric people and has been occupied by the Havasupai, "people of the blue-green waters," for the last 800 years.

2. The long, narrow strip of relatively level land located in the Grand Canyon, separating the inner gorge from the upper canyon and following the course of the Colorado River.

floor of the main canyon. I had no rope with me—only my walking stick. But I was hungry and thirsty, as always. I started down.

For a while everything went well. The floor of the little canyon began as a bed of dry sand, scattered with rocks. Farther down a few boulders were wedged between the walls; I climbed over and under them. Then the canyon took on the slickrock[3] character—smooth, sheer, slippery sandstone carved by erosion into a series of scoops and potholes which got bigger as I descended. In some of these basins there was a little water left over from the last flood, warm and fetid water under an oily-looking scum, condensed by prolonged evaporation to a sort of broth, rich in dead and dying organisms. My canteen was empty and I was very thirsty but I felt that I could wait.

I came to a lip on the canyon floor which overhung by twelve feet the largest so far of these stagnant pools. On each side rose the canyon walls, roughly perpendicular. There was no way to continue except by dropping into the pool. I hesitated. Beyond this point there could hardly be any returning, yet the main canyon was still not visible below. Obviously the only sensible thing to do was to turn back. I edged over the lip of stone and dropped feet first into the water.

Deeper than I expected. The warm, thick fluid came up and closed over my head as my feet touched the muck at the bottom. I had to swim to the farther side. And here I found myself on the verge of another drop-off, with one more huge bowl of green soup below.

This drop-off was about the same height as the one before, but not over-hanging. It resembled a children's playground slide, concave and S-curved, only steeper, wider, with a vertical pitch in the middle. It did not lead directly into the water but ended in a series of steplike ledges above the pool. Beyond the pool lay another edge, another drop-off into an unknown depth. Again I paused, and for a much longer time. But I no longer had the option of turning around and going back. I eased myself into the chute[4] and let go of everything—except my faithful stick.

I hit rock bottom hard, but without any physical injury. I swam the stinking pond dog-paddle[5] style, pushing the heavy scum away from my face, and crawled out on the far side to see what my fate was going to be.

Fatal. Death by starvation, slow and tedious. For I was looking straight down an overhanging cliff to a rubble pile of broken rocks eighty feet below.

After the first wave of utter panic had passed I began to try to think. First of all I was not going to die immediately, unless another flash flood came down the gorge; there was the pond of stagnant water on hand to save me from thirst and a man can live, they say, for thirty days or more without food. My sun-bleached bones, dramatically sprawled at the bottom of the chasm, would provide the diversion of the picturesque for future wanderers—if any man ever came this way again.

My second thought was to scream for help, although I knew very well there could be no other human being within miles. I even tried it but the sound of that anxious shout, cut short in the dead air within the canyon walls, was so

3. A term used in the Southwest to refer to smooth, consolidated, and hardened sand dunes.
4. A waterfall or steep descent in a river.

5. A simple swimming style, often used by children.

inhuman, so detached as it seemed from myself, that it terrified me and I didn't attempt it again.

I thought of tearing my clothes into strips and plaiting a rope. But what was I wearing?—boots, socks, a pair of old and ragged blue jeans, a flimsy T-shirt, an ancient and rotten sombrero[6] of straw. Not a chance of weaving such a wardrobe into a rope eighty feet long, or even twenty feet long.

How about a signal fire? There was nothing to burn but my clothes; not a tree, not a shrub, not even a weed grew in this stony cul-de-sac. Even if I burned my clothing the chances of the smoke being seen by some Hualapai Indian[7] high on the south rim were very small; and if he did see the smoke, what then? He'd shrug his shoulders, sigh, and take another pull from his Tokay[8] bottle. Furthermore, without clothes, the sun would soon bake me to death.

There was only one thing I could do. I had a tiny notebook in my hip pocket and a stub of pencil. When these dried out I could at least record my final thoughts. I would have plenty of time to write not only my epitaph but my own elegy.[9]

But not yet.

There were a few loose stones scattered about the edge of the pool. Taking the biggest first, I swam with it back to the foot of the slickrock chute and placed it there. One by one I brought the others and made a shaky little pile about two feet high leaning against the chute. Hopeless, of course, but there was nothing else to do. I stood on the top of the pile and stretched upward, straining my arms to their utmost limit and groped with fingers and fingernails for a hold on something firm. There was nothing. I crept back down. I began to cry. It was easy. All alone, I didn't have to be brave.

Through the tears I noticed my old walking stick lying nearby. I took it and stood it on the most solid stone in the pile, behind the two topmost stones. I took off my boots, tied them together and hung them around my neck, on my back. I got up on the little pile again and lifted one leg and set my big toe on the top of the stick. This could never work. Slowly and painfully, leaning as much of my weight as I could against the sandstone slide, I applied more and more pressure to the stick, pushing my body upward until I was again stretched out full length above it. Again I felt about for a fingerhold. There was none. The chute was smooth as polished marble.

No, not quite that smooth. This was sandstone, soft and porous, not marble, and between it and my wet body and wet clothing a certain friction was created. In addition, the stick had enabled me to reach a higher section of the S-curved chute, where the angle was more favorable. I discovered that I could move upward, inch by inch, through adhesion and with the help of the leveling tendency of the curve. I gave an extra little push with my big toe—the stones collapsed below, the stick clattered down—and crawled rather like a snail or slug, oozing slime, up over the rounded summit of the slide.

The next obstacle, the overhanging spout twelve feet above a deep plunge pool, looked impossible. It *was* impossible, but with the blind faith of despair

6. A broad-brimmed hat common in Spain and Spanish America.
7. "People of the tall pine," the Hualapai are a Native American people living along the pine-clad southern side of the Grand Canyon.
8. Tokay is a sweet wine, often available in cheap or inexpensive forms.
9. An epitaph is a short text inscribed on a tombstone, honoring a deceased person; an elegy is a mournful poem, especially a funeral song or a lament for the dead.

I slogged into the water and swam underneath the drop-off and floundered around for a while, scrabbling at the slippery rock until my nerves and tiring muscles convinced my numbed brain that *this was not the way*. I swam back to solid ground and lay down to rest and die in comfort.

Far above I could see the sky, an irregular strip of blue between the dark, hard-edged canyon walls that seemed to lean toward each other as they towered above me. Across that narrow opening a small white cloud was passing, so lovely and precious and delicate and forever inaccessible that it broke the heart and made me weep like a woman, like a child. In all my life I had never seen anything so beautiful.

The walls that rose on either side of the drop-off were literally perpendicular. Eroded by weathering, however, and not by the corrasion[1] of rushing floodwater, they had a rough surface, chipped, broken, cracked. Where the walls joined the face of the overhang they formed almost a square corner, with a number of minute crevices and inch-wide shelves on either side. It might, after all, be possible. What did I have to lose?

When I had regained some measure of nerve and steadiness I got up off my back and tried the wall beside the pond, clinging to the rock with bare toes and fingertips and inching my way crabwise toward the corner. The watersoaked, heavy boots dangling from my neck, swinging back and forth with my every movement, threw me off balance and I fell into the pool. I swam out to the bank, unslung the boots and threw them up over the drop-off, out of sight. They'd be there if I ever needed them again. Once more I attached myself to the wall, tenderly, sensitively, like a limpet,[2] and very slowly, very cautiously, worked my way into the corner. Here I was able to climb upward, a few centimeters at a time, by bracing myself against the opposite sides and finding sufficient niches for fingers and toes. As I neared the top and the overhang became noticeable I prepared for a slip, planning to push myself away from the rock so as to fall into the center of the pool where the water was deepest. But it wasn't necessary. Somehow, with a skill and tenacity I could never have found in myself under ordinary circumstances, I managed to creep straight up that gloomy cliff and over the brink of the drop-off and into the flower of safety. My boots were floating under the surface of the little puddle above. As I poured the stinking water out of them and pulled them on and laced them up I discovered myself bawling again for the third time in three hours, the hot delicious tears of victory. And up above the clouds replied—thunder.

I emerged from that treacherous little canyon at sundown, with an enormous fire in the western sky and lightning overhead. Through sweet twilight and the sudden dazzling flare of lightning a I hiked back along the Tonto Bench, bellowing the *Ode to Joy*.[3] Long before I reached the place where I could descend safely to the main canyon and my camp, however, darkness set in, the clouds opened their bays and the rain poured down. I took shelter under a ledge in a shallow cave about three feet high—hardly room to sit up in. Others had been here before: the dusty floor of the little hole was littered with the droppings of birds, rats, jackrabbits, and coyotes.

---

1. The wearing away of rock by the constant flow of water.
2. Common name for numerous kinds of saltwater and freshwater snails.

3. A famous theme in the final movement of German composer and pianist Ludwig van Beethoven's (1770–1827) Ninth Symphony (1824).

There were also a few long gray pieces of scat with a curious twist at one tip—cougar? I didn't care. I had some matches with me, sealed in paraffin (the prudent explorer); I scraped together the handiest twigs and animal droppings and built a little fire and waited for the rain to stop.

It didn't stop. The rain came down for hours in alternate waves of storm and drizzle and I very soon had burnt up all the fuel within reach. No matter. I stretched out in the coyote den, pillowed my head on my arm and suffered through the long long night, wet, cold, aching, hungry, wretched, dreaming claustrophobic nightmares. It was one of the happiest nights of my life.

1968

BARRY LOPEZ

B arry Lopez's "The Raven" is a difficult piece of writing to categorize. In its specific attention to details of the desert landscape and creatures, it belongs to the genre of nature writing for which Lopez (b. 1945) is so well known (for example, his award winning books *Arctic Dreams*, 1986, and *Of Wolves and Men*, 2004). But like much of Lopez's writing, "The Raven" is clearly not a simple factual description of ravens. Embedded in the piece are what we might call "raven tales"—fables or stories about the life and behaviors of a bird whose symbolic importance in indigenous cultures is widespread. And, in fact, the book in which this piece first appeared, *Desert Notes: Reflections in the Eye of a Raven* (1976), bore the subtitle "Short Stories." But as Lopez himself has pointed out, "the distinction between fiction and nonfiction, though logical and even useful, is not as important as the distinction between an authentic and inauthentic story." "The Raven" is an authentic story about the desert landscape and its inhabitants and, equally important, a story that creates in the writer and the reader an authentic sense of wonder. In its presentation of a natural world deeply connected to myth and storytelling there are clear affinities between this piece and the work of Native American writers like Louise Erdrich and Sherman Alexie.

Lopez is an intimate observer of the landscape he writes about in "The Raven." He grew up in rural Southern California and as a child spent time in the Mojave desert. His interest in the relationships between landscapes and human culture has taken him on travels to both remote and populated parts of the world.

The Raven

I am going to have to start at the other end by telling you this: there are no crows in the desert. What appear to be crows are ravens. You must examine the crow, however, before you can understand the raven. To forget the crow completely, as some have tried to do, would be like trying to understand the one who stayed without talking to the one who left. It is important to make note of who has left the desert.

To begin with, the crow does nothing alone. He cannot abide silence and he is prone to stealing things, twigs and bits of straw, from the nests of his neighbors. It is a game with him. He enjoys tricks. If he cannot make up his mind the crow will take two or three wives, but this is not a game. The crow is very accommodating and he admires compulsiveness.

Crows will live in street trees in the residential areas of great cities. They will walk at night on the roofs of parked cars and peck at the grit; they will scrape the pinpoints of their talons across the steel and, with their necks outthrust, watch for frightened children listening in their beds.

Put all this to the raven: he will open his mouth as if to say something. Then he will look the other way and say nothing. Later, when you have forgotten, he will tell you he admires the crow.

The raven is larger than the crow and has a beard of black feathers at his throat. He is careful to kill only what he needs. Crows, on the other hand, will search out the great horned owl, kick and punch him awake, and then, for roosting too close to their nests, they will kill him. They will come out of the sky on a fat, hot afternoon and slam into the head of a dozing rabbit and go away laughing. They will tear out a whole row of planted corn and eat only a few kernels. They will defecate on scarecrows and go home and sleep with 200,000 of their friends in an atmosphere of congratulation. Again, it is only a game; this should not be taken to mean that they are evil.

There is however this: when too many crows come together on a roost there is a lot of shoving and noise and a white film begins to descend over the crows' eyes and they go blind. They fall from their perches and lie on the ground and starve to death. When confronted with this information, crows will look past you and warn you vacantly that it is easy to be misled.

The crow flies like a pigeon. The raven flies like a hawk He is seen only at a great distance and then not very clearly. This is true of the crow too, but if you are very clever you can trap the crow. The only way to be sure what you have seen is a raven is to follow him until he dies of old age, and then examine the body.

Once there were many crows in the desert. I am told it was like this: you could sit back in the rocks and watch a pack of crows working over the carcass of a coyote. Some would eat, the others would try to squeeze out the vultures. The raven would never be seen. He would be at a distance, alone, perhaps eating a scorpion.

There was, at this time, a small alkaline water hole at the desert's edge. Its waters were bitter. No one but crows would drink there, although they drank sparingly, just one or two sips at a time. One day a raven warned someone about the dangers of drinking the bitter water and was overheard by a crow. When word of this passed among the crows they felt insulted. They jeered and raised insulting gestures to the ravens. They bullied each other into drinking the alkaline water until they had drunk the hole dry and gone blind.

The crows flew into canyon walls and dove straight into the ground at forty miles an hour and broke their necks. The worst of it was their cartwheeling across the desert floor, stiff wings outstretched, beaks agape, white eyes ballooning, surprising rattlesnakes hidden under sage bushes out of the noonday sun. The snakes awoke, struck and held. The wheeling birds strew them across the desert like sprung traps.

When all the crows were finally dead, the desert bacteria and fungi bored into them, burrowed through bone and muscle, through aqueous humor[1] and feathers until they had reduced the stiff limbs of soft black to blue dust.

1. The thick watery substance filling the space between the lens and the cornea of the eye.

After that, there were no more crows in the desert. The few who watched from a distance took it as a sign and moved away.

Finally there is this: one morning four ravens sat at the edge of the desert waiting for the sun to rise. They had been there all night and the dew was like beads of quicksilver on their wings. Their eyes were closed and they were as still as the cracks in the desert floor.

The wind came off the snow-capped peaks to the north and ruffled their breath feathers. Their talons arched in the white earth and they smoothed their wings with sleek, dark bills. At first light their bodies swelled and their eyes flashed purple. When the dew dried on their wings they lifted off from the desert floor and flew away in four directions. Crows would never have had the patience for this.

If you want to know more about the raven: bury yourself in the desert so that you have a commanding view of the high basalt[2] cliffs where he lives. Let only your eyes protrude. Do not blink—the movement will alert the raven to your continued presence. Wait until a generation of ravens has passed away. Of the new generation there will be at least one bird who will find you. He will see your eyes staring up out of the desert floor. The raven is cautious, but he is thorough. He will sense your peaceful intentions. Let him have the first word. Be careful: he will tell you he knows nothing.

If you do not have the time for this, scour the weathered desert shacks for some sign of the raven's body. Look under old mattresses and beneath loose floorboards. Look behind the walls. Sooner or later you will find a severed foot. It will be his and it will be well preserved.

Take it out in the sunlight and examine it closely. Notice that there are three fingers that face forward, and a fourth, the longest and like a thumb, that faces to the rear. The instrument will be black but no longer shiny, the back of it sheathed in armor plate and the underside padded like a wolf's foot.

At the end of each digit you will find a black, curved talon. You will see that the talons are not as sharp as you might have suspected. They are made to grasp and hold fast, not to puncture. They are more like the jaws of a trap than a fistful of ice picks. The subtle difference serves the raven well in the desert. He can weather a storm on a barren juniper limb; he can pick up and examine the crow's eye without breaking it.

1976

---

2. A common volcanic rock, usually fine-grained due to the rapid cooling of lava.

JAMAICA KINCAID

Jamaica Kincaid was born on the island of Antigua in the West Indies in 1949; at seventeen she felt she had to "rescue herself" from an oppressive cultural and family situation and came to New York as an *au pair* (she calls herself "a servant"). Writing, she has said, was for her "a matter of saving my life." In 1973 she changed her birth name of Elaine Cynthia Potter Richardson to Jamaica Kincaid, because, she said, her family disapproved of her writing. After she left Antigua she did not see her mother again for twenty years. When she began a career as a writer she became a regular contributor to the *New Yorker* magazine. Her first book, *Annie John* (1983), is an autobiographical coming-of-age novel, as is *Lucy* (1990), a fictional version of her coming to New York. Her other work includes a book about Antigua (*A Small Place*, 1988), a memoir (*My Brother*, 1998), and two books on gardening, one of her passions.

"Girl," which first appeared in the *New Yorker* in 1978, is one all-but-uninterrupted sentence in which a West Indian mother instructs her daughter on how to be the "proper" young woman she is certain her daughter is not. Although the daughter twice tries to interject, she's unable to change what is essentially monologue into dialogue. Kincaid has said that the voice in the story is "my mother's voice exactly over many years" and that, as a child, "a powerless person," she spoke infrequently. Like the other pieces collected in *At the Bottom of the River* (1983), "Girl" resists classification. Its implicit narrative makes it story; its strong rhythm and vivid images make it poetry. Simultaneously, like an essay it documents issues of gender and power. And, like much of this writer's work, it is rooted in autobiography. "I am so happy to write that I don't care what you call it," she has said. The mother/daughter relationship in "Girl" is one of Kincaid's earliest explorations of her ongoing and self-proclaimed "obsessive theme" as a writer: "the relationship between the powerful and the powerless."

Girl

Wash the white clothes on Monday and put them on the stone heap; wash the color clothes on Tuesday and put them on the clothesline to dry; don't walk barehead in the hot sun; cook pumpkin fritters[1] in very hot sweet oil; soak your little cloths right after you take them off; when buying cotton to make yourself a nice blouse, be sure that it doesn't have gum[2] on it, because that way it won't hold up well after a wash; soak salt fish[3] overnight before you cook it; is it true that you sing benna[4] in Sunday school?; always eat your food in such a way that it won't turn someone else's stomach; on Sundays try to walk like a lady and not like the slut you are so bent on becoming; don't sing benna in Sunday school; you mustn't speak to wharf-rat[5] boys, not even to give directions; don't eat fruits on the street—flies will follow you; *but I don't sing benna on Sundays at all and never in Sunday school*; this is how to sew on a button; this is how to make a buttonhole for the button you have just sewed on; this is how to hem a dress when you see the hem coming down and so to prevent yourself from looking like the slut I know you are so bent on becoming; this is how you iron your father's khaki shirt so that it doesn't have a crease; this is how you iron your father's khaki pants so that they don't have a crease; this is how you grow okra[6]—far from the house, because okra tree harbors red ants; when you are growing dasheen,[7] make sure it gets plenty of water or else it makes your throat itch when you are eating it; this is how you

1. A Caribbean dish made from fried calabaza, or West Indian pumpkin.
2. A naturally occurring, viscous resin found in the woody parts of plants.
3. A popular West Indian dish of dried and salted codfish sautéed with spices.
4. A calypso-like music characterized by a call-and-response format; it was used as a form of folk communication to spread gossip and other local news across the islands of the British West Indies in the early 20th century.
5. Regarding an individual who lives by stealing from ships or warehouses near wharves.
6. Vegetable thought to be of African origin, grown in tropical and warm temperate climates, often cooked in soups and stews or served raw.
7. The edible, starchy, tuberous root of taro, a tropical plant.

sweep a corner; this is how you sweep a whole house; this is how you sweep a yard; this is how you smile to someone you don't like too much; this is how you smile to someone you don't like at all; this is how you smile to someone you like completely; this is how you set a table for tea; this is how you set a table for dinner; this is how you set a table for dinner with an important guest; this is how you set a table for lunch; this is how you set a table for breakfast; this is how to behave in the presence of men who don't know you very well, and this way they won't recognize immediately the slut I have warned you against becoming; be sure to wash every day, even if it is with your own spit; don't squat down to play marbles—you are not a boy, you know; don't pick people's flowers—you might catch something; don't throw stones at blackbirds; because it might not be a blackbird at all; this is how to make a bread pudding;[8] this is how to make doukona;[9] this is how to make pepper pot;[1] this is how to make a good medicine for a cold; this is how to make a good medicine to throw away a child before it even becomes a child; this is how to catch a fish; this is how to throw back a fish you don't like, and that way something bad won't fall on you; this is how to bully a man; this is how a man bullies you; this is how to love a man, and if this doesn't work there are other ways, and if they don't work don't feel too bad about giving up; this is how to spit up in the air if you feel like it, and this is how to move quick so that it doesn't fall on you; this is how to make ends meet; always squeeze bread to make sure it's fresh; *but what if the baker won't let me feel the bread?*; you mean to say that after all you are really going to be the kind of woman who the baker won't let near the bread?

1978, 1983

---

8. A dessert made from leftover bread.
9. A Caribbean pudding made from plantain and wrapped in a plantain leaf.

1. A Caribbean meat stew, strongly flavored with cinnamon, hot peppers, and cassareep, a special sauce made from the cassava root.

DOROTHY ALLISON

The central fact of my life," Dorothy Allison writes, "is that I was born in 1949 in Greenville, South Carolina, the bastard daughter of a white woman from a desperately poor family." The title of her first book, *Trash* (1988), a collection of short stories, deliberately appropriates the contemptuous slur directed toward her family and all those whose poverty is seen, she writes, as "somehow oddly deserved." Her novel *Bastard Out of Carolina* (1989), a fictional account of her experience as the first child of a fifteen-year-old unwed mother who worked as a waitress, is a fierce and passionate articulation of the devastating effects of social class and its link to sexual abuse and violence. An activist on feminist and gay/lesbian issues, Allison has been writer-in-residence at Emory University in Atlanta, Georgia, as well as Davidson College in Davidson, North Carolina, and Columbia College in Chicago.

The selection below comes from "Stubborn Girls and Mean Stories," Allison's introduction to a second edition of *Trash* (2002). In this piece "mean" and "stubborn" are terms of praise implying survival and resilience. "'Now that's mean,'" her mama says with a smile after Allison has sent her one of her stories. "I want it mean," Allison replies. Writing for Allison becomes an act of setting "moment to moment a small piece of stubbornness against an ocean of ignorance and obliteration." "Stubborn Girls and Mean Stories" takes its place beside classic documents of the devastating effects of poverty such as James Agee and Walker Evan's *Let Us Now Praise Famous Men* (1941) as well as accounts (such as Eudora Welty's) in which a writer describes how and why she came to be a writer.

From Stubborn Girls and Mean Stories

Introduction

The central fact of my life is that I was born in 1949 in Greenville, South Carolina,[1] the bastard daughter of a white woman from a desperately poor family, a girl who had left the seventh grade the year before, worked as a waitress, and was just a month past fifteen when she birthed me. That fact, the inescapable impact of being born in a condition of poverty that this society finds shameful, contemptible, and somehow oddly deserved, has had dominion over me to such an extent that I have spent my life trying to overcome or deny it. My family's lives were not on television, not in books, not even comic books. There was a myth of the poor in this country, but it did not include us, no matter how I tried to squeeze us in. There was this concept of the "good" poor, and that fantasy had little to do with the everyday lives my family had survived. The good poor were hardworking, ragged but clean, and intrinsically honorable. We were the bad poor. We were men who drank and couldn't keep a job; women, invariably pregnant before marriage, who quickly became worn, fat, and old from working too many hours and bearing too many children; and children with runny noses, watery eyes, and the wrong attitudes. My cousins quit school, stole cars, used drugs, and took dead-end jobs pumping gas or waiting tables. I worked after school in a job provided by Lyndon Johnson's War on Poverty,[2] stole books I could not afford. We were not noble, not grateful, not even hopeful. We knew ourselves despised. What was there to work for, to save money for, to fight for or struggle against? We had generations before us to teach us that nothing ever changed, and that those who did try to escape failed.

Everything I write comes out of that very ordinary American history. There is no story in which my family is not background, even as I have moved very far from both Greenville, South Carolina, and the poverty to which I was born. I remain my mother's bastard girl, a woman who treasures her handmade family, my own adopted bastard child and the lover/partner who has nurtured and provoked me for more than fifteen years. We become what we did not intend, and still the one thing I know for sure is that only my sense of humor will sustain me.

Stories I began as a girl seem different to me when I read them now. It is almost as if I did not write them, as if that writer were another person—which of course she is. Twenty and twenty-five years ago when I first began to publish stories, I was a different person—not just younger but more girlish

1. South Carolina's sixth largest city, located upstate in the foothills of the Appalachian Mountains.
2. The "War on Poverty" is a phrase used by President Lyndon B. Johnson (1908–1973), during his 1964 State of the Union address in response to a rising national poverty rate, which led to the establishment of the Office of Economic Opportunity to administer the local application of federal funds targeting poverty.

than it is easy for me to admit today. I grew up writing these stories. I made peace with my family. I forgave myself and some of the people I had held in such contempt—most of all those I loved. That forgiveness took place in large part through the writing of these stories, in a process of making peace with the violence of my childhood, in owning up to it and finding a way to talk about it that did not make me more ashamed of myself or those I loved.

* * *

Before I published any of my own stories, I read a great many stories by people just as passionate about writing as I was, and I learned something from everyone I read—sometimes most important what I should not try to write. I began in the tradition of Muriel Rukeyser,[3] aching to break the world open with what I had to say on the page. There were specific feelings I wanted the stories to create, realizations I wanted people to experience. Sometimes it was grief I wanted to provoke, sometimes anger, almost always a spur to action, to change. I wanted the world to be different in my lifetime, and I truly believed that stories were one way to help that happen. I did not begin with craft, I began with strong feelings and worked toward craft. I wanted to be good and I wanted to be effective, and these are not always the same thing. Sometimes I was trying to write a poem, but the thing would not pare down enough to anything less than narrative. Sometimes I was so angry, I wrote to stop my own rage. Mostly I was angry, and drunk on words, the sound of words more than the way they looked on the page. It is quite literally the case that I wrote out loud, reading the stories out loud over and over until they were closer to what I wanted.

"If I die tomorrow, I want to have gotten this down."

That is how many of these stories started. Once in a while, I had read someone else's story and put it down in rage, beginning my own to refuse the one that had so confounded me. Going back into these stories, I remember those moments even when I no longer remember the actual stories I was refuting. Taylor Caldwell stories,[4] I called them in an early journal—stories in which poor Southern characters were framed as if they were brain-damaged, or morally insufficient, or just damn stupid.

"We are not stupid. We do pretty well with what we have." I'd set out to put that on the page—but often I would go south. By that I mean I would not wind up where I intended. I started "Meanest Woman Ever Left Tennessee" to work out in my own mind what it must have been like to have been my grandmother—and her mother, my great-grandma about whom I knew almost nothing, except that her children hated her and that she had lived a long time. How'd that work? I wondered, and made up a fictional Mattie Lee, a pretend Shirley. I gave the children names that actually figured in my grandmother's conversations—names of cousins, second cousins, and lost uncles. I worked it out as if it were a movie, or the kind of story people in my family simply would not tell. Contrary to the myth of Southern families passing stories along on the porch, people in my family kept secrets and

3. American poet and political activist (1913–1980), known for her poems about equality, feminism, social justice, and Judaism.

4. One of the pen names of Janet Miriam Holland (1900–1985), an Anglo-American novelist and prolific author of popular fiction

only hinted at what might have happened. Some days I think the way to make a storyteller is to refuse to tell her what happened—as my mama and aunts did with me. I had to make up my great-grandmother, and I did it in a story that was originally to be about her daughter—a story I started when I was still in college, and my mother told me my grandmother had died—but three months after the funeral was past, and long past any hope I might have had of going to Greenville, attending the funeral or learning anything about how she had died.

"In a ditch," my Uncle Jack told me a decade later. "Had a stroke halfway between our house and your Uncle Bo's. Just lay down and died."

"Oh." I just stood there.

"Oh." I was living in Tallahassee then, in a feminist collective household,[5] and fiercely determined to learn more about my grandmother, my aunts, even legendary Great-grandma Shirley. But my uncle's brutal comment was all I gathered in that visit, and almost as soon as I asked about it, one of my aunts denied that was how it happened.

"She didn't die down there. She died in the hospital two whole days later. She just fell in that ditch and lay there awhile before we went out and found her."

Maybe that was the story I should have written, but it was not. By the time I got back to my big complicated household, I was working on the story of what Grandma Mattie Lee might have been like as a girl. What if? And I was in it, watching Shirley beat on the steps with that broom handle. Would I have made Mattie Lee so heroic if my own mother had not hidden her death from me, if my uncle had not spoken so brutally? Maybe. Still, what I wrote felt right on the page, and from this distance that seems the primary fact. I did a lot of things because it felt right on the page, or sounded right when read out loud in an empty room. I did not finish that story in Tallahassee. I did not finish that story till Brooklyn; fully fifteen years after my grandmother's death. Even then, I think I finished it because I fell in love with that teenage girl, her mouth full of white and her eyes full of fire. It worked well enough that it was another of the stories my mama would never talk to me about. "Now that's mean," my mama said about one of the stories I sent her. She smiled and gave a little shudder when she said it. That is what I intended, I told her. I want it mean. I did not say that I also wanted the story to be about love and compassion. For that sometimes I had to dig deeper, into the muscle of character. Still, I think you can tell that I loved my impossible grandmother with my whole heart, her black brows and wide face, her bulldog glare and frank inclination to tell me things my mother never intended me to learn. I knew she worked her children the way her mother had worked her, putting them out to pick strawberries for neighboring farmers and pocketing the money to buy snuff. I knew she was quick to slap and full of desperation, but I knew also that in the context of how she had been raised and what she had survived, she was almost gentle, almost sweet-tempered. But not quite. I had sweet-tempered cousins and I saw them get ground down. I had gentle aunts and it seemed they almost disappeared out of their own lives. Is it any wonder that when I set out to

---

5. A group of individuals who are motivated by a common interest (feminism, in this case), work together on specific projects to further this common objective, and tend to make decisions on an egalitarian basis.

write stories, I made up women like my grandmother, like my great-grandmother? Troublesome, angry, complicated women with secretive, unpredictable natures—that is who you will find in my stories—and little girls who were not me. What are these stories about? Shame and outrage, pride and stubbornness, and the vital necessity of a sense of humor. I wrote to release indignation and refuse humiliation, to admit fault and to glorify the people I loved who were never celebrated. I wrote to celebrate. I wrote to take a little revenge, and sometimes to make clear that revenge was not what I was doing. Always, I tried not to use the flat metallic language of politics and preaching, but sometimes I knew no other way to frame what I had to say.

*　*　*

Now for a word on "trash." I originally claimed the label "trash" in self-defense. The phrase had been applied to me and to my family in crude and hateful ways. I took it on deliberately, as I had "dyke"[6]—though I have to acknowledge that what I heard as a child was more often the phrase "white trash." As an adult I saw all too clearly the look that would cross the face of any black woman in the room when that particular term was spoken. It was like a splash of cold water, and I saw the other side of the hatefulness in the words. It took me right back to being a girl and hearing the uncles I so admired spew racist bile and callous homophobic insults. Some phrases cannot be reclaimed. I gave that one up and took up the simpler honorific. By my twenties, that was what I heard most often anyway. Even rednecks get sensitized to insults, abandon some and cultivate others. I have not been called white trash in two decades, but only a couple years ago, I heard myself referred to as "that trash" in a motel corridor in the central valley in California.

In 1988, I titled this short story collection *Trash* to confront the term and to claim it honorific. In 2002, Trash still suits me, even though I live over here in California among people who are almost postconscious. In Sonoma County it makes more sense to call myself a Zen redneck, or just a dyke mama. What it comes down to is that I use "trash" to raise the issue of who the term glorifies as well as who it disdains. There are not simple or direct answers on any of these questions, and it is far harder to be sure your audience understands the textured lay of what you are doing—specially if you are in Northern California rather than Louisiana, and in 2002 rather than 1988. And of course these days I feel like there is a nation of us—displaced Southerners and children of the working class. We listen to Steve Earle, Mary J. Blige, and k.d. lang.[7] We devour paperback novels and tell evil mean stories, value stubbornness above patience and a sense of humor more than a college education. We claim our heritage with a full appreciation of how often it has been disdained.

And let me promise you, you do not want to make us angry.

2002

6. Slang term referring to a lesbian regardless of the individual's actual sexual identity; originally a derogatory label for a masculine woman.
7. Steve Earle (b. 1955), American singer-songwriter known for his rock and country music as well as his political activism; Mary J. Blige (b.

1971), American singer, producer, songwriter, actress, and rapper; k.d. lang (b. 1961), Canadian pop and country singer-songwriter also known as an activist for animal rights, gay rights, and Tibetan human rights.

JOHN CRAWFORD

The Last True Story I'll Ever Tell (2006) is, like many war stories, a narrative that speaks for itself. Its author restricts information about himself to the tale. Biographical data that others might find interesting are withheld; the author's date of birth, for instance, is undisclosed. Only the facts relating to his service in Iraq and its aftermath are revealed: in 2002, one semester shy of graduating with a college degree financed by his service in the Florida National Guard, John Crawford was called to active duty and readied for combat. His truthful account cannot help but recall earlier fictional models, from the Civil War (Ambrose Bierce's "Occurrence at Owl Creek Bridge") to Vietnam (Tim O'Brien's *Going after Cacciato*), a reminder that the horrors of warfare stretch even nonfictive prose to its creative limits. Reprinted here is the last chapter from Crawford's book.

The Last True Story I'll Ever Tell

There were trees everywhere. That's all I remember thinking: towering green giants smiling down on the world. My foot slid down a little farther on the gas pedal and my dad's old truck responded in turn, roaring up to eighty-five. The windows were up and the air conditioner blew civilization into my face. On the radio was some new band I hadn't even heard of, but it didn't matter. The old paved road I drove on was full of potholes that threatened to sack me in, but that didn't matter either. Everything important was self-contained. My life was complete, better than it had ever been before, and I couldn't even begin to ruin it by putting it into words.

My wife sat next to me, red hair cradling her doll face as her lips mouthed the words to a song I hadn't heard before. She looked at me, and her eyes twinkled. They were hazel today; yesterday I had thought they were green; it all depended on her mood, I guess. She smiled and put her hand on top of mine. The vibration of the gearshift coursed like an electrical current between us when we touched, and it made my heart tingle.

"God, I missed you so much," I whispered barely audibly over the other noises that cycloned around us.

"I know, baby, I missed you too." My wife put her arm under mine and pulled herself close, her head resting warmly on my shoulder. Her eyes looked through the bug-covered windshield at the road ahead as she wondered where we were going. My own were clouded by tears of happiness. When I was a boy I wasn't allowed to cry, but I guess crying from sheer joy is acceptable.

Stephanie may have wondered where we were going on this windy stretch of blacktop. I had driven this road a thousand times in my childhood and had dreamed of it a thousand more while I was in Iraq. I was home.

We were going into my hometown, a tiny speck of a city south of Jacksonville. Our only claim to fame was the annual Blue Crab Festival. Every Memorial Day, hundreds of thousands of tourists flock to Palatka for the fresh seafood, entertainment, and most important, the beer tent. Tourists, stomachs full from too many crustaceans and arms tired from carrying pieces of carved driftwood and homemade jam, would stop by for one drink and spend the rest of the evening and their wallets there.

Parking was hard to find that time of year, but locals always have tricks, and I was no different. I pulled into the darkened parking lot of Saint Monica's Catholic Church. The engine sputtered to a stop, an occasional clanking continuing as we gathered our effects and stepped out into the shadows behind old Father Joe's house. No tow truck would venture here unless he wanted an earful from the elderly Irish priest.

I reached out in the darkness and found a loving hand. Together we ventured out into the bustling avenue. The craft stores that ventured for a mile in either direction were mostly closed. It was near ten at night, and the remaining food for sale had been swimming in grease all day like tadpoles in a mud puddle. Next to the mural of Billy Graham[1] we turned east toward the riverfront. As we walked, I saw familiar faces. We smiled and nodded to each other—some kid I rode a bus with, another who had suffered through high school trigonometry with me. There was no reason to say hi. Nothing ever changed in my hometown; there was nothing new to talk about.

My wife was from the North. Well, not strictly. Most people don't consider DC to be particularly up there, but when you grow up in Florida, if it snows, it's the North. I looked over at my angel and saw she was gawking, mouth half open, at my battered town and its residents. Most of the tourists go home fairly early, and the locals who spend their days hiding in shantytowns come out like roaches. It wasn't her first visit to Palatka, but it was her first Blue Crab Festival, and that takes some getting used to. People staggered by with no teeth. A man with a hunchback talked to his one-armed girlfriend. A policeman sat sipping a beer and flirted with a seventeen-year-old dropout. I couldn't help broadening my smile and taking a deep breath of stale beer and fried food. For a second I watched it all fade away into the slums, tans, and reek of Baghdad. Smoke and rotten meat tickled my nose. I shook my head. That couldn't happen; I was home.

"John Fucking Crawford!" I swiveled around on my heels and into a bear hug from Kris.

"Kris, what's up?"

He gave Stephanie a hug too. They had met at the wedding, although I wasn't sure that she approved of my Palatka friends. They were all hard-partying guys, and Kris stood out among them, as I had once.

"Where's everyone at?"

"In the beer tent. C'mon, we saved you a seat."

The beer tent was the unequivocal center of the world during Blue Crab. In reality, the whole festival was an excuse to erect a circus tent full of beer-dispensing vixens and tired bands playing tired songs.

The night felt different, though—everything was more colorful and alive. Kris led me to the table where Quint and Joe sat with their wives. They both laughed out loud and gave me hugs when I approached. I laughed, uncomfortable with all the attention, but it sure was good to see them. Quint had been the popular one in school and all the girls had craved his attention. His wife, Amanda, perched on his shoulder and fed off his smile. She

---

1. American Christian evangelist (b. 1918).

scarcely acknowledged the rest of us. If I was unsure how Stephanie felt about my friends, there was no doubt how Amanda viewed Quint's friends.

Next to them were Joe and Jamila. The three of us were closer than the rest because we had gone to Florida State at the same time. Joe was the smartest of us, but still managed to pull off hanging with us. He met Jamila at a bar in Tallahassee; I had been there when they met. Joe had told me to stay away, that she was his the moment they met, and a few years later they were married and Joe was still entranced with her.

There were plenty of hugs and smiles around, and a scantily clad blonde with a soft keg attached to her back came around and filled all our beers for a dollar.

"So I hear you guys just got back from Europe?" I started to say, provoking a long, partially boring tale of exotic cities and cultures. I wanted to catch up on a year and a half's worth of gossip, but the rest of the table was more interested in watching Tony's band play. I hadn't heard them in years, and they had gotten really good.

The beer kept coming like a horror-movie villain, always right behind you. Life was good, my friends were there, my wife sat next to me, her hand resting on my thigh under the table as we smiled at everyone and laughed. We downed drink after drink and talked about the time I nearly flipped my first truck not twenty minutes after it was bought.

We decided to go to Quint's farm the next day and do some shooting, sans the women. Tony's band was kicking, and people were getting up to dance or crowd the stage. The place was full of gleeful noises, young girls giggled and flirted, and old men told fish stories. Lovers whispered and laughed around us. I looked around and felt like pumping my fist in the air. I was home.

"So . . . we spent the last summer in Europe and we told you about that. Tell us about your summer, John?" Joe asked, his eyes on mine, trying to read me.

"Summer, my ass. It fucking sucked."

"Yeah, whatever. C'mon, man, what was it like?" Kris jumped in.

"Tell us a war story." Quint threw in. "Did you shoot anyone?" The rest of the table cheered in agreement and leaned forward over their plastic cups in anticipation. Even my wife looked at me expectantly. I had always been a storyteller, and they were excited to hear what yarn I would give them about this one.

"You guys don't want to hear a war story. None of them make any fucking sense. I'll tell you guys all you want tomorrow." But they wouldn't give up. They badgered, pestered, and hounded me until they saw me breaking.

I leaned over and took a cigarette from Quint's pack, which rested in the center of the table.

"Lemme get a cigarette."

"I suppose you want a light too? Next you'll be taking the fillings outta my fucking teeth." Everyone laughed at Quint's joke except me.

I arrived in An Nasiriyah[2] on March 22. Third Infantry Division had come through an hour earlier and smoldering bodies blackened the sides of the road. In their rush north, the invaders had simply blown through

---

2. City in Iraq on the Euphrates River 225 miles southeast of Baghdad.

whatever opposition they had met, but bypassed much of the city. We came in with the First Marine Expeditionary Force and were immediately bogged down by heavy fighting. The marines were taking heavy casualties inside the city, while my platoon sat just outside city limits guarding an ammunition supply point that had previously belonged to the Eleventh Iraqi Infantry Division. They had popped smoke at the first sign of American armor. The eggs and flour were still damp on the kitchen counter. Human shit crawled out of the corners to get underneath your boots. No one really noticed it very much, though; we were all preoccupied with staring openmouthed at the cache of weapons we had found. There were warehouses literally full of rifles, grenades, missiles, mortars, and rocket-propelled grenades. It was one of those sights that overwhelm the mind by just going on as far as the eye can see.

The area we had to secure was too big for one platoon, and we spent most of the time as a quick reactionary force speeding down dusty roads after looters or guerrilla soldiers sneaking in for resupply. We did this for about a week, just high-speed chases through the desert after rag-clad hajjis.[3] The modern buildings of Nasiriyah loomed on one horizon, while Abraham's temple reached toward the sky in the other direction. We were in the biblical city of Ur,[4] and I remember being impressed with that. It was still very early in the war.

The place was a slum, though. Bedouins herded goats past us, paying no more attention to us than we did them. Mudbrick houses broke up the skyline. Donkey carts and starving people milled about, rummaging through the belongings of the dead. It was a sight one would expect to find after stepping out of a time machine. Aside from the very occasional beat-up taxicab, it was like looking at a portrait from five thousand years ago. The smell was what I remember most. Burned human flesh combined with diesel and shit. There were bodies all over the place, and although we ran into a few live ones, most of the combatants had long ago left. Some of the guys took pictures, but that wasn't for me. I had no urge to reminisce later over photos of meat on the ground.

We were smack dab in the center of the fertile crescent,[5] except it wasn't nearly as fertile as I had imagined. On one side of the road there were fields of super-green crops, and then, like a dog at the end of its leash, they would stop and turn into lifeless desert. There was no happy reception from the Iraqis. We were greeted with indifference. No one clapped or waved flags. They just stared at us and waited for us to leave. We raided nearby houses and buildings looking for soldiers hiding there. We were excited, ready to get things over with and go home. We were itching. It had been more than two months since any of us had talked to loved ones or received any mail. We were on two meals a day plus water ration, and on top of that we were eating sand, drinking sand. Sand was in every orifice of our bodies. At some point, you begin to imagine that you're made of sand. It gets into you, the desert, not physically, but really into your soul until you're just pissed off.

There was a complex of bunkers to our north, and my squad moved out one morning to clear them. They were empty, but in one room we came upon

---

3. Specifically, a Muslim who has made the pilgrimage to Mecca; U.S. soldiers in Iraq used the term to refer to any Iraqi, especially a combatant.
4. Ancient Sumerian capital and religious center, presently known as Muqayyar; the Bible names Ur as the birthplace and early home of Abraham.

5. The region stretching from Egypt's Nile Valley northward to the Levant (modern-day Israel, Lebanon, and Syria) and then southeastward to include Mesopotamia (modern-day Iraq); the Fertile Crescent is thought to be the birthplace of agriculture and civilization.

a large map overlay. Twice as tall as me and from one corner of the room to the other, it marked every Iraqi unit position south of the Tigris River. We called it in, and the commander told us to take it and Charlie Mike[6]—continue mission.

There was nothing else of interest, and before long we returned, drenched in sweat, to the perimeter. The company commander took one look at that map and decided that it needed to be taken to the division headquarters in what is now Tallil Air Force Base. Back then it was just a mechanized battalion, some Special Forces guys, and a few rear-echelon motherfuckers. Regardless, our company commander thought he would get all sorts of kudos for the map *he* had found, so he loaded up in another Humvee[7] with a goofy first lieutenant who looked like he couldn't run a Boy Scout troop, and together we went toward Tallil. They were moving ahead of us, and the sun was slowly painting the desert red as it set.

Staff Sergeant Connel was driving, Specialist Ramirez was in the back with a 240 golf machine gun, and I rode in the passenger seat with my M-249 squad automatic weapon as flank security. The Humvees we drove in were unarmored. You could throw a rock through them if you had a good enough arm, and hell, we didn't even have doors on. There we were, driving thirty-five miles an hour through an area that later that night would be nicknamed Ambush Alley because a young maintenance female got taken prisoner. Best way to earn medals in the army, after all—get lost or be an officer. Do both at the same time and you might even get a high school named after you.

On the right side of the road was the desert. The huts and hovels had sheets flapping in front of the door, light from kerosene lanterns peeking out. Chickens and goats ran free, while young girls and old ladies tried to finish up the daily chores before darkness fell. They stepped mindlessly over the bodies, washing clothes and maintaining the facade that they lived in complete normalcy.

The men, meanwhile, were content to sit on their stoops smoking cigarettes and drinking beer. The little boys emulated them by taking it easy as well. They frolicked about, skipping among the stones. There was no danger in the air, so it was with a total lack of fear that I noticed a group of little boys playing on the left side of the road. There were three, all about eight or nine years old. They stood knee deep in crops, their ragged clothes blowing in the wind around their emaciated bodies. I was about to wave cordially when the center one reached up and pointed his finger at the commander's Humvee in front of us. The sun was setting behind them, and as we rolled up, that finger became the front sight post of an AK-47.[8] Anyone who has ever seen one knows there's nothing else to mistake it for with its thick metal triangle; there's no other rifle in the world that looks like that.

"Fuck!" I yelled to no one.

"He's got a fucking AK!" I yelled again.

It was on the opposite side of the vehicle from me, so there was little I could do except shout a warning. Sergeant Connel slammed on the brakes. The tires squealed and struggled against the pavement, and our screeching halt came with a black rubbery smell catching up with us. Ramirez, on the machine gun in the back, never even got to point in that direction. The sudden stop caused him to fly forward halfway over the cab, his gun banging noisily on the hood.

Connel's rifle sling was snagged on something in the vehicle, and despite his tugs and frantic curses he couldn't free it. Without doors or seat belts, I slid easily out of the Humvee and had my feet in the dirt before the stop was even complete. I slammed my saw onto the hood with a clank. The bipod legs on my weapon were still up and in the locked position, but the boys weren't very far away, so accuracy wasn't too much of a problem.

Our sudden stop had caused quite a commotion, and all three boys were looking at us now. Their eyes wide with wonder. The one holding the rifle slowly turned it toward me. It seemed so slow the way he moved, but I suppose that was just the way I remember everything happening. My safety was already off, and I had him in the middle of my sight picture.

Why don't they run? Most likely they didn't realize that in a tenth of a second their bodies would be ripped apart, shredded by a hundred bullets manufactured a world away in Cleveland or somewhere. They couldn't have known that that very night the dogs that scavenged the desert would be tearing out their entrails and that they would be unrecognizable to the morning.

I held my breath and steadied on the hood of that vehicle as best I could. They were silhouetted black against the sunset, and I could clearly see the entire barrel assembly of the rifle with a thirty-round magazine locked into the bottom. The muzzle was almost on me, and I had already hesitated too long. While they stood on the swelling bloody sun, I applied pressure to the trigger.

I don't know if that was before or after I realized that the rest of the rifle was missing. The trigger was gone, as was the buttstock and bolt. Someone had killed a hajji there the day before and just run over his rifle with their track, rendering it useless. That kid couldn't have shot spitballs through it even if he had wanted to.

No one at the table said a word; our circle had become a pool of awkward silence. Stephanie squeezed my leg under the table in support, but I didn't move.

"It's no big deal, man, you can just tell us a story some other time," Joe said reassuringly. The table began to resurrect; cups were refilled, cigarettes lit. Tony's band had stopped playing and they were now introducing all the members. The chattering in the background was coming back, growling into a great screeching howl. I wanted to stay and talk, but couldn't. After a few more halfhearted attempts to laugh, we left.

My wife and I were silent as we passed the church on our way back to the car. I remembered being an altar boy when I was, as Father Joe described me, "a wee lad." He used to place this oversized Bible on my head and read from it to the congregation as if I were some form of human lectern. The churchgoers would snicker, incensing me, but I was just a little boy then. I was a man now, and I was fairly sure that book wouldn't fit on my head anymore. What did it matter, though? I was home.

A crashing boom broke the night air and I jumped up on my cot with a start. It took me a moment to realize where I was. Pearson and Hightower were already up, throwing on body armor and grabbing weapons to defend the perimeter. I wiped sleep from my eyes. I had been dreaming, nothing more. It was just a vision of what home could or should be.

What I'm about to write is true. Utterly true. The first thing I wrote for this book was a fiction short story I wrote while still in Iraq. It was all about returning home and finding myself in a world where no one understood my experience, but they were all there to support me. My wife was on my arm, telling me that no matter what she loved me. We would have children soon, and the rest of my life would be wonderful. I was wiser in that story than I am now. Like Joseph Campbell's[9] hero with a thousand faces, I returned victorious. I told tales of my exploits and people listened. They cared.

It wasn't until I got back that truth engulfed me like a storm cloud. Dreams and truth are never intertwined.

I spent a few months drifting around friends' houses, from one couch to the next. When I finally got enough money to get an apartment again, I kept getting kicked out.

I was evicted from one place I was renting because I have a dog, a big one. He sleeps with me at night when I'm drunk and can't understand why I'm alone. Dogs don't turn their backs on you, that's another truth. I moved five times in five months.

Most days I was sick. It was a lingering, wasting sickness that comes only when you have nothing left. There are people out there who really don't know why they get up in the morning; it's sad, and that's how you know it's true.

In my dream, my wife never told me that things would have been better off if I had just never come home. In reality, I agree with her.

This is a true story. You can tell because it makes your stomach turn. I am home now, and I will never again write a true story.

9. American scholar and writer (1904–1987), best known for his work in comparative mythology beginning with his first book, *The Hero with a Thousand Faces* (1949).

JOAN DIDION

Joan Didion's collection of essays on the 1960s counterculture, *Slouching Toward Bethlehem* (1968), made her famous and established her as a practitioner of "The New Journalism." Her second essay collection *The White Album* (1979) mixes autobiography with cultural events in Los Angeles in the 1960s (the book's title refers to the 1968 double album by the Beatles, which had no graphics or text other than the band's name). These widely influential books confirmed Didion's reputation as a shrewd and edgy cultural observer and literary stylist. She has also published several novels, including *Play It As It Lays* (1970) and *Democracy* (1984).

A native Californian, Joan Didion (b. 1934) moved to New York as a young woman, where she worked for *Vogue* magazine and, in 1964, married the novelist John Gregory Dunne. In the mid-1960s the couple moved to Los Angeles, where they spent the next 20 years. They collaborated on several screenplays and became a glamorous couple whose talents were sought after in Hollywood. In the 1980s they moved back to New York, where Didion continued her work as a screenwriter, novelist, and nonfiction author.

The Year of Magical Thinking (2005) is Didion's account of the year following the sudden death from cardiac arrest of her husband of forty years. In this book Didion makes herself and her experience of grief the factual center of the book; in a sense she makes herself a case study for the craziness of grief, for the "magical thinking" that assumes, for example, that if you don't let someone tell you a person is dead, then he isn't really dead. The precision of the book's analysis, with its extensive display of medical research, makes *The Year of Magical Thinking* an autobiographical account unlike most others.

Quintana Roo Dunne, John Gregory Dunne, and Joan Didion at home in Malibu in 1976.

Five days before her husband's death, their daughter, Quintana Roo, whom they adopted in 1966, was hospitalized for pneumonia and fell into septic shock and then a coma (two months before the publication of *The Year of Magical Thinking*, Quintana Roo died of pancreatitis). In the selection that appears below, Didion provides an account of the evening of her husband's death precise enough to be called, at first, clinical. However, the restrained, minimalist style in which she delivers her acute observation can be read as her way of controlling and holding off potentially overwhelming feelings. "We tell stories in order to live," *The White Album* begins. In this excerpt from *The Year of Magical Thinking* we experience the writer using all of the tools at her disposal to make sense of an experience that, as she writes, changed everything.

From The Year of Magical Thinking

December 30, 2003, a Tuesday.
We had seen Quintana in the sixth-floor ICU at Beth Israel North.[1]
  We had come home.
  We had discussed whether to go out for dinner or eat in.
  I said I would build a fire, we could eat in.
  I built the fire, I started dinner, I asked John[2] if he wanted a drink.
  I got him a Scotch and gave it to him in the living room, where he was reading in the chair by the fire where he habitually sat.
  The book he was reading was by David Fromkin, a bound galley of *Europe's Last Summer: Who Started the Great War in 1914?*[3]

---

1. New York City hospital located on Manhattan's Upper East Side. "ICU": The Intensive Care Unit is a specialized department in many hospitals that provides life support or organ support systems in patients who are critically ill and require intensive monitoring.

2. John Gregory Dunne, American novelist, screenwriter, and literary critic (1932–2003), was Joan Didion's husband from 1964 until his death.
3. An account of the underpinnings of World War I by David Fromkin, a noted author, lawyer, and historian.

I finished getting dinner, I set the table in the living room where, when we were home alone, we could eat within sight of the fire. I find myself stressing the fire because fires were important to us. I grew up in California, John and I lived there together for twenty-four years, in California we heated our houses by building fires. We built fires even on summer evenings, because the fog came in. Fires said we were home, we had drawn the circle, we were safe through the night. I lit the candles. John asked for a second drink before sitting down. I gave it to him. We sat down. My attention was on mixing the salad.

John was talking, then he wasn't.

At one point in the seconds or minute before he stopped talking he had asked me if I had used single-malt Scotch[4] for his second drink. I had said no, I used the same Scotch I had used for his first drink. "Good," he had said. "I don't know why but I don't think you should mix them." At another point in those seconds or that minute he had been talking about why World War One was the critical event from which the entire rest of the twentieth century flowed.

I have no idea which subject we were on, the Scotch or World War One, at the instant he stopped talking.

I only remember looking up. His left hand was raised and he was slumped motionless. At first I thought he was making a failed joke, an attempt to make the difficulty of the day seem manageable.

I remember saying *Don't do that.*

When he did not respond my first thought was that he had started to eat and choked. I remember trying to lift him far enough from the back of the chair to give him the Heimlich.[5] I remember the sense of his weight as he fell forward, first against the table, then to the floor. In the kitchen by the telephone I had taped a card with the New York–Presbyterian[6] ambulance numbers. I had not taped the numbers by the telephone because I anticipated a moment like this. I had taped the numbers by the telephone in case someone in the building needed an ambulance.

Someone else.

I called one of the numbers. A dispatcher asked if he was breathing. I said *Just come.* When the paramedics came I tried to tell them what had happened but before I could finish they had transformed the part of the living room where John lay into an emergency department. One of them (there were three, maybe four, even an hour later I could not have said) was talking to the hospital about the electrocardiogram[7] they seemed already to be transmitting. Another was opening the first or second of what would be many syringes for injection. (Epinephrine? Lidocaine? Procainamide?[8] The names came to mind but I had no idea from where.) I remember saying that he might have choked. This was dismissed with a finger swipe: the airway was clear. They seemed now to be using defibrillating paddles,[9] an attempt

---

4. High-quality, unblended whiskey distilled in Scotland, using malted barley as the only grain ingredient.
5. Abdominal thrusts to help a person choking clear the blocked airway by forcing air from the lungs.
6. Hospital in New York City, considered among the best in the world.
7. A noninvasive test using skin electrodes to check for problems with the electrical activity of your heart.

8. Procainamide: A pharmaceutical agent used to suppress fast rhythms of the heart (cardiac arrhythmias). "Epinephrine": also, adrenaline; a hormone and neurotransmitter that increases the heart rate, contracts blood vessels, and dilates air passages. "Lidocaine": common local anesthetic and anti-arrhythmic drug.
9. Paddles which, when placed on a patient's chest, deliver a therapeutic surge of electricity to restore normal electrical activity in the heart.

to restore a rhythm. They got something that could have been a normal heartbeat (or I thought they did, we had all been silent, there was a sharp jump), then lost it, and started again.

"He's still fibbing," I remember the one on the telephone saying.

"V-fibbing,"[1] John's cardiologist said the next morning when he called from Nantucket. "They would have said 'V-fibbing.' V for ventricular."

Maybe they said "V-fibbing" and maybe they did not. Atrial fibrillation[2] did not immediately or necessarily cause cardiac arrest. Ventricular did. Maybe ventricular was the given.

I remember trying to straighten out in my mind what would happen next. Since there was an ambulance crew in the living room, the next logical step would be going to the hospital. It occurred to me that the crew could decide very suddenly to go to the hospital and I would not be ready. I would not have in hand what I needed to take. I would waste time, get left behind. I found my handbag and a set of keys and a summary John's doctor had made of his medical history. When I got back to the living room the paramedics were watching the computer monitor they had set up on the floor. I could not see the monitor so I watched their faces. I remember one glancing at the others. When the decision was made to move it happened very fast. I followed them to the elevator and asked if I could go with them. They said they were taking the gurney down first, I could go in the second ambulance. One of them waited with me for the elevator to come back up. By the time he and I got into the second ambulance the ambulance carrying the gurney was pulling away from the front of the building. The distance from our building to the part of New York–Presbyterian that used to be New York Hospital is six crosstown blocks. I have no memory of sirens. I have no memory of traffic. When we arrived at the emergency entrance to the hospital the gurney was already disappearing into the building. A man was waiting in the driveway. Everyone else in sight was wearing scrubs. He was not. "Is this the wife," he said to the driver, then turned to me. "I'm your social worker," he said, and I guess that is when I must have known.

"I opened the door and I seen the man in the dress greens and I knew. I immediately knew." This was what the mother of a nineteen-year-old killed by a bomb in Kirkuk said on an HBO documentary quoted by Bob Herbert[3] in the *New York Times* on the morning of November 12, 2004. "But I thought that if, as long as I didn't let him in, he couldn't tell me. And then it—none of that would've happened. So he kept saying, 'Ma'am, I need to come in.' And I kept telling him, 'I'm sorry, but you can't come in.'"

When I read this at breakfast almost eleven months after the night with the ambulance and the social worker I recognized the thinking as my own.

2005

---

1. Ventricular fibrillation, a condition in which there is uncoordinated contraction of the cardiac muscle of the ventricles in the heart.
2. The most common of abnormal heart rhythms, involving the uncoordinated quivering of the heart muscles of the two upper chambers, or atria, of the heart.

3. American journalist and op-ed columnist for the *New York Times* (b. 1945) who frequently writes about poverty, the Iraq war, racism, and political apathy toward racial issues. "Kirkuk": city in Iraq, invaded by American and British military forces in March 2003. "HBO": Home Box Office, a cable television network.

EDWIDGE DANTICAT

Edwidge Danticat was born in Port-au-Prince, the capital of Haiti, in 1969. Her novels *Breath, Eyes, Memory* (1994) and *The Farming of Bones* (1998), as well as her collection of stories, *Krik? Krak!* (1995—the title comes from a Haitian chant), draw on her experiences as a Haitian American. Danticat was two years old when her father left Haiti to make a better life for the family in the United States; two years later, her mother left to join him. For the next eight years Danticat and her brother remained in Haiti under the care of their uncle Joseph, a Baptist minister who founded his own church and school in Port-au-Prince. She then emigrated to the United States to be reunited with her parents. In 2004, after violence destroyed her uncle's church and put his life in jeopardy, Joseph entered the United States asking for temporary asylum but was detained in Miami by Department of Homeland Security officials suspicious of his plea. During questioning, Joseph collapsed but was refused treatment at the time. The next day he was taken to a Florida hospital where he died. In October 2007 Danticat testified on this issue before the House Judiciary Subcommittee on Immigration, Citizenship Refuges, Border Security, and International Law. Like many creative nonfiction writers, Danticat uses personal narrative to illuminate larger issues: the political and economic situation in Haiti, the challenges facing immigrants to the United States, and the need to reform the practices of immigration detainee medical care.

   Brother, I'm Dying is a memoir partly of the writer's childhood in Haiti and, more particularly, of the interconnected lives of her uncle and father, who, after leaving Haiti, ran a car-service business in New York and died from pulmonary fibrosis soon after his brother's death. When the adult Danticat, now pregnant with her first child, listens to her gravely ill father respond to the question "Have you enjoyed your life?" by speaking of his children and family, she recalls living as a child with her uncle when the family would regularly receive letters from her father in the United States. This selection captures Danticat's exploration of what words can and cannot say, a question at the heart of this writer's work.

From Brother, I'm Dying

Listening to my father, I remembered a time when I used to dream of smuggling him words. I was eight years old and Bob and I were living in Haiti with his oldest brother, my uncle Joseph, and his wife. And since they didn't have a telephone at home—few Haitian families did then—and access to the call centers was costly, we had no choice but to write letters. Every other month, my father would mail a half-page, three-paragraph missive addressed to my uncle. Scribbled in his minuscule scrawl, sometimes on plain white paper, other times on lined, hole-punched notebook pages still showing bits of fringe from the spiral binding, my father's letters were composed in stilted French,[1] with the first paragraph offering news of his and my mother's health, the second detailing how to spend the money they had wired for food, lodging, and school expenses for Bob and myself, the third section concluding abruptly after reassuring us that we'd be hearing from him again before long.

---

1. That is, the formal French taught in Haitian schools, rather than the vernacular Creole of everyday life.

Later I would discover in a first-year college composition class that his letters had been written in a diamond sequence, the Aristotelian *Poetics*[2] correspondence, requiring an opening greeting, a middle detail or request, and a brief farewell at the end. The letter-writing process had been such an agonizing chore for my father, one that he'd hurried through while assembling our survival money, that this specific epistolary formula, which he followed unconsciously, had offered him a comforting way of disciplining his emotions.

"I was no writer," he later told me. "What I wanted to tell you and your brother was too big for any piece of paper and a small envelope."

Whatever restraint my father showed in his letters was easily compensated for by Uncle Joseph's reactions to them. First there was the public reading in my uncle's sparsely furnished pink living room, in front of Tante[3] Denise, Bob and me. This was done so there would be no misunderstanding as to how the money my parents sent for me and my brother would be spent. Usually my uncle would read the letters out loud, pausing now and then to ask my help with my father's penmanship, a kindness, I thought, a way to include me a step further. It soon became obvious, however, that my father's handwriting was as clear to me as my own, so I eventually acquired the job of deciphering his letters.

Along with this task came a few minutes of preparation for the reading and thus a few intimate moments with my father's letters, not only the words and phrases, which did not vary greatly from month to month, but the vowels and syllables, their tilts and slants, which did. Because he wrote so little, I would try to guess his thoughts and moods from the dotting of his *i*'s and the crossing of his *t*'s, from whether there were actual periods at the ends of his sentences or just faint dots where the tip of his pen had simply landed. Did commas split his streamlined phrases, or were they staccato,[4] like someone speaking too rapidly, out of breath?

For the family readings, I recited my father's letters in a monotone, honoring what I interpreted as a secret between us, that the impersonal style of his letters was due as much to his lack of faith in words and their ability to accurately reproduce his emotions as to his caution with Bob's and my feelings, avoiding too-happy news that might add to the anguish of separation, too-sad news that might worry us, and any hint of judgment or disapproval for my aunt and uncle, which they could have interpreted as suggestions that they were mistreating us. The dispassionate letters were his way of avoiding a minefield, one could have set off from a distance without being able to comfort the victims.

Given all this anxiety, I'm amazed my father wrote at all. The regularity, the consistency of his correspondence now feels like an act of valor. In contrast, my replies, though less routine—Uncle Joseph did most of the writing— were both painstakingly upbeat and suppliant. In my letters, I bragged about my good grades and requested, as a reward for them, an American doll at Christmas, a typewriter or sewing machine for my birthday, a pair of "real" gold earrings for Easter. But the things I truly wanted I was afraid to ask for, like when I would finally see him and my mother again. However, since my uncle read and corrected all my letters for faulty grammar and spelling, I wrote for his eyes more than my father's, hoping that even after the vigor-

2. The earliest surviving work of dramatic and literary theory, written by Aristotle (384–322 B.C.E.), which analyzes poetry in terms of its essential elements.

3. Aunt (French).

4. A form of musical articulation, signifying an unconnected note, short and detached.

ous editing, my father would still decode the longing in my childish cursive slopes and arches, which were so much like his own.

The words that both my father and I wanted to exchange we never did. These letters were not approved, in his case by him, in my case by my uncle. No matter what the reason, we have always been equally paralyzed by the fear of breaking each other's heart. This is why I could never ask the question Bob did. I also could never tell my father that I'd learned from the doctor that he was dying. Even when they mattered less, there were things he and I were too afraid to say.

2007

SHERMAN ALEXIE
b. 1966

Except for one great-grandparent, Sherman Alexie's lineage is Native American: Coeur d'Alene on his father's side; Colville, Flathead, and Spokane on his mother's. The cities of Coeur d'Alene (Idaho) and Spokane (Washington) mark the interior northwest corner of the contiguous forty-eight states, the place where Alexie's poetry, fiction, and cinematic work is sometimes set. Yet his interest in Native American culture ranges widely, to include other tribes such as the Navajo and regions throughout the West and Southwest. Raised on the Spokane reservation at Wellpinit, Washington, Alexie thrived in the cultural immersion that secondary education at Reardan High School, some distance from home, provided—especially the popular culture that would later infuse his work. Hence both words in the designation "Native American" figure prominently in how he sees himself as a writer.

Equal doses of trouble and humor characterize Alexie's work. Having survived hydrocephalus (a cerebrospinal abnormality) as a child and alcoholism as a young adult, he drew on his college experience as an undergraduate at Gonzaga University in Spokane and Washington State University in Pullman to find a literary voice, drawing on inspirations as diverse as John Steinbeck's fiction and the Native American poetry collected by Joseph Bruchac in the anthology *Songs from This Earth on Turtle's Back* (1983). In 1992 he published his own first work, *The Business of Fancydancing: Stories and Poems*, with one of America's most prominent small presses, Hanging Loose (Brooklyn, New York).

When *The Business of Fancydancing* was published, a review in the *New York Times* called Alexie "one of the major lyric voices of our time." "I was a 25-year-old Spokane Indian guy working as a secretary at a high school exchange program," he has written. "I thought 'Great! Where do I go from here?'"

Alexie has continued telling stories through poetry, fiction, and screenwriting. *Reservation Blues* (1994) was his first novel, followed by *Indian Killer* in 1996. *Flight* (2007) shows the influence of Kurt Vonnegut, from its device of time travel to its reinvention of history from a comparative point of view. Presented broadly, even comically, his stories often draw on simple incidents. His storytelling offers a tragicomic vision of contemporary Native American life, notably in his National Book Award–winning novel *The Absolutely True Diary of a Part-Time Indian* (2007), in the stories of his several collections, and in his several volumes of poetry. College educated and street-smart ("I'm a rez kid who's gone urban"), irreverent and also dead serious, Alexie resembles the trickster figure of Crow in his poem "Crow Testament."

The narrative power of his poems has a furious energy. Although some of his work, like the villanelle "Sister Fire, Brother Smoke," takes traditional forms, most of his poems are open and improvisational, frequently and effectively using repetition and parallelism. The title of Alexie's 2000 collection, *One Stick Song*, offers an apt image for his work; it refers to a gambling game in which sticks function like chips. When down to one stick, he explains, "You're desperate," and a "One Stick Song" is "a desperate celebration, a desperate attempt to save yourself, putting everything you have into one song." The best of Alexie's poems, like "The Exaggeration of Despair," make facing up to grief and anger an act of survival. The intensity of this effort is especially evident when he reads from or recites his work. A brilliant performer, sliding between humor, anger, and pain, he makes a poetry reading a dynamic event. It is no wonder that his interest in performance has turned him to stand-up comedy as well.

Popular audiences know Alexie from the 2002 film he wrote and directed, *The Business of Fancydancing*, and especially his 1998 film *Smoke Signals*, a major Hollywood production he scripted from material in his story collection *The Lone Ranger and Tonto Fistfight in Heaven* (1993). These stories and the movies drawn from them cover the range of contemporary Native American experiences. As one of his characters says, Native Americans have "a way of surviving. But it's almost like Indians can easily survive the big stuff. Mass murder, loss of language and land rights. It's the small things that hurt the most. The white waitress who wouldn't take an order, Tonto, the Washington Redskins." "This Is What It Means to Say Phoenix, Arizona" is typical of both the collection's and the movie's sometimes raucous blending of the sentimental and the ridiculous. Family structures have been set askew by the imposition of a Reservation system, a system all the more confining in the social conditions of current times. Can tribal structures ameliorate these problems? In this story and elsewhere, Alexie's answers vary from comic to tragic.

Married with two children and living in Seattle, Alexie has used his work to address issues from national politics to family crises.

At Navajo Monument Valley Tribal School

from the photograph
by Skeet McAuley

the football field rises
to meet the mesa. Indian boys
gallop across the grass, against

the beginning of their body.
On those Saturday afternoons,   5
unbroken horses gather to watch

their sons growing larger
in the small parts of the world.
Everyone is the quarterback.

There is no thin man in a big hat   10
writing down all the names
in two columns: winners and losers.

This is the eternal football game,
Indians versus Indians. All the Skins
in the wooden bleachers fancydancing,   15

Navajo Monument Valley playing field, where "the football field rises / to meet the mesa." Photograph by Skeet McAuley.

stomping red dust straight down
into nothing. Before the game is over,
the eighth-grade girls' track team

comes running, circling the field,
their thin and brown legs echoing   20
wild horses, wild horses, wild horses.

1992

Pawn Shop

I walk into the bar, after being gone for a while, and it's empty. The
Bartender tells me all the Indians are gone, do I know where they went?
I tell him I don't know, and I don't know, so he gives me a beer just for
being Indian, small favors, and I wonder where all the Skins disappeared
to, and after a while, I leave, searching the streets, searching storefronts,   5
until I walk into a pawn shop, find a single heart beating under glass, and
I know who it used to belong to, I know all of them.

1992

Crow Testament[1]

1.

Cain lifts Crow, that heavy black bird
and strikes down Abel.[2]

---

1. Crow, like Raven, is a trickster figure in many
Native American cultures.

2. In Genesis, Cain kills his brother, Abel. They
are the sons of Adam and Eve.

Damn, says Crow, I guess
this is just the beginning.

2.

The white man, disguised   5
as a falcon, swoops in
and yet again steals a salmon
from Crow's talons.

Damn, says Crow, if I could swim
I would have fled this country years ago.   10

3.

The Crow God as depicted
in all of the reliable Crow bibles
looks exactly like a Crow.

Damn, says Crow, this makes it
so much easier to worship myself.   15

4.

Among the ashes of Jericho,[3]
Crow sacrifices his firstborn son.

Damn, says Crow, a million nests
are soaked with blood.

5.

When Crows fight Crows   20
the sky fills with beaks and talons.

Damn, says Crow, it's raining feathers.

6

Crow flies around the reservation
and collects empty beer bottles

but they are so heavy   25
he can carry only one at a time.

So, one by one, he returns them
but gets only five cents a bottle.

Damn, says Crow, redemption
is not easy.   30

---

3. This biblical city, famous for its great walls, was the first town attacked by the Israelites under Joshua, after they crossed the Jordan River.

7.

Crow rides a pale horse
into a crowded powwow
but none of the Indians panic.

Damn, says Crow, I guess
they already live near the end of the world.   35

2000

JHUMPA LAHIRI
b. 1967

When Jhumpa Lahiri writes, her setting is quite literally the world—focused sometimes here and sometimes there, but always with global implications. This orientation is a factor of her times. Unlike children of earlier immigrant generations, Lahiri did not face the pressures of assimilating into an American society apart from and in some cases above other cultures. Instead, international trade, travel, and communications have made global culture a practical reality. In "Sexy," one of Lahiri's most wide-ranging yet deeply penetrating stories, her protagonist listens to a sad tale about a friend's "cousin's husband." The bad news, "a wife's worst nightmare," is being conveyed in Boston, where the friends live, but it involves a flight from Delhi to Montreal stopping at Heathrow Airport outside London. Four locations in two hemispheres an ocean and a continent apart indicate the world that people with family backgrounds in India share when they become Americans. Geographical barriers become much more easily manageable thanks to cell phones and e-mail. Education, employment, friendships, and romantic relationships span the world. Films from India are viewed with American pop songs in mind and Chinese cuisine in the stomach, all, flavorful as they are, seeming as natural as the lives being lived among such givens.

The flavor of Lahiri's fiction defies categorization, other than being dependent on no single national ingredient. A visit to Boston's Mapparium (a giant globe viewed from inside) or Museum of Fine Arts is less a field trip through region and history than a comfortable part of her characters' way of living, a reminder of the larger culture they share.

The author's Bengali parents parted from their large extended family when they moved from Calcutta to London, where Lahiri was born. Following a normal progression in the former British Commonwealth, Lahiri's parents then relocated to the United States, where they worked as educators in Rhode Island while she studied at Barnard College and Boston University, concentrating on literature and creative writing and ending with a Ph.D. Her first stories reflect how much of her family's past had to be conveyed to her via storytelling, such as in "When Mr. Pirzada Came to Dine," where a ten-year-old in America learns about political troubles in India from a visiting family friend. To the youngster, it sounds exotic, but no more so than the situation experienced by a pair of Indian newlyweds, in "This Blessed House," who are alternately intrigued and mystified by fundamentalist Christian curios left behind by the previous tenants of their new home. Much of Lahiri's work, first collected in *Interpreter of Maladies* (1999) and extended in *Unaccustomed*

Earth (2008), involves discoveries of this nature, in which she is particularly adept at portraying the learning process of someone acting without monocultural constraint. The curiosity of children or young adults is a hallmark of her style.

In 2003, having married, become a mother, and settled in the Park Slope area of Brooklyn, New York, a neighborhood popular with writers, Lahiri published her novel *The Namesake*. Like her earlier work, it contrasts cultural assimilation with curiosity about the values, beliefs, and practices of a preceding generation. But here a certain amount of anger and confusion come into play, as the protagonist, Gogol Ganguli, is uncomfortable with how the private first name his parents have used for him at home has become his public name as well, all without his understanding its personal (much less literary) significance. Lahiri had been saddled with "Jhumpa" as a first name by her teachers, who found it easier to pronounce than her other two given names, either of which would have been more appropriate for formal use. But while Lahiri's enforced assimilation didn't bother her, Ganguli's does, although much of his discomfort is comic, such as when he assumes that a sociologist's anagrammatical reference to "ABCDs" means not "multiculturals" but "American-born confused deshi" (India countrymen). In fact, Ganguli doesn't even know what "deshi" properly means, just that his parents customarily refer to India as "desh." He "never thinks of India as desh. He thinks of it as Americans do, as India." Other contrasts, such as arranged marriages versus modern ones, are handled with more gravity. But this too helps the protagonist in his process of understanding who he is, something not possible until he comprehends who his parents are.

The following text is from *Interpreter of Maladies* (1999).

Sexy

It was a wife's worst nightmare. After nine years of marriage, Laxmi told Miranda, her cousin's husband had fallen in love with another woman. He sat next to her on a plane, on a flight from Delhi to Montreal, and instead of flying home to his wife and son, he got off with the woman at Heathrow.[1] He called his wife, and told her he'd had a conversation that had changed his life, and that he needed time to figure things out. Laxmi's cousin had taken to her bed.

"Not that I blame her," Laxmi said. She reached for the Hot Mix she munched throughout the day, which looked to Miranda like dusty orange cereal. "Imagine. An English girl, half his age." Laxmi was only a few years older than Miranda, but she was already married, and kept a photo of herself and her husband, seated on a white stone bench in front of the Taj Mahal,[2] tacked to the inside of her cubicle, which was next to Miranda's. Laxmi had been on the phone for at least an hour, trying to calm her cousin down. No one noticed; they worked for a public radio station,[3] in the fundraising department, and were surrounded by people who spent all day on the phone, soliciting pledges.

"I feel worst for the boy," Laxmi added. "He's been at home for days. My cousin said she can't even take him to school."

"It sounds awful," Miranda said. Normally Laxmi's phone conversations—mainly to her husband, about what to cook for dinner—distracted Miranda

---

1. International airport near London.
2. Muslim mausoleum near Agra, India, built on a monumental scale in the mid-17th century by Emperor Shah Jahan for his favorite wife, Mum-taz Mahal.
3. Noncommercial, listener-supported, often oriented toward arts and culture in its broadcasting.

as she typed letters, asking members of the radio station to increase their annual pledge in exchange for a tote bag or an umbrella. She could hear Laxmi clearly, her sentences peppered every now and then with an Indian word, through the laminated wall between their desks. But that afternoon Miranda hadn't been listening. She'd been on the phone herself, with Dev, deciding where to meet later that evening.

"Then again, a few days at home won't hurt him." Laxmi ate some more Hot Mix, then put it away in a drawer. "He's something of a genius. He has a Punjabi mother and a Bengali[4] father, and because he learns French and English at school he already speaks four languages. I think he skipped two grades."

Dev was Bengali, too. At first Miranda thought it was a religion. But then he pointed it out to her, a place in India called Bengal, in a map printed in an issue of *The Economist*.[5] He had brought the magazine specially to her apartment, for she did not own an atlas, or any other books with maps in them. He'd pointed to the city where he'd been born, and another city where his father had been born. One of the cities had a box around it, intended to attract the reader's eye. When Miranda asked what the box indicated, Dev rolled up the magazine, and said, "Nothing you'll ever need to worry about," and he tapped her playfully on the head.

Before leaving her apartment he'd tossed the magazine in the garbage, along with the ends of the three cigarettes he always smoked in the course of his visits. But after she watched his car disappear down Commonwealth Avenue,[6] back to his house in the suburbs, where he lived with his wife, Miranda retrieved it, and brushed the ashes off the cover, and rolled it in the opposite direction to get it to lie flat. She got into bed, still rumpled from their lovemaking, and studied the borders of Bengal. There was a bay below and mountains above. The map was connected to an article about something called the Gramin Bank.[7] She turned the page, hoping for a photograph of the city where Dev was born, but all she found were graphs and grids. Still, she stared at them, thinking the whole while about Dev, about how only fifteen minutes ago he'd propped her feet on top of his shoulders, and pressed her knees to her chest, and told her that he couldn't get enough of her.

She'd met him a week ago, at Filene's.[8] She was there on her lunch break, buying discounted pantyhose in the Basement. Afterward she took the escalator to the main part of the store, to the cosmetics department, where soaps and creams were displayed like jewels, and eye shadows and powders shimmered like butterflies pinned behind protective glass. Though Miranda had never bought anything other than a lipstick, she liked walking through the cramped, confined maze, which was familiar to her in a way the rest of Boston still was not. She liked negotiating her way past the women planted at every turn, who sprayed cards with perfume and waved them in the air; sometimes she would find a card days afterward, folded in her coat pocket,

---

4. Punjab, state in northern India; Bengal, former province of India, now a region that includes Bengal State and East Bengal, the latter part of Bangladesh.
5. Weekly British magazine of news and commentary.
6. Major thoroughfare in Boston.

7. Properly the Grameen Bank, which provides credit to the poorest classes in rural Bangladesh as a means of fighting poverty and promoting social economic development.
8. A department store. Filene's Basement, downstairs, is a renowned discount store.

and the rich aroma, still faintly preserved, would warm her as she waited on cold mornings for the T.[9]

That day, stopping to smell one of the more pleasing cards, Miranda noticed a man standing at one of the counters. He held a slip of paper covered in a precise, feminine hand. A saleswoman took one look at the paper and began to open drawers. She produced an oblong cake of soap in a black case, a hydrating mask, a vial of cell renewal drops, and two tubes of face cream. The man was tanned, with black hair that was visible on his knuckles. He wore a flamingo pink shirt, a navy blue suit, a camel overcoat with gleaming leather buttons. In order to pay he had taken off pigskin gloves. Crisp bills emerged from a burgundy wallet. He didn't wear a wedding ring.

"What can I get you, honey?" the saleswoman asked Miranda. She looked over the tops of her tortoiseshell glasses, assessing Miranda's complexion.

Miranda didn't know what she wanted. All she knew was that she didn't want the man to walk away. He seemed to be lingering, waiting, along with the saleswoman, for her to say something. She stared at some bottles, some short, others tall, arranged on an oval tray, like a family posing for a photograph.

"A cream," Miranda said eventually.

"How old are you?"

"Twenty-two."

The saleswoman nodded, opening a frosted bottle. "This may seem a bit heavier than what you're used to, but I'd start now. All your wrinkles are going to form by twenty-five. After that they just start showing."

While the saleswoman dabbed the cream on Miranda's face, the man stood and watched. While Miranda was told the proper way to apply it, in swift upward strokes beginning at the base of her throat, he spun the lipstick carousel. He pressed a pump that dispensed cellulite gel and massaged it into the back of his ungloved hand. He opened a jar, leaned over, and drew so close that a drop of cream flecked his nose.

Miranda smiled, but her mouth was obscured by a large brush that the saleswoman was sweeping over her face. "This is blusher Number Two," the woman said. "Gives you some color."

Miranda nodded, glancing at her reflection in one of the angled mirrors that lined the counter. She had silver eyes and skin as pale as paper, and the contrast with her hair, as dark and glossy as an espresso bean, caused people to describe her as striking, if not pretty. She had a narrow, egg-shaped head that rose to a prominent point. Her features, too, were narrow, with nostrils so slim that they appeared to have been pinched with a clothespin. Now her face glowed, rosy at the cheeks, smoky below the brow bone. Her lips glistened.

The man was glancing in a mirror, too, quickly wiping the cream from his nose. Miranda wondered where he was from. She thought he might be Spanish, or Lebanese. When he opened another jar, and said, to no one in particular, "This one smells like pineapple," she detected only the hint of an accent.

"Anything else for you today?" the saleswoman asked, accepting Miranda's credit card.

"No thanks."

The woman wrapped the cream in several layers of red tissue. "You'll be very happy with this product." Miranda's hand was unsteady as she signed the receipt. The man hadn't budged.

9. Metropolitan Transit Authority (MTA), Boston's subway system.

"I threw in a sample of our new eye gel," the saleswoman added, handing Miranda a small shopping bag. She looked at Miranda's credit card before sliding it across the counter. "Bye-bye, Miranda."

Miranda began walking. At first she sped up. Then, noticing the doors that led to Downtown Crossing,[1] she slowed down.

"Part of your name is Indian," the man said, pacing his steps with hers.

She stopped, as did he, at a circular table piled with sweaters, flanked with pinecones and velvet bows. "Miranda?"

"Mira. I have an aunt named Mira."

His name was Dev. He worked in an investment bank back that way he said, tilting his head in the direction of South Station.[2] He was the first man with a mustache, Miranda decided, she found handsome.

They walked together toward Park Street station,[3] past the kiosks that sold cheap belts and handbags. A fierce January wind spoiled the part in her hair. As she fished for a token in her coat pocket, her eyes fell to his shopping bag. "And those are for her?"

"Who?"

"Your Aunt Mira."

"They're for my wife." He uttered the words slowly, holding Miranda's gaze. "She's going to India for a few weeks." He rolled his eyes. "She's addicted to this stuff."

Somehow, without the wife there, it didn't seem so wrong. At first Miranda and Dev spent every night together, almost. He explained that he couldn't spend the whole night at her place, because his wife called every day at six in the morning, from India, where it was four in the afternoon. And so he left her apartment at two, three, often as late as four in the morning, driving back to his house in the suburbs. During the day he called her every hour, it seemed, from work, or from his cell phone. Once he learned Miranda's schedule he left her a message each evening at five-thirty, when she was on the T coming back to her apartment, just so, he said, she could hear his voice as soon as she walked through the door. "I'm thinking about you," he'd say on the tape. "I can't wait to see you." He told her he liked spending time in her apartment, with its kitchen counter no wider than a breadbox, and scratchy floors that sloped, and a buzzer in the lobby that always made a slightly embarrassing sound when he pressed it. He said he admired her for moving to Boston, where she knew no one, instead of remaining in Michigan, where she'd grown up and gone to college. When Miranda told him it was nothing to admire, that she'd moved to Boston precisely for that reason, he shook his head. "I know what it's like to be lonely," he said, suddenly serious, and at that moment Miranda felt that he understood her—understood how she felt some nights on the T, after seeing a movie on her own, or going to a bookstore to read magazines, or having drinks with Laxmi, who always had to meet her husband at Alewife station[4] in an hour or two. In less serious moments Dev said he liked that her legs were longer than her torso, something he'd observed the first time she walked across a room naked. "You're the first," he told her, admiring her from the bed. "The first woman I've known with legs this long."

---

1. Major interchange of MTA subway lines.
2. MTA commuter hub for lines from the south suburbs.
3. MTA stop in the business district.
4. MTA stop in Cambridge, Massachusetts, across the Charles River from Boston.

Dev was the first to tell her that. Unlike the boys she dated in college, who were simply taller, heavier versions of the ones she dated in high school, Dev was the first always to pay for things, and hold doors open, and reach across a table in a restaurant to kiss her hand. He was the first to bring her a bouquet of flowers so immense she'd had to split it up into all six of her drinking glasses, and the first to whisper her name again and again when they made love. Within days of meeting him, when she was at work, Miranda began to wish that there were a picture of her and Dev tacked to the inside of her cubicle, like the one of Laxmi and her husband in front of the Taj Mahal. She didn't tell Laxmi about Dev. She didn't tell anyone. Part of her wanted to tell Laxmi, if only because Laxmi was Indian, too. But Laxmi was always on the phone with her cousin these days, who was still in bed, whose husband was still in London, and whose son still wasn't going to school. "You must eat something," Laxmi would urge. "You mustn't lose your health." When she wasn't speaking to her cousin, she spoke to her husband, shorter conversations, in which she ended up arguing about whether to have chicken or lamb for dinner. "I'm sorry," Miranda heard her apologize at one point. "This whole thing just makes me a little paranoid."

Miranda and Dev didn't argue. They went to movies at the Nickelodeon and kissed the whole time. They ate pulled pork and cornbread in Davis Square,[5] a paper napkin tucked like a cravat into the collar of Dev's shirt. They sipped sangria at the bar of a Spanish restaurant, a grinning pig's head presiding over their conversation. They went to the MFA[6] and picked out a poster of water lilies for her bedroom. One Saturday, following an afternoon concert at Symphony Hall, he showed her his favorite place in the city, the Mapparium[7] at the Christian Science center, where they stood inside a room made of glowing stained-glass panels, which was shaped like the inside of a globe, but looked like the outside of one. In the middle of the room was a transparent bridge, so that they felt as if they were standing in the center of the world. Dev pointed to India, which was red, and far more detailed than the map in *The Economist.* He explained that many of the countries, like Siam and Italian Somaliland,[8] no longer existed in the same way; the names had changed by now. The ocean, as blue as a peacock's breast, appeared in two shades, depending on the depth of the water. He showed her the deepest spot on earth, seven miles deep, above the Mariana Islands.[9] They peered over the bridge and saw the Antarctic archipelago[1] at their feet, craned their necks and saw a giant metal star overhead. As Dev spoke, his voice bounced wildly off the glass, sometimes loud, sometimes soft, sometimes seeming to land in Miranda's chest, sometimes eluding her ear altogether. When a group of tourists walked onto the bridge, she could hear them clearing their throats, as if through microphones. Dev explained that it was because of the acoustics.

Miranda found London, where Laxmi's cousin's husband was, with the woman he'd met on the plane. She wondered which of the cities in India Dev's wife was in. The farthest Miranda had ever been was to the Bahamas once when she was a child. She searched but couldn't find it on the glass

---

5. MTA stop near Tufts University in a formerly working-class, now upscale neighborhood.
6. Museum of Fine Arts (Boston).
7. Large walk-through globe that maps the earth as stars and planets would be seen in a

planetarium.
8. Presently Thailand and Somalia.
9. Island chain in the western Pacific Ocean.
1. Group of islands northwest of the Antarctic Peninsula.

panels. When the tourists left and she and Dev were alone again, he told her to stand at one end of the bridge. Even though they were thirty feet apart, Dev said, they'd be able to hear each other whisper.

"I don't believe you," Miranda said. It was the first time she'd spoken since they'd entered. She felt as if speakers were embedded in her ears.

"Go ahead," he urged, walking backward to his end of the bridge. His voice dropped to a whisper. "Say something." She watched his lips forming the words; at the same time she heard them so clearly that she felt them under her skin, under her winter coat, so near and full of warmth that she felt herself go hot.

"Hi," she whispered, unsure of what else to say.

"You're sexy," he whispered back.

At work the following week, Laxmi told Miranda that it wasn't the first time her cousin's husband had had an affair. "She's decided to let him come to his senses," Laxmi said one evening as they were getting ready to leave the office. "She says it's for the boy. She's willing to forgive him for the boy." Miranda waited as Laxmi shut off her computer. "He'll come crawling back, and she'll let him," Laxmi said, shaking her head. "Not me. If my husband so much as looked at another woman I'd change the locks." She studied the picture tacked to her cubicle. Laxmi's husband had his arm draped over her shoulder, his knees leaning in toward her on the bench. She turned to Miranda. "Wouldn't you?"

She nodded. Dev's wife was coming back from India the next day. That afternoon he'd called Miranda at work, to say he had to go to the airport to pick her up. He promised he'd call as soon as he could.

"What's the Taj Mahal like?" she asked Laxmi.

"The most romantic spot on earth." Laxmi's face brightened at the memory. "An everlasting monument to love."

While Dev was at the airport, Miranda went to Filene's Basement to buy herself things she thought a mistress should have. She found a pair of black high heels with buckles smaller than a baby's teeth. She found a satin slip with scalloped edges and a knee-length silk robe. Instead of the pantyhose she normally wore to work, she found sheer stockings with a seam. She searched through piles and wandered through racks, pressing back hanger after hanger, until she found a cocktail dress made of a slinky silvery material that matched her eyes, with little chains for straps. As she shopped she thought about Dev, and about what he'd told her in the Mapparium. It was the first time a man had called her sexy, and when she closed her eyes she could still feel his whisper drifting through her body, under her skin. In the fitting room, which was just one big room with mirrors on the walls, she found a spot next to an older woman with a shiny face and coarse frosted hair. The woman stood barefoot in her underwear, pulling the black net of a body stocking taut between her fingers.

"Always check for snags," the woman advised.

Miranda pulled out the satin slip with scalloped edges. She held it to her chest.

The woman nodded with approval. "Oh yes."

"And this?" She held up the silver cocktail dress.

"Absolutely," the woman said. "He'll want to rip it right off you."

Miranda pictured the two of them at a restaurant in the South End[2] they'd been to, where Dev had ordered foie gras and a soup made with champagne and raspberries. She pictured herself in the cocktail dress, and Dev in one of his suits, kissing her hand across the table. Only the next time Dev came to visit her, on a Sunday afternoon several days since the last time they'd seen each other, he was in gym clothes. After his wife came back, that was his excuse: on Sundays he drove into Boston and went running along the Charles. The first Sunday she opened the door in the knee-length robe, but Dev didn't even notice it; he carried her over to the bed, wearing sweatpants and sneakers, and entered her without a word. Later, she slipped on the robe when she walked across the room to get him a saucer for his cigarette ashes, but he complained that she was depriving him of the sight of her long legs, and demanded that she remove it. So the next Sunday she didn't bother. She wore jeans. She kept the lingerie at the back of a drawer, behind her socks and everyday underwear. The silver cocktail dress hung in her closet, the tag dangling from the seam. Often, in the morning, the dress would be in a heap on the floor; the chain straps always slipped off the metal hanger.

Still, Miranda looked forward to Sundays. In the mornings she went to a deli and bought a baguette and little containers of things Dev liked to eat, like pickled herring, and potato salad, and tortes of pesto and mascarpone cheese. They ate in bed, picking up the herring with their fingers and ripping the baguette with their hands. Dev told her stories about his childhood, when he would come home from school and drink mango juice served to him on a tray, and then play cricket by a lake, dressed all in white. He told her about how, at eighteen, he'd been sent to a college in upstate New York during something called the Emergency,[3] and about how it took him years to be able to follow American accents in movies, in spite of the fact that he'd had an English-medium education. As he talked he smoked three cigarettes, crushing them in a saucer by the side of her bed. Sometimes he asked her questions, like how many lovers she'd had (three) and how old she'd been the first time (nineteen). After lunch they made love, on sheets covered with crumbs, and then Dev took a nap for twelve minutes. Miranda had never known an adult who took naps, but Dev said it was something he'd grown up doing in India, where it was so hot that people didn't leave their homes until the sun went down. "Plus it allows us to sleep together," he murmured mischievously, curving his arm like a big bracelet around her body.

Only Miranda never slept. She watched the clock on her bedside table, or pressed her face against Dev's fingers, intertwined with hers, each with its half-dozen hairs at the knuckle. After six minutes she turned to face him, sighing and stretching, to test if he was really sleeping. He always was. His ribs were visible through his skin as he breathed, and yet he was beginning to develop a paunch. He complained about the hair on his shoulders, but Miranda thought him perfect, and refused to imagine him any other way.

At the end of twelve minutes Dev would open his eyes as if he'd been awake all along, smiling at her, full of a contentment she wished she felt herself. "The best twelve minutes of the week." He'd sigh, running a hand along the backs of her calves. Then he'd spring out of bed, pulling on his sweatpants and lacing up his sneakers. He would go to the bathroom and brush his teeth with his index finger, something he told her all Indians

---

2. Trendy Boston neighborhood.
3. State of internal emergency declared in 1975 by Indira Gandhi (1917–1984), prime minister of India, that allowed her to rule by decree until 1977, when she was defeated in an election.

knew how to do, to get rid of the smoke in his mouth. When she kissed him good-bye she smelled herself sometimes in his hair. But she knew that his excuse, that he'd spent the afternoon jogging, allowed him to take a shower when he got home, first thing.

Apart from Laxmi and Dev, the only Indians whom Miranda had known were a family in the neighborhood where she'd grown up, named the Dixits. Much to the amusement of the neighborhood children, including Miranda, but not including the Dixit children, Mr. Dixit would jog each evening along the flat winding streets of their development in his everyday shirt and trousers, his only concession to athletic apparel a pair of cheap Keds. Every weekend, the family—mother, father, two boys, and a girl—piled into their car and went away, to where nobody knew. The fathers complained that Mr. Dixit did not fertilize his lawn properly, did not rake his leaves on time, and agreed that the Dixits' house, the only one with vinyl siding, detracted from the neighborhood's charm. The mothers never invited Mrs. Dixit to join them around the Armstrongs' swimming pool. Waiting for the school bus with the Dixit children standing to one side, the other children would say "The Dixits dig shit," under their breath, and then burst into laughter.

One year, all the neighborhood children were invited to the birthday party of the Dixit girl. Miranda remembered a heavy aroma of incense and onions in the house, and a pile of shoes heaped by the front door. But most of all she remembered a piece of fabric, about the size of a pillowcase, which hung from a wooden dowel at the bottom of the stairs. It was a painting of a naked woman with a red face shaped like a knight's shield. She had enormous white eyes that tilted toward her temples, and mere dots for pupils. Two circles, with the same dots at their centers, indicated her breasts. In one hand she brandished a dagger. With one foot she crushed a struggling man on the ground. Around her body was a necklace composed of bleeding heads, strung together like a popcorn chain. She stuck her tongue out at Miranda.

"It is the goddess Kali,"[4] Mrs. Dixit explained brightly, shifting the dowel slightly in order to straighten the image. Mrs. Dixit's hands were painted with henna, an intricate pattern of zigzags and stars. "Come please, time for cake."

Miranda, then nine years old, had been too frightened to eat the cake. For months afterward she'd been too frightened even to walk on the same side of the street as the Dixits' house, which she had to pass twice daily, once to get to the bus stop, and once again to come home. For a while she even held her breath until she reached the next lawn, just as she did when the school bus passed a cemetery.

It shamed her now. Now, when she and Dev made love, Miranda closed her eyes and saw deserts and elephants, and marble pavilions floating on lakes beneath a full moon. One Saturday, having nothing else to do, she walked all the way to Central Square,[5] to an Indian restaurant, and ordered a plate of tandoori chicken. As she ate she tried to memorize phrases printed at the bottom of the menu, for things like "delicious" and "water" and "check, please." The phrases didn't stick in her mind, and so she began to stop from time to time in the foreign-language section of a bookstore in Kenmore Square,[6] where she studied the Bengali alphabet in the Teach Yourself series. Once she went so far as to try to transcribe the Indian part of her name, "Mira," into her

4. Hindu goddess of destruction.
5. In Cambridge.
6. In Boston.

Filofax,[7] her hand moving in unfamiliar directions, stopping and turning and picking up her pen when she least expected to. Following the arrows in the book, she drew a bar from left to right from which the letters hung; one looked more like a number than a letter, another looked like a triangle on its side. It had taken her several tries to get the letters of her name to resemble the sample letters in the book, and even then she wasn't sure if she'd written Mira or Mara. It was a scribble to her, but somewhere in the world, she realized with a shock, it meant something.

During the week it wasn't so bad. Work kept her busy, and she and Laxmi had begun having lunch together at a new Indian restaurant around the corner, during which Laxmi reported the latest status of her cousin's marriage. Sometimes Miranda tried to change the topic; it made her feel the way she once felt in college, when she and her boyfriend at the time had walked away from a crowded house of pancakes without paying for their food, just to see if they could get away with it. But Laxmi spoke of nothing else. "If I were her I'd fly straight to London and shoot them both," she announced one day. She snapped a papadum in half and dipped it into chutney.[8] "I don't know how she can just wait this way."

Miranda knew how to wait. In the evenings she sat at her dining table and coated her nails with clear nail polish, and ate salad straight from the salad bowl, and watched television, and waited for Sunday. Saturdays were the worst because by Saturday it seemed that Sunday would never come. One Saturday when Dev called, late at night, she heard people laughing and talking in the background, so many that she asked him if he was at a concert hall. But he was only calling from his house in the suburbs. "I can't hear you that well," he said. "We have guests. Miss me?" She looked at the television screen, a sitcom that she'd muted with the remote control when the phone rang. She pictured him whispering into his cell phone, in a room upstairs, a hand on the doorknob, the hallway filled with guests. "Miranda, do you miss me?" he asked again. She told him that she did.

The next day, when Dev came to visit, Miranda asked him what his wife looked like. She was nervous to ask, waiting until he'd smoked the last of his cigarettes, crushing it with a firm twist into the saucer. She wondered if they'd quarrel. But Dev wasn't surprised by the question. He told her, spreading some smoked whitefish on a cracker, that his wife resembled an actress in Bombay named Madhuri Dixit.[9]

For an instant Miranda's heart stopped. But no, the Dixit girl had been named something else, something that began with P. Still, she wondered if the actress and the Dixit girl were related. She'd been plain, wearing her hair in two braids all through high school.

A few days later Miranda went to an Indian grocery in Central Square which also rented videos. The door opened to a complicated tinkling of bells. It was dinnertime, and she was the only customer. A video was playing on a television hooked up in a corner of the store: a row of young women in harem pants were thrusting their hips in synchrony on a beach.

"Can I help you?" the man standing at the cash register asked. He was eating a samosa,[1] dipping it into some dark brown sauce on a paper plate.

7. Loose-leaf personal organizer, manufactured by the Filofax Company in England.
8. Thick, sweet, spicy sauce used as a condiment. "Papadum": crisp lentil wafer.
9. Indian film actress (b. 1967) renowned for her beauty.
1. Deep-fried turnover filled with vegetables or ground meat.

Below the glass counter at his waist were trays of more plump samosas, and what looked like pale, diamond-shaped pieces of fudge covered with foil, and some bright orange pastries floating in syrup. "You like some video?"

Miranda opened up her Filofax, where she had written "Mottery Dixit." She looked up at the videos on the shelves behind the counter. She saw women wearing skirts that sat low on the hips and tops that tied like bandannas between their breasts. Some leaned back against a stone wall, or a tree. They were beautiful, the way the women dancing on the beach were beautiful, with kohl-rimmed eyes and long black hair. She knew then that Madhuri Dixit was beautiful, too.

"We have subtitled versions, miss," the man continued. He wiped his fingertips quickly on his shirt and pulled out three titles.

"No," Miranda said. "Thank you, no." She wandered through the store, studying shelves lined with unlabeled packets and tins. The freezer case was stuffed with bags of pita bread and vegetables she didn't recognize. The only thing she recognized was a rack lined with bags and bags of the Hot Mix that Laxmi was always eating. She thought about buying some for Laxmi, then hesitated, wondering how to explain what she'd been doing in an Indian grocery.

"Very spicy," the man said, shaking his head, his eyes traveling across Miranda's body. "Too spicy for you."

By February, Laxmi's cousin's husband still hadn't come to his senses. He had returned to Montreal, argued bitterly with his wife for two weeks, packed two suitcases, and flown back to London. He wanted a divorce.

Miranda sat in her cubicle and listened as Laxmi kept telling her cousin that there were better men in the world, just waiting to come out of the woodwork. The next day the cousin said she and her son were going to her parents' house in California, to try to recuperate. Laxmi convinced her to arrange a weekend layover in Boston. "A quick change of place will do you good," Laxmi insisted gently, "besides which, I haven't seen you in years."

Miranda stared at her own phone, wishing Dev would call. It had been four days since their last conversation. She heard Laxmi dialing directory assistance, asking for the number of a beauty salon. "Something soothing," Laxmi requested. She scheduled massages, facials, manicures, and pedicures. Then she reserved a table for lunch at the Four Seasons. In her determination to cheer up her cousin, Laxmi had forgotten about the boy. She rapped her knuckles on the laminated wall.

"Are you busy Saturday?"

The boy was thin. He wore a yellow knapsack strapped across his back, gray herringbone trousers, a red V-necked sweater, and black leather shoes. His hair was cut in a thick fringe over his eyes, which had dark circles under them. They were the first thing Miranda noticed. They made him look haggard, as if he smoked a great deal and slept very little, in spite of the fact that he was only seven years old. He clasped a large sketch pad with a spiral binding. His name was Rohin.

"Ask me a capital," he said, staring up at Miranda.

She stared back at him. It was eight-thirty on a Saturday morning. She took a sip of coffee. "A what?"

"It's a game he's been playing," Laxmi's cousin explained. She was thin like her son, with a long face and the same dark circles under her eyes. A rust-colored coat hung heavy on her shoulders. Her black hair, with a few strands of gray at the temples, was pulled back like a ballerina's. "You ask him a country and he tells you the capital."

"You should have heard him in the car," Laxmi said. "He's already memorized all of Europe."

"It's not a game," Rohin said. "I'm having a competition with a boy at school. We're competing to memorize all the capitals. I'm going to beat him."

Miranda nodded. "Okay. What's the capital of India?"

"That's no good." He marched away, his arms swinging like a toy soldier. Then he marched back to Laxmi's cousin and tugged at a pocket of her overcoat. "Ask me a hard one."

"Senegal," she said.

"Dakar!" Rohin exclaimed triumphantly, and began running in larger and larger circles. Eventually he ran into the kitchen. Miranda could hear him opening and closing the fridge.

"Rohin, don't touch without asking," Laxmi's cousin called out wearily. She managed a smile for Miranda. "Don't worry, he'll fall asleep in a few hours. And thanks for watching him."

"Back at three," Laxmi said, disappearing with her cousin down the hallway. "We're double-parked."

Miranda fastened the chain on the door. She went to the kitchen to find Rohin, but he was now in the living room, at the dining table, kneeling on one of the director's chairs. He unzipped his knapsack, pushed Miranda's basket of manicure supplies to one side of the table, and spread his crayons over the surface. Miranda stood over his shoulder. She watched as he gripped a blue crayon and drew the outline of an airplane.

"It's lovely," she said. When he didn't reply, she went to the kitchen to pour herself more coffee.

"Some for me, please," Rohin called out.

She returned to the living room. "Some what?"

"Some coffee. There's enough in the pot. I saw."

She walked over to the table and sat opposite him. At times he nearly stood up to reach for a new crayon. He barely made a dent in the director's chair.

"You're too young for coffee."

Rohin leaned over the sketch pad, so that his tiny chest and shoulders almost touched it, his head tilted to one side. "The stewardess let me have coffee," he said. "She made it with milk and lots of sugar." He straightened, revealing a woman's face beside the plane, with long wavy hair and eyes like asterisks. "Her hair was more shiny," he decided, adding, "My father met a pretty woman on a plane, too." He looked at Miranda. His face darkened as he watched her sip. "Can't I have just a little coffee? Please?"

She wondered, in spite of his composed, brooding expression, if he were the type to throw a tantrum. She imagined his kicking her with his leather shoes, screaming for coffee, screaming and crying until his mother and Laxmi came back to fetch him. She went to the kitchen and prepared a cup for him as he'd requested. She selected a mug she didn't care for, in case he dropped it.

"Thank you," he said when she put it on the table. He took short sips, holding the mug securely with both hands.

Miranda sat with him while he drew, but when she attempted to put a coat of clear polish on her nails he protested. Instead he pulled out a paperback world almanac from his knapsack and asked her to quiz him. The countries were arranged by continent, six to a page, with the capitals in boldface, followed by a short entry on the population, government, and other statistics. Miranda turned to a page in the Africa section and went down the list.

"Mali," she asked him.

"Bamako," he replied instantly.

"Malawi."

"Lilongwe."

She remembered looking at Africa in the Mapparium. She remembered the fat part of it was green.

"Go on," Rohin said.

"Mauritania."

"Nouakchott."

"Mauritius."

He paused, squeezed his eyes shut, then opened them, defeated. "I can't remember."

"Port Louis," she told him.

"Port Louis." He began to say it again and again, like a chant under his breath.

When they reached the last of the countries in Africa, Rohin said he wanted to watch cartoons, telling Miranda to watch them with him. When the cartoons ended, he followed her to the kitchen, and stood by her side as she made more coffee. He didn't follow her when she went to the bathroom a few minutes later, but when she opened the door she was startled to find him standing outside.

"Do you need to go?"

He shook his head but walked into the bathroom anyway. He put the cover of the toilet down, climbed on top of it, and surveyed the narrow glass shelf over the sink which held Miranda's toothbrush and makeup.

"What's this for?" he asked, picking up the sample of eye gel she'd gotten the day she met Dev.

"Puffiness."

"What's puffiness?"

"Here," she explained, pointing.

"After you've been crying?"

"I guess so."

Rohin opened the tube and smelled it. He squeezed a drop of it onto a finger, then rubbed it on his hand. "It stings." He inspected the back of his hand closely, as if expecting it to change color. "My mother has puffiness. She says it's a cold, but really she cries, sometimes for hours. Sometimes straight through dinner. Sometimes she cries so hard her eyes puff up like bullfrogs."

Miranda wondered if she ought to feed him. In the kitchen she discovered a bag of rice cakes and some lettuce. She offered to go out, to buy something from the deli, but Rohin said he wasn't very hungry, and accepted one of the rice cakes. "You eat one too," he said. They sat at the table, the rice cakes between them. He turned to a fresh page in his sketch pad. "You draw."

She selected a blue crayon. "What should I draw?"

He thought for a moment. "I know," he said. He asked her to draw things in the living room: the sofa, the director's chairs, the television, the telephone. "This way I can memorize it."

"Memorize what?"

"Our day together." He reached for another rice cake.

"Why do you want to memorize it?"

"Because we're never going to see each other, ever again."

The precision of the phrase startled her. She looked at him, feeling slightly depressed. Rohin didn't look depressed. He tapped the page. "Go on."

And so she drew the items as best as she could—the sofa, the director's chairs, the television, the telephone. He sidled up to her, so close that it was sometimes difficult to see what she was doing. He put his small brown hand over hers. "Now me."

She handed him the crayon.

He shook his head. "No, now draw me."

"I can't," she said. "It won't look like you."

The brooding look began to spread across Rohin's face again, just as it had when she'd refused him coffee. "Please?"

She drew his face, outlining his head and the thick fringe of hair. He sat perfectly still, with a formal, melancholy expression, his gaze fixed to one side. Miranda wished she could draw a good likeness. Her hand moved in conjunction with her eyes, in unknown ways, just as it had that day in the bookstore when she'd transcribed her name in Bengali letters. It looked nothing like him. She was in the middle of drawing his nose when he wriggled away from the table.

"I'm bored," he announced, heading toward her bedroom. She heard him opening the door, opening the drawers of her bureau and closing them.

When she joined him he was inside the closet. After a moment he emerged, his hair disheveled, holding the silver cocktail dress. "This was on the floor."

"It falls off the hanger."

Rohin looked at the dress and then at Miranda's body. "Put it on."

"Excuse me?"

"Put it on."

There was no reason to put it on. Apart from in the fitting room at Filene's she had never worn it, and as long as she was with Dev she knew she never would. She knew they would never go to restaurants, where he would reach across a table and kiss her hand. They would meet in her apartment, on Sundays, he in his sweatpants, she in her jeans. She took the dress from Rohin and shook it out, even though the slinky fabric never wrinkled. She reached into the closet for a free hanger.

"Please put it on," Rohin asked, suddenly standing behind her. He pressed his face against her, clasping her waist with both his thin arms. "Please?"

"All right," she said, surprised by the strength of his grip.

He smiled, satisfied, and sat on the edge of her bed.

"You have to wait out there," she said, pointing to the door. "I'll come out when I'm ready."

"But my mother always takes her clothes off in front of me."

"She does?"

Rohin nodded. "She doesn't even pick them up afterward. She leaves them all on the floor by the bed, all tangled.

"One day she slept in my room," he continued. "She said it felt better than her bed, now that my father's gone."

"I'm not your mother," Miranda said, lifting him by the armpits off her bed. When he refused to stand, she picked him up. He was heavier than she expected, and he clung to her, his legs wrapped firmly around her hips, his head resting against her chest. She set him down in the hallway and shut the door. As an extra precaution she fastened the latch. She changed into the dress, glancing into the full-length mirror nailed to the back of the door. Her ankle socks looked silly, and so she opened a drawer and found the stockings. She searched through the back of the closet and slipped on the high heels with the tiny buckles. The chain straps of the dress were as light as paper clips against her collarbone. It was a bit loose on her. She could not zip it herself.

Rohin began knocking. "May I come in now?"

She opened the door. Rohin was holding his almanac in his hands, muttering something under his breath. His eyes opened wide at the sight of her. "I need help with the zipper," she said. She sat on the edge of the bed.

Rohin fastened the zipper to the top, and then Miranda stood up and twirled. Rohin put down the almanac. "You're sexy," he declared.

"What did you say?"

"You're sexy."

Miranda sat down again. Though she knew it meant nothing, her heart skipped a beat. Rohin probably referred to all women as sexy. He'd probably heard the word on television, or seen it on the cover of a magazine. She remembered the day in the Mapparium, standing across the bridge from Dev. At the time she thought she knew what his words meant. At the time they'd made sense.

Miranda folded her arms across her chest and looked Rohin in the eyes. "Tell me something."

He was silent.

"What does it mean?"

"What?"

"That word. 'Sexy.' What does it mean?"

He looked down, suddenly shy. "I can't tell you."

"Why not?"

"It's a secret." He pressed his lips together, so hard that a bit of them went white.

"Tell me the secret. I want to know."

Rohin sat on the bed beside Miranda and began to kick the edge of the mattress with the backs of his shoes. He giggled nervously, his thin body flinching as if it were being tickled.

"Tell me," Miranda demanded. She leaned over and gripped his ankles, holding his feet still.

Rohin looked at her, his eyes like slits. He struggled to kick the mattress again, but Miranda pressed against him. He fell back on the bed, his back straight as a board. He cupped his hands around his mouth, and then he whispered, "It means loving someone you don't know."

Miranda felt Rohin's words under her skin, the same way she'd felt Dev's. But instead of going hot she felt numb. It reminded her of the way she'd felt at the Indian grocery, the moment she knew, without even looking at a picture, that Madhuri Dixit, whom Dev's wife resembled, was beautiful.

"That's what my father did," Rohin continued. "He sat next to someone he didn't know, someone sexy, and now he loves her instead of my mother."

He took off his shoes and placed them side by side on the floor. Then he peeled back the comforter and crawled into Miranda's bed with the almanac. A minute later the book dropped from his hands, and he closed his eyes. Miranda watched him sleep, the comforter rising and falling as he breathed. He didn't wake up after twelve minutes like Dev, or even twenty. He didn't open his eyes as she stepped out of the silver cocktail dress and back into her jeans, and put the high-heeled shoes in the back of the closet, and rolled up the stockings and put them back in her drawer.

When she had put everything away she sat on the bed. She leaned toward him, close enough to see some white powder from the rice cakes stuck to the corners of his mouth, and picked up the almanac. As she turned the pages she imagined the quarrels Rohin had overheard in his house in Montreal. "Is she pretty?" his mother would have asked his father, wearing the same bathrobe she'd worn for weeks, her own pretty face turning spiteful. "Is she sexy?" His father would deny it at first, try to change the subject. "Tell me," Rohin's mother would shriek, "tell me if she's sexy." In the end his father would admit that she was, and his mother would cry and cry, in a bed surrounded by a tangle of clothes, her eyes puffing up like bullfrogs. "How could you," she'd ask, sobbing, "how could you love a woman you don't even know?"

As Miranda imagined the scene she began to cry a little herself. In the Mapparium that day, all the countries had seemed close enough to touch, and Dev's voice had bounced wildly off the glass. From across the bridge, thirty feet away, his words had reached her ears, so near and full of warmth that they'd drifted for days under her skin. Miranda cried harder, unable to stop. But Rohin still slept. She guessed that he was used to it now, to the sound of a woman crying.

On Sunday, Dev called to tell Miranda he was on his way. "I'm almost ready. I'll be there at two."

She was watching a cooking show on television. A woman pointed to a row of apples, explaining which were best for baking. "You shouldn't come today."

"Why not?"

"I have a cold," she lied. It wasn't far from the truth; crying had left her congested. "I've been in bed all morning."

"You do sound stuffed up." There was a pause. "Do you need anything?"

"I'm all set."

"Drink lots of fluids."

"Dev?"

"Yes, Miranda?"

"Do you remember that day we went to the Mapparium?"

"Of course."

"Do you remember how we whispered to each other?"

"I remember," Dev whispered playfully.

"Do you remember what you said?"

There was a pause. "'Let's go back to your place.'" He laughed quietly. "Next Sunday, then?"

The day before, as she'd cried, Miranda had believed she would never forget anything—not even the way her name looked written in Bengali. She'd fallen asleep beside Rohin and when she woke up he was drawing an airplane on the copy of *The Economist* she'd saved, hidden under the bed. "Who's Devajit Mitra?" he had asked, looking at the address label.

Miranda pictured Dev, in his sweatpants and sneakers, laughing into the phone. In a moment he'd join his wife downstairs, and tell her he wasn't going jogging. He'd pulled a muscle while stretching, he'd say, settling down to read the paper. In spite of herself, she longed for him. She would see him one more Sunday, she decided, perhaps two. Then she would tell him the things she had known all along: that it wasn't fair to her, or to his wife, that they both deserved better, that there was no point in it dragging on.

But the next Sunday it snowed, so much so that Dev couldn't tell his wife he was going running along the Charles. The Sunday after that, the snow had melted, but Miranda made plans to go to the movies with Laxmi, and when she told Dev this over the phone, he didn't ask her to cancel them. The third Sunday she got up early and went out for a walk. It was cold but sunny, and so she walked all the way down Commonwealth Avenue, past the restaurants where Dev had kissed her, and then she walked all the way to the Christian Science center. The Mapparium was closed, but she bought a cup of coffee nearby and sat on one of the benches in the plaza outside the church, gazing at its giant pillars and its massive dome, and at the clear-blue sky spread over the city.

1999

JUNOT DÍAZ
b. 1968

The people of two neighborhoods inspire most of Junot Díaz's fiction: those living in Villa Juana, a district of Santo Domingo in the Dominican Republic, and others residing in the London Terrace area of Palin, New Jersey. Born on the last day of 1968, Díaz lived in Villa Juana for his first five years, a time when his father was away working in the United States. Just before his fifth birthday he joined his father in New Jersey. Becoming an American did not mark a division in his life, nor would it as a source for his writing. Instead, Díaz appreciates the rich duality of any immigrant's experience. Narratives set in the Dominican Republic show characters ever mindful of what is happening among their relations on the North American mainland, and the young people in his New Jersey stories speak an English heavily laced with Dominican slang and live in a manner still marked by their Caribbean heritage. Not so much people of two worlds, Díaz's characters are creatures of a new world fashioned by multicultural factors and ultimately shaped by their own ingenuity.

The stories collected in *Drown* (1996) show the influence of two authors whose work Díaz read in college, Sandra Cisneros and Toni Morrison. Majoring in English at Kean College and Rutgers University, Díaz profited from a "living-and-learning" residence hall program that provided an immersion in both creative writing and literary studies. From Cisneros's fiction he learned how a neighborhood, such as the one she depicted in *The House on Mango Street* (1984), can be as vital and vibrant a creation as any character—how the neighborhood itself can be a character in the writer's imagination, a technique Díaz would later develop in his own manner. Morrison's novels popular during Díaz's undergraduate years (1988–92) are especially strong in privileging the novelist as creator of an otherwise unwritten minority history, a theme the younger writer would extend to the immigrant's experience of living in two worlds, neither of which conform to dominant cultural models. At the same time Díaz was paying for his education by working numerous part-time jobs that he recalls as roles customarily reserved for adult Latinos recently arrived in the

United States, such as in the service industries (washing dishes, delivering pool tables) and in a steel plant. An MFA in creative writing from Cornell University followed in 1995, by which time Díaz had published many of the stories collected in *Drown*, including several in such prestigious venues as the *New Yorker* and the *Paris Review*. Díaz lives in New York City, where he remains active in the Dominican community; at the Massachusetts Institute of Technology he teaches creative writing in the Program in Writing and Humanistic Studies.

The fact that Díaz's novel, *The Brief Wondrous Life of Oscar Wao* (2007), appeared eleven years after *Drown* is indicative of his painstaking writing method. A winner of both the 2008 Pulitzer Prize for fiction and the National Book Critics Circle Award for the best novel of 2007, *The Brief Wondrous Life of Oscar Wao* presents a character who fulfills Díaz's professed goal of challenging "the type of protagonist that many of the young male Latino writers I knew were writing," as the author told Meghan O'Rourke of *Slate* in the wake of his awards. In a similar discussion with Jaime Perales Contreras of the bilingual *Literal* magazine, Díaz explained that his title character's name was prompted by a young Mexican literature student's pronunciation of Oscar Wilde's name. "Spanglish" is the slang term for such colorful mixtures of Spanish and English, and as a poetry of sorts it contributes to the texture and rhythm of Díaz's narration. As O'Rourke puts it, his fiction "is propelled by its attention to the energetic hybridity of American life," stretching from the questions of identity and inclusion dealt with in the stories of *Drown* to the complexities of a multicultural boyhood depicted in the novel. Throughout Díaz's work "authority" is an ever-present concern, from the memories of Oscar Wao's family suffering under the Trujillo dictatorship in the Dominican Republic to the contested nature of various narrative accounts with which young Oscar struggles in his American high school.

The following text is the title story from the 1996 collection *Drown*.

Drown

My mother tells me Beto's home, waits for me to say something, but I keep watching the TV. Only when she's in bed do I put on my jacket and swing through the neighborhood to see. He's a pato[1] now but two years ago we were friends and he would walk into the apartment without knocking, his heavy voice rousing my mother from the Spanish of her room and drawing me up from the basement, a voice that crackled and made you think of uncles or grandfathers.

We were raging then, crazy the way we stole, broke windows, the way we pissed on people's steps and then challenged them to come out and stop us. Beto was leaving for college at the end of the summer and was delirious from the thought of it—he hated everything about the neighborhood, the break-apart buildings, the little strips of grass, the piles of garbage around the cans, and the dump, especially the dump.

I don't know how you can do it, he said to me. I would just find me a job anywhere and go.

Yeah, I said. I wasn't like him. I had another year to go in high school, no promises elsewhere.

Days we spent in the mall or out in the parking lot playing stickball, but nights were what we waited for. The heat in the apartments was like something heavy that had come inside to die. Families arranged on their porches, the glow from their TVs washing blue against the brick. From my family

---

1. Dominican slang (pejorative) for a gay man (literally, "duck" in Spanish).

apartment you could smell the pear trees that had been planted years ago, four to a court, probably to save us all from asphyxiation. Nothing moved fast, even the daylight was slow to fade, but as soon as night settled Beto and I headed down to the community center and sprang the fence into the pool. We were never alone, every kid with legs was there. We lunged from the boards and swam out of the deep end, wrestling and farting around. At around midnight abuelas,[2] with their night hair swirled around spiky rollers, shouted at us from their apartment windows. ¡Sinvergüenzas![3] Go home!

I pass his apartment but the windows are dark; I put my ear to the busted-up door and hear only the familiar hum of the air conditioner. I haven't decided yet if I'll talk to him. I can go back to my dinner and two years will become three.

Even from four blocks off I can hear the racket from the pool—radios too—and wonder if we were ever that loud. Little has changed, not the stink of chlorine, not the bottles exploding against the lifeguard station. I hook my fingers through the plastic-coated hurricane fence. Something tells me that he will be here; I hop the fence, feeling stupid when I sprawl on the dandelions and the grass.

Nice one, somebody calls out.

Fuck me, I say. I'm not the oldest motherfucker in the place, but it's close. I take off my shirt and my shoes and then knife in. Many of the kids here are younger brothers of the people I used to go to school with. Two of them swim past, black and Latino, and they pause when they see me, recognizing the guy who sells them their shitty dope. The crackheads have their own man, Lucero, and some other guy who drives in from Paterson,[4] the only full-time commuter in the area.

The water feels good. Starting at the deep end I glide over the slick-tiled bottom without kicking up a spume or making a splash. Sometimes another swimmer churns past me, more a disturbance of water than a body. I can still go far without coming up. While everything above is loud and bright, everything below is whispers. And always the risk of coming up to find the cops stabbing their searchlights out across the water. And then everyone running, wet feet slapping against the concrete, yelling, Fuck you, officers, you puto sucios,[5] fuck you.

When I'm tired I wade through to the shallow end, past some kid who's kissing his girlfriend, watching me as though I'm going to try to cut in, and I sit near the sign that runs the pool during the day. *No Horseplay, No Running, No Defecating, No Urinating, No Expectorating.* At the bottom someone has scrawled in *No Whites, No Fat Chiks* and someone else has provided the missing *c.* I laugh. Beto hadn't known what expectorating meant though he was the one leaving for college. I told him, spitting a greener by the side of the pool.

Shit, he said. Where did you learn that?

I shrugged.

Tell me. He hated when I knew something he didn't. He put his hands on my shoulders and pushed me under. He was wearing a cross and cutoff jeans. He was stronger than me and held me down until water flooded my nose and throat. Even then I didn't tell him; he thought I didn't read, not even dictionaries.

2. Grandmothers (Spanish).
3. Shameless, brazen ones (Spanish).
4. City in northern New Jersey.
5. Dirty whores (Spanish).

We live alone. My mother has enough for the rent and groceries and I cover the phone bill, sometimes the cable. She's so quiet that most of the time I'm startled to find her in the apartment. I'll enter a room and she'll stir, detaching herself from the cracking plaster walls, from the stained cabinets, and fright will pass through me like a wire. She has discovered the secret to silence: pouring café without a splash, walking between rooms as if gliding on a cushion of felt, crying without a sound. You have traveled to the East and learned many secret things, I've told her. You're like a shadow warrior.

And you're like a crazy, she says. Like a big crazy.

When I come in she's still awake, her hands picking clots of lint from her skirt. I put a towel down on the sofa and we watch television together. We settle on the Spanish-language news: drama for her, violence for me. Today a child has survived a seven-story fall, busting nothing but his diaper. The hysterical baby-sitter, about three hundred pounds of her, is head-butting the microphone.

It's a goddamn miraclevilla,[6] she cries.

My mother asks me if I found Beto. I tell her that I didn't look.

That's too bad. He was telling me that he might be starting at a school for business.

So what?

She's never understood why we don't speak anymore. I've tried to explain, all wise-like, that everything changes, but she thinks that sort of saying is only around so you can prove it wrong.

He asked me what you were doing.

What did you say?

I told him you were fine.

You should have told him I moved.

And what if he ran into you?

I'm not allowed to visit my mother?

She notices the tightening of my arms. You should be more like me and your father.

Can't you see I'm watching television?

I was angry at him, wasn't I? But now we can talk to each other.

Am I watching television here or what?

Saturdays she asks me to take her to the mall. As a son I feel I owe her that much, even though neither of us has a car and we have to walk two miles through redneck territory to catch the M15.[7]

Before we head out she drags us through the apartment to make sure the windows are locked. She can't reach the latches so she has me test them. With the air conditioner on we never open windows but I go through the routine anyway. Putting my hand on the latch is not enough—she wants to hear it rattle. This place just isn't safe, she tells me. Lorena got lazy and look what they did to her. They punched her and kept her locked up in her place. Those morenos[8] ate all her food and even made phone calls. Phone calls!

That's why we don't have long-distance, I tell her but she shakes her head. That's not funny, she says.

She doesn't go out much, so when she does it's a big deal. She dresses up, even puts on makeup. Which is why I don't give her lip about taking her to

6. Slang term for "miraculous" in "Spanglish," an amalgamation of Spanish and English as spoken in some Hispanic communities.
7. Bus route in the New Brunswick area of New Jersey.
8. Dark-skinned persons (Spanish).

the mall even though I usually make a fortune on Saturdays, selling to those kids going down to Belmar or out to Spruce Run.

I recognize like half the kids on the bus. I keep my head buried in my cap, praying that nobody tries to score. She watches the traffic, her hands somewhere inside her purse, doesn't say a word.

When we arrive at the mall I give her fifty dollars. Buy something, I say, hating the image I have of her, picking through the sale bins, wrinkling everything. Back in the day, my father would give her a hundred dollars at the end of each summer for my new clothes and she would take nearly a week to spend it, even though it never amounted to more than a couple of t-shirts and two pairs of jeans. She folds the bills into a square. I'll see you at three, she says.

I wander through the stores, staying in sight of the cashiers so they won't have reason to follow me. The circuit I make has not changed since my looting days. Bookstore, record store, comic-book shop, Macy's. Me and Beto used to steal like mad from these places, two, three hundred dollars of shit in an outing. Our system was simple—we walked into a store with a shopping bag and came out loaded. Back then security wasn't tight. The only trick was in the exit. We stopped right at the entrance of the store and checked out some worthless piece of junk to stop people from getting suspicious. What do you think? we asked each other. Would she like it? Both of us had seen bad shoplifters at work. All grab and run, nothing smooth about them. Not us. We idled out of the stores slow, like a fat seventies car. At this, Beto was the best. He even talked to mall security, asked them for directions, his bag all loaded up, and me, standing ten feet away, shitting my pants. When he finished he smiled, swinging his shopping bag up to hit me.

You got to stop that messing around, I told him. I'm not going to jail for bullshit like that.

You don't go to jail for shoplifting. They just turn you over to your old man.

I don't know about you, but my pops hits like a motherfucker.

He laughed. You know my dad. He flexed his hands. The nigger's got arthritis.

My mother never suspected, even when my clothes couldn't all fit in my closet, but my father wasn't that easy. He knew what things cost and knew that I didn't have a regular job.

You're going to get caught, he told me one day. Just you wait. When you do I'll show them everything you've taken and then they'll throw your stupid ass away like a bad piece of meat.

He was a charmer, my pop, a real asshole, but he was right. Nobody can stay smooth forever, especially kids like us. One day at the bookstore, we didn't even hide the drops. Four issues of the same *Playboy* for kicks, enough audio books to start our own library. No last-minute juke either. The lady who stepped in front of us didn't look old, even with her white hair. Her silk shirt was half unbuttoned and a silver horn necklace sat on the freckled top of her chest. I'm sorry fellows, but I have to check your bag, she said. I kept moving, and looked back all annoyed, like she was asking us for a quarter or something. Beto got polite and stopped. No problem, he said, slamming the heavy bag into her face. She hit the cold tile with a squawk, her palms slapping the ground. There you go, Beto said.

Security found us across from the bus stop, under a Jeep Cherokee. A bus had come and gone, both of us too scared to take it, imagining a plainclothes waiting to clap the cuffs on. I remember that when the rent-a-cop tapped his nightstick against the fender and said, You little shits better come out here real slow, I started to cry. Beto didn't say a word, his face stretched out and gray, his hand squeezing mine, the bones in our fingers pressing together.

Nights I drink with Alex and Danny. The Malibou Bar is no good, just wash-outs and the sucias[9] we can con into joining us. We drink too much, roar at each other and make the skinny bartender move closer to the phone. On the wall hangs a cork dartboard and a Brunswick Gold Crown[1] blocks the bath-room, its bumpers squashed, the felt pulled like old skin.

When the bar begins to shake back and forth like a rumba, I call it a night and go home, through the fields that surround the apartments. In the distance you can see the Raritan,[2] as shiny as an earthworm, the same river my homeboy goes to school on. The dump has long since shut down, and grass has spread over it like a sickly fuzz, and from where I stand, my right hand directing a colorless stream of piss downward, the landfill might be the top of a blond head, square and old.

In the mornings I run. My mother is already up, dressing for her housecleaning job. She says nothing to me, would rather point to the mangu[3] she has prepared than speak.

I run three miles easily, could have pushed a fourth if I were in the mood. I keep an eye out for the recruiter who prowls around our neighborhood in his dark K-car.[4] We've spoken before. He was out of uniform and called me over, jovial, and I thought I was helping some white dude with directions. Would you mind if I asked you a question?

No.

Do you have a job?

Not right now.

Would you like one? A real career, more than you'll get around here?

I remember stepping back. Depends on what it is, I said.

Son, I know somebody who's hiring. It's the United States government.

Well. Sorry, but I ain't Army material.

That's exactly what I used to think, he said, his ten piggy fingers buried in his carpeted steering wheel. But now I have a house, a car, a gun and a wife. Discipline. Loyalty. Can you say that you have those things? Even one?

He's a southerner, red-haired, his drawl so out of place that the people around here laugh just hearing him. I take to the bushes when I see his car on the road. These days my guts feel loose and cold and I want to be away from here. He won't have to show me his Desert Eagle[5] or flash the photos of the skinny Filipino girls sucking dick. He'll only have to smile and name the places and I'll listen.

When I reach the apartment, I lean against my door, waiting for my heart to slow, for the pain to lose its edge. I hear my mother's voice, a whisper from the kitchen. She sounds hurt or nervous, maybe both. At first I'm terrified that Beto's inside with her but then I look and see the phone cord, swinging lazily. She's talking to my father, something she knows I disapprove of. He's in Florida now, a sad guy who calls her and begs for money. He swears that if she moves down there he'll leave the woman he's living with. These are lies, I've told her, but she still calls him. His words coil inside of her, wrecking her

9. Sluts (Spanish).
1. Pool table.
2. River in New Jersey.
3. Dominican dish made from plantains with

butter, salt, pepper, and water.
4. A Chrysler Corporation automobile popular as a fleet vehicle.
5. A semi-automatic military pistol.

sleep for days. She opens the refrigerator door slightly so that the whir of the compressor masks their conversation. I walk in on her and hang up the phone. That's enough, I say.

She's startled, her hand squeezing the loose folds of her neck. That was him, she says quietly.

On school days Beto and I chilled at the stop together but as soon as that bus came over the Parkwood hill I got to thinking about how I was failing gym and screwing up math and how I hated every single living teacher on the planet.

I'll see *you* in the p.m., I said.

He was already standing on line. I just stood back and grinned, my hands in my pockets. With our bus drivers you didn't have to hide. Two of them didn't give a rat fuck and the third one, the Brazilian preacher, was too busy talking Bible to notice anything but the traffic in front of him.

Being truant without a car was no easy job but I managed. I watched a lot of TV and when it got boring I trooped down to the mall or the Sayreville library, where you could watch old documentaries for free. I always came back to the neighborhood late, so the bus wouldn't pass me on Ernston and nobody could yell Asshole! out the windows. Beto would usually be home or down by the swings, but other times he wouldn't be around at all. Out visiting other neighborhoods. He knew a lot of folks I didn't—a messed-up black kid from Madison Park, two brothers who were into that N.Y. club scene, who spent money on platform shoes and leather backpacks. I'd leave a message with his parents and then watch some more TV. The next day he'd be out at the bus stop, too busy smoking a cigarette to say much about the day before.

You need to learn how to walk the world, he told me. There's a lot out there.

Some nights me and the boys drive to New Brunswick. A nice city, the Raritan so low and silty that you don't have to be Jesus to walk over it. We hit the Melody and the Roxy, stare at the college girls. We drink a lot and then spin out onto the dance floor. None of the chicas[6] ever dance with us, but a glance or a touch can keep us talking shit for hours.

Once the clubs close we go to the Franklin Diner, gorge ourselves on pancakes, and then, after we've smoked our pack, head home. Danny passes out in the back seat and Alex cranks the window down to keep the wind in his eyes. He's fallen asleep in the past, wrecked two cars before this one. The streets have been picked clean of students and townies and we blow through every light, red or green. At the Old Bridge Turnpike we pass the fag bar, which never seems to close. Patos are all over the parking lot, drinking and talking.

Sometimes Alex will stop by the side of the road and say, Excuse me. When somebody comes over from the bar he'll point his plastic pistol at them, just to see if they'll run or shit their pants. Tonight he just puts his head out the window. Fuck you! he shouts and then settles back in his seat, laughing.

That's original, I say.

6. Girls (Spanish).

He puts his head out the window again. Eat me, then!

Yeah, Danny mumbles from the back. Eat me.

Twice. That's it.

The first time was at the end of that summer. We had just come back from the pool and were watching a porn video at his parents' apartment. His father was a nut for these tapes, ordering them from wholesalers in California and Grand Rapids. Beto used to tell me how his pop would watch them in the middle of the day, not caring a lick about his moms, who spent the time in the kitchen, taking hours to cook a pot of rice and gandules.[7] Beto would sit down with his pop and neither of them would say a word, except to laugh when somebody caught it in the eye or the face.

We were an hour into the new movie, some vaina[8] that looked like it had been filmed in the apartment next door, when he reached into my shorts. What the fuck are you doing? I asked, but he didn't stop. His hand was dry. I kept my eyes on the television, too scared to watch. I came right away, smearing the plastic sofa covers. My legs started shaking and suddenly I wanted out. He didn't say anything to me as I left, just sat there watching the screen.

The next day he called and when I heard his voice I was cool but I wouldn't go to the mall or anywhere else. My mother sensed that something was wrong and pestered me about it, but I told her to leave me the fuck alone, and my pops, who was home on a visit, stirred himself from the couch to slap me down. Mostly I stayed in the basement, terrified that I would end up abnormal, a fucking pato, but he was my best friend and back then that mattered to me more than anything. This alone got me out of the apartment and over to the pool that night. He was already there, his body pale and flabby under the water. Hey, he said. I was beginning to worry about you.

Nothing to worry about, I said.

We swam and didn't talk much and later we watched a Skytop crew pull a bikini top from a girl stupid enough to hang out alone. Give it, she said, covering herself, but these kids howled, holding it up over her head, the shiny laces flopping just out of reach. When they began to pluck at her arms, she walked away, leaving them to try the top on over their flat pecs.

He put his hand on my shoulder, my pulse a code under his palm. Let's go, he said. Unless of course you're not feeling good.

I'm feeling fine, I said.

Since his parents worked nights we pretty much owned the place until six the next morning. We sat in front of his television, in our towels, his hands bracing against my abdomen and thighs. I'll stop if you want, he said and I didn't respond. After I was done, he laid his head in my lap. I wasn't asleep or awake, but caught somewhere in between, rocked slowly back and forth the way surf holds junk against the shore, rolling it over and over. In three weeks he was leaving. Nobody can touch me, he kept saying. We'd visited the school and I'd seen how beautiful the campus was, with all the students drifting from dorm to class. I thought of how in high school our teachers loved to crowd us into their lounge every time a space shuttle took off from Florida. One teacher, whose family had two grammar schools named after it, compared us to the shuttles. A few of you are going to make it. Those are the

---

7. Pigeon peas (Spanish).   8. Dominican slang for "stuff" (Spanish).

orbiters. But the majority of you are just going to burn out. Going nowhere. He dropped his hand onto his desk. I could already see myself losing altitude, fading, the earth spread out beneath me, hard and bright.

I had my eyes closed and the television was on and when the hallway door crashed open, he jumped up and I nearly cut my dick off struggling with my shorts. It's just the neighbor, he said, laughing. He was laughing, but I was saying, Fuck this, and getting my clothes on.

I believe I see him in his father's bottomed-out Cadillac, heading towards the turnpike, but I can't be sure. He's probably back in school already. I deal close to home, trooping up and down the same dead-end street where the kids drink and smoke. These punks joke with me, pat me down for taps, sometimes too hard. Now that strip malls line Route 9, a lot of folks have part-time jobs; the kids stand around smoking in their aprons, name tags dangling heavily from pockets.

When I get home, my sneakers are filthy so I take an old toothbrush to their soles, scraping the crap into the tub. My mother has thrown open the windows and propped open the door. It's cool enough, she explains. She has prepared dinner—rice and beans, fried cheese, tostones.[9] Look what I bought, she says, showing me two blue t-shirts. They were two for one so I bought you one. Try it on.

It fits tight but I don't mind. She cranks up the television. A movie dubbed into Spanish, a classic, one that everyone knows. The actors throw themselves around, passionate, but their words are plain and deliberate. It's hard to imagine anybody going through life this way. I pull out the plug of bills from my pockets. She takes it from me, her fingers soothing the creases. A man who treats his plata[1] like this doesn't deserve to spend it, she says.

We watch the movie and the two hours together makes us friendly. She puts her hand on mine. Near the end of the film, just as our heroes are about to fall apart under a hail of bullets, she takes off her glasses and kneads her temples, the light of the television flickering across her face. She watches another minute and then her chin lists to her chest. Almost immediately her eyelashes begin to tremble, a quiet semaphore. She is dreaming, dreaming of Boca Raton, of strolling under the jacarandas[2] with my father. You can't be anywhere forever, was what Beto used to say, what he said to me the day I went to see him off. He handed me a gift, a book, and after he was gone I threw it away, didn't even bother to open it and read what he'd written.

I let her sleep until the end of the movie and when I wake her she shakes her head, grimacing. You better check those windows, she says. I promise her I will.

9. Flattened fried plantains, a side dish in the Dominican Republic.
1. Slang term for money (literally, "silver" in Spanish).
2. Flowering trees native to the tropics.

Selected Bibliographies

BEGINNINGS TO 1700

Reference Works

For early American writers in English, the basic resource is *American Writers before 1800: A Biographical and Critical Dictionary* (1983), 3 vols., edited by James A. Levernier and Douglas R. Wilmes, supplemented by *American Prose to 1820: A Guide to Information Sources* (1979), edited by Donald Yannella and John H. Roch. Useful guidance on obscure figures can still be found in Evert A. and George L. Duyckinck, *Cyclopedia of American Literature* (1855), 2 vols. Lists of early publications include Charles Evans, *American Bibliography: A Chronological Dictionary of All Books, Pamphlets and Periodical Publications Printed in the United States of America . . .* Volume 1: *1639–1729* (1903) for items issued in what became the United States; and, for items issued there and elsewhere, Joseph Sabin and Wilberforce Eames, *Biblioteca Americana: A Dictionary of Books Relating to America* (1868–1936), 29 vols. Evans is updated in Clifford K. Shipton and James E. Mooney, *National Index of American Imprints through 1800* (1969), 2 vols. William Matthews and Roy Harvey Pearce, *American Diaries: An Annotated Bibliography of American Diaries Written Prior to the Year 1861* (1945) lists over three hundred diaries from before 1700; Matthews, *American Diaries in Manuscript, 1580–1954: A Descriptive Bibliography* (1974), adds three dozen others. Harold S. Jantz, *The First Century of New England Verse* (1944) contains a full bibliography.

Histories

The first history of early American literature, although it covers only works written in English and for that and other reasons is heavily devoted to New England, remains in many ways the best: Moses C. Tyler, *A History of American Literature, 1607–1765* (1878). This is updated by more recent and more inclusive surveys, such as the first two parts of *The Cambridge History of American Literature,* Volume 1: *1590–1820* (1994), edited by Sacvan Bercovitch and Cyrus R. K. Patell. Given the involvement of much early American writing in the large-scale expansion of Europe in the first imperial age, considerable insight can be gained from major studies of that historical process.

For the basic outline of European expansion westward, Samuel Eliot Morison's *The European Discovery of America* (1971–74), 2 vols., is useful. For North America, David Beers Quinn's thorough *North America from Earliest Discovery to First*

Settlements (1977) and his *England and the Discovery of America, 1481–1620* (1973) give detailed narrative and analysis, as does Gary Nash's *Red, White, and Black: The People of Early America* (1974). Edmundo O'Gorman's insightful *The Invention of America* (1961) shifts the discussion away from the geographical discoveries of Renaissance Europe and toward the cultural responses that those discoveries called forth, a theme followed as well in J. H. Elliot's brief *The Old World and the New, 1492–1650* (1970) and in Stephen Greenblatt's *Marvelous Possessions: The Wonder of the New World* (1991). Roy Harvey Pearce's *Savagism and Civilization: A Study of the Indian and the American Mind* (1953; 1988) goes from 1609 to the mid-nineteenth century and serves as an indispensable starting point for the literary impact of the Native American on "the American mind." In a related vein, Alfred W. Crosby traces the biological exchanges between the hemispheres in his influential *The Columbian Exchange: Biological and Cultural Consequences of 1492* (1972), while Carl O. Sauer takes up the question of how the Caribbean was altered after 1492 in *The Early Spanish Main* (1966). A similar project is carried out for New England in William Cronon's excellent *Changes in the Land: Indians, Colonists, and the Ecology of New England* (1983); for the South, see Timothy Silver, *A New Face on the Countryside: Indians, Colonists, and Slaves in the South Atlantic Forests, 1500–1800* (1990).

Theory and Criticism

Among books that deal with the verbal shape of the early documents, William Carlos Williams's *In the American Grain* (1925) gives brief but evocative guidance. Howard Mumford Jones places early American culture in the context of Renaissance Europe in *O Strange New World: American Culture, the Formative Years* (1964). In *The Machine in the Garden: Technology and the Pastoral Ideal in America* (1964), Leo Marx offers insightful readings of some Renaissance texts (such as Shakespeare's *The Tempest*) that reflect on the new lands suddenly opened to the Old World; responses to the New World (and a reading, again, of *The Tempest*) are considered in Eric Cheyfitz's *The Poetics of Imperialism: Translation and Colonization from "The Tempest" to "Tarzan"* (expanded ed., 1997). A feminist perspective guides Annette Kolodny's *The Lay of the Land; Metaphor as Experience and History in American Life and Letters* (1975), and the opening chapters of Richard Drinnon's *Facing West: The Metaphysics of Indian-Hating and Empire-Building* (1980) offer a psychohistorical perspective. Francis Jennings's *The Founders of America* (1994) and Daniel Richter's *Facing East from Indian Country: A Native History of Early America* (2001) are important revisionist histories. William C. Spengemann argues for the centrality of early American texts in the transformation of Western writing generally in *The Adventurous Muse: The Poetics of American Fiction, 1789–1900* (1977), John Seelye offers ingenious readings of many early texts in *Prophetic Waters: The River in Early American Life and Literature* (1977), and Wayne Franklin gives attention to sixteenth-century works in *Discoveries, Explorers, Settlers: The Diligent Writers of Early America* (1979). Gordon Sayre's *"Les Sauvages Américains": Representations of Native Americans in French and English Colonial Literature* (1997) offers fresh comparative readings of English and French texts and the codes they developed for depicting encounters with Native American peoples.

Some coverage of Dutch colonial culture is provided by Ellis L. Raesly's *Portrait of New Netherland* (1945); it can be supplemented by Donna Merwick's case studies *Possessing Albany, 1630–1710, The Dutch and English Experiences* (1990) and *Death of a Notary: Conquest and Change in Colonial New York* (1999). Henry C. Murphy's *Anthology of New Netherland* (1865) remains the single best source of translated texts (with biographical sketches) of three seventeenth-century writers. German immigrant experience and writings from the seventeenth century are briefly treated in Henry A. Pochmann's *German Culture in America, 1600–1900, Philosophical and Literary Influences* (1957). John J. Stoudt's *Pennsylvania German Poetry, 1685–1830* (1955), surveys one form of expression in depth. The texts and introductory materials and notes in the following volumes of the *Original Narratives of Early American History* series remain useful for non-English (and in some cases English) writers: *Narratives of New Netherland, 1609–1664* (1909), edited by J. Franklin Jameson; *Journal of Jasper Danckaerts* (1913), edited by Jameson and Bartett Burleigh James; *Narratives of Early Pennsylvania, West New Jersey, and Delaware, 1630–1707* (1912), edited by Albert Cook Myers; *The Spanish Explorers in the Southern United States, 1528–1543* (1907), edited by Frederick W. Hodge; *Spanish Exploration in the Southwest, 1542–1706* (1916), edited by Herbert Eugene Bolton; and *Early Narratives of the Northwest, 1634–1699* (1917), edited by Louise P. Kellogg.

The classic study of the Puritans remains Perry Miller's *The New England Mind: The Seventeenth Century* (1939) and *The New England Mind: From Colony to Province* (1953). Useful essays by Miller are included in *Errand into the Wilderness* (1956) ("The Marrow of Puritan Divinity" and "From Edwards to Emerson" are especially important). Miller and Thomas H. Johnson edited the anthology *The Puritans: A Sourcebook of Their Writings* in 1938 (rev. ed., 1963), which contains useful introductions. A valuable collection is *Seventeenth-Century American Poetry* (1968), compiled by Harrison T. Meserole. Peter White edited *Puritan Poets and Poetics* in 1985. Patricia Caldwell discusses Puritan "relations" (accounts of conversions or spiritual autobiographies) in *The Puritan Conversion Narrative* (1983). Other books of general interest are Edmund S. Morgan's *Visible Saints: The History of a Puritan Idea* (1963), Kenneth B. Murdock's *Literature and Theology in Colonial New England* (1949), and Larzer Ziff's *Puritans in America: New Culture in a New World* (1973). On Puritan historians, see Peter Gay's *Loss of Mastery* (1966) and David Levin's *In Defense of Historical Literature* (1967). Sacvan Bercovich edited a useful collection of essays on the Puritans in *The American Puritan Imagination: Essays in Revaluation* (1974); it contains a good selected bibliography. Another useful revaluation of Puritans that brings together some hard-to-come-by essays is Michael McGiffert's *Puritanism and the American Experience* (1969). Some of the best accounts of the intellectual and cultural life of the seventeenth century are to be found in the biographies of writers included in this anthology. One important study of a writer not included is Edmund Morgan's life of Ezra Stiles, *The Gentle Puritan* (1962).

William Bradford

Bradford awaits a new editor of his history and other works, including his poems. Larry Anderson's *William Bradford's Books* (2003) is a major new study of the creation and the history of Plymouth. For a discussion of Puritan historians, including Bradford, see Kenneth B. Murdock's *Literature and Theology in Colonial New England* (1949), and David Levin's "William Bradford: The Value of Puritan Historiography," in E. H. Emerson's *Major Writers of Early American Literature* (1972).

Anne Bradstreet

The standard edition is now Jeannine Hensley's *The Works of Anne Bradstreet* (1967), with an introduction by Adrienne Rich. Students interested in textual variants will want to consult *The Complete Works* (1981), edited by J. R. McElrath Jr. and Allen P. Robb. Useful critical discussions may be found in Josephine K. Piercy's *Anne Bradstreet* (1965), Elizabeth W. White's *Anne Bradstreet: The Tenth Muse* (1971), Ann Stanford's *Anne Bradstreet: The Worldly Puritan* (1974), and Rosamond Rosenmeier's *Anne Bradstreet* (1991). Jeffrey Hammond's *Sinful Self, Saintly Self* (1993) is useful on Wigglesworth and Taylor as well as Bradstreet.

Álvar Núñez Cabeza de Vaca

An excellent colloquial translation of *La Relación* is Cyclone Covey's *Cabeza de Vaca's Adventures in the Unknown Interior of America* (1961; 1983). This relies on studies of Cabeza de Vaca's itinerary by Cleve Hallenbeck, *Álvar Núñez Cabeza de Vaca: The Journey* and Route of the First European to Cross the Continent of North America, 1534–1536 (1940; 1971) and Carl O. Sauer's Sixteenth-Century North America (1971). Two translations of La Relación are The Account: Álvar Núñez Cabeza de Vaca's Relación (1993), translated by Martin A. Favata and José Fernández; and Castaways: The Narrative of Álvar Núñez Cabeza de Vaca (1993), edited by Enrique Pupo-Walker and translated by Frances M. López-Morillas. Morris Bishop's The Odyssey of Cabeza de Vaca (1933) treats the whole of the life, including the later South American episodes. Cabeza de Vaca's Río de la Plata narrative, Commentarios (1555), was translated by Luis L. Dominguez in The Conquest of the River Plate (1891). A fictional account of Estevánico, the Moorish slave who was one of the four survivors of the Cabeza de Vaca party, is offered in Daniel Panger's Black Ulysses (1982). Interesting later notes on Cabeza de Vaca and Estevánico are to be found in the various narratives of the Coronado expedition collected in George Parker Winship and Frederick Webb Hodge's The Journey of Francisco Vázquez de Coronado, 1540–1542 (1933; 1990).

Christopher Columbus

Cecil Jane's Select Documents Illustrating the Four Voyages of Columbus (1930–33; 1988) is the best bilingual edition of various writings. It does not include the "journal" of the first voyage, which survives only in summaries and unreliable transcriptions by others. The best text of that problematic work is Oliver Dunn and James E. Kelley's bilingual The Diario of Christopher Columbus's First Voyage to America, 1492–93 (1989); on the problems associated with this text (and others), see David Heninge's In Search of Columbus: The Sources for the First Voyage (1991). Biographies include Samuel Eliot Morison's now somewhat dated Admiral of the Ocean Sea (1942) and Kirkpatrick Sale's contentious The Conquest of Paradise: Christopher Columbus and the Columbian Legacy (1990). James Axtell's After Columbus (1988) and Beyond 1492 (1992) offer excellent and broad coverage of key topics.

Iroquois Creation Story

First published in 1851, Lewis Henry Morgan's League of the Iroquois (1972, with an introduction by William Fenton) remains useful as an introduction to Iroquoian culture. Daniel K. Richter's The Ordeal of the Longhouse: The Peoples of the Iroquois League in the Era of European Colonization (1992) covers the basic elements of Iroquois language, culture, and history and begins with an overview of Iroquois cosmogonic myths that builds on the work of

William Fenton, whose "This Island, the World on the Turtle's Back," Journal of American Folklore, 75 (1962), is a rich analysis of Iroquois mythology. Seneca ethnologist Arthur C. Parker's Seneca Myths and Folk Tales, Buffalo Historical Society Publications No. 27 (1923), is also useful. A modern reconstruction of these materials may be found in John C. Mohawk's Iroquois Creation Story: John Arthur Gibson's and J. N. B. Hewitt's Myth of the Earth Grasper (2005). For David Cusick, see Susan Kalter's "Finding a Place for David Cusick in Native American Literary History" (2002) and Maureen Konkle's Writing Indian Nations (2004).

Cotton Mather

Kenneth Silverman's The Life and Times of Cotton Mather (1984) supersedes earlier biographies such as that of Barrett Wendell (1891), but the introduction to Kenneth B. Murdock's Selections from Cotton Mather (1926) is still useful. In addition to Silverman's biography, interested students will want to read David Levin's Cotton Mather: The Young Life of the Lord's Remembrancer (1978) and Robert Middlekauff's The Mathers: Three Generations of Puritan Intellectuals (1971). Sacvan Bercovich has written about Mather in Major Writers of Early American Literature (1972), edited by E. H. Emerson, and in his influential book The Puritan Origins of the American Self (1975).

Mary Rowlandson

Richard Slotkin's Regeneration through Violence (1973) contains a useful discussion of Rowlandson's captivity. See also R. H. Pearce's "The Significance of the Captivity Narrative," American Literature 19 (1947). Neal Salisbury's edition (1997) of the Narrative has a fine introduction.

John Smith

A definitive edition of Smith's many writings is The Complete Works of Captain John Smith (1986), edited by Philip Barbour in 3 vols. The single best book on Smith is Everett H. Emerson's Captain John Smith (1971), but for a more expansive treatment of Smith's life the student can turn to Bradford Smith's Captain John Smith, His Life and Legend (1953) and Philip L. Barbour's The Three Worlds of Captain John Smith (1964). A useful descriptive bibliography can be found in American Prose to 1820 (1979), edited by Donald Yanella and John H. Roche.

Edward Taylor

The long standard edition The Poems of Edward Taylor (1960) is by Donald E. Stanford. This should now be used in tandem with *Edward Taylor's God Determinations and Preparatory Meditations. A Critical Edition* (2003), by Daniel Patterson. Taylor's *Diary* (1964) was edited by Francis Murphy and his *Christographia* sermons (1962) and *Treatise Concerning the Lord's Supper* (1966) by Norman S. Grabo, who has also written the best critical biography (1961, rev. ed. 1988). Thomas M. Davis and Virginia L. Davis edited *The Minor Poetry* (1981) with an informative introduction. Thomas Davis also published *A Reading of Edward Taylor* (1992). Important critical studies include William J. Scheick's *The Will and the Word* (1974), Karen E. Rowe's *Saint and Singer* (1986), and Jeffrey Hammond's *Sinful Self, Saintly Self* (1993).

Roger Williams
There are a number of distinguished studies of Williams, but the best of these are Perry Miller's *Roger Williams: His Contribution to the American Tradition* (1953), Ola E. Winslow's *Roger Williams* (1957), Edmund S.

Morgan's *Roger Williams: The Church and the State* (1967), and Henry Chupack's *Roger Williams* (1969). *The Complete Writings of Roger Williams* (1963) includes a valuable essay by Perry Miller as an introduction to vol. 7.

John Winthrop
The standard edition of *The Journal* is that edited by Richard S. Dunn, James Savage, and Laetitia Yeandle (1996). It contains a valuable introduction by Dunn. Dunn and Yeandle prepared an abridged and modernized edition of *The Journal* (1966). *The Winthrop Papers, 1498–1654* (1929–) is a multivolume series in progress published under the auspices of the Massachusetts Historical Society, Boston. Richard S. Dunn's *Puritans and Yankees: The Winthrop Dynasty of New England* (1962) and Edmund S. Morgan's *The Puritan Dilemma: The Story of John Winthrop* (1958) are among the best critical and biographical studies. For a more sympathetic account of Mrs. Hutchinson see Philip F. Gura's *A Glimpse of Sion's Glory* (1984).

AMERICAN LITERATURE 1700–1820

Reference Works

The first volume of Savcan Bercovitch's *The Cambridge History of American Literature* (1994) serves as a rich guide to the literature of this period. Hugh Amory and David D. Hall's edited *A History of the Book in America*, volume 1 (2000) recounts the history of print culture through the eighteenth century.

Histories

David S. Shields's *Civil Tongues and Polite Letters in America* (1997) treats eighteenth-century club and manuscript culture. His *Oracles of Empire: Poetry, Politics, and Commerce in British America* (1990) covers transatlantic poetry. The religious history of the period, and particularly the importance of the Great Awakening, is covered in Alan Heimert's *Religion and the American Mind* (1966) and Jon Butler's *Awash in a Sea of Faith* (1990), while Frank Lambert's *Inventing the Great Awakening* (1999) explains the significance of print culture to the religious revivals. Kenneth Silverman's *A Cultural History of the American Revolution* (1976), Michael Kammen's *A Season of Youth* (1978), and Russel B. Nye's *The Cultural Life of the New Nation* (1960) offer useful overviews of literary and artistic culture. Henry F. May's *The American Enlightenment* (1976) provides a similar service for philosophical issues. Women's evolving roles in the New Nation are treated in Mary Beth Norton's *Liberty's Daughters* (1980) and *Founding Mothers and Daughters* (1996) and Linda Kerber's *Women of the Republic* (1980). Gordon Wood's magisterial *The Creation of the American Republic* (1969) and *The Radicalism of the American Revolution* (1996) are the chief guides to the political history.

Criticism

Emory Elliot's *Revolutionary Writers* (1982) offers useful criticism of the major work of several eighteenth-century writers, while Julia Stern's *The Plight of Feeling* (1997) treats sentiment as a moral and philosophical category in fiction. On the American novel, Cathy S. Davidson's *Revolution and the Word* (1986) is seminal, while Jeffrey H. Richards's *Theater Enough* (1991) and *Drama, Theatre, and Identity in the New Republic* (2005) and Walter J. Meserve's *An Emerging Entertainment* (1977) treat drama. Michael Warner's *Letters of the Republic* (1990) discusses the relation of literature to the emergence of the public sphere. A good study of African American authors of the Atlantic Rim is Vincent Carretta and Philip Gould's edited *Genius in Bondage* (1996), and Gould also has contributed *Barbaric Traffic* (2003). William C. Dowling's *Poetry and Ideology in Revolutionary Connecticut* (1990) is the best treatment of the Connecticut Wits and their milieu.

Charles Brockden Brown

Harry R. Warfel's biography *Charles Brockden Brown: American Gothic Novelist* (1949) can be supplemented with David Lee Clark's *Charles Brockden Brown: Pioneer Voice of America* (1952). Good studies of Brown's complete works are Steven Watts's *The Romance of Real Life: Charles Brockden Brown and the Origins of American Culture* (1994), Bill Christophersen's *The Apparition in the Glass: Charles Brockden Brown's American Gothic* (1993), and Norman S. Grabo's *The Coincidental Art of Charles Brockden Brown* (1981). Caleb Crain's *American Sympathy: Men Friendship, and Literature in the New Nation* (2001) focuses on sexuality in his novels, and Mark Kamrath's *The Historicism of Charles Brockden Brown: Radical History and the Early Republic* (2010) focuses on nation building. The standard edition of his works has been published by Kent State University Press (1977–87). See also Michael Cody's *Charles Brockden Brown and the Literary Magazine: Cultural Journalism in the Early American Republic* (2004), and Philip Barnard, Mark Kamrath, and Steven Shapiro's edited *Revising Charles Brockden Brown: Culture, Politics, and Sexuality in the Early Republic* (2004). Robert S. Levine includes a chapter on Brown in his *Dislocating Race and Nation: Episodes in Nineteenth-Century American Literary Nationalism* (2008); an opposing view is found in John Carlos Rowe's *Literary Culture and U.S. Imperialism: From the Revolution to World War II* (2000). Brown's novel *Wieland* is available in a Norton Critical Edition, edited by Bryan Waterman in 2010; a useful new edition of Brown's novels is edited by Shapiro and Barnard.

J. Hector St. John de Crèvecoeur

Sketches of Eighteenth Century America, More Letters of St. John de Crèvecoeur (1925) was edited by H. L. Bourdin and co-workers. *Eighteenth Century Travels in Pennsylvania and New York* (1962) was edited by P. G. Adams. The best biographies are by Thomas Philbrick (1970) and Gay Wilson Allen and Roger Asselineau (1987).

Jonathan Edwards

Yale University Press has published a complete edition of the works of Jonathan Edwards's 26 vols. (1957–2008). Some of the editors of this project have issued *A Jonathan Edwards Reader* (1995), the best single-volume collection of Edwards's writings. Also useful are two recent collections of essays: Nathan O. Hatch and Harry S. Stout's edited *Jonathan Edwards and the American Experience* (1988) and Stephen J. Stein's edited *Jonathan Edwards's Writings* (1996). David Levin's *Jonathan Edwards: A Profile* (1969) includes Samuel Hopkins's *Life and Character of the Late Rev. Mr. Jonathan Edwards* (1765). Perry Miller's *Jonathan Edwards* (1949) and essays included in *Errand into the Wilderness* (1956) are indispensable. The best biographies are George Marsden's *Jonathan Edwards: A Life* (2003) and Philip F. Gura's *Jonathan Edwards: America's Evangelical* (2005). Daniel B. Shea Jr. includes a discussion of the *Personal Narrative* in his *Spiritual Autobiography in Early America* (1968). Patricia J. Tracy Considers the implications of his career in *Jonathan Edwards, Pastor* (1980).

Olaudah Equiano

The Interesting Narrative was edited by Werner Sollors in a Norton Critical Edition in 2001. Sidney Kaplan in *The Black Presence in the Era of the American Revolution, 1770–1800* (1973) discusses the American publication of Equiano's *Narrative*. Vincent Carretta assembles the evidence concerning Equiano's birth in *Equiano, the African* (2005).

The Federalist
A very useful introduction to *The Federalist* papers is found in Benjamin Fletcher Wright's edition of 1961. On Alexander Hamilton, see Ron Chernow's *Alexander Hamilton* (2004); on James Madison, see Jack N. Ralsove's *James Madison and the Creation of the American Republic* (1990); on John Jay, see Walter Stahr's *John Jay: Founding Father* (2005).

Benjamin Franklin
The Papers of Benjamin Franklin are being published by Yale University Press, which in 2002 brought out Edmund S. Morgan's biography, *Benjamin Franklin*. A good selection of Franklin's writings may be found in *Benjamin Franklin: Representative Selection* (1936), edited by F. L. Mott and C. L. Jorgensen. The standard biography is J. A. Leo Lemay's *The Life of Benjamin Franklin* (2006), 3 vols. Useful critical studies include Bruce I. Granger's *Benjamin Franklin, an American Man of Letters* (1964), Robert Middlekauff's *Benjamin Franklin and His Enemies* (1996), and Alfred O. Aldridge's *Benjamin Franklin and Nature's God* (1967). See also David Levin's "The Autobiography of Benjamin Franklin: The Puritan Experimenter in Life and Art," *Yale Review* 53 (1964). A famous unfavorable response to Franklin can be found in D. H. Lawrence's *Studies in Classic American Literature* (1923). Franklin's early years are discussed in A. B. Tourtellot's *Benjamin Franklin: The Boston Years* (1977). Francis Jennings wrote *Benjamin Franklin, Politician* (1996), and Nian-Sheng Huang surveys two hundred years of American response to Franklin in *Benjamin Franklin in America* (1994).

Philip Freneau
The standard edition of *The Poems of Philip Freneau* is that of F. L. Pattee, 3 vols. (1902–07). Lewis Leary, who edited *The Last Poems of Philip Freneau* (1945), wrote the best biography, *That Rascal Freneau: A Study in Literary Failure* (1941). A very useful introduction to Freneau can be found in Harry H. Clark's edition of *Philip Freneau: Representative Selections* (1929). Richard C. Vitzhum offers a study of Freneau's lyrics in *Land and Sea* (1978).

Thomas Jefferson
Princeton University Press is currently engaged in publishing the *Papers of Thomas Jefferson*. The best biography is Dumas Malone's 6-vol. *Jefferson and His Time* (1948–81). Malone's article on Jefferson in *The Dictionary of American Biography* (1933) is very helpful. Useful critical studies include M. D. Peterson's *Thomas Jefferson and the New Nation* (1970), Garry Wills's *Inventing America: Jefferson's Declaration of Independence* (1978), and Pauline Maier's *American Scripture* (1997). Jefferson's Monticello is the subject of a distinguished study by William Howard Adams (1983). Joseph J. Ellis's *American Sphinx: The Character of Thomas Jefferson* is an important addition to Jefferson biography (1997) and Jay Fliegelman's *Declaring Independence* (1993) to the critical literature. Annette Gordon-Reed discusses Jefferson's mistress in *The Hemingses of Monticello: An American Family* (2008).

Sarah Kemble Knight
A useful biographical sketch by Sidney Gunn can be found in *The Dictionary of American Biography* (1933). G. P. Winship's edition of the *Private Journal* (1920) contains Theodore Dwight's original introduction to the first edition (1825).

Judith Sargent Murray
A modern reprint of *The Gleaner* is available with an introduction by Nina Baym (1992). *Selected Writings* (1995), edited by Sharon M. Harris, offers useful commentary on Murray's work. The best biographical study is Sheila L. Skemp's *First Lady of Letters: Judith Sargent Murray and the Struggle for Female Independence* (2009).

Samson Occom
The *Collected Writings of Samson Occom, Mohegan: Leadership and Literature in Eighteenth-Century Native America* (2006) has been edited by Joanna Brooks and Robert Warrior. Brooks's *American Lazarus: Religion and the Rise of African and Native American Literatures* (2003) is also useful on Occom, as is Hilary Wyss's *Writing Indians: Literacy, Christianity, and Native Community in Early America* (2000). Occom's "Short Narrative" was first published by Berndt Peyer in *The Elders Wrote: An Anthology of Early Prose by North American Indians, 1768–1931* in 1982, and it is still worth consulting. Peyer's *The Tutor'd Mind: Indian Missionary-Writers in Antebellum America* (1997) continues to be useful.

Thomas Paine
Moncure D. Conway, who edited *The Writings of Thomas Paine,* (1894–96) 4 vols., wrote the best life of Paine (1892). H. H. Clark's *Thomas Paine: Representative Selections* (1944) contains a very helpful introduction. Crane Brinton's entry in *The Dictionary of American Biography* (1933) is justly admired. Cecil Kenyon's "Where Paine Went Wrong," *American Political Science Review* 45 (1951), is a challenging critical assessment, as is Eric Foner's

Tom Paine and Revolutionary America (1976). More recent biographies are by David F. Hawke (1974) and John Keane (1995).

Phillis Wheatley
The best edition of the poems is that edited by Julian D. Mason (1966; rev. ed. 1989).

Shirley Graham's The Story of Phillis Wheatley (1969) and William G. Allen's Wheatley, Banneker, and Horton (1970) are useful critical biographies. William H. Robinson edited Critical Essays (1982). Also see John C. Shields's Phillis Wheatley's Poetics of Liberation: Backgrounds and Contexts (2008).

AMERICAN LITERATURE 1820–1865

Reference Works

For basic information on writers and writings of this period, see Philip W. Leininger's 1995 updating of James D. Hart's Oxford Companion to American Literature; and the four-volume Oxford Encyclopedia of American Literature (2004), edited by Jay Parini. The entries on authors in the 1999 American National Biography are mostly excellent; each ANB entry on a writer concludes with a brief guide to his or her surviving papers, to major editions, and to the most reliable biographies. Gale's multivolume Dictionary of Literary Biography is also worth consulting. Richard M. Ludwig and Clifford A. Nault Jr.'s Annals of American Literature: 1602–1983 (1983) and Daniel S. Burt's The Chronology of American Literature (2004) provide useful timelines and detailed year-by-year listings of publications in the United States.

For scholarship and criticism on writers in this anthology, the best bibliographical resource is the annual American Literary Scholarship; many research libraries have access to both the print and the online versions. Before the latest ALS comes out, students may consult the articles, reviews, and advertisements in journals such as American Literature, American Literary History, ESQ: A Journal of the American Renaissance, African American Review, Studies in American Indian Literature, Legacy: A Journal of American Women Writers, and Nineteenth-Century Literature. Also invaluable is the annual MLA International Bibliography, which, like ALS, is available both in print and online versions. Clarence Gohdes and Sanford E. Marovitz's Bibliographical Guide to the Literature of the U.S.A. (1984) remains useful, especially to students interested in the history of scholarship and criticism. On developments in the field, see Caroline F. Levander and Robert S. Levine's A Companion to American Literary Studies (2011) and Russ Castronovo's The Oxford Handbook to Nineteenth-Century American Literature (2011).

The Web has revolutionized bibliographical, textual, historical, and critical studies in American literature. While it is important to keep in mind that some websites are considerably more reliable than others, and that archives can be short-lived, one can still recognize the crucial importance of digital archives for American literary scholarship in the twenty-first century. The best overview site on American literature is Donna M. Campbell's American Authors, Timelines, Literary Movements <wsu.edu/~campbelld/>. This digital archive makes available just about all of the main websites devoted to American authors, while providing information on chronologies and literary history. Also useful is PAL: Perspectives in American Literature—A Research *and Reference Guide* <www.csustan.edu/english/reuben/pal/table.html>. The Library of Congress's *American Memory* archive <loc.gov/index.html> provides images and rare texts, as does the New York Public Library's Schomburg Center for Research in Black Culture <nypl.org/locations/schomburg>. Other sites worth consulting are Northeastern University's archive on nineteenth-century American women writers <scribblingwomen.org/>; the University of North Carolina's archive on slave narratives <docsouth.unc.edu/neh/index.html>; and the Wright American Fiction archive, 1851–75 <letrs.indiana.edu/web/w/wright2/>, which makes available nearly three thousand full texts. Finally, many hard-to-find texts relating to U.S. literary, cultural, and political history can be found in the *Making of America* archive being developed jointly at Cornell University and the University of Michigan <hti.umich.edu/m/moagrp/> and <cdl.library.cornell.edu/moa/>.

Histories

The *Literary History of the United States* (1948, 1974), edited by Robert E. Spiller et al., includes some still useful guides to writers and topics. The *Columbia Literary History of the United States* (1988), under the general editorship of Emory Elliott, is an excellent one-volume history. Greil Marcus and Werner Sollors's provocative *A New Literary History of America* (2009) offers short, punchy essays on authors, texts, cultural events, and literary movements. Sacvan Bercovitch is general editor of the *Cambridge History of American Literature*, now the best resource for a comprehensive literary historical overview. Volume 2, *1820–1865* (1994), consists of monograph-length sections by four contributors: Michael Davitt Bell on "Conditions of Literary Vocation," Eric J. Sundquist on "The Literature of Expansion and Race," Barbara L. Packer on "The Transcendentalists," and Jonathan Arac on "Narrative Forms"; and Volume 4, *Nineteenth-Century Poetry: 1800–1910* (2004), consists of monograph-length sections by two contributors: Barbara Packer on "American Verse Traditions, 1800–1855," and Shira Wolosky on "Poetry and Public Discourse, 1820–1910." *The Cambridge History of the American Novel* (2011), edited by Leonard Cassuto et al., includes up-to-date essays on antebellum novelists; see also Shirley Samuels's *A Companion to American Fiction, 1780–1865* (2004). Also useful is *The Columbia History of the American Novel* (1991), under the general editorship of Emory Elliott; and Gregg Crane's *The Cambridge Introduction to the Nineteenth-Century American Novel* (2007).

Eric L. Haralson's *Encyclopedia of American Poetry: The Nineteenth Century* (1998) is a companion to John Hollander's two-volume anthology, *American Poetry: The Nineteenth Century* (1993). On drama see the *Cambridge History of American Theatre: Beginnings to 1870*, edited by Don B. Wilmeth and Christopher Bigsby (1998). The *Oxford Companion to African American Literature* (1997) is edited by William L. Andrews, Frances Smith Foster, and Trudier Harris, with a foreword by Henry Louis Gates Jr.; see also Blyden Jackson's *A History of Afro-American Literature: The Long Beginnings, 1746–1895* (1989), Audrey A. Fisch's *The Cambridge Companion to the African*

American Slave Narrative (2007), and Gene Andrew Jarrett's *A Companion to African American Literature* (2010). Other useful works are the volumes of Frank Luther Mott's *History of American Magazines* (1938, 1968), Mott's *American Journalism: A History of Newspapers in the United States* (1950), Edward E. Chielens's *American Literary Magazines: The Eighteenth and Nineteenth Centuries* (1986), Louis D. Rubin Jr.'s *The History of Southern Literature* (1985, 1990), Joseph M. Flora and Lucinda H. MacKethan's *The Companion to Southern Literature: Themes, Genres, Places, People, Movements, and Motifs* (2002), Cathy Davidson and Linda Wagner-Martin's *Oxford Companion to Women's Writing in the United States* (1995), and Denise D. Knight's *Nineteenth-Century American Women Writers: A Bio-Bibliographical Critical Source Book* (1997). On Transcendentalism, see Charles Capper and Conrad Edick Wright's *Transient and Permanent: The Transcendentalist Movement and Its Contexts* (1999), Joel Myerson's *Transcendentalism: A Reader* (2000), Philip F. Gura's *American Transcendentalism: A History* (2007), and Myerson, Sandra Harbert Petrulionis, and Laura Dassow Walls's *The Oxford Handbook of Transcendentalism* (2010). Also useful are Bruce Burgett and Glenn Hendler's *Keywords for American Cultural Studies* (2007) and Karen Halttunen's *A Companion to American Cultural History* (2008).

Literary Criticism

For a sampling of classic works in the field, see D. H. Lawrence's *Studies in Classic American Literature* (1923), F. O. Matthiessen's *American Renaissance: Art and Expression in the Age of Emerson and Whitman* (1941), Richard Chase's *The American Novel and Its Tradition* (1957), Leslie A. Fiedler's *Love and Death in the American Novel* (1960), Leo Marx's *The Machine in the Garden: Technology and the Pastoral Ideal in America* (1964), and Richard Poirier's *A World Elsewhere: The Place of Style in American Literature* (1966). Other influential works include Lawrence Buell's *Literary Transcendentalism: Style and Vision in the American Renaissance* (1973), Richard Slotkin's *Regeneration through Violence: The Mythology of the American Frontier, 1600–1860* (1973), Michael Davitt Bell's *The Development of American Romance: The Sacrifice of Relation* (1980), Annette Kolodny's *The Land before Her: Fantasy and Experience of the American Frontiers, 1630–1860* (1984), Jane Tompkins's *Sensational Designs: The Cultural Work of American Fiction, 1790–1860* (1985), Buell's *New England Literary Culture: From Revolution through Renaissance* (1986), George Dekker's *The American Historical Romance* (1988), Larry J. Reynolds's *European Revolutions and the American Renaissance* (1988), David S. Reynolds's *Beneath the American Renaissance: The Subversive Imagination in the Age of Emerson and Melville* (1989), Robert S. Levine's *Conspiracy and Romance: Studies in Brockden Brown, Cooper, Hawthorne, and Melville* (1989), David Leverenz's *Manhood and the American Renaissance* (1989), Nicholas Bromell's *By the Sweat of the Brow: Literature and Labor in Antebellum America* (1993), Priscilla Wald's *Constituting Americans: Cultural Anxiety and Narrative Form* (1995), Nina Baym's *American Women Writers and the Work of History, 1790–1860* (1995), Teresa A. Goddu's *Gothic America: Narrative, History, and Nation* (1997), Mary

Loeffelholz's, *From School to Salon: Reading Nineteenth-Century American Women's Poetry* (2004), Max Cavitch's *American Elegy: The Poetry of Mourning from the Puritans to Whitman* (2007), Christopher Castiglia's *Interior States: Institutional Consciousness and the Inner Life of Democracy in the Antebellum United States* (2008), and Paul Gilmore's *Aesthetic Materialism: Electricity and American Romanticism* (2008).

Discussions of the early national and antebellum literary marketplace can be found in William Charvat's *The Profession of Authorship in America, 1800–1870* (1968), Michael T. Gilmore's *American Romanticism and the Marketplace* (1985), Susan Coultrap-McQuin's *Doing Literary Business: American Women Writers in the Nineteenth Century* (1990), Michael Winship's *American Literary Publishing in the Mid-Nineteenth Century* (1995), Meredith L. McGill's *American Literature and the Culture of Reprinting, 1834–1853* (2003), and Trish Loughran's *The Republic in Print: Print Culture in the Age of U.S. Nation-Building, 1770–1870* (2007). On connections between law and literature, see Robert A. Ferguson's *Law and Letters in American Culture* (1984), Brook Thomas's *Cross-Examinations of Law and Literature: Cooper, Hawthorne, Stowe, and Melville* (1987) and *Civic Myths: A Law-and-Literature Approach to Citizenship* (2007), and Gregg D. Crane's *Race, Citizenship, and Law in American Literature* (2002). For discussions of transatlantic and hemispheric perspectives, see Robert Weisbuch's *Atlantic Double-Cross: American Literature and British Influence in the Age of Emerson* (1986), Paul Giles's *Transatlantic Insurrections: British Culture and the Formation of American Literature, 1730–1860* (2001), Anna Brickhouse's *Transamerican Literary Relations and the Nineteenth-Century Public Sphere* (2004), Gretchen Murphy's *Hemispheric Imaginings: The Monroe Doctrine and Narratives of U.S. Empire* (2005), Leonard Tennenhouse's *The Importance of Feeling English: American Literature and the British Diaspora, 1750–1850* (2007), Meredith L. McGill's *The Traffic in Poems: Nineteenth-Century Poetry and Transatlantic Exchange* (2008), and Caroline F. Levander and Robert S. Levine's *Hemispheric American Studies* (2008). Questions of empire and imperialism have been taken up by a number of critics; see, for example, John Carlos Rowe's *Literary Culture and U.S. Imperialism: From the Revolution to World War II* (2000), Amy Kaplan's *The Anarchy of Empire in the Making of U.S. Culture* (2002), and Laura Doyle's *Freedom's Empire: Race and the Rise of the Novel in Atlantic Modernity, 1640–1940* (2008).

Much recent criticism has been inspired by work on gender and race and the recovery of neglected writings by women, African Americans, and Native Americans. Nina Baym's *Women's Fiction: A Guide to Novels by and about Women in America, 1820–1870* (1978, 1993 with a new preface) and Mary Kelley's *Private Woman, Public Stage: Literary Domesticity in Nineteenth-Century America* (1984) have been especially influential. On the sometimes overlapping concerns of domesticity, sentimentalism, and sympathy in nineteenth-century U.S. writing, see Gillian Brown's *Domestic Individualism: Imagining Self in Nineteenth-Century America* (1990), Baym's *Feminism and American Literary History* (1992), Lora Romero's *Home Fronts: Domesticity and Its Critics in the Antebellum United States* (1997), Elizabeth Young's *Disarming the Nation: Women's Writing and the American Civil War* (1999), Glenn Hendler's *Public Sentiments: Structures of Feeling in Nineteenth-Century American Literature* (2001), Cindy Weinstein's *Family, Kinship, and Sympathy in Nineteenth-Century American Literature* (2004), Melissa J. Homestead's *American Women Authors and Literary Property, 1822–1869* (2005), and Elizabeth Barnes's *Love's Whipping Boy: Violence and Sentimentality in the American Imagination* (2011). Key works in the study of race and slavery in antebellum writing include Houston A. Baker Jr.'s *The Journey Back: Issues in Black Literature and Criticism* (1980), Henry Louis Gates Jr.'s *Figures in Black: Words, Signs, and the "Racial Self"* (1987), William L. Andrews's *To Tell a Free Story: The First Century of Afro-American Autobiography, 1760–1865* (1986), Dana D. Nelson's *The Word in Black and White: Reading "Race" in American Literature, 1638–1867* (1992), Karen Sánchez-Eppler's *Touching Liberty: Abolition, Feminism, and the Politics of the Body* (1993), Eric J. Sundquist's *To Wake the Nations: Race in the Making of American Literature* (1993), John Ernest's *Resistance and Reformation in Nineteenth-Century American Literature* (1995), Carla L. Peterson's *"Doers of the Word": African-American Women Speakers and Writers in the North (1830–1880)* (1995), Russ Castronovo's *Fathering the Nation: American Genealogies of Slavery and Freedom* (1995), Leonard Cassuto's *The Inhuman Race: The Racial Grotesque in American Literature and Culture* (1997), Rafia Zafar's *African Americans Write American Literature, 1760–1870* (1997), Dickson D. Bruce Jr.'s *The Origins of African American Literature, 1680–1865* (2001), Susan M. Ryan's *The Grammar of Good Intentions: Race and the Antebellum Culture of Benevolence* (2003), Maurice S. Lee's *Slavery, Philosophy, and American Literature, 1830–1860* (2005), Caroline F. Levander's *Cradle of Liberty: Race, the Child, and National Belonging from Thomas Jefferson to W. E. B. Du Bois* (2006), Robert S. Levine's *Dislocating Race and Nation: Episodes in Nineteenth-Century American Literary Nationalism* (2008), Ian Frederick Finseth's *Shades of Green: Visions of Nature in the Literature of American Slavery, 1770–1860* (2009), and John Ernest's *Chaotic Justice: Rethinking African American Literary History* (2009). For important critical work in Native American studies, see Lucy Maddox's *Removals: Nineteenth-Century American Indian Literature and the Politics of Indian Affairs* (1991), Arnold Krupat's *Ethnocriticism: Ethnography, History, Literature* (1992), Helen Carr's *Inventing the American Primitive: Politics, Gender and the Representation of Native American Literary Traditions, 1789–1936* (1996), Cheryl Walker's *Indian Nation: Native American Literature and Nineteenth-Century Nationalisms* (1997), John M. Coward's *The Newspaper Indian: Native American Identity in the Press, 1820–90* (1999), Neil Schmitz's *White Robe's Dilemma: Tribal History in American Literature* (2001), Maureen Konkle's *Writing American Indian Nations: Native Intellectuals and the Politics of Historiography, 1827–1863* (2004), Daniel Justice's *Our Fire Survives the Storm: A Cherokee Literary History* (2006), Krupat's *All That Remains: Varieties of Indigenous Expression* (2009), and Scott Richard Lyons's *X-Marks: Native Signatures of Assent* (2010).

Louisa May Alcott
Some of Alcott's work never went out of print, and much of the rest has been republished. Madeleine B. Stern has played a pioneering role in the recovery of Alcott's larger canon, including the sensation fiction that Alcott published anonymously. Key editions include Stern's *Behind a Mask: The Unknown Thrillers of Louisa May Alcott* (1975); Elaine Showalter's *Alternative Alcott* (1988); Daniel Shealy, Stern, and Joel Myerson's *Louisa May Alcott: Selected Fiction* (1990) and *Freaks of Genius: Unknown Thrillers of Louisa May Alcott* (1991); Elizabeth Lennox Keyser's *Whispers in the*

Dark: The Fiction of Louisa May Alcott (1993); Shealy's *Louisa May Alcott's Fairy Tales and Fantasy Stories* (1992); Sarah Elbert's *Louisa May Alcott on Race, Sex, and Slavery* (1997); Stern's *Louisa May Alcott Unmasked: Collected Thrillers* (1995) and *Louisa May Alcott: From Blood and Thunder to Hearth and Home* (1998); Keyser's *The Portable Louisa May Alcott* (2000); and Stern's *L. M. Alcott: Signature of Reform* (2002). The Library of America's *Little Women, Little Men, Jo's Boys*, edited by Showalter, was published in 2005; and the Norton Critical Edition of *Little Women*, edited by Anne K. Phillips and Gregory Eiselein, appeared in 2003. Stern's edition of *A Modern Mephistopheles* (1877) appeared in 1987; Joy S. Kasson's edition of *Work* (1873) appeared in 1994; and Elbert's edition of *Moods* (1864; revised 1882) appeared in 1991. Myerson and Daniel Shealy, with Stern as associate, edited *The Selected Letters of Louisa May Alcott* (1987) and *The Journals of Louisa May Alcott* (1989); and Shealy edited *Literary Women Abroad: The Alcott Sisters' Letters from Europe, 1870–1871* (2008). Ednah D. Cheney's *Louisa May Alcott: Her Life, Letters, and Journals* (1889) was reprinted in 1980. Stern's important biography, *Louisa May Alcott* (1950, 1978), was republished in 1996 in a revised edition, *Louisa May Alcott: A Biography*. Two excellent recent biographies are John Matteson's *Eden's Outcasts: The Story of Louisa May Alcott and Her Father* (2007) and Harriet Reisen's *Louisa May Alcott: The Woman behind Little Women* (2009). For primary texts bearing on biography, see Shealy's *Alcott in Her Own Time: A Biographical Chronicle of Her Life, Drawn from Recollections, Interviews, and Memoirs* (2005).

On critical reception, see Beverly Lyon Clark's *Louisa May Alcott: The Contemporary Reviews* (2004). An excellent resource for Alcott's most famous novel is Janice M. Alberghene and Clark's *Little Women and the Feminist Imagination: Criticism, Controversy, Personal Essays* (1999). Also useful is Eiselein and Phillips's *The Louisa May Alcott Encyclopedia* (2001). Important critical work includes Stern's *Critical Essays on Louisa May Alcott* (1984), Sarah Elbert's *A Hunger for Home: Louisa May Alcott and "Little Women"* (1987), Keyser's *Whispers in the Dark: The Fiction of Louisa May Alcott* (1993), Anne E. Boyd's *Writing for Immortality: Women and the Emergence of High Literary Culture in America* (2004), Susan S. Williams's *Reclaiming Authorship: Literary Women in America, 1850–1900* (2006), and Michelle Ann Abate's *Tomboys: A Literary and Cultural History* (2008).

William Apess

Barry O'Connell's *On Our Own Ground: The Complete Writings of William Apess, a Pequot* (1992) is the indispensable starting point for a study of Apess. O'Connell's *A Son of the Forest and Other Writings* (1997), a selection from Apess' work, has an updated introduction that provides some new material. Arnold Krupat has chapters on Apess in *The Voice in the Margin* (1989) and *Ethnocriticism* (1992); more recently he has considered "William Apess as Public Intellectual" in *All That Remains* (2009). Berndt Peyer's chapter on Apess in *The Tutor'd Mind* (1997) is valuable, as are the reflections of Hilary Wyss in "Captivity and Conversion: William Apess, Mary Jemison, and Narratives of Racial Identity," *American Indian Quarterly* (1999). Maureen Konkle has a chapter on Apess in her *Writing Indian Nations* (2004), and Robert Warrior offers a "Eulogy" for William Apess in his *The People and the Word: Reading Native Nonfiction* (2005). Michael Elliott's "Indians, Incorporated," *American Literary History* (2007), is also worth consulting. Most recent—and extremely interesting—is Lisa Brooks's chapter, "Regenerating the Village Dish: William Apess and the Mashpee Woodland Revolt," in her book *The Common Pot: The Recovery of Native Space in the Northeast* (2008).

William Cullen Bryant

William Cullen Bryant II and Thomas G. Voss edited *The Letters of William Cullen Bryant* (1975–92) in six volumes. Earlier biographies are superseded by Albert F. McLean's *William Cullen Bryant* (1989). Bryant's poetry has not been edited according to modern standards, but the edition of his *Poetical Works* (1878) published at his death is a useful starting point. His newspaper writing had been buried in the files of the *New York Evening Post* until William Cullen Bryant II republished selected editorials in *Power for Sanity* (1994). For a good collection of Bryant's major writings, see Frank Gado and Nicholas B. Stevens's *William Cullen Bryant: An American Voice* (2006). An excellent recent study is Gilbert H. Muller's *William Cullen Bryant: Author of America* (2008). Bernard Duffey's *Poetry in America: Expression and Its Values in the Times of Bryant, Whitman, and Pound* (1978) remains provocative.

James Fenimore Cooper

James Franklin Beard was editor-in-chief of a long-planned and, after 1979, fast-appearing edition, *The Writings of James Fenimore Cooper*, published by the State University of New York. Excellent volumes of *The Pioneers* and *The Last of the Mohicans*, and many of Cooper's other works, have already appeared as part of an edition with forty-eight proposed volumes. Beard also edited the indispensable six-volume *Letters and Journals of James Fenimore Cooper* (1960–68). Wayne Franklin's biography should become standard; see the first volume, *James Fenimore Cooper: The Early Years* (2007). For good overviews, see James Grossman's *James Fenimore Cooper* (1949) and Robert Emmet Long's *James Fenimore Cooper* (1990). Essential background is in Alan Taylor's *William Cooper's Town: Power and Persuasion on the Frontier of the Early American Republic* (1995), a biography of Cooper's father.

Critical reception is surveyed in George Dekker and John P. McWilliams's *Fenimore Cooper: The Critical Heritage* (1973). For collections of essays, see Robert Clark's *James Fenimore Cooper: New Critical Essays* (1985), W. M. Verhoeven's *James Fenimore Cooper: New Historical and Literary Contexts* (1993), and Leland S. Person's *Historical Guide to James Fenimore Cooper* (2006). Useful critical work includes McWilliams's *Political Justice in a Republic: James Fenimore Cooper's America* (1972), H. Daniel Peck's *A World by Itself: The Pastoral Moment in Cooper's Fiction* (1977), Wayne Franklin's *The New World of James Fenimore Cooper* (1982), James D. Wallace's *Early Cooper and His Audience* (1986), Charles Hansford Adams's *"The Guardian of the Law": Authority and Identity in James Fenimore Cooper* (1990), and Geoffrey Rans's *Cooper's Leatherstocking Series, A Secular Reading* (1991). For up-to-date scholarship, see the essays in *Literature in the Early Republic: Annual Studies on Cooper and His Contemporaries* (2009–present), edited by Matthew Wynn Sivils and Jeffrey Walker.

Rebecca Harding Davis

In 1972, Tillie Olson's Feminist Press edition of *Life in the Iron Mills*, accompanied by Olson's "A Biographical Interpretation," helped to revive Davis's critical reputation. Up to that time, Davis had mainly been known through writings about her son, the author-celebrity Richard Harding Davis. Rebecca Harding Davis published an autobiographical volume, *Bits of Gossip*, in 1904. Useful critical studies include Sharon M. Harris's *Rebecca Harding Davis and American Realism* (1991), Jane Atteridge Rose's *Rebecca Harding Davis* (1993), Jean Pfaelzer's *Parlor Radical: Rebecca Harding Davis and the Origins of American Social Realism* (1996), and William Dow's *Narrating Class in American Fiction* (2009). A groundbreaking article is Janice Milner Lasseter's "The Censored and Uncensored Literary Lives of *Life in the Iron-Mills*," *Legacy* 20 (2003): 175–89. Davis's 1862 novel *Margret Howth* is available in a 1990 edition with an afterword by Jean Fagan Yellin. Cecelia Tichi edited a cultural edition of *Life in the Iron-Mills* (1998). There are three excellent collections of Davis's writings: Jean Pfaelzer's *A Rebecca Harding Davis Reader* (1995), Janice Milner Lasseter and Sharon M. Harris's *Rebecca Harding Davis: Writing Cultural Autobiogra-*

phy (2001), and Harris and Robin L. Cadwallader's *Rebecca Harding Davis's Stories of the Civil War Era: Selected Writings from the Borderlands* (2010).

Emily Dickinson

Three volumes of *The Poems of Emily Dickinson* (1955) were edited by Thomas H. Johnson; and Johnson and Theodora Ward edited three companion volumes of *The Letters of Emily Dickinson* (1958). R. W. Franklin's *The Manuscript Books of Emily Dickinson* (1981) provides, in two volumes, facsimile reproductions of the poems Dickinson left at her death in fascicles. R. W. Franklin's three-volume *Poems of Emily Dickinson: Variorum Edition* (1998) augments and updates Johnson's three-volume *Poems*. In 1999 Franklin published the one-volume *The Poems of Emily Dickinson: Reading Edition*. Important biographies include Richard B. Sewall's *The Life of Emily Dickinson* (1974), Cynthia Griffin Wolff's *Emily Dickinson* (1986), Alfred Habegger's *My Wars Are Laid Away in Books: The Life of Emily Dickinson* (2001), Brenda Wineapple's *White Heat: The Friendship of Emily Dickinson and Thomas Wentworth Higginson* (2008), and Lyndall Gordon's *Lives Like Loaded Guns: Emily Dickinson and Her Family's Feuds* (2010). Jay Leyda's *The Years and Hours of Emily Dickinson* (1960) provides two volumes of documents, such as excerpts from family letters. Additional documents can be found in Polly Longsworth's *The World of Emily Dickinson* (1990) and Ellen Louise Hart and Martha Nell Smith's *Open Me Carefully: Emily Dickinson's Intimate Letters to Susan Huntington Dickinson* (1998).

Research tools include Joseph Duchac's *The Poems of Emily Dickinson: An Annotated Guide to Commentary Published in English, 1890–1977* (1979), and the continuation (published in 1993) covering 1978–89; Karen Dandurand's *Dickinson Scholarship: An Annotated Bibliography 1969–1985* (1988), and the treasure trove compiled by Willis J. Buckingham (drawing on Mabel Loomis Todd's scrapbooks), *Emily Dickinson's Reception in the 1890s* (1989). Also useful are Jane Donahue Eberwein's *An Emily Dickinson Encyclopedia* (1998) and Sharon Leiter's *Critical Companion to Emily Dickinson: A Literary Reference to Her Life and Work* (2007). The *Dickinson Electronic Archives* <emilydickinson.org>, directed by Martha Nell Smith with Ellen Louise Hart, Lara Vetter, and Marta Werner, offer access to Dickinson's manuscripts, out-of-print volumes about Dickinson, and never-before-published writings by various family members. Another valuable research tool is Martha Nell Smith and Lara Vetter's *Emily Dickinson's Correspondences: A Born-Digital Textual Inquiry* (2008).

Edited collections of critical essays provide an excellent introduction to Dickinson studies. See Susan Juhasz's *Feminist Critics Read Emily Dickinson* (1983); Judith Farr's *Emily Dickinson: A Collection of Critical Essays* (1996); Gudrun Grabher, Roland Hagenbüchle, and Cristanne Miller's *The Emily Dickinson Handbook* (1998, 2006); Wendy Martin's *The Cambridge Companion to Emily Dickinson* (2002); Vivian R. Pollak's *A Historical Guide to Emily Dickinson* (2004); Martha Nell Smith and Mary Loeffelholz's *A Companion to Emily Dickinson* (2008); and Jane Donahue Eberwein and Cindy MacKenzie's *Reading Emily Dickinson's Letters: Critical Essays* (2009). Important studies include Paula Bennett's *Emily Dickinson: Woman Poet* (1990), Judith Farr's *The Passion of Emily Dickinson* (1992), Martha Nell Smith's *Rowing in Eden: Rereading Emily Dickinson* (1992), Sharon Cameron's *Choosing Not Choosing: Dickinson's Fascicles* (1993), Domhnall Mitchell's *Emily Dickinson: Monarch of Perception* (2000), Eleanor Elson Heginbotham's *Reading the Fascicles of Emily Dickinson* (2003), and Virginia Walker Jackson's *Dickinson's Misery: A Theory of Lyric Reading* (2005). For a lively engagement with Dickinson's poetry from a celebrated close reader, see Helen Vendler's *Dickinson: Poems and Commentaries* (2010).

Frederick Douglass

The definitive edition of Douglass's writings is under the editorship of John Blassingame and John R. McKivigan; six volumes have appeared since 1979. The Library of America's *Frederick Douglass: Autobiographies*, edited by Henry Louis Gates Jr., contains *Narrative of the Life of Frederick Douglass, An American Slave, Written by Himself* (1845), *My Bondage and My Freedom* (1855), and *Life and Times of Frederick Douglass* (1892). William L. Andrews's *The Oxford Frederick Douglass Reader* (1996) offers an excellent selection and a perceptive introduction. Philip S. Foner edited *The Life and Writings of Frederick Douglass* in five volumes (1950–75). In addition, Andrews and William S. McFeely have edited a Norton Critical Edition of the *Narrative* (1997).

The standard biography is William S. McFeely's *Frederick Douglass* (1991), but it should be supplemented by Benjamin Quarles's *Frederick Douglass* (1948), Dickson J. Preston's *Young Frederick Douglass* (1980), David W. Blight's *Frederick Douglass's Civil War* (1989), Maria Diedrich's *Love Across the Color Lines: Ottilie Assing and Frederick Douglass* (1999), and John Stauffer's *Giants: The Parallel Lives of Frederick Douglass and Abraham Lincoln* (2008). Waldo E. Martin Jr.'s *The Mind of Frederick Douglass* (1984) offers a full-scale intellectual history and remains among the best books in Douglass studies.

Important essays on Douglass can be found in Eric J. Sundquist's *Frederick Douglass: New Literary and Historical Essays* (1990), William L. Andrews's *Critical Essays on Frederick Douglass* (1991), Bill E. Lawson and Frank M. Kirkland's *Frederick Douglass: A Critical Reader* (1999), Robert S. Levine and Samuel Otter's *Frederick Douglass and Herman Melville: Essays in Relation* (2008), and Maurice S. Lee's *The Cambridge Companion to Frederick Douglass* 2009). A useful reference work is *The Frederick Douglass Encyclopedia* (2010), edited by Julius E. Thompson, James L. Conyers Jr., and Nancy J. Dawson. Valuable critical studies include Houston A. Baker Jr.'s *Blues, Ideology, and Afro-American Literature* (1984), William L. Andrews's *To Tell a Free Story: The First Century of Afro-American Autobiography, 1760–1865* (1986), Eric J. Sundquist's *To Wake the Nations: Race in the Making of American Literature* (1993), John Ernest's *Resistance and Reformation in Nineteenth-Century African-American Literature* (1995), Robert S. Levine's *Martin Delany, Frederick Douglass, and the Politics of Representative Identity* (1997), Maggie M. Sale's *The Slumbering Volcano: American Slave Ship Revolts and the Production of Rebellious Masculinity* (1997), Maurice O. Wallace's *Constructing the Black Masculine: Identity and Ideality in African American Men's Literature and Culture, 1775–1995* (2002), William Jeremiah Moses's *Creative Conflict in African American Thought: Frederick Douglass, Alexander Crummell, Booker T. Washington, W. E. B. Du Bois, and Marcus Garvey* (2004), James Colaiaco's *Frederick Douglass and the Fourth of July* (2006), and Robert B. Stepto's *A Home Elsewhere: Rereading African American Classics in the Age of Obama* (2010).

Ralph Waldo Emerson

An outstanding achievement in Emerson scholarship is the edition of *Journals and Miscellaneous Notebooks*, 16 vols. (1960–82), edited by William H. Gilman et al. For a one-volume introduction to the journals, see Joel Porte's *Emerson in His Journals* (1982); a fuller selection is available in the Library of America's two-volume *Selected Journals* (2010), edited by Lawrence Rosenwald. Stephen E. Whicher, Robert E. Spiller, and Wallace E. Williams edited *The Early Lectures of Ralph Waldo Emerson*, 3 vols. (1959–72); Ronald A. Bosco and Joel Myerson edited *The Later Lectures of Ralph Waldo Emerson, 1843–1871* (2001). The *Complete Sermons of Ralph Waldo Emerson* (1989) is available in four volumes, under the editorship of Albert J. von Frank. Merton M. Sealts Jr. and Alfred R. Ferguson edited *"Nature": Origin, Growth, Meaning* (1969), which Sealts updated and revised (1979). Ralph L. Rusk and Eleanor M. Tilton edited the ten-volume *Letters* (1939,

1990–95); a welcome distillation is Joel Myerson's *Selected Letters of Ralph Waldo Emerson* (1997). Len Gougeon and Myerson edited *Emerson's Antislavery Writings* (1995); Joel Porte edited the Library of America's *Emerson: Essays and Lectures* (1993); and Kenneth S. Sachs edited *Political Writings / Emerson* (2008).

The most detailed biography is still Ralph L. Rusk's *The Life of Ralph Waldo Emerson* (1949), but see also Gay Wilson Allen's *Waldo Emerson* (1981) and especially Robert D. Richardson's *Emerson: The Mind on Fire* (1995). Phyllis Cole's *Mary Moody Emerson and the Origins of Transcendentalism: A Family History* (1998) explores the crucial influence of Emerson's aunt on his life and thought. Albert J. von Frank compiled *An Emerson Chronology* (1993); Joel Myerson edited *Emerson and Thoreau: The Contemporary Reviews* (1992) and prepared *Ralph Waldo Emerson: A Descriptive Bibliography* (1982); and Robert E. Burkholder edited *Ralph Waldo Emerson: An Annotated Bibliography of Criticism, 1980–1991* (1994).

For critical essays, see Burkholder and Myerson's *Critical Essays on Ralph Waldo Emerson* (1983), Lawrence Buell's *Ralph Waldo Emerson: A Collection of Critical Essays* (1993), Myerson's *A Historical Guide to Ralph Waldo Emerson* (1999), Ronald A. Bosco and Myerson's *Emerson Bicentennial Essays* (2006), Arthur S. Lothstein and Michael Brodrick's *New Morning: Emerson in the Twenty-first Century* (2008), John Lysaker and William Rossi's *Emerson and Thoreau: Figures of Friendship* (2010), and Branka Arsić and Cary Wolfe's *The Other Emerson* (2010). Joel Porte and Saundra Morris edited both the *Cambridge Companion to Ralph Waldo Emerson* (1999) and the Norton Critical Edition of *Ralph Waldo Emerson: Prose and Poetry* (2001). Important critical studies include Len Gougeon's *Virtue's Hero: Emerson, Antislavery, and Reform* (1990), Christopher Newfield's *The Emerson Effect: Individualism and Submission in America* (1996), Eduardo Cadava's *Emerson and the Climates of History* (1997), Lawrence Buell's *Emerson* (2003), Kris Fresonke's *West of Emerson: The Design of Manifest Destiny* (2003), Joel Porte's *Consciousness and Culture: Emerson and Thoreau Reviewed* (2004), Randall Fuller's *Emerson's Ghosts: Literature, Politics, and the Making of Americanists* (2007), Neil Dolan's *Emerson's Liberalism* (2009), and Branka Arsić's *On Leaving: A Reading in Emerson* (2010).

Margaret Fuller

There are substantial collections of Fuller's writings: Bell Gale Chevigny's *The Woman and the Myth: Margaret Fuller's Life and Writings* (1976, 1994), Larry J. Reynolds and Susan Belasco Smith's *"These Sad but Glorious Days": Dispatches from Europe 1846–1850* (1992), Jeffrey Steele's *The Essential Margaret Fuller* (1992), Mary Kelley's *The Portable Margaret Fuller* (1994), and Judith Mattson Bean and Joel Myerson's *Margaret Fuller, Critic: Writings for the New-York Tribune, 1844–1846* (2000). Robert N. Hudspeth's edition of Fuller's *Letters* is complete in six volumes (1983–94). Susan Belasco Smith edited *Summer on the Lakes in 1843* (1990), and Larry J. Reynolds edited a Norton Critical Edition of *Woman in the Nineteenth Century* (1997). Madeleine B. Stern's pioneering *The Life of Margaret Fuller* (1942, 1991) should be supplemented by Joseph J. Deiss's *The Roman Years of Margaret Fuller* (1969) and Eve Kornfeld's *Margaret Fuller: A Brief Biography with Documents* (1997). The standard biography is now Charles Capper's *Margaret Fuller: An American Romantic Life*, vol. 1: *The Private Years* (1994), and vol. 2: *The Public Years* (2002); but see also Meg McGavran's *Margaret Fuller, Wandering Pilgrim* (2008). Myerson edited *Fuller in Her Own Time: A Biographical Chronicle of Her Life, Drawn from Recollections, Interviews, and Memoirs* (2008). Important criticism includes Christina Zwarg's *Feminist Conversations: Fuller, Emerson, and the Play of Reading* (1995), Jeffrey Steele's *Transfiguring America: Myth, Ideology, Mourning in Margaret Fuller's Writing* (2001), Bruce Mills's *Poe, Fuller, and the Mesmeric Arts* (2006), and Charles Capper and Cristina Giorcelli's edited collection, *Margaret Fuller: Transatlantic Crossings in a Revolutionary Age* (2007).

Frances Ellen Watkins Harper

The best introduction to Harper is Frances Smith Foster's *A Brighter Day Coming: A Frances Watkins Harper Reader* (1990). Maryemma Graham edited Harper's *Complete Poems* (1988), and Foster edited *Three Rediscovered Novels by Frances E. W. Harper* (2000) and Harper's *Iola Leroy* (1988). On the racial dynamics of "The Two Offers," see Gene Andrew Jarrett's *African American Literature beyond Race* (2006). Good critical commentary on Harper can be found in Hazel V. Carby's *Reconstructing Womanhood: The Emergence of the Afro-American Woman Novelist* (1987), Joan R. Sherman's *Invisible Poets: Afro-Americans of the Nineteenth Century* (1989), Foster's *Written by Herself: Literary Production of Early African-American Women Writers* (1993), Carla L. Peterson's *"Doers of the Word": African-American Women Speakers and Writers in the North (1830–1880)* (1995), John Ernest's *Resistance and Reformation in Nineteenth-Century African-American Literature* (1995), and Janet Sinclair Gray's *Race and Time: American Women's Poetics from Antislavery to Racial*

Modernity (2004). For a biographical overview, see Melba Joyce Boyd's *Discovered Legacy: Politics and Poetics in the Life of Frances E. W. Harper, 1825–1911* (1994).

Nathaniel Hawthorne

The Centenary Edition of the Works of Nathaniel Hawthorne (1962–97), published by the Ohio State University Press, is now complete and offers a comprehensive scholarly edition of Hawthorne's letters, journals, children's writings, romances, stories and sketches, and nonfiction. For a good selection from the voluminous notebooks, see Robert Milder and Randall Fuller's *The Business of Reflection: Hawthorne in His Notebooks* (2009). An excellent recent biography is Brenda Wineapple's *Hawthorne: A Life* (2003); this should be supplemented with James Mellow's *Nathaniel Hawthorne in His Times* (1980) and T. Walter Herbert's *Dearest Beloved: The Hawthornes and the Making of the Middle-Class Family* (1993). Also useful is Ronald A. Bosco and Jillmarie Murphy's *Hawthorne in His Own Time: A Biographical Chronicle of His Life, Drawn from Recollections, Interviews, and Memoirs* (2007).

John L. Idol and Buford Jones edited *Hawthorne: The Contemporary Reviews* (1994); see also B. Bernard Cohen's *The Recognition of Nathaniel Hawthorne* (1969), J. Donald Crowley's *Hawthorne: The Critical Heritage* (1970), and Gary Scharnhorst's *Nathaniel Hawthorne: An Annotated Bibliography of Comment and Criticism before 1900* (1988). For critical essays see Michael J. Colacurcio's *New Essays on "The Scarlet Letter"* (1985), Millicent Bell's *New Essays on Hawthorne's Major Tales* (1993), Claudia D. Johnson's *Understanding "The Scarlet Letter": A Student Casebook to Issues, Sources, and Historical Documents* (1995), John L. Idol Jr. and Melissa Ponder's *Hawthorne and Women: Engendering and Expanding the Hawthorne Tradition* (1999), Larry J. Reynolds's *A Historical Guide to Nathaniel Hawthorne* (2001), Richard H. Millington's *The Cambridge Companion to Nathaniel Hawthorne* (2004), Bell's *Hawthorne and the Real: Bicentennial Essays* (2005), and Jana L. Argersinger and Leland S. Person's *Hawthorne and Melville: Writing a Relationship* (2008). Person's Norton Critical Edition of *The Scarlet Letter and Other Writings* (2005) collects a wide range of primary and secondary texts; see also James McIntosh's Norton Critical Edition of *Nathaniel Hawthorne's Tales* (1987) and Robert S. Levine's Norton Critical Edition of *The House of the Seven Gables* (2006).

The scholarship on Hawthorne is rich and voluminous. A good starting point is Leland S. Person's *The Cambridge Introduction to Nathaniel Hawthorne* (2007). Important studies include Frederick Crews's *The Sins of the Fathers: Hawthorne's Psychological Themes* (1966), Michael Davitt Bell's *Hawthorne and the Historical Romance of New England* (1971), Nina Baym's *The Shape of Hawthorne's Career* (1976), Michael J. Colacurcio's *The Province of Piety: Moral History in Hawthorne's Early Tales* (1984), Richard Brodhead's *The School of Hawthorne* (1986), Baym's *The Scarlet Letter: A Reading* (1986), Gordon Hutner's *Secrets and Sympathy: Forms of Disclosure in Hawthorne's Novels* (1988), Sacvan Bercovitch's *The Office of the Scarlet Letter* (1991), Joel Pfister's *The Production of Personal Life: Class, Gender, and the Psychological in Hawthorne's Fiction* (1991), Richard H. Millington's *Practicing Romance: Narrative Form and Cultural Engagement in Hawthorne's Fiction* (1992), Samuel Chase Coale's *Mesmerism and Hawthorne* (1998), Clark Davis's *Hawthorne's Shyness: Ethics, Politics, and the Question of Engagement* (2005), and Larry J. Reynolds's *Devils and Rebels: The Making of Hawthorne's Damned Politics* (2008).

Washington Irving

The Complete Works of Washington Irving (1969–), organized under the editorship of Henry A. Pochmann, was continued by Herbert L. Kleinfield, then by Richard Dilworth Rust. The introductory essays to this edition provide an excellent history of Irving's career. Three volumes of Irving's writings are available in the Library of America series: *History, Tales, and Sketches* (1983), *Bracebridge Hall; Tales of a Traveller; The Alhambra* (1991), and *Three Western Narratives* (2004). The standard biographies are Stanley T. Williams's *Life of Washington Irving* (1935) and William L. Hedges's *Washington Irving: An American Study 1802–1832* (1965), though these need to be supplemented by Andrew Burstein's *The Original Knickerbocker: The Life of Washington Irving* (2007) and Brian Jay Jones's *Washington Irving: An American Original* (2008). On reception and critical debate, see Andrew B. Myers's *A Century of Commentary on the Works of Washington Irving* (1976), Edwin and Ralph M. Aderman's *Critical Essays on Washington Irving* (1990), and James Tuttleton's *Washington Irving: The Critical Reaction* (1993). An important study is Jeffrey Rubin-Dorsky's *Adrift in the Old World: The Psychological Pilgrimage of Washington Irving* (1988).

Harriet Jacobs

Jean Fagin Yellin's pioneering edition of *Incidents in the Life of a Slave Girl* (1987), with biography, interpretation, and annotation, has been reissued (2000) with Harriet's brother John S. Jacobs's 1861 "A True Tale of Slavery." Frances Smith Foster and Nellie Y. McKay edited a Norton Critical Edition of *Incidents*

(2001). Yellin's *Harriet Jacobs: A Life* (2004) should remain the standard biography for some time to come. An essential resource is the two-volume *The Harriet Jacobs Family Papers* (2008), edited by Yellin et al. For critical discussion, see Rafia Zafar and Deborah M. Garfield's edited collection, *Harriet Jacobs and "Incidents in the Life of a Slave Girl": New Critical Essays* (1996). Additional commentary may be found in Valerie Smith's *Self-Discovery and Authority in Afro-American Narrative* (1987), Karen Sánchez-Eppler's *Touching Liberty: Abolition, Feminism, and the Politics of the Body* (1993), Frances Smith Foster's *Written by Herself: Literary Production by African American Women, 1746–1892* (1993), Jennifer Fleischner's *Mastering Slavery: Memory, Family, and Identity in Women's Slave Narratives* (1996), and Carla Kaplan's *The Erotics of Talk: Women's Writing and Feminist Paradigms* (1996). On Lydia Maria Child's editing of *Incidents*, see Carolyn L. Karcher's *Lydia Maria Child: A Cultural Biography* (1994) and Bruce Mills's *Cultural Reformations: Lydia Maria Child and the Literature of Reform* (1994).

Abraham Lincoln

The most comprehensive collection is *The Collected Works of Abraham Lincoln* (1953), 9 vols., edited by Roy P. Basler et al. The best introductions to Lincoln as a writer are Andrew Delbanco's *The Portable Abraham Lincoln* (1992) and Fred Kaplan's *Lincoln: The Biography of a Writer* (2008). Books on Lincoln constitute a library in themselves. For a sampling, see Steven B. Oates's *With Malice toward None: The Life of Abraham Lincoln* (1977), James M. McPherson's *Abraham Lincoln and the Second American Revolution* (1990), Garry Wills's *Lincoln at Gettysburg: The Words That Remade America* (1992), Harry V. Jaffa's *A New Birth of Freedom: Abraham Lincoln and the Coming of the Civil War* (2000), John Channing Briggs's *Lincoln's Speeches Reconsidered* (2005), and John Stauffer's *Giants: The Parallel Lives of Frederick Douglass and Abraham Lincoln* (2008). Excellent recent edited collections include Harold Holzer's *The Lincoln Anthology: Great Writers on His Life and Legacy from 1860 to Now* (2008), Eric Foner's *Our Lincoln: New Perspectives on Lincoln and His World* (2008), and Henry Louis Gates Jr.'s *Lincoln on Race and Slavery* (2009).

Henry Wadsworth Longfellow

The fullest biography is still the two-volume *Life of Henry Wadsworth Longfellow* (1886–87), written and edited by the poet's brother, Samuel Longfellow; this should be supplemented by Charles C. Calhoun's *Longfellow: A Rediscovered Life* (2003). Andrew Hilen's *The Letters of Henry Wadsworth Longfellow*

(1966–82) is invaluable, revealing much that Samuel Longfellow suppressed. Lawrence Buell edited *Selected Poems* (1988), and J. D. McClatchy edited the Library of America's *Henry Wadsworth Longfellow: Poems and Other Writings* (2000). Still useful are Edward Wagenknecht's edition of *Mrs. Longfellow: Selected Letters and Journals of Fanny Appleton Longfellow (1817–1861)* (1956), Newton Arvin's *Longfellow* (1963), and Wagenknecht's *Henry Wadsworth Longfellow, His Poetry and Prose* (1986). Important discussions of Longfellow and the literary marketplace may be found in William Charvat's *The Profession of Authorship in America, 1800–1870* (1968) and Christopher Irmscher's provocative *Longfellow Redux* (2006). For good introductions to Longfellow as a poet, see Dana Gioia, "Longfellow in the Aftermath of Modernism," in *The Columbia History of American Poetry* (1993), and Robert L. Gale's *A Henry Wadsworth Longfellow Companion* (2003).

Herman Melville

The Northwestern-Newberry Edition of *The Writings of Herman Melville* (1968–), edited by Harrison Hayford, Hershel Parker, and G. Thomas Tanselle, is standard. The Parker-Hayford revised and updated Norton Critical Edition of *Moby-Dick* (2001) contains much new documentary information. Dan McCall has a Norton Critical Edition of *Melville's Short Novels* (2002). Parker and Mark Niemayer have edited a Norton Critical Edition of *The Confidence-Man* (2nd edition, 2006). Jay Leyda's monumental compilation of documents, *The Melville Log* (1951; reprinted 1969, with a supplement), is being expanded by Parker. Parker's magisterial *Herman Melville: A Biography, 1819–1851* (1996) and *Herman Melville: A Biography, 1851–1891* (2002) provide a wealth of new information about Melville and his family. For a good shorter life, see Andrew Delbanco's *Melville: His World and Work* (2005). Stanton Garner's *The Civil War World of Herman Melville* (1993) remains of great value, and the "Historical Notes" in the Northwestern-Newberry volumes contain essential biographical, historical, and textual scholarship. Nineteenth-century biographical accounts are reprinted and analyzed in Merton M. Sealts Jr.'s *The Early Lives of Melville* (1974). Sealts's *Melville's Reading* (1988), primarily a list of books known to have been in Melville's possession, should be supplemented by Mary K. Bercaw's *Melville's Sources* (1987). Brian Higgins and Parker compiled *Herman Melville: The Contemporary Reviews* (1995). Basic research tools are Higgins's *Herman Melville: An Annotated Bibliography, 1846–1930* (1979) and *Herman Melville: A Reference Guide,*

1931–1960 (1987). See also Gail H. Coffler's *Melville's Allusions to Religion: A Comprehensive Index and Glossary* (2002).

Edited collections of critical essays and reviews provide excellent introductions to a range of Melville criticism; see John Bryant's *A Companion to Melville Studies* (1986), Robert Milder's *Critical Essays on Melville's "Billy Budd, Sailor"* (1989), Robert Burkholder's *Critical Essays on Herman Melville's "Benito Cereno"* (1992), Brian Higgins and Hershel Parker's *Critical Essays on Herman Melville's "Moby-Dick"* (1992), Myra Jehlen's *Herman Melville: A Collection of Critical Essays* (1994), John Bryant and Robert Milder's *Melville's Evermoving Dawn: Centennial Essays* (1997), Robert S. Levine's *The Cambridge Companion to Herman Melville* (1998), Donald Yannella's *New Essays on "Billy Budd"* (2002), Giles Gunn's *A Historical Guide to Herman Melville* (2005), Wyn Kelly's *A Companion to Herman Melville* (2006), John Bryant, Mary K. Bercaw, and Timothy Marr's *Ungraspable Phantom: Essays on Moby-Dick* (2006), Robert S. Levine and Samuel Otter's *Frederick Douglass and Herman Melville: Essays in Relation* (2008), Jana L. Argersinger and Leland S. Person's *Hawthorne and Melville: Writing a Relationship* (2008), and Samuel Otter and Geoffrey Sanborn's *Melville and Aesthetics* (2011). Visually stunning and illuminating are Robert K. Wallace's *Melville and Turner: Spheres of Love and Fright* (1992) and Elizabeth A. Schultz's *Unpainted to the Last: "Moby-Dick" and Twentieth-Century American Art* (1995). Among the most influential recent works in Melville studies are Wai-chee Dimock's *Empire for Liberty: Melville and the Poetics of Individualism* (1989), John Bryant's *Melville and Repose: The Rhetoric of Humor in the American Renaissance* (1993), Wyn Kelley's *Melville's City* (1996), Elizabeth Renker's *Strike through the Mask: Herman Melville and the Scene of Writing* (1996), Samuel Otter's *Melville's Anatomies* (1999), Robert Milder's *Exiled Royalties: Melville and the Life We Imagine* (2006), Hershel Parker's *Melville: The Making of the Poet* (2008), and Sterling Stuckey's *African Culture and Melville's Art: The Creative Process in "Benito Cereno" and "Moby-Dick"* (2009). A good starting point is Kelley's *Herman Melville: An Introduction* (2008).

Edgar Allan Poe

There is no complete modern scholarly edition of Poe, although there are a number of facsimile reprints of early editions as well as modern volumes of the poems edited by Floyd Stovall (1965) and Thomas O. Mabbott (1969). Burton R. Pollin continued Mabbott's long-projected edition of the *Collected Writings*; the first volume appeared in 1981. Patrick F.

Quinn's Library of America *Edgar Allan Poe: Poetry and Tales* (1984) is an excellent one-volume collection; and G. R. Thompson's Library of America *Edgar Allan Poe: Essays and Revisions* (1984) makes many elusive documents readily available. See also G. R. Thompson's Norton Critical Edition of *The Selected Writings of Edgar Allan Poe* (2004) and Stuart Levine and Susan F. Levine's *Edgar Allan Poe, Critical Theory: The Major Documents* (2009). John W. Ostrom edited *The Letters of Edgar Allan Poe* (1966). Partly because of forgeries and calumnies by Poe's literary executor, Rufus Griswold, Poe biography has remained enmeshed in legends. John Carl Miller's *Building Poe Biography* (1977) lucidly traces the gradual emergence of knowledge about Poe. The best recent biography is Kenneth Silverman's *Edgar A. Poe* (1991), but that should be supplemented by Dwight Thomas and David K. Jackson's essential *The Poe Log: A Documentary Life of Edgar Allan Poe, 1809–1849* (1987) and Benjamin Franklin Fisher's *Poe in His Own Time: A Biographical Chronicle of His Life, Drawn from Recollections, Interviews, and Memoirs* (2010). J. R. Hammond's *An Edgar Allan Poe Chronology* (1998) is also useful. Two good handbooks are Frederick S. Frank and Anthony Magistrale's *The Poe Encyclopedia* (1997) and Dawn B. Sova's *Critical Companion to Edgar Allan Poe* (2007). Elizabeth Wiley prepared a *Concordance to the Poetry of Edgar Allan Poe* (1989).

Poe's early reputation is traced in Eric Carlson's *The Recognition of Edgar Allan Poe* (1966) and Jean Alexander's *Affidavits of Genius: Edgar Allan Poe and the French Critics, 1847–1924* (1971). Modern collections of criticism, such as I. M. Walker's *Edgar Allan Poe: The Critical Heritage* (1986), are largely superseded by Graham Clarke's four-volume *Edgar Allan Poe: Critical Assessments* (1991). Valuable recent collections include Kenneth Silverman's *New Essays on Poe's Major Tales* (1993), Shawn Rosenheim and Stephen Rachman's *The American Face of Edgar Allan Poe* (1995), Eric W. Carlson's *A Companion to Poe Studies* (1996), J. Gerald Kennedy's *A Historical Guide to Edgar Allan Poe* (2001), Kennedy and Liliane Weissberg's *Romancing the Shadow: Poe and Race* (2001), and Kevin J. Hayes's *The Cambridge Companion to Edgar Allan Poe* (2002). Recent studies include Jonathan Elmer's *Reading at the Social Limit: Affect, Mass Culture, and Edgar Allan Poe* (1995), Terence Whalen's *Edgar Allan Poe and the Masses: The Political Economy of Literature in Antebellum America* (1999), Meredith L. McGill's *American Literature and the Culture of Reprinting, 1834–1853* (2003), Scott Peeples's *The Afterlife of Edgar Allan Poe* (2004), Eliza Richards's *Gender and the Politics of*

Reception in Poe's Circle (2004), Richard Kopley's *Edgar Allan Poe and the Dupin Mysteries* (2008), and Douglas Anderson's *Pictures of Ascent in the Fiction of Edgar Allan Poe* (2009). For good short introductions, see Benjamin F. Fisher's *The Cambridge Introduction to Edgar Allan Poe* (2008) and Kevin J. Hayes's *Edgar Allan Poe* (2009). Daniel Hoffman's *Poe Poe Poe Poe Poe Poe Poe* (1972) continues to entertain and instruct.

Harriet Beecher Stowe

The Writings of Harriet Beecher Stowe (1896, 1967), in sixteen volumes, though not complete, is comprehensive enough to represent Stowe's literary range. The Library of America's volume contains *Uncle Tom's Cabin, The Minister's Wooing,* and *Oldtown Folks* (1982). Elizabeth Ammons edited a Norton Critical Edition of *Uncle Tom's Cabin* (1994; 2nd edition 2010), and Joan D. Hedrick edited *The Oxford Harriet Beecher Stowe Reader* (1999). Stowe's second antislavery novel, *Dred: A Tale of the Great Dismal Swamp* (1856), is available in an edition edited by Robert S. Levine (2006). Bibliographical resources include Margaret Holbrook Hildreth's *Harriet Beecher Stowe: A Bibliography* (1976) and Jean Ashton's *Harriet Beecher Stowe: A Reference Guide* (1977).

Joan D. Hedrick's *Harriet Beecher Stowe: A Life* (1994) is the standard biography. Two earlier biographies focusing on Stowe's religious ideas remain useful: Robert Forrest Wilson's *Crusader in Crinoline* (1941) and Charles H. Foster's *The Rungless Ladder: Harriet Beecher Stowe and New England Puritanism* (1954, 1970). A good family biography is Milton Rugoff's *The Beechers: An American Family* (1981), which should be supplemented by Barbara A. White's *The Beecher Sisters* (2003). See also Susan Belasco's *Stowe in Her Own Time: A Biographical Chronicle of Her Life, Drawn from Recollections, Interviews, and Memoirs* (2009). Thomas R. Gossett's *"Uncle Tom's Cabin" and American Culture* (1985) is invaluable; see also Sarah Meer's *Uncle Tom Mania: Slavery, Minstrelsy, and Transatlantic Culture in the 1850s* (2005). Useful collections of critical essays include Elizabeth Ammons's *Critical Essays on Harriet Beecher Stowe* (1980); Eric Sundquist's *New Essays on "Uncle Tom's Cabin"* (1986); Mason I. Lowance Jr., Ellen E. Wesbrook, and R. C. De Prospo's *The Stowe Debate: Rhetorical Strategies in "Uncle Tom's Cabin"* (1994); Cindy Weinstein's *The Cambridge Companion to Harriet Beecher Stowe* (2004); and Ammons's *Harriet Beecher Stowe's Uncle Tom's Cabin: A Casebook* (2007).

Specialized critical studies dealing wholly or in part with Stowe include Edwin Bruce Kirkham's *The Building of "Uncle Tom's Cabin"* (1977), Gillian Brown's *Domestic Individualism: Imagining Self in Nineteenth-Century America* (1992), Marianne Noble's *The Masochistic Pleasures of Sentimental Literature* (2000), and Susan M. Ryan's *The Grammar of Good Intentions: Race and the Antebellum Culture of Benevolence* (2003). Stephen Railton has developed a superb website, *Uncle Tom's Cabin and American Culture* <iath.virginia.edu/utc/>.

Henry David Thoreau

The Princeton Edition of Thoreau's writings (1971–) is standard. Of the volumes published so far, *Walden* (1971), edited by J. Lyndon Shanley, should be supplemented by Shanley's *The Making of "Walden"* (1957, 1966) and Jeffrey S. Cramer's *Walden: A Fully Annotated Edition* (2004). See also the Norton Critical Edition edited by William Rossi (3rd edition 2008). The Princeton Edition of Thoreau's writings includes the journals (1981–); for an excellent selection, see *I to Myself: An Annotated Selection from the Journal of Henry D. Thoreau* (2007), edited by Cramer. The bulk of Thoreau's letters can be found in Carl Bode and Walter Harding's *Correspondence of Henry David Thoreau* (1958), supplemented by Kenneth W. Cameron's *Companion to Thoreau's Correspondence* (1964). The Library of America has made available *Collected Essays and Poems* (2001), edited by Elizabeth Hall Witherell. Raymond R. Borst compiled *The Thoreau Log: A Documentary Life of Henry David Thoreau, 1817–1862* (1992); see also Richard Schneider's *Henry David Thoreau: A Documentary Volume* (2004). The most reliable narrative biography is still Walter Harding's *The Days of Henry Thoreau: A Biography* (1965); for an excellent intellectual biography, see Robert D. Richardson's *Henry Thoreau: A Life of the Mind* (1986).

Walter Harding's *Thoreau Handbook* (1959) was revised by Harding and Michael Meyer (1980). Essential is Robert Sattelmeyer's *Thoreau's Reading: A Study in Intellectual History with Bibliographical Catalogue* (1988). Gary Scharnhorst compiled *Henry David Thoreau: An Annotated Bibliography of Comment and Criticism before 1900* (1992). Thoreau's reputation is surveyed in Michael Meyer's *Several More Lives to Live: Thoreau's Political Reputation in America* (1977), Joel Myerson's *Emerson and Thoreau: The Contemporary Reviews* (1992), and Scharnhorst's *Henry David Thoreau: A Case Study in Canonization* (1993). Good collections of critical essays include Myerson's *The Cambridge Companion to Henry David Thoreau* (1995), William E. Cain's *A Historical Guide to Henry David Thoreau* (2000), Sandra Harbert Petrulionis and Laura Dassow Walls's *More Day to Dawn: Thoreau's "Walden" for the Twenty-first Century* (2007), Jack Turner's *A Political Companion to Henry David Thoreau* (2009), and John T. Lysaker and William Rossi's *Emerson and Thoreau: Figures of Friendship* (2010). Three critical books related by their interest in Thoreau's compositional process and literary professionalism are Stephen Adams and Donald Ross Jr.'s *Revising Mythologies: The Composition of Thoreau's Major Works* (1988), Steven Fink's *Prophet in the Marketplace: Thoreau's Development as a Professional Writer* (1992), and Robert Milder's *Reimagining Thoreau* (1995). Lawrence Buell's *The Environmental Imagination* (1995), which has a major section on Thoreau, is a classic in a new field of study; see also Robert F. Sayre's *Thoreau and the American Indians* (1977) and Walls's *Seeing New Worlds: Henry David Thoreau and Nineteenth-Century Natural Science* (1995). Recent critical work includes Alan D. Hodder's *Thoreau's Ecstatic Witness* (2001), Joel Porte's *Consciousness and Culture: Emerson and Thoreau Reviewed* (2004), David M. Robinson's *Natural Life: Thoreau's Worldly Transcendentalism* (2004), and Sharon Mariotti's *Thoreau's Democratic Withdrawal: Alienation, Participation, and Modernity* (2010). For an illuminating new perspective on Walden Pond, see Elise Virginia Lemire's *Black Walden: Slavery and Its Aftermath in Concord, Massachusetts* (2009).

Walt Whitman

The study of Whitman has been revolutionized by the *Walt Whitman Hypertext Archive* <whitman.archive.org>, directed by Kenneth M. Price and Ed Folsom. Before going to the printed sources listed below, students should explore this huge and superbly organized archive, which includes a lengthy and reliable biographical essay by Folsom and Price, all the known contemporary reviews, all the known photographs, the various editions of *Leaves of Grass* and other of Whitman's writings, and a current bibliography of scholarship and criticism.

The Collected Writings of Walt Whitman was under the general editorship of Gay Wilson Allen; part of this edition is *Walt Whitman: The Correspondence* (1961–69), a six-volume set with two supplements (1990–91), edited by Edwin H. Miller. Essential, in three volumes, is *"Leaves of Grass": A Textual Variorum of the Printed Poems* (1980), edited by Sculley Bradley, Harold W. Blodgett, Arthur Golden, and William White; see also Michael Moon's Norton Critical Edition of *Leaves of Grass* (2002). Important documents can be found in *Notebooks and Unpublished Prose Manuscripts* (1984), edited by Edward F. Grier in six volumes. The first volume of Whitman's *Journalism*, edited by Herbert Bergman, Douglas A. Noverr, and Edward J. Recchia, appeared in 1998. For Whitman's temperance novel, *Franklin Evans, or The Inebriate: A Tale of the Times* (1842), see Christopher Castiglia and

Glenn Hendler's informative edition (2007); and Ed Folsom has edited a new facsimile edition (2010) of Whitman's 1870 *Democratic Vistas*. Valuable editions of documentary materials include Joel Myerson's *Whitman in His Own Time: A Biographical Chronicle of His Life, Drawn from Recollections, Memoirs, and Interviews, Friends and Associates* (1991, rev. 2000), and Myerson's *Walt Whitman: A Documentary Volume* (2000). The last of nine volumes of Horace Traubel's *With Walt Whitman in Camden*, edited by Jeanne Chapman and Robert Macisaac, appeared in 1996; an excellent starting place is Gary Schmidgall's *Intimate with Walt: Selections from Whitman's Conversations with Horace Traubel, 1888–1892* (2001).

The standard biography is still Gay Wilson Allen's *The Solitary Singer* (1967). It should be supplemented by Justin Kaplan's *Walt Whitman: A Life* (1980), David S. Reynolds's *Walt Whitman's America: A Cultural Biography* (1995), Gary Schmidgall's *Walt Whitman: A Gay Life* (1998), Jerome Loving's *Walt Whitman: The Song of Himself* (1999), and Ed Folsom and Kenneth M. Price's *Re-scripting Walt Whitman: An Introduction to His Life and Work* (2005). On the Civil War period, see Roy Morris Jr.'s *The Better Angel: Walt Whitman in the Civil War* (2000), and Ted Genoways's *Walt Whitman and the Civil War* (2009); and for a good biographical and critical overview, see M. Jimmie Killingsworth's *The Cambridge Introduction to Walt Whitman* (2007).

On Whitman's critical reception, see Graham Clarke's four-volume *Walt Whitman: Critical Assessments* (1996) and Kenneth M. Price's *Walt Whitman: The Contemporary Reviews* (1996). Valuable collections of critical essays include Robert K. Martin's *The Continuing Presence of Walt Whitman: The Life after the Life* (1992); Gay Wilson Allen and Ed Folsom's *Walt Whitman and the World* (1995); Ezra Greenspan's *The Cambridge Companion to Walt Whitman* (1995); Betsy Erkkila and Jay Grossman's *Breaking Bounds: Whitman and American Cultural Studies* (1996); David S. Reynolds's *A Historical Guide to Walt Whitman* (2000); Donald D. Kummings's *A Companion to Walt Whitman* (2006); Susan Belasco, Ed Folsom, and Kenneth M. Price's *Leaves of Grass: The Sesquicentennial Essays* (2007); and David Haven Blake and Michael Robertson's *Walt Whitman: Where the Future Becomes Present* (2008). Important critical work includes Betsy Erkkila's *Whitman the Political Poet* (1989), Kenneth M. Price's *Whitman and Tradition* (1990), Michael Moon's *Disseminating Whitman: Revision and Corporeality in "Leaves of Grass"* (1991), Ezra Greenspan's *Walt Whitman and the American Reader* (1991), Ed Folsom's *Walt Whitman's Native Representations* (1994), Martin Klammer's *Whitman, Slavery, and the Emergence of "Leaves of Grass"*

(1995), Vivian R. Pollack's *The Erotic Whitman* (2000), Jay Grossman's *Reconstituting the American Renaissance: Emerson, Whitman, and the Poetics of Representation* (2003), M. Wynn Thomas's *Transatlantic Connections: Whitman U.S., Whitman U.K.* (2005), David Haven Blake's *Walt Whitman and the Culture of American Celebrity* (2006), Michael Robertson's *Worshipping Whitman: The Whitman Disciples* (2008), and Edward Whitley's *American Bards: Walt Whitman and Other Unlikely Candidates for National Poet* (2010). Kenneth M. Price's *To Walt Whitman, America* (2004) traces Whitman's continuing impact on U.S. literary culture.

John Greenleaf Whittier
Brenda Wineapple has edited a recent collection of Whittier's *Selected Poems* (2004), but see also Robert Penn Warren's *John Greenleaf Whittier's Poetry: An Appraisal and a Selection* (1971). An interesting collection of Whittier's nonfiction is Edwin Harrison Cady and Harry Hayden Clark's *Whittier on Writers and Writing: The Uncollected Critical Writings* (1971). Samuel T. Pickard's *Life and Letters of John Greenleaf Whittier* (1894) was superseded by *John Greenleaf Whittier: Friend of Man* (1949), John B. Pickard's *John Greenleaf Whittier: An Introduction and Interpretation* (1961), Pickard's three-volume *Letters of John Greenleaf Whittier* (1975), and Roland H. Woodwell's *John Greenleaf Whittier: A Biography* (1985). For a bibliographical guide, see Albert J. von Frank's *Whittier: A Comprehensive Annotated Bibliography* (1976). Pickard edited a collection of criticism, *Memorabilia of John Greenleaf Whittier* (1968), but even more useful is Jayne K. Kribbs's *Critical Essays on John Greenleaf Whittier* (1980).

AMERICAN LITERATURE 1865–1914

Reference Works

Many useful sources are now online, including the *International MLA Bibliography*; "A Brief Timeline of American Literature and Events, 1620–1920" <www.wsu.edu/~campbelld/amlit/>; and "PAL: Perspectives in American Literature—A Research and Reference Guide" <www.csustan.edu/english/reuben/pal/table.html>. Author biographies are available in the *Dictionary of Literary Biography*, the *American National Biography*, and Jay Parini's *American Writers: A Collection of Literary Biographies* (2003). General resources for the period include *Encyclopedia of American Cultural and Intellectual History*, edited by Mary Kupiec Cayton and Peter W. Williams (2001); *A Companion to American Fiction, 1865–1914*, edited by Robert Paul Lamb and G. R. Thompson (2005); *A Companion to the Regional Literatures of America*, edited by Charles L. Crow (2003); Denise D. Knight and Emmanuel S. Nelson's *Nineteenth-Century American Women Writers: A Bio-Bibliographical Critical Sourcebook* (1997); Sharon M. Harris's *American Women Prose Writers, 1870–1920* (2000), which includes biographical information; Trudier Harris and Thadious M. Davis's *Afro-American Writers before the Harlem Renaissance* (1986); *African American Writers*, 2nd edition, edited by Valerie Smith (2001); Xiaohuang Yin's *Chinese American Literature since the 1850s* (2006), which traces representations of Chinese American identity, especially in tales of interracial marriage in the fiction of Sui Sin Far and others; A. LaVonne Brown Ruoff's *American Indian Literatures: An Introduction, Bibliographic Review, and Selected Bibliography* (1990); Andrew Wiget's *Handbook of Native American Literature* (1996); *Native American Writers of the United States* (1997), edited by Kenneth Roemer; and *Hispanic Literature of the United States: A Comprehensive Reference*, edited by Nicolás Kannelos (2003). Still useful is the *Oxford Companion to American Literature*, edited by James D. Hart and Phillip Leiniger (1995). Richard M. Ludwig and Clifford Nault, Jr.'s *Annals of American Literature, 1602–1983* (1989) is a good source for locating major works in their cultural contexts. The annual *American Literary Scholarship* (also online) provides critical commentary on a wide range of scholarly books and articles; for guidance to recent books on American literature in this period, see the chapters on "Themes, Topics, Criticism" and "Nineteenth-Century Literature."

Literary Histories

The ongoing, eight-volume *Cambridge History of American Literature* (Sacvan Bercovitch, general editor) addresses literary genres and periods. A useful introduction to the novel of this period is David Minter's *A Cultural History of the American Novel: Henry James to William Faulkner* (1996); see also the relevant chapters in Gregg Crane's *The Cambridge Introduction to the Nineteenth-Century American Novel* (2007). American poetry is covered in Alan Shucard, Fred Moramarco, and William Sullivan's *Modern American Poetry, 1865–1950* (1989), and Robert Shulman's *Social Criticism and Nineteenth-Century American Poetry, 1865–1950* (1989). A provocative one-volume reference work is *A New Literary History of America* (2009), edited by Greil Marcus and Werner Sollors (2009). Important studies of American literary history and culture during the 1865–1914 period include Nancy Bentley's *Frantic Panoramas: American Literature and Mass Culture, 1870–1920* (2009), Susan L. Mizruchi's *The Rise of Multicultural America* (2008), Russ Castronovo's *Beautiful Democracy: Aesthetics and Anarchy in a Global Era* (2007), Molly Crumpton Winter's *American Narratives: Multiethnic Writing in the Age of Realism* (2007), James C. Davis's *Commerce in Color: Race, Consumer Culture, and American Literature 1893–1933* (2007), Claudia Stokes's *Writers in Retrospect: The Rise of American Literary History* (2006), Caroline F. Levander's *Cradle of Liberty: Race, the Child, and National Belonging from Thomas Jefferson to W. E. B. Du Bois* (2006), Loren Glass's *Authors, Inc.: Literary Celebrity in the Modern United States, 1880–1980* (2004), Robert Dale Parker's *The Invention of Native American Literature* (2003), Gregg D. Crane's *Race, Citizenship, and Law in American Literature* (2002), Glenn Hendler's *Public Sentiments: Structures of Feeling in Nineteenth-Century America* (2001), John Carlos Rowe's *Literary Culture and U.S. Imperialism: From the Revolution to World War II* (2000), Orm Överland's *Immigrant Minds, American Identities: Making the United States Home, 1870–1930* (2000), Gavin Jones's *Strange Talk: The Politics of Dialect Literature in Gilded Age America* (1999), Richard Slotkin's *The Fatal Environment: The Myth of the Frontier in the Age of Industrialization, 1800–1890* (1985), and Alan Trachtenberg's *The Incorporation of America: Culture and Society in the Gilded Age* (1982).

Studies of American women writers include Dale M. Bauer's *Sex Expression and American Women Writers, 1860–1940* (2009); *Before They Could Vote: American Women's Autobiographical Writing, 1819–1919*, edited by Sidonie A. Smith and Julia Watson (2006); Susan S. Williams's *Reclaiming Authorship: Literary Women in America, 1850–1900* (2006); Martha H. Patterson's *Beyond the Gibson Girl: Reimagining the American New Woman,*

1895–1915 (2005); Suzanne Bost's *Mulattas and Mestizas: Representing Mixed Identities in the Americas, 1850–2000* (2003); *The Cambridge Companion to Nineteenth-Century American Women's Writing* (2001), edited by Dale M. Bauer and Philip Gould; Elsa Nettels's *Language and Gender in American Fiction: Howells, James, Wharton, and Cather* (1997); and Elizabeth Ammons's *Conflicting Stories: American Women Writers at the Turn into the Twentieth Century* (1992). Hazel V. Carby's *Reconstructing Womanhood: The Emergence of the Afro-American Woman Novelist* (1988) discusses Pauline Hopkins and Ida B. Wells-Barnett. For African American writers see also Gene Andrew Jarrett's *Deans and Truants: Race and Realism in African American Literature* (2007); Jennifer C. James's *A Freedom Bought with Blood: African American War Literature from the Civil War to World War II* (2007); *Post-Bellum, Pre-Harlem: African American Literature and Culture, 1877–1919* (2006), edited by Barbara McCaskill and Caroline Gebhard; Eric J. Sundquist's *To Wake the Nations: Race in the Making of American Literature* (1993); Toni Morrison's *Playing in the Dark: Whiteness and the Literary Imagination* (1992); Dickson D. Bruce, Jr.'s *Black American Writing from the Nadir: The Evolution of a Literary Tradition, 1877–1915*; Bernard W. Bell's *The Afro-American Novel and Its Tradition* (1987); and Wilson J. Moses's *The Golden Age of Black Nationalism, 1850–1925* (1978, reprinted 1988).

Realism and naturalism are discussed in *The Cambridge Companion to American Realism and Naturalism: Howells to London*, edited by Donald Pizer (1995); see also Pizer's *American Naturalism and the Jews: Garland, Norris, Dreiser, Wharton, and Cather* (2008) and *Realism and Naturalism in Nineteenth-Century American Literature* (1984), along with his edited collection *Documents of American Realism and Naturalism* (1998). Other important work on realism and naturalism includes Jane F. Thrailkill's *Affecting Fictions: Mind, Body, and Emotion in American Literary Realism* (2007), Jennifer L. Fleissner's *Women, Compulsion, Modernity: The Moment of American Naturalism* (2004), Henry Wonham's *Playing the Races: Ethnic Caricature and American Literary Realism* (2004), Bert Bender's *Evolution and "the Sex Problem": American Narratives during the Eclipse of Darwinism* (2004), Michael A. Elliott's *The Culture Concept: Writing and Difference in the Age of Realism* (2002), Barbara Hochman's *Getting at the Author: Reimagining Books and Reading in the Age of American Realism* (2001), Phillip Barrish's *American Literary Realism, Critical Theory, and Intellectual Prestige, 1880–1990* (2001), Brook Thomas's *American Literary Realism and the Failed Promise of Contract* (1997), David E. Shi's *Facing Facts: Realism in American Thought and Culture, 1850–1920* (1995), Tom Quirk and Gary Scharnhorst's edited *American Realism and the Canon* (1994), Kenneth Warren's *Black and White Strangers: Race and American Literary Realism* (1993), Michael Davitt Bell's *The Problem of American Realism: Studies in the Cultural History of a Literary Idea* (1993), Amy Kaplan's *The Social Construction of American Realism* (1988), Walter Benn Michaels's *The Gold Standard and the Logic of Naturalism* (1987), June Howard's *Form and History in American Literary Naturalism* (1985), and Warner Berthoff's classic *The Ferment of Realism* (1965).

On regionalism see Philip Joseph's *American Literary Regionalism* (2007); *American Literary Geographies: Spatial Practice and Cultural Production, 1500–1900*, edited by Martin Brückner and Hsuan L. Hsu (2007); Judith Fetterley and Marjorie Pryse's *Writing Out of Place: Regionalism, Women, and*

American Literary Culture (2003); Donna M. Campbell's *Resisting Regionalism: Gender and Naturalism in American Fiction, 1885–1915* (1998); *Breaking Boundaries: New Perspectives on Women's Regional Writing* (1997), edited by Sherrie A. Inness and Diana Royer; and Josephine Donovan's *New England Local Color Literature: A Women's Tradition* (1983). On Western writing in particular, see Nina Baym's *Women Writers of the American West, 1833–1927* (2011), Nathaniel Lewis's *Unsettling the Literary West: Authenticity and Authorship* (2003), Noreen Groover Lape's *West of the Border: The Multicultural Literature of the Western American Frontiers* (2000), Bonney MacDonald's *Updating the Literary West* (1997), and Glen A. Love's *New Americans: The Westerner and the Modern Experience in the American Novel* (1982).

Ambrose Bierce

The fullest edition of Bierce's writings is *Collected Works of Ambrose Bierce* (1909–12), edited by Walter Neale. *The Short Fiction of Ambrose Bierce, 3 Volumes: A Comprehensive Edition* (2006), edited by S. T. Joshi, Lawrence I. Berkove, and David E. Schultz, brings together all of Bierce's known short fiction with helpful introductions, extensive annotations, textual variants, and a section of Bierce's prefaces to his published short fiction. Joshi and Schultz also edited *The Fall of the Republic and Other Political Satires* (2000), *The Unabridged Devil's Dictionary* (2000), and *A Much Misunderstood Man: Selected Letters of Ambrose Bierce* (2003). *Phantoms of a Blood-Stained Period: The Complete Civil War Writings of Ambrose Bierce*, is edited by Russell Duncan and David J. Klooster (2002); Robert C. Evans edited *"An Occurrence at Owl Creek Bridge": An Annotated Critical Edition* (2003). Bierce's poetry is collected in *Poems of Ambrose Bierce*, edited by M. E. Grenander (1996). The largest collection of Bierce's letters is available in Bertha C. Pope's edition of *The Letters of Ambrose Bierce* (1921).

Robert L. Gale surveys Bierce's life and work in *An Ambrose Bierce Companion* (2001). S. T. Joshi and David E. Schultz edited *Ambrose Bierce: An Annotated Bibliography of Primary Sources* (1999). Prior to Lawrence I. Berkove's fine critical biography, *A Prescription for Adversity: The Moral Art of Ambrose Bierce* (2002), the standard critical biography had been Paul Fatout's still useful *Ambrose Bierce, the Devil's Lexicographer* (1951). Also useful is Joshi and Schultz's *A Sole Survivor: Bits of Autobiography* (1999). On Bierce and the Civil War, see Roy Morris, Jr.'s *Ambrose Bierce: Alone in Bad Company* (1996), Brian Thomenson's *Shadows of Blue & Gray: The Civil War Writings of Ambrose Bierce* (2003), Donald T. Blume's *Ambrose Bierce's Civilians and Soldiers in Context: A Critical Study* (2004), and David M. Owens's *The Devil's Topographer: Ambrose Bierce and the American War Story* (2006). Cathy N. Davidson's *The Experimental Fictions of Ambrose Bierce: Structuring the Ineffable* (1984) remains an important work; Davidson also edited *Critical Essays on Ambrose Bierce* (1982).

Abraham Cahan

There is no collected edition of Cahan's many writings in English, Russian, and Yiddish. Isaac Metzker edited *A Bintel Brief: Sixty Years of Letters from the Lower East Side to the Jewish Daily Forward* (1971). Moses Rischin's *Grandma Never Lived in America: The New Journalism of Abraham Cahan* (1985) features an extensive and informative introduction. Cahan's *"The Imported Bridegroom" and Other Stories of the New York Ghetto* (1898) was reprinted with an introduction by Bernard G. Richards in 1970. The *Rise of David Levinsky: A Novel* (1917) was reprinted with a superb introduction and notes by Jules Chametzky (1993). More recently, Cahan is represented in Stanford Sternlicht's 2007 reference book, *Masterpieces of Jewish American Literature*. No full-scale biography of Cahan has been published, but there are accounts of his life in Irving Howe's *World of Our Fathers* (1976), Ronald Sanders's *The Downtown Jews: Portraits of an Immigrant Generation* (1969), and John Higham's still valuable *Strangers in the Land: Patterns of American Nativism, 1860–1925* (1955). Sanford Marovitz's *Abraham Cahan* (1996) is the best introduction to Cahan's life and work; Jules Chametsky's *From the Ghetto: The Fiction of Abraham Cahan* (1977) is the best critical study. David Fine's chapter on Cahan in *The City of the Immigrant and American Fiction, 1880–1920* (1977) provides a good overview. Louis Harap's *Creative Awakening: The Jewish Presence in Twentieth Century American Literature: 1900–1940s* (1987) is worth consulting, as is Allen Guttman's *The Jewish Writer in America: Assimilation and the Crisis of Identity* (1971) and Hana Wirth-Nesher's *Call it English: The Languages of Jewish American Literature* (2006).

Charles W. Chesnutt

Werner Sollors edited the Library of America's *Charles W. Chesnutt: Stories, Novels and Essays* (2002). *Charles W. Chesnutt: Essays and*

Speeches, edited by Joseph R. McElrath, Jr., Robert C. Leitz III, and Jesse S. Crisler (1999), presents all of Chesnutt's known nonfiction. McElrath, Leitz, and Crisler have also edited *An Exemplary Citizen: Letters of Charles W. Chesnutt, 1906–1932* (2002). Sylvia L. Render edited *The Short Fiction of Charles W. Chesnutt* (1974); Richard H. Brodhead edited *The Journals of Charles W. Chesnutt* (1993), as well as *The Conjure Woman and Other Conjure Tales* (1993); and William L. Andrews edited *The Collected Stories of Charles W. Chesnutt* (1992). In 2002 *The Marrow of Tradition* was issued as a Bedford Cultural Edition, edited by Nancy Bentley and Sandra Gunning. *The Portable Charles W. Chesnutt,* edited by Andrews and Henry Louis Gates, Jr., appeared in 2008.

Chesnutt's daughter, Helen M. Chesnutt, published the first full-length biography, *Charles Waddell Chesnutt: Pioneer of the Color Line* (1952). William L. Andrews's *The Literary Career of Charles W. Chesnutt* (1980) is a useful critical biography. Marjorie Pryse and Hortense J. Spillers's *Conjuring: Black Women, Fiction, and Literary Tradition* (1985) and Jane Campbell's *Mythic Black Fiction: The Transformation of History* (1986) contain useful contextual material on Chesnutt. A more specialized study is Ernestine Williams Pickens's *Charles W. Chesnutt and the Progressive Movement* (1994). Eric J. Sundquist's *To Wake the Nations* (1993) treats Chesnutt at length. Other valuable critical studies include Robert B. Stepto's *Charles Chesnutt: The Uncle Julius Stories* (1984), Henry Wonham's *Charles W. Chesnutt: A Study of the Short Fiction* (1998), Charles Duncan's *The Absent Man: The Narrative Craft of Charles W. Chesnutt* (1998), Dean McWilliams's *Charles W. Chesnutt and the Fictions of Race* (2002), Matthew Wilson's *Whiteness in the Novels of Charles W. Chesnutt* (2004), Ryan Simmons's *Chesnutt and Realism: A Study of the Novels* (2006), and David Murray's *Matter, Magic, and Spirit: Representing Indian and African American Belief* (2007). Two edited essay collections provide especially good introductions to Chesnutt criticism: Joseph R. McElrath's *Critical Essays on Charles W. Chesnutt* (1999), and David Garrett Izzo and Maria Orban's *Charles Chesnutt Reappraised: Essays on the First Major African American Fiction Writer* (2009).

Kate Chopin

Per Seyersted edited *The Complete Works of Kate Chopin* (1969) in two volumes; he also published *Kate Chopin: A Critical Biography* (1969). Emily Toth's *Unveiling Kate Chopin* (1999), which incorporates material from Chopin's later discovered diaries and manuscripts, is now the standard biography. Barbara C. Ewell's *Kate Chopin* (1986) and *Kate Chopin: A Literary Life* by Nancy Walker (2001) are good introductions to the life and work. Important new essay collections are *The Cambridge Companion to Kate Chopin* (2008), edited by Janet Beer; *Kate Chopin in the Twenty-First Century: New Critical Essays* (2008), edited by Heather Ostman; and *Awakenings: The Story of the Kate Chopin Revival* (2009), edited by Bernard Koloski. Robert C. Evans's *Kate Chopin's Short Fiction: A Critical Companion* (2001) is also useful.

Nancy A. Walker edited *Kate Chopin: The Awakening, Complete Authoritative Text with Biographical and Historical Contexts* (1993); Margo Culley edited the second edition of the Norton Critical Edition of *The Awakening* (1994). Susan Disheroon Green, David Caudle, and Emily Toth compiled *Kate Chopin: An Annotated Bibliography of Critical Works* (1999). Seyersted and Toth edited *A Kate Chopin Miscellany* (1980), a collection of unpublished short fiction, poems, and letters. Bernard J. Kosloski brought out an edition of Chopin's two most important collections of short stories, *"Bayou Folk" and "A Night in Acadie"* (1999).

Critical studies of Chopin's writings include Wendy Martin's edited collection *New Essays on The Awakening* (1988); Lynda S. Boren and Sara deSaussure's edited collection *Kate Chopin Reconsidered: Beyond the Bayou* (1992); Joyce Dyer's *The Awakening: A Novel of Beginnings* (1993); Bernard J. Kosloski's *Kate Chopin: A Study of the Short Fiction* (1996); and Janet Beer's comparative *Kate Chopin, Edith Wharton and Charlotte Perkins Gilman: Studies in Short Fiction* (2005).

Samuel L. Clemens
See Mark Twain.

Stephen Crane

Fredson Bowers is the textual editor of *The Works of Stephen Crane* (1969–76); J. C. Levenson edited The Library of America volume, *Crane: Prose and Poetry* (1996). The fourth edition of the Norton Critical Edition of *The Red Badge of Courage,* edited by Eric Carl Link and Donald Pizer, was published in 2007. R. W. Stallman and Lillian Gilkes's *Stephen Crane: Letters* (1960) was followed and to some extent superseded by *The Correspondence of Stephen Crane* (1988), edited by Stanley Wertheim and Sorrentino. Joseph Katz edited both *The Portable Stephen Crane* (1969) and *The Poems of Stephen Crane: A Critical Edition* (1966). Patrick K. Dooley compiled *Stephen Crane: An Annotated Bibliography of Secondary Scholarship* (1992), a research tool now annually updated by Dooley in *Stephen Crane Studies.* Useful biographical resources include Linda H. Davis's *Badge of Courage: The Life of*

Stephen Crane (1998); *The Crane Log: A Documentary Life of Stephen Crane, 1871–1900* (1994), edited by Wertheim and Sorrentino; Christopher Benfey's *The Double Life of Stephen Crane: A Biography* (1992); and *Stephen Crane: A Critical Biography* (1950), by the poet John Berryman. Sorrentino's *Stephen Crane Remembered* (2006) collects writings by Crane's friends, colleagues, and contemporaries. Wertheim edited the comprehensive *A Stephen Crane Encyclopedia* (1997).

Edwin H. Cady's *Stephen Crane* (1980) provides a good critical introduction to Crane's life and work. Other studies of interest include James Nagel's *Stephen Crane and Literary Impressionism* (1980), Chester L. Wolford's *The Anger of Stephen Crane: Fiction and the Epic Tradition* (1983), David Halliburton's *The Color of the Sky: A Study of Stephen Crane* (1991), Patrick K. Dooley's *The Pluralistic Philosophy of Stephen Crane* (1993), Michael Robertson's *Stephen Crane, Journalism, and the Making of Modern American Literature* (1997), Bill Brown's *The Material Unconscious: American Amusement, Stephen Crane and the Economics of Play* (1997), George E. Monteiro's *Stephen Crane's Blue Badge of Courage* (2000), Keith Gandal's *Class Representation in Modern Fiction and Film* (2007), and John Fagg's *On the Cusp: Stephen Crane, George Bellow, and Modernism* (2009). Donald Pizer edited and introduced *Critical Essays on Stephen Crane's The Red Badge of Courage* (1990). Claudia Durst Johnson edited *Understanding the Red Badge of Courage* (1998).

Theodore Dreiser
There is no complete edition of Dreiser's writings, although one is in progress from the University of Pennsylvania Press, edited by James L. W. West III and Neda Westlake. Among the books published in the series are *Sister Carrie*, edited by John C. Berkey and Alice M. Winters (1981); *American Diaries: 1902–1926*, edited by Thomas P. Riggio (1983); and a restored edition of *Jennie Gerhardt*, edited by West (1992). Important resources include Robert H. Elias's three-volume *Letters of Theodore Dreiser* (1959); Donald Pizer's *Theodore Dreiser: A Selection of Uncollected Prose* (1977); *Theodore Dreiser: Interviews*, edited by Frderick E. Rusch, Pizer, and Riggio (2004); the Norton Critical Edition of *Sister Carrie*, edited by Pizer (2006); Pizer's *A Picture and a Criticism of Life: New Letters* (2008); and Riggio's *Letters to Women: New Letters* (2009). The standard biographies are Jerome Loving's *The Last Titan: A Life of Theodore Dreiser* (2005) and Richard Lingeman's two-volume *Theodore Dreiser: At the Gates of the City, 1891–1907* (1986) and *Theodore Dreiser: An American Journey, 1908–1945* (1990).

Useful critical books include Richard Lehan, *Theodore Dreiser: His World and His Novels* (1974); Donald Pizer, *The Novels of Theodore Dreiser* (1976); Philip Gerber, *Theodore Dreiser Revisited* (1992); Louis J. Zanine, *Mechanism and Mysticism: The Influence of Science on the Thought and Work of Theodore Dreiser* (1993); Clare Virginia Eby, *Dreiser and Veblen: Saboteurs of the Status Quo* (1999); Pizer, *Literary Masters: Theodore Dreiser* (2000); and Mary Hricko, *The Genesis of the Chicago Renaissance: Theodore Dreiser, Langston Hughes, Richard Wright, and James T. Farrell* (2009). See also Miriam Gogol's edited collection *Theodore Dreiser: Beyond Naturalism* (1995), Yoshinobo Hakutani's edited *Theodore Dreiser and American Culture: New Readings* (2000), and Leonard Cassuto and Clare Eby's *The Cambridge Companion to Theodore Dreiser* (2004).

W. E. B. Du Bois
Herbert Aptheker's *The Complete Published Works of W. E. B. Du Bois* (1973–1986), in thirty-six volumes, offers a comprehensive collection of Du Bois's writings. Useful shorter collections include Philip S. Foner's *W. E. B. Du Bois Speaks: Speeches and Addresses* (1970); Eric Sundquist's *The Oxford W. E. B. Du Bois Reader* (1995); and the Library of America volume, *Du Bois: Writings*, edited by Nathan Huggins (1996). Herbert Aptheker edited the three-volume *The Correspondence of W. E. B. Du Bois* (1973–1978), the four-volume *Writings by W. E. B. Du Bois in Periodicals Edited by Others* (1982), *Selections from Phylon* (1980), and the two-volume *Selections from the Crisis* (1972). Other good collections are Phil Zuckerman's *The Social Theory of W. E. B. Du Bois* (2004), Amy Helene Kirschke's *Art in Crisis: W. E. B. Du Bois and the Art of the Crisis Magazine* (2006), and Robert Wortham's *W. E. B. Du Bois and the Sociological Imagination: A Reader, 1897–1914* (2009). Important biographies of Du Bois include Arnold Rampersad's *The Art and Imagination of W. E. B. Du Bois* (1976); Jack B. Moore's *W. E. B. Du Bois* (1981); and David Levering Lewis's now standard two-volume *W. E. B. Du Bois: Biography of a Race, 1868–1919* (1993) and *W. E. B. Du Bois: The Fight for Equality and the American Century, 1919–1963* (2000).

The centennial publication of *The Souls of Black Folk* is addressed in Dolan Hubbard's edited collection, *The Souls of Black Folk: One Hundred Years Later* (2003), and in Chester Fontenot and Mary Alice Morgan's edited *W. E. B. Du Bois and Race: Essays Celebrating the Centennial Publication of The Souls of Black Folk* (2001). Critical studies of Du Bois's politics and art include Manning Marable's

W. E. B. Du Bois: Black Radical Democrat (1986), Eric J. Sundquist's *To Wake the Nations: Race in the Making of American Literature* (1993), Keith E. Byerman's *Seizing the World: History, Art, and Self in the Work of W. E. B. Du Bois* (1994), Adolph L. Reed, Jr.'s *W. E. B. Du Bois and American Political Thought* (1995), Shannon Zamir's *W. E. B. Du Bois and American Thought, 1888–1903* (1995), Shawn Michelle Smith's *Photography on the Color Line: W. E. B. Du Bois, Race, and Visual Culture* (2004), Derek Alridge's *The Educational Thought of W. E. B. Du Bois: An Intellectual History* (2008), and Jonathon S. Kahn's *Divine Discontent: The Religious Imagination of W. E. B. Du Bois* (2009). Edited collections of essays are good starting points; see William L. Andrews's *Critical Essays on W. E. B. Du Bois* (1985), Gerald Horne and Mary Young's *W. E. B. Du Bois: An Encyclopedia* (2001), Mary Keller and Chester J. Fontenot's *Re-Cognizing W. E. B. Du Bois in the 21st Century: Essays on W. E. B. Du Bois* (2007), Susan Gillman and Alys Eve Weinbaum's *Next to the Color Line: Gender, Sexuality, and W. E. B. Du Bois* (2007), and Shamoon Zamir's *The Cambridge Companion to W. E. B. Du Bois* (2008).

Paul Laurence Dunbar
Important editions include *The Collected Poetry of Paul Laurence Dunbar* (1993), edited by Joanne M. Braxton, and *The Complete Stories of Paul Laurence Dunbar* (2006), edited by Gene Andrew Jarrett. Also useful is a 1999 reprint of *The Life and Works of Paul Laurence Dunbar: Containing His Complete Poetical Works, His Best Short Stories, Numerous Anecdotes, and a Complete Biography*, originally compiled and introduced by William Dean Howells in 1907. (Jarrett's *Deans and Truants: Race and Realism in African American Literature* [2007] has an excellent chapter on Dunbar and Howells.) Other useful editions include *In His Own Voice: The Dramatic and Other Uncollected Works of Paul Laurence Dunbar* (2002), edited by Herbert Woodward Martin and Ronald Primeau, with a foreword by Henry Louis Gates, Jr., and *The Collected Novels of Paul Laurence Dunbar* (2009), edited by Herbert Woodward Martin, Ronald Primeau, and Gene Andrew Jarrett. For a good biography, see Felton O. Best's *Crossing the Color Line: A Biography of Paul Laurence Dunbar, 1872–1906* (1996). Illuminating discussions of Dunbar's writings can be found in Peter Revell's *Paul Laurence Dunbar* (1979), Gayle Jones's *Liberating Voices* (1991), Keith D. Leonard's *Fettered Genius: The African American Bardic Poet from Slavery to Civil Rights* (2006), and Jennifer C. James's *Freedom Bought with Blood* (2007). A special issue of *African American Review* (summer 2007) marked the centenary

of Dunbar's death with a collection of excellent, up-to-date essays on Dunbar's life and art.

Sui Sin Far (Edith Maud Eaton)
The only substantial collection of Sui Sin Far's writing is *"Mrs. Spring Fragrance" and Other Writings* (1995), edited by Amy Ling and Annette White-Parks. White-Parks has also published *Sui Sin Far/Edith Maude Eaton: A Literary Biography* (1995), with a chronological listing of her writings. Historical and critical work on Sui Sin Far includes Elaine Kim, *Asian American Literature: An Introduction to the Writings and Their Social Context* (1982); William F. Wu, *The Yellow Peril: Chinese Americans in American Fiction, 1850–1940* (1982); Judy Yung, *Chinese Women of America* (1986); Mary Dearborn, *Pocahontas's Daughters: Gender and Ethnicity in American Culture* (1986); Amy Ling, *Between Worlds: Women Writers of Chinese Ancestry* (1990); and Susan Coultrap-McQuin, *Doing Literary Business: American Women Writers in the Nineteenth Century* (1990). Two books published in 2001 add to the scholarship on Sui Sin Far and her sister: Diana Birchall's *Onoto Watanna: The Story of Winnifred Eaton*, and Dominika Ferens's *Edith and Winnifred Eaton: Chinatown Missions and Japanese Romances*. Elizabeth Ammons's *Conflicting Stories* (1992) has a chapter on "Mrs. Spring Fragrance"; see also the chapter on Sui Sin Far in Molly Crumpton Winter's *American Narratives: Multiethnic Writing in the Age of Realism* (2007).

Mary E. Wilkins Freeman
The best collection of Freeman's work is *Selected Stories of Mary E. Wilkins Freeman* (1983), edited and introduced by Marjorie Pryse. Brent L. Kendrick edited *The Infant Sphinx: Collected Letters of Mary E. Wilkins Freeman* (1985); Charles Johanningsmeier edited a 2002 reprinting of Freeman's 1894 novel *Pembroke*; and Mary R. Reichard edited *A Mary Wilkins Freeman Reader* (1997). Perry D. Westbrook's *Mary Wilkins Freeman* (1988) provides a good introduction to Freeman's life and writings; Leah Blatt Glasser's *In a Closet Hidden: The Life and Work of Mary E. Wilkins Freeman* (1996) also contributes to biographical and critical scholarship. Other books with discussions of Freeman include Judith Fetterley and Marjorie Pryse's anthology *American Women Regionalists: 1850–1910* (1992), Reichard's *Mary Wilkins Freeman: A Study of the Short Story* (1998), John Idol and Melinda Ponder's *The Unfortunate Fall: Women and Genteel Poverty in the Fiction of Hawthorne and Freeman* (1999), Reichardt's *A Web of Relationship: Women in the Short Fiction of Mary Wilkins Freeman* (2007), and

Roxanne Harde's edited *Narratives of Community: Women's Short Story Sequences* (2007). See also the Mary E. Wilkins Freeman special issue of *American Transcendental Quarterly*, guest edited by Shirley Marchalonis (1999).

Charlotte Perkins Gilman

Reprints of Gilman's writings include *The Living of Charlotte Perkins Gilman: An Autobiography*, edited by Ann J. Lane (1975); *Herland*, edited by Lane (1979); *The Charlotte Perkins Gilman Reader*, edited by Lane (1980); *Herland and Selected Stories by Charlotte Perkins Gilman*, edited by Barbara Solomon (1992); *Charlotte Perkins Gilman: Her Progress Toward Utopia with Selected Writings*, edited by Carol Farley Kessler (1994); and *Women and Economics: A Study of the Economic Relation Between Men and Women as a Factor in Social Evolution*, edited by Michael Kimmel (1998). Gary Scharnhorst's *Charlotte Perkins Gilman: A Bibliography* (2003) is indispensable. Ann J. Lane's critical biography, *To Herland and Beyond: The Life and Work of Charlotte Perkins Gilman* (1990), is standard, though it should be supplemented by Cynthia J. Davis's *Charlotte Perkins Gilman: A Biography* (2010). Mary A. Hill's *Charlotte Perkins Gilman: The Making of a Radical Feminist* (1980) and her *Endure: The Diaries of Charles Walter Stetson* (1985) illuminate Gilman's early years. Hill also edited *A Journey from Within: The Love Letters of Charlotte Perkins Gilman, 1897–1900* (1995). Denise D. Knight edited the two-volume *The Diaries of Charlotte Perkins Gilman* (1994).

Critical books include Judith A. Allen's *The Feminism of Charlotte Perkins Gilman: Sexualities, Histories, Progressivism* (2009), Denise D. Knight's *Charlotte Perkins Gilman: A Study of the Short Fiction* (1997), Sheryl L. Meyering's *Charlotte Perkins Gilman: The Woman and Her Work* (1989), Polly Wynn Allen's *Building Domestic Liberty: Charlotte Perkins Gilman's Architectural Feminism* (1988), and Gary Scharnhorst's *Charlotte Perkins Gilman* (1985). Cynthia J. Davis and Knight have edited *Charlotte Perkins Gilman and Her Contemporaries: Literary and Intellectual Contexts* (2004). Joanne B. Karpinski edited *Critical Essays on Charlotte Perkins Gilman* (1992). For good comparative studies, see Janet Beer's *Kate Chopin, Edith Wharton and Charlotte Perkins Gilman: Studies in Short Fiction* (2005), Beth Sutton-Ramspeck's *Raising the Dust: The Literary Housekeeping of Mary Ward, Sarah Grand, and Charlotte Perkins Gilman* (2004), and Alys Eve Weinbaum's *Wayward Reproductions: Genealogies of Race and Nation in Transatlantic Modern Thought* (2004). Jill Rudd and Val Gough's edited collection,

Charlotte Perkins Gilman: Optimist Reformer (1999), and Heather Ostman's *Kate Chopin in the Twenty-First Century: New Critical Essays* (2008) offer a wide range of critical and theoretical perspectives.

Critical casebooks on "The Yellow Wallpaper" include Catherine Golden's *The Captive Imagination: A Casebook on "The Yellow Wallpaper"* (1991); Julie Bates Dock's *The Legend of "The Yellow Wallpaper": A Documentary Casebook* (1998); and Dock's *Charlotte Perkins Gilman's "The Yellow Wall-Paper" and the History of Its Publication and Reception: A Critical Edition and Documentary Casebook* (1998).

Bret Harte

The most complete collection is *The Works of Bret Harte* in twenty-five volumes (1914). Harte's poetry may be found in *The Complete Poetical Works of Bret Harte* (1899). Geoffrey Bret Harte edited *The Letters of Bret Harte* (1926); *Selected Letters of Bret Harte* appeared in 1997, edited by Gary Scharnhorst and Robert L. Gale. Scharnhorst also edited Bret Harte's *California* (1990) and coedited (with Lawrence I. Berkove) *The Old West in the Old World: Lost Plays by Bret Harte and Sam Davis* (2006). Scharnhorst's critical biography, *Bret Harte: Opening the American Literary West* (2000), anlayzes Harte's life, career, and reception; Axel Nissen's biography, *Bret Harte: Prince and Pauper* (2000), should also be consulted. Patrick Morrow's *Bret Harte: Literary Critic* (1979) offers a judicious account of Harte's sometimes injudicious literary criticism. The best bibliography is Scharnhorst's *Bret Harte: A Bibliography* (1995). Provocative discussions of Harte can be found in Chis Packard's *Queer Cowboys and Other Erotic Male Friendships in Nineteenth-Century American Literature* (2005) and Joanna Levin's *Bohemia in America, 1858–1920* (2010).

William Dean Howells

Indiana University Press's *A Selected Edition of W. D. Howells* now amounts to thirty volumes. Howells's letters can be found in *The Correspondence of Samuel L. Clemens and William Dean Howells, 1972–1910* (1960), edited by Henry Nash Smith and William M. Gibson; *Life in Letters of William Dean Howells* (1928), edited by his daughter Mildred Howells; and the *John Hay-Howells Letters* (1980), edited by George Monteiro and Brenda Murphy. Ruth Bardon's *Selected Short Stories of William Dean Howells* was published in 1997. Other collections include *Interviews with William Dean Howells* (1973), compiled by Ulrich Halfmann; John W. Crowley's *The Mask of Fiction: Essays of W. D. Howells* (1989); *The Early Prose Writings of William Dean Howells* (1990), edited by Thomas Wortham;

three volumes of *Selected Criticism* (1992), edited by David Nordloh; and *Staging Howells: Plays and Correspondence* (1994), edited by Lawrence Barrett, George Arms, Mary Beth Whidden, and Gary Scharnhorst. An up-to-date bibliography can be found at the William Dean Howells Society website: <www.wsu.edu/~campbelld/howells/recent.htm>.

The important early biographies of Howells are Edwin H. Cady's *The Road to Realism: The Early Years, 1837–1885* (1956) and *The Realist at War: The Mature Years, 1885–1920* (1958); Van Wyck Brooks's *Howells: His Life and Work* (1959); and Kenneth S Lynn's *William Dean Howells: An American Life* (1971). More recently, John W. Crowley published *The Dean of American Letters: The Late Career of William Dean Howells* (2005) and Susan Goodman and Carl Dawson brought out *William Dean Howells: A Writer's Life* (2005). Useful critical studies of Howells's writings include Elizabeth Stevens Prioleau's *The Circle of Eros: Sexuality in the Work of William Dean Howells* (1983), Crowley's *The Black Heart's Truth: The Early Career of W. D. Howells* (1985), Elsa Nettels's *Language, Race, and Social Class in Howells's America* (1988), Amy Kaplan's *The Social Construction of American Realism* (1988), Edwin H. Cady and Louis Budd's collection *On Howells: The Best Articles from American Literature* (1993), Gregory J. Stratman's *Speaking for Howells: Charting the Dean's Career through the Language of His Characters* (2001), Susan Goodman's *American Novelists and Manners, 1880–1940* (2003), Rob Davidson's *The Master and the Dean: The Literary Criticism of Henry James and William Dean Howells* (2005), and Dohra Ahmad's *Landscapes of Hope: Anti-Colonial Utopianism in America* (2009). A special issue of *American Literary Realism*, introduced by Jesse Crisler, was devoted to Howells (2006).

Henry James

The Novels and Tales of Henry James (The New York Edition), in twenty-six volumes, originally published in 1907–17, was reissued 1962–65. Other collections of James's diverse writings are available in R. P. Blackmur's *The Art of the Novel* (1935) (which collects James's prefaces to the works in the New York Edition), F. O. Matthiessen and Kenneth B. Murdoch's *The Notebooks of Henry James* (1947), Leon Edel's *The Complete Plays of Henry James* (1949), F. W. Dupee's edition of the three volumes of *Henry James: Autobiography* (1956), Morris Shapiro's *Selected Literary Criticism* (1963), and Pierre A. Walker's *Henry James on Culture: Collected Essays on Politics and the American Social Scene* (1999). James's novels, short stories, and literary essays are collected in multiple volumes of the Library of America

series. *Tales of Henry James* (2005) was published as a Norton Critical Edition, edited by Christof Wegelin and Henry B. Wonham. Leon Edel is the editor of the five-volume *The Letters of Henry James* published between 1974 and 1984. Philip Horne has published *Henry James: A Life in Letters* (1999), with half of the nearly 300 selections previously unpublished, and Susan E. Gunter and Steven H. Jobe have edited *Dearly Beloved Friends: Henry James's Letters to Younger Men* (2001), which contains a number of previously unpublished letters. Pierre A. Walker, Gred Zacharias, and Alfred Habegger edited two volumes in the ongoing complete edition of James's letters (2009). *The New York Stories of Henry James* (2006), edited by Colm Tóibín, offers eight tales; *The Portable Henry James* (2003) is edited by John Auchard. Two useful bibliographies are *A Bibliography of Henry James* (1999), edited by Edel, Dan H. Laurence, and James Rambeau; and Judith E. Funston's *Henry James: A Reference Guide, 1975–1987* (1991). Lawrence Raw's *Adapting Henry James to the Screen: Gender, Fiction and Film* (2006) offers a detailed history of film adaptations of James's works, twenty-eight in all. John R. Bradley edited *Henry James on Stage and Screen* (2000), and Susan M. Griffin edited *Henry James Goes to the Movies* (2001).

Leon Edel's five-volume opus *Henry James* (1953–72) remains the standard biography. Sheldon N. Novick published *Henry James: The Mature Master* (2007) as a follow-up to his 1996 *Henry James: The Young Master*, recasting James as an active and engaged artist rather than a lonely observer of life. Like Edel, he argues that James was the leading novelist of his generation. Fred Kaplan's *Henry James: The Imagination of Genius, A Biography* (1999) relies almost exclusively on the letters and diaries of James and his associates. R. W. B. Lewis studied the James family in *The Jameses* (1993), as did F. O. Matthiessen's earlier *The James Family* (1947). Other biographical studies include Edwin Sill Fussell's *The Catholic Side of Henry James* (1993), Kenneth Graham's *Henry James: A Literary Life* (1995), Carol Holly's *Intensely Family: The Inheritance of Family Shame and the Autobiographies of Henry James* (1995), and Lyndall Gordon's *A Private Life of Henry James: Two Women and His Art* (1999), which looks at James's relationships with his cousin Minnie Temple and friend Constance Fenimore Woolson. James's later career is illuminated by Lyall H. Powers's edition of Theodora Bosanquet's memoir, *Henry James at Work* (2006), originally published in 1924. Among the best of the immense number of critical studies of James are Ruth Bernard Yeazell's *Language and Knowledge in the Late Novels of Henry James* (1976), Charles Robert

Anderson's *Person, Place, and Thing in Henry James's Novels* (1977), Daniel Mark Fogel's *Henry James and the Structure of the Romantic Imagination* (1981), John Carlos Rowe's *The Theoretical Dimensions of Henry James* (1984), Sharon Cameron's *Thinking in Henry James* (1989), Alfred Habegger's *Henry James and the "Woman Business"* (1989), Millicent Bell's *Meaning in Henry James* (1991), Ross Posnock's *The Trial of Curiosity: Henry James, William James, and the Challenge of Modernity* (1991), Adeline R. Tintner's *The Cosmopolitan World of Henry James: An Intertextual Study* (1991), Wendy Graham's *Henry James's Thwarted Love* (1999), Eric Haralson's *Henry James and Queer Modernity* (2003), Leland Person's *Henry James and the Suspense of Masculinity* (2003), J. Hillis Miller's *Literature As Conduct: Speech Acts in Henry James* (2005), Hazel Hutchison's *Seeing and Believing: Henry James and the Spiritual World* (2006), Elaine Pigeon's *Queer Impressions: Henry James's Art of Fiction* (2006), Victoria Coulson's *Henry James, Women and Realism* (2007), Kendall Johnson's *Henry James and the Visual* (2007), and Amy Tucker's *The Illustration of the Master: Henry James and the Magazine Revolution* (2010).

Useful edited collections of critical essays include Graham Clark's *Henry James: Critical Assessments* (1991), Daniel Mark Fogel's *A Companion to Henry James Studies* (1993), Peter Rawlings's *Critical Essays on Henry James* (1993), Jonathan Freedman's *The Cambridge Companion to Henry James* (1998), Joseph Dewey's *The Finer Thread, The Tighter Weave: New Essays on the Short Fiction* (2001), Peggy McCormack's *Questioning the Master: Gender and Sexuality in Henry James's Writings* (2000), David Garrett Izzo and Daniel T. O'Hara's *Henry James Against the Aesthetic Movement: Essays on the Middle and Late Fiction* (2006), and Greg Zacharias's *A Companion to Henry James* (2008).

Sarah Orne Jewett

Jewett's *Stories and Tales* were published in seven volumes in 1910; a selection, *The Best Stories of Sarah Orne Jewett* (1925), was edited in two volumes with a foreword by Willa Cather. Richard Cary edited *The Uncollected Short Stories of Sarah Orne Jewett* (1971), as well as *Sarah Orne Jewett: Letters* (1967). The Library of America's edition of Jewett's *Novels and Stories* (1994), edited by Michael Davitt Bell, reprints three novels and thirty stories. Paula Blanchard's *Sarah Orne Jewett: Her World and Her Work* (2002) is an informative biography; a good introductory study is Josephine Donovan's *Sarah Orne Jewett* (1980). Perry D. Westbrook's *Acres of Flint: Sarah Orne Jewett and Her Contemporaries* (1981),

Gwen L. Nagel's *Critical Essays on Sarah Orne Jewett* (1984), Louis A. Renza's "A White Heron" and the Question of Minor Literature (1985), and Sarah Way Sherman's *Sarah Orne Jewett: An American Persephone* (1989) are useful. For more recent critical work, see Joseph Church's *Transcendent Daughters in Jewett's Country of the Pointed Firs* (1995), Margaret Roman's *Sarah Orne Jewett: Reconstructing Gender* (1997), Karen L. Kilcup and Thomas S. Edwards's *Jewett and Her Contemporaries: Reshaping the Canon* (1999), Paul R. Petrie's *Conscience and Purpose: Fiction and Social Consciousness in Howells, Jewett, Chesnutt, and Cather* (2005), and Mitchell Robert Breitwieser's *National Melancholy: Mourning and Opportunity in Classic American Literature* (2007).

Jack London

Useful editions include the three-volume *Letters of Jack London* (1988) and the three-volume *Complete Short Stories of Jack London* (1993), both edited by Earle Labor, Robert C. Leitz III, and I. Milo Shepard. Editions of material otherwise difficult to track down are *Jack London Reports* (1970; essays and newspaper articles), edited by King Hendricks and Irving Shepard; *No Mentor but Myself: Jack London on Writers and Writing* (1999), edited by Dale L. Walker and Jeanne Campbell Reesman; the Library of America *Jack London: Novels and Stories* (1982), edited by Donald Pizer; and *The Portable Jack London* (1994), edited by Earle Labor. Jonah Raskin's *The Radical Jack London: Writings on War and Revolution* (2008) offers a selection of London's political writings. *The Road (Subterranean Lives)* (2006), edited by Todd Depastino, collects nine of London's essays from his days as a hobo, many first published in *Cosmopolitan* during 1907–08. Dan Wichlan edited *Jack London: The Unpublished and Uncollected Articles and Essays* and *The Complete Poetry of Jack London*, both published in 2008. Bibliographical work on London has languished since the publication of Joan Sherman's *Jack London: A Reference Guide* (1977) and Hensley C. Woodbridge, John London, and George H. Tweney's *Jack London: A Bibliography* (1966). The Jack London Online Collection is managed by Roy Tennant and Clarice Stasz at Sonoma State University: <www.london.sonoma.edu>.

Russ Kingman's *Jack London: A Definitive Chronology* (1992) and *A Pictorial Life of Jack London* (1979) are factually reliable and useful. A new critical biography of London with an emphasis on his racial ambivalences is Jeanne Campbell Reesman's *Jack London's Racial Lives* (2009). Critical books and collections of essays include Franklin Walker's *Jack*

London and the Klondike: The Genesis of an American Writer (1966; rpt. 2005), James McClintock's White Logic: Jack London's Short Stories (1975; rpt. 1997 as Jack London's Strong Truths: A Study of the Short Stories), Jacqueline Tavernier-Courbin's Critical Essays on Jack London (1983), Charles N. Watson Jr.'s The Novels of Jack London: A Reappraisal (1983), Earle Labor and Jeanne Campbell Reesman's Jack London: Revised Edition (1994), Susan Nuernberg's The Critical Response to Jack London (1995), Leonard Cassuto and Reesman's edited collection Rereading Jack London (1996), Jonathan Auerbach's Male Call: Becoming Jack London (1996), Reesman's Jack London: A Study of the Short Fiction (1998), Sara S. Hodson and Reesman's edited collection Jack London: One Hundred Years a Writer (2002), Gina Rossetti's Imagining the Primitive in Naturalist and Modernist Literature (2006), and Daniel Métraux's The Asian Writings of Jack London (2010).

Mark Twain

As the center for authoritative editions of his writings, The Mark Twain Papers at the University of California at Berkeley has been producing annotated volumes since the 1960s. Their editions to date, including Adventures of Huckleberry Finn (2003), Mysterious Stranger Manuscripts (1969), A Connecticut Yankee in King Arthur's Court (1983), Roughing It (1996), and several volumes of Mark Twain's Letters and his Notebooks and Journals, are scholarly landmarks. For Twain books that have yet to receive this treatment, however, a good recourse is the series The Oxford Mark Twain (1997), edited by Shelley Fisher Fishkin. Essentially facsimiles of all first editons of Twain works published in his lifetime or soon after, the series is important because in the years when Clemens was head of his own publishing company, he could control everything that was produced with "Mark Twain" on the cover—including the numerous illustrations in his most famous books. These facsimiles show what American readers encountered when these books were fresh on the market, and help readers understand how Mark Twain included printed images in the creative process.

There are three encyclopedic recent guides to Twain's life and works: Gregg Camfield's The Oxford Companion to Mark Twain (2003), R. Kent Rasmussen's two-volume Critical Companion to Mark Twain: A Literary Reference to His Life and Work (2007), and Rasmussen's shorter and earlier Mark Twain: A to Z (1995). Also worth consulting are Forrest G. Robinson's The Cambridge Companion to Mark Twain (1995) and Peter Messent

and Louis J. Budd's A Companion to Mark Twain (2005). Much briefer introductions to Twain's work and his literary legacy include Peter Messent's The Cambridge Introduction to Mark Twain (2007) and Stephen Railton's Mark Twain: A Short Introduction (2004).

Because the life of Samuel Clemens has become an American novel and legend in its own right, biographies abound; the 2010 centenary of his death brought a fresh wave, including Jerome Loving's Mark Twain: The Adventures of Samuel Clemens (2010) and Michael Shelden's Mark Twain: Man in White (2010). Also recent and well received is Ron Powers's Mark Twain: A Life (2005). These comprehensive narratives make use of journals and letters, and also a welter of previous retellings of the Twain story, including Justin Kaplan's still-reliable Mr. Clemens and Mark Twain (1966) and Albert Bigelow Paine's very early, extensive, but doubtfully authoritative Mark Twain: A Biography (1912). The 2002 Ken Burns documentary film produced for PBS (as part of the American Lives series) provides a strong visual impression of the man, his upbringing, his family, his adventures, and his world. Other accounts of Clemens center on the Hannibal boyhood, the adventures in the West, the episodes of European and worldwide travel, and life on the lecture circuit; lately, much attention has concentrated on the final decade of his life. Recent revelations and opinions about this period include Laura Skandera Trombley's Mark Twain's Other Woman: The Hidden Story of His Final Years (2010) and Karen Lystra's Dangerous Intimacy: The Untold Story of Mark Twain's Final Years (2006). Both of these build upon Hamlin Hill's Mark Twain: God's Fool (1973) and Van Wyck Brooks's The Ordeal of Mark Twain (1920), decisive works in transforming an author into an archetypal "wounded" American celebrity. Twain's anti-imperialism at the turn of the century has also recently engaged critics; for a good collection, see Following the Equator and Anti-Imperialist Essays, edited by Fred Kaplan (1996).

Other biographical studies emphasize the imaginative experience, the business realities, and the cultural contexts of Mark Twain in his most productive years; notable among these are Victor Doyno's Writing Huck Finn: Mark Twain's Creative Process (1993), Everett Emerson's Mark Twain: A Literary Life (2000), Bruce Michelson's Printer's Devil: Mark Twain and the American Publishing Revolution (2006), and Roy Morris Jr.'s Lighting Out for the Territory: How Samuel Clemens Headed West and Became Mark Twain (2010).

Louis J. Budd's Our Mark Twain: The Making of His Public Personality (1983) describes how Twain's reputation expanded, with embellishments, in the opening decades of the twentieth century. See also Shelley Fisher Fishkin's recent Library of America volume on the international response to Twain: *The Mark Twain Anthology: Great Writers on His Life and Works* (2010). The most influential studies of Twain's wit and humor include James M. Cox's *Mark Twain: The Fate of Humor* (1966), David E. E. Sloane's *Mark Twain as a Literary Comedian* (1979), Bruce Michelson's *Mark Twain on the Loose: A Comic Writer and the American Self* (1995), and Linda Morris's *Gender Play in Mark Twain: Cross-Dressing and Transgression* (2007). For controversies about *Huckleberry Finn* as a "great" American novel, see Tom Quirk's *Coming to Grips With Huckleberry Finn* (1993), Shelley Fisher Fishkin's *Lighting Out for the Territory: Reflections on Mark Twain and American Culture* (1996), and Jonathan Arac's *Huckleberry Finn as Idol and Target* (1997). The first volume of a new edition of *Autobiography of Mark Twain*, published by the University of California Press in 2010, became a national best seller.

Booker T. Washington

Louis R. Harlan edited *The Booker T. Washington Papers* in fourteen volumes (1972–89). William L. Andrews edited a Norton Critical Edition of *Up From Slavery* (1996). Louis R. Harlan's two-volume biography, *Booker T. Washington: The Making of a Black Leader, 1865–1901* (1972) and *Booker T. Washington: The Wizard of Tuskegee, 1901–1915* (1983), is standard, but it should be supplemented by Michael Rudelph West's *The Education of Booker T. Washington: American Democracy and the Idea of Race Relations* (2006), Michael Bieze's *Booker T. Washington and the Art of Self-Representation* (2008), and Robert J. Norell's *Up from History: The Life of Booker T. Washington* (2009). Robert B. Stepto's chapter on Washington's *Up From Slavery*, in *Behind the Veil: A Study of Afro-American Narrative* (1979), is a classic analysis, as is James M. Cox's "Autobiography and Washington" in his *Recovering Lost Ground: Essays in American Autobiography* (1989). Also worth consulting are James Olney's essay on Frederick Douglass and Washington in Deborah McDowell and Arnold Rampersad's edited collection, *Slavery and the Literary Imagination* (1989); Kevern Verney's *The Art of the Possible: Booker T. Washington and Black Leadership in the United States, 1881–1925* (2001); Houston A. Baker, Jr.'s *Turning South Again: Re-Thinking Modernism/Re-Reading Booker T.* (2001); Wilson Jeremiah Moses's *Creative Conflict in African American Thought: Frederick Douglass, Alexander Crummell, Booker T. Washington, W. E. B. Du Bois, and Marcus Garvey* (2005);

and Rebecca Carroll's edited collection *Uncle Tom or New Negro?: African Americans Reflect on Booker T. Washington and Up From Slavery 100 Years Later* (2006).

Edith Wharton

R. W. B. Lewis edited *The Collected Short Stories of Edith Wharton* (1988) in two volumes. Frederick Wegener edited *Edith Wharton: The Uncollected Critical Writings* (1991), and Laura Rattray edited *The Unpublished Writings of Edith Wharton* (2009). The Library of America published several volumes of Wharton's works (1986, 1990, 2001), including novels, novellas, stories, and poems. *The Correspondence of Edith Wharton and Macmillan, 1901–1930* (2007), edited by Shafquat Towheed, helps to illuminate Wharton's relationship with her publisher. R. W. B. Lewis's groundbreaking *Edith Wharton: A Biography* appeared in 1975, and Cynthia Griffin Wolff's critical biographical study, *A Feast of Words: The Triumph of Edith Wharton*, followed in 1977. Two more recent biographies are also excellent: Shari Benstock's *No Gifts from Chance: A Biography of Edith Wharton* (1994) and Hermione Lee's *Edith Wharton* (2007). George Ramsden's *Edith Wharton's Library: A Catalogue* (1999) inventories about half of her library—more than 2,200 books. Janet Beer and Elizabeth Nolan's *Edith Wharton* (2006) is a reference work about contemporary views of the author. On reception, see also James W. Tuttleton, Kristin O. Lauer, and Margaret P. Murray's *Edith Wharton: The Contemporary Reviews* (1992) and Helen Killoran's *The Critical Reception of Edith Wharton* (2001).

Book-length critical studies include Gary H. Lindberg's *Edith Wharton and the Novel of Manners* (1975), Elizabeth Ammons's *Edith Wharton's Argument with America* (1980), Susan Goodman's *Edith Wharton's Women* (1990), Goodman's *Edith Wharton's Inner Circle* (1994), Donna Campbell's *Resisting Regionalism: Gender and Naturalism in American Fiction, 1885–1915* (1997), Carol Singley's *Edith Wharton: Matters of Mind and Spirit* (1998), Hildegard Hoeller's *Edith Wharton's Dialogue with Realism and Sentimental Fiction* (2000), Jill M. Kress's *The Figure of Consciousness: William James, Henry James, and Edith Wharton* (2002), Julie Olin-Ammentorp, *Edith Wharton's Writings from the Great War* (2004), Emily J. Orlando's *Edith Wharton and the Visual Arts* (2007), Jennifer Haytock's *Edith Wharton and the Conversations of Literary Modernism* (2008), Jennie A. Kassanoff's *Edith Wharton and the Politics of Race* (2008), Judith P. Saunders's *Reading Edith Wharton through a Darwinian Lens: Evolutionary Biological Issues in Her Fiction* (2009), and Pamela

Knight's *The Cambridge Introduction to Edith Wharton* (2009). A useful reference work is Sarah Bird Wright and Clare Colquitt's *Edith Wharton A to Z* (1998). For wide-ranging collections of essays, see Alfred Bendixen and Annette Zilversmit's *Edith Wharton: New Critical Essays* (1992), Millicent Bell's *The Cambridge Companion to Edith Wharton* (1995), Colquitt, Goodman, and Candace Waid's *A Forward Glance: New Essays on Edith Wharton* (1999), and Singley's *Historical Guide to Edith Wharton* (2003).

Zitkala Ša (Gertrude Simmons Bonnin)
Dexter Fisher's 1986 edition of Zitkala Ša's *American Indian Stories* (1921) includes an expert and insightful introduction to this collection of autobiography, fiction, and nonfiction prose. P. Jane Hafen helpfully edited a number of Zitkala Ša's works in *Dreams and Thunder: Stories, Poems and "The Sun Dance Opera"* (2001). Dexter Fisher's *Zitkala Ša: The Evolution of a Writer* (1979) and Dorothea M. Susag's *Zitkala-Ša (Gertrude Simmons Bonnin): A Power(full) Literary Voice* (1993) are among the few critical and biographical studies. See also Patricia Okker's "Native American Literatures and the Canon" in Tom Quirk and Gary Scharnhost's collection *American Realism and the Canon* (1995). Cathy Davidson and Ada Norris's edited volume, *Zitkala Ša: American Indian Stories, Legends, and Other Writings* (2003) has an excellent introduction and notes.

AMERICAN LITERATURE 1914–1945

Reference Works and Histories

Chapters on the period may be consulted in the *Columbia Literary History of the United States* (1988), general editor Emory Elliott; the *Columbia History of the American Novel* (1991), general editor Emory Elliot; the *Columbia History of American Poetry* (1993), edited by Jay Parini; *The History of Southern Literature* (1985), edited by Louis D. Rubin et al.; *A Literary History of the American West* (1987); and A. LaVonne Brown Ruoff's *American Indian Literature* (1990). Relevant volumes in the eight-volume *Cambridge History of American Literature* are volume 5, *Poetry and Criticism, 1900–1950* (2003), edited by Sacvan Bercovitch, and volume 6, *Prose Writing, 1910–1950* (2002), edited by Sacvan Bercovitch and Cyrus R. Patell. Other reference works include the *Cambridge Companion to Native American Literature* (2005), edited by Joy Porter and Kenneth Roemer; *A Companion to the Literature and Culture of the American South* (2004), edited by Richard Grey and Owen Robinson; and *An Interethnic Companion to Asian American Literature* (1996), edited by King-Kok Cheung. Reference works dedicated to the period and some of its important movements include *A Companion to Modernist Literature and Culture,* edited by David Bradshaw and Kevin J. H. Dettmar (2006); the *Cambridge Companion to American Modernism* (2005), edited by Walter Kalaidjian; the *Cambridge Companion to the Harlem Renaissance,* edited by George Hutchinson (2007); *A Companion to Twentieth-Century Poetry,* edited by Neil Roberts (2001); *A Companion to Twentieth-Century American Fiction,* edited by David Seed (2010); the *Cambridge Companion to Modernist Poetry,* edited by Alex Davis and Lee M. Jenkins (2007); and *A Companion to Twentieth-Century American Drama* (2005), edited by David Krasner.

For early histories of the period authored by critics who were active in the rise of modernism, see Malcolm Cowley, *Exile's Return* (1951), *After the Genteel Tradition: American Writers, 1910–1930* (1964), and *A Second Flowering: Works and Days of the Lost Generation* (1973); and Edmund Wilson,

The Shores of Light: A Literary Chronicle of the Twenties and Thirties (1952). Other important early surveys include Alfred Kazin's *On Native Grounds: An Interpretation of Modern American Prose Literature* (1942); Maxwell Geismer's *Writers in Crisis: The American Novel between Two Wars* (1942); Frederick J. Hoffman's *The Twenties: American Writing in the Postwar Decade*; Harold Clurman's *The Fervent Years: The Story of the Group Theatre and the Thirties* (1957); Walter Rideout's *The Radical Novel in the United States, 1900–1954* (1956); Joseph Wood Krutch's *The American Drama Since 1918* (1957), Daniel Aaron's *Writers on the Left* (1961), Louis D. Rubin's *Writers of the Modern South* (1963); Howard Taubman's *The Making of the American Theater* (1965); Warren French's *The Social Novel at the End of an Era* (1966); Dale Kramer's *Chicago Renaissance: The Literary Life in the Midwest, 1910–1930* (1966); Brooks Atkinson's *Broadway: Nineteen Hundred to Nineteen Seventy* (1970); Nathan I. Huggins's *Harlem Renaissance* (1971); Hugh Kenner's *The Pound Era* (1971); and Kenner's *A Homemade World: The American Modernist Writers* (1975).

General books on literary and cultural history appearing since 1980 include Marcus Klein's *Foreigners: The Making of American Literature, 1900–1940* (1981); David Levering Lewis's *When Harlem Was in Vogue* (1981); Daniel J. Singal's *The War Within: From Victorian to Modernist Thought in the South 1919–1945* (1982); Shari Benstock's *Women of the Left Bank: Paris 1900–1940* (1986); *Modernism and the Harlem Renaissance* (1987), edited by Houston Baker Jr.; Cecilia Tichi's *Shifting Gears: Technology, Literature, Culture in Modernist America* (1987); Joan Shelley Rubin's *The Making of Middlebrow Culture* (1992); Mary Loeffelholz's *Experimental Lives: Women and Literature, 1900–1945* (1992); Michael North's *The Dialect of Modernism: Race, Language and Twentieth-Century Literature* (1994); George Chauncey's *Gay New York: Gender, Urban Culture, and the Making of the Gay Male World, 1980–1940* (1994); George Hutchinson's *The Harlem Renaissance in Black and White* (1995); Cheryl Wall's *Women of the Harlem Renaissance* (1995); Walter Benn Michaels's *Our America* (1995); Ann Douglas's *Terrible Honesty: Mongrel Manhattan in the 1920s* (1995); Ross Posnock's *Color and Culture: Black Writers and the Making of the Modern Intellectual* (1998); William J. Maxwell's *New Negro, Old Left: African-American Writing and Communism between the Wars* (1999); Christine Stansell's *American Moderns: Bohemian New York and the Creation of a New Century* (1999); David G. Nicholls's *Conjuring the Folk: Forms of Modernity in African America* (2000); Michael Szalay's *New Deal Modernism: American Literature and the Invention of the Welfare State* (2000); Edward Pavlic's *Crossroads Modernism: Descent and Emergence in African-American Literary Culture* (2002); Catherine Turner's *Marketing Modernism between the Two World Wars* (2003); Michael Soto's *The Modernist Nation: Generation, Renaissance, and Twentieth-Century American Literature* (2004); Tim Armstrong's *Modernism: A Cultural History* (2005); Joseph B. Entim's *Sensational Modernism: Experimental Fiction and Photography in Thirties America* (2007); and Daphne Lamothe's *Inventing the New Negro: Narrative, Culture, and Ethnography* (2008).

Literary Theory and Criticism

For an introduction to the ideas of literary criticism during the period, see Rene Wellek's *A History of Modern Criticism: American Criticism, 1900–1950,* Vol. 7 (1987) and Vincent B. Leitch's *American Literary Criticism from the 30s to the 80s* (1988). Gordon Hutner's *American Literature, American Culture* (1998) reprints a number of critical statements from the period. Gerald's Graff's *Professing Literature: An Institutional History* (1987), Lawrence H. Schwartz's *Creating Faulkner's Reputation: The Politics of Modern Literary Criticism* (1988), and Mark Jancovich's *The Cultural Politics of the New Criticism* (1994) analyze aspects of American literary criticism in the period and its aftermath.

Theoretical treatments of modernism (often in international perspectives) include Andreas Huyssen's *After the Great Divide: Modernism, Mass Culture, Postmodernism* (1986), Ashadur Eyssteinsson's *The Concept of Modernism* (1991), Joseph N. Riddel's *The Turning Word: American Literary Modernism and Continental Theory* (1996), Leonard Diepeveen's *The Difficulties of Modernism* (2003), Michael Trask's *Cruising Modernism: Class and Sexuality in American Literature and Social Thought* (2003), Susan McCabe's *Cinematic Modernism: Modernist Poetry and Film* (2005), and Robert Scholes's *Paradoxy of Modernism* (2006).

Criticism of poetry published since 1980 includes M. L. Rosenthal and Sally M. Gall's *The Modern Poetic Sequence: The Genius of Modern Poetry* (1984), William Drake's *The First Wave: Women Poets in America, 1914–1945* (1987), Albert Gelpi's *A Coherent Splendor: The American Poetic Renaissance, 1910–1950* (1987), Lisa M. Steinman's *Made in America: Science, Technology, and American Modernist Poets* (1987), Maureen Honey's edited *Shadowed Dreams: Women's Poetry of the Harlem Renaissance* (1989), Cary Nelson's *Repression and Recovery: Modern American Poetry and the Politics of Cultural Memory, 1910–1945* (1989), Elisa New's *Fictions of Form in American Poetry* (1993), Frank Lentricchia's *Modernist Quartet* (1994), Elizabeth Gregory's, *Quotation and Modern America Poetry: Imaginary Gardens with Real Toads* (1996), Rachel Blau DuPlessis's *Genders, Races, and Religious Cultures in Modern American Poetries, 1908–1934* (2001), Merrill Cole's *The Other Orpheus: A Poetics of Modern Homosexuality* (2003), Jennifer Ashton's *From Modernism to Postmodernism: American Poetry and Theory in the Twentieth Century* (2005), Rachel Potter's *Modernism and Democracy: Literary Culture, 1900–1930* (2006), and Charles Altieri's *The Art of Twentieth-Century American Poetry: Modernism and After* (2006).

Critical studies of fiction published since 1980 include Hazel V. Carby's *Reconstructing Womanhood: The Emergence of the Afro-American Woman Novelist* (1987), Linda Wagner-Martin's *The Modern American Novel, 1914–1945* (1990), J. Gerald Kennedy's *Imagining Paris* (1993), Barbara Foley's *Radical Representations: Politics and Form in U.S. Proletarian Fiction, 1929–41* (1993), David Minter's *A Cultural History of the American Novel* (1994), Laura Hapke's *Daughters of the Great Depression: Women, Work, and Fiction in the American 1930s* (1995), and Gordon Hutner's *What America Read: Taste, Class, and the Novel, 1920–1960* (2009).

Critical studies of drama published since 1980 include C. W. E. Bigsby's *A Critical Introduction to Twentieth-Century American Drama*, Vol. 1, *1900–1940* (1985), Ethan Mordden's *The American Theatre* (1981), Brenda Murphy's *American Realism and American Drama, 1880–1940* (1987), David Krasner's *A Beautiful Pageant: African American Theatre, Drama, and Performance in the Harlem Renaissance, 1910–1927* (2002), and Julia A. Walker's *Expressionism and Modernism in the American Theatre: Bodies, Voices, Words* (2005).

Sherwood Anderson

There is no collected edition of Anderson's writing. In addition to works mentioned in the author's headnote, Anderson published *The Modern Writer* (1925); *Sherwood Anderson's Notebook* (1925); *Alice and the Lost Novel* (1929); *Nearer the Grass Roots* (1929); *The American Country Fair* (1930); and *Home Town* (1940). The Norton Critical Edition of *Winesburg, Ohio* (1996), edited by Charles E. Modlin and Ray Lewis White, includes background materials and critical essays, as does the edition edited by John H. Ferres (1996). White edited a variorum edition of *Winesburg, Ohio* (1997) as well as *Sherwood Anderson's Memoirs: A Critical Edition* (1969). *The Letters of Sherwood Anderson* (1953) were edited by Howard Mumford Jones and Walter Rideout. See also *Sherwood Anderson: Selected Letters* (1984), edited by Charles E. Modlin and *Letters to Bab: Sherwood Anderson to Marietta D. Finley, 1916–1933* (1985). A two-volume biography by Walter Rideout is *Sherwood Anderson: A Writer in America* (2006–7). For critical commentary see *Sherwood Anderson: A Collection of Critical Essays* (1974), edited by Walter Rideout; *New Essays on Winesburg, Ohio* (1990), edited by John W. Crowley; Allen Papinchak's *Sherwood Anderson: A Study of the Short Fiction* (1992); Judy Jo Small's *A Reader's Guide to the Short Stories of Sherwood Anderson* (1994); Ray Lewis White's *Winesburg, Ohio: An Exploration* (1990), and Clarence Lindsay's *Such a Rare Thing: The Art of Sherwood Anderson's Winesburg, Ohio* (2009).

Willa Cather

Cather's volume of verse, *April Twilights* (1903; rev. 1923; reissued with an introduction by Bernice Slote, 1990, and her collection of essays, *Not under Forty* (1936), supplement the standard edition of her fiction, *The Novels and Stories of Willa Cather* (1937–41). Her tales and novels were published in two volumes by the Library of America with notes by Sharon O'Brien (1987, 1990). A scholarly edition of *My Ántonia* (1994), with background materials, was edited by Charles Mignon with Kari Ronning; a scholarly edition of *Youth and the Bright Medusa* (2009) was edited by Mark J. Madigan with Frederick M. Link, Charles Mignon, Judith Boss, and Kari Ronning. *The Selected Letters of Willa Cather* (2013) were edited by Andrew Jewell and Janis Stout. Other sources include *Willa Cather on Writing* (1949); *Writings from Willa Cather's Campus Years* (1950), edited by James Shively; and *The Kingdom of Art: Willa Cather's First Principles and Critical Statements* (1967), edited by Bernice Slote. William M. Curtin collected articles and reviews in the two-volume *The World and the Parish* (1970). Personal memoirs include Edith Lewis's *Willa Cather Living* (1953, 2000) and Elizabeth Sergeant's *Willa Cather: A Memoir* (1953, 1992). Janis P. Stout's *A Calendar of the Letters of Willa Cather* (2002) and the biography *Willa Cather: The Writer and Her World* (2000) are worthwhile. *Willa: The Life of Willa Cather* (1982), by Phyllis C. Robinson, is a full-length biography, as is *Willa Cather: A Literary Life* (1987), by James Woodress. Sharon O'Brien's *Willa Cather: The Emerging Voice* (1987) concentrates on Cather's early years.

Critical studies of Cather are David Stouck's *Willa Cather's Imagination* (1975), Marilyn Arnold's *Willa Cather's Short Fiction* (1984) and *Willa Cather: A Reference Guide* (1986), Susan J. Rosowski's *The Voyage Perilous: Willa Cather's Romanticism* (1986), Sally P. Harvey's *Redefining the American Dream: The Novels of Willa Cather* (1995), Joseph R. Urgo's *Willa Cather and the Myth of American Migration* (1995), Guy Reynolds's *Willa Cather in Context* (1996), O'Brien's *New Essays on My Ántonia* (1999), Ann Romines's *Willa Cather's Southern Connection* (2000), Joan Acocella's *Willa Cather and the Politics of Criticism* (2000), and David Porter's *On the Divide: The Many Lives of Willa Cather* (2008) on her relationship to the literary marketplace. Janis P. Stout edited *Willa Cather and Material Culture: Real-World Writing and Writing the Real World* (2005). Also useful is *Violence, the Arts, and Willa Cather* (2007), ed. Joseph R. Urgo and Merrill Maguire Skaggs.

Hart Crane

Langdon Hammer edited *Hart Crane: Complete Poems and Selected Letters* (2006) for the Library of America. Crane's *Collected Poems*, edited by his friend Waldo Frank, appeared in 1933. *Correspondence between Hart Crane and Waldo Frank* (1998) was edited by Steve

H. Cook. Other sources of primary and bibliographical material are *My Land, My Friends: The Selected Letters of Hart Crane* (1997), edited by Langdon Hammer and Brom Weber; *Hart Crane: An Annotated Critical Bibliography* (1970), edited by Joseph Schwartz; and *Hart Crane: A Descriptive Bibliography* (1972), edited by Joseph Schwartz and Robert C. Schweik. Gary Lane compiled *A Concordance to the Poems of Hart Crane* (1972). Biographies of Crane are John Unterecker's *Voyager: A Life of Hart Crane* (1969), Paul Mariani's *The Broken Tower: A Life of Hart Crane* (2000), and Clive Fisher's *Hart Crane: A Life* (2002).

Useful earlier studies are R. W. B. Lewis's *The Poetry of Hart Crane* (1967), Monroe K. Spears's *Hart Crane* (1965), and Hunce Voelcker's *The Hart Crane Voyages* (1967). See also Richard P. Sugg's *Hart Crane's "The Bridge"* (1976), Helge Norman Nilsen's *Hart Crane's Divided Vision: An Analysis of "The Bridge"* (1980), Edward Brunner's *Hart Crane and the Making of "The Bridge"* (1984), Paul Giles's *Hart Crane: The Contexts of The Bridge* (1986), Thomas E. Yingling's *Hart Crane and the Homosexual Text* (1990), Brian M. Reed's *Hart Crane: After His Lights* (2006), and Daniel Gabriel's *Hart Crane and the Modernist Epic: Canon and Genre Formation in Crane, Pound, Eliot and Williams* (2007).

Countee Cullen

Cullen's groundbreaking anthology of 1927, *Caroling Dusk,* was reissued in 1993. His poetry volume, *Color,* originally published in 1925, was also reissued in 1993. *My Soul's High Song,* a collection of his writings edited by Gerald Early, appeared in 1991. Earlier work of interest includes Helen J. Dinger's *A Study of Countee Cullen* (1953), Margaret Perry's *A Bio-Bibliography of Countee P. Cullen* (1969), Blanche E. Ferguson's *Countee Cullen and the Negro Renaissance* (1966), and Alan R. Shucard's *Countee Cullen* (1984). A recent article is Marisa Parham's "Hughes, Cullen, and the In-sites of Loss" in *ELH* (Summer 2007).

E. E. Cummings

Complete Poems 1904–62, edited by George J. Firmage, was published in 1991. Firmage also edited *Three Plays and a Ballet* (1967). Cummings's prose fiction includes *The Enormous Room* (1922) and *EIMI* (1933). *E. E. Cummings: A Miscellany Revised* (1965), edited by Firmage, contains previously uncollected short prose pieces. *Six Nonlectures* (1953) consists of the talks that Cummings delivered at Harvard in the same year. A gathering of works is *Another E. E. Cummings* (1999), edited by Richard Kostceanetz. *Selected Letters of E. E. Cummings* (1969) was edited by F. W. Dupee and George Stade. George J. Firmage edited *E. E.*

Cummings: A Bibliography (1960). Barry Ahearn edited *The Correspondence of Ezra Pound and E. E. Cummings* (1996).

Several of Cummings's earlier individual works have been reedited by Firmage in the Cummings Typescript Editions. These include *Tulips & Chimneys* (1976); *No Thanks* (1978); *The Enormous Room,* including illustrations by Cummings (1978); *ViVa* (1979); *XAIPE* (1979); and *Etcetera,* the unpublished poems (1983).

A biography is *Dreams in the Mirror* (1979, 1994), by Richard S. Kennedy. Early studies include Norman Friedman's *E. E. Cummings: The Growth of a Writer* (1964), Robert E. Wegner's *The Poetry and Prose of E. E. Cummings* (1965), and Rushworth Kidder's *E. E. Cummings, An Introduction to the Poetry* (1979). See also Cary Lane's *I Am: A Study of E. E. Cummings' Poems* (1976) and Richard S. Kennedy's *E. E. Cummings Revisited* (1994). Norman Friedman edited *E. E. Cummings: A Collection of Critical Essays* (1972) and authored *(Re)Valuing Cummings: Further Essays on the Poet* (1996).

Hilda Doolittle (H.D.)

The poetry through 1944 has been collected and edited by Louis L. Martz in *Collected Poems 1912–1944* (1983). *Collected Poems of H.D.* was published in 1925. Subsequent volumes of poetry include *Red Rose for Bronze* (1931); the trilogy of war poems *The Walls Do Not Fall* (1944), *Tribute to the Angels* (1945), and *The Flowering of the Rod* (1946); the dramatic monologue *Helen in Egypt* (1961); the major collection of her late poems, *Hermetic Definition* (1972); and the long poem *Vale Ave* (1992). H.D.'s other book-length verse dramas are *Hippolytus Temporizes* (1927) and the translation of Euripides' *Ion* (1937). *Palimpsest* (1926), *Hadylus* (1928), *Bid Me to Live* (1961), *HERmione* (1981), and *Asphodel* (1992), edited by Robert Spoo, compose her major prose fiction. *By Avon River* (1949) celebrates Shakespeare in prose and verse. *Tribute to Freud* (1956) is her account of her psychoanalysis by Freud. Also important are two autobiographical works: *End to Torment* (1979) and *The Gift* (1982, complete edition 1998). Michael Boughn compiled *H.D.: A Bibliography, 1905–1990* (1993). *Richard Aldington and H.D.: The Early Years in Letters* (1992), edited by Caroline Zilboorg, collects correspondence.

Herself Defined: The Poet H.D. and Her World (1984), by Barbara Guest, is a biography, while *H.D.: The Career of That Struggle* (1986), by Rachel Blau DuPlessis, *Psyche Reborn: The Emergence of H.D.* (1981), by Susan S. Friedman, and *H.D.: The Life and Work of an American Poet* (1982), by Janice S. Robinson, combine biography and literary analysis. Among critical books are Gary Burnett's *H. D.: Between Image and Epic*, *The Mysteries of Her Poetics* (1990), Friedman's *Penelope's Web: Gender, Modernity, and H.D.'s Fiction* (1990), Eileen Gregory's *H.D. and Hellenism* (1997), Diana Collecott's *H.D and Sapphic Modernism* (1999), Georgia Taylor's *H.D. and the Public Sphere of Modernist Women Writers 1913–1946* (2001), and Adalaide Morris's *How to Live/What to Do: H.D.'s Cultural Poetics* (2003).

T. S. Eliot

Eliot's poetic works have been collected in *Collected Poems, 1909–1962* (1963) and *The Complete Poems and Plays of T. S. Eliot* (1969). *Inventions of the March Hare: Poems 1909–1917* (1997), edited by Christopher Ricks, contains early, previously unpublished poetry. The indispensable manuscript to *The Waste Land* is in *The Waste Land: A Facsimile and Transcript of the Original Drafts Including the Annotations of Ezra Pound* (1971), edited by Valerie Eliot. Michael North edited a Norton Critical Edition of *The Waste Land* (2001), and Lawrence Rainey edited *The Annotated Waste Land with Eliot's Contemporary Prose* (2005). Important critical writings include *The Use of Poetry and the Use of Criticism* (1933), *Poetry and Drama* (1951), *The Three Voices of Poetry* (1953), *On Poetry and Poets* (1957), and *To Criticize the Critic and Other Writings* (1965). Three volumes of social commentary are *After Strange Gods* (1934), *The Idea of a Christian Society* (1939), and *Notes toward the Definition of Culture* (1948). Valerie Eliot edited *The Letters of T. S. Eliot, Vol. 1: 1898–1922* (1988). J. L. Dawson edited *Concordance to the Complete Poems and Plays of T. S. Eliot* (1995). Good biographies are Peter Ackroyd's *T. S. Eliot: A Life* (1984), Lyndall Gordon's *T. S. Eliot: An Imperfect Life* (1998, 2000), an updating of her earlier biographies, and James E. Miller, Jr., *T. S. Eliot: The Making of an American Poet, 1888–1922* (2005).

Influential earlier studies of Eliot include F. O. Matthiessen's *The Achievement of T. S. Eliot* (rev. 1947), Helen Gardner's *The Art of T. S. Eliot* (1950), Hugh Kenner's *The Invisible Poet* (1959), Northrop Frye's *T. S. Eliot* (1963), and Stephen Spender's *T. S. Eliot* (1976).

Among numerous critical studies are Helen Gardner's *The Composition of Four Quartets* (1978), Derek Traversi's *T. S. Eliot: The Longer Poems* (1976), Louis Menand's *Discovering Modernism: T. S. Eliot and His Context* (1987), Jewel Spears Brooker and Joseph Bentley's *Reading "The Waste Land": Modernism and the Limits of Interpretation* (1990), Brooker's *Mastery and Escape: T. S. Eliot and the Dialectic of Modernism* (1994), A. David Moody's *Thomas Stearns Eliot, Poet* (1994), Anthony Julius's *T. S. Eliot, Anti-Semitism, and Literary Form* (1996), Ronald Schuchard's *Eliot's Dark Angel: Intersections of Life and Art* (2001), David Chintz's *T. S. Eliot and the Cultural Divide* (2003), and Craig Raine's *T. S. Eliot* (2006). Moody also edited the useful *Cambridge Companion to T. S. Eliot* (1994). For collections of critical essays about Eliot, see *T. S. Eliot: A Collection of Criticism* (1974), edited by Linda W. Wagner (1974); *T. S. Eliot: The Modernist in History* (1991), edited by Ronald Bush; and *Gender, Desire, and Sexuality in T. S. Eliot* (2004), edited by Cassandra Laity and Nancy K. Gish. Gareth Reeves's *T. S. Eliot's "The Waste Land"* (1994) is a comprehensive introduction to the poem.

Donald C. Gallup compiled the standard bibliography, *T. S. Eliot: A Bibliography* (rev. 1969).

William Faulkner

The Library of America issued Faulkner's novels in four volumes: *1930–1935* (1985); *1936–1940* (1990); *1942–1954* (1994); and *1957–1962* (1999). In addition to volumes mentioned in the author's headnote are *Early Prose and Poetry* (1962), edited by Carvel Collins (1962); *Dr. Martino and Other Stories* (1934); *Pylon* (1935); *The Unvanquished* (1938); *Intruder in the Dust* (1948); *Knight's Gambit* (1949); *Collected Stories of William Faulkner* (1950); *Requiem for a Nun* (1951); *Notes on a Horsethief* (1951); *Big Woods* (1955); and *Essays, Speeches, and Public Letters* (rev. 2004), edited by James B. Meriwether. Transcripts of discussions and interviews with Faulkner include *Faulkner at Nagano* (1956), edited by Robert A. Jelliffe; *Faulkner in the University* (1959), edited by Frederick L. Gwynn and Joseph L. Blotner; *Faulkner at West Point* (1964), edited by Joseph L. Fant and Robert Ashley (1964); and *The Lion in the Garden* (1968), edited by Meriwether and Michael Millgate. Letters are collected in *The Faulkner-Cowley File* (1961), edited by Malcolm Cowley (1961), and *Selected Letters of William Faulkner* (1977), edited by Joseph L. Blotner. Noel Polk has produced editions of several Faulkner novels based on study of the manuscripts. David Minter has published a Norton Critical Edition of *The Sound and the Fury* (1994), and Michael Gorra has published one of *As I Lay Dying* (2010).

Faulkner: A Biography, 2 vols. (1974), by Blotner has been condensed and updated in *Faulkner* (1984). Two shorter biographies based on Blotner's work are *William Faulkner: His Life and Work* (1980), by David Minter, and *Faulkner: The Transfiguration of Biography* (1979), by Judith Wittenberg.

Comprehensive guides are *Faulkner's World: A Directory of His People and Synopsis of*

Actions in His Published Works (1988), by Thomas E. Connolly; and *A William Faulkner Encyclopedia* (1999), edited by Robert W. Hamblin and Charles E. Peek. Teresa Towner's *Cambridge Introduction to William Faulkner* (2008) and Richard Moreland's edited *Companion to William Faulkner* are useful. Influential early studies include Cleanth Brooks's *William Faulkner: The Yoknapatawpha Country* (1963) and Hyatt H. Waggoner's *William Faulkner: From Jefferson to the World* (1959). Later studies include John T. Irwin's *Doubling and Incest, Repetition and Revenge: A Speculative Reading of Faulkner* (1975), Thadious M. Davis's *Faulkner's "Negro": Art and the Southern Context* (1983), Eric J. Sundquist's *Faulkner: The House Divided* (1983), Robert Dale Parker's *Faulkner and the Novelistic Imagination* (1985), Warwick Wadlington's *Reading Faulknerian Tragedy* (1987) and *As I Lay Dying: Stories out of Stories* (1992), Stephen M. Ross's *Fiction Inexhaustible Voice: Speech and Writing in Faulkner* (1989), Minrose C. Gwin's *The Feminine and Faulkner: Reading (beyond) Sexual Difference* (1990), André Bleikasten's *The Ink of Melancholy: Faulkner's Novels from "The Sound and the Fury" to "Light in August"* (1990), Richard Moreland's *Faulkner and Modernism: Rereading and Rewriting* (1990), Joel Williamson's *William Faulkner and Southern History* (1993), Diane Roberts's *Faulkner and Southern Womanhood* (1994), David Minter's *Faulkner's Questioning Narratives: Fiction of His Major Phase, 1929–42* (2001), and Philip Weinstein's *Becoming Faulkner: The Art and Life of William Faulkner* (2010).

Edited collections of critical essays include Louis J. Budd and Edwin Cady's *On Faulkner* (1989), Linda Wagner-Martin's *Faulkner: Six Decades of Criticism* (2002), and Annette Trefzer's *Global Faulkner: Faulkner and Yoknapatawpha, 2006* (2009).

F. Scott Fitzgerald

Fitzgerald's novels are *This Side of Paradise* (1920), *The Beautiful and Damned* (1922), *The Great Gatsby* (1925), *Tender Is the Night* (1934; rev. 1939; rpt. 1953), and the unfinished *The Last Tycoon* (1941). His collections of stories are *Flappers and Philosophers* (1921), *Tales of the Jazz Age* (1922), *All the Sad Young Men* (1926), and *Taps at Reveille* (1935). Two recent editions of his fiction are the Library of America's *Novels and Stories 1920–1922* (2000) and Matthew J. Bruccoli and Judith Baughman's *Before Gatsby: The First Twenty-Six Stories* (2001). The nine-volume Cambridge Edition of Fitzgerald's works (1991–2008) includes his novels, story collections, and *My Lost City: Personal Essays, 1920–1940* (2005). A satirical play, *The Vegetable, or From Presidents to Postman,* was published in 1923. Among collections of Fitzgerald's writings are *F. Scott Fitzgerald in His Own Time: A Miscellany* (1971), edited by Jackson R. Bryer and Bruccoli, and *Afternoon of an Author* (1957), edited by Arthur Mizener. *The Crack-Up* (1945), edited by Edmund Wilson, collects essays, notebook entries, and letters from the 1930s; youthful work is collected in *F. Scott Fitzgerald: The Princeton Years; Selected Writings, 1914–1920* (1966), edited by Chip Defaa.

The fullest collection of letters is *Correspondence of F. Scott Fitzgerald* (1980), edited by Bruccoli and Margaret M. Duggan. Other volumes of letters are *Dear Scott/Dear Max: The Fitzgerald-Perkins Correspondence* (1971), edited by John Kuehl and Jackson R. Bryer, *As Ever, Scott Fitz* (1972), edited by Bruccoli and Jennifer McCabe Atkinson (letters between Fitzgerald and his literary agent, Harold Ober), and *Dear Scott, Dearest Zelda: The Love Letters of F. Scott and Zelda Fitzgerald* (2002), edited by Jackson R. Bryer and Cathy W. Barks. Fitzgerald's biographies include Bruccoli's *Some Sort of Epic Grandeur: The Life of F. Scott Fitzgerald* (1981), Scott Donaldson's *Fool for Love: F. Scott Fitzgerald, A Biographical Portrait* (1983), James Mellow's *Invented Lives* (1984), Jeffrey Myers's *Scott Fitzgerald* (2000), and Andrew Turnbull's *Scott Fitzgerald* (2001).

Among guides are Robert Gale's *An F. Scott Fitzgerald Encyclopedia* (1998), Linda Pelzer's *Student Companion to F. Scott Fitzgerald* (2001), *A Historical Guide to F. Scott Fitzgerald* (2004), edited by Kirk Curnutt, and Curnutt's *Cambridge Introduction to F. Scott Fitzgerald* (2007). Critical studies include Milton R. Stern's *The Golden Moment: The Novels of F. Scott Fitzgerald* (1970), Brian Way's *F. Scott Fitzgerald and the Art of Social Fiction* (1980), John Kuehl's *F. Scott Fitzgerald, a Study of the Short Fiction* (1991), and Scott Donaldson's *Fitzgerald and Hemingway: Works and Days.* Among collections of critical essays are *The Short Stories of F. Scott Fitzgerald: New Approaches in Criticism* (1983), edited by Jackson R. Bryer; *New Essays on "The Great Gatsby,"* edited by Bruccoli; *The Cambridge Companion to F. Scott Fitzgerald,* edited by Ruth Prigozy (2001); and *F. Scott Fitzgerald in the Twenty-First Century* (2003), edited by Jackson R. Bryer, Prigozy, and Milton B. Stern.

Robert Frost

The Poetry of Robert Frost (1969) incorporated *Complete Poems* (1949) and Frost's last volume, *In the Clearing* (1962). The Library of America issued Frost's *Collected Poems, Prose, and Plays* (1995). Mark Richardson edited *The Collected Prose of Robert Frost* (2007), and Robert Faggen *The Notebooks of Robert Frost* (2007). Important collections of letters appear in *Selected Letters of Robert Frost* (1964), edited by Thompson; *The Letters of Robert Frost to Louis Untermeyer* (1963); and Margaret Anderson, *Robert Frost and John Bartlett: The Record of a Friendship* (1963). Conversations and interviews with Frost include Edward C. Lathem's *Interviews with Robert Frost* (1966), Reginald L. Cook's *The Dimensions of Robert Frost* (1964), Daniel Smythe's *Robert Frost Speaks* (1954), and Louis Mertin's *Robert Frost: Life and Talks—Walking* (1965).

Lawrance Thompson completed two volumes of the authorized biography: *Robert Frost: The Early Years, 1874–1915* (1966) and *Robert Frost: The Years of Triumph, 1915–1938* (1970). The third volume, *Robert Frost, the Later Years,* was completed by Richard Winnick (1976), and Lathem produced a shorter version of the biography in *Robert Frost: A Biography* (1981). Other biographies are Jeffrey Meyers's *Robert Frost* (1996) and Jay Parini's *Robert Frost: A Life* (1999). William H. Pritchard in *Frost: A Literary Life Reconsidered* (1984) is interested in the poet's art, not his personal life. James L. Potter's *Robert Frost Handbook* (1980) is a useful guide; Lathem produced a concordance to Frost's poetry (1994).

A brief critical introduction is Mordecai Marcus's *The Poems of Robert Frost* (1991). Specialized critical studies are Richard Poirier's *Robert Frost, The Work of Knowing* (1977, reissued with new material in 1990), John C. Kemp's *Robert Frost and New England: The Poet as Regionalist* (1979), George Monteiro's *Robert Frost and the New England Renaissance* (1988), Mario D'Avanzo's *A Cloud of Other Poets: Robert Frost and the Romantics* (1990), Judith Oster's *Toward Robert Frost* (1991), George Bagby's *Frost and the Book of Nature* (1993), and Mark Richardson's *Robert Frost: The Poet and His Poetics* (1997). Collections of critical essays include *On Frost* (1991), edited by Edwin H. Cady and Louis J. Budd, and Robert Faggen's *Cambridge Companion to Robert Frost* (2001).

Susan Glaspell
Plays by Susan Glaspell—including *Trifles, The Outside, The Verge,* and *Inheritors*—appeared in 1987. Another collection is *"Lifted Masks" and Other Works* (1993). *Major Novels of Susan Glaspell,* edited by Martha C. Carpenter, was published in 1995. Two biographies are Arthur E. Waterman's *Susan Glaspell* (1966) and Barbara O. Rajkowska's *Susan Glaspell: A Critical Biography* (2000). Critical studies include Marcia Noe's *Susan Glaspell: Voice from the Heartland* (1983), Veronica A. Makowsky's *Susan Glaspell's Century of American Women: A Critical Interpretation of Her Work* (1993), J. Ellen Gainor's *Susan Glaspell in Context: American Theater, Culture, and Politics, 1915–48* (2001), and Brenda Murphy's *The Province-*

town Players and the Culture of Modernity (2005). A collection of critical essays is *Susan Glaspell: Essays on Her Theater and Fiction* (1995), edited by Linda Ben-Zvi.

Ernest Hemingway
There is no collected edition of Hemingway's writings. In addition to works mentioned in the author's headnote, his fiction includes *Today Is Friday* (1926) and *God Rest You Merry Gentlemen* (1933). His tribute to Spain, *The Spanish Earth,* and his play *The Fifth Column* appeared in 1938, the latter in a collection *The Fifth Column and the First Forty-nine Stories.* His journalism has been collected in *The Wild Years* (1962), edited by Gene Z. Hanrahan, and *By-Line: Ernest Hemingway, Selected Articles and Dispatches of Four Decades* (1967), edited by William White. His *Complete Poems* (1992) has been edited by Nicholas Gerogiannis. Audre Hanneman's *Ernest Hemingway: A Comprehensive Bibliography* (1967) is thorough. Scribners published *The Complete Short Stories of Ernest Hemingway* (1987).

The authorized biography is Carlos Baker's *Ernest Hemingway: A Life Story* (1969). Jeffrey Meyers's *Hemingway: A Biography* (1985) and Kenneth S. Lynn's *Hemingway* (1987) are important. Michael Reynolds's detailed volumes include *The Young Hemingway* (1986), *Hemingway: The Paris Years* (1989), *Hemingway: The 1930s* (1997), and *Hemingway: The Final Years* (1999). *The Hemingway Women* (1983), by Bernice Kert, tells about Hemingway's mother, wives, and lovers; *Fame Became of Him: Hemingway as Public Writer* (1984), by John Raeburn, compares the life with the public image.

A Reader's Guide to the Short Stories of Ernest Hemingway (1989), by Paul Smith, is useful; Peter B. Messent's *Ernest Hemingway* (1992) is a good overview. For collections of critical essays on Hemingway, see *Ernest Hemingway: Eight Decades of Criticism* (2009), edited by Linda Wagner-Martin; *New Critical Approaches to the Short Stories of Ernest Hemingway* (1991), edited by Jackson J. Benson; *The Cambridge Companion to Hemingway* (1996), edited by Scott Donaldson; and *A Historical Guide to Ernest Hemingway* (2001), edited by Wagner-Martin. Specialized studies include Wirt Williams's *The Tragic Art of Ernest Hemingway* (1982), Mark Spilka's *Hemingway's Quarrel with Androgyny* (1990), Robert W. Trogdon's *The Lousy Racket: Hemingway, Scribners, and the Business of Literature* (2007), and Amy L. Strong's *Race and Identity in Hemingway's Fiction* (2008).

Langston Hughes
A sixteen-volume standard edition of Hughes's complete works appeared in 2001–03. Arnold

Rampersad and David Roessel edited *The Collected Poems of Langston Hughes* (1994), including *The Weary Blues* (1926), *Fine Clothes to the Jew* (1927), *The Dream Keeper and Other Poems* (1932), *Scottsboro Limited: Four Poems and a Play in Verse* (1932), *Montage of a Dream Deferred* (1951), and *The Panther and the Lash: Poems of our Times* (1967). His short stories were edited by Akiba Sullivan Harper (1996). Faith Berry edited *Good Morning Revolution: Uncollected Social Protest Writings by Langston Hughes* (1973). *Mule Bone* (1991), which he co-authored with Zora Neale Hurston, has been edited with contextual materials by George Houston Pope and Henry Louis Gates Jr. Hughes's autobiographical volumes include *The Big Sea* (1940) and *I Wonder as I Wander* (1956); both were reissued in 1993. Charles H. Nichols edited *Arna Bontemps–Langston Hughes, Letters 1925–1967* (1980).

Early biographies of Hughes include Charlemae Rollins's *Black Troubador: Langston Hughes* (1970) and James S. Haskins's *Always Movin' On: The Life of Langston Hughes* (1976). Faith Berry's *Langston Hughes: Before and Beyond Harlem* (1983, 1995) contains much about Hughes's life to 1940. Arnold Rampersad's two-volume *Life of Langston Hughes—* Vol. I, 1902–1941: *I, Too, Sing America* (1986), and Vol. II, 1941–1967: *I Dream a World* (1988)—is definitive.

Thomas A. Mikolyzk compiled *Langston Hughes: A Bio-Bibliography* (1990). Contemporary reviews were collected by Letitia Dace (1997). Full-length critical studies are Onwuchekwa Jemie's *Langston Hughes: An Introduction to the Poetry* (1976), Richard K. Barksdale's *Langston Hughes: The Poet and His Critics* (1977), Steven C. Tracy's *Langston Hughes and the Blues* (1988), and R. Baxter Miller's *The Art and Imagination of Langston Hughes* (1989). Essay collections include *Langston Hughes, Black Genius: A Critical Evaluation* (1972), edited by Therman B. O'Daniel; *Langston Hughes: Critical Perspectives Past and Present* (1993), edited by Henry Louis Gates Jr. and K. A. Appiah; *Langston Hughes: The Man, His Art, and His Continuing Influence* (1995), edited by C. James Trotman; and *A Historical Guide to Langston Hughes* (2003), edited by Steven C. Tracy. Peter Mandelik and Stanley Schatt's *A Concordance to the Poetry of Langston Hughes* (1975) is useful.

Zora Neale Hurston

Robert Hemenway's *Zora Neale Hurston, A Literary Biography* (1977) initiated the Hurston revival; her work is mostly available in paperback editions. A recent biography is Valerie Boyd's *Wrapped in Rainbows: The Life of Zora Neale Hurston* (2003). The Library of America published Hurston's writing in two volumes: *Novels and Stories* (1995) and *Folklore, Memoirs, and Other Writings* (1995); Jean Lee Cole and Charles Mitchell edited *Collected Plays* (2008). Her letters were edited by Carla Kaplan (2002). Book-length studies include Karla C. F. Holloway's *The Character of the Word: The Texts of Zora Neale Hurston* (1987), John Lowe's *Jump at the Sun: Zora Neale Hurston's Cosmic Comedy* (1994), Deborah G. Plant's *Every Tub Must Sit on Its Own Bottom: The Philosophy and Politics of Zora Neale Hurston* (1995), Margaret Genevieve West's *Zora Neale Hurston and American Literary Culture* (2005), and Lovalerie King's *Cambridge Introduction to Zora Neale Hurston* (2008). Hurston is linked to other writers in Cheryl A. Wall's *Women of the Harlem Renaissance* (1995), Carla Kaplan's *The Erotics of Talk: Women's Writing and Feminist Paradigms* (1996), and Trudier Harris's *The Power of the Porch: The Storyteller's Craft in Zora Neale Hurston, Gloria Naylor, and Randall Kenan* (1996). Collections of essays are *New Essays on "Their Eyes Were Watching God"* (1990), edited by Michael Awkward; *Zora Neale Hurston: Critical Perspectives Past and Present* (1993), edited by Henry Louis Gates Jr. and K. A. Appiah; and *Critical Essays on Zora Neale Hurston* (1998), edited by Gloria L. Cronin.

Amy Lowell

Lowell's complete poems were published in 1955. Ferris Greenslet, who was her editor at Houghton Mifflin, has written an excellent family chronicle from the first settler to Amy Lowell, *The Lowells and Their Seven Worlds* (1945). Additional biographical material may be found in S. Foster Damon's *Amy Lowell: A Chronicle, with Extracts from Her Correspondence* (1935), and *Florence Ayscough and Amy Lowell: Correspondence of a Friendship* (1945), edited by Harley Farnsworth MacNair. Critical estimates of Lowell include Jean Gould's *Amy: The World of Amy Lowell and the Imagist Movement* (1975), Glenn Richard Ruihley's *The Thorn of a Rose: Amy Lowell Reconsidered* (1975), and Richard Benvenuto's *Amy Lowell* (1985). Mary E. Galvin's *Queer Poetics: Five Modernist Women Writers* (1999) includes Lowell. Adrienne Munich and Melissa Bradshaw edited *Amy Lowell, American Modern* (2004).

Mina Loy

There is no scholarly edition of Loy's writing. Roger L. Conover's edition of *The Lost Lunar Baedeker* (1996) is the fullest collection of Loy's work currently in print; it includes some prose in addition to poetry. Carolyn Burke's *Becoming Mina Loy* (1996) remains the only biography. Virginia M. Kouidis's *Mina Loy: American Modernist Poet* (1980) for many years was the only full-length study. A more recent collection of essays is Maeera Schreiber and Keith Tuma's *Mina Loy: Woman and Poet* (1998). Cristanne Miller's *Cultures of Modernism: Marianne Moore, Mina Loy, and Else Lasker-Schüler* (2005) examines Loy along with other women modernists, as does Alex Goody's *Modernist Articulations: A Cultural Study of Djuna Barnes, Mina Loy, and Gertrude Stein* (2007).

Claude McKay

Volumes of McKay's poetry include *Songs of Jamaica* (1912), *Constab Ballads* (1912), *Spring in New Hampshire and Other Poems* (1920)—published in England—and *Harlem Shadows* (1922). William J. Maxwell edited the *Complete Poems* (2004), including many poems previously uncollected. Books of prose published in his lifetime include the novels *Home to Harlem* (1928), *Banjo* (1929), and *Banana Bottom* (1933); a short story collection, *Gingertown* (1932, 1991); an autobiography, *A Long Way from Home* (1937), and an essay collection, *Harlem: Negro Metropolis* (1940). Collections brought out after McKay's death include *Selected Poems* (1953), *The Dialect Poetry of Claude McKay* (1972), *The Passion of Claude McKay: Selected Poetry and Prose* (1973); two books of short stories, *Trial By Lynching* (1977) and *My Green Hills of Jamaica* (1979); and an essay collection, *The Negro in America* (1979).

Three good biographies are James R. Giles's *Claude McKay* (1976), Wayne F. Cooper's *Claude McKay: Rebel Sojourner in the Harlem Renaissance* (1987, 1996), and Tyrone Tillery's *Claude McKay: A Black Poet's Struggle for Identity* (1992). A collection of interpretive essays is *Claude McKay: Centennial Studies* (1992), edited by A. L. McLeod. General works with material on McKay include Harold Cruse's still valuable *The Crisis of the Negro Intellectual* (1967), Kenneth Ramchand's *The West Indian Novel and Its Background* (1970; rev. ed. 2004), Nathan I. Huggins's *Harlem Renaissance* (1971), Addison Gayle's *The Way of the New World: The Black Novel in America* (1975), David Levering Lewis's *When Harlem Was in Vogue* (1981), Bernard W. Bell's *The Afro-American Novel and Its Tradition* (1987), and George Hutchinson's *The Harlem Renaissance in Black and White* (1995). Contrasting treatments of McKay's poetry are in Winston James's *A Fierce Hatred of Injustice: Claude McKay's Jamaican Poetry of Rebellion* (2001) and Josh Gosciak's *The Shadowed Country: Claude McKay and the Romance of the Victorians* (2006).

Marianne Moore

Each collection of Moore's verse excluded some earlier poems while subjecting others to extensive revisions and changes in format. Her separate volumes include *Poems* (1921); *Observations* (1924); *The Pangolin and Other Verse* (1936); *What Are Years?* (1941); *Nevertheless* (1944); *Like a Bulwark* (1956); *O to Be a Dragon* (1959); and *Tell Me, Tell Me* (1966). Collections include *Selected Poems* (1935); *Collected Poems* (1951); and *The Complete Poems of Marianne Moore* (1967, repr. 1981, 1987), which included selections from her translation of *The Fables of La Fontaine* (1954). Grace Shulman's *The Poems of Marianne Moore* (2003) is now the fullest edition. Patricia C. Willis has brought together Moore's published prose in *The Complete Prose of Marianne Moore* (1986). Moore's correspondence with Robert Lowell is published in *Becoming a Poet* (1991), by David Kalstone; her relation to Wallace Stevens is considered by Robin G. Schulze in *The Web of Friendship* (1995). The only biography is *Marianne Moore: A Literary Life* (1990), by Charles Molesworth. Bonnie Costello edited *The Selected Letters of Marianne Moore* (1997). Book-length studies include Bernard F. Engel's *Marianne Moore* (1963, rev. 1989), Costello's *Marianne Moore: Imaginary Possessions* (1982), John M. Slatin's *The Savage's Romance: The Poetry of Marianne Moore* (1986), Grace Schulman's *Marianne Moore: The Poetry of Engagement* (1987), Margaret Holley's *The Poetry of Marianne Moore: A Study in Voice and Value* (1987), Cristanne Miller's *Questions of Authority* (1995), Linda Leavell's *Marianne Moore and the Visual Arts* (1995), and Elisabeth W. Joyce's *Cultural Critique and Abstraction: Marianne Moore and the Avant-Garde* (1998). Bethany Hickock's *Degrees of Freedom: American Women Poets and the Women's College, 1905–1955* (2008) connects Moore with Elizabeth Bishop and Sylvia Plath. Essay collections include *Marianne Moore, Woman and Poet* (1990), edited by Patricia Willis, and *Critics and Poets on Marianne Moore: "A Right Good Salvo of Barks"* (2005), edited by Leavell, Miller, and Schulze. Craig S. Abbott compiled *Marianne Moore: A Descriptive Bibliography* in 1977. Gary Lane's *A Concordance to the Poems of Marianne Moore* appeared in 1972.

Eugene O'Neill

The Library of America collected O'Neill's plays in three volumes, *Complete Plays 1913–1920, Complete Plays, 1920–1931*, and *Complete Plays 1932–1943* (1988). The standard biography of O'Neill is still that of Arthur and Barbara Gelb, *O'Neill* (1962, rev. 2000). Other biographical treatments are L. Schaeffer's *O'Neill, Son and Artist* (1973, 1990) and Stephen A. Bloch's *Eugene O'Neill: Beyond Mourning and Tragedy* (1999). *The Theatre We Worked For: The Letters of Eugene O'Neill to*

Kenneth Macgowan (1982), edited by Jackson R. Bryer, documents O'Neill's attitudes to the theater of his day. Brenda Murphy's *O'Neill: Long Day's Journey Into Night* (2001) provides a production history. Bryer and Travis Bogard edited *Selected Letters of Eugene O'Neill* (1994). *Conversations with Eugene O'Neill* (1990) is edited by Mark W. Estrin. Literary analysis of O'Neill's plays can be found in Bogard's *Contour in Time: The Plays of Eugene O'Neill* (1972, rev. 1987), Michael Manheim's *Eugene O'Neill's New Language of Kinship* (1982), Judith E. Barlow's *Final Acts: The Creation of Three Late O'Neill Plays* (1985), Kurt Eisen's *The Inner Strength of Opposites* (1994; on O'Neill's techniques), Joel Pfister's *Staging Depth: Eugene O'Neill and the Politics of Psychological Discourse* (1995), Donald Gallup's *Eugene O'Neill and His Eleven-Play Cycle* (1998), Doris Alexander's *Eugene O'Neill's Last Plays: Separating Art from Autobiography* (2005), and John Patrick Diggins's *Eugene O'Neill's America: Desire Under Democracy* (2007).

Essay collections include *Eugene O'Neill's Century* (1991), edited by Richard F. Moorton Jr.; *The Critical Response to Eugene O'Neill* (1993), edited by John H. Houchin; and *The Cambridge Companion to Eugene O'Neill* (1998), edited by Michael Manheim.

Katherine Anne Porter

Primary sources include *Ship of Fools* (1962); *The Collected Stories of Katherine Anne Porter* (1965); *The Collected Essays and Occasional Writings of Katherine Anne Porter* (1970); *The Never-Ending Wrong* (1977), about the Sacco and Vanzetti case; *Letters* (1990), edited by Isabel Bayley; *"This Strange, Old World" and Other Book Reviews by Katherine Anne Porter* (1991), edited by Darlene Harbour Unrue; *Uncollected Early Prose of Katherine Anne Porter* (1993), edited by Ruth M. Alvarez and Thomas F. Walsh; and *Katherine Anne Porter's Poetry* (1996), edited by Unrue.

Biographies are Joan Givner's *Katherine Anne Porter, A Life* (1982, rev. 1991) and Unrue's *Katherine Anne Porter: The Life of an Artist* (2005). Givner also edited *Katherine Anne Porter: Conversations* (1987). *A Bibliography of the Works of Katherine Anne Porter*, edited by Louise Waldrip and Shirley Ann Bauer, appeared in 1969.

Critical studies include Jane Krause DeMouy's *Katherine Anne Porter's Women: The Eye of Her Fiction* (1983), Unrue's *Truth and Vision in Katherine Anne Porter's Fiction* (1985), Willene and George Hendrick's *Katherine Anne Porter* (rev. 1988), Thomas F. Walsh's *Katherine Anne Porter and Mexico: The Illusion of Eden* (1992), Robert H. Brinkmeyer's *Katherine Anne Porter's Artistic Development* (1993), Janis P. Stout's *Katherine Anne Porter, A Sense of the Times* (1995), and Mary Titus's *The Ambivalent Art of Katherine Anne Porter* (2005). Unrue edited *Critical Essays on Katherine Anne Porter* (1997).

Ezra Pound

Pound's early poetry, from *A Lume Spento* (1908) through *Ripostes* (1912), is in the authoritative *Collected Early Poems of Ezra Pound* (1976), edited by Michael King. The same volumes, along with later volumes *Hugh Selwyn Mauberley* and *Homage to Sextus Propertius*, are collected in *Personae: The Collected Shorter Poems* (rev. ed. 1949; 2nd rev. ed. 1990). The New Directions edition of *The Cantos* (1993) is definitive. The most important of Pound's critical writings are *The Spirit of Romance* (rev. 1952); *Gaudier-Brzeska: A Memoir* (1916); *Instigations* (1920); *Make It New* (1934); *The ABC of Reading* (1934); *Guide to Kulchur* (1938); and *Patria Mia* (1950). His criticism has been collected in *Literary Essays of Ezra Pound* (1954), edited by T. S. Eliot; *Selected Prose, 1909–1965* (1973), edited by William Cookson (1973); and *Ezra Pound's Poetry and Prose Contributions to Periodicals* (1991), prefaced and arranged by Lea Baechler, A. Walton Litz, and James Longenback in eleven volumes. *Ezra Pound Speaking: Radio Speeches of World War II* (1978), edited by Leonard W. Doob, collects his wartime radio addresses. D. D. Paige edited *The Letters of Ezra Pound, 1907–1941* (1950). Other correspondence is collected in *Ezra Pound and Dorothy Shakespear: Their Letters, 1909–1914* (1984), edited by Omar Pound and A. Walton Litz; *Pound/Lewis: The Letters of Ezra Pound and Wyndham Lewis* (1985), edited by Timothy Materer; *Ezra Pound and James Loughlin* (1994), edited by David M. Gordon; and *Pound/Cummings: The Correspondence of Ezra Pound and E. E. Cummings*, edited by Barry Ahearn. Reviews of Pound are collected in Eric Homberger's *Ezra Pound: The Critical Heritage* (1973, 1997).

James J. Wilhelm's three-volume biography includes *The American Roots of Ezra Pound* (1985), *Ezra Pound in London and Paris, 1908–1925* (1990), and *Ezra Pound: The Tragic Years, 1925–1972* (1994). Also useful are Noel Stock's *The Life of Ezra Pound* (1970, 1982), C. David Haymann's *Ezra Pound, The Last Rower: A Political Profile* (1976), Humphrey Carpenter's *A Serious Character: The Life of Ezra Pound* (1988), and Wendy Stallard Flory's *The American Ezra Pound* (1989). *The Roots of Treason: Ezra Pound and the Secrets of St. Elizabeth* (1984), by E. Fuller Torrey, focuses on Pound's trial and incarceration.

Hugh Kenner's *The Pound Era* (1972) has been influential. Good introductions are Christine Brooke-Rose's *A ZBC of Ezra Pound* (1971) and James Knapp's *Ezra Pound* (1972). For *The Cantos* see the *Annotated Index to the Cantos of Ezra Pound* (1957) (through Canto LXXXIV), edited by John H. Edwards and William W. Vasse; George Dekker's *The Cantos of Ezra Pound* (1963); Noel Stock's *Reading the Cantos* (1967); Ronald Bush's *The Genesis of Pound's Cantos* (1976); Wilhelm's *The Later Cantos of Ezra Pound* (1977); Lawrence S. Rainey's *Ezra Pound and the Monument of Culture* (1991); Carrol F. Terrill's *A Companion to the Cantos of Ezra Pound* (1993); George Kearn's *Guide to Ezra Pound's Selected Cantos* (1980); Anthony Woodward's *Ezra Pound and "The Pisan Cantos"* (1980); and William Cookson's updated *Guide to the Cantos of Ezra Pound* (2001). *Ezra Pound and Italian Fascism* (1991), by Tim Redman, addresses the poet's politics; as does *Pound in Purgatory: From Economic Realism to Anti-Semitism* (1999), by Leon Surette. Cultural approaches to Pound include Michael Coyle's *Ezra Pound, Popular Genres, and the Discourse of Culture* (1995), Daniel Tiffany's *Radio Corpse* (1995), and Rebecca Beasley, *Ezra Pound and the Visual Culture of Modernism* (2007). Marjorie Perloff's *The Dance of the Intellect* (1996) studies poetry in the Pound tradition; Jacob Korg's *Winter Love: Ezra Pound and H. D.* (2003) is a comparative study. Andrew Gibson edited *Pound in Multiple Perspective: A Collection of Critical Essays* (1993) and Ira B. Nadel edited *The Cambridge Companion to Ezra Pound* (1999).

Edwin Arlington Robinson

Collected Poems of Edwin Arlington Robinson (1921) was enlarged periodically through 1937. In addition to shorter verse, Robinson wrote long narrative poems, including the Arthurian trilogy of *Merlin* (1917), *Lancelot* (1920), and *Tristrum* (1927). Other books include *Roman Bartholomew* (1923), *The Man Who Died Twice* (1924), *Cavender's House* (1929), *The Glory of the Nightingales* (1930), *Matthias at the Door* (1931), *Talifer* (1933), *Amaranth* (1934), and *King Jasper* (1935). Ridgely Torrence compiled *Selected Letters* (1940). Denham Sutcliffe edited *Untriangulated Stars: Letters of Edwin Arlington Robinson to Harry de Forest Smith, 1890–1905* (1947). Richard Cary edited *Edwin Arlington Robinson's Letters to Edith Brower* (1968).

Scott Donaldson's *Edwin Arlington Robinson: A Poet's Life* (2007) is comprehensive. Richard Cary documented *The Early Reception of Edwin Arlington Robinson* (1974). Introductions to Robinson's work include Wallace L. Anderson's *Edwin Arlington Robinson: A Critical Introduction* (1967), Hoyt C. Franchere's *Edwin Arlington Robinson* (1968), and Louis O. Coxe's *Edwin Arlington Robin-*

son: The Life of Poetry (1969). Ellsworth Barnard edited *Edwin Arlington Robinson: Centenary Essays* (1969). Other collections are *Appreciation of Edwin Arlington Robinson: Twenty-eight Interpretive Essays* (1969), edited by Richard Cary; and *Edwin Arlington Robinson: A Collection of Critical Essays* (1970), edited by Francis Murphy. Richard Hoffpair's *The Contemplative Poetry of Edwin Arlington Robinson, Robert Frost, and Yvor Winters* (2002) links Robinson to other poets.

Carl Sandburg

The Complete Poems of Carl Sandburg (1950) was revised and expanded in 1970. *Breathing Tokens* (1978), edited by Margaret Sandburg, prints unpublished poems. *Billy Sunday and Other Poems* (1993), edited by George and Willene Hendrick, contains some of his unpublished, uncollected, and unexpurgated poems. In addition to eight full-length volumes of poetry, Sandburg wrote a Pulitzer Prize–winning study of Abraham Lincoln: *Abraham Lincoln: The Prairie Years*, 2 vols. (1926), and *Abraham Lincoln: The War Years*, 4 vols. (1939), two collections of journalism and social commentary, *Rootabaga Stories* for children, a novel, and a book of American folk songs. *Fables, Foibles and Foobles* (1988), edited by George Hendrick, is a selection of unpublished humorous pieces. *More Rootabagas* (1993), edited by Hendrick, contains stories for children. *Selected Poems* (1996) was edited by George and Willene Hendrick. *The Letters of Carl Sandburg* (1968, 1988) was edited by Herbert Mitgang. *The Poet and the Dream Girl: The Love Letters of Lilian Steichen and Carl Sandburg* (1987, 1999) was edited by Margaret Sandburg.

Always the Young Strangers (1953) and *Ever the Winds of Chance* (1983), edited by Margaret Sandburg and George Hendrick, are segments of Sandburg's autobiography. A full-scale biography is Penelope Niven's *Carl Sandburg: A Biography* (1991). Critical studies include Richard Crowder's *Carl Sandburg* (1964) and Philip R. Yannella's *The Other Carl Sandburg* (1996).

Gertrude Stein

The Library of America published Stein's writings in two volumes: 1903–32 and 1932–46 (1998). *The Yale Edition of the Unpublished Writings of Gertrude Stein* (1951–58), edited by Carl Van Vechten, contains eight volumes of poetry, prose fiction, portraits, essays, and miscellany. The Norton Critical Edition of *Three Lives and Q.E.D.* (2005), edited by Marianne DeKoven, supplies critical and biographical contexts. Among publications in Stein's lifetime are *Tender Buttons* (1914) and prose fiction, including *Three Lives* (1909),

The Making of Americans (1925), *Lucy Church Amiably* (1930), *Ida: A Novel* (1941), and *Brewsie and Willie* (1946). *Geography and Plays* (1922), *Operas and Plays* (1932), and *Last Operas and Plays* (1949, 1995), edited by Carl Van Vechten, contain dramatic pieces. Biographical material and portraits of Stein's contemporaries may be found in *The Autobiography of Alice B. Toklas* (1933), *Portraits and Prayers* (1934); *Everybody's Autobiography* (1937), and *Wars I Have Seen* (1945). Other works, including meditations, essays, sketches, and sociolinguistic treatises, are *Useful Knowledge* (1928), *How to Write* (1931), *Lectures in America* (1935), *Narration: Four Lectures by Gertrude Stein* (1935), *What Are Masterpieces* (1940), and *Four in America* (1947). Donald C. Gallup edited *Fernhurst, Q.E.D. and Other Early Writings by Gertrude Stein* (1971) and also a collection of letters to Stein, *The Flowers of Friendship* (1953). Her correspondence with Mabel Dodge Luhan is edited by Patricia R. Everett (1996) and with Thornton Wilder by Edward Burns and Ulla E. Dydo (1996). *Baby Precious Always Shines* (2000), edited by Kay Tarner, has selected love letters written between Stein and her partner, Alice B. Toklas. *Gertrude Stein: An Annotated Bibliography* (1979) was compiled by Maureen R. Liston.

W. G. Rogers's *When This You See Remember Me: Gertrude Stein in Person* (1948) and Alice B. Toklas's *What Is Remembered* (1963) are reminiscences of Stein by friends. Biographies include Howard Greenfield's *Gertrude Stein: A Biography* (1973), James R. Mellow's *Charmed Circle: Gertrude Stein and Company* (1974), Janet Hobhouse's *Everybody Who Was Anybody* (1989), Linda Wagner-Martin's *Favored Strangers: Gertrude Stein and Her Family* (1995), Brenda Wineapple's *Sister Brother: Gertrude and Leo Stein* (1996), and Janet Malcolm's *Two Lives: Gertrude and Alice* (2007).

Critical studies include Robert B. Haas's *A Primer for the Gradual Understanding of Gertrude Stein* (1971), Richard Bridgman's *Gertrude Stein in Pieces* (1970), Wendy Steiner's *Exact Resemblance to Exact Resemblance: The Literary Portraiture of Gertrude Stein* (1978), Marianne DeKoven's *A Different Language: Gertrude Stein's Experimental Writing* (1983), Randa Kay Dubnick's *The Structure of Obscurity: Gertrude Stein, Language, and Cubism* (1984), Lisa Ruddick's *Reading Gertrude Stein: Body, Text, Gnosis* (1990), Jane P. Bowers's *Gertrude Stein* (1993), Linda Watts's *Gertrude Stein: A Study of the Short Fiction* (1999), Barbara Will's *Gertrude Stein, Modernism, and the Problem of "Genius"* (2000), Steven Meyer's *Irresistible Dictation: Gertrude Stein and the Correlations of Writing and Science* (2001), and Dana Cairns Watson's *Gertrude Stein and the Essence of What Hoppens* (2005). Bruce

Kellner edited the useful *Gertrude Stein Companion* (1988). A collection of critical essays, edited by Richard Kostelanetz, is *Gertrude Stein Advanced* (1990).

John Steinbeck

The Library of America issued three volumes of Steinbeck's work, *Novels and Stories 1932–1937* (1994), *The Grapes of Wrath and Other Writings* (1996), and *Novels 1942–1952* (2002). Two biographies are *The True Adventures of John Steinbeck, Writer* (1984), by Jackson J. Benson, and *John Steinbeck* (1995), by Jay Parini. Elaine Steinbeck and Robert Wallsten edited *Steinbeck: A Life in Letters* (1975). Critical studies of Steinbeck include R. S. Hughes's *Beyond the Red Pony: A Reader's Guide to Steinbeck's Complete Short Stories* (1987), John H. Timmerman's *The Dramatic Landscape of Steinbeck's Short Stories* (1990), and Warren French's *John Steinbeck's Fiction Revisited* (1994). R. David edited *John Steinbeck: A Collection of Critical Essays* (1972); other collections are *Rediscovering Steinbeck* (1989), edited by Cliff Lewis and Carroll Britch; *Critical Essays on Steinbeck's* Grapes of Wrath (1989), edited by John Ditsky; *Short Novels of John Steinbeck* (1990), edited by Jackson J. Benson; *John Steinbeck: The Contemporary Reviews* (1996), edited by Joseph R. McElrath Jr., Jesse S. Crisler, and Susan Shillinglaw; *Steinbeck and the Environment: Interdisciplinary Approaches* (1997), edited by Susan F. Beegel; and *Beyond Boundaries: Rereading John Steinbeck* (2002), edited by Shillinglaw and Kevin Hearle.

Wallace Stevens

The Collected Poems of Wallace Stevens was published in 1954. *Opus Posthumous* (1957, rev. 1989) by Milton J. Bates includes previously uncollected poems, plays, and essays. *The Necessary Angel: Essays on Reality and the Imagination* (1951) is Stevens's prose statement on poetry. The Library of America issued his *Collected Poetry and Prose* (1997). Other resources are *Letters of Wallace Stevens* (1966, 1996), edited by Holly Stevens; *The Contemplated Spouse: The Letters of Wallace Stevens to Elsie* (2006), edited by J. Donald Blount; *Concordance to the Poetry of Wallace Stevens* (1963), edited by Thomas Walsh; and *Wallace Stevens: A Descriptive Bibliography* (1973), compiled by J. M. Edelstein.

Joan Richardson's *Wallace Stevens: The Early Years, 1879–1923* (1986) chronicles the poet's youth and her *Wallace Stevens: The Later Years, 1923–1955* (1988) completes the story. Another biography is Tony Sharpe's *Wallace Stevens: A Literary Life* (2000). A. Walton Litz's *Introspective Voyager: The Poetic Development of Wallace Stevens* (1972) traces

Stevens's thought and style through his early and middle years. Harold Bloom's *Wallace Stevens: The Poems of Our Climate* (1977) considers intellectual influences on Stevens; Joseph N. Riddle's *The Clairvoyant Eye: The Poetry and Poetics of Wallace Stevens* (1969, 1991) reads many individual poems. Other good full-length studies include Eleanor Cook's *Poetry, Word-Play, and Word-War in Wallace Stevens* (1988) and Cook's *A Reader's Guide to Wallace Stevens* (2007), James Longenbach's *Wallace Stevens: The Plain Sense of Things* (1991), Daniel Schwarz's *Narrative and Representation in the Poetry of Wallace Stevens* (1993), Alan Filreis's *Modernism from Left to Right* (1994), and Janet McCann's *Wallace Stevens Revisited* (1995). Jacqueline Vaught Brogan's *The Violence Within/The Violence Without: Wallace Stevens and the Emergence of a Revolutionary Poetics* (2003) and Malcolm Woodland's *Wallace Stevens and the Apocalyptic Mode* (2005) consider the relation of Stevens's poetry to war. Albert Gelpi collects essays on the poet in *Wallace Stevens: The Poetics of Modernism* (1990); other collections are *Critical Essays on Wallace Stevens* (1988), edited by Steven Gould Axelrod and Helen Deese, *Wallace Stevens and the Feminine* (1993), edited by Melita Schaum, and *Wallace Stevens Across the Atlantic* (2008), edited by Bart Eeckhout and Edward Ragg.

Jean Toomer

Toomer's published works include *Cane* (1923, repr. 1975, pub. also in a Norton Critical Edition, 2011), *Essentials* (1931), *Portage Potential* (1932), and an address, "The Flavor of Man" (1949). His *Collected Poems*, edited by Robert B. Jones and Margery Toomer Latimer, were published in 1988. *A Jean Toomer Reader* (1993), containing previously unpublished writings, was edited by Frederik L. Rusch; Robert B. Jones edited *Selected Essays and Literary Criticism* (1996). Mark Whalan edited *The Letters of Jean Toomer, 1919–1924* (2005). Brian Joseph Benson and Mabel Mayle Dillard's *Jean Toomer* (1980); Nellie Y. McKay's *Jean Toomer, Artist: A Study of His Literary Life and Work, 1894–1936* (1984); and Cynthia Earl Kerman and Richard Eldridge's *The Lives of Jean Toomer: A Hunger for Wholeness* (1989) are biographies. Studies include *Jean Toomer and the Terrors of American History* (1998), by Charles Scruggs and Lee Van De Marr, and *Split-Gut Song: Jean Toomer and the Poetics of Modernity* (2005), by Karen Ford Jackson. Whalan's *Race, Manhood, and Modernism in America: The Short Story Cycles of Sherwood Anderson and Jean Toomer* (2007) is a comparative study. Essay collections are *Jean Toomer: A Critical Evaluation* (1988), edited by Therman B. O'Daniel, and *Jean Toomer and*

the Harlem Renaissance, edited by Geneviève Faber and Michel Faith (2000).

William Carlos Williams

Williams's poems were first collected in three volumes: *Collected Earlier Poems of William Carlos Williams* (1951), *Collected Later Poems of William Carlos Williams* (1950), and *Pictures from Brueghel* (1962). More recent are *The Collected Poems of William Carlos Williams, Vol. 1, 1909–1939* (1996), edited by A. Walton Litz and Christopher MacGowan, and *Vol. 2, 1939–1962* (1988), edited by Mac-Gowan (1988). *Paterson's* five books, published individually between 1946 and 1958, were issued in one volume in 1963 and reedited by MacGowan (1992). *Kora in Hell,* Williams's volume of prose poetry, is in the collection *Imaginations* (1970), edited by Webster Schott, along with essays, fiction, and creative prose. Williams's short stories are collected in *Make Light of It* (1950) and again, with several additions, in *The Farmers' Daughters* (1961). His novels are *A Voyage to Pagany* (1928), *White Mule* (1937), *In the Money* (1940), and *The Build Up* (1946). His dramatic pieces were published together in *Many Loves and Other Plays* (1961). Important essays are contained in *In the American Grain* (1925, 1940); *Selected Essays of William Carlos Williams* (1954); and *Imaginations* (1970), edited by Webster Schott. Williams's prose also includes *The Autobiography of William Carlos Williams* (1951); a book of recollections dictated to Edith Heal, *I Wanted to Write a Poem* (1958); and *Yes, Mrs. Williams* (1959), a portrait of the poet's mother. J. C. Thirlwall edited *The Selected Letters of William Carlos Williams* (1957). Selections from the Pound–Williams correspondence, edited by Hugh Witemeyer, appeared in 1996. Letters between Williams and Denise Levertov, edited by MacGowan, appeared in 1998. Barry Ahearn edited *The Correspondence of William Carlos Williams and Louis Zukofsky* (2003). *The Humane Particulars: The Collected Letters of William Carlos Williams and Kenneth Burke* (2003) was edited by James H. East. Emily Mitchell Wallace compiled *A Bibliography of William Carlos Williams* (1968). Reed Whittemore's *William Carlos Williams: Poet from Jersey* (1975) is a critical biography, as is Paul Mariani's more detailed *William Carlos Williams: A New World Naked* (1981).

James E. Breslin's *William Carlos Williams: An American Artist* (1970) is a still-useful overview. Other general introductions are Thomas R. Whitaker's *William Carlos Williams* (1989) and Kelli A. Larson's *Guide to the Poetry of William Carlos Williams* (1995). Among specialized studies are Mike Weaver's *William Carlos Williams: The American Background*

(1971), Joseph N. Riddel's *The Inverted Bell: Modernism and the Counter-Poetics of William Carlos Williams* (1974), Henry M. Sayre's *The Visual Text of William Carlos Williams* (1983), Ann W. Fisher-Wirth's *William Carlos Williams and Autobiography: The Woods of His Own Nature* (1989), Ron Callan's *William Carlos Williams and Transcendentalism* (1992), T. Hugh Crawford's *Modernism, Medicine, and William Carlos Williams* (1993), Brian A. Bremen's *William Carlos Williams and the Diagnostics of Culture* (1993), Peter Halter's *The Revolution in the Visual Arts and the Poetry of William Carlos Williams* (1994), Donald W. Markos's *Ideas in Things* (1994), Barry Ahearn's *William Carlos Williams and Alterity* (1994), Julio Marzan's *The Spanish American Roots of William Carlos Williams* (1994), Stanley Koehler's *Countries of the Mind: The Poetry of William Carlos Williams* (1998), and John Beck's *Writing the Radical Center: William Carlos Williams, John Dewey, and American Cultural Politics,* (2001).

Linda Wagner's *The Prose of William Carlos Williams* (1970) and Robert Coles's *William Carlos Williams: The Knack of Survival in America* (1975) discuss Williams's prose. For *Paterson,* see Joel Conarroe's *William Carlos Williams' Paterson: Language and Landscape* (1970) and Benjamin Sankey's *A Companion to William Carlos Williams's Paterson* (1971). Paul Mariani's *William Carlos Williams: The Poet and His Critics* (1975) considers Williams's critical reception, as does *William Carlos Williams, The Critical Heritage* (1980, 1997), edited by Charles Doyle. *Critical Essays on Wallace Stevens* was edited by Steven Gould Axelrod and Helen Deese (1988).

Richard Wright

Wright's fiction includes *Uncle Tom's Children* (1938), *Native Son* (1940), *The Outsider* (1953), and *Eight Men* (1961). *Black Boy* (1945) is his autobiography; *White Man, Listen!* (1957) is an important work of nonfiction. The Library of America has published his writings in two volumes, including an unexpurgated version of *Native Son* (1991). For a complete bibliography of his writings, see *Richard Wright: A Primary Bibliography* (1982), compiled by Charles T. Davis and Michel Fabre. A good example of reviews can be found in *Richard Wright: The Critical Reception* (1978), edited by John M. Reilly; a massive bibliography of Wright criticism around the world has been assembled by Keneth Kinnamon (1988). Kinnamon and Michel Fabre edited *Conversations with Richard Wright* (1993). The best critical biography is Fabre's *The Unfinished Quest of Richard Wright* (1993); see also Margaret Walker's *Richard Wright, Daemonic Genius* (1993) and Hazel Rowley's *Richard Wright: The Life and Times* (2001). Critical studies include Russell C. Brignano's *Richard Wright: An Introduction to the Man and His Works* (1970), Kinnamon's *The Emergence of Richard Wright* (1972), Fabre's *Richard Wright: Books and Writers* (1990), and his essays in *The World of Richard Wright* (2007), and Robert Butler's *Native Son: The Emergence of a New Black Hero* (1991). Abdul R. Jan Mohamed's *The Death-Bound-Subject: Richard Wright's Archaeology of Death* (2005) is an ambitious theoretical study. Collections of criticism are Yoshinobu Hakutani's *Critical Essays on Richard Wright* (1982); *Richard Wright: Critical Perspectives Past and Present* (1993), edited by Henry Louis Gates Jr. and K. A. Appiah; *The Critical Response to Richard Wright* (1995), edited by Robert J. Butler; *Richard Wright: A Collection of Critical Essays* (1995), edited by Arnold Rampersad; and Kinnamon's *Critical Essays on Richard Wright's Native Son* (1997).

AMERICAN LITERATURE SINCE 1945

Reference Works and Histories

James L. Harner's *Literary Research Guide* (1993, updated online) is a valuable resource. James D. Hart's *Oxford Companion to American Literature,* 5th ed. (1983), Jack Saltzman's *The Cambridge Handbook of American Literature* (1986), and the annual volumes of *American Literary Scholarship* (currently edited by David J. Nordloh and Gary Scharnhorst) identify authors and trends. Of broader scope are editor Emory Elliott's *The Columbia Literary History of the United States* (1988) and *The Columbia History of the American Novel* (1991), together with editor Jay Parini's *The Columbia History of American Poetry* (1993). Sacvan Bercovitch is general editor of the multivolume, ongoing *Cambridge History of American Literature.* Don B.

Wilmeth has edited the *Cambridge Guide to American Theatre* (1996). The vast *Dictionary of Literary Biography*, under the supervision of Matthew J. Bruccoli, the Scribners *American Writers* series, edited by Jay Parini, and vol. 2 of David Perkins's *History of Modern Poetry* (1976) offer wide coverage of specific authors. An indispensable reference guide for poetry is *Contemporary Poets*, 7th ed. (2000), edited by Thomas Riggs. Specific areas are treated by editors Joel Shatzky and Michael Taub's *Contemporary Jewish-American Novelists: A Bio-Critical Sourcebook* (1997), Darryl Dickson-Carr's *The Columbia Guide to Contemporary African American Fiction* (2005), editor Eric Cheyfitz's *The Columbia Guide to American Indian Literatures of the United States since 1945* (2006), and José F. Aranda Jr.'s *When We Arrive: A New Literary History of Mexican America* (2003). Steven Conner's *The Cambridge Companion to Postmodernism* (2004) provides a guide to the cultural contexts of the period. Useful introductory series are the University of South Carolina Press's *Understanding . . .* volumes, the Twayne United States Authors series, Methuen's Contemporary Writers, the University Press of Mississippi's *Conversations with . . .* , the *Critical Essays* books from G. K. Hall Publishers, the Greenwood Press *Critical Response* series, and the *Modern Critical Views* collections edited by Harold Bloom. The University of Michigan's *Poets on Poetry* series offers volumes in which poets comment on their own and others' work.

Literary Theory and Criticism

Theoretical overviews are provided by Christian Moraru in *Memorious Discourse: Reprise and Representation in Postmodernism* (2005) and Stacey Olster in *The Trash Phenomenon: Contemporary Literature, Popular Culture, and the Making of the American Century* (2003). The critic and theorist Marjorie Perloff has written a series of books that provide theoretical overviews and studies of the poetry of the period: *The Poetics of Indeterminacy* (1981), *The Dance of the Intellect* (1985), *Radical Artifice: Writing in the Age of Media* (1991), and *21st-Century Modernism: The New Poetics* (2001). Playwrights and their work are studied by Sanford Sternlicht in *A Reader's Guide to Modern American Drama* (2002), Thomas S. Hischak in *American Theatre: A Chronicle of Comedy and Drama, 1969–2000* (2001), Christopher Bigsby in *Contemporary American Playwrights* (1999), and Herbert Blau in *The Dubious Spectacle: Extremities of the Theater, 1976–2000* (2002). Histories of specific movements in poetry are explored in Michael Palmer's *The San Francisco Renaissance* (1991) and David Lehmann's *The Last Avant-Garde: The Making of the New York School of Poets* (1998). A more general history appears in Robert von Hallberg's *American Poetry and Culture 1945–1980* (1985). The history of poetry may also be traced through statements on poetics: *Poetics of the New American Poetry* (1973), edited by Donald Allen, was groundbreaking, and *Twentieth-Century American Poetry* (2004), edited by Dana Gioia, David Mason, and Meg Schoerke, gathers statements on poetics from throughout the period. Fiction's development is traced in detail in Kathryn Hume's *American Dream, American Nightmare: Fiction since 1960* (2000) and Marc Chénetier's *Beyond Suspicion: New*

American Fiction since 1960 (1996). Mark McGurl traces the impact of creative writing programs on fiction in *The Program Era* (2009), while Samuel Cohen focuses on a key decade in *After the End of History: American Fiction in the 1990s* (2009). The development of poetry in the period is examined in Dana Gioia's *Disappearing Ink: Poetry at the End of Print Culture* (2004), Christopher MacGowan's *Twentieth-Century American Poetry* (2004), Stephen Fredman's *A Concise Companion to Twentieth-Century American Poetry* (2005), Jennifer Ashton's *From Modernism to Postmodernism: American Poetry and Theory in the Twentieth Century* (2006), and Charles Altieri's *The Art of Twentieth-Century American Poetry: Modernism and After* (2006). Among the useful collections of literary criticism that focus on poetry of the period are Sherman Paul's *The Lost America of Love* (1981), J. D. McClatchy's *White Paper* (1990), Helen Vendler's *The Music of What Happens* (1988) and *Soul Says* (1995), Lynn Keller's *Re-Making It New* (1987), Vernon Shetley's *After the Death of Poetry* (1993), Peter Stitt's *Uncertainty and Plenitude: Five Contemporary Poets* (1997), Charles Altieri's *Postmodernisms Now* (1998), Thomas Travisano's *Mid-Century Quartet* (1999), and Adam Kirsch's *The Wounded Surgeon: Confession and Transformation in Six American Poets* (2005). Political implications are examined by Alan Nadel in *Containment Culture: American Narratives, Postmodernism, and the Atomic Age* (1995), while Wendy Steiner exlores the controversy over sexual elements in *The Scandal of Pleasure* (1995). Politics in poetry is explored in Mutlu Konuk's *Politics and Form in Postmodern Poetry* (1995), Tim Wood's *The Poetics of the Limit: Ethics and Politics in Modern and Contemporary American Poetry* (2002), and Walter Kalaidjian's *The Edge of Modernism: American Poetry and the Traumatic Past* (2006).

Two important studies from a feminist perspective are Nancy J. Peterson's *Against Amnesia: Contemporary Women Writers and the Crisis of Historical Memory* (2001) and Linda S. Kauffman's *Bad Girls and Sick Boys: Fantasies in Contemporary Art and Culture* (1998). A feminist approach to the study of poetry can be found in *Gendered Modernisms: American Women Poets and Their Readers* (1996), edited by Margaret Dickie and Thomas Travisano. Jean Wyatt considers social issues in *Risking Difference: Identification, Race, and Community in Contemporary Fiction and Feminism* (2004). Multiculturalism concerns Martha J. Cutter in *Lost and Found in Translation: Contemporary Ethnic American Writing and the Politics of Language Diversity* (2005), Paula M. L. Moya in *Learning from Experience: Minority Identities, Multicultural Struggles* (2002), Robert Jackson in *Seeking the Region in American Literature and Culture* (2005), and A. Robert Lee in *Multicultural American Literature: Comparative Black, Native, Latino/a and Asian American Fictions* (2003). Multiculturalism in poetry is the subject of Satya Mohanty's *Literary Theory and the Claims of History: Postmodernism, Objectivity and Multicultural Politics* (1997). Cassie Premo Steele's *We Heal from Memory: Sexton, Lorde, Anzaldúa, and the Poetry of Witness* (2000) treats women poets across the divisions of ethnicity. African American writing is the focus in Bernard W. Bell's *The Contemporary African American Novel: Its Folk Roots and Modern Literary Branches* (2004), Cheryl A. Wall's *Worrying the Line: Black Women Writers, Lineage, and Literary Tradition* (2005), Suzanne W. Jones's *Race Mixing: Southern Fiction since the Sixties* (2004), and James W. Coleman's *Faithful Vision: Treatments of the*

Sacred, Spiritual, and Supernatural in Twentieth-Century African American Fiction (2006). *Black Women Writers (1950–1980): A Critical Evaluation*, edited by Mari Evans, explores African American novelists and poets from a feminist perspective. *African American Theater: A Cultural Companion* (2008) by Gloria Dickerson covers the subject in a narrative manner. African American poetry is examined in Joanne Gabbin's *The Furious Flowering of African American Poetry* (1999) and Alden Lynn Nielsen's *Black Chant: Languages of African-American Postmodernism* (1992). Chicano/a work is treated by Charles M. Tatum in *Chicano Popular Culture* (2001), Mary Pat Brady in *Extinct Lands, Temporal Geographies: Chicana Literature and the Urgency of Space* (2002), Elisabeth Mermann-Jozwiak in *Postmodern Vernaculars: Chicana Literature and Postmodern Rhetoric* (2005), Tey Diana Rebolledo in *The Chronicles of Panchita Villa and Other Guerrilleras* (2005), Ramon Saldívar in *Chicano Narrative* (1990), and Ellie D. Hernandez in *Postnationalism in Chicanal/o Literature and Culture* (2009). Deborah L. Madsen's *Understanding Contemporary Chicana Literature* (2000) examines the work of women poets.

Transnational Asian American Literature: Sites and Transits (2006), edited by Shirley Geok-lin Lim, et al., includes essays covering issues from immigration to feminism and globalism. More general concerns occupy David Leiwei Li in *Imagining the Nation: Asian American Literature and Cultural Consent* (1998). Jinqui Ling reconciles conflicting approaches of cultural study and nationalist impulses in *Narrating Nationalisms: Ideology and Form in Asian American Literature* (1998). Xiaojing Zhou studies Asian American poetry in *The Ethics of Poetics of Alterity in Asian American Poetry* (2006), and Guiyou Huang has edited a resource guide to poets, *Asian American Poets: A Bio-Bibliographical Critical Sourcebook* (2002). Arnold Krupat's *Red Matters: Native American Studies* (2002) looks beyond nationalism, indigenism, and cosmopolitanism to gauge Native American literature's importance to the ethical and intellectual heritage of the West. Catherine Rainwater's *Dreams of Fiery Stars: The Transformation of Native American Fiction* (1999) offers strong artistic analysis. John Lloyd Purdy's *Writing Indian, Native Conversations* (2009) combines criticism and dialogue. Kenneth Lincoln's *Sing with the Heart of a Bear: Fusions of Native and American Poetry, 1890–1999* (1999) stresses poetry's flexible and adaptable nature rather than its conformity to rigid ethnic and literary categories. Robin Riley First's *The Heart Is a Drum: Continuance and Resistance in American Indian Poetry* (2000) provides cultural and historical readings of a wide range of poems.

Especially useful for understanding how and why contemporary writers produce their work is the critical interview, the exploratory technique for which was pioneered by Joe David Bellamy in his *The New New Fiction: Interviews with Innovative American Writers* (1974) and which has been perfected by Larry McCaffery, who with various coeditors has produced a series of extensive, insightful, and critically developed dialogues with important authors of the past four decades: *Anything Can Happen* (1983), *Alive and Writing* (1987), *Across the Wounded Galaxies* (1990), and *Some Other Frequency* (1996). Over the years the *Paris Review* has conducted a series of interviews, "Writers at Work," that includes some of the most important writers of this period. These interviews are now available on the *Paris Review* website. The University of Michigan series, *Poets on Poetry*, includes interviews as well as essays (for individual volumes, consult the bibliographies of specific poets). Other valuable sources for interviews with poets are *Black Women Writers at Work* (1988), edited by Claudia Tate, *Survival This Way: Interviews with American Indian Poets* (1987), edited by Joseph Bruchac, and *Truthtellers of the Time: Interviews with Contemporary Women Poets* (1998), edited by Janet Palmer Mullaney.

The rapidly expanding genre of creative nonfiction has produced a variety of collections that suggest the characteristics and range of the form, including John D'Agata's *The Next American Essay* (2002) and Lee Gutman's series, *The Best Creative Nonfiction* (2010, 2008, 2007), as well as his preceding collection, *In Fact* (2004). David Shields's provocative book, *Reality Hunger* (2010), offers a version of a manifesto for a wide range of work by creative nonfiction writers.

A considerable amount of material, some of it useful, can be found on the Internet, including websites that offer audio versions of writers reading from their work. The Academy of American Poets' poets.org is the best general site for poetry and includes an audio component and links to other resources. The Internet Public Library offers "Native American Authors" at www.ipl .org/div/natam/.

Edward Abbey

A prolific writer, Abbey published numerous nonfiction works of environmental writing as well as eight novels. Among his nonfiction works are *Desert Solitaire: A Season in the Wilderness* (1968), *Slickrock: The Canyon Country of Southeast Utah* (1971), *Cactus Country* (1973), *The Journey Home* (1977), *The Hidden Canyon: A River Journey* (1977), *Abbey's Road* (1979), *Desert Images* (1979), *Down the River* (1982), and *Beyond the Wall: Essays from Outside* (1984). Two volumes with selections from Abbey's journals are *A Voice Crying in the Wilderness: Notes from a Secret Journal* (1989) and *Confessions of a Barbarian: Selections from the Journals of Edward Abbey, 1951–1989* (1995). Abbey's best-known work of fiction is his novel *The Monkey Wrench Gang* (1975). An anthology, *The Best of Edward Abbey*, appeared in 1988. His poetry is collected in *Earth Apples: The Poetry of Edward Abbey* (1994). *Edward Abbey: A Voice in the Wilderness* (1993), produced and directed by Eric Temple, is a documentary film about Abbey's life. Among the critical discussions of Abbey's work are Anne Ronald's *The New West of Edward Abbey* (1982), John Cooley's edited collection, *Earthly Words: Essays on Contemporary American Nature and Environmental Writers* (1994), James I. McClintock's *Nature's Kindred Spirits: Aldo Leopold, Joseph Wood Krutch, Edward Abbey, Annie Dillard, and Gary Snyder* (1994), Peter Quigley's *Coyote in the Maze: Tracking Edward Abbey in a World of Words* (1998), and John M. Cahalan's important biography, *Edward Abbey: A Life* (2001).

Sherman Alexie

Alexie's novels are *Reservation Blues* (1995), *Indian Killer* (1996), and *The Absolutely True Diary of a Part-Time Indian* (2007). His story collections are *The Lone Ranger and Tonto Fistfight in Heaven* (1993, adapted as a film script for *Smoke Signals* in 1998). *The Toughest Indian in the World* (2000), *Ten Little Indians* (2003), and *War Dances* (2007). His poetry collections are *The Business of Fancydancing* (1992), *I Would Steal Horses* (1992), *First Indian on the Moon* (1993), *Old Shirts and New Skins* (1993), *Seven Mourning Songs for the Cedar Flute I Have Yet to Learn to Play* (1994), *Water Flowing Home* (1996), *The Man Who Loves Salmon* (1998), *One Stick Song* (2000), *Il powwow della fine del mondo* (2005), *Dangerous Astronomy* (2005), and *Face* (2009). He wrote and directed the movie *The Business of Fancydancing* (2000).

Daniel Grassian provides critical analysis in *Understanding Sherman Alexie* (2005).

Dorothy Allison

Allison's fiction includes *Trash: Short Stories* (1988), *Bastard Out of Carolina* (1992), *Two or Three Things I Know for Sure* (1995). A nonfiction collection, *Skin: Talking About Sex, Class, and Literature*, appeared in 1994. Allison has also published a collection of poems, *The Women Who Hate Me: Poetry 1980–1990* (1991). Two valuable pieces are "Moving toward Truth: An Interview with Dorothy Allison," *The Kenyon Review* 16.4 (Autumn 1994): 71–83, and an interview in the online journal *Salon* (1998), at www.salon.com.

Kathleen Wilkinson's "Dorothy Allison: The Value of Redemption" is a critical discussion that appears in *Curve* magazine (2009).

Julia Alvarez

Alvarez's novels are *How the García Girls Lost Their Accents* (1991), *In the Time of the Butterflies* (1994), *¡Yo!* (1997), *In the Name of Salomé* (2000), *Saving the World* (2006), and *Return to Sender* (2009). Her poetry collections are *The Housekeeping Book* (1984), *Homecoming* (1984, revised 1996), *The Other Side / El Otro Lado* (1995), *Seven Trees* (1998), and *The Woman I Kept to Myself* (2004). *Something to Declare* (1998) gathers her essays. *Once Upon a Quinceañera: Coming of Age in the USA* (2007) is nonfiction. *How Tía Lola Came to Stay* (2001), *A Cafecito Story* (2002), *Before We Were Free* (2002), and *A Gift of Gracias* (2005) are books for children and young adults.

Kelli Lyon Johnson presents a critical analysis in *Julia Alvarez: Writing a New Place on the Map* (2005).

Gloria Anzaldúa

Borderlands/La Frontera (1987) includes memoir, historical analysis, and narrative poetry. Anzaldúa has also written several novels: *La Prieta* ("The Dark One") (1997), and (for children) *Prietita Has a Friend—Prietita Tiene un Amigo* (1991), *Friends from the Other Side—Amigos del Otra Lado* (1993), and *Prietita and the Ghost Woman—Prietita y La Llorona* (1996). She is the editor of *Making Face, Making Soul / Haciendo Caras: Creative and Critical Perspectives by Feminists of Color* (1990), and (with Cherríe Moraga) coedited *This Bridge Called My Back: Writings by Radical Women of Color* (1981). In 2002 she coedited, with AnaLouise Keating, *This Bridge We Call Home: Radical Visions for Transformation*.

Anzaldúa's work is studied by Deborah L. Madsen in *Understanding Contemporary Chicana Literature* (2000). Sonia Sandívar-Hull in *Feminism on the Border: Chicana Politics and Literature* (2000), Paula M. L. Moya in *Learning from Experience: Minority Identities, Multicultural Struggles* (2002), Catrióna Rueda Esquibel in *With Her Machete in Her Hand: Reading Chicana Lesbians* (2006), and AnaLouise Keating in *Extremundos / Between Worlds* (2008).

John Ashbery

Ashbery's volumes of poetry include *Some Trees* (1956), *The Tennis Court Oath* (1962), *Rivers and Mountains* (1966), *The Double Dream of Spring* (1970), *Three Poems* (1972), *Self-Portrait in a Convex Mirror* (1975), *Houseboat Days* (1977), *As We Know* (1979), *Shadow Train* (1981), *A Wave* (1984), *Selected Poems*

(1985), *April Galleons* (1988), *Flow Chart* (1991), *And the Stars Were Shining* (1994), *Can You Hear, Bird* (1995), *Girls on the Run* (1999), *Your Name Here* (2000), *Chinese Whispers* (2002), *Where Shall I Wander* (2005), and *A Worldly Country* (2007). *Notes From the Air* (2007) is a selection of his later poems. Ashbery is now represented in the Library of America series by *John Ashbery: Collected Poems 1956–87* (2008). Ashbery's Charles Eliot Norton Lectures on Poetry appear in *Other Traditions* (2000), and he has also published *Selected Prose* (2004).

Among useful critical essays are David Kalstone's *Five Temperaments* (1977) and John Shoptaw's book-length study of Ashbery's poetry, *On the Outside Looking Out* (1994). David K. Kermani's *John Ashbery: A Comprehensive Bibliography* (1975) is indispensable and amusing. See also *Beyond Amazement: New Essays on John Ashbery* (1980), edited by David Lehman, Charles Altieri's *Postmodernisms Now* (1998), and John Emil Vincent's *John Ashbery and You: His Later Books* (2007).

James Baldwin

Baldwin's novels are *Go Tell It on the Mountain* (1953), *Giovanni's Room* (1956), *Another Country* (1962), *Tell Me How Long the Train's Been Gone* (1968), *If Beale Street Could Talk* (1974), and *Just Above My Head* (1979). His other books are a collection of short stories, *Going to Meet the Man* (1965); a volume of nonfiction prose, *The Price of the Ticket* (1985); and two plays, *Blues for Mr. Charlie* (1964) and *The Amen Corner* (1968).

James Campbell's *Talking at the Gates: A Life of James Baldwin* (1991) is a biographical study. Critical interpretations include Lynn Orilla Scott's *James Baldwin's Later Fiction: Witness to the Journey* (2002) and Clarence E. Hardy III's *James Baldwin's God: Sex, Hope and Crisis in Black Holiness Culture* (2003). Further essays are found in editor D. Quentin Miller's *Reviewing James Baldwin: Things Not Seen* (2000). Baldwin's nonfiction has been gathered as *Collected Essays* (1998) and *The Cross of Redemption* (2010).

Amiri Baraka (LeRoi Jones)

Poetry volumes include *Preface to a Twenty Volume Suicide Note* (1961), *The Dead Lecturer* (1964), *Black Magic* (1969), *Hard Facts* (1975), *Transbluesency* (1995), *Funk Lore* (1996), and *Somebody Blew Up America* (2003). *Eulogies* (1996) uses poetry and prose to memorialize friends. Baraka authored four books on music: *Blues People* (1963), *Black Music* (1968), and *The Music: Reflections on Jazz and Blues* (1987), and *Digging: The Afro-American Soul of American Classical Music* (2009). His essays are collected in

Home (1966), *Raise Race Rays Raze* (1971), and *Selected Plays and Prose of Amiri Baraka / LeRoi Jones* (1979). Baraka produced three important anthologies: *The Moderns* (1963), *Black Fire* (1968, with Larry Neal), and *Confirmation: An Anthology of African American Women* (1983), with Amina Baraka. In 1984 he published *The Autobiography of LeRoi Jones / Amiri Baraka*. Baraka was also a dramatist. His play *Dutchman and the Slave* (1964) was published as a combined edition, as was *The Baptism & The Toilet* (1967). *Four Black Revolutionary Plays* (1969) includes *Experimental Death Unit #1, A Black Mass, Great Goodness of Life*, and *Madheart*. *The Motion of History and Other Plays* (1978) gathers the title work with *Slave Ship* and *S-1*. *The System of Dante's Hell* (1965) is a novel; *Tales* (1967) is a collection of short stories, as is *Tales of the Out & the Gone* (2006).

Early but still useful studies are *Baraka: The Renegade and the Mask* (1976) by Kimberly W. Benston and *Amiri Baraka / LeRoi Jones: The Quest for a "Populist Modernism"* (1978) by Werner Sollors. William J. Harris has written *The Poetry and Poetics of Amiri Baraka: The Jazz Aesthetic* (1985) and edited *The LeRoi Jones / Amiri Baraka Reader* (1991), supplying introductory literary history and a bibliography. Ross Posnock's *Color and Culture* (1998) locates the author's thought; Jerry Gafio Watt's *Amiri Baraka: The Politics and Art of a Black Intellectual* (2001) is comprehensive. Baraka's first wife, Hettie Cohen, has authored a memoir, *How I Became Hettie Jones* (1990).

Saul Bellow

Bellow is the author of fourteen novels and novellas: *Dangling Man* (1944), *The Victim* (1947), *The Adventures of Augie March* (1953), *Seize the Day* (1956), *Henderson the Rain King* (1959), *Herzog* (1964), *Mr. Sammler's Planet* (1970), *Humboldt's Gift* (1975), *The Dean's December* (1982), *More Die of Heartbreak* (1987), *A Theft* (1989), *The Bellarosa Connection* (1989), *The Actual* (1997), and *Ravelstein* (2000). His short stories appear in three collections: *Mosby's Memoirs* (1968), *Him with His Foot in His Mouth* (1984), and *Something to Remember Me By* (1991), and are joined by an additional story in *Collected Stories* (2001). A play, *The Last Analysis*, was produced in New York in 1964 and published the following year. *To Jerusalem and Back* (1976) is a personal account of his activities in Israel. *It All Adds Up* (1994) draws on Bellow's essays dating back to 1948. In 2010 Bellow's *Letters* appeared, edited by Benjamin Taylor.

James Atlas's *Bellow: A Biography* (2000) is exhaustive yet critically focused. Malcolm Bradbury provides the best concise introduction to this author's major work in *Saul Bellow* (1982), while in *Saul Bellow: Drumlin Wood-chuck* (1980) fellow writer Mark Harris offers an insightful portrait of Bellow as a professional figure. John J. Clayton's *Saul Bellow: In Defense of Man* (1979) celebrates the author's stressfully tested humanism, while Ellen Pifer's *Saul Bellow: Against the Grain* (1990) argues for his culturally atypical belief in the transcendent soul, as does M. A. Quayum's *Saul Bellow and American Transcendentalism* (2004). Gender is Gloria L. Cronin's focus in *A Room of His Own: In Search of the Feminine in the Novels of Saul Bellow* (2001). In *Saul Bellow: Vision and Revision* (1984) Daniel Fuchs examines manuscripts and letters to establish Bellow's Dostoyevskian engagement with issues of character. Julia Eichelberger sums up his work in *Prophets of Recognition* (1999).

John Berryman

Berryman's *Collected Poems: 1937–1971* appeared in 1991; *John Berryman: Selected Poems*, in 2004. *Homage to Mistress Bradstreet* (1956) and a selection of his *Short Poems* (1948) were issued together as a paperback in 1968. His other volumes of poetry include *77 Dream Songs* (1964); *Berryman's Sonnets* (1967); *His Toy, His Dream, His Rest* (1968); *Love and Fame* (1970; rev. 1972); *Delusions, Etc.* (1972); and a posthumous volume, *Henry's Fate* (1977). Berryman's critical biography, *Stephen Crane*, appeared in 1950, and a collection of his short fiction and literary essays was issued under the title *The Freedom of the Poet* (1976). Berryman's unfinished novel about his alcoholism, *Recovery*, appeared in 1973.

Valuable critical introductions to Berryman's poetry can be found in Helen Vendler's *The Given and the Made* (1995) and Thomas Travisano's *Midcentury Quartet* (1999). Paul Mariani's *Dream Song: The Life of John Berryman* (1996) and Eileen Simpson's *Poets in Their Youth* (1982) are useful biographical studies.

Elizabeth Bishop

Bishop's poems are available in *The Complete Poems 1927–1979* (1983). *The Collected Prose* (1984) includes memoirs and stories, especially the memory-based story "In the Village," invaluable for a reading of her poems. A remarkable selection of Bishop's correspondence, *One Art* (1994), was edited by her friend and publisher, Robert Giroux, and *Words in the Air: The Complete Correspondence between Elizabeth Bishop and Robert Lowell*, edited by Thomas Travisano and Saskia Hamilton, documents one of the great literary friendships in twentieth century poetry. Reproductions of Bishop's watercolor paintings appear in *Exchanging Hats* (1996). Alice Quinn edited *Edgar Allan Poe & The Juke-Box: Uncollected Poems, Drafts, and*

Fragments (2006). Bishop also translated from the Portuguese *The Diary of Helena Morley* (1957, 1977, 1991), an enchanting memoir of provincial life in Brazil.

Useful critical essays on Bishop appear in Seamus Heaney's *The Redress of Poetry* (1995), Lorrie Glodensohn's *Elizabeth Bishop: The Biography of a Poetry* (1992), and David Kalstone's *Becoming a Poet* (1989). *Elizabeth Bishop and Her Art*, edited by Lloyd Schwartz and Sybil P. Estess (1983), includes two interviews as well as essays. A provocative essay on Bishop appears in Adrienne Rich's *Blood, Bread and Poetry* (1986). Among the most valuable of the many critical studies are Brett C. Miller's important biography, *Elizabeth Bishop: Life and the Memory of It* (1993); *Elizabeth Bishop: The Geography of Gender* (1993), a collection of essays edited by Marilyn Lombardi; *Conversations with Elizabeth Bishop* (1996), edited by George Monteiro; and Thomas Travisano's *Midcentury Quartet* (1999). Candace MacMahon's *Elizabeth Bishop: A Bibliography* (1980) is indispensable.

Gwendolyn Brooks

Brooks's volumes of poetry include *A Street in Bronzeville* (1945), *Annie Allen* (1949), *In the Time of Detachment, In the Time of Cold* (1965), *In the Mecca* (1968), *Riot* (1969), *Family Pictures* (1970), *Aloneness* (1972), *Aurora* (1972), *Beckonings* (1975), *To Disembark* (1981), *Winnie* (1989), and *Children Coming Home* (1991). Many of her poems are collected in *Selected Poems* (1999), *The Essential Gwendolyn Brooks* (2005), and the *Gwendolyn Brooks CD Poetry Collection* (2005). She has also written prose autobiographies, *Report from Part One* (1972) and *Report from Part Two* (1996).

Other useful biographical material appears in *A Life Distilled*, edited by M. K. Mootry and others. Valuable discussions of Brooks's poetry appear in *Black Women Writers (1950–1980)*, edited by Mari Evans (1984). Stephen Wright's *On Gwendolyn Brooks: Reliant Contemplation* (1996), Harold Bloom's *Gwendolyn Brooks* (2000), and Martha E. Rhynes's *Gwendolyn Brooks: Poet from Chicago* (2003) are recent critical studies. An interview with Brooks appears in Janet Mullaney's *Truthtellers of the Times: Interviews with Contemporary Women Poets* (1998). Brooks and Gloria Jean Wade Gayles published *Conversations with Gwendolyn Brooks* (2002).

Raymond Carver

Principal collections of Carver's extensive short fiction are *Put Yourself in My Shoes* (1974), *Will You Please Be Quiet, Please?* (1976), *Furious Seasons* (1977), *What We Talk About When We Talk About Love* (1981), *The Pheasant* (1982), *Cathedral* (1983), and *Where I'm Calling From* (1988). *Fires* (1983) is a sampling of essays, poems, and narratives. Carver's uncollected work has been edited by William L. Stull as *No Heroics, Please* (1991), expanded as *Call If You Need Me* (2000). The Library of America's *Collected Stories* (2009), edited by William L. Stull and Maureen P. Carroll, includes drafts of stories before changes were introduced by Gordon Lish. Throughout his career Carver published poetry as well, the bulk of which appears in several volumes from *Near Klamath* (1968) to *A New Path to the Waterfall* (1989); *All of Us* (1998) collects all his poems.

Arthur M. Saltzman's *Understanding Raymond Carver* (1988) looks beyond the author's apparent realism, as does Randolph Runyon's *Reading Raymond Carver* (1992). Carver's return to traditionalism is celebrated by Kirk Nesset in *The Stories of Raymond Carver* (1995). Editors Sandra Lee Kleppe and Robert Miltner present a wide variety of critical commentaries in *New Paths to Raymond Carver* (2008). Sam Halpert sifts through comments by Carver's associates in *Raymond Carver: An Oral Biography* (1995). The standard biography is *Raymond Carver: A Writer's Life* (2009) by Carol Sklenicka.

John Cheever

Cheever's seven volumes of short stories, which appeared between 1943 and 1973, are assembled in *The Stories of John Cheever* (1978); *The Uncollected Stories of John Cheever* appeared posthumously in 1988. His novels are *The Wapshot Chronicle* (1957), *The Wapshot Scandal* (1964), *Bullet Park* (1969), *Falconer* (1977), and *Oh What a Paradise It Seems* (1982). *The Letters of John Cheever*, edited by his son, Benjamin Cheever, was published in 1988. *The Journals of John Cheever* (1991) was edited by Robert Gottlieb.

Scott Donaldson's *John Cheever* (1988) is a full-length biography. *Home before Dark* (1984), by his daughter, Susan Cheever, is a personal memoir. Francis J. Bosha has edited *The Critical Response to John Cheever* (1994). Samuel Chase Coale provides an overview in *John Cheever* (1977), while George W. Hunt explores religious dimensions in *John Cheever: The Hobgoblin Company of Love* (1983). The stories are given close study by James Eugene O'Hara in *John Cheever: A Study of the Short Fiction* (1989).

Sandra Cisneros

The House on Mango Street (1984) has been described as both interrelated short stories and a novel, whereas *Woman Hollering Creek* (1991) collects more evidently independent short stories. *Caramello* (2002) is a novel. Cisneros has published two major collections of poetry, *My Wicked Wicked Ways* (1987) and

Loose Woman (1994). Her *Hairs/Pelitos* (1994), written in English and accompanied by a Spanish text translated by Liliana Valenzuela, is a narrative for children.

Jean Wyatt's *Risking Difference* (2004) focuses on *Women Hollering Creek*. Ramón Saldíva discusses Cisneros's fiction in *Chicano Narrative* (1990), as do Tey Diana Rebolledo in *Women Singing in the Snow* (1995) and Sonia Saldivár-Hull in *Feminism on the Border* (2000). An extensive dialogue with her appears in *Interviews with Writers of the Post-Colonial World* (1992), edited by Feroza Jussawalla and Reed Way Dasenbrock.

Lucille Clifton

Clifton's volumes of poetry are *Good Times* (1969), *Good News About the Earth* (1972), *An Ordinary Woman* (1974), *Two-Headed Woman* (1980), *Good Woman: Poems and a Memoir 1969–1980* (1987), *Next: New Poems* (1987), *Quilting: Poems 1987–1990* (1991), *The Book of Light* (1993), *The Terrible Stories: Poems* (1995), *Blessing the Boats: New and Selected Poems, 1988–2000* (2000), *Mercy* (2004) and *Voices* (2008). Her memoir, *Generations* (1976), provides a valuable context for her work. Clifton's books for children include *The Black BC's* (1970), *Some of the Days of Everett Anderson* (1970), *The Boy Who Didn't Believe in Spring* (1973), *Don't You Remember* (1973), *All Us Come Cross the Water* (1973), *Good, Says Jerome* (1973), *Everett Anderson's Year* (1974; illustrated by Ann Grifalconi), *The Times They Used to Be* (1974), *My Brother Fine With Me* (1975), *Amifika* (1978), *The Lucky Stone* (1979), *My Friend Jacob* (1980), *Sonora Beautiful* (1981), *Everett Anderson's Goodbye* (1983), *Some of the Days of Everett Anderson* (1987), *Everett Anderson's Nine Month Long* (1987), *Everett Anderson's Christmas Coming* (1991; illustrated by Jan Spivey Gilchrist), *Everett Anderson's Friend* (1992), *Everett Anderson's 1-2-3* (1992; illustrated by Ann Grifalconi), *Three Wishes* (1994), *El Nino Que No Creia En La Primavera* (1996), and *Dear Creator: A Week of Poems for Young People and Their Teachers* (1997).

Critical discussions of her work include Hilary Holiday's *Wild Blessings: The Poetry of Lucille Clifton* (2004). Mary Jane Lupton has published *Lucille Clifton: Her Life and Letters* (2006).

Billy Collins

Collections of Collins's poetry include *The Apple That Astonished Paris* (1988), *Questions about Angels* (1991), *The Art of Drowning* (1995), *Picnic, Lightning* (1998), *Sailing Alone Around the World: New and Selected Poems* (2001), *Nine Horses* (2002), *The Trouble with Poetry, and Other Poems* (2005), and *Ballistics* (2008). *The Best Cigarette* (1997), an audiobook, provides a chance to hear Collins reading thirty-three of his poems. He selected and introduced the anthologies *Poetry 180: A Turning Back to Poetry* (2003) and *180 More: Extraordinary Poems for Everyday Life* (2005).

Critical discussion of Collins's work appears in David Baker's *Heresy and the Ideal: On Contemporary Poetry* (2000).

Edwidge Danticat

Danticat has published both fiction and nonfiction. Her nonfiction works include *After the Dance: A Walk Through Carnival in Jacmel, Haiti* (2002) and *Brother, I'm Dying* (2007). She also edited *The Butterfly's Way: Voices from the Haitian Dyaspora in the United States* (2003). Her fiction includes *Krik? Krak!* (1996), *The Farming of Bones* (1998), and *The Dew Breaker* (1994), as well as the young adult novels *Breath, Eyes, Memory* (1994), *Behind the Mountains* (2002), and *Anacaona: Golden Flower, Haiti, 1490* (2005). A video, audio, and print transcript of her 2011 interview on Democracy Now, "The Immigrant Artist at Work," can be found on the program's website www.democracynow.org. Critical discussion of Danticat's work can be found in Meredith M. Gadsby's *Sucking Salt: Caribbean Women Writers, Migration, and Survival* (2006).

Junot Díaz

Drown (1996) collects Díaz's short stories; *The Brief Wondrous Life of Oscar Wao* (2007) is his novel.

Jacquelyn Loss studies Díaz's fiction in *Latino and Latina Writers* (2003), edited by Alan West–Durán, as do Raphael Dalleo and Elena Machado Sáez in *The Latino/a Canon and the Emergence of a Post-Sixties Literature* (2007). Díaz's cultural context is examined by Lucia Suarez in *The Tears of Hispaniola: Haitian and Dominican Diaspora Memory* (2006).

Joan Didion

Didion's long and varied career as a writer includes works of both fiction and nonfiction as well as multiple screenplays. Among her nonfiction volumes are *We Tell Ourselves Stories in Order to Live: Collected Nonfiction* (2006), which includes work from *The White Album* (1979), *Salvador* (1983), *Miami* (1987), *After Henry* (1992), *Political Fictions* (2001), *Where I Was From* (2003), *Fixed Ideas: America Since 9.11* (2003). Another collection of her work, *Vintage Didion*, appeared in 2004. Her creative nonfiction memoir, *The Year of Magical Thinking*, appeared in 2005. Didion's novels include *Run, River* (1963), *Play It As It Lays* (1970), *A Book of Common Prayer* (1977), *Democracy* (1984), and *The Last Thing He*

Wanted (1996). Among her screenplays are *The Panic in Needle Park* (1971), *Play It As It Lays* (1972), *A Star Is Born* (1976), *True Confessions* (1981), and *Up Close and Personal* (1996). Two interviews with Didion have appeared in the *Paris Review*, one in 1978; a second, "The Art of Nonfiction" (2006), is available online at www.parisreview.org. Critical discussion of Didion's work can be found in James N. Still's "The Minimal Self: Joan Didion's Journalism of Survival" in *Literary Selves: Autobiography and Contemporary American Nonfiction* (1993) and Doug Underwood's *Journalism and the Novel: Truth and Fiction, 1700–2000* (2008).

Rita Dove

Dove has published eight volumes of poetry: *The Yellow House on the Corner* (1980), *Museum* (1983), *Thomas and Beulah* (1986), *Grace Notes* (1989), *Selected Poems* (1993), *Mother Love* (1995), *On the Bus with Rosa Parks* (1999), *American Smooth* (2004), and *Sonata Mulattica* (2009). She has also published a collection of fiction; *Fifth Sunday* (1985); a novel, *Through the Ivory Gate* (1992); and a valuable collection of essays, *The Poet's World* (1995). *Conversations with Rita Dove*, edited by Earl G. Ingersol, appeared in 2003.

Therese Steffen's critical study *Crossing Color: Transcultural Space and Place in Rita Dove's Poetry, Fiction, and Drama* appeared in 2001; Malin Pereira's *Rita Dove's Cosmopolitanism*, in 2003; and Pat Righelato's *Understanding Rita Dove*, in 2006.

Ralph Ellison

In his lifetime Ellison published three books: a novel, *Invisible Man* (1952), and two volumes of essays, *Shadow and Act* (1964) and *Going to the Territory* (1986). The latter materials are combined with other nonfiction in *The Collected Essays of Ralph Ellison* (1995), edited by John F. Callahan with a preface by Saul Bellow. Fragments of his novel in progress are noted in the bibliography to Mark Busby's *Ralph Ellison* (1991) in the Twayne United States Authors series; *Flying Home and Other Stories* (1997) gathers thirteen short stories written between 1937 and 1954, six of which were previously unpublished. In 1999 Callahan, as Ellison's literary executor, drew on manuscripts to assemble *Juneteenth* as a posthumous novel, a fuller version of which is presented by Callahan and editor Adam Bradley as *Three Days Before the Shooting . . .* (2010). Robert G. O'Meally edited *Living with Music: Ralph Ellison's Jazz Writings* (2001). *Trading Twelves: The Selected Letters of Ralph Ellison and Albert Murray*, edited by Murray and Callahan, appeared in 2000.

The centrality of Ellison's first novel to his other work is explained by Edith Shor in *Visible Ellison: A Study of Ralph Ellison's Fiction* (1993). Political interests shape the critical essays collected by Lucas E. Morel in *Ralph Ellison and the Raft of Hope* (2004), as does music in Horace A. Porter's *Jazz Country: Ralph Ellison in America* (2001). Julia Eichelberger's *Prophets of Recognition* (1999) considers his larger impact. *Jazz Country: Ralph Ellison's America* (2001) by Horace A. Porter relates the author's jazz background to his novels and essays. *Ulysses in Black* (2008) by Patrice D. Rankin considers Ellison's debts to the classics. Political influences are studied by Barbara Foley in *Wrestling with the Left: The Making of Ralph Ellison's* Invisible Man (2010). Arnold Rampersand's *Ralph Ellison* (2007) is a comprehensive biography. The author's lifelong growth is measured by Adam Bradley in *Ralph Ellison's Progress* (2010).

Louise Erdrich

Erdrich's novels are *Love Medicine* (1984), *The Beet Queen* (1986), *Tracks* (1988), *The Bingo Palace* (1994), *Tales of Burning Love* (1996), *The Antelope Wife* (1998), *The Last Report on the Miracles at Little No Horse* (2001), *The Master Butcher's Singing Club* (2003), *Four Souls* (2004), *The Painted Drum* (2005), *The Plague of Doves* (2008), and *Shadow Tag* (2010). *The Red Convertible* (2009) collects her short stories. For children she has written *Grandmother's Pigeon* (1996), *The Birchbark House* (1999), *The Game of Silence* (2005), and *The Porcupine Years* (2008). *The Blue Jay's Dance: A Birth Year* (1995) is her account of becoming a mother, *Birds and Islands in Ojibwe Country* (2003) is a memoir. With Michael Dorris she coauthored *The Crown of Columbus* (1991), a novel. Her poetry collections are *Jacklight* (1984), *Baptism of Desire* (1989), and *Original Fire* (2003).

Erdrich's fiction is treated by Louis Owens in *Other Destinies: Understanding the American Indian Novel* (1992), in the essays edited by Allan Chavkin in *The Chippewa Landscape of Louise Erdrich* (1999), and Peter G. Beidler and Gay Barton in *A Reader's Guide to the Novels of Louise Erdrich* (2006).

Allen Ginsberg

Ginsberg's *Collected Poems, 1947–1980* appeared in 1984, *White Shroud: Poems, 1980–1985* in 1986, and *Death and Fame: Poems 1993–1997* in 1999. His individual volumes, with the exception of *Empty Mirror* (early poems collected in 1961), have been issued in the now unmistakable City Lights paperbacks. They include *Howl and Other Poems* (1956), *Kaddish and Other Poems, 1958–1960* (1961), *Reality Sandwiches* (1963), *Planet News, 1961–1967* (1968), *The Fall of America, Poems of These States, 1965–1971* (1973), and

Mind Breaths, Poems 1972–1977 (1977). *Cosmopolitan Greetings* appeared in 1995 and *Selected Poems 1947–1995* in 1996. *Deliberate Prose: Selected Essays, 1952–1995* (2000) is a useful complement to the poetry. Ginsberg published a great number of pages from his journals, dealing with his travels, such as the *Indian Journals* (1970). *Allen Verbatim* (1974) includes transcripts of some of his lectures on poetry. In 1977 he published *Letters: Early Fifties Early Sixties* and in 1980 *Composed on the Tongue: Literary Conversations 1967–1977*, edited by Donald Allen. Ginsberg's interviews are collected in *Spontaneous Mind: Selected Interviews, 1958–1996* (2001).

Jane Kramer's *Allen Ginsberg in America* (1969) is a brilliant documentary piece on Ginsberg in the 1960s. *On the Poetry of Allen Ginsberg*, edited by Lewis Hyde (1980), is a collection of essays by different hands. Michelle Kraus has published *Allen Ginsberg: An Annotated Bibliography, 1969–1977* (1980). Bill Morgan has published *The Works of Allen Ginsberg 1941–1994: A Descriptive Bibliography* (1995) and *The Response to Allen Ginsberg 1926–1994: A Bibliography of Secondary Sources* (1996).

Joy Harjo

Harjo's collections of poetry include two chap-books, *The Last Song* (1975) and *What Moon Drove Me to This* (1979), and the volumes *She Had Some Horses* (1983), *In Mad Love and War* (1990), *The Woman Who Fell from the Sky* (1996), *A Map to the Next World* (2000), and *How We Became Human: New and Selected Poems 1975–2001* (2002). In *Secrets from the Center of the World* (1989) she wrote the text to accompany Steven Strom's photographs of the particulars of the southwestern landscape. She has also edited an anthology of Native American women's writing, *Reinventing the Enemy's Language: Contemporary Native Women's Writing of North America* (1997).

Laura Coltelli has edited a valuable collection of interviews with Harjo, *The Spiral of Memory* (1990). Commentary on the contexts of Harjo's work appears in Paula Gunn Allen's *The Sacred Hoop: Recovering the Feminine in American Indian Traditions* (1986) and Norma Wilson's *The Nature of Native American Poetry* (2001).

Robert Hayden

Hayden's *Collected Poems* appeared in 1985; his *Collected Prose* appeared the previous year. Both were edited by Frederick Glaysher.

Fred M. Fetrow's *Robert Hayden* (1984) is a critical study of Hayden's work. Essays on Hayden's work appear in the journals *Antioch Review* (1997) and *MELUS* (1998) and in

Harold Bloom's edited volume *Robert Hayden* (2005).

Randall Jarrell

Jarrell's *Complete Poems* was published in 1969, and a *Selected Poems* appeared in 1991. A selection of Jarrell's brilliant critical essays is available in *No Other Book* (1999), edited by Brad Leithauser. His novel satirizing American academic life, *Pictures from an Institution*, appeared in 1954.

Some of the most valuable commentary on Jarrell's life and work is to be found in a memorial volume of essays edited by Robert Lowell, Peter Taylor, and Robert Penn Warren, *Randall Jarrell, 1914–1965* (1967). William Pritchard's fine *Randall Jarrell: A Literary Life* (1990) illumines Jarrell's life and work, as does Mary Randall's *Remembering Randall* (1999). Critical discussion of Jarrell's work appears in Thomas Travisano's *Midcentury Quartet* (1999).

Jack Kerouac

Kerouac's novels are *The Town and the City* (1950), *On the Road* (1957), *The Subterraneans* (1958), *The Dharma Bums* (1958), *Doctor Sax* (1959), *Maggie Cassidy* (1959), *Tristessa* (1960), *Big Sur* (1962), *Visions of Gerard* (1963), *Desolation Angels* (1965), *Vanity of Duluoz* (1968), *Pic* (1971), and *Visions of Cody* (1972). His works of nonfiction are *The Scripture of the Golden Eternity* (1960), *Lonesome Traveler* (1960), *Book of Dreams* (1960), and *Satori in Paris* (1966). An important first draft has been restored by editor Howard Cunnell in *On the Road: The Original Scroll* (2007). His poems are collected in *Mexico City Blues* (1959), *Scattered Poems* (1971), *Heaven & Other Poems* (1977), and *San Francisco Blues* (1983). In 2004 Douglas Brinkley edited *Windblown World: The Journals of Jack Kerouac, 1947–1954*.

John Tytell's *Naked Angels: The Lives and Literature of the Beat Generation* (1983) includes Kerouac in his historical and critical context. Stylistic analyses are undertaken by Regina Weinrich in *The Spontaneous Prose of Jack Kerouac* (1987) and Michael Hrebeniak in *Action Writing: Jack Kerouac's Wild Form* (2006). More specifically thematic is James T. Jones's *Jack Kerouac's Duluoz Legend: The Mythic Form of an Autobiographical Fiction* (1999). Kerouac's friend Carolyn Cassady has written a memoir, *Off the Road* (1990), as has Edie Kerouac-Parker, *You'll Be Okay: My Life with Jack Kerouac* (2007). Biographies include Barry Gifford and Lawrence Lee's *Jack's Book: Jack Kerouac in the Lives and Words of His Friends* (1978), Tom Clark's *Jack Kerouac* (1984), Gerald Nicosia's *Memory Babe* (1983), and Ann Charter's *Jack Kerouac* (1987). Charters also prepared *A Bibliography of Works by Jack Kerouac* (1975). Kerouac's papers are housed in the Berg Collection of the New York Public Library.

Martin Luther King Jr.

Dr. King's published writings, sermons, speeches, unpublished writings, and most significant correspondence have been collected by editor Clayborne Carson in *The Papers of Martin Luther King, Jr.* (1985). The originals of these and other materials are housed in the Martin Luther King Jr. Research and Education Institute at Stanford University, which also maintains the King Document Search Access (OKRA) database.

Roger Bruns has authored *Martin Luther King, Jr.: A Biography* (2006). Taylor Branch studies Dr. King's social and political context in *At Canaan's Edge: America in the King Years, 1965–68* (2006). Eric J. Sundquist offers specific analysis in *King's Dream: The Legacy of Martin Luther King's "I Have a Dream" Speech* (2009).

Maxine Hong Kingston

The Woman Warrior (1976) and *China Men* (1980) were first received as autobiography, though Kingston scholars now recognize important fictive elements. *Tripmaster Monkey: His Fake Book* (1989) is more obviously a novel. Essays Kingston wrote in 1978 appear as *Hawai'i One Summer* (1999). *The Fifth Book of Peace* (2003) incorporates remembered pages of a lost novel with sections of conventional memoir. *I Love a Broad Margin to My Life* (2011) is an autobiography that uses poetry to address concerns of the author's aging.

Shirley Geok-Lim edited *Approaches to Teaching Kingston's "The Woman Warrior"* (1991); also helpful is Sidonie Smith's *A Poetics of Women's Autobiography: Marginality and the Fictions of Self-Representation* (1987). More cognizant of fiction's role in Kingston's writing is *Articulate Silences: Hisaye Yamamoto, Maxine Hong Kingston, and Joy Kogawa* (1993) by King-Kok Cheung and *Writing Tricksters* (1997) by Jeanne Rosier Smith. Cultural identity features in Martha J. Cutter's *Lost and Found in Translation* (2005).

Jamaica Kincaid

Kincaid has published both fiction and nonfiction, including memoirs and gardening books. Her books include a collection of short pieces variously categorized as stories, prose poems, or memoirs, *At the Bottom of the River* (1984), and the novels, *Annie John* (1985), *Lucy* (1990), and *Mr. Potter* (2002), as well as the fictional memoir *The Autobiography of My Mother* (1995). *My Brother* (1997) is a searing account of her brother's death from AIDS.

Kincaid is a passionate gardener; she is the editor of *My Favorite Plant: Writers and Gardeners on the Plants They Love* (editor; 1998) and the author of *My Garden* (1999) and *Among Flowers: A Walk in the Himalayas* (2005). Her essay, *"On Seeing England for the First Time"* (*Harper's* magazine, August 1991) is a brilliant postcolonial document. An interview in the online journal *Salon* can be found at www.salon.com. Critical discussion of Kincaid's work includes Moira Ferguson's *Jamaica Kincaid: Where the Land Meets the Body* (1994), Lisa Paravisini-Gebert's *Jamaica Kincaid: A Critical Companion* (1999), Justin D. Edwards's *Understanding Jamaica Kincaid* (2007), and Mary Ellen Snodgrass's *Jamaica Kincaid: A Literary Companion* (2008).

Yusef Komunyakaa

Komunyakaa's poetry appears in *Lost in the Bonewheel Factory* (1979), *Copacetic* (1984), *I Apologize for the Eyes in My Head* (1986), *Dien Cai Dau* (1987), *Magic City* (1992), *Neon Vernacular: New and Selected Poems* (1993), *Thieves of Paradise* (1998), *Talking Dirty to the Gods* (2000), *Pleasure Dome* (2001), *Taboo: The Wishbone Trilogy, Part I* (2004), and *Warhorses* (2008). With Martha Collins he has translated Nguyen Quang Thieu's *The Insomnia of Fire* (1992). With Sascha Feinstein he has edited *The Jazz Poetry Anthology* (1991) and *The Second Set: The Jazz Poetry Anthology, Volume 2* (1996). In 2000 he published *Blue Notes: Essays, Interviews, and Commentaries.*

Critical discussions of his work include Angela M. Salas's *Flashback Through the Heart: The Poetry of Yusef Komunyakaa* (2004).

Jhumpa Lahiri

Lahiri's collections of stories are *Interpreter of Maladies* (1999) and *Unaccustomed Earth* (2008); her first novel is *The Namesake* (2003).

Criticism of her fiction is found in *Transnational Asian American Literature: Sites and Transits* (2006), edited by Shirley Geok-lin Lim, et al., and in *Literary Gestures: The Aesthetic in Asian American Writers* (2007), edited by Rocío G. Davis and Sue-Im Lee.

Li-Young Lee

Lee's volumes of poetry are *Rose* (1986), *The City in Which I Love You* (1990), *A Book of My Nights* (2001), and *Behind My Eyes* (2008). A memoir, *The Winged Seed*, appeared in 1995.

Gerald Stern's foreword to *Rose* provides useful biographical material about Lee's family. Available on videotape, as part of the series *The Power of the Word*, is "Voices of Memory," in which Bill Moyers conducts a valuable interview with Lee. An interview with Lee appears in *Words Matter: Conversations with Asian American Writers* (2000), edited by King-Kok Cheung. *Breaking the Alabaster Jar: Conversation with Li-Young Lee*, edited by Earl G. Ingersol (2006), is a collection of interviews.

Denise Levertov
Some of Levertov's poems have been gathered in *Collected Earlier Poems 1940–1960* (1979). *The Selected Poems of Denise Levertov* appeared in 2002. Her individual volumes include *The Double Image* (1946), *Here and Now* (1957), *Overland to the Islands* (1958), *With Eyes at the Back of Our Heads* (1960), *The Jacob's Ladder* (1962), *O Taste and See* (1964), *The Sorrow Dance* (1967), *Relearning the Alphabet* (1970), *To Stay Alive* (1971), *Footprints* (1972), *The Freedom of the Dust* (1973), *Life in the Forest* (1978), *Candles in Babylon* (1982), *Oblique Prayers* (1984), *Breathing the Water* (1987), *A Door in the Hive* (1989), *Evening Train* (1992), *Tesserae* (1995), and *The Great Unknowing: Last Poems* (1999). *Making Peace* (2005) is a posthumous collection edited by Peggy Rosenthal. *The Poet in the World* (1973) and *Light Up the Cave* (1981) include essays on her own work, memoirs, reviews of other poets, and some theoretical essays. *New and Selected Essays* appeared in 1992.

Conversations with Denise Levertov (1998) is a collection of interviews. James E. Breslin's *From Modern to Contemporary: American Poetry 1945–1965* (1984) contains a discussion of Levertov. Linda Wagner-Martin edited *Critical Essays on Denise Levertov* (1990), and Anne Little edited *Denise Levertov: New Perspectives* (2000).

Barry Lopez
Lopez is a prolific writer and has published numerous works of fiction and nonfiction; as is the case with many creative nonfiction writers, his work often combines these genres. Among his environmental and travel writings are *Of Wolves and Men* (1978), the award-winning *Arctic Dreams: Imagination and Desire in a Northern Landscape* (1986), *Crossing Open Ground* (1988), *The Rediscovery of North America* (1991), *About This Life: Journeys on the Threshold of Memory* (1998), and *Home Ground: Language for an American Landscape* (2010). He mixes fact and fictional techniques in *Desert Notes: Reflections in the Eye of a Raven* (1976), *River Notes: The Dance of Herons* (1979), *Crow and Weasel* (1990), *Field Notes: The Grace Note of the Canyon Wren* (1994), and *Lessons from the Wolverine* (1997). *Winter Count* (1981) is a collection of stories and *Resistance* (2004) is a novel. Useful interviews with Lopez can be found in Christian Martin's "On Resistance: An Interview with Barry Lopez" in *The Georgia Review* (Spring 2006) and Mike Newell's *No Bottom: In Conversation with Barry Lopez* (2008). Critical discussion of Lopez's work includes Scot Slovic's *Seeking Awareness in American Nature Writing: Henry Thoreau, Annie Dillard, Edward Abbey, Wendell Berry, and Barry Lopez* (1992) and Willliam H. Rueckert's essay, "Barry Lopez and the Search for a Dignified and Honorable Relationship with Nature," in *Earthly Words: Essays on Contemporary American Nature and Environmental Writers*, edited by John Cooley (1994).

Audre Lorde
The Collected Poems of Audre Lorde (1997) brings together Lorde's poetry from *Cables to Rage* (1970), *New York Head Shop and Museum* (1975), *The Black Unicorn* (1978), and *Our Dead behind Us* (1986). A collection of essays and speeches, *Sister Outsider* (1984), provides a powerful context for reading her work. Her autobiographical writing includes *The Cancer Journals* (1980) and *Zami: A New Spelling of My Name* (1982).

Critical studies of Lorde's work appear in *Black Women Writers*, edited by Mari Evans (1984), and Cassie Steele's *We Heal From Memory: Sexton, Lorde, Anzaldúa, and the Poetry of Witness* (2000). An interview with Lorde appears in *Women Writers at Work* (1998), edited by George Plimpton.

Robert Lowell
Lowell's books of verse include *Lord Weary's Castle* (1946), *The Mills of the Kavanaughs* (1951), *Life Studies* (1959), *Imitations* (1961), *For the Union Dead* (1964), *Near the Ocean* (1967), *Notebook* (1969; rev. and exp. 1970), *The Dolphin* (1973), *For Lizzie and Harriet* (1973), and *History* (1973). For the stage Lowell adapted Racine's *Phaedra* (1961) and Aeschylus's *Prometheus Bound* (1969) as well as versions of Hawthorne and Melville stories grouped under the title *The Old Glory* (1965). His *Collected Prose* (1987) is an indispensable companion to Lowell's poetry and contains valuable essays on the work of other writers.

Among the many useful critical works on Lowell are Stephen Yenser's *Circle to Circle* (1975), Steven Axelrod's *Robert Lowell: Life and Art* (1978), and Thomas Travisano's *Midcentury Quartet* (1999). *Robert Lowell: A Collection of Critical Essays* (1968), edited by Thomas Parkinson, includes an important interview with the poet, and *The Critical Response to Robert Lowell* (1999), edited by Steven Gould Axelrod, provides an overview of criticism on the work. A partial bibliography of Lowell's work can be found in Jerome Mazzaro's *The Achievement of Robert Lowell, 1939–1959* (1960). Ian Hamilton's biography,

Robert Lowell, appeared in 1982. An edition of Lowell's letters, edited by Saskia Hamilton, appeared in 2005 and provides a valuable context for his work. *Words in the Air: The Complete Correspondence Between Elizabeth Bishop and Robert Lowell*, edited by Thomas Travisano and Saskia Hamilton (2008), documents one of the great literary friendships in twentieth century poetry.

Arthur Miller

Miller's earlier plays—*All My Sons*, *Death of a Salesman*, *The Crucible*, *A Memory of Two Mornings*, and *A View from the Bridge*—are brought together in *Arthur Miller's Collected Plays* (1957), which also includes a lengthy and useful introduction. Later dramas are available in *Collected Plays, 1957–1981* (1981) and thereafter separately, including *Danger, Memory!* (1987), *The Archbishop's Ceiling: The American Clock* (1989), *The Ride Down Mt. Morgan* (1992), *Broken Glass* (1994), *The Last Yankee* (1994), and *The Price* (2002). *Focus* (1945) is a novel; short fiction is collected in *The Misfits and Other Stories* (1987), *Homely Girl, a Life, and Other Stories* (1997), and *Presence* (2007); *The Misfits* (1961) is a screenplay. *Echoes Down the Corridor: Collected Essays, 1944–2000* appeared in 2000. Harold Clurman edited *The Portable Arthur Miller* in 1971, and Robert A. Martin edited *The Theater Essays of Arthur Miller* in 1978. Miller published an account of the production of *Death of a Salesman* in China in 1984 and an autobiography, *Timebends: A Life*, in 1987.

Martin Gottfried's *Arthur Miller: His Life and Work* (2003) is the major biography. The best recent analysis of Miller's work is found in Christopher Bigsby's *Arthur Miller, 1915–1962* (2010), supplemented by Bigsby's *Arthur Miller: A Critical Study* (2005) and his edited *The Cambridge Companion to Arthur Miller* (1997). Also helpful are the materials commissioned by Steven R. Centola for the edited volume *The Achievement of Arthur Miller: New Essays* (1995). Specifics are handled by Brenda Murphy in *Miller: Death of a Salesman* (1995), by Matthew C. Rodané in *Approaches to Teaching Miller's Death of a Salesman* (1995), and in the materials edited by Eric J. Sterling for *Arthur Miller's Death of a Salesman* (2008).

N. Scott Momaday

Momaday's autobiographical works begin with *The Journey to Tai-me* (1967) and continue with *The Way to Rainy Mountain* (1969) and *The Names: A Memoir* (1976), supplemented by *The Man Made of Words: Essays, Stories, Passages* (1997). *House Made of Dawn* (1968), *The Ancient Child* (1989), and *In the Bear's House* (1999) are novels. In 1999 he published *Circle of Wonder: A Native American Christmas Story*. His poems appear in *Angle of Geese* (1974), *Before an Old Painting of the Crucifixion, Carmel Mission, June 1960* (1975), and *The Gourd Dancer* (1976). *In the Presence of the Sun: Stories and Poems 1961–1991* was published in 1992 with illustrations by the author. *Three Plays: The Indolent Boys, Children of the Sun, The Moon in Two Windows* appeared in 2008. Momaday has also written books for children, edited editions of writers, and written the commentary for photographer David Muench's *Colorado: Summer, Fall, Winter, Spring* (1973).

Book-length studies of Momaday include *N. Scott Momaday: The Cultural and Literary Background* (1985) by Matthias Schubnell and *Reading, Learning, and Teaching N. Scott Momaday* (2007) by Jim Charles. Of the many interviews with Momaday, early and worthy is Joseph Bruchac's "The Magic of Words: An Interview with N. Scott Momaday," in *Survival This Way: Interviews with American Indian Poets* (1987), edited by Bruchac. Louis Owens's "N. Scott Momaday," in *This Is about Vision: Interviews with Southwestern Writers* (1990), edited by William Balassi, John F. Crawford, and Annie O. Eysturoy, also offers quite a good interview. Kenneth M. Roemer edited *Approaches to Teaching Momaday's "The Way to Rainy Mountain"* (1988), which is useful. Arnold Krupat's *The Voice in the Margin: Native American Literature and the Canon* (1989) compares autobiographical writing of Momaday and Leslie Marmon Silko. Susan Scarberry-Garcia's *Landmarks of Healing: A Study of "House Made of Dawn"* (1990,) fills in some of the multitribal mythic context. Gerald Vizenor edited *Narrative Chance: Postmodern Discourse on Native American Indian Literatures* (1989), with three articles on Momaday. A fine account, focused on *House Made of Dawn*, is in Louis Owens's *Other Destinies: Understanding the American Indian Novel* (1992), supplemented by Scott B. Vickers's work in *Native American Identities* (1998).

Toni Morrison

Morrison's novels are *The Bluest Eye* (1970), *Sula* (1974), *Song of Solomon* (1977), *Tar Baby* (1981), *Beloved* (1987), *Jazz* (1992), *Paradise* (1998), *Love* (2003), and *A Mercy* (2008). A play, *Dreaming Emmett*, was produced in 1986. Morrison is the author of *Playing in the Dark: Whiteness and the Literary Imagination* (1992) and editor of *Racing Justice, Engendering Power: Essays on Anita Hill, Clarence Thomas, and the Construction of Social Reality* (1992). Her *Lecture and Speech of Acceptance upon the Award of the Nobel Prize for Literature* was published in 1994.

Book-length studies include Trudier Harris's *Fictions and Folklore: The Novels of Toni Morrison* (1991), Denise Heinze's *The Dilemma of "Double-Consciousness": Toni Morrison's Novels* (1993), Gurleen Grewal's *Circles of Sorrow, Lines of Struggle* (1998), John N. Duvall's *The Identifying Fictions of Toni Morrison* (2000), J. Brooks Bouson's *Quiet As It's Kept* (2000), Andrea Reilly's *Toni Morrison and Motherhood* (2004), Susan Neal Mayberry's *Can't Love What I Criticize: The Masculine and Morrison* (2007), Karen F. Stein's *Reading, Learning, Teaching Toni Morrison* (2009), K. Zauditu-Salassie's *African Spiritual Traditions in the Novels of Toni Morrison* (2009), and Evelyn Jaffe Schreiber's *Race, Trauma, and Home in the Novels of Toni Morrison* (2010). In *Deans and Truants: Race and Realism in African American Literature* (2007) Gene Andrew Jarrett pays close attention to "Recitatif." Henry Louis Gates Jr. and K. A. Appiah have edited *Toni Morrison: Critical Perspectives Past and Present* (1993). *Toni Morrison: An Annotated Bibliography* (1987) has been compiled by David L. Middleton.

Flannery O'Connor

O'Connor's novels and stories (edited by Sally Fitzgerald) are a volume in the *Library of America series* (1988). Her novels are *Wise Blood* (1952) and *The Violent Bear It Away* (1960). Two collections of stories, *A Good Man Is Hard to Find* (1955) and *Everything That Rises Must Converge* (1965), are included with earlier uncollected stories in *Complete Stories* (1971). Her letters are collected in *The Habit of Being: The Letters of Flannery O'Connor* (1979). *The Presence of Grace, and Other Book Reviews* (1983) collects some of her critical prose, as does *Mystery and Manners* (1969), edited by Sally Fitzgerald and Robert Fitzgerald.

Jean W. Cash provides a biography in *Flannery O'Connor: A Life* (2003), as does Brad Gooch in *Flannery* (2009). Studies of O'Connor's fiction include Jon Lance Bacon's *Flannery O'Connor and Cold War Culture* (1993), Lorine M. Gertz's *Flannery O'Connor, Literary Theologian* (2000), Richard Giannone's *Flannery O'Connor, Hermit Novelist* (2000), Sarah Gordon's *Flannery O'Connor: The Obedient Imagination* (2000), *Flannery O'Connor's Radical Reality* (2006), edited by Jan Nordby Grettund and Karl-Heinz Westarp, and Donald E. Hardy's *The Body in Flannery O'Connor's Fiction* (2007). *Flannery O'Connor: A Descriptive Bibliography* (1981) was compiled by David Farmer.

Sylvia Plath

Plath's books of poetry include *The Colossus and Other Poems* (1962), *Ariel* (1966), *Crossing the Water* (1971), and *Winter Trees* (1972). Her novel *The Bell Jar* was first published in England in 1963. Plath's mother, Aurelia Schober Plath, selected and edited the useful *Letters Home: Correspondence 1950–63* (1975). Karen Kukil edited *The Unabridged Journals of Sylvia Plath, 1950–1962* (2000). Among the biographical and critical studies of Plath's work are Judith Kroll's *Chapters in a Mythology* (1976), Anne Stevenson's *Bitter Fame: The Undiscovered Life of Sylvia Plath* (1988), Linda Wagner-Martin's *Sylvia Plath: A Biography* (1987), Jacqueline Rose's *The Haunting of Sylvia Plath* (1993), Diane Middlebrook's *Sylvia Plath* (1998), and Christina Britzolakis's *Sylvia Plath and the Theatre of Mourning* (1999). *The Cambridge Introduction to Sylvia Plath*, by Jo Gill, appeared in 2008.

Thomas Pynchon

Pynchon's novels are *V.* (1963), *The Crying of Lot 49* (1966), *Gravity's Rainbow* (1973), *Vineland* (1990), *Mason & Dixon* (1997), *Against the Day* (2006) and *Inherent Vice* (2009). *Slow Learner* (1984) collects early stories.

Book-length studies are William M. Plater's *The Grim Phoenix: Reconstructing Thomas Pynchon* (1978), Thomas H. Schaub's *Pynchon, The Voice of Ambiguity* (1981), and David Seed's *The Fictional Labyrinths of Thomas Pynchon* (1988). Alan N. Brownlie studies the author's first three novels in *Thomas Pynchon's Narratives: Subjectivity and the Problems of Knowing* (2000), while the fourth and fifth novels are analyzed in Geoffrey Green, Donald J. Greiner, and Larry McCaffery's edited *The Vineland Papers* (1993) and Brooke Horvath and Irving Malin's edited *Pynchon and Mason & Dixon* (2000), respectively. New critical essays are collected by Niran Abbas in *Thomas Pynchon: Reading from The Margins* (2003) and Ian D. Copestake in *American Postmodernity: Essays on the Recent Fiction of Thomas Pynchon* (2003). The author's work is integrated with the canon by John A. McClure in *Partial Faiths: Postmodern Fiction in the Age of Pynchon and Morrison* (2007).

Adrienne Rich

The Fact of a Doorframe: Poems 1950–2001 (2002) draws from *A Change of World* (1951), *The Diamond Cutters* (1955), *Snapshots of a Daughter-in-Law* (1963), *Necessities of Life* (1966), *Leaflets* (1969), *The Will to Change* (1971), *Diving into the Wreck* (1973), *The Dream of a Common Language* (1978), *A Wild Patience Has Taken Me This Far* (1981), *Your Native Land, Your Life* (1986), *Time's Power: Poems 1985–1988* (1989), *An Atlas of the Difficult World: Poems 1988–1991* (1991), *Dark Fields of the Republic: Poems 1991–1995*

(1995), *Midnight Salvage: Poems 1995–1998* (1999), *Fox: Poems 1998–2000* (2001), *The School among the Ruins: 2000–2004* (2004), and *Telephone Ringing in the Labyrinth: Poems 2004–2006* (2007). Several valuable collections gather Rich's essays, lectures, and speeches: *On Lies, Secrets, and Silence* (1979), *Blood, Bread, and Poetry* (1986), *What Is Found There?: Notebooks on Poetry and Politics* (1993), *Arts of the Possible* (2001), *Poetry and Commitment: An Essay* (2007), and *A Human Eye: Essays on Art in Society* (2009). Rich is also the author of an important study, *Of Woman Born: Motherhood as Experience and Institution* (1976).

Valuable critical essays and an interview appear in *Adrienne Rich's Poetry* (1975), edited by Barbara Charlesworth Gelpi and Albert Gelpi. Other studies are *Reading Adrienne Rich* (1984), edited by Jane Roberta Cooper; Paula Bennett's *My Life, a Loaded Gun: Female Creativity and Feminist Poetics* (1986); Margaret Dickie's *Stein, Bishop, & Rich: Lyrics of Love, War, & Place* (1997); and Molly McQuade's *By Herself: Women Reclaim Poetry* (2000).

Theodore Roethke

The Collected Poems of Theodore Roethke was published in 1966. *Dirty Dinkey and Other Creatures: Poems for Children*; edited by B. Roethke and Stephen Lushington, appeared in 1973. Useful comments on poetic tradition and his own poetic practice are to be found in several collections of Roethke's prose: *On the Poet and His Craft: Selected Prose of Theodore Roethke* (1965), edited by Ralph J. Mills Jr.; *Straw for the Fire: From the Notebooks of Theodore Roethke, 1948–63* (1972), edited by David Wagoner; and *The Selected Letters of Theodore Roethke* (1970), edited by Mills.

Among the useful studies of Roethke's work are *Theodore Roethke: Essays on the Poetry* (1965), edited by Arnold Stein, and Laurence Lieberman's *Beyond the Muse of Memory: Essays on Contemporary Poets* (1995). Allan Seager's *The Glass House* (1968) contains useful biographical material.

Philip Roth

Roth's fiction consists of *Goodbye, Columbus* (1959)—a novella and five short stories—and the following novels: *Letting Go* (1962), *When She Was Good* (1967), *Portnoy's Complaint* (1969), *Our Gang* (1971), *The Breast* (1972), *The Great American Novel* (1973), *My Life as a Man* (1974), *The Professor of Desire* (1977), *The Ghost Writer* (1979), *Zuckerman Unbound* (1981), *The Anatomy Lesson* (1983), *The Counterlife* (1987), *Deception* (1990), *Operation Shylock* (1993), *Sabbath's Theater* (1995), *American Pastoral* (1997), *I Married a Communist* (1998), *The Human Stain* (2000), *The Dying Animal* (2001), *The Plot against America* (2004), *Everyman* (2006), *Exit Ghost* (2007), *Indignation* (2008), *The Humbling* (2009), and *Nemesis* (2010). *Reading Myself and Others* (1975) is a collection of essays and interviews. *The Facts: A Novelist's Autobiography* (1988) is Roth's memoir. A memoir of his father, *Patrimony*, was published in 1991.

Philip Roth (1982) by Hermione Lee is an excellent introduction, as is *Understanding Philip Roth* (1990) by Murray Baumgarten and Barbara Gottfried. *Philip Roth and the Jews* (1996) by Alan Cooper considers religious and cultural dimensions of the author's work. The broad sweep of Roth's career is covered by James D. Bloom in *The Literary Bent* (1997), by Mark Shechner in *Up Society's Ass, Copper: Reading Philip Roth* (2003), and by Deborah Shostak in *Philip Roth—Countertexts, Counterhues* (2004). Elaine B. Safer's *Mocking the Age: The Later Novels of Philip Roth* (2006) discusses his experiments in narrative, while Ross Posnock handles controversy in *Philip Roth's Rude Truth* (2005). David Bramer provides an overview in *Philip Roth* (2007).

Anne Sexton

Sexton's books of poems include *To Bedlam and Part Way Back* (1960), *All My Pretty Ones* (1962), *Live or Die* (1966), *Love Poems* (1969), *Transformations* (1971), *The Book of Folly* (1973), *The Death Notebooks* (1974), and *The Awful Rowing toward God* (1975). *Complete Poems* appeared in 1981.

Diane Wood Middlebrook's biography, *Anne Sexton* (1991), and Sexton's *A Self-Portrait in Letters* (1977) give useful biographical material. Important interviews and critical essays are to be found in J. D. McClatchy's *Anne Sexton: The Artist and Her Critics* (1978) and Diane Hume George's *Sexton: Selected Criticism* (1988). An interview with Sexton appears in *Women Writers at Work* (1998), edited by George Plimpton.

Leslie Marmon Silko

Silko's novels are *Ceremony* (1977), *Almanac of the Dead* (1991), and *Gardens in the Dunes* (1999). *Storyteller* (1981) includes prose poems and related short stories. *Laguna Woman* (1974), *Voices Under One Sky* (1994), and *Rain* (1996) are books of poetry. *Yellow Woman and a Beauty of the Spirit* (1996) consists of Silko's essays on contemporary Native American life. *Lullaby*, coauthored with Frank Chin, was dramatically adapted and produced in San Francisco in 1976. *The Delicacy and Strength of Lace*, a collection of letters between Silko and the poet James Wright, edited by Anne Wright, was published in 1985. Silko's work also appeared in *Yellow Woman* (1993), edited by Melody Graulich.

Leslie Mormon Silko (1980) by Per Seyersted is an introduction to her work. *Four American Indian Literary Masters* (1982) by Alan R. Veile is also relevant, as are Louise K. Barnett and James L. Thorson's edited *Leslie Marmon Silko* (1999), Catherine Rainwater's *Dreams of Fiery Stars* (1999), Rosemary A. King's *Border Influences from the Mexican War to the Present* (2001), and Claudia Sadowsky-Smith's *Border Fictions* (2008).

Gary Snyder

Snyder's poems have been published by several different presses, often with duplication of poems. *Riprap*, originally published in 1959, is most easily obtained in *Riprap and Cold Mountain Poems* (1965, 1991). *Myths and Texts* first appeared in 1960. *The Blue Sky* first appeared in 1969 and reappeared in *Six Sections of Mountains and Rivers without End plus One* (1970). Other volumes include *The Back Country* (1968), *Regarding Wave* (1970), *Turtle Island* (1974), *Axe Handles* (1983), *Left Out in the Rain: New Poems 1947–1985* (1986), *No Nature: New and Selected Poems* (1992), and *Danger on Peaks* (2004). In 1996 Snyder published the completion of *Mountains and Rivers without End*. He has also published important prose collections dealing with ecology, such as *Earth House Hold* (1969) and *A Place in Space: Ethics, Aesthetics, and Watersheds* (1995). A gathering of Snyder's prose and poetry appears in *The Gary Snyder Reader* (1999). *The Real Work: Interviews and Talks 1964–1979*, edited by William Scott McLean, appeared in 1980. Another essay collection, *Back on Fire*, appeared in 2007.

Helpful critical discussion of Snyder's work can be found in Sherman Paul's *In Search of the Primitive* (1986) and Patrick Murphy's *A Place for Wayfaring: The Poetry and Prose of Gary Snyder* (2000). An interview with Snyder appears in the *Paris Review* 141 (1996).

Cathy Song

Song's poetry collections are *Picture Bride* (1983), *Frameless Windows, Squares of Light* (1988), *School Figures* (1994), *The Land of Bliss* (2000), and *Cloud Moving Hands* (2007).

Discussion of Song's work appears in *Conversations and Contestations* (2000), edited by Ruth Hsu and Cynthia Franklin.

Art Spiegelman

Spiegelman's books include *The Complete Mr. Infinity* (1970), *The Viper Vicar of Vice, Villany, and Vickedness* (1972), *Zip-a-Tune and More Melodies* (1972), *Ace Hole, Midget Detective* (1974), *Every Day Has Its Dog* (1979), *Work and Turn* (1979), *Two-Fisted Painters* (1980), *Maus, A Survivor's Tale: My Father Bleeds History* (1986), *Maus II, A Survivor's Tale: And Here My Troubles Began* (1991), *Open Me . . . I'm a Dog!* (1997), *In the Shadow of No Towers* (2004), and *Breakdowns* (2008).

Comic Books as History: The Narrative Art of Jack Jackson, Art Spiegelman, and Harvey Pekar (1989) by Joseph Witek locates Spiegelman's importance in the evolution of underground comics and the graphic novel. A broader view is found in Charles Hatfield's *Alternative Comics: An Emerging Literature* (2005). Alan Rosen analyzes *Maus* in *Sounds of Defiance: The Holocaust, Multilingualism, and the Problem of English* (2005), as do contributors to Jeet Heer and Kent Worcester's *A Comic Studies Reader* (2009).

John Updike

Updike's novels are *The Poorhouse Fair* (1959), *Rabbit, Run* (1960), *The Centaur* (1963), *Of the Farm* (1965), *Couples* (1968), *Rabbit Redux* (1971), *A Month of Sundays* (1975), *Marry Me* (1976), *The Coup* (1978), *Rabbit Is Rich* (1981), *The Witches of Eastwick* (1984), *Roger's Version* (1986), *S.* (1988), *Rabbit at Rest* (1990), *Memories of the Ford Administration* (1992), *Brazil* (1994), *In the Beauty of the Lilies* (1996), *Toward the End of Time* (1997), *Gertrude and Claudius* (2000), *Seek My Face* (2002), *Villages* (2004), *Terrorist* (2006), and *The Widows of Eastwick* (2008). Collections of short fiction are *The Same Door* (1959), *Pigeon Feathers* (1962), *Olinger Stories: A Selection* (1964), *The Music School* (1966), *Bech: A Book* (1970), *Museums and Women* (1972), *Too Far to Go: The Maples Stories* (1979), *Problems* (1979), *Bech Is Back* (1982), *Trust Me* (1987), *The Afterlife* (1994), *Bech at Bay* (1998), *Licks of Love* (2000), and *My Father's Tears* (2009). Stories from 1953 to 1975 are presented thematically in *The Early Stories* (2003). Updike's poems are gathered in *Collected Poems 1953–1993* (1993), drawing on the individual volumes *The Carpentered Hen* (1958), *Telephone Poles* (1963), *Midpoint* (1969), *Tossing and Turning* (1977), and *Facing Nature* (1985); *Americana: and Other Poems* (2001) and *Endpoint* (2009) are newer work. Reviews and literary essays appear in *Assorted Prose* (1965, *Picked-Up Pieces* (1975), *Hugging the Shore* (1983), *Odd Jobs* (1991), *More Matter* (1999), and *Due Considerations* (2007). *Self-Consciousness* (1989) is a memoir, *Just Looking* (1989) and *Still Looking* (2005) are art criticism, and *Golf Dreams* (1996) collects the author's essays on his favorite sport. *Buchanan Dying* (1974) is a play meant for reading rather than for stage production. Updike has authored five books for children: *The Magic Flute* (1962), *The Ring* (1964), *A Child's Calendar* (1965), *Bottom's Dream* (1969), and *A Helpful Alphabet of Friendly Objects* (1995).

Donald J. Greiner's thorough examination

of the early canon appears in his *John Updike's Novels* (1984) and *The Other John Updike: Poems/Short Stories/Prose/Plays* (1981). Longer views are taken by James A. Schiff in *John Updike Revisited* (1998) and by William Pritchard in *Updike: America's Man of Letters* (2000). Peter J. Bailey pursues theological matters in *Rabbit (Un)Redeemed: The Drama of Belief in John Updike's Fiction* (2006). Jack De Bellis has prepared *The John Updike Encyclopedia* (2007) and (with Michael Broomfield) *John Updike: A Bibliography* (2007). Updike's papers have been deposited in The Houghton Library at Harvard University.

Alice Walker

Walker's novels are *The Third Life of Grange Copeland* (1970), *Meridian* (1976), *The Color Purple* (1982), *The Temple of My Familiar* (1989), *Possessing the Secret of Joy* (1992), *By the Light of My Father's Smile* (1998), and *Now Is the Time to Open Your Heart* (2004). Her short-story collections are *In Love and Trouble* (1973), *You Can't Keep a Good Woman Down* (1981), and *The Way Forward Is with a Broken Heart* (2000). Poetry collections are *Once* (1986), *Five Poems* (1972), *Revolutionary Petunias* (1973), *Good Night, Willie Lee, I'll See You in the Morning* (1969), *Horses Make a Landscape Look More Beautiful* (1984), *Her Blue Body Everything We Know* (1991), *Absolute Trust in the Goodness of the Earth* (2003), and *A Poem Traveled Down My Arm* (2003). Her *Collected Poems* appeared in 2005. Walker's literary essays are collected in *In Search of Our Mothers' Gardens* (1983), *Living by the Word* (1988), and *Anything We Love Can Be Saved* (2000); she has also written *Warrior Marks: Female Genital Mutilation and the Sexual Blinding of Women* (1987, with Pratibha Parmar), *The Same River Twice: Honoring the Difficult: A Meditation on Life, Spirit, Art, and the Making of the Film* The Color Purple *Ten Years Later* (1996), *We Are the Ones We Have Been Waiting For* (2006), and *Overcoming Speechlessness: A Poet Encounters the Horror in Rwanda, Eastern Congo, and Palestine/Israel* (2010). Her books for children include an illustrated version of *To Hell with Dying* (1988), *Finding the Green Stone* (1991), and a biography, *Langston Hughes, American Poet* (1974).

Evelyn C. White's *Alice Walker: A Life* (2004) is a comprehensive biography. Good samplings of scholarship on Walker fill two volumes: editors Henry Louis Gates Jr. and K. Anthony Appiah's *Alice Walker: Critical Perspectives Past and Present* (1993) and editor Lillie P. Howard's *Alice Walker and Zora Neale Hurston: The Common Bond* (1993). *Alice Walker* (2000) is Maria Lauret's book-length study.

Eudora Welty

Welty's novels are *The Robber Bridegroom* (1942), *Delta Wedding* (1947), *The Ponder Heart* (1954), *Losing Battles* (1970), and *The Optimist's Daughter* (1972). Her *Collected Stories* (1980) draws from the volumes *A Curtain of Green* (1941), *The Wide Net* (1943), *Music from Spain* (1948), *The Golden Apples* (1949), *The Bride of Innisfallen* (1955), and *Thirteen Stories* (1965). Later volumes are *Moon Lake* (1980) and *Retreat* (1981). *A Flock of Guinea Hens Seen from a Car* (1970) is poetry; among Welty's many volumes of nonfiction prose are *The Eye of the Story: Selected Essays and Reviews* (1978), *One Writer's Beginnings* (1984), and *A Writer's Eye: Collected Book Reviews* (1994).

Ann Waldron published *Eudora: A Writer's Life* in 1998. Susan Marrs completes the picture in *Eudora Welty: A Biography* (2005) and *One Writer's Imagination: The Fiction of Eudora Welty* (2002). Good introductions are available in Gail Mortimer's *Daughter of the Swan: Love and Knowledge in Eudora Welty's Fiction* (1994), *Eudora Welty's Aesthetics of Place* (1994) by Jan Nordby Gretlund, and Ruth D. Weston's *Gothic Traditions and Narrative Techniques in the Fiction of Eudora Welty* (1994). *Eudora Welty: A Bibliography* by Noel Polk appeared in 1994.

Tennessee Williams

Most of Williams's plays are collected in the seven-volume *The Theatre of Tennessee Williams* (1971–81). Some later dramas are available in separate editions; a few others are still to be published. Other writings include a novel, *The Roman Spring of Mrs. Stone* (1950); short stories printed in several volumes and finally brought together in *Collected Stories* (1986), edited by Gore Vidal; a volume of screenplays, *Stopped Rocking* (1984); and poems collected as *In the Winter of Cities* (1964) and *Androgyne, Mon Amour* (1977). *Where I Live: Selected Essays*, edited by Christine R. Day and Bob Woods, appeared in 1978.

Williams's *Memoirs* (1975) is interestingly revelatory but is not a reliable biographical guide; neither is Dotson Rader's *Tennessee: Cry of the Heart* (1985). Donald Spoto's *A Kindness of Strangers: The Life of Tennessee Williams* (1985) is workmanlike; a historically sound treatment is *Tennessee Williams: Everyone Else Is an Audience* (1993) by Ronald Hayman. More theoretically inclined is Nicholas Pagan's *Rethinking Literary Biography: A Postmodern Approach* (1993). Judith J. Thompson provides a Jungian analysis of the plays and identifies structural patterns in *Tennessee Williams' Plays: Memory, Myth, and Symbol* (1987, rev. 2002). Time relationships are explored by Patricia Schroeder in *The Presence of the Past* in *Modern American Drama* (1989). Philip G. Kolin edited *Tennessee Williams: A Guide to Research and Performance* (1998); Matthew C. Rodané prepared *The Cambridge Companion to Tennessee Williams*. George E. Crandell compiled *Tennessee Williams: A Descriptive Bibliography* (1995). *The Selected Letters of Tennessee Williams, Volume I, 1920–1945* (2000) was edited by Albert J. Devlin and Nancy M. Tischler. Margaret Bradham Thornton has edited Williams's *Notebooks* (2007).

James Wright
Above the River (1990) collects the work in Wright's individual volumes: *The Green Wall* (1956), *Saint Judas* (1963), *Shall We Gather at the River* (1968), *Moments of the Italian Sum-* *mer* (1976), *To a Blossoming Pear Tree* (1977), and *This Journey* (1982). An edition of his *Collected Prose*, edited by Anne Wright, appeared in 1983. Some of Wright's translations from the Spanish and German are available in *Twenty Poems of Georg Trakl* (1963), *Twenty Poems of Cesar Vallejo* (1964), and *Twenty Poems of Pablo Neruda* (with Robert Bly, 1968).

The best critical discussions of Wright's work appear in the essays collected in *The Pure Clear Word: Essays on the Poetry of James Wright* (1982), edited by Dave Smith, and in Laurence Lieberman's *Beyond the Muse of Memory* (1995). *A Wild Perfection: The Selected Letters of James Wright*, edited by Annie Wright and Saundra Rose Maley, appeared in 2005.

PERMISSIONS ACKNOWLEDGMENTS

IMAGE CREDITS

COLOR INSERT CREDITS

TEXT CREDITS

Index